BOOKS IN PRINT®

1989–90

BOOKS IN PRINT · 42nd · EDITION

This edition of BOOKS IN PRINT was
prepared by R. R. Bowker's Database
Publishing Group in collaboration with the
Publication Systems Department.

Peter Simon, Vice President, Database Publishing Group
Albert Simmonds, Managing Editor
Doreen Gravesande, Senior Editor
Dereck Rousch, Senior Editor
Joan Russell, Senior Associate Editor, Quality Control
Frank Accurso and Allan Baptiste, Senior Associate Editors
Domonique Fernandez, Vincent Fiorillo,
Gene Gold, Yvonne Holness, Malcolm MacDermott,
Myriam Nunez, Raymond Padilla,
Beverly Palacio, George Tibbetts,
Joseph Tondi and Mark Worrell, Assistant Editors.

Michael Gold, Director, Systems Development
Jack Murphy, Computer Operations Manager.

BOOKS IN PRINT®

1989–90

VOLUME 7

OUT OF PRINT

OUT OF STOCK INDEFINITELY

R.R. BOWKER
New York

Published by R. R. Bowker a division of Reed Publishing (USA) Inc.

International Standard Book Numbers: Set 0-8352-2740-5
Vol. 1 0-8352-2741-3, Vol. 2 0-8352-2742-1
Vol. 3 0-8352-2744-8, Vol. 4 0-8352-2745-6
Vol. 5 0-8352-2746-4, Vol. 6 0-8352-2747-2
Vol. 7 0-8352-2748-0
Vol. 8 0-8352-2749-9
International Standard Serial Number 0068-0214
Library of Congress Catalog Card Number 4-12648

Printed and bound in the United States of America

8 Volume Set

ISBN 0-8352-2740-5

9 780835 227407

CONTENTS

PREFACE

In publishing Volume 7 of *Books In Print*, R.R. Bowker provides current information that answers the bookseller's and book buyer's crucial question: *"Is the book out-of-print?"* This addition to *Books In Print* has also accomplished a significant step in book buyer, bookseller and publisher relations in its forthright presentation of publisher-verified information on out-of-print and out-of-stock status for the period July 1988-June 1989.

This volume should dramatically increase the efficiency and economy of book reference and acquisitions functions. Hundreds of thousands of dollars are wasted each year in attempts to purchase books which are no longer available from the publisher. In addition to contributing to rising book acquisitions costs, unfulfilled book orders cause patron dissatisfaction and a breakdown of vital services in bookstores and libraries.

This compilation of out-of-print and out-of-stock titles is the result of several mailings to 30,000 *Books In Print* publishers, as well as the electronic transfer of data from publishers directly into the BIPS database. OP and OSI status, as reported by publishers to the editors of *Books In Print,* means that the title in question is unavailable for purchase from that particular publisher. It does not necessarily mean that rights have reverted to the author(s), since that is a matter of interpretation in the particular contracts involved. Additionally, these titles may still be available in the stock of some bookstores and wholesalers.

In compiling this information Bowker has established an out-of-print status notation on over 95,000 titles declared OP/OSI since BIP 1988-89.

Titles reported only as OS (out-of-stock) as opposed to OSI (out-of-stock indefinitely) are not included in *Volume 7,* but remain in *Books In Print, Volumes 1-6.* (These titles often come back into print after a short time span, and therefore are never listed with the inactive listings.)

While it was a primary goal in the preparation of this volume to provide as much information as possible on out-of-print and out-of-stock titles, there are some publishers who have decided not to participate, for various reasons. These publishers are listed below:

Apollo Editions
Ballinger Publishing Company
Basic Books, Inc.
Cambridge University Press
Cellar Book Shop
Dial Books for Young Readers
E. P. Dutton
Harper & Row Junior Books
Harper & Row Publishers, Inc.
J. B. Lippincott Company
Lodestar Books
Oxford University Press
Philosophical Research Society, Inc.
Scarecrow Press, Inc.
Sovereign Press
Theatre Arts Books
Thomas Y. Crowell Company
Ultramarine Publishing Company, Inc.
Walker & Company
Western Publishing Company, Inc.
Williams & Wilkins Company

HOW TO USE VOLUME 7

Volume 7 of Books in Print, which appears for the first time in this edition, includes approximately 95,000 titles which have been declared by the publisher as out-of-print or out-of-stock since July, 1988. It includes two main indexes, author and title. Also included are several indexes which provide information on OP/OSI resources. In cases where publishers have indicated that titles may be produced on demand, we have made indications in the price field. A list of these on-demand houses is provided. This special Resources section listing was designed to identify, for the users of *Volume 7,* those companies who may have stock for books declared out-of-print, or be in a position to fulfill orders.

ALPHABETICAL ARRANGEMENT OF AUTHOR AND TITLE INDEXES

Within each index entries are filed alphabetically by word, with the following exceptions:

Initial articles of titles in English, French, German, Italian and Spanish are deleted from the title index.

M', Mc and *Mac* are filed as if they were *Mac* and are interfiled with other names beginning with *Mac;* for example, Macan, MacAnally, Macardle, McAree, McArthur, Macarthur, M'Aulay, Macaulay, McAuley. Within a specific name grouping *Mc* and *Mac* are interfiled according to the given name of the author; for example, Macdonald, Agnes; McDonald, Alexander; Macdonald, Anne L; McDonald, Austin F.; MacDonald, Betty. Compound names are listed under the first part of the name, and cross-references appear under the last part of the name.

Entries beginning with initial letters (whether authors' given names or titles) are filed first, e.g., Smith, H.C., comes before Smith, Harold A.; B E A M A Directory comes before Baal, Babylon.

Numerals, including year dates, are written out in most cases and are filed alphabetically:

Seven Years in Tibet
Seventeen
Seventeen famous operas
Seventeen-Fifteen to the present
Seventeen party book
Seventeen reader
Seventeenth century

U.S., UN, Dr., Mr., and St. are filed as though they were spelled out. In the author index, however, "Dr. Seuss" files as "Dr. Seuss" rather than "Doctor Seuss" or "Seuss."

SPECIAL NOTE ON HOW TO FIND AN AUTHOR'S COMPLETE LISTING

In sorting author listings by computer it is not possible to group the entire listing for an author together unless a standard spelling and format for each name is used. If an author's name is given in various forms by the contributing publishers, his listings in the author index may be divided into several groups.

Variant forms of an author's first and middle names may not be adjacent in the filing sequence, as in: Aiken, Conrad and Aiken, Conrad P. or Jung, C. G. or Jung, Carl G. For most surnames, variant forms of entry will fall close together, but for the most common surnames (Smith, Brown, etc.) it is suggested you check specifically for all variant forms of first and middle names.

Foreign names which may or may not be given with a prefix will not be adjacent in the filing sequence, such as, Balzac and de Balzac and Goethe or von Goethe. German names with umlauts may appear in two alphabets because of the varying treatment of the umlauted vowel; Müller, F. Max or Mueller, F. Max. Acronyms for names of corporate authors may appear in two or more groups of listing if one form is presented with no space between initials—UNESCO, and another with spaces, U N E S C O.

You will find cross-references to the variant forms of an author's name wherever we anticipated that his listings might not be filed together.

INFORMATION INCLUDED IN TITLE ENTRY

Entries in the title index include the following bibliographic information, when available: author, co-author, editor, co-editor, translator, co-translator, title, number of volumes, edition, Library of Congress number, series information, language if other than English, whether or not illustrated, grade range, year of publication, type of binding if other than cloth over boards, the price the entry carried when it was declared out-of-print, International Standard Book Number, publisher's order number, imprint and publisher. When an entry includes the prices for both the hardcover and paperback editions, the publication date within the entry refers to the hardcover binding; however, when the paperback binding is the only one included in the entry, the publication date is the paperback publication date. (Information on the International Standard Book Numbering System in the United States and other English-speaking countries is available from R. R. Bowker.)

GENERAL EDITORIAL POLICIES

In order to insure that the essential information in these listings is uniform, complete, and easy to find, the following editorial policies have been maintained:

When two authors or editors are responsible for a book, full bibliographic information is included in the author entry for the author or editor named first, and a cross-reference directs the user from the second author or editor to the primary entry; e.g., Wilson, Robert E., jt. auth. see Fensch, E.A. If more than two authors or editors are responsible for a certain publication, only the name of the first is given followed by *et al.*

Titles of single volumes as part of a set are given if the volumes are sold singly. Some series are also listed in the Title Index.

The Bible, the Book of Common Prayer, catechisms, hymnals and books of this type cannot always be recorded with full description. Since incomplete information is misleading, the user of this book is directed to the appropriate publisher's trade lists.

Most prices are list prices. Lack of uniformity in publishers' data prohibits indicating trade discounts. An "a" follows some of the trade edition prices and indicates that a specially priced library edition is available; "t" indicates a tentative price; "g" a guaranteed binding on a juvenile title; and "x" a short discount—20%, or less. Short discount information is generally supplied by publishers to Bowker for each publication. However, all publishers do not uniformly supply this information and Bowker can only transmit this information when it is provided. PLB indicates a publishers' library binding. YA indicates that a title may be used for young adults. An "i" following the price indicates an invoice price. Specific policies for such titles should be obtained from the individual publishers.

Publishers' and distributors' names, in most instances, are abbreviated. A key to these abbreviations will be found in the *Key to Publishers' & Distributors' Abbreviations* immediately following the Author Index in Volume 3. Entries in this Key are arranged alphabetically by the abbreviations used in the bibliographic entries. A complete listing is provided, which contains: abbreviation used, company name, editorial address(es), ordering addresses(es), telephone number(s), toll-free telephone numbers(s), imprints, ISBN prefix(es). Standard Address Number(s) (SAN), and business affiliation.

For example:

> **Abingdon** *(Abingdon Pr., 0-687).* Div. of United Methodist Publishing Hse. 201 Eighth Ave., S., Nashville, TN 37202 (SAN 201-0054)Tel 615-749-6290; Toll free: 800-251-3320; 1015 Visco Dr., Nashville, TN 37210 (SAN 699-9956). Imprints: Apex Books (Apex); Ferstival Books (Festival)

If a bibliographic entry contains a "Pub. by" note after the ISBN, the title should not be ordered from the publisher, but from the company whose abbreviation appears at the end of the entry. For example, the title below should be ordered from Kluwer Academic.

> **Reichardt, W.** Acoustics Dictionary. Date not set. lib. bdg. 28.50 (ISBN 90-247-2707-3, Pub. by Martinus Nijhoff Netherlands). Kluwer Academic.

The SAN (Standard Address Number) is a unique identification code for each address of each organization in or served by the book industry.

KEY TO ABBREVIATIONS

a — after price, specially priced library edition available
abr. — abridged
adpt. — adapted
Amer. — American
annot. — annotation(s), annotated
ans. — answer(s)
app. — appendix
approx. — approximately
assn. — association
auth. — author
bd. — bound
bdg. — binding
bds. — boards
bibl(s). — bibliography(ies)
bk(s). — book, books
bklet(s) — booklets
Bro. — Brother
coll. — college
comm. — commission, committee
co. — company
cond. — condensed
comp(s). — compiler(s)
corp. — corporation
dept. — department
diag(s). — diagram(s)
dir. — director
disk — software disk or diskette
dist. — distributed
Div. — Division
doz. — dozen
ea. — each
ed. — editor, edited, edition
eds. — editions, editors
educ. — education
elem. — elementary
ency. — encyclopedia
Eng. — English
enl. — enlarged
exp. — expurgated
fac. — facsimile
fasc. — fascicule
fict. — fiction
fig(s). — figure(s)
for. — foreign
Fr. — French
frwd. — foreword
g — after price, guaranteed binding
gen. — general
Ger. — German
Gr. — Greek
gr. — grade, grades
hdbk. — handbook
i — invoice price—see publisher for specific pricing policies
ISBN — International Standard Book Number
i.t.a. — initial teaching alphabet
Illus. — illustrated, illustration(s), illustrator(s)
in prep. — in preparation
incl. — includes, including
inst. — institute
intro. — introduction
Ital. — Italian
Jr. — Junior
jt. auth. — joint author
jt. ed. — joint editor
k — kindergarten audience level
l.p. — long playing
ltd. ed. — limited edition
lab. — laboratory
lang(s). — language(s)
Lat. — Latin
lea. — leather
lib. — library
lit. — literature, literary
math. — mathematics
mod. — modern
mor. — morocco
MS, MSS — manuscript, manuscripts
natl. — national
no., nos. — number, numbers
o.p. — out of print
orig. — original text, not a reprint (paperback)
o.s.i. — out of stock indefinitely
pap. — paper
photos — photographs, photographer
PLB — publisher's library binding (juvenile)
Pol. — Polish
pop. ed. — popular edition
Port. — Portuguese
prep. — preparation
probs. — problems
prog. bk. — programmed book
ps — preschool audience level
pseud. — pseudonym
pt(s). — part, parts
pub. — published, publisher, publishing
pubn. — publication
ref(s). — reference(s)
repr. — reprint
reprod(s). — reproduction(s)
rev. — revised
rpm. — revolution per minute (phono records)
Rus. — Russian
SAN — Standard Address Number
S&L — Signed and Limited
s.p. — school price
scp — single copy Direct to the Consumer Price
sec. — section
sel. — selected
ser. — series
Soc. — Society
sols. — solutions
Span. — Spanish
Sr. (after given name) — Senior
Sr. (before given name) — Sister
St. — Saint
subs. — subsidiary
subsc. — subscription
suppl. — supplement
tech. — technical
text ed. — text edition
tr. — translator, translated, translation
univ. — university
vol(s). — volume, volumes
wkbk. — workbook
x — after price, short discount (20% or less)
YA — young adult audience level
yrbk. — yearbook

ARRANGEMENT AND CONTENT OF ENTRIES, OUT OF PRINT RESOURCES

Section I—Retailers

Listing retail outlets in the United States and Canada, this section is arranged geographically by state or province and city. City headings carry population statistics (from the 1980 census of the United States, and from **The Canadian Almanac and Directory** for Canada) and the telephone area code. Under each city bookstores are arranged alphabetically by name. Businesses bearing the name of the owner are alphabetized under the person's last name. Stores which carry the name of a literary character or historical personality are alphabetized by the first name.

Each bookstore entry provides store name, street and mailing address, and telephone number. Also listed is information on types of books carried and subject specialties. To the right of each entry, the major category of books stocked is shown.

Section II—Wholesalers

This section contains entries for wholesalers, jobbers, and distributors of trade books and magazines. Publishers who distribute solely their own publications have been omitted from this section. Information on these firms can be found in R.R. Bowker's annual **Publishers, Distributors & Wholesalers of the U.S.**

LIST OF ABBREVIATIONS

acad—academic, academy
acctg—accounting
accts—accounts
adv—advertising
Afr—Africa(n)
agr—agriculture
Alb—Albania(n)
alt—alternative
Am—America(n)
Amer—Americana
ann—annual(ly)
anthrop—anthropology
antq—antiques
appr libr collec—appraises library collections
archaeol—archaeology
archit—architecture
astrol—astrology
astron—astronomy
autg—autographs
auth—author(s)
av mat—audiovisual material
Ave—Avenue
bibliog—bibliography
biog—biography
biol—biology
biper—back issue periodicals
(bk)s—book(s)
bkst—bookstore(s)
bldg—building
Blvd—Boulevard
econ—economics
educ—education
EEur—East Europe
EGer—East Germany
elem—elementary
el-hi—elementary & high school
encycl—encyclopedia
Eng—England, English
eng—engineering
espec—especially
Eur—Europe(an)
exec—executive
exp—export(s)
ext—extension
fac ed—facsimile edition
fict—fiction
1st ed—first edition
for lang—foreign language(s)
Fr—France, French
geneal—genealogy
geol—geology
Ger—Germany
govt—government
Gr—Greece, Greek
gr cds—greeting cards
hb—hardbound
Hebr—Hebrew
hist—history
hort—horticulture
hp—higher priced
Hq—Headquarters
math—mathematics
mech—mechanic(s, al)
med—medical, medicine
merch—merchandise
metaphys—metaphysical, metaphysics
Mex—Mexico
mgr—manager
mgt—management
mil—military
mm—mass market
mod—modern
mss—manuscripts
mus—music(al)
musicol—musicology
nat hist—natural history
Neth—Netherlands
newspr—newspapers
nonfict—nonfiction
Norw—Norway, Norwegian
numis—numismatic(s)
nutrit—nutrition
o&r—old & rare
oceanog—oceanography
off equip—office furniture & supplies
off sup—office supplies
op—out of print
oper—operated, operates
orig—original
ornith—ornithology
rel—religion, religious (C-Catholic, J-Jewish P-Protestant)
rel gd—religious goods
remd—remainder(s)
remd dir—remainders dealer
reprod—reproductions
restr—restricted
Rom—Romanian
Rte—Route
Russ—Russia(n)
s&s—sidelines & services
SAfr—South Africa
SAm—South America
Scand—Scandinavia(n)
sch—school
sci—science
sci-tech—science-technology
S/Ctr—Shopping Center
sec—secondary
secy—secretary
sem—seminary
serv—service(s)
sh mus—sheet music
soc—social
social—sociology
Sp—Spain, Spanish
spec—special
Sq—Square
SS—Sunday School

bnd—binding(s)
bot—botany
br—branch(es)
Bulg—Bulgaria(n)
bus—business
Can—Canada, Canadian
cat 3x ann—catalog 3 times annually
cds—cards
Celt—Celtic
ch—church
chts—charts
chem—chemistry
chmn—chairman
class—classical
Co—Company
col—college
ctr—center
Czech—Czechoslovakia(n)
Den—Denmark
dent—dentistry
Dept—Department
dict—dictionaries
dir—director
Div—Division
doc—document
Dr—Drive
Hwy—Highway
hydrol—hydrology
ichthyol—ichthyology
illus—illustration(s)
imp—import(s)
Inc—Incorporated
incunab—incunabula
indep—independent(ly)
indust—industrial, industry
ins—insurance
int—international
Isr—Israel
Ital—Italian, Italy
Jap—Japan(ese)
juv—juvenile
Kor—Korea(n)
lang—language(s)
LDS—Church of Jesus Christ of Latter Day Saints (Mormons)
libr—libraries, library
lit—literary, literature
Lith—Lithuania(n)
Ltd—Limited
ltd ed—limited edition
mag—magazines
mat—material
ov tr—overhead transparencies
papbk—paperback(s)
per—periodicals
Pers—Persia(n)
pharm—pharmacy
pharmaceut—pharmaceutical
Phil—Philippines
philat—philately
philos—philosophy
photog—photography
Pkwy—Parkway
Pl—Place
Pol—Poland, Polish
polit—political, politics
Port—Portugal, Portuguese
prbnd—prebind(s)
pres—president
psychiat—psychiatry
psychol—psychology
pub—public
publ—publish(er) (ing), publication(s)
pvt—private
Rd—Road
rec—records
ref—reference
St—Street
Sta—Station
staty—stationery
subj—subject(s)
subs—subscription, subsidiary
SUNY—State University of New York
sup—supplies
supvr—supervisor
Swed—Sweden, Swedish
Switz—Switzerland
tech—technical
theol—theology
Tib—Tibet(an)
Tpk—Turnpike
transp—transportation
treas—treasurer
Turk—Turkey, Turkish
tv—television
UK—United Kingdom
Univ—University
vet med—veterinary medicine
vpres—vice president
WGer—West Germany
xmas cds—Christmas cards
Yugo—Yugoslavia(n)
zool—zoology

*Information obtained from secondary sources

BOOKS IN PRINT

1989-90

VOLUME 7

O.P.-O.S.I.

TITLES

A

A & The or William T. C. Baumgarten Comes to Town. Ellen Raskin. (Illus.). (gr. 1-4). 1970. PLB 4.95 o.p. (ISBN 0-689-20609-7). Macmillan.

A Comprehensive Treatise on Inorganic & Theoretical Chemistry see Comprehensive Treatise on Inorganic & Theoretical Chemistry.

A Course in Practical Spirituality see How to Change Attitudes & Emotions.

A. D. France Two. Ed. by RotoVision Staff. (Illus.). 376p. pap. 55.00 o.p. (ISBN 0-8230-5799-2). Watson-Guptill.

A. E. Gallatin Collection: Museum of Living Art. Ed. by A. E. Gallatin. (Illus.). 156p. 1954. 5.00 o.p. (ISBN 0-87633-028-6). Phila Mus Art.

A. E. Housman: The Scholar-Poet. Perceval Graves. (Encore Edition). 5.95 o.p. (ISBN 0-684-17678-5). Scribner.

A. E. Nordenskiold Collection in Helsinki University Library: Annotated Catalogue of Maps Made up to 1800, Vol. 1, Atlases A-J. Ed. by Ann-Mari Mickwitz & Leena Miekkavaara. 1979. text ed. 80.00x o.p. (ISBN 0-391-01393-9). Humanities.

A for Anything. Damon Knight. 1980. pap. 1.95 o.p. (ISBN 0-380-48553-2, 48553). Avon.

A for Effort. Joyce Sloan. (gr. 9 up). 1966. pap. 0.75 o.p. (ISBN 0-377-80101-1). Friendship Pr.

A. Garner's Book of Brit Fairy Tales. Date not set. (ISBN 0-385-29425-5). Delacorte.

A-Ha in Their Own Words. (Illus.). 32p. (Orig.). 1986. pap. 5.95 o.p. (ISBN 0-88188-478-2, Pub. by Robus Bks). H Leonard Pub Corp.

A. Hoen on Stone: E. Weber & Co. & A. Hoen & Co. Exhibition Catalogue. Lois B. McCauley. LC 79-87284. (Illus.). 1969. 7.00 o.s.i. (ISBN 0-938420-02-X). Md Hist.

A. I. B. S. Directory of Bio-Science Departments & Facilities in the United States & Canada. 2nd ed. Ed. by Peter Gray. LC 75-33761. 1975. 66.00 o.p. (ISBN 0-12-786589-6). Acad Pr.

A Is for Aggravation: Alphabet Book. Elizabeth Wetzel. LC 82-83566. 224p. 1983. pap. 6.95 o.p. (ISBN 0-689-70649-9, Atheneum). Macmillan.

A Is for Alibi: A Kinsey Millhone Mystery. Sue Grafton. LC 81-7128. 256p. 1982. 12.95 o.p. (ISBN 0-03-059048-5). H Holt & Co.

A Is for Always: An ABC Book. Joan W. Anglund. LC 68-15423. (Illus.). (ps-2). 1968. 2.50 o.p. (ISBN 0-15-200670-2, HJ). HarBraceJ.

A. J. Cronin: A Reference Guide. Dale Salwak. 1982. lib. bdg. 32.50 o.p. (ISBN 0-8161-8595-6, Hall Reference). G K Hall.

A. J.'s Tax Court - Who Won, Who Lost & Why. A. J. Cook & Jacquelene Ross. LC 86-29659. (Illus.). 288p. 1987. 16.95 o.p. (ISBN 0-918518-55-5, St Luke TN); pap. 10.95 o.p. (ISBN 0-918518-53-9). Peachtree Pubs.

A la Recherche du Temps Perdu see Oeuvres.

A... My Name Is Alice. Joan M. Silver & Julianne Boyd. 64p. 1985. pap. 3.95 o.p. (ISBN 0-380-89853-5, Bard). Avon.

A-P Classic. McGraw.

A. Philip Randolph: A Biographical Portrait. Jervis Anderson. LC 73-12847. (Illus.). 398p. 1974. pap. 4.45 o.p. (ISBN 0-15-671710-7, Harv). HarBraceJ.

A Propos! Communication et Culture: Un Debut. Anne Slack & Marlies Mueller. LC 82-82509. 1983. text ed. 36.36 o.p. (ISBN 0-395-33167-6). HM.

A-Team, No. 3: When You Comin' Back, Range Rider? Charles Heath. 208p. (Orig.). 1984. pap. 2.50 o.p. (ISBN 0-440-10027-5). Dell.

A to Z of Soft Animals. Carolyn Hall. (Illus.). 128p. 1986. 14.95 o.p. (ISBN 0-671-61397-9). P-H.

A-Twenty Havoc at War. Encore ed. Hess. 6.95 o.p. (ISBN 0-684-17708-0). Scribner.

A. W. Tozer: A Twentieth Century Prophet. David J. Fant, Jr. LC 64-21945. (Illus.). 180p. 1964. pap. 4.95 o.p. (ISBN 0-87509-048-6). Chr Pubns.

A-Z Guide for New Mothers. Jayne Garrison. 96p. 1986. pap. 1.95 o.p. (ISBN 0-8423-0008-2). Tyndale.

A-Z Industrial Salesmanship. John Fenton. 1975. text ed. 23.50x o.p. (ISBN 0-434-90559-3); pap. text ed. 16.95x o.p. (ISBN 0-434-90560-7). Trans-Atl Phila.

A-Z of Astronomy. Patrick Moore. (Encore Edition). (Illus.). 1977. pap. 1.95 o.p. (ISBN 0-684-16913-4, SL700, ScribT). Scribner.

A-10 Thunderbolt II. Dana Bell. (Warbirds Illustrated Ser.: No. 40). (Illus.). 72p. (Orig.). 1986. pap. 9.95 o.p. (ISBN 0-85368-772-2, Pub. by Arms & Armour). Sterling.

AA Atlas of Ireland. (Illus.). 64p. 1988. pap. 7.95 o.p. (ISBN 0-86145-596-7, Pub. by British Tour). Salem Hse Pubs.

AA Big Road Atlas of Britain. (Illus.). 94p. 1985. pap. 12.95 o.p. (ISBN 0-86145-238-0, Pub. by Automobile Assn Brit). Salem Hse Pubs.

AA Big Road Atlas of Britain: Nineteen Eighty-Six Edition. rev. ed. 84p. 1986. pap. 12.95 o.p. (ISBN 0-86145-320-4, Pub. by Automobile Assn Brit). Salem Hse Pubs.

AA BTA Touring Map of Great Britain. rev. ed. pap. 7.95 o.p. (ISBN 0-86145-000-0, Pub. by British Tour). Salem Hse Pubs.

AA Camping & Caravanning in Britain. rev. ed. 304p. 1985. pap. 11.95 o.p. (ISBN 0-86145-247-X, Pub. by Automobile Assn Brit). Salem Hse Pubs.

AA Guesthouses, Farmhouses & Inns in Britain. (AA Accommodation Guides Ser.). 416p. 1986. pap. 12.95 o.p. (ISBN 0-86145-305-0, Pub. by Automobile Assn Brit). Salem Hse Pubs.

AA Guesthouses, Farmhouses & Inns in Europe. rev. ed. (Illus.). 192p. 1986. pap. 11.95 o.p. (ISBN 0-86145-312-3, Pub. by Automobile Assn Brit). Salem Hse Pubs.

AA Hotels & Restaurants in Britain. rev. ed. 752p. 1985. pap. 15.95 o.p. (ISBN 0-86145-246-1, Pub. by Automobile Assn Brit). Salem Hse Pubs.

A.A. Llega a Su Mayor Edad. 338p. (Span.). 1975. pap. 3.15 o.p. (ISBN 0-916856-10-0). AAWS.

AA Pocket Guide to London. (Illus.). 176p. 1988. pap. 7.95 o.p. (ISBN 0-86145-528-2, Pub. by British Tour). Salem Hse Pubs.

AA Regional Touring Guide Wales. 160p. 1988. pap. 19.95 o.p. (ISBN 0-86145-499-5, Pub. by British Tour). Salem Hse Pubs.

AA Touring England. (Illus.). 600p. 1988. 69.95 o.p. (ISBN 0-86145-619-X, Pub. by British Tour). Salem Hse Pubs.

AA Touring Map of Western Europe. Automobile Association Staff. (Illus.). 1981. pap. 8.95 o.p. (ISBN 0-86145-001-9, Pub. by British Tour). Salem Hse Pubs.

AA Traveller's Guide to Europe. rev. ed. 416p. pap. 14.95 o.p. (ISBN 0-86145-251-8, Pub. by Automobile Assn Brit). Salem Hse Pubs.

AA Traveller's Guide to Europe. rev. ed. (Illus.). 200p. 1986. pap. 16.95 o.p. (ISBN 0-86145-310-7, Pub. by Automobile Assn Brit). Salem Hse Pubs.

AAAS Annual Meeting Abstracts of Papers: 154th National Meeting, 1988. Compiled by Barbara C. Klein-Helmuth. 120p. 1988. pap. 5.00 o.p. AAAS.

AAAS Annual Meeting Abstracts of Papers: 153rd National Meeting, 1987. Ed. by Barbara C. Klein-Helmuth & David Savold. 116p. 1987. pap. 3.00 o.p. AAAS.

AAAS Annual Meeting Program - 154th National Meeting, February 1988. Ed. by A. Herschman. 122p. 1988. pap. 5.00 o.p. AAAS.

AAAS Annual Meeting Program - 1987. Ed. by A. Herschman. 138p. 1987. pap. 3.00 o.p. AAAS.

AAAS Handbook Nineteen Eighty-Eight to Eighty-Nine: Officers, Organization, Activities. Ed. by AAAS Staff. 180p. 1988. pap. 3.75 o.p. AAAS.

AAAS Handbook Nineteen Eighty-Seven to Eighty-Eight: Officers, Organization, Activities. Ed. by AAAS Staff. 169p. 1987. pap. 3.75 o.p. AAAS.

AAAS Report IX: Research & Development, FY 1985. Intersociety Working Group Staff. Ed. by Shapley & Teich. 284p. 1984. pap. 10.00 o.p. (ISBN 0-87168-265-6). AAAS.

AAAS Report VIII: Research & Development, FY 1984. Intersociety Working Group Staff. Ed. by Shapley et al. 255p. 1983. pap. 5.00 o.p. (ISBN 0-87168-260-5). AAAS.

AAAS Report X: Research & Development FY 1986. Intersociety Working Group Staff. Ed. by Shapley et al. 270p. 1985. pap. text ed. 15.00 o.p. (ISBN 0-87168-272-9). AAAS.

AACR Two & the Catalog: Theory-Structure-Changes. Wesley Simonton & Marilyn J. McClaskey. LC 81-11757. 78p. 1981. pap. 9.50 o.p. (ISBN 0-87287-267-X). Libs Unl.

AACR Two Headings: A Five-Year Projection of Their Impact on Catalogs. Arlene T. Dowell. LC 82-9927. (Research Studies in Library Science: No. 17). 145p. 1982. lib. bdg. 25.00 o.p. (ISBN 0-87287-330-7). Libs Unl.

AAHPERD Youth Fitness Test Manual. 1976. 4.25 o.p. (ISBN 0-88314-214-7). AAHPERD.

AAMI Nineteenth Annual Meeting Proceedings. annual 120p. (Orig.). 1984. pap. text ed. 6.00 o.p. (ISBN 0-910275-34-3). Assn Adv Med Instrn.

A&P Mechanics Airframe Question Book. Federal Aviation Administration Staff. (Aviation Maintenance Training Course Ser.). 96p. 1986. pap. 3.50 o.p. (ISBN 0-89100-288-X, EA-FAA-T-8080-12A). IAP.

Aardvark to Zebra. Lois Boncer. LC 84-6899. (Illus.). 224p. (Orig.). 1984. pap. 14.95 o.p. (ISBN 0-8329-0306-X). New Century.

Aaron Copland. Arthur Berger. LC 79-136055. (Illus.). 1971. Repr. of 1953 ed. lib. bdg. (ISBN 0-8371-5205-4, BEAC). Greenwood.

Aaron Copland. Arthur V. Berger. 120p. Repr. of 1971 ed. lib. bdg. 39.00 o.p. (Pub. by Am Repr Serv). Reprint Servs.

Aaron to Zipfel. Rich Marazzi & Len Fiorito. (Illus.). 608p. 1985. pap. 4.95 o.p. (ISBN 0-380-89694-X). Avon.

Aaron's Christmas Donkey. Lois W. Johnson. LC 74-79364. (Illus.). 32p. (gr. 1 up). 1974. 3.95 o.p. (ISBN 0-8066-1425-0, 10-0120, Augsburg). Augsburg Fortress.

AAU Official Code Directory 1987. softcover 7.00 o.p. (ISBN 0-89710-047-6). AAU Pubns.

Ab Initio Calculation of Phonon Spectra. Ed. by J. T. Devreese & V. E. Van Doren. 312p. 1983. 49.50x o.p. (ISBN 0-306-41119-9, Plenum Pr). Plenum Pub.

Abacs or Nomograms. A. Giet. (Illus.). 1956. (ISBN 0-8022-0591-7). Philos Lib.

Abbot. Walter Scott. 1969. Repr. of 1906 ed. 14.95x o.p. (ISBN 0-460-00124-8, DEL-04000, Evman). Biblio Dist.

ABC. Fitzgerald. (Dear God Kids Ser.). 1985. 3.95 o.s.i. (ISBN 0-671-50677-3). S&S.

ABC. Jan Pienkowski. (Concept Bks.). (Illus.). 32p. (ps-k). 1981. 3.95 o.s.i. (ISBN 0-671-44454-9, Little Simon). S&S.

ABC, an Alphabet Book. Photos by Thomas Matthiesen. (Illus.). 64p. (gr. 3 up). 1981. 3.95 o.p. (ISBN 0-448-41054-0, G&D); PLB 3.09 o.p. (ISBN 0-448-13607-4, G&D). Putnam Pub Group.

ABC & Counting Rhymes. (gr. k-3). 1963. 0.79 o.p. (ISBN 0-8431-4100-X). Wonder.

ABC & XYZ of Bee Culture. 38th ed. A. I. Root. (Illus.). 738p. 1982. 24.95 o.s.i. (ISBN 0-684-17479-0, ScribT). Scribner.

ABC & XYZ of Bee Culture. 39th ed. A. I. Root. (Illus.). 738p. 1983. 24.95 o.s.i. (ISBN 0-684-18024-3, ScribT). Scribner.

ABC Bible Characters. J. M. Stifle. (ps-1). 1982. pap. 1.75 o.p. (ISBN 0-570-04062-0, 56-1365). Concordia.

ABC Bible Stories. J. M. Stifle. (ps-1). 1982. pap. 1.75 o.p. (ISBN 0-570-04063-9, 56-1366). Concordia.

ABC Board Shape Book. (Board Shape Bks.). (Illus.). (ps). 1985. bds. 1.69 o.s.i. (ISBN 0-517-46319-9). Outlet Bk Co.

ABC Book about Jesus. J. M. Stifle. (ps-k). 1981. pap. 1.75 o.p. (ISBN 0-570-04054-X, 56-1715). Concordia.

ABC for the Library. Mary Little. LC 75-6825. (Illus.). 32p. (ps-1). 1975. 5.95 o.s.i. (ISBN 0-689-30467-6, Atheneum). Macmillan.

ABC of Church Music. Stephen Rhys & King Palmer. LC 73-83175. 1969. 7.50 o.s.i. (ISBN 0-8008-0010-9, Crescendo). Taplinger.

ABC of Democracy. Adolph Kreisberg. (ISBN 0-8022-0891-6). Philos Lib.

ABC of Ear, Nose & Throat. Huldman. 51p. 1981. pap. 10.50x o.p. (ISBN 0-7279-0078-1, Pub. by British Med Assoc UK). Taylor & Francis.

ABC of Endocrinology. K. J. Catt. 154p. 1972. 15.00 o.p. (ISBN 0-316-13190-3). Little.

ABC of Healthy Travel. Rev. ed. E. Walker & G. Williams. 39p. 1983. pap. 10.50 o.p. (ISBN 0-7279-0140-0, Pub. by British Med Assoc UK). Taylor & Francis.

ABC of Hypertension. 44p. 1981. pap. 11.50x o.p. (ISBN 0-7279-0074-9, Pub. by British Med Assoc UK). Taylor & Francis.

ABC of Lettering & Printing Types. Erik Lindegren. 1976. 25.00 o.s.i. (ISBN 0-8008-0011-7, Pentalic). Taplinger.

ABC of Monsters. Deborah Niland. (Illus.). (gr. k-2). 1978. text ed. 6.95 o.p. (ISBN 0-07-046560-6). McGraw.

ABC of One to Seven. H. Bernard Valman. 108p. 1982. pap. 20.50x o.p. (ISBN 0-7279-0086-2, Pub. by British Med Assoc UK). Taylor & Francis.

ABC of the Federal Reserve System. 12th ed. Edwin W. Kemmerer. LC 70-138118. (Illus.). 1971. Repr. of 1950 ed. lib. bdg. 22.50x o.p. (ISBN 0-8371-5694-7, KEFR). Greenwood.

ABCDEFGHIJKLMNOPQRSTUVWXYZ. Thomas M. Disch. 79p. 1981. pap. 6.95 o.p. (ISBN 0-686-72558-1). Small Pr Dist.

ABC's. Lawrence Henry. Ed. by Kate Klimo. (Learn with E.T. Ser.). (Illus.). 24p. 1983. pap. 1.90 o.s.i. (ISBN 0-671-46439-6, Little). S&S.

ABC's of Air Travel. George Davidson. LC 84-71960. (Illus.). 90p. (Orig.). 1984. pap. 2.50 ea. o.p. (ISBN 0-931921-00-7). ABC's Air.

ABC's of Athletic Injuries & Conditioning. Albert B. Ferguson & Jay Bender. LC 64-18772. 262p. 1970. Repr. of 1964 ed. 9.95 o.p. (ISBN 0-88275-017-8). Krieger.

ABC's of AutoCAD. Alan R. Miller. 350p. (Orig.). 1988. pap. 21.95 o.p. (ISBN 0-89588-498-4). Sybex.

ABC's of Christian Faith. James D. Smart. 1968. pap. 3.25 o.s.i. (ISBN 0-664-24820-9, Westminster). Westminster John Knox.

ABC's of Developing Software: A Primer on Essentials of Software Development. Sheldon D. Softky. (Illus.). 130p. 1985. pap. 13.95 o.p. W Kaufmann.

ABC's of Electronics. 3rd ed. Farl J. Waters. LC 77-93167. 1984. pap. 12.95 o.p. (ISBN 0-672-21507-1). Sams.

ABC's of Faith, Bk. 4. Francine O'Connor & Kathryn Boswell. (Illus.). (gr. 1-4). 1981. pap. 1.95 o.p. (ISBN 0-89243-138-5). Liguori Pubns.

ABC'S of IRA'S: The Complete Guide to Individual Retirement Accounts. William J. Grace, Jr. 1984. pap. 3.95 o.p. (ISBN 0-440-50398-1, Dell Trade Pbks). Dell.

ABC's of Lotus 1-2-3: A Step-by-Step Guide. Bill Kling. (Illus.). 432p. 1984. pap. 18.95 o.s.i. (ISBN 0-673-15996-5). Scott F.

ABC's of Microsoft WORD. Alan R. Neibauer. 321p. (Orig.). 1988. pap. 18.95 o.p. (ISBN 0-89588-497-6). Sybex.

ABC's of MS-DOS. Alan R. Miller. 224p. (Orig.). 1986. pap. 17.95 o.p. (ISBN 0-89588-395-3). Sybex.

ABC's of PC-DOS. Alan R. Miller. 231p. (Orig.). 1987. pap. 17.95 o.p. (ISBN 0-89588-438-0). Sybex.

ABC's of Prescription Drugs. Edward Edelson. LC 86-19845. 288p. 1987. 12.95 o.s.i. (ISBN 0-385-18558-8). Doubleday.

ABC's of Reloading. 2nd ed. Dean A. Grennell. LC 73-91588. (Illus.). 288p. 1980. pap. 9.95 o.p. (ISBN 0-695-81415-X). DBI.

ABC's of Reloading. 3rd ed. Dean A. Grennell. LC 73-91588. (Illus.). 288p. (Orig.). 1985. pap. 12.95 o.p. (ISBN 0-910676-84-4). DBI.

ABC's of Selling. Charles Futrell. LC 84-81731. 1988. pap. 24.95x o.p. (ISBN 0-256-03304-8). Irwin.

ABC's of S.T.D. A Guide to Sexually Transmitted Diseases. Alan Meltzer. (Illus.). 120p. 1983. pap. 4.95 o.p. (ISBN 0-920792-19-7). Eden Pr.

ABC's of the IBM PC. Joan Lasselle & Carol Ramsay. LC 83-61383. (Illus.). 143p. 1983. pap. 13.95 o.p. (ISBN 0-89588-102-0). SYBEX.

ABC's of 1-2-3. Chris Gilbert & Laurie Williams. 227p. 1984. pap. 15.95 o.p. (ISBN 0-89588-168-3). SYBEX.

Abdominal Pain. Donald J. Currie. (Illus.). 1979. text ed. 21.95 o.p. (ISBN 0-07-014942-9). McGraw.

Abdominal Ultrasonography. 2nd ed. Ed. by Barry B. Goldberg. LC 84-2257. 528p. 1984. 57.50x o.p. (ISBN 0-471-08569-3, Pub. by Wiley Med). Wiley.

Abduction. Gerd C. Seeber. LC 81-47465. 272p. 1983. 16.50 o.p. (ISBN 0-03-059404-9). H Holt & Co.

Abdul Haris Nasution: A Political Biography. C. L. Penders & Ulf Sundhaussen. LC 84-22010. (Illus.). 312p. 1985. text ed. 37.50 o.p. (ISBN 0-7022-1709-3). U of Queensland Pr.

Abe Lincoln, Make It Right! Dorothy F. Richards. LC 78-7690. (Illus.). (gr. k-4). 1978. PLB 7.95 o.p. (ISBN 0-89565-033-9). Childs World.

Abecedarium Philosophicum. A. Owen Barfield. 1986. pap. 2.50 o.p. (ISBN 0-916786-90-0). St George Bk Serv.

Abel, No. 13. Louise Bernikow. 1982. pap. 2.75 o.s.i. (ISBN 0-345-30212-5). Ballantine.

Abel-Baker-Charley. John R. Maxim. 1983. 15.45 o.p. (ISBN 0-395-34409-3). HM.

Abelard. Cedric H. Whitman. LC 65-22057. 1965. 10.50x o.s.i. (ISBN 0-674-00100-1). Harvard U Pr.

Abelian Categories with Applications to Rings & Modules. N. Popescu. (London Mathematical Society Monographs). 1973. 82.50 o.p. (ISBN 0-12-561550-7). Acad Pr.

Abelian Group Theory: Proceedings of the 2nd New Mexico State University Bicentennial Conference on Abelian Group, Held at Las Cruces, New Mexico, Dec. 9-12 1976. Ed. by D. M. Arnold et al. (Lecture Notes in Mathematics: Vol. 616). 1977. pap. text ed. 26.00 o.p. (ISBN 0-387-08447-9). Springer-Verlag.

Abelian Groups & Modules. Ed. by R. Gobel et al. (CISM International Centre for Mechanical Sciences Ser.: Vol. 287). (Illus.). xii, 531p. 1985. pap. 40.60 o.p. (ISBN 0-387-81847-2). Springer-Verlag.

Abel's Daughter. Rachel Maddux. 1978. pap. 1.75 o.p. (ISBN 0-380-39040-X, 39040). Avon.

Abenteuer Eines Brotbeutels und Andere Geschichten. Heinrich Boll. Ed. by Richard Plant. (Ger). 1958. pap. 2.25x o.p. (ISBN 0-393-09459-6, NortonC). Norton.

Abenteuer Im Wattenmeer. Stefan De Haan. Ed. by John H. Brown. 1971. pap. 4.48 o.p. (ISBN 0-395-12501-4). HM.

Abhumanisme. Jacques Audiberti. 232p. 1955. 9.95 o.p. (ISBN 0-686-54479-X). French & Eur.

Abide in Me: A Pocket Guide to Daily Scriptural Prayer. David Rosage. 240p. 1987. text ed. 7.95 o.p. (ISBN 0-89283-363-7). Servant.

Abiding Appalachia: Where Mountain & Atom Meet. Marilou B. Thompson-Awiakta. LC 78-12970. (Illus.). 94p. 1978. 8.95 o.s.i. (ISBN 0-918518-09-1, St Luke TN); pap. 8.95 o.p. (ISBN 0-918518-15-6). Peachtree Pubs.

Abilene, Texas. (Panel Advisory Service Report Ser.). 63p. 1981. pap. 10.00 o.p. (ISBN 0-317-06735-4, A-11). Urban Land.

Abilene: The Key City. Juanita D. Zachry. LC 86-7818. (Illus.). 128p. 1986. 22.95 o.p. (ISBN 0-89781-150-X). Windsor Pubns Inc.

Abnormal & Clinical Psychology: An Introductory Text. J. E. Orme. LC 84-45285. 240p. 1984. 31.00 o.p. (ISBN 0-7099-1939-5, Pub. by Croom Helm Ltd); pap. 16.00 o.p. (ISBN 0-7099-1940-9). Routledge Chapman & Hall.

Abnormal Behavior: A Guide to Information Sources. Ed. by Henry Leland & Marilyn W. Deutsch. LC 80-65. (Psychology Information Guide Ser.: Vol. 5). 280p. 1980. 68.00x o.p. (ISBN 0-8103-1416-9). Gale.

Abnormal Behavior: Perspectives in Conflict. 2nd ed. Richard R. Price. LC 77-20504. 1978. pap. 18.95 o.p. (ISBN 0-03-089964-8, HoltC). HR&W.

Abnormal Behaviors: Outlined Reference. Jim Smith. LC 83-1074. 176p. (Orig.). 1983. pap. text ed. 14.00 o.p. (ISBN 0-8191-3031-1). U Pr of Amer.

Abnormal Offenders, Delinquency & the Criminal Justice System. Ed. by John Gunn & David P. Farrington. LC 81-14657. (Current Research in Forensic Psychiatry & Psychology Ser.: Vol. 1). 384p. 1982. 79.95x o.p. (ISBN 0-471-28047-X, Pub. by Wiley-Interscience). Wiley.

Abnormal Postural Reflex Activity Caused by Brain Lesions. 2nd ed. B. Bobath. (Illus.). 1976. pap. 12.50 o.s.i. (ISBN 0-433-03332-0). E J Brill USA.

Abnormal Psychology. Ed. by Thomas R. Coleman. 185p. 1974. text ed. 29.95x o.p. (ISBN 0-8290-2134-5). Irvington.

Abnormal Psychology. rev. ed. Raleigh M. Drake. (Quality Paperback Ser.: No. 101). 193p. 1972. pap. 4.95 o.p. (ISBN 0-8226-0101-X). Littlefield.

Abnormal Psychology. Judith E. Gallatin. 1982. text ed. (ISBN 0-02-475510-9). Macmillan.

Abnormal Psychology. David C. Rimm & John W. Somervill. 696p. 1977. 32.40 o.p. (ISBN 0-12-588840-6); instrs'manual 13.50i o.p. (ISBN 0-12-588842-2). Acad Pr.

Abnormal Psychology. 5th ed. Irwin G. Sarason & Barbara R. Sarason. (Illus.). 608p. 1987. text ed. (ISBN 0-13-000381-6). P-H.

Abnormal Psychology, A Perspectives Approach. James D. Smrtic. 234p. (Orig.). 1980. pap. text ed. 11.95 o.p. Avery Pub.

Abnormal Psychology & Modern Life. 7th ed. James C. Coleman & James N. Butcher. 1984. text ed. write for info. o.p. (ISBN 0-673-15886-1). Scott F.

Abnormal Psychology: Changing Concepts. 2nd ed. Melvin Zax & Emory L. Cowen. LC 75-38894. 1976. text ed. 19.95 o.p. (ISBN 0-03-089517-0, HoltC). HR&W.

Abnormal Psychology: The Problem of Maladaptive Behavior. 4th ed. Irwin J. Sarason & Barbara R. Sarason. (Illus.). 544p. 1984. text ed. (ISBN 0-13-000638-6). P-H.

Abode of an Unknown God: A Study of Ancient Egypt & the Significance of the Great Pyramid. Lois M. Shaw. (Illus.). 96p. 1980. 5.00 o.p. (ISBN 0-682-49585-9). Exposition-Phoenix.

Abode of Life. Lee Corey. (Gregg Press Science Fiction - Star Trek Ser.). 208p. 1986. lib. bdg. 11.95x o.p. (ISBN 0-8398-2931-0, Gregg). G k Hall.

Abolition of Slavery in Brazil: 1880-1888. Robert B. Toplin. LC 79-139329. 1975. 10.00x o.s.i. (ISBN 0-689-10500-2, Atheneum); pap. text ed. 4.25x o.s.i. (ISBN 0-689-70526-3, NL34). Macmillan.

Abolition or Reform? The Metropolitan Counties & the GLC. Norman Flynn et al. LC 84-24384. (Local Government Briefings Ser.). 120p. 1985. text ed. 34.95x o.p. (ISBN 0-04-352119-3). Unwin Hyman.

Abolitionists. Dan Lacy. 1978. text ed. 9.95 o.p. (ISBN 0-07-035753-6). McGraw.

Aboriginal & Spanish Colonial Trinidad: A Study in Cultural Contact. L. Newson. 1976. 59.50 o.p. (ISBN 0-12-517450-0). Acad Pr.

Aboriginal Music: Education for Living: Cross Cultural Experiences from South Australia. Catherine J. Ellis. LC 83-10630. (Scholars Library). (Illus.). 236p. 1985. text ed. 37.50x o.p. (ISBN 0-7022-1992-4). U of Queensland Pr.

Aboriginal Place Names of New York. William M. Beauchamp. LC 68-17915. 342p. 1972. Repr. of 1907 ed. 44.00x o.p. (ISBN 0-8103-3231-0). Gale.

Aboriginal Sign Languages of the Americas & Australia. Ed. by D. J. Umiker-Sebeok & T. A. Sebeok. Incl. Vol. 1. North America - Classic Comparative Perspectives. LC 78-1303. 474p (ISBN 0-306-31073-2); Vol. 2. The Americas & Australia. LC 78-1303. 480p (ISBN 0-306-31081-3). 1978. 75.00x ea. o.p. (Plenum Pr). Plenum Pub.

Abortion: An Eternal Social & Moral Issue. Ed. by Mark A. Siegel et al. (Information Aids Ser.). 88p. 1986. pap. 15.95 o.p. (ISBN 0-936474-54-8). Info Plus TX.

Abortion & the Christian: What Every Believer Should Know. John J. Davis. 125p. 1984. pap. 4.95 o.p. (ISBN 0-8010-2964-3). Baker Bk.

Abortion Papers: Inside the Abortion Mentality. Bernard N. Nathanson. LC 83-81126. 240p. 1983. 14.95 o.p. (ISBN 0-8119-0593-4). Fell.

Abortion Papers: Inside the Abortion Mentality. Bernard N. Nathanson. 240p. 1984. pap. 9.95 o.p. (ISBN 0-8119-0685-X). Fell.

Abortion Parley. Ed. by James Burtchaell. 352p. 20.00 o.p. (LL9009). Sheed & Ward MO.

Abortion Politics. McGraw.

Abortion Politics: Private Morality & Public Policy. Frederick S. Jaffe et al. LC 80-17035. 224p. 1981. text ed. 29.95 o.p. (ISBN 0-07-032189-2). McGraw.

Abortion: Sexual Suicide. Jacky Hertz. 35p. (Orig.). 1971. pap. 0.35 o.p. (ISBN 0-913382-09-4, 105-22). Prow Bks-Franciscan.

Abortion: The Catholic Debate in America. Hans Lotstra. 340p. 1985. 39.50x o.s.i. (ISBN 0-8290-0728-8). Irvington.

Abortion, The Claims of the Body & the Deceit of "Choice" Vivian De Danois. (Illus.). 1978. deluxe ed. 117.50 o.p. (ISBN 0-930582-10-1). Gloucester Art.

Abounding in Hope: A Family of Faith at Work through the Lutheran World Federation. Charles P. Lutz. LC 85-1216. 144p. (Orig.). 1985. pap. 5.95 o.p. (ISBN 0-8066-2158-3, 10-0123, Augsburg). Augsburg Fortress.

About Antiques. Ella S. Bowles. LC 70-174011. (Tower Bks). (Illus.). 272p. 1971. Repr. of 1929 ed. 40.00x o.p. (ISBN 0-8103-3921-8). Gale.

About Bats: A Chiropteran Symposium. Ed. by Bob H. Slaughter & Dan W. Walton. LC 71-138650. (No. 11). (Illus.). 352p. (Orig.). 1970. pap. 11.95x o.p. (ISBN 0-87074-107-1). SMU Press.

About Bolton. Esther K. Whitcomb. (Illus.). xi, 463p. 1988. 35.00 o.p. (ISBN 1-55613-105-4). Heritage Bk.

About Face: An Hour a Week to Radiant Skin & Flawless Make-Up. Jeffrey Bruce & Sherry S. Cohen. (Illus.). 160p. 1985. pap. 8.95 o.p. (ISBN 0-399-51112-1, Perigee). Putnam Pub Group.

About Old Story-Tellers. Donald G. Mitchell. LC 75-159859. 237p. 1979. Repr. of 1877 ed. 45.00x o.p. (ISBN 0-8103-3732-0). Gale.

About People for a Special Time. Gladys S. Stump. 1981. pap. 7.95 o.p. (ISBN 0-8163-0353-3). Pacific Pr Pub Assn.

About Your Brain. Seymour Simon & Dennis Kendrick. 64p. 1981. text ed. 8.95 o.p. (ISBN 0-07-057437-5). McGraw.

Above Every Name: The Lordship of Christ & Social Systems. Ed. by Thomas E. Clarke. LC 80-82082. (Woodstock Studies). 312p. (Orig.). 1980. pap. 8.95 o.p. (ISBN 0-8091-2338-X). Paulist Pr.

Above Los Angeles. Robert Cameron. LC 76-28657. 1977. 24.95 o.p. (ISBN 0-918684-03-X). Cameron & Co.

Above San Francisco, Vol. II. Robert Cameron. LC 70-103848. 1977. 19.95 o.p. (ISBN 0-918684-05-6). Cameron & Co.

Abraham Lincoln. Norman Kolpas. Ed. by Eleanor Nichols. (Great Leaders Ser.). (Illus.). 69p. 1981. text ed. 7.95 o.p. (ISBN 0-07-035265-8). McGraw.

Abraham Lincoln. Emil Ludwig. (Black & Gold Lib). (Illus.). 1949. 7.95 o.p. (ISBN 0-87140-884-8). Liveright.

Abraham Lincoln: From His Own Words & Contemporary Accounts. Ed. by Roy E. Appleman. (National Park Service Source Ser.: Bk. 2). (Illus.). 55p. 1942. pap. 2.25 o.p. (S/N 024-005-00156-5). USGPO.

Abraham Lincoln: The Prairie Years. Carl Sandburg. LC 28-5762. 1939. Boxed Set. 80.00 o.s.i. (ISBN 0-15-100779-9). HarBraceJ.

Abraham Lincoln: The Prairie Years & the War Years. Carl Sandburg. 1939. 6 vols. 240.00 o.s.i. (ISBN 0-15-102570-3). HarBraceJ.

Abraham Lincoln: The Prairie Years & the War Years. rev. ed. Carl Sandburg. LC 74-122389. (Illus.). 640p. (1 Vol.). 1970. Repr. of 1954 ed. 17.95 o.s.i. (ISBN 0-15-100640-7). HarBraceJ.

Abraham Lincoln: The War Years, 4 Vols. Carl Sandburg. LC 39-27998. 1939. Set. 160.00 o.s.i. (ISBN 0-15-101610-0); Vols. 1 & 2. 80.00 o.s.i. (ISBN 0-15-101608-9); Vols. 3 & 4. 80.00 o.s.i. (ISBN 0-15-101609-7). HarBraceJ.

Abroad in England. Frank Entwisle. (Illus.). 1983. 14.50 o.p. (ISBN 0-393-01755-9). Norton.

Absent in the Spring. Mary Westmacott. LC 70-150379. 256p. 1981. pap. 5.95 o.p. (ISBN 0-87795-350-3, Arbor Hse). Morrow.

Absenteeism: A Selective Bibliography. Lorna Peterson. (Public Administration Ser.: P 1724). 11p. 1985. 2.00 o.p. (ISBN 0-89028-494-6). Vance Biblios.

Absolute Being. Jorge Tallet. 74p. 1959. (ISBN 0-8022-1687-0). Philos Lib.

Absolute Liberty: A Selection from the Articles & Papers of Caroline Robbins. Ed. by Barbara Taft. LC 82-1725. (Studies in British History & Culture Ser.: Vol. VIII). 460p. 1982. 32.50 o.p. (ISBN 0-208-01955-3, Archon). Shoe String.

Absolute Nothingness: Foundations for a Buddhist-Christian Dialogue. Hans Waldenfels. Tr. by James W. Heisig from Ger. LC 80-81442. Orig. Title: Absolutes Nichts. 224p. 1980. pap. 8.95 o.p. (ISBN 0-8091-2316-9). Paulist Pr.

Absolute Surrender: A Guide to the Spirit-Filled Life. Andrew Murray. 142p. 1987. pap. 3.95 o.p. (ISBN 0-310-55132-3, 19013P). Zondervan.

Absolutely Definite Philosophy for the Intelligence of Contemporary Man. Paul W. Wintercross. (Illus.). 1980. deluxe ed. 117.75 o.p. (ISBN 0-89266-221-2). Am Classical Coll Pr.

Absolutely, Positively Overnight. Robert A. Sigafoos. LC 83-9482. (Illus.). 192p. (Orig.). 1983. pap. 9.95 o.p. (ISBN 0-918518-27-X, St Luke TN). Peachtree Pubs.

Absoluteness of Christianity & the History of Religions. Ernst Troeltsch. LC 74-133242. 1971. 7.95 o.p. (ISBN 0-8042-0462-4, John Knox). Westminster John Knox.

Absolutes Nichts see Absolute Nothingness: Foundations for a Buddhist-Christian Dialogue.

Absorbed Monolayers on Solid Surfaces. G. A. Somorjai & M. A. Van Hove. LC 67-11280. (Structure & Bonding Ser.: Vol. 38). (Illus.). 1979. 39.30 o.p. (ISBN 0-387-09582-9). Springer-Verlag.

Absorption Spectra, Vols. 18 & 19. Lang. 1974. Vol. 18. 95.50 o.p. (ISBN 0-12-436318-0); Vol. 19. 95.50 o.p. (ISBN 0-12-436319-9). Acad Pr.

Abstract Algebra. Violet H. Larney. LC 75-28495. 1975. text ed. write for info. o.p. (ISBN 0-87150-209-7, PWS 1711, Prindle). PWS-Kent Pub.

Abstract Algebra: An Active Learning Approach. Neil A. Davidson & Frances F. Gulick. LC 75-19537. (Illus.). 1976. text ed. 22.75 o.p. (ISBN 0-395-20663-4). HM.

Abstract Harmonic Analysis: Vol. 1, Structure of Topological Groups, Integration Theory, Group Representations. E. Hewitt & K. A. Ross. (Grundlehren der Mathematischen Wissenschaften Ser.: Vol. 115). 1963. 54.30 o.p. (ISBN 0-387-02983-4). Springer-Verlag.

Abstract Inference. Ulf Grenander. LC 80-22016. (Probability & Mathematical Statistics Ser.). 526p. 1981. 49.95x o.p. (ISBN 0-471-08267-8). Wiley.

Abstract Non Linear Wave Equations. M. C. Reed. (Lecture Notes in Mathematics: Vol. 507). 128p. 1976. pap. 13.00 o.p. (ISBN 0-387-07617-4). Springer-Verlag.

Abstracts of Methods Used to Assess Fish Quality. S. Jhaveri & J. Montecalvo, Jr. (Technical Report Ser.: No. 69). 104p. 1978. 3.00 o.p. (ISBN 0-938412-00-0, P777). Sea Grant Pubns.

Abstracts of Papers: Proceedings of the 9th International Conference on Cartography, College Park, MD, 1978. International Conference on Cartography Staff. 96p. 1978. 9.00 o.p. (ISBN 0-317-32442-X, C100). Am Congrs Survey.

Abstracts of Presentations: Proceedings. Deutsche Gesellschaft Fur Biophysik, Annual Meeting, Konstanz, October 1979. Ed. by G. Adam & G. Stark. 1979. pap. 19.00 o.p. (ISBN 0-387-09684-1). Springer-Verlag.

Abstracts of the Second International Congress on Child Abuse & Neglect. International Congress on Child Abuse & Neglect, 2nd, London 1978. Ed. by A. White Franklin. LC 78-41195. 1979. pap. 70.00 o.p. (ISBN 0-08-023438-0). Pergamon.

Abstracts of the Twelfth CINP Congress, Gothenberg, Sweden, 22-26 June, 1980. 400p. 1980. 70.00 o.p. (ISBN 0-08-026383-6). Pergamon.

Absurd. A. P. Hinchliffe. (Critical Idiom Ser.). 105p. 1969. pap. 5.50 o.p. (ISBN 0-416-14540-X, NO.2233). Routledge Chapman & Hall.

Absurdity, Insecurity & Despair. James Park. (Existential Freedom Ser.: No. 8). 1975. pap. 5.00x o.p. (ISBN 0-89231-008-1). Existential Bks.

Abuse This Word. Patrick Cosgrove & Lawrence Hussar. (Illus.). 1980. pap. 3.95 o.p. (ISBN 0-380-76117-3, 76117-3). Avon.

Abysmal Gloom. Robert Adams. (Illus.). 32p. 1984. bds. 11.95 laminated o.p. (ISBN 0-584-62073-X). Salem Hse Pubs.

AC Electric Locomotives of the British Rail. Brian Webb & John Duncan. (Illus.). 1979. 24.95 o.p. (ISBN 0-7153-7663-2). David & Charles.

AC 61-82 ATP Rotorcraft: Helicopter Flight Test Guide. Date not set. pap. 2.75 o.p. Aviation.

Academic Achievement Job. Wise. (Out Disc Econ One Ser.). 1979. text ed. 19.00 o.p. (ISBN 0-8240-4146-1). Garland Pub.

Academic Ambitions & Library Development: The American Bureau of Industrial Research & the State Historical Society of Wisconsin, 1904-18. John C. Colson. (Occasional Papers: No. 159). 53p. 1983. pap. 3.00 o.p. (ISBN 0-317-59006-5). U of Ill Lib Info Sci.

Academic American Encyclopedia, 21 vols. rev. ed. Ed. by Ann Ranson. LC 85-27032. (Illus.). 1987. text ed. write for info. o.p. (ISBN 0-7172-2020-6). Grolier Inc.

Academic Architecture & the Work of Paul Schweikher: A Selected Bibliography. Bibliographic Research Library Staff. (Architecture Ser.: A 1392). 8p. 1985. 2.00 o.p. (ISBN 0-89028-402-4). Vance Biblios.

Academic Degrees. Walter C. Eells & Harold A. Haswell. LC 70-128397. 332p. Repr. of 1960 ed. 35.00x o.p. (ISBN 0-8103-3015-6). Gale.

Academic English. Lee D. Rossi & Michael Gasser. 300p. 1983. pap. text ed. (ISBN 0-13-000950-4). P-H.

Academic Festival Overtures. Daryl Hine. LC 84-45704. 208p. 1985. 20.00 o.p. (ISBN 0-689-11573-3, Atheneum). pap. 10.95 o.p. (ISBN 0-689-11580-6, Atheneum). Macmillan.

Academic Microfile. 1983. 720.00 o.p. Learned Info.

Academic Murder. Dorsey Fiske. 256p. 1987. pap. 3.50 o.p. (ISBN 1-55547-179-X). Critics Choice Paper.

Academic Status Survey. 340p. 1981. 17.00 o.p. (ISBN 0-8389-6737-X). Assn Coll & Res Libs.

Academic Testing & the Consumer. Ed. by Scarvia B. Anderson & Louisa V. Coburn. LC 81-48587. (Testing & Measurement Ser.: No. 16). 1982. 13.95x o.p. Jossey-Bass.

Academic Tribes. Hazard Adams. 1976. 8.95 o.p. (ISBN 0-87140-623-3); pap. 3.95 o.p. (ISBN 0-87140-111-8). Liveright.

Academic Who's Who 1975-76: University Teachers in the British Isles in the Arts, Education & Social Sciences. 2nd ed. 784p. 1975. 45.00x o.p. (ISBN 0-8103-2020-7). Gale.

Academic Year: A Novel. 2nd ed. D. J. Enright. 1987. 15.95 o.p. (ISBN 0-907675-29-8, Pub. by Buchan & Enright England). Seven Hills Bk Dists.

Academica: Plato, Philip of Opus, & the Pseudo-Platonic Epinomis. Leonardo Taran. LC 74-78092. (Memoirs Ser.: Vol. 107). 1975. 20.00 o.p. (ISBN 0-87169-107-8). Am Philos.

Academics in the Eighties. James Everett & Leland Entrekin. 156p. 1986. 26.00 o.p. (ISBN 0-949614-23-8, Pub. by Croom Helm UK). Routledge Chapman & Hall.

Academics in the Eighties. James Everett & Leland Entrekin. 156p. 1987. lib. bdg. 33.00x o.p. (Pub. by Croom Helm UK). Routledge Chapman & Hall.

Academy of Terror. Steven Charles. (Private School Ser.: No. 2). (YA) (gr. 7 up). pap. 2.50 o.p. (ISBN 0-671-60327-2). Archway.

Acadia: The Geography of Early Nova Scotia to 1760. Andrew H. Clark. (Illus.). 470p. 1969. 30.00x o.p. (ISBN 0-299-05080-7). U of Wis Pr.

Acapulco. Burt Hirschfeld. LC 79-169925. 1971. 7.50 o.p. (ISBN 0-87795-021-0, Arbor Hse). Morrow.

Accelerated Cooling of Steel. Ed. by P. D. Southwick. LC 86-8533. (Illus.). 606p. 1986. 110.00 o.p. (ISBN 0-87339-020-2). Minerals Metals.

Accelerated Growth Planning: Profit Improvement Strategies for Consumer, Industrial, & Service Business Game Plans. Mack Hanan. LC 77-13201. (Illus.). 1978. text ed. 29.95 o.p. (ISBN 0-07-025971-2). McGraw.

Accelerator Health Physics. H. Wade Paterson & Ralph H. Thomas. 1973. 59.50 o.p. (ISBN 0-12-547150-5). Acad Pr.

Accent Buyer's Guide: 1986-87 Edition. 5th ed. 10.00 o.p. (1460). Cheever Pub.

Accent Guide: One Hundred Fifty-One Tax Deductions You Can Take. Gregory Thomsen & Paul M. McInerny. (Orig.). 1982. pap. 3.50 o.p. (ISBN 0-915708-14-0). Cheever Pub.

Accent Onliving Buyers Guide, 1986-87: Your Number One Source of Information on Products for the Disabled. 5th ed. Betty Garee. 152p. 1985. pap. 10.00 o.p. Cheever Pub.

Accented Russian Reader. Ed. by Horace G. Lunt. 1957. text ed. 34.40x o.p. (ISBN 90-2791-014-6). Mouton.

Acceptable Inequalities. Ian Bowen. 148p. 1970. 6.50x o.p. (ISBN 0-7735-0101-0, Pub. by McGill Canada). U of Toronto Pr.

Acceptable Losses. Irwin Shaw. LC 82-72056. 1982. 14.95 o.p. (ISBN 0-87795-437-2, Arbor Hse). Morrow.

Access. Richard S. Wurman. (Access Guidebooks). (Illus.). 184p. 1986. pap. 14.95 o.p. Access Pr.

Accessibility: The Rural Challenge. Malcolm J. Moseley. (Illus.). 1979. 32.00x o.p. (ISBN 0-416-71220-7, NO.2328). Routledge Chapman & Hall.

Accessible Wilderness. George Cowles. 110p. (Orig.). 1985. pap. 6.95 o.s.i. (ISBN 0-934318-50-6). Falcon Pr MT.

Accessioning: Registration, Documentation, & Filing. rev. ed. Kevin W. Sandifer. Ed. by Rowland P. Gill. (Layman's Guide to Religious Archival Science Ser.: No. 2). 1985. pap. text ed. 2.50x o.s.i. (ISBN 0-910653-07-0, 8101-H). Archival Servs.

ACCH Resource Directory. 100p. 1985. 13.50 o.p. (ISBN 0-318-18154-1); members 9.00 o.p. (ISBN 0-318-18155-X). Assn Care Child.

Accident. Elie Wiesel. Tr. by Ann Borchardt. 128p. 1985. pap. 6.95 o.p. (ISBN 0-8090-1525-0). Hill & Wang.

Accident Analysis, Ride Quality, Driver Education & Behavior Research. (Transportation Research Record Ser.). 68p. 1978. 4.40 o.p. (ISBN 0-309-02812-4). Transport Res Bd.

Accident at Three Mile Island: The Need for Change, the Legacy of TMI. Ed. by John G. Kemeny. (Illus.). 201p. 1980. 55.00 o.p. (ISBN 0-08-025949-9); pap. 50.00 o.p. (ISBN 0-08-025946-4). Pergamon.

Accident Case & Family Law Guide: A Dialoque & Translation Between Attorney & the Spanish Client. Iris Lippe. 138p. 1984. 19.95 o.p. (ISBN 0-910531-06-4). Wolcotts.

Accident Causation. Society of Automotive Engineers Staff. LC 80-65072. 1980. 28.00 o.p. (ISBN 0-89883-232-2, SP461). Soc Auto Engineers.

Accident Facts 1987. (Illus.). 106p. 1987. pap. 13.10 o.p. (ISBN 0-87912-137-8, 02167). Natl Safety Coun.

Accident of Birth. Edith Begner. 1977. pap. 1.95 o.p. (ISBN 0-380-00990-0, 32672). Avon.

Accident Prevention on Board Ship at Sea & in Port. 4th ed. 1984. 11.40 o.p. (ISBN 92-2-101837-7). Intl Labour Office.

Accident Prevention on Board Ship at Sea & in Port: An ILO Code of Practice. 5th ed. xi, 188p. 1986. 14.00 o.p. Intl Labour Office.

Accidental Death of an Anarchist. Dario Fo. pap. 4.95 o.p. (ISBN 0-413-15610-9). Heinemann Ed.

Accidental Hypothermia. MacLean & Emslie. (Illus.). 488p. 1977. 56.75 o.p. (ISBN 0-632-00831-8, B-3067-3). Mosby.

Accidental Tourist. Anne Tyler. (General Ser.). 464p. 1986. lib. bdg. 18.95 o.s.i. (ISBN 0-8161-4055-3, Large Print Bks). G K Hall.

Accidents: Causes, Prevention & Services. Kenneth S. Cliff. LC 84-9567. 301p. 1984. 29.95 o.p. (ISBN 0-7099-0792-3, Pub. by Croom Helm Ltd). Routledge Chapman & Hall.

Accidents, Compensation & the Law. 3rd ed. P. S. Atiyah. (Law in Context Ser.). xxiv, 695p. 1980. 47.00x o.p. (ISBN 0-297-77754-8, Pub. by Weidenfeld & Nicolson England). Rothman.

Acclimatization. Steve Van Matre. 7.00 o.p. Inst Earth.

Acclimatizing. Steve Van Matre. 8.00 o.p. (ISBN 0-87603-016-9). Inst Earth.

Accompagnes de la Flute. Jean Giono. (Illus.). 148p. 1959. 125.00 o.p. (ISBN 0-686-53947-8). French & Eur.

Accomplices. Georges Simenon. Tr. by Bernard Frechtman. 1977. pap. 2.25 o.p. (ISBN 0-15-602670-8, Harv). HarBraceJ.

According to Hoyle. rev. ed. Ed. by Richard L. Frey. 1981. pap. 2.95 o.p. (ISBN 0-449-23652-8, Crest). Fawcett.

According to John: The New Look at the Fourth Gospel. Archibald M. Hunter. LC 69-14199. 1969. pap. 2.95 o.s.i. (ISBN 0-664-24850-0, Westminster). Westminster John Knox.

Account Book for Farm & Ranch Management. 7th ed. Kent D. Olson et al. 128p. 1989. text ed. write for info. o.p. Burgess MN Intl.

Account Book for Farm & Ranch Management. 6th ed. Delane E. Welsch et al. 128p. 1985. text ed. write for info. o.p. (ISBN 0-8087-3775-9). Burgess MN Intl.

Account of An Expedition from Pittsburgh to the Rocky Mountains, Performed in the Years 1819 & 1820, 2 vols. Compiled by Edwin James. LC 68-55198. 1970. Repr. of 1823 ed. Set. lib. bdg. 24.75x o.p. (ISBN 0-8371-8599-8, JAPI). Greenwood.

Account of the Cultivation & Manufacture of Tea in China. Samuel Ball. LC 78-74309. (Modern Chinese Economy Ser.). 382p. 1980. lib. bdg. 51.00 o.p. (ISBN 0-8240-4250-6). Garland Pub.

Account of the Ottoman Conquest of Egypt in the Year A. H. 922 (A. D. 1516) Ibn Iyas. Tr. by W. H. Salmon from Arabic. LC 79-2867. 117p. 1980. Repr. of 1921 ed. 15.25 o.s.i. (ISBN 0-8305-0040-5). Hyperion Conn.

Account of the Polynesian Race: Its Origin & Migration, 3 vols. in 1. Abraham Fornander. LC 69-13505. (Illus.). 1980. Repr. of 1878 ed. Set. 37.50 o.p. (ISBN 0-8048-0002-2). C E Tuttle.

Account of the State of Agriculture & Grazing in New South Wales. James Atkinson. (Illus.). 184p. 1975. Repr. of 1826 ed. 21.00x o.p. (ISBN 0-424-06960-1, Pub by Sydney U Pr). Intl Spec Bk.

Accountability & Prisons: Opening up a Closed World. Ed. by John Vagg & Mike Maguire. 250p. 1986. text ed. 36.00 o.p. (ISBN 0-317-39830-X, 9774, Pub. by Tavistock England). Routledge Chapman & Hall.

Accountability in Development, National & International: How to Have Development with the Least Bureacracy. (Leslie Sawhney Programme Ser.). 160p. 1982. text ed. 18.95x o.p. (ISBN 0-7069-1429-5, Pub. by Vikas India). Advent NY.

Accountancy & the British Economy, Eighteen Forty to Nineteen Eighty: The Evolution of Ernst & Whitney. Edgar Jones. (Illus.). 288p. 1981. 47.50 o.p. (ISBN 0-7134-3776-6, Pub. by Batsford England). David & Charles.

Accountant's Desk Handbook. 2nd rev. ed. Albert P. Ameiss & Nicholas A. Kargas. 437p. 1981. text ed. 49.95 o.p. (ISBN 0-13-001461-3). P-H.

Accountants' Liability: 1981. Practising Law Institute Staff & Dan L. Goldwasser. LC 81-80633. (Litigation & Administrative Practice Ser.). 404p. 1981. write for info. o.p. PLI.

Accountants' Liability 1984. (Litigation & Administrative Practice, Course Handbook Ser. 1983-1984). 435p. 1984. 15.00 o.p. (ISBN 0-686-80266-7, H4-4918). PLI.

Accounting, Vol. 6. Compiled by James W. Dean & Richard Schwindt. 232p. 1985. 14.00 o.p. (ISBN 0-88024-106-3). Eno River Pr.

Accounting: An Introduction. K. W. Perry. 1971. text ed. 33.95 o.p. (ISBN 0-07-049425-8). McGraw.

Accounting & Fianancing for Motor Carriers. Philip C. Cheng. LC 83-48661. 448p. 1984. 49.00x o.p. (ISBN 0-669-07340-7). Lexington Bks.

Accounting & Financial Management. National Association of Home Builders Staff. 68p. 1985. pap. 24.00 o.p. (ISBN 0-86718-232-6). Nat Assn H Build.

Accounting & Information Systems Study Manual: Canadian CEBS Course 6. Dalhousie University Staff. 300p. (Orig.). 1986. pap. 45.00 wkbk. o.p. (ISBN 0-89154-310-4). Intl Found Employ.

Accounting & Management Action. 2nd ed. Jack C. Gray & Kenneth S. Johnston. (Illus.). 1977. text ed. 34.95 o.p. (ISBN 0-07-024216-X). McGraw.

Accounting & the Lawyer. 303p. 1980. 3.00 o.p. (ISBN 0-318-02379-2). ICLE Georgia.

Accounting: Concepts & Applications. Paul R. Berney & Stanley J. Gartska. 1984p. 42.95 o.p. (ISBN 0-256-02964-4). Irwin.

Accounting Cycle: A Self-Study Review Program. Harry R. Mathis. 210p. 1986. pap. text ed. 16.95 o.p. (ISBN 0-89917-472-8, Pub. by Coll Town Pr). Tichenor Pub.

Accounting Desk Book. 6th ed. William H. Behrenfeld. 1979. 49.50 o.p. (ISBN 0-87624-009-0, Inst Busn Plan). P-H.

Accounting Desk Book. 7th ed. Douglas L. Blensly & Tom M. Plank. LC 82-6231. 448p. 1983. text ed. 54.50 o.p. (ISBN 0-87624-010-4, Inst Busn Plan). P-H.

Accounting Desk Book. 5th ed. Stephen R. Novak. LC 73-11994. 500p. 1977. 29.95 o.p. (ISBN 0-87624-008-2, Inst Busn Plan). P-H.

Accounting Essentials. Neal Margolis & N. Paul Harmon. LC 72-4756. (Self-Teaching Guides Ser.). 308p. 1972. pap. text ed. 10.95 o.p. (ISBN 0-471-56867-8, Pub. by Wiley Pr). Wiley.

Accounting Experience with the Apple II Microcomputer: A Service Firm. Kelley. 1983. pap. 17.95t o.p. (ISBN 0-256-02955-5). Irwin.

Accounting Experience with the IBM Microcomputer: A Merchandising Firm. Jane Kelley. 1985. 21.95x o.p. (ISBN 0-256-03438-9). Irwin.

Accounting Experience with the IBM Microcomputer: A Service Firm. 2nd ed. Kelley. 1985. pap. 21.95x o.p. (ISBN 0-256-03437-0). Irwin.

Accounting, Finance, & Taxation: A Basic Guide for Small Business. C. Richard Baker & Rick S. Hayes. LC 79-16481. 384p. 1983. 24.95 o.p. (ISBN 0-8436-0784-X); pap. 14.95 o.p. (ISBN 0-8436-0859-5). Van Nos Reinhold.

Accounting for Control & Decisions. Holmes et al. Irwin.

Accounting for Employee Benefits. (Financial Report Survey Ser.: No. 14). 1977. pap. 10.00 o.p. (ISBN 0-685-92034-8). Am Inst CPA.

Accounting for Franchise Fee Revenue. 1973. pap. 3.50 o.p. (ISBN 0-685-36115-2). Am Inst CPA.

Accounting for Government & Non-Profit Entities. 7th ed. Leon E. Hay. 1985. 43.95x o.p. (ISBN 0-256-03194-0). Irwin.

Accounting for Income Taxes: An Interpretation of APB Opinion No. 11. Donald J. Bevis & Raymond E. Perry. 76p. 1969. pap. 10.00 o.p. (ISBN 0-685-03111-X). Am Inst CPA.

Accounting for Industrial Management. R. Sidebotham. 1964. 50.00 o.p. (ISBN 0-08-009892-4); pap. 50.00 o.p. (ISBN 0-08-009891-6). Pergamon.

Accounting for Inflation in U. K. Farmer. 1980. pap. 20.95 o.p. (ISBN 0-85258-199-8). Van Nos Reinhold.

Accounting for Non-Profit Organizations. 2nd ed. Emerson O. Henke. LC 77-5120. 211p. 1977. pap. 9.95x o.p. (ISBN 0-534-00543-8). PWS-Kent Pub.

Accounting for Owners & Managers. Merwin Leven. LC 80-19502. 175p. 1980. 50.00 o.p. (ISBN 0-932648-16-9). Boardroom.

Accounting for Research & Development. J. Batty. 237p. 1976. text ed. 26.95x o.p. (ISBN 0-686-70288-3, Pub. by Busn Bks England). Gower Pub Co.

Accounting for Software. Robert W. McGee. LC 83-73712. 225p. 1984. 35.00 o.p. (ISBN 0-87094-468-1). Dow Jones-Irwin.

Accounting for the Middle Manager. Dale L. Flesher & Tonya K. Flesher. 462p. 1980. 21.95 o.p. (ISBN 0-442-23875-4). Van Nos Reinhold.

Accounting Fundamentals for Non-Financial Executives. Allen Sweeny. LC 78-173320. 1972. 14.95 o.p. (ISBN 0-8144-5286-8). AMACOM.

Accounting in Action. 80p. 1983. pap. 7.50 o.p. (ISBN 0-686-84205-7). Am Inst CPA.

Accounting in Developing Countries: A Framework for Standard Setting. Felix E. Amenkhienan. Ed. by Richard N. Farmer. LC 85-20892. (Research for Business Decisions Ser.: No. 82). 114p. 1985. 39.95 o.p. (ISBN 0-8357-1717-8). UMI Res Pr.

Accounting in the Public Sector. Ed. by Robert W. Ingram. 417p. (Orig.). 1980. pap. text ed. 15.00x o.p. (ISBN 0-89832-005-4); pap. 17.00 o.p. Pub Horizons.

Accounting Information Systems: Concepts & Practice for Effective Decision Making. 2nd ed. Stephen A. Moscove & Mark G. Simkin. LC 83-16842. 721p. 1984. (ISBN 0-471-88354-9). Wiley.

Accounting Principles. 5th ed. Robert N. Anthony & James S. Reece. 1983. 35.95 o.p. (ISBN 0-256-02785-4). Irwin.

Accounting Principles. 4th ed. Hermanson et al. 1989. 35.95 o.p. (ISBN 0-256-03415-X). Irwin.

Accounting Principles. 2nd ed. Roger H. Hermanson et al. 1983. 32.95x o.p. (ISBN 0-256-02872-9); study guide, vol. 1 10.95x o.p. (ISBN 0-256-02873-7); study guide. vol. 2 10.95 o.p. (ISBN 0-256-02933-4); working papers, bk. 1 11.95 o.p. (ISBN 0-256-02874-5); working papers, bk. 2 11.95 o.p. (ISBN 0-256-02875-3); practice set 9.95x o.p. (ISBN 0-256-02876-1); practice set 9.95x o.p. (ISBN 0-256-02877-X); practice set 9.95x o.p. (ISBN 0-256-02878-8). Irwin.

Accounting Principles. Donald F. Istvan & Clarence G. Avery. (Illus.). 1095p. 1979. text ed. 23.95 o.p. (ISBN 0-15-500420-4, HC); working papers (2) 7.95 o.p. HarBraceJ.

Accounting Principles for Midmanagement. Tonya K. Flesher & Dale L. Flesher. LC 78-62620. (Accounting Ser.). 454p. 1980. text ed. 29.95 o.p. (ISBN 0-8273-1628-3); instr's. guide 11.00 o.p. (ISBN 0-8273-1629-1). Delmar.

Accounting Principles-Working Papers: Group B, Chapters 1-12. 2nd ed. Ronald Thacker. 1979. pap. text ed. (ISBN 0-13-002832-0). P-H.

Accounting Problem for Manual Solution. Holmes et al. Irwin.

Accounting Profession: Years of Trial, 1969-1980. Wallace E. Olson. 307p. 1982. 27.50 o.p. (ISBN 0-686-90407-9, 051036). Am Inst CPA.

Accounting Reports Today U. K. Rowe. 1983. pap. 19.95 o.p. (ISBN 0-85258-232-3). Van Nos Reinhold.

Accounting Sampler. 3rd ed. T. J. Burns & Harvey S. Hendrickson. 1976. text ed. 24.95 o.p. (ISBN 0-07-009202-8). McGraw.

Accounting Standards: Complete 1984 Edition. Financial Accounting Standards Board. 1952p. 1984. text ed. 30.90 o.p. (ISBN 0-07-079459-6). McGraw.

Accounting Standards: Current Text (as of June 1, 1985), Complete Edition. Financial Accounting Standards Board. 1985. Set. text ed. 28.90 shrink-wrapped o.p. (ISBN 0-07-020936-7). McGraw.

Accounting Standards: Current Text (as of June 1, 1985) General Standards. Financial Accounting Standards Board. 1985. text ed. 15.95 o.p. (ISBN 0-07-020941-3). McGraw.

Accounting Standards: Current Text-General Standards. Financial Accounting Standards Board. 1440p. 1984. text ed. 18.95 o.p. (ISBN 0-07-020916-2); text ed. 11.95 o.p. (ISBN 0-07-020917-0). McGraw.

Accounting Standards: Original Pronouncements-Complete Edition. Financial Accounting Standards Board. 2304p. 1984. text ed. 30.90 o.p. (ISBN 0-07-079460-X). McGraw.

Accounting Standards: Original Pronouncements; July 1973-June 1, 1984. Financial Accounting Standards Board. 1664p. 1984. text ed. 20.95 o.p. (ISBN 0-07-020919-7). McGraw.

Accounting Standards: Original Pronouncements-Through June 1973. Financial Accounting Standards Board. 640p. 1984. text ed. 9.95 o.p. (ISBN 0-07-020918-9). McGraw.

Accounting System for Real Estate Brokers. 79p. 10.00 o.p. (ISBN 0-318-15165-0, 111-321). Natl Assoc Realtors.

Accounting Systems & Procedures see Accounting Ten-Twelve.

Accounting Ten-Twelve, 4 pts. Max H. Freeman et al. Incl. Pt. 1. Elements of Financial Records. 1968. pap. 4.56 o.p. (ISBN 0-07-022021-2); pap. text ed. 4.56 o.p. (ISBN 0-07-022025-5); Pt. 2. Accounting Systems & Procedures. text ed. (ISBN 0-07-022022-0); Pt. 3. Special Accounting Procedures. text ed. 5.04 o.p. (ISBN 0-07-022023-9); Pt. 4. Business Data Processing Fundamentals. text ed. (ISBN 0-07-022024-7). 1968. text ed. (ISBN 0-07-022018-2, G). McGraw.

Accounting: Text & Cases. 7th ed. Robert N. Anthony & James S. Reece. 1983. 41.95x o.p. (ISBN 0-256-02787-0). Irwin.

Accounting Theory. Ahmed Belkaoui. 318p. 1981. pap. text ed. 14.25 o.p. (ISBN 0-15-500470-0, HC). HarBraceJ.

Accounting Theory & Practice. Albert K. Francisco & Kenneth A. Smith. LC 87-62077. (CPA Examination Review Ser.). 728p. 1988. pap. text ed. 33.95 o.p. (ISBN 0-932276-74-1). Prof Pubns CA.

Accounts & Papers Relating to Mary Queen of Scots. Ed. by Allan J. Crosby. 1967. Repr. of 1867 ed. 19.00 o.p. (ISBN 0-384-10235-2). Johnson Repr.

Accreditation Manual for Hospitals: 1986 Edition. 336p. 1985. pap. 50.00 o.s.i. (ISBN 0-86688-089-5, H-86). Joint Comm Hlthcare.

Accreditation Manual for Hospitals: 1987 Edition. LC 86-81878. 324p. 1986. pap. 50.00 o.s.i. (ISBN 0-86688-104-2). Joint Comm Hlthcare.

Accreditation Manual for Hospitals: 1988 Edition. 367p. 1987. 55.00 o.s.i. (ISBN 0-86688-128-X). Joint Comm Hlthcare.

Accreditation Manual for Long Term Care Facilities 1984. 113p. 1983. pap. 25.00 o.s.i. (ISBN 0-86688-059-3). Joint Comm Hlthcare.

Accredited Resident Manager Profile, 1984. Ed. by Kenneth Anderson. 24p. (Orig.). Date not set. pap. 16.95 o.p. (ISBN 0-912104-76-7, 966). Inst Real Estate.

Acculturation in the Americas: Proceedings of the International Congress of Americanists, 29th. Americanists Staff. Ed. by Sol Tax. LC 67-18218. (Illus.). 333p. 1967. Repr. of 1952 ed. 25.00 o.p. (ISBN 0-8154-0230-9). Cooper Sq.

Accumulation of Capital--An Anti-Critique: Imperialism & the Accumulation of Capital. Rosa Luxemburg & Nikolai Bukharin. Ed. by Kenneth J. Tarbuck. Tr. by Rudolf Wichmann from Ger. LC 72-81768. 368p. 1972. 9.50 o.p. (ISBN 0-85345-265-2); pap. 5.95 o.p. (ISBN 0-85345-291-1). Monthly Rev.

Accuracy of Flow Measurements by Laser Doppler Methods: Proceedings of the LDA Symposium, Copenhagen, 1975. LDA-Symposium Staff. Ed. by P. Buchhave et al. LC 76-53089. (Illus.). 1976. text ed. 55.00 o.p. (ISBN 0-89116-040-X). Hemisphere Pub.

ACEC Computer User Listing. 176p. 1983. pap. 30.00 o.p. (ISBN 0-686-48373-1); pap. 30.00 members o.p. (ISBN 0-686-48374-X). Am Consul Eng.

ACEC International Engineering Directory. 161p. 1984. 15.00 o.p. (61); members 15.00 o.p. Am Consul Eng.

ACEC Membership Directory, 1984-85. American Consulting Engineers Council Staff. 413p. 1983. 50.00 o.p. (ISBN 0-686-60620-5). Am Consul Eng.

ACEC Membership Directory, 1987-1988. 500p. 1987. 140.00 o.p. (60). Am Consul Eng.

Acenaphthylene, Acenaphthene, Fluorene, & Fluoranthene. (American Petroleum Institute Monograph). 57p. 1981. 8.00 o.p. (ISBN 0-317-33085-3, 822-71500). Am Petroleum.

Aces High. William Hughes. 1976. pap. 1.50 o.p. (ISBN 0-380-00788-6, 30692). Avon.

Acetylthiocholinesterase Distribution in the Brain Stem of the Cat. E. Ramon-Moliner. LC 72-94301. (Advances in Anatomy, Embryology, & Cell Biology Ser.: Vol. 46, Pt. 4). (Illus.). 53p. 1972. pap. 16.60 o.p. (ISBN 0-387-06036-7). Springer-Verlag.

Achievement & Task Motivation. Ed. by J. H. Van Den Bercken et al. xii, 268p. (Orig.). 1986. pap. text ed. 25.00 o.p. (ISBN 90-265-0739-9, Pub. by Swets & Zeitlinger (Netherlands)). CJ Hogrefe Pubs.

Achievement of Galileo. Ed. by James Brophy & Henry Paolucci. 1962. pap. 7.95x o.p. (ISBN 0-8084-0389-3). New Coll U Pr.

Achievements of Biblical Religion: A Prolegomenon to Old Testament Theology. Simon J. De Vries. LC 83-3614. 558p. (Orig.). 1983. lib. bdg. 43.00 o.p. (ISBN 0-8191-3140-7); pap. text ed. 23.50 o.p. (ISBN 0-8191-3141-5). U Pr of Amer.

Achieving an Affordable Defense: A Military Strategy to Guide Military Spending. 1987. write for info. o.p. Comm Natl Security.

Achieving an Affordable Defense: A Military Strategy to Guide Military Spending. Stephen Daggett & Jo. L. Husbands. (Military Budget Studies). (Illus.). 45p. (Orig.). 1987. pap. write for info. o.p. (ISBN 0-937115-07-X). Comm Natl Security.

Achieving Classroom Communication Through Self Analysis. Theodore Parson. 1976. leader's kit (instructor's manual, worktext, audiotape cassettes, instruction sheets) 21.50 o.p. (ISBN 0-574-23040-8, 13-6040); group leader's manual 4.95 o.p. (ISBN 0-574-23042-4, 13-6042); worktext 8.95 o.p. (ISBN 0-574-23041-6, 13-6041); studio kit (worktext, audiotape, instruction sheet) 17.50 o.p. (ISBN 0-574-23045-9, 3-6045); pre-recorded audiotape cassette 9.95 o.p. (ISBN 0-686-77229-6, 13-6043). SRA.

Achieving "Due Responsibility" Perspectives on the American Presidency. League of Women Voters Education Fund Staff. (Federalist Papers Reexamined: No. 4). 37p. 1977. pap. 1.00 o.p. (ISBN 0-89959-040-3, 331). LWV US.

Achieving Promises: A Spiritual Guide for the Transitions of Life. William F. Kraft. LC 81-10496. 132p. 1981. pap. 6.95 o.s.i. (ISBN 0-664-24384-3, Westminster). Westminster John Knox.

Achieving Sex Equity in Vocational Education: A Crack in the Wall. League of Women Voters Education Fund Staff. 36p. 1982. 2.50 o.p. (ISBN 0-89959-329-1, 493). LWV US.

Achieving Success in College. Irwin L. Joffe. 239p. 1982. pap. text ed. (ISBN 0-534-01032-6). Wadsworth Pub.

Achieving Success in Manufacturing Management. Charles Hoitash. LC 80-51544. (Manufacturing Update Ser.). (Illus.). 260p. 1980. 35.00 o.p. (ISBN 0-87263-055-2). SME.

Achieving Wellness Through Risk Taking: The End of Boredom. Mark Crookse. LC 85-90954. (Illus.). 224p. 1986. 15.00 o.p. (ISBN 0-682-40249-4). Exposition-Phoenix.

Acid Base Homeostasis of the Brain Extracellular Fluid & the Respiratory Control System. Ed. by H. H. Loeschke. LC 75-22546. (Illus.). 234p. 1976. 22.50 o.p. (ISBN 0-88416-131-5). Year Bk Med.

Acid Dreams: The CIA, LSD & the Sixties Rebellion. Martin A. Lee & Bruce Shlain. (History & Sociology Ser.). 343p. 1986. pap. 13.95 o.p. (ISBN 0-394-62081-X, Ever). Grove.

Acid Drop. Sara George. LC 75-10754. 192p. 1975. 6.95 o.p. (ISBN 0-689-10673-4, Atheneum). Macmillan.

Acid Earth: The Global Threat of Acid Pollution. LC 86-139577. 1985. 7.75 o.p. (ISBN 0-905347-61-7). C I D E.

Acid: LSD Today. 1984. pap. 0.25 o.p. (ISBN 0-89230-181-3). Do it Now.

Acid Rain. Ross Howard & Michael Perley. (Paperback Ser.). (Illus.). 208p. 1982. pap. text ed. 6.95 o.p. (ISBN 0-07-030546-3). McGraw.

Acid Rain in Europe & North America: National Responses to an International Problem - Final Report. German Marshall Fund of the United States Staff et al. LC 83-1466. 1983. 14.00 o.p. (ISBN 0-911937-01-3). Environ Law Inst.

Acid Rain: Planning for the Eighties. Michael J. Zimmer & James A. Thompson, Jr. (Illus.). 311p. 1983. 3-ring binder 85.00 o.p. (ISBN 0-86587-118-3). Gov Insts.

Acid Rain: The Georgia Situation. James E. Kundell. LC 84-7403. 20p. (Orig.). 1984. pap. 4.50 o.p. (ISBN 0-89854-097-6). U of Ga Inst Govt.

Acidic Proteins of the Nucleus. Ed. by Ivan L. Cameron & James R. Jeter, Jr. 1974. 74.50 o.p. (ISBN 0-12-156930-6). Acad Pr.

Ackerley Letters. Ed. by Neville Braybrooke. LC 74-32313. (Illus.). 392p. 1975. 15.00 o.p. (ISBN 0-15-150858-5). HarBraceJ.

Ackroyd. Jules Feiffer. 1978. pap. 1.95 o.p. (ISBN 0-380-39347-6, 39347). Avon.

Acne: Morphogenesis & Treatment. G. Plewig & A. M. Kligman. (Illus.). 360p. 1979. 65.00 o.p. (ISBN 0-387-07212-8). Springer-Verlag.

Acolyte. Thea Astley. 158p. 1980. pap. 10.95x o.p. (ISBN 0-7022-1540-6). U of Queensland Pr.

Acorn BASIC Manual. Lynne Mass & Thomas M. Kemnitz. LC 85-437. (Kids Working with Computers Ser.). (Illus.). 48p. (gr. 2 up). 1985. lib. bdg. 11.27 o.p. (ISBN 0-516-08421-6). Childrens.

Acoustic & Vibrational Communication in Insects: Proceedings of Two Symposia at the Seventeenth International Congress of Entomology. Klaus Kalmring & Norbert Elsner. (Illus.). 230p. 1985. pap. text ed. 42.00x o.p. (ISBN 3-489-65936-8). Parey Sci Pubs.

Acoustic Emission: Proceedings of the Symposium, held in Bad Nauheim, West Germany, 1979. Ed. by German Society of Metallurgy Staff. Tr. by A. R. Nicoll. (Illus.). 385p. 1980. lib. bdg. 63.00 o.p. (ISBN 3-88355-030-2, Pub. by DGM Metallurgy Germany). IR Pubns.

Acoustic Surface Waves. A. A. Oliner. LC 77-17957. (Topics in Applied Physics Ser.: Vol. 24). (Illus.). 1978. 64.00 o.p. (ISBN 0-387-08575-0). Springer-Verlag.

Acoustic Transducers. Ed. by Ivor D. Groves, Jr. LC 81-4113. (Benchmark Papers in Acoustics Ser.: Vol. 14). 391p. 1982. 55.95 o.p. (ISBN 0-87933-387-1). Van Nos Reinhold.

Acoustic Waveguides: Applications to Oceanic Science. C. Allan Boyles. LC 83-17000. 321p. 1984. 51.95x o.p. (ISBN 0-471-88771-4). Wiley.

Acoustical Foundations of Music. John Backus. 312p. Repr. of 1969 ed. lib. bdg. 49.00 o.p. (Pub. by Am Repr Serv). Reprint Servs.

Acoustics. Ed. by R. Bruce Lindsay. LC 72-90974. (Benchmark Papers in Acoustics Ser.: Vol. 2). 465p. 1982. 62.95 o.p. (ISBN 0-87933-015-5). Van Nos Reinhold.

Acoustics: An Introducton to Its Physical Principles & Applications. Allan D. Pierce. (Illus.). 656p. 1981. text ed. 49.95x o.p. (ISBN 0-07-049961-6). McGraw.

ACP Review Manual: Foundations of an Information System Career. Kenniston W. Lord, Jr. (Illus.). 1024p. 1987. pap. 34.95 o.p. (ISBN 0-8306-2889-4, 2889, TAB-TPR). TAB Bks.

Acquiring & Serving Computer Clients. Computer Law Institute Staff & ALI-ABA, Committee on Continuing Professional Education. LC 84-60195. 1984. 25.00 o.p. Mass CLE.

Acquiring Ball Skill. H. T. Whiting. (Illus.). 118p. 1970. pap. 5.00 o.p. (ISBN 0-8121-0290-8). Lea & Febiger.

Acquiring Conversational Competence. Elinor Ochs & Bambi B. Schieffelin. (Language, Education & Society Ser.). 256p. 1983. 24.95x o.p. (ISBN 0-7100-9459-0). Routledge Chapman & Hall.

Acquiring or Selling the Privately Held Company '87. Howard L. Shecter. LC 86-62253. (Corporate Law & Practice Course Handbook Ser.: No. 559). 430p. 1987. 45.00 o.p. (ISBN 0-317-57192-3, B46789). PLI.

Acquisition & Analysis of Pictorial Data: Proceedings, Vol. 48. Society of Photo-Optical Instrumentation Engineers Staff. 1975. 28.00 o.p. (ISBN 0-89252-060-4). SPIE.

Acquisition of Communicative Competence. Ed. by Richard L. Schiefelbusch & Joanne Pickar. LC 84-2286. 560p. 1984. text ed. 29.00x o.p. (ISBN 0-8391-1989-5, 1323). Pro Ed.

Acquisition of Maps & Charts Published by the United States Government. Jane G. Low. (Occasional Papers: No. 125). 36p. 1976. pap. 2.00 o.p. (ISBN 0-317-58962-8). U of Ill Lib Info Sci.

Acquisition of Noncompetitive Federal Oil & Gas Leases on the Public Domain. Robert G. Vernon. (Illus.). 1963. write for info. o.p. Columbia Law.

Acquisition of Skill. Ed. by Edward A. Bilodeau. 1966. 58.50 o.p. (ISBN 0-12-099150-0). Acad Pr.

Acquisition of Syntax in Bilingual Children. Carolyn Kessler. LC 72-76735. 109p. 1971. pap. 4.95 o.p. (ISBN 0-87840-157-1). Georgetown U Pr.

Acquisitions & Mergers 1984: Tactics & Techniques, 1984. Practising Law Institute Staff & Melvin Katz. (Corporate Law & Practice Course Handbook Ser.: No. 451). 560p. 1984. 40.00 o.p. (B4-6652). PLI.

Acquisitions & Mergers 1985: Tactics, Techniques, & Recent Developments. Melvin Katz & Ronald M. Loeb. 862p. 1985. 15.00 o.p. (B4-6722). PLI.

Acquisitions-Circulation Interface. Ed. by Sharon M. Edge. 104p. 1981. pap. 13.00 o.p. (ISBN 0-08-026761-0). Pergamon.

Acquisitive Society. Richard H. Tawney. LC 28-30737. 188p. 1955. pap. 4.95 o.p. (ISBN 0-15-602846-8, Harv). HarBraceJ.

ACRL University Library Statistics 1983-84. Ed. by Sandy Whiteley. 55p. (Orig.). 1985. pap. 15.00 o.p. (ISBN 0-8389-6892-9). Assn Coll & Res Libs.

Acronyms, Initialisms, & Abbreviations Dictionary, Vol. 1. 12th ed. Ed. by Julie E. Towell & Helen E. Sheppard. 3104p. 1987. Set. 190.00x o.p. (ISBN 0-8103-2505-5). Gale.

Acropolis of Athens As Described by Pausanias & Other Writers: Inscriptions & Archaeological Evidences. O. Jahn & A. Michaelis. (Illus.). 1976. 30.00 o.p. Ares.

Across China-China Pictorial Photos over 35 Years. Ed. by Zhang Yunlei et al. Tr. by Deng Xin from Chinese. (Illus.). 192p. (Orig.). 1985. pap. 24.95 o.p. (ISBN 0-8351-1688-3). China Bks.

Across the High Frontier. Lundgren. Date not set. pap. 3.95 o.p. Aviation.

Across the Limpopo: A Family's Hazardous 4,000-mile Journey Through Africa. Michael Nicholson. 220p. 1986. 14.95 o.p. (ISBN 0-86051-304-1, Pub. by by Tarquin). Parkwest Pubns.

Across the Night. J. E. Jacoby. 128p. 1959. (ISBN 0-8022-0786-3). Philos Lib.

Across the Pacific: An Inner History of American-East Asian Relations. Akira Iriye. LC 67-19202. 1967. 9.75 o.p. (ISBN 0-15-103209-2). HarBraceJ.

Across the Pacific: An Inner History of American-East Asian Relations. Akira Iriye. LC 67-19202. 347p. 1969. pap. 6.95 o.p. (ISBN 0-15-602790-9, Harv). HarBraceJ.
Across the Sea of Suns. Gregory Benford. 480p. 1984. 15.50 o.s.i. (ISBN 0-671-44668-1, Timescape). PB.
Across the Soviet Union. F. Kohler. 1979. 6.45 o.p. (ISBN 0-8285-1896-3, Pub. by Progress Pubs USSR). Imported Pubns.
Acrostic Mysteries. Henry Sleasar. 1985. pap. 4.95 o.p. (ISBN 0-380-89854-3). Avon.
Acrostics for the Connoisseur, No. 1. 128p. 1982. pap. 3.95 o.p. (ISBN 0-448-14813-7, G&D). Putnam Pub Group.
Acrostics for the Connoisseur, No. 3. Charles Preston. 128p. 1983. pap. 3.95 o.p. (ISBN 0-399-50830-9, G&D). Putnam Pub Group.
Acrostics for the Connoisseur, No. 4. 1984. pap. 3.95 o.p. (ISBN 0-399-50974-7, G&D). Putnam Pub Group.
ACS Directory of Graduate Research. 1230p. 1983. 43.00 o.p. (ISBN 0-8412-0797-6). Am Chemical.
Act Natural. Bruce Hugman. 95p. 1977. text ed. 9.75x o.p. (ISBN 0-7199-0933-3, Pub. by Bedford England); pap. (ISBN 0-7199-0934-1). Gower Pub Co.
Act of Being: Towards a Theory of Acting. Charles Marowitz. LC 74-5821. (Illus.). 1978. 11.95 o.p. (ISBN 0-8008-0015-X); pap. 5.95 o.s.i. (ISBN 0-8008-0016-8). Taplinger.
Act of Congress. Eugene Eidenberg & Roy D. Morey. 1969. 6.50x o.p. (ISBN 0-393-05331-8, NortonC); pap. 4.95x o.p. (ISBN 0-393-09692-0). Norton.
Act of Darkness. large print ed. Frances King. LC 84-6535. 554p. 1984. Repr. of 1983 ed. 14.95 o.p. (ISBN 0-89621-534-2). Thorndike Pr.
Act of Writing. Jessie Rehder & Wallace Kaufman. 350p. 1969. pap. text ed. write for info. o.p. (ISBN 0-02-399170-4). Macmillan.
Act Thin, Stay Thin: New Ways to Lose Weight & Keep It off. Richard B. Stuart. 1977. 12.95 o.p. (ISBN 0-393-08805-7). Norton.
Actes et Paroles: Avant et Pendant l'Exil, Vol. 1. Victor Hugo. (Illus.). 9.95 o.p. (ISBN 0-686-54051-4). French & Eur.
Actes et Paroles: Avant, Pendant et Depuis l'Exil, Vol. 2. 2nd ed. Victor Hugo. 9.95 o.p. (ISBN 0-686-54052-2). French & Eur.
Acting-In: Practical Applications of Psychodramatic Methods. Howard A. Blatner. (Illus.). 160p. 1973. pap. text ed. 12.95 o.p. (ISBN 0-8261-1400-8). Springer Pub.
Acting Is Believing: A Basic Method. 4th ed. Charles J. McGaw & Gary Blake. LC 79-21527. 272p. 1980. text ed. 24.95 o.p. (ISBN 0-03-021671-0, HoltC). HR&W.
Actinides: Electronic Structure & Related Properties, 2 vols. Ed. by A. J. Freeman & J. B. Darby. Vol. 1. 1974. 98.00 o.p. (ISBN 0-12-266701-8); Vol. 2. 1974. 98.00 o.p. (ISBN 0-12-266702-6). Acad Pr.
Actinides in Perspective: Proceedings of the Conference Held at Pacific Grove, CA, Sept. 10-15, 1981. Ed. by N. M. Edelstein. (Illus.). 620p. 1982. 110.00 o.p. (ISBN 0-08-029193-7). Pergamon.
Actinomycetales: Characteristics & Practical Importance. Ed. by G. Sykes & F. A. Skinner. (Society for Applied Bacteriology Symposium Ser.: No. 2). 1973. 82.00 o.p. (ISBN 0-12-679950-4). Acad Pr.
Actinomycetes Biology. Ed. by Librado Ortiz-Ortiz et al. 1984. 39.95 o.p. (ISBN 0-12-528620-1). Acad Pr.
Action Against Abuse: Handbook for Battered Women & their Advocates. Mid-Hudson Chapter of the Guild. 1985. Natl Lawyers Guild.
Action & Existence: Anarchism for Business Administration. Pierre Guillet de Montoux. 294p. 1983. 64.95 o.p. (ISBN 0-471-10217-2). Wiley.
Action for Human Settlements. C. I. Doxiadis. (Illus.). 1977. 12.95x o.p. (ISBN 0-393-08361-6). Norton.
Action, Gesture & Symbol: The Emergence of Language. Ed. by Andrew Lock. 1979. 112.00 o.p. (ISBN 0-12-454050-3). Acad Pr.
Action in the Liturgy. Walter Lowrie. 1952. (ISBN 0-8022-1001-5). Philos Lib.
Action of Insulin on Cells. Maurice E. Krahl. (Illus.). 1961. 49.50 o.p. (ISBN 0-12-424550-1). Acad Pr.
Action Planning & Responsive Design: Issues of Housing, Building, Planning & Development in the Third World. Ed. by S. Groak. 350p. 1984. pap. 74.00 o.p. (ISBN 0-08-031310-8). Pergamon.
Action Systems: An Introduction to the Analysis of Complex Behavior. David D. Clarke & Jill Crossland. 160p. 1985. 35.00 o.p. (ISBN 0-416-36120-X, 4175); pap. 12.95 o.p. (ISBN 0-416-36130-7, 4176). Routledge Chapman & Hall.
Action Theory. Ed. by John A. Meacham. 220p. 1985. pap. 25.25x o.p. (ISBN 3-8055-3895-2). Transaction Pubs.
Action with the Elderly: A Handbook for Relatives & Friends. Kenneth M. Keddie. 1978. 34.00 o.p. (ISBN 0-08-021442-8); pap. 13.00 o.p. (ISBN 0-08-021441-X). Pergamon.
Actions & Events: Perspectives on the Philosophy of Donald Davidson. Ed. by Ernest LePore & Brian McLaughlin. 528p. 1986. lib. bdg. 60.00x o.p. (ISBN 0-631-14451-X). Basil Blackwell.
Actions & Remedies, 2 vols. Ed. by Charles Friend. 1984. 60.00 o.p. Callaghan.
Actions to Implement the Recommendations of the Presidential Commission on the Space Shuttle Challenger Accident, Report to the President. (Illus.). 61p. (Orig.). 1986. pap. 3.00 o.p. (ISBN 0-318-21276-5, S/N 033-000-00990-9). USGPO.
Activated Sludge Process: Fundamentals of Operation. David R. Junkins & Kevin J. Deeny. LC 82-70699. (Illus.). 260p. 1983. 16.95 o.p. (ISBN 0-250-40506-7). Butterworth.
Activation of Energy. Pierre Teilhard De Chardin. LC 75-142104. (Helen & Kurt Wolff Bk). 1971. 7.50 o.p. (ISBN 0-15-103276-9). HarBraceJ.
Activation of Grignard Reagents by Transition Metal Compounds. H. Felkin & G. Swierczewski. 1976. pap. 15.50 o.p. (ISBN 0-08-020465-1). Pergamon.
Active Birth. Janet Balaskas. 1983. text ed. 14.95 o.p. (ISBN 0-07-003546-6); pap. text ed. 6.95 o.p. (ISBN 0-07-003545-8). McGraw.
Active Carbons. Bansal. Ed. by Stoeckl Donnet. 1988. 125.00 o.p. (ISBN 0-8247-7842-1). Dekker.
Active Experiments in Space Plasmas. Ed. by C. T. Russell. (Advances in Space Research: Vol. 1, No. 2). (Illus.). 468p. 1981. pap. 72.00 o.p. (ISBN 0-08-027158-8). Pergamon.
Active Filter Design. Date not set. (ISBN 0-8104-0959-3). Sams.
Active Filters for Communication & Instrumentation. P. Bowron & F. W. Stephenson. (Illus.). 320p. 1979. text ed. 27.00 o.p. (ISBN 0-07-084086-5). McGraw.
Active Filters for Integrated Circuits. W. E. Heinlein & W. H. Holmes. 1974. 65.50 o.p. (ISBN 0-387-91070-0). Springer Verlag.
Active Man & the Christ. Robert K. Hudnut. LC 72-75650. 128p. (Orig.). 1972. pap. 0.50 o.p. (ISBN 0-8006-0119-X, 1-119, Fortress). Augsburg Fortress.
Active Network & Feedback Amplifier Theory. Chen. 481p. 1980. 51.00 o.p. (ISBN 0-89116-478-2). Hemisphere Pub.
Active Network Feedback Amplifier Theory. Chen Wai-Kai. LC 79-16997. (Illus.). 550p. 1980. text ed. 49.95 o.p. (ISBN 0-07-010779-3). McGraw.
Active Nitrogen. A. Nelson Wright & Carl A. Winkler. (Physical Chemistry Ser.: Vol. 14). 1968. 103.50 o.p. (ISBN 0-12-765150-0). Acad Pr.
Active Touch-The Mechanism of Recognition of Objects by Manipulation: A Multidisciplinary Approach. Ed. by G. Gordon. 1978. 91.00 o.p. (ISBN 0-08-022647-7); pap. 51.00 o.p. (ISBN 0-08-022667-1). Pergamon.
Active Transport Through Animal Cell Membranes. P. G. Le Fevre. (Protoplasmatologia: Vol. 8, Pt. 7a). (Illus.). 1955. pap. 33.70 o.p. (ISBN 0-387-80387-4). Springer-Verlag.
Activism that Makes Sense: Congregations & Community Organization. Gregory F. Pierce. LC 83-82016. (Orig.). 1984. pap. 6.95 o.p. (ISBN 0-8091-2600-1). Paulist Pr.
Activities & Games. Lucy C. LeGros. (Illus.). 42p. (Orig.). (gr. k-4). 1980. pap. 4.95 o.p. (ISBN 0-937306-02-9). Creat Res NC.
Activities & Spaces: Dimensional Data for Housing Design. John Noble. (Illus.). 32p. 1983. pap. 9.95 o.p. (ISBN 0-85139-745-X). Nichols Pub.
Activities Desk Book for Teaching Arithmetic Skills. Joan M. Higley. 219p. 1983. text ed. 16.50x o.p. (ISBN 0-13-003517-3, Parker). P-H.
Activities for School-Age Child Care. Rosalie Blau et al. LC 77-91044. (Illus.). 85p. 1977. pap. text ed. 4.00 o.p. (ISBN 0-912674-57-1, NAEYC #214). Natl Assn Child Ed.
Activities for Teaching Mathematics to Low Achievers. Daisy Howell et al. LC 73-93330. (Illus.). 1974. pap. 1.00 o.p. (ISBN 0-87805-052-3). U Pr of Miss.
Activities for Teaching Metrics in Kindergarden. Sam E. Brown. LC 77-95155. 1978. pap. text ed. 9.00 o.p. (ISBN 0-8191-0462-0). U Pr of Amer.
Activities for the Christian Family Handbook (Paths of Life) Gaynell B. Cronin. LC 79-92007. 1980. pap. 2.95 o.p. (ISBN 0-8091-2273-1). Paulist Pr.
Activities Handbook for Teachers of Young Children. 3rd ed. Doreen J. Croft & Robert D. Hess. LC 79-90365. 1980. pap. 16.95 o.p. (ISBN 0-395-28698-0). HM.
Activities Handbook for the Teaching of Psychology, Vol. 3. cancelled o.s.i. (ISBN 1-55798-046-2, 4280070). Am Psychol.
Activities in Ceramics. Vernon D. Seeley & Robert L. Thompson. (Illus.). 1956. pap. 4.60 o.p. (ISBN 0-87345-161-9). Glencoe.
Activity & Experience: Sources of English Informal Education. Lydia A. Smith. LC 73-22313. (Illus.). 240p. 1976. 12.00x o.p. (ISBN 0-87586-047-8). Agathon.
Activity Guide for Salesmanship. Joel Podell et al. 1979. pap. text ed. 12.00 o.p. (ISBN 0-394-32210-X, RanC). Random.
Activity-Oriented Mathematics. William E. Schall. 1976. pap. text ed. write for info. o.p. (ISBN 0-87150-173-2, PWS 1392, Prindle). PWS-Kent Pub.
Activity Puzzles. 1983. pap. 1.75 o.s.i. (ISBN 0-345-30890-5). Ballantine.
Actor. Robert J. Conley. LC 87-13482. (Double D Western Ser.). 192p. 1987. 12.95 o.s.i. (ISBN 0-385-23956-4). Doubleday.
Actor at Work. 3rd ed. Robert L. Benedetti. (Illus.). 1981. text ed. 28.67 o.p. (ISBN 0-13-003673-0). P-H.
Actors & Singers, Vol. 5. Richard Wagner. 1967. Repr. of 1896 ed. Broude.
Actors Talk about Acting. Ed. by Lewis Funke & John Booth. 1961. pap. 1.95 o.p. (ISBN 0-380-01006-2, 15602, Bard). Avon.
Actress to Actress. Rita Gam. (Illus.). 224p. 1986. 17.95 o.p. (ISBN 0-941130-23-1). Lyons & Burford.
Acts, Vol. V. Beacon Bible Expositions Staff. 6.95 o.p. (ISBN 0-8010-0679-1). Baker Bk.
Acts: A Good News Commentary. David J. Williams. LC 83-48427. (Good News Commentary Ser.). 448p. 1985. pap. 12.95 o.p. (ISBN 0-06-069451-3). HarpR.
Acts: An Inductive Study. Irving L. Jensen. 256p. 1973. pap. 8.95 o.p. (ISBN 0-8024-0138-4). Moody.
Acts & the History of Earliest Christianity. Martin Hengel. LC 79-8893. 160p. 1980. 9.95 o.p. (ISBN 0-8006-0630-2, 1-630, Fortress); pap. 7.50 o.p. (ISBN 0-8006-1876-9, 1-1876). Augsburg Fortress.
Acts of Joanna. Anne Ortlund. 160p. 1982. 7.95 o.p. (ISBN 0-8499-0283-5). Word Bks.
Acts of Mercy. Bill Pronzini & Barry Malzberg. 1981. pap. 2.25 o.p. (ISBN 0-505-51617-9, Pub. by Tower Bks). Dorchester Pub Co.
Acts of the Anti-Slavery Apostles. Parker Pillsbury. LC 70-92758. 1969. Repr. of 1883 ed. 35.00x o.p. (ISBN 0-8371-2183-3, PIA&, Pub. by Negro U Pr). Greenwood.
Acts of the Apostles. Robert E. Tourville. 439p. 1983. 17.95 o.s.i. (ISBN 0-912981-00-8); pap. 14.95 o.p. Hse Bon Giovanni.
Acts of Theft. Arthur A. Cohen. LC 79-1818. 1980. 10.00 o.p. (ISBN 0-15-103334-X). HarBraceJ.
Acts Trilogy: Birth of the Body; Growth of the Body; Triumph of the Body, 3 vols. Ray Stedman. 1981. Boxed Set. 12.95 o.p. (ISBN 0-88449-078-5, VH 013). Vision Hse.
Actuator Disk Theory: Discontinuities in Thermo-Fluid Dynamics. J. H. Horlock. (Illus.). 1979. text ed. 62.00 o.p. (ISBN 0-07-030360-6). McGraw.
Acupressure Techniques: For the Self Treatment of Minor Ailments. Hans Ewald. 96p. (Orig.). 1984. pap. 6.95 o.p. (ISBN 0-7225-0433-0). Inner Tradit.
Acupuncture & the Life Energies. Sidney Rose-Neil. 160p. 1981. pap. 8.95 o.s.i. (ISBN 0-88231-121-2). ASI Pubs Inc.
Acupuncture Energy in Health & Disease: A Practical Guide for Advanced Students. Henry Woollerton & Colleen J. McLean. (Illus.). 128p. (Orig.). 1983. pap. 6.95 o.p. (ISBN 0-7225-0482-9, Pub. by Thorsons Pubs England). Sterling.
Acupuncture for Patients. Teruo Matsumoto & Bruce A. Levy. (Illus.). 120p. 1975. pap. 13.25x o.p. (ISBN 0-398-03250-5). C C Thomas.
Acupuncture for Physicians. Teruo Matsumoto. (Illus.). 224p. 1974. 24.00x o.p. (ISBN 0-398-02958-X). C C Thomas.
Acupuncture in Medical Practice. Louise Wensel. (Illus.). 320p. 1980. text ed. 27.95 o.p. (ISBN 0-8359-0128-9). Appleton & Lange.
Acupuncture Made Easy. Acupuncture Research Institute Staff. 1976. 9.50 o.p.; pap. 6.95 o.p. Borden.
Acupuncture Therapy: Clinical Diagnosis & Treatment. Ysohiaki Omura. (Illus.). 288p. 1985. pap. 29.95 o.p. (ISBN 0-87040-582-9). Japan Pubns USA.
Acute Hand Injuries: A Multispecialty Approach. Ed. by Francis G. Wolfort. LC 79-90896. 1980. text ed. 34.50 o.p. (ISBN 0-316-95112-9). Little.
Acute Inflammation. 2nd ed. J. V. Hurley. LC 82-14793. (Illus.). 157p. 1983. text ed. 42.50 o.p. (ISBN 0-443-02507-X). Churchill.
Acute Leukemias. Ed. by T. Buchner et al. (Haematology & Blood Transfusion Ser.: Vol. 30). (Illus.). 740p. 1987. pap. 137.20 o.p. (ISBN 0-387-16556-8). Springer-Verlag.
Acute Pancreatitis: An Interdisciplinary Synopsis. Ed. by Louis Hollender et al. Orig. Title: Akute Pankreatitis. (Illus.). 170p. 1983. text ed. 34.50 o.p. (ISBN 0-8067-0841-7). Urban & S.
Acute Respiratory Care. Kathy L. Emanuelson & Mary J. Desmore. LC 81-50072. (Series in Critical Care Nursing). (Illus.). 216p. (Orig.). 1981. pap. text ed. 15.95 o.p. (ISBN 0-471-88804-4). Wiley.
Ad Hoc Consultation on the Value of Non-Protein Nitrogen for Ruminants: Report. 1971. pap. 14.00 o.p. (F1086, FAO). UNIPUB.
Ad Reinhardt, Paintings & Watercolors. Ed. by Pace Gallery Publications Staff. (Illus.). 9p. (Orig.). 1981. portfolio format 8.00 o.p. (ISBN 0-938608-33-9). Pace Pubns.
ADA: An Advanced Introduction Including Reference Manual for the Ada Programming Language. Narain Gehani. (Illus.). 672p. 1984. text ed. 38.33 o.p. (ISBN 0-13-003997-7). P-H.
Ada: Concurrent Programming. Narain Gehani. (Illus.). 272p. 1984. pap. text ed. 38.00 o.p. (ISBN 0-13-004011-8). P-H.
Ada or Ardor: A Family Chronicle. Vladimir Nabokov. (McGraw-Hill Paperback Ser.). 612p. 1980. pap. text ed. 12.95 o.p. (ISBN 0-07-045723-9). McGraw.
Ada Programming Language. 2nd. ed. Ian Pyle. LC 84-17817. (Illus.). 336p. (Orig.). 1985. pap. text ed. 35.00 o.p. (ISBN 0-13-003906-3). P-H.
Adam & Eve Fantasy. Jess E. Weiss. 80p. 1985. 8.00 o.p. (ISBN 0-682-40262-1). Exposition-Phoenix.
Adam Bede. George Eliot. 1978. 14.95x o.p. (ISBN 0-460-00027-6, Evman); pap. 3.50x o.p. (ISBN 0-460-01027-1). Biblio Dist.
Adam Experiment. Geoffrey Simmons. LC 77-93098. 1978. 8.95 o.p. (ISBN 0-87795-185-3, Arbor Hse). Morrow.
Adam Names the Animals. (Baker Flip & Find Bks.). (Illus.). (ps-2). 1986. 2.95 o.p. (ISBN 0-8010-3529-5). Baker Bk.
Adam Sleep. Winfred Van Atta. 192p. 1981. pap. 2.25 o.p. (ISBN 0-380-53744-3, 53744). Avon.
Adam Smith & the Wealth of Nations, 1776-1976: Bicentennial Essays. Ed. by F. Glahe. LC 77-91609. 1978. pap. 8.95x o.p. Univ Pr Colo.
Adam Smith: Man of Letters & Economist. Clyde E. Dankert. LC 74-80675. 1974. text ed. 10.00 o.p. (ISBN 0-682-48020-7, University). Exposition-Phoenix.
Adam Smith's Daughters. Dorothy Lampen Thomson. LC 72-97724. 1973. 6.00 o.p. (ISBN 0-682-47675-7, University). Exposition-Phoenix.
Adam Style In America. Sterling Boyd. Ed. by S. J. Freedberg. LC 85-11451. (Outstanding Dissertations in Fine Arts Ser.). (Illus.). 780p. 1985. Repr. of 1964 ed. 75.00 o.p. (ISBN 0-8240-6864-5). Garland Pub.
Adam User's Guide. A. J. Bell & E. Q. Bell. 336p. 1984. 7.95 o.p. (ISBN 0-89303-300-6). Brady Bks.
Adam, Where Art Thou. Ralph S. Cannon. 288p. 1988. 12.95 o.p. (ISBN 0-8062-3058-4). Carlton.
Adam's at Bat. Paul Weinman. 16p. 1987. pap. 1.00 o.p. (ISBN 0-318-23498-X). Samisdat.
Adams Chronicles: Four Generations of Greatness. Jack Shepherd. (Illus.). 448p. 1987. 29.95 o.p. (ISBN 0-316-78500-8); pap. 17.95 o.p. (ISBN 0-316-78501-6). Little.
Adam's Companion. Ramsey J. Benson & Jack B. Rochester. 400p. 1984. pap. 9.95 o.p. (ISBN 0-380-87650-7, 87650-7). Avon.
Adam's Daughter. Faye Ashley. 496p. (Orig.). 1982. pap. 3.50 o.p. (ISBN 0-8439-1071-2, Pub. by Leisure Bks CT). Dorchester Pub Co.
Adams Family Correspondence: December 1761-March 1778, 2 vols. Ed. by Lyman H. Butterfield et al. LC 63-14964. (Adams Paper). (Illus.). 1965. pap. 2.95 ea. o.p. (Atheneum); o.p. vol. 1 o.p. (ISBN 0-689-70036-9, TAP 5). Vol. 2 (ISBN 0-689-70037-7, TAP 6). Macmillan.
Adams Federalists. Manning Dauer, Jr. LC 84-12995. xxiii, 381p. 1984. Repr. of 1953 ed. lib. bdg. 48.50x o.p. (ISBN 0-313-22663-6, DAAD). Greenwood.
Adaptation-Level Theory: A Symposium. M. H. Appley. 1971. 63.00 o.p. (ISBN 0-12-059250-9). Acad Pr.
Adaptation to Work: An Exploration of Processes & Outcomes. William L. Ashley et al. 82p. 1980. 5.50 o.p. (ISBN 0-318-22013-X, SN31). Natl Ctr Res Voc Ed.
Adaptations to Terrestial Environments. Ed. by N. S. Margaris et al. LC 83-13713. 256p. 1983. 52.50x o.p. (ISBN 0-306-41468-6, Plenum Pr). Plenum Pub.

Adaptations Within Antarctic Ecosystems: Proceedings of the Third SCAR Symposium on Antarctic Biology. Ed. by George Llano. LC 76-21500. 1296p. 1977. 19.95x o.p. (ISBN 0-87201-000-7). Gulf Pub.

Adapted Physical Education: A Practitioner's Guide. Lowell F. Masters & Allen A. Mori. LC 82-20672. 408p. 1983. 36.00 o.p. (ISBN 0-89443-669-4). Aspen Pub.

Adaptibility of the Vascular Wall: Proceedings. Ed. by Z. Reinis. (Illus.). 650p. 1980. 87.40 o.p. (ISBN 0-387-09907-7). Springer-Verlag.

Adapting Government to Regional Needs: Report of the Conference on Bay Area Regional Organization, April 18, 1970. Ed. by Stanley Scott & Harriet Nathan. LC 72-634806. (Orig.). 1971. pap. 5.50x o.p. (ISBN 0-87772-079-7). UCB IGS.

Adapting Work Sites for People with Disabilties: Ideas from Sweden. 3rd ed. Ed. by Ake Olsson. (International Exchange of Experts & Information in Rehabilitation Ser.: No. 20). 260p. 1983. 5.00 o.p. (ISBN 0-939986-32-9). World Rehab Fund.

Adaptive Behavior Curriculum: Prescriptive Behavior Analyses for Moderately, Severely, & Profoundly Handicapped Students, Vol. 2. Ed. by Dorothy Popovich & Sandra L. Laham. LC 80-39511. 332p. (Orig.). 1982. pap. text ed. 21.95 o.p. (ISBN 0-933716-17-6, 176). P H Brookes.

Adaptive Brain, 2 vols. Ed. by S. Grossberg. (Advances in Psychology Ser.: No. 42). Set. 132.50 o.p. (ISBN 0-444-70119-2, North Holland); Vol. 1: Cognition, Learning, Reinforcement & Rhythm; 498p. 79.50 o.p. (ISBN 0-444-70117-6); Vol. 2, Vision, Speech, Language & Motor Contol; 514p. 79.50 o.p. (ISBN 0-444-70118-4). Elsevier.

Adaptive Control. Ed. by B. D. Anderson & L. Ljung. 232p. 1984. pap. 44.00 o.p. (ISBN 0-08-031660-3). Pergamon.

Adaptive Control Processes: A Guided Tour. Richard E. Bellman. (Rand Corporation Research Studies). 1961. 50.00x o.p. (ISBN 0-691-07901-3). Princeton U Pr.

Adaptive Education: Individual Diversity & Learning. Robert Glaser. LC 76-56081. (Principles of Educational Psychology Ser.). 1977. pap. text ed. 6.95 o.p. (ISBN 0-03-015291-7, HoltC). HR&W.

Adaptive Functions of Imagery: Proceedings of the Center for Research in Cognition & Effect, 3rd, Conference, New York City, 1971. Center for Research in Cognition & Effect Staff. Ed. by Sydney J. Segal. 1971. 52.50 o.p. (ISBN 0-12-635450-2). Acad Pr.

Adaptive Information Processing: An Introductory Survey. J. R. Sampson. LC 76-8470. (Texts & Monographs in Computer Science Ser.). (Illus.). 1976. 25.00 o.p. (ISBN 0-387-07739-1). Springer-Verlag.

Adaptive Reuse of School Buildings: A Bibliography. Mary E. Huls. (Architecture Ser.: A 1475). 6p. 1985. 2.00 o.p. (ISBN 0-89028-605-1). Vance Biblios.

Add Life to Your Years. Frank S. Caprio. 192p. 1975. 6.95 o.p. (ISBN 0-8065-0472-2, Pub. by Citadel Pr). Carol Pub Group.

Addict Aftercare: Recovery Training & Self-Help. Fred Zackon et al. (DHHS Publication ADM 85-1341 Treatment Research Monograph). 212p. 1985. pap. 7.00 o.p. (ISBN 0-318-22499-2, S/N 017-024-01228-9). USGPO.

Addicted Society. Joel Fort. LC 81-8918. 160p. 1982. pap. 5.95 o.p. (ISBN 0-394-17889-0, E814, Ever). Grove.

Addicted Society: Pleasure-Seeking & Punishment Revisited. Joel Fort. LC 80-8918. 224p. 1981. 10.95 o.s.i. (ISBN 0-394-52234-6, GP848). Grove.

Addicted to Suicide: A Woman Struggling to Live. Mary Savage. 144p. 1979. text ed. 18.95x o.p. (ISBN 0-87073-906-9); pap. text ed. 5.95x o.p. (ISBN 0-87073-907-7). Schenkman Bks Inc.

Addiction. Ed. by Peter G. Bourne. 1974. 29.95 o.p. (ISBN 0-12-119535-X). Acad Pr.

Addiction Research & Treatment Converging Trends: Proceedings. Coatesville-Jefferson Conference on Addiction, 1st, October 1977. Ed. by E. L. Gottheil et al. LC 78-23703. 1979. 29.00 o.p. (ISBN 0-08-023025-3). Pergamon.

Addictions. Margaret O. Hyde. 1978. text ed. 9.95 o.p. (ISBN 0-07-031645-7). McGraw.

Adding a Dimension. Isaac Asimov. 1975. pap. 1.50 o.p. (ISBN 0-380-00278-7, 36871, Discus). Avon.

Adding Machine. Burroughs. (ISBN 0-8050-0000-3). Seaver Bks.

Addison Mizner: The Palm Beach Architect. Donald H. Dyal. (Architecture Ser.: Bibliography A 1341). 1985. pap. 2.00 o.p. (ISBN 0-89028-311-7). Vance Biblios.

Addison-Wesley Book of Apple Software 1983. Ed. by Jeffrey Stanton & John Dickey. (Microbook Popular Ser.). 402p. 1983. pap. text ed. 19.95 o.p. (ISBN 0-201-10285-4). Addison-Wesley.

Addison-Wesley Book of Atari Software 1983. Ed. by Jeffery Stanton et al. 288p. 1983. pap. 19.95 o.p. (ISBN 0-201-10286-2). Addison-Wesley.

Addition & Subtraction. Philip Lutgendorf. LC 79-730038. (Illus.). 1978. pap. text ed. 159.00 o.s.i. (ISBN 0-89290-092-X, A508-SATC). Soc for Visual.

Addition & Subtraction Logarithms: Gaussian Tables. William W. Johnson. 1943. 3.00 o.p. (ISBN 0-685-19461-2). Powner.

Additive Migration from Plastics into Food. T. R. Crompton. 1979. 65.00 o.p. (ISBN 0-08-022465-2). Pergamon.

Address Book: How to Reach Anyone Who's Anyone. Michael Levine. LC 83-24980. 224p. 1984. pap. 6.95 o.p. (ISBN 0-399-50988-7, Perigee); pap. 71.40 sets of 12 o.p. (ISBN 0-399-51048-6). Putnam Pub Group.

Address Book: How to Reach Anyone Who's Anyone. Michael Levine. 220p. 17.95x o.p. (ISBN 0-87196-872-X). Facts on File.

Addresses upon the American Road: 1955-1960. Herbert Hoover. LC 61-5290. 415p. 1968. 7.50 o.p. (ISBN 0-87004-065-0). Caxton.

Adelasia Ed Aleramo & Exve. Mayer. (Italian Opera Ser., 1810-1840). 1987. text ed. 85.00 o.p. (ISBN 0-8240-6560-3). Garland Pub.

Adeline, A Child of Yani. Virgil S. Powell. (Illus.). 1979. 9.00 o.p. (ISBN 0-682-49416-X, Banner). Exposition-Phoenix.

Adeline Mowbray: Or, The Mother & Daughter. Mrs. Opie. (Mothers of the Novel Reprints Ser.). 352p. 1986. pap. 8.95 o.p. (ISBN 0-86358-085-8, 80858). Routledge Chapman & Hall.

Adelphi Experiment. Date not set. 4.95 o.p. Coun Soc Wk Ed.

Adelphoe see Brothers.

Adept. 1983. pap. 12.95 o.s.i. (ISBN 0-913922-81-1). Dawn Horse Pr.

Adequate Earth. Donald Finkel. LC 72-78285. 1972. pap. 2.95 o.p. (ISBN 0-689-10512-6, Atheneum). Macmillan.

Adhesion Between Polymers & Concrete. H. Rainer Sasse. 784p. 1987. 140.00 o.p. (ISBN 0-412-29050-2, 1128, Pub. by Chapman & Hall England). Routledge Chapman & Hall.

Adhesion in Biological Systems. Ed. by Richard S. Manly. 1970. 66.00 o.p. (ISBN 0-12-469050-5). Acad Pr.

Adhesion Science & Technology. Lieng-Huang Lee. Incl. Pt. A. 470p (ISBN 0-306-36493-X); Pt. B. 456p (ISBN 0-306-36494-8). LC 75-35744. (Polymer Science & Technology Ser.: Vols. 9A & 9B). 1975. write for info. o.p. (Plenum Pr). Plenum Pub.

Adhesive Bonding: Techniques & Applications. Charles V. Cagle. 1968. write for info. o.p. (P&RB). McGraw.

Adhesives in Building Constrution. Robert H. Gillespie et al. (Agriculture Handbook Ser.: No. 516). (Illus.). 160p. 1987. pap. 6.50 o.p. (ISBN 0-318-22654-5, S/N 001-000-03712-9). USGPO.

Adhesives Technology: Developments Since 1979. Ed. by Marcia Gutcho. LC 82-19096. (Chemical Technology Review: No. 215). (Illus.). 452p. 1983. 48.00 o.p. (ISBN 0-8155-0921-9). Noyes.

Adieu Gary Cooper. Romain Gary. (Coll. Soleil). 13.95 o.p. (ISBN 0-685-34122-4). Schoenhof.

Adieu Volodia. Simone Signoret. Tr. by Stanley Hochman from Fr. LC 85-19572. 448p. 1986. 18.45 o.p. (ISBN 0-394-54927-9). Random.

Adieux: A Farewell to Sartre. Simone De Beauvoir. Tr. by Patrick O'Brian. LC 83-19327. 453p. 1984. 19.45 o.p. (ISBN 0-394-53035-7). Pantheon.

Adirondack Canoe Waters: North Flow. 2nd, rev. ed. Paul Jamieson. LC 86-17397. (Illus.). 320p. 1986. pap. 10.95 o.p. (ISBN 0-935272-38-0). ADK Mtn Club.

Adirondack Canoe Waters: South & West Flow. Alec Proskine. LC 84-18616. (Illus.). 137p. 1986. pap. 9.95 o.p. (ISBN 0-935272-23-2). ADK Mtn Club.

Adirondack Pilgrimage. Paul Jamieson. LC 86-20685. (Illus.). 248p. 1986. 29.50 o.p. (ISBN 0-935272-36-4). ADK Mtn Club.

Adirondack Sampler: Day Hikes for All Seasons. rev ed. Bruce Wadsworth. LC 88-10860. (Illus.). 128p. 1986. pap. 5.95 o.p. (ISBN 0-935272-33-X). ADK Mtn Club.

Adjectives Will Cost You Extra. Garry Trudeau. (He's Never Heard of You, Either Ser.: Bk. I). 128p. 1982. pap. 2.25 o.p. (ISBN 0-449-24505-5, Crest). Fawcett.

Adjudicating Alleged Unethical Conduct: A Simulation. Jane P. Cutler. 33p. 1982. 4.50 o.p. (ISBN 0-317-67646-6). Natl Assn Soc Wkrs.

Adjusting to An Older Work Force. Lois F. Copperman & Frederick D. Keast. 192p. 1983. 24.95 o.p. (ISBN 0-442-21493-6). Van Nos Reinhold.

Adjustment & Growth in a Changing World. 2nd ed. Vince Napoli & James M. Kilbride. (Illus.). 507p. 1984. text ed. 35.00 o.p. (ISBN 0-314-85280-8). West Pub.

Adjustment in the Urban System: The Tasman Bridge Collapse & Its Effects on Metropolitan Hobart. Lee & L. J. Wood. (Progress in Planning Ser.: Vol. 15, Pt. 2). 85p. 1981. pap. 16.25 o.p. (ISBN 0-08-026810-2). Pergamon.

Adjustment: Pathways to Personal Growth. Stephen Worchel & George R. Goethals. (Illus.). 512p. 1985. pap. text ed. (ISBN 0-13-004136-X). P-H.

Adjustment Problems in Children. Alexander Tolor & Margaret C. Deignan. 160p. (Orig.). 1985. pap. text ed. 10.50x o.p. (ISBN 0-87562-083-3). Spec Child.

Adjustment to Physical Handicap & Illness. rev. ed. Roger G. Barker et al. LC 53-7245. (Social Science Research Council Bulletin Ser.). 1953. pap. 35.00 o.p. (ISBN 0-527-03284-0). Kraus Repr.

Adjustment, Trade & Growth in Developed & Developing Countries. (Illus.). 1979. pap. 7.50 o.p. (ISBN 0-685-94613-4, G119, GATT). UNIPUB.

ADLA Four: The Forty First Competition Sponsored by the Art Directors Club of Los Angeles. (Illus.). 246p. 1988. 39.95 o.p. (ISBN 0-8230-5767-4). Madison Square.

ADLA 2. Art Directors Club of Los Angeles. (Illus.). 253p. 1986. 39.95 o.p. (ISBN 0-942604-12-1). Madison Square.

Adler Years, 1954-1981. San Francisco Opera Staff. 120p. (Orig.). 1981. pap. 14.95 o.p. (ISBN 0-89174-041-4). Comstock Edns.

Adler's Physiology of the Eye: Clinical Application. 7th ed. Robert A. Moses. LC 80-16862. (Illus.). 763p. 1980. 52.95 o.p. (ISBN 0-8016-3541-1). Mosby.

Administering Instructional Media Programs. Carlton W. Erickson. LC 68-12281. (Illus.). 1968. text ed. write for info. o.p. (ISBN 0-02-333980-2, 33398). Macmillan.

Administration in the Public Sector. 2nd ed. Harold F. Gortner. LC 86-7204. 428p. 1986. Repr. of 1981 ed. text ed. 19.50 o.p. (ISBN 0-89874-947-6). Krieger.

Administration of Archives. J. H. Hodson. LC 72-163642. 224p. 1972. 55.00 o.p. (ISBN 0-08-016676-8). Pergamon.

Administration of Civil Justice in England & Wales. R. W. Vick & C. F. Schoolbred. LC 67-31508. 1968. text ed. 25.00 o.p. (ISBN 0-08-013299-5); pap. text ed. 8.75 o.p. (ISBN 0-08-013285-5). Pergamon.

Administration of Continuing Education. Adult Education Association Staff. 438p. 6.50 o.p. (ISBN 0-317-36198-8). A A A C E.

Administration of Economic Development Programs: Baselines for Discussion, No. 1. Frwd. by John D. Montgomery. (Lincoln Institute Monograph: No. 79-2). 1979. pap. text ed. 6.00 o.s.i. (ISBN 0-686-28288-4). Lincoln Inst Land.

Administration of Economic Development Programs: Baselines for Discussion, No. 4. Frwd. by John D. Montgomery. (Lincoln Institute Monograph: No. 79-5). 1979. pap. text ed. 6.00 o.s.i. (ISBN 0-686-28291-4). Lincoln Inst Land.

Administration of Economic Development Programs: Baselines for Discussion, No. 5. Frwd. by John D. Montgomery. (Lincoln Institute Monograph: No. 79-6). 1979. pap. text ed. 6.00 o.s.i. (ISBN 0-686-28292-2). Lincoln Inst Land.

Administration of Education in the Asian Region. (Illus.). 252p. (Orig.). 1974. pap. 8.50 o.p. (ISBN 0-685-51932-5, UB3, UB). UNIPUB.

Administration of Justice. 4th ed. Paul B. Weston & Kenneth M. Wells. (Illus.). 240p. 1981. pap. text ed. (ISBN 0-13-006395-9). P-H.

Administration of Lord Elgin in India, Eighteen Ninety-Four to Eighteen Ninety-Nine. P. L. Malhotra. 1979. text ed. 16.95x o.p. (ISBN 0-7069-0747-7, Pub. by Vikas India). Advent NY.

Administration of PE & Athletics. 2nd ed. Reuben B. Frost & Stanley J. Marshall. 480p. 1981. pap. text ed. write for info. o.p. (ISBN 0-697-07171-5). Wm C Brown.

Administration of Physical Education & Sports Programs. Lawrence E. Horine. 360p. 1985. text ed. 27.95 o.p. (ISBN 0-03-060552-0). SCP.

Administration of Special Education. Clifford E. Howe. 300p. 1981. text ed. 24.95 o.p. (ISBN 0-89108-106-2). Love Pub Co.

Administration of the Federal Reserve System: A Bibliographical Overview of Its Board of Governors, Federal Reserve Banks & Monetary Policy. Coppa & Avery Consultants Staff. (Public Administration Ser.: P 1734). 11p. 1985. 2.00 o.p. (ISBN 0-89028-504-7). Vance Biblios.

Administrative Finance. R. W. Morell. LC 81-40367. (Illus.). 260p. (Orig.). 1982. lib. bdg. 29.75 o.p. (ISBN 0-8191-2050-2); pap. text ed. 13.50 o.p. (ISBN 0-8191-2051-0). U Pr of Amer.

Administrative History of the Federal Government: Recent Journal Articles, 1980-1982. Dale E. Casper. (Public Administration Ser.: P 1668). 9p. 1985. 2.00 o.p. (ISBN 0-89028-378-8). Vance Biblios.

Administrative Improvement Methods. Donald B. Sparks. LC 72-93689. 187p. 1973. 10.95x o.p. (ISBN 0-87201-002-3). Gulf Pub.

Administrative Inflation & Public Policy. Gardiner Means. 1959. 5.00 o.p. (ISBN 0-910136-04-1). Anderson Kramer.

Administrative Justice & Supplementary Benefits. Melvin Herman. 68p. 1972. pap. text ed. 5.00x o.p. (ISBN 0-7135-1711-5, Pub. by Bedford England). Gower Pub Co.

Administrative Justice & the Unemployed. Julian Fulbrook. (Studies in Labour & Social Law: Vol. 1). 356p. 1978. lib. bdg. 32.00x o.p. (ISBN 0-7201-0555-2). Mansell.

Administrative Law. Joseph A. Clifford. 30p. 1963. pap. 1.50 o.p. (ISBN 0-87526-001-2). Gould.

Administrative Law: Cases & Materials. 4th ed. Louis L. Jaffe & Nathaniel L. Nathanson. 1976. 28.00 o.p. (ISBN 0-316-45606-3). Little.

Administrative Law in the American Political System. Kenneth F. Warren. (Illus.). 638p. 1982. text ed. 35.25 o.p. (ISBN 0-314-63306-5). West Pub.

Administrative Law: The Formal Process. Peter Woll. 1974. 33.00x o.p. (ISBN 0-520-02802-3). U of Cal Pr.

Administrative Leadership in the Community College. Joseph Foresi, Jr. LC 74-76025. 1974. 6.00 o.p. (ISBN 0-682-47961-6, University). Exposition-Phoenix.

Administrative Manual of Policies & Procedures for Long Term Care Facilities. Depaul & Mount St. Vincent Center. LC 75-21141. (Orig.). 1976. pap. 10.00 o.p. (ISBN 0-87125-028-4). Cath Health.

Administrative Manual of Saint Johns Hospital: Springfield, Illinois. St. Johns Hospital Staff. LC 75-1931. 1975. pap. 10.00 o.p. (ISBN 0-87125-026-8). Cath Health.

Administrative Process. James M. Landis. LC 73-17952. 160p. 1974. Repr. lib. bdg. 22.50x o.p. (ISBN 0-8371-7284-5, LAAP). Greenwood.

Administrative Reforms of Frederick William First of Prussia. Reinhold A. Dorwart. LC 70-138221. 1971. Repr. of 1953 ed. lib. bdg. 25.00x o.p. (ISBN 0-8371-5578-9, DOAR). Greenwood.

Administrative Reorganization of Mississippi Government: A Study in Politics. Thomas E. Kynerd. LC 77-8799. 1978. 3.00 o.p. (ISBN 0-87805-038-8). U Pr of Miss.

Administrative "Revolution" in Whitehall: A Study in the Politics of Administrative Change in British Central Government since the 1950's. G. K. Fry. 218p. 1981. 25.00 o.p. (ISBN 0-7099-1010-X, Pub. by Croom Helm Ltd). Routledge Chapman & Hall.

Administrative Skills for the Manager. Ronald S. Burke. LC 82-72868. 275p. 1982. ringed binder 29.95x o.p. (ISBN 0-87094-348-0). Dow Jones-Irwin.

Administrative Waltz or Ten Commandments for the Administrator. G. Singer & M. Wallace. 1976. 35.00 o.p. (ISBN 0-08-020985-8); pap. 35.00 o.p. (ISBN 0-08-019614-4). Pergamon.

Administrator & Educational Facilities. Jack Davis & E. E. Loveless. LC 80-1445. 272p. 1981. lib. bdg. 28.50 o.p. (ISBN 0-8191-1391-3); pap. text ed. 13.50 o.p. (ISBN 0-8191-1392-1). U Pr of Amer.

Administrators & Reading. Thorsten R. Carlson. 275p. 1972. text ed. 10.95 o.p. (ISBN 0-15-500780-7, HC). HarBraceJ.

Administrator's Guide to Equitable Opportunity in Vocational Educational. Stanley B. Cohen & Denie Denniston. 76p. cancelled o.s.i. (ISBN 0-318-15394-7, RD208). Natl Ctr Res Voc Ed.

Administrator's Handbook: For Community Health & Home Care Services. 2nd ed. 480p. 1984. pap. text ed. 145.00 o.p. (ISBN 0-88737-066-7, 21-1943). Natl League Nurse.

Admirable Warrior: Guerrero Admirable; el Mariscal Sucre, Luchador Por la Independencia Sudamericana. John P. Hoover. Tr. by Alicia C. De Reed. LC 77-12944. (Illus.). 1977. 15.00 o.p. (ISBN 0-87917-061-1). Ethridge.

Admiral of the Fleet, Earl Beatty: The Last Naval Hero. Stephen Roskill. LC 80-19778. 1981. 19.95 o.p. (ISBN 0-689-11119-3, Atheneum). Macmillan.

Admiralty in a Nutshell. Frank L. Maraist. LC 83-16838. (Nutshell Ser.). 390p. 1983. pap. text ed. 10.95 o.p. (ISBN 0-314-76098-9). West Pub.

Admission & Academic Placement of Students from Hong Kong, Malaysia, Philippines & Singapore: Report of the 1979 NAFSA, AACRO & JCOW Workshop. Ed. by Homer Higbee & Margaret K. Winters. 237p. 1980. 2.50 o.s.i. (ISBN 0-317-36685-8, P001-80). NAFSA Washington.

Admission Standards & Admission Processes of Medical Technology Programs. Doris J. Holter. LC 84-24627. 80p. 1985. pap. text ed. 11.00 o.p. (ISBN 0-89189-176-5, 45-9-018-00). Am Soc Clinical.

Admission to Residential Care. P. Brearley et al. 1980. 25.00x o.p. (ISBN 0-422-76930-4, NO.2019, Pub. by Tavistock). Routledge Chapman & Hall.

Admit Desire. Catherine Lanigan. (Avon Romance Ser.). 352p. 1983. pap. 2.95 o.p. (ISBN 0-380-81810-8, 81810-8). Avon.

Adobe & Rammed Earth Buildings: Design & Construction. Paul G. McHenry. LC 83-10397. 217p. 1984. 45.50 o.p. (ISBN 0-471-87677-1, Pub. by Wiley-Interscience). Wiley.

Adobe Building: A Revision of A-76. Mary Vance. (Architecture Ser.: A 1380). 20p. 1985. 3.00 o.p. (ISBN 0-89028-390-7). Vance Biblios.

Adol Feminists Portraits. Bakerman & De Marr. (Reference Ser.). 1983. text ed. 28.00 o.p. (ISBN 0-8240-9136-1). Garland Pub.

Adolescence. W. Eastwood Atwater. (Illus.). 448p. 1983. pap. text ed. (ISBN 0-13-008631-2). P-H.

Adolescence. Harold E. Jones. (National Society for the Study of Education Yearbooks Ser: No. 43, Pt. 1). 1944. pap. text ed. 4.50x o.s.i. (ISBN 0-226-59983-3). U of Chicago Pr.

Adolescence: A Farewell to Childhood. Louise J. Kaplan. LC 84-5486. 1984. 17.45 o.p. (ISBN 0-671-45395-5). S&S.

Adolescence & Early Adulthood. Judith Stevens-Long & Nancy J. Cobb. 506p. 1983. text ed. 27.95 o.p. (ISBN 0-87484-507-6). Mayfield Pub.

Adolescence in Literature. Ed. by Thomas W. Gregory. LC 77-17719. (English & Humanities Ser.). 1978. pap. text ed. 18.95 o.p. (ISBN 0-582-28045-1). Longman.

Adolescence of Zhenya Lyvers. Boris Paternak. 96p. 1961. (ISBN 0-8022-1282-4). Philos Lib.

Adolescence: Psychology, Psychopathology, & Psychotherapy. Derek Miller. LC 73-81211. 556p. 1974. 25.00x o.p. (ISBN 0-87668-101-1). Aronson.

Adolescence Today: Sex Roles & the Search for Identity. David R. Matteson. 1975. 14.50x o.p. (ISBN 0-256-01731-X). Brooks-Cole.

Adolescent. 5th ed. Rice. 608p. 1986. 38.00 o.p. (ISBN 0-205-10465-7). Allyn.

Adolescent & His World. Irene M. Josselyn. 124p. 1952. pap. 5.00 o.p. (ISBN 0-87304-019-8). Family Serv.

Adolescent Behavior Disorders: Foundations & Contemporary Concerns, Advances in Child Behavioral Analysis & Therapy, Vol. III. Paul Karoly & John J. Steffen. LC 83-47801. 336p. 1984. 39.00x o.p. (ISBN 0-669-05641-3). Lexington Bks.

Adolescent Dermatology. Lawrence M. Solomon et al. LC 77-78574. (Major Problems in Clinical Pediatrics Ser.: Vol. 19). (Illus.). 1978. text ed. write for info. o.p. (ISBN 0-7216-8492-0). Saunders.

Adolescent Development. Berzonsky. 1981. write for info. o.p. (ISBN 0-02-471360-0). Macmillan.

Adolescent Development. 4th ed. Elizabeth B. Hurlock. 1973. text ed. 34.95 o.p. (ISBN 0-07-031457-8). McGraw.

Adolescent Development. Richard M. Lerner & Graham B. Spanier. (Illus.). 1980. text ed. 29.95 o.p. (ISBN 0-07-037186-5). McGraw.

Adolescent Medicine: Selected Topics. Ed. by I. R. Shenker. (Illus.). 1978. text ed. 35.00 o.p. (ISBN 0-913258-53-9). Thieme Med Pubs.

Adolescent, Other Citizens, & Their High Schools. Task Force, 1974 Staff. 1975. text ed. 19.95 o.p. (ISBN 0-07-062918-8); pap. text ed. 2.65 o.p. (ISBN 0-07-062920-X). McGraw.

Adolescent Peer Pressure: Theory, Corelates, & Program Implications for Drug Abuse Prevention. 120p. 1981. pap. 4.00 o.p. (ISBN 0-318-11752-5, S/N 017-024-01110-0). USGPO.

Adolescent Personality & Behavior: MMPI Patterns of Normal, Delinquent, Dropout & Other Outcomes. Starke R. Hathaway & Elio D. Monachesi. LC 63-23057. 1963. 16.95 o.p. (ISBN 0-8166-0310-3). U of Minn Pr.

Adolescent Relations with Mothers, Fathers, & Friends. James Youniss & Jacqueline Smollar. LC 84-28067. viii, 202p. 1985. 25.00x o.s.i. (ISBN 0-226-96487-6). U of Chicago Pr.

Adolescent Suicidal Behavior: A Family Systems Model. Roma J. Heillig. Ed. by Peter E. Nathan. LC 83-3594. (Research in Clinical Psychology Ser.: No. 7). 170p. 1983. 37.95 o.p. (ISBN 0-8357-1390-3). Univ Microfilms.

Adolescent Suicide. David K. Curran. (Series in Death Education, Aging & Health Care). 250p. 1987. 39.95 o.p. (ISBN 0-89116-618-1). Hemisphere Pub.

Adolescent Years. 2nd ed. William W. Wattenberg. (Illus.). 1973. text ed. 18.95 o.p. (ISBN 0-15-501387-4, HC). HarBraceJ.

Adolescents: Behavior & Development. 2nd ed. Boyd R. McCandless & Richard H. Coop. LC 78-26507. 1979. text ed. 30.95 o.p. (ISBN 0-03-021456-4, HoltC). HR&W.

Adolescents with Reading Disability-- A Search for Early Causes: Warning: Educational Theory May Be Dangerous to Your Child's Reading Development. John A. Maus. LC 77-78205. 1977. 5.50 o.p. (ISBN 0-682-48848-8, University). Exposition-Phoenix.

Adolf Bastian & the Psychic Unity of Mankind: The Foundations of Anthropology in Nineteen Century Germany. Klaus-Peter Koepping. LC 82-7076. (Scholars' Library). (Illus.). 272p. 1983. text ed. 34.50x o.p. (ISBN 0-7022-1870-7). U of Queensland Pr.

Adolf Hitler: Faces of a Dictator. Heinrich Hoffmann. LC 68-24392. 1969. 9.50 o.p. (ISBN 0-15-103551-2). HarBraceJ.

Adonde? y Como? I. Akimushkin. 375p. (Span.). 1973. 5.95 o.p. (ISBN 0-8285-1462-3, Pub. by Mir Pubs USSR). Imported Pubns.

Adopted Jane. Helen F. Daringer. LC 47-30260. (Illus.). 225p. (gr. 4-8). 1947. 6.25 o.p. (ISBN 0-15-201395-4, HJ). HarBraceJ.

Adopted Jane. Helen F. Daringer. LC 47-30260. (Illus.). 225p. (gr. 3-7). 1973. pap. 1.25 o.p. (ISBN 0-15-602950-2, VoyB). HarBraceJ.

Adoption Book. Sheila Macmanus. (Orig.). 1984. pap. 4.95 o.p. (ISBN 0-8091-2578-1). Paulist Pr.

Adoption in Eastern Oceania. Ed. by Vern Carroll. LC 77-89650. (Association for Social Anthropology in Oceania Monographs: No. 1). (Illus.). 432p. 1970. text ed. 17.50x o.p. (ISBN 0-87022-110-8). UH Pr.

Adoption: The Grafted Tree. Laurie Wishard & William R. Wishard. 208p. 1981. pap. 3.50 o.p. (ISBN 0-380-55640-5, 55640-5, Discus). Avon.

Adoptions Without Agencies: A Study of Independent Adoptions. William Meezan et al. LC 77-99283. 237p. 1977. 12.50 o.s.i. (ISBN 0-87868-174-4, 1906); pap. 13.50 o.p. (ISBN 0-87868-190-6). Child Welfare.

Adore the Lord: Adoration Viewed Through the Old Testament. Ernest Lussier. LC 78-20783. 1979. 6.95 o.p. (ISBN 0-8189-0380-5). Alba.

Adrenal Cortex: Physiological Function & Disease. Don H. Nelson. LC 79-64776. (Major Problems in Internal Medicine Ser.: Vol. 18). (Illus.). 281p. 1980. text ed. write for info. o.p. (ISBN 0-7216-6733-3). Saunders.

Adrenergic Nerves of the Normal & Atrophied Heart. Franz Borchard. Ed. by Wolfgang Bergmann & Wilhelm Doerr. Tr. by H. J. Hirsch from Ger. LC 77-92112. (Normal & Pathologic Anatomy Ser.). (Illus.). 72p. 1978. pap. 24.50 o.p. (ISBN 0-88416-240-0). Year Bk Med.

Adriaen Coorte: A Unique Late Seventeenth Century Dutch Still-Life Painter. L. J. Bol. (Illus.). 1977. text ed. 28.50x o.p. (ISBN 90-232-1516-8). Humanities.

Adrian Mole Diaries: A Novel. Sue Townsend. LC 86-226. 368p. 1986. 14.95 o.p. (ISBN 0-394-55298-9). Grove.

Adrian Piper: Reflections, 1967-1987. Alternative Museum Staff. LC 87-70603. (Illus., Orig.). 1987. pap. 8.00 o.p. (ISBN 0-932075-15-0). Alternative Mus.

Adriatic: A Sea-Guide to Venice, the Italian Shore & the Dalmatian Coast. H. M. Denham. (Illus.). 1977. 19.95 o.p. (ISBN 0-393-03204-3). Norton.

Adrift. Steven Callahan. LC 86-5826. 350p. 1986. 16.95 o.p. (ISBN 0-89621-719-1). Thorndike Pr.

Adrift. Tristan Jones. 288p. 1983. pap. 2.95 o.p. (ISBN 0-380-62455-9, 62455-9, Discus). Avon.

Adrift in Space & Other Stories. George Zebrowski et al. Ed. by Roger Elwood. LC 73-21476. (Illus.). 48p. (gr. 4-8). 1974. PLB 3.95g o.p. (ISBN 0-8225-0951-2). Lerner Pubns.

Adsorption & Collective Paramagnetism. Pierce W. Selwood. 1962. 54.00 o.p. (ISBN 0-12-636550-4). Acad Pr.

Adsorption from Solution. Ed. by R. H. Ottewill. 1983. 43.50 o.p. (ISBN 0-12-530980-5). Acad Pr.

Adsorptive Bubble Separation Techniques. Robert Lemlich. 1972. 85.00 o.p. (ISBN 0-12-443350-2). Acad Pr.

Adtimchiolan Chreidimh. Ed. by R. L. Thomson. 1978. 15.00x o.p. (ISBN 0-7073-0041-X, Pub. by Scot Acad Pr). Longwood Pub Group.

Adult & Immature Tabanidae (Diptera) of California. Woodrow W. Middlekauff & Robert S. Lane. (Bulletin of the California Insect Survey: Vol. 22). 1980. pap. 18.95x o.p. (ISBN 0-520-09604-5). U of Cal Pr.

Adult Baptism & the Catechumenate. Ed. by Johannes Wagner. LC 67-19979. (Concilium Ser.: Vol. 22). 204p. 1967. 7.95 o.p. (ISBN 0-8091-0000-2). Paulist Pr.

Adult Basic Education. ERIC Clearinghouse on Adult, Career, & Vocational Education Staff. 57p. 1983. 4.95 o.p. (ISBN 0-318-22016-4, BB66). Natl Ctr Res Voc Ed.

Adult Development. Calvin A. Colarusso & Robert A. Nemiroff. 300p. 1981. 22.50 o.p. Da Capo.

Adult Development: The Differentiation of Experience. Susan K. Whitbourne & Comilda Weinstock. LC 78-23558. 1979. text ed. 29.95 o.p. (ISBN 0-03-017741-3, HoltC). HR&W.

Adult, Education & Public Policy. Michael O'Keefe. 70p. (Orig.). 1977. pap. text ed. 5.00 o.p. (ISBN 0-8191-5839-9, Pub. by Aspen Inst for Humanistic Studies). U Pr of Amer.

Adult Education Dissertation Abstracts. 311p. 1963. 8.50 o.p. (ISBN 0-317-32113-7). A A A C E.

Adult Education Dissertation Abstracts 1963-1967. Ed. by Roger DeCrow. Nehume League. 1970. 8.50 o.p. (ISBN 0-88379-001-7). A A A C E.

Adult Education for the Handicapped. Gordon A. Larson. 37p. 1982. 4.25 o.p. (ISBN 0-318-22019-9, IN240). Natl Ctr Res Voc Ed.

Adult Education in Developing Countries. 2nd ed. Edwin Townsend-Coles. 1977. 23.00 o.p. (ISBN 0-08-021293-X). Pergamon.

Adult Education: Principles, Practice & Prospects. C. L. Kundu. 112p. 1984. text ed. 12.95x o.p. (ISBN 0-86590-259-3, Pub. by Sterling Pubs India). Apt Bks.

Adult Educator: A Handbook for Staff Development. Harry G. Miller & John R. Verduin. LC 78-67244. (Building Blocks of Human Potential Ser.). 178p. 1979. 19.00x o.p. (ISBN 0-87201-233-6). Gulf Pub.

Adult English Two. John Chapman. (Illus.). 1978. pap. text ed. (ISBN 0-13-008839-0). P-H.

Adult Guide to Beginning Piano & Basic Musicianship. Milton Friedman. (Illus.). 1979. pap. text ed. 28.00 ref. o.p. (ISBN 0-13-008797-1). P-H.

Adult Health Management: Guidelines for Nurse Practitioners. Thompson et al. 1983. pap. text ed. 19.95 o.p. (ISBN 0-8359-0160-2). Appleton & Lange.

Adult Learning: A Design for Action: A Comprehensive International Survey. Ed. by Bud L. Hall & Roby Kidd. 1978. 85.00 o.p. (ISBN 0-08-022245-5). Pergamon.

Adult Learning & Education. Ed. by Malcolm Tight. 336p. 1983. pap. 12.95 o.p. (ISBN 0-7099-2449-6, Pub. by Croom Helm Ltd). Routledge Chapman & Hall.

Adult Learning & Public Broadcasting. Ed. by Marilyn Kressel. (Orig.). 1980. pap. text ed. 6.50 o.p. (ISBN 0-87117-096-5). Am Assn Comm Jr Coll.

Adult Life Cycle Trainer Manual & Reader. Vivian R. McCoy et al. 250p. (Orig.). 1978. pap. 20.00 spiral bdg. o.p. (ISBN 0-936352-07-8). U of KS Cont Ed.

Adult Life: Developmental Processes. Judith Stevens-Long. LC 78-71610. (Illus.). 549p. 1984. pap. 24.95 o.p. (ISBN 0-87484-577-7); instr's. manual avail. o.p. Mayfield Pub.

Adult Literacy & Broadcasting: The BBC's Experience. David Hargreaves. 257p. 1980. 39.50 o.p. (ISBN 0-89397-089-1). Nichols Pub.

Adult Literacy Education in the United States. Wanda D. Cook. LC 76-58957. 149p. 1977. pap. 4.50 o.p. (ISBN 0-87207-934-1). Intl Reading.

Adult Psychiatric Nursing. 2nd ed. Jeanette Lancaster. (Current Clinical Nursing Ser). 1984. pap. 23.75 o.p. Med Exam.

Adult Vocational ESL. Jo Ann Crandall. (Language in Education Ser.: No. 22). 51p. 1986. pap. text ed. 6.67 o.p. (ISBN 0-13-008996-6). P-H.

Adult-Youth Guide on "The Nations of Southern Africa" John S. Kerr. (Orig.). 1976. pap. 1.95 o.p. (ISBN 0-377-00051-5). Friendship Pr.

Adultery. Lauvenia Willingham. 1985. 7.95 o.p. (ISBN 0-533-06181-4). Vantage.

Adultery Can Be Funny. Joel Rothman. (Illus.). 74p. 1985. pap. 2.95 o.p. (ISBN 0-86051-219-3). Parkwest Pubns.

Adults & Their Parents in Family Therapy: A New Direction in Treatment. Lee Headley. LC 77-13990. 194p. 1977. 32.50x o.p. (ISBN 0-306-31087-2, Plenum Pr). Plenum Pub.

Adults Going to the Hospital. Harold Geist & C. F. Hawkins. LC 66-22695. (Illus.). 31p. 1966. pap. 4.10x o.p. (ISBN 0-87424-203-7). Western Psych.

Adults Teaching Adults: Principles & Strategies. John R. Verduin, Jr. et al. LC 77-9259. 199p. 1977. 19.50 o.p. (ISBN 0-89384-015-7). Univ Assocs.

Advance Agents of American Destiny. Roy F. Nichols. LC 79-25886. 254p. 1980. Repr. of 1956 ed. lib. bdg. 35.00x o.p. (ISBN 0-313-22123-5, NIAA). Greenwood.

Advanced Accounting. 3rd ed. Floyd A. Beams. (Illus.). 928p. 1985. text ed. (ISBN 0-13-010091-9). P-H.

Advanced Accounting. 3rd ed. Andrew A. Haried et al. 981p. 1985. (ISBN 0-471-88009-4). Wiley.

Advanced Accounting. Hoyle. 1984. 34.95 o.p. (ISBN 0-256-03067-7). Irwin.

Advanced Accounting: Concepts & Practice. Arnold J. Pahler & Joseph E. Mori. 1026p. 1981. text ed. 24.75 o.p. (ISBN 0-15-501815-9, HC). HarBraceJ.

Advanced Accounting: Concepts & Practices. 2nd ed. Arnold J. Pahler & Joseph E. Mori. 1056p. 1985. text ed. 34.00x o.p. (ISBN 0-15-501820-5, HC). HarBraceJ.

Advanced Accounting: Theory & Practice. James B. Cameron et al. LC 78-69529. (Illus.). 1979. text ed. 49.56 o.p. (ISBN 0-395-27446-X). HM.

Advanced Actuation, Controls, & Integration for Aerospace Vehicles. 1985. 25.00 o.p. (ISBN 0-89883-729-4, P 170). Soc Auto Engineers.

Advanced Airbrushing Techniques Made Simple. Carl Caiati. (Illus.). 144p. 1985. pap. 14.60 o.p. (ISBN 0-8306-1955-0, 1955). TAB Bks.

Advanced Aluminum & Titanium Structures (AD-02) Ed. by J. W. Goodman. 52p. 1981. 14.00 o.p. (ISBN 0-686-34473-1, H00193). ASME.

Advanced Antitrust Workshop: Fifteenth Annual Workshop, Vol. 478. Practising Law Institute Staff. 382p. 1985. pap. 40.00 o.p. (ISBN 0-317-27478-3, #B4-6698). PLI.

Advanced Applesoft Techniques with Sound & Graphics. Walt Gehman & Lee E. Sumner, Jr. (Illus.). 176p. (Orig.). 1985. 19.95 o.p. (ISBN 0-8306-0892-3, 1892); pap. 12.60 o.p. (ISBN 0-8306-1892-9). TAB Bks.

Advanced B & W Darkroom Book. Bob Nadler. (Illus.). 80p. 1979. pap. 8.95 o.p. (ISBN 0-8174-2947-6, Amphoto). Watson-Guptill.

Advanced BASIC: Structured Programming for Microcomputers. Edward J. Coburn. 336p. 1986. pap. 21.95 o.p. (ISBN 0-8273-2481-2). Delmar.

Advanced Business BASIC for Microcomputers. Chao C. Chien. (Irwin Series in Information & Decision Sciences). (Illus.). 343p. 1985. pap. text ed. 25.95x o.p. (ISBN 0-256-03175-4). Irwin.

Advanced Business Models with 1- 2- 3. Stanley R. Trost. LC 84-51215. 190p. 1984. pap. 17.95 o.p. (ISBN 0-89588-159-4). SYBEX.

Advanced Calculus. Hans Sagan. 676p. 1974. text ed. 22.50 o.p. (ISBN 0-395-17090-7). HM.

Advanced Cases in Marketing Management. Edward C. Bursk & Stephen A. Grayser. LC 68-24633. (Foundations of Marketing Ser). (Orig.). 1968. pap. text ed. 19.00 ref. ed. o.p. (ISBN 0-13-011320-4). P-H.

Advanced Chapter 11 Bankruptcy Practice, Vol. III. Ed. by Thomas J. Salerno. 415p. 1987. lexitone 45.00 o.p. (ISBN 0-941161-29-3). PES Inc WI.

Advanced Chapter 11 Bankruptcy Practice, Vol. IV. Ed. by Thomas J. Salerno. 607p. 1987. lexitone 45.00 o.p. (ISBN 0-941161-30-7). PES Inc WI.

Advanced Chapter 11 Bankruptcy Practice, Vol. V. Ed. by Thomas J. Salerno. 572p. 1987. lexitone 45.00 o.p. (ISBN 0-941161-31-5). PES Inc WI.

Advanced Chapter 11 Bankruptcy Practice, VI. Ed. by Thomas J. Salerno. 550p. (Orig.). 1987. lexitone 45.00 o.p. (ISBN 0-941161-32-3). PES Inc WI.

Advanced COBOL: A Structured Approach. Gerry Manning. 480p. 1985. pap. text ed. 25.00 o.p. (ISBN 0-394-33071-4, RanC). Random.

Advanced College Course on How to Become a Great Actor, 2 vols. International Foundation for Theatrical Research Staff. (Illus.). 243p. 1984. Repr. 226.75 o.p. (ISBN 0-89901-179-9). Found Class Reprints.

Advanced Composites. Business Communications Staff. 191p. 1985. pap. 1750.00 o.p. (ISBN 0-89336-442-8, P-023R). BCC.

Advanced Computer Design. J. Iliffe. 1981. text ed. 47.00 o.p. (ISBN 0-13-011254-2). P-H.

Advanced Computer Graphics: Economics, Techniques & Applications. Ed. by R. D. Parslow & R. Elliot Green. LC 77-137740. 1230p. 1971. 155.00x o.p. (ISBN 0-306-30517-8, Plenum Pr). Plenum Pub.

Advanced Concepts in Arrhythmias. Henry J. Marriott & Mary H. Conover. LC 82-3447. (Illus.). 354p. 1982. 33.95 o.p. (ISBN 0-8016-3110-6). Mosby.

Advanced Converters & Near Breeders: Proceedings of the Wingspread Conference, Racine, Wisconsin, 1975. Ed. by P. J. Howe. 1976. 45.00 o.p. (ISBN 0-08-020523-2). Pergamon.

Advanced Cost Accountancy. J. Batty. 512p. (Orig.). 1978. pap. 24.00x o.p. (ISBN 0-7121-0168-3). Trans-Atl Phila.

Advanced Data Communications. Gary A. Shade. (Orig.). 1984. pap. spiral bdg. o.p. (ISBN 0-88006-088-3, CC7418). Wayne Green Ent.

Advanced Development Techniques for dBASE II & dBASE III. Pacer Business Automation Staff & David Duchesneau. 250p. (Orig.). 1985. pap. 28.95 o.p. (ISBN 0-912677-73-2). Tate Pub.

Advanced Dynamics for Engineers. Bruce J. Torby. 426p. 1984. text ed. 41.95 o.p. (ISBN 0-03-063366-4). H Holt & Co.

Titles

Advanced Economic Theory. 6th ed. M. L. Jhingan. 742p. 1984. text ed. 40.00x o.p. (ISBN 0-7069-2676-5, Pub. by Vikas India). Advent NY.

Advanced Electric Circuits. A. M. Brookes. 1966. 22.00 o.p. (ISBN 0-08-011610-8); pap. 50.00 o.p. (ISBN 0-08-011609-4). Pergamon.

Advanced Engineering Mathematics. 5th ed. Erwin Kreyszig. 988p. 1983. (ISBN 0-471-86251-7). Wiley.

Advanced Engineering Thermodynamics. 2nd ed. Rowland S. Benson. 1977. 55.00 o.p. (ISBN 0-08-020719-7); pap. 17.00 o.p. (ISBN 0-08-020718-9). Pergamon.

Advanced Excel Solutions. David K. Simerly. 253p. (Orig.). 1986. pap. 19.95 o.p. (ISBN 0-89588-389-9). Sybex.

Advanced Fibers & Composites for Elevated Temperatures: Proceedings of the AIME Annual Meeting, New Orleans, 1979. AIME Staff. Ed. by Iqbal Ahmad & Bryan Norton. (Illus.). 253p. 36.00 o.p. (ISBN 0-89520-366-9); members 24.00 o.p. (ISBN 0-317-34855-8); student members 14.00 o.p. (ISBN 0-317-34856-6). ASM.

Advanced Fibrous Reinforced Composites Symposium, San Diego, 9-11 November 1966: Proceedings. (Science of Advanced Materials & Process Engineering Ser., Vol. 10). 530p. 25.00 o.p. (ISBN 0-938994-10-7). SAMPE.

Advanced German. rev. ed. A. Russon & L. J. Russon. 1976. pap. text ed. 11.25 o.p. (ISBN 0-582-35245-2). Longman.

Advanced Ground Instructor Written Test Guide. Federal Aviation Administration Staff. 88p. 1980. pap. text ed. 4.50 o.p. (ISBN 0-939158-24-8). Flightshops.

Advanced Immigration Workshop, 1984. (Litigation & Administrative Practice Course Handbook Ser.). 409p. 1984. 15.00 o.p. (ISBN 0-686-79958-5, H4-4931). PLI.

Advanced Industrial Electronics. 2nd ed. Noel M. Morris. LC 83-25538. 1984. text ed. 11.95 o.p. (ISBN 0-07-084694-4). McGraw.

Advanced Industrial Selling. David A. Stumm. 240p. 1981. 17.95 o.p. (ISBN 0-8144-5665-0). AMACOM.

Advanced Inorganic Chemistry: A Comprehensive Text. 4th ed. F. Albert Cotton & Geoffrey Wilkinson. LC 79-22506. 1396p. 1980. 38.50x o.p. (ISBN 0-471-02775-8). Wiley.

Advanced Laboratory Manual for Nutrition Research. G. Krishna & S. K. Ranjhan. 150p. write for info. o.p. (ISBN 0-7069-1125-3, Pub by Vikas India). Advent NY.

Advanced Machine Code Techniques for the BBC Micro. A. P. Stephenson & D. J. Stephenson. (Illus.). 260p. (Orig.). 1984. pap. 15.95 o.p. (ISBN 0-246-12227-7, Pub. by Granada England). Sheridan.

Advanced Mass Spectrometry: Applications in Organic & Analytical Chemistry. U. P. Schlunegger. LC 80-40512. (Illus.). 150p. 1980. 40.00 o.p. (ISBN 0-08-023842-4). Pergamon.

Advanced Materials for Pressure Vessel Service with Hydrogen at High Temperature & Pressures. M. Semchyshen. (MPC-18). 288p. 1982. 50.00 o.p. (H00227). ASME.

Advanced Materials Research: A Guide to R&D Centers. Technical Insights, Inc. Staff. LC 84-51895. 285p. 1984. 270.00 o.p. (ISBN 0-914993-05-4). Tech Insights.

Advanced Mathematics for Engineers. A. D. Myskis. 794p. 1975. 12.50 o.p. (ISBN 0-8285-0700-7, Pub. by Mir Pubs USSR). Imported Pubns.

Advanced Methods for Solving Differential Equations. Ed. by Research & Education Association Staff. LC 82-80750. (Illus.). 352p. (Orig.). 1982. pap. text ed. 13.30 o.s.i. (ISBN 0-87891-541-9). Res & Educ.

Advanced Methods of Data Exploration & Modelling. B. S. Everitt & G. Dunn. LC 83-292. xix, 253p. 1983. text ed. 25.00x o.p. (ISBN 0-435-82294-2). Heinemann Ed.

Advanced Modern Food & Beverage Service. William L. Kahrl. (Illus.). 1977. text ed. 27.67 o.p. (ISBN 0-13-011353-0). P-H.

Advanced MS-DOS Programming: The Microsoft Guide for Assembly Language & C Programmers. Ray Duncan. 496p. 1986. pap. 22.95 o.p. (ISBN 0-914845-77-2). Microsoft.

Advanced Mycology. A. K. Sarbhoy. 231p. 1983. text ed. 25.00 o.p. (ISBN 0-317-64507-2, Pub. by Messers Today & Tomorrow Printers & Publishers). Scholarly Pubns.

Advanced Nuclear Energy Systems: Proceedings, American Nuclear Society Conference, Pittsburgh, March 14-17, 1976. 600p. soft 55.00 o.p. (ISBN 0-317-33006-3, 700015). Am Nuclear Soc.

Advanced Nuclear Systems for Portable Power in Space. National Research Council. 60p. 1983. pap. 13.50x o.p. (ISBN 0-309-03427-2). Natl Acad Pr.

Advanced Organic Chemistry. 2nd ed. Jerry March. (Advanced Chemistry Ser.). (Illus.). 1977. text ed. 59.95 o.p. (ISBN 0-07-040247-7). McGraw.

Advanced Pipe & Tube Welding. Ed. by F. W. Copleston et al. (Engineering Craftsmen Ser.: No. F21). (Illus.). 1970. spiral bdg. 45.00x o.p. Trans-Atl Phila.

Advanced Pipework. S. Bane et al. (Illus.). 213p. 1979. spiral 48.00 o.p. Trans Atl Phila.

Advanced Placement & College Level Examinations in English: Analysis & Interpretation of Literature. James W. Morrison et al. LC 77-14209. (Illus.). 1978. pap. text ed. 4.95 o.p. (ISBN 0-668-04406-3, 4406). Arco.

Advanced Plasma Theory. Ed. by M. N. Rosenbluth. (Italian Physical Society Ser.: Course 25). 1964. 82.50 o.p. (ISBN 0-12-368825-6). Acad Pr.

Advanced Portrait Photography. Roger W. Hicks. (Illus.). 192p. 1988. 29.95 o.p. (ISBN 0-7137-1677-0, Pub. by Blandford Pr England). Sterling.

Advanced Power Training. Ron Marchini & Leo Fong. (Specialties Ser.). (Illus., Orig.). 1983. pap. 9.95 o.p. (ISBN 0-89750-093-8, 430). Ohara Pubns.

Advanced Problems & Methods for Space Flight Optimization. B. F. De Veubeke. 1969. 75.00 o.p. (ISBN 0-08-013290-1). Pergamon.

Advanced Process Control. W. Harmon Ray. (Chemical Engineering Ser.). (Illus.). 1981. text ed. 48.95 o.p. (ISBN 0-07-051250-7). McGraw.

Advanced Processing Methods for Titanium: Proceedings. TMS-AIME Fall Meeting, Louisville, 1981. Ed. by Dennis F. Hasson & C. Howard Hamilton. (Illus.). 320p. 36.00 o.p. (ISBN 0-89520-395-2); members 24.00 o.p. (ISBN 0-317-36222-4); students 12.00 o.p. (ISBN 0-317-36223-2). ASM.

Advanced Program Implementation for dBASE II & dBASE III. Pacer Business Automation Staff et al. 250p. (Orig.). 1985. pap. 28.95 o.p. (ISBN 0-912677-72-4). Tate Pub.

Advanced Programmer's Guide Featuring dBASE III & dBASE II. L. Castro & T. Rettig. 1985. pap. text ed. 28.95 o.p. (ISBN 0-07-912605-7). McGraw.

Advanced Programmer's Guide Featuring dBASE III Plus. L. Castro. 1986. pap. text ed. 28.95 o.p. (ISBN 0-07-912723-1). McGraw.

Advanced Programming & Problem Solving with PASCAL. G. Michael Schneider & Steven C. Bruell. LC 81-1344. 506p. 1981. 36.95 o.p. (ISBN 0-471-07876-X). Wiley.

Advanced Programming for the BBC Micro. Mike James & S. M. Gee. (Illus.). 203p. (Orig.). 1984. pap. 13.95 o.p. (ISBN 0-246-12158-0, Pub. by Granada England). Sheridan.

Advanced Programming for the Model 100. Carl Oppedahl. (Illus., Orig.). 1984. pap. 14.95 o.p. (ISBN 0-88006-078-6, BK7413). Wayne Green Ent.

Advanced Quilting. Elsie Svennas. (Illus.). 144p. 1980. 4.95 o.p. (ISBN 0-684-16612-7, ScribT). Scribner.

Advanced Racing Tactics. Stuart H. Walker. (Illus.). 368p. 1976. 24.95 o.p. (ISBN 0-393-03184-5). Norton.

Advanced Reactors: Physics, Design, & Economics: Proceedings, International Conference, Atlanta, Georgia, Sept. 1974. Ed. by J. M. Kallfelz & R. A. Karam. LC 75-4642. 864p. 1975. 71.00 o.p. (ISBN 0-08-019610-1). Pergamon.

Advanced Reading Inventory: Grade Seven Through College. Jerry L. Johns. 100p. 1981. wire coil o.p. (ISBN 0-697-06058-6). Wm C Brown.

Advanced Restorative Dentistry. 2nd ed. Lloyd Baum & Richard B. McCoy. (Illus.). 580p. 1984. write for info. o.p. (ISBN 0-7216-1599-6). Saunders.

Advanced Sheet Metal Skills. Philip M. Johnston & Murray Liebowitz. LC 76-14088. 1978. pap. 16.95 o.p. (ISBN 0-8273-1239-3); instr's. guide 7.70 o.p. (ISBN 0-8273-1240-7). Delmar.

Advanced Soil Mechanics. Braja Das. (Illus.). 528p. 1983. text ed. 50.95 o.p. (ISBN 0-07-015416-3). McGraw.

Advanced Structural Analysis: Worked Examples. 260p. 1978. pap. text ed. 42.00x o.p. (ISBN 0-258-97030-8, Pub. by Granada England). Gower Pub Co.

Advanced Structured COBOL. Gary S. Popkin. LC 82-21278. 512p. 1983. pap. text ed. write for info. o.p. (ISBN 0-534-01394-5). PWS-Kent Pub.

Advanced Sugar Chemistry. Robert S. Shallenberger. (Illus.). 1982. 67.95 o.s.i. (ISBN 0-87055-399-2). AVI.

Advanced System Analysis & Design for dBASE II & dBASE III. Luis Castro et al. 250p. (Orig.). 1985. pap. 29.95 cancelled o.p. (ISBN 0-912677-71-6). Tate Pub.

Advanced Techniques for Characterizing Hydrogen in Metals: Proceedings. TMS-AIME Fall Meeting, Louisville, 1981. Ed. by N. F. Fiore & B. J. Berkowitz. (Illus.). 260p. 32.00 o.p. (ISBN 0-89520-394-4); members 20.00 o.p. (ISBN 0-317-36224-0); students 10.00 o.p. (ISBN 0-317-36225-9). ASM.

Advanced Techniques for Characterizing Microstructures. Ed. by F. W. Wiffen & J. A. Spitznagel. (Illus.). 510p. 50.00 o.p. (ISBN 0-89520-390-1); members 32.00 o.p. (ISBN 0-317-36226-7); students 16.00 o.p. (ISBN 0-317-36227-5). ASM.

Advanced Techniques for Material Investigation & Fabrication Symposium: Proceedings, Cocoa Beach FL, 5-7 November 1968. (Science of Advanced Materials & Process Engineering Ser., Vol. 14). 1200p. 20.00 o.p. (ISBN 0-938994-14-X). SAMPE.

Advanced Techniques in AutoCAD. Robert M. Thomas. 407p. (Orig.). 1987. pap. 26.95 o.p. (ISBN 0-89588-437-2). Sybex.

Advanced Techniques in Automobile Accident Litigation. Neil Shayne. (Litigation & Administrative Practice Ser.). (Illus.). 1983. 45.00 o.p. (H4-4908). PLI.

Advanced Techniques in Biological Electron Microscopy. Ed. by J. K. Koehler. LC 72-96041. (Illus.). 300p. 1973. 38.00 o.p. (ISBN 0-387-06049-9). Springer-Verlag.

Advanced Techniques in dBASE II. Alan Simpson. LC 85-50466. 395p. 1985. pap. 22.95 o.p. (ISBN 0-89588-228-0). SYBEX.

Advanced Techniques in dBASE III. Alan Simpson. LC 85-71774. 505p. 1985. pap. 22.95 o.p. (ISBN 0-89588-282-5). SYBEX.

Advanced Techniques in Framework. Alan Simpson. LC 85-61339. 320p. 1985. pap. 22.95 o.p. (ISBN 0-89588-246-9). SYBEX.

Advanced Techniques in Microsoft WORD. Alan R. Neibauer. 537p. (Orig.). 1987. pap. 21.95 o.p. (ISBN 0-89588-416-X). Sybex.

Advanced Techniques in Ocular Surgery. Frederick A. Jakobiec & Jesse Sigelman. (Illus.). 350p. 1984. write for info. o.p. (ISBN 0-7216-1047-1). Saunders.

Advanced Techniques in Turbo Pascal. Charles C. Edwards. 309p. (Orig.). 1987. pap. 19.95 o.p. (ISBN 0-89588-350-3). Sybex.

Advanced Techniques in WordPerfect. Kay Y. Nelson. 474p. (Orig.). 1987. pap. 19.95 o.p. (ISBN 0-89588-431-3). Sybex.

Advanced Techniques in WordStar 2000. John Donovan. 350p. (Orig.). 1987. pap. 21.95 o.p. (ISBN 0-89588-418-6). Sybex.

Advanced Tennis. 3rd ed. Chet Murphy. (Physical Education & Activities Ser). 120p. 1982. pap. text ed. write for info. o.p. (ISBN 0-697-07189-8). Wm C Brown.

Advanced Topics on Radiosensitizers of Hypoxic Cells. Ed. by A. Breccia et al. LC 82-427. (NATO ASI Series A, Life Sciences: Vol. 43). 296p. 1982. 59.50x o.p. (ISBN 0-306-40915-1, Plenum Pr); Two-volume set. with Nitroimide notes 89.00 o.p. (Plenum Pr). Plenum Pub.

Advanced Torts: Cases & Materials. Peter B. Kutner & Osborne M. Reynolds. Carolina Acad Pr.

Advanced Treatment & Reclamation of Wastewater. S. H. Jenkins. 1978. pap. 110.00 flexi-cover o.p. (ISBN 0-08-022937-9). Pergamon.

Advanced Turbo Pascal: Programming & Techniques. Herbert Schildt. (Illus.). 350p. (Orig.). 1986. pap. text ed. 19.95 o.p. (ISBN 0-07-881220-8). Osborne-McGraw.

Advanced Turbo Prolog. Herbert Schildt. (Illus.). 300p. (Orig.). 1986. pap. text ed. 19.95 o.p. (ISBN 0-07-881007-8). Osborne-McGraw.

Advanced Typewriting. S. J. Wanous et al. 1981. text ed. write for info. o.p. (ISBN 0-538-14530-7, N53). SW Pub.

Advanced UNIX Programming. Marc J. Rochkind. 265p. 1985. text ed. 37.33 o.p. (ISBN 0-13-011818-4); pap. 34.95 o.p. (ISBN 0-13-011800-1). P-H.

Advanced Will Drafting, 1984. (Tax Law & Estate Planning Ser.). 322p. 1984. 45.00 o.p. (D4-5166). PLI.

Advanced Work Measurement. Delmar W. Karger & Walton C. Hancock. LC 82-935. (Illus.). 321p. 1982. 36.95x o.p. (ISBN 0-8311-1140-2). Indus Pr.

Advancement of Ecology: Proceedings of the All India Symposium, Muzaffarnagar, Dec. 1976. All India Symposium Staff. Ed. by V. P. Agarwal & V. K. Sharma. (Current Trends in Life Sciences: Vol. 4). xxii, 218p. 1978. 22.50 o.p. (ISBN 0-88065-005-2, Pub. by Messers Today & Tomorrow Printers & Publishers). Scholarly Pubns.

Advancement of Learning. Reginald Hill. LC 85-17139. 254p. 1985. 14.95 o.s.i. (ISBN 0-88150-053-4, Foul Play). Countryman.

Advancement of Local Government in New South Wales, 1906 to the Present. F. A. Larcombe. (History of Local Government in New South Wales Ser., 1931 to the Present: Vol. 3). 1978. 43.00x o.p. (ISBN 0-424-00037-7, Pub. by Sydney U Pr). Intl Spec Bk.

Advances & Technical Standards in Neurosurgery, Vol. 4. N. A. Lassan. LC 74-10499. 1977. 46.00 o.p. (ISBN 0-387-81423-X). Springer-Verlag.

Advances & Trends in Structural & Solid Mechanics: Proceedings of the Symposium, Washington D.C., October 4-7, 1982. Ed. by A. K. Noor & J. M. Housner. 587p. 1983. 180.00 o.p. (ISBN 0-08-029990-3). Pergamon.

Advances in Activation Analysis, Vols. 1-2. Ed. by J. M. Lenihan & S. J. Thomson. Vol. 1. 1969. 45.00 o.p. (ISBN 0-12-000401-1); Vol 2. 1972. 65.00 o.p. (ISBN 0-12-000402-X). Acad Pr.

Advances in Aerospace Structures & Materials, 1982. Ed. by R. M. Laurenson & U. Yuceoglu. (AD-03). 1982. 30.00 o.p. (H00240). ASME.

Advances in Allergology & Applied Immunology: Proceedings of the International Congress of Allergology, 10th, Jerusalem, Israel, Nov., 1979. International Congress of Allergology Staff. Ed. by A. Oehling et al. (Illus.). 680p. 1980. 230.00 o.p. (ISBN 0-08-025519-1). Pergamon.

Advances in Analytical Toxicology, Vol. 1. Ed. by R. Baselt. LC 83-73098. (Illus.). 286p. 1984. text ed. 42.50 o.p. (ISBN 0-931890-15-2, Biomed Pubns). Year Bk Med.

Advances in Animal & Comparative Physiology: Proceedings of the 28th International Congress of Physiological Sciences, Budapest, 1980. G. Pethes & V. L. Frenyo. LC 80-41894. (Advances in Physiological Sciences: Vol. 20). (Illus.). 400p. 1981. 71.00 o.p. (ISBN 0-08-027341-6). Pergamon.

Advances in Applied Microbiology, Vol. 19. Ed. by D. Perlman. (Serial Publication Ser.). 1975. 99.50 o.p. (ISBN 0-12-002619-8). Acad Pr.

Advances in Applied Solid State Science, Supplement, 2A: Silicon Integrated Circuits. Ed. by D. Kahng. (Serial Publication). 1981. 77.00 o.p. (ISBN 0-12-002954-5). Acad Pr.

Advances in Artificial Hip & Knee Joint Technology. Ed. by M. Schaldach & D. Hohmann. (Engineering in Medicine Ser: Vol. 2). 1976. 41.00 o.p. (ISBN 0-387-07728-6). Springer-Verlag.

Advances in Behavior Research & Therapy, Vol. 3. Ed. by S. Rachman & T. Wilson. (Illus.). 206p. 1982. 125.00 o.p. (ISBN 0-08-029671-8). Pergamon.

Advances in Behavior Research & Therapy, Vol. 4. Ed. by S. Rachman & T. Wilson. (Illus.). 282p. 1984. 125.00 o.p. (ISBN 0-08-031502-X). Pergamon.

Advances in Behavior Research & Therapy, Vol. 5. Ed. by S. Rachman & T. Wilson. (Illus.). 258p. 1985. 145.00 o.p. (ISBN 0-08-032327-8). Pergamon.

Advances in Behaviour Research & Therapy, Vol. 1, Pt. 1. Ed. by H. J. Eysenck & S. Rachman. 1977. pap. 23.00 o.p. (ISBN 0-08-022257-9). Pergamon.

Advances in Behaviour Research & Therapy, Vol. 2. Ed. by S. Rachman. (Illus.). 186p. 1980. 100.00 o.p. (ISBN 0-08-027110-3). Pergamon.

Advances in Behaviour Research & Therapy, Vol. 6. Ed. by S. Rachman & T. Wilson. (Illus.). 270p. 1986. 132.00 o.p. (ISBN 0-08-034143-8, Pub. by PPL). Pergamon.

Advances in Biochemical Engineering, Vol. 1. Ed. by T. K. Ghose & A. Fiechter. LC 71-152360. (Illus.). 1971. 32.00 o.p. (ISBN 0-387-05400-6). Springer-Verlag.

Advances in Biochemical Engineering, Vol. 2. Ed. by A. Fiechter et al. LC 72-152360. (Illus.). 220p. 1973. 32.50 o.p. (ISBN 0-387-06017-0). Springer-Verlag.

Advances in Bioengineering: 1979. Ed. by M. K. Wells. 200p. 1979. 24.00 o.p. (ISBN 0-317-33578-2, G00155); members 12.00 o.p. (ISBN 0-317-33579-0). ASME.

Advances in Biomedical Engineering, Vol. VII. Ed. by J. H. Brown. LC 71-141733. 1979. 93.50 o.p. (ISBN 0-12-004907-4); 68.00 o.p. (ISBN 0-12-004976-7). Acad Pr.

Advances in Biomedical Engineering, Vol. 4. Ed. by J. H. Brown. (Serial Publication Ser.). 1974. 93.50 o.p. (ISBN 0-12-004904-X). Acad Pr.

Advances in Biomedical Engineering, Vol. 4. Y. Miura et al. (Illus.). 1976. 38.00 o.p. (ISBN 0-387-07747-2). Springer-Verlag.

Advances in Biomedical Engineering, Vol. 5. J. H. Brown. (Serial Publication Ser.). 1975. 93.50 o.p. (ISBN 0-12-004905-8). Acad Pr.

Advances in Biomedical Engineering, Vol. 6. Ed. by J. H. Brown & James F. Dickson. 1976. 93.50 o.p. (ISBN 0-12-004906-6); lib. ed. 94.50 o.p. (ISBN 0-12-004974-0). Acad Pr.

Advances in Bioprocess Technology: Industrial-Specialty Chemicals via Biological Sources-Routes. Technical Insights, Inc. Staff. LC 85-50348. (Emerging Technologies Ser.: No. 14). (Illus.). 265p. 1985. 670.00 o.p. (ISBN 0-914993-12-7). Tech Insights.

Advances in Biotechnology: Fermentation & Yeasts--Proceedings of the 6th International Fermentation Symposium-5th International Symposium on Yeasts, London, Canada, July 20-25, 1980, 4 vols. Moo-Young. (Illus.). 2900p. 1981. Set. 695.00 o.p. (ISBN 0-08-025365-2); Vol. 1. 155.00 o.p. (ISBN 0-08-025383-0); Vol. 2. 180.00 o.p. (ISBN 0-08-025384-9); Vol. 3. 150.00 o.p. (ISBN 0-08-025385-7); Vol. 4. 175.00 o.p. (ISBN 0-08-025382-2). Pergamon.

Advances in Cancer Chemotherapy, Vol. 1. Rosowsky. 1979. 65.00 o.p. (ISBN 0-8247-6806-X). Dekker.

Advances in Cancer Research, Vol. 35. Ed. by George Klein & Sidney Weinhouse. (Serial Publication Ser.). 1981. 92.50 o.p. (ISBN 0-12-006635-1). Acad Pr.

Advances in Carbohydrate Chemistry & Biochemistry, Vol. 33. Ed. by Ward Pigman & Derek Horton. 1976. 94.50 o.p. (ISBN 0-12-007233-5); 94.00 o.p. (ISBN 0-12-007278-5). Acad Pr.

Advances in Cardiovascular Nursing. Julie A. Shinn & Marilyn K. Douglas. 1985. 39.55 o.p. (ISBN 0-87189-105-0). Aspen Pub.

Advances in Cellular Neurobiology, Vol. 4. Ed. by S. Fedoroff & L. Hertz. (Serial Publication Ser.). 420p. 1983. 92.50 o.p. (ISBN 0-12-008304-3). Acad Pr.

Advances in Cement Technology: Critical Reviews & Case Studies on Manufacturing, Quality Control, Optimization & Use. Ed. by S. N. Ghosh. (Illus.). 775p. 1982. 195.00 o.p. (ISBN 0-08-028670-4). Pergamon.

Advances in Chemical Physics, Vol. 18. Ed. by I. Prigogine et al. 321p. 1970. 35.50 o.p. (ISBN 0-471-69923-3, John Wiley). Krieger.

Advances in Chemical Physics, Vol. 21. Ed. by I. Prigogine et al. 816p. 1971. 44.50 o.p. (ISBN 0-471-40066-1). Krieger.

Advances in Chemical Physics, Vols. 19-20 & 22-25. Ed. by I. Prigogine et al. Incl. Vol. 19. 1971 (ISBN 0-471-69924-1); Vol. 20. 1971 (ISBN 0-471-69925-X); Vol. 22. 1972 (ISBN 0-471-69926-8); Vol. 23. 1973 (ISBN 0-471-69927-6); Vol. 24. 1973 (ISBN 0-471-69929-2); Vol. 25. 1974 (ISBN 0-471-69930-6). LC 58-9935. 35.50 ea. o.p. (Pub. by Wiley). Krieger.

Advances in Chemical Physics, Vol. 57. I. Prigogine & Stuart A. Rice. (Advances in Chemical Physics Ser.: 2-007). 467p. 1984. 105.00x o.p. (ISBN 0-471-87830-8, Pub. by Wiley-Interscience). Wiley.

Advances in Climatic Physiology. Ed. by S. Itoh et al. LC 72-78342. (Illus.). 416p. 1972. 39.90 o.p. (ISBN 0-387-05826-5). Springer-Verlag.

Advances in Comparative Physiology & Biochemistry, Vols. 1-4. Ed. by O. E. Lowenstein. 88.00 ea. o.p. Vol. 1, 1962 (ISBN 0-12-011501-8). Vol. 2, 1966 (ISBN 0-12-011502-6). Vol. 3, 1968 (ISBN 0-12-011503-4). Vol. 4, 1971 (ISBN 0-12-011504-2). Vols. 5-7, 1978. Vol. 7 (ISBN 0-12-011507-7). Acad Pr.

Advances in Complex Function Theory. Ed. by W. E. Kirwan & L. Zalcman. LC 75-45187. (Lecture Notes in Mathematics Ser: Vol. 505). 1976. pap. 16.00 o.p. (ISBN 0-387-07548-8). Springer-Verlag.

Advances in Composite Materials: Proceedings of the Third International Conference on Composite Materials, Paris, France, 26-29 August, 1980, 2 vols. Ed. by A. R. Bunsell et al. LC 80-40997. 2000p. 1980. Set. 500.00 o.p. (ISBN 0-08-026717-3). Pergamon.

Advances in Computer-Assited Learning: Selected Proceedings from the CAL 85 Symposium. P. R. Smith. 260p. 1986. 45.00 o.p. (ISBN 0-08-031813-4, Pub. by PPL). Pergamon.

Advances in Computer Chess in 3 Parts: Proceedings of the International Conference on Advances in Computer Chess, London, UK, April, 1981. International Conference on Advances in Computer Chess Staff. Ed. by M. R. Clarke. LC 78-309646. (Pergamon Chess Ser.). 182p. 1982. 50.00 o.p. (ISBN 0-08-026898-6). Pergamon.

Advances in Computer System Security. Ed. by Rein Turn. LC 81-65989. (Illus.). 403p. (Orig.). 1981. pap. text ed. 42.00 o.p. (ISBN 0-89006-096-7). Artech Hse.

Advances in Computer Technology, 2 vols. Ed. by Ali Seireg. Incl. Vol. I. Industry; Energy; Robots & Manipulators; Mini & Micro Software; Application & Design. 480p (H00173); Vol. II. Microprocessor; Automotive Development; Systems; Data Base; Finite Elements; Graphics; Education; Manufacturing; Management; Language Standards; Personal Computing. 492p (H00174). 1980. text ed. 60.00 ea. o.p. (ISBN 0-317-02542-2). ASME.

Advances in Corrosion Science & Technology. Ed. by M. G. Fontana & R. W. Staehle. Incl. Vol. 1. 384p. 1970 (ISBN 0-306-39501-0); Vol. 2. 354p. 1972 (ISBN 0-306-39502-9); Vol. 3. 432p. 1973 (ISBN 0-306-39503-7); Vol. 4. 340p. 1974 (ISBN 0-306-39504-5); Vol. 5. 408p. 1976 (ISBN 0-306-39505-3); Vol. 6. 278p. 1976 (ISBN 0-306-39506-1); Vol. 7. 376p. 1980 (ISBN 0-306-39507-X). LC 76-107531. (Illus.). each 69.50x o.p. (Plenum Pr). Plenum Pub.

Advances in Cryogenic Engineering, Vol. 25. Ed. by K. D. Timmerhaus & H. A. Snyder. LC 57-35598. (Illus.). 868p. 1980. 95.00x o.p. (ISBN 0-306-40504-0, Plenum Pr). Plenum Pub.

Advances in Cryogenic Engineering, Vol. 26. Ed. by A. F. Clark & R. P. Reed. LC 57-35598. 718p. 1981. 95.00x o.p. (ISBN 0-306-40531-8, Plenum Pr). Plenum Pub.

Advances in Cryogenic Engineering, Vol. 27. Ed. by R. W. Fast. LC 57-35598. 1252p. 1982. 125.00x o.p. (ISBN 0-306-41103-2, Plenum Pr). Plenum Pub.

Advances in Cryogenic Engineering, Vol. 28. Ed. by R. P. Reed & A. F. Clark. LC 57-35598. 944p. 1982. 110.00x o.p. (ISBN 0-306-41104-0, Plenum Pr). Plenum Pub.

Advances in Cytopharmacology: Proceedings of the International Symposium on Cell Biology & Cytopharmacology, 1st, Vol. 1. International Symposium on Cell Biology & Cytopharmacology Staff. Ed. by F. Clementi & B. Ceccarelli. LC 70-84115. (Illus.). 493p. 1971. 79.50 o.p. (ISBN 0-911216-09-X). Raven.

Advances in Data Communications Management, Vol. 1. Thomas A. Rullo. (Advances Library in EDP Management Ser.). 210p. 1980. 56.00 o.p. (ISBN 0-471-25998-5). Wiley.

Advances in Data Processing Management, Vol. 1. Ed. by Thomas A. Rullo. LC 81-640185. 207p. 1980. 56.95 o.p. (ISBN 0-471-25993-4). Wiley.

Advances in Disease Prevention, Vol. I. Charles B. Arnold et al. 320p. 1981. text ed. 35.00 o.p. (ISBN 0-8261-2830-0). Springer Pub.

Advances in Electronics & Electron Physics, Vol. 43. Ed. by L. Marton. 1977. 99.50 o.p. (ISBN 0-12-014643-6). Acad Pr.

Advances in Enzyme Technology: Artificial & Semisynthetic Designed Enzymes. Technical Insights, Inc. Staff. LC 84-51898. (Emerging Technologies Ser.: No. 12). 181p. 1984. 580.00 o.p. (ISBN 0-914993-08-9). Tech Insights.

Advances in Enzymology & Related Areas of Molecular Biology, Vol. 57. Ed. by Alton Meister. 513p. 1985. 67.50 o.p. (ISBN 0-471-89011-1). Wiley.

Advances in Enzymology & Related Areas of Molecular Biology, Vol. 58. Alton Meister. 389p. 1986. 57.50 o.p. (ISBN 0-471-88013-2). Wiley.

Advances in Experiential Social Processes. Ed. by Cary L. Cooper & Clayton Alderfer. LC 77-22060. (Advances in Experimental Social Processes Ser.: Vol. 1). 225p. 1978. 59.95 o.p. (ISBN 0-471-99546-0, Pub. by Wiley-Interscience). Wiley.

Advances in Experimental Clinical Psychology. Henry E. Adams & William K. Boardman. 230p. 1972. 55.00 o.p. (ISBN 0-08-016399-8). Pergamon.

Advances in Experimental Social Psychology, Vol. 19. Leonard Berkowitz. (Serial Publication). 1985. pap. 24.95 o.p. (ISBN 0-12-000010-5). Acad Pr.

Advances in Fetal Physiology: Reviews in Honor of G. C. Liggins. Ed. by P. D. Gluckman et al. (Research in Perinatal Medicine Ser.: No. VIII). (Illus.). 1989. 102.50x o.p. (ISBN 0-916859-41-X). Perinatology.

Advances in Fracture Research: Proceedings of the 5th International Conference on Fracture, 1981, Cannes, France, 6 vols. D. Francois. LC 80-41879. (International Series on the Strength & Fracture of Materials & Structures). 3000p. 1981. Set. 665.00 o.p. (ISBN 0-08-025428-4). Pergamon.

Advances in Free Radical Chemistry, 4 vols. Ed. by G. H. Williams. Vol. 2, 1967. 93.50 o.p. (ISBN 0-12-017002-7); Vol. 3, 1969. 93.50 o.p. (ISBN 0-12-017003-5); Vol. 4, 1972. 93.50 o.p. (ISBN 0-12-017004-3); Vol. 5, 1975. 93.50 o.p. (ISBN 0-12-017005-1). Acad Pr.

Advances in Fuzzy Set Theory & Applications. Ed. by M. M. Gupta et al. 753p. 1979. 158.00 o.p. (ISBN 0-444-85372-3, North Holland). Elsevier.

Advances in Game Theory. Ed. by Melvin Dresher et al. (Annals of Mathematics Studies, Vol. 52). 86.50 o.p. (ISBN 0-691-07902-1). Princeton U Pr.

Advances in Genetics, Development, & Evolution of Drosophila. Ed. by Seppo Lakovaara. LC 82-9154. 480p. 1982. 79.50x o.p. (ISBN 0-306-41106-7, Plenum Pr). Plenum Pub.

Advances in High Temperature Chemistry. Ed. by LeRoy Eyring. Vol. 1. 1967. 93.50 o.p. (ISBN 0-12-021501-2); Vol. 2. 1969. 93.50 o.p. (ISBN 0-12-021502-0); Vol. 3.1971. 93.50 o.p. (ISBN 0-12-021503-9); Vol. 4.1972.. 93.50 o.p. (ISBN 0-12-021504-7). Acad Pr.

Advances in Human Clinical Nutrition. Ed. by Joseph J. Vitale. (Illus.). 232p. 1982. text ed. 26.00 o.p. (ISBN 0-88416-219-2). Year Bk Med.

Advances in Human Genetics, Vols. 1-10. Ed. by Harry Harris & Kurt Hirschhorn. Incl. Vol. 1. 352p. 1970. 49.50x o.p. (ISBN 0-306-39601-7); Vol. 2. 330p. 1971. 49.50x o.p. (ISBN 0-306-39602-5); Vol. 3. 464p. 1972. 49.50x o.p. (ISBN 0-306-39603-3); Vol. 4. 424p. 1974. 49.50x o.p. (ISBN 0-306-39604-1); Vol. 5. 398p. 1975. 49.50x o.p. (ISBN 0-306-39605-X); Vol. 6. 396p. 1976. 49.50x o.p. (ISBN 0-306-39606-8); Vol. 7. 274p. 1976. 49.50x o.p. (ISBN 0-306-39607-6); Vol. 8. 458p. 1977. 49.50x o.p. (ISBN 0-306-39608-4); Vol. 9. 394p. 1979. 59.50x (ISBN 0-306-40219-X, Plenum Pr); Vol. 10. 412p. 1980. 59.50x (ISBN 0-306-40386-2, Plenum Pr). LC 77-84583. (Illus.). Plenum Pub.

Advances in Image Processing & Pattern Recognition. Ed. by V. Cappellini & R. Marconi. 340p. 1986. 116.00 o.p. (ISBN 0-444-70068-4, North-Holland). Elsevier.

Advances in Immunology, Vols. 1-29. Ed. by W. H. Taliaferro & J. H. Humphrey. Incl. Vol. 1. 1961. 75.00 (ISBN 0-12-022401-1); Vol. 2. 1963. 75.00 (ISBN 0-12-022402-X); Vol. 3. Ed. by F. J. Dixon, Jr. & J. H. Humphrey. 1963. 70.00 (ISBN 0-12-022403-8); Vol. 4. 1964. 70.00 (ISBN 0-12-022404-6); Vol. 5. 1966. 70.00 (ISBN 0-12-022405-4); Vol. 6. 1967. 75.00 (ISBN 0-12-022406-2); Vol. 7. Ed. by F. J. Dixon, Jr. & Henry G. Kunkel. 1967. 70.00 (ISBN 0-12-022407-0); Vol. 8. 1968. 70.00 (ISBN 0-12-022408-9); Vol. 9. 1968. 70.00 (ISBN 0-12-022409-7); Vol. 10. 1969. 70.00 (ISBN 0-12-022410-0); Vol. 11. 1969. 70.00 (ISBN 0-12-022411-9); Vol. 12. 1970. 70.00 (ISBN 0-12-022412-7); Vol. 13. 1971. 70.00 (ISBN 0-12-022413-5); Vol. 14. 1971. 70.00 (ISBN 0-12-022414-3); Vol. 15. 1972. 70.00 (ISBN 0-12-022415-1); Vol. 16. 1973. 70.00 (ISBN 0-12-022416-X); Vol. 17. 1973. 70.00 (ISBN 0-12-022417-8); Vol. 18. 1974. 70.00 (ISBN 0-12-022418-6); Vol. 19. 1974. 70.00 (ISBN 0-12-022419-4); Vol. 20. 1975. 70.00 (ISBN 0-12-022420-8); Vol. 21. 1975. 70.00 (ISBN 0-12-022421-6); Vol. 22. 1976. 70.00 (ISBN 0-12-022422-4); Vol. 23. 1976. 70.00 (ISBN 0-12-022423-2); Vol. 24. 1976. 70.00 (ISBN 0-12-022424-0); Vol. 25. 1978. 66.00 (ISBN 0-12-022425-9); Vol. 26. Ed. by Henry G. Kunkel & E. J. Dixon. 1978. 67.50 (ISBN 0-12-022426-7); Vol. 27. 1979. 60.00 (ISBN 0-12-022427-5); Vol. 28. 1980. 65.00 (ISBN 0-12-022428-3); Vol. 29. 1980. 60.00 (ISBN 0-12-022429-1). LC 61-17057. 1980. 57.00 o.p. (ISBN 0-686-66773-5); 60.00 o.p. (ISBN 0-12-022430-5). Acad Pr.

Advances in Immunopharmacology: Proceedings of the First International Conference on Immunopharmacology, 29 July-1 August 1980, Brighton. J. Hadden et al. (Illus.). 538p. 1981. 105.00 o.p. (ISBN 0-08-026384-4); pap. 48.00 o.p. (ISBN 0-08-027974-0). Pergamon.

Advances in Infrared & Raman Spectroscopy, Vol. 5. Ed. by R. J. Clark & R. E. Hester. 404p. 1978. casebound 171.00 o.p. (ISBN 0-471-25636-6, Pub. by Wiley Heyden). Wiley.

Advances in Insect Population Control by the Sterile-Male Technique. (Technical Reports Ser.: No. 44). (Illus.). 79p. (Orig.). 1965. pap. 13.50 o.p. (ISBN 92-0-115065-2, IDC44, IAEA). UNIPUB.

Advances in Instrumentation: Proceedings of the ISA Conference & Exhibit, 39th, Vol. 39. Instrument Society of America Staff. LC 56-29277. 1984. pap. text ed. 105.00x set o.p. (ISBN 0-87664-827-8); Pt. 1, 656 pgs. pap. text ed. 58.00x o.p. (ISBN 0-87664-825-1); Pt. 2, 800 pgs. pap. text ed. 60.00x o.p. (ISBN 0-87664-826-X). Instru Soc.

Advances in Instrumentation: Proceedings of the ISA International Conference & Exhibit, Philadelphia, Pa., Oct., 1982, 3 pts, Vol. 37. Instrument Society of America Staff. LC 56-29277. (Orig.). 1982. Set. pap. text ed. 95.00x o.p. (ISBN 0-87664-709-3); pap. text ed. 35.00x ea. o.p. Pt. 1; 528p (ISBN 0-87664-700-X). Pt. 2; 560p (ISBN 0-87664-701-8). Pt. 3; 664p (ISBN 0-87664-702-6). Instru Soc.

Advances in Instrumentation: Proceedings of the 38th ISA Conference & Exhibit, 1983, 2 pts, Vol. 38. Instrument Society of America Staff. LC 56-29277. 1983. Set. pap. text ed. 95.00x o.p. (ISBN 0-87664-779-4); Pt. 1, 722pp. pap. text ed. 55.00x o.p. (ISBN 0-87664-780-8); Pt. 2, 790pp. pap. text ed. 55.00x o.p. (ISBN 0-87664-781-6). Instru Soc.

Advances in Internal Medicine & Pediatrics, Vol. 37. Ed. by F. K. Port et al. LC 43-32964. 1975. 85.00 o.p. (ISBN 0-387-07040-0). Springer-Verlag.

Advances in Laser Spectroscopy, Vol. I. Ed. by Bruce A. Garetz & John R. Lombardi. 245p. 1982. 75.00x o.p. (ISBN 0-471-26185-8). Wiley.

Advances in Linear Free-Energy Relationships. Ed. by N. B. Chapman & J. Shorter. LC 78-161305. 448p. 1972. 65.00x o.p. (ISBN 0-306-30566-6, Plenum Pr). Plenum Pub.

Advances in Liquid Crystal Research & Applications: Proceedings of the Third Liquid Crystal Conference of the Socialist Countries, Budapest, 27-31 August 1979. Ed. by L. Bata. 1000p. 1981. 260.00 o.p. (ISBN 0-08-026191-4). Pergamon.

Advances in Macromolecular Chemistry. Ed. by W. M. Pasika. Vol. 1. 1968. 36.00 o.p. (ISBN 0-12-025201-5); Vol. 2. 1970. 25.00 o.p. (ISBN 0-12-025202-3). Acad Pr.

Advances in Management Education. Ed. by John Beck & Charles Cox. LC 80-40117. 360p. 1980. 73.95x o.p. (ISBN 0-471-27775-4, Pub. by Wiley-Interscience). Wiley.

Advances in Manufacturing Systems - Research & Development. J. Peklenik. 196p. 1971. 60.00 o.p. (ISBN 0-08-016497-8). Pergamon.

Advances in Medical Imaging & Related Dosimetry: International School of Radiation Damage Protection & Anomalies. Ed. by A. Brill et al. 600p. 1988. 74.00 o.p. (ISBN 9971-50-191-0). World Scientific Pub.

Advances in Metal Processing. Ed. by John J. Burke & Volker Weiss. LC 81-439. (Sagamore Army Materials Research Conference Ser.: Vol. 25). 398p. 1981. 69.50x o.p. (ISBN 0-306-40651-9, Plenum Pr). Plenum Pub.

Advances in Microbiology of the Sea, Vol. 1. Ed. by M. Droop & F. Wood. 1968. 69.00 o.p. (ISBN 0-12-027801-4). Acad Pr.

Advances in Microelectronics: Review Papers from the 12th Yugoslav Conference on Microelectronics, Yugoslavia, 7-9 May 1984. Ed. by N. D. Stojadinovic. 176p. 1984. pap. 50.00 o.p. (ISBN 0-08-031162-8). Pergamon.

Advances in Mineral Processing. Intro. by P. Somasundaran. LC 85-63668. (Illus.). 756p. 1986. 68.50x o.p. (ISBN 0-87335-050-2). SMM&E Inc.

Advances in Monetary Economics. Ed. by David Currie. LC 85-2130. 240p. 1985. 34.50 o.p. (ISBN 0-7099-3443-2, Pub. by Croom Helm Ltd). Routledge Chapman & Hall.

Advances in Myocardiology, Vol. 3. Ed. by E. Chazov et al. LC 80-643989. 670p. 1982. 95.00x o.p. (ISBN 0-306-40876-7, Plenum Med Bk). Plenum Pub.

Advances in Myocardiology, Vol. 4. Ed. by E. Chazov et al. LC 80-643989. 664p. 1983. 95.00x o.p. (ISBN 0-306-40877-5, Plenum Med Bk). Plenum Pub.

Advances in Neurosurgery, Vol. 4. Ed. by R. Wuellenweber et al. LC 76-57741. 1977. pap. 48.00 o.p. (ISBN 0-387-08100-3). Springer-Verlag.

Advances in Neurotoxicology: Proceedings of the International Congress on Neurotoxicology, Varese, 27-30 September 1979. Ed. by L. Manzo. (Illus.). 404p. 1980. 105.00 o.p. (ISBN 0-08-024953-1). Pergamon.

Advances in Nuclear Engineering Computational Methods: International Meeting, Knoxville, Tennessee. 905p. 1985. 75.00 o.p. (ISBN 0-89448-117-7, 700100). Am Nuclear Soc.

Advances in Oral Biology. Ed. by Peter H. Staple. Vol. 1. 1964. 82.50 o.p. (ISBN 0-12-030501-1); Vol. 2. 1966. 82.50 o.p. (ISBN 0-12-030502-X); Vol. 3. 1968. 82.50 o.p. (ISBN 0-12-030503-8); Vol. 4. 1970. 75.00 o.p. (ISBN 0-12-030504-6). Acad Pr.

Advances in Oral Radiology. Ed. by Allan B. Reiskin. LC 79-21095. (Post Graduate Dental Handbook Ser.: Vol. 9). 330p. 1980. text ed. 38.00 o.p. (ISBN 0-88416-165-X). Year Bk Med.

Advances in Organic Geochemistry, 1964-1966: Proceedings. Ed. by G. D. Hobson. 1970. 145.00 o.p. (ISBN 0-08-012758-4). Pergamon.

Advances in Organic Geochemistry, 1968: Proceedings. P. A. Schenck. 1969. 155.00 o.p. (ISBN 0-08-006628-3). Pergamon.

Advances in Organic Geochemistry 1979: Proceedings of the 9th International Meeting on Organic Geochemistry Held at Newcastle-Upon-Tyne, England, Sept. 1979. Ed. by A G. Douglas & J. R. Maxwell. LC 80-41078. (International Series in Earth Sciences: Vol. 36). (Illus.). 750p. 1981. 200.00 o.p. (ISBN 0-08-024017-8). Pergamon.

Advances in Organic Geochemistry, 1971. H. R. Von Gaertner & H. Wehner. 1972. 185.00 o.p. (ISBN 0-08-017598-8). Pergamon.

Advances in Pacemaker Technology. Ed. by M. Schaldach & S. Furman. (Engineerining in Medicine: Vol. 1). 575p. 1975. 35.00 o.p. (ISBN 0-387-07360-4). Springer-Verlag.

Advances in Parasitology, Vol. 17. Ed. by W. H. Lumsden. LC 62-22124. (Serial Publication). 1980. 96.00 o.p. (ISBN 0-12-031717-6). Acad Pr.

Advances in Pathology (Anatomic & Clinical) Laboratory Medicine: Proceedings of the Triennial World Congress of the World Association of Societies of Pathology, 11th, Jerusalem, Israel, Sept. 20-25, 1981. World Association of Societies of Pathology Staff & E. Levy. (Illus.). 542p. 1982. Vol. 1. 175.00 o.p. (ISBN 0-08-028878-2); Set. 365.00 o.p. (ISBN 0-08-029777-3); Vol. 2. 195.00 o.p. (ISBN 0-08-028879-0). Pergamon.

Advances in Pharmaceutical Sciences. H. S. Bean et al. Vol. 1. 1964. (ISBN 0-12-032301-X); Vol. 2. 1967. 99.00 o.p. (ISBN 0-12-032302-8); Vol. 3. 1971. (ISBN 0-12-032303-6); Vol. 4 1975. 121.00 o.p. (ISBN 0-12-032304-4). Acad Pr.

Advances in Pharmacology & Therapeutics: Proceedings of Eighth International Congress of Pharmacology, Tokyo, Japan, 19-24 July 1981, Ser. II, Vol. 3. Ed. by H. Yoshida et al. (Illus.). 346p. 1982. 105.00 o.p. (ISBN 0-08-028023-4). Pergamon.

Advances in Pharmacology & Therapeutics: Proceedings of the Eighth International Congress of Pharmacology, Tokyo, Japan, 19-24 July, 1981, Series No. 2, Vol. 4. Ed. by H. Yoshida & Y. Gigihara. (Illus.). 310p. 1982. 105.00 o.p. (ISBN 0-08-028024-2). Pergamon.

Advances in Pharmacology & Therapeutics: Proceedings of the Eighth International Congress of Pharmacology, Tokyo, Japan, July 19-24, 1981, Series No. 2, Vol. 5. Ed. by H. Yoshida et al. (Illus.). 380p. 1982. 105.00 o.p. (ISBN 0-08-028025-0). Pergamon.

Advances in Pharmacology & Therapeutics: Proceedings of 8th International Congress of Pharmacology, Tokyo, Japan, July 19-24, 1981, Series No. 2, Vol. 6. Ed. by H. Yoshida et al. (Illus.). 310p. 1982. 105.00 o.p. (ISBN 0-08-028026-9). Pergamon.

Advances in Photochemistry, Vol. 9. Ed. by James N. Pitts, Jr. et al. 566p. 1974. 49.50 o.p. (ISBN 0-471-69092-9). Krieger.

Advances in Physical Chemistry: Current Developments in Electrochemistry & Corrosion. Y. Kolotyrkin. 191p. 1982. pap. 6.45 o.p. (ISBN 0-8285-2304-5, Pub. by Mir Pubs USSR). Imported Pubns.

Advances in Physiological Sciences: Kidney & Body Fluids. Ed. by L. Takacs. LC 80-42187. (International Union of Physiological Sciences Ser.). (Illus.). 672p. 1981. 100.00 o.p. (ISBN 0-08-026824-2, PBL). Pergamon.

Advances in Polymer Science. Ed. by Z. A. Rogovin et al. 340p. 1974. text ed. 65.00x o.p. (ISBN 0-7065-1439-4, Pub. by Keter Pub Jerusalem). Coronet Bks.

Advances in Polymer Science, Vol. 15. G. Henrici-Olive et al. Ed. by H. J. Cantow. LC 61-642. (Illus.). iii, 155p. 1974. 46.10 o.p. (ISBN 0-387-06910-0). Springer-Verlag.

Advances in Polymer Science: Macro-Conformation of Polymers, Vol. 18. P. A. Small et al. LC 61-642. (Illus.). 150p. 1975. text ed. 43.00 o.p. (ISBN 0-387-07252-7). Springer-Verlag.

Advances in Polymer Science: Polymerization, Vol. 17. A. Casale et al. Ed. by H. J. Cantow. LC 61-642. (Illus.). 120p. 1975. 35.00 o.p. (ISBN 0-387-07111-3). Springer-Verlag.

Advances in Programming Non-Numerical Applications to Computing Machines. Ed. by L. Fox. 1966. 55.00 o.p. (ISBN 0-08-011356-7). Pergamon.

Advances in Quantum Electronics. Ed. by D. W. Goodwin. Vol. 1, 1970. 60.50 o.p. (ISBN 0-12-035001-7); Vol. 2, 1974. 66.00 o.p. (ISBN 0-12-035002-5); Vol. 3, 1975. 129.00 o.p. (ISBN 0-12-035003-3). Acad Pr.

Advances in Radiation Processing: Transactions of the Second International Meeting on Radiation Processing Held at Miami, Florida 22-26 Oct. 1978, 2 vols, Vol. 14, No. 1-3 & 4-6. Ed. by Joseph Silverman. 948p. 1980. Set. pap. 160.00 o.p. (ISBN 0-08-025025-4). Pergamon.

Advances in Radio Research, 2 Vols. Ed. by John A. Saxton. 1964. Vol. 1. 52.50 o.p. (ISBN 0-12-036001-2); Vol. 2. 55.00 o.p. (ISBN 0-12-036002-0). Acad Pr.

Advances in Research on the Strength & Fracture of Materials, 6 Vols. D. M. Taplin. Incl. Vol. 1. An Overview. 1978. 145.00 o.p. (ISBN 0-08-022136-X); Vol. 2a. Physical Metallurgy of Fracture. 1978. 145.00 o.p. (ISBN 0-08-022138-6); Vol. 2b. Fatigue. 1978. 145.00 o.p. (ISBN 0-08-022140-8); Vol. 3a. 1978. 145.00 o.p. (ISBN 0-08-022142-4); Vol. 3b. Applications & Non-Metals. 1978. 145.00 o.p. incl. index (ISBN 0-08-022144-0). 1978. 695.00 o.p. (ISBN 0-08-022130-0). Pergamon.

Advances in Sex Hormone Research, Vol. 4. Ed. by John A. Thomas. Radhey L. Singhal. LC 79-25717. (Illus.). 376p. 1980. text ed. 35.00 o.p. (ISBN 0-8067-1914-1). Urban & S.

Advances in Small Computer Technology. M. Healey. 35p. 1981. pap. 28.60x o.p. (ISBN 0-686-97774-2, Online Coferences England). Gower Pub Co.

Advances in Social Theory & Methodology: Towards a Integration of Micro & Macro-Sociology. Ed. by K. Knorr-Cetina & A. Cicourel. 320p. 1981. 29.95x o.p. (ISBN 0-7100-0946-1); pap. 12.95x o.p. (ISBN 0-7100-0947-X). Routledge Chapman & Hall.

Advances in Solid-Liquid Flow in Pipes & Its Application. Ed. by I. Zandi. LC 77-120000. 1971. 80.00 o.p. (ISBN 0-08-015767-X). Pergamon.

Advances in Solution Chemistry. Ed. by I. Bertini et al. LC 80-28783. 398p. 1981. 75.00x o.p. (ISBN 0-306-40638-1, Plenum Pr). Plenum Pub.

Advances in Source Coding: Courses & Lectures. T. Berger & L. D. Davisson. (CISM (International Centre for Mechanical Sciences) Ser.: Vol. 166). (Illus.). 71p. 1975. pap. 9.00 o.p. (ISBN 0-387-81302-0). Springer-Verlag.

Advances in Structural Composites Symposium: Proceedings, Anaheim CA, 10-12 October 1967. (Science of Advanced Materials & Process Engineering Ser., Vol. 12). 840p. 20.00 o.p. (ISBN 0-938994-12-3). SAMPE.

Advances in Surface Treatments: Technology, Applications, Effects, Vol. 1. Ed. by A. Niku-Lari. (Illus.). 240p. 1984. 70.00 o.p. (ISBN 0-08-031126-1). Pergamon.

Advances in Test Measurement see Instrumentation in the Aerospace Industry, Vol. 30: Proceedings of the International Instrumentation Symposium, 30th, 1984.

Advances in the Analysis of Air Contaminants: Reprint Ser. (Vol. 11). 56p. 1980. 7.50 o.p. (ISBN 0-318-12238-3, RS-11); members 6.00 o.p. (ISBN 0-318-12239-1). Air & Waste.

Advances in the Management of Cleft Palate. Edwards et al. (Illus.). 1981. text ed. 45.00 o.p. (ISBN 0-443-01601-1). Churchill.

Advances in the Teaching of Modern Languages, Vol. 2. Ed. by G. Mathieu. 1966. 34.00 o.p. (ISBN 0-08-011840-2). Pergamon.

Advances in Theoretical Physics, 2 Vols. Ed. by Keith A. Brueckner. Vol. 1 1965. 75.50 o.p. (ISBN 0-12-038501-5); Vol. 2 1968. 66.00 o.p. (ISBN 0-12-038502-3). Acad Pr.

Advances in Thermal Spraying: Proceedings of the International Thermal Spraying Conference, 11th, September 8-12, 1986, Montreal, Canada. Ed. by Welding Institute of Canada. (Illus.). 936p. 1986. 230.00 o.p. (ISBN 0-08-031878-9, PBI). Pergamon.

Advances in Titanium Welding. Ed. by W. A. Baeslack & D. F. Hasson. (Reproduction on Demand UMI) o.s.i. Minerals Metals.

Advances in Topical Corticosteroid Therapy: Proceedings of the International Symposium, Amsterdam, Sept., 1975. Ed. by M. K. Polano et al. (Dermatologica: Suppl. 1, Vol. 152). (Illus.). 210p. 1976. 32.75 o.p. (ISBN 3-8055-2309-2). S Karger.

Advances in Tuberculosis Research, Vol. 17. Ed. by H. Birkhaeuser et al. (Bibliotheca Tuberculosea et Medicinae Thoracalis: No. 26). 1970. 57.50 o.p. (ISBN 3-8055-0364-4). S Karger.

Advances in Tunnelling & Subsurface Technology & Use. International Tunnelling Association. 1980. pap. 40.00 o.p. (ISBN 0-08-025446-2). Pergamon.

Advances in Vacuum Science & Technology: Proceedings of the Israeli Vacuum Congress, 5th, Israel, April, 1978. Israeli Vacuum Congress Staff. Ed. by J. Yarwood & Y. Margoninski. 1979. pap. 15.75 o.p. (ISBN 0-08-024238-3). Pergamon.

Advances in World Archaeology, Vol. 4. Ed. by Fred Wendorf & Angela E. Close. (Serial Publication). 1985. 71.50 o.p. (ISBN 0-12-039904-0). Acad Pr.

Advances in X-Ray Analysis, Vol. 20. Ed. by Howard F. McMurdie. LC 58-35928. 622p. 1977. 85.00x o.p. (ISBN 0-306-38120-6, Plenum Pr). Plenum Pub.

Advances in X-Ray Analysis, Vol. 21. Ed. by Charles S. Barrett et al. LC 58-35928. 342p. 1978. 59.50x o.p. (ISBN 0-306-38421-3, Plenum Pr). Plenum Pub.

Advances in X-Ray Analysis, Vol. 22. Ed. by Gregory J. McCarthy et al. LC 58-35928. 510p. 1979. 79.50x o.p. (ISBN 0-306-40163-0, Plenum Pr). Plenum Pub.

Advances in X-Ray Analysis, Vol. 23. Ed. by John S. Rhodes et al. LC 58-35928. 408p. 1980. 72.50x o.p. (ISBN 0-306-40435-4, Plenum Pr). Plenum Pub.

Advances in X-Ray Analysis, Vol. 24. Ed. by D. K. Smith et al. LC 58-35928. 448p. 1981. 75.00x o.p. (ISBN 0-306-40734-5, Plenum Pr). Plenum Pub.

Advances in X-Ray Analysis, Vol. 25. Ed. by John C. Russ & Charles S. Barrett. LC 58-35928. 416p. 1982. 72.50x o.p. (ISBN 0-306-41008-7, Plenum Pr). Plenum Pub.

Advances on the AIDS Horizon. 2nd ed. Lauren Russel. 88p. 1988. pap. 9.95 o.p. (ISBN 0-942028-40-6). R D Anderson.

Advances on the AIDS Horizon: 1986. Margaret Greenough. 60p. 1986. pap. text ed. 14.00 Home Study Course o.p. (ISBN 0-942028-22-8); reference book 4.95 o.p. (ISBN 0-942028-23-6). R D Anderson.

Advancing Frontiers of Mycology & Plant Pathology: Prof. K. S. Bhargava Commemoration Volume. Ed. by K. S. Bilgrami & R. S. Misra. (Illus.). xxvi, 330p. 1982. 50.00 o.p. (ISBN 0-88065-222-5, Pub. by Messers Today & Tomorrow Printers & Publishers). Scholarly Pubns.

Advancing the Two-Year College. Ed. by Peter S. Bryant & Jane A. Johnson. LC 81-48480. (Institutional Advancement Ser.: No. 15). 1982. pap. 13.95x o.p. (ISBN 0-87589-899-8). Jossey-Bass.

Advent. Richard Sanden. 1978. 4.00 o.p. (ISBN 0-682-48823-2). Exposition-Phoenix.

Advent & Christmas Resource Book. L. Koopman. 1982. pap. 7.95 o.p. (ISBN 0-941850-04-8). Liturgical Pubns.

Advent-Christmas. Paul J. Achtemeier & J. Leland Mebust. Ed. by Elizabeth Achtemeier et al. LC 79-7377. (Proclamation 2: Aids for Interpreting the Lessons of the Church Year, Ser. B). 64p. (Orig.). 1981. pap. 3.75 o.p. (ISBN 0-8006-4060-8, 1-4060, Fortress). Augsburg Fortress.

Advent-Christmas. Frederick H. Borsch & Davie Napier. Ed. by Elizabeth Achtemeier et al. LC 79-7377. (Proclamation 2: Aids for Interpreting the Lessons of the Church Year, Ser. A). 64p. (Orig.). 1980. pap. 3.75 o.p. (ISBN 0-8006-4091-8, 1-4091, Fortress). Augsburg Fortress.

Advent-Christmas. Reginald H. Fuller. Ed. by Elizabeth Achtemeier et al. LC 79-7377. (Proclamation 2: Aids for Interpreting the Lessons of the Church Year, Ser. C). 64p. 1979. pap. 3.75 o.p. (ISBN 0-8006-4079-9, 1-4079, Fortress). Augsburg Fortress.

Advent-Christmas. Thor Hall & James L. Price. LC 74-24899. (Proclamation 1: Aids for Interpreting the Lessons of the Church Year, Ser. B). 64p. 1974. pap. 2.95 o.p. (ISBN 0-8006-4071-3, 1-4071, Fortress). Augsburg Fortress.

Advent-Christmas. Gerard S. Sloyan. LC 84-18756. (Proclamation 3 C Ser.). 64p. 1985. pap. 3.75 o.p. (ISBN 0-8006-4125-6, 1-4125, Fortress). Augsburg Fortress.

Advent-Christmas. Bruce Vawter. LC 84-18756. (Proclamation 3A Ser.). 64p. 1986. pap. 3.75 o.p. (ISBN 0-8006-4117-5, 1-4117, Fortress). Augsburg Fortress.

Advent-Christmas. David B. Watermulder & Gerhard Krodel. LC 73-79329. (Proclamation 1: Aids for Interpreting the Lessons of the Church Year, Ser. C). 64p. 1973. pap. 2.95 o.p. (ISBN 0-8006-4051-9, 1-4051, Fortress). Augsburg Fortress.

Advent-Christmas. Samuel Wylie & John L. McKenzie. LC 74-76924. (Proclamation 1: Aids for Interpreting the Lessons of the Church Year, Ser. A). 64p. 1974. pap. 2.95 o.p. (ISBN 0-8006-4061-6, 1-4061, Fortress). Augsburg Fortress.

Advent-Christmas: Series B. Walter Brueggemann. LC 84-6020. (Proclamation 3: Aids for Interpreting the Lessons of the Church Year Ser.). 64p. 1984. pap. 3.75 o.p. (ISBN 0-8006-4101-9, 1-4101, Fortress). Augsburg Fortress.

Advent Landmarks: From a Preacher's Notebook. Robert D. Hershey. LC 75-13034. 64p. 1975. pap. 0.50 o.p. (ISBN 0-8006-1211-6, 1-1211, Fortress). Augsburg Fortress.

Advent of Modernism: Post-Impressionism & North American Art 1900-1918. William C. Agee & Peter Morrin. LC 85-82270. (Illus.). 200p. (Orig.). 1986. pap. 22.50 o.p. (ISBN 0-939802-24-4). High Mus Art.

Adventist Evangelist's Diary. large print ed. Pearl Brians. 27p. 1985. pap. 5.00 o.p. (ISBN 0-914009-25-7). VHI Library.

Adventists & Labor Unions in the U. S. Robert Kistler. Ed. by Gerald Wheeler. LC 83-13664. (Illus.). 127p. (Orig.). 1984. pap. 9.95 o.p. (ISBN 0-8280-0221-5). Review & Herald.

Adventure Education. David E. Wood & James C. Gillis. 56p. 1979. pap. 1.39 o.p. (ISBN 0-8106-1677-7). NEA.

Adventure Holidays Nineteen Eighty-Eight. Ed. by David Stevens. 176p. 1987. pap. 9.95 o.p. (ISBN 0-907638-82-1, Pub. by Vacation-Work England). Writers Digest.

Adventure Holidays, Nineteen Eighty-Seven. Ed. by David Stevens. 176p. (Orig.). 1986. pap. 8.95 o.p. (ISBN 0-907638-70-8, Pub. by Vacation-Work England). Writers Digest.

Adventure Holidays 1984. Ed. by Gillian Nineham. 208p. 1983. pap. 7.95 o.p. (ISBN 0-907638-24-4, Pub. by Vacation Wk). Writers Digest.

Adventure Holidays 1985. Ed. by Gillian Nineham. 208p. (Orig.). 1984. pap. 8.95 o.p. (ISBN 0-907638-35-X, 3009, Pub. by Vacation Work Pub). Writers Digest.

Adventure in Analysis. Edmund W. Gagnier. 704p. 1954. (ISBN 0-8022-0557-7). Philos Lib.

Adventure in Renewal. A. Donald Davies. LC 74-80384. (Orig.). 1974. pap. 2.95 o.p. (ISBN 0-8192-1170-2). Morehouse Pub.

Adventure in TV Land. Elizabeth J. Hanchett. (gr. k-6). 1977. 6.50 o.p. (ISBN 0-682-48950-6). Exposition-Phoenix.

Adventure of Becoming One. Louis Caldwell. (Ultra Bks.). 80p. 1981. 5.95 o.p. (ISBN 0-8010-2334-3). Baker Bk.

Adventure of Giving. Bill Stafford. Ed. by Ted Griffin. 128p. (Orig.). 1985. pap. 4.95 o.p. (ISBN 0-8423-0036-8). Tyndale.

Adventure of the Ecoplasmic Man. Daniel Stashower. LC 84-20552. 224p. 1985. 12.95 o.p. (ISBN 0-688-04189-2). Morrow.

Adventure of the Peerless Peer. Philip Jose Farmer. 112p. 1974. 5.50 o.p. (ISBN 0-915230-06-2). Rue Morgue.

Adventure on Padre Island. Aleda Renken. LC 75-5945. (Haley Adventure Bks.). (Illus.). 96p. (gr. 3-7). 1975. pap. 1.00 o.p. (ISBN 0-570-07231-X, 39-1029). Concordia.

Adventure Pack, No. 1: Three Introductory Adventures for TimeLords. Greg Porter & Roger Campbell. (Illus.). 24p. (Orig.). 1987. pap. 3.95 saddlestitch o.p. (ISBN 0-943891-01-9). Blacksburg Tactical.

Adventure: Queen of the Windjammers. Joe Garland & Jim Sharp. LC 85-70646. (Illus.). 208p. 1984. 24.95 o.p. (ISBN 0-89272-206-1). Down East.

Adventure Together: Teacher's Manual. W. Imbiorski. 60p. 1974. pap. 3.00 o.p. (ISBN 0-915388-03-0, Buckley Pubns). ACTA Pubns.

Adventure Travel Abroad. Pat Dickerman. (Illus.). 224p. 1986. pap. 12.95 o.p. (ISBN 0-03-008564-0, Owl Bks). H Holt & Co.

Adventure Travel in North America. Pat Dickerman. (Illus.). 224p. 1986. pap. 12.95 o.p. (ISBN 0-03-008563-2, Owl Bks). H Holt & Co.

Adventure Vacation Catalog. Specialty Travel Index Publishers Staff. (Illus.). 382p. 1984. pap. 15.95 o.s.i. (ISBN 0-671-50770-2). S&S.

Adventures & Discourses of Captain John Smith. John Ashton. LC 76-78108. (Illus.). 332p. 1969. Repr. of 1883 ed. 35.00x o.p. (ISBN 0-8103-3565-4). Gale.

Adventures at Green Knowe, 5 vols. Lucy M. Boston. Incl. Children of Green Knowe. Repr. of 1955 ed; Treasure of Green Knowe. Repr. of 1958 ed; River at Green Knowe. Repr. of 1959 ed; Stranger at Green Knowe. Repr. of 1961 ed; Enemy at Green Knowe. Repr. of 1964 ed. (Illus.). (gr. 4-7). 1979. Boxed Set. pap. 9.95 o.p. (ISBN 0-15-603246-5, VoyB). HarBraceJ.

Adventures at Mountain Haven. Lloyd Fezler. LC 84-60868. 1984. pap. 3.95 o.p. (ISBN 0-89051-098-9). Master Bks.

Adventures in Christian Living & Learning: A Resource Book for Use with Retarded Persons, Pt. 2. Ed. by Doris Monroe. (Cooperative Ser: Curriculum Materials for the Mentally Retarded). (Illus., Orig.). (gr. 6-10). 1970. pap. 1.25 ea. o.p. (ISBN 0-8042-1140-X, John Knox); tchrs' ed. 2.50 ea. o.p. (ISBN 0-8042-1141-8). Westminster John Knox.

Adventures in Church Growth. Roger L. Dudley & Des Cummings, Jr. Ed. by Gerald Wheeler. LC 83-16089. (Illus.). 160p. (Orig.). 1983. pap. 8.95 o.p. (ISBN 0-8280-0228-2). Review & Herald.

Adventures in Error. Vilhialmur Stefansoon. LC 71-121210. 314p. 1970. Repr. of 1936 ed. 35.00x o.p. (ISBN 0-8103-3838-6). Gale.

Adventures in Fern Hollow. John Patience. (Illus.). 64p. (ps-1). 1985. 2.98 o.s.i. (ISBN 0-517-45856-X). Outlet Bk Co.

Adventures in Immortality. George Gallup, Jr. & William Procter. 1982. text ed. 12.95 o.p. (ISBN 0-07-022754-3). McGraw.

Adventures in the Alaskan Skin Trade. John Hawkes. LC 85-11795. 364p. 1985. 17.45 o.p. (ISBN 0-671-47304-2). S&S.

Adventures in the Philosophy of Religion. Robert Leet Patterson. 1977. 5.50 o.p. (ISBN 0-682-48827-5, University). Exposition-Phoenix.

Adventures in Tranquility. Esther Matson. 116p. 1954. (ISBN 0-8022-1084-8). Philos Lib.

Adventures in Two Worlds. A. J. Cronin. 1956. 7.95 o.p. (ISBN 0-316-16155-1). Little.

Adventures in Understanding. David Grayson. (Illus.). 288p. 1989. Repr. of 1925 ed. pap. 12.95 incl. dust jacket o.p. (ISBN 1-55838-110-4). R H Pub.

Adventures of a Ballet Historian. Ivor Guest. LC 81-70096. (Illus.). 144p. 1982. 29.95 o.p. (ISBN 0-87127-131-1, Pub. by Dance Horiz). Princeton Bk Co.

Adventures of a Cheap Antiquer. Arline Beitler. 1979. pap. 1.95 o.p. (ISBN 0-380-42804-0, 42804). Avon.

Adventures of a Cork-Screw, Seventeen Seventy-Five. Ed. by Michael F. Shugrue. (Flowering of the Novel, 1740-1775 Ser: Vol. 107). 1975. lib. bdg. 61.00 o.p. (ISBN 0-8240-1206-2). Garland Pub.

Adventures of a Jesuit, Seventeen Seventy-One. Ed. by Michael F. Shugrue. (Flowering of the Novel, 1740-1775 Ser: Vol. 94). 1975. lib. bdg. 61.00 o.p. (ISBN 0-8240-1193-7). Garland Pub.
Adventures of a Mathematician. S. M. Ulam. LC 75-20133. (Illus.). 320p. 1983. pap. 7.95 o.s.i. (ISBN 0-684-15064-6, ScribT). Scribner.
Adventures of a Yiddish Lecturer. Abraham Shulman. LC 79-28734. 1980. 7.95 o.p. (ISBN 0-8298-0391-2). Pilgrim NY.
Adventures of an Author: Written by Himself and a Friend, 2 vols. in 1. Ed. by Michael F. Shugrue. (Flowering of the Novel, 1740-1775 Ser: Vol. 77). 1975. lib. bdg. 61.00 o.p. (ISBN 0-8240-1176-7). Garland Pub.
Adventures of Arthur & Edmund: A Tale of Two Seals. Bonte Duran. LC 83-71900. (Illus.). 32p. (ps-3). 1984. 10.95 o.s.i. (ISBN 0-689-50295-8, M K McElderry). Macmillan.
Adventures of Augie March. Saul Bellow. 1977. pap. 3.50 o.p. (ISBN 0-380-00961-7, 64600-5). Avon.
Adventures of Binkie, Dog Extraordinaire. Claire Bryant. (gr. k-6). 1978. 4.50 o.p. (ISBN 0-682-49164-0). Exposition-Phoenix.
Adventures of Conan Doyle: The Life of the Creator of Sherlock Holmes. Charles Higham. (Illus.). 1976. 12.95 o.p. (ISBN 0-393-07507-9). Norton.
Adventures of Dan & Mark. S. Norman Strandholt. (gr. 1-4). 1978. 4.00 o.p. (ISBN 0-682-49070-9). Exposition-Phoenix.
Adventures of Don Quixote see also Don Quixote.
Adventures of Don Quixote. Miguel Cervantes de Saavedra. Ed. by Olive Jones. Tr. by J. M. Cohen from Span. LC 79-23512. (Illus.). 1980. 10.95 o.p. (ISBN 0-416-87910-1, NO.0189). Routledge Chapman & Hall.
Adventures of Gingerbee. Vicki R. Davies. 35p. (gr. 1-3). 1986. 4.95 o.p. (ISBN 0-533-06670-0). Vantage.
Adventures of Huckleberry Finn see also Huckleberry Finn.
Adventures of Huckleberry Finn. Samuel Clemens. (Illus.). 352p. 1984. 11.95 o.p. (ISBN 0-396-08253-X). Dodd.
Adventures of Huckleberry Finn. Mark Twain. 352p. 1960. pap. 2.95 o.p. (ISBN 0-440-30028-2, LE). Dell.
Adventures of John-John the Mouse That Turned into a Puppy. Joseph Mendoskin & Margaret Mendoskin. 32p. 1987. 6.95 o.p. (ISBN 0-8062-3024-X). Carlton.
Adventures of Mao on the Long March. Frederic Tuten. 1971. 5.95 o.p. (ISBN 0-8065-0248-7, Pub. by Citadel Pr). Carol Pub Group.
Adventures of Marco Polo. Demi. LC 81-13216. (Illus.). 32p. (gr. k-2). 1982. 6.95 o.p. (ISBN 0-03-061263-2). H Holt & Co.
Adventures of Mark Twain. Jerry Allen. 12.00 o.p. (ISBN 0-8446-0453-4). Peter Smith.
Adventures of Nanabush: Ojibway Indian Stories. Ed. by Emerson Coatsworth & David Coatsworth. LC 79-89499. (Illus.). 96p. (gr. 3-7). 1980. 10.95 o.p. (ISBN 0-689-50162-5, Atheneum). Macmillan.
Adventures of Paddy Pork. John S. Goodall. LC 68-26425. (Illus.). (gr. k-3). 1968. 5.95 o.p. (ISBN 0-15-201589-2, HJ). HarBraceJ.
Adventures of Pinocchio. Carlo Collodi. (Illus.). (gr. 4-6). 1982. pap. 5.95 o.p. (ISBN 0-448-11001-6, G&D); Companion Lib. Ed. 2.95 o.p. (ISBN 0-448-05471-X); deluxe ed. 11.95 o.p. (ISBN 0-448-06001-9). Putnam Pub Group.
Adventures of Pinocchio: Tale of a Puppet. C. Collodi, pseud. Tr. by M. L. Rosenthal. LC 83-801. (Illus.). 256p. (gr. 3 up). 1983. 17.50 o.p. (ISBN 0-688-02267-7). Lothrop.
Adventures of Ricky the Brave. Anne Ferrington. LC 85-3215. (Chumble Chums Ser.). (Illus.). 32p. (ps-3). 1987. 5.95 o.s.i. (ISBN 0-394-87882-5, BYR). Random.
Adventures of Robin Hood & His Merry Outlaws. (Greenwich House Classic Library). (YA) (gr. 2-6). 4.98 o.s.i. (ISBN 0-517-43602-7). Outlet Bk Co.
Adventures of Robinson Crusoe see also Robinson Crusoe.
Adventures of Sherlock Holmes. Arthur Conan Doyle. pap. 2.50 o.p. (ISBN 0-425-07501-X). Berkley Pub.
Adventures of Sidney & Fred Or When Two Bears Go to Play. Doris Beck. (Illus.). 116p. (Orig.). (ps-5). 1985. pap. 9.95 o.p. (ISBN 0-934875-03-0). Couturier Pr.
Adventures of Stanley Kane. S. J. Goldberg & V. Chess. LC 73-75320. (gr. 5 up). 1973. 6.50 o.p. (ISBN 0-15-201599-X, HJ). HarBraceJ.
Adventures of Telemachus, 2 vols. Fenelon & Francois De Salignac De La Mothe. Ed. by Ronald Paulson. LC 78-60835. (Novel 1720-1805 Ser.: Vol. 1). 1979. lib. bdg. 75.00 o.p. (ISBN 0-8240-3650-6). Garland Pub.
Adventures of the Borrowers, 4 vols. Mary Norton. (Illus.). 784p. (gr. 4 up). 1975. Set. pap. 11.95 o.p. (ISBN 0-15-613605-8, VoyB). HarBraceJ.
Adventures of the Stainless Steel Rat. Harry Harrison. 1984. pap. 3.95 o.s.i. (ISBN 0-425-09531-2, Medallion). Berkley Pub.
Adventures of Tom Sawyer see also Tom Sawyer.
Adventures of Tom Sawyer. Samuel L. Clemens. (Illus.). 352p. 1984. 12.95 o.p. (ISBN 0-396-08254-8). Dodd.
Adventures of Tom Sawyer. Mark Twain. LC 62-19420. (Illus.). (gr. 4-6). deluxe ed. 11.95 o.p. (ISBN 0-448-06002-7, G&D); PLB 3.79 o.p. (ISBN 0-448-03264-3). Putnam Pub Group.
Adventures of Tom Sawyer. Mark Twain. Ed. by Wendy Barish. LC 62-19420. (Illus.). 288p. 1982. 14.50 o.s.i. (ISBN 0-671-43791-7). Wanderer Bks.
Adventures of Tom Sawyer. Mark Twain. 48p. (Orig.). 1988. pap. 9.95 o.p. (ISBN 1-55651-877-3); audiocassette tape incl. o.p. (ISBN 1-55651-878-1). Cram Cassettes.
Adventures of Tom Sawyer & Huckleberry Finn. Mark Twain. (gr. 3 up). 1948. pap. 11.95 o.p. (ISBN 0-448-06000-0, G&D). Putnam Pub Group.
Adventures of Tony, David & Marc: Reading from A-Z. Lenchen Coleman De Vane. (Illus.). 1976. 6.95 o.p. (ISBN 0-682-48435-0); tchr's. manual 4.00 o.p. (ISBN 0-682-48677-9). Exposition-Phoenix.
Adventures of Tumbletin the Robot. Veronica P. Towey. (Illus.). 36p. (gr. 1-3). 1984. 4.95 o.p. (ISBN 0-533-06075-3). Vantage.
Adventures of Wee Willy Wiley. Ria Foster. (Illus.). 64p. (gr. k-4). 1980. 5.00 o.p. (ISBN 0-682-49552-2). Exposition-Phoenix.
Adventures of Wilbur H. Worm & His Friends. Colleen M. Payton. 1983. 4.95 o.p. (ISBN 0-8062-2254-9). Carlton.
Adventures of Young & Impressionable Manko As He Meets His Jungle Friends see Manko of Mankoland.
Adventures, Rhymes & Designs. Vachel Lindsay. LC 68-27399. (Illus.). 1968. 12.95x o.p. (ISBN 0-87130-011-7); pap. 6.95 o.p. (ISBN 0-87130-012-5). Eakins.
Adventures with a Hand Lens. Richard Headstrom. 11.25 o.p. (ISBN 0-8446-5479-5). Peter Smith.
Adventurous Spirits: Australian Migrant Society in Pre-Cession Fiji. John Young. LC 84-7218. (Illus.). 417p. 1985. text ed. 37.50x o.p. (ISBN 0-7022-1704-2). U Of Queensland Pr.
Adventurous Traveler's Guide. Leo LeBon. 1985. pap. 14.95 o.p. (ISBN 0-671-60447-3, Fireside). S&S.
Adverbs, Vowels, & Other Objects of Wonder. James D. McCawley. LC 78-11608. xii, 304p. 1985. pap. text ed. 10.00x o.s.i. (ISBN 0-226-55616-6). U of Chicago Pr.
Adverse Consequences for the Enjoyment of Human Rights of Political, Military, Economic & Other forms of Assistance Given to the Racist & Colonialist Regime of South Africa. 164p. 1985. 19.00 o.p. (ISBN 92-1-154046-1, E.85.XIV.4). UN.
Adverse Selection in the Labor Market. Bruce C. Greenwald. LC 78-75052. (Outstanding Dissertations in Economics Ser.). 1979. lib. bdg. 36.00 o.p. (ISBN 0-8240-4130-5). Garland Pub.
Adversity & Grace: Studies in Recent American Literature. Ed. by Nathan A. Scott, Jr. LC 68-16717. (Essays in Divinity Ser: Vol. 4). 1968. lib. bdg. 9.50x o.s.i. (ISBN 0-226-74283-0). U of Chicago Pr.
Adversus Nationes Libri Seven, Bk. 7. Afer Arnobius. (Corpus Scriptorum Ecclesiasticorum Latinorum, Vol. 4). 31.00 o.p. Johnson Repr.
Advertising. 5.00 o.p. (E.79.II.A.2). UN.
Advertising. Kenneth A. Longman. (Illus.). 1971. text ed. 12.75 o.p. (ISBN 0-15-501901-5, HC). HarBraceJ.
Advertising & Promotion for Professional Pharmacy Practice. W. L. Fitzgerald et al. 238p. 1983. pap. 25.00 o.s.i. (ISBN 0-910769-20-6). Am Coll Apothecaries.
Advertising & Promotion: Management & Strategy. Belch & Belch. (Illus.). 687p. 1989. 35.95 o.p. (ISBN 0-8016-0630-6). Mosby.
Advertising & the New Electronic Media. (Reports Ser.: No. 539). 160p. 1983. 985.00x o.p. (ISBN 0-88694-539-9). Intl Res Dev.
Advertising Career Directory, 1986: 24 Top Industry Leaders. Intro. by Bart Cummings. (Career Directory Ser.). 334p. (Orig.). 1986. 24.95 o.p. (ISBN 0-934829-00-4). Career Pr Inc.
Advertising Career Directory: 1987. rev. ed. Ed. by Ron Fry. (Career Directory Ser.). 335p. 1987. text ed. 34.95 o.p. (ISBN 0-934829-16-0); pap. text ed. 26.95 o.p. (ISBN 0-934829-10-1); Special Bookstore Edition Distributed by Williamson Publishing Co. pap. 17.95 o.p. (ISBN 0-934829-04-7). Career Pr Inc.
Advertising Design in Japan, Vol. 21. Ed. by Rikuyo-Sha Staff. (Illus.). 368p. 1986. 55.00 o.s.i. (ISBN 4-897-37056-6, Pub. by Rikuyo-Sha Japan). Bks Nippan.
Advertising Design in Japan, No. 22. Ed. by Rikuyo-sha. 390p. 1988. 55.00 o.p. (ISBN 4-897-37065-5). Bks Nippan.
Advertising: How to Write the Kind That Works. David L. Malickson & John W. Nason. LC 76-18310. (Illus.). 320p. 1977. 12.50 o.s.i. (ISBN 0-684-14770-X, ScribT); pap. 7.95 o.s.i. (ISBN 0-684-14771-8, ScribT). Scribner.
Advertising: Its Role in Modern Marketing. 5th ed. S. Watson Dunn & Arnold M. Barban. LC 81-67231. 710p. 1982. text ed. 28.00x o.p. (ISBN 0-03-060049-9); instr's manual with transparencies & test bank 16.00 o.p. (ISBN 0-03-060051-0). Dryden Pr.
Advertising Law Anthology Index (1987) Ed. by Donald J. Hoyes. (National Law Anthology Ser.). 120p. 1987. pap. text ed. 29.95x o.s.i. (ISBN 0-914250-31-0). Intl Lib.
Advertising Law Handbook. 2nd ed. Diana Woolley. 196p. 1976. text ed. 21.00x o.p. (ISBN 0-220-66306-8, Pub. by Busn Bks England). Gower Pub Co.
Advertising Layouts: Ad Kit 2. Larry Notman. (Illus.). 1977. pap. text ed. 5.00x o.p. Newspaper Serv.
Advertising Management. 2nd ed. David A. Aaker & John G. Myers. (Illus.). 560p. 1982. pap. text ed. (ISBN 0-13-016006-7). P-H.
Advertising Management. William S. Sachs. 656p. 1983. text ed. write for info. o.p. (ISBN 0-02-405000-8). Macmillan.
Advertising: Mass Communication in Marketing. 3rd ed. James E. Littlefield & C. A. Kirkpatrick. (Illus.). 1970. text ed. 19.50 o.p. (ISBN 0-395-04802-8, 3-33465). HM.
Advertising Photography in Chicago, 1985. Ed. by Alfred De Bat. (Illus.). 150p. 1985. pap. 30.00 o.p. (ISBN 0-917001-01-X). R Silver.
Advertising Practices. Francis S. King. LC 81-68551. (Illus.). 240p. (Orig.). 1983. pap. text ed. 17.95 o.p. (ISBN 0-8273-1702-6); instr's. guide 6.00 o.p. (ISBN 0-8273-1703-4). Delmar.
Advertising, Prices & Consumer Reaction: A Dynamic Analysis. John M. Scheidell. 1978. pap. 7.00 o.p. (ISBN 0-8447-3309-1). Am Enterprise.
Advertising World of Norman Rockwell. Donald Stoltz & Marshall Stoltz. 244p. 1984. 39.95 o.p. (ISBN 0-942604-04-0). Madison Square.
Advise & Consent. Allen Drury. 1977. pap. 2.50 o.p. (ISBN 0-380-01007-0, 52340). Avon.
Advising California Partnerships. California Continuing Education of the Bar Staff & Curtis M. Karplus. LC 74-620089. (California Practice Book Ser.: No. 64). xiii, 443p. 1975. 75.00 o.p. (ISBN 0-88124-035-4). Cal Cont Ed Bar.
Advising Pennsylvania Municipalities. 230p. 1984. 35.00 o.p. (ISBN 0-318-03925-7, 274). PA Bar Inst.
Advisory Councils: A Theoretical & Practical Guide for Program Planners. Jacquelyn M. Cole & Maurice F. Cole. (Illus.). 224p. 1983. text ed. 37.00 o.p. (ISBN 0-13-018184-6). P-H.
Advisory Opinions of the Grievance Commission of the Board of Overseers of the Bar. 150p. three ringbinder 25.00, o.p. (ISBN 0-89442-042-9). Tower Pub Co.
Advocacy: Art Pleadi. 1983. text ed. 75.00 o.p. (ISBN 0-07-023331-4). McGraw.
Advocacy: Risk & Reality. Mary F. Kohnke. LC 82-6460. (Illus.). 204p. 1982. pap. text ed. 18.95 o.p. (ISBN 0-8016-2721-4). Mosby.
AED African Financial Directory. Middle East Economic Digest Staff. 400p. (Orig.). 1987. pap. 90.00x o.p. (ISBN 0-946510-18-0). Lynne Rienner.
Aegean: A Sea-Guide to Its Coasts & Islands. rev., 3rd ed. H. M. Denham. (Illus.). 1976. 19.95 o.p. (ISBN 0-393-03197-7). Norton.
Aegean Turkey. George E. Bean. (Illus.). 1980. 17.50 o.p. (ISBN 0-393-01328-6). Norton.
Aekyung's Dream. Min Paek. LC 78-59168. (Fifth World Tales Ser.). (Illus.). 24p. (gr. 2-9). 1979. pap. 5.95 korean bilingual ed. o.p. (ISBN 0-89239-018-2, Imprenta de Libros Infantiles). Childrens Book Pr.
Aeneid of Virgil. 48p. (Orig.). 1988. pap. 9.95 o.p. (ISBN 1-55651-000-4); cassette o.p. (ISBN 1-55651-001-2). Cram Cassettes.
Aeration in Wastewater Treatment ('71) Water Pollution Control Federation Staff. (Manual of Practice Ser.: No. 5). 90p. (Orig.). 1971. pap. 9.50 o.p. (ISBN 0-943244-05-6). Water Pollution.
Aerial Banner Towing. Alan C. Taylor. (Illus.). 224p. 1982. pap. 7.95 o.p. (ISBN 0-8306-2303-5, 2303). TAB Bks.
Aerial Espionage: Secret Intelligence Flights by East & West. Dick Van Der Aart. (Arco Military Bk.). (Illus.). 176p. 1986. 19.95 o.p. (ISBN 0-671-61952-7). Arco.
Aerial Surveys, Geometrics, Surface Drainage, Ecological Impacts, & Safety Appurtenances. (Transportation Research Record Ser.). 58p. 1979. 3.40 o.p. (ISBN 0-309-02991-0). Transport Res Bd.
Aerial Techniques for Environmental Monitoring: Proceedings, American Nuclear Society Topical Meeting, Las Vegas, March 7-11, 1977. 270p. pap. 23.00 o.p. (ISBN 0-89448-103-7, 700026). Am Nuclear Soc.
Aero Aviation College Directory. M. George Mandis. LC 83-73370. 272p. 1984. 12.95 o.p. (ISBN 0-8168-3029-0, 23029, TAB-Aero). TAB Bks.
Aero-Thermodynamics & Flow in Turbomachines. Michael H. Vavra. LC 74-9545. 626p. 1974. Repr. of 1960 ed. 44.00 o.p. (ISBN 0-88275-189-1). Krieger.
Aero-Thermodynamics of Steam Turbines. Ed. by W. E. Steltz & A. M. Donaldson. 1981. 24.00 o.p. (ISBN 0-686-34474-X, H00203). ASME.
Aerobic Biological Treatment of Waste Waters. Arthur W. Busch. LC 70-155639. 418p. 1971. 39.00x o.p. (ISBN 0-87201-008-2). Gulf Pub.
Aerobic Gram-Negative Bronchopneumonias: Proceedings of the Symposium, Brussels, Sept. 22, 1978. Aerobic Gram-Negative Bronchopneumonias Symposium Staff. Ed. by J. Thys et al. LC 79-42759. (Illus.). 120p. 1980. 46.00 o.p. (ISBN 0-08-025533-7). Pergamon.
Aerobic Pas de Deux. Lorraine Katterhenry. (Educational Dance Score Registry Ser.: No. 6). (Illus.). 28p. 1983. dance score 12.00 o.s.i. (ISBN 0-932582-33-8). Dance Notation.
Aerobicise. Ron Harris & Penelope Bloch. 1986. pap. 10.95 o.p. (ISBN 0-671-55186-8, Fireside). S&S.
Aerobie Book. John Cassidy. (Illus., Orig.). 1985. pap. 12.95 incl. aerobie o.p. (ISBN 0-932592-11-2). Klutz Pr.
Aerobiology: The Ecological Systems Approach. Ed. by Robert L. Edmonds. LC 78-23769. (US-IBP Synthesis Ser.: Vol. 10). 386p. 1982. 43.95 o.p. (ISBN 0-87933-346-4). Van Nos Reinhold.
Aerodynamics, 2 vols. N. U. Krasnov. 942p. 1985. 20.95 o.p. (ISBN 0-8285-3119-6, Pub. by Mir Pubs USSR). Imported Pubns.
Aerodynamics for Engineers. John J. Bertin & Michael L. Smith. (Illus.). 1979. text ed. 54.00 o.p. (ISBN 0-13-018234-6). P-H.
Aerodynamics of Transportation. Ed. by T. Morel & C. Dalton. 256p. 1979. 30.00 o.p. (ISBN 0-317-33406-9, G00147); members 15.00 o.p. (ISBN 0-317-33407-7). ASME.
Aerodynamics: The Science of Fluid in Motion. 2nd ed. John E. Allen. (Illus.). 205p. 1982. text ed. 39.50 o.p. (ISBN 0-07-001074-9). McGraw.
Aerofilms Book of London from the Air. Paul Johnson. (Illus.). 176p. 1984. 22.95 o.p. (ISBN 0-03-071918-6). H Holt & Co.
Aerograph Four: Convair B-58. J. Miller. 136p. 40.00 o.p. (ISBN 0-942548-27-2). Aerofax.
Aeromedicine for Aviators. Keith Read. 80p. 1982. 30.00x o.p. (ISBN 0-9504543-1-1, Pub. by Airlife England). State Mutual Bk.
Aeronautics in China, AAS4. Ed. by Jerry Grey. LC 81-19083. (Illus.). 199p. 1981. 20.00 o.p. (ISBN 0-915928-59-0). AIAA.
Aeroplane or a Grave. Brian Peachment. 1974. pap. text ed. 1.85 o.s.i. (ISBN 0-08-017841-3). Pergamon.
Aeroplanes & Aero-Engines. J. H. Clark. (Illus.). 1957. (ISBN 0-8022-0254-3). Philos Lib.
Aerosol Science. Ed. by Charles N. Davies. 1967. 99.00 o.p. (ISBN 0-12-205650-7). Acad Pr.
Aerosols in Science, Medicine & Technology: Proceedings of the Tenth Annual Conference of the Association for Aerosol Research (Gesellschaft fur Aerosolforschung), Bologna, Italy, 14-17 September 1982. Ed. by H. Fissan. 225p. 1983. pap. 32.00 o.p. (ISBN 0-08-030260-2). Pergamon.
Aerosols: Research, Risk Assessment & Control Strategies. S. D. Lee et al. LC 86-20065. (Illus.). 1221p. 1986. 125.00 o.p. (ISBN 0-87371-051-7). Lewis Pubs Inc.
Aerospace & Test Measurement Proceedings Index: Index of Proceedings from Instrumentation in the Aerospace Industry, Vols. 1-24, Fundamentals of Aerospace Intrumentation, Vols. 1-10 & Advances in Test Measurement, Vols. 11-15, 1980. Instrument Society of America Staff. LC 79-52762. 198p. 1980. pap. text ed. 30.00x o.p. (ISBN 0-87664-445-0). Instru Soc.
Aerospace Dictionary. Frank Gaynor. 272p. 1960. (ISBN 0-8022-0569-0). Philos Lib.
Aerospace Environment. T. Beer & M. D. Kucherawy. (Wykeham Science Ser.: No. 36). 170p. 1975. 8.60x o.p. (ISBN 0-8448-1163-7, Pub. by Crane Russak & Co). Taylor & Francis.
Aerospace Observation Techniques. Ed. by H. T. Verstappen. 100p. 1975. pap. 23.00 o.p. (ISBN 0-08-019665-9). Pergamon.
Aerospace Technology & Commercial Nuclear Power, AAS 7. LC 82-18402. 20.00 o.p. (ISBN 0-915928-69-8). AIAA.
Aerospace Technology & Marine Transport, AAS3. LC 79-22220. (Illus.). 146p. 1979. 20.00 o.p. (ISBN 0-915928-34-5). AIAA.

Aerostructures, Selected Papers of Nicholas J. Hoff. Ed. by R. B. Testa. LC 77-164024. 1974. 50.00 o.p. (ISBN 0-08-016834-5). Pergamon.

Aerothermodynamics of Gas Turbines & Rocket Propulsion. Gordon C. Oates. LC 84-11152. (Illus.). 412p. 1984. 49.50 o.p. (ISBN 0-915928-87-6). AIAA.

Aeschylus & Sophocles: Their Work & Influence. J. T. Sheppard. LC 63-10270. (Our Debt to Greece & Rome Ser). 1970. Repr. of 1930 ed. 18.50x o.p. (ISBN 0-8154-0205-8). Cooper Sq.

Aesop's Fables. Aesop. LC 33-31662. (Dent's Illustrated Children's Classics Ser.). (Illus.). 171p. (gr. 4 up). 1975. Repr. of 1961 ed. 11.00x o.p. (ISBN 0-460-05049-4, BKA 01565, Pub. by J. M. Dent England). Biblio Dist.

Aesop's Fables. Date not set. 9.95 o.p. Ideals.

Aesop's Fables. Valerius Babrius. Tr. by Denison B. Hull from Gr. LC 60-14237. 112p. 1974. pap. 2.95 o.s.i. (ISBN 0-226-03384-8, P577, Phoen). U of Chicago Pr.

Aesop's Fables. Illus. by Gaynor Chapman. LC 71-175551. (Illus.). (gr. k-4). 1972. 5.50 o.p. (ISBN 0-689-30024-7, Atheneum). Macmillan.

Aesthetic Dimensions of Religious Education. Gloria Durka & Joanmarie Smith. LC 78-65903. 252p. 1979. pap. 8.50 o.p. (ISBN 0-8091-2164-6). Paulist Pr.

Aesthetic Impulse. M. Ross. 250p. 1984. 38.00 o.p. (ISBN 0-08-030234-3, 3400-3, 2600-2); pap. 19.25 o.p. (ISBN 0-08-030233-5). Pergamon.

Aesthetic Obsession: A Portrait of Sir William Eden. Wall Wilkes. (Illus.). 100p. 1986. 24.95 o.p. (ISBN 0-85362-222-1, Oriel). Routledge Chapman & Hall.

Aesthetic Realism Acting Lesson. Eli Siegel. 1970. pap. 2.95x o.p. (ISBN 0-911492-21-6). Aesthetic Realism.

Aesthetic Rhinoplasty. Jack H. Sheen. LC 78-27554. (Illus.). 618p. 1978. text ed. 145.00 o.p. (ISBN 0-8016-4575-1). Mosby.

Aesthetic Theory. T. W. Adorno. Tr. by G. Lenhardt from Ger. (International Library of Phenomenology & Moral Sciences). 480p. 1984. 49.95X o.p. (ISBN 0-7100-9204-0). Routledge Chapman & Hall.

Aesthetic Venture: Virginia Woolf's Poetics of the Novel. S. P. Mittal. (Ajanta Series in Aesthetics: Vol. 4). 200p. 1985. text ed. 15.00x o.p. (ISBN 0-391-03175-9). Humanities.

Aestheticism & Decadence: A Selective Annotated Bibliography. LC 76-52676. (Library of Humanities Reference Bks.: No. 82). 1977. lib. bdg. 29.00 o.p. (ISBN 0-8240-9891-9). Garland Pub.

Aesthetics & Criticism. Harold Osborne. 368p. 1955. (ISBN 0-8022-1248-4). Philos Lib.

Aesthetics & History. Bernhard Berenson. LC 52-1732. 242p. 1955. Repr. 49.00 o.p. (ISBN 0-403-03882-0). Somerset Pub.

Aesthetics & Poetics. Y. Barabash. 292p. 1977. 6.95 o.p. (ISBN 0-8285-0189-0, Pub. by Progress Pubs USSR). Imported Pubns.

Aesthetics & Technology in Building. Pier L. Nervi. Tr. by R. Einaudi. LC 65-16686. (Charles Eliot Norton Lectures Ser: 1961-1962). (Illus.). 1965. 16.00x o.s.i. (ISBN 0-674-00701-8). Harvard U Pr.

Aesthetics & the Sociology of Art. Janet Wolff. (Controversies in Sociology Ser.: No. 14). 128p. 1982. text ed. 34.00x o.p. (ISBN 0-04-301152-7); pap. text ed. 12.95x o.p. (ISBN 0-04-301153-5). Unwin Hyman.

Aesthetics & Theory of Art. Max Dessoir. Tr. by Stephen A. Emery. LC 68-22680. 454p. 1970. text ed. 22.50x o.p. (ISBN 0-8143-1383-3). Wayne St U Pr.

Aesthetics of Gyorgy Lukacs. Bela Kiralyfalvi. LC 74-22401. (Essays in Literature Ser.). 180p. 1975. 25.00x o.p. (ISBN 0-691-07205-1). Princeton U Pr.

Aesthetics of Indian Folk Dance. P. Banerji. (Illus.). 1983. text ed. 35.00x o.p. (ISBN 0-391-02913-4). Humanities.

Aesthetics: Problems in the Philosophy of Criticism. Monroe C. Beardsley. 1958. text ed. 16.95 o.p. (ISBN 0-15-501976-7, HC). HarBraceJ.

Aesthetisch-Plastische Operationen in der Gynaekologie: Proceedings of the Schweizerische Gesellschaft fuer Gynakologie, Bericht Ueber die Jahresversammlung, Lugano, June 30 - July 2, 1977. Schweizerische Gesellschaft fuer Gynaekologie Staff. Ed. by E. Dreher. (Gynaekologische Rundschau: Vol. 18, No. 1). (Illus., Fr., Ger. & Ital.). 1978. 23.50 o.p. (ISBN 3-8055-2908-2). S Karger.

Affair at Santa Marguerita. Barbara Tori. 1974. pap. 1.50 o.p. (ISBN 0-380-01008-9, 19471). Avon.

Affair of Doctors. Francis Rickett. LC 75-11145. 1975. 8.95 o.p. (ISBN 0-87795-109-8, Arbor Hse). Morrow.

Affair of the Blood-Stained Egg Cosy. James Anderson. 256p. 1978. pap. 2.95 o.p. (ISBN 0-380-01919-1, 63826-6). Avon.

Affairs at Thrush Green. Miss Read. 1984. 13.45 o.p. (ISBN 0-395-36554-6). HM.

Affect & Memory: A Reformulation. S. Dutta & R. N. Kanunga. LC 75-8628. 148p. 1975. 50.00 o.p. (ISBN 0-08-018270-4). Pergamon.

Affecting Presence: An Essay in Humanistic Anthropology. Robert P. Armstrong. LC 75-107090. (Illus.). 235p. 1971. 22.95 o.p. (ISBN 0-252-00104-4). U of Ill Pr.

Affectionately Eve. Upton Sinclair. 14.95 o.p. New Coll U Pr.

Affectionately, F. D. R. James Roosevelt & Sidney Shalett. LC 75-22309. (Illus.). 394p. 1975. Repr. of 1959 ed. lib. bdg. 22.50x o.p. (ISBN 0-8371-8329-4, ROAF). Greenwood.

Affective Education for Special Children & Youth. Ed. by William C. Morse et al. LC 80-65499. 128p. (Orig.). pap. 6.50 o.p. (ISBN 0-86586-104-8). Coun Exc Child.

Affective Education: Strategies for Experiential Learning see Fifty Strategies for Experiential Learning: Book One.

Affectivity & Learning see Science of Education.

Affiche De Cinema. Jean L. Capitaine & Balthazar Charton. (Illus.). 159p. (Orig., Fr.). 1983. pap. 40.00 o.p. (ISBN 0-317-06234-4, 2390099, Pub. by Editions de l'Amateur FR). Seven Hills Bk Dists.

Affinity. Katherine Hale. 1979. pap. 1.95 o.p. (ISBN 0-380-40907-0, 40907). Avon.

Affinity Chromatography & Biological Recognition (Symposium) Irwin M. Chaiken et al. 1983. 45.00 o.p. (ISBN 0-12-166580-1). Acad Pr.

Affinity Chromatography: Proceedings of an International Symposium Held in Vienna, 1977. Ed. by O. Hoffman-Ostenhof et al. LC 78-40289. 1978. 93.00 o.p. (ISBN 0-08-022632-9). Pergamon.

Affirmation of God: A World Treasury of Quotations about the Meaning of the Divine. David M. White. 1985. 24.95 o.p. (ISBN 0-02-626590-7). MacMillan.

Affirmations of Judaism. J. H. Hertz. 338p. 1975. 9.95 o.p. (ISBN 0-900689-54-4). Soncino Pr.

Affirmative Action & the Woman Worker: Guidelines for Personnel Management. Jennie Farley. LC 78-11719. 1979. 15.95 o.p. (ISBN 0-8144-5498-4). AMACOM.

Affirmative Action Compliance Kit. Peter Reid. 1980. pap. 125.00 o.p. (ISBN 0-917386-45-0). Exec Ent Pubns.

Affirmative Action Compliance Kit: EEO Dictionary. Peter Reid. 1980. pap. 10.00 o.p. (ISBN 0-917386-35-3). Exec Ent Pubns.

Affirmative Action Compliance Kit: Reference Guide. Peter Reid. 1980. pap. 15.00 o.p. (ISBN 0-917386-34-5). Exec Ent Pubns.

Affirmative Action Compliance Kit: Working Manual. Peter Reid. 1980. pap. 75.00 o.p. (ISBN 0-917386-33-7). Exec Ent Pubns.

Affirmative Action in Higher Education: A Sourcebook. Lois Vanderwaert. LC 80-9041. 225p. 1982. lib. bdg. 52.00 o.p. (ISBN 0-8240-9313-5). Garland Pub.

Affirming the Family in an Urban World. James A. Speer. 1978. 1.00 o.p. (ISBN 0-911802-42-8). Free Church Pubns.

Affluence & the Christian. Hendrik Van Oyen. Ed. by Franklin Sherman. Tr. by Frank Clarke. LC 66-24863. (Facet Bks.). 1966. pap. 0.50 o.p. (ISBN 0-8006-3034-3, 1-3034, Fortress). Augsburg Fortress.

Affluent Society. 3rd rev. ed. John Kenneth Galbraith. 1976. 15.95 o.p. (ISBN 0-395-24375-0); pap. 2.95 o.p. (ISBN 0-395-12689-4). HM.

Affordable Chic: Tours of Factory Clothing Outlets in San Francisco. 2nd ed. Victoria Goff & Viktoria Sparks-Forrester. (Illus.). 1987. pap. 4.95 o.p. (ISBN 0-9615416-0-1). RND Pub.

Affordable Computer: Microcomputer Applications in Business & Industry. new ed. Claire Summer & Walter A. Levy. LC 78-24672. 1979. 13.95 o.p. (ISBN 0-8144-5493-3). AMACOM.

Affordable Furs: Combining Fur & Leather with Knitting. Janet W. Mysse. LC 83-62505. (Illus.). 150p. 1983. 34.50 o.s.i. (ISBN 0-934318-21-2). Falcon Pr MT.

Afghan Syndrome: How to Live with Soviet Power. Bhabani Sen Gupta. 368p. 1982. text ed. 35.00x o.p. (ISBN 0-7069-1349-3, Pub. by Vikas India). Advent NY.

Afghanistan. L. Fischer. (Geomedical Monograph Ser.: Vol. 2). (Illus., Ger. & Eng.). 1968. 32.20 o.p. (ISBN 0-387-04266-0). Springer-Verlag.

Afghanistan. Masatoshi Konishi. LC 69-16367. (This Beautiful World Ser.: Vol. 7). (Illus.). 1969. pap. 4.95 o.p. (ISBN 0-87011-071-3). Kodansha.

Afghanistan: Between the Past & the Future. L. Nikolayev. 207p. 1986. pap. 3.95 o.p. (ISBN 0-8285-3245-1, Pub. by Progress Pubs USSR). Imported Pubns.

Afghanistan: Highway of Conquest. Arnold Fletcher. LC 81-20233. (Illus.). vii, 325p. 1982. Repr. of 1965 ed. lib. bdg. 38.50x o.p. (ISBN 0-313-23349-7, FLAF). Greenwood.

Afghanistan in Crisis. K. P. Misra. 1981. 18.95x o.p. (ISBN 0-89891-003-X, Pub. by Vikas India). Advent NY.

Afghanistan Today. Boris Petkov. 98p. 1984. text ed. 10.50x o.p. (ISBN 0-86590-170-8, Pub. by Sterling Pubs India). Apt Bks.

Afghans: Traditional & Modern. Bonita Bray. (Illus.). 1977. o. p. 9.95 o.p. (ISBN 0-517-53104-6); pap. 2.98 o. s. i. o.p. (ISBN 0-517-53105-4). Crown.

Afocha: A Link Between Community & Administration in Harar Ethiopia. Peter Koehn & Sidney R. Waldron. LC 78-27903. (Foreign & Comparative Studies Program African Ser.: No. 31). (Illus.). 120p. 1978. pap. 7.00x o.p. (ISBN 0-915984-53-9). Syracuse U Foreign Comp.

Afoot in the Field of Men. Pat E. Taylor. 108p. (Orig.). 1983. 10.95 o.p. (ISBN 0-941720-14-4); pap. 5.95x o.p. Slough Pr TX.

Afreeka Brass. Mwatabu S. Okantah. 28p. (Orig.). 1983. pap. 3.50 o.p. (ISBN 0-914946-41-2). Cleveland St Univ Poetry Ctr.

Africa. Ed. by Phyllis M. Martin & Patrick O'Meara. LC 77-74450. (Midland Bks.: No. 218). (Illus.). 512p. 1978. 25.00x o.p. (ISBN 0-253-30210-2); pap. 12.50x o.p. (ISBN 0-253-20218-3). Ind U Pr.

Africa. Waldemar A. Nielsen. LC 65-27530. (New York Times Byline Books). (Orig.). 1966. pap. 3.25x o.p. (ISBN 0-689-10213-5, Atheneum). Macmillan.

Africa. rev. ed. Benjamin E. Thomas et al. LC 80-69172. (World Cultures Ser.). (Illus.). (gr. 6 up). 1981. text ed. 13.70 ea. 1-4 copies o.p. (ISBN 0-88296-143-8); text ed. 10.96 ea. 5 or more copies o.p.; tchrs'. guide 4.96 o.p. (ISBN 0-88296-362-7). Gateway Pr MI.

Africa. Sanford J. Ungar. 544p. 1986. pap. 12.95 o.s.i. (ISBN 0-671-62809-7, Touchstone Bks). S&S.

Africa: A Season for Hope. Ed. by W. Dayton Roberts. LC 85-25618. (Illus.). 128p. 1986. pap. 5.95 o.s.i. (ISBN 0-8307-1120-1, 5418732). Regal.

Africa: A Study Geography for Advanced Students. 2nd ed. John M. Pritchard. (Illus.). 1979. pap. text ed. 16.95 o.p. (ISBN 0-582-64636-7). Longman.

Africa & After. Victor Kelleher. LC 82-20043. 218p. 1983. text ed. 17.95 o.p. (ISBN 0-7022-1791-3); 9.95 o.p. (ISBN 0-7022-1801-4). U of Queensland Pr.

Africa & Europe: From Partition to Interdependence or Dependence? Ed. by Amadu Sesay. 272p. 1986. 43.00 o.p. (ISBN 0-7099-4406-3, Pub. by Croom Helm Ltd). Routledge Chapman & Hall.

Africa & Her Children: An Introduction to the Origin of Civilization. Harry Armorer. 64p. 1979. 6.00 o.p. (ISBN 0-682-49356-2). Exposition-Phoenix.

Africa & International Crises. Robert W. Brown et al. LC 76-17820. (Foreign & Comparative Studies Program, Eastern Africa Ser.: No. 22). 106p. 1976. pap. text ed. 5.50x o.p. (ISBN 0-915984-19-9). Syracuse U Foreign Comp.

Africa & South America. rev. ed. William D. Allen et al. LC 77-87337. (World Cultures Ser). (Illus.). (gr. 6 up). 1978. text ed. 12.43 ea. 1-4 copies, 5 or more 9.94 o.p. (ISBN 0-88296-166-7); tchrs'. guide 8.94 o.p. (ISBN 0-686-85952-9). Gateway Pr MI.

Africa & the International Political System. Ed. by Timothy M. Shaw & Sola Ojo. LC 80-6242. (Illus.). 308p. (Orig.). 1982. lib. bdg. 33.75 o.p. (ISBN 0-8191-2233-5); pap. text ed. 15.25 o.p. (ISBN 0-8191-2234-3). U Pr of Amer.

Africa & the Middle East see Developing Areas: A Classed Bibliography of the Joint Bank-Fund Library, World Bank Group & International Monetary Fund.

Africa Explored: Europeans in the Dark Continent, 1769-1889. Christopher Hibbert. (Illus.). 1983. 17.00 o.p. (ISBN 0-393-01760-5). Norton.

Africa: From Independence to Tomorrow. David Hapgood. LC 71-103074. 1970. pap. text ed. 2.75x o.p. (ISBN 0-689-70225-6, 157, Atheneum). Macmillan.

Africa in the Wider World. D. Brokensha & M. Crowder. 1967. 75.00 o.p. (ISBN 0-08-012673-1); pap. 75.00 o.p. (ISBN 0-08-012672-3). Pergamon.

Africa in World Politics. Vernon McKay. LC 73-11866. 468p. 1974. Repr. of 1963 ed. lib. bdg. 22.50x o.p. (ISBN 0-8371-7100-8, MCAW). Greenwood.

Africa Index to Continental Periodical Literature: Covering 1979-1980, Vols. 4 & 5. Ed. by Colin Darch. 392p. 1983. lib. bdg. 62.00 o.p. (ISBN 3-598-21822-2). K G Saur.

Africa of the Heart: A Personal Journey. Joseph Hone. 1986. 16.95 o.p. (ISBN 0-688-04859-5, Pub. by Beech Tree Bks). Morrow.

Africa on a Shoestring. 3rd ed. Geoff Crowther. 700p. 1985. pap. 14.95 o.p. (ISBN 0-908086-89-X). Lonely Planet.

Africa on a Shoestring. 4th ed. Geoff Crowther. (Illus.). 752p. (Orig.). 1989. pap. 14.95 o.p. Lonely Planet.

Africa or Death. A. G. Mondini. (Illus.). 1964. 5.00 o.p. (ISBN 0-8198-0007-4). Dghtrs St Paul.

Africa Policy Update. Jane W. Jacqz. 43p. (Orig.). 1978. pap. text ed. 3.95 o.p. (ISBN 0-87855-727-X). Transaction Pubs.

Africa: Regional Study. rev. ed. Fred Burke. (World Regional Studies). (gr. 7 up). 1974. text ed. 8.80 o.p. (ISBN 0-395-03112-5). HM.

Africa: Regional Study. rev. ed. Hyman Kublin. 1974. pap. 10.32 o.p. (ISBN 0-395-17716-2). HM.

Africa South: Contemporary Writings. Ed. by Mothobi Mutloatse. (Africa Writes Ser.: No. 243). (Orig.). pap. text ed. 7.50x o.p. (ISBN 0-435-90243-1). Heinemann Ed.

Africa South of the Sahara. Howard Turner. 235p. (Orig.). 1986. pap. text ed. 16.95 o.p. (ISBN 0-582-58524-4). Longman.

Africa South of the Sahara: A Bibliography for Undergraduate Libraries. University of the State of New York, Foreign Area Materials Center Staff. Ed. by Peter Duignan. LC 76-151802. (Occasional Publications Ser: No. 12). 105p. 1971. 8.95 o.s.i. (ISBN 0-87272-019-5). Brodart.

Africa South of the Sahara: Index to Periodical Literature, First Supplement. Library of Congress Staff. 1973. lib. bdg. 110.00 o.p. (ISBN 0-8161-1048-4, Hall Library). G K Hall.

Africa South of the Sahara: Index to Periodical Literature, Third Supplement. Intro. by Angel D. Batiste. 314p. 1985. 15.00 o.p. (ISBN 0-8444-0507-8, S/N 030-000-00170-2). USGPO.

Africa South of the Sahara: Index to Periodical Literature, 1900-1970, 4 vols. Library of Congress Staff. 1974. Set. 365.00 o.p. (ISBN 0-8161-0892-7, Hall Library). G K Hall.

Africa South of the Sahara, Nineteen Eighty-Seven. 16th ed. 1100p. 1986. 145.00x o.p. (ISBN 0-946653-21-6, Pub. by Europa England). Intl Pubns Serv.

Africa South of the Sahara, Nineteen Eighty-Eight. 17th ed. 1140p. 1987. 160.00x o.p. (ISBN 0-946653-34-8, Pub. by Europa England). Gale.

Africa South of the Sahara 1986. 1089p. 1985. 135.00 o.p. (ISBN 0-946653-08-9, Pub. by England). Taylor & Francis.

Africa That Never Was: Four Centuries of British Writing about Africa--an Anthropological View Contrasting the Africa of Fact & the Africa of Fiction. Dorothy Hammond & Alta Jablow. LC 78-77035. 251p. 1978. text ed. 39.50x o.p. (ISBN 0-8290-0151-4); pap. text ed. 19.95x o.p. (ISBN 0-8290-0152-2). Irvington.

Africa: The Nile Route. K. Naylor. 160p. (Orig.). 1983. pap. 11.95 o.p. (Lascelles). Bradt Ent.

Africa: The People & Politics of an Emerging Continent. Sanford J. Ungar. 1985. 21.45 o.s.i. (ISBN 0-671-42010-0). S&S.

Africa: The Year of the Students. Colin Legum. (Current Affairs Ser.). 28p. 1972. pap. 3.50 o.p. (ISBN 0-8419-0101-5). Holmes & Meier.

Africa Today see Know Africa.

Africa Today: Its Peoples & Comtempory Cultures. Daniel Boamah-Wiafe. 334p. 1987. pap. text ed. 23.95 o.p. (ISBN 0-8403-4254-3). Kendall Hunt.

Africa View. Julian S. Huxley. LC 68-23300. 1968. Repr. of 1931 ed. lib. bdg. 35.00x o.p. (ISBN 0-8371-0112-3, HUAV). Greenwood.

Africa Who's Who see Know Africa.

Africa: Year of Great Decision. Colin Legum. (Current Affairs Ser.). 62p. 1972. pap. 3.50 o.p. Holmes & Meier.

African: A Photographic Essay on Black Women of Ghana & Nigeria. Joseph Franklin. LC 77-81436. 1977. 9.95 o.p. (ISBN 0-685-99392-2, Pub. by Wallingford Bks). Chulainn Press.

African Achievement & Tragedy see Tarikh.

African Adventures. Lloyd Fezler. LC 84-60869. 1984. pap. 3.95 o.p. (ISBN 0-89051-099-7). Master Bks.

African Animals. Yukio Togawa. LC 79-100629. (This Beautiful World Ser.: Vol. 14). (Illus., Orig.). 1970. pap. 4.95 o.p. (ISBN 0-87011-108-6). Kodansha.

African Animals Through African Eyes. Janet D'Amato & Alex D'Amato. LC 70-154970. (Illus.). 64p. (gr. 4 up). 1971. lib. bdg. 4.79 o.p. (ISBN 0-671-32426-8). Messner.

African Artistry: Technique & Aesthetics in Yoruba Sculpture. Henry J. Drewal. Ed. by Kelly Morris. LC 80-81184. (Illus.). 100p. (Orig.). 1980. pap. 7.00 o.p. (ISBN 0-939802-03-1). High Mus Art.

African Bees of the Genera Ceratina, Halictus & Megachile. T. D. Cockerell. xvi, 245p. 1937. 21.50x o.p. (ISBN 0-565-00151-5, Pub. by Brit Mus Nat Hist England). Sabbot-Natural Hist Bks.

African Book World & Press: A Directory. 3rd ed. Ed. by Hans Zell & Carol Bundy. 313p. 1984. 78.00x o.p. (ISBN 0-905450-10-8). K G Saur.
African Child & His Environment. R. O. Ohuche & B. Otaala. 1981. 15.00 o.p. (ISBN 0-08-025671-6). Pergamon.
African Child & His Environment. R. O. Ohuche & B. Otaala. (Studies Ser.: Vol. 3). 97p. 1981. pap. 10.00 o.p. (UNEP058, UNEP). UNIPUB.
African Christian Spirituality. Ed. by Aylward Shorter. LC 79-23063. 160p. (Orig.). 1980. pap. 1.74 o.p. (ISBN 0-88344-011-3). Orbis Bks.
African Countries & Cultures. Hornburger. 1985. 13.95 o.s.i. (ISBN 0-679-20507-1). McKay.
African Development & Europe. T. Burley & P. Tregear. 1970. 35.00 o.p. (ISBN 0-08-006669-0); pap. 35.00 o.p. (ISBN 0-08-006670-4). Pergamon.
African Development Bank: Problems of International Cooperation. Kwame D. Fordwor. LC 80-24607. (Pergamon Policy Studies on International Development). 300p. 1981. 90.00 o.p. (ISBN 0-08-026339-9). Pergamon.
African Experience see Tree Where Man Was Born.
African Experience in the American Marketplace: A Comparative Study of Cultural Philosophy. K. C. Anyanwu. 128p. 1983. pap. 5.00 o.p. (ISBN 0-682-49976-5, University). Exposition-Phoenix.
African Fabric Crafts: Sources of African Design & Technique. Esther W. Dendel. LC 72-6627. (Illus.). 160p. 1974. 10.95 o.s.i. (ISBN 0-8008-0150-4). Taplinger.
African Furniture & Household Objects. Roy Sieber. LC 79-5340. (Illus.). 280p. 1980. 37.50x o.p. (ISBN 0-253-11927-8); pap. 20.00x o.p. (ISBN 0-253-28242-X). Ind U Pr.
African Genesis. Robert Ardrey. LC 61-15889. (Illus.). 1961. 9.95 o.p. (ISBN 0-689-10013-2, Atheneum). Macmillan.
African Herdboy: A Story of the Masai. Jean Bothwell. LC 76-117615. (Illus.). (gr. 4-6). 1970. 5.25 o.p. (ISBN 0-15-201630-9, HJ). HarBraceJ.
African Homicide & Suicide. Ed. by Paul Bohannan. LC 59-13873. 1967. pap. text ed. 2.95x o.p. (ISBN 0-689-70018-0, 109, Atheneum). Macmillan.
African Hunter. James Mellon. LC 74-16351. (Illus.). 544p. 1975. 39.95 o.p. (ISBN 0-15-103954-2). HarBraceJ.
African in Germany. Martin O. Ijere. 1975. 5.00 o.p. (ISBN 0-682-48386-9). Exposition-Phoenix.
African in Greenland. Tete-Michel Kpomassie. Tr. by James Kirkup. LC 82-21235. (Illus.). 320p. 1983. 14.95 o.p. (ISBN 0-15-105589-0). HarBraceJ.
African Influence in the United Nations, 1967-1975: The Politics & Techniques of Gaining Compliance to U. N. Principles & Resolutions. Gregory L. Wilkins. LC 80-5735. 263p. (Orig.). 1981. lib. bdg. 29.75 o.p. (ISBN 0-8191-1424-3); pap. text ed. 13.25 o.p. (ISBN 0-8191-1425-1). U Pr of Amer.
African International Legal History. (UNITAR Studies Ser.). pap. 15.00 o.p. (UN76/15/ST9, UN). UNIPUB.
African Leadership & European Domination see Tarikh.
African Music. (Illus.). 154p. (Orig.). 1973. pap. 27.50 o.p. (ISBN 0-685-31875-3, UM31, UNESCO). UNIPUB.
African Music in Ghana. J. H. Kwabena Nketia. 148p. Repr. of 1963 ed. lib. bdg. 39.00 o.p. (Pub. by Am Repr Serv). Reprint Servs.
African Muslims in Antebellum America: A Sourcebook. Allan D. Austin. LC 80-9045. 500p. 1983. lib. bdg. 83.00 o.p. (ISBN 0-8240-9317-8). Garland Pub.
African Odyssey on Wheels: Twenty Thousand Miles Through East & Central Africa Without a Plan. Frederick H. Halpern. (Illus.). 1978. 12.50 o.p. (ISBN 0-682-49142-X). Exposition-Phoenix.
African Opposition in South Africa: The Failure of Passive Resistance. Edward Feit. LC 67-24130. (Publications Ser.: No. 57). 1967. 12.95x o.p. (ISBN 0-8179-1571-0). Hoover Inst Pr.
African Personality. 29p. 1980. pap. 5.00 o.p. (ISBN 92-808-0136-8, TUNU062, UNU). UNIPUB.
African Philosophy: A Historico-Hermeneutical Investigation of the Conditions of Its Possibility. Theophilus Okere. 156p. (Orig.). 1983. text ed. 25.50 o.p. (ISBN 0-8191-3023-0); pap. text ed. 10.25 o.p. (ISBN 0-8191-3024-9). U Pr of Amer.
African Poison Murders. Elspeth Huxley. LC 75-44985. (Crime Fiction Ser). 1976. Repr. of 1939 ed. lib. bdg. 21.00 o.p. (ISBN 0-8240-2377-3). Garland Pub.
African Politics: The Corruption of Power. Ken C. Kotecha & Robert W. Adams. LC 81-40155. 479p. 1981. lib. bdg. 34.75 o.p. (ISBN 0-8191-1564-9); pap. text ed. 18.75 o.p. (ISBN 0-8191-1565-7). U Pr of Amer.
African Presence in Early Asia. Ed. by Ivan Van Sertima. LC 85-8529. 168p. (Orig.). 1985. pap. text ed. 10.00x o.p. (ISBN 0-88738-637-7). Transaction Pubs.
African Rhythm & African Sensibility. John M. Chernoff. LC 79-189. 1980. lib. bdg. 20.00x o.s.i. (ISBN 0-226-10344-7). U of Chicago Pr.
African Success Story: The Ivory Coast. Marc Bernheim & Evelyne Bernheim. LC 72-84772. (Illus.). (gr. 7 up). 1970. 6.95 o.p. (ISBN 0-15-201650-3, HJ). HarBraceJ.
African Textiles. John Picton & John Mack. (Illus.). 160p. 1979. 28.50 o.p. (ISBN 0-7141-1552-5, Pub. by Brit Mus); pap. 18.50 o.p. (ISBN 0-7141-1553-3). Textile Mus.
African Theology En Route: Papers from the Pan-African Conference of Third World Theologians, December 17-23, 1977, Accra, Ghana. Ed. by Kofi Appiah-Kubi & Sergio Torres. LC 78-10604. 224p. (Orig.). 1978. pap. 10.95 o.p. (ISBN 0-88344-010-5). Orbis Bks.
African Trio: Talatala, Tropic Moon, Aboard the Aquitaine. Georges Simenon. 1979. 9.95 o.p. (ISBN 0-15-103955-0). HarBraceJ.
African Ungulates: A Comparative Review of Their Ethology & Behavioral Ecology. W. Leuthold. Ed. by D. S. Farner. LC 76-44535. (Zoophysiology & Ecology Ser.: Vol. 8). (Illus.). 1977. 46.00 o.p. (ISBN 0-387-07951-3). Springer-Verlag.
African Voices. Ed. by Howard Sergeant. LC 73-80849. 156p. 1974. 7.50 o.p. (ISBN 0-88208-016-4). Chicago Review.
African Widows. Michael C. Kirwen. LC 78-15870. (Illus.). 246p. (Orig.). 1979. pap. 2.24 o.p. (ISBN 0-88344-009-1). Orbis Bks.
African Wings: Poems. Craig Williamson. 1969. 4.00 o.p. (ISBN 0-8065-0236-3, Pub. by Citadel Pr). Carol Pub Group.
Africana Conference Paper Index, 2 vols. 1982. Set. lib. bdg. 189.00 o.p. (ISBN 0-8161-1309-2, Hall Library). G K Hall.
Africanderisms. Charles Pettman. LC 68-18007. 600p. 1968. Repr. of 1913 ed. 53.00x o.p. (ISBN 0-8103-3289-2). Gale.
Africans: A Triple Heritage. Ali A. Mazrui. 1986. 29.95 o.p. (ISBN 0-316-55200-3). Little.
Africans Knew. Tillie S. Pine & Joseph Levine. (Illus.). (gr. 1-4). 1967. text ed. 7.95 o.p. (ISBN 0-07-050076-2). McGraw.
Africa's Shared Water Resources: Legal & Institutional Aspects of the Nile, Niger & Senegal River Systems. Bonaya Godana. LC 85-8370. 370p. 1985. lib. bdg. 30.00x o.p. (ISBN 0-931477-44-1). Lynne Rienner.
Afrika Korps. George Balin. (Illus.). 64p. (Orig.). 1985. pap. 9.95 o.p. (ISBN 0-85368-692-0, Pub. by Arms & Armour). Sterling.
Afro-American History: Primary Sources. Ed. by Thomas R. Frazier. (Shorter ed.). 1971. pap. text ed. 2.73 o.p. (ISBN 0-15-502051-X, HC). HarBraceJ.
Afro-American Literature: An Introduction. Robert Hayden et al. 1971. pap. text ed. 10.95 o.p. (ISBN 0-15-502075-7, HC). HarBraceJ.
Afro-American Literature: Fiction. Ed. by William Adams et al. (Afro-American Literature Ser). (gr. 9-12). 1970. pap. 10.40 o.p. (ISBN 0-395-01977-X). HM.
Afro-American Literature: Nonfiction. Ed. by William Adams et al. (Afro-American Literature Ser.). (gr. 9-12). 1970. pap. 8.40 o.p. (ISBN 0-395-01979-6). HM.
Afro-American Literature: Poetry. Ed. by William Adams et al. (Afro-American Literature Ser.). (gr. 10-12). 1970. pap. 7.56 o.p. (ISBN 0-395-01975-3). HM.
Afro-American Tradition in Decorative Arts. John M. Vlach. LC 77-19326. (Illus.). 184p. 1978. pap. 12.00x o.p. (ISBN 0-910386-39-0, Pub. by Cleveland Mus Art). Ind U Pr.
Afro-Asian Culture Studies. rev. ed. Geller Rosenfeld. LC 78-23785. (Illus.). 1979. text ed. 17.95 o.p. (ISBN 0-8120-5322-2); pap. 12.95 o.p. (ISBN 0-8120-0993-2). Barron.
Afro-Asian Movement: Ideology & Foreign Policy of the Third World. David Kimche. 1973. casebound 16.95x o.p. (ISBN 0-87855-161-1). Transaction Pubs.
Afro-Spanish American Authors, an Annotated Bibliography of Criticism. Richard L. Jackson. LC 79-7928. (Garland Reference Library of the Humanities). 175p. 1980. lib. bdg. 24.00 o.p. (ISBN 0-8240-9529-4). Garland Pub.
Afrocommunism. rev. ed ed. David Ottaway & Marina Ottaway. LC 80-24289. (New Library of African Affairs Ser.). 280p. 1986. text ed. 29.50 o.p. (ISBN 0-8419-0664-5, Africana); pap. text ed. 16.95 o.p. (ISBN 0-8419-0699-8). Holmes & Meier.
After a Famous Victory. Lucilla Andrews. 1985. 12.95 o.p. (ISBN 0-8166-0102-X, Large Print Bks). G K Hall.
After a Funeral. Diana Athill. 176p. 1986. 15.45 o.s.i. (ISBN 0-89919-454-0). Ticknor & Fields.
After a Loss in Pregnancy: Help for Families Affected by a Miscarriage, a Still Birth, or a Newborn's Death. Nancy Berezin. (Illus.). 224p. (Orig.). 1982. pap. 9.95 o.p. (ISBN 0-671-25525-8, Fireside). S&S.
After Alienation: American Novels in Mid-Century. Marcus Klein. LC 77-92757. (Midway Reprint). 1978. pap. text ed. 13.00x o.s.i. (ISBN 0-226-43953-4). U of Chicago Pr.
After Candlemas. Ruth M. Arthur. LC 73-84820. (Illus.). 128p. (gr. 5-9). 1974. 5.25 o.p. (ISBN 0-689-30129-4, Atheneum). Macmillan.
After Death, What? William B. Ward. LC 65-10754. (Orig.). 1965. pap. 1.95 o.p. (ISBN 0-8042-3352-7, John Knox). Westminster John Knox.
After Eighteen Eighty Three: One Hundred Years of Organized Veterinary Medicine in Pennsylvania. Ray Thompson. (Illus.). 256p. 1982. (ISBN 0-7216-1039-0). Saunders.
After Einstein: Proceedings of the Einstein Centennial Celebration, Memphis State University, March 14-16, 1979. Einstein Centennial Celebration Staff. Ed. by Peter Barker & Cecil G. Shugart. LC 80-27347. (Illus.). 1981. 24.95x o.p. (ISBN 0-87870-095-1). Memphis St Univ.
After Eli. Terry Kay. LC 80-27577. 288p. 1981. 10.95 o.p. (ISBN 0-395-30854-2). HM.
After Fifteen Years. Leon Jaworski. LC 61-14514. 167p. 1961. 12.00x o.p. (ISBN 0-87201-017-1). Gulf Pub.
After Fifty Pharmacy: An Easy-to-Understand Guide to Prescription & Nonprescription Medications. Ann Kepler et al. 272p. 1987. pap. 9.95 o.p. (ISBN 0-8092-4770-4). Contemp bks.
After Freedom: A Cultural Study in the Deep South. Hortense Powdermaker. LC 68-16415. (Studies in American Negro Life). 1968. pap. 3.45 o.p. (ISBN 0-689-70160-8, NL3, Atheneum). Macmillan.
After Goliath. R. V. Cassill. LC 84-16225. 224p. 1985. 14.45 o.p. (ISBN 0-89919-325-0). Ticknor & Fields.
After Great Pain: The Inner Life of Emily Dickinson. John Cody. LC 79-148937. 1971. 27.95 o.s.i. (ISBN 0-674-00878-2, Belknap Pr). Harvard U Pr.
After Hours. Edwin Torres. 1982. pap. 2.75 o.p. (ISBN 0-380-60731-X, 60731). Avon.
After Imperialism: The Search for a New Order in the Far East, 1921-1931. Akira Iriye. LC 65-22052. 1969. pap. text ed. 5.95x o.p. (ISBN 0-689-70105-5, 147, Atheneum). Macmillan.
After Innocence: Visions of the Fall in Modern Literature. Terry Otten. LC 81-11538. (Critical Essays in Modern Literature Ser.). 243p. 1982. 23.95x o.p. (ISBN 0-8229-3453-1). U of Pittsburgh Pr.
After Its Kind. rev. ed. Byron C. Nelson. (Illus.). 1967. pap. 5.95 o.p. (ISBN 0-87123-008-9). Bethany Hse.
After Law School? Finding a Job in a Tight Market. Saul Miller. 1978. pap. 7.95 o.p. (ISBN 0-316-57362-0). Little.
After Leningrad: A Diary of Survival During World War Two. Elena Skrjabina. (Soviet Union at War Ser.: Vol. 2). 195p. 1978. 24.95 o.p. (ISBN 0-8093-0856-8). Transaction Pubs.
After Midnight. Irmgard Keun. 160p. 1987. Repr. of 1937 ed. 18.95 o.p. (ISBN 0-575-03656-7, Pub. by Gollancz England). David & Charles.
After My House Burned Down. Elaine Ward. 88p. (Orig.). 1982. pap. 6.95 o.s.i. (ISBN 0-940754-11-8). Ed Ministries.
After School Is Out see Getting along Series of Skills.
After School Secret. Linda Barr. (Illus.). 96p. (gr. 4-7). 1987. 2.25 o.s.i. (ISBN 0-87406-230-6). Willowisp Pr.
After-Summer Seed. Ed. by John Hollow. (Illus.). viii, 149p. 1978. pap. 6.00x o.s.i. (ISBN 0-931332-02-8). Wedgestone Pr.
After-Tax Money Income Estimates of Households 1984. 5th annual ed. Charles T. Nelson. (Current Population Reports Series P-23, Special Studies Ser.: No. 147). (Illus.). 55p. (Orig.). 1986. pap. 2.75 o.p. (ISBN 0-318-21635-3, S/N 003-001-91564-2). USGPO.
After the Affair. Alexis Rotella. (Illus.). 30p. (Orig.). pap. 3.95 o.p. (ISBN 0-934536-19-8). Merging Media.
After the Bugles. Elmer Kelton. (Nightingale Paperbacks Ser.). 288p. 1987. pap. 11.95 o.p. (ISBN 0-8161-4326-9, Large Print Bks). G K Hall.
After the Dream. Charles Kaufman. (Orig.). 1977. pap. 1.75 o.p. (ISBN 0-380-01105-0, 32912). Avon.
After the First Death. Robert Cormier. 224p. 1980. pap. 2.50 o.p. (ISBN 0-380-48652-0, Flare). Avon.
After the Flood. P. C. Jersild. Tr. by Lone T. Blecher & George Blecher. LC 85-278. 256p. 1986. 15.95 o.p. (ISBN 0-688-04902-8). Morrow.
After the Goat Man. Betsy Byars. (Illus.). 126p. (gr. 3-5). 1976. pap. 1.25 o.p. (ISBN 0-380-00437-2, 53314-6, Camelot). Avon.
After the Lost Generation. John W. Aldridge. 1985. 6.95 o.p. (ISBN 0-87795-757-6, Arbor Hse); pap. 6.95 o.p. (ISBN 0-87795-723-1). Morrow.
After the Preaching, the Praying & the Shouting, What Then? Thirty-Two Sermons. Alexander Montgomery. (Illus.). 1978. 6.00 o.p. (ISBN 0-682-49167-5). Exposition-Phoenix.
After the Race. Marvin Elkoff. 1983. 14.50 o.p. (ISBN 0-671-47033-7). S&S.
After the Reunion. Rona Jaffe. 336p. 1985. 17.95 o.p. (ISBN 0-385-29413-1). Delacorte.
After the Revolution: Profiles of Early American Culture. Joseph J. Ellis. (Illus.). 1979. 19.95 o.p. (ISBN 0-393-01253-0). Norton.
After the Revolution: The Smithsonian History of Everyday Life in the 18th Century. Barbara Smith. LC 85-42853. 240p. 1987. pap. 8.95 o.p. (ISBN 0-394-74638-4). Pantheon.
After the Second Oil Crisis: Energy Policies in Europe, America, & Japan. Wilfrid L. Kohl. LC 81-47023. 256p. 1982. 32.50x o.p. (ISBN 0-669-04547-0). Lexington Bks.
After the Storm. Margaret Johnson. 224p. 1987. pap. 5.95 o.p. (ISBN 0-310-47201-6, 15566P). Zondervan.
After Therapy What? Proceedings of the John G. Finch Symposium on Psychology & Religion, 1nd. John G. Finch Symposium on Psychology & Religion Staff & Thomas C. Oden. (Illus.). 224p. 1974. 22.50x o.p. (ISBN 0-398-03105-3). C C Thomas.
After You Receive Power. Philip E. Weeks. LC 74-80380. 128p. (Orig.). 1975. pap. 2.95 o.p. (ISBN 0-8192-1185-0). Morehouse Pub.
After You've Said I Do. Dwight H. Small. 1976. pap. 2.95 o.s.i. (ISBN 0-515-09678-4). Jove Pubns.
Afterglow. Judith Plowden. 1979. pap. 2.25 o.p. (ISBN 0-8439-0665-0, Pub. by Leisure Bks CT). Dorchester Pub Co.
Afterlife. Colin Wilson. 272p. 1987. pap. 16.95 o.p. (ISBN 0-385-23765-0, Dolp). Doubleday.
Aftermath. Ladislas Farago. 1975. pap. 1.95 o.p. (ISBN 0-380-00407-0, 25387). Avon.
Aftermath: A Soldier's Return from Vietnam. Frederick Downs, Jr. LC 83-42659. 224p. 1984. 12.45 o.p. (ISBN 0-393-01769-9). Norton.
Aftermath of Revolution: British Policy Toward the United States, 1783-1795. Charles R. Ritcheson. LC 77-86328. 520p. 1969. 19.95x o.p. (ISBN 0-87074-100-4). SMU Press.
Afternoon Sun. David Pryce-Jones. LC 86-9068. 224p. 1986. 15.95 o.s.i. (ISBN 1-55584-006-X). Weidenfeld.
Aftershocks: A Tale of Two Victims. David H. Bain. 320p. 1980. 11.95 o.p. (ISBN 0-416-00681-7, NO.0179). Routledge Chapman & Hall.
Agadir. Artur Lundkvist. Tr. by William Jay Smith & Leif Sjoberg. LC 80-15978. (International Poetry Ser.: Vol. 2). (Illus.). xiii, 57p. 1979. 12.95x o.p. (ISBN 0-8214-0444-X); pap. 7.95 o.p. (ISBN 0-8214-0561-6). Ohio U Pr.
Against Gravity: Poems. Donald E. Axinn. LC 86-271. 96p. 1986. 12.50 o.s.i. (ISBN 0-394-55342-X). Grove.
Against Gravity: Poems Nineteen Eighty-Two to Nineteen Eighty-Five. Donald E. Axinn. LC 86-271. 96p. 1986. pap. 5.95 o.p. (ISBN 0-394-62198-0, Ever). Grove.
Against Infinity. Gregory Benford. 240p. 1983. 14.50 o.p. (Timescape). PB.
Against Liquidationism. V. I. Lenin. 346p. 1973. 3.45 o.p. (ISBN 0-8285-0068-1, Pub. by Progress Pubs USSR). Imported Pubns.
Against Revisionism. V. I. Lenin. 604p. 1976. 4.95 o.p. (ISBN 0-8285-0069-X, Pub. by Progress Pubs USSR). Imported Pubns.
Against Socialist Ill. Date not set. (ISBN 0-8052-3963-4). Random.
Against the Current: Reform & Experimentation in Higher Education. Ed. by Richard M. Jones & Barbara L. Smith. 389p. 1984. 22.95 o.p. (ISBN 0-87073-648-5); pap. 11.95 o.p. (ISBN 0-87073-649-3). Schenkman Bks Inc.
Against the Fall of Night see Lion of Comarre.
Against the Grain: Coming through Mid-Life Crises. David Maitland. 208p. 1981. pap. 8.95 o.p. (ISBN 0-8298-0675-X). Pilgrim NY.
Against the Grain: The Dilemma of Project Food Aid. Tony Jackson & Deborah Eade. (Illus.). 132p. pap. 9.95 o.s.i. (ISBN 0-85598-063-X). Inst Food & Develop.
Against the Moon. Jane G. Rushing. 1979. pap. 1.95 o.p. (ISBN 0-380-42812-1, 42812). Avon.
Against the Night, the Stars: The Science Fiction of Arthur C. Clarke. John Hollow. LC 82-23366. 208p. 1983. 14.95 o.p. (ISBN 0-15-103966-6). HarBraceJ.
Against the Odds. David J. Keddy. 1987. 6.50 o.p. (ISBN 0-8062-2489-4). Carlton.
Against the Stream. Karl Barth. (Illus.). 252p. 1954. (ISBN 0-8022-0072-9). Philos Lib.
Against the Stream. James Hawley. 256p. 1983. pap. 4.95 o.p. (ISBN 0-380-63693-X, 63693-X, Bard). Avon.

Against the Wind: Screenplay. Bronwyn Binns & Ian Jones. (Australian Theatre Workshop Ser.). 1978. pap. text ed. 8.00x o.p. (ISBN 0-686-65307-6). Heinemann Ed.

Against Trotskyism. Ed. by A. A. Solovyov. 406p. 1972. 4.10 o.p. (ISBN 0-8285-0391-5, Pub. by Progress Pubs USSR). Imported Pubns.

Agaperos. Grady Nutt. LC 77-71722. (Illus.). (YA) (gr. 7-12). 1977. pap. 4.95 o.p. (ISBN 0-8054-5327-X, 4253-27). Broadman.

Agatha Christie: An Autobiography. Agatha Christie. 1978. pap. 3.95 o.p. (ISBN 0-345-27646-9); 3.95 o.p. (ISBN 0-345-31310-0). Ballantine.

Agatha Christie Crossword Puzzle Book. Randall Toye & Judith H. Gaffney. 132p. (Orig.). 1981. pap. 6.95 o.p. (ISBN 0-03-059158-9). H Holt & Co.

Agatha Moudio's Son. Francis Bebey. Tr. by Joyce A. Hutchinson from Fr. LC 72-96591. 160p. (Orig.). 1973. pap. 3.95 o.p. (ISBN 0-88208-038-5). Chicago Review.

Agatha's Friends. Thomas Houser. 224p. 1983. pap. 2.50 o.p. (ISBN 0-380-82222-9, 82222-9). Avon.

Age. Hortense Calisher. LC 86-34005. 128p. 1987. 14.95 o.s.i. (ISBN 1-55584-132-5). Weidenfeld.

Age & Generation. Mike O'Donnell & Patrick McNeill. LC 85-4792. (Society Now Ser.). 160p. 1985. pap. text ed. 6.50 o.p. (ISBN 0-422-79360-4, 9591, Pub. by Tavistock England). Routledge Chapman & Hall.

Age de Raison. Jean-Paul Sartre. 310p. 1945. 9.95 o.p. (ISBN 0-686-54971-6). Schoenhof.

Age de Raison see Chemins de la liberte.

Age Discrimination Workshop Nineteen Eighty-Five: State & Federal Litigation. Age Discrimination Workshop Staff et al. LC 85-196202. (Litigation & Administrative Practice Ser.). 640p. 1985. 15.00 o.p. (ISBN 0-317-39965-9, H44974). PLI.

Age, Learning Ability & Intelligence. Ed. by Richard L. Sprott. 176p. 1980. 21.95 o.p. (ISBN 0-442-27895-0). Van Nos Reinhold.

Age Like This: Nineteen Twenty to Nineteen Forty see Collected Essays, Journalism, & Letters of George Orwell.

Age of Access: Information Technology & Social Revolution. Colin Cherry. Ed. by William Edmondson. LC 85-16675. (New Information Technology Ser.). 192p. 1985. 34.50 o.p. (ISBN 0-7099-3458-0, Pub. by Croom Helm Ltd). Routledge Chapman & Hall.

Age of Adam. James Lees-Milne. LC 48-3247. 184p. 1947. Repr. 39.00x o.p. (ISBN 0-403-08606-X). Somerset Pub.

Age of Austerity. Ed. by Michael Sissons & Philip French. LC 75-45350. 349p. 1976. Repr. of 1963 ed. lib. bdg. 22.50x o.p. (ISBN 0-8371-8732-X, SIAA). Greenwood.

Age of Cameras. Edward Holmes. (Illus.). 160p. 1987. 22.50 o.p. (ISBN 0-85242-346-2, Pub. by Fountain Pr UK). Seven Hills Bk Dists.

Age of Capital. Eric J. Hobsbawm. LC 75-29583. 1975. 17.50 o.s.i. (ISBN 0-684-14450-6, ScribT). Scribner.

Age of Caravaggio. Mina Gregori et al. (Illus.). 368p. 1985. 19.95 o.p. (ISBN 0-87099-380-1); pap. 9.95 o.p. (ISBN 0-87099-382-8). Metro Mus Art.

Age of Dante. Vittorini. pap. 2.25 o.p. (ISBN 0-8065-0307-6, Pub. by Citadel Pr). Carol Pub Group.

Age of Discovery: 1400-1600. David Arnold. (Lancaster Pamphlets Ser.). 50p. 1984. pap. 3.95 o.p. (ISBN 0-416-36040-8, NO. 3982). Routledge Chapman & Hall.

Age of Elegance. Intro. by Madeleine Ginsburg. (Illus., Orig.). 1985. pap. 9.95 o.p. (ISBN 0-948107-11-1, Pub. by Victoria & Albert Mus UK). Faber & Faber.

Age of Equipoise. William L. Burn. 1965. pap. 3.95x o.p. (ISBN 0-393-00319-1, Norton Lib). Norton.

Age of Exuberance, Fifteen Hundred to Seventeen Hundred. Michael Reed. (Making of Britain Ser.). (Illus.). 320p. 1986. text ed. 29.95 o.p. (ISBN 0-7100-9803-0). Routledge Chapman & Hall.

Age of Goethe: An Anthology of German Literature 1749-1832. Ed. by Stuart Atkins. LC 70-681. (Illus., Ger.). 1969. text ed. 21.50 o.p. (ISBN 0-395-04119-8, 3-01600). HM.

Age of Great Cities. Robert Vaughan. (The Development of Industrial Society Ser.). 384p. 1971. Repr. of 1843 ed. 32.50x o.p. (ISBN 0-7165-1597-0, BBA 02147, Pub. by Irish Academic Pr Ireland). Biblio Dist.

Age of Great Cities. Robert Vaughan. (Studies in Urban History). 376p. 1969. Repr. of 1842 ed. 27.50x o.p. (ISBN 0-7130-0019-8, Pub. by Woburn Pr England). Biblio Dist.

Age of Illusion: Politics & Art in France, 1918-1940. Douglas Johnson & Madeleine Johnson. LC 86-26153. (Illus.). 160p. 1987. 30.00 o.p. (ISBN 0-8478-0788-6). Rizzoli Intl.

Age of Inigo Jones. James Lees-Milne. 242p. 1953. Repr. 39.00x o.p. (ISBN 0-403-03878-2). Somerset Pub.

Age of Keynes. Robert Lekachman. LC 66-12014. 336p. 1975. pap. text ed. 3.95 o.p. (ISBN 0-07-037154-7). McGraw.

Age of Lloyd George: The Liberal Party & British Politics, 1880-1929. 2nd ed. Kenneth O. Morgan. (Historical Problems: Studies & Documents). 1978. pap. text ed. 15.95x o.p. (ISBN 0-04-942093-3). Unwin Hyman.

Age of Louis Fourteenth. Voltaire. 1969. Repr. of 1926 ed. 14.95x o.p. (ISBN 0-460-00780-7, Evman). Biblio Dist.

Age of Miracles. Morton Kelsey. LC 78-74095. 80p. 1979. pap. 2.45 o.p. (ISBN 0-87793-169-0). Ave Maria.

Age of Reagan. Alexander Cockburn & James Ridgeway. 350p. 1987. 18.95 o.p. (ISBN 0-86091-176-4, A0799, Pub. by Verso). Routledge Chapman & Hall.

Age of Recovery: The Fifteenth Century. Jerah Johnson & William A. Percy. LC 76-10816. (Development of Western Civilization Ser.). (Illus.). 156p. 1970. pap. 6.95x o.p. (ISBN 0-8014-9858-9). Cornell U Pr.

Age of Reformation. E. Harris Harbison. LC 82-2985. (Development of Western Civilization Ser.). xiv, 145p. 1982. Repr. of 1955 ed. lib. bdg. 35.00x o.p. (ISBN 0-313-23555-4, HAAGR). Greenwood.

Age of Reptiles. Edwin H. Colbert. (World Naturalist Ser.). 1966. pap. 4.95 o.p. (ISBN 0-393-00374-4, Norton Lib). Norton.

Age of Roosevelt: The Crisis of the Old Order, Vol. 1. Arthur M. Schlesinger, Jr. 1957. 12.95 o.p. (ISBN 0-395-08159-9); pap. 5.95 o.p. (ISBN 0-395-08388-5). HM.

Age of the Cosmos. Harold S. Slusher. LC 79-92722. (ICR Technical Monograph). 1980. pap. 6.95 o.p. (ISBN 0-932766-03-X, Inst Creation). Master Bks.

Age of the Dream Palace: Cinema & Society in Britain 1930-1939. Jeffrey Richards. (Cinema & Society Ser.). (Illus.). 352p. 1984. 29.95 o.p. (ISBN 0-7100-9764-6). Routledge Chapman & Hall.

Age of the Earth. Harold S. Slusher & Thomas P. Gamwell. LC 78-70530. (ICR Technical Monograph). 1978. pap. 5.95 o.p. (ISBN 0-932766-02-1, Inst Creation). Master Bks.

Age of the Enlightened Despot: Sixteen Sixty to Seventeen Eighty-Nine. rev. ed. Arthur H. Johnson & C. T. Atkinson. LC 75-8719. 1978. Repr. of 1964 ed. lib. bdg. 35.00x o.p. (ISBN 0-8371-7999-8, JOED). Greenwood.

Age of the Enlightenment: Studies Presented to Theodore Besterman. Theodore Besterman. Ed. by W. H. Barber et al. (Illus.). 468p. 1967. 15.00x o.p. (ISBN 0-87471-217-3). Rowman.

Age of the Moguls. Stewart H. Holbrook. 1985. pap. 8.95 o.s.i. (ISBN 0-517-55679-0). Crown.

Age of the Solar System. Harold S. Slusher & Stephen J. Robertson. LC 78-70529. (ICR Technical Monograph). 1978. pap. 7.95 o.p. (ISBN 0-932766-01-3, Inst Creation). Master Bks.

Age of Trust: How to Prevent Future War. Starnes R. Wellborn. 1974. 6.00 o.p. (ISBN 0-682-47872-5). Exposition-Phoenix.

Age of Uncertainty. John Kenneth Galbraith. 1978. 17.95 o.p. (ISBN 0-395-24900-7); pap. 9.95 o.p. (ISBN 0-395-25947-9). HM.

Age of Wonders. Aharon Appelfeld. Tr. by Dalya Bilu from Hebrew. LC 81-47318. 224p. 1981. 12.95 o.s.i. (ISBN 0-87923-402-4). Godine.

Age Reduction System: A Complete Program to Help Slow, Halt, or Retard Aging. Richard C. Kaufman. LC 84-42933. 322p. 1985. 18.95 o.p. (ISBN 0-89256-285-4). Rawson Assocs.

Aged Man Remembers April. Raymond P. Fischer. LC 85-13495. 48p. 1985. lib. bdg. 7.95 o.p. (ISBN 0-87483-000-1). August Hse.

Aged Poor in England & Wales. Charles Booth. LC 79-56948. (English Working Class Ser.). 1980. lib. bdg. 53.00 o.p. (ISBN 0-8240-0103-6). Garland Pub.

Agee: His Life Remembered. Ed. by Ross Spears & Jude Cassidy. (Illus.). 208p. 1985. 19.95 o.p. (ISBN 0-03-060079-0). H Holt & Co.

Ageing in Industry. F. Le Gros & Agnes C. Dunne. 160p. 1957. (ISBN 0-8022-0252-7). Philos Lib.

Ageless Ageing: The Natural Way to Stay Young. Leslie Kenton. 376p. Repr. of 1985 ed. 17.95 o.s.i. (ISBN 0-394-55552-X). Grove.

Agency, Associations, Employment, Licensing & Partnerships: Cases, Statutes & Analysis. 3rd ed. Alfred F. Conard et al. LC 82-82863. (University Casebook Ser.). 656p. 1982. pap. 20.00 o.p. (ISBN 0-88277-080-2). Foundation Pr.

Agency Management Manual: Continuing Manual (Looseleaf) Emmett Vaughn. Ed. by The Merrit Company Staff. 1700p. 1987. 150.00 o.p. (ISBN 0-317-59921-6). Merritt Co.

Agency N. Y. Louis A. Kass. 1965. pap. 2.25 o.p. (ISBN 0-87526-002-0). Gould.

Agenda for Biblical People. Jim Wallis. LC 75-36745. 160p. (Orig.). 1976. pap. 6.68i o.p. (ISBN 0-06-069236-7, RD146). HarpR.

Agenda for Institutional Change. Ed. by Leslie Wagner. 200p. 1982. 18.00x o.p. (ISBN 0-900868-85-6, Open Univ Pr). Taylor & Francis.

Agenda for Theology. Thomas C. Oden. LC 78-19506. 1979. pap. text ed. 11.00 o.p. (ISBN 0-06-066347-2). HarpR.

Agent. Bill Adler & David R. Slavitt. LC 85-16038. 264p. 1986. 16.95 o.p. (ISBN 0-385-23007-9). Doubleday.

Agent in Place. Helen MacInnes. LC 75-44165. 339p. 1976. 8.95 o.s.i. (ISBN 0-15-103967-4). HarBraceJ.

Agent in Place: The Wennerstrom Affair. Thomas Whiteside. 160p. 1983. pap. 2.50 o.s.i. (ISBN 0-345-30326-1). Ballantine.

Agent of Byzantium. Harry Turtledove. (Isaac Asimov Presents Ser.). 1987. 15.95 o.p. (ISBN 0-86553-183-8). Congdon & Weed.

Agent Orange & the Vietnam Veteran: An Annotated Bibliography. Caroline D. Harnly. LC 85-141261. (Public Administration Ser.: Bibliography P 1623). 160p. 1985. pap. 18.25 o.p. (ISBN 0-89028-293-5). Vance Biblios.

Agent Orange on Trial: Mass Toxic Disasters in the Courts. Peter H. Schuck. LC 86-7360. 352p. 1986. 25.00x o.p. (ISBN 0-674-01025-6, Belknap Pr). Harvard U Pr.

Agents of Change: A Study in Police Reform. Hans Toch. LC 73-78120. 437p. 1974. 17.95 o.p. (ISBN 0-470-87606-9); pap. 6.95x o.p. (ISBN 0-470-87607-7). Halsted Pr.

Agents of Change: The Development & Practice of Management Consultancy. Patricia Tisdall. (Illus.). 192p. 1983. 22.95 o.p. (ISBN 0-434-91961-6, Pub. by W. Heinemann Ltd). David & Charles.

Ages & Dispensations. Frank M. Boyd. 112p. 1955. pap. 1.50 o.p. (ISBN 0-88243-463-2, 02-0463). Gospel Pub.

Aggregate Economic Analysis. 5th ed. Joseph P. McKenna. LC 76-19362. 336p. 1977. text ed. 29.95x o.p. (ISBN 0-03-089707-6). Dryden Pr.

Aggregates-Building Materials: Monographs. Mary Vance. LC 85-141715. (Architecture Ser.: Bibliography A 1329). 1985. pap. 3.75 o.p. (ISBN 0-89028-279-X). Vance Biblios.

Aggregating Behavior & Exploitation of Subterranean Habitat by Gravid Eastern Mild Snakes (Lampropeltis T. triangulum) Robert W. Henderson. (Contributions in Biology & Geology: No. 32). 1980. 1.00 o.p. (ISBN 0-89326-056-8). Milwaukee Pub Mus.

Aggregation & Averaging. Irving H. Siegel. 33p. 1968. pap. 1.95 o.p. (ISBN 0-911558-45-4). W E Upjohn.

Aggression: A Social Learning Analysis. Albert Bandura. (P-H Social Learning Ser). (Illus.). 368p. 1973. text ed. 34.00 ref. ed. o.p. (ISBN 0-13-020743-8). P-H.

Aggression & Criminality of Adolescence. Emanuel J. Martinez. 1979. 7.50 o.p. (ISBN 0-682-49224-8, University). Exposition-Phoenix.

Aggression in the Schools: Bullies & Whipping Boys. Dan Olweus. (Series in Clinical & Community Psychology). 218p. 1978. 41.95x o.p. (ISBN 0-470-99361-8). Halsted Pr.

Aghvook, White Eskimo. Charles J. Keim. LC 68-28823. (Illus.). 313p. 1969. U of Alaska Pr.

Aging. Ed. by Geraldine M. Emerson. (Benchmark Papers in Human Physiology: Vol. 11). 1977. 61.50 o.p. (ISBN 0-12-786420-2). Acad Pr.

Aging & Estrogens. Ed. by P. A. Van Keep & C. Lauritzen. (Frontiers of Hormone Research: Vol. 2). (Illus.). 1973. 30.00 o.p. (ISBN 3-8055-1606-1). S Karger.

Aging & Mental Health. Robert N. Butler & Myrna I. Lewis. LC 82-22404. (Mosby Medical Library). (Illus.). 386p. 1983. pap. 8.95 o.p. (ISBN 0-8016-1002-8). Mosby.

Aging Brain: Physiological & Pathophysiological Aspects. Ed. by S. Hoyer. (Experimental Brain Research: Supplementum 5). (Illus.). 281p. 1982. 47.00 o.p. (ISBN 0-387-11394-0). Springer-Verlag.

Aging Game: Success, Sanity & Sex after Sixty. Barbara G. Anderson. LC 79-18293. (McGraw-Hill Paperbacks Ser.). 252p. 1981. pap. text ed. 4.95 o.p. (ISBN 0-07-001761-1). McGraw.

Aging Game: Success, Sanity & Sex After Sixty. Barbara G. Anderson. LC 79-18293. 1979. text ed. 12.95 o.p. (ISBN 0-07-001760-3). McGraw.

Aging in America. CQ Inc. Staff. 105p. 1988. 10.95 o.p. (ISBN 0-87187-501-2). Congr Quarterly.

Aging in Developing Societies: A Reader in Third World Gerontology, Volume Two. Ed. by John H. Morgan. ii, 161p. (Orig.). 1985. pap. 9.95x o.p. (ISBN 0-932269-16-8). Wyndham Hall.

Aging in Nonhuman Primates. Douglas M. Bowden. (Primate Behavior & Development Ser.). 1979. 38.95 o.p. (ISBN 0-442-20734-4). Van Nos Reinhold.

Aging-in-Place: Five Housing Alternatives for the Elderly. Patricia B. Pollak. (Architecture Ser.: A 1490). 9p. 1985. 2.00 o.p. (ISBN 0-89028-620-5). Vance Biblios.

Aging Is Not for Sissies. Terry Schuckman. LC 74-34139. 1975. 5.95 o.s.i. (ISBN 0-664-20725-1, Westminster); pap. 2.95 o.s.i. (ISBN 0-664-24818-7, Westminster). Westminster John Knox.

Aging, Isolation & Resocialization. Ed. by Ruth Bennett. 224p. 1980. 21.95 o.p. (ISBN 0-442-20661-5). Van Nos Reinhold.

Aging of America & the Role of the Academic Health Center. Andreopoulos. 1988. price not set o.p. (ISBN 0-471-63472-7). Churchill.

Aging of Connective & Skeletal Tissue. Ed. by Arthur Engel & Tage Larsson. (Illus.). 336p. 1969. text ed. 25.00x o.p. Coronet Bks.

Aging of Connective Tissue. David A. Hall. 1976. 51.50 o.p. (ISBN 0-12-319150-5). Acad Pr.

Aging Parents. Ed. by Pauline K. Ragan. LC 78-66073. 1979. pap. 14.00x o.p. (ISBN 0-88474-087-0, 05746-0). Lexington Bks.

Aging: Recent Advances & Creative Responses. Ed. by Alan Butler. LC 85-17481. 311p. 1985. 24.50 o.p. (ISBN 0-7099-3927-2, Pub. by Croom Helm Ltd). Routledge Chapman & Hall.

Aging: Spiritual Perspectives. Ed. by Francis Tiso et al. 320p. 1982. pap. 9.95 o.p. (ISBN 0-941850-03-X). Liturgical Pubns.

Aging Together, Serving Together: A Guide to Congregational Planning for the Aging. Fredrick J. Schenk & James V. Anderson. LC 10-185. 40p. (Orig.). 1982. pap. 3.50 o.p. (ISBN 0-8066-1963-5, 10-0185, Augsburg). Augsburg Fortress.

Aging, Vol. 3 (incl. 1986-87 Supplements) Ed. by Eleanor C. Goldstein. (Social Issues Resources Ser.). 1987. 30.00 o.p. (ISBN 0-89777-084-6). Soc Issues.

Aging, 1988-89. 6th ed. Harold Cox. LC 78-645208. (Annual Editions Ser.). (Illus.). 256p. 1988. pap. text ed. 9.95 o.p. (ISBN 0-87967-662-0). Dushkin Pub.

Agitations: Letters to the Press, 1875-1950. George Bernard Shaw. Ed. by Dan H. Laurence & James Rambeau. LC 82-40256. 391p. 1985. 22.50 o.p. (ISBN 0-8044-2493-4). Ungar.

Aglow in the Kitchen. Aglow Staff. 160p. 1976. 4.95 o.p. (ISBN 0-930756-21-5, 532001). Aglow Pubns.

Agonia De una Dictadura: Cronica Nicaraguense. O. Ignatiev & G. Borovik. 190p. (Span.). 1980. pap. 1.95 o.p. (ISBN 0-8285-2268-5, Pub. by Progress Pubs USSR). Imported Pubns.

Agony of a Dictatorship. O. Ignatiev & G. Borovik. 159p. 1980. pap. 1.95 o.p. (ISBN 0-8285-1596-4, Pub. by Progress Pubs USSR). Imported Pubns.

Agony of Alcholism & How I Overcome It. Bill C. Judge. 1979. 7.00 o.p. (ISBN 0-682-49267-1). Exposition-Phoenix.

Agoraphobia. Ruth H. Vose. 208p. 1981. 21.00 o.p. (ISBN 0-571-11752-X); pap. 9.95 o.p. (ISBN 0-571-11753-8). Faber & Faber.

Agoraphobia: Coping with the World Outside. Muriel Frampton. (Life Crisis Bk.). 96p. (Orig.). 1984. pap. 7.99 o.p. (ISBN 0-85500-213-1, Pub. by Turnstone Pr England). Sterling.

Agrarian Change in Egypt: An Anatomy of Rural Poverty. Samir Radwan & Eddy Lee. LC 85-11356. 160p. 1985. 27.50 o.p. (ISBN 0-7099-4214-1, Croom Helm Ltd). Routledge Chapman & Hall.

Agrarian Development & Modernization in the Philippines. Dov Weintraub et al. 1973. 4.95 o.p. (ISBN 0-87855-264-2); pap. text ed. 2.95 o.p. (ISBN 0-87855-673-7). Transaction Pubs.

Agrarian Development in Peasant Economies. E. S. Clayton. 1964. text ed. 16.50 o.p. (ISBN 0-08-010562-9); pap. 7.75 o.p. (ISBN 0-08-010561-0). Pergamon.

Agrarian Evolution in a Multiform Structure Society: Experience of Independent India. V. G. Rastyannikov. Tr. by Konstantin A. Kostrov from Rus. 373p. 1981. 32.50x o.p. (ISBN 0-7100-0755-8). Routledge Chapman & Hall.

Agrarian Landscape Terms: A Glossary for Historical Geography Ser. I. H. Adams. (Special Publication of the Institute of British Geographers: No. 9). 1980. 26.00 o.p. (ISBN 0-12-044180-2). Acad Pr.

Agrarian Policies & Rural Poverty in Africa: Second Impression, 1985. International Labour Office Staff. Ed. by Dharam Ghai & Samir Radwan. (WEP Study Ser.). ix, 311p. (Orig.). 1985. 21.40 o.p. (ISBN 92-2-103109-8); pap. 15.70 o.p. (ISBN 92-2-103100-4). Intl Labour Office.

Agrarian Policy of the Chinese Communist Party, Nineteen Twenty-One to Nineteen Fifty-Nine. Chao Kuo-Chun. LC 77-14587. 1977. Repr. of 1960 ed. lib. bdg. 35.00x o.p. (ISBN 0-8371-9861-5, CHAP). Greenwood.

Agrarian Reform & Rural Poverty: Egypt, 1952-1975. 91p. 1977. pap. 8.55 o.p. (ISBN 0-686-39954-9, ILO67, ILO). UNIPUB.

Agrarian Reform in Ethiopia. Dessalegn Rahmato. 105p. 1985. pap. write for info. o.p. (Africana). Holmes & Meier.

Agreement Establishing the Common Fund for Commodities. 30p. 1981. pap. 4.00 o.p. (UN81/2D8, UN). UNIPUB.

Agreement on Government Procurement. 30p. (Eng., Fr. & Span.). 1980. pap. 5.00 o.p. (ISBN 0-686-63027-0, G133, GATT). UNIPUB.

Agreement on Implementation of Article Six of the General Agreement on Tariffs & Trade. 28p. (Eng., Fr. & Span.). 1980. pap. 5.00 o.p. (ISBN 0-686-63028-9, G130, GATT). UNIPUB.

Agreement on Import Licensing Procedures. 12p. (Eng., Fr. & Span.). 1980. pap. 5.00 o.p. (ISBN 0-686-63029-7, G137, GATT). UNIPUB.

Agreement on Interpretation & Application of Articles VI, XVI, & XXIII of the General Agreement on Tariffs & Trade. 40p. (Eng., Fr. or Span.). 1980. pap. 5.00 o.p. (ISBN 0-686-63030-0, G135, GATT). UNIPUB.

Agreement on Technical Barriers to Trade. 31p. (Eng., Fr. & Span.). 1980. pap. 5.00 o.p. (ISBN 0-686-63031-9, G136, GATT). UNIPUB.

Agreement on the Implementation of Article Seven of the General Agreement on Tariffs & Trade & Protocol. 48p. (Eng., Fr. & Span.). 1980. pap. 6.50 o.p. (ISBN 0-686-63032-7, G131, GATT). UNIPUB.

Agreement on Trade in Civil Aircraft. 22p. (Eng., Fr. & Span.). 1980. pap. 5.00 o.p. (ISBN 0-686-63033-5, G134, GATT). UNIPUB.

Agreements for Arms Control: A Critical Survey. J. Goldblat. 388p. 1982. 41.00x o.p. (ISBN 0-85066-229-X). Taylor & Francis.

Agreements of International Organizations & the Vienna Convention on the Law of Treaties: Oesterreich, Zeitschrift fuer Oeffentiliches Recht Suppl. 1. Ed. by K. Lamenek. 1971. pap. 39.00 o.p. (ISBN 0-387-81010-2). Springer-Verlag.

Agreements Regarding Bovine Meat. (Illus.). 11p. (Eng., Fr. & Span.). 1980. pap. 5.00 o.p. (ISBN 0-686-63035-1, G138, GATT). UNIPUB.

Agreements Registered with the IAEA. Incl. 6th Edition. pap. 14.00 o.p. (ISP422, IAEA). UNIPUB; 7th Edition. 248p. 1978. pap. 28.00 o.p. (ISBN 92-0-176081-7, ISP485, IAEA). UNIPUB; 8th Edition. 253p. 1981. pap. 32.00 (ISBN 92-0-176081-7). UNIPUB. (Legal Ser.: No. 3). UNIPUB.

Agreements Relating to the Framework for the Conduct of International Trade. 22p. (Eng., Fr. & Span.). 1980. pap. 5.00 o.p. (ISBN 0-686-63034-3, G132, GATT). UNIPUB.

AGREP - Permanent Inventory of Agricultural Research Projects in the European Communities: AGREP Base Volumes & Supplement, 2 vols. 385p. 1983. Set. pap. 166.00 o.p. CAB Intl.

AGREP - Permanent Inventory of Agricultural Research Projects in the European Communities, 2 vols. 1982. Set. pap. 124.00 o.p. (ISBN 0-85198-512-2). Vol. I, Main List: Research Projects. Vol. II, Indexes. CAB Intl.

AGREP - Permanent Inventory of Agricultural Research Projects in the European Communities: Supplement. 385p. 1983. pap. text ed. 60.00 o.p. CAB Intl.

Agri-Finance: Banks, Farmers, & Agricultural Policy. Mary E. Huls. (Public Administration Ser.: P 1690). 8p. 1985. 2.00 o.p. (ISBN 0-89028-420-2). Vance Biblios.

Agribusiness in the Americas: The Political Economy of Corporate Agriculture. Roger Burbach & Patricia Flynn. LC 80-17114. 314p. 1980. 16.00 o.s.i. (ISBN 0-85345-535-X); pap. 7.50 o.s.i. (ISBN 0-85345-536-8). Monthly Rev.

Agricide. Date not set. (ISBN 0-8052-4013-6). Random.

Agricultural Administration in the United States: A Bibliographical Overview of Administrative Practices, Price Supports & Models. Coppa & Avery Consultants Staff. (Public Administration Ser.: P 1735). 11p. 1985. 2.00 o.p. (ISBN 0-89028-505-5). Vance Biblios.

Agricultural & Food Chemistry: Past, Present, Future. Roy Teranishi. (Illus.). 1978. 49.95 o.p. (ISBN 0-87055-231-7). AVI.

Agricultural Change & the Peasant Economy of South China. Evelyn S. Rawski. LC 77-173407. (East Asian Ser: No. 66). (Illus.). 280p. 1972. 18.50x o.s.i. (ISBN 0-674-01210-0). Harvard U Pr.

Agricultural Chemical New Product Development Review. rev. ed. 1988. pap. 300.00 o.p. (ISBN 0-913702-41-2). Thomson Pubns.

Agricultural Chemicals, Bk. One, 1985-86: Insecticides, Acaracides, & Ovicides. rev. ed. W. T. Thomson. 250p. 1985. pap. 16.50 perfect bdg. o.p. Thomson Pubns.

Agricultural Chemicals, Bk. Two, 1986-87: Herbicides. rev. ed. W. T. Thomson. 260p. 1986. pap. 16.50 perfect bdg. o.p. Thomson Pubns.

Agricultural Chemicals, Book I: Insecticides. rev. ed. W. T. Thomson. 260p. 1986. pap. 16.50 o.p. (ISBN 0-913702-31-5). Thomson Pubns.

Agricultural Chemicals, Book III: Fumigants, Growth Regulators, Repellents, Rodenticides. rev. ed. W. T. Thomson. 190p. 1986. pap. 16.50 o.p. Thomson Pubns.

Agricultural Chemistry in Two Vols. Ed. by B. A. Yagodin. 758p. 1984. 16.95 o.s.i. (ISBN 0-8285-2820-9, Pub. by Mir Pubs USSR). Imported Pubns.

Agricultural Choice & Change: Decision Making in a Costa Rican Community. Peggy F. Barlett. (Illus.). 208p. 1982. 30.00 o.p. (ISBN 0-8135-0936-X). Rutgers U Pr.

Agricultural Computer Programming: A Practical Guide. Richard A. Levins & W. Charles Walden. (Illus.). 128p. 1984. pap. 15.95 o.p. (ISBN 0-13-018862-X). P-H.

Agricultural Credit in Africa: Report of the FAO-Finland Regional Seminar on Agricultural Credit in Africa. (TF-RAF Ser.: No. 66). 1977. pap. 15.00 o.p. (ISBN 92-5-100227-4, F680, FAO). UNIPUB.

Agricultural Credit Legislation in Selected Developing Countries. (Legislative Studies: No. 6). 144p. 1974. pap. 7.50 o.p. (ISBN 92-5-101979-7, F1019, FAO). UNIPUB.

Agricultural Economics & Agribusiness. 3rd ed. Gail L. Cramer & Clarence W. Jensen. LC 84-19546. 441p. 1985. (ISBN 0-471-87871-5). Wiley.

Agricultural Economy of Northumberland & Durham in the Period 1640-1750. Paul Brassley. LC 84-45996. (British Economic History Ser.). 230p. 1985. lib. bdg. 28.00 o.p. (ISBN 0-8240-6676-6). Garland Pub.

Agricultural Education Curriculum. ERIC Clearinghouse on Adult, Career, & Vocational Education Staff. 62p. 1983. 4.95 o.p. (ISBN 0-318-22024-5, BB62). Natl Ctr Res Voc Ed.

Agricultural Engineers' Handbook. C. B. Richey et al. 1961. text ed. 72.50 o.p. (ISBN 0-07-052617-6). McGraw.

Agricultural Enterprises Management in an Urban-Industrial Society: A Guide to Information Sources. Ed. by Portia Christian. LC 76-27856. (Management Information Guide Ser.: No. 34). 328p. 1978. 68.00x o.p. (ISBN 0-8103-0834-7). Gale.

Agricultural Extension: A Reference Manual. 2nd ed. Ed. by Burton E. Swanson. 262p. 1985. pap. 24.75 o.p. (ISBN 92-5-101504-X, F2673, FAO). UNIPUB.

Agricultural Extension in Surinam: Communication Patterns & Their Organizational Structure. (Agricultural Research Reports: No. 864). 1977. pap. 36.00 o.p. (ISBN 90-220-0625-5, XS31822 1, PUDOC). UNIPUB.

Agricultural Extension Systems in Some African & Asian Countries. Peter von Blankenburg. (Economic & Social Development Papers: No. 46). 75p. 1985. pap. 7.50 o.p. (ISBN 92-5-101461-2, F2683, FAO). UNIPUB.

Agricultural Extension Worldwide: Issues, Practices & Emerging Priorities. Ed. by W. M. Rivera & Susan G. Schram. 304p. 1987. lib. bdg. 30.00x o.p. (ISBN 0-317-64374-6, Pub. by Croom Helm UK). Routledge Chapman & Hall.

Agricultural Finance. 7th ed. Warren F. Lee et al. iii, 438p. 1980. text ed. 24.95x o.p. (ISBN 0-8138-0050-1). Iowa St U Pr.

Agricultural Finance: An Introduction to Micro & Macro Concepts. John B. Penson, Jr. & David A. Lins. (Illus.). 1980. text ed. 34.00 o.p. (ISBN 0-13-018903-0). P-H.

Agricultural Food Policy Review: Commodity Program Perspectives. (Agricultural Economic Report Ser.: No. 530). 259p. 1985. pap. 12.00 o.p. (ISBN 0-318-21693-0, S/N 001-019-00486-0). USGPO.

Agricultural Geography: Problems in Modern Geography. John R. Tarrant. 1980. 32.50 o.p. (ISBN 0-7153-6286-0). David & Charles.

Agricultural Growth in Japan, Taiwan, Korea, & the Philippines. 404p. 1979. 22.00 o.p. (APO82, APO). UNIPUB.

Agricultural Hand Tools. Roy Brigden. (Shire Album Ser.: No. 100). (Illus.). 32p. 1985. pap. 3.50 o.p. (ISBN 0-85263-630-X, Pub. by Shire Pubns England). Seven Hills Bk Dists.

Agricultural Impacts on Ground Water Conference, 1986: Proceedings. LC 86-23734. 1986. 43.75 o.p. (ISBN 0-318-23004-6). Natl Water Well.

Agricultural Land Preservation: A Review of State Programs. 173p. 1982. 5.00 o.s.i. (ISBN 1-55516-435-8). Natl Conf State Legis.

Agricultural Law, 2 vols. 10th ed. John H. Davidson. LC 81-1964. (Environmental Publications). 1035p. 1983. text ed. 180.00 o.p. (ISBN 0-07-015432-5). Shepards-McGraw.

Agricultural Marketing: Strategy & Pricing Policy. Dieter Elz. 140p. 1986. 18.95 o.p. (BK0830). World Bank.

Agricultural Notebook. 17th ed. Ed. by R. J. Halley. 1982. text ed. 70.00 o.p. (ISBN 0-408-10701-4). Butterworth.

Agricultural Options: Trading Puts & Calls in the New Grain & Livestock Futures Market. George Angell. 272p. 1986. 21.85 o.p. (ISBN 0-8144-5822-X). AMACOM.

Agricultural Organizations & Economic & Social Development in Rural Areas. Xavier Flores. 1971. 18.20 o.p. (ISBN 92-2-100104-0). Intl Labour Office.

Agricultural Physics. C. W. Rose. 1966. text ed. 17.75 o.p. (ISBN 0-08-011885-2); pap. text ed. 12.00 o.p. (ISBN 0-08-011884-4). Pergamon.

Agricultural Policy in an Affluent Society. Ed. by Vernon W. Ruttan et al. (Problems of the Modern Economy Ser.). 1969. 7.50x o.p. (ISBN 0-393-05274-5, NortonC); pap. text ed. 5.95x o.p. (ISBN 0-393-09839-7). Norton.

Agricultural Price Policies & the Developing Countries. George S. Tolley et al. LC 81-47614. (World Bank Research Publication Ser.). 272p. 1983. text ed. 25.00x o.p. (ISBN 0-8018-2704-3). Johns Hopkins.

Agricultural Process Engineering. 3rd ed. Henderson. 1976. 32.95 o.s.i. (ISBN 0-87055-212-0). Van Nos Reinhold.

Agricultural Research Centers, 2 vols. 8th ed. Ed. by Nigel Harvey. 1138p. 1986. Set. 395.00x o.p. (ISBN 0-582-90033-6, Pub. by Longman). Gale.

Agricultural Research Policy. Vernon W. Ruttan. LC 81-16396. 354p. 1982. 32.50x o.p. (ISBN 0-8166-1101-7); pap. 14.95 o.p. (ISBN 0-8166-1102-5). U of Minn Pr.

Agricultural Research Policy & Development. V. W. Ruttan. (FAO Research & Technology Paper: No. 2). 249p. 1987. pap. text ed. 24.75 o.p. (ISBN 0-317-69440-5, F3129). Intl Labour Office.

Agricultural Stagnation under Population Pressure: The Case of Bangladesh. Alia Ahmad. LC 84-902023. 246p. 1984. text ed. 27.95x o.p. (ISBN 0-7069-2577-7, Pub. by Vikas India). Advent NY.

Agricultural Statistics: A Handbook for Developing Countries. N. M. Idaikkadar. (Illus.). 1979. text ed. 35.00 o.p. (ISBN 0-08-023388-0); pap. text ed. 11.50 o.p. (ISBN 0-08-023387-2). Pergamon.

Agricultural Statistics, 1985. (Illus.). 561p. 1985. pap. 16.00 o.p. (ISBN 0-318-20414-2, S/N 001-000-04443-5). USGPO.

Agricultural Technology in Developing Countries. A. L. Mac Donald. 236p. 1976. text ed. 32.00x o.p. (ISBN 90-237-6259-2, Gower England). Gower Pub Co.

Agricultural Waste Management. Raymond Loehr. 1974. 49.95 o.p. (ISBN 0-12-455250-1). Acad Pr.

Agriculture & the Development Process: A Study of Punjab. D. P. Chaudhri & Ajit K. Dasgupta. LC 84-27507. 216p. 1985. 34.50 o.p. (ISBN 0-7099-3408-4, Pub. by Croom Helm Ltd). Routledge Chapman & Hall.

Agriculture, Biomass, Wind, New Developments see Sharing the Sun.

Agriculture Biotechnology: Strategies for National Competitiveness. National Research Council U. S. Committee on a National Strategy for Biotechnology in Agriculture. LC 87-12181. 205p. 1987. pap. 14.95 o.p. (ISBN 0-317-65245-1). Natl Acad Pr.

Agriculture Cooperatives: A Case Study of Punjab. Manohar S. Gill. viii, 560p. 1984. text ed. 45.00x o.p. (ISBN 0-7069-2371-5, Pub. by Vikas India). Advent NY.

Agriculture, Food & Nutrition Sciences Division: The First Five Years. IDRC, Ottawa Staff. 49p. 1977. pap. 5.00 o.p. (ISBN 0-88936-130-4, IDRC89, IDRC). UNIPUB.

Agriculture in America, Sixteen Twenty-Two-Eighteen Sixty: Printed Works in the Collections of the American Philosophical Society, the Historical Society of Pennsylvania, the Library Company of Philadelphia. Andrea J. Tucher. LC 83-49300. 264p. 1984. lib. bdg. 56.00 o.p. (ISBN 0-8240-8967-7). Garland Pub.

Agriculture in the Australian Economy. D. Williams. 1967. 21.00x o.p. (ISBN 0-424-05300-4, Pub by Sydney U Pr). Intl Spec Bk.

Agriculture in the Australian Economy. 2nd ed. D. B. Williams. 422p. 1982. pap. text ed. 45.00 o.p. (ISBN 0-424-00092-X, Pub. by Sydney U Pr). Intl Spec Bk.

Agriculture in Western Europe: Challenge & Response, 1880-1980. 2nd ed. Michael Tracy. (Illus.). 500p. 1982. pap. text ed. 30.50x o.p. (ISBN 0-246-11446-0, Pub. by Granada England). Gower Pub Co.

Agriculture, the Countryside & Land Use: An Economic Critique. J. K. Bowers & P. C. Cheshire. LC 83-13069. 224p. 1983. pap. 11.95 o.p. (ISBN 0-416-31830-4, NO. 3925). Routledge Chapman & Hall.

Agrochemicals in Soils: Selected Papers. Soil Chemistry, Soil Fertility & Soil Clay Mineralogy Commissions of the International Society of Soil Science, 13-18 July 1976, Jerusalem. Ed. by A. Banin & U. Kafkafi. LC 79-41750. 500p. 1980. 115.00 o.p. (ISBN 0-08-025914-6). Pergamon.

Ah, Bewilderness: Muddling Through Life. Mary Z. Gray. LC 83-45512. 288p. 1984. 14.95 o.s.i. (ISBN 0-689-11432-X, Atheneum). Macmillan.

Ah, but Your Land Is Beautiful. Alan Paton. 208p. 1982. lib. bdg. 22.50 o.p. (ISBN 0-684-17336-0, ScribT). Scribner.

Ah! Jeunesse. Georges Courteline. 190p. 1965. 8.95 o.p. (ISBN 0-686-54626-1). French & Eur.

Ah Q & Others: Selected Stories of Lusin. Chou Shu-Jen. Tr. by Chi-Chen Wang from Chinese. LC 75-143310. 1971. Repr. of 1941 ed. lib. bdg. 35.00x o.p. (ISBN 0-8371-5965-2, CHAQ). Greenwood.

AHA. Rex Whistler. 1979. 5.95 o.p. (ISBN 0-395-28051-6). HM.

AHFS Drug Information, Nineteen Eighty-Seven. rev. ed. Ed. by Gerald K. McEvoy. xvi, 2091p. 1987. text ed. 55.00 o.p. (ISBN 0-930530-71-3). Am Soc Hosp Pharm.

AHFS Drug Information, 1988. rev. ed. Ed. by Gerald K. McEvoy. 2200p. 1988. pap. text ed. 65.00 o.p. (ISBN 0-930530-80-2). Am Soc Hosp Pharm.

Ahrends, Burton & Koralek, Architects: A Bibliography. Mary Vance. (Architecture Ser.: A 1453). 7p. 1985. 2.00 o.p. (ISBN 0-89028-543-8). Vance Biblios.

AIAA Journal, Vol. 25. Ed. by George W. Sutton. 1987. 235.00 o.p. (ISBN 0-317-66160-4). AIAA.

AIAA Roster, 1987. 450p. 1987. 79.95 o.p. (ISBN 0-317-43147-1). AIAA.

AIAA Test Pilots' Aviation Workshop, 1981. 94p. 15.00 o.p. (ISBN 0-915928-54-X, P813). AIAA.

AIChE Accumulative Salary Survey of Member Chemical Engineers. 1971-1980. LC 81-3530. 14p. 1981. pap. 25.00 o.p. (ISBN 0-8169-0200-3, X-96). Am Inst Chem Eng.

Aid in Africa. Guy Arnold. 250p. 1979. 32.50 o.p. (ISBN 0-89397-062-X). Nichols Pub.

Aid to Africa. I. M. Little. 1964. 3.30 o.p. (ISBN 0-08-010938-1). Pergamon.

Aid to Clinical Surgery. 3rd ed. Dudley. (Illus.). 1984. pap. text ed. 16.50 o.p. (ISBN 0-443-02684-X). Churchill.

Aid to Russia, Nineteen Forty-One to Nineteen Forty-Six: Strategy, Diplomacy, the Origins of the Cold War. George C. Herring, Jr. LC 72-10545. 364p. 1973. 40.00x o.p. (ISBN 0-231-03336-2); pap. 17.00x o.p. (ISBN 0-231-08348-3). Columbia U Pr.

Aiding Ambulatory Patients. Ed. by Patti Urosevich & Barbara McVan. LC 82-21253. (Nursing Photobook Ser.). (Illus.). 160p. 1983. 17.95 o.p. (ISBN 0-916730-49-2). Springhouse Pub.

AIDS. Rubicon Consulting Staff. 1985. 3-ring text 395.00 o.p. (ISBN 0-938124-10-2). Rubicon.

AIDS: A Guide to Survival. Peter Tatchell. 143p. (Orig.). 1986. pap. 6.95 o.p. (ISBN 0-317-52710-X, Pub. by GMP England). Alyson Pubns.

AIDS: A Manager's Guide. Victor Schachter et al. LC 86-50479. 71p. write for info. o.p. (ISBN 0-88057-595-6). Exec Ent Pubns.

AIDS-Acquired Immune Deficiency Syndrome-& Other Manifestations of HIV Infection: Epidemiology, Etiology, Immunology, Clinical Manifestations, Pathology, Control, Treatment & Prevention. Ed. by Gary P. Wormser et al. LC 86-33308. (Illus.). 1103p. 1987. 98.00 o.p. (ISBN 0-8155-1108-6). Noyes.

AIDS & Health Related Issues, an OTA Survey. Jill Eden et al. 64p. (Orig.). 1988. pap. 2.75 o.p. (S/N 052-003-01093-3). USGPO.

AIDS & Immune Deficiency: Macrobiotic Approach. Michio Kushi & Martha C. Cottrell. LC 86-81560. (Illus.). 320p. 1987. 16.95 o.p. (ISBN 0-87040-680-9). Japan Pubns USA.

AIDS Crisis, Vol. 1 (Incl. 1986-87 Supplements) Ed. by Eleanor C. Goldstein. (Social Issues Resources Ser.). 80p. 1987. binder 60.00 o.p. (ISBN 0-89777-840-5). Soc Issues.

AIDS Hysteria. Arthur F. Ide. (Illus.). 117p. (Orig.). 1986. pap. 5.95 o.p. (ISBN 0-930383-08-7). Monument Pr.

AIDS in Children, Adolescents & Heterosexual Adults: An Interdisciplinary Approach. Ed. by R. F. Schinazi & A. J. Nahmias. 500p. 1988. 80.00 o.p. (ISBN 0-444-01315-6). Elsevier.

AIDS in Correctional Facilities: Issues & Options. Theodore M. Hammett & Monique Sullivan. (Issues & Practices in Criminal Justice Ser.). 222p. 1986. pap. 11.00 o.p. (ISBN 0-318-20085-6, S/N 027-000-01250-7). USGPO.

Aids Package. Edmond Locklear, Jr. 192p. 1987. 11.95 o.p. (ISBN 0-8062-3077-0). Carlton.

AIDS: The Medical Mystery. Frederick P. Siegal & Marta Siegal. LC 83-48298. 196p. 1983. 19.50 o.p. (ISBN 0-394-53505-7, GP 883). Grove.

AIDS: The Medical Mystery. Frederick P. Siegal & Marta Siegal. LC 83-48298. 196p. 1983. pap. 12.50 o.s.i. (ISBN 0-394-62496-3, E876, Ever). Grove.

Aids to Endocrinology. John C. Stevenson & Pritpal Chahal. LC 85-6659. (Illus.). 158p. 1985. pap. 7.50 o.p. (ISBN 0-443-02968-7). Churchill.

Aids to Independence: A Guide to Products for the Disabled & Elderly. Irene Crawford. (Illus.). 120p. (Orig.). 1985. pap. 11.95 o.p. (ISBN 0-88908-608-7, 9536). ISC Pr.

Aids to Orthopaedics. Malcolm F. Macnicol. LC 84-7605. (Aids to... Ser.). 193p. (Orig.). 1984. pap. text ed. 10.00 o.p. (ISBN 0-443-03045-6). Churchill.

Aids to Postgraduate Surgery. 2nd ed. Meirion Thomas & John S. Belstead. (Aids to Ser.). 1982. pap. text ed. 12.00 o.p. (ISBN 0-443-02514-2). Churchill.

Aids to Teaching & Learning. H. E. Coppen. 1968. text ed. 29.00 o.p. (ISBN 0-08-012905-6); pap. text ed. 14.25 o.p. (ISBN 0-08-012904-8). Pergamon.

Aids to Undergraduate Surgery. 2nd ed. P. M. Mowschenson. 1983. pap. text ed. 10.00 o.p. (ISBN 0-443-02987-3). Churchill.

AIDS: Your Questions Answered. Richard B. Fisher. 128p. (Orig.). 1984. pap. 3.95 o.p. (ISBN 0-907040-29-2, Pub. by GMP England). Alyson Pubns.

AIF Uranium Seminar: Set of Papers. (Technical & Economic Reports: Uranium). 1983. 100.00 o.p. (ISBN 0-318-02245-1). US Coun Energy Awareness.

Aigle a Deux Tetes see Theatre.

Aiki. John Gilbert. 288p. pap. 3.95 o.p. (ISBN 0-671-64198-0). Archway.

Ailments of Aging: From Symptom to Treatment. Manuel M. Villaverde & C. Wright Macmillan. 816p. 1980. 42.95 o.p. (ISBN 0-442-25108-4). Van Nos Reinhold.

Aim & Structure of Physical Theory. Pierre Duhem. LC 53-6383. 1962. pap. text ed. 5.95x o.s.i. (ISBN 0-689-70064-4, 13, Atheneum). Macmillan.

AIM-FAR, 1987: Complete Combined Edition. Tab-Aero Staff. 1987. 16.95 o.p. (ISBN 0-8306-8438-7, 24387); pap. 11.95 o.p. (ISBN 0-8306-8387-9). TAB Bks.

Aim for a Job As an Electronic Technician. Rev. ed. John E. Keefe. LC 67-11254. (Aim High Vocational Guidance Ser.). (gr. 7up). 1978. PLB 9.97 o.p. (ISBN 0-8239-0451-2). Rosen Group.

Aim for a Job in a Business Office. Phyllis Peck & Gilbert J. Konkel. (Aim High Vocational Guidance Ser.). (YA) (gr. 7-12). 1980. PLB 9.97 o.p. (ISBN 0-8239-0391-5). Rosen Group.

Aim for a Job in a Medical Laboratory. rev. ed. Moira D. Reynolds. LC 70-183733. (Aim High Vocational Guidance Ser.). (Illus.). 144p. (gr. 7 up). 1982. PLB 9.97 o.p. (ISBN 0-8239-0261-7). Rosen Group.

Aim for a Job in a Small Business Occupation. James Hahn & Lynn Hahn. (Aim High Ser.). (Illus.). 128p. 1980. lib. bdg. 9.97 o.p. (ISBN 0-8239-0500-4). Rosen Group.

Aim for a Job in Appliance Repair. James Hahn & Lynn Hahn. (Aim High Ser.). 128p. 1982. lib. bdg. 9.97 o.p. (ISBN 0-8239-0541-1). Rosen Group.

Aim for a Job in Cartooning. Adeline Fixman. (Aim High Vocational Guidance Ser.). (gr. 7 up). 1976. PLB 9.97 o.p. (ISBN 0-8239-0355-9). Rosen Group.

Aim for a Job in Cattle Ranching. Oren Arnold. LC 78-153810. (Aim High Vocational Guidance Ser.). (Illus.). (gr. 7 up). 1972. PLB 9.97 o.p. (ISBN 0-8239-0245-5). Rosen Group.

Aim for a Job in Drafting. Fred J. Delong. LC 68-10505. (Aim High Vocational Guidance Ser.). (gr. 7 up). 1976. PLB 9.97 o.p. (ISBN 0-8239-0365-6). Rosen Group.

Aim for a Job in the Allied Health Field. Rev. ed. Fenton Keyes. LC 73-91273. (Aim High Vocational Guidance Ser.). (Illus.). 140p. (gr. 7-12). 1979. PLB 9.97 o.p. (ISBN 0-8239-0297-8). Rosen Group.

Aim for a Job in the Construction Industry. Rev. ed. Lynn Hahn & James Hahn. (Aim High Ser.). 144p. 1982. lib. bdg. 9.97 o.p. (ISBN 0-8239-0427-X). Rosen Group.

Aim for a Job in the Iron & Steel Industry. rev. ed. John W. Sullivan. LC 67-12977. (Aim High Vocational Guidance Ser.). (gr. 7-12). 1982. PLB 9.97 o.p. (ISBN 0-8239-0427-X). Rosen Group.

Aim for a Job in the Printing Trade. James Hahn & Lynn Hahn. (Illus.). (gr. 7-12). 1979. PLB 9.97 o.p. (ISBN 0-8239-0470-9). Rosen Group.

Aim for a Job in the Record Business. Rick Mitz. (Aim High Vocational Guidance Ser.). (YA) (gr. 7-12). 1977. PLB 9.97 o.p. (ISBN 0-8239-0384-2). Rosen Group.

Aim for a Job in Watchmaking. Rev. ed. Benjamin Lipton. LC 67-10289. (Aim High Vocational Guidance Ser.). (Illus.). (gr. 7-12). 1978. PLB 9.97 o.p. (ISBN 0-8239-0453-9). Rosen Group.

Aim for a Job in Welding. Thomas Berg. LC 67-10290. (Aim High Vocational Guidance Ser.). (Illus.). (gr. 7-12). 1978. PLB 9.97 o.p. (ISBN 0-8239-0465-2). Rosen Group.

Aim for a Job with the Telephone Company. James Hahn & Lynn Hahn. (Aim High Vocational Guidance Ser.). (Illus.). (YA) (gr. 7-12). 1979. PLB 9.97 o.p. (ISBN 0-8239-0440-7). Rosen Group.

Aim for a Job Working with Your Hands. Ronald Todd & Karen R. Todd. (Aim High Vocational Guidance Ser.). (Illus.). 140p. (gr. 7-12). 1975. PLB 9.97 o.p. (ISBN 0-8239-0323-0). Rosen Group.

Aim, 1988. Aviation Supplies & Academics Staff. 1988. pap. 6.95 o.p. (ISBN 0-940732-55-6, Pub. by ASA). Aviation.

Aimbe, the Pastor. Paulias Matane. 1979. 12.50 o.p. (ISBN 0-682-49230-2). Exposition-Phoenix.

Aims & Techniques of Group Teaching. 4th ed. M. L. Abercrombie. 92p. Date not set. pap. 14.00 o.p. (ISBN 0-900868-70-8, Open Univ Pr). Taylor & Francis.

Aims of Education. L. M. Brown. LC 76-120600. 1970. pap. text ed. 8.95x o.p. (ISBN 0-8077-1129-2). Tchrs Coll.

Aims of Education Restated. John White. 192p. 1982. O.P. 18.95x o.p. (ISBN 0-7100-0941-0); pap. 9.95x o.p. (ISBN 0-7100-0998-4). Routledge Chapman & Hall.

Ainslie's Complete Guide to Thoroughbred Racing. rev. ed. Tom Ainslie. 1979. 23.50 o.p. (ISBN 0-671-24632-1). S&S.

Ainslie's Complete Guide to Thoroughbred Racing. 3rd, rev. ed. Tom Ainslie. (Illus.). 384p. 1986. 18.45 o.p. (ISBN 0-671-62414-8). S&S.

Ainslie's New Complete Guide to Harness Racing. rev. ed. Tom Ainslie. 1981. 17.95 o.p. (ISBN 0-671-25257-7). S&S.

Ain't I a Wonder & Ain't You a Wonder Too. Jess Lair. 1981. pap. 2.95 o.p. (ISBN 0-449-23688-9, Crest). Fawcett.

Ain't That Mad. Terence E. Jackson. 40p. 1986. 6.50 o.p. (ISBN 0-8062-2913-6). Carlton.

Ainu Life & Lore: Echoes of a Departing Race. John Batchelor. Repr. of 1927 ed. 37.00 o.p. (ISBN 0-384-03528-0). Johnson Repr.

Air. E. B. Shieldrop. 1958. (ISBN 0-8022-1553-X). Philos Lib.

Air & Satellite Communications. Ed. by Lee M. Paschall & Stephen J. Andriole. LC 84-72110. (AFCEA Signal Magazine C3I Ser.: Vol. II). (Illus.). 373p. 1985. 29.95 o.p. (ISBN 0-916159-03-5). AFCEA Intl Pr.

Air Chemistry & Radioactivity. C. E. Junge. (International Geophysics Ser.: Vol. 4). 1963. 77.00 o.p. (ISBN 0-12-392150-3). Acad Pr.

Air Conditioning & Energy Conservation. Ed. by A. F. Sherratt. (Illus.). 287p. 1980. 69.50 o.s.i. (ISBN 0-89397-071-9, Pub. by Architectural Pr). Nichols Pub.

Air Conditioning Sheet Metal Layout. 3rd ed. Joseph J. Kaberlein. cancelled o.s.i. (ISBN 0-02-819440-3). Glencoe.

Air Disasters. Stanley Stewart. (Illus.). 240p. 1987. 19.95 o.s.i. (ISBN 0-87052-385-6). Hippocrene Bks.

Air Instrument Surgery, Vol. One: Cranial Surgery, Intracranial Surgery, Temperol Bone Surgery, Vertebral Surgery. Ed. by R. M. Hall. (Illus.). 1970. 70.80 o.p. (ISBN 0-387-05311-5). Springer-Verlag.

Air Instrument Surgery, Vol. Three: Facial, Oral & Reconstructive Surgery. Ed. by R. M. Hall. LC 70-132149. (Illus.). xiii, 242p. 1973. 53.10 o.p. (ISBN 0-387-06182-7). Springer-Verlag.

Air Leadership: Proceedings of a Conference at Bolling Air Force Base, Apr. 13-14, 1986. Ed. by Wayne Thompson. LC 86-18196. (USAF Warrior Ser.). 168p. (Orig.). 1986. pap. 6.50 o.p. (ISBN 0-912799-37-4, S/N 008-070-00580-8). USGPO.

Air Monitoring Methods for Industrial Contaminants. David A. Halliday. LC 83-73097. (Illus.). 420p. 1983. text ed. 48.00 o.p. (ISBN 0-931890-12-8, Biomed Pubns). Year Bk Med.

Air Pollution. Virginia Brodine. Ed. by Barry Commoner. (Environmental Issues Ser.). (Illus.). 1973. pap. text ed. 7.95 o.p. (ISBN 0-15-502112-5, HC). HarBraceJ.

Air Pollution. R. S. Scorer. 1968. pap. 17.50 o.p. (ISBN 0-08-012275-2). Pergamon.

Air Pollution. R. S. Scorer. 1968. 35.00 o.p. (ISBN 0-08-013345-2). Pergamon.

Air Pollution along the United States-Mexico Border. Ed. by Howard G. Applegate & C. Richard Bath. LC 74-80108. 1974. 6.00 o.p. (ISBN 0-87404-051-5). Tex Western.

Air Pollution & Energy in Australia: Economic & Policy Implications. Alan Gilpin & Hanns Hartmann. LC 81-17355. (East-West Environment & Policy Institute Research Report Ser.: No. 6). v, 63p. (Orig.). 1981. pap. text ed. 3.00 o.p. (ISBN 0-86638-028-0). EW Ctr HI.

Air Pollution & Its Control. rev ed. Wayne T. Sproull. LC 77-98962. 1972. text ed. 7.00 o.p. (ISBN 0-682-47490-8, Banner). Exposition-Phoenix.

Air Pollution Control Equipment: Selection, Design, Operation & Maintenance. Ed. by Louis Theodore & Anthony J. Buonicore. (Illus.). 640p. 1982. text ed. 53.33 o.p. (ISBN 0-13-021154-0). P-H.

Air Pollution Control for Hospitals & Other Medical Facilities. Louis Theodore. LC 80-19352. 336p. 1981. 24.50 o.p. (ISBN 0-8240-7132-8). Krieger.

Air Pollution Control in the Iron & Steel Industry: Proceedings, San Francisco, Ca., Jan 1981. Air Pollution Control Association Specialty Conference. 208p. 1981. 15.00 o.p. (ISBN 0-318-12240-5, SP-39); members 12.00 o.p. (ISBN 0-318-12241-3). Air & Waste.

Air Pollution Control Technology. Robert M. Bethea. (Environmental Engineering Ser). 1978. 44.95 o.p. (ISBN 0-442-20715-8). Van Nos Reinhold.

Air Pollution-Health & Management: Proceedings of the Joint IIASA-WHO-EURO Workshop, Laxenburg, Austria, 27-30 July, 1982. Ed. by W. Klug et al. M. J. Suess. 176p. 1984. pap. 46.00 o.p. (ISBN 0-08-031429-5). Pergamon.

Air Pollution in Donora: An Analysis of the Extreme Effects of Smog. U. S. Public Health Service. 1970. Repr. of 1949 ed. (ISBN 0-08-022310-9). Pergamon.

Air Pollution Meteorology. Air Pollution Control Association. (APCA Reprint Ser.: Vol. 7). 112p. 1977. 9.00 o.p. (ISBN 0-318-12243-X, RS-7); members 6.00 o.p. (ISBN 0-318-12244-8). Air & Waste.

Air Pollution: Proceedings, International Symposium on the Chemical Aspects of Air Pollution, Held in Cortina D'ampezzo, Italy, 9-10 July, 1969. Ed. by V. Cantuti. 134p. 1976. 32.00 o.p. (ISBN 0-08-020721-9). Pergamon.

Air Pollution, Pt. B: Prevention & Control. J. O. Ledbetter. (Environmental Health Engineering Textbooks Ser.: Vol. 2). 300p. 1974. 35.00 o.p. (ISBN 0-8247-1406-7). Dekker.

Air Portfolios No. 1: Boeing 737. P. R. Smith. 64p. 1987. 8.95 o.p. (ISBN 0-7106-0424-6). Janes Info Group.

Air Portfolios No. 2: Shorts 330 & 360. P. R. Smith. 64p. 1987. 8.95 o.p. (ISBN 0-7106-0425-4). Janes Info Group.

Air Portfolios No. 3: Douglas DC-9 & McDonnell Douglas MD-80. P. R. Smith. 64p. 1987. 8.95 o.p. (ISBN 0-7106-0427-0). Janes Info Group.

Air Portfolios No. 4: Airbus A300 & 310. P. R. Smith. 64p. 1987. 8.95 o.p. (ISBN 0-7106-0428-9). Janes Info Group.

Air Portfolios, No. 5: Boeing 727. P. R. Smith. (Air Portfolios Ser.). (Illus.). 64p. 1987. 9.95 o.p. (ISBN 0-7106-0474-2). Janes Info Group.

Air Portfolios, No. 6: DeHavilland Canada DHC-6, DHC-7, & DHC-8. P. R. Smith. (Air Portfolios Ser.). (Illus.). 64p. 1987. 9.95 o.p. (ISBN 0-7106-0473-4). Janes Info Group.

Air Power: A Concise History. 2nd, rev. & exp. ed. Robin Higham. (Illus.). 184p. 1984. pap. text ed. 15.00x o.p. (ISBN 0-89745-058-2). Sunflower U Pr.

Air Quality Analysis in Transportation Planning. (Transportation Research Record Ser.). 82p. 1978. 5.00 o.p. (ISBN 0-309-02809-4). Transport Res Bd.

Air Quality Management: Qualifying Benefits. Gordon L. Brady & Blair T. Bower. LC 81-17478. (East-West Environment & Policy Institute Research Report Ser.: No. 7). v, 25p. (Orig.). 1981. pap. text ed. 3.00 o.p. (ISBN 0-86638-029-9). EW Ctr HI.

Air Resource Management Primer. Mackenzie L. Davis. 260p. 1973. pap. text ed. 17.00 o.p. (ISBN 0-87262-055-7). Am Soc Civil Eng.

Air Sampling, Quality Control & Concrete. (Transportation Research Record Report Ser.). 66p. 1976. 3.20 o.p. (ISBN 0-309-02554-0). Transport Res Bd.

Air Traffic Control Specialist Employment Guide. St. John. 236p. 1989. pap. 14.95 o.p. Buckeye Aviat Bk.

Air Transportation. 8th ed. Robert M. Kane & Allen D. Vose. (Illus.). 1981. perfect bdg. 17.95 o.p. (ISBN 0-8403-2639-4). Kendall Hunt.

Air Transportation: A Management Perspective. Alexander T. Wells. 540p. 1984. text ed. 31.00x o.p. (ISBN 0-534-03397-0). Wadsworth Pub.

Air War: One Volume Edition. Edward Jablonski. LC 78-8213. (Illus.). 1979. pap. 29.95 o.p. (ISBN 0-385-14279-X). Doubleday.

Air Water Pollution Control. BNA Environment & Safety Services Staff. write for info. o.p. BNA.

Airborne Electronic Warfare: History, Weapons & Tactics. Martin Streetly. (Illus.). 208p. 1988. 45.00 o.p. (ISBN 0-7106-0538-2). Janes Info Group.

Airborne Soldier. John Weeks. (Illus.). 192p. 1986. pap. 14.95 o.p. (ISBN 0-7137-1702-5, Pub. by Blandford Pr England). Sterling.

Airborne Warfare. James M. Gavin. LC 80-65183. (Airborne Ser.: No. 10). (Illus.). 186p. 1980. Repr. of 1947 ed. 17.50 o.p. (ISBN 0-89839-029-X). Battery Pr.

Airbrush Art in Japan. Ed. by Graphic-Sha Staff. (Illus.). 178p. 1986. 25.00 o.p. (ISBN 0-8161-8811-4, Pub. by Graphic-Sha Pub Co Ltd Japan). G K Hall.

Airbrush Art in Japan. Ed. by Graphic-Sha Staff. (Illus.). 178p. (Orig.). 1987. pap. 32.95 o.p. (ISBN 4-766-10317-3, Pub. by Graphic-Sha Japan). Bks Nippan.

Airbrush Art in Japan. Ed. by Graphic-Sha Staff. (No. 2). (Illus.). 160p. (Orig.). 1987. pap. 32.95 o.p. (ISBN 4-766-10383-1, Pub. by Graphic Sha Japan). Bks Nippan.

Airbrush Illustrations by Twelve Japanese Illustrators. (Graphic-Sha Bks.). (Illus.). 1984. 32.95 o.p. (ISBN 4-7661-0268-1). Bks Nippan.

Airbrush Illustrations by Twelve Japanese Illustrators. 2nd ed. Graphic-Sha Staff. (Illus.). 180p. 1986. pap. 32.95 o.p. (ISBN 4-766-10262-2, Pub. by Graphic Sha Japan). Bks Nippan.

Airbrushing. Carl Caiati. (Illus.). 160p. (Orig.). 1984. pap. 14.60 o.p. (ISBN 0-8306-0155-4, 1555). TAB Bks.

Airbrushing in Rendering. Eiji Mitooka. LC 84-13098. (Illus.). 144p. 1984. pap. 37.95 o.p. (ISBN 0-442-26082-2). Van Nos Reinhold.

Aircraft Communications Systems. J. H. Grover. 128p. 1958. (ISBN 0-8022-0640-9). Philos Lib.

Aircraft Crash Litigation 1984. Practice Law Institute Staff & Mark A. Domcroft. LC 83-62215. (Litigation Course Handbook Ser.: No. 267). (Illus.). 349p. 1984. 15.00 o.p. (H44952). PLI.

Aircraft Erecting. Ed. by T. Airey et al. (Engineering Craftsmen: No. H34). (Illus.). 1977. spiral bdg. 39.95x o.p. (ISBN 0-85083-413-9). Trans-Atl Phila.

Aircraft Fatigue: Design, Operational & Economic Aspects. Ed. by J. Y. Mann & I. S. Milligan. LC 71-125094. 570p. 1973. 125.00 o.p. (ISBN 0-08-017526-0). Pergamon.

Aircraft Gas Turbine Powerplants. Charles E. Otis. (Aviation Technician Training Course Ser.). (Illus.). 202p. 1979. pap. text ed. 9.95 o.p. (ISBN 0-89100-095-X, EA-TEP-1). IAP.

Aircraft Inspection, Repair & Alterations: AC 43.13-1A & 43.13-2A. Federal Aviation Administration Staff. 449p. pap. 13.50 o.p. (ISBN 0-89100-081-X, EA-AC43-13,1A & 2A). IAP.

Aircraft of the Soviet Union. Bill Gunston. (Illus.). 416p. 1983. 45.00 o.p. (ISBN 0-85045-445-X, Pub. by Osprey England). Motorbooks Intl.

Aircraft Piston Engines: From the Manly Baltzer to the Continental Tiara. Herschel Smith. (Aviation Ser.). (Illus.). 264p. 1981. text ed. 28.95 o.p. (ISBN 0-07-058472-9). McGraw.

Aircraft Stability & Control. A. W. Babister. 1962. 116.00 o.p. (ISBN 0-08-009550-X). Pergamon.

Aircraft Structures. David J. Peery. (Illus.). 1950. text ed. 36.00 o.p. (ISBN 0-07-049195-X, C). McGraw.

Aircraft Structures for Engineering Students. T. Megson. 494p. 1972. pap. 29.00x o.p. (ISBN 0-8448-0592-0, Pub. by Crane Russak & Co). Taylor & Francis.

Aircraft Today. J. W. Taylor. 110p. 1955. (ISBN 0-8022-1702-8). Philos Lib.

Aircraft Turbocharging. Paul Garrison. (Illus.). 144p. 1982. pap. 5.95 o.p. (ISBN 0-8306-2306-X, 2306). TAB Bks.

Aircraft Versus Aircraft: The Illustrated Story of Fighter Pilot Combat since 1914. Norman Franks. LC 86-905. (Illus.). 192p. 1986. 19.95 o.p. (ISBN 0-02-540620-5). Macmillan.

Aircrew Stress in Wartime Operations. Ed. by E. J. Dearnaley & P. B. War. 1979. 60.00 o.p. (ISBN 0-12-207750-4). Acad Pr.

Airfinance Annual: 1987-88. 4th ed. 250p. pap. cancelled o.s.i. (ISBN 0-8002-4107-X). Intl Pubns Serv.

Airframe & Power Plant Mechanics: General Handbook. (Advisory Circular Ser.: No. 65-9A). (Illus.). 559p. 1976. pap. 18.00 o.p. (ISBN 0-318-21913-1, S/N 050-007-00379-0). USGPO.

Airframe & Powerplant Mechanics Airframe Writen Test Guide. rev. ed. Federal Aviation Administration Staff. 109p. 1981. pap. text ed. 5.50 o.p. (ISBN 0-939158-20-5). Flightshops.

Airframe & Powerplant Mechanics General Written Test Guide. rev. ed. Federal Aviation Administration Staff. 95p. 1981. pap. text ed. 5.50 o.p. (ISBN 0-939158-19-1). Flightshops.

Airframe & Powerplant Mechanics: Powerplant Handbook. rev. ed. (Advisory Circular 65-12A). (Illus.). 510p. 1976. pap. 12.00 o.p. (ISBN 0-318-18722-1, S/N 050-007-00373-1). USGPO.

Airframe & Powerplant Mechanic's Powerplant Written Test Guide. rev. ed. Federal Aviation Administration Staff. 90p. 1981. pap. text ed. 5.50 o.p. (ISBN 0-939158-21-3). Flightshops.

Airframe & Systems Fitting. 2nd ed. Ed. by C. J. Green et al. (Engineering Craftsmen: No. H9). (Illus.). 1973. spiral bdg. 39.95x o.p. (ISBN 0-85083-218-7). Trans-Atl Phila.

Airframe Mechanic. rev. ed. Dale Crane. (Capstan Guide: Fast-Track Method Ser.). 176p. pap. text ed. cancelled o.s.i. Av Suppl & Acad.

Airgun Book. John Walter. (Illus.). 128p. 1988. 29.95 o.p. (ISBN 0-85368-882-6, Pub. by Arms & Armour). Sterling.

Airline Competition: A Study of the Effects of Competition on the Quality & Price of Airline Service & the Self-Sufficiency of the United States Domestic Airlines. F. W. Gill & G. L. Bates. 1949. 175.00 o.p. (ISBN 0-08-018738-2). Pergamon.

Airline Deregulation Handbook. Jeffrey R. Miller. LC 81-80687. 84p. (Orig.). 1981. pap. 6.95 o.p. (ISBN 0-916032-12-4). Delmar.

Airline Economics. Ed. by George W. James. (Illus.). 352p. 1981. 45.00x o.p. (ISBN 0-669-04909-3). Lexington Bks.

Airline Pilot Employment Interview. Clark St. John. 69p. 1988. pap. 10.95 o.p. (ISBN 0-942397-03-7). Buckeye Aviat Bk.

Airline Pilot Employment Test Guide. rev. ed. St. John. (Illus.). 105p. 1989. pap. 14.95 o.p. Buckeye Aviat Bk.

Airline Pilot Employment Test Guide. 2nd, rev. ed. Clark St. John. (Illus.). 104p. 1987. spiral 14.95 o.p. (ISBN 0-942397-00-2). Buckeye Aviat Bk.

Airline Planning: Corporate, Financial, & Marketing. Nawal K. Taneja. LC 80-8736. 224p. 1982. 37.00x o.p. (ISBN 0-669-04346-X). Lexington Bks.

Airline Price Policy: A Study of Airline Passenger Fares. P. W. Cherington. 1958. Repr. of 1958 ed. 120.00 o.p. (ISBN 0-08-018739-0). Pergamon.

Airline Transport Pilot, Airplane FAR, Pt. 135: Helicopter-VFR, Helicopter-IFR, Gyroplane-VFR, Question Book. (Illus.). 242p. 1986. pap. 9.50 o.p. (ISBN 0-318-20002-3, S/N 050-007-00721-3). USGPO.

Airline Transport Pilot, Airplane, Practical Test Guide (Ac 61-77) Federal Aviation Administration Staff. 1974. pap. text ed. 3.00 o.p. (ISBN 0-686-74081-5, Pub. by Astro). Aviation.

Airline Transport Pilot-Airplane Written Test Guide: Air Carrier. rev. ed. Federal Aviation Administration Staff. 189p. 1980. pap. text ed. 7.00 o.p. (ISBN 0-939158-16-7). Flightshops.

Airline Transport Pilot Test - Part 121. 1988. 23.95 o.p. (ISBN 0-940732-22-X, ASA-ATP121A). Av Suppl & Acad.

Airline Transport Pilot Test Book - Part 135. 1988. 16.95 o.p. (ISBN 0-940732-33-5, ASA-ATP135B). Av Suppl & Acad.

Airling.... & Other Poems. Gerald E. Clarke. 1977. 5.00 o.p. (ISBN 0-8233-0256-3). Golden Quill.

Airman's Information Manual. 248p. 6.75 o.p. (ISBN 0-8168-1362-0, TAB-Aero). TAB Bks.

Airman's Information Manual. 23rd, rev. ed. Federal Aviation Administration Staff. Ed. by Walter P. Winner. LC 70-164372. (Illus.). 304p. 1988. pap. 6.95 o.p. (ISBN 0-916413-08-X). Aviation.

Airman's Information Manual, 1987. TAB-Aero Staff. 288p. (Orig.). 1987. pap. 6.95 o.p. (ISBN 0-317-61102-X, 21367, TAB-Aero). TAB Bks.

Airman's Odyssey. Antoine de Saint-Exupery. LC 43-51284. 1943. 9.50 o.p. (ISBN 0-15-104081-8). HarBraceJ.

Airman's War 1914-1918. Peter Liddle. (Illus.). 224p. 1987. 21.95 o.p. (ISBN 0-7137-1592-8, Pub. Blandford Pr England). Sterling.

Airplanes. (Preschool Puppet Board Bks.). (Illus.). 7p. (ps-1). 1973. 2.50 o.p. (ISBN 0-448-09733-8, G&D). Putnam Pub Group.

Airplanes & Income Tax. Daniel J. O'Conner. 75p. 1987. pap. 12.95 o.p. (ISBN 0-9613218-3-0). Aviation.

Airplanes: From the Dawn of Light to the Present Day. Enzo Angelucci. LC 72-12755. (Illus.). 288p. 1973. text ed. 24.95 o.p. (ISBN 0-07-001807-3). McGraw.

Airport Adventure. Bonnie West. LC 81-68855. (Carolrhoda Mini-Mysteries Ser.). (Illus.). 32p. (gr. 1-4). 1982. PLB 5.95 o.p. (ISBN 0-87614-172-6). Carolrhoda Bks.

Airport People. Norton J. Hughes. (Inflation Fighter Ser.). 192p. 1982. pap. 1.50 o.s.i. (ISBN 0-8439-1149-2, Pub. by Leisure Bks CT). Dorchester Pub Co.

Airports of Baja California & North Western Mexico. 17th ed. Arnold D. Senterfitt. 384p. 1987. pap. 24.95 o.p. (ISBN 0-937260-02-9). Aviation.

Airscream. John Bruce. LC 77-13572. 1978. 8.95 o.p. (ISBN 0-689-10843-5, Atheneum). Macmillan.

Airwar over Great Britain Nineteen Fourteen to Nineteen Eighteen. (Vintage Warbirds Ser.: No.7). (Illus.). 64p. 1987. pap. 9.95 o.p. (ISBN 0-85368-804-4, Pub. by Arms & Armour). Sterling.

Airwar over the Pacific. Robert C. Stern. (Warbirds Illustrated Ser.: No. 36). (Illus.). 68p. (Orig.). 1986. pap. 9.95 o.p. (ISBN 0-85368-735-8, Pub. by Arms & Armour). Sterling.

AIS New Car Cost Guide 1985. Ed. by Christine Boldt. 250p. 1985. loose-leaf binder 73.00 o.p. (ISBN 0-88098-056-7). H M Gousha.

Ait 'Atta of Southern Morocco: Daily Life & Recent History. David Hart. 219p. 1985. lib. bdg. 32.50x o.p. Lynne Rienner.

AKA. Tristan Jones. 224p. 1983. pap. 3.50 o.p. (ISBN 0-380-64196-8, 64196). Avon.

A.K.A. A Cosmic Fable. Rob Swigart. 1978. 8.95 o.p. (ISBN 0-395-26306-9); pap. 4.95 o.p. (ISBN 0-395-26384-0). HM.

A.K.A. Chip Harrison. Lawrence Block. (Foul Play Press Ser.). 368p. 1983. pap. 5.95 o.p. (ISBN 0-88150-001-1, Foul Play Pr). Countryman.

Akamba from Within: Egalitarianism in Social Relations. Joseph Muthiani. LC 72-94858. 1973. 6.00 o.p. (ISBN 0-682-47620-X, University). Exposition-Phoenix.

AKA's World of Pure Bred Dog. Date not set. (ISBN 0-87605-406-8). Howell Bk.

Akavak: An Eskimo Journey. James Houston. LC 68-26426. (Illus.). (gr. 3-5). 1968. 7.95 o.p. (ISBN 0-15-201729-1, HJ). HarBraceJ.

Akbar. M. Mujeeb. (gr. 6-9). 1969. pap. 1.00 o.s.i. (ISBN 0-88253-350-9). Ind-US Inc.

AKEL: The Communist Party of Cyprus. T. W. Adams. LC 70-126963. (Studies Ser.: No. 27). 284p. 1971. 10.95x o.p. (ISBN 0-8179-3271-2). Hoover Inst Pr.

Akhmatova i Blok. Vladimir N. Toporov. (Modern Russian Literature & Culture, Studies & Texts: Vol. 5). 202p. (Rus.). 1981. pap. 10.00 o.p. (ISBN 0-933884-16-8). Berkeley Slavic.

Akiba. Marcus Lehmann. Tr. by Joseph Leftwich. (gr. 7 up). 7.95 o.p. (ISBN 0-87306-120-9). Feldheim.

Akin to Slavery: Prison Labor in South Africa. Allen Cook. 81p. 1982. 2.00 o.p. (ISBN 0-317-36648-3). Africa Fund.

Akiviak. Kaare Rodahl. 1979. 9.95 o.p. (ISBN 0-393-01181-X). Norton.

Akkadian Influences on Aramaic. Stephen A. Kaufman. LC 74-16674. (Assyriological Studies Ser: No. 19). xviii, 196p. 1975. pap. text ed. 10.00x o.s.i. (ISBN 0-226-62281-9, AS19). U of Chicago Pr.

Aktuell & Interessant, 3 vols. Heinz Griesbach. 78p. (Ger.). 1975. Vol. 1,Die Deutschsprachigen Laender, 80 p. 5.50 o.p. (ISBN 3-468-49561-7); Vol 2: Die Laender der Bundesrepublik Deutschland, 80p. 5.50 o.p. (ISBN 3-468-49661-3); Vol 3, Einigestaedte der Bundesrepublik Deutschland,80p. 5.50 o.p. (ISBN 3-468-49761-X). Langenscheidt.

Aktuelle Probleme der Otorhinolaryngologie. Ed. by U. Fisch. (ORL: Vol. 38, Suppl. 1). 1976. 40.00 o.p. (ISBN 3-8055-2394-7). S Karger.

Akute Pankreatitis see Acute Pancreatitis: An Interdisciplinary Synopsis.

Al Ganna wa'l Mugana I (Songs & Singers) Tr. by Arthur Wormhoudt from Arabic. (Arab Translation Ser.: No. 86). 160p. (Orig.). 1986. pap. 6.50x o.p. (ISBN 0-916358-38-0). Wormhoudt.

Al Ganna wa'l Muganna II (Songs & Singers) Tr. by Arthur Wormhoudt from Arabic. (Arab Translation Ser.: No. 88). 160p. (Orig.). 1986. pap. 6.50x o.p. (ISBN 0-916358-40-2). Wormhoudt.

Al Ghazali: On the Duties of Brotherhood. Tr. by Muhtar Holland. LC 76-8057. 96p. 1979. 15.95 o.p. (ISBN 0-87951-046-3); pap. 7.95 o.p. (ISBN 0-87951-083-8). Overlook Pr.

Al-Islam bain Jahl 'Abna'ihi wa Ajz Ulama'ihi. Abdul Q. Audah. 79p. (Orig., Arabic.). 1980. pap. 1.55x o.s.i. (ISBN 0-939830-12-4, Pub. by IIFSO Kuwait). New Era Pubns MI.

Al Looks for a Job see Getting along Series of Skills.

Al Muslimun Wa al Badil al Hadari: "Muslims & the Civilizational Alternative" monograph ed. Taha Jabir al Alwani. 38p. (Arabic.). Date not set. pap. text ed. 2.00 o.s.i. IIIT VA.

Al-Mustaqbal li-hadha ad-Din. Sayyid Qutb. 118p. (Orig., Arabic.). 1978. pap. 2.35x o.s.i. (ISBN 0-939830-16-7, Pub. by IIFSO Kuwait). New Era Pubns MI.

Al-Serat: The Imam Husayn Conference Number, Published in Association with the Muhammadi Trust. 273p. 1988. pap. text ed. 25.00 o.p. (ISBN 0-7103-0235-5). Routledge Chapman & Hall.

ALA Handbook of Organization & Membership Directory, 1987-1988. American Library Association Staff. 906p. 1987. pap. text ed. 20.00x o.p. (ISBN 0-8389-5706-4). ALA.

ALA Handbook of Organization, 1987-1988. American Library Association Staff. 326p. 1987. pap. text ed. 10.00x o.p. (ISBN 0-8389-5705-6). ALA.

ALA Publications Checklist 1988. Ed. by RuthAnn Jones & Emily Melton. 80p. 1988. pap. text ed. 3.00x o.p. (ISBN 0-8389-7177-6). ALA.

ALA Survey of Librarian Salaries, 1986. Mary J. Lynch. 90p. 1986. pap. text ed. 40.00x o.p. (ISBN 0-8389-3335-1). ALA.

Alabama Business Directory, 1988-89. American Directory Publishing Co., Inc. Staff. 1075p. (Orig.). 1988. pap. 95.00 o.p. (ISBN 0-944316-17-4). Amer Directory.

Alabama: Conflict of Laws. 8.50 o.p. (ISBN 0-686-90619-5). Am Law Inst.

Alabama Constitutional Commission: A Pragmatic Approach to Constitutional Revision. William H. Stewart, Jr. LC 74-24627. 144p. 1975. 10.75 o.p. (ISBN 0-8173-4725-9). U of Ala Pr.

Alabama: Contracts. 9.50 o.p. (ISBN 0-686-90621-7). Am Law Inst.

Alabama Criminal Code. Michie Company Editorial Staff. (State Publications Ser.). 850p. 1986. 21.50x o.p. (ISBN 0-87473-263-8). Michie Co.

Alabama Football: The Crimson Tide. Clyde Bolton. LC 72-91388. (College Sports Ser.). 1982. 10.95 o.p. Strode.

Alabama Mining & Manufacturing Directory, 1987-88. 784p. 1987. pap. 63.00 o.p. (ISBN 0-318-22792-4). Manufacturers.

Alabama: Property, Vols. 1-5. 13.50 o.p. (ISBN 0-686-90625-X). Am Law Inst.

Alabama Rules Annotated. Michie Company Editorial Staff. 1200p. 1987. 30.00x o.p. (ISBN 0-87473-272-7). Michie Co.

Alabama Rules of Court. 736p. 1986. pap. 17.75 o.p. (ISBN 0-314-24951-6). West Pub.

Alabama Showdown: The Football Rivalry Between Auburn & Alabama. Geoffrey Norman. (Illus.). 256p. 1986. 18.95 o.p. (ISBN 0-8050-0081-X). H Holt & Co.

Alabama United States Senators. Elbert Watson. LC 81-52625. 1982. 12.95 o.p. (ISBN 0-87397-081-0). Strode.

Alain Robbe-Grillet. John Fletcher. LC 83-13077. (Contemporary Writers Ser.). 92p. 1983. pap. 4.75 o.p. (ISBN 0-416-34420-8, NO.3749). Routledge Chapman & Hall.

Alameda - Santa Clara Counties Street Guide & Directory 1988. Thomas Bros. Maps Staff. (Illus.). 320p. 1988. pap. 18.95 o.p. (ISBN 0-88130-267-8). Thomas Bros Maps.

Alameda-Contra Costa Counties Street Atlas Combination 1985. Thomas Bros. Maps Staff (Illus.). 324p. pap. 17.50 o.p. (ISBN 0-88130-113-2). Thomas Bros Maps.

Alameda-Contra Costa Counties Street Atlas Combination: 1987. rev. ed. Thomas Bros. Maps Staff. (Illus.). 324p. 1986. pap. 19.95 o.p. Thomas Bros Maps.

Alameda-Contra Costa Counties Street Guide & Directory, 1988. Thomas Bros. Maps Staff. (Illus.). 314p. 1987. pap. 19.95 o.p. (ISBN 0-88130-266-X). Thomas Bros Maps.

Alameda County Public Schools: How Are They Doing? (1984) Lillian S. Clancy. (How Are They Doing Ser.). 80p. (Orig.). 1984. pap. 11.95 o.p. (ISBN 0-939580-08-X). CA Schl Surveys.

Alameda County Street Atlas 1985. Thomas Bros. Maps Staff. (Illus.). 194p. pap. 9.95 o.p. (ISBN 0-88130-112-4). Thomas Bros Maps.

Alameda County Street Atlas: 1987. rev. ed. Thomas Bros. Maps Staff. (Illus.). 201p. 1986. pap. 11.95 o.p. (ISBN 0-88130-209-0). Thomas Bros Maps.

Alameda County Street Guide & Directory, 1988. Thomas Bros. Maps Staff. (Illus.). 178p. 1988. pap. 11.95 o.p. (ISBN 0-88130-265-1). Thomas Bros Maps.

Alameda-Santa Clara Counties Street Atlas & Directory, 1987. rev. ed. Thomas Bros. Maps Staff. (Illus.). 322p. 1987. pap. 18.95 o.p. (ISBN 0-88130-207-4). Thomas Bros Maps.

Alameda-Santa Clara Counties Street Atlas 1985. Thomas Bros. Maps Staff. (Illus.). 266p. pap. 17.00 o.p. (ISBN 0-88130-114-0). Thomas Bros Maps.

Alamo House: Women Without Men, Men Without Brains. Sarah Bird. 1986. 15.45 o.p. (ISBN 0-393-02323-0). Norton.

Alamo Tree. Ernest Brawley. 432p. 1984. 17.45 o.p. (ISBN 0-671-45088-3). S&S.

Alan Ayckbourn. Michael Billington. LC 83-49373. (Modern Dramatists Ser.). 224p. 1984. 19.50 o.p. (ISBN 0-394-53856-0, GP893). Grove.

Alan Ayckbourn. Michael Billington. LC 83-49373. (Modern Dramatists Ser.). 224p. 1984. pap. 9.95 o.p. (ISBN 0-394-62051-8, E908, Ever). Grove.

Alan Garner's Book of British Fairy Tales. Alan Garner. LC 85-4586. (Illus.). 160p. (ps-3). 1985. 16.95 o.p. (ISBN 0-385-29425-5). Delacorte.

Alan Turing: The Enigma. Andrew Hodges. (Illus.). 576p. 1983. 24.45 o.s.i. (ISBN 0-671-49207-1). S&S.

Alanbrooke. David Fraser. LC 81-69156. 1982. 19.95 o.p. (ISBN 0-689-11267-X, Atheneum). Macmillan.

Alaska. Paul C. Johnson. LC 74-78594. (This Beautiful World Ser: Vol. 50). (Illus.). 120p. 1974. pap. 5.25 o.p. (ISBN 0-87011-234-1). Kodansha.

Alaska. Patricia Kindle & Susan Finney. (Gifted Learning Ser.). (Illus.). 64p. (gr. 4-8). 1985. wkbk. 6.95 o.p. (ISBN 0-86653-293-5). Good Apple.

Alaska: A Travel Survival Kit. Jim DuFresne. (Illus.). 176p. (Orig.). 1983. pap. 6.95 o.p. (ISBN 0-908086-44-X). Lonely Planet.

Alaska Almanac, 1986. 10th ed. Ed. by Alaska Northwest Publishing Staff. (Illus.). 200p. (Orig.). 1986. pap. 5.95 o.p. (ISBN 0-88240-243-9). Alaska Northwest.

Alaska Almanac 1989: Facts about Alaska. Alaska Northwest Books Staff. (Illus.). 230p. 1989. pap. 6.95 o.p. (ISBN 0-88240-244-7). Alaska Northwest.

Alaska Angling Guide. Ed. by Marty Sherman. (Illus.). 80p. 1986. 6.95 o.p. (ISBN 0-936608-43-9). F Amato Pubns.

Alaska Angling Guide 1987. Ed. by Marty Sherman. (Illus.). 75p. 1987. pap. 4.95 o.p. (ISBN 0-936608-37-4). F Amato Pubns.

Alaska Catalog: Living, Working & Traveling in the Northland. Ed. by Elizabeth Johannsen. LC 77-76351. (Illus.). 1977. pap. 6.95x o.p. (ISBN 0-918792-01-0). Otter Pr.

Alaska: Eighteen Sixty-Seven to Nineteen Fifty-Nine. Robert N. DeArmond. (Alaska Historical Commission Studies in History: No. 18). (Illus.). 20p. (Orig.). 1981. pap. 3.00 o.p. (ISBN 0-943712-02-5). Alaska Hist.

Alaska: High Roads to Adventure. Photos by George F. Mobley. Ed. by Donald J. Crump. LC 76-692. (Special Publications: Series 11, No. 3). (Illus.). 1976. 7.95 o.p. (ISBN 0-87044-188-4); lib. bdg. 9.50 o.p. (ISBN 0-87044-193-0). Natl Geog.

Alaska: Memoir of a Vanishing Frontier. Dan Saunders. 1975. pap. 1.50 o.p. (ISBN 0-380-00471-2, 21360). Avon.

Alaska Milepost 1987. Alaska Northwest Publishing Staff. 1987. pap. 14.95 o.p. (ISBN 0-88240-211-0). Alaska Northwest.

Alaska Native Languages: A Bibliographical Catalogue - Part One: Indian Languages. Michael E. Krauss & Mary Jane McGary. (Alaska Native Language Center Research Papers Ser.: No. 3). (Illus.). viii, 455p. 1980. pap. 20.00 o.p. (ISBN 0-933769-33-4). Alaska Native.

Alaska: Promises to Keep. Robert B. Weeden. 1978. 9.95 o.p. (ISBN 0-395-27123-1). HM.

Alaska: The Embattled Frontier. George Laycock. (Audubon Library: Vol. 1). 1971. 7.95 o.p. (ISBN 0-395-12345-3). HM.

Alaska: Travel Guide. 3rd ed. Sunset Magazine & Books Editors. LC 77-90724. (Illus.). 112p. 1978. pap. 7.95 o.p. (ISBN 0-376-06035-2, Sunset Bks). Sunset-Lane.

Alaska Wilderness Milepost 1988. Alaska Northwest Publishing Staff. (Illus.). 400p. 1988. pap. 14.95 o.s.i. (ISBN 0-88240-287-0). Alaska Northwest.

Alaska Yukon Caribou. facsimile ed. Olaus Marie. (Shorey Historical Ser.). (Illus.). 118p. pap. 9.95 o.s.i. (ISBN 0-8466-0165-6, S165). Shorey.

Alaska-Yukon Handbook: A Gypsy Guide to the Inside Passage & Beyond. David Stanley. Ed. by Deke Castleman & Diane Hume. (Illus.). 230p. (Orig.). 1984. pap. 7.95 o.p. (ISBN 0-9603322-5-1). Moon Pubns CA.

Alaskan Gold Fields. Sam C. Dunham. (Northern History Library). (Illus.). 64p. 1984. pap. 5.95 o.s.i. (ISBN 0-88240-260-9). Alaska Northwest.

Alaskan Poker Stories. Kenneth Gilbert. (Shorey Historical Ser.). (Illus.). 48p. pap. 4.95 o.s.i. (ISBN 0-8466-0281-4, S281). Shorey.

Alaska's Inside Passage. Kim Heacox. 1987. pap. 7.95 o.p. (ISBN 0-917859-14-6). Sunrise SBCA.

Alaska's Southeast: Touring the Inside Passage. Sarah Eppenbach. (Illus.). 296p. (Orig.). 1983. pap. 11.95 o.p. (ISBN 0-914718-79-7). Pacific Search.

Alaska's Southeast: Touring the Inside Passage. 2nd, rev. ed. Sarah Eppenbach. LC 84-253640. (Illus.). 315p. 1985. pap. 11.95 o.p. (ISBN 0-914718-97-5). Globe Pequot.

Alban Berg. Karen Monson. 1979. 15.00 o.p. (ISBN 0-395-27762-0). HM.

Titles

Albanian-English, English-Albanian Dictionary. Nelo Drizari. LC 57-9330. (Albanian & Eng.). 35.00 o.p. (ISBN 0-8044-0130-6). Ungar.

Albany: Capital City on the Hudson. John McEneney. 247p. 1981. 24.95 o.s.i. (ISBN 0-89781-025-2). Windsor Pubns Inc.

Albear: The Dog Who Could Talk. Carlos. (Illus.). 64p. (gr. k-2). 1981. 5.00 o.p. (ISBN 0-682-49748-7). Exposition-Phoenix.

Albergo Empedocle & Other Early Writings. E. M. Forster. Ed. by George H. Thomson. LC 79-162435. 1971. 7.95 o.p. (ISBN 0-87140-540-7). Liveright.

Albert Bierstadt. Matthew Baigell. (Illus.). 84p. sewn bdg. 25.00 o.p. (ISBN 0-317-54911-1). Apollo.

Albert C-One-Thirty & the Blue Angels' A-4 Skyhawk Jets. Nettie Brown. (Illus.). 64p. 1981. pap. 4.00 o.p. (ISBN 0-682-49802-5). Exposition-Phoenix.

Albert Camus. Phillip H. Rhein. (World Authors Ser.). 1969. lib. bdg. 13.95 o.p. (ISBN 0-8057-2196-7, Twayne). G K Hall.

Albert Camus 1980. Ed. by Raymond Gay-Crosier. LC 80-22240. 330p. (Orig., Fr.). 1980. pap. 16.00 o.p. (ISBN 0-8130-0691-0). U Presses Fla.

Albert Durer Master Printmaker. Museum of Fine Arts, Boston. LC 87-80023. (Illus.). xxiv, 295p. 1988. Repr. of 1971 ed. lib. bdg. 75.00 o.p. (ISBN 0-317-66599-5). Hacker.

Albert Einstein: World Scientist. Irving Gerber. (American Destinty Ser. Jewish Americans). (Illus.). 1979. of 10 12.95 set o.p. (ISBN 0-87594-185-0). Book Lab.

Albert Schweitzer: The Story of His Life. Jean Pierhal. 1957. (ISBN 0-8022-1975-6). Philos Lib.

Albert Schweitzer's Mission: Healing & Peace. Norman Cousins. 1985. 16.45 o.p. (ISBN 0-393-02238-2). Norton.

Albert Speer: The End of a Myth. Matthias Schmidt. Tr. by Joachim Neugroschel. 288p. 1986. pap. 7.95 o.p. (ISBN 0-02-006600-7, Collier). Macmillan.

Albert the Alphabetical Elephant. Roger Hargreaves. LC 81-84548. (Illus.). 32p. (ps-1). 1982. 3.95 o.p. (ISBN 0-448-12319-3, G&D). Putnam Pub Group.

Alberta Homestead: Chronicle of a Pioneer Family. Sarah E. Roberts. Ed. by Lathrop E. Roberts. (M. K. Brown Range Life Ser.: No. 10). (Illus.). 282p. 1971. 14.95 o.p. (ISBN 0-292-70143-8). U of Tex Pr.

Alberta the Gorilla. (Zoo Babies Ser.). 16p. (gr. k-6). 1982. pap. 1.25 o.p. (ISBN 0-8249-8036-0). Ideals.

Alberti's Church of San Sebastiano in Mantua. Richard E. Lamoureux. Ed. by Sydney J. Freedberg. LC 78-74370. (Oustanding Dissertations in the Fine Arts Ser.). (Illus.). 1979. lib. bdg. 46.00 o.p. (ISBN 0-8240-3958-0). Garland Pub.

Alberto Sani: An Artist Out of His Time. Bernhard Berenson. LC 70-138202. (Illus.). 115p. 1972. Repr. of 1950 ed. lib. bdg. 35.00x o.p. (ISBN 0-8371-5555-X, BEAS). Greenwood.

Albion in China: The First British Football Tour to China in Pictures. D. Kingsley & F. Taylor. (Illus.). 1979. pap. 9.75 o.p. (ISBN 0-08-024496-3). Pergamon.

Albrecht Durer: Paintings, Prints, Drawings. Peter Strieder. (Illus.). 400p. sewn bdg. 60.00 o.s.i. (ISBN 0-317-54958-8). Apollo.

Album de Vers Anciens see Poesies.

Albumin: Structure, Function & Uses. Ed. by Victor Rosenoer et al. 1977. 100.00 o.p. (ISBN 0-08-019603-9). Pergamon.

Albums of Early Life. Stanley Kauffmann. LC 80-14481. 204p. 1980. 10.95 o.p. (ISBN 0-89919-015-4). Ticknor & Fields.

Alchemist. Ben Jonson. Ed. by F. M. Mares. 1978. pap. 7.95 o.p. (ISBN 0-416-71830-2, NO.2255). Routledge Chapman & Hall.

Alchemists. Geary Gravel. 1984. pap. 2.95 o.s.i. (ISBN 0-345-31397-6, Del Rey). Ballantine.

Alchemists Through the Ages, Vol. 25. Arthur E. Waite. LC 76-130814. (Spiritual Science Library). (Illus.). 320p. Repr. of 1970 ed. lib. bdg. 20.00 cancelled o.s.i. (ISBN 0-89345-035-9). Garber Comm.

Alchemy: A Bibliography of English Language Writings. Alan Pritchard. 400p. 1980. 75.00x o.p. (ISBN 0-7100-0472-9). Routledge Chapman & Hall.

Alchemy of Happiness. Hazrat Inayat Khan. (Sufi Message of Hazrat Inayat Khan Ser.: Vol. 6). 262p. 1979. 14.95 o.s.i. (ISBN 90-6077-953-3, Pub. by Servire BV Netherlands). Hunter Hse.

Alchemy: The Secret of Art. Klossowski. De Rola. (Art & the Cosmos Ser.). (Illus.). 128p. 1973. pap. 4.95 o.p. (ISBN 0-380-01012-7, 16907). Avon.

Alcibiades Reexamined. Edmund F. Bloedow. 96p. (Orig.). 1973. pap. text ed. 26.00x o.p. (ISBN 3-515-00270-7, Pub. by Franz Steiner). Coronet Bks.

Alcohol, Vol. 4, (Including 1987 Supplements) Ed. by Eleanor C. Goldstein. 1988. 15.00 o.p. (ISBN 0-89777-130-3). Soc Issues.

Alcohol & Abnormal Protein Biosynthesis, Biochemical & Clinical. Ed. by M. A. Rothschild et al. 550p. 1975. 71.00 o.p. (ISBN 0-08-017708-5). Pergamon.

Alcohol & Aggression. Ed. by Paul F. Brain. LC 85-22437. 256p. 1985. 37.75 o.p. (ISBN 0-7099-0691-9, Pub. by Croom Helm Ltd). Routledge Chapman & Hall.

Alcohol & Aldehyde Metabolizing Systems, 3 vols. Ed. by Ronald G. Thurman et al. (Johnson Foundation Colloquia Ser.). 1974. Vol. 1. 77.00 o.p. (ISBN 0-12-691450-8); Vol. 2, 1978. 77.00 o.p. (ISBN 0-12-691402-8); Vol. 3, 1977. 77.00 o.p. (ISBN 0-12-691403-6); Set. (ISBN 0-686-77325-X). Acad Pr.

Alcohol & Health: Fifth Special Report to the United States Congress. 170p. 1983. pap. 5.00 o.p. (ISBN 0-318-11754-1, S/N 017-024-01199-1). USGPO.

Alcohol & Opiates: Neurochemical & Behavioral Mechanisms. Ed. by K. Blum. 1977. 55.00 o.p. (ISBN 0-12-108450-7). Acad Pr.

Alcohol & Pregnancy: Why They Don't Mix. American Medical Association Staff. 15p. (Orig.). 1984. pap. 1.50 o.p. (ISBN 0-89970-272-4, OP-245). AMA.

Alcohol & Substance Abuse. Stephen P. Apthorp. 288p. 1985. 19.95 o.p. (ISBN 0-8192-1375-6); pap. 11.95 o.p. (ISBN 0-8192-1372-1). Morehouse Pub.

Alcohol As a Crutch. Shirley Schwarzrock & C. Gilbert Wrenn. (Coping with Ser.). (Illus.). (gr. 7-12). 1971. pap. text ed. 3.00 o.p. (ISBN 0-913476-17-X). Am Guidance.

Alcohol, Drugs, & Arbitrition: Concepts & Questions. Arnold M. Zack & Ricard I. Bloch. LC 79-84539. 84p. 1980. pap. 9.95/7.95 o.p. (ISBN 0-943001-10-2). Am Arbitration.

Alcohol, Drugs & School-Leavers. Martin A. Plant et al. 208p. 1985. text ed. 36.00 o.p. (ISBN 0-422-78260-2, 4011, Pub. by Tavistock England). Routledge Chapman & Hall.

Alcohol Fuels: Options for Developing Countries. National Research Council, Board on Science & Technology for International Development & Griff Shay. 109p. 1983. pap. text ed. 8.95x o.p. (ISBN 0-309-03386-1). Natl Acad Pr.

Alcohol: Our Favorite Drug. Royal College of Psychiatrists Staff. (Illus.). 224p. 1987. 45.00 o.p. (ISBN 0-422-61110-7, 1136, Pub. by Tavistock England); pap. 15.95 o.p. (ISBN 0-422-61120-4, 1151, Pub. by Tavistock England). Routledge Chapman & Hall.

Alcohol Problems. 59p. 1982. pap. 14.00x o.p. (ISBN 0-7279-0094-3, Pub. by British Med Assoc UK). Taylor & Francis.

Alcohol Problems in Employment. Ed. by Brian D. Hore & Martin A. Plant. (Illus.). 208p. 1981. 35.00 o.p. (ISBN 0-7099-1202-1, Pub. by Croom Helm Ltd). Routledge Chapman & Hall.

Alcohol Programs for Higher Education. James Dean & Bill Bryan. 11.00 o.p. (ISBN 1-55620-000-5, 72612C). Am Assn Coun Dev.

Alcohol-Proof of What? Essie E. Lee. LC 75-45149. 192p. (gr. 7 up). 1976. lib. bdg. 8.79 o.s.i. (ISBN 0-671-32789-5). Messner.

Alcohol y la Familia. P. Frank. 1981. pap. 1.50 o.p. (ISBN 0-89243-139-3). Liguori Pubns.

Alcohol, Youth & the State: Drinking Practices, Controls & Health Education. Nicholas Dorn. 280p. 1983. 35.00 o.p. (ISBN 0-7099-0243-3, Pub. by Croom Helm Ltd). Routledge Chapman & Hall.

Alcoholic & the Help He Needs. Max Glatt. LC 73-16957. 194p. 1974. 7.95 o.s.i. (ISBN 0-8008-0165-2). Taplinger.

Alcoholic Liver Disease: Pathobiology, Epidemiology & Clinical Aspects. Ed. by Pauline Hall. 270p. 1985. 42.50 o.p. (ISBN 0-471-82469-0). Wiley.

Alcoholic Patient: Diagnosis & Management. Morris E. Chafetz. 240p. 1983. casebound 31.95 o.p. (ISBN 0-87489-276-7). Med Economics.

Alcoholics & Business: Problems, Costs, Solutions. new ed. Joseph F. Follmann, Jr. LC 75-40270. 256p. 1976. 12.95 o.p. (ISBN 0-8144-5410-0). AMACOM.

Alcoholism: A Treatment Manual. Wayne Poley et al. LC 78-13435. 159p. 1979. 15.95x o.p. (ISBN 0-470-26523-X). Halsted Pr.

Alcoholism, Alcohol Abuse & Related Problems: Opportunities for Research. Institute of Medicine, Division of Health Promotion & Disease Prevention Staff & National Research Council Staff. 1980. pap. text ed. 8.75x o.p. (ISBN 0-309-03097-8). Natl Acad Pr.

Alcoholism: An Inherited Disease. Peter L. Petrakis. (DHHS Publication: No. ADM 85-1426). 47p. (Orig.). 1985. pap. 1.25 o.p. (ISBN 0-318-20001-5, S/N 017-024-01273-4). USGPO.

Alcoholism: It's Psychology & Cure. Frederick B. Rea. 130p. 1956. (ISBN 0-8022-1314-6). Philos Lib.

Alcoholism: Modern Psychological Approaches to Treatment. Eva M. Blum & Richard H. Blum. LC 67-13278. (Social & Behavioral Science Ser.). 1967. 29.95x o.p. (ISBN 0-87589-005-9). Jossey-Bass.

Alcoholism: Treatable Illness. J. G. Strachan. 1972. 15.00 o.p. (ISBN 0-685-11990-4). E J Brill USA.

Alcoholisms: Detection, Diagnosis & Assessment. George Jacobson. LC 75-10497. 414p. 1976. text ed. 39.95 o.p. (ISBN 0-87705-268-9). Human Sci Pr.

Alcohols & Derivatives, 2 vols. Ed. by J. Tremolieres. 1970. Set. 155.00 o.p. (ISBN 0-08-006937-1). Pergamon.

Alcohols with Water. A. S. Burton. Ed. by A. F. Barton. (Solubility Data Ser.: Vol. 15). 465p. 1984. 110.00 o.p. (ISBN 0-08-025276-1). Pergamon.

Alcools. Guillaume Apollinaire. (Illus.). deluxe ed. 500.00 o.p. (ISBN 0-685-37177-8). French & Eur.

Aldehydes in Biological Systems: Their Natural Occurence & Biological Activities. E. Schauenstein et al. (Advanced Biochemistry Ser.). 205p. 1977. 29.00x o.p. (ISBN 0-85086-059-8, NO.2949, Pub. by Pion England). Routledge Chapman & Hall.

Aldehydes-Photometric Analysis, 5 vols. Eugene Sawicki & Carole R. Sawicki. (Analysis of Organic Materials Ser.). 1975. Vol. 1. 76.00 o.p. (ISBN 0-12-620501-9); Vol. 2. 82.00 o.p. (ISBN 0-12-620502-7); Vol. 3, 1976. 76.00 o.p. (ISBN 0-12-620503-5); Vol. 4. 1977. 60.50 o.p.; Vol. 5, 1978. 117.00 o.p. (ISBN 0-12-620505-1). Acad Pr.

Alder Gulch. Ernest Haycox. 1984. lib. bdg. 13.95 o.p. (ISBN 0-8161-3550-9, Large Print Bks). G K Hall.

Aldo Applesauce. Johanna Hurwitz. 1983. pap. 1.95 o.p. (ISBN 0-590-62329-X). Scholastic Inc.

Aldo Ice Cream. Johanna Hurwitz. (Illus.). (gr. 3-5). 1982. pap. 1.75 o.p. (ISBN 0-671-43940-5). Archway.

Aldo Van Eyck. Lamia Doumato. (Architecture Ser.: Bibliography A-1303). 1985. pap. 2.00 o.p. (ISBN 0-89028-233-1). Vance Biblios.

Aldosterone. Edith Glaz & Paul Vecsei. LC 70-138666. 628p. 1971. 145.00 o.p. (ISBN 0-08-013368-1). Pergamon.

Aldous Huxley. Donald Wyatt. (Critical Heritage Ser.). 320p. 1985. pap. 15.00 o.p. (ISBN 0-7102-0591-0). Routledge Chapman & Hall.

Aldous Huxley & Eastern Wisdom. B. L. Chakoo. 308p. 1981. text ed. 17.50x o.p. (ISBN 0-391-02910-X). Humanities.

Aldous Huxley: The Critical Heritage. Ed. by Donald Watt. (Critical Heritage Ser.). 1975. 30.00x o.p. (ISBN 0-7100-8114-6). Routledge Chapman & Hall.

Aldous Huxley: Vedantic & Buddhistic Influences. Kishore Gandhi. 256p. 1980. text ed. 15.00x o.p. (ISBN 0-391-02024-2). Humanities.

Alec Clifton-Taylor's Buildings of Delight. Ed. by Denis Moriarty. (Illus.). 260p. 1988. 34.95 o.p. (ISBN 0-575-03701-6, Pub. by Gollancz England). David & Charles.

Aleck Maury, Sportsman. Caroline Gordon. LC 74-164531. 1972. Repr. of 1934 ed. 18.50x o.p. (ISBN 0-8154-0400-X). Cooper Sq.

Alejo Carpentier: The Pilgrim at Home. Robert Gonzalez-Echevarria. LC 76-28013. 304p. 1977. 29.50x o.p. (ISBN 0-8014-1029-0). Cornell U Pr.

Alessandro Stradella's "Esule dalle sfere" Cantata for the Souls of Purgatory. Ed. by Eleanor F. McCrickard. Tr. by Aldo Scaglione from Ital. LC 82-17544. (Early Musical Masterworks). xi, 144p. 1983. 27.00x o.p. (ISBN 0-8078-1536-5). U of NC Pr.

Aleutian Indian & English Dictionary. facsimile ed. Charles A. Lee. 23p. (Aleut.). pap. 9.95 o.s.i. (ISBN 0-8466-0101-X, SJS101). Shorey.

Aleutian Islands: Their People & Natural History. facsimile ed. Collins et al. (Illus.). 157p. pap. 15.00 o.s.i. (ISBN 0-8466-0186-9, S186). Shorey.

Aleutians. Ed. by Alaska Geographic Staff. LC 80-17331. (Alaska Geographic Ser.: Vol. 7, No. 3). (Illus.). 224p. (Orig.). 1980. pap. 14.95 o.s.i. (ISBN 0-88240-145-9). Alaska Northwest.

Alex Icicle: A Romance in Ten Torrid Chapters. Robert Kaplow. LC 84-10740. 192p. (gr. 5-9). 1984. 11.45 o.p. (ISBN 0-395-36230-X). HM.

Alex Katz. Robert Rosenblum & Richard Marshall. LC 85-31460. (Illus.). 168p. 1987. 40.00 o.p. (ISBN 0-8478-0717-7); pap. 25.00 o.p. (ISBN 0-8478-0840-8). Rizzoli Intl.

Alexander & the Terrible, Horrible, No Good, Very Bad Day. Judith Viorst. LC 72-75289. 32p. (gr. k-4). 1976. pap. 2.95 o.s.i. (ISBN 0-689-70428-3, Aladdin). Macmillan.

Alexander Archipenko. Nehama Guralink & Katherine J. Michaelson. LC 86-18118. (Illus.). 160p. 1987. pap. 19.95 o.p. (ISBN 0-87663-510-9). Universe.

Alexander Blok: Selected Poems. Ed. by Avril Pyman. LC 67-31506. 388p. 1972. 46.00 o.p. (ISBN 0-08-012185-3). Pergamon.

Alexander Conspiracy: A Life of A. I. Zhelybov. David Footman. LC 74-57. Orig. Title: Red Prelude. (Illus.). 370p. 1974. Repr. of 1944 ed. 12.95 o.p. (ISBN 0-912050-47-0, Library Pr). Open Court.

Alexander Hamilton: A Biography. Jacob E. Cooke. (Illus.). 288p. 1982. 17.95 o.s.i. (ISBN 0-684-17344-1, ScribT). Scribner.

Alexander Hamilton & the Constitution. Clinton Rossiter. LC 64-11540. 1964. 9.50 o.p. (ISBN 0-15-104215-2). HarBraceJ.

Alexander I of Russia, the Man Who Defeated Napoleon. Leonid I. Strakhovsky. 1971. Repr. of 1947 ed. lib. bdg. 35.00x o.p. (ISBN 0-8371-4034-X, STAL). Greenwood.

Alexander Pope. Bonamy Dobree. 1952. (ISBN 0-8022-0406-6). Philos Lib.

Alexander Solzhenitsyn. Steven Allaback. LC 77-92765. 1978. 9.95 o.s.i. (ISBN 0-8008-0167-9). Taplinger.

Alexander Solzhenitsyn. Andrej Kodjak. (World Author Ser.). 1978. lib. bdg. 14.95 o.s.i. (ISBN 0-8057-6320-1, Twayne). G K Hall.

Alexander Technique. E. Maisel. 5.95 o.p. (ISBN 0-8216-0053-2, Pub. by Univ Bks). Carol Pub Group.

Alexander to Actium: An Essay on the Historical Evolution of Hellenistic Age, Vol. 1. Peter Green. Ed. by Anthony W. Bulloch et al. (Hellenistic Culture & Society Ser.). cancelled o.s.i. (ISBN 0-520-05611-6). U of Cal Pr.

Alexander Vesnisn & Russian Constructivism. Selim O. Khan-Magomedov. 1987. 55.00 o.p. (ISBN 0-8478-0773-8). Rizzoli Intl.

Alexander's Care of the Patient in Surgery. 7th ed. Barbara J. Gruendemann & Margaret H. Meeker. LC 82-8212. (Illus.). 848p. 1983. text ed. 45.95 cloth o.p. (ISBN 0-8016-4147-0). Mosby.

Alexandra Kollontai: Selected Writings. Alexandra Kollontai. Ed. & tr. by Alix Holt. LC 77-88786. 336p. 1978. 12.95 o.p. (ISBN 0-88208-092-X). Chicago Review.

Alexandre Dumas Pere: A Bibliography of Works Published in French, 1825-1900. Douglas Munro. 1981. lib. bdg. 61.00 o.p. (ISBN 0-8240-9361-5). Garland Pub.

Alexandre Dumas Pere: A Bibliography of Works Translated into English to 1910. Douglas Munro. LC 77-83381. (Library of Humanities Reference Bks.: No. 110). 1978. lib. bdg. 43.00 o.p. (ISBN 0-8240-9836-6). Garland Pub.

Alexandre-Gabriel Decamps (1803-1860, 2 vols. Dewey F. Mosby. LC 76-23651. (Outstanding Dissertations in the Fine Arts - 2nd Series - 19th Century). (Illus.). 1977. Repr. of 1973 ed. Set. lib. bdg. 155.00 o.p. (ISBN 0-8240-2714-0). Garland Pub.

Alexandrian Christianity. Ed. by J. E. Oulton & Henry Chadwick. LC 54-10257. (Library of Christian Classics). 472p. 1977. pap. 8.95 o.s.i. (ISBN 0-664-24153-0, Westminster). Westminster John Knox.

Alexandrinische Akzentuationssystem Unter Zugrundelegung der Theoretischen Lehren der Grammatik. Bernhard Laum. Repr. of 1928 ed. 41.00 o.p. (ISBN 0-384-31620-4). Johnson Repr.

Alexis Lichine's Guide to the Wines & Vineyards of France. rev. ed. Alexis Lichine. LC 81-48101. 508p. 1982. 19.95 o.p. (ISBN 0-394-52506-X); pap. 9.95 o.p. (ISBN 0-394-70890-3). Knopf.

Alexis Lichine's Guide to the Wines & Vineyards of France. 3rd ed. Alexis Lichine. 1986. 24.50 o.p. (ISBN 0-394-55335-7); pap. 14.95 o.p. (ISBN 0-394-74440-3). Knopf.

Alexis Lichine's New Encyclopedia of Wines & Spirits. 3rd ed. Alexis Lichine. LC 80-22385. (Illus.). 734p. 1981. 39.50 o.s.i. (ISBN 0-394-51781-4). Knopf.

Alfabetische Catalogus Van De Boeken En Brochures Van Het International: Alphabetical Catolog of the Books & Pamphlets of the International Institute of Social History, 12 vols. Institut Voor Sociale Geschiedenis Staff. 1970. Set. lib. bdg. 1220.00 o.p. (ISBN 0-8161-0807-2, Hall Library). G K Hall.

Alfabetische Catalogus Van De Boeken En Brochures Van Het Internationaal Instituut Voor Sociale Geschiedenis (Alphabetical Catalog of the Books & Pamphlets of the International Institute of Social History) Amsterdam, 1st Suppl, 2 vols. Instituut voor Sociale Geschiedenis Staff. 1975. Set. lib. bdg. 250.00 o.p. (ISBN 0-8161-1033-6, Hall Library). G K Hall.

Alfalfa, Beans & Clover. Joan E. Rahn. LC 76-67. (Illus.). 128p. (gr. 4-6). 1976. 6.50 o.s.i. (ISBN 0-689-30528-1, Atheneum). Macmillan.

Alferd G. Packer: Cannibal! Victim? Ervan F. Kushner. (Illus.). 320p. pap. 10.95 o.p. (ISBN 0-939650-03-7). R H Pub.

Alfons Spies: Militat Omnis Amons see Bruno Lier: Ad Topica Carminum Amatorium Symbolae.

Alfonso Reyes & Spain: His Dialogue with Unamuno, Valle-Inclan, Ortega y Gasset, Jimenez, & Gomez de la Serna. Barbara B. Aponte. 216p. 1972. 15.00x o.p. (ISBN 0-292-70300-7). U of Tex Pr.

Alfred de Musset: A Reference Guide. Patricia J. Siegel. 1982. lib. bdg. 55.00 o.p. (ISBN 0-8161-8233-7, Hall Reference). G K Hall.

Alfred Hitchcock Movie Quiz Book. Bryan Brown. (Illus.). 1986. pap. 8.95 o.p. (ISBN 0-399-51221-7). Putnam Pub Group.

Alfred Hitchcock's Tales to Be Read with Caution. Ed. by Eleanor Sullivan. 1979. 9.95 o.s.i. (ISBN 0-8037-0343-0). Davis Pubns.

Alfred Hitchcock's Tales to Fill You with Fear & Trembling. Ed. by Eleanor Sullivan. 1980. 9.95 o.s.i. (ISBN 0-8037-0392-9). Davis Pubns.

Alfred Hitchcock's Tales to Scare You Stiff. Ed. by Eleanor Sullivan. 1978. 8.95 o.s.i. (ISBN 0-8037-0135-7). Davis Pubns.

Alfred Hitchcock's Tales to Send Chills Down Your Spine. Ed. by Eleanor Sullivan. 1979. 8.95 o.s.i. (ISBN 0-8037-0342-2). Davis Pubns.

Alfred Jarry & Guillaume Apollinaire. Claude Schumacher. LC 84-82355. (Modern Dramatists Ser.). 196p. 1985. 22.50 o.s.i. (ISBN 0-394-54501-X, GP-958). Grove.

Alfred Jarry & Guillaume Apollinaire. Claude Schumacher. LC 84-82355. (Modern Dramatists Ser.). pap. 7.95 o.s.i. (ISBN 0-394-62358-4, E-974, Ever). Grove.

Alfred Jensen: Paintings & Works on Paper. Guggenheim, Solomon R., Foundation Staff. (Illus.). 80p. (Orig.). 1985. pap. 18.50 o.p. (ISBN 0-89207-051-X). S R Guggenheim.

Alfred Mansfeld, Architect (Israel) Florita Z. Louis de Malave. (Architecture Ser.: A 1393). 5p. 1985. 2.00 o.p. (ISBN 0-89028-403-2). Vance Biblios.

Alfred Marshall: Critical Assessments, 4 vols. Ed. by John C. Wood. 1828p. 1982. Set. 495.00 o.p. (ISBN 0-7099-2705-3, Pub. by Croom Helm Ltd). Routledge Chapman & Hall.

Alfred Stevens, 1817-1875. Susan Beattie. (Illus.). 48p. (Orig.). 1984. pap. 3.95 o.p. (ISBN 0-901486-88-4, Pub. by Victoria & Albert Mus UK). Faber & Faber.

Alfred Stieglitz: An American Seer. Dorothy Norman. LC 72-5048. (Illus.). 256p. 1978. 35.00 o.p. (ISBN 0-89381-035-5); pap. 17.50 o.p. (ISBN 0-89381-036-3). Aperture.

Alfred Werner: Founder of Coordination Chemistry. George B. Kauffmann. (Illus.). 1966. pap. 27.20 o.p. (ISBN 0-387-03577-X). Springer-Verlag.

Algae Abstracts: A Guide to the Literature, 3 vols. Compiled by Office of Water Resources Research Staff. Incl. Vol. 1. To 1969. LC 73-84004. 586p. 1973. 95.00x (ISBN 0-306-67181-6); Vol. 2. 1970 to 1972. 694p. 1973. 95.00x (ISBN 0-306-67182-4); Vol. 3. 1972 to 1974. 890p. 1976. 95.00x (ISBN 0-306-67183-2). IFI Plenum). Plenum Pub.

Algal Taxonomy in India. Y. S. Sarma & Khan. (International Bio-Science Ser.: No. 6). 168p. 1980. 12.00 o.p. (ISBN 0-88065-184-9, Pub. by Messers Today & Tomorrow Printers & Publishers). Scholarly Pubns.

Algebra. Harley Flanders & Justin J. Price. 1975. text ed. 15.95 o.p. (ISBN 0-12-259666-8); instr's. manual 3.00 o.p. (ISBN 0-12-259669-2). Acad Pr.

Algebra. 2nd ed. Harley Flanders & Justin J. Price. 1981. text ed. 27.95 o.s.i. (ISBN 0-03-057801-9, CBS C); instr's manual 11.95 o.s.i. (ISBN 0-03-058633-X); study guide 11.95 o.s.i. (ISBN 0-03-058634-8). SCP.

Algebra, Vol. 1. L. Redei. 1967. 200.00 o.p. (ISBN 0-08-010954-3). Pergamon.

Algebra: An Elementary Approach. 2nd ed. Allen R. Angel. (Illus.). 448p. 1988. text ed. (ISBN 0-13-020819-1). P-H.

Algebra & Trigonometry. Thomas A. Davis. (Illus.). 1972. text ed. 14.95 o.p. (ISBN 0-15-502150-8, HC). HarBraceJ.

Algebra & Trigonometry. Walter Fleming & Dale E. Varberg. (Illus.). 1980. text ed. (ISBN 0-13-021824-3). P-H.

Algebra & Trigonometry. 2nd ed. Walter Fleming & Dale E. Varberg. (Illus.). 576p. 1984. text ed. (ISBN 0-13-021535-X). P-H.

Algebra & Trigonometry. Vivian S. Groza & Gene Sellers. 1982. pap. 29.95 o.p. (ISBN 0-03-060107-X, CBS C). SCP.

Algebra & Trigonometry. Thomas W. Hungerford & Richard Mercer. 1982. text ed. 32.95 o.p. (ISBN 0-03-059519-3). HR&W.

Algebra & Trigonometry. Murphy et al. 550p. 1983. text ed. 24.00 o.p. (ISBN 0-15-502135-4, HC). HarbraceJ.

Algebra & Trigonometry. Bernard J. Rice & Jerry D. Strange. text ed. write for info. o.p. (ISBN 0-87150-286-0, Prindle). PWS-Kent Pub.

Algebra & Trigonometry. Arnold R. Steffensen & L. Murphy Johnson. 1981. pap. text ed. write for info. o.p. (ISBN 0-673-15371-1). Scott F.

Algebra & Trigonometry: A Pre-Calculus Approach. 2nd ed. Max A. Sobel & Norbert Lerner. (Illus.). 608p. 1983. text ed. (ISBN 0-13-021634-8). P-H.

Algebra for College Students. 2nd ed. Bernard Kolman & Arnold Shapiro. 1986. text ed. 23.00 o.p. (ISBN 0-12-417900-2); instr's manual 10.00 o.p. (ISBN 0-12-417901-0). Acad Pr.

Algebra for College Students. Michael G. Murphy & Kenneth E. Oberhoff. 390p. 1982. text ed. 18.50 o.p. (ISBN 0-15-502160-5, HC). HarBraceJ.

Algebra for the Practical Worker. J. E. Thompson. 288p. 1982. pap. 11.95 o.s.i. (ISBN 0-442-28273-7). Van Nos Reinhold.

Algebra: Its Elements & Structure, Bk. 1. 3rd rev. ed. Max A. Sobel & J. Houston Banks. (gr. 9). 1976. text ed. 28.88 o.p. (ISBN 0-07-059581-X). McGraw.

Algebra of Representations of Some Finite Groups. L. C. Biedenharn et al. (Rice University Studies: Vol. 54, No. 2). 68p. 1968. pap. 10.00x o.p. (ISBN 0-89263-196-1). Rice Univ.

Algebra Programmed, Pt. 2. 2nd ed. Robert H. Alwin & Robert D. Hackworth. (Illus.). 1978. pap. text ed. (ISBN 0-13-022020-5). P-H.

Algebra Programmed, Pt. 3. 2nd ed. Robert H. Alwin et al. 1980. pap. text ed. (ISBN 0-13-021931-2). P-H.

Algebra Programmed, Pt. 1. 2nd ed. Robert H. Alwin & Robert D. Hackworth. (Illus.). 1978. pap. text ed. (ISBN 0-13-022038-8). P-H.

Algebra Simplified & Self-Taught. David Frieder. LC 83-2843. 144p. (Orig.). 1983. pap. 5.95 o.p. (ISBN 0-668-05797-1, 5797). Arco.

Algebraic Analysis of Storage Fragmentation. Terry Betteridge. Ed. by Harold Stone. LC 82-11194. (Computer Science: Systems Programming Ser.: No. 15). 232p. 1983. 44.95 o.p. (ISBN 0-8357-1364-4). UMI Res Pr.

Algebraic & Geometric Topology: Proceedings of a Symposium Held at Santa Barbara in Honor of Raymond L. Wilder, July 25-29, 1977. Ed. by K. C. Millett. LC 78-15091. (Lecture Notes in Mathematics: Vol. 664). 1978. pap. 16.00 o.p. (ISBN 0-387-08920-9). Springer-Verlag.

Algebraic Coding Theory: History & Development. Ed. by Ian F. Blake. LC 73-9627. (Benchmark Papers in Electrical Engineering & Computer Science: Vol. 3). 413p. 1982. 54.95 o.p. (ISBN 0-87933-038-4). Van Nos Reinhold.

Algebraic Geometry: Proceedings: Summer Meeting, Copenhagen, August 7-12, 1978. Ed. by K. Lonsted. (Lecture Notes in Mathematics: Vol. 732). 1979. pap. 38.00 o.p. (ISBN 0-387-09527-6). Springer-Verlag.

Algebraic Geometry: Proceedings, Tromso Symposium, June 27-July 8,1977. Ed. by L. D. Olson. (Lecture Notes in Mathematics: Vol. 687). 1978. pap. 18.00 o.p. (ISBN 0-387-08954-3). Springer-Verlag.

Algebraic Introduction to Mathematical Logic. D. W. Barnes & J. M. Mack. LC 74-22241. (Graduate Texts in Mathematics Ser.: Vol. 22). (Illus.). 230p. 1975. 23.10 o.p. (ISBN 0-387-90109-4). Springer-Verlag.

Algebraic K-Theory. Ed. by M. R. Stein. (Lecture Notes in Mathematics Ser.: Vol. 551). 1977. soft cover 23.00 o.p. (ISBN 0-387-07996-3). Springer-Verlag.

Algebraic K-Theory 3: Hermitian K-Theory & Geometric Applications. Ed. by H. Bass. LC 73-13421. (Lecture Notes in Mathematics: Vol. 343). xv, 572p. 1973. pap. 27.00 o.p. (ISBN 0-387-06436-2). Springer-Verlag.

Algebraic Methods in Pattern Recognition: Proceedings of the CISM, Department of Automation & Information, Academy of Sciences, Warsaw, 1971. CISM (International Center for Mechanical Sciences), Department of Automation & Inforamation Staff. Ed. by J. Kulikowsky. (CISM Pubns. Ser.: No. 85). (Illus.). 82p. 1973. pap. 12.40 o.p. (ISBN 0-387-81128-1). Springer-Verlag.

Algebraic Number Field: L Functions & Galois Properties. Ed. by A. Frohlich. 1977. 120.00 o.p. (ISBN 0-12-268960-7). Acad Pr.

Algebraic Number Theory. Ed. by J. W. Cassels & A. Frohlich. 384p. 1976. 50.50 o.p. (ISBN 0-12-163250-4); pap. 34.50 o.p. (ISBN 0-12-163251-2). Acad Pr.

Algebraic Number Theory. I. N. Stewart & D. O. Tall. LC 78-31625. 200p. 1979. pap. 16.95x o.p. (ISBN 0-412-16000-5, NO.6273, Pub. by Chapman & Hall). Routledge Chapman & Hall.

Algebraic Number Theory. 2nd ed. Edwin Weiss LC 76-5803. xii, 275p. 1976. 19.95 o.p. (ISBN 0-8284-0293-0). Chelsea Pub.

Algebraic Spaces. D. Knutson. (Lecture Notes in Mathematics: Vol. 203). 1971. pap. 14.00 o.p. (ISBN 0-387-05496-0). Springer-Verlag.

Algebraic Theories. E. G. Manes. LC 75-11991. (Graduate Texts in Mathematics: Vol. 26). 374p. 1976. text ed. 36.00 o.p. (ISBN 0-387-90140-X). Springer-Verlag.

Algebraic Theory of Machines, Languages & Semigroups. Michael A. Arbib. LC 68-18654. 1968. 84.00 o.p. (ISBN 0-12-059050-6). Acad Pr.

Algebraic Topology-Homotopy & Homology. R. M. Switzer. (Grundlehren der Mathematischen Wissenschaften Ser.: Vol. 212). 526p. 1975. 74.00 o.p. (ISBN 0-387-06758-2). Springer-Verlag.

Algeria. David W. Mise. (World Education Ser.). (Illus.). 160p. (Orig.). 45.50 o.p. (ISBN 0-317-65049-1); xerographic 39.50 o.p. (ISBN 0-317-65050-5). Am Assn Coll Registrars.

Algeria, Mali, Morocco, & Tunisia see Surveys of African Economies.

Algic Researches: Comprising Inquiries Respecting the Mental Characteristics of the North American Indians. Henry Schoolcraft. LC 78-66498. (Classic Anthropology Ser.). 429p. Date not set. text ed. 80.00 o.p. (ISBN 0-8240-9642-8). Garland Pub.

ALGOL Sixty Compilation & Assessment. B. Wichmann. (Automatic Programming Information Centre Studies in Data Processing). 1974. 70.00 o.p. (ISBN 0-12-748250-4). Acad Pr.

Algonquian & Iroquois Crafts for You to Make. Jane D'Amato & Alex D'Amato. LC 79-15487. (Illus.). 96p. (gr. 3 up). 1979. lib. bdg. 10.79 o.s.i. (ISBN 0-671-32979-0). Messner.

Algorithms for Some Design Automation Problems. James P. Cohoon. Ed. by Harold Stone. LC 84-24101. (Computer Science: Computer Architecture & Design Ser.: No. 3). 113p. 1985. 34.95 o.p. (ISBN 0-8357-1615-5). UMI Res Pr.

Algrave Travel. Berlitz Editors. (Travel Guides Ser.). 1980. pap. 4.95 o.p. (ISBN 0-317-12095-6, Berlitz). Macmillan.

Alhambra. Oleg Grabar. 1978. 22.95x o.p. (ISBN 0-674-01556-8). Harvard U Pr.

Ali. Mary L. O'Neill. 1968. 3.95 o.p. (ISBN 0-689-20318-7, Atheneum). Macmillan.

Ali, a Persian Yankee. Maxine A. Miller. LC 65-18664. (Illus.). 247p. 1965. 4.95 o.p. (ISBN 0-87004-104-5). Caxton.

Ali Baba & the Forty Thieves. (Derrydale Fairytale Library). (Illus.). (ps-3). 1985. 2.98 o.s.i. (ISBN 0-517-28801-X). Outlet Bk Co.

Alias David Bowie. Peter Gillman & Leni Gillman. LC 86-33482. 1987. 19.95 o.p. (ISBN 0-8050-0390-8). H Holt & Co.

Alias the Saint. Leslie Charteris. (Saint Ser.). 160p. 1980. pap. 1.95 o.s.i. (ISBN 0-441-01350-3). Ace Bks.

Alibi of Guilt. Philip Daniels. 176p. 1986. pap. 2.95 o.p. (ISBN 0-931773-96-2). Critics Choice Paper.

Alice in Bibleland. George Wills. 1953. (ISBN 0-8022-1892-X). Philos Lib.

Alice in Wonderland see New Method Supplementary Readers: Bestseller Pack.

Alice in Wonderland: Through the Looking Glass. Lewis Carroll. (Classics Ser.). (Illus.). 346p. (gr. 2 up). 1984. Repr. of 1940 ed. Boxed Set. 25.00 o.p. (ISBN 0-88088-903-9, 889039). Peter Pauper.

Alice James: A Biography. Jean Strouse. 384p. 1980. 15.00 o.p. (ISBN 0-395-27787-6). HM.

Alice, Let's Eat: Further Adventures of a Happy Eater. Calvin Trillin. LC 79-11070. 1979. pap. 3.95 o.s.i. (ISBN 0-394-74171-4, Vin). Random.

Alice Trumbull Mason. Una Johnson. LC 85-50576. (Illus.). 60p. 1985. 12.50 o.s.i. (ISBN 0-8008-0160-1). Taplinger.

Alice's Adventures in Wonderland. Lewis Carroll. Bd. with Through the Looking Glass. LC 82-242973. (Reader's Request). 1980. PLB 10.95 o.p. (ISBN 0-8161-3070-1, Large Print Bks). G K Hall.

Alice's Adventures in Wonderland. Lewis Carroll. LC 82-242973. (Illus.). 160p. (gr. 3 up). 1985. 3.98 o.p. (ISBN 0-517-55591-3). Crown.

Alice's Adventures in Wonderland. Lewis Carroll. LC 82-242973. (Illus.). 120p. (gr. 4-6). 1985. 14.95 o.p. (ISBN 0-03-002037-9, Owl Bks). H Holt & Co.

Alice's Adventures in Wonderland & Through the Looking Glass. Lewis Carroll. Ed. by Wendy Barish. (Illus.). 256p. 1982. 14.50 o.s.i. (ISBN 0-671-43788-7). Wanderer Bks.

Alice's Adventures in Wonderland (Pennyroyal-California Edition) Lewis Carroll. LC 82-242973. (Illus.). 148p. (gr. 8 up). 1982. 29.95 o.p. (ISBN 0-520-04815-6); deluxe ed. 225.00 o.p. (ISBN 0-520-04820-2). U of Cal Pr.

Alice's Adventures Under Ground. Lewis Carroll. LC 85-80635. (Illus.). 1986. pap. 12.95 o.p. (ISBN 0-03-006113-X). H Holt & Co.

Alicia's Trump. Joseph Mathewson. 224p. 1980. pap. 2.25 o.p. (ISBN 0-380-76521-7, 76521). Avon.

Alien Encounter. Flanna Devin. 1981. pap. 1.95 o.p. (ISBN 0-8439-0898-X, Pub. by Leisure Bks CT). Dorchester Pub Co.

Alien Encounters. Ed. by Jan H. Finder. LC 81-50227. 256p. 1982. 11.95 o.s.i. (ISBN 0-8008-0168-7). Taplinger.

Alien Entities. Lester Sumrall. 232p. (Orig.). 1984. pap. 6.95 o.p. (ISBN 0-89274-320-4). Harrison Hse.

Alien Heat. Michael Moorcock. 1977. pap. 1.50 o.p. (ISBN 0-380-01749-0, 34611-7). Avon.

Alien Realms: Eight Excursions Beyond Human Space. Timothy B. Brown. (Traveler Ser.). (Illus.). 49p. (Orig.). 1986. pap. 7.00 o.p. (ISBN 0-943580-09-9). Game Designers.

Alien: The Movie Novel. Ed. by Richard J. Anobile. 1979. pap. 8.95 o.p. (ISBN 0-380-46631-7, 46631-7). Avon.

Alienation. Ian Everton. 210p. (Orig.). 1982. pap. 7.50 o.p. (ISBN 0-907040-10-1, Pub. by GMP England). Alyson Pubns.

Alienation & Authenticity. Brian Baxter. 240p. 1982. 35.00 o.p. (ISBN 0-422-78280-7, NO. 3708, Pub. by Tavistock). Routledge Chapman & Hall.

Alienation As a Concept in the Social Sciences: A Trend Report & Bibliography Prepared for the International Sociological Association Under the Auspices of the International Committee for Social Science Information & Documentation. Peter C. Ludz. (Current Sociology-la Sociologie Contemporaine: Vol. 21, No. 1). 1975. pap. 7.20x o.p. (ISBN 90-2797-841-7). Mouton.

Alienation: Concept, Term, & Meaning. Ed. by Frank A. Johnson. LC 72-7702. 1973. 41.00 o.p. (ISBN 0-12-785381-2). Acad Pr.

Alienation of Modern Man. Fritz Pappenheim. LC 59-15331. 1959. pap. 7.00 o.s.i. (ISBN 0-85345-005-6). Monthly Rev.

Alienation: Problems of Meaning, Theory, & Method. Ed. by Felix R. Geyer & David Schweitzer. 288p. 1981. 28.00x o.p. (ISBN 0-7100-0835-X). Routledge Chapman & Hall.

Alienation Theories: A General Systems Approach. R. F. Geyer. LC 79-42780. (Systems Science & World Library). 212p. 1980. 83.00 o.p. (ISBN 0-08-024298-7); pap. 37.00 o.p. (ISBN 0-08-024297-9). Pergamon.

Aliens among Us. Ruth Montgomery. LC 84-26565. 272p. 1985. 15.95 o.p. (ISBN 0-399-13065-9). Putnam Pub Group.

Alimentary Tract & Abdominal Wall (Colon, Rectum, & Anus, Pt. 3. 4th ed. Ian P. Todd & L. P. Fielding. (Operative Surgery Ser.). 672p. 1984. text ed. 114.95 o.p. (ISBN 0-8016-4407-0). Mosby.

Alinor. Roberta Gellis. (Roselynde Chronicles Ser.). 1984. lib. bdg. 13.95 o.p. (ISBN 0-8398-2861-6, Gregg). G K Hall.

Ali's Dream: The Story of Baha'u'llah. John Hatcher. (Illus.). 260p. 18.50 o.p. (ISBN 0-85398-092-6); pap. 8.95 o.p. (ISBN 0-85398-093-4). G Ronald Pub.

Alishar Huyuk, Seasons of 1928-1929, Pt. 2. Erich F. Schmidt. LC 30-14678. (Researches in Anatolia Ser: Vol. 5). 1933. 20.00x o.p. (ISBN 0-226-62116-2, OIP20). U of Chicago Pr.

Alistair in Outer Space. Marilyn Sadler. LC 84-4896. (Illus.). 48p. (gr. k-3). 1984. 12.95 o.s.i. (ISBN 0-13-022369-7). P-H.

Alistair's Elephant. Marilyn Sadler. LC 82-23091. (Illus.). 32p. (gr. k-3). 1983. 11.95 o.s.i. (ISBN 0-13-022756-0). P-H.

Alive & Taking Names. Colette Inez. LC 77-86351. 74p. 1977. 7.95x o.p. (ISBN 0-8214-0377-X); pap. 4.95 o.p. (ISBN 0-8214-0393-1, 82-82758). Ohio U Pr.

Alkali Metal, Alkaline-Earth Metal & Ammonium Halides in Amide Solvents. Ed. by Scrosati & Colin A. Vincent. (IUPAC Solubility Data Ser.: Vol. 11). 374p. 1980. 110.00 o.p. (ISBN 0-08-023917-X). Pergamon.

Alkali Metal Complexes with Organic Ligands. Ed. by J. D. Dunitz et al. LC 67-11280. (Structure & Bonding Ser.: Vol. 16). (Illus.). iii, 189p. 1973. pap. 40.00 o.p. (ISBN 0-387-06423-0). Springer-Verlag.

Alkali Metal Coolants: Proceedings. (Proceedings Ser.). (Illus.). 786p. 1967. pap. 50.25 o.p. (ISBN 0-686-93180-7, ISP143, IAEA). UNIPUB.

Alkali Metal Handling & Systems Operating Techniques. J. W. Mausteller. LC 67-26578. 241p. 1967. 12.00 o.p. (ISBN 0-685-58266-3, 450007). Am Nuclear Soc.

Alkaline Earth Metal Halates. Ed. by H. Miyamoto et al. 352p. 1983. 130.00 o.s.i. (ISBN 0-08-029213-5). Pergamon.

Alkaline Ring Complexes in Africa: Proceedings of the International Conference Held in Zaria, Nigeria, Dec. 6-10, 1983. Ed. by R. Black & P. Boden. 286p. 1985. pap. 51.00 o.p. (ISBN 0-08-032613-7, Pub by PPL). Pergamon.

Alkaloid Biology & Metabolism in Plants. G. R. Waller & E. K. Nowacki. LC 76-30903. (Illus.). 312p. 1978. 45.00x o.p. (ISBN 0-306-30981-5, Plenum Pr). Plenum Pub.

Alkan, the Enigma. Ronald Smith. 1977. 7.95 o.s.i. (ISBN 0-8008-0169-5, Crescendo). Taplinger.

Alkan: The Music, Vol. 2. Ronald Smith. (Illus.). 256p. 1987. 19.95 o.s.i. (ISBN 0-8008-0170-9, Crescendo). Taplinger.

All Aboard for Wales! Essye Price Flaten. (Illus.). (YA) (gr. 7 up). 1979. 5.00 o.p. (ISBN 0-682-49265-5). Exposition-Phoenix.
All About Adolescence. Charles G. Brook. LC 85-16936. 152p. 1985. pap. 14.00 o.p. (ISBN 0-471-90860-6, Dist. by A R Liss). Wiley.
All about Baseball. George Sullivan. (Illus.). 128p. (gr. 4 up). 1988. PLB 11.95 o.p. (ISBN 0-396-09326-4). Dodd.
All about Cats As Pets. Marjorie Zaum. LC 81-813. (Illus.). 96p. (gr. 3 up). 1981. lib. bdg. 9.29 o.p. (ISBN 0-671-33099-3). Messner.
All about Chess & Computers. David Levy & Monroe Newborn. LC 82-12497. (Computer Chess Ser.). 146p. 1982. pap. text ed. 23.95 o.p. (ISBN 0-914894-75-7, Computer Sci Pr). W H Freeman.
All about Dinosaurs. (Illus.). (gr. k-5). 1985. 2.98 o.s.i. (ISBN 0-517-47996-6). Outlet Bk Co.
All about Drugs & Alcohol: A Kid's Quiz. (Illus.). 1983. pap. 0.25 o.p. (ISBN 0-89230-148-1). Do it Now.
All about Geneva. Scott Charles. 261p. 1985. pap. 14.95 o.p. (ISBN 2-8257-0122-X, Pub. by Georg Switzerland). Bradt Ent.
All About Hands. Elizabeth E. Watson. LC 81-50676. (Happy Day Bks.). (Illus.). 24p. (Orig.). (ps-1). 1981. pap. 1.59 o.p. (ISBN 0-87239-460-3, 3593). Standard Pub.
All about Home Satellite Television. Rick Cook & Frank Vaughan. (Illus.). 336p. (Orig.). 1983. 19.95 o.p. (ISBN 0-8306-0519-3); pap. 13.15 o.p. (ISBN 0-8306-1519-9, 1519). TAB Bks.
All about Lawns. Michael R. MacCaskey. Ed. by Ortho Books Editorial Staff. LC 79-52995. (Illus.). 96p. 1980. pap. 5.95 ea. o.p. Midwest-Northeast Ed (ISBN 0-917102-83-5). Southern Ed (ISBN 0-917102-84-3). Western Ed (ISBN 0-917102-77-0). Ortho.
All about Letters. rev. ed. 64p. 1982. 2.50 o.p. (ISBN 0-8141-0113-5). NCTE.
All about Love. Henry V. Sattler. o.p. (ISBN 0-913631-03-5). Anastasia VA.
All about Love. Stirrup Associates, Inc. Staff. Ed. by Cheryl M. Phillips & Bonnie C. Harvey. LC 84-50915. (Child's Paraphrase Ser.). (Illus.). 32p. (ps). 1984. pap. 1.49 o.p. (ISBN 0-937420-16-6). Stirrup Assoc.
All about Mail Order: Facts, Trends, Key Data. Maxwell H. Sroge. 60p. 1987. perf. bd. 19.95 o.p. (ISBN 0-942674-05-7). Sroge M.
All About Me Books. rev. ed. Margaret W. Hudson. 1973. pap. 1.75x boys' ed. o.p. (ISBN 0-88323-000-3, 101); pap. 1.75x girls' ed. o.p. (ISBN 0-88323-001-1, 102). Pendergrass Pub.
All about Meat. Leon Lobel & Stanley Lobel. Ed. by Inez M. Krech. LC 77-3322. (Illus.). 1977. pap. 6.95 o.p. (ISBN 0-15-604600-8, Harv). HarBraceJ.
All About Medicare. Rev. ed. 63p. (Orig.). 1987. pap. 5.25 o.p. (ISBN 0-87218-451-X). Natl Underwriter.
All about Medicare. The National Underwriter Co. Staff & William W. Thomas, III. 64p. (Orig.). 1988. pap. 5.50 o.p. (ISBN 0-87218-460-9). Natl Underwriter.
All about Permanent Hair Removal. Sophie K. Horchem. LC 76-11436. 1976. pap. 5.00 o.p. (ISBN 0-8283-1671-6). Branden Pub Co.
All about Roses. Ed. by Ortho Books Staff. LC 76-29248. 1977. pap. 5.95 o.p. (ISBN 0-917102-23-1). Ortho.
All About Selected American Restaurants. Gen Saito. (Illus.). 300p. (Orig.). 1984. pap. 49.95 o.s.i. (ISBN 4-785-80080-1, Pub. by Shotenkenchiku-Sha Japan). Bks Nippan.
All About the Birds & Bees & Other Stinging Satire. Marion Sargent. 1979. 4.00 o.p. (ISBN 0-682-49279-5). Exposition-Phoenix.
All about the Commodore 64, Vol. 1. Craig Chamberlain. 237p. (Orig.). 1984. pap. 14.95 o.p. (ISBN 0-942386-40-X). Compute Pubns.
All about the Commodore 64, Vol. 2. Craig Chamberlain. Ed. by Compute! Publications, Inc. Staff. 491p. (Orig.). 1985. pap. 16.95 o.p. (ISBN 0-942386-45-0). Compute Pubns.
All about the Royal Family. Phoebe Hichens. 1983. pap. 7.95 o.p. (ISBN 0-380-64816-4, 64816). Avon.
All about the Telescope. P. Klushansev. 70p. 1981. 5.95 o.p. (ISBN 0-8285-1966-8, Pub. by Progress Pubs USSR). Imported Pubns.
All about Tomatoes. Walter Doty & A. Cort Sinnes. Ed. by Lammers Susan. LC 76-29249. (Illus.). 96p. (Orig.). 1981. pap. 6.95 o.p. (ISBN 0-917102-97-5). Ortho.
All about Toy Dogs. Date not set. (ISBN 0-87605-321-5). Howell Bk.
All about Your Money. Dan Fitzgibbon. LC 83-15608. (Illus.). 148p. (gr. 6 up). 1984. 11.95 o.s.i. (ISBN 0-689-31031-5, Atheneum Childrens Bks). Macmillan.
All American Chinese Cookbook. Lucy C. McHale & Joyce Goldberg. LC 80-15767. 144p. (Orig.). 1980. pap. 8.95 o.p. (ISBN 0-8437-3363-2). Hammond Inc.
All Animation. (Big Little Bks.: No. 76). (Illus.). 350p. 1984. 6.95 o.p. (ISBN 0-318-02712-7). Bks Nippan.
All Around the Farm. Alice Low. LC 83-62379. (Illus.). 16p. (gr. k-2). 1984. board 2.95 o.s.i. (ISBN 0-394-85955-3, BYR). Random.
All-Around-the-House Art & Craft Book. Patricia Z. Wirtenberg. (Illus.). (gr. 1 up). 1974. pap. 3.95 o.p. (ISBN 0-395-19974-3, Sandpiper). HM.
All-Around-The-House Art & Craft Book. Patricia Z. Wirtenberg. (gr. 5 up). 1974. 6.95 o.p. (ISBN 0-395-07209-3). HM.
All-Asia Guide. 14 ed. 704p. 1986. pap. 20.00 o.p. (ISBN 962-7010-25-1, Pub. by FER). Taylor & Francis.
All Because of Jill. Teri Martini. LC 75-44167. 154p. (gr. 7-9). 1976. 6.95 o.s.i. (ISBN 0-664-32589-0, Westminster). Westminster John Knox.
All but Impossible! An Anthology of Locked Room & Impossible Crime Stories. Mystery Writers of America Members. Ed. by Edward D. Hoch. LC 81-8718. (Joan Kahn Bk). 372p. 1981. 14.95 o.p. (ISBN 0-89919-045-6). Ticknor & Fields.
All Change. Sheila Groves & Gordon Stowell. (Tortoise Tales Ser.). (Orig.). (ps-2). 1981. pap. 0.79 o.p. (ISBN 0-8010-3773-5). Baker Bk.
All Clear: An Everyday Guide to Total Skin Care. Treila Krueger. LC 84-12502. (Illus.). 180p. (Orig.). 1984. pap. 8.95 o.p. (ISBN 0-932620-39-6). Betterway Pubns.
All Color Book of the Body. P-H.
All Color Book of the Earth. P-H.
All-Color Encyclopedia of International Cooking. LC 88-2681. (Illus.). 400p. 1988. 34.95 o.p. (ISBN 0-89535-207-9). Knapp Pr.
All Drawn by Horses. James Arnold. LC 79-51087. (Illus.). 1985. 30.95 o.s.i. (ISBN 0-7153-7682-9). David & Charles.
All Dreams Never Die. James C. Conant. 1977. 4.50 o.p. (ISBN 0-682-48920-4). Exposition-Phoenix.
All Ends Up. Gina Wilson. LC 83-25300. 160p. (gr. 6 up). 1984. 13.95 o.p. (ISBN 0-571-13196-4). Faber & Faber.
All Fall Down. James L. Herlihy. 1977. pap. 1.75 o.p. (ISBN 0-380-01707-5, 33829). Avon.
All Fifty-Two Cards: How to Reconstruct the Concealed Hands at the Bridge Table. rev. ed. Marshall Miles. (Illus.). 176p. 1982. pap. 6.95 o.p. (ISBN 0-682-49897-1, Banner). Exposition-Phoenix.
All for Love. Patricia Gallagher. 400p. 1983. pap. 2.95 o.p. (ISBN 0-380-77818-1, 83816-8). Avon.
All Four Engines Have Failed: Flight BA 009 & the "Jakarta Incident" Betty Tootell. (Illus.). 192p. 1985. 20.95 o.p. (ISBN 0-233-97758-9, Pub. by A Deutsch England). David & Charles.
All God's Children. Arthur Lyons. LC 82-2931. 224p. 1982. pap. 3.95 o.p. (ISBN 0-03-060394-3, Owl Bks). H Holt & Co.
All Hands Aboard Scrimshawing. Marius Barbeau. (Illus.). 1973. pap. 4.95 o.p. (ISBN 0-87577-030-4). Peabody Mus Salem.
All in an African Lifetime. Wilfred Grenville-Grey. (Orig.). 1971. pap. 1.50 o.p. (ISBN 0-377-11221-6). Friendship Pr.
All in Good Time. Edward Ormondroyd. LC 75-1688. (Illus.). 208p. (gr. 4-7). 1975. 7.95 o.p. (ISBN 0-395-27697-7, Pub. by Parnassus). HM.
All in the Day's Work. Ida M. Tarbell. (Non-Fiction Ser.). (Illus.). 412p. 1985. pap. 8.95 o.p. (ISBN 0-8398-2881-0, Gregg). G K Hall.
All in the Family: Animal Species Around the World. Gilda Berger. (Science Is What & Why Bk.). (Illus.). 48p. (gr. 7-10). 1981. PLB 6.99 o.p. (ISBN 0-698-30730-5, Coward). Putnam Pub Group.
All Italy: The Book of Everything Italian. Ed. by Francesca Manisco. LC 86-42765. (Illus.). 208p. 1986. 35.00 o.p. (ISBN 0-89471-385-X); pap. 14.95 o.p. (ISBN 0-89471-386-8). Running Pr.
All Japan: The Catalogue of Everything Japanese. Oliver Statler. 1984. pap. 15.95 o.p. (Quill). Morrow.
All Maine All Poultry Cookbook. Ed. by Loana Shibles & Annie Rogers. LC 76-52261. (All Maine Cooking Ser.). (Illus.). 184p. 1977. pap. 3.95 o.p. (ISBN 0-89272-091-3, 458). Down East.
All Monsters & Heroes. (Big Little Bks.: No. 1). (Illus.). 350p. 1984. 6.95 o.p. (ISBN 0-318-02684-8). Bks Nippan.
All My Patients Are under the Bed. Louis J. Camuti. 1980. 14.50 o.s.i. (ISBN 0-671-24271-7). S&S.
All My Pretty Ones. Anne Sexton. 1973. pap. 3.95 o.p. (ISBN 0-395-08177-7). HM.
All New Best of the Mini Page. Betty Debnam. LC 82-71458. (Illus.). 144p. (ps-6). 1982. pap. text ed. 7.95 o.p. (ISBN 0-8362-4210-6). Andrews & McMeel.
All New Complete Book of Bicycling. rev. ed. Eugene A. Sloane. (Illus.). 1981. 19.95 o.s.i. (ISBN 0-671-24967-3). S&S.
All New Complete Book of Bicycling. rev. ed. Eugene A. Sloane. (Illus.). 736p. 1983. pap. 13.95 o.s.i. (ISBN 0-671-49430-9, Fireside). S&S.
All Our Children: The American Family Under Pressure. Kenneth Keniston & Carnegie Council on Children Staff. LC 77-74800. (Illus.). 1977. 10.95 o.p. (ISBN 0-15-104611-5). HarBraceJ.
All Our Secrets Are the Same: New Fiction from Esquire. Ed. by Gordon Lish. 1977. pap. 6.95 o.p. (ISBN 0-393-08748-4). Norton.
All Our Tomorrows. Patricia Boatner. 384p. 1988. pap. 3.95 o.p. (ISBN 0-380-75020-1). Avon.
All Our Yesterdays. Stuart Buchan. (gr. 6 up). 1987. pap. 2.25 o.p. (ISBN 0-373-98006-X). Harlequin Bks.
All Over. Edward Albee. LC 71-162965. 1971. 5.95 o.p. (ISBN 0-689-10425-1, Atheneum). Macmillan.
All People Are Famous. Harold Clurman. LC 74-13820. (Illus.). 327p. 1974. 8.95 o.p. (ISBN 0-15-104775-8). HarBraceJ.
All Quiet on the Western Front. Erich M. Remarque. 48p. (Orig.). 1989. pap. 9.95 o.p. (ISBN 1-55651-008-X); audiocassette tape incl. o.p. (ISBN 1-55651-009-8). Cram Cassettes.
All Sail Set: A Romance of the Flying Cloud. Armstrong Sperry. LC 84-47650. (Illus.). 192p. (gr. 4 up). pap. 8.95 o.s.i. (ISBN 0-87923-523-3). Godine.
All Signs Rising. Elbert Wade. 74p. 1984. 5.95 o.p. (ISBN 0-317-66051-9, 2555-01). Am Fed Astrologers.
All Six Career Directories. pap. 144.95 o.p. (ISBN 0-934829-38-1). Career Pr Inc.
All Six Career Directories. text ed. 184.95 o.p. (ISBN 0-934829-46-2). Career Pr Inc.
All-Stars: All Star Baseball Book. Nick Acocella & Donald Dewey. 304p. 1986. pap. 3.95 o.p. (ISBN 0-380-89879-9). Avon.
All Suite Hotels. Pamela Lanier. 1987. pap. 11.95 o.p. (ISBN 0-912528-70-2). John Muir.
All That Glitters & the Shadowed Chase. Chuck Mongomery. cancelled o.s.i. Dragon Tree.
All That Is Solid Melts into Air. Marshall Berman. 1983. pap. 6.75 o.p. (ISBN 0-671-45700-4, Touchstone Bks). S&S.
All That Is Solid Melts into Air: The Experience of Modernity. Marshall Berman. LC 81-16640. 1982. 16.95 o.p. (ISBN 0-671-24602-X). S&S.
All That Jazz & More: The Complete Book of Jazz Dancing. Christy Lane. LC 82-83944. (Illus.). 240p. (Orig.). 1983. pap. 21.95 o.s.i. (ISBN 0-88011-124-0, 0124). Leisure Pr.
All That Money & No Cash. Donald L. Clugston. (Illus.). 128p. 1981. 7.50 o.s.i. (ISBN 0-682-49678-2). Exposition-Phoenix.
All the Answers to All Your Questions About Training Pointing Dogs. Paul Long. LC 74-81251. (Illus.). 85p. 1974. pap. 5.95 o.p. (ISBN 0-9601034-1-4). Lyons & Burford.
All the Cats in the World. Sonia Levitin. LC 81-20036. (Illus.). 32p. (ps-3). 1982. 14.95 o.p. (ISBN 0-15-202396-8, HJ). HarBraceJ.
All: The Collected Short Poems, 1923-1958. Louis Zukofsky. 1965. 6.00 o.p. (ISBN 0-393-04197-2). Norton.
All the Colors of Darkness. Lloyd Biggle, Jr. 1975. pap. 1.25 o.p. (ISBN 0-685-54123-1, LB2956K, Pub. by Leisure Bks CT). Dorchester Pub Co.
All the Desk's a Stage. Drina Kay. LC 81-83806. 144p. (gr. 1-6). 1982. pap. text ed. 5.95 o.p. (ISBN 0-86530-003-8, IP-038). Incentive Pubns.
All the Divine Names & Titles in the Bible. Herbert Lockyer. 308p. 1975. 17.95 o.p. (ISBN 0-310-28040-0, 10077). Zondervan.
All the Fathers: The Fein Family Story. Howard Portnoy. LC 85-40719. (Illus.). 352p. 1944. 18.45 o.p. (ISBN 0-394-54915-5, Pub. by Villard Bks). Random.
All the Games Kids Like. rev. ed. Dianne S. Barad. 229p. 1983. pap. text ed. 24.95 o.p. (ISBN 0-88450-876-5, 7013-B). Communication Skill.
All the Happy Families: Exploring the Varieties of Family Life. P. Bohannan. 224p. 1985. text ed. 16.95 o.p. (ISBN 0-07-006432-6). McGraw.
All the Justice I Could Afford. Eugene B. Goodman. Ed. by Howard E. Sandum. LC 82-22300. 272p. 1983. 16.95 o.p. (ISBN 0-15-104778-2). HarBraceJ.
All the Little Bunnies. Elizabeth Bridgman. LC 76-28815. 48p. (ps-2). 1977. 5.95 o.p. (ISBN 0-689-50068-8, Atheneumn). Macmillan.
All the Lonely People: Life in a Single Room Occupancy Hotel. Robert Hamburger. LC 82-19128. 352p. 1983. 15,45 o.p. (ISBN 0-89919-159-2). Ticknor & Fields.
All The Olympians: A Biographical Portrait of the Irish Literary Renaissance. Ulick O'Connor. (Illus.). 292p. 1984. 18.95 o.s.i. (ISBN 0-689-11490-7, Atheneum). Macmillan.
All the President's Men. Bob Woodward & Carl Bernstein. 1974. 12.95 o.s.i. (ISBN 0-671-21781-X). S&S.
All the Presidents Plus: An Insight into Moments of History Through Biorhythms. August W. Schara. (Illus.). 1978. 9.50 o.p. (ISBN 0-682-48872-0). Exposition-Phoenix.
All the Pretty Horses. Susan Jeffers. 1985. pap. 2.50 o.p. (ISBN 0-590-33629-0). Scholastic Inc.
All the Sky Together. Florence E. Randall. LC 83-2604. 240p. (gr. 5-9). 1983. 11.95 o.s.i. (ISBN 0-689-30996-1, Atheneum Childrens Bks). Macmillan.
All the Strange Hours: The Excavation of a Life. Loren Eiseley. LC 75-22433. 1975. pap. 8.95 o.s.i. (ISBN 0-684-14868-4, SL690, ScribT). Scribner.
All the Summer Voices. Barbara Corcoran. LC 73-76316. (Illus.). 208p. (gr. 5-9). 1973. 6.25 o.p. (ISBN 0-689-30107-3, Atheneum). Macmillan.
All the World Is Kin. Bernice E. Hicks. LC 82-2086. (Illus.). 224p. 1982. 13.95 o.p. (ISBN 0-87961-116-2); pap. 7.95 o.p. (ISBN 0-87961-117-0). Naturegraph.
All These Lutherans: Three Paths Toward a New Lutheran Church. Todd Nichol. LC 86-3638. (Illus.). 128p. (Orig.). 1986. pap. 6.95 o.p. (ISBN 0-8066-2208-3, 10-0228, Augsburg). Augsburg Fortress.
All These to Teach: Essays in Honor of C. A. Robertson. Ed. by Robert A. Bryan et al. LC 65-23168. 1965. 6.50 o.p. (ISBN 0-8130-0030-0). U Presses Fla.
All Things Wise & Wonderful. Pasadena Art Alliance Staff. 1975. pap. 5.95 o.p. (ISBN 0-937042-00-5). Pasadena Art.
All This Is Ended: The Life & Times of Her Highness Begum Sumroo. Vera Chatterjee. 1979. 12.50x o.p. (ISBN 0-7069-0719-1, Pub. by Vikas India). Advent NY.
All Those Girls in Love with Horses. Robert Vavra. LC 81-82876. (Illus.). 240p. 1981. 39.95 o.p. (ISBN 0-688-00649-3). Morrow.
All Those Tomorrows: An Autobiography. Mai Zetterling. (Illus.). 256p. 1986. Repr. of 1985 ed. 16.95 o.p. (ISBN 0-394-55602-X). Grove.
All Through the Town. Alice Low. LC 83-62378. (Illus.). 16p. (gr. k-2). 1984. board 2.95 o.s.i. (ISBN 0-394-85954-5, BYR). Random.
All-Time All-Star Baseball Book. Bart Acocella et al. 368p. 1985. pap. 3.95 o.p. (ISBN 0-380-89530-7). Avon.
All Time All Stars. Ed. by Tom Murray. LC 76-53400. 1977. 9.95 o.p. (ISBN 0-689-10791-9, Atheneum). Macmillan.
All Too Soon. Andrea Edwards. 368p. 1985. pap. 3.50 o.p. (ISBN 0-380-89512-9). Avon.
All Trivia. Smith. 1945. 2.75 o.p. (ISBN 0-15-105046-5). HarBraceJ.
All Trivia. Logan P. Smith. LC 84-19. 216p. 1984. 7.70 o.p. (ISBN 0-89919-285-8). Ticknor & Fields.
All-Valence Electrons S. C. F. Calculations. F. Boschke & O. Leary. LC 51-5497. (Topics in Current Chemistry: Vol. 15, Pt. 4). (Illus.). 1970. pap. 27.20 o.p. (ISBN 0-387-05102-3). Springer-Verlag.
Allart van Everdingen. Alice I. Davies. LC 77-94692. (Outstanding Dissertations in the Fine Arts Ser.). 1978. lib. bdg. 77.00 o.p. (ISBN 0-8240-3223-3). Garland Pub.
Alleged Discrepancies of the Bible. John W. Haley. (Direction Bks.). 1977. pap. 7.95 o.p. (ISBN 0-8010-4171-6). Baker Bk.
Allegoresis: The Craft of Allegory in Medieval Literature. Russell J. Stephen. (Reference Library of the Humanities). 246p. 1988. lib. bdg. 33.00 o.p. Garland Pub.
Allegories of the Virtues & Vices in Medieval Art. Adolf Katzenellenbogen. (Warburg Institute Studies: Vol. 10). Repr. of 1939 ed. 32.00 o.p. (ISBN 0-8115-1388-2). Kraus Repr.
Allegory. John MacQueen. (Critical Idiom Ser.: Vol. 14). 1970. pap. 5.50x o.p. (ISBN 0-416-08050-2, NO.2347). Routledge Chapman & Hall.
Allegory & Mirror: Tradition & Structure in Middle English Literature. James I. Wimsatt. LC 71-101376. 1970. 26.50x o.p. (ISBN 0-672-63502-X). Irvington.
Allen-Barker-Hines Peripheral Vascular Diseases. 5th ed. John L. Juergens et al. LC 78-65379. (Illus.). 981p. 1980. text ed. write for info. o.p. (ISBN 0-7216-5229-8). Saunders.
Allen Lane: King Penguin. Jack Morpurgo. 320p. 1980. 25.00 o.p. (ISBN 0-09-139690-5, NO.0218, Pub. by Hutchinson England). Routledge Chapman & Hall.
Allende Years: A List of Chilean Imprints in Selected U. S. Libraries, 1970-1973. Latin American Collection, Yale University Staff. 1977. lib. bdg. 27.00 o.p. (ISBN 0-8161-7972-7, Hall Reference). G K Hall.
Allergies & You. Shelia L. Burns. LC 79-26637. (Illus.). 64p. (gr. 4 up). 1980. lib. bdg. 9.29 o.p. (ISBN 0-671-33044-6). Messner.
Allergy. M. H. Lessof. LC 84-5243. 474p. 1984. 55.00 o.p. (ISBN 0-471-90479-1). Wiley.

Allergy Encyclopedia. Ed. by Craig T. Norback & Asthma & Allergy Foundation of America Staff. (Mosby Medical Library). 256p. 1982. pap. 7.95 o.p. (ISBN 0-8016-3717-1). Mosby.

Allergy: Immunological & Clinical Aspects. 2nd ed. M. H. Lessof et al. 1987. (ISBN 0-471-90927-0). Wiley.

Allergy: Principles & Practice, Vols. I & II. 2nd ed. Ed. by Elliott Middleton, Jr. et al. (Illus.). 1760p. 1983. 160.00 o.p. (ISBN 0-8016-3482-2). Mosby.

Alley Cat. Yves Beauchemin. Tr. by Sheila Fischman. 464p. 1986. 17.95 o.p. (ISBN 0-8050-0157-3). H Holt & Co.

Alley Oop! Marianna Mayer. LC 84-15730. (Illus.). 32p. (ps-2). 1985. 7.95 o.p. (ISBN 0-03-070496-0). H Holt & Co.

Alliance. Gerald N. Lund. LC 83-14359. 329p. 1983. 11.95 o.p. (ISBN 0-87747-982-8). Deseret Bk.

Alliance: America, Europe, Japan-Makers of the Post-War World. Richard J. Barnet. (Illus.). 544p. 1983. 19.25 o.p. (ISBN 0-671-42502-1). S&S.

Alliance: America, Europe, Japan-Makers of the Postwar World. Richard J. Barnet. 528p. 1985. pap. 10.95 o.p. (ISBN 0-671-54184-6, Touchstone Bks). S&S.

Allied Health Education Directory. 16th ed. American Medical Association Staff. LC 79-644041. 313p. 1988. pap. 27.95 o.s.i. (ISBN 0-89970-312-7, OP220-8). AMA.

Allied Health Education Directory. 15th ed. Ed. by William R. Burrows & Hannah H. Hedrick. LC 79-644041. x, 300p. 1987. 25.95 o.p. (ISBN 0-89970-270-8, OP-220-7). AMA.

Allied Health Education in Michigan: Labor Market Information for Counselors & Administrators. Rodger Lawson. 141p. 1973. pap. 2.75 o.p. (ISBN 0-911558-51-9). W E Upjohn.

Allied Health Professions Admission Test (AHPAT) Practice Examination Number 4 - Annotated Answers. David M. Tarlow. 20p. 1986. pap. 4.95 o.p. Datar Pub.

Allied Health Professions Admissions Test. Donald E. Taylor. LC 84-348. 208p. (Orig.). 1984. pap. 12.95 o.p. (ISBN 0-668-05816-1). Arco.

Allied Occupation of Japan 1945-1952 & Japanese Religions. W. P. Woodard. (Illus.). 1972. 40.00 o.p. (ISBN 0-88431-002-7). E J Brill USA.

Allied Tanks Italy, World War II. Bryan Perrett. (Tanks Illustrated Ser.: No. 20). (Illus.). 64p. (Orig.). 1986. pap. 9.95 o.p. (ISBN 0-85368-780-3, Pub. by Arms & Armour). Sterling.

Allied Tanks North Africa, World War II. Bryan Perrett. (Tanks Illustrated Ser.: No. 21). (Illus.). 64p. (Orig.). 1986. pap. 9.95 o.p. (ISBN 0-85368-775-7, Pub. by Arms & Armour). Sterling.

Alligator Pie. Dennis Lee. (Illus.). 64p. (gr. k-3). 1975. 6.95 o.p. (ISBN 0-395-21596-X). HM.

Alligator's Song. Robert Tallon. LC 80-19522. (Illus.). 48p. (ps-3). 1981. 5.95 o.s.i. (ISBN 0-8193-1043-3); PLB 5.95 o.s.i. (ISBN 0-8193-1044-1). Parents.

Allistar: Journey Through a Mind. Kurt W. Aigner. LC 84-90092. 101p. 1985. 8.95 o.p. (ISBN 0-533-06159-8). Vantage.

Alliterative Morte Arthure: A Reassessment of the Poem. Ed. by Karl H. Goller. (Arthurian Studies: II). 186p. 1981. 45.00 o.p. (ISBN 0-85991-075-X, Pub. by Boydell & Brewer). Longwood Pub Group.

Alloy & Microstructural Design. Ed. by John K. Tien et al. 1976. 91.50 o.p. (ISBN 0-12-690850-8). Acad Pr.

Allure. Cheryl Durant. 272p. 1988. pap. 3.95 o.p. (ISBN 0-380-75009-0). Avon.

Allusions Cultural, Literary, Biblical, & Historical: A Thematic Dictionary. Ed. by Laurance Urdang. 1982. 70.00x o.p. (ISBN 0-8103-1124-0). Gale.

Allyn & Bacon Transparencies for Management. 1987. (ISBN 0-205-10537-8). Allyn.

Alma-Ata: A Guide. I. Malyar. 62p. 1983. 6.95 o.p. (ISBN 0-8285-2626-5, Pub. by Raduga Pubs USSR). Imported Pubns.

Alma Mahler: Muse to Genius. Karen Monson. 1983. 18.45 o.p. (ISBN 0-395-32213-8). HM.

Alma Tadema's Spring. rev. ed. Burton B. Fredericksen. LC 78-78201. (Illus.). 32p. 1979. pap. 5.00 o.p. (ISBN 0-89236-013-5). J P Getty Trust.

Almanac & Traveler's Guide to Lotteries. Ed. by Lottery Player's Magazine Staff. (LOMAP Ser.: Vol. 2). (Illus.). 250p. 1987. pap. 14.95 o.p. (ISBN 0-936918-05-5). Intergalactic NJ.

Almanac for Computers, 1987. 11th ed. LeRoy Doggett & Helena I. Guertler. 101p. (Orig.). 1986. pap. 4.75 o.p. (ISBN 0-318-21650-7, S/N 008-054-00127-1). USGPO.

Almanac for Music Lovers. Elizabeth C. Moore. LC 70-167078. (Tower Bks). xiv, 606p. 1972. Repr. of 1940 ed. 48.00x o.p. (ISBN 0-8103-3940-4). Gale.

Almanac of American Letters. Randy F. Nelson. LC 80-27571. (Illus.). 341p. (Orig.). 1981. 16.95x o.p. (ISBN 0-86576-018-7); pap. 9.95 o.p. (ISBN 0-86576-008-X). W Kaufmann.

Almanac of Dates. Linda Millgate. LC 76-27408. 1977. pap. 8.95 o.p. (ISBN 0-15-145773-5, Harv). HarBraceJ.

Almanac of Words at Play. Willard R. Espy. (Illus.). pap. 7.95 o.s.i. (ISBN 0-317-60344-2). Crown.

Almanac, 1981. 1981. 7.95 o.s.i. RWCPH.

Almanac, 1985. 1985. 7.95 o.s.i. RWCPH.

Almanac, 1986. 1986. 8.95 o.s.i. RWCPH.

Almanac, 1988. 1988. write for info. o.s.i. RWCPH.

Almond Blossom Fairy. Fay Marden. LC 86-20667. (Flower Fairy Story Bks.). (Illus.). 24p. (gr. k-3). 1987. 7.95 o.p. (ISBN 0-87226-140-9). P Bedrick Bks.

Almoran & Hamet: An Oriental Tale 1761, 2 vols. in 1. John Hawkesworth. Ed. by Michael F. Shugrue. (Flowering of the Novel, 1740-1775 Ser: Vol. 57). 1975. lib. bdg. 61.00 o.p. (ISBN 0-8240-1156-2). Garland Pub.

Almost a Famous Person. Herb Michelson. LC 79-2766. 1980. 9.95 o.p. (ISBN 0-15-105069-4). HarBraceJ.

Almost Chosen People see Lincoln's Religion.

Almost Compleat Angler. Timothy Benn. 96p. 1986. 20.00 o.p. (ISBN 0-575-03713-X). Lyons & Burford.

Almost Dark. Charlie McDade. LC 84-9037. 368p. 1983. 14.95 o.p. (ISBN 0-15-105071-6). HarBraceJ.

Almost Everyone's Guide to Economics. John Kenneth Galbraith & Nicole Salinger. 1978. 8.95 o.p. (ISBN 0-395-27117-7). HM.

Almost Everywhere: Odysseys to Unusual Places. Wilbur M. Rabinowitz. (Illus.). 1985. 19.95 o.p. (ISBN 0-682-40222-2). Exposition-Phoenix.

Almost Famous. David Small. 1983. pap. 4.50 o.p. (ISBN 0-380-65722-8, 65722, Bard). Avon.

Almost Grown: A Christian Guide for Parents of Teenagers. James Oraker & Char Meredith. LC 78-20585. 192p. 1982. pap. 6.95 o.p. (ISBN 0-06-066398-7, RD 380). HarpR.

Almost Innocent. Sheila Bosworth. LC 85-11990. 320p. 1984. 16.45 o.s.i. (ISBN 0-671-50365-0). S&S.

Almost Midnight: The Story of a Powerful, Black Religious Leader Told by the Women Who Loved Him. Don Belton. LC 85-30753. 224p. 1986. 14.95 o.p. (ISBN 0-688-06342-X, Pub. by Beech Tree Bks). Morrow.

Almost Murder. Raymond Hughes. 1979. 8.00 o.p. (ISBN 0-682-49437-2). Exposition-Phoenix.

Almost Periodic Differential Equations. A. M. Fink. (Lecture Notes in Mathematics: Vol. 377). viii, 336p. 1974. pap. 23.00 o.p. (ISBN 0-387-06729-9). Springer-Verlag.

Almost-Periodic Functions & Functional Equations. G. Prouse & L. Amerio. LC 72-112713. viii, 183p. 1971. 24.00 o.p. (ISBN 0-387-90119-1). Springer-Verlag.

Almost Twelve. Kenneth N. Taylor. 59p. 1968. pap. 2.95 o.s.i. (ISBN 0-8423-0060-0). Tyndale.

Almost Year. Florence E. Randall. (Illus.). (gr. 5-9). 1971. 5.95 o.p. (ISBN 0-689-20652-6, Atheneum). Macmillan.

Almuerzo en la Hierba. Arcadio Diaz Quinones. LC 81-68088. (Nave Y El Puerto Ser.). 174p. (Span.). 1982. pap. 6.95 o.p. (ISBN 0-940238-42-X). Ediciones Huracan.

Alone. Daniel Gillis. (Illus.). 1978. 8.95 o.p. (ISBN 0-393-03217-5). Norton.

Alone Again. Richard Krebs. LC 77-84085. 1978. 7.95 o.p. (ISBN 0-8066-1610-5, 10-0241, Augsburg); pap. 6.95 o.p. (ISBN 0-8066-1611-3, 10-0240). Augsburg Fortress.

Alone & Beginning Again. Nancy K. Johnson. 128p. 1982. pap. 6.95 o.p. (ISBN 0-8170-0951-5). Judson.

Alone in the Valley. Kenneth W. Baker. 280p. 1987. text ed. 18.95 o.s.i. (ISBN 0-317-58718-8). Exposition-Phoenix.

Alone, Unarmed, but Safe! An Illustrated Guide to Judo Defense. Buddy Clark & Craig Davis. (Illus.). 128p. 1981. 8.00 o.p. (ISBN 0-682-49712-6); pap. 5.00 o.p. (ISBN 0-682-49711-8). Exposition-Phoenix.

Alone with Others. Stephen Batchelor. Ed. by Hannelore Rosset. LC 82-21054. (Grove Press Eastern Philosophy & Religion Ser.). 144p. 1983. pap. 8.95 o.p. (ISBN 0-394-62457-2, E843, Ever). Grove.

Along a Dark Path. Velda Johnston. 303p. 1987. lib. bdg. 14.95x o.p. (ISBN 0-8161-4035-9, Large Print Bks). G K hall.

Along Came the Witch: A Journal of the 1960's. Helen Bevington. LC 75-31653. 216p. 1976. 8.95 o.p. (ISBN 0-15-105080-5). HarBraceJ.

Along the Great Rivers. Gordon Cooper. 160p. 1953. (ISBN 0-8022-0296-9). Philos Lib.

Along the Number Twenty Line: Reminiscences of the Vancouver Waterfront. Rolf Knight. (Illus.). 231p. 1980. pap. 6.50 o.p. (ISBN 0-919888-25-9). Left Bank.

Along the Shore. Elizabeth F. Weidner. (Illus.). 64p. 1985. 6.00 o.p. (ISBN 0-682-40239-7). Exposition-Phoenix.

Along Wit's Trail: The Humor & Wisdom of Ronald Reagan. Ed. by L. William Troxler. 1984. pap. 5.95 o.p. (ISBN 0-03-072019-2, Owl Bks). H Holt & Co.

Alongside Night. J. Neil Schulman. 256p. 1987. pap. 3.50 o.p. (ISBN 0-380-75281-6). Avon.

Alpha & the Dirty Baby. Brock Cole. (Illus.). (ps-12). 1988. 13.95 o.p. (ISBN 0-374-30241-3). FS&G.

Alpha-Andrenoceptor Blockers in Cardiovascular Disease. Ed. by Helge Refsum & Ole D. Mjos. LC 84-23307. (Illus.). 328p. 1985. text ed. 79.50 o.p. (ISBN 0-443-03334-X). Churchill.

Alpha Brain Waves. Jodi Lawrence. 1972. pap. 1.75 o.p. (ISBN 0-380-01014-3, 27839). Avon.

Alpha Centauri. Robert Siegel. LC 82-70916. 256p. 1981. pap. 5.95 o.p. (ISBN 0-89107-242-X, Crossway Bks). Good News.

Alpha List. Ted Allbeury. 228p. 1979. 9.95 o.p. (ISBN 0-416-00771-6, NO.0197). Routledge Chapman & Hall.

Alphabet. David Diringer. 1958. (ISBN 0-8022-0401-5). Philos Lib.

Alphabet & Elements of Lettering. rev. ed. Frederic W. Goudy. 13.50 o.p. (ISBN 0-8446-2145-5). Peter Smith.

Alphabet Book of Feelings. Maria Valeri. 1984. 4.95 o.p. (ISBN 0-533-05743-4). Vantage.

Alphabet for Young Eckists. Jean Lucchese. (Illus.). 30p. (gr. k-1). 1984. pap. 4.95 o.p. (ISBN 0-88155-033-7, 0270). Illum Way Pub.

Alphabet Is Fun. S. V. Kologrivova & T. S. Zalmanova. 111p. 1986. pap. 7.95 o.p. (ISBN 0-8285-3025-4, Pub. by Rus Lang Pubs USSR). Imported Pubns.

Alphabet of Beauty & Other Poems. Harriet R. Stimson. 1979. pap. 4.00 o.p. (ISBN 0-682-49442-9). Exposition-Phoenix.

Alphabet of Creation. Date not set. pap. (ISBN 0-8052-0359-1). Random.

Alphabet of God. Nora E. Larson. LC 81-66071. (Illus.). 56p. (Orig.). (gr. 1-4). 1981. pap. 4.00 o.p. (ISBN 0-87516-450-1). DeVorss.

Alphabetic As a Science. Walter Durfee. 1957. Philos Lib.

Alphabetical Arrangement of Main Entries from the Shelf List of the Union Theological Seminary Library, 10 Vols. Union Theological Seminar Library Staff. 1960. Set. 1415.00 o.p. (ISBN 0-8161-0595-2, Hall Library). G K Hall.

Alphabetical Catalog of the Books & Pamphlets of the International Institute of Social History: Library Catalogs-Bibliography Guides 2nd Supplement. International Institute of Social History, Amstersdam Staff. 1979. lib. bdg. 410.00 o.p. (ISBN 0-8161-0297-X, Hall Library). G K Hall.

Alphabetical Order & Donkeys' Years. Michael Frayn. 165p. 1977. pap. 6.95 o.p. (ISBN 0-413-37990-6, NO.3003). Heinemann Ed.

Alphabetischer Katalog der Bibliothek des Johann Gottfried Herder-Instituts: Second Supplement. Herder, Johann Gottfried Institut Staff. 1981. lib. bdg. 365.00 o.p. (ISBN 0-8161-0277-5, Hall Library). G K Hall.

Alphabetischer Katalog der Bibliothek, 5 Vols. Herder, Johann Gottfried Institut Staff. 1964. Set. lib. bdg. 495.00 o.p. (ISBN 0-8161-0698-3, Hall Library); First Suppl. 1971. 2 Vol. Set. lib. bdg. 215.00 o.p. (ISBN 0-8161-0808-0). G K Hall.

Alphabets Go to the Park. Roger Knights. Ed. by Kate Klimo. (Lettermen Ser.). (Illus.). 32p. (ps-3). 1982. pap. 1.40 o.s.i. (ISBN 0-671-45039-5, Little Simon). S&S.

Alphabets Old & New for the Use of Craftsmen. 3rd ed. Lewis F. Day. LC 68-23148. 312p. 1968. Repr. of 1910 ed. 30.00x o.p. (ISBN 0-8103-3301-5). Gale.

Alphabetum Romanum. 50p. 100.00 o.p. (ISBN 0-8115-0911-7). Kraus Repr.

Alphabots. Jonathan Gathrid. Ed. by Erin B. Gathrid. (Illus.). 28p. (ps). bds. 4.95 o.p. (ISBN 0-915391-01-5, Pub. by Mad Hatter Bks). Slawson Comm.

Alphagraphics. Virginia Smith. (Illus.). 1978. pap. 2.95 o.p. (ISBN 0-684-15978-3, ScribT). Scribner.

Alphonse Mucha: The Complete Posters & Panels. Jack Rennert & Alain Weill. LC 84-9022. (Illus.). 405p. 1984. lib. bdg. 83.00 o.s.i. (ISBN 0-8161-8719-3, Hall Reference). G K Hall.

Alphonse, That Bearded One. Natalie S. Carlson. LC 54-5151. (Illus.). (gr. k-3). 1954. 7.95 o.p. (ISBN 0-15-202648-7, HJ). HarBraceJ.

Alquonquin Wits. Ed. by Robert E. Drennan. (Illus.). 176p. 1975. pap. 2.95 o.p. (ISBN 0-8065-0464-1, Pub. by Citadel Pr). Carol Pub Group.

Alson Skinner Clark. Jean Stern. LC 83-62425. (Illus.). 115p. 1983. lib. bdg. 30.00 o.p. (ISBN 0-317-19153-5). Petersen Pub.

ALTA WILL Source Workbook. 197p. 1983. 27.50x o.p. ALA.

Altar Guild: A Guide for the Ministry of Liturgical Preparations. S. Anita Stauffer. 64p. 1978. pap. 2.95 o.p. (ISBN 0-8006-1321-X, 1-1321, Fortress). Augsburg Fortress.

Altars of Venus. (Grove Press Victorian Library). 1986. pap. 3.95 o.p. (ISBN 0-394-62242-1, BC). Grove.

Altbabylonische Privatbriefe. Ed. & tr. by Simon K. Landersdorfer. Repr. of 1908 ed. Johnson Repr.

Altchristliche Basiliken und Lokaltraditionen in Sudjudaa. Andreas E. Mader. pap. 19.00 o.p. (ISBN 0-384-35000-3). Johnson Repr.

Altenglische Bearbeitung der Erzahlung von Appolonius von Tyrus. Robert Markisch. (Ger). 13.00 o.p. (ISBN 0-685-02196-3); pap. 8.00 o.p. (ISBN 0-685-02197-1). Johnson Repr.

Alterations in Food Production. Dietrich Knorr. 1983. 29.95 o.p. (ISBN 0-442-24860-1). Van Nos Reinhold.

Altere Ethnographica aus Nordamerika im Berliner Museum fuer Voelkerkunde. Walter Krickeberg. Repr. of 1954 ed. 25.00 o.p. (ISBN 0-384-30450-8). Johnson Repr.

Altering Course. Richard J. Vogt. 1979. 10.95 o.p. (ISBN 0-393-03230-2). Norton.

Altering Medicaid Provider Reimbursement Methods. John Holahan et al. (Medicaid Cost Containment Ser.). 215p. 1977. pap. 8.50x o.p. (ISBN 0-87766-197-9, 17800). Urban Inst.

Alternate Conceptions of Work in Society & the Nursing Profession. Ed. by Carol Lindeman. 225p. (Orig.). 1988. pap. 20.00 o.p. (ISBN 0-922148-00-7). AACN.

Alternate Language for Public: Sector Labor Contracts see Issues in the Public Employee Relations Library: Series 5.

Alternating Current. Octavio Paz. (ISBN 0-8050-0188-3). Seaver Bks.

Alternative, 3 vols, No. 5. Non-Violent Revolution Committee. 1968. Repr. of 1951 ed. lib. bdg. 11.00x o.p. (ISBN 0-8371-9124-6, AL00). Greenwood.

Alternative Adult Education. Hayden Roberts. (International Perspectives on Adult & Continuing Education Ser.). 176p. 1988. lib. bdg. 45.00 o.p. (ISBN 0-415-00603-1). Routledge Chapman & Hall.

Alternative Careers for Ph.D.s in the Humanities: A Selected Bibliography. Elizabeth A. Flynn & Christine F. Donaldson. LC 82-3399. 41p. (Orig.). 1982. pap. 6.50x o.p. (ISBN 0-87352-099-8). Modern Lang.

Alternative Development Strategies & Appropriate Technology: Science Policy for an Equitable World Order. Romesh K. Diwan & Dennis Livingston. (Pergamon Policy Studies). 1979. 65.00 o.p. (ISBN 0-08-023891-2). Pergamon.

Alternative Frameworks for Analysis. Ed. by Doreen B. Massey & P. W. Batey. (London Papers in Regional Science). 168p. 1977. pap. 12.50x o.p. (ISBN 0-85086-061-X, NO.2915, Pub. by Pion England). Routledge Chapman & Hall.

Alternative Fuels: Chemical Energy Resources. E. M. Goodger. LC 80-11796. 238p. 1980. 57.95 o.p. (ISBN 0-470-26952-9). Halsted Pr.

Alternative Fuels for Maritime Use. Maritime Transportation Research Board Staff & National Research Council Staff. 1983. pap. text ed. 11.25 o.p. (ISBN 0-309-03088-9). Natl Acad Pr.

Alternative Health Care Delivery System: The Individual Practice Association. 38p. 1980. pap. 2.25 o.p. (ISBN 0-89970-243-0, OP-203). AMA.

Alternative Health Care for Women. Patsy Wescott & Leyardia Black. LC 87-19432. 192p. 1987. pap. 10.95 o.s.i. (ISBN 0-89281-245-1). Inner Tradit.

Alternative Home Heating. Dan Browne. LC 79-3445. (Illus.). 208p. (Orig.). 1980. 12.95 o.s.i. (ISBN 0-03-041531-4, Owl Bks.); pap. 9.95 o.s.i. (ISBN 0-03-041536-5). H Holt & Co.

Alternative I Ching. Derek Walters. (Illus.). 224p. (Orig.). 1987. pap. 9.99 o.p. (ISBN 0-85030-659-0, Pub. by Aquarian Pr). Sterling.

Alternative Learning Environments. Ed. by Gary J. Coates. LC 74-1268. (Community Development Ser: Vol. 7). (Illus.). 387p. 1982. 39.95 o.p. (ISBN 0-87933-037-6). Van Nos Reinhold.

Alternative Medicines: Popular & Policy Perspectives. Ed. by J. Warren Salmon. 305p. 1984. 33.00 o.p. (ISBN 0-422-78700-0, NO. 9327, Pub. by Tavistock England); pap. 12.95 o.p. (ISBN 0-422-78710-8, NO. 9183). ROutledge Chapman & Hall.

Alternative Multimodal Passenger Transportation Systems: Comparative Economic Analysis. (National Cooperative Highway Research Program Report). 68p. 1973. 4.00 o.p. (ISBN 0-309-02203-7). Transport Res Bd.

Alternative Roles. National Association of Women Deans & Counselors. 1973. pap. 6.00 o.p. (ISBN 0-686-09579-0). Natl Assn Women.

Titles

Titles

Alternative Sentencing, Nineteen Seventy-Nine to Nineteen Eighty-Four: A Selective Bibliography. Mary E. Huls. (Public Administration Ser.: Bibliography P 1625). 1985. pap. 2.00 o.p. (ISBN 0-89028-295-1). Vance Biblios.

Alternative Siting Requirements & Practices for Nuclear Power Plants (AIF-NESP 018) Dames & Moore. (National Environmental Studies Project: NESP Reports). 300p. 1980. 45.00 o.p. (ISBN 0-318-13551-5); to NESP sponsors 15.00 o.p. (ISBN 0-318-13552-3). US Coun Energy Awareness.

Alternative Sources of Event Data on Zambian Foreign Policy. Timothy M. Shaw & Douglas G. Anglin. LC 81-2274. (Foreign & Comparative Studies Program, African Ser.: No. 36). 1981. pap. text ed. 5.00x o.p. (ISBN 0-915984-60-1). Syracuse U Foreign Comp.

Alternative Work Schedules, Pts. 2 & 3: Permanent Part-Time & the Compressed Workweek. Stanley D. Nollen & Virginia H. Martin. LC 78-17323. 1978. pap. 10.00 o.p. (ISBN 0-8144-3134-8). AMACOM.

Alternatives & Consequences of Actions: An Essay on Certain Fundamental Notions in Teleological Ethics. Lars Bergstrom. 141p. (Orig.). 1966. pap. text ed. 20.00x o.p. Coronet Bks.

Alternatives for the On-Site Retention of Low-Level Radwaste at Nuclear Power Plants (AIF-NESP-015R) NUS Corporation Staff. (National Environmental Studies Project: NESP Reports). 280p. 1980. 60.00 o.p. (ISBN 0-318-13553-1); to NESP sponsors 20.00 o.p. (ISBN 0-318-13554-X). US Coun Energy Awareness.

Alternatives in Development: Is Europe Responding to Third World Needs? Ed. by J. West. 1974. 35.00 o.p. (ISBN 0-08-018169-4). Pergamon.

Alternatives in Print: An International Catalog of Books, Pamphlets, Periodicals & Audiovisual Materials. 6th ed. American Library Association Task Force on Alternatives in Print of the Social Responsibilities Round Table Staff. LC 76-54384. 668p. 1980. 48.00 o.p. (ISBN 0-918212-20-0). Neal-Schuman.

Alternatives in Print, 77-78. 5th ed. Ed. by American Library Association, Social Responsibilities Round Table Staff. LC 76-54384. 1977. 12.95 o.p. (ISBN 0-912078-50-2); pap. 8.95 o.p. (ISBN 0-912078-49-9). Volcano Pr.

Alternatives to Mental Hospital Treatment. Ed. by L. I. Stein & M. A. Test. LC 77-17576. 336p. 1978. 50.00x o.p. (ISBN 0-306-31120-8, Plenum Pr). Plenum Pub.

Alternatives to Piaget: Critical Essays on the Theory. Ed. by Linda S. Siegel. 1977. 24.00 o.p. (ISBN 0-12-641950-7). Acad Pr.

Alternatives to the Current Use of Nitrite in Foods. Assembly of Life Sciences, National Research Council. 280p. 1982. pap. text ed. 12.95x o.p. (ISBN 0-309-03277-6). Natl Acad Pr.

Alternatives to the Present Tax System for Increasing Saving & Investment. American Institute of Certified Public Accountants, Federal Taxation Division Staff. LC 86-102606. (Illus.). vi, 64p. 1985. 8.00 o.p. Am Inst CPA.

Altitude of Prayer. Joel S. Goldsmith. Ed. by Lorainne Sinkler. LC 74-25082. 160p. 1975. 9.45 o.p. (ISBN 0-06-063171-6). HarpR.

Alto & Tango. Claire Schumacher. LC 83-13381. 32p. (ps-1). 1984. PLB 10.88 o.p. (ISBN 0-688-02740-7). Morrow.

Altogether Lovely. Charlene Johnson. LC 60-5292. (gr. 8-12). 1960. pap. 1.00 o.p. (ISBN 0-8006-1205-1, Fortress). Augsburg Fortress.

Alton-Loki: Dual Personality. Alton H. Hilden. 80p. 1986. 6.95 o.p. (ISBN 0-8062-2969-1). Carlton.

Altostniederfraenkischen Psalmenfragmente: Die Lipsius'schen Glossen & Die Altsuedmittelfraenkischen Psalmenfragmente. Ed. by William L. Van Helten. 222p. 1970. 30.00 o.p. (ISBN 0-384-22230-7). Johnson Repr.

Altsinaitische Forschungen, Epigraphisches und Historisches. Hubert Grimme. 1937. pap. 15.00 o.p. (ISBN 0-384-20050-8). Johnson Repr.

Aluminium-Lithium Alloys III. Ed. by C. Baker et al. 640p. 1986. text ed. 79.00x o.p. (ISBN 0-904357-80-5, Pub. by Inst Metals). Gower Pub Co.

Aluminum Construction. Mary Vance. (Architecture Ser.: Bibliography A 1354). 1985. pap. 2.00 o.p. (ISBN 0-89028-324-9). Vance Biblios.

Aluminum-Lithium Alloys II: Proceedings, Monterey, California, 1983. Ed. by E. A. Starke, Jr. & T. H. Sanders, Jr. LC 83-83124. (Illus.). 692p. 1984. 62.00 o.p. (ISBN 0-89520-472-X). Minerals Metals.

Aluminum-Lithium Alloys: Proceedings. Stone Mountain, Georgia, 1980. Ed. by T. H. Sanders, Jr. & E. A. Starke, Jr. (Illus.). 377p. 36.00 o.p. (ISBN 0-89520-373-1); members 22.00 o.p. (ISBN 0-317-36232-1); student members 12.00 o.p. (ISBN 0-317-36233-X). ASM.

Alumni College Movement. Linda Carl. 63p. 1977. 10.50 o.p. (ISBN 0-89964-001-X). Coun Adv & Supp Ed.

Alvar Aalto Furniture. Alvar Aalto. Ed. by Juhani Pallasmaa. (Illus.). 179p. 1985. 27.50 o.p. (ISBN 0-262-13206-0). MIT Pr.

Alvin Fernald, Mayor for a Day. Clifford B. Hicks. LC 70-80325. (Illus.). (gr. 3-6). 1970. reinforced bdg. 5.95 o.p. (ISBN 0-03-089895-1). H Holt & Co.

Alvin Fernald, Superweasel. Clifford B. Hicks. LC 73-21828. (Illus.). 160p. (gr. 3-6). 1974. reinforced bdg. 6.95 o.p. (ISBN 0-03-012326-7). H Holt & Co.

Alvin Fernald, TV Anchorman. Clifford B. Hicks. LC 80-11415. (Illus.). 144p. (gr. 4-7). 1980. 9.95 o.p. (ISBN 0-03-046521-4). H Holt & Co.

Alvin Steadfast on Vernacular Island. Frank Jacobs. LC 78-20692. (Illus.). 1979. 5.95 o.p. (ISBN 0-8008-0173-3); pap. 2.95 o.s.i. (ISBN 0-8008-0174-1). Taplinger.

Alvin's Secret Code. Clifford B. Hicks. LC 63-15141. 160p. (gr. 4-6). 1963. 6.50 o.p. (ISBN 0-03-089736-X). H Holt & Co.

Always. rev. ed. Trevor Meldal-Johnsen. 1979. pap. 3.50 o.p. (ISBN 0-380-41897-5, 64147-X). Avon.

Always a Rainbow. Anita M. Willison. 1984. 10.00 o.p. (ISBN 0-682-40142-0). Exposition-Phoenix.

Always April. I. B. Stoner. 80p. 1986. 7.95 o.p. (ISBN 0-8062-2817-2). Carlton.

Always Keep Him Laughing. Molly Katz. (Candlelight Ecstasy Ser.: No. 383). (Orig.). 1985. pap. 2.25 o.p. (ISBN 0-440-10331-2). Dell.

Always Live Better Than Your Clients. Isadore Barmash. (Illus.). 224p. 1983. 15.95 o.p. (ISBN 0-396-08216-5). Dodd.

Always on Sunday. Peggy Whedon. 1980. 12.95 o.p. (ISBN 0-393-01407-X). Norton.

Always on the Offense. Mike Schmidt & Barbara Walder. LC 80-69764. 256p. 1982. 12.95 o.p. (ISBN 0-689-11165-7, Atheneum). Macmillan.

Always with Honour. P. N. Wrangel. 9.95 o.p. (ISBN 0-8315-0065-4). Speller.

Am Eng Tod G-9 PE. 2nd ed. Date not set. (ISBN 0-07-025319-6). McGraw.

Am Eng Tod Gr 10. 2nd ed. Date not set. (ISBN 0-07-025320-X). McGraw.

Am Eng Tod Gr 12. 2nd ed. Date not set. (ISBN 0-07-025322-6). McGraw.

Am Eng Tod Gr 7. 2nd ed. Date not set. (ISBN 0-07-025317-X). McGraw.

Am Eng Tod Gr 8. 2nd ed. Date not set. (ISBN 0-07-025318-8). McGraw.

Am Eng Tod Gr 9. Date not set. (ISBN 0-07-025287-4). McGraw.

Am Eng Tod G7 TMK. 2nd ed. Date not set. (ISBN 0-07-025347-1). McGraw.

Am Eng Tod G8 TMK. 2nd ed. Date not set. (ISBN 0-07-025348-X). McGraw.

Am Eng Tod G9 TMK. 2nd ed. Date not set. (ISBN 0-07-025339-0). McGraw.

Am Eng Tod TMK G9. Date not set. (ISBN 0-07-025272-6). McGraw.

Am Eng Tod TMK 10. Date not set. (ISBN 0-07-025273-4). McGraw.

Am Eng Tod TMK 11. Date not set. (ISBN 0-07-025274-2). McGraw.

Am Eng Tod 10 TMK. 2nd ed. Date not set. (ISBN 0-07-025340-4). McGraw.

Am Eng Tod 11 TMK. 2nd ed. Date not set. (ISBN 0-07-025341-2). McGraw.

Am Eng Tod 12 TMK. 2nd ed. Date not set. (ISBN 0-07-025342-0). McGraw.

Am I Blue? Living with Diabetes & Dammit, Having Fun! Elaine Stritch. LC 84-6041. 144p. 1984. 10.95 o.p. (ISBN 0-87131-428-2). M Evans.

Am I Losing My Faith? William E. Hulme. LC 71-133035. (Pocket Counsel Bks.). 56p. (Orig.). 1971. pap. 1.75 o.p. (ISBN 0-8006-0154-8, 1-154, Fortress). Augsburg Fortress.

Am I Still Visible? A Woman's Triumph over Anorexia Nervosa. Sandra H. Heater. LC 83-6902. 140p. (Orig.). 1983. 10.95 o.p. (ISBN 0-932620-51-5, White Hall Bks); pap. 6.95 o.p. (ISBN 0-932620-50-7, White Hall Bks). Betterway Pubns.

Am Seguliah: A Treasured People. Eli L. Cooper. LC 82-91010. 148p. 1984. 10.00 o.p. (ISBN 0-533-05673-X). Vantage.

AMA Book of Skin & Hair Care. Ed. by Linda Schoen. 1978. pap. 3.50 o.p. (ISBN 0-380-01871-3, 65979-4). Avon.

AMA Drug Evaluations. 3rd rev. ed. American Medical Association & American Medical Association. LC 76-9254. (Illus.). 1977. students & AMA members 27.50 o.p. (ISBN 0-88416-175-7); 37.50 o.p. (ISBN 0-685-76990-9). Year Bk Med.

AMA Handbook on Alcoholism. LC 87-70251. 100p. 1987. (ISBN 0-89970-235-X). AMA.

AMA Handbook on Drug Abuse. LC 87-70252. 350p. 1987. (ISBN 0-89970-236-8). AMA.

Amador County (CA) History. 3rd ed. Ed. by J. L. Sargent. (Illus.). 128p. 1985. Repr. of 1977 ed. 10.00 o.p. Cenotto Pubns.

Amanda-Miranda. Richard Peck. 544p. 1981. pap. 2.95 o.p. (ISBN 0-380-53850-4, 53850-5). Avon.

Amant Rendu Cordelier a l'Observance d'Amours. Martial D'Auvergne. (Societe Des Anciens Textes Francais Ser: Vol. 15). (Fr). 1881. 25.00 o.p. (ISBN 0-686-76885-X); pap. 19.00 o.p. Johnson Repr.

Amasis Painter & His World: Vase Painting in Sixth-Century B. C. Athens. Dietrich Von Bothmer. LC 85-12590. (Illus.). 248p. 1985. 40.00 o.p. (ISBN 0-500-23443-4). Thames Hudson.

Amateur. Robert Littell. 1982. pap. 3.25 o.p. (ISBN 0-440-10119-0). Dell.

Amateur Acting & Stage Encyclopedia. D. J. Smith. (Illus.). 188p. 1961. (ISBN 0-8022-1590-4). Philos Lib.

Amateur Corpse. Simon Brett. 1986. pap. 3.50 o.p. (ISBN 0-440-10185-9). Dell.

Amateur Gunsmithing. Desmond Mills & Mike Barnes. 1987. 36.00 o.p. (Pub. by Boydell & Brewer). Longwood Pub Group.

Amateur Radio Advanced Class License Study Guide. 3rd ed. James Kyle et al. 1982. pap. 9.95 o.p. (ISBN 0-8306-1327-7, 1327). TAB Bks.

Amateur Radio General Class License Study Guide. 3rd ed. James Kyle et al. 1985. pap. 12.95 o.p. (ISBN 0-8306-1351-X, 1351). TAB Bks.

Amateur Radio, Super Hobby. Vince Luciani. LC 83-25544. (Illus.). 288p. 1984. pap. text ed. 9.95 o.p. (ISBN 0-07-038959-4). McGraw.

Amateurs. David Halberstam. LC 85-2940. (Illus.). 160p. 1985. 14.95 o.p. (ISBN 0-688-04948-6). Morrow.

Amazed by Grace. David Redding. 1986. 10.95 o.p. (ISBN 0-8007-1480-6). Revell.

Amazing Amazeman & The Hydrozoid Attack: A Super-Maze Adventure. Vladimir Koziakin. 112p. 1983. pap. 1.95 o.p. (ISBN 0-380-83352-2, 83352). Avon.

Amazing Amazeman in a Super Maze Adventure. Vladimir Koziakin. 112p. 1982. pap. 1.95 o.p. (ISBN 0-380-81547-8, 81547-8). Avon.

Amazing Amazeman vs. the Spider Queen. Vladimir Koziakin. 1983. pap. 1.95 o.p. (ISBN 0-380-82149-4, 82149). Avon.

Amazing Book. Tony Salerno. (Amazing Bible Ser.). 48p. (ps-2). 1987. 9.95 o.p. (ISBN 0-8407-6723-4). Nelson.

Amazing Brain. Robert E. Ornstein & Richard F. Thompson. (Illus.). 1984. 16.45 o.p. (ISBN 0-395-35486-2). HM.

Amazing D. Randall MacRae. James W. Ingles. (Orig.). 1984. pap. 4.95 o.p. (ISBN 0-8024-0469-3). Moody.

Amazing Days. Randy Harelson. LC 78-73727. (Illus.). 256p. (gr. k-6). 1979. pap. 8.95 spiral bound o.p. (ISBN 0-89480-071-X, 249). Workman Pub.

Amazing Facts about Prehistoric Animals. Gyles Brandreth. LC 80-1085. (Amazing Facts Bks.). (Illus.). 32p. (gr. 4-6). 1986. pap. 3.50 o.p. (ISBN 0-385-17019-X). Doubleday.

Amazing Grace: John Newton's Story. John Pollock. LC 78-3142. 192p. 1981. 10.95i o.p. (ISBN 0-06-066653-6). HarpR.

Amazing Herschell Gordon Lewis & His World of Exploitation Films. Daniel Krogh & John McCarty. (Illus.). 180p. (Orig.). 1983. pap. 14.95x o.p. (ISBN 0-938782-03-7). Fantaco.

Amazing Home Remedy: The Natural Hot Water Washing Method for Relief from Hemorrhoid. Jan. (Illus., Orig.). pap. 5.50 o.p. (ISBN 0-682-40126-9). Exposition-Phoenix.

Amazing Laser. Ben Bova. LC 75-161697. (Franklin Institute Bk). (Illus.). (gr. 7-10). 1971. 5.95 o.p. (ISBN 0-664-32502-5, Westminster); pap. 2.95 o.s.i. (ISBN 0-664-34003-2, Westminster). Westminster John Knox.

Amazing Love. Corrie Ten Boom. (Orig.). 1982. pap. 2.50 o.s.i. (ISBN 0-515-06735-0). Jove Pubns.

Amazing Monsters: Verses to Thrill & Chill. Ed. by Robert Fisher. Tr. & illus. by Rowena Allen. (Illus.). 96p. (ps-5). 1982. 9.95 o.p. (ISBN 0-571-11850-X). Faber & Faber.

Amazing Trains of the World. Roland Berry & Frank Moses. (Illus.). 32p. (gr. 3-6). 1986. 14.95 o.p. (ISBN 0-241-10967-1, Pub. by Hamish Hamilton England). David & Charles.

Amazing 3-D. Hal Morgan & Daniel Symmes. (Illus.). 1982. pap. 14.95 o.p. (ISBN 0-316-58283-2). Little.

Amazon. Brian Kelly & Mark London. 400p. 1983. 15.95 o.p. (ISBN 0-15-105463-0). HarBraceJ.

Amazon. Brian Kelly & Mark London. 1985. pap. 9.95 o.p. (ISBN 0-03-003668-2, Owl Bks). H Holt & Co.

Amazon Journey: An Anthropologist's Year Among Brazil's Mekranoti Indians. Dennis Werner. 288p. 1984. 16.45 o.p. (ISBN 0-671-49290-X). S&S.

Amazons. Cleo Birdwell. LC 80-80241. 400p. 1980. 12.95 o.p. (ISBN 0-03-055426-8). H Holt & Co.

Ambassador. Andre Brink. 1986. 16.45 o.s.i. (ISBN 0-671-61934-9). Summit Bks.

Ambassadors. Henry James. 1971. pap. 2.50x o.p. (ISBN 0-460-01987-2, DEL-04008, Evman). Biblio Dist.

Ambassador's Journal: A Personal Account of the Kennedy Years. John Kenneth Galbraith. LC 69-15012. 1969. 10.00 o.p. (ISBN 0-395-07708-7). HM.

Ambassador's Women. Catherine Gaskin. 512p. 1986. 18.95 o.p. (ISBN 0-684-18661-6). Scribner.

Ambassador's Women. Catherine Gaskin. 640p. 1987. pap. 4.50 o.p. (ISBN 0-380-70174-X). Avon.

Amber, a Very Personal Cat. Gladys Taber. 160p. 1983. pap. 5.95 o.p. (ISBN 0-940160-20-X). Parnassus Imprints.

Amber Sword of World's End. Michael P. Price. LC 86-50105. (Advanced Dungeons & Dragons (R) One-On-One (TM) Adventure Gamebooks). 1986. 5.95 o.p. (ISBN 0-88038-287-2). TSR Inc.

Amber: The Golden Gem of the Ages. Patty C. Rice. 1980. 28.50 o.p. (ISBN 0-442-26138-1). Van Nos Reinhold.

Ambidextrous Universe: Mirror Asymmetry & Time-Reversed Worlds. rev. ed. Martin Gardner. (Illus.). 1979. pap. 4.95 o.p. (ISBN 0-684-15790-X, ScribT). Scribner.

Ambient. Jack Womack. LC 86-15784. 272p. 1987. 15.95 o.s.i. (ISBN 1-55584-082-5). Weidenfeld.

Ambiguous Iroquois Empire. Francis Jennings. (Illus.). 1984. 24.45 o.p. (ISBN 0-393-01719-2). Norton.

Ambitions. Audrey Howard. 544p. 1987. 19.95 o.p. (ISBN 0-02-555080-2). Macmillan.

Ambivalent Force. 2nd ed. Arthur Niederhoffer & Abraham S. Blumberg. LC 75-26614. 1976. pap. text ed. 15.95 o.p. (ISBN 0-03-014226-1, HoltC). HR&W.

Ambler. Fred Halliday. 240p. 1986. pap. 3.50 o.p. (ISBN 0-931773-51-2). Critics Choice Paper.

Amboy Dukes. Irving Shulman. 192p. 1986. pap. 2.95 o.p. (ISBN 0-931773-56-3). Critics Choice Paper.

Ambrose Caliver: Adult Education & Civil Servant. Walter G. Daniel. 1966. 2.00 o.p. (ISBN 0-88379-032-7). A A A C E.

Ambrosia. Rosanne Kohake. 1985. pap. 3.95 o.p. (ISBN 0-380-89734-2). Avon.

Ambulance: The Story of Emergency Transportation of Sick & Wounded Through the Centuries. Katherine T. Barkley. (Illus.). 1978. 8.50 o.p. (ISBN 0-682-48983-2). Exposition-Phoenix.

Ambulatory Care: Problems of Cost & Access. Stuart H. Altman et al. LC 82-49054. (University Health Policy Consortium Ser.). 256p. 1983. 30.00x o.p. (ISBN 0-669-06401-7). Lexington Bks.

Ambulatory Health Care Scoring Guidelines. 68p. pap. cancelled o.s.i. (ISBN 0-86688-152-2). Joint Comm Hlthcare.

Ambulatory Health Care Standards Manual, 1986. 80p. 1985. pap. 25.00 o.s.i. (ISBN 0-86688-093-3, ACH-504). Joint Comm Hlthcare.

Ambulatory Pediatrics for Nurses. 2nd ed. Marie S. Brown & Mary A. Murphy. LC 80-12462. (Illus.). 624p. 1981. text ed. 35.95 o.p. (ISBN 0-07-008291-X). McGraw.

Ambush. Samuel L. Marshall. (Vietnam War Ser.: No. 2). (Illus.). 242p. 1982. Repr. of 1969 ed. 16.95x o.p. (ISBN 0-89839-070-2). Battery Pr.

Ambush at Jubilo Junction. Leslie Ernenwein. 1976. pap. 0.95 o.p. (ISBN 0-685-69142-X, LB361, Pub. by Leisure Bks CT). Dorchester Pub Co.

Ambush at Vermejo. Jim Boss. (Living Books). 320p. (Orig.). 1985. pap. 3.95 o.p. (ISBN 0-8423-0091-0). Tyndale.

AMC Field Guide to Trail Building & Maintenance. 2nd ed. Robert Proudman & Reuben Rajala. LC 82-121206. (Illus.). 288p. 1981. pap. 8.95 o.s.i. (ISBN 0-910146-30-6). AMC Books.

AMC Guide to Country Walks Near Boston. Alan Fisher. (Illus.). 180p. (Orig.). 1976. pap. 6.95 o.p. (ISBN 0-910146-07-1). AMC Books.

AMC Guide to Mount Desert Island & Acadia National Park. 3rd ed. AMC Maine Mountain Guide Book Committee. (Illus.). 40p. 1984. pap. 3.50 o.p. (ISBN 0-910146-52-7). AMC Books.

AMC Guide to Mt. Washington & the Presidential Range. rev. & 3rd ed. White Mountain Guide Book Committee. 160p. 1983. pap. 6.95 o.p. (ISBN 0-910146-50-0). AMC Books.

AMC Maine Mountain Guide. 5th ed. AMC Maine Mountain Guide Book Committee. (Illus.). 308p. 1985. pap. 10.95 o.p. (ISBN 0-910146-54-3). AMC Books.
AMC Massachusetts-Rhode Island Trail Guide. 5th ed. Ed. by Massachusetts-Rhode Island Guidebook Committee. LC 78-108996. (Illus.). 480p. 1982. pap. 12.95 o.s.i. (ISBN 0-910146-38-1). AMC Books.
AMC, Nineteen Seventy Five to Nineteen Eighty-Two. Chilton Automotives Editorial Staff. 1982. pap. 13.50 o.s.i. (ISBN 0-8019-7199-3). Chilton.
AMC River Guide I: Vol. 1: Maine. 2nd ed. AMC River Guide Committee. Ed. by Roioli Schweiker. (AMC River Guide Ser.). (Illus.). 234p. (Orig.). 1980. pap. 7.95 o.p. (ISBN 0-910146-24-1). AMC Books.
AMC River Guide: New Hampshire & Vermont. (AMC River Guides Ser.). (Illus.). 272p. 1983. pap. 9.95 o.p. (ISBN 0-910146-49-7). AMC Books.
AMC Service-Repair Handbook: Pacer, Gremlin, Hornet-1971-1980. Jeff Robinson. Ed. by Jeff Robinson. (Illus.). pap. 11.95 o.p. (ISBN 0-89287-139-3, A129). Clymer Pub.
AMD: Proceedings, Vol. 7. Structural Optimization Symposium Staff. 162p. 1974. 18.00 o.p. (ISBN 0-685-48054-2, I00042). ASME.
AMDG--A History of Canisius College 1883-1913: Under the New York State Regents' Charter, on Washington Street, Buffalo. Thomas E. Harney. 1981. 10.00 o.p. (ISBN 0-682-49658-8). Exposition-Phoenix.
Amelia. Kathryn Douglas. 256p. (Orig.). 1985. pap. 2.95 o.s.i. (ISBN 0-345-31103-5). Ballantine.
Amelia Bedelia & Her Wacky World, 4 vols. 1986. Boxed Set. pap. 11.80 o.p. (ISBN 0-380-75238-7, Camelot). Avon.
Amelia Earhart: The Myth & the Reality. Dick Strippel. LC 76-186486. 1972. 7.50 o.p. (ISBN 0-682-47447-9, Banner). Exposition-Phoenix.
Amelia Gayle Gorgas: A Biography. Mary T. Johnston & Elizabeth J. Lipscomb. LC 77-18889. 191p. 1978. 12.95 o.p. (ISBN 0-8173-5235-X). U of Ala Pr.
Amelia Quackenbush. Sharlya Gold. LC 73-7129. (gr. 3-6). 1979. 5.95 o.p. (ISBN 0-395-28856-8, Clarion). HM.
Amelioration of the Human Environment: IGU Congress, Moscow, 1976, Proceedings, Pt. 1. Ed. by Yuri Medvedkov. 1977. pap. 23.00 o.p. (ISBN 0-08-021322-7). Pergamon.
Amen, Brother Ben: A Mississippi Collection of Children's Rhymes. Marice C. Brown. LC 78-32017. 1979. pap. text ed. 5.00 o.p. (ISBN 0-87805-094-9). U Pr of Miss.
Amendment That Refused to Die: Amendment XIV. Howard N. Meyer. LC 77-88587. 1978. pap. 6.95x o.p. (ISBN 0-8070-5419-4, BP575). Beacon Pr.
Amerasia, 11 vols, No. 7. Incl. Vol. 1. lib. bdg. 29.00 (ISBN 0-313-21611-8, AM01); Vol. 2. lib. bdg. 29.00 (ISBN 0-313-21612-6, AM02); Vol. 3. lib. bdg. 29.00 (ISBN 0-313-21613-4, AM03); Vol. 4. lib. bdg. 29.00 (ISBN 0-313-21614-2, AM04); Vol. 5. lib. bdg. 29.00 (ISBN 0-313-21615-0, AM05); Vol. 6. lib. bdg. 29.00 (ISBN 0-313-21616-9, AM06); Vol. 7. lib. bdg. 29.00 (ISBN 0-313-21617-7, AM07); Vol. 8. lib. bdg. 29.00 (ISBN 0-313-21618-5, AM08); Vol. 9. lib. bdg. 29.00 (ISBN 0-313-21619-3, AM09); Vols. 10 & 11. lib. bdg. 29.00 (ISBN 0-313-21620-7, AM10). 1968. Repr. of 1947 ed. 260.00x o.p. (ISBN 0-8371-9125-4, AM00). Greenwood.
America & Lewis Hine. Alan Tractenberg. LC 77-70068. (Illus.). 144p. 1977. 25.00 o.p. (ISBN 0-89381-008-8). Aperture.
America & the Origins of the Cold War. Ed. by James V. Compton. LC 71-169722. (New Perspectives in History Ser). (Orig.). 1972. pap. 5.25 o.p. (ISBN 0-395-12080-2). HM.
America & the Third World. J. S. Girling. (Illus.). 1980. 26.95x o.p. (ISBN 0-7100-0318-8). Routledge Chapman & Hall.
America & the World, 1978. Ed. by William P. Bundy. (Pergamon Policy Studies). 260p. 1979. text ed. 43.00x o.p. (ISBN 0-08-023896-3); pap. text ed. 9.75 o.p. (ISBN 0-08-023895-5). Pergamon.
America & the World, 1979. Ed. by William P. Bundy. (Pergamon Policy Studies, Foreign A). 281p. 1980. 85.00 o.p. (ISBN 0-08-025952-9); pap. 85.00 o.p. (ISBN 0-08-025951-0). Pergamon.
America & the World, 1980. (Pergamon Policy Studies on International Politics). 1981. 85.00 o.p. (ISBN 0-08-027515-X); pap. 85.00 o.p. (ISBN 0-08-027514-1). Pergamon.
America & the World, 1981. Ed. by William P. Bundy. (Pergamon Policy Studies on International Politics Ser.). 294p. 1982. text ed. 40.00 o.p. (ISBN 0-08-028834-0, K125); pap. text ed. 9.75 o.p. (ISBN 0-08-028827-8). Pergamon.
America & the World, 1982. Ed. by Foreign Affairs Staff & William P. Bundy. 300p. 1983. 46.00 o.p. (ISBN 0-08-030132-0); pap. 85.00 o.p. (ISBN 0-08-030131-2). Pergamon.
America & the World, 1983. Ed. by William Bundy. (Pergamon Policy Studies on International Politics). 275p. 1984. pap. 8.95 o.p. (ISBN 0-08-031592-5). Pergamon.
America & the World, 1984. Ed. by William G. Hyland. 275p. 1985. pap. 8.95 o.p. (ISBN 0-08-032375-8). Pergamon.
America & the World 1985. Ed. by William G. Hyland. (America & the World Ser.). 300p. 1986. pap. 8.95 o.p. (ISBN 0-08-033183-1, K125, Pub. by PPI). Pergamon.
America at Mid-Century. (Our Nations Heritage Ser.). Date not set. (ISBN 0-07-375408-0). McGraw.
America by Car. 20th ed. Norman D. Ford. (Illus.). 1986. pap. 7.95 o.p. (ISBN 0-685-65735-3). Allsport Pub.
America: Christian or Pagan. Don R. Pegram. 1982. pap. 1.25 o.p. (ISBN 0-89265-082-6). Randall Hse.
America Five Cent. (Our Nations Heritage Ser.). Date not set. (ISBN 0-07-375430-7). McGraw.
America Five Centuries. (Our Nations Heritage Ser.). Date not set. (ISBN 0-07-375409-9). McGraw.
America Has a Better Team: The Remarkable Story of Bill Walsh & San Francisco's Super Bowl Champion 49ers. Glenn Dickey. (Illus.). 168p. 1982. 14.95 o.p. (ISBN 0-936602-48-1); pap. 9.95 o.p. (ISBN 0-936602-47-3). Kampmann.
America Hxatal: Two Books of a Poem. Sterling K. Webb. 44p. (Orig.). 1978. lib. bdg. 25.00 o.p. (ISBN 0-916908-32-1); pap. 5.00 o.p. (ISBN 0-916908-10-0). Place Herons.
America in Europe: A History of the New World in Reverse. German Arciniegas. Tr. by Gabriela Arciniegas & Victoria Arana. LC 85-21924. 288p. 1986. 19.95 o.p. (ISBN 0-15-105555-6). HarBraceJ.
America in Miniatures: How to Make Models of Early American Houses & Furniture. C. J. Maginley. LC 76-13002. 1976. 10.00 o.p. (ISBN 0-15-105587-4). HarBraceJ.
America in Modern Italian Literature. Donald Heiney. 278p. 1965. 40.00 o.p. (ISBN 0-8135-0471-6). Rutgers U Pr.
America in Our Time: From World War II to Nixon--What Happened & Why. Godfrey Hodgson. (YA) 1978. pap. 10.96 o.p. (ISBN 0-394-72517-4, Vin). Random.
America in the Twenties: A History. Geoffrey Perrett. 1982. 20.25 o.p. (ISBN 0-671-25107-4). S&S.
America in the Twenties: A History. Geoffrey Perrett. 592p. 1983. pap. 9.50 o.s.i. (ISBN 0-671-25108-2, Touchstone). S&S.
America in the Twentieth-Century: A History. James T. Patterson. 1976. Part One: A History To 1945; 361p. pap. text ed. 14.00 o.p. (ISBN 0-15-502222-9, HC); Part two: A History Since 1939;266p. pap. text ed. 12.75 o.p. (ISBN 0-15-502223-7). HarBraceJ.
America in the Twentieth Century: A History. 2nd. ed. James T. Patterson. 516p. 1983. pap. 20.00 net o.p. (ISBN 0-15-502224-5, HC). HarBraceJ.
America in the Twentieth Century: A History. James T. Patterson. 1976. 18.95 o.p. (ISBN 0-15-502221-0). HarbraceJ.
America in Time. American Heritage Dictionary Editors. (Illus.). 1977. 9.95 o.p. (ISBN 0-395-25408-6). HM.
America in Transition: Implications for Employee Benefits. Ed. by Dallas L. Salisbury. LC 82-8770. 97p. (Orig.). 1982. pap. 14.00 o.p. (ISBN 0-86643-026-1). Employee Benefit.
America in World War Two. (Our Nations Heritage Ser.). Date not set. (ISBN 0-07-375407-2). McGraw.
America in World War Two. (Our Nations Heritage Ser.). Date not set. (ISBN 0-07-375428-5). McGraw.
America in Yiddish Poetry: An Anthology. Ed. by Jehiel B. Cooperman. Tr. by Sarah C. Cooperman. 1967. 10.00 o.p. (ISBN 0-682-46879-7, Banner). Exposition-Phoenix.
America Inside Out: At Home & Abroad from Roosevelt to Reagan. David Schoenbrun. (Illus.). 486p. 1984. text ed. 17.95 o.p. (ISBN 0-07-055473-0). McGraw.
America Is My Neighborhood. Willard Scott & Daniel Paisner. (Illus.). 240p. 1987. 16.45 o.s.i. (ISBN 0-671-62585-3). S&S.
America Is Not All Traffic Lights: Poems of the Midwest. Alice Fleming. 84p. (gr. 7 up). 1976. 12.45i o.p. (ISBN 0-316-28590-0). Little.
America Latina: Cooperacion Regional y Problemas del Desarrollo. N. Zaitsev. 291p. (Span.). 1983. 4.95 o.p. (ISBN 0-8285-2589-7, Pub. by Progress Pubs USSR). Imported Pubns.
America Latina en Su Arquitectura. (America Latina En Su Cultura Ser.). 1976. pap. 24.25 o.p. (ISBN 92-3-301245-X, U19, UNESCO). UNIPUB.
America Latina: Expansion del Imperialismo y Crisis de la Via Capitalista de Desarrollo. P. Boyko. 259p. (Span.). 5.45 o.p. (ISBN 0-8285-1412-7, Pub. by Progress Pubs USSR). Imported Pubns.
America Latina: Nacionalismo, Democracia y Revolucion. V. Chertijin et al. 188p. (Span.). 1978. pap. 4.95 o.p. (ISBN 0-8285-1675-8, Pub. by Progress Pubs USSR). Imported Pubns.
America Now. Marvin Harris. 1982. pap. 7.95 o.s.i. (ISBN 0-671-45701-2, Touchstone Bks). S&S.
America on Trial. Richard K. Tanaka. (Illus.). 176p. 1987. 9.75 o.p. (ISBN 0-8062-2783-4). Carlton.
America Plans for Space: A Reader Based on the National Defense University Space Symposium. LC 86-12646. 209p. (Orig.). 1986. pap. 6.00 o.p. (ISBN 0-318-21277-3, S/N 008-020-01068-5). USGPO.
America Rediscovered. William E. Pulliam et al. Incl. Its Economic Life. 1977. pap. 11.60 o.p. (ISBN 0-395-21949-3); Its Foreign Affairs. 1977. pap. 8.60 o.p. (ISBN 0-395-21952-3); Its People. 1977. pap. 11.60 o.p. (ISBN 0-395-21950-7); Its Political Life. 1977. pap. 10.72 o.p. (ISBN 0-395-21951-5). LC 75-28704. 1977. pap. 11.88 tchr's. guide o.p. (ISBN 0-395-21948-5). HM.
America the Beautiful: A Collection of Best-loved Patriotic Songs. Tom Glazer. LC 86-755066. (Illus.). 64p. (gr. k up). 1987. pap. 12.95 o.p. (ISBN 0-385-24074-0, Zephyr-BFYR). Doubleday.
America the Raped. Gene Marine. 1984. pap. 1.25 o.p. (ISBN 0-380-01015-1, 09373, Discus). Avon.
America World Power. (Our Nations Heritage Ser.). Date not set. (ISBN 0-07-375404-8). McGraw.
American Academy in Rome, 1894-1969. Alan Valentine & Lucia Valentine. LC 72-92663. 237p. 1973. 20.00x o.p. (ISBN 0-8139-0444-7). U Pr of Va.
American Adviser in Late Yi Korea: The Letters of Owen Nickerson Denny. Robert R. Swartout, Jr. LC 83-5042. (Illus.). xii, 195p. 1984. pap. 22.50x o.p. (ISBN 0-8173-0189-5). U of Ala Pr.
American Album. Oliver Jensen et al. LC 85-15046. (Illus.). 342p. 1985. 45.00 o.p. (ISBN 0-8281-3075-2, Dist. by H M); pap. 19.95 o.p. Am Heritage.
American Amusement Park: An Annotated Bibiography. Glenna Dunning. (Architecture Ser.: Bibliography A 1318). 48p. 1985. pap. 7.50 o.p. (ISBN 0-89028-268-4). Vance Biblios.
American & Soviet Relations Since Detente: The Framework. Terry L. Heyns. LC 86-23838. (Illus.). 267p. 1987. pap. 8.00 o.p. (ISBN 0-317-62917-4, S-N 008-020-01097-9). USGPO.
American Antique Weather Vanes. A. B. Westervelt & W. T. Westervelt. 1983. 13.00 o.p. (ISBN 0-8446-5941-X). Peter Smith.
American Appeasement: United States Foreign Policy & Germany 1933-1938. Arnold A. Offner. LC 69-13767. 1969. 24.50x o.s.i. (ISBN 0-674-01840-0, Belknap Pr). Harvard U Pr.
American Approach to Foreign Policy. Dexter Perkins. LC 62-11400. 1968. pap. text ed. 2.95x o.p. (ISBN 0-689-70154-3, 123, Atheneum). Macmillan.
American Architects from the Civil War to the First World War: A Guide to Information Sources. Ed. by Lawrence Wodehouse. LC 73-17525. (Art & Architecture Information Guide Ser.: Vol. 3). 356p. 1976. 68.00x o.p. (ISBN 0-8103-1269-7). Gale.
American Architectural Iron: A Selected Bibliography. Anthony G. White. (Architecture Ser.: A 1407). 7p. 1985. 2.00 o.p. (ISBN 0-89028-437-7). Vance Biblios.
American Army Life: An Historic Portrait of the American Soldier from Colonial Times to the Present. John R. Elting. (Illus.). 352p. 1982. 35.00 o.s.i. (ISBN 0-684-17500-2, ScribT). Scribner.
American Art see **American Etchings.**
American Art Criticism: 1910-1939, No. 5. Peninah R. Y. Petruck. LC 79-575499. (Outstanding Dissertations in the Fine Arts Ser.). 310p. 1981. text ed. 40.00 o.p. (ISBN 0-8240-3939-4). Garland Pub.
American Art Directory. 51st ed. Ed. by Bowker, R. R., Staff. 721p. 1986. 94.50 o.p. (ISBN 0-8352-2218-7). Bowker.
American Art Directory. 50th ed. Ed. by Jaques Cattell Press Staff. 721p. 1984. 85.00 o.p. (ISBN 0-8352-1876-7). Bowker.
American Art Galleries: The Illustrated Guide to Their Art & Artists. Ed. by Les Krantz. (Illus.). 304p. 1985. 24.95 o.p. (ISBN 0-8160-0089-1); pap. 16.95 o.p. (ISBN 0-8160-0090-5). Facts on File.
American Art, Nineteen Thirty-Four to Nineteen Fifty-Six: Selections from the Whitney Museum of American Art. Montgomery Museum of Fine Arts Staff. Ed. by Diane J. Gingold. LC 78-54064. (Illus.). 1978. pap. 6.00 o.p. (ISBN 0-89280-009-7). Montgomery Mus.
American Art Theory, 1945-1970. Stewart Buettner. Ed. by Donald Kuspit. LC 81-1812. (Studies in Fine Arts: Art Theory, No. 1). 226p. 1981. 42.95 o.p. (ISBN 0-8357-1178-1). UMI Res Pr.
American Artists. 3rd ed. 610p. 1986. 125.00 o.p. Apollo.
American Artists Today in Black, Vol. I. Hobie L. Williams. Ed. by Mosezelle White & Bobby Roberts, II. LC 80-53573. 87p. (Orig.). 1981. pap. text ed. 7.95x o.s.i. (ISBN 0-936026-11-1). R&M Pub Co.
American Artists Today in Black & White, Vol. II. Hobie L. Williams. Ed. by Mosezelle White & Bobby Roberts, III. LC 80-53573. 87p. (Orig.). 1982. pap. text ed. 7.95 o.s.i. (ISBN 0-936026-12-X). R&M Pub Co.
American As Reformer. 2nd ed. Arthur M. Schlesinger, Jr. LC 50-14677. 1968. 9.95x o.s.i. (ISBN 0-674-01950-4). Harvard U Pr.
American Association of Architectural Bibliographers' Papers, Vol. 1. Ed. by William B. O'Neal. Incl. Henry-Russell Hitchcock. James H. Grady; Walter Gropius. Carol Shillaber; Philip C. Johnson. William O'Neal; Early Architecture of Virginia. Frederick D. Nichols. LC 65-14273. 128p. 1965. 13.50x o.p. (ISBN 0-8139-0003-4). U Pr of Va.
American Association of Architectural Bibliographers' Papers, Vol. 2. Ed. by William B. O'Neal. Incl. Sibyl Moholy-Nagy. Philip C. Johnson & William B. O'Neal; Holabird & Roche. William Rudd; Early Architecture of Virginia. Frederick D. Nichols. LC 65-14273. 113p. 1966. 13.50x o.p. (ISBN 0-8139-0004-2). U Pr of Va.
American Association of Architectural Bibliographers' Papers, Vol. 3. Ed. by William B. O'Neal. Incl. Walter Gropius. LC 65-14273. 138p. 1966. 13.50x o.p. (ISBN 0-8139-0005-0). U Pr of Va.
American Association of Architectural Bibliographers' Papers, Vol. 4. Ed. by William B. O'Neal. Incl. Carroll L. V. Meeks. William B. O'Neal & Frederick D. Nichols; Charles-Louis Clerisseau. Thomas J. McCormick; Library at Biltmore. Stapleton D. Gooch; International Expositions, 1851-1900. Julia F. Davis. LC 65-14273. 130p. 1967. 13.50x o.p. (ISBN 0-8139-0006-9). U Pr of Va.
American Association of Architectural Bibliographers' Papers, Vol. 5. Ed. by William B. O'Neal. Incl. Henry-Russell Hitchcock. James H. Grady; Architectural Comment in American Magazines, 1783-1815. J. Meredith Neil; The Adam Style in America, 1770-1820. Sterling M. Boyd; Calvert Vaux. John D. Sigle; Alvar Aalto. Peter W. Beal. LC 65-14273. 106p. 1968. 13.50x o.p. (ISBN 0-8139-0007-7). U Pr of Va.
American Association of Architectural Bibliographers' Papers, Vol. 6. Ed. by William B. O'Neal. Incl. Jefferson As an Architect. William B. O'Neal. LC 65-14273. (Illus.). 150p. 1969. 13.50x o.p. (ISBN 0-8139-0281-9). U Pr of Va.
American Association of Architectural Bibliographers' Papers, Vol. 7. Ed. by William B. O'Neal. Incl. Sir Nikolaus Pevsner. John R. Barr. LC 65-14273. 124p. 1970. 13.50x o.p. (ISBN 0-8139-0299-1). U Pr of Va.
American Association of Architectural Bibliographers' Papers, Vol. 9. Ed. by William B. O'Neal. Incl. Supplement to the Bibliography of Walter Gropius. Ed. by Ise Gropius; Bibliography of Works About Sir Christopher Wren. Ed. by Gail G. Stringer; Benjamin Henry Latrobe. Ed. by Paul F. Norton; Frank Lloyd Wright in Print 1959-1970. Compiled by James Muggenberg. LC 65-14273. 132p. 1972. 13.50x o.p. (ISBN 0-8139-0391-2). U Pr of Va.
American Association of Architectural Bibliographers' Papers, Vol. 10. Ed. by William B. O'Neal. Incl. A Bibliography of Antonio Gaudi & the Catalan Movement, 1870-1930. Compiled by George R. Collins & Maurice E. Farinas. LC 65-14273. 1973. 15.00x o.p. (ISBN 0-8139-0477-3). U Pr of Va.
American Association of Architectural Bibliographers Papers, Vol. 11: Index to Papers 1-10. Ed. by William B. O'Neal. LC 65-14273. 1975. 17.50x o.p. (ISBN 0-8139-0608-3). U Pr of Va.
American at Random: Q. & A. Jerome B. Agel. LC 83-70474. (Illus.). 192p. 1983. 7.95 o.p. (ISBN 0-87795-455-0, Arbor Hse). Morrow.
American Attitude Towards Indian Nationalist Movement. Diwakar P. Singh. xvi, 352p. 1974. 15.00x o.p. (ISBN 0-88386-335-9). South Asia Bks.

American Attitudes Towards Health Maintenance Organizations. Louis Harris. (Louis Harris Publications Ser.). 1981. lib. bdg. 29.00 o.p. (ISBN 0-8240-9374-7). Garland Pub.

American Autobiography: The Prophetic Mode. G. Thomas Couser. Date not set. price not set o.p. U of Mass Pr.

American Automobiles of the Fifties & Sixties. Alberto Martinez & Jean-Loup Nory. (Illus.). 187p. 1986. 14.98 o.p. (ISBN 0-87938-226-0, Pub. by Edns Presse AudioVisual France). Motorbooks Intl.

American Ballad Operas. Ed. by Walter H. Rubsamen. LC 74-4466. (Ballad Opera Ser.). 1974. lib. bdg. 61.00 o.p. (ISBN 0-8240-0927-4). Garland Pub.

American Bar Association Section of Family Law 1987 Annual Meeting Compendium. America Bar Association Section of Family Law. 686p. (Orig.). 1987. pap. 50.00 o.p. (ISBN 0-941161-40-4). PES Inc WI.

American Bestiary. Anne Folsom & Otto Von Frisch. LC 76-20554. 1976. 5.95 o.p. (ISBN 0-15-105573-4). HarBraceJ.

American Biking Atlas & Touring Guide. Sue Browder. LC 75-8816. (Illus.). 320p. 1974. pap. 7.95 o.p. (ISBN 0-911104-36-4, 048). Workman Pub.

American Bird Decoys. William Mackey, Jr. LC 65-19954. (Illus.). 272p. 1979. Repr. of 1965 ed. 19.95 o.p. (ISBN 0-916838-20-X). Schiffer.

American Black Chamber. Herbert O. Yardley. (Espionage Intelligence Library: No. 1). 256p. 1981. pap. 2.75 o.s.i. (ISBN 0-345-29867-5). Ballantine.

American Black Spiritual & Gospel Songs from Southeast Georgia: A Comparative Study. Jacqueline C. Djedje. (CAAS Monographs: No. VII). 105p. 1978. pap. 3.95 o.s.i. (ISBN 0-934934-16-9). UCLA CAAS.

American Blood. John Nichols. LC 86-25616. 1987. 17.95 o.p. (ISBN 0-8050-0374-6). H Holt & Co.

American Book Auction Catalogues, 1713-1934. Ed. by George L. McKay. 592p. 1967. Repr. of 1937 ed. 43.00x o.p. (ISBN 0-8103-3311-2). Gale.

American Book Design & William Morris. Susan O. Thomson. LC 77-8733. (Illus.). 258p. 1977. 39.95 o.p. (ISBN 0-8352-0984-9). Bowker.

American Book Prices Current, Vol. 92. Ed. by Katharine K. Leab & Daniel J. Leab. 1000p. 1986. 92.95 o.p. (ISBN 0-914022-19-9). Bancroft Parkman.

American Book Prices Current, Vol. 93. Ed. by Katharine K. Leab & Daniel J. Leab. 1987. 93.95 o.p. (ISBN 0-914022-20-2). Bancroft Parkman.

American Book Publishing Record Annual Cumulative, 1978. LC 66-19741. 1186p. 1979. 59.00x o.p. (ISBN 0-8352-1134-7). Bowker.

American Book Trade Directory 1986. 32nd ed. 1986. lib. bdg. 129.95 o.p. (ISBN 0-8352-2234-9). Bowker.

American Book Trade Directory, 1987-1988. 33rd ed. Ed. by Bowker, R. R., Co. Staff. 1773p. 1987. 149.95 o.p. (ISBN 0-8352-2338-8). Bowker.

American Breweries. Donald Bull et al. LC 83-73558. 400p. 1984. pap. 17.95 o.p. (ISBN 0-9601190-6-X). Bullworks.

American Buffalo. David Mamet. LC 77-78079. 1978. 10.00 o.p. (ISBN 0-394-50229-9, GP810). Grove.

American Building: The Historical Forces That Shaped It. James M. Fitch. (Illus.). 1966. 15.00 o.p. (ISBN 0-395-07680-3). HM.

American Building Two: The Environmental Forces That Shape It. James M. Fitch. 1972. 20.00 o.p. (ISBN 0-395-12681-9). HM.

American Bullion in the European World Trade 1600-1800. Arthur Attman. (Acta Regiae Societatis Scientiarum Humaniora Ser.: No. 26). 115p. (Orig.). 1986. pap. text ed. 29.00x o.p. (ISBN 0-317-65620-1). Coronet Bks.

American Bureaucracy. Peter Woll. (Orig.). 1963. pap. 2.95x o.p. (ISBN 0-393-09595-9, NortonC). Norton.

American Business: An Introduction. 3rd ed. Ferdinand F. Mauser & David J. Schwartz. 1974. text ed. 18.95 o.p. (ISBN 0-15-502273-3, HC). HarBraceJ.

American Business: An Introduction. 5th ed. Ferdinand F. Mauser & David J. Schwartz. (Illus.). 598p. 1982. text ed. 21.50 o.p. (ISBN 0-15-502295-4, HC). HarbraceJ.

American Business Dictionary. H. Lazarus. 548p. 1957. (ISBN 0-8022-0941-6). Philos Lib.

American Business Encounters. Roger E. Olsen. Ed. by Gerry Ryan. (Illus.). 96p. (Orig.). 1982. pap. text ed. 5.95 o.p. (ISBN 0-88084-053-6). Alemany Pr.

American Business History. Herman E. Krooss & Charles Gilbert. 352p. 1972. pap. text ed. 24.00 ref ed. o.p. (ISBN 0-13-024083-4). P-H.

American Capitalism: The Concept of Countervailing Power. John Kenneth Galbraith. LC 80-65363. 222p. 1980. 35.00 o.p. (ISBN 0-87332-178-2). M E Sharpe.

American Captain. Edison Marshall. 1976. pap. 1.75 o.p. (ISBN 0-380-00827-0, 30932). Avon.

American Car Spotter's Guide 1940-1965. rev. ed. Tad Burness. LC 78-14879. (Spotter's Guide Ser.). (Illus.). 1978. pap. 16.95 o.p. (ISBN 0-87938-057-8). Motorbooks Intl.

American Catalogue. Ed. by Bruce Johnson. 1976. pap. 5.45 o.p. (ISBN 0-380-00590-5, 28613, Flare). Avon.

American Catholic Experience: A History from Colonial Times to the Present. Jay P. Dolan. LC 84-26026. 504p. 1985. 19.95 o.s.i. (ISBN 0-385-15206-X). Doubleday.

American Catholicism & European Immigrants (1900-1924) Richard M. Linkh. LC 74-79914. vii, 200p. 1975. pap. 9.95 o.p. (ISBN 0-913256-17-X). Ctr Migration.

American Chair: Three Centuries of Style. Robert Bishop. (Illus.). 526p. sewn bdg. 27.50 o.p. (ISBN 0-317-54996-0). Apollo.

American Challenge. Jean-J. Servan-Schreiber. Tr. by Ronald Steel from Fr. LC 68-19793. 1979. pap. 5.95 o.s.i. (ISBN 0-689-70586-7, 249, Atheneum). Macmillan.

American Cheese. Laura Chenel & Linda Siegfried. (Illus.). 256p. 1988. 18.95 o.p. Aris Bks.

American Children of Krsna: Case Studies in Cultural Anthropology. Francine J. Daner. LC 75-15616. 1976. pap. text ed. 9.95 o.p. (ISBN 0-03-013546-X, HoltC). HR&W.

American Choice: The Muriel Kallis. Ed. by William S. Lieberman. LC 81-4006. (Steinberg Newman Collection). (Illus.). 168p. 1981. pap. 1.50 o.p. (ISBN 0-87099-270-8). Metro Mus Art.

American Christmases: From the Puritans to the Victorians. Eugenia L. Tennant. 1975. 10.00 o.p. (ISBN 0-682-48358-3, Banner). Exposition-Phoenix.

American Church. Vergilus Ferm. 1953. (ISBN 0-8022-0484-8). Philos Lib.

American Cinema: Directors & Directions, 1929-1968. Andrew Sarris. LC 81-22385. 383p. 1982. Repr. of 1968 ed. lib. bdg. 31.50 o.p. (ISBN 0-374-97031-9, Octagon). Hippocrene Bks.

American Circus. Wilton Eckley. 1984. lib. bdg. 14.95 o.s.i. (ISBN 0-8057-9017-9, Twayne). G K Hall.

American City. Stuart A. Queen. LC 73-138175. (Illus.). 383p. 1972. Repr. of 1953 ed. lib. bdg. 35.00x o.p. (ISBN 0-8371-5632-7, QUAC). Greenwood.

American City: From the Civil War to the New Deal. Giorgio Ciucci et al. Tr. by Barbara L. La Penta from Ital. (Illus.). 580p. 1979. pap. text ed. 19.95 o.p. (ISBN 0-262-53044-9). MIT Pr.

American Civil-Military Decisions. Ed. by Harold Stein. LC 62-16825. 706p. 1963. 35.00 o.p. (ISBN 0-8173-4707-0). U of Ala Pr.

American Class Structure: A New Synthesis. Dennis Gilbert & Joseph A. Kahl. 1982. pap. 18.00x o.p. (ISBN 0-256-02678-5). Wadsworth Pub.

American Class System: An Introduction to Social Stratification. Daniel W. Rossides. LC 75-31001. (Illus.). 480p. 1976. text ed. 17.50 o.p. (ISBN 0-395-20624-3). HM.

American Classrooms. Catherine Wagner. Catherine Wagner. (Illus.). 96p. 1988. pap. 25.00 o.p. (ISBN 0-89381-338-9). Aperture.

American Cockroach. W. J. Bell & K. G. Adiyodi. 1981. 85.00 o.p. (ISBN 0-412-16140-0, NO. 6557, Pub. by Chapman & Hall). Routledge Chapman & Hall.

American College. P. F. Valentine. (ISBN 0-8022-1758-3). Philos Lib.

American College Faculty Members: Nineteen Sixty-Three. Joe L. Spaeth. (Report Ser.: No. 106). 1966. 6.00x o.p. (ISBN 0-932132-06-5). NORC.

American College Novel: An Annotated Bibliography. John E. Kramer, Jr. 1981. lib. bdg. 51.00 o.p. (ISBN 0-8240-9365-8). Garland Pub.

American College Testing Program (ACT) 9th ed. Eve Steinberg. LC 81-2727. 384p. 1981. lib. bdg. 12.00 o.p. (ISBN 0-668-05145-0); pap. 7.95 o.p. (ISBN 0-668-05151-5). Arco.

American Colonial Painting: Materials for a History. Waldron P. Belknap, Jr. Ed. by Charles C. Sellers. LC 59-10313. (Illus.). 398p. 1960. boxed 32.50x o.s.i. (ISBN 0-674-02250-5, Belknap Pr). Harvard U Pr.

American Combat Planes. 3rd & enl. ed. Ray Wagner. LC 77-16952. (Illus.). 608p. 1982. pap. 14.95 o.p. (ISBN 0-385-13120-8). Doubleday.

American Communism: A Critical Analysis of Its Origins, Development & Programs. James O'Neal & G. A. Werner. LC 75-138170. 416p. 1972. Repr. of 1947 ed. lib. bdg. 22.50x o.p. (ISBN 0-8371-5627-0, ONAC). Greenwood.

American Constitution. 5th ed. Alfred H. Kelly & Winfred Harbison. 1976. 19.95x o.p. (ISBN 0-393-09176-7, NortonC). Norton.

American Constitutional Custom. Burleigh C. Rodick. 1953. (ISBN 0-8022-1362-6). Philos Lib.

American Constitutional Law: Introductory Essays & Selected Cases. 7th ed. Alpheus T. Mason et al. 704p. 1983. pap. text ed. (ISBN 0-13-024695-6). P-H.

American Correctional Association, 114th Annual Congress: Proceedings. Ed. by Patricia Millard & Darlene Megahan. 150p. (Orig.). 1984. pap. 10.00 o.p. (ISBN 0-942974-68-9). Am Correctional.

American Costume Dolls: How to Make & Dress Them. Nina R. Jordan. LC 41-51603. (Illus.). (gr. 3-7). 1941. 6.50 o.p. (ISBN 0-15-203006-9, HJ). HarBraceJ.

American Counterpoint: Slavery & Racism in the North & South. C. Vann Woodward. 17.50 o.p. (ISBN 0-8446-6087-6). Peter Smith.

American Country. Shields Potter. (Illus.). 1986. pap. 19.95 o.p. (ISBN 0-317-60351-5). Crown.

American Country Dances of the Revolutionary Era: Seventeen Seventy-Five to Seventeen Ninety-Five. 2nd, rev. ed. Kate V. Keller & Ralph Sweet. 53p. 1976. 3.00x o.p. (ISBN 0-686-26758-3). Conn Hist Soc.

American Country Houses of the Guilded Age. Arnold Lewis. 1983. 15.50 o.p. (ISBN 0-8446-5947-9). Peter Smith.

American Craft Today. Paul. J. Smith & Edward Lucie-Smith. LC 86-11063. (Illus.). 328p. 1986. 45.00 o.p. (ISBN 1-55584-014-0). Weidenfeld.

American Criminal Procedure, Cases & Commentary: 1986 Supplement. 2nd ed. Stephen A. Saltzburg. (American Casebook Ser.). 310p. 1986. 8.95 o.p. (ISBN 0-314-28600-4). West Pub.

American Criminal Procedure Cases & Commentary: 1987 Supplement. 2nd ed. Stephen A. Saltzburg. (American Casebook Ser.). 390p. 1987. pap. text ed. 9.95 o.p. (ISBN 0-314-61005-7). West Pub.

American Criminal Procedure, Cases & Commentary. 2nd ed. Stephen A. Saltzburg. LC 83-19780. (American Casebook Ser.). 1193p. 1983. text ed. 32.95 o.p. (ISBN 0-314-76068-7). West Pub.

American Culture & Society since the Nineteen Thirties. Christopher Brookeman. 192p. 1984. 22.00x o.p. (ISBN 0-8052-3939-1). Schocken.

American Culture since the Nineteen Thirties. Date not set. (ISBN 0-8052-3939-1). Random.

American Days: A Play. Stephen Poliakoff. 65p. 1974. pap. 4.95 o.p. (ISBN 0-413-46890-9, NO.2579). Heinemann Ed.

American Defense Policy from Eisenhower to Kennedy: The Politics of Changing Military Requirements, 1957-1961. Richard A. Aliano. LC 74-27709. xi, 309p. 1975. 18.50x o.p. (ISBN 0-8214-0181-5); pap. 8.95x o.p. (ISBN 0-8214-0406-7). Ohio U Pr.

American Department of the British Government, 1768-1782. Margaret Spector. 1972. lib. bdg. 18.00x o.p. (ISBN 0-374-97535-3, Octagon). Hippocrene Bks.

American Diabetes Association & the American Dietetic Association Family Cookbook, Vol. II. American Diabetes Association Staff & American Dietetic Association Staff. (Illus.). 400p. 1984. 15.95 o.p. (ISBN 0-13-024910-6). P-H.

American Dictionary of Printing & Bookmaking. Ed. by W W. Pasko. LC 66-27215. 600p. 1967. Repr. of 1894 ed. 42.00x o.p. (ISBN 0-8103-3345-7). Gale.

American Dietetic Association Family Cookbook. American Diabetes Association Staff & American Dietetic Association Staff. LC 80-16722. 320p. 1980. 15.95 o.p. (ISBN 0-13-024901-7). P-H.

American Diplomacy. rev. & enl. ed. Robert H. Ferrell. (Illus.). 1969. 11.50x o.p. (ISBN 0-393-09861-3, NortonC). Norton.

American Diplomacy & the War of the Pacific. Herbert Millington. 1972. lib. bdg. 16.00x o.p. (ISBN 0-374-95725-8, Octagon). Hippocrene Bks.

American Diplomacy During the World War. Charles Seymour. LC 74-12649. 1975. Repr. of 1934 ed. lib. bdg. 35.00x o.p. (ISBN 0-8371-7746-4, SEAD). Greenwood.

American Diplomacy in the Great Depression: Hoover-Stimson Foreign Policy, 1929-1933. Robert H. Ferrell. (Illus.). 1970. pap. 2.25 o.p. (ISBN 0-393-00511-9, Norton Lib). Norton.

American Diplomatic Memoirs: A Bibliography. Amos Lakos. (Public Administration Ser.: P 1750). 12p. 1985. 2.00 o.p. (ISBN 0-89028-530-6). Vance Biblios.

American Drama & Its Critics: A Collection of Critical Essays. Ed. by Alan S. Downer. LC 65-24424. (Midway Reprint Ser). 1976. pap. text ed. 15.00x o.s.i. (ISBN 0-226-16061-0). U of Chicago Pr.

American Dramatists Nineteen Eighteen to Nineteen Forty. Ed. by Bernard F. Dukore. (Modern Dramatists Ser.). 224p. 1984. 19.50 o.p. (ISBN 0-394-54293-2, GP948). Grove.

American Dramatists 1918-1945. Ed. by Bernard F. Dukore. (Modern Dramatists Ser.). 224p. 1984. pap. 7.95 o.p. (ISBN 0-394-62340-1, E-963, Ever). Grove.

American Eagle. (Everything Bks.). 128p. 1983. pap. 2.98 o.p. (ISBN 0-913428-75-2). Landfall Pr.

American Earthquake: A Documentary of the Twenties & Thirties. Edmund Wilson. 576p. 1979. pap. 7.95 o.p. (ISBN 0-374-51507-7). FS&G.

American Ecclesiastes. Richard Batman. LC 84-10726. (Illus.). 384p. 1985. 24.95 o.p. (ISBN 0-15-105578-5). HarBraceJ.

American Economic History. Robert C. Puth. 485p. 1983. text ed. 32.95 o.s.i. (ISBN 0-03-050556-9). Dryden Pr.

American Economic History. Kenneth H. Smith. LC 75-84415. (Real World of Economics Ser.). (Illus.). (gr. 5-11). 1970. PLB 4.95 o.p. (ISBN 0-8225-0612-2). Lerner Pubns.

American Economic History: A Guide to Information Sources. Ed. by William K. Hutchinson. LC 73-17577. (Economic Information Guide Ser.: Vol. 16). 312p. 1980. 68.00x o.p. (ISBN 0-8103-1287-5). Gale.

American Economics Series. Attiyeh & Lumsden. (gr. 10-12). 1972. pap. text ed. 9.00 each incl. 7 texts, plus 1 suppl. o.p. (ISBN 0-8449-0700-6); tchrs' manual 2.00 o.p. (ISBN 0-8449-0704-9); test 2.00 o.p. Carroll CA.

American Economy We Need: But Won't Get from the Republicans or the Democrats. John B. Anderson. LC 83-48832. 370p. 1984. 17.95 o.p. (ISBN 0-689-11464-8, Atheneum). Macmillan.

American Electorate. Bruce A. Campbell. LC 78-31154. 1979. pap. text ed. 11.95 o.p. (ISBN 0-275-85770-0, HoltC). HR&W.

American Electorate: A Historical Bibliography. LC 83-12229. (Research Guides: No. 8). 388p. 1984. lib. bdg. 34.00 o.p. (ISBN 0-87436-372-1). ABC-Clio.

American Electrician's Handbook. 10th ed. Terrell Croft et al. 1664p. 1981. text ed. 57.50 o.p. (ISBN 0-07-013931-8). McGraw.

American Encyclopaedia of Printing. Ed. by J. Luther Ringwalt & John Bidwell. LC 78-74411. (Nineteenth-Century Book Arts & Printing History Ser.: Vol. 21). (Illus.). 1980. lib. bdg. 80.00 o.p. (ISBN 0-8240-3895-9). Garland Pub.

American Engineer in China. William B. Parsons. LC 78-74326. (Modern Chinese Economy Ser.). 315p. 1980. lib. bdg. 40.00 o.p. (ISBN 0-8240-4256-5). Garland Pub.

American Engineers of the Nineteenth Century: A Biographical Index. Christine M. Roysdon & Linda A. Khatri. LC 77-83371. (Reference Library of Social Science). 1978. lib. bdg. 39.00 o.p. (ISBN 0-8240-9827-7). Garland Pub.

American English: Grammatical Structure, 4 Bks. Harvey Nadler & Leonard R. Marelli. (Integrated Series for International Students). 1971. Bk. I. pap. 11.75 o.p. (ISBN 0-395-31009-1); Bk. II. pap. 10.50 o.p. (ISBN 0-395-31010-5); Bk. III. pap. 10.50 o.p. (ISBN 0-395-31011-3); Bk. IV. pap. 10.00 o.p. (ISBN 0-395-30992-1). HM.

American English: Guided Composition Paper. Harvey Nadler & Leonard R. Marelli. (Integrated Series for International Students). 1984. pap. 12.75 o.p. (ISBN 0-395-30995-6); Readings I. pap. 6.25 o.p. (ISBN 0-395-30997-2); Readings II. pap. 6.25 o.p. (ISBN 0-395-30998-0); Readings III. pap. 6.25 o.p. (ISBN 0-395-30999-9). HM.

American English: Pronunciation & Dictation. Harvey Nadler & Leonard R. Marelli. (Integrated Series for International Students). 1971. pap. 8.50 o.p. (ISBN 0-395-30994-8). HM.

American Ephemeris for the 20th Century: 1900 to 2000. Rev. ed. Neil F. Michelsen. (American Ephemeris Ser.). 608p. (Orig.). 1983. Midnight. pap. 15.95 o.p. (ISBN 0-917086-19-8). Noon (ISBN 0-917086-20-1). A C S Pubns Inc.

American Ephemeris 1971 to 1980. Neil F. Michelsen. 1976. pap. 5.00 o.p. (ISBN 0-917086-02-3, Pub. by Astro Computing Serv.). Whitford Pr.

American Ephemeris 1977. 1978. pap. 1.00 o.p. (ISBN 0-917086-09-0, Pub. by Astro Computing Serv.). Whitford Pr.

American Etchings. S. R. Koehler. Bd. with American Art. LC 75-28876. (Art Experience in Late 19th Century America Ser.: Vol. 12). (Illus.). 1978. Repr. of 1886 ed. lib. bdg. 88.00 o.p. (ISBN 0-8240-2236-X). Garland Pub.

American Ethnic Groups. Ed. by Thomas Sowell. 254p. 1978. pap. 14.50 o.p. (ISBN 0-87766-210-X, 16100). Urban Inst.

American Expansion in the Late 19th Century. Ed. by J. R. Hollingsworth. (American Problem Ser.). 128p. 1968. pap. 5.95 o.p. (ISBN 0-03-067240-6). Krieger.

American Express: An Unauthorized History. Peter Z. Grossman. (Illus.). 384p. 1987. 19.95 o.p. (ISBN 0-517-56238-3). Crown.

American Express Pocket Guide to Hong Kong, Singapore, Bangkok. (American Express Pocket Travel Guides). (Illus.). 1988. pap. 9.95 o.p. Prentice Hall Pr.

American Express Pocket Guide to London. rev. ed. (American Express Pocket Travel Guides Ser.). 1986. 8.95 o.p. (ISBN 0-671-62014-2). S&S.

American Express Pocket Guide to New York. rev. ed. (American Express Pocket Travel Guides Ser.). (Illus.). 250p. 1986. 8.95 o.p. (ISBN 0-671-62015-0). S&S.

American Express Pocket Guide to Paris. rev. & enl. ed. (American Express Pocket Travel Guides). 1986. pap. 8.95 o.p. (ISBN 0-671-62016-9). P-H.

American Express Pocket Guide to Spain. Herbert B. Livesay. (American Express Pocket Travel Guides). (Illus.). 1984. pap. 8.95 o.p. (ISBN 0-671-50028-7). S&S.

American Express Pocket Guides to Mexico. James Tickell. (Illus.). 1984. pap. 8.95 o.p. (ISBN 0-671-50026-0). S&S.

American Express Pocket Travel Guide to Tokyo. (Illus.). 250p. 1988. 9.95 o.p. (ISBN 0-317-64609-5). Prentice Hall Pr.

American Expressions. R. B. Costello. 192p. 1981. text ed. 10.95 o.p. (ISBN 0-07-047137-1). McGraw.

American Extremes. Daniel Cosio Villegas. Tr. by Americo Paredes from Span. LC 64-11188. (Texas Pan American Ser.). Orig. Title: Extremos de America. 243p. 1964. pap. 6.95x o.p. (ISBN 0-292-70069-5). U of Tex Pr.

American Fairy Tales. L. Frank Baum. (Illus.). 13.25 o.p. (ISBN 0-8446-5731-X). Peter Smith.

American Falls. John C. Batchelor. 1985. 16.45 o.p. (ISBN 0-393-02211-0). Norton.

American Family Cookbook. Melanie DeProft. 832p. 1981. pap. 10.95 o.p. (ISBN 0-671-43884-0, Fireside). S&S.

American Family History: A Historical Bibliography. LC 84-2955. (Research Guides: No. 12). 282p. 1984. lib. bdg. 34.00 o.p. (ISBN 0-87436-380-2). ABC-Clio.

American Farm. Maisie Conrat & Richard Conrat. 1977. 17.50 o.p. (ISBN 0-395-25105-2, Co-Pub. by HM); pap. 9.95 o.p. (ISBN 0-395-25359-4). Calif Hist.

American Fashion Designs by Wilson Folmar. Montgomery Museum of Fine Arts Staff. Ed. by Katherine Campbell. LC 78-61234. (Illus.). 48p. 1978. pap. 5.00 o.p. (ISBN 0-89280-011-9). Montgomery Mus.

American Federal Executive. William L. Warner et al. LC 75-11487. 405p. 1975. Repr. of 1963 ed. lib. bdg. 22.50x o.p. (ISBN 0-8371-8207-7, WAAF). Greenwood.

American Fiction: New Readings. Ed. by Richard Gray. LC 83-2810. (Critical Studies). 240p. 1983. text ed. 28.50x o.p. (ISBN 0-389-20370-X, 07242). B&N Imports.

American Fiction, Nineteen Twenty to Nineteen Forty. Joseph W. Beach. LC 60-8197. 1972. pap. text ed. 3.25x o.p. (ISBN 0-689-70289-2, 172, Atheneum). Macmillan.

American Fictional Hero, Vol. 4. Ramachandra B. Rao. (English Language & Literature Ser.). 96p. 1979. text ed. 10.50x o.p. (ISBN 0-391-02543-0). Humanities.

American Film Exhibition & an Analysis of the Motion Picture Industry's Market Structure, 1963-1980. Gary R. Edgerton. Ed. by Garth S. Jowett. LC 81-48343. (Dissertations on Film Ser.). 235p. 1982. lib. bdg. 36.00 o.p. (ISBN 0-8240-5100-9). Garland Pub.

American Film Studios. Gene Fernett. 1988. lib. bdg. 35.00x o.p. McFarland & Co.

American Firehouse: An Architectural & Social History. Rebecca Zurier. LC 82-73304. (Illus.). 288p. 1982. 35.00 o.s.i. (ISBN 0-89659-314-2). Abbeville Pr.

American Firms Importing from the People's Republic of China. Ed. by Joan M. Richards. 93p. 1982. pap. text ed. 60.00x o.p. (ISBN 0-8103-2038-X, Pub. by Natl Coun US-China). Gale.

American Flying Boats: A Pictorial Survey. Ed. by D. Bradford Barton Ltd. 1981. 25.00x o.p. (ISBN 0-686-97136-1, Pub. by D B Barton England). State Mutual Bk.

American Folk Art: Expressions of a New Spirit. Museum of American Folk Art Staff. LC 83-60191. (Illus.). 146p. 1985. 29.95x o.s.i. (ISBN 0-87663-461-7); pap. 19.95 o.p. (ISBN 0-87663-863-9). Universe.

American Food & California Wine. Barbara Kafka. Ed. by Gladys Topkis. LC 81-68837. (Great American Cooking Schools Ser.). (Illus.). 84p. 1981. pap. 5.95 o.p. (ISBN 0-941034-00-3). I Chalmers.

American Football: The Records. Miles Aiken & Peter Rowe. (Illus.). 144p. (Orig.). 1987. pap. 14.95 o.p. (ISBN 0-85112-839-4, Pub. by Guinness Superlatives England). Sterling.

American Forecaster Nineteen Eighty-Eight: The First No-Nonsense Authority on the Future. Kim Long. 192p. 1987. pap. 5.95 o.p. (ISBN 0-89471-556-9). Running Pr.

American Forecaster, 1986. Long & Reim. LC 86-10062. 192p. (Orig.). 1986. 5.95 o.p. (ISBN 0-89471-414-7). Running Pr.

American Foreign Policy. 2nd ed. Valentine J. Belfiglio. (Illus.). 152p. 1983. pap. text ed. 12.25 o.p. (ISBN 0-8191-2677-2). U Pr of Amer.

American Foreign Policy. enl. ed. Henry A. Kissinger. 250p. 1974. 6.95 o.p. (ISBN 0-393-05525-6); pap. 3.95x o.p. (ISBN 0-393-09264-X). Norton.

American Foreign Policy: A History. 2nd ed. Thomas G. Paterson & J. G. Clifford. 1983. Vol. I, 304. pap. text ed. 14.50 o.p. (ISBN 0-669-04567-5); Vol. II, 496. pap. text ed. 15.50 o.p. (ISBN 0-669-04566-7). Heath.

American Foreign Policy since World War II. 10th ed. John Spanier. LC 84-25190. 353p. 1985. pap. text ed. 18.95 o.p. (ISBN 0-03-001093-4, HoltC). HR&W.

American Foreign Policy: Three Essays. Henry A. Kissinger. 1949. pap. 1.45x o.p. (ISBN 0-393-09853-2, NortonC). Norton.

American Freedom & the Radical Right. Edward L. Ericson. LC 81-71132. 128p. 1982. 9.95 o.p. (ISBN 0-8044-5355-1); pap. 6.95 o.p. (ISBN 0-8044-6141-4). Ungar.

American Frontier Life: Early Western Painting & Prints. Ron Tyler et al. (Illus.). 204p. 1987. 45.00 o.p. (ISBN 0-89659-691-5). Abbeville Pr.

American Frontiers: The Photographs of Timothy H. O'Sullivan 1867-1874. Joel Snyder. LC 81-66768. (Illus.). 120p. 1982. ltd. ed. 250.00 o.p. (ISBN 0-89381-094-0). Aperture.

American Fur Trade in the Far West, 2 vols. Hiram M. Chittenden. LC 73-21914. (Illus.). 1976. Repr. of 1935 ed. Set. lib. bdg. 75.00x o.p. (ISBN 0-678-01035-8). Kelley.

American Furniture & Its Makers. Ed. by Ian M. Quimby. LC 64-7642. (Winterthur Portfolio: No. 13). 1979. 20.00 o.s.i. (ISBN 0-226-92139-5). U of Chicago Pr.

American Furniture of the Colonial Period. Marvin D. Schwartz. LC 76-18763. (Illus.). 110p. 1976. 1.95 o.p. (ISBN 0-87099-149-3). Metro Mus Art.

American Furniture: The Federal Period. Montgomery. 497p. 150.00 o.p. (ISBN 0-317-54994-4). Apollo.

American Gardens in the Eighteenth Century: "For Use or for Delight" Ann Leighton. 1976. 17.50 o.p. (ISBN 0-395-24764-0). HM.

American Genealogist: Being a Catalogue of Family Histories, a Bibliography of American Genealogy or a List of the Title Pages of Books & Pamphlets on Family History. 5th ed. LC 74-34247. 406p. 1975. Repr. of 1900 ed. 60.00x o.p. (ISBN 0-8103-4151-4). Gale.

American Geological Literature 1669-1850. Ed. by R. M. Hazen & M. Hindle Hazen. LC 79-25898. 448p. 1982. 44.95 o.p. (ISBN 0-87933-371-5). Van Nos Reinhold.

American Ghost. Chester Aaron. LC 72-88166. (Illus.). 192p. (Orig.). (gr. 5 up). 1973. 5.95 o.p. (ISBN 0-15-203050-6, HJ). HarBraceJ.

American Girls Handy Book. Lina Beard & Adelia Beard. LC 69-11086. (Illus.). (gr. 2-8). 1968. Repr. of 1888 ed. 12.50 o.p. (ISBN 0-8048-0008-1). C E Tuttle.

American Glass. Helen McKearin & George S. McKearin. (Illus.). 1941. 22.50 o.s.i. (ISBN 0-517-00111-X). Crown.

American Government. Gayle Avant. (College Outlines Ser). 1978. pap. 4.95 o.s.i. (ISBN 0-671-08051-2). Monarch Pr.

American Government. Charles V. Hamilton. 1982. text ed. write for info. o.p. (ISBN 0-673-15220-0); write for info. study guide o.p. (ISBN 0-673-15572-2). Scott F.

American Government. 3rd ed. Arthur J. Hughes. (gr. 9-12). cancelled o.s.i. (ISBN 0-02-644560-3, 64448); cancelled o.s.i. (ISBN 0-02-644490-9, 64449). Glencoe.

American Government. 2nd ed. Michael A. Krasner & Stephen G. Chabersky. 1982. text ed. write for info. o.p. (ISBN 0-02-366270-0). Macmillan.

American Government. 3rd ed. Walter E. Volkomer. (Illus.). 448p. 1983. pap. text ed. (ISBN 0-13-027292-2). P-H.

American Government. 4th ed. Walter E. Volkomer. (Illus.). 432p. 1986. pap. text ed. (ISBN 0-13-027335-X). P-H.

American Government & Politics Today. Steffen W. Schmidt et al. (Illus.). 708p. 1985. text ed. 33.50 o.p. (ISBN 0-314-85294-8). West Pub.

American Government & Politics Today: Essentials. Barbara A. Bardes et al. (Illus.). 578p. (Orig.). 1986. pap. text ed. 31.50 o.p. (ISBN 0-314-96078-3); instr's manual avail. o.p. (ISBN 0-314-99663-X); study guide 11.75 o.p. (ISBN 0-314-98327-9). West Pub.

American Government: Incomplete Conquest. Brief ed. Theodore J. Lowi. LC 76-41099. 1977. 17.95 o.p. (ISBN 0-03-019886-0, HoltC). HR&W.

American Government: Policy & Politics. Neal Tannahill & Wendell M. Bedichek. 1985. pap. text ed. write for info. o.p. (ISBN 0-673-15838-1); write for info. study guide o.p. (ISBN 0-673-18098-0). Scott F.

American Government, Politics & Policymaking. 2nd ed. David R. Berman. LC 82-61096. (Illus.). 1983. text ed. 13.95x o.p. (ISBN 0-913530-31-X). Palisades Pub.

American Government: Strategy & Choice. Peter H. Aranson. 1981. text ed. write for info. o.p. (ISBN 0-316-04940-9); tchr's. ed. avail. o.p. (ISBN 0-316-04941-7). Scott F.

American Government Today. rev. ed. Gaylon L. Caldwell & Robert Lawrence. (Illus.). 1969. 8.25x o.p. (ISBN 0-393-09864-8, NortonC). Norton.

American Graphic Art. Frank Weitenkampf. LC 74-6198. 448p. 1974. Repr. of 1912 ed. 45.00x o.p. (ISBN 0-8103-4020-8). Gale.

American Grilles. Salmieri Frattolillo. LC 79-1859. (Illus.). 1979. 12.95 o.p. (ISBN 0-15-105588-2); pap. 8.95 o.p. (ISBN 0-15-605589-9, Harv). HarBraceJ.

American Guide to U. S. Coins 1986. rev. & updated ed. Charles F. French. 1985. pap. 4.95 o.p. (ISBN 0-671-60368-X, Fireside). S&S.

American Guide to U. S. Coins, 1988 Edition. Charles F. French. (Illus.). 192p. 1987. pap. 5.95 o.s.i. (ISBN 0-671-64577-3, Fireside). S&S.

American Heart Association Cookbook. 3rd rev. ed. Ed. by Mary Winston & Ruthe Eshleman. (Illus.). 1979. 12.95 o.p. (ISBN 0-679-50902-X). McKay.

American Heritage Book of Indians. William Brandon. Ed. by Alvin M. Josephy, Jr. LC 61-14871. (Illus.). 1961. 10.98 o.p. (ISBN 0-8281-0301-1, B038R1-08). Am Heritage.

American Heritage Guide to Antiques. Mary Durant. LC 72-111653. 1970. pap. text ed. 4.95 o.p. (ISBN 0-07-018346-5). McGraw.

American Heritage History of the Great West. David Lavender. Ed. by Alvin M. Josephy, Jr. LC 65-23041. (Illus.). 416p. 1973. Repr. 24.95 o.p. (ISBN 0-8281-0303-8). Am Heritage.

American Heritage History of the Indian Wars. Robert M. Utley & Wilcomb E. Washburn. LC 77-23044. (Illus.). 352p. 1977. Repr. slipcased 39.95 o.p. (ISBN 0-8281-0203-1); 12.95 o.p. (ISBN 0-8281-0202-3). Am Heritage.

American Heritage Picture History of the Civil War. American Heritage Editors & Bruce Catton. LC 60-10751. 1960. 24.95 o.p. (ISBN 0-385-00907-0, Pub. by Am Heritage). Doubleday.

American Heritage Short History of the Civil War. Bruce Catton. 288p. 1982. pap. 2.95 o.p. (ISBN 0-440-30123-8, LE). Dell.

American High School Band. George Taylor. (YA) (gr. 7-12). 1977. PLB 9.97 o.p. (ISBN 0-8239-0387-7). Rosen Group.

American Historian: A Social-Intellectual History of the Writing of the American Past. Harvey Wish. LC 82-21150. viii, 366p. 1983. Repr. of 1960 ed. lib. bdg. 48.50x o.p. (ISBN 0-313-23847-2, WHAM). Greenwood.

American Historical Views on Staffordshire China. 3rd ed. Ellouise B. Larsen. (Illus.). 16.50 o.p. (ISBN 0-8446-5213-X). Peter Smith.

American History after Eighteen Sixty-Five. 8th ed. Ray A. Billington. (Quality Paperback: No. 27). 364p. (Orig.). 1979. pap. 3.95 o.p. Littlefield.

American History: Major Controversies Reviewed. Richard Kezirian. 176p. 1982. pap. text ed. 11.95 o.p. (ISBN 0-8403-2921-0). Kendall-Hunt.

American History Suppy, No. 1. Date not set. pap. (ISBN 0-8052-0775-9). Random.

American History, 1987-88, Vol. 1. 10th ed. Robert J. Maddox. LC 74-187540. (Annual Editions Ser.). (Illus.). 224p. 1988. pap. text ed. 9.95 o.p. (ISBN 0-87967-669-8). Dushkin Pub.

American History, 1987-88, Vol. 2. 10th ed. Robert J. Maddox. LC 75-20755. (Annual Editions Ser.). (Illus.). 256p. 1988. pap. text ed. 9.95 o.p. (ISBN 0-87967-670-1). Dushkin Pub.

American Home: A Historical Background of General Works. Lamia Doumato. (Architecture Ser.: A 1367). 21p. 1985. 3.00 o.p. (ISBN 0-89028-357-5). Vance Biblios.

American Home All-Purpose Cookbook. American Home Editors. LC 66-23272. (Illus.). 572p. 1978. pap. 7.95 o.p. (ISBN 0-87131-268-9). M Evans.

American Home Garden Book & Plant Encyclopedia. American Home Editors. LC 63-19657. (Illus.). 512p. 1964. pap. 8.95 o.p. (ISBN 0-87131-035-X). M Evans.

American Hospital Association Guide to the Health Care Field. 1987. pap. 150.00 o.p. (ISBN 0-87258-452-6, AHA-010087). Am Hospital.

American Humor: A Study of the National Character. Constance Rourke. LC 31-7953. 1971. pap. 3.95 o.p. (ISBN 0-15-605590-2, HB213, Harv). HarBraceJ.

American Illustration Showcase, Vol. 9. American Showcase Staff. (Illus.). 536p. 1986. pap. 29.95 o.p. (ISBN 0-8230-0184-9). Watson-Guptill.

American Illustration Showcase, 8. Ed. by Ira Shapiro. (Illus.). 388p. 1985. pap. 24.95 o.s.i. (ISBN 0-931144-31-0). Am Showcase.

American Illustration Showcase, 9. (Illus.). 536p. 1986. pap. 29.95 o.s.i. (ISBN 0-931144-35-3). Am Showcase.

American Impressions: Prints since Pollock. Riva Castleman. LC 84-47690. (Illus.). 195p. 1985. 39.50 o.s.i. (ISBN 0-394-53683-5). Knopf.

American in Europe. Egon Larsen. 224p. 1954. (ISBN 0-8022-0928-9). Philos Lib.

American in the Making: The Life Story of an Immigrant. M. E. Ravage. 12.00 o.p. (ISBN 0-8446-0231-0). Peter Smith.

American Indian Authors. N. Scott Momaday. Ed. by William Adams. (Multi-Ethnic Literature Ser.). (gr. 9-12). 1976. pap. 9.44 o.p. (ISBN 0-395-24040-9). HM.

American Indian Craft Inspirations. Janet D'Amato & Alex D'Amato. LC 72-83734. (Illus.). 224p. 1972. 7.95 o.p. (ISBN 0-87131-031-7). M Evans.

American Indian Culture: A Selective Bibliography of Bibliographies. Frank J. Dolak. (Public Administration Ser.: P 1778). 7p. 1985. 2.00 o.p. (ISBN 0-89028-578-0). Vance Biblios.

American Indian Gestural Code Based on Universal American Indian Hand Talk. Ed. by M. Skelly. LC 79-19202. 528p. 1979. 69.50 o.p. (ISBN 0-444-00333-9, Biomedical Pr); pap. 37.25 o.p. (ISBN 0-444-00331-2, Biomedical Pr). Elsevier.

American Indian in Higher Education, 1975-76 to 1984-85. Judith E. Fries. (CS Ser.: No. 87-321). (Illus.). 38p. 1987. pap. 2.00 o.p. (S/N 065-000-00286-8). USGPO.

American Indian Law. William C. Canby, Jr. LC 81-3066. (Nutshell Ser.). 288p. 1981. pap. text ed. 9.95 o.p. (ISBN 0-314-59473-6). West Pub.

American Indian: Past & Present. 2nd ed. Roger I. Nichols & George R. Adams. 283p. 1981. pap. text ed. 9.00 o.p. (ISBN 0-394-34200-3, RanC). Random.

American Indian Poetry: An Anthology of Songs & Chants. Ed. by George W. Cronyn. LC 73-133483. 1970. pap. 5.95 o.p. (ISBN 0-87140-226-2). Liveright.

American Indian Policy in the Jacksonian Era. Ronald N. Satz. LC 73-94119. (Illus.). xii, 351p. 1975. 14.95x o.p. (ISBN 0-8032-0823-5); pap. 7.50x o.p. (ISBN 0-8032-5848-8, BB 628, Bison). U of Nebr Pr.

American Industry in International Competition: Government Policies & Corporate Strategies. Ed. by John Zysman & Laura Tyson. LC 82-22044. 436p. 1984. 42.50x o.p. (ISBN 0-8014-9297-1); pap. 19.95 o.p. Cornell U Pr.

American Industry: Structure, Conduct, Performance. 5th ed. Richard E. Caves. LC 82-495. (Illus.). 160p. 1982. pap. text ed. (ISBN 0-13-027656-1). P-H.

American Jewish Album: From Sixteen Fifty-Four to the Present. Allon Schoener. LC 83-42934. (Illus.). 352p. 1983. 45.00 o.p. (ISBN 0-8478-0500-X); 200.00 o.p. limited leatherbound ed. (ISBN 0-8478-0521-2); pap. 25.00 o.p. (ISBN 0-8478-0592-1). Rizzoli Intl.

American Jewish Year Book, 1979, Vol. 79. LC 99-4040. 1979. 15.00 o.p. Am Jewish Comm.

American Jewry & the Civil War. Bertram W. Korn. LC 61-65874. (Temple Bk). 1970. pap. 4.50 o.p. (ISBN 0-689-70245-0, T19, Atheneum). Macmillan.

American Journey: Traveling with Tocqueville in Search of Democracy in America. Richard Reeves. 1982. 15.50 o.p. (ISBN 0-671-24746-8). S&S.

American Judaism. rev. ed. Nathan Glazer. LC 57-8574. (Chicago History of American Civilization Ser). 1973. lib. bdg. 12.50x o.s.i. (ISBN 0-226-29839-6); pap. text ed. 7.50x o.s.i. (ISBN 0-226-29841-8, CHAC7). U of Chicago Pr.

American Judaism: The Religion & Religious Institutions of the Jewish People in the United States. Joseph Leiser. LC 78-26230. 1979. Repr. of 1925 ed. lib. bdg. 35.00x o.p. (ISBN 0-313-20879-4, LEAJ). Greenwood.

American Judiciary: Will a Uniform System Help? Ed. by Mark A. Siegel et al. 78p. 1983. pap. 13.95 o.p. (ISBN 0-936474-33-5). Info Plus TX.

American Kaleidoscope. Julius Toldi. 430p. 1960. (ISBN 0-8022-1729-X). Philos Lib.

American Kaleidoscope. Wang Tsomin. Ed. & tr. by Duan Liancheng. (Illus.). 470p. 1986. 9.95 o.p. (ISBN 0-8351-1792-8). China Bks.

American Karate: A Complete Fitness Training & Self-Defense Program for Everyday Life. Don Quine. 1986. pap. 9.95 o.p. (ISBN 0-671-55260-0, Fireside). S&S.

American Kennel Club, Eighteen Eighty-Four to Nineteen Eighty-Four. Date not set. (ISBN 0-87605-404-1). Howell Bk.

American Kennel Club, 1884-1984: A Source Book. American Kennel Club Staff. Ed. by Charles A. O'Neill. LC 85-24915. (Illus.). 299p. 1985. 22.95 o.p. (ISBN 0-87605-256-1). Howell Bk.

American Labor & European Politics: The AFL As a Transnational Force. Roy Godson. LC 76-491. 230p. 1976. 17.50x o.p. (ISBN 0-8448-0919-5, Pub. by Crane Russak & Co); pap. 12.00x o.p. (ISBN 0-8448-0920-9). Taylor & Francis.

American Labor Movement. Leon Litwack. 192p. 1986. pap. 6.95 o.p. (ISBN 0-671-62827-5, Touchstone Bks). S&S.

American Labor Sourcebook. Bernard Rifkin. 1979. text ed. 78.00 o.p. (ISBN 0-07-052830-6). McGraw.

American Land Planning Law, 8 vols. Norman Williams, Jr. LC 73-94339. 475.00 o.p. Callaghan.

American Landmarks: Historic Properties of the National Trust for Historic Preservation. 72p. pap. 5.95 o.p. (ISBN 0-89133-093-3). Preservation Pr.

American Landscape Painting: An Interpretation. Wolfgang Born. LC 71-100222. Repr. of 1948 ed. lib. bdg. 29.75x o.p. (ISBN 0-8371-3253-3, BOAL). Greenwood.

American Landscapes. John Szarkowski. 1981. pap. 5.00 o.p. Museum Mod Art.

American Language Today, Checklist 1. Nachbar. Date not set. (ISBN 0-07-045751-4). McGraw.

American Language Today, Checklist 2. Nachbar. Date not set. (ISBN 0-07-045753-0). McGraw.

American Language Today, Checklist 5. Nachbar. Date not set. (ISBN 0-07-045755-7). McGraw.

American Language Today L-4 Te. Nachbar. Date not set. (ISBN 0-07-045784-0). McGraw.

American Language Today L-5 Te. Nachbar. Date not set. (ISBN 0-07-045785-9). McGraw.

American Language Today Lev 6. Nachbar. Date not set. (ISBN 0-07-045776-X). McGraw.

American Language Today LV3 Te. Nachbar. Date not set. (ISBN 0-07-045783-2). McGraw.

American Left in the Twentieth Century. John P. Diggins. (History of U. S. Ser). 1973. pap. text ed. 6.95 o.p. (ISBN 0-15-502308-X, HC). HarBraceJ.

American Library Directory, 1980. 33rd ed. Ed. by Jaques Cattell Press. LC 23-3581. 1836p. 1980. 54.95 o.p. (ISBN 0-8352-1251-3). Bowker.

American Library Directory, 1987-1988, 2 vols. 40th ed. Ed. by Bowker, R. R., Co. Staff. 2386p. 1987. Set. 149.95 o.p. (ISBN 0-8352-2339-6). Vol. 1 (ISBN 0-8352-2420-1). Vol. 2 (ISBN 0-8352-2422-8). Bowker.

American Library History: 1876-1976. Ed. by Howard W. Winger. (Library Trends Ser: Vol. 25, No. 1). 416p. 1976. 8.00x o.p. (ISBN 0-87845-045-9); pap. 5.00x o.s.i. (ISBN 0-87845-057-2). U of Ill Lib Info Sci.

American Life. Jeb S. Magruder. LC 74-78466. (Illus.). 352p. 1974. 10.00 o.p. (ISBN 0-689-10603-3, Atheneum). Macmillan.

American Lit Relit. Richard Armour. 1970. pap. text ed. 2.95 o.p. (ISBN 0-07-002283-6). McGraw.

American Literary Yearbook, Vol. 1. LC 68-21521. 290p. 1968. Repr. of 1919 ed. 40.00x o.p. (ISBN 0-8103-3149-7). Gale.

American Literature & the Dream. Frederic I. Carpenter. 228p. 1956. (ISBN 0-8022-0214-4). Philos Lib.

American Literature As an Expression of the National Mind. rev. ed. Russell Blankenship. LC 72-85845. xvii, 731p. 1973. Repr. of 1949 ed. lib. bdg. 29.50x o.p. (ISBN 0-8154-0432-8). Cooper Sq.

American Literature in Context II, 1830-1865. Brian Harding. 247p. 22.00 o.p. (ISBN 0-416-73900-8, NO. 3655); pap. 10.95 o.p. (ISBN 0-416-73910-5, NO. 3656). Routledge Chapman & Hall.

American Literature Survey. Ed. by Milton R. Stern & Seymour L. Gross. Incl. Vol. 1. Colonial & Federal to 1800. 672p. 1978. pap. text ed. 5.95 o.p. (ISBN 0-14-015085-4); Vol. 2. The American Romantics 1800-1860. Pref. by Van W. Brooks. 720p. 1977. pap. text ed. 5.95 o.p. (ISBN 0-14-015086-2); Vol. 3. Nation & Region, 1860-1900. Pref. by Howard M. Jones. 736p. 1977. pap. text ed. 4.95 o.p. (ISBN 0-14-015087-0); Vol. 4. The Twentieth Century. Pref. by Malcolm Cowley. 736p. 1977. pap. text ed. 6.95 o.p. (ISBN 0-14-015088-9). LC 74-3690. (Viking Portable Library). 1977. pap. Penguin.

American Literature to Nineteen Hundred. Intro. by Lewis Leary. (Great Writers Library). 340p. pap. 9.95 o.p. (ISBN 0-312-34711-1). Academy Chi Pubs.

American Lithographers, 1900-1960: The Artists & Their Printers. Clinton Adams. LC 83-51034. (Illus.). 238p. 1983. 65.00 o.p. (ISBN 0-8263-0660-8). U of NM Pr.

American Local Color Stories. Ed. by Harry R. Warfel & G. H. Orians. LC 72-127599. 846p. 1971. Repr. of 1941 ed. lib. bdg. 25.00x o.p. (ISBN 0-8154-0345-3). Cooper Sq.

American Look. Jaclyn Smith. 192p. 1986. pap. 9.95 o.p. (ISBN 0-671-61439-8, Fireside). S&S.

American Made. Shylah Boyd. 416p. 1975. 10.00 o.p. (ISBN 0-374-10416-6). FS&G.

American Magic: Codes, Ciphers & the Defeat of Japan. Ronald Lewin. (Illus.). 347p. 1982. 14.95 o.p. (ISBN 0-374-10417-4). FS&G.

American Mail-Order Gourmet: The Catalog of Hundreds of Hard-to-Find Delectable Delights. Mark Smith & Naomi Black. LC 86-10032. (Illus.). 128p. 1986. 24.95 o.p. (ISBN 0-89471-388-4); pap. 12.95 o.p. (ISBN 0-89471-389-2). Running Pr.

American Medical Directory, 5 vols. American Medical Association. LC 7-10295. (Vol. 5 is the Directory of Women Physicians). 1979. Set. 225.00 o.p. (ISBN 0-88416-274-5). Vol. 1 (ISBN 0-88416-275-3). Vol. 2 (ISBN 0-88416-276-1). Vol. 3 (ISBN 0-88416-277-X). Vol. 4 (ISBN 0-88416-278-8). Vol. 5 (ISBN 0-88416-279-6). Year Bk Med.

American Medical Directory, 4 vols. 30th ed. 1986. Set of 4 vols. 400.00 o.p. (ISBN 0-89970-210-4, OP-128-6). AMA.

American Medical Directory: Update to the 27th Edition. American Medical Association. 814p. 1981. text ed. 75.00 o.p. (ISBN 0-88416-351-2). Year Bk Med.

American Medical Ethnobotany: A Reference Dictionary. Daniel E. Moerman. LC 76-24771. (Reference Library of Social Science: Vol. 34). 1977. lib. bdg. 73.00 o.p. (ISBN 0-8240-9907-9). Garland Pub.

American Men & Women of Science, 8 vols. 16th ed. Ed. by Jacques Cattell Press Staff. 1986. Set. 595.00 o.p. (ISBN 0-8352-2221-7). Bowker.

American Men & Women of Science: Physical & Biological Sciences, 7 vols. 15th ed. Ed. by Jaques Cattell Press Staff. 7010p. 1982. Set. 495.00 o.p. (ISBN 0-8352-1413-3); 85.00 ea. o.p. Bowker.

American Menus-Winter. Elizabeth E. Swanson & Clyde H. Eller. LC 85-72354. (Illus.). 50p. (Orig.). 1988. pap. 3.00 o.s.i. (ISBN 0-933190-14-X). Clyde Pr.

American Metric Handbook. R. J. Lytle. 1981. text ed. 23.50 o.p. (ISBN 0-07-039277-3). McGraw.

American Military: Opposing Viewpoints. Ed. by David L. Bender. LC 85-8050. (Opposing Viewpoints Ser.). (Illus.). 160p. (Orig.). 1983. lib. bdg. 14.95 o.p. (ISBN 0-89908-342-0); pap. text ed. 7.95 o.p. (ISBN 0-89908-317-X). Greenhaven.

American Mosaic: Intermediate-Advanced ESL Reader. Anna H. Live & Suzanne H. Sandkowsky. LC 79-16352. 1980. pap. text ed. (ISBN 0-13-028126-3). P-H.

American Mountain People. Ed. by Donald J. Crump. LC 73-829. (Special Publications Series 8: No. 1). (Illus.). 1973. avail. only from Natl. Geog. 7.95 o.p. (ISBN 0-87044-126-4). Natl Geog.

American Multinationals & American Interests. C. Fred Bergsten et al. LC 77-91786. 1978. 32.95 o.p. (ISBN 0-8157-0920-X); pap. 16.95 o.p. (ISBN 0-8157-0919-6). Brookings.

American Myths & Legends, 2 vols. Charles M. Skinner. LC 78-175743. (Illus.). 718p. 1975. Repr. of 1903 ed. Set. 75.00x o.p. (ISBN 0-8103-4036-4). Gale.

American Narrow-Gauge. John Krause. LC 78-12544. (Illus.). 256p. 1978. 30.95 o.p. (ISBN 0-87095-059-2). Gldn West Bks.

American Nation. 5th ed. John D. Hicks et al. LC 72-137994. (Illus.). 1971. text ed. 19.50 o.p. (ISBN 0-395-04621-1, 3-24749). HM.

American National Dictionary for Information Systems. American National Standards Committee, X3, Information Processing System. LC 83-73087. 350p. 1984. 40.00 o.p. (ISBN 0-87094-503-3). Dow Jones-Irwin.

American National Government. 3rd ed. Robert S. Ross. 1981. pap. 22.50 o.p. (ISBN 0-395-30717-1). HM.

American National Security: Policy & Process. Rev. ed. Amos A. Jordan & William J. Taylor. LC 83-49194. 640p. 1984. pap. text ed. 14.95x o.p. (ISBN 0-8018-3214-4). Johns Hopkins.

American National Standard for Basic Criteria for Indexes, Z39.4. American National Standards committee 239 on LIbrary Work & Information Sciences. 1984. 8.00 o.p. ANSI.

American Nationalism: An Interpretative Essay. Hans Kohn. LC 79-24317. xi, 272p. 1980. Repr. of 1957 ed. lib. bdg. 35.00x o.p. (ISBN 0-313-22231-2, KOAM). Greenwood.

American Naval Heritage in Brief. 2nd ed. Paolo E. Coletta. LC 79-6603. 689p. 1980. 33.75 o.p. (ISBN 0-8191-0927-4); pap. 14.75 o.p. (ISBN 0-8191-0928-2). U Pr of Amer.

American Naval Heritage in Brief. Paolo E. Coletta. 1978. pap. text ed. 15.00 o.p. (ISBN 0-8191-0390-X). U Pr of Amer.

American Negro Dilemma. Robert E. Davis. 1955. (ISBN 0-8022-0361-2). Philos Lib.

American Neighbors. rev. ed. Ed. by John P. Augelli. LC 79-53985. (American Neighbors Ser.). (Illus.). (gr. 5 up). 1980. text ed. 16.18 1-4 copies o.p. (ISBN 0-88296-085-7); text ed. 12.94 5 or more copies o.p. (ISBN 0-88296-085-7); tchrs'. guide 6.96 o.p. (ISBN 0-88296-353-8). Gateway Pr MI.

American Neighbors. rev. ed. Ed. by John P. Augelli. LC 81-71296. (American Neighbors Ser.). (Illus.). (gr. 5 up). 1982. text ed. 16.18 o.p. (ISBN 0-88296-086-5); tchr's. guide 6.96 o.p. (ISBN 0-88296-354-6). Gateway Pr MI.

American Neutrality, Trial & Failure. Charles G. Fenwick. LC 78-138609. 190p. 1975. Repr. of 1940 ed. lib. bdg. 35.00x o.p. (ISBN 0-8371-5719-6, FEAN). Greenwood.

American Newsfilm, 1914-1919: The Underexposed War. David H. Mould. Ed. by Garth S. Jowett. LC 81-48349. (Dissertations on Film Ser.). 320p. 1983. lib. bdg. 48.00 o.p. (ISBN 0-8240-5107-6). Garland Pub.

American Newspaperman. Bernard A. Weisberger. LC 61-8647. (Chicago History of American Civilization Ser.). (Illus.). 1961. lib. bdg. 10.00x o.s.i. (ISBN 0-226-89138-0). U of Chicago Pr.

American Novel To-Day: A Social & Psychological Study. Regis Michaud. LC 77-2571. 1977. Repr. of 1928 ed. lib. bdg. 27.50x o.p. (ISBN 0-8371-9553-5, MIAN); microfiche o.p. (ISBN 0-8371-9606-X); fiche & cloth o.p. (ISBN 0-8371-9605-1). Greenwood.

American Nuclear Society. Topical Meeting. Irradiation Experimentation in Fast Reactors, Jackson Lake Lodge, September 10-12, 1973: Proceedings. 512p. pap. 14.00 o.p. (ISBN 0-317-33034-9, 700008). Am Nuclear Soc.

American Nuclear Society Transactions: Nuclear Power-Option for the World European Nuclear Society '79 Conference. 665p. pap. 42.00 o.p. (ISBN 0-317-32987-1, 140004). Am Nuclear Soc.

American Nuclear Society Transactions: Nuclear Power Plant Construction, Operation, & Development, 2nd Conference. Pacific Basin Conference Staff. 335p. pap. 48.00 o.p. (ISBN 0-317-32988-X, 140003). Am Nuclear Soc.

American Nuclear Society Transactions: Proceedings of the Transfer of Nuclear Energy Iran Conference. American Nuclear Society Staff. 167p. 38.00 o.p. (ISBN 0-317-32989-8, 140002). Am Nuclear Soc.

American Oak Furniture Styles & Prices. Robert W. Swedberg & Harriett Swedberg. 160p. pap. 10.95 o.p. (ISBN 0-87069-363-8). Wallace-Homestead.

American Oblique: Writing about the American Experience. Joseph F. Trimmer & Robert Kettler. LC 75-31025. (Illus.). 416p. 1976. pap. 19.95 o.p. (ISBN 0-395-21917-5). HM.

American Pages. Bozhidar Bozhilov. Tr. by Cornelia Bozhilova. LC 80-83427. (International Poetry: Vol. 5). 40p. 1981. 11.95x o.p. (ISBN 0-8214-0596-9); pap. 6.95 o.p. (ISBN 0-8214-0597-7). Ohio U Pr.

American Painting: A Guide to Information Sources. Sydney S. Keaveney. LC 73-17522. (Art & Architecture Information Guide Ser.: Vol. 1). 274p. 1974. 68.00x o.p. (ISBN 0-8103-1200-X). Gale.

American Paintings in the Museum of Fine Arts, Boston, 2 vols. LC 68-27634. 697p. 1969. Set. 40.00 o.p. (ISBN 0-686-47016-8). Apollo.

American Paintings of the Sixties & Seventies, the Real-the Ideal-the Fantastic: Selections from the Whitney Museum of American Art. Mitchell D. Kahan. LC 80-80977. (Illus.). 88p. 1980. pap. 8.00 o.p. (ISBN 0-89280-015-1). Montgomery Mus.

American Past: A Survey of American History, 1 Vol, Pts. One & Two. Joseph R. Conlin. Incl. Pt. One. Survey of American History to 1877. 462p. 1984. pap. text ed. 16.00 o.p. (ISBN 0-15-502310-1); Pt. Two. Survey of American History Since 1865. 514p. 1984. pap. text ed. 16.00 o.p. (ISBN 0-15-502311-X). 910p. 1984. text ed. 24.75 o.p. (ISBN 0-15-502309-8, HC). HarBraceJ.

American People: A Study in National Character. rev. ed. Geoffrey Gorer. 1964. pap. 3.25x o.p. (ISBN 0-393-00262-4, Norton Lib). Norton.

American People & Science Policy: The Role of Public Attitudes in the Policy Process. Jon D. Miller. (Illus.). 176p. 1983. 45.00 o.p. (ISBN 0-08-028064-1). Pergamon.

American Period Interiors in Miniature. Kate D. Klavan. (Illus.). 275p. 1984. 35.00 o.p. (ISBN 0-684-18002-2, ScribT). Scribner.

American Philanthropy. Robert H. Bremner. LC 60-7246. (Midway Reprint Ser.). x, 230p. 1982. pap. text ed. 11.00x o.s.i. (ISBN 0-226-07328-9). U of Chicago Pr.

American Philanthropy: A Guide for South Africans. 122p. 1988. 10.00 o.p. IRRC Inc DC.

American Philanthropy in the Near East, 1820-1960. Robert L. Daniel. LC 74-81451. xii, 322p. 1970. 15.00x o.p. (ISBN 0-8214-0063-0). Ohio U Pr.

American Philatelic Periodicals. Chester M. Smith, Jr. 1978. 14.00 o.p. (ISBN 0-686-24133-9). Am Philatelic Society.

American Photography Showcase, 8. Ed. by Ira Shapiro. (Illus.). 638p. 1985. pap. 39.95 o.s.i. (ISBN 0-931144-29-9). Am Showcase.

American Photography Showcase, 9. (Illus.). 496p. 1986. pap. 32.50 o.s.i. (ISBN 0-931144-37-X). Am Showcase.

American Photography Three. Ed. by Edward Booth-Clibborn. (Illus.). 208p. 1987. 49.50 o.p. (ISBN 0-8109-1860-9). Abrams.

American Pieced Quilts. Jonathan Holstein. 1974. pap. 3.45 o.p. (ISBN 0-380-00091-1, 21279, Flare). Avon.

American Pistol & Revolver Design & Performance. L. R. Wallack. LC 77-20219. 1978. 19.95 o.p. (ISBN 0-8329-2552-7, Pub. by Winchester Pr). New Century.

American Place-Names. Alfred H. Holt. LC 68-26574. 224p. 1969. Repr. of 1938 ed. 38.00x o.p. (ISBN 0-8103-3235-3). Gale.

American Planner. Donald A. Krueckeberg. 1983. 29.95 o.p. (ISBN 0-416-33360-5, NO.3707). Routledge Chapman & Hall.

American Poets, Eighteen Eighty to Nineteen Forty-Five: First Series. Ed. by Peter Quartermain. (Dictionary of Literary Biography Ser.: Vol. 45). 514p. 1985. 98.00x o.p. (ISBN 0-8103-1723-0). Gale.

American Political Dictionary. 6th ed. Jack C. Plano & Milton Greenberg. 1982. 18.95 o.p. (ISBN 0-03-061514-3); pap. 14.95 o.p. (ISBN 0-03-060127-4). H Holt & Co.

American Political Experience: An Introduction to Government. 3rd ed. David V. Edwards. (Illus.). 704p. 1985. text ed. (ISBN 0-13-028325-8). P-H.

American Political Experience: Learning Guide. 3rd ed. David V. Edwards. 256p. 1985. pap. text ed. (ISBN 0-13-028390-8). P-H.

American Political System. H. M. Roelofs & Gerald L. Houseman. 640p. 1983. text ed. write for info. o.p. (ISBN 0-02-402720-0). Macmillan.

American Political System: A Radical Approach. 4th ed. Edward S. Greenberg. 1986. pap. text ed. write for info. o.p. (ISBN 0-673-39442-5); tchr's. ed. avail. o.p. Scott F.

American Politics & the Constitution. Walker. LC 77-16337. 1978. pap. 5.95 o.p. (ISBN 0-87872-161-4). PWS-Kent Pub.

American Politics: Changing Expectations. 2nd ed. Ronald E. Pynn. LC 83-7880. 620p. 1983. text ed. 22.50 pub net o.p. (ISBN 0-534-02813-6). Brooks-Cole.

American Politics: Playing the Game. Susan Rouder. LC 76-13962. (Illus.). 1977. pap. 15.95 o.p. (ISBN 0-395-24971-6). HM.

American Politics: The Promise of Disharmony. Samuel P. Huntington. (Belknap Ser.). (Illus.). 368p. 1981. 22.50x o.p. (ISBN 0-674-03020-6, Belknap Pr). Harvard U Pr.

American Poor. Ed. by John A. Schiller. LC 81-52271. 240p. (Orig.). 1982. pap. 11.95 o.p. (ISBN 0-8066-1903-1, 10-0310, Augsburg). Augsburg Fortress.

American Popular Culture: A Historical Bibliography. Ed. by Arthur F. Wertheim. LC 82-24285. (Clio Bibliography Ser.: No. 14). 246p. 1984. lib. bdg. 68.00 o.p. (ISBN 0-87436-049-8). ABC-Clio.

American Porcelain. Lloyd Herman. LC 81-124691. (Illus.). 150p. 1980. pap. 14.95 o.p. (ISBN 0-917304-60-8). Timber.

American Premium Guide to Baseball Cards, 1880-1981. Ron Erbe. (Illus.). 768p. 1982. pap. 14.95 o.p. (ISBN 0-89689-026-0). Bks Americana.

American Premium Guide to Electric Trains: Identifications & Values. Richard O'Brien. 304p. (Orig.). 1982. pap. 10.95 o.p. (ISBN 0-89689-038-4). Bks Americana.

American Premium Guide to Olde Cameras. David Sharbrough. (Illus.). 160p. (Orig.). 1983. pap. 9.95 o.p. (ISBN 0-89689-037-6, 1399). Bks Americana.

American Premium Guide to Pocket Knives. Jim Sargent. 294p. 1986. pap. 14.95 o.p. (ISBN 0-89689-056-2, 1686). Bks Americana.

American Premium Record Guide Identification & Values: 1915-1965. 2nd ed. Les R. Docks. (Illus.). 326p. 1982. pap. 14.95 o.p. (ISBN 0-89689-023-6). Bks Americana.

American Presidency. rev. ed. Clinton Rossiter. LC 60-5436. 1961. pap. 2.95 o.p. (ISBN 0-15-605598-8, HB35, Harv). HarBraceJ.

American Presidents. 6th ed. David C. Whitney. LC 85-7076. (Illus.). 576p. 1986. 14.95 o.s.i. (ISBN 0-385-18557-X). Doubleday.

American Presidents & American Presidency: A Bibliography, 2 vols. 1987. Set. 220.00 o.p. (ISBN 0-87187-434-2). Congr Quarterly.

American Primitive: John & Abigail. William Gibson. LC 77-184721. 1972. 5.95 o.p. (ISBN 0-689-10447-2, Atheneum). Macmillan.

American Primitive Painting. Jean Lipman. (Illus.). 16.75 o.p. (ISBN 0-8446-4574-5). Peter Smith.

American Primitives in Needlepoint. Brande Ormond. 1977. 12.95 o.p. (ISBN 0-395-25485-X). HM.

American Prisoners & Ex-Prisoners: Their Writings: An Annotated Bibliography of Published Works, 1798-1981. H. Bruce Franklin. LC 82-11682. 64p. 1982. pap. 5.95 o.p. (ISBN 0-88208-147-0). Chicago Review.

American Pronunciation see Society's Work.

American Prophet's Record: The Diaries & Journals of Joseph Smith. Ed. by Scott H. Faulring. 600p. 1987. 50.00 o.p. (ISBN 0-941214-55-9). Signature Bks.

American Prospect: Insights into Our Next One Hundred Years. Henry F. Thoma. 1977. 7.95 o.p. (ISBN 0-395-25354-3); pap. 3.95 o.p. (ISBN 0-395-25405-1). HM.

American Protestantism & a Jewish State. Hertzel Fishman. LC 72-3746. (Schaver Publication Fund for Jewish Studies Ser). 250p. 1973. 24.95x o.p. (ISBN 0-8143-1481-3). Wayne St U Pr.

American Psychiatric Association Biographical Directory, 1983. LC 63-12595. 1460p. 1983. 89.95x o.p. (ISBN 0-89042-182-X, 42-182-X); pap. 59.95x o.p. (ISBN 0-89042-181-1, 42-181-1). Am Psychiatric.

American Public Opinion: Cumulative Index, 1981-85. 160p. 1987. 25.00 o.p. (ISBN 0-913577-15-4). Opinion Res.

American Public Policy: A Citizen's Guide. Kenneth M. Dolbeare. 1982. text ed. 19.95x o.p. (ISBN 0-07-017405-9). McGraw.

American Pupils of Jean-Leon Gerome. H. Barbara Weinberg. LC 84-72686. (Anne Burnett Tandy Lectures in American Civilization: No. 5). (Illus.). 128p. 1984. text ed. 24.95x o.p. (ISBN 0-88360-049-8, Dist by Univ of Texas Pr). Amon Carter.

American Puritanism: Faith & Practice. Darrett B. Rutman. 1977. pap. 3.45x o.p. (ISBN 0-393-00842-8, Norton Lib). Norton.

American Quartet: A Novel about the Mortal Link between Four Marked Presidents of the United States. Warren Adler. LC 81-70030. 1982. 13.95 o.p. (ISBN 0-87795-365-1, Arbor Hse). Morrow.

American Quest. Clinton Rossiter. LC 76-142095. (Fund for the Republic Ser.). 1971. 9.50 o.p. (ISBN 0-15-106110-6). HarBraceJ.

American Realism: Twentieth-Century Drawings & Watercolors. Alvin Martin. LC 85-13481. (Illus.). 240p. 1985. pap. 22.50 o.p. (ISBN 0-918471-04-4). San Fran MOMA.

American Recipe Collection. Ed. & intro. by Sandy Lesberg. (Orig.). 1988. Eastern Edition, 340pp. pap. 9.95 o.p. (ISBN 0-317-67347-5); Western Edition, 330pp. pap. 9.95 o.p. (ISBN 0-317-67348-3). Fell.

American Religion & Philosophy: A Guide to Information Sources. Ed. by Ernest R. Sandeen & Frederick Hale. LC 73-17562. (American Studies Information Guide: Vol. 5). 400p. 1978. 68.00x o.p. (ISBN 0-8103-1262-X). Gale.

American Religious Depression 1925-1935. Robert T. Handy. Ed. by Richard C. Wolf. LC 68-31338. (Facet Bks.). (Orig.). 1968. pap. 0.50 o.p. (ISBN 0-8006-3048-3, 1-3048, Fortress). Augsburg Fortress.

American Religious Experiment: Piety & Practicality. Ed. by Clyde L. Manschreck & Barbara B. Zikmund. LC 76-7199. (Studies in Ministry & Parish Life). 128p. 1976. 13.95x o.p. (ISBN 0-913552-06-2); pap. 7.95x o.p. (ISBN 0-913552-07-0). Exploration Pr.

American Religious Values & the Future of America. Ed. by Rodger Van Allen. LC 76-15894. 224p. 1978. 6.50 o.p. (ISBN 0-8006-0486-5, 1-486, Fortress). Augsburg Fortress.

American Reporters on the Western Front, 1914 to 1918. Emmet Crozier. LC 80-19400. (Illus.). xii, 299p. 1980. Repr. of 1959 ed. lib. bdg. 35.00x o.p. (ISBN 0-313-22655-5, CRAR). Greenwood.

American Revolution. Compiled by John Shy. LC 72-178292. (Goldentree Bibliographies in American History Ser.). 152p. (Orig.). 1973. pap. 6.95x o.s.i. (ISBN 0-88295-532-2). Harlan Davidson.

American Revolution: Changing Perspectives. Ed. by William Fowler & Wallace Coyle. LC 79-88424. (Illus.). 245p. 1979. pap. 10.95x o.p. (ISBN 0-930350-21-9). NE U Pr.

American Revolution: Changing Perspectives. Ed. by William M. Fowler & Wallace Coyle. LC 79-88424. (Illus.). 245p. 1979. text ed. 20.95x o.p. (ISBN 0-930350-03-0). NE U Pr.

American Revolution, in Its Political & Military Aspects: 1763-1783. Eric Robson. 1966. pap. 3.95 o.p. (ISBN 0-393-00382-5, Norton Lib). Norton.

American Revolution, Seventeen Seventy-Five to Seventeen Eighty-Three. Clorinda Clarke. Ed. by Marjorie Reeves. (Then & There Ser.). (Illus.). 100p. (Orig.). (gr. 7-12). 1964. pap. text ed. 4.95x o.p. (ISBN 0-582-20398-8). Longman.

American Rivers: A Natural History. Bill Thomas. (Illus.). 1978. 14.98 o.p. (ISBN 0-393-08838-3). Norton.

American Romance. John Casey. LC 74-20348. 1977. 9.95 o.p. (ISBN 0-689-10770-6, Atheneum). Macmillan.

American Rose. Julia Markus. 320p. 1981. 11.95 o.p. (ISBN 0-395-30229-3). HM.

American-Russian Rivalry in the Far East. Edward H. Zabriskie. LC 72-11484. (Illus.). 226p. 1973. Repr. of 1946 ed. lib. bdg. 29.75x o.p. (ISBN 0-8371-6666-7, ZAAR). Greenwood.

American Saga: The Story of Helen Thomas & Simon Flexner. James T. Flexner. (Illus.). 488p. 1984. 24.95 o.p. (ISBN 0-316-28611-7). Little.

American Saints & Seers: American-Born Religions & the Genius Behind Them. Edward Rice. LC 81-15293. (Illus.). 240p. (gr. 7 up). 1982. 11.95 o.s.i. (ISBN 0-02-775980-6, Four Winds). Macmillan.

American Search: Readings in American History. Henry Waltmann et al. (gr. 11-12). 1976. pap. text ed. 15.00x o.p. (ISBN 0-88334-094-1). Ind Sch Pr.

American Secondary School Curriculum. 2nd ed. Leonard H. Clark & Raymond L. Klein. (Illus.). 544p. 1972. text ed. write for info. o.p. (ISBN 0-02-322580-7, 32258). Macmillan.

American Sextet. Warren Adler. LC 82-72050. 256p. 1982. 13.95 o.p. (ISBN 0-87795-414-3, Arbor Hse). Morrow.

American Sextet. Warren Adler. 256p. 1986. pap. 3.75 o.p. (ISBN 0-931773-44-X). Critics Choice Paper.

American Sexual Dilemma. Ed. by William L. O'Neill. (American Problem Studies). 122p. 1972. pap. text ed. 6.50 o.p. (ISBN 0-03-086650-2, Pub. by HR&W). Krieger.

American Ships of the Colonial & Revolutionary Periods. John F. Millar. (Illus.). 1979. 24.95 o.p. (ISBN 0-393-03222-1). Norton.

American Short Fiction: Readings & Criticism. Ed. by James K. Bowen & Richard Van Der Beets. 476p. 1970. pap. text ed. write for info. o.p. (ISBN 0-02-313010-5). Macmillan.

American Short Story: Continuity & Change 1940-1975. rev. 2nd. enl. ed. William Peden. LC 75-23089. 1975. 7.95 o.p. (ISBN 0-395-20720-7). HM.

American Shotgun Design & Performance. L. R. Wallack. LC 77-21886. 1977. 11.50 o.p. (ISBN 0-8329-2366-4, Pub. by Winchester Pr). New Century.

American Silver Flatware. Noel D. Turner. LC 68-27217. (Illus.). 473p. 1971. 37.50 o.s.i. (ISBN 0-498-06580-4). A S Barnes.

American Skin. Peter Viertel. 256p. 1984. 15.45 o.p. (ISBN 0-395-34647-9). HM.

American Society, Inc. 2nd ed. Maurica Zeitlin. 1977. pap. 14.95 o.p. (ISBN 0-395-30776-7). HM.

American Society of Journalists & Authors, 1984: A Listing of Professional Free-Lance Writers. ASJA Publications Committee. 84p. 1983. pap. 40.00 o.p. (ISBN 0-9612200-0-7). Am Soc Jrnl & Auth.

American Songbag. Ed. by Carl Sandburg. LC 28-681. (Illus.). 1936. 9.95 o.p. (ISBN 0-15-106287-0). HarBraceJ.

American South: A Brief History. Monroe L. Billington. LC 73-13275. 1971. pap. text ed. 9.95x o.p. (ISBN 0-684-12324-X, ScribC). Scribner.

American Southwest. Ed. by Harrap Limited Staff. 1986. pap. 49.75X o.p. (ISBN 0-245-54176-4, Pub. by Harrap Ltd England). State Mutual Bk.

American Space: The Centennial Years, 1865-1876. John B. Jackson. (Illus.). 256p. 1972. 7.95 o.p. (ISBN 0-393-06321-6); pap. 4.95x o.p. (ISBN 0-393-09382-4). Norton.

American Spiders. 2nd ed. Willis J. Gertsch. 320p. 1978. 38.95 o.p. (ISBN 0-442-22649-7). Van Nos Reinhold.

American Spirit. Ed. by Henry S. Commager & Stephen M. Doherty. (Illus.). 352p. 1985. 49.50 o.p. (ISBN 0-8109-1838-2). Abrams.

American Story. Richard H. Kelner. LC 81-90620. 1983. 7.95 o.p. (ISBN 0-533-05253-X). Vantage.

American Subsidiaries of German Firms 1986. 17th ed. Ed. by German American Chamber of Commerce Staff. 300p. (Ger. & Eng.). 1986. spiral 65.00 o.p. (ISBN 0-86640-022-2). German Am Chamber.

American Subsidiaries of German Firms-Tochtergesellschaften Deutscher Unternehmen In U. S. A. 16th ed. Ed. by German American Chamber of Commerce Staff. 264p. (Ger. & Eng.). 1984. (ISBN 0-86640-017-6). German Am Chamber.

American Survival Guide: How to Survive in Your Toxic Environment. Edward J. Bergin & Ronald E. Grandon. (Illus.). 512p. 1984. pap. 11.95 o.p. (ISBN 0-380-87460-1, 87460-1). Avon.

American Survivors: Cities & Other Scenes. Karen Gerard. LC 84-6634. 352p. 1985. 22.95 o.p. (ISBN 0-15-106304-4). HarBraceJ.

American System of Government. 3rd ed. Ernest S. Griffith. 1976. 13.95x o.p. (ISBN 0-416-70400-X, NO.2738); pap. 13.95x o.p. (ISBN 0-416-70410-7, NO.2739). Routledge Chapman & Hall.

American Taste. James Villas. 1983. pap. 7.95 o.p. (ISBN 0-87795-513-1, Arbor Hse). Morrow.

American Taste of Japan. Elizabeth Andoh. LC 85-10558. 345p. 1985. 24.95 o.p. (ISBN 0-688-04369-0). Morrow.

American Taste: The American Palate Coast-to-Coast. James Villas. LC 81-71690. 1982. 15.00 o.p. (ISBN 0-87795-406-2, Arbor Hse). Morrow.

American Teacher in Early Meiji Japan. Edward Beauchamp. (Asian Studies at Hawaii: No. 17). 176p. 1976. pap. text ed. 8.00x o.p. (ISBN 0-8248-0404-X). UH Pr.

American Teen: 13 Steps to Beauty. Fashion Academy Staff. (Illus.). 160p. (Orig.). 1988. pap. 16.95 o.p. (ISBN 0-937359-08-4). HDL Pubs.

American Theatre Annual, 1978-1979. Ed. by Catharine R. Hughes. (Illus.). 192p. 1980. 66.00x o.p. (ISBN 0-8103-0418-X, Incorporates New York Theatre Annual). Gale.

American Theatre Annual, 1979-1980. Ed. by Catharine R. Hughes. (Illus.). 288p. 1981. 66.00x o.p. (ISBN 0-8103-0419-8). Gale.

American Thought from Puritanism to Pragmatism & Beyond: A Greenwood Archival Edition. 2nd ed. Isaac W. Riley. 1970. Repr. of 1923 ed. lib. bdg. 65.00x o.p. (ISBN 0-8371-2391-7, RIAT). Greenwood.

American Topics: A Reading Vocabulary Text for Speakers of ESL. Robert C. Lugton. (Illus.). 1978. pap. text ed. (ISBN 0-13-029561-2). P-H.

American Touch in Micronesia. David Nevin. 1977. 9.95 o.p. (ISBN 0-393-05617-1). Norton.

American Tradition in the Arts. Richard McLanathan. LC 65-21032. 1968. 15.00 o.p. (ISBN 0-15-106323-0). HarBraceJ.

American Tradition in the Arts. Richard McLanathan. LC 65-21032. (Illus.). 494p. 1969. pap. text ed. 8.75 o.p. (ISBN 0-15-502595-3, HC). HarBraceJ.

American Traditional: A Comprehensive Guide to Home Decorating the Ethan Allen Way. Genevieve Fernandez. (Illus.). 320p. 1984. 24.45 o.p. (ISBN 0-671-47687-4). S&S.

American Tramp & Underworld Slang. Godfrey Irwin. LC 75-149783. 263p. 1971. Repr. of 1931 ed. 40.00x o.p. (ISBN 0-8103-3748-7). Gale.

American Treasure & the Price Revolution in Spain, 1501-1650. Earl J. Hamilton. 1965. lib. bdg. 31.50x o.p. (ISBN 0-374-93420-7, Octagon). Hippocrene Bks.

American Tropic. David A. Kaufelt. 624p. pap. 4.50 o.p. (ISBN 0-671-52883-1). Archway.

American Urban Education: Inquiries into Changing Patterns. Alfred Lightfoot. 142p. 1970. pap. text ed. 6.95x o.p. (ISBN 0-8290-1603-1). Irvington.

American Values in Transition: A Reader. Robert C. Bannister. 368p. 1972. pap. text ed. 6.95 o.p. (ISBN 0-15-502596-1, HC). HarBraceJ.

American Variations see Persian Words in English.

American Vernacular Design, Eighteen Seventy to Nineteen Forty: An Illustrated Glossary. Herbert Gottfried & Jan Jennings. (Illus.). 288p. 1985. pap. 27.95 o.p. (ISBN 0-442-22739-6). Van Nos Reinhold.

American Verse of the Nineteenth Century. Ed. by Richard Gray. 234p. 1973. 13.50x o.p. (ISBN 0-460-10250-8, DEL 05224, Evman). Biblio Dist.

American Victorian Architecture: A Survey of the 70's & 80's in Contemporary Photographs. Arnold Lewis & Keith Morgan. 15.50 o.p. (ISBN 0-8446-5217-2). Peter Smith.

American War Ballads & Lyrics, Vol. II. Ed. by George C. Eggleston. LC 77-94084. (Granger Poetry Library). (Illus.). 286p. 1982. Repr. of 1889 ed. 24.75x o.p. (ISBN 0-89609-230-5). Roth Pub Inc.

American War of Independence. R. E. Evans. LC 76-22413. (Cambridge Topic Bks.). (Illus.). (gr. 5-10). 1977. PLB 8.95 o.p. (ISBN 0-8225-1201-7). Lerner Pubns.

American War Songs. National Society of Colonial Dames of America Staff. LC 73-156922. 1974. Repr. of 1925 ed. 34.00x o.p. (ISBN 0-8103-3722-3). Gale.

American Way of Life: An Introduction to the Study of Contemporary Society. 2nd ed. Harry E. Barnes. LC 72-138200. (Illus.). 1971. Repr. of 1950 ed. lib. bdg. (ISBN 0-8371-5553-3, BAAW). Greenwood.

American Way of Life Need Not Be Hazardous to Your Health. John W. Farquhar. (Illus.). 208p. 1979. 12.95 o.p. (ISBN 0-393-06443-3); pap. 6.95 o.p. (ISBN 0-393-00963-7). Norton.

American Weather Book. dual ed. David M. Ludlum. (Illus.). 352p. 1982. 14.95 o.p. (ISBN 0-395-32049-6); pap. 8.95 o.p. (ISBN 0-395-32122-0). HM.

American West. Michael L. Tate. 100p. 1981. pap. 26.00 o.p. (ISBN 0-08-026758-0). Pergamon.

American West in the Thirties. Arthur Rothstein. (Illus.). 16.25 o.p. (ISBN 0-8446-5911-8). Peter Smith.

American Whaleman: Life & Labor in the Whaling Industry. Elmo P. Hohman. (Illus.). 1928. 15.00x o.p. (ISBN 0-686-17393-7). R S Barnes.

American Wildlife & Plants: A Guide to Wildlife Food Habits. Alexander C. Martin et al. 15.75 o.p. (ISBN 0-8446-2536-1). Peter Smith.

American Wine. Anthony Dias-Blue. LC 84-28631. (Illus.). 1985. pap. 29.95 o.p. (ISBN 0-385-19191-X, Dial). Doubleday.

American Wing: A Guide. Marshall B. Davidson. (Illus.). 176p. 1980. pap. 9.95 o.p. (ISBN 0-87099-238-4). Metro Mus Art.

American Wing in the Metropolitan Museum of Art. Marshall B. Davidson & Elizabeth Stillinger. LC 85-7250. (Illus.). 352p. 1985. 49.50 o.s.i. (ISBN 0-394-54847-7). Knopf.

American Woman. Kati Marton. 1987. 15.45 o.p. (ISBN 0-393-02420-2). Norton.

American Woman in Colonial & Revolutionary Times, 1565-1800. Eugenie A. Leonard & Sophie Drinker. LC 74-27221. 169p. 1975. Repr. of 1962 ed. lib. bdg. 35.00 o.p. (ISBN 0-8371-7883-5, LEAW). Greenwood.

American Woman's Complete Sewing Book. rev. ed. Ida R. Duncan. 1961. 6.95 o.p. (ISBN 0-87140-946-1). Liveright.

American Woman's Cookbook. Ed. by Ruth Berolzheimer. 1974. pap. 1.95 o.p. (ISBN 0-380-00124-1, 20610). Avon.

American Women Artists: From Early Indian Times to the Present. Charlotte S. Rubinstein. (Illus.). 570p. 1982. lib. bdg. 39.95 o.p. (ISBN 0-8161-8535-2, Hall Reference). G K Hall.

American Women Artists from Early Indian Times to the Present. Charlotte S. Rubinstein. (Illus.). 560p. sewn bdg. 43.95 o.s.i. (ISBN 0-317-54860-3). Apollo.

American Women in Politics. Barbara J. Nelson. LC 82-49142. 220p. 1983. lib. bdg. 46.00 o.p. (ISBN 0-8240-9139-6). Garland Pub.

American Women: The Report. U. S. President's Commission on the Status of Women. Ed. by Margaret Mead & Frances B. Kaplan. LC 75-33325. 1976. Repr. of 1965 ed. 17.95 o.p. (ISBN 0-89201-004-5). Zenger Pub.

American Women: Three Decades of Change. Suzanne M. Bianchi & Daphne Spain. (CDS-80-8. Special Demographic Analyses). (Illus.). 43p. (Orig.). 1983. pap. 3.50 o.p. (ISBN 0-318-22494-1, S/N 003-024-05743-3). USGPO.

American Writer & the Great Depression. Ed. by Harvey Swados. LC 65-23009. (Illus., Orig.). 1966. pap. (ISBN 0-02-418470-5, AHS63). Macmillan.

American Yoga. Ed. by Deena Brown. LC 79-6156. (Illus.). 144p. (Orig.). 1981. pap. 9.95 o.p. (ISBN 0-394-17649-9, E751, Ever). Grove.

Americanization of the Synagogue, 1820-1870. Leon A. Jick. LC 75-18213. (Illus.). 260p. 1976. 28.00x o.p. (ISBN 0-87451-119-4). U Pr of New Eng.

Americans: A Brief History. 2nd ed. Henry Bedford et al. 1976. One vol. ed. 14.95 o.p. (ISBN 0-15-502603-8). HarbraceJ.

Americans: A Brief History, 1 vol. ed. 3rd ed. Henry F. Bedford & Trevor Colbourn. 622p. 1980. pap. text ed. 16.00 o.p. (ISBN 0-15-502613-5, HC). HarBraceJ.

Americans: A Brief History, Pt. 1. 2nd ed. Henry Bedford et al. 1976. 9.95 o.p. (ISBN 0-15-502604-6). HarbraceJ.

Americans: A Brief History, Pt. 2. 2nd ed. Henry Bedford et al. 1976. 9.95 o.p. (ISBN 0-15-502605-4). HarbraceJ.

Americans & Chinese Reform & Revolution, 1898-1922: The Role of Private Citizens in Diplomacy. Key R. Chong. 322p. (Orig.). 1984. lib. bdg. 29.00 o.p. (ISBN 0-8191-4032-5); pap. text ed. 15.50 o.p. (ISBN 0-8191-4033-3). U Pr of Amer.

Americans & Drug Abuse. Christian Kryder & Stephen P. Strickland. 76p. (Orig.). 1977. pap. text ed. 7.00x o.p. (ISBN 0-8191-5902-6, Pub. by Aspen Inst for Humanistic Studies). U Pr of Amer.

Titles

Americans & the Soviet Experiment, 1917-1933. Peter G. Filene. LC 67-11669. 1967. 27.00x o.s.i. (ISBN 0-674-03100-8). Harvard U Pr.
Americans & Their Schools. E. V. Johanningmeir. 328p. 1980. pap. 20.95 o.p. (ISBN 0-395-30640-X). HM.
Americans Betrayed. Morton Grodzins. (Midway Reprint Ser.). xviii, 445p. 1974. pap. text ed. 17.50x o.s.i. (ISBN 0-226-30940-1). U of Chicago Pr.
American's Guide to Britain. Robin W. Winks. LC 77-23341. 1977. pap. 6.95 o.p. (ISBN 0-684-15189-8, ScribT). Scribner.
American's Guide to Britain. rev. ed. Robin W. Winks. (Illus.). 432p. 1984. pap. 9.95 o.p. (ISBN 0-684-18067-7, ScribT). Scribner.
Americans Import Merit: Origins of the United States Civil Service System & the Influence of the British Model. Richard E. Titlow. LC 78-65352. 1978. pap. text ed. 16.75 o.p. (ISBN 0-8191-0655-0). U Pr of Amer.
Americans in Conflict: The Civil War & Reconstruction. David Lindsey. 208p. 1974. pap. 14.50 o.p. (ISBN 0-395-14068-4). HM.
America's Backpacking Book. rev. ed. Raymond Bridge. 1981. Encore Ed. 6.95 o.p. (ISBN 0-684-16872-3, ScribT). Scribner.
America's Best Recipes: State Fair Blue Ribbon Winners. Peter C. Hanley & Rosemary A. Hanley. 288p. 1983. 16.45i o.p. (ISBN 0-316-34339-0); pap. 10.45 o.p. (ISBN 0-316-34336-6). Little.
America's Burke: The Mind of Thomas Hutchinson. William Pencak. 258p. (Orig.). 1982. lib. bdg. 31.25 o.p. (ISBN 0-8191-2626-8); pap. text ed. 14.00 o.p. (ISBN 0-8191-2627-6). U Pr of Amer.
America's Cup, 1987: The Official Record. Bob Fisher & Bob Ross. (Illus.). 256p. 35.00 o.p. (ISBN 0-8050-0580-3). H Holt & Co.
America's Dizzy Dean. Curt Smith. LC 77-29060. 1978. 4.95 o.p. (ISBN 0-8272-0014-5). CBP.
America's Ethan Allen. Stewart Holbrook. (Illus.). 96p. (gr. 4-6). 1976. PLB 8.95 o.p. (ISBN 0-395-24449-8); pap. 3.95 o.p. (ISBN 0-395-24908-2, Sandpiper). HM.
America's Favorite Backyard Birds. Kit Harrison & George H. Harrison. (Illus.). 256p. 1983. 17.45 o.s.i. (ISBN 0-671-46411-6). S&S.
America's Favorite National Parks. Michael Frome. (Illus.). 75p. (Orig.). 1987. pap. 5.95 o.p. (ISBN 0-528-84591-8). Rand McNally.
America's Flying Book. Ed. by Flying Magazine Editors. LC 72-1213. (Illus.). 320p. 1972. encore ed. 5.95 o.p. (ISBN 0-684-16540-6, ScribT). Scribner.
America's Grand Resort Hotels: Eighty Classic Resorts in the United States & Canada. Rod Fensom. LC 84-48888. (Illus.). 224p. (Orig.). 1985. pap. 10.95 o.p. (ISBN 0-88742-022-2). Globe Pequot.
America's Greatest Walks: A Traveler's Guide to One Hundred Scenic Adventures. Gary Yanker & Carol Tarlow. LC 85-28708. (Illus.). 288p. 1986. pap. Addison-Wesley.
America's Handyman Book. 2nd, rev. ed. Family Handyman Magazine Editors. (Illus.). 1979. 16.95 o.s.i. (ISBN 0-684-16296-2, ScribT). Scribner.
America's Hardwood Forests: Opportunities Unlimited. LC 83-60910. 352p. (Orig.). 1983. pap. 17.00 o.p. (ISBN 0-939970-19-8, SAF 83-04). Soc Am Foresters.
America's House of Lords: An Inquiry into the Freedom of the Press. Harold L. Ickes. LC 74-5784. 214p. 1974. Repr. of 1939 ed. lib. bdg. 35.00x o.p. (ISBN 0-8371-7498-8, ICAH). Greenwood.
America's Housing: Prospects & Problems. Ed. by George Sternlieb & James W. Hughes. LC 80-10700. 480p. 1980. pap. text ed. 15.00 o.p. (ISBN 0-88285-063-6). Ctr Urban Pol Res.
America's Literary Revolt. Michael Yatron. 1959. (ISBN 0-8022-1948-9). Philos Lib.
America's Management Challenge: Capitalizing on Change. William B. Miller. LC 83-70785. 336p. 1983. 16.50 o.p. (ISBN 0-8019-7395-3). Chilton.
America's Mark Twain. May McNeer. (gr. 4-6). 1974. 6.95 o.p. (ISBN 0-395-19842-9). HM.
America's Meeting Places. Redtree Associates Staff. 288p. 1984. 35.00 o.p. (ISBN 0-87196-995-5, 995-5). Facts on File.
America's Moment: Nineteen Eighteen. Arthur Walworth. 1977. 14.95x o.p. (ISBN 0-393-05591-4). Norton.
America's Near West: U. S. - Japan Relations in Perspective. Kenneth W. Dam. 1984. 3.00 o.s.i. (ISBN 0-317-06767-2). Japan Soc.
America's One Hundred One Most High Falutin', Big Talkin' Knee Slappin', Golly Whoppers & Tall Tales: The Best of the Burlington Liars' Club. Ed. by Robert G. Deindorfer. LC 80-51618. (Illus.). 128p. (Orig.). 1980. pap. 3.95 o.p. (ISBN 0-89480-136-8, 244). Workman Pub.
America's Paul Revere. Esther Forbes. (Illus.). 48p. (gr. 4-6). 1976. PLB 8.95 o.p. (ISBN 0-395-06767-7); pap. 2.95 o.p. (ISBN 0-395-24907-4). HM.
America's Place in the World Economy. Brenda Forman. LC 69-11494. (Curriculum Related Bks.). 1969. 5.50 o.p. (ISBN 0-15-203168-5, HJ). HarBraceJ.
America's Priceless Heritage, the King James Version of the Bible. John Wahnert. 1978. 4.00 o.p. (ISBN 0-682-48996-4). Exposition-Phoenix.
America's Problems: Social Issues & Public Policy. Elliot Currie et al. 1984. write for info. o.p. (ISBN 0-673-39569-3). Scott F.
America's Public Lands: Politics, Economics, & Administration. Conference on the Public Land Law Review Commission Report, Dec. 1970. Ed. by Harriet Nathan. LC 72-4850. (Illus.). 395p. (Orig.). 1972. pap. 7.00x o.p. (ISBN 0-87772-084-3). UCB IGS.
America's Revolutionary Spirit: The Evangelical Religious Heritage of the Nation. John R. Terry. 1977. 12.50 o.p. (ISBN 0-682-48888-7, University). Exposition-Phoenix.
America's Robert E. Lee. Henry Steele Commager & Lynd Ward. (Illus.). (gr. 7-9). 10.95 o.p. (ISBN 0-395-06707-3). HM.
America's Second Century: Topical Readings, 1865-Present. Alfers et al. 392p. 1984. pap. text ed. 11.95 o.p. (ISBN 0-8403-3157-6). Kendall-Hunt.
America's Struggle Against Poverty, 1900-1980. James T. Patterson. LC 81-4620. (Illus.). 320p. 1981. text ed. 18.50x o.p. (ISBN 0-674-03120-2). Harvard U Pr.
America's Third Century. Norman Macrae. (Orig.). 1976. pap. text ed. 7.95 o.p. (ISBN 0-15-502609-7, HC). HarBraceJ.
America's Vice-Presidents: Our First Forty-Three Vice-Presidents & How They Got to Be Number Two. Diana D. Healy. LC 83-45490. (Illus.). 192p. 1984. 15.95 o.p. (ISBN 0-689-11454-0, Atheneum). Macmillan.
America's Wildlife Sampler. Thomas B. Allen et al. LC 82-60674. (Illus.). 208p. 1988. Repr. of 1982 ed. 21.95 o.p. (ISBN 0-912186-45-3). Natl Wildlife.
Amerika. Date not set. (ISBN 0-8052-3002-5). Random.
Amerique au Jour le Jour: Voyages. Simone De Beauvoir. 9.95 o.p. (ISBN 0-685-37185-9). Schoenhof.
Amers see Oeuvre Poetique.
Ames Fortes. Jean Giono. 1958. pap. 8.50 o.p. (ISBN 0-685-10993-3). Schoenhof.
Amfiparnasso. Orazio Vecchi. Ed. by Robert Eitner. (Publikation aelterer praktischer und theoretischer Musikwerke Ser.: Vol. XXVI). (Ger. & Ital.). 1967. Repr. of 1902 ed. Broude.
Ami, C'est Quelqu'un Qui T'Aime. Joan W. Anglund. LC 65-14113. (Illus.). 1965. 2.95 o.p. (ISBN 0-15-292770-0, HJ). HarBraceJ.
AMI-Rowe Jukeboxes Nineteen Twenty-Nine to Nineteen Eighty-Eight. Frank Adams. 200p. (Orig.). 1988. 29.95 o.p. (ISBN 0-939971-18-6). AMR Pub Co.
Amiga's Programmer's Handbook. Eugene P. Mortimore. LC 85-63784. 529p. (Orig.). 1986. pap. 24.95 o.p. (ISBN 0-89588-343-0). Sybex.
Amigo. Byrd B. Schweitzer. LC 63-18124. (Illus.). 48p. (gr. k-3). 1973. pap. 2.95 o.s.i. (ISBN 0-02-044950-X, Collier). Macmillan.
Amiloride & Epithelial Sodium Transport. Ed. by A. W. Cuthbert et al. LC 79-251. (Illus.). 202p. 1979. text ed. 22.50 o.p. (ISBN 0-8067-0311-3). Urban & S.
Amine Oxidases in Clinical Research. V. Z. Gorkin. LC 82-18132. (Illus.). 300p. 1982. 115.00 o.p. (ISBN 0-08-025523-X). Pergamon.
Amino Acid Analysis. John M. Rattenbury. LC 81-2917. 380p. 1981. 96.95x o.p. (ISBN 0-470-27141-8). Halsted Pr.
Aminoacids, Peptides & Proteins: An Introduction. 1st English ed. Hans-Dieter Jakubke & Hans Jeschkeit. Tr. by G. P. Cotterrell & J. H. Jones. LC 77-23945. 336p. 1978. 54.95x o.p. (ISBN 0-470-99279-4). Halsted Pr.
Aminocyclitol Antibiotics. Ed. by Kenneth L Rinehart, Jr. & Tetsuo Suami. LC 80-10502. (ACS Symposium Ser.: No. 125). 1980. 44.95 o.p. (ISBN 0-8412-0554-X). Am Chemical.
Aminoglycoside Ototoxicity. Stephen A. Lerner et al. 1981. text ed. 39.00 o.p. (ISBN 0-316-52130-2). Little.
Amiodarone & Arrhythmias: Based on the Scientific Symposium Sponsored by the International Society & Federation of Cardiology. Ed. by D. M. Krikler & W. J. McKenna. (Illus.). 100p. 1983. 26.00 o.p. (ISBN 0-08-029798-6). Pergamon.
Amish People: Plain Living in a Complex World. Carolyn Meyer. LC 75-28272. 152p. (gr. 7 up). 1976. 8.95 o.p. (ISBN 0-689-50041-6, Atheneum). Macmillan.
Amish Society. 3rd ed. John A. Hostetler. LC 79-23823. 432p. 1980. pap. 25.00x o.p. (ISBN 0-8018-2333-1). Johns Hopkins.
Ammahabas. Bill Hotchkiss. LC 82-14217. 1983. 15.45 o.p. (ISBN 0-393-01718-4). Norton.
AMO Profile. Institute of Real Estate Management Staff. (Illus.). 22p. 15.95 o.p. Inst Real Estate.
Amoco Cadiz Oil Spill. Ed. by M. F. Spooner. (Illus.). 1979. pap. 9.25 o.p. (ISBN 0-08-023830-0). Pergamon.
Amon Carter Museum: Nineteen Sixty-One to Nineteen Seventy-Seven. Amon Carter Museum Staff. LC 77-81806. (Illus.). 47p. 1977. pap. 3.50 o.p. (ISBN 0-88360-028-5). Amon Carter.
Among Birches. Rebecca Hill. LC 85-21476. 352p. 1986. 17.95 o.p. (ISBN 0-688-06165-6). Morrow.
Among Lions: The Battle for Jerusalem, June 5-7, 1967. J. Robert Miskin. (War Library). 432p. 1983. pap. 4.95 o.s.i. (ISBN 0-345-29673-7). Ballantine.
Among Lions: The Definitive Account of the 1967 Battle for Jerusalem. J. Robert Moskin. LC 81-71671. (Illus.). 1982. 16.95 o.p. (ISBN 0-87795-377-5, Arbor Hse). Morrow.
Among the Ashes: Six SF Horror Stories. C. D. Huneycutt. 92p. (Orig.). 1983. pap. 4.80X o.p. (ISBN 0-915153-02-5). Gold Star Pr.
Among the Bantu Nomads. John T. Brown. LC 77-79270. (Illus.). 1969. Repr. of 1926 ed. 35.00x o.p. (ISBN 0-8371-1466-7, BRB&, Pub. by Negro U Pr). Greenwood.
Among the Indians: Four Years on the Upper Missouri, 1858-1862. Henry A. Boller. Ed. by Milo M. Quaife. LC 76-100810. (Illus.). xvi, 370p. 1972. pap. 7.95 o.p. (ISBN 0-8032-5714-7, BB 514, Bison). U of Nebr Pr.
Amor Est Sensus Quidam Peculiaris. Joan W. Anglund. Tr. by G. M. Lyne. LC 68-25184. (Illus., Lat.). (gr. 8 up). 1968. 2.50 o.p. (ISBN 0-15-203231-2, HJ). HarBraceJ.
Amori d'Apollo e di Dafne. Francesco Cavalli. Ed. by Howard M. Brown. LC 76-21071. (Italian Opera 1640-1770 Ser.). 1978. lib. bdg. 77.00 o.p. (ISBN 0-8240-2600-4). Garland Pub.
Amorite Personal Names in the Mari Texts: A Structural & Lexical Study. Herbert B. Huffmon. 320p. 1965. 37.00x o.p. (ISBN 0-8018-0283-0). Johns Hopkins.
Amorous Adventures of a Japanese Gentleman. 13.95 o.p. (ISBN 0-394-55387-X). Grove.
Amorous Adventures of a Japanese Gentleman. LC 86-80042. (Classics of the Victorian Imagination Ser.). pap. 7.95 o.p. (ISBN 0-394-62214-6, Ever). Grove.
Amorous Adventures of Moll Flanders see also Moll Flanders.
Amorous Drawings of the Marquis Von Bayros. Franz Von Bayros. LC 83-49388. 240p. 1984. pap. 12.50 o.p. (ISBN 0-394-62054-2, E926, Ever). Grove.
Amorous Leander. Alan Hunter. 1985. 12.95 o.p. (ISBN 0-317-53045-3, Large Print Bks). G K Hall.
Amos among the Prophets: Composition & Theology. Robert B. Coote. LC 80-8054. 144p. 1981. pap. 5.95 o.p. (ISBN 0-8006-1400-3, 1-1400, Fortress). Augsburg Fortress.
Amos (Neighborhood Bible Study) Marilyn Kunz & Catherine Schell. 64p. 1978. pap. 2.95 o.p. (ISBN 0-8423-0067-8). Tyndale.
Amos R. Anderson: The Lone Wolf of Boston Post Road. Frank D. Singewald. (Illus.). 1985. pap. 5.00 o.p. (ISBN 0-682-40255-9). Exposition-Phoenix.
Amos the Prophet: The Man & His Background. Hans W. Wolff. Ed. by John Reumann. Tr. by Foster McCurley from Ger. LC 72-87062. 110p. 1973. pap. 2.95 o.p. (ISBN 0-8006-0012-6, 1-12, Fortress). Augsburg Fortress.
Amos Zook: A Garden of Lights & Gravities. (Illus.). 1982. 0.50 o.p. (ISBN 0-913883-07-7). Madison Art.
Amour Sacre, Amour Profane; Autour de l'Heptameron. Febure. (Coll. Idees). pap. 4.50 o.p. (ISBN 0-685-34188-7). Schoenhof.
Amphetamines: Medical & Psychological Studies. Francis A. Whitlock et al. 1974. 28.50x o.p. (ISBN 0-8422-7129-5). Irvington.
Amphibian Development: New Research, 2 vols. Incl. Vol. 1. Ed. by James N. Dumont et al; Vol. 2. Ed. by P. Grippo et al (ISBN 0-8422-7250-X). 1977. text ed. 29.00x ea. o.p. Irvington.
Amphibians & Reptiles of Great Smoky Mountains National Park. James E. Huheey & Arthur Stupka. LC 67-21108. (Illus.). 1967. pap. 4.95 o.p. (ISBN 0-87049-077-X). U of Tenn Pr.
Amphibians & Reptiles of the Carolinas & Virginia. Bernard S. Martof et al. LC 79-11790. (Illus.). 264p. 1980. 16.95 o.p. (ISBN 0-8078-1389-3). U of NC Pr.
Amphibians of New England. Anne O. Epple. LC 82-73602. (Illus.). 1983. pap. 7.95 o.p. (ISBN 0-89272-159-6). Down East.
Amphiboles: Crystal Chemistry, Phase Relations & Occurence. W. G. Ernst. (Minerals, Rocks & Inorganic Materials Ser.: Vol. 1). (Illus.). 1968. 20.40 o.p. (ISBN 0-387-04267-9). Springer-Verlag.
Amphigorey. Edward Gorey. (Illus.). 1980. 12.95 o.p. (ISBN 0-399-50433-8, Perigee). Putnam Pub Group.
Amphigorey Too. Edward Gorey. (Illus.). 224p. 1980. 9.95 o.p. (ISBN 0-399-50420-6, Perigee). Putnam Pub Group.
Amphion see Poesies.
Amphoto Guide to Backpacking Photography. Susan Lariviere & Ted Schiffman. (Illus.). 168p. 1981. 12.95 o.p. (ISBN 0-8174-3520-4, Amphoto); pap. 7.95 o.p. (ISBN 0-8174-3519-0). Watson-Guptill.
Amphoto Guide to Cameras. Hubert C. Birnbaum. (Illus.). 184p. 1978. 10.95 o.p. (ISBN 0-8174-2444-X, Amphoto); pap. 7.95 o.p. (ISBN 0-8174-2117-3). Watson-Guptill.
Amrita Sher-Gil. N. Iqbal Singh. (Illus.). 208p. 1984. text ed. 40.00x o.p. (ISBN 0-7069-2474-6, Vikas India). Advent NY.
Amsterdam. Carole Chester. (Rand McNally Pocket Guide). (Illus.). 95p. 1986. pap. 5.95 o.p. (ISBN 0-528-84846-1). Rand McNally.
Amsterdam School: Dutch Expressionist Architecture 1915-1930. Ed. by Wim De Wit. LC 83-72390. (Illus.). 172p. 1984. 27.50 o.p. (ISBN 0-262-04074-3). MIT Pr.
Amsterdam Travel Guide. Berlitz Editors. (Travel Guides for English Speakers). 1977. pap. 4.95 o.p. (ISBN 0-02-969010-2, Berlitz). Macmillan.
Amsterdam, Twelve Seventy-Five - Nieuw Amsterdam, Sixteen Twenty-Five - New York, Nineteen Seventy-Five. Werner Lowenhardt. (Illus., Dutch & Eng.). 1975. 20.00 o.s.i. E J Brill USA.
Amsterdam: Where to Go, 3 vols. G. A. Vries. (Illus.). 1974. Set. incl. a record 30.00 o.s.i. (ISBN 0-685-58561-1). E J Brill USA.
Amtrak Railway System: A Periodical Bibliography of an Inter-City Transportation Network. Glenna Dunning. (Public Administration Ser.: P 1660). 18p. 1985. 3.00 o.p. (ISBN 0-89028-370-2). Vance Biblios.
Amulet. Michael McDowell. 352p. 1979. pap. 2.50 o.p. (ISBN 0-380-40584-9, 40584). Avon.
Amulets & Superstitions. E. Wallis Budge. 15.75 o.p. (ISBN 0-8446-5676-3). Peter Smith.
Amulets, Charms & Talismans, How to Make: What They Mean & How to Use Them. Deborah Lippman & Paul Colin. LC 73-89758. (Illus.). 208p. 1985. 8.95 o.p. (ISBN 0-87131-135-6); pap. 4.95 o.p. (ISBN 0-87131-151-8). M Evans.
Amusemens De Spa; or, the Gallantries of the Spaw in Germany, Pt. 1. Karl L. Pollnitz. LC 78-170597. (Foundations of the Novel Ser.: Vol. 67). 1973. lib. bdg. 61.00 o.p. (ISBN 0-8240-0579-1). Garland Pub.
Amy Jean. Lorinda Hagen. 1976. pap. 1.75 o.p. (ISBN 0-505-51151-7, Pub. by Tower Bks). Dorchester Pub Co.
Amy Jean. Lorinda Hagen. 256p. 1982. pap. 2.75 o.p. (ISBN 0-505-51848-1, Pub. by Tower Bks). Dorchester Pub Co.
Amyloidosis. Ed. by Otto Wegelius & Amos Pasternack. 1977. 104.00 o.p. (ISBN 0-12-741350-2). Acad Pr.
Amyntas. Andre Gide. 224p. 1926. 4.95 o.p. (ISBN 0-686-56060-4). Schoenhof.
Amyotrophic Lateral Sclerosis: Recent Research Trends. Ed. by John M. Andrews et al. 1977. 32.50 o.p. (ISBN 0-12-059750-0). Acad Pr.
An Duanaire Sixteen Hundred to Nineteen Hundred: Poems of the Dispossessed. Ed. by Sean O. Tuama. Tr. by Thomas Kinsella from Irish. (Illus.). 382p. (Do not add a slash to the title). 1985. pap. 10.95 o.p. (ISBN 0-937702-02-1). Irish Bks Media.
Anabaptists & Religious Liberty in the Sixteenth Century. Harold S. Bender. Ed. by Charles S. Anderson. LC 73-99611. (Facet Bks). 1970. pap. 0.50 o.p. (ISBN 0-8006-3058-0, 1-3058, Fortress). Augsburg Fortress.
Anabase see Oeuvre Poetique.
Anacapa Island. Ed. by Lois W. Roberts. 1982. pap. 7.50 o.p. (ISBN 0-87461-040-0). McNally & Loftin.
Anaerobic Bacteria: Selected Topics. Ed. by Dwight W. Lambe et al. LC 80-18505. 324p. 1980. 59.50x o.p. (ISBN 0-306-40546-6, Plenum Pr). Plenum Pub.
Anaesthesia-Review 3. Ed. by Leon Kaufman. (Illus.). 216p. 1985. pap. text ed. 27.75 o.p. (ISBN 0-443-03202-5). Churchill.
Anais Nin. Nancy Scholar. LC 83-26583. (United States Authors Ser.: No. 460). 175p. 1984. lib. bdg. 14.95 o.s.i. (ISBN 0-8057-7400-9, Twayne). G K Hall.
Anais Nin Reader. Ed. by Philip Jason. 1976. pap. 3.95 o.p. (ISBN 0-380-00074-1, 65003-7). Avon.
Anal Pleasure & Health. 2nd ed. Jack Morin. (Illus.). 256p. 1984. 14.00 o.p. (ISBN 0-940208-00-8, Yes Press); pap. 9.50 o.p. (ISBN 0-940208-01-6). Down There Pr.
Analgesic Drugs. Parkhouse & Pleuvry. (Illus.). 168p. 1979. pap. 17.50 o.p. (ISBN 0-632-00433-9, B-37686). Mosby.
Analgetics. Ed. by George De Stevens. (Medicinal Chemistry Ser.: Vol. 5). 1965. 100.00 o.p. (ISBN 0-12-212150-3). Acad Pr.
Analog Electronics for Microcomputer Systems. Goldsbrough et al. LC 83-61062. 440p. 1983. pap. 19.95 o.p. (ISBN 0-672-21821-6). Sams.

Analog Integrated Circuits. Ed. by A. B. Grebene. LC 78-59636. 448p. cancelled o.s.i. (ISBN 0-87942-114-2, PC01099). Inst Electrical.

Analogies: A Visual Approach to Writing. Anthony Garcia & Robert Myers. (Illus.). 256p. 1974. text ed. 21.95 o.p. (ISBN 0-07-022825-6). McGraw.

Analyse des Processus Sociaux. Ed. by Francois Chazel et al. (Methods De la Sociologie: No. 3). (Illus.). 1970. pap. 14.00x o.p. (ISBN 90-2796-297-9). Mouton.

Analyse Structurale et Exegese Biblique. Roland Barthes et al. 128p. 1973. 17.50 o.p. (ISBN 0-686-53927-3). French & Eur.

Analyses for Soil-Structure Interaction Effects for Nuclear Power Plants: Proceedings, American Nuclear Society, Ad Hoc Group on Soil-Structure Interaction. 155p. pap. 16.00 o.p. (ISBN 0-317-33044-6, 700043). Am Nuclear Soc.

Analyses of Satisfaction, Vol. 3. Ed. by Maynard W. Shelly. 1972. 27.50x o.p. (ISBN 0-8422-5010-7). Irvington.

Analyses of Satisfaction, Vol. 1. Ed. by Maynard W. Shelly. 1972. 27.50x o.p. (ISBN 0-8422-5008-5). Irvington.

Analyses of Satisfaction, Vol. 2. Ed. by Maynard W. Shelly. 1972. 27.50x o.p. (ISBN 0-8422-5009-3). Irvington.

Analysis & Computation of Electric & Magnetic Field Problems. 2nd ed. K. J. Binns & P. J. Lawrenson. 1973. 90.00 o.p. (ISBN 0-08-016638-5). Pergamon.

Analysis & Decision in Regional Policy. Ed. by I. G. Cullen. (London Papers in Regional Science). 232p. 1979. 19.50x o.p. (ISBN 0-85086-070-9, NO.2936, Pub. by Pion England). Routledge Chapman & Hall.

Analysis & Design of Certain Quantitative Multiresponse Experiments. S. N. Roy et al. 314p. 1971. 38.00 o.p. (ISBN 0-08-006917-7). Pergamon.

Analysis & Design of Structural Sandwich Panels. H. G. Allen. 1969. 75.00 o.p. (ISBN 0-08-012870-X); pap. 75.00 o.p. (ISBN 0-08-012869-6). Pergamon.

Analysis & Estimates. Ed. by Roy Godson. (Intelligence Requirements for the 1980's: Vol. 2). 224p. 1980. pap. 7.50 o.p. (ISBN 0-87855-827-6). Transaction Pubs.

Analysis & Evaluation of Conceptual Models of Nursing. Jacqueline Fawcett. LC 83-5340. 307p. 1983. 22.00x o.p. (ISBN 0-8036-3409-9). Davis Co.

Analysis & Identification of Polymers, International Symposium, FBI Academy, Quantico, Virginia, July 31-August 2, 1984: Proceedings. (Illus.). 84p. 1986. pap. 9.50 o.p. (ISBN 0-932115-02-0, S/N 027-000-01265-5). USGPO.

Analysis & Optimization of Stochastic Systems. Ed. by O. L. R. Jacobs et al. (IMA Conference Ser.). 1980. 94.00 o.p. (ISBN 0-12-378680-0). Acad Pr.

Analysis & Optimization of Systems: Proceedings. Ed. by A. Bensoussan & J. L. Lions. (Lecture Notes in Control & Information Sciences Ser.: Vol. 28). 999p. 1980. pap. 66.00 o.p. (ISBN 0-387-10472-0). Springer-Verlag.

Analysis & Optimization of Systems: Proceedings of the Sixth International Conference on Analysis & Optimization of Systems, Nice, June 19-22, 1983. Ed. by A. Bensoussan & J. L. Lions. (Lecture Notes in Control & Information Sciences,: Vol. 62, Pt. 1). (Illus.). xix, 591p. 1984. pap. 36.70 o.p. (ISBN 0-387-13551-0). Springer-Verlag.

Analysis & Prediction in International Mediation. (United Nations Peaceful Settlement Ser.). 2.50 o.p. (ISBN 92-1-157004-2, E.75.XV.PS/2). UN.

Analysis Cartel Market. Marshalla. (Out Disc Econ One Ser.). 1979. text ed. 43.00 o.p. (ISBN 0-8240-4052-X). Garland Pub.

Analysis Design & Construction of Double Layer Grids. Z. S. Makowski. LC 81-6982. 414p. 1981. 102.95 o.p. (ISBN 0-470-27274-0). Halsted Pr.

Analysis, Design, & Evaluation of Man-Machine Systems: Proceedings of the IFAC-IFIP-IEA-IFORS Symposium, Baden-Baden, Brd, Sept., 1982. IFAC-IFIP-IEA-IFORS Symposium Staff & G. Johannsen. Ed. by J. E. Rijnsdorp. (IFAC Proceedings Ser.). 434p. 1983. 130.00 o.p. (ISBN 0-08-029348-4). Pergamon.

Analysis for Financial Management. Robert C. Higgins. LC 82-73628. 325p. 1983. 29.95 o.p. (ISBN 0-87094-377-4). Dow Jones-Irwin.

Analysis for Financial Management. Robert C. Higgins. 1984. 18.95x o.p. (ISBN 0-256-03004-9). Irwin.

Analysis in Euclidian Space. Kenneth Hoffman. 1975. text ed. 45.67 o.p. (ISBN 0-13-032656-9). P-H.

Analysis of Alternative Vesting Requirements for Private Pensions. Employee Benefit Research Institute Staff. 35p. (Orig.). 1980. stapled cover 10.00 o.p. (ISBN 0-86643-011-3). Employee Benefit.

Analysis of Assaults on Police Officers in Forty-Six South Central Cities. James L. Regens et al. (Criminal Justice Policy & Administration Research Ser: No. 5). 23p. 1974. pap. 1.50 o.p. (ISBN 0-686-20781-5). Univ OK Gov Res.

Analysis of Bank Financial Statements. Oliver G. Wood & Robert J. Porter. 1979. 22.95 o.p. (ISBN 0-442-29537-5). Van Nos Reinhold.

Analysis of Binary Data. D. R. Cox. 1970. 16.95 o.p. (ISBN 0-412-15340-8, NO.6065, Pub. by Chapman & Hall). Routledge Chapman & Hall.

Analysis of Coniferous Forest Ecosystems in the Western United States. Ed. by Robert L. Edmonds. LC 80-26699. (US-IBP Synthesis Ser.: Vol. 14). 448p. 1982. 49.95 o.p. (ISBN 0-87933-382-0). Van Nos Reinhold.

Analysis of Dreams. Medard Boss. 224p. 1958. (ISBN 0-8022-0158-X). Philos Lib.

Analysis of Drugs & Meta-Bolites by Gas Chromotography-Mass Spectometry: Analgesics, Local Anesthetics, & Antibiotics, Vol. 5. B. J. Gudzinowicz & M. J. Gudzinowicz. 1978. 99.75 o.p. (ISBN 0-8247-6651-2). Dekker.

Analysis of Drugs & Metabolites by Gas Chromatography-Mass Spectometry: Antipsychotic, Antiemetic & Antidepressant Drugs, Vol. 3. B. J. Gudzinowicz. 1977. 99.75 o.p. (ISBN 0-8247-6586-9). Dekker.

Analysis of Drugs & Metabolites by Gas Chromatography-Mass Spectometry: Central Nervous Stimulants, Vol. 4. Benjamin Gudzinowicz & Michael Gudzinowicz. 1978. 99.75 o.p. (ISBN 0-8247-6614-8). Dekker.

Analysis of Drugs & Metabolites by Gas Chromatography-Mass Spectometry: Natural, Pyrolytic & Metabolic Products of Tobacco & Marijuana, Vol. 7. 1980. 99.75 o.p. (ISBN 0-8247-6861-2). Dekker.

Analysis of Drugs & Related Compounds by Gas Chromotography-Mass Spectometry: Respiratory Gases, Volatile Anesthetics, Ethyl Alcohol, & Related Toxicological Materials, Vol. 1. Michael J. Gudzinowicz & Benjamin J. Gudzinowicz. 1977. 99.75 o.p. (ISBN 0-8247-6576-1). Dekker.

Analysis of Drugs & Related Compounds by Gas Chromotography-Mass Spectometry: Hypnotics, Anticonvulsants & Sedatives, Vol. 2. Michael J. Gudzinowicz & Benjamin J. Gudzinowicz. 1977. 99.75 o.p. (ISBN 0-8247-6585-0). Dekker.

Analysis of Drugs, Vol. 6: Cardiovascular, Antihypertensive, Hypoglycemic & Thyroid-Related Agents. Gudzinowicz. 1979. 99.75 o.p. (ISBN 0-8247-6757-8). Dekker.

Analysis of Electric Circuits. 2nd ed. Egon Brenner & M. Javid. (Electrical & Electronic Engineering Ser.). 1967. text ed. 36.00 o.p. (ISBN 0-07-007630-8). McGraw.

Analysis of Frequency Data. Shelby J. Haberman. LC 74-7558. (Statistical Research Monographs). (Midway Reprints). 1977. pap. text ed. 17.00x o.s.i. (ISBN 0-226-31185-6). U of Chicago Pr.

Analysis of International Relations. 2nd ed. Karl W. Deutsch. (Foundations of Modern Political Science Ser.). 1977. pap. text ed. (ISBN 0-13-033217-8). P-H.

Analysis of Knowledge & Valuation. C. I. Lewis. LC 47-20878. (Paul Carus Lecture Ser.). 610p. 1971. 19.95 o.p. (ISBN 0-87548-093-4); pap. 7.95 o.p. (ISBN 0-87548-094-2). Open Court.

Analysis of Linear Circuits. Charles M. Close. 716p. 1966. text ed. 31.25 o.p. (ISBN 0-15-502610-0, HC, HC). HarBraceJ.

Analysis of Natural Gas Contracts, Vol. 3: Contract Provisions Covering Production of New Gas. (DOE-EIA: No. 0505). 147p. 1987. pap. 7.00 o.p. (ISBN 0-317-62820-8, S-N 061-003-00526-8). USGPO.

Analysis of NMR Spectra. R. A. Hoffman et al. LC 70-156999. (NMR-Basic Principles & Progress: Vol. 5). (Illus.). 1971. 38.00 o.p. (ISBN 0-387-05427-8). Springer-Verlag.

Analysis of Nuclear Power Reactor, Decomissioning Costs. Stone & Webster Engineering Corporation Staff. (National Environmental Studies Project AIF-Inforum). 300p. 1981. 60.00 o.p. (ISBN 0-318-13555-8, AIF-NESP-021); NESP sponsors 25.00 o.p. (ISBN 0-318-13556-6). US Coun Energy Awareness.

Analysis of Officer Characteristics & Police Assaults Among Selected South Central Cities. C. Kenneth Meyer et al. (Criminal Justice Policy & Administration Research Ser.: No. 6). 1974. pap. 1.00 o.p. (ISBN 0-686-21836-1). Univ OK Gov Res.

Analysis of Organoaluminium & Organozinc Compounds. T. R. Crompton. 1968. text ed. 60.00 o.p. (ISBN 0-08-012578-6). Pergamon.

Analysis of Pavement Systems. (Transportation Research Record Ser.). 98p. 1978. 5.40 o.p. (ISBN 0-309-02811-6). Transport Res Bd.

Analysis of Pesticide Residues, Vol. 58. H. Anson Moye. (Chemical Analysis: A Series of Monographs on Analytical Chemistry & Its Applications). 467p. 1981. 95.00 o.p. (ISBN 0-471-05461-5). Krieger.

Analysis of Police Assailants in Albuquerque. Denise L. Heller. (Criminal Justice Policy & Administration Research Ser: No. 10). 23p. 1974. pap. 1.50 o.p. (ISBN 0-686-20782-3). Univ OK Gov Res.

Analysis of Project Finance in Developing Countries. Charles Harvey. x, 171p. (Orig.). 1983. pap. text ed. 17.50x o.p. (ISBN 0-435-84391-5). Heinemann Ed.

Analysis of Regional Structure: Essays in Honour of August Losch. Ed. by R. Funck & J. B. Parr. (Karlsruhe Papers in Regional Science). 168p. 1978. pap. 13.50x o.p. (ISBN 0-85086-068-7, NO.2961, Pub. by Pion England). Routledge Chapman & Hall.

Analysis of Response in Crop & Livestock Production. 2nd ed. John L. Dillon. 1977. 34.00 o.p. (ISBN 0-08-021118-6); pap. 55.00 o.p. (ISBN 0-08-021115-1). Pergamon.

Analysis of Structural Learning: Monograph. Malcolm A. Jeeves & Brain Green. 1984. 67.00 o.p. (ISBN 0-12-382080-4). Acad Pr.

Analysis of Temperate Forest Ecosystems. Ed. by D. E. Reichle. LC 70-103020. (Ecological Studies, Analysis & Synthesis: Vol. 1). (Illus.). 1970. 29.00 o.p. (ISBN 0-387-04793-X). Springer-Verlag.

Analysis of the Determinants of Occupational Upgrading. D. Leigh. LC 78-3343. (Inst. for Research on Poverty Monograph). 1978. 19.50 o.p. (ISBN 0-12-442850-9). Acad Pr.

Analysis of the Report of the New York State Bar Association for Implementing the American Bar Association's Proposal Relative to Loyalty Among Lawyers. National Lawyers Guild, NYC Chapter Staff. LC 84-220412. 1954. Natl Lawyers Guild.

Analysis of the SMP Policy: A Line-by-Line Explanation of the Special Multi-Peril Policy. George E. Guinane. 20.00 o.p. (ISBN 0-686-31022-5, 26625). Rough Notes.

Analysis of the 1977 University of California Union List of Serials. Barbara Radke & Mike Berger. (UCULAP Paper: No. 78-3). 1978. 7.00 o.p. (ISBN 0-686-87253-3). UCDLA.

Analysis of Triglycerides. Carter Litchfield. 1972. 80.00 o.p. (ISBN 0-12-451950-4). Acad Pr.

Analysis of Vertebrate Structure. 2nd ed. Milton Hildebrand. LC 81-13049. 654p. 1982. (ISBN 0-471-09058-1). Wiley.

Analysis Repair & Individuation. Kenneth Lambert. (Library of Analytical Psychology Ser.: No. 5). 1981. 36.00 o.p. (ISBN 0-12-434640-5). Acad Pr.

Analysis, Treatment & Disposal of Ferricyanide in Photographic Effluents - A Compendium: A Compenchum. Eastman Kodak Company. LC 79-57024. 72p. 1980. pap. 5.75 o.p. (ISBN 0-87985-244-5, J-54). Eastman Kodak.

Analytic Capacity & Measure. J. Garnett. LC 72-93416. (Lecture Notes in Mathematics: Vol. 297). (Illus.). 1973. pap. 11.00 o.p. (ISBN 0-387-06073-1). Springer-Verlag.

Analytic Chemistry of the Condensed Phosphates. S. Greenfield & S. Clift. LC 74-32261. 1975. 55.00 o.p. (ISBN 0-08-018174-0). Pergamon.

Analytic Functions. R. Nevanlinna. Tr. by P. Emig. (Grundlehren der Mathematischen Wissenschaften: Vol. 162). (Illus.). 1970. 49.20 o.p. (ISBN 0-387-04834-0). Springer-Verlag.

Analytic Geometry. V. A. Ilyin et al. 232p. 1985. 7.95 o.s.i. (Pub. by Mir Pubs USSR). Imported Pubns.

Analytic Geometry. Edwin J. Purcell. LC 58-5609. (Century Mathematics Ser.). (Illus.). 1958. 39.50x o.p. (ISBN 0-89197-605-1). Irvington.

Analytic Techniques in Urban & Regional Planning: With Applications in Public Administration & Affairs. John W. Dickey & Thomas M. Watts. (Illus.). 1978. text ed. 49.95 o.p. (ISBN 0-07-016798-2). McGraw.

Analytical Applications of Complex Equilibria. J. Inczedy. LC 75-25687. (Analytical Chemistry Ser.). 415p. 1976. 129.00x o.p. (ISBN 0-470-42713-2). Halsted Pr.

Analytical Applications of 1, 10-Phen'-antroline & Related Compounds. A. A. Schilt. 1969. 50.00 o.p. (ISBN 0-08-012877-7). Pergamon.

Analytical Bibliography of Universal Collected Biography. Ed. by Phyllis M. Riches. 1980. Repr. 130.00x o.p. (ISBN 0-8103-0168-7). Gale.

Analytical Chemistry in Space. R. E. Wainerdi. 1970. 90.00 o.p. (ISBN 0-08-006887-1). Pergamon.

Analytical Chemistry of Molybdenum & Tungsten. W. T. Elwell & D. F. Wood. 292p. 1971. 80.00 o.p. (ISBN 0-08-016673-3). Pergamon.

Analytical Chemistry of Nickel. C. L. Lewis & L. Ott. 1970. 70.00 o.p. (ISBN 0-08-015876-5). Pergamon.

Analytical Chemistry of Organic Halogen Compounds. L. Mazor. LC 75-5934. 400p. 1976. 81.00 o.p. (ISBN 0-08-017903-7). Pergamon.

Analytical Chemistry of Phosphorus Compounds. Ed. by M. Halmann. LC 70-37170. (Chemical Analysis Ser.: Vol. 37). 862p. 1972. 64.50 o.p. (ISBN 0-471-34558-X, Pub. by John Wiley). Krieger.

Analytical Chemistry of Plutonium. M. S. Milyukova. (Analytical Chemistry of the Elements). 440p. 1971. 41.95x o.p. (ISBN 0-470-60415-8). Halsted Pr.

Analytical Chemistry of Zirconium & Hafnium. A. K. Mukherji. LC 71-109236. 1970. 100.00 o.p. (ISBN 0-08-006886-3). Pergamon.

Analytical Experimental Physics. 3rd ed. Michael Ference, Jr. et al. LC 55-5124. (Illus.). 1956. lib. bdg. 17.50x o.s.i. (ISBN 0-226-24299-4). U of Chicago Pr.

Analytical Index. 3rd rev. ed. (Text of the General Agreement on Trade and Tarriffs). (Orig.). 1970. pap. 18.00 o.p. (ISBN 0-685-11717-0, G97, GATT). UNIPUB.

Analytical Index to the Ballad-Entries (1557-1709) in the Registers of the Company of Stationers of London. London Stationers' Company Staff. LC 67-1586. xviii, 346p. Repr. of 1967 ed. 35.00x o.p. (ISBN 0-8103-5019-X). Gale.

Analytical Index to the Ballad-Entries, 1557-1709, in the Register of the Company of Stationers London. London Stationers' Company Staff. (Studies in Philology: Vol. 21, No. 1). 1967. Repr. of 1924 ed. 12.00 o.p. (ISBN 0-384-33510-1). Johnson Repr.

Analytical Mechanics. 3rd ed. Grant R. Fowles. LC 76-57839. 1977. text ed. 41.95 o.p. (ISBN 0-03-089725-4, HoltC). HR&W.

Analytical Methods for Glycerol. M. R. Ashworth. 1979. 84.00 o.p. (ISBN 0-12-065050-9). Acad Pr.

Analytical Methods for Organic Cyano Groups. M. F. Ashworth. 1971. 40.00 o.p. (ISBN 0-08-016191-X). Pergamon.

Analytical Methods in Clinical Chemistry. Ed. by L. J. Kricka. (Illus.). 96p. 1984. pap. 28.00 o.p. (ISBN 0-08-031453-8). Pergamon.

Analytical Photogrammetry. Sanjib K. Ghosh. LC 79-1063. (Illus.). 1979. 55.00 o.p. (ISBN 0-08-023883-1). Pergamon.

Analytical Physiology of Cells & Developing Organisms. Ed. by B. Goodwin. 1977. 70.50 o.p. (ISBN 0-12-289360-3). Acad Pr.

Analytical Planning: The Organization of Systems. T. L. Saaty. LC 85-3475. (International Series in Modern Applied Mathematics & Computer Science: Vol. 7). 215p. 1985. 48.00 o.p. (ISBN 0-08-032599-8). Pergamon.

Analytical Potential of the Current Population Survey for Manpower & Employment Research. J. Morton. 71p. 1965. pap. 0.75 o.p. (ISBN 0-911558-20-9). W E Upjohn.

Analytical Procedures for Therapeutic Drug Monitoring & Emergency Toxicology. Randall C. Baselt. LC 79-50639. 328p. 1980. text ed. 40.00 o.p. (ISBN 0-931890-03-9, Biomed Pubns). Year Bk Med.

Analytical Spectroscopy: A Polychrome Branch of Science: Proceedings of the Twenty-third Colloquim International, including the 10th International Conference on Atomic Spectroscopy, Amsterdam, 26 June-1 July 1983. 1984 ed. Ed. by P. W. Boumans. 224p. 1984. pap. 61.00 o.p. (ISBN 0-08-031403-1). Pergamon.

Analytical Spectroscopy: Theory & Applications: Dedicated to Velmer Fassel. Ed. by R. Kniseley. 434p. 1986. pap. 96.25 o.p. (ISBN 0-08-033929-8, Pub. by PPL). Pergamon.

Analytical Survey of the Bible. Gerald H. Twombly. pap. 5.95 o.p. (ISBN 0-88469-120-9). BMH Bks.

Analytical Techniques in Environmental Chemistry: Proceedings of the International Congress, Barcelona, November 27-30, 1978. International Congress on Analytical Techniques in Environmental Chemistry Staff. Ed. by J. Albaiges. LC 79-41670. 1980. 165.00 o.p. (ISBN 0-08-023809-2). Pergamon.

Analytical Techniques in Environmental Chemistry 2: Proceedings of the International Congress, 2nd, Barcelona, Spain, November, 1981. International Congress on Analytical Techniques in Environmental Chemistry Staff & J. Albaiges. LC 82-15047. (Series on Environmental Science: Vol. 7). (Illus.). 482p. 1982. 120.00 o.p. (ISBN 0-08-028740-9). Pergamon.

Analytische Geometrie der Ebene und Des Raumes. R. Fueter. (Mathematische Reihe Ser.: No. 2). 180p. (Ger.). 1945. 21.95x o.p. (ISBN 0-8176-0130-9). Birkhauser.

Analyze Your Personality Through Color. Alfred W. Munzert. (Test Yourself Ser.). 1980. pap. 3.95 o.p. (ISBN 0-671-34036-0). Monarch Pr.

Titles

Analyzed Bible. Campbell G. Morgan. 256p. 1984. Isaiah I. pap. 5.95 o.p. (ISBN 0-8010-6171-7); Isaiah 2. pap. 5.95 o.p. (ISBN 0-8010-6172-5). Baker Bk.

Analyzed Bible. Campbell G. Morgan. Matthew. 6.95 o.p. (ISBN 0-8010-6159-8); Romans. pap. 5.95 o.p. (ISBN 0-8010-6149-0). Baker Bk.

Analyzer of Medical-Biological Words: A Clarifying Dissection of Medical Terminology, Showing How It Works, for Medics, Paramedics, Students, & Visitors from Foreign Countries. J. E. Schmidt. 224p. 1973. 13.25 o.p. (ISBN 0-398-02682-3). C C Thomas.

Analyzing Activity Areas: An Ethnoarchaeological Study of the Use of Space. Susan Kent. LC 83-14492. (Illus.). 275p. 1984. 24.95x o.p. (ISBN 0-8263-0718-3); pap. 12.95x o.p. (ISBN 0-8263-0719-1). U of NM Pr.

Analyzing Commercial & Multi-Family Real Estate Transactions 1982. (Real Estate Law & Practice Ser. 1982-83). 737p. 1982. 45.00 o.p. (N4-4399). PLI.

Analyzing Deviance. James D. Orcutt. 416p. 1983. pap. text ed. (ISBN 0-534-10741-9). Wadsworth Pub.

Analyzing Medical Records. 147p. 1988. 50.00 o.p. (ISBN 0-318-03916-8, 426). PA Bar Inst.

Analyzing Multivariate Data. Paul E. Green. 1978. text ed. 33.75 o.p. (ISBN 0-03-020786-X). Dryden Pr.

Analyzing Options for Local Institutional Development. Norman Uphoff. (Special Series on Local Institutional Development: No. 1). 49p. (Orig.). 1985. pap. text ed. 5.50 o.p. (ISBN 0-86731-108-8). Cornell CIS RDC.

Analyzing Prose. Richard A. Lanham. LC 82-20488. 255p. 1983. text ed. 12.95 o.s.i. (ISBN 0-684-17834-6). Scribner.

Analyzing Psychotherapy. Solomon Katzenelbogen. 1958. (ISBN 0-8022-0829-0). Philos Lib.

Analyzing Research Data: The Basics of Biomedical Research. Marks. LC 82-77764. 224p. 1982. 27.95 o.p. (ISBN 0-317-63767-3). Krieger.

Analyzing the Impact of Regulatory Change in Public Utilities. Ed. by Michael A. Crew. LC 83-48674. 208p. 1984. 29.00x o.p. (ISBN 0-669-07341-5). Lexington Bks.

Analyzing Urban Service Distributions: New Concepts & New Measures. Ed. by Richard C. Rich. LC 80-7690. (Policy Studies Organization Bk.). 272p. 1982. 30.00x o.p. (ISBN 0-669-03766-4). Lexington Bks.

Ananda Marga: Serving the People of North America. Ananda Marga Editors. (Illus.). 24p. (Orig.). 1982. pap. 1.00 o.s.i. (ISBN 0-88476-022-7). Ananda Marga.

Anaphora & Semantic Interpretation. Tanya Reinhart. (Illus.). 200p. 1983. 31.00 o.p. (ISBN 0-7099-2237-X, Pub. by Croom Helm Ltd). Routledge Chapman & Hall.

Anaphora in Natural Language Understanding: A Survey. G. Hirst. (Lecture Notes in Computer Science: Vol. 119). 126p. 1981. pap. 12.00 o.p. (ISBN 0-387-10858-0). Springer Verlag.

Anaphora or Great Eucharistic Prayer: An Eirenical Study in Liturgical History. Walter H. Frere. (Church Historical Society, London, New Ser.: No. 25). Repr. of 1938 ed. 50.00 o.p. (ISBN 0-8115-3149-X). Kraus Repr.

Anarchism. Denis Fauvel Rouif et al. 1982. lib. bdg. 20.00 o.p. (ISBN 3-598-10442-1). K G Saur.

Anarchism & Anarcho-Syndicalism: Selections. Karl Marx & Friedrich Engels. LC 72-82080. 388p. 1972. 8.50 o.p. (ISBN 0-7178-0348-1); pap. 3.25 o.p. (ISBN 0-7178-0349-X). Intl Pubs Co.

Anarchism & the Mexican Working Class, 1860-1931. John M. Hart. LC 77-16210. (Illus.). 259p. 1978. pap. 14.95x o.p. (ISBN 0-292-70331-7). U of Tex Pr.

Anarchism in France: The Case of Octave Mirbeau. Reg Carr. 1977. lib. bdg. 14.95x o.p. (ISBN 0-7735-0301-3, Pub. by McGill Canada). U of Toronto Pr.

Anarchist Handbook: The Materials & Production of Improvised Weapons. R. Wells. (Criminology Ser.). 1986. lib. bdg. 79.95 o.p. (ISBN 0-8490-3688-7). Gordon Pr.

Anarchist Women: Eighteen Seventy to Nineteen Twenty. Margaret Marsh. (American Civilization Ser.). (Illus.). 256p. 1980. 29.95 o.p. (ISBN 0-87722-202-9). Temple U Pr.

Anarchists of Casa Viejas. Jerome R. Mintz. LC 81-19696. xvi, 336p. 1984. pap. 10.95 o.s.i. (ISBN 0-226-53107-4). U of Chicago Pr.

Anasazi Subsistence & Settlement on White Mesa, San Juan County, Utah. Ed. by William S. Davis et al. LC 85-13346. (Illus.). 644p. (Orig.). 1985. lib. bdg. 42.75 o.p. (ISBN 0-8191-4800-8); pap. text ed. 26.00 o.p. (ISBN 0-8191-4801-6). U Pr of Amer.

Anatole & the Pied Piper. Eve Titus & Paul Galdone. 1979. text ed. 9.95 o.p. (ISBN 0-07-064897-2). McGraw.

Anatoly Karpov's Games As World Champion 1975-1977. K. J. O'Connell & David Levy. 1978. pap. 20.95 o.p. (ISBN 0-7134-0227-X, Pub. by Batsford England). David & Charles.

Anatomia y Fisiologia Humanas. V. G. Tatarinov. 364p. (Span.). 1980. 10.00 o.p. (ISBN 0-8285-1660-X, Pub. by Mir Pubs USSR). Imported Pubns.

Anatomic Foundation of Neuroradiology of the Brain. 2nd ed. McClure Wilson. 1972. 31.00 o.p. (ISBN 0-316-94413-0). Little.

Anatomic Studies on the Arthrodiran Head. E. Stensio. (Illus.). 419p. (Orig.). 1963. pap. text ed. 67.50x o.p. Coronet Bks.

Anatomical Atlas of Chinese Acupuncture Points. Shandong Medical College Staff. (Illus.). 265p. 1982. 50.00 o.p. (ISBN 0-8351-0954-2). China Bks.

Anatomical Basis of Dentistry. Bernard Liebgott. (Illus.). 528p. 1982. write for info. o.p. (ISBN 0-7216-5784-2). Saunders.

Anatomical Drawings from the Royal Library Windsor Castle. Leonardo Da Vinci. 1984. 55.00 o.p. (ISBN 0-8016-1278-0). Mosby.

Anatomical Kinesiology: A Programmed Text. Jerry N. Barham & William L. Thomas. (Illus., Prog. Bk.). 1969. pap. text ed. write for info. o.p. (ISBN 0-02-306010-7, 30601). Macmillan.

Anatomical Organization of the Suprasylvian Gyrus of the Cat. C. J. Heath & E. G. Jones. LC 79-177566. (Advances in Anatomy, Embryology & Cell Biology: Vol. 45, Pt. 3). (Illus.). 65p. 1971. pap. 27.20 o.p. (ISBN 0-387-05596-7). Springer-Verlag.

Anatomy & Life Drawing. Don Davy. LC 77-91042. 1978. pap. 4.95 o.s.i. (ISBN 0-8008-0196-2, Pentalic). Taplinger.

Anatomy & Physiology: A Laboratory Manual. James Crouch & Micheline Carr. LC 76-56507. (Illus.). 369p. 1977. spiral bdg. 19.95 o.p. (ISBN 0-87484-356-1). Mayfield Pub.

Anatomy & Physiology: A Self Instructional Course, 5 vols. Cambridge Communication, Ltd. Staff. LC 84-4977. (Illus.). 1985. Set. pap. text ed. 32.00 o.p. (ISBN 0-443-03395-1); Bk. 1. The Human Body & the Reproductive System. pap. text ed. 6.50 o.p. (ISBN 0-443-03170-3); Bk. 2. The Endocrine Glands & the Nervous System. pap. text ed. 6.50 o.p. (ISBN 0-443-03206-8); Bk. 3. The Locomotor System & the Special Senses. pap. text ed. 6.50 o.p. (ISBN 0-443-03207-6); Bk. 4. The Respiratory System & the Cardiovascular System. pap. text ed. 6.50 o.p. (ISBN 0-443-03208-4); Bk. 5. The Urinary System & the Digestive System. pap. text ed. 6.50 o.p. (ISBN 0-443-03209-2). Churchill.

Anatomy & Physiology Applied to Nursing. 6th ed. Janet T. Riddle. LC 84-21413. (Livingstone Nursing Text Ser.). (Illus.). 196p. 1985. pap. text ed. 12.00 o.p. (ISBN 0-443-03030-8). Churchill.

Anatomy & Physiology for Physiotherapists. 2nd ed. Moffatt & Mottram. 1986. 21.00 o.p. (ISBN 0-8016-3506-3). Mosby.

Anatomy & Physiology Laboratory Manual. 11th ed. Catherine P. Anthony & Gary A. Thibodeau. (Illus.). 284p. 1983. pap. text ed. 14.95 o.p. (ISBN 0-8016-0279-3). Mosby.

Anatomy for Artists. Reginald Marsh. (Illus.). 13.25 o.p. (ISBN 0-8446-5702-6). Peter Smith.

Anatomy of a Comprehensive Employee Relations Program see Issues in the Public Employee Relations Library: Series 2.

Anatomy of a Jury: The System on Trial. Seymour Wishman. LC 85-40845. 300p. 1986. 17.95 o.s.i. (ISBN 0-8129-1260-8, Dist. by Random House). Times Bks.

Anatomy of a Park Plan: The Essentials of Recreation Area Design. A. J. Rutledge. 1971. text ed. 41.50 o.p. (ISBN 0-07-054347-X). McGraw.

Anatomy of Accounting. 3rd ed. A. D. Barton. LC 83-7015. 1984. text ed. 30.00x o.p. (ISBN 0-7022-1863-4); pap. text ed. 19.95x o.p. (ISBN 0-7022-1460-4). U of Queensland Pr.

Anatomy of Achievement Motivation. Heinz Heckhausen. (Personality & Psychopathology Ser.: Vol. 1). 1967. 65.00 o.p. (ISBN 0-12-336350-0). Acad Pr.

Anatomy of an Egyptian Intellectual: Yahya Haqqi. Miriam Cooke. LC 83-70809. 188p. 1984. 24.00 o.p. (ISBN 0-89410-395-4); pap. 14.00 o.p. (ISBN 0-89410-396-2). Three Continents.

Anatomy of Bibliomania. Holbrook Jackson. 1978. Repr. of 1950 ed. lib. bdg. 49.00x o.p. (ISBN 0-374-94128-9, Octagon). Hippocrene Bks.

Anatomy of Change: The Menninger Foundation Report on Testing the Effects of Psychotherapy. Ed. by Stephen Appelbaum. LC 77-5382. (Illus.). 334p. 1977. 42.50x o.p. (ISBN 0-306-31002-3, Plenum Pr). Plenum Pub.

Anatomy of Communism. Andrew Scott. 1952. (ISBN 0-8022-1523-8). Philos Lib.

Anatomy of Decision. Mirek Karasek. LC 84-90239. 177p. 1985. 14.95 o.p. (ISBN 0-533-06284-5). Vantage.

Anatomy of Food Service Design 1. Ed. by Jule Wilkinson. LC 75-5730. (Illus.). 224p. 1983. 29.95 o.p. (ISBN 0-8436-0569-3). Van Nos Reinhold.

Anatomy of Freedom. Henry P. Fairchild. 1957. (ISBN 0-8022-0466-X). Philos Lib.

Anatomy of Human Destructiveness. new ed. Erich Fromm. LC 73-3698. 448p. 1973. pap. 6.95 o.p. (ISBN 0-03-018451-7). H Holt & Co.

Anatomy of Job Loss: The How, Why & Where of Employment Decline. Doreen Massey & Richard Meegan. 280p. 1982. 26.00x o.p. (ISBN 0-416-32350-2, NO. 3692); pap. 13.95x o.p. (ISBN 0-416-32360-X, NO. 3693). Routledge Chapman & Hall.

Anatomy of Leadership: Princes, Heroes & Supermen. Eugene E. Jennings. 1972. pap. text ed. 5.95 o.p. (ISBN 0-07-032449-2). McGraw.

Anatomy of Literature. Robert Foulke & Paul Smith. 1124p. 1972. text ed. 13.50 o.p. (ISBN 0-15-502710-7, HC). HarBraceJ.

Anatomy of Paleocortex: A Critical Review. R. Pigache. LC 73-146518. (Advances in Anatomy, Embryology & Cell Biology: Vol. 43, Pt. 6). (Illus.). 1970. 22.50 o.p. (ISBN 0-387-05083-3). Springer-Verlag.

Anatomy of Poetry. Rev. ed. Majorie Boulton. 1983. pap. 6.95 o.p. (ISBN 0-7100-9087-0). Routledge Chapman & Hall.

Anatomy of the Aeroplane. Darrol Stinton. 321p. 1980. text ed. 36.75x o.p. (ISBN 0-246-11447-9, Pub. by Granada England). Gower Pub Co.

Anatomy of the Horse. George Stubbs. 19.00 o.p. (ISBN 0-8446-5663-1). Peter Smith.

Anatomy of the Human Orbit & Accessory Organs of Vision. Ernest S. Whitnall. LC 78-27070. (Classics in Ophthalmology Ser.). (Illus.). 1979. Repr. of 1932 ed. Set. 199.50 o.p. (ISBN 0-88275-934-5); Set. lib. bdg. 37.50 o.p. (ISBN 0-88275-840-3). Krieger.

Anatomy of the Laboratory Mouse. Margaret J. Cook. 1976. 47.50 o.p. (ISBN 0-12-186956-3). Acad Pr.

Anatomy of the Sacred: An Introduction to Religion. James C. Livingston. 734p. 1987. text ed. write for info. o.p. (ISBN 0-02-371370-4). Macmillan.

Anatomy of the SS State. Helmut Krausnick & Martin Broszat. 304p. pap. 7.95 o.p. (ISBN 0-586-08028-7, Pub. by Granada England). Academy Chi Pubs.

Anatomy: PreTest Self-Assessment & Review. 3rd ed. PreTest Service Inc. & Ernest W. April. (Basic Science Ser.). 260p. 1983. text ed. 12.95 o.p. (ISBN 0-07-051931-5). McGraw.

Anatomy: PreTest Self-Assessment & Review. 4th ed. PreTest Service, Inc. Staff. (Illus.). 260p. 1985. 14.95 o.p. (ISBN 0-07-051940-4). McGraw-Pretest.

Anaximander, Heraclitus, Parmenides, Plotinus, Lao-Tzu, Nagarjuna. Karl Jaspers. Ed. by Hannah Arendt. Tr. by Ralph Manheim from Ger. LC 74-4335. (From the Great Philosophers Ser.: Vol. No. 2). 160p. 1974. pap. 3.25 o.p. (ISBN 0-15-607500-8, Harv). HarBraceJ.

Anbrunch, Vols. 1-4. Ed. by Otto Schneider & I. B. Neumann. 77.00 o.p. (ISBN 0-317-44545-6). Kraus Repr.

Ancestral Lines Revised. Carl Boyer, 3rd. LC 81-68273. 666p. 1981. 42.00 o.p. (ISBN 0-936124-05-9). C Boyer.

Anchor Anthology of Jacobean Drama see Jacobean Drama: An Anthology.

Anchor Companion to the Orchestra. Norman Del Mar. LC 87-1359. 288p. 1987. pap. 19.95 o.p. (ISBN 0-385-24081-3, Anchor Pr); pap. 10.95 o.p. (ISBN 0-385-24082-1, Anchor Pr). Doubleday.

Anchor of the Soul. Samuel Jardine. 1978. pap. 1.95 o.p. (ISBN 0-937396-05-2). Walterick Pubs.

Anchoring Systems. Ed. by Michael E. McCormick. 1979. 36.00 o.p. (ISBN 0-08-022694-9). Pergamon.

Anchors. N. E. Upham. (Album Ser.: No. 110). (Illus.). 32p. (Orig.). 1983. pap. 3.50 o.p. (ISBN 0-85263-636-9, Pub. by Shire Pubns England). Seven Hills Bk Dists.

Anchorwoman's Story. Christine Craft. 228p. (Orig.). 1986. pap. 8.95 o.p. Capra Pr.

Ancien Regime. C. B. Behrens. (History of European Civilization Library). (Illus.). 215p. 1967. pap. text ed. 9.50 o.p. (ISBN 0-15-502750-6, HC). HarBraceJ.

Ancien Royaume Du Congo Des Origines a la Fin Du XIXe Siecle. W. G. Randles. (Civilisations & Societes: No. 14). (Illus.). 1968. pap. 23.00x o.p. (ISBN 90-2796-259-6). Mouton.

Ancient Agricultural Implements. Sian Rees. (Shire Archaeology Ser.: No. 15). (Illus.). 72p. 1981. pap. 5.95 o.p. (ISBN 0-85263-535-4, Pub. by Shire Pubns England). Seven Hills Bk Dists.

Ancient & Modern Rome. Rodolfo Lanciani. LC 63-10278. (Our Debt to Greece & Rome Ser). 169p. Repr. of 1930 ed. 18.50x o.p. (ISBN 0-8154-0131-0). Cooper Sq.

Ancient & Oriental Music (by) Romain Goldron. A. Louis Burkhalter. 121p. Repr. of 1968 ed. lib. bdg. 39.00 o.p. (Pub. by Am Repr Serv). Reprint Servs.

Ancient Architecture in Beijing. Zhou Yi et al. (Illus.). 47p. (Orig.). 1985. pap. 14.95 o.p. (ISBN 0-8351-1637-9). China Bks.

Ancient Art from Cyprus: The Ringling Collection. Ed. by Norma Kershaw. LC 83-80443. (Illus.). 80p. 1983. pap. 1.00 o.p. (ISBN 0-916758-11-7). Ringling Mus Art.

Ancient Art of Self-Healing. Harbhajan Singh Khalsa. Ed. by Siri Amir Singh Khalsa. 150p. Repr. lib. bdg. cancelled o.s.i. (ISBN 0-8095-6110-7). Borgo Pr.

Ancient Art: Pre-Greek & Greek Art. LC 76-14063. (Garland Library of the History of Art). 1977. lib. bdg. 61.00 o.p. (ISBN 0-8240-2412-5). Garland Pub.

Ancient Athens. E. J. Sheppard. Ed. by Marjorie Reeves. (Then & There Ser.). (Illus.). 110p. (gr. 7-12). 1967. pap. text ed. 4.95x o.p. (ISBN 0-582-20406-2). Longman.

Ancient Aztalan. Samuel A. Barrett. LC 70-11394. 1970. Repr. of 1933 ed. lib. bdg. 35.00x o.p. (ISBN 0-8371-4624-0, BAAA). Greenwood.

Ancient Boats. Sean McGrail. (Shire Archaeology Ser.: No. 31). (Illus.). 64p. 1983. pap. 5.95 o.p. (ISBN 0-85263-626-1, Pub. by Shire Pubns England). Seven Hills Bk Dists.

Ancient Burial-Mounds of England. L. V. Grinsell. LC 73-13037. (Illus.). 278p. 1975. Repr. of 1953 ed. lib. bdg. 35.00x o.p. (ISBN 0-8371-7101-6, GRAB). Greenwood.

Ancient Burials of Metallic Foundation: Documents in Stone Boxes. H. Curtis Wright. (Occasional Papers: No. 157). 42p. 1982. pap. 3.00 o.p. (ISBN 0-317-59004-9). U of Ill Lib Info Sci.

Ancient China's Technology & Science. Institute of National Science Staff & Chinese Academy of Science Staff. (China Knowledge Ser.). (Illus.). 632p. (Orig.). 1983. 16.95 o.p. (ISBN 0-8351-1235-7); pap. 9.95 o.p. (ISBN 0-8351-1001-X). China Bks.

Ancient Chinese Toys & Ornaments. Tian Yuan. Tr. by Liu Li from Chinese. (Illus.). 55p. 1983. text ed. 7.95 o.p. (ISBN 0-8351-1508-9). China Bks.

Ancient Constitution & the Feudal Law: A Study of English Historical Thought in the 17th Century. J. G. Pocock. 1967. pap. 3.95x o.p. (ISBN 0-393-00387-6, Norton Lib). Norton.

Ancient Crete & Mycenae. James Bolton. Ed. by Marjorie Reeves. (Then & There Ser.). (Illus.). 96p. (YA) (gr. 7-12). 1968. pap. text ed. 4.95x o.p. (ISBN 0-582-20415-1). Longman.

Ancient Education. William Smith. 1955. (ISBN 0-8022-1602-1). Philos Lib.

Ancient Egypt: A Survey. Elfriede Preger. LC 78-54099. (Illus.). 1978. pap. 6.95 o.s.i. (ISBN 0-89708-001-7). And Bks.

Ancient Egyptian Alchemy. Jack Lindsay. Ed. by John O'Quinn. 44p. 1981. pap. text ed. 6.95 o.s.i. (ISBN 0-9609802-4-5). Life Science.

Ancient Egyptians: How They Lived & Worked. Jill Kamil. LC 76-42175. 1977. 15.95 o.p. (ISBN 0-8023-1267-5). Dufour.

Ancient Europe: From the Beginnings of Agriculture to Classical Antiquity. Stuart Piggott. LC 64-21369. (Illus.). 1966. lib. bdg. 33.95x o.p. (ISBN 0-202-33002-8). Aldine de Gruyter.

Ancient Glass: Ancient & Islamic Glass in the Carnegie Museum of Natural History. Andrew Oliver, Jr. LC 80-67130. (Illus.). 156p. 1980. 5.00 o.p. (ISBN 0-911239-03-0); pap. 3.50 o.p. (ISBN 0-911239-04-9). Carnegie Mus.

Ancient Glass in the Freer Gallery of Art. Richard Ettinghausen. (Illus.). 1962. pap. 3.00x o.p. (ISBN 0-934686-14-9). Freer.

Ancient Greek: A Structural Programme. C. Douglas Ellis & Albert Schachter. (Illus.). 1528p. 1973. wkbk. 30.00x o.p. (ISBN 0-7735-0196-7, Pub. by McGill Canada). U of Toronto Pr.

Ancient Greek Gadgets & Machines. Robert S. Brumbaugh. LC 75-3983. (Illus.). 152p. 1975. Repr. of 1966 ed. lib. bdg. 35.00x o.p. (ISBN 0-8371-7427-9, BRGG). Greenwood.

Ancient Greeks. Moses I. Finley. 1977. pap. 5.95 o.p. (ISBN 0-14-020812-7, Pelican). Penguin.

Ancient Hawaiian Civilization. rev. ed. E. Craighill Handy et al. LC 65-23709. (gr. 9 up). 1965. 16.50 o.p. (ISBN 0-8048-0023-5). C E Tuttle.

Ancient Herbs in the J. Paul Getty Museum. Jeanne D'Andrea. LC 82-81306. (Illus.). 96p. 1982. pap. 10.00 o.p. (ISBN 0-89236-035-6). J P Getty Trust.

Ancient History of Western Asia, India, & Crete. Bedrich Hronzny. 1954. (ISBN 0-8022-0753-7). Philos Lib.

Ancient India. 2nd. ed. Romila Thapar. 1969. pap. 2.00 o.s.i. (ISBN 0-88253-275-8). Ind-US Inc.

Ancient Indian Magic & Folklore: An Introduction. Margaret Stutley. LC 79-13211. (Illus.). 1980. write for info. o.p. (ISBN 0-87773-712-6). Shambhala Pubns.

Ancient Law. Henry J. Maine. 1972. Repr. of 1917 ed. 12.95x o.p. (ISBN 0-460-00734-3, Evman). Biblio Dist.

Ancient Lives: Daily Life in Egypt of the Pharaohs. John Romer. LC 84-12908. (Illus.). 256p. 1984. 18.95 o.s.i. H Holt & Co.

Ancient, Medieval, & Modern Christianity. Charles A. Guignebert. 1961. 10.00 o.p. (ISBN 0-8216-0032-X, Pub. by Univ Bks). Carol Pub Group.

Ancient Mind & Its Heritage, 2 vols. Elmer G. Suhr. Incl. Vol. 1. Exploring the Primitive, Egyptian & Mesopotamian Cultures. 1959. text ed. 5.00 o.p. (ISBN 0-682-40097-1); Vol. 2. Exploring the Hebrew, Hindu, Greek & Chinese Cultures. 1960. text ed. 5.00 o.p. (ISBN 0-682-40098-X). University). Exposition-Phoenix.

Ancient Mirrors of Womanhood: A Treasury of Goddess & Heroine Lore from Around the World, 2 vols. Merlin Stone. LC 83-73164. (Illus.). 425p. 1984. 22.50x o.p. (ISBN 0-8070-6718-0); pap. 11.95 o.p. (ISBN 0-8070-6719-9, BP676). Beacon Pr.

Ancient Mysteries Described. William Hone. LC 67-23905. (Illus.). 302p. 1969. Repr. of 1823 ed. 35.00x o.p. (ISBN 0-8103-3444-5). Gale.

Ancient Myths & Biblical Faith. Foster R. McCurley. LC 82-48589. 208p. 1983. pap. 12.95 o.p. (ISBN 0-8006-1696-0, 1-1696, Fortress). Augsburg Fortress.

Ancient Myths & Early History of Japan. Michiko Y. Aoki. LC 73-82081. 1974. text ed. 7.00 o.p. (ISBN 0-682-47774-5, University). Exposition-Phoenix.

Ancient of Days. Michael Bishop. LC 84-28324. 310p. 1985. 15.95 o.p. (ISBN 0-87795-724-X, Arbor Hse). Morrow.

Ancient Ones. Janet Lewis. (Illus.). 1979. pap. 7.50 o.p. (ISBN 0-931832-12-8). Fithian Pr.

Ancient Persian Bronzes in the Adam Collection. P. R. Moorey. 208p. 1974. 36.00 o.p. (ISBN 0-571-10216-6). Faber & Faber.

Ancient Records & the Structure of Genesis. P. J. Wiseman. Ed. by D. J. Wiseman. 160p. 1985. pap. 6.95 o.p. (ISBN 0-8407-7502-4). Nelson.

Ancient Regime. Hippolyte A. Taine. 11.75 o.p. (ISBN 0-8446-1434-3). Peter Smith.

Ancient Religions. Vergilius Ferm. Orig. Title: Forgotten Religions. 408p. (ISBN 0-8022-0485-6). Philos Lib.

Ancient Roman Construction in Italy from the Prehistoric Period to Augustus. Marion E. Blake. (Carnegie Institution Publication Ser.: No. 570). (Illus.). 1968. Repr. of 1947 ed. 75.00 o.p. (ISBN 0-527-08850-1). Kraus Repr.

Ancient Rome. rev. ed. Robert Payne. LC 79-95730. Orig. Title: Horizon Book of Ancient Rome. 1971. pap. text ed. 6.95 o.p. (ISBN 0-07-048937-8). McGraw.

Ancient Rome. 2nd ed. Nicholas Sherwin-White. (Then & There Ser.). (Illus.). 1978. pap. text ed. 4.95x o.p. (ISBN 0-582-21574-9). Longman.

Ancient Songs & Ballads, from the Reign of King Henry Second to the Revolution. Joseph Ritson. LC 67-23930. 528p. 1968. Repr. of 1877 ed. 43.00x o.p. (ISBN 0-8103-3417-8). Gale.

Ancient Sparta. K. M. Chrimes. 1952. (ISBN 0-8022-0245-4). Philos Lib.

Ancient Sun: Proceedings of the Conference on the Ancient Sun: Fossil Record in the Earth, Moon & Meteorites, Boulder Colorado, October 16-19, 1979. Compiled by Lunar & Planetary Institute Staff. LC 80-20084. (Geochimica & Cosmochimica Acta: Suppl. 13). 500p. 1981. 75.00 o.p. (ISBN 0-08-026324-0). Pergamon.

Ancient Synagogue Excavations at Khirbet Shema, Upper Galilee, Israel, 1970-1972. Joint Expedition to Khirbet Shema Staff & Eric M. Meyers. LC 76-40864. pap. 117.00 o.p. (ISBN 0-317-42147-6, 2026210). UMI Res Pr.

Ancient Theatre. Ericka Simon. 64p. 1982. 17.95x o.p. (ISBN 0-416-32520-3, NO. 3617); pap. 7.95x o.p. (ISBN 0-416-32530-0, NO. 3618). Routledge Chapman & Hall.

Ancient World. Thomas W. Africa. (Illus., Orig.). 1969. pap. 16.95 o.p. (ISBN 0-395-04095-7). HM.

Ancient World: A Social & Cultural History. D. Brendan Nagle. (Illus.). 1979. pap. text ed. (ISBN 0-13-036400-2). P-H.

And after the Journey. Georgette W. Amowitz. (Educational Dance Score Registry Ser.: No. 9). (Illus.). 14p. 1984. dance score 20.00 o.s.i. (ISBN 0-932582-38-9). Dance Notation.

And All the Stars a Stage. James Blish. 1976. pap. 2.25 o.p. (ISBN 0-380-00013-X, 61739-0). Avon.

And Crown Thy Good. Philip Davis. 1952. (ISBN 0-8022-0360-4). Philos Lib.

And Everything Nice: The Story of Sugar, Spice & Flavoring. Elizabeth K. Cooper. LC 66-12588. (Illus.). (gr. 3-7). 1966. 5.50 o.p. (ISBN 0-15-203498-6, HJ). HarBraceJ.

And God Bless Uncle Harry & His Roommate Jack Who We Are Not Supposed to Talk About. Christopher Street Magazine Editors. 1978. pap. 2.95 o.p. (ISBN 0-380-01897-7, 37291-6). Avon.

And God Wants People. Mary L. Lacy. LC 62-11717. 1976. pap. 1.25 o.p. (ISBN 0-8042-3594-5, John Knox). Westminster John Knox.

And He Had Compassion on Them: The Christian & World Hunger. Task Force on World Hunger Staff. (Illus.). 1979. pap. text ed. 3.50 o.p. (ISBN 0-933140-00-2). CRC Pubns.

And It Rained. Ellen Raskin. LC 69-18967. (Illus.). (gr. k-4). 1969. PLB 6.95 o.p. (ISBN 0-689-20587-2, Anetheum). Macmillan.

And Me, Coyote! Betty Baker. LC 82-7134. (Illus.). 32p. (gr. k-4). 1982. 8.95 o.s.i. (ISBN 0-02-708280-6). Macmillan.

And More by Andy Rooney. Andrew A. Rooney. LC 82-45183. 256p. 1982. 12.95 o.s.i. (ISBN 0-689-11316-1, Atheneum). Macmillan.

And Music at the Close: Stravinsky's Last Years, a Personal Memoir. Lillian Libman. (Illus.). 400p. 1972. 12.50 o.p. (ISBN 0-393-02113-0). Norton.

And Not to Yield: An Autobiography. Ella Winter. LC 63-15320. 1963. 5.95 o.p. (ISBN 0-15-106820-8). HarBraceJ.

And Now a Word from Our Creator. Thomas G. Savage. LC 72-1370. 1972. 5.95 o.p. (ISBN 0-8294-0213-6). Loyola.

And Now... the News. Mike Wolverton. LC 77-76872. 136p. 1977. 19.00x o.p. (ISBN 0-87201-041-4). Gulf Pub.

And Pastures New: A Collection of Poems. Melville Cane. LC 56-5333. 1956. 4.00 o.p. (ISBN 0-15-106838-0). HarBraceJ.

And Perhaps: The Story of Ruth Dayan. Ruth Dayan & Helga Dudman. LC 72-79920. 1973. 6.95 o.p. (ISBN 0-15-106845-3). HarBraceJ.

And Sarah Laughed: The Status of Woman in the Old Testament. John H. Otwell. LC 76-54671. 222p. 1977. pap. 8.95 o.s.i. (ISBN 0-664-24126-3, Westminster). Westminster John Knox.

And Scatter the Proud. Lewis W. Green. LC 78-88672. 447p. 1969. 4.98 o.p. (ISBN 0-910244-54-5). Blair.

And So to Murder. Carter Dickson. (Black Dagger Crime Ser.). 1987. text ed. 14.95x o.p. (ISBN 0-86220-703-7, Pub. by Firecrest Pub Ltd). Prescott Pr Nh.

And Still in the Running: A Horse Called Port Conway Lane. Barbara W. Prabhu. LC 83-22129. 64p. (gr. 7 up). 1984. lib. bdg. 9.79 o.s.i. (ISBN 0-671-46940-1). Messner.

And Still the Earth. Ignacio D. Brandao. 384p. 1985. pap. 4.95 o.p. (ISBN 0-380-89874-8, Bard). Avon.

And the Angels Wept. Farley Freeman. 1985. 9.95 o.p. (ISBN 0-533-06597-6). Vantage.

And the Children Played. Patricia Joudry. LC 75-2790. 1975. 9.95 o.p. (ISBN 0-912766-16-6); pap. 5.95 o.p. (ISBN 0-88776-160-7). Tundra Bks.

And the Truth Shall Set You Free. Eleanor I. Moore. (Illus.). 1980. 15.00 o.p. (ISBN 0-682-49344-9). Exposition-Phoenix.

And They Also Kick You When You're Down: An Irreverent Guide to the Way the Real World Works. Donald G. Smith. 224p. 1984. 15.95 o.p. (ISBN 0-396-08411-7). Dodd.

And They Called Him Amos: The Story of John Amos Comenius-a Woodcut in Words. Florence H. Anastasas. LC 73-86540. 1973. 10.00 o.p. (ISBN 0-682-47814-8, University). Exposition-Phoenix.

And Yet They Come: Portuguese Immigration from the Azores to the United States (1820-1978) Jerry Williams. 1982. pap. 14.95 o.s.i. (ISBN 0-913256-57-9). Ctr Migration.

Andalusian Diplomatic Relations with Western Europe During the Umayyad Period. Abdurraham Hajji. 28.00x o.p. (ISBN 0-86685-014-7). Intl Bk Ctr.

Andean Pact Technology Policies. Junta del Acuerdo de Cartagena Staff. 58p. 1976. pap. 5.00 o.p. (ISBN 0-88936-077-4, IDRC60, IDRC). UNIPUB.

Anders Nygren. Thor Hall. (Makers of the Modern Theological Mind Ser.). 1978. 8.95 o.p. (ISBN 0-8499-0098-0). Word Bks.

Anders Nygren. Thor Hall. 230p. 1984. pap. text ed. 8.95 o.p. (ISBN 0-8499-3004-9, 3004-9). Word Bks.

Andersen on Financial Planning: How to Increase & Preserve Your Money No Matter How Much You Make. Carl E. Andersen. 250p. 1985. 19.95 o.p. (ISBN 0-87094-663-3). Dow Jones-Irwin.

Andersen on Mutual Funds: The Investor's Game Plan for Building Personal Wealth. Carl E. Andersen. 174p. 1984. 16.50 o.p. (ISBN 0-673-15931-0). Scott F.

Andersen's Fairy Tales. Hans Christian Andersen. LC 58-6191. (Illus.). 300p. 1983. 15.50 o.s.i. (ISBN 0-671-47559-2). Wanderer Bks.

Andersen's Symphony Tips & Tricks. 2nd ed. Dick Andersen & Janet McBeen. Orig. Title: Symphony Encore: Program Notes. 321p. (Orig.). 1986. pap. 19.95 o.p. (ISBN 0-89588-342-2). Sybex.

Anderson Tapes. Lawrence Sanders. 1983. pap. 3.50 o.p. (ISBN 0-425-07503-6). Berkley Pub.

Anderson's Alice: Walter Anderson Illustrates Alice's Adventures in Wonderland by Lewis Carroll. Lewis Carroll. LC 83-14643. (Illus.). 128p. (gr. 2). 1983. 14.95 o.p. (ISBN 0-87805-188-0). U Pr of Miss.

Andosols. Kim H. Tan. 1984. 66.95 o.p. (ISBN 0-442-28282-6). Van Nos Reinhold.

Andre Gide. rev. ed. Albert J. Guerard. LC 74-88805. 1969. 25.00x o.p. (ISBN 0-674-03525-9). Harvard U Pr.

Andre Kertesz: The Manchester Collection. (Illus.). 185p. pap. 25.00 o.p. (ISBN 0-89381-210-2). Aperture.

Andre Norton: A Primary & Secondary Bibliography. Roger C. Schlobin. 1979. lib. bdg. 15.00 o.p. (ISBN 0-8161-8044-X, Hall Reference). G K Hall.

Andre Simon's Wines of the World. 2nd ed. Serena Sutcliffe. (Illus.). 1981. text ed. 35.00 o.p. (ISBN 0-07-057423-5). McGraw.

Andreae & the Formula of Concord. Robert Kolb. 1977. pap. 8.50 o.p. (ISBN 0-570-03741-7, 12-2645). Concordia.

Andreas Schleiermacher's Bibliographic Classification & Its Relationship to the Dewey Decimal & Library of Congress Classifications. Gordon Stevenson. (Occasional Papers: No. 136). 22p. 1978. pap. 2.00 o.p. (ISBN 0-317-58976-8). U of Ill Lib Info Sci.

Andrew & Tobias. J. I. Stewart. 1980. 12.95 o.p. (ISBN 0-393-01405-3). Norton.

Andrew Jackson. Margaret L. Coit. (Illus.). (gr. 7-9). 1965. 7.95 o.p. (ISBN 0-395-06698-0). HM.

Andrew Johnson & Reconstruction. Eric L. McKitrick. LC 60-5467. 1964. pap. text ed. 13.00x o.s.i. (ISBN 0-226-56046-5). U of Chicago Pr.

Andrew Marvell: A Reference Guide. Dan S. Collins. 1981. lib. bdg. 36.50 o.p. (ISBN 0-8161-8017-2, Hall Reference). G K Hall.

Andrew Marvell: Complete Poetry. Ed. by George D. Lord. 318p. 1984. pap. 5.95x o.p. (ISBN 0-460-01358-0, DEL-05071, Pub. by Evman England). Biblio Dist.

Andrew Murray & His Message. W. M. Douglas. (Christian Biography Ser.). 336p. 1981. pap. 5.95 o.p. (ISBN 0-8010-2908-2). Baker Bk.

Andrew Project. James Taylor. LC 85-42826. (Illus.). 108p. (Orig.). 1985. pap. 1.95 o.s.i. (ISBN 0-8042-0461-6, John Knox). Westminster John Knox.

Andrew Young: Champion of the Poor. Paul Westman. LC 82-25106. (Taking Part Ser.). (Illus.). 48p. (gr. 3 up). 1983. PLB 9.95 o.p. (ISBN 0-87518-239-9). Dillon.

Andro, Star of Bethlehem. Anne Claire. Ed. by Patricia Mahany. LC 82-62727. (Happy Day Bks.). (Illus.). 24p. (ps-2). 1983. pap. 1.59 o.p. (ISBN 0-87239-631-2, 3551). Standard Pub.

Androgens & Anti-Androgen Therapy. Ed. by S. L. Jeffcoate. LC 81-19712. (Wiley Series on Current Topics in Reproductive Endocrinoogy). 188p. 1982. 45.00 o.p. (ISBN 0-471-10154-0, Dist. by A R Liss). Wiley.

Androgynous Trollope: Attitudes to Women Amongst Early Victorian Novelists. Rajiva Wijesinha. LC 81-40260. 360p. 1982. lib. bdg. 30.50 o.p. (ISBN 0-8191-2060-X); pap. text ed. 16.25 o.p. (ISBN 0-8191-2061-8). U Pr of Amer.

Android at Arms. Andre Norton. LC 77-152695. 253p. (gr. 7 up). 1971. 6.50 o.p. (ISBN 0-15-203497-8, HJ). HarBraceJ.

Android Design. Martin Weinstein. (Illus.). 248p. (Orig.). 1981. pap. 13.95 o.p. (ISBN 0-8104-5192-1). Sams.

Andromache. Richard Wilbur & Racine. LC 82-47658. (Illus.). 114p. 1982. 10.95 o.p. (ISBN 0-15-107052-0). HarBraceJ.

Andropov File. Martin Ebon. 304p. 1983. text ed. 16.95 o.p. (ISBN 0-07-018861-0). McGraw.

Androscoggin River Valley: Gateway to the White Mountains. Denman B. Wight. LC 67-18141. 1967. 12.75 o.p. (ISBN 0-8048-0024-3). C E Tuttle.

Andy. Phyllis A. Wood. LC 76-130526. (Hiway Bk: A High Interest-Low Reading Level Book). (gr. 9 up). 1971. 4.95 o.s.i. (ISBN 0-664-32485-1, Westminster). Westminster John Knox.

Andy Adams: His Life & Writings. Wilson M. Hudson. LC 64-16632. (Illus.). 292p. 1964. 15.95 o.p. (ISBN 0-87074-080-6). SMU Press.

Andy Ant Coloring Book. (Illus.). 64p. (gr. 1 up). 1988. pap. 1.49 o.s.i. (ISBN 0-8423-0321-9). Tyndale.

Andy Capp: Man of the Hour. Reginald Smythe. 1984. pap. 1.95 o.s.i. (ISBN 0-449-12749-4, GM). Fawcett.

Andy Capp: This Is War, No. 40. Reginald Smythe. (Orig.). 1986. pap. 2.25 o.s.i. (ISBN 0-449-12962-4, GM). Fawcett.

Andy Jackson's Water Well. William O. Steele. LC 59-7282. (Illus.). (gr. 1-5). 1959. 4.50 o.p. (ISBN 0-15-203364-5, HJ). HarBraceJ.

Andy Lang's Remodeling Handbook. Andy Lang. LC 78-17860. (Home Construction Ser.). (Illus.). 96p. 1979. pap. 4.95 o.p. (ISBN 0-8437-3413-2). Hammond Inc.

Anecdotes & Traditions, Illustrative of Early English History & Literature. Ed. by William J. Thoms. Repr. of 1848 ed. 19.00 o.p. (ISBN 0-384-60310-6). Johnson Repr.

Anecdotes, Observations & Characters of Books & Men: Collected from the Conversation of Mr. Pope & Other Eminent Persons of His Time. Joseph Spence. LC 65-10024. (Centaur Classics Ser.). 308p. 1964. 15.00x o.p. (ISBN 0-8093-0167-9). S Ill U Pr.

Anemia: Facts about Low Blood. David Steinberg. LC 81-50840. 224p. (Orig.). 1981. pap. 7.95 o.p. (ISBN 0-03-059678-5, HoltC). HR&W.

ANEP European Petroleum Yearbook, 1987, Vol. 20. 520p. 1987. 150.00x o.p. (ISBN 0-8002-4197-5). Intl Pubns Serv.

Anesthesia Equipment: Performance, Classification & Safety. P. Schreiber. LC 73-175908. (Anesthesiology & Resuscitation. Vol. 59). (Illus.). 231p. 1972. pap. 26.50 o.p. (ISBN 0-387-05624-6). Springer-Verlag.

Anesthesia Machine. Clayton Petty. (Illus.). 234p. 1987. text ed. 29.50 o.p. (ISBN 0-317-60700-6). Churchill.

Aneurysmal Subarachnoid Hemorrhage: Report of the Cooperative Study. Adolph L. Sahs et al. LC 81-2354. (Illus.). 388p. 1981. text ed. 38.00 o.p. (ISBN 0-8067-1861-7). Urban & S.

Anfang der Bescheidenheit. Wolfgang Pehnt. (Illus.). 270p. (Ger.). 1983. pap. 30.00 o.p. (ISBN 3-7913-0627-8, Pub. by Prestel). TeNeues.

Ange Aux Entrailles. Jacques Audiberti. 164p. 1964. 7.95 o.p. (ISBN 0-686-54480-3). French & Eur.

Ange-Jacques Gabriel. Christopher Tadgell. (Studies in Architecture: Vol. 19). (Illus.). 1978. 100.00 o.s.i. (ISBN 0-8390-0224-6). Abner Schram Ltd.

Angel. Elizabeth Taylor. 1985. 13.95 o.p. (ISBN 0-317-53048-8, Large Print Bks). G K Hall.

Angel Eyes. Loren D. Estleman. 1981. 11.95 o.p. (ISBN 0-395-31558-1). HM.

Angel for Paradise. Jack Canon. (Paradise Ser.). 1979. pap. 1.95 o.p. (ISBN 0-441-02278-2). Ace Bks.

Angel: Gypsy Hustler. David Hanna. 1976. pap. 1.25 o.s.i. (ISBN 0-8439-0376-7, Pub. by Leisure Bks CT). Dorchester Pub Co.

Angel in the Parlor: Five Stories & Eight Essays. Nancy Willard. LC 83-4307. 352p. 1983. 22.95 o.p. (ISBN 0-15-107181-0). HarBraceJ.

Angel: New Poems. Frank Lima. 1976. 6.95 o.p. (ISBN 0-87140-617-9); pap. 2.95 o.p. (ISBN 0-87140-109-6). Liveright.

Angel of the East & a Winter's Day. Gale E. Church. 48p. 1987. 6.95 o.p. (ISBN 0-8062-2377-4). Carlton.

Angel Range. John Reese. 1976. pap. 0.95 o.p. (ISBN 0-685-72360-7, LB386NK, Pub. by Leisure Bks CT). Dorchester Pub Co.

Angel Speaks Again. Jonathan Gabriel. 1985. 7.95 o.p. (ISBN 0-533-06537-2). Vantage.

Angel Unaware. Dale E. Rogers. 8.95 o.p. (ISBN 0-8007-0439-8); pap. 1.50 o.p. (ISBN 0-8007-8001-9, Spire Bks). Revell.

Angelic Avengers. Isak Dinesen. LC 75-12973. viii, 304p. 1975. Repr. of 1947 ed. 8.95 o.s.i. (ISBN 0-226-15290-1). U. of Chicago Pr.

Angelica. Samuel A. Schreiner, Jr. LC 78-57323. 1978. 9.95 o.p. (ISBN 0-87795-194-2, Arbor Hse). Morrow.

Angelina's Adventure. Arleta Richardson. (Illus.). 27p. (Orig.). (gr. 1-3). 1988. pap. 3.00 o.p. (ISBN 0-89367-129-0). Light & Life.

Angelina's Birthday & Address Book. Katharine Holabird. (Illus.). 64p. (gr. k-12). 1986. 7.95 o.p. (ISBN 0-517-55808-4, C N Potter Bks). Crown.

Angels. Michael Daley. 16p. 1986. pap. 5.00 o.p. (ISBN 0-911287-08-6). Blue Begonia.

Angels. Denis Johnson. LC 83-47782. 224p. 1983. 12.45 o.s.i. (ISBN 0-394-53225-2). Knopf.

Angels & Other Strangers: Family Christmas Stories. Katherine Paterson. (Illus.). 132p. (gr. 1-8). 1980. pap. 1.95 o.p. (ISBN 0-380-51144-4, Camelot). Avon.

Angels & Their Mission. Jean Danielou. x, 118p. 1987. pap. 7.50 o.p. (ISBN 0-87061-056-2). Chr Classics.

Angels in Pinafores. Alice L. Humphreys. 5.50 o.p. (ISBN 0-8042-2256-8, John Knox). Westminster John Knox.

Angels Look the Same. Norman D. Hunter. 1976. 4.00 o.p. (ISBN 0-682-48470-9). Exposition-Phoenix.

Angels Must Have Smiled. 2nd ed. William Armstrong. LC 70-101346. (Illus.). 144p. (Orig.). (ps up). 1969. pap. 1.00 o.p. (ISBN 0-913452-01-7). Jesuit Bks.

Angels of Doom. Leslie Charteris. (Saint Ser.). (Illus.). 320p. 1982. pap. 2.50 o.s.i. (ISBN 0-441-74875-9). Ace Bks.

Angels of Double Faces. Rufus O. Abio. 1977. 8.00 o.p. (ISBN 0-682-48338-9). Exposition-Phoenix.

Angels of September. Andrew M. Greeley. 672p. 1986. pap. 12.95 o.p. (ISBN 0-8161-4120-7, Large Print Bks). G K Hall.

Angel's Share. Heather X. Graham. (Candlelight Supreme Ser.: No. 94). (Orig.). 1985. pap. 2.75 o.s.i. (ISBN 0-440-10350-9). Dell.

Angels, Their Origin, Nature, Mission & Destiny. Howard A. Blazer. 64p. 1974. pap. 2.50x o.p. (ISBN 0-88428-034-9). Parchment Pr.

Angels Unawares: Twentieth Century Portraits. T. S. Matthews. LC 85-4779. 1985. 17.45 o.p. (ISBN 0-89919-378-1). Ticknor & Fields.

Anger see Hunger & Thirst & Other Plays.

Anger & Assertiveness in Pastoral Care. David W. Augsburger. Ed. by Howard J. Clinebell & Howard W. Stone. LC 78-14660. (Creative Pastoral Care & Counseling Ser.). 96p. 1979. pap. 0.50 o.p. (ISBN 0-8006-0562-4, 1-562, Fortress). Augsburg Fortress.

Anger in Love. Samuel Southard. LC 73-7997. 96p. 1973. pap. 2.45 o.s.i. (ISBN 0-664-24975-2, Westminster). Westminster John Knox.

Anger: The Misunderstood Emotion. Carol Tavris. 1983. 15.50 o.s.i. (ISBN 0-671-25094-9). S&S.

Angie: The Story of a Mischievous Scottie. Ernestine B. McLelland. LC 85-91007. (Illus.). 32p. (gr. 1). 1985. 5.50 o.p. (ISBN 0-682-40198-6). Exposition-Phoenix.

Angina Pectoris. 2nd ed. Desmond G. Julian. LC 84-7098. (Illus.). 233p. 1985. 79.00 o.p. (ISBN 0-443-02269-0). Churchill.

Angiography in Trauma: A Work Atlas. Yoram Ben-Menachem. (Illus.). 350p. 1981. text ed. write for info. o.p. (ISBN 0-7216-1733-6). Saunders.

Angiography of the Mesencephalon: Normal & Pathological Findings. A. Wackenheim & J. P. Braun. LC 73-124076. (Illus.). 1970. 65.20 o.p. (ISBN 0-387-05266-6). Springer-Verlag.

Angiography-Scintigraphy: Proceedings. The European Association of Radiology Symposium, Mainz, 1970. Ed. by L. Diethelm. LC 72-76759. (Illus.). 550p. 1972. 56.70 o.p. (ISBN 0-387-05804-4). Springer-Verlag.

Angiotensin Converting Enzyme Inhibitors: Mechanisms of Action & Clinical Implications. Z. P. Horowitz. LC 81-388. (Illus.). 472p. 1981. text ed. 37.50 o.p. (ISBN 0-8067-0821-2). Urban & S.

Angkor Wat. Michio Fujioka. LC 71-158641. (This Beautiful World Ser.: Vol. 29). (Illus.). 138p. (Orig.). 1972. pap. 4.95 o.p. (ISBN 0-87011-156-6). Kodansha.

Anglais En Afrique. (Programmes et Methodes D'enseignement). (Illus.). 132p. (Fr.). 1975. pap. 6.60 o.p. (ISBN 0-685-53916-4, UNESCO). UNIPUB.

Angle of Ascent: New and Selected Poems. Robert Hayden. 131p. 1975. 0.00 o.p.; pap. 3.95 o.p. (ISBN 0-87140-106-1). Liveright.

Angler's Guide to Plug & Bait Casting: A Complete Manual of Revolving-Spool Tackle & How to Use It. C. Boyd Pfeiffer. LC 85-6433. (Illus.). 224p. 1985. pap. 12.95 o.p. (ISBN 0-8329-0315-9, Pub. by Winchester Pr). New Century.

Anglican Cycle of Prayer, 1988. Ed. by Charles H. Long. (Partners in Prayer Ser.). (Illus.). 128p. 1987. pap. 1.75 o.s.i. (ISBN 0-88028-067-0). Forward Movement.

Anglican Orders (English) The Bull of His Holiness Leo XIII, September 13, 1896, & the Answer to the Archbishops of England March 29, 1897. (Church Historical Society, London, Ser.: No. 12). pap. 40.00 o.p. Kraus Repr.

Anglican Orders (Latin) The Bull of His Holiness Leo XIII, September 13, 1896, & the Answer to the Archbishops of England March 29, 1897. (Church Historical Society, London, Ser.: No. 13). Repr. of 1932 ed. 40.00 o.p. (ISBN 0-8115-3136-8). Kraus Repr.

Angling: Fundamental Principles. Barrie Rickards. 318p. 1986. 26.00 o.p. (ISBN 0-85115-441-7, Pub. by Boydell & Brewer). Longwood Pub Group.

Anglo-American Cataloging Rules: One Year Later. Ed. by John T. Corrigan. (CLA Studies in Librarianship: No. 6). (Illus.). 61p. pap. 8.00 o.p. (ISBN 0-87507-023-X). Cath Lib Assn.

Anglo-American Cataloguing Rules. 2nd ed. Ed. by Michael Gorman & Paul W. Winkler. LC 78-13789. 640p. 1978. 30.00x o.p. (ISBN 0-8389-3210-X); pap. text ed. 20.00x o.p. (ISBN 0-8389-3211-8); looseleaf Lib Bdg o.p. 12.50 o.p. (ISBN 0-8389-3230-4). ALA.

Anglo-American Cataloguing Rules: Revisions 1985. rev ed. Joint Steering Committee for Revision of AACR2. LC 85-30634. 50p. 1986. 4.00x o.p. (ISBN 0-8389-3324-6). ALA.

Anglo-American Legal System, Readings & Cases in Itroduction to. Edgar Bodenheimer et al. LC 80-18757. (American Casebook). 161p. 1980. pap. text ed. 10.95 o.p. (ISBN 0-8299-2103-6). West Pub.

Anglo-American Realm. 2nd ed. Otis P. Starkey et al. (Geography Ser.). (Illus.). 384p. 1975. text ed. 38.95 o.p. (ISBN 0-07-060872-5). McGraw.

Anglo-American Trends in Restitution. Gareth Jones. 1978. pap. 4.00 o.p. (ISBN 9-0268-0981-6, Pub. by Kluwer Law Netherlands). Kluwer Academic.

Anglo-American Understanding: Eighteen Ninety-Eight to Nineteen Hundred Three. Charles S. Campbell, Jr. LC 79-25199. (Illus.). vii, 385p. 1980. Repr. of 1957 ed. lib. bdg. 35.00x o.p. (ISBN 0-313-22162-6, CAAA). Greenwood.

Anglo-Irish Studies, No. 3. Ed. by P. J. Drudy. 1977. text ed. 12.50x o.p. (ISBN 0-391-00820-X). Humanities.

Anglo-Norman England Ten Sixty-Six to Eleven Sixty-Six. Marjorie Chibnall. 248p. 1986. 45.00x o.p. (ISBN 0-631-13234-1). Basil Blackwell.

Anglo-Norman Political Songs. Ed. by Isabel S. Aspin. 30.00 o.p. (ISBN 0-384-02201-4); pap. 24.00 o.p. (ISBN 0-384-02202-2). Johnson Repr.

Anglo-Saxon Architecture. Mary Kerr & Nigel Kerr. (Shire Archaeology Ser.: No. 18). (Illus.). 1983. pap. 5.95 o.p. (ISBN 0-85263-570-2, Pub. by Shire Pubns England). Seven Hills Bk Dists.

Anglo-Saxon England. Lloyd Laing & Jennifer Laing. (Britain Before the Conquest Ser.). 256p. 1983. pap. 9.95 o.p. (ISBN 0-586-08371-5, Pub. by Granada England). Academy Chi Pubs.

Anglo-Saxon Sculpture. James Lang. (Shire Archaeology Ser.: No. 38). (Illus.). 64p. (Orig.). 1984. pap. 5.50 o.p. (ISBN 0-85263-679-2, Pub. by Shire Pubns England). Seven Hills Bk Dists.

Anglo-Saxon World. Ed. by Kevin Crossley-Holland. LC 82-24331. (Illus.). 200p. 1983. text ed. 25.00x o.p. (ISBN 0-389-20367-X). B&N Imports.

Angola: A Country Study. Ed. by Irving Kaplan. LC 79-21789. (Area Handbook Ser.: No. 550-59). (Illus.). 386p. 1979. 11.00 o.p. (ISBN 0-318-21921-2, S/N 008-020-00816-8). USGPO.

Angola: Five Centuries of Conflict. Lawrence W. Henderson. LC 79-5089. (Africa in the Modern World Ser.). (Illus.). 256p. 1979. 24.50x o.p. (ISBN 0-8014-1247-1). Cornell U Pr.

Angolan Revolution: Exile Politics & Guerrilla Warfare, 1962-1976, Vol. II. John A. Marcum. LC 69-11310. 1978. 50.00x o.p. (ISBN 0-262-13136-6). MIT Pr.

Angry Arthur. Hiawyn Oram. LC 82-80196. (Illus.). 32p. (ps-3). 1982. 11.95 o.p. (ISBN 0-15-203547-8, HJ). HarBraceJ.

Angry Eye: A Comment on Life & Letters. Max Harris. 1974. 65.00 o.p. (ISBN 0-08-017373-X). Pergamon.

Angry Giants of Troll Mountain. Don A. Torgersen. LC 80-12515. (Troll & Gnome Stories). (Illus.). 32p. (gr. k-4). 1980. PLB 9.95 o.p. (ISBN 0-516-03409-X); pap. 3.50 o.p. (ISBN 0-516-43409-8). Childrens.

Angry People. Amerigo Fasulo. 1984. 11.95 o.p. (ISBN 0-533-05961-5). Vantage.

Angry Town of Pawnee Bluffs. Lewis B. Patten. (Large Print Bks.). 245p. 1986. lib. bdg. 13.95x o.p. (ISBN 0-8161-3897-4). G K Hall.

Angry West: A Vulnerable Land & Its Future. Richard D. Lamm & Michael McCarthy. 192p. 1982. 13.95 o.p. (ISBN 0-395-32066-6). HM.

Anguish of Change. Louis Harris. 1974. pap. text ed. 5.95x o.p. (ISBN 0-393-09315-8). Norton.

Anhydrobiosis. Ed. by John H. Crowe & James S. Clegg. LC 73-12354. (Benchmark Papers in Biological Concepts: Vol. 2). 477p. 1982. 59.95 o.p. (ISBN 0-87933-039-2). Van Nos Reinhold.

Animal. Tony Conrad & Barbara Broughel. (Illus.). 24p. 1984. pap. 6.00 o.p. (ISBN 0-939784-09-2). CEPA Gall.

Animal Architecture. Karl Frisch. Tr. by Lisbeth Gombrich. (Helen & Kurt Wolff Bk.). 1976. 12.95 o.p. (ISBN 0-15-107251-5); pap. 7.95 o.p. (ISBN 0-15-607520-2, Harv). HarBraceJ.

Animal Band. (Fun Time Pop-Ups Ser.). (Illus.). (ps-1). 1.98 o.p. (ISBN 0-517-48301-7); pap. 1.98 o.p. (ISBN 0-517-46818-2). Outlet Bk Co.

Animal Behavior: An Evolutionary Approach. 3rd, rev. ed. John Alcock. LC 83-14420. (Illus.). 380p. 1984. text ed. 32.95x o.p. (ISBN 0-87893-021-3). Sinauer Assocs.

Animal Behavior: Concepts, Processes, & Methods. 2nd ed. Lee C. Drickamer & Stephen H. Vessey. 619p. 1986. text ed. (ISBN 0-87150-919-9). Wadsworth Pub.

Animal Book. Marc Harrison. (Bible Look-n-Learn Ser.). (ps). 1987. bds. 3.95 o.p. (ISBN 0-8407-6708-0). Nelson.

Animal Builders. Kenneth Lilly. LC 83-61970. (Animal Board Bks.). (Illus.). 10p. (ps). 1984. 2.95 o.p. (ISBN 0-394-86373-9, BYR). Random.

Animal Cafe. John Stadler. LC 80-15072. (Illus.). 32p. (gr. k-2). 1980. 9.95 o.s.i. (ISBN 0-02-786600-9). Bradbury Pr.

Animal Cell Culture & Virology. Ed. by Robert J. Kuchler. LC 74-833. (Benchmark Papers in Microbiology Ser.: Vol. 6). 461p. 1982. 59.95 o.p. (ISBN 0-87933-081-3). Van Nos Reinhold.

Animal Climbers. Kenneth Lilly. LC 83-61968. (Animal Board Bks.). (Illus.). 10p. (ps). 1984. 2.95 o.p. (ISBN 0-394-86374-7, BYR). Random.

Animal Crackers. Bracken. (Platt & Munk Cricket Bks.). (Illus.). 24p. (ps-3). 1979. 2.50 o.p. (ISBN 0-448-46531-0, G&D); PLB 3.59 o.p. (ISBN 0-448-13071-8). Putnam Pub Group.

Animal Crackers in My Soup. LaVerne Subblefield. 48p. (gr. 1-6). 1986. 6.00 o.p. (ISBN 0-8062-2801-6). Carlton.

Animal Dads Take Over. Jonathan M. Shebar & Sharon S. Shebar. LC 80-25332. (Illus.). 64p. (gr. 3-6). 1981. lib. bdg. 7.59 o.s.i. (ISBN 0-671-34003-4). Messner.

Animal Discrimination Learning. Ed. by R. M. Gilbert & N. S. Sutherland. 1969. 79.50 o.p. (ISBN 0-12-283250-7). Acad Pr.

Animal Ecology. C. S. Elton. 1966. pap. 8.95x o.p. (ISBN 0-412-20080-5, NO.6098, Pub. by Chapman & Hall). Routledge Chapman & Hall.

Animal Electroencephalography. W. R. Klemm. 1969. 71.00 o.p. (ISBN 0-12-414150-1). Acad Pr.

Animal Fact: Animal Fable. Seymour Simon. LC 78-14866. (Illus.). (gr. k-3). 1979. PLB 11.95 o.s.i. (ISBN 0-517-53474-6); pap. 4.95 o.s.i. (ISBN 0-517-53794-X). Crown.

Animal Family Album. Tony Palazzo. (Illus.). (gr. k-3). 1967. PLB 8.95 PLB o.p. (ISBN 0-87460-091-X). Lion Bks.

Animal Family: The Fascinating Variety of Parenthood, from the Courtship Displays to the Day the Children Leave Home. Philip Whitfield. (Illus.). 1980. 21.95 o.p. (ISBN 0-393-01304-9). Norton.

Animal Farm. George Orwell. Tr. by Iryna Dycko. LC 84-50503. 98p. (Ukrainian.). 1984. 5.00 o.s.i. (ISBN 0-914834-53-3). Smoloskyp.

Animal Fiero y Tierno. Angelamaria Davila. LC 81-68085. 68p. 1981. pap. 5.50 o.p. (ISBN 0-940238-50-0). Ediciones Huracan.

Animal Folklore, Myth & Legend. Anthony Wootton. (Illus.). 160p. 1987. 21.95 o.p. (ISBN 0-7137-1617-7, Pub. by Blandford Pr England). Sterling.

Animal Friends. Fitzgerald. (Dear God Kids Ser.). 1985. 3.95 o.s.i. (ISBN 0-671-50679-X). S&S.

Animal Friends. Zokeisha. (Puffies Ser.). (Illus.). 8p. (ps). 1982. pap. 3.40 o.s.i. (ISBN 0-671-44843-9, Little Simon). S&S.

Animal Go Bye-Bye. Louise Gikow. (Can You Imagine Ser.). (Illus.). 32p. (ps-2). 1986. pap. 1.95 o.p. (ISBN 0-517-56190-5). Crown.

Animal Hormones, Pt. 1: Control of Growth & Metamorphosis. P. M. Jenkin. LC 60-8977. 1970. 90.00 o.p. (ISBN 0-08-015648-7). Pergamon.

Animal Husbandry. Ruth Hayes. (Illus.). 54p. 1986. pap. 3.95 o.p. (ISBN 0-933457-11-1). Real Comet.

Animal Husbandry Heresies. Allan Fraser. 192p. 1960. (ISBN 0-8022-0531-3). Philos Lib.

Animal Identifcation: Insects, Vol. 3. D. Hollis. 160p. 1980. 73.95 o.p. (ISBN 0-471-27767-3, Pub. by Wiley-Interscience). Wiley.

Animal Invaders. Alvin Silverstein & Virginia Silverstein. LC 73-84835. (Illus.). 128p. (gr. 4-6). 1974. 6.95 o.p. (ISBN 0-689-30146-4, Atheneum). Macmillan.

Animal Jumpers. Kenneth Lilly. LC 83-61969. (Animal Board Bks.). (Illus.). 10p. (ps). 1984. 2.95 o.p. (ISBN 0-394-86375-5, BYR). Random.

Animal Life. 96p. (gr. 4-7). 1987. pap. 3.50 o.p. (ISBN 0-528-87855-7, Checkerboard Pr). Macmillan.

Animal Magnetism & the Life Energy. Jerome Eden. 1974. 8.50 o.p. (ISBN 0-682-48045-2). Exposition-Phoenix.

Animal Memory. Ed. by Werner K. Honig & Henry James. 1971. 59.00 o.p. (ISBN 0-12-355050-5). Acad Pr.

Animal Migration & Navigation. Philip Street. LC 75-30276. (Illus.). 1976. 9.95 o.s.i. (ISBN 0-684-14516-2, ScribT). Scribner.

Animal Mind - Human Mind: Report on the Dahlem Workshop. Ed. by D. R. Griffin. (Dahlem Workshop Report Ser.: Vol. 21). (Illus.). 427p. 1982. 29.00 o.p. (ISBN 0-387-11330-4). Springer-Verlag.

Animal Models & Hypoxia: Proceedings of an International Symposium on Animal Models & Hypoxia, Held at Weisbaden, FRG, on 19 November 1979. V. Stefanovich. (Advances in Biosciences Ser.: Vol. 30). (Illus.). 138p. 1981. 40.00 o.p. (ISBN 0-08-025911-1). Pergamon.

Animal Models for the Study of Herpes Virus Associated Malignancy, Vol. 2. Ed. by Harry C. Hinze et al. LC 73-20281. 156p. 1974. text ed. 26.50x o.p. (ISBN 0-8422-7180-5). Irvington.

Animal Models in Alcohol Research: Proceedings of the International Conference, June 4-8, 1979. International Conference Held in Helsinki Staff et al. Ed. by K. Eriksson. LC 80-40103. 1980. 84.00 o.p. (ISBN 0-12-240650-8). Acad Pr.

Animal Models in Dental Research. Juan M. Navia. LC 75-29252. 496p. 1977. 32.50 o.p. (ISBN 0-8173-2302-3). U of Ala Pr.

Animal Models of Comparative & Developmental Aspects of Immunity & Disease: Proceedings. International Symposium of the American Society of Zoologists, Toronto, December 27-30, 1977. Ed. by M. Eric Gershwin & Edwin L. Cooper. LC 78-15022. 1978. 62.00 o.p. (ISBN 0-08-022648-5). Pergamon.

Animal Nutrition. 3rd ed. P. McDonald et al. 480p. 1986. pap. 41.95 o.p. (ISBN 0-470-20544-X, Co-Pub. with Longman). Wiley.

Animal Nutrition & Feeding Practices in India. S. K. Ranjhan. (Illus.). 339p. 1977. 25.00x o.p. (ISBN 0-7069-0509-1, Pub. by Vikas India). Advent NY.

Animal People. Gale Cooper. (Illus.). 224p. 1983. 15.45 o.p. (ISBN 0-395-32198-0); pap. 8.70 o.p. (ISBN 0-395-34838-2). HM.

Animal Plant & Microbial Toxins. Ed. by Y. Sawai. 1975. pap. 19.75 o.p. (ISBN 0-08-019965-8). Pergamon.

Animal Population Dynamics. R. Moss et al. LC 82-9531. 1982. 7.50 o.p. (ISBN 0-412-22240-X, NO. 2297, Pub. by Chapman & Hall). Routledge Chapman & Hall.

Animal Production: Multilingual Illustrated Dictionary. 5th ed. (Illus.). 488p. 1986. pap. text ed. 24.95x o.p. (ISBN 3-924333-37-8). Agribookstore.

Animal Reproduction, No. 3. Ed. by Beltsville Symposia in Agricultural Research Staff. LC 78-65535. (Beltsville Symposia in Agricultural Research). (Illus.). 434p. 1979. 45.95 o.p. (ISBN 0-470-26672-4). Halsted Pr.

Animal Rhymes. Illus. by Blanche F. Wright. (The Real Mother Goose Mini Boxed Set Ser.). (Illus.). (ps-1). 1987. bds. 5.95 o.p. (ISBN 0-02-689016-X, Checkerboard Pr). Macmillan.

Animal Ribosomes: Experimental Studies of the Last Five Years. Guiseppe Attardi et al. 200p. 1972. text ed. 22.50x o.p. (ISBN 0-8422-7012-4). Irvington.

Animal Runners. Kenneth Lilly. LC 83-61971. (Animal Board Bks.). (Illus.). 10p. (ps). 1984. 2.95 o.p. (ISBN 0-394-86376-3, BYR). Random.

Animal Science: Reproduction, Climate, Meat & Wool. N. T. Yeates et al. 2296p. 1975. 95.00 o.p. (ISBN 0-08-018209-7). Pergamon.

Animal Structure & Function. 2nd ed. Donald R. Griffin & A. Novick. LC 70-77810. (Modern Biology Ser). 1970. pap. text ed. 16.95 o.p. (ISBN 0-03-077505-1, HoltC). HR&W.

Animal Superstars: Biggest, Strongest, Fastest, Smartest. Russell Freeman. (Illus.). (gr. 5 up). 1981. 10.95 o.s.i. (ISBN 0-13-037648-5). P-H.

Animal Swimmers. Kenneth Lilly. LC 83-61967. (Animal Board Bks.). (Illus.). 10p. (ps). 1984. 2.95 o.p. (ISBN 0-394-86377-1, BYR). Random.

Animal Things We Say. Darryl Lyman. LC 82-10026. 274p. 1983. 12.50 o.p. (ISBN 0-8246-0291-9). Jonathan David.

Animal Thinking. Donald R. Griffin. LC 83-12892. 256p. 1984. text ed. 18.50x o.p. (ISBN 0-674-03712-X). Harvard U Pr.

Animal Thought. Stephen Walker. (International Library of Psychology Ser.). 280p. 1982. 35.00x o.p. (ISBN 0-7100-9037-4). Routledge Chapman & Hall.

Animal Vision. (Nature Watch Ser.). (Illus.). 64p. (gr. 5 up). 1988. 13.95 o.p. Facts On File.

Animal Walk: Make Way for the Horses, Lions, Camels, & Bears in This Spectacular Grand-Entry Parade! Sue Dreamer. (Illus.). 16p. (ps-k). 1986. press-out concertina bk. 6.70i o.p. (ISBN 0-316-19198-1). Little.

Animal Weapons. Philip Street. LC 74-153075. (Illus.). 1971. 7.95 o.s.i. (ISBN 0-8008-0265-9). Taplinger.

Animales Que Ayudan. S. P. Russell. Orig. Title: Four Legged Helpers. 132p. 1.10 o.s.i. (ISBN 0-311-38510-9). Casa Bautista.

Animals, Aging, & the Aged. Leo K. Bustad. (Wesley W. Spink Lectures in Comparative Medicine Ser.). (Illus.). 227p. 1981. 19.50x o.p. (ISBN 0-8166-0997-7). U of Minn Pr.

Animals & Monsters. Alan Dent. LC 72-13625. (World of Shakespeare Ser: Vol. 1). 160p. 1973. 5.50 o.s.i. (ISBN 0-8008-0274-8). Taplinger.
Animals & Pets in Pastel. Sally Michel. (Leisure Arts Ser.: No. 24). (Illus.). 32p. (Orig.). 1984. pap. 2.95 o.p. (ISBN 0-89134-085-8). North Light Bks.
Animals Around Us. Thompson & Swallow. (Animal World Ser.). (gr. 3-6). 1978. 12.95 o.s.i. (ISBN 0-86020-188-0, Usborne-Hayes). EDC.
Animals As Friends: A Head Keeper Remembers London Zoo. James Alldis. LC 73-5275. (Illus.). 128p. 1973. 5.95 o.s.i. (ISBN 0-8008-0271-3). Taplinger.
Animals As Monitors of Environmental Pollutants. Institute of Laboratory Animal Resources Staff & National Research Council Staff. 1979. pap. text ed. 18.75x o.p. (ISBN 0-309-02871-X). Natl Acad Pr.
Animals at the Zoo. Ed. by Kate Klimo. (Baby Animals Board Bks.). (Illus.). 10p. 1982. 1.95 o.s.i. (ISBN 0-671-45152-9, Little Simon). S&S.
Animals I Love & Other Stories. Rasheed Mohammed. (Illus.). (gr. k-4). 1978. 4.00 o.p. (ISBN 0-682-48948-4). Exposition-Phoenix.
Animals in Art. Ana M. Berry. LC 79-162506. (Tower Bks.). (Illus.). 100p. 1971. Repr. of 1929 ed. 40.00x o.p. (ISBN 0-8103-3900-5). Gale.
Animals in Research: New Perspectives in Animal Experimentation. David Sperlinger. LC 80-49974. 373p. 1981. 77.95 o.p. (ISBN 0-471-27843-2, Pub. by Wiley-Interscience). Wiley.
Animals in the Classroom: A Book for Teachers. Elementary Science Study Staff. 1970. text ed. 14.40 o.p. (ISBN 0-07-017706-6). McGraw.
Animals in the Country. Ed. by Kate Klimo. (Baby Animals Board Bks.). (Illus.). 10p. 1982. 1.95 o.s.i. (ISBN 0-671-45153-7, Little Simon). S&S.
Animals in the Jungle. Ed. by Kate Klimo. (Baby Animals Board Bks.). (Illus.). 10p. 1982. 1.95 o.s.i. (ISBN 0-671-45154-5, Little Simon). S&S.
Animals in the Wild: Elephant. Mary Hoffman. LC 83-21157. (Picturebacks Ser.). (Illus.). 24p. (ps-3). 1984. pap. 1.95 saddle-stitched bdg. o.p. (ISBN 0-394-86553-7, Pub. by BYR). Random.
Animals in the Wild: Monkey. Mary Hoffman. LC 83-21158. (Picturebacks Ser.). (Illus.). 24p. (ps-3). 1984. pap. 1.95 saddle-stitched bdg. o.p. (ISBN 0-394-86554-5, Pub. by BYR). Random.
Animals in the Wild: Tiger. Mary Hoffman. LC 83-19236. (Picturebacks Ser.). (Illus.). 24p. (ps-3). 1984. pap. 1.95 saddle-stitched bdg. o.p. (ISBN 0-394-86556-1, Pub. by BYR). Random.
Animals in the Woods. Michele C. Roosevelt. LC 80-54770. (Board Bks.). (Illus.). 14p. (ps). 1981. bds. 3.50 o.p. (ISBN 0-394-84810-1). Random.
Animals of the Deserts. Sylvia A. Johnson. LC 75-27754. (Lerner Wildlife Library). (Illus.). 28p. (gr. 4 up). 1976. PLB 7.95 o.p. (ISBN 0-8225-1279-3). Lerner Pubns.
Animals of the Night. Tony Palazzo. LC 70-87744. (Illus.). (gr. k-3). 1970. PLB 9.95 o.p. (ISBN 0-87460-094-4). Lion Bks.
Animals of the Ocean. Ed. by Kate Klimo. (Baby Animals Board Bks.). (Illus.). 10p. 1982. 1.95 o.s.i. (ISBN 0-671-45155-3, Little Simon). S&S.
Animals of the Polar Regions. Sylvia A. Johnson. LC 75-27753. (Lerner Wildlife Library). (Illus.). 28p. (gr. 4 up). 1976. PLB 7.95 o.p. (ISBN 0-8225-1281-5). Lerner Pubns.
Animals on the Farm. Ed. by Kate Klimo. (Baby Animals Board Bks.). (Illus.). 10p. 1982. 1.95 o.s.i. (ISBN 0-671-45151-0, Little Simon). S&S.
Animals That Migrate. Caroline Arnold. LC 82-1253. (On My Own Bks.). (Illus.). 56p. (gr. k-4). 1982. lib. bdg. 8.95 o.p. (ISBN 0-87614-194-7). Carolrhoda Bks.
Animals with Human Faces: A Guide to Animal Symbolism. Beryl Rowland. LC 70-173657. (Illus.). 1973. 22.50x o.p. (ISBN 0-87049-136-9). U of Tenn Pr.
Animated Film. rev. ed. Ralph Stephenson. LC 72-1785. (International Film Guide Ser). (Illus.). 224p. 1981. pap. 5.95 o.s.i. (ISBN 0-498-01202-6). A S Barnes.
Animation Book. Kit Laybourne. 1978. 15.95 o.p. (ISBN 0-517-53389-8); pap. 16.95 o.p. (ISBN 0-517-52946-7). Crown.
Animation, Games, & Graphics for the Timex 1000. Tony Fabbri. (Personal Computing Ser.). (Illus.). 240p. 1984. pap. 13.95 o.p. (ISBN 0-13-037318-4). P-H.
Animation, Games, & Sound for the Apple II-IIe. Tony Fabbri. (P-H Personal Computing Ser.). (Illus.). 144p. 1984. incl. disk 33.95 o.p. (ISBN 0-13-037276-5); pap. 17.95 incl. cassette o.p. (ISBN 0-13-037284-6). P-H.
Animation, Games & Sound for the IBM Personal Computer. Tony Fabbri. (Illus.). 224p. 1983. pap. 19.50 o.p. (ISBN 0-13-037689-2). P-H.
Animation, Games & Sound for the TI 99-4A. Tony Fabbri. (Prentice-Hall Personal Computing Ser.). (Illus.). 224p. 1984. pap. 17.50 o.p. (ISBN 0-13-037227-7). P-H.
Animation, Games, & Sounds for the Commodore 64. Tony Fabbri. (Personal Computing Ser.). (Illus.). 224p. 1984. pap. 16.95 o.p. (ISBN 0-13-037375-3). P-H.
Animation Magic with Your IBM PC & PCjr. Ron Person. LC 84-22639. 250p. 1984. pap. text ed. 16.95 o.p. (ISBN 0-07-881145-7). Osborne-McGraw.
Animation Rurale & Rural Development: The Experience of Senegal. Sheldon Gellar et al. (Special Series on Animation Rurale: No. 2). 211p. (Orig.). 1980. pap. text ed. 11.05 o.p. (ISBN 0-86731-042-1). Cornell CIS RDC.
Animations of Mortality. Terry Gilliam & Lucinda Cowel. LC 78-60982. (Illus.). 1978. pap. 9.95 o.p. (ISBN 0-413-39380-1, NO.0066). Routledge Chapman & Hall.
Animator's Workbook. Tony White. (Illus.). 160p. 1986. 27.50 o.p. (ISBN 0-8230-0228-4). Watson-Guptill.
Anime Idols. (Big Little Bks.: No. 164). (Illus.). 350p. 1984. 6.95 o.p. (ISBN 0-318-02743-7). Bks Nippan.
Anioma's Attainment of Humanity. Osodi E. Echezonam. 104p. 1985. 7.00 o.p. (ISBN 0-682-49996-X). Exposition-Phoenix.
Anionic Surfactants, Pt. 1. Ed. by Warner M. Linfield. (Surfactants Science Ser.: Vol. 7). 328p. 1976. 89.75 o.p. (ISBN 0-8247-6158-8). Dekker.
Anita Desai. R. S. Sharma. (Indian Writers Ser.: Vol. 18). 1981. 12.00 o.s.i. (ISBN 0-86578-071-4). Ind-US Inc.
Anitya. Paul Twitchell. (Illus.). 1969. 6.95 o.p. (ISBN 0-914766-01-5). Illum Way Pub.
Ankle Injuries. Isadore G. Yablon et al. LC 82-14761. (Illus.). 288p. 1983. text ed. 37.50 o.p. (ISBN 0-443-08095-X). Churchill.
Ankylosing Spondylitis. Andrei Calin & James F. Fries. (Contemporary Patient Management Ser.). 1978. spiral 14.00 o.p. (ISBN 0-87488-887-5). Med Exam.
Ann Radcliffe in Relation to Her Time. C. F. McIntyre. LC 74-91186. (Yale Studies in English Ser.: No. 62). 104p. 1970. Repr. of 1920 ed. 18.00 o.p. (ISBN 0-208-00915-9, Archon). Shoe String.
Anna. Margaret Graham. (Living Bks). 488p. 1986. pap. 4.50 o.p. (ISBN 0-8423-0020-1). Tyndale.
Anna. Dagfinn Gronoset. 1977. pap. 1.50 o.s.i. (ISBN 0-8439-0458-5, Pub. by Leisure Bks CT). Dorchester Pub Co.
Anna. C. Vereketi. 48p. 1987. 6.95 o.p. (ISBN 0-8062-2975-6). Carlton.
Anna & Dula. Robert Vavra. LC 66-8703. (Illus.). (gr. 2 up). 1966. 5.25 o.p. (ISBN 0-15-203570-2, HJ). HarBraceJ.
Anna Freud Research Library of the Reiss-Davis Child Study Center. 1978. lib. bdg. 185.00 o.p. (ISBN 0-8161-0086-1, Hall Library). G K Hall.
Anna Held & Flo Ziegfeld. Liane Carrera. 1979. 10.00 o.p. (ISBN 0-682-49309-0). Exposition-Phoenix.
Anna to the Infinite Power. Mildred Ames. LC 80-28459. 204p. (gr. 7 up). 1981. 13.95 o.s.i. (ISBN 0-684-16855-3, Pub. by Scribner). Macmillan.
Annabelle Starr, E.S.P. Lila Perl. 160p. (gr. 4-6). 1984. pap. 2.25 o.p. (ISBN 0-671-50350-2). Archway.
Annals of Flowerland. Kathleen I. Oldham. LC 81-90561. 147p. 1982. 7.95 o.p. (ISBN 0-533-05235-1). Vantage.
Annals of Jamaica, 2 vols. George W. Bridges. LC 76-106830. 1971. Repr. of 1827 ed. Set. 38.00x o.p. (ISBN 0-8371-3452-8, BJA&, Pub. by Negro U Pr). Greenwood.
Annals of Stanislaus County. Jack Brotherton. LC 82-83514. (Illus.). 180p. 1982. 22.95 o.p. (ISBN 0-934136-29-7). Western Tanager.
Anna's Book. Compiled by Fynn. 1987. 12.95 o.p. (ISBN 0-8050-0430-0). H Holt & Co.
Anna's Magic Broom. Barbara Westman. LC 77-4831. (Illus.). 32p. (gr. k-3). 1977. PLB 7.95 o.p. (ISBN 0-395-25783-2). HM.
Anna's Tree Swing. Del Aven. LC 81-65799. (gr. k-3). 1981. bds. 5.95 o.p. (ISBN 0-8054-4268-5, 4242-68). Broadman.
Anne Carroll Moore: A Biography. Frances C. Sayers. LC 72-78291. (Illus.). 320p. 1972. 8.95 o.p. (ISBN 0-689-10523-1, Atheneum). Macmillan.
Anne Frank: A Portrait in Courage. Ernst Schnabel. LC 58-12702. (Illus.). 1958. 7.50 o.p. (ISBN 0-15-107527-1). HarBraceJ.
Anne Frank: A Portrait in Courage. Ernst Schnabel. LC 53-12702. 1967. pap. 0.65 o.p. (ISBN 0-15-607530-X, Harv). HarBraceJ.
Anne Frank: A Short Life. Johanna Hurwitz. 1988. 10.95 o.p. JPS Phila.
Anne Frank Remembered: The Story of Miep Gies, Who Helped to Hide the Frank Family. Miep Gies & Alison L. Gold. 1987. 17.45 o.s.i. (ISBN 0-671-54771-2). S&S.
Anne Goldthwaite: Eighteen Sixty-Nine to Nineteen Forty-Four. Ed. by Diane J. Gingold. LC 77-74790. (Illus.). 1977. pap. 5.00 o.p. (ISBN 0-89280-006-2). Montgomery Mus.
Anne Sexton: A Self-Portrait in Letters. Ed. by Linda G. Sexton & Lois Ames. 1979. pap. 6.95 o.s.i. (ISBN 0-395-27763-9). HM.
Anne Sexton: A Self-Portrait in Letters. Ed. by Linda G. Sexton & Lois Ames. 1977. 15.00 o.p. (ISBN 0-395-25727-1). HM.
Anneau d'Amethyste see Romans et Contes.
Annemieke: Poems & Illustrations. 1982. 5.00 o.p. (ISBN 0-682-49807-6). Exposition-Phoenix.
Annie. Leonore Fleischer. 1982. pap. 2.50 o.s.i. (ISBN 0-345-30451-9). Ballantine.
Annie Annie. Molly Cone. LC 69-19937. (Illus.). (gr. 5-9). 1973. 8.95 o.p. (ISBN 0-395-06705-7). HM.
Annie: Herald of Home Missions. Eva B. Lloyd. (Orig.). 1981. pap. 1.95 o.p. (ISBN 0-8054-9502-9). Broadman.
Annie's Secret. Crystal Earnhardt. Ed. by Raymond H. Woolsey. 96p. (gr. 6). 1989. pap. 6.95 o.p. (ISBN 0-8280-0460-9). Review & Herald.
Anno Domini. George Barker. LC 82-25160. 56p. 1983. pap. 8.95 o.p. (ISBN 0-571-13026-7). Faber & Faber.
Annointed. Z'ev B. Halevi. 1987. pap. 9.95 o.p. (ISBN 1-85063-050-X, Pub. by Routledge UK). Routledge Chapman & Hall.
Anno's Britain. Mitsumasa Anno. (Illus.). 48p. 1982. 11.95 o.p. (ISBN 0-399-20861-5, Philomel); pap. 5.95 o.p. Putnam Pub Group.
Annotated & Enlarged Edition of Ernst Steiger's Precentennial Bibliography, "The Periodical Literature of the United States of America" Karl J. Arndt. LC 79-25836. 1980. lib. bdg. 60.00 o.p. (ISBN 0-527-03668-4). Kraus Intl.
Annotated BASIC: A New Technique for Neophytes, Vol. 1. Gregory R. Glau et al. Ed. by Nan McCarthy & Chris Crocker. 160p. (Orig.). 1981. pap. 10.95 o.p. (ISBN 0-88006-028-X, BK 7384). Wayne Green Ent.
Annotated BASIC: A New Technique for Neophytes, Vol. 2. Dave Brickner et al. Ed. by Nan McCarthy & Chris Crocker. (Illus.). 125p. 1982. pap. 10.95 o.p. (ISBN 0-88006-037-9, BK 7385). Wayne Green Ent.
Annotated Bibliographies of Mineral Deposits in Africa Asia (Exclusive of the U. S. S. R.) & Australasia. J. D. Ridge. 545p. 1976. 110.00 o.p. (ISBN 0-08-020459-7). Pergamon.
Annotated Bibliography see Creativity in the Life Cycle.
Annotated Bibliography of Canada's Major Authors, Vol. 2: Margaret Atwood, Leonard Cohen, Archibald Lampman, E. J. Pratt, & Al Purdy. Ed. by Robert Leeker. 1981. 31.50 o.p. (ISBN 0-8161-8552-2, Hall Reference). G K Hall.
Annotated Bibliography of Cryptography. David Shulman. LC 75-24077. (Reference Library of the Humanities: Vol. 37). 390p. 1976. lib. bdg. 55.00 o.p. (ISBN 0-8240-9974-5). Garland Pub.
Annotated Bibliography of French Language & Literature. Fernande Bassan et al. LC 75-24079. (Reference Library of the Humanities: Vol. 26). 300p. 1976. lib. bdg. 40.00 o.p. (ISBN 0-8240-9986-9). Garland Pub.
Annotated Bibliography of Greek & Roman Art, Architecture, & Archaeology. William D. Coulson. LC 75-24081. (Reference Library of the Humanities: Vol. 28). 135p. 1976. lib. bdg. 25.00 o.p. (ISBN 0-8240-9984-2). Garland Pub.
Annotated Bibliography of Homosexuality, 2 vols. Vern L. Bullough et al. LC 75-24106. (Reference Library of Social Science: Vol. 22). 1000p. 1976. Set. lib. bdg. 107.00 o.p. (ISBN 0-8240-9959-1). Garland Pub.
Annotated Bibliography of Indian Painting Through the Ages. R. Nath. 1982. 60.00 o.p. E J Brill USA.
Annotated Bibliography of John Dryden: Text & Studies, 1949-1973. John A. Zamonski. LC 74-22231. 160p. 1975. lib. bdg. 25.00 o.p. (ISBN 0-8240-1059-0). Garland Pub.
Annotated Bibliography of John Updike Criticism 1967-73: & a Checklist of His Works. Michael A. Olivas. LC 74-13951. 1975. lib. bdg. 24.00 o.p. (ISBN 0-8240-1053-1). Garland Pub.
Annotated Bibliography of Moravia Criticism in Italy & the English-Speaking World. Ferdinando P. Alfonsi & Sandra R. Alfonsi. LC 75-24084. (Reference Library of the Humanities: Vol. 30). 500p. 1976. lib. bdg. 34.00 o.p. (ISBN 0-8240-9982-6). Garland Pub.
Annotated Bibliography of Pharmacy Practice Contributions in Primary Health Care. 1981. 5.00 o.p. (ISBN 0-686-83879-3). AACP Alexandria.
Annotated Bibliography of Shakespearean Burlesques, Parodies & Travesties. Henry E. Jacobs & Claudia D. Johnson. LC 75-24087. (Reference Library of the Humanities: Vol. 41). 200p. 1976. lib. bdg. 41.00 o.p. (ISBN 0-8240-9964-8). Garland Pub.
Annotated Bibliography of Texts on Writing Skills: Grammar, Composition, Rhetoric, Technical Writing. Shannon Burns et al. LC 75-24096. (Reference Library of the Humanities: Vol. 38). 250p. 1976. lib. bdg. 34.00 o.p. (ISBN 0-8240-9968-0). Garland Pub.
Annotated Bibliography of the British Army, Sixteen Sixty to Nineteen Fourteen. A. P. Bruce. LC 75-23072. (Reference Library of Social Science: Vol. 14). 255p. 1976. lib. bdg. 34.00 o.p. (ISBN 0-8240-9988-5). Garland Pub.
Annotated Bibliography of the Literature on American Indians Published in State Historical Society Publications: New England & Middle Atlantic States. Arlene B. Hirschfelder. LC 82-17213. 376p. 1982. lib. bdg. 70.00 o.p. (ISBN 0-527-40889-1). Kraus Intl.
Annotated Bibliography of Twentieth Century Critical Studies of Women & Literature, 1660-1800. Paula R. Backscheider & Felicity A. Nussbaum. LC 76-24746. (Reference Library of the Humanities Ser.: Vol. 64). 1977. lib. bdg. 43.00 o.p. (ISBN 0-8240-9934-6). Garland Pub.
Annotated Bibliography on Taxation As an Instrument of Land Planning Policy. Ed. by Michael M. Bernard. (Monograph: No. 80-8). 90p. 1980. pap. text ed. 4.00 o.s.i. (ISBN 0-686-29504-8). Lincoln Inst Land.
Annotated Checklist of Osleriana. Earl F. Nation et al. LC 75-44711. (Illus.). 289p. 1976. 27.50x o.p. (ISBN 0-87338-186-6). Kent St U Pr.
Annotated Checklist of the Biota of the Coastal Zone of South Carolina. Richard G. Zingmark. LC 78-110686. xii, 364p. 1978. text ed. 19.50x o.s.i. (ISBN 0-87249-373-3); pap. text ed. 9.95x o.p. (ISBN 0-87249-374-1). U of SC Pr.
Annotated Gilbert & Sullivan, Vol. 2. Ed. & intro. by Ian Bradley. (Music Ser.). 520p. 1984. pap. 10.95 o.s.i. (ISBN 0-14-070849-9). Penguin.
Annotated Guide to the Works of Dorothy L. Sayers. R. B. Harmon & M. A. Burger. LC 76-52666. (Reference Library of the Humanities Ser.: Vol. 80). 1977. lib. bdg. 40.00 o.p. (ISBN 0-8240-9896-X). Garland Pub.
Annotated Lolita. Vladimir Nabokov. Ed. & intro. by Alfred Appel, Jr. 1970. pap. text ed. 12.95 o.p. (ISBN 0-07-045730-1). McGraw.
Annotated Oscar Wilde. Ed. by Montgomery Hyde. (Illus.). 480p. 1982. 25.00 o.p. (ISBN 0-517-54745-7, C N Potter Bks). Crown.
Annotated Walden. Henry David Thoreau. Ed. by Philip V. Stern. (Illus.). 512p. 1971. 15.00 o.p. (ISBN 0-517-50402-2, C N Potter Bks). Crown.
Annual Bibliography of British & Irish History: Publications of 1982 Vol. 8. Ed. by G. Elton. 1982. text ed. 45.00 o.p. (ISBN 0-391-02942-8). Humanities.
Annual Conference Abstracts, 10th, Boston see Annual Conference Abstracts, 11th, Philadelphia.
Annual Conference Abstracts, 11th, Philadelphia. Incl. Annual Conference Abstracts, 12th, Cleveland. 56p. 1984. 3.50 (ISBN 0-317-36388-3); Annual Conference Abstracts, 13th, Los Angeles. 84p. 1985. 5.00 (ISBN 0-317-36389-1); Annual Conference Abstracts, 14th, New York. 72p. 1986. 5.00; Annual Conference Abstracts, 9th, San Francisco. 26p. 2.50 o.p.; Annual Conference Abstracts, 10th, Boston. 48p. 3.50; Annual Conference Abstracts, 15th, Washington D. C. 64p. 1987. 5.00; Annual Conference Abstracts, 16th, Dallas. 48p. 1988. 7.00. 56p. 1983. 3.50 o.p. (ISBN 0-317-36387-5). Art Libs Soc.
Annual Conference Abstracts, 12th, Cleveland see Annual Conference Abstracts, 11th, Philadelphia.
Annual Conference Abstracts, 13th, Los Angeles see Annual Conference Abstracts, 11th, Philadelphia.
Annual Conference Abstracts, 14th, New York see Annual Conference Abstracts, 11th, Philadelphia.
Annual Conference Abstracts, 15th, Washington D. C. see Annual Conference Abstracts, 11th, Philadelphia.
Annual Conference Abstracts, 16th, Dallas see Annual Conference Abstracts, 11th, Philadelphia.
Annual Conference Abstracts, 9th, San Francisco see Annual Conference Abstracts, 11th, Philadelphia.

Titles

Annual Conference of the American Academy of Advertising: Proceedings. 1977. pap. 20.00x o.p. (ISBN 0-931030-00-5). Am Acad Advert.
Annual Editions: Aging. 4th ed. Harold Cox. LC 78-645208. (Annual Editions Ser.). (Illus.). 256p. 1985. pap. text ed. 8.95x o.p. (ISBN 0-87967-549-7). Dushkin Pub.
Annual Editions: American Government, 1985-86. 15th ed. Bruce Stinebrickner. LC 76-180265. (Annual Editions Ser.). (Illus.). 288p. 1985. pap. text ed. 8.95 o.p. (ISBN 0-87967-575-6). Dushkin Pub.
Annual Editions: American Government 1988-1989. rev., 18th ed. Ed. by Bruce Stinebricker. LC 76-180265. (Illus.). 256p. 1988. pap. text ed. 9.95 o.p. (ISBN 0-87967-722-8). Dushkin Pub.
Annual Editions: American History, Vol. I. 8th ed. Robert J. Maddox. LC 74-187540. (Illus.). 224p. 1985. pap. text ed. 8.95 o.p. (ISBN 0-87967-572-1). Dushkin Pub.
Annual Editions: American History, Vol. II. 8th ed. Robert J. Maddox. LC 75-20755. (Annual Editions Ser.). (Illus.). 256p. 1985. pap. text ed. 8.95 o.p. (ISBN 0-87967-573-X). Dushkin Pub.
Annual Editions: Anthropology, 1985-86. 8th ed. Elvio Angeloni. LC 74-84595. (Annual Editions Ser.). (Illus.). 256p. (Orig.). 1985. pap. text ed. 8.95 o.p. (ISBN 0-87967-577-2). Dushkin Pub.
Annual Editions: Biology. 4th ed. John Crane. LC 84-30680. (Annual Editions Ser.). (Illus.). 256p. 1984. pap. text ed. 8.95 o.p. (ISBN 0-87967-484-9). Dushkin Pub.
Annual Editions: Business-Management, 1985-86. 6th ed. Joseph G. Mattingly, Jr. LC 73-30680. (Annual Editions Ser.). (Illus.). 256p. 1985. pap. text ed. 8.95 o.p. (ISBN 0-87967-551-9). Dushkin Pub.
Annual Editions: Comparative Politics, 1985-1986. 3rd ed. LC 83-647654. (Annual Editions Ser.). (Illus.). 288p. pap. 8.95 o.p. (ISBN 0-87967-590-X). Dushkin Pub.
Annual Editions: Criminal Justice, 1985-86. 9th ed. John J. Sullivan & Joseph L. Victor. LC 77-640116. (Annual Editions Ser.). (Illus.). 288p. 1978. pap. text ed. 8.95 o.p. (ISBN 0-87967-571-3). Dushkin Pub.
Annual Editions: Drugs, Society & Behavior, 1986-87. 1986. 8.95 o.p. (ISBN 0-87967-612-4). Dushkin Pub.
Annual Editions: Early Childhood Education, 1985-86. 7th ed. Judy S. McKee. LC 77-640114. (Annual Editions Ser.). (Illus.). 256p. 1985. pap. text ed. 8.95 o.p. (ISBN 0-87967-538-1). Dushkin Pub.
Annual Editions: Early Childhood Education, 1988-1989. Judy S. McKee & Karen M. Paciorek. LC 77-640114. 156p. 1988. pap. text ed. 9.95 o.p. Dushkin Pub.
Annual Editions: Economics, 1985-86. 14th ed. Reuben Slesinger & Glen Beeson. LC 78-942037. (Annual Editions Ser.). (Illus.). 288p. 1985. pap. text ed. 8.95 o.p. (ISBN 0-87967-579-9). Dushkin Pub.
Annual Editions: Educating Exceptional Children. 3rd ed. LC 79-644171. (Annual Editions Ser.). (Illus.). 256p. (Orig.). (gr. 11 up). 1985. pap. text ed. 8.95x o.p. (ISBN 0-87967-593-4). Dushkin Pub.
Annual Editions: Education, 1985-86. 12th ed. Fred Schultz. LC 73-78580. (Annual Editions Ser.). (Illus.). 256p. 1985. pap. text ed. 8.95 o.p. (ISBN 0-87967-584-5). Dushkin Pub.
Annual Editions: Educational Psychology, 1985-1986. 2nd ed. Fredric Linder & James H. McMillan. LC 82-640517. (Illus.). 256p. 1985. pap. 8.95x o.p. (ISBN 0-87967-553-5). Dushkin Pub.
Annual Editions: Environment, 1985-86. 5th ed. John Allen. LC 79-644216. (Annual Editions Ser.). (Illus.). 256p. (gr. 12). 1985. pap. text ed. 8.95 o.p. (ISBN 0-87967-570-5). Dushkin Pub.
Annual Editions: Geography, 1986-87. Gerald R. Pitzl. 1986. 8.95 o.p. (ISBN 0-87967-615-9). Dushkin Pub.
Annual Editions: Global Issues, 1985-1986. Robert Jackson. (Annual Editions Ser.). (Illus.). 256p. 1985. pap. text ed. 8.95 o.p. (ISBN 0-87967-557-8). Dushkin Pub.
Annual Editions: Health, 1985-86. 7th ed. LC 81-643582. (Annual Editions Ser.). (Illus.). 256p. 1985. pap. text ed. 8.95 o.p. (ISBN 0-87967-591-8). Dushkin Pub.
Annual Editions: Human Development, 1985-86. 13th ed. Hiram E. Fitzgerald. Ed. by Michael Wairawen. LC 72-91973. (Annual Editions Ser.). (Illus.). 288p. 1985. pap. text ed. 8.95 o.p. (ISBN 0-87967-583-7). Dushkin Pub.
Annual Editions: Human Sexuality, 1985-86. 10th ed. Ollie Pocs. LC 75-20756. (Annual Editions Ser.). (Illus.). 256p. 1985. pap. 8.95 o.p. (ISBN 0-87967-582-9). Dushkin Pub.
Annual Editions: Macroeconomics, 1985-86. 5th ed. John Pisciotta. LC 72-180264. (Annual Editions Ser.). 256p. 1985. pap. text ed. 8.95 o.p. (ISBN 0-87967-576-4). Dushkin Pub.
Annual Editions: Marketing, 1985-86. 7th ed. LC 73-78578. (Annual Editions Ser.). (Illus.). 256p. 1985. pap. text ed. 8.95 o.p. (ISBN 0-87967-555-1). Dushkin Pub.
Annual Editions: Marriage & Family, 1985-86. 11th ed. Ollie Pocs & Robert H. Walsh. LC 74-884596. (Annual Editions Ser.). (Illus.). 256p. 1985. pap. text ed. 8.95 o.p. (ISBN 0-87967-589-6). Dushkin Pub.
Annual Editions: Personal Growth & Behavior, 1985-86. 6th ed. LC 75-20757. (Annual Editions Ser.). (Illus.). 1985. pap. text ed. 8.95 o.p. (ISBN 0-87967-574-8). Dushkin Pub.
Annual Editions: Psychology, 1985-86. 15th ed. Hiram E. Fitzgerald & Michael Walraven. LC 79-180263. (Annual Editions Ser.). (Illus.). 288p. 1985. pap. text ed. 8.95 o.p. (ISBN 0-87967-578-0). Dushkin Pub.
Annual Editions: Social Problems, 1985-86. 13th ed. Leroy Barnes. LC 73-78577. (Annual Editions Ser.). (Illus.). 256p. 1985. pap. text ed. 8.95 o.p. (ISBN 0-87967-585-3). Dushkin Pub.
Annual Editions: Sociology, 1985-86. 14th ed. Kurt Finsterbush. LC 72-76876. (Annual Editions Ser.). (Illus.). 1985. pap. text ed. 8.95 o.p. (ISBN 0-87967-580-2). Dushkin Pub.
Annual Editions: State & Local Government, 1985-1986. 2nd ed. Bruce Stinebrickner. (Annual Editions Ser.). (Illus.). 288p. pap. text ed. 8.95 o.p. (ISBN 0-87967-588-8). Dushkin Pub.
Annual Editions: Third World 1988-89. Ed. by Jeffrey M. Elliot. (Annual Editions Ser.). (Illus.). 256p. 1988. pap. text ed. 9.95 o.p. (ISBN 0-87967-707-4). Dushkin Pub.
Annual Editions: Western Civilization, Vol. I. 3rd ed. William Hughes. LC 82-645823. (Illus.). 224p. 1985. pap. 8.95 o.p. (ISBN 0-87967-586-1). Dushkin Pub.
Annual Editions: World Politics, 1985-86. 6th ed. Suzanne P. Ogden. (Illus.). 288p. 1985. pap. 8.95 o.p. (ISBN 0-87967-581-0). Dushkin Pub.
Annual Educational Conference Proceedings: 1982 Focus on Education, Vol. 24. Ed. by Becky A. Wright. 485p. 1983. text ed. 35.00 o.p. (ISBN 0-89154-201-9). Intl Found Employ.
Annual Energy Outlook, 1987, with Projections to 2000. (Illus.). 72p. 1988. pap. 3.50 o.p. (S/N 061-003-00565-9). USGPO.
Annual Energy Review, 1985. (Illus.). 297p. 1986. pap. 14.00 o.p. (S/N 061-003-00483-1). USGPO.
Annual Energy Review, 1986. (EIA Ser.: No. 0384(86)). (Illus.). 300p. 1987. pap. 14.00 o.p. (ISBN 0-318-22875-0, S/N 061-003-00524-1). USGPO.
Annual Fertilizer Review. annual Incl. 1971. 191p. 1973. pap. 20.25 (F46, FAO). UNIPUB; 1970. 176p. 1971. pap. 13.75 (F1452, FAO). UNIPUB; 1973. 139p. 1974. pap. 19.50 (ISBN 92-5-001691-3, F48, FAO). UNIPUB; 1974. 205p. 1975. pap. 17.50 (ISBN 92-5-001692-1, F49, FAO). UNIPUB; 1975. (Illus.). 205p. 1976. pap. 17.50 (ISBN 92-5-000069-3, F50, FAO). UNIPUB; 1976. (Statistics Ser.: No. 5). 111p. 1977. pap. 12.75 (ISBN 92-5-000335-8, F1226, FAO). UNIPUB; 1977. (Statistics Ser.: No. 19). 115p. 1978. pap. 12.75 (ISBN 92-5-000605-5, F1488, FAO). UNIPUB. UNIPUB.
Annual Guide to Public Policy Experts, 1985. Ed. by Robert Huberty & Catherine Ludwig. 263p. 1985. 5.95 o.p. Heritage Found.
Annual Meeting Proceedings, 1986 New Directions - Advancement Through Knowledge. AAMI Staff. 112p. 1986. pap. text ed. 35.00 o.p. (ISBN 0-910275-57-2). Assn Adv Med Instrn.
Annual of Power & Conflict, 1979-1980. Ed. by Institute for the Study of Conflict Staff. 465p. 1980. 50.00x o.p. (ISBN 0-8448-1386-9, Pub. by Crane Russak & Co). Taylor & Francis.
Annual of Power & Conflict, 1981-82. 11th ed. Institute for the Study of Conflict, London Staff. LC 77-370326. 485p. 1982. 77.50x o.p. (ISBN 0-8002-2888-X). Intl Pubns Serv.
Annual of the Year's Best Science Fiction, 6th. Ed. by Judith Merril. 1981. pap. 2.50 o.s.i. (ISBN 0-671-83601-3). S&S.
Annual Produce Marketing Almanac. 228p. 1987. 50.00 o.p. Produce Mktg Assn.
Annual Register of Grant Support: 1984-85. 18th ed. 825p. 1984. 69.50 o.s.i. (ISBN 0-8379-1911-8). Marquis.
Annual Register, 1981. Ed. by H. V. Hodson. 600p. 1982. 75.00x o.p. (ISBN 0-8103-2029-0, Pub. by Longman). Gale.
Annual Report of the Commisioner & Chief Counsel of the Internal Revenue Service **see Internal Revenue Service, 1986 Annual Report.**
Annual Report of the Illinois State Historical Library. Illinois State Historical Society Staff. Ed. by Michael J. Devine. 1985. write for info. o.p. (ISBN 0-912226-18-8). Ill St Hist Soc.
Annual Report on Exchange Arrangements & Exchange Restrictions. ix, 560p. 1987. pap. 15.00 o.s.i. (ISBN 0-939934-97-3). Intl Monetary.
Annual Report on Wood Protection, 1953-1954. Ed. by G. Becker & G. Theden. vi, 219p. 1955. 29.10 o.p. (ISBN 0-387-01928-6). Springer-Verlag.
Annual Report on Wood Protection, 1957-1958. Ed. by G. Becker & G. Theden. v, 433p. 1966. 62.00 o.p. (ISBN 0-387-03339-4). Springer-Verlag.
Annual Report, 1952. 1952. pap. 40.00 o.p. (ISBN 0-686-30730-5). Munger Oil.
Annual Report, 1953. 1953. pap. 40.00 o.p. (ISBN 0-686-30731-3). Munger Oil.
Annual Report, 1954. 1954. pap. 40.00 o.p. (ISBN 0-686-30732-1). Munger Oil.
Annual Report, 1955. 1955. pap. 40.00 o.p. (ISBN 0-686-30733-X). Munger Oil.
Annual Report, 1981. 11th ed. Association of Research Libraries, Office of Management Studies. Assn Res Lib.
Annual Report, 1982. 12th ed. Association of Research Libraries, Office of Management Studies. Assn Res Lib.
Annual Reports in Inorganic & General Syntheses, Vol. 1. Ed. by Kurt Niedenzu & Hans Zimmer. 1973. 54.00 o.p. (ISBN 0-12-040701-9). Acad Pr.
Annual Reports in Inorganic & General Syntheses, Vol. 5. Ed. by Hans Zimmer. 1977. 70.50 o.p. (ISBN 0-12-040705-1). Acad Pr.
Annual Reports in Medicinal Chemistry, Vol. 14. Ed. by Hans-Jurgen Hess. LC 66-26843. (Serial Publication). 1979. 65.00 o.p. (ISBN 0-12-040514-8). Acad Pr.
Annual Review in Automatic Programming, Vol. 9C. Ed. by M. I. Halpern. (Illus.). 222p. 1981. 68.00 o.p. (ISBN 0-08-020242-X). Pergamon.
Annual Review of Chronopharmacology, Vol. 2. Ed. by A. Reinberg et al. (Illus.). 334p. 1986. 108.00 o.p. (ISBN 0-08-034135-7, Pub. by PPL). Pergamon.
Annual Review of Engineering Industries & Automation. Incl. 1979. 63p. 1981. pap. 8.00 (UN81/2E16). UNIPUB; 1980. 114p. 1983. pap. text ed. 13.50 (UN82/2E18). UNIPUB; 1981. 82p. 1984. pap. 11.00 (UN83/2E20). UNIPUB; 1982. 78p. 1985. pap. 11.00 (UN84/2E12 5091). UNIPUB. (Economic Commission for Europe Ser.). UNIPUB.
Annual Review of Information Science & Technology, Vol. 20. Ed. by Martha E. Williams. LC 66-25096. (American Society for Information Science Ser.). 360p. 1985. 52.50 o.p. (ISBN 0-86729-175-3). Knowledge Indus.
Annual Review of Information Science & Technology, 1968, Vol. 3. Ed. by Carlos A. Cuadra. LC 66-25096. (Illus.). 457p. 1968. 45.00 o.p. (ISBN 0-685-94669-X). Knowledge Indus.
Annual Review of Information Science & Technology, 1969, Vol. 4. Ed. by Carlos A. Cuadra & Ann W. Luke. LC 66-25096. 547p. 1969. 45.00 o.p. (ISBN 0-85229-147-7). Knowledge Indus.
Annual Review of Information Science & Technology, 1970, Vol. 5. Ed. by Carlos A. Cuadra & Ann W. Luke. LC 66-25096. 468p. 1970. 45.00 o.p. (ISBN 0-85229-156-6). Knowledge Indus.
Annual Review of Information Science & Technology, 1972, Vol. 7. Ed. by Carlos A. Cuadra & Ann W. Luke. LC 66-25096. (Illus.). 606p. 1972. 45.00 o.p. (ISBN 0-87715-206-3). Knowledge Indus.
Annual Review of Information Science & Technology, 1973, Vol. 8. Ed. by Carlos A. Cuadra & Ann W. Luke. LC 66-25096. 411p. 1973. 45.00 o.p. (ISBN 0-87715-208-X). Knowledge Indus.
Annual Review of Information Science & Technology, 1974, Vol. 9. Ed. by Carlos A. Cuadra & Ann W. Luke. LC 66-25096. (Illus.). 457p. 1974. 45.00 o.p. (ISBN 0-87715-209-8). Knowledge Indus.
Annual Review of Information Science & Technology, 1977, Vol. 12. Ed. by Martha E. Williams. LC 66-25096. 361p. 1977. 45.00 o.p. (ISBN 0-914236-11-3). Knowledge Indus.
Annual Review of Information Science & Technology, 1978, Vol. 13. Ed. by Martha E. Williams. LC 66-25096. 386p. 1978. 45.00 o.p. (ISBN 0-914236-21-0). Knowledge Indus.
Annual Review of Information Science & Techology, 1979, Vol. 14. Ed. by Martha E. Williams. LC 66-25096. 375p. 1979. 45.00 o.p. (ISBN 0-914236-44-X). Knowledge Indus.
Annual Review of Information Science & Technology, 1980, Vol. 15. Ed. by Martha E. Williams. LC 66-25096. 413p. 1980. 45.00 o.p. (ISBN 0-914236-65-2). Knowledge Indus.
Annual Review of Information Science & Technology, 1981, Vol. 16. Ed. by Martha E. Williams. LC 66-25096. 422p. 1981. 45.00x o.p. (ISBN 0-914236-90-3). Knowledge Indus.
Annual Review of Information Science & Technology, 1982, Vol. 17. Ed. by Martha E. Williams. LC 66-25096. 367p. 1982. 45.00x o.p. (ISBN 0-86729-032-3). Knowledge Indus.
Annual Review of Information Science & Technology, 1983, Vol. 18. Ed. by Martha E. Williams. LC 66-25096. 447p. 1983. 45.00x o.p. (ISBN 0-86729-050-1). Knowledge Indus.
Annual Review of Information Science & Technology, 1984, Vol. 19. Ed. by Martha E. Williams. LC 66-25096. 417p. 1984. 50.00x o.p. (ISBN 0-86729-093-5). Knowledge Indus.
Annual Review of Psychology, Vol. 31. Ed. by M. R. Rosenzweig & L. W. Porter. LC 50-13143. (Illus.). 1980. text ed. 27.00 o.s.i. (ISBN 0-8243-0231-1). Annual Reviews.
Annual Review of Psychology, Vol. 32. Ed. by M. R. Rosenzweig & L. W. Porter. LC 50-13143. (Illus.). 1981. text ed. 27.00 o.s.i. (ISBN 0-8243-0232-X). Annual Reviews.
Annual Review of the Social Sciences of Religion, Vol. 1. Ed. by Joachim Matthes et al. 1977. pap. 23.20x o.p. (ISBN 90-279-7794-1). Mouton.
Annual Review of the Social Sciences of Religion, Vol. 2, 1978. Ed. by Joachim Mathes et al. 1978. pap. text ed. 23.20x o.p. (ISBN 0-686-27014-2). Mouton.
Annual Review of the Social Sciences of Religion, Vol. 3, 1979. Ed. by Joachim Matthes et al. 1979. pap. text ed. 26.00x o.p. (ISBN 0-686-27015-0). Mouton.
Annual Review of United Nations Affairs, 1950, 1952, 1954, 1955-56, 1959, 1960-61, 19964-65, 1968-69 & 1973. 17.50 o.p. Oceana.
Annual Reviews Reprints. Compiled by L. J. Mullins. Incl. Cell Membranes, 1975-1977. LC 78-55105. (Illus.). 1978. pap. text ed. 12.00 (ISBN 0-8243-2501-X). (Illus.). Annual Reviews.
Annual Reviews Reprints: Immunology, 1977-1979. Compiled by Irving Weissman. (Illus.). 1980. soft cover 12.00 o.p. (ISBN 0-8243-2502-8). Annual Reviews.
Annual Statement Studies, 1987. 416p. 49.50 o.s.i. (ISBN 0-936742-32-1). Robt Morris Assocs.
Annual Statistical Bulletin, 1980. 15th ed. Ed. by Organization of the Petroleum Exporting Countries (OPEC) Staff. LC 74-640556. (Illus.). 193p. (Orig.). 1981. pap. 30.00x o.p. (ISBN 0-8002-2970-3). Intl Pubns Serv.
Annual Statistical Bulletin, 1981. 16th ed. OPEC Staff. LC 74-640556. (Illus.). 236p. (Orig.). 1982. pap. 30.00x o.p. (ISBN 0-8002-3125-2). Intl Pubns Serv.
Annual Summary of Information on Natural Disasters. Incl. 1966. (No. 1). (Illus.). 81p. 1970. pap. 9.25 (U22, UNESCO). UNIPUB; 1967. (Illus.). 66p. 1967. pap. 5.25 (U23, UNESCO). UNIPUB; 1968. (Illus.). 72p. 1968. pap. 5.00 (U24, UNESCO). UNIPUB; 1969. (Illus.). 73p. 1969. pap. 5.00 (U25, UNESCO). UNIPUB; 1971. LC 72-83612. (No. 6). 82p. 1971. pap. 5.25 (ISBN 92-3-101042-5, U27, UNESCO). UNIPUB; Vol. 9, 1974. Earthquakes, Tsunamis, Volcanic Eruptions, Landslides, Avalanches. (Illus.). 99p. 1976. pap. 7.00 (ISBN 92-3-001369-2, U30, UNESCO). UNIPUB. UNIPUB.
Annual Summary of Information on Natural Disasters: 1972, No. 7. 106p. (Orig.). 1974. pap. 5.25 o.p. (ISBN 0-685-50559-6, U28, UNESCO). UNIPUB.
Annual Summary of Investigations Relating to Reading: July 1, 1982 to June 30, 1983. Ed. by Sam Weintraub et al. (IRA Bk: No. 961). 352p. 1984. 20.00 o.p. (ISBN 0-317-14164-3). Intl Reading.
Annual Survey of Bankruptcy Law: 1979-1984. William Norton, Jr. 86.00 o.p. (ISBN 0-317-11806-4). Callaghan.
Annuale Mediaevale, Vols. 12-17. Ed. by Herbert H. Petit. 200p. (Orig.). 1971-75. pap. text ed. 10.50 ea o.p.; Vol. 12. pap. text ed. 10.00x o.p.; pap. text ed. 10.50x o.p. Vol. 14 (ISBN 0-391-00463-8). Vol. 16. pap. text ed. 10.50x o.p. (ISBN 0-391-00536-7); Vol. 17. pap. text ed. 15.00x o.p. (ISBN 0-391-01219-3). Humanities.
Annuale Mediaevale, Vol. 18. Ed. by Frank T. Zbozny. 1978. pap. text ed. 13.50x o.p. (ISBN 0-391-01220-7). Humanities.
Annuale Mediaevale, Vol. 19. Ed. by Frank Zbozny. 97p. 1979. pap. text ed. 13.50x o.p. Humanities.
Annuale Mediaevale, Vol. 20. Ed. by Frank Zbozny et al. 122p. 1981. pap. text ed. 13.50x o.p. (ISBN 0-391-02694-1). Humanities.
Annuale Mediaevale, Vol. 21. Ed. by B. A. Beranek & H. Petik. 138p. 1982. 13.50x o.p. (ISBN 0-686-82238-2). Humanities.
Annuale Mediaevale, Vol. 22. Ed. by B. A. Beranek. 126p. 1985. pap. text ed. 28.50x o.p. (ISBN 0-317-26979-8). Humanities.
Annunciation from the Right: From Early Christian Times to the Sixteenth Century. Don Denny. LC 76-23611. (Outstanding Dissertations in the Fine Arts - 2nd Ser. - Fifteenth Century). (Illus.). 1977. Repr. of 1965 ed. lib. bdg. 55.00 o.p. (ISBN 0-8240-2683-7). Garland Pub.

Anodes for Electrowinning: Proceedings, AIME Annual Meeting, Los Angeles, 1984. Ed. by D. J. Robinson & S. E. James. LC 84-60151. (Illus.). 113p. 1984. pap. 17.00 o.p. (ISBN 0-89520-474-6). Minerals Metals.

Anodic Oxidation. Sidney Ross et al. (Organic Chemistry Ser.). 1975. 88.00 o.p. (ISBN 0-12-597650-X). Acad Pr.

Anomeric Effect: Origins & Consequences. Ed. by Derek Horton & Walter A. Szarek. LC 78-26407. (ACS Symposium Ser.: No. 87). 1979. 24.95 o.p. (ISBN 0-8412-0470-5). Am Chemical.

Anonymous Christ: Jesus As Savior in Modern Theology. Lee E. Snook. LC 86-14117. 192p. (Orig.). 1986. pap. 11.95 o.p. (ISBN 0-8066-2220-2, 10-0370, Augsburg). Augsburg Fortress.

Anonymous: Enquire Within. Facsimile ed. 386p. 1978. 8.95 o.p. (ISBN 0-374-14853-8). FS&G.

Anopheline Names: Their Derivations & Histories see Thomas Say Foundation Publications.

Anorexia Nervosa & Bulimic Disorders: Current Perspectives: Proceedings of the Conference on Anorexia Nervosa & Related Disorders Held at University College, Swansea, Wales, on 3-7 September 1984. Ed. by G. I. Szmukler et al. 458p. 1986. 135.00 o.p. (ISBN 0-08-032704-4, PBL). Pergamon.

Another Autumn & Other Poems. Robert E. Witt. 1977. 4.00 o.p. (ISBN 0-682-48890-9). Exposition-Phoenix.

Another Beautiful Day: The All-New 1986 Rod McKuen Book of Days, Databook & Diary. Rod McKuen. (Illus.). 192p. 1984. 12.45 o.p. (ISBN 0-06-250580-7). HarpR.

Another Beginning. Sian James. 216p. 1981. 9.95 o.p. (ISBN 0-395-30535-7). HM.

Another Birth. Forugh Farrokhzad. Tr. by Hasan Javadi & Susan Sallee. 144p. (Orig.). 1981. pap. 10.00 o.p. (ISBN 0-89410-361-X). Three Continents.

Another Chance: Post War America, 1945-1985. 2nd ed. James B. Gilbert. 332p. 1986. pap. text ed. (ISBN 0-534-10539-4). Wadsworth Pub.

Another Hurdle: The Making of an Olympic Champion. David Hemery. LC 76-364. (Illus.). (YA) (gr. 9 up). 1976. 9.95 o.s.i. (ISBN 0-8008-0233-0). Taplinger.

Another Land. Richard Vasquez. 288p. 1982. pap. 2.75 o.p. (ISBN 0-380-79400-4, 79400-4). Avon.

Another Life. Derek Walcott. LC 81-51675. 192p. 1982. pap. 7.50 o.p. (ISBN 0-89410-279-6). Three Continents.

Another Life: A Novel in Two Parts. J. W. Etherington. LC 83-90938. 315p. 1985. 14.95 o.p. (ISBN 0-533-05946-1). Vantage.

Another Life: The House on the Embankment. Yuri Trifonov. Tr. by Michael Glenny from Rus. 368p. 1983. 16.50 o.p. (ISBN 0-671-24266-0). S&S.

Another Life-the House on the Embankment: Novellas. Yuri Trifonov. Tr. by Michael Glenny. 1986. pap. 8.95 o.p. (ISBN 0-671-60603-4, Touchstone). S&S.

Another Look at the Campus Culture. National Association for Women Deans, Administrators & Counselors. 1980. pap. 6.00 o.p. (ISBN 0-686-28002-4). Natl Assn Women.

Another Man's Poison: The Life & Writings of Columnist George Frazier. Charles Fountain. LC 84-13709. (Illus.). 288p. (Orig.). 1984. pap. 12.95 o.p. (ISBN 0-87106-857-5); casebound 17.95 o.p. (ISBN 0-87106-863-X). Globe Pequot.

Another Marvelous Thing. Laurie Colwin. LC 85-45588. 144p. 1986. 13.95 o.p. (ISBN 0-394-55128-1). Knopf.

Another Mother Tongue: Gay Words, Gay Worlds. Judy Grahn. LC 83-45953. 324p. 1984. 19.95 o.p. (ISBN 0-8070-6716-4); pap. 9.95 o.p. (ISBN 0-8070-6717-2, BP701). Beacon Pr.

Another Name for Madness. Marion Roach. LC 85-4297. 241p. 1985. 14.45 o.p. (ISBN 0-395-35373-4). HM.

Another Side of the Blues: Seven Stories. Charles Wilder. (Orig.). 1980. pap. 6.00 o.p. (ISBN 0-682-49543-3). Exposition-Phoenix.

Another Step Forward. University of Florida Staff. 1978. 2.00 ea. o.p. (ISBN 0-318-22027-X). Mainstreaming Handicapped Students into the Regular Classroom (SN21-A). Characteristics of Handicapped Students (SN21-B). A System of Management (SN21-C). Evaluation & Placement (SN21-D). Architectural Considerations for a Barrier Free Environment (SN21-E). Set. 8.25 o.p. (SN21). Natl Ctr Res Voc Ed.

Another Story: Women & the Falklands War. Jean Carr. 192p. 1984. 19.95 o.p. (ISBN 0-241-11391-1, Pub. by Hamish Hamilton England); pap. 10.95 o.p. (ISBN 0-241-11354-7, Pub. by Hamish Hamilton England). David & Charles.

Another War, Another Peace. Ronald J. Glasser. 256p. 1985. 14.70 o.s.i. (ISBN 0-671-50767-2). Summit Bks.

Ansatze Zum Geschichtlichen und Politischen Denken Im Kiewer Russland. Werner Philipp. (Ger). Repr. of 1940 ed. 14.00 o.p. (ISBN 0-384-46235-9). Johnson Repr.

Anschluss Movement in Austria & Germany, 1918-1919 & the Paris Peace Conference. Alfred D. Low. LC 74-78094. (Memoirs Ser.: Vol. 103). (Illus.). 1974. pap. 15.00 o.p. (ISBN 0-87169-103-5). Am Philos.

Ansel Adams: An Autobiography. (Illus.). 1985. 60.00 o.p. Little.

Ansel Adams: Classics Images. 1986. 29.95 o.p. Little.

Ansel Adams the Eloquent Light. Nancy Newhall. LC 80-68714. (Illus.). 176p. 1980. 75.00 o.s.i. (ISBN 0-89381-066-5). Aperture.

Anselm & Nicholas of Cusa. Karl Jaspers. Ed. by Hannah Arendt. Tr. by Ralph Manheim from Ger. LC 74-4484. (From the Great Philosophers: Vol. No. 2). 208p. 1974. pap. 3.50 o.p. (ISBN 0-15-607600-4, HB289, Harv). HarBraceJ.

ANSI COBOL Programming. 2nd ed. J. Saxon & W. Englander. 1977. pap. text ed. (ISBN 0-13-037770-8). P-H.

Answer As a Man. Taylor Caldwell. 480p. 1982. pap. 3.95 o.p. (ISBN 0-449-24467-9, Crest). Fawcett.

Answer As a Man. Taylor Caldwell. (General Ser.). 1984. lib. bdg. 15.95 o.p. (ISBN 0-8161-3746-3, Large Print Bks); pap. 11.95 o.p. (ISBN 0-8161-3766-8). G K Hall.

Answer Back. Donald Finkel. LC 68-17382. 1968. 4.50 o.p. (ISBN 0-689-10086-8, Atheneum); pap. 1.95 o.p. (ISBN 0-689-10087-6). Macmillan.

Answer in the Tide. Elisabeth Ogilvie. LC 77-26012. 1978. text ed. 9.95 o.p. (ISBN 0-07-047664-0). McGraw.

Answer Is the Spirit. R. E. White. LC 79-23825. 168p. 1980. pap. 6.50 o.s.i. (ISBN 0-664-24311-8, Westminster). Westminster John Knox.

Answer to Divorce. Norman Wright. LC 76-52831. (Answer Ser.). 1977. pap. 1.95 o.p. (ISBN 0-89081-033-8, 0338). Harvest Hse.

Answer to Submission & Decision Making. Norman Wright. pap. 1.95 o.p. (ISBN 0-89081-078-8). Harvest Hse.

Answers to Questions About Old Jewelry (1840-1950) Jeanenne Bell. (Illus.). 304p. (Orig.). 1982. pap. 9.95 o.p. (ISBN 0-89689-033-3). Bks Americana.

Answers to the Study Guide for CFP 3. R. Robert Rackley. (CFP Answers Ser.). 1985. pap. text ed. 40.00 o.p. (ISBN 0-88171-095-4). Insurance Achiev.

Antacids in the Eighties. Ed. by F. Halter. (Illus.). 160p. 1982. text ed. 22.00 o.p. (ISBN 0-8067-0831-X). Urban & S.

Antarctic Hazard. W. Ross Cockrill. 230p. 1957. (ISBN 0-8022-0275-6). Philos Lib.

Antarctic Year: Brabant Island Expedition. Chris Furse. (Illus.). 192p. 1986. 22.50 o.p. (ISBN 0-7099-1058-4, Pub. by Croom Helm UK). Routledge Chapman & Hall.

Antarctica. Emil Schulthess. 1960. 15.00 o.p. (ISBN 0-671-03510-X). S&S.

Antebellum Charleston Dramatists. Charles S. Watson. LC 75-30635. (Illus.). 192p. 1976. 14.00 o.p. (ISBN 0-8173-6001-8). U of Ala Pr.

Antebellum Plantation at Stone Mountain Park. Norman Shavin. (Illus.). 52p. 1985. pap. 3.50 o.p. (ISBN 0-910719-11-X). Capricorn Corp.

Antenatal Care. 11th ed. J. C. Browne et al. LC 77-1557. (Illus.). 1978. 35.00 o.p. (ISBN 0-443-01476-0). Churchill.

Antenna Book. 14th ed. (Illus.). 328p. 1982. 12.50 o.p. (ISBN 0-87259-003-8); pap. 8.00 o.p. (ISBN 0-87259-414-9). Am Radio.

Antennas & Propagation (ICAP 83) Institute of Electrical Engineers (UK) Staff & Peter Perogrinus, Ltd. (IEE Conference Publication Ser.: No. 219). 861p. 1983. pap. 142.00 o.s.i. (ISBN 0-85296-270-3, IC219). Inst Elect Eng.

Anterior Pituitary. Ed. by A. Tixier-Vidal & Marilyn G. Farquhar. 1975. 80.50 o.p. (ISBN 0-12-692050-8). Acad Pr.

Anterior Segment Fluorescein Angiography. Michael H. Kottow. LC 77-16572. 268p. 1978. 27.50 o.p. (ISBN 0-683-04757-4). Krieger.

Anthologized Poetry of Loula D. Constandinidou. Loula D. Constandinidou. Tr. by Maria Hogan. 1979. 4.00 o.p. (ISBN 0-682-49268-X). Exposition-Phoenix.

Anthology for Musical Analysis. 3rd ed. Charles Burkhart. LC 78-15566. 1979. pap. text ed. 27.95 o.p. (ISBN 0-03-018866-0, HoltC). HR&W.

Anthology of American Poetry. Ed. by G. Gesner. (Avenel Home Library). 720p. 1983. 8.98 o.s.i. (ISBN 0-517-38557-0, Avenel). Outlet Bk Co.

Anthology of Andres Bello. Ed. by OAS, General Secretariat. Tr. by Barbara D. Huntley & Pilar Liria. (Cultural Ser.). 259p. 1981. pap. 8.00 o.p. OAS.

Anthology of Bells: The Bell Collectors' Treasury of Verses. Ed. by Dorothy M. Warren. LC 78-66999. (Illus.). 1979. 8.95 o.p. (ISBN 0-682-49185-3). Exposition-Phoenix.

Anthology of Brazilian Modernist Poetry. G. Pontiero. 1969. 26.00 o.p. (ISBN 0-08-013327-4); pap. text ed. 12.50 o.p. (ISBN 0-08-013326-6). Pergamon.

Anthology of Children's Literature. 5th ed. Edna Johnson et al. 1977. text ed. 29.95 o.p. (ISBN 0-395-24554-0). HM.

Anthology of German Poetry from Holderlin to Rilke. Ed. by Angel Flores. 12.75 o.p. (ISBN 0-8446-1185-9). Peter Smith.

Anthology of I Ching. W. A. Sherrill & W. K. Chu. 256p. 1983. pap. 8.95 o.p. (ISBN 0-7100-9520-1). Routledge Chapman & Hall.

Anthology of Indo-English Poetry. Gauri Deshpande. 162p. 1975. pap. text ed. 2.50 o.s.i. (ISBN 0-88253-455-6). Ind-US Inc.

Anthology of Irish Verse: The Poetry of Ireland from Mythological Times to the Present. rev. ed. Ed. by Padraic Colum. (Black & Gold Lib). 1972. pap. 5.95 o.p. (ISBN 0-87140-273-4). Liveright.

Anthology of Japanese Literature: Earliest Era to Mid-Nineteenth Century. Ed. by Donald Keene. 1960. pap. 13.95 o.p. (ISBN 0-394-17221-3, E216, Ever). Grove.

Anthology of Jesus. James Marchant. Ed. by Warren W. Wiersbe. LC 80-25038. 382p. 1981. Repr. of 1926 ed. 12.95 o.p. (ISBN 0-8254-4015-7). Kregel.

Anthology of Longer Scottish Poems, Vol. 1. Ed. by F. Riddy & P. Bawcutt. 448p. 1987. 29.95 o.p. (ISBN 0-7073-0328-1, Pub. by Scot Acad Pr); pap. 13.95 o.p. (ISBN 0-7073-0509-8). Longwood Pub Group.

Anthology of Longer Scottish Poems, Vol. 2. Ed. by D. Hewitt et al. 418p. 1987. 29.95 o.p. (ISBN 0-7073-0329-X, Pub. by Scot Acad Pr); pap. 13.95 o.p. (ISBN 0-7073-0510-1). Longwood Pub Group.

Anthology of Orthopaedics. Mercer Rang. 1977. Repr. 31.50 o.p. (ISBN 0-443-00408-0). Churchill.

Anthology of Russian Plays, Vol. 2 see Twentieth-Century Russian Plays: An Anthology.

Anthology of Twentieth Century Music. Mary H. Wennerstrom. 1969. pap. text ed. 31.00 o.p. (ISBN 0-13-038489-5). P-H.

Anthology of Verse. Kathleen Finnerty. 1978. 3.50 o.p. (ISBN 0-682-49102-0). Exposition-Phoenix.

Anthony Adverse. Hervey Allen. 1977. 12.95 o.s.i. (ISBN 0-03-028400-7). H Holt & Co.

Anthony Burgess: The Artist As Novelist. Geoffrey Aggeler. LC 78-12200. (Illus.). 245p. 1979. 19.50 o.p. (ISBN 0-8173-7106-0). U of Ala Pr.

Anthony Burns, a History. Charles E. Stevens. Repr. of 1856 ed. lib. bdg. 35.00x o.p. (ISBN 0-8371-2724-6, SBU&). Greenwood.

Anthony Caro. William Rubin. LC 74-21725. (Illus.). 196p. 1975. 17.50 o.p. (ISBN 0-87070-275-0); pap. 7.95 o.p. (ISBN 0-87070-276-9). Museum Mod Art.

Anthony Merry Redivivus: A Reappraisal of the British Minister to the United States, 1803-6. Malcom Lester. LC 77-20910. 161p. 1978. 16.95x o.p. (ISBN 0-8139-0750-0). U Pr of Va.

Anthony Trollope. Donald Smalley. (Critical Heritage Ser.). 592p. 1985. pap. 15.00 o.p. (ISBN 0-7102-0593-7). Routledge Chapman & Hall.

Anthony Van Leeuwenhoek & His Little Animals. Anthony Van Leeuwenhoek. pap. 7.50 o.p. (ISBN 0-486-60594-9). Dover.

Anthony Wayne, Washington's General. Adele DeLeeuw & Cateau DeLeeuw. LC 74-1130. (Illus.). (gr. 5-9). 1974. 5.50 o.s.i. (ISBN 0-664-32547-5, Westminster). Westminster John Knox.

Anthracyclines: Current Status & New Developments. Ed. by Stanley T. Crooke & Steven D. Reich. 1980. 58.50 o.p. (ISBN 0-12-197780-3). Acad Pr.

Anthropod Phylogeny. Ayodhya P. Gupta. 768p. 1979. 44.95 o.p. (ISBN 0-442-22973-9). Van Nos Reinhold.

Anthropological Imagination. Muriel Dimen-Schein. (McGraw-Hill Paperbacks Ser.). 1977. 8.95 o.p. (ISBN 0-07-016986-1); pap. text ed. 4.95 o.p. (ISBN 0-07-016985-3). McGraw.

Anthropological Report on the Edo-Speaking Peoples of Nigeria, 2 vols. Northcote W. Thomas. LC 70-82082. (Illus.). 1970. Repr. of 1910 ed. Set. 28.00x o.p. (ISBN 0-8371-3807-8, THE&, Pub. by Negro U Pr). Greenwood.

Anthropological Resources & Teaching. Ed. by Marion J. Rice et al. (Special Issues of the Arthropology & Education Quarterly Ser.: Vol. 8, No. 1). 1977. 7.50 o.s.i. (ISBN 0-317-66331-3). Am Anthro Assn.

Anthropologist at Work. Margaret Mead. 1973. pap. 4.45 o.p. (ISBN 0-380-01022-4, 16857). Avon.

Anthropology. 4th ed. Carol R. Ember & Melvin Ember. (Illus.). 624p. 1985. text ed. (ISBN 0-13-037045-2). P-H.

Anthropology. J. White. (Illus.). 192p. 1955. (ISBN 0-8022-1859-8). Philos Lib.

Anthropology: A Cultural Perspective. James P. Spradley & David W. McCurdy. LC 74-23259. 400p. 1980. pap. text ed. 21.00 o.p. (ISBN 0-394-34411-1). Random.

Anthropology: A General Introduction. Victor Barnouw. 507p. 1979. pap. text ed. (ISBN 0-534-10467-3). Wadsworth Pub.

Anthropology & Education: A Selected Bibliography. Katherine Murray. (Multicultural Research Guides Ser.). 10p. 2.00 o.p. (ISBN 0-317-65382-2). I N Thut World Educ Ctr.

Anthropology & Ethics: The Quest for Moral Understanding. rev. ed. Abraham Edel & May Edel. 280p. 1970. casebound 12.95 o.p. (ISBN 0-87855-098-4). Transaction Pubs.

Anthropology & Marxism. James W. Wessman. LC 80-14042. 370p. 1980. 18.95x o.p. (ISBN 0-87073-708-2); pap. text ed. 11.95 o.p. (ISBN 0-87073-709-0). Schenkman Bks Inc.

Anthropology & the Old Testament. J. W. Rogerson. LC 78-71043. 1979. 8.95 o.p. (ISBN 0-8042-0083-1, John Knox). Westminster John Knox.

Anthropology: Biology & Race. Alfred L. Kroeber. LC 63-12159. 1963. pap. 2.65 o.p. (ISBN 0-15-607804-X, Harv). HarBraceJ.

Anthropology for the Eighties: Introductory Readings. Ed. by Johnetta B. Cole. LC 81-69764. pap. text ed. 115.95 o.p. (ISBN 0-02-906430-9). Free Pr.

Anthropology Full Circle. Ino Rossi et al. LC 74-33027. 444p. (Orig.). 1977. pap. text ed. 15.95 o.p. (ISBN 0-275-89200-X, HoltC). HR&W.

Anthropology in Museums of Canada & the United States. Cornelius Osgood. (Publications in Museology Ser.: No. 7). 109p. 1979. 7.50 o.p. (ISBN 0-89326-048-7). Milwaukee Pub Mus.

Anthropology of Dance. Anya P. Royce. LC 77-74428. (Midland Bks.: No. 235). (Illus.). 256p. 1977. pap. 7.95x o.p. (ISBN 0-253-20235-3); 22.50x o.p. (ISBN 0-253-30752-X). Ind U Pr.

Anthropology of Medicine: From Culture to Method. Ed. by Lola Romanucci-Ross et al. (Illus.). 416p. 1983. text ed. 44.95x o.s.i. (ISBN 0-03-062192-5); pap. text ed. 19.95x o.s.i. (ISBN 0-89789-013-2). Bergin & Garvey.

Anthropology of Power: Ethnographic Studies from Asia, Oceania & New World. Ed. by Raymond D. Fogelson & Richard N. Adams. (Studies in Anthropology). 1977. 33.00 o.p. (ISBN 0-12-261550-6). Acad Pr.

Anthropology of Saint John of Damascus. Constance N. Tsirpanlis. 64p. 1980. pap. 3.00 o.p. (ISBN 0-686-36332-9). EO Pr.

Anthropology of the Desert West: Essays in Honor of Jesse D. Jennings. Ed. by Carol J. Condie & Don D. Fowler. (Anthropological Papers: No. 110). (Illus.). 440p. 1986. 30.00x o.p. (ISBN 0-87480-246-6); pap. 15.00x o.p. (ISBN 0-87480-248-2). U of Utah Pr.

Anthropology of the Old Testament. Hans W. Wolff. Tr. by Margaret Kohl from Ger. LC 74-21591. 304p. 1981. pap. 10.95 o.p. (ISBN 0-8006-1500-X, 1-1500, Fortress). Augsburg Fortress.

Anthropology: Study Guide & Workbook. 4th ed. Dennis Werner. 192p. 1985. pap. text ed. (ISBN 0-13-037086-X). P-H.

Anthropology: The Biocultural View. Francis E. Johnston & Henry A. Selby. 600p. 1978. text ed. write for info. o.p. (ISBN 0-697-07587-7). Wm C Brown.

Anthropology, 1988-89. 11th, rev. ed. Elvio Angeloni. LC 74-84595. (Annual Editions Ser.). (Illus.). 256p. 1988. pap. text ed. 9.95 o.p. (ISBN 0-87967-713-9). Dushkin Pub.

Anti-Authoritarian Personalities, Vol. 21. William P. Kreml. LC 76-28746. 1977. 34.00 o.p. (ISBN 0-08-021063-5). Pergamon.

Anti-Bolshevik Communism. Paul Mattick. LC 78-68639. 244p. 1979. 35.00 o.p. (ISBN 0-87332-135-9). M E Sharpe.

Anti-Coloring Book of Red-Letter Days. Susan Striker. (Anti- Coloring Bks.). (Illus.). 64p. (Orig.). (gr. 2 up). 1981. pap. 3.95 o.p. (ISBN 0-03-057873-6). H Holt & Co.

Anti-Communist Myths in Left Disguise. Robert Steigerwald. LC 76-54854. Orig. Title: Marxistische Klassenanalyse Oder Spatburgerliche Mythen. 100p. 1977. pap. 1.75 o.p. (ISBN 0-7178-0479-8). Intl Pubs Co.

Anti-Corruption Manual for Administrators in Law Enforcement. Richard H. Ward & Robert McCormack. 1979. pap. 4.95 o.p. (ISBN 0-89444-010-1). John Jay Pr.

Anti-Dumping & Countervailing Duties. (Eng. & Fr.). 1958. pap. 7.50 o.p. (ISBN 0-686-93151-3, G105, GATT). UNIPUB.

Anti-Equilibrium. J. Kornai. LC 75-134644. 402p. 1971. 92.00 o.p. (ISBN 0-444-10122-5, North-Holland); pap. 22.00 o.p. (ISBN 0-444-10342-2). Elsevier.

Anti-Infective Therapy. Ed. by Gerald L. Mandell et al. LC 85-3135. 516p. 1985. 22.00 o.p. (ISBN 0-471-80442-8, Pub. by Wiley Med). Wiley.

Anti-Inflamatory Agents: Chemistry & Pharmacology, Vols. 1 & 2. Ed. by Robert A. Scherrer & Michael W. Whitehouse. 1974. Vol. 1. 96.00 o.p. (ISBN 0-12-623901-0); Vol. 2. 96.00 o.p. (ISBN 0-12-623902-9). Acad Pr.

Anti-Judaism in Christian Theology. Charlotte Klein. Tr. by Edward Quinn. LC 76-62600. 192p. 1978. 4.50 o.p. (ISBN 0-8006-0488-1, 1-488, Fortress). Augsburg Fortress.

Anti-Mormonism in Idaho, Eighteen Seventy-Two to Ninety-Two. Merle W. Wells. LC 77-89975. (Studies in Mormon History Ser.: No. 4). 1978. pap. 7.95 o.p. (ISBN 0-8425-0904-6). Brigham.

Anti-Nuclear Attitudes in New Zealand & Australia. Dora Alves. (National Security Affairs Monograph Ser.). (Illus.). 108p. (Orig.). 1985. pap. 2.25 o.p. (ISBN 0-318-19999-8, S/N 008-020-01053-7). USGPO.

Anti-Scepticism: Or, Notes upon Each Chapter of Mr. Locke's Essay Concerning Humane Understanding. Henry Lee. LC 83-48571. (Philosophy of John Locke Ser.). 342p. 1978. lib. bdg. 46.00 o.p. (ISBN 0-8240-5606-X). Garland Pub.

Anti-Semitism in the New Testament? Samuel Sandmel. LC 77-15245. 192p. 1978. 9.95 o.p. (ISBN 0-8006-0521-7, 1-521, Fortress). Augsburg Fortress.

Anti-Tussive Agents, 3 vols. H. Salem & D. M. Aviado. 1970. Set. 210.00 o.p. (ISBN 0-08-013340-1). Pergamon.

Antiarrhythmic Action: The Puzzle of Perhexiline. William Vaughan. LC 80-40429. 1980. 54.50 o.p. (ISBN 0-12-715180-X). Acad Pr.

Antibiotic Choice: The Importance of Colonisation Resistance. Dirk Van der Waij. (Antimicrobial Chemotherapy Research Studies Ser.). 132p. 1983. 59.95x o.p. (ISBN 0-471-90165-2, Pub. by Research Studies Press). Wiley.

Antibiotic Therapy in Obstetrics & Gynecology. Ronald S. Gibbs & Alan J. Weinstein. LC 80-23095. 228p. 1981. pap. 23.50 o.p. (ISBN 0-471-06003-8, Pub. by John Wiley). Krieger.

Antibiotics for Surgical Infections. P. J. Sanderson. LC 82-21751. (Antimicrobial Chemotherapy Ser.). 262p. 1983. 57.00 o.p. (ISBN 0-471-90109-1, Res Stud Pr). Wiley.

Antibiotics in Clinical Medicine Case Studies. Samuel Pegram & Joseph Johnson. 1981. text ed. 35.00 o.p. (ISBN 0-87488-190-0); pap. text ed. 29.50 o.p. (ISBN 0-87488-197-8). Med Exam.

Antibiotika Erzeugende Virus-Ahnliche Faktoren in Bakterien see Multiplication of Viruses.

Anticancer Drug Development. Ed. by P. Hilgard & K. Hellman. (Proceedings of the 1st International Symposium on Management & Realization of Anticancer Drug Development Held in Granada, Spain March 25-26, 1982). (Illus.). 1982. 65.00 o.p. (ISBN 84-499-6141-6). E J Brill USA.

Anticholinesterase Agents. A. G. Karczmar. 1970. 125.00 o.p. (ISBN 0-08-006633-X). Pergamon.

Antichrist. Friedrich Nietzsche. 1986. 9.00 o.p. (ISBN 0-317-53257-X). Noontide.

Anticoagulants & Myocardial Infraction: A Reappraisal. Ed. by T. W. Meade. 272p. 1985. 54.00 o.p. (ISBN 0-471-90442-2, Dist. by A R Liss). Wiley.

Anticomunismo Moderno, Politica y Ideologica. O. Reinhold et al. 366p. (Span.). 1976. 7.95 o.p. (ISBN 0-8285-1745-2, Pub. by Progress Pubs USSR). Imported Pubns.

Anticonvulsant Drugs, Vols. 1-2. Ed. by J. Mercier. LC 72-8044. 1973. Vol. 1. 100.00 o.p. (ISBN 0-08-016840-X); Vol. 2. 81.00 o.p. (ISBN 0-08-017245-8). Pergamon.

Antifibrinolytic Drugs: Chemistry, Pharmacology & Clinical Usage. D. Ogston. LC 84-13099. 180p. 1985. pap. 30.00 o.p. (ISBN 0-471-90562-3, Dist. by A R Liss). Wiley.

Antigens, Lymphoid Cells & the Immune Response. G. J. Nossal & G. L. Ada. LC 71-137602. (Monographs on Immunology: Vol. 1). 1971. 83.00 o.p. (ISBN 0-12-521950-4). Acad Pr.

Antigone see Theatre.

Antigrav: Cosmic Comedies by SF Masters. Ed. by Philip Strick. LC 75-26328. 192p. 1976. 8.50 o.s.i. (ISBN 0-8008-0237-3). Taplinger.

Antigua & Barbuda: Economic Report. 102p. 1985. 5.00 o.p. (ISBN 0-8213-0628-6, 0628). World Bank.

Antihypertensive Agents. Ed. by Emil Schlittler. (Medicinal Chemistry: Vol. 7). 1967. 89.50 o.p. (ISBN 0-12-625650-0). Acad Pr.

Antimalarial Agents: Chemistry & Pharmacology. Paul E. Thompson & Leslie M. Werbel. 1972. 85.00 o.p. (ISBN 0-12-688950-3). Acad Pr.

Antimemoires. Andre Malraux. 1967. 27.95 o.p. (ISBN 0-685-11009-5). Schoenhof.

Antimetabolites in Biochemistry, Biology & Medicine: Proceedings, Prague, 1978. Ed. by J. Skoda & P. Langen. (Federation of European Biochemical Societies Symposium: Vol. 57). (Illus.). 1979. 93.00 o.p. (ISBN 0-08-024384-3). Pergamon.

Antineoplastic Agents. William A. Remers. LC 83-12411. (Chemistry & Pharmacology of Drugs: A Series of Monographs: 1-406). 269p. 1984. 75.00 o.p. (ISBN 0-471-08080-2, Pub. by Wiley-Interscience). Wiley.

Antioch Humor Test. Mindess et al. 176p. 1985. pap. 5.95 o.p. (ISBN 0-380-89620-6). Avon.

Antiochus: A Novel. Walter K. Price & John Gillies. 396p. 1982. pap. 4.95 o.p. (ISBN 0-8024-0249-6). Moody.

Antiplane Elastic Systems. L. M. Milne-Thomson. (Ergebnisse der Angewandten Mathematik: Vol. 8). (Illus.). 1962. pap. 37.20 o.p. (ISBN 0-387-02805-6). Springer-Verlag.

Antipolitics. George Konrad. Tr. by Richard E. Allen. 1987. pap. 9.95 o.s.i. (ISBN 0-8050-0357-6). H Holt & Co.

Antique Airplanes. Chris Sorensen & Flying Magazine Editors. LC 78-11272. (Encore Edition). (Illus.). 1979. 9.95 o.p. (ISBN 0-684-16927-4, ScribT). Scribner.

Antique Cats for Collectors. Katherine M. McClinton. (Illus.). 180p. 1973. 19.95 o.p. (ISBN 0-7188-2150-5, Pub. by Lutterworth Pr UK). Seven Hills Bk Dists.

Antique Collector's Guide. David Benedictus. LC 80-69368. 1981. 14.95 o.p. (ISBN 0-689-11146-0, Atheneum). Macmillan.

Antique Ethnic Furniture with Prices. Lyndon C. Viel. (Illus.). 168p. pap. 14.95 o.p. (ISBN 0-87069-403-0). Wallace-Homestead.

Antique Fishing Reels: Your Illustrated Guide to Identifying & Understanding U. S. Patented Models Through 1920. Steven K. Vernon. (Illus.). 192p. 1985. 19.95 o.p. (ISBN 0-8117-0108-5). Stackpole.

Antique Humour. Joel Rothman. (Illus.). 80p. (Orig.). 1985. pap. 2.95 o.p. (ISBN 0-86051-238-X). Parkwest Pubns.

Antique Pistols Collection, Fourteen Hundred to Eighteen Sixty. James Frith & Ronald Andrews. 25.00 o.p. (ISBN 0-87556-677-4). Saifer.

Antique Plane Guide. 2nd ed. Peter M. Bowers. 1985. pap. 6.95 o.p. (ISBN 0-8306-2285-3, 2285). TAB Bks.

Antique Spoons: A Collector's Guide. Victor Houart. LC 82-207350. (Illus.). 144p. 1985. 16.95 o.s.i. (ISBN 0-285-62499-7, Pub. by Souvenir Pr Ltd Uk). Seven Hills Bk Dists.

Antique Toy Trains: The Hobby of Collecting Old Toy Trains. Howard Godel. 1976. 25.00 o.p. (ISBN 0-682-48600-0). Exposition-Phoenix.

Antique Trader Antiques & Collectibles Price Guide. Ed. by Catherine Murphy. LC 84-71864. (Illus.). 908p. 1984. pap. 11.95 o.p. (ISBN 0-930625-00-5). Babka Pub.

Antique Trader Antiques & Collectibles Price Guide. 2nd ed. Ed. by Catherine Murphy. LC 85-71173. (Illus.). 908p. 1985. pap. 11.95 o.p. (ISBN 0-930625-01-3). Babka Pub.

Antique Trader Antiques & Collectibles Price Guide. 3rd ed. Ed. by Catherine Murphy. (Illus.). 908p. 1986. pap. 11.95 o.p. (ISBN 0-930625-02-1). Babka Pub.

Antique Trader Antiques & Collectibles Price Guide. 4th ed. Ed. by Catherine Murphy & Kyle Husfloen. (Illus.). 908p. 1987. pap. 11.95 o.p. (ISBN 0-930625-03-X). Babka Pub.

Antiques & Art: How to Know, Buy & Use Them. Howard L. Katzander. 1977. 35.00 o.p. (ISBN 0-385-01091-5). Doubleday.

Antiques Care & Repair Handbook. Albert Jackson & David Day. LC 83-48845. (Illus.). 255p. 1984. 18.45 o.p. (ISBN 0-394-53492-1). Knopf.

Antiquitates Culinariae: Or, Curious Tracts Relating to the Culinary Affairs of the Old English. Richard Warner. (Illus.). 137p. 1982. 75.00x o.p. (ISBN 0-907325-05-X, Pub. by Prospect England). U Pr of Va.

Antiquites Egyptiennes De Zagreb: Catalogue Raisonne Des Antiquites Egyptiennes Conservees Au Musee Archeologique De Zagreb En Yougoslavie. Janine Monnet Saleh. (Illus.). 1970. 50.40x o.p. (ISBN 90-2796-980-9). Mouton.

Antiquities of the Irish Countryside. 5th ed. Sean P. O'Riordain. (Illus.). 1979. 33.00x o.p. (ISBN 0-416-85630-6, NO.2354); pap. 10.95x o.p. (ISBN 0-416-85610-1, NO.2355). Routledge Chapman & Hall.

Antisemitism & the Foundations of Christianity. Ed. by Alan T. Davies. LC 79-65620. 276p. 1979. pap. 8.95 o.p. (ISBN 0-8091-2219-7). Paulist Pr.

Antislavery Newspapers & Periodicals: Annotated Index of Letters, 1817 - 1871, Vol. III: 1836-1854. John W. Blassingame & Mae G. Henderson. 1981. lib. bdg. 83.50 o.p. (ISBN 0-8161-8558-1, Hall Reference). G K Hall.

Antislavery: The Crusade for Freedom in America. Dwight L. Dumond. (Illus.). 1966. pap. 2.45x o.p. (ISBN 0-393-00370-1, Norton Lib). Norton.

Antislavery Vanguard: New Essays on the Abolitionists. Ed. by Martin Duberman. 1965. 40.00x o.p. (ISBN 0-691-04505-4); pap. 12.50 o.p. (ISBN 0-691-00552-4). Princeton U Pr.

Antitrust & Regulated Industries. David C. Hjelmfelt. LC 84-22016. (Wiley Federal Practice: A Law Ser.). 465p. 1985. 75.00 o.p. (ISBN 0-471-89166-5). Wiley.

Antitrust & the Economics of the Market: Text, Readings, Cases. Les Seplaki. 690p. 1982. pap. text ed. 16.00 o.p. (ISBN 0-15-502860-X, HC). HarBraceJ.

Antitrust Casebook. William Breit & Kenneth G. Elzinga. 400p. 1982. pap. 13.95 o.p. (ISBN 0-03-060147-9). Dryden Pr.

Antitrust Law Handbook, 1987. William C. Holmes. 1987. pap. 58.50 o.p. (ISBN 0-87632-537-1). Clark Boardman.

Antitrust Law: Nineteen Eighty-Six Supplement. Phillip E. Areeda & Herbert Hovenkamp. (Orig.). 1986. pap. 80.00 o.p. (ISBN 0-316-05066-0). Little.

Antitrust Litigation, Vol. 470. Practising Law Institute Staff. 236p. 1985. pap. 40.00 o.p. (ISBN 0-317-27462-7, #B4-6705). PLI.

Antitrust Update. 1984. (ISBN 0-88129-148-X). Wash Bar CLE.

Antiviral Chemotherapy: Design of Inhibitors of Viral Functions. Ed. by K. K. Gauri. LC 81-12858. 1981. 58.50 o.p. (ISBN 0-12-277720-4). Acad Pr.

Antiviral Mechanisms. Ed. by Morris Pollard. (Perspectives in Virology: Vol. 9). 1975. 71.00 o.p. (ISBN 0-12-560565-X). Acad Pr.

Antoine's Restaurant Cookbook. Roy F. Guste, Jr. (Illus.). 1980. pap. 9.95 o.p. (ISBN 0-393-00027-3). Norton.

Anton Chekhov. Laurence Senelick. Ed. by Bruce King & Adele King. LC 85-47545. (Modern Dramatists Ser.). 188p. 1986. 27.50 o.p. (ISBN 0-394-54717-9). Grove.

Anton Chekhov. Laurence Senelick. Ed. by Bruce King & Adele King. LC 85-47545. (Modern Dramatists Ser.). 188p. 1986. pap. 11.95 o.s.i. (ISBN 0-394-62066-6). Grove.

Anton Makarenko: His Life & His Work in Education. M. Gorky et al. 393p. 1976. 4.95 o.p. (ISBN 0-8285-0421-0, Pub. by Progress Pubs USSR). Imported Pubns.

Anton Raphael Mengs & Neoclassicism. Thomas Pelzel. LC 78-74375. (Fine Arts Dissertations, Fourth Ser.). (Illus.). 1980. lib. bdg. 33.00 o.p. (ISBN 0-8240-3962-9). Garland Pub.

Anton Reiser. (ISBN 0-88355-583-2). Hyperion Conn.

Antonin Artaud. pap. 1.65 o.p. (ISBN 0-380-12062-3). Avon.

Antonin Cyril Stojan: Apostle of Church Unity. Ludvik Nemec. LC 83-70817. (Illus.). 256p. 1983. pap. 11.95 o.p. (ISBN 0-89944-068-1). Don Bosco Multimedia.

Antonin Dvorak. Karel Hoffmeister. Tr. by Rosa Newmarch. 1970. Repr. of 1928 ed. lib. bdg. 35.00x o.p. (ISBN 0-8371-3946-5, HOAD). Greenwood.

Antonin Dvorak. Otaker Sourek. 138p. 1954. (ISBN 0-8022-1612-9). Philos Lib.

Antonin Dvorak, His Achievement. Ed. by Viktor Fischl. LC 78-104263. 1970. Repr. of 1943 ed. lib. bdg. 35.00x o.p. (ISBN 0-8371-3922-8, FIAD). Greenwood.

Antonio Gramsci: Conservative Schooling for Radical Politics. Harold Entwistle. (Routledge Education Bks.). 1979. 21.00x o.p. (ISBN 0-7100-0333-1); pap. 9.50x o.p. (ISBN 0-7100-0334-X). Routledge Chapman & Hall.

Antonio Jacobsen: The Checklist. Illus. by Antonio N. Jacobsen. (Illus.). 350p. 75.00 o.s.i. (ISBN 0-317-54907-3). Apollo.

Antonio Machado. Ricardo Gullon et al. LC 85-764181. 73p. 1976. pap. 10.00 o.p. Society Sp & Sp-Am.

Antonio Panizzi As Administrator. Barbara McCrimmon. (Occasional Papers: No. 68). 15p. 1963. pap. 1.00 o.p. (ISBN 0-317-58846-X). U of Ill Lib Info Sci.

Antonio's Revenge. John Marston. Ed. by Reavley Gair. (Revels Plays Ser.). 1978. text ed. 15.00x o.p. (ISBN 0-8018-2012-X). Johns Hopkins.

Antony & Cleopatra see also Tragedy of Antony & Cleopatra.

Antony & Cleopatra. William Shakespeare. 48p. (Orig.). 1989. pap. 9.95 o.p. (ISBN 1-55651-002-0); audiocassette tape incl. o.p. (ISBN 1-55651-003-9). Cram Cassettes.

Antrieb und Hemmung bei Toetungsdelikten. (Schriftenreihe des Instituts fuer Konfliktforschung: Heft 9). x, 124p. 1982. pap. 13.50 o.p. (ISBN 3-8055-3604-6). S Karger.

Ants of Colorado: Their Ecology, Taxonomy & Geographic Distribution. Robert E. Gregg. LC 62-63446. (Illus.). 1963. 23.50x o.p. (ISBN 0-87081-027-8). Univ Pr Colo.

Anubis Gates. Tim Powers. 416p. 1985. pap. 3.95 o.s.i. (ISBN 0-441-02382-7, Pub. by Ace Science Fiction). Ace Bks.

Anvil of Passion. Jack Hoffenberg. 1977. pap. 1.95 o.p. (ISBN 0-380-01024-0, 35261). Avon.

Anwendung des Simulationsmodells BAYMO 70 auf die Stadtentwicklungsplanung, Vol. 1. Werner Schulein. (Interdisciplinary Systems Research Ser.: No. 43). 136p. (Ger.). 1980. pap. 20.95x o.p. (ISBN 0-8176-0968-7). Birkhauser.

Anwendung des Simulationsmodells BAYMO 70 auf die Stadtentwicklungsplanung, Vol. 2. Peter Eulenberger. (Interdisciplinary Systems Research Ser.: No. 44). 94p. (Ger.). 1980. pap. 18.95x o.p. (ISBN 0-8176-0969-5). Birkhauser.

Anwendung des Simulationsmodells BAYMO 70 auf die Stadtentwicklungsplanung, Vol. 3. Werner Schuclein & Peter Eulenberger. (Interdisciplinary Systems Research Ser.: No. 45). 138p. (Ger.). 1980. pap. 20.95x o.p. (ISBN 0-8176-0970-9). Birkhauser.

Anxiety & Depression: The Adaptive Emotions. Charles G. Costello. 1976. text ed. 12.50x o.p. (ISBN 0-7735-0255-6, Pub. by McGill Canada). U of Toronto Pr.

Anxiety & Panic Attacks: Their Cause & Cure; The Life Plus Five-Point Program for Conquering Fear. Robert Handly & Pauline Neff. LC 84-61931. 241p. 1985. 16.95 o.p. (ISBN 0-89256-276-5). Rawson Assocs.

Anxiety Disease & How to Overcome It. David V. Sheehan. 224p. 1984. 15.95 o.p. (ISBN 0-684-18047-2, ScribT). Scribner.

Anxious Search: The Way to Universal Self. A. R. Arasteh. 1984. pap. 12.50 o.p. E J Brill USA.

Any Child Can Write: How to Improve Your Child's Writing Skills. Harvey S. Wiener. LC 77-26707. 1978. text ed. 9.95 o.p. (ISBN 0-07-069035-9). McGraw.

Any Children? Bil Keane. (Family Circus Ser.). (Illus.). 1982. pap. 1.95 o.p. (ISBN 0-449-14116-0, GM). Fawcett.

Any Day of Your Life. David Kherdian. LC 75-4381. 64p. 1975. 14.95 o.p. (ISBN 0-87951-034-X); pap. 8.95 o.p. (ISBN 0-87951-062-5). Overlook Pr.

Any Fool Can Be a Pig Farmer. 2nd ed. James Robertson. (Illus.). 155p. 1981. 17.95 o.p. (ISBN 0-85236-111-4, Pub. by Farming Pr UK). Diamond Farm Bk.

Any Four Women... Could Rob the Bank of Italy. Ann Cornelisen. LC 83-4342. 288p. 1983. 15.95 o.p. (ISBN 0-03-063254-4). H Holt & Co.

Any Man's Death. Loren D. Estleman. 224p. 1987. pap. 3.95 o.p. (ISBN 0-445-40588-0). Mysterious Pr.

Any Miracle God Wants to Give. Danny E. Morris. 1974. pap. 1.25x o.p. (ISBN 0-8358-0314-7). Upper Room.

Anything Book. Bernard H. Porter. 1986. 42.50 o.p. (ISBN 0-317-55109-4). Bern Porter.

Anything Box. Zenna Henderson. 1977. pap. 1.50 o.p. (ISBN 0-380-01745-8, 55293-0). Avon.

Anything Can Happen: Interviews with Contemporary American Novelists. Ed. by Thomas LeClair & Larry McCaffery. LC 82-2867. (Illus.). 320p. 1983. pap. 19.95 o.p. (ISBN 0-252-00970-3). U of Ill Pr.

Anything for a Friend. Ellen Conford. (gr. 5-7). 1981. pap. 2.25 o.s.i. (ISBN 0-671-54314-8); pap. 1.95 o.s.i. (ISBN 0-671-56069-7). Archway.

Anything Goes: An Educator's Guide for Working with Parents & Citizens. Anne Henderson. 80p. (Orig.). 1985. pap. 10.00 o.p. (ISBN 0-934460-26-4). NCCE.

Anywhere: Anywhen. Ed. by Sylvia L. Engdahl. LC 76-5485. 324p. (gr. 6-12). 1976. 8.95 o.p. (ISBN 0-689-30537-0, Atheneum). Macmillan.

Anzio Beachhead Twenty-Second of January to Twenty-Fifth of May 1944. Ed. by Historical Division, Department of the Army. (Combat Arms Ser.: 12th). (Illus.). 160p. 1986. Repr. of 1947 ed. 25.00 o.p. (ISBN 0-89839-088-5). Battery Pr.

Anzio: The Gamble That Failed. Martin Blumenson. 1986. pap. 3.50 o.p. (ISBN 0-440-10353-3). Dell.

AORN Standards & Recommended Practices for Perioperative Nursing. 36p. 1987. 12.00 o.p. (ISBN 0-939583-26-7). Assn Oper Rm Nurses.

Aortic Alterations in Rabbits Following Sheathing with Silastic & Polyethylene Tubes, Vol. 60. F. Huth et al. Incl. Radioactively Labeled Iododeoxyuridine in the Study of Experimental Liver Regeneration. K. Buerki et al; Human Placental Villitides: A Review of Chronic Intrauterine Infection. G. Altshuler & P. Russel; Ultrastructural Pathology of the Adrenal Glands Incushing's Syndrome. H. Mitschke & W. Saeger; DNA in Human Tumors: A Cytophotometric Study. N. Boehm & W. Sandritter. (Current Topics in Pathology Ser). (Illus.). 260p. 1975. 93.30 o.p. (ISBN 0-387-07434-1). Springer-Verlag.

Aortic Dissection. Robert M. Doroghazi & Eve E. Slater. (Illus.). 352p. 1983. text ed. 60.00 o.p. (ISBN 0-07-017767-8). McGraw.
APA Map: Indonesia. Insight Guides Staff. 1985. pap. 6.95 o.p. (ISBN 0-13-457383-8). P-H.
APA Map: Malaysia. Insight Guides Staff. 1985. pap. 6.95 o.p. (ISBN 0-13-548256-9). P-H.
APA Map: Nepal. Insight Guides Staff. 1985. pap. 6.95 o.p. (ISBN 0-13-611146-7). P-H.
APA Map: Sri Lanka. Insight Guides Staff. 1985. pap. 6.95 o.p. (ISBN 0-13-839952-2). P-H.
Apache Agent: The Story of John P. Clum. Woodworth Clum. LC 77-14135. (Illus.). xvi, 297p. 1978. pap. 5.95 o.p. (ISBN 0-8032-5886-0, BB 654, Bison). U of Nebr Pr.
Apache Country. John R. Browne. (Golden West Ser.). 1978. pap. 1.50 o.s.i. (ISBN 0-8439-0520-4, Pub. by Leisure Bks CT). Dorchester Pub Co.
Apache Indians, Vol. IX. Averam B. Bender. Ed. by David A. Horr. (American Indian Ethnohistory Ser.). 1974. lib. bdg. 51.00 o.p. (ISBN 0-8240-0711-5). Garland Pub.
Apache Indians, Vol. III. Gerald. Incl. Aboriginal Use & Occupation of Certain Lands by Tigua, Manso & Suma Indians. Rex E. Gerald; History & Administration of the Tigua Indians of Ysleta Del Sur During the Spanish Colonial Period. Myra E. Jenkins; Apache Ethnohistory: Government, Land & Indian Policies Relative to Lipan, Mescalero & Tigua Indians. Kenneth F. Neighbours. (American Indian Ethnohistory Ser: Indians of the Southwest). (Illus.). 1974. lib. bdg. 51.00 o.p. (ISBN 0-8240-0717-4). Garland Pub.
Apache Indians, Vol. VI. B. L. Gordon et al. Ed. by David A. Horr. (American Indian Ethnohistory Ser.). 1975. lib. bdg. 51.00 o.p. (ISBN 0-8240-0708-5). Garland Pub.
Apache Indians: A Study of the Apache Indians, Vol. I. Albert H. Schroeder. (American Indian Ethnohistory Ser: Indians of the Southwest). 1975. lib. bdg. 51.00 o.p. (ISBN 0-8240-0715-8). Garland Pub.
Apache Moon. John Durham. (Lythway Ser.). 208p. 1988. lib. bdg. 17.50x o.p. (ISBN 0-7451-0715-X, Pub. by Chivers Pr UK). G K Hall.
Apaches. Oakley Hall. 544p. 1986. 18.45 o.p. (ISBN 0-671-50643-9). S&S.
Apartheid Book. Roger Omond. 231p. (Orig.). 1986. pap. 4.95 o.p. (ISBN 0-14-052375-8). Penguin.
Apartheid: Proceedings of the International Labour Conference, 64th Session, 1978. International Labour Office Staff. 54p. 8.55 o.p. (ISBN 92-2-101942-X, ILC 64/I/SPECIAL REPORT). Intl Labour Office.
Apartheid's Army in Namibia: South Africa's Illegal Military Occupation. 74p. 1981. 1.35 o.p. (ISBN 0-317-36665-3). Africa Fund.
Apartment Farmer. Duane Newcomb. 1977. pap. 1.75 o.p. (ISBN 0-380-00975-7, 32524). Avon.
Apartments, Townhouses & Condominiums. 3rd ed. Architectural Record Magazine Editors. (Architectural Record Ser.). (Illus.). 224p. 1981. text ed. 51.50 o.p. (ISBN 0-07-002356-5). McGraw.
Apatite: Its Crystal Chemistry, Mineralogy, Utilization, & Biologic Occurrences. D. McConnell. LC 72-88060. (Applied Mineralogy Ser.: Vol. 5). (Illus.). 111p. 1973. 45.00 o.p. (ISBN 0-387-81095-1). Springer-Verlag.
Apeiron of Anaximander. Paul Seligman. LC 72-7510. 181p. 1974. Repr. of 1962 ed. lib. bdg. 22.50x o.p. (ISBN 0-8371-6518-0, SEAP). Greenwood.
Aperture, No. 77. J. Williams et al. 1977. pap. 12.50 o.s.i. (ISBN 0-89381-013-4). Aperture.
Aperture, No. 81. 1978. 12.50 o.p. (ISBN 0-89381-027-4). Aperture.
APHA Drug Names. Ed. by L. Luan Corrigan. Janet Shoff. LC 78-78275. 1979. softcover 18.00 o.p. (ISBN 0-917330-24-2). Am Pharm Assn.
Aphasia. Libby Kumin. LC 77-70099. (Cliffs Speech & Hearing Ser.). (Illus.). 1978. pap. text ed. 3.95 o.p. (ISBN 0-8220-1816-0). Cliffs.
Aphasia Theory & Therapy: Selected Lectures & Papers of Hildred Schuell. 2nd ed. Hildred Schuell. Ed. by Luther F. Sies. LC 82-20228. (Illus.). 344p. 1983. pap. text ed. 14.50 o.p. (ISBN 0-8191-2768-X). U Pr of Amer.
Aphids of the Rocky Mountain Region see **Thomas Say Foundation Publications.**
Aphra Behn. Frederick M. Link. (English Authors Ser.). Repr. lib. bdg. 6.95 o.p. (ISBN 0-686-77207-5). Irvington.
Aphrodite's Cave. N. Richard Nash. 480p. (Orig.). 1982. pap. 3.50 o.p. (ISBN 0-380-55970-6). Avon.
API Guide to Prepaid Legal Services: The Insiders View. 146p. 1984. 45.00 o.s.i. (ISBN 0-317-40250-1, 2-013). Am Prepaid.
APO Annual Report. Incl. 1982. 140p. 1983. pap. 7.50 o.p. (ISBN 92-833-1507-3, APO145, APO). UNIPUB; 1983. 142p. 1985. pap. 7.50 (ISBN 92-833-1508-1, APO162, APO). UNIPUB. UNIPUB.
Apocalypse Brigade. Alfred Coppel. LC 81-47459. 320p. 1981. 12.95 o.p. (ISBN 0-03-059532-0). H Holt & Co.
Apocalypse Delayed: The Story of Jehovah's Witnesses. M. James Penton. 432p. 1985. 29.95 o.p. (ISBN 0-8020-2540-4). U of Toronto Pr.
Apocalypse En Francais Au XIIIE, 2 Vols. Repr. of 1900 ed. Set. 116.00 o.p. (ISBN 0-384-04215-5). Johnson Repr.
Apocalypse: Visions from the Book of Revelations in Western Art. Frederick Van Der Meer. (Illus.). 367p. 1979. 85.00 o.p. (ISBN 0-933516-03-7, Pub. by Alpine Bk Co). Eastview.
Apocalyptic: Ancient & Modern. D. S. Russell. LC 78-54561. 96p. 1978. pap. 4.25 o.p. (ISBN 0-8006-1342-2, 1-1342, Fortress). Augsburg Fortress.
Apocalyptics: Cancer & the Big Lie - How Environmental Politics Controls What We Know About Cancer. Edith Efron. 512p. 1984. 19.45 o.p. (ISBN 0-671-41743-6). S&S.
Apochryphal Birth Stories, 2 Vols. Tr. by I. B. Horner & Padmanabh S. Jaini. (Pali Text Society). 1986. Vol. I, 400 pgs. lib. bdg. 42.50 o.p. (ISBN 0-86013-233-1). Vol. II, 300 pgs. Routledge Chapman & Hall.
Apollo: The Magazine of the Arts: Vols. 1-90, London, 1925-1969. 11502.00 o.p.; pap. 10980.00 o.p. Kraus Repr.
Apollonian Poems. Arthur Freeman. LC 61-9254. (Orig.). 1961. pap. 1.65 o.p. (ISBN 0-689-10091-4, Atheneum). Macmillan.
Apologie de Raimond Sebond. Michel de Montagne. 1967. 4.95 o.p. (ISBN 0-686-54773-X). Schoenhof.
Apologies to the Iroquois: With a Study of the Mohawks in High Street. Edmund Wilson & Joseph Mitchell. 1978. Repr. of 1959 ed. lib. bdg. 19.50x o.p. (ISBN 0-374-98648-7, Octagon). Hippocrene Bks.
Apology for Actors. Thomas Heywood. Bd. with Refutation of the 'Apology for Actors' John Greene. LC 74-170415. (English Stage Ser.: Vol. 12). 1973. lib. bdg. 61.00 o.p. (ISBN 0-8240-0595-3). Garland Pub.
Apology for Wonder. Sam Keen. LC 69-17017. 1969. pap. 6.95i o.p. (ISBN 0-06-064261-0, RD 58). HarpR.
Apostate. Ashley Aasheim. 240p. 1987. pap. 3.50 o.p. (ISBN 1-55547-181-1). Critics Choice Paper.
Apostle. John Pollock. Orig. Title: Man Who Shook the World. 244p. 1972. pap. 7.95 o.p. (ISBN 0-88207-233-1). Victor Bks.
Apostle: A Life of Paul. John Pollock. 312p. 1985. 12.95 o.p. (ISBN 0-89693-368-7). Victor Bks.
Apostle Paul Speaks to Us Today. Rolston Holmes. LC 79-87735. (Bible Speaks to Us Today Ser.). 1979. pap. 4.25 o.p. (ISBN 0-8042-0202-8, John Knox). Westminster John Knox.
Apostle Peter Speaks to Us Today. Holmes Rolston. LC 76-44974. (Bible Speaks to Us Today Ser.). 1977. pap. 3.45 o.p. (ISBN 0-8042-0201-X, John Knox). Westminster John Knox.
Apostles & Prophets: Medicine for Society's Ills. Frederick Eberson. LC 76-42861. 1977. 6.00 o.p. (ISBN 0-682-48694-9, University). Exposition-Phoenix.
Apostles' Creed: In the Light of Today's Questions. Wolfhart Pannenberg. Tr. by M Kohl. LC 72-5767. 186p. 1972. 9.95 o.s.i. (ISBN 0-664-20947-5, Westminster). Westminster John Knox.
Apostles for Our Time: Thoughts on Apostolic Spirituality. Andre Simonet. Tr. by M. Angeline Bouchard from Fr. LC 77-8537. 1977. pap. 4.95 o.p. (ISBN 0-8189-0354-6). Alba.
Apostles of the Self-Made Man. John G. Cawelti. LC 65-25123. 1968. pap. text ed. 4.95x o.s.i. (ISBN 0-226-09865-6, P292, Phoen). U of Chicago Pr.
Apostolic Church in the New Testament. David M. Stanley. LC 65-19453. 500p. 1965. 7.95 o.p. (ISBN 0-8091-0002-9). Paulist Pr.
Apostolic Interpretation of History: A Commentary on Acts 13: 16-41. C. A. Joachim Pillai. 1980. 9.00 o.p. (ISBN 0-682-49404-6, University). Exposition-Phoenix.
Apotheosis & after Life. Eugenia Strong. (Select Bibliographies Reprint Ser.). 1982. Repr. of 1915 ed. lib. bdg. 29.00 o.p. (ISBN 0-8290-0844-6). Irvington.
Appalachian Andy. Mary G. Stallard. 40p. 1987. 6.75 o.p. (ISBN 0-8062-2890-3). Carlton.
Appalachian Mountains. Photos by Clyde Smith. LC 80-65134. (Belding Imprint Ser.). (Illus.). 160p. (Text by Wilma Dykeman & Stokley Dykeman). 1980. 29.50 o.s.i. (ISBN 0-912856-59-9). Gr Arts Ctr Pub.
Appalachian Trail. Photos by Michael Warren. LC 78-75107. (Illus.). 96p. (Text by Sandra Kocher). 1979. 12.95 o.s.i. (ISBN 0-912856-45-9). Gr Arts Ctr Pub.
Appalachian Trail. Photos by Michael Warren. LC 78-75107. (Illus.). 103p. (Text by Sandra Kocher). 1985. pap. 12.95 o.s.i. (ISBN 0-932575-06-4). Gr Arts Ctr Pub.
Appalachian Valley: Case Studies in Cultural Anthropology. George L. Hicks. LC 76-728. 1976. pap. text ed. 9.95 o.p. (ISBN 0-03-077305-9, HoltC). HR&W.
Appalachians. Maurice G. Brooks. (Illus.). 1965. 11.95 o.p. (ISBN 0-395-07458-4). HM.
Apparent & Intrinsic Organization of Laminated Structures in the Brain. Ed. by O. Creutzfeld. (Experimental Brain Research, Suppl. 1). (Illus.). 1977. soft cover 34.30 o.p. (ISBN 0-387-07923-8). Springer-Verlag.
Apparitions. Noel Scanlon. 208p. 1986. pap. 2.95 o.p. (ISBN 0-931773-57-1). Critics Choice Paper.
Apparitions & Survival of Death. Raymond Bayless. 7.95 o.p. (ISBN 0-8216-0202-0, Pub. by Univ Bks). Carol Pub Group.
Apparitions of Our Blessed Mother in Cuapa, Nicaragua. Pablo A. Vega. 1984. pap. 1.00 o.p. (ISBN 0-911988-59-9). Ami Pr.
Appeal of Fascism. Alastair Hamilton. 1973. pap. 2.25 o.p. (ISBN 0-380-01025-9, 16691, Discus). Avon.
Appeal That Was Never Made: The Allies, Scandinavia, & the Finnish Winter War, 1939-1940. Jukka Nevakivi. 1977. lib. bdg. 14.00x o.p. (ISBN 0-7735-0262-9, Pub. by McGill Canada). U of Toronto Pr.
Appeal to the Heart. J. Marlin. LC 85-12386. 138p. (gr. 7 up). 1986. 13.95 o.p. (ISBN 0-448-47769-6, G&D). Putnam Pub Group.
Appeal to the Men of Great Britain on Behalf of Women. Mary Hays. Ed. by Gina Luria. LC 74-8547. (Feminist Controversy in England, 1788-1810 Ser.). 1975. lib. bdg. 61.00 o.p. (ISBN 0-8240-0868-5). Garland Pub.
Appealing Appetizers. Ed. by Annette Gohlke. LC 82-83968. 64p. 1982. pap. 3.95 o.s.i. Reiman Assocs.
Appeals to the Second Circuit: Rules of the 2nd Circuit & Federal Rules of Appellate Procedure. 5th ed. 179p. 1985. 15.00 o.p. (ISBN 0-317-29486-5). Fed Legal Pubn.
Appearing. Penny E. Wheeler. LC 79-16298. (Orion Ser.). 1979. pap. 4.95 o.p. (ISBN 0-8127-0231-X). Review & Herald.
Appeasement: A Study in Political Decline, 1933-34. Alfred L. Rowse. 1963. pap. 2.95x o.p. (ISBN 0-393-00139-3, Norton Lib). Norton.
Appel: Initiation au Francais. Jacqueline Ollivier & Michelle Morran. 538p. 1983. text ed. 24.00 o.p. (ISBN 0-15-502930-4, HC). HarBraceJ.
Appellate Advocacy (2-84) Institute for Continuing Legal Education (New Jersey) Staff & Aaron Dines. LC 84-149485. 1985. incl. cassettes 70.00 o.p. NJ Inst CLE.
Appellate Litigation. Richardson R. Lynn. LC 84-19703. 542p. 1985. 75.00x o.p. (ISBN 0-471-89623-3); pap. 25.00x o.p. (ISBN 0-471-89622-5). Wiley.
Appellate Litigation: A Virginia Law Practice System. Randolph W. Church. 250p. 1982. looseleaf with forms 75.00 o.p. (ISBN 0-87215-510-2). Michie Co.
Appellate Practice in the United States. Robert L. Stern. 568p. 1981. text ed. 49.00 o.p. (ISBN 0-87179-352-0, 0352). BNA.
Appendix with Supplementary Notes. Edmund H. Fellowes. (Tudor Church Music Ser.). 1963. Repr. of 1948 ed. 50.00x o.p. Broude.
Appetizers. Bon Appetit Magazine Editors. LC 82-13083. (Cooking with Bon Appetit Ser.). (Illus.). 144p. 1984. 12.95 o.p. (ISBN 0-89535-105-6). Knapp Pr.
Appians Darstellung Des Zweiten Punischen Krieges. Alfred Klotz. pap. 8.00 o.p. (ISBN 0-384-29880-X). Johnson Repr.
Applause Catalog, 1987. 160p. 1987. pap. 4.00 o.p. (ISBN 0-317-59727-2). Applause Theatre Bk Pubs.
Apple. Mosbysorts. 1984. 250.00 o.p. (ISBN 0-8016-3843-7). Mosby.
Apple a Day. Judith Barrett. LC 73-76315. (Illus.). 32p. (gr. k-3). 1973. 3.95 o.p. (ISBN 0-689-30105-7). Macmillan.
Apple a Day. Tennessee Nurses' Association Staff. Ed. by Shirley Burd & Linda S. White. (Illus.). 272p. 1981. pap. 10.95 o.p. (ISBN 0-939114-32-1). Wimmer Bks.
Apple & Pear. Sue Tarsky. (Look & Say Ser.). (Illus.). 32p. 1983. 1.50 o.s.i. (ISBN 0-671-47656-4, Little Simon). S&S.
Apple & the Arrow. Mary Buff & Conrad Buff. (Illus.). (gr. 3-7). 1974. reinforced bdg. 6.95 o.p. (ISBN 0-395-18591-2). HM.
Apple & the Arrow. Mary Buff & Conrad Buff. (Illus.). 80p. (gr. 3-6). 1974. pap. 1.25 o.p. (ISBN 0-395-19969-7, Sandpiper). HM.
Apple & the Spectroscope. Thomas R. Henn. 1966. pap. 3.95x o.p. (ISBN 0-393-09703-X, NortonC). Norton.
Apple BASIC Made Easy. David A. Gardner & Marianne L. Gardner. (Illus.). 224p. 1984. text ed. 28.00 o.p. (ISBN 0-13-038928-5); pap. 20.95 o.p. (ISBN 0-13-038910-2). P-H.
Apple BASIC Manual. Lynne Mass & Thomas M. Kemnitz. LC 85-394. (Kids Working with Computers Ser.). (Illus.). 48p. (gr. 2 up). 1985. lib. bdg. 11.27 o.p. (ISBN 0-516-08422-4). Childrens.
Apple Bloom. Marjorie Lawrence. LC 85-91073. 80p. (YA) (gr. 7 up). 1986. 10.00 o.p. (ISBN 0-682-40289-3). Exposition-Phoenix.
Apple Connection. James W. Coffron. LC 82-50620. (Illus.). 263p. 1982. pap. 15.95 o.p. (ISBN 0-89588-085-7, C405). SYBEX.
Apple Country Interurban. Kenneth G. Johnsen. LC 79-15270. (Illus.). 130p. 1979. 11.00 o.p. (ISBN 0-87095-074-6). Gldn West Bks.
Apple CP-M Book. Murray Arnow. LC 85-2393. 164p. 1985. pap. 5.95 o.p. (ISBN 0-673-18068-9). Scott F.
Apple Crunch. Frederic V. Huber. 1982. pap. 2.95 o.p. (ISBN 0-380-60699-2). Avon.
Apple Dining & Entertainment Club. Louis Cimino. Ed. by Marc Dozier & Michael Ryan. 116p. (Orig.). Date not set. pap. 9.95 o.p. (ISBN 0-943711-00-2). Apple Dining.
Apple for the Doctor. Mary Essex, pseud. 1985. 13.50 o.p. (ISBN 0-317-53046-1, Large Print Bks). G K Hall.
Apple for the Teacher: Fundamentals of Instructional Computing. George Culp & Herbert Nickles. 225p. 1983. pap. write for info. o.p. Brooks-Cole.
Apple Graphics & Sound Book. Jonathan Erickson & William D. Cramer. 256p. (Orig.). 1985. pap. text ed. 15.95 o.p. (ISBN 0-07-881167-8, 167-3). Osborne McGraw.
Apple II Applications. Marvin L. De Jong. LC 83-61064. 240p. 1983. pap. text ed. 13.95 o.p. (ISBN 0-672-22035-0, 22035). Sams.
Apple II Assembly Language. Marvin L. De Jong. LC 82-50015. 336p. 1982. pap. 15.95 o.p. (ISBN 0-672-21894-1). Sams.
Apple II for Kids from Eight to Eighty. Zabinski & Mazzola. LC 83-51232. 160p. 1984. pap. 10.95 o.p. (ISBN 0-672-22297-3). Sams.
Apple II Interfacing. Jonathan S. Titus et al. LC 81-84282. 208p. 1981. pap. 11.95 o.p. (ISBN 0-672-21862-3, 21862). Sams.
Apple II Micro TSP. 1983. pap. text ed. 19.95 o.p. (ISBN 0-07-025667-5). McGraw.
Apple IIc: A Practical Guide. Thomas Blackadar. LC 84-51440. 197p. 1984. pap. 12.95 o.p. (ISBN 0-89588-241-8). SYBEX.
Apple IIc User's Handbook. Weber Systems, Inc. Staff. 320p. 1985. pap. 14.95 o.p. (ISBN 0-345-32001-8). Ballantine.
Apple IIe Personal Computer for Beginners. Seamus Dunn & Valerie Morgan. 260p. 1984. pap. 24.95 o.p. (ISBN 0-13-038969-2). P-H.
Apple IIe Programmer's Reference Guide. David L. Heiserman. LC 84-50059. 368p. 1984. pap. 21.95 o.p. (ISBN 0-672-22299-X). Sams.
Apple Island. Gladys Fullbrook. 1985. 12.50 o.p. (ISBN 0-317-53049-6, Large Print Bks). G K Hall.
Apple LOGO Manual. Lynne Mass & Thomas M. Kemnitz. LC 85-408. (Kids working with Computers Ser.). (Illus.). 48p. (gr. 2 up). 1985. lib. bdg. 11.27 o.p. (ISBN 0-516-08423-2). Childrens.
Apple LOGO Programming Primer. Martin & Donald Martin. LC 84-50735. 454p. 1984. pap. 19.95 o.p. (ISBN 0-672-22342-2). Sams.
Apple Macintosh Book. 2nd ed. Cary Lu. 448p. 1985. pap. 19.95 o.p. (ISBN 0-914845-66-7). Microsoft.
Apple Macintosh User's Handbook. Weber Systems, Inc. Staff. 304p. (Orig.). 1984. pap. 9.95 o.p. (ISBN 0-345-31840-4). Ballantine.
Apple Pascal Games. Douglas Hergert & Joseph T. Kalash. LC 81-16577. (Illus.). 371p. 1981. pap. 15.95 o.p. (ISBN 0-89588-074-1, P360). SYBEX.
Apple Pie Adventure of an Apple Pie. 3.00 o.p. (ISBN 0-486-22413-9); pap. 1.75 o.p. (ISBN 0-486-21722-1). Dover.
Apple Registered Computer Directory: Hardware, Software & Peripherals. Kelly-Grimes Corporation Staff. LC 84-17427. (Kelly-Grimes Buyers Guide Ser.: 1-702). 469p. 1985. pap. 26.95 o.p. (ISBN 0-471-87818-9, Pub. by Wiley Pr). Wiley.
Apple Sliced: Studies of New York City. Ed. by Vernon Boggs et al. 368p. 1984. text ed. 34.95 o.p. (ISBN 0-03-063213-7); pap. 16.95 o.p. (ISBN 0-89789-016-7). Bergin & Garvey.
Apple Soft Subroutine Cookbook. David D. Busch. (Illus.). 208p. 1985. pap. 12.95 o.p. (ISBN 0-89303-322-7). Brady Bks.
Apple Software: Rating the Best. Consumer Guide Editors & Roe R. Adams, III. LC 83-73275. 154p. 1984. spiral bdg. 1.00 o.p. (ISBN 0-517-42475-4). Outlet Bk Co.
Apple Tree, Lean Down. Mary E. Pearce. 1983. pap. 4.50 o.s.i. (ISBN 0-345-30460-8). Ballantine.
Apple Trees at Olema. Robert Hass. 190p. 1989. 15.95 o.p. Ecco Pr.

Apple Writer Tutor: A Step-by-Step Tutorial on Apple Writer IIe-II-III. Barry Leshowitz. 276p. 1985. pap. 9.95 spiralbound o.p. (ISBN 0-673-18012-3). Scott F.

Apple's Europe: An Uncommon Guidebook. R. W. Apple, Jr. LC 85-48292. (Illus.). 450p. 1986. 14.95 o.p. (ISBN 0-689-11607-1, Atheneum). Macmillan.

Apples of Gold. June Hornsby & Jean Evans. LC 84-61281. 128p. (Orig.). 1984. pap. 6.95 o.p. (ISBN 0-89051-106-3). Master Bks.

Apples on a Stick. Barbara Michels & Bettye White. (Illus.). (gr. 3-6). 1983. 10.95 o.p. (ISBN 0-698-20567-7, Coward). Putnam Pub Group.

Apples: Uses for the Apple. Recycling Consortium Staff. 14p. 1984. pap. text ed. 1.95 o.p. (Pub. by Recycling Consort). Prosperity & Profits.

Applesoft BASIC: From the Ground Up. H. Mullish & D. Kruger. (Illus.). 240p. 1984. pap. text ed. 10.95 o.p. (ISBN 0-07-044034-4, BYTE Bks). McGraw.

Applesoft BASIC Primer for the Apple II Plus, IIe, & IIc. Jo Lynne Jones & Howard Greenfield. LC 84-19937. (Computers in Education Ser.). 74p. 1985. pap. 9.95 o.p. (ISBN 0-88175-047-6, Computer Sci Pr); diskette 20.00 o.p. (ISBN 0-88175-048-4). W H Freeman.

Applesoft for the Apple IIe. George Blackwood & Brian Blackwood. LC 83-50833. 304p. 1983. pap. 19.95 o.p. (ISBN 0-672-22259-0). Sams.

Applesoft Language. 2nd ed. Brian D. Blackwood & George H. Blackwood. LC 83-60172. 288p. 1983. pap. 14.95 o.p. (ISBN 0-672-22073-3). Sams.

AppleWorks: Boosting Your Business with Integrated Software. Charles Rubin. LC 85-10576. (Illus.). 320p. (Orig.). 1985. pap. 16.95 o.p. (ISBN 0-914845-47-0). Microsoft.

AppleWorks for Educators: A Beginners Workbook. Linda Rathje. 214p. 1986. 18.00 o.p. (ISBN 0-924667-30-3). Intl Council Comp.

AppleWorks: Tips & Techniques. Robert Ericson. LC 85-62543. 373p. (Orig.). 1985. pap. 18.95 o.p. (ISBN 0-89588-303-1). Sybex.

Appleworks User's Handbook. Richard Rose. LC 85-13729. 200p. 1985. pap. 15.95 o.p. (ISBN 0-938862-09-X). Weber Systems.

Appley Dapply's Nursery Rhymes. Beatrix Potter. (Illus.). (ps-2). 1917. 4.95 o.p. (ISBN 0-7232-0613-9). Warne.

Appliance Service Handbook. George Meyerink. (Illus.). 464p. 1973. text ed. 40.00x ref. ed. o.p. (ISBN 0-13-038844-0). P-H.

Applicable Finite Mathematics. David S. Moore & James W. Yackel. 432p. 1974. text ed. 24.95 o.p. (ISBN 0-395-17771-5). HM.

Applicable Mathematics of Non-Physical Phenomena. Ed. by F. Oliveira-Pinto & B. W. Connolly. LC 81-20140. (Ellis Horwood Series in Mathematics and its Applications). 269p. 1982. 68.95x o.p. (ISBN 0-470-27297-X). Halsted Pr.

Application Design Handbook for Distributed Systems: For Distributed Systems. Robert L. Patrick. LC 79-27205. (Illus.). 285p. 1983. 29.95 o.p. (ISBN 0-8436-1601-6). Van Nos Reinhold.

Application Junction. 1984. 19.95 o.p. (ISBN 0-912677-09-0). Tate Pub.

Application Modules, Vol. I. Center for Occupational Research & Development Staff. (Unified Technical Concepts Ser.). (Illus.). 653p. 1983. pap. text ed. 18.00 o.p. (ISBN 1-55502-162-X). Ctr Res & Dev.

Application of Behaviour Modification. Ed. by Travis Thompson & William S. Dockens. 1975. 82.00 o.p. (ISBN 0-12-689550-3). Acad Pr.

Application of Biological Markers to Carcinogen Testing. Ed. by Harry A. Milman & Stewart Sell. LC 83-19097. (Environmental Science Research: Vol. 29). 528p. 1983. 85.00x o.p. (ISBN 0-306-41490-2, Plenum Pr). Plenum Pub.

Application of Computers & Operations Research in the Mineral Industry: 17th International Symposium. Ed. by T. B. Johnson & R. J. Barnes. LC 82-70016. (Illus.). 806p. 1982. text ed. 35.00x o.p. (ISBN 0-89520-293-X). SMM&E Inc.

Application of Computers & Operations Research in the Mineral Industry (APCOM), 19th International Symposium. Ed. by R. V. Ramani. (APCOM Ser.). (Illus.). 912p. 1986. 63.50x o.p. (ISBN 0-87335-058-8, 058-8). SMM&E Inc.

Application of Economic Analysis to Transportation Problems: Six Reports. (Transportation Research Record Ser.). 67p. 1975. 3.20 o.p. (ISBN 0-309-02456-0). Transport Res Bd.

Application of Finite Difference Equations to Shell Analysis. M. Soare. 1968. 110.00 o.p. (ISBN 0-08-010214-X). Pergamon.

Application of GPSS Five to Discrete System Simulation. Geoffrey Gordon. (Illus.). 336p. 1975. text ed. 50.00 o.p. (ISBN 0-13-039057-7). P-H.

Application of Interactive Graphics in Citizen Participation: Five Reports. (Transportation Research Record Ser.). 49p. 1975. 2.40 o.p. (ISBN 0-309-02457-9). Transport Res Bd.

Application of Invariant Imbedding to Reactor Physics. Akinao Shimizu & Katsutada Aoki. (Nuclear Science & Technology Ser). 1972. 60.50 o.p. (ISBN 0-12-640150-0). Acad Pr.

Application of Measurement to Health & Physical Education. 5th ed. H. Harrison Clarke. (Illus.). 464p. 1976. pap. text ed. (ISBN 0-13-039024-0). P-H.

Application of Meteoro Logy to Safety at Nuclear Plants. (Safety Ser.: No. 29). (Illus.). 29p. (Fr. & Eng.). 1969. pap. 6.25 o.p. (ISBN 92-0-223169-9, IAEA). UNIPUB.

Application of Nuclear Techniques in Geothermal Investigations. Ed. by E. Barbier. 192p. 1983. pap. 61.00 o.p. (ISBN 0-08-030269-6, 2304, 1506, 1901). Pergamon.

Application of Nuclear Techniques to Geothermal Studies: Proceedings. Ed. by E. Barbier. 1978. pap. 94.00 o.p. (ISBN 0-08-021670-6). Pergamon.

Application of Nuclear Techniques to the Study of Amorphous Metals: Supplement No. 1. (Atomic Energy Review Ser.). 294p. 1981. pap. 23.25 o.p. (ISBN 0-686-78893-1, IAERS1/81, IAEA). UNIPUB.

Application of On-Line Analytical Instrumentation to Process Control. Robert M. Arthur. LC 82-70694. 222p. 1982. 42.95 o.p. (ISBN 0-250-40539-3). Butterworth.

Application of Optical Instrumentation in Medicine I: Proceedings. Society of Photo-Optical Instrumentation Engineers, Staff. 258p. 1972. 10.00 o.p. (ISBN 0-89252-046-9). SPIE.

Application of Optical Instrumentation: Proceedings, Vol. 47. Society of Photo-Optical Instrumentation Engineers Staff. 1975. 15.00 o.p. (ISBN 0-89252-059-0). SPIE.

Application of Systems Analysis Irrigation, Drainage & Flood Control: A Manual for Engineers & Water Technologists. Ed. by International Commission on Irrigation & Drainage, New Delhi, India. (Water Development, Supply & Management Ser.: Vol. 11). (Illus.). 1980. 60.00 o.p. (ISBN 0-08-023425-9); pap. 60.00 o.p. (ISBN 0-08-023431-3). Pergamon.

Application of the Geometrical Theory of Diffraction to Terrestrial LF Radio Wave Propagation. R. M. Jones. (Mitteilungen Aus Dem Max-Planck-Institut Fuer Aeronomie: No. 37). (Illus.). 1968. pap. 5.90 o.p. (ISBN 0-387-04272-5). Springer-Verlag.

Application of Videotape to the Teaching of Reading: Implications for Global Education. Richard Kritzer. 1976. 4.00 o.p. (ISBN 0-682-48530-6, University). Exposition-Phoenix.

Application Prototyping: A Project Management Perspective. Bernard H. Boar. (AMA Management Briefings Ser.). 1985. 10.00 o.p. (ISBN 0-8144-2312-4). AMACOM.

Applications & Research in Information Systems & Sciences: Proceedings of the International Conference, 1st, Patras, Greece, August 1976, 3 vols. new ed. International Conference on Information Sciences & Systems Staff. Ed. by Demetrios G. Lainiotis & Nicolaos Tzannes. LC 77-15000. (Illus.). 920p. 1977. Set. pap. text ed. 168.00 o.p. (ISBN 0-89116-160-0). Hemisphere Pub.

Applications & Theory of Petri Nets. Ed. by A. Pagnoni & G. Rozenberg. (Informatik-Fachberichte: vol. 66). 315p. 1983. pap. 16.10 o.p. (ISBN 0-387-12309-1). Springer-Verlag.

Applications in Bayesian Decision Processes. Ed. by Samuel R. Honston et al. 79p. 1975. pap. text ed. 4.75x o.p. (ISBN 0-8422-0484-9). Irvington.

Applications in Word & Information Processing. Alan R. Neibauer. LC 84-17533. 352p. 1984. pap. text ed. 23.95 o.p. (ISBN 0-8273-2400-6); instr's. guide 12.00 o.p. (ISBN 0-8273-2401-4). Delmar.

Applications of Algebraictopology, Graphs & Networks: The Picard-Lefschetz Theory & Feynman Integrals. S. Lefschetz. LC 75-6924. (Applied Mathematical Sciences Ser.: Vol. 16). (Illus.). 200p. 1975. pap. 27.00 o.p. (ISBN 0-387-90137-X). Springer-Verlag.

Applications of Ambient Energy in Buildings. Ed. by A. F. Sherratt. 200p. 1984. 55.00x o.p. (ISBN 0-419-12790-9, NO. 6809). Routledge Chapman & Hall.

Applications of Chemical Analysis: Lab Manual. Robert D. Braun & Fred H. Walters. 384p. 1982. text ed. 21.95 o.p. (ISBN 0-07-007282-5). McGraw.

Applications of College Mathematics: Management, Life, & Social Sciences. Donald L. Stancl & Mildred L. Stancl. 736p. 29.00 o.p. (ISBN 0-669-03860-1); instr's. guide 2.00 o.p. (ISBN 0-669-03861-X); computer problem solving 7.00 o.p. (ISBN 0-669-03881-4). Heath.

Applications of Computers Laboratory Manual. Michael A. Soderstrand. 48p. 1982. 5.95 o.p. (ISBN 0-8403-2663-7). Kendall-Hunt.

Applications of Conditioning Theory. Ed. by Graham Davey. (Psychology in Progress Ser.). 1981. 25.00x o.p. (ISBN 0-416-73560-6, NO.3459); pap. 11.50x o.p. (ISBN 0-416-73570-3, 3458). Routledge Chapman & Hall.

Applications of Electronics. 2nd ed. Bernard Grob & Milton S. Kiver. 1966. text ed. 39.95 o.p. (ISBN 0-07-024930-X). McGraw.

Applications of Energy: Nineteenth Century. Ed. by B. R. Lindsay. (Benchmark Papers in Energy: Vol. 2). 1976. 78.50 o.p. (ISBN 0-12-786961-1). Acad Pr.

Applications of GaAs MESFETs. Robert Soares et al. LC 83-71124. (Illus.). 554p. 1983. 72.00 o.p. (ISBN 0-89006-120-3). Artech Hse.

Applications of Holography & Optical Data Processing: Proceedings of an International Conference, Jerusalem, 1976. Ed. by E. Marom et al. 1977. 180.00 o.p. (ISBN 0-08-021625-0). Pergamon.

Applications of Integral Transforms in the Theory of Elasticity. I. N. Sneddon. (International Center for Mechanical Sciences: Vol. 220). (Illus.). 1978. pap. 44.90 o.p. (ISBN 0-387-81342-X). Springer-Verlag.

Applications of Ion Beams to Metals. Ed. by S. T. Picraux et al. LC 74-4395. 706p. 1974. 105.00x o.p. (ISBN 0-306-30781-2, Plenum Pr). Plenum Pub.

Applications of Lasers in Materials Processing. Ed. by Edward A. Metzbower. 1979. 36.00 o.p. (ISBN 0-87170-084-0). ASM.

Applications of Liquid Crystals. G. Meier et al. (Illus.). 160p. 1975. pap. 33.10 o.p. (ISBN 0-387-07302-7). Springer-Verlag.

Applications of Methods of Functional Analysis to Problems in Mechanics. Ed. by P. Germain & B. Nayroles. LC 76-5454. (Lecture Notes in Mathematics Ser: Vol. 503). 1976. pap. 27.00 o.p. (ISBN 0-387-07629-8). Springer-Verlag.

Applications of Minicomputers to Library & Related Problems. Clinic on Library Applications of Data Processing Proceedings, 1974. Ed. by F. W. Lancaster. LC 65-1841. 195p. 1974. 7.00x o.p. (ISBN 0-87845-041-6). U of Ill Lib Info Sci.

Applications of Nonlinear Programming to Optimization & Control: Proceedings of the IFAC Symposium, 4th, San Francisco, California, June, 1983. IFAC Symposium Staff & H. E. Rauch. LC 83-21936. (IFAC Proceedings). 230p. 1983. 55.00 o.p. (ISBN 0-08-030574-1). Pergamon.

Applications of Nuclear Magnetic Resonance Spectroscopy in Organic Chemistry. 2nd ed. L. M. Jackman & S. Sternhell. 1978. 120.00 o.p. (ISBN 0-08-012542-5); pap. 120.00 o.p. (ISBN 0-08-022953-0). Pergamon.

Applications of Number Theory to Numerical Analysis: Proceedings of the Centre for Research in Mathematics, University of Montreal Symposium, Sept. 1971. Centre for Research in Mathematics, University of Montreal Symposium Staff. Ed. by S. K. Zaremba. 1972. 71.00 o.p. (ISBN 0-12-775950-6). Acad Pr.

Applications of Numerical Heat Transfer. Nogotov. 142p. 1978. 51.50 o.p. (ISBN 0-89116-500-2). Hemisphere Pub.

Applications of Numerical Methods to Forming Processes: AMD, Vol. 28. Ed. by Harry Armen. R. F. Jones, Jr. 208p. 1978. 30.00 o.p. (ISBN 0-685-66790-1, H00111). ASME.

Applications of Numerical Methods to Heat Transfer. E. F. Nogotov. (Illus.). 1978. text ed. 52.00 o.p. (ISBN 0-07-046852-4). McGraw.

Applications of Space Developments II: Selected Papers of the International Astronautical Congress, Tokyo, Japan, September 22-27, 1980. International Astronautical Congress Staff & L. G. Napolitano. 310p. 1981. pap. 77.00 o.p. (ISBN 0-08-028676-3). Pergamon.

Applications of the Electromagnetic Reciprocity Principle. C. D. Monteath. 1973. 40.00 o.p. (ISBN 0-08-016895-7). Pergamon.

Applied Abstract Analysis. Jean-Pierre Aubin. LC 77-2382. (Pure & Applied Mathematics Ser.). 263p. 1977. 47.50x o.p. (ISBN 0-471-02146-6, Pub. by Wiley-Interscience). Wiley.

Applied Algebra for the Computer Sciences. Arthur Gill. (Illus.). 416p. 1976. text ed. 58.00 o.p. (ISBN 0-13-039222-7). P-H.

Applied Analysis for Physicists & Engineers. B. J. Rice & Jerry D. Strange. 1972. write for info. o.p. (ISBN 0-87150-137-6, PWS 1051, Prindle). PWS-Kent Pub.

Applied Anthropology: A Practical Guide. Erve Chambers. 300p. 1985. pap. text ed. 31.00 o.p. (ISBN 0-13-039371-1). P-H.

Applied Atomic Energy. Fearnside et al. (Illus.). 164p. 1954. (ISBN 0-8022-0478-3). Philos Lib.

Applied Atomic Spectroscopy, 2 vols. Ed. by E. L. Grove. Incl. Vol. 1. 332p. 59.50x (ISBN 0-306-33905-6); Vol. 2. 364p. 59.50x (ISBN 0-306-33906-4). LC 77-17444. (Modern Analytical Chemistry Ser.). (Illus.). 1978. 95.00x set o.p. (Plenum Pr). Plenum Pub.

Applied Automata Theory. Ed. by Julius T. Tou. LC 68-26634. (Electrical Science Ser.). 1969. 88.00 o.p. (ISBN 0-12-696230-8). Acad Pr.

Applied Business Communication. Robert C. Cornwell & Darwin W. Manship. 300p. 1978. text ed. write for info. o.p. (ISBN 0-697-08025-0). Wm C Brown.

Applied Consumption Analysis. 2nd, rev. & enl. ed. L. Phlips. (Advanced Textbooks in Economics: Vol. 5). 324p. 1983. 45.00 o.p. (ISBN 0-444-86531-4, North-Holland); pap. 30.00 o.p. (ISBN 0-444-86657-4). Elsevier.

Applied Contemporary Chemistry. 2nd ed. John A. Markisz & Martin P. Levine. (Illus.). 1979. lab manual 10.95 o.p. (ISBN 0-89529-020-0). Avery Pub.

Applied Control Theory. J. R. Leigh. (IEE Control Engineering Ser.: No. 18). 220p. 1987. casebound 68.00 o.p. (ISBN 0-906048-72-9, CE018). Inst Elect Eng.

Applied Cross-Cultural Psychology: Proceedings of the 2nd Conference, Kingston, Ont., August 6-10, 1974. International Conference of Selected Papers Staff. Ed. by J. W. Berry & W. Lonner. 340p. (Orig.). 1975. pap. text ed. 21.00 o.p. (ISBN 0-686-27809-7, Pub. by Swets & Zeitlinger Netherlands). CJ Hogrefe Pubs.

Applied Digital Control: Theory, Design & Implementation. J. R. Leigh. (Illus.). 448p. 1985. pap. text ed. 45.00 o.p. (ISBN 0-13-040189-7). P-H.

Applied Dynamic Programming. Richard E. Bellman & S. Dreyfus. (Rand Corporation Research Studies). 1962. 45.00x o.p. (ISBN 0-691-07913-7). Princeton U Pr.

Applied Econometrics. Megnad Desai. (Illus.). 1976. text ed. 27.50 o.p. (ISBN 0-07-016541-6). McGraw.

Applied Electrical Systems for Construction. Robert K. Clidero & Kenneth H. Sharpe. 1982. 32.95 o.s.i. (ISBN 0-442-21660-2). Van Nos Reinhold.

Applied Electronics. Carl Weick. 1976. text ed. 43.95 o.p. (ISBN 0-07-069012-X). McGraw.

Applied Electronics for Veterinary Medicine & Animal Physiology. W. R. Klemm. (Illus.). 484p. 1976. 60.00x o.p. (ISBN 0-398-03477-X). C C Thomas.

Applied Engineering Statistics for Practicing Engineers. Lawrence Mann, Jr. LC 76-129578. 184p. 1983. pap. 14.95 o.p. (ISBN 0-8436-0317-8). Van Nos Reinhold.

Applied Finite Element Analysis: An Apple II Implementation. R. D. Cooke. 448p. 1986. pap. (ISBN 0-471-82337-6). Wiley.

Applied Finite Mathematics. Dalton Hunkins & Larry Mugridge. LC 80-29563. 538p. 1981. 21.00 o.p. (ISBN 0-87150-306-9, Prindle). PWS-Kent Pub.

Applied Finite Mathematics with Calculus. Howard Anton & Bernard Kolman. 760p. 1978. 17.75 o.p. (ISBN 0-12-059560-5); SBP 24.00 o.p. Acad Pr.

Applied Foodservice Sanitation. 3rd ed. National Institute for Food Service Industry Staff. LC 85-70715. 320p. 1985. text ed. 18.95 o.p. (ISBN 0-697-00315-9). Wm C Brown.

Applied Forecasting Methods. N. Thomopoulos. 1980. text ed. 51.00 o.p. (ISBN 0-13-040139-0). P-H.

Applied Functional Analysis. Jean-Pierre Aubin. LC 78-20896. (Pure & Applied Mathematics Ser.). 423p. 1979. 48.50x o.p. (ISBN 0-471-02149-0, Pub. by Wiley-Interscience). Wiley.

Applied Gamma-Ray Spectrometry. 2nd rev. ed. F. Adams & R. Dams. LC 79-114847. 1970. 190.00 o.p. (ISBN 0-08-006888-X). Pergamon.

Applied Geochronology. E. I. Hamilton. 1965. 46.00 o.p. (ISBN 0-12-321450-5). Acad Pr.

Applied Group Theory. A. P. Cracknell. 1968. 105.00 o.p. (ISBN 0-08-013328-2); pap. 105.00 o.p. (ISBN 0-08-012286-8). Pergamon.

Applied Headspace Gas Chromatography. B. Kolb. 224p. 1980. 63.95 o.p. (ISBN 0-471-25838-5, Pub. by Wiley Heyden). Wiley.

Applied Historical Studies. Ed. by Michael Drake. 1973. pap. 9.50x o.p. (ISBN 0-416-79110-7, NO.2171). Routledge Chapman & Hall.

Applied Human Relations: An Organizational Approach. 2nd ed. Jack Halloran. (Illus.). 496p. 1983. pap. text ed. (ISBN 0-13-040808-5); Study guide. pap. text ed. (ISBN 0-13-040790-9). P-H.

Applied Kinesiology. 2nd ed. Clayne R. Jensen & Gordon W. Schultz. (Health Ed., Phys. Ed., & Recreation Ser.). (Illus.). 1976. text ed. 32.95 o.p. (ISBN 0-07-032463-8, C). McGraw.

Applied Leica Technique. Gunter Osterloh. Tr. by Rolf Fricke from Ger. (Illus.). 300p. 1986. 29.95 o.p. (ISBN 3-524-68014-3). Seven Hills Bk Dists.

Applied Linear Algebra. 2nd ed. Ben Noble & James W. Daniel. (Illus.). 1977. text ed. (ISBN 0-13-041343-7). P-H.

Applied Linear Regression Analysis. John Neter & William Wasserman. 1983. 36.95x o.p. (ISBN 0-256-02547-9). Irwin.

Applied Market & Social Research. Bradley. 1980. pap. 23.95 o.p. (ISBN 0-442-30438-2). Van Nos Reinhold.

Applied Market & Social Research. Ute Bradley. 1982. 45.95 o.s.i. (ISBN 0-442-30437-4). Van Nos Reinhold.

Applied Marketing. Donald Sciglimpaglia. 216p. 1984. pap. text ed. (ISBN 0-471-88025-6). Wiley.

Applied Marketing Research. Donald Sciglimpaglia & William G. Zikmund. 240p. 1982. pap. text ed. 15.95x o.s.i. (ISBN 0-03-057634-2); instr's manual 20.00 o.s.i. (ISBN 0-03-061817-7). Dryden Pr.

Applied Math: I. Resource Systems International Staff. 1982. pap. text ed. 15.00 o.p. (ISBN 0-8359-0140-8, Reston). P-H.

Applied Math: II. Resource Systems International Staff. 1982. pap. text ed. 15.00 o.p. (ISBN 0-8359-0141-6, Reston). P-H.

Applied Math: III. Resource Systems International Staff. 1982. pap. text ed. 15.00 o.p. (ISBN 0-8359-0142-4, Reston). P-H.

Applied Math: IV. Resource Systems International Staff. 1982. pap. text ed. 15.00 o.p. (ISBN 0-8359-0143-2, Reston). P-H.

Applied Math: V. Resource Systems International Staff. 1982. pap. text ed. 15.00 o.p. (ISBN 0-8359-0144-0, Reston). P-H.

Applied Mathematical Analysis. Stanley I. Grossman. 677p. 1986. text ed. (ISBN 0-534-05766-7). Wadsworth Pub.

Applied Mathematics: For Business, Economics & the Social Sciences. Ann J. Hughes. 1983. text ed. 34.95x o.p. (ISBN 0-256-02829-X); pap. text ed. 11.50x student wkbk. o.p. (ISBN 0-256-03086-3). Irwin.

Applied Mathematics for the Management, Life, & Social Sciences. Stanley I. Grossman. 778p. 1985. text ed. (ISBN 0-534-04239-2). Wadsworth Pub.

Applied Mechanics. 2nd ed. D. Titherington & J. G. Rimmer. 192p. 1982. text ed. 9.00 o.p. (ISBN 0-07-084659-6). McGraw.

Applied Mechanics of Materials. Joseph E. Shigley. (Illus.). 1975. text ed. 42.00 o.p. (ISBN 0-07-056845-6). McGraw.

Applied Methods in the Theory of Nonlinear Oscillations. V. M. Starzhinskii. 1980. 8.95 o.p. (ISBN 0-8285-1802-5, Pub. by Mir Pubs USSR). Imported Pubns.

Applied Metric Math. Resource Systems International Staff. 1982. pap. text ed. 15.00 o.p. (ISBN 0-8359-0139-4, Reston). P-H.

Applied Mining Geology. Ed. by A. J. Erickson, Jr. LC 84-81473. (Illus.). 222p. 1984. pap. 35.00 o.p. (ISBN 0-89520-431-2, 431-2). SMM&E Inc.

Applied Mining Geology: Ore Reserve Estimation, No. 3. Ed. by Donald E. Ranta. LC 86-61399. (Illus.). 202p. (Orig.). 1986. pap. 43.50x o.p. (ISBN 0-87335-060-X). SMM&E Inc.

Applied Modern Algebra. Larry L. Dornhoff & Franz E. Hohn. (Illus.). 1978. write for info. o.p. (ISBN 0-02-329980-0). Macmillan.

Applied Multivariate Statistical Analysis. Richard A. Johnson & Dean W. Wichern. 750p. 1982. pap. text ed. (ISBN 0-13-041400-X). P-H.

Applied Nomography, Vol. 2. Javier F. Kuong. LC 65-18920. 116p. 1968. 25.00x o.p. (ISBN 0-87201-586-6). Gulf Pub.

Applied Nomography, Vol. 3. Javier Kuong. LC 65-18920. 126p. 1969. 25.00x o.p. (ISBN 0-87201-587-4). Gulf Pub.

Applied Nonparametric Statistics. Wayne W. Daniel. LC 77-74515. (Illus.). 1978. text ed. 35.50 o.p. (ISBN 0-395-25795-6). HM.

Applied Numerical Analysis. Melvin J. Maron. 1982. text ed. write for info. o.p. (ISBN 0-02-475670-9). Macmillan.

Applied Numerical Modeling: Proceedings of the First International Conference, Held at the University of Southampton, 11-15 July, 1977. Ed. by C. A. Brebbia. LC 77-11141. 713p. 1978. 73.95x o.p. (ISBN 0-470-99271-9). Wiley.

Applied Oceanography. Joseph M. Bishop. LC 83-26091. (Ocean Engineering: A Wiley Ser.). 252p. 1984. 32.95x o.p. (ISBN 0-471-87445-0, Pub. by Wiley-Interscience). Wiley.

Applied Optimal Design: Mechanical & Structural Systems. Edward J. Haug & Jasbir S. Arora. LC 79-11437. 506p. 1979. 59.95x o.p. (ISBN 0-471-04170-X, Pub. by Wiley-Interscience). Wiley.

Applied Pharmacology for the Dental Hygienist. Barbara Requa & Sam V. Holroyd. LC 81-14168. (Illus.). 348p. 1981. pap. 25.50 o.p. (ISBN 0-8016-2239-5). Mosby.

Applied Physics. 2nd ed. Paul E. Tippens. (Illus.). 1978. text ed. 31.00 o.p. (ISBN 0-07-064961-8). McGraw.

Applied Physics see Physics Programs.

Applied Physiology of the Mouth. LaVelle. 368p. 1975. 27.00 o.p. (ISBN 0-7236-0362-6, Pub. by John Wright UK). Butterworth.

Applied Price Theory. Cotton M. Lindsay. 634p. 1984. text ed. 33.95 o.s.i. (ISBN 0-03-056129-9); instr.'s manual 19.95 o.s.i. (ISBN 0-03-056131-0). Dryden Pr.

Applied Psychology: Adjustments in Living & Work. 2nd ed. B. V. Gilmer. (Illus.). 464p. 1975. text ed. 33.95 o.p. (ISBN 0-07-023210-5). McGraw.

Applied Radionuclide Metrology: Proceedings of the International Committee for Radionuclide Metrology Seminar, Geel, Belgium, 16-17 May 1983. Ed. by G. C. Mann et al. (International Journal of Applied Radiation & Isotopes Ser.: Vol. 34, No. 8). 286p. 1984. pap. 28.00 o.p. (ISBN 0-08-030271-8). Pergamon.

Applied Research in Aging: A Guide to Methods & Research. Charles S. Harris et al. (Gerontology Ser.). 1983. text ed. 14.95 o.p. (ISBN 0-316-79282-9); pap. text ed. 8.95 o.p. (ISBN 0-316-79283-7). Scott F.

Applied Research in Education. Ed. by E. Wayne Courtney. (Quality Paperback Ser.: No. 92). (Orig.). 1965. pap. 3.50 o.p. (ISBN 0-8226-0092-7). Littlefield.

Applied Science in the Casting of Metals. K. Strauss. 1970. 135.00 o.p. (ISBN 0-08-015711-4). Pergamon.

Applied Sciences Research & Utilization of Lunar Resources. F. J. Malina. 1970. 70.00 o.p. (ISBN 0-08-015565-0). Pergamon.

Applied Statistical Decision Theory. Howard Raiffa & Robert Schlaifer. LC 60-11282. 1961. 15.95x o.p. (ISBN 0-87584-017-5, Dist. by Harper & Row Pubs., Inc.). Harvard Busn.

Applied Statistics & Analytic Techniques for Public Administrators. Meier & Brudney. 1981. write for info. o.p. (ISBN 0-686-77661-5, Duxbury Pr). PWS-Kent Pub.

Applied Statistics for Engineers. C. Wilson. (Illus.). 148p. 1972. 28.00 o.p. (ISBN 0-85334-529-5, Pub. by Elsevier Applied Sci England). Elsevier.

Applied Stream Sanitation. 2nd ed. Clarence J. Velz. LC 83-23555. 800p. 1984. 85.00x o.p. (ISBN 0-471-86416-1). Wiley.

Applied Structured WATFIV. Roy Ageloff & Richard Mojena. 619p. 1984. pap. text ed. (ISBN 0-534-03079-3). Wadsworth Pub.

Applied Surgical Pathology. Stuart & Samuel. (Illus.). 1120p. 1975. 108.00 o.p. (ISBN 0-632-08800-1, B-4646-4). Mosby.

Applied Systems & Cybernetics: Proceedings of the International Congress on Applied Systems Research & Cybernetics, Acapulco, Mexico, Dec. 12-16, 1980, 6 Vols. Ed. by George E. Lasker. Incl. Vol. 1. The Quality of Life: Systems Approaches. 600p. 1981. 155.00 o.p. (ISBN 0-08-027198-7); Vol. 2. Systems Concepts, Models & Methodology. 540p. 1981. 140.00 o.p. (ISBN 0-08-027199-5); Vol. 3. Human Systems, Sociocybernetics, Management & Organizations. 580p. 1981. 150.00 o.p. (ISBN 0-08-027200-2); Vol. 4. Systems Research in Health Care, Biocybernetics & Ecology. 425p. 1981. 115.00 o.p. (ISBN 0-08-027201-0); Vol. 5. Systems Approaches to Computer Science & Mathematics. 670p. 1981. 175.00 o.p. (ISBN 0-08-027202-9); Vol. 6. Fuzzy Sets & Systems, Possibility Theory, & Special Topics in Systems Research. 670p. 1981. 155.00 o.p. (ISBN 0-08-027203-7). 1981. Set. 655.00 o.p. (ISBN 0-08-027196-0). Pergamon.

Applied Technical Mathematics. Merwin J. Lyng et al. LC 77-76423. (Illus.). 1978. text ed. 24.95 o.p. (ISBN 0-395-25429-9). HM.

Applied Therapeutic Drug Monitoring, Vol. 1. Ed. by T. Moyer & R. Boeckx. LC 82-72107. 239p. 1982. pap. text ed. 15.00 o.p. (ISBN 0-915274-19-1). Am Assn Clinical Chem.

Applied Therapeutics: The Clinical Use of Drugs. 3rd ed. Ed. by Brian S. Katcher & Lloyd Y. Young. LC 82-73291. (Illus.). 1983. pap. 55.00x o.p. (ISBN 0-915486-05-9). Applied Therapeutics.

Applied Thermoluminescence Dosimetry. Ed. by M. Oberhofer & A. Scharmann. (Illus.). 410p. 1981. 106.00x o.p. (ISBN 0-85274-544-3, Pub. by A Hilger UK). Taylor & Francis.

Applied Time Series Analysis, No. 2. Ed. by D. F. Findley. LC 78-9007. 1978. 54.50 o.p. (ISBN 0-12-257250-5). Acad Pr.

Applied Underwater Acoustics. D. G. Tucker & B. K. Gazey. 1966. text ed. 29.00 o.p. (ISBN 0-08-011817-8); pap. text ed. 15.00 o.p. (ISBN 0-08-011816-X). Pergamon.

Applied Urban Analysis: A Critique & Synthesis. Ian Cullen. (Orig.). 1985. 28.00x o.p. (ISBN 0-416-36430-6, 4082); pap. 14.95x o.p. (ISBN 0-416-36440-3, 4083). Routledge Chapman & Hall.

Applied Welfare Economics & Public Policy. Richard E. Just et al. (Illus.). 448p. 1982. text ed. (ISBN 0-13-043398-5). P-H.

Apply Yourself: Writing College Applications That Get Results. Susan D. Van Raalte. (Orig.). 1985. pap. 6.95 o.s.i. (ISBN 0-449-90131-9, Columbine). Fawcett.

Applying Automated Inspection. Society of Manufacturing Engineers Staff. Ed. by T. Pryor & W. North. 263p. 1985. 35.00 o.p. (ISBN 0-87263-194-X). SME.

Applying Behavior Analysis Procedures with Children & Youth. Beth Sulzer-Azaroff. Ed. by G. Roy Mayer. LC 77-371. 1977. text ed. 33.95 o.p. (ISBN 0-03-039711-1, HoltC). HR&W.

Applying Data Structures. Theodore G. Lewis & Marilyn Z. Smith. LC 75-25004. (Illus.). 1976. text ed. 27.95 o.p. (ISBN 0-395-24060-3). HM.

Applying Ethics: A Text with Readings. 2nd ed. Vincent Barry. 421p. 1985. pap. text ed. (ISBN 0-534-03687-2). Wadsworth Pub.

Applying Psychology in Organizations. Frank Blacker & Sylvia Shimmin. 160p. 1984. pap. 5.95 o.p. (ISBN 0-416-33680-9, NO. 9180). Routledge Chapman & Hall.

Applying Psychology: Understanding People. Robert C. Beck. (Illus.). 480p. 1982. text ed. (ISBN 0-13-043463-9). P-H.

Applying the Gospel: Suggestions for Christian Social Action in the Local Church. new ed. William M. Pinson. LC 75-8374. 160p. 1975. pap. 6.95 o.p. (ISBN 0-8054-6306-2). Broadman.

Applying the Systems Approach to Urban Development. Jack W. Lapatra. LC 73-11942. (Community Development Ser.: Vol. 5). 296p. 1982. pap. 22.95 o.p. (ISBN 0-87933-298-0). Van Nos Reinhold.

Applying to Colleges & Universities in the United States: A Handbook for International Students. LC 85-3496. 310p. (Orig.). 1985. pap. 11.95 o.p. (ISBN 0-87866-273-1). Petersons Guides.

Applying to Graduate School: A Student's Guide. Marliss G. Strange & Jack W. Bennett. 160p. 1985. pap. 6.95 o.p. (ISBN 0-668-06273-8). Arco.

Appointing & Removal Power of the President of the United States. Charles E. Morganston. LC 75-35372. (U. S. Government Documents Program Ser.). 224p. 1976. Repr. of 1929 ed. lib. bdg. 22.50x o.p. (ISBN 0-8371-8611-0, MOAR). Greenwood.

Appointment Calendar for Psychologists & Other Mental Health Professionals, 1988. 156p. 1987. pap. 15.50 o.p. (ISBN 0-317-60693-X). Ohio Psych Pub.

Appointment with Death. Agatha Christie. 192p. 1981. pap. 2.95 o.p. (ISBN 0-440-10246-4). Dell.

Appomatox. Burleigh C. Rodick. 1965. (ISBN 0-8022-1361-8). Philos Lib.

Appomattox & Other Poems. Robert A. Merritt. 1979. 5.00 o.p. (ISBN 0-682-49184-5). Exposition-Phoenix.

Appraisal of Real Estate. rev. ed. 752p. 18.00 o.p. (ISBN 0-318-15169-3, 21-1005). Natl Assoc Realtors.

Appraiser & Real Estate Feasibility Studies. 57p. 3.50 o.p. (ISBN 0-318-15171-5). Natl Assoc Realtors.

Appraiser's Handbook: A Unique Guide to Appraising Land, Buildings & Machinery with Specialized Information for Industrial Engineers. E. B. Fallon. LC 74-21441. 1975. 50.00 o.p. (ISBN 0-682-48191-2, Banner). Exposition-Phoenix.

Appraising the Boss: An Annotated Bibliography for Librarians. Lorna Peterson. (Public Administration Ser.: P 1680). 7p. 1985. 2.00 o.p. (ISBN 0-89028-410-5). Vance Biblios.

Appreciating Poetry. Richard P. Sugg. 1975. pap. 18.95 o.p. (ISBN 0-395-19375-3). HM.

Appreciation of Architecture: Landscape & Buildings. K. Lindley. (Illus.). 58p. 1972. 4.65 o.p. (ISBN 0-08-015677-0). Pergamon.

Apprentices in Love. Mark Gibbard. 128p. 1974. 4.25 o.p. (ISBN 0-8192-1166-4). Morehouse Pub.

Apprenticeship Fund Institutes: Proceedings, Nov. 21-24, 1982, Holliwood Fl. Becky A. Wright. 62p. pap. text ed. 9.00 o.p. (ISBN 0-89154-202-7). Intl Found Employ.

Apprenticeship in the United States: Implications for Vocational Education Research & Development. Robert W. Glover. 20p. 1980. 2.20 o.p. (ISBN 0-318-22034-2, OC66). Natl Ctr Res Voc Ed.

Apprenticeships in America. rev. ed. Harry Kursh. 1965. 5.95 o.p. (ISBN 0-393-08530-9). Norton.

Approach to Economics. Ludwig H. Mai. (Quality Paperback: No. 83). (Orig.). 1970. pap. 1.50 o.p. (ISBN 0-8226-0083-8). Littlefield.

Approach to Engineering Mathematics. A. H. Douglas. 1971. pap. 35.00 o.p. (ISBN 0-08-016016-6). Pergamon.

Approach to Teaching Autistic Children. Ed. by Margaret P. Everard. 156p. 1976. text ed. 17.75 o.p. (ISBN 0-08-020895-9); pap. text ed. 7.00 o.p. (ISBN 0-08-019923-2). Pergamon.

Approach to Technical Translation. C. A. Finch. 1969. pap. text ed. 3.50 o.p. (ISBN 0-08-013425-4). Pergamon.

Approaches to Assertion Training. John M. Whiteley & John V. Flowers. 1978. 8.50 o.p. (ISBN 1-55620-001-3, 71001C). Am Assn Coun Dev.

Approaches to Clay Modelling. John Scott & Eric Fisher. LC 75-8414. (Craft Approaches Ser). (Illus.). 80p. 1975. 7.50 o.s.i. (ISBN 0-8008-0281-0). Taplinger.

Approaches to Collage. Warren Farnworth. LC 75-42539. (Illus.). (YA) (gr. 4 up). 1976. 9.95 o.s.i. (ISBN 0-8008-0280-2). Taplinger.

Approaches to Criminal Justice Training. John Fay. 264p. (Orig.). 1979. pap. 12.00x o.p. (ISBN 0-89854-051-8). U of GA Inst Govt.

Approaches to Earth Survey Problems Through the Use of Space Techniques. P. Bock. 1977. 130.00 o.p. (ISBN 0-08-021996-9). Pergamon.

Approaches to Insanity: A Philosophical & Sociological Study. Jeff Coulter. 180p. 1973. 24.95x o.p. (ISBN 0-85520-049-9); pap. 14.95x o.p. (ISBN 0-85520-048-0). Basil Blackwell.

Approaches to Language. R. Harris. LC 82-12390. (Language & Communication Library: Vol. 4). (Illus.). 192p. 1983. 28.00 o.p. (ISBN 0-08-028910-X). Pergamon.

Approaches to Modern Embroidery. Margaret Beautement. LC 75-8416. (Craft Approaches Ser). (Illus.). 80p. 1975. 7.50 o.s.i. (ISBN 0-8008-0283-7). Taplinger.

Approaches to Morality: Readings in Ethics from Classical Philosophy to Existentialism. Ed. by Jesse A. Mann & Gerald F. Kreyche. (Harbrace Ser. in Philosophy). 1966. text ed. 12.95 o.p. (ISBN 0-15-502910-X, HC). HarBraceJ.

Approaches to Organizing. Ed. by Robert T. Golembiewski. LC 81-70133. (PAR Classics: Vol. III). 1981. 11.95 o.s.i. (ISBN 0-936678-03-8). Am Soc Pub Admin.

Approaches to Painting. Leo Walmsley. LC 75-8417. (Craft Approaches Ser). (Illus.). 80p. 1975. 7.50 o.s.i. (ISBN 0-8008-0284-5). Taplinger.

Approaches to Personality Theory. David Peck & David Whitlow. (Essential Psychology Ser.). 1975. pap. 4.50x o.p. (ISBN 0-416-82810-8, NO.2363). Routledge Chapman & Hall.

Approaches to Printing. John Lancaster. LC 75-8419. (Craft Approaches Ser). 80p. 1975. 7.50 o.s.i. (ISBN 0-8008-0285-3). Taplinger.

Approaches to Psychology. Ed. by John Medcof & John Roth. 354p. 1980. pap. 11.50x o.p. (ISBN 0-458-94140-9, NO.6447). Routledge Chapman & Hall.

Approaches to the Informal Evaluation of Reading. John J. Pikulski & Timothy Shanahan. 128p. 1982. pap. text ed. 6.00 o.p. (ISBN 0-87207-528-1). Intl Reading.

Approaches to Ulysses: Ten Essays. Ed. by Thomas F. Staley & Bernard Benstock. LC 76-123093. 1970. 29.95x o.p. (ISBN 0-8229-3209-1). U of Pittsburgh Pr.

Approaches to Welfare. Ed. by Philip Bean & Stewart MacPherson. 300p. 1983. 28.95x o.p. (ISBN 0-7100-9423-X); pap. 15.95x o.p. (ISBN 0-7100-9424-8). Routledge Chapman & Hall.

Approaches with Emotionally Disturbed Children. Ed. by Bruce T. Saunders. LC 74-76038. (Illus.). 1974. text ed. 20.00 o.p. (ISBN 0-682-47883-0, University). Exposition-Phoenix.

Approaching Maximal Leadership Conflict for Domination of the World. Marcellus Simkovich. (Illus.). 1979. deluxe ed. 68.75x o.p. (ISBN 0-930008-22-7). Inst Econ Pol.

Approaching Seven Major Political Revolutions Which Will Transform Radically the World. Oswald M. Steinmiller. (Illus.). 137p. 1983. 97.85x o.p. (ISBN 0-86722-030-9). Inst Econ Pol.

Appropiate Building Materials for Low Cost Housing. Ed. by International Council for Building Research & Documentation Staff & International Union of Testing & Research Labs for Materials & Structures Staff. 550p. 1983. 55.00 o.p. (ISBN 0-419-13280-5, NO.6876). Routledge Chapman & Hall.

Appropriate Building Materials: A Catalogue of Potential Solutions. Roland Stulz. (Illus.). 324p. 1983. pap. 19.50x o.p. (ISBN 0-903031-90-6, Pub. by Intermed Tech England). Intermediate Tech.

Appropriate Building Materials for Low Cost Housing, Vol. 2. International Council for Building Research Studies & Documentation Staff. Ed. by International Union of Testing & Research Labs for Materials & Structures Staff. 312p. 1985. (ISBN 0-419-13430-1, 9572, Pub. by E & FN Spon England). Routledge Chapman & Hall.

Appropriate Technology for Employment Creation in the Food Processing & Drink Industries of Developing Countries: Report III of the Food Products & Drink Industries, 2nd Tripartite Technical Meeting, Geneva, 1978. Food Products & Drink Industries, Second Tripartite Technical Meeting Staff. 88p. 1978. 10.50 o.p. (ISBN 92-2-101880-6, FAD/2/III). Intl Labour Office.

Appropriate Technology Organizations: A Worldwide Directory. Ed. by Center for Business Information Staff. LC 83-43053. 150p. 1984. pap. 29.95x o.p. (ISBN 0-89950-098-6). McFarland & Co.

Approximate Molecular Orbital Theory. J. A. Pople & D. L. Beveridge. 1970. text ed. 52.95 o.p. (ISBN 0-07-050512-8). McGraw.

Approximate Stochastic Behavior of n-Server Service Systems with Large n. G. F. Newell. (Lecture Notes in Economics & Mathematical Systems: Vol. 87). (Illus.). vii, 118p. 1973. pap. 13.00 o.p. (ISBN 0-387-06366-8). Springer-Verlag.

Approximation. Hans J. Schadlich. Tr. by Richard Winston & Clara Winston. LC 78-22271. 1980. Repr. of 1977 ed. 8.95 o.p. (ISBN 0-15-107847-5). HarBraceJ.

Approximation of Continuous Functions by Positive Linear Operators. R. A. De Vore. LC 72-91891. (Lecture Notes in Mathematics: Vol. 293). viii, 289p. 1972. pap. 13.00 o.p. (ISBN 0-387-06038-3). Springer-Verlag.

Approximation Theory. A. Talbot. 1970. 56.50 o.p. (ISBN 0-12-682250-6). Acad Pr.

Approximations for Digital Computers. Cecil Hastings. (Rand Corporation Research Studies). 1955. 31.50x o.p. (ISBN 0-691-07914-5). Princeton U Pr.

Aprende en Espanol y en Ingles: Level One-Reader A. Alicia Castroleal. (Aprende en Espanol y en Ingles Ser.). (Illus., Span.). (gr. 1-2). 1979. text ed. (ISBN 0-88345-409-2). Prentice ESL.

Aprende en Espanol y en Ingles: Level One-Reader B. Alicia Castroleal. (Aprende en Espanol y en Ingles Ser.). (Illus., Span.). 1979. text ed. (ISBN 0-88345-410-6). Prentice ESL.

Aprende en Espanol y en Ingles: Level 1-Reader A. Alicia Castroleal & Diamantina V. Suarez. 1979. pap. text ed. (ISBN 0-88345-388-6); tchr's. guide o.p. (ISBN 0-88345-390-8). Prentice ESL.

Aprende en Espanol y en Ingles: Readiness Level. Suarez & Castroleal. (gr. k-1). 1978. (ISBN 0-88345-364-9); tchr's. guide o.p. (ISBN 0-88345-365-7); cassettes, teacher's manuals & spirit masters 100.00 o.p. (ISBN 0-685-78815-6). Prentice ESL.

Apricot Bed. Margaret Yorke. (Lythway Ser.). 1987. lib. bdg. 17.50x o.p. (ISBN 0-7451-0585-8, Pub. by Chivers Pr UK). G K Hall.

Apricots at Midnight. Adele Geras. LC 82-1728. (Illus.). 144p. (gr. 4-6). 1982. 10.95 o.s.i. (ISBN 0-689-30921-X, Atheneum). Macmillan.

April Age. Lavinia Russ. LC 74-18194. 128p. (gr. 6 up). 1975. 5.25 o.p. (ISBN 0-689-30431-5, Atheneum). Macmillan.

April Fool. Mary B. Christian. LC 81-3782. (Ready-to-Read Ser.). (Illus.). 48p. (gr. 1-4). 1981. 8.95 o.s.i. (ISBN 0-02-718280-0). Macmillan.

April Ghost. Marjory Hall. LC 75-17932. 186p. (gr. 6-9). 1975. 6.50 o.s.i. (ISBN 0-664-32578-5, Westminster). Westminster John Knox.

April Harvest. Lillian Budd. 304p. 1980. pap. 2.25 o.p. (ISBN 0-380-49593-7, 49593). Avon.

April Snow. Lillian Budd. 1979. pap. 1.95 o.p. (ISBN 0-380-45401-7, 45401-7). Avon.

April Twilights (Nineteen Hundred Three) rev. ed. Willa Cather. Ed. by Bernice Slote. LC 62-8899. (Illus.). xlviii, 88p. 1968. 14.95x o.p. (ISBN 0-8032-0011-0). U of Nebr Pr.

Aprocrine Glands & the Breast. Marshall B. Craigmyle. LC 85-621. 82p. 1985. text ed. 45.00 o.p. (ISBN 0-471-90506-2, Dist. by A R Liss). Wiley.

Aprons Instead of Uniforms: The Practice of Printing, 1776-1787. Rollo G. Silver. 1977. pap. 5.00x o.p. (ISBN 0-912296-19-4, Dist. by U Pr of Va). Am Antiquarian.

AQTST - Aquifer Test Analyses with a Hand-Held Calculator. 1982. 18.75 o.p. (ISBN 0-318-23050-X). Natl Water Well.

AQTST-Aquifer Test Analysis with a Hand-Held Calculator. 18.75 o.p. (ISBN 0-318-02531-0). Natl Water Well.

Aquarian Odyssey: A Nineteen Sixties Album. Don Snyder. (Illus.). 1980. 19.95 o.p. (ISBN 0-87140-639-X); pap. 9.95 o.p. (ISBN 0-87140-126-6). Liveright.

Aquarium Fish from Around the World. Klaus Paysan. LC 73-102892. (Nature & Man Ser.). (Illus.). (gr. 5-12). 1970. PLB 9.95 o.p. (ISBN 0-8225-0561-4). Lerner Pubns.

Aquatic Aide: A Guidebook for Water Safety Instruction. Mary L. Oppenheim. (Illus.). 1982. 7.50 o.p. (ISBN 0-682-49764-9). Exposition-Phoenix.

Aquatic Vegetation & Its Use & Control. 135p. 1982. pap. 10.00 o.p. (ISBN 92-3-101082-4, U1212, UNESCO). UNIPUB.

Aquatics. Ed. by Charlotte Piper & Dorothy Lewis. (Illus.). 150p. 1983. pap. text ed. 11.95 o.p. (ISBN 0-89582-135-4). Morton Pub.

Aqui, Alla y Aculia: Conversacion y Composicion. Fausto Vergara et al. LC 83-12356. 199p. 1984. pap. 15.95 o.p. (ISBN 0-471-87371-3). Wiley.

Aqui Mismo. Kenneth R. Scholberg & Diana E. Scholberg. (Illus.). 288p. (Orig.). 1980. pap. text ed. 9.95 o.p. (ISBN 0-88377-148-9). Newbury Hse.

Aquitaine Progression. Robert Ludlum. 1985. lib. bdg. 19.95 o.p. (ISBN 0-8161-3873-7, Large Print Bks); pap. 11.95 o.p. (ISBN 0-8161-3907-5, Large Print Bks). G K Hall.

Arab. G. Lee Tippin. 206p. 1986. pap. 3.50 o.p. (ISBN 1-55547-121-8). Critics Choice Paper.

Arab Ba'th Socialist Party History, Ideology, & Organization. Kamel S. Abu Jaber. LC 66-25181. 1966. 11.95x o.p. (ISBN 0-8156-0051-8). Syracuse U Pr.

Arab Directory for Commerce, Industry & Liberal Professions in the Arab Countries 1977-1978 (1977) 25th ed. Ed. by Joseph N. Halabi. (Eng., Arabic. & Fr.). 1978. 150.00 o.p. (ISBN 0-685-01103-8). E J Brill USA.

Arab Industrial Integration: A Strategy for Development. Elias T. Ghantus. (Illus.). 240p. 1982. 36.50 o.p. (ISBN 0-7099-1117-3, Pub. by Croom Helm Ltd). Routledge Chapman & Hall.

Arab-Israeli Conflict. Schools Council History 13-16 Project Staff. (Modern World Problems Ser.). (Illus.). 1979. lib. bdg. 12.95 o.p. (ISBN 0-912616-68-7); pap. text ed. 6.95 o.p. (ISBN 0-912616-67-9). Greenhaven.

Arab-Israeli Wars: War & Peace in the Middle East, from the War of Independence Through Lebabon. Chaim Herzog. LC 83-5846. (Illus.). 464p. 1982. 19.50 o.p. (ISBN 0-394-50379-1); pap. 8.95 o.p. (ISBN 0-394-71746-5, Vin). Random.

Arab Left. Tareq Y. Ismael. LC 76-48136. 1976. 24.95x o.p. (ISBN 0-8156-0124-7); pap. 7.95x o.p. (ISBN 0-8156-0125-5). Syracuse U Pr.

Arab Mind. rev. ed. Raphael Patai. 448p. 1983. 24.95 o.p. (ISBN 0-684-17809-5, ScribT); pap. 15.95 o.p. (ISBN 0-684-17810-9). Scribner.

Arab Mind Considered: A Need for Understanding. John Laffin. LC 75-5042. 1975. 8.95 o.s.i. (ISBN 0-8008-0294-2). Taplinger.

Arab Periodicals & Serials: A Classified Directory. Mohammed M. Aman. LC 78-68242. (Reference Library of Social Sciences Ser.). 1979. 44.00 o.p. (ISBN 0-8240-9816-1). Garland Pub.

Arab Press: News Media & Political Process in the Arab World. William A. Rugh. (Illus.). 224p. 1979. 9.95x o.p. (ISBN 0-8156-2191-4); pap. 6.95 o.p. (ISBN 0-8156-0159-X). Syracuse U Pr.

Arab Refugee Problem. Joseph B. Schechtman. 1952. (ISBN 0-8022-1500-9). Philos Lib.

Arab Republic of Egypt Military Decorations & Medals. David V. Olson. 60p. 1987. pap. 10.00 o.p. WW Milit Exch.

Arab Society: Continuity & Change. Ed. by Samih K. Farsoun. LC 85-19446. 144p. 1985. 29.95 o.p. (ISBN 0-7099-1082-7, Pub. by Croom Helm Ltd). Routledge Chapman & Hall.

Arab Sruggle for Economic Independence. M. Ata Alla. 271p. 1974. 4.95 o.p. (ISBN 0-8285-2221-9, Pub. by Progress Pubs USSR). Imported Pubns.

Arab World & Iran in Trade with the U. S. A., U. K., EEC, Comecon, Japan & the Third World: 1978. Arab World & Iran Business Guides. 1978. pap. 10.00 o.p. (ISBN 0-931000-06-8). Suburban Pub CT.

Arab World: Libraries & Librarianship 1960-1976; a Bibliography. Veronica S. Pantelidis. 116p. 1979. pap. 18.00x o.p. (ISBN 0-7201-0821-7). Mansell.

Arabella & Mr. Crack. Dick Gackenbach. LC 81-15670. (Illus.). 32p. (gr. k-3). 1982. 8.95 o.s.i. (ISBN 0-02-735770-8). Macmillan.

Arabia: A Journey Through the Labyrinth. Jonathan Raban. 1980. pap. 7.75 o.p. (ISBN 0-671-25057-4, Touchstone). S&S.

Arabian Essays. Ghazi A. Algosaibi. 120p. 1982. 19.95x o.p. (ISBN 0-7103-0019-0, Kegan Paul). Routledge Chapman & Hall.

Arabian Essays. Ghazi A. Algosaibi. 120p. 1985. pap. 10.95x o.p. (ISBN 0-7103-0126-X, Kegan Paul). Routledge Chapman & Hall.

Arabian Gulf States: Their Legal & Political Status. H. M. Al Bahanna. 428p. 1979. 33.00x o.p. (ISBN 0-86010-174-6). Graham & Trotman.

Arabian Nights. Heather X. Graham. (Candlelight Ecstasy Supreme Ser.: No. 37). 288p. (Orig.). 1984. pap. 2.50 o.s.i. (ISBN 0-440-10214-6). Dell.

Arabian Peninsula. Time-Life Books Editors. (Library of Nations Ser.). (Illus.). 160p. (YA) (gr. 7 up). 1985. lib. bdg. 23.93 o.p. Time-Life.

Arabian Studies, No. 5. Ed. by R. B. Serjeant & R. L. Bidwell. 1980. Repr. 30.00x o.p. (ISBN 0-7735-0511-3, Pub. by McGill Canada). U of Toronto Pr.

Arabic Computer Dictionary: English-Arabic, Arabic-English. Ernest Kay. 336p. 1986. 67.50 o.p. (ISBN 0-7102-0457-4, 04574). Routledge Chapman & Hall.

Arabic Dictionary of Civil Engineering: English-Arabic, Arabic-English. Ernest Kay. 276p. 1986. text ed. 85.00 o.p. (ISBN 0-7102-0429-9). Routledge Chapman & Hall.

Arabic-English Dictionary. F. Steingass. 69.00 o.p. (ISBN 0-317-14640-8). Kazi Pubns.

Arabic Proverbs: Or the Manners & Customs of the Modern Egyptian, Illustrated from Their Proverbial Sayings Current at Cairo. Tr. by J. L. Burckhardt from Arabic. 1984. pap. 12.50 o.p. (ISBN 0-7007-0185-0). E J Brill USA.

Arabic Reader I: An Introduction to Phonology & Script. R. M. Rammuny et al. 206p. (Orig.). 1981. pap. 7.95x o.s.i. (ISBN 0-939830-19-1); cassettes 32.10 o.s.i. (ISBN 0-939830-09-4). New Era Pubns MI.

Arabic Words in English see Needed Words.

Arable Holdings. F. R. Higgins. 60p. 1971. Repr. of 1933 ed. 15.00x o.p. (ISBN 0-7165-1377-3, BBA 02061, Pub. by Cuala Press Ireland). Biblio Dist.

Arabs in Israel. Sabri Jiryis. Tr. by Inea Bushnaq. LC 75-15347. 314p. 1977. pap. 5.95 o.p. (ISBN 0-85345-406-X). Monthly Rev.

Arafat: The Man & the Myth. Thomas Kiernan. 288p. 1976. 9.95 o.p. (ISBN 0-393-07503-6). Norton.

Arakawa: The Mechanism of Meaning. Arakawa & Madeline H. Gins. (Art Bks. by Artists). (Illus.). 1979. 20.00 o.p.; pap. 12.50 o. p. o.p. (ISBN 0-8109-2165-0). Abrams.

Aran Islands. Daphne Pochin-Mould. (Island Set). (Illus.). 171p. 1973. 19.95 o.p. (ISBN 0-7153-5782-4). David & Charles.

Arapaho Spirit. Jane Toombs. (American Indians Ser.: No. 13). 320p. (Orig.). 1983. pap. 2.95 o.p. (ISBN 0-440-00272-9, Emerald). Dell.

Arara: The Capital of the Ticuna Indians of the Colombian Amazon. Gabriel Medina Tellez. (Illus.). 1979. pap. 6.00 o.p. (ISBN 0-682-49296-5, University). Exposition-Phoenix.

Ararat. Elgin Groseclose. 464p. 1977. pap. 2.95 o.p. (ISBN 0-89191-078-6, 11445). Cook.

Ararat. Robert Houston. 400p. 1982. pap. 3.50 o.p. (ISBN 0-380-80937-0, 80937-0). Avon.

Arator: The Codices. Ed. by A. P. McKinlay. 1942. 8.00x o.p. (ISBN 0-910956-18-9). Medieval Acad.

Arbitration & the Federal Sector Advocate: A Practical Guide. Francis J. Loevi, Jr. & Roger P. Kaplan. LC 82-71917. 88p. 1982. pap. 8.00 o.p. (ISBN 0-943001-13-7). Am Arbitration.

Arbitration & the Law, Nineteen Eighty-Six: General Counsel's Annual Report. 342p. 1987. 50.00 o.p. (ISBN 0-943001-19-6). Am Arbitration.

Arbitration & the Law, 1983. American Arbitration Association Staff. Ed. by Linda Miller. LC 81-70413. (AAA General Counsel's Report). 374p. 1984. 30.00 o.p. (ISBN 0-943001-00-5); pap. 30.00 o.p. (ISBN 0-317-59663-2). Am Arbitration.

Arbitration & the Law, 1984. Ed. by Michael F. Hoellering et al. LC 81-70413. (General Counsel's Report). 342p. 1985. 30.00 o.p. (ISBN 0-943001-01-3); pap. 30.00 o.p. Am Arbitration.

Arbitration & the Law, 1985. American Arbitration Association Staff. Ed. by Linda Miller & Margaret Doyle. LC 81-70413. (AAA General Counsel Report). 326p. 1986. 30.00 o.p. (ISBN 0-943001-11-0). Am Arbitration.

Arbitration Guide. Raymond L. Britton. (Illus.). 304p. 1982. text ed. 66.00 three-ring binder o.p. (ISBN 0-13-043984-3). P-H.

Arbitration in the Schools. Robert Coulson. LC 85-73739. 151p. 1986. pap. 6.95 o.p. (ISBN 0-943001-08-0). Am Arbitration.

Arbitration Law in Europe. Ed. by International Chamber of Commerce Staff. 368p. 1981. 65.00 o.p. (ISBN 0-318-12368-1). Am Arbitration.

Arbitration of Drug & Alcohol Disputes: A Casebook. Robert Coulson. 1987. pap. 9.95 o.p. (ISBN 0-943001-20-X). Am Arbitration.

Arbitration of Real Estate Valuation Disputes. Ed. by Gerald M. Levy. 246p. 1987. pap. 14.95 o.p. (ISBN 0-943001-21-8). Am Arbitration.

Arbitration Procedure. Ed. by Institution of Civil Engineers Staff. 50p. 1976. 7.25x o.p. (ISBN 0-7277-0032-4, Pub. by T Telford UK). Am Soc Civil Eng.

Arbor House Book of Cartooning. Mort Gerberg. LC 81-71666. (Illus.). 1983. 16.95 o.p. (ISBN 0-87795-372-4, Arbor Hse); pap. 9.95 o.p. (ISBN 0-87795-399-6). Morrow.

Arbor House Celebrity Book of Horror Stories. Ed. by Martin H. Greenberg. 600p. 1982. 20.95 o.p. (ISBN 0-87795-373-2, Arbor Hse); pap. 8.95 o.p. (ISBN 0-87795-400-3). Morrow.

Arbor House Celebrity Book of the Greatest Stories Ever Told. Ed. by Martin H. Greenberg & Charles G. Waugh. 512p. 1983. 15.95 o.p. (ISBN 0-87795-448-8, Arbor Hse); pap. 7.95 o.p. (ISBN 0-87795-449-6). Morrow.

Arbor House Necropolis -- Voodoo! Mummy! Ghoul! Bill Pronzini. 850p. 1981. pap. 10.95 o.p. (ISBN 0-87795-338-4, Arbor Hse). Morrow.

Arbor House Treasure of Detective & Mystery Stories from the Great Pulps. Ed. by Bill Pronzini. 356p. 1983. 15.95 o.p. (ISBN 0-87795-451-8, Arbor Hse); pap. 7.95 o.p. (ISBN 0-87795-452-6). Morrow.

Arbor House Treasure of True Crime. John Dunning. 1985. 18.95 o.p. (ISBN 0-87795-679-0, Arbor Hse). Morrow.

Arbor House Treasury of Great Science Fiction Short Novels. Ed. by Robert Silverberg & Martin H. Greenberg. LC 80-66764. 1980. 19.95 o.p. (ISBN 0-87795-284-1, Arbor Hse); pap. 7.95 o.p. (ISBN 0-87795-295-7). Morrow.

Arbor House Treasury of Great Western Stories. Ed. by Bill Pronzini. Martin H. Greenberg. LC 82-72052. 1982. 17.95 o.p. (ISBN 0-87795-439-9, Arbor Hse); pap. 8.95 o.p. (ISBN 0-87795-410-0). Morrow.

Arbor House Treasury of Horror & the Supernatural. Ed. by Bill Pronzini et al. LC 80-70220. 512p. (Orig.). 1981. 19.95 o.p. (ISBN 0-87795-309-0, Arbor Hse); pap. 8.95 o.p. (ISBN 0-87795-319-8). Morrow.

Arbor House Treasury of Modern Science Fiction. Ed. by Martin H. Greenberg & Robert Silverberg. LC 79-54005. 1980. 19.95 o.p. (ISBN 0-87795-246-9, Arbor Hse); pap. 8.95 o.p. (ISBN 0-87795-266-3). Morrow.

Arbor House Treasury of Mystery & Suspense. Ed. by Bill Pronzini & Barry N. Malzberg. LC 81-67525. 1982. 20.95 o.p. (ISBN 0-87795-349-X, Arbor Hse); pap. 9.95 o.p. (ISBN 0-87795-348-1). Morrow.

Arbor House Treasury of Nobel Prize Winners. Ed. by Martin H. Greenberg & Charles G. Waugh. 294p. 1984. 15.95 o.p. (ISBN 0-87795-511-5, Arbor Hse); pap. 7.95 o.p. (ISBN 0-87795-613-8). Morrow.

Arbor House Treasury of Science Fiction Masterpieces. Ed. by Robert Silverberg & Martin H. Greenberg. 1983. 16.95 o.p. (ISBN 0-87795-445-3, Arbor Hse); pap. 8.95 o.p. (ISBN 0-87795-446-1). Morrow.

Arc Physics. M. F. Hoyaux. LC 68-24015. (Applied Physics & Engineering Ser.: Vol. 8). (Illus.). 1969. 41.00 o.p. (ISBN 0-387-04054-4). Springer-Verlag.

Arc Plasma Technology in Materials Science. D. A. Gerdeman & N. L. Hecht. (Applied Mineralogy: Vol. 3). (Illus.). 1973. 45.00 o.p. (ISBN 0-387-81041-2). Springer-Verlag.

Arc Welding: Equipment. Resource Systems International Staff. 1982. pap. text ed. 15.00 o.p. (Reston). P-H.

Arc Welding: Gas Metal (Mig) Resource Systems International Staff. 1982. pap. text ed. 15.00 o.p. (ISBN 0-8359-0304-4, Reston). P-H.

Arc Welding: Gas Tungsten (Tig) Resource Systems International Staff. 1982. 15.00 o.p. (ISBN 0-8359-0305-2, Reston). P-H.

Arc Welding: Other Processes. Resource Systems International Staff. 1982. pap. text ed. 15.00 o.p. (ISBN 0-8359-0306-0, Reston). P-H.

Arc Welding: Shielded Metal I. Resource Systems International Staff. 1982. pap. text ed. 15.00 o.p. (ISBN 0-8359-0307-9, Reston). P-H.

Arc Welding: Shielded Metal II. Resource Systems International Staff. 1982. pap. text ed. 15.00 o.p. (ISBN 0-8359-0309-5, Reston). P-H.

Arcade Games for the Commodore 64. Fanfare House Inc., Staff. 194p. 1985. FPT 32.95 o.p. (ISBN 0-03-001049-7). HR&W.

Arcadia Story. Marjorie Russell. LC 85-40651. 265p. 1985. pap. 9.95 o.p. (ISBN 0-938232-83-5, Dist. by Baker & Taylor Co.). Winston-Derek.

Arcana of Astrology. W. J. Simmonite. LC 74-6220. (Illus.). 476p. 1974. pap. 5.95 o.p. (ISBN 0-87877-026-7). Newcastle Pub.

Arch of Septimius Severus in the Roman Forum. R. Brilliant. 270p. 1987. 48.00x o.s.i. (ISBN 0-271-00451-7). Pa St U Pr.

Archaeologia Britannica: An Account of the Languages, Histories & Customs of the Original Inhabitants of Great Britain from Collections: Glossography, Vol. I. Edward Lhuyd. 484p. 1971. Repr. of 1707 ed. text ed. 40.00x o.p. (ISBN 0-7165-0031-0, BBA 04712, Pub. by Irish Academic Pr England). Biblio Dist.

Archaeological Encyclopedia of the Holy Land. rev. ed. Ed. by Avraham Negev. (Illus.). 416p. 1986. 24.95 o.p. (ISBN 0-8407-7523-7). Nelson.

Archaeological Excavations along Route 24 Near Zuni, New Mexico. Kathleen E. Gratz. (Research Ser.). 130p. 1977. pap. 4.50 o.p. (RS-7). Mus Northern Ariz.

Archaeological Investigations along the Navajo-McCullough Transmission Line, Southern Utah & Northern Arizona. Kathleen Moffit et al. (Research Ser.). 200p. 1978. 5.95 o.p. (RS-10). Mus Northern Ariz.

Archaeological Investigations at the Hedgepeth Hills Petroglyph Site. J. Simon Bruder. (Research Ser.). 317p. pap. 8.50 o.p. (RS-28). Mus Northern Ariz.

Archaeological Investigations at the Kingfish Site, St. Clair County, Illinois. N. H. Lopinot et al. LC 82-50285. (Center for Archaeological Investigations Research Paper: No. 25). (Illus.). xiii, 220p. (Orig.). 1982. pap. 19.95 o.p. (ISBN 0-88104-001-0). Center Archaeo.

Archaeological Investigations at the Milar Site, Alexander County, Illinois. Charles R. Cobb & Richard W. Jefferies. (Center for Archaeological Investigations Research Paper: No. 40). (Illus.). viii, 54p. (Orig.). 1983. 11.80 o.p. (ISBN 0-88104-011-8). Center Archaeo.

Archaeological Investigations at the Riebling Site, Monroe County, Illinois. Michael S. Nassaney. (Center for Archaeological Investigations Research Paper: No. 41). (Illus.). viii, 55p. (Orig.). 1983. pap. 11.85 o.p. (ISBN 0-88104-012-6). Center Archaeo.

Archaeological Investigations at the Roos Site, St. Clair County, Illinois. Marilyn J. Bender & Paul A. Webb. (Center for Archaeological Investigations Research Paper: No. 43). (Illus.). viii, 58p. 1984. pap. 11.60 o.p. (ISBN 0-88104-015-0). Center Archaeo.

Archaeological Reconnaissance of Monument Valley in Northeastern Arizona. James A. Neely & Alan P. Olson. (Research Ser.). 98p. 1977. pap. 3.50 o.p. (RS-3). Mus Northern Ariz.

Archaeological Survey of Exchange Lands & Timber Sales in the Shawnee National Forest, Southern Illinois, 1982. James S. Penny, Jr. (Center for Archaeological Investigations Research Paper: No. 42). (Illus.). ix, 132p. (Orig.). 1983. 15.60 o.p. (ISBN 0-88104-013-4). Center Archaeo.

Archaeology: A Brief Introduction. 2nd ed. Brian M. Fagan. 1982. pap. text ed. write for info. o.p. (ISBN 0-673-39003-9). Scott F.

Archaeology: A Reference Handbook. Ed. by Alan E. Day. LC 77-21938. 319p. 1978. 28.00 o.p. (ISBN 0-208-01672-4, Linnet). Shoe String.

Archaeology & Cultural Resources Management: Selected Topics. Kurt R. Moore. (Public Administration Ser.: P 1754). 23p. 1985. 3.75 o.p. (ISBN 0-89028-534-9). Vance Biblios.

Archaeology of Canals. P. J. Ransom. (Illus.). 240p. 1980. pap. 10.50 o.p. (ISBN 0-317-02475-2, Pub. by World's Work). David & Charles.

Archaeology of Gardens. Christopher Taylor. (Archaeology Ser.: No. 30). (Illus.). 64p. 1983. pap. 5.95 o.p. (ISBN 0-85263-625-3, Pub. by Shire Pubns England). Seven Hills Bk Dists.

Archaeology of India. D. P. Agrawal. (Scandinavian Institute of Asian Studies Monograph: No.46). (Illus.). 294p. 1982. pap. text ed. 18.50x o.p. Humanities.

Archaeology of Late Celtic Britain & Ireland, c.400-1200 A.D. Lloyd Laing. 512p. 1975. 55.00x o.p. (ISBN 0-416-65970-5, NO.2281); pap. 20.00x o.p. (ISBN 0-416-82360-2, NO.2282). Routledge Chapman & Hall.

Archaeology of Lower Central America. Ed. by Frederick W. Lange & Doris Z. Stone. LC 83-21747. (School of American Research Advanced Seminar Ser.). (Illus.). 490p. 1984. 45.00x o.p. (ISBN 0-8263-0717-5). U of NM Pr.

Archaeology of Medieval Ireland. T. B. Barry. 304p. 1987. PLB 49.95x o.p. (ISBN 0-416-30360-9). Routledge Chapman & Hall.

Archaeology of Mesopotamia: From the Old Stone Age to the Persian Conquest. Seton Lloyd. 1980. pap. 8.95 o.p. (ISBN 0-500-79007-8). Thames Hudson.

Archaeology of Powell Plateau: Regional Interaction at Grand Canyon. Richard W. Effland et al. LC 81-82376. 59p. 1981. pap. 5.00 o.p. (ISBN 0-938216-16-3). GCNHA.

Archaeology of the Central Mississippi Valley. Dan F. Morse & Phyllis A. Morse. LC 82-22734. (New World Archaeological Record Series). 1983. 39.50 o.p. (ISBN 0-12-508180-4). Acad Pr.

Archaic Dictionary. William R. Cooper. LC 73-76018. 688p. 1969. Repr. of 1876 ed. 75.00x o.p. (ISBN 0-8103-3885-8). Gale.

Archbishop Romero: Martyr of Salvador. Placido Erdozain. Tr. by John McFadden & Ruth Warner. LC 81-2007. Orig. Title: Monsenor Romero: Martis de la Iglesia Popular. (Illus.). 128p. (Orig.). 1981. pap. 4.95 o.p. (ISBN 0-88344-019-9). Orbis Bks.

Archean: Search for the Beginning. Ed. by G. J. McCall. LC 76-11015. 1977. 85.00 o.p. (ISBN 0-12-787025-3). Acad Pr.

Archeological Theory & Practice. Ed. by D. E. Strong. 1973. 76.00 o.p. (ISBN 0-12-785811-3). Acad Pr.

Archeology of the Death Valley Salt Pan. Alice Hunt. (Illus.). xvi, 313p. 1960. Repr. 31.00 o.p. (ISBN 0-384-24920-5). Johnson Repr.

Archeology of the New Testament: The Life of Jesus & the Beginning of the Early Church. Jack Finegan. LC 69-18059. (Illus.). 1970. 60.00x o.p. (ISBN 0-691-03534-2); pap. 10.50x o.p. (ISBN 0-691-02000-0). Princeton U Pr.

Archer Armadillo's Secret Room. Marilyn Singer. LC 84-20087. (Illus.). 32p. (ps-2). 1985. 9.95 o.s.i. (ISBN 0-02-782700-3). Macmillan.

Archer County History. Jack Loftin. 1979. 25.00 o.p. (ISBN 0-89015-227-6). Eakin Pr.

Archer's Digest. 3rd ed. Ed. by Cheri Elliott. LC 77-148722. (Illus.). 288p. 1982. pap. 11.95 o.p. (ISBN 0-910676-40-2). DBI.

Archery Equipment Illustrated. Ed. by Bow & Arrow Magazine Staff & Jack Lewis. LC 84-71762. (Illus.). 256p. (Orig.). 1984. pap. 10.95 o.p. (ISBN 0-910676-79-8). DBI.

Arches & Short Span Bridges. S. Leliavsky. (Design Textbooks in Civil Engineering: Vol. 7). (Illus.). 250p. 1982. 45.00 o.p. (ISBN 0-412-22560-3, NO. 6686, Pub. by Chapman & Hall England). Routledge Chapman & Hall.

Archetypes: A Natural History of the Self. Anthony Stevens. 448p. 1982. 16.50 o.p. (ISBN 0-688-00785-6). Morrow.

Archetypes: The Persistence of Unifying Patterns. Elemire Zola et al. LC 81-13164. (Helen & Kurt Wolff Bks.). 156p. 1982. 10.95 o.p. (ISBN 0-15-107878-5). HarbraceJ.

Archibald Macleish: A Checklist. Edward J. Mullaly. LC 72-619620. (Serif Ser.: No. 26). 100p. 1973. 10.00x o.p. (ISBN 0-87338-132-7). Kent St U Pr.

Archie's Acrobats. Date not set. (ISBN 0-8052-3878-6). Random.

Archipenko: A Study of the Early Works, 1908-1920. Katherine J. Michaelsen. LC 76-23644. (Outstanding Dissertations in the Fine Arts - 2nd Series - 20th Century). (Illus.). 1977. Repr. of 1975 ed. lib. bdg. 73.00 o.p. (ISBN 0-8240-2712-4). Garland Pub.

Architect & the Computer - Design, Office Automation, & Building Management: A Bibliography of Recent Periodical Literature. Carole Cable. (Architecture Ser.: A 1445). 9p. 1985. 2.00 o.p. (ISBN 0-89028-515-2). Vance Biblios.

Architect-Client Relationship. Mary Vance. (Architecture Ser.: Bibliography A-1301). 1985. pap. 2.00 o.p. (ISBN 0-89028-231-5). Vance Biblios.

Architect in Practice. 6th ed. Arthur J. Willis & W. N. George. 333p. 1974. text ed. 17.25x o.p. (ISBN 0-258-96959-8, Pub. by Granada England). Gower Pub Co.

Architect: The Life & Work of Charles W. Moore. David Littlejohn. 1984. 22.95 o.s.i. (ISBN 0-03-063829-1, William Abrahams Bk). H Holt & Co.

Architecte et l'Empereur d'Assyrie. Fernando Arrabal. 320p. 1971. pap. 4.95 o.p. (ISBN 0-686-54448-X). French & Eur.

Architects' Contracts: A Bibliography. Mary Vance. LC 85-141173. (Architecture Ser.: Bibliography A 1352). 1985. pap. 2.00 o.p. (ISBN 0-89028-322-2). Vance Biblios.

Architect's Data: The Handbook of Building Types, 2nd (International) English Edition. Ernst Neufert. LC 80-40644. 433p. 1980. 95.00x o.p. (ISBN 0-470-26947-2). Halsted Pr.

Architect's Detail Sheets: First Series. Edward D. Mills. 1956. (ISBN 0-8022-1120-8). Philos Lib.

Architect's Detail Sheets: Second Series. Edward D. Mills. 230p. 1955. (ISBN 0-8022-1121-6). Philos Lib.

Architect's Detail Sheets: Third Series. Edward D. Mills. 1956. (ISBN 0-8022-1122-4). Philos Lib.

Architect's Guide to Energy Conservation. Seymour Jarmul. (Illus.). 1980. text ed. 29.95 o.p. (ISBN 0-07-032296-1). McGraw.

Architect's Guide to Facility Programming. American Institute of Architects Staff. 304p. 1981. text ed. 41.95 o.p. (ISBN 0-07-001490-6). McGraw.

Architect's Guide to Law & Practice. Bob Greenstreet & Karen Greenstreet. LC 82-24852. 1984. 24.95 o.p. (ISBN 0-442-22823-6). Van Nos Reinhold.

Architect's Handbook. David K. Ballast. LC 83-13795. 315p. 1983. text ed. 59.95 o.p. (ISBN 0-13-044677-7, Busn). P-H.

Architects, Legal Status, Laws, Etc. Mary Vance. (Architecture Ser.: Bibliography A 1351). 1985. pap. 2.25 o.p. (ISBN 0-89028-321-4). Vance Biblios.

Architects: The Noted & the Ignored. Niels L. Prak. LC 83-6988. 242p. 1984. 49.95x o.p. (ISBN 0-471-90203-9). Wiley.

Architect's Yearbook, No. 7. Trevor Dannat. 224p. 1956. (ISBN 0-8022-0337-X). Philos Lib.

Architect's Yearbook, No. 8. Trevor Dannat. 1958. (ISBN 0-8022-0338-8). Philos Lib.

Architectural Acoustics. Ed. by Thomas D. Northwood. (Benchmark Papers in Acoustics: Vol. 10). 1977. 80.50 o.p. (ISBN 0-12-787145-4). Acad Pr.

Architectural Aesthetics. Lamia Doumato. (Architecture Ser.: A 1433). 12p. 1985. 2.00 o.p. (ISBN 0-89028-483-0). Vance Biblios.

Architectural & Building Trades Dictionary. 3rd ed. R. Putnam & G. E. Carlson. (Illus.). 510p. 1974. pap. 17.48 o.p. (ISBN 0-8269-0402-5). Am Technical.

Architectural & Perspective Designs. Guiseppe G. Bibiena. (Illus.). 16.50 o.p. (ISBN 0-8446-1676-1). Peter Smith.

Architectural Antiques. Alan Robertson. (Illus.). 160p. 1987. 25.00 o.p. (ISBN 0-87701-500-7). Chronicle Bks.

Architectural Color. Tom Porter. (Illus.). 128p. 1985. pap. 19.95 o.p. (ISBN 0-8230-7042-5). Watson-Guptill.

Architectural Common Sense Site, Vol. 1. R. Dike. 1983. 28.95 o.p. (ISBN 0-442-21364-6); pap. 18.95 o.p. (ISBN 0-442-21805-2). Van Nos Reinhold.

Architectural Daylighting: A Recent Bibliography. Anthony G. White. (Architecture Ser.: A 1364). 6p. 1985. 2.00 o.p. (ISBN 0-89028-354-0). Vance Biblios.

Architectural Design: Monographs. Mary Vance. (Architecture Ser.: Bibliography A-1299). 21p. 1985. pap. 3.00 o.p. (ISBN 0-89028-229-3). Vance Biblios.

Architectural Detailing Simplified. Caleb Hornbostel. (Illus.). 160p. 1985. text ed. 30.00 o.p. (ISBN 0-13-044173-2). P-H.

Architectural Digest California Interiors. Ed. by Paige Rense. LC 79-84685. (Worlds of Architectural Digest Ser.). (Illus.). 1979. 14.95 o.p. (ISBN 0-89535-032-7). Knapp Pr.

Architectural Digest, Celebrity Homes. Ed. by Paige Rense. LC 77-84047. (Illus.). 1977. 35.00x o.p. (ISBN 0-89535-001-7). Knapp Pr.

Architectural Digest Historic Interiors. Ed. by Paige Rense. LC 77-84683. (Worlds of Architectural Digest Ser.). (Illus.). 1979. 14.95 o.p. (ISBN 0-89535-033-5). Knapp Pr.

Architectural Digest New York Interiors. Ed. by Paige Rense. LC 79-84686. (Worlds of Architectural Digest Ser.). (Illus.). 1979. 14.95 o.p. (ISBN 0-89535-031-9). Knapp Pr.

Architectural Digest Traditional Interiors. Ed. by Paige Rense. LC 79-84682. (Worlds of Architectural Digest Ser.). (Illus.). 1979. 14.95 o.p. (ISBN 0-89535-034-3). Knapp Pr.

Architectural Drafting & Construction. 3rd ed. Ernest R. Weidhaas. 1985. 53.00 o.p. (ISBN 0-205-08405-2, 328405). Allyn.

Architectural Drafting & Design. 5th ed. Ernest R. Weidhaas. LC 84-24583. 528p. 1985. 53.00 o.p. (ISBN 0-205-08407-9, 328407). Allyn.

Architectural Drawing & Light Construction. 2nd ed. Edward J. Muller. (Illus.). 480p. 1976. text ed. 34.00 o.p. (ISBN 0-13-044578-9). P-H.

Architectural Drawings-Collections: A Selected Bibliography. Anthony G. White. LC 85-140862. (Architecture Ser.: Bibliography A 1348). 1985. pap. 2.00 o.p. (ISBN 0-89028-318-4). Vance Biblios.

Architectural Education: A Selective Bibliography, 1961-1984. Frank J. Dolak. (Architecture Ser.: A 1516). 15p. 1985. 2.25 o.p. (ISBN 0-89028-666-3). Vance Biblios.

Architectural Fabric Structures: The Use of Tensioned Fabric Structures by Federal Agencies. National Research Council. LC 84-62844. 87p. 1985. pap. text ed. 8.75x o.p. (ISBN 0-309-03493-0). Natl Acad Pr.

Architectural Graphic Standards. 7th ed. American Institute Architects Staff et al. LC 80-18151. 785p. 1981. 130.00 o.p. (ISBN 0-471-04683-3). Wiley.

Architectural Graphics. Frank Ching. 1975. 15.95 o.p. (ISBN 0-442-21530-4); pap. 9.95 o.p. (ISBN 0-442-21531-2). Van Nos Reinhold.

Architectural Graphics. 2nd ed. C. Leslie Martin. (Illus.). 1970. text ed. write for info. o.p. (ISBN 0-02-376570-4). Macmillan.

Architectural Guide to Wood Construction, Preservation, Conservation, Restoration & Framing. Coppa & Avery Consultants Staff. (Architecture Series: Bibliography: A-1312). 11p. 1985. pap. 2.00 o.p. (ISBN 0-89028-242-0). Vance Biblios.

Architectural Heritage of Newport, Rhode Island: 1640-1915. 2nd ed. A. F. Downing & V. J. Scully, Jr. (Illus.). 1967. 19.95 o.p. (ISBN 0-517-09719-2, American Legacy pr.). Crown.

Architectural History of Canterbury Cathedral. Francis Woodman. 1982. 45.00 o.p. (ISBN 0-7100-0752-3). Routledge Chapman & Hall.

Architectural History of King's College Chapel. Francis Woodman. (Illus.). 200p. 1985. 75.00 o.p. (ISBN 0-7100-9871-5). Routledge Chapman & Hall.

Architectural Illustration. L. Dudley. 1977. text ed. 37.33 o.p. (ISBN 0-13-044610-6). P-H.

Architectural Photography. Joseph W. Molitor. LC 76-6537. 174p. 1976. 34.50 o.p. (ISBN 0-471-61312-6, JW). Krieger.

Architectural Photography of Hedrich-Blessing. Ed. by Robert A. Sobieszek. LC 82-12014. (Illus.). 92p. 1984. 25.00 o.p. (ISBN 0-03-061554-2). H Holt & Co.

Architectural Presentation by Rendering. Satochiro Tsujimoto. (Illus.). 116p. 1986. 32.95 o.p. (ISBN 4-766-10277-0, Pub. by Graphic Sha Japan). Bks Nippan.

Architectural Presentation Techniques. William W. Atkin. 196p. 1982. pap. 14.95 o.p. (ISBN 0-442-21074-4). Van Nos Reinhold.

Architectural Preservation in the United States, 1941-1975: A Bibliography of Federal, State, & Local Government Publications. Richard Tubesing. (Reference Library of the Humanities: Vol. 61). (LC 76-024740). 1978. lib. bdg. 58.00 o.p. (ISBN 0-8240-9937-0). Garland Pub.

Architectural Rendering: The Technique of Contemporary Presentation. 2nd ed. Albert O. Halse. (Illus.). 323p. 1973. text ed. 71.50 o.p. (ISBN 0-07-025628-4). McGraw.

Architectural Research. Ed. by James C. Snyder. 336p. 1984. 41.95 o.p. (ISBN 0-442-28211-7). Van Nos Reinhold.

Architectural Stained Glass. Brian Clarke. LC 79-211. (Illus.). 1979. text ed. 43.50 o.p. (ISBN 0-07-011264-9). McGraw.

Architecture. Alfred M. Brooks. LC 63-10303. (Our Debt to Greece & Rome Ser). Repr. of 1930 ed. 18.50x o.p. (ISBN 0-8154-0032-2). Cooper Sq.

Architecture: A Short History. rev. ed. Joseph Watterson. (Illus.). 1968. 16.95x o.p. (ISBN 0-393-04295-2, NortonC). Norton.

Architecture & Community: Building of the Islamic World Today. Ed. by Renata Holod & Darl Rastorfer. LC 83-71377. (Illus.). 256p. 1983. 40.00 o.p. (ISBN 0-89381-123-8). Aperture.

Architecture & Critical Imagination. Wayne Attoe. 188p. 1978. 54.95x o.p. (ISBN 0-471-99574-6, Pub. by Wiley-Interscience). Wiley.

Architecture & Interior Design of Beauty Salons: A Periodical Bibliography. Mary E. Huls. (Architecture Ser.: A 1487). 5p. 1985. 2.00 o.p. (ISBN 0-89028-617-5). Vance Biblios.

Architecture & Models in Data Base Management: Proceedings of the IFIP-TC-2 Working Conference, 4th, Nice, January, 1977. Ed. by G. M. Nijssen. 326p. 1977. 79.00 o.p. (ISBN 0-7204-0758-3, North-Holland). Elsevier.

Architecture & Politics in Germany, 1918-1945. Barbara M. Lane. LC 67-22867. (Illus.). 1968. 20.00x o.s.i. (ISBN 0-674-04350-2). Harvard U Pr.

Architecture & the Urban Experience. Raymond J. Curran. 240p. 1983. 36.95 o.p. (ISBN 0-442-21208-9). Van Nos Reinhold.

Architecture & Writings of Diana Agrest & Mario Gandelsonas. Carole Cable. (Architecture Ser.: A 1494). 6p. 1985. 2.00 o.p. (ISBN 0-89028-624-8). Vance Biblios.

Architecture for Adult Education. Commission of Architecture of AEA. 74p. 1953. 3.00 o.p. (ISBN 0-88379-008-4). A A A C E.

Architecture for People. Ed. by Byron Mikellides. LC 79-48067. (Illus.). 196p. 1980. 18.95 o.p. (ISBN 0-03-057491-9); pap. 9.95 o.p. (ISBN 0-03-057489-7). H Holt & Co.

Architecture for Worship. Edward A. Sovik. LC 73-78254. (Illus.). 112p. (Orig.). 1973. pap. 6.95 o.p. (ISBN 0-8066-1320-3, 10-0425, Augsburg). Augsburg Fortress.

Architecture in America: A Pictorial History, 2 vols. G. E. Smith. Intro. by Marshal B. Davidson. (Illus.). 1976. 19.95 ea. o.p. (ISBN 0-393-04453-X, Pub. by American Heritage Co.). Norton.

Architecture in Continuity: Building in the Islamic World Today. Sherban Cantacuzino. LC 85-47828. (Illus.). 256p. 1985. 45.00 o.p. (ISBN 0-89381-187-4); pap. 22.50 o.p. (ISBN 0-89381-196-3). Aperture.

Architecture in Pakistan. Kamil K. Mumtaz. (Illus.). 212p. 1987. 20.00 o.s.i. (ISBN 0-89381-245-5). Aperture.

Architecture in the American Southwest & the Work of John Gaw Meem: A Selected Bibliography. Bibliographic Research Library Staff. (Architecture Ser.: A 1401). 7p. 1985. 2.00 o.p. (ISBN 0-89028-431-8). Vance Biblios.
Architecture: Italian Renaissance. Date not set. (ISBN 0-8052-0134-3). Random.
Architecture Librarianship: A Selective Bibliography. Edward H. Teague. (Architecture Ser.: Bibliography A 1349). 1985. pap. 2.00 o.p. (ISBN 0-89028-319-2). Vance Biblios.
Architecture Nineteen Seventy to Nineteen Eighty in Switzerland. 2nd ed. Werner Blaser. (Illus.). 168p. (Eng., Ger. & Fr.). 1982. 15.95 o.p. (ISBN 3-7643-1311-0). Birkhauser.
Architecture of Ancient Greece. 3rd ed. William B. Dinsmoor. (Illus.). 424p. 1975. Repr. 18.95x o.p. (ISBN 0-393-04412-2). Norton.
Architecture of Ancient Rome: An Account of Its Historic Development. William J. Anderson & Richard P. Spiers. LC 27-24681. 202p. Repr. cancelled o.s.i. (ISBN 0-403-08618-3). Somerset Pub.
Architecture of Cognition. John R. Anderson. (Cognitive Science Ser.: No. 5). (Illus.). 352p. 1983. text ed. 32.00x o.p. (ISBN 0-674-04425-8). Harvard U Pr.
Architecture of Concurrent Programs. P. Brinch-Hanson. 1977. text ed. 59.00 o.p. (ISBN 0-13-044628-9). P-H.
Architecture of Distributed Computer Systems. G. V. Bochmann. (Lecture Notes in Computer Sciences: Vol. 77). 238p. 1980. pap. 14.00 o.p. (ISBN 0-387-09723-6). Springer-Verlag.
Architecture of Embassies. Coppa & Avery Consultants Staff. (Architecture Ser.: A 1385). 9p. 1985. 2.00 o.p. (ISBN 0-89028-395-8). Vance Biblios.
Architecture of Erik Gunnar Asplund. Stuart Wrede. (Illus.). 280p. 1980. pap. 17.95 o.p. (ISBN 0-262-73068-5). MIT Pr.
Architecture of Houston, Texas: A Bibliography of Articles, 1978 to 1983, An Update to Architecture Ser: Bibliography A-2. Carole Cable. (Architecture Ser.: Bibliograpy A 1325). 1985. pap. 2.00 o.p. (ISBN 0-89028-275-7). Vance Biblios.
Architecture of India-Buddhist & Hindu. Satish Grover. (Illus.). 1980. text ed. 40.00x o.p. (ISBN 0-7069-0685-3, Pub. by Vikas India). Advent NY.
Architecture of India: Islamic. Satish Grover. (Illus.). 280p. 1981. text ed. 45.00x o.p. (ISBN 0-7069-1130-X, Pub. by Vikas India). Advent NY.
Architecture of John Wellborn Root. Donald Hoffmann. LC 72-4008. (Studies in Nineteenth-Century Architecture). (Illus.). 288p. 1973. 32.50x o.p. (ISBN 0-8018-1371-9). Johns Hopkins.
Architecture of Johnson-Burgee: A Selected Bibliography. Bibliographic Research Library Staff. (Architecture Ser.: A 1394). 6p. 1985. 2.00 o.p. (ISBN 0-89028-404-0). Vance Biblios.
Architecture of Mexico & Central America: Monographs Published 1970-1984. Mary Vance. (Architecture Ser.: A 1481). 18p. 1985. 3.00 o.p. (ISBN 0-89028-611-6). Vance Biblios.
Architecture of Pipelined Computers. Peter M. Kogge. LC 80-26122. (Advanced Computer Science Ser.). (Illus.). 352p. 1981. text ed. 52.95 o.p. (ISBN 0-07-035237-2). McGraw.
Architecture of Ralph Erskine. Peter Collymore. 178p. 1982. text ed. 39.95x o.p. (ISBN 0-246-11250-6, Pub. by Granada England). Gower Pub Co.
Architecture of Sir Christopher Wren. Viktor Furst. LC 56-36662. 244p. 1956. Repr. 49.00 o.p. (ISBN 0-686-01441-3). Somerset Pub.
Architecture of South America: Monographs Published 1970-1984. Mary Vance. (Architecture Ser.: A 1480). 26p. 1985. 3.75 o.p. (ISBN 0-89028-610-8). Vance Biblios.
Architecture of the Caribbean. John N. Lewis. (Illus.). 1984. 20.00 o.p. (ISBN 0-913962-68-6, M686P). Am Inst Arch.
Architecture of the Renaissance. Leonardo Benevolo. Tr. by Judith Landry. (Illus.). 1077p. 67.50 o.p. (ISBN 0-7100-8036-0). Routledge Chapman & Hall.
Architecture of Tibet: An Introductory Bibliography. Edward H. Teague. (Architecture Ser.: A 1382). 7p. 1985. 2.00 o.p. (ISBN 0-89028-392-3). Vance Biblios.
Architecture of Videotex Systems. Jan Gecsei. (Illus.). 320p. 1983. text ed. 48.00 o.p. (ISBN 0-13-044776-5). P-H.
Architecture: Perspective Shadows & Reflections. Dik Vrooman. 151p. 1983. 22.95 o.p. (ISBN 0-442-28825-5). Van Nos Reinhold.
Architecture, San Francisco: The Guide. John Woodbridge & Sally Woodbridge. LC 82-14291. (Illus.). 208p. 1982. pap. 10.95 o.p. (ISBN 0-89286-204-1, One Hund One Prods). Ortho.
Architecture, Society & Space-The High-Density Question Re-Examined. A. R. Cuthbert. (Illus.). 90p. 1985. pap. 22.00 o.p. (ISBN 0-08-033227-7, Pub. by PPL). Pergamon.
Archival Choices: Managing the Historical Record in an Age of Abundance. Ed. by Nancy E. Peace. LC 81-48395. 176p. 1984. 29.00x o.p. (ISBN 0-669-05354-6). Lexington Bks.
Archive Buildings & Equipment. Michel Duchein. (ICA Handbook Ser.). (Illus.). 201p. 1977. pap. text ed. 17.00 o.p. (ISBN 3-7940-3780-4). K G Saur.
Archives & Manuscript Repositories in the U. S. S. R., Moscow & Leningrad: Supplement I; Biographical Addenda. Patricia K. Grimsted. 218p. 1980. 31.50x o.p. (ISBN 0-691-05290-5). Princeton U Pr.
Archives Jean Piaget: Catalog of the Jean Piaget Archives. University of Geneva Staff. 1975. lib. bdg. 78.00 o.p. (ISBN 0-8161-1184-7, Hall Library). G K Hall.
Archives of American Art: Collection of Exhibition Catalogs. 1979. lib. bdg. 100.00 o.s.i. (ISBN 0-8161-0251-1, Hall Library). G K Hall.
Arctic Air Chemistry: Proceedings of the Second Symposium, Graduate School of Oceanography, University of Rhode Island, 6-8 May 1980. Ed. by K. A. Rahn. (Atmospheric Environment: Vol. 15, No. 8). iv, 172p. 1981. pap. 36.00 o.p. (ISBN 0-08-026288-0). Pergamon.
Arctic & Alpine Environments. Jack D. Ives & Roger G. Barry. LC 74-2673. (Illus.). 980p. 1974. 150.00x o.p. (ISBN 0-416-65980-2, NO.2250). Routledge Chapman & Hall.
Arctic & Tropical Arboviruses. Ed. by Edouard Kurstak. 1979. 38.50 o.p. (ISBN 0-12-429765-X). Acad Pr.
Arctic Archaeology: An Annotated Bibliography & History. Albert A. Dekin, Jr. LC 75-5120. (Reference Library of Natural Science: No. 1). (Illus.). 200p. 1978. lib. bdg. 37.00 o.p. (ISBN 0-8240-1084-1). Garland Pub.
Arctic Cat: Snowmobile Service-Repair, 1974-1979. Eric Jorgensen. (Illus.). pap. 11.95 o.p. (ISBN 0-89287-172-5, X951). Clymer Pub.
Arctic Ecosystem: The Coastal Tundra at Barrow, Alaska. Ed. by J. Brown et al. LC 78-22901. (US-IBP Synthesis Ser.: Vol. 12). 571p. 1982. 45.95 o.p. (ISBN 0-87933-370-7). Van Nos Reinhold.
Arctic Life of Birds & Mammals Including Man. L. Irving. LC 72-79584. (Zoophysiology & Ecology, Ser.: Vol. 2). (Illus.). 200p. 1973. 33.00 o.p. (ISBN 0-387-05801-X). Springer-Verlag.
Arctic Manual. Vilhjalmur Stefansson. LC 74-10378. (Illus.). 556p. 1974. Repr. of 1944 ed. lib. bdg. 30.00x o.p. (ISBN 0-8371-7682-4, STARM). Greenwood.
Arctic Mission. Jill Burrell & Maurice Burrell. 1974. 1.60 o.s.i. (ISBN 0-08-017621-6). Pergamon.
Arctic Solitudes. Admiral Lord Mountevans. (Illus.). 160p. 1953. (ISBN 0-8022-1160-7). Philos Lib.
Arctic Whaling Diary: The Journal of Captain George Comer in Hudson Bay 1903-1905. Ed. by W. Gillies Ross. 304p. 1984. 29.95x o.p. (ISBN 0-8020-5618-0). U of Toronto Pr.
Arctic World. Fred Bruemmer et al. Ed. by William E. Taylor, Jr. LC 85-2051. (Illus.). 256p. 1985. 39.95 o.p. (ISBN 0-87156-842-X). Sierra.
Arden of Feversham. (Royal Shakespeare Company Playtext Ser.). 48p. 1983. pap. 3.95 o.p. (ISBN 0-413-53430-8, NO. 3905). Heinemann Ed.
Ardrossan, County of Strathcona, Alberta, Canada. Nu-West Development Corporation Ltd. (Panel Advisory Service Reports). 1980p. 10.00 o.p. (ISBN 0-317-36120-1, A10). Urban Land.
Are All the Giants Dead? Mary Norton. LC 78-6622. (Illus.). (gr. 4-6). 1978. pap. 2.50 o.p. (ISBN 0-15-607888-0, VoyB). HarBraceJ.
Are Pesticides Really Necessary? Keith C. Barrons. LC 80-54684. 245p. 1981. pap. 6.95 o.p. (ISBN 0-89526-888-4). Regnery Gateway.
Are Religious Cults Dangerous? Carol Coulter. 112p. 1984. pap. 8.95 o.p. (ISBN 0-85342-722-4, Pub. by Mercier Pr Ireland). Irish Bks Media.
Are Those Your Good Pants? Parker et al. 128p. (Orig.). 1981. pap. 1.75 o.s.i. (ISBN 0-449-14390-2, GM). Fawcett.
Are We All Nazis? Hans Askenasy. 1978. 8.95 o.p. (ISBN 0-8184-0248-2). Carol Pub Group.
Are We Alone? Robert T. Rood & James S. Trefil. (Illus.). 272p. 1983. pap. 7.95 o.s.i. (ISBN 0-684-17842-7, ScribT). Scribner.
Are We There Yet? Diane Vreuls. 1976. pap. 1.25 o.p. (ISBN 0-380-00565-4, 28746). Avon.
Are You Happy? & Other Questions Lovers Ask. Edward Koren. LC 78-53922. (Illus.). 1978. 3.95 o.p. (ISBN 0-394-50271-X). Pantheon.
Are You Happy? Some Answers to the Most Important Question in Your Life. Dennis Wholey. 1986. 16.45 o.s.i. (ISBN 0-395-40779-6). HM.
Are You in the Right Job? James Boulgarides & Mary Fischer. 128p. 1984. pap. 7.95 o.p. (ISBN 0-671-50222-0). Monarch Pr.
Are You Listening? Henrietta Gambill. LC 84-7026. (Illus.). 32p. (ps-k). 1984. lib. bdg. 2.95 o.p. (ISBN 0-89693-221-4). Dandelion Hse.
Are You Listening? R. Nichols & L. A. Stevens. 1957. text ed. 14.95 o.p. (ISBN 0-07-046475-8). McGraw.
Are You Looking for God? Edmund A. Steimle. LC 57-5757. 1957. pap. 1.85 o.p. (ISBN 0-8006-1792-4, Fortress). Augsburg Fortress.
Are You Nobody? Paul Tournier. pap. 2.95 o.p. (ISBN 0-8042-3356-X, John Knox). Westminster John Knox.
Are You Now or Have You Ever Been in the FBI Files? How to Secure & Interpret Your FBI Files. Ann Buitrago & Leon A. Immerman. LC 79-6155. (Illus.). 227p. 1981. pap. 7.95 o.p. (ISBN 0-394-17647-2, E750, Ever). Grove.
Are You Saved? Answers to the Awkward Question. Thomas H. Troeger. LC 79-14402. 132p. 1979. pap. 6.95 o.s.i. (ISBN 0-664-24267-7, Westminster). Westminster John Knox.
Are You Tough Enough? An Insider's View of Washington Power Politics. Anne M. Burford & John Greenya. (Illus.). 304p. 1985. text ed. 16.95 o.p. (ISBN 0-07-008940-X). McGraw.
Are Your Lights On? How to Figure Out What the Problem Really Is. Don C. Gause & Gerald M. Weinberg. 157p. (Orig.). 1982. pap. text ed. 9.95 o.p. Scott F.
Arena. Norman Bogner. 1980. pap. 3.25 o.p. (ISBN 0-440-10369-X). Dell.
Arfive. A. B. Guthrie, Jr. 1971. 5.95 o.p. (ISBN 0-395-11076-9). HM.
Argent. Emile Zola. 1960. pap. 7.95 o.p. (ISBN 0-685-23957-8). Schoenhof.
Argentina: A Country Study. 3rd ed. Ed. by James D. Rudolph. LC 86-3616. (DA Pam 550-73. Area Handbook Ser.). 437p. 1986. 17.50 o.p. (ISBN 0-318-22490-9, S/N 008-020-01093-6). USGPO.
Argentina & the United States, 1810-1960. Harold F. Peterson. LC 62-21414. 627p. 1964. 49.50x o.p. (ISBN 0-87395-010-0). State U NY Pr.
Argentina, the Peronist Myth: An Essay on the Cultural Decay in Argentina After the Second World War. Roberto Aizcorbe. LC 74-34506. 1975. 10.00 o.p. (ISBN 0-682-48232-3, University). Exposition-Phoenix.
Argentina's Foreign Policy, 1930-62. Alberto C. Paz & Gustavo E. Ferrari. Tr. by J. J. Kennedy. 1966. 22.95x o.p. (ISBN 0-268-00010-7). U of Notre Dame Pr.
Argentine Journal. Jo Ann Lordahl. 1987. Lat Am Lit Rev Pr.
Argentine Radicalism. Peter G. Snow. 137p. 1965. pap. 7.00 o.p. (ISBN 0-87745-016-1). U of Iowa Pr.
Argia. Antonio Cesti. Ed. by Howard M. Brown. LC 76-21082. (Italian Opera 1640-1770 Ser.: Vol. 3). 1978. lib. bdg. 77.00 o.p. (ISBN 0-8240-2602-0). Garland Pub.
Argo: Poems. R. F. Willetts. (Illus.). 48p. (Orig.). 1985. pap. 9.95x o.p. (ISBN 0-85362-221-3, Oriel). Routledge Chapman & Hall.
Argon: Gas Solubilities. Clever. (IUPAC Solubility Data Ser.: Vol. 4). (Illus.). 348p. 1980. 110.00 o.p. (ISBN 0-08-022353-2). Pergamon.
Arguing for Socialism: Theoretical Considerations. Andrew Levine. (Critical Social Thought Ser.). 280p. 1984. 23.50x o.p. (ISBN 0-7100-9931-2). Routledge Chapman & Hall.
Argument: The Logic of the Fallacies. Woods. 1982. text ed. 12.95 o.p. (ISBN 0-07-548026-3). McGraw.
Argumentation & Debate: Critical Thinking for Reasoned Decision Making. 6th ed. Austin J. Freeley. 427p. 1986. text ed. write for info. o.p. (ISBN 0-534-05526-5). Wadsworth Pub.
Aria. Brown Meggs. LC 77-81588. 1978. 10.95 o.p. (ISBN 0-689-10832-X, Atheneum). Macmillan.
Ariadne Clue. Carol Clemeau. 176p. 1983. pap. 2.50 o.s.i. (ISBN 0-345-30736-4). Ballantine.
Arid Land Irrigation in Developing Countries: Environmental Problems & Effects. Ed. by E. Barton Worthington. 1977. 185.00 o.p. (ISBN 0-08-021588-2). Pergamon.
Arid Zone Irrigation. Ed. by B. Yaron et al. LC 73-76816. (Ecological Studies Ser.: Vol. 5). (Illus.). 500p. 1973. 52.30 o.p. (ISBN 0-387-06206-8). Springer-Verlag.
Ariel. Lawrence Block. LC 79-87835. 1980. 9.25 o.p. (ISBN 0-87795-234-5, Arbor Hse). Morrow.
Aries. Julia Parker. (Pocket Guides to Astrology 1982 Ser.). (Orig.). 1981. pap. 4.95 o.p. (ISBN 0-671-43442-X). S&S.
Aris, the Christmas Wolf. Phillip Scardina. 1987. 6.00 o.p. (ISBN 0-8062-2590-4). Carlton.
Arise Jerusalem: Parish Advent Program, Advent Family Handbook. Ed. by Jean M. Heisberger. LC 78-70425. 1978. pap. text ed. 1.25 o.p. (ISBN 0-8091-9179-2). Paulist Pr.
Aristocrats of the Trees. Ernest H. Wilson. (Illus.). 279p. 1974. Repr. of 1930 ed. 6.95 o.p. (ISBN 0-486-20038-8). Dover.
Aristocrats of the Trees. Ernest H. Wilson. (Illus.). 9.00 o.p. (ISBN 0-8446-5100-1). Peter Smith.
Aristophanes: Acharnians. C. E. Graves. 210p. 1982. Repr. of 1905 ed. 15.25 o.p. (ISBN 0-86292-003-5, Pub. by Bristol Classical UK). Focus Info Gr.
Aristotle on the Art of Poetry. 2nd ed. Ingram Bywater. LC 78-66550. (Ancient Philosophy Ser.). 435p. 1980. lib. bdg. 53.00 o.p. (ISBN 0-8240-9607-X). Garland Pub.
Aristotle's De Partibus Animalium: Critical & Literary Commentaries. Ingemar During. LC 78-66548. (Ancient Philosophy Ser.). 223p. 1980. lib. bdg. 26.00 o.p. (ISBN 0-8240-9602-9). Garland Pub.
Aristotle's Physics. Aristotle. Tr. by Richard Hope. LC 61-5498. xiv, 242p. 1961. pap. 6.25x o.p. (ISBN 0-8032-5093-2, BB 122, Bison). U of Nebr Pr.
Aristotle's Prior & Posterior Analytics: A Revised Text with Introduction & Commentary. W. D. Ross. LC 78-66588. (Ancient Philosophy Ser.). 700p. 1980. lib. bdg. 80.00 o.p. (ISBN 0-8240-9587-1). Garland Pub.
Arithmefun. Kids' Stuff People Staff. (Illus.). 80p. (gr. 1-3). 1982. pap. text ed. 5.95 o.p. (ISBN 0-86530-002-X, IP-02X). Incentive Pubns.
Arithmetic. 3rd ed. Jack Barker et al. 1983. pap. text ed. 27.95 o.p. (ISBN 0-03-062397-9). HR&W.
Arithmetic. Vivian S. Groza. 1982. 27.95 o.p. (ISBN 0-03-060109-6, CBS C); instr's manual 10.95 o.p. (ISBN 0-03-060111-8). SCP.
Arithmetic: A Text-Workbook. Charles D. Miller & Stanley A. Salzman. 1981. pap. text ed. write for info. o.p. (ISBN 0-673-15274-X). Scott F.
Arithmetic: An Applied Approach. Richard N. Aufmann & Vernon C. Barker. LC 77-77005. (Illus.). 1978. pap. 20.50 o.p. (ISBN 0-395-25791-3). HM.
Arithmetic & Beginning Algebra. 2nd ed. Allyn J. Washington. 1984. 24.95 o.p. (ISBN 0-8053-9540-7). Benjamin-Cummings.
Arithmetic Applied Mathematics. Donald Greenspan. LC 80-40295. (Illus.). 172p. 1980. 41.00 o.p. (ISBN 0-08-025047-5); pap. 16.00 o.p. (ISBN 0-08-025046-7). Pergamon.
Arithmetic Enrichment Activities for Elementary School Children. Joseph Crescimbeni. 1965. text ed. 14.95x o.p. (ISBN 0-13-046177-6, Parker). P-H.
Arithmetic for Billy Goats. Donald Barr. LC 66-21608. (Illus.). (gr. 3-6). 1966. 4.95 o.p. (ISBN 0-15-203867-1, HJ). HarBraceJ.
Arithmetic for the Practical Worker. 4th ed. J. E. Thompson. 272p. 1982. pap. 9.95 o.p. (ISBN 0-442-28275-3). Van Nos Reinhold.
Arithmetic of Dosages & Solutions: A Programmed Presentation. 6th ed. Laura K. Hart. (Illus.). 82p. 1985. 14.95 o.p. (ISBN 0-8016-2089-9). Mosby.
Arithmetic on Elliptic Curves with Complex Multiplication. B. H. Cross. (Lecture Notes in Mathematics Ser.: Vol. 776). 1980. pap. 13.00 o.p. (ISBN 0-387-09743-0). Springer-Verlag.
Arithmetic Review for Electronics. Nelson M. Cooke & Herbert F. Adams. 1968. text ed. 26.50 o.p. (ISBN 0-07-012516-3). McGraw.
Arithmetic Simplified & Self-Taught. The Arco Editorial Board. 144p. 1985. pap. 5.95 o.p. (ISBN 0-668-06468-4). Arco.
Arithmetic That We Need. Thomas Mooney. 1966. pap. 2.75x o.p. (ISBN 0-88323-003-8, 104); tchr's. key 2.75x o.p. (ISBN 0-88323-004-6, 105). Pendergrass Pub.
Arithmetic the Easy Way. Williams. (Easy Way Ser.). 240p. (gr. 6-12). 1982. pap. 8.95 o.p. (ISBN 0-8120-2621-7). Barron.
Arithmetics Groups. J. E. Humphreys. (Lecture Notes in Mathematics: Vol. 789). 158p. 1980. pap. 15.00 o.p. (ISBN 0-387-09972-7). Springer-Verlag.
Arizona: Agency. 8.50 o.p. (ISBN 0-686-90627-6). Am Law Inst.
Arizona Clan. Zane Grey. LC 85-469. 1984. pap. 2.95 o.s.i. (ISBN 0-671-50296-4). PB.
Arizona II. Photos by Josef Muench. LC 79-51787. (Belding Imprint Ser.). (Illus.). 128p. (Text by Tom Cooper). 1979. 29.50 o.s.i. (ISBN 0-912856-48-3). Gr Arts Ctr Pub.
Arizona Index: A Subject Index to Periodical Articles About the State, 2 vols. Ed. by University of Arizona Library Staff. 1978. lib. bdg. 177.00 o.p. (ISBN 0-8161-0090-X, Hall Library). G K Hall.
Arizona Industrial Minerals. 1975. 15.80 o.p. (ISBN 0-942218-00-0). Minobras.
Arizona Manufacturers Directory, 19877-88. 196p. 1987. pap. 65.00 o.p. (ISBN 0-318-02843-3). Manufacturers.

Arizona Museums. Mildred M. Fischer & Al Fischer. 88p. 1985. pap. 5.00 o.p. (ISBN 0-914846-19-1). Golden West Pub.

Arizona No-Fault Divorce. Van O'Steen & John R. Bates. (Illus.). 1983. Repr. of 1976 ed. folio 19.95 o.p. (ISBN 0-935810-08-0). Primer Pubs.

Arizona Property & Casualty. 1985. write for info. o.p. Merritt Co.

Arizona Supplement for Modern Real Estate Practice. 4th ed. Charles E. Myler, Jr. LC 83-24440. 174p. 1984. pap. text ed. 10.95 o.p. (ISBN 0-88462-487-0, 1510-25, Real Estate Ed). Longman Finan.

Arizona Trails. 2nd ed. David Mazel. LC 84-52658. (Illus.). 320p. 1985. pap. 13.95 o.p. (ISBN 0-89997-051-6). Wilderness Pr.

Arizona: Travel Guide. 5th ed. Sunset Editors. LC 78-53677. (Illus.). 112p. 1978. pap. 8.95 o.p. (ISBN 0-376-06057-3, Sunset Bks.). Sunset-Lane.

Arizona: Trusts. 8.50 o.p. (ISBN 0-686-90629-2). Am Law Inst.

Arizona's Red Rock Country: Seasons in Oak Creek Canyon & Sedona. Larry Russell. LC 83-63311. (Western Horizons Bk.). (Illus.). 72p. 1984. pap. 11.95 o.p. (ISBN 0-87358-353-1). Northland.

Ark. Margot Benary-Isbert. LC 52-13677. (gr. 7 up). 1953. 6.50 o.p. (ISBN 0-15-203901-5, HJ). HarBraceJ.

Ark. Margot Benary-Isbert. Tr. by Clara Winston & Richard Winston. LC 52-13677. (gr. 7 up). 1966. pap. 1.95 o.p. (ISBN 0-15-607921-6, VoyB). HarBraceJ.

Ark: A Provocative & Challenging Look at Religion. David R. Kibby. 1980. 5.00 o.p. (ISBN 0-682-49573-5). Exposition-Phoenix.

Ark of Noah. David Fasold. (Illus.). 336p. 1988. 18.95 o.p. (ISBN 0-8007-7206-7). Wynwood Pr.

Ark of the North. Paul Durcan. 1982. 8.95 o.p. (ISBN 0-906897-42-4); pap. 7.95 o.p. (ISBN 0-906897-41-6). Dufour.

Arkansas: An Illustrated History of the Land of Opportunity. C. Fred Williams. Ed. by Susan Wells. LC 86-22376. (Illus.). 384p. 1986. 29.95 o.p. (ISBN 0-89781-182-8). Windsor Pubns Inc.

Arkansas Court Rules. Michie Company Editorial Staff. (State Practice Publications Ser.). 1001p. 1987. Annual subscription. pap. 35.00x o.p. (ISBN 0-87473-282-4). Michie Co.

Arkansas Criminal Code. Michie Company Editorial Staff. (State Practices Publications Ser.). 940p. 1985. pap. 27.50x o.p. (ISBN 0-87215-858-6). Michie Co.

Arkansas Directory of Industries, 1988. 312p. 1988. pap. 50.00 o.p. (ISBN 0-318-22793-2). Manufacturers.

Arkansas: Learning Activities for Elementary Students. Robert L Cornish & Aleta M. Mabry. 1983. 15.00x o.p. (ISBN 0-931510-13-9). Hi Willow.

Arkansas Traveller: Adapted for Today's Readers. Liz S. Parkhurst. LC 82-70162. (Illus.). 44p. 1982. 7.95 o.p. (ISBN 0-935304-43-6). August Hse.

Arkansas: Trusts. 8.50 o.p. (ISBN 0-686-90631-4). Am Law Inst.

Armada. Bryce Walker & Time-Life Books Editors. (Seafarers Ser.). (Illus.). 176p. 1981. 13.95 o.p. (ISBN 0-8094-2697-8). Time-Life.

Armageddon in Prime Time. George Bailey. 1984. pap. 3.95 o.p. (ISBN 0-380-89598-6). Avon.

Armageddon Rag. George R. Martin. 1983. 15.50 o.s.i. (ISBN 0-671-47526-6, Pub. by Poseidon). S&S.

Armance. Stendhal. Ed. by Martineau. 1962. pap. 7.50 o.p. (ISBN 0-685-11013-3). Schoenhof.

Armchair Aviator. John Thorn. (Illus.). 320p. 1983. 19.95 o.s.i. (ISBN 0-684-18014-6, ScribT). Scribner.

Armchair Basic. (ISBN 0-07-931092-3). McGraw.

Armchair Detective, 5 vols. Incl. Vol. 18, No. 3. 1985 (ISBN 0-89296-327-1); Vol. 18, No. 4. 1985 (ISBN 0-89296-328-X); Vol. 19, No. 1. 1986 (ISBN 0-89296-329-8); Vol. 19, No. 2. 1986 (ISBN 0-89296-330-1); Vol. 19, No. 3. 1986 (ISBN 0-89296-331-X). (Illus.). 6.00 ea. o.p. (Pub by Hill & Wang). FS&G.

Armchair Mountaineer: The Triumphs & Tragedies of Ascent, from Fact & Fiction. Ed. by David Reuther & John Thorn. (Illus.). 320p. 1985. 19.95 o.s.i. (ISBN 0-684-18198-3, ScribT). Scribner.

Armed & Alone: The American Security Dilemma. Dean W. Rudoy. LC 72-91425. 96p. 1972. pap. 1.95 o.p. (ISBN 0-8076-0667-7). Braziller.

Armed Criminal in America: A Survey of Incarcerated Felons. James D. Wright & Peter H. Rossi. (National Institute of Justice Research Report). 58p. 1985. pap. 2.50 o.p. (ISBN 0-318-18725-6, S/N 027-000-01240-0). USGPO.

Armed Forces of Latin America: Their Histories, Development, Present Strength & Military Potential. Adrian J. English. (Illus.). 480p. 1985. 50.00 o.p. (ISBN 0-7106-0321-5). Janes Info Group.

Armed Forces of the Soviet State: A Soviet View. A. A. Grechko. (Soviet Military Thought Ser.: No. 12). 349p. (Orig.). 1977. pap. 7.00 o.p. (ISBN 0-318-21916-6, S/N 008-070-00379-1). USGPO.

Armed Struggle in Italy: A Chronology. Tr. by Jean Weir from Ital. (Anarchist Pamphlets Ser.: No. 4). 94p. (Orig.). 1979. pap. 3.00 o.p. (ISBN 0-317-67944-9). Left Bank.

Armees Revolutionnaires, 2 Vols. Richard Cobb. (Societe Mouvements Sociaux et Ideologies Etudes 3: No. 3). 1961. Set. pap. text ed. 50.40x o.p. (ISBN 90-2796-235-9). Mouton.

Armenian Cause. Yves Ternon. LC 84-23228. 1985. pap. 15.00x o.p. (ISBN 0-88206-503-3). Caravan Bks.

Armenian Community. Sarkis Atamian. 1955. (ISBN 0-8022-0043-5). Philos Lib.

Armenian Jewelry Art. Ed. by H. Sharamanyan. 222p. 1983. 15.00 o.p. (ISBN 0-8285-2717-2, Pub. by Sovetakan Grogh USSR). Imported Pubns.

Armenian Miniatures of the Thirteenth & Fourteenth Centuries. E. Korkhmazian. 140p. 1984. 40.00 o.p. (ISBN 0-8285-2902-7, Pub. by Aurora Pubs USSR). Imported Pubns.

Armies & Politics in Latin America. Ed. by Abraham F. Lowenthal. LC 76-17832. 1985. 17.50x o.p. (ISBN 0-8419-0281-X); pap. 12.50 o.s.i. (ISBN 0-8419-0282-8). Holmes & Meier.

Armies Encamped in the Fields Beyond the Unfinished Avenues: Prose Poems. rev. & expanded ed. Morton Marcus. (Illus.). pap. 5.95 o.p. Brown Bear.

Armistice 1918. Harry R. Rudin. LC 67-15927. (Illus.). vii, 442p. 1967. Repr. of 1944 ed. 37.50 o.p. (ISBN 0-208-00280-4, Archon). Shoe String.

Armorial General Precede d'un Dictionnaire des Termes du Blason, Pt. 1. Johannes B. Rietstap. (Fr.). 1934. 135.00 o.p. (ISBN 0-686-56594-0, M-7298, Pub. by Olms). French & Eur.

Armoured Fighting Vehicles of the World. rev. ed. Christopher Foss. LC 77-74717. (Illus.). 1978. 8.95 o.p. (ISBN 0-684-15225-8, ScribT). Scribner.

Armoury in the Moscow Kremlin. L. Kharlamova. 135p. 1982. 6.95 o.p. (ISBN 0-8285-2342-8, Pub. by Aurora Pubs USSR). Imported Pubns.

Arms & the State: Civil-Military Elements in National Policy. W. Millis. (Twentieth Century Fund Ser.). Repr. of 1958 ed. 10.00 o.p. (ISBN 0-527-02829-0). Kraus Repr.

Arms & Uniforms: The Age of Chivalry, 3 vols. Liliane Funcken & Fred Funcken. 1983. Vol. I, 102p. pap. 8.95 o.p. (ISBN 0-13-046276-4); Vol. II, 109p. pap. 8.95 o.p. (ISBN 0-13-046292-6); Vol. III, 104p. pap. 8.95 o.p. (ISBN 0-13-046326-4); Vol. I. 17.95 o.p. (ISBN 0-13-046284-5); Vol. II. 17.95 o.p. (ISBN 0-13-046318-3); Vol. III. 17.95 o.p. (ISBN 0-13-046334-5). P-H.

Arms Control: Issues for the Public. Ed. by Louis Henken. LC 61-14148. 1961. 3.50 o.p. (ISBN 0-936904-00-3); pap. 1.95 o.p. (ISBN 0-936904-25-9). Am Assembly.

Arms Limitation: Plans for Europe Before 1914. Incl. Report on the Limitation of Armaments. Paul Estournelles De Constant; Limitation of Naval & Military Expenditure. Paul Estournelles De Constant; On the Reduction of Continental Armies. a Proposel. Adolf Fischhof; A Propos Du Desarmement. Augustin Hamon. LC 75-147537. (Library of War & Peace; Control & Limitation of Arms). 1973. lib. bdg. 46.00 o.p. (ISBN 0-8240-0322-5). Garland Pub.

Arms, Men, & Military Budgets: Issues for Fiscal Year 1981. Francis P. Hoeber et al. LC 79-93071. 186p. (Orig.). 1980. pap. 6.95 o.p. (ISBN 0-87855-804-7). Transaction Pubs.

Arms of Valor. Pavlo Shandruk. 6.00 o.p. (ISBN 0-8315-0066-2). Speller.

Arms Race: A Programme for World Disarmament. Philip J. Noel-Baker. LC 60-10966. 603p. 1960. pap. 17.50 o.p. (ISBN 0-379-00085-7). Oceana.

Arms Race Kills Even Without War. Dorothee Soelle. LC 82-48543. 128p. 1983. pap. 1.95 o.p. (ISBN 0-8006-1701-0, Fortress). Augsburg Fortress.

Arms Race: Opposing Viewpoints. Ed. by David L. Bender. LC 85-7685. (Opposing Viewpoints Ser.). 1982. lib. bdg. 14.95 o.p. (ISBN 0-89908-339-0); pap. 7.95 o.p. (ISBN 0-89908-314-5). Greenhaven.

Arms Trade Registers. Stockholm International Peace Research Institute (SIPRI) Staff. LC 75-868. 186p. 1975. text ed. 30.00x o.p. (ISBN 0-262-19138-5). MIT Pr.

Arms Transfers & U. S. Foreign & Military Policy. Alvin Cotrell et al. LC 80-50062. (Significant Issues Ser.: Vol. 1, No. 7). 72p. (Orig.). 1987. pap. 9.75 o.p. (ISBN 0-8191-6076-8, Pub. by CSIS). U Pr of Amer.

Army Exploration in the American West, 1803-1863. William H. Goetzmann. LC 79-14764. (Illus.). xx, 489p. 1979. 32.50x o.p. (ISBN 0-8032-2103-7); pap. 9.95 o.p. (ISBN 0-8032-7003-8, BB 716, Bison). U of Nebr Pr.

Army Gunships in Vietnam. Bob Chenowith. (Warbirds Illustrated Ser.: No. 47). (Illus.). 72p. (Orig.). 1988. pap. 9.95 o.p. (ISBN 0-85368-854-0, Pub. by Arms & Armour). Sterling.

Army in Exile: The Story of the Second Polish Corps. W. Anders. (Allied Forces Ser.: No. 1). (Illus.). 319p. 1981. Repr. of 1949 ed. 18.95 o.p. (ISBN 0-89839-043-5). Battery Pr.

Army of Francis Joseph. Gunther E. Rothenberg. LC 75-16051. 312p. 1976. 12.00 o.p. (ISBN 0-911198-41-5). Purdue U Pr.

Army of Israel. Moshe Pearlman. (ISBN 0-8022-1295-6). Philos Lib.

Army on the Powder River. facs. ed. Robert A. Murray. 1972. pap. 3.00 o.p. (ISBN 0-88342-203-4). Old Army.

Army Staff Officer's Guide. Glen R. Johnson & Fred M. Walker. LC 74-11834. 298p. 1975. 21.00x o.p. (ISBN 0-87201-046-5). Gulf Pub.

Army Uniforms of World War One. Andrew Mollo. (Illus.). 138p. 1987. pap. 12.95 o.p. (ISBN 0-7137-1928-1, Pub. by Blandford Pr England). Sterling.

Arnie & a House Full of Company. Margarete S. Corbo & Diane M. Barras. (Illus.). 240p. 1985. 11.70 o.p. (ISBN 0-395-38167-3). HM.

Arnie & a House Full of Company. Margarete S. Corbo & Diane M. Barras. (Large Print Bks (General Ser.)). 335p. 1986. lib. bdg. 15.95 o.p. (ISBN 0-8161-4077-4). G K Hall.

Arnie, the Darling Starling. Margaret E. Corbo & Diane M. Barras. (General Ser.). 1984. lib. bdg. 12.95 o.p. (ISBN 0-8161-3638-6, Large Print Bks). G K Hall.

Arnie, the Darling Starling. Margarete S. Corbo & Diane M. Barras. (Illus.). 288p. 1983. 9.70 o.p. (ISBN 0-395-34390-9). HM.

Arnold Bennett: A Biography. Margaret Drabble. (Hall Nonfiction Paperbacks). 440p. 1986. pap. 11.95 o.p. (ISBN 0-8398-2903-5). G K Hall.

Arnold Bennett: An Annotated Bibliography, 1887-1932. Anita Miller. LC 75-42919. (Reference Library of the Humanities Ser.: Vol. 46). 1977. lib. bdg. 109.00 o.p. (ISBN 0-8240-9954-0). Garland Pub.

Arnold Bennett: The Critical Heritage. James Hepburn. (Critical Heritage Ser.). 576p. 1981. 48.50x o.p. (ISBN 0-7100-0512-1). Routledge Chapman & Hall.

Arnold Flaten: Sculptor. Ed. by Karen Foget. LC 74-14168. 128p. 1974. 15.00 o.p. (ISBN 0-8066-1452-8, 10-0430). Augsburg Fortress.

Arnold Palmer's Complete Book of Putting. Arnold Palmer & Peter Dobereiner. LC 85-48135. (Illus.). 192p. 1986. 24.95 o.p. (ISBN 0-689-11624-1, Atheneum). Macmillan.

Arnold Schoenberg. Hans H. Stuckenschmidt. Tr. by H. Searle from Ger. LC 77-81649. (Illus.). 1978. 20.00 o.s.i. (ISBN 0-02-872480-1). Schirmer Bks.

Arnold: The Education of a Body Builder. Arnold Schwarzenegger & Douglas K. Hall. (Illus.). 1977. 14.95 o.s.i. (ISBN 0-671-22879-X). S&S.

Arnold Toynbee & the Crisis of the West. Marvin Perry. LC 81-40162. 138p. 1982. 25.50 o.p. (ISBN 0-8191-2025-1); pap. 9.50 o.p. (ISBN 0-8191-2026-X). U Pr of Amer.

Arnold's Bodybuilding for Men. Arnold Schwarzenegger & Bill Dobbins. 1981. 17.50 o.s.i. (ISBN 0-671-25613-0). S&S.

Arnold's Bodyshaping for Women. Arnold Schwarzenegger. 1979. 14.95 o.s.i. (ISBN 0-671-24301-2). S&S.

Ar'n't I a Woman? Female Slaves in the Plantation South. Deborah G. White. 1985. 18.45 o.p. (ISBN 0-393-02217-X). Norton.

Aromaticity, Pseudoaromaticity, Antiaromaticity. Ed. by E. D. Bergmann & B. Pullman. LC 79-134838. 1971. 84.00 o.p. (ISBN 0-12-091040-3). Acad Pr.

Aromatics & Derivatives see Petrochemical Manufacturing & Marketing Guide.

Around & Beyond the Confines of Art. Philip Metman. 1985. 10.00x o.p. (ISBN 0-317-61994-2, Guild of Pastoral Psych). State Mutual Bk.

Around Brisbane: Including Gold Coast, Sunshine Coast & Toowoomba. Sallyanne Atkinson. (Illus.). 1979. pap. 7.45 o.p. (ISBN 0-7022-1166-4). U of Queensland Pr.

Around Lake Michigan. Jean Komaiko et al. 1980. pap. 7.95 o.p. (ISBN 0-395-29127-5). HM.

Around the Corner. Virginia Sorensen. LC 78-158005. (Illus.). (gr. 4-6). 1971. 5.95 o.p. (ISBN 0-15-204000-5, HJ). HarBraceJ.

Around the World in Eighty Ways. Hans G. Guggenheim. 128p. (Orig.). 1981. pap. 6.00 o.p. (ISBN 0-682-49683-9). Exposition-Phoenix.

Around the World in Seventy-Eight Days. Nicholas Coleridge. 224p. 1985. text ed. 14.95 o.p. (ISBN 0-07-011699-7). McGraw.

Around the Year with C. S. Lewis & His Friends. Ed. by Kathryn Lindskoog. 384p. 1986. 12.95 o.s.i. (ISBN 0-8378-5126-2). Gibson.

Arousers. Merle L. Browne. LC 74-80702. 1974. 6.95 o.p. (ISBN 0-87795-064-4, Arbor Hse). Morrow.

Arranged Marriage. Inge Trachtenberg. 272p. 1975. 6.95 o.p. (ISBN 0-393-08705-0). Norton.

Arrangement. Elia Kazan. 1974. pap. 1.75 o.p. (ISBN 0-380-01027-5, 21352). Avon.

Arrangement & Description of Archival Materials. Hugh Taylor. (ICA Handbook Ser.). 181p. 1980. pap. text ed. 20.00 o.p. (ISBN 3-598-20272-5). K G Saur.

Arrangement Regarding International Trade in Textiles. (Eng., Fr. & Span.). 1966. pap. 5.00 o.p. (ISBN 0-686-93153-X, G67, GATT). UNIPUB.

Arranging Flowers for the Church. rev. ed. Oleta S. Moffitt. 1977. pap. 2.25 o.p. (ISBN 0-8006-1837-8, 1-1837, Fortress). Augsburg Fortress.

Array Processing. Ed. by S. Haykin. LC 79-11772. (Benchmark Papers in Electrical Engineering & Computer Science: Vol. 22). 362p. 1982. 64.95 o.p. (ISBN 0-87933-351-0). Van Nos Reinhold.

Arrest of Vessels. 2nd ed. Maritime & Transport Law Committee. write for info. o.p. Kluwer Academic.

Arrest, Search & Seizure. Lawrence C. Waddington. LC 73-7366. (Criminal Justice Ser). 320p. 1974. text ed. write for info. o.p. (ISBN 0-02-478940-2). Macmillan.

Arrest Warrant Forms, March 1982: Replacement Pages for the Second Edition. Ed. by Joan G. Brannon & Robert L. Farb. 69p. 1982. 5.00 o.p. (ISBN 0-686-39457-7). Institute Government.

Arrhythmias Case Studies. Lester Jacobson & Nora Goldschlager. 1978. spiral 23.00 o.p. (ISBN 0-87488-070-X). Med Exam.

Arrighi's Running Hand. Tr. by Paul Standard from Ital. LC 78-58412. 1979. pap. 4.95 o.s.i. (ISBN 0-8008-0323-X, Pentalic). Taplinger.

ARRL Antenna Anthology. American Radio Relay League. LC 78-71955. 1979. 4.00 o.p. (ISBN 0-87259-775-X). Am Radio.

ARRL Code Kit. 8.00 o.p. (ISBN 0-87259-901-9). Am Radio.

ARRL Field Resource Directory. 1986. 10.00 o.p. (ISBN 0-87259-032-1). Am Radio.

ARRL Handbook, 1988. 21.00 o.p. (ISBN 0-87259-065-8). Am Radio.

ARRL Repeater Directory. 1986. 3.00 o.p. (ISBN 0-87259-026-7). Am Radio.

Arrow of Gold. Joseph Conrad. 1968. pap. 1.95 o.p. (ISBN 0-393-00458-9, Norton Lib). Norton.

Arrow Street Guide Atlas of Jacksonville & Duval Co., FL. 1978. 6.25 o.p. (ISBN 0-913450-40-5). Arrow Pub.

Arrow Street Guide of Berkshire County. Ed. by Arrow Pub Staff. 1976. pap. 2.25 o.p. (ISBN 0-913450-29-4). Arrow Pub.

Arrow Street Guide of Cleveland. Ed. by Arrow Pub. Staff. 1983. 3.95 o.p. (ISBN 0-913450-28-6). Arrow Pub.

Arrow Street Guide of Metro Ottawa-Hull, Canada. 1977. 2.25 o.p. (ISBN 0-913450-35-9). Arrow Pub.

Arrow Street Guide of Springfield, MA. 1973. 1.95 o.p. (ISBN 0-317-67374-2). Arrow Pub.

Arrow Street Guide of the North Shore. Ed. by Arrow Pub Staff. 1976. pap. 2.50 o.p. (ISBN 0-913450-30-8). Arrow Pub.

Arrow Street Guide of Worcester, MA. 1975. 3.50 o.p. (ISBN 0-913450-27-8). Arrow Pub.

Arrow Zip Code Directory. Ed. by Arrow Pub Staff. 1976. pap. 2.95 o.p. (ISBN 0-913450-33-2). Arrow Pub.

Arrowhead Farm: 300 Years of New England Husbandry & Cooking. Pauline C. Harrell et al. LC 83-10111. (Illus.). 240p. 1984. 17.95 o.p. (ISBN 0-914378-98-8); pap. 12.95 o.s.i. (ISBN 0-914378-99-6). Countryman.

Arrows of Desire. Geoffrey Household. Ed. by Edward Weeks & Upton Brady. LC 85-28938. 136p. 1986. 12.95 o.p. (ISBN 0-87113-045-9). Atlantic Monthly.

Arrowsmith. Sinclair Lewis. LC 25-78. (Modern Classic Ser.). 1949. 5.95 o.p. (ISBN 0-15-108216-2). HarBraceJ.

Arsenal of Democracy II: American Military Power in the 1980s & the Origins of the New Cold War. rev. ed. Tom Gervasi. LC 80-993. (Illus.). 272p. (Orig.). 1981. pap. 12.95 o.p. (ISBN 0-394-17662-6, E760, Ever). Grove.

Arsenal: Understanding Weapons in the Nuclear Age. Kosta Tsipis. (Illus.). 320p. 1984. 16.50 o.p. (ISBN 0-671-44073-X). S&S.

Arson! John Barracato & Peter Michelmore. (Illus.). 1976. 8.95 o.p. (ISBN 0-393-08744-1). Norton.

Arson. Elizabeth Tackler. 224p. 1985. pap. 2.95 o.p. (ISBN 0-931773-31-8). Critics Choice Paper.

Art: A History of Painting, Sculpture, Architecture. 2nd ed. Frederick Hartt. LC 84-12380. (Illus.). 1012p. 1985. 49.50 o.p. (ISBN 0-8109-1824-2). Abrams.

Art: A History of Painting, Sculpture, Architecture, Vol. II. 2nd ed. Frederick N. Hartt. LC 84-12380. (Abrams Bk.). (Illus.). 544p. 1985. pap. text ed. 26.95 o.p. (ISBN 0-13-047382-0). P-H.

Art Adventures: Shapes, Bk. 2. Sandra M. Zawadzki. (Art Adventure Ser.). (Illus.). 48p. (gr. k-6). 1985. wkbk. 5.95 o.p. (ISBN 0-86653-298-6). Good Apple.

Art Adventures: Textures, Bk. 3. Sandra M. Zawadzki. (Art Adventure Ser.). (Illus.). 48p. (gr. k-6). 1985. wkbk. 5.95 o.p. (ISBN 0-86653-300-1). Good Apple.

Art: African American. Samella Lewis. (Illus.). 246p. (Orig.). 1978. pap. text ed. 16.75 o.p. (ISBN 0-15-503410-3, HC). HarBraceJ.

Art America. Mary Ann Tighe & Elizabeth E. Lang. (Illus.). 1977. text ed. 36.95 o.p. (ISBN 0-07-064607-4); pap. text ed. 19.95 o.p. (ISBN 0-07-064601-5). McGraw.

Art: An Introduction. 2nd ed. Dale G. Cleaver. (Illus.). 1972. pap. text ed. 9.50 o.p. (ISBN 0-15-503431-6, HC). HarBraceJ.

Art: An Introduction. 3rd ed. Dale G. Cleaver. LC 76-16436. (Illus.). 440p. 1977. pap. text ed. 15.25 o.p. (ISBN 0-15-503432-4, HC). HarBraceJ.

Art: An Introduction. 4th ed. Dale G. Cleaver. (Illus.). 469p. 1985. pap. text ed. 22.00 net o.p. (ISBN 0-15-503433-2, HC). HarBraceJ.

Art & Analysis: An Essay Toward Theory in Aesthetics. Edward G. Ballard. 219p. 1957. Repr. 25.00x o.p. (ISBN 0-403-08903-4). Somerset Pub.

Art & Antique Restorers Handbook. Savage. 140p. 1954. (ISBN 0-8022-1494-0). Philos Lib.

Art & Architecture Book Guide: 1974. Art & Architecture Book Guide Editors. 1978. lib. bdg. 95.00 o.p. (ISBN 0-8161-6806-7, Biblio Guides). G K Hall.

Art & Architecture of Japan. rev. ed. R. Paine & A. Soper. (Pelican History of Art Ser.: No. 8). 1956. 39.50 o.p. (ISBN 0-607-13395-3, Pelican). Penguin USA.

Art & Artists of Our Time, 3 vols. Clarence Cook. Ed. by H. Barbara Weinberg. LC 75-28881. (Art Experience in Late 19th Century America Ser.: Vol. 15). (Illus.). 1978. Repr. of 1888 ed. Set. lib. bdg. 303.00 o.p. (ISBN 0-8240-2239-4). Garland Pub.

Art & Civilization. 2nd ed. Bernard S. Myers. 1967. text ed. 50.95 o.p. (ISBN 0-07-044251-7). McGraw.

Art & Culture of the Cyclades in the Third Millennium B. C. Ed. by Jurgen Thimme. Tr. by A. Cornford & P. Getz-Preziosi. LC 77-84340. (Illus.). 1978. 90.00x o.s.i. (ISBN 0-226-79499-7). U of Chicago Pr.

Art & Faith. Jacques Maritain. (ISBN 0-8022-1055-4). Philos Lib.

Art & Human Experience. Pamela Rydzewski. 1967. text ed. 27.00 o.p. (ISBN 0-08-012136-5). Pergamon.

Art & Human Values. Bertram Jessup & M. Rader. (Illus.). 1975. text ed. 28.67 o.p. (ISBN 0-13-046821-5). P-H.

Art & Illusion: A Study in the Psychology of Pictorial Presentation. 2nd ed. Ernst H. Gombrich. (Bollingen Ser.: Vol. 35). (A. W. Mellon Lecture No. 5). 1961. 63.00x o.p. (ISBN 0-691-09785-2); pap. 14.50x o.p. (ISBN 0-691-01750-6, 156). Princeton U Pr.

Art & Imagination of W. E. B. Dubois. Arnold Rampersad. 1976. 21.00x o.s.i. (ISBN 0-674-04711-7). Harvard U Pr.

Art & Ingenuity of the Woodstove. Jan Adkins. 1980. pap. 7.95 o.p. (ISBN 0-89696-096-X, An Everest House Book). Dodd.

Art & Inquiry. Berel Lang. LC 74-18240. 227p. 1975. text ed. 21.50x o.p. (ISBN 0-8143-1531-3). Wayne St U Pr.

Art & Life of J. W. Waterhouse RA 1849-1917. Anthony Hobson. (Illus.). 208p. 1987. 39.95 o.p. (ISBN 0-86294-013-3, Pub. by Trefoil Bks Ltd UK). Seven Hills Bk Dists.

Art & Material Culture in the Paintings of Akbar's Court. Som P. Verma. (Illus.). 1978. text ed. 25.00x o.p. (ISBN 0-7069-0595-4). Humanities.

Art & Morality. Kitaro Nishida. Tr. by D. A. Dilworth & V. H. Viglielmo. 227p. 1973. 14.00x o.p. (ISBN 0-8248-0256-X, Eastwest Ctr). UH Pr.

Art & Music: An Introduction. Dale G. Cleaver & John M. Eddins. (Illus.). 568p. (Orig.). 1977. pap. text ed. 14.50 o.p. (ISBN 0-15-503437-5, HC). HarBraceJ.

Art & Philosophy. rev. ed. Joseph Margolis. (Eclipse Bks.). 250p. 1979. text ed. 25.00x o.p. (ISBN 0-391-00645-2). Humanities.

Art & Poetry. Jacques Maritain. (ISBN 0-8022-1056-2). Philos Lib.

Art & Politics, Vol. 4. Richard Wagner. 1967. Repr. of 1895 ed. 22.50x o.p. Broude.

Art & Politics in the Weimar Republic: The New Sobriety, 1917-1933. John Willett. LC 78-51805. (Illus.). 1979. 17.95 o.p. (ISBN 0-394-49628-0). Pantheon.

Art & Practice of Public Administration: Papers by Louis J. Kroeger. Louis J. Kroeger. Ed. by Harriet Nathan. LC 78-634565. (Illus.). 332p. (Orig.). 1971. pap. 5.75x o.p. (ISBN 0-87772-077-0). UCB IGS.

Art & Science: A Study of Alberti, Pierodella Francesca & Giorgione. Adrian D. Stokes. LC 50-2168. 1949. Repr. 39.00x o.p. (ISBN 0-403-07226-3). Somerset Pub.

Art & Science of Dental Caries Research. Ed. by Robert S. Harris. LC 68-18670. 1968. 79.00 o.p. (ISBN 0-12-327350-1). Acad Pr.

Art & Science of Effective Thinking. George R. Lyman. (Illus.). 1979. 117.75 o.p. (ISBN 0-89266-208-5). Am Classical Coll Pr.

Art & Science of Meditation. Ed. by L. K. Misra. 112p. 1976. pap. 3.95 o.p. (ISBN 0-89389-018-9). Himalayan Pubs.

Art & Technique of Prayer. Ferdinand Valentine. (Overview Studies: No. 9). 1969. pap. 0.50x o.p. (ISBN 0-87343-049-2). Magi Bks.

Art & Technique of Soaring. Richard A. Wolters. 1971. text ed. 19.95 o.p. (ISBN 0-07-071560-2). McGraw.

Art & Technology. Ed. by Rene Berger & Lloyd Eby. LC 85-21552. (Illus.). 422p. 1986. 29.95 o.p. (ISBN 0-89226-029-7, Pub. by ICUS). Paragon Hse.

Art & the Excited Spirit: America in the Romantic Period. D. Huntington. (Illus.). 150p. 1972. pap. 3.50 o.p. (ISBN 0-912303-06-9). Michigan Mus.

Art & the Reformation. George G. Coulton. LC 69-15789. (Illus.). xxii, 662p. 1969. Repr. of 1928 ed. 48.50 o.p. (ISBN 0-208-00738-5, Archon). Shoe String.

Art & Theological Imagination. John W. Dixon, Jr. (Illus.). 1978. 12.95 o.p. (ISBN 0-8164-0397-X). HarpR.

Art As Revelation: The Role of Art in Human Existence. Frank A. Wilson. (Illus.). 296p. 1981. text ed. 20.00x o.p. (ISBN 0-87663-359-9). Universe.

Art at Auction-Sotheby 85-86. 48.00 o.p. (ISBN 0-317-57524-4). Editions Pub.

Art Boggs, Private Investigator. Matt Scheele. (Illus.). 96p. 1981. 6.00 o.p. (ISBN 0-682-49766-5). Exposition-Phoenix.

Art Book of Pencil Sketching. Vladimir Greenhall. (Illus.). 101p. 1984. 97.45x o.p. (ISBN 0-86650-098-7). Gloucester Art.

Art Chronicles: 1954-1966. Frank O'Hara. LC 74-77526. (Illus.). 176p. 1975. 15.00 o.p. (ISBN 0-8076-0755-X). Braziller.

Art Deco Furniture: The French Designers. Alastair Duncan. LC 84-81003. (Illus.). 192p. 1984. 35.00 o.p. (ISBN 0-03-000099-8). H Holt & Co.

Art deco Les Maitres du Mobilier. Pierre Kjellberg. (Illus.). 182p. (Fr.). 1981. 70.00 o.p. (ISBN 2-85917-019-7, 2390019, Pub. by Editions de l'Amateur FR). Seven Hills Bk Dists.

Art Deco: Monographs. Mary Vance. (Architecture Ser.: Bibliography A-1313). 15p. 1985. pap. 2.25 o.p. (ISBN 0-89028-243-9). Vance Biblios.

Art Directors Annual, 64th. Ed. by Miriam L. Solomon. (Illus.). 816p. 1985. 44.95 o.p. (ISBN 0-937414-05-0). R Silver.

Art Directors Index to Illustrators, No. 7. Ed. by Brian Morris. (Illus.). 400p. 1987. 59.50 o.p. (ISBN 2-88046-062-X, Pub. by Rotovision). R Silver.

Art Directors' Index to Illustrators, No. 7. Ed. by RotoVision Staff. (Illus.). 428p. 1987. 59.50 o.p. (ISBN 0-8230-5787-9). Watson-Guptill.

Art Directors' Index to Illustrators, No. 8. (Illus.). 320p. 1988. 59.95 o.p. (ISBN 0-8230-5771-2). Watson-Guptill.

Art Education, Civilization & the 21st Century: A Researcher's Reflections on the National Endowment for the Arts' Report to Congress. Brent Wilson. 16p. 1988. pap. 10.00 o.p. (ISBN 0-937652-47-4). Natl Art Ed.

Art Fakes & Forgeries. F. Mendax. Tr. by H. S. Whitman. (Illus.). 222p. 1956. (ISBN 0-8022-1101-1). Philos Lib.

Art Flick's Master Fly Tying Guide. rev. ed. Art Flick. LC 83-63027. (Illus.). 208p. 1983. pap. 17.95 o.p. (ISBN 0-8329-0243-8). Lyons & Burford.

Art Flicks New Streamside Guide to Naturals & Them Imitations. Art Flicks Editors. LC 83-5744. (Illus.). 176p. 1983. pap. 9.95 o.p. (ISBN 0-8329-0331-0). Lyons & Burford.

Art for Children's Liturgy: What You Need & How To Do It. Marge Tuthill. LC 82-60855. 1982. pap. 4.95 o.p. (ISBN 0-8091-2478-5). Paulist Pr.

Art for Elementary Classrooms. G. Hubbard. 1982. pap. text ed. (ISBN 0-13-047274-3). P-H.

Art for the Masses 1911-1917: A Radical Magazine & its Artists. Rebecca Zurier. (Illus.). 180p. (Orig.). 1985. pap. 20.00 o.p. (ISBN 0-89467-036-0). Yale Art Gallery.

Art Gallery of Armenia. M. Mikaelian. 159p. 1984. pap. 9.95 o.p. (ISBN 0-8285-2936-1, Pub. by Aurora Pubs USSR). Imported Pubns.

Art History: A Study Guide. Joyce M. Smith. Tr. by Janet F. Masters. (Illus.). 256p. 1982. pap. text ed. (ISBN 0-13-047324-3). P-H.

Art in a Democratic Society. Mann. LC 77-84919. 1977. 9.95 o.p. (ISBN 0-87972-087-5). Bowling Green.

Art in America: A Critical & Historical Sketch. S. G. Benjamin. Ed. by H. Barbara Weinberg. LC 75-28872. (Art Experience in Late 19th Century America Ser.: Vol. 8). (Illus.). 1976. Repr. of 1880 ed. lib. bdg. 70.00 o.p. (ISBN 0-8240-2232-7). Garland Pub.

Art in Coinage. C. H. Sutherland. (Illus.). 228p. 1956. Philos Lib.

Art in Context. Jack A. Hobbs. (Illus.). 336p. 1975. pap. text ed. 13.95 o.p. (ISBN 0-15-503469-3, HC). HarBraceJ.

Art in Context. 2nd ed. Jack A. Hobbs. 320p. 1980. 15.25 o.p. (ISBN 0-15-503470-7, HC). HarBraceJ.

Art in Everyday Life. 4th ed. Harriet I. Goldstein & Vetta Goldstein. (Illus.). 1954. text ed. write for info. o.p. (ISBN 0-02-344480-0, 34448). Macmillan.

Art in Needlework: A Book about Embroidery. Lewis F. Day & Mary Buckle. LC 74-159927. 290p. Repr. of 1900 ed. 34.00x o.p. (ISBN 0-8103-3062-8). Gale.

Art in Painting. Barnes. 1937. 8.25 o.p. (ISBN 0-15-108491-2). HarBraceJ.

Art in Society. Ken Baynes. LC 74-21587. (Illus.). 288p. 1975. 85.00 o.p. (ISBN 0-87951-027-7). Overlook Pr.

Art in the Early Church. Walter Lowrie. (Illus.). 1969. pap. 5.95 o.p. (ISBN 0-393-00493-7, Norton Lib). Norton.

Art in the Life of the Northwest Coast Indians. Erna Gunther. (Illus.). 274p. (Orig.). 1966. pap. 12.95 o.p. (ISBN 0-89955-345-1, Pub. by Portland Art). Intl Spec Bk.

Art in the Lives of Persons with Special Needs. 40p. 6.00 o.p. (ISBN 0-937652-07-5). Natl Art Ed.

Art Institute of Chicago: The Stock Exchange Trading Room. John Vinci. LC 77-72950. (Illus.). 64p. (Orig.). 1977. pap. 2.95 o.p. (ISBN 0-86559-026-5). Art Inst Chi.

Art Is for Children. Eugenia M. Oole. LC 79-54126. 144p. 1980. pap. 5.50 o.p. (ISBN 0-8066-1750-0, 10-0435, Augsburg). Augsburg Fortress.

Art Law: Representing Artists, Dealers & Collectors. Robert E. Duffy. LC 77-86511. 1988. text ed. 45.00 o.p. (ISBN 0-685-86794-3, G1-0647). PLI.

Art Life of William Rimmer: Sculptor, Painter, & Physician. Truman H. Bartlett. LC 68-27718. (Library of American Art Ser.). (Illus.). 1970. Repr. of 1890 ed. lib. bdg. 35.00 o.p. (ISBN 0-306-71166-4). Da Capo.

Art Museum As Educator. Ed. by Barbara Newsom. LC 76-14301. 1978. 70.00x o.p. (ISBN 0-520-03248-9); pap. 14.95 o.p. (ISBN 0-520-03249-7); pap. 40.00 o.p. (ISBN 0-520-04166-6). U of Cal Pr.

Art Nouveau: An Anthology of Design & Illustration from the Studio. Edmund V. Gillon. LC 73-82624. (Illus.). 13.50 o.p. (ISBN 0-8446-0644-8). Peter Smith.

Art Nouveau Belgium-France. Yvonne Brunhammer et al. LC 76-1649. 1976. 20.00 o.p. (ISBN 0-914412-11-6). Inst for the Arts.

Art Nouveau Book in Britain. John R. Taylor. LC 79-53860. (Illus.). 176p. 1980. 24.95 o.s.i. (ISBN 0-8008-0366-3). Taplinger.

Art Nouveau Decorative Ironwork: 137 Photographs. Theodore Menten. (Illus.). 19.00 o.p. (ISBN 0-8446-5904-5). Peter Smith.

Art Nouveau Jewelry by Rene Lalique. T. Gomes Ferreira & Mary P. Proddow. Ed. by B. J. Bradley. Tr. by Nancy Freeman. LC 85-80544. (Illus.). 120p. (Orig.). 1985. 12.50 o.p. (ISBN 0-88397-086-4). Intl Exhibitions.

Art Nouveau Postcards. Giovanni Fanelli & Ezio Godoli. LC 87-6184. (Illus.). 384p. 1987. 50.00 o.p. (ISBN 0-8478-0832-7). Rizzoli Intl.

Art Nouveau Style in Jewelry, Metalwork, Glass, Ceramics, Textiles, Architecture & Furniture. Ed. by Roberta Waddell. 16.25 o.p. (ISBN 0-8446-5660-7). Peter Smith.

Art of A. Henry Nordhausen. Laurence E. Schmeckebier. LC 80-20077. (Illus.). 168p. 1980. 45.00 o.p. (ISBN 0-914016-73-3). Phoenix Pub.

Art of American Indian Cooking. Jean Anderson & Yeffe Kimball. 1986. pap. 7.95 o.p. (ISBN 0-671-61987-X, Fireside). S&S.

Art of Appropriation. Alternative Museum Staff. LC 85-72795. (Illus.). 1985. pap. 5.00 o.p. (ISBN 0-932075-03-7). Alternative Mus.

Art of Archerie. facs. ed. Gervase Markham. LC 68-16503. 268p. (Limited ed. of 400). 1968. Repr. of 1634 ed. casebound 15.00 o.p. (ISBN 0-87387-017-4). Shumway.

Art of Architecture. A. E. Richardson & Hector O. Corfiato. (Illus.). 744p. 1956. (ISBN 0-8022-1337-5). Philos Lib.

Art of Argument. Giles St. Aubyn. LC 85-9739. 128p. 1985. pap. 6.95 o.s.i. (ISBN 0-8008-0369-8). Taplinger.

Art of Arranging Artificial Flowers. Larry Porricelli. (Illus.). 160p. 1987. 24.95 o.p. (ISBN 0-671-62131-9). S&S.

Art of Asia. Helen Rubissow. (Illus.). 1954. (ISBN 0-8022-1404-5). Philos Lib.

Art of Bedouin Jewelery: A Saudi Arabian Profile. Heather C. Ross. (Illus.). 132p. 1982. 50.00 o.p. (ISBN 0-7103-0032-8, Kegan Paul). Routledge Chapman & Hall.

Art of Being a Man. J. Allan Petersen. 1974. pap. 1.25 o.p. (ISBN 0-8423-0085-6). Tyndale.

Art of Blackwork Embroidery. Rosemary Drysdale. (Illus.). 160p. 1982. pap. 12.95 o.s.i. (ISBN 0-684-17642-4, ScribT). Scribner.

Art of Budget Cooking: The Minute Rice Cookbook. Celebrity Kitchens Staff. 1976. pap. 1.50 o.p. (ISBN 0-380-00692-8, 29207). Avon.

Art of Byzantium & the Medieval West: Selected Studies. Ernst Kitzinger. Ed. by W. Eugene Kleinbauer. LC 75-34728. (Illus.). 448p. 1976. 27.50x o.p. (ISBN 0-253-31055-5). Ind U Pr.

Art of Calligraphy: A Practical Guide. Marie Angel. (Illus.). 1978. pap. 7.95 o.s.i. (ISBN 0-684-15518-4, ScribT). Scribner.

Art of Captain Cook's Voyages, Vol. III: The Voyage of the Resolution & the Discovery, 1776-1780, 2 vols. Rudiger Joppien & Bernard Smith. (Illus.). 660p. 1988. Set. 200.00 o.p. Yale U Pr.

Art of Central Asia: The Stein Collection in the British Museum, Textiles, Sculpture & Other Arts, Vol. 3. Roderick Whitfield. LC 81-80657. (Illus.). 340p. 1985. 425.00 o.p. (ISBN 0-87011-556-1). Kodansha.

Art of Chanderi: A Study of the Fifthteen Century Monuments of Chanderi. R. Nath. 1980. 17.50x o.p. (Pub. by Ambika India). South Asia Bks.

Art of Chinese Paper Folding: For Young & Old. Maling Soong. LC 48-6198. (Illus.). (gr. 1-5). 1946. 6.50 o.p. (ISBN 0-15-204080-3, HJ). HarBraceJ.

Art of Color & Design. 2nd ed. Maitland E. Graves. (Illus.). 1951. text ed. 45.95 o.p. (ISBN 0-07-024119-8). McGraw.

Art of Communication: A Self-Help Course in Basics. Dorothy M. Peed. 1978. 10.00 o.p. (ISBN 0-682-48796-1, University). Exposition-Phoenix.

Art of Computer Management: How Small Firms Can Increase Their Productivity & Profits with Personal Computers. Jim McNitt. 256p. 1984. 15.45 o.p. (ISBN 0-671-46471-X). S&S.

Art of Cooking for Two. Coralie Castle & Astrid Newton. LC 76-6892. (Illus.). 192p. (Orig.). 1976. pap. 7.95 o.p. (ISBN 0-912238-76-3, One Hund One Prods). Ortho.

Art of Counterpoint. Gioseffo Zarlino. Tr. by Guy A. Marco & Claude V. Palisca. (Illus.). 1976. pap. 5.95 o.p. (ISBN 0-393-00833-9, Norton Lib). Norton.

Art of Creative Writing. Lajos Egri. 1968. pap. 5.95 o.s.i. (ISBN 0-8065-0200-2, C263, Pub. by Citadel Pr). Carol Pub Group.

Art of Crusher Joe. (Illus.). 100p. 1984. 15.95 o.p. (ISBN 0-318-02748-8). Bks Nippan.

Art of Damaging: A Sequel. Rustom S. Davar & Dhun R. Davar. (Illus.). 1979. 15.00x o.p. (ISBN 0-7069-0783-3, Pub. by Vikas India). Advent NY.

Art of Decision-Making: Seven Steps to Achieving More Effective Results. John D. Arnold. Orig. Title: Make up Your Mind. 1980. pap. 8.95 o.p. (ISBN 0-8144-7537-X). AMACOM.

Art of Destructive Management: What Hath Man Wrought. Edward N. Hall. LC 82-99974. 107p. 1984. 8.95 o.p. (ISBN 0-533-05601-2). Vantage.

Art of Digital Design: An Introduction to Top-Down Design. David E. Winkel & Franklin P. Prosser. (Illus.). 1980. text ed. 44.67 o.p. (ISBN 0-13-046607-7). P-H.

Art of Drawing. Chaet. 27.50 o.p. (ISBN 0-03-042101-2). H Holt & Co.

Art of Drawing. Philip Rawson. (Illus.). 160p. 1983. text ed. 34.00 o.p. (ISBN 0-13-047266-2); pap. text ed. (ISBN 0-13-047341-3). P-H.

Art of Drawing on Stone, Giving a Full Explanation of the Various Styles of the Different Methods to Be Employed to Ensure Success, & of the Modes of Correcting, As Well As of the Several Causes of Failure. Charles J. Hullmandel. LC 78-74392. (Nineteenth-Century Book Arts & Printing History Ser.: Vol. 7). 1982. lib. bdg. 26.00 o.p. (ISBN 0-8240-3881-9). Garland Pub.

Art of Ecstasy: Teresa, Bernini & Crashaw. Robert T. Petersson. LC 79-108825. (Illus.). 1970. pap. text ed. 3.95x o.p. (ISBN 0-689-70515-8, 206, Atheneum). Macmillan.

Art of Egg Decorating. Allan Stacey. 128p. 1982. 19.95x o.p. (ISBN 0-7100-9026-9). Routledge Chapman & Hall.

Art of Egg Decorating. Allan Stacey. (Illus.). 128p. 1984. pap. 9.95 o.p. (ISBN 0-7100-9027-7). Routledge Chapman & Hall.

Art of Electronic Music. Compiled by Tom Dorter & Greg Armbruster. LC 85-60142. (Illus.). 320p. 1985. 25.00 o.p. (ISBN 0-688-03105-6). Morrow.

Art of Falconry. G. Lascelles. 176p. 12.50 o.p. (ISBN 0-87556-647-2). Saifer.

Art of Fine Baking. Paula Peck. 320p. 1984. pap. 7.95 o.p. (ISBN 0-671-20611-7, Fireside). S&S.

Art of Fishing with Worms & Other Live Bait. Harold F. Blaisdell. 1977. 14.00 o.s.i. (ISBN 0-394-40039-9). Knopf.

Art of Getting Even. Gary Brodsky. 128p. (Orig.). 1988. pap. 2.95 o.p. (ISBN 1-55547-249-4). Critics Choice Paper.

Art of Greek Cookery. St. Paul's Greek Orthodox Church Women Staff. LC 63-18214. (Illus.). 13.95 o.p. (ISBN 0-385-03793-7). Doubleday.

Art of Grit: Ken Kesey's Fiction. M. Gilbert Porter. LC 81-69835. (Literary Frontiers Editions). 112p. pap. text ed. 8.95 o.p. (ISBN 0-8262-0368-X). U of Mo Pr.

Art of Hanging Loose in an Uptight World. Kenneth J. Olson. LC 74-19787. (Illus.). 132p. 1974. pap. 4.95 o.p. (ISBN 0-89019-021-6). Norwalk Pr.

Art of Heraldry. Carl-Alexander Von Volborth. (Illus.). 224p. 1987. 80.00 o.p. (ISBN 0-7137-1390-9, Pub. by Blandford Pr England). Sterling.

Art of Inner Listening. J. K. Crum. 1975. pap. 2.95 o.s.i. (PV092). Jove Pubns.

Art of Instructing the Jury. Robert L. McBride. 545p. 1969. text ed. 49.75 o.p. (ISBN 0-87084-553-5). Anderson Pub Co.

Art of James Thurber. Richard C. Tobias. LC 68-20938. vi, 196p. 1969. 13.50x o.p. (ISBN 0-8214-0058-4). Ohio U Pr.

Art of Japanese Management. Richard T. Pascale & Anthony G. Althos. 1981. 11.95 o.p. (ISBN 0-671-22539-1). S&S.

Art of Jeet-Kung-Tao. Jack K. Tsirakis. 1977. 10.00 o.p. (ISBN 0-682-48507-1, Banner). Exposition-Phoenix.

Art of Judaic Needlework: Traditional & Contemporary Designs. Ita Aber. (Illus.). 1979. 17.50 o.p. (ISBN 0-684-16239-3); pap. 3.95 encore o.p. (ISBN 0-684-17684-X). Scribner.

Art of Korean Cooking. Harriet Morris. LC 59-10408. (Illus., Orig.). 1959. pap. 5.75 o.p. (ISBN 0-8048-0036-7). C E Tuttle.

Art of La Celestina. Stephen Gilman. LC 76-49053. 1977. Repr. of 1956 ed. lib. bdg. 24.75x o.p. (ISBN 0-8371-9349-4, GILC). Greenwood.

Art of Lacemaking. Ann Collier. (Illus.). 96p. 1987. 29.95 o.s.i. (ISBN 0-7153-8846-0). David & Charles.

Art of Leadership: Skill-Building Techniques That Produce Results. Lin K. Bothwell. (Illus.). 255p. 1983. 18.95 o.p. (ISBN 0-13-047100-3); pap. 11.95 o.p. (ISBN 0-13-047092-9). P-H.

Art of Learning. Z. Pietrasinski. 1969. text ed. 23.00 o.p. (ISBN 0-08-012019-9). Pergamon.

Art of Listening: The Creative Hearer in Language, Literature & Popular Culture. Ed. by Graham McGregor & Robert S. White. 256p. 1986. 34.50 o.p. (ISBN 0-7099-4654-6, Pub. by Croom Helm Ltd). Routledge Chapman & Hall.

Art of Literary Research. 2nd, rev. ed. Richard D. Altick. 1975. 11.95x o.p. (ISBN 0-393-09227-5, NortonC); text ed. 5.95x o.p. (ISBN 0-393-09590-8). Norton.

Art of Living & Other Stories. John Gardner. pap. 3.50 o.s.i. (ISBN 0-345-30371-7). Ballantine.

Art of Living Treasure Chest: The 75 Best & Most Inspiring Art of Living Essays. Wilfred A. Peterson. 1977. pap. 8.95 o.p. (ISBN 0-671-22847-1, Fireside). S&S.

Art of Managing People. Philip Hunsacker & Anthony J. Alessandra. (Illus.). 1980. 15.95 o.p. (ISBN 0-13-047472-X, Spec); pap. 9.95 o.p. (ISBN 0-13-047464-9, Spec). P-H.

Art of Managing Technical Project. Melvin Silverman. (Illus.). 304p. 1987. text ed. 43.00 o.p. (ISBN 0-13-047010-4). P-H.

Art of Melody. Arthur C. Edwards. 296p. 1956. (ISBN 0-8022-0434-1). Philos Lib.

Art of Mosaics. Michael Avi-Yonah. LC 72-10793. (Lerner Archaeology Ser.). (Illus.). 96p. (gr. 5). 1975. PLB 8.95 o.p. (ISBN 0-8225-0828-1). Lerner Pubns.

Art of Nausicaa. (Illus.). 1984. 24.95 o.s.i. (ISBN 0-318-02749-6). Bks Nippan.

Art of Netsuke Carving. Masatoshi. LC 81-80659. (Illus.). 236p. 1981. 100.00 o.p. (ISBN 0-87011-480-8). Kodansha.

Art of Norval Morrisseau. Lister Sinclair & Jack Pollack. (Illus.). 1979. 50.00 o.p. (ISBN 0-458-93820-3, NO.0130). Routledge Chapman & Hall.

Art of Officiating Sports. 3rd ed. John W. Bunn. 1967. text ed. 27.67 o.p. (ISBN 0-13-047803-2). P-H.

Art of Painting. Leonardo Da Vinci. 224p. 1957. (ISBN 0-8022-0354-X). Philos Lib.

Art of Painting on Porcelain. Georges Miserez-Schira. LC 74-6404. (Creative Crafts Ser.). Orig. Title: Peinture Sur Porcelaine. (Illus.). 136p. 1974. 19.95 o.p. (ISBN 0-8019-6155-6). Chilton.

Art of Papermaking, 1890. Alexander Watt. (Illus.). 240p. 1983. pap. 20.00 o.p. (ISBN 0-87556-581-6). Saifer.

Art of Pastoral Conversation. Gaylord Noyce. LC 81-82350. 128p. 1982. pap. 7.95 o.s.i. (ISBN 0-8042-1131-0, John Knox). Westminster John Knox.

Art of Persuasion. 2nd ed. Wayne C. Minnick. LC 68-58412. (Illus.). 1968. text ed. 14.50 o.p. (ISBN 0-395-04924-5, 3-37936). HM.

Art of Persuasion in Greece. George Kennedy. (History of Rhetoric Ser.: Vol. 3). 350p. 1963. 38.00x o.p. (ISBN 0-691-06008-8); 119.50 set o.p.; 32.00x o.p. (ISBN 0-691-03566-0). Princeton U Pr.

Art of Philip Larkin. Simon Petch. (Sydney Studies in Literature). 144p. 1892. 7.50x o.p. (ISBN 0-424-00090-3, Pub. by Sydney U Pr Australia). Intl Spec Bk.

Art of Philosophizing & Other Essays. Bertrand Russell. 118p. 1968. (ISBN 0-8022-1415-0). Philos Lib.

Art of Poland. Irena Piotrowska. (ISBN 0-8022-1980-2). Philos Lib.

Art of Power & Control Selling: The Salesman's Bible. Calvin Hill. 1980. 12.50 o.p. (ISBN 0-682-49547-6). Exposition-Phoenix.

Art of Pre-Columbian Mexico: An Annotated Bibliography of Works in English. Aubyn Kendall. (Institute of Latin American Studies Guides & Bibliographies Ser.: No. 5). (Illus.). 129p. 1973. pap. 5.95x o.p. (ISBN 0-292-70304-X). U of Tex Pr.

Art of Pre-Hispanic MesoAmerica: An Annotated Bibliography. Janet C. Berlo. (Reference Publications in Art History). 272p. 1985. lib. bdg. 39.00 o.s.i. (ISBN 0-8161-8562-X). G K Hall.

Art of Preaching. Arthur Allen. (ISBN 0-8022-0020-6). Philos Lib.

Art of Presenting Food: Everyone's Perfect Cooking Companion. Sallie Y. Williams. LC 86-5367. (Illus.). 216p. 1986. pap. 15.95 o.p. (ISBN 0-688-06665-8). Hearst Bks.

Art of Primitive People. J. T. Hooper & C. A. Burland. (Illus.). 180p. 1954. (ISBN 0-8022-0740-5). Philos Lib.

Art of Recruiting Volunteers. Mark Senter, III. 96p. 1983. pap. 9.95 o.p. (ISBN 0-88207-297-8). Victor Bks.

Art of Return of the Jedi. 1983. 29.50 o.s.i. (ISBN 0-345-31254-6). Ballantine.

Art of Rock & Roll. Charles T. Brown. (Illus.). 208p. 1983. pap. text ed. (ISBN 0-13-047076-7). P-H.

Art of Russia. Helen Rubissow. (ISBN 0-8022-1405-3). Philos Lib.

Art of Scenic Photography: Technical & Aesthetic Guidelines for the Creative Photographer. Tom Grill & Mark Scanlon. (Illus.). 144p. 1982. 22.50 o.p. (ISBN 0-8174-3538-7, Amphoto). Watson-Guptill.

Art of Science Writing. Dale Worsley & Bernadette Mayer. (Illus.). 224p. (Orig.). 1989. pap. 12.95 o.p. (ISBN 0-915924-20-X). Tchrs & Writers Coll.

Art of Science Writing: A Guide for Teachers & Students. Dale Worsley & Bernadette Mayer. 224p. (Orig.). (YA) (gr. 9 up). 1989. pap. 12.95 o.p. (ISBN 0-915924-20-X). Tchrs & Writers Coll.

Art of Scientific Investigation. rev. ed. W. I. Beveridge. 1957. 8.95x o.p. (ISBN 0-393-06287-2, NortonC). Norton.

Art of Sculpture. 2nd ed. Herbert Read. (Bollingen Ser.: Vol. 35). (Illus., A. W. Mellon Lecture, No. 3). 1961. 41.00x o.p. (ISBN 0-691-09786-0); pap. 11.50x o.p. (ISBN 0-691-01811-1). Princeton U Pr.

Art of Selfishness: How to Deal with the Tyrants & Tyrannies in Your Life. David Seabury. 1966. 8.95 o.p. (ISBN 0-671-05460-0). S&S.

Art of Selling Intangibles: How to Make a Million Investing Other People's Money. Le Roy Gross. LC 81-11349. (Illus.). 302p. 1982. 29.95 o.p. (ISBN 0-13-048777-5). NY Inst Finance.

Art of Shuriken Jutsu: The Samurai Skill of Throwing Stars & Spikes. rev. ed. Michael Finn. (Illus.). 88p. 1985. pap. text ed. 12.00 o.p. (ISBN 0-87364-376-3). Paladin Pr.

Art of Silhouette. Desmond Coke. LC 73-110809. (Illus.). 240p. 1970. Repr. of 1913 ed. 40.00x o.p. (ISBN 0-8103-3549-2). Gale.

Art of Spying. Ronald Seth. 1957. (ISBN 0-8022-1534-3). Philos Lib.

Art of Teaching Christian Doctrine. rev. ed. Johannes Hofinger. 1962. 14.95 o.p. (ISBN 0-268-00015-8). U of Notre Dame Pr.

Art of the Aqualung. Robert Gruss. 72p. 1956. (ISBN 0-8022-0642-5). Philos Lib.

Art of the Chinese Potter. R. L. Hobson & A. L. Hetherington. 1983. 16.50 o.p. (ISBN 0-8446-5948-7). Peter Smith.

Art of the Edge: European Frames 1300-1900. Richard R. Brettel. LC 86-72239. (Illus.). 124p. 1986. pap. 14.95 o.p. (ISBN 0-86559-062-1). Art Inst Chi.

Art of the Embroiderer: Charles Germain de Saint-Aubin, Designer to King Louis XV. Charles G. Saint-Aubin. Tr. by Nikki Scheuer from Fr. LC 82-24943. (Illus.). 192p. 1983. slipcased 30.00 o.s.i. (ISBN 0-87923-480-6). Godine.

Art of the Forger. Christopher Wright. 160p. 1985. 13.95 o.p. (ISBN 0-396-08568-7). Dodd.

Art of the Painted Finish for Furniture & Decoration. Isabel O'Neil. (Illus.). 1971. 19.95 o.p. (ISBN 0-688-01070-9). Morrow.

Art of the Possible: Diplomatic Alternatives in the Middle East. Michael Reisman. 1970. 22.50x o.p. (ISBN 0-691-05635-8); pap. 9.50x o.p. (ISBN 0-691-01059-5). Princeton U Pr.

Art of the Times. Ed. by Jean-Claude Suares. (Illus.). 1973. pap. 4.45 o.p. (ISBN 0-380-01029-1, 17863-X). Avon.

Art of the Tin Toy. David Pressland. (Illus.). 224p. 1983. 39.95 o.s.i. (ISBN 0-904568-04-0, Pub. by New Cavendish England). Schiffer.

Art of the West in the Middle Ages, Vol. 1: Romanesque. Henri Focillon. Tr. by Donald King from Fr. (Landmarks in Art History Ser.). (Illus.). 332p. 1980. Paperback Ser. pap. 14.95 o.p. (ISBN 0-8014-9191-6). Cornell U Pr.

Art of the 1930's: The Age of Anxiety. Edward Lucie-Smith. (Illus.). 264p. 35.00 o.s.i. (ISBN 0-317-54948-0). Apollo.

Art of Thinking. Dagobert D. Runes. 90p. 1961. (ISBN 0-8022-1423-1). Philos Lib.

Art of Three-Dimensional Design: How to Create Space Figures. Louis Wolchonok. (Illus.). 14.00 o.p. (ISBN 0-8446-0968-4). Peter Smith.

Art of Tribes & Early Kingdoms. Richard F. Townsend. Ed. by Elizabeth A. Pratt. LC 83-73267. (Illus.). 72p. 1984. pap. 3.00 o.p. (ISBN 0-86559-055-9). Art Inst Chi.

Art of Understanding Your Mate: With Leader's Guide. Cecil Osborne. pap. 4.95 o.p. (ISBN 0-310-30602-7, 10476P). Zondervan.

Art of Verga. David Woolf. 1977. pap. 16.00x o.p. (ISBN 0-424-00040-7, Pub by Sydney U Pr). Intl Spec Bk.

Art of War. Christian Feest. (Tribal Art Ser.). (Illus.). 96p. 1980. pap. 10.95 o.p. (ISBN 0-500-06010-X). Thames Hudson.

Art Partronage of Maria de' Medici. Deborah Marrow. Ed. by Ann S. Harris. LC 82-1951. (Studies in Baroque Art History: No. 4). 192p. 1982. 42.95 o.p. (ISBN 0-8357-1303-2). UMI Res Pr.

Art Programs in Higher Education: A Directory-Survey in the U. S. & Canada. 156p. 1988. 15.00 o.p. (ISBN 0-937652-37-7). Natl Art Ed.

Art Sales: From Early in the 18th Century to Early in the 20th Century, 3 vols. Algernon Graves. 1137p. Set. sewn bdg. 50.00 o.s.i. (ISBN 0-317-54939-1). Apollo.

Art Sans Oeuvre ou L'Anonymat dans les Arts Contemporains. Trinh Thi Minh-ha. (Fr.). 1982. 10.00x o.p. (ISBN 0-936968-02-8). Intl Bk Ctr.

Art, Society, Revolution: Russia, 1917-1921. Nils A. Nilsson. 272p. 1980. pap. text ed. 25.00x o.p. (ISBN 0-391-01939-2). Humanities.

Art That Is Life: The Arts & Crafts Movement in America, 1875-1920. Ed. by Wendy Kaplan. LC 86-63192. (Illus.). 416p. 1987. 50.00 o.p. (ISBN 0-87846-278-3); pap. 29.95 o.p. (ISBN 0-87846-265-1). Mus Fine Arts Boston.

Art Thoughts: The Experiences & Observations of an American Amateur in Europe. James J. Jarves. Ed. by H. Barbara Weinberg. LC 75-28866. (Art Experience in Late 19th Century America Ser.: Vol. 2). (Illus.). 1976. Repr. of 1869 ed. lib. bdg. 45.00x o.p. (ISBN 0-8240-2226-2). Garland Pub.

Art Through the Ages. 6th ed. Helen Gardner. (Illus.). 1969. text ed. 5.50 o.p. (ISBN 0-15-522710-6, HC). HarBraceJ.

Art Today: An Introduction to the Visual Arts. 5th ed. Ray Faulkner et al. LC 69-19919. (Illus.). 1974. pap. text ed. 26.95 o.p. (ISBN 0-03-089627-4, HoltC). HR&W.

Art Treasures of America, 3 vols. Edward Strahan. LC 75-28871. (Art Experience in Late 19th Century America Ser.: Vol. 7). (Illus.). 1977. Set. lib. bdg. 351.00 o.p. (ISBN 0-8240-2231-9). Garland Pub.

Art, Wisdom & the Pursuit of Excellence. Leo A. Foley. 200p. (Orig.). 1986. lib. bdg. 26.00 o.p. (ISBN 0-8191-5125-4); pap. text ed. 12.00 o.p. (ISBN 0-8191-5126-2). U Pr of Amer.

Arterial Pollution: An Integrated View on Atherosclerosis. Ed. by H. Peeters & G. A. Gresham. LC 82-24586. (NATO ASI Series A, Life Sciences: Vol. 58). 432p. 1983. 75.00x o.p. (ISBN 0-306-41243-8, Plenum Press). Plenum Pub.

Arterial Pressure & Hypertension. Arthur C. Guyton. LC 79-67792. (Circulatory Physiology Ser.: Vol. III). (Illus.). 564p. 1980. text ed. write for info. o.p. (ISBN 0-7216-4362-0). Saunders.

Arteries & Arterial Blood Flow. C. M. Rodkiewicz. (CISM, Courses & Lectures: No. 270). (Illus.). 417p. 1983. pap. 36.00 o.p. (ISBN 0-387-81635-6). Springer-Verlag.

Artful Dodger. Tommy Lasorda & David Fisher. LC 85-3890. (Illus.). 1985. 15.95 o.p. (ISBN 0-87795-716-9, Arbor Hse). Morrow.

Artful Egg. James McClure. 1986. pap. 3.95 o.p. (ISBN 0-394-72126-8). Pantheon.

Arthritis & Allied Conditions: A Textbook of Rheumatology. 10th ed. Ed. by Daniel J. McCarty. LC 84-9748. (Illus.). 1773p. 1985. text ed. 110.00 o.p. (ISBN 0-8121-0925-2). Lea & Febiger.

Arthritis & Folk Medicine. D. C. Jarvis. 1981. pap. 2.50 o.p. (ISBN 0-449-24160-2, Crest). Fawcett.

Arthritis Book of Water Exercise. Judy Jetter & Nancy Kadlec. LC 84-6523. (Illus.). 106p. 1985. 12.95 o.p. (ISBN 0-03-070714-5). H Holt & Co.

Arthritis Helpbook: What You Can Do for Your Arthritis. Kate Lorig & James F. Fries. (Illus.). 160p. 1980. 11.95 o.p. (ISBN 0-201-03796-3); pap. 8.95 o.p. (ISBN 0-201-03797-1). Addison-Wesley.

Arthritis: Its Cause & Cure. Harry W. Joedicke. 1980. 7.50 o.p. (ISBN 0-682-49553-0). Exposition-Phoenix.

Arthrodesis in the Restoration of Working Ability. Ed. by George Chapchal. LC 75-18932. (Illus.). 248p. 1975. lib. bdg. 19.50 o.p. (ISBN 0-88416-055-6). Year Bk Med.

Arthrography of the Knee Joint. C. J. Thijn. (Illus.). 1979. 61.00 o.p. (ISBN 0-387-09129-7). Springer-Verlag.

Arthur & the Purple Panic. Alan Coren. LC 83-61281. (Illus.). 64p. (gr. 4-6). 1984. 6.50 o.p. (ISBN 0-88186-001-8). Parkwest Pubns.

Arthur C. Clarke. Ed. by Joseph D. Olander & Martin H. Greenberg. LC 76-11052. (Writers of the 21st Century Ser.). (YA) (gr. 11 up). 1977. 12.95 o.s.i. (ISBN 0-8008-0402-3); pap. 5.95 o.s.i. (ISBN 0-8008-0401-5). Taplinger.

Arthur C. Clarke's July 20, 2019: Life in the 21st Century. Arthur C. Clarke. LC 86-12618. (Illus.). 256p. 1986. 24.95 o.p. (ISBN 0-02-525800-1). Macmillan.

Arthur C. Clarke's Venus Prime, Vol. 2: Maelstrom. Paul Preuss. 1988. pap. 94.80 o.s.i. (ISBN 0-380-75687-0). Avon.

Arthur Dove & Duncan Phillips: Artist & Patron. Sasha M. Newman. Ed. by Kathleen A. Lynch et al. LC 81-8493. 1981. text ed. 35.00 o.p.; pap. text ed. 18.00 o.p. (ISBN 0-686-36420-1). Phillips Coll.

Arthur Fiedler & the Boston Pops. Harry E. Dickson. 276p. 1981. 12.95 o.p. (ISBN 0-395-30524-1). HM.

Arthur Frommer's Guide to Amsterdam & Holland, 1985-1986. 1984. pap. 4.95 o.p. (ISBN 0-671-52466-6). Prentice Hall Pr.

Arthur Frommer's Guide to Athens. 1984. pap. 4.95 o.p. (ISBN 0-671-52467-4). Prentice Hall Pr.

Arthur Frommer's Guide to Athens, 1983-84. 224p. 1982. pap. 3.95 o.p. (ISBN 0-671-45418-8). Prentice Hall Pr.

Arthur Frommer's Guide to Atlantic City. 1984. pap. 4.95 o.p. (ISBN 0-671-52471-2). Prentice Hall Pr.

Arthur Frommer's Guide to Boston. 1984. pap. 4.95 o.p. (ISBN 0-671-52416-X). Prentice Hall Pr.

Arthur Frommer's Guide to Boston, 1983-84. 224p. 1982. pap. 3.95 o.p. (ISBN 0-671-45385-8). Prentice Hall Pr.

Arthur Frommer's Guide to Dublin & Ireland. 1984. pap. 4.95 o.p. (ISBN 0-671-52418-6). Prentice Hall Pr.

Arthur Frommer's Guide to Dublin & Ireland, 1983-84. 215p. 1982. pap. 3.95 o.p. (ISBN 0-671-45387-4). Prentice Hall Pr.

Arthur Frommer's Guide to Hawaii. 1984. pap. 4.95 o.p. (ISBN 0-671-52417-8). Prentice Hall Pr.

Arthur Frommer's Guide to Hawaii, 1983-84. 220p. 1983. pap. 3.95 o.p. (ISBN 0-671-45386-6). Prentice Hall Pr.

Arthur Frommer's Guide to Las Vegas. 1984. pap. 4.95 o.p. (ISBN 0-671-52653-7). Prentice Hall Pr.

Arthur Frommer's Guide to Las Vegas, 1983-84. 220p. 1982. pap. 3.95 o.p. (ISBN 0-671-45114-6). Prentice Hall Pr.

Arthur Frommer's Guide to Lisbon, Madrid & Costa del Sol, 1983-84. 224p. 1982. pap. 3.95 o.p. (ISBN 0-671-44796-3). Prentice Hall Pr.

Titles

Arthur Frommer's Guide to Lisbon, Madrid & Costa del Sol. 1984. pap. 4.95 o.p. (ISBN 0-671-52421-6). Prentice Hall Pr.

Arthur Frommer's Guide to London. 1984. pap. 4.95 o.p. (ISBN 0-671-52423-2). Prentice Hall Pr.

Arthur Frommer's Guide to London, 1983-84. 224p. 1982. pap. 3.95 o.p. (ISBN 0-671-44794-7). Prentice Hall Pr.

Arthur Frommer's Guide to Los Angeles. 1984. pap. 4.95 o.p. (ISBN 0-671-52652-9). Prentice Hall Pr.

Arthur Frommer's Guide to Los Angeles, 1983-84. 224p. 1982. pap. 3.95 o.p. (ISBN 0-671-45112-X). Prentice Hall Pr.

Arthur Frommer's Guide to Mexico City & Acapulco. 1984. pap. 4.95 o.p. (ISBN 0-671-52424-0). Prentice Hall Pr.

Arthur Frommer's Guide to Mexico City & Acapulco, 1983-84. 1982. pap. 3.95 o.p. (ISBN 0-671-45298-3). Prentice Hall Pr.

Arthur Frommer's Guide to Montreal & Quebec City. 1984. pap. 4.95 o.p. (ISBN 0-671-52425-9). Prentice Hall Pr.

Arthur Frommer's Guide to Montreal-Quebec, 1983-84. 1982. pap. 3.95 o.p. (ISBN 0-671-45296-7). Prentice Hall Pr.

Arthur Frommer's Guide to New Orleans. 1984. pap. 4.95 o.p. (ISBN 0-671-52415-1). Prentice Hall Pr.

Arthur Frommer's Guide to New Orleans, 1983-84. 224p. 1982. pap. 3.95 o.p. (ISBN 0-671-45388-2). Prentice Hall Pr.

Arthur Frommer's Guide to New York. 1984. pap. 4.95 o.p. (ISBN 0-671-52426-7). Prentice Hall Pr.

Arthur Frommer's Guide to New York, 1983-84. 224p. 1982. pap. 3.95 o.p. (ISBN 0-671-45389-0). Prentice Hall Pr.

Arthur Frommer's Guide to Orlando, Disney World & EPCOT. 1984. pap. 4.95 o.p. (ISBN 0-671-52429-1). Prentice Hall Pr.

Arthur Frommer's Guide to Orlando, Disney World & EPCOT. Marylyn Springer. (Illus.). 224p. 1983. 3.95 o.p. (ISBN 0-671-46918-5). Prentice Hall Pr.

Arthur Frommer's Guide to Paris. 1984. pap. 4.95 o.p. (ISBN 0-671-52427-5). Prentice Hall Pr.

Arthur Frommer's Guide to Paris, 1983-84. 224p. 1982. pap. 3.95 o.p. (ISBN 0-671-44795-5). Prentice Hall Pr.

Arthur Frommer's Guide to Philadelphia, 1985-1986. 1984. pap. 4.95 o.p. (ISBN 0-671-52470-4). Prentice Hall Pr.

Arthur Frommer's Guide to Philadelphia & Atlantic City, 1983-84. Hal M. Lewis. (Illus.). 224p. 1982. pap. 3.95 o.p. (ISBN 0-671-45414-5). Prentice Hall Pr.

Arthur Frommer's Guide to Rome, 1983-84. 224p. 1982. pap. 3.95 o.p. (ISBN 0-671-44918-4). Prentice Hall Pr.

Arthur Frommer's Guide to Rome, 1985-1986. 224p. 1984. pap. 4.95 o.p. (ISBN 0-671-52428-3). Prentice Hall Pr.

Arthur Frommer's Guide to San Francisco, 1983-84. 224p. 1982. pap. 3.95 o.p. (ISBN 0-671-45113-8). Prentice Hall Pr.

Arthur Frommer's Guide to San Francisco, 1985-1986. 224p. 1984. pap. 4.95 o.p. (ISBN 0-671-52654-5). Prentice Hall Pr.

Arthur Frommer's Guide to Washington, D. C., 1983-84. 224p. 1982. pap. 3.95 o.p. (ISBN 0-671-45384-X). Prentice Hall Pr.

Arthur Frommer's Guide to Washington, D. C., 1985-1986. 224p. 1984. pap. 4.95 o.p. (ISBN 0-671-52456-9). Prentice Hall Pr.

Arthur Gets What He Spills. Louise Armstrong. LC 78-32029. (Let Me Read Ser.). (Illus.). (gr. 6-10). 1979. 4.95 o.p. (ISBN 0-15-204106-0, HJ); pap. 1.95 o.p. (ISBN 0-15-607945-3, VoyB). HarBraceJ.

Arthur Machen: A Bibliography. Henry Danielson. LC 79-149784. 69p. 1971. Repr. of 1923 ed. 35.00x o.p. (ISBN 0-8103-3682-0). Gale.

Arthur Miller. Neil Carson. LC 81-84704. (Modern Dramatists Ser.). 184p. (Orig.). 1982. pap. 6.95 o.p. (ISBN 0-394-17966-8, E-794, Ever). Grove.

Arthur Miller: A Reference Guide. John H. Ferres. 1979. lib. bdg. 30.50 o.p. (ISBN 0-8161-7822-4, Hall Reference). G K Hall.

Arthur O. Lovejoy: An Annotated Bibliography. Daniel J. Wilson. LC 82-11744. (Garland Bibiliographies of Modern Critics & Critical Schools Ser.). 211p. 1982. lib. bdg. 36.00 o.p. (ISBN 0-8240-9257-0). Garland Pub.

Arthur Penn: A Guide to Reference & Resources. Joel S. Zuker. 1979. lib. bdg. 28.00 o.p. (ISBN 0-8161-8116-0, Hall Reference). G K Hall.

Arthur Versus the Rest. Alan Coren. LC 83-61280. (Illus.). 64p. (gr. 3-5). 1985. 6.50 o.p. (ISBN 0-88186-000-X). Parkwest Pubns.

Arthurian Chronicles: A Paraphrase of Wace's "Roman De Brut" Robert Wace & Layamon. Tr. by Eugene Mason. 1976. Repr. of 1912 ed. 8.95x o.p. (ISBN 0-460-00578-2, Evman); pap. 3.50x o.p. (ISBN 0-460-01578-8, Evman). Biblio Dist.

Arthurian Literature IV. Ed. by Richard Barber. LC 83-640196. 178p. 1985. 39.95x o.p. (ISBN 0-389-20432-3, BNB-07318). B&N Imports.

Arthur's Eyes. Marc Brown. (Illus.). 32p. (gr. 1-3). 1981. pap. 2.25 o.p. (ISBN 0-380-53389-8, 70000-X, Camelot). Avon.

Arthur's Kingdom of Adventures: The World of Malory's Morte Darthur. Muriel Whitaker. (Arthurian Studies: No. X). (Illus.). 144p. 1984. 45.00 o.p. (ISBN 0-85991-165-9, Pub. by Boydell & Brewer). Longwood Pub Group.

Arthur's Last Stand. Alan Coren. LC 79-14052. (Illus.). (gr. 4-6). 1979. 12.45i o.p. (ISBN 0-316-15742-2). Little.

Arthur's Nose. Marc Brown. (Illus.). 32p. (gr. 1-3). 1981. pap. 2.25 o.p. (ISBN 0-380-53397-9, 68940-5, Camelot). Avon.

Arthur's Valentine. Marc Brown. (Snuggle & Read Story Bks.). (Illus.). 32p. (Orig.). (ps-3). 1982. pap. 1.95 o.p. (ISBN 0-380-57075-0, 57075-0, Camelot). Avon.

Articles on Library Instruction in Colleges & Universities, 1876-1932. John M. Tucker. (Occasional Papers: No. 143). 45p. 1980. pap. 3.00 o.p. (ISBN 0-317-58994-6). U of Ill Lib Info Sci.

Articulate Images: The Sister Arts from Hogarth to Tennyson. Ed. by Richard Wendorf. LC 83-5798. (Illus.). 283p. 1983. 29.50x o.p. (ISBN 0-8166-1143-2). U of Minn Pr.

Articulate Mammal: An Introduction to Psycholinguistics. Jean Aitchison. (Illus.). 1978. pap. text ed. 4.95 o.p. (ISBN 0-07-000736-5). McGraw.

Articulation & Voice: Improving Oral Communication. Robert G. King & Eleanor M. Di Michael. (Illus.). 1978. pap. write for info. o.p. (ISBN 0-02-364250-5). Macmillan.

Articulation Disorders. John E. Bernthal & Nicholas W. Bankson. (Illus.). 352p. 1981. text ed. (ISBN 0-13-049072-5). P-H.

Articulation Learning. William M. Diedrich & Jeff Bangert. LC 80-18405. (Illus.). 368p. 1980. text ed. 34.00 o.p. (ISBN 0-316-18707-0). College-Hill.

Articulation Worksheets: For Remediation & Carryover of Speech & Language Skills. Margaret F. Smith. 70p. 1981. 3-ring binder 24.95 o.p. (ISBN 0-88450-737-8, 2080-B). Communication Skill.

Articulos y Ensayos. Jose J. Vargas. Ed. by Anibal Vargas-Baron. 1963. 3.50 o.p. (ISBN 0-87114-010-1). U of Oreg Bks.

Artifact in Social Science Research. Anton J. Nederhof. text ed. cancelled o.s.i. (ISBN 0-8290-1064-5). Irvington.

Artificial Family: A Consideration of Artificial Insemination by Donor. R. Snowden & G. D. Mitchell. 138p. 1981. 29.95 o.p. (ISBN 0-04-176001-8). Unwin Hyman.

Artificial Groundwater Discharge. L. Huisman. 330p. 1982. 64.95 o.p. (ISBN 0-470-20498-2, Co-Pub. with Longman). Wiley.

Artificial Intelligence. Business Communications Staff. 1988. 2450.00 o.p. (ISBN 0-89336-659-5, G-086R). BCC.

Artificial Intelligence. Neill Graham. LC 78-26512. (Illus.). 1979. 12.95 o.p. (ISBN 0-8306-9835-3); pap. 9.70 o.p. (ISBN 0-8306-1076-6, 1076). TAB Bks.

Artificial Intelligence. International Resource Development, Inc. Staff. 167p. 1983. 1650.00x o.p. (ISBN 0-88694-552-6). Intl Res Dev.

Artificial Intelligence. Stevens. 1985. 14.95 o.p. (ISBN 0-8104-6327-X). Sams.

Artificial Intelligence. Time-Life Books Editors. (Understanding Computers Ser.). 128p. (YA) (gr. 7 up). 1986. 19.93 o.p.; lib. bdg. 23.93 o.p. Time-Life.

Artificial Intelligence & Design. Louis Steinberg & Christopher Tong. (Illus.). 80p. 1988. pap. text ed. 12.00x o.p. (ISBN 0-929280-19-9). Amer Artificial.

Artificial Intelligence & Legal Information. C. Ciampi & A. A. Martino. 1984. 147.50 o.p. (ISBN 0-444-86413-X). Elsevier.

Artificial Intelligence Applications in Hardware Diagnosis. Matthew Ginsberg & Narinder Singh. (Illus.). 85p. 1988. pap. text ed. 12.00x o.p. (ISBN 0-929280-23-7). Amer Artificial.

Artificial Intelligence, Bad Honnef, FRG 1982: Proceedings. Ed. by W. Wahlster. (Informatik Fachberichte Ser.: Vol. 58). 246p. 1983. pap. 12.30 o.p. (ISBN 0-387-11960-4). Springer-Verlag.

Artificial Intelligence in Medicine. Ed. by Ramesh Patil. 116p. 1988. pap. text ed. 20.00x o.p. (ISBN 0-929280-03-2). Amer Artificial.

Artificial Intelligence Reports from Bolt, Beranek & Newman. Comtex Staff. 1984. (ISBN 0-471-82286-8). Wiley.

Artificial Intelligence Reports from Carnegie Mellon University. Comtex Staff. 1984. (ISBN 0-471-82289-2). Wiley.

Artificial Intelligence Reports from Carnegie Mellon University, Pt. 1. Comtex Staff. 1984. (ISBN 0-471-82288-4). Wiley.

Artificial Intelligence Reports from Carnegie Mellon University, Pt. 2. Comtex Staff. 1984. (ISBN 0-471-82287-6). Wiley.

Artificial Intelligence Reports from the University of Pennsylvania. Comtex Staff. 1984. (ISBN 0-471-82283-3). Wiley.

Artificial Intelligence Reports from Yale University. Comtex Staff. 1985. (ISBN 0-471-82285-X). Wiley.

Artificial Kidney. 123p. 1968. pap. 24.00 o.p. (ISBN 0-8169-0273-9, S-84). Am Inst Chem Eng.

Artificial Larynx. Yvan Lebrun et al. (Neurolinguistics Ser.: Vol. 1). 90p. 1973. pap. text ed. 18.50 o.p. (ISBN 90-265-0173-0, Pub. by Swets & Zeitlinger Netherlands). CJ Hogrefe Pubs.

Artificial Particle Beams in Space Plasma Studies. Ed. by Bjorn Grandal. LC 82-470. (NATO ASI Series B, Physics: Vol. 79). 722p. 1982. 105.00x o.p. (ISBN 0-306-40985-2, Plenum Pr). Plenum Pub.

Artificial Persons: The Formation of Character in the Tragedies of Shakespeare. J. Leeds Barroll. LC 73-13991. 1974. 21.95x o.p. (ISBN 0-87249-294-X); pap. text ed. 12.95x o.p. (ISBN 0-87249-377-6). U of SC Pr.

Artificial Recharge of Groundwater. Takashi Asano. LC 84-14296. 800p. 1985. text ed. 79.95 o.p. (ISBN 0-250-40549-0). Butterworth.

Artificial Selection & Development of Evolutionary Theory. Ed. by Carl J. Bajema. LC 80-10784. (Benchmark Papers in Systematic & Evolutionary Biology: Vol. 4). 384p. 1982. 52.95 o.p. (ISBN 0-87933-369-3). Van Nos Reinhold.

Artificial Ventilation: Technical, Biological & Clinical Aspects. Ed. by J. P. Payne & J. A. Bushman. LC 80-40391. 1980. 58.00 o.p. (ISBN 0-12-547960-3). Acad Pr.

Artificial Vision for Robots. Ed. by I. Aleksander. (Illus.). 234p. 1984. 37.50 o.p. (ISBN 0-412-00451-8, NO. 9001, Pub. by Chapman & Hall New York). Routledge Chapman & Hall.

Artificially Arranged Scenes: The Films of Georges Meiles. John Frazer. 1979. lib. bdg. 32.50 o.s.i. (ISBN 0-8161-8368-6, Hall Reference). G K Hall.

Artisan Elite in Victorian Society: Kentish London 1840-1880. Geoffrey Crossick. 306p. 1978. 26.50x o.p. (ISBN 0-8476-6098-2). Rowman.

Artisans & Sans-Culottes. Gwyn A. Williams. LC 69-14476. (Foundations of Modern History Ser). 1969. pap. text ed. 3.95x o.p. (ISBN 0-393-09832-X, NortonC). Norton.

Artisans, Peasants & Proletarians 1760-1860: Essays Presented to Gwyn A. Williams. Ed. by Clive Emsley & James Walvin. LC 85-17498. 224p. 1985. 34.50 o.p. (ISBN 0-7099-3635-4, Pub. by Croom Helm Ltd). Routledge Chapman & Hall.

Artist. Jan De Hartog. LC 63-7801. (YA) 1963. 5.00 o.p. (ISBN 0-689-00012-X, Atheneum). Macmillan.

Artist. Norman Garbo. 1978. 12.95 o.p. (ISBN 0-393-08790-5). Norton.

Artist & the Quilt. Ed. by Charlotte Robinson. LC 83-47775. 1983. 24.45 o.p. (ISBN 0-394-53220-1); pap. 12.95 o.p. (ISBN 0-394-71560-8). Knopf.

Artist As Photographer. Marina Vaizey. (Illus.). 1982. 25.00 o.p. (ISBN 0-03-062427-4). H Holt & Co.

Artist of the Floating World. Kazuo Ishiguro. 208p. 1986. 15.95 o.p. (ISBN 0-399-13119-1). Putnam Pub Group.

Artistic America, Tiffany Glass & Art Nouveau. Samuel Bing. (Illus.). 288p. 1970. pap. 11.95 o.p. (ISBN 0-262-52025-7). MIT Pr.

Artistic & Romantic Chronicle of the New England Seacoast, 2 vols. Charles Boardman. (Illus.). 251p. 1986. Set. 189.45 o.p. (ISBN 0-86650-184-3). Gloucester Art.

Artistic Applications of Classical Criteria to the Decoration of Walls, 2 vols. Mark W. McClelland. (Illus.). 301p. 1985. Set. 237.45 o.p. (ISBN 0-86650-135-5). Gloucester Art.

Artistic Truth & Dialectics of Creative Work. V. Novikov. 342p. 1981. 10.00 o.p. (ISBN 0-8285-2296-0, Pub. by Progress Pubs USSR). Imported Pubns.

Artistry of Shakespeare's Prose. 2nd ed. Brian Vickers. (Library Reprints Ser.). 464p. 1980. 55.00x o.p. (ISBN 0-416-72570-8, NO.2820). Routledge Chapman & Hall.

Artistry of the Mentally Ill. H. Prinzhorn. Tr. by E. Von Brockdorff from Ger. LC 70-162403. (Illus.). 1972. 59.50 o.s.i. (ISBN 0-387-05508-8). Springer-Verlag.

Artists & Enemies: Three Novellas. Arthur A. Cohen. 1987. 17.95 o.p. (ISBN 0-317-56201-0). Godine.

Artists & People. Y. Greer Thiel. (Illus.). 327p. 1959. (ISBN 0-8022-1710-9). Philos Lib.

Artist's Contracts of the Early Renaissance. Hannelore Glasser. LC 76-23624. (Outstanding Dissertations in the Fine Arts - 2nd Series - 15th Century). (Illus.). 1977. Repr. of 1965 ed. lib. bdg. 68.00 o.p. (ISBN 0-8240-2694-2). Garland Pub.

Artists Exhibited in Wales, Nineteen Forty-Five to Nineteen Seventy-Four. Kirstine B. Dunthorne. 344p. 1980. pap. 20.95x o.p. (ISBN 0-9500455-8-6, Pub. by Welsh Art Wales). Intl Spec Bk.

Artist's Guide to Living by Your Brush Alone. Edna W. Piersol. Ed. by Fritz Henning. LC 83-15123. (Illus.). 154p. (Orig.). 1983. pap. 9.95 o.p. (ISBN 0-89134-063-7, Pub. by North Light Pub). Writers Digest.

Artists in Print: An Introduction to Prints & Printmaking. Pat Gilmour. LC 83-61268. (Illus.). 144p. 1984. pap. 16.95 o.p. (ISBN 0-88186-500-1). Parkwest Pubns.

Artists in the Making. Frank X. Barron. LC 72-77220. 256p. 1972. 44.00 o.p. (ISBN 0-12-785042-2). Acad Pr.

Artist's Manual. Stan Smith. 1988. 19.98 o.p. (ISBN 0-8317-4251-8). Smith Pubs.

Artist's Market, 1983. Ed. by Sally A. Davis. 528p. 1982. 14.95 o.p. (ISBN 0-89879-084-0). Writers Digest.

Artist's Market, 1984. Ed. by Sally A. Davis. 528p. 1983. 14.95 o.p. (ISBN 0-89879-121-9). Writers Digest.

Artist's Market, 1985. Sally A. Davis. 528p. 1984. 15.95 o.p. (ISBN 0-89879-152-9). Writers Digest.

Artist's Market, 1986. Ed. by Diana L. Martin-Hoffman. 576p. 1985. 16.95 o.p. (ISBN 0-89879-200-2, 1047). Writers Digest.

Artist's Market '87. Susan Conner. 576p. 1986. 16.95 o.p. (ISBN 0-89879-246-0). Writers Digest.

Artist's Market 88. Ed. by Susan Conner. 624p. 1987. 18.95 o.p. (ISBN 0-89879-275-4). Writers Digest.

Artist's Notebook: The Life & Art of Merritt Mauzey. Merritt Mauzey. Ed. by Gordon Weaver. (Illus.). 1979. 21.50 o.p. (ISBN 0-87870-066-8). Memphis St Univ.

Artists Observed. Elaine A. King. 160p. 1986. pap. 17.95 o.p. (ISBN 0-8109-2325-4). Abrams.

Artists of American Folk Music: The Legends of Traditional Folk, the Stars of the Sixties, the Virtuosi of New Acoustic Music. Ed. by Phil Hood. (Illus.). 160p. (Orig.). 1986. pap. 12.95 o.p. (ISBN 0-688-05916-3, Quill). Morrow.

Artists of the Book, Nineteen Eighty-Eight: A Facet of Modernism. Ed. by Frances Barna. (Illus.). 1988. pap. 5.00 o.s.i. (ISBN 0-934552-53-3). Boston Athenaeum.

Artists of the Tudor Court: The Portrait Miniature Rediscovered, 1520-1620. Roy Strong. (Illus.). 168p. (Orig.). 1984. pap. 15.95 o.p. (ISBN 0-905209-34-6, Pub. by Victoria & Albert Mus UK). Faber & Faber.

Artist's Silk Screen Manual. Andrew B. Gardner. LC 73-22737. (Craft Books Ser.). (Illus.). 192p. 1976. pap. 9.95 o.p. (ISBN 0-448-11593-X, G&D). Putnam Pub Group.

Arts: A Way of Knowing. Ed. by M. Ross. LC 83-13208. (Curriculum Issues of Education Ser.: Vol. 4). 248p. 1983. 65.00 o.p. (ISBN 0-08-030180-0). Pergamon.

Arts Administration. John Pick. 256p. 1980. pap. 15.95x o.p. (ISBN 0-419-11540-4, NO.2067, Pub. by E & FN Spon). Routledge Chapman & Hall.

Arts & Aesthetics: An Agenda for the Future. Stanley S. Madeja. 422p. 1977. 24.95 o.p. (ISBN 0-87855-355-X). Transaction Pubs.

Arts & Crafts of the Austral Islands: A Special Exhibition, 17 December 1968 to 30 April 1969. Martin A. Brunor. 1969. pap. 2.00 o.p. (ISBN 0-87577-018-5). Peabody Mus Salem.

Arts & Crafts of Turkestan: Bauhaus. Frank Whitford. LC 83-50527. (Illus.). 216p. (Orig.). 1984. pap. 9.95 o.p. Thames-Hudson.

Arts & Humanity. Charles W. Cooper. 1952. (ISBN 0-8022-0295-0). Philos Lib.

Arts & Ideas. 6th ed. William Fleming. LC 79-20123. 502p. 1980. pap. text ed. 26.95 o.p. (ISBN 0-03-046531-1, HoltC). HR&W.

Arts & the Schools. Jerome J. Hausman. (IDEA Study of Schooling in the United States Ser.). (Illus.). 332p. 1980. text ed. 21.15 o.p. (ISBN 0-07-027225-5). McGraw.

Arts As an Industry: Their Economic Importance to the New York-New Jersey Metropolitan Region. 151p. 1983. 12.00 o.p. (ISBN 0-89062-153-5, Pub. by Alliance for the Arts). Pub Ctr Cult Res.

Arts, Cognition, & Basic Skills. Ed. by Stanley S. Madeja. 263p. 1978. 24.95 o.p. (ISBN 0-87855-356-8). Transaction Pubs.

Arts Education Advocacy. 88p. 1976. 3.00 o.p. (ISBN 0-937652-08-3). Natl Art Ed.

Arts in America: A Bibliography, 4 vols. Ed. by Bernard Karpel. 2700p. Set. 240.00 o.p. (ISBN 0-317-54873-5). Apollo.

Arts in Cultural Diversity. International Society for Education through Art Staff. 304p. (Orig.). pap. 35.95 o.p. (ISBN 0-275-91511-5, B1511). Praeger.

Arts in Education Partners: Schools & Their Communities. JDR 3rd Fund Staff. (Illus.). 128p. 1976. pap. 6.00 o.s.i. (ISBN 0-317-32504-3, NO. 165). Am Council Arts.

Arts in Education Source Book: A View from the JDR 3rd Fund. Kathryn Bloom et al. (Illus.). 249p. pap. cancelled o.s.i. (ISBN 0-9604224-0-4). Am Council Arts.
Arts in Ireland: A Chronological Survey. Christopher Fitz-Simon. 256p. 1982. text ed. 45.00x o.p. (ISBN 0-391-02578-3, Pub. by Gill & Macmillan Ireland). Humanities.
Arts in the Economic Life of the City. Urban Innovations Group, Inc. Staff. LC 79-29764. (Illus.). 150p. (Orig.). pap. text ed. cancelled o.s.i. (ISBN 0-915400-16-2, 1550). Am Council Arts.
Arts of a Vanished Era. Whatcom Museum of History & Art Staff. LC 68-9204. (Whatcom Museum Ser.). (Illus.). 64p. 1968. pap. 5.00 o.p. (ISBN 0-295-95576-7). U of Wash Pr.
Arts of Asia at the Time of American Independence. LC 75-42866. (Illus.). 1976. pap. 3.00 o.p. (ISBN 0-934686-16-5). Freer.
Arts of China. rev. ed. Michael Sullivan. LC 76-44639. (Illus.). 1978. 20.00 o.p. (ISBN 0-520-03366-3); pap. 16.95 o.p. (ISBN 0-520-03367-1). U of Cal Pr.
Arts of China, Vol. 1: Neolithic Cultures to the T'ang Dynasty. Terukazu Akiyama et al. LC 68-17454. (Illus.). 1973. 89.00 o.p. (ISBN 0-87011-064-0). Kodansha.
Arts of China, Vol. 3: Paintings in Chinese Museums. Yoshio Yonezawa et al. LC 68-17454. (Illus.). 1973. 89.00 o.p. (ISBN 0-87011-128-0). Kodansha.
Arts of Thailand: A Handbook of the Architecture, Sculpture, & Painting of Thailand. Indiana University Staff. LC 74-31411. 1975. Repr. of 1960 ed. lib. bdg. 0.25x o.p. (ISBN 0-8371-7884-3, IUAT). Greenwood.
Arts of the Beautiful. Etienne H. Gilson. LC 76-42284. 1976. Repr. of 1965 ed. lib. bdg. 69.50x o.p. (ISBN 0-8371-9294-3, GIAB). Greenwood.
Arturo Toscanini: Genius of Conducting. Irving Gerber. (American Destiny Ser.: Jewish Americans). (Illus.). 1979. of 10 12.95 set o.p. (ISBN 0-87594-189-3). Book Lab.
Artworks. Ed. by David Spicer. LC 78-13298. (Brooks Memorial Gallery Bks.). (Illus.). 1979. pap. 3.95 o.p. (ISBN 0-918518-10-5, St Luke TN). Peachtree Pubs.
Arun: A National History of the World's Deepest Valley. Edward W. Cronin, Jr. 1979. 10.95 o.p. (ISBN 0-395-26299-2). HM.
Arykosia. George D. Sovey. 448p. 1988. 18.95 o.p. (ISBN 0-8062-3044-4). Carlton.
As a Little Child. Nora E. Larson. LC 81-66072. (Illus.). 56p. (Orig.). (gr. 1-4). 1981. pap. 4.00 o.p. (ISBN 0-87516-451-X). DeVorss.
As a Man Thinketh. James Allen. 4.95 o.p. (ISBN 0-529-05908-8, F12); pap. 2.95 o.p. (ISBN 0-529-05906-1, D6). World Bible.
As a Tree Grows: Reflections on Growing in the Image of Christ. W. Phillip Keller. 96p. 1985. pap. 3.50 o.p. (ISBN 0-89283-248-7, Pub. by Vine Books). Servant.
As Close As Possible. Bruce L. Baker et al. LC 77-81502. 1977. text ed. 13.95 o.p. (ISBN 0-316-07827-1); pap. text ed. 9.95 o.p. (ISBN 0-316-07829-8). Little.
As Equals & As Sisters: Feminism, the Labor Movement, & the Women's Trade Union League of New York. Nancy S. Dye. LC 80-16751. 208p. 1981. text ed. 23.00x o.p. (ISBN 0-8262-0318-3). U of Mo Pr.
As Far As You Can Go Without a Passport: The View from the End of the Road. Tom Bodett. LC 85-13478. 143p. 1985. 11.95 o.p. (ISBN 0-201-10661-2). Addison-Wesley.
As France Goes. David Schoenbrun. LC 55-8033. 1968. pap. 3.25 o.p. (ISBN 0-689-70174-8, 128, Atheneum). Macmillan.
As He Saw It. Elliott Roosevelt. LC 74-9044. 170p. 1974. Repr. of 1946 ed. lib. bdg. 22.50x o.p. (ISBN 0-8371-7609-3, ROHS). Greenwood.
As I Lay Dying. William Faulkner. 48p. (Orig.). 1989. pap. 9.95 o.p. (ISBN 1-55651-004-7); audiocassette tape incl. o.p. (ISBN 1-55651-005-5). Cram Cassettes.
As I Please: Nineteen Forty-Three to Nineteen Forty-Five see Collected Essays, Journalism, & Letters of George Orwell.
As I Walked Down New Grub Street. Walter Allen. LC 81-69852. vi, 278p. 1982. 15.00x o.s.i. (ISBN 0-226-01433-9). U of Chicago Pr.
As I Walked out One Midsummer Morning. Laurie Lee. (Illus.). 256p. 1969. 14.95 o.s.i. (ISBN 0-233-96117-8). Andre Deutsch.
As I Walked Out One Midsummer Morning. Laurie Lee. LC 85-11459. (Illus.). 1985. Repr. of 1969 ed. 22.00 o.p. (ISBN 0-393-02233-1). Norton.
As I Was Crossing Boston Common. Norma Farber & Arnold Lobel. (Illus.). 32p. (ps-1). 1982. pap. 5.95 o.p. (ISBN 0-916870-43-X). Creative Arts Bk.
As I Was Going Down Sackville Street. Oliver S. Gogarty. LC 37-4752. 1967. pap. 2.25 o.p. (ISBN 0-15-609004-X, Harv). HarBraceJ.
As I Was Saying. Lynn Ashby. Ed. by Scott Lubeck. 272p. 1984. 14.95 o.p. (ISBN 0-932012-29-9). Texas Month Pr.
As I Was Saying: A Chesterton Reader. Ed. by Robert Knille. 352p. 1985. 19.95 o.p. (ISBN 0-8028-3597-X). Eerdmans.
As If after Sex. Joseph Torchia. 192p. 1983. 13.95 o.p. (ISBN 0-03-062858-X). H Holt & Co.
As If by Magic. Patti Newman. 31p. (gr. 3-5). 1985. 4.95 o.p. (ISBN 0-533-06323-X). Vantage.
As It Happenith to the Fool. Carol Jeffrey. 1985. 10.00x o.p. (ISBN 0-317-61996-9, Gulid of Pastoral Psych). State Mutual Bk.
As It Was: An Inside View of Politics & Power in the Fifties & Sixties. Henry C. Lodge. 1976. 8.95 o.p. (ISBN 0-393-05597-3). Norton.
As Lonely As Franz Kafka. Marthe. 1982. 14.95 o.p. (ISBN 0-15-109058-0). HarbraceJ.
As Long As the Grass Shall Grow. R. J. Lenarcic. 1973. pap. text ed. 8.95x o.p. (ISBN 0-8422-0232-3). Irvington.
As Once to Birth I went New I Am Taken Back. Harry Brody. 1981. 3.00 o.s.i. (ISBN 0-317-61631-5). New Collage.
As Others See Vocational Education. Ann R. Nunez & Jill F. Russell. 1982. A Survey of the National Association of Manufacturers, 25p. 3.75 o.p. (ISBN 0-318-22036-9, RD225A); A Survey of the National Conference of State Legislators, 28p. 3.75 o.p. (ISBN 0-318-22037-7, RD225B); Set. 7.25 o.p. (ISBN 0-318-22038-5, RD225). Natl Ctr Res Voc Ed.
As the Earth Turns. Gladys H. Carroll. 1978. 12.95 o.p. (ISBN 0-393-08830-8). Norton.
As the Lord Revealed It to Me. Robert D. Boyd. 1976. 4.00 o.p. (ISBN 0-682-48500-4). Exposition-Phoenix.
As the Twig Is Bent: Readings in Early Childhood Education. Ed. by Robert H. Anderson & Harold G. Shane. LC 71-135675. 1972. pap. 11.50 o.p. (ISBN 0-395-11218-4, 3-01135). HM.
As the Twig Is Bent: Sketches of a Bittersweet Life. Winifred Foley. LC 77-92766. 1978. 9.95 o.s.i. (ISBN 0-8008-0421-X). Taplinger.
As We Forgive Those. Elisabeth Elliot. 16p. 1982. pap. 1.50 o.p. (ISBN 0-89107-255-1). Good News.
As We Remember Mother. Ruth Stout. 1975. 6.00 o.p. (ISBN 0-682-48352-4). Exposition-Phoenix.
As You Believe. Barbara Dewey. LC 85-7370. 208p. 1985. 18.95 o.p. (ISBN 0-933123-01-9). Bartholomew Bks.
As You Like It. William Shakespeare. 48p. (Orig.). 1989. pap. 9.95 o.p. (ISBN 1-55651-006-3); audiocassette tape incl. o.p. (ISBN 1-55651-007-1). Cram Cassettes.
As You Like It: An Old-Spelling & Old-Meaning Edition. William Shakespeare. Ed. by Christiane Trauvetter. 222p. cancelled o.s.i. (ISBN 3-533-02227-7). Adlers Foreign Bks.
As You Recover. Douglas Elliott. 32p. 1984. pap. 1.25 o.p. (ISBN 0-8010-3414-0). Baker Bk.
As You Sow: Three Studies in the Social Consequences of Agribusiness. Walter Goldschmidt. LC 77-84435. 560p. 1978. 16.50x o.s.i. (ISBN 0-916672-10-7, Pub. by Allanheld); pap. text ed. 7.95x o.s.i. (ISBN 0-916672-11-5). Rowman.
As Your Acknowledged Leader: The Best of Lynn Ashby. Lynn Ashby. Ed. by Barbara Rodriguez. 281p. 1983. 12.95 o.p. (ISBN 0-932012-64-7). Texas Month Pr.
Asa Gray. A. Hunter Dupree. LC 59-12967. (Illus.). 1968. pap. text ed. 3.95x o.p. (ISBN 0-689-70066-0, 132, Atheneum). Macmillan.
Asad - The Sphinx of Damascus: A Political Biography. Moshe Ma'oz. LC 87-36539. 224p. 1988. 19.95 o.p. (ISBN 1-55584-062-0). Weidenfeld.
Asahel: A Novel. Aharon Megged. Tr. by Robert Whitehill & Susan C. Lilly. LC 81-8822. 256p. 1982. 11.95 o.s.i. (ISBN 0-8008-0410-4). Taplinger.
Asbestos: Medical & Legal Aspects. Barry Castleman. LC 84-10825. 608p. 1984. 55.00 o.p. (ISBN 0-15-100002-6, Pub. by Law & Business). HarBraceJ.
Asbestos Properties, Applications & Hazards: (Properties of Materials: Saftey & Environmental Factors, Vol. 1. L. Michaels & S. S. Chissick. LC 78-16535. 553p. 1979. 146.00 o.p. (ISBN 0-471-99698-X, Pub. by Wiley-Interscience). Wiley.
Asbestos Waste Management Guidance: Generation, Transport, Disposal. (Illus.). 32p. 1985. pap. 1.00 o.p. (ISBN 0-318-22491-7, S/N 055-000-00248-7). USGPO.
ASCE Guide to Employment Conditions for Civil Engineers. (Manual & Report on Engineering Practice Ser.: No. 55). 24p. 1980. pap. 7.00x o.p. (ISBN 0-87262-229-0). Am Soc Civil Eng.
Ascending Flame, Descending Dove: An Essay on Creative Transcendence. Roger Hazelton. LC 75-9649. 128p. 1975. pap. 3.75 o.s.i. (ISBN 0-664-24767-9, Westminster). Westminster John Knox.
Ascension. Harvey R. Brunelle. 320p. 1986. 14.95 o.p. (ISBN 0-8062-2897-0). Carlton.
Ascent into Hell. Andrew M. Greeley. 633p. 1983. lib. bdg. 18.50 o.p. (ISBN 0-8161-3588-6, Large Print Bks). G K Hall.
Ascent of Man: An Introduction to Human Evolution. David Pilbeam. (Illus.). 224p. 1972. pap. text ed. write for info. o.p. (ISBN 0-02-395270-9). Macmillan.
Ascent of Mount Fuji. Chingiz Aitmatov & Kaltai Mukhamedzhanov. 212p. 1975. pap. 4.95 o.p. (ISBN 0-374-51215-9). FS&G.
Ascent to Excellence in Catholic Education: A Guide to Effective Decision-Making. Mary-Angela Harper. 278p. 1980. 9.55 o.p. (ISBN 0-318-00777-0). Natl Cath Educ.
Ascent to Power: Wran & the Media. Brian Dale. (Illus.). 156p. 1986. pap. 12.95 o.p. (ISBN 0-86861-944-2). Unwin Hyman.
Ascent: Two Lives Explored. Edmund Hillary & Peter Hillary. LC 86-16600. (Illus.). 224p. 1986. 18.95 o.p. (ISBN 0-385-19831-0). Doubleday.
Ascent, 1984: The Mountaineering Experience in Word & Image. Ed. by Steve Roper & Allen Steck. LC 84-5379. (Illus.). 208p. 1984. 25.00 o.s.i. (ISBN 0-87156-826-8). Sierra.
Ascorbinsaeure in der Pflanzenzelle. H. Metzner. Bd. with Vitamin C in the Animal Cell. G. H. Bourne. (Protoplasmatologia: Vol. 2B, Pt. 2b). (Illus.). iv, 159p. (Eng. & Ger.). 1957. pap. 44.30 o.p. (ISBN 0-387-80453-6). Springer-Verlag.
ASEAN-Japan Industrial Co-operation: An Overview. Ed. by M. K. Xhng & R. Hirono. 144p. 1985. text ed. 17.50x o.p. (ISBN 9971-902-53-2). Gower Pub Co.
ASEAN-Japan Relations: Investment. Ed. by Sueo Sekiguchi. 284p. (Orig.). 1984. pap. text ed. 28.50 o.p. (ISBN 9971-902-62-1, Pub. by Inst Southeast Asian Stud). Gower Pub Co.
ASEAN-Japan Relations: Trade & Development. Ed. by Narongchai Akrasanee. (Institute Southeast Asian Studies). 200p. (Orig.). 1984. pap. text ed. 26.00x o.p. (ISBN 9971-902-63-X). Gower Pub Co.
Asepsis in Surgery: Its Special Application to Orthopedics. R. Orozco. Tr. by E. Garaza from Span. (Illus.). 1976. 52.00 o.p. (ISBN 0-387-92110-9). Springer-Verlag.
Asgard Solution. James Marino. 384p. 1983. pap. 3.50 o.p. (ISBN 0-380-84145-2, 84145-2). Avon.
Ash Staff. Paul Fisher. LC 79-11731. (gr. 4-6). 1979. 8.95 o.p. (ISBN 0-689-30708-X, Atheneum). Macmillan.
Ash Tallman, the Wages of Sin: No. 3. Tom Lord. 192p. 1984. pap. 2.25 o.p. (ISBN 0-380-87197-1, 87197). Avon.
ASHA Membership Directory, 1986-87. Ed. by Frederick T. Spahr & Alfred K. Kawana. 780p. pap. 50.00 o.p. (ISBN 0-910329-32-X). Am Speech Lang Hearing.
Ashanti Doll. Francis Bebey. Tr. by Joyce Hutchinson. LC 76-52658. 192p. 1977. 7.50 o.p. (ISBN 0-88208-075-X). Chicago Review.
Ashby. Date not set. (ISBN 0-8052-3907-3). Random.
Asher B. Durand: A Documentary Catalogue of the Narrative & Landscape Paintings. David B. Lawall. LC 76-24754. (Reference Library of the Humanities Ser.: Vol. 74). (Illus.). 414p. 1978. lib. bdg. 67.00 o.p. (ISBN 0-8240-9923-0). Garland Pub.
Asher Brown Durand: His Art & Art Theory in Relations to His Times. David B. Lawall. LC 76-23635. (Outstanding Dissertations in the Fine Arts Ser.). 800p. 1977. lib. bdg. 118.00 o.p. (ISBN 0-8240-2704-3). Garland Pub.
Ashes of Gold. Kshitij Mohan. (Writers Workshop Redbird Ser.). 39p. 1975. 8.00 o.s.i. (ISBN 0-88253-502-1); pap. text ed. 4.80 o.s.i. (ISBN 0-88253-501-3). Ind-US Inc.
Ashes of Sin. Eleanor Lamb. 128p. 1987. text ed. 13.95 o.p. (ISBN 0-682-40345-8). Exposition-Phoenix.
Ashkenazy: Beyond Frontiers. Jasper Parrott & Vladimir Ashkenazy. LC 84-6211. (Illus.). 256p. 1985. 14.95 o.p. (ISBN 0-689-11505-9, Atheneum). Macmillan.
Ashton-Tate Developer's Registry. Ashton-Tate Staff. 1000p. (Orig.). 1987. pap. 24.95 o.p. (ISBN 0-317-59758-2). Tate Pub.
Asi Es la Vida. Anson C. Piper. 1958. 5.95x o.p. (ISBN 0-393-09508-8, NortonC). Norton.
Asia - Reference Works: A Select Annotated Guide. Ed. by G. Raymond Nunn. 382p. 1980. Repr. of 1971 ed. text ed. 59.00x o.p. (ISBN 0-7201-0921-3). Mansell.
Asia: A Regional & Economic Geography. 12th ed. L. Dudley Stamp. 1967. 55.00x o.p. (ISBN 0-416-30400-1, NO.2523). Routledge Chapman & Hall.
Asia & Oceania see Developing Areas: A Classed Bibliography of the Joint Bank-Fund Library, World Bank Group & International Monetary Fund.
Asia Banking Almanac: 1986. 6th ed. 1986. 125.00 o.p. (ISBN 0-8002-4109-6). Intl Pubns Serv.
Asia: Half the Human Race, a Viewer's Guide. Ed. by Terry E. Lautz & Fay Willey. (Illus.). 105p. (Orig.). 1979. pap. text ed. 3.50x o.p. (ISBN 0-936876-06-9). LRIS.
Asia Through the Back Door. Rick Steves & John Gottberg. (Illus.). 384p. (Orig.). 1986. pap. 11.95 o.p. (ISBN 0-912528-58-3). John Muir.
Asia Yearbook, 1987. 28th ed. 280p. 1987. pap. 35.00 o.p. (ISBN 0-8002-4099-5, Pub. by FER). Taylor & Francis.
Asia Yearbook, 1988. 1988. 34.95 o.p. (ASYE08). China Bks.
Asia 101: History, Art & Culture for the Traveler. John Gottberg. (Illus.). 352p. pap. cancelled o.s.i. (ISBN 0-912528-81-8). John Muir.
Asian & Pacific Short Stories. Compiled by Cultural & Social Centre, Asian & Pacific Council. LC 73-93869. 1974. 6.75 o.p. (ISBN 0-8048-1125-3). C E Tuttle.
Asian Christian Theology: Emerging Themes. rev. ed. Ed. by Douglas J. Elwood. LC 80-21228. 342p. 1980. pap. 14.95 o.s.i. (ISBN 0-664-24354-1, Westminster). Westminster John Knox.
Asian Drama: An Inquiry into the Poverty of Nations, 3 vols. Gunnar Myrdal. LC 75-162556. (Twentieth Century Fund Ser.). 1968. Vols. 1 & 3. write for info. o.p. (ISBN 0-527-02832-0); Vol. 2. 16.00 o.p. (ISBN 0-527-02776-6). Kraus Repr.
Asian Flavors. Kay Shimizu. LC 70-164869. 1971. 7.00 o.p. (ISBN 0-682-47305-7, Banner). Exposition-Phoenix.
Asian Highland Societies: An Anthropological Perspective. Ed. by Christoph Von Furer-Haimendorf. 265p. 1981. text ed. 32.50x o.p. (ISBN 0-391-02250-4). Humanities.
Asian Ideas of East & West: Tagore & His Critics in Japan, China, & India. Stephen N. Hay. LC 73-89972. (East Asian Ser.: No. 40). 1970. text ed. 32.00x o.s.i. (ISBN 0-674-04975-6). Harvard U Pr.
Asian-Pacific Security: Emerging Challenges & Responses. Ed. by Young W. Kihl & Lawrence E. Grinter. LC 85-25631. 280p. 1986. lib. bdg. 36.50x o.p. (ISBN 0-931477-51-4). Lynne Rienner.
Asian States & the Development of International Law. Ed. by R. P. Anand. 1986. text ed. 35.00x o.p. (ISBN 0-7069-2981-0, Pub. by Vikas India). Advent NY.
Asians in America. H. Brett Melendy. (American Immigrant Ser.). 340p. 1981. pap. 9.95 o.p. (ISBN 0-88254-513-2). Hippocrene Bks.
Asia's New Giant: How the Japanese Economy Works. Ed. by Hugh Patrick & Henry Rosovsky. 1976. 26.95 o.p. (ISBN 0-8157-6934-2); pap. 21.95 o.p. (ISBN 0-8157-6933-4). Brookings.
Asiatic Mode of Production: Science & Politics. Ed. by Anne M. Bailey. (Illus.). 1981. pap. 15.95x o.p. (ISBN 0-7100-0738-8). Routledge Chapman & Hall.
Asiatic Wild Horse. Erna Mohr. Tr. by Daphne M. Goodall. (Illus.). 14.95 o.p. (ISBN 0-85131-013-3, Dist. by Sporting Book Center). S R Smith Sporting Bks.
Asimov on Science Fiction. Isaac Asimov. 320p. 1982. pap. 2.95 o.p. (ISBN 0-380-58511-1, 58511-1, Discus). Avon.
Ask & It Shall Be Given. Donald T. Kauffman. 48p. 1986. 6.95 o.p. (ISBN 0-8378-5095-9). Gibson.
Ask Beth: You Can't Ask Your Mother. Elizabeth Winship. 1976. 9.95 o.p. (ISBN 0-395-13656-3); pap. 4.95 o.p. (ISBN 0-395-24759-4). HM.
Ask Claude Pepper. Claude Pepper. LC 83-40138. 264p. 1984. pap. 7.95 o.p. (ISBN 0-385-19270-3). Doubleday.
Ask Erica. Erica Wilson. (Illus.). 1977. Encore ed. 0.95 o.p. (ISBN 0-684-17685-8, ScribT). Scribner.
Ask for Love & They Give You Rice Pudding. Bradford Angier & Barbara Corcoran. 160p. (gr. 7 up). 1977. 6.95 o.s.i. (ISBN 0-395-25300-4). HM.
Ask for Me Tomorrow. Margaret Millar. 1978. pap. 1.50 o.p. (ISBN 0-380-01805-5, 35618). Avon.
Ask Me If I Care. H. B. Gilmore. LC 84-91813. 192p. (Orig.). 1985. pap. 2.50 o.p. (ISBN 0-449-70073-9, Juniper). Fawcett.
Ask Me Tomorrow. James G. Cozzens. LC 40-11104. (Modern Classic Ser.). 1952. 11.95 o.s.i. (ISBN 0-15-109041-6). HarBraceJ.
Ask of the Wind. J. J. McKenna. 240p. 1980. pap. 1.95 o.p. (ISBN 0-380-75812-1, 75812). Avon.
Asking for Trouble. Donald Woods. LC 80-69643. 1981. 12.95 o.p. (ISBN 0-689-11159-2, Atheneum). Macmillan.

Asking for Trouble: What It Means to Be a Vice-Chancellor Today. Amrik Singh. 280p. 1984. text ed. 30.00x o.p. (ISBN 0-7069-2575-0, Pub. by Vikas India). Advent NY.
Asking Questions: A Classroom Model for Teaching the Bible. D. Bruce Lockerbie. 1980. pap. 7.95 o.p. (ISBN 0-8010-5640-3). Baker Bk.
Asking the Fathers. Aelred Squire. 250p. 1973. pap. 5.95 o.p. (ISBN 0-8192-1221-0). Morehouse Pub.
Asking the Hard Questions. Eugene B. Hines. LC 85-19528. 1986. pap. 4.95 o.p. (ISBN 0-8054-5013-0). Broadman.
ASLIB Directory: Information Sources in the Social Sciences, Medicine & the Humanities, Vol. 2. 4th ed. Ed. by Ellen M. Codlin. 871p. 1981. 135.00x o.p. (ISBN 0-85142-130-X, Pub. by Aslib England). Gale.
ASME-ANS International Conference on Advanced Nuclear Energy Systems, 1976. 638p. 1976. pap. 55.00 o.p. (ISBN 0-685-78340-5, H00099). ASME.
ASME Handbook: Engineering Tables. American Society of Mechanical Engineers Staff. 1956. text ed. 98.00 o.p. (ISBN 0-07-001516-3). McGraw.
ASME Steam Tables in SI (Metric) Units for Instructional Use, 1977. 19p. 1977. pap. text ed. 3.00 o.p. (ISBN 0-685-86854-0, H00093). ASME.
A.S.P. Technical Papers: 48th Annual Meeting, 1982. 619p. 1982. pap. text ed. 12.00 (7.00 member) o.p. (ISBN 0-937294-37-3). ASP & RS.
ASPA Handbook of Personnel & Industrial Relations: Employee & Labor Relations, Vol. 3. 2nd, rev. ed. Ed. by Dale Yoder, Jr. & Herbert G. Heneman, Jr. LC 79-15194. (Illus.). 232p. 1979. pap. text ed. 18.00 o.p. (ISBN 0-87179-305-9, 0305). BNA.
Asparagus. Nancy Hewitt. LC 77-3483. (Edible Garden Ser.). (Illus.). 1977. pap. 2.50 o.s.i. (ISBN 0-89286-114-2, One Hund One Prods). Ortho.
Asparagus, Asparagus, Ah Sweet Asparagus. Faye Kicknosway. LC 81-16233. (Illus.). 48p. 1981. signed 35.00 o.p. (ISBN 0-915124-55-6, Pub. by Toothpaste); pap. 7.50 o.p. (ISBN 0-915124-56-4). Coffee Hse.
ASPCA Guide to Pet Care. Diana Henley et al. LC 74-114389. (Illus.). 1970. pap. 1.25 o.s.i. (ISBN 0-8008-0453-8). Taplinger.
Aspects Financiers du Systeme de Prets aux Etudiants en Colombie. 61p. (Orig., Fr.). 1975. pap. 4.25 o.p. (ISBN 92-803-2064-5, U41, UNESCO). UNIPUB.
Aspects of American English. 2nd ed. Elizabeth M. Kerr & Ralph M. Aderman. (Orig.). 1971. pap. text ed. 7.95 o.p. (ISBN 0-15-503821-4, HC). HarBraceJ.
Aspects of Assimilation & Accumulation of Nitrate in Some Cultivated Plants. (Agricultural Research Reports: No. 843). 1975. pap. 10.25 o.p. (ISBN 90-220-0586-0, PDC199, PUDOC). UNIPUB.
Aspects of Boston. William Berchen & Ursula Berchen. 1976. pap. 9.95 o.p. (ISBN 0-395-20549-2). HM.
Aspects of British Politics, 1904-1919. D. Collins. 1966. 27.00 o.p. (ISBN 0-08-010987-X); pap. 95.00 o.p. (ISBN 0-08-010986-1). Pergamon.
Aspects of Care in Labour. J. M. Beazley & M. O. Lobb. LC 83-7357. (Current Reviews in Obstetrics & Gynaecology Ser.: Vol. 6). (Illus.). 142p. (Orig.). 1983. pap. text ed. 20.00 o.p. (ISBN 0-443-02927-X). Churchill.
Aspects of Composition. Billie A. Inman & Ruth Gardner. 1970. pap. text ed. 9.95 o.p. (ISBN 0-15-503840-0, HC). HarBraceJ.
Aspects of Constructibility. K. J. Devlin. (Lecture Notes in Mathematics: Vol. 354). 240p. 1973. pap. 16.00 o.p. (ISBN 0-387-06522-9). Springer-Verlag.
Aspects of Current International Debt Problems: Is the Problem Insolvency or Illiquidity? Jefferson, Thomas, Center Foundation Staff & Roger E. Shields. LC 85-167620. (G. Warren Nutter Lectures in Political Economy). Date not set. write for info. o.p. (ISBN 0-8447-1373-2). Am Enterprise.
Aspects of Deep Sea Biology. N. B. Marshall. 1955. (ISBN 0-8022-1065-1). Philos Lib.
Aspects of Developmental & Comparative Immunology I: First Congress of Developmental & Comparative Immunology, 27 July-1 August 1980, Aberdeen. Ed. by J. B. Solomon. (Illus.). 580p. 1981. 150.00 o.p. (ISBN 0-08-025922-7). Pergamon.
Aspects of Diagenesis. Ed. by Peter A. Scholle & Paul R. Schluger. (Special Publication Ser.: No. 26). 443p. 1979. 26.00 o.p. (ISBN 0-918985-06-4, 26). SEPM.
Aspects of Epilepsy & Psychiatry. Ed. by Tom G. Bolwig. Michael R. Trimble. 256p. 1986. 42.00 o.p. (ISBN 0-471-90932-7, Dist. by A R Liss). Wiley.
Aspects of European History, 1494-1789. Stephen J. Lee. (Illus.). 1978. 29.95x o.p. (ISBN 0-416-70930-3, NO.2288); pap. 13.50 o.p. (NO.2289). Routledge Chapman & Hall.
Aspects of European History: 1789-1980. Stephen J. Lee. LC 82-6310. 340p. 1982. 25.00x o.p. (ISBN 0-416-73170-8, 3721); pap. 12.50x o.p. (ISBN 0-416-73180-5, 3722). Routledge Chapman & Hall.
Aspects of Eve: Poems. Linda Pastan. 56p. 1975. 6.95 o.p. (ISBN 0-87140-608-X); pap. 3.95 o.p. (ISBN 0-87140-102-9). Liveright.
Aspects of Indian Art. Ed. by Pratapaditya Pal. LC 72-94766. (Illus.). 282p. (Orig.). 1972. 40.00x o.p. (ISBN 90-04-03625-3). LA Co Art Mus.
Aspects of Islam in Post-Colonial Indonesia: Five Essays. C. A. Van Nieuwenhuijze. 1958. 23.75x o.p. (ISBN 0-686-21860-4). Mouton.
Aspects of Jewish Prayer. Faye Pye. 1985. 10.00x o.p. (ISBN 0-317-61997-7, Guild of Pastoral Psych). State Mutual Bk.
Aspects of Language. 2nd ed. Dwight Bolinger. 320p. 1975. pap. text ed. 8.75 o.p. (ISBN 0-15-503868-0, HC). HarBraceJ.
Aspects of Language. Dwight Bolinger. 1968. pap. text ed. 9.95 o.p. (ISBN 0-15-503865-6, HC). HarBraceJ.
Aspects of Law Affecting the Paramedical Professions. John D. Finch. 208p. (Orig.). 1984. pap. 11.95 o.p. (ISBN 0-571-13272-3). Faber & Faber.
Aspects of Love. E. Aniello Spezio. 1985. 13.95 o.p. (ISBN 0-682-40264-8). Exposition-Phoenix.
Aspects of Memory. Ed. by Michael M. Gruneberg & Peter Morris. 1978. 18.95x o.p. (ISBN 0-416-70550-2, NO.2217); pap. 12.50x o.p. (ISBN 0-416-71350-5, NO.2741). Routledge Chapman & Hall.
Aspects of Molybdenum & Related Chemistry. Ed. by F. L. Boschke. LC 78-13469. (Topics in Current Chemistry Ser.: Vol. 76). (Illus.). 1978. 49.00 o.p. (ISBN 0-387-08986-1). Springer-Verlag.
Aspects of Motion Perception. Paul A. Kolers. LC 73-188746. 232p. 1972. 50.00 o.p. (ISBN 0-08-016843-4). Pergamon.
Aspects of Neural Ontogeny. Arthur F. Hughes. 1968. 58.00 o.p. (ISBN 0-12-360550-4). Acad Pr.
Aspects of Neuroendocrinology: Proceedings. International Symposium on Neurosecretion, Kiel, 1969. Ed. by W. Bargmann & B. Scharrer. (Illus.). 1970. 85.00 o.p. (ISBN 0-387-04772-7). Springer-Verlag.
Aspects of Occupational Health. Ed. by W. M. Dixon & Susan M. Price. (Illus.). 208p. (Orig.). 1984. pap. 11.95 o.p. (ISBN 0-571-13203-0). Faber & Faber.
Aspects of Organic Photochemistry. W. M. Horspool. 1976. 76.00 o.p. (ISBN 0-12-356650-9). Acad Pr.
Aspects of Protein Biosynthesis, Pt. A. Ed. by C. B. Anfinsen. 1970. 79.50 o.p. (ISBN 0-12-058701-7). Acad Pr.
Aspects of Pyschotherapeutic Processes. Erik Gotlind. 132p. 1971. text ed. 22.50x o.p. Coronet Bks.
Aspects of Simulation & Gaming: An Anthology of SAGSET Journal Volumes. Ed. by Jacquetta Megarry. 200p. 1977. 35.00 o.p. (ISBN 0-85038-075-8). Nichols Pub.
Aspects of Soviet Policy Toward Latin America. Ed. by Stephen T. Cheston & Bernard Loeffke. LC 74-7328. 147p. 1974. 19.50x o.p. (ISBN 0-8422-5183-9); pap. text ed. 9.50x o.p. (ISBN 0-8422-0411-3). Irvington.
Aspects of Terpenoid Chemistry & Biochemistry: Proceedings. Phytochemical Society. Ed. by T. W. Goodwin. 1971. 68.00 o.p. (ISBN 0-12-289840-0). Acad Pr.
Aspects of the Blues Tradition. Paul Oliver. 294p. Repr. of 1970 ed. lib. bdg. 39.00 o.p. (Pub. by Am Repr Serv). Reprint Servs.
Aspects of the Dying Process. Michael Wilding. (Paperback Prose Ser). 124p. 1972. 14.95x o.p. (ISBN 0-7022-0734-9); pap. 7.95x o.p. (ISBN 0-7022-0762-4). U of Queensland Pr.
Aspects of the Grammar of Focus in English. Adrian Akmajian. Ed. by Jorge Hankamer. LC 78-66534. (Outstanding Dissertations in Linguistics Ser.). 1979. 45.00 o.p. (ISBN 0-8240-9691-6). Garland Pub.
Aspects of the K Through Twelve Culture. National Association for Women Deans, Administrators, & Counselors. 1977. pap. 6.00 o.p. (ISBN 0-686-19041-6). Natl Assn Women.
Aspects of the Kadiweu Language. Glyn Griffiths & Cynthia Griffiths. 200p. 1976. pap. 5.20x o.p. (ISBN 0-88312-369-X). Summer Inst Ling.
Aspects of the Novel. E. M. Forster. LC 27-23181. 1947. 9.95 o.p. (ISBN 0-15-109179-X). HarBraceJ.
Aspects of the Presidency. John Hersey. LC 79-27694. 267p. 1980. 11.95 o.p. (ISBN 0-89919-012-X). Ticknor & Fields.
Aspects of the Theory of Bounded Integral Operators in LSRP-Spaces. G. O. Okikiolu. 1971. 95.00 o.p. (ISBN 0-12-525150-5). Acad Pr.
Aspects of Twentieth Century Music. Richard P. Delone et al. (Illus.). 541p. 1975. text ed. 34.00 o.p. (ISBN 0-13-049346-5). P-H.
Aspects-Radar Signal Processing. Bernard Lewis et al. 1986. text ed. 66.00 o.p. Artech Hse.
Aspekte: First-Year German Reader. 3rd ed. Robert E. Helbling et al. (Ger.). 1983. text ed. 31.95 o.p. (ISBN 0-03-062506-8); instr's. manual 19.95 o.p. (ISBN 0-03-062592-0); lab manual-exercise manual 13.95 o.p. (ISBN 0-03-062508-4); tapes avail. o.p. (ISBN 0-03-062509-2). HR&W.
Aspen: Ecology & Management in the Western United States. Norbert V. DeByle & Robert P. Winokur. (Illus.). 268p. 1985. pap. 8.50 o.p. (ISBN 0-318-19998-X, S/N 001-001-00617-3). USGPO.
Asphalt Concrete Pavement Design & Evaluation: Six Reports. (Transportation Research Report Ser.). 83p. 1974. 3.60 o.p. (ISBN 0-309-02366-1). Transport Res Bd.
Asphalt Pavement Engineering. Hugh A. Wallace & J. R. Martin. 1967. text ed. 48.50 o.p. (ISBN 0-07-067923-1). McGraw.
Asphalt Properties & Performance: Six Reports. (Transportation Research Record Ser.). 65p. 1975. 3.20 o.p. (ISBN 0-309-02399-8). Transport Res Bd.
Asphalt Technology & Construction: Practices Instructors Guide. 544p. 45.00 o.p. (ISBN 0-318-13386-5, ES-1). Asphalt Inst.
Asphalts, Aggregates, Mixes & Stress-Absorbing Membranes. (Transportation Research Report Ser.). 68p. 1976. 2.60 o.p. (ISBN 0-309-02564-8). Transport Res Bd.
Aspirin Age: 1919-1941. Isabel Leighton. 1968. pap. 12.95 o.s.i. (ISBN 0-671-20062-3, Touchstone Bks). S&S.
Assasin Prepares. N. J. McIver. LC 87-33070. (Crime Club Ser.). 192p. 1988. 12.95 o.p. (ISBN 0-385-24329-4). Doubleday.
Assassination American Style. John Hurley. 209p. (Orig.). 1980. pap. 3.95 o.p. (ISBN 0-933990-03-0). Canterbury Pr.
Assassination of Jesse James by the Coward Robert Ford. Ron Hansen. 368p. 1984. pap. 3.95 o.s.i. (ISBN 0-345-29626-5). Ballantine.
Assassination on Embassy Row. John Dinges & Saul Landau. (McGraw-Hill Paperbacks Ser.). 432p. 1981. pap. text ed. 5.95 o.p. (ISBN 0-07-016998-5). McGraw.
Assassins: No. 14. Lee Falk. (Phantom Ser.). 1975. pap. 0.95 o.p. (ISBN 0-380-00298-1, 23283). Avon.
Assassins' World. Lauran Paine. LC 74-5814. (Illus.). 212p. 1975. 9.50 o.s.i. (ISBN 0-8008-0473-2). Taplinger.
Assault in Norway. Thomas Gallagher. LC 74-20958. 252p. 1975. 6.95 o.p. (ISBN 0-15-109582-5). HarBraceJ.
Assault on Fellawi. Cain Cabot. 1976. pap. 1.50 o.p. (ISBN 0-380-00718-5, 28969). Avon.
Assault on Kolchak. Alan Caillou. 1976. pap. 1.50 o.p. (ISBN 0-380-00688-X, 28191). Avon.
Assay of Protein & Polypeptide Hormones. H. Van Cauwenberge & P. Franchimont. LC 76-108930. 1970. 60.00 o.p. (ISBN 0-08-015685-1). Pergamon.
Assembler Language for Application Programming. Don H. Stabley. (Illus.). 700p. 1982. 35.00 o.p. (ISBN 0-89433-176-0). Petrocelli.
Assemblers, Compilers, & Program Translation. Peter Calingaert. LC 78-21905. (Computer Software Engineering Ser.). 270p. 1979. 29.95 o.p. (ISBN 0-914894-23-4, Computer Sci Pr). W H Freeman.
Assembly at Westminster: Reformed Theology in the Making. John H. Leith. LC 72-11162. 128p. (Orig.). 1973. pap. 6.95 o.p. (ISBN 0-8042-0885-9, John Knox). Westminster John Knox.
Assembly Cookbook for the Apple II-IIe. Don Lancaster. LC 82-50247. 408p. 1984. pap. 21.95 o.p. (ISBN 0-672-22331-7). Sams.
Assembly Language for IBM Compatible Processors: A Systematic Approach. Herbert Berry. LC 83-23828. 354p. 1984. pap. text ed. write for info o.p. (ISBN 0-87150-695-5, 8200). PWS-Kent Pub.
Assembly Language Primer for the IBM PC. Robert Lafore. (Plume-Waite Computer Ser.). (Illus.). 1984. pap. 21.95 o.p. (ISBN 0-452-25497-3, Plume). NAL.
Assembly Language Programmer's Guide. TMS32010, 1983, 160 pp. 19.95 o.p. (ISBN 0-317-27325-6, SPRU002B); TMS99000, 1983, 322 pp. 13.35 o.p. (ISBN 0-317-27326-4, SPOU001); TMS7000, 1983, 160 pp. 8.00 o.p. (ISBN 0-317-27327-2, SPNU002B). Tex Instr Inc.
Assembly Language: Programming for the Atari Computer. Mark Chasin. (BYTE Book). 1984. pap. text ed. 15.95 o.p. (ISBN 0-07-010679-7). Mcgraw.
Assembly Language Programming for the Control Data 6000 Series & the Cyber Series. Ralph Grishman. Date not set. pap. 15.00 o.p. (ISBN 0-686-46118-5). Algorithmics.
Assembly Language Programming for the PDP-11. Harvey Shapiro. 349p. 1984. text ed. 27.95 o.p. (ISBN 0-87484-704-4). Mayfield Pub.
Assembly Language Programming for the IBM Systems 360 & 370 for OS-DOS. 2nd ed. Michael D. Kudlick. 624p. 1983. pap. write for info. o.p. (ISBN 0-697-08166-4); instr's. manual avail. o.p. (ISBN 0-697-08184-2). Wm C Brown.
Assembly Language Programming for the 65816 & 65802. Michael Fischer. (Illus.). 425p. (Orig.). 1986. pap. text ed. 21.95 o.p. (ISBN 0-07-881235-6). Osborne-McGraw.
Assembly Language Programming: 6502. Lance Leventhal et al. 640p. (Orig.). 1979. pap. text ed. 19.95 o.p. (ISBN 0-07-931027-3). Osborne-McGraw.
Assembly Language Programming: 68000. Gerry Kane et al. 624p. 1981. pap. text ed. 19.95 o.p. (ISBN 0-07-931062-1, 62-1). Osborne-McGraw.
Assembly Language Safari on the IBM PC: First Explorations. John Socha. (Illus.). 384p. 1984. pap. 16.95 o.p. (ISBN 0-89303-321-9); bk. & diskette 56.95 o.p. (ISBN 0-89303-294-8); diskette 40.00 o.p. (ISBN 0-89303-295-6). Brady Bks.
Assembly Language Techniques on the IBM-PC. Alan R. Miller. LC 86-61058. 358p. (Orig.). 1986. pap. 22.95 o.p. (ISBN 0-89588-309-0). Sybex.
Assembly Principles. F. B. Hole. Ed. by R. P. Daniel. 40p. pap. 3.50 o.p. (ISBN 0-88172-141-7). Believers Bkshelf.
Assertion Training: A Facilitator's Guide. Colleen Kelley. LC 78-69787. 382p. 1979. pap. 11.95 o.p. (ISBN 0-88390-146-3). Univ Assocs.
Assertive Discipline: Competency-Based Resource Materials & Guidelines. Lee Canter & Marlene Canter. (Illus.). 1979. wkbk. 6.95 o.s.i. (ISBN 0-9608978-1-X). Lee Canter & Assocs.
Assertiveness at Work: A Practical Guide to Handling Awkward Situations. Ken Back & Kate Back. (Illus.). 176p. 1982. text ed. 23.95 o.p. (ISBN 0-07-084576-X). McGraw.
Assertiveness at Work: How to Increase Your Personal Power on the Job. Kathleen Adams & Linda MacNeilage. (Illus.). 266p. 1982. 15.95 o.p. (ISBN 0-13-049502-6); 7.95 o.p. (ISBN 0-13-049494-1). P-H.
Assertiveness for Managers. Diana Cawood. 208p. (Orig.). pap. 8.95 o.s.i. (ISBN 0-88908-562-5, 9516). ISC Pr.
Asses vs. Jackasses. William G. Long. (Illus.). 136p. 1969. 2.95 o.p. (ISBN 0-317-56411-0). Touchstone Oregon.
Assessing & Developing Management Skills: Perception, Vol. 1. Cabot Jaffee. 204p. 1983. ring-bound 39.95 o.p. (ISBN 0-8436-0791-2). Van Nos Reinhold.
Assessing Athletics & Physical Education Programs: A Manual with Reproducible Forms. Kenneth A. Penman & Samuel H. Adams. 312p. 1980. pap. write for info. o.p. (ISBN 0-205-06616-X, Pub. by Longwood Div). Wm C Brown.
Assessing Biological Diversity in the United States: Data Considerations. LC 86-600513. (OTA-BP-F-39 Background Paper, United States Office of Technology Assessment Ser.: No. 2). (Illus.). 78p. 1986. pap. 2.75 o.p. (ISBN 0-318-20432-0, S/N 052-003-01031-3). USGPO.
Assessing Children with Special Needs: A Practical Guide for the Use of Psychological, Behavioral, & Educational Measures. Thomas Mahan & Aline Mahan. LC 80-27106. (Orig.). 1981. pap. text ed. 21.95 o.p. (ISBN 0-03-052981-6). HR&W.
Assessing Children's Language: Guidelines for Teachers. Andrew Stibbs. 1980. pap. text ed. 5.50x o.p. (ISBN 0-7062-3853-2). Boynton Cook Pubs.
Assessing Children's Language in Naturalistic Contexts. Nancy J. Lund & Judith F. Duchan. 368p. 1983. pap. text ed. (ISBN 0-13-049668-5). P-H.
Assessing Country Risk. 172p. 1981. 88.00x o.p. (ISBN 0-8002-3407-3). Intl Pubns Serv.
Assessing Employer Satisfaction with Vocational Education Graduates. F. Marion Asche & Daniel E. Vogler. 41p. 1980. 3.25 o.p. (ISBN 0-318-22039-3, IN204). Natl Ctr Res Voc Ed.
Assessing Experimental Learning in Career Education. Sharon Malak et al. 124p. 7.75 o.p. (ISBN 0-318-15397-1, RD 165). Natl Ctr Res Voc Ed.
Assessing Lawyer Evaluation & Partnership Decisions after Hishon V. King & Spaulding. Practising Law Institute Staff & Stanley J. Brown. LC 85-61808. (Commercial Law & Practice Course Handbook Ser.: No. 359). (Illus.). 176p. 1985. 15.00 o.p. (A44121). PLI.

Assessing Performance Appraisal. Marshall Sashkin. LC 81-51733. 143p. 1981. pap. 18.50 o.p. (ISBN 0-88390-171-4). Univ Assocs.

Assessing Personality. Robert R. Holt. 1971. pap. text ed. 10.95 o.p. (ISBN 0-15-503982-2, HC). HarBraceJ.

Assessing the Effectiveness of Advertising. Jack Potter & Mark Lowell. 281p. 1975. text ed. 31.50x o.p. (ISBN 0-220-69730-2, Pub. by Busn Bks England). Gower Pub Co.

Assessing the Effectiveness of Library Service. Rosemary R. Du Mont & Paul F. Du Mont. (Occasional Papers: No. 152). 24p. 1981. pap. 3.00 o.p. (ISBN 0-317-58998-9). U of Ill Lib Info Sci.

Assessing the United Nations Sale of Assessments: Is It Fair? Is It Equitable? United Nations Institute for Training & Research Staff. (UNITAR Policy & Efficacy Studies: No. 9). 59p. 1983. pap. 5.00 o.p. (ISBN 0-686-44046-3, UN82/15PE9, UNITAR). UNIPUB.

Assessing Vital Functions Accurately. 2nd ed. Ed. by Susan Williams & Barbara McVan. LC 83-20023. (New Nursing Skillbook Ser.: Vol. 3). (Illus.). 192p. 1983. text ed. 14.95 o.p. (ISBN 0-916730-65-4). Springhouse Pub.

Assessing Your Patients. Ed. by Jean Robinson & Barbara McVan. LC 80-36819. (Nursing Photobook Ser.). (Illus.). 160p. 1980. text ed. 17.95 o.p. (ISBN 0-916730-24-7). Springhouse Pub.

Assessment & Collection of Data on Post-Harvest Foodgrain Losses. (Economic & Social Development Papers: No. 13). 76p. (Eng., Fr. & Span.). 1980. pap. 7.50 o.p. (ISBN 92-5-100934-1, F2072, FAO). UNIPUB.

Assessment & Mitigation of Earthquake Risk. (Natural Hazards Ser.: No. 1). 341p. 1978. pap. 13.00 o.p. (ISBN 92-3-101451-X, U843, UNESCO). UNIPUB.

Assessment Centers for Supervisors & Managers in Public Administration: A Selective Checklist. Lorna Peterson. (Public Administration Ser.: P 1770). 9p. 1985. 2.00 o.p. (ISBN 0-89028-570-5). Vance Biblios.

Assessment in American Higher Education: Issues & Contexts. Terry W. Hantle & John Harris. Ed. by Clifford Adelman. (OR 86-301 Ser.). (Illus.). 1986. pap. 4.50 o.p. (ISBN 0-318-21328-1, S/N 065-000-00256-6). USGPO.

Assessment in Higher Education. John Heywood. LC 76-12786. 289p. 1977. 86.00x o.p. (ISBN 0-471-99404-9, Pub. by Wiley-Interscience). Wiley.

Assessment in Special & Remedial Education. John Salvia & James E. Ysseldyke. LC 77-72891. (Illus.). 1978. text ed. 20.30 o.p. (ISBN 0-395-25073-0). HM.

Assessment in Special & Remedial Education. 2nd ed. John Salvia & James E. Ysseldyke. (Illus.). 576p. 1981. text ed. 28.50 o.p. (ISBN 0-395-29694-3). HM.

Assessment in Special Education. John T. Neisworth. LC 82-11455. 233p. 1982. 33.50 o.p. (ISBN 0-89443-808-5). Aspen Pub.

Assessment of Fertility & Contraception in Seven Philippine Provinces: 1975. Wilhelm Flieger & Imelda Pagtolun-an. LC 81-17443. (Papers of the East-West Population Institute: No.77). x, 154p. (Orig.). 1981. pap. text ed. 3.00 o.p. (ISBN 0-86638-014-0). EW Ctr HI.

Assessment of Health Effects at Chemical Waste Disposal Sites. Ed. by William W. Lowrance. LC 81-15397. (Illus.). 172p. (Orig.). 1982. pap. text ed. 15.00 o.p. (ISBN 0-86576-025-X). W Kaufmann.

Assessment of Hearing Loss & Handicap in Adults. W. G. Noble. 1978. 39.95 o.p. (ISBN 0-12-520050-1). Acad Pr.

Assessment of Immune Status by the Leukocyte Adherence Inhibition Test. Ed. by D. M. Thomson. LC 82-3984. 380p. 1982. 65.50 o.p. (ISBN 0-12-689750-6). Acad Pr.

Assessment of Logging Costs from Forest Inventories in the Tropics, 2 Parts. Incl. Vol. 1. Principles & Methodology. 56p. UNIPUB; Vol. 2. Data Collections & Calculations. 76p (ISBN 92-5-100599-0). UNIPUB. (Forestry Papers: No. 10). (Eng., Fr. & Span.). 1978. Set. pap. 13.25 o.p. (ISBN 0-686-93608-6, F1492, FAO). UNIPUB.

Assessment of Major Hazards. Institution of Chemical Engineers Staff. 1982. 66.00 o.s.i. (ISBN 0-08-028768-9). Pergamon.

Assessment of Maternal Nutrition. 2nd ed. 25p. 1982. 3.00 o.p. (ISBN 0-686-36512-7). Am Coll Obstetric.

Assessment of Multihandicapped & Developmentally Disabled Children. Ruth K. Mulliken & John J. Buckley. LC 83-3739. 343p. 1983. 34.00 o.p. (ISBN 0-89443-876-X). Aspen Pub.

Assessment of Organic Intellectual Impairment. J. McFie. 1976. 47.50 o.p. (ISBN 0-12-481950-8). Acad Pr.

Assessment of Pulmonary Function. Ed. by Alfred P. Fishman. 416p. 1980. text ed. 32.00 o.p. (ISBN 0-07-021117-5). McGraw.

Assessment of Radioactive Contamination in Man. (Proceedings Ser.). (Illus.). 698p. (Orig.). 1972. pap. 63.00 o.p. (ISBN 92-0-020072-9, ISP290, IAEA). UNIPUB.

Assessment of Short-Range Transit Planning in Selected U. S. Cities. Ronald Kirby et al. 82p. (Orig.). 1980. pap. text ed. 6.00x o.p. (ISBN 0-87766-274-6). Urban Inst.

Assessment of Skeletal Maturity & Prediction of Adult Height: TW 2 Method. J. M. Tanner et al. 1976. 55.50 o.p. (ISBN 0-12-683350-8). Acad Pr.

Assessment of the Child in Primary Health Care. John H. Gundy. (Illus.). 208p. 1981. text ed. 14.95 o.p. (ISBN 0-07-025197-5). McGraw.

Assessment of the Newborn: A Guide for the Practitioner. Mohsen Zisi et al. 425p. 1983. text ed. 61.00 o.p. (ISBN 0-316-98754-9). Little.

Assessment, Schools & Society. Patricia Broadfoot. 1979. 19.95x o.p. (ISBN 0-416-71570-2, NO.2854). Routledge Chapman & Hall.

Asset in Black. Casey Prescott. 1985. 15.95 o.p. (ISBN 0-87795-661-8, Arbor Hse). Morrow.

Asset in Black. Casey Prescott. 400p. 1986. pap. 3.95 o.p. (ISBN 0-380-69962-1). Avon.

Asset Management: Answers to Questions on Subject Matter for the Learning Guide, CEBS Course 7. 3rd ed. 1984. pap. 18.00 o.p. (ISBN 0-89154-242-6). Intl Found Employ.

Asset Management: Learning Guide CEBS Course 7. 3rd ed. 1984. Spiral bdg. 18.00 o.p. (ISBN 0-89154-241-8). Intl Found Employ.

Asset Securitization Handbook. Ed. by Phillip L. Zweig. 400p. 1988. 47.50 o.p. (ISBN 0-317-67954-6). Dow Jones-Irwin.

Assets of the Information Society see Understanding U. S. Information Policy.

Assignment--Moon Girl. Edward S. Aarons. 1977. pap. 1.50 o.s.i. (ISBN 0-449-13856-9, GM). Fawcett.

Assignment & Matching Problems: Solution Methods with FORTRAN-Programs. R. E. Burkhard & U. Derigs. (Lecture Notes in Economics & Mathematical Systems Ser.: Vol. 184). 148p. 1980. pap. 18.00 o.p. (ISBN 0-387-10267-1). Springer-Verlag.

Assignment: Burma. Lee O. Miller. (Orig.). 1980. pap. 1.75 o.p. (ISBN 0-505-51498-2, Pub. by Tower Bks). Dorchester Pub Co.

Assignment in the Philippines: Dramatic Accounts from Jared & Marilee Barker. Marti Hefley. (Orig.). 1984. pap. 7.95 o.p. (ISBN 0-8024-0265-8). Moody.

Assignment: Suspense. Helen MacInnes. LC 61-7253. 1961. 9.50 o.s.i. (ISBN 0-15-109731-3). HarBraceJ.

Assimil Junior. (Fr.). 15.00 o.p. (ISBN 0-685-36086-5). French & Eur.

Assimil Language Courses: English for Children - Assimil Junior. Assimil. 15.95 o.p. (ISBN 0-686-56110-4); accompanying records & tapes 99.50 o.p. (ISBN 0-686-56111-2). French & Eur.

Assist One, Two & Three. rev. ed. Octavia Milton. 140p. 1983. pap. text ed. 24.95 o.p. (ISBN 0-88450-859-5, 4696-B). Communication Skill.

Assisted Circulation. Ed. by F. Unger. (Illus.). 1979. 120.00 o.p. (ISBN 0-387-09308-7). Springer-Verlag.

Assisted Job Search for the Insured Unemployed. David W. Stevens. 112p. 1974. pap. 5.95 o.p. (ISBN 0-911558-26-8). W E Upjohn.

Assisted Ventilation of the Neonate. Jay P. Goldsmith & Edward H. Karotkin. LC 80-53489. (Illus.). 390p. 1981. text ed. write for info. o.p. (ISBN 0-7216-4154-7). Saunders.

Associate Degree Campaign Kit. 1985. 12.50 o.p. (1017). Am Assn Comm Jr Coll.

Associate Degree Education for Nursing, 1986-87. 47p. 1987. 5.95 o.p. (ISBN 0-88737-344-5, 23-1309). Natl League Nurse.

Associated Press Stylebook. Associated Press. 1977. 12.95 o.p. (ISBN 0-89328-016-X). Lorenz Corp.

Associates. John J. Osborn, Jr. 1979. 8.95 o.p. (ISBN 0-395-27097-9). HM.

Association Executive Compensation Study 1987. American Society of Association Executives Staff. 68p. 1987. pap. 100.00 o.p. (ISBN 0-88034-016-9). Am Soc Assn Execs.

Association for the Advancement of Medical Instrumentation 22nd Annual Meeting: Proceedings (1987) AAMI Staff. 96p. 1987. pap. text ed. 35.00 o.p. (ISBN 0-910275-71-8). Assn Adv Med Instrn.

Association Meetings & Conventions in the 1990s. Robert H. Smith. 91p. Date not set. GBC Binding. 30.00 o.p. (ISBN 0-88034-018-5). Am Soc Assn Execs.

Association of Income & Educational Achievement. Roy L. Lassiter, Jr. LC 66-63922. (University of Florida Social Sciences Monographs: No. 30). (Illus.). 1966. pap. 3.50 o.p. (ISBN 0-8130-0141-2). U Presses Fla.

Associative Memory: A System-Theoretical Approach. T. Kohonen. (Communication & Cybernetics Ser.: Vol. 17). 1978. 33.00 o.p. (ISBN 0-387-08017-1). Springer-Verlag.

Assumptions & Purchase Money Mortgages (A plus PMM) Stephen R. Mettling. (Residential Financing Resource Library). 49p. 1982. pap. 6.50 o.s.i. (ISBN 0-88462-137-5, 1905-16, Real Estate Ed). Longman Finan.

Assurance. R. Gene Reynolds. 128p. 1982. pap. 3.95 o.p. (ISBN 0-8423-0088-0). Tyndale.

Assured Survival: How to Stop the Nuclear Arms Race. Ben Bova. 341p. 1984. 15.45 o.p. (ISBN 0-395-36405-1). HM.

Astaire & Rogers. Suzanne Topper. (Illus.). 1976. pap. 1.50 o.p. (ISBN 0-8439-0380-5, LB380DK, Pub. by Leisure Bks CT). Dorchester Pub Co.

Asthma in Children. R. S. Jones. LC 76-12027. (Illus.). 278p. 1976. 22.50 o.p. (ISBN 0-88416-028-9). Year Bk Med.

Asthma Is Curable. Jacob J. Robbins. 1965. 6.00 o.p. (ISBN 0-682-43045-5, University). Exposition-Phoenix.

Asthma: Physiology, Immunopharmacology & Treatment, Vol. 2. Ed. by L. M. Lichtenstein et al. 1978. 71.00 o.p. (ISBN 0-12-448502-2). Acad Pr.

Asthma Research: Clinical Studies. Felicidad Cua-Lim et al. 204p. 1974. text ed. 29.00x o.p. (ISBN 0-8422-7172-4). Irvington.

Astral Journey. Herbert B. Greenhouse. 1976. pap. 1.95 o.p. (ISBN 0-380-00611-1, 28928). Avon.

Astride a Dolphin. L. Zhukovitsky. 330p. 1971. pap. 4.45 o.p. (ISBN 0-8285-1078-4, Pub. by Progress Pubs USSR). Imported Pubns.

Astro-Palmistry. Cyrus Abayakoon. LC 75-7187. (Illus.). 1975. 20.00 o.p. (ISBN 0-88231-012-7). ASI Pubs Inc.

Astroblemes-Cryptoexplosion Structures. Ed. by G. J. H. McCall. LC 79-10991. (Benchmark Papers in Geology: Vol. 50). 437p. 1982. 63.95 o.p. (ISBN 0-87933-342-1). Van Nos Reinhold.

Astrolabes of the World, 2 vols. in one. Robert T. Gunther. (Illus.). 100.00 o.p. (ISBN 0-87556-604-9). Saifer.

Astrologer in the Underground. Andrzej Busza. Tr. by Jagna Boraks & Micheal Bullock. 61p. 1970. 6.95 o.p. (ISBN 0-8214-0073-8). Ohio U Pr.

Astrologer's Forecasting Workbook. Lloyd Cope. LC 82-73127. 182p. 1982. 16.95 o.p. (ISBN 0-86690-041-1, C2642-014). Am Fed Astrologers.

Astrological Almanac for 1986. Lynne Palmer. LC 85-71485. 160p. 11.00 o.p. (ISBN 0-86690-291-0). Am Fed Astrologers.

Astrological Almanac for 1987. Lynne Palmer. LC 86-70793. 156p. 1986. 11.00 o.p. (ISBN 0-86690-318-6, 2361-01). Am Fed Astrologers.

Astrological Almanac, 1988: With 4 Months of 1987. Lynne Palmer. 192p. 1987. 11.00 o.p. (ISBN 0-317-61634-X). Am Fed Astrologers.

Astrological Foundation of Stock Market Price Movements. Alfred Verleyson. (Illus.). 99p. 1989. 57.75 o.p. (ISBN 0-86654-288-4). Inst Econ Finan.

Astrological Keywords. Manly P. Hall. 1959. (ISBN 0-8022-0659-X). Philos Lib.

Astrological Let Me Be Book. Florence Nelson. (Illus.). 1977. pap. 2.50 o.s.i. (ISBN 0-918328-01-2). Carma.

Astrology & Alchemy: Two Fossil Sciences. Mark Graubard. 360p. 1953. (ISBN 0-8022-0620-4). Philos Lib.

Astrology & Past Lives. Mary Devlin. 12.95 o.p. (ISBN 0-317-42956-6). Whitford Pr.

Astrology & Romance. Elsbeth Ebertin. Tr. by D. G. Nelson from Ger. LC 73-90428. (Illus.). 132p. 1973. Repr. of 1936 ed. 7.95 o.p. (ISBN 0-88231-002-X). ASI Pubs Inc.

Astrology & the Modern Psyche: An Astrologer Looks at Depth Psychology. Dane Rudhyar. LC 76-21583. 1976. pap. 11.95 o.s.i. (ISBN 0-916360-05-9). CRCS Pubns CA.

Astrology Annual Reference Book 1985. 224p. 1984. 12.50 o.p. (ISBN 0-318-17792-7, 2556-06). Am Fed Astrologers.

Astrology Books in Print. Para Research, Inc. 128p. (Orig.). 1981. pap. 3.95 o.s.i. (ISBN 0-914918-25-7). Whitford Pr.

Astrology for Everyone. Evangeline Adams. LC 81-3107. 1981. pap. 7.95 o.p. (ISBN 0-396-07985-7). Dodd.

Astrology for the Aquarian Age. Alexandra Mark. 1973. pap. 4.95 o.p. (ISBN 0-671-21678-3, Fireside). S&S.

Astrology: How & Why It Works. Marc E. Jones. LC 76-84580. (Illus.). 364p. 1977. pap. 2.95 o.p. (ISBN 0-87773-108-X). Shambhala Pubns.

Astrology in the Renaissance. Eugenio Garin. Tr. by Carolyn Jackson & June Allen. 160p. 1983. 21.95 o.p. (ISBN 0-7100-9259-8). Routledge Chapman & Hall.

Astrology in the Renaissance: The Zodiac of Life. Eugenio Garin. 160p. 1986. text ed. 9.95 o.p. (ISBN 0-7100-9484-1). Routledge Chapman & Hall.

Astrology Software Buyer's Guide. Richard Nolle. 44p. 1986. 4.00 o.p. (ISBN 0-86690-322-4). Am Fed Astrologers.

Astrology: The Celestial Mirror. Warren Kenton. (Art & the Cosmos Ser.). (Illus.). 128p. 1974. pap. 4.95 o.p. (ISBN 0-380-01037-2, 18721-3). Avon.

Astrology: Trash & Treasure. Dai Circe. 1976. 6.00 o.p. (ISBN 0-682-48574-8). Exposition-Phoenix.

Astronautics for Peace & Human Progress: Proceedings of the International Astronautical 29th Congress, Dubrovnik, October 1-8, 1978. International Astronautical Congress Staff. Ed. by L. G. Napolitano. LC 79-40049. (Illus.). 1979. 130.00 o.p. (ISBN 0-08-024732-6). Pergamon.

Astronomia para los Ninos. B. Levin & Lidia Radlova. 36p. 1985. pap. 2.99 o.p. (ISBN 0-8285-3087-4, Pub. by Raduga Pubs USSR). Imported Pubns.

Astronomical Almanac for the Year 1987. 547p. 1986. text ed. 18.00 o.p. (ISBN 0-11-886925-6, S/N 008-054-00124-6). USGPO.

Astronomical Calendar, 1988. Guy Ottewell. 1987. pap. 12.00 huge atlas-size bk. o.p. (ISBN 0-934546-18-5). Astron Wkshp.

Astronomical Dictionary: In Six Languages. Josip Kleczek. (Eng., Fr., Ger., Ital., Rus. & Czech.). 1962. 105.00 o.p. (ISBN 0-12-411950-6). Acad Pr.

Astronomical Discovery. Herbert H. Turner. (Illus.). 12.00 o.p. (ISBN 0-8446-3096-9). Peter Smith.

Astronomical Objects for Southern Telescopes. 2nd ed. E. J. Hartung. (Illus.). 248p. 1987. pap. 18.00 o.p. (ISBN 0-522-84281-X, Pub. by Melbourne U Pr). Intl Spec Bk.

Astronomical Phenomena for the Year 1988. 74p. (Orig.). 1986. pap. 3.00 o.p. (ISBN 0-318-21278-1, S/N 008-054-00123-8). USGPO.

Astronomical Phenomena for the Year 1989. (Illus.). 73p. 1987. pap. 3.00 o.p. (ISBN 0-318-22651-0, S/N 008-054-00125-4). USGPO.

Astronomical Techniques. Ed. by William A. Hiltner. LC 62-9113. (Midway Reprint Ser., Stars & Stellar Systems: Vol. 2). (Illus.). 1962. 29.00x o.p. (ISBN 0-226-45963-2). U of Chicago Pr.

Astronomical Telescopes & Observatories for Amateurs. Ed. by Patrick Moore. (Illus.). 256p. 1973. 7.95 o.p. (ISBN 0-393-06395-X). Norton.

Astronomy. Dinah Moche. LC 77-27367. (Self-Teaching Guides Ser.). 1978. pap. text ed. 10.95 o.p. (ISBN 0-471-01764-7). Wiley.

Astronomy & Astrophysics Abstracts, Vol. 13: Literature 1975, Pt. 1. Ed. by S. Boehme et al. viii, 632p. 1976. 58.00 o.p. (ISBN 0-387-07492-9). Springer-Verlag.

Astronomy & Astrophysics Abstracts, Vol. 18: Literature 1976, Pt. 2. Ed. by S. Boehme et al. x, 859p. 1977. 58.00 o.p. (ISBN 0-387-08319-7). Springer-Verlag.

Astronomy & Astrophysics Abstracts, Vol. 19: Literature 1977, Pt. 1. Ed. by S. Boehme et al. viii, 732p. 1977. 66.00 o.p. (ISBN 0-387-08555-6). Springer-Verlag.

Astronomy & Astrophysics Abstracts, Vol. 20: Literature 1977, Pt. 2. Ed. by S. Boehme et al. viii, 786p. 1978. 65.00 o.p. (ISBN 0-387-08838-5). Springer-Verlag.

Astronomy & Telescopes: A Beginner's Handbook. Robert J. Traister & Susan E. Harris. (Illus.). 192p. 1983. 19.95 o.p. (ISBN 0-8306-0419-7, 1419); pap. 14.60 o.p. (ISBN 0-8306-1419-2). TAB Bks.

Astronomy & the Imagination: A New Approach to Experience of the Stars. Norman Davidson. LC 84-15995. (Illus.). 237p. 1985. 25.00 o.p. (ISBN 0-7102-0371-3). Routledge Chapman & Hall.

Astronomy Encyclopedia. (Encyclopedia Ser.). (Illus.). 144p. (gr. 4 up). 1987. Repr. 12.95 o.s.i. (ISBN 0-02-688538-7, Checkerboard Pr). Macmillan.

Astronomy for the Younger Set. Jean Dunn. (gr. 1-5). 1984. 7.95 o.p. (ISBN 0-533-05825-2). Vantage.

Astronomy from Space: Proceedings of the Topical Meeting of the COSPAR Interdisciplinary Scientific Commission E (Meetings E3, E4, & E5) of the COSPAR 25th Plenary Meeting held in Graz, Austria, 25 June - 7 July 1984. Ed. by G. G. Fazio et al. (Illus.). 220p. 1985. pap. 54.00 o.p. (ISBN 0-08-033192-0, PUb by PPL). Pergamon.

Astronomy: From the Earth to the Universe. 2nd ed. Jay M. Pasachoff. 1983. pap. text ed. 33.25 o.s.i. (ISBN 0-03-058419-1, CBS C). SCP.

Astronomy Now. Jay M. Pasachoff. 1978. pap. text ed. 32.95 o.p. (ISBN 0-7216-7100-4, CBS C); instr's manual 7.95 o.p. (ISBN 0-03-057251-7). SCP.

Astronomy: The Cosmic Journey. 1987 ed. William K. Hartmann. 548p. 1987. text ed. (ISBN 0-534-07938-5). Wadsworth Pub.

Astrotherapy: Astrology & the Realization of the Self. Gregory Szanto. 225p. (Orig.). 1987. pap. 11.95 o.p. (ISBN 1-85063-059-3, Pub. by Routledge UK). Routledge Chapman & Hall.

Astrowheeling: Space-Age Twirling. Charles R. Schroeder. (Illus.). (gr. 7-12). 1979. pap. text ed. 6.95 o.p. (ISBN 0-87870-074-9). Memphis St Univ.

Asundered: Biblical Teachings on Divorce & Remarriage. Robert Kysar & Myrna Kaysar. LC 77-79591. 1978. 7.95 o.p. (ISBN 0-8042-1096-9, John Knox). Westminster John Knox.

ASU's Annual Conference on Micros in Education. Janie Hydrick & Maurice Miller. LC 87-5171. (Illus.). 323p. 1987. 35.00 o.p. (ISBN 0-88175-169-3, Computer Sci Pr). W H Freeman.

Asylees & Refugees: Strategies for Representation. National Immigration Project. 1982. 25.00 o.p. Natl Lawyers Guild.

Asymptotic Behavior & Stability Problems in Ordinary Differential Equations. 3rd ed. L. Cesari. LC 76-157246. (Ergebnisse der Mathematik & Ihrer Grenzgeniete: Vol. 16). (Illus.). 1971. 34.40 o.p. (ISBN 0-387-05435-9). Springer-Verlag.

Asymptotic Methods in Nonlinear Wave Theory. A. Jeffrey. 272p. 1982. 44.95 o.p. (ISBN 0-470-20506-7, Co-Pub. with Longman). Wiley.

At Dawn We Slept: The Untold Story of Pearl Harbor. Gordon W. Prange. 848p. 1981. text ed. 22.95 o.p. (ISBN 0-07-050669-8). McGraw.

At Her Age. Marian Novick. 304p. 1986. 15.95 o.s.i. (ISBN 0-684-18459-1, ScribT). Scribner.

At Her Age. Marian Novick. 358p. 1986. lib. bdg. 16.95x o.p. (ISBN 0-8161-4010-3, Large Print Bks). G K Hall.

At Home. Eric Hill. LC 82-60627. (Eric Hill's Baby Bear Bks.). (Illus.). 14p. (ps-k). 1983. pap. 2.50 o.s.i. (ISBN 0-394-85638-4). Random.

At Home in the Thrush Green. Read. 1986. 16.45 o.p. (ISBN 0-395-41224-2). HM.

At Kindergarten. 1978. pap. 1.95 o.p. (ISBN 0-8351-0542-3). China Bks.

At Least a Thousand Things to Do. Cherrie Farnette et al. LC 77-83655. (Kids & Careers Ser.). (Illus.). 112p. (gr. 2-6). 1977. pap. text ed. 6.95 o.p. (ISBN 0-913916-53-6, IP 53-6). Incentive Pubns.

At Mother's Request: A True Story of Money, Murder, & Betrayal. Jonathan Coleman. LC 84-45616. (Illus.). 640p. 1985. 19.95 o.p. (ISBN 0-689-11547-4, Atheneum). Macmillan.

At Peace with Failure. Duane Mehl. LC 83-721141. 128p. (Orig.). 1984. pap. 5.95 o.p. (ISBN 0-8066-2058-7, 10-0472, Augsburg). Augsburg Fortress.

At Seventy: A Journal. May Sarton. (Illus.). 344p. 1984. 15.45 o.p. (ISBN 0-393-01838-5). Norton.

At Swords' Points. Andre Norton. LC 54-8575. (gr. 7 up). 1954. 5.75 o.p. (ISBN 0-15-283893-7, HJ). HarBraceJ.

At the Bend in the River: The Story of Evansville. Kenneth P. McCutchan. LC 82-50191. (Illus.). 144p. 1982. 22.95 o.s.i. (ISBN 0-89781-060-0). Windsor Pubns Inc.

At the Border. Robert Hemenway. LC 83-45503. 256p. 1984. 14.95 o.p. (ISBN 0-689-11441-9, Atheneum). Macmillan.

At the Center. Norma G. Rosen. 1982. 12.95 o.p. (ISBN 0-395-31263-9). HM.

At the Crossroads. Daniel E. Lewis. 64p. 1980. 6.50 o.p. (ISBN 0-682-49631-6). Exposition-Phoenix.

At the Crossroads of the Earth & the Sky: An Andean Cosmology. Gary Urton. (Latin American Monograph Ser.: No. 55). (Illus.). 268p. 1981. pap. 30.00x o.p. (ISBN 0-292-70349-X). U of Tex Pr.

At the Edge of the Body. Erica Jong. LC 78-14950. 1979. 7.95 o.p. (ISBN 0-03-044881-6); pap. 3.95 o.p. (ISBN 0-03-049201-7). H Holt & Co.

At the Feet of Mahatma Gandhi. Rajendra Prasad. LC 79-156204. 1971. Repr. of 1961 ed. lib. bdg. 35.00x o.p. (ISBN 0-8371-6154-1, PRMG). Greenwood.

At the Feet of Mahtma Gandhi. Rajendra Prasad. 360p. 1956. (ISBN 0-8022-2012-6). Philos Lib.

At the Feet of Ski Ramakrishna. Vijnananda. 66p. 1985. pap. 1.50 o.p. (ISBN 0-87481-225-9, Pub. by Ramakrishna Math Madras India). Vedanta Pr.

At the Foot of Blue Mountains: Stories by Tajik Authors. S. Niyasi. 262p. 1985. 8.95 o.p. (ISBN 0-8285-2909-4, Pub. by Raduga Pubs USSR). Imported Pubns.

At the Gates of Spiritual Science. Rudolf Steiner. 1976. pap. 5.50 o.p. (ISBN 0-85440-306-X, Pub by Steinerbooks). Anthroposophic.

At the Hands of Another. Arthur Lyons. LC 82-21315. (Rinehart Suspense Novel). 240p. 1983. 13.50 o.s.i. (ISBN 0-03-059616-5). H Holt & Co.

At the Hands of Another. Arthur Lyons. LC 82-21315. 240p. 1986. pap. 3.95 o.s.i. (ISBN 0-03-008533-0, Owl Bks). H Holt & Co.

At the Home Front in War & Life: Confessions of a Lawyer. Charles E. Pendleton. 1978. 15.00 o.p. (ISBN 0-682-48982-4). Exposition-Phoenix.

At the Other End of Australia: The Commonwealth & the Northern Territory 1911-1978. P. F. Donovan. LC 83-21746. (Illus.). 277p. 1985. 35.00 o.p. (ISBN 0-7022-1914-2). U of Queensland Pr.

At the Piano with Faure. Marguerite Long. LC 79-63623. (Illus.). 1981. 11.95 o.s.i. (ISBN 0-8008-0505-4, Crescendo). Taplinger.

At the Sign of the Barber's Pole. William Andrews. LC 74-77164. 136p. 1969. Repr. of 1904 ed. 35.00x o.p. (ISBN 0-8103-3846-7). Gale.

At the Table of the Grail: Magic & the Use of Imagination. 2nd ed. Ed. by John Mathews. 224p. 1987. pap. 10.95 o.p. (ISBN 1-85063-081-X, Pub. by Routledge UK). Routledge Chapman & Hall.

At the Table of the Grail: Magic & the Use of Imagination. John Matthews. 224p. (Orig.). 1984. pap. 10.95 o.p. (ISBN 0-7100-9938-X). Routledge Chapman & Hall.

At the Zoo. 1981. pap. 3.50 o.p. (ISBN 0-8351-0805-8). China Bks.

At Your Word, Lord. William L. Vaswig. LC 81-52272. 128p. (Orig.). 1982. pap. 6.95 o.p. (ISBN 0-8066-1904-X, 10-0498, Augsburg). Augsburg Fortress.

AT-6 Harvard. Len Morgan. Ed. by Ernest J. Gentle. LC 65-26763. (Famous Aircraft Ser.). (Illus.). 64p. 1985. pap. 7.95 o.p. (ISBN 0-8168-5661-3, 25661, TAB-Aero). TAB Bks.

ATA-MSC Software Directory: American Trucking Associations Management Systems Committee July 1987. American Trucking Associations, Management Systems Department. 45p. 1988. pap. text ed. 30.00 o.p. (ISBN 0-88711-089-4). Am Trucking Assns.

AT&T Computer Software Guide. AT&T Computer Information Systems, Inc. Staff. 1985. 19.95 o.p. (ISBN 0-8359-9276-4, Reston). P-H.

AT&T 6300: A Comprehensive User's Manual. Frederick Holtz. (Illus.). 256p. 1985. 22.95 o.p. (ISBN 0-8306-0920-2, 1920); pap. 16.60 o.p. (ISBN 0-8306-1920-8). TAB Bks.

Atari BASIC. XL ed. Bob Albrecht et al. LC 84-20803. 388p. 1985. pap. 16.95 o.p. (ISBN 0-471-80726-5). Wiley.

Atari BASIC Manual. Lynne Mass & Thomas M. Kemnitz. LC 85-395. (Kids Working with Computers Ser.). (Illus.). 48p. (gr. 2 up). 1985. lib. bdg. 11.27 o.p. (ISBN 0-516-08424-0). Childrens.

Atari BASIC Programs in Minutes. Stanley R. Trost. LC 83-51097. (Illus.). 171p. (Orig.). 1984. pap. 12.95 o.p. (ISBN 0-89588-143-8). SYBEX.

Atari Book of Games. Mike James et al. 156p. 1985. pap. text ed. 12.95 o.p. (ISBN 0-07-881159-7). Osborne-McGraw.

Atari Diskguide. 1983. pap. text ed. 4.00 o.p. (ISBN 0-07-047852-X). McGraw.

Atari Diskguide. (ISBN 0-07-931095-8). McGraw.

ATARI Programming... with Fifty-Five Programs. Linda M. Schreiber. (Illus.). 256p. (Orig.). 1982. 21.95 o.p. (ISBN 0-8306-1385-4); pap. 14.15 o.p. (ISBN 0-8306-1485-0, 1485). TAB Bks.

Atari Software: Rating the Best. Consumer Guide Editors. LC 83-737274. 154p. 1984. spiral bdg. 1.00 o.p. (ISBN 0-517-42474-6). Outlet Bk Co.

Atari ST Peeks & Pokes. S. Dittrich. 200p. 1986. pap. 16.95 o.p. (ISBN 0-916439-56-9). Abacus Soft.

Atari ST User's Guide. John Heilborn. (Illus.). 225p. (Orig.). 1986. pap. text ed. 15.95 o.p. (ISBN 0-07-881185-6). Osborne-McGraw.

Atari ST User's Handbook. Weber Systems, Inc. Staff. 300p. (Orig.). 1986. pap. 9.95 o.p. (ISBN 0-938862-40-5). Weber Systems.

Atari User's Guide: BASIC & Graphics for the Atari 400, 800, 1200. Mark Ellis & Robert Ellis. 288p. 1984. pap. 14.95 o.p. (ISBN 0-89303-323-5). Brady Bks.

Atariba & Niguayona. Harriet Rohmer. LC 76-17495. (Fifth World Tales Ser.). (Illus.). (gr. 2-9). 1976. pap. 5.95 spanish bilingual ed. o.p. (ISBN 0-89239-007-7, Imprenta de Libros Infantiles). Childrens Book Pr.

Ataxia Telangiectasia: A Cellular & Molecular Link Between Cancer, Neuropathology & Immune Deficiency. Ed. by B. A. Bridges & D. G. Harnden. LC 81-13146. 424p. 1982. 50.00x o.p. (ISBN 0-471-10055-2, Dist. by A R Liss). Wiley.

ATF Arson Investigative Guide. 156p. (Orig.). 1986. pap. 7.00 spiral bdg. o.p. (ISBN 0-318-20086-4, S/N 048-012-00085-0). USGPO.

Atheis. Achdiat Mihardja. Tr. by R. J. Maguire. (Asian & Pacific Writing Ser., No. 1). 192p. 1972. 17.95x o.p. (ISBN 0-7022-0766-7); pap. 8.50x o.p. (ISBN 0-7022-0765-9). U of Queensland Pr.

Athenian Citizen. Mabel Lang. (Excavations of the Athenian Agora Picture Bks.: No. 4). (Illus.). 1960. pap. 3.00x o.p. (ISBN 0-87661-604-X). Am Sch Athens.

Athenian Half-Century, 478-431 B.C. A. French. Tr. by A. French. LC 71-145645. (Sources in Ancient History). (Illus.). 120p. 1971. pap. 15.00x o.p. (ISBN 0-424-06220-8, Pub. by Sydney U Pr). Intl Spec Bk.

Athens & Attica. Date not set. (ISBN 0-13-049891-2). P-H.

Athens Ascendant. George D. Wilcoxon. (Illus.). 288p. 1979. text ed. 16.75 o.p.; pap. text ed. 10.95x o.p. (ISBN 0-8138-1130-9). Iowa St U Pr.

Athenum Woordenboek: Espanol-Holandes, Holandes-Espanol. 382p. (Span. & Dutch.). 1979. pap. 5.25 o.p. (ISBN 84-303-0801-6, S-35068). French & Eur.

Atherosclerosis & Its Origin. Ed. by Maurice Sandler & Geoffrey H. Bourne. 1963. 88.00 o.p. (ISBN 0-12-618250-7). Acad Pr.

Athlete's Guide to Agents. Robert H. Ruxin. LC 82-47781. (Midland Bks.: No. 290). 176p. 1983. 15.00x o.p. (ISBN 0-253-10400-9); pap. 6.95X o.p. (ISBN 0-253-20290-6). Ind U Pr.

Athletes: The Paintings of Joe Wilder, M. D. Wilder. 1985. 45.00 o.p. (ISBN 0-8016-5445-9). Mosby.

Athletic Fitness: The Athlete's Guide to Training & Conditioning. Dewey Schurman. LC 75-76762. 256p. 1975. 7.95 o.p. (ISBN 0-689-10663-7, Atheneum). Macmillan.

Athletic Injuries to the Head, Neck, & Face. Ed. by Joseph S. Torg. LC 81-11784. (Illus.). 300p. 1982. text ed. 32.50 o.p. (ISBN 0-8121-0810-8). Lea & Febiger.

Athletic Injury Assessment. Booher & Thibodeau. 1984. text ed. 30.95 o.p. (ISBN 0-8016-0711-6). Mosby.

Athletic Massage. Rich Phaigh & Paul Perry. 144p. 1984. 14.70 o.p. (ISBN 0-671-52565-4). S&S.

Athletics for Life: Sports Doctor's Program for Safe & Enjoyable Aerobic Conditioning. Kenneth Forsythe & Neil Feineman. 224p. (Orig.). 1986. 17.45 o.p. (ISBN 0-671-53123-9). S&S.

Athol Fugard. Dennis Walder. LC 84-82354. (Modern Dramatists Ser.). 192p. 1985. 22.50 o.p. (ISBN 0-394-54500-1, GP-957). Grove.

Athol Fugard. Dennis Walder. (Modern Dramatists Ser.). 1985. pap. 7.95 o.p. (ISBN 0-394-62230-8, E-973, Ever). Grove.

Atiyah-Singer Index Theorem: An Introduction. P. Shanahan. (Lecture Notes in Mathematics: Vol. 638). (Illus.). 1978. pap. 18.00 o.p. (ISBN 0-387-08660-9). Springer-Verlag.

ATLA Masters at Work, I. Ed. by Robert W. Rifkin. LC 83-83407. (Illus.). 728p. (Orig.). 1984. pap. 65.00 o.p. (ISBN 0-941916-13-8, 41B). Assn Trial Ed.

Atlan Revisited: The War of the Gods. George Mitrovic. LC 84-90082. 156p. 1985. 11.95 o.p. (ISBN 0-533-06152-0). Vantage.

Atlanta. Milt Machlin. 544p. 1986. pap. 3.95 o.p. (ISBN 0-931773-70-9). Critics Choice Paper.

Atlanta Braves. Martin. LC 82-17106. (Baseball Today Ser.). 48p. (gr. 4 up). 1982. Repr. of 1987 ed. 11.95 o.p. (ISBN 0-87191-852-8). Creative Ed.

Atlanta Falcons. James Rothaus. (NFL Today Ser.). (Illus.). 48p. (gr. 4-12). 1981. PLB 8.95 o.p. (ISBN 0-87191-808-0); pap. 4.25 o.p. (ISBN 0-89812-254-6). Creative Ed.

Atlanta Hawks. Jim Moore. (NBA Today Ser.). 48p. (gr. 4 up). 1984. PLB 10.54 o.p. (ISBN 0-87191-970-2). Creative Ed.

Atlanta Job Atlas & Business Directory. rev ed. Mark Torghele. 240p. 1987. pap. 10.95 o.s.i. (ISBN 0-943003-00-8). Atlanta Job Atlas.

Atlanta Job Atlas & Business Directory. 3rd, rev. ed. Mark Torghele. 175p. 1987. pap. text ed. 10.95 o.s.i. (ISBN 0-943003-01-6). Atlanta Job Atlas.

Atlanta Job Atlas & Business Directory. 5th, rev. ed. Mark Torghele. 194p. 1989. pap. text ed. 10.95 o.p. Atlanta Job Atlas.

Atlanta Professional Women's Directory, 1986. 5th ed. 1985. 4.00 o.p. (ISBN 0-935197-00-1). Atlanta Pro.

Atlanta Restaurant Guide. Harold V. Shumacher. LC 82-10134. 272p. (Orig.). 1982. pap. 4.95 o.s.i. (ISBN 0-88289-248-7). Pelican.

Atlanta: Triumph of a People. 2nd, rev. ed. Norman Shavin & Bruce Galphin. (Illus.). 400p. 1985. 29.95 o.s.i. (ISBN 0-910719-12-8). Capricorn Corp.

Atlanta University Publications, Nos. 1-11, 2 Vols. Ed. by W. E. B. Dubois. 1968. Set. lib. bdg. 34.00x o.p. (ISBN 0-374-92356-6, Octagon). Hippocrene Bks.

Atlantic Community in Crisis: A Redefinition of the Transatlantic Relationship. Ed. by Walter F. Hahn & Robert L. Pflatzgraff, Jr. (Pergamon Policy Studies). 386p. 1979. 100.00 o.p. (ISBN 0-08-023003-2). Pergamon.

Atlantic Crossing. Melvin Maddocks & Time-Life Books Editors. (Seafarers Ser.). (Illus.). 176p. 1981. 13.95 o.p. (ISBN 0-8094-2726-5). Time Life.

Atlantic Crossing Guide. RCC Pilotage Foundation Staff. 1983. 29.45 o.p. (ISBN 0-393-03283-3). Norton.

Atlantic Disaster. Richard Garrett. 304p. 1987. 26.50 o.p. (ISBN 0-907675-57-3, Pub. by Buchan & Enright England). Seven Hills Bk Dists.

Atlantic Puffin. David Boag & Mike Alexander. (Illus.). 128p. 1987. 29.95 o.p. (ISBN 0-7137-1734-3, Pub. by Blandford Pr England). Sterling.

Atlantis Fire. Gary Goshgarian. 1981. pap. 2.75 o.p. (ISBN 0-380-56093-3, 56093). Avon.

Atlantis Reconsidered: A New Look at the Ancient Deluge Legends & an Analysis of Mysterious Modern Phenomena. Michael Baran. 96p. 1981. 7.00 o.s.i. (ISBN 0-682-49761-4). Exposition-Phoenix.

Atlantis Rising. Brad Steiger. 220p. (Orig.). 1973. pap. 1.50 o.p. (ISBN 0-440-11182-X). Dell.

Atlas & Glossary of Primary Sedimentary Structures. F. J. Pettijohn & P. E. Potter. (Illus., Eng., Span., Fr. & Ger.). 1964. 47.00 o.p. (ISBN 0-387-03194-4). Springer-Verlag.

Atlas-Data Abstract for the United States & Selected Areas, Fiscal Year 1986. (Illus.). 98p. (Orig.). 1986. pap. 9.50 o.p. (ISBN 0-318-22461-5, S/N 008-000-00468-4). USGPO.

Atlas des Maladies Renales. G. Williams. Tr. by Micheline Levy. (Atlas Karger en Couleur: No. 4). (Illus.). 240p. 1974. 43.50 o.p. (ISBN 3-8055-1639-8). S Karger.

Atlas of Acute Hand Injuries. S. C. Sandzen, Jr. LC 79-21848. (Illus.). 456p. 1980. 95.00 o.p. (ISBN 0-88416-030-0, Dist. by McGraw). Year Bk Med.

Atlas of Ancient History. Colin McEvedy. (Maps). (YA) (gr. 9 up). 1967. pap. 6.95 o.p. (ISBN 0-14-070832-4). Penguin.

Atlas of Angiography. Ed. by K. E. Loose & R. J. A. M. Van Dongen. LC 75-16100. (Illus.). 444p. 1976. 65.00 o.p. (ISBN 0-88416-060-2). Year Bk Med.

Atlas of Applied Human Histology: The Identification of Tissues by Light Microscopy for Students, Residents, & Pathologists. J. D. Reid. (Illus.). 224p. 1982. 34.00 o.p. (ISBN 0-398-04590-9). C C Thomas.

Atlas of Bacterial Flagellation. Einar Leifson. (Illus.). 1959. 42.00 o.p. (ISBN 0-12-441650-0). Acad Pr.

Atlas of British Politics. Robert J. Waller. LC 84-675366. 206p. 1985. pap. 29.00 o.p. (ISBN 0-7099-3609-5, Pub. by Croom Helm Ltd). Routledge Chapman & Hall.

Atlas of British Railway History. Michael Freeman & Derek Aldcroft. LC 85-16645. 128p. 1985. 24.95 o.p. (ISBN 0-7099-0542-4, Pub. by Croom Helm Ltd). Routledge Chapman & Hall.

Atlas of Cancer Mortality in the People's Republic of China. 278p. 1982. 240.00 o.p. (ISBN 0-08-028850-2). Pergamon.

Atlas of Canine Surgical Techniques. Bedford. 1985. 39.50 o.p. (ISBN 0-632-01154-8, B-0576-8). Mosby.

Atlas of Carotid Angiography. Mutsumasa Takahashi. LC 77-91589. (Illus.). 525p. 1977. 105.00 o.p. (ISBN 0-89640-022-0). Igaku-Shoin.

Atlas of Children's Growth: Normal Variation & Growth Disorders. Ed. by J. M. Tanner & R. H. Whitehouse. LC 77-8381. 206p. 1982. 439.00 o.s.i. (ISBN 0-12-683340-0). Acad Pr.

Atlas of Coloscopy. F. P. Rossini. 1977. 70.00 o.p. (ISBN 0-387-91133-2). Springer-Verlag.

Atlas of Comparative Primate Hematology. H. J. Huser. 1970. 97.50 o.p. (ISBN 0-12-362750-8). Acad Pr.

Atlas of Dental Radiographic Anatomy. 2nd ed. Myron J. Kasle. LC 76-20937. 256p. 1983. pap. 28.95 o.p. (ISBN 0-7216-1036-6). Saunders.

Atlas of Diagnostic Cytology. C. Gompel. LC 77-27068. 237p. 1978. 80.00x o.p. (ISBN 0-471-02278-0). Wiley.

Atlas of Drought in Britain Nineteen Seventy-Five to Nineteen Seventy-Six. Ed. by J. C. Doornkamp et al. (Institute of British Geographers). 1983. 36.50 o.p. (ISBN 0-12-220780-7). Acad Pr.

Atlas of Economic Structure & Policies, Vol. 2. P. S. Florence. LC 68-30840. 1970. 40.00 o.p. (ISBN 0-08-013218-9). Pergamon.

Atlas of EEC Affairs. R. Hudson. LC 84-501. 100p. 1984. 29.95 o.p. (ISBN 0-416-30910-0, NO.4174); pap. 14.95 o.p. (ISBN 0-416-30920-8, NO.3921). Routledge Chapman & Hall.

Atlas of Electron Spin Resonance Spectra. Benon H. Bielski & Janusz M. Gebicki. 1967. 113.00 o.p. (ISBN 0-12-096650-6). Acad Pr.

Atlas of Hand Surgery, Vol. 1. Robert A. Chase. LC 72-79907. (Illus.). 438p. 1973. text ed. write for info. o.p. (ISBN 0-7216-2495-2). Saunders.

Atlas of Histology. E. E. Dodd. 1979. text ed. 50.00 o.p. (ISBN 0-07-017230-7). McGraw.

Atlas of Human Anatomy. Johannes Sobotta. Ed. by Frank H. Figge & Walter J. Hild. Incl. Vol. 1. Regions, Bones, Ligaments & Muscles. 290p. text ed. 39.50 (ISBN 0-8067-1719-X); Vol. 2. Visceral Anatomy (Cardiovascular, Lymphatic, Digestive, Respiratory & Urogenital Systems) 255p. text ed. 39.50 (ISBN 0-8067-1729-7); Vol. 3. Central Nervous System, Autonomic Nervous System, Sense Organs & Skin, Peripheral Nerves & Vessels. 366p. text ed. 45.00 (ISBN 0-8067-1739-4). (Illus.). 1978. Repr. of 1974 ed. 112.00 o.p. (ISBN 0-686-77287-3). Urban & S.

Atlas of Human Cross-Sectional Anatomy. Donald R. Cahill & Matthew J Orland. LC 83-13613. (Illus.). 139p. 1984. text ed. 29.50 o.p. (ISBN 0-8121-0890-6). Lea & Febiger.

Atlas of Human Embryology. Trent D. Stephens. (Illus.). 1980. pap. text ed. write for info. o.p. (ISBN 0-02-417150-6). Macmillan.

Atlas of Human Histology. 5th ed. Mariano S. Di Fiore. LC 81-8164. (Illus.). 267p. 1981. text ed. 21.50 o.p. (ISBN 0-8121-0756-X). Lea & Febiger.

Atlas of Infertility Surgery. 2nd ed. Grant W. Patton & Robert W. Kistner. 353p. text ed. 87.00 o.p. Little.

Atlas of Intrauterine Contraception. Russel J. Thomsen. LC 81-23748. (Illus.). 176p. 1982. text ed. 64.75 o.p. (ISBN 0-89116-246-1). Hemisphere Pub.

Atlas of Irish History. 2nd ed. Ruth D. Edwards. (Illus.). 180p. 1981. 11.50x o.p. (ISBN 0-416-08110-X, 6497); pap. 10.50 o.p. (ISBN 0-416-08120-7, 6496). Routledge Chapman & Hall.

Atlas of Isothermal Transformation & Cooling Transformation Diagrams. 1977. 71.00 o.p. (ISBN 0-87170-043-3). ASM.

Atlas of London. E. Jones & D. J. Sinclair. 1968. 220.00 o.p. (ISBN 0-08-013255-3). Pergamon.

Atlas of Mammalian Chromosomes, Vol. 10. T. C. Hsu & K. Benirschke. (Illus.). 1977. looseleaf 51.70 o.p. (ISBN 0-387-90273-2). Springer-Verlag.

Atlas of Mammography. J. Gershon-Cohen. LC 70-108918. (Illus.). 1970. 70.00 o.p. (ISBN 0-387-05106-6). Springer-Verlag.

Atlas of Mankind. Rand McNally & Company Staff. (Illus.). 208p. 1982. 35.00 o.p. (ISBN 0-528-83085-6). Rand McNally.

Atlas of Medical Anatomy. Jan Langman & M. W. Woerdeman. LC 81-51356. 523p. 1981. pap. write for info. o.p. (ISBN 0-7216-5622-6). Saunders.

Atlas of Medical Anatomy. Jan Langman & M. W. Woerdman. LC 75-22735. (Illus.). 1978. text ed. write for info. o.p. (ISBN 0-7216-5626-9). Saunders.

Atlas of Medical Anatomy. Jan Longman & M. W. Woerdeman. 523p. 1981. pap. 14.95 o.p. (ISBN 0-03-059656-4, HoltC). HR&W.

Atlas of Modern History to Eighteen Fifteen. Colin McEvedy. (Orig., Maps). 1973. pap. 6.95 o.p. (ISBN 0-14-070841-3). Penguin.

Atlas of Mortality from Selected Diseases in England & Wales 1968-1978. M. J Gardner et al. 96p. 1985. 110.00 o.p. (ISBN 0-471-90622-0, Dist. by A R Liss). Wiley.

Atlas of Normal Radiographs of the Skull. Walther Bergerhoff. (Eng., Ger., Fr. & Span.). 1961. 99.20 o.p. (ISBN 0-387-02637-1). Springer-Verlag.

Atlas of Obstetric & Gynecologic Ultrasound. Dennis A. Sarti. (Illus.). 240p. 1984. text ed. 39.95 o.p. (ISBN 0-8161-2262-8, G2262, Hall Medical). G K Hall.

Atlas of Operations in Soft Tissue Sarcomas. C. Karakousis. 480p. 1985. text ed. 135.00 o.p. (ISBN 0-07-033285-1). McGraw.

Atlas of Orthopaedic Surgery. 2nd ed. Louis A. Goldstein & Robert C. Dickerson. LC 80-25987. (Illus.). 660p. 1981. text ed. 127.00 cloth o.p. (ISBN 0-8016-1884-3). Mosby.

Atlas of Orthotics: Biomechanical Principles & Application. 2nd ed. American Academy of Orthopaedic Surgeons Staff. 1985. 75.00 o.p. (ISBN 0-8016-0072-3). Mosby.

Atlas of Pathologic Anatomy. W. Doerr et al. LC 75-16097. (Illus.). 318p. 1975. 97.50 o.p. (ISBN 0-88416-063-7). Year Bk Med.

Atlas of Pedodontics. 2nd ed. John M. Davis et al. (Illus.). 425p. 1980. (ISBN 0-7216-2977-6). Saunders.

Atlas of Radiographic Anatomy of the Dog & Cat. 4th, rev., enl. ed. H. Schebitz & H. Wilkens. (Illus.). 244p. 1987. lib. bdg. 130.00x o.p. (ISBN 3-489-56416-2). Parey Sci Pubs.

Atlas of Radiographic Anatomy of the Horse. 3rd ed. H. Schebitz & H. Wilkens. (Illus.). 100p. 1979. (ISBN 0-7216-7964-1). Saunders.

Atlas of Sectional Anatomy. Philomena McGrath & P. Mills. (Illus.). viii, 238p. 1984. 54.75 o.p. (ISBN 3-8055-3624-0). S Karger.

Atlas of Sectional Human Anatomy: Frontal, Sagittal & Horizontal Planes, 2 vols. J. G. Korite & H. Sick. Incl. Vol. 1. Head, Neck, Thorax. 175p (ISBN 0-8067-1031-4); Vol. 2. Abdomen, Pelvis. 171p (ISBN 0-8067-1032-2). LC 82-13558. (Illus.). 1983. text ed. 98.00 ea. o.p.; Set. text ed. 185.00 o.p. (ISBN 0-8067-1030-6). Urban & S.

Atlas of Skin Biopsy: Diagnosis by Light & Immuno Microscopy of Vesico-Bullous, Connective Tissue Disorders & Vasculitis of the Skin. Raghunath P. Misra & I. Daniel Sanusi. (Illus.). 120p. 1983. 28.00x o.p. (ISBN 0-398-04744-8). C C Thomas.

Atlas of Standard Surgical Procedures. Ed. by William V. McDermott, Jr. LC 82-12714. (Illus.). 193p. 1983. text ed. 47.50 o.p. (ISBN 0-8121-0842-6). Lea & Febiger.

Atlas of Steroid Spectra. Walter Neudert & H. Roepke. Tr. by J. B. Leane. (Illus., Eng. & Ger.). 1965. 116.00 o.p. (ISBN 0-387-03376-9). Springer-Verlag.

Atlas of Surgical Approaches to the Bones of the Horse. Dennis W. Milne & Simon Turner. (Illus.). 210p. 1979. (ISBN 0-7216-6362-1). Saunders.

Atlas of Surgical Exposures of the Extremities. Sam W. Banks & Harold Laufman. LC 52-12872. (Illus.). 1973. (ISBN 0-7216-1530-9). Saunders.

Atlas of the Anatomy of the Ear. Branislav Vidic & Ronan O'Rahilly. LC 70-151688. (Illus.). 1971. write for info. incl. slides o.p. (ISBN 0-7216-9806-9). Saunders.

Atlas of the Central Nervous System in Sectional Planes: Selected Myelin Stained Sections of the Human Brain & Spinal Cord. Susanna Zuleger & Jochen Staubesand. LC 77-2159. (Illus.). 104p. 1977. pap. text ed. 14.50 o.p. (ISBN 0-8067-2201-0). Urban & S.

Atlas of the Frog's Brain. Milena Kemali & Valentino Braitenberg. LC 68-9507. (Illus.). 1969. 68.90 o.p. (ISBN 0-387-04579-1). Springer-Verlag.

Atlas of the Historical Geography of the U. S. Charles O. Paullin. Ed. by John K. Wright. LC 75-14058. (Carnegie Institution of Washington Ser.: No. 4). (Illus.). 162p. 1975. Repr. of 1932 ed. lib. bdg. 135.25x o.p. (ISBN 0-8371-8208-5, PAHG). Greenwood.

Atlas of the Land. Karen W. Fonstad. LC 85-6203. (Illus.). 176p. 1985. 19.95 o.p. (ISBN 0-345-31431-X, Del Rey); pap. 9.95 o.p. (ISBN 0-345-31433-6, Del Rey). Ballantine.

Atlas of the Planets. Paul Doherty. LC 80-12347. (Illus.). 144p. 1980. text ed. 19.95 o.p. (ISBN 0-07-017341-9). McGraw.

Atlas of the Presidents. rev. ed. Donald E. Cooke. LC 81-6525. (Hammond Profile Ser.). (Illus.). 96p. (gr. 6 up). 1984. 9.95 o.p. (ISBN 0-8437-1045-4). Hammond Inc.

Atlas of the Presidents. rev. ed. Donald E. Cooke. LC 81-6525. (Profile Ser.). (Illus.). 96p. (gr. 6 up). 1989. 10.95 o.p. Hammond Inc.

Atlas of the World's Railways. Brian Hollingsworth. (Illus.). 352p. 1982. 14.95 o.p. (ISBN 0-8119-0468-7, Pub. by Bison Bks.). Fell.

Atlas of Ultrasonic Diagnosis in Obstetrics & Gynecology. K. H. Schlensker. LC 75-16104. (Illus.). 162p. 1975. 20.00 o.p. (ISBN 0-88416-127-7). Year Bk Med.

Atlas of Utah. Ed. by Wayne L. Wahlquist et al. (Illus.). 298p. 1982. lib. bdg. 49.95 o.p. (ISBN 0-8425-1831-2). Brigham.

Atlas of Vertebrate Cells in Tissue Culture. Ed. by George G. Rose. 1971. 81.00 o.p. (ISBN 0-12-596856-6). Acad Pr.

Atlas of World Affairs. 7th ed. A. Boyd. LC 83-675921. (Illus.). 200p. 1983. 17.95 o.p. (ISBN 0-416-32370-7, NO. 3923); pap. 8.95 o.p. (ISBN 0-416-32380-4, NO. 3922). Routledge Chapman & Hall.

Atlas of World History. Ed. by R. I. Moore. (Illus.). 192p. 1984. 14.95 o.p. (ISBN 0-528-83114-3). Rand McNally.

Atlas of Wrist & Hand Fractures. S. C. Sandzen, Jr. LC 75-12036. (Illus.). 446p. 1981. 59.00 o.p. (ISBN 0-88416-032-7). Year Bk Med.

Atlas of Xeroradiography. Lothar Schertel et al. LC 76-14693. (Illus.). 1977. text ed. write for info. o.p. (ISBN 0-7216-7970-6). Saunders.

Atlas Text Language: Standard 416-1984. 2nd ed. 777p. 1985. 78.00 o.p. (ISBN 0-471-82745-2, SHO9696). IEEE Comp Soc.

Atmosphere: An Introduction to Meteorology. Frederick K. Lutgens & Edward J. Tarbuck. (Illus.). 496p. 1982. text ed. (ISBN 0-13-050120-4). P-H.

Atmosphere: An Introduction to Meteorology. 3rd ed. Frederick K. Lutgens & Edward J. Tarbuck. (Illus.). 576p. 1986. text ed. (ISBN 0-13-049917-X). P-H.

Atmosphere & Ocean: Our Fluid Environments. J. G. Harvey. LC 77-377903. 143p. 1978. pap. 19.50x o.p. (ISBN 0-8448-1293-5, Pub. by Crane Russak & Co). Taylor & Francis.

Atmosphere of Venus: Recent Findings: Proceedings of Workshop III of the COSPAR 25th Plenary Meeting Held in Graz, Austria, 28 June-2 July 1984. Ed. by G. M. Keating et al. (Illus.). 208p. 1985. pap. 54.00 o.p. (ISBN 0-08-033223-4, Pub. by PPL). Pergamon.

Atmosphere, Weather & Climate. 4th ed. Roger G. Barry & R. J. Chorley. 425p. 1982. 38.00x o.p. (ISBN 0-416-33690-6, NO. 3748); pap. 14.95x o.p. (ISBN 0-416-33700-7, 3740). Routledge Chapman & Hall.

Atmosphere, Weather & Climate. John G. Navarra. LC 78-1791. 520p. 1979. text ed. 29.95x o.s.i. (ISBN 0-7216-6661-2). SCP.

Atmospheric Dispersion Modeling. (APCA Reprint Ser.: Vol. 10). 87p. 1980. 10.00 o.p. (ISBN 0-318-12245-6, RS-10); members 8.00 o.p. (ISBN 0-318-12246-4). Air & Waste.

Atmospheric Dispersion Modeling for Emergency Preparedness. Environmental Research & Technology, Inc. Staff. (National Environmental Studies Project: NESP Reports). 60p. 1981. 45.00 o.p. (ISBN 0-318-13561-2, AIF-NESP-022); NESP sponsors 15.00 o.p. (ISBN 0-318-13562-0). US Coun Energy Awareness.

Atmospheric Emergencies: Existing Capabilities & Future Needs. National Research Council (U. S.) Transportation Research Board. LC 83-13464. (Transportation Research Record Ser.: No. 902). 1983. 6.40x o.p. (ISBN 0-309-03516-3). Natl Acad Pr.

Atmospheric Motion & Air Pollution: An Introduction for Students of Engineering & Science. Richard A. Dobbins. LC 79-952. 344p. 1979. 65.00 o.p. Krieger.

Atmospheric Pollution. 3rd rev. ed. A. R. Meetham. 1964. 15.15 o.p. (ISBN 0-08-010143-7). Pergamon.

Atmospheric Spectroscopy: Proceedings of the International Workshop SERC Rutherford Appleton Laboratory, Chilton, Didcot, Oxon, U. K., July 19-21, 1983. Ed. by G. E. Hunt & J. Ballard. (Illus.). 120p. 1985. pap. 83.00 o.p. (ISBN 0-08-030278-5). Pergamon.

Atom & the Energy Revolution. N. Lansdell. (Illus.). 200p. 1959. (ISBN 0-8022-0926-2). Philos Lib.

Atom Bomb & the Future of Man. Karl Jaspers. Tr. by E. B. Ashton. LC 60-7237. xiv, 342p. 1984. pap. 10.95 o.s.i. (ISBN 0-226-39482-4). U of Chicago Pr.

Atom Bomb Spies. H. Montgomery Hyde. LC 80-65998. (Illus.). 1980. 14.95 o.p. (ISBN 0-689-11075-8, Macmillan). Macmillan.

Atom Story. J. G. Feinberg. 1953. (ISBN 0-8022-0480-5). Philos Lib.

Atomic Absorption Spectrophotometry. 2nd ed. W. T. Elwell & J. A. Gidley. 1966. 28.00 o.p. (ISBN 0-08-012063-6). Pergamon.

Atomic Absorption Spectroscopy. 2nd rev. & enl. ed. James W. Robinson. 200p. 1975. 39.75 o.p. (ISBN 0-8247-6249-5). Dekker.

Atomic Absorption Spectroscopy, Vol. 25. 2nd ed. Morris Slavin. LC 78-16257. (Chemical Analysis: Series of Monographs on Analytical Chemistry & Its Applications: Vol. 25). 193p. 1978. 47.00x o.p. (ISBN 0-471-79652-2, Pub. by Wiley-Interscience). Wiley.

Atomic Absorption Spectroscopy: Past, Present & Future, Pt. 2: To Commemorate the 25th Anniversary of Alan Walsh's Landmark Paper in Spectrochimica Acta. Ed. by P. W. Boumans. (Spectrochimica Acta B: Vol. 36, No. 5). iv, 92p. 1981. pap. 19.25 o.p. (ISBN 0-08-026287-2). Pergamon.

Atomic Absorption Spectroscopy-Past, Present & Future: To Commemorate the 25th Anniversary of Alan Walsh's Landmark Paper in Spectrochimica Acta. P. W. Boumans. 248p. 1981. pap. 39.00 o.p. (ISBN 0-08-026267-8). Pergamon.

Atomic Absorption Spectroscopy: Proceedings of an International Conference, Sheffield, U. K., 1969. International Union of Pure & Applied Chemistry. 152p. 1976. 33.00 o.p. (ISBN 0-08-020727-8). Pergamon.

Atomic Age & Our Biological Future. H. V. Bronsted. 1958. (ISBN 0-8022-0183-0). Philos Lib.

Atomic & Ionic Impact Phenomena on Metal Surfaces. Manfred Kaminsky. (Illus.). 1965. 50.80 o.p. (ISBN 0-387-03410-2). Springer-Verlag.

Atomic & Molecular Collision Theory. Ed. by Franco A. Gianturco. LC 81-15362. (NATO ASI Series B, Physics: Vol. 71). 514p. 1982. 85.00x o.p. (ISBN 0-306-40807-4, Plenum Pr). Plenum Pub.

Atomic & Molecular Physics of Controlled Thermonuclear Fusion. Ed. by Charles J. Joachain & Douglas E. Post. LC 83-11128. (NATO ASI Series B, Physics: Vol. 101). 586p. 1983. 89.50x o.p. (ISBN 0-306-41398-1, Plenum Pr). Plenum Pub.

Atomic & Molecular Polarizability. K. D. Sen. 300p. 1989. 48.00 o.p. (ISBN 9971-50-571-1); pap. 29.00 o.p. (ISBN 9971-50-572-X). World Scientific Pub.

Atomic & Molecular Processes in Controlled Thermonuclear Fusion. Ed. by M. R. McDowell & A. M. Ferendeci. LC 80-238. (NATO ASI Series B, Physics: Vol. 53). 506p. 1980. 85.00x o.p. (ISBN 0-306-40424-9, Plenum Pr). Plenum Pub.

Atomic & Nuclear Chemistry: Atomic Theory & the Structure of the Atom, Vol. 1. T. Peacocke. 1968. 40.00 o.p. (ISBN 0-08-012524-7); pap. 40.00 o.p. (ISBN 0-08-012525-5). Pergamon.

Atomic & Nuclear Methods in Fossil Energy Research. Ed. by Royston H. Filby et al. LC 81-21169. 518p. 1982. 79.50x o.p. (ISBN 0-306-40899-6, Plenum Pr). Plenum Pub.

Atomic Bomb. Joan Solomon. (Science in a Social Context Ser.). 1986. pap. 6.95x o.p. (ISBN 0-631-91000-X). Basil Blackwell.

Atomic Bomb Shelters & Blast-Resistant Building: A Selective Bibliography of Periodical Literature. Carole Cable. (Architecture Ser.: A 1441). 7p. 1985. 2.00 o.p. (ISBN 0-89028-511-X). Vance Biblios.

Atomic Energy. E. C. Roberson & A. Radcliff. (Illus.). 142p. 1956. (ISBN 0-8022-1357-X). Philos Lib.

Atomic Energy in Agriculture. W. E. Dick. (Illus.). 160p. 1958. (ISBN 0-8022-0396-5). Philos Lib.

Atomic Energy in Medicine. K. E. Halnam. (Illus.). 151p. 1957. (ISBN 0-8022-0666-2). Philos Lib.

Atomic Energy Research at Harwell. K. E. Jay. 150p. 1955. (ISBN 0-8022-0795-2). Philos Lib.

Atomic Energy Review - Thorium: Physico-Chemical Properties of Its Compounds & Alloys. (Special Issue Ser.: No. 5). (Illus.). 241p. 1975. pap. 21.75 o.p. (ISBN 92-0-149075-5, IAER5, IAEA). UNIPUB.

Atomic Energy Review: Commemorative Issue. 102p. 1967. pap. 7.50 o.p. (ISBN 92-0-079067-4, IAER4C, IAEA). UNIPUB.

Atomic Energy Review Cumulative Index, Vol. 1-10, 1963-72. 70p. 1973. pap. (ISP/66, IAEA). UNIPUB.

Atomic Energy Review, Special Issue No. 5: Thorium: Physico-Chemical Properties of Its Compounds & Alloys. (Illus.). 241p. 1975. pap. 21.75 o.p. (ISBN 92-0-149075-5, IAER5, IAEA). UNIPUB.

Atomic Energy: The Story of Nuclear Science. Irene D. Jaworski & Alexander Joseph. LC 60-13702. (Illus.). 1961. 4.95 o.p. (ISBN 0-15-204438-8, HJ). HarBraceJ.

Atomic Physics of Highly Ionized Atoms. Ed. by R. Marrus. LC 83-8081. (NATO ASI Series B, Physics: Vol. 96). (Illus.). 580p. 1983. 89.50x o.p. (ISBN 0-306-41356-6, Plenum Pr). Plenum Pub.

Atomic Physics 7. Ed. by Daniel Kleppner & Francis M. Pipkin. LC 72-176581. 584p. 1981. 95.00x o.p. (ISBN 0-306-40650-0, Plenum Pr). Plenum Pub.

Atomic Physics 8. Ed. by I. Lindgren et al. LC 72-176581. 604p. 1983. 95.00x o.p. (ISBN 0-306-41361-2, Plenum Pr). Plenum Pub.

Atomic Spectroscopy in Japan. Ed. by K. Fuwa et al. (Journal Spectrochimica Acta Ser.: No. 36). 160p. 1981. pap. 19.25 o.p. (ISBN 0-08-028731-X). Pergamon.

Atomic Theory for Students of Metallurgy. W. Hume-Rothery & B. R. Cole. 438p. 1969. 30.00 o.p. (ISBN 0-85066-099-8). Taylor & Francis.

Atoms & Energy. H. S. Massey. (Illus.). 180p. 1956. (ISBN 0-8022-1080-5). Philos Lib.

Atoms & Molecules in Astrophysics. Ed. by T. R. Carson & M. J. Roberts. (NATO Advanced Study Institute Volume Ser.). 1973. 59.50 o.p. (ISBN 0-12-161050-0). Acad Pr.

Atoms at Work. George P. Bischof. LC 51-100007. (Illus.). (gr. 5-8). 1951. 4.50 o.p. (ISBN 0-15-204617-8, HJ). HarBraceJ.

Atoms, Men, & God. Paul Sabine. 1953. (ISBN 0-8022-1463-0). Philos Lib.

Atoms of Thought. George Santayana. 352p. 1954. Philos Lib.

Atonement. Albert Barnes. LC 80-65582. 1980. pap. 8.95 o.p. (ISBN 0-87123-016-X, 210016). Bethany Hse.

Atonement of the Death of Christ. H. D. McDonald. 352p. 1985. pap. 19.95 o.p. (ISBN 0-8010-6194-6). Baker Bk.

Atonement: The Origins of the Doctrine in the New Testament. Martin Hengel. Tr. by John Bowden from Ger. LC 80-2384. 132p. 1981. pap. 7.95 o.p. (ISBN 0-8006-1446-1, 1-1446, Fortress). Augsburg Fortress.

Atrium Buildings. Richard Saxon. 1983. 55.95 o.p. (ISBN 0-442-28045-9). Van Nos Reinhold.

Atrocious Two. Sheila Greenwald. (Illus.). 1978. 6.95 o.p. (ISBN 0-395-26451-0). HM.

Attachments. Judith Rossner. 1977. 9.95 o.p. (ISBN 0-671-22591-X). S&S.

Attack & Counterattack: The Texas-Mexican Frontier, 1842. Joseph M. Nance. (Illus.). 764p. 1964. 35.00x o.p. (ISBN 0-292-73168-X). U of Tex Pr.

Attack of the Insecticons. Lynn Beach. (Transformers Find Your Fate Junior Ser.: No. 3). 80p. (Orig.). (gr. 4 up). 1985. pap. 1.95 o.p. (ISBN 0-345-32671-7). Ballantine.
Attack of the Mutants: A Thundercats Adventure. Ann Hodgman. LC 85-2015. (Illus.). 32p. (gr. 5-8). 1985. 4.95 o.s.i. (ISBN 0-394-87452-8, BYR). Random.
Attack of Thomas Cooke see Popeiana.
Attack on Big Business. J. D. Glover. Repr. of 1954 ed. 21.50 o.s.i. (ISBN 0-08-022304-4). Pergamon.
Attack on Corporate America: The Corporate Issues Sourcebook. Law & Economics Center, University of Miami School of Law Staff. (Illus.). 1978. text ed. 34.50 o.p. (ISBN 0-07-036693-4). McGraw.
Attack on the King. Eric Affabee. (Wizards, Warriors & You Ser.: No. 16). (Illus.). 112p. (YA) (gr. 5 up). 1986. pap. 2.95 o.p. (ISBN 0-380-75045-7). Avon.
Attempt at a Russian Bibliography or a Complete Dictionary of Works Printed in Church Slavonic & Russian from the Introduction of Printing in 1813, 2 Vols. V. S. Sopikov. 195.00 o.p. (ISBN 0-87556-323-6). Saifer.
Attending Ob-Gyn Patients. Ed. by Patricia R. Urosevich & Barbara McVan. LC 82-15627. (Nursing Photobook Ser.). (Illus.). 160p. 1982. 17.95 o.p. (ISBN 0-916730-48-4). Springhouse Pub.
Attention, Arousal & the Orientation Reaction. R. Lynn. 1966. 29.00 o.p. (ISBN 0-08-011524-1); pap. text ed. 14.25 o.p. (ISBN 0-08-013840-3). Pergamon.
Attention Deficit Disorders: Diagnostic, Cognitive & Therapeutic Understanding. Ed. by L. Bloomingdale. 240p. 1984. 35.00 o.p. (ISBN 0-88331-111-9). Luce.
Attic & Baroque Prose Style: The Anti-Ciceronian Movement, Four Essays. J. Max Patrick et al. 1966. pap. 10.50x o.p. (ISBN 0-691-01293-8). Princeton U Pr.
Attic Bilingual Vases & Their Painters. Beth Cohen. LC 77-94689. (Outstanding Dissertations in the Fine Arts Ser.). 1978. lib. bdg. 97.00 o.p. (ISBN 0-8240-3220-9). Garland Pub.
Attila the Pun: A Magic Moscow Book. Daniel M. Pinkwater. LC 80-28504. (Illus.). 80p. (gr. 3-7). 1981. 7.95 o.s.i. (ISBN 0-02-774410-8, Four Winds). Macmillan.
Attitude, Ego-Involvement & Change. Ed. by Carolyn W. Sherif & Muzafer Sherif. LC 74-27184. 1976. Repr. of 1967 ed. lib. bdg. 24.75x o.p. (ISBN 0-8371-7894-0, SHAE). Greenwood.
Attitudes & Reading. J. Estill Alexander & Ronald C. Filler. (Reading Aids Ser.). 80p. (Orig.). 1976. pap. text ed. 4.50 o.p. (ISBN 0-87207-222-3). Intl Reading.
Attitudes, Conflict & Social Change. Ed. by Bert King & Elliot McGinnies. 1972. 24.95 o.p. (ISBN 0-12-407750-1). Acad Pr.
Attitudes to Class in the English Novel: From Walter Scott to David Storey. Mary Eagleton & David Pierce. 1980. 17.95 o.s.i. (ISBN 0-500-51002-4). Thames Hudson.
Attitudes to Toxicology in the European Economic Community. LC 87-23118. 250p. 1988. (ISBN 0-471-91769-9). Wiley.
Attitudes Toward Persons with Disabilities: A Compendium of Related Literature. John G. Schroedel. LC 78-62049. 182p. 1978. 8.25 o.p. (ISBN 0-686-38794-5). Human Res Ctr.
Attlee. Kenneth Harris. (Illus.). 1983. 27.00 o.p. (ISBN 0-393-01815-6). Norton.
Attorney Conspiracy. C. Terry Cline, Jr. LC 82-72059. 375p. 1983. 15.50 o.p. (ISBN 0-87795-371-6, Arbor Hse). Morrow.
Attorney for the Damned. Ed. by Arthur Weinberg & William O. Douglas. 576p. 1983. pap. 9.50 o.p. (ISBN 0-671-49251-9, Touchstone). S&S.
Attorneys & Agents Registered to Practice Before the United States Patent & Trademark Office: 1987. Annual ed. 376p. 1987. pap. 17.00 o.p. (ISBN 0-318-23540-4, 003-004-00629-3). USGPO.
Attorney's Guide to Agricultural Real Estate Transactions. Pennsylvania Bar Institute Staff. 305p. 1983. 20.00 o.p. (ISBN 0-318-02180-3, 228). PA Bar Inst.
Attorney's Guide to Effective Discovery Techniques. Walter Barthold. 304p. 1974. text ed. 26.50 o.p. (ISBN 0-13-050484-X, Busn). P-H.
Attorney's Guide to Restitution. Graham Douthwaite. 1977. text ed. 40.00x including 1986 suppl. o.s.i. (ISBN 0-87473-095-3, A Smith Co). Michie Co.
Attorney's Handbook on Division Nine. California Continuing Education of the Bar Staff & Harry C. Sigman. LC 75-620125. 200p. 1976. 15.00 o.p. (ISBN 0-88124-043-5). Cal Cont Ed Bar.
Attracting, Feeding & Housing Wild Birds: With Project Plans. Phyllis Moorman. (Illus.). 154p. 1985. 15.95 o.p. (ISBN 0-8306-0755-2, 1755); pap. 8.70 o.p. (ISBN 0-8306-1755-8). TAB Bks.
Attractiveness of God: Essays in Christian Doctrine. R. P. Hanson. LC 73-5345. 208p. 1973. 9.95 o.p. (ISBN 0-8042-0473-X, John Knox). Westminster John Knox.
Attribute Grammar for the Semantic Analysis of Ada. J. Uhl et al. (Lecture Notes in Computer Science Ser.: Vol. 139). 511p. 1982. pap. 24.00 o.p. (ISBN 0-387-11571-4). Springer-Verlag.
Atypical Mycobacteria & Human Mycobacteriosis. John S. Chapman. LC 77-1824. (Current Topics in Infectious Diseases Ser.). (Illus.). 216p. 1977. 45.00x o.p. (ISBN 0-306-30997-1, Plenum Med Bk). Plenum Pub.
Au & Ag Heap & Dump Leaching Practice. J. Brent Hisket. LC 84-71234. (Illus.). 162p. text ed. 30.00x o.p. (ISBN 0-89520-425-8, 425-8). SMM&E Inc.
Au Bonheur des Dames. Emile Zola. 1957. pap. 9.50 o.p. (ISBN 0-685-23950-0). Schoenhof.
Au Jour le Jour: A French Review. 2nd ed. Jean Sareil & William Ryding. LC 73-18083. 240p. 1974. text ed. 25.95 o.p. (ISBN 0-13-052977-X). P-H.
Aubade. Carl Wolz. (Educational Dance Score Registry Ser.: No. 7). (Illus.). 19p. 1984. dance score 10.00 o.s.i. (ISBN 0-932582-39-7). Dance Notation.
Auburn-Alabama Joke Book. S. C. Lee. LC 74-21104. 1982. pap. 2.95 o.p. (ISBN 0-87397-241-4). Strode.
Auction: A Modern Novel, 1760, 2 vols. in 1. Mrs. A. Woodfin. Ed. by Michael F. Shugrue. (Flowering of the Novel, 1740-1775 Ser: Vol. 54). 1975. lib. bdg. 61.00 o.p. (ISBN 0-8240-1153-8). Garland Pub.
Auction Yearlings of 1978. pap. 10.00 o.p. (ISBN 0-936032-02-2). Blood-Horse.
Auctioneer. Joan Samson. 304p. 1977. pap. 2.75 o.p. (ISBN 0-380-00842-4, 57810-7). Avon.
Auctions of 1981. Ed. by Blood-Horse, Inc. Staff. (Blood-Horse Annual Supplement Ser.). (Illus.). 300p. (Orig.). 1982. pap. 10.00 o.p. (ISBN 0-936032-50-2). Blood-Horse.
Auctions of 1985. (Annual Supplement to the Blood-Horse Ser.). 525p. (Orig.). 1986. pap. 21.50 o.p. (ISBN 0-936032-89-8). Blood-Horse.
Auctions of 1986: Annual Supplement. 525p. 1987. pap. 21.50 o.p. (ISBN 0-939049-06-6). Blood Horse.
Auden in Love. Dorothy J. Farnan. LC 85-10505. (Illus.). 269p. 1984. 17.45 o.p. (ISBN 0-671-50418-5). S&S.
Audi Service-Repair Handbook: Fox--1973-1979. Jeff Rogbinson. (Illus.). pap. 11.95 o.p. (ISBN 0-89287-155-5, A132). Clymer Pub.
Audi Service-Repair Handbook: 100 LS Series, 1970-1977. 2nd ed. Ed. by Jeff Robinson. (Illus.). pap. 12.95 o.p. (ISBN 0-89287-096-6, A131). Clymer Pub.
Audi 4000S, 4000CS & Coupe GT Offical Factory Repair Manual: 1984-1987. Audi of America Inc. LC 86-73081. 1320p. (Orig.). 1987. pap. 69.95 o.p. (ISBN 0-8376-0348-X). Bentley.
Audi 5000s Official Factory Repair Manual: 1984-1985: Gasoline Models including Wagon & Turbo. Volkswagen of America, Inc. (Illus.). 400p. 1985. pap. 44.95 o.p. (ISBN 0-8376-0347-1). Bentley.
Audiences, Messages, Speakers: An Introduction to Human Communication. John L. Vohs & Gerald P. Mohrmann. 224p. 1975. text ed. 12.95 o.p. (ISBN 0-15-504286-6, HC). HarBraceJ.
Audio Blue Book, 1986. 630p. Date not set. 125.00 o.p. (ISBN 0-932089-07-0). Orion Res.
Audio Blue Book, 1987. Ed. by Orion Research Corporation Staff. 700p. 1986. 125.00 o.p. (ISBN 0-932089-12-7). Orion Res.
Audio Frequency Testers. Ronald Ives et al. Ed. by Sandy Cole. (Seventy-Three Test Equipment Library: Vol. 2). 78p. 1976. pap. 4.95 o.p. (ISBN 0-88006-011-5, LB 7360). Wayne Green Ent.
Audio Sweetening for Film & TV. Milton C. Hubatka & Frederick Hull. (Illus.). 288p. 1986. 29.00 o.p. (ISBN 0-8306-1994-1, NO. 1994). Tab Bks.
Audio-Tutorial Introduction to Chemistry. Paul J. Santiago. Incl. Metric System; Signed Numbers & Solving Simple Linear Equations. 1975. 47.00 o.p. tape (ISBN 0-395-17746-4); Definition of Chemistry; Chemical Classification of Matter. 1975. 47.00 o.p. tape (ISBN 0-395-17747-2); Sub-Atomic Structures of the Isotopes. 1975. 47.00 o.p. tape (ISBN 0-395-17748-0); Periodic Table; Bonding of Atoms. 1975. 47.00 o.p. tape (ISBN 0-395-17749-9); Writing Formulas for Ionic Compounds; Calculating Formula Weights & Percentage Compositions. 1975. 47.00 o.p. tape (ISBN 0-395-17750-2); The Mole Concept; Balancing a Chemical Equation. 1975. 47.00 o.p. tape (ISBN 0-395-17751-0); Calculation of the Simplest Formula for a Compound; Weight-Weight Problems. 1975. 47.00 o.p. tape (ISBN 0-395-17752-9); Kinetic Molecular Theory of Matter & the Gas Laws; General Gas Law Equation. 1975. 47.00 o.p. tape (ISBN 0-395-17753-7); Volume-Volume & Weight-Volume Problems; Density of Gas at S.T.P.; Solutions. 1975. 47.00 o.p. (ISBN 0-395-17754-5); Definition of Electrolites, Acids, Bases, & Salts; Single Replacement Reactions. 1975. 47.00 o.p. tape (ISBN 0-395-17755-3); Double Replacement Reactions; Neutralization. 1975. 47.00 o.p. tape (ISBN 0-395-17756-1). 1975. pap. 16.50 chemical prob. wkbk. o.p. (ISBN 0-395-17745-6). HM.
Audio-Video ICs. 1987. 105.00 o.p. DATA Busn Pub.
Audio-Visual-Motor Training with Pattern Cards. Edith Klasen. 1970. pap. text ed. 8.95 o.p. (ISBN 0-917962-16-8). T H Peek.
Audio Visuals for Real Estate Instruction. 84p. 2.00 o.p. (ISBN 0-318-15173-1, 111-230). Natl Assoc Realtors.
AudioCraft: An Introduction to the Tools & Techniques of Audio Production. Randy Thom et al. (Illus.). 183p. 1982. pap. text ed. 15.00 o.p. (ISBN 0-941209-00-8). Natl Fed Com Broad.
Audiological Assessment. 2nd ed. Darrell E. Rose. 1977. text ed. (ISBN 0-13-050815-2). P-H.
Audiovisual, Draughting, Office, Reproduction & Other Ancillary Equipment & Supplies: Equipment Planning Guide for Vocational & Technical Training & Education Programmes. International Labour Office, Geneva Staff. (No. 15). (Illus.). 279p. (Orig.). 1982. pap. 22.80 o.p. (ISBN 92-2-102112-2). Intl Labour Office.
Audiovisual Idea Book for Churches. Mary Jensen & Andrew Jensen. LC 73-88612. 160p. (Orig.). 1974. pap. 5.50 o.p. (ISBN 0-8066-1415-3, 10-0500, Augsburg). Augsburg Fortress.
Audiovisual Primer. rev. ed. Michael Goudket. LC 72-93755. (Illus.). 77p. 1974. pap. text ed. 3.50x o.p. (ISBN 0-8077-2437-8). Tchrs Coll.
Audit Criteria for Drug Utilization Review, Vol. 1. Jacalyn Henricks. 182p. 1981. pap. text ed. 40.00 spiral bound o.p. (ISBN 0-930530-18-7). Am Soc Hosp Pharm.
Audit Criteria for Drug Utilization Review, Vol. 2. Jacalyn Henricks. 124p. 1983. pap. 30.00 spiral bound o.p. (ISBN 0-930530-35-7). Am Soc Hosp Pharm.
Audit Guide for the Community Bank. Bank Administration Institute Staff. 28p. 1977. 18.00 o.p. (200). Bank Admin Inst.
Audit Problem: Crafters, Inc. Arthur W. Holmes & David C. Burns. 1980. pap. 21.95x o.p. (ISBN 0-256-02162-7). Irwin.
Audit Report. J. Shaw. 1980. 29.95 o.p. (ISBN 0-442-27540-4). Van Nos Reinhold.
Audit Standards in the Public Sector: An Analysis of Comparative Experience. 132p. 1987. 15.00 o.p. (ISBN 92-1-123108-6, E.87.II.H.2). UN.
Auditing. Albert K. Francisco & Kenneth A. Smith. LC 87-62076. (CPA Examination Review Ser.). 416p. 1988. pap. text ed. 22.95 o.p. (ISBN 0-932276-76-8). Prof Pubns CA.
Auditing. 7th ed. Leslie R. Howard. 332p. (Orig.). 1978. pap. text ed. 18.95x o.p. (ISBN 0-7121-0178-0, Pub. by Macdonald & Evans England). Trans-Atl Phila.
Auditing. 4th ed. Ed. by Jack C. Robertson & Frederick G. Davis. 1985. text ed. 40.95x o.p. (ISBN 0-256-03274-2). Irwin.
Auditing: Philosophy & Technique. John W. Cook & Gary M. Winkle. LC 75-31033. (Illus.). 512p. 1976. text ed. 18.25 o.p. (ISBN 0-395-20660-X). HM.
Auditing: Philosophy & Technique. 2nd ed. John W. Cook & Gary M. Winkle. LC 79-88718. (Illus.). 1981. text ed. 27.95 o.p. (ISBN 0-395-28660-3); suppl. test bank 1.25 o.p. HM.
Auditing: Standards & Procedures. 9th ed. Arthur W. Holmes & David C. Burns. 1979. 37.95x o.p. (ISBN 0-256-02163-5). Irwin.
Auditing Standards & Procedures Manual 1986-87. Douglas R. Carmichael & Martin Benis. (Professional Accounting & Business Ser.). 1986. pap. 75.00 o.p. (ISBN 0-471-85642-8). Wiley.
Auditing the Data Processing Function. Richard W. Lott. (Illus.). 1980. 17.95 o.p. (ISBN 0-8144-5527-1). AMACOM.
Auditing: Theory & Practice. C. William Thomas & Emerson O. Henke. LC 82-21262. 992p. 1983. text ed. write for info. o.p. (ISBN 0-534-01388-0). PWS-Kent Pub.
Audition for Murder. P. M. Carlson. 225p. 1985. pap. 2.75 o.p. (ISBN 0-380-89538-2). Avon.
Auditor Independence & Systems Design. Larry E. Rittenberg. LC 77-79366. (Modern Concepts of Internal Auditing Ser.). 1977. pap. 3.50 o.p. (ISBN 0-89413-053-6). Inst Inter Aud.
Auditor Risk & Legal Liability. Kent E. St. Pierre. Ed. by Richard N. Farmer. LC 82-21744. (Research for Business Decisions Ser.: No. 59). 136p. 1983. 42.95 o.p. (ISBN 0-8357-1395-4). UMI Res Pr.
Auditorium Acoustics. R. Mackenzie. (Illus.). x, 231p. 1975. 52.00 o.p. (ISBN 0-85334-646-1, Pub. by Elsevier Applied Sci England). Elsevier.
Auditor's Study & Evaluation of Internal Control in EDP Systems. 1977. pap. 6.00 o.p. (ISBN 0-685-58472-0). Am Inst CPA.
Auditory & Reading Comprehension Exercises in French. Mary Bernstein. (gr. 10-12). 1964. pap. 1.25 o.p. (ISBN 0-88345-021-6, 17466); tchrs. ed. 2.50 o.p. (ISBN 0-88345-022-4, 17467). Prentice ESL.
Auditory Disorders. Susan Jerger & James Jerger. 187p. 1981. text ed. 20.95 o.p. (ISBN 0-316-46140-7). Little.
Auditory Management of Hearing-Impaired Children. Mark Ross & Thomas G. Giolas. LC 78-6114. (Perspectives in Audiology Ser.). (Illus.). 394p. 1978. text ed. 19.00x o.p. (ISBN 0-8391-1246-7, 1320). Pro Ed.
Auditory Perception: Diagnosis & Development for Language & Reading Abilities. Thomas Oakland & Fern C. Williams. LC 79-158860. 175p. (Orig.). 1971. pap. 9.00x o.p. (ISBN 0-87562-028-0). Spec Child.
Auditory Processing & Learning Disabilities. Donald L. Rampp. LC 79-55973. (Cliffs Speech & Hearing Ser.). (Illus., Orig.). 1980. pap. text ed. 4.95 o.p. (ISBN 0-8220-1830-6). Cliffs.
Auditory, Reading & Dialogue Comprehension Exercises in Spanish. Susanne Vasi & Joseph Tomasino. (gr. 9-12). 1973. pap. text ed. 2.95 cancelled o.p. (ISBN 0-88345-025-9, 18113); tchr's manual 3.50 o.p. (ISBN 0-88345-026-7, 18135); cassettes 40.00 o.p. (ISBN 0-685-48110-7). Prentice ESL.
Audubon Notebook. Illus. by John J. Audubon. LC 81-10637. lib. bdg. 15.90 o.p. (ISBN 0-89471-149-0); pap. 5.95 o.p. (ISBN 0-89471-148-2). Running Pr.
Audubon Society Book of Marine Wildlife. Les Line & George Reiger. (Audobon Society Bks.). (Illus.). 1980. 35.00 o.p. (ISBN 0-8109-0672-4). Abrams.
Audubon Society Field Guide to the Natural Places of the Northeast: Inland, Vol. II. Stephen Kulik et al. 364p. 1984. pap. 11.95 o.p. (ISBN 0-394-72282-5). Pantheon.
Auerbach Will. Stephen Birmingham. 416p. 1985. 16.95 o.p. (ISBN 0-316-09646-6). Little.
Auferstehung see Resurrection.
Aufgaben und Lehrsatze Aus der Analysis see Problems & Theorems in Analysis, Vol. 2: Theory of Functions, Zeros, Polynomials, Determinants, Number Theory, Geometry.
Augmenting Economic Measures of Well-Being. Ed. by M. L. Moon & Eugene Smolensky. 1977. 24.50 o.p. (ISBN 0-12-504640-5). Acad Pr.
Augsburg Confession: A Contemporary Commentary. George W. Forell. LC 68-25798. (Orig.). 1968. pap. 6.95 o.p. (ISBN 0-8066-0815-3, 10-0518, Augsburg). Augsburg Fortress.
Augsburg Confession: Anniversary Edition. Tr. by Theodore G. Tappert. 64p. 1980. pap. 1.95 o.p. (ISBN 0-8006-1385-6, 1-1385, Fortress). Augsburg Fortress.
Augsburg Sermons: Gospels - Series A. LC 74-77679. 288p. 1974. 13.50 o.p. (ISBN 0-8066-1430-7, 10-0526, Augsburg). Augsburg Fortress.
Augsburg Sermons: Gospels - Series B. LC 75-2844. 288p. 1975. 14.25 o.p. (ISBN 0-8066-1489-7, 10-0527, Augsburg). Augsburg Fortress.
Augsburg Sermons: Gospels - Series C. LC 73-78262. 1973. 11.50 o.p. (ISBN 0-8066-9485-8, 10-0525, Augsburg). Augsburg Fortress.
Augsburg Sermons Lesser Festivals: Sermons for the 27 Lesser Festivals on Texts from the New Lectionary & Calendar. LC 77-72465. 1977. 11.95 o.p. (ISBN 0-8066-1582-6, 10-0528, Augsburg). Augsburg Fortress.
August, Die She Must. Barbara Corcoran. LC 83-15657. 180p. (gr. 5-9). 1984. 11.95 o.s.i. (ISBN 0-689-31012-9, Atheneum Childrens Bks). Macmillan.

August Nineteen Ninety-Nine. Frank H. Stuckert. 1978. 7.00 o.p. (ISBN 0-682-48947-6). Exposition-Phoenix.

August Sander. Illus. by August Sander. LC 77-70069. (The Aperture History of Photography Ser.). (Illus.). 96p. 1978. 25.00 o.p. Aperture.

August Sander: Citizens of the Twentieth Century, Portrait Photographs, 1892-1952. Ed. by Gunther Sander. Tr. by Linda Keller from Ger. (Illus.). 560p. 1986. 55.00 o.p. (ISBN 0-262-19248-9). MIT Pr.

August Strindberg. Margery Morgan. Ed. by Bruce King & Adele King. LC 85-47546. (Modern Dramatists Ser.). 172p. 1986. 27.50 o.s.i. (ISBN 0-394-54716-0). Grove.

August Strindberg. Margery Morgan. Ed. by Bruce King & Adele King. LC 85-47546. (Modern Dramatists Ser.). 172p. 1986. pap. 11.95 o.s.i. (ISBN 0-394-62065-8, Ever). Grove.

Augusta Played. Kelly Cherry. 1979. 9.95 o.p. (ISBN 0-395-27573-3). HM.

Augustan England. Geoffrey Holmes. 352p. 1982. text ed. 45.00 o.p. (ISBN 0-04-942178-6). Unwin Hyman.

Augustans & Romantics, Sixteen Eighty-Nine to Eighteen Thirty. 2nd rev. ed. Henry V. Dyson & John E. Butt. Repr. of 1950 ed. 39.00x o.p. (ISBN 0-403-03061-7). Somerset Pub.

Auguste Lepere: Peintre et Graveur. Charles Saunier. (Illus.). 284p. (Orig., Fr.). 1982. pap. 85.00 o.s.i. (ISBN 0-915346-47-8). A Wofsy Fine Arts.

Augustus & Lady Maude: A Victorian Novel. LC 85-70898. (Victorian Library). 224p. (Orig.). 1985. pap. 3.95 o.s.i. (ISBN 0-394-62070-4, BC). Grove.

Augustus Saint-Gaudens: Master Sculptor. Kathryn Greenthal. (Reference Publications - Visual Arts Ser.). (Illus.). 1985. lib. bdg. 49.50 o.s.i. (ISBN 0-8161-8789-4). G K Hall.

Aujourd'hui. Raymond Ortali. (Orig., Fr.). 1976. pap. text ed. 8.75 o.p. (ISBN 0-15-504303-X, HC). HarBraceJ.

Aung San. Aung San Suu Kyi. LC 84-194440. (Leaders of Asia Ser.). 1984. pap. 4.95 o.p. (ISBN 0-318-12096-8). U of Queensland Pr.

Aunt Agatha Plays Tournament Bridge. Freddie North. 176p. 1984. 19.95 o.p. (ISBN 0-571-13341-X); pap. 7.95 o.p. (ISBN 0-571-13342-8). Faber & Faber.

Aunt Bernice. Jack Gantos. LC 77-17858. (Illus.). (gr. k-3). 1978. reinforced bdg. 6.95 o.p. (ISBN 0-395-26461-8). HM.

Aunt Erma's Cope Book. Erma Bombeck. 1984. pap. 3.50 o.p. (ISBN 0-449-20758-7, Crest). Fawcett.

Aunt Jeanne. Georges Simenon. Tr. by Geoffrey Sainsbury from Fr. LC 82-21359. 160p. 1983. 13.95 o.p. (ISBN 0-15-109792-5). HarBraceJ.

Aunt Mary's Wonderland: Short Stories for Children. Mary S. English. LC 84-204943. (ps-2). 1984. 7.50 o.p. (ISBN 0-682-40228-1). Exposition-Phoenix.

Aunt Maude & le Faisan d'Or. Barbara Devor. 1981. 6.00 o.p. (ISBN 0-682-49563-8). Exposition-Phoenix.

Aunt Vinnie's Invasion. Karin Anckarsvard. LC 62-17039. (Illus.). 128p. (gr. 5 up). 1962. 4.50 o.p. (ISBN 0-15-204621-6, HJ). HarBraceJ.

Aura of Roses. Carol Kluz. 40p. 1986. 5.75 o.p. (ISBN 0-8062-2766-4). Carlton.

Auraria: Where Denver Began. Don D. Etter. LC 72-85656. (Illus.). 100p. 1980. pap. 11.95 o.p. (ISBN 0-87081-093-6). Univ Pr Colo.

Aurora Floyd, 3 vols. Ed. by Robert L. Wolff. LC 79-50468. (Mary Elizabeth Braddon Ser.: Vol. 1). 1979. Set. lib. bdg. 138.00 o.p. (ISBN 0-8240-4350-2). Garland Pub.

Aus Nah und Fern. 2nd ed. L. B. Foltin. 1972. pap. 8.75 o.p. (ISBN 0-395-04464-2). HM.

Aus Unserer Zeit. 3rd. ed. Ed. by Ian Loram & Leland Phelps. LC 78-141590. 423p. (Ger.). 1972. pap. text ed. 11.95x o.p. (ISBN 0-393-09389-1). Norton.

Auschwitz & the Allies. Martin Gilbert. (Illus.). 368p. 1982. 15.95 o.p. (ISBN 0-03-059284-4); pap. 8.50 o.p. (ISBN 0-03-057058-1). H Holt & Co.

Ausfuehrliches Namenregister und Sachregister Mit Genauem Inhalsverzeichnis der Seither Erschienene Baende 1-90 see Leben des Bischofs Benno der Zweiter von Osnabruck.

Auspices. Cid Corman. (Orig.). 1978. limited signed ed. 35.00 o.p. (ISBN 0-915316-59-5); pap. 6.00 o.p. (ISBN 0-915316-58-7). Pentagram.

Austin & Mabel: The Amherst Affair & Love Letters of Austin Dickinson & Mabel Loomis Todd. Polly Longsworth. pap. 10.95 o.p. (ISBN 0-03-003862-6, Owl Bks). H Holt & Co.

Austin A30 & A35. Kim Henson. (Super Profile Ser.). (Illus.). 56p. 1985. 8.95 o.p. (ISBN 0-85429-469-4, Pub. by G T Foulis Ltd). Haynes Pubns.

Austin Seven. Chris Harvey. (Classic Car Ser.: No. 11). (Illus.). 256p. 1985. 29.95 o.p. (ISBN 0-946609-04-7, Pub. by Oxford Ill Pr). Haynes Pubns.

Austin, Texas. Andy Clausen. 1981. lib. bdg. 18.00 o.p. (ISBN 0-916908-33-X); pap. 3.50 o.p. (ISBN 0-916908-16-X). Place Herons.

Austin: The Texas Monthly Guidebook. Richard Zelade. Ed. by Scott Lubeck. 272p. 1984. pap. 9.95 o.p. (ISBN 0-932012-69-8). Texas Month Pr.

Austral English. Edward E. Morris. LC 68-18003. 550p. 1968. Repr. of 1898 ed. 65.00x o.p. (ISBN 0-8103-3287-6). Gale.

Australia. (Post Guides Ser.). (Illus.). 144p. (Orig.). 1987. pap. 8.95 o.p. (ISBN 962-10-0039-4). Hunter Pub NY.

Australia. Time-Life Books Editors. (Library of Nations Staff). (Illus.). 160p. (YA) (gr. 7 up). 1985. lib. bdg. 23.93 o.p. Time-Life.

Australia - A Geography: Space & Society, Vol. 2. 2nd ed. Ed. by D. N. Jeans. (Illus.). 436p. 1987. 55.00 o.p. (ISBN 0-424-00120-9, Pub. by Sydney U Pr); pap. 35.00 o.p. (ISBN 0-424-00125-X, Pub. by Sydney U Pr). Intl Spec Bk.

Australia - A Geography: The Natural Environment, Vol. 1. 2nd ed. Ed. by D. N. Jeans. (Illus.). 347p. 1986. 55.00 o.p. (ISBN 0-424-00114-4, Pub. by Sydney U Pr); pap. 35.00 o.p. (ISBN 0-424-00124-1, Pub. by Sydney U Pr). Intl Spec Bk.

Australia: A Travel Survival Kit. 3rd ed. Tony Wheeler. (Illus.). 576p. (Orig.). 1983. pap. 12.95 o.p. (ISBN 0-908086-39-3). Lonely Planet.

Australia & America: 1788-1972. L. G. Churchward. 290p. 1981. 16.95 o.p. (ISBN 0-88208-202-7, Alternative Publishing Cooperative Ltd). Chicago Review.

Australia & Nuclear War. Ed. by M. A. Denborough. LC 84-148159. 224p. 1985. 34.50 o.p. (ISBN 0-949614-05-X, Pub by Croom Helm Ltd); pap. 15.50 o.p. (ISBN 0-949614-09-2, Pub. by Croom Helm Ltd). Routledge Chapman & Hall.

Australia & the Colonial Question at the United Nations. W. J. Hudson. LC 79-86488. (Illus.). 1970. 8.00x o.p. (ISBN 0-8248-0096-6, Eastwest Ctr). UH Pr.

Australia & the Jewish Refugees, 1933-48. Michael Blakeney. 335p. 1985. 29.95 o.p. (ISBN 0-949614-18-1, Pub. by Croom Helm Ltd). Routledge Chapman & Hall.

Australia & the League of Nations. Ed. by W. J. Hudson. 224p. 1980. 36.00x o.p. (ISBN 0-424-00084-9, Pub. by Sydney U Pr Australia). Intl Spec Bk.

Australia in Twenty-Two Days. John Gottberg. (Twenty-Two Days Ser.). (Illus.). 136p. (Orig.). 1987. pap. 6.95 o.p. (ISBN 0-912528-75-3). John Muir.

Australia National Bib. 1985. 86.00x o.p. (ISBN 0-8002-3914-8, Natl Library Aust). Intl Pubns Serv.

Australia on Twenty Five Dollars Day. 247p. 1984. pap. 9.95 o.p. (ISBN 0-671-46798-0). Prentice Hall Pr.

Australia, Papua & New Guinea. Ed. by W. J. Hudson. 198p. 1971. pap. 16.00x o.p. (ISBN 0-424-06280-1, Pub. by Sydney U Pr). Intl Spec Bk.

Australian & New Zealand Library Resources. Robert B. Downs. 164p. 1979. 43.00x o.p. (ISBN 0-7201-0913-2). Mansell.

Australian Architecture, 1901 to 1951: Sources of Modernism. Ed. by Donald L. Johnson. 240p. 1980. 43.00x o.p. (ISBN 0-424-00071-7, Pub. by Sydney U Pr Australia). Intl Spec Bk.

Australian Bibliography: A Guide to Printed Sources of Information. D. H. Borchardt. 284p. 1978. 70.00 o.p. (ISBN 0-08-020551-8); pap. 70.00 o.p. (ISBN 0-08-020550-X). Pergamon.

Australian Birds in Colour. Keith Hindwood. (Illus.). 1967. 10.00x o.p. (ISBN 0-8248-0066-4, Eastwest Ctr). UH Pr.

Australian Capital Cities: Historical Essays. J. W. McCarty & C. B. Schedvin. pap. 17.00x o.p. (ISBN 0-424-00048-2, Pub. by Sydney U Pr). Intl Spec Bk.

Australian Christian Play. Janell G. Dyer. 1986. 11.95 o.p. (ISBN 0-533-06485-6). Vantage.

Australian Company: Studies in Strategy & Structure. W. J. Byrt. 171p. 1981. 20.00 o.p. (ISBN 0-7099-0615-3, Pub. by Croom Helm Ltd). Routledge Chapman & Hall.

Australian Conference on Electrochemistry, 1st. Ed. by J. A. Friend. 1965. 235.00 o.p. (ISBN 0-08-010501-7). Pergamon.

Australian Crustaceans in Colour. Anthony Healy & John C. Yaldwyn. LC 74-138064. (Illus.). 1971. 7.45 o.p. (ISBN 0-8048-0957-7). C E Tuttle.

Australian Encyclopedia. Ed. by John Shaw. (Illus.). 864p. 1985. 49.95 o.p. G K Hall.

Australian Financial System after the Campbell Report. J. O. Perkins. 152p. 1982. pap. 14.00x o.p. (ISBN 0-522-84253-4, Pub. by Melbourne U Pr Australia). Intl Spec Bk.

Australian Finches. Curt A. Enehjelm. Tr. by U. Erich Friese from Ger. Orig. Title: Australische Prachtfinken. (Illus.). 1979. 5.95 o.p. (ISBN 0-87666-987-9, KW-O27). TFH Pubns.

Australian Mining, Minerals & Oil. Ed. by Alan Deans. 610p. 1984. 110.00x o.p. (ISBN 0-317-04431-1, NO. 5060). Routledge Chapman & Hall.

Australian National Bibliography, 1981. 21st ed. National Library of Australia Staff. LC 63-33739. 1231p. 1982. 67.50x o.p. (ISBN 0-8002-3014-0). Intl Pubns Serv.

Australian Parrots. 2nd ed. Joseph M. Forshaw. (Illus.). 224p. 1980. 75.00 o.p. (ISBN 0-686-62188-3); write for ltd. ed. o.p. Eastview.

Australian Parsonage: The Settler & the Savage in Western Australia. Mrs. Edward Millet. 415p. 1982. 35.00x o.p. (ISBN 0-85564-191-6, Pub. by U of W Austral Pr). Intl Spec Bk.

Australian Patchwork & Applique. Nan Bosler. 36p. (Orig.). 1985. pap. 5.95 o.p. (ISBN 0-86417-004-1, Pub. by Kangaroo Pr). Intl Spec Bk.

Australian Policies & Attitudes Toward China. Henry S. Albinski. 1966. 52.50x o.p. (ISBN 0-691-03004-9). Princeton U Pr.

Australian Science Fiction. Ed. by Van Iken. 320p. 1984. 16.95 o.s.i. (ISBN 0-89733-104-4); pap. 8.95 o.s.i. (ISBN 0-89733-103-6). Academy Chi Pubs.

Australian Social Security Today. Ed. by T. H. Kewley. 233p. 1980. 31.00x o.p. (ISBN 0-424-00067-9, Pub. by Sydney U Pr Australia). Intl Spec Bk.

Australian Town Planning: Uniformity & Change. Rev., 2nd ed. A. S. Fogg. 601p. 1983. text ed. 27.50x o.p. (ISBN 0-7022-1951-7). U of Queensland Pr.

Australian Unions. D. W. Rawson & Sue Wrightson. 123p. 1985. 19.95 o.p. (ISBN 0-949614-13-0, Pub. by Croom Helm Ltd). Routledge Chapman & Hall.

Australian Ways. Ed. by Lenore Manderson. 240p. 1985. text ed. 24.95x o.p. (ISBN 0-86861-703-2); pap. text ed. 12.95x o.p. (ISBN 0-86861-671-0). Unwin Hyman.

Australians & British: Social & Political Connections. Ed. by J. D. Miller. 228p. 1986. 29.00 o.p. (ISBN 0-949614-36-X, Pub. by Croom Helm UK). Routledge Chapman & Hall.

Australia's Outlook on Asia. Werner Levi. LC 78-26904. 1979. Repr. of 1958 ed. lib. bdg. 35.00x o.p. (ISBN 0-313-20897-2, LEAO). Greenwood.

Australische Prachtfinken see Australian Finches.

Austria. Bill Harris. 1988. 15.95 o.s.i. (ISBN 0-517-65125-4). Crown.

Austria: A Phaidon Cultural Guide. Phaidon Press Limited Staff. 560p. 1985. 17.95 o.p. (ISBN 0-13-053836-1). P-H.

Austria & Switzerland. Shirley Harrison & John Harrison. LC 82-61195. (Pocket Guide Ser.). (Illus.). 1983. pap. 5.95 o.p. (ISBN 0-528-84892-5). Rand McNally.

Austria-Hungary & Great Britain, 1908-1914. Alfred F. Pribram. LC 70-138174. 328p. 1972. Repr. of 1951 ed. lib. bdg. 35.00x o.p. (ISBN 0-8371-5631-9, PRAG). Greenwood.

Austria, Switzerland & Italy. (AA Road Map Ser.). Date not set. (ISBN 0-86145-018-3, Pub. by Auto Assn England). Salem Hse Pubs.

Austrian Achievement: 1700-1800. Ernst Wangermann. (History of European Civilization Library). (Illus.). 216p. 1973. pap. text ed. 6.95 o.p. (ISBN 0-15-504337-4, HC). HarBraceJ.

Austro-German Relations in the Anschluss Era. Radomir Luza. 432p. 1975. 52.50x o.p. (ISBN 0-691-07568-9). Princeton U Pr.

Auswertung und Deutung des EKG 11. Auflage. A. H. Lemmerz & R. R. Schmidt. (Illus.). 1976. pap. 32.75 o.p. (ISBN 3-8055-0548-5). S Karger.

Authentic Arthritis Diet & the Problem of Alkalosis. Victor J. Manley. 1986. 10.95 o.p. (ISBN 0-533-06674-3). Vantage.

Authentic Counselor. 2nd ed. John J. Pietrofesa et al. 1978. pap. 20.50 o.p. (ISBN 0-395-30697-3). HM.

Authentic Pasta Book. Fred Plotkin. 1985. 16.45 o.p. (ISBN 0-671-50909-8). S&S.

Authentic Preaching. Arndt L. Halvorson. LC 81-52269. 192p. (Orig.). 1982. pap. 9.95 o.p. (ISBN 0-8066-1901-5, 10-0535, Augsburg). Augsburg Fortress.

Authenticity & Learning: Nietzsche's Educational Philosophy. David E. Cooper. (International Library of the Philosophy of Education). 200p. 1983. 24.95X o.p. (ISBN 0-7100-9552-X). Routledge Chapman & Hall.

Author & Classified Catalogues of the Royal Botanic Gardens Library, 9 vols. Royal Botanic Gardens Library Staff, Kew, England. 1973. lib. bdg. 495.00 author 5 vols. o.p. (ISBN 0-8161-1086-7, Hall Library); lib. bdg. 415.00 4 vols. o.p. (ISBN 0-8161-1087-5). G K Hall.

Author & Subject Catalogues of the Library of the Peabody Museum of Archaeology & Ethnology, Second Supplement, 6 vols. Harvard University, Peabody Museum of Archaeology & Ethnology Staff. 1972. Set. 835.00 o.p. (ISBN 0-8161-0960-5, Hall Library). G K Hall.

Author & Subject Catalogues of the Library of the Peabody Museum of Archaeology & Ethnology, 54 vols. Harvard University, Peabody Museum of Archaeology & Ethnology Staff. 1970. Set. lib. bdg. 5825.00 o.p. (ISBN 0-8161-0647-9, Hall Library). G K Hall.

Author & Subject Catalogues of the Library of the Peabody Museum of Archaeology & Ethnology, Third Supplement, 7 vols. Harvard University, Peabody Museum of Archaeology & Ethnology Staff. 1975. Set. lib. bdg. 965.00 o.p. (ISBN 0-8161-1168-5, Hall Library). G K Hall.

Author & Subject Catalogues of the Library of the Peabody Museum of Archaeology & Ethnology: Fourth Supplement, 7 vols. Peabody Museum of Archaeology & Ethnology Editors. 1979. lib. bdg. 980.00 set o.p. (ISBN 0-8161-0253-8, Hall Library). G K Hall.

Author! Author! Ed. by Richard Findlater. 300p. 1984. 16.95 o.p. (ISBN 0-571-13377-0); pap. 7.95 o.p. (ISBN 0-571-13409-2). Faber & Faber.

Author Bibliography of English Language Fiction in the Library of Congress Through 1950, 8 vols. 1976. Set. 790.00 o.p. (ISBN 0-8161-0966-4, Hall Library). G K Hall.

Author Biographies Master Index. 2nd ed. 1664p. 1984. 225.00x o.p. (ISBN 0-8103-0662-X). Gale.

Author Biography Master Index 2nd Edition Supplement. Ed. by Barbara McNeil. 409p. 1986. 105.00x o.p. (ISBN 0-8103-1088-0). Gale.

Author Catalog of the Library of the New York Academy of Medicine, 43 Vols. New York Academy of Medicine Staff. 1970. Set. lib. bdg. 3900.00 o.p. (ISBN 0-8161-0829-3, Hall Library). G K Hall.

Author Catalog of the Library of the New York Academy of Medicine, 1st Suppl, 4 vols. New York Academy of Medicine Staff. 1974. Set. lib. bdg. 495.00 o.p. (ISBN 0-8161-0851-X, Hall Library). G K Hall.

Author Catalog of the Peruvian Collection of the National Library of Peru, 6 vols. National Library of Peru Staff. Ed. by Maria C. De Gaviria. 1979. Set. lib. bdg. 685.00 o.p. (ISBN 0-8161-0250-3, Hall LIbrary). G K Hall.

Author from a Savage People. Bette Pesetsky. (Hall Fiction Paperbacks Ser.). 208p. 1986. pap. 5.95 o.p. (ISBN 0-8398-2904-3). G K Hall.

Author, Subject & Manuscript Catalogs of the Sophia Smith Collection (Women's History Archive, 7 vols. Smith College, Sophia Smith Collection Staff. 1975. Set. lib. bdg. 655.00 o.p. (ISBN 0-8161-0001-2, Hall Library). G K Hall.

Author-Title & Chronological Catalogs of Americana, 1493-1860, in the William L. Clements Library, 7 vols. University of Michigan, Ann Arbor, Clements, William L., Library Staff. 1970. Set. 645.00 o.p. (ISBN 0-8161-0874-9, Hall Library). G K Hall.

Author-Title & Subject Catalogs of the Centers for Disease Control Library. Disease Control Centers, for Atlanta, Georgia Staff. 1983. lib. bdg. 780.00 o.p. (ISBN 0-8161-0395-X, Hall Library). G K Hall.

Author-Title & Subject Catalogs of the Ethel Percy Andrus Gerontology Center, 2 vols. University of Southern California Staff. 1976. Set. lib. bdg. 200.00 o.p. (ISBN 0-8161-1095-6, Hall Library). G K Hall.

Author-Title Catalog, 35 Vols. John Crerar Library Staff. 1970. Set. 3460.00 o.p. (ISBN 0-8161-0728-9, Hall Library). G K Hall.

Author-Title Catalog of the Baker Library, 22 vols. Harvard University, Graduate School of Business Administration Staff. 1971. Set. 2475.00 o.p. (ISBN 0-8161-0893-5, Hall Library). G K Hall.

Author-Title Catalog of the Department Library: First Supplement. U. S. Department of Health, Education & Welfare, Washington, D. C. Staff. Incl. Author-Title Catolog, 7 vols. lib. bdg. 765.00 (ISBN 0-8161-1109-X). 1973 (Hall Library). G K Hall.

Author-Title Catalog of the Department Library, 29 vols. Ed. by U. S. Department of Health, Education & Welfare, Washington, D. C. Staff. 1970. Set. 2865.00 o.p. (ISBN 0-8161-0717-3, Hall Library). G K Hall.

Author-Title Catalog of the Francis A. Countway Library of Medicine for Imprints Through 1959, 10 vols. Harvard Medical Library Staff & Boston Medical Library Staff. 8104p. 1973. Set. lib. bdg. 1595.00 o.p. (ISBN 0-8161-1024-7, Hall Library). G K Hall.

Authoritarian Personality. T. W. Adorno et al. 1969. pap. 9.95 o.p. (ISBN 0-393-00492-9, N492, Norton Lib). Norton.

Titles

Authority: A Philosophical Analysis. Ed. by R. Baine Harris. LC 75-11666. 224p. 1976. 15.50 o.s.i. (ISBN 0-8173-6620-2); pap. 7.95 o.s.i. (ISBN 0-8173-6621-0). U of Ala Pr.
Authority & the Individual. Bertrand Russell. (Unwin Paperbacks Ser.). 1977. pap. 3.95 o.p. (ISBN 0-04-170030-9). Unwin Hyman.
Authority Control in the University of California Union Catalog. rev. ed. Dorothy McPherson. (Working Paper: No. 9). 1980. 5.00 o.p. (ISBN 0-686-87250-9). UCDLA.
Authority in Social Casework. R. Foren & R. Bailey. 1968. pap. 80.00 o.p. (ISBN 0-08-012962-5). Pergamon.
Authority of Experience: Essays in Feminist Criticism. Ed. by Arlyn Diamond & Lee Edwards. LC 76-8755. 320p. 1977. 17.50x o.p. (ISBN 0-87023-220-7). U of Mass Pr.
Authority of Experts: Studies in History & Theory. Ed. by Thomas L. Haskell. LC 83-48173. (Interdisciplinary Studies in History Ser.). 320p. 1984. 22.50x o.p. (ISBN 0-253-31079-2). Ind U Pr.
Authority of the Bible & the Rise of the Modern World. Henning G. Reventlow. Tr. by John Bowden from Ger. LC 83-48921. 688p. 1984. 19.95 o.p. (ISBN 0-8006-0288-9, 1-288, Fortress). Augsburg Fortress.
Author's Guide. Little, Brown & Co. College Division Staff. pap. 3.95 o.p. (ISBN 0-316-15183-1). Little.
Autism & Severe Psychopathology: Advances in Child Behavioral Analysis Therapy, Vol. II. Ed. by John J. Steffen & Paul Karoly. LC 82-47799. 352p. 1982. 35.00x o.p. (ISBN 0-669-05639-1). Lexington Bks.
Autism: Diagnosis, Current Research & Management. Ed. by Ritvo et al. LC 76-1931. 1976. 25.00 o.p. (ISBN 0-88331-112-7). Luce.
Autistic Children: Teaching, Community & Research Approaches. Ed. by Brian Roberts & Barbara Furneaux. (Special Needs in Education Ser.). 1977. 19.95x o.p. (ISBN 0-7100-8704-7). Routledge Chapman & Hall.
Auto Album. Tad Burness. (Illus.). 175p. 1983. pap. 6.70 o.p. (ISBN 0-395-33966-9). HM.
Auto Body Repair for the Do-It-Yourselfer. Advanced Learning, Inc. LC 76-1132. 1976. pap. 6.95 o.p. (ISBN 0-672-23238-3, Pub. by Audel). Macmillan.
Auto-Carto Seven: International Syposium on Computer Assisted Cartography. Intro. by Steven J. Vogel. (Illus.). 599p. (Orig.). 1985. pap. 33.00 o.p. (ISBN 0-937294-65-9). ASP & RS.
Auto Carto 5: International Symposium on Computer-Assisted Cartography, Jan. 1983. 752p. 1983. (14.00 member) 19.00 o.p. (ISBN 0-937294-44-6). ASP & RS.
Auto Compendium. Eric V. Masterman. LC 85-73333. (Illus.). 256p. 1986. pap. 9.95 o.s.i. (ISBN 0-9615753-5-2). Arcas Pr.
Auto-Immunity in the Endocrine System. R. Volpe. (Endocrinology Monographs: Vol. 20). (Illus.). 210p. 1981. 52.00 o.p. (ISBN 0-387-10677-4). Springer-Verlag.
Auto-Instructional Text in Correct Writing, Form A. 2nd ed. Eugenia Butler et al. 416p. 1976. pap. text ed. 13.95 o.p. (ISBN 0-669-95844-1). Heath.
Auto Mechanics. Jay Webster. LC 79-2488. 576p. (gr. 10-12). text ed. cancelled o.s.i. (ISBN 0-02-829770-9); cancelled o.s.i. (ISBN 0-02-829780-6); cancelled o.s.i. (ISBN 0-02-829790-3). Glencoe.
Auto Racing. Charles I. Coombs. LC 73-153770. (Illus.). (gr. 5-9). 1971. 11.75 o.p. (ISBN 0-688-21053-8); PLB 8.59 o.p. (ISBN 0-688-31053-2). Morrow.
Auto Racing U. S. A., 1986: The Year in Review. Ed. by Leslie A. Taylor. 1987. 39.95 o.p. (ISBN 0-942103-00-9). Enterprise Del.
Auto Repairs for Dummies. D. Sclar. LC 75-45103. (Illus.). 300p. 1976. (ISBN 0-07-055870-1, GB); (ISBN 0-07-055871-X). McGraw.
Autobiographies of Noah Webster: From the Letters & Essays, Memoir & Diary. Intro. by Richard M. Rollins. 350p. 1989. text ed. 29.95x o.p. (ISBN 0-87249-574-4). U of SC Pr.
Autobiography. 2nd ed. M. K. Gandhi. 1979. pap. 10.00 o.p. E J Brill USA.
Autobiography & Imagination: Studies in Self-Scrutiny. John Pilling. 200p. 1981. 21.95x o.p. (ISBN 0-7100-0730-2). Routledge Chapman & Hall.
Autobiography: Journey East, Journey West, 1907 to 1937, Vol. I. Mircea Eliade. Tr. by Mac L. Ricketts. LC 80-8357. 352p. pap. 9.57 o.p. (ISBN 0-06-062144-3, RD 480). HarpR.
Autobiography of a Boy. G. S. Street. LC 76-19978. (Decadent Consciousness Ser.: Vol. 23). 1977. Repr. of 1894 ed. lib. bdg. 46.00 o.p. (ISBN 0-8240-2772-8). Garland Pub.
Autobiography of a Chinese Girl. Hsieh Ping-Ying. 224p. 1986. pap. 8.95 o.p. (ISBN 0-86358-052-1, Pandora Pr). Routledge Chapman & Hall.
Autobiography of a Yogi. 3rd ed. P. Yogananda. 1951. (ISBN 0-8022-1950-0). Philos Lib.
Autobiography of Alice B. Toklas. Gertrude Stein. LC 79-92497. 1980. o.s. 6.95 o.p. (ISBN 0-394-60487-3). Modern Lib.
Autobiography of an American Communist: A Personal View of a Political Life, 1925-1975. Peggy Dennis. LC 77-23607. (Illus.). 288p. 1977. 12.95 o.p. (ISBN 0-88208-081-4); pap. 5.95 o.s.i. (ISBN 0-88208-090-3). Chicago Review.
Autobiography of Eleanor Roosevelt. Eleanor Roosevelt. LC 84-9093. 456p. 1984. pap. 9.95 o.p. (ISBN 0-8398-2851-9, Gregg). G K Hall.
Autobiography of G. K. Chesterton, Vol. XVI. G. K. Chesterton. LC 85-81511. (Illus.). 341p. 1988. pap. 14.95 o.p. Ignatius Pr.
Autobiography of Guibert, Abbot of Nogent-Sous-Coucy. Guibert De Nogent. Tr. by C. C. Bland from Lat. LC 79-11248. 1980. Repr. of 1926 ed. lib. bdg. 35.00x o.p. (ISBN 0-313-21460-3, GUAU). Greenwood.
Autobiography of John Fitch. Ed. by Frank D. Prager. LC 76-8596. (Memoirs Ser.: Vol. 113). (Illus.). 1976. pap. 10.00 o.p. (ISBN 0-87169-113-2). Am Philos.
Autobiography of Lincoln Steffens. Lincoln Steffens. LC 67-7897. (Illus.). 1949. 2.50 o.p. (ISBN 0-15-110283-X). HarBraceJ.
Autobiography of Madame Guyon. Jeanne Guyon. (Shepherd Illustrated Classic Ser.). (Illus.). 5.95 o.p. (ISBN 0-317-52076-8). Christian Bks.
Autobiography of Maxim Gorky, 3 vols. in 1. Maxim Gorky. Tr. by Isidore Schneider. Incl. My Childhood; In the World; My Universities. 13.25 o.p. (ISBN 0-8446-2143-9). Peter Smith.
Autobiography of Miss Jane Pittman. Ernest J. Gaines. LC 86-24381. 255p. 1987. 16.95 o.p. (ISBN 0-385-24017-1). Doubleday.
Autobiography of Prayer. Albert E. Day. 1979. pap. 3.95x o.p. (ISBN 0-8358-0384-8). Upper Room.
Autobiography of Rudolf Jordan. Rudolf Jordan. LC 80-70948. (Illus.). 256p. 1981. 10.95 o.p. (ISBN 0-8119-0415-6). Fell.
Autobiography of St. Ignatius Loyola, with Related Documents. St. Ignatius Loyola. Tr. by Joseph F. O'Callaghan. 16.00 o.p. (ISBN 0-8446-5240-7). Peter Smith.
Autobiography of Venerable Marie of the Incarnation. Tr. by John J. Sullivan. 1964. 3.95 o.p. (ISBN 0-8294-0076-1). Loyola.
Autobiography of Wilhelm Stekel. Wilhelm Stekel. 1950. 6.95 o.p. (ISBN 0-87140-847-3). Liveright.
Autobiography of Will Rogers. Will Rogers. Ed. by Donald Day. 1980. pap. 1.50 o.p. (ISBN 0-380-00213-2, 34397). Avon.
Autobiography: Volume I, Journey East, Journey West 1907-1937. Mircea Eliade. LC 80-8357. 352p. 1981. 17.50i o.p. (ISBN 0-06-062142-7). HarpR.
Autobot Alert! Judith B. Stamper. (Transformers Find Your Fate Junior Ser.: No. 7). (Orig.). (gr. 4 up). 1986. pap. 2.50 o.p. (ISBN 0-345-33388-8, Pub. by Ballantine Trade). Ballantine.
Autobot's Secret Weapon. (Transformer Hardcover Storybks.). (Illus.). 48p. (ps up). 1985. bds. 5.95 o.p. (ISBN 0-517-55904-8). Crown.
AutoCAD Standards for Architects & Engineers. John Albright & Elizabeth Schaeffer. (Illus.). 480p. 1989. cancelled o.s.i. (ISBN 0-934035-55-5); 14.95 o.s.i. (ISBN 0-934035-56-3). New Riders Pub.
Autocourse 1984-1985. Mike Hamilton. (Racing Annual Ser.). (Illus.). 256p. 1985. 39.95 o.p. (ISBN 0-905138-32-5, Pub. by Hazelton England). Motorbooks Intl.
AUTOFACT Europe: Proceedings. Society of Manufacturing Engineers Staff. 1985. write for info. o.p. (ISBN 0-87263-197-4). SME.
AUTOFACT Europe '84: Proceedings. Society of Manufacturing Engineers Staff. 1984. 45.00 o.p. (ISBN 0-87263-123-0). SME.
AUTOFACT Six: Proceedings. Society of Manufacturing Engineers Staff. 1984. 68.00 o.p. (ISBN 0-87263-161-3). SME.
Autographensammler - Lebenslaenglich. Rudolf F. Kallir. (Illus.). 1977. 18.70x o.p. (ISBN 3-7611-0518-5). M S Rosenberg.
Autographs & Manuscripts: A Collector's Manual. Ed. by Edmund Berkeley, Jr. (Illus.). 1978. 24.95 o.s.i. (ISBN 0-684-15622-9, ScribR). Scribner.
Autohypnosis: A Step-by-Step Guide to Self-Hypnosis. Ronald Shone. (Illus.). 160p. (Orig.). 1983. pap. 6.95 o.p. (ISBN 0-8069-7790-6). Sterling.
Autoimmune Aspects of Endocrine Disorders. Ed. by A. Pinchera & D. Doniach. (Serono Symposia Ser.: No. 33). 1981. 115.00 o.p. (ISBN 0-12-556750-2). Acad Pr.
Autoimmunity & the Thyroid. Ed. by Paul G. Walfish et al. 1985. 48.50 o.p. (ISBN 0-12-731950-6). Acad Pr.
Autoimmunity: Genetic, Immunologic, Virologic & Clinical Aspects. Ed. by N. Talal. 1978. 104.00 o.p. (ISBN 0-12-682350-2). Acad Pr.
Autoloading Pistols: Gun Digest Book Of. Dean A. Grennell. LC 83-72348. (Illus.). 288p. (Orig.). 1983. pap. 11.95 o.p. (ISBN 0-910676-59-3). DBI.
Autologous Transfusion. Ed. by S. Gerald Sandler & Arthur J. Silvergleid. 1983. 16.00 o.p. (ISBN 0-914404-89-X). Am Assn Blood.
Automach Australia 1985: Proceedings. Society of Manufacturing Engineers Staff. 1985. 55.00 o.p. (ISBN 0-87263-191-5). SME.
Automania: Man & the Motor Car. Julian Pettifer & Nigel Turner. LC 84-48260. (Illus.). 288p. 1984. 19.95 o.p. (ISBN 0-316-70371-0). Little.
Automata, Languages, & Programming: Aarhus, Denmark 1982. Ed. by M. Nielsen & E. M. Schmidt. (Lecture Notes in Computer Science: Vol. 140). 614p. 1982. pap. 27.60 o.p. (ISBN 0-387-11576-5). Springer-Verlag.
Automata Theory. Ed. by E. R. Caianiello. (Spring School Lectures, 1964). 1966. 55.00 o.p. (ISBN 0-12-154550-4). Acad Pr.
Automata Theory & Modeling of Biological Systems. M. L. Tsetlin. (Mathematics in Science & Engineering Ser.). 1973. 77.00 o.p. (ISBN 0-12-701650-3). Acad Pr.
Automated Architect. N. Cross. (Research in Planning & Design Ser.). 178p. 1977. text ed. 18.95x o.p. (ISBN 0-85086-057-1, NO.2934, Pub. by Pion England). Routledge Chapman & Hall.
Automated Deduction Conference: Proceedinngs of Conference, 6th, New York, 1982. Ed. by D. W. Loveland. (Lecture Notes in Computer Science Ser.: Vol. 138). 389p. 1982. pap. 20.00 o.p. (ISBN 0-387-11558-7). Springer-Verlag.
Automated Financial Systems: How to Computerize a Business. Emily R. Myers. LC 83-16194. 192p. 1984. pap. text ed. 24.95 o.p. (ISBN 0-07-044169-3). McGraw.
Automated Guided Vehicle Systems. Thomas Muller. 290p. 1982. 41.00 o.p. (ISBN 0-317-18025-8). Robot Inst Am.
Automated Inventory Management for the Distributor. Gordon Graham. LC 80-17655. 234p. 1983. 24.95 o.p. (ISBN 0-8436-0794-7). Van Nos Reinhold.
Automated Microcode Synthesis. Robert A. Mueller. Ed. by Harold Stone. LC 83-24095. (Computer Science: Computer Architecture & Design Ser.: No. 1). 134p. 1984. 42.95 o.p. (ISBN 0-8357-1498-5). UMI Res Pr.
Automated Performance Optimization of Custom Integrated Circuits. Stephen Trimberger. Ed. by Harold Stone. LC 86-6918. (Computer Science: Very Large Scale Integration Ser.: No. 2). 152p. 1986. 47.95 o.p. (ISBN 0-8357-1747-X). UMI Res Pr.
Automated Process Control Systems: Concepts & Hardware. Ronald P. Hunter. (Illus.). 1978. text ed. 40.00 ref. ed. o.p. (ISBN 0-13-054502-3). P-H.
Automated Structural Analysis: An Introduction. W. R. Spillers. (Pergamon Unified Engineering Ser.: Vol. 7). 182p. 1972. 34.00 o.p. (ISBN 0-08-016782-9). Pergamon.
Automatic & Concealable Firearms Design Book, III. Paladin Press Staff. (Illus.). 64p. 1982. pap. 12.00 o.p. (ISBN 0-87364-224-4). Paladin Pr.
Automatic & Concealable Firearms Design Book, Vol. I. (Illus.). 40p. 1979. pap. text ed. 12.00 o.p. (ISBN 0-87364-165-5). Paladin Pr.
Automatic & Semi-Automatic Gearboxes for Heavy Commercial Vehicles. 175p. 1978. 27.00 o.p. (ISBN 0-85298-392-1, MEP-71). Soc Auto Engineers.
Automatic Control in Desalination & the Oil Industry, Appropriate Applications: Proceedings of the Al Fateh-IFAC Workshop, 1st, Tripoli, Libya, May 1980. Al Fateh Staff & IFAC Staff. Ed. by H. El Hares & T. Dali. LC 81-23412. (Illus.). 209p. 1982. 65.00 o.p. (ISBN 0-08-028698-4, A115, A135). Pergamon.
Automatic Control System. 4th ed. Benjamin C. Kuo. (Illus.). 720p. 1982. text ed. 53.33 o.p. (ISBN 0-13-054817-0). P-H.
Automatic Interpretation & Classification of Images. Ed. by A. Grasselli. (NATO Advanced Study Institute Ser.). 1969. 81.50 o.p. (ISBN 0-12-295850-0). Acad Pr.
Automatic Potentiometric Titrations. Gyula Svehla. 1978. 81.00 o.p. (ISBN 0-08-021590-4). Pergamon.
Automatic Shelving & Book Retrieval: A Contribution Toward a Progressive Philosophy of Library Service for a Research Library. Stanley Humenuk. (Occasional Papers: No. 78). 29p. 1966. pap. 1.00 o.p. (ISBN 0-317-58860-5). U of Ill Lib Info Sci.
Automatic Test Equipment: Hardware, Software & Management. Ed. by Fred Liguori. LC 74-18892. (Illus.). 264p. 1974. 27.70 o.p. (ISBN 0-87942-049-9, PC00364). Inst Electrical.
Automatic Titrators. John P. Phillips. 1959. 58.50 o.p. (ISBN 0-12-553456-6). Acad Pr.
Automatic Transmissions. Commercial Trades Institute Staff. 1972. text ed. 19.95 o.p. (ISBN 0-07-012375-6, G). McGraw.
Automatic Transmissions Workbook on Service & Repair. Howard Tucker. LC 80-67593. (Automotive Technology Ser.). (Illus.). 64p. (Orig.). 1982. pap. text ed. 9.78 o.p. (ISBN 0-8273-1894-4). Delmar.
Automatic Turning Machines. 2nd ed. Ed. by J. E. Matthews et al. (Engineering Craftsmen Ser.: No. H30/3). (Illus.). 1978. spiral bdg 43.50x o.p. (ISBN 0-85083-405-8). Trans-Atl Phila.
Automatic Vehicle Locating System. Edward N. Skomal. 336p. 1981. 41.95 o.p. (ISBN 0-442-24495-9). Van Nos Reinhold.
Automating Apartheid: Computers in South Africa. 70p. 1986. Repr. of 1982 ed. 3.50 o.p. (ISBN 0-317-55998-2). Africa Fund.
Automation. John Diebold. 224p. 1983. 14.95 o.p. (ISBN 0-8144-5756-8). AMACOM.
Automation & Control in Transport. F. T. Barwell. 1972. 45.00 o.p. (ISBN 0-08-016962-7). Pergamon.
Automation & Management. James R. Bright. Repr. of 1958 ed. 30.00 o.s.i. (ISBN 0-08-022293-5). Pergamon.
Automation & Reorganization of Technical Public Services: Kit & Flyer No. 112. 95p. 1985. 20.00 o.p. (ISBN 0-318-18190-8); members 10.00 o.p. (ISBN 0-318-18191-6). OMS.
Automation, Cybernetics, & Society. F. H. George. (Illus.). 300p. 1959. (ISBN 0-8022-0576-3). Philos Lib.
Automation in Buildings. Mary Vance. LC 85-141117. (Architecture Ser.: Bibliograpphy A 1332). 1985. pap. 2.00 o.p. (ISBN 0-89028-282-X). Vance Biblios.
Automation in Libraries. 2nd ed. Richard T. Kimber & A. Boyd. 1974. 60.00 o.p. (ISBN 0-08-017969-X). Pergamon.
Automation, Mechanization & Data Handling in Microbiology. Ed. by A. Baillie & R. J. Gilbert. (Society for Applied Bacteriology Technical Ser.: No. 4). 1970. 54.50 o.p. (ISBN 0-12-073650-0). Acad Pr.
Automation, Production Systems & Computer-Aided Manufacturing. Mikell P. Groover. 1980. text ed. 46.00 o.p. (ISBN 0-13-054668-2). P-H.
Automation Technology for Management & Productivity Advancements Through CAD-CAM & Engineering Data Handling: Proceedings of the Automation Technology Symposium, 3rd, Monterey, Calif, Sept. 1981. Automation Technology Symposium Staff. Ed. by Peter C. Wang. (Illus.). 336p. 1983. text ed. 48.00 o.p. (ISBN 0-13-054593-7). P-H.
Automatische Rechenplanfertigung Bei Programmgesteuerten Rechenmaschinen. H. Rutishauser. 45p. (Ger.). 1961. pap. 8.95x o.p. (ISBN 0-8176-0322-0). Birkhauser.
Automechanics. 3rd ed. Herb Ellinger. (Illus.). 592p. 1983. text ed. 33.00 o.p. (ISBN 0-13-054767-0). P-H.
Automobile Choice & Its Energy Implications. Ed. by Charles Lave. (Illus.). 137p. 1981. pap. 49.50 o.p. (ISBN 0-08-027397-1). Pergamon.
Automobile Garages: A Bibliographic Overview. Coppa & Avery Consultants Staff. LC 85-143841. (Architecture Ser.: Bibliography A-1309). 11p. 1985. pap. 2.00 o.p. (ISBN 0-89028-239-0). Vance Biblios.
Automobile Year: No. 29, 1981-1982, No. 29. (Illus.). 1982. 39.95 o.p. (ISBN 2-88001-105-1). Norton.
Automobile Year, 1984-85. 32nd ed. (Illus.). 228p. 1985. 39.95 o.p. (ISBN 2-8265-0098-8, Pub. by Editions Twenty Four Heures (Switzerland)). Motorbooks Intl.
Automobiles of America: Milestones, Pioneers, Roll Call, Highlights. 4th, rev. ed. Motor Vehicle Manufacturers Association of the United States Staff. (Illus.). 301p. 1974. pap. 9.95 o.p. (ISBN 0-8143-1515-1). Wayne St U Pr.
Automotive Aerodynamics. Society of Automotive Engineers Staff. LC 78-57059. 282p. 1978. Eighteen papers. 50.00 o.p. (ISBN 0-89883-104-0, PT 16). Soc Auto Engineers.
Automotive Air Conditioning Handbook: Installation, Maintenance & Repair. John E. Traister. (Illus.). 280p. 1978. 9.95 o.p. (ISBN 0-8306-9980-5); pap. 10.60 o.p. (ISBN 0-8306-1020-0, 1020). TAB Bks.
Automotive Application of Sensors: Proceedings of the Automotive Engineering Congress, 1978. Society of Automotive Engineers Staff. 72p. 1978. pap. 28.00 o.p. (ISBN 0-89883-199-7, SP427). Soc Auto Engineers.
Automotive Body Repair & Refinishing. William H. Crouse & Donald L. Anglin. (Illus.). 1979. text ed. 29.95 o.p. (ISBN 0-07-014791-4). McGraw.
Automotive Brakes: Text-Lab Manual. 1st ed. Sheldon L. Abbott. pap. cancelled o.s.i.; cancelled o.s.i. (ISBN 0-02-810160-X). Glencoe.
Automotive Chassis & Accessory Circuits. Mathias F. Brejcha & Clifford L. Samuels. LC 76-14835. (Illus.). 1977. pap. text ed. 32.00 o.p. (ISBN 0-13-055475-8). P-H.

Automotive Collision Work. 4th ed. Edward D. Spicer. (Illus.). 1972. pap. 15.96 o.p. (ISBN 0-8269-0022-4). Am Technical.

Automotive Consultant Directory, 1988. 1988. 18.00 o.p. (ISBN 0-89883-756-1, CD88). Soc Auto Engineers.

Automotive Diagnosis & Tune-up. Guy F. Wetzel. (gr. 9-12). 1974. text ed. 19.96 o.p. (ISBN 0-87345-100-7). Glencoe.

Automotive Diagnosis & Tune-up: A Text-Workbook. 2nd ed. James A. Johnson. (Automotive Technology Ser.). (Illus.). 1977. text ed. 22.85 o.p. (ISBN 0-07-032593-6). McGraw.

Automotive Diesels. Edward Ralbovsky. LC 84-19956. 288p. 1985. pap. text ed. 23.95 o.p. (ISBN 0-8273-2217-8); instr's. guide 8.00 o.p. (ISBN 0-8273-2218-6). Delmar.

Automotive Electronics. (Conference Publications: No. 229). 278p. 1983. pap. 71.00 o.s.i. (ISBN 0-85296-283-5, IC229). Inst Elect Eng.

Automotive Electronics & Electrical Equipment. 9th ed. William H. Crouse. LC 79-24438. (Illus.). 1981. text ed. 26.80 o.p. (ISBN 0-07-014831-7). McGraw.

Automotive Emission Control & Tune-up Procedures. 3rd ed. Ignition Manufacturers Institute Staff. (Illus.). 1980. text ed. 22.95 o.p. (ISBN 0-13-054791-3); pap. text ed. 28.67 o.p. (ISBN 0-13-054783-2). P-H.

Automotive Encyclopedia. Rev ed. William K. Toboldt & Larry Johnson. (Illus.). 840p. 1983. text ed. 23.60 o.p. (ISBN 0-87006-436-3). Goodheart.

Automotive Engine Repair. Ivan D. Hinerman. LC 77-81911. 512p. pap. text ed. cancelled o.s.i. (ISBN 0-02-818600-1); cancelled o.s.i. (ISBN 0-686-61256-6). Glencoe.

Automotive Engines. 5th ed. William H. Crouse & Donald L. Anglin. (Automotive Technology Ser.). 1975. text ed. 22.60 o.p. (ISBN 0-07-014602-0). McGraw.

Automotive Fuel Injection Systems: A Technical Guide. 2nd ed. Jan Norbye. LC 81-16833. (Illus.). 182p. 1988. pap. 14.95 o.p. (ISBN 0-87938-139-6). Motorbooks Intl.

Automotive Handbook. Intel Staff. 1200p. 1988. pap. 20.00 o.p. (ISBN 1-55512-030-X, 231792-002). Intel Corp.

Automotive History Collection of the Detroit Public Library: A Simplified Guide to Its Holdings, 2 Vols. Detroit Public Library Staff. 1966. Set. 200.00 o.p. (ISBN 0-8161-0718-1, Hall Library). G K Hall.

Automotive History of Lucky Kellerman. Steve Heller. LC 87-14816. 256p. (Orig.). 1987. pap. 9.95 o.p. (ISBN 0-930031-09-1). Chelsea Green Pub.

Automotive Mechanics. 7th ed. William H. Crouse & Donald L. Anglin. (Illus.). 640p. (gr. 11-12). 1975. text ed. 33.95 o.p. (ISBN 0-07-014535-0). McGraw.

Automotive Power Trains Systems. J. Webster. (Illus.). 296p. 1982. pap. 16.96 o.p. (ISBN 0-8269-0250-2). Am Technical.

Automotive Shop Safety. Rev. ed. Peter Novellino. LC 75-735758. 1987. wkbk. 6.00 o.p. (ISBN 0-8064-0087-0, 411); audio visual pkg. 299.00 o.p. (ISBN 0-8064-0088-9). Bergwall.

Automotive Systems Fuel Lubrication & Cooling. H. Ellinger. 1976. pap. text ed. 32.00 o.p. (ISBN 0-13-055269-0). P-H.

Automotive Transmissions. Sheldon L. Abbott. 320p. pap. text ed. cancelled o.s.i. (ISBN 0-02-810170-7); cancelled o.s.i. (ISBN 0-02-810180-4). Glencoe.

Autonomismo Puertorriqueno. Mariano Negron-Portillo. LC 81-70981. (Coleccion Semilla Ser.). (Illus.). 96p. 1981. pap. 4.95 o.p. (ISBN 0-940238-65-9). Ediciones Hura.

Autonomy & Control at the Workplace: Contexts for Job Redesign. Ed. by John E. Kelly & Chris W. Clegg. (Illus.). 214p. 1982. 29.50 o.p. (ISBN 0-7099-0410-X, Pub. by Croom Helm Ltd). Routledge Chapman & Hall.

Autopilots, Flight Directors & Flight-Control Systems. Paul Garrison. (Illus.). 160p. (Orig.). 1985. pap. 12.60 o.p. (ISBN 0-8306-2356-6, 2356). TAB Bks.

Autopsy of Traditional Real Estate Financing. Stephen R. Mettling. (Residential Financing Resource Library). 16p. (Orig.). 1981. pap. 6.50 o.s.i. (ISBN 0-88462-126-X, 1905-03, Real Estate Ed). Longman Finan.

Autoradiography for Biologists. Ed. by P. B. Gahan. 1972. 38.00 o.p. (ISBN 0-12-273250-2). Acad Pr.

Autoradiography of Diffusible Substances. Ed. by Lloyd J. Roth & Walter Stumpf. 1969. 79.50 o.p. (ISBN 0-12-598550-9). Acad Pr.

Autosegmental Phonology. John A. Goldsmith. Ed. by Jorge Hankamer. LC 78-67735. (Outstanding Dissertations in Linguistics Ser.). 1979. 26.00 o.p. (ISBN 0-8240-9673-8). Garland Pub.

Autumn. A. G. Mojtabai. 1982. 9.70 o.p. (ISBN 0-395-32051-8). HM.

Autumn Grasses & Water: Motifs in Japanese Art. Karen L. Brock. 1983. 25.00 o.s.i. (ISBN 0-317-06768-0); pap. 15.00 o.p. (ISBN 0-317-06769-9). Japan Soc.

Autumn in April. Essie Summers. (Nightingale Ser.). 305p. 1987. pap. 11.95x o.p. (ISBN 0-8161-4190-8, Large Print Bks.). G K Hall.

Autumn in the Enchanted Forest. (Enchanted Forest Ser.). (Illus.). (ps-1). 1985. 2.98 o.s.i. (ISBN 0-517-46979-0). Outlet Bk Co.

Autumn Leaves. Andre Gide. 1956. (ISBN 0-8022-0585-2). Philos Lib.

Autumn of Central Paris: The Defeat of Town Planning, 1850-1970. Anthony Sutcliffe. (Studies in Urban History: No. 1). (Illus.). 1971. 20.00x o.p. (ISBN 0-7735-0115-0, McGill Canada). U of Toronto Pr.

Autumn Wind: A Selection from the Poems of Issa. Tr. by Lewis Mackenzie. LC 83-48874. (Illus.). 126p. 1984. pap. 4.95 o.p. (ISBN 0-87011-657-6). Kodansha.

Auxology: Human Growth in Health & Disorder. L. Gedda. Ed. by P. Parisi. (Serono Symposia Ser.). 1978. 79.50 o.p. (ISBN 0-12-279050-2). Acad Pr.

Available Light. Ed. by Mike Stensvold. LC 80-83130. (Petersen's Photographic Library: Vol. 4). (Illus.). 160p. (Orig.). 1980. pap. 8.95 o.p. (ISBN 0-8227-4042-7). Petersen Pub.

Avalon. Anya Seton. 1965. 10.00 o.p. (ISBN 0-395-08170-X). HM.

Avant Gardener: A Handbook & Sourcebook of All That's New & Useful in Gardening. Thomas Powell & Betty Powell. LC 74-34599. 320p. 1975. 12.95 o.p. (ISBN 0-395-20460-7); pap. 6.95 o.p. (ISBN 0-395-20506-9). HM.

Avatar of Night: The Hidden Side of Sai Baba. Tal Brooke. 392p. 1982. pap. text ed. 6.95x o.p. (ISBN 0-686-91763-4, Pub. by Vikas India). Advent NY.

Aven Nelson of Wyoming. Roger L. Williams. LC 83-71133. 1984. 29.50 o.p. (ISBN 0-87081-147-9). Univ Pr Colo.

Avenging Angels. Linwood Carson. 1976. pap. 1.50 o.p. (ISBN 0-8439-0408-9, LB408, Pub. by Leisure Bks CT). Dorchester Pub Co.

Avenging Saint. Leslie Charteris. (Saint Ser.). 256p. 1979. pap. 1.95 o.s.i. (ISBN 0-441-03655-4). Ace Bks.

Aventine. Lee Killough. 160p. 1981. pap. 1.95 o.s.i. (ISBN 0-345-29521-8, Del Rey). Ballantine.

Aventuras De Pepito. Wm. Armstrong. Tr. by Arturo Igartua & Wm. Armstrong. (Armstrong Spanish Cartoons Ser.: Vol. 1). (Illus.). 48p. (Orig., Span. & Eng.). (gr. 1-10). 1973. pap. 1.00 o.p. (ISBN 0-913452-23-8). Jesuit Bks.

Aventures de France et Quelques Autres Contines. Ginette Laroque. (Illus.). 64p. (Fr.). 1983. 5.50 o.p. (ISBN 0-682-49988-9). Exposition-Phoenix.

Avenue of Stone. Pamela H. Johnson. LC 73-3966. 1974. 7.95 o.s.i. (ISBN 0-684-13442-X, ScribT). Scribner.

Avenue of the Righteous. Peter Hellman. LC 80-66001. (Illus.). 1980. 11.95 o.p. (ISBN 0-689-11109-6, Atheneum). Macmillan.

Average American Book: An up-to-the Minute Look at the Traits, Habits, Tastes, Life Styles & Attitudes of the American People. Barry Tarshis. LC 79-50964. 1979. 12.95 o.p. (ISBN 0-689-11010-3, Atheneum). Macmillan.

Average Man Against Superior Man. Osias L. Schwarz. Philos Lib.

Aversive Conditioning & Learning. Ed. by F. Robert Brush. LC 70-127680. 1971. 86.00 o.p. (ISBN 0-12-137950-7). Acad Pr.

Averted Threat. Gershon Kranzler. saddle-stitched 5.00 o.p. (ISBN 0-87559-129-9). Shalom.

Averting Armageddon. Gordon Thomas & Max Morgan-Witts. LC 84-10101. 360p. 1984. 18.95 o.p. (ISBN 0-385-18985-0). Doubleday.

Avery Index to Architectural Periodicals: 1987, 4 vols. Avery Memorial Library, Columbia University. 2800p. 1988. 325.00x o.p. (ISBN 0-8161-0460-3, Hall Library). G K Hall.

Avery Index to Architectural Periodicals, 15 vols. 2nd ed. Columbia University Editors. 1975. Set. lib. bdg. 1485.00 o.p. (ISBN 0-8161-1067-0, Hall Library). G K Hall.

Avery Index to Architectural Periodicals, First Supplement. 2nd ed. Columbia University Editors. 1978. lib. bdg. 145.00 o.p. (ISBN 0-8161-0018-7, Hall Library). G K Hall.

Avery Index to Architectural Periodicals: Third Supplement. Columbia University Editors. 1979. lib. bdg. 145.00 o.p. (ISBN 0-8161-0282-1, Hall Library). G K Hall.

Avi Names His Price. Sheindel Weinbach. (Illus.). (gr. 2-5). 1976. 6.95 o.p. (ISBN 0-87306-119-5). Feldheim.

Avian Orientation & Navigation. K. Schmidt-Koenig. 1979. 55.50 o.p. (ISBN 0-12-626550-X). Acad Pr.

Aviation & Space Dictionary. 6th ed. Gentle & Riethmaier. 262p. Date not set. 19.95 o.p. TAB Bks.

Aviation, Environment & World Order. S. Bhatt. 196p. 1980. text ed. 17.50x o.p. (ISBN 0-391-01809-4). Humanities.

Aviation Europe 1987-88. 40th ed. 1987. pap. 95.00 o.p. (ISBN 0-85499-894-2). Intl Pubns Serv.

Aviation Forecasting, Planning, & Operations. (Transportation Research Report Ser.). 79p. 1979. 4.40 o.p. (ISBN 0-309-02987-2). Transport Res Bd.

Aviation Ground Operation Safety Handbook. 3rd ed. LC 77-74161. 132p. 1977. 24.25 o.p. (ISBN 0-87912-028-2, 129.62). Natl Safety Coun.

Aviation in South Africa. Herman Potgieter. 160p. 32.50 o.p. (ISBN 0-7106-0423-8). Janes Info Group.

Aviation Law for Pilots. 4th ed. S. E. Taylor & H. A. Parmar. 143p. 1983. 17.50x o.p. (ISBN 0-246-12052-5, Pub. by Granada England). Gower Pub Co.

Aviation Maintenance Law. Fred Biehler. 172p. 1975. text ed. 19.95 o.p. (ISBN 0-89100-067-4, EA-AML-2). pap. 17.95 o.p. (ISBN 0-89100-061-5, EA-AML-1). IAP.

Aviation Mechanic Airframe Question Book Including Answers, Explanations & References. 176p. (Orig.). 1986. pap. text ed. 8.75 o.p. (ISBN 0-89100-289-8, EA-FAA-T-8080-12AX). IAP.

Aviation Mechanic, Airframe, Question Book. (FAA-T-8080-12A Ser.). (Illus.). 92p. 1986. pap. 3.50 o.p. (ISBN 0-318-19553-4, S/N 050-007-00725-6). USGPO.

Aviation Mechanic Airframe Test Guide. Aviation Supplies & Academics Staff. 1986. pap. 8.95 o.p. (AMA-B, Pub. by ASA). Aviation.

Aviation Mechanic, General, Question Book. (FAA-T-8080-10A Ser.). 70p. (Orig.). 1986. pap. 2.75 o.p. (ISBN 0-318-19554-2, S/N 050-007-00723-0). USGPO.

Aviation Mechanic Powerplant Question Book Including Answers, Explanations & References. (Aviation Maintenance Ser.). 167p. 1986. pap. text ed. 8.75 o.p. (ISBN 0-89100-284-7, EA-FAA-T-8080-11AX). IAP.

Aviation Mechanic, Powerplant, Question Book. (FAA-T-8080-11A Ser.). (Illus.). 88p. 1986. pap. 3.50 o.p. (ISBN 0-318-19555-0, S/N 050-007-00724-8). USGPO.

Aviation Mechanic Powerplant Question Book. Federal Aviation Administration Staff. (Aviation Maintenance Training Course Ser.). (Illus.). 80p. 1986. pap. 3.50 o.p. (ISBN 0-89100-285-5, EA-FAA-T-8080-11A). IAP.

Aviation Mechanics General Question Book Including Answers, Explanations & References. 112p. 1986. pap. text ed. 7.95 o.p. (ISBN 0-89100-287-1, EA-FAA-T-8080-10AX). IAP.

Aviation Mechanics General Question Book. Federal Aviation Administration Staff. (Aviation Maintenance Training Course Ser.). 64p. 1986. pap. 2.75 o.p. (ISBN 0-89100-286-3, EA-FAA-T-8080-10A). IAP.

Aviation Medicine. Richard M. Harding & F. John Mills. 148p. 1984. pap. 13.00x o.p. (ISBN 0-7279-0145-1, Pub. by British Med Assoc UK). Taylor & Francis.

Aviation-Space Dictionary. 6th ed. E. J. Gentle & L. W. Reithmaier. LC 80-67567. (Illus.). 1980. 19.95 o.p. (ISBN 0-8168-3002-9, 23002, TAB-Aero). TAB Bks.

Aviation Telephone Directory: Atlantic & Eastern States. 1987. pap. 11.95 o.p. Aviation.

Aviation Telephone Directory: Midcontinent States. 1987. pap. 11.95 o.p. Aviation.

Aviation Telephone Directory: Pacific & Western States. 369p. 1987. pap. 11.95 o.p. Aviation.

Aviation Telephone Directory: Southwestern & Gulf States. 1987. pap. 11.95 o.p. Aviation.

Aviation's Mr. Sam. James Haggerty. LC 74-78958. 1974. 1.00 o.p. (ISBN 0-8168-3100-9, 23100, TAB-Aero). TAB Bks.

Aviator. Ernest K. Gann. LC 80-68543. 1981. 10.95 o.p. (ISBN 0-87795-299-X, Arbor Hse). Morrow.

Aviatrix. Elinor Smith. (Illus.). 288p. 1981. 13.95 o.p. (ISBN 0-15-110372-0). HarBraceJ.

Avicenna & the Visionary Recital. Henry Corbin. Tr. by Willard R. Trask from Fr. (Dunquin Ser.: No. 13). 314p. 1980. pap. 16.50 o.p. (ISBN 0-88214-213-5). Spring Pubns.

Avoidance of Baldness. Joseph Rego. 128p. 1982. 7.00 o.p. (ISBN 0-682-49839-4). Exposition-Phoenix.

Avoiding Malpractice for the California Nurse. 2nd ed. Robert D. Anderson. 112p. 1982. pap. text ed. 26.99 Home Study Course o.p. (ISBN 0-942028-03-1); Reference Book 15.00 o.p. (ISBN 0-942028-07-4). R D Anderson.

Avon Bottle Encyclopedia. 10th ed. Bud Hastins. (Illus.). 1984. 19.95 o.p. Avons Res.

Avon Seven: Avons Collections Handbook & Price Guide to Avon Bottles. (Illus.). 1981. pap. 22.95 o.p. (ISBN 0-931864-07-0). Avons Res.

Avon Superstars: Kevin McHale, Michael Jordan. Jordan Deutsch. 80p. 1987. pap. 2.50 o.p. (ISBN 0-380-75312-X). Avon.

Avon Superstars: Marcus Allen, Jim McMahon. Jordan Deutsch. (Illus.). 80p. (Orig.). 1986. pap. 2.50 o.p. (ISBN 0-380-75227-1, Camelot). Avon.

Avro Vulcan. Robert Jackson. (Illus.). 192p. (Orig.). 1987. pap. 12.95 o.p. (ISBN 0-85260-010-0, Pub. by PSL P Stephens). Sterling.

Awake & Sing. 1974. 15.00 o.p. (ISBN 0-686-23316-6). Rochester Folk Art.

Awake in Nightmare - Jonestown: The Only Eyewitness Account. Ethan Feinsod. 1981. 14.95 o.p. (ISBN 0-393-01431-2). Norton.

Awakened Conscience: Studies in Commonwealth Literature. Ed. by C. D. Narasimhaiah. 1978. text ed. 32.50x o.p. (ISBN 0-391-00920-6). Humanities.

Awakened Minority see Mexican Americans.

Awakened One: The Life & Work of Bhagwan Shree Rajneesh. Vasant Joshi. LC 81-48209. 210p. 1982. pap. 7.64i o.p. (ISBN 0-06-064205-X, RD 392). HarpR.

Awakening. Fay Young. 64p. 1981. 5.00 o.p. (ISBN 0-682-49701-0). Exposition-Phoenix.

Awakening Interest in Science During the First Century of Printing, 1450-1550. Margaret B. Stillwell. LC 78-114982. 399p. 1970. 25.00x o.p. (ISBN 0-8139-0935-X, Bibliographical Soc. of Amer). U Pr of Va.

Awakening Minorities: American Indians, Mexican Americans & Puerto Ricans. Ed. by John R. Howard. 1972. text ed. o.p. (ISBN 0-87855-055-0); pap. text ed. 3.95x o.p. (ISBN 0-87855-548-X). Transaction Pubs.

Awakening Mystical Consciousness. Joel S. Goldsmith. Ed. by Lorraine Sinkler. LC 79-3601. 176p. 1980. 10.45 o.p. (ISBN 0-06-063174-0). HarpR.

Awakening Nightmare: A Breakthrough in Treating the Mentally Ill. 1972. 9.95 o.p. (ISBN 0-686-67702-1). Exposition-Phoenix.

Awakening of Alice. Violet Winspear. (Nightingale Paperbacks Ser.). 254p. 1984. pap. 8.95 o.p. (ISBN 0-8161-3567-3, Large Print Bks). G K Hall.

Awakening of Faith. Ashvagosha. Ed. by Alan H. Walton. Tr. by Timothy Richard. 1967. 5.00 o.p. (ISBN 0-8216-0013-3, Pub. by Univ Bks). Carol Pub Group.

Awakening of Intelligence. J. Krishnamurti. 1976. pap. 3.95 o.p. (ISBN 0-380-00462-3, 63560-7, Discus). Avon.

Awakening of the Human Spirit. Hazrat Inayat Khan. LC 82-80091. (Collected Works of Hazat Inayat Khan). 224p. (Orig.). 1982. pap. 8.95 o.p. (ISBN 0-930872-27-4, 1014P). Omega Pr NY.

Awakening the Slower Mind. V. Bruce. 1969. 60.00 o.p. (ISBN 0-08-006387-X); pap. 60.00 o.p. (ISBN 0-08-006386-1). Pergamon.

Award World Atlas. (Illus.). 1986. 20.00 o.s.i. (ISBN 0-8437-1022-5). Hammond Inc.

Awarding College Credit for Non-College Learning: A Guide to Current Practices. Peter Meyer. LC 74-28918. (Higher Education Ser.). 1975. 24.95x o.p. (ISBN 0-87589-254-X). Jossey-Bass.

Awards, Honors & Prizes--Supplement. 6th ed. Ed. by Gita Siegman. 200p. 1986. pap. 88.00x o.p. (ISBN 0-8103-0448-1). Gale.

Awards, Honors & Prizes, Vol. 1: United States & Canada. 6th ed. Ed. by Gita Siegman. LC 78-16691. 950p. 1985. 145.00x o.p. (ISBN 0-8103-0445-7). Gale.

Awards, Honors & Prizes, Vol. 2: International & Foreign. 6th ed. Ed. by Gita Siegman. 800p. 1986. 170.00x o.p. (ISBN 0-8103-0446-5). Gale.

Awareness of Awareness see Science of Education.

Awareness Trap: Self-Absorption Instead of Social Change. Edwin M Schur. LC 77-1243. 1977. pap. text ed. 3.95 o.p. (ISBN 0-07-055661-X). McGraw.

Away in a Manger. Nussbaumer. 1965. 4.25 o.p. (ISBN 0-15-204735-2, HJ). HarBraceJ.

Awful Rowing Toward God. Anne Sexton. LC 74-23618. 96p. 1975. o.s. 8.95 o.p. (ISBN 0-395-20365-1); pap. 5.50 o.p. (ISBN 0-395-20366-X). HM.

Awkward Age. Henry James. 1969. pap. 3.95 o.p. (ISBN 0-393-00285-3, Norton Lib.). Norton.

Axe-Age, Wolf-Age: A Selection of Norse Myths. Kevin C. Holland. (Illus.). (gr. 6 up). 1986. 11.95 o.p. (ISBN 0-317-61636-6). Andre Deutsch.

Axe-Time, Sword-Time. Barbara Corcoran. LC 75-29468. 192p. (gr. 5-9). 1976. 6.95 o.p. (ISBN 0-689-30498-6, Atheneum). Macmillan.

Axiom of Constructibility: A Guide for the Mathematician. K. J. Devlin. LC 77-17119. (Lecture Notes in Mathematics Ser.: Vol. 617). 1977. pap. 14.00 o.p. (ISBN 0-387-08520-3). Springer-Verlag.

Axiomatic Models of Bargaining. A. E. Roth. (Lecture Notes in Economics & Mathematical Systems Ser.: Vol. 170). 1979. pap. 13.00 o.p. (ISBN 0-387-09540-3). Springer-Verlag.

Axiomatic Set Theory. G. Takeuti & W. Zaring. LC 72-85950. (Graduate Texts in Mathematics Ser.: Vol. 8). 226p. 1973. text ed. 25.50 o.p. (ISBN 0-387-90051-9); pap. text ed. 21.00 o.p. (ISBN 0-387-90050-0). Springer-Verlag.

Axis. Clive Irving. LC 79-55609. 1980. 12.95 o.p. (ISBN 0-689-11044-8, Atheneum). Macmillan.

Ayesha: The Return of She. H. Rider Haggard. (Forgotten Fantasy Library: Vol. 14). 360p. 1977. Repr. of 1905 ed. pap. 5.95 o.p. (ISBN 0-87877-113-1). Newcastle Pub.

Ayisha. H. Noga. LC 72-82179. 1972. 6.50 o.p. (ISBN 0-87795-048-2, Arbor Hse). Morrow.

Ayshire & Other Whitework. Margaret Swain. (Album Ser.: No. 88). (Illus.). 32p. (Orig.). 1983. pap. 3.50 o.p. (ISBN 0-85263-589-3, Pub. by Shire Pubns England). Seven Hills Bk Dists.

Aztec. Gary Jennings. LC 79-55608. (Illus.). 1980. 15.95 o.p. (ISBN 0-689-11045-6, Atheneum). Macmillan.

Aztec Downfall. Jessie B. McGaw. 64p. 1986. 7.95 o.p. (ISBN 0-8062-2992-6). Carlton.

Aztec Studies II: Sierra Nahuat Word Structure. Dow F. Robinson. (Publications in Linguistics & Related Fields Ser.: No. 22). 186p. 1970. pap. 2.00 o.s.i. (ISBN 0-88312-024-0); microfiche (2) 4.00 o.p. (ISBN 0-88312-424-6). Summer Inst Ling.

B

B A R T. Ron Silliman. 28p. (Orig.). pap. 3.00 o.p. (ISBN 0-937013-09-9). Potes Poets.

B & T Cell Tumors: Symposium. Ed. by Ellen S. Vitetta. LC 82-13948. 583p. 1982. 71.00 o.p. (ISBN 0-12-722380-0). Acad Pr.

B-52 Strato Fortress at War. Jeff Ethell & Joe Christy. 1981. encore ed. 5.50 o.p. (ISBN 0-684-16980-0, ScribT). Scribner.

Baba of Karo. Mary Smith. 300p. 1955. (ISBN 0-8022-1601-3). Philos Lib.

Babar the King. facsimile ed. Jean De Brunhoff. LC 85-30273. (Illus.). 48p. (ps). 1986. 14.95 o.s.i. (ISBN 0-394-88245-8, BYR). Random.

Babe. Joan Smith. (General Ser.). 1980. lib. bdg. 13.95 o.p. (ISBN 0-8161-3112-0, Large Print Bks). G K Hall.

Babe. Marianne Wiggins. (Orig.). 1975. pap. 3.45 o.p. (ISBN 0-380-00239-6, 21840, Equinox). Avon.

Babees' Book: Medieval Manners for the Young. Ed. by Edith Rickert. LC 66-30209. (Medieval Library). (Illus.). 203p. Repr. of 1926 ed. 18.50x o.p. (ISBN 0-8154-0193-0). Cooper Sq.

Babelism: Social Problems of the Watergate Era. J. M. Sanchez-Perez. LC 73-91102. 1974. 6.50 o.p. (ISBN 0-682-47873-3). Exposition-Phoenix.

Babes in Toyland. Illus. & retold by Toby Bluth. (ps up). 1986. 5.95 o.p. (ISBN 0-8249-8149-9). Ideals.

Babeuf Plot: The Making of a Republican Legend. David Thomson. LC 75-27687. (Illus.). 112p. 1975. Repr. of 1947 ed. lib. bdg. 22.50x o.p. (ISBN 0-8371-8466-5, THBP). Greenwood.

Babies, Breastfeeding & Bonding. Ina M. Gaskin. (Illus.). 240p. 1987. 39.95 o.p. (ISBN 0-89789-135-X); pap. 12.95 o.p. (ISBN 0-89789-134-1). Bergin & Garvey.

Babies Need Books. Dorothy Butler. LC 80-14027. 1980. 9.95 o.s.i. (ISBN 0-689-11112-6, Atheneum). Macmillan.

Babies Need Books: How Books Can Help Your Child Become a Happy & Involved Human Being. Dorothy Butler. LC 80-14027. 192p. 1985. pap. 5.95 o.s.i. (ISBN 0-689-70682-0, 322, Atheneum). Macmillan.

Baboushka. Arthur Scholey. (Illus.). 22p. (gr. 1-6). 1983. 4.95 o.p. (ISBN 0-89107-281-0, Crossway Bks). Good News.

Baboushka & the Three Kings. Ruth Robbins. (Illus.). 28p. (gr. k-3). 1960. Repr. PLB 4.95 o.p. (ISBN 0-395-27672-1). HM.

Baby & Child Care. rev. ed. Benjamin Spock & Michael B. Rothenberg. 1985. pap. 4.95 o.s.i. (ISBN 0-671-49451-1). PB.

Baby Animals. Zokeisha. (Puppet Story Board Bks.). (Illus.). 12p. (ps-2). 1981. 2.95 o.s.i. (ISBN 0-671-42645-1, Little Simon). S&S.

Baby Animals see My Toys, My First Book, Baby Animals, the Farm.

Baby Bear. Illus. by Carolyn Bracken. (Tuck-A-Toy Bks.). (Illus.). 7p. (ps). 1985. 3.95 o.p. (ISBN 0-8407-6664-5). Nelson.

Baby Ben Gets Dressed. Harriet Ziefert. LC 84-61323. (Baby Ben Bks.). (Illus.). 16p. (ps). 1985. pap. 3.95 o.s.i. (ISBN 0-394-87025-5, BYR). Random.

Baby Book. 10th, rev. ed. Better Homes & Gardens Editors. 9.95 o.p. (ISBN 0-696-00021-0). BH&G.

Baby Boutique. Date not set. pap. 5.98 o.p. (ISBN 0-317-03196-1). Gick.

Baby Called John see What the Bible Tells Us: Third Series.

Baby Chase. Tony Kornheiser. LC 82-73025. 224p. 1983. 12.95 o.p. (ISBN 0-689-11354-4, Atheneum). Macmillan.

Baby Doll. Carroll Baker. 320p. 1985. pap. 3.95 o.p. (ISBN 0-440-10431-9). Dell.

Baby Doll: An Autobiography. Carroll Baker. (Illus.). 1983. 15.95 o.p. (ISBN 0-87795-558-1, Arbor Hse). Morrow.

Baby Dolphin. Paul Harvey. (ps). 1985. 1.95 o.s.i. (ISBN 0-671-55661-4, Little Simon). S&S.

Baby Elephant & the Secret Wishes. Sesyle Joslin & Leonard Weisgard. LC 62-14244. (Illus.). (gr. k-3). 1962. 6.50 o.p. (ISBN 0-15-205156-2, HJ). HarBraceJ.

Baby Food Book. Alma Payne. (Illus.). 1977. pap. 4.95 o.p. (ISBN 0-316-69543-2). Little.

Baby in the Icebox: And Other Short Fiction. James M. Cain. Ed. by Roy Hoopes. LC 80-28900. 320p. 1981. 14.95 o.p. (ISBN 0-03-058501-5). H Holt & Co.

Baby Is Baptized. Stuart R. Oglesby. pap. 2.95 o.p. (ISBN 0-8042-1536-7, John Knox). Westminster John Knox.

Baby Island. Carol R. Brink. 1973. pap. 0.95x o.s.i. (ISBN 0-02-041890-6, Collier). Macmillan.

Baby Jesus' Birthday. Nancy Irland. (Cut & Color Bks.). (Illus.). 16p. (Orig.). (gr. k-3). 1982. pap. 0.95 o.p. (ISBN 0-87239-585-5, 2389). Standard Pub.

Baby Love: Too Young for Love But Not for Making Babies. Joyce Maynard. 224p. 1982. pap. 2.95 o.p. (ISBN 0-380-59550-8, 60129-X). Avon.

Baby Massage: Parent-Child Bonding Through Touching. Amelia D. Auckett. LC 82-2172. (Illus.). 128p. (Orig.). 1982. 12.95 o.p. (ISBN 0-937858-09-9); pap. 6.95 o.p. (ISBN 0-937858-07-2). Newmarket.

Baby Needs Shoes. Dale Carlson. LC 74-75556. (Illus.). 160p. (gr. 5-7). 1974. 6.95 o.p. (ISBN 0-689-30404-8, Atheneum). Macmillan.

Baby Owl. Yasuko Funazaki. (Illus.). 32p. (ps). 1979. 7.95 o.p. (ISBN 0-416-30721-3, NO.0206). Routledge Chapman & Hall.

Baby Piggy's Purse. Illus. by Lauren Attinello. (Cuddle Doll Bks.). (Illus.). 12p. (ps). 1986. 3.95 o.s.i. (ISBN 0-394-87988-0). Random.

Baby Sitters. John Salisbury. LC 77-88910. 1978. 9.95 o.p. (ISBN 0-689-10852-4, Atheneum). Macmillan.

Baby-Sitting: A Concise Guide. Rubie Saunders. (Illus.). (gr. 7-9). 1974. pap. 1.50 o.s.i. (ISBN 0-671-56012-3). Archway.

Baby Talk. D. Leb Tannenbaum. (Illus.). 32p. (gr. 1-3). 1981. pap. 1.95 o.p. (ISBN 0-380-76935-2, 76935-2, Camelot). Avon.

Baby, That Was Rock & Roll: The Legendary Leiber & Stoller. Robert Palmer. LC 78-7102. (Illus.). 1978. pap. 6.95 o.p. (ISBN 0-15-610155-6, Harv). HarBraceJ.

Baby the Lost Legend. David L. Miller. (gr. 3 up). 1985. 6.95 o.s.i. (ISBN 0-671-54091-2, Little Simon). S&S.

Baby Travel. 335p. (Orig.). 1987. pap. 11.95 o.p. (ISBN 0-87052-378-3). Hippocrene Bks.

Babylon & the Old Testament. Andre Parrott. 166p. 1958. (ISBN 0-8022-1268-9). Philos Lib.

Babylon Is Everywhere: The City As Man's Fate. Wolf Schneider. Tr. by Ingeborg Sammet & John Oldenburg. LC 75-26220. (Illus.). 400p. 1976. Repr. of 1963 ed. lib. bdg. 24.25x o.p. (ISBN 0-8371-8402-9, SCBE). Greenwood.

Babylonian Talmud. Leo Auerbach. 288p. (ISBN 0-8022-0045-1). Philos Lib.

Babylonischen Kudurru Als Urkundenform. Franz X. Steinmetzer. Repr. of 1922 ed. 22.00 o.p. (ISBN 0-384-57850-0). Johnson Repr.

Baby's Animal Book. Hildegarde Ford. (Illus.). (ps-1). 1976. 6.95 o.p. (ISBN 0-8054-4150-6, 4241-50). Broadman.

Baby's First Book about Creation. L'Ann Carwell. (Illus.). (ps-1). 1979. 1.25 o.p. (ISBN 0-570-08000-2, 56-1325). Concordia.

Baby's First Year. Gordon Bourne. (Gift Book Ser.). (Illus.). 48p. 1987. 9.95 o.s.i. (ISBN 0-87226-145-X). P Bedrick Bks.

Baby's Lullabies. Freeman. (ps). bds. 3.95 o.s.i. (ISBN 0-448-03088-8, G&D). Putnam Pub Group.

Baby's Opera. Walter Crane. (Illus.). 56p. 1981. pap. 6.95 o.s.i. (ISBN 0-671-42551-X). Windmill Bks.

Baby's Playground. Eloise Wilkin. (Baby's World Board Bks.). (Illus.). 12p. (ps). 1985. 2.95 o.p. (ISBN 0-448-10428-8, G&D). Putnam Pub Group.

Baby's Seasons. (Platt & Munk Teddy Board Bks.). (Illus.). 12p. (ps). 1978. 3.95 o.p. (ISBN 0-448-40871-6, G&D). Putnam Pub Group.

Babysitter. Andrew Coburn. 1979. 9.95 o.p. (ISBN 0-393-01189-5). Norton.

Baccalaureate Education in Nursing 1986-1987. 50p. 1987. pap. 5.95 o.p. (ISBN 0-88737-345-3, 15-1311). Natl League Nurse.

Bacchylides: Complete Poems. Bacchylides. Tr. by Robert Fagles. LC 75-14595. 1976. Repr. of 1961 ed. lib. bdg. 22.50x o.p. (ISBN 0-8371-8221-2, BACP). Greenwood.

Bachelor Fatherhood. Michael McFadden. 1978. pap. 1.75 o.p. (ISBN 0-441-04620-7). Ace Bks.

Bachelorhood: Tales of the Metropolis. Phillip Lopate. 1985. 6.95 o.p. (ISBN 0-87795-693-6, Arbor Hse). Morrow.

Bachelors Anonymous. P. G. Wodehouse. 192p. 1974. 6.95 o.p. (ISBN 0-671-21741-0). S&S.

Bachman's Law. Richard Thorman. 1981. 12.95 o.p. (ISBN 0-393-01443-6). Norton.

Bach's Passions. Paul Steinitz. (Illus.). 1979. 5.95 o.p. (ISBN 0-684-16229-6, ScribT); Encore ed. 5.95 o.p. (ISBN 0-684-17516-9). Scribner.

Bacillariophyta: Diatomeae. Friedrich Hustedt. (Suesswasserflora Mitteleuropas Ser.: Vol. 10). (Illus.). 466p. (Ger.). 1976. 60.00x o.p. (ISBN 3-87429-111-1). Lubrecht & Cramer.

Back Book: The Complete Health & Exercise Program to Cure Your Aching Back. Cal Del Pozo. (Illus.). 1983. pap. 6.95 o.p. (ISBN 0-87795-515-8, Arbor Hse). Morrow.

Back Road Caller. Bob Arnold. (Juniper Bk.: No. 48). 1985. pap. 6.00 o.p. (ISBN 1-55780-047-2). Juniper Pr WI.

Back Roads & City Streets: Weekend Getaways in & Around Georgia. Colin Bessonette. LC 83-63500. (Illus.). 150p. (Orig.). 1984. pap. 6.95 o.p. (ISBN 0-931948-54-1). Peachtree Pubs.

Back Roads of California. 2nd ed. Sunset Magazine & Books Editors. LC 76-40552. (Illus.). 208p. 1977. pap. 10.95 o.p. (ISBN 0-376-05014-4, Sunset Bks). Sunset-Lane.

Back Room in Somers Town. John Malcolm. 160p. 1985. 12.95 o.s.i. (ISBN 0-684-18301-3, ScribT). Scribner.

Back School & Other Conservative Approaches to Low Back Pain. Arthur H. White. LC 82-12541. (Illus.). 191p. 1983. text ed. 39.95 o.p. (ISBN 0-8016-5423-8). Mosby.

Back to Basics. Burton Y. Pines. 320p. 1982. 13.50 o.p. (ISBN 0-688-01117-9). Morrow.

Back to Basics. Vic Willoughby. 120p. pap. 6.50 o.p. (ISBN 0-85429-288-8, F288). Haynes Pubns.

Back to Battle. Max Hennessy. LC 79-55585. 1980. 10.95 o.p. (ISBN 0-689-11042-1, Atheneum). Macmillan.

Back to Methuselah. George Bernard Shaw. (Plays Ser.). 1972. pap. 5.95 o.p. (ISBN 0-14-048011-0). Penguin.

Back to Normal: Living Your Life to Prevent Back Pain. Richard Lonnetto & Gayle Kumchy. LC 86-4450. 192p. 1986. 9.95 o.p. (ISBN 0-385-19410-2). Doubleday.

Back to the Eighties. Jack Ohman. (Illus.). 98p. 1986. pap. 5.95 o.s.i. (ISBN 0-671-63041-5, Fireside). S&S.

Back Toward Lisbon. Allison Cole. 224p. 1985. 14.95 o.p. (ISBN 0-396-08708-6). Dodd.

Backache, Stress & Tension. Hans Krauss. 1978. pap. 5.95 o.p. (ISBN 0-671-24214-8, Fireside). S&S.

Backbench Opinion in the House of Commons, 1945-1955. Hugh B. Berrington. 1973. 70.00 o.p. (ISBN 0-08-016748-9). Pergamon.

Backfire. Clive Egleton. LC 79-63906. 1979. 9.95 o.p. (ISBN 0-689-10990-3, Atheneum). Macmillan.

Backfire: A History of How American Culture Led Us into Vietnam & Made Us Fight the Way We Did. Loren Baritz. LC 84-22625. 416p. (Orig.). 1985. 17.95 o.p. (ISBN 0-688-04185-X). Morrow.

Backgammon for Blood. Bruce Becker. 1976. pap. 2.95 o.p. (ISBN 0-380-00384-8). Avon.

Background of Colonial American Portraiture. Louisa Dresser. 1966. pap. 6.00x o.p. (ISBN 0-912296-20-8, Dist. by U Pr of Va). Am Antiquarian.

Background of Hispanic-American Law: Legal Sources & Juridical Literature of Spain. John T. Vance. LC 79-1622. 1980. Repr. of 1937 ed. 21.50 o.s.i. (ISBN 0-88355-926-9). Hyperion Conn.

Background of Luther's Doctrine of Justification in Late Medieval Theology. Bengt Hagglund. Ed. by Charles S. Anderson. LC 78-152367. (Facet Bks.). 1971. pap. 1.00 o.p. (ISBN 0-8006-3063-7, 1-3063, Fortress). Augsburg Fortress.

Background of Passion Music. Basil Smallman. 128p. 1957. (ISBN 0-8022-1589-0). Philos Lib.

Background Paper on Income for the Nineteen Seventy-One White House Conference on Aging. Yung-Ping Chen. 1971. 3.00 o.p. (ISBN 0-89215-054-8). U Cal LA Indus Rel.

Background Papers on Industry's Changing Role in Health Care Delivery. Ed. by R. H. Egdahl. LC 77-13611. (Springer Series on Industry & Health Care: No. 3). 1977. 60.00 o.p. (ISBN 0-387-90290-2). Springer-Verlag.

Background Studies for History of Education. Ed. by Joseph Kirschner et al. 175p. 1971. pap. text ed. 6.00x o.p. (ISBN 0-8422-0146-7). Irvington.

Background to Bitterness. Henry Gibbs. 260p. 1956. (ISBN 0-8022-0578-X). Philos Lib.

Background to Buckling. H. G. Allen & P. S. Bulson. (Illus.). 1980. text ed. 62.95x o.p. (ISBN 0-07-084100-4). McGraw.

Background to Eastern Europe. F. B. Singleton. 1965. text ed. 11.55 o.p. (ISBN 0-08-011209-9); pap. 6.05 o.p. (ISBN 0-08-011208-0). Pergamon.

Background to Migraine: Proceedings. Migraine Symposium, 2nd, London, 1967. Ed. by R. Smith. (Illus.). 1969. 6.00 o.p. (ISBN 0-387-91028-X). Springer-Verlag.

Background to Migraine: Proceedings. Migraine Symposium, 3rd, London, 1969. Ed. by A. L. Cochrane. (Illus.). 1970. 7.60 o.p. (ISBN 0-387-91035-2). Springer-Verlag.

Background to Migraine: Proceedings. Migraine Symposium, 4th, London, 1971. Ed. by J. N. Cumings. (Illus.). 1971. 8.00 o.p. (ISBN 0-387-91086-7). Springer-Verlag.

Background to Migraine: Proceedings. Migraine Symposium, 5th, London, 1972. Ed. by J. N. Cumings. 1973. 26.00 o.p. (ISBN 0-387-91115-4). Springer Verlag.

Backgrounds in Music Theory. Maurice Whitney. 1954. pap. 7.95 o.s.i. (ISBN 0-02-872870-X). Schirmer Bks.

Backpack Fishing. Charles J. Farmer. LC 73-20839. (Illus.). 224p. 1976. pap. 6.95 o.p. (ISBN 0-89149-018-3). Jolex.

Backpacker's Africa. 2nd ed. Hilary Bradt. (Backpacker's Guide Ser.). (Illus.). 192p. 1987. pap. 12.95 o.p. (ISBN 0-9505797-9-3). Hunter Pub NY.

Backpacker's Digest. 3rd ed. Cheri Elliott. LC 72-97509. (Illus.). 288p. (Orig.). 1981. pap. 9.95 o.p. (ISBN 0-910676-21-6, 6536). DBI.

Backpacking. (Agriculture Department Program Aid: No. 1239). (Illus.). 1981. pap. 3.50 o.p. (ISBN 0-318-22493-3, S/N 001-000-04247-5). USGPO.

Backpacking & Trekking in Chile & Argentina. Hilary Bradt & John Pilkington. LC 80-68116. (Backpacker Guide Ser.). (Illus.). 144p. 1980. pap. 7.95 o.p. (ISBN 0-9505797-7-7). Bradt Ent.

Backpacking in North America: The Great Outdoors. Hilary J. Bradt & George N. Bradt. (Backpacker Guide Ser.). (Illus.). 1980. pap. 7.95 o.p. (ISBN 0-9505797-4-2). Bradt Ent.

Backpacking Is for Me. Art Thomas. LC 80-12847. (Sports for Me Bks.). (Illus.). 48p. (gr. 2-5). 1980. PLB 7.95 o.p. (ISBN 0-8225-1095-2). Lerner Pubns.

Backstage Handbook: An Illustrated Almanac of Technical Information. Paul Carter. (Illus.). 264p. 1988. pap. 12.95 o.p. (ISBN 0-911747-09-5). Broadway Pr.

Backstop Ace. Dick Friendlich. (gr. 7-10). 1961. 4.25 o.s.i. (ISBN 0-664-32246-8, Westminster). Westminster John Knox.

Backward Glance. D. J. Steans. 240p. 1983. 12.00 o.p. (ISBN 0-682-49964-1). Exposition-Phoenix.

Backward Look. Daniel Lang. 1979. text ed. 8.95 o.p. (ISBN 0-07-036239-4). McGraw.

Backward Look: Germans Remember. Daniel Lang. (McGraw-Hill Paperbacks Ser.). (Illus.). 144p. (Orig.). 1981. pap. text ed. 4.95 o.p. (ISBN 0-07-036241-6). McGraw.

Backyard Bird Watcher. George H. Harrison. 1979. 17.45 o.s.i. (ISBN 0-671-22664-9). S&S.

Backyard Birder's Journal. Howard Blume. LC 86-3873. (Illus.). 256p. (Orig.). 1987. pap. 12.95 o.p. (ISBN 0-87156-767-9). Sierra.

Backyard Insects. Millicent E. Selsam & Ronald Goor. LC 82-18390. (Illus.). 40p. (gr. k-3). 1983. 12.95 o.s.i. (ISBN 0-02-781820-9, Four Winds). Macmillan.

Backyard Stonebuilder: Fourteen Projects for the Weekend Mason. Charles Long. (Illus.). 160p. (Orig.). 1985. pap. 9.95 o.p. (ISBN 0-920197-19-1, Pub. by Summerhill CN). Sterling.

Backyard Vegetable Gardening for the Beginner. Hugh Wiberg. LC 70-171918. 1971. 5.00 o.p. (ISBN 0-682-47329-4, Banner). Exposition-Phoenix.

Backyards & Tiny Gardens. Judith Berrisford. 160p. 1977. pap. 5.95 o.p. (ISBN 0-571-10837-7). Faber & Faber.

Bacon Is Shake-Speare. Edwin Durning-Lawrence. LC 78-97330. Repr. of 1910 ed. lib. bdg. 35.00x o.p. (ISBN 0-8371-2894-3, DUBS). Greenwood.

Bacteria & Complement. Ed. by M. Loos. (Current Topics in Microbiology & Immunology: Vol. 121). (Illus.). 208p. 1985. 49.50 o.p. (ISBN 0-387-15877-4). Springer-Verlag.

Bacterial Adherence see Queues: Receptors & Recognition Series B.

Bacterial Chemotaxis. (Landmark Ser.). 1979. 24.00x o.p. (ISBN 0-8422-4106-X). Irvington.

Bacterial Membranes & Walls. Ed. by Loretta Leive. (Microbiology Ser.: Vol. 1). 520p. 1973. 99.75 o.p. (ISBN 0-8247-6085-9). Dekker.

Bacterial Nutrition. Ed. by Herman C. Lichstein. LC 82-11720. (Benchmark Papers in Microbiology: Vol. 19). 377p. 1983. 54.95 o.p. (ISBN 0-87933-439-8). Van Nos Reinhold.

Bacterial Physiology. John R. Sokatch. 1969. 96.00 o.p. (ISBN 0-12-654250-3). Acad Pr.

Bacterial Spore. G. Gould & A. Hurst. 1969. 95.00 o.p. (ISBN 0-12-293650-7). Acad Pr.

Bacterial Taxonomy. D. Jones & M. Goodfellow. (Outline Studies in Biology). 1985. pap. 7.50 o.p. (ISBN 0-412-13140-4, NO.6414, Pub. by Chapman & Hall England). Routledge Chapman & Hall.

Bacterial Transformation. Archer. 1973. 71.50 o.p. (ISBN 0-12-059450-1). Acad Pr.

Bacteriocins. P. Reeves. LC 77-188625. (Molecular Biology, Biochemistry & Biophysics Ser.: Vol. 11). (Illus.). 164p. 1973. 36.00 o.p. (ISBN 0-387-05735-8). Springer-Verlag.

Bacteriophages. John Douglas. 1975. 18.95x o.p. (ISBN 0-412-12630-3, NO.6087, Pub. by Chapman & Hall); pap. 11.50 o.p. (ISBN 0-412-12640-0, NO.6088). Routledge Chapman & Hall.

Bacth Party: A History from Its Origins to 1966. John F. Devlin. LC 75-41903. (Publications Ser.: No. 156). 372p. 1976. 12.95x o.p. Hoover Inst Pr.

Bad at the Bijou. William R. Horner. LC 82-17222. (Illus.). 173p. 1982. lib. bdg. 19.95x o.p. (ISBN 0-89950-060-9). McFarland & Co.

Bad Communist. Max Crawford. LC 78-20637. 1979. 8.95 o.p. (ISBN 0-15-110440-9). HarBraceJ.

Bad Company. Liza Cody. 260p. 1982. 11.95 o.s.i. (ISBN 0-684-17760-9, ScribT). Scribner.

Bad Dreams. Anthony Haden-Guest. 480p. 1982. pap. 3.95 o.s.i. (ISBN 0-345-30720-8). Ballantine.

Bad Dreams of a Good Girl. Susan Shreve. 92p. (gr. 2-5). 1983. pap. 2.25 o.p. (ISBN 0-380-63966-1, 63966-1, Camelot). Avon.

Bad Earth: Enviromental Degradation in China. Vaclav Smil. LC 83-14821. (Illus.). 236p. 1984. 35.00 o.p. (ISBN 0-87332-230-4); pap. 15.95 o.p. (ISBN 0-87332-253-3). M E Sharpe.

Bad Girls. Mary Flanagan. LC 84-24493. 237p. 1985. 12.95 o.p. (ISBN 0-689-11593-8, Atheneum). Macmillan.

Bad Guys' Quote Book. Robert Singer. 128p. 1984. pap. 2.50 o.p. (ISBN 0-380-87346-X, 87346-X). Avon.

Bad Karma: A True Story of Obsession, & Murder. Deborah Blum. LC 85-48129. (Illus.). 320p. 1986. 17.95 o.p. (ISBN 0-689-11617-9, Atheneum). Macmillan.

Bad Lands. Oakley Hall. LC 77-15839. 1978. 10.95 o.p. (ISBN 0-689-10823-0, Atheneum). Macmillan.

Bad News, Vol. 1. Glasgow University, Media Group Staff. 326p. 1976. 30.50x o.p. (ISBN 0-7100-8489-7); pap. 17.95x o.p. (ISBN 0-7100-0792-2). Routledge Chapman & Hall.

Bad News: The Best of Esquire Magazine's Dubious Achievements, 1961-1984. 144p. 1984. pap. 6.95 o.p. (ISBN 0-380-85712-X, 85712). Avon.

Bad Night at Dry Creek. Cameron Judd. 1981. pap. 1.75 o.p. (ISBN 0-8439-0894-7, Pub. by Leisure Bks CT). Dorchester Pub Co.

Bad Room. Christopher C. Gilmore. 256p. 1983. pap. 3.50 o.p. (ISBN 0-380-82669-0, 82669-0). Avon.

Bad Sisters. Emma Tennant. 176p. 1980. pap. 1.95 o.p. (ISBN 0-380-48280-0, 48280). Avon.

Baden Powell: A Family Album. Heather Baden-Powell. (Illus.). 148p. 1986. 22.50 o.p. (ISBN 0-87052-315-5). Hippocrene Bks.

Badenheim Nineteen Thirty-Nine. Aharon Appelfeld. (General Ser.). 1981. lib. bdg. 11.95 o.p. (ISBN 0-8161-3205-4, Large Print Bks). G K Hall.

Badger's Illustrated Catalogue of Cast-Iron Architecture. Daniel D. Badger. 1983. 16.50 o.p. (ISBN 0-8446-5938-X). Peter Smith.

Badges & Distinctive Insignia of the Multinational Force & Observers (MFO) David V. Olson. 250p. 1986. pap. 10.00 o.p. (ISBN 0-9609690-6-3). WW Milit Exch.

Badges of the British Army: Eighteen-Twenty to the Present. Fred Wilkinson. (Illus.). 80p. 1987. 14.95 o.p. (ISBN 0-85368-789-7, Pub. by Arms & Armour). Sterling.

Badlands Run. Greene Lambard & Sharleen Lambard. LC 86-91768. (Car Wars Adventure Gamebook: No. 4). 192p. (Orig.). 1987. pap. 2.95 o.p. (ISBN 0-88038-444-1). TSR Inc.

Baedeker's Egypt. (Illus.). 1985. 27.50 o.p. Hippocrene Bks.

Bael Tatpauopoos und Die Kerube Des Ezechiel. Ed. by Simon K. Landersdorfer. pap. 8.00 o.p. (ISBN 0-384-31200-4). Johnson Repr.

Baelund Transformations, the Inverse Scattering Method, Solutions, & Their Applications. Ed. by R. M. Miura. (Lecture Notes in Mathematics Ser.: Vol. 515). 1976. pap. 17.00 o.p. (ISBN 0-387-07687-5). Springer-Verlag.

Bag of Wind. Gerald Rose. 32p. 1984. bds. 9.95 Laminated o.p. (ISBN 0-370-30537-X, Pub. by Bodley Head). Salem Hse Pubs.

Bagpipes & Tunings. Theodor H. Podnos. LC 73-94129. (Detroit Monographs in Musicology: No. 3). 1974. 10.00 o.p. (ISBN 0-911772-52-9); pap. 2.00 o.p. (ISBN 0-89990-005-4). Harmonie Pk Pr.

Bahama Crisis. Desmond Bagley. 256p. 1983. 13.50 o.s.i. (ISBN 0-671-43453-5). Summit Bks.

Bahasa Indonesia for Beginners, Bk. 2. 2nd ed. Purwanto Danusugondo. 1969. pap. 15.00x o.p. (ISBN 0-424-00018-0, Pub. by Sydney U Pr). Intl Spec Bk.

Bahian Adventure. Harold Geist. 128p. 1982. 8.95 o.p. (ISBN 0-682-49868-8). Exposition-Phoenix.

Bahnar Dictionary. John Banker et al. 202p. (Orig.). 1979. pap. 9.00x o.s.i. (ISBN 0-88312-997-3); microfiche (3) 9.00 o.s.i. (ISBN 0-88312-933-7). Summer Inst Ling.

Bahrain. Middle East Economic Digest Staff. Ed. by John Whelan. (MEED Practical Guides Ser.). (Illus.). 190p. (Orig.). 1983. pap. 16.95x o.p. (ISBN 0-9505211-7-5). Lynne Rienner.

Bahrain Nineteen Twenty to Nineteen Forty-Five: Britain, the Shaikh & the Administration. Mahdi A. Al-Tajir. 304p. 1987. lib. bdg. 52.50X o.p. (ISBN 0-7099-5122-1, Pub. by Croom Helm UK). Routledge Chapman & Hall.

BAI Survey of the Check Collection System. 1987. 60.00 o.p. (ISBN 1-55520-072-9, 604). Bank Admin Inst.

Baidarka. George Dyson. LC 86-10912. (Illus.). 212p. (Orig.). 1988. pap. 24.95 o.p. (ISBN 0-88240-315-X, 731). Alaska Northwest.

Bailey & the Bearcat. Gene Olson. (gr. 7-10). 1964. 3.50 o.s.i. (ISBN 0-664-32327-8, Westminster). Westminster John Knox.

Bailments Law of New York, 1962. Gould Editorial Staff. 1962. pap. text ed. 1.50x o.p. (ISBN 0-87526-004-7). Gould.

Bailout: America's Billion Dollar Gamble on the "New" Chrysler Corporation. Reginald Stuart. LC 80-70279. (Illus.). 210p. (Orig.). 1981. pap. 6.95 o.s.i. (ISBN 0-89708-050-5). And Bks.

Baja Book. Tom Miller & Elmar Baxter. (Illus.). 1974. pap. 7.95x o.p. (ISBN 0-914622-01-3). Baja Trail.

Baja Book II. Tom Miller & Elmar Baxter. (Illus.). 1985. pap. 9.95x o.p. (ISBN 0-914622-03-X). Baja Trail.

Baja Oklahoma. Dan Jenkins. LC 81-65996. 1981. 12.95 o.p. (ISBN 0-689-11173-8, Atheneum). Macmillan.

Baker. Educational Research Council of America Staff. Ed. by Theodore N. Ferris & John P. Marchak. (Real People at Work Ser.: Q). (Illus.). 36p. 1977. 2.70 o.p. (ISBN 0-89247-124-7, 9615). Changing Times.

Baker Street Dozen: Sir Arthur Conan Doyle's Thirteen Favorite Sherlock Holmes Stories. Ed. by P J. Doyle & E. W. McDiarmid. 352p. 1987. 16.95 o.p. (ISBN 0-86553-187-0). Congdon & Weed.

Baker's Flower Quick Mix Cookbook. Kaye Manning. LC 84-28232. (Illus.). 216p. 1985. pap. 9.95 o.p. (ISBN 0-932620-42-6). Betterway Pubns.

Baker's Nickel. William S. Cohen. Ed. by Maria D. Guarnaschelli. LC 86-8409. 100p. 1986. 10.95 o.p. (ISBN 0-688-06549-X). Morrow.

Baker's Ohio School Law Guide 1981-1986. Robert T. Baker. 120.00 o.p. (ISBN 0-317-57010-2). Anderson Pub Co.

Baker's Ohio School Law Handbook, 1987-88. 1987. 40.00 o.p. (ISBN 0-317-57012-9). Anderson Pub Co.

Baker's Pocket Treasury of Religious Verse. Compiled by Donald T. Kauffman. (Direction Bks.). 384p. 1980. pap. 4.95 o.p. (ISBN 0-8010-5417-6). Baker Bk.

Bakery Business. W. B. Park. LC 83-8000. (Illus.). 32p. (gr. 1-3). 1983. PLB 10.45i o.p. (ISBN 0-316-69078-3). Little.

Bakery Restaurant Cookbook. Louis Szathmary. 256p. 1983. 14.95 o.p. (ISBN 0-8436-2195-8). Van Nos Reinhold.

Bakke Case: The Politics of Inequality. Joel Dreyfuss & Charles Lawrence, III. 1979. 8.95 o.p. (ISBN 0-15-110536-7). HarBraceJ.

Bakke Case: The Politics of Inequality. Joel Dreyfuss & Charles Lawrence, III. LC 78-22249. 1979. pap. 3.95 o.p. (ISBN 0-15-616782-4, Harv). HarBraceJ.

Bakunin's Writings. M. A. Bakunin. Repr. of 1947 ed. 25.00 o.p. (ISBN 0-527-04600-0). Kraus Repr.

Bal du Comte d'Orgel. Raymond Radiguet. 1959. pap. 3.95 o.p. (ISBN 0-686-54717-9). Schoenhof.

Balance, A Tried & Tested Formula for Church Growth. Ira North. 1983. pap. 5.95 o.p. (ISBN 0-89225-270-7). Gospel Advocate.

Balance Book: A Guide for Teachers. 2nd ed. Elementary Science Study Staff. 1975. text ed. 23.76 o.p. (ISBN 0-07-018575-1). McGraw.

Balance of Payments for the Thirteen Colonies 1768-1772. James F. Shepherd. Ed. by Stuart Bruchey. LC 84-45427. (American Economic History Ser.). 194p. 1985. lib. bdg. 29.00 o.p. (ISBN 0-8240-6671-5). Garland Pub.

Balance of Payments Statistics Yearbook. International Monetary Fund Staff. 12.00 o.s.i. (ISBN 1-55775-003-3). Intl Monetary.

Balance Pan Chain Pk. Date not set. (ISBN 0-07-521128-9). McGraw.

Balance Pkg. Date not set. (ISBN 0-07-521230-7). McGraw.

Balance Sheets & the Lending Banker. 5th ed. J. H. Clemens. LC 78-670081. 1977. 17.50x o.p. (ISBN 0-905118-15-4). Intl Pubns Serv.

Balanced Life. E. Hans Freund. 1960. (ISBN 0-8022-0541-0). Philos Lib.

Balanchine's Ballerinas: Conversations with the Muses. Robert Tracy & Sharon DeLano. (Illus.). 192p. 1983. 24.00 o.p. (ISBN 0-671-46146-X, Linden Pr). S&S.

Balanchine's Tchaikovsky: Interviews with George Balanchine. Solomon Volkov. Tr. by Antonina W. Bouis from Rus. 208p. 1985. 19.45 o.p. (ISBN 0-671-49875-4). S&S.

Balanchine's Tchaikovsky: Interviews With George Balanchine. Solomon Volkov. 1986. pap. 9.95 o.p. (ISBN 0-671-62255-2, Touchstone Bks). S&S.

Balancing Act. Rebecca Larson. (Going For It Ser.: No. 2). 1985. pap. 2.50 o.p. (ISBN 0-380-89900-0). Avon.

Balancing Act. Paul R. Satran. (Finding Mr. Right Ser.). 1983. pap. 2.75 o.p. (ISBN 0-380-83659-9, 83659-9). Avon.

Balancing Act: A Handbook for Working Mothers. Niki Scott. LC 78-10166. 1978. pap. 4.95 o.p. (ISBN 0-8362-6404-5). Andrews & McMeel.

Balancing Act II: A Career & a Family. rev. ed. Jayme Curley et al. LC 81-38524. 300p. 1981. pap. 8.95 o.p. (ISBN 0-914091-08-5). Chicago Review.

Bald Eagle's Flying Shadow: A Fourth of July Celebration. Louise Phillips. (Illus.). 64p. (gr. 2-4). 1984. 14.95 o.p. (ISBN 0-682-40193-5). Exposition-Phoenix.

Baldicer: A Simulation Game on Feeding the World's People. Georgeann Wilcoxson. (Awareness Games Ser). 1970. 30.00x o.p. (ISBN 0-8042-1150-7, John Knox). Westminster John Knox.

Baldios (Movie) (Big Little Bks.: No. 104). (Illus.). 350p. 1984. 6.95 o.p. (ISBN 0-318-02724-0). Bks Nippan.

Baldios (T.V.) (Big Little Bks.: No. 103). (Illus.). 350p. 1984. 6.95 o.p. (ISBN 0-318-02723-2). Bks Nippan.

Baldwin Thwarts the Opposition: The British General Election of 1935. Tom Stannage. 320p. 1980. 29.95 o.p. (ISBN 0-7099-0341-3, Pub. by Croom Helm Ltd). Routledge Chapman & Hall.

Baldwin's Ohio Legal Forms, 6 vols. (Baldwin's Ohio Practice Ser.). 5730p. 1973. Set. annual 360.00 o.p. (ISBN 0-8322-0003-4). Banks-Baldwin.

Baldwin's Ohio School Law Handbook. Ed. by Squire et al. 808p. 1987. pap. 45.00 o.p. (ISBN 0-8322-0202-9). Banks-Baldwin.

Balfour Conspiracy. Ian St. James. LC 80-69378. 1981. 10.95 o.p. (ISBN 0-689-11140-1, Atheneum). Macmillan.

Bali & Lombok: A Travel Survival Kit. 2nd ed. Mary Covernton et al. (Illus.). 224p. (Orig.). 1989. pap. 7.95 o.p. (ISBN 0-908086-91-1). Lonely Planet.

Balkan Cookbook. (Illus.). 287p. 1988. 24.95 o.s.i. (ISBN 0-87052-695-2). Hippocrene Bks.

Balkans in Our Time. rev. ed. Robert L. Wolff. 1978. pap. text ed. 11.95x o.p. (ISBN 0-393-09010-8). Norton.

Ball. David Lloyd. (First Words Ser.). (Illus.). 32p. (ps-3). 1983. 1.50 o.s.i. (ISBN 0-671-47105-8, Little Simon). S&S.

Ballad. Alan Bold. (Critical Idiom Ser.). 1979. 5.50x o.p. (ISBN 0-416-70890-0, NO.2035); pap. 5.25x o.p. (ISBN 0-416-70900-1, NO.2036). Routledge Chapman & Hall.

Ballad & the Plough. David K. Cameron. 256p. 1987. pap. 12.95 o.p. (ISBN 0-575-04076-9, Pub. by Gollancz England). David & Charles.

Ballad & the Source. Rosamond Lehmann. LC 74-17030. 312p. 1975. pap. 3.95 o.s.i. (ISBN 0-15-610260-9, Harv). HarBraceJ.

Ballad-Drama of Medieval Japan. James T. Araki. LC 76-50314. 1977. pap. 4.25 o.p. (ISBN 0-8048-1279-9). C E Tuttle.

Ballad of Sexual Dependency. Nan Goldin. (Illus.). 140p. (Orig.). 1989. pap. 19.95 o.p. (ISBN 0-89381-339-7). Aperture.

Ballad of the Sad Cafe. Edward A. Albee & Carson McCullers. LC 63-23325. 1963. 4.95 o.p. (ISBN 0-685-26843-8, Atheneum); pap. 2.65 o.p. (ISBN 0-685-26844-6). Macmillan.

Ballad of the Sad Cafe see Collected Short Stories.

Ballade of the Scottysshe Kynge. John Skelton. LC 67-23927. 104p. 1969. Repr. of 1882 ed. 35.00x o.p. (ISBN 0-8103-3461-5). Gale.

Ballads & Songs Collected by the Missouri Folk-Lore Society. 2nd ed. Ed. by Henry M. Belden. LC 55-7519. 554p. 1973. 55.00x o.p. (ISBN 0-8262-0142-3). U of Mo Pr.

Ballads, Blues & Swan Songs. William Wiser. LC 81-66032. 1982. 10.95 o.p. (ISBN 0-689-11188-6, Atheneum). Macmillan.

Ballads of Books. Ed. by Brander Matthews. LC 70-141032. 174p. 1971. Repr. of 1887 ed. 35.00x o.p. (ISBN 0-8103-3384-8). Gale.

Ballads of the Big California Woman. Jeanie Keltner. 224p. (Orig.). 1982. pap. 4.95 o.p. (ISBN 0-380-79061-0, 79061-0). Avon.

Ballet Collection. Compiled by Dance Notation Bureau Staff. (Illus.). 32p. (Orig.). 1980. pap. text ed. 8.50 o.p. (ISBN 0-932582-25-7). Dance Notation.

Ballet Techniques for the Male Dancer. Nikolai I. Tarasov. LC 82-46042. (Illus.). 448p. 1985. 24.95 o.p. (ISBN 0-385-18448-4). Doubleday.

Ballooning Adventures of Paddy Pork. John S. Goodall. LC 69-18625. (Illus.). (gr. 4-6). 1969. 5.95 o.p. (ISBN 0-15-205693-9, HJ). HarBraceJ.

Balloonist. MacDonald Harris. 1977. pap. 1.95 o.p. (ISBN 0-380-01739-3, 34504). Avon.

Ballot Question in Nineteenth Century English Politics. Bruce L. Kinzer. Ed. by Peter Stansky & Leslie Hume. LC 81-48361. (Modern British History Ser.). 300p. 1982. lib. bdg. 43.00 o.p. (ISBN 0-8240-5157-2). Garland Pub.

Ballots & Fence Rails: Reconstruction on the Lower Cape Fear. W. McKee Evans. (Illus.). 328p. 1974. pap. 7.95 o.p. (ISBN 0-393-00711-1, Norton Lib). Norton.

Ballots & Trade Union Democracy. Roderick Martin & Roger Undy. 280p. 1984. text ed. 45.00x o.p. (ISBN 0-631-13539-1). Basil Blackwell.

Ballots & Trade Union Democracy. Roderick Martin & Roger Undy. 280p. 1986. pap. 14.95x o.p. (ISBN 0-631-13541-3). Basil Blackwell.

Ballpoint Bananas & Other Jokes for Children. Charles Keller. (Illus.). (gr. 3-7). 1976. pap. 5.95 o.s.i. (ISBN 0-13-055517-7, Pub. by Treehouse). P-H.

Ballylee: The Tower Poems with Letter by George Yeats. William Butler Yeats & George Yeats. (Illus.). 48p. 1983. 70.00 o.p. (ISBN 0-317-12323-8). Press Alley.

Balthazar, the Black & Shining Prince. Alvin L. Ben-Moring. LC 74-8177. (Illus.). (gr. 7 up). 1974. 4.95 o.s.i. (ISBN 0-664-32554-8, Westminster). Westminster John Knox.

Balthus. Sabine Rewald. Ed. by Kathleen Howard. LC 83-26560. (Orig.). 1984. pap. 4.95 o.p. (Dist. by Harry N. Abrams Co.) (ISBN 0-87099-366-6). Metro Mus Art.

Balthus. Skira-Rizzoli Staff & Jean Leymarie. LC 82-60071. (Illus.). 156p. 1982. pap. 17.50 o.p. (ISBN 0-8478-0458-5). Rizzoli Intl.

Baltimore Orioles. rev. ed. Hinz. LC 82-239149. (Baseball Today Ser.). 48p. (gr. 4 up). 1982. PLB 9.95 o.p. (ISBN 0-87191-853-6). Creative Ed.

Baltimore: The Nineteenth Century Black Capital. Leroy Graham. 346p. (Orig.). 1982. lib. bdg. 32.00 o.p. (ISBN 0-8191-2624-1); pap. text ed. 15.25 o.p. (ISBN 0-8191-2625-X). U Pr of Amer.

Balzac En Sa Touraine. Honore De Balzac & Marie Helene Richard. (Illus.). 68p. 1975. 9.95 o.p. (ISBN 0-686-53868-4). French & Eur.

Bama under Bear: Alabama's Family Tides. rev. ed. Tommy Ford. (College Sports Ser.: Football). (Illus.). 288p. 1983. 10.95 o.p. (ISBN 0-87397-251-1). Strode.

Bamboo Bed. William Eastlake. 336p. 1985. pap. 3.50 o.p. (ISBN 0-380-69966-4). Avon.

Bamboo Cradle. Avraham Schwartlbaum. 1988. write for info. o.p. Feldheim.

Bamboo Fire: An Anthropologist in New Guinea. William E. Mitchell. (Illus.). 1979. 9.95 o.p. (ISBN 0-393-06436-0); pap. 3.95 o.p. (ISBN 0-393-95085-9). Norton.

Bamboo of Japan: Splendor in Four Seasons. Shinji Takama. (Illus.). 92p. (Orig.). 1986. pap. 19.95 o.p. (ISBN 0-87040-707-4). Japan Pubns USA.

Banana Bits. Steven Kroll. (Snuggle & Read Story Bks.). (Illus.). 32p. (Orig.). (ps-3). 1982. pap. 1.95 o.p. (ISBN 0-380-79111-0, 79111-0, Camelot). Avon.

Bananas Move to the Ceiling. Esther Manes & Stephen Manes. LC 82-17519. (Easy-Read Story Bks.). (Illus.). 32p. (gr. k-3). 1983. 3.95 o.p. (ISBN 0-531-03575-1). Watts.

Banares: The Sacred City of India. Raghubir Singh. (Illus.). 1987. 40.00 o.p. (ISBN 0-500-24132-5). Thames Hudson.

Bancroft Library, Catalog of Printed Books, 22 Vols. Ed. by University of California, Berkeley Staff. 1970. Set. 1980.00 o.p. (ISBN 0-8161-0678-9, Hall Library). G K Hall.

Bancroft Library, University of California, Berkeley: Catalog of Printed Books, Third Supplement. Bancroft Library University of California, Berkeley Editors. (Library Catalogs-Bib. Guides). 1979. lib. bdg. 830.00 o.p. (ISBN 0-8161-1163-4, Hall Library). G K Hall.

Band Theory of Metals. S. L. Altmann. 1970. 70.00 o.p. (ISBN 0-08-015602-9); pap. 70.00 o.p. (ISBN 0-08-015601-0). Pergamon.

Bandit of the Black Hills. Max Brand. (Gunsmoke Western Ser.). 176p. 1988. text ed. 12.95 o.p. (ISBN 0-85997-862-1, Pub. by Firecrest Pub Ltd). Prescott Pr NH.

Banditry in Islam: Case Studies in Morocco, Algeria & the Pakistan North West Frontier. David M. Hart. 80p. 1987. lib. bdg. 14.95 o.p. (ISBN 0-906559-22-7). Lynne Rienner.
Bangalle. Stephen Cosgrove. (Illus.). 1136p. 1977. 1.50 o.p. French & Eur.
Bangladesh: A Traveller's Guide. Don Yeo. (Illus.). 200p. (Orig.). 1984. pap. 11.95 o.p. (ISBN 0-903909-21-9, Pub. by Roger Lascelles England). Bradt Ent.
Bangladesh: Current Trends & Development Issues. Carl A. Jayarajah. x, 116p. 1979. 10.00 o.p. (ISBN 0-686-36100-8, RC-7904). World Bank.
Bangladesh: The First Decade. Marcus Franda. 1982. 24.00x o.p. (ISBN 0-8364-0891-8). South Asia Bks.
Bangladesh: The First Decade. Marcus Franda. LC 81-19639. 1981. 9.95 o.p. (ISBN 0-88333-006-7). U Field Staff Intl.
Banjangi. F. Staschewski. Repr. of 1917 ed. 15.00 o.p. (ISBN 0-384-57550-1). Johnson Repr.
Banjo of the Bush: The Life & Times of A. B. "Banjo" Paterson. 2nd ed. Clement Semmler. LC 84-3550. (Illus.). 264p. 1984. 25.00 o.p. (ISBN 0-7022-1756-5). U of Queensland Pr.
Banjo's Brand. Larry Chatham. (Lythway Ser.). 1987. lib. bdg. 16.50x o.p. (ISBN 0-7451-0578-5, Pub. by Chivers Pr UK). G K Hall.
Banjos: The Tsumura Collection. Akira Tsumura. LC 83-80219. (Illus.). 132p. 1984. 39.95 o.p. (ISBN 0-87011-605-3). Kodansha.
Bank Book: How to Get the Most for Your Banking Dollars. Naphtali Hoffman & Stephen Brobreck. Ed. by Jack Gillis. LC 85-27271. 200p. 1986. pap. 5.95 o.p. (ISBN 0-15-610676-0, Harv). HarBraceJ.
Bank Cash Compensation Survey 1987. 243p. 1987. 90.00 o.p. (ISBN 1-55520-013-3, 451). Bank Admin Inst.
Bank Letter Writing Handbook. 400p. 1987. 48.00 o.p. (ISBN 0-317-66092-6, 408). Bank Admin Inst.
Bank of Boston Two Hundred: A History of New England's Leading Bank, Seventeen Eighty-Four - Nineteen Eighty-Four. Ben A. Williams, Jr. LC 82-23431. 466p. 1984. 27.00 o.p. (ISBN 0-395-34432-8). HM.
Bank of England Operations Eighteen Ninety to Nineteen Fourteen. Richard S. Sayers. 1970. Repr. of 1936 ed. lib. bdg. 22.50x o.p. (ISBN 0-8371-4329-2, SABE). Greenwood.
Bank Reconciliation Projects. 2nd ed. Robert J. McCullough & Kenneth Everard. pap. cancelled o.s.i. (ISBN 0-02-830770-4); cancelled o.s.i. (ISBN 0-02-830780-1). Glencoe.
Bank Records: A Guide to Management & Retention. Bank Administration Institute. 68p. 1982. 12.00 o.p. (331). Bank Admin Inst.
Bank Register: 1986. 1954p. 1986. 150.00 o.p. (ISBN 0-8002-4055-3). Intl Pubns Serv.
Bank Robbers Wrote My Diary. Harry McCormick & Mary Carey. (Illus.). 144p. 1985. 10.95 o.p. (ISBN 0-89015-464-3). Eakin Pr.
Bank Security. Ralph E. Anderson. 1982. text ed. 32.95 o.p. (ISBN 0-409-95038-6). Butterworth.
Bankei Zen. Ed. by Yoshito S. Hakeda. Tr. by Peter Haskel. LC 83-81372. (Eastern Bks.). 240p. 1985. 27.50 o.p. (ISBN 0-394-53524-3, GP 886). Grove.
Bankei Zen. Ed. by Yoshito S. Hakeda. Tr. by Peter Haskel. LC 83-81372. (Eastern Bks.). 1985. pap. 9.95 o.p. (ISBN 0-394-62493-9, E-272, Ever). Grove.
Banker. Dick Francis. 1983. 9.95 o.p. (ISBN 0-8161-3604-1, Large Print Bks). G K Hall.
Banker's Guide to Financial Statements. 2nd ed. Thomas J. O'Malia. LC 82-8786. 348p. 1982. 45.00 o.p. (ISBN 0-87267-038-4). Bank Admin Inst.
Banker's Handbook. rev. ed. Ed. by William H. Baughn & Charls E. Walker. LC 77-89797. 1978. 65.00 o.p. (ISBN 0-87094-154-2). Dow Jones-Irwin.
Banking see Money & Banking.
Banking & Financial Deregulation: A Blessing or a Curse? Eugene B. Mapel. 96p. 1984. 12.95 o.p. (ISBN 0-682-40200-1). Exposition-Phoenix.
Banking & Financial Institutions Law in a Nutshell. William A. Lovett. LC 83-23277. (Nutshell Ser.). 409p. 1983. pap. text ed. 10.95 o.p. (ISBN 0-314-78557-4). West Pub.
Banking Automation, 1970-71, 2 vols. Ed. by Geoffrey W. Dummer et al. 1971. 505.00 o.p. (ISBN 0-08-016120-0). Pergamon.
Banking Dictionary. Ed. by Swiss Association of Bank Employees Staff. 264p. (Eng. & Fr.). 1984. pap. text ed. 30.00 o.p. (ISBN 3-258-03340-4, Pub. by P Haupt CH). Gower Pub Co.
Banking Is Serious Business:(Don't You Believe It) Ernest O. LaCroix. 1979. 5.00 o.p. (ISBN 0-682-49449-6). Exposition-Phoenix.
Banking Laws & Regulations. 200p. 1987. 22.00 o.p. (ISBN 0-317-66100-0, 129). Bank Admin Inst.
Banking Management. James B. Bexley. LC 78-53195. 192p. 1978. 19.00x o.p. (ISBN 0-87201-054-6). Gulf Pub.
Banking on the Biosphere. 1979. 10.00 o.p. (ISBN 0-905347-10-2). C I D E.
Banking Problems under the UCC. Practising Law Institute Staff & Hillman William C. LC 82-61809. (Commercial Law & Practice Course Handbook Ser.: No. 286). (Illus.). 407p. 1982. 40.00 o.p. (A4-4043). PLI.
Bankrolling Ballots: The Role of Business in Financing State Ballot Question Campaigns. Steve Lydenberg. 90p. 1976. 1.00 o.p. CEP.
Bankrupt & Other Plays. David Mercer. 1981. 6.95 o.p. (ISBN 0-413-29940-6, NO.2597). Heinemann Ed.
Bankruptcy Code Amendments - a Utility in Chapter 11: First Annual New England Bankruptcy Conference. New England Bankruptcy Conference Staff & Massachusetts Continuing Legal Education, Inc. Staff. LC 84-61789. write for info. o.p. Mass CLE.
Bankruptcy Code Reexamined & Updated, Vol. 1. University of Colorado, Boulder School of Law Staff & American Law Institute-American Bar Association Committee on Continuing Professional Education. LC 83-233698. (ALI-ABA Course of Study Materials Ser.). Date not set. price not set o.p. Am Law Inst.
Bankruptcy Code, Rules & Forms, Including: Federal Rules of Civil Procedure & Federal Rules of Evidence, 1987 Edition. West's Editorial Staff. 1255p. 1987. pap. text ed. write for info. o.p. (ISBN 0-314-38368-9). West Pub.
Bankruptcy Code, Rules & Official Forms: Law School & C.L.E. Edition, 1984 Edition Revision As Amended to July 10, 1984. West Publishing Company Staff. 602p. 1984. pap. 9.95 o.p. (ISBN 0-314-85273-5). West Pub.
Bankruptcy Code, Rules & Official Forms, 1987. Law School ed. West's Editorial Staff. 816p. 1987. pap. text ed. 12.95 o.p. (ISBN 0-314-38235-6). West Pub.
Bankruptcy, Do It Yourself. 3rd ed. Janice Kosel. Ed. by Ralph Warner. LC 80-81774. 194p. 1984. pap. 19.95 o.p. (ISBN 0-917316-76-2). Nolo Pr.
Bankruptcy: Do It Yourself. 5th., rev. ed. Janice Kosel. 184p. 1987. pap. 17.95 o.p. (ISBN 0-87337-043-0). Nolo Pr.
Bankruptcy: Do It Yourself. 6th, rev. ed. Janice Kosel. 200p. 1988. pap. 17.95 o.p. (ISBN 0-87337-071-6). Nolo Pr.
Bankruptcy Law Handbook. Richard I. Aaron. 1987. 45.00 o.p. (ISBN 0-87632-538-X). Clark Boardman.
Bankruptcy Practice & Procedure 1985, 2 vols. 1430p. 1985. 15.00 o.p. (A4-4130). PLI.
Bankruptcy Practice for Bank Counsel 1985, 2 vols. 1181p. 1985. 15.00 o.p. (B4-6721). PLI.
Bankruptcy Practice for Bank Counsel, 1983. Practising Law Institute Staff et al. LC 83-182435. (Corporate Law & Practice Course Handbook Ser.: No. 418). 1072p. 1983. 40.00 o.p. (B4-6651). PLI.
Bankruptcy: Problem, Process, Reform. David T. Stanley et al. LC 79-161592. 270p. 1971. 11.95 o.p. (ISBN 0-8157-8098-2). Brookings.
Banks & Their Borrowers: New Opportunities in Financial Services. Practising Law Institute Staff & Carl D. Lobell. LC 84-61951. (Corporate Law & Practice Course Handbook Ser.: No. 462). (Illus.). 912p. 1984. 15.00 o.p. (B46699). PLI.
Banks, the SEC, & Regulatory Agencies: Enforcement & Civil Litigation Developments, Vol. 476. Practising Law Institute Staff. 1069p. 1985. pap. 15.00 o.p. (ISBN 0-317-27475-9, #B4-6707). PLI.
Banksias, Vol. 1. C. Rosser & A. S. George. LC 81-66685. 1982. 1965.00 o.p. (ISBN 0-12-598001-9); 1750.00 o.p. (ISBN 0-12-598011-6). Acad Pr.
Banlieue de Paris a l'Aurore, Mouvement Brownien. Michel Butor. (Coll. Huit). 18.50 o.p. (ISBN 0-685-37243-X). French & Eur.
Bannaman Legacy. Catherine Cookson. 528p. 1985. 18.45 o.s.i. (ISBN 0-671-53024-0). Summit Bks.
Banner in the Sky. James R. Ullman. (gr. 7-9). 1967. pap. 1.75 o.p. (ISBN 0-671-56081-6); 2.95 o.p. Archway.
Banner in the Sky. James R. Ullman. 256p. (gr. 7-10). 1984. pap. 2.95 o.p. (ISBN 0-671-54629-5). Archway.
Bannerman. Jay Flynn. 1976. pap. 1.25 o.s.i. (ISBN 0-8439-0389-9, LB389, Pub. by Leisure Bks CT). Dorchester Pub Co.
Bannerman. Jay Flynn. 192p. 1982. pap. 2.25 o.p. (ISBN 0-8439-1119-0, Pub. by Leisure Bks CT). Dorchester Pub Co.
Bannerman Border Incident. Jay Flynn. 1976. pap. 1.25 o.p. (ISBN 0-8439-0401-1, LB401, Pub. by Leisure Bks CT). Dorchester Pub Co.
Banners & Flags: How to Sew a Celebration. Margot C. Blair & Cathleen Ryan. LC 77-2246. (Illus.). 1977. 16.95 o.p. (ISBN 0-15-110560-X); pap. 7.95 o.p. (ISBN 0-15-610678-7, Harv). HarBraceJ.
Banners & Mobiles & Odds & Ends. Vienna. (Illus.). 40p. (Orig.). 1973. pap. 2.50 o.p. (ISBN 0-8192-1147-8). Morehouse Pub.
Banquet. Carolyn Slaughter. LC 83-24204. 192p. 1984. 13.45 o.p. (ISBN 0-89919-274-2). Ticknor & Fields.
Banquet Business. Arno B. Schmidt. 256p. 1983. 26.95 o.p. (ISBN 0-8436-2147-8). Van Nos Reinhold.
Banquet of the Word: Bible Study Based on the Sunday Readings. Thomas Welbers. LC 86-60891. 358p. 1986. pap. 17.95 o.p. (ISBN 0-89390-073-7). Resource Pubns.
Banquets & Beggers: Dramas & Meditations on Six Parables. W. A. Poovey. LC 74-77672. 128p. (Orig.). 1974. pap. 2.25 o.p. (ISBN 0-8066-1419-6, 10-0540, Augsburg); (ISBN 0-8066-1420-X, 10-0541). Augsburg Fortress.
Bantu Bureaucracy: A Century of Political Evolution Among the Basoga of Uganda. Lloyd A. Fallers. LC 65-10270. 1965. lib. bdg. 12.50x o.s.i. (ISBN 0-226-23678-1). U of Chicago Pr.
Bantu Bureaucracy: A Century of Political Evolution Among the Basoga of Uganda. Lloyd A. Fallers. LC 65-10270. 1965. pap. text ed. 2.25x o.s.i. (ISBN 0-226-23680-3, P197, Phoen). U of Chicago Pr.
Bantu Folklore. Matthew L. Hewat. LC 77-129948. 1970. Repr. of 1906 ed. lib. bdg. 22.50x o.p. (ISBN 0-8371-4992-4, HBF&, Pub. by Negro U Pr). Greenwood.
Bantu Heritage. Henri P. Junod. LC 78-107510. (Illus.). 1970. Repr. of 1938 ed. 35.00x o.p. (ISBN 0-8371-3780-2, JUB&, Pub. by Negro U Pr). Greenwood.
Bantu-Speaking Peoples of Southern Africa. Ed. by W. D. Hammond-Tooke. (Illus.). 298p. 1980. pap. 35.00 o.p. (ISBN 0-7100-0708-6). Routledge Chapman & Hall.
Baptism: A Pastoral Perspective. Eugene L. Brand. LC 75-2827. 128p. (Orig.). 1975. pap. 4.50 o.p. (ISBN 0-8066-1472-2, 10-0545, Augsburg). Augsburg Fortress.
Baptism in the New Testament. Oscar Cullmann. LC 78-6937. 84p. 1978. pap. 5.95 o.s.i. (ISBN 0-664-24219-7, Westminster). Westminster John Knox.
Baptismal Names. 4th ed. Joseph L. Weidenhan. LC 68-26618. 352p. 1968. Repr. of 1931 ed. 46.00x o.p. (ISBN 0-8103-3136-5). Gale.
Baptist Answers Reviewed. C. R. Nichol. Date not set. pap. 1.95 o.p. (ISBN 0-915547-51-1). Abilene Christ U.
Baptistery of Pisa. Christine Smith. LC 77-94715. (Outstanding Dissertations in the Fine Arts Ser.). (Illus.). 432p. 1978. lib. bdg. 53.00 o.p. (ISBN 0-8240-3249-7). Garland Pub.
Baptists & the Bible. Russ Bush & Tom Nettles. LC 80-11694. 1980. 14.95 o.p. (ISBN 0-8024-0466-9); pap. 10.95 o.p. (ISBN 0-8024-0474-X). Moody.
Bar & Party Guide, Complete Guide to Mixing Drinks. Edie Hilton. 1.50 o.p. (ISBN 0-87067-486-2). Borden.
Bar Code Book. Richard G. Lloyd. (Applied Information Technology Ser.). (Illus.). 65p. Date not set. pap. text ed. 6.95 o.p. (ISBN 0-939303-11-6). Educ Lrn Syst.
Bar Joint Denture. Eugene J. Dolder & Gustav T. Durrer. (Illus.). 150p. 1978. 48.00 o.p. (ISBN 0-931386-02-0). Quint Pub Co.
Bar Mitzvah. Stuart Schoenfeld et al. LC 85-4412. (Illus.). 192p. 1985. 50.00 o.p. (ISBN 0-385-19826-4). Doubleday.
Bar Mitzvah Mother's Manual. Alice K. Lanckton. (Illus.). 304p. 1986. pap. 6.95 o.p. (ISBN 0-87052-283-3). Hippocrene Bks.
Barbados. (Population Profiles: No. 9). 39p. 1978. pap. 5.00 o.p. (ISBN 0-685-42365-4, UNFPA15, UNFPA). UNIPUB.
Barbara Cartland: An Authorized Biography. Gwen Robyns. 514p. 1985. lib. bdg. 17.95 o.p. (ISBN 0-8161-3943-1, Large Print Bks). G K Hall.
Barbara Morgan. Intro. by Peter Bunnell. LC 72-92282. (Illus.). 160p. pap. 6.95 o.p. (ISBN 0-88360-037-4). Amon Carter.
Barbara Walters: Today's Woman. Jason Bonderoff. 1975. pap. 1.50 o.p. (ISBN 0-8439-0306-6, Pub. by Leisure Bks CT). Dorchester Pub Co.
Barbara Wooton: Social Science & Public Policy. Ed. by Philip Bean & David Whynes. 280p. 1986. text ed. 55.00 o.p. (ISBN 0-422-79690-5, 9786, Pub. by Tavistock England). Routledge Chapman & Hall.
Barbara's World of Horses & Ponies. Barbara Woodhouse. LC 83-20372. (Illus.). 120p. 1984. 14.70 o.s.i. (ISBN 0-671-46141-9). Summit Bks.
Barbarossa Red. Dennis Jones. 368p. 1985. 16.95 o.p. (ISBN 0-316-47292-1). Little.
Barbarous Coast. Ross Macdonald. 192p. 1975. 2.95 o.s.i. (ISBN 0-553-24268-7); pap. 2.95 o.s.i. (ISBN 0-553-12249-5). Bantam.
Barbary Coast: Algeria Under the Turks. John B. Wolf. (Illus.). 1979. 19.95x o.p. (ISBN 0-393-01205-0). Norton.
Barbary Coast Tong. Tom Cutter. (Tracker Ser.: No. 6). 144p. 1985. pap. 2.25 o.p. (ISBN 0-380-89583-8). Avon.
Barbecue Cook Book. 5th ed. Sunset Editors. LC 78-70272. (Illus.). 96p. 1979. pap. 5.95 o.p. (ISBN 0-376-02079-2, Sunset Bks). Sunset-Lane.
Barbed Wire on the Isle of Man. Alexander Ramati. LC 79-3361. 252p. 1980. 10.95 o.p. (ISBN 0-15-110671-1). HarBraceJ.
Barbeque & Smoke Cookery. rev. ed. Maggie Waldron. LC 82-24683. (Illus.). 192p. 1983. pap. 7.95 o.p. (ISBN 0-89286-211-4, One Hund One Prods). Ortho.
Barber of Seville. Pierre-Augustin Beaumarchais. Ed. & tr. by Brobury P. Ellis. LC 65-27803. (Crofts Classics Ser). 1966. pap. 1.25x o.s.i. (ISBN 0-88295-009-6). Harlan Davidson.
Barber's Shop. rev. & enl. ed. Richard W. Proctor. LC 74-79753. (Illus.). 280p. 1971. Repr. of 1883 ed. 35.00x o.p. (ISBN 0-8103-3036-9). Gale.
Barbiturates: The Oblivion Express. 1984. pap. 0.25 o.p. (ISBN 0-89230-184-8). Do It Now.
Barbra Streisand: The Woman, the Myth, the Music. Shaun Considine. 1986. pap. 4.50 o.p. (ISBN 0-440-10464-5). Dell.
Barcelona Travel Guide. Berlitz Editors. (Travel Guides Ser.). 1976. pap. 4.95 o.p. (ISBN 0-317-12101-4, Berlitz). Macmillan.
Bard: The Odyssey of the Irish. Morgan Llywelyn. LC 84-6645. 463p. 1984. 16.45 o.p. (ISBN 0-395-35352-1). HM.
Bardot, Deneuve, Fonda: An Autobiography. Roger Vadim. 416p. 1986. 17.45 o.p. (ISBN 0-671-53007-0). S&S.
Bard's Theme. Robert Emmert Gray. 1977. 5.00 o.p. (ISBN 0-682-48961-1). Exposition-Phoenix.
Bareback. Merrilee Steiner. (Going for It Ser.: No. 5). 1986. pap. 2.50 o.p. (ISBN 0-380-89903-5, Flare). Avon.
Barefoot Brigade. Douglas C. Jones. LC 82-892. 320p. 1984. 15.50 o.s.i. (ISBN 0-03-060041-3, Owl Bks); pap. 5.95 o.s.i. (ISBN 0-03-000434-9). H Holt & Co.
Barefoot Doctor's Manual: The Cloudburst Press Edition. LC 81-12401. (Illus.). 384p. 1981. pap. 14.95 o.s.i. (ISBN 0-914842-52-8). Madrona Pubs.
Barefoot in Arcadia: Memories of a More Innocent Era. Louis B. Wright. LC 74-11038. (Illus.). xii, 176p. 1981. pap. 12.95 o.p. (ISBN 0-87249-414-4). U of SC Pr.
Barely Undercover. M. Arthur Bogen. (Burchardt & Decker Mystery Ser.). 112p. (Orig.). (gr. 7 up). 1983. pap. 2.25 o.p. (ISBN 0-380-85217-9, 85217-9, Flare). Avon.
Bargain Bride. Evelyn S. Lampman. LC 76-46567. 192p. (gr. 7 up). 1977. 8.95 o.p. (ISBN 0-689-50075-0, Atheneum). Macmillan.
Bargain Hunting in Los Angeles. rev. ed. Barbara Partridge. 352p. pap. 10.95 o.p. (ISBN 0-87905-267-8). Gibbs Smith Pub.
Bargain Hunting in Sacramento. 2nd ed. Victoria Goff. (Illus.). pap. 4.95 o.p. (ISBN 0-9615416-1-X). RND Pub.
Bargain Hunting in the Bay Area. 4th ed. Sally Socolich. pap. 5.95 o.p. (ISBN 0-914728-40-7). Wingbow Pr.
Bargain Hunting in the Bay Area. 5th ed. Sally Socolich. (ISBN 0-914728-48-2). Wingbow Pr.
Bargain Price Offers & Similar Marketing Practices. OECD Staff. (Illus., Orig.). 1980. pap. text ed. 6.00 o.p. (ISBN 92-64-12033-5, 24-80-01-1). OECD.
Bargain Shopper's Guide to Northern New England. Margaret A. Marden. LC 81-66701. 208p. (Orig.). 1981. pap. 7.95 o.p. (ISBN 0-89272-122-7, PIC474). Down East.
Bargaining & Dispute Resolution Curricula: A Sourcebook, Vol. 12. Compiled by James W. Dean & Richard Schwindt. 238p. 1985. 14.00 o.p. (ISBN 0-88024-112-8). Eno River Pr.
Bargaining Behavior: Beitraege zur Experimentellen Wirtschaftsordnung. Heinz Sauermann. cancelled o.s.i. (ISBN 3-163-40972-5). Adlers Foreign Bks.
Barge Book. Jerry Bushey. LC 83-7746. (Carolrhoda Photo Bks.). (Illus.). 32p. (gr. k-4). 1984. lib. bdg. 9.95 o.p. (ISBN 0-87614-205-6). Carolrhoda Bks.
Bargello Antics. Encore ed. Dorothy Kaestner. (Illus.). 1980. 16.95 o.p. (ISBN 0-684-15995-3); pap. 2.50 o.p. (ISBN 0-684-15996-1, ScribT). Scribner.
Barham Downs, 2 vols. Robert Bage. Ed. by Ronald Paulson. LC 78-60850. (Novel 1720-1805 Ser.: Vol. 9). 1979. Set. lib. bdg. 75.00 o.p. (ISBN 0-8240-3658-1). Garland Pub.
Barhebraeus' Scholia on the Old Testament Pt. 1: Genesis 2nd Samuel. Ed. by Martin Sprengling & William C. Graham. LC 32-461. (Oriental Institute Pubns. Ser: No. 13). 1931. 28.00x o.p. (ISBN 0-226-62107-3). U of Chicago Pr.

Barkham Burroughs' Encyclopaedia of Astounding Facts & Useful Information 1889-1986 Date Book. Barkham Burroughs. Ed. by Miggs Burroughs. (Illus.). 110p. 1985. pap. 4.95 o.p. (ISBN 0-9610994-2-9). Brayden.

Barking Deer. Jonathan Rubin. 336p. 1982. pap. 3.25 o.p. (ISBN 0-380-61135-X, 68437-3). Avon.

Barkley Come Home. Marilyn D. Anderson. (Illus.). 96p. (gr. 3-5). 1985. 2.25 o.s.i. (ISBN 0-87406-027-3). Willowisp Pr.

Barn. Randolph Scott. 1979. 5.00 o.p. (ISBN 0-682-49399-6). Exposition-Phoenix.

Barnaby: Wanted: A Fairy Godmother, Vol. 1. Crockett Johnson. 224p. 1985. pap. 2.95 o.s.i. (ISBN 0-345-32673-3, Del Rey). Ballantine.

Barnet & Stubbs's: Practical Guide to Writings with Additional Readings. 4th ed. Sylvan Barnet & Marcia Stubbs. 1983. pap. text ed. 14.95 o.p. (ISBN 0-316-08153-1). Little.

Barnett Newman. Harold Rosenberg. (Contemporary Artists Ser.). 1985. 75.00 o.p. (ISBN 0-8109-1360-7). Abrams.

Barney & the UFO. Margaret G. Clark. LC 79-52046. (Illus.). (gr. 4 up). 1979. 8.95 o.p. (ISBN 0-396-07711-0). Dodd.

Barney Buck & the Buck of Goober Holler. (Barney Buck Ser.). 224p. (gr. 4-7). 1985. 3.50 o.p. (ISBN 0-8423-0129-1). Tyndale.

Barney Buck & the Flying Solar Cycle. Gilbert Morris. (Barney Buck Ser.). 144p. (gr. 4-7). 1985. 3.50 o.p. (ISBN 0-8423-0131-3). Tyndale.

Barney Buck & the Phantom of the Circus. Gilbert Morris. (Barney Buck Ser.). 192p. (gr. 4-7). 1985. 3.50 o.p. (ISBN 0-8423-0132-1). Tyndale.

Barney Buck & the Rough Rider Special. Gilbert Morris. (Barney Buck Ser.). 208p. (Orig.). (gr. 6-8). 1985. pap. 3.95 o.p. (ISBN 0-8423-0134-8). Tyndale.

Barney Buck & the World's Wackiest Wedding. Gilbert Morris. (Barney Buck Ser.). 160p. (Orig.). (gr. 6-8). 1986. pap. 3.95 o.p. (ISBN 0-8423-0339-1). Tyndale.

Barns of Wisconsin. Jerold W. Apps. LC 77-5472. (Illus.). 1977. pap. 10.00 o.p. (ISBN 0-915024-14-4). WI Trails.

Barnstormers. Don Dwiggins. (Illus.). 144p. 1982. pap. 5.95 o.p. (ISBN 0-8306-2297-7, 2297). TAB Bks.

Baron of Beacon Hill: A Biography of John Hancock. William M. Fowler. 1980. 15.00 o.p. (ISBN 0-395-27619-5). HM.

Baron of the Bull Pen. Dick Friendlich. (gr. 7-10). 1955. 4.75 o.s.i. (ISBN 0-664-32115-1, Westminster). Westminster John Knox.

Baroness. Henri Troyat. 1961. 4.50 o.p. (ISBN 0-671-06760-5). S&S.

Baroque & Rococo. A. C. Sewter. LC 73-152765. (History of Art Ser.). (Illus.). 1972. 6.95 o.p. (ISBN 0-15-110691-6). HarBraceJ.

Baroque Arsenal. Mary Kaldor. (American Century Ser.). 294p. 1981. 17.95 o.p. (ISBN 0-8090-2812-3); pap. 7.25 o.p. (ISBN 0-8090-1501-3). Hill & Wang.

Baroque Concerto. Arthur Hutchings. 363p. Repr. of 1961 ed. lib. bdg. 49.00 o.p. (Pub. by Am Repr Serv). Reprint Servs.

Baroque Painters. John Canaday. 1972. pap. 2.95 o.p. (ISBN 0-393-00665-4, Norton Lib). Norton.

Baroque: Principles, Styles, Modes, Themes. Germain Bazin. (Illus.). 368p. 1978. pap. text ed. 12.95 o.p. (ISBN 0-393-09055-8). Norton.

Baroreceptors & Hypertension. Ed. by P. Kezdi. 1967. 115.00 o.p. (ISBN 0-08-012488-7). Pergamon.

Barracuda. Irving Greenfield. LC 77-90660. 1978. 8.95 o.p. (ISBN 0-87795-188-8, Arbor Hse). Morrow.

Barracudas. Keefe Brasselle. 1975. pap. 1.50 o.p. (ISBN 0-380-01040-2, 14639). Avon.

Barrier. Hilda B. Powicke. (Orig.). 1964. pap. 0.95 o.p. (ISBN 0-377-80151-8). Friendship Pr.

Barrier Coextruded Plastic Systems: Markets, Developments, Technologies. Business Communications Staff. 187p. 1986. 1750.00 o.p. (ISBN 0-89336-364-2, P-085). BCC.

Barrier Island Migration: An Annotated Bibliography. Stephen F. Leatherman. LC 84-243221. (Public Administration Ser.: P-1696). 54p. 1985. pap. 8.25 o.p. (ISBN 0-89028-426-1). Vance Biblios.

Barrier Methods of Contraception. Elizabeth B. Connell & Howard J. Tatum. LC 84-71598. 1985. 8.65 o.p. (ISBN 0-917634-17-9). Creative Infomatics.

Barriers & Hazards in Counseling. Dorothy E. Johnson & Mary J. Vestermark. LC 73-14990. (Orig.). 1972. pap. 22.36 o.p. (ISBN 0-395-04694-7). HM.

Barriers to Belief. Norman F. Langford. (Layman's Theological Library). 1958. pap. 1.45 o.s.i. (ISBN 0-664-24010-0, Westminster). Westminster John Knox.

Barriers to Ecumenism: The Holy See & the World Council on Social Questions. Thomas S. Derr. LC 82-18761. 112p. (Orig.). 1983. pap. 7.95 o.p. (ISBN 0-88344-031-8). Orbis Bks.

Barrington Moore Jr. A Critical Appraisal. Dennis Smith. LC 82-19197. 224p. (Orig.). 1983. lib. bdg. 29.95 o.p. (ISBN 0-87332-241-X); pap. text ed. 12.95 o.p. (ISBN 0-87332-242-8). M E Sharpe.

Barron's Compact Guide to Colleges. Ed. by Barron's College Division Staff. 384p. (gr. 10-12). 1986. pap. 4.95 o.p. (ISBN 0-8120-3654-9). Barron.

Barron's Guide to Law Schools. 7th ed. Epstein et al. 488p. 1986. pap. 10.95 o.p. (ISBN 0-8120-3651-4). Barron.

Barron's Guide to Law Schools. 6th ed. Elliott M. Epstein et al. LC 84-9316. 1984. 8.95 o.p. (ISBN 0-8120-2772-8). Barron.

Barron's Guide to Medical & Dental Schools. 2nd ed. Saul Wischnitzer. LC 85-11056. 320p. (gr. 12). 1985. pap. 9.95 o.p. (ISBN 0-8120-2788-4). Barron.

Barron's Guide to the Best, Most Popular, & Most Exciting Colleges. 4th ed. Ed. by Barron's College Division Staff. LC 81-17573. 416p. (gr. 10-12). 1986. pap. 9.95 o.p. (ISBN 0-8120-3652-2). Barron.

Barron's Guide to the Most Prestigious Colleges. 4th ed. Ed. by Barron's College Division Staff. LC 81-17573. 272p. (gr. 10-12). 1986. pap. 9.95 o.p. (ISBN 0-8120-3653-0). Barron.

Barron's Guide to the Most Prestigious College. 1982. pap. 6.95 o.p. (ISBN 0-8120-2606-3). Barron.

Barron's How to Prepare for Civil Service Examinations: Clerks, Stenographers, Typists. 4th ed. Edwin Riemer & Louis Leibling. LC 80-26402. (Barron's Educational Ser.). 405p. 1981. pap. text ed. 8.95 o.p. (ISBN 0-8120-2033-2). Barron.

Barron's How to Prepare for College Entrance Examinations (SAT) 12th, rev. ed. Samuel C. Brownstein & Mitchel Weiner. LC 78-9661. 704p. (gr. 11-12). 1984. 23.95 o.p. (ISBN 0-8120-5550-0); pap. 8.95 o.p. (ISBN 0-8120-2773-6). Barron.

Barron's How to Prepare for the Advanced Placement Examination - Biology. 2nd ed. Gabrielle Edwards & Marion Cimmino. Ed. by Maurice Bleifeld. (gr. 10-12). 1982. pap. 8.95 o.p. (ISBN 0-8120-2328-5). Barron.

Barron's How to Prepare for the Advanced Placement Examination - English. Max Nadel & Arthur Sherrer. LC 81-7972. 320p. (gr. 9-12). 1984. pap. text ed. 8.95 o.p. (ISBN 0-8120-2901-1). Barron.

Barron's How to Prepare for the Advanced Placement Examination-Mathematics. 2nd. ed. Shirley O. Hockett. (gr. 10-12). 1983. pap. text ed. 9.95 o.p. (ISBN 0-8120-2071-5). Barron.

Barron's How to Prepare for the American College Testing Program (ACT) rev., 6th ed. Murray Shapiro et al. LC 79-20856. (gr. 11-12). 1985. pap. text ed. 8.95 o.p. (ISBN 0-8120-3499-6). Barron.

Barron's How to Prepare for the California High School Proficiency Examination (CHSPE) 2nd ed. Sharon Green & Michael Siemon. LC 77-10521. 1983. pap. 8.95 o.p. (ISBN 0-8120-2327-7). Barron.

Barron's How to Prepare for the California High School Proficiency Examination (CHSPE) 3rd ed. Sharon Green & Michael Siemon. 1988. pap. 9.95 o.p. (ISBN 0-8120-3953-X). Barron.

Barron's How to Prepare for the Certified Public Accountant Examination. 2nd ed. Robert Beekman et al. 640p. 1986. pap. 14.95 o.p. (ISBN 0-8120-3635-2). Barron.

Barron's How to Prepare for the Civil Service Examinations. Jerry Bobrow. 224p. 1986. pap. 8.95 o.p. (ISBN 0-8120-2862-7). Barron.

Barron's How to Prepare for the College Board Achievement Tests - French. 3rd ed. Louis Cabat et al. LC 75-151972. (gr. 11-12). 1981. pap. 7.95 o.p. (ISBN 0-8120-0941-X). Barron.

Barron's How to Prepare for the College Board Achievement Tests -- Chemistry. 2nd ed. Joseph Mascetta. LC 81-887. (gr. 10-12). 1981. pap. text ed. 8.95 o.p. (ISBN 0-8120-2069-3). Barron.

Barron's How to Prepare for the College Board Achievement Tests - Social Studies - American History. rev. ed. David Midgeley. LC 77-3941. (gr. 9-12). 1982. pap. text ed. 7.95 o.p. (ISBN 0-8120-2552-0). Barron.

Barron's How to Prepare for the College Board Achievement Tests - Mathematics Level I. 3rd rev. ed. James J. Rizzuto. 240p. (gr. 11-12). 1982. pap. text ed. 8.95 o.p. (ISBN 0-8120-2344-7). Barron.

Barron's How to Prepare for the Graduate Management Admission Test (GMAT) 6th ed. Stephen Hilbert & Eugene Jaffe. LC 81-3536. 576p. 1984. pap. text ed. 8.95 o.p. (ISBN 0-8120-2868-6). Barron.

Barron's How to Prepare for the Graduate Record Examination (GRE) 7th ed. Brownstein & Weiner. LC 78-15175. 544p. 1985. text ed. 12.95 o.p. (ISBN 0-8120-5417-2); pap. text ed. 8.95 o.p. (ISBN 0-8120-2927-5). Barron.

Barron's How to Prepare for the Miller Analogies Test (MAT) 3rd ed. Robert J. Sternberg. LC 81-10762. 1981. pap. text ed. 6.95 o.p. (ISBN 0-8120-2325-0). Barron.

Barron's How to Prepare for the National Teachers Examinations-Common Exam: Education in the Elementary School. Albertina A. Weinlander. LC 70-110468. 1984. pap. 9.95 o.p. (ISBN 0-8120-2203-3). Barron.

Barron's How to Prepare for the New Medical College Admission Test (MCAT) 4th ed. Brown. 1983. pap. 8.95 o.p. (ISBN 0-8120-2608-X). Barron.

Barron's How to Prepare for the New Medical College Admission Test (MCAT) Hugo Seibel & Kenneth E. Guyer. LC 80-15470. pap. text ed. 7.95 o.p. (ISBN 0-8120-2190-8). Barron.

Barron's How to Prepare for the Preliminary Scholastic Aptitude Test - National Merit Scholarship Q Test (PSAT - NMSQT) 5th ed. Brownstein & Weiner. 336p. 1982. pap. 7.95 o.p. (ISBN 0-8120-2336-6). Barron.

Barron's How to Prepare for the Real Estate Licensing Examination -- Salesperson & Broker. J. Bruce Lindeman & Jack P. Friedman. LC 78-17332. 1983. pap. text ed. 8.95 o.p. (ISBN 0-8120-2351-X). Barron.

Barron's How to Prepare for the Test of English as a Foreign Language--TOEFL. 5th ed. Pamela J. Sharpe. 368p. 1986. pap. 10.95 o.p. (ISBN 0-8120-2964-X). Barron.

Barron's How to Prepare for the TOEFL: Test of English As a Foreign Language. 4th ed. Pamela J. Sharpe. LC 79-65306. (gr. 11-12). 1983. pap. text ed. 9.95 o.p. (ISBN 0-8120-2361-7). Barron.

Barron's Profiles of American Colleges: Descriptions of the Colleges, Vol. 1. rev. ed. Barron's Educational Series, Inc. College Division Staff. LC 81-21243. 1088p. 1982. 25.95 o.p. (ISBN 0-8120-5449-0); pap. 11.95 o.p. (ISBN 0-8120-2459-1). Barron.

Barrons Profiles of American Colleges: The Northeast. 6th. ed. Barron's Educational Series, Inc., College Division Staff. 336p. (gr. 10-12). 1984. pap. 7.95 o.p. (ISBN 0-8120-2795-7). Barron.

Barron's Three-Year Sequence for High School Mathematics. Ed. by Lester Schlumpf. 250p. (gr. 9-12). 1981. Course I. pap. text ed. 4.95 o.p. (ISBN 0-8120-3205-5); Course II. pap. text ed. 4.95 o.p. (ISBN 0-8120-3126-1); Course III. pap. text ed. 4.95 o.p. (ISBN 0-8120-3128-8). Barron.

Barron's Verbal Aptitude Workbook for College Entrance Examinations. rev. ed. Mitchel Weiner. (gr. 10-12). 1983. pap. text ed. 7.95 o.p. (ISBN 0-8120-2434-6). Barron.

Barron's Vocabulary Builder: A Systematic Plan for Building a Vocabulary, Testing Progress & Applying Knowledge. 9th, rev. ed. Samuel C. Brownstein & Mitchel Weiner. LC 75-14340. (Orig.). (gr. 9-12). 1982. pap. 6.95 o.p. (ISBN 0-8120-2449-4). Barron.

Barry Sheene. Nick Harris. (Profiles Ser.). (Illus.). 63p. (gr. 4-6). 1982. 9.95 o.p. (ISBN 0-241-10851-9, Pub. by Hamish Hamilton England). David & Charles.

Bartender's Guide to the Best Mixed Drinks. Kappa. (Eng. & Japanese.). bds. 2.75 o.p. (ISBN 0-8048-0056-1). C E Tuttle.

Bartholomew World Atlas. rev. ed. Illus. by Bartholomew's Cartographic Staff. (Illus.). 168p. 1982. 35.00 o.p. (ISBN 0-7028-0404-5). Hammond Inc.

Bartok Studies. Ed. by Todd Crow. LC 76-257. (Detroit Reprints in Music). 1976. 15.00 o.p. (ISBN 0-911772-78-2). Harmonie Pk Pr.

Bartolome Mitre: Historian of the Americas. John L. Robinson. LC 81-43802. 128p. (Orig.). 1982. lib. bdg. 25.00 o. p. o.p. (ISBN 0-8191-2505-9); pap. text ed. 10.00 o.p. (ISBN 0-8191-2506-7). U Pr of Amer.

Bartolomeo Cavaceppi, Eighteenth-Century Restorer. Seymour Howard. LC 79-57504. (Outstanding Dissertations in the Fine Arts Ser.: No. 5). 450p. 1982. lib. bdg. 67.00 o.p. (ISBN 0-8240-3935-1). Garland Pub.

Baruch Ata Befi Hataf: Illustrated Prayers & Blessings for Young Children. Illus. by Zev Lipman. (Illus.). (ps-1). 4.95 o.p. (ISBN 0-685-84974-0). Feldheim.

Baruch Spinoza & Western Democracy. Joseph Dunner. 140p. 1955. (ISBN 0-8022-0425-2). Philos Lib.

Barundi Eine Volkerkundliche Sudie aus Deutch-Ostafrika. Hans H. Meyer. (Classics of Anthropology Ser.). 48.00 o.p. (ISBN 0-8240-9638-X). Garland Pub.

Barye Bronzes, a Catalogue Raisonne. Stuart Pivar. (Illus.). 284p. 1981. Repr. of 1970 ed. 89.50 o.s.i. (ISBN 0-902028-30-8). Antique Collect.

Baryshnikov: From Russia to the West. Gennady Smakov. (Illus.). 244p. 1981. 17.95 o.p. (ISBN 0-374-10908-7); pap. 10.95 o.p. (ISBN 0-374-51705-3). FS&G.

Baryshnikov in Russia. Nina Alovert. Tr. by Irene Huntoon from Rus. LC 83-13012. 224p. 1984. 30.00 o.p. (ISBN 0-03-062589-0). H Holt & Co.

Basaltic Volcanism on Terrestrial Planets: Proceedings of the Lunar & Planetary Institute, Houston, Texas. Lunar & Planetary Institute Staff. (Illus.). 1200p. 1982. 325.00 o.p. (ISBN 0-08-028086-2). Pergamon.

Basalts & Phase Diagrams: An Introduction to the Quantitative Use of Phase Diagrams in Igneous Petrology. S. A. Morse. (Illus.). 400p. 1980. 42.00 o.p. (ISBN 0-387-90477-8). Springer-Verlag.

Base Catalyzed Reactions of Hydrocarbons & Related Compounds. Herman Hines & Wayne M. Stalick. 587p. 1977. 85.00 o.p. (ISBN 0-12-557150-X). Acad Pr.

Base Metal Oxide Catalysts for the Petrochemical, Petroleum, & Chemical Industries. Happel et al. (Firm orders only). 495.00 o.p. (ISBN 0-8247-6437-4). Dekker.

Baseball. Ed. by Richard Grossinger. (Illus.). 232p. (Orig.). 1971. pap. 10.00 o.p. (ISBN 0-913028-11-8). North Atlantic.

Baseball. Walter Iooss & Roger Angell, Jr. (Illus.). 160p. 1984. 24.95 o.p. (ISBN 0-8109-0711-9). Abrams.

Baseball-Access. Richard S. Wurman. (Guidebook Ser.). (Illus.). 72p. 1984. pap. 4.95 o.p. (ISBN 0-915461-00-5). Access Pr.

Baseball & the Cold War: Being a Soliloquy on the Necessity of Baseball. Howard Senzel. Ed. by Okrent. LC 76-27427. 1977. 10.00 o.p. (ISBN 0-15-110693-2). HarBraceJ.

Baseball Bear. Michael J. Pellowski. (Illus.). 24p. (gr. k-4). 1987. 1.95 o.p. (ISBN 0-87406-148-2). Willowisp Pr.

Baseball Becky. Michael H. Dessent. 128p. (gr. 4-8). 1982. 8.95 o.p. (ISBN 0-916392-80-5); pap. 5.95 o.p. (ISBN 0-916392-97-X). Oak Tree Pubns.

Baseball Card Engagement Book, 1987. Michael Gershman. 1986. pap. 7.95 o.s.i. (ISBN 0-395-41455-5). HM.

Baseball Catalog. rev. ed. Dan Schlossberg. 320p. 1981. pap. 7.95 o.p. (ISBN 0-8246-0271-4). Jonathan David.

Baseball Catalog. Dan Schlossberg. LC 77-29025. (Illus.). 320p. 1983. pap. 8.95 o.p. (ISBN 0-8246-0293-5). Jonathan David.

Baseball Catalogue. Dan Schlossberg. 1979. 16.95 o.p. (ISBN 0-8246-0227-7). Jonathan David.

Baseball Dope Book, 1984. 464p. 1984. pap. 7.95 o.p. (ISBN 0-89204-151-X). Sporting News.

Baseball Encyclopedia Update. 1987. pap. 7.95 o.p. (ISBN 0-02-029501-4). Macmillan.

Baseball Guide, 1984. 470p. 1984. pap. 9.95 o.p. (ISBN 0-89204-149-8). Sporting News.

Baseball, My Way. Joe Morgan. Ed. by Joel H. Cohen. LC 76-11532. 160p. (gr. 7 up). 1976. 8.95 o.p. (ISBN 0-689-10739-0, Atheneum). Macmillan.

Baseball Reader: Favorites from the Fireside Book of Baseball. C. Einstein. 384p. 1983. pap. text ed. 8.95 o.p. (ISBN 0-07-019531-5). McGraw.

Baseball: Records, Stars, Feats, & Facts. Louis Phillips. LC 79-87525. (Illus.). (gr. 4-7). 1979. 2.95 o.p. (ISBN 0-15-205718-8, HJ). HarBraceJ.

Baseball Register, 1984. 560p. 1984. pap. 9.95 o.p. (ISBN 0-89204-148-X). Sporting News.

Baseball Rule Book, 1984. 1984. 2.50 o.s.i. (ISBN 0-89204-153-6). Sporting News.

Baseball Trades & Acquisitions, Nineteen Fifty to Nineteen Seventy-Nine. Richard S. Kubik. 124p. 1981. 10.00 o.p. (ISBN 0-682-49676-6). Exposition-Phoenix.

Baseball Trivia Puzzler, No. 1. Robert Kelly. (Orig.). 1981. pap. 1.95 o.p. (ISBN 0-440-00393-8). Dell.

Baseball Winter: The Off-Season Life of the Summer Game. Terry Pluto & Jeffrey Neuman. 320p. 1986. 16.95 o.p. (ISBN 0-02-597760-1). Macmillan.

Baseball Wit. Bill Adler. LC 85-19495. (Illus.). 1986. 9.95 o.p. (ISBN 0-517-55831-9). Crown.

Baseball's Golden Dozen. Joseph Bruno. 1976. 8.50 o.p. (ISBN 0-682-48564-0, Banner). Exposition-Phoenix.

Baseball's Great Tragedy: The Story of Carl Mays, Submarine Pitcher. Bob McGarigle. LC 72-72480. 1972. 6.00 o.p. (ISBN 0-682-47450-9, Banner). Exposition-Phoenix.

Baseball's Greatest Records, Streaks & Feats. Harvey Frommer. LC 82-45939. 208p. 1983. 13.95 o.s.i. (ISBN 0-689-11385-4, Atheneum). Macmillan.

Baseball's Home-Run Hitters. Richard Rainbolt. LC 74-27473. (Sports Heroes Library). (Illus.). 72p. (gr. 5-11). 1975. PLB 7.95 o.p. (ISBN 0-8225-1055-3). Lerner Pubns.

Baseball's Hottest Hitters. Nathan Aaseng. LC 83-711. (Sports Heroes Library). (Illus.). 80p. (gr. 4up). 1983. PLB 7.95 o.p. (ISBN 0-8225-1331-5). Lerner Pubns.

Baseball's Top Teams since 1920. Howard Sinner. 1988. 8.95 o.p. (ISBN 0-317-67805-1). Pharos Bks NY.

Bases Du Pacifisme. Alfred H. Fried. LC 76-147580. (Library of War & Peace; Int'l. Organization, Arbitration & Law). 1980. lib. bdg. 46.00 o.p. (ISBN 0-8240-0487-6). Garland Pub.

Bases of Economic Geography. 2nd ed. Ronald R. Boyce. LC 77-21382. 1978. text ed. 25.95 o.p. (ISBN 0-03-019496-2, HoltC). HR&W.

Bases of Modern Librarianship. C. M. White. 1964. 35.00 o.p. (ISBN 0-08-010627-7). Pergamon.

Bases of Yoga. Sri Aurobindo. 168p. 1979. pap. 2.00 o.p. (ISBN 0-89071-288-3, Pub. by Sri Aurobindo Ashram India). Aurobindo Assn.

BASEX. Paul Warme. LC 79-775. 1979. pap. text ed. 10.95 o.p. (ISBN 0-07-068290-9, BYTE Bks). McGraw.

Basic see Fate of French-E in English: The Plural of Nouns Ending in-th.

Basic Accounting. 2nd ed. J. O. Magee. 352p. 1979. pap. text ed. 16.95x o.p. (ISBN 0-7121-0284-1, Pub. by Macdonald & Evans England). Trans-Atl Phila.

Basic Accounting & Budgeting for Long Term Care Facilities. Jerry L. Rhodes. 460p. 1983. 29.95 o.p. (ISBN 0-8436-0795-5). Van Nos Reinhold.

Basic Accounting & Budgeting for Nursing Homes. 152p. 15.95 o.p. (ISBN 0-318-12739-3, 901-00022); members 11.95 o.p. (ISBN 0-318-12740-7, CAT. NO. 901-00021). Am Health Care Assn.

Basic Accounting & Cost Accounting. 2nd ed. Eugene L. Grant & L. F. Bell. 1964. text ed. 34.95 o.p. (ISBN 0-07-024094-9). McGraw.

Basic Actions of Sex Steroids on Target Organs: Proceedings of the International Seminar on Reproductive Physiology & Sexual Endocrinology, 3rd, Brussels, 1970. International Seminar on Reproductive Physiology & Sexual Endocrinology Staff. Ed. by P. O. Hubinont et al. 1971. 38.00 o.p. (ISBN 3-8055-1156-6). S Karger.

Basic Algebra. M. N. Manougian. 1981. text ed. 25.95 o.s.i. (ISBN 0-03-019711-2, CBS C). SCP.

Basic Algebra. E. Wainwright Martin, Jr. (Plaid Ser.). 1970. pap. 10.95 o.p. (ISBN 0-87094-332-4). Dow Jones-Irwin.

BASIC: An Introduction to Computer Programming with the Apple. Robert J. Bent & George C. Sethares. 1983. pub net 22.00 o.p. (ISBN 0-534-01370-8, 82-20572). Brooks-Cole.

Basic Analytical Chemistry. L. Pataki & E. Zapp. (Analytical Chemistry Ser.: Vol. 2). (Illus.). 1981. 77.00 o.p. (ISBN 0-08-023850-5); pap. 32.00 o.p. (ISBN 0-08-026271-6). Pergamon.

Basic & Advanced Cooking for Pathfinders: A Youth Enrichment Skill. Lou Gattis, III. (Illus.). 20p. (Orig.). (gr. 5-6). 1986. pap. 5.00 tchrs. ed. o.p. (ISBN 0-936241-12-8). Cheetah Pub.

Basic & Applied Dental Biochemistry. R. Williams & J. Elliott. (Illus.). 1978. pap. text ed. 25.00 o.p. (ISBN 0-443-01880-4). Churchill.

BASIC & Chemistry. Leonard Soltzberg et al. 1975. pap. 16.50 o.p. (ISBN 0-395-21720-2). HM.

Basic Animal Nutrition & Feeding. 2nd ed. D. C. Church & W. G. Pond. 403p. 1982. pap. (ISBN 0-471-87514-7). Wiley.

Basic Animation Stand Techniques. Brian G. Salt. LC 76-40298. 1977. 60.00 o.p. (ISBN 0-08-021368-5). Pergamon.

Basic Applied Logic. Kenton Machina. 1982. text ed. write for info. o.p. (ISBN 0-673-15359-2). Scott F.

Basic Approach to Executive Decision Making. Alfred R. Oxenfeldt et al. (Illus.). 1978. 14.95 o.p. (ISBN 0-8144-5467-4). AMACOM.

Basic Approach to Executive Decision Making. Alfred R. Oxenfeldt et al. LC 73-1369. 240p. 1981. pap. 7.95 o.p. (ISBN 0-8144-7551-5). AMACOM.

Basic Approach to Structured BASIC. 2nd ed. Henry Mullish. LC 82-11073. 375p. 1982. pap. 27.95 o.p. (ISBN 0-471-06071-2). Wiley.

Basic Arc Welding. 3rd ed. Ivan H. Griffin et al. LC 76-4309. 1977. pap. text ed. 8.95 o.p. (ISBN 0-8273-1250-4); instr's. guide 4.50 o.p. (ISBN 0-8273-1251-2). Delmar.

Basic Arithmetic with Applications. Lawrence Trivieri. 400p. 1981. pap. text ed. 24.00 o.p. (ISBN 0-87150-322-0, 33L 2562, Prindle). PWS-Kent Pub.

Basic Aspects of Psychoanalytic Group Therapy. Peter Kutter. Tr. by Angela Molnos. (International Library of Group Psychotherapy & Group Process Ser.). 112p. (Orig., Ger.). 1982. pap. 10.95x o.p. (ISBN 0-7100-9244-X). Routledge Chapman & Hall.

Basic Aspects of Receptor Biochemistry: Proceedings, Vienna, Austria, 1982. Ed. by M. Goldstein et al. (Journal of Neural Transmission Supplementum: Vol. 18). 380p. 1983. pap. 58.80 o.p. (ISBN 0-387-81733-6). Springer-Verlag.

Basic Audiometry: Including Impedance Measurement. Thomas G. Giolas & Kenneth Randolph. LC 76-7113. (Cliffs Speech & Hearing Ser.). (Illus.). 1977. pap. text ed. 4.95 o.p. (ISBN 0-8220-1813-6). Cliffs.

Basic Auto Repair Manual. 8th rev. ed. Ed. by Spence Murray. LC 75-18057. (Basic Repair & Maintenance Ser.). (Illus.). 384p. 1977. pap. 5.95 o.p. (ISBN 0-8227-5011-2). Petersen Pub.

Basic Automotive Troubleshooting. 2nd, rev ed. Ed. by Don Whitt. LC 74-76521. (Basic Repair & Maintenance Manuals Ser.). (Illus.). 1977. pap. 6.95 o.p. (ISBN 0-8227-5012-0). Petersen Pub.

Basic Band Repertory: British Band Classics from the Conductor's Point of View. Frederick Fennell. 1980. pap. 6.00 o.p. (ISBN 0-686-29444-0). Instrumental Co.

Basic BASIC-English Dictionary: For the Apple, IBM-PC, Commodore 64, VIC-20, Atari, TRS-80, TRS-80 Color Computer, TI 99-4A, PET & Timex-Sinclair. Larry Noonan. (Illus.). 288p. 1985. pap. 3.95 o.p. (ISBN 0-918398-54-1). Weber Systems.

BASIC Beginnings. Susan D. Lipscomb & Margaret A. Zuanich. (Illus.). 96p. (gr. 2-6). 1983. pap. 2.50 o.p. (ISBN 0-380-83774-9, Camelot). Avon.

Basic Behavioral Statistics. Robert E. Gehring. LC 77-78447. (Illus.). 1978. text ed. 29.95 o.p. (ISBN 0-395-24684-9). HM.

Basic Bible Doctrines. Millard F. Day. 1953. pap. 3.95 o.p. (ISBN 0-8024-0239-9). Moody.

Basic Bibliography of Science & Technology. McGraw-Hill Editors. 1966. text ed. 25.00 o.p. (ISBN 0-07-045218-0). McGraw.

Basic Blueprint Reading & Sketching. C. Thomas Olivo et al. LC 76-56490. 1978. text ed. 16.95 o.p. (ISBN 0-8273-2141-4); pap. text ed. 11.95 o.p. (ISBN 0-8273-2050-7); instr's. guide o.s.i. 3.00 o.p. Delmar.

Basic Blueprint Reading for Practical Applications. John E. Traister. (Illus.). 304p. 1983. write for info. o.p.; pap. 13.60 o.p. (ISBN 0-8306-0146-5, 1546). TAB Bks.

Basic Body Repair & Refinishing for the Weekend Mechanic. Carl Caiati. (Illus.). 192p. 1984. pap. 11.60 o.p. (ISBN 0-8306-2122-9, 2122). TAB Bks.

Basic Bodywork & Painting. 5th ed. Ed. by Brice Caldwell & Craig Caldwell. LC 73-79967. (Illus.). 192p. (Orig.). 1981. pap. 9.95 o.p. (ISBN 0-8227-5057-0, Dist. by Kampmann). Petersen Pub.

Basic Book of Fingerweaving. Esther W. Dendel. (Illus.). 1974. 8.95 o.p. (ISBN 0-671-21697-X). S&S.

Basic Botany. Claire Skellern & Paul Rogers. (Illus.). 208p. (Orig.). 1977. pap. text ed. 16.95x o.p. (ISBN 0-7121-0255-8, Pub. by Macdonald & Evans England). Trans-Atl Phila.

Basic Bridge. Ron Klinger. 1978. pap. 11.95 o.p. (ISBN 0-575-02637-5, Pub. by Gollancz England). David & Charles.

Basic Building Craft Science. Alf Fulcher et al. 164p. 1981. text ed. 14.50x o.p. (Pub. by Granada England). Gower Pub Co.

Basic Business English. R. Barry. 1981. pap. text ed. (ISBN 0-13-057208-X). P-H.

Basic Business Logistics. Ronald H. Ballou. (Illus.). 1978. pap. text ed. (ISBN 0-13-057364-7). P-H.

Basic Business Math & Electronic Calculators. 3rd ed. Ronald Merchant. 306p. 1983. pap. text ed. 16.95x o.p. (ISBN 0-89863-069-X). Star Pub CA.

Basic Business Mathematics. John Ernest & Charlotte Ernest. 1977. text ed. write for info. o.p. (ISBN 0-02-472610-9). Macmillan.

Basic Business Mathematics. 3rd ed. Gerald Pintel & Jay Diamond. (Illus.). 240p. 1982. pap. text ed. (ISBN 0-13-057380-9). P-H.

Basic Calculus with Applications. Burton Rodin. 1978. text ed. write for info. o.p. (ISBN 0-673-16224-9). Scott F.

Basic Cams, Valves & Exhaust Systems. 4th rev. ed. Ed. by Spence Murray. LC 70-902. (Basic Repair & Maintenance Ser.). (Illus.). 192p. 1977. pap. 4.95 o.p. (ISBN 0-8227-5010-4, Dist. by Kampmann). Petersen Pub.

Basic Car Care Illustrated. 2nd ed. Ed. by Allen D. Bragdon. (Illus.). 528p. 1980. 19.95 o.p. (ISBN 0-87851-523-2); pap. 13.00 o.p. (ISBN 0-87851-520-8). Hearst Bks.

Basic Carpentry Illustrated. Sunset Editors. LC 72-77140. (Illus.). 88p. 1972. pap. 4.95 o.p. (ISBN 0-376-01014-2, Sunset Bks). Sunset-Lane.

Basic Carrier Telephony. 3rd, rev. ed. David Talley. (Illus.). (gr. 10 up). 1977. pap. 9.25 o.p. (ISBN 0-8104-5848-9); exam 0.50 o.p. (ISBN 0-8104-0727-2); final exam 0.50 o.p. (ISBN 0-8104-0728-0). Sams.

Basic Carrier Telephony. 3rd, rev. ed. David Talley. 218p. 1977. 15.95 o.p. (ISBN 0-686-98107-3). Telecom Lib.

Basic Cases in Public International Law. A. Dunlap. 1971. pap. text ed. 14.95x o.p. (ISBN 0-8290-1388-1). Irvington.

Basic Chemistry. 4th ed. William S. Seese & Guida H. Daub. (Illus.). 656p. 1985. text ed. (ISBN 0-13-057811-8); pap. text ed. (ISBN 0-13-057852-5). P-H.

Basic Chemistry for the Health Sciences. Ralph J. Fessenden & Joan S. Fessenden. 1984. text ed. 45.00 o.s.i. (ISBN 0-205-08016-2, 688016); instr's. manual avail. o.s.i. (ISBN 0-205-08029-4); write for info. o.s.i. (ISBN 0-205-08017-0, 688017). Allyn.

Basic Chemistry: Laboratory Experiments. 4th ed. Charles H. Corwin. (Illus.). 272p. 1985. pap. text ed. (ISBN 0-13-057845-2). P-H.

Basic Chemistry of Textile Coloring & Finishing. Cockett & Hilton. 196p. 1956. (ISBN 0-8022-0272-1). Philos Lib.

Basic Chemistry of Textile Preparation. Cockett & Hilton. 196p. 1956. (ISBN 0-8022-0273-X). Philos Lib.

Basic Chemistry: Problems Book. M. E. Schaff & B. R. Siebring. 64p. 1982. saddle stitched 3.95 o.p. (ISBN 0-8403-2819-2). Kendall-Hunt.

Basic Christian Faith. C. Donald Cole. LC 84-72008. 256p. (Orig.). 1985. pap. 6.95 o.p. (ISBN 0-89107-338-8, Crossway Bks). Good News.

Basic Circuit Analysis. Gerald J. Kirwin & Stephen Grodzinsky. LC 79-88449. (Illus.). 1980. text ed. 53.96 o.p. (ISBN 0-395-28488-0). HM.

Basic Clinical Pharmacokinetics. Michael E. Winter. LC 80-69785. (Illus.). 1980. 22.00x o.p. (ISBN 0-915486-04-0). Applied Therapeutics.

Basic Coastal Engineering. Robert M. Sorensen. LC 77-29256. (Ocean Engineering Ser.). 227p. 1978. 39.95 o.p. (ISBN 0-471-81370-2, Pub. by Wiley-Interscience). Wiley.

Basic College Mathematics: An Applied Approach. 2nd ed. Richard N. Aufmann & Vernon C. Barker. LC 81-84253. 1983. pap. 29.25 o.p. (ISBN 0-395-31679-0). HM.

Basic Composition see Theme & Paragraph.

Basic Computational Math. V. F. Dyachenko. 125p. 1979. pap. 4.95 o.p. (ISBN 0-8285-1593-X, Pub. by Mir Pubs USSR). Imported Pubns.

Basic Computational Techniques for Engineers. R. A. Adey & C. A. Brebbia. LC 83-5739. 208p. 1983. 29.50 o.p. (ISBN 0-471-88970-9, Pub. by Wiley-Interscience). Wiley.

Basic Computer Logic. John Scott. LC 80-5074. (The Lexington Books Series in Computer Science). 256p. 1981. 26.50x o.p. (ISBN 0-669-03706-0). Lexington Bks.

BASIC Computer Programs in Science & Engineering. Jules H. Gilder. 256p. 1980. pap. 10.95 o.p.; 2 apple disks 39.95_incl. o.p. Sams.

Basic Computing for Civil Engineers 0685. W. Jenkins. 1983. pap. 15.95 o.s.i. (ISBN 0-442-30559-1). Van Nos Reinhold.

Basic Concepts & Applications. William K. Holstein & John P. Seagle. 1987. pap. 26.95 o.p. (ISBN 0-317-61135-6). Irwin.

Basic Concepts in Anatomy & Physiology: A Programmed Presentation. 4th ed. Catherine P. Anthony & Gary A. Thibodeau. LC 79-19392. (Illus.). 222p. 1979. pap. text ed. 17.95 o.p. (ISBN 0-8016-0260-2). Mosby.

Basic Concepts in Sociology. Max Webber. 1962. (ISBN 0-8022-1825-3). Philos Lib.

Basic Concepts of Algebraic Topology. F. H. Croom. LC 77-16092. 1978. 23.00 o.p. (ISBN 0-387-90288-0). Springer-Verlag.

Basic Concepts of Chemistry. 3rd ed. Alan Sherman et al. LC 83-81614. 576p. 1984. text ed. 45.56 o.p. (ISBN 0-395-34491-3). HM.

Basic Concepts of Chemistry. 2nd ed. Alan Sherman et al. LC 79-88447. (Illus.). 1980. text ed. 27.50 o.p. (ISBN 0-395-28153-9). HM.

Basic Concepts of Elementary Mathematics. 3rd ed. John M. Peterson. 1978. text ed. write for info. o.p. (ISBN 0-87150-247-X, PWS 2011, Prindle). PWS-Kent Pub.

Basic Concepts of Elementary Mathematics. 4th ed. John M. Peterson & James E. Smith. 1982. text ed. 24.00 o.p. (ISBN 0-87150-333-6, 2661, Prindle). PWS-Kent Pub.

Basic Concepts of Sociology. Max Weber. Orig. Title: Basic Sociology. 1962. pap. 3.95 o.p. (66, Pub. by Citadel Pr). Carol Pub Group.

Basic Construction Blueprint Reading. Mark W. Huth. LC 79-50919. (gr. 9). 1980. pap. text ed. 13.50 o.p. (ISBN 0-8273-1865-0); instr's. guide 6.00 o.p. (ISBN 0-8273-1866-9). Delmar.

Basic Conversational French. 7th ed. Julian Harris & Andre Leveque. LC 81-20166. 1982. text ed. 26.95 o.p. (ISBN 0-03-060112-6, HoltC); instr's. manual 19.95 o.p. (ISBN 0-03-060117-7); lab manual 11.95 o.p. (ISBN 0-03-060113-4). HR&W.

Basic Conversational Italian. 2nd ed. Cecilia Bartoli & Pina Swenson. LC 77-15655. (Ital.). 1979. text ed. 26.95 o.p. (ISBN 0-03-021681-8). HR&W.

Basic Conversational Spanish. rev. ed. Gregory G. LaGrone. 1974. text ed. 27.95 o.p. (ISBN 0-03-089250-3, HoltC). HR&W.

Basic Corporate Taxation - Nineteen Eighty-Two Pocket Part. 3rd ed. Douglas A. Kahn. 87p. 1982. write for info. o.p. (ISBN 0-314-68840-4); 1982 supplement 4.95 o.p. (ISBN 0-314-67869-7). West Pub.

Basic Cost Accounting Concepts. Henry R. Anderson & Mitchell H. Raiborn. LC 76-12017. (Illus.). 720p. 1977. text ed. 45.16 o.p. (ISBN 0-395-20646-4). HM.

Basic Course in Design. rev. ed. Ray Prohaska. LC 80-10766. 96p. 1980. pap. 12.95 o.p. (ISBN 0-89134-031-9). North Light Bks.

Basic Course in Real Estate. 130p. 3.00ea. o.p. (ISBN 0-318-15174-X, 111-222); bulk rates avail. o.p. Natl Assoc Realtors.

Basic Creditors' & Debtors' Rights in Florida. Florida Bar Staff. LC 88-83609. 365p. 1988. casebound 50.00 o.p. (ISBN 0-910373-27-2, 225). Fl Bar Legal Ed.

Basic Documentation for Tariff Study, 3 vols. (Eng. & Fr.). 1970. pap. 50.00 Set o.p. (G55, GATT). UNIPUB.

Basic Documents of International Organization. Samuel Shih-Tsai Chen. LC 76-187538. 300p. 1971. pap. text ed. 8.50x o.p. (ISBN 0-8422-0195-5). Irvington.

Basic Documents on Commercial Arbitration. The Eastman Arbitration Library. LC 85-155440. 1988. 10.00 o.p. Am Arbitration.

Basic Drafting for Interior Designers. William E. Miller. 120p. 1982. 19.95 o.p.; pap. 14.95 o.p. (ISBN 0-442-26177-2). Van Nos Reinhold.

Basic Drawing. Date not set. (ISBN 0-8052-3924-3). Random.

Basic Drug Calculations. 2nd ed. Meta Brown & Joyce Mulholland. LC 79-10785. 190p. 1984. pap. 15.95 o.p. (ISBN 0-8016-0863-5). Mosby.

Basic Economic Concepts: Macroeconomics. 2nd ed. Werner Sichel & Peter Eckstein. 1980. pap. 16.50 o.p. (ISBN 0-395-30746-5). HM.

Basic Education & Agricultural Extension: Costs, Effects & Alternatives. Hilary Perraton et al. (Working Paper Ser.: No. 564). 308p. 1983. 15.00 o.p. (ISBN 0-8213-0176-4, WP 0564). World Bank.

Basic Electric Circuit Analysis. 2nd ed. David E. Johnson et al. (Illus.). 592p. 1984. text ed. (ISBN 0-13-060111-X). P-H.

Basic Electric Circuits. 2nd ed. A. M. Brookes. LC 75-8774. 368p. 1975. 95.00 o.p. (ISBN 0-08-018310-7); pap. text ed. 35.00 o.p. (ISBN 0-08-018309-3). Pergamon.

Basic Electrical Engineering & Instrumentation for Engineers. 2nd ed. E. C. Bell & R. W. Whitehead. 487p. 1981. pap. text ed. 22.00x o.p. (ISBN 0-258-97051-0, Pub. by Granada England); pap. 14.75 o.p. Gower Pub Co.

Basic Electricity, 5 Vols. rev. ed. Van Valkenburgh et al. (Illus.). 1978. combined ed. 27.50 o.p. (ISBN 0-8104-0881-3); Set. pap. 29.25 o.p. (ISBN 0-8104-0875-9); pap. 6.40 ea. o.p.; Vol. 1, Rev. Ed. pap. (ISBN 0-8104-0876-7); Vol. 2, Rev. Ed. pap. (ISBN 0-8104-0877-5); Vol. 3, Rev. Ed. pap. (ISBN 0-8104-0878-3). Vol. 5,rev. pap. (ISBN 0-8104-0880-5). Sams.

Basic Electromagnetic Theory. D. T. Paris & F. K. Hurd. LC 68-8775. (Physical & Quantum Electronic Ser.). (Illus.). 1969. text ed. 45.00 o.p. (ISBN 0-07-048470-8). McGraw.

Basic Electronic Switching for Telephone Systems. David Talley. 240p. 1982. 15.95 o.p. (ISBN 0-686-98106-5). Telecom Lib.

Basic Electronics. 4th ed. Bernard Grob. (Illus.). (gr. 11-12). 1977. text ed. 43.95 o.p. (ISBN 0-07-024923-7, G). McGraw.

Basic Electronics, 6 Vols. Van Valkenburgh et al. (Illus.). 1959. combined cloth 25.95 o.p. (ISBN 0-8104-0049-9); Set. pap. 31.80 o.p. (ISBN 0-8104-0048-0); Vol. 1. pap. 5.30 o.p. (ISBN 0-8104-0041-3); Vols. 2-6. pap. 5.30 ea. o.p.; Vol. 2. pap. (ISBN 0-8104-0042-1); Vol. 3. pap. (ISBN 0-8104-0043-X); Vol. 4. pap. (ISBN 0-8104-0044-8); Vol. 5. pap. (ISBN 0-8104-0045-6); Vol. 6. pap. (ISBN 0-8104-0046-4). Sams.

Basic Electronics: A Text-Lab Manual. 4th ed. Paul B. Zbar. 1976. text ed. 19.25 o.p. (ISBN 0-07-072761-9). McGraw.

Basic Electronics Course. Norman H. Crowhurst. LC 75-178692. 1972. 11.95 o.p. (ISBN 0-8306-2588-7); pap. 13.95 o.p. (ISBN 0-8306-1588-1, 588). TAB Bks.

Basic Electronics for Instrumentation. Peter H. Sydenham. Ed. by Sorin Davidovici. LC 82-80222. 284p. 1982. pap. text ed. 32.50x o.p. (ISBN 0-87664-565-1). Instru Soc.

Basic Electronics for Scientists. 3rd ed. James J. Brophy. (Illus.). 1977. text ed. 42.95 o.p. (ISBN 0-07-008107-7). McGraw.

Basic Electronics Technology. Alvis J. Evans et al. Ed. by Gerald Luecke & Kenneth M. Krone. (Electronic Technology Ser.). (Illus.). 464p. 1985. text ed. 19.95 o.p. (ISBN 0-672-27022-6, LCB8601). Sams.

Basic Electronics Theory with Projects & Experiments. Delton T. Horn. LC 81-9207. (Illus.). 532p. 1981. 19.95 o.p. (ISBN 0-8306-0020-5); pap. 15.50 o.p. (ISBN 0-8306-1338-2). TAB Bks.

Basic Engineering Elements, 14 vols. Incl. Vol. 1. Reading Engineering Drawings; Vol. 2. Limits & Fits; Vol. 3. Calculations; Vol. 4. Micrometers; Vol. 5. Linear, Bore, Slip & Vernier Gauges; Vol. 6. Ferrous & Non-Ferrous Metals; Vol. 7. Drills, Reamers & Contebores; Vol. 8. Boring Bars & Heads; Vol. 9. Turning Tools; Vol. 10. Thread Cutting; Vol. 11. Screwed Joints; Vol. 12. Speeds & Feeds; Vol. 13. Coolant Equipment; Vol. 14. Safety. (Illus.). 1978. Set. 55.00x o.p. (ISBN 0-89563-000-1). Trans-Atl Phila.

Basic Engineering Principles. 2nd ed. James A. Merkel. (Illus.). 1983. 24.95 o.p. (ISBN 0-87055-421-2). AVI.

Basic English: International Second Language. rev. ed. Charles K. Ogden. Ed. by E. C. Graham. LC 68-28654. 1968. 8.95 o.p. (ISBN 0-15-110695-9). HarBraceJ.

Basic Environmental Problems of Man in Space: Proceedings of the Fifth International Symposium, Washington, D.C., 1973. Ed. by A. Graybiel. 1976. 95.00 o.p. (ISBN 0-08-021067-8). Pergamon.

Basic Estate Planning & Administration. Pennsylvania Bar Institute Staff. 237p. 1985. 30.00 o.p. (ISBN 0-318-19023-0, 298). PA Bar Inst.

BASIC Exercises for the IBM Personal Computer. J. P. Lamoitier. LC 82-60234. (Illus.). 251p. (Orig.). 1982. pap. 13.95 o.p. (ISBN 0-89588-088-1). SYBEX.

Basic Experimental Chemistry: A Laboratory Manual for Beginning Students. rev. ed. Christian Anderson & J. L. Hawes. 1971. pap. 24.95 o.p. (ISBN 0-8053-0222-0). Benjamin-Cummings.

BASIC Explorer for the Commodore 64. Lee Berman & Ken Leonard. (Illus.). 200p. 1984. pap. text ed. 11.95 o.p. (ISBN 0-07-881139-2). Osborne-McGraw.

Basic Factors for the Treatment & Disposal of Radioactive Wastes. (Safety Ser.: No. 24). (Illus.). 41p. 1967. pap. 9.50 o.p. (ISBN 0-686-93169-6, ISP170, IAEA). UNIPUB.

Basic Facts about the United Nations. 2.75 o.p. (ISBN 92-1-100254-0, E.84.I.12). UN.

Basic Facts of Fractures. Browne. (Illus.). 208p. 1983. pap. 17.50 o.p. (ISBN 0-632-00854-7, B-0776-0). Mosby.

Basic Finance: An Introduction to Money & Financial Management. Herbert B. Mayo. (Illus.). 1978. text ed. 28.95 o.s.i. (ISBN 0-7216-6209-9). HR&W.

Basic Financial Accounting. Robert Bowman. 440p. 1983. pap. text ed. 26.50x o.p. (ISBN 0-7131-0729-4). Trans-Atl Phila.

Basic Financial Management. rev. ed. Curtis W. Symonds. (Illus.). 1979. 13.95 o.p. (ISBN 0-8144-5481-X). AMACOM.

Basic Financial Management. rev. ed. Curtis W. Symonds. (Illus.). 216p. 1981. pap. 7.95 o.p. (ISBN 0-8144-7563-9). AMACOM.

Basic Fluid Power. Dudley A. Pease. 1967. pap. text ed. 36.33 ref. ed. o.p. (ISBN 0-13-061432-7). P-H.

Basic Foil Fencing. Charles Simonian. (Orig.). 1982. pap. text ed. 8.95 o.p. (ISBN 0-8403-2726-9, 40272602). Kendall-Hunt.

Basic Food Microbiology. abr. ed. George J. Banwart. (Illus.). 1981. 37.95 o.p. (ISBN 0-87055-322-4). AVI.

Basic Food Microbiology. unabridged ed. Ed. by George J. Banwart. (Illus.). 1979. 49.95 o.p. (ISBN 0-87055-385-2). AVI.

Basic Foods. 2nd ed. June C. Gates. LC 80-26409. 636p. 1981. text ed. 28.95 o.p. (ISBN 0-03-049846-5, HoltC). HR&W.

BASIC for Business. Douglas Hergert. LC 81-85955. (Illus.). 223p. 1982. pap. 12.95 o.p. (ISBN 0-89588-080-6, B390). SYBEX.

BASIC for Everyone. Thomas Worth. (Illus.). 368p. 1976. pap. text ed. (ISBN 0-13-061481-5). P-H.

BASIC for Microcomputers: Apple, TRS-80, PET. Roger Haigh & Loren Radford. 300p. 1982. pap. text ed. write for info. o.p. (ISBN 0-87150-334-4, 8050). PWS-Kent Pub.

BASIC for Microcomputers: Apple, TRS-80, PET. Roger W. Haigh & Loren E. Radford. 337p. 1983. 28.95 o.p. (ISBN 0-442-27843-8). Van Nos Reinhold.

Basic Framework for Economic Analysis. 2nd ed. Richard H. Leftwich. 1984. 19.95 o.p. (ISBN 0-256-03068-5); wkbk. 8.95 o.p. (ISBN 0-256-03069-3). Irwin.

Basic Framework for Economics. Richard H. Leftwich. 1980. pap. 12.95x o.p. (ISBN 0-256-02309-3); student wkbk. 5.50x o.p. (ISBN 0-256-02358-1). Irwin.

BASIC Fun with Adventure Games. Susan D. Lipscomb & Margaret A. Zuanich. (Illus.). 112p. (gr. 4-7). 1984. pap. 2.95 o.p. (ISBN 0-380-87486-5, Camelot). Avon.

BASIC Fun with Graphics: The Apple Computer Way. Susan D. Lipscomb & Margaret A. Zuanich. 124p. (ps up). 1983. pap. 3.95 o.p. (ISBN 0-380-85043-5, Camelot). Avon.

BASIC Fun with Graphics: The Atari Computer Way. Susan D. Lipscomb & Margaret A. Zuanich. 124p. (ps up). 1983. pap. 3.95 o.p. (ISBN 0-380-85050-8, 85050-8, Camelot). Avon.

BASIC Fun with Graphics: The IBM-PC Computer Way. Susan D. Lipscomb & Margaret A. Zuanich. 124p. (ps up). 1983. pap. 3.95 o.p. (ISBN 0-380-85068-0, 85068, Camelot). Avon.

Basic Grammar & Usage. Penelope Choy. 199p. (Orig.). 1978. pap. text ed. 9.95 o.p. (ISBN 0-15-504926-7, HC). HarBraceJ.

Basic Grammar & Usage. alt. ed. Penelope Choy. 199p. 1980. pap. text ed. 12.95 o.p. (ISBN 0-15-504928-3, HC). HarBraceJ.

Basic Grammar Guide: Advanced Practice for Competency & Proficiency Exams, 3 of 3 vol. ser. Loretta Pastva. LC 81-7936. (Illus.). 224p. 1982. lib. bdg. 10.00 o.p. (ISBN 0-668-05471-9, 5471); pap. 5.95 o.p. (ISBN 0-668-05294-5, 5294). Arco.

Basic Grammar Guide: Intermediate Practice for Competency & Proficiency Exams, 2 of 3 vol. ser. Loretta Pastva. LC 81-7933. (Illus.). 128p. 1982. lib. bdg. 8.00 o.p. (ISBN 0-668-05480-8, 5480); pap. 4.95 o.p. (ISBN 0-668-05273-2, 5273). Arco.

Basic Grammar of Modern English. Bruce L. Liles. 1979. text ed. (ISBN 0-13-061853-5). P-H.

Basic Ground Instructor Written Test Guide. Federal Aviation Administration Staff. 113p. 1980. pap. text ed. 4.75 o.p. (ISBN 0-939158-23-X). Flightshops.

Basic Guide to Data Communications. Ray Sarch. 361p. 1986. pap. text ed. 37.95 o.p. (ISBN 0-07-054728-9). McGraw.

Basic Guide to Photography. 2nd ed. Lou Jacobs, Jr. Ed. by Mike Stensvold. LC 73-79969. (Photography How-to Ser.). (Illus.). (gr. 8-12). 1980. pap. 5.95 o.p. (ISBN 0-8227-4038-9). Petersen Pub.

Basic Guide to Plastics in Packaging. Stanley Sacharow & Roger C. Griffin, Jr. LC 72-91986. 224p. 1983. 29.95 o.p. (ISBN 0-8436-1208-8). Van Nos Reinhold.

Basic Guide to Record Keeping & Taxes. rev., 8th ed. Toys 'n Things Press Staff. Ed. by Tom Copeland. (Business Ideas for Family Day Care Providers Ser.). 40p. (Orig.). 1986. pap. 6.50 o.p. (ISBN 0-934140-33-2). Toys 'n Things.

Basic Guitar. Guitar Player Magazine Editors. (Guitar Player Basic Library). 128p. (Orig.). 1984. pap. 9.95 o.p. (ISBN 0-88188-293-3, HL00183050). H Leonard Pub Corp.

Basic Handbook of Foreign Exchange: A Guide to Foreign Exchange Dealing. C. Tygier. 1984. 120.00 o.p. (ISBN 0-8002-3169-4). Intl Pubns Serv.

Basic Health, Bk. 1. Nancy Lobb. 1987. pap. 4.00 o.p. (ISBN 0-88323-231-6, 244). Pendergrass Pub.

Basic Heat Transfer. M. Necati Ozisik. 1976. text ed. 42.00 o.p. (ISBN 0-07-047980-1). McGraw.

Basic History of Art. 2nd ed. H. W. Janson et al. (Illus.). 444p. 1981. pap. text ed. 25.95 o.p. (ISBN 0-13-062356-3). P-H.

Basic Home Repairs. T. Jeff Williams & Ortho Books Editorial Staff. LC 79-52989. (Illus.). 112p. (Orig.). 1980. pap. 5.95 o.p. (ISBN 0-917102-82-7). Ortho.

Basic Home Wiring. (Illus.). 96p. 1987. 6.95 o.p. (ISBN 0-376-01095-9). Sunset-Lane.

Basic Hospital Financial Management. Donald R. Beck. LC 80-19598. 300p. 1981. text ed. 39.50 o.p. (ISBN 0-89443-329-6). Aspen Pub.

Basic Hotel Front Office Procedures. Peter F. Renner. LC 80-17905. 280p. 1983. pap. 20.95 o.p. (ISBN 0-8436-2190-7). Van Nos Reinhold.

Basic Ideas of Science of Mind. Ernest Holmes. 96p. 1957. pap. 4.50 o.p. (ISBN 0-911336-23-0). Sci of Mind.

Basic Ignition & Electrical Systems. 5th rev. ed. Ed. by Jon C. Jay. LC 73-79968. (Basic Repair & Maintenance Ser.). (Illus.). (gr. 9-12). 1977. pap. 6.95 o.p. (ISBN 0-8227-5014-7). Petersen Pub.

Basic Immunology & Its Medical Application. 2nd ed. James T. Barrett. LC 80-14328. (Illus.). 320p. 1980. text ed. 25.95 o.p. (ISBN 0-8016-0495-8). Mosby.

Basic Income Tax. 240p. 1984. 25.00 o.p. (ISBN 0-88129-138-2). Wash Bar CLE.

Basic Inferential Statistics. Maurice C. Bryson & Robert L. Heiny. 1981. write for info. o.p. (ISBN 0-87150-282-8, 2211, Prindle). PWS-Kent Pub.

Basic Instrumentation for Engineers & Physicists. A. M. Brookes. 1968. text ed. 16.25 o.p. (ISBN 0-08-012538-7); pap. text ed. 6.50 o.p. (ISBN 0-08-012537-9). Pergamon.

Basic Instruments & Selected Documents: 1st Through 24th Supplements. annual General Agreement on Tariffs & Trade Staff. Incl. First. 1953. pap. 5.00 (ISBN 0-685-48339-8, G71). UNIPUB; Second. 1954. pap. 5.00 (ISBN 0-685-48340-1, G72). UNIPUB; Third. 1955. pap. 5.00 (ISBN 0-685-48341-X, G73). UNIPUB; Fourth. 1956. pap. 5.00 (ISBN 0-685-48342-8, G74). UNIPUB; Fifth. 1957. pap. 5.00 (ISBN 0-685-48343-6, G75). UNIPUB; Sixth. 1958. pap. 5.00 (ISBN 0-685-48344-4, G76). UNIPUB; Seventh. 1959. pap. 5.00 (ISBN 0-685-48345-2, G77). UNIPUB; Eighth. 1960. pap. 8.00 (ISBN 0-685-48346-0, G78). UNIPUB; Ninth. 1961. pap. 9.50 (ISBN 0-685-48347-9, G79). UNIPUB; Tenth. 1962. pap. 9.50 (ISBN 0-685-48348-7, G80). UNIPUB; Eleventh. 1963. pap. 8.00 (ISBN 0-685-48349-5, G81). UNIPUB; Twelfth. 1964. pap. 8.00 (ISBN 0-685-48350-9, G82). UNIPUB; Thirteenth. 1965. pap. 9.50 (ISBN 0-685-48351-7, G83). UNIPUB; Fourteenth. 1966. pap. 9.50 (ISBN 0-685-48352-5, G84). UNIPUB; Fifteenth. 1968. pap. 12.00 (ISBN 0-685-48353-3, G99). UNIPUB; Sixteenth. 1969. pap. 12.00 (ISBN 0-685-48354-1, G85). UNIPUB; Seventeenth. 1970. pap. 13.00 (ISBN 0-685-48355-X, G86). UNIPUB; Eighteenth. 1972. pap. 15.00 (ISBN 0-685-48356-8, G87). UNIPUB; Nineteenth. 1973. pap. 15.00 (ISBN 0-685-48357-6, G88). UNIPUB; Twentieth. 1974. pap. text ed. 18.50 (ISBN 0-686-52225-7, G89). UNIPUB; Twenty-First. 167p. 1975. pap. text ed. 18.50 (ISBN 0-685-57615-9, G90). UNIPUB; Twenty-Second. 112p. 1976. pap. text ed. 18.50 (ISBN 0-685-76007-3, G91). UNIPUB; Twenty-Third. 1977. pap. text ed. 18.50 (ISBN 0-685-59476-9, G92). UNIPUB; Twenty-Fourth. 1978. pap. text ed. 18.50 (ISBN 0-685-60672-4, G118). UNIPUB; Twenty-Fifth. pap. 18.50 (G123, GATT). UNIPUB; Twenty-Six. 393p. 1980. pap. 24.50 (G141, GATT). UNIPUB; Twenty-Seventh. 257p. 1981. pap. 18.50 (G149, GATT). UNIPUB; Twenty-Ninth. 235p. 1983. pap. text ed. 18.50 (ISBN 92-870-1007-2, G158). UNIPUB; Thirtieth. 272p. 1985. pap. 18.50 (ISBN 92-870-1010-2, G163, GATT). UNIPUB. (Basic Instruments & Selected Documents Ser.). (Orig., Eng. & Fr.). pap. (GATT). UNIPUB.

Basic Integrated Circuits. Myles H. Marks. (Illus.). 432p. 1986. 26.95 o.p. (ISBN 0-8306-0409-X, 2609); pap. 16.60 o.p. (ISBN 0-8306-0509-6, 2609P). Tab Bks.

Basic Intensive Psychotherapy. William H. Reid. LC 79-24337. 1980. 20.00 o.p. (ISBN 0-87630-227-4). Brunner-Mazel.

Basic Investments. Herbert B. Mayo. 544p. 1980. text ed. 32.95 o.s.i. (ISBN 0-03-054691-5); instr's. manual 10.00 o.s.i. (ISBN 0-03-056801-3). Dryden Pr.

Basic Issues in Econometrics. Arnold Zellner. LC 83-24285. (Illus.). 320p. 1984. lib. bdg. 48.00x o.s.i. (ISBN 0-226-97983-0). U of Chicago Pr.

Basic Issues in the Philosophy of Time. Ed. by Eugene Freeman & Wilfrid Sellars. LC 73-128197. (Monist Library of Philosophy Ser.). 241p. 1971. 19.95 o.p. (ISBN 0-87548-078-0). Open Court.

Basic Issues of American Democracy. 8th ed. Samuel Hendel & Hillman Bishop. 1976. pap. text ed. (ISBN 0-13-062521-3). P-H.

Basic Italian. 5th ed. Charles Speroni & Carlo L. Golino. 441p. 1981. text ed. 25.95 o.p. (ISBN 0-03-058174-5, HoltC); wkbk. 11.95 o.p. (ISBN 0-03-058176-1); lab manual 11.95 o.p. (ISBN 0-03-058177-X); tapes 350.00 o.p. (ISBN 0-03-058178-8). HR&W.

Basic Judaism. Milton Steinberg. LC 47-30768. (Modern Classic Ser.). 1949. 5.95 o.p. (ISBN 0-15-110697-5). HarBraceJ.

Basic Karate. E. G. Bartlett. (Illus.). 96p. 1980. 13.95 o.p. (ISBN 0-571-11435-0); pap. 7.95 o.p. (ISBN 0-571-11436-9). Faber & Faber.

Basic Labor Law. 2nd ed. New Jersey Institute for Continuing Legal Education Staff & Thomas J. Savage. LC 83-181751. iii, 441p. 0.00 o.p. NJ Inst CLE.

Basic Laws of Electromagnetism. I. E. Irodov. 309p. 1986. 7.95 o.p. (ISBN 0-8285-3194-3, Pub. by Mir Pubs USSR). Imported Pubns.

Basic Learning Processes in Childhood. Hayne W. Reese. LC 74-25530. 1976. pap. text ed. 7.95 o.p. (ISBN 0-03-013216-9, HoltC). HR&W.

Basic Library for Bible Students. Warren W. Wiersbe. (Orig.). 1981. pap. 2.95 o.p. (ISBN 0-8010-9641-3). Baker Bk.

Basic Library Skills: A Short Course. Carolyn Wolf & Richard Wolf. LC 81-4865. (Illus.). 137p. 1981. pap. 9.95x o.p. (ISBN 0-89950-018-8). McFarland & Co.

Basic Limbic System Anatomy of the Rat. Ed. by Leonard W. Hamilton. LC 76-46401. (Illus.). 168p. 1976. 35.00x o.p. (ISBN 0-306-30925-4, Plenum Pr). Plenum Pub.

Basic Linear Algebra with Applications. Garfield C. Schmidt. LC 79-16225. (Applied Mathematics Ser.). 536p. 1980. text ed. 17.50 o.p. (ISBN 0-89874-000-2). Krieger.

Basic Macroeconomics. 3rd ed. Edwin G. Dolan. LC 82-72175. 400p. 1983. pap. text ed. 19.95x o.s.i. (ISBN 0-03-062407-X). Dryden Pr.

Basic Management: An Experience Based Approach. rev. ed. Hyler J. Bracey et al. 1981. pap. 20.95x o.p. (ISBN 0-256-02572-X). Irwin.

Basic Marketing: A Managerial Approach. Canadian Edition. 4th ed. J. E. McCarthy & Stanley J. Shapiro. 1986. text ed. 45.00x o.p. (ISBN 0-256-03725-6); learning aid 17.50 o.p. (ISBN 0-256-03726-4). Irwin.

Basic Maternity Nursing. 5th ed. Persis M. Hamilton. (Illus.). 369p. 1983. pap. text ed. 19.95 o.p. (ISBN 0-8016-2042-2). Mosby.

Basic Mathematic Skills. Sheer. 1979. pap. text ed. 5.95 o.p. (ISBN 0-07-055226-6). McGraw.

Basic Mathematics. Dennis D. Airey. 1976. coil bdg. 10.95 o.p. (ISBN 0-88252-021-0). Paladin Hse.

Basic Mathematics. 3rd ed. Marion W. Keller & James H. Zant. LC 78-69602. (Illus.). 1979. pap. 21.95 o.p. (ISBN 0-395-27050-2); pap. 22.95 instr's annotated ed. o.p. (ISBN 0-395-27051-0). HM.

Basic Mathematics. Richard Steinhoff. LC 72-5310. 224p. 1973. text ed. 36.95 o.p. (ISBN 0-07-061123-8, +007). McGraw.

Basic Mathematics: An Individualized Approach, 6, Modules 1-6. Joanna Burris. 1974. write for info. o.p. (ISBN 0-87150-172-4, PWS 1381-6, Prindle). PWS-Kent Pub.

Basic Mathematics & Computer Techniques for Coal Preparation & Mining. Ed. by Kenneth K. Humphreys & Joseph W. Leonard. (Energy, Power, & Environment Ser.: Vol. 17). (Illus.). 248p. 1983. 55.00 o.p. (ISBN 0-8247-1884-4). Dekker.

Basic Mathematics for Administration. F. Parker Fowler, Jr. & E. W. Sandberg. LC 83-94. 358p. 1983. Repr. of 1962 ed. text ed. 24.95 o.p. (ISBN 0-89874-613-2). Krieger.

Basic Mathematics for Radio & Electronics. Colebrook. 320p. 1957. (ISBN 0-8022-0280-2). Philos Lib.

Basic Mathematics for Technical Occupations. Ronald L. Bohuslov. (Illus.). 480p. 1976. text ed. (ISBN 0-13-063396-8). P-H.

Basic Mathematics for Technicians. C. W. Schofield. (Illus.). 1977. pap. text ed. 22.00x o.p. (ISBN 0-7131-3379-1). Trans-Atl Phila.

Basic Mathematics for the Biological & Social Sciences. F. H. Marriott. LC 73-99863. 1970. 22.00 o.p. (ISBN 0-08-006663-1); pap. 60.00 o.p. (ISBN 0-08-006664-X). Pergamon.

Basic Mathematics: Second Series-Form A. Marion W. Keller & James H. Zant. (Orig.). (gr. 9 up). 1972. pap. 12.50 o.p. (ISBN 0-395-04715-3, 3-29333); ans. 1.00 o.p. (ISBN 0-685-12132-1, 3-29334). HM.

Basic Mathematics: What Every College Student Should Know. Shirley Hockett. (Illus.). 1977. pap. text ed. (ISBN 0-13-063446-8). P-H.

Basic Mechanisms in Hearing. Ed. by Aage R. Moller & Pamela Boston. 1973. 49.95 o.p. (ISBN 0-12-504250-7). Acad Pr.

Basic Mechanisms of Ocular Motility & Their Clinical Implications. Ed. by G. Lennerstrand & P. Bach-Y-Rita. 1975. 170.00 o.p. (ISBN 0-08-018885-0). Pergamon.

Basic Meeting Manual: For Officers & Members of Any Organization. Ed. by Nelson Reference Books Staff. 408p. 1986. 15.95 o.p. (ISBN 0-8407-4154-5). Nelson.

Basic Methods of Organic Microanalysis. V. A. Klimova. 228p. 1977. 5.95 o.p. (Pub. by Mir Pubs USSR). Imported Pubns.

Basic Microbiology with Applications. 2nd ed. Thomas D. Brock & Katherine M. Brock. (Illus.). 1978. text ed. (ISBN 0-13-065284-9). P-H.

Basic Microeconomics. 3rd ed. Edwin G. Dolan. LC 82-72174. 464p. 1983. pap. text ed. 19.95x o.s.i. (ISBN 0-03-062406-1). Dryden Pr.

Basic Microprocessors & Sixty-Eight Hundred. Ron Bishop. 1979. pap. 21.95 o.p. (ISBN 0-8104-0758-2). Sams.

Basic Microsoft BASIC. James S. Coan. 256p. pap. 16.95 o.p. (6263). Sams.

BASIC Microsoft: Basic for the Macintosh. Coan. 256p. (gr. 10-12). 1985. 18.95 o.p. (ISBN 0-317-39991-8). Sams.

Basic Microwaving. Barbara Methven. LC 79-113264. (Microwaving Cooking Library). (Illus.). 160p. 1978. 15.95 o.p. (ISBN 0-86573-501-8); pap. 12.95 o.p. (ISBN 0-86573-521-2). Cy De Cosse.

Basic Music: Functional Musicianship for the Non-Music Major. 5th ed. Robert E. Nye & Bjorner Bergethon. (Illus.). 240p. 1981. pap. text ed. (ISBN 0-13-065672-0). P-H.

Basic-Needs Approach to Development: Some Issues Regarding Concepts & Methodology. D. P. Ghai et al. 113p. 1980. pap. 10.50 o.p. (ISBN 92-2-101801-6, ILO69, ILO). UNIPUB.

Basic Needs, Poverty & Government Policies in Sri Lanka. World Employment Program Study. 176p. 1981. pap. 10.00 o.p. (ISBN 92-2-102316-8, ILO164, ILO). UNIPUB.

Basic Neurophysiology. Beverly Bishop. (Illus.). 1982. pap. 25.50 o.p. (ISBN 0-87488-600-7). Med Exam.

Basic Numerical Mathematics, Vol. 2: Numerical Algebra. John Todd. 1978. 42.00 o.p. (ISBN 0-12-692402-3). Acad Pr.

Basic of Bead Stringing. David Champion. 40p. 1985. pap. 3.95 o.p. (ISBN 0-317-68273-3). Borjay.

Basic Oral Spanish. Joseph W. Barlow. (Illus.). 1947. text ed. 16.95x o.p. (ISBN 0-89197-042-8); pap. text ed. 9.95x o.p. (ISBN 0-89197-043-6). Irvington.

Basic Oxyacetylene Welding. 3rd ed. Ivan H. Griffin et al. LC 76-4307. 1977. pap. 8.95 o.p. (ISBN 0-8273-1252-0); instr's. guide 5.00 o.p. (ISBN 0-8273-1253-9). Delmar.

Basic Pathophysiology: A Conceptual Approach. 2nd ed. Maureen W. Groer & Maureen E. Shekleton. LC 82-3579. (Illus.). 643p. 1983. pap. text ed. 31.95 o.p. (ISBN 0-8016-2023-6). Mosby.

Basic Pediatric Nursing. 4th ed. Persis M. Hamilton. LC 81-18887. (Illus.). 584p. 1982. pap. text ed. 17.95 o.p. (ISBN 0-8016-2040-6). Mosby.

Basic Pen & Ink Sketching for Pathfinders: A Youth Enrichment Skill. Lee Evans. (Illus., Orig.). pap. 4.95 o.p. (ISBN 0-317-61551-3). Cheetah Pub.

Basic Petroleum Geology. Peter K. Link. (Illus.). 426p. 1988. 40.00 o.p. (ISBN 0-930972-01-5, P-7140). Oil & Gas.

Basic Petroleum Geology. 2nd ed. Peter K. Link. 425p. 1987. 40.00 o.p. Oil & Gas.

Basic Physical Chemistry. Walter J. Moore. (Illus.). 768p. 1983. text ed. (ISBN 0-13-066019-1). P-H.

Basic Physical Chemistry Calculations. 2nd ed. H. E. Avery & D. J. Shaw. (Illus.). 1980. pap. 14.95 o.p. (ISBN 0-408-70936-7). Butterworth.

Basic Physical Chemistry: Solutions Manual. W. Moore. 192p. 1983. pap. text ed. (ISBN 0-13-066027-2). P-H.

Basic Physical Science for Technicians. A. B. Pollard & C. W. Schofield. (Illus.). 1977. pap. 20.00x o.p. (ISBN 0-7131-3384-8). Trans-Atl Phila.

Basic Physics in Diagnostic Ultrasound. Joseph L. Rose & B. B. Goldberg. 340p. 1979. 41.20 o.p. (ISBN 0-318-17213-5, 335). Am Soc Nondestructive.

Basic Piano for the College Student. 4th ed. Alex H. Zimmerman et al. 240p. 1982. plastic comb o.p. (ISBN 0-697-03518-2). Wm C Brown.

Basic Plumbing. Harry Slater & Lee Smith. LC 77-85751. 1979. pap. text ed. 13.50 o.p. (ISBN 0-8273-1204-0); instr's. guide 6.00 o.p. (ISBN 0-8273-1205-9). Delmar.

Basic Principles & Calculations in Chemical Engineering. 4th ed. David M. Himmelblau. (Illus.). 656p. 1982. text ed. 58.00 o.p. (ISBN 0-13-066498-7). P-H.

Basic Principles of Automatic Control Theory: Special Linear & Nonlinear Systems. A. A. Voronov. 319p. 1984. 9.95 o.p. (ISBN 0-8285-2985-X, Pub. by Mir Pubs USSR). Imported Pubns.

Basic Principles of Electronics, Vol. 2: Semiconductors. J. Jenkins & W. H. Jarvis. 1971. 35.00 o.p. (ISBN 0-08-016118-9); pap. 65.00 o.p. (ISBN 0-08-016119-7). Pergamon.

Basic Principles of Genetics. M. Feldman. (Biocore Ser: Unit 7). 1974. pap. text ed. 15.00 o.p. (ISBN 0-07-005337-5). McGraw.

Basic Principles of Nucleic Chemistry. Ts'o. 1974. Vol. 1. 90.50 o.p. (ISBN 0-12-701901-4); Vol. 2, 1974. 85.00 o.p. (ISBN 0-12-701902-2). Acad Pr.

Basic Principles of Oral Radiography. Myron J. Kasle & Robert Langlais. (Exercises in Dental Radiology Ser.: Vol. 4). (Illus.). 200p. 1981. text ed. write for info. o.p. (ISBN 0-7216-5291-3). Saunders.

Basic Problems of Philosophy. 4th ed. Daniel J. Bronstein et al. LC 79-179449. 656p. 1972. text ed. (ISBN 0-13-067637-3). P-H.

Basic Procedures in Family Practice: An Illustrated Manual. Ed. by Harry E. Mayhew & Leroy A. Rodgers. LC 84-7971. 276p. 1984. 18.95 o.p. (ISBN 0-471-87913-4, Pub. by Wiley Med). Wiley.

BASIC Programming. 3rd ed. John G. Kemeny & Thomas E. Kurtz. LC 79-20683. 334p. 1980. pap. text ed. 28.95x o.p. (ISBN 0-471-01863-5). Wiley.

BASIC Programming. Donald D. Spencer. LC 82-17689. (Illus.). 224p. 1983. pap. 9.95 o.s.i. (ISBN 0-684-18039-1, ScribT). Scribner.

BASIC: Programming Byte-by-Byte. Bijan Mashaw. 1985. pap. 23.95 o.p. (ISBN 0-87484-692-7). Mayfield Pub.

BASIC Programming for Business. Irvine F. Forkner. (Illus.). 288p. 1977. pap. text ed. (ISBN 0-13-066423-5). P-H.

BASIC Programming for Kids--& Grown-ups, Too! Stephen D. Savas & E. S. Savas. 100p. (Orig.). (gr. 1-9). 1984. spiral bdg. 9.95 o.p. (ISBN 0-88006-085-9, BK7415). Wayne Green Ent.

BASIC Programming for the IBM Personal Computer. Harriet H. Morrill. (Microcomputer Bookshelf Ser.). 175p. (Orig.). 1983. pap. 17.45 o.p. (ISBN 0-316-58402-9); tchr's. manual avail. o.p. (ISBN 0-316-58403-7). Scott F.

BASIC Programming Solutions for Manufacturing. J E. Nicks. (Illus.). 298p. 1982. 34.00 o.p. (ISBN 0-87263-076-5). SME.

BASIC Programs for the ATARI 600XL & 800XL. Timothy O. Knight. (Illus.). 120p. 1984. 14.95 o.p. (ISBN 0-8306-0726-9, 1726); 24.50 o.p.; pap. 8.70 o.p. (ISBN 0-8306-1726-4). TAB Bks.

Basic Psychology. 4th ed. L. Dodge Fernald & Peter S. Fernald. LC 77-78910. (Illus.). 1979. pap. 23.95 o.p. (ISBN 0-395-25826-X). HM.

Basic Psychology. Henry Gleitman. 500p. 1982. text ed. 28.95x o.p. (ISBN 0-393-95254-1). Norton.

Basic Psychology: Selected Readings. Ed. by George Morelli. 275p. 1969. pap. text ed. 9.95x o.p. (ISBN 0-8422-0006-1). Irvington.

Basic Reading Instruction. Ed. by Paul M. Hollingsworth & Patrick Kelly. 156p. 1969. text ed. 6.00x o.p. (ISBN 0-686-80329-9). Irvington.

Basic Reading Inventory. 3rd ed. (Reading Ser.). 1986. pap. 11.95 o.p. (ISBN 0-8403-3429-X). Kendall-Hunt.

Basic Readings in Geographic Information Systems. Duane F. Marble et al. 250p. 1984. looseleaf 32.95x o.p. (ISBN 0-913913-00-6). Spad Sys.

Basic Readings in Medical Sociology. Ed. by David Tuckett & Joseph M. Kaufert. 1978. pap. text ed. 13.95x o.p. (ISBN 0-422-76290-3, NO. 2554, Pub. by Tavistock England). Routledge Chapman & Hall.

Basic Rehabilitation Techniques: A Self-Instructional Guide. 2nd. ed. Robert D. Sine et al. LC 80-25506. 268p. 1981. text ed. 29.75 o.p. (ISBN 0-89443-342-3). Aspen Pub.

Basic Robotic Concepts. John M. Holland. LC 83-60173. (Blacksburg Continuing Education Ser.). (Illus.). 272p. 1983. pap. text ed. 19.95 o.p. (ISBN 0-672-21952-2). Sams.

Basic Roof Framing. Benjaming Barnow. (Illus.). 192p. 1986. 19.95 o.p. (ISBN 0-8306-0677-7, 2677); pap. 11.60 o.p. (ISBN 0-8306-2677-8). Tab Bks.

Basic Science for Dental Auxiliaries. Clarinda E. Olson. (Illus.). 1980. pap. text ed. 23.95 ref. ed. o.p. (ISBN 0-13-069245-X). P-H.

Basic Science for Nurses. 2nd ed. W. Ryan & M. Pedder. 256p. 1983. text ed. 17.50 o.p. (ISBN 0-07-072939-5). McGraw.

Basic Science in Obstetrics & Gynaecology: A Textbook for MRCOG, Pt. 1. Ed. by John Dewhurst et al. LC 84-19977. (Illus.). 256p. (Orig.). 1986. pap. text ed. 24.00 o.p. (ISBN 0-443-02287-9). Churchill.

Basic Shop Measurement. Ed. by National Machine Tool Builders Association Staff & K. O. Hoffman. LC 83-3510. (NMTBA Shop Practices Ser.: No. 1-471). 192p. 1983. pap. text ed. 13.95 o.p. (ISBN 0-471-07842-5); Special Ed. (ISBN 0-471-89032-4). Wiley.

Basic Skills: A Plan for Your Child, A Program for All Children. Herbert R. Kohl. 1982. 12.95 o.p. (ISBN 0-316-50136-0, Pub. by Atlantic Monthly Pr). Little.

Basic Sleep Mechanisms. Ed. by Olga Petre-Quadens & John D. Schlag. (NATO Advanced Study Institute Ser.). 1974. 75.50 o.p. (ISBN 0-12-552950-3). Acad Pr.

Basic Slovak. Josef Mistrik. 1985. 10.50 o.p. (ISBN 0-317-57001-3). E J Brill USA.

Basic Sociology see Basic Concepts of Sociology.

Basic Solid-State Electronics: Information Reception, Vol. 4. Van Valkenburgh, Nooger & Neville, Inc. Staff. 196p. 1986. pap. text ed. 10.50 o.p. (ISBN 0-8104-0888-0). Sams.

Basic Solid-State Electronics: Information System Building Blocks, Vol.1. Van Valkenburgh, Nooger & Neville, Inc. Staff. 148p. 1986. pap. text ed. 10.50 o.p. (ISBN 0-8104-0885-6). Sams.

Basic Speech. 3rd ed. Jon Eisenson & Paul H. Boase. (Illus.). 448p. 1975. text ed. write for info. o.p. (ISBN 0-02-331870-8, 33187). Macmillan.

Basic Spelling Skills. 2nd ed. Learning Technology, Inc. Staff. Ed. by Alton L. Raygor. (Basic Skills Ser.). 1980. text ed. 21.95 o.p. (ISBN 0-07-044415-3). McGraw.

Basic Stamp Collecting for Pathfinders: A Youth Enrichment Skill. George Register. (Illus., Orig.). 1987. pap. 4.95 o.p. (ISBN 0-317-61540-8). Cheetah Pub.

Basic Statistics: A Modern Approach. Morris Hamburg. LC 73-13184. (Illus.). 451p. 1974. text ed. 20.95 o.p. (ISBN 0-15-505105-9, HC). HarBraceJ.

Basic Statistics: A Modern Approach. 2nd ed. Morris Hamburg. 496p. 1979. text ed. 20.00 o.p. (ISBN 0-15-505109-1, HC). HarBraceJ.

Basic Statistics: An Introduction to Problem Solving with Your Personal Computer. Jerry W. O'Dell. LC 84-8804. (Illus.). 462p. (Orig.). 1984. 21.95 o.p. (ISBN 0-8306-0759-5); pap. 15.60 o.p. (ISBN 0-8306-1759-0, 1759). TAB Bks.

Basic Statistics for Business & Economics. 3rd ed. Paul G. Hoel & Raymond J. Jessen. LC 81-19739. (Probability & Mathematical Statistics-Applied-Applied Probabilty & Statistics Section Ser.). 629p. 1982. 36.95 o.p. (ISBN 0-471-09829-9). Wiley.

Basic Statistics for Education & the Behavioral Sciences. Sharon L. Weinberg & Kenneth P. Goldberg. LC 78-56433. (Illus.). 1979. text ed. 31.95 o.p. (ISBN 0-395-26853-2). HM.

Basic Statistics for Medical & Social Science Students. 2nd ed. A. E. Maxwell. 1978. pap. 7.95 o.p. (ISBN 0-412-15580-X, NO. 6194, Pub. by Chapman & Hall). Routledge Chapman & Hall.

Basic Statistics for Social Research. 2nd ed. Dean Champion. 1981. text ed. write for info. o.p. (ISBN 0-02-320600-4). Macmillan.

Basic Statistics for the Behavioral Sciences. Kenneth D. Hopkins & Gene V. Glass. LC 77-10877. (Educational, Measurement, Research & Statistics Ser.). (Illus.). 1978. pap. text ed. (ISBN 0-13-069377-4). P-H.

Basic Statistics of the European Community, 1984. 22nd ed. 1985. 15.00 o.p. (ISBN 0-8002-3875-3). Intl Pubns Serv.

Basic Steps in Planning Nursing Research. 2nd ed. Pamela J. Brink & Marilynn T. Wood. LC 82-17426. 304p. 1983. pap. text ed. 22.50 o.p. (ISBN 0-534-01241-8). Jones & Bartlett.

Basic Studies Reading & Word Skills. rev. ed. Raymond W. Hodges et al. 1984. 17.00x o.s.i. (ISBN 0-913310-19-0). PAR Inc.

Basic Surgical Techniques. 2nd ed. R. M. Kirk. 1978. pap. text ed. 12.95 o.p. (ISBN 0-443-01775-1). Churchill.

Basic Suturing. Romm. 1986. 20.00 o.p. (ISBN 0-8016-4297-3). Mosby.

Basic Swedish Word List. Martin S. Allwood & Inga Wilhelmsen. LC 47-26851. (Swedish Language Textbooks). 1947. pap. 0.75x o.p. (ISBN 0-8006-1081-4, 1-1081, Fortress). Augsburg Fortress.

Basic Technical Mathematics. Thomas C. Crooks & Harry L. Hancock. 1969. text ed. write for info. o.p. (ISBN 0-02-325640-0, 32564). Macmillan.

Basic Technical Mathematics. Leffin et al. LC 80-23384. 402p. 1981. text ed. write for info. o.p. (ISBN 0-87150-298-4, 2341, Prindle). PWS-Kent Pub.

Basic Technical Mathematics with Calculus. Ralph H. Hannon. LC 76-20934. (Illus.). 1978. text ed. 24.95 o.s.i. (ISBN 0-7216-4497-X). SCP.

Basic Techniques in Ecological Farming. Stuart Hill & Pierre Ott. 365p. 1983. 20.95x o.p. (ISBN 0-8176-1374-9). Birkhauser.

Basic Techniques of Preparative Organic Chemistry. W. Sabel. 1967. pap. 9.25 o.p. (ISBN 0-08-012307-4). Pergamon.

Basic Telephone Switching Systems. 2nd ed. David Talley. 1979. pap. 10.50 o.p. (ISBN 0-8104-5687-7). Sams.

Basic Television 1972, British Edition, 3 pts. Van Valkenburgh, Nooger & Neville, Inc. Staff. text ed. write for info. o.p.; Set. text ed. 14.40 o.p. (ISBN 0-685-25404-6); Foreign language eds. text ed. write for info. o.p. Brolet.

Basic Textiles: A Learning Package. Carol H. Siewert et al. 228p. 1973. pap. 24.95 o.p. (ISBN 0-395-14220-2). HM.

Basic Thalamic Structure & Function: Proceedings of the Downstate Medical Center Conference, Brooklyn, 1971 Staff. Downstate Medical Center Conference, Brooklyn, 1971. Ed. by W. Riss et al. (Brain, Behavior & Evolution: Vol. 6, Nos. 1-6). (Illus.). 350p. 1972. pap. 77.50 o.p. (ISBN 3-8055-1491-3). S Karger.

Basic Theory of Structures. J. S. Browne. 1966. 27.00 o.p. (ISBN 0-08-011654-X); pap. text ed. 12.75 o.p. (ISBN 0-08-011653-1). Pergamon.

Basic Theory of Waveguide Junctions & Introductory Microwave Network Analysis. D. M. Kerns & R. W. Beatty. 1967. text ed. 18.50 o.p. (ISBN 0-08-012064-4). Pergamon.

Basic Tig & Mig Welding. 2nd ed. I. H. Griffin et al. LC 76-14085. 1977. pap. text ed. 9.50 o.p. (ISBN 0-8273-1260-1); instr's. guide o.s.i. 2.20 o.p. (ISBN 0-8273-1262-8). Delmar.

Basic Tips on the GED. 2nd ed. Rockowitz et al. (Test Preparation Ser.). 1984. pap. 3.95 o.p. (ISBN 0-8120-2764-7). Barron.

Basic Tips on the SAT. 3rd ed. Samuel C. Brownstein & Mitchel Weiner. 1984. 3.95 o.p. (ISBN 0-8120-2463-X). Barron.

Basic Training for Kicking. Pu Gill Gwon. LC 81-85161. (Ser. 415). (Illus., Orig.). 1981. pap. 9.50 o.p. (ISBN 0-89750-078-4). Ohara Pubns.

Basic Training: What to Expect & How to Prepare. Robert F. Collins. Ed. by Ruth Rosen. (Military Opportunities Ser.). (YA) (gr. 7 up). 1988. lib. bdg. 14.95 o.p. (ISBN 0-8239-0833-X). Rosen Group.

Basic Tricks for the Apple. Allen L. Wyatt. LC 83-50830. 144p. 1983. pap. 8.95 o.p. (ISBN 0-672-22208-6). Sams.

Basic Tricks for the IBM. Allen L. Wyatt. LC 83-51185. 136p. 1984. pap. 7.95 o.p. (ISBN 0-672-22250-7). Sams.

Basic Tune-up & Test Equipment. 2nd rev. ed. Ed. by Kalton C. Lahue. LC 74-78228. (Basic Repair & Maintenance Manuals Ser.). (Illus.). 1978. pap. 6.95 o.p. (ISBN 0-8227-5018-X). Petersen Pub.

Basic Two Phase Flow Modeling in Reactor Safety & Performance: EPRI Workshop Held at Tampa, Fla. 27 Feb.--2 March 1979. Ed. by G. Hetsroni. 170p. 1980. pap. 55.00 o.p. (ISBN 0-08-026160-4). Pergamon.

Basic Uniform Commercial Code Teaching Materials. 2d ed. David G. Epstein & James A. Martin. LC 83-1153. (American Casebook Ser.). 667p. 1983. text ed. 36.95 o.p. (ISBN 0-314-71764-1). West Pub.

Basic Upholstery Repair & Restoration. Robert J. McDonald. (Illus.). 184p. 1989. pap. 15.95 o.p. (ISBN 0-7134-5973-5, Pub. by Batsford England). David & Charles.

Basic Values on Single Span Beams: Tables for Calculating Continuous Beams & Frame Constructions, Including Prestressed Beams. Gunter Baum. (Illus.). 1966. 28.00 o.p. (ISBN 0-387-03464-1). Springer-Verlag.

Basic Vibration Control. T. C. Bramer et al. 1978. pap. 19.95x o.p. (ISBN 0-419-11440-8, NO. 6265, Pub. by E & FN Spon England). Routledge Chapman & Hall.

Basic Voice Training for Speech. 2nd ed. Elise Hahn et al. 1957. text ed. 14.95 o.p. (ISBN 0-07-025505-9). McGraw.

Basic Water Treatment for Application Worldwide. 2nd ed. George Smethurst. 224p. 1979. 27.00 o.p. (ISBN 0-7277-0071-5, Pub. by T Telford UK). Am Soc Civil Eng.

BASIC with Style: Programming Proverbs. Paul Nagin & Henry F. Ledgard. (gr. 10 up). 1978. pap. text ed. 8.75 o.p. (ISBN 0-8104-5115-8). Sams.

Basic Writer & Reader. Irwin Griggs & Robert Llewellyn. LC 70-171888. 528p. (Orig.). 1972. pap. 14.50 o.p. (ISBN 0-442-22276-9). Krieger.

Basic Writing Skills: Preparation for Competency Tests. Carlin Kindilien. LC 81-10819. 160p. (Orig.). 1981. pap. 4.95 o.p. (ISBN 0-668-05264-3, 5264). Arco.

Basically Bach: A Three Hundredth Birthday Celebration. Herbert Kupferberg. (Illus.). 208p. 1985. text ed. 12.95 o.p. (ISBN 0-07-035646-7). McGraw.

BASICally Kaypro: Programming the 2, 4 & 10. Joseph K. Rensin & Larry J. Goldstein. (Illus.). 288p. 1984. 16.95 o.p. (ISBN 0-89303-360-X). Brady Bks.

Basics in Folk Art & Tole, Bk. 2. Joyce Howard. (Illus.). 52p. (Orig.). pap. 5.95 cancelled o.s.i. (ISBN 0-917119-18-5, 45-1041). Priscillas Pubns.

Basics of American Politics. 4th ed. Gary Wasserman. 1985. pap. text ed. write for info. o.p. (ISBN 0-673-39488-3). Scott F.

Basics of Anesthesia. Robert K. Stoelting & Ronald D. Miller. LC 84-12084. (Illus.). 480p. 1984. text ed. 30.00 o.p. (ISBN 0-443-08281-2). Churchill.

Basics of BASIC. Alfredo Gomez. 1983. pap. text ed. 20.95 o.p. (ISBN 0-03-063069-X). HR&W.

Basics of Electric Appliance Servicing. B. Scharff. 1976. text ed. 34.95 o.p. (ISBN 0-07-055141-3). McGraw.

Basics of Financial Management. Robert Hartl. 576p. 1986. 38.00 o.p. (ISBN 0-205-11547-0, H1547-2); 15.00 o.p. (ISBN 0-205-11548-9, H1548-0). studypak IBM disk, 1989 16.00 o.p. (H15514); Apple disk 16.00 o.p. (H15522). Allyn.

Basics of Successful Business Management. William R. Osgood. 304p. 1981. 19.95 o.p. (ISBN 0-8144-5641-3). AMACOM.

Basics of Supervisory Management: Mastering the Art of Effective Supervision. James M. Black. 256p. 1975. text ed. 47.95 o.p. (ISBN 0-07-005513-0). McGraw.

Basil & Josephine Stories. F. Scott Fitzgerald. Ed. by John Kuehl & Jackson R. Bryer. LC 73-1120. 320p. 1973. 8.95 o.s.i. (ISBN 0-684-13398-9, ScribT). Scribner.

Basil Brush Goes Boating. Peter Firmin. (Basil Brush Ser.). (Illus.). 48p. (gr. 1-4). 1982. pap. 3.95 o.s.i. (ISBN 0-13-066803-6, Pub. by Treehouse). P-H.

Basil Reader Approach to Reading. Robert C. Aukerman. 339p. 1981. write for info. o.p. (ISBN 0-02-304940-5). Macmillan.
Basis Doppler Echocardiography. Ed. by Joseph Kisslo et al. (Clinics in Diagnostic Ultrasound Ser.: Vol. 17). (Illus.). 224p. 1985. text ed. 35.00 o.p. (ISBN 0-443-08431-9). Churchill.
Basis for Marketing Decisions Through Controlled Motivation Research. Louis Cheskin. 1961. 6.95x o.p. (ISBN 0-87140-965-8). Liveright.
Basis of Motor Control. Ragnar Granit. 1970. 89.50 o.p. (ISBN 0-12-295350-9). Acad Pr.
Basis of Scientific Thinking. Samuel Reiss. 1961. (ISBN 0-8022-1323-5). Philos Lib.
Basket Faire. 4.98 o.p. (ISBN 0-317-38612-3). Gick.
Basket Work of the Aborigines. facsimile ed. Otis Mason. (Shorey Indian Ser.). (Illus.). 83p. pap. 5.95 o.s.i. (ISBN 0-8466-4005-8, 15). Shorey.
Basketball. 2nd ed. Frances H. Ebert & Billye A. Cheatum. LC 76-8573. (Illus.). 282p. 1977. pap. text ed. 15.95 o.p. (ISBN 0-7216-3306-4). SCP.
Basketball My Way. Nancy Lieberman & Harvey Frommer. (Illus.). 192p. 1982. 12.95 o.s.i. (ISBN 0-684-17012-4, ScribT); pap. 6.95 o.s.i. (ISBN 0-684-18203-3). Scribner.
Basketball Skillbook. Earl Monroe & Wes Unseld. Ed. by Ray Siegener. LC 72-862687. (Illus.). 1973. 7.95 o.p. (ISBN 0-689-10528-2, Atheneum). Macmillan.
Basketball's Amoeba Defense: A Complete Multiple System. Fran Webster. LC 83-23654. 264p. 1984. text ed. 19.95x o.p. (ISBN 0-13-069139-9, Parker). P-H.
Basketball's Pro-Set Playbook: The Complete Offensive Arsenal. Harry L. Harkins. LC 82-3487. 188p. 1982. text ed. 16.95 o.p. (ISBN 0-13-056366-8, Parker). P-H.
Basketmaker's Art: Contemporary Baskets & Their Makers. Ed. by Rob Pulleyn. LC 86-82336. (Illus.). 180p. 1986. 26.95 o.s.i. (ISBN 0-937274-28-3, Dist. by Sterling Publishing Co.). Lark Bks.
Basketry Book. Sherry De Leon. LC 77-2777. (Illus.). 1978. 12.95 o.p. (ISBN 0-03-017866-5); pap. 7.95 o.p. (ISBN 0-03-042851-3). H Holt & Co.
Basketwork Through the Ages. Henry H. Bobart. LC 72-171354. 192p. 1971. Repr. of 1936 ed. 35.00x o.p. (ISBN 0-8103-3400-3). Gale.
Baskin: Sculpture, Drawings, Prints. Leonard Baskin. LC 73-132198. 1970. 25.00 o.p. (ISBN 0-8076-0577-8). Braziller.
Basque. Mario Saltarelli. (Descriptive Grammars Ser.). 300p. 1988. lib. bdg. 65.95x o.p. (ISBN 0-317-64387-8, Pub. by Croom Helm UK). Routledge Chapman & Hall.
Basque Americans: A Guide to Information Sources. Ed. by William A. Douglass & Righard W. Etulain. (Ethnic Studies Information Guide Ser.: Vol. 6). 184p. 1981. 68.00x o.p. (ISBN 0-8103-1469-X). Gale.
Bass. Robert H. Boyle & Elgin Ciampi. (Illus.). 144p. 1980. 27.50 o.p. (ISBN 0-393-01379-0). Norton.
Bass Fishing Fundamentals. Ken Schultz. (Illus.). 272p. 1982. 14.95 o.p. (ISBN 0-686-97485-9). Exposition-Phoenix.
Bassoon & Contrabassoon. Lyndesay G. Langwill. (Illus.). 1966. 10.95x o.p. (ISBN 0-393-02098-3, NortonC). Norton.
Bastard Angel. Barrie Keeffe. 64p. 1989. pap. 4.95 o.p. (ISBN 0-413-47160-8). Heinemann Ed.
Bastard Child. George W. Perkins. 200p. 1985. 10.95 o.p. (ISBN 0-533-06358-2). Vantage.
Bastion. Anthony Esler. 320p. 1987. pap. 3.95 o.p. (ISBN 1-55547-187-0). Critics Choice Paper.
Bastoor. Mehrdad Bahar. LC 70-128811. (Illus.). (gr. k-5). 1972. PLB 4.95g o.p. (ISBN 0-87614-015-0). Carolrhoda Bks.
Basutoland: Its Legends & Customs. Minnie Martin. LC 75-88997. Repr. of 1903 ed. 35.00x o.p. (ISBN 0-8371-1756-9, MAK&, Pub. by Negro U Pr). Greenwood.
Bat. Nina Leen. LC 75-32252. (Illus.). 80p. (gr. 5-12). 1976. 7.50 o.s.i. (ISBN 0-03-015581-9). H Holt & Co.
Batavus Moped Owner Service-Repair: 1976-1978. Ed Scott. (Illus., Orig.). pap. 6.00 o.p. (ISBN 0-89287-199-7, M438). Clymer Pub.
Batch One: Computer Programming Problems. National Computing Centre, Ltd. Staff. LC 72-97126. (Computers & People Ser.). 46p. 1973. pap. 8.50x o.s.i. (ISBN 0-85012-089-6). Intl Pubns Serv.
Bates Family. Reginald Ottley. LC 69-18627. (gr. 4-6). 1969. 4.50 o.p. (ISBN 0-15-205726-9, HJ). HarBraceJ.
Bath. Edith Sitwell. LC 78-24153. 1980. Repr. of 1932 ed. lib. bdg. 35.00 o.p. (ISBN 0-313-20815-8, SIBT). Greenwood.
Bath Color & Activity Book. Carole Marsh. (Carole Marsh Bks.). (Illus.). 20p. (Orig.). (gr. 1-12). 1986. pap. 5.00 o.p. (ISBN 0-935326-73-1). Gallopade Pub Group.
Bath Cookbook. Carole Marsh. (Carole Marsh Bks.). (Illus.). 63p. (Orig.). 1986. pap. 7.95 o.p. (ISBN 0-935326-98-7). Gallopade Pub Group.
Bathrooms. Steven Kroll. (Snuggle & Read Story Bks.). (Illus.). 32p. (Orig.). (ps-3). 1982. pap. 1.95 o.p. (ISBN 0-380-79103-X, 79103-X, Camelot). Avon.
Bathrooms. Sunset Editors. LC 80-80856. (Illus.). 80p. (Orig.). 1980. pap. 3.95 o.p. (ISBN 0-376-01326-5, Sunset Bks). Sunset-Lane.
Bathtime. David Lloyd. LC 83-182399. (Time to Talk Ser.). (Illus.). 32p. (ps-2). 1983. 1.50 o.s.i. (ISBN 0-671-47107-4, Little Simon). S&S.
Bathtime on Sesame Street. Sesame Street Staff. Ed. by Janet Schulman. LC 82-80571. (Little Pops). (Illus.). 12p. (ps-3). 1983. pap. 2.50 o.s.i. (ISBN 0-394-85449-7). Random.
Bathtime Pals: A Bathtime Play Book. (Learning Curves Bks.). (Illus.). 4p. (ps-1). 1987. pap. 3.95 o.p. (ISBN 0-553-18330-3). Bantam.
Bathtub Physics. Hy Ruchlis. LC 67-18545. (Curriculum Related Bks.). (Illus.). (gr. 5 up). 1967. 4.95 o.p. (ISBN 0-15-205730-7, HJ). HarBraceJ.
Batman. Elliot S. Maggin. (Super Powers Which Way Bks.). (gr. 8-12). 1983. pap. 1.95 o.p. (ISBN 0-671-47565-7). Archway.
Baton Twirling Unlimited. Susan D. Orr. LC 81-82409. (Illus.). 268p. 1981. pap. 14.95 o.p. (ISBN 0-915088-27-4). C Hungness.
Bats. Davey Johnson & Peter Golenbock. 1986. 16.95 o.p. (ISBN 0-399-13120-5). Putnam Pub Group.
Batter & Breading. Suderman. 1983. 37.95 o.p. (ISBN 0-87055-435-2). Van Nos Reinhold.
Batter & Breading Technology. Darrel R. Suderman & Frank E. Cunningham. (Illus.). 1983. 37.95 o.p. (ISBN 0-87055-434-4). AVI.
Batter My Heart. Robb Murray. (Orion Ser.). 192p. 1980. pap. 4.95 o.p. (ISBN 0-8127-0301-4). Review & Herald.
Battered Child. 3rd rev. enl. ed. C. Henry Kempe & Ray E. Helfer. LC 80-14329. (Illus.). xviii, 440p. 1982. pap. text ed. 16.00x o.s.i. (ISBN 0-226-43039-1). U of Chicago Pr.
Battered Child. 3rd rev. ed. C. Henry Kempe & Ray E. Helfer. LC 80-14329. (Illus.). 1980. lib. bdg. 35.00x o.s.i. (ISBN 0-226-43038-3). U of Chicago Pr.
Battered Spouses. Nick Miller. 69p. 1975. pap. text ed. 5.00x o.p. (ISBN 0-7135-1936-3, Pub. by Bedford England). Gower Pub Co.
Battered Women: A Psychosociological Study of Domestic Violence. Ed. by Maria Roy. 1979. 14.95 o.p. (ISBN 0-442-27201-4); pap. 18.95 o.p. (ISBN 0-442-25645-0). Van Nos Reinhold.
Batteries & Bulbs Two: Student's Book. Elementary Science Study Staff. (gr. 5-9). 1971. text ed. 33.20 o.p. (ISBN 0-07-017713-9). McGraw.
Batteries: Lead Acid Batteries & Electric Vehicles, Vol. 2. Ed. by Karl Kordesch. 536p. 1977. 110.00 o.p. (ISBN 0-8247-6489-7). Dekker.
Batting Ninth for the Braves. Nathan Aaseng. (Pennypinchers Ser.). 132p. (Orig.). (gr. 3-6). 1982. pap. 2.95 o.p. (ISBN 0-89191-708-X). Cook.
Battle Creek: The Place Behind the Products: An Illustrated History. Peter J. Schmitt & Larrie B. Massie. (Illus.). 136p. 1984. 19.95 o.s.i. (ISBN 0-89781-117-8). Windsor Pubns Inc.
Battle Cry of Freedom: The United States 1848-1877. H. Jeremy Packard. (Illus.). 288p. 1983. pap. text ed. 6.75 o.p. (ISBN 0-88334-165-4). Ind Sch Pr.
Battle Drive. Barbara Siegel & Scott Siegel. (Transformers Find Your Fate Junior Ser.: No. 2). 80p. (Orig.). (gr. 4 up). 1985. pap. 1.95 o.p. (ISBN 0-345-32670-9). Ballantine.
Battle for Barbie. Reva A. Smith. Ed. by Gerald Wheeler. LC 83-21318. (Banner Bks.). (Illus.). 159p. (Orig.). (gr. 3 up). 1984. pap. 6.95 o.p. (ISBN 0-8280-0164-2). Review & Herald.
Battle for Creation: Acts, Facts, Impacts, Vol. 2. Henry M. Morris & Duane T. Gish. LC 74-75429. (Illus.). 1976. pap. 5.95 o.p. (ISBN 0-89051-020-2). Master Bks.
Battle for Democracy. Rexford G. Tugwell. 1969. Repr. of 1935 ed. lib. bdg. 35.00x o.p. (ISBN 0-8371-1862-X, TUDE). Greenwood.
Battle for Gaul. Julius Caesar. Tr. by Anne Wiseman & Peter Wiseman. LC 79-54955. (Illus.). 216p. 1980. 17.95 o.s.i. (ISBN 0-87923-306-0). Godine.
Battle for Investment Survival. rev. ed. Gerald M. Loeb. 1972. pap. 8.95 o.p. (ISBN 0-671-21304-0, Fireside). S&S.
Battle for Religious Liberty. Lynn Buzzard & Samuel Ericcson. (Issues & Insight Ser.). (Orig.). 1982. pap. 6.95 o.p. (ISBN 0-89191-552-4, 55525). Cook.
Battle for Rome. W. G. Jackson. 1978. pap. 1.95 o.p. (ISBN 0-441-04859-5). Ace Bks.
Battle for the Trinity: The Debate over Inclusive God-Language. Donald G. Bloesch. 1985. 10.95 o.p. (ISBN 0-89283-230-4, Pub. by Vine Books). Servant.
Battle in the River of Heaven. Ding Yuzheng. (Monkey Ser.: No. 13). (Illus.). 70p. (Orig.). 1987. pap. 7.95 o.p. (ISBN 0-8351-1582-8). China Bks.
Battle of Britain. Julia Markl. LC 84-7396. (Turning Points of World War II Ser.). (Illus.). 96p. 1984. lib. bdg. 11.90 o.p. (ISBN 0-531-04861-6). Watts.
Battle of Gabhra. Ed. by Nicholas O'Kearney. 176p. Repr. of 1854 ed. 21.00 o.p. (ISBN 0-384-42995-5). Johnson Repr.
Battle of Hamburg: Allied Forces Against a German City in 1943. Martin Middlebrook. 1981. 4.95 o.p. (ISBN 0-684-16727-1, ScribT). Scribner.
Battle of Ideas in the Modern World. V. Kovtunov. 364p. 1979. 7.95 o.p. (ISBN 0-8285-1499-2, Pub. by Progress Pubs USSR). Imported Pubns.
Battle of Moscow. Albert Steaton. (War Bks.). 320p. 1985. pap. 3.95 o.s.i. (ISBN 0-515-08345-3). Jove Pubns.
Battle of the Crater: Eyewitness Accounts of the Civil War. John C. Featherstone. 40p. Date not set. pap. 12.50 o.p. (ISBN 0-87651-998-2). Southern U Pr.
Battle Pay. Peter McCurtin. (Soldier of Fortune Ser.). 1978. pap. 1.50 o.p. (ISBN 0-505-51233-5, Pub. by Tower Bks). Dorchester Pub Co.
Battle Road. Steve Jackson. LC 86-90223. (Car Wars Gamebook Ser.: No. 1). 192p. (Orig.). 1986. pap. 2.95 o.p. (ISBN 0-88038-297-X). TSR Inc.
Battle Your Bank & Win. Edward F. Mrkvicka, Jr. 224p. 1984. 12.95 o.p. (ISBN 0-688-03952-9). Morrow.
Battleground of Freedom: South Carolina in the Revolution. Nat Hilborn & Sam Hilborn. LC 70-143042. (Illus.). 256p. 1970. 19.95 o.p. (ISBN 0-87844-000-3). Sandlapper Pub Co.
Battlelines: World War I Posters from the Bowman Gray Collection. Libby Chenault. LC 87-72897. (Illus.). xii, 210p. 1988. pap. 24.95 o.p. (ISBN 0-8078-4215-X, Pub. by Rare Bk Coll). U of NC Pr.
Battlement Garden. Walter C. Hodges. LC 79-15849. (Illus.). (gr. 6 up). 1980. 10.95 o.p. (ISBN 0-395-29184-4, Clarion). HM.
Battles in the Monsoon: Campaigning in the Central Highlands, Vietnam, Summer 1966. Samuel L. Marshall. (Vietnam War Ser.: No. 5). (Illus.). 408p. 1984. Repr. of 1966 ed. 18.95x o.p. (ISBN 0-89839-075-3). Battery Pr.
Battleship Potemkin. Sergei Eisenstein. 1978. pap. 7.95 o.p. (ISBN 0-380-30460-0, 30460-0). Avon.
Battleships of the Grand Fleet: A Pictorial Review of British Battleships & Battlecruisers, 1906-1921. W. P. Trotter & R. A. Burt. LC 81-86414. (Illus.). 96p. 1982. 21.95 o.p. (ISBN 0-87021-916-2); bulk rates avail. o.p. Naval Inst Pr.
Battling for the National Parks. George B. Hartzog. 1989. pap. 10.95 o.p. Moyer Bell Limited.
Batty, Bloomers & Boycott: A Little Etymology of Eponymous Words. Rosie Boycott. LC 83-71477. 128p. 1983. 8.95 o.p. (ISBN 0-911745-12-2). P Bedrick Bks.
Baugeschichtliche Untersuchungen am Stadtrand von Pompeji. Ferdinand Noack & Karl Lehmann-Hartleben. (Denkmaeler Antiker Architektur, Vol. 2). (Illus.). xii, 245p. (Ger.). Repr. of 1936 ed. 182.00x o.p. (ISBN 3-11-004986-4). De Gruyter.
Bausell Home Learning Guide: Teach Your Child to Write. R. Barker Bausell et al. 1981. write for info. o.p. (ISBN 0-03-057666-0). Saunders.
Bausell Home Learning Guide: Teach Your Child Math. R. Barker Bausell et al. LC 81-50842. 256p. (Orig.). 1981. pap. 12.95 o.p. (ISBN 0-03-059652-1, HoltC). HR&W.
Bavarian Royal Castles. (Panorama Bks.). (Illus., Fr.). 4.95 o.p. (ISBN 0-685-11036-2). French & Eur.
Bay Area Counties Public Schools: How Are They Doing? 1985. Lillian S. Clancy. (California Public Schools Ser.: Vol. 5). 360p. 1984. pap. 23.95 o.p. (ISBN 0-939580-23-3). CA Schl Surveys.
Bay Area Counties Public Schools, 1986, Vol. 5. Lillian S. Clancy. (California Public Schools: How Are They Doing? Ser.). 400p. (Orig.). 1985. pap. 24.95 o.p. (ISBN 0-939580-32-2). CA Schl Surveys.
Bay Area Counties Public Schools, 1987, Vol. 5. Lillian S. Clancy. (California Public Schools: How Are They Doing? Ser.). 400p. (Orig.). 1987. pap. 24.95 o.p. (ISBN 0-939580-41-1). CA Schl Surveys.
Bay Area Counties Public Schools, 1988, Vol. 5. Lillian S. Clancy. (California Public Schools: How Are They Doing? Ser.). 400p. (Orig.). 1988. pap. 29.95 o.p. (ISBN 0-939580-49-7). CA Schl Surveys.
Bay Area Public Schools: How Are They Doing? (1984) Lillian S. Clancy. (How Are They Doing Ser.). 330p. (Orig.). 1984. pap. 17.95 o.p. (ISBN 0-939580-05-5). CA Schl Surveys.
Bay Bib: Rhode Island Marine Bibliography, 2 vols. (Marine Technical Reports: Nos. 70 & 71). Set. 5.00 o.p. (ISBN 0-686-34464-2); keyword in context index 2.00 o.p. (ISBN 0-938412-02-7). Sea Grant Pubns.
Bay Boy or the Autobiography of a Youth of Massachusetts Bay by Royall Tyler. Ed. by Martha R. Wright. 1978. 5.00 o.p. (ISBN 0-682-49180-2). Exposition-Phoenix.
Bay of Lions. Ned Calmer. LC 78-72924. 1980. 9.95 o.p. (ISBN 0-87795-214-0, Arbor Hse). Morrow.
Bay of Pigs. Haynes Johnson. (Illus.). 1964. 10.50 o.p. (ISBN 0-393-04263-4). Norton.
Bayesian Analysis in Economic Theory & Time Series Analysis. C. A. Holt & R. W. Shore. (Studies in Bayesian Econometrics: Vol. 2). 1987. 63.50 o.p. (ISBN 0-317-65940-5). Elsevier.
Bayesian Full Information Structural Analysis. Juan-Antonio Morales. LC 70-155592. (Lecture Notes in Operation Research: Vol. 43). 1971. pap. 10.70 o.p. (ISBN 0-387-05417-0). Springer-Verlag.
Bazaar. Susan Wood. LC 80-14985. 64p. 1981. 10.95 o.p. (ISBN 0-03-057856-6, Owl Bk); pap. 5.95 o.p. (ISBN 0-03-057709-8). H Holt & Co.
Bazaar Stall. Monica Stuart & Gill Soper. 64p. 1979. pap. 6.95 o.p. (ISBN 0-571-11289-7). Faber & Faber.
BBC Micro Add-On Guide. Philip Gardner et al. (Illus.). 160p. (Orig.). 1985. pap. 13.95 o.p. (ISBN 0-00-383009-8, Pub. by Collins England). Sheridan.
BBC Micro Gamemaster. Kay Ewban et al. (Illus.). 159p. (Orig.). 1984. pap. 11.95 o.p. (ISBN 0-246-12581-0, Pub. by Granada England). Sheridan.
BBC Micro Graphics & Sound. Steve Money. (Illus.). 170p. 1983. pap. 13.95 o.p. (ISBN 0-246-12156-4, Pub. by Granada England). Sheridan.
BBC Micro Machine Code Portfolio. Bruce Smith. (Illus.). 212p. (Orig.). 1985. pap. 15.95 o.p. (ISBN 0-246-12643-4, Pub. by Granada England). Sheridan.
BBC Micro Wargaming. Owen Bishop & Audrey Bishop. (Illus.). 170p. (Orig.). 1985. pap. 15.95 o.p. (ISBN 0-00-383000-4, Pub. by Collins England). Sheridan.
BBC Microcomputer for Beginners. Seamus Dunn & Valerie Morgan. 1984. pap. 15.95 o.p. (ISBN 0-13-069328-6). P-H.
B.B.L.'s Recommendations for Pronouncing Doubtful Words see Needed Words.
BCG Vaccine: Tuberculosis-Cancer. Sol R. Rosenthal. LC 77-94883. (Illus.). 410p. 1980. 36.00 o.p. (ISBN 0-88416-213-3). Year Bk Med.
BCTV: Bibliography on Cable Television 1983. Communications Library Staff. 75p. (Orig.). 1988. pap. 35.00x o.p. (ISBN 0-934339-08-2, 1983). Comm Lib.
Be a Better Parent. Mary M. Kern. LC 79-9098. 160p. 1979. pap. 6.95 o.s.i. (ISBN 0-664-24271-5, Westminster). Westminster John Knox.
Be a Better Reader, Canadian Ed, Bks. 1-3. Nila B. Smith. Ed. by M. Jenkinson et al. (YA) (gr. 7-12). 1963. Bk. 1. pap. text ed. 2.75 o.p.; Bk. 2. pap. text ed. 2.75 o.p. (ISBN 0-13-072652-4); Bk. 3. pap. text ed. 2.75 o.p. (ISBN 0-685-19077-3). P-H.
Be a Rockhound. Martin L. Keen. LC 79-1769. (Illus.). 64p. (gr. 3 up). 1979. lib. bdg. 8.29 o.p. (ISBN 0-671-32820-4). Messner.
Be an EQ Traveler. Girl Scouts of the U. S. A. Staff. (gr. 1-8). 1971. pap. 0.10 o.p. (ISBN 0-88441-122-2, 19-966). Girl Scouts USA.
Be As You Are: The Teachings of Sri Ramana Maharshi. Ed. by David Godman. 256p. 1985. pap. 8.95 o.p. (ISBN 1-85063-006-2, Ark Paperbks). Routledge Chapman & Hall.
Be Fit Through Your Forties. Eric Taylor. (Illus.). 144p. (Orig.). 1987. pap. 7.95 o.p. (ISBN 0-7137-1844-7, Pub. by Javelin). Sterling.
Be Forever Yamato, Vol. 1. (This is Animation Ser.: No. 2). (Illus.). 125p. 1984. 7.95 o.p. (ISBN 0-318-02665-1). Bks Nippan.
Be Good to Your Body. Trent Busby. 1977. 8.95 o.p. (ISBN 0-8065-0558-3, Pub. by Citadel Pr). Carol Pub Group.
Be Good to Yourself. John MacKenzie. (Illus.). 156p. 1981. 7.95 o.p. (ISBN 0-89496-027-X); pap. 4.95 o.p. (ISBN 0-89496-026-1). Ross Bks.
Be Happy - You Are Loved! Robert H. Schuller. LC 86-20854. 224p. 1986. 15.95 o.p. (ISBN 0-8407-5517-1). Nelson.
Be It Ever So Humble. Daisy Hepburn. LC 83-24603. (Life with Spice Bible Study Ser.). 1984. 2.95 o.s.i. (ISBN 0-8307-0943-6, 6101805). Regal.
Be Mine. Daisy Hepburn. LC 83-24618. (Life with Spice Bible Study Ser.). 1984. 2.95 o.s.i. (ISBN 0-8307-0944-4, 6101817). Regal.
Be My Friend. Segal. 1.95 o.p. (ISBN 0-8065-0308-4, Pub. by Citadel Pr); pap. 1.10 o.p. (ISBN 0-685-38413-6). Carol Pub Group.

Titles

Be My Friend: The Art of Good Relationships. Patricia Sternberg. LC 83-10254. 192p. 1983. pap. 8.95 o.s.i. (ISBN 0-664-26007-1, Westminster). Westminster John Knox.

Be My Love. Harriett Hinsdale. 1980. pap. 0.95 o.p. (ISBN 0-380-01041-0, 17590). Avon.

Be Reconciled. Rolland Stair. 48p. 1981. softcover 0.75 o.p. (ISBN 0-8146-1233-4). Liturgical Pr.

Be Somebody: A Biography of Marguerite Rawalt. Judith Paterson. 288p. 1986. 16.95 o.p. (ISBN 0-89015-551-8). Eakin Pr.

Be Still & Know. Bhagwan Shree Rajneesh. Ed. by Ma Yoga Anurag. (Question & Answer Ser.). (Illus.). 364p. (Orig.). 1981. pap. 9.95 o.p. (ISBN 0-88050-511-7). Chidvilas Inc.

Be the Boss: Start & Run Your Own Service Business. Sandi Wilson. 256p. 1985. pap. 5.95 o.p. (ISBN 0-380-89634-6). Avon.

Be the Person You're Meant to Be. Jerry Greenwald. 1974. 6.95 o.p. (ISBN 0-671-21629-5). S&S.

Be Ye Transformed. Elizabeth S. Turner. 1969. 6.95 o.p. (ISBN 0-87159-008-5). Unity School.

Be Your Own Doctor. William Utrecht. 91p. 1921. pap. text ed. 7.95 o.s.i. (ISBN 0-88697-042-3). Life Science.

Be Your Own Rose Expert. D. G. Hessayon & Harry Wheatcroft. 35p. 1977. pap. 2.50 o.p. (ISBN 0-8119-0358-3). Fell.

Beach Boats of Britain. Robert Simper. LC 84-149827. (Illus.). 156p. 1984. 27.00 o.p. (ISBN 0-85115-195-7, Pub. by Boydell & Brewer). Longwood Pub Group.

Beach Book. Nancy Bruning. LC 80-28390. (Illus.). 224p. (Orig.). 1981. pap. 8.95 o.p. (ISBN 0-395-30523-3). HM.

Beach Boys Silver Anniversary. John Milward. Ed. by Ilene Cherna. LC 84-21112. (Illus.). 240p. 1985. pap. 15.95 o.p. (ISBN 0-385-19650-4, Dolp). Doubleday.

Beach Glass. John Gabel. (Cleveland Poets Ser.: No. 22). 29p. 1979. 2.50 o.p. (ISBN 0-914946-18-8). Cleveland St Univ Poetry Ctr.

Beach Hotels of the World. Jack White. Ed. by David Hogan. LC 85-61335. (Illus.). 220p. 1987. 30.00 o.p. (ISBN 0-317-56030-1). Authors Unltd.

Beach of Morning: A Walk in West Africa. Stephen Pern. (Illus.). 224p. 1984. 22.95 o.p. (ISBN 0-340-26236-2, Pub. by Hodder & Stoughton UK). David & Charles.

Beach Processes & Sedimentation. Paul D. Komar. (Illus.). 464p. 1976. text ed. (ISBN 0-13-072595-1). P-H.

Beach Towels. Marilyn Sachs. (Illus.). 76p. (gr. 5 up). 1984. pap. 2.25 o.p. (ISBN 0-380-68825-5, 68825-5, Flare). Avon.

Beach Towns - A Walker's Guide to L.A.'s Beach Communities: Detailed Walking Tours of Ten Beach Communities from Santa Monica to Long Beach. Robert J. Pierson. LC 84-19912. (Illus.). 160p. (Orig.). 1985. pap. 7.95 o.p. (ISBN 0-87701-312-8). Chronicle Bks.

Beachcombers. Helen Cresswell. LC 72-57348. 144p. (gr. 5 up). 1972. 9.95 o.s.i. (ISBN 0-02-725470-4). Macmillan.

Beaches of Maui County. John R. Clark. LC 80-13857. (Illus.). 172p. 1980. pap. 9.95 o.p. (ISBN 0-8248-0694-8). UH Pr.

Beacon Bible Commentary, 10 vols. Set. 149.50 o.p. (ISBN 0-8010-0675-9). Baker Bk.

Beagle Brigade. Innes Hamilton. 1980. 10.00 o.p. (ISBN 0-682-49532-8). Exposition-Phoenix.

Beagle qui a du Chien. Charles M. Schulz. (Fr.). pap. 5.95 o.s.i. (ISBN 0-03-061653-0). H Holt & Co.

Beam & Fiber Optics. J. A. Arnaud. (Quantum Electronics Ser.). 1976. 91.00 o.p. (ISBN 0-12-063250-0). Acad Pr.

Beam Engines. 1982 ed. T. E. Crowley. (Albums Ser.: No. 15). (Illus.). 32p. pap. 3.50 o.p. (ISBN 0-85263-595-8, Pub. by Shire Pubns England). Seven Hills Bk Dists.

Beam Pkg Beams & H. Date not set. (ISBN 0-07-521222-6). McGraw.

Beams & Framed Structures. 2nd ed. J. Heyman. LC 74-2234. 160p. 1974. 35.00 o.p. (ISBN 0-08-017945-2); pap. 35.00 o.p. (ISBN 0-08-017946-0). Pergamon.

Beams of Illumination from the Divine Revelation. Shaykh F. Haeri. 340p. 1987. pap. 18.95 o.p. (ISBN 0-7103-0219-3, 02193, Kegan Paul). Routledge Chapman & Hall.

Bean & the Scene. Barbara Westman. (Illus.). 1975. pap. 2.50 o.p. (ISBN 0-517-52113-X). Barre.

Bean Cuisine: A Culinary Guide for the Ecogourmet. Beverly White. (Illus.). 158p. pap. 5.95 o.p. (ISBN 0-7100-8759-4). Routledge Chapman & Hall.

Bean Feast: An International Legumes Cookbook. Valerie Turvey. LC 79-5447. (Illus.). 160p. 1979. pap. 5.95 o.s.i. (ISBN 0-89286-158-4, One Hund One Prods). Ortho.

Beans of Egypt Maine. Carolyn Chute. 353p. 1985. lib. bdg. 14.95 o.p. (ISBN 0-8161-3956-3, Large Print Bks). G K Hall.

Beansprout Book. Gay Courter. (Illus.). 1977. pap. 2.95 o.p. (ISBN 0-671-22947-8, Fireside). S&S.

Bear, a Bobcat & Three Ghosts. Anne Rockwell. LC 77-5084. (Ready-to-Read Ser.). (Illus.). (gr. 1-4). 1977. 6.95 o.s.i. (ISBN 0-02-777460-0). Macmillan.

Bear & I: The Story of the World's Most Famous Caddie. Angelo Argea & Jolee Edmondson. LC 79-63844. (Illus.). 1979. 7.95 o.p. (ISBN 0-689-10983-0, Atheneum). Macmillan.

Bear Attacks. Stephen Herrero. LC 85-165. 288p. 1985. 15.95 o.p. (ISBN 0-8329-0377-9). Lyons & Burford.

Bear-Claw Range. Frank Bosworth. (Lythway Ser.). 1987. lib. bdg. 16.50x o.p. (ISBN 0-7451-0576-9, Pub. by Chivers Pr UK). G K Hall.

Bear Hunt. Anthony Browne. LC 79-21964. (Illus.). 24p. (ps-2). 1980. 8.95 o.p. (ISBN 0-689-30733-0, Atheneum). Macmillan.

Bear on the Doorstep. Jane Flory. (Illus.). 32p. (gr. k-3). 1980. 6.95 o.p. (ISBN 0-395-29239-5). HM.

Bear Shadow. Frank Asch. LC 84-18250. (Illus.). 32p. (gr. k-8). 1985. 12.95 o.s.i. (ISBN 0-13-071580-8). P-H.

Bear Who Slept Thru Xmas. Date not set. incl. cassette 8.95 o.p. Ideals.

Bear Who Slept Thru Xmas. Date not set. incl. cassette & toy 14.95 o.p. Ideals.

Beard & Victims: Two Plays. Michael McClure. LC 84-48293. 196p. 1985. 12.95 o.s.i. (ISBN 0-394-54132-4, GP-932). Grove.

Beards. Reginald Reynolds. LC 75-34138. 302p. 1976. pap. 3.95 o.p. (ISBN 0-15-610845-3, Harv). HarBraceJ.

Beard's Roman Women. Anthony Burgess. 1976. text ed. 8.95 o.p. (ISBN 0-07-008960-4). McGraw.

Bear's Autumn. Keizaburo Tejima. Date not set. 12.95 o.p. (ISBN 0-310-57010-7, 16101). Zondervan.

Bear's Bargain. Frank Asch. (Illus.). 32p. (ps-2). 1985. 11.95 o.s.i. (ISBN 0-13-071606-5). P-H.

Bears, Bibles & a Boy. Jesse D. Roberts. (Illus.). 1961. 4.95 o.p. (ISBN 0-393-07408-0). Norton.

Bear's House. E. Raud. 32p. 1984. pap. 0.99 o.p. (ISBN 0-8285-2912-4, Pub. by Raduga Pubs USSR). Imported Pubns.

Bears of Blue River. Charles Major. (Illus.). 277p. (gr. 3 up). 1983. pap. 5.95 o.p. (ISBN 0-913428-37-X). Landfall pr.

Bear's Story. Richard Fowler. (Stand-Up Stories Ser.). (Illus.). 24p. (gr. k). 1985. pap. 1.95 o.p. (ISBN 0-448-07854-6, G&D). Putnam Pub Group.

Bearskinner. Jacob Grimm & Wilhelm K. Grimm. LC 77-92742. (Illus.). 32p. (gr. 1-4). 1978. 8.95 o.p. (ISBN 0-689-50123-4, Atheneum). Macmillan.

Beast. Hugh Fleetwood. LC 78-72979. 1979. 7.95 o.p. (ISBN 0-689-10956-3, Atheneum). Macmillan.

Beast Master. Andre Norton. LC 59-8955. 1959. 5.75 o.p. (ISBN 0-15-206049-9, HJ). HarBraceJ.

Beast of Heaven. Victor Kelleher. LC 83-21726. 205p. 1985. 10.00 o.p. (ISBN 0-7022-1795-6). U Of Queensland Pr.

Beast of Revelation Thirteen: The Number of a Man Six Threescore & Six? or Six Threescore to the Power & Six? Equals Nine? Lee Dawkins. 68p. 1982. 5.00 o.p. (ISBN 0-682-49887-4). Exposition-Phoenix.

Beast on the Brink. Betty Levin. (Illus.). 160p. (gr. 5-7). 1980. pap. 1.95 o.p. (ISBN 0-380-76141-6, 76141-6, Camelot). Avon.

Beast or Angel? Choices That Make Us Human. Rene Dubos. LC 74-10737. (Scribner Library of Contemporary Classics). 240p. 1984. pap. 7.95 o.p. (ISBN 0-684-14436-0, ScribT). Scribner.

Beast Within. Edward Levy. LC 78-73871. 1981. 12.50 o.p. (ISBN 0-87795-225-6, Arbor Hse). Morrow.

Beastly Buildings: Architecture for Animals. Lucinda Lambton. Ed. by Joyce Johnson. LC 85-73156. (Illus.). 192p. 1984. 19.95 o.p. (ISBN 0-87113-066-1). Atlantic Monthly.

Beastly Law. Fenton Bresler. (Illus.). 128p. 1987. 13.95 o.p. (ISBN 0-7153-8828-2). David & Charles.

Beastly Riddles: Fishy, Flighty & Buggy, Too. Joseph Low. LC 83-856. (Illus.). 48p. (gr. 1-3). 1983. 9.95 o.s.i. (ISBN 0-02-761380-1). Macmillan.

Beasts, Ballads, & Bouldingisms. Kenneth E. Boulding. Ed. by Richard P. Beilock. LC 79-65223. 200p. 1980. 12.95 o.p. (ISBN 0-87855-339-8). Transaction Pubs.

Beat Inflation Strategy. Roger Klein & William Wolman. 1977. pap. 4.95 o.p. (ISBN 0-671-23080-8). PB.

Beat It, Burn It, Drown It. Suzanne Hilton. LC 73-11318. (Illus.). 128p. (gr. 7 up). 1974. 5.95 o.s.i. (ISBN 0-664-32538-6, Westminster). Westminster John Knox.

Beat the Drum: Independence Day Has Come. Ed. by Lee B. Hopkins. LC 76-46542. (Illus.). (gr. 1-5). 1977. 4.75 o.p. (ISBN 0-15-206050-2, HJ). HarBraceJ.

Beat the Links. Bill Olson & Lo Linkert. LC 78-59843. (Sports Library). (Illus., Orig.). 1978. 8.95 o.p. (ISBN 0-89149-040-X); pap. 6.95 o.p. (ISBN 0-89149-039-6). Jolex.

Beat the Racetrack. William T. Ziemba & Donald B. Hausch. 1984. 22.95 o.p. (ISBN 0-15-111275-4). HarBraceJ.

Beating Job Burnout. Beverly Potter. (Illus.). 204p. 1980. 11.95 o.p. (ISBN 0-936602-02-3). Kampmann.

Beating the Break-up Habit. Dick Purnell. 128p. (Orig.). 1983. pap. 5.95 o.p. (ISBN 0-89840-059-7). Heres Life.

Beatitude Saints. Daniel Morris. LC 83-62423. 128p. (Orig.). 1984. pap. 2.45 o.p. (ISBN 0-87973-615-1, 615). Our Sunday Visitor.

Beatitudes for the Balmy: And Other Poems. Bentley Barnabas. 1985. 6.95 o.p. (ISBN 0-682-40211-7). Exposition-Phoenix.

Beatlemania: Nineteen Sixty-Seven to Nineteen Seventy, Vol. II. The Beatles. 127p. 1967. pap. 7.95 o.s.i. (ISBN 0-89524-110-2, 1308). Cherry Lane.

Beatlemania: Nineteen Sixty-Three to Nineteen Sixty-Six, Vol. I. The Beatles. 128p. 1963. pap. 7.95 o.s.i. (ISBN 0-89524-109-9, 1307). Cherry Lane.

Beatlemania: The History of the Beatles on Film. Bill Harry. 192p. 1985. pap. 9.95 o.p. (ISBN 0-380-89557-9). Avon.

Beatles A-Z: John Lennon, Paul McCartney, George Harrison & Ringo Starr. Goldie Friede et al. (Illus.). 1981. pap. 8.95 o.p. (ISBN 0-416-00781-3, NO.0203). Routledge Chapman & Hall.

Beatles Complete Easy Guitar. Ed. by Milton Okun. 312p. (Orig.). 1982. pap. 14.95 o.s.i. (ISBN 0-89524-160-9). Cherry Lane.

Beatles Conquer America. Dezo Hoffman. 160p. 1985. pap. 12.95 o.p. (ISBN 0-380-89805-5). Avon.

Beatles Illustrated Lyrics, Vol. 1. Ed. by Alan Aldridge. (Illus.). 160p. (Orig.). (gr. 7 up). 1980. pap. 9.95 o.p. (ISBN 0-440-50503-8, Dell Trade Pbks). Dell.

Beatles Illustrated Lyrics, Vol. 11. Ed. by Alan Aldridge. 128p. (Orig.). (gr. 7 up). 1980. pap. 9.95 o.p. (ISBN 0-440-50504-6, Dell Trade Pbks). Dell.

Beatles in Their Own Words. Compiled by Miles. 1979. pap. 6.95 o.p. (ISBN 0-399-41013-9, Delilah). Putnam Pub Group.

Beatles on Record. Mark Wallgren. LC 82-10305. (Illus.). 336p. 1982. pap. 9.50 o.p. (ISBN 0-671-45682-2, Fireside). S&S.

Beatles: The Long & Winding Road, a History of the Beatles on Record. Neville Stannard. 240p. (Orig.). 1984. pap. 7.95 o.p. (ISBN 0-380-85704-9, 85704). Avon.

Beatles: Working Class Heroes, Vol. 2. Neville Stannard & John Tobler. 240p. (Orig.). 1984. pap. 9.95 o.p. (ISBN 0-380-89334-7). Avon.

Beaton. Ed. & text by James Danziger. LC 86-45038. (Illus.). 256p. 1986. pap. 14.95 o.p. (ISBN 0-8050-0024-0). H Holt & Co.

Beatrice. Intro. by Patrick Henden. LC 81-48545. 208p. (Orig.). 1982. pap. 3.95 o.p. (ISBN 0-394-17973-0, B472, BC). Grove.

Beatrice Doesn't Want to. Laura J. Numeroff. LC 81-447. (Easy-Read Story Bks.). (Illus.). 32p. (gr. k-3). 1981. 3.95 o.p. (ISBN 0-686-76377-7). Watts.

Beatrice; or, the Unknown Relatives, 1852. Catherine Sinclair. Ed. by Robert L. Wolff. LC 75-453. (Victorian Fiction Ser.). 1975. lib. bdg. 73.00 o.p. (ISBN 0-8240-1532-0). Garland Pub.

Beatrice Webb: A Life. Kitty Muggeridge & Ruth Adam. (Illus.). 280p. 1983. pap. 7.95 o.s.i. (ISBN 0-89733-088-9). Academy Chi Pubs.

Beatrix: Le Livre de Poche Classique. Honore De Balzac. pap. 9.95 o.p. (ISBN 0-685-34070-8). Schoenhof.

Beatrix Potter, Children's Storyteller. Patricia D. Frevert. Ed. by Ann Redpath. (People to Remember Ser.). (Illus.). 32p. (gr. 4 up). 1981. PLB 8.95 o.p. (ISBN 0-87191-801-3). Creative Ed.

Beaujolais: The Complete Guide. Guy Jacquemont & Paul Mereaud. 1987. 29.95 o.p. (ISBN 0-316-45598-9). Little.

Beautiful Biblical Beams. Charles Russell Storer. 1980. 5.00 o.p. (ISBN 0-682-49567-0). Exposition-Phoenix.

Beautiful California Missions. Lee Foster. Ed. by Robert D. Shangle. LC 78-102341. (Illus.). 72p. 1986. pap. 8.95 o.p. (ISBN 0-915796-22-8); 12.95 o.p. (ISBN 0-915796-23-6). Beautiful Am.

Beautiful Embroidery Designs. Ondori Publishing Company Staff. LC 81-80835. (Illus.). 104p. (Orig.). 1981. pap. 9.50 o.p. (ISBN 0-87040-500-4). Japan Pubns USA.

Beautiful Flagellants of New York. LC 79-155136. (Classics of the Victorian Imagination Ser.). 168p. 1985. pap. 6.95 o.p. (ISBN 0-394-62095-X, Ever). Grove.

Beautiful Girl. Alice Adams. 240p. 1980. pap. 2.95 o.s.i. (ISBN 0-671-83218-2). WSP.

Beautiful Idaho. 2nd ed. Paul M. Lewis. LC 79-779. (Illus.). 72p. 1984. 14.95 o.p. (ISBN 0-89802-415-3); pap. 8.95 o.p. (ISBN 0-89802-414-5). Beautiful Am.

Beautiful Ireland. John Freeman. 1988. 7.98 o.p. (ISBN 0-8317-0737-2, Gallery Bks). Smith Pubs.

Beautiful Lofty People. Helen Bevington. LC 73-15426. 1974. 7.95 o.p. (ISBN 0-15-111310-6). HarBraceJ.

Beautiful Maryland. James F. Waesche. Ed. by Robert D. Shangle. LC 79-22530. (Illus.). 72p. 1980. 12.95 o.p. (ISBN 0-915796-65-1); pap. 6.95 o.p. (ISBN 0-915796-64-3). Beautiful Am.

Beautiful My Mane in the Wind. Catherine Petroski. LC 82-12120. (Illus.). 32p. (gr. 1 up). 1983. 9.70 o.p. (ISBN 0-395-33074-2). HM.

Beautiful Necessity. new ed. Claude Bragdon. LC 77-17454. (Illus.). 1978. pap. 3.75 o.s.i. (ISBN 0-8356-0507-8, Quest). Theos Pub Hse.

Beautiful Oregon Coast. Paul M. Lewis. LC 78-102344. (Illus.). 48p. 1986. pap. 5.95 o.p. (ISBN 0-89802-444-7). Beautiful Am.

Beautiful Seattle. rev. ed. Ann Rule. (Illus.). 72p. 1986. 16.95 o.p. (ISBN 0-89802-071-9); pap. 8.95 o.p. (ISBN 0-89802-070-0). Beautiful Am.

Beautiful Skin. Gail Gross & Honora Finkelstein. (Orig.). 1985. pap. 8.95 o.p. (ISBN 0-449-90108-4, Columbine). Fawcett.

Beautiful Strangers. Rod McKuen. 1981. 9.95 o.p. (ISBN 0-671-43614-7). S&S.

Beautiful Switzerland-Merveillevse Suisse. Ed. by Herbert Maeder & Armin Och. (Illus., Fr. & Eng.). 1975. 35.00 o.s.i. (ISBN 3-7263-6186-3). E J Brill USA.

Beautiful Yosemite National Park. 3rd ed. Robin Will. LC 79-15850. (Illus.). 80p. 1986. 16.95 o.p. (ISBN 0-89802-069-7); pap. 8.95 o.p. (ISBN 0-89802-068-9). Beautiful Am.

Beauty & the Beast. (Derrydale Fairytale Library). (Illus.). (ps-3). 1985. 2.98 o.s.i. (ISBN 0-517-28802-8). Outlet Bk Co.

Beauty & the Beast. Ed McBain. LC 82-11896. 228p. 1983. 13.50 o.p. (ISBN 0-03-062198-4). H Holt & Co.

Beauty & the Beast. Illus. by Freire Wright. (Illus.). 32p. (gr. 1 up). 1985. 14.95 o.p. (ISBN 0-7182-6091-0, Pub. by Kaye & Ward). David & Charles.

Beauty & the Beast: The Coevolution of Plants & Animals. Susan T. Grant. LC 84-10609. (Illus.). 224p. 1984. 14.95 o.p. (ISBN 0-684-18186-X, ScribT). Scribner.

Beauty & the Mission of the Teacher. William J. Castleman. 144p. 1982. 7.50 o.p. (ISBN 0-682-49853-X, University). Exposition-Phoenix.

Beauty Begins at Forty: How to Look Your Best for a Lifetime. Barbara Coffey. (Illus.). 257p. 1984. 15.95 o.p. (ISBN 0-03-063817-8). H Holt & Co.

Beauty Book. Rubie Saunders. Ed. by Wendy Barish. (Just for Teens Ser.). 160p. (gr. 10 up). 1983. pap. 3.40 o.s.i. (ISBN 0-671-46271-7). Wanderer Bks.

Beauty Book. Rubie Saunders. LC 82-16949. (Teen Survival Library). (Illus.). 160p. (YA) (gr. 7 up). 1983. lib. bdg. 9.29 o.p. (ISBN 0-671-46743-3). Messner.

Beauty Is My Business: The ABC's of Successful Salon Management. Joseph J. Vizzini. LC 74-76042. 1974. 6.50 o.p. (ISBN 0-682-47952-7, Banner). Exposition-Phoenix.

Beauty of Holiness. J. Baines Atkinson. 160p. 1953. (ISBN 0-8022-0044-3). Philos Lib.

Beauty of Running. Gayle Baron & Kim Chapin. LC 79-3343. (Illus.). 256p. 1980. 12.95 o.p. (ISBN 0-15-111401-3). HarBraceJ.

Beauty Principal: The Beauty Program for Life. Victoria Principal. 224p. 1984. 17.45 o.p. (ISBN 0-671-49643-3). S&S.

Beauty Through Health: From the Edgar Cayce Readings. Lawrence M. Steinhart. LC 73-91501. 1974. 7.95 o.p. (ISBN 0-87795-078-4, Arbor Hse). Morrow.

Beauty Through Health: From the Edgar Cayce Readings. Lawrence M. Steinhart. 1983. pap. 5.25 o.p. (ISBN 0-87795-518-2, Arbor Hse). Morrow.

Beaver Year. Irene Brady. LC 75-38907. (Illus.). 48p. (gr. 1-5). 1976. PLB 8.95 o.p. (ISBN 0-395-24208-8). HM.

Because God Cares: Messages 1980. Wallace E. Fisher. LC 80-67791. 112p. (Orig.). 1980. pap. 4.75 o.p. (ISBN 0-8066-1852-3, 10-0566, Augsburg). Augsburg Fortress.

Because I Love You. Alice J. Davidson. (Illus.). 128p. 1981. 12.95 o.p. (ISBN 0-8007-1281-1). Revell.

Because of a Flower. Lorus Milne & Margery Milne. LC 74-19292. (gr. 4-6). 1975. 6.95 o.p. (ISBN 0-689-30452-8, Atheneum). Macmillan.

Because of the Wind in the Wheat. Clara P. Schultz. LC 85-51800. 54p. (Orig.). 1985. pap. 6.95x o.p. (ISBN 0-932269-67-2). Wyndham Hall.

Because We Are. Mildred P. Walter. LC 83-987. 192p. (gr. 6 up). 1983. 10.25 o.p. (ISBN 0-688-02287-1). Lothrop.

Becker-Shaffer's Diagnosis & Therapy of the Glaucomas. 5th ed. Allan E. Kolker & John Hetherington, Jr. LC 82-14126. (Illus.). 590p. 1983. 64.50 o.p. (ISBN 0-8016-2723-0). Mosby.

Beckett in the Theatre: The Author as Practical Playwright & Director. Dougald McMillan & Martha Fehsenfeld. (Illus.). 352p. 1989. 35.00 o.p.; pap. 19.95 o.p. (ISBN 0-7145-4151-6). Riverrun NY.

Beckett the Shape Changer. Ed. by Katharine Worth. 1975. 18.95x o.p. (ISBN 0-7100-8123-5). Routledge Chapman & Hall.

Become an Ex-Smoker. Brian G. Danaher & Edward Lichtenstein. LC 78-1679. (Self-Management Psychology Ser.). (Illus.). 1978. 11.95 o.p. (ISBN 0-13-072249-9, Spec); 5.95 o.p. (ISBN 0-13-072231-6, Spec). P-H.

Becoming a Christian. Lewis J. Sherrill & Helen H. Sherrill. 1943. pap. 2.95 o.s.i. (ISBN 0-8042-1548-0, John Knox). Westminster John Knox.

Becoming a City: From Fishing Village to Manufacturing Center. Margaret D. Uroff. LC 68-13813. (Curriculum-Related Bks.). (Illus.). (gr. 5-9). 1968. 4.95 o.p. (ISBN 0-15-206169-X, HJ). HarBraceJ.

Becoming a Member of the Presbyterian Church. Stuart R. Oglesby. pap. 2.95 o.p. (ISBN 0-8042-1560-X, John Knox). Westminster John Knox.

Becoming a Poet. David Kalstone. 208p. Date not set. 16.95 o.p. (ISBN 0-374-10960-5). FS&G.

Becoming a Professional Model. Larry Goldman. LC 85-18571. (Illus.). 256p. (Orig.). 1986. 22.95 o.p. (ISBN 0-688-04765-3, Pub. by Beech Tree Bks). Morrow.

Becoming a Prophetic Community. J. Elliott Corbett & Elizabeth S. Smith. LC 80-17618. 201p. (Orig.). 1980. pap. 7.95 o.p. (ISBN 0-8042-0784-4, John Knox). Westminster John Knox.

Becoming Comprehensive: Case Histories. Ed. by E. Halsall. 1970. 27.00 o.p. (ISBN 0-08-015820-X); pap. 17.00 o.p. (ISBN 0-08-015819-6). Pergamon.

Becoming Myself. James D. McGuire. (Illus., Orig.). (gr. 3-4). 1968. pap. 2.95 o.p. (ISBN 0-8042-9715-0, John Knox). Westminster John Knox.

Becoming One Flesh. Denise L. Carmody & John T. Carmody. LC 84-50841. 160p. (Orig.). 1984. pap. 6.95 o.p. (ISBN 0-8358-0486-0). Upper Room.

Becoming One Flesh. Steven M. Nelson & Frank L. Starkey. 1979. pap. 2.95 o.p. (ISBN 0-89536-354-2, 0229). CSS of Ohio.

Becoming Parents: Preparing for the Emotional Changes of First-Time Parenthood. Sandra S. Jaffe & Jack Viertel. LC 79-63794. 352p. 1985. pap. 8.95 o.p. (ISBN 0-689-70685-5, 325, Atheneum). Macmillan.

Becoming Psychiatrists. Donald Light, Jr. 1980. 18.95 o.p. (ISBN 0-393-01168-2). Norton.

Becoming Psychiatrists: The Professional Transformation of Self. Donald Light. 448p. 1982. 8.95 o.p. (ISBN 0-393-00078-8). Norton.

Becoming Visible: Women in European History. Renate Bridenthal & Claudia Koonz. LC 76-11978. 1977. pap. 19.50 o.p. (ISBN 0-395-24477-3). HM.

Bed Airobics for Seniors & Lazy Juniors. Lena Ross. 48p. 1987. 5.95 o.p. (ISBN 0-8062-2853-9). Carlton.

Bed & Breakfast - California: A Selective Guide. 2nd ed. Linda K. Bristow. (Illus.). 240p. 1985. pap. 8.95 o.p. (ISBN 0-87701-332-2). Chronicle Bks.

Bed & Breakfast, American Style. rev. ed. Norman T. Simpson. LC 81-65526. (Illus.). 350p. 1983. pap. 9.95 o.p. (ISBN 0-912944-77-3). Berkshire Traveller.

Bed & Breakfast, American Style. rev. & enl. ed. Ed. by Norman T. Simpson. LC 81-65526. (Illus.). 436p. 1984. pap. 10.95 o.p. (ISBN 0-912944-92-7). Berkshire Traveller.

Bed & Breakfast: California. Linda Bristow. LC 82-22086. (Illus.). 180p. 1983. pap. 7.95 o.p. (ISBN 0-87701-196-6). Chronicle Bks.

Bed & Breakfast Guide: East Coast. Roberta Gardner. 128p. 1984. pap. 9.95 o.p. (ISBN 0-671-50845-8). S&S.

Bed & Breakfast Guide: West Coast. Courtia Worth. 128p. 1984. pap. 9.95 o.p. (ISBN 0-671-52451-8). S&S.

Bed & Breakfast Homes Directory: Homes Away from Home, West Coast. 4th ed. Diane Knight. Ed. by Suzy Blackaby. LC 85-81398. (Illus.). 240p. 1986. pap. 8.95 o.p. (ISBN 0-942902-03-3). Knighttime Pubns.

Bed & Breakfast in Britain. Date not set. (ISBN 0-86145-772-2, Pub. by Auto Assn England). Salem Hse Pubs.

Bed & Breakfast in Europe. Date not set. (Pub. by Auto Assn England). Salem Hse Pubs.

Bed & Breakfast in New England. Bernice Chesler. LC 87-8499. (Voyager Book Ser.). 512p. 1987. pap. 12.95 o.p. (ISBN 0-87106-754-4). Globe Pequot.

Bed & Breakfast in the Mid-Atlantic States. Bernice Chesler. LC 87-8482. (Voyager Book Ser.). 352p. 1987. pap. 10.95 o.p. (ISBN 0-87106-756-0). Globe Pequot.

Bed & Breakfast in the Northeast: From Maine to Washington, D. C., 300 Selected B&B's. Bernice Chesler. LC 83-48194. (Illus.). 512p. (Orig.). pap. (ISBN 0-87106-917-2). Globe Pequot.

Bed & Breakfast Inns of New England. Deborah Patton. Ed. by Mark Corsey. LC 86-51016. (Yankee Guidebook Ser.). 192p. (Orig.). 1987. pap. 9.95 o.p. (ISBN 0-89909-124-5). Yankee Bks.

Bed Book. Mark Dittrick. LC 79-1856. (Illus.). 1980. pap. 8.95 o.p. (ISBN 0-15-611322-8, Harv). HarBraceJ.

Bed-Knob & Broomstick. Mary Norton. LC 57-11341. (Illus.). (gr. 3-7). 1957. 10.95 o.s.i. (ISBN 0-15-206228-9, HJ). HarBraceJ.

Bed-Wetting: Origins & Treatment. rev. ed. Warren B. Baller. 300p. 1975. 35.00 o.p. (ISBN 0-08-017859-6). Pergamon.

Bedeutung Franzoesischer Dichter in Werk und Weltbild Stefan Georges. Freya Hobohm. 1931. pap. 10.00 o.p. (ISBN 0-384-23720-7). Johnson Repr.

Bedeutungsentwicklung der, Ag 5. Marco K. Mincoff. (Ger). 18.00 o.p. (ISBN 0-384-39020-X); pap. 13.00 o.p. (ISBN 0-685-02056-8). Johnson Repr.

Bedeviled. Thomas Cullinan. 1979. pap. 1.95 o.p. (ISBN 0-380-44560-3, 44560). Avon.

Bedita's Bad Day. Eros Keith. LC 71-161278. (Illus.). (ps-2). 1971. 5.95 o.s.i. (ISBN 0-87888-036-4). Bradbury Pr.

Bedroom & Bath Storage. Sunset Magazine & Books Editors. LC 81-82870. (Illus.). 80p. (Orig.). 1982. pap. 5.95 o.p. (ISBN 0-376-01121-1, Sunset Bks). Sunset-Lane.

Bedroom in a Country Cottage. Elspeth. 1973. pap. 1.50 o.p. (ISBN 0-87588-079-7, 187). Hobby Hse.

Beds of Nails & Roses: Witty Obervations on Enjoying Life As a Modern Woman. Irma Kurtz. 192p. 1983. 13.95 o.p. (ISBN 0-396-08202-5). Dodd.

Bedside Diagnosis. 12th ed. Charles Seward & David Mattingly. LC 84-12094. (Illus.). 425p. 1985. pap. 36.00 o.p. (ISBN 0-443-02666-1). Churchill.

Bedside Hollywood. Ed. by Robert Atwan & Bruce Forer. (Illus.). 300p. 1986. 24.95 o.p. (ISBN 0-918825-11-3); pap. 12.95 o.p. (ISBN 0-918825-30-X, Dist. by Kampmann & Co.). Moyer Bell Limited.

Bedside Manners. Crenshaw. 336p. 1983. text ed. 14.95 o.p. (ISBN 0-07-013581-9). McGraw.

Bedside Manners: The Troubled History of Doctors & Patients. Edward Shorter. 336p. 1986. 18.45 o.p. (ISBN 0-671-53254-5). S&S.

Bedside Manners: The Troubled History of Doctors & Patients. Edward Shorter. 320p. 1987. pap. 9.95 o.s.i. (ISBN 0-671-63309-0, Touchstone Bks). S&S.

Bedside Nursing Techniques in Medicine & Surgery. 2nd ed. Audrey L. Sutton. LC 69-12891. 1969. pap. write for info. o.p. (ISBN 0-7216-8666-4). Saunders.

Bedside Pediatrics: Diagnostic Evaluation of the Child. Mohsen Ziai. 1983. 71.00 o.p. (ISBN 0-316-98752-2). Little.

Bedtime Rhymes. Illus. by Blanche F. Wright. (Real Mother Goose Mini Boxed Sets Ser.). (Illus.). (ps-1). 1987. bds. 5.95 o.p. (ISBN 0-02-689017-8, Checkerboard Pr). Macmillan.

Bedtime Stories. Zokeisha. (Puppet Story Board Bks.). (Illus.). 12p. (ps-2). 1981. 2.95 o.s.i. (ISBN 0-671-42644-3, Little Simon). S&S.

Bedtime Story. Les Marcs. LC 85-91005. 1985. 9.00 o.p. (ISBN 0-682-40220-6). Exposition-Phoenix.

Bee. Peter Z. Cohen. LC 74-19197. (Illus.). 192p. (gr. 2-4). 1975. PLB 6.95 o.p. (ISBN 0-689-30445-5, Atheneum). Macmillan.

Bee Keepers Encyclopedia. Alexander S. Deans. LC 75-23248. (Illus.). 194p. 1979. Repr. of 1949 ed. 65.00x o.p. (ISBN 0-8103-4176-X). Gale.

Bee Says Buzzzz. Carla Dijs & Kees Moerbeek. LC 86-80651. (Illus.). 10p. (ps-k). 1986. 4.95 o.p. (ISBN 0-8050-0136-0). H Holt & Co.

Beef Housing & Equipment Handbook. 3rd ed. Midwest Plan Service Engineers Staff. (Illus.). 84p. 1975. pap. 5.00 o.p. (ISBN 0-89373-003-3, MWPS-6). Midwest Plan Serv.

Beef Management & Production: A Practical Guide for Farmers & Students. Derek H. Goodwin. 200p. (Orig.). 1982. pap. text ed. 10.95x o.p. (ISBN 0-09-127061-8, Hutchinson & Co). Gower Pub Co.

Beef, Veal, Lamb & Pork. Ed. by Bon Appetit. 144p. 1985. 12.95 o.p. (ISBN 0-517-55467-4). Knapp Pr.

Beef, Veal, Lamb & Pork. Bon Appetit Magazine Editors. LC 84-19405. (Cooking with Bon Appetit Ser.). (Illus.). 1985. 12.95 o.p. (ISBN 0-89535-138-2). Knapp Pr.

Beekeeping. John F. Adams. 1980. pap. 1.75 o.p. (ISBN 0-380-01043-7, 48124-3). Avon.

Beekeeping: The Gentle Craft. John Adams. 192p. 1988. pap. 8.95 o.p. (ISBN 0-8007-7200-8). Wynwood Pr.

Beekman Place. Bruce Nicolaysen. (Novel of New York Ser.: Vol. 3). 576p. 1982. pap. 3.50 o.p. (ISBN 0-380-79673-2, 79673-2). Avon.

Beep! Beep! I'm a Jeep! A Toddler's Book of "Let's Pretend" Felice Haus. LC 85-62036. (Great Big Board Books Ser.). (Illus.). 14p. (ps). 1986. bds. 3.95 o.s.i. (ISBN 0-394-88000-5). Random.

Bees, Beekeeping, Honey & Pollination. Walter L. Gojmerac. (Illus.). 1980. 26.95 o.s.i. (ISBN 0-87055-342-9). AVI.

Beet Queen. Louise Erdrich. LC 86-4788. 338p. 1986. 16.45 o.p. (ISBN 0-03-070612-2). HR&W.

Beethoven As I Knew Him. Anton F. Schindler. Ed. by Donald W. MacArdle. Tr. by Constance S. Jolly. (Illus.). 552p. 1972. pap. 6.95 o.p. (ISBN 0-393-00638-7, Norton Lib). Norton.

Beethoven by Berlioz. Tr. by Ralph De Sola. LC 74-84541. 1975. pap. 2.95 o.s.i. (ISBN 0-8008-0711-1, Crescendo). Taplinger.

Beethoven Encyclopedia. Paul Nettl. 336p. 1956. (ISBN 0-8022-1190-9). Philos Lib.

Beethoven: Impressions by His Contemporaries. Oscar G. Sonneck. 231p. Repr. of 1967 ed. lib. bdg. 39.00 o.p. (Pub. by Am Repr Serv). Reprint Servs.

Beethoven Reader. Ed. by Denis Arnold & Nigel Fortune. LC 77-139374. (Illus.). 1971. 25.00x o.p. (ISBN 0-393-02149-1). Norton.

Beethoven Studies. Ed. & pref. by Alan Tyson. (Illus.). 256p. 1973. 10.00x o.p. (ISBN 0-393-02168-8). Norton.

Beethoven: The Sonatas for Piano & Violin. Max Rostal. (Illus.). 219p. 29.95 o.s.i. (ISBN 0-907689-05-1, Pub. by Toccata Pr UK); pap. 15.95 o.s.i. (ISBN 0-907689-06-X, Pub. by Toccata Pr UK). David & Charles.

Beethoveniana: Aufsaetze und Mitteilungen, 3 vols. in 1. Gustav Nottebohm. (Ger). 1970. Repr. of 1872 ed. 35.00 o.p. (ISBN 0-384-42030-3). Johnson Repr.

Beethoven's Missa Solemnis. Roger Fiske. (Illus.). 1979. 5.95 o.p. (ISBN 0-684-17519-3, ScribT). Scribner.

Beetlecreek. William Demby. 223p. 1972. Repr. of 1950 ed. 7.50x o.p. (ISBN 0-911860-12-6). Chatham Bkseller.

Beetles. Wilfrid S. Bronson. LC 63-15397. (Illus.). (gr. 5 up). 1963. 5.50 o.p. (ISBN 0-15-206260-2, HJ). HarBraceJ.

Befana: A Christmas Story. Ann Rockwell. LC 74-75570. (Illus.). 48p. (gr. 1-4). 1974. 6.95 o.p. (ISBN 0-689-30438-2, Atheneum). Macmillan.

Before a Battle & Other Poems. Paul Oppenheimer. LC 67-19204. 50p. 1967. 9.95 o.p. (ISBN 0-15-111602-4). HarBraceJ.

Before Adam. Jack London. (Illus.). 242p. 1982. pap. 5.95 o.s.i. (ISBN 0-932458-09-2). Star Rover.

Before & After Dinner Cookbook. Charlotte McNamara & Leonore Howell. LC 77-5374. (Illus.). 1977. 10.95 o.p. (ISBN 0-689-10824-9, Atheneum). Macmillan.

Before Columbus. Muriel Batherman. (Illus.). 32p. (gr. k-3). 1981. 8.95 o.p. (ISBN 0-395-30088-6). HM.

Before Columbus: Who Discovered America? Harry E. Neal. LC 81-11331. (Illus.). 96p. (gr. 3-6). 1981. lib. bdg. 9.79 o.p. (ISBN 0-671-42404-1). Messner.

Before Divorce. John M. Vayhinger. Ed. by William E. Hulme. LC 72-171512. (Pocket Counsel Bks). 56p. 1972. pap. 1.75 o.p. (ISBN 0-8006-1106-3, 1-1106, Fortress). Augsburg Fortress.

Before Divorce: A Handbook for Relationships. Susan W. Kalashian. Ed. by Helen Graves. 102p. 1987. pap. 7.95 o.p. (ISBN 1-55523-051-2). Winston-Derek.

Before Honor. Eugene B. McDaniel & James L. Johnson. LC 75-20213. 1982. Repr. of 1975 ed. 8.95 o.p. (ISBN 0-8054-5901-4). Broadman.

Before I Go Out on the Road. Grace Butcher. (Poets Ser.: No. 20). (Orig.). 1979. pap. 3.50 o.p. (ISBN 0-914946-15-3). Cleveland St Univ Poetry Ctr.

Before I Was Born. Carolyn Nystrom. (gr. 1-3). 1984. 8.95 o.p. (ISBN 0-89107-283-7, Crossway Bks). Good News.

Before Kampuchea: Preludes to Tragedy. Milton Osborne. 200p. (Orig.). 1985. pap. text ed. 13.95 o.p. Unwin Hyman.

Before My Life Began. Jay Neugeboren. 1985. 18.45 o.p. (ISBN 0-671-54372-5). S&S.

Before Nightfall. Harriet W. Holden. LC 85-90070. 88p. 1985. 7.95 o.p. (ISBN 0-533-06590-9). Vantage.

Before the Armada: The Emergence of the English Nation, 1485-1588. R. B. Wernham. 1972. pap. 6.95x o.p. (ISBN 0-393-00616-6, Norton Lib). Norton.

Before the Crying Ends. John Hughes. LC 77-5014. 1977. 7.95 o.p. (ISBN 0-8076-0865-3). Braziller.

Before the Deluge. Otto Friedrich. 1973. pap. 1.95 o.p. (ISBN 0-380-01044-5, 15859). Avon.

Before the Industrial Revolution: European Society & Economy, 1000-1700. Carlo M. Cipolla. (Illus.). 1976. 12.95x o.p. (ISBN 0-393-05538-8); pap. 4.95x o.p. (ISBN 0-393-09255-0). Norton.

Before the Judge. Jerry B. Jenkins. (Bradford Family Adventures Ser.). (Illus.). 128p. (gr. 3-6). 1986. 2.95 o.p. (ISBN 0-87403-094-3, 2924). Standard Pub.

Before the Lamps Went Out. Esme C. Wingfield-Stratford. LC 78-12081. 1979. Repr. of 1945 ed. lib. bdg. 35.00 o.p. (ISBN 0-313-21067-5, WSBL). Greenwood.

Before the Law: An Introduction to the Legal Process. 2nd ed. John J. Bonsignore et al. LC 78-69606. (Illus.). 1979. pap. 19.95 o.p. (ISBN 0-395-27514-8). HM.

Before the Moon Dies. Christa Weber. 1984. pap. 1.50 o.p. (ISBN 9971-972-15-8). OMF Bks.

Before the Storm: Soviet Ukrainian Fiction of the 1920s. George Luckyj. Tr. by Yuri Tkacz from Ukrainian. 265p. 1986. lib. bdg. 30.00 o.p. (ISBN 0-88233-521-9); pap. 10.50 o.p. (ISBN 0-88233-522-7). Ardis Pubs.

Before the Supreme Court: The Story of Belva Ann Lockwood. Terry Dunnahoo. LC 73-22057. (Illus.). 192p. (gr. 4-7). 1974. 7.95 o.p. (ISBN 0-395-18520-3). HM.

Before the War: Nineteen Hundred Eight to Nineteen Thirty-Nine: An Autobiography in Pictures. Illus. by John S. Goodall. LC 81-65810. (Illus.). 64p. 1981. 9.95 o.p. (ISBN 0-689-50203-6, Atheneum). Macmillan.

Before the World Was. Ilona E. Richardson. 1979. pap. 4.00 o.p. (ISBN 0-682-49358-9). Exposition-Phoenix.

Before Their Diaspora: A Photographic History of the Palestinians, 1876-1948 (Arabic Edition) Walid Khalidi. (Illus.). 352p. (Arabic.). 1987. 40.00 o.p.; pap. text ed. 27.50 o.p. (ISBN 0-88728-169-9). Inst Palestine.

Before You Say a Word: The Executive Guide to Effective Communication. Myles Martel. 218p. 1983. 19.95 o.p. (ISBN 0-13-071613-8, Busn). P-H.

Begehungsort Im Internationalen Strafrecht Deutschlands, Englands und der Vereinigten Staaten Von Amerika. Lothar Bergmann. (Neue Koelner Rechtswissenschaftliche Abhandlungen Ser.: Vol. 48). (Ger). 1966. pap. 18.00x o.p. (ISBN 3-11-001077-1). De Gruyter.

Beggar on Horseback: The Autobiography of Thomas D. Cabot. Thomas D. Cabot. LC 78-70524. (Illus.). 1979. 12.50 o.s.i. (ISBN 0-87923-268-4). Godine.

Beggar's Gulch. Cameron Judd. (Orig.). 1980. pap. 1.75 o.p. (ISBN 0-8439-0733-9, Pub. by Leisure Bks CT). Dorchester Pub Co.

Begin at the Beginning: Teaching Basic Response Patterns. Daniel B. Overbeck. 64p. 1981. pap. text ed. 10.95 o.p. (ISBN 0-88450-742-4, 2086-B). Communication Skill.

Beginner Book of Things to Make. Robert Lopshire. LC 64-22011. (Beginner Bks.: No. 37). (Illus.). (gr. k-3). 1977. 5.95 o.p. (ISBN 0-394-83493-3); lib. bdg. 6.99 o.p. (ISBN 0-394-93493-8). Beginner.

Beginner's Bookshelf, 8 vols. (gr. k up). 1982. Ferguson.

Beginner's Computer Dictionary. Elizabeth S. Wall & Alexander C. Wall. (Illus.). 80p. (Orig.). (gr. 2-5). 1984. pap. 2.25 o.p. (ISBN 0-380-87114-9, 87114-9, Camelot). Avon.

Beginner's Computer Handbook. (gr. 5-9). 1984. pap. 6.95 o.p. (ISBN 0-86020-694-7). EDC.

Beginner's Guide to Amateur Radio. American Radio Relay League Inc., Staff. (Illus.). 208p. 1982. text ed. 35.00 o.p. (ISBN 0-13-072157-3); pap. 17.95 o.p. (ISBN 0-13-072140-9). P-H.

Beginner's Guide to American Bonsai. Jerald P. Stowell. LC 77-15372. 1978. 22.95 o.p. (ISBN 0-87011-326-7). Kodansha.

Beginner's Guide to Buying a Personal Computer. Richard Mansfield et al. Ed. by Compute! Magazine Staff. (Illus.). 90p. (Orig.). 1983. pap. 3.95 o.p. (ISBN 0-942386-22-1). Compute Pubns.

Beginner's Guide to Computer Logic. Gerald Stapleton. LC 70-155978. (Illus.). 1971. pap. 7.95 o.p. (ISBN 0-8306-0548-7, 548). TAB Bks.

Beginner's Guide to Computers & Microprocessors--with Projects. C. K. Adams. (Illus.). (gr. 10 up). 1978. 15.95 o.p. (ISBN 0-8306-9890-6); pap. 8.95 o.p. (ISBN 0-8306-1015-4, 1015). TAB Bks.

Beginner's Guide to Electricity & Electrical Phenomena. W. Edmund Hood. (Illus.). 256p. (Orig.). 1984. 15.95 o.p. (ISBN 0-8306-0507-X); pap. 9.95 o.p. (ISBN 0-8306-1507-5, 1507). TAB Bks.

Beginners Guide to Electronics. Terence L. Squires. 192p. 1968. (ISBN 0-8022-1628-5). Philos Lib.

Beginner's Guide to Investing. Dick Golfberg. 190p. 1985. pap. 11.95 o.p. (ISBN 0-317-61654-4). Invest Info.

Beginner's Guide to Microprocessors. 2nd ed. Charles M. Gilmore. (Illus.). 224p. 1984. 14.95 o.p. (ISBN 0-8306-0695-5, 1695); pap. 9.95 o.p. (ISBN 0-8306-1695-0). TAB Bks.

Beginner's Guide to TV Repair. 2nd ed. George Zwick. (Illus.). 1979. 14.95 o.p. (ISBN 0-8306-9758-6); pap. 9.95 o.p. (ISBN 0-8306-1013-8, 1013). TAB Bks.

Beginner's Guide to Zen & the Art of Windsurfing. 2nd ed. Frank Fox et al. (Illus.). 160p. 1985. pap. 6.95 o.p. (ISBN 0-934965-01-3). Amber Co Pr.

Beginner's Handbook in Biological Transmission Electron Microscopy. 2nd ed. Brenda Weakley. 252p. 1981. 27.75 o.p. (ISBN 0-443-02091-4). Churchill.

Beginner's Handbook of IC Projects. David L. Heiserman. (Illus.). 272p. 1981. pap. 17.50 o.p. (ISBN 0-13-074286-4); pap. text ed. 32.00 o.p. (ISBN 0-13-074229-5). P-H.

Beginner's Investment Handbook: One Hundred & Two Ways to Invest One Thousand or Less...& Make It Pay. Christopher Elias. 1984. 15.95 o.p. (ISBN 0-87795-519-0, Arbor Hse); pap. 6.95 o.p. (ISBN 0-87795-568-9). Morrow.

Beginner's Natural Food Cookbook. new ed. Judith Goeltz & Patricia Lazenby. 192p. (Orig.). 1975. pap. 5.95 o.p. (ISBN 0-89036-048-0). Hawkes Pub Inc.

Beginner's Workbook to Safe & Profitable Investing. M. Ann Trainer. 1977. 6.00 o.p. (ISBN 0-682-48876-3). Exposition-Phoenix.

Beginning Algebra. Ignacio Bello & Jack Britton. LC 75-12485. 450p. 1976. text ed. 25.95 o.p. (ISBN 0-7216-1688-7). HR&W.

Beginning Algebra. 3rd ed. Alfonse Gobran. 400p. 1983. text ed. 23.00 o.p. (ISBN 0-87150-349-2, 2741, Prindle). PWS-Kent Pub.

Beginning Algebra. 4th ed. Margaret L. Lial & Charles D. Miller. 1984. text ed. write for info. o.p. (ISBN 0-673-15890-X). Scott F.

Beginning & End in the Bible. Claus Westermann. Ed. by John Reumann. Tr. by Keith Crim from Ger. LC 72-75659. (Facet Bks.). 46p. (Orig.). 1972. pap. 1.00 o.p. (ISBN 0-8006-3071-8, 1-3071, Fortress). Augsburg Fortress.

Beginning & Intermediate Gymnastics. William L. Cornelius. (Illus.). 112p. 1983. pap. text ed. 9.95x o.p. (ISBN 0-89582-134-6). Morton Pub.

Beginning Backpacking. Tony Freeman. LC 80-12379. (Sports & Hobbies Ser.). (Illus.). 48p. (gr. 3 up). 1980. PLB 10.60 o.p. (ISBN 0-516-04372-2); pap. 2.95 o.p. (ISBN 0-516-44372-0). Childrens.

Beginning BASIC. D. Keith Carver. 260p. pap. Brooks-Cole.

Beginning Bicycle Racing. Fred Matheny. Ed. by Ed Pavelka. (Illus.). 229p. 1981. pap. 9.95 o.p. (ISBN 0-941950-01-8). Vitesse Pr.

Beginning Bicycle Racing. rev. ed. Fred Matheny. Ed. by Ed Pavelka. LC 83-50041. (Illus.). 237p. 1983. 12.95 o.p. (ISBN 0-941950-04-2). Vitesse Pr.

Beginning Blacksmithing, with Projects. Jim Converse. (Illus.). 288p. 1986. 18.95 o.p. (ISBN 0-8306-0351-4, 2651); pap. 12.60 o.p. (ISBN 0-8306-0451-0, 2651P). Tab Bks.

Beginning Composition Through Pictures. J. B. Heaton. (English As a Second Language Bk.). (Illus.). 1975. pap. text ed. 5.95 o.p. (ISBN 0-582-55519-1). Longman.

Beginning Conductor. Hugo D. Marple. (Illus.). 320p. 1972. text ed. 41.95 o.p. (ISBN 0-07-040456-9). McGraw.

Beginning Indonesian, 2 pts. John U. Wolff. 562p. 1980. 25.00 set o.p. Pt. 1 (ISBN 0-87727-513-0). Pt. 2 (ISBN 0-87727-514-9). Cornell SE Asia.

Beginning Indonesian Through Self-Instruction. 2nd, rev. ed. John U. Wolff et al. 877p. 1986. 25.00 o.p. (ISBN 0-87727-518-1). Cornell SE Asia.

Beginning Lessons in English. new rev. ed. Robert J. Dixson & Isobel Fisher. (Illus., Orig.). (gr. 9 up). 1971. pap. text ed. 3.50 o.p. (ISBN 0-88345-013-5, 17974). Prentice ESL.

Beginning Math. (E. T. Practice Workbooks). (Illus.). 48p. 1983. pap. 2.40 o.s.i. (ISBN 0-671-47681-5, Little Simon). S&S.

Beginning Model Rocketry. Charles W. Mitchell & Joseph E. Riley. 1971. pap. 5.00 o.p. (ISBN 0-87012-116-2). McClain.

Beginning of Seership: Astral Projection, Clairvoyance & Prophecy. Vincent N. Turvey. LC 69-16355. (Library of Mystic Arts Ser). 1969. 4.95 o.p. (ISBN 0-8216-0055-9, Pub. by Univ Bks). Carol Pub Group.

Beginning of Systematic Bibliography. 2nd ed. Theodore Besterman. LC 72-79199. 81p. 1936-40. Repr. 25.00 o.p. (ISBN 0-403-03317-9). Somerset Pub.

Beginning of the Long Dash: A History of Timekeeping in Canada. Malcolm M. Thomson. 1978. 25.00x o.p. (ISBN 0-8020-5383-1). U of Toronto Pr.

Beginning of the World of Books: 1450-1470. Margaret B. Stillwell. LC 79-185917. 112p. 1972. 10.00x o.p. (ISBN 0-8139-0936-8, Bibliographical Soc. of America.). U Pr of Va.

Beginning Place. Ursula K. Le Guin. (Spectra Ser.). 192p. 1987. pap. 2.95 o.p. (ISBN 0-553-26282-3, Spectra). Bantam.

Beginning Programming on the IBM PC. (ISBN 0-672-22251-5). Sams.

Beginning Reading. (E.T. Practice Workbooks). (Illus.). 48p. 1983. pap. 2.40 o.s.i. (ISBN 0-671-47680-7, Little Simon). S&S.

Beginning Readings in French. Edward E. Milligan. (Orig.). 1961. pap. text ed. write for info. o.p. (ISBN 0-02-381360-1). Macmillan.

Beginning Social Work Research. Morton L. Arkava. 300p. 1983. pap. 26.00 o.p. (ISBN 0-205-07815-X); pap. 24.00 scp. o.p. Allyn.

Beginning Statistics. G. Zirkel & Robert Rosenfeld. 1975. text ed. 26.00 o.p. (ISBN 0-07-072840-2, C). McGraw.

Beginning String Class Method. 4th. ed. Arthur C. Edwards. 192p. 1985. write for info. wire coil o.p. (ISBN 0-697-00295-0). Wm C Brown.

Beginning Structured COBOL. 2nd ed. D. Keith Carver. LC 84-11340. (Computer Science Ser.). 500p. 1984. pap. text ed. 22.00 pub net o.p. (ISBN 0-534-03795-X). Brooks-Cole.

Beginning Structured COBOL 2D. D. Keith Carver. 433p. 1984. pap. (ISBN 0-534-03795-X). Brooks-Cole.

Beginning Teacher: A Practical Guide to Problem Solving. Robert J. Krajewski & R. Baird Shuman. 128p. 1979. pap. 7.95 o.p. (ISBN 0-8106-1489-8). NEA.

Beginning Your Marriage see Camino Hacia el Amor.

Beginnings. Eugene Johnson. 122p. 1984. 8.95 o.p. (ISBN 0-533-06141-5). Vantage.

Beginnings. Ed. by Gwendolyn Reed. (gr. 6-10). 1971. PLB 5.95 o.p. (ISBN 0-689-20653-4, Atheneum). Macmillan.

Beginnings. Betty J. Wylie. 160p. 1984. pap. 2.95 o.p. (ISBN 0-345-31617-7). Ballantine.

Beginnings & Beyond: Foundations in Early Childhood Education. Ann Gordon & Kathryn W. Browne. LC 84-23000. 512p. 1985. text ed. 29.95 o.p. (ISBN 0-8273-2282-8); instr's. guide 8.00 o.p. (ISBN 0-8273-3411-7). Delmar.

Beginnings & Endings. Ed. by James Campbell et al. (Themepaks Ser.). (gr. 1-6). 1977. 4.95 o.p. (ISBN 0-8042-1455-7, John Knox). Westminster John Knox.

Beginnings & Other Poems. David D. Licciardi. LC 84-90251. 50p. 1985. 5.95 o.p. (ISBN 0-533-06289-6). Vantage.

Beginnings of Christology, together with The Lord's Supper. Willi Marxsen. Tr. by Paul J. Achtemeier & Lorenz Nieting. LC 79-7384. 128p. 1979. pap. 5.95 o.p. (ISBN 0-8006-1372-4, 1-1372, Fortress). Augsburg Fortress.

Beginnings of English Literature to Skelton, Fifteen Nine. 2nd rev. ed. William L. Renwick & Harold Orton. Repr. of 1952 ed. 59.00x o.p. (ISBN 0-403-03075-7). Somerset Pub.

Beginnings of Human Life. E. Blechschmidt. Tr. by Transemantics, Inc. LC 77-16658. (Heidelberg Science Library). (Illus.). 1977. pap. 23.10 o.p. (ISBN 0-387-90249-X). Springer-Verlag.

Beginnings of Modern American Psychiatry: The Ideas of Harry Stack Sullivan. Patrick Mullahy. 1973. pap. 4.95 o.p. (ISBN 0-395-17228-4, 78, SenEd). HM.

Beginnings of Modernization in the Middle East: The Nineteenth Century. Ed. by William R. Polk & Richard L. Chambers. LC 68-16712. (Publications of the Center for Middle Eastern Studies). 1968. lib. bdg. 25.00x o.s.i. (ISBN 0-226-67425-8). U of Chicago Pr.

Beginnings of Monkey. Xu Li. (Monkey Ser.: No. 1). (Illus.). 74p. (gr. 3 up). 1985. pap. 7.95 o.p. (ISBN 0-8351-1317-5). China Bks.

Beginnings of the Church. Stuart D. Currie. (Illus.). (gr. 3-4). 1967. pap. 3.45 o.p. (ISBN 0-8042-9451-8, John Knox). Westminster John Knox.

Beginnings of the Church. Megan McKenna & Darryl Ducote. LC 78-71533. (Followers of the Way Ser.: Vol. 6). (gr. 9-12). 1980. 22.50 o.p. (ISBN 0-8091-9547-X); cassette 7.50 o.p. (ISBN 0-8091-7671-8). Paulist Pr.

Beginnings of Visual Photochemistry: Translations & Biographies in Honor of F. Boll & F. W. Kuhne. Ed. by T. Shipley. 1978. 35.00 o.p. (ISBN 0-08-021534-3). Pergamon.

Beginnings of Writing. 2nd, rev. ed. Charles Temple. 288p. (Orig.). 1988. pap. text ed. 19.50 o.p. (ISBN 0-205-11107-6). Allyn.

Beginnings: The Orientation of New Teachers. Katherine Egan. 20p. 1981. 2.40 o.p. (ISBN 0-686-39892-0). Natl Cath Educ.

Beginnings to Fifteen Fifty-Eight. Intro. by Allan MacLaine. (Great Writers Library). 86p. pap. 5.95 o.p. (ISBN 0-312-34700-6). Academy Chi Pubs.

Beginnings Without End. Sam Keen. LC 75-9321. 1977. pap. 3.95i o.p. (ISBN 0-06-064265-3, RD 245). HarpR.

Behaving Badly. Catherine Heath. LC 84-24039. 224p. 1985. 14.95 o.s.i. (ISBN 0-8008-0713-8). Taplinger.

Behavior. William G. Van Der Kloot. LC 68-13741. (Illus.). 1968. pap. text ed. 4.95x o.p. (ISBN 0-03-067725-4). Irvington.

Behavior Analysis of Child Development. Sidney W. Bijou & Donald M. Baer. (Child Psychology Ser.). 1978. Reference ed. pap. text ed. 13.67 o.p. (ISBN 0-13-066712-9). P-H.

Behavior & Ecology of Wolves. new ed. Erich Klinghammer. LC 77-89306. (Illus.). 1979. lib. bdg. 69.00 o.p. (ISBN 0-8240-7019-4, Garland STPM Pr). Garland Pub.

Behavior & Evolution. Jean Piaget. Tr. by Donald Nicholson-Smith from Fr. LC 77-88762. 1978. 10.00 o.p. (ISBN 0-394-41810-7); pap. 2.95 o.p. (ISBN 0-394-73588-9). Pantheon.

Behavior & Psychological Man: Essays in Motivation & Learning. Edward C. Tolman. 1951. pap. 1.95 o.p. (ISBN 0-520-01271-2). U of Cal Pr.

Behavior & Rehabilitation. 2nd ed. Butler & Rosenthal. 208p. 1978. pap. 20.00 o.p. (ISBN 0-7236-0489-4, Pub. by John Wright UK). Butterworth.

Behavior & Taxonomy of the Epicauta Maculata Group (Coleoptera: Meloidae) J. D. Pinto. (UC Publications in Entomology: Vol. 89). 1980. pap. 25.00x o.p. (ISBN 0-520-09616-9). U of Cal Pr.

Behavior & Training of Dogs & Puppies. Louis L. Vine. LC 77-1387. 1979. 5.95 o.p. (ISBN 0-668-04156-0); pap. 2.50 o.p. (ISBN 0-668-04162-5). Arco.

Behavior As an Ecological Factor. David E. Davis. LC 79-3006. (Benchmark Papers in Ecology Ser.: Vol. 2). 390p. 1982. 57.95 o.p. (ISBN 0-87933-132-1). Van Nos Reinhold.

Behavior-Genetic Analysis. Ed. by J. Hirsch & T. R. McGuire. LC 81-13323. (Benchmark Papers in Behavior: Vol. 16). 393p. 1982. 52.95 o.p. (ISBN 0-87933-419-3). Van Nos Reinhold.

Behavior in Organizations: A Multi-Dimensional View. 2nd ed. Robert E. Coffey et al. LC 74-12372. (Illus.). 608p. 1975. pap. text ed. 37.33 o.p. (ISBN 0-13-073148-X). P-H.

Behavior in the Insect World. Lorus J. Milne & Margery Milne. (Illus.). 129p. 1980. 12.95 o.p. (ISBN 0-684-16627-5, ScribT). Scribner.

Behavior Influence & Personality. L. Krasner & L. P. Ullmann. LC 72-9583. 1973. text ed. 19.95 o.p. (ISBN 0-03-056155-8, HoltC). HR&W.

Behavior Management in Dentistry for Children. Gerald Z. Wright. LC 74-31840. (Illus.). 266p. 1975. write for info. o.p. (ISBN 0-7216-9608-2). Saunders.

Behavior Modification. 1976. 7.50 o.p. (ISBN 0-8144-6960-4). AMACOM.

Behavior Modification. Richard Camellion. LC 78-2209. 140p. 1978. pap. 10.00 o.p. (ISBN 0-87364-100-0). Paladin Pr.

Behavior Modification. 2nd ed. W. Edward Craighead et al. LC 80-83115. 576p. 1981. text ed. 38.36 o.p. (ISBN 0-395-29721-4). HM.

Behavior Modification: Applications to Education. Ed. by Fred S. Keller & Emilio Ribes-Inesta. 1974. 24.95 o.p. (ISBN 0-12-403950-2). Acad Pr.

Behavior Modification for Counseling Centers: A Guide to Program Development. John L. Shelton. (ACPA Publications). 1976. pap. 9.00 nonmembers o.p. (ISBN 0-911547-06-1, 72163W34); pap. 7.00 members o.p. (ISBN 0-686-34279-8). Am Assn Coun Dev.

Behavior Modification for People with Mental Handicaps. 2nd ed. Ed. by William Yule. Janet Carr. 320p. 1987. text ed. 25.00x o.p. (ISBN 0-7099-2918-8, Pub. by Croom Helm). Routledge Chapman & Hall.

Behavior Modification in Children: Case Studies & Illustrations from a Summer Camp. Henry C. Rickard & Michael Dinoff. LC 73-22589. 192p. 1974. 14.75 o.p. (ISBN 0-8173-2701-0). U of Ala Pr.

Behavior Modification in the Human Services: A Systematic Introduction to Concepts & Applications. Martin Sundel & Sandra S. Sundel. (Illus.). 320p. 1982. pap. text ed. (ISBN 0-13-073916-2). P-H.

Behavior Modification in the Natural Environment. Roland Tharp & Ralph Wetzel. LC 75-91418. 1970. 82.00 o.p. (ISBN 0-12-686050-5). Acad Pr.

Behavior Modification: Issues & Extensions. Ed. by Sidney W. Bijou & Emilio Ribes-Inesta. 1972. 35.50 o.p. (ISBN 0-12-097650-1). Acad Pr.

Behavior Modification: Principles, Issues & Applications. W. Edward Craighead et al. LC 75-25003. (Illus.). 608p. 1976. text ed. 19.50 o.p. (ISBN 0-395-21924-8). HM.

Behavior Modification: Procedures for School Personnel. Beth Sulzer-Azaroff & G. Roy Mayer. LC 75-172794. 316p. (Orig.). 1972. pap. text ed. 21.95 o.p. (ISBN 0-03-089029-2, HoltC). HR&W.

Behavior Modification: What It Is & How to Do It. Garry Martin & Joseph Pear. (Illus.). 496p. 1983. pap. text ed. 32.00 o.p. (ISBN 0-13-072082-8). P-H.

Behavior of Insonated Metals see Radiation Damage: Proceedings of CISM, Department for Mechanics of Defamable Bodies, Univ. of Vienna, 1970.

Behavior of Matter: Laboratory Experiments in Introductory Chemistry. Sydney S. Biechler. (Illus., Orig.). 1970. pap. 8.70 o.p. (ISBN 0-395-04189-9, 3-03750). HM.

Behavior of Non-Human Primates: Modern Research Trends. Ed. by Allan M. Schrier et al. Vol. 1, 1965. 49.50 o.p. (ISBN 0-12-629101-2); Vol. 2, 49.50 o.p. (ISBN 0-12-629102-0); Vol. 3, 1971. 49.50 o.p. (ISBN 0-12-629103-9); Vol. 4, 1971. 49.50 o.p. (ISBN 0-12-629104-7). Acad Pr.

Behavior of Prices & Output in India. Isher J. Ahluwalia. 1979. 16.00x o.p. (ISBN 0-8364-0508-0). South Asia Bks.

Behavior: Reflexes & Conditioned Reflexes, Pt. 1, Vol. 1. George L. Geis & William C. Stebbins. (Illus., Program bk). 1965. pap. text ed. 8.95x o.p. (ISBN 0-89197-478-4). Irvington.

Behavior System. Clark L. Hull. LC 73-8149. (Illus.). 372p. 1974. Repr. of 1952 ed. lib. bdg. 27.50x o.p. (ISBN 0-8371-6955-0, HUBS). Greenwood.

Behavior Therapist. Carl E. Thoresen. 1980. 5.95 o.p. (ISBN 1-55620-002-1, 71007C). Am Assn Coun Dev.

Behavior Therapy & Beyond. Arnold A. Lazarus. (Psychology Ser.). (Illus.). 300p. 1971. text ed. 40.95 o.p. (ISBN 0-07-036800-7). McGraw.

Behavioral Assessment: A Practical Handbook. Ed. by Michel Hersen & Alan S. Bellack. 1981. text ed. 61.00 o.p. (ISBN 0-08-025956-1); pap. text ed. 21.00 o.p. (ISBN 0-08-025955-3). Pergamon.

Behavioral Assessment of Severe Developmental Disablities. Michael D. Powers & Jan S. Handleman. LC 84-16878. 228p. 1984. 33.00 o.p. (ISBN 0-89443-863-8). Aspen Pub.

Behavioral Assessment: Recent Advances in Methods, Concepts, & Applications. Stephen N. Haynes & C. Chrisman Wilson. LC 79-88775. (Social & Behavioral Science Ser.). 1980. text ed. 39.95x o.p. (ISBN 0-87589-439-9). Jossey-Bass.

Behavioral Basis of Design: Selected Papers, Bk. 1. Ed. by Peter Suedfeld & James A. Russell. LC 76-11594. (Community Development Ser.: Vol. 28). 1982. 37.95 o.p. (ISBN 0-87933-248-4). Van Nos Reinhold.

Behavioral Concepts & Nursing Throughout the Lifespan. Sharon L. Roberts. 1978. ref. 19.95x o.p. (ISBN 0-13-074559-6); pap. text ed. 21.95x o.p. (ISBN 0-13-074567-7). P-H.

Behavioral Concepts & the Critically Ill Patient. Sharon Roberts. 1976. 24.95 o.p. (ISBN 0-13-074476-X). Appleton & Lange.

Behavioral Concepts in Management. 3rd ed. David Hampton. (Contemporary Thought in Mngt. Ser.). 1978. pap. text ed. (ISBN 0-534-00576-4). Brooks-Cole.

Behavioral Enrichment in the Zoo. Hal Markowitz. 208p. 1982. 32.95 o.p. (ISBN 0-442-25125-4). Van Nos Reinhold.

Behavioral Intervention in Human Problems. Ed. by Henry C. Rickard. LC 76-112398. 434p. 1972. 110.00 o.p. (ISBN 0-08-016327-0); pap. 110.00 o.p. (ISBN 0-08-017737-9). Pergamon.

Behavioral Interviewing for Adult Disorders. Peter H. Wilson et al. 200p. 1988. text ed. 52.50 o.p. (ISBN 0-415-00111-0); pap. text ed. 19.95 o.p. (ISBN 0-415-00112-9). Routledge Chapman & Hall.

Behavioral Medicine: Clinical Applications. Susan S. Pinkerton et al. LC 81-11417. (Wiley Series on Personality Processes). 376p. 1982. 40.95 o.p. (ISBN 0-471-05619-7, Pub. by Wiley-Interscience). Wiley.

Behavioral Modification & Cognitive-Affective Processes. Ed. by Lu Hsien. 97p. 1971. pap. text ed. 5.95x o.p. (ISBN 0-8422-0167-X). Irvington.

Behavioral Neuroscience: An Introduction. Carl W. Cotman & Robert Jenson. 1979. instr's. manual 13.50 o.p. (ISBN 0-12-191655-3). Acad Pr.

Behavioral Orientations Toward Party Leadership & System Norms: An Exploratory Analysis. Lelan E. McLemore. (Legislative Research Ser: No. 11). 46p. 1975. pap. 3.50 o.p. (ISBN 0-686-20783-1). Univ OK Gov Res.

Behavioral Patterns in Internal Audit Relationships. Fredrick E. Mints. 1972. pap. text ed. 13.50 o.p. (ISBN 0-89413-040-4). Inst Inter Aud.

Behavioral Pediatrics: Psychological Aspects of Child Health Care. Stanford Friedman & Robert A. Hoekelman. (Illus.). 448p. 1980. text ed. 21.00 o.p. (ISBN 0-07-022426-9). McGraw.

Behavioral Principles in the Practice of Management. William E. Scott & Phillip M. Podsakoff. LC 84-15181. (Series in Management). 222p. 1985. (ISBN 0-471-06248-0). Wiley.

Behavioral Science & Educational Administration: 63rd Yearbook. Ed. by Daniel E. Griffiths. (National Society for the Study of Education Ser: No. 63, Pt. II). (Illus.). xii, 368p. 1974. pap. text ed. 4.50x o.s.i. (ISBN 0-226-60076-9). U of Chicago Pr.

Behavioral Science & Human Factors in Power Plant Applications. C. D. Gaddy et al. (Illus.). 138p. 1980. spiral bdg. 49.50x o.p. (ISBN 0-87683-140-4). GP Pub.

Behavioral Science & Human Survival. Ed. by Milton Schwebel. LC 65-12297. (Orig.). 1965. pap. 4.95x o.p. (ISBN 0-8314-0005-6). Sci & Behavior.

Behavioral Science & Nursing Theory. Powhatan Wooldridge et al. LC 82-14394. (Illus.). 240p. 1983. pap. text ed. 19.95 o.p. (ISBN 0-8016-5623-0). Mosby.

Behavioral Science & the Secret Service: Toward the Prevention of Assassination. National Research Council Institute of Medicine Staff. 193p. 1981. pap. text ed. 9.95 o.p. (ISBN 0-309-03225-3). Natl Acad Pr.

Behavioral Science Approaches to Employee Relations see Issues in the Public Employee Relations Library: Series 3.

Behavioral Science for the Boreds. Frederick S. Sierles. 88p. (Orig.). 1987. pap. text ed. 9.95 o.p. (ISBN 0-940780-07-0). MedMaster.

Behavioral Sex Differences in Non-Human Primates. G. Mitchell. (Primate Behavior & Development Ser.). 1979. 41.95 o.p. (ISBN 0-442-24594-7). Van Nos Reinhold.

Behavioral Treatment of Alcoholism. P. M. Miller. 1976. 50.00 o.p. (ISBN 0-08-019519-9); pap. 50.00 o.p. (ISBN 0-08-019518-0). Pergamon.

Behavioral Treatment of Disease. Ed. by Richard S. Surwit & Redford B. Williams, Jr. (NATO Conference Series III, Human Factors: Vol. 19). 482p. 1982. 70.00x o.p. (ISBN 0-306-41114-8, Plenum Pr). Plenum Pub.

Behavioral Treatments of Obesity: A Practical Handbook. Ed. by John P. Foreyt. 1977. 34.00 o.p. (ISBN 0-08-019902-X). Pergamon.

Behaviour Analysis in Educational Psychology. Ed. by Kevin Whendall & Frank Merrett. 288p. 1986. 25.00 o.p. (ISBN 0-7099-3689-3, Pub. by Croom Helm UK). Routledge Chapman & Hall.

Behaviour & Design of Steel Structures. N. S. Trahair. 1977. pap. 29.95x o.p. (ISBN 0-412-14900-1, 6292, Pub. by Chapman & Hall). Routledge Chapman & Hall.

Behaviour & Rehabilitation. 2nd ed. R. Butler & G. Rosenthal. 1985. 21.00 o.p. (ISBN 0-7236-0824-5). Butterworth.

Behaviour Modification in the Classroom. Alex Harrop. 160p. 1983. pap. text ed. 14.95 o.s.i. (ISBN 0-340-28172-3). Princeton Bk Co.

Behaviour of Centrioles & the Structure & Formation of the Achromatic Figure. H. A. Went. (Protoplasmatologia: Vol. 6, Pt. G1). (Illus.). 1966. pap. 30.70 o.p. (ISBN 0-387-80783-7). Springer-Verlag.

Behaviour Patterns of Blood-Sucking Flies. E. C. Muirhead-Thomson. (Illus.). 240p. 1982. 73.00 o.p. (ISBN 0-08-025497-7). Pergamon.

Behaviour Problems in Schools: An Evaluation of Support Centres. Peter Mortimore et al. LC 85-127067. 155p. (Orig.). 1984. pap. 15.50 o.p. (ISBN 0-7099-1770-8, Pub. by Croom Helm Ltd). Routledge Chapman & Hall.

Behaviour Studies in Psychiatry. S. J. Hutt & C. Hutt. 1970. 55.00 o.p. (ISBN 0-08-015780-7). Pergamon.

Behaviour Therapy Nursing. Philip J. Barker. 276p. 1982. pap. 17.00 o.p. (ISBN 0-7099-0637-4, Pub. by Croom Helm Ltd). Routledge Chapman & Hall.

Behavioural Aspects of Parasite Transmission. Ed. by E. V. Canning & C. A. Wright. 1973. 47.50 o.p. (ISBN 0-12-158650-2). Acad Pr.

Behavioural Ecology: An Evolutionary Approach. 2nd, rev ed. Ed. by John R. Krebs & Nicholas B. Davies. LC 83-20267. (Illus.). 500p. text ed. cancelled o.s.i. (ISBN 0-87893-132-5); pap. text ed. cancelled o.s.i. (ISBN 0-87893-133-3). Sinauer Assocs.

Behavioural Problems in Geography Revisited. Ed. by Kevin R. Cox & Reginald G. Golledge. 1982. 29.95x o.p. (ISBN 0-416-72430-2, NO. 3533); pap. 14.95x o.p. (ISBN 0-416-72440-X, NO. 3534). Routledge Chapman & Hall.

Behavioural Travel Modelling. Ed. by David Hensher & Peter Stopher. 640p. 1979. 99.00 o.p. (ISBN 0-85664-819-1, Pub. by Croom Helm Ltd). Routledge Chapman & Hall.

Behcet's Syndrome: Clinical & Immunological Features. Ed. by T. Lehner & C. G. Barnes. LC 79-41307. 1980. 78.00 o.p. (ISBN 0-12-442680-8). Acad Pr.

Behind Closed Doors. Bob Woolf. LC 75-41850. 1976. 9.95 o.p. (ISBN 0-689-10712-9, Atheneum). Macmillan.

Behind Closed Doors: Politics in the Public Interest. Edward N. Costikyan. LC 66-123599. 269p. 1968. pap. 5.75 o.p. (ISBN 0-15-611681-2, Harv). HarBraceJ.

Behind Closed Doors: Secret Papers on the Failure of Romanian-Soviet Negotiations 1931-1932. Ed. by Walter M. Bacon, Jr. LC 77-78050. (Archival Documentation Publications Ser.: No. 180). (Illus.). 228p. 1979. 17.50x o.p. (ISBN 0-8179-6801-6). Hoover Inst Pr.

Behind Closed Doors: Wheeling & Dealing in the Banking World. Hope Lampert. LC 86-47683. 384p. 1986. 18.95 o.p. (ISBN 0-689-11747-7, Atheneum). Macmillan.

Behind Enemy Lines: America Spies & Saboteurs in World War II. Milton J. Shapiro. LC 77-25527. 192p. (gr. 7 up). 1978. lib. bdg. 8.79 o.s.i. (ISBN 0-671-32830-1). Messner.

Behind the Ballots: The Personal History of a Politician. James A. Farley. LC 78-114521. (Illus.). 392p. 1972. Repr. of 1938 ed. lib. bdg. 25.00x o.p. (ISBN 0-8371-4738-7, FABB). Greenwood.

Behind the Circus Tent. Leland Jacobs & Allan Jacobs. LC 67-15703. (Illus.). (gr. k-5). 1967. PLB 3.95g o.p. (ISBN 0-8225-0259-3). Lerner Pubns.

Behind the Dial. Bob Grove. Ed. by Rich Force. 57p. (Orig.). 1977. pap. 4.95 o.p. (ISBN 0-88006-001-8, BK 7307). Wayne Green Ent.

Behind the Door. Giorgio Bassani. LC 72-75413. (Helen & Kurt Wolff Bk.). 1972. 5.95 o.p. (ISBN 0-15-111697-0). HarBraceJ.

Behind the Door. E. J. Lype, pseud. LC 66-26969. 1967. (ISBN 0-8022-1006-6). Philos Lib.

Behind the Forbidden Door: Travels in Unknown China. Tiziano Terzani. (Illus.). 1986. 17.95 o.p. (ISBN 0-03-008508-X). H Holt & Co.

Behind the Forbidden Door: Travels in Unknown China. Tiziano Terzani. LC 86-3093. (Owl Bks.). 1988. pap. 8.95 o.p. (ISBN 0-8050-0794-6). H Holt & Co.

Behind the Front Page: Organizational Self-Renewal in Metropolition Newspapers. Chris Argyris. LC 73-22558. (Social & Behavioral Science Ser.). 320p. 1974. 27.95x o.p. (ISBN 0-87589-223-X). Jossey-Bass.

Behind the Great Wall: A Photographic Essay on China. Mary Cross & Theodore Cross. LC 79-1742. (Illus.). 1979. 25.00 o.p. (ISBN 0-689-11018-9, Atheneum). Macmillan.

Behind the Lines: Cartoons. Tony Auth. 1977. 9.95 o.p. (ISBN 0-395-25789-1); pap. 4.95 o.p. (ISBN 0-395-25946-0). HM.

Behind the Lines in the Southern Confederacy. Charles W. Ramsdell. Ed. by Wendell H. Stephenson. 1969. Repr. of 1944 ed. lib. bdg. 22.50x o.p. (ISBN 0-8371-2218-X, RABL). Greenwood.

Behind the Mirror: A Search for a Natural History of Human Knowledge. Konrad Lorenz. Tr. by Ronald Taylor. LC 76-55029. (Helen & Kurt Wolff Bk.). (Illus.). 288p. 1977. 10.00 o.s.i. (ISBN 0-15-111699-7). HarBraceJ.

Behind the Scenes in American Government. 6th ed. Peter Woll. 1987. pap. text ed. (ISBN 0-673-39494-8). Scott F.

Behind the Screen see Scoop.

Behind the Veil in Arabia: Women in Oman. Unni Wikan. LC 81-18622. (Illus.). 384p. 1982. text ed. 34.50x o.p. (ISBN 0-8018-2729-9). Johns Hopkins.

Behind the Walls of Terra. Philip Jose Farmer. 1977. pap. 2.50 o.p. (ISBN 0-441-05374-2). Ace Bks.

Behind the War in Eritrea. Ed. by Basil Davidson et al. 150p. 1981. pap. text ed. 8.95x o.p. (ISBN 0-85124-302-9). Barber Pr.

Behold His Love. Basilea Schlink. 144p. 1973. pap. 3.95 o.p. (ISBN 0-87123-039-9). Bethany Hse.

Behold the Lamb. R. Kent Hughes. 180p. 1984. pap. 6.95 o.p. (ISBN 0-88207-623-X). Victor Bks.

Behold the Man. R. Kent Hughes. LC 84-50144. 180p. 1984. pap. 6.95 o.p. (ISBN 0-89693-379-2). Victor Bks.

Behold the Man. Michael Moorcock. 1976. pap. 2.25 o.p. (ISBN 0-380-00637-5, 39982-2). Avon.

Behrman's Neonatal-Perinatal Medicine: Diseases of the Fetus & Infant. 3rd ed. Avroy A. Fanaroff & Richard J. Martin. LC 82-6371. (Illus.). 1216p. 1982. text ed. 80.00 o.p. (ISBN 0-8016-0580-6). Mosby.

Beijing: The Treasures of an Ancient Capital. 1987. 90.00 o.p. (BE0000). China Bks.

Being a Boss. Cheryl Reimold. (Clear & Simple Ser.). (Orig.). 1984. pap. 3.95 o.p. (ISBN 0-440-50595-X, Dell Trade Pbks). Dell.

Being a Christian When the Chips Are Down. Helmut Thielicke. Tr. by H. George Anderson from Ger. LC 78-54562. 128p. 1979. 7.95 o.p. (ISBN 0-8006-0541-1, 1-541, Fortress). Augsburg Fortress.

Being a Loving Wife. Ed. by Jeanne Hunt. LC 82-48422. (Christian Reader Ser.). 128p. (Orig.). 1983. pap. 5.72i o.p. (ISBN 0-06-061386-6, RD/438). HarpR.

Being a Man: The Paradox of Masculinity. Donald Bell. 168p. 1984. pap. 5.95 o.p. (ISBN 0-15-611686-3, Harv). HarBraceJ.

Being a Success at Who You Are. Andre Bustanoby. 1986. pap. 2.95 o.p. (ISBN 0-310-45381-X, 9172P). Zondervan.

Being a Well Woman. Miriam Stoppard. (Illus.). 1982. 19.95 o.p. (ISBN 0-03-060606-3). H Holt & Co.

Being an Actor. Simon Callow. (Illus.). 224p. 1985. 15.95 o.p. (ISBN 0-413-52440-X, NO. 9187). Heinemann Ed.

Being & Nothingness. Jean-Paul Sartre. 1965. pap. 5.95 o.s.i. (ISBN 0-8065-0195-2, 156, Pub. by Citadel Pr). Carol Pub Group.

Being & the Messiah: The Message of St. John. Jose P. Miranda. Tr. by John Eagleson from Span. LC 77-5388. Orig. Title: Ser y el Mesias. 253p. (Orig.). 1977. 8.95x o.p. (ISBN 0-88344-027-X); pap. 4.95x o.p. (ISBN 0-88344-028-8). Orbis Bks.

Being Bernard Berenson. Meryle Secrest. LC 78-31433. (Illus.). 480p. pap. 15.95 o.p. (ISBN 0-03-018411-8). H Holt & Co.

Being Human. David Deamer. 1981. text ed. 32.95 o.s.i. (ISBN 0-03-022076-9, CBS C); instr's manual 19.95 o.s.i. (ISBN 0-03-045036-5). SCP.

Being Human: The Nature of Spiritual Experience. Ranald Macaulay & Jerram Barrs. LC 77-11365. 1978. pap. 10.95 o.p. (ISBN 0-87784-796-7). Inter-Varsity.

Being Intimate: A Guide to Successful Relationships. John Amodeo & Kris Amodeo. 192p. 1986. pap. 12.95 o.p. (ISBN 1-85063-037-2, 30372). Routledge Chapman & Hall.

Being Jewish in America. Date not set. (ISBN 0-8052-3692-9). Random.

Being Number One: Rebuilding the U. S. Economy. Gail G. Schwartz & Pat Choate. 160p. 1980. 22.00x o.p. (ISBN 0-669-04308-7). Lexington Bks.

Being Religious in America: The Deepening Crises over Public Faith. Erling Jorstad. LC 86-3360. 128p. (Orig.). 1986. pap. 7.95 o.p. (ISBN 0-8066-2222-9, 10-0585, Augsburg). Augsburg Fortress.

Being the Best. Denis Waitley. 224p. 1987. 14.95 o.p. (ISBN 0-8407-9071-6). Oliver-Nelson.

Beirut Pipeline. Ray Alan. 242p. 1980. 10.95 o.p. (ISBN 0-374-11018-2). FS&G.

Beitrag Z. Kenntnis D. Trutzwaffen D. Indonesier, Suedseevoelker U. Indianer. George Friederici. Repr. of 1915 ed. 15.00 o.p. (ISBN 0-384-16910-4). Johnson Repr.

Beitrag zur Desmidieenflora von Sued-Holstein und der Hansestadt Hamburg. K. Foerster. (Illus.). 160p. 1970. pap. text ed. 15.00x o.p. (ISBN 3-7682-0676-9). Lubrecht & Cramer.

Beitrage Zur Kulturgeschichte der Afrikanischen Feldarbeit. Walter G. Beck. Repr. of 1943 ed. 19.00 o.p. (ISBN 0-384-03705-4). Johnson Repr.

Beitray Zur Ethrologie Von Bouganville und Buka. Ernest Frizzi. Repr. of 1914 ed. 10.00 o.p. (ISBN 0-384-17020-X). Johnson Repr.

Bel Ami. Guy De Maupassant. Ed. by Delaisement. 1960. pap. 3.95 o.p. (ISBN 0-685-11039-7). Schoenhof.

Bel Indifferent. Jean Cocteau. 9.95 o.p. (ISBN 0-686-54513-3). French & Eur.

Bela Bartok Letters. Bela Bartok. 466p. Repr. of 1971 ed. lib. bdg. 59.00 o.p. (Pub. by Am Repr Serv). Reprint Servs.

Belden, the White Chief: Or, Twelve Years among the Wild Indians of the Plains from the Diaries & Manuscripts of George P. Belden. facsimile ed. Ed. by James S. Brisbin. LC 73-92900. (Illus.). xxvi, 513p. 1974. Repr. of 1870 ed. 10.95 o.p. (ISBN 0-8214-0150-5). Ohio U Pr.

Belfast: The Making of the City. J. C. Bockett et al. (Illus.). 188p. 1983. 25.95 o.p. (ISBN 0-86281-100-7, Pub. by Appletree Pr). Irish Bks Media.

Belgian Congo & the Berlin Act. Arthur B. Keith. LC 73-109329. 1970. Repr. of 1919 ed. 35.00x o.p. (ISBN 0-8371-3599-0, KEB&, Pub. by Negro U Pr). Greenwood.

Belgium & Luxembourg. 6th ed. John Tomes. (Blue Guides Ser.). (Illus.). 1983. 24.95 o.p. (ISBN 0-393-01656-0); pap. 15.95 o.p. (ISBN 0-393-30063-3). Norton.

Belief, Change & Forms of Life. D. Z. Phillips. LC 85-27080. (Library of Philosophy & Religion). 144p. 1986. text ed. 29.95x o.p. (ISBN 0-391-03385-9). Humanities.

Beliefs & Their Engrammes: Revised & Tested on the QE-2 World Cruise. J. M. Sanchez-Perez. 1975. 7.50 o.p. (ISBN 0-682-48266-8). Exposition-Phoenix.

Believer's Bible Companion. Larry Huggins. 32p. (Orig.). 1984. pap. 1.95 o.p. (ISBN 0-89274-314-X, HH-314). Harrison Hse.

Believers Incorporated: The Message of Ephesians for Evangelical Outreach. Walter R. Wietzke. LC 76-27073. 1977. pap. 3.95 o.p. (ISBN 0-8066-1553-2, 10-0650, Augsburg). Augsburg Fortress.

Believing in God. Daniel Jenkins. LC 56-9576. (Layman's Theological Library). 1965. pap. 1.45 o.s.i. (ISBN 0-664-24004-6, Westminster). Westminster John Knox.

Believing the Impossible Before Breakfast. Ernest Lee Stoffel. LC 76-44977. 1977. 6.95 o.p. (ISBN 0-8042-2246-0, John Knox). Westminster John Knox.

Belinda. Maria Edgeworth. (Mothers of the Novel Reprint Ser.). 480p. 1986. pap. 7.95 o.p. (ISBN 0-86358-074-2). Routledge Chapman & Hall.

Belinda. Anne Rampling, pseud. LC 67-10449. 352p. 1986. 17.95 o.p. (ISBN 0-87795-826-2). Morrow.

Belinda's Ball. Joan Bodger & Mark Thurman. LC 80-18324. (Illus.). 48p. 1981. PLB 9.95 o.s.i. (ISBN 0-689-30836-1, Atheneum). Macmillan.

Belize. Ralph L. Woodward, Jr. (World Bibliographical Ser.: No. 21). 229p. 1980. 31.25 o.p. (ISBN 0-903450-41-0). ABC-Clio.

Bell, Book & Scandal. 2nd ed. P. Hamilton Pollock. 1978. 12.00 o.p. (ISBN 0-682-49000-8). Exposition-Phoenix.

Bell Harry & Other Poems. Christopher Hassall. LC 64-2396. 1964. 9.95 o.p. (ISBN 0-15-111790-X). HarBraceJ.

Bella. Jilly Cooper. 192p. 1981. pap. 2.25 o.s.i. (ISBN 0-449-24473-3, Crest). Fawcett.

Bella Mastera, Pt. 2. Ezerskaya. 1986. 6.95 o.s.i. RWCPH.

Bellary Bay. John Welcome. LC 79-51523. 1979. 10.95 o.p. (ISBN 0-689-11013-8, Atheneum). Macmillan.

Belle Catherine. Juliette Benzoni. 1978. pap. 1.95 o.p. (ISBN 0-380-36525-1, 36525). Avon.

Belle Epoque Exhibition Checklist. Paul M. Ettesvold. Ed. by Amy Horbar. 24p. (Orig.). 1983. pap. 2.95 o.p. (ISBN 0-87099-342-9). Metro Mus Art.

Belle et la Bete. Jean Cocteau. (Illus.). 256p. 1975. 23.50 o.p. (ISBN 0-686-54514-1). French & Eur.

Belle Image. Marcel Ayme. 1972. pap. 8.95 o.p. (ISBN 0-686-51901-9). French & Eur.

Belle of Amherst. William Luce. 1976. 6.95 o.p. (ISBN 0-395-24980-5). HM.

Belli Files. Melvin Belli. 275p. 1982. 14.95 o.p. (ISBN 0-13-077974-1, Busn). P-H.

Belli for Your Malpractice Defense. Melvin M. Belli, Sr. & John Carlova. 1986. casebound 32.95 o.p. (ISBN 0-87489-380-1). Med Economics.

Bellini. Leslie Orrey. (Master Musicians Ser.: No. M137). (Illus.). 1973. pap. 7.95 o.p. (ISBN 0-8226-0705-0). Littlefield.

Bellini. Leslie Orrey. (Master Musicians Ser.). (Illus.). 188p. 1969. 17.95x o.p. (ISBN 0-460-03132-5, Pub. by J. M. Dent England). Biblio Dist.

Bell's Acrostic Dictionary. W. M. Baker. LC 77-141772. 288p. 1971. Repr. of 1927 ed. 35.00x o.p. (ISBN 0-8103-3379-1). Gale.

Belly Dancer. 1983. pap. text ed. 9.95 o.p. (ISBN 0-07-070811-8). McGraw.

Belonging. James Campbell et al. (gr. 1-6). 1977. 4.95 o.p. (ISBN 0-8042-1456-5, John Knox). Westminster John Knox.

Belonging. Virginia M. Scott. LC 85-31135. (Illus.). viii, 200p. 1986. 11.95 o.p. (ISBN 0-930323-14-9, Pub. by K Green Pubns). Gallaudet Univ Pr.

Beloved Captain. Jo Ann Simon. 320p. 1988. pap. 3.95 o.p. (ISBN 0-380-89771-7). Avon.

Beloved Rebel. Chet Cunningham. 1978. pap. 1.95 o.p. (ISBN 0-8439-0550-6, Pub. by Leisure Bks CT). Dorchester Pub Co.

Below the Belt: Unarmed Combat for Women. Bradley J. Steiner. LC 76-1353. (Illus.). 180p. 1976. pap. 16.95 o.p. (ISBN 0-87364-034-9). Paladin Pr.

Belshazzar: A Cat's Story for Humans. Chaim Bermant. 64p. 1982. pap. 2.50 o.p. (ISBN 0-380-58560-X, 58560-X). Avon.

Belshazzar: Prince of Babylon, 4 pts. Florence H. Anastasas. (Illus.). 304p. 1982. 15.00 o.p. (ISBN 0-682-49818-1, University). Exposition-Phoenix.

Titles

Belt Conveyors for Bulk Materials. 2nd ed. Conveyor Equipment Manufacturers Association Staff. LC 78-31987. 384p. 1983. 36.95 o.p. (ISBN 0-8436-1008-5). Van Nos Reinhold.

Belt of Gold. Cecelia Holland. 1987. pap. 6.95 o.p. (ISBN 0-345-34108-2). Ballantine.

Beltran: Basque Sheepman of the American West. Beltran Paris. As told to William A. Douglass. LC 79-20311. (Basque Book Ser.). (Illus.). 186p. 1979. 11.95 o.p. (ISBN 0-87417-054-0). U of Nev Pr.

Beluga: Investigation of the Species. S. E. Kleinenberg et al. 376p. 1966. text ed. 76.00x o.p. (ISBN 0-7065-0507-7, Pub. by Keter Pub Jerusalem). Coronet Bks.

Bemba: An African Adventure. Andree Clair. Tr. by Marie Ponsot. LC 62-13332. (Illus.). (gr. 4-6). 1966. pap. 0.60 o.p. (ISBN 0-15-611816-5, AVB37, VoyB). HarBraceJ.

Bemisia Tabaci. Ed. by M. J. Cock. 122p. 1986. pap. 10.45 o.p. (ISBN 0-85198-575-0). CAB Intl.

Ben-Gurion: Prophet of Fire. Dan Kurzman. 1983. 19.25 o.p. (ISBN 0-671-23094-8). S&S.

Ben Gurion: Prophet of Fire. Dan Kurzman. 544p. 1984. pap. 10.95 o.p. (ISBN 0-671-52821-1, Touchstone Bks). S&S.

Ben Hall Bushranger. D. J. Shiel. LC 82-21904. (Illus.). 231p. 1984. 19.95 o.p. (ISBN 0-7022-1722-0). U of Queensland Pr.

Ben Jonson & the Language of Prose Comedy. Jonas A. Barish. 1970. pap. 2.45x o.p. (ISBN 0-393-00554-2, Norton Lib). Norton.

Ben Jonson: His Vision & Art. Alexander Leggatt. 300p. 1981. 42.00 o.p. (ISBN 0-416-74660-8, NO. 3477). Routledge Chapman & Hall.

Ben Jonson's Non-Dramatic Works: A Reference Guide. David C. Judkins. 1982. lib. bdg. 36.50 o.p. (ISBN 0-8161-8036-9, Hall Reference). G K Hall.

Ben Jonson's Plays: An Introduction. Robert E. Knoll. LC 64-17220. (Illus.). xviii, 206p. 1965. 18.95x o.p. (ISBN 0-8032-0094-3). U of Nebr Pr.

Ben Lexcen: The Man, the Keel & the Cup. Bruce Stannard. (Illus.). 200p. 1984. 14.95 o.p. (ISBN 0-571-13396-7). Faber & Faber.

Ben-Yehuda's English-Hebrew Hebrew-English Dictionary. (Eng. & Hebrew.). (gr. 8-12). 1983. pap. 4.95 o.s.i. (ISBN 0-671-47211-9). PB.

Benares. Henry Wilson. LC 85-50546. (Illus.). 120p. 1985. 29.95 o.p. (ISBN 0-500-24123-6). Thames Hudson.

Bench Woodwork. rev. ed. John Feirer. (Illus.). 255p. 1978. encore ed 8.85 o.p. (ISBN 0-684-17520-7, ScribT). Scribner.

Bend Sinister. Vladimir Nabokov. LC 73-5990. 256p. 1974. pap. text ed. 8.95 o.p. (ISBN 0-07-045710-7). McGraw.

Bend with the Wind. Elisabeth Moore. LC 78-31664. 1981. 14.95 o.s.i. (ISBN 0-87949-142-6). Ashley Bks.

Beneath an Opal Moon. Eric Van Lustbader. 1983. pap. 2.75 o.s.i. (ISBN 0-425-07040-9). Berkley Pub.

Beneath Another Sun. Marjory Hall. LC 77-110081. (gr. 7-10). 1970. 4.75 o.s.i. (ISBN 0-664-32472-X, Westminster). Westminster John Knox.

Beneath the Eagle's Eye. Franklin H. Smith. 136p. 1988. 10.95 o.p. (ISBN 0-8062-3063-0). Carlton.

Beneath the Fur. Stanley Bloom. 1979. 7.00 o.p. (ISBN 0-682-49349-X). Exposition-Phoenix.

Beneath the Mask. 2nd ed. Christopher F. Monte. LC 79-20214. 739p. 1979. text ed. 32.95x o.p. (ISBN 0-03-049016-2, HoltC). HR&W.

Beneath the Moors. Brian Lumley. LC 74-78130. 156p. 1974. 6.00 o.p. (ISBN 0-87054-066-1). Arkham.

Beneath the Red Banner. Lao She. Tr. by Don J. Cohn from Chinese. (Panda Ser.). 215p. (Orig.). 1982. pap. 4.95 o.p. (ISBN 0-8351-1026-5). China Bks.

Beneath the Wheel. Hermann Hesse. Tr. by Michael Roloff from Ger. 192p. 1968. pap. 7.95 o.p. (ISBN 0-374-50748-1). FS&G.

Benedict Arnold: The Dark Eagle. Brian Boylan. (Illus.). 266p. 1973. 7.95 o.p. (ISBN 0-393-07471-4). Norton.

Benedictine Cartoons. Wm. Armstrong. (Armstrong Cartoon Ser.). (Illus., Orig.). 1973. pap. 1.00 o.p. (ISBN 0-913452-25-4). Jesuit Bks.

Benefactor. Susan Sontag. 274p. 1963. 8.95 o.p. (ISBN 0-374-11092-1); pap. 7.95 o.p. (ISBN 0-374-52056-9). FS&G.

Benefactor. Susan Sontag. 280p. 1987. pap. 7.95 o.p. (ISBN 0-374-52056-9). FS&G.

Beneficiation of Mineral Fines. Ed. by P. Somasundaran & N. Arbiter. LC 79-91945. (Illus.). 406p. (Orig.). 1979. pap. text ed. 10.00x o.p. (ISBN 0-89520-259-X). SMM&E Inc.

Benefit-Cost Analysis of Air-Pollution Control. Robert Halvorsen & Michael G. Ruby. LC 78-19587. (Illus.). 288p. 1981. 31.50x o.p. (ISBN 0-669-02647-6). Lexington Bks.

Benefit of Environmental Satellites to Offshore Industries. A. Leibert. 116p. (Orig.). 1980. pap. text ed. 80.95x o.p. (ISBN 0-903796-67-8, Pub. by Online Conferences England). Gower Pub Co.

Benefit Plan Professionals Institute: Proceedings, June 20-23, 1982, Lake Tahoe, Nev. Ed. by Becky A. Wright. 82p. (Orig.). 1982. pap. 10.00 o.p. (ISBN 0-89154-199-3). Intl Found Employ.

Benefit Plans Disputes: Arbitration Case Stories. Morris Stone. 92p. 3.50 o.p. Am Arbitration.

Benefits. Zoe Fairbairns. 224p. 1983. pap. 2.95 o.p. (ISBN 0-380-63164-4, 63164-4, Bard). Avon.

Benefits Processing Institute Proceedings. December 8-11, 1982, Orlando, Florida. Ed. by Mary E. Brennan. 61p. (Orig.). 1983. pap. text ed. 10.00 o.p. (ISBN 0-89154-203-5). Intl Found Employ.

Benelux & Germany. (AA Road Map Ser.). (Illus.). Date not set. (ISBN 0-86145-017-5, Pub. by Auto Assn England). Salem Hse Pubs.

Benevolent Man: A Life of Ralph Allen of Bath. Benjamin Boyce. LC 67-11667. (Illus.). 1967. 23.50x o.s.i. (ISBN 0-674-06650-2). Harvard U Pr.

Bengal Famine of Nineteen Forty-Three: The American Response. M. S. Venkataramani. 1977. text ed. 10.00x o.p. (ISBN 0-686-77719-0, Pub. by Vikas India). Advent NY.

Benicia: Portrait of an Early California Town. Robert Bruegmann. LC 79-15642. (Illus.). 162p. 1980. pap. 8.95 o.s.i. (ISBN 0-89286-152-5, One Hund One Prods). Ortho.

Benin: An African Kingdom & Culture. Kit Elliot. LC 78-56810. (Cambridge Topic Bks.). (Illus.). (gr. 5-10). 1978. PLB 8.95 o.p. (ISBN 0-8225-1211-4). Lerner Pubns.

Benito Perez Galdos: Tormento. Ed. by Eamon J. Rodgers. 1978. text ed. 29.00 o.p. (ISBN 0-08-018089-2); pap. text ed. 14.00 o.p. (ISBN 0-08-018088-4). Pergamon.

Benjamin Britten. Donald Mitchell & Hans Keller. (Illus.). 428p. 1953. (ISBN 0-8022-1125-9). Philos Lib.

Benjamin Disraeli, Earl of Beaconsfield. Cecil Roth. 1952. (ISBN 0-8022-1382-0). Philos Lib.

Benjamin Franklin. Ingri D'Aulaire & Edgar P. D'Aulaire. (Illus.). (gr. 1-4). 1950. 11.95 o.s.i. (ISBN 0-385-07219-8); PLB o.p. (ISBN 0-385-07603-7). Doubleday.

Benjamin Franklin. Raymond J. Seeger. LC 73-7981. 200p. 1973. 26.00 o.p. (ISBN 0-08-017648-8). Pergamon.

Benjamin Franklin. John Tottle. (gr. 4-6). 1958. text ed. 6.84 o.p. (ISBN 0-395-01748-3, Piper). HM.

Benjamin Franklin. Carl C. Van Doren. LC 73-8566. (Illus.). 845p. 1973. Repr. of 1938 ed. lib. bdg. 47.25x o.p. (ISBN 0-8371-6964-X, VABF). Greenwood.

Benjamin Franklin: A Perspective see Exhibition Catalogues from the Fogg Art Museum.

Benjamin Franklin, Printer. John C. Oswald. LC 74-3020. 262p. 1974. Repr. of 1917 ed. 48.00x o.p. (ISBN 0-8103-3642-1). Gale.

Benjamin Franklin's "Good House" Claude-Anne Lopez. (National Park Service Handbook Ser.: No. 114). (Illus.). 65p. 1982. pap. 3.25 o.p. (ISBN 0-318-21928-X, 024-005-00907-8). USGPO.

Benjamin Henry Latrobe see American Association of Architectural Bibliographers' Papers.

Benjamin Rabbit & the Bad Dream. Irene Keller & Dick Keller. (Illus.). 32p. (gr. k-6). 1986. 3.95 o.p. (ISBN 0-8249-8153-7). Ideals.

Benjamin Rabbit & the Fire Chief. Irene Keller. (Illus.). 48p. (gr. k-5). 1986. 3.95 o.p. (ISBN 0-8249-8161-8). Ideals.

Benjamin Rabbit & the Stranger Danger. Irene Keller. LC 84-28673. (Illus.). 32p. (gr. k-6). 1985. 3.95 o.p. (ISBN 0-8249-8100-6). Ideals.

Benjamin West: A Biography. Robert C. Alberts. 1978. 20.00 o.p. (ISBN 0-395-26289-5). HM.

Benjamin's Balloon. Janet Quin-Harkin. LC 78-11225. (Illus.). 48p. (ps-3). 1979. 5.95 o.s.i. (ISBN 0-8193-0976-1); PLB 5.95 o.s.i. (ISBN 0-8193-0977-X). Parents.

Benjamin's Book. Alan Baker. LC 82-4605. (Illus.). 32p. (ps-1). 1983. 13.00 o.p. (ISBN 0-688-01697-9). Lothrop.

Benji & Zax: A Maze Story Book. Illus. by Katherine Wilson-Heaney. (Saturday Morning Bks.). (Illus.). 24p. (gr. 2-6). 1983. pap. 1.95 o.p. (ISBN 0-89954-233-6). Antioch Pub Co.

Benmussa Directs: Portrait of Dora by Helene Cixous & the Singular Life of Albert Nobbs by Simone Benmussa. Simone Benmussa. Tr. by Anita Barrows & Barbara Wright. 128p. 1985. 10.95 o.p. (ISBN 0-7145-3764-0). Riverrun Ny.

Benn's Media Directory, 1986, 2 vols. 1986. 208.00 set o.p. (ISBN 0-86382-028-X). Intl Pubns Serv.

Benny. Barbara Cohen. LC 77-242. (gr. 3-7). 1977. 7.25 o.p. (ISBN 0-688-41804-X); PLB 11.88 o.p. (ISBN 0-688-51804-4). Lothrop.

Bent. Martin Sherman. 1980. pap. 2.50 o.p. (ISBN 0-380-75754-0, 60181-8, Bard). Avon.

Bent World: Essays on Religion & Culture. Ed. by John R. May. 224p. (Orig.). 1986. pap. 24.25 o.p. (ISBN 0-8191-5614-0, Pub. by College Theology Society). U Pr of Amer.

Benteen-Gold Letters on Custer & His Last Battle. Ed. by John M. Carroll. 1974. 35.00 o.p. (ISBN 0-87140-580-6). Liveright.

Bentham's Theory of Fictions. Charles K. Ogden. (Quality Paperback: No. 202). 161p. 1959. pap. 3.95 o.p. (ISBN 0-8226-0202-4). Littlefield.

Bentley Farm Cook Book. Virginia W. Bentley. LC 74-13108. 368p. 1975. pap. 13.45 o.p. (ISBN 0-395-19394-X). HM.

Benya Krik, the Gangster & Other Stories. Issac Babel. Ed. by Avrahahm Yarmolinsky. LC 70-101637. 128p. 1987. pap. 4.95 o.s.i. (ISBN 0-8052-0244-7). Schocken.

Benzodiazepines Divided: A Multidisciplinary Review. Ed. by M. R. Trimble. 329p. 1983. 59.95 o.p. (ISBN 0-471-90199-7). Wiley.

Benzofurans, Vol. 29. Ahmed Mustafa. LC 73-4780. (Heterocyclic Compounds Ser.). 514p. 1974. 62.50 o.p. (ISBN 0-471-38207-8, John Wiley). Krieger.

Beobachtung und Beurteilung von Kindern und Jugendlichen. 13th ed. H. Thomae. (Psychologische Praxis: Band 15). (Illus.). vi, 90p. 1980. soft cover 8.00 o.p. (ISBN 3-8055-1526-X). S Karger.

Beowulf. 48p. 1988. pap. 9.95 o.p. (ISBN 1-55651-075-8); audiocassette tape incl. o.p. (ISBN 1-55651-076-4). Cram Cassettes.

Beowulf: An Edition with Manuscript Spacing Notation & Graphotactic Analyses. Robert D. Stevick. LC 75-1201. (Reference Library of the Humanities: No. 20). 300p. 1975. lib. bdg. 46.00 o.p. (ISBN 0-8240-1090-6). Garland Pub.

Beowulf to Beatles & Beyond. 2nd ed. David R. Pichaske. 1981. pap. text ed. (ISBN 0-02-395390-X). Macmillan.

Berbers & Blacks: Impressions of Morocco, Timbuktu & the Western Sudan. David P. Barrows. LC 70-129938. (Illus.). 1970. Repr. of 1927 ed. lib. bdg. 22.50 o.p. (ISBN 0-8371-1003-3, BBB&, Pub. by Negro U Pr). Greenwood.

Bereaved Husband. Clell Edgar Bowman. 1976. 8.00 o.p. (ISBN 0-682-48519-5). Exposition-Phoenix.

Berenice, Princess of Judea. K. Kolby. 21.95x o.p. New Coll U Pr.

Berenstain Bears & the Messy Room. Stan Berenstain & Janice Berenstain. (First Time Book & Puppet Packages Ser.). (Illus.). 32p. (ps-1). 1987. pap. 2.95 o.s.i. (ISBN 0-394-88892-8, BYR). Random.

Berenstain Bears Forget Their Manners. Stan Berenstain & Janice Berenstain. LC 84-43156. (First Time Book & Puppet Packages). (Illus.). 32p. (ps-1). 1988. pap. 2.95 o.s.i. (ISBN 0-394-89798-6, BYR). Random.

Berenstains' Baby Book. Stan Berenstain & Janice Berenstain. (Illus.). 192p. 1983. 12.95 o.p. (ISBN 0-87795-509-3, Arbor Hse). Morrow.

Berger Building Cost File 1987. S. Berger et al. 288p. (Orig.). 1987. pap. 30.00 o.p. (ISBN 0-934041-14-8). Craftsman.

Berger Building Cost File 1988. S. Berger et al. 286p. (Orig.). 1987. pap. 30.00 o.p. (ISBN 0-934041-31-8). Craftsman.

Bergmann's Linear Integral Operator Method in the Theory of Compressible Fluid Flows. M. Z. Von Krzywoblocki. (Illus.). 1960. 40.20 o.p. (ISBN 0-387-80546-X). Springer-Verlag.

Berkeley: The Central Arguments. A. C. Grayling. 232p. 1986. 26.95 o.p. (ISBN 0-8126-9037-0). Open Court.

Berkeley Working Papers on South & Southeast Asia: Vol. 1, 1975-1976. Center for South & Southeast Asia Studies Staff. (Occasional Papers of the Center for South & Southeast Asia Studies). 498p. 1983. pap. text ed. 23.50 o.p. (ISBN 0-8191-3115-6, Co-pub. by Ctr S SE Asia). U Pr of Amer.

Berlin, Alexanderplatz. Alfred Doblin. Tr. by Eugene Jolas. LC 58-8957. 1958. pap. 11.95 o.p. (ISBN 0-8044-6120-1). Ungar.

Berlin: Contemporary Writing from Berlin. Ed. by Mitch Cohen. LC 77-642342. (Rockbottom Specials Ser.). (Illus., Eng. & Ger.). 1983. 20.00x o.p. (ISBN 0-930012-23-2); pap. 12.00x o.p. (ISBN 0-930012-22-4). Bandanna Bks.

Berlin Fugle. J. C. Winters. 1985. pap. 3.95 o.p. (ISBN 0-380-89866-7). Avon.

Berlin Game. Len Deighton. (General Ser.). 1984. lib. bdg. 16.95 o.p. (ISBN 0-8161-3685-8, Large Print Bks). G K Hall.

Berlin Game. Len Deighton. 320p. 1984. pap. 4.50 o.p. (ISBN 0-345-31498-0). Ballantine.

Berlin Police Force in the Weimar Republic, 1918-1933. Liang Hsi-Huey. LC 74-85452. (Illus.). 1970. 35.00x o.p. (ISBN 0-520-01603-3). U of Cal Pr.

Berlin: Story of a Battle. Andrew Tully. LC 76-56788. (Illus.). 1977. Repr. of 1963 ed. lib. bdg. 22.50x o.p. (ISBN 0-8371-9431-8, TUBS). Greenwood.

Berlin Travel Guide. Berlitz Editors. (Travel Guides for English Speakers Ser.). 1983. pap. 6.95 o.p. (ISBN 0-02-969040-4, Berlitz). Macmillan.

Berlin Tunnel, Twenty-One. Donald Lindquist. 1978. pap. 2.95 o.p. (ISBN 0-380-01843-8, 78394-0). Avon.

Berlin Wall: Kennedy, Khrushchev & a Showdown in the Heart of Europe. Norman Gelb. LC 86-5898. (Illus.). 384p. 1987. 19.45 o.s.i. (ISBN 0-8129-1218-7). Times bks.

Berlioz & the Romantic Century, 2 Vols. Jacques Barzun. Repr. of 1969 ed. lib. bdg. 108.00 o.p. (Pub. by Am Repr Serv). Reprint Servs.

Berlitz Arabic for Travellers. Berlitz Editors. 192p. (Arabic.). 1975. 4.95 o.p. (ISBN 0-02-964180-2, Berlitz); pap. 4.95 o.p. Macmillan.

Berlitz Arabic for Your Trip. 192p. 1982. 8.95 o.p. (Berlitz). Macmillan.

Berlitz Chinese for Travellers. Berlitz Editors. 192p. 1981. pap. 4.95 o.p. (ISBN 0-686-93010-X, Berlitz); pap. 4.95 o.p. (ISBN 0-02-964210-8). Macmillan.

Berlitz Editors. 192p. 1982. 8.95 o.p. (ISBN 0-02-965470-X, Berlitz). Macmillan.

Berlitz European Menu for Travellers. Berlitz Editors. 192p. 1975. pap. 4.95 o.p. (ISBN 0-686-93020-7, Berlitz); pap. 4.95 o.p. (ISBN 0-02-964200-0). Macmillan.

Berlitz French for Your Trip. Berlitz Editors. 192p. 1982. 8.95 o.p. (ISBN 0-02-965160-3, Berlitz). Macmillan.

Berlitz German for Your Trip. Berlitz Editors. 192p. 1982. 8.95 o.p. (ISBN 0-02-965170-0, Berlitz). Macmillan.

Berlitz Greek for Your Trip. Berlitz Editors. 192p. 1982. 8.95 o.p. (ISBN 0-02-965480-7, Berlitz). Macmillan.

Berlitz Italian for Your Trip. Berlitz Editors. 192p. 1982. 8.95 o.p. (Berlitz). Macmillan.

Berlitz Latin-American Spanish for Your Trip. Berlitz Editors. 192p. 1982. 8.95 o.p. (Berlitz). Macmillan.

Berlitz Spanish for Your Trip. Berlitz Editors. 192p. 1982. 8.95 o.p. (Berlitz). Macmillan.

Berlitz Travel Guide: London. Berlitz Editors. (Illus.). 128p. 1978. pap. 4.95 o.p. (ISBN 0-02-969320-9, Berlitz). Macmillan.

Berlitz Travel Guide: Paris. Berlitz Editors. (Illus.). 128p. 1978. pap. 4.95 o.p. (ISBN 0-02-969430-2, Berlitz). Macmillan.

Berlitz Travel Guide: Rome. Berlitz Editors. (Illus.). 128p. 1976. pap. 6.95 o.p. (ISBN 0-02-969470-1, Berlitz). Macmillan.

Berlitz Travel Guide: Southern Caribbean. Berlitz Editors. (Illus.). 128p. 1982. pap. 4.95 o.p. (ISBN 0-686-92930-6, Berlitz). Macmillan.

Berlitz Travel Guide to Corfu. Berlitz Editors. 1977. pap. 4.95 o.p. (ISBN 0-02-969080-3, Berlitz). Macmillan.

Berlitz Travel Guide to Costa Brava. Berlitz Editors. 1977. pap. 4.95 o.p. (ISBN 0-02-969110-9, Berlitz). Macmillan.

Berlitz Travel Guide to Costa Dorada & Barcelona. Berlitz Editors. 1977. pap. 4.95 o.p. (ISBN 0-02-969150-8, Berlitz). Macmillan.

Berlitz Travel Guide to Crete. Berlitz Editors. 1977. pap. 4.95 o.p. (ISBN 0-02-969600-3, Berlitz). Macmillan.

Berlitz Travel Guide to Istria. Berlitz Editors. 1977. pap. 4.95 o.p. (ISBN 0-02-969170-2, Berlitz). Macmillan.

Berlitz Travel Guide to Moscow. Berlitz Editors. 1976. pap. 4.95 o.p. (ISBN 0-02-969300-4, 0-02-96930, Berlitz). Macmillan.

Berlitz Travel Guide to Venice. Berlitz Editors. 1977. pap. 4.95 o.p. (ISBN 0-02-969560-0, Berlitz). Macmillan.

Berlitz Travel Guide: Virgin Islands. Berlitz Editors. (Illus.). 128p. 1977. pap. 4.95 o.p. (Berlitz). Macmillan.

Berlitz Travel Kits: China. Berlitz Editors. 1986. pap. 19.95 o.p. (ISBN 0-02-964790-8, Berlitz); one-hour cassette incl. o.p. Macmillan.

Berlitz Travel Kits: France. Berlitz Editors. 1985. 14.95 o.p. (ISBN 0-02-964740-1, Berlitz). Macmillan.

Berlitz Travel Kits: Great Britain. Berlitz Editors. 1985. 14.95 o.p. (ISBN 0-02-964730-4, Berlitz). MacMillan.

Berlitz Travel Kits: Hong Kong. Berlitz Editors. 1986. 19.95 o.p. (ISBN 0-02-964810-6, Berlitz); one-hour cassette incl. o.p. Macmillan.

Berlitz Travel Kits: Italy. Berlitz Editors. 1985. 14.95 o.p. (ISBN 0-02-964760-6, Berlitz). MacMillan.

Berlitz Travel Kits: Japan. Berlitz Editors. 1986. 19.95 o.p. (ISBN 0-02-964800-9, Berlitz); one-hour cassette incl. o.p. Macmillan.

Berlitz Travel Kits: Mexico. Berlitz Editors. 1985. 14.95 o.p. (ISBN 0-02-964710-X, Berlitz). MacMillan.
Berlitz Travel Kits: Singapore. Berlitz Editors. 1986. 14.95 o.p. (ISBN 0-02-964820-3, Berlitz); one-hour cassette incl. o.p. Macmillan.
Berlitz Travel Kits: Spain. Berlitz Editors. 1985. 14.95 o.p. (ISBN 0-02-964720-7, Berlitz). MacMillan.
Berlitz Travel Kits: Switzerland. Berlitz Editors. 1985. 19.95 o.p. (ISBN 0-02-964750-9, Berlitz). MacMillan.
Berlitz Travel Kits: Thailand. Berlitz Editors. 1986. 14.95 o.p. (ISBN 0-02-964870-X, Berlitz); one-hour cassette incl. o.p. Macmillan.
Bernard Baruch: The Adventures of a Wall Street Legend. James Grant. 384p. 1985. pap. 9.95 o.p. (ISBN 0-671-41887-4, Touchstone Bks). S&S.
Bernard M. Baruch: The Adventures of a Wall Street Legend. James Grant. (Illus.). 352p. 1983. 19.25 o.p. (ISBN 0-671-41886-6). S&S.
Bernard Shaw. Eric Bentley. 288p. 1976. pap. 3.95 o.p. (ISBN 0-393-00818-5, N818, Norton Lib). Norton.
Bernard Shaw & Alfred Douglas: A Correspondence. George Bernard Shaw & Alfred Douglas. Ed. by Mary Hyde. LC 82-5567. (Illus.). 280p. 1982. 24.50 o.p. (ISBN 0-89919-128-2). Ticknor & Fields.
Berne Convention for the Protection of Literary & Artistic Works: Texts, 1968 Supplement (Stockholm Act, 1967) 1968. loose leaf bdg. 7.50 o.p. (ISBN 0-686-53124-8, WIPO6, WIPO). UNIPUB.
Bernoulli Seventeen Thirteen, Bayes Seventeen Sixty-Three, Laplace Eighteen Thirteen: Proceedings, Anniversary Vol. International Research Seminar - Berkeley - 1963. Ed. by Lucien M. Lecam & Jerzy Neyman. (Illus.). 1965. pap. 17.20 o.p. (ISBN 0-387-03260-6). Springer-Verlag.
Berrigans: A Bibliography of Published Works by Daniel, Philip, & Elizabeth Berrigan. Anne Klejment. LC 78-68214. (Garland Reference Library of Humanities: No. 154). 1979. lib. bdg. 36.00 o.p. (ISBN 0-8240-9788-2). Garland Pub.
Berry Cookbook. Kyle D. Fulwiler. LC 81-1877. 110p. 1981. pap. 5.95 o.p. (ISBN 0-914718-59-2). Pacific Search.
Berserker Throne. Fred Saberhagen. 1985. 14.70 o.p. (ISBN 0-671-55836-6). S&S.
Berserker Throne. Fred Saberhagen. 1985. pap. 6.95 o.p. (ISBN 0-671-50387-1, Fireside). S&S.
Bert & Barney. Ned Delaney. (Illus.). (gr. k-3). 1979. PLB 7.95 o.p. (ISBN 0-395-28377-9). HM.
Bertaud Model: A Model for the Analysis of Alternatives for Low-Income Shelter in the Developing World. PADCO, Inc. Staff & World Bank Staff. (Urban Development Technical Paper: No. 2). 153p. 1981. pap. 8.00 o.p. (ISBN 0-686-39777-0, UD-0002). World Bank.
Bertelsmann Woerterbuch Deutsch-Franzoesisch, Franzoesisch-Deutsch. Karl Knauer. 640p. (Ger. & Fr.). 1974. 17.50 o.p. (ISBN 3-570-01486-X, M-7307, Pub. by Bertelsmann Lexikon VVA). French & Eur.
Berthe Morisot. Kathleen Adler & Tamar Garb. LC 86-29287. 128p. 1987. 29.95 o.p. (ISBN 0-8014-2053-9). Cornell U Pr.
Bertolt Brecht: Poems - 1913-1956. Bertolt Brecht. Ed. by John Willett & Ralph Manheim. 627p. 1987. 29.95 o.p. (ISBN 0-416-00081-9, 0126); pap. 14.95 o.p. (ISBN 0-416-00091-6, 0127). Routledge Chapman & Hall.
Bertrand of Brittany: Biography of Messire du Guesclin. Roger Vercel. Tr. by M. Saunders. 1934. 39.50x o.p. (ISBN 0-686-83487-9). Elliots Bks.
Bertrand Russell. H. W. Leggett. 1950. (ISBN 0-8022-0952-1). Philos Lib.
Bertrand Russell & His World. Ronald Clark. LC 81-50617. (Illus.). 1981. 14.95 o.p. (ISBN 0-500-13070-1). Thames Hudson.
Bertrand Russell's Dictionary of Mind, Matter, & Morals. Lester Denon. 304p. 1952. (ISBN 0-8022-1413-4). Philos Lib.
Beryllium. Ed. by Herbert E. Stokinger. (Atomic Energy Commission Monographs). 1966. 23.50 o.p. (ISBN 0-12-671850-4). Acad Pr.
Beschreibung der Bekanntesten Kupfermunzen, 7 Vols. Joseph Neumann. (Illus.). 1858-72. Set. 175.00 o.p. (ISBN 0-384-41160-6); Vol. 1-6. 25.00 ea. o.p.; Vol. 7 Index. 30.00 o.p. (ISBN 0-685-13352-4). Johnson Repr.
Beseiged. Thomas Cullinan. 1973. pap. 1.25 o.p. (ISBN 0-380-01049-6, 15453). Avon.
Beside Still Waters. Mrs. Glen Karssen. 160p. 1985. 10.95 o.p. (ISBN 0-89109-536-5). NavPress.
Besprechungen. Adolph Muschg. (Poly Ser.: No. 10). 148p. (Ger.). 1982. 13.95 o.p. (ISBN 0-8176-1156-8). Birkhauser.
Bess of Hardwick. David N. Durant. LC 77-24459. 1978. 10.95 o.p. (ISBN 0-689-10835-4, Atheneum). Macmillan.
Bess W. Truman. Margaret Truman. 720p. 1987. lib. bdg. 21.95 o.p. (ISBN 0-8161-4179-7, Large Print Bks); pap. 13.95x o.p. (ISBN 0-8161-4180-0, Large Print Bks). G K Hall.
Bessemer & Lake Erie Railroad, 1869-1969. Roy C. Beaver. LC 73-97230. (Illus.). 200p. 1969. 20.95 o.p. (ISBN 0-87095-033-9). Gldn West Bks.
Best American Short Stories. Martha Foley. 1975. Vol. 1. 10.00 o.p. (ISBN 0-395-20719-3); Vol. 2. 10.00 o.p. (ISBN 0-395-24770-5). HM.
Best American Short Stories Nineteen Eighty. Ed. by Stanley Elkin & Shannon Ravenel. 496p. 1980. 12.95 o.p. (ISBN 0-395-29446-0). HM.
Best American Short Stories Nineteen Eighty-Two. Ed. by John Gardner. 1982. 14.45 o.p. (ISBN 0-395-32207-3). HM.
Best American Short Stories of Nineteen Seventy-Nine. Ed. by Joyce Carol Oates & Shannon Ravenel. 1979. 11.95 o.p. (ISBN 0-395-27769-8). HM.
Best American Short Stories, 1971. Ed. by Martha Foley & David Burnett. 1971. 7.50 o.p. (ISBN 0-395-12709-2). HM.
Best American Short Stories 1973. Ed. by Martha Foley. 1973. 8.95 o.p. (ISBN 0-395-17119-9). HM.
Best American Short Stories 1974. Ed. by Martha Foley. LC 16-11387. 400p. 1974. 9.95 o.p. (ISBN 0-395-19415-6). HM.
Best American Short Stories 1978. Ed. by Theodore Solotaroff & Shannon Ravenel. 1978. 11.95 o.p. (ISBN 0-395-27104-5). HM.
Best American Short Stories, 1981. Ed. by Hortense Calisher & Shannon Ravenel. 1981. 12.95 o.p. (ISBN 0-395-31259-0). HM.
Best American Short Stories 1983. Ann Tyler & Shannon Ravenel. 1983. 14.45 o.p. (ISBN 0-395-34428-X); pap. 7.70 o.p. (ISBN 0-395-34844-7). HM.
Best American Short Stories 1984. Ed. by John Updike & Shannon Ravenel. 1984. 14.45 o.p. (ISBN 0-395-35413-7); pap. 8.70 o.p. (ISBN 0-395-36512-0). HM.
Best American Short Stories 1986. Ed. by Raymond Carver & Shannon Ravenel. 1986. 15.45 o.p. (ISBN 0-395-38399-4); pap. 8.70 o.p. (ISBN 0-395-38398-6). HM.
Best Bars of New York: Two Hundred & Fifty of the Most Exciting Watering Holes in Manhattan. Caroline Latham. 204p. (Orig.). 1984. pap. 8.95 o.p. (ISBN 0-399-51083-4, Perigee). Putnam Pub Group.
Best Basketball Booster. S. C. Lee. LC 72-91390. (Strode Superstar Ser.). (Illus.). 134p. (gr. 3-6). 1974. 4.95 o.p. (ISBN 0-87397-040-3). Strode.
Best Baths. Creative Homeowner Press Editors. LC 80-67154. (Illus., Orig.). 1980. 22.95 o.p. (ISBN 0-932944-19-1); pap. 6.95 o.p. (ISBN 0-932944-20-5). Creative Homeowner.
Best Bed & Breakfast in the World. Rev. ed. Sigourney Welles & Jill Darbey. LC 82-83265. 318p. 1984. pap. 10.95 o.p. (ISBN 0-88742-002-8). Globe Pequot.
Best Bed & Breakfast in the World: England, Scotland & Wales. Sigourney Welles & Jill Darbey. LC 85-45807. 340p. 1988. pap. 12.95 o.p. (ISBN 0-87106-789-7). Globe Pequot.
Best Bed & Breakfast in the World: United Kingdom, 1987 Edition. Sigourney Welles & Jill Darbey. (Illus.). 315p. 1987. pap. 11.95 o.p. (ISBN 0-88742-102-4). Globe Pequot.
Best Bed & Breakfast in the World 1986: The United Kingdom & Ireland. Sigourney Welles & Jill Darbey. LC 85-45807. 340p. 1986. pap. 10.95 o.p. (ISBN 0-88742-070-2). Globe Pequot.
Best Bike Rides Around Portland. Anndy Wiselogle & Virginia Church. (Illus.). 118p. (Orig.). 1987. pap. text ed. 8.95 o.p. (ISBN 0-9618290-0-1). Bicycle Commuter.
Best Biker Fiction, No. 3. Ed. by Easyriders Staff. (Paisano Bks.). 224p. (Orig.). 1984. pap. 2.95 o.p. (ISBN 0-440-01832-3). Dell.
Best Book of Framework. Alan Simpson. 1985. pap. 17.95 o.p. (ISBN 0-672-22421-6). Sams.
Best Book of Symphony. Alan Simpson. 1985. pap. 21.95 o.p. (ISBN 0-672-22420-8). Sams.
Best Books, 6 Vols. 3rd. ed. William S. Sonnenschein. LC 68-58760. 3809p. 1969. Repr. of 1935 ed. Set. 350.00x o.p. (ISBN 0-8103-3362-7). Gale.
Best Christmas Pageant Ever. Barbara Robinson. (Illus.). 96p. (gr. 5 up). 1979. pap. 2.95 o.p. (ISBN 0-380-48066-2, Flare). Avon.
Best Christmas Pageant Ever. Barbara Robinson. (Illus.). 96p. (gr. 3-5). 1979. pap. 2.25 o.p. (ISBN 0-380-00769-X, Camelot). Avon.
Best Dad Is a Good Lover. Charlie W. Shedd. 1978. pap. 1.75 o.p. (ISBN 0-380-01931-0, 37804). Avon.
Best English see Needed Words.
Best European Travel Tips. 5th ed. John Whitman. 226p. 1987. 6.95 o.s.i. (ISBN 0-671-63625-1). P-H.
Best Ever How-to-Get-a-Job Book. Richard H. Stansfield. LC 80-967. 176p. 1980. 10.95 o.s.i. (ISBN 0-8019-6974-3); pap. 6.95 o.p. (ISBN 0-8019-6975-1). Chilton.
Best Evidence. David Lifton. 1982. pap. 6.95 o.p. (ISBN 0-440-00586-8). Dell.
Best Excuse. Donald Carroll. 176p. 1983. 14.95 o.p. (ISBN 0-698-11219-9, Coward). Putnam Pub Group.
Best Film Plays Nineteen Forty-Five. John Gassner & Dudley Nicholas. Ed. by Bruce S. Kupelnick. LC 76-52103. (Classics of Film Literature Ser.). 1978. lib. bdg. 39.00 o.p. (ISBN 0-8240-2876-7). Garland Pub.
Best Film Plays, Nineteen Forty-Three to Forty-Four. John Gassner & Dudley Nichols. LC 76-52102. (Classics of Film Literature Ser.: Vol. 11). (Illus.). 1977. Repr. of 1945 ed. lib. bdg. 39.00 o.p. (ISBN 0-8240-2875-9). Garland Pub.
Best Fire Pictures of Nineteen Eighty-Five. Ed. by Mary Quinlan. LC 86-60372. (Illus.). 128p. (Orig.). 1986. pap. 24.95 o.p. (ISBN 0-933341-44-X). Quinlan Pr.
Best Foods of Russia see Cooking from the Caucasus.
Best Foods of Russia: Culinary Classics from the Caucasus. Sonia Uvezian. LC 76-12463. (Illus.). 1976. 8.95 o.p. (ISBN 0-15-111905-8). HarBraceJ.
Best Fragments from France. Bruce Bairnsfather. Ed. by Valmai Holt & Tonie Holt. (Illus.). 1983. pap. 9.95 o.p. (ISBN 0-903852-40-3, Pub. by Milestone Pubns UK). Seven Hills Bk Dists.
Best Friends. Archie Parrish & John Parrish. 192p. 1986. 10.95 o.p. (ISBN 0-8407-9057-0). Oliver-Nelson.
Best Health Ideas I Know: My Personal Plan for Living. Robert Rodale. 1983. pap. 1.50 o.p. (ISBN 0-380-00360-0, 24513). Avon.
Best Intentions: The Education & Killing of Edmund Perry. Robert S. Anson. LC 86-10150. (Illus.). 224p. 1987. 17.45 o.s.i. (ISBN 0-394-55274-1). Random.
Best Is Yet to Be. Kurt Rommel. Tr. by David L. Scheidt from Ger. LC 74-26327. (Illus.). 80p. 1975. pap. 0.50x o.p. (ISBN 0-8006-1096-2, Fortress). Augsburg Fortress.
Best is Yet to Be. Philip D. Wheaton. 249p. 1983. 14.95 o.p. (ISBN 0-396-08235-1). Dodd.
Best I've Read. Walter A. Weiss. 1973. text ed. 16.50x o.p. (ISBN 0-8422-5138-3); pap. text ed. 9.50x o.p. (ISBN 0-8422-0359-1). Irvington.
Best Judo. Isao Inokuma & Nobuyuki Sato. LC 79-84656. (Illus.). 256p. 1979. 24.95 o.p. (ISBN 0-87011-381-X). Kodansha.
Best Karate: Kata: Heian & Tekki. Masatoshi Nakayama. LC 77-74829. (Best Karate Ser.: Vol. 5). 1979. pap. 11.95 o.p. (ISBN 0-87011-379-8). Kodansha.
Best Laid Plans. Elaine R. Chase. (Finding Mr. Right Ser.). 224p. 1983. pap. 2.75 o.p. (ISBN 0-380-82743-3, 82743-3). Avon.
Best Laid Plans. Gail Parent. 1981. pap. 2.75 o.s.i. (ISBN 0-345-29480-7). Ballantine.
Best Lawyers in America. Steven Naifeh & Gregory W. Smith. 1984. pap. 8.95 o.p. (ISBN 0-399-51068-0, Perigee). Putnam Pub Group.
Best-Loved Bible Stories: Old Testament & New Testament, 2 vols. Ed. by World Book, Inc. Staff. LC 79-55309. (Illus.). 90p. (gr. 4-8). 1980. write for info. o.p. (ISBN 0-7166-2059-6). World Bk.
Best Loved Recipes of the American People. Ida B. Allen. LC 81-43453. 648p. 1982. pap. 8.95 o.p. (ISBN 0-385-18015-2, Dolp). Doubleday.
Best Loved Short Stories of Jesse Stewart. Jesse Stewart. Intro. by H. Edward Richardson. 448p. 1982. text ed. 14.95 o.p. (ISBN 0-07-062305-8). McGraw.
Best Mysteries of Isaac Asimov. Isaac Asimov. LC 85-31199. (Illus.). 360p. 1986. 17.95 o.s.i. (ISBN 0-385-19783-7). Doubleday.
Best Mystery & Suspense Plays of the Modern Theatre. Ed. by Stanley Richards. 1979. pap. 7.95 o.p. (ISBN 0-380-46466-7, 46466). Avon.
Best of Bon Appetit. Date not set. pap. (ISBN 0-89535-043-2). Knapp Pr.
Best of Bon Appetit. Bon Appetit Magazine Editors. LC 79-2384. (Illus.). 1979. 19.95 o.p. (ISBN 0-89535-008-4). Knapp Pr.
Best of Bon Appetit, Vol 1. Bon Appetit Magazine Editors. LC 85-7620. (Illus.). 1985. 9.95 o.p. (ISBN 0-89535-164-1). Knapp Pr.
Best of Bon Appetit, Vol. 2. Bon Appetit Magazine Editors. LC 85-7620. (Illus.). 1985. 9.95 o.p. (ISBN 0-89535-165-X). Knapp Pr.
Best of Book Bonanza. Lee B. Hopkins. LC 79-20668. 243p. 1979. professional ed. 18.95 o.p. (ISBN 0-03-056714-9, HoltC); pap. 14.95 o.p. (ISBN 0-03-052681-7). HR&W.
Best of Both Worlds: A Guide to Home-Based Careers. Joan W. Anderson. LC 82-4283. 188p. (Orig.). 1982. 10.95 o.p. (ISBN 0-932620-14-0); pap. 6.95 o.p. (ISBN 0-932620-13-2). Betterway Pubns.
Best of Bret Harte. Wilhemina Harper. Ed. by Aimee Peters. (Illus.). 8.95 o.p. (ISBN 0-395-07778-8). HM.
Best of C. G. Chappell. Clovis G. Chappell. (Best Ser.). 240p. 1984. pap. 5.95 o.p. (ISBN 0-8010-2500-1). Baker Bk.
Best of C. L. Moore. Ed. by Lester Del Rey. LC 77-5293. 1977. Repr. of 1976 ed. 9.95 o.s.i. (ISBN 0-8008-0722-7). Taplinger.
Best of California: Some People, Places & Institutions of the Most Exciting State in the Nation, as Featured in California Magazine, 1976-1986. Ed. by California Magazine Staff & Harold Hayes. 320p. (Orig.). 1986. pap. 9.95 o.p. (ISBN 0-88496-245-8). Capra Pr.
Best of Cold Foods. Ed. by H P Books Staff. LC 85-60201. (Illus.). 240p. 1985. 17.95 o.p. (ISBN 0-89586-336-7). Price Stern.
Best of Colorado. Susan Kaye. LC 88-18714. (Illus.). 150p. (Orig.). 1986. pap. 8.95 o.p. (ISBN 0-87108-703-0). Pruett.
Best of Cooking for All Occasions. Christian Teubner & Annette Wolter. LC 86-81047. 192p. 1986. 9.95 o.p. (ISBN 0-89586-243-3). Price Stern.
Best of Country Music: A Guide to 750 Great Albums. John Morthland. LC 83-14238. (Illus.). 456p. 1984. pap. 14.95 o.p. (ISBN 0-385-19192-8, Dolp). Doubleday.
Best of Dwight L. Moody. Ed. by Dwight L. Moody & Ralph G. Turnbull. (Best Ser.). 1979. pap. 6.95 o.p. (ISBN 0-8010-6216-0). Baker Bk.
Best of Educational Software for the Commodore 64. Gary G. Bitter & Kay Gore. LC 84-51976. 250p. 1984. pap. 16.95 o.p. (ISBN 0-89588-223-X). SYBEX.
Best of Everything. Rona Jaffe. 1976. pap. 2.25 o.p. (ISBN 0-380-00581-6, 54221). Avon.
Best of "Food & Wine" Food & Wine Magazine Editors. LC 84-12415. (Illus.). 240p. 1984. 19.95 o.p. (ISBN 0-385-19619-9). Doubleday.
Best of France. rev. ed. Henri Gault & Christian Millau. LC 85-17445. (Illus.). 624p. 1986. pap. 14.95 o.p. (ISBN 0-517-55402-X). Crown.
Best of France. Christian Millau. (Illus.). 608p. 1982. 22.95 o.p. (ISBN 0-517-54772-4); pap. 13.95 o.p. (ISBN 0-517-54773-2). Crown.
Best of Friends. Josephine H. Aldridge. LC 60-18901. (Illus.). (gr. k-2). 1963. PLB 4.95 o.p. (ISBN 0-395-27693-4, Pub. by Parnassus). HM.
Best of Friends. David Roth. LC 82-23378. 208p. (gr. 7 up). 1983. 10.45 o.p. (ISBN 0-395-33889-1). HM.
Best of Friends: Profiles of Men & Friendship. David T. Michaelis. LC 84-22316. (Illus.). 320p. 1985. pap. 7.95 o.p. (ISBN 0-688-03933-2, Quill). Morrow.
Best of Friends, the Worst of Enemies: Womens Hidden Power over Women. Eva L. Margolies. LC 84-26066. 336p. 1985. 16.95 o.p. (ISBN 0-385-27872-1, Dial). Doubleday.
Best of Gracian. Thomas G. Corvan. 96p. 1964. (ISBN 0-8022-0305-1). Philos Lib.
Best of H. A. Ironside. H. A. Ironside. 1981. pap. 4.95 o.p. (ISBN 0-87213-394-X). Loizeaux.
Best of Hagar the Horrible. Dik Browne. (Illus.). 240p. 1985. pap. 10.95 o.p. (ISBN 0-03-005599-7). H Holt & Co.
Best of Instaration 1976. (Illus.). 115p. pap. 16.00 o.p. (ISBN 0-317-53258-8). Noontide.
Best of Instaration 1977. 127p. 1986. pap. 16.00 o.p. (ISBN 0-317-53259-6). Noontide.
Best of Italian Cooking, Texas Style: Cav Valentine. Belfiglio. 104p. 1985. 11.95 o.p. (ISBN 0-89015-459-7). Eakin Pr.
Best of Italy. Henri Gault & Christian Millau. 1984. pap. 13.95 o.p. (ISBN 0-517-55032-6). Crown.
Best of Jazz: Basin Street to Harlem. Humphrey Lyttelton. LC 79-13159. (Illus.). 1979. 8.95 o.s.i. (ISBN 0-8008-0727-8, Crescendo). Taplinger.
Best of Jazz I: Basin Street to Harlem, 1917-1930. Humphrey Lyttelton. LC 79-131598. (Illus.). 214p. 1982. pap. 5.95 o.s.i. (ISBN 0-8008-0729-4, Crescendo). Taplinger.
Best of Jazz II: Enter the Giants, 1931-1944. Humphrey Lyttelton. LC 81-21418. (Illus.). 239p. 1982. 10.95 o.s.i. (ISBN 0-8008-0728-6, Crescendo). Taplinger.
Best of Jazz II: Enter the Giants, 1931-1944. Humphrey Lyttleton. LC 81-21418. (Illus.). 239p. 1983. pap. 6.95 o.s.i. (ISBN 0-8008-0731-6, Crescendo). Taplinger.
Best of Jenny's Kitchen: Cooking Naturally with Vegetables. Jennifer Raymond. 192p. 1982. pap. 4.95 o.p. (ISBN 0-380-58461-1, 58461-1). Avon.

Best of Joe Weider's Muscle & Fitness Women's Weight Training & Bodybuilding Training Tips & Routines. Joe Weider & Betty Weider. (Illus.). 128p. 1982. 15.50 o.p. (ISBN 0-8092-5755-6); pap. 7.95 o.p. (ISBN 0-8092-5754-8). Contemp Bks.

Best of L. A. The L.A. Weekly's Guide to the Very Best That Los Angeles Has to Offer. L. A. Weekly Staff. Ed. by Mary B. Crain. LC 84-3139. 160p. (Orig.). 1984. pap. 7.95 o.p. (ISBN 0-87701-306-3). Chronicle Bks.

Best of London. rev. ed. Henry Gault & Christian Millau. (Illus.). 1986. pap. 13.95 o.p. (ISBN 0-517-55956-0). Crown.

Best of Los Angeles. Henri Gault & Christian Millau. 1984. pap. 13.95 o.p. (ISBN 0-517-55034-2). Crown.

Best of Marion Zimmer Bradley. Ed. by Martin H. Greenberg. 367p. 1985. 16.95 o.s.i. (ISBN 0-89733-165-6); pap. 6.95 o.p. (ISBN 0-89733-166-4). Academy Chi Pubs.

Best of Modern Humor. Mordecai Richler. LC 83-48102. 400p. 1983. 17.95 o.p. (ISBN 0-394-51531-5). Knopf.

Best of New York. Henri Gault & Christian Millau. 384p. 1982. 5.98 o.p. (ISBN 0-517-54770-8); pap. 11.95 o.p. (ISBN 0-517-54771-6). Crown.

Best of New York. rev. & updated ed. Henri Gault & Christian Millau. 1984. pap. 13.95 o.p. (ISBN 0-517-55328-7). Crown.

Best of Old Cars, 3 Vols. Old Cars Editors. LC 78-51020. (Illus.). 1978. Vol.1. pap. 10.95 o.s.i. (ISBN 0-87341-017-3); Vol.2. pap. 8.95 o.s.i. (ISBN 0-87341-040-8); Vol.3. pap. 11.95 o.s.i. (ISBN 0-87341-041-6). Krause Pubns.

Best of Old Cars, Vol. 4. LC 78-51020. (Illus.). 550p. 1983. pap. 11.95 o.s.i. (ISBN 0-87341-033-5). Krause Pubns.

Best of Old Cars, Vol. 6. Ed. by Old Cars Editors. LC 79-88062. (Illus.). 1600p. 1987. pap. 11.95 o.s.i. (ISBN 0-87341-098-X). Krause Pubns.

Best of Paris. rev. ed. Henri Gault & Christian Millau. 1986. pap. 14.95 o.p. (ISBN 0-517-55401-1). Crown.

Best of Paris. Gault Millau. LC 82-13064. 608p. 1982. 22.95 o.p. (ISBN 0-517-54774-0); pap. 14.95 o.p. (ISBN 0-517-54775-9). Crown.

Best of Photojournalism, 5: People, Places, & Events of 1979. National Press Photographers Association Staff. LC 77-81586. (National Press Photographers Association, University of Missouri Journalism School Ser.). (Illus.). 256p. 1980. 24.95 o.p. (ISBN 0-8262-0321-3). U of Mo Pr.

Best of Polish Cooking: Recipes for Entertaining & Special Occasions. Karen West. 132p. 1983. 9.95 o.p. (ISBN 0-88254-863-8). Hippocrene Bks.

Best of Sail Cruising: A Selection of Articles from Sail Magazine. (Illus.). 1978. 11.95 o.p. (ISBN 0-393-03227-2). Norton.

Best of Sail Magazine. Ed. by Sail Magazine. (Illus.). 13.95 o.p. (ISBN 0-393-03261-2). Norton.

Best of Sail Trim: A Selection of Articles from Sail Magazine. 1975. 14.95 o.p. (ISBN 0-393-03189-6). Norton.

Best of Smithsonian. LC 81-6534. (Illus.). 320p. 1981. 27.50 o.p. (ISBN 0-89599-007-5, Dist. by Crown). Smithsonian Bks.

Best of Smithsonian. Smithsonian Magazine Editors. 320p. 1981. 27.50 o.p. (ISBN 0-517-54526-8, Harmony). Crown.

Best of Store Designs. (Illus.). 240p. 1987. 49.95 o.p. (ISBN 0-317-65501-9, 60-5676). Natl Ret Merch.

Best of Store Designs. The National Retail Merchants Association Staff & The Institute of Store Planners' Store Interior Design Competition Staff. LC 85-6445. (Illus.). 240p. 1986. 55.00 o.p. (ISBN 0-86636-012-3). PBC Intl Inc.

Best of Store Designs Two. National Retail Merchants Association Staff. Ed. by Carol Denby. LC 86-9448. (Library of Applied Design). (Illus.). 256p. 1986. 55.00 o.p. (ISBN 0-86636-015-8). PBC Intl Inc.

Best of Sydney J. Harris. Sydney J. Harris. LC 75-28012. 1975. 10.00 o.p. (ISBN 0-395-21980-9). HM.

Best of the Old Farmer's Almanac. Will Forpe. (Illus.). 1977. 16.95 o.p. (ISBN 0-8246-0209-9). Jonathan David.

Best of the Old Farmer's Almanac. Ed. by Will Forpe. LC 78-6656. (Illus.). 1978. pap. 4.95 o.p. (ISBN 0-15-611863-7, Harv). HarBraceJ.

Best of the Outer Banks. Carole M. Longmeyer. (Lost Colony Collection Ser.). (Illus.). 200p. (Orig.). 1983. pap. 5.00 o.p. (ISBN 0-935326-43-X). Gallopade Pub Group.

Best of the Proceedings Microcomputers in Education Conferences 1982-84. Ed. by Donna Craighead & Gary G. Bitter. LC 84-23098. (Computers in Education Ser.). 189p. 1984. 30.00 o.p. (ISBN 0-88175-092-1, Computer Sci Pr). W H Freeman.

Best of the West, 2 vols. Ed. by Reader's Digest Editors. LC 75-10496. (Illus.). 1246p. 1976. 17.97 o.p. (ISBN 0-89577-027-X). RD Assn.

Best of the West: The Texas Monthly Guidebook. Ron Butler. Ed. by Barbara Rodriquez. 224p. 1983. 9.95 o.p. (ISBN 0-932012-54-X). Texas Month Pr.

Best of These Days. Ed. by Larry M. Correu. LC 82-13415. 132p. 1983. 8.95 o.s.i. (ISBN 0-664-21391-X, Westminster). Westminster John Knox.

Best of Tombstone Humor. Richard De'ath. (Illus.). 192p. (Orig.). 1988. pap. 5.95 o.p. (ISBN 0-7137-1995-8, Pub. by Javelin England). Sterling.

Best of Try This One. Ed. by Thom Schultz. (Illus.). 80p. (Orig.). 1977. pap. 5.95 o.p. (ISBN 0-936664-01-0). Group Pub.

Best of Walter A. Maier. Paul L. Maier. 1980. pap. 7.95 o.p. (ISBN 0-570-03823-5, 12-2786). Concordia.

Best Place in the World: A Wrinkles Storybook. Toni Scribner. LC 86-6555. 12p. (ps-1). 1986. 4.95 o.s.i. (ISBN 0-394-88431-0, BYR). Random.

Best Places see Northwest Best Places.

Best Places to Kiss in the Northwest. Paula Begoun. 128p. 1986. pap. 7.95 o.p. (ISBN 0-9615514-1-0). Beginning Pr.

Best Places to Stay in New England. Christina Tree & Bruce Shaw. LC 85-27058. (Gambit Guides Ser.). (Illus.). 354p. (Orig.). 1986. pap. 9.95 o.p. (ISBN 0-916782-74-3, Dist. by Kampmann & Co.). Harvard Common Pr.

Best Plays. Anton Chekhov. Tr. by Stark Young. LC 56-8837. 6.95 o.p. (ISBN 0-394-60459-8). Modern Lib.

Best Plays of Racine: Andromaque, Britannicus, Phaedre, Athalia. Jean Racine. Tr. by Lacy Lockert from Fr. 1936. pap. 12.95x o.p. (ISBN 0-691-01251-2). Princeton U Pr.

Best Practices: How to Avoid Surprises in the World's Most Complicated Technical Process, the Transition from Development to Production. Ed. by Douglas O. Patterson. (NAVSO P-6071 Ser.). (Illus.). 326p. 1986. pap. 19.00 o.p. (ISBN 0-317-47014-0, S/N 008-050-00234-4). USGPO.

Best Pubs of Great Britain, 1987-1988. Compiled by Neil Hanson. Orig. Title: Good Beer Guide, 1986. (Illus.). 320p. 1986. pap. 9.95 o.p. (ISBN 0-88742-104-0). Globe Pequot.

Best Recipes from the Backs of Boxes, Bottles, Cans & Jars. Ceil Dyer. LC 79-17925. (Illus.). 194p. 1982. text ed. 11.95 o.p. (ISBN 0-07-018551-4); pap. text ed. 5.95 o.p. (ISBN 0-07-018550-6). McGraw.

Best Recipes Yearbook 1987. Better Homes & Gardens Editors. 1987. 18.95 o.p. (ISBN 0-696-02129-3). BH&G.

Best Reference Books 1981-1985. Ed. by Bohdan S. Wynar. LC 86-15316. xxii, 504p. 1986. lib. bdg. 45.00 o.p. (ISBN 0-87287-554-7). Libs Unl.

Best Restaurants & Others: Washington, D. C. rev. ed. Phyllis C. Richman. LC 82-18897. (Best Restaurants Ser.). (Illus.). 272p. (Orig.). 1982. pap. 4.95 o.p. (ISBN 0-89286-200-9, One Hund One Prods). Ortho.

Best Restaurants Chicago & Suburbs. rev. ed. Illus. by Sherman Kaplan. LC 82-8173. (Best Restaurants Ser.). (Illus.). 272p. (Orig.). 1983. pap. 4.95 o.p. (ISBN 0-89286-201-7, One Hund One Prods). Ortho.

Best Restaurants Florida's Gold Coast. Robert W. Tolf. LC 79-3723. (Best Restaurant Ser.). (Illus.). 222p. (Orig.). 1979. pap. 3.95 o.p. (ISBN 0-89286-161-4, One Hund One Prods). Ortho.

Best Restaurants Los Angeles. Colman Andrews. LC 82-8173. (Best Restaurants Ser.). (Illus.). 224p. (Orig.). 1982. pap. 4.95 o.p. (ISBN 0-89286-203-3, One Hund One Prods). Ortho.

Best Restaurants, Los Angeles. rev. ed. Colman Andrews. LC 84-7491. (Best Restaurants Ser.). (Illus.). 272p. 1984. pap. 4.95 o.p. (ISBN 0-89286-236-X, One Hund One Prods). Ortho.

Best Restaurants New England. Patricia Brooks. LC 80-16277. 211p. (Orig.). 1980. pap. write for info. o.p. (One Hund One Prods). Ortho.

Best Restaurants New York. rev. ed. Stendhal. LC 80-18846. 225p. 1980. pap. 3.95 o.p. (ISBN 0-89286-167-3, One Hund One Prods). Ortho.

Best Restaurants New York. Stendhal. LC 78-9420. (Best Restaurant Ser.). (Illus.). pap. 3.95 o.p. (ISBN 0-89286-137-1, One Hund One Prods). Ortho.

Best Restaurants of Los Angeles & Southern California. Ed. by California Critic Editors. LC 78-18227. (Best Restaurants Ser.). (Illus.). 1978. pap. write for info. o.p. (One Hund One Prods). Ortho.

Best Restaurants of San Francisco & Northern California. Ed. by California Critic Editors. LC 75-14337. (Best Restaurants Ser.). (Illus.). 1977. pap. 2.95 o.p. (ISBN 0-89286-117-7, One Hund One Prods). Ortho.

Best Restaurants of Texas. Texas Critic Editors. LC 76-45456. (Best Restaurants Series). (Illus.). 200p. (Orig.). 1976. pap. 2.95 o.p. (ISBN 0-89286-106-1, One Hund One Prods). Ortho.

Best Restaurants of the Pacific Northwest: Pacific Northwest. Bob Rubenstein. LC 76-15698. (Best Restaurants Ser.). (Illus.). 204p. 1976. pap. 2.95 o.p. (ISBN 0-912238-85-2, One Hund One Prods). Ortho.

Best Restaurants, Orange County. Herb Baus. LC 82-81766. (Best Restaurants Ser.). (Illus.). 224p. (Orig.). 1982. pap. 4.95 o.p. (ISBN 0-89286-199-1, One Hund One Prods). Ortho.

Best Restaurants Orange County. rev., exp. ed. Herb Baus. LC 84-7491. (Best Restaurants Ser.). (Illus.). 240p. 1984. pap. 4.95 o.p. (ISBN -089286-235-1, One Hund One Prods). Ortho.

Best Restaurants Orange County. 3rd ed. Herb Baus. LC 87-7656. (Best Restaurants Ser.). (Illus.). 216p. 1987. pap. 4.95 o.p. (ISBN 0-89286-267-X, One Hund One Prods). Ortho.

Best Restaurants: Philadelphia. rev. ed. Elaine Tait. LC 85-10656. (Illus.). 225p. 1985. pap. 4.95 o.p. (ISBN 0-89286-248-3, TX907T34-1985, One Hund One Prods). Ortho.

Best Restaurants Philadelphia & Environs. rev. ed. Elaine Tait. LC 81-38386. (Best Restaurants Ser.). (Illus.). 225p. 1981. pap. 4.95 o.p. (ISBN 0-89286-189-4, One Hund One Prods). Ortho.

Best Restaurants Philadelphia & Environs. Elaine Tait. LC 79-12551. (Best Restaurant Ser.). (Illus.). 236p. 1979. pap. 3.95 o.p. (ISBN 0-89286-150-9, One Hund One Prods). Ortho.

Best Restaurants San Francisco Bay Area. 5th, rev. ed. Jacqueline Killeen & Sharon Silva. (Best Restaurants Ser.). (Illus.). 240p. (Orig.). 1986. pap. 4.95 o.p. (ISBN 0-89286-260-2, One Hund One Prods). Ortho.

Best Restaurants San Francisco Bay Area. Jacqueline Killeen et al. LC 84-7536. (Best Restaurants Ser.). 200p. 1984. pap. 4.95 o.p. (ISBN 0-89286-216-5, One Hund One Prods). Ortho.

Best Restaurants Southern New England. Patricia Brooks. LC 83-61463. (Best Restaurants Ser.). (Illus.). 200p. 1983. pap. 4.95 o.p. (ISBN 0-89286-214-9, One Hund One Prods). Ortho.

Best Restaurants Washington D. C. & Environs. Phyllis C. Richman. LC 80-11923. 256p. (Orig.). 1980. pap. 3.95 o.p. (ISBN 0-89286-166-5, One Hund One Prods). Ortho.

Best Restaurants: Washington D.C. & Environs. 3rd ed. Phyllis C. Richman. LC 85-10658. (Illus.). 272p. (Orig.). 1985. pap. 4.95 o.p. (ISBN 0-89286-249-1, TX907.C547-1985, One Hund One Prods). Ortho.

Best Science Fiction of Issac Asimov. Isaac Asimov. LC 85-31200. 336p. 1986. 17.95 o.s.i. (ISBN 0-385-19782-9). Doubleday.

Best Sellers. Stephen Lewis. 320p. 1981. pap. 2.50 o.s.i. (ISBN 0-8439-0960-9, Pub. by Leisure Bks CT). Dorchester Pub Co.

Best Sellers: Popular Fiction of the 1970s. John Sutherland. 272p. 1981. 21.95x o.p. (ISBN 0-7100-0750-7). Routledge Chapman & Hall.

Best SF of the Year, No. 15. Terry Carr. 384p. 1987. 22.95 o.p. (ISBN 0-575-03912-4, Pub. by Gollancz England). David & Charles.

Best Shotguns Ever Made in America: Seven Vintage Doubles to Shoot & to Treasure. Michael McIntosh. 1981. 17.95 o.s.i. (ISBN 0-684-16825-1, ScribT). Scribner.

Best Sports Stories, 1987. Ed. by Tom Barnidge. LC 45-35124. (Best Sport Stories Ser.). 287p. 1987. 16.95 o.p. (ISBN 0-89204-244-3); pap. 10.95 o.p. (ISBN 0-89204-243-5). Sporting News.

Best Team Money Could Buy. Steve Jacobson. LC 77-15349. 1978. 9.95 o.p. (ISBN 0-689-10856-7, Atheneum). Macmillan.

Best Things in New York Are Free. Marian Hamilton. (Illus.). 560p. (Orig.). 1985. pap. 10.95 o.p. (ISBN 0-916782-75-1). Harvard Common Pr.

Best Times. B. B. Hiller & Neil W. Hiller. 144p. (Orig.). 1986. pap. 2.50 o.p. (ISBN 0-380-75059-7, Flare). Avon.

Best True Ghost Stories of the 20th Century. David C. Knight. LC 83-23075. (Illus.). 160p. 1984. 11.95 o.s.i. (ISBN 0-13-071895-5). P-H.

Best Value Britain. Date not set. (ISBN 0-86145-637-8, Pub. by Auto Assn England). Salem Hse Pubs.

Best Vegetable Recipes from Woman's Day. Woman's Day Editors. 224p. 1980. 10.95 o.p. (ISBN 0-395-27594-6). HM.

Best Way Out. K. Follis Cheatham. LC 81-47528. 168p. 1982. 9.95 o.p. (ISBN 0-15-206741-8, HJ). HarBraceJ.

Best Way to Lose. Janet Dailey. (Nightingale Paperbacks). 1985. pap. 9.95 o.p. (ISBN 0-8161-3699-8, Large Print Bks). G K Hall.

Best Way to Plan Your Day. Robert W. Bell & D. Bruce Lockerbie. 320p. 1989. pap. 4.50 o.p. (ISBN 0-8423-1631-0). Tyndale.

Best Way to Ripton. Maggie S. Davis. LC 82-2940. (Illus.). 32p. (ps-3). 1982. 8.95 o.p. (ISBN 0-8234-0459-5). Holiday.

Best Ways to Make Money. 2nd ed. 87p. 1987. 5.95 o.p. (ISBN 0-88908-650-8). ISC Pr.

Best Western Stories of Lewis B. Patten. Ed. by Bill Pronzini & Martin H. Greenberg. LC 86-26144. (Western Writers Ser.). 184p. 1987. 18.95 o.p. (ISBN 0-8093-1358-8). S Ill U Pr.

Best Western Stories of Steve Frazee. Ed. by Bill Pronzini & Martin H. Greenberg. (Western Writers Ser.). 219p. 1984. 16.95 o.p. (ISBN 0-8093-1174-7). S Ill U Pr.

Best Western Stories of Wayne D. Overholser. Wayne D. Overholser. Ed. by Bill Pronzini & Martin H. Greenberg. LC 83-20111. (Western Writers Ser.). 224p. 1984. 16.95 o.p. (ISBN 0-8093-1145-3). S Ill U Pr.

Best, Worst, Least & Most: The U. S. Book of Rankings. Clark S. Judge. LC 79-2768. 1980. pap. 5.95 o.p. (ISBN 0-15-611865-3, Harv). HarBraceJ.

Best Years-Nineteen Forty-Five to Nineteen Fifty. Joseph C. Goulden. LC 75-41852. 1976. 12.95 o.p. (ISBN 0-689-10708-0, Atheneum). Macmillan.

Bestiaire. Guillaume Apollinaire. (Coll. Les Peintres du Livre). (Illus.). deluxe ed. 24.95 o.p. (ISBN 0-685-37178-6). French & Eur.

Bestiaire ou Cortege d'Orphee. Guillaume Apollinaire. Tr. by Lauren Shakely from Fr. LC 77-23500. (Illus.). 88p. 1977. 4.95 o.p. (ISBN 0-87099-165-5). Metro Mus Art.

Bestiaires. Henri De Montherlant. (Coll. Soleil). 1957. 13.95 o.p. (ISBN 0-685-11046-X). Schoenhof.

Bestiaires. Henry de Montherlant. 1972. 3.95 o.p. (ISBN 0-686-54804-3). Schoenhof.

Bestiary. Stephan M. Sechi & J. Andrew Keith. (Atlantean Trilogy). (Illus.). 140p. 1986. pap. 14.00 o.p. (ISBN 0-9610770-7-7). Bard Games.

Bestiary-Bestiario. Pablo Neruda & Antonio Frasconi. Tr. by Elsa Neuberger. LC 65-11991. (Illus.). 1965. 12.50 o.p. (ISBN 0-15-111910-4). HarBraceJ.

Bestiary-Bestiario. Pablo Neruda & Antonio Frasconi. Tr. by Elsa Neuberger from Span. LC 74-6154. (Illus.). 48p. 1974. pap. 3.95 o.p. (ISBN 0-15-611860-2, Harv). HarBraceJ.

Best's Five Year Historical Exhibits. Best, A. M., Staff. 300p. 1986. pap. 165.00 o.p. A M Best.

Best's Flit Compend. Best, A. M., Staff. 630p. 1986. 20.00 o.p. A M Best.

Beta Lactamases. Ed. by J. M. Hamilton-Miller & J. T. Smith. 1979. 109.00 o.p. (ISBN 0-12-321550-1). Acad Pr.

Betcha Didn'tNo. Andrew B. Courts. 208p. 1988. 10.95 o.p. (ISBN 0-8062-3018-5). Carlton.

Betes Libres et Prisonnieres. Colette. 219p. 1958. 8.95 o.p. (ISBN 0-686-54563-X). French & Eur.

Bething's Folly. Barbara Metzger. 176p. 1982. pap. 2.50 o.p. (ISBN 0-380-61143-0, 61143-0). Avon.

Betrayal. Harold Pinter. LC 78-65251. 1979. 10.00 o.p. (ISBN 0-394-50525-5, GP818). Grove.

Betrayal. Harold Pinter. LC 78-65251. 1979. pap. 6.95 o.p. (ISBN 0-394-17084-9, E724, Ever). Grove.

Betrayal of Innocence. David B. Peters. 160p. 1986. 11.95 o.p. (ISBN 0-8499-0502-8, 0502-8). Word Bks.

Betrayed. Amalie Skram. Tr. by Aileen Hennes. (Mothers of the Novel Ser.). 162p. 1987. 22.50 o.p. (ISBN 0-86358-114-5, 81145, Pub. by Pandora Pr); pap. 8.95 o.p. (ISBN 0-86358-099-8, 80998, Pub. by Pandora Pr). Routledge Chapman & Hall.

Betrayed by F. Scott Fitzgerald. Ron Carlson. 1977. 7.95 o.p. (ISBN 0-393-08775-1). Norton.

Betrayed by Rita Hayworth. Manuel Puig. 1978. pap. 1.65 o.p. (ISBN 0-380-01054-2, 36020, Bard). Avon.

Betrayers of the Truth. William Broad & Nicholas Wade. LC 82-10583. 1983. 14.50 o.p. (ISBN 0-671-44769-6). S&S.

Betrothed. Alessandro Manzoni. Tr. by Archibald Colquhoun. 1983. pap. text ed. 7.95x o.p. (ISBN 0-460-11999-0, Evman). Biblio Dist.

Betsy & Peter Are Different. Gunilla Wolde. LC 78-66265. (Betsy Bks.). (Illus.). (ps). Date not set. 1.95 o.p. (BYR); lib. bdg. write for info. o.p. (ISBN 0-394-95423-8). Random.

Betsy & the Vacuum Cleaner. Gunilla Wolde. LC 78-66266. (Betsy Bks.). (Illus.). (ps). Date not set. 1.95 o.p. (ISBN 0-394-85426-8, BYR); lib. bdg. write for info. o.p. (ISBN 0-394-95426-2). Random.

Betsy Byars Boxed Set. Betsy Byars. (gr. 5-8). 1979. pap. 7.50 o.p. (ISBN 0-380-46748-8, 46748-8, Camelot). Avon.

Bette Davis: A Biography in Photographs. Christopher Nickens. LC 84-22279. (Illus.). 224p. 1985. pap. 14.95 o.p. (ISBN 0-385-19675-X, Dolp). Doubleday.

Bette Davis: A Celebration. Alexander Walker. 1986. 22.50 o.p. (ISBN 0-316-91846-6). Little.

Better, Better Body Book. Marge Frank & Nancy Linton. LC 85-11851. 1985. pap. 10.95 o.p. (ISBN 0-310-42741-X, 12736P). Zondervan.

Better Boat Handling. Des Sleightholme. LC 82-19210. (Illus.). 178p. 1983. 15.00 o.p. (ISBN 0-915160-30-7). Seven Seas.

Better Business Writing for Bigger Profits. Courtland L. Bovee. 1970. text ed. 10.00 o.p. (ISBN 0-682-47127-5, University). Exposition-Phoenix.

Better Health Through Natural Healing: How to Get Well Without Drugs or Surgery. Ross Trattler. 640p. 1985. text ed. 24.95 o.p. (ISBN 0-07-065141-8). McGraw.

Better Homes & Gardens Baby Book. Better Homes & Gardens Editors. 1977. pap. 3.95 o.p. (ISBN 0-553-23821-3). Bantam.

Better Homes & Gardens Best-Recipes Yearbook: 1985. Better Homes & Gardens Editors. 192p. 1985. 14.95 o.p. (ISBN 0-696-02105-6). BH&G.

Better Homes & Gardens Crockery Cooker Cook Book. Better Homes & Gardens Editors. LC 75-40624. (Illus.). 96p. 1976. 6.95 o.p. (ISBN 0-696-01020-8). BH&G.

Better Homes & Gardens Easy Bazaar Crafts. Better Homes & Gardens Editors. 6.95 o.p. (ISBN 0-696-01390-8). BH&G.

Better Homes & Gardens Low-Salt Cooking. Better Homes & Gardens Editors. (Illus.). 96p. 1984. 6.95 o.p. (ISBN 0-696-01320-7). BH&G.

Better Homes & Gardens Microwave Cook Book. Better Homes & Gardens Editors. LC 75-38241. (Illus.). 96p. 1976. 6.95 o.p. (ISBN 0-696-01035-6). BH&G.

Better Homes & Gardens, 1984: Best-Recipes Yearbook. Better Homes & Gardens Editors. (Illus.). 192p. 1984. 14.95 o.p. (ISBN 0-696-02099-8). BH&G.

Better Listening. Hans Fantel. 192p. 1983. pap. 6.95 o.s.i. (ISBN 0-684-17892-3, ScribT). Scribner.

Better Listening: A Practical Guide to Stereo Equipment for the Home. Hans Fantel. (Illus.). 192p. 1982. 15.95 o.s.i. (ISBN 0-684-17298-4, ScribT). Scribner.

Better Maintenance: Measuring Quality, Training Personnel, Snow Fences & Deicing Chemicals, Planting & Patching; Nine Reports. (Transportation Research Record Ser.). 94p. 1974. 4.00 o.p. (ISBN 0-309-02299-1). Transport Res Bd.

Better Photography. Lester Loeb. (ISBN 0-8022-0988-2). Philos Lib.

Better Place I Know. Helen Cannon. 1979. pap. 2.25 o.p. (ISBN 0-380-75002-3, 75002). Avon.

Better Sport Skating. Richard Arnold. (Illus.). 96p. 1983. 12.95 o.p. (ISBN 0-7182-1467-6, Pub. by Kaye & Ward). David & Charles.

Better Sweaters: The Step-by-Step Guide to Drafting Your Own Patterns. Mari Dembrow. (Illus.). 128p. 1986. pap. 11.95 o.p. (ISBN 0-671-61395-2). P-H.

Better Telephoning: A Plan to Improve Your Telephone Technique. Vera Gough & B. R. Grier. 1970. pap. 4.20 o.p. (ISBN 0-08-006822-7). Pergamon.

Better Tennis for Boys & Girls. Harry Hopman. LC 76-165672. (Illus.). (gr. 7 up). 1972. PLB 8.95 o.p. (ISBN 0-396-06365-9). Dodd.

Better Than Laughter. Chester Aaron. LC 73-181536. 160p. (gr. 5 up). 1972. 5.75 o.p. (ISBN 0-15-206950-X, HJ). HarBraceJ.

Better World-The Great Schism: Stalinism & the American Intellectuals. William L. O'Neill. 497p. 1983. pap. 9.50 o.p. (ISBN 0-671-49267-5, Touchstone). S&S.

Better Writing for Professionals: A Concise Guide. Carol Gelderman. (PROCOM Ser.). 128p. 1984. pap. 9.95 o.p. (ISBN 0-673-15563-3). Scott F.

Betty Boop. Max Fleischer. 1975. pap. 3.45 o.p. (ISBN 0-380-00294-9). Avon.

Betty Crocker's Kitchen Secrets. General Mills Staff. (Illus.). 1983. 12.00 o.p. (ISBN 0-394-52306-7). Random.

Betty Miles, 5 vols. 1983. Set. pap. 13.20 o.s.i. (ISBN 0-380-84913-5). Avon.

Betty White in Person. Betty White. 1988. pap. 3.95 o.p. (ISBN 0-7701-0985-3). PaperJacks US.

Between Anvil & Forge: Pictorial Rememberances of the Blacksmith Shop. Angela Fannin & Jerry Fannin. Ed. by Melissa Roberts. (Illus.). 116p. 1987. pap. 9.95 o.p. (ISBN 0-89015-595-X). Eakin Pr.

Between Capitalism & Socialism: Essays in Political Economics. Robert L. Heilbroner. 1983. 13.00 o.p. (ISBN 0-8446-6035-3). Peter Smith.

Between Continents-Between Seas: Precolumbian Art of Costa Rica. (Illus.). 240p. 1981. pap. 19.95 o.p. (ISBN 0-89558-088-8, Co-pub. by Abrams). Detroit Inst Arts.

Between Conviction & Sentence: The Process of Mitigation. Joanna Shapland. 192p. 1981. 28.95x o.p. (ISBN 0-7100-0945-3). Routledge Chapman & Hall.

Between Dances: Maggie Adams' Eighteenth Summer. Karen S. Dean. 176p. 1982. pap. 2.50 o.p. (ISBN 0-380-79285-0, Flare). Avon.

Between East & West: A History of the Jews of North Africa. Andre N. Chouraqui. Tr. by Michael M. Bernet from Fr. LC 68-19610. (Temple Bks). 1973. pap. 4.65 o.p. (ISBN 0-689-70346-5, T26, Atheneum). Macmillan.

Between Flops: A Biography of Preston Sturges. James Curtis. LC 81-48009. (Illus.). 352p. 1982. 15.95 o.p. (ISBN 0-15-111932-5). HarBraceJ.

Between Gogol & Sevcenko: Polarity in the Literary Ukraine, 1798-1847. George S. Luckyj. 439p. cancelled o.s.i. (ISBN 3-7705-0388-0). Adlers Foreign Bks.

Between Health & Illness: New Notions on Stress & the Nature of Well Being. Barbara Brown. 256p. 1984. 14.45 o.p. (ISBN 0-395-34634-7). HM.

Between Heaven & Earth. abr ed. Otto Ludwig. Tr. by Muriel Almon. LC 64-20047. 1964. 7.00 o.p. (ISBN 0-8044-2559-0); pap. 3.95x o.p. (ISBN 0-8044-6453-7). Ungar.

Between Heaven & Earth. Franz Werfel. Tr. by Maxim Newmark. 252p. 1944. (ISBN 0-8022-1851-2). Philos Lib.

Between Jesus & Paul. Martin Hengel. LC 83-48003. 256p. 1983. pap. 6.95 o.p. (ISBN 0-8006-1720-7, Fortress). Augsburg Fortress.

Between Life & Death. Robert Kastenbaum. LC 79-17760. (Death & Suicide Ser.: Vol. 1). 192p. 1979. text ed. 19.50 o.p. (ISBN 0-8261-2540-9). Springer Pub.

Between Life & Death: The Letters of Krystyna Wituskiej. Tr. by Sanzen Suemitsu. 1977. 4.00 o.p. (ISBN 0-682-48865-8, Banner). Exposition-Phoenix.

Between McAlpine & Polaris: A Social Inscape Study. George G. Giarchi. 256p. (Orig.). 1984. pap. 25.00x o.p. (ISBN 0-7100-9435-3). Routledge Chapman & Hall.

Between Neurology & Psychiatry. Ed. by Michael R. Trimble. 220p. 1985. 85.75x o.p. (ISBN 3-8055-4023-X). Transaction Pubs.

Between Ocean & Empire: An Illustrated History of Long Island. Robert McKay & Carol Traynor. LC 85-26605. 304p. 1985. 24.95 o.p. (ISBN 0-89781-143-7). Windsor Pubns Inc.

Between Ourselves: Letters Between Mothers & Daughters. Karen Payne. 352p. 1983. 16.45 o.p. (ISBN 0-395-33969-3). HM.

Between Peace & War: The Nature of International Crisis. Richard N. Lebow. LC 80-21982. 368p. 1981. pap. 30.00x o.p. (ISBN 0-8018-2311-0). Johns Hopkins.

Between Pets & People: The Importance of Animal Companionship. Alan Beck & Aaron Katcher. (Illus.). 204p. 1984. pap. 8.95 o.p. (ISBN 0-399-51069-9, Perigee). Putnam Pub Group.

Between Tears & Laughter. Mulk R. Anand. 171p. 1974. pap. 2.75 o.s.i. (ISBN 0-88253-311-8). Ind-US Inc.

Between the Devil & the Sea: The Life of James Forten. Brenda A. Johnston. LC 74-5603. 128p. (gr. 5 up). 1974. 6.75 o.p. (ISBN 0-15-206965-8, HJ). HarBraceJ.

Between the Eyes. Ralph Steadman. 1986. 14.95 o.s.i. (ISBN 0-671-62949-2). Summit Bks.

Between the Sexes. Lisa S. Cahill. 160p. (Orig.). 1985. pap. 7.95 o.p. (ISBN 0-8091-2711-3). Paulist Pr.

Between the Thunder & the Sun. Alfred Coppel. LC 77-147228. 1971. 7.95 o.p. (ISBN 0-15-111950-3). HarBraceJ.

Between the Tides. Philip Street. (Illus.). 176p. 1953. (ISBN 0-8022-1666-8). Philos Lib.

Between Thimbles & Thumb. Shirley Botsford. LC 78-16332. (Illus.). 1979. 14.95 o.p. (ISBN 0-03-017501-1); pap. 8.95 o.p. (ISBN 0-03-050546-1). H Holt & Co.

Between Two Plenums: China's Intraleadership Conflict, 1959-1962. Ellis Joffe. (Michigan Monographs in Chinese Studies: No. 22). 72p. 1975. pap. 6.00 o.p. (ISBN 0-89264-022-7). U of Mich Ctr Chinese.

Between Two Revolutions: Islandmagee County Antrim, Seventeen Ninety-Eight to Nineteen Twenty. Donald H. Akenson. LC 79-12899. (Illus.). 221p. 1979. 22.50 o.p. (ISBN 0-208-01827-1, Archon). Shoe String.

Between Two Rivers: Union County Literature Today. Ed. by Penny Harter & William J. Higginson. 112p. (Orig.). 1980. pap. 4.95 o.p. (ISBN 0-89120-017-7). From Here.

Between Two Worlds: A Guide for Those Beginning to Be Religious. Diogenes Allen. LC 76-12395. 1977. pap. 5.95 o.p. (ISBN 0-8042-1168-X, John Knox). Westminster John Knox.

Between Two Worlds: An Introduction to Geography. 2nd ed. Robert A. Harper & Theodore H. Schmudde. LC 77-76418. (Illus.). 1978. text ed. 27.95 o.p. (ISBN 0-395-25164-8). HM.

Between Two Worlds: The Life of a Young Pole in Russia 1939-46. K. S. Karol. LC 86-14254. (New Republic Bks). (Illus.). 374p. 1987. 19.95 o.p. (ISBN 0-8050-0099-2). H Holt & Co.

Between Two Worlds: Victorian Ambivalence about Progress. Bruce McPherson. LC 82-23814. 92p. (Orig.). 1983. lib. bdg. 23.00 o.p. (ISBN 0-8191-2972-0); pap. text ed. 8.50 o.p. (ISBN 0-8191-2973-9). U Pr of Amer.

Between Walden & the Whirlwind. Jean Fleming. (Christian Character Library). 133p. 1985. hdbk. 8.95 o.p. (ISBN 0-89109-520-9). NavPress.

Between Wars & Other Poems. Anne Halley. Date not set. price not set o.p. U of Mass Pr.

Between Wind & Water. Brace. 1977. pap. 3.95 o.p. (ISBN 0-89272-029-8). Down East.

Between Wind & Water. Gerald W. Brace. (Illus.). 1966. 5.95 o.p. (ISBN 0-393-08537-6). Norton.

Beulah Land. Lonnie Coleman. 1980. pap. 1.95 o.p. (ISBN 0-440-11393-8). Dell.

Beverage Management & Bartending. Peter E. Van Kleek. 164p. 1983. pap. 14.95 o.p. (ISBN 0-8436-2209-1). Van Nos Reinhold.

Beverage Trends in America, 1960-2000. Marvin R. Shanken. (Illus.). 236p. 1984. pap. 895.00 o.p. (ISBN 0-918076-24-2). M Shanken Comm.

Beverly: An Autobiography. Beverly Sills & Larry Linderman. LC 86-47567. 400p. 1987. 19.95 o.p. (ISBN 0-553-05173-3). Bantam.

Beware of Socialism. 2nd ed. Bhagwan Shree Rajneesh. Ed. by Sambuddha Swami Anand Maitreya. LC 84-42804. (Early Discourses & Writings Ser.). 288p. 1984. pap. 3.95 o.p. (ISBN 0-88050-706-3). Chidvilas Inc.

Beware the Months of Fire. Patrick Lane. LC 74-75922. (House of Anansi Poetry Ser.: No. 32). 100p. 1974. 2.00 o.p. (ISBN 0-88784-133-3, Pub. by Hse Anansi Pr Canada); pap. 5.95 o.p. (ISBN 0-88784-032-9). U of Toronto Pr.

Beware the Smiling Stranger. Mitchell Dana. 1977. pap. 1.25 o.p. (ISBN 0-380-00830-0, 30965). Avon.

Beware When Elephants Sneeze. Alice J. Davidson. (Good Little Books for Good Little Children). 32p. (ps-3). 1986. 6.95 o.s.i. (ISBN 0-8378-5086-X). Gibson.

Bewick Collector, 2 Vols. Thomas Hugo. LC 67-24353. (Illus.). 978p. 1968. Repr. of 1866 ed. Set Incl. Suppl. 65.00x o.p. (ISBN 0-8103-3491-7). Gale.

Beyond. I. A. Richards. LC 73-18249. 1974. 10.00 o.p. (ISBN 0-15-111985-6). HarBraceJ.

Beyond a Portrait. Photos by Dorothy Norman & Alfred Stieglitz. Mark Holborn. LC 80-70144. 72p. 1984. 20.00 o.p. (ISBN 0-89381-143-2). Aperture.

Beyond a Reasonable Doubt. C. W. Grafton. LC 75-44977. (Crime Fiction Ser). 1976. Repr. of 1940 ed. lib. bdg. 21.00 o.p. (ISBN 0-8240-2371-4). Garland Pub.

Beyond Baby Fat: Weight-Loss Plans for Children & Teenagers. Francis S. Goulart. LC 84-28948. 208p. 1985. text ed. 15.95 o.p. (ISBN 0-07-023831-6). McGraw.

Beyond Barriers. William J. Pomeroy. 32p. 1983. pap. 2.00 o.p. (ISBN 0-931122-33-3). West End.

Beyond Beauty. Arlene Dahl. 1980. 11.95 o.p. (ISBN 0-671-24555-4). S&S.

Beyond Belief: Essays on Religion in a Post-Traditional World. Robert N. Bellah. LC 77-109058. 1970. 8.95x o.p. (ISBN 0-06-060774-2, RD-129). HarpR.

Beyond Biblical Criticism: Encountering Jesus Christ in the Scripture. Arthur Wainwright. LC 81-85327. 153p. 1982. pap. 9.99 o.p. (ISBN 0-8042-0027-6, John Knox). Westminster John Knox.

Beyond Broadcasting: Into the Cable Age. Timothy Hollins. LC 84-125713. (British Film Institute Bks.). 396p. 1984. pap. 15.95 o.p. (ISBN 0-85170-148-5). U of Ill Pr.

Beyond Brokenness. Louis A. Smith & Joseph R. Barndt. (Orig.). 1980. pap. 2.95 o.p. (ISBN 0-377-00100-7). Friendship Pr.

Beyond Charted Space: A Search for Stolen Treasure. Lewell L. Sorenson. LC 84-90206. 185p. 1985. 10.95 o.p. (ISBN 0-533-06262-4). Vantage.

Beyond Cinderella: The Modern Woman's Guide to Finding a Prince. Nita Tucker. 220p. 1987. pap. 11.95 o.p. (ISBN 0-916682-57-9). Outdoor Empire.

Beyond Class Images: Explorations in the Structure of Social Consciousness. Howard H. Davis. (Social Analysis Ser.). 213p. 1979. 32.00 o.p. (ISBN 0-85664-801-9, Pub. by Croom Helm Ltd). Routledge Chapman & Hall.

Beyond Counseling & Therapy. 2nd ed. Robert R. Carkhuff & Bernard G. Berenson. LC 76-16184. 295p. 1977. text ed. 23.95 o.p. (ISBN 0-03-089812-9, HoltC). HR&W.

Beyond Courage. Clay Blair. (War Library). 208p. 1983. pap. 2.95 o.p. (ISBN 0-345-30824-7). Ballantine.

Beyond Culture. Lionel Trilling. LC 79-11660. 204p. 1979. pap. 4.95 o.p. (ISBN 0-15-611891-2, Harv). HarBraceJ.

Beyond Desire. Sherwood Anderson. (Black & Gold Library). (Illus.). 1970. 6.95 o.p. (ISBN 0-87140-991-7); pap. 2.45 o.p. (ISBN 0-87140-206-8). Liveright.

Beyond Dialogue: Toward a Mutual Transformation of Christianity & Buddhism. John B. Cobb, Jr. LC 82-8389. 176p. 1982. pap. 8.95 o.p. (ISBN 0-8006-1647-2, 1-1647, Fortress). Augsburg Fortress.

Beyond Diplomacy. Atlantic Council's Special Committee on Intergovernmental Organization & Reorganization. 81p. 1975. pap. text ed. 4.50 o.p. (ISBN 0-87855-744-X). Transaction Pubs.

Beyond Domination: An Essay in the Political Philosophy of Education. Patricia White. LC 83-9507. (International Library of the Philosophy of Education). 183p. 1984. 23.95x o.p. (ISBN 0-7100-9765-4). Routledge Chapman & Hall.

Beyond Drugs. Stanley Einstein. LC 73-7940. 1975. 28.00 o.p. (ISBN 0-08-017767-0); pap. 75.00 o.p. (ISBN 0-08-017768-9). Pergamon.

Beyond East & West. John C. Wu. 388p. 1980. 5.95 o.p. (ISBN 0-89955-182-3, Pub. by Mei Ya China). Intl Spec Bk.

Beyond Easy Believism. Gary Collins. 197p. 1985. pap. 8.95 o.p. (ISBN 0-8499-3025-1, 3025-1). Word Bks.

Beyond Empiricism: Philosophy of Science in Sociology. Andrew Tudor. (Monographs in Social Theory). 224p. (Orig.). 1982. pap. 9.95x o.p. (ISBN 0-7100-0925-9). Routledge Chapman & Hall.

Beyond Glamour: A Guide to Nude Photography. Michelle Busselle. (Illus.). 192p. 1987. 24.95 o.p. (ISBN 0-7137-1650-9, Pub. by Blandford Pr England). Sterling.

Beyond God the Father. Mary Daly. 1974. pap. 6.95 o.p. (ISBN 0-8070-4165-3). Beacon Pr.

Beyond God the Father: Toward a Philosophy of Women's Liberation. Mary Daly. LC 73-6245. 256p. 1973. pap. 8.95 o.p. (ISBN 0-8070-1503-2, BP488). Beacon Pr.

Beyond History: The Methods of Prehistory. Bruce G. Trigger. Ed. by George Spindler & Louise Spindler. (Case Studies in Cultural Anthropology). 132p. 1988. pap. text ed. 9.95x o.p. (ISBN 0-8290-0588-9). Irvington.

Beyond Ideology: Religion & the Future of Western Civilization. Ninian Smart. LC 81-47429. 368p. 1981. 15.86i o.p. (ISBN 0-06-067402-4). HarpR.

Beyond Inspiration. Stephen B. Stum. 128p. 1984. 5.95 o.p. (ISBN 0-87159-011-5). Unity School.

Beyond Media: New Approaches to Mass Communications. Ed. by Richard W. Budd & Brent D. Ruben. 292p. 1979. pap. text ed. 14.95x o.p. (ISBN 0-317-39902-0). Transaction Pubs.

Beyond Metaphysics? The Hermeneutic Circle in Contemporary Continental Philosophy. John Llewelyn. (Contemporary Studies in Philosophy & the Human Sciences). 256p. 1985. text ed. 25.00x o.p. (ISBN 0-391-03115-5). Humanities.

Beyond Mindstorms: Teaching with IBM Logo. Joyce Tobias. 432p. 1985. pap. text ed. 21.45 o.p. (ISBN 0-03-071722-1, HoltC). HR&W.

Beyond Nakedness. Paul Abelman. (Illus.). 112p. 1985. 11.95 o.p. (ISBN 0-317-06236-0); pap. 8.95 o.p. (ISBN 0-910550-52-2). Elysium.

Beyond Necessity: Art in the Folk Tradition. Kenneth L. Ames. (Illus.). 1978. 14.95x o.p. (ISBN 0-393-04499-8). Norton.

Beyond Nihilism: Albert Camus's Contribution to Political Thought. Fred H. Willhoite, Jr. LC 68-13449. x, 230p. 1968. 27.50 o.p. (ISBN 0-8071-0828-6). La State U Pr.

Beyond Normality: The Predictive Value & Efficiency of Medical Diagnosis. Robert S. Galen & S. Raymond Gambino. LC 75-25915. 237p. 1975. 38.50 o.p. (ISBN 0-471-29047-5, Pub. by Wiley Medical). Wiley.

Beyond Our Limitations. Tracy Lay. 1955. (ISBN 0-8022-0938-6). Philos Lib.

Beyond Peek-a-Boo & Pat-a-Cake: Activities for Baby's First Year. Evelyn M. Munger & Susan J. Bowdon. 208p. 1980. 10.95 o.p. (ISBN 0-8329-1439-8). New Century.

Beyond Power: On Women, Men & Morals. Marilyn French. 708p. 1985. 19.45 o.s.i. (ISBN 0-671-49959-9). Summit Bks.

Beyond Reason. Margaret Trudeau. (Illus.). 253p. 1979. 16.50x o.p. (ISBN 0-8464-1198-9). Beekman Pubs.

Beyond Reason: How Miracles Can Change Your Life. Pat Robertson & William Proctor. LC 84-61470. 192p. 1984. 12.95 o.p. (ISBN 0-688-02214-6). Morrow.

Beyond Schenkerism: The Need for Alternatives in Music Analysis. Eugene Narmour. LC 76-25632. 1977. lib. bdg. 23.00x o.s.i. (ISBN 0-226-56847-4). U of Chicago Pr.

Titles

Beyond Sugar & Spice: How Women Learn, Grow. Caryl Rivers & Rosalind Barnett. 282p. 1981. pap. 2.95 o.s.i. (ISBN 0-345-29010-0). Ballantine.
Beyond Surrender. Jo Ann Wendt. 384p. (Orig.). 1982. pap. 2.95 o.p. (ISBN 0-380-79038-6, 79038-6). Avon.
Beyond Survival: Emerging Dimensions of Indian Economy. Pranab Mukherjee. 250p. 1984. text ed. 27.95x o.p. (ISBN 0-7069-2658-7, Pub. by Vikas India). Advent NY.
Beyond the Balance Sheet: Evaluating Profit Potential. James Lines. LC 74-5512. 166p. 1974. 26.95x o.p. (ISBN 0-470-53906-2). Halsted Pr.
Beyond the Bath: A Dreamer's Guide. Thomas Cowan. LC 83-61775. (Illus.). 128p. (Orig.). 1983. lib. bdg. 19.80 o.p. (ISBN 0-89471-224-1); pap. 8.95 o.p. (ISBN 0-89471-223-3). Running Pr.
Beyond the Battlefield: American Military Professionalism. Sam C. Sarkesian. LC 80-27027. (Pergamon Policy Studies on International Politics). 1981. text ed. 75.00 o.p. (ISBN 0-08-027178-2). Pergamon.
Beyond the Bedroom Wall. Larry Woiwode. 1976. pap. 1.95 o.p. (ISBN 0-380-00684-7, 47670-3, Bard). Avon.
Beyond the Best Interests of the Child. Joseph Goldstein et al. LC 79-7630. 1980. 17.95 o.p. (ISBN 0-02-912200-7); pap. 7.95 o.p. (ISBN 0-02-912190-6). Free Pr.
Beyond the Blue Event Horizon, No. 2. Frederik Pohl. 1980. pap. 3.95 o.p. (ISBN 0-345-35046-4, Del Rey). Ballantine.
Beyond the Body. Susan J. Blackmore. 272p. pap. 5.95 o.s.i. (ISBN 0-586-08428-2, Pub. by Granada England). Academy Chi Pubs.
Beyond the Body. Sandra Gibson. 1979. pap. 2.25 o.p. (ISBN 0-505-51340-4, Pub. by Tower Bks). Dorchester Pub Co.
Beyond the Body: The Human Double & the Astral Planes. Benjamin Walker. 1977. 16.95 o.p. (ISBN 0-7100-7808-0); pap. 6.95 o.p. (ISBN 0-7100-8581-8). Routledge Chapman & Hall.
Beyond the Courtroom: A Comparative Analysis of Misdemeanor Sentencing, Executive Summary. 37p. 1984. 2.25 o.p. (ISBN 0-318-23091-7, 027-000-01213-2). USGPO.
Beyond the Dream. Ira Berkow. LC 75-16761. 1975. 6.95 o.p. (ISBN 0-689-30489-7, Atheneum). Macmillan.
Beyond the Energy Crisis-Opportunity & Challenge: Proceedings of the ICEUM, 3rd, Berlin, October 26-30, 1981, 4 vols. International Conference on Energy Use Management Staff & R. Fazzolari. 2500p. 1981. 555.00 o.p. (ISBN 0-08-027589-3). Pergamon.
Beyond the Facts, Acts. Pat McGeachy. (Orig.). 1973. pap. 1.95 o.p. (ISBN 0-377-03051-1). Friendship Pr.
Beyond the Flag. C. Buonanno. (Orig.). 1981. pap. 1.95 o.p. (ISBN 0-505-51616-0, Pub. by Tower Bks). Dorchester Pub Co.
Beyond the Flames. Sarah C. Cunningham. 320p. (Orig.). 1985. pap. 10.00 o.p. (ISBN 0-914339-06-0). P E Randall Pub.
Beyond the Freeze: The Road to Nuclear Sanity. Union of Concerned Scientists Staff et al. LC 82-72504. (Orig.). 1982. pap. 6.95x o.p. (ISBN 0-8070-0484-7, BP646). Beacon Pr.
Beyond the Gates of Death: A Biblical Examination of Evidence for Life After Death. Hans Schwarz. LC 80-67805. 136p. 1981. pap. 7.95 o.p. (ISBN 0-8066-1868-X, 10-0647, Augsburg). Augsburg Fortress.
Beyond the General Hospital Patient: Investigations in Consultation Psychiatry. Hengeveld. 1983. pap. text ed. 17.00 o.p. (ISBN 90-265-0488-8, Pub. by Swets & Zeitlinger Netherlands). CJ Hogrefe Pubs.
Beyond the Gunsights: One Arab Family in the Promised Land. Yoella Har-Shefi. 1980. 9.95 o.p. (ISBN 0-395-27614-4). HM.
Beyond the Hiss Case: The FBI, Congress, & the Cold War. Ed. by Athan G. Theoharis. 350p. 1982. 29.95 o.p. (ISBN 0-87722-241-X). Temple U Pr.
Beyond the Hundredth Meridian. Wallace Stegner. 1962. pap. 5.95 o.p. (ISBN 0-395-08369-9, 20, SenEd). HM.
Beyond the Inhabited World: Roman Britain. Anthony Thwaite. LC 76-17526. (Illus.). (gr. 6 up). 1979. 8.95 o.s.i. (ISBN 0-395-28926-2, Clarion). HM.
Beyond the Kitchen: A Dreamer's Guide. Thomas Cowan. LC 84-42923. (Illus.). 128p. (Orig.). 1985. 24.95 o.p. (ISBN 0-89471-303-5); pap. 12.95 o.p. (ISBN 0-89471-306-X). Running Pr.
Beyond the Lighthouse: English Women Novelists in the 20th Century. Margaret Crosland. LC 81-5638. 256p. 1982. 14.95 o.s.i. (ISBN 0-8008-0734-0). Taplinger.
Beyond the Looking Glass: Reflections of Alice & Her Family. Colin Gordon. LC 83-8556. (Illus.). 246p. 1983. 19.95 o.p. (ISBN 0-15-112022-6). HarBraceJ.
Beyond the Moon. Paolo Maffei. 1980. pap. 7.95 o.p. (ISBN 0-380-48744-6, 48744-6). Avon.
Beyond the Mountain. William Dieter. LC 84-45052. 320p. 1985. 13.95 o.p. (ISBN 0-689-11477-X, Atheneum). Macmillan.
Beyond the New Morality: The Responsibilities of Freedom. Germain Grisez & Russell Shaw. LC 73-17772. 240p. 1974. 14.95 o.p. (ISBN 0-268-00533-8); pap. 3.25x o.p. (ISBN 0-268-00534-6). U of Notre Dame Pr.
Beyond the Post-Modern Mind. Huston Smith. 208p. 1982. 14.95 o.p. (ISBN 0-8245-0457-7). Crossroad NY.
Beyond the Post-Modern Mind. Huston Smith. LC 84-40511. 218p. 1985. pap. 7.95 o.s.i. (ISBN 0-8356-0592-2). Theos Pub Hse.
Beyond the Revolution: Bolivia Since 1952. Ed. by James M. Malloy & Richard S. Thorn. LC 77-135848. (Pitt Latin American Ser). 1971. 40.95x o.p. (ISBN 0-8229-3220-2). U of Pittsburgh Pr.
Beyond the Senses: A Report on Psychical Research in the Sixties. Paul Tabori & Phyllis Raphael. LC 70-185482. (Frontiers of the Unknown Ser.). 226p. 1972. 6.50 o.s.i. (ISBN 0-8008-0735-9). Taplinger.
Beyond the Sixth Game. Peter Gammons. (Illus.). 280p. 1985. 15.45 o.s.i. (ISBN 0-395-35345-9). HM.
Beyond the Sociology of Development. Ed. by Ivar Oxaal et al. (International Library of Sociology). 1975. 25.00x o.p. (ISBN 0-7100-8049-2); pap. 12.95x o.p. (ISBN 0-7100-8050-6). Routledge Chapman & Hall.
Beyond the Strawberry Patch. Rose S. Bell. Ed. by Helen Graves. LC 85-20210. 132p. 1985. pap. 5.95 o.s.i. (ISBN 0-938232-76-2, Dist. by Baker & Taylor Co.). Winston-Derek.
Beyond the Tomorrow Mountains. Sylvia L. Engdahl. LC 72-86934. 264p. (gr. 7 up). 1973. 7.95 o.p. (ISBN 0-689-30084-0, Atheneum). Macmillan.
Beyond the Visible: The Triumph Over Yourself...Life & Emotions. Paul Molow & Doree Molow. 192p. 1981. 10.00 o.p. (ISBN 0-682-49739-8). Exposition-Phoenix.
Beyond the Wild Wood: The World of Kenneth Grahame. Peter Green. LC 83-5553. (Illus.). 224p. 17.95 o.p. (ISBN 0-87196-740-5). Facts on File.
Beyond Tomorrow. Fern Michaels. (Nightingale Ser.). 1985. pap. 9.95 o.p. (ISBN 0-8161-3741-2, Large Print Bks). G K Hall.
Beyond Trivia: Expanded Answers to America's Most Loved Trivia Game. Jerome B. Agel. 674p. 1985. pap. 8.95 o.p. (ISBN 0-671-54128-5). S&S.
Beyond Vengeance. J. L. Bouma. 1979. pap. 1.75 o.p. (ISBN 0-8439-0703-7, Pub. by Leisure Bks CT). Dorchester Pub Co.
Beyond Violence. Jiddu Krishnamurti. LC 72-9875. 176p. 1973. pap. 6.95 o.p. (ISBN 0-06-064839-2, RD 61). HarpR.
Beyond Within: The LSD Story. rev. ed. Sidney Cohen. LC 64-25848. 1967. 6.95 o.p. (ISBN 0-689-10056-6, Atheneum). Macmillan.
Beyond Words. Ed. by Lester Alexander. LC 76-29896. (Illus.). 1977. 8.95 o.p. (ISBN 0-03-020871-8); pap. 5.95 o.p. (ISBN 0-03-016911-9). H Holt & Co.
Beyond Words: Mystical Fancy in Children's Literature. James E. Higgins. LC 71-96760. 1970. pap. 7.95x o.p. (ISBN 0-8077-1517-4). Tchrs Coll.
BF Beading of a Wate. Date not set. (ISBN 0-07-017461-X). McGraw.
BF Bean Sprouts. Date not set. (ISBN 0-07-017459-8). McGraw.
BF Bones X Ray MP. Date not set. (ISBN 0-07-017454-7). McGraw.
BF Candle Burning TE. Date not set. (ISBN 0-07-017457-1). McGraw.
BF Candle Burning 2. Date not set. (ISBN 0-07-017456-3). McGraw.
BF Draw with Templates. Helsel. Date not set. (ISBN 0-07-028008-8). McGraw.
BF Lettering. Helsel. Date not set. (ISBN 0-07-028005-3). McGraw.
BF Mech Drawing Loop. Helsel. Date not set. (ISBN 0-07-079743-9). McGraw.
BF Paramecium. Date not set. (ISBN 0-07-017476-8). McGraw.
BF Revolved Sect. Helsel. Date not set. (ISBN 0-07-028016-9). McGraw.
BF Sand Pend 2 Draw. Date not set. (ISBN 0-07-017472-5). McGraw.
BF Sand Pend 5 Pour. Date not set. (ISBN 0-07-017475-X). McGraw.
BF Sketching Circles. Helsel. Date not set. (ISBN 0-07-028002-9). McGraw.
BF Surface Devel Par. Helsel. Date not set. (ISBN 0-07-028018-5). McGraw.
BF Trichoderma Growth. Date not set. (ISBN 0-07-017468-7). McGraw.
BF U Bones X Ray MP. Date not set. (ISBN 0-07-017453-9). McGraw.
BF Vorticella. Date not set. (ISBN 0-07-017483-0). McGraw.
BF 1 Pt Persp Draw. Helsel. Date not set. (ISBN 0-07-028023-1). McGraw.
BG Sketching Lines. Helsel. Date not set. (ISBN 0-07-028001-0). McGraw.
BGIS Level 2 TE. 4th ed. Date not set. (ISBN 0-07-033902-3). McGraw.
BGIS Level 3 TE. 4th ed. Date not set. (ISBN 0-07-033903-1). McGraw.
BGIS Level 5 TE. 4th ed. Date not set. (ISBN 0-07-033905-8). McGraw.
BGIS Level 6 TE. 4th ed. Date not set. (ISBN 0-07-033906-6). McGraw.
BGIS Level 6 Text. 4th ed. Date not set. (ISBN 0-07-033896-5). McGraw.
BGIS Level 8 TE. 4th ed. Date not set. (ISBN 0-07-033908-2). McGraw.
BGIS LV 1 Workbook TE. 4th ed. Date not set. (ISBN 0-07-033921-X). McGraw.
BGIS LV 3 Webmast. Date not set. (ISBN 0-07-033604-0). McGraw.
BGIS LV 6 Workbook TE. 4th ed. Date not set. (ISBN 0-07-033926-0). McGraw.
BGIS LV 8 Workbook TE. 4th ed. Date not set. (ISBN 0-07-033928-7). McGraw.
Bhabani Bhattacharya. K. R. Chandrasekharan. (Indian Writers Ser.). 1976. 8.50 o.s.i. (ISBN 0-89253-505-9). Ind-US Inc.
Bhutan: A Kingdom of the Eastern Himalayas. Francoise Pommaret-Imaeda & Yoshiro Imaeda. Tr. by Ian Noble. LC 84-23610. (Illus.). 176p. 1985. 49.95 o.p. (ISBN 0-87773-321-X, 54540-0). Shambhala Pubns.
Bi-Sexual Man or Evolution of the Sexes. 2nd ed. Buzzacott & Wymore. (Illus.). 83p. 1912. pap. 8.95 o.s.i. (ISBN 0-88697-012-1). Life Science.
Bias & the Pious: The Relationship Between Prejudice & Religion. James E. Dittes. LC 72-90263. (Study of Generations Paperbacks Ser). 104p. 1973. pap. 1.95 o.p. (ISBN 0-8066-1311-4, 10-0670, Augsburg). Augsburg Fortress.
Bib Sac Reader. John F. Walvoord & Roy B. Zuck. (Orig.). 1983. pap. 8.95 o.p. (ISBN 0-8024-0459-6). Moody.
Bible: A Modern Understanding. J. Lindblom. Tr. by Eric H. Wahlstrom from Swedish. LC 72-91525. 208p. 1973. pap. 3.95 o.p. (ISBN 0-8006-0125-4, 1-125, Fortress). Augsburg Fortress.
Bible Activities for Kids, No. 6. Donna L. Pape et al. 62p. (Orig.). (gr. 2-7). 1982. 2.50 o.p. (ISBN 0-87123-276-6, 210276). Bethany Hse.
Bible Activity Fun for Kids. Mary E. Lysne. 24p. (gr. 1-3). 1983. pap. 1.69 o.p. (ISBN 0-87239-693-2, 2363). Standard Pub.
Bible Adventures. Ruth Odor. (Flip-a-Bible-Story Bks.). (Illus.). 16p. (Orig.). (ps-4). 1982. pap. 3.95 o.p. (ISBN 0-87239-561-8, 2735). Standard Pub.
Bible & American Arts & Letters. Ed. by Giles Gunn. LC 83-5634. (Bible in American Culture Ser.). 256p. 1983. 15.95 o.p. (ISBN 0-8006-0613-2, 1-613, Fortress). Augsburg Fortress.
Bible & American Law, Politics, & Political Rhetoric. Ed. by James T. Johnson. LC 83-16327. (Bible in American Culture Ser.: No. 4). 216p. 1985. 14.95 o.p. (ISBN 0-8006-0614-0, 1-614, Fortress). Augsburg Fortress.
Bible & Ethics in the Christian Life. Bruce C. Birch & Larry L. Rasmussen. LC 76-3856. 224p. 1976. pap. 9.95 o.p. (ISBN 0-8066-1524-9, Augsburg, 10-0702). Augsburg Fortress.
Bible & I. E. M. Blaiklock. 128p. (Orig.). 1983. pap. 3.95 o.p. (ISBN 0-87123-298-7). Bethany Hse.
Bible & Popular Culture in America. Ed. by Allene S. Phy. LC 83-11548. (Bible in American Culture Ser.). 256p. 1984. 15.95 o.p. (ISBN 0-8006-0735-X, Fortress). Augsburg Fortress.
Bible & Recent Archaeology. Dame Kathleen Kenyon. LC 78-4089. (Illus.). 1979. pap. 8.95 o.p. (ISBN 0-8042-0010-6, John Knox). Westminster John Knox.
Bible & Social Reform. Ed. by Ernest R. Sandeen. LC 81-71386. (Bible in American Culture Ser.). 196p. 1982. 12.95 o.p. (ISBN 0-8006-0611-6, 1-611, Fortress). Augsburg Fortress.
Bible & the Faiths of Men. Vinjamuri E. Devadutt. (Orig.). 1967. pap. 1.25 o.p. (ISBN 0-377-37011-8). Friendship Pr.
Bible & the Human Quest. Algernon O. Steele. 256p. 1957. (ISBN 0-8022-1633-1). Philos Lib.
Bible & the Reader: An Introduction to Literary Criticism. Edgar V. McKnight. LC 85-4603. 176p. 1985. pap. 2.95 o.p. (ISBN 0-8006-1872-6, 1-1872, Fortress). Augsburg Fortress.
Bible Animals. Ed. by Patricia Mahany. (Classroom Activity Bks.). (Illus., Orig.). (ps-k). 1984. pap. 2.95 o.p. (ISBN 0-87239-715-7, 2445). Standard Pub.
Bible Answers to Man's Questions on Demons. 2nd ed. Kenneth E. Hagin. 1987. pap. 1.00 o.p. (ISBN 0-89276-029-X). Hagin Ministries.
Bible Answers Us with Pictures. Christa Meves. Tr. by Hal Taussig from Ger. LC 76-49909. (Illus.). 1977. pap. 5.95 o.s.i. (ISBN 0-664-24130-1, Westminster). Westminster John Knox.
Bible Babies. Ed. by Patricia Mahany. (Classroom Activity Bks.). (Illus.). 48p. (Orig.). (ps-k). 1984. pap. 2.95 o.p. (ISBN 0-87239-716-5, 2446). Standard Pub.
Bible Between Fundamentalism & Philosophy. Henry P. Hamann. LC 80-65558. 80p. 1980. pap. 3.50 o.p. (ISBN 0-8066-1803-5, 10-0701, Augsburg). Augsburg Fortress.
Bible, Christian & Latter Day Saints. Gordon Lewis. pap. 1.25 o.p. (ISBN 0-8010-5567-9). Baker Bk.
Bible, Christians & Jehovah's Witnesses. Gordon Lewis. pap. 1.95 o.p. (ISBN 0-8010-5568-7). Baker Bk.
Bible Creative: John. Dennis C. Benson. 312p. 1983. 14.95 o.s.i. (ISBN 0-936664-12-6). Group Pub.
Bible Encyclopedia for Children. Cecil Northcott. (Illus.). (gr. 1-10). 1964. 8.95 o.s.i. (ISBN 0-664-20494-5, Westminster). Westminster John KNox.
Bible: Fact, Fiction, Fantasy, Faith. H. N. Dukes. 178p. (Orig.). 1987. pap. 8.00 o.p. (ISBN 0-682-40337-7). Exposition-Phoenix.
Bible for Bartenders. Greg Gorris. 243p. 1977. 6.50 o.p. (ISBN 0-682-48847-X). Exposition-Phoenix.
Bible for Children, with Songs & Plays, Vol. I, Vol. II: Old Testament, New Testament. Ed. by J. L. Klink. (Illus.). (gr. 4-7). 1968. 4.95 o.s.i. (ISBN 0-664-20798-7, Westminster); pap. 4.95 o.s.i. (Westminster). Westminster John Knox.
Bible for Children, with Songs & Plays, Vol. 2: New Testament. J. L. Klink. Tr. by Patricia Crampton. LC 68-10178. (Illus.). (gr. 1 up). 1969. 4.95 o.s.i. (ISBN 0-664-20820-7, Westminster). Westminster John Knox.
Bible for Today. Ed. by Richard Herkes. (Illus.). 1979. pap. 4.95 o.s.i. (ISBN 0-664-24264-2, Westminster). Westminster John Knox.
Bible for Today's Church. Robert A. Bennett & O. C. Edwards. (Church's Teaching Ser.: Vol. 2). 320p. 1979. 5.95 o.p. (ISBN 0-8164-0419-4); pap. 4.95 o.p. (ISBN 0-8164-2215-X); users guide 1.50 o.p. (ISBN 0-8164-2222-2). HarpR.
Bible Games for Teams & Groups. Judene Leon. (Illus.). 64p. 1984. pap. 6.95 o.p. (ISBN 0-86683-832-5). HarpR.
Bible Hero Stories. Joe Maniscalco. LC 74-28725. (Illus.). 144p. (gr. 3-6). 1975. 6.95 o.p. (ISBN 0-87239-036-5, 2746). Standard Pub.
Bible Heroes. Ruth Odor. (Flip-a-Bible-Story Bks.). (Illus.). 16p. (Orig.). (ps-4). 1982. pap. 3.95 o.p. (ISBN 0-87239-562-6, 2736). Standard Pub.
Bible in American Education. Ed. by David L. Barr & Nicholas Piediscalzi. LC 81-71385. (Bible in American Culture Ser.). 196p. 1982. text ed. 12.95 o.p. (ISBN 0-8006-0612-4, 1-612, Fortress). Augsburg Fortress.
Bible in the Classroom. Alan T. Dale. 96p. (Orig.). 1973. pap. 4.95 o.p. (ISBN 0-8192-1151-6). Morehouse Pub.
Bible in the Making. Geddes MacGregor. LC 82-17499. 318p. 1983. pap. 15.25 o.p. (ISBN 0-8191-2810-4). U Pr of Amer.
Bible Journeys. Dick Orr & David L. Bartlett. 80p. 1980. pap. 4.95 o.p. (ISBN 0-8170-0898-5). Judson.
Bible Keys for Today's Family. Knofel Staton. LC 83-9239. 144p. (Orig.). 1984. pap. 2.95 o.p. (ISBN 0-87239-669-X, 41024). Standard Pub.
Bible Learning Fun for Kids. Mary E. Lysne. 24p. (gr. 4-8). 1983. pap. 1.50 o.p. (ISBN 0-87239-694-0, 2364). Standard Pub.
Bible of the World. Ed. by Robert O. Ballou et al. 1415p. 1980. pap. 5.50 o.p. (ISBN 0-380-01057-7, 17350). Avon.
Bible Pop-O-Rama Books. Joann Scheck. Incl. God Loves His People. 2.50 o.p. (ISBN 0-8066-1505-2, 10-2580); When Jesus Was a Baby. 2.95 (ISBN 0-8066-1521-4, 10-7062); Jesus Tells a Story. 2.95 o.p. (ISBN 0-8066-1512-5, 10-3540); Jesus Does Great Things. 2.95 o.p. (ISBN 0-8066-1511-7, 10-3500). (Illus.). 12p. (gr. 3 up). 1976 (Augsburg). Augsburg Fortress.
Bible Programs & Dramas for Children. Carol Richardson. 64p. (Orig.). 1983. pap. 2.95 o.p. (ISBN 0-87239-665-7, 3350). Standard Pub.
Bible Puzzle Trails. Helen Sattler. (Pelican Activity Ser.). 32p. (gr. 3-7). 1977. pap. 0.89 o.p. (ISBN 0-8010-7900-4). Baker Bk.
Bible Questions Answered. Hazel Buffinger. 40p. 1987. 6.95 o.p. (ISBN 0-8062-3038-X). Carlton.
Bible Quiz: Five Hundred Questions & Answers with Bible References. Hazel C. Rapp. 1976. 4.00 o.p. (ISBN 0-682-48580-2). Exposition-Phoenix.
Bible Quizzes for Everybody. Frederick Hall. (Quiz & Puzzle Bks.). 150p. 1980. pap. 3.95 o.p. (ISBN 0-8010-4032-9). Baker Bk.
Bible Research. rev. ed. Kenneth P. Malmin. (Illus.). 149p. 1979. Repr. of 1976 ed. notebk. 11.95 o.p. (ISBN 0-914936-33-6). Bible Temple.

Bible Sharing: How to Grow in the Mystery of Christ. John Burke. LC 79-15006. (Orig.). 1979. pap. 5.95 o.p. (ISBN 0-8189-0386-4). Alba.

Bible Speaks Again. Tr. by Annebeth Mackie. LC 79-75400. (Dutch). 1969. pap. 4.95 o.p. (ISBN 0-8066-0931-1, 10-0704, Augsburg). Augsburg Fortress.

Bible Stories. Charles M. Sheldon. LC 74-4817. (Illus.). 1978. pap. 4.95 o.p. (ISBN 0-448-14612-6, G&D). Putnam Pub Group.

Bible Stories & You. Gail Fargo. 1954. (ISBN 0-8022-0474-0). Philos Lib.

Bible Stories for Children. 32p. (gr. k-5). 1981. pap. 3.95 o.p. (ISBN 0-8249-8017-4). Ideals.

Bible Stories for Children. (Illus.). 20p. (gr. k-5). 1985. incl. cassette 8.95 o.p. (ISBN 0-8249-8121-9). Ideals.

Bible Stories for Everyone. Ed. by Daughters of St. Paul. 1956. 6.00 o.p. (ISBN 0-8198-0008-2); pap. 5.00 o.p. (ISBN 0-8198-0009-0). Dghtrs St Paul.

Bible Stories in Action for Children. Richard S. Robbins. (gr. k-4). 1981. 4.50 o.p. (ISBN 0-89536-475-1, 0209). CSS of Ohio.

Bible Stories Reader. Robert L. Larson. 1985. 8.95 o.p. (ISBN 0-533-06749-9). Vantage.

Bible Stories to Live By. V. Gilbert Beers & Ronald A. Beers. LC 82-84616. (Illus.). 192p. (gr. 3-6). 1983. 12.95 o.p. (ISBN 0-89840-044-9). Heres Life.

Bible Student's English-Greek Concordance & Greek-English Dictionary. James Gall. (Paperback Reference Library). 376p. 1983. pap. 9.95 o.p. (ISBN 0-8010-3795-6). Baker Bk.

Bible Study Source Book: New Testament. Ed. by Robert C. Walton. LC 80-82195. 240p. 1981. pap. 4.99 o.p. (ISBN 0-8042-0009-2, John Knox). Westminster John Knox.

Bible Study Source Book: Old Testament. Ed. by Robert C. Walton. LC 80-82194. 216p. 1981. pap. 4.99 o.p. (ISBN 0-8042-0008-4, John Knox). Westminster John Knox.

Bible That Wouldn't Burn. L. Ulmer. LC 39-1094. 1983. pap. 1.50 o.p. (ISBN 0-570-03634-8). Concordia.

Bible Verses to Remember. Julianne Booth. (gr. 2-5). 1982. pap. 1.25 o.p. (ISBN 0-570-04061-2, 56-1364). Concordia.

Bible Who Am I? Patricia S. Mahany. (Stick-On Activity & Coloring Bks.). (Illus.). 16p. (gr. k-3). 1983. pap. 1.50 o.p. (ISBN 0-87239-687-8, 2367). Standard Pub.

Bible Wisdom for Modern Living: Arranged by Subject. Ed. by David Brown. 400p. 1986. 17.95 o.p. (ISBN 0-671-62545-4). S&S.

Bible Word Chain Puzzles. William C. Hendricks & Glenn Van Noord. (Quiz & Puzzle Bks.). 96p. (Orig.). 1981. pap. 2.95 o.p. (ISBN 0-8010-4238-0). Baker Bk.

Bible's Legacy for Womanhood. Edith Deen. 1976. pap. (ISBN 0-515-09586-9). Jove Pubns.

Biblia lo Dice. Ed. by Jorge Diaz & Nelly De Gonzalez. (Illus.). 120p. (Span.). 1986. Repr. of 1984 ed. spiral bdg. 3.95 o.p. (ISBN 0-311-11453-9). Casa Bautista.

Biblia Pauperum. 50p. 250.00 o.p. (ISBN 0-8115-0909-5). Kraus Repr.

Biblical Approaches to Pastoral Counseling. Donald Capps. LC 81-11473. 214p. 1981. pap. 9.95 o.s.i. (ISBN 0-664-24388-6, Westminster). Westminster John Knox.

Biblical Archaeology. abr ed. G. Ernest Wright. 1961. pap. 3.45 o.s.i. (ISBN 0-664-24306-1, Westminster). Westminster John Knox.

Biblical Archaeology. rev. ed. G. Ernest Wright. LC 57-5020. (Illus.). 292p. 1963. 27.50 o.s.i. (ISBN 0-664-20420-1, Westminster). Westminster John Knox.

Biblical Basis for Ministry. Ed. by Earl E. Shelp & Ronald H. Sunderland. Paul J. Achtmeier et al. LC 81-920. 238p. 1981. pap. 9.50 o.s.i. (ISBN 0-664-24371-1, Westminster). Westminster John Knox.

Biblical Chants. A. W. Binder. 128p. 1959. (ISBN 0-8022-0128-8). Philos Lib.

Biblical Christian Marriage. Cliff Edwards. LC 76-44973. 1977. 6.95 o.p. (ISBN 0-8042-1100-0, John Knox). Westminster John Knox.

Biblical Doctrine of Immortality. S. D. Salmond. 718p. lib. bdg. 24.95 o.p. (ISBN 0-8254-5225-2). Kregel.

Biblical Inspiration. Bruce Vawter. (Theological Resources Ser). 1971. 9.95 o.s.i. (ISBN 0-664-20914-9, Westminster). Westminster John Knox.

Biblical Interpretation & the Church: The Problem of Contextualization. Ed. by D. A. Carson. 232p. 1985. pap. 7.95 o.p. (ISBN 0-8407-7501-6). Nelson.

Biblical Interpreter: An Agrarian Bible in an Industrial Age. Richard L. Rohrbaugh. LC 78-54560. 132p. 1978. pap. 4.95 o.p. (ISBN 0-8006-1346-5, 1-1346, Fortress). Augsburg Fortress.

Biblical Mosaic: Changing Perspectives. Ed. by Robert M. Polzin & Eugene Rothman. LC 81-67307. (Semeia Studies). 1982. pap. 9.95 o.p. (ISBN 0-8006-1510-7, Fortress). Augsburg Fortress.

Biblical Perspectives on Death, No. 5. Lloyd R. Bailey, Sr. Ed. by Walter Brueggemann & John R. Donahue. LC 78-145661. (Overtures to Biblical Theology Ser.). 180p. 1978. pap. 8.95 o.p. (ISBN 0-8006-1530-1, 1-1530, Fortress). Augsburg Fortress.

Biblical Prints. Sadao Watanabe. (Illus.). 1986. deluxe ed. 100.00 o.p. (ISBN 0-8028-3635-6). Eerdmans.

Biblical Separation Defended. Gary G. Cohen. 1966. pap. 3.50 o.p. (ISBN 0-87552-147-9). Presby & Reformed.

Biblical Structuralism: Method & Subjectivity in the Study of Ancient Texts. Robert M. Polzin. Ed. by William A. Beardslee. LC 76-15895. (Semeia Studies). 224p. 1977. pap. 5.95 o.p. (ISBN 0-8006-1506-9, 1-1506, Fortress). Augsburg Fortress.

Biblical Studies: Essays in Honor of William Barclay. Ed. by Johnston R. McKay & James F. Miller. LC 76-6943. 1976. 12.50 o.s.i. (ISBN 0-664-20760-X, Westminster). Westminster John Knox.

Biblical Theology in Crisis. Brevard S. Childs. LC 74-96698. 256p. 1970. 9.50 o.s.i. (ISBN 0-664-20882-7, Westminster). Westminster John Knox.

Biblical View of Reality: The Bible & Christian Ethics. David N. Duke. ii, 59p. 1985. pap. text ed. 6.95x o.p. (ISBN 0-932269-05-2). Wyndham Hall.

Biblioclasm. Marc Drogin. (Illus.). 224p. cancelled o.s.i. (ISBN 0-8390-0368-4, Littlefield & Schram). Abner Schram Ltd.

Bibliografa Californica: Supplement. Alexander S. Taylor. Ed. by Dave Basso. (Great Abstracts Ser.). 26p. (Orig.). 1983. pap. text ed. 17.95 o.p. (ISBN 0-936332-17-4). Falcon Hill Pr.

Bibliografia Chicana: A Guide to Information Sources. Ed. by Arnulfo D. Trejo. LC 74-11562. (Ethnic Studies Information Guide Ser.: Vol. 1). 210p. 1975. 68.00x o.p. (ISBN 0-8103-1311-1). Gale.

Bibliografia General de la Literatura Latinoamericana. (Orig., Span.). 1973. pap. 6.75 o.p. (ISBN 0-685-39009-8, U46, UNESCO). UNIPUB.

Bibliographer's Manual of English Literature, 8 Vols. William T. Lowndes. LC 66-28042. 3466p. 1967. Repr. of 1864 ed. 220.00x o.p. (ISBN 0-8103-3217-5). Gale.

Bibliographia Cartesiana: A Critical Guide to the Descartes Literature (1800-1960) G. Sebba. 1964. 50.00 o.s.i. (ISBN 0-685-11995-5). E J Brill USA.

Bibliographic Essays on the Architecture of the Ancient City of Rome, No. 45: The City of Rome, No. 41: City Walls. James Phillips. (Architecture Ser.: A 1376). 10p. 1985. 2.00 o.p. (ISBN 0-89028-366-4). Vance Biblios.

Bibliographic Essays on the Architecture of the Ancient City of Rome, No. 44: The City of Rome, No. 40: City Gates: Porta Ostiensis - Porta Viminalis. James Phillips. (Architecture Ser.: A 1375). 12p. 1985. 2.00 o.p. (ISBN 0-89028-365-6). Vance Biblios.

Bibliographic Essays on the Architecture of the Ancient City of Rome, No. 43: The City of Rome, No. 39: City Gates: General Works - Porta Nomentana. James Phillips. (Architecture Ser.: A 1374). 13p. 1985. 2.00 o.p. (ISBN 0-89028-364-8). Vance Biblios.

Bibliographic Essays on the Architecture of the Ancient City of Rome, No. 42: The City of Rome, No. 38: Funerary Monuments: Sepulcrum Pomponii Hylae - Vatican Cemetery. James Phillips. (Architecture Ser.: A 1373). 17p. 1985. 2.25 o.p. (ISBN 0-89028-363-X). Vance Biblios.

Bibliographic Essays on the Architecture of the Ancient City of Rome, No. 41: The City of Rome, No. 37: Funerary Monuments: Sepulcretum-Sepulcrum Lucilii Paeti. James Phillips. (Architecture Ser.: A 1372). 17p. 1985. 2.25 o.p. (ISBN 0-89028-362-1). Vance Biblios.

Bibliographic Essays on the Architecture of the Ancient City of Rome, No. 40: The City of Rome, No. 36: Funerary Monuments: Ustrina, General Works on Tombs, Mausolea, & Pyramids. James Phillips. (Architecture Ser.: A 1371). 18p. 1985. 3.00 o.p. (ISBN 0-89028-361-3). Vance Biblios.

Bibliographic Guide for Prosecutors. 83p. 1981. 10.50 o.p. (ISBN 0-318-15269-X). Natl Coll DA.

Bibliographic Guide to Art & Architecture: 1975. Bibliographic Guide Editors. 1977. lib. bdg. 145.00 o.p. (ISBN 0-8161-6809-1, Biblio Guides). G K Hall.

Bibliographic Guide to Art & Architecture: 1981, 2 vols. Bibliographic Guide Editors. 1982. Set. lib. bdg. 145.00 set o.p. (ISBN 0-8161-6950-0, Biblio Guides). G K Hall.

Bibliographic Guide to Art & Architecture: 1978, 2 vols. Bibliographic Guide Editors. 1979. Set. lib. bdg. 145.00 o.p. (ISBN 0-8161-6847-4, Biblio Guides). G K Hall.

Bibliographic Guide to Art & Architecture: 1980, 2 vols. Bibliographic Guide Editors. 1981. Set. lib. bdg. 145.00 o.p. (ISBN 0-8161-6881-4, Biblio Guides). G K Hall.

Bibliographic Guide to Art & Architecture: 1976. Bibliographic Guide Editors. 1978. lib. bdg. 145.00 o.p. (ISBN 0-8161-6821-0, Biblio Guides). G K Hall.

Bibliographic Guide to Art & Architecture: 1982. Bibliographic Guide Editors. 1983. lib. bdg. 130.00 o.p. (ISBN 0-8161-6967-5, Biblio Guides). G K Hall.

Bibliographic Guide to Black Studies: 1977. Bibliographic Guide Editors. 1977. lib. bdg. 85.00 o.p. (ISBN 0-8161-6834-2, Biblio Guides). G K Hall.

Bibliographic Guide to Black Studies: 1978. Bibliographic Guide Editors. 1978. lib. bdg. 85.00 o.p. (ISBN 0-8161-6848-2, Biblio Guides). G K Hall.

Bibliographic Guide to Black Studies: 1981. Bibliographic Guide Editors. 1982. lib. bdg. 85.00 o.p. (ISBN 0-8161-6951-9, Biblio Guides). G K Hall.

Bibliographic Guide to Black Studies: 1980. Bibliographic Guide Editors. 1981. lib. bdg. 75.00 o.p. (ISBN 0-8161-6882-2, Biblio Guides). G K Hall.

Bibliographic Guide to Black Studies: 1982. Bibliographic Guide Editors. 1983. lib. bdg. 85.00 o.p. (ISBN 0-8161-6968-3, Biblio Guides). G K Hall.

Bibliographic Guide to Black Studies, 1984. Bibliographic Guide Editors. (Bibliographic Guides Ser.). 1984. 95.00 o.p. (ISBN 0-8161-7002-9). G K Hall.

Bibliographic Guide to Business & Economics: 1979, 3 vols. Bibliographic Guide Editors. 1979. Set. lib. bdg. 325.00 o.p. (ISBN 0-8161-6865-2, Biblio Guides). G K Hall.

Bibliographic Guide to Business & Economics: 1978, 3 vols. Bibliographic Guide Editors. 1978. Set. lib. bdg. 325.00 o.p. (ISBN 0-8161-6849-0, Biblio Guides). G K Hall.

Bibliographic Guide to Business & Economics: 1981, 3 vols. Bibliographic Guide Editors. 1982. Set. lib. bdg. 325.00 o.p. (ISBN 0-8161-6952-7, Biblio Guides). G K Hall.

Bibliographic Guide to Business & Economics: 1975, 2 vols. Bibliographic Guide Editors. 1976. Set. lib. bdg. 325.00 o.p. (ISBN 0-8161-6811-3, Biblio Guides). G K Hall.

Bibliographic Guide to Business & Economics: 1976, 3 vols. Bibliographic Guide Editors. 1976. Set. lib. bdg. 325.00 o.p. (ISBN 0-8161-6823-7, Biblio Guides). G K Hall.

Bibliographic Guide to Business & Economics: 1977, 3 vols. Bibliographic Guide Editors. 1977. Set. lib. bdg. 325.00 o.p. (ISBN 0-8161-6835-0, Biblio Guides). G K Hall.

Bibliographic Guide to Business & Economics: 1980, 3 vols. Bibliographic Guide Editors. 1981. Set. lib. bdg. 325.00 o.p. (ISBN 0-8161-6883-0, Biblio Guides). G K Hall.

Bibliographic Guide to Business & Economics: 1982, 3 Vols. Bibliographic Guide Editors. 1983. Set. lib. bdg. 325.00 o.p. (ISBN 0-8161-6983-7, Biblio Guides). G K Hall.

Bibliographic Guide to Conference Publications: 1979, 2 vols. Bibliographic Guide Editors. 1979. Set. lib. bdg. 180.00 o.p. (ISBN 0-8161-6866-0, Biblio Guides). G K Hall.

Bibliographic Guide to Conference Publications: 1978, 2 vols. Bibliographic Guide Editors. 1979. Set. lib. bdg. 180.00 o.p. (ISBN 0-8161-6850-4, Biblio Guides). G K Hall.

Bibliographic Guide to Conference Publications: 1981, 2 vols. Bibliographic Guide Editors. 1982. Set. lib. bdg. 180.00 o.p. (ISBN 0-8161-6953-5, Biblio Guides). G K Hall.

Bibliographic Guide to Conference Publications: 1975. Bibliographic Guide Editors. 1976. lib. bdg. 180.00 o.p. (ISBN 0-8161-6812-1, Biblio Guides). G K Hall.

Bibliographic Guide to Conference Publications: 1976, 2 vols. Bibliographic Guide Editors. 1978. Set. lib. bdg. 180.00 o.p. (ISBN 0-8161-6824-5, Biblio Guides). G K Hall.

Bibliographic Guide to Conference Publications: 1980, 2 vols. Bibliographic Guide Editors. 1981. Set. lib. bdg. 180.00 o.p. (ISBN 0-8161-6884-9, Biblio Guides). G K Hall.

Bibliographic Guide to Conference Publications: 1982, 2 vols. Bibliographic Guide Editors. 1983. Set. lib. bdg. 190.00 o.p. (ISBN 0-8161-6969-1, Biblio Guides). G K Hall.

Bibliographic Guide to Dance: 1975, 2 vols. Bibliographic Guide Editors. 1976. Set. lib. bdg. 200.00 o.p. (ISBN 0-8161-6813-X, Biblio Guides). G K Hall.

Bibliographic Guide to Dance: 1979, 2 vols. Bibliographic Guide Editors. 1980. Set. lib. bdg. 200.00 o.p. (ISBN 0-8161-6867-9, Biblio Guides). G K Hall.

Bibliographic Guide to Dance: 1980, 2 vols. Bibliographic Guide Editors. 1981. Set. lib. bdg. 200.00 o.p. (ISBN 0-8161-6885-7, Biblio Guides). G K Hall.

Bibliographic Guide to Dance: 1981, 2 vols. Bibliographic Guide Editors. 1982. Set. lib. bdg. 200.00 o.p. (ISBN 0-8161-6954-3, Biblio Guides). G K Hall.

Bibliographic Guide to Dance: 1982. 1983. lib. bdg. 205.00 o.s.i. (ISBN 0-8161-6970-5, Biblio Guides). G K Hall.

Bibliographic Guide to Dance: 1986, 2 vols. 1505p. 1987. 372.00 o.p. (ISBN 0-8161-7039-8, Pub. by Biblio Guides). G K Hall.

Bibliographic Guide to Education: 1979. Bibliographic Guide Editors. 1980. lib. bdg. 135.00 o.p. (ISBN 0-8161-6868-7, Biblio Guides). G K Hall.

Bibliographic Guide to Education: 1980. Bibliographic Guide Editors. 1981. lib. bdg. 135.00 o.p. (ISBN 0-8161-6880-6, Biblio Guides). G K Hall.

Bibliographic Guide to Education: 1981. Bibliographic Guide Editors. 1982. lib. bdg. 135.00 o.p. (ISBN 0-8161-6955-1, Biblio Guides). G K Hall.

Bibliographic Guide to Education: 1982. Bibliographic Guide Editors. 1983. lib. bdg. 158.00 o.p. (ISBN 0-8161-6971-3, Biblio Guides). G K Hall.

Bibliographic Guide to Education: 1983. Bibliographic Guide Editors. 1984. lib. bdg. 150.00 o.p. (ISBN 0-8161-6998-5). G K Hall.

Bibliographic Guide to Government Publications - U. S. 1980, 2 vols. Bibliographic Guide Editors. 1981. Set. lib. bdg. 275.00 o.p. (ISBN 0-8161-6887-3, Biblio Guides). G K Hall.

Bibliographic Guide to Government Publications - U. S. 1976, 2 vols. Bibliographic Guide Editors. 1976. Set. lib. bdg. 275.00 o.p. (ISBN 0-8161-6826-1, Biblio Guides). G K Hall.

Bibliographic Guide to Government Publications - U. S. 1981, 2 vols. Bibliographic Guide Editors. 1982. Set. lib. bdg. 275.00 o.p. (ISBN 0-8161-6957-8, Biblio Guides). G K Hall.

Bibliographic Guide to Government Publications - U. S. 1975, 2 vols. Bibliographic Guide Editors. 1976. Set. lib. bdg. 275.00 o.p. (ISBN 0-8161-6814-8, Biblio Guides). G K Hall.

Bibliographic Guide to Government Publications - U. S. 1979, 2 vols. Bibliographic Guide Editors. 1979. Set. 275.00 o.p. (ISBN 0-8161-6870-9, Biblio Guides). G K Hall.

Bibliographic Guide to Government Publications - U. S. 1978, 2 vols. Bibliographic Guide Editors. 1978. Set. lib. bdg. 275.00 o.p. (ISBN 0-8161-6853-9, Biblio Guides). G K Hall.

Bibliographic Guide to Government Publications - U. S. 1977, 2 vols. Bibliographic Guide Editors. 1977. Set. lib. bdg. 275.00 o.p. (ISBN 0-8161-6839-3, Biblio Guides). G K Hall.

Bibliographic Guide to Government Publications-Foreign: 1976, 2 vols. Bibliographic Guide Editors. 1977. Set. lib. bdg. 275.00 o.p. (ISBN 0-8161-6827-X, Biblio Guides). G K Hall.

Bibliographic Guide to Government Publications-Foreign: 1980, 2 vols. Bibliographic Guide Editors. 1981. Set. lib. bdg. 275.00 o.p. (ISBN 0-8161-6886-5, Biblio Guides). G K Hall.

Bibliographic Guide to Government Publications-Foreign: 1981, 2 vols. Bibliographic Guide Editors. 1982. Set. lib. bdg. 290.00 o.p. (ISBN 0-8161-6956-X, Biblio Guides). G K Hall.

Bibliographic Guide to Government Publications-Foreign: 1978, 2 vols. Bibliographic Guide Editors. 1979. Set. lib. bdg. 275.00 o.p. (ISBN 0-8161-6854-7, Biblio Guides). G K Hall.

Bibliographic Guide to Government Publications-Foreign: 1979, 2 vols. Bibliographic Guide Editors. 1980. Set. lib. bdg. 275.00 o.p. (ISBN 0-8161-6869-5, Biblio Guides). G K Hall.

Bibliographic Guide to Government Publications-Foreign: 1977, 2 vols. Bibliographic Guide Editors. 1978. Set. lib. bdg. 275.00 o.p. (ISBN 0-8161-6840-7, Biblio Guides). G K Hall.

Bibliographic Guide to Government Publications-Foreign: 1982, 2 vols. Bibliographic Guide Editors. 1983. Set. lib. bdg. 295.00 o.p. (ISBN 0-8161-6972-1, Biblio Guides). G K Hall.

Bibliographic Guide to Government Publications, Foreign 1987. New York Public Library Staff. (Bibliographics Guides). 2070p. 1988. 450.00 o.s.i. (ISBN 0-8161-7064-9). G K Hall.

Bibliographic Guide to Government Publications: U. S. 1987. New York Public Library Staff. (Bibliographic Guides). 1560p. 1988. 395.00 o.s.i. (ISBN 0-8161-7063-0). G K Hall.

Bibliographic Guide to Government Publications-U.S. 1982, 2 vols. Bibliographic Guide Editors. 1983. Set. lib. bdg. 310.00 o.p. (ISBN 0-8161-6973-X, Biblio Guides). G K Hall.

Bibliographic Guide to Latin American Studies, 3 vols. 1986. 445.00 o.s.i. (ISBN 0-8161-7025-8). G K Hall.

Bibliographic Guide to Latin American Studies: 1981, 3 vols. Bibliographic Guide Editors. 1982. Set. lib. bdg. 340.00 o.p. (ISBN 0-8161-6958-6, Biblio Guides). G K Hall.

Bibliographic Guide to Latin American Studies: 1979, 3 vols. Bibliographic Guide Editors. 1980. Set. lib. bdg. 325.00 o.p. (ISBN 0-8161-6872-5, Biblio Guides). G K Hall.

Bibliographic Guide to Latin American Studies: 1980, 3 vols. Bibliographic Guide Editors. 1981. Set. lib. bdg. 325.00 o.p. (ISBN 0-8161-6888-1, Biblio Guides). G K Hall.

Bibliographic Guide to Latin American Studies: 1982, 3 vols. Bibliographic Guide Editors. 1983. Set. lib. bdg. 368.00 o.p. (ISBN 0-8161-6974-8, Biblio Guides). G K Hall.

Bibliographic Guide to Latin American Studies: 1983. Bibliographic Guide Editors. 1984. lib. bdg. 350.00 o.p. (ISBN 0-8161-6985-3). G K Hall.

Bibliographic Guide to Law: 1977, 2 vols. Bibliographic Guide Editors. 1977. Set. lib. bdg. 200.00 o.p. (ISBN 0-8161-6841-5, Biblio Guides). G K Hall.

Bibliographic Guide to Law: 1978, 2 vols. Bibliographic Guide Editors. 1978. Set. lib. bdg. 200.00 o.p. (ISBN 0-8161-6856-3, Biblio Guides). G K Hall.

Bibliographic Guide to Law: 1979, 2 vols. Bibliographic Guide Editors. 1979. Set. lib. bdg. 200.00 o.p. (ISBN 0-8161-6873-3, Biblio Guides). G K Hall.

Bibliographic Guide to Law: 1980, 2 vols. Bibliographic Guide Editors. 1981. Set. lib. bdg. 200.00 o.p. (ISBN 0-8161-6889-X, Biblio Guides). G K Hall.

Bibliographic Guide to Law: 1981, 2 vols. Bibliographic Guide Editors. 1982. Set. lib. bdg. 200.00 o.p. (ISBN 0-8161-6959-4, Biblio Guides). G K Hall.

Bibliographic Guide to Law: 1982, 3 vols. Bibliographic Guide Editors. 1983. Set. lib. bdg. 335.00 o.p. (ISBN 0-8161-6975-6, Biblio Guides). G K Hall.

Bibliographic Guide to Law, 1983, 2 vols. Bibliographic Guide Editors. 1983. Set. 225.00 o.p. (ISBN 0-8161-6984-5). G K Hall.

Bibliographic Guide to Law: 1986, 2 vols. 1440p. 1987. 278.00 o.p. (ISBN 0-8161-7044-4, Pub. by Biblio Guides). G K Hall.

Bibliographic Guide to Law: 1987. 1987. 299.00 o.s.i. (ISBN 0-8161-7055-X). G K Hall.

Bibliographic Guide to Maps & Atlases: 1981. Bibliographic Guide Editors. 1982. lib. bdg. 150.00 o.p. (ISBN 0-8161-6960-8, Biblio Guides). G K Hall.

Bibliographic Guide to Maps & Atlases: 1980. Bibliographic Guide Editors. 1981. lib. bdg. 150.00 o.p. (ISBN 0-8161-6890-3, Biblio Guides). G K Hall.

Bibliographic Guide to Maps & Atlases: 1982. Bibliographic Guide Editors. 1983. lib. bdg. 158.00 o.p. (ISBN 0-8161-6976-4, Biblio Guides). G K Hall.

Bibliographic Guide to Maps & Atlases 1987. New York Public Library Staff. (Bibliographic Guides). 1020p. 1988. 275.00 o.s.i. (ISBN 0-8161-7060-6). G K Hall.

Bibliographic Guide to Music: 1980. Bibliographic Guide Editors. 1981. lib. bdg. 125.00 o.p. (ISBN 0-8161-6891-1, Biblio Guides). G K Hall.

Bibliographic Guide to Music: 1981. Bibliographic Guide Editors. 1982. lib. bdg. 125.00 o.p. (ISBN 0-8161-6961-6, Biblio Guides). G K Hall.

Bibliographic Guide to Music: 1982. Bibliographic Guide Editors. 1983. lib. bdg. 125.00 o.p. (ISBN 0-8161-6977-2, Biblio Guides). G K Hall.

Bibliographic Guide to North American History: 1980. Bibliographic Guide Editors. 1981. lib. bdg. 158.00 o.p. (ISBN 0-8161-6892-X, Biblio Guides). G K Hall.

Bibliographic Guide to North American History: 1978. Bibliographic Guide Editors. 1979. lib. bdg. 150.00 o.p. (ISBN 0-8161-6855-5, Biblio Guides). G K Hall.

Bibliographic Guide to North American History: 1979. Bibliographic Guide Editors. 1980. lib. bdg. 150.00 o.p. (ISBN 0-8161-6871-7, Biblio Guides). G K Hall.

Bibliographic Guide to North American History: 1982. Bibliographic Guide Editors. 1983. lib. bdg. 158.00 o.p. (ISBN 0-8161-6978-0, Biblio Guides). G K Hall.

Bibliographic Guide to North American History 1987. New York Public Library Staff. (Bibliographic Guides). 875p. 1988. 250.00 o.s.i. (ISBN 0-8161-7065-7). G K Hall.

Bibliographic Guide to Psychology: 1975. Bibliographic Guide Editors. 1976. lib. bdg. 95.00 o.p. (ISBN 0-8161-6818-0, Biblio Guides). G K Hall.

Bibliographic Guide to Psychology: 1976. Bibliographic Guide Editors. 1977. lib. bdg. 95.00 o.p. (ISBN 0-8161-6830-X, Biblio Guides). G K Hall.

Bibliographic Guide to Psychology: 1977. Bibliographic Guide Editors. 1978. lib. bdg. 95.00 o.p. (ISBN 0-8161-6844-X, Biblio Guides). G K Hall.

Bibliographic Guide to Psychology: 1978. Bibliographic Guide Editors. 1979. lib. bdg. 95.00 o.p. (ISBN 0-8161-6859-8, Biblio Guides). G K Hall.

Bibliographic Guide to Psychology: 1979. Bibliographic Guide Editors. 1980. lib. bdg. 95.00 o.p. (ISBN 0-8161-6876-8, Biblio Guides). G K Hall.

Bibliographic Guide to Psychology: 1980. Bibliographic Guide Editors. 1981. lib. bdg. 100.00 o.p. (ISBN 0-8161-6893-8, Biblio Guides). G K Hall.

Bibliographic Guide to Psychology: 1981. Bibliographic Guide Editors. 1982. lib. bdg. 95.00 o.p. (ISBN 0-8161-6963-2, Biblio Guides). G K Hall.

Bibliographic Guide to Psychology: 1982. Bibliographic Guide Editors. 1983. lib. bdg. 100.00 o.p. (ISBN 0-8161-6979-9, Biblio Guides). G K Hall.

Bibliographic Guide to Psychology: 1984. Bibliographic Guide Editors. (Bibliographic Guides Ser.). 1984. lib. bdg. 130.00 o.s.i. (ISBN 0-8161-7013-4). G K Hall.

Bibliographic Guide to Soviet & East European Studies, 3 vols. 1986. 445.00 o.s.i. (ISBN 0-8161-7031-2). G K Hall.

Bibliographic Guide to Soviet & East European Studies: 1981, 3 vols. Bibliographic Guide Editors. 1982. Set. lib. bdg. 295.00 o.p. (ISBN 0-8161-6964-0, Biblio Guides). G K Hall.

Bibliographic Guide to Soviet & East European Studies: 1980, 3 vols. Bibliographic Guide Editors. 1981. Set. lib. bdg. 295.00 o.p. (ISBN 0-8161-6894-6, Biblio Guides). G K Hall.

Bibliographic Guide to Soviet & East European Studies: 1982, 2 vols. Bibliographic Guide Editors. 1983. Set. lib. bdg. 295.00 Set o.p. (ISBN 0-8161-6980-2, Biblio Guides). G K Hall.

Bibliographic Guide to Soviet & East European Studies: 1979, 2 vols. New York Public Library, Research Libraries Staff & Library of Congress, Research Libraries Staff. 1980. Set. lib. bdg. 295.00 o.p. (ISBN 0-8161-6877-6, Biblio Guides). G K Hall.

Bibliographic Guide to Soviet & East European Studies 1987. New York Public Library Staff. (Bibliographic Guides). 2390p. 1988. lib. bdg. 495.00 o.s.i. (ISBN 0-8161-7066-5). G K Hall.

Bibliographic Guide to Technology: 1976, 2 vols. Bibliographic Guide Editors. 1977. Set. lib. bdg. 225.00 o.p. (ISBN 0-8161-6831-8, Biblio Guides). G K Hall.

Bibliographic Guide to Technology: 1978, 2 vols. Bibliographic Guide Editors. 1979. lib. bdg. 225.00 o.p. (ISBN 0-8161-6861-X, Biblio Guides). G K Hall.

Bibliographic Guide to Technology: 1979, 2 vols. Bibliographic Guide Editors. 1980. Set. lib. bdg. 195.00 o.p. (ISBN 0-8161-6878-4, Biblio Guides). G K Hall.

Bibliographic Guide to Technology: 1980, 2 vols. Bibliographic Guide Editors. 1981. Set. lib. bdg. 225.00 o.p. (ISBN 0-8161-6895-4, Biblio Guides). G K Hall.

Bibliographic Guide to Technology: 1981, 2 vols. Bibliographic Guide Editors. 1982. Set. lib. bdg. 225.00 o.p. (ISBN 0-8161-6965-9, Biblio Guides). G K Hall.

Bibliographic Guide to Technology: 1982, 2 vols. Bibliographic Guide Editors. 1983. Set. lib. bdg. 263.00 o.p. (ISBN 0-8161-6981-0, Biblio Guides). G K Hall.

Bibliographic Guide to Technology: 1987. New York Public Library Staff. (Bibliographic Guides). 1040p. 1988. lib. bdg. 325.00 o.s.i. (ISBN 0-8161-7062-2). G K Hall.

Bibliographic Guide to Theatre Arts: 1976. Bibliographic Guide Editors. 1977. lib. bdg. 100.00 o.p. (ISBN 0-8161-6832-6, Biblio Guides). G K Hall.

Bibliographic Guide to Theatre Arts: 1980. Bibliographic Guide Editors. 1981. lib. bdg. 125.00 o.p. (ISBN 0-8161-6896-2, Biblio Guides). G K Hall.

Bibliographic Guide to Theatre Arts: 1981. Bibliographic Guide Editors. 1982. lib. bdg. 125.00 o.p. (ISBN 0-8161-6966-7, Biblio Guides). G K Hall.

Bibliographic Guide to Theatre Arts: 1982. Bibliographic Guide Editors. 1983. lib. bdg. 125.00 o.p. (ISBN 0-8161-6982-9, Biblio Guides). G K Hall.

Bibliographic Guide to Theatre Arts: 1986. 260p. 1987. 168.00 o.s.i. (ISBN 0-8161-7051-7, Pub. by Biblio Guides). G K Hall.

Bibliographic Index to Romance Philology, Vols. 1-25. Mark G. Littlefield. 1974. 50.00x o.p. (ISBN 0-520-02455-9). U of Cal Pr.

Bibliographic Instruction Handbook. 68p. 1979. 10.00 o.p. (ISBN 0-8389-6729-9). Assn Coll & Res Libs.

Bibliographic Specifications for Consolidation of Records. Katharina Klemperer. (Working Paper: No. 2). 1978. 5.00 o.p. (ISBN 0-686-87241-X). UCDLA.

Bibliographic Specifications for Display: University of California Union Catalog. rev. ed. Arjun Aiyer et al. (Working Paper: No. 1). 1979. 5.00 o.p. (ISBN 0-686-87236-3). UCDLA.

Bibliographic Specifications for MARC Card Conversion Processing. rev. ed. (Working Paper: No. 4). 1979. 5.00 o.p. (ISBN 0-686-87244-4). UCDLA.

Bibliographic Specifications for Processing Campus OCLC Records. Dorothy McPherson. (Working Paper: No. 3, Revision 1). 1980. 5.00 o.p. (ISBN 0-686-87243-6). UCDLA.

Bibliographic Specifications for Processing Campus RLIN Records. Dorothy McPherson. (Working Paper: No. 8). 1980. 5.00 o.p. (ISBN 0-686-87249-5). UCDLA.

Bibliographic Utilities: A Guide for the Special Librarian. Ed. by James K. Webster. 32p. 1980. pap. 4.25 o.p. SLA.

Bibliographical Account of English Theatrical Literature. Robert W. Lowe. LC 66-27665. 384p. 1966. Repr. of 1888 ed. 46.00x o.p. (ISBN 0-8103-3216-7). Gale.

Bibliographical Exhibitions: Monographs. Mary Vance. LC 85-140875. (Architecture Ser.: Bibliography A 1350). 1985. pap. 3.00 o.p. (ISBN 0-89028-320-6). Vance Biblios.

Bibliographical Guide to Dance, 1985, 2 vols. Ed. by New York Public Library Staff. 1986. 290.00 o.s.i. (ISBN 0-8161-7021-5, Pub. by Biblio Guides). G K Hall.

Bibliographical Guide to Disaster Planning, Management, Insurance & the Case of Bhopal, India. Coppa & Avery Consultants Staff. (Public Administration Ser.: P 1803). 10p. 1985. 2.00 o.p. (ISBN 0-89028-633-7). Vance Biblios.

Bibliographical Guide to Education, 1985. Ed. by New York Public Library Staff. 1986. 235.00 o.s.i. (ISBN 0-8161-7022-3, Pub. by Biblio Guides). G K Hall.

Bibliographical Guide to Psychology, Pt. 1. 1984. 115.00 o.p. (ISBN 0-8161-6991-8, Pub. by Biblio Guides). G K Hall.

Bibliographical Inventory to the Early Music in the Newberry Library, Chicago, Illinois. Newberry Library, Chicago Staff. Ed. by D. W. Krummel. 1977. lib. bdg. 78.00 o.p. (ISBN 0-8161-0042-X, Hall Library). G K Hall.

Bibliographical Notes on Histories & Inventions & Books of Secrets, 2 vols. in 1. John Ferguson. 1983. 60.00 o.p. (ISBN 0-87556-494-1). Saifer.

Bibliographical Society of America, Nineteen Hundred Four to Nineteen Seventy-Nine: A Retrospective Collection. LC 80-14334. 557p. 1980. 20.00x o.p. U Pr of Va.

Bibliographie Courante D'Articles de Periodiques Posterieurs a 1944 Sur les Problems Politiques, Economiques et Sociaux: Dixieme Supplement, 2 vols. Fondation Nationale des Sciences Politiques, Paris, France Staff. (Bib.Guides). Orig. Title: Index to Post-1944 Periodical Articles on Political Economic & Social Problems - Tenth Supplement. 1979. Set. lib. bdg. 290.00 o.p. (ISBN 0-8161-0298-8, Hall Library). G K Hall.

Bibliographie de la Peninsule du Quebec-Labrador, 2 Vols. Universite Laval, Centre d'Etudes Nordiques, Quebec Staff. Compiled by Alan Cooke & Fabien Caron. 1970. Set. 198.00 o.p. (ISBN 0-8161-0758-0, Hall Library). G K Hall.

Bibliographies for African Studies 1980-1983. Ed. by Yvette Scheven. LC 83-162633. 300p. 1984. lib. bdg. 36.00 o.p. (ISBN 3-598-10487-1). K G Saur.

Bibliographies of the E. S. A, Vol. 2. 1983. pap. 2.50 o.p. (ISBN 0-318-02796-8). Entomol Soc.

Bibliography & Index of U. S. Geological Survey Publications Relating to Coal: January 1971 Through June 1978. Flora K. Walker. 80p. (Orig.). 1980. pap. 4.00 o.p. (ISBN 0-913312-44-4). Am Geol.

Bibliography & Index, Vol. 18: Part I, Authors. Harvard University Graduate School of Design, Laboratory for Computer Graphics & Spatial Analysis Staff. (Harvard Library of Computer Graphics, Mapping Collection). 73p. 1981. pap. 15.95 o.p. (ISBN 0-8122-1198-7). U of Pa Pr.

Bibliography & Index, Vol. 19: Part II, Bibliography & Key-Word-in-Context. Laboratory for Computer Graphics & Spatial Analysis, Harvard University Graduate School of Design Staff. (Harvard Library of Computer Graphics, Mapping Collection). 99p. 1981. pap. 15.95 o.p. (ISBN 0-8122-1199-5). U of Pa Pr.

Bibliography of Afghanistan. K. S. McLachlan & W. Whittaker. 671p. 1985. lib. bdg. 43.50x o.p. Lynne Rienner.

Bibliography of African Languages & Linguistics. John D. Murphy & Harry Goff. LC 71-98990. 147p. 1969. pap. 14.95 o.p. (ISBN 0-8132-0496-8). Cath U Pr.

Bibliography of American Historical Societies. 2nd ed. rev. ed. Appleton P. Griffin. LC 67-480. 1374p. 1966. Repr. of 1907 ed. 75.00x o.p. (ISBN 0-8103-3080-6). Gale.

Bibliography of American Numismatic Auction Catalogues, 1828-1875. E. J. Attinelli. LC 75-32394. (Illus.). 1976. Repr. of 1875 ed. 35.00x o.p. (ISBN 0-88000-072-4). Quarterman.

Bibliography of Aquatic Flowering Plants of Ohio. Ronald L. Stuckey. 1973. 1.00 o.p. (ISBN 0-86727-066-7). Ohio Bio Survey.

Bibliography of Astronomy 1970 to 1979. Robert A. Seal & Sarah S. Martin. LC 81-20877. 407p. 1982. text ed. 37.50x o.p. (ISBN 0-87287-280-7). Libs Unl.

Bibliography of Australian Medicine Seventeen Ninety to Nineteen Hundred. Edward Ford. (Illus.). 1976. 48.00x o.p. (ISBN 0-424-00022-9, Pub. by Sydney U Pr). Intl Spec Bk.

Bibliography of Business & Economic Forecasting. Ed. by R. Fildes & D. Dews. 432p. 35.00x o.p. (ISBN 0-87196-555-0). Facts on File.

Bibliography of Business Ethics, 1971-1975. Donald G. Jones. LC 76-52486. 207p. 1977. 14.95x o.p. (ISBN 0-8139-0711-X). U Pr of Va.

Bibliography of C Language. Mark Cooper. 56p. (Orig.). 1987. pap. 14.95 o.p. (ISBN 0-945473-41-9). Algo Pub.

Bibliography of California Indians: Archaelogy, Ethnography, Indian History. Robert Heizer & Albert B. Elsasser. LC 76-52687. (Reference Library of Social Science: Vol. 48). 280p. 1977. lib. bdg. 41.00 o.p. (ISBN 0-8240-9866-8). Garland Pub.

Bibliography of Cartography, 5 vols. Library of Congress, Washington, D. C., Geography & Map Division Staff. 1973. Set. lib. bdg. 360.00 o.p. (ISBN 0-8161-1008-5, Hall Library). G K Hall.

Bibliography of Cartography, First Supplement. Library of Congress, Washington, D. C., Geography & Map Division Staff. 1980. lib. bdg. 260.00 o.p. (ISBN 0-8161-0259-7, Hall Library). G K Hall.

Bibliography of Ceramics & Glass. Ed. by Larry L. Hench & B. A. McEldowney. LC 67-7492. 15.00 o.p. (ISBN 0-916094-17-0). Am Ceramic.

Bibliography of Computer Applications in Music. Stefan M. Kostka. (Music Indexes & Bibliographies: No. 7). 1974. pap. 5.00 o.p. (ISBN 0-913574-07-4). Eur-Am Music.

Bibliography of David Hume & of Scottish Philosophy from Francis Hutcheson to Lord Balfour. T. E. Jessop. LC 82-48333. (Philosophy of David Hume Ser.). 295p. 1983. lib. bdg. 36.00 o.p. (ISBN 0-8240-5411-3). Garland Pub.

Bibliography of Dickensian Criticism, Eighteen Thirty-Six to Nineteen Seventy-Four. R. C. Churchill. LC 75-5119. (Reference Library of the Humanities: No. 12). 300p. 1975. lib. bdg. 48.00 o.p. (ISBN 0-8240-1083-3). Garland Pub.

Bibliography of Discographies, Vol. III: Popular Music. Michael H. Gray & Gerald D. Gibson. 200p. 1983. 55.00 o.p. (ISBN 0-8352-1683-7). Bowker.

Bibliography of Doctoral Dissertations, India: Biological Sciences. 1975. 25.00x o.p. (ISBN 0-88386-661-7). South Asia Bks.

Bibliography of Doctoral Dissertations, India: Humanities. 1975. 25.00x o.p. (ISBN 0-88386-662-5). South Asia Bks.

Bibliography of Doctoral Dissertations, India: Physical Sciences. 1975. 30.00x o.p. (ISBN 0-88386-663-3). South Asia Bks.

Bibliography of Edith, Osbert & Sacheverell Sitwell. 2nd ed. Richard Fifoot. LC 75-31654. 432p. 1971. 39.50 o.p. (ISBN 0-208-01233-8, Archon). Shoe String.

Bibliography of Edith, Osbert, & Sacherevell Sitwell. 2nd, rev. ed. Richard Fifoot. 432p. 60.00x o.p. (Pub by St Paul's Bliographics, England). U Pr of Va.

Bibliography of Education. Will S. Monroe. LC 68-30661. 228p. 1968. Repr. of 1897 ed. 35.00x o.p. (ISBN 0-8103-3337-6). Gale.

Bibliography of English Source Materials for the Study of Modern Hindi Literature. Gordon C. Roadarmel. (Occasional Papers: No. 4). 110p. 1983. pap. text ed. 12.25 o.p. (ISBN 0-8191-3116-4, Co-pub. by Ctr S SE Asia). U Pr of Amer.

Bibliography of George Cumberland (1754-1848) G. E. Bentley, Jr. LC 74-34010. (Reference Library of the Humanities: No. 11). (Illus.). 153p. 1975. lib. bdg. 28.00 o.p. (ISBN 0-8240-1082-5). Garland Pub.

Bibliography of Hispanic Dictionaries: Catalan, Galician, Spanish, Spanish in Latin America & the Philippines. M. Fabri. 1979. pap. 45.00 o.s.i. (ISBN 0-686-77969-X). E J Brill USA.

Bibliography of International Geographical Congresses, 1871-1976. George Kish. 1979. lib. bdg. 36.50 o.p. (ISBN 0-8161-8226-4, Hall Reference). G K Hall.

Bibliography of John Brown. Donald D. Eddy. LC 72-185918. (Illus.). 210p. 1971. 7.50x o.p. (ISBN 0-8139-0937-6, Bibliographical Society of America). U Pr of Va.

Bibliography of Language Arts Materials for Native North Americans, 1965-74. G. Edward Evans et al. (American Indian Bibliographic Ser.). 283p. 1977. pap. 5.00 o.p. (ISBN 0-935626-13-1). U Cal AISC.

Bibliography of Literary Reviews in British Periodicals 1798-1820 see Romantics Reviewed: A Collection in Depth of Periodical Reviews (1793-1830,.

Bibliography of Middle Scots Poets. William Geddie. (Scottish Text Society Publications Ser: No. 61). 1969. Repr. of 1912 ed. 43.00 o.p. (ISBN 0-384-17975-4). Johnson Repr.

Bibliography of Netherlandic Dictionaries: Dutch-Flemish. Frans M. Claes. 1980. lib. bdg. 55.00 o.p. (ISBN 3-601-00048-2). Kraus Intl.

Bibliography of Numerical Models for Tidal Rivers, Estuaries & Coastal Waters. Robert Gordon & Malcolm Spaulding. (Marine Technical Report Ser.: No. 32). 1974. pap. 2.00 o.p. (ISBN 0-938412-03-5). Sea Grant Pubns.

Bibliography of Nursing Literature: Holdings of the Royal College of Nursing, London, Vol. 4, 1977-1980. Frances Walsh. 336p. 1985. 70.00 o.p. (ISBN 0-85365-906-0, Pub. by Library Assn Pub London). ALA.

Bibliography of Ohio Paleobotany. Robert C. Romans & Patricia S. McCann. 1974. 1.00 o.p. (ISBN 0-86727-073-X). Ohio Bio Survey.

Bibliography of Pennsylvania History. Norman B. Wilkinson. LC 58-9079. 826p. 1957. 9.95 o.p. (ISBN 0-911124-07-1). Pa Hist & Mus.

Bibliography of Primary Sources for Nineteenth Century Tropical Africa, As Recorded by Explorers, Missionaries, Traders, Travelers, Administrators, Military Men, Adventurers & Others. Robert L. Hess & Dalvan M. Coger. LC 71-185241. (Bibliographical Ser.: No. 47). 800p. 1972. 35.00x o.p. (ISBN 0-8179-2471-X). Hoover Inst Pr.

Bibliography of Printing. F. C. Bigmore. 1982. 75.00x o.p. (ISBN 0-87556-157-8). Saifer.

Bibliography of Psychohistory. Lloyd De Mause et al. LC 75-5140. (Reference Library of Social Science: No. 6). 200p. 1975. lib. bdg. 22.00 o.p. (ISBN 0-8240-9999-0). Garland Pub.

Bibliography of Published Research of the World Employment Programme. 6th ed. ILO Staff. vii, 177p. 1986. pap. 10.50 o.p. (ISBN 92-2-105464-0). Intl Labour Office.

Bibliography of Published Works by Kenneth E. Boulding. Compiled by Vivian Wilson. LC 82-74149. 1985. 15.00x o.p. (ISBN 0-87081-140-1). Univ Pr Colo.

Bibliography of Quantitative Ecology. V. Schultz et al. 1976. 54.00 o.p. (ISBN 0-12-787430-5). Acad Pr.

Bibliography of Research: Health Care Programs. Employee Benefit Research Institute Staff. LC 81-12521. 584p. 1981. loose-leaf 25.00 o.p. (ISBN 0-86643-021-0). Employee Benefit.

Bibliography of Research: Retirement Income & Capital Accumulation Programs. Employee Benefit Research Institute Staff. LC 81-12484. 403p. 1981. loose-leaf 25.00 o.p. (ISBN 0-86643-022-9). Employee Benefit.

Bibliography of Robert Watt. Robert Watt. LC 68-28119. 74p. 1968. Repr. of 1950 ed. 35.00x o.p. (ISBN 0-8103-3323-6). Gale.

Bibliography of Shelley Studies: 1823-1950. Clement Dunbar. LC 75-24093. (Reference Library of the Humanities: Vol. 32). 363p. 1976. lib. bdg. 43.00 o.p. (ISBN 0-8240-9980-X). Garland Pub.

Bibliography of Skiing Studies. 7th ed. 130p. 1984. pap. text ed. 15.00 o.p. (ISBN 0-89478-082-4). U CO Busn Res Div.

Bibliography of Skiing Studies. 6th ed. C. R. Goeldner & K. Dicke. 1982. pap. text ed. 10.00 o.p. (ISBN 0-89478-068-9). U CO Busn Res Div.

Bibliography of Society, Ethics & the Life Sciences, Nineteen Seventy-Six to Seventy-Seven. Sharmon Sollitto & Robert M. Veatch. Rev. by Nancy Taylor. LC 73-160650. (Reference Library of Social Science: Vol. 37). 1977. lib. bdg. 19.00 o.p. (ISBN 0-8240-9875-7). Garland Pub.

Bibliography of Sources for the Study of Ancient Greek Music. Thomas J. Mathiesen. (Music Indexes & Bibliographies: No. 10). 1974. pap. 5.00 o.p. (ISBN 0-913574-10-4). Eur-Am Music.

Bibliography of Soymilk, from 1500 to 1988. William Shurtleff & Akiko Aoyagi. (Bibliographies of Soybeans & Soyfoods Ser.). 228p. (Orig.). 1988. pap. text ed. 121.00 spiral bdg. o.p. (ISBN 0-933332-40-8). Soyfoods Center.

Bibliography of Studies in Hindi Language & Linguistics. Narindar K. Aggarwal. 1978. 14.00x o.p. (ISBN 0-8364-0172-7). South Asia Bks.

Bibliography of Technology for the Law Firm: Computers & the Law. Joseph J. Galin. LC 86-109582. (Public Administration Ser.: P 1674). 1985. 2.00 o.p. (ISBN 0-89028-384-2). Vance Biblios.

Bibliography of Telecommunications & Development. Heather Hudson. 1988. text ed. 40.00 o.p. Artech Hse.

Bibliography of Tempeh, from 1815 to 1988. William Shurtleff & Akiko Aoyagi. (Bibliographies of Soya Ser.). 107p. (Orig.). 1988. pap. 76.00 spiral bdg. o.p. (ISBN 0-933332-39-4). Soyfoods Center.

Bibliography of the History of Agriculture in the U. S. Everett E. Edwards. LC 66-27834. 320p. 1967. Repr. of 1930 ed. 40.00x o.p. (ISBN 0-8103-3102-0). Gale.

Bibliography of the Literature on North American Climates of the Past Thirteen Thousand Years. Donald K. Grayson. LC 75-5131. (Reference Library of Natural Science: No. 2). 160p. 1975. lib. bdg. 22.00 o.p. (ISBN 0-8240-9992-3). Garland Pub.

Bibliography of the Natural History of Newfoundland & Labrador. M. Laird. 1980. 95.50 o.p. (ISBN 0-12-434050-4). Acad Pr.

Bibliography of the Seventeenth Century Novel in France. R. C. Williams. 355p. 25.00 o.p. (ISBN 0-87556-717-7). Saifer.

Bibliography of the State of Maine. Ed. by Bangor Public Library Editors. 1970. 100.00 o.p. (ISBN 0-8161-0636-3, Hall Library). G K Hall.

Bibliography of the Works of Antoine Lavoisier: Bibliography of the Works of Antoine Lavoisier: Seventeen Forty-Three to Seventeen Ninety-Four. Dennis I. Duveen & H. S. Klickstein. (Illus.). 491p. 1954. 37.50x o.p. (ISBN 0-8464-0192-4). Beekman Pubs.

Bibliography of the Works of Dorothy L. Sayers. Colleen B. Gilbert. LC 78-18795. 263p. 1978. 29.50 o.p. (ISBN 0-208-01755-0, Archon). Shoe String.

Bibliography of the Writings of Henry E. Sigerist. Ed. by Genevieve Miller. 120p. 1966. 7.50x o.p. (ISBN 0-7735-0035-9, McGill Canada). U of Toronto Pr.

Bibliography of the Writings of Walter H. Pater. S. Wright. LC 74-30448. (Reference Library of the Humanities: No. 6). (Illus.). 216p. 1975. lib. bdg. 31.00 o.p. (ISBN 0-8240-1062-0). Garland Pub.

Bibliography of Theoretical Population Genetics. Joseph Felsenstein. LC 81-264. 866p. 1982. 61.95 o.p. (ISBN 0-87933-397-9). Van Nos Reinhold.

Bibliography of Theses & Dissertations Relevant to Pharmacy Administration 1970-1974. Ed. by Dewey D. Gardner. 1976. 5.00 o.p. (ISBN 0-937526-01-0). AACP Alexandria.

Bibliography of Tofu & Tofu Products, from A.D. 950 to 1988. Compiled by William Shurtleff & Akiko Aoyagi. (Bibliographies of Soya Ser.). 270p. (Orig.). 1988. pap. text ed. 143.00 spiral bdg. o.p. (ISBN 0-933332-42-4). Soyfoods Center.

Bibliography of Unfinished Books in the English Language. Albert R. Corns. Ed. by Archibald Sparke. LC 67-28093. 278p. 1968. Repr. of 1915 ed. 40.00x o.p. (ISBN 0-8103-3208-6). Gale.

Bibliography of Works About Sir Christopher Wren see American Association of Architectural Bibliographers' Papers.

Bibliography of Writings by & about Sir Reginald Theodore Bloomfield, 1856 to 1942. Carole Cable. (Architecture Ser.: Bibliography A 1342). 1985. pap. 2.00 o.p. (ISBN 0-89028-312-5). Vance Biblios.

Bibliography on Chemical Cleaning of Metals (TPC-6) Vol. 1. 101p. 1978. 20.00 o.p. (ISBN 0-915567-96-2, 52135). Natl Corrosion Eng.

Bibliography on Economic Analysis for Parks & Recreation. Henry N. McCarl & David McConnell. (Public Administration Ser.: P 1709). 28p. 1985. 4.50 o.p. (ISBN 0-89028-459-8). Vance Biblios.

Bibliography on German Settlements in Colonial North America. Emil Meynen. LC 66-25870. 676p. 1966. Repr. of 1937 ed. 70.00x o.p. (ISBN 0-8103-3336-8). Gale.

Bibliography on Herbs, Herbal Remedies, Natural Foods, & Unconventional Treatment. Theodora Andrews et al. LC 82-128. 339p. 1982. lib. bdg. 30.00 o.p. (ISBN 0-87287-288-2). Libs Unl.

Bibliography on Land Pooling - Readjustment - Redistribution for Planned Urban Development in Asian-Pacific Countries. 2nd ed. R. W. Archer. (Public Administration Ser.: P 1794). 23p. 1985. 3.75 o.p. (ISBN 0-89028-594-2). Vance Biblios.

Bibliography on Molding of Pulp. (Bibliographic Ser.: No. S4). 98p. 1966. 9.00 o.p. (ISBN 0-317-34340-8). Inst Paper Chem.

Bibliography on the Constitutions of Nigeria. Oluremi Jegede. LC 81-83448. 78p. 1981. pap. 15.00 o.p. (ISBN 0-379-20739-7). Oceana.

Bibliopegia; or, the Art of Bookbinding in All Its Branches. John A. Arnett. Ed. by John Bidwell. LC 78-74390. (Nineteenth-Century Book Arts & Printing History Ser.: Vol. 5). (Illus.). 1980. lib. bdg. 33.00 o.p. (ISBN 0-8240-3879-7). Garland Pub.

Biblioteca Chimica; Catalog of the Alchemical & Pharmaceutical Books in the Library of James Young, 2 vols. John Ferguson. 1100p. 125.00 o.p. (ISBN 0-87556-493-3). Saifer.

Biblioteca Juvenil Oxford, 8 vols. (Span.). Set. 79.95 o.p. (ISBN 0-686-57360-9, S-50473). French & Eur.

Bibliotheca Americana: Catalogue of the John Carter Brown Library in Brown University, Short-Title List of Additions, Books Printed 1471-1700. John Carter Brown Library Staff. LC 73-7121. 73p. 1973. 10.00x o.p. (ISBN 0-87057-141-9). U Pr of New Eng.

Bibliotheca Bacchica Wine & Cooking Bibliography, 2 vols in 1. Andre Simon. 45.00x o.p. (ISBN 0-87556-158-6). Saifer.

Bibliotheca Canadensis: A Bio-Bibliographical Manual of Canadian Literature. Henry J. Morgan. LC 68-27177. 424p. 1968. Repr. of 1867 ed. 60.00x o.p. (ISBN 0-8103-3151-9). Gale.

Bibliotheca Gastronomica. Andre Simon. 210p. 65.00 o.p. (ISBN 0-87556-672-3). Saifer.

Bibliotheca Osleriana. Ed. by W. W. Francis et al. 1969. 85.00 o.p. (ISBN 0-7735-9050-1, McGill Canada). U of Toronto Pr.

Bibliotheca Scriptorum Graecorum et Romanorum Teubneriana. (Lat.). cancelled o.s.i. Adlers Foreign Bks.

Bibliotheca Vinaria. R. W. Shirley. 340p. Repr. of 1913 ed. 125.00 o.p. (ISBN 0-317-03769-2). Saifer.

Bibliotheca Washingtoniana. William S. Baker. LC 67-14022. 200p. 1967. Repr. of 1889 ed. 35.00x o.p. (ISBN 0-8103-3318-X). Gale.

Bicentennial Guide to Greater Cincinnati: A Portrait of Two Hundred Years. Geoffrey J. Giglierano et al. (Illus.). 650p. Date not set. o.p. (ISBN 0-911497-08-0). Cinc Hist Soc.

Bicentennial of Materials: Proceedings, 8th National SAMPE Technical Conference, Seattle, October 1976. 502p. 1976. 40.00 o.p. (ISBN 0-318-16532-5). SAMPE.

Bicentennial Papers: Toward Economic Reconstruction, Vol. I. Miklos Szabo-Pelsoczi. LC 76-27823. 1976. 20.00 o.p. (ISBN 0-682-48625-6, University). Exposition-Phoenix.

Bicentennial Tragedy: An Indictment of the Law. John R. Tucker. 1977. 8.00 o.p. (ISBN 0-682-48588-8). Exposition-Phoenix.

Bicknell's Victorian Buildings: Floor Plans & Elevations for 45 Houses & Other Structures. A. J. Bicknell. 16.00 o.p. (ISBN 0-8446-5737-9). Peter Smith.

Bicycle Escape Routes. Philip Van Valkenberg & Doug Shidell. LC 74-29551. (Illus., Orig.). 1975. pap. 4.50 o.p. (ISBN 0-915024-04-7). WI Trails.

Bicycle Planning: Policy & Practice. Mike Hudson et al. 192p. 1982. 85.00 o.p. (ISBN 0-89397-120-0). Nichols Pub.

Bicycle Rider's Bible. Jeff Marshall. LC 79-6868. (Outdoor Bible Ser.). (Illus.). 176p. 1981. pap. 4.50 o.p. (ISBN 0-385-15134-9). Doubleday.

Bicycles & Bicycling: A Guide to Information Sources. Ed. by Mark Schultz & Barbara Schultz. LC 79-22839. (Sports, Games, & Pastimes Information Guide Ser.: Vol. 6). 320p. 1979. 68.00x o.p. (ISBN 0-8103-1448-7). Gale.

Bicycles up Kilimanjaro. Nick Crane & Richard Crane. (Illus.). 160p. 1986. 14.95 o.p. (ISBN 0-946609-27-6, Pub. by Oxford Ill Pr). Haynes Pubns.

Bicycling Fuel: Nutrition for Bicyclists. Richard Rafoth. Ed. by Paddy Monk. (Illus.). 128p. (Orig.). Date not set. pap. 6.95 o.p. (ISBN 0-933201-17-6). Bicycle Books.

Bicycling Notes. LC 76-29515. 1976. flexible plastic 3.95 o.p. (ISBN 0-916890-46-5). Mountaineers.

Bicycling the Backroads Around Puget Sound. 2nd ed. Erin Woods & Bill Woods. LC 81-11133. (Illus.). 224p. 1981. pap. 9.95 o.p. (ISBN 0-89886-039-3). Mountaineers.

Bicyclist's Guide to Yellowstone National Park. Gene Colling. (Illus.). 64p. (Orig.). 1984. pap. 3.95 o.p. (ISBN 0-934318-15-8). Falcon Pr MT.

Bidders. John Baxter. 1980. pap. 3.50 o.s.i. (ISBN 0-425-10603-9). Berkley Pub.

Bidri Ware. Susan Stronge. 1984. 17.95 o.p. (ISBN 0-905209-63-X, Pub. by Victoria & Albert Mus UK). Faber & Faber.

Bienvenue Chez Nous-Welcome to Our Town. Guy Bailey. (Illus.). 1978. 3.95 o.p. (ISBN 0-88776-111-9). Tundra Bks.

Big & Little. Botho Strauss. Tr. by Anne Cattaneo from Ger. LC 78-27794. 192p. 1979. 15.00 o.p. (ISBN 0-374-11254-1); pap. 6.95 o.p. (ISBN 0-374-51511-5). FS&G.

Big & Little: A Wrinkles Book of Opposites. Photos by Anita Shevett & Steve Shevett. LC 86-62246. (Wrinkles Board Bks.). (Illus.). 12p. (ps-1). 1987. 2.95 o.s.i. (ISBN 0-394-88679-8, BYR). Random.

Big Band Jazz: From the Beginnings to the Fifties. Ed. by Gunther Schuller & Martin Williams. (Smithsonian Collection of Recordings Ser.). 52p. Boxed Set. incl. booklet & 6 cassettes 41.95 o.p. (ISBN 0-252-01180-5); Boxed Set. incl. booklet & 6 LPs 41.95 o.p. (ISBN 0-252-01179-1). U of Ill Pr.

Big Beautiful Book of Hors D'Oeuvres. Julia Weinberg. Ed. by S. Wyler. LC 82-62408. (Illus.). 1979. 14.95 o.s.i. (ISBN 0-8329-0196-2). New Century.

Big Beauty Book: Glamour for the Fuller-Figure Woman. Ann Harper & Glenn Lewis. (Illus.). 256p. 1983. 17.50 o.s.i. (ISBN 0-03-060561-X). H Holt & Co.

Big Beauty Book: Glamour for the Fuller-Figure Woman. Ann Harper & Glenn Lewis. 1984. pap. 8.95 o.p. (ISBN 0-03-071061-8). H Holt & Co.

Big Ben. David Walker. LC 74-82477. (Illus.). (gr. 3-7). 1969. 5.95 o.p. (ISBN 0-395-07167-4). HM.

Big Ben Hood. Emanuel Fried. LC 87-50361. 320p. (Orig.). 1987. 10.95 o.p.; pap. 9.95 o.p. (ISBN 0-938838-20-2). Textile Bridge.

Big Bill Haywood & the Radical Union Movement. Joseph R. Conlin. LC 79-80015. (Men & Movements Ser). (Illus.). 1969. 15.95x o.p. (ISBN 0-8156-2140-X). Syracuse U Pr.

Big Bob. Georges Simenon. Tr. by Eileen M. Lowe. LC 81-47557. 180p. 1981. 11.95 o.p. (ISBN 0-15-112075-7). HarBraceJ.

Big Book of Applique. Virginia Avery. (Illus.). 176p. 1982. 17.50 o.s.i. (ISBN 0-684-15623-7, ScribT); pap. 12.95 o.s.i. (ISBN 0-684-17422-7). Scribner.

Big Book of Auto Repair: 1982 Edition. Ed. by Kalton C. Lahue. (Illus.). 896p. (Orig.). 1981. pap. 14.95 o.p. (ISBN 0-8227-5067-8). Petersen Pub.

Big Book of Classic Fairy Stories. Craik. 1987. 9.98 o.p. (ISBN 0-517-63792-8). Crown.

Big Book of Fondues. Eva Klever & Ulrich Klever. (Illus.). 128p. 1984. 10.95 o.p. (ISBN 0-8120-5454-7). Barron.

Big Book of Horses. Edward L. Chase. (Illus.). (gr. 4-6). 1964. 1.95 o.p. (ISBN 0-448-02241-9, G&D); PLB 2.99 o.p. (ISBN 0-448-03692-4). Putnam Pub Group.

Big Book of Marine Electronics. Frederick Graves. LC 85-22196. (Illus.). 300p. 1986. 29.95 o.p. (ISBN 0-915160-86-2). Seven Seas.

Big Book of Real Trucks. Elizabeth Cameron. (Grosset Picture Bks.). (gr. 1-5). 1970. 2.95 o.p. (ISBN 0-448-02240-0, G&D). Putnam Pub Group.

Big Book of Wild Animals. Felix Sutton. (Illus.). 32p. (gr. k-3). 1982. 3.95 o.p. (ISBN 0-448-04243-6, G&D); PLB 3.99 o.p. (ISBN 0-448-03657-6). Putnam Pub Group.

Big Boys. Max Ehrlich. 288p. 1981. 12.95 o.p. (ISBN 0-395-30525-X). HM.

Big Broadcast 1920-1950. Frank Buxton & Bill Owen. (Illus.). 301p. 1980. pap. 4.45 o.p. (ISBN 0-380-01058-5, 16683). Avon.

Big Brother & the Holding Company: The World Behind Watergate. Ed. by Steve Weissman. LC 78-90631. 349p. 1974. 14.00 o.p. (ISBN 0-87867-050-5). Ramparts.

Big Brother's Indian Programs: With Reservations. S. A. Levitan. 1971. pap. text ed. 12.95 o.p. (ISBN 0-07-037391-4). McGraw.

Big Bucks. Ernest Tidyman. 320p. 1983. pap. 2.95 o.p. (ISBN 0-380-64931-4, 64931-4). Avon.

Big Bucks: The True, Outrageous Story of the Plymouth Mail Robbery... & How They Got Away With It. Ernest Tidyman. 320p. 1982. 14.95 o.p. (ISBN 0-393-01459-2). Norton.

Big Burn: The Northwest's Forest Fire of 1910. Stan B. Cohen & Donald C. Miller. LC 78-51507. (Illus.). 96p. 1978. pap. 5.95 o.p. (ISBN 0-933126-04-2). Pictorial Hist.

Big Business Leaders in America. W. Lloyd Warner & James Abegglen. LC 55-8545. 1963. pap. 1.25 o.p. (ISBN 0-689-70198-5, 21, ATheneum). Macmillan.

Big Cats & Other Animals: Their Beauty, Dignity & Survival. Joseph R. Spies. Ed. by Kathy Leth. (Illus.). 160p. 34.95 o.s.i. (ISBN 0-8119-0737-6). Fell.

Big Cheese. Eve Bunting. LC 76-45381. (Illus.). 48p. (gr. 2-5). 1977. 8.95 o.s.i. (ISBN 0-02-715370-3). Macmillan.

Big Chill: How the Reagan Administration, Corporate America, & Religious Conservatives Are Subverting Free Speech & the Public's Right to Know. Eve Pell. LC 83-71942. 281p. 1986. pap. 10.95 o.p. (ISBN 0-8070-6161-1, BP705). Beacon Pr.

Big-City Police: An Urban Institute Study. Robert M. Fogelson. 1979. 27.00x o.p. (ISBN 0-674-07281-2); pap. 9.95x o.p. (ISBN 0-674-07295-2). Harvard U Pr.

Titles

Big Day for Scepters. Stephen Krensky. LC 76-41185. (Illus.). 128p. (gr. 3-7). 1977. 5.95 o.p. (ISBN 0-689-30567-2, Atheneum). Macmillan.
Big Deal in Veragua. Pablo Morales. 1979. pap. 1.50 o.s.i. (ISBN 0-8439-0632-4, Pub. by Leisure Bks CT). Dorchester Pub Co.
Big Doc's Girl. Mary Medearis. 192p. 1986. pap. 2.95 o.p. (ISBN 1-55547-112-9). Critics Choice Paper.
Big Drops: Ten Legendary Rapids. Robert O. Collins & Roderick Nash. LC 78-5821. (Illus.). 240p. 1978. 18.50 o.s.i. (ISBN 0-87156-217-0). Sierra.
Big Eight: Inside America's Largest Accounting Firms. Mark Stevens. 256p. 1981. pap. write for info. o.p. (ISBN 0-02-614420-4). Macmillan.
Big Enchilada. L. A. Morse. (Sam Hunter Mystery Ser.). 224p. (Orig.). 1982. pap. 2.50 o.p. (ISBN 0-380-77602-2, 87809-7). Avon.
Big Fat Cat Book. Ronald Searle. 1982. 12.95 o.p. (ISBN 0-316-77898-2). Little.
Big Fat Red Juicy Apple Cook Book. Ed. by Judith Bosley. (Illus.). 112p. (Orig.). 1985. pap. 5.95 o.p. (ISBN 0-930809-00-9). Grand Bks Inc.
Big Fearon Early Learning Book. Jean Marzollo & Beth Savage. (Makemaster Bk.). (ps-2). 1981. pap. 17.95 o.p. (ISBN 0-8224-4476-3). D S Lake Pubs.
Big Fish. Thomas Perry. 288p. 1985. 15.95 o.s.i. (ISBN 0-684-18367-6, ScribT). Scribner.
Big Game Hunting Around the World. Bert Klineburger & Vernon W. Hurst. LC 75-98959. 1969. 15.00 o.p. (ISBN 0-682-47038-4). Exposition-Phoenix.
Big Green-Out. Sol Yurick. 1983. 15.95 o.p. (ISBN 0-87795-503-4, Arbor Hse). Morrow.
Big Gus & Little Gus. Lee Lorenz. (Illus.). 32p. (ps-3). 1982. 10.95x o.s.i. (ISBN 0-13-077875-3). P-H.
Big It. Alfred B. Guthrie, Jr. 1985. pap. 2.50 o.s.i. (ISBN 0-345-32753-5). Ballantine.
Big Kids' Mother Goose: Christian Counselor Finds New Insights in Old Stories. William A. Miller. LC 75-22722. (Illus.). 112p. 1976. pap. 3.95 o.p. (ISBN 0-8066-1500-1, 10-0715, Augsburg). Augsburg Fortress.
Big Little Dinosaur. (gr. k-3). 0.79 o.p. (ISBN 0-8431-4141-7). Wonder.
Big Man & Other Stories. Martha Kelley. 1979. 4.50 o.p. (ISBN 0-682-49308-2). Exposition-Phoenix.
Big Morning Blues. Gordon Williams. 1977. pap. 1.50 o.s.i. (ISBN 0-8439-0428-3, LB428, Pub. by Leisure Bks CT). Dorchester Pub Co.
Big Paddle. Robin Moore. LC 77-90661. 1978. 9.95 o.p. (ISBN 0-87795-178-0, Arbor Hse). Morrow.
Big Paul's School Bus. Paul Nichols. (Illus.). (ps-3). 1981. 8.95x o.s.i. (ISBN 0-13-076091-9). P-H.
Big Phil's Kid. M. M. Parker. 224p. 1985. pap. 2.50 o.p. (ISBN 0-380-69931-1, Flare). Avon.
Big Picnic & Other Meals in the New Testament. Lee H. Bristol. LC 75-13455. (Illus.). 96p. 1975. 4.95 o.p. (ISBN 0-8042-2286-X, John Knox). Westminster John Knox.
Big Powers & Small Nations: A Case Study of United States-Liberian Relations. Hassan B. Sisay. LC 84-25780. (Illus.). 212p. (Orig.). 1985. lib. bdg. 26.75 o.p. (ISBN 0-8191-4507-6); pap. text ed. 12.50 o.p. (ISBN 0-8191-4508-4). U Pr of Amer.
Big Questions: A Short Introduction to Philosophy. Robert C. Solomon. (Cambridge Studies in Criminology: No. XLVI). 266p. (Orig.). 1982. pap. text ed. 11.25 o.p. (ISBN 0-15-505410-4, HC). HarBraceJ.
Big Red Barn. Eve Bunting. LC 78-12186. (Let Me Read Ser.). (Illus.). 32p. (ps-3). 1979. 4.95 o.p. (ISBN 0-15-207145-8, HJ). HarBraceJ.
Big Road Atlas of Europe. (Illus.). 126p. (Orig.). 1983. pap. 12.95 o.p. (ISBN 0-86145-151-1, Pub. by Automobile Assn Brit). Salem Hse Pubs.
Big Room: Forty-Eight Portraits from the Golden Age. Guy Peellaert & Michael Herr. 176p. 1986. 24.95 o.s.i. (ISBN 0-671-63028-8). Summit Bks.
Big Score. Burt Hirschfeld. (Orig.). 1984. pap. 2.95 o.p. (ISBN 0-440-00398-9, Emerald). Dell.
Big Sister Tells Me That I'm Black. Arnold Adoff. LC 75-32249. (Illus.). 32p. (gr. k-4). 1976. reinforced bdg. 5.95 o.p. (ISBN 0-03-014546-5). H Holt & Co.
Big Sky. Alfred B. Guthrie, Jr. 13.95 o.p. (ISBN 0-395-07762-1, 44, SenEd); pap. 9.95 o.p. (ISBN 0-395-08393-1). HM.
Big Sleep. Raymond Chandler. 1978. pap. 3.95 o.p. (ISBN 0-394-72631-6, Vin). Random.
Big Steal. Tony Marzano & Painter E. Powell. 288p. 1980. 10.95 o.p. (ISBN 0-395-28150-4). HM.
Big Tax Savings for Small Business. Joseph R. Oliver. LC 82-71426. 1982. 24.95 o.p. (ISBN 0-913864-68-4). Enterprise Del.
Big Things from Little Computers: A Layperson's Guide to Personal Computing. Dale Peterson. (Illus.). 224p. 1982. pap. 20.95 o.p. (ISBN 0-13-077859-1). P-H.
Big Time: How Success Really Works in 14 Top Business Careers. Glenn Kaplan. LC 82-8311. 384p. 1984. 16.95 o.p. (ISBN 0-312-92052-0); pap. 8.95 o.p. (ISBN 0-312-92053-9). Congdon & Weed.
Big V. William Pelfrey. 192p. 1984. pap. 2.95 o.p. (ISBN 0-380-67074-7, 67074). Avon.
Big Winds, Glass Mornings, Shadows Cast by Stars: Poems, 1972-1980. rev. ed. Morton Marcus. 80p. pap. 5.95 o.p. Brown Bear.
Big Words for Big Shooters. John E. Rose, Jr. 272p. (Orig.). 1982. pap. 6.95 o.p. (ISBN 0-89696-151-6, Everest House Book). Dodd.
Bigfoot: America's Number One Monster. Daniel Cohen. (Archway Hi-Lo Bks.). (Illus.). (gr. 4 up). 1982. pap. 1.75 o.p. (ISBN 0-671-44224-4). Archway.
Bigger Secrets: More Than 125 Things They Prayed You'd Never Find Out. William Poundstone. 1986. 15.45 o.p. (ISBN 0-395-38477-X). HM.
Biggest Christmas Tree on Earth. Fernando Krahn. (Illus.). 32p. (gr. 1-3). 1987. 7.70 o.p. (ISBN 0-317-60236-5). Little.
Biggest Company on Earth: A Profile of AT&T. Sonny Kleinfield. LC 80-13095. 352p. 1981. 14.95 o.s.i. (ISBN 0-03-045326-7). H Holt & Co.
Biggest Company on Earth: A Profile of AT&T. Sonny Kleinfield. LC 80-13095. 336p. (Orig.). 1982. pap. 8.25 o.p. (ISBN 0-03-061483-X, Owl Bks). H Holt & Co.
Biggest Game in Town. A. Alvarez. 200p. 1983. 13.45 o.p. (ISBN 0-395-33964-2). HM.
Biggest Shadow in the Zoo. Jack Kent. LC 80-25517. (Illus.). 48p. (ps-3). 1981. 5.95 o.s.i. (ISBN 0-8193-1047-6); PLB 5.95 o.s.i. (ISBN 0-8193-1048-4). Parents.
Biggest Victory. Alfred Slote. (gr. 3-7). 1977. pap. 1.95 o.p. (ISBN 0-380-00907-2, 52787, Camelot). Avon.
Bigness Complex: Industry, Labor, & Government in the American Economy. Walter Adams & James Brock. LC 86-42624. (Illus.). 384p. 1986. 22.45 o.s.i. (ISBN 0-394-54721-7). Pantheon.
Bike Fever. Lee Gutkind. 1974. pap. 1.50 o.p. (ISBN 0-380-00046-6, 19497). Avon.
Bikers: Birth of a Modern-Day Outlaw. Maz Harris. LC 85-10157. (Illus.). 128p. (Orig.). 1985. pap. 9.95 o.p. (ISBN 0-571-13510-2). Faber & Faber.
Bikes. (Fact Bks). 96p. (gr. 4-7). 1987. pap. 3.50 o.p. (ISBN 0-528-87138-2, Checkerboard Pr). Macmillan.
Biking Alone Around the World. J. Hart Rosdail. LC 72-86591. 1973. 10.00 o.p. (ISBN 0-682-47541-6, Banner). Exposition-Phoenix.
Bilateral Treaties in Force Between the U. S. A. & Italy, 2 vols. Emanuele Turco. 1270p. 1975. text ed. 95.00x o.p. (ISBN 0-8377-1201-7). Rothman.
Bild Als Naar. Ferdinand Avenarius. LC 70-147679. (Library of War & Peace; Artists on War). 1972. lib. bdg. 46.00 o.p. (ISBN 0-8240-0436-1). Garland Pub.
Bilharziasis. International Academy Of Pathology. Ed. by F. K. Mostofi. (Illus.). 1967. 32.00 o.p. (ISBN 0-387-03737-3). Springer-Verlag.
Biliary Tract. Ed. by L. H. Blumgart. LC 82-4532. (Clinical Surgery International Ser.: Vol. 5). (Illus.). 293p. 1983. text ed. 48.00 o.p. (ISBN 0-443-02322-0). Churchill.
Bilingual Child: Research & Analysis of Existing Educational Themes. Ed. by Antonio Simoes, Jr. 1976. 35.50 o.p. (ISBN 0-12-644050-6). Acad Pr.
Bilingual Education: A Reappraisal of Federal Policy. Ed. by Keith A. Baker. Adriana A. Kenter. LC 82-48040. 272p. 1982. 29.00x o.p. (ISBN 0-669-05885-8). Lexington Bks.
Bilingual Guide to Business & Professional Correspondence: English-French. J. Harvard. 1969. text ed. 28.00 o.p. (ISBN 0-08-015973-7); pap. text ed. 12.50 o.p. (ISBN 0-08-015594-4). Pergamon.
Bilingual Schooling in the United States, 2 vols. Theodore Andersson & Mildred Boyer. LC 76-5907. 1976. Repr. of 1970 ed. 42.50 set o.p. (ISBN 0-87917-050-6). Ethridge.
Bilingual Special Education Interface. Leonard M. Baca & Hermes Cervantes. 450p. 1984. pap. text ed. 26.95 o.p. (ISBN 0-675-20584-0). Merrill.
Bilingualism & Bilingual Education: A Comparative Study. E. Glyn Lewis. LC 79-55982. 471p. 1980. 35.00x o.p. (ISBN 0-8263-0532-6). U of NM Pr.
Bill Bailey Came Home. William A. Bailey et al. LC 73-79904. 183p. 1973. 7.95 o.p. (ISBN 0-87421-061-5); pap. 5.95 o.p. (ISBN 0-87421-092-5). Utah St U Pr.
Bill Haymes Songbook. Bill Haymes. (Illus.). 64p. 1984. pap. 7.95 o.p. (ISBN 0-935304-69-X). August Hse.
Bill James Baseball Abstract 1983. Bill James. 224p. (Orig.). 1983. pap. 6.95 o.s.i. (ISBN 0-345-30367-9). Ballantine.
Bill Neal's Southern Cooking. Bill Neal. LC 85-1170. (Illus.). xiv, 233p. 1985. 15.95 o.p. (ISBN 0-8078-1649-3). U of NC Pr.
Bill of Rights Then & Now: Perspectives on Individual Liberty. League of Women Voters Education Fund Staff. (Federalist Papers Reexamined: No. 2). 1976. pap. 1.00 o.p. (ISBN 0-89959-038-1, 377). LWV US.
Bill Pickett: First Black Rodeo Star. Sibyl Hancock. LC 76-41741. (Let Me Read Ser). (Illus.). (gr. k-3). 1977. pap. 1.95 o.p. (ISBN 0-15-207393-0, VoyB). HarBraceJ.
Bill Pickett: First Black Rodeo Star. Sibyl Hancock & Lorinda B. Cauley. LC 76-41741. (Let Me Read Ser.). (Illus.). (gr. 1-5). 1977. 4.95 o.p. (ISBN 0-15-207392-2, HJ). HarBraceJ.
Bill Severn's Impromptu Magic. Bill Severn. (Illus.). 192p. 1984. pap. 6.95 o.s.i. (ISBN 0-684-18074-X, ScribT). Scribner.
Billboard Book of Top Forty Hits: 1955 to Present. Joel Whitburn. LC 83-71259. (Illus.). 509p. 1983. pap. 14.95 o.p. (ISBN 0-8230-7511-7, Billboard Bks). Watson-Guptill.
Billboard Book of Top Forty Hits: 1955 to Present. rev. ed. Joel Whitburn. (Illus.). 528p. 1985. 14.95 o.p. (ISBN 0-8230-7518-4). Watson-Guptill.
Billboard's Top One Thousand, 1955-1986. Joel Whitburn. (Illus.). 144p. (Orig.). 1986. pap. 5.95 o.p. (ISBN 0-88188-475-8). H Leonard Pub Corp.
Billboard's Top Two Thousand: 1955-1985. Joel Whitburn. 140p. 1985. pap. text ed. 30.00 o.p. (ISBN 0-89820-056-3). Record Research.
Billiards at Half-Past Nine. Heinrich Boll. 1976. pap. 3.95 o.p. (ISBN 0-380-00280-9, Bard). Avon.
Billie & Berley's Best of Quilting. Billie Horine & Kimberley Channel. 48p. 1986. 6.95 o.p. (ISBN 0-8062-3023-1). Carlton.
Billing & Collections, Vol. 5. A. Zeigler. (Illus.). 1979. pap. 21.95 o.p. (ISBN 0-87489-154-X). Med Economics.
Billing & Collections see Doctors' Administrative Program.
Billions. Ian K. Martin. LC 79-55611. 192p. 1980. 8.95 o.p. (ISBN 0-689-11050-2, Atheneum). Macmillan.
Billy Budd & Typee. Herman Melville. 48p. (Orig.). 1988. pap. 9.95 o.p. (ISBN 1-55651-077-2); audiocassette tape incl. o.p. (ISBN 1-55651-078-0). Cram Cassettes.
Billy Budd, Sailor, & Other Stories. Herman Melville. Ed. by Harold Beaver. Incl. Bartlby; Cock-a-Doodle-Doo; Encantada; Bell Tower; Benito Cereno; John Marr; Daniel Orme. (English Library Ser.). 466p. 1968. pap. 2.50 o.p. (ISBN 0-14-043029-6). Penguin.
Billy Graham-Evangelist to the World: An Authorized Biography. John Pollock. LC 79-62949. (Illus.). 352p. 1980. pap. 4.95i o.p. (ISBN 0-06-066692-7, RD 324). HarpR.
Billy Idol. (Metal Mania Ser.). (Illus.). 32p. (gr. 4-12). 1985. 4.95 o.p. (ISBN 0-88188-343-3, Robus Books). H Leonard Pub Corp.
Billy Idol. Kate Russell. LC 84-25807. (gr. 3-7). 1985. lib. bdg. 8.79 o.p. (ISBN 0-671-55479-4). Messner.
Billy Jack. Frank Christina & Teresa Christina. 1973. pap. 1.25 o.p. (ISBN 0-380-01062-3, 26351). Avon.
Billy Mitchell: Crusader for Air Power. new ed. Alfred F. Hurley. LC 74-22831. (Midland Bks.: No. 180). (Illus.). 204p. 1975. 15.00x o.p. (ISBN 0-253-31203-5); pap. 6.95x o.p. (ISBN 0-253-20180-2). Ind U Pr.
Billy 'n' Bear Go to a Birthday Party see Billy 'n' Bear Series.
Billy 'n' Bear Go to Church see Billy 'n' Bear Series.
Billy 'n' Bear Go to Sunday School see Billy 'n' Bear Series.
Billy 'n' Bear Go to the Doctor see Billy 'n' Bear Series.
Billy 'n' Bear Go to the Grocery Store see Billy 'n' Bear Series.
Billy 'n' Bear Series. Robin Gunn. Incl. Billy 'n' Bear Go to Sunday School (ISBN 0-570-08900-X, 56-1546); Billy 'n' Bear Go to Church (ISBN 0-570-08901-8, 56-1547); Billy 'n' Bear Go to the Grocery Store (ISBN 0-570-08902-6, 56-1548); Billy 'n' Bear Go to a Birthday Party (ISBN 0-570-08903-4, 56-1549); Billy 'n' Bear Go to the Doctor (ISBN 0-570-08904-2, 56-1550); Billy 'n' Bear Visit Grandma & Grandpa (ISBN 0-570-08905-0, 56-1551). (Illus.). 24p. (Orig.). (gr. 2-5). 1985. pap. 3.95 ea. o.p. (ISBN 0-317-20512-9). Concordia.
Billy 'n' Bear Visit Grandma & Grandpa see Billy 'n' Bear Series.
Billy Ray & the Good News. Frank Roderus. LC 87-8876. (Double D Western Ser.). 192p. 1987. 12.95 o.p. (ISBN 0-385-23517-8). Doubleday.
Billy the Brave. Anne-Marie Chapouton. (Illus.). (ps-k). 1986. 7.70 o.p. HR&W.
Billy the Kid. Edwin Corle. LC 79-4930. (Zia Books). 306p. 1979. pap. 8.95 o.p. (ISBN 0-8263-0509-1). U of NM Pr.
Billy the Kid, Chicken Gizzards & Other Tales. James A. Perkins. LC 77-87775. (Illus.). 1977. pap. 4.00 o.s.i. (ISBN 0-936014-04-0). Dawn Valley.
Billyball. Billy Martin & Phil Pepe. LC 86-29057. (Illus.). 288p. 1987. 16.95 o.p. (ISBN 0-385-23491-0). Doubleday.
Billy's Army. Nicolas Babcock. LC 81-69129. (Illus.). 256p. 1982. 14.95 o.p. (ISBN 0-689-11242-4, Atheneum). Macmillan.
Billy's Shoes. Gen LeRoy. Tr. by J. Winslow Higginbottom. (Illus.). (gr. 1-3). 1981. text ed. 9.95 o.p. (ISBN 0-07-037201-2). McGraw.
Bilog 2. Robert Mislevy & R. Darrell Bock. pap. 11.00 o.p. (ISBN 0-89498-012-2). Sci Ware.
Binary & Multiple Systems of Stars. A. H. Batten. LC 72-88026. 288p. 1973. 70.00 o.p. (ISBN 0-08-016986-4). Pergamon.
Binary Brain: Artificial Intelligence in the Age of Electronics. David Ritchie. 224p. 1984. 14.45i o.p. (ISBN 0-316-74730-0, 747300). Little.
Binaural Hearing Aids. Andreas Markides. 1977. 73.00 o.p. (ISBN 0-12-472650-X). Acad Pr.
Binding Spell. Elizabeth Arthur. 352p. 1988. (ISBN 0-395-47096-X). HM.
Bingity Bangity School Bus. (gr. k-3). 1978. 0.79 o.p. (ISBN 0-8431-4101-8). Wonder.
Bingo, Gallant Reindeer Dog. Bernard F. Ederer. (Illus.). 1977. 7.50 o.p. (ISBN 0-682-48887-9). Exposition-Phoenix.
Bins & Bunkers for Handling Bulk Materials. W. Reisner & M. Eisenhart Rothe. (Series on Rock & Soil Mechanics). (Illus.). 1976. pap. 24.00x o.p. (ISBN 0-87849-001-9, Trans Tech Pubns (BRD)). Gower Pub Co.
Bio-Babel: Can We Survive the New Biology? Allen R. Utke. LC 77-79595. 1977. 11.95 o.p. (ISBN 0-8042-0786-0, John Knox). Westminster John Knox.
Bio-Imagery Method of Breast Enlargement & Waist Reduction. Craig Stratton. 251p. 1982. 12.95 o.p. (ISBN 0-943154-00-6). Longman Trade.
Bio of a Space Tyrant: Mercenary. Piers Anthony. (Science Fiction Ser.: Vol. II). 373p. 1985. lib. bdg. 13.95 o.p. (ISBN 0-8398-2901-9, Gregg). G K Hall.
Bio of a Space Tyrant: Politician. Piers Anthony. (Science Fiction Ser.: Vol. III). 345p. 1985. lib. bdg. 13.95 o.p. (ISBN 0-8398-2902-7, Gregg). G K Hall.
Bio of a Space Tyrant: Refugee. Piers Anthony. (Science Fiction Ser.: Vol. I). 312p. 1985. lib. bdg. 13.95 o.p. (ISBN 0-8398-2900-0, Gregg). G K Hall.
Bioactive Microbial Products: Search & Discovery. J. D. Bu'Lock et al. (Special Publications of the Society for General Microbiology: No. 6). 1982. 32.50 o.p. (ISBN 0-12-140750-0). Acad Pr.
Biochemical & Biological Engineering Science. Ed. by N. Blakebrough. 32.00 o.p. (ISBN 0-12-103601-4); Vol. 2. 1969. 56.00 o.p. (ISBN 0-12-103602-2). Acad Pr.
Biochemical & Clinical Aspects of Ketone Body Metabolism. Ed. by H. D. Soling & C. D. Seufert. LC 76-52978. (Illus.). 280p. 1978. 34.50 o.p. (ISBN 0-88416-144-7). Year Bk Med.
Biochemical & Clinical Aspects of Neuropeptides: Synthesis, Processing, & Gene Structure. Gerhard Koch & Dietmar Richter. LC 83-22381. 1983. 41.50 o.p. (ISBN 0-12-417320-9). Acad Pr.
Biochemical & Clinical Aspects of Oxygen. Ed. by Winslow S. Caughey. LC 79-23522. 1979. 39.95 o.p. (ISBN 0-12-164380-8). Acad Pr.
Biochemical & Immunological Taxonomy of Animals. Ed. by C. A. Wright. 1975. 84.00 o.p. (ISBN 0-12-765350-3). Acad Pr.
Biochemical Applications of Mass Spectrometry: First Supplementary Volume. George R. Waller & Otis C. Dermer. LC 79-24388. 1279p. 1980. 251.50x o.p. (ISBN 0-471-03810-5, Pub. by Wiley-Interscience). Krieger.
Biochemical Aspects of New Protein Food. Ed. by J. Adler-Nissen & B. O. Eggum. LC 77-30603. (Federation of European Biochemical Societies Ser.). 228p. 1978. 73.00 o.p. (ISBN 0-08-022625-6). Pergamon.
Biochemical Aspects of Reactions on Solid Supports. Ed. by George R. Stark. 1971. 60.50 o.p. (ISBN 0-12-663950-7). Acad Pr.
Biochemical Aspects of Renal Function: Proceedings of a Symposium Held in Honour of Professor Sir Hans Krebs FRS, at Merton College, Oxford, 16-19 September 1979. Ed. by D. B. Ross & W. G. Guder. (Illus.). 340p. 1980. pap. 67.00 o.p. (ISBN 0-08-025517-5). Pergamon.
Biochemical Aspects of Tumour Growth. V. S. Shapot. 334p. 1980. 11.00 o.p. (ISBN 0-8285-0006-1, Pub. by Mir Pubs USSR). Imported Pubns.

Biochemical Characterization of Lymphokines: Proceedings of the Second International Lymphokine Workshop. Ed. by Alain L. De Weck et al. LC 80-289. 1980. 76.50 o.p. (ISBN 0-12-213950-X). Acad Pr.

Biochemical Correlates of Brain Structure & Function. Ed. by A. N. Davison. 1977. 99.00 o.p. (ISBN 0-12-206650-2). Acad Pr.

Biochemical Ecology of Water Pollution. Patrick Dugan. LC 74-26780. 170p. 1972. pap. 17.95x o.p. (ISBN 0-306-20012-0, Plenum Pr). Plenum Pub.

Biochemical Ecology of Water Pollution. Patrick R. Dugan. LC 74-26780. 170p. 1972. 35.00x o.p. (ISBN 0-306-30540-2, Plenum Pr); pap. 17.95x o.p. (Plenum Pr). Plenum Pub.

Biochemical Education. Ed. by Charles F. Bryce. (Illus.). 220p. 1981. 33.00 o.p. (ISBN 0-7099-0600-5, Pub. by Croom Helm Ltd). Routledge Chapman & Hall.

Biochemical Factors Concerned in the Functional Activity of the Nervous System. Ed. by D. Richter. 1969. pap. 42.00 o.p. (ISBN 0-08-013311-8). Pergamon.

Biochemical Fluorescence: Concepts, Vol. 1. Ed. by R. F. Chen & H. Edelhoch. 424p. 1975. 85.00 o.p. (ISBN 0-8247-6222-3). Dekker.

Biochemical Individuality: The Basis for the Genetotrophic Concept. Roger J. Williams. LC 56-12578. (Illus.). 228p. 1969. pap. 5.95x o.p. (ISBN 0-292-70022-9). U of Tex Pr.

Biochemical Mechanisms of Liver Injury. Ed. by T. F. Slater. 1979. 130.50 o.p. (ISBN 0-12-649150-X). Acad Pr.

Biochemical Methods in Red Cell Genetics. Ed. by Jorge Yunis. 1969. 84.00 o.p. (ISBN 0-12-775140-8). Acad Pr.

Biochemical Microcalorimetry. H. D. Brown. 1969. 78.00 o.p. (ISBN 0-12-136150-0). Acad Pr.

Biochemical Phylogeny of the Protists. Ed. by Mark A. Ragan & David J. Chapman. 1978. 61.00 o.p. (ISBN 0-12-575550-3). Acad Pr.

Biochemical Predestination. D. Kenyon & G. D. Steinman. (Illus.). 1969. text ed. 14.50 o.p. (ISBN 0-07-034126-5). McGraw.

Biochemical Toxicology of Insecticides. Ed. by R. D. O'Brien & Izuru Yamamoto. 1970. 46.50 o.p. (ISBN 0-12-523935-1). Acad Pr.

Biochemical Values in Clinical Medicine. 7th ed. Eastham. 266p. 1978. pap. 24.00 o.p. (ISBN 0-7236-0502-5, Pub. by John Wright UK). Butterworth.

Biochemistry. Ed. by F. L. Boschke. (Topics in Current Chemistry Ser.: Vol. 83). (Illus.). 1979. 56.00 o.p. (ISBN 0-387-09312-5). Springer-Verlag.

Biochemistry. A. S. Mildvan et al. LC 67-11280. (Structure & Bonding Ser.: Vol. 20). 180p. 1975. 43.00 o.p. (ISBN 0-387-07053-2). Springer-Verlag.

Biochemistry. Michael Yudkin & Robin Offord. 1975. text ed. 34.95 o.p. (ISBN 0-395-17199-7). HM.

Biochemistry & Biophysics of Mitochondrial Membranes: Proceedings. Biochemistry & Biophysics of Mitochondrial Membranes Symposium Staff. Ed. by G. F. Azzone. 1972. 85.00 o.p. (ISBN 0-12-068950-2). Acad Pr.

Biochemistry & Function of Phagocytes. Ed. by F. Rossi & P. Patriarca. LC 81-19251. (Advances in Experimental Medicine & Biology, Ser.: Vol. 141). 716p. 1982. 110.00x o.p. (ISBN 0-306-40887-2, Plenum Pr). Plenum Pub.

Biochemistry & Genetics of Yeasts: Pure & Applied Aspects. Ed. by Metry Bacila et al. LC 78-21898. 1978. 71.00 o.p. (ISBN 0-12-071250-4). Acad Pr.

Biochemistry & Neurology. Ed. by H. F. Bradford & C. D. Marsden. 304p. 1976. pap. 52.50 o.p. (ISBN 0-12-123750-8). Acad Pr.

Biochemistry & Pharmacology of Antibacterial Agents. R. A. Williams & Z. L. Kruk. (Illus.). 89p. 1981. pap. 10.00 o.p. (ISBN 0-85664-858-2, Pub. by Croom Helm Ltd). Routledge Chapman & Hall.

Biochemistry & Physiology of Bone, 4 vols. 2nd ed. Ed. by Geoffrey Bourne. Vol. 1 1972. 83.00 o.p. (ISBN 0-12-119201-6); Vol. 2 1972. 97.00 o.p. (ISBN 0-12-119202-4); Vol. 3 1972. 104.00 o.p. (ISBN 0-12-119203-2); Vol. 4 1976. 110.00 o.p. (ISBN 0-12-119204-0). Acad Pr.

Biochemistry & Physiology of Tetrahymena. Donald L. Hill. (Cell Biology Ser). 1972. 54.50 o.p. (ISBN 0-12-348350-6). Acad Pr.

Biochemistry & Physiology of the Cell: An Introductory Text. 2nd ed. N. A. Edwards & K. A. Hassall. 1980. text ed. 52.00 o.p. (ISBN 0-07-084097-0). McGraw.

Biochemistry for Blood Bankers. Ed. by Steven R. Pierce & Susan M. Steane. 156p. 1983. 16.00 o.p. (ISBN 0-914404-88-1). Am Assn Blood.

Biochemistry I. Ed. by F. L. Boschke. (Topics in Current Chemistry Ser.: Vol. 78). (Illus.). 1979. 57.00 o.p. (ISBN 0-387-09218-8). Springer-Verlag.

Biochemistry Laboratory Techniques. Sterling Chaykin. LC 76-52458. (Illus.). 178p. 1977. Repr. of 1966 ed. lib. bdg. 12.50 o.p. (ISBN 0-88275-517-X). Krieger.

Biochemistry of Aging. M. S. Kanungo. LC 79-41522. 1980. 84.00 o.p. (ISBN 0-12-396450-4). Acad Pr.

Biochemistry of Antimicrobial Action. 3rd ed. Ed. by T. J. Franklin & G. A. Snow. 1981. 44.00x o.p. (ISBN 0-412-22440-2, NO. 2239, Pub. by Chapman & Hall); pap. 22.00x o.p. (ISBN 0-412-22450-X, NO. 6540). Routledge Chapman & Hall.

Biochemistry of Cancer. 2nd ed. Jesse P. Greenstein. 1954. 77.00 o.p. (ISBN 0-12-300550-7). Acad Pr.

Biochemistry of Characterized Neurons. Ed. by Neville N. Osborne. LC 76-55379. 1978. 81.00 o.p. (ISBN 0-08-021503-3). Pergamon.

Biochemistry of Chloroplasts, 2 vols. Ed. by T. W. Goodwin & T. W. Goodwin. 1966-67. Vol. 1. 75.50 o.p. (ISBN 0-12-289861-3); Vol. 2. Acad Pr.

Biochemistry of Foreign Compounds. D. V. Parke. 1968. 70.00 o.p. (ISBN 0-08-012202-7). Pergamon.

Biochemistry of Human Cancer. Oscar Bodansky. 1975. 94.00 o.p. (ISBN 0-12-109850-8). Acad Pr.

Biochemistry of Nucleic Acids. 9th ed. R. L. Adams & R. H. Burdon. 420p. 1981. 49.95x o.p. (ISBN 0-412-22680-4, NO. 6532, Pub. by Chapman & Hall England); pap. 23.00x o.p. (ISBN 0-412-22690-1, NO. 6531). Routledge Chapman & Hall.

Biochemistry of Oxygen: Proceedings. Gesellschaft Fuer Biologische Chemie, 19th Colloquium, Mossbach-Baden, 1968. Ed. by B. Hess & H. Straudinger. (Illus.). viii, 360p. (Fr., Ger. & Eng.). 1968. pap. 58.50 o.p. (ISBN 0-387-04067-6). Springer-Verlag.

Biochemistry of Parasites: Proceedings of Satellite Conference of the 13th Annual Meeting of the Federation of European Biochemical Societies (FEBS), Jerusalem, August 1980. Ed. by Gerald M. Slutzky. (Illus.). 236p. 1981. 60.00 o.p. (ISBN 0-08-026381-X). Pergamon.

Biochemistry of Silicon & Related Problems. Ed. by G. Bendz & I. Lindqvist. LC 77-29160. 604p. 1978. 95.00x o.p. (ISBN 0-306-33710-X, Plenum Pr). Plenum Pub.

Biochemistry of the Brain. Sudhir Kumar. (Illus.). 1980. 160.00 o.p. (ISBN 0-08-021345-6). Pergamon.

Biochemistry of the Glycosidic Linkage: An Integrated View, Proceedings. Ed. by Romano Piras & Horatio G. Piras. 1972. 74.50 o.p. (ISBN 0-12-557250-6). Acad Pr.

Biochemistry of the Poliomyelitis Viruses. E. Kovacs. 1964. 70.00 o.p. (ISBN 0-08-010111-9). Pergamon.

Biochemistry of the Retina. Ed. by Clive N. Graymore. (Illus.). 1965. 33.00 o.p. (ISBN 0-12-297150-7). Acad Pr.

Biochemistry of Thermophily. Ed. by S. Marvin Friedman. LC 78-23214. 1978. 65.50 o.p. (ISBN 0-12-268250-5). Acad Pr.

Biochemistry: PreTest Self-Assessment & Review. 3rd ed. PreTest Service, Inc. & F. Chlapowski. (PreTest Basic Science Review Bk.). 184p. 1983. text ed. 12.95 o.p. (ISBN 0-07-051932-3). McGraw.

Biochemistry: PreTest Self-Assessment & Review. 4th ed. PreTest Service, Inc. Staff. (Illus.). 184p. 1985. pap. 14.95 o.p. (ISBN 0-07-051942-0). McGraw-Pretest.

Biochemistry up-to-Date. Eric F. Powell. 1963. pap. 3.50 o.p. (ISBN 0-85032-098-4, Pub. C. W. Daniel Co. Ltd.). Formur Intl.

Biocolloids & Their Interactions with Special Reference to Coacervates & Related Systems. H. L. Booij & H. G. Bungenberg De Jong. (Protoplasmatologia: Vol. 1, Pt. 2). (Illus.). 1956. 46.70 o.p. (ISBN 0-387-80421-8). Springer-Verlag.

Biocompatible Products for Humans. Business Communications Staff. 245p. 1984. 1750.00 o.p. (ISBN 0-89336-362-6, GB-072). BCC.

Bioelectrochemistry. Ed. by Hendrik Keyzer & Felix Gutmann. LC 80-14838. 444p. 1980. 75.00x o.p. (ISBN 0-306-40453-2, Plenum Pr). Plenum Pub.

Bioelectronics. Albert Szent-Gyorgyi. 1968. 27.00 o.p. (ISBN 0-12-680945-3). Acad Pr.

Bioenergetics & Metabolism of Green Algae, 2 vols. Marcia Brody et al. LC 74-515. 1974. Vol. 1. text ed. 24.50x o.p. (ISBN 0-8422-7200-3); Vol. 2. text ed. 24.50x o.p. (ISBN 0-8422-7201-1). Irvington.

Bioenergetics: The Molecular Basis of Biological Energy Transformations. 2nd ed. Albert L. Lehninger. (Biology Teaching Monograph). 1971. pap. text ed. 21.95 o.p. (ISBN 0-8053-6103-0). Benjamin-Cummings.

Bioengineering & Rehabilitation: Windows of Opportunity Past, Present & Future. (NASA EP-216 Ser.). (Illus.). 52p. 1985. pap. 4.50 o.p. (ISBN 0-318-11759-2, S/N 033-000-00945-3). USGPO.

Bioengineering: Proceedings of the Ninth Northeast Conference, March, 1981, Rutgers University, Piscataway, New Jersey. Ed. by Walter Welkowitz. (Illus.). 432p. 1981. 110.00 o.p. (ISBN 0-08-027207-X). Pergamon.

Bioethical Decision Making: Releasing Religion from the Spiritual. Barbara Ann D. Swyhart. LC 75-13040. 128p. 1975. 1.00x o.p. (ISBN 0-8006-0418-0, Fortress). Augsburg Fortress.

Bioethics. 2nd ed. Thomas Shannon. LC 76-18054. 646p. 1976. pap. 14.95 o.p. (ISBN 0-8091-1970-6). Paulist Pr.

Bioethics: A Guide to Information Sources. Ed. by Doris M. Goldstein. (Health Affairs Information Guide Ser.: Vol. 8). 384p. 1982. 68.00x o.p. (ISBN 0-8103-1502-5). Gale.

Biofeedback. Wilfred I. Hume. Ed. by D. F. Horrobin. (Biofeedback Research Review Ser.: Vol. II). 74p. 1980. Repr. of 1976 ed. 24.95 o.p. (ISBN 0-87705-966-7). Human Sci Pr.

Biofeedback. Wilfred I. Hume. Ed. by D. F. Horrobin. (Biofeedback Research Review Ser.: Vol. I). 126p. 1977. Repr. of 1976 ed. 24.95 o.p. (ISBN 0-87705-965-9). Human Sci Pr.

Biofeedback: A Survey of the Literature. Francine Butler. LC 78-6159. 352p. 1978. 80.00x o.p. (ISBN 0-306-65173-4, IFI Plenum). Plenum Pub.

Biogenesis-Evolution-Homeostasis: A Symposium by Correspondence. Ed. by A. Locker. LC 72-96743. (Illus.). 190p. 1973. pap. 33.00 o.p. (ISBN 0-387-06134-7). Springer-Verlag.

Biogenesis of Antibiotic Substances: Proceedings. Ed. by Zdenko Vanek & Z. Hostalek. 1965. 65.50 o.p. (ISBN 0-12-713850-1). Acad Pr.

Biogenesis of Mitochondria: Transcriptional, Translational & Genetic Aspects, Proceedings. Ed. by A. M. Kroon & C. Saccone. 1974. 71.50 o.p. (ISBN 0-12-426750-5). Acad Pr.

Biogenesis of Plant Cell Wall Polysaccharides: Proceedings of the American Chemical Society, 164th National Meeting. American Chemical Society Staff. Ed. by Frank Loewus. 1973. 103.50 o.p. (ISBN 0-12-455350-8). Acad Pr.

Biogeography. James H. Brown & Arthur C. Gibson. LC 82-14124. (Illus.). 643p. 1983. 37.95 o.p. (ISBN 0-8016-0824-4). Mosby.

Biograph Bulletins: 1908-1912. Ed. by Eileen Bowser. 1973. lib. bdg. 40.00x o.p. (ISBN 0-374-90638-6, Octagon). Hippocrene Bks.

Biographia Britannica Literaria, 2 vols. Thomas Wright. LC 68-22061. 1090p. 1968. Repr. of 1842 ed. Set. 75.00x o.p. (ISBN 0-8103-3154-3). Gale.

Biographical & Historical Index of American Indians & Persons Involved in Indian Affairs, 8 Vols. Ed. by U. S. Department of the Interior, Washington, D. C. Staff. 1970. 855.00 o.p. (ISBN 0-8161-0716-5, Hall Library). G K Hall.

Biographical Concordance of the New Testament. Madison D. Cook. 216p. 1984. pap. 8.95 o.p. (ISBN 0-87213-089-4). Loizeaux.

Biographical Dictionary of American Architects Deceased. Henry F. Withey & Elsie R. Withey. 1970. Repr. of 1956 ed. 28.50 o.p. (ISBN 0-912158-11-5). Hennessey.

Biographical Dictionary of Japanese Art. Ed. by Yutaka Tazawa. LC 81-82717. 825p. 1982. 65.00 o.s.i. (ISBN 0-87011-488-3). Kodansha.

Biographical Dictionary of Japanese History. Ed. by Seiichi Iwao. Tr. by Burton Watson from Japanese. LC 76-9359. 655p. 1978. 55.00 o.s.i. (ISBN 0-87011-274-0). Kodansha.

Biographical Dictionary of Philadelphia Architects & Master Builders: 1760-1930. Sandra L. Tatman & Roger W. Moss. 1984. lib. bdg. 99.50 o.p. (ISBN 0-8161-0437-9, Hall Reference). G K Hall.

Biographical Dictionary of the British Colonial Governor, Vol. 1: Africa. Anthony Kirk-Greene. LC 80-81949. 256p. 1980. 31.95x o.p. (ISBN 0-8179-2611-9). Hoover Inst Pr.

Biographical Dictionary of the Federal Judiciary. Ed. by Harold Chase et al. LC 76-18787. (Illus.). 408p. 1976. 98.00x o.p. (ISBN 0-8103-1125-9). Gale.

Biographical Directory of the South Carolina Senate, 3 Vols. N. Louise Bailey et al. 1986. 34.95 ea. o.p. Vol. 1, 500p (ISBN 0-87249-479-9). Vol. 2, 500p (ISBN 0-87249-480-2). Vol. 3, 500p (ISBN 0-87249-489-6). 3 vol set 100.00x, o.p. (ISBN 0-87249-490-X). U of SC Pr.

Biographical Index of British Engineers in the 19th Century. S. Peter Bell. LC 75-5114. (Reference Library of the Social Sciences: Vol. 5). 206p. 1975. lib. bdg. 37.00 o.p. (ISBN 0-8240-1078-7). Garland Pub.

Biographical Notes Upon Botanists, 3 Vols. New York Botanical Garden Library Staff. 1974. Set. 338.00 o.p. (ISBN 0-8161-0695-9, Hall Library). G K Hall.

Biographie universelle ancienne et moderne, 45 Vols. 2nd ed. Joseph F. Michaud. Repr. of 1843 ed. Set. cancelled o.s.i. (ISBN 3-201-00016-7). Adlers Foreign Bks.

Biography. Alan Shelston. (Critical Idiom Ser.). 1977. text ed. 5.50x o.p. (ISBN 0-416-83680-1, NO.2502); 4.95x o.p. (ISBN 0-416-83690-9, NO.2503). Routledge Chapman & Hall.

Biography see Popeiana.

Biography Almanac. 3rd ed. Ed. by Susan L. Stetler. 1986. 90.00x set o.p. (ISBN 0-8103-2142-4); vol. 1 & 2 1771 pgs 52.00x o.p. (ISBN 0-8103-2143-2); vol. 3 925 pgs 52.00x o.p. (ISBN 0-8103-2144-0). Gale.

Biography in the Eighteenth Century: Publications of the McMaster University Association for 18th Century Studies. J. D. Browning. LC 80-14652. (Vol. 8). 207p. 1980. 31.00 o.p. (ISBN 0-8240-4007-4). Garland Pub.

Biography of a Bank: The Story of Bank of America N. T. & S. A. Marquis James. LC 77-109291. (Illus.). 1971. Repr. of 1954 ed. lib. bdg. 28.00x o.p. (ISBN 0-8371-3834-5, JABI). Greenwood.

Biography of a Bar Harbor Summer Cottage. Frank Matter. (Illus., Orig.). 1985. pap. 5.95 o.p. (ISBN 0-934745-02-1). Acadia Pub Co.

Biography of Alice B. Toklas. Linda Simon. 1978. pap. 2.95 o.p. (ISBN 0-380-39073-6, 54650-7, Discus). Avon.

Biography of an Idea. Ruth N. Anshen. 240p. (Orig.). 1986. 18.95 o.p. (ISBN 0-918825-29-6, Dist. by Kampmann & Co.). Moyer Bell Limited.

Biography of Edward Marsh. Christopher Hassall. LC 59-11654. (Illus.). 1959. 6.75 o.p. (ISBN 0-15-112215-6). HarBraceJ.

Biography of William Faulkner. Frederick Karl. 1988. price not set o.p. Weidenfeld.

BioLab Book. Lundy Pentz. LC 82-49066. 144p. 1983. pap. text ed. 9.95x o.p. (ISBN 0-8018-2512-1). Johns Hopkins.

Biologic & Clinical Effects of Low-Frequency Magnetic & Electric Fields. Ed. by J. G. Llaurado et al. (Illus.). 384p. 1974. 49.25x o.p. (ISBN 0-398-03024-3). C C Thomas.

Biological Activities of Steroids in Relation to Cancer: Proceedings. Ed. by Gregory Pincus & E. Vollmer. 1960. 88.00 o.p. (ISBN 0-12-557068-6). Acad Pr.

Biological Amplification Systems in Immunology. Ed. by N. K. Day & R. A. Good. LC 76-56828. (Comprehensive Immunology Ser.: Vol. 2). (Illus.). 340p. 1977. 59.50x o.p. (ISBN 0-306-33102-0, Plenum Med Bk). Plenum Pub.

Biological & Biomedical Applications of Isoelectric Focusing. Ed. by Nicholas Catsimpoolas & James Drysdale. LC 77-10776. (Biological Separations Ser.). (Illus.). 366p. 1977. 59.50x o.p. (ISBN 0-306-34603-6, Plenum Pr). Plenum Pub.

Biological & Physical Basis of Psychosomatic Disease: Based on Papers Presented at a Conference on Psychological Load & Stress in the Work Environment, Bergen, Norway, 1980. Ed. by H. Ursin & R. Murison. (Illus.). 304p. 1982. 75.00 o.p. (ISBN 0-08-029774-9). Pergamon.

Biological & Psychological Background to Education. C. G. Hussell & A. F. Laing. 1967. 18.75 o.p. (ISBN 0-08-012195-0); pap. 11.75 o.p. (ISBN 0-08-012194-2). Pergamon.

Biological & Social Analysis of a Mississippian Cemetery from Southeast Missouri: The Turner Site 23b21a. Thomas K. Black. (Anthropological Papers Ser.: No. 68). (Illus.). 170p. (Orig.). 1980. pap. 6.00x o.p. (ISBN 0-932206-81-6). U Mich Mus Anthro.

Biological Approaches to Cancer Chemotherapy: Proceedings. Ed. by Robert J. Harris. 1961. 66.00 o.p. (ISBN 0-12-327156-8). Acad Pr.

Biological Aspects of Human Sexuality. 2nd ed. Herant Katchadourian & Donald T. Lunde. 224p. 1980. pap. text ed. 14.95 o.p. (ISBN 0-03-055396-2, HoltC). HR&W.

Biological Aspects of Rare Plant Conservation. Ed. by Hugh Synge. LC 80-42067. 592p. 1981. 118.95 o.p. (ISBN 0-471-28004-6, Pub. by Wiley-Interscience). Wiley.

Biological Aspects of Schizophrenia & Addiction. Gwynneth Hemmings. LC 81-16040. 277p. 1982. 71.95 o.p. (ISBN 0-471-10117-6, Pub. by Wiley-Interscience). Wiley.

Biological Balance & Thermal Modification see Towards a Plan of Actions for Mankind.

Biological Basis of Medicine, Vols. 2-6. Ed. by E. E. Bittar & N. Bittar. Vol. 2 1969. 89.50 o.p. (ISBN 0-12-102702-3). Vol. 3 1969. 79.50 o.p. (ISBN 0-12-102703-1); Vol. 4 1969. 68.50 o.p. (ISBN 0-12-102704-X); Vol. 5 1969. 89.50 o.p. (ISBN 0-12-102705-8); Vol. 6 1970. 99.50 o.p. (ISBN 0-12-102706-6). Acad Pr.

Biological Control. Ed. by C. B. Huffaker. LC 79-157149. (Illus.). 530p. 1971. 65.00x o.p. (ISBN 0-306-30532-1, Plenum Pr). Plenum Pub.

Biological Control. Ed. by C. B. Huffaker. LC 74-619. 530p. 1977. pap. 22.50x o.p. (ISBN 0-306-20008-2, Plenum Pr). Plenum Pub.

Biological Control of Nitrogen in Wastewater Treatment. D. Barnes & P. Bliss. 150p. 1983. 42.00 o.p. (ISBN 0-419-12350-4, NO. 6765, E & FN Spon). Routledge Chapman & Hall.

Biological Control of Weeds: A World Catalogue of Agents & Their Target Weeds. Ed. by M. H. Julien. 108p. 1982. pap. text ed. 17.50 o.p. (ISBN 0-85198-494-0). CAB Intl.

Biological Diversity. 50p. 4.00 o.s.i. (ISBN 0-318-13863-8). Ctr Action Endangered.

Biological Dosimetry: Cytometric Approaches to Mammalian Systems. Ed. by W. G. Eisert & M. L. Mendelsohn. (Illus.). 380p. 1984. pap. 45.00 o.p. (ISBN 0-387-12790-9). Springer-Verlag.

Biological Effect of DDT in Lower Organisms. Maria L. Dinamarca et al. LC 73-12476. 238p. 1974. text ed. 29.50x o.p. (ISBN 0-8422-7120-1). Irvington.

Biological Energy Conservation. 2nd ed. C. W. Jones. (Outline Studies in Biology). 1981. pap. 8.50 o.p. (ISBN 0-412-13970-7, NO. 6489, Pub. by Chapman & Hall). Routledge Chapman & Hall.

Biological Energy Resources. Malcolm Slesser & Chris Lewis. LC 79-10255. (Energy Ser.). 250p. 1979. 18.95x o.p. (ISBN 0-419-11340-1, NO. 6250, Pub. by E & FN Spon England); pap. text ed. 18.95x o.p. (ISBN 0-419-12570-1, NO. 6709). Routledge Chapman & Hall.

Biological Factors in Materials Deterioration. (Illus.). 59p. 30.00 o.p. (52292). Natl Corrosion Eng.

Biological Foundations & Human Nature. Miriam Balaban. (Aharon Katzir-Katchalsky Lectures Ser.). 1984. 47.00 o.p. (ISBN 0-12-076150-5). Acad Pr.

Biological Functions of Carbohydrates. David J. Candy. LC 80-18668. (Tertiary Level Biology Ser.). 197p. 1980. 54.95x o.p. (ISBN 0-470-27038-1). Halsted Pr.

Biological Functions of Microtubules & Related Structure: Proceedings, 13th Oji International Seminar, Tokyo, Japan, December, 1981. Ed. by Hikoichi Sakai & Hideo Mohri. LC 82-11609. 1982. 47.00 o.p. (ISBN 0-12-615080-X). Acad Pr.

Biological Hazards: The Hidden Threat. A. Price. 96p. 1982. pap. 6.95 o.p. (ISBN 0-442-30703-9). Van Nos Reinhold.

Biological Horizons in Surface Science. Ed. by L. M. Prince & D. F. Sears. 1973. 89.50 o.p. (ISBN 0-12-565850-8). Acad Pr.

Biological Hydroxylation Mechanisms: Proceedings. Biochemical Society Symposium, 34th. Ed. by G. S. Boyd & R. M. Smellie. 1973. 49.50 o.p. (ISBN 0-12-121850-3). Acad Pr.

Biological Identification with Computers. Ed. by R. J. Pankhurst. (Systematics Association Ser.). 1975. 82.50 o.p. (ISBN 0-12-544850-3). Acad Pr.

Biological Markers in Mental Disorders: Proceedings of the Symposium Held in Milan, Italy, June 1983. Ed. by S. Garattini & G. Tognoni. 200p. 1985. pap. 36.00 o.p. (ISBN 0-08-031848-7). Pergamon.

Biological Markers in Psychiatry & Neurology: Symposium on Biological Markers in Psychiatry & Neurology, Ochsner Clinic, New Orleans, U. S. A., 8-10 May 1981. Ed. by E. Usdin & I. Hanin. 544p. 1982. 110.00 o.p. (ISBN 0-08-027987-2). Pergamon.

Biological Mechanisms of Attachment: The Comparative Morphology & Bioengineering of Organs for Linkage, Suction, & Adhesion. W. Nachtigall. Tr. by M. A. Biederman-Thorson. LC 73-17936. (Illus.). 194p. 1974. 49.50 o.p. (ISBN 0-387-06550-4). Springer-Verlag.

Biological Methods of Prospecting for Minerals. R. R. Brooks. LC 82-21819. 322p. 1983. 53.95 o.p. (ISBN 0-471-87400-0). Wiley.

Biological Monitoring in Water Pollution. J. Cairns, Jr. (Illus.). 144p. 1982. 40.00 o.p. (ISBN 0-08-028730-1). Pergamon.

Biological Monitoring Methods for Industrial Chemicals. Randall C. Baselt. LC 79-56927. 312p. 1980. text ed. 55.00 o.p. (ISBN 0-931890-04-7, Biomed Pubns). Year Bk Med.

Biological Order & Brain Organization: Selected Works of W. R. Hess. Ed. by K. Akert. (Illus.). 347p. 1981. 77.60 o.p. (ISBN 0-387-10551-4). Springer-Verlag.

Biological Paths to Energy Self-Reliance. Russell E. Anderson. 400p. 1982. pap. 18.95 o.p. (ISBN 0-442-20872-3). Van Nos Reinhold.

Biological Principles of Tissue Banking. R. Klen. (Illus.). 273p. 1982. 87.00 o.p. (ISBN 0-08-024413-0). Pergamon.

Biological Processes Design for Wastewater Treatment. Clifford W. Randall & Larry D. Benefield. (Environmental Sciences Ser.). (Illus.). 1980. text ed. 40.33 o.p. (ISBN 0-13-076406-X). P-H.

Biological Relevance of Immune Suppression Induced by Therapeutic & Environmental Chemicals. J. Dean & M. Padarathsingh. 346p. 1981. 42.95 o.p. (ISBN 0-442-24429-0). Van Nos Reinhold.

Biological Response Mediators & Modulators (Symposium) Ed. by J. Thomas August. (John Jacob Abel Symposium on Drug Development). 1983. 45.50 o.p. (ISBN 0-12-068050-5). Acad Pr.

Biological Response Modifiers in Human Oncology & Immunology. Ed. by Thomas Klein et al. LC 83-13410. (Advances in Experimental Medicine & Biology Ser.: Vol. 166). 334p. 1983. 59.50x o.p. (ISBN 0-306-41391-4, Plenum Pr). Plenum Pub.

Biological Rhythms & Behavior. Julien Mendlewicz & Herman Meir van Praag. 154p. 1983. pap. 53.95x o.p. Transaction Pubs.

Biological Rhythms & Human Performance. Ed. by W. P. Colquhoun. 1971. 76.00 o.p. (ISBN 0-12-182050-5). Acad Pr.

Biological Rhythms in Birds: Neural & Endocrine Aspects. Ed. by Y. Tanabe et al. 373p. 1980. 55.00 o.p. (ISBN 0-387-10311-2). Springer-Verlag.

Biological Science. 3rd ed. William T. Keeton. (Illus.). 1980. text ed. 35.95x o.p. (ISBN 0-393-95021-2); pap. 2.95x tchr's manual o.p. (ISBN 0-393-95031-X). Norton.

Biological Science: Demonstration - Recitation Guide. Vicente D. Villa et al. (Illus.). 77p. 1980. pap. 6.95 lab manual o.p. (ISBN 0-89459-118-5). Hunter Textbks.

Biological Science for Elementary Teachers: Laboratory Manual. Albert Ruesink & Malcolm Slovin. 1979. pap. text ed. 8.95x o.s.i. (ISBN 0-89917-318-7). TIS Inc.

Biological Sciences. Valerie Kay. (Developing Reading Skills Ser.). (Illus.). 92p. 1984. pap. text ed. 6.95 o.p. (ISBN 0-08-031063-X). Alemany Pr.

Biological Structure & Function: Proceedings, 2 Vols. I U B - I U B S Joint Symposium - 1st - Stockholm - 1960. Ed. by T. W. Goodwin & Olov Lindberg. 1961. Vol. 1. 57.50 o.p. (ISBN 0-12-289851-6). Acad Pr.

Biological Structures & Coupled Flows. Ed. by Avraham Oplatka & Miriam Balaban. 1983. 44.00 o.p. Acad Pr.

Biological Studies of Mental Processes. Ed. by David Caplan. (Illus.). 1980. 37.50x o.p. (ISBN 0-262-03061-6). MIT Pr.

Biological Techniques in Electron Microscopy. Ed. by D. F. Parsons. 1970. 44.50 o.p. (ISBN 0-12-545550-X). Acad Pr.

Biological Transmission of Disease Agents: Proceedings. Symposium of the Entymological Society of America - Atlantic City - 1960. Ed. by K. Maramorosch. 1962. 32.50 o.p. (ISBN 0-12-470250-3). Acad Pr.

Biologically Active Principles of Natural Products. Wolfgang Voelter & Doyle C. Doves. (Illus.). 319p. 1985. text ed. 27.95 o.p. (ISBN 0-86577-144-8). Thieme Med Pubs.

Biology. 2nd ed. Karen Arms & Pamela S. Camp. 1982. text ed. 36.95 o.p. (ISBN 0-03-059961-X, CBS C); instr's manual 13.95 o.p. (ISBN 0-03-059962-8); study guide 13.95 o.p. (ISBN 0-03-059966-0). SCP.

Biology. 4th ed. Helena Curtis. LC 82-83895. (Illus.). 1983. text ed. 43.95x o.p. (ISBN 0-87901-186-6); study guide 9.95x o.p. (ISBN 0-87901-187-4); lab topics in biology. 15.95x o.p. (ISBN 0-87901-103-3). Worth.

Biology. Clyde F. Herreid. (Illus.). 1978. write for info. o.p. (ISBN 0-02-353780-9). Macmillan.

Biology. Leland G. Johnson. 1215p. 1982. text ed. write for info. o.p. (ISBN 0-697-04706-7). Wm C Brown.

Biology: A Contemporary View. Thomas A. Steyaert. (Illus.). 512p. 1975. text ed. 37.95 o.p. (ISBN 0-07-061346-X). McGraw.

Biology: An Introduction. K. Johnson et al. 1984. 40.95 o.p. (ISBN 0-8053-7887-1); study guide 14.95 o.p. (ISBN 0-8053-7888-X); instr's guide 6.95 o.p. (ISBN 0-8053-7889-8); transparencies 150.00 o.p. (ISBN 0-8053-7891-X). Benjamin-Cummings.

Biology & Chemistry of Basement Membranes. Ed. by Nicholas A. Kefalides. 1978. 39.95 o.p. (ISBN 0-12-403150-1). Acad Pr.

Biology & Knowledge. Jean Piaget. Tr. by Beatrix Walsh from Fr. LC 70-157421. 1974. pap. text ed. 5.45 o.s.i. (ISBN 0-226-66776-6, P508, Phoen). U of Chicago Pr.

Biology & Man. George G. Simpson. LC 69-12045. 175p. 1969. 5.95 o.p. (ISBN 0-15-112362-4). HarBraceJ.

Biology & Management of Capricornis & Related Mountain Antelopes. Ed. by Hiroaki Soma. 416p. 1987. lib. bdg. 99.95 o.p. (ISBN 0-7099-4458-6, Pub. by Croom Helm UK). Routledge Chapman & Hall.

Biology & Management of Mountain Ungulates. Ed. by Sandro Lovari. LC 84-21239. (Illus.). 271p. 1985. 43.00 o.p. (ISBN 0-7099-1688-4, Pub. by Croom Helm Ltd). Routledge Chapman & Hall.

Biology & Neurophysiology of the Conditioned Reflex & Its Role in Adaptive Behavior. Peter K. Anokhin. Tr. by Samuel A. Corson. LC 73-744. 592p. 1977. 145.00 o.p. (ISBN 0-08-017160-5); pap. 145.00 o.p. (ISBN 0-08-021516-5). Pergamon.

Biology & Pathology of Nerve Growth. H. Mei Liu. LC 81-3630. 1981. 53.50 o.p. (ISBN 0-12-452960-7). Acad Pr.

Biology & Radiobiology of Anucleate Systems, 2 vols. Ed. by Silvano Bonotto et al. 1972. Vol. 1. 46.50 o.p. (ISBN 0-12-115001-1); Vol. 2. 50.50 o.p. (ISBN 0-12-115002-X). Acad Pr.

Biology Encyclopedia. (Encyclopedia Ser.). (Illus.). 144p. (gr. 4 up). 1985. 14.95 o.s.i. (ISBN 0-02-689198-0, Checkerboard Pr). Macmillan.

Biology, History & Natural Philosophy. Ed. by Allan D. Breck & Wolfgang Yourgrau. LC 74-774. 370p. 1974. pap. 6.95x o.p. (ISBN 0-306-20009-0, Rosetta). Plenum Pub.

Biology in the Laboratory. William T. Keeton et al. 1970. pap. 9.95x o.p. (ISBN 0-393-09943-1). Norton.

Biology in the Modern World. 2nd ed. Tommy E. Wynn. 178p. 1979. pap. 9.95x lab manual o.p. (ISBN 0-89459-052-9). Hunter Textbks.

Biology in Transition: A Critical Inquiry. Harry Lehman. 1978. 8.50 o.p. (ISBN 0-682-48973-5, University). Exposition-Phoenix.

Biology, Including Modern Biology in Review. Maurice Bleifeld. 1981. pap. 7.95 o.p. (ISBN 0-8120-2345-5). Barron.

Biology Lab Text. 2nd ed. Robert H. Brown & Roy H. Wishard. 1986. pap. text ed. 28.95 o.p. (ISBN 0-8403-3872-4). Kendall-Hunt.

Biology Laboratory Manual. Charlie J. Salter. (Illus.). 142p. 1979. lab manual 6.95x o.p. (ISBN 0-89459-046-4). Hunter Textbks.

Biology of a Marine Copepod: Calanus Finmarchicus (Gunnerus) S. M. Marshall & A. P. Orr. (Illus.). vii, 195p. 1972. Repr. of 1955 ed. 21.00 o.p. (ISBN 0-387-05677-7). Springer-Verlag.

Biology of a Neotropical Glass Frog, Centrolenella Fleischmanni (Boettger), with Special Reference to its Frogfly Associates. Jaime Villa. (Contributions in Biology & Geology Ser.: No. 55). (Illus.). 60p. 1984. 8.50 o.p. (ISBN 0-89326-098-3). Milwaukee Pub Mus.

Biology of Acetabularia: Proceedings. Ed. by Jean Brachet & S. Bonotto. 1970. 65.50 o.p. (ISBN 0-12-123360-X). Acad Pr.

Biology of Aging. Ed. by John A. Behnke et al. LC 78-19012. (Illus.). 400p. 1978. 27.50x o.p. (ISBN 0-306-31139-9, Plenum Pr). Plenum Pub.

Biology of Agricultural Systems. C. R. Spedding. 1975. 68.00 o.p. (ISBN 0-12-656550-3). Acad Pr.

Biology of Amphibian Tumors. Ed. by M. Mizell. LC 72-101624. (Recent Results in Cancer Research Special Supplement). (Illus.). 1969. 106.00 o.p. (ISBN 0-387-04430-2). Springer-Verlag.

Biology of Benthic Organisms: 11th European Symposium on Marine Biology, Galway, Ireland. Ed. by B. F. Keegan & P. O. Ceidigh. 1977. 155.00 o.p. (ISBN 0-08-021378-2). Pergamon.

Biology of Bone Marrow Transplantation. Ed. by Robert P. Gale & C. Fred Fox. (ICN-UCLA Symposia on Molecular & Cellular Biology Ser.: Vol. 17). 1980. 76.50 o.p. (ISBN 0-12-273960-4). Acad Pr.

Biology of Bryozoans. Ed. by Robert M. Woollacott & Russell L. Zimmer. 1977. 79.00 o.p. (ISBN 0-12-763150-X). Acad Pr.

Biology of Cancer. 2nd ed. E. J. Ambrose & F. J. Roe. LC 74-26860. 315p. 1975. 84.95x o.p. (ISBN 0-470-02527-1). Halsted Pr.

Biology of Fibroblast. Ed. by E. Kulonen. 1974. 104.00 o.p. (ISBN 0-12-428950-9). Acad Pr.

Biology of Gestation, 2 Vols. N. S. Assali. 1968. Vol. 1. 84.00 o.p. (ISBN 0-12-065401-6); Vol. 2. 84.00 o.p. (ISBN 0-12-065402-4). Set (ISBN 0-686-76852-3). Acad Pr.

Biology of Halophytes. Yoav Waisel. (Physiological Ecology Ser). 1972. 80.50 o.p. (ISBN 0-12-730850-4). Acad Pr.

Biology of Human Personality. G. Mangan. (International Series in Experimental Psychology: Vol. 25). 470p. 1982. 105.00 o.p. (ISBN 0-08-026781-5). Pergamon.

Biology of Hydra. Ed. by Allison L. Burnett. 1973. 79.50 o.p. (ISBN 0-12-145950-0). Acad Pr.

Biology of Imaginal Disks. H. Ursprung & R. Noethiger. LC 72-75723. (Results & Problems in Cell Differentiation: Vol. 5). (Illus.). 189p. 1972. 25.00 o.p. (ISBN 0-387-05785-4). Springer-Verlag.

Biology of Memory. Ed. by Karl Pribram & Donald Braodbent. 1970. 58.00 o.p. (ISBN 0-12-564350-0). Acad Pr.

Biology of Microorganisms. 4th ed. Thomas D. Brock et al. (Illus.). 868p. 1984. text ed. (ISBN 0-13-078113-4). P-H.

Biology of Mosses. D. H. Richardson. LC 81-3029. 220p. 1981. pap. 34.95x o.p. (ISBN 0-470-27190-6). Halsted Pr.

Biology of Nematodes: Current Studies. R. Behme et al. LC 72-8856. 219p. 1972. text ed. 24.50x o.p. (ISBN 0-8422-7043-4). Irvington.

Biology of Nutrition, Pts. 1-2. Ed. by R. N. Fiennes. Incl. Pt. 1. The Evolution & Nature of Living Systems; Pt. 2. The Organizations & Nutritional Methods of Life Forms. 688p. 1972. Set. 185.00 o.p. (ISBN 0-08-016470-6). Pergamon.

Biology of Physical Activity. Dee Edington & V. Reggie Edgerton. LC 75-26095. (Illus.). 352p. 1976. text ed. 21.95 o.p. (ISBN 0-395-18579-3). HM.

Biology of Plankton. Thomas A. Clarke et al. 206p. 1972. text ed. 29.00x o.p. (ISBN 0-8422-7016-7). Irvington.

Biology of Plant Litter Decomposition, 2 vols. Ed. by C. H. Dickinson & G. J. Pugh. 1974. Vol. 1. 91.00 o.p. (ISBN 0-12-215001-5); Vol. 2. 140.00 o.p. (ISBN 0-12-215002-3). Acad Pr.

Biology of Pseudoscorpions. Peter Weygoldt. LC 78-82300. (Books in Biology Ser: No. 6). (Illus.). 1969. text ed. 13.50x o.s.i. (ISBN 0-674-07425-4). Harvard U Pr.

Biology of Reinforcement: Facet of Brain Stimulation Reward. Ed. by Aryeh Routtenberg. (Behavioral Biology Ser.). 1980. 35.00 o.p. (ISBN 0-12-599350-1). Acad Pr.

Biology of RNA. J. L. Sirlin. 1972. 79.50 o.p. (ISBN 0-12-646950-4). Acad Pr.

Biology of RNA-Tumor Viruses. Howard M. Temin. (Perspectives of Current Research Ser.). 318p. 1974. text ed. 29.50x o.p. (ISBN 0-8422-7237-2). Irvington.

Biology of Tetrahymena. Alfred M. Elliot. LC 73-12911. 508p. 1982. 69.95 o.p. (ISBN 0-87933-013-9). Van Nos Reinhold.

Biology of the Anthropod Cuticle, 2 vols. in 1, Vols. 4-5. A. C. Neville. LC 74-30175. (Zoophysiology & Ecology Ser). (Illus.). 500p. 1975. 87.00 o.p. (ISBN 0-387-07081-8). Springer-Verlag.

Biology of the Arthropod Cuticle. Charles Neville. Ed. by J. J. Head. LC 78-51261. (Carolina Biology Readers Ser.: No. 103). (Illus.). 16p. (gr. 10 up). 1978. pap. 1.80 o.p. (ISBN 0-89278-303-6, 45-9703). Carolina Biological.

Biology of the Cancer Cell. Karl Letnansky. LC 81-80907. (Illus.). 434p. 1980. 76.50 o.p. (ISBN 0-89640-052-2). Igaku-Shoin.

Biology of the Cell. 2nd ed. Stephen L. Wolfe. 544p. 1981. text ed. (ISBN 0-534-00900-X). Wadsworth Pub.

Biology of the Cyclostomes. M. W. Hardisty. LC 79-40803. 350p. 1979. 75.00x o.p. (ISBN 0-412-14120-5, NO.6142, Pub. by Chapman & Hall England). Routledge Chapman & Hall.

Biology of the Kinetoplastida, Vol. I. Ed. by W. H. R. Lumsden & D. A. Evans. 1976. 122.00 o.p. (ISBN 0-12-460201-0). Acad Pr.

Biology of the Lymphokines. Ed. by Stanley Cohen et al. LC 78-825. 1979. 75.50 o.p. (ISBN 0-12-178250-6). Acad Pr.

Biology of the Male Gamete: Linnean Society Supplement No. 1 to the Biological Journal, Vol. 7. Ed. by J. G. Duckett & P. A. Racey. 1975. 125.00 o.p. (ISBN 0-12-223050-7). Acad Pr.

Biology of the Nemerteans of the Atlantic Coast of North America. Wesley R. Coe. 1943. pap. 59.50x o.p. (ISBN 0-686-51347-9). Elliots Bks.

Biology of the Nocardiae. Ed. by M. Goodfellow. 1976. 125.50 o.p. (ISBN 0-12-289650-5). Acad Pr.

Biology of the Race Problem. Wesley C. George. 72p. 1979. pap. 2.00x o.p. (ISBN 0-911038-76-0, 132). Noontide.

Biology of the Reptilia: Morphology D, Vol.4. Ed. by Carl Gans & Thomas Parsons. 1974. 150.00 o.p. (ISBN 0-12-274604-X). Acad Pr.

Biology of Turbellaria. Jacob Shapira et al. (Illus.). 220p. 1973. text ed. 39.50x o.p. (ISBN 0-8422-7085-X). Irvington.

Biology of Turbellaria: Experimental Advances, II. Teiichi Betchaku et al. LC 72-13502. 1973. 29.50x o.p. (ISBN 0-8422-7112-0). Irvington.

Biology One Hundred One Laboratory Manual. Richard N. Trelease et al. 1982. pap. text ed. 8.95 o.p. (ISBN 0-8403-2745-5). Kendall-Hunt.

Biology: The Essential Principles. Tom M. Graham. LC 81-53071. 736p. 1982. text ed. 33.95x o.p. (ISBN 0-03-057838-8). SCP.

Biology: The Unity & Diversity of Life. 4th ed. Cecie Starr & Ralph Taggart. 776p. 1987. text ed. (ISBN 0-534-06924-X). Wadsworth Pub.

Biology, 1988-89. 5th, rev. ed. Ed. by Phyllis C. Braun. LC 74-30680. (Annual Editions Ser.). (Illus.). 256p. 1988. pap. text ed. 9.95 o.p. (ISBN 0-87967-709-0). Dushkin Pub.

Biomarkers, Genetics & Cancer. Henry T. Lynch & Hoda Anton-Guirgis. (Illus.). 192p. 1985. 50.95 o.p. (ISBN 0-442-24958-6). Van Nos Reinhold.

Biomass As a Nonfossil Fuel Source. Ed. by Donald L. Klass. LC 80-26044. (ACS Symposium Ser.: No. 144). 1981. 44.95 o.p. (ISBN 0-8412-0599-X). Am Chemical.

Biomass for Energy in the Developing Countries: Current Role-Potential-Problems-Prospects. D. O. Hall et al. (Illus.). 200p. 1982. 55.00 o.p. (ISBN 0-08-028689-5). Pergamon.

Biomass Utilization. Ed. by Wilfred A. Cote. LC 83-9585. (NATO ASI Series A, Life Sciences: Vol. 67). 742p. 1983. 115.00x o.p. (ISBN 0-306-41376-0, Plenum Pr). Plenum Pub.

Biomaterials in Reconstructive Surgery. Rubin. 1982. 99.95 o.p. (ISBN 0-8016-4232-9). Mosby.

Biomaterials, 1980, Vol. 3. Ed. by George D. Winter et al. LC 81-15923. (Advances in Biomaterials Ser.). 221p. 1982. 110.00x o.p. (ISBN 0-471-10126-5, Pub. by Wiley-Interscience). Wiley.

Biomechanics of Women's Gymnastics. Gerald S. George. 1980. text ed. 30.00 o.p. (ISBN 0-13-077461-8). P-H.

Biomechanics 3: Proceedings of the International Seminar on Biomechanics, 3rd, Rome, 1971. International Seminar on Biomechanics Staff. Ed. by S. Cerquiglini et al. (Medicine & Sport Ser.: Vol 8). 512p. 1973. 106.75 o.p. (ISBN 3-8055-1406-9). S Karger.

Biomedical Applications of Immobilized Enzymes & Proteins, 2 vols. Ed. by T. M. Chang. Incl. Vol. 1. 448p. 1977. 69.50x (ISBN 0-306-34311-8); Vol. 2. 380p. 1977. 69.50x (ISBN 0-306-34312-6). LC 76-56231. (Illus., Plenum Pr). Plenum Pub.

Biomedical Aspects of Botulism. Ed. by George Lewis. LC 81-19119. 1981. 52.00 o.p. (ISBN 0-12-447180-3). Acad Pr.

Biomedical Aspects of Drug Dependence: International Biomedical Research Symposium on Drug Dependence, Tangier, Morocco, 11-15 October 1982. Ed. by A. A. Badawy. (Illus.). 120p. 1984. pap. 22.00 o.p. (ISBN 0-08-030785-X). Pergamon.

Biomedical Aspects of Lactation. Stuart Patton & Robert G. Jensen. 1976. pap. 17.50 o.p. (ISBN 0-08-020192-X). Pergamon.

Biomedical Engineering I: Recent Developments. Proceedings of the First Southern Biomedical Engineering Conference, Shreveport, Louisiana, U. S. A., June 7-8, 1982. Louisiana State University Medical Center, Subrata Saha Staff. (Illus.). 432p. 1982. pap. 105.00 o.p. (ISBN 0-08-028826-X, H220). Pergamon.

Biomedical Engineering II: Recent Developments: Second Southern Biomedical Engineering Conference, Proceedings, September 26-27, 1983, San Antonio, Texas, U. S. A. Ed. by C. William Hall. 448p. 1983. pap. 110.00 o.p. (ISBN 0-08-030145-2, 11/3). Pergamon.

Biomedical Engineering IV: Recent Developments: Proceedings of the Fourth Southern Biomedical Engineering Conference, Jackson, MS, U. S. A. October 11-12, 1985. Ed. by B. W. Sauer. (Illus.). 300p. 1985. pap. 98.00 o.p. (ISBN 0-08-033137-8, Pub. by PPI). Pergamon.

Biomedical Psychiatric Therapeutics. John L. Sullivan. 256p. 1984. text ed. 45.00 o.p. (ISBN 0-409-95151-X). BUtterworth.

Biomedical Sciences Instrumentation: Proceedings of the Rocky Mountain Bioengineering International Symposium, 19th, 1982. Instrument Society of America Staff. LC 66-21220. 144p. 1982. pap. text ed. 24.00x o.p. (ISBN 0-87664-681-X). Instru Soc.

Biomedical Sciences Instrumentation: Proceedings of the Rocky Mountain Bioengineering International Symposium, 16th, Denver, Colorado, 1979, Vol. 15. Instrument Society of America Staff. LC 66-21220. 120p. 1979. pap. text ed. 19.00x o.p. (ISBN 0-87664-442-6). Instru Soc.

Biomedical Sciences Instrumentation: Proceedings of the Rocky Mountain Bioengineering International Symposium, 17th, Colorado Springs, Colorado, 1980, Vol. 16. Instrument Society of America Staff. LC 66-21220. 159p. 1980. pap. text ed. 24.00x o.p. (ISBN 0-87664-481-7). Instru Soc.

Biomedical Sciences Instrumentation: Proceedings of the Rocky Mountain Bioengineering International Symposium, 18th, Laramie, Wyoming, 1981, Vol. 17. Instrument Society of America Staff. LC 66-21220. 128p. 1981. pap. text ed. 24.00x o.p. (ISBN 0-87664-522-8). Instru Soc.

Biomedical Scientists & Public Policy. Ed. by H. H. Fudenberg & V. L. Melnick. LC 78-15052. 260p. 1978. 35.00x o.p. (ISBN 0-306-40085-5, Plenum Pr). Plenum Pub.

Biomedical Technology in Hospital Diagnosis. Ed. by T. Elder & W. Neill. LC 74-189281. 528p. 1972. 170.00 o.p. (ISBN 0-08-015576-6). Pergamon.

Biomedical Telemetry. Ed. by C. A. Caceres. 1965. 84.50 o.p. (ISBN 0-12-153850-8). Acad Pr.

Biomembranes, Architecture, Biogenesis, Bioenergetics & Differentiation. Lester Packer. 1974. 55.00 o.p. (ISBN 0-12-543440-5). Acad Pr.

Biometeorological Survey: Human Biometeorology, 1973-1978, 2 vols, Vol. 1. Ed. by S. W. Tromp & J. J. Bouma. (Biometeorology Survey Ser.: Pt. A). 257p. 1979. 128.00x o.p. (ISBN 0-471-26063-0, Pub. by Wiley Heyden). Wiley.

Biometeorology: Ninth International Biometeorological Congress held in Osnabruck & Stuttgart-Hohenheim 1981, Vol. 8, Pts. 1 & 2. Ed. by D. Overdieck et al. 540p. 1983. pap. text ed. 55.00 o.p. (ISBN 90-265-0384-9, Pub. by Swets Pub Serv Holland). Swets North Am.

Biometeorology: Proceedings of the 7th Congress, College Park, MD, 1975, Vol. 6. International Biometeorological Congress Staff. Ed. by H. E. Landsberg. 380p. (Supplements to vol. 19 & 20 of the international journal of biometeorology). 1976. pap. text ed. 77.50 o.p. (ISBN 90-265-0241-9, Pub. by Swets Pub Serv Holland). Swets North Am.

Biometeorology Seven: Proceedings of the Eighth International Biometeorological Congress 9-15 September 1979, Supplement to Volume 24 of the International Journal of Biometeorology, No.7, Pt.1. Ed. by Z. Zemel & N. St. G. Hyslop. vi, 150p. 1980. pap. text ed. 44.75 o.p. (ISBN 90-265-0349-0). Swets North Am.

Biometeorology Seven: Proceedings, of the International Biometerological Congress 8th, Sept.9-15, 1979, Pt. 2. Biometerological Congress Staff. Ed. by Z. Zemel & N. Hyslop. 1981. pap. text ed. 44.75 o.p. (ISBN 90-265-0350-4). Swets North Am.

Biometeorology Seven: Proceedings, Supplement to Volume 24, of the International Journal of Biometeorology of the 8th Congress, September 9-15, 1979, Pts. 1 & 2. International Biometeorological Congress Staff. Ed. by Z. Zemel & N. Hyslop. 1981. pap. text ed. 78.95 o.p. (ISBN 90-265-0354-7). Swets North Am.

Biometerology-2: Proceedings, International Bioclimatological Congress - 3rd, Pts. 1 & 2. Ed. by S. W. Tromp & W. H. Weihe. 1967. 275.00 o.p. (ISBN 0-08-011045-2). Pergamon.

Biomolecular Structure & Function. Ed. by Paul F. Agris. 1978. 66.00 o.p. (ISBN 0-12-043950-6). Acad Pr.

Biomolecular Structure, Conformation, Function & Evolution, 2 vols. R. Srinivasan. Incl. Vol. 1. Diffraction & Related Studies; Vol. 2. Physico-Chemical & Theoretical Studies. 1981. Set. 405.00 o.p. (ISBN 0-08-023187-X). Pergamon.

Bionic Joke Book. Jim Simon. 1976. pap. 1.25 o.p. (ISBN 0-8439-0406-2, LB406, Pub. by Leisure Bks CT). Dorchester Pub Co.

Bionic People Are Here. Arthur S. Freese. LC 78-8253. (Illus.). (gr. 7-9). 1979. text ed. 8.95 o.p. (ISBN 0-07-022133-2). McGraw.

Biophysical Aspects of Cardiac Muscle. Ed. by Martin Morad & Susan Smith. 1978. 29.95 o.p. (ISBN 0-12-506150-1). Acad Pr.

Biophysical Aspects of Cerebral Circulation. Ed. by Yu E. Moskalenko. LC 78-41243. (Illus.). 174p. 1980. 73.00 o.p. (ISBN 0-08-022672-8). Pergamon.

Biophysics. M. V. Volkenshtein. 640p. 1983. 12.95 o.p. (ISBN 0-8285-2405-X, Pub. by Mir Pubs USSR). Imported Pubns.

Biophysics Progression: Some Physical, Mathematical & Logical Aspects, Vol. 37, No. 1. A. Noble. LC 50-11295. (Illus.). 48p. 1981. pap. 28.00 o.p. (ISBN 0-08-027133-2). Pergamon.

Biopolitics & International Values: Investigating Liberal Norms. Ralph Pettman. LC 80-22926. (PPS on International Politics). 196p. 1981. 30.00 o.p. (ISBN 0-08-026329-1); pap. 50.00 o.p. (ISBN 0-08-026328-3). Pergamon.

Biopolitics: Ethological & Physiological Approaches. Ed. by Meredith W. Watts. LC 80-84284. (Methodology of Social & Behavioral Science Ser.: No. 7). 1981. pap. text ed. 13.95x o.p. (ISBN 0-87589-851-3). Jossey-Bass.

Biopolymers. Business Communications Staff. 1988. pap. 2250.00 o.p. (ISBN 0-89336-608-0, C-054). BCC.

Biopolymers. Alan G. Walton & John Blackwell. (Molecular Biology Ser). 1973. 99.00 o.p. (ISBN 0-12-734350-4). Acad Pr.

Biopsy Pathology of the Breast. J. Sloane. 284p. 1985. 40.00 o.p. (ISBN 0-471-83760-1). Wiley.

Biopsy Pathology of the Oesophagus, Stomach & Duodenum. D. W. Day. 1986. 45.00 o.p. (ISBN 0-471-01046-4). Wiley.

Biopsychology of Development. Ethel Tobach et al. 1971. 89.00 o.p. (ISBN 0-12-691750-7). Acad Pr.

Biorheology: Abstracts of the Second International Congress, No. 2. Ed. by A. Copley. 1975. pap. 29.00 o.p. (ISBN 0-08-019962-3). Pergamon.

Biorheology: Proceedings of the Second International Congress. Ed. by A. Copley. 1975. pap. 47.00 o.p. (ISBN 0-08-019963-1). Pergamon.

Biorhythms at Your Fingertips. James Roche. 128p. (Orig.). 1986. pap. 5.95 o.p. (ISBN 0-7137-1562-6, Pub. by Javelin England). Sterling.

Bios: Process & Diversity. Ed. by Barbara Crandall-Stotler & Katherine Jacobson. 1983. wire coil 14.95 o.p. (ISBN 0-8403-3125-8). Kendall-Hunt.

BIOSIS Previews Search Guide. rev. ed. 703p. 1987. looseleaf binder 90.00 o.p. (ISBN 0-916246-16-7). BIOSIS.

Biosphere & Politics. G. Khozin. 176p. 1979. pap. 5.45 o.p. (ISBN 0-8285-0429-6, Pub. by Progress Pubs USSR). Imported Pubns.

Biosphere: The Realm of Life. Robert A. Wallace et al. 1984. text ed. write for info. o.p. (ISBN 0-673-16603-1); write for info. study guide o.p. (ISBN 0-673-16632-5). Scott F.

Biostatistics Casebook. Ed. by Rupert G. Miller et al. LC 79-25405. (Applied Probability & Statistics Ser.). 256p. 1980. pap. 22.95x o.p. (ISBN 0-471-06258-8, Pub. by Wiley-Interscience). Wiley.

Biostatistics in Pharmacology. Ed. by A. L. Delaunois. LC 78-40220. (International Encyclopedia of Pharmacology & Therapeutics Ser.). 1979. 260.00 o.p. (ISBN 0-08-023168-3). Pergamon.

Biostratigraphy of Fossil Plants: Sucessional & Paleoecological Analyses. Ed. by D. L. Dilcher & T. N. Taylor. LC 79-27418. 259p. 1982. 39.95 o.p. (ISBN 0-87933-373-1). Van Nos Reinhold.

Biosynthesis, Modification & Processing of Cellular & Viral Polyproteins. Gebhard Koch & Dietmar Richter. 1980. 48.00 o.p. (ISBN 0-12-417560-0). Acad Pr.

Biosynthesis of Anematic Isoprenoids. M. F. Grundon. 1978. pap. 15.50 o.p. (ISBN 0-08-020469-4). Pergamon.

Biosynthesis of Aromatic Compounds. Ulrich Weiss & J. Michael Edwards. LC 78-1496. 728p. 1980. 65.50x o.p. (ISBN 0-471-92690-6, Pub by Wiley-Interscience). Wiley.

Biosynthesis of Ergot Alkaloids & Related Compounds. Ed. by Heinz C. Floss. 1976. pap. 15.50 o.p. (ISBN 0-08-021232-8). Pergamon.

Biosynthesis of Natural Products Polylketides, Terpenoids, Steroids & Phenepropanoids. P. Manitto. LC 80-41739. 548p. 1981. 130.00x o.p. (ISBN 0-470-27100-0). Halsted Pr.

Biosynthesis of Secondary Metabolites. R. B. Herbert. 1981. 40.00 o.p. (ISBN 0-412-16370-5, NO.6501, Pub. by Chapman & Hall England); pap. 16.95 o.p. (ISBN 0-412-16380-2, NO.6500). Routledge Chapman & Hall.

Biosynthesis of Vitamins & Related Compounds. T. W. Goodwin. 1963. 58.00 o.p. (ISBN 0-12-289858-3). Acad Pr.

Biosynthetic Products for Cancer Chemotherapy, Vol. 1. George R. Pettit. LC 76-54146. (Illus.). 228p. 1977. 49.50x o.p. (ISBN 0-306-37687-3, Plenum Pr). Plenum Pub.

Biosynthetic Products for Cancer Chemotherapy, Vol. 2. Ed. by George R. Pettit & Gordon M. Cragg. LC 76-54146. 160p. 1978. 49.50x o.p. (ISBN 0-306-37688-1, Plenum Pr). Plenum Pub.

Biota of the West Flower Garden Bank. Ed. by Thomas Bright & Linda Pequegnat. LC 74-10372. 436p. 1974. 25.00x o.p. (ISBN 0-87201-058-9). Gulf Pub.

Biotech: Proceedings. International Conference on the Commercial Applications & Implementations of Biotechnology Staff. 1100p. (Orig.). 1983. pap. text ed. 210.00x o.p. (ISBN 0-86353-000-1, Pub. by Online Conferences England). Gower Pub Co.

Biotechnical Slope Protection: Economic Methods for Earth Support & Erosion Control. Donald Gray & Andrew Leiser. 432p. 1982. 34.95 o.p. (ISBN 0-442-21222-4). Van Nos Reinhold.

Biotechnology. Ed. by A. Fiechter. (Advances in Biochemical Engineering: Vol. 7). (Illus.). 1977. 39.00 o.p. (ISBN 0-387-08397-9). Springer-Verlag.

Biotechnology & Waste Treatment: Proceedings of a Workshop Sponsored by the United Nations Environment Programme Held at the University of Waterloo, Canada, July 27-31, 1981. United Nations Environment Programme Staff & M. Moo-Young. 84p. 1982. pap. 40.00 o.p. (ISBN 0-08-028784-0). Pergamon.

Biotechnology Directory 1985. Jim Coombs. 464p. 1985. pap. 130.00x o.p. (ISBN 0-943818-06-0, Stockton Pr). Groves Dict Music.

Biotechnology Directory 1986. J. Coombs. 500p. 1986. pap. 140.00x o.p. (ISBN 0-943818-20-6, Stockton Pr). Groves Dict Music.

Biotechnology Directory 1988. J. Coombs & Y. R. Alston. LC 83-12138. 524p. 1987. pap. 150.00x o.p. (ISBN 0-935859-13-6, Stockton Pr). Groves Dict Music.

Biotechnology Emerges: The Key Years, 1973-1980. Janice K. Mandel. 295.00 o.p. (ISBN 0-89947-019-X, EIC Intell). Bowker.

Biotechnology in Food. Business Communications Staff. 1988. 2650.00 o.p. (ISBN 0-89336-653-6, C-099). BCC.

Biotechnology in Western Europe. Robert T. Yuan. 276p. (Orig.). 1987. pap. 13.00 o.p. (ISBN 0-317-62828-3, S/N 003-009-00509-4). USGPO.

Biotechnology: Perspectives, Policies, & Issues. Ed. by Indra Vasil. 25.00 o.p. (ISBN 0-317-64592-7). U Presses Fla.

Biotelemetry III. Ed. by T. B. Fryer & H. A. Miller. 1976. 65.00 o.p. (ISBN 0-12-269250-0). Acad Pr.

Biotutorial: A Modular Program for Introductory Biology. Student Laboratory Guide. Edward Samuels. 1975. pap. 12.25 o.p. (ISBN 0-395-17855-X). HM.

Bipartisanship in the United States. Chester C. Maxey. LC 64-15396. 1965. 6.95 o.p. (ISBN 0-87004-101-0). Caxton.

Birch Bark Poems of Charles F. Lummis. Dudley Gordon. (Illus.). 29p. 1969. 10.00 o.p. (ISBN 0-317-11688-6). Dawsons.

Birch's Emergencies in Medical Practice. 11th ed. Ed. by Colin Ogilvie. (Illus.). 1981. text ed. 72.00 o.p. (ISBN 0-443-01983-5). Churchill.

Birchwood. John Banville. 176p. 1973. 5.95 o.p. (ISBN 0-393-08572-4). Norton.

Bird Alphabet Book. Jerry Pallotta. LC 86-64019. (Illus.). 32p. Date not set. 10.95 o.p. (ISBN 0-933341-94-6); pap. 5.95 o.p. (ISBN 0-933341-65-2). Quinlan Pr.

Bird Faunas of Africa & Its Islands. R. E. Moreau. 1967. 74.50 o.p. (ISBN 0-12-506650-3). Acad Pr.

Bird Finder's Three Year Notebook. rev. ed. Paul S. Eriksson. LC 75-15198. (Illus.). 288p. 1982. plastic comb 9.95 o.p. (ISBN 0-8397-1028-3). Eriksson.

Bird in Medieval Manuscripts. Date not set. (ISBN 0-8052-3818-2). Random.

Bird in My Bed. Anne D. Graham. LC 72-155090. (Illus.). 1971. 6.95 o.s.i. (ISBN 0-8008-0745-6). Taplinger.

Bird Infirmary. Eva Engholm. LC 72-6617. (Illus.). 1973. 6.95 o.s.i. (ISBN 0-8008-0742-1). Taplinger.

Bird Keeping. Jurgen Nicolai. Tr. by Petra Bleher from Ger. (Illus.). 96p. 1980. 4.95 o.p. (ISBN 0-87666-997-6, KW-034). TFH Pubns.

Bird Migration. Christopher Mead. LC 82-15385. (Illus.). 224p. 1983. 19.95 o.p. (ISBN 0-87196-694-8). Facts on File.

Bird Neighbour. Wang Yanrong. (Illus.). 26p. (gr. 1-3). 1984. pap. text ed. 3.50 o.p. (ISBN 0-8351-1412-0). China Bks.

Bird of Life, Bird of Death: A Naturalist's Journey Through a Land of Political Turmoil. Jonathan E. Maslow. 256p. 1986. 17.45 o.p. (ISBN 0-671-52738-X). S&S.

Bird of Paper: Poems of Vicente Aleixandre. Vicente Aleixandre. Tr. by Willis Barnstone & David Garrison. (International Poetry Ser.: Vol. 6). viii, 75p. 1982. lib. bdg. 16.95x o.p. (ISBN 0-8214-0661-2); pap. 10.95 o.p. (ISBN 0-8214-0662-0, 82-84325). Ohio U Pr.

Bird Populations in East Central Illinois: Fluctuations, Variations, & Development over a Half-Century. S. Charles Kendeigh. LC 81-16073. (Illinois Biological Monographs: No. 52). (Illus.). 152p. 1982. pap. 14.50 o.p. (ISBN 0-252-00955-X). U of Ill Pr.

Birdless Summer. Han Suyin. 350p. 1985. pap. 6.95 o.p. (ISBN 0-586-03769-1, Pub. by Granada England). Academy Chi Pubs.

Birdman of Alcatraz. Thomas E. Gaddis. 266p. 1987. pap. 6.95 o.p. (ISBN 0-575-03710-5, Pub. by Gollancz England). David & Charles.

Birdman of St. Petersburg. Tom Shachtman. LC 81-82019. (Illus.). 96p. (gr. 5-9). 1981. 8.95 o.s.i. (ISBN 0-02-782530-2). Macmillan.

Birds: A Brief Anthology of Poems & Prose. Winston Elstob. 1971. pap. 7.00 o.s.i. (ISBN 0-686-02016-2). Turtles Quill.

Birds & Bee of Education. Thomas A. Smith. LC 73-77587. 1973. 5.50 o.p. (ISBN 0-682-47676-5, University). Exposition-Phoenix.

Birds & How They Function. Philip S. Callahan. LC 79-2109. (Illus.). 160p. (YA) (gr. 7 up). 1979. 8.95 o.p. (ISBN 0-8234-0363-7). Holiday.

Birds & Men: American Birds in Science, Art, Literature, & Conservation, 1800-1900. Robert H. Welker. LC 55-11608. (Illus.). 1966. pap. 2.45 o.p. (ISBN 0-689-70202-7, 82, Atheneum). Macmillan.

Birds: Brain & Behavior. Ed. by Irving Goodman & Martin Schein. 1974. 65.00 o.p. (ISBN 0-12-290350-1). Acad Pr.

Birds' Christmas Carol. Kate D. Wiggin. 96p. 1987. pap. 2.95 o.p. (ISBN 0-345-34379-4, Pub. by Ballantine Epiphany). Ballantine.

Birds for All Seasons. Jeffery Boswall. (Illus.). 160p. 1988. 19.95 o.p. (ISBN 0-563-20453-2, Pub. by BBC). Parkwest Pubns.

Birds' Homes. Ju Zi. (Illus.). 36p. (Orig.). (gr. 3-4). 1982. 4.50 o.p. (ISBN 0-8351-1129-6); pap. 3.50 o.p. (ISBN 0-8351-1123-7). China Bks.

Birds in Egg - Eggs in Bird. G. Olsson. 523p. 1980. 19.50x o.p. (ISBN 0-85086-077-6, NO.6338, Pub. by Pion England). Routledge Chapman & Hall.
Birds in Legend, Fable & Folklore. Ernest Ingersoll. LC 68-26576. 304p. 1968. Repr. of 1923 ed. 40.00x o.p. (ISBN 0-8103-3548-4). Gale.
Birds in Peril: A Guide to the Endangered Birds of the United States & Canada. John P. Mackenzie. 1977. 14.95 o.p. (ISBN 0-395-25855-3). HM.
Bird's Nest. Shirley Jackson. 288p. 1986. pap. 5.95 o.p. (ISBN 0-87795-833-5). Morrow.
Birds New to Britain & Ireland. Ed. by J. T. Sharrock. (Illus.). 1983. 25.00 o.p. (ISBN 0-85661-033-X, Pub. by T & A D Poyser England). Buteo.
Birds of a Feather. Pat Spencer. 136p. (Orig.). 1984. pap. 3.95 o.p. (ISBN 0-86760-015-2, Pub. by Albatross Bks). Meyer Stone Bks.
Birds of America. Mary McCarthy. 352p. 1981. pap. 3.95 o.p. (ISBN 0-380-55459-3, 55459, Bard). Avon.
Birds of Aristophanes. Dudley Fitts. LC 57-5294. 1957. 4.95 o.p. (ISBN 0-15-112767-0). HarBraceJ.
Birds of New Zealand & Outlying Islands. M. F. Soper. 216p. 1986. 29.95 o.p. (ISBN 0-7233-0724-5, Pub. by Whitcoulls NZ). Intl Spec Bk.
Birds of Paradise. Johanna Luchting. 1977. 10.00 o.p. (ISBN 0-682-48803-8). Exposition-Phoenix.
Birds of Passage. Bernice Rubens. Ed. by J. Silberman. 224p. 1982. 12.95 o.s.i. (ISBN 0-671-44798-X). Summit Bks.
Birds of Prey. Parry & Putnam. 1979. 29.95 o.p. (ISBN 0-671-25151-1). S&S.
Birds of Summer. Zilpha K. Snyder. LC 82-13756. 204p. (gr. 7 up). 1983. 10.95 o.s.i. (ISBN 0-689-30967-8, Atheneum Childrens Bks). Macmillan.
Birds of the Eastern Forest, 2 vols. James F. Lansdowne. (Illus.). 1968. 35.00 ea. o.p.; Vol. 1. 35.00 o.p. (ISBN 0-395-07888-1); Vol. 2. 35.00 o.p. (ISBN 0-395-10950-7). HM.
Birds of the Northern Forest. James F. Lansdowne. (Illus.). 1966. 35.00 o.p. (ISBN 0-395-07887-3). HM.
Birds of the Northern Rockies. Tom J. Ulrich. LC 84-2048. (Illus.). 180p. (Orig.). 1985. pap. 7.95 o.p. (ISBN 0-87842-169-6). Mountain Pr.
Birds of the West Coast, Vol. 1. James F. Lansdowne. 1976. 6.00 o.p. (ISBN 0-395-24580-X). HM.
Birds of the West Coast, Vol. 2. James F. Lansdowne. 1980. 6.00 o.p. (ISBN 0-395-29546-7). HM.
Birds of Winter. Theodore Vrettos. 1980. 9.95 o.p. (ISBN 0-395-29455-X). HM.
Birds of Yorkshire. John R. Mather. LC 85-17065. (Illus.). 500p. 1986. 69.00 o.p. (ISBN 0-7099-3510-2, Pub. by Croom Helm Ltd). Routledge Chapman & Hall.
Birds on a Banana Tree or How Not to Retire & Move to Florida. Selina Thomson. 1978. 7.50 o.p. (ISBN 0-682-49014-8). Exposition-Phoenix.
Birdseye Writing Skills: Punctuation. Beverley Dietz. LC 83-62439. (gr. 4-6). 1983. pap. 5.95 o.p. (ISBN 0-8224-0723-X). D S Lake Pubs.
Birdstones. Jane L. Curry. LC 77-3392. 228p. (gr. 5-9). 1977. 6.95 o.p. (ISBN 0-689-50089-0, Atheneus). Macmillan.
Birdwatcher's Activity Book. Donald S. Heintzelman. (Illus.). 256p. 1983. pap. 11.95 o.p. (ISBN 0-8117-2152-3). Stackpole.
Birdwatching with American Women: A Selection of Nature Writings. Compiled by Deborah Strom. LC 85-8822. (Illus.). 1986. 17.45 o.p. (ISBN 0-393-02270-6). Norton.
Birmingham since Eighteen Eighty-Five. Thomas H. Blake. Date not set. 6.50 o.p. (ISBN 0-87651-202-3). Southern U Pr.
Birmingham Since 1885. Birmingham Historical Society Staff & Thomas H. Blake. 1972. pap. 6.50 o.p. (ISBN 0-87651-202-3). Southern U Pr.
Birnbaum Haggadah. Philip Birnbaum. (Illus.). 160p. 1976. 5.95 o.s.i. (ISBN 0-88482-908-1); pap. 3.95 o.s.i. (ISBN 0-88482-912-X). Hebrew Pub.
Birnbaum's Canada, 1986. Steve Birnbaum. 688p. 1985. pap. 11.70 o.p. (ISBN 0-395-39401-5). HM.
Birnbaum's Caribbean, 1986. Steve Birnbaum. 688p. 1985. pap. 11.70 o.p. (ISBN 0-395-39406-6). HM.
Birnbaum's Disneyland, 1986. Steve Birnbaum. 160p. 1985. pap. 5.95 o.p. (ISBN 0-395-39405-8). HM.
Birnbaum's Europe for Business Travelers, 1986. Steve Birnbaum. 560p. 1985. pap. 7.70 o.p. (ISBN 0-395-39403-1). HM.
Birnbaum's Europe, 1986. Steve Birnbaum. 1232p. 1985. pap. 13.45 o.p. (ISBN 0-395-39398-1). HM.
Birnbaum's France, 1986. Steve Birnbaum. 784p. 1985. pap. 11.70 o.p. (ISBN 0-395-39402-3). HM.
Birnbaum's Great Britain & Ireland 1986. Steve Birnbaum. 1985. pap. 11.70 o.p. (ISBN 0-395-39399-X). HM.
Birnbaum's Hawaii, 1986. Steve Birnbaum. 456p. 1985. pap. 11.70 o.p. (ISBN 0-395-39396-5). HM.
Birnbaum's Mexico, 1986. Steve Birnbaum. 528p. 1985. pap. 11.70 o.p. (ISBN 0-395-39407-4). HM.
Birnbaum's South America, 1986. Steve Birnbaum. 784p. 1985. pap. 11.70 o.p. (ISBN 0-395-39397-3). HM.
Birnbaum's United States, 1986. Steve Birnbaum. 848p. 1985. pap. 11.70 o.p. (ISBN 0-395-39400-7). HM.
Birth. Caterine Milinaire. Ed. by Joseph Berger. (Illus.). 350p. 1974. 12.95 o.p. (ISBN 0-517-51455-9, Harmony); pap. 8.95 o.p. (ISBN 0-517-51456-7). Crown.
Birth: An Anthology of Ancient Texts, Songs, Prayers & Stories. Ed. by David Meltzer. LC 80-82441. (Illus.). 288p. 1981. 17.50 o.p. (ISBN 0-86547-004-9); pap. 12.50 o.p. (ISBN 0-86547-005-7). N Point Pr.
Birth & Development of Ornament. F. Edward Hulme. LC 79-78173. (Illus.). xii, 352p. 1974. Repr. of 1893 ed. 44.00x o.p. (ISBN 0-8103-4026-7). Gale.
Birth & Our Bodies: Exercises & Meditations for the Childbearing Year & Preparation for Active Birth. Paddy O'Brian. (Illus.). 160p. 1986. pap. 7.95 o.p. (ISBN 0-86358-047-5, 80475). Routledge Chapman & Hall.
Birth Control & Abortion. Christopher Tietze et al. 289p. 1972. text ed. 29.00x o.p. (ISBN 0-8422-7004-3). Irvington.
Birth Control Book. Howard I. Shapiro. 1981. pap. 3.95 o.p. (ISBN 0-380-56986-8, 65136-X). Avon.
Birth Control in Jewish Law: Marital Relations, Contraception, & Abortion As Set Forth in the Classic Texts of Jewish Law. David M. Feldman. LC 79-16712. 1980. Repr. of 1968 ed. lib. bdg. 35.00x o.p. (ISBN 0-313-21297-X, FEBC). Greenwood.
Birth Defects & Drugs in Pregnancy. O. P. Heinonen et al. LC 75-16094. 582p. 1982. 58.00 o.p. (ISBN 0-88416-034-3). Year Bk Med.
Birth Defects & Speech-Language Disorders. Shirley N. Sparks. LC 83-23917. (Illus.). 190p. 1984. pap. 23.50 o.p. (ISBN 0-316-80493-2). College-Hill.
Birth Defects: Risks & Consequences. Ed. by Sally Kelly et al. 1976. 65.50 o.p. (ISBN 0-12-403450-0). Acad Pr.
Birth of a First Child: Towards an Understanding of Femininity. Dana Breen. (Illus.). 1975. pap. 11.95x o.p. (ISBN 0-422-74340-2, NO.2770, Pub. by Tavistock England). Routledge Chapman & Hall.
Birth of an Island. Francois Clement. 1977. pap. 1.75 o.p. (ISBN 0-380-00952-8, 32284). Avon.
Birth of Neurosis: Myth, Malady & the Victorians. George F. Drinka. (Illus.). 400p. 1984. 21.45 o.p. (ISBN 0-671-44999-0). S&S.
Birth of Neurosis: Myth, Malady & the Victorians. George F. Drinka. 1985. pap. 10.95 o.p. (ISBN 0-671-60448-1, Touchstone Bks.). S&S.
Birth of the Gospel. W. B. Smith. 1956. (ISBN 0-8022-1603-X). Philos Lib.
Birth of the Hospital in the Byzantine Empire. Timothy S. Miller. LC 84-26111. (Henry E. Sigerist Supplements to the Bulletin of the History of Medicine, New Ser.: No. 10). 304p. 1985. text ed. 28.50x o.p. (ISBN 0-8018-2676-4). Johns Hopkins.
Birth of the Irish Free State, 1921-1923. Joseph M. Curran. LC 79-4088. 400p. 1980. 25.00 o.p. (ISBN 0-8173-0013-9). U of Ala Pr.
Birth of the Israel Air Force. Monty Jacobs. (Illus.). 1954. 3.00 o.p. (ISBN 0-914080-43-1). Shulsinger Sales.
Birth of the Studio. (Illus.). 176p. 1977. pap. 12.50 o.p. (ISBN 0-902028-44-8). Antique Collect.
Birth of the United States, 1763-1816. Isaac Asimov. LC 73-19514. (Illus.). 288p. (gr. 7 up). 1974. 6.95 o.s.i. (ISBN 0-395-18451-7). HM.
Birth of Western Economy: Economic Aspects of the Dark Ages. Robert LaTouche. Tr. by E. M. Wilkinson. 368p. 1981. 49.95x o.p. (ISBN 0-416-32090-2, NO.3582). Routledge Chapman & Hall.
Birth Reborn. Michael Odent. Tr. by Juliette Levin & Jane Pincus. (Illus.). 1984. 14.45 o.p. (ISBN 0-394-52901-4). Pantheon.
Birth Stories: The Experience Remembered. Ed. by Janet I. Ashford. LC 84-17017. (Birth Ser.). (Illus.). 208p. (Orig.). 1984. 20.95 o.p. (ISBN 0-89594-150-3); pap. 8.95 o.p. (ISBN 0-89594-149-X). Crossing Pr.
Birth to Rebirth. Brad McClennan. 1976. 4.00 o.p. (ISBN 0-682-48526-8). Exposition-Phoenix.
Birthday Bear & the Runaway Skateboard. Michael J. Pellowski. (Illus.). 24p. (gr. k-3). 1987. 1.95 o.s.i. (ISBN 0-87406-177-6). Willowisp Pr.
Birthday Book. Suzanne Green. LC 86-16619. (Perlorians Ser.). (Illus.). 32p. (ps-k). 1987. 5.95 o.p. (ISBN 0-385-23505-4); pap. 5.95 o.p. (ISBN 0-385-24006-6). Doubleday.
Birthday of the Infanta & Other Stories by Oscar Wilde. Oscar Wilde. LC 81-1402. (Illus.). 80p. (gr. 2 up). 14.95 o.p. (ISBN 0-689-30850-7, Atheneum). Macmillan.
Birthday Party. Nicoletta Costa. (Molly & Tom Bks.). (Illus.). 16p. (gr. k-1). 1984. 3.50 o.p. (ISBN 0-448-23404-1, G&D). Putnam Pub Group.
Birthday Party Book. Ed. by Whitcoullls Publishers Staff. 40p. 1986. pap. 2.95 o.p. (ISBN 0-7233-0777-6, Pub. by Whitcoulls NZ). Intl Spec Bk.
Birthday Present for Mama. Nicole Lorian. (Step into Reading Book & Cassette Library). 48p. (gr. 1-3). 1986. book & cassette 5.95 o.s.i. (ISBN 0-394-88338-1, BYR). Random.
Birthdays. rev. ed. 1973. 4.95 o.p. (ISBN 0-8066-1336-X, 10-0750, Augsburg). Augsburg Fortress.
Birthplace Tables of Houses. Walter A. Koch & Elisabeth Schaeck. LC 75-22416. 1975. 12.00 o.p. (ISBN 0-88231-020-8); pap. text ed. 10.00 o.p. (ISBN 0-88231-021-6). ASI Pubs Inc.
Birthpyre. Larry Brand. 288p. 1980. pap. 2.25 o.p. (ISBN 0-380-76539-X, 76539). Avon.
Birthquakes. Norman C. Habel. LC 73-88339. (Illus.). 112p. 1974. 1.00 o.p. (ISBN 0-8006-0075-4, Fortress). Augsburg Fortress.
Bisexual Option. Fred Klein. LC 77-90662. (Priam). 1979. pap. 4.95 o.p. (ISBN 0-87795-244-2, Arbor Hse). Morrow.
Bisexual Option: A Concept of One Hundred Percent Intimacy. Fred Klein. LC 77-9062. 1978. 8.95 o.p. (ISBN 0-87795-179-9, Arbor Hse). Morrow.
Bishop Barlow's Consecration & Archbishop Parker's Register: With Some New Documents. Claude Jenkins. (Church Historical Society London New Ser.: No. 17). Repr. of 1935 ed. 20.00 o.p. (ISBN 0-8115-3140-6). Kraus Repr.
Bishop in the Back Seat. Clarissa Watson. LC 79-2115. 1980. 9.95 o.p. (ISBN 0-689-11012-X, Atheneum). Macmillan.
Bishops & Bluestockings. Helen Fletcher. 192p. 1986. 12.95 o.p. (ISBN 0-86358-075-0, Pandora Pr); pap. 5.95 o.p. (ISBN 0-86358-071-8). Routledge Chapman & Hall.
Bishop's Daughter: A Chronicle of Certain Personal Events Written by Miss Mellissa Worthing of Hans Town, London to Mollify Her Mind & Chasten Her Spirit in a Time of Great Tribulation. Ray Russell. (Summerfield Saga Ser.: Vol. 2). 311p. 1981. 12.95 o.p. (ISBN 0-395-31562-X). HM.
Bishop's Landing. Richard Forsythe. 1980. pap. 2.75 o.p. (ISBN 0-8439-0824-6, Pub. by Leisure Bks CT). Dorchester Pub Co.
Bismarck, Gladstone, & the Concert of Europe. William N. Medlicott. Repr. of 1956 ed. lib. bdg. 90.50x o.p. (ISBN 0-8371-0567-6, AEMECE). Greenwood.
Bistrota: Collection of Stories. Vera Efremova. 1987. 6.95 o.s.i. RWCPH.
Bit by Bit: An Illustrated History of Computers. Stan Augarten. LC 84-2508. 304p. 1984. 29.45 o.p. (ISBN 0-89919-268-8); pap. 17.45 o.p. (ISBN 0-89919-302-1). Ticknor & Fields.
Bit of a Rebel: The Life & Work of George Arnold Wood (1865-1928) R. M. Crawford. (Illus.). 368p. 1976. 33.00x o.p. (ISBN 0-424-00005-9, Pub by Sydney U Pr). Intl Spec Bk.
Bit of a Star, Media Women...Their Fine Points & Phobias. Photos by Dave L. Travis. (Illus.). 106p. 1987. 16.50 o.p. (ISBN 0-901023-34-5, Pub. by Fountain Pr UK). Seven Hills Bk Dists.
Bitches & Abdicators. Toni Scalia. Ed. by Herb Katz. LC 85-1636. 228p. 1985. 12.95 o.p. (ISBN 0-87131-455-X). M Evans.
Bite of Eve's Apple: And Other Stories. Frances H. Mulliken. 1982. pap. 10.00 o.p. (ISBN 0-8309-0348-8). Herald Hse.
Biting the Hand That Feeds Me: Days of Binging, Purging, & Recovery. Lisa Messinger. pap. 8.95 o.p. (ISBN 0-87879-525-1, Pub. by Arena Press). Acad Therapy.
Bits & Pieces. Blaise W. Liffick. (Orig.). 1980. pap. text ed. 10.95 o.p. (ISBN 0-07-037828-2, BYTE Bks). McGraw.
Bits 'n Bytes about Computing: A Computer Literacy Primer. Rachelle S. Heller & C. Dianne Martin. LC 82-2515. (Computer in Education Ser.). 174p. 1982. text ed. 23.95 o.p. (ISBN 0-914894-26-9, Computer Sci Pr). W H Freeman.
Bits 'n Bytes about Computing for Everyone. Rachelle Heller & Dianne Martin. write for info. o.s.i. (ISBN 0-914894-92-7, Computer Sci Pr). W H Freeman.
Bits 'n Bytes Gazette. Rachelle S. Heller & C. Dianne Martin. (Computers in Education Ser.). (Illus.). 72p. 1983. pap. text ed. 10.95 o.p. (ISBN 0-88175-074-3, Computer Sci Pr). W H Freeman.
Bits O' This & That. Frank A. Collins. 1978. 4.00 o.p. (ISBN 0-682-48995-6). Exposition-Phoenix.
Bits of Americana: Whirly-Girlys to Country Gossip. Phyllis Van Swearingen. (Illus.). 80p. 1983. 5.50 o.p. (ISBN 0-682-49939-0). Exposition-Phoenix.
Bits of Faith & Love & Fun. Mary Jane Meyer. 1977. 4.50 o.p. (ISBN 0-682-48975-1). Exposition-Phoenix.
Bits of Paradise. F. Scott Fitzgerald & Zelda Fitzgerald. LC 74-4648. 392p. 1974. encore ed. 2.49 o.p. (ISBN 0-684-13902-2, ScribT). Scribner.
Bits of Paradise. Zelda Fitzgerald & F. Scott Fitzgerald. 1976. pap. 1.95 o.p. (ISBN 0-671-80250-X, 80250). PB.
Bitter Dreams. Dolores Hughes. 480p. 1984. pap. 3.95 o.s.i. (ISBN 0-8439-2093-9, Pub. by Leisure Bks CT). Dorchester Pub Co.
Bitter Graces. Terrence Ross. 192p. 1980. pap. 2.25 o.p. (ISBN 0-380-76208-0, 76208-0). Avon.
Bitter Harvest: A History of California Farmworkers, 1870-1941. Cletus E. Daniel. LC 80-25664. 368p. 1981. 36.50x o.p. (ISBN 0-8014-1284-6). Cornell U Pr.
Bitter is the Hawk's Path. Jean McCord. LC 71-154756. 1972. 4.50 o.p. (ISBN 0-689-20682-8, Atheneum). Macmillan.
Bitter Passion, Sweet Love. Patricia Ott. (Orig.). 1981. pap. 2.95 o.p. (ISBN 0-505-51718-3, Pub. by Tower Bks). Dorchester Pub Co.
Bitter Pecos. W. W. Southard. 1985. lib. bdg. 13.95 o.p. (ISBN 0-8161-3799-4, Large Print Bks). G K Hall.
Bitter Pills. David Mason & Fran Dyller. 224p. 1977. 10.00 o.p. (ISBN 0-8065-0531-1, Pub. by Citadel Pr). Carol Pub Group.
Bitter Promise. Ila D. Youngblood. 256p. 1982. pap. 2.50 o.p. (ISBN 0-380-79343-1, 79343). Avon.
Bitter Shield: Book II - The Story of Canada. Dennis Adair & Janet Rosenstock. 288p. (Orig.). 1982. pap. 2.95 o.p. (ISBN 0-380-79053-X, 79053-X). Avon.
Bitter-Sweet Recollections. Barbara Brokhoff. 1983. 6.50 o.p. (ISBN 0-89536-638-X, 0238). CSS of Ohio.
Bitter Water. Charles Popell. LC 84-60870. 1984. pap. 5.95 o.p. (ISBN 0-89051-097-0). Master Bks.
Bittersweet. Denise Robins. 1977. pap. 1.25 o.p. (ISBN 0-380-00874-2, 31419). Avon.
Bittersweet Afternoons. Fiona Harrowe. 288p. 1984. pap. 2.75 o.s.i. (ISBN 0-345-31256-2). Ballantine.
Bittersweet Love. Betty R. Headapohl. 240p. 1984. 3.50 o.p. (ISBN 0-8423-0181-X). Tyndale.
Bittersweet: True Stories of Decisions That Shaped Eternal Paths. Mike Berger. LC 80-81505. 124p. 1980. 6.95 o.p. (ISBN 0-88290-144-3). Horizon Utah.
Bituminous Concrete Materials, Mixtures, & Additives. (Transportation Research Report Ser.). 53p. 1977. 4.00 o.p. (ISBN 0-309-02688-1). Transport Res Bd.
Bituminous Emulsions for Highway Pavements. (National Cooperative Highway Research Program Synthesis of Highway Practice). 76p. 1975. 4.80 o.p. (ISBN 0-309-02337-8). Transport Res Bd.
Bituminous Materials & Skid Resistance. (Transportation Research Report Ser.). 68p. 1979. 3.80 o.p. (ISBN 0-309-02959-7). Transport Res Bd.
Bituminous Materials, Mixtures & Performance. (Transportation Research Report Ser.). 52p. 1978. 3.00 o.p. (ISBN 0-309-02840-X). Transport Res Bd.
Bituminous Mixtures, Aggregates & Pavements: Six Reports. (Transportation Research Report Ser.). 63p. 1975. 3.00 o.p. (ISBN 0-309-02454-4). Transport Res Bd.
Bix: Man & Legend. Richard M. Sudhalter & Philip R. Evans. (Illus.). 1975. pap. 6.95 o.p. (ISBN 0-02-872500-X). Schirmer Bks.
Bizarre Murders. Gilda Berger & Melvin Berger. LC 82-42880. (Illus.). 96p. (YA) (gr. 7 up). 1983. lib. bdg. 9.79 o.s.i. (ISBN 0-671-45583-4). Messner.
Bizet. rev. ed. Winton Dean. (Master Musicians Ser.: No. M170). (Illus.). 306p. 1975. pap. 7.95 o.p. (ISBN 0-8226-0706-9). Littlefield.
Black Activism. Robert H. Brisbane. LC 74-2892. 336p. 1974. 10.00 o.p. (ISBN 0-8170-0619-2); pap. 9.50 o.p. (ISBN 0-8170-0674-5). Judson.
Black Africa: The Economic & Cultural Basis for a Federated State. rev. ed. Cheikh A. Diop. LC 87-71876. 180p. 1987. pap. 7.95 o.p. (ISBN 0-86543-058-6, Joint Publication with Lawrence Hill & Co.). Africa World.
Black Alibi. Cornell Woolrich. 224p. 1982. pap. 2.25 o.s.i. (ISBN 0-345-30707-0). Ballantine.

Black America: A Study of the Ex-Slave - His Late Master. William L. Clowes. LC 78-109322. 1970. Repr. of 1891 ed. 35.00x o.p. (ISBN 0-8371-3588-5, CBA&, Pub. by Negro U Pr). Greenwood.

Black American. William Hough. 64p. 1986. 6.95 o.p. (ISBN 0-8062-2963-2). Carlton.

Black American Inventors. C. R. Gibbs. 188p. (YA) (gr. 6-12). 1988. pap. 8.95 o.p. (ISBN 0-87460-367-6). Lion Bks.

Black American Literature. V. Shourie. 266p. 1984. text ed. 23.00x o.p. Coronet Bks.

Black Americans & the Supreme Court. Ed. by Arnold M. Paul. LC 73-186567. (American Problem Studies). 140p. 1972. pap. text ed. 6.50 o.p. (ISBN 0-03-084009-0, Pub. by HR&W). Krieger.

Black Americans & the White Man's Burden, 1898-1903. Willard B. Gatewood, Jr. LC 75-9945. (Blacks in the New World Ser). 363p. 1975. 29.95 o.p. (ISBN 0-252-00475-2). U of Ill Pr.

Black Americans in North Carolina & the South. Ed. by Jeffrey J. Crow & Flora J. Hatley. LC 83-21762. (Illus.). xix, 200p. 1984. 19.95x o.p. (ISBN 0-8078-1593-4). U of NC Pr.

Black & Blue Magic. Zilpha K. Snyder. LC 66-12850. (Illus.). 192p. (gr. 3-7). 1966. Spartan ed. 5.95 o.p. (ISBN 0-689-30075-1, Atheneum); pap. 0.95 o.p. (ISBN 0-689-70313-9). Macmillan.

Black & White, 2 vols, No. 5. League of American Writers Staff. 1970. Repr. of 1940 ed. Set. 28.00x o.p. (ISBN 0-8371-9132-7, BW00). Greenwood.

Black & White in School: Trust, Tension, or Tolerance. Janet W. Schofield. LC 82-9117. 272p. 1982. 35.95 o.s.i. (ISBN 0-275-90898-4, C0898). Praeger.

Black-&-White Processing Using Kodak Chemicals. Eastman Kodak Company Staff. LC 73-82620. (Illus.). 52p. 1986. pap. 6.95 o.s.i. (ISBN 0-87985-312-3, J-1). Eastman Kodak.

Black & White Shaded Drawing. Valerie Jacobs. (Illus.). 64p. 1975. pap. 5.50 o.p. (ISBN 0-85440-295-0, Pub. by Steinerbooks). Anthroposophic.

Black Angel. Cornell Woolrich. 256p. 1982. pap. 2.25 o.s.i. (ISBN 0-345-30664-3). Ballantine.

Black Apache. Clay Fisher. 224p. (Orig.). 1988. pap. 2.95 o.p. (ISBN 0-553-27240-3). Bantam.

Black Apostles at Home & Abroad: Afro-Americans & the Christian Mission from the Revolution to Reconstruction. Ed. by David W. Wills & Richard Newman. 420p. 1982. lib. bdg. 46.00 o.p. (ISBN 0-8161-8482-8, Hall Reference). G K Hall.

Black Bag Owner's Manual I: Spookcentre. 90p. 1978. pap. 8.00 o.p. (ISBN 0-87364-149-3). Paladin Pr.

Black Bag Owner's Manual II: The Hit Parade. 100p. 1979. pap. 8.00 o.p. (ISBN 0-87364-157-4). Paladin Pr.

Black Beauty. Anna Sewell. LC 59-12495. (Illus.). (gr. 4-6). pap. 10.95 o.p. (ISBN 0-448-06007-8, G&D); PLB 3.79 o.p. (ISBN 0-448-13450-0, G&D); lib. bdg. 2.95 o.p. (ISBN 0-448-05457-4, G&D). Putnam Pub Group.

Black Beauty see New Method Supplementary Readers: Bestseller Pack.

Black Bishop: Samuel Adjai Crowther. Jesse Page. LC 75-106783. (Illus.). 1979. Repr. of 1908 ed. 35.00x o.p. (ISBN 0-8371-4610-0, PBB&, Pub. by Negro U Pr). Greenwood.

Black Bloomers & Han-Ga-Ber. Eleanor V. Lampert. 64p. 1986. 6.75 o.p. (ISBN 0-8062-2725-7). Carlton.

Black Body-Rdr Ed. (ISBN 0-679-72424-9, Villard). Random.

Black Bondage in the North. Edgar J. McManus. LC 72-12425. (Illus.). 250p. 1973. 12.95x o.p. (ISBN 0-8156-0091-7). Syracuse U Pr.

Black Book: 1987. Marty Goldstein & Stuart Waldman. 1987. 100.00 o.p. (ISBN 0-916098-23-0). Creat Black Bk.

Black Box. R. G. Austin. (Which Way Bks.). 1983. pap. 1.95 o.p. Archway.

Black Business & Professional Woman: Selected References of Achievement (A Tribute to the 50th Year of the National Association of Negro Business & Professional Women's Clubs, Inc.) Rosalind G. Bauchum. (Public Administration Ser.: P 1776). 11p. 1985. 2.00 o.p. (ISBN 0-89028-576-4). Vance Biblios.

Black Camel. Earl D. Biggers. 224p. 1987. pap. 3.95 o.p. (ISBN 0-445-40215-6). Mysterious Pr.

Black Canyon of the Gunnison: A Guide & Reference Book. John Dolson. LC 82-531. (Illus.). 80p. (Orig.). 1982. pap. 4.95 o.p. (ISBN 0-87108-622-0). Pruett.

Black Capitalism: Strategy for Business in the Ghetto. Theodore L. Cross. LC 72-80268. 1971. pap. 3.95 o.p. (ISBN 0-689-70266-3, 174, Atheneum). Macmillan.

Black Cat see Heinemann Guided Readers.

Black Champions of the Gridiron: O. J. Simpson & Leroy Keyes. A. S. Young. LC 76-8810. (Curriculum-Related Bks). (gr. 4-6). 1969. 5.50 o.p. (ISBN 0-15-208399-5, HJ). HarBraceJ.

Black Children: Their Roots, Culture, & Learning Styles. Janice E. Hale. 200p. (Orig.). 1982. pap. text ed. 9.95 o.p. (ISBN 0-8425-2092-9). Brigham.

Black Cop: A Biography of Tilmon O'Bryant. Ina R. Friedman. LC 73-20142. (Illus.). 160p. (gr. 7-11). 1974. 5.95 o.s.i. (ISBN 0-664-32546-7, Westminster). Westminster John Knox.

Black Curtain. Cornell Woolrich. 160p. 1982. pap. 2.25 o.s.i. (ISBN 0-345-30490-X). Ballantine.

Black Diamonds Gathered in Darkey Homes of the South. Edward A. Pollard. LC 68-55909. 1969. Repr. of 1859 ed. lib. bdg. 22.50x o.p. (ISBN 0-8371-0617-6, POD&, Pub. by Negro U Pr). Greenwood.

Black Dog, Red Dog. Stephen Dobyns. (National Poetry Ser.). 84p. 1984. 7.95 o.s.i. (ISBN 0-03-071077-4). H Holt & Co.

Black Dragon River. Grace L. McGary. LC 83-90849. 231p. 1984. 12.95 o.p. (ISBN 0-533-05862-7). Vantage.

Black Dwarf, 12 vols. Incl. Vol. 1. lib. bdg. 44.00 (ISBN 0-313-21506-5, BD01); Vol. 2. 44.00 (ISBN 0-313-21507-3, BD02); Vol. 3. lib. bdg. 44.00 (ISBN 0-313-21508-1, BD03); Vol. 4. lib. bdg. 50.00 (ISBN 0-313-21509-X, BD04); Vol. 5. lib. bdg. 50.00 (ISBN 0-313-21510-3, BD05); Vol. 6. lib. bdg. 50.00 (ISBN 0-313-21511-1, BD06); Vol. 7. lib. bdg. 50.00 (ISBN 0-313-21512-X, BD07); Vol. 8. lib. bdg. 50.00 (ISBN 0-313-21513-8, BD08); Vol. 9. lib. bdg. 50.00 (ISBN 0-313-21514-6, BD09); Vol. 10. lib. bdg. 50.00 (ISBN 0-313-21515-4, BD10); Vol. 11. lib. bdg. 44.00 (ISBN 0-313-21516-2, BD11); Vol. 12. lib. bdg. 44.00 (ISBN 0-313-21517-0, BD12). 1970. Repr. of 1824 ed. Set. lib. bdg. 505.00x o.p. (ISBN 0-8371-9133-5, BD00). Greenwood.

Black Easter. James Blish. 176p. 1982. pap. 2.50 o.p. (ISBN 0-380-59568-0, 59568-0). Avon.

Black Enterprise with the Third World. Edeward Adegbite. 1985. 5.75 o.p. (ISBN 0-8062-2372-3). Carlton.

Black Experience in Big Business. Harold E. Byrd. (Illus.). 1977. 6.50 o.p. (ISBN 0-682-48901-8). Exposition-Phoenix.

Black Experience in Children's Audiovisual Materials. 32p. 1973. pap. 1.00 o.p. (ISBN 0-87104-610-5, Branch Lib). NY Pub Lib.

Black Experience in Children's Books. Barbara Rollock. 1984. pap. 3.00 o.p. (ISBN 0-87104-665-2, Dist. by Branch Lib.). NY Pub Lib.

Black Experience: Soul. Ed. by Lee Rainwater. 186p. 1970. pap. (ISBN 0-87855-512-9). Transaction Pubs.

Black Fairy Tales. Ed. by Terry Berger. LC 70-75517. (Illus.). (gr. 3-7). 1969. PLB 5.95 o.p. (ISBN 0-689-20622-4, Atheneum Childrens Bk); pap. 3.50 o.p. (ISBN 0-689-70402-X). Macmillan.

Black Feeling, Black Talk-Black Judgement. Nikki Giovanni. LC 70-119846. 1970. 6.95 o.p. (ISBN 0-688-30294-7). Morrow.

Black Fire. Sonni Cooper. (Gregg Press Science Fiction - Star Trek Ser.). 224p. 1986. lib. bdg. 11.95x o.p. (ISBN 0-8398-2935-3, Gregg). G K Hall.

Black Flag: A Look Back at the Strange Case of Nicola Sacco & Bartolomeo Vanzetti. Brian Jackson. 208p. 1981. 21.95x o.p. (ISBN 0-7100-0897-X). Routledge Chapman & Hall.

Black Foremothers TG. Date not set. (ISBN 0-07-020434-9). McGraw.

Black Foremothers: Three Lives. Dorothy Sterling. (Women's Lives-Women's Work Ser.). (Illus.). 192p. (gr. 11 up). 1979. pap. 9.95 o.p. (ISBN 0-317-66235-X). Feminist Pr.

Black Goddess & the Unseen Real. Redgrove Peter. 1988. 17.95 o.p. (ISBN 0-8021-1054-1). Grove.

Black Grail. Damien Broderick. 320p. 1986. pap. 3.50 o.p. (ISBN 0-380-89977-9). Avon.

Black Hand: A Chapter in Ethnic Crime. Thomas M. Pitkin & Francesco Cordasco. (Quality Paperback Ser: No. 333). (Illus.). 1977. pap. 4.95 o.p. (ISBN 0-8226-0333-0). Littlefield.

Black Heart. Eric Van Lustbader. 1984. pap. 4.50 o.p. (ISBN 0-449-21151-7, Crest). Fawcett.

Black Hills Badlands. Mike Link & Craig Blacklock. (Illus.). 120p. 1980. 18.95 o.p. (ISBN 0-318-04123-5); pap. 9.95 o.p. (ISBN 0-89658-018-0). Voyageur Pr.

Black Hills Believables. John Hafnor. LC 83-82162. 112p. 1983. 4.95 o.p. (ISBN 0-934318-27-1). Falcon Pr Mt.

Black Holes. Walter Sullivan. 352p. 1983. pap. 4.50 o.p. (ISBN 0-446-32288-1). Warner Bks.

Black Holes, Quasars, & the Universe. Harry L. Shipman. LC 75-19535. (Illus.). 384p. 1976. text ed. 16.95 o.p. (ISBN 0-395-24342-4); pap. 8.50 o.p. (ISBN 0-395-20615-4). HM.

Black Holes, Quasars, & the Universe. 2nd ed. Harry L. Shipman. (Illus.). 1980. text ed. 26.95 o.p. (ISBN 0-395-29302-2); pap. 21.95 o.p. (ISBN 0-395-28499-6). HM.

Black Holes: The End of the Universe? John Taylor. (YA) (gr. 7 up). 1978. pap. 2.25 o.p. (ISBN 0-380-00327-9, 46805-0). Avon.

Black House. Paul Theroux. LC 74-6135. 256p. 1974. 6.95 o.p. (ISBN 0-395-19400-8). HM.

Black Images of America, 1784-1870. Leonard I. Sweet. (Essays in American History Ser). 1976. pap. text ed. 2.95 o.p. (ISBN 0-393-09195-3). Norton.

Black Is Beautiful but Grey Is Gorgeous. Catherine Liska. 1979. 5.00 o.p. (ISBN 0-682-49461-5). Exposition-Phoenix.

Black Lamb & Grey Falcon. Rebecca West. Penguin USA.

Black Leather Jacket. Mick Farren. LC 85-18541. 96p. 1986. 19.95 o.p. (ISBN 0-89659-591-9). Abbeville Pr.

Black Lights: Inside the World of Professional Boxing. Thomas Hauser. 272p. 1985. text ed. 16.95 o.p. (ISBN 0-07-027217-4). McGraw.

Black-Man of Zinacantan: A Central American Legend. Sarah C. Blaffer. (Texas Pan American Ser). (Illus.). 210p. 1972. 13.95x o.p. (ISBN 0-292-70701-0). U of Tex Pr.

Black Manhattan. James Weldon Johnson. LC 68-9823. (Studies in American Negro Life Ser.). 1968. pap. text ed. 5.95x o.p. (ISBN 0-689-70112-8, NL9, Atheneum). Macmillan.

Black Man's Burden. William H. Holtzclaw. LC 76-100293. Repr. of 1915 ed. 35.00x o.p. (ISBN 0-8371-2932-X, HOM&, Pub. by Negro U Pr). Greenwood.

Black Man's Place in South Africa. Peter Nielsen. LC 70-109347. 1970. Repr. of 1922 ed. 35.00x o.p. (ISBN 0-8371-3619-9, NIB&, Pub. by Negro U Pr). Greenwood.

Black Market. James Patterson. LC 85-26834. 365p. 1986. 17.45 o.p. (ISBN 0-671-61087-2). S&S.

Black Mask Boys. Ed. by William F. Nolan. LC 84-14778. 288p. 1985. 16.95 o.p. (ISBN 0-688-03966-9). Morrow.

Black Mask Boys: Masters in the Hard-Boiled School of Detective Fiction. William F. Nolan. 272p. 1987. Repr. 8.95 o.p. (ISBN 0-89296-931-8). Mysterious Pr.

Black Media in America: A Bibliography & Resource Guide. George H. Hill. 352p. 1984. lib. bdg. 50.00 o.p. (ISBN 0-8161-8610-3, Hall Reference). G K Hall.

Black Men in Chains: Narratives by Escaped Slaves. Ed. by Charles H. Nichols. LC 72-78320. 320p. 1972. o. p. 8.95 o.p. (ISBN 0-88208-003-2); pap. 5.95 o.p. (ISBN 0-88208-004-0). Chicago Review.

Black Mesa. Zane Grey. LC 85-17430. 1984. pap. 2.95 o.s.i. (ISBN 0-671-52637-5). PB.

Black Metropolis, Vol. 1. St. Clair Drake & Horace R. Cayton. LC 73-12271. (Illus.). 1970. pap. 2.85 o.p. (ISBN 0-15-613050-5, H078, Harv). HarBraceJ.

Black Metropolis, Vol. 2. St. Clair Drake & Horace R. Cayton. LC 73-12271. (Illus.). 1970. pap. 2.85 o.p. (ISBN 0-15-613051-3, HO79, Harv). HarBraceJ.

Black Military Experience in the American West. Ed. by John M. Carroll. 1974. pap. 3.95 o.p. (ISBN 0-87140-285-8). Liveright.

Black Military Experience in the American West. Ed. by John M. Carroll. LC 76-137866. (Illus.). 1971. 17.50 o.p. (ISBN 0-87140-519-9). Liveright.

Black Mountain Boy. Vada Carlson & Gary Witherspoon. 81p. Date not set. price not set o.s.i. (ISBN 0-89019-008-9). Navajo Curr.

Black Music of Two Worlds. John S. Roberts. (Illus., Orig.). 1985. pap 8.95 o.p. (ISBN 0-688-05278-9). Riverrun NY.

Black Mutiny. 3.45 o.p. Pilgrim NY.

Black November: The Nineteen Eighteen Influenza Epidemic in New Zealand. Geoffrey Rice. 29.95 o.p. (ISBN 0-86861-595-1). Unwin Hyman.

Black Paradise: The Rastafarian Movement. Peter B. Clarke. 112p. 1986. pap. 11.95 o.p. (ISBN 0-85030-428-8). Newcastle Pub.

Black Parents Handbook: A Guide to Healthy Pregnancy, Birth & Child Care. Clara J. McLaughlin. LC 75-43986. (Illus.). 220p. 1976. pap. 5.95 o.p. (ISBN 0-15-613100-5, Harv). HarBraceJ.

Black Parents Handbook: A Guide to the Facts of Pregnancy, Birth & Child Care. Clara J. McLaughlin. LC 75-43986. (Illus.). 1976. 10.00 o.p. (ISBN 0-15-113185-6). HarBraceJ.

Black Poet. Richard Walser. LC 66-18817. 1967. (ISBN 0-8022-1801-6). Philos Lib.

Black Political Theology. J. Deotis Roberts, Sr. LC 74-4384. 1974. pap. 3.95 o.s.i. (ISBN 0-664-24988-4, Westminster). Westminster John Knox.

Black Princess & Other Stories. A. V. Bharath. (Illus.). 96p. 1967. 1.00 o.s.i. (ISBN 0-88253-413-0). Ind-US Inc.

Black Progress: Reality or Illusion. Ed. by Carol C. Collins. 192p. 1986. 24.95 o.p. (ISBN 0-87196-968-8). Facts on File.

Black Prophet. William Carleton. 408p. 1972. Repr. of 1899 ed. 25.00x o.p. (ISBN 0-7165-1798-1, BBA 02225, Pub by Irish Academic Pr). Biblio Dist.

Black Reality. Parnell Turrentine, Jr. 72p. 1986. 6.50 o.p. (ISBN 0-8062-2618-8). Carlton.

Black Resource Guide. LC 85-91077. 1986. 25.00 o.p. (ISBN 0-9608374-3-4); pap. 15.00 o.p. (ISBN 0-9608374-4-2). Black Resource.

Black Resource Guide. 5th ed. Robert B. Johnson. (Illus.). 216p. 1985. 25.00 o.p. (ISBN 0-9608374-2-6). Black Resource.

Black Rock. Ralph Connor. 1973. pap. 0.95 o.p. (ISBN 0-380-01065-8, 17301). Avon.

Black Roots in Southeastern Connecticut 1650-1900: A Guide to Information Sources. Ed. by James M. Rose & Barbara Brown. (Genealogy & Local History Ser.: Vol. 8). 750p. 1980. 68.00x o.p. (ISBN 0-8103-1411-8). Gale.

Black Sands: A History of the Mineral Sand Mining Industry in Eastern Australia. I. W. Morley. (Illus.). 278p. 1982. text ed. 39.95x o.p. (ISBN 0-7022-1633-X). U of Queensland Pr.

Black Satin. Eleanor M. Woodard. 40p. 1987. 6.95 o.p. (ISBN 0-8062-3017-7). Carlton.

Black South African Views on Disinvestment. Meg Voorhes. 36p. 1986. 25.00 o.p. (ISBN 0-317-52536-0). IRRC Inc DC.

Black Spaniel Mystery. Betty Cavanna. (gr. 5-9). 1945. 5.50 o.s.i. (ISBN 0-664-32003-1, Westminster). Westminster John Knox.

Black Sportsmen. Ernest Cashmore. 224p. (Orig.). 1982. pap. 13.95x o.p. (ISBN 0-7100-9054-4). Routledge Chapman & Hall.

Black Square & Compass: 200 Years of Prince Hall Freemasonry. rev. ed. Joseph A. Walkes, Jr. LC 79-112352. 192p. 1981. text ed. 12.50 o.p. (ISBN 0-88053-061-8, M 324). Macoy Pub.

Black Star Rising. Frederik Pohl. LC 84-24204. 304p. 1986. 15.95 o.p. (ISBN 0-345-31903-6, Del Rey); pap. 3.50 o.p. (ISBN 0-345-31902-8, Del Ray). Ballantine.

Black Struggles. Alphonse Jenkins, Sr. 1978. 4.00 o.p. (ISBN 0-682-49121-7). Exposition-Phoenix.

Black Studies: Pedagogy & Revolution; A Study of Afro-American Studies & the Liberal Arts Tradition through the Discipline of Afro-American Literature. Johnnella E. Butler. LC 80-67213. 162p. 1981. lib. bdg. 25.50 o.p. (ISBN 0-8191-1568-1); pap. text ed. 10.25 o.p. (ISBN 0-8191-1569-X). U Pr of Amer.

Black Sun. Edward Abbey. 160p. 1982. pap. 2.50 o.p. (ISBN 0-380-58503-0, 58503-0). Avon.

Black Sun. James Tarabilda. 1980. pap. 2.25 o.p. (ISBN 0-8439-0767-3, Pub. by Leisure Bks CT). Dorchester Pub Co.

Black Swan. Thomas Mann. Tr. by Willard R. Trask. LC 79-24136. 160p. 1980. pap. 2.95 o.p. (ISBN 0-15-613128-5, Harv). HarBraceJ.

Black Task Force Report. Ed. by Anita J. Delaney. LC 78-24566. (Project on Ethnicity Ser.). 37p. 1979. pap. 4.00 o.p. (ISBN 0-87304-171-2). Family Serv.

Black Tents of Arabia. Carl Raswan. 240p. 1971. 9.95 o.p. (ISBN 0-374-11416-1). FS&G.

Black Theology Exposed. Robert L. Jordan. LC 81-90503. (Illus.). 92p. 1983. 8.95 o.p. (ISBN 0-533-05215-7). Vantage.

Black Triumvirate. Benjamin H. Levin. 1972. 6.95 o.p. (ISBN 0-8065-0268-1, Pub. by Citadel Pr). Carol Pub Group.

Black Ulysses. Daniel Panger. LC 82-3517. (Illus.). vi, 402p. 1982. 16.95 o.p. (ISBN 0-8214-0660-4); pap. 6.95 o.p. (ISBN 0-8214-0680-9). Ohio U Pr.

Black Velvet Gown. Catherine Cookson. 368p. 1984. 16.45 o.s.i. (ISBN 0-671-46788-3). Summit Bks.

Black Walnut for Profit: A Guide to Risks & Rewards. 2nd ed. Bruce Thompson. 285p. 1978. pap. text ed. 12.95x o.p. (ISBN 0-917304-40-3). Timber.

Black Weather. Berton Roueche. LC 84-28398. 1985. 5.95 o.p. (ISBN 0-87795-713-4, Arbor Hse). Morrow.

Black Wheel. Abraham Merritt & Hannes Bok. 288p. 1981. pap. 2.50 o.p. (ISBN 0-380-55822-X, 55822). Avon.

Black-White Income Differentials: Empirical Studies & Policy. S. Masters. 1975. 22.50 o.p. (ISBN 0-12-479050-X). Acad Pr.

Black Woman in America: Sex, Marriage & the Family. Robert Staples. LC 72-95280. 287p. 1973. 21.95x o.s.i. (ISBN 0-911012-55-9); pap. 11.95x o.s.i. (ISBN 0-88229-420-2). Nelson-Hall.

Black Woman's Career Guide. Beatryce Nivens. LC 80-1816. (Illus.). 456p. 1982. 24.95 o.p. (ISBN 0-385-15095-4); pap. 12.95 o.p. (ISBN 0-385-15096-2, Anchor Pr). Doubleday.

Black Women & Religion. Marilyn Richardson. 1980. 17.50 o.p. (ISBN 0-8161-8087-3, Hall Reference). G K Hall.

Black Worker. Sterling D. Spero & Abram L. Harris. LC 68-16419. (Studies in American Negro Life). 1968. pap. text ed. 4.95x o.p. (ISBN 0-689-70185-3, NL7, Atheneum). Macmillan.

Black Writers-White Audience: A Critical Approach to African Literature. Phanuel A. Egejuru. 1978. 12.50 o.p. (ISBN 0-682-48977-8, University). Exposition-Phoenix.

Black Zion. David Jenkins. LC 75-2174. 285p. 1975. 10.95 o.p. (ISBN 0-15-113193-7). HarBraceJ.

Blackballed. Michael Mewshaw. LC 86-47664. 320p. 1986. 16.95 o.p. (ISBN 0-689-11837-6, Atheneum). Macmillan.

Blackbeard's Ghost. Ben Stahl. (Illus.). 192p. (gr. 4-6). 1965. 7.95 o.p. (ISBN 0-395-07115-1). HM.

Blackberry Winter. Margaret Mead. 337p. 1973. pap. 5.95 o.p. (ISBN 0-671-43299-0). WSP.

Blackbird. Steve MacKenzie. (Seals Ser.: No. 2). 192p. (Orig.). 1987. pap. 2.50 o.p. (ISBN 0-380-75190-9). Avon.

Blackboard Jungle. Evan Hunter. 1976. pap. 1.75 o.p. (ISBN 0-380-00859-9, 31260). Avon.

Blackboard Jungle. Evan Hunter. 1984. pap. 6.95 o.p. (ISBN 0-87795-600-6, Arbor Hse). Morrow.

Blackboard Jungle. Evan Hunter. 1985. lib. bdg. 18.95 o.p. (ISBN 0-8161-3862-1, Large Print Bks). G K Hall.

Blackbriar. William Sleator. (YA) (gr. 7 up). 1975. pap. 0.95 o.p. (ISBN 0-380-00248-5, 30247-0). Avon.

Blackfoot Ambush. Catherine Weber. (American Indians Ser.: No. 2). 368p. (Orig.). 1981. pap. 2.75 o.p. (ISBN 0-440-00590-6, Banbury). Dell.

Blacks & Metropolitan Governance: The Stakes of Reform. Willis D. Hawley. LC 72-5145. 34p. (Orig.). 1972. pap. 1.50x o.p. (ISBN 0-87772-153-X). UCB IGS.

Blacks & the Law. Ed. by Jack Greenberg & Richard D. Lambert. LC 72-93252. (Annals of the American Academy of Political & Social Science: No. 407). 250p. 1973. 15.00 o.p. (ISBN 0-87761-163-7); pap. 8.95 o.p. (ISBN 0-87761-162-9). Am Acad Pol Soc Sci.

Blacks & the Populist Revolt: Ballots & Bigotry in the "New South" Gerald H. Gaither. LC 75-6904. (Illus.). 269p. 1977. 19.75 o.p. (ISBN 0-8173-4726-7). U of Ala Pr.

Blacks in the United States: A Geographic Perspective. George A. Davis & O. Fred Donaldson. 1975. pap. 8.50 o.p. (ISBN 0-395-14066-8). HM.

Blacks in These Sea Islands. Carline S. Robinson. LC 84-90301. 129p. 1985. 12.95 o.p. (ISBN 0-533-06343-4). Vantage.

Blacks in White America Since 1865: Issues & Interpretations. Ed. by Robert C. Twombly. LC 77-141930. 1971. pap. 8.95x o.p. (ISBN 0-679-30018-X, Pub. by MacKay). Longman.

Blackwater, I: The Flood. Michael McDowell. 1983. pap. 2.95 o.p. (ISBN 0-380-81489-7, 81489-7). Avon.

Blackwater, II: The Levee. Michael McDowell. 1983. pap. 2.95 o.p. (ISBN 0-380-82206-7, 82206-7). Avon.

Blackwater, III: The House. Michael McDowell. 176p. (Orig.). 1983. pap. 2.95 o.p. (ISBN 0-380-82594-5, 82594-5). Avon.

Blackwater, IV: The War. Michael McDowell. 192p. 1983. pap. 2.95 o.p. (ISBN 0-380-82776-X, 82776-X). Avon.

Blackwater, VI: Rain. Michael McDowell. 1983. pap. 2.95 o.p. (ISBN 0-380-82792-1, 82792-1). Avon.

Blaedud the Birdman. Vera Chapman. 1980. pap. 1.95 o.p. (ISBN 0-380-45070-4, 45070). Avon.

Blaiklock's Handbook to the Bible. E. M. Blaiklock. 256p. 1981. pap. 6.95 o.p. (ISBN 0-8007-5055-1, Power Bks). Revell.

Blaise Pascal: The Genius of His Thought. Roger Hazelton. LC 73-21951. 224p. 1975. 7.50 o.s.i. (ISBN 0-664-20999-8, Westminster). Westminster John Knox.

Blake & the Assimilation of Chaos. G. Gallant. LC 78-51165. 1978. 25.50x o.p. (ISBN 0-691-06367-2). Princeton U Pr.

Blake Dictionary: The Ideas & Symbols of William Blake. S. Foster Damon. LC 65-18187. (Illus.). 472p. 1965. 45.00x o.p. (ISBN 0-87057-088-9). U Pr of New Eng.

Blake: Selected Poems & Letters. William Blake. Ed. by J. Bronowski. (Poets Ser.). 1958. pap. 4.95 o.p. (ISBN 0-14-042042-8). Penguin.

Blake's Illustrations to the Divine Comedy. Albert S. Roe. LC 77-4443. (Illus.). 1977. Repr. of 1953 ed. lib. bdg. 46.75x o.p. (ISBN 0-8371-9595-0, ROBIL). Greenwood.

Blake's Night: William Blake & the Idea of Pastoral. David Wagenknecht. LC 72-92123. (Illus.). 321p. 1973. 24.50x o.s.i. (ISBN 0-674-07635-4, Belkap Pr). Harvard U Pr.

Blam: The Explosion of Pop, Minimalism & Performance, 1958-1964. Barbara Haskell. LC 84-7304. (Illus.). 160p. 1984. 27.00 o.p. (ISBN 0-393-01935-7). Norton.

Blanche & Smitty, Bk. 1. Michele Malkin. 32p. (YA) 1988. pap. 3.95 o.p. (ISBN 0-553-05424-4). Bantam.

Blanche & Smitty's Summer Vacation. Michele Malkin. 32p. 1988. pap. 3.50 o.p. (ISBN 0-553-05478-3). Bantam.

Blanda, Alive & Kicking. Wells Twombly. 1973. pap. 1.25 o.p. (01067-4). Avon.

Blandford Family Quiz Book 2. Elizabeth Young. 130p. (Orig.). 1986. pap. 2.95 o.p. (ISBN 0-7137-1621-5, Pub. by Javelin England). Sterling.

Blanding's Practical Physical Distribution. new ed. Warren Blanding. LC 78-63404. 1978. 37.50 o.p. (ISBN 0-87408-010-X). Intl Thom Trans Pr.

Blanket That Had to Go. Nancy E. Cooney. (Illus.). 32p. (gr. 4-8). 1981. 8.95 o.p. (ISBN 0-399-20716-3, Putnam); pap. 5.95 o.p. (ISBN 0-399-21054-7, Putnam). Putnam Pub Group.

Blast, 2 vols, No. 5. 1970. Repr. of 1917 ed. Set. lib. bdg. 27.00x o.p. (ISBN 0-8371-9134-3, BL00). Greenwood.

Blast off with BASIC Games for Your Commodore 64. David D. Busch. LC 83-25682. (Illus.). 1984. pap. 12.95 o.p. Brady Bks.

Blasting Operations. Gary B. Hemphill. (Illus.). 1980. text ed. 48.50 o.p. (ISBN 0-07-028093-2). McGraw.

Blaze & the Gray Spotted Pony. Clarence W. Anderson. LC 68-10997. (Illus.). (ps-2). 1968. 10.95 o.s.i. (ISBN 0-02-701150-X); pap. 2.95 o.s.i. (ISBN 0-02-041480-3, Collier). Macmillan.

Blaze & the Indian Cave. Clarence W. Anderson. LC 64-14529. (Illus.). (gr. 1-3). 1971. 11.95 o.s.i. (ISBN 0-02-702470-9). Macmillan.

Blaze & the Mountain Lion. Clarence W. Anderson. LC 59-22393. (gr. 1-3). 1969. 10.95 o.s.i. (ISBN 0-02-702630-2). Macmillan.

Blazing Air. Oswald Wynd. LC 81-5671. (Joan Kahn Bk). 324p. 1981. 12.95 o.p. (ISBN 0-89919-047-2). Ticknor & Fields.

Blazing Embers. Deborah Camp. (Avon Romance Ser.). 368p. 1987. pap. 3.95 o.p. (ISBN 0-380-75126-7). Avon.

Bleaching Earths. M. K. Hasruddin Siddiqui. 1968. 31.00 o.p. (ISBN 0-08-012738-X). Pergamon.

Bledding Sorrow. Marilyn Harris. 408p. 1977. pap. 2.75 o.p. (ISBN 0-380-00936-6, 53181-X). Avon.

Bleeders Come First. Colin Douglas. LC 79-64156. 1979. 8.95 o.s.i. (ISBN 0-8008-0816-9). Taplinger.

Bleeding Between the Lines. Eliot Asinof. LC 78-14181. 1979. 9.95 o.p. (ISBN 0-03-047536-8). H Holt & Co.

Bleeding Disorders. Jessica Lewis et al. (Contemporary Patient Management Ser.). 1978. spiral 16.00 o.p. (ISBN 0-87488-891-3). Med Exam.

Bleeding Heart. Marilyn French. 416p. 1985. pap. 4.95 o.p. (ISBN 0-345-33284-9). Ballantine.

Bleeding Heart. Marilyn French. LC 79-26346. 1980. 12.95 o.s.i. (ISBN 0-671-44784-X). Summit Bks.

Bleeding Orange. Pender Murphy. LC 85-90985. 160p. 1985. 12.50 o.p. (ISBN 0-682-40273-7). Exposition-Phoenix.

Bleeding Soul Ame. Ojaovo I. Otu. 64p. 1981. 4.00 o.p. (ISBN 0-682-49763-0). Exposition-Phoenix.

Blend-It. Cecelia Pollack & Diane Glasser. (Intersensory Reading Program). (Illus.). 48p. (gr. k-3). 1976. wkbk 2.95 o.p. (ISBN 0-87594-143-5). Book-Lab.

Bleomycin: Chemical, Biochemical & Biological Aspects. Ed. by S. H. Hecht. LC 79-4295. (Illus.). 1979. 69.00 o.p. (ISBN 0-387-90395-X). Springer-Verlag.

Bleomycin: Current Status & New Developments. Ed. by Stephen K. Carter et al. 1978. 60.50 o.p. (ISBN 0-12-161550-2). Acad Pr.

Bless This Day: A Book of Prayer for Children. Ed. by Elfrida Vipont. LC 57-10352. (Illus.). (gr. 1 up). 1958. 5.95 o.p. (ISBN 0-15-208734-6, HJ). HarBraceJ.

Bless This House: American Palace No. 1. Evan H. Rhodes. (Orig.). 1982. pap. 3.25 o.s.i. (ISBN 0-425-05457-8). Berkley Pub.

Blessed Are Your Eyes. Bessie Beihl. pap. 1.00 o.p. (ISBN 0-87516-131-6). DeVorss.

Blessed Athanasia. Alexander Priklonsky. (Illus.). 55p. Date not set. pap. 2.50 o.p. St Herman AK.

Blessed Be the Bond: Christian Perspectives on Marriage & Family. William J. Everett. LC 84-48712. 144p. 1985. pap. 6.95 o.p. (ISBN 0-8006-1831-9, 1-1831, Fortress). Augsburg Fortress.

Blessed John the Wonderworker. Seraphim Rose & Abbot Herman. (Illus.). 480p. Date not set. pap. 15.00 o.p. St Herman AK.

Blessed Virgin. Clifford Stevens. LC 84-60745. 160p. 1985. pap. 6.95 o.p. (ISBN 0-87973-704-2, 704). Our Sunday Visitor.

Blessing: In the Bible & the Life of the Church, No. 3. Claus Westermann. Ed. by Walter Brueggeman & John R. Donahue. Tr. by Keith Crim from Ger. LC 78-54564. (Overtures to Biblical Theology Ser.). 144p. 1978. pap. 8.95 o.p. (ISBN 0-8006-1529-8, 1-1529, Fortress). Augsburg Fortress.

Blessing Outside Us. Hilda Morley. Ed. by Peter Kaplan. 3.50x o.s.i. (ISBN 0-915176-19-X). Pourboire.

Blessing Way. Tony Hillerman. (YA) (gr. 7 up). 1978. pap. 2.95 o.p. (ISBN 0-380-39941-5). Avon.

Blessings of Temple Marriage. George McCune. 1974. pap. 4.95 o.p. (ISBN 0-89036-040-5). Hawkes Pub Inc.

Blest Be the Tie That Frees. Ken Berven. LC 73-83784. 104p. 1973. pap. 2.95 o.p. (ISBN 0-8066-1337-8, 10-0775, Augsburg). Augsburg Fortress.

Blick & Einsicht: Intermediate German. W. A. Von Schmidt & H. Hinrichs. 1983. 17.50 o.p. (ISBN 0-8384-1231-9). Heinle & Heinle.

Blind Date. Jerzy Kosinski. 1977. 8.95 o.p. (ISBN 0-395-25781-6). HM.

Blind Landing. Bjorn K. Paulsson. Tr. by Constance F. Toverud from Norwegian. LC 77-161388. 123p. (gr. 7 up). 1972. 5.95 o.p. (ISBN 0-15-208770-2, HJ). HarBraceJ.

Blind Owl. Sadegh Hedayat. Tr. by D. P. Costello. 1970. pap. 1.95 o.s.i. (ISBN 0-394-17445-3, B205, BC). Grove.

Blind Spot. Austin Hall & Homer E. Flint. 256p. 1987. 15.00 o.p. (ISBN 0-947898-57-3). Kraus Repr.

Blind Trust: The Human Crisis in Airline Safety. John J. Nance. LC 85-13709. (Illus.). 448p. 1986. 17.95 o.p. (ISBN 0-688-05360-2). Morrow.

Blinded by the Light. Robin Brancato. LC 78-4583. (YA) (gr. 7-12). 1978. 7.95 o.p. (ISBN 0-394-83721-5); lib. bdg. 7.99 o.p. (ISBN 0-394-93721-X). Knopf.

Blinkety Blanks, 1 & 2. Ruby Maschke. Ed. by Arthur L. Zapel. (Illus., Orig.). (gr. 6-12). 1981. 3.95 set o.p. (ISBN 0-916260-10-0). Meriwether Pub.

Bliss & Bluster. Janwillem Van de Wetering. (Illus.). 128p. (Orig.). 1982. pap. 7.95 o.p. (ISBN 0-395-31839-4). HM.

Blithewold, Bristol, Rhode Island. Alice D. Pardee. LC 78-60477. (Illus.). 1978. write for info o.p. (ISBN 0-917218-10-8). A Mobray Inc.

Blitz. Hetty B. Beatty. (Illus.). 144p. (gr. 3-6). 1974. pap. 0.95 o.p. (ISBN 0-395-18565-3, Sandpiper). HM.

Blizzard! Jerry Jenkins. (Bradford Family Adventures Ser.). (Illus.). 112p. (gr. 3-6). 1985. 2.95 o.p. (ISBN 0-87239-942-7, 2992). Standard Pub.

Blockade Busters. Ralph Barker. (Illus.). 1977. 8.95 o.p. (ISBN 0-393-05609-0). Norton.

Bloedel Reserve: Gardens in the Forest. Lawrence Kresiman. LC 88-71534. (Illus.). 112p. (Orig.). 1988. 30.00 o.p.; pap. 20.00 o.p. Bloedel Reserve.

Blond Baboon. Janwillem Van De Wetering. 1978. 7.95 o.p. (ISBN 0-395-26307-7). HM.

Blonde Eckbert. Ludwig Tieck & Brentano. Ed. by Margaret E. Atkinson. (German Text Ser.). 114p. 1952. pap. 9.95x o.p. (ISBN 0-631-01560-4). Basil Blackwell.

Blonds. Barbara Sloan-White & Charles R. Woods. 96p. 1984. pap. 12.95 o.p. (ISBN 0-671-50881-4, Fireside). S&S.

Blood & Guts in High School. Kathy Acker. (Illus.). 176p. 1984. pap. 7.95 o.p. (ISBN 0-394-62334-7, E-959, Ever). Grove.

Blood & Guts in High School. Kathy Acker. 176p. (Orig.). 1989. pap. 9.95 o.s.i. (ISBN 0-8021-3193-X). Grove.

Blood & Guts: The True Story of General George S. Patton, U. S. A. John Devaney. LC 82-60636. (Illus.). 96p. (gr. 4 up). 1982. lib. bdg. 9.79 o.p. (ISBN 0-671-44273-2). Messner.

Blood & Ice. Liz Lochhead. 34p. 1983. pap. 5.95 o.p. (ISBN 0-907540-23-6, NO.3989). Routledge Chapman & Hall.

Blood & Lungs. Gwynne Vevers. LC 83-18757. (Your Body Ser.). (Illus.). 24p. (gr. 1-4). 1984. 8.25 o.p. (ISBN 0-688-02823-3); PLB 7.63 o.p. (ISBN 0-688-02824-1). Lothrop.

Blood & Roses. Bernice Grohskopf. LC 78-14583. (gr. 6-10). 1979. 8.95 o.p. (ISBN 0-689-30681-4, Atheneum). Macmillan.

Blood & Tissue Antigens: A Symposium Volume. Ed. by David Aminoff. 1970. 92.50 o.p. (ISBN 0-12-057050-5). Acad Pr.

Blood Banking in a Changing Environment. Ed. by Dennis Smith & John Judd. (Illus.). 117p. 1984. text ed. 18.00 o.p. (ISBN 0-914404-99-7). Am Assn Blood.

Blood, Brains & Beer: An Autobiography. David Ogilvy. LC 77-76541. 1978. 7.95 o.p. (ISBN 0-689-10809-5, Atheneum). Macmillan.

Blood Brothers. Harry Tegnaeus. 182p. 1953. (ISBN 0-8022-1703-6). Philos Lib.

Blood Coagulation Disorders. F. R. Matthias. 345p. 1987. pap. 23.90 o.p. (ISBN 0-387-17813-9). Springer-Verlag.

Blood Coast: A Novel of South Florida. Michael H. Gora. 1980. 12.50 o.p. (ISBN 0-682-49606-5, Banner). Exposition-Phoenix.

Blood Feud. Edward Hannibal & Robert Boris. 320p. 1983. pap. 2.95 o.s.i. (ISBN 0-345-31238-4). Ballantine.

Blood for Blood. Julian Gloag. LC 85-8741. 302p. 1985. 15.95 o.p. (ISBN 0-03-006012-5). H Holt & Co.

Blood Group Antigens & Diseases. Ed. by George Garratty. 145p. 1983. 16.00 o.p. (ISBN 0-914404-96-2). Am Assn Blood.

Blood Group O. David Brierley. 208p. 1984. 9.70 o.s.i. (ISBN 0-671-47754-4). Summit Bks.

Blood Group Substances: Their Chemistry & Immunochemistry. Elvin A. Kabat. 1956. 78.50 o.p. (ISBN 0-12-392850-8). Acad Pr.

Blood in the Furrows: A Historical Novel. Ingrid Clairmont & Leonard Clairmont. (Illus.). 1979. 12.00 o.p. (ISBN 0-682-49504-2, Banner). Exposition-Phoenix.

Blood in the Snow. Marlene F. Shyer. (Illus.). 144p. (gr. 3-7). 1975. 5.95 o.p. (ISBN 0-395-21929-9). HM.

Blood Knife. Jack Slade. (Sundance Ser: No. 25). 1979. 1.75 o.p. (ISBN 0-8439-0626-X, Pub. by Leisure Bks CT). Dorchester Pub Co.

Blood-Line: A Translation of Gustav Wied's Slaegten. J. C. Sandeman. 1983. 10.00 o.p. (ISBN 0-533-05504-0). Vantage.

Blood Lord. Hugh Seidman. LC 73-10546. 1974. 5.95 o.p. (ISBN 0-385-08172-3). Small Pr Dist.

Blood-Membrane Internation in Extracorporeal Circuits. Ed. by L. W. Henderson & D. Chenoweth. (Journal: Blood Purification Ser.: Vol. 5, No. 2-3, 1987). (Illus.). 96p. 1987. 46.00 o.p. (ISBN 0-317-61284-0). S Karger.

Blood Music. Greg Bear. LC 84-24351. 248p. 1985. 14.95 o.p. (ISBN 0-87795-720-7, Arbor Hse). Morrow.

Blood of Amber. Roger Zelazny. LC 86-3530. 224p. 1986. 14.95 o.p. (ISBN 0-87795-829-7, Arbor Hse). Morrow.

Blood of an Englishman. James McClure. (International Crime Ser.). 1982. pap. 2.95 o.p. (ISBN 0-394-71019-3). Pantheon.

Blood of His Servants: The True Story of One Man's Search for His Family's Friend & Executioner. Malcolm C. MacPherson. LC 83-40089. (Illus.). 310p. 1984. 16.95 o.p. (ISBN 0-8129-1098-2). Times Bks.

Blood of Paradise. Stephen Goodwin. 1985. pap. 3.95 o.p. (ISBN 0-380-69890-0). Avon.

Blood of Sheep: Composition & Function. M. H. Blunt. (Illus.). 250p. 1975. 43.00 o.p. (ISBN 0-387-07234-9). Springer-Verlag.

Blood of the Air. Philip Lamantia. LC 74-105925. (Writing Ser: No. 25). 56p. (Orig.). 1970. pap. 2.25 o.p. (ISBN 0-87704-013-3). Four Seasons Foun.

Blood of the Cross: Understanding the Mystery of Redemption. Andrew Murray. 96p. 1987. pap. 3.95 o.p. (ISBN 0-310-55112-9, 19011P). Zondervan.

Blood of the Falcon, No. 222. Nick Carter. 208p. pap. 2.75 o.s.i. (ISBN 0-441-57291-X, Pub. by Charter). Ace Bks.

Blood of the Land. Rex Weyler. LC 82-2349. (Illus.). 304p. 1982. 16.95 o.p. (ISBN 0-89696-134-6, Everest House Book). Dodd.

Blood Offerings. Robert SanSouci. 368p. (Orig.). 1985. pap. 3.75 o.s.i. (ISBN 0-8439-2185-4, Pub. by Leisure Bks CT). Dorchester Pub Co.

Blood on the Bosom Devine. Thomas Kyd. LC 75-44988. (Crime Fiction Ser). 1976. Repr. of 1948 ed. lib. bdg. 21.00 o.p. (ISBN 0-8240-2380-3). Garland Pub.

Blood Platelets in Man & Animals, 2 vols. B. Maupin. 1969. Set. 250.00 o.p. (ISBN 0-08-006405-1). Pergamon.

Blood Policy & Technology. LC 85-601151. (Illus.). 247p. 1985. pap. 7.50 o.p. (ISBN 0-318-22489-5, S/N 052-003-00977-3). USGPO.

Blood Pressure Levels in Persons 18-74 Years of Age in 1974-80 & the Trends in Blood Pressure from 1960-1980 in the United States. Terence Drizd. LC 85-32032. (Vital & Health Statistics Data from the National Health Survey Ser.: Vol. 11, No. 234). (Illus.). 74p. 1986. pap. 3.75 o.p. (S/N 017-022-00963-3). USGPO.

Blood Relations. E. E. Kophal. 1984. 9.50 o.p. (ISBN 0-8062-2280-8). Carlton.

Blood Relations. Leonard Mosley. LC 79-55584. (Illus.). 1980. 17.50 o.p. (ISBN 0-689-11055-3, Atheneum). Macmillan.

Blood Replacement. U. F. Gruber. Tr. by L. Oxtoby & R. F. Armstrong. LC 69-16845. (Illus.). 1969. 25.00 o.p. (ISBN 0-387-04496-5). Springer-Verlag.

Blood River Gold. Swain Adams. (Orig.). 1981. pap. 1.95 o.p. (ISBN 0-505-51628-4, Pub. by Tower Bks). Dorchester Pub Co.

Blood Rubies. Axel Young. (Orig.). 1982. pap. 2.95 o.p. (ISBN 0-380-79392-X, 79392-X). Avon.

Blood Secrets. Craig Jones. 1979. pap. 2.25 o.s.i. (ISBN 0-345-28238-8). Ballantine.
Blood Solstice. James H. Kunstler. LC 85-16043. 240p. 1986. 15.95 o.p. (ISBN 0-385-19697-0). Doubleday.
Blood Stripe. William Blankenship. 400p. 1987. pap. 3.95 o.p. (ISBN 0-380-75284-0). Avon.
Blood Suckers. Judith Schoder. LC 81-10999. (Jem Bks.). (Illus.). 64p. (Teens reading on a 2-3rd grade level). (gr. 2-3). 1981. lib. bdg. 9.29 o.s.i. (ISBN 0-671-43778-X). Messner.
Blood Sun in Jerusalem. Herbert G. Wittels. 416p. 1984. 16.95 o.p. (ISBN 0-682-40180-3). Exposition-Phoenix.
Blood Tango. Robert Houston. 272p. 1984. pap. 3.95 o.p. (ISBN 0-380-85506-2, 85506). Avon.
Blood Tie. Mary L. Settle. (Signature Editions Ser.). 400p. 1986. pap. 7.95 o.p. (ISBN 0-684-18662-4). Scribner.
Blood Tie. Mary Lee Settle. 1977. 10.95 o.p. (ISBN 0-395-25401-9). HM.
Blood Transfusion Therapy: A Problem Oriented Approach. Napier. 1987. (ISBN 0-471-91283-2, Dist. by A R Liss). Wiley.
Blood Vessels & Lymphatics. Ed. by David I. Abramson. 1962. 98.00 o.p. (ISBN 0-12-042550-5). Acad Pr.
Blood Viscosity in Heart Disease & Cancer: Proceedings. Ed. by L. Dintenfass & L. Dintenfass. (Illus.). 192p. 1981. 51.00 o.p. (ISBN 0-08-024954-X). Pergamon.
Blood Vote. Jack Lindsay. LC 84-25709. 373p. 1985. 15.95 o.p. (ISBN 0-7022-1838-3). U of Queensland Pr.
Blood Will Tell. Gary Cartwright. LC 78-22246. 1979. 10.95 o.p. (ISBN 0-15-169961-5). HarBraceJ.
Blood Will Tell. Miles Napier. pap. (ISBN 0-85131-254-3, NL51, Dist. by Miller). S R Smith Sporting Bks.
Bloodbrothers. Richard Price. LC 75-40369. 1976. 8.95 o.p. (ISBN 0-395-24303-3). HM.
Bloodheart Royal. Richard Tresillian. (Illus.). 288p. 1988. 18.95 o.p. (ISBN 0-7126-9553-2, Pub. by Century Hutchinson). David & Charles.
Bloodmoon. Robert Kalish. 1985. pap. 2.95 o.p. (ISBN 0-380-89732-6). Avon.
Bloodrun. Robert Kalish. 208p. (Orig.). 1984. pap. 2.75 o.p. (ISBN 0-380-88021-0). Avon.
Bloodstar. Tom Topor. 1978. 9.95 o.p. (ISBN 0-393-08829-4). Norton.
Bloodstock Sales Analysis, 1962. Compiled by Bernard J. O'Sullivan. 1.00 o.p. (ISBN 0-85131-058-3, NL51, Dist. by Miller). S R Smith Sporting Bks.
Bloodtide. Robert Kalish. 176p. 1985. pap. 2.95 o.p. (ISBN 0-380-89521-8). Avon.
Bloody Crossroads: Where Literature & Politics Meet. Norman Podhoretz. 206p. 1986. 16.45 o.s.i. (ISBN 0-671-61891-1). S&S.
Bloody Crossroads: Where Literature & Politics Meet. Norman Podhoretz. 224p. 1987. pap. 8.95 o.s.i. (ISBN 0-671-63314-7, Touchstone Bks). S&S.
Bloody Grass. Hobe Gilmore. 1977. pap. 1.50 o.s.i. (ISBN 0-8439-0469-0, Pub. by Leisure Bks CT). Dorchester Pub Co.
Bloomfield. Horace Robinson. 464p. 1987. 12.95 o.p. (ISBN 0-8062-2813-X). Carlton.
Bloomingdales. Maxine Brady. LC 80-15867. (Illus.). 256p. 1980. 25.00 o.p. (ISBN 0-15-113219-4). HarBraceJ.
Bloomsbury: A House of Lions. Leon Edel. 1980. pap. 2.75 o.p. (ISBN 0-380-50005-1, 50005-1). Avon.
Bloomsbury Heritage: Their Mothers & Their Aunts. Elizabeth F. Boyd. LC 76-422. (Illus.). 1976. 10.50 o.s.i. (ISBN 0-8008-0821-5). Taplinger.
Bloomsday Book: A Guide Through Joyce's Ulysses. Harry Blamires. (Orig.). 1966. pap. 13.50 o.p. (ISBN 0-416-69500-0, NO.2092). Routledge Chapman & Hall.
Bloomsday for Maggie. May McNeer. LC 75-44359. (Illus.). 256p. (gr. 9 up). 1976. 7.95 o.p. (ISBN 0-395-24388-2). HM.
Blow a Bugle at Catfish Bend. Ben L. Burman. 132p. (gr. 3-5). 1981. pap. 1.95 o.p. (ISBN 0-380-53504-1, 53504-1, Camelot). Avon.
Blow a Wild Bugle for Catfish Bend. Ben L. Burman. LC 67-12429. (Illus.). (gr. 6 up). 3.95 o.s.i. (ISBN 0-8008-0825-8). Taplinger.
Blow by Blow: The Memories of a Musical Rogue & Vagabond. Archie Camden. (Illus.). 208p. 1983. text ed. 15.00x o.p. (ISBN 0-87663-421-8). Universe.
Blow Flies of North America see Thomas Say Foundation Publications.
Blow the Trumpet in Zion. Richard Booker. LC 85-62152. 208p. (Orig.). pap. cancelled o.s.i. (ISBN 0-932081-02-9). Victory Hse.
Blow Your Horn. Jeffrey P. Davidson. 16.95 o.p. (ISBN 0-317-67104-9). AMACOM.
Blowpipe Analysis. J. Landauer. 1984. pap. 8.95 o.p. (ISBN 0-917914-19-8). Lindsay Pubns.
Blue & White Devils: A Personal Memoir & History of the Third Infantry Division in World War II. Hugh A. Scott. (Twenty-Fifth Release in the Divisional Ser.). (Illus.). 173p. 1984. 16.95 o.p. (ISBN 0-89839-074-5). Battery Pr.
Blue Angels: An Illustrated History. Rosario Rausa. (Illus.). 1979. 14.50 o.s.i. (ISBN 0-911721-82-7, Pub. by Moran). Aviation.
Blue Book Nineteen Seventy-Six: Leaders of the English-Speaking World, 2 vols. LC 73-13918. 1876p. 1979. Set. 130.00x o.p. (ISBN 0-8103-0216-0). Gale.
Blue Book of American Antiques: A Price Guide to Americana Collectibles. Paul Fellows. 256p. 1989. pap. 9.95 o.p. Wynwood Pr.
Blue Book of Dolls & Values. 5th ed. Jan Foulke. 364p. 1982. pap. 5.95 o.p. (ISBN 0-87588-189-0, 232). Hobby Hse.
Blue Book of Dolls & Values. 8th ed. Jan Foulke. (Illus.). 364p. (Orig.). 1984. pap. 12.95 o.p. (ISBN 0-87588-228-5, 2864). Hobby Hse.
Blue Book of Questions & Answers for Second Mate, Chief Mate & Master. 3rd ed. W. A. MacEwen. LC 62-15957. (Illus.). 320p. 1969. pap. 10.00x o.p. (ISBN 0-87033-007-1). Cornell Maritime.
Blue Brotherhood. Ernest O. Zimmerman. 352p. (Orig.). 1981. pap. 2.75 o.p. (ISBN 0-8439-0986-2, Pub. by Leisure Bks CT). Dorchester Pub Co.
Blue Chair. Joyce Thompson. 256p. 1977. pap. 1.75 o.p. (ISBN 0-380-01656-7, 78386, Bard). Avon.
Blue Chip Salary Study, 1988. American Society of Association Executives Staff. 1988. GBC Binding. 100.00 o.p. (ISBN 0-88034-020-7). Am Soc Assn Execs.
Blue Coats-Black Skin: The Black Experience in New York City Police Department Since 1891. James I. Alexander. 1978. 6.95 o.p. (ISBN 0-682-49031-8, University). Exposition-Phoenix.
Blue-Collar Workers & Politics: A French Paradox. Richard A. DeAngelis. (Illus.). 286p. 1982. 28.00 o.p. (ISBN 0-7099-0815-6, Pub. by Croom Helm Ltd). Routledge Chapman & Hall.
Blue Cut Job. Tom Cutter. (Tracker Ser.). 192p. 1983. pap. 2.25 o.p. (ISBN 0-380-84483-4, 84483). Avon.
Blue Eye Shadow Should Be Illegal: A Beautifully Different Makeup Manual. Paula Begoun. (Illus.). 128p. (Orig.). 1985. pap. 7.95 o.p. (ISBN 0-9615514-0-2). Beginning Pr.
Blue Eyes. Jerome Charyn. 1977. pap. 2.95 o.p. (ISBN 0-380-00882-3, 55467). Avon.
Blue Flame. Joseph Gilmore. 296p. 1985. pap. 3.75 o.p. (ISBN 0-317-66391-7). Critics Choice Paper.
Blue Guide - Ireland. 1979. 27.95 o.p. (ISBN 0-528-84633-7); pap. 19.95 o.p. (ISBN 0-528-84632-9). Rand McNally.
Blue Guide - Moscow & Leningrad. 1980. 39.95 o.p. (ISBN 0-528-84611-6); pap. 24.95 o.p. (ISBN 0-528-84607-8). Rand McNally.
Blue Guide - Sicily. 1981. 33.95 o.p. (ISBN 0-528-84622-1); pap. 19.95 o.p. (ISBN 0-528-84621-3). Rand McNally.
Blue Guide - Venice. 1980. 33.95 o.p. (ISBN 0-528-84613-2); pap. 19.95 o.p. (ISBN 0-528-84609-4). Rand McNally.
Blue Guide - Wales. 1979. 39.95 o.p. (ISBN 0-528-84631-0); pap. 23.95 o.p. (ISBN 0-528-84630-2). Rand McNally.
Blue Highways. William L. Moon. (General Ser.). 756p. 1983. lib. bdg. 19.95 o.p. (ISBN 0-8161-3596-7, Large Print Bks). G K Hall.
Blue Highways: A Journey into America. William L. Moon. 1983. pap. 3.95 o.p. (ISBN 0-449-20432-4). Fawcett.
Blue Hills. Fanny Howe. 128p. (Orig.). (YA) (gr. 7 up). 1981. pap. 1.95 o.p. (ISBN 0-380-78998-1, 78998-1, Flare). Avon.
Blue Horse & Other Night Poems. Siv Cedering-Fox. LC 78-12793. (Illus.). 32p. (ps-3). 1979. 8.95 o.s.i. (ISBN 0-395-28952-1, Clarion). HM.
Blue Jeans. Jonathan Rosenbloom. LC 76-20739. (Illus.). 64p. (gr. 3-5). 1976. lib. bdg. 8.29 o.s.i. (ISBN 0-671-32798-4). Messner.
Blue Leader. Walter Wager. LC 78-67778. 1979. 9.95 o.p. (ISBN 0-87795-206-X, Arbor Hse). Morrow.
Blue Light. James M. Godard. (Orig.). 1964. pap. 1.95 o.p. (ISBN 0-8042-9614-6, John Knox). Westminster John Knox.
Blue Messiah. James D. Horan. 1976. pap. 1.95 o.p. (ISBN 0-380-00138-1, 30676). Avon.
Blue Misty Monsters. Catherine Sefton. (Illus.). 106p. (gr. 3-5). 1986. 12.95 o.p. (ISBN 0-571-13564-1). Faber & Faber.
Blue Moon. Parris A. Bonds. 369p. 1986. lib. bdg. 17.95x o.p. (ISBN 0-8161-4087-1, Large Print Bks). G K Hall.
Blue Moon. Walter Wager. LC 79-87837. 1980. 9.95 o.p. (ISBN 0-87795-235-3, Arbor Hse). Morrow.
Blue Murder. Walter Wager. LC 80-67622. 1981. 11.95 o.p. (ISBN 0-87795-286-8, Arbor Hse). Morrow.
Blue Mystery. Margot Benary-Isbert. LC 57-6558. (gr. 4-7). 1957. 5.95 o.p. (ISBN 0-15-209092-4, HJ). HarBraceJ.
Blue Mystery. Margot Benary-Isbert. LC 57-6558. (Illus.). (gr. 4-7). 1965. pap. 3.95 o.p. (ISBN 0-15-613225-7, VoyB). HarBraceJ.
Blue Oboe: A Book of Poems. David Garrison. vi, 43p. 1984. pap. 6.95x o.p. (ISBN 0-932269-14-1). Wyndham Hall.
Blue Pencil Warriors: Censorship & Propaganda in World War II. John Hilvert. LC 83-12345. 1984. text ed. 27.95 o.p. (ISBN 0-7022-1953-3). U of Queensland Pr.
Blue Plaque Guide to London. Caroline Dakers. (Illus.). 318p. 1982. 17.95 o.p. (ISBN 0-393-01528-9). Norton.
Blue Ribbon University. George N. Belknap. 1976. pap. 1.25 o.p. (ISBN 0-87114-082-9). U of Oreg Bks.
Blue Ridge Mountain Pleasures: An A-Z Guide to North Georgia, Western North Carolina & the Upcountry of South Carolina. Donald C. Wenberg. LC 84-72967. (Illus.). 280p. (Orig.). 1985. pap. 8.95 o.p. (ISBN 0-88742-051-6). Globe Pequot.
Blue Ridge Trolly: The Hagerstown & Frederick Railway. Herbert Harwood. LC 73-97231. 17.95 o.p. (ISBN 0-87095-034-7). Gldn West Bks.
Blue Rose. Gerda Klein. LC 74-9383. (Illus.). 64p. (gr. 3-7). 1974. 12.00 o.s.i. (ISBN 0-88208-047-4); pap. 5.95 o.s.i. (ISBN 0-88208-048-2). Chicago Review.
Blue Sky Laws: State Regulation of Securities 1985, Vol. 473. Practising Law Institute Staff. 701p. 1985. pap. 40.00 o.p. (ISBN 0-317-27467-8, B4-6708). PLI.
Blue Smoke. Dorothy Lyons. LC 53-7867. (Illus.). (gr. 6 up). 1968. pap. 1.95 o.p. (ISBN 0-15-613275-3, VoyB). HarBraceJ.
Blue Trees, Red Sky. Norma Klein. LC 75-2545. (Illus.). 96p. (gr. 2-5). 1975. lib. bdg. 5.99 o.s.i. (ISBN 0-394-93108-4). Pantheon.
Blue Water: A Guide to Self Reliant Sailboat Cruising. Robert Griffith & Nancy Griffith. (Illus.). 1979. 17.95 o.p. (ISBN 0-393-03239-6). Norton.
Blue Water, Green Skipper. Stuart Woods. (Illus.). 1977. 9.95 o.p. (ISBN 0-393-03203-5). Norton.
Blue Wren. Belinda Brooker. (Illus.). 23p. 1985. 6.95 o.p. (ISBN 0-85564-233-5, Pub. by U of W Austral Pr). Intl Spec Bk.
Bluebeard. Date not set. (ISBN 0-385-29590-1). Delacorte.
Bluebeard. Max Frisch. Tr. by Geoffrey Skelton. LC 82-21250. 144p. 1983. 10.95 o.p. (ISBN 0-15-113200-3). HarBraceJ.
Bluebeard. Kurt Vonnegut, Jr. 312p. 1987. pap. 17.95 o.p. (ISBN 0-385-29590-1); pap. 100.00 signed ltd. slipcased ed. o.p. (ISBN 0-385-29609-6). Delacorte.
Bluebeard's Egg & Other Stories. Margaret Atwood. 1986. 16.45 o.s.i. (ISBN 0-395-40424-X). HM.
Blueberry Cake That Little Fox Baked. Andrea Da Rif. LC 84-444. (Illus.). 32p. (ps-3). 1984. 10.95 o.s.i. (ISBN 0-689-50307-5, M K McElderry). Macmillan.
Blueberry Troll. Tricia Springstubb. LC 81-3872. (Carolrhoda on My Own Bks.). (Illus.). 48p. (gr. k-3). 1981. PLB 8.95 o.p. (ISBN 0-87614-167-X, AACR2). Carolrhoda Bks.
Bluegrass Banjo Method. Neil Griffin. 1976. pap. 5.95 o.p. (ISBN 0-89328-005-4). Lorenz Corp.
Bluegrass Complete: Complete Words, Music & Guitar Chords for Eighty-Nine Songs. Creative Concepts. (Illus.). 192p. (Orig.). pap. 9.95 o.s.i. (ISBN 0-486-24503-9). Dover.
Blueprint for Health. Mary Ann Howard. 176p. (Orig.). 1985. pap. 4.95 o.p. (ISBN 0-310-42151-9, 12776P). Zondervan.
Blueprint for Progress in Tax Administration of New York State Tax Laws. Internal Revenue Service Staff. (Illus.). 262p. (Orig.). 1984. pap. 18.00 o.s.i. (ISBN 0-89831-002-4). SagaPr.
Blueprint for Success: Community Mobilization for Dropout Prevention. 32p. 1987. 4.00 o.p. (ISBN 0-8106-7010-0). NEA.
Blueprint Reading: Boilermaker. Resource Systems International Staff. 1982. pap. text ed. 15.00 o.p. (ISBN 0-8359-0511-X, Reston). P-H.
Blueprint Reading, Checking & Testing, 2 Pts. 3rd ed. Otto A. Steinike. (Illus.). (gr. 9-10). 1956. Pt. 1. pap. text ed. 5.00 o.p. (ISBN 0-87345-080-9); Pt. 2. text ed. 5.00 o.p. (ISBN 0-87345-082-5). Glencoe.
Blueprint Reading for Industry. Rev. ed. Walter C. Brown. LC 82-20949. 345p. 1983. spiral bdg. 15.00 o.p. (ISBN 0-87006-429-0). Goodheart.
Blueprint Reading for Machine Technology. Hale Rayshich & McGuire. 1985. pap. text ed. 22.00 o.p. (ISBN 0-534-01383-X, 77F6040, PWS-Kent Ser Tech). PWS-Kent Pub.
Blueprint Reading for Plumbers: Residential & Commercial. 2nd, rev. ed. Bartholomew D'Arcangelo et al. LC 78-24844. (Blueprint Reading Ser.). 1980. pap. text ed. 17.50 o.p. (ISBN 0-8273-1367-5); instr's. guide 8.00 o.p. (ISBN 0-8273-1368-3). Delmar.
Blueprint Reading for the Machine Trades. Russel R. Schultz. (Illus.). 304p. 1981. pap. text ed. 29.00 o.p. (ISBN 0-13-077727-7). P-H.
Blueprint Reading for the Welding Trade. Darrell C. Lockhart. LC 83-14690. 206p. 1984. pap. text ed. (ISBN 0-471-86844-2). Wiley.
Blueprint Reading for Welders. 3rd ed. A. E. Bennett & L. Siy. LC 82-46005. 304p. 1983. text ed. 15.95 o.p. (ISBN 0-8273-2144-9). Delmar.
Blueprint Reading: Tanks & Vessels. Resource Systems International Staff. 1982. pap. text ed. 15.00 o.p. (ISBN 0-8359-0512-8, Reston). P-H.
Blueprint Series, Vol. 1. PhotoGraphic Magazine Editors et al. LC 73-82543. (Photography How-to Ser.). (Illus.). 80p. (Orig.). 1973. pap. 3.95 o.p. (ISBN 0-8227-0032-8). Petersen Pub.
Blueprint Series, Vol. 2. Ed. by Mike Stensvold. LC 73-82543. (Photography How-to Ser.). (Illus.). 1978. pap. 3.95 o.p. (ISBN 0-8227-4017-6). Petersen Pub.
Blueprints. Lloyd Elder. LC 84-7634. 1984. 7.50 o.p. (ISBN 0-8054-6581-2). Broadman.
Blueprints: Building Educational Programs for People Who Care for Children. Ed. by Susan Middleton. (Illus.). 238p. pap. 9.50x o.p. (ISBN 0-934140-16-2). Toys N Things.
Blues a la Gauche. Ann L. Rodiger. (Educational Dance Score Registry Ser.: No. 5). (Illus.). 42p. 1982. Dance Score. 25.00 o.s.i. (ISBN 0-932582-34-6). Dance Notation.
Blues Brothers: Private. Judith Jacklin. 1980. pap. 7.95 o.p. (ISBN 0-399-50476-1, Perigee). Putnam Pub Group.
Blues Brothers Souvenir Songbook. 7.95 o.p. (ISBN 0-89524-111-0). Cherry Lane.
Blues for Julie. Andy Martin & Joseph Greene. (Photo Stories 1). (Illus.). 46p. pap. text ed. 4.95 o.p. (ISBN 0-582-79806-X). Longman.
Blues Line: A Collection of Blues Lyrics. Compiled by Eric Sackheim. LC 68-87912. (Illus.). 1975. pap. 14.95 o.s.i. (ISBN 0-02-872260-4). Schirmer Bks.
Blues of the Sky: Interpreted from the Original Hebrew Book of Psalms. David Rosenberg. LC 76-9991. 53p. 1976. 6.00 o.p. (ISBN 0-06-067009-6). SUN.
Blues: The British Connection. Bob Brunning. (Illus.). 256p. (Orig.). 1987. pap. 14.95 o.p. (ISBN 0-7137-1836-6, Pub. by Blandford Pr England). Sterling.
Blunder! How U. S. Gave Away Nazi Supersecrets. Tom Agoston. (Illus.). 224p. 1985. 15.95 o.p. (ISBN 0-396-08556-3). Dodd.
Blunted Lance. Max Hennessy. LC 81-66019. 1981. 10.95 o.p. (ISBN 0-689-11220-3, Atheneum). Macmillan.
BMDP-83: Biomedical Computer Programs, P-Series. rev. ed. Ed. by W. J. Dixon & M. B. Brown. 1983. pap. text ed. 19.95x o.p. (ISBN 0-520-04408-8). U Of Cal Pr.
BMW 500 & 600 cc Twins, 1955-1969: Service-Repair-Performance. Ed. by Eric Jorgensen. (Illus.). pap. 13.95 o.p. (ISBN 0-89287-224-1, M308). Clymer Pub.
BMX Bear. Patty Hayman. (Illus.). 24p. (gr. k-2). 1985. 1.50 o.p. (ISBN 0-87406-011-7). Willowisp Pr.
BMX Freestyle. Dave Spurdens. (Illus.). (gr. 7 up). 1985. 7.95 o.p. (ISBN 0-8069-4184-7); pap. 3.95 o.p. (ISBN 0-8069-6204-6). Sterling.
BNA's Directory of State Courts, Judges & Clerks: A State-by-State Listing. Compiled by BNA Library Staff & Kamla J. King. 444p. 1986. pap. 45.00 o.p. (ISBN 0-87179-514-0, 0514). BNA.
Bo. Bo Derek & John Derek. Date not set. pap. 9.95 o.s.i. (ISBN 0-671-41155-1). PB.
Bo the Orangutan. Georgeanne Irvine. (Zoo Babies Ser.). (Illus.). 16p. (Orig.). (gr. k-6). 1983. pap. 1.25 o.p. (ISBN 0-8249-8052-2). Ideals.
Board & Financial Management. B. Prodham. 175p. 1979. text ed. 34.00 o.p. (ISBN 0-220-66354-8, Pub. by Business Books England). Gower Pub Co.
Board & Table Game Antiques. R. C. Bell. (Album Ser.: No. 60). (Illus.). 32p. (Orig.). 1983. pap. 2.95 o.p. (ISBN 0-85263-538-9, 3380029, Pub. by Shire Pubns England). Seven Hills Bk Dists.
Board & the Presentation of Financial Information to Management. J. Batty. 340p. 1978. text ed. 39.25x o.p. (ISBN 0-220-66352-1, Pub. by Busn Bks England). Gower Pub Co.
Board Member of a Social Agency: Responsibilities & Functions. LC 57-8122. 1957. pap. 6.75 o.p. (ISBN 0-87868-146-9, AM-10). Child Welfare.
Boarding Party. James Leasor. 1979. 8.95 o.p. (ISBN 0-395-27217-3). HM.

Titles

Boards of Directors: A Study of Current Practices in Board Management & Board Operations in Voluntary Hospitals, Health & Welfare Organizations. Greater New York Fund, Inc. Staff. LC 74-8586. 266p. 1974. lib. bdg. 17.50 o.p. (ISBN 0-379-00275-2). Oceana.

Boards: Purposes, Organization, Procedures. Tilman R. Smith. LC 78-62628. 64p. 1978. pap. 1.95 o.p. (ISBN 0-8361-1862-6). Herald Pr.

Boat & Marine Equipment Theft: Summary Report of a 1979 National Workshop. Ed. by N. W. Ross & D. W. Nixon. (Marine Memo Ser.: No. 64). 48p. 1980. 2.00 o.p. (ISBN 0-686-36981-5, P838). Sea Grant Pubns.

Boat Building Techniques Illustrated. Richard Birmingham. LC 83-81366. (Illus.). 320p. 1984. 32.45 o.p. (ISBN 0-87742-176-5, B144). Intl Marine.

Boatbuilding One-Off in Fiberglass. Allan H. Vaitses. LC 82-48431. (Illus.). 304p. 1984. pap. 8.95 o.p. (ISBN 0-87742-156-0, B142). Intl Marine.

Boaters & Broomsticks. Lionel Wyld. (Illus.). 128p. 1987. 9.95 o.p. (ISBN 0-932052-45-2). North Country.

Boater's Guide to Biscayne Bay: Miami to Jewfish Creek. George L. Sites. LC 75-173322. (Illus.). 1971. spiral bdg. 4.95 o.p. (ISBN 0-87024-233-4). U of Miami Pr.

Boatman's Bible. Damon C. Fenwick. 1985. 24.95 o.p. (ISBN 0-8306-9925-2, 1231); pap. 16.95 o.p. TAB Bks.

Boatopia. Francoise LeGrand. LC 85-80263. (Illus.). 128p. 1986. Repr. 15.95 o.p. (ISBN 0-688-06163-X). Morrow.

Boats Against the Current. John Logue. 1987. 16.95 o.p. (ISBN 0-316-53220-7). Little.

Boatwatch. Max W. Averitt. (Encore Edition). (Illus., Orig.). 1979. pap. 1.95 o.p. (ISBN 0-684-17689-0, SL854, ScribT). Scribner.

Bob Bondurant on High Performance Driving. Bob Bondurant & John Blakemore. LC 82-10624. (Illus.). 144p. 1982. pap. 11.95 o.p. (ISBN 0-87938-158-2). Motorbooks Intl.

Bob Pierce: This One Thing I Do. Franklinn Graham & Jeanette Lockerbie. 1983. 10.95 o.p. (ISBN 0-8499-0097-2). Word Bks.

Bob Smith's Complete Guide to Harbors, Anchorages & Marinas. Robert H. Smith. LC 81-69410. (Southern California Ser.: Vol. I). (Illus.). 230p. 1984. 19.95 o.p. (ISBN 0-941786-00-5). C Bks.

Bob Smith's Complete Guide to Harbors, Anchorages & Marinas. Robert H. Smith. LC 85-71734. (Northern California Ser.: Vol. II). (Illus.). 230p. 1984. 19.95 o.p. (ISBN 0-941786-02-1). C Bks.

Bobbed Wire VI Bible. Jack Glover. 1976. 7.95 o.p. (ISBN 0-89015-105-9). Eakin Pr.

Bobbin Lace, First Series: Les Dentelles Aux Fuseaux, 3 pts. rev. ed. Tr. & intro. by Mary McPeek. LC 73-18373. (Illus.). 255p. 1974. Repr. Set. 78.00x o.p. (ISBN 0-8103-3955-2); 25 corner patterns incl. o.p. Gale.

Bobbi's New Year. Joan Solomon. (Illus.). (ps-3). 1980. 10.95 o.p. (ISBN 0-241-10214-6, Pub. by Hamish Hamilton England). David & Charles.

Bobbsey Twins & the Cedar Camp Mystery. Laura L. Hope. (Bobbsey Twins Ser.: Vol. 14). (gr. 1-4). 1967. 4.50 o.p. (ISBN 0-448-08014-1, G&D). Putnam Pub Group.

Bobbsey Twins & the Four-Leaf Clover Mystery. rev. ed. Laura L. Hope. (Bobbsey Twins Ser.: Vol. 19). (Illus.). (gr. 1-4). 1968. 4.50 o.p. (ISBN 0-448-08019-2, G&D). Putnam Pub Group.

Bobbsey Twins & Their Camel Adventure. Laura L. Hope. (Bobbsey Twins Ser.: Vol. 59). (gr. 1-4). 1966. 2.95 o.p. (ISBN 0-448-18059-6, G&D). Putnam Pub Group.

Bobs, Kipling's General: The Life of Field-Marshall Earl Roberts of Kandahar, VC. W. H. Hannah. LC 72-3642. (Illus.). 263p. (Orig.). 1972. 27.50 o.p. (ISBN 0-208-01139-0, Archon). Shoe String.

Bodhi Kalpa. 1978p. pap. 1.00 o.s.i. (ISBN 0-686-95470-X). Ananda Marga.

Bodie Bonanza: The True Story of a Flamboyant Past. Warren Loose. 1971. 10.00 o.p. (ISBN 0-682-47273-5, Lochinvar). Exposition-Phoenix.

Bodily Communication. Michael Argyle. 400p. 1988. lib. bdg. 65.00 o.p. (ISBN 0-416-38140-5); pap. 17.95 o.p. (ISBN 0-416-38150-2). Routledge Chapman & Hall.

Body. Don Johnson. LC 83-70653. 1983. 13.95 o.p. (ISBN 0-8070-2900-9). Beacon Pr.

Body & Mind in Zulu Medicine: An Ethnography of Health & Disease in Nyuswa-Zulu Thought & Practice. Harriet Ngubane. (Studies in Anthropology Ser.). 1977. 64.00 o.p. (ISBN 0-12-518250-3). Acad Pr.

Body & Soul. (Candlelight Ecstasy Supreme Ser.: No. 13). 288p. (Orig.). 1984. pap. 2.50 o.p. (ISBN 0-440-10759-8). Dell.

Body & Soul. J. P. Smith. 224p. 1987. 15.95 o.p. (ISBN 0-8021-0020-1). Grove.

Body by Jake. Jake Steinfeld & Melissa Miller. (Illus.). 1984. 16.45 o.p. (ISBN 0-671-50321-9). S&S.

Body C. T. Adrian K. Dixon. (Illus.). 176p. (Orig.). 1983. pap. text ed. 29.50 o.p. (ISBN 0-443-02956-3). Churchill.

Body Code: The Meaning in Movement. Warren Lamb & Elizabeth Watson. 1985. pap. 8.95 o.p. (ISBN 0-7102-0533-3). Routledge Chapman & Hall.

Body Consciousness. Seymour Fisher. LC 74-9264. 176p. 1974. Repr. 17.50x o.p. (ISBN 0-87668-181-X). Aronson.

Body Count. Ted Meyer. 176p. 1982. 8.50 o.p. (ISBN 0-682-49840-8). Exposition-Phoenix.

Body Culture. Roger Turner & Al Green. (Illus.). 208p. (Orig.). 1986. pap. 9.95 o.p. (ISBN 0-920197-14-0, Pub. by Summerhill CN). Sterling.

Body Fat & Physical Fitness. Jana Parizkova. Tr. by K. Osancova from Czech. (Illus.). 280p. 1977. 32.50 o.p. (ISBN 90-247-1925-9, Pub. by Nijhoff). Year Bk Med.

Body Fluids & Electrolytes: A Programmed Presentation. 4th ed. Norma J. Weldy. (Illus.). 192p. 1983. pap. 15.95 o.p. (ISBN 0-8016-5397-5). Mosby.

Body Fluids in Pediatrics: Medical, Surgical, & Neonatal Disorders of Acid-Base Status, Hydration & Oxygenation. Ed. by Robert W. Winters. (Illus.). 1973. 40.00 o.p. (ISBN 0-316-94741-5). Little.

Body Flying for Skydivers. rev. & 2nd ed. Dave Howeski. Ed. by Michael Truffer. (Illus.). 200p. 1987. pap. 12.95 o.p. (ISBN 0-9607814-2-0). AeroGraphics.

Body Has Its Reasons. Therese Bertherat & Carol Bernstein. 1979. pap. 2.95 o.p. (ISBN 0-380-44321-X, 61788-9). Avon.

Body: Images of the Nude in Art. Edward Lucie-Smith. (Illus.). 1981. 14.98 o.p. (ISBN 0-500-23339-X). Thames Hudson.

Body, Land & Spirit: Health & Healing in Aboriginal Society. Janice Reid. (Illus.). 241p. 1985. pap. 10.95x o.p. (ISBN 0-7022-1779-4). U of Queensland Pr.

Body Language of Children. Suzanne Szasz. (Illus.). 1978. 14.95 o.p. (ISBN 0-393-01171-2). Norton.

Body, Mind, & Creativity. Blackhurst. 1954. Philos Lib.

Body, Mind & Sugar. E. M. Abrahamson & A. W. Pezet. (YA) (gr. 7 up). 1977. pap. 4.95 o.p. (ISBN 0-380-00903-X, 64964-0). Avon.

Body, Mind & Sugar. E. M. Abrahamson & A. W. Pezet. 3.95x o.p. (ISBN 0-380-47415-8). Cancer Control Soc.

Body of America: An Insider's Journey Through the Bumps & Pumps, Groans & Moans, Pecs & Wrecks, Sweat & Sex of the Fitness Explosion. Blair Sabol. 1986. 14.95 o.p. (ISBN 0-87795-807-6). Morrow.

Body Principal: The Exercise Program for Life. Victoria Principal. (Illus.). 224p. 1983. 16.50 o.s.i. (ISBN 0-671-46684-4). S&S.

Body Purification. Brown Landone. 71p. pap. text ed. 8.95 o.s.i. (ISBN 0-88697-043-1). Life Science.

Body Quantum: The New Physics of Body, Mind, & Health. Fred A. Wolf. (Illus.). 352p. 1986. 19.95 o.p. (ISBN 0-02-630890-8). Macmillan.

Body Reveals. Ron Kurtz & Hector Prestera. LC 75-66800. 160p. (Orig.). 1976. pap. 9.57 o.p. (ISBN 0-06-066680-3, RD139). HarpR.

Body Rhythm: The Circadian Rhythms Within You. Lee Weston. LC 79-1854. 1979. 8.95 o.p. (ISBN 0-15-113338-7). HarBraceJ.

Body Rub. Mark Andrews. 1976. pap. 1.50 o.p. (ISBN 0-8439-0419-4, Pub. by Leisure Bks CT). Dorchester Pub Co.

Body Shop: Scandinavian Exercises for Relaxation. Gerda Hinrichsen. LC 73-16958. (Illus.). 192p. 1974. 7.95 o.s.i. (ISBN 0-8008-0871-1). Taplinger.

Body Structures & Functions. 5th ed. Elvira Ferris & Esther G. Skelley. LC 77-83347. 160p. 1979. pap. 15.95 o.p. (ISBN 0-8273-1322-5); instr's. guide o.s.i. 3.00 o.p. (ISBN 0-8273-1323-3); slides packet 85.00 o.p. (ISBN 0-8273-1821-9). Delmar.

Body Structures & Functions. 5th ed. Elvira B. Ferris & Esther G. Skelley. 1979. 19.95 o.p. (ISBN 0-442-21481-2). Van Nos Reinhold.

Body Surrounded by Water. Eric Wright. (Inspector Charlie Salter Mystery Ser.). 208p. 1987. 14.95 o.p. (ISBN 0-684-18873-2). Scribner.

Body Temperature: Regulation, Drug Effects, & Theraputic Implications. Lomax & Schonbaum. (Modern Pharmacology-Toxicology Ser.: Vol. 16). 1979. 110.00 o.p. (ISBN 0-8247-6655-5). Dekker.

Body Tensor Fields in Continuum Mechanics. Arthur S. Lodge. 1975. 85.00 o.p. (ISBN 0-12-454950-0). Acad Pr.

Body Weight Control: The Physiology, Clinical Treatment & Prevention of Obesity. Ed. by A. E. Bender & L. J. Brookes. LC 86-17561. (Illus.). 294p. 1987. text ed. 55.50 o.p. (ISBN 0-443-03688-8). Churchill.

Bodyline. Paul Wheeler. LC 84-45032. 216p. 1984. 12.95 o.p. (ISBN 0-689-11498-2, Atheneum). Macmillan.

Bodymind Liberation: Achieving Holistic Health. Robert H. Woody. 172p. 1980. 17.25 o.p. (ISBN 0-398-04055-9). C C Thomas.

Bodysense: The Hazard Free Fitness Program for Men & Women. Sue Luby & Richard A. St. Onge. (Illus.). 300p. 1986. pap. 17.95 o.p. (ISBN 0-571-12546-8). Faber & Faber.

Bodywork: Look Good - Keep Fit - Feel Great. Christina Barth. 1987. pap. 9.95 o.p. (ISBN 0-668-06401-3). Arco.

Bodyworkbook. Herbert Haessler & Raymond Harris. 1980. pap. 6.95 o.p. (ISBN 0-380-75309-X, 75309-X). Avon.

Boeing P-26 "Peashooter" Edward Maloney. LC 72-85152. (Aero Ser.: Vol. 22). (Illus.). 1973. pap. 5.95 o.p. (ISBN 0-8168-0584-9, 20584, TAB-Aero). TAB Bks.

Boeing P12, F4B. Aero Publishers, Inc., Aeronautical Staff et al. LC 66-17554. (Aero Ser.: Vol. 5). 1966. pap. 5.95 o.p. (ISBN 0-8168-0516-4, 20516, TAB-Aero). TAB Bks.

Boeing-727: Flight Engineer Written Test Guide. C. St. John. 75p. 1988. pap. 12.95 o.p. (ISBN 0-942397-05-3). Buckeye Aviat Bk.

Boeing 747. Hiroshi Seo. (Illus.). 84p. 1984. 10.95 o.p. (ISBN 0-7106-0304-5). Janes Info Group.

Boeuf Clandestin. Marcel Ayme. (Illus.). deluxe ed. 61.25 o.p. (ISBN 0-685-37181-6). French & Eur.

Bogart. David Hanna. (Orig.). 1976. pap. 1.50 o.p. (ISBN 0-685-62586-9, LB322, Pub. by Leisure Bks CT). Dorchester Pub Co.

Bogmail. Patrick McGinley. LC 80-26135. (Joan Kahn Bk.). 264p. 1981. 10.95 o.p. (ISBN 0-89919-031-6). Ticknor & Fields.

Bohemian Girl: Blanche Yurka's Theatrical Life. Blanche Yurka. LC 79-81449. xii, 306p. 1970. 11.95 o.p. (ISBN 0-8214-0071-1). Ohio U Pr.

Bohemians of the Latin Quarter. Henri Murger. LC 76-50140. 1983. Repr. of 1905 ed. 25.00x o.p. (ISBN 0-86527-221-2). Fertig.

Boies's Fundamentals of Otolaryngology: A Textbook of Ear, Nose & Throat Diseases. 5th ed. George L. Adams et al. LC 75-44601. (Illus.). 1978. text ed. write for info. o.p. (ISBN 0-7216-1035-8). Saunders.

Boiler: Installation. Resource Systems International Staff. 1982. pap. text ed. 15.00 o.p. (ISBN 0-8359-0556-X, Reston). P-H.

Boiler Operator's Guide. Harry M. Spring. 1980. text ed. 29.50 o.p. (ISBN 0-07-060510-6, P&RB). McGraw.

Boiler: Repair & Maintenance. Resource Systems International Staff. 1982. pap. text ed. 15.00 o.p. (ISBN 0-8359-0557-8, Reston). P-H.

Boiler Room Questions & Answers. 2nd ed. Alex Higgins & Stephen M. Elonka. (Illus.). 384p. 1976. text ed. 45.00 o.p. (ISBN 0-07-028754-6). McGraw.

Boiler Systems & Components I. Resource Systems International Staff. 1982. pap. text ed. 15.00 o.p. (ISBN 0-8359-0560-8, Reston). P-H.

Boiler Systems & Components II. Resource Systems International Staff. 1982. pap. text ed. 15.00 o.p. (ISBN 0-8359-0562-4, Reston). P-H.

Boilermaker Hand Tools. Resource Systems International Staff. 1982. pap. text ed. 15.00 o.p. (Reston). P-H.

Boilermaker Power Tools. Resource Systems International Staff. 1982. pap. text ed. 15.00 o.p. (ISBN 0-8359-0559-4, Reston). P-H.

Boilers. C. Shields. 1961. text ed. 79.50 o.p. (ISBN 0-07-056801-4). McGraw.

Boiling Phenomena, 2 vols. D. Van Stralen & Robert Cole. LC 78-10484. (Series in Thermal & Fluids Engineering). (Illus.). 1979. Vol. 1. text ed. 58.95 o.p. (ISBN 0-07-067611-9); Vol. 2. text ed. 58.95 o.p. (ISBN 0-07-067612-7); Set. text ed. 97.50 o.p. (ISBN 0-07-079189-9). McGraw.

Boiling Point. H. P. Lovecraft et al. 18p. (Orig.). 1985. pap. 1.50 o.p. (ISBN 0-318-04709-8). Necronomicon.

Boiling Water Reactor Transient Response. (Illus.). 102p. 1979. Set. 295.00x o.p. (ISBN 0-87683-063-7); text ed. 40.00x spiral bdg. o.p. (ISBN 0-87683-064-5); Videotape 1: Reactor Plant Startup. 90.00x o.p. (ISBN 0-87683-065-3); Videotape 2: Turbine Trip. 90.00x o.p. (ISBN 0-87683-066-1); Videotape 3: Reactor Coolant Leakage. 650.00x o.p. (ISBN 0-87683-067-X); Videotape 4: Feedwater Malfunctions. 90.00x o.p. (ISBN 0-87683-068-8). GP Pub.

Boise: An Illustrated History. Merle Wells. (Illus.). 208p. 1982. 22.95 o.s.i. (ISBN 0-89781-042-2). Windsor Pubns Inc.

Bold & Magnificient Dream: America's Founding Years, 1492-1815. Bruce Catton & William B. Catton. LC 77-25581. (Illus.). 1978. 6.50 o.s.i. (ISBN 0-385-00341-2). Doubleday.

Bold Blades Flashing. Lorinda Hagen. 1979. pap. 2.25 o.p. (ISBN 0-8439-0689-8, Pub. by Leisure Bks CT). Dorchester Pub Co.

Bold Blades Flashing. Lorinda Hagen. 320p. 1983. pap. 3.25 o.p. (ISBN 0-8439-2050-5, Pub. by Leisure Bks CT). Dorchester Pub Co.

Bold Conquest. Virginia Henley. 1983. pap. 3.50 o.p. (ISBN 0-380-84830-9, 84830). Avon.

Bold Destiny. Douglass Elliot. 1983. pap. 2.95 o.s.i. (ISBN 0-345-29824-1). Ballantine.

Bold in the Spirit: Erling Jorstad. LC 74-77681. (Lutheran Charismatic Renewal in America Today). 128p. (Orig.). 1974. pap. 3.50 o.p. (ISBN 0-8066-1432-3, 10-0780, Augsburg). Augsburg Fortress.

Bold Ones. Gardner Fox. 1976. pap. 1.25 o.p. (ISBN 0-685-72571-5, LB398, Pub. by Leisure Bks CT). Dorchester Pub Co.

Bold Stroke for a Wife. Susannah Centlivre. Ed. by Thalia Stathas. LC 67-12640. (Regents Restoration Drama Ser.). xxvi, 112p. 1968. 12.50x o.p. (ISBN 0-8032-0351-9); pap. 2.95xo. p. o.p. (ISBN 0-8032-5351-6, BB 267, Bison). U of Nebr Pr.

Boldest Dream: The Story of Twelve Who Climbed Mount Everest. Rick Ridgeway. LC 78-14080. (Illus.). 1979. 10.95 o.p. (ISBN 0-15-113432-4). HarBraceJ.

Boletes & Related Groups in South America. Rolf Singer. (Illus.). pap. 12.50x o.p. (ISBN 3-7682-0212-7). Lubrecht & Cramer.

Bolivar: A Continent & Its Destiny. J. L. Salcedo-Bastardo. Ed. & tr. by Annella McDermott. (Illus.). 216p. 1986. text ed. 39.95x o.p. (ISBN 0-391-03400-6); pap. text ed. 12.50x o.p. (ISBN 0-391-03399-9). Humanities.

Bolivia: Post Report. (State Department Publication 9226. Department & Foreign Services Ser.: No. 268). (Illus.). 19p. (Orig.). 1986. pap. 1.00 o.p. (ISBN 0-318-20090-2, S/N 044-000-02111-1). USGPO.

Bolognese Drawings in North American Collections 1500-1800. Mary Cazort & Catherine Johnson. (National Gallery of Canada Ser.). (Illus.). 304p. 1982. pap. 35.00 o.s.i. (ISBN 0-226-56295-6). U of Chicago Pr.

Bolshevik Revolution: A Social History of the Russian Revolution. Marc Ferro. 368p. 1985. pap. 13.95 o.p. (ISBN 0-7102-0550-3). Routledge Chapman & Hall.

Boltzmann Equation (Theory & Applications) Proceedings of the Symposium, Vienna, 1972. Boltzmann Equation Symposium Staff. Ed. by E. G. Cohen & W. Thirring. LC 73-76978. (Acta Physica Austriaca: Suppl. 10). (Illus.). xii, 642p. 1973. 87.40 o.p. (ISBN 0-387-81137-0). Springer-Verlag.

Bomb & European Security. Guido Vigeveno. LC 83-48137. (Illus.). 152p. 1983. 12.95x o.p. (ISBN 0-253-31208-6); pap. 6.95x o.p. (ISBN 0-253-21220-0). Ind U Pr.

Bomb in the Bible: An Incredible Look at the Prophecies Concerning Nuclear War. David M. Tyler. 1979. 6.00 o.p. (ISBN 0-682-49228-0). Exposition-Phoenix.

Bomb Squad. Mark Andrews. 1977. pap. 1.50 o.s.i. (ISBN 0-8439-0453-4, Pub. by Leisure Bks CT). Dorchester Pub Co.

Bomb Two. Don Henderson. 1987. 14.95 o.p. (ISBN 0-907675-13-1, Pub. by Buchan & Enright England). Seven Hills Bk Dists.

Bombed, Buzzed, Smashed, or... Sober. John Langone. 160p. (YA) (gr. 7 up). 1979. pap. 1.95 o.p. (ISBN 0-380-43653-1, 52456-2, Flare). Avon.

Bomber. Bobbye Goddard. 1979. 6.50 o.p. (ISBN 0-682-49486-0). Exposition-Phoenix.

Bomber. Ben Samuel. LC 84-91392. 220p. 1985. 12.95 o.p. (ISBN 0-533-06467-8). Vantage.

Bombers in Blue: PB4Y-2 Privateers & PB4Y-1 Liberators. Frederick A. Johnsen. (Illus.). 1979. pap. 3.95 o.p. (ISBN 0-911721-53-3, Pub. by Bomber). Aviation.

Bombs Away. (Danger Mouse Lift-the-Flap Bks.). 16p. (ps-3). 1986. 5.95 o.p. (ISBN 0-316-14707-9). Little.

Bon Appetit Too Busy to Cook? Bon Appetit Magazine Editors. LC 81-5959. (Illus.). 224p. 1981. 19.95 o.p. (ISBN 0-89535-049-1). Knapp Pr.

Bon Marche: Bourgeois Culture & the Department Store, 1869 to 1920. Michael B. Miller. LC 80-36797. (Illus.). 250p. 1980. 20.50x o.p. (ISBN 0-691-05321-9). Princeton U Pr.

Bonapartes. Felix Markham. LC 75-3637. (Illus.). 224p. 1975. 14.95 o.s.i. (ISBN 0-8008-0874-6). Taplinger.

Bond Graph Techniques for Dynamic Systems in Engineering & Biology. Dean Karnopp et al. 1979. pap. 34.00 o.p. (ISBN 0-08-025056-4). Pergamon.

Bond of Blood. Roberta Gellis. 1976. pap. 2.50 o.p. (ISBN 0-380-00713-4, 55764-2). Avon.

Bond of Love. Created by Rosemary Joyce. (Dream Girls Ser.: No. 4). (YA) (gr. 7 up). pap. 2.50 o.p. (ISBN 0-671-62114-9). Archway.

Bond Portfolio Immunization. Michael R. Granito. LC 83-49012. 256p. 1984. 32.00x o.p. (ISBN 0-669-07660-0). Lexington Bks.

Bonding & Structure. Ed. by F. L. Boschke. (Topics in Current Chemistry: Vol. 63). (Illus.). 160p. 1976. 42.00 o.p. (ISBN 0-387-07605-0). Springer-Verlag.

Bonding: Relationships in the Image of God. Donald Joy. LC 84-27121. 192p. 1985. 9.95 o.p. (ISBN 0-8499-0440-4, 0440-4). Word Bks.

Bonds Investments in the Eighties. Jim Reilly. 272p. 1982. 28.95 o.p. (ISBN 0-442-27532-3). Van Nos Reinhold.

Bonds of Matrimony. Elizabeth Hunter. (Nightingale Paperbacks). 1985. pap. 9.95 o.p. (ISBN 0-8161-3869-9, Large Print Bks). G K Hall.

Bondswoman. Caryl Ledner. 1978. pap. 1.95 o.p. (ISBN 0-380-01781-4, 35154). Avon.

Bone & Mineral Research Annual, Vol. 2. W. Peck. 1984. 109.50 o.p. (ISBN 0-444-90337-2, I-498-83). Elsevier.

Bone Biopsy. Ed. by Jennifer Jowsey. LC 77-8647. (Topics in Bone & Mineral Disorders Ser.). (Illus.). 158p. 1977. 35.00x o.p. (ISBN 0-306-31045-7, Plenum Med Bk). Plenum Pub.

Bone Disease in the Elderly. C. R. Paterson & W. J. MacLennan. LC 84-3716. (Disease Management in the Elderly Ser.). 1000p. 1984. 47.50 o.p. (ISBN 0-471-90298-5, Dist. by A R Liss). Wiley.

Bone Implant Interface: Workshop Report. Ed. by Jack Lewis & Jorge O. Galante. (Illus.). 256p. 1985. 18.00 o.p. (ISBN 0-89203-009-7). Amer Acad Ortho Surg.

Bone Is Pointed. Arthur Upfield. LC 75-46003. (Crime Fiction Ser.). 1976. Repr. of 1938 ed. lib. bdg. 21.00 o.p. (ISBN 0-8240-2395-1). Garland Pub.

Bone Marrow Transplantation. Ed. by Roy S. Weiner et al. 160p. 1983. 16.00 o.p. (ISBN 0-914404-95-4). Am Assn Blood.

Bone of Space. Seung Sahn. LC 82-2476. (Wheel Ser.: No. 2). (Illus.). 86p. (Orig.). 1982. pap. 6.95 o.p. (ISBN 0-87704-053-2). Four Seasons Foun.

Bone Planet. Louis Hammer. (Illus.). 32p. 1967. 5.00 o.p. Kayak.

Bone Repair & Fracture Healing in Man. Simon Sevitt. (Current Problems in Orthopaedics Ser.). (Illus.). 300p. 1981. text ed. 42.00 o.p. (ISBN 0-443-01806-5). Churchill.

Bone-Sculpture. Agha S. Ali. (Writers Workshop Redbird Ser.). 32p. 1975. text ed. 8.00 o.s.i. (ISBN 0-89253-535-0); pap. text ed. 3.00 o.s.i. (ISBN 0-88253-727-X). Ind-US Inc.

Bone Tumors in Children. Ed. by Norman Jaffe et al. LC 77-94881. (Progress in Pediatric Hematology & Oncology Ser.). 284p. 1979. 27.50 o.p. (ISBN 0-88416-142-0). Year Bk Med.

Bones. Elementary Science Study Staff. (gr. 4-6). 1967. text ed. 8.96 picture bk. o.p. (ISBN 0-07-018496-8). McGraw.

Bones: Ancient Men & Modern Myths. Lewis R. Binford. LC 80-81776. (Studies in Archaeology). 1981. 39.50 o.p. (ISBN 0-12-100035-4). Acad Pr.

Bones & Feathers. Cecil Rajendra. (Writing in Asia Ser.). 1978. pap. text ed. 5.00x o.p. (ISBN 0-686-60333-8). Heinemann Ed.

Bones & Skeletons. Brenda Thompson & Rosemary Giesen. LC 76-22420. (First Fact Bks.). (Illus.). (gr. k-3). 1977. PLB 4.95 o.p. (ISBN 0-8225-1352-8). Lerner Pubns.

Bones of Contention: Controversies in the Search for Human Origins. Roger Lewin. LC 87-9541. (Illus.). 384p. 1987. 19.45 o.s.i. (ISBN 0-671-52688-X). S&S.

Bones of God. Stephen Leigh. 304p. (Orig.). 1986. pap. 3.50 o.p. (ISBN 0-380-89961-2). Avon.

Bones Wizard. Alan Ryan. LC 87-20057. (Science Fiction Ser.). (Illus.). 192p. 1988. 12.95 o.s.i. (ISBN 0-385-24223-9). Doubleday.

Bonfire! Rope Jackson. 112p. 1983. 7.00 o.p. (ISBN 0-682-49947-1). Exposition-Phoenix.

Bonhomme et la Grosse Bete qui avait des Escailles sur le Dos. Laurent de Brunhoff. (Illus.). 1975. 12.95 o.p. (ISBN 0-686-54145-6). French & Eur.

Bonkers Is a Preventable Disease. Kevin Leman. 192p. 1986. 10.95 o.p. (ISBN 0-8007-1506-3). Revell.

Bonn: The Capital of West Germany in Photographs. 3rd, rev. & enl. ed. H. Lutzeler. (Illus.). 1985. 35.00 o.s.i. (ISBN 3-7885-0278-9). E J Brill USA.

Bonnard: The Late Paintings. Ed. by Sasha M. Newman. (Illus.). 1986. pap. 24.95 o.s.i. (ISBN 0-500-27400-2). Thames Hudson.

Bonne Chanson. Paul Verlaine. Bd. with Romances sans Paroles; Sagesse. 1963. pap. 3.95 o.p. (ISBN 0-685-35919-0, 1116, Pub. by Livre De Poche). Schoenhof.

Bonnie Prudden's after Fifty Fitness Guide. Bonnie Prudden. LC 86-40107. (Illus.). 384p. 1986. 19.45 o.p. (ISBN 0-394-54964-3, Pub. by Villard Bks). Random.

Bonsai Tree. Meira Chand. LC 82-19615. 240p. 1983. 12.45 o.p. (ISBN 0-89919-166-5). Ticknor & Fields.

Bonus Years. Mildred Tengbom. LC 74-14180. 160p. (Orig.). 1975. pap. 3.95 o.p. (ISBN 0-8066-1463-3, 10-0782, Augsburg). Augsburg Fortress.

Bonzo Beaver. Arthur Crowley. (Illus.). 32p. (gr. k-3). 1980. PLB 7.95 o.p. (ISBN 0-395-29081-3). HM.

Boo to a Goose. Joseph Low. LC 74-18188. (Illus.). 32p. (ps-3). 1975. 5.95 o.p. (ISBN 0-689-50009-2, Atheneum). Macmillan.

Boo! Who? Colin Hawkins & Jacqui Hawkins. LC 83-80071. (Illus.). 16p. (ps-1). 1984. 8.95 o.p. (ISBN 0-03-063929-8). H Holt & Co.

Boogey Man. Arthur Crowley. LC 77-18517. (Illus.). (gr. k-3). 1978. reinforced bdg. 8.95 o.p. (ISBN 0-395-26458-8). HM.

Boogeyman. Ronald Koertge. 1980. 9.95 o.p. (ISBN 0-393-01296-4). Norton.

Book. Eurakia. 1979. 6.00 o.p. (ISBN 0-682-49354-6). Exposition-Phoenix.

Book about Bringing Up Children. Y. Azarov. 319p. 1983. 7.95 o.p. (Pub. by Progress Pubs USSR). Imported Pubns.

Book Auctions in England in the Seventeenth Century. John Lawler. LC 68-30614. 288p. 1968. Repr. of 1898 ed. 35.00x o.p. (ISBN 0-8103-3310-4). Gale.

Book Availability & the Library User. Michael K. Buckland. LC 74-8682. 220p. 1975. 23.00 o.p. (ISBN 0-08-017709-3); pap. 11.50 o.p. (ISBN 0-08-018160-0). Pergamon.

Book Bag Treasury of Literary Quizzes. Ed. by Washington Post Book World Editors. (Illus.). 192p. 1984. pap. 6.95 o.p. (ISBN 0-684-18129-0, ScribT). Scribner.

Book Bait: Detailed Notes on Adult Books Popular with Young People. 3rd ed. Compiled by Elinor Walker. LC 78-21067. 1979. pap. 7.50x o.p. (ISBN 0-8389-0279-0). ALA.

Book Burning. Cal Thomas. LC 83-70319. 180p. 1983. pap. 6.95 o.p. (ISBN 0-89107-284-5, Crossway Bks). Good News.

Book Clubs & Printing Societies of Great Britain & Ireland. Harold H. Williams. LC 68-26622. 140p. 1971. Repr. of 1929 ed. 46.00x o.p. (ISBN 0-8103-3749-5). Gale.

Book Dealer's & Collectors' Year-Book & Diary 1985. 250p. 1984. pap. 12.95 o.p. (ISBN 0-900661-35-6, Sheppard Press Limited England). Seven Hills Bk Dists.

Book Dealers' & Collectors' Year-Book & Diary 1986. 8th ed. 250p. 1985. pap. 12.95 o.p. (ISBN 0-900661-39-9, Sheppard Press Limited England). Seven Hills Bk Dists.

Book Dealers in North America, 1983-85. (ISBN 0-900661-28-3). Intl Pubns Serv.

Book for a Friend. Dorothy J. Olzendam. 1978. 4.95 o.p. (ISBN 0-8323-0321-6). Binford-Metropolitan.

Book for Grandmothers. Ruth Goode. (Paperbacks Ser.). 1977. pap. text ed. 3.95 o.p. (ISBN 0-07-023740-9). McGraw.

Book for Jodan. Marcia Newfield. LC 74-18192. (Illus.). 48p. (gr. 2-5). 1975. 8.95 o.p. (ISBN 0-689-50010-6, Atheneumn). Macmillan.

Book for Mom. Katharine Short. (Illus.). 62p. 5.95 o.p. (ISBN 0-85648-867-4). Lion USA.

Book: Its History & Development. Cyril Davenport. LC 79-164212. (Tower Bks.). (Illus.). viii, 266p. 1971. Repr. of 1930 ed. 37.00x o.p. (ISBN 0-8103-3944-7). Gale.

Book IX-Prophacies Fulfilled. Rebecca Daniels. (Life of Jesus Ser.). 32p. (YA) (gr. 7-12). 1984. wkbk. 3.95 o.p. (ISBN 0-86653-230-7). Good Apple.

Book-Lover's Enchiridion. Alexander Ireland. LC 78-76113. 534p. 1969. Repr. of 1888 ed. 40.00x o.p. (ISBN 0-8103-3895-5). Gale.

Book of a Thousand Tongues. Eric M. North. LC 73-174087. (Tower Bks). 400p. 1972. Repr. of 1938 ed. 46.00x o.p. (ISBN 0-8103-3948-X). Gale.

Book of Abraham. Marek Halter. Tr. by Lowell Blair. LC 85-17582. 768p. 1985. 19.95 o.p. (ISBN 0-03-071887-2). H Holt & Co.

Book of American Figure Painters. Mariana G. Van Rensselaer. Ed. by H. Barbara Weinberg. LC 75-28875. (Art Experience in Late 19th Century America Ser.: Vol. 11). (Illus.). 1977. Repr. of 1886 ed. lib. bdg. 88.00 o.p. (ISBN 0-8240-2235-1). Garland Pub.

Book of Animals. 472p. 1000.00 o.p. Kraus Repr.

Book of Badminton. E. Choong & F. Brundle. (Illus.). 128p. 1956. (ISBN 0-8022-0244-6). Philos Lib.

Book of BASIC. Arleen G. Schwartz & Dorothy Jabarin. 230p. (Orig.). 1984. pap. 12.95 o.p. (ISBN 0-942386-61-2). Compute Pubns.

Book of Beauty. John Hadfield. (Illus.). 224p. 1977. 15.00 o.p. (ISBN 0-85115-137-X, Pub. by Boydell & Brewer). Longwood Pub Group.

Book of British Towns. Automobile Association of England. (Illus.). 1979. 22.95 o.p. (ISBN 0-393-01232-8). Norton.

Book of Business Knowledge. rev. ed. LC 83-11754. 1983. 50.00 o.p. (ISBN 0-932648-62-2). Boardroom.

Book of Cacti & Other Succulents. Claude Chidamian. (Illus.). 260p. 1984. pap. 13.95 o.p. (ISBN 0-917304-90-X). Timber.

Book of Ceremonial Magic. A. E. Waite. (Illus.). 384p. 1988. 39.95 o.p. (ISBN 0-7126-1421-4, Pub. by Century Hutchinson). David & Charles.

Book of Child Care: The Complete Guide for Today's Parents. Hugh Jolly. LC 84-10756. (Illus.). 688p. 1984. 19.95 o.p. (ISBN 0-15-113460-X). HarBraceJ.

Book of Christian Faith: Questions & Answers for the Twentieth Century. Johann C. Hampe. Tr. by Edwin H. Robertson. LC 80-65549. 248p. (Orig.). 1980. pap. 8.75 o.p. (ISBN 0-8066-1794-2, 10-0784, Augsburg). Augsburg Fortress.

Book of Contemplation. Dagobert D. Runes. 1957. (ISBN 0-8022-1425-8). Philos Lib.

Book of Country Living. Ed. by Susan Osborn & Jeffrey Weiss. LC 81-47462. (Illus.). 192p. 1982. pap. write for info. o.p. (ISBN 0-03-059613-0). H Holt & Co.

Book of Craftsmen: The Story of Man's Handiwork Through the Ages. Marjory Bruce. LC 70-185352. (Illus.). 322p. 1974. Repr. of 1937 ed. 40.00x o.p. (ISBN 0-8103-3960-9). Gale.

Book of Cryptic Puzzles, No 2. Eugene T. Maleska. 64p. 1983. pap. 5.75 o.s.i. (ISBN 0-671-45875-2, Fireside). S&S.

Book of Daniel. Andre Lacocque. LC 78-2036. 1978. 19.95 o.p. (ISBN 0-8042-0090-4, John Knox). Westminster John Knox.

Book of Days. National Gallery Staff. (Illus.). 160p. (Orig.). 1979. 8.95 o.p. (ISBN 0-03-052711-2). H Holt & Co.

Book of Delights. rev. ed. John Hadfield. (Illus.). 224p. 1977. 15.00 o.p. (ISBN 0-85115-138-8, Pub. by Boydell & Brewer). Longwood Pub Group.

Book of Dreams. Michael Waldecki. 1979. pap. 4.00 o.p. (ISBN 0-682-49428-3). Exposition-Phoenix.

Book of English Desserts. Constance Chambers. (Illus.). 1965. 19.95 o.p. (ISBN 0-911202-01-3). Radio City.

Book of English Proverbs, with Origins & Explanations. Vere H. Collins. LC 73-16945. 144p. 1974. Repr. of 1959 ed. lib. bdg. 29.75x o.p. (ISBN 0-8371-7242-X, COEN). Greenwood.

Book of Enoch: Or One Enoch. 2nd ed. Ed. & R. H. Charles. 331p. pap. 16.95 o.s.i. (ISBN 0-88697-009-1). Life Science.

Book of Epigrams. Dimitris Tsaloumas. Tr. by Philip Grundy from Gr. LC 84-22003. 207p. 1985. 14.95 o.p. (ISBN 0-7022-1837-5). U of Queensland Pr.

Book of Esther. Tr. by Aryeh Kaplan. 268p. 8.95 o.s.i. (ISBN 0-686-27543-8); pap. 6.45 o.s.i. (ISBN 0-940118-21-1). Maznaim.

Book of Fairies. Beatrice Phillpotts. (Illus.). 1979. pap. 8.95 o.s.i. (ISBN 0-345-28092-X). Ballantine.

Book of Fairs. Helen Augur. LC 75-159875. (Tower Bks). (Illus.). 326p. 1972. Repr. of 1939 ed. 43.00x o.p. (ISBN 0-8103-3927-7). Gale.

Book of Fame. Richard J. Anobile. 1981. pap. 7.95 o.p. (ISBN 0-449-90044-4, Columbine). Fawcett.

Book of Family Prayer. Robert E. Webber. LC 86-5243. 288p. 1986. 17.95 o.p. (ISBN 0-8407-5479-5). Nelson.

Book of Family Therapy. Andrew Ferber et al. 1973. pap. 10.95 o.s.i. (ISBN 0-395-17227-6, 77, SenEd). HM.

Book of Famous Wits. Walter C. Jerrold. LC 77-155086. 342p. 1971. Repr. of 1912 ed. 40.00x o.p. (ISBN 0-8103-3757-6). Gale.

Book of Five Rings. Miyamoto Musashi. 1983. 6.98 o.p. (ISBN 0-517-41528-3). Crown.

Book of Floating: Exploring the Private Sea. Michael Hutchison. LC 83-25040. (Illus.). 258p. 1984. 14.95 o.p. (ISBN 0-688-03117-X). Morrow.

Book of Flower Arranging: For Fresh, Dried, & Artificial Flowers. Mary Forsell. (Illus.). 128p. 1987. 15.95 o.p. (ISBN 0-89471-527-5). Running Pr.

Book of Folly. Anne Sexton. LC 72-3839. 1973. 5.95 o.p. (ISBN 0-395-14014-5); pap. 3.95 o.p. (ISBN 0-395-14075-7). HM.

Book of Genesis. Charles F. Pfeiffer. (Shield Bible Study). (Orig.). pap. 2.95 o.p. (ISBN 0-8010-6906-8). Baker Bk.

Book of God. Baruch Spinoza. 128p. 1958. (ISBN 0-8022-1617-X). Philos Lib.

Book of Great Breakfasts & Brunches. Terence Janericco. 272p. 1983. 21.95 o.p. (ISBN 0-8436-2264-4). Van Nos Reinhold.

Book of Health. 3rd abr. ed. R. Lee Clark & Russell W. Cumley. LC 77-76457. 1977. pap. 8.95 o.p. (ISBN 0-15-613548-5, Harv). HarBraceJ.

Book of Herb Cookery. Irene B. Hoffmann. LC 53-11357. 272p. 1975. pap. 3.95 o.p. (ISBN 0-395-20675-8). HM.

Book of Hours of Pannonhalma, Vols. I & II. Szabo & Elizabeth Floris-Soltesz. write for info. o.s.i. Newbury Bks.

Book of Incomes. Gerald Krefetz & Philip Gittelman. LC 81-47472. 224p. 1982. 12.95 o.p. (ISBN 0-03-059897-4); pap. 6.95 o.p. (ISBN 0-03-056848-X). H Holt & Co.

Book of Jamaica. Russell Banks. 1980. 10.95 o.p. (ISBN 0-395-29085-6). HM.

Book of Jewish Thoughts. Ed. by Joseph H. Hertz. 1976. Repr. 9.95 o.s.i. (ISBN 0-8197-0252-8). Bloch.

Book of Jewish Values. Louis Jacobs. (Limited Editions Reprints). 160p. 1984. pap. text ed. 6.95 o.p. (ISBN 0-940646-06-4, 83-21278). Rossel Bks.

Book of Life. James T. Clark. 1981. 4.00 o.p. (ISBN 0-682-49138-1). Exposition-Phoenix.

Book of London. Date not set. (ISBN 0-86145-329-8, Pub. by Auto Assn England). Salem Hse Pubs.

Book of Lost Tales, Vol. 2. J. R. R. Tolkien. Ed. by Christopher Tolkien. LC 83-12782. 1984. 16.45 o.p. (ISBN 0-395-36614-3). HM.

Book of Love. John Hadfield. (Illus.). 223p. 1978. 15.00 o.p. (ISBN 0-85115-139-6, Pub. by Boydell & Brewer). Longwood Pub Group.

Book of Love, Vol. I. Lisa Layne & Paul Sinn. (Illus.). 80p. 1984. pap. 4.80 o.p. (ISBN 0-671-50056-2, Fireside). S&S.

Book of Low Fire Ceramics. Harvey Brody. LC 79-944. (Illus.). 176p. (Orig.). 1980. 18.95 o.p. (ISBN 0-03-042116-0); pap. 11.95 o.p. (ISBN 0-03-042111-X). H Holt & Co.

Book of Macrobiotics: The Universal Way of Health & Happiness. Michio Kushi. LC 76-29341. (Illus.). 176p. (Orig.). 1977. pap. 11.95 o.p. (ISBN 0-87040-381-8). Japan Pubns USA.

Book of Magic. John Mulholland. LC 63-9766. (Encore Edition). 1963. pap. 1.95 o.p. (ISBN 0-684-16914-2, ScribT). Scribner.

Book of Mary: Prayers in Honor of the Blessed Virgin Mary. Rev. ed. 40p. (Orig.). 1987. pap. 1.95 o.p. (ISBN 0-317-60066-4). US Catholic.

Book of Merlin: Insight from the Merlin Conference. Ed. by R. J. Stewart. (Illus.). 192p. 1987. 24.95 o.p. (ISBN 0-7137-1945-1, Pub. by Blandford Pr England). Sterling.

Book of Merlyn. T. H. White. 1984. pap. 2.95 o.s.i. (ISBN 0-425-09450-2). Berkley Pub.

Book of Merlyn: The Unpublished Conclusion to "The Once & Future King" T. H. White. LC 77-3454. (Illus.). 159p. 1977. pap. 14.95 o.p. (ISBN 0-292-70718-5). U of Tex Pr.

Book of Microwave Cookery. Sonia Allison. (Illus.). 128p. 1987. 16.95 o.p. (ISBN 0-7153-8884-3). David & Charles.

Book of Mormon: It Begins with a Family. LC 83-73118. 270p. 1983. 8.95 o.p. (ISBN 0-87747-987-9). Deseret Bk.

Book of Nahum. Walter A. Maier. (Thornapple Commentaries). 392p. 1980. pap. 6.95 o.p. (ISBN 0-8010-6098-2). Baker Bk.

Book of Nasty Legends. Paul Smith. (Illus.). 109p. 1984. 14.95x o.p. (ISBN 0-7102-0004-8); pap. 8.95 o.p. (ISBN 0-7102-0140-0). Routledge Chapman & Hall.

Book of Nations see World Book Desk Reference Set.

Book of Nonsense. Edward Lear. LC 80-5355. (Illus.). 60p. (gr. 4 up). 1980. 4.95 o.p. (ISBN 0-87099-241-4, Co-pub by Viking Pergion Inc.). Metro Mus Art.

Book of Nonsense. Edward Lear et al. 1975. 14.95x o.p. (ISBN 0-460-00806-4, Evman); pap. 5.95x o.p. (ISBN 0-460-01806-X, Evman). Biblio Dist.

Book of Nonsense. Edward Lear et al. 200p. 1984. pap. 5.95x o.p. (ISBN 0-460-11806-4, Pub. by Evman England). Biblio Dist.

Book of Noodles: Stories of Simpletons. William A. Clouston. LC 67-24351. 288p. 1969. Repr. of 1888 ed. 35.00x o.p. (ISBN 0-8103-3519-0). Gale.

Book of Numbers. Raymond St. Jaques. 1970. pap. 1.50 o.p. (ISBN 0-380-01070-4, 15990). Avon.

Book of Nursery Songs & Rhymes. Sabine Baring-Gould. LC 68-23135. 1969. Repr. of 1895 ed. 30.00x o.p. (ISBN 0-8103-3471-2). Gale.

Book of One's Own: People & Their Diaries. Thomas Mallon. LC 84-8666. 293p. 1984. 15.45 o.p. (ISBN 0-89919-242-4). Ticknor & Fields.

Book of Perks. James R. Baehler. 1984. pap. 7.95 o.p. (ISBN 0-03-071073-1). H Holt & Co.

Book of Personal Computers & Games. Consumer Guide Editors. 54p. 1984. spiral bdg. 1.00 o.p. (ISBN 0-517-41595-X, Pub. by Beekman Hse). Outlet Bk Co.

Book of Phoebe. Mary-Ann T. Smith. LC 84-13715. 288p. 1985. 15.95 o.p. (ISBN 0-385-19673-3). Doubleday.

Book of Poems. L. Martynov. 229p. 1979. 6.45 o.p. (ISBN 0-8285-1559-X, Pub. by Progress Pubs USSR). Imported Pubns.

Book of Poems Dedicated to the Dream...of Love. Charlotte Fawls. 1979. 4.00 o.p. (ISBN 0-682-49458-5). Exposition-Phoenix.

Titles

Book of Political Quotes. J. Green. 256p. 1983. pap. text ed. 8.95 o.p. (ISBN 0-07-024354-9). McGraw.

Book of Poverbs. Rosenzweig. LC 65-19205. 128p. 1965. (ISBN 0-8022-1378-2). Philos Lib.

Book of Practical Candle Magic. Leo Vinci. LC 86-34292. 128p. 1986. lib. bdg. 19.95x o.p. (ISBN 0-8095-7028-9). Borgo Pr.

Book of Prayers. Katherine E. Charitonuk. LC 84-91336. 189p. 1985. 8.95 o.p. (ISBN 0-533-06433-3). Vantage.

Book of Problems in Ordinary Differential Equations. M. L. Krasnov et al. 332p. 1981. 6.80 o.s.i. (ISBN 0-8285-1925-0, Pub. by Mir Pubs USSR). Imported Pubns.

Book of Puzzlements. Date not set. (ISBN 0-8052-3786-0). Random.

Book of Puzzles. Tyler. (Brain Benders Ser.). (gr. 2-5). 1980. 10.95 o.p. (ISBN 0-86020-440-5, Usborne-Hayes). EDC.

Book of Rock Lists. Dave Marsh & Kevin Stein. 672p. (Orig.). (gr. 7 up). 1981. pap. 9.95 o.p. (ISBN 0-440-57580-X, Dell Trade Pbks). Dell.

Book of Royal Lists. Craig Brown & Lesley Cunliffe. 292p. (Orig.). 1983. 15.50 o.s.i. (ISBN 0-671-46507-4); pap. 6.95 o.s.i. (ISBN 0-671-47282-8). Summit Bks.

Book of Russian Idioms Illustrated. M. I. Dubrovin. LC 79-40433. (Illus.). 328p. 1981. 10.75 o.p. (ISBN 0-08-023594-8). Pergamon.

Book of Salads. Sonia Uvezian. LC 77-23838. (Illus.). 1977. pap. 6.95 o.p. (ISBN 0-89286-126-6, One Hund One Prods). Ortho.

Book of Scottish Ballads. Ed. by David Buchan. 232p. 1985. pap. 8.95 o.p. (ISBN 0-7102-0539-2). Routledge Chapman & Hall.

Book of Scripts. 2nd ed. Alfred Fairbank. (Illus.). 48p. 1977. pap. 6.50 o.p. (ISBN 0-571-11080-0). Faber & Faber.

Book of Sex Lists. Compiled by Albert B. Gerber. 1984. pap. 3.95 o.s.i. (ISBN 0-345-30831-X). Ballantine.

Book of Sharks: A Complete Illustrated Natural History of the Sharks of the World. Richard Ellis. LC 82-23333. (Illus.). 256p. 1983. 29.95 o.p. (ISBN 0-15-113462-6); pap. 14.95 o.p. (ISBN 0-15-613552-3, Harv). HarBraceJ.

Book of Silence. Lawrence Watt-Evans. (Lords of Dus Ser.: Bk. 4). 336p. 1984. pap. 3.50 o.p. (ISBN 0-345-30880-8). Ballantine.

Book of Similes. Roger Baldwin & Ruth Paris. (Illus.). 132p. 1982. 14.95x o.p. (ISBN 0-7100-9285-7); pap. 7.95 o.p. (ISBN 0-7100-9456-6). Routledge Chapman & Hall.

Book of Solo Games. Gyles Brandreth. LC 84-340. (Illus.). 238p. 1984. 15.95 o.p. (ISBN 0-911745-53-X). P Bedrick Bks.

Book of Songs. Tr. by Arthur Waley. 1960. pap. 9.95 o.s.i. (ISBN 0-394-17331-7, E209, Ever). Grove.

Book of Spells. Marc De Pascale. LC 70-163218. (Illus.). 1978. pap. 4.95 o.s.i. (ISBN 0-8008-0934-3). Taplinger.

Book of Stillmeadow. Gladys Taber. (General Ser.). 1984. lib. bdg. 15.95 o.p. (ISBN 0-8161-3717-X, Large Print Bks). G K Hall.

Book of Studies in Plant Form: With Some Suggestions for Their Application to Design. A. E. Lilley & W. Midgley. LC 70-89276. (Tower Bks.). (Illus.). xvi, 150p. 1972. Repr. of 1896 ed. 35.00x o.p. (ISBN 0-8103-3947-1). Gale.

Book of Surrender. Emmanuel Paine & Wingate Paine. 192p. 1987. pap. 8.95 o.p. (ISBN 0-317-62399-0). Prentice Hall Pr.

Book of Texas Days. Ron Stone. LC 85-14341. (Illus.). 288p. 1985. 19.95 o.p. (ISBN 0-940672-30-8). Shearer Pub.

Book of Texas Lists. Ed. by Anne Dingus. 1982. 220 pp. 15.00, o.p. (ISBN 0-932012-17-5); pap. 6.95 o.p. 208 pp. (ISBN 0-932012-41-8). Texas Month Pr.

Book of the Beasts. Ramon Lull. Tr. by E. Allison Peers from Catalan. LC 76-48438. (Library of World Literature Ser.). 1978. Repr. of 1927 ed. 15.00 o.s.i. (ISBN 0-88355-572-7). Hyperion Conn.

Book of the Black Bass II: Ou Achigan Deux. James B. Potts. (Illus.). 144p. 1982. 9.00 o.p. (ISBN 0-682-49878-5, Banner). Exposition-Phoenix.

Book of the Car. 3rd ed. Automobile Association of England. (Illus.). 1977. 22.95 o.p. (ISBN 0-393-08774-3). Norton.

Book of the Car. (Illus.). 440p. 1973. 17.50 o.p. (ISBN 0-393-08676-3). Norton.

Book of the City of Ladies. Christine De Pizan. Tr. by E. J. Richards from Fr. (Illus.). 336p. 1982. 17.95 o.p. (ISBN 0-89255-061-9). Persea Bks.

Book of the Courtier. Baldassare Castiglione. Tr. by Thomas Hoby. 1975. 12.95x o.p. (ISBN 0-460-10807-7, Evman); pap. 4.95x o.p. (ISBN 0-460-11807-2, Evman). Biblio Dist.

Book of the Dead. E. A. Budge. (Illus.). 992p. 1985. pap. 9.95 o.p. (ISBN 1-85063-020-8, Ark Paperbks). Routledge Chapman & Hall.

Book of the Dead. Intro. by E. A. Budge. 1977. pap. 12.95 o.p. (ISBN 0-8065-0591-5, Pub. by Citadel Pr). Carol Pub Group.

Book of the Dead: An English Translation of the Chapters, Hymns, Etc., of the Theban Recension. 2nd ed. E. A. Budge. (Illus.). 1969. 35.00 o.p. (ISBN 0-7100-1128-8). Routledge Chapman & Hall.

Book of the Dead: Egyptian Literature. rev. ed. Ed. by Wallis E. Budge. (Illus.). 417p. pap. 22.95 o.s.i. (ISBN 0-88697-013-X). Life Science.

Book of the Hackle. Frank Elder. 1979. 16.95 o.p. (ISBN 0-7073-0223-4, Pub. by Scot Acad Pr). Longwood Pub Group.

Book of the Lion. Elizabeth Daly. 160p. (Orig.). 1985. pap. 2.95 o.p. (ISBN 0-553-24883-9). Bantam.

Book of the Night. Rhoda Lerman. LC 83-22848. 1984. 16.95 o.p. (ISBN 0-03-071081-2). H Holt & Co.

Book of the Popes. Tr. by Louise R. Loomis. 1965. lib. bdg. 19.50x o.p. (ISBN 0-374-95093-8, Octagon). Hippocrene Bks.

Book of the Royal Wedding. Alastair Burnet. 128p. 1986. 14.95 o.s.i. (ISBN 0-671-63303-1). Summit Bks.

Book of the Secrets of Enoch. Ed. by R. H. Charles. 100p. pap. 11.95 o.s.i. (ISBN 0-88697-010-5). Life Science.

Book of the Sonnet: Poems & Criticism. Ed. by Martin Kallich et al. LC 72-125263. 214p. 1972. text ed. 26.00x o.p. (ISBN 0-8290-0156-5); pap. text ed. o.p. Irvington.

Book of the Violin. Ed. by Dominic Gill. 256p. 1984. 37.50 o.p. (ISBN 0-8478-0548-4). Rizzoli Intl.

Book of Ultimates. J. Caldwell. 160p. 1983. pap. text ed. 6.95 o.p. (ISBN 0-07-009608-2). McGraw.

Book of United States Navy Ships. rev. ed. M. D. Van Orden. LC 73-7097. (Illus.). (gr. 5 up). 1979. 8.95 o.p. (ISBN 0-396-07661-0). Dodd.

Book of U. S. Postal Exams: How to Score 95-100 & Get a 20,000 a Year Job. Veltisezar B. Bautista. LC 85-72726. (Illus.). 184p. 1986. pap. 10.00 o.p. (ISBN 0-931613-01-9). Bkhaus.

Book of Urizen. William Blake. LC 78-58217. (Illus.). 102p. 1978. pap. 15.00 o.p. (ISBN 0-87773-131-4, 73629-X). Shambhala Pubns.

Book of Virgil Finlay. Gerry De La Ree. (Illus.). 1976. pap. 4.95 o.p. (ISBN 0-380-00770-3, 30585). Avon.

Book of Why. Robert L. Shook. LC 83-126. (Illus.). 160p. 1983. 9.95 o.p. (ISBN 0-8437-3335-7). Hammond Inc.

Book of Winners. Claire Walter. LC 79-14237. 1979. pap. 8.95 o.p. (ISBN 0-15-697208-5, Harv). HarBraceJ.

Book of World-Famous Music Classical, Popular & Folk. James J. Fuld. 688p. Repr. of 1971 ed. lib. bdg. 79.00 o.p. (Pub. by Am Repr Serv). Reprint Servs.

Book on C. R. E. Berry & B. A. Meekings. (Computer Science Ser.). (Illus.). 210p. (Orig.). 1984. pap. text ed. 24.00x o.p. (ISBN 0-333-36821-5, Pub. by Macmillan England). Scholium Intl.

Book Publishing Career Directory, 1986: 20 Top Book Publishing Professionals. Intro. by Samuel S. Vaughan. (Career Directory Ser.). 268p. (Orig.). 1986. pap. 24.95 o.p. (ISBN 0-934829-02-0). Career Pr Inc.

Book Publishing Career Directory: 1987. rev. ed. Ed. by Ron Fry. (Career Directory Ser.). 280p. 1987. text ed. 34.95 o.p. (ISBN 0-934829-19-5); pap. text ed. 26.95 o.p. (ISBN 0-934829-13-6); Special Bookstore Edition Distributed by Williamson Publishing Co. pap. 17.95 o.p. (ISBN 0-934829-07-1). Career Pr Inc.

Book Publishingm 1984, 2 vols. Ed. by Henry R. Kaufman. (Nineteen Eighty-Three to Eighty-Four Patents, Copyrights, Trademark & Literary PropertyCourse Handbook). 865p. (Orig.). 1984. pap. text ed. 15.00 o.p. (ISBN 0-686-78753-6, G4-3747). PLI.

Book Review Index: Annual Cumulation, 1985. Ed. by Gary C. Tarbert & Barbara Beach. LC 65-9908. 1096p. 1984. 170.00x o.p. (ISBN 0-8103-0575-5). Gale.

Book Review Index, 1987: Periodical Issues, No. 2. Ed. by Barbara Beach. 1987. 170.00x o.p. (ISBN 0-8103-2496-2). Gale.

Book Reviewing. Ed. by Sylvia E. Kamerman. LC 78-9390. 1978. 12.00 o.p. (ISBN 0-87116-113-3). Writer.

Book Society. Graham Watson. LC 79-55587. 1980. 10.95 o.p. (ISBN 0-689-11060-X, Atheneum). Macmillan.

Book: That Which Has Been & That Which Shall Be, Bk. I. Sharon A. Taylor. LC 84-91294. 74p. 1985. 7.95 o.p. (ISBN 0-533-06386-8). Vantage.

Bookbinding & the Care of Books. Douglas Cockerell. 1978. pap. 9.95 o.s.i. (ISBN 0-8008-0946-7, Pentalic). Taplinger.

Bookbinding As a Handcraft. Manly Banister. LC 75-14522. (Illus.). 160p. (Orig.). 1986. pap. 8.95 o.p. (ISBN 0-8069-6352-2). Sterling.

Bookdealers' & Collectors' Year-Book & Diary, 1984. Sheppard Press, Ltd. 163p. 1983. 12.00 o.p. (ISBN 0-900661-31-3, Sheppard England). Seven Hills Bk Dists.

Bookdealers in India, Pakistan, Etc. Compiled by Sheppard Press, Ltd., Staff. 1985. 7.50 o.p. (ISBN 0-900661-14-3, Pub. by Sheppard England). Seven Hills Bk Dists.

Bookdealers in North America: A Directory of Dealers in Secondhand & Antiquarian Books in Canada & the United States of America, 1983-1985. 9th ed. Compiled by Sheppard Press, Ltd. Staff. 371p. 1983. 25.00 o.p. (ISBN 0-900661-28-3, Pub. by Sheppard England). Seven Hills Bk Dists.

Booker T. Washington Papers, Vol. 13: 1914-15, 13 vols. Booker T. Washington. Ed. by Louis R Harlan et al. (Illus.). 1984. Set. 364.00 o.p.; Vol. 13, 592p. 35.00 o.p. U of Ill Pr.

Bookies & Bettors: Two Hundred Years of Gambling. Richard Sasuly. LC 81-7139. 288p. 1982. 15.50 o.s.i. (ISBN 0-03-053756-8). H Holt & Co.

Bookkeeping & Tax Reports see Doctors' Administrative Program.

Bookman's Concise Dictionary. F. C. Avis. 1956. Philos Lib.

Books about the Book: A Guide to Biblical Reference Works. John R. Kohlenberger, III. 272p. 1986. pap. 10.95 o.p. (ISBN 0-310-39341-8, 6287P). Zondervan.

Books & Articles on South Carolina History: A List for Laymen. Lewis P. Jones. LC 70-133844. (Tricentennial Booklet: No. 8). xiv, 106p. 1970. pap. 4.95 o.p. (ISBN 0-87249-207-9). U of SC Pr.

Books & History. Robert B. Downs. LC 74-620006. (Monograph: No. 13). 83p. 1974. 5.00x o.p. (ISBN 0-87845-039-4). U of Ill Lib Info Sci.

Books & Periodicals. Nuchine Nobari. 376p. 1987. 125.00 o.p. (ISBN 0-317-65176-5). Learned Info.

Books & Portraits: Some Further Selections from the Literary & Biographical Writings of Virginia Woolf. Virginia Woolf. LC 77-85206. 240p. 1978. 10.00 o.p. (ISBN 0-15-113478-2). HarBraceJ.

Books for Catholic Elementary Schools. Eileen Noonan. pap. 2.50 o.p. (ISBN 0-87507-024-8). Cath Lib Assn.

Books for Public Libraries. 3rd. ed. Ed. by Constance Koehn. 381p. 1982. 20.00x o.p. (ISBN 0-8389-0328-2). ALA.

Books for Religious Education in Catholic Secondary Schools. rev. ed. Compiled by Eileen F. Noonan. ii, 18p. 1986. pap. 5.00 o.p. (ISBN 0-87507-039-6). Cath Lib Assn.

Books for the Teen Age, 1985 Annual. 1985. pap. 2.00 o.p. (ISBN 0-87104-670-9, Branch Lib). NY Pub Lib.

Books for the Teen Age, 1986 Annual. 1987. pap. 5.00 o.p. (ISBN 0-87104-686-5, Branch Lib). NY Pub Lib.

Books for the Teen Age, 1987 Annual. 1988. pap. 5.00 o.p. (ISBN 0-87104-690-3, Branch Libraries). NY Pub Lib.

Books for World Explorers Series, No. 5. (gr. 3-8). 1984. Set of 4. 34.00 o.p. (ISBN 0-87044-501-4, 00501); Set of 4. PLB 27.80 o.p. (ISBN 0-87044-506-5, 00506). Natl Geog.

Books for You, 1985: A Booklist for Senior High Students. Ed. by Donald R. Gallo. LC 85-21666. 360p. (Orig.). (YA) (gr. 9-12). 1985. pap. 9.75 o.p. (ISBN 0-8141-0363-4). NCTE.

Books in American History: A Basic List for High Schools & Junior Colleges. 2nd ed. John E. Wiltz & Nancy C. Cridland. LC 80-8766. (Midland Bks.: No. 266). 128p. 1981. 15.00x o.p. (ISBN 0-253-15255-0); pap. 5.95x o.p. (ISBN 0-253-20266-3). Ind U Pr.

Books in Bottles: The Curious in Literature. William G. Clifford. LC 70-78125. 194p. 1971. Repr. of 1926 ed. 35.00x o.p. (ISBN 0-8103-3791-6). Gale.

Books in Chains & Other Bibliographical Papers. William Blades. LC 68-30610. 272p. 1968. Repr. of 1892 ed. 35.00x o.p. (ISBN 0-8103-3298-1). Gale.

Books in English on the Soviet Union, 1917-73: A Bibliography. David L. Jones. LC 75-6887. (Reference Library of Social Science: No. 3). 200p. 1975. lib. bdg. 47.00 o.p. (ISBN 0-8240-1061-2). Garland Pub.

Books in Print Supplement, 1987-88, 2 vols. Ed. by Bowker, R. R., Co. Staff. 3077p. 1988. Set. 139.95 o.p. (ISBN 0-8352-2429-5). Bowker.

Books in Print 1987-88, 7 vols. Ed. by Bowker, R. R., Co. Staff. 13017p. 1987. Set. 249.95 o.p. (ISBN 0-8352-2370-1); microfiche, full year sub. 625.00 o.p. (ISBN 0-8352-2398-1). Bowker.

Books, Libraries, & Research. Mary Hauer et al. 1983. pap. text ed. 14.95 o.p. (ISBN 0-8403-3067-7, 40306703). Kendall-Hunt.

Books of Blood, Vols. I-III. Clive Barker. (Illus.). 476p. 1985. Repr. of 1984 ed. 30.00 o.s.i. (ISBN 0-910489-14-9). Scream Pr.

Books of the Pilgrims. Lawrence D. Geller & Peter J. Gomes. LC 74-30056. (Reference Library of the Humanities: No. 13). (Illus.). 100p. 1975. lib. bdg. 25.00 o.p. (ISBN 0-8240-1065-5). Garland Pub.

Books of William Morris. H. Buxton Forman. 45.00x o.p. (ISBN 0-87556-290-6). Saifer.

Books on Tape Catalog, 1988. Ed. by Books on Tape, Inc. Staff. 1987. 5.00 o.p. (ISBN 0-913369-05-5). Bks on Tape.

Books Out of Print, 1983-87, 3 vols. Ed. by Bowker, R. R., Staff. 3403p. 1988. Set. 99.95 o.p. (ISBN 0-8352-2394-9). Bowker.

Bookshelves & Cabinets. Sunset Magazine & Books Editors. LC 74-76541. (Illus.). 96p. (Orig.). 1974. pap. 5.95 o.p. (ISBN 0-376-01085-1, Sunset Bks). Sunset-Lane.

Bookshops of London. rev. ed. Dianna Stephenson. 120p. (Orig.). 1985. pap. 9.95 o.p. (ISBN 0-933982-30-5, Lascelles). Bradt Ent.

Bookstore Book. Robert Egan. 1979. pap. 5.95 o.p. (ISBN 0-380-46474-8, 46474-8). Avon.

Bookstore Planning & Design. Ken White. (Illus.). 192p. 1982. text ed. 51.50 o.p. (ISBN 0-07-069851-1). McGraw.

Boomerang Book. John Cassidy. (Illus.). 64p. (Orig.). 1985. pap. 12.95 incl. boomerang o.p. (ISBN 0-932592-07-4). Klutz Pr.

Boomerang Conspiracy. Michael Stanley. 1977. pap. 1.95 o.p. (ISBN 0-380-01803-9, 35535). Avon.

Boomerang: How to Throw, Catch, & Make It. Benjamin Ruhe & Eric Darnell. LC 85-40523. (Illus.). 96p. (Orig.). 1985. pap. 9.95 o.p. (ISBN 0-89480-935-0). Workman Pub.

Boomerang Hunter. Jim Kjelgaard. (YA) 1978. pap. 1.25 o.p. (ISBN 0-380-01911-6, 37408, Camelot). Avon.

Boomerang: The Works of Valentyn Moroz. Ed. by Yaroslav Bihun. LC 74-77633. 1974. 5.75 o.s.i. (ISBN 0-914834-00-2); soft-cover 3.75 o.s.i. Smoloskyp.

Boomkitchwatt. Don Hendrie, Jr. LC 72-88011. 269p. (Orig.). 1972. pap. 2.95 o.p. (ISBN 0-912528-04-4). John Muir.

Boots. David Lloyd. (First Words Ser.). (Illus.). 32p. (ps-2). 1983. 1.50 o.s.i. (ISBN 0-671-47106-6, Little Simon). S&S.

Boots the Kitten. Margaret S. Pursell. Tr. by Dyan Hammarberg from Fr. LC 76-1277. (Animal Friends Bks). (Illus.). 24p. (gr. k-4). 1976. PLB 5.95 o.p. (ISBN 0-87614-066-5). Carolrhoda Bks.

Booze Battle. Ruth Maxwell. 1986. pap. 3.50 o.p. (ISBN 0-345-33851-0). Ballantine.

Booze, Books & the Big Deuce. LC 78-60523. 1978. 4.95 o.p. (ISBN 0-932212-12-3). Avery Color.

Booze Who: Intoxicating Humour. Joel Rothman. (Illus.). 80p. 1985. pap. 2.95 o.p. (ISBN 0-86051-237-1). Parkwest Pubns.

Border. Douglas K. Hall. (Illus.). 252p. 1988. 35.00 o.p. (ISBN 0-89659-685-0). Abbeville Pr.

Border Boom Town: Ciudad Jaurez since 1848. Oscar J. Martinez. LC 77-26161. (Illus.). 263p. 1978. 18.50x o.p. (ISBN 0-292-70723-1). U of Tex Pr.

Border Crossings. Greg Pape. LC 77-15731. (Pitt Poetry Ser.). 1978. 15.95x o.p. (ISBN 0-8229-3369-1); pap. 6.95 o.p. (ISBN 0-8229-5289-0). U of Pittsburgh Pr.

Border Guns. John Durham. 1985. 12.95 o.p. (ISBN 0-317-53059-3, Large Print Bks). G K Hall.

Border Patrol. Clifford A. Perkins. Ed. by Nancy Dickey & C. L. Sonnichsen. 1978. 14.00 o.p. (ISBN 0-87404-058-2). Tex Western.

Border Riders. Robert Steelman. (Gunsmoke Western Ser.). 160p. 1988. text ed. 12.95 o.p. (ISBN 0-85997-858-3, Pub. by Firecrest Pub Ltd). Prescott Pr NH.

Border Security - Anti-Infiltration Operations FM 31-55. U. S. Army Staff. 68p. 1978. pap. 10.00 o.p. (ISBN 0-87364-121-3). Paladin Pr.

Border South States: People, Politics & Power in the Five States of the Border South. Neal R. Peirce. (Illus.). 1975. 12.95 o.p. (ISBN 0-393-05531-0). Norton.

Border Terrier. Anne Roslin-Williams. (Illus.). 211p. 1988. 22.95 o.p. (ISBN 0-85493-118-X, Pub. by Gollancz England). David & Charles.

Border War on Drugs. LC 87-619802. (OTA Ser.: No. 0-336). (Illus.). 70p. (Orig.). 1987. pap. 3.25 o.p. (ISBN 0-318-22879-3, S/N 052-003-01057-7). USGPO.

Borderland. Neil Claremon. 1976. pap. 1.75 o.p. (ISBN 0-380-00679-0, 29736). Avon.

Borderlands of Science. Alfred Still. (ISBN 0-8022-1648-X). Philos Lib.

Borderline Patient. Roy R. Grinker, Sr. & Beatrice Werble. LC 84-45089. 240p. 1983. 25.00x o.p. (ISBN 0-87668-676-5). Aronson.

Borderline Patient. Arlene R. Wolberg. LC 72-10235. 1982. 37.50 o.p. Thieme Med Pubs.

Bordo see Precipice.

Borgeois Anonymous. Date not set. (ISBN 0-8052-0754-6). Random.

Borges' Ultraist Movement & Its Poets. Thrope Running. 1982. 13.00x o.p. (ISBN 0-936968-03-6). Intl Bk Ctr.

Borgias. Marion Johnson. LC 80-29150. (Illus.). 224p. 1981. 19.95 o.p. (ISBN 0-03-059576-2). H Holt & Co.

Boris Pil'niak: A Soviet Writer in Conflict with the State. Vera T. Reck. 288p. 1975. 12.50x o.p. (ISBN 0-7735-0237-8, McGill Canada); pap. 6.00 o.p. (ISBN 0-7735-0248-3). U of Toronto Pr.

Boris Podrecca. Boris Podrecca & Wilfried Wang. LC 87-80604. (Illus.). 68p. 1987. pap. 15.00 o.p. (ISBN 0-8478-0836-X). Rizzoli Intl.

Bormann Receipt. Madelaine Duke. 1979. pap. 2.25 o.p. (ISBN 0-441-07095-7). Ace Bks.

Born Again & Growing. J. Kenneth Grider. 118p. 1982. pap. 3.50 o.p. (ISBN 0-8341-0758-9). Beacon Hill.

Born-Again Politics: The New Christian Right in America. Robert Zwier. (Illus.). 132p. 1982. pap. 4.95 o.p. (ISBN 0-87784-828-9). Inter-Varsity.

Born Again Radical. Don Benedict. LC 82-9100. 240p. (Orig.). 1982. pap. 7.95 o.p. (ISBN 0-8298-0371-8). Pilgrim NY.

Born Againism: Perspectives on a Movement. Eric W. Gritsch. LC 81-70595. 112p. 1982. pap. 1.95 o.p. (ISBN 0-8006-1625-1, 1-1625, Fortress). Augsburg Fortress.

Born Carpenter. Thom Roberts. LC 87-37191. 256p. 1988. 16.95 o.p. (ISBN 1-55584-071-X). Weidenfeld.

Born Early: The Story of a Premature Baby. Mary E. Avery & Georgia Litwack. (Illus.). 160p. 1983. 15.95 o.p. (ISBN 0-316-05865-3). Little.

Born Exile: George Gissing. Gillian Tindall. LC 74-6387. 304p. 1974. 10.00 o.p. (ISBN 0-15-113594-0). HarBraceJ.

Born for Battle. 3rd ed. R. Arthur Mathews. 1980. pap. 2.95 o.p. (ISBN 0-85363-143-3). OMF Bks.

Born in Sorrow: An Essay Concerning Human Nature. Gunars Berzins. 1984. 8.50 o.p. (ISBN 0-533-05830-9). Vantage.

Born into Eternity. George N. Snelling. 1978. 4.00 o.p. (ISBN 0-682-49217-5). Exposition-Phoenix.

Born of a Woman: Selected & New Poems. Etheridge Knight. 1980. 10.95 o.p. (ISBN 0-395-29199-2); pap. 5.95 o.p. (ISBN 0-395-29200-X). HM.

Born on the Circus. Fred Powledge. LC 76-2449. (Illus.). 96p. (gr. 5-6). 1976. 7.95 o.p. (ISBN 0-15-209970-0, HJ). HarBraceJ.

Born Out of Season. Melvin T. Chambers. 1978. 5.50 o.p. (ISBN 0-682-49063-6). Exposition-Phoenix.

Born Primitive in the Philippines. Severino N. Luna. Ed. & frwd. by Irene Murphy. LC 75-23290. (Illus.). 160p. 1975. 8.95x o.p. (ISBN 0-8093-0746-4). S Ill U Pr.

Born to Heal. Ruth Montgomery. 224p. 1985. pap. 3.50 o.p. (ISBN 0-449-20670-X). Fawcett.

Born to Live. T. C. Mann et al. LC 73-82091. 1973. 5.50 o.p. (ISBN 0-682-47761-3). Exposition-Phoenix.

Born to Pay: The New Politics of Aging in America. Phillip Longman. 1987. 17.45 o.s.i. (ISBN 0-395-38369-2). HM.

Born to Win: A Life-Long Struggle to Capture the America's Cup. John Bertrand. LC 85-5863. (Illus.). 385p. 1985. 19.95 o.p. (ISBN 0-688-04349-6, Pub. by Marine Bks). Morrow.

Born Too Soon. Robert Marion. LC 84-28682. 360p. 1985. 16.95 o.p. (ISBN 0-385-19833-7). Doubleday.

Borobudur: The Buddhist Monument of Java. D. Chihara. (Illus.). 1971. 80.00 o.s.i. (ISBN 0-685-79813-5). E J Brill USA.

Boron & Refractory Borides. Ed. by V. I. Matkovick. LC 77-5056. 1977. 120.00 o.p. (ISBN 0-387-08181-X). Springer-Verlag.

Boron Chemistry Four: Fourth International Meeting on Boron Chemistry, Salt Lake City & Snowbird, Utah, 8-13 July 1979. Robert W. Parry & Goji Kodama. (IUPAC Symposium Ser.). 150p. 1980. 85.00 o.p. (ISBN 0-08-025256-7). Pergamon.

Boron Chemistry-3. Ed. by Noth & H. North. 1977. 35.00 o.p. (ISBN 0-08-021206-9). Pergamon.

Boron in Steel: Proceedings of the TMS-AIME Fall Meeting Symposium, Milwaukee, WI, Sept. 16-20, 1979. TMS-AIME Fall Meeting Symposium Staff. Ed. by J. E. Morral & S. K. Banerji. LC 80-81828. (Proceedings). 215p. 1980. 10.00 o.p. (ISBN 0-89520-363-4). Minerals Metals.

Borromini's San Carlo Alle Quattro Fontane: A Study in Multiple Form & Architectural Symbolism. Leo Steinberg. LC 75-23815. (Outstanding Dissertations in the Fine Arts - 17th Century). (Illus.). 300p. 1976. lib. bdg. 50.00 o.p. (ISBN 0-8240-2008-1). Garland Pub.

Borrowed Water: A Book of American Haiku. Los Altos Writers Roundtable Staff. LC 66-26103. (Illus.). (gr. 9 up). 1966. 3.95 o.p. (ISBN 0-8048-0070-7). C E Tuttle.

Borrowing & Lending Technology: A World Bank Glossary. 64p. (Eng., Span. & Fr.). 1985. 8.50 o.p. (ISBN 0-8213-0365-1, BK 0365). World Bank.

Borrowing Money: A Reference Book of Math, Strategies & Information. 2nd ed. Roger Bennitt. 132p. 1987. pap. 15.00 o.p. (ISBN 0-934311-25-0). Intl Wealth.

Borzoi College Reader. 5th ed. Charles Muscatine & Marlene Griffith. 1983. pap. text ed. 13.00 o.p. (ISBN 0-394-33261-X, KnopfC). Knopf.

Bosch. Carl Linfert. LC 71-149853. (Library Great Painters). (Illus.). 136p. 1971. 45.00 o.p. (ISBN 0-8109-0043-2). Abrams.

Bosoms & Bras & Me. Twylla Witt. 1977. 4.50 o.p. (ISBN 0-682-48699-X). Exposition-Phoenix.

Bosporus Bridge. W. C. Brown et al. 96p. 1976. pap. 7.25x o.p. (ISBN 0-7277-0039-1, Pub. by T Telford UK). Am Soc Civil Eng.

Boss Cat. Kristin Hunter. (gr. 2-5). 1981. pap. 0.95 o.p. (ISBN 0-380-00196-9, 21873, Camelot). Avon.

Boss Nineteen Seventy-Six: Proceedings of an International Conference on the Behavior of Off-Shore Structures, Norwegian Institute of Technology, Trondheim, 2-5 August 1976. Ed. by J. Kuvas. LC 77-75338. 1977. pap. 245.00 o.p. (ISBN 0-08-021739-7). Pergamon.

Boss of Panamint. Leslie Ernenwein. 1975. pap. 0.95 o.p. (ISBN 0-685-59189-1, LB313, Pub. by Leisure Bks CT). Dorchester Pub Co.

Bosses & Reformers: Urban Politics in America, 1880-1920. Ed. by Blaine A. Brownell & Warren E. Stickle. LC 72-4798. (New Perspectives in History Ser.). 250p. (Orig.). 1973. pap. 9.50 o.p. (ISBN 0-395-14050-1, 3-41025). HM.

Boss's Encyclopedia. Boardroom's Experts & Editors. LC 83-2498. 600p. 1984. 60.00 o.p. (ISBN 0-932648-39-8). Boardroom.

Boston. Arthur S. Harris, Jr. LC 74-29557. (This Beautiful World Ser.: Vol. 53). (Illus.). 150p. 1975. pap. 4.95 o.p. (ISBN 0-87011-244-9). Kodansha.

Boston Adventure. Jean Stafford. LC 44-40176. 1944. 4.95 o.p. (ISBN 0-15-113610-6). HarBraceJ.

Boston Bay Mysteries & Other Tales. Edward R. Snow. LC 77-10901. (Illus.). 1977. bds. 8.95 o.s.i. (ISBN 0-396-07505-3). Dodd.

Boston Celtics. Dan Zadra. (NBA Today Ser.). (Illus.). 48p. (gr. 4 up). 1984. PLB 10.45 o.p. (ISBN 0-87191-971-0). Creative Ed.

Boston: City on a Hill. Andrew Buni & Alan Rogers. (Illus.). 240p. 1984. 24.95 o.s.i. (ISBN 0-89781-090-2). Windsor Pubns Inc.

Boston College High School: 1863-1983. David J. Loftus. LC 84-80029. (Illus.). 230p. (Orig.). 1984. 25.00 o.p. (ISBN 0-9611268-2-5, Pub. by A C Getchell). Quinlan Pr.

Boston Economy During the Civil War. Ed. by Frank Feidel & Ernest May. (Harvard Dissertations in American History & Political Science Ser.). 440p. 1989. lib. bdg. 75.00 o.p. (ISBN 0-8240-5144-0). Garland Pub.

Boston Furniture of the Eighteenth Century. Ed. by Walter M. Whitehill et al. LC 74-8139. 1974. 25.00x o.p. (ISBN 0-685-56093-7, Colonial Soc. of Massachusetts). U Pr of Va.

Boston Globe Cookbook. rev. ed. Margaret D. Murphy. Ed. by Gail Perrin. LC 81-82608. (Illus.). 326p. 1981. pap. 10.95 o.p. (ISBN 0-87106-048-5). Globe Pequot.

Boston Ice Cream Lover's Guide: A Heavenly Tour of over 55 of the Hub's Finest Ice Cream Shops. Yadin Kaufmann & Lori Kaufmann. LC 84-24555. (Illus.). 128p. 1985. pap. (ISBN 0-201-12690-7). Addison-Wesley.

Boston in Your Pocket. 2nd ed. (City in Your Pocket Ser.). 128p. 1983. pap. 2.50 o.p. (ISBN 0-8120-2694-2). Barron.

Boston, Nineteen Eighty-Seven to Nineteen Eighty-Eight. (Frommer's City Guides). 224p. 5.95 o.p. (ISBN 0-671-62354-0). Prentice Hall Pr.

Boston Picture Book. Barbara Westman & Herbert Kenny. LC 74-3079. 48p. 1974. 8.95 o.p. (ISBN 0-395-19336-2); pap. 2.95 o.p. (ISBN 0-395-20574-3). HM.

Boston Red Sox. Martin. LC 82-13977. (Baseball Today Ser.). 48p. (gr. 4 up). 1982. PLB 10.45 o.p. (ISBN 0-87191-854-4). Creative Ed.

Boston Red Sox: Seventy-Fifth Anniversary History, 1901-1975. Ellery H. Clark, Jr. LC 75-17066. (Illus.). 1975. 7.50 o.p. (ISBN 0-682-48317-6, Banner). Exposition-Phoenix.

Boston Sports Trivia. Bernard Corbett. LC 85-70069. (Illus.). 213p. (Orig.). 1985. pap. 7.95 o.s.i. (ISBN 0-933341-02-4). Quinlan Pr.

Boston Symphony Cookbook. Boston Symphony Orchestra Staff. 1983. 18.45 o.p. (ISBN 0-395-33118-8). HM.

Bostonians. Ed. by Alfred Habegger. 496p. 1976. pap. text ed. write for info. o.p. (ISBN 0-02-348560-4). Macmillan.

Boston's Immigrants. Oscar Handlin. LC 59-7653. (Illus.). 1968. pap. text ed. 3.25x o.p. (ISBN 0-689-70086-5, 118, Atheneum). Macmillan.

Boston's Locke-Ober Cafe. Ned Bradford & Pam Bradford. LC 77-15871. (Illus.). 1978. 12.95 o.p. (ISBN 0-689-10865-6, Atheneum). Macmillan.

Boswell in Extremes: 1776-1778. James Boswell. Ed. by Charles M. Weis & Frederick A. Pottle. 1970. text ed. 28.50 o.p. (ISBN 0-07-069059-6, P&RB). McGraw.

Botanical Bibliographies: Guide to Bibliographic Materials Applicable to Botany. L. H. Swift. 800p. 1974. Repr. of 1970 ed. lib. bdg. 132.00x o.p. (ISBN 3-87429-076-X). Lubrecht & Creamer.

Botanical Index to the Journal of Henry David Thoreau. Ray Angelo. 203p. 1984. pap. 12.95 o.p. (ISBN 0-87905-182-5). Gibbs Smith Pub.

Botanical Names for English Readers. Randal H. Alcock. LC 73-174935. 258p. 1971. Repr. of 1876 ed. 40.00x o.p. (ISBN 0-8103-3823-8). Gale.

Botanist at Bay. John Sherwood. 176p. 1985. 13.95 o.s.i. (ISBN 0-684-18432-X, ScribT). Scribner.

Botany: A Human Concern. David Rayle & Hale Wedberg. 1975. text ed. 18.40 o.p. (ISBN 0-395-20112-8). HM.

Both-And: A Balanced Apologetic. Ronald Mayers. 1984. pap. 11.95 o.p. (ISBN 0-8024-0226-7). Moody.

Bothie: The Text of 1848. Arthur H. Clough. Ed. by Patrick Scott. (Victorian Texts: No. 4). 1977. 19.95x o.p. (ISBN 0-7022-1153-2); pap. 10.95x o.p. (ISBN 0-7022-1163-X). U of Queensland Pr.

Botswana, Lesotho, Swaziland, Burundi, Equatorial Guinea, & Rwanda see Surveys of African Economies.

Bottgersteinzeug, Yixing, Und Andere Rote Ware. Neuwirth Waltraud. (Illus.). 407p. (Orig.). 1982. pap. 35.00 o.p. (ISBN 3-900282-20-X, Pub. by Waltraud Neuwirth). Seven Hills Bk Dists.

Bottle Book. Richard Fike. (Illus.). 256p. 1987. pap. 24.95 o.p. (ISBN 0-87905-218-X, Peregrine Smith). Gibbs Smith Pub.

Bottle Collector's Price List: For Embossed, Ink & Pontil-Scarred Bottles. Robert J. Ashton. LC 74-186480. 1972. 6.00 o.p. (ISBN 0-682-47442-8, Banner); pap. 3.95 o.p. (ISBN 0-682-47443-6). Exposition-Phoenix.

Bottle of Psychology. Donal Na Greine. (Illus.). 64p. 1981. 5.00 o.p. (ISBN 0-682-49679-0). Exposition-Phoenix.

Bottom Fishing. Frank Woolner & Henry Lyman. LC 84-1061. (Illus.). 128p. (Orig.). 1984. pap. 7.95 o.p. (ISBN 0-8329-0363-9). Lyons & Burford.

Bottom Line Issues in Retailing. Randy L. Allen. LC 83-45388. 204p. 1984. 16.95 o.s.i. (ISBN 0-8019-7410-0); pap. 12.50 o.p. Chilton.

Boubouroche, Lidoire et Potiron. Georges Courteline. 189p. 1964. 8.95 o.p. (ISBN 0-686-54628-8). French & Eur.

Boucher's Complete Paintings, 2 vols. Alexandre Ananoff. (Illus., Fr.). 1988. Set. 625.00 o.p. (ISBN 1-55660-012-7); Vol. 1, 415 p. Vol. 2, 366 p. A Wofsy Fine Arts.

Bought for a Dollar & Other Exciting Stories of China. Elsie B. Ezzo. 96p. 1969. pap. 1.25 o.p. (ISBN 0-88243-505-1, 02-0505). Gospel Pub.

Boulez. Joan Peyser. LC 76-20884. (Illus.). 1978. pap. 5.95 o.p. (ISBN 0-02-871810-0). Schirmer Bks.

Boulez. Joan Peyser. LC 76-20884. 1976. 12.95 o.p. (ISBN 0-02-871700-7). Schirmer Bks.

Bouncing Back: Finding Acceptance in the Face of Rejection. William Coleman. (Orig.). 1985. pap. 4.95 o.p. (ISBN 0-89081-455-4). Harvest Hse.

Bound by Love. Catherine Lanigan. 432p. 1981. pap. 2.95 o.p. (ISBN 0-380-79046-7, 79046-7). Avon.

Bound by Love: The Sweet Trap of Daughterhood. Lucy Gilbert & Paula Webster. LC 81-65760. 200p. 1983. 13.50 o.p. (ISBN 0-8070-3250-6); pap. 9.95 o.p. (ISBN 0-8070-6711-3, BP 658). Beacon Pr.

Bound for Success. Nancy Foreman. 1985. pap. 6.95 o.p. (ISBN 0-671-55547-2, Pub. by Fireside). S&S.

Bound over: Indentured Servitude & American Conscience. John Van der Zee. 1985. 18.45 o.p. (ISBN 0-671-54118-8). S&S.

Boundaries. Roberta Silman. 272p. 1982. pap. 2.95 o.p. (ISBN 0-380-59501-X, 59501-X, Flare). Avon.

Boundary Conditions & Global Management. Guido Loero. 1975. 45.50 o.p. (ISBN 0-12-455050-9). Acad Pr.

Boundary Element Method for Engineers. Carlos A. Brebbia. 189p. 1978. Repr. 43.00 o.p. (ISBN 0-931215-00-5). Computational Mech MA.

Boundary Element Methods in Engineering Science. P. K. Banerjee & R. Butterfield. 512p. 1981. text ed. 42.00 o.p. (ISBN 0-07-084120-9). McGraw.

Boundary Layer Climates. T. R. Oke. 1978. 39.95x o.p. (ISBN 0-416-70520-0, NO.6297); pap. 22.00x0 o.p. (ISBN 0-416-70530-8, NO.6298). Routledge Chapman & Hall.

Boundary Layer Research: Proceedings of the International Union of Theoretical & Applied Mechanics Symposium, Freiberg, 1957. International Union of Theoretical & Applied Mechanics Staff. Ed. by H. Goertler. (Illus.). 1957. 67.90 o.p. (ISBN 0-387-02273-2). Springer-Verlag.

Boundary Theory for Symmetric Markov Processes. M. L. Silverstein. (Lecture Notes in Mathematics: Vol. 516). 1976. pap. 20.00 o.p. (ISBN 0-387-07688-3). Springer-Verlag.

Boundary Waters Canoe Area: The Western Region, Vol. I. 3rd ed. Robert Beymer. LC 85-40197. (Illus.). 176p. 1985. pap. 9.95 o.p. (ISBN 0-89997-053-2). Wilderness Pr.

Boundless Horizons: Portrait of a Pioneer Woman Scientist. Icie G. Hoobler. (Illus.). 240p. 1982. 15.00 o.p. (ISBN 0-682-49834-3, Banner). Exposition-Phoenix.

Bountiful Bread: Basics to Brioches. Lynn Kutner. Ed. by Barbara Spiegel. LC 81-68840. (Great American Cooking Schools Ser.). (Illus.). 84p. 1982. pap. 5.95 o.p. (ISBN 0-941034-03-8). I Chalmers.

Bounty Guns. Luke Short. 1986. pap. 2.95 o.p. (ISBN 0-440-10758-X). Dell.

Bourbon Democracy in Alabama, 1874-1890. Allen J. Going. LC 71-141279. (Illus.). 256p. 1972. Repr. of 1951 ed. lib. bdg. 22.50x o.p. (ISBN 0-8371-5876-1, GOBD). Greenwood.

Bourgeois Gentilhomme see also Would-Be Gentleman.

Bourreau. Pierre Boulle. 208p. 1954. 9.95 o.p. (ISBN 0-686-54098-0). French & Eur.

Bovine Excrement. Ron Campbell. LC 84-91313. 51p. 1985. 6.95 o.p. (ISBN 0-533-06404-X). Vantage.

Bovine Medicine & Surgery, Vols. I & II. Ed. by H. E. Amstutz. LC 80-68110. (Illus.). 1272p. 1980. 39.50 o.p. (ISBN 0-939674-06-8). Am Vet Pubns.

Bovine Surgery: The Library of Veterinary Practice. Weaver. 1986. 9.50 o.p. (ISBN 0-8016-5361-4). Mosby.

Bow & Finger Magic. Gaylord Yost. 2.50 o.p. (ISBN 0-913650-56-0). CPP Belwin.

Bow & the Lyre: The Poem, The Poetic Revelation, Poetry & History. Octavio Paz. Tr. by Ruth L. Simms from Span. LC 73-3479. (Texas Pan American Ser). 293p. 1973. pap. 9.95 o.p. (ISBN 0-292-70709-6). U of Tex Pr.

Bow: Its History, Manufacture & Use. Henry Saint-George. (Strad Library: No. III). (Illus.). 144p. 1970. Repr. of 1896 ed. 12.50 o.p. (ISBN 0-8450-2582-1). Broude.

Bow Tie Book: Learn to Tie It, Wear It, Love It. Mario Sartori. 16p. 1986. pap. 5.95 o.p. (ISBN 0-671-62364-8, Fireside). S&S.

Bowdrie's Law. Louis L'Amour. LC 85-824. 1985. lib. bdg. 13.95 o.p. (ISBN 0-8161-3878-8, Large Print Bks). G K Hall.

Bowerman System. Chris Walsh. (Illus.). 72p. (Orig.). 1983. pap. 9.50 o.p. (ISBN 0-911521-07-0). Tafnews.

Bowhunting for Whitetail & Mule Deer. new ed. M. R. James. LC 73-20851. 224p. 1976. pap. 6.95 o.p. (ISBN 0-89149-019-1). Jolex.

Bowie. Jerry Hopkins. 320p. 1986. 9.95 o.p. (ISBN 0-02-060750-4, Collier). Macmillan.

Bowker Annual, 1987. Ed. by Margaret Spier. 800p. 1987. 89.95 o.p. (ISBN 0-8352-2333-7). Bowker.

Bowker-Bantam Complete Sourcebook of Personal Computing 1984. LC 83-15596. 750p. 1983. 24.95 o.p. (ISBN 0-8352-1767-1, Co-Pub. by Bantam). pap. 18.95 o.p. (ISBN 0-8352-1765-5, Co-Pub. by Bantam) (ISBN 0-553-34086-7). Bowker.

Bowker's Complete Sourcebook of Personal Computing 1985. 700p. 1984. pap. 19.95 o.p. (ISBN 0-8352-1931-3). Bowker.

Bowker's Law Books & Serials in Print, 1988, 3 vols. Ed. by Bowker, R. R., Staff. 3213p. 1988. 425.00 o.p. (ISBN 0-8352-2413-9). Bowker.

Bowl, Bama, Bowl. Al Browning. LC 77-91209. (College Sports Ser.). 1981. 10.95 o.p. (ISBN 0-87397-138-8). Strode.

Bowl of Saki. rev., 4th ed. Hazrat Inayat Khan. LC 78-65653. 128p. (Orig.). 1979. pap. 5.95 o.p. (ISBN 0-900217-12-X, Pub. by Sufi Pub Co England). Hunter Hse.

Bowling. Nelson Burton, Jr. Ed. by Jerry Levine. LC 72-94249. (Illus.). 1973. 6.95 o.p. (ISBN 0-689-10540-1, Atheneum). Macmillan.

Bowling. 3rd ed. Richard T. Mackey. LC 80-82563. (Illus.). 89p. 1980. pap. text ed. 6.95 o.p. (ISBN 0-87484-513-0). Mayfield Pub.

Bowling. 3rd ed. Carol Schunk. LC 75-19857. (Physical Activities Ser.). (Illus.). 106p. 1983. pap. text ed. 10.95 o.p. (ISBN 0-03-062447-9). H Holt & Co.

Box. Edward Albee. Bd. with Quotations from Chairman Mao Tse-Tung. LC 69-15501. 1969. 4.50 o.p. (ISBN 0-689-10007-8, Atheneum). Macmillan.

Box Two Hundred Four. Hilda A. Johnson. 1984. 11.95 o.p. (ISBN 0-533-05698-5). Vantage.

Box 44, Monrovia. Nona Freeman. Ed. by Mary H. Wallace. (Illus.). 224p. 1983. pap. 5.95 o.p. (ISBN 0-912315-09-1). Word Aflame.

Boxer. Anna K. Nicholas. (Illus.). 288p. 1984. text ed. 16.95 o.p. (ISBN 0-86622-028-3, PS-813). TFH Pubns.

Boxer Catastrophe. Chester C. Tan. 1971. pap. 2.25 o.p. (ISBN 0-393-00575-5, Norton Lib). Norton.

Boxful of Spirits: Adventures of a Film-Maker in Africa. Leslie Woodhead. (Illus.). 250p. 1989. 29.95 o.p. (ISBN 0-434-87788-3, Pub. by W Heinemann Ltd). David & Charles.

Boxing Dictionary. F. C. Avis. 128p. 1958. (ISBN 0-8022-0047-8). Philos Lib.

Boxing for Beginners. Jim Fitzgerald. LC 79-1989. (Illus.). 1980. 7.95 o.p. (ISBN 0-689-10991-1, Atheneum). Macmillan.

Boxing for Beginners. Jim Fitzgerald. LC 79-1989. (Illus.). 1983. pap. 6.95 o.p. (ISBN 0-689-70661-8, 304, Atheneum). Macmillan.

Boy Alone. Reginald Ottley. LC 66-11204. (Illus.). (gr. 4-7). 1966. 6.95 o.p. (ISBN 0-15-210682-0, HJ). HarBraceJ.

Boy & the Forest. Will & Nicolas. LC 64-11571. (Illus.). 40p. (gr. k-3). 1964. 4.95 o.p. (ISBN 0-15-210683-9, HJ). HarBraceJ.

Boy & the Otter. A. R. Lloyd. LC 84-27965. 1985. 14.95 o.p. (ISBN 0-03-004434-0). H Holt & Co.

Boy Friend. Jane Sorenson. (Jennifer Bks.). 144p. (gr. 5-8). 1985. 2.95 o.p. (ISBN 0-87239-931-1, 2981). Standard Pub.

Boy from Nowhere. Margaret Hinxman. (Lythway Ser.). 1987. lib. bdg. 17.50x o.p. (ISBN 0-7451-0609-9, Pub. by Chivers Pr UK). G K Hall.

Boy Had a Mother Who Bought Him a Hat. Karla Kuskin. (Illus.). 32p. (gr. k-3). 1976. 8.95 o.p. (ISBN 0-395-24740-3). HM.

Boy in the Forest. E. Shim. 146p. 1979. 4.95 o.p. (ISBN 0-8285-1572-7, Pub. by Progress Pubs USSR). Imported Pubns.

Boy Named Mary Jane, & Other Silly Verse. William Cole. (Illus.). 64p. (gr. 3-5). 1979. pap. 1.50 o.p. (ISBN 0-380-45955-8, 45955-8, Camelot). Avon.

Boy of the Islands. William Lipkind. LC 54-5154. (Illus.). (gr. 2-5). 1955. 5.95 o.p. (ISBN 0-15-211061-5, HJ). HarBraceJ.

Boy on Horseback. Lincoln Steffens. LC 35-27284. (Illus.). (gr. 7 up). 1935. 5.50 o.p. (ISBN 0-15-210882-3, HJ). HarBraceJ.

Boy on the Run. Bianca Bradbury. LC 74-22486. 128p. (gr. 3-6). 1979. 5.95 o.p. (ISBN 0-395-28848-7, Clarion). HM.

Boy Scouts: An American Adventure. Robert W. Peterson. LC 84-16748. (Illus.). 256p. 1985. pap. 12.95 o.p. (ISBN 0-8281-1174-X, Dist. by H M). Am Heritage.

Boy Soldier. John H. Hall. 64p. 1987. 6.95 o.p. (ISBN 0-8062-2980-2). Carlton.

Boy Thirteen: Reflections on Death. Jerry A. Irish. LC 74-22318. 1975. 3.95 o.s.i. (ISBN 0-664-20720-0, Westminster). Westminster John Knox.

Boy Who Could Find Anything. Joan L. Nixon. LC 77-15061. (gr. k-3). 1978. 5.95 o.p. (ISBN 0-15-210697-9, HJ). HarBraceJ.

Boy Who Could Find Anything. Joan L. Nixon. LC 77-15061. (Let Me Read Ser.). (Illus.). 64p. (ps-3). 1978. pap. 3.95 o.p. (ISBN 0-15-613748-6, VoyB). HarBraceJ.

Boy Who Could Fly. Robert Newman. (Illus.). 1976. pap. 1.25 o.p. (ISBN 0-380-00747-9, 53306-5, Camelot). Avon.

Boy Who Couldn't Talk. Lulu Hathaway. (Illus.). (gr. 3-8). 1968. pap. 1.75 o.p. (ISBN 0-377-14701-X). Friendship Pr.

Boy Who Cried Wolf. Katherine Evans. LC 60-8429. (Illus.). (gr. k-2). 1960. PLB 9.50 o.p. (ISBN 0-8075-0863-2). A Whitman.

Boy Who Drew Sheep. Anne Rockwell. LC 72-86948. 48p. (gr. 4-6). 1973. 4.50 o.p. (ISBN 0-689-30097-2, Atheneum). Macmillan.

Boy Who Picked the Bullets Up. Charles Nelson. 432p. 1982. pap. 3.95 o.p. (ISBN 0-380-60301-2, 69658). Avon.

Boy Who Sailed Round the World Alone. Robin Graham & Derek Gill. 192p. 1985. 8.95 o.p. (ISBN 0-8499-0477-3, 0477-3). Word Bks.

Boy Who Turned into a TV Set. Stephen Manes. (Illus.). 32p. (Orig.). (gr. 2-5). 1983. pap. 2.50 o.p. (ISBN 0-380-62000-6, Camelot). Avon.

Boy with a Harpoon. William Lipkind. LC 52-6911. (Illus.). (gr. 2-5). 1952. 4.50 o.p. (ISBN 0-15-210703-7, HJ); PLB 3.56 o.p. HarBraceJ.

Boy with a Pack. Stephen W. Meader. LC 39-27870. (Illus.). (gr. 7 up). 1939. 5.95 o.p. (ISBN 0-15-211240-5, HJ). HarBraceJ.

Boy with the Helium Head. Phyllis R. Naylor. LC 82-1807. (Illus.). 32p. (ps-3). 1982. 11.95 o.s.i. (ISBN 0-689-30934-1, Atheneum Childrens Bks). Macmillan.

Boy Without a Name. Penelope Lively. LC 74-28699. (Illus.). 48p. (gr. 3-6). 1975. 5.95 o.p. (ISBN 0-395-27679-9, Pub. by Parnassus); PLB 4.77 o.p. (ISBN 0-87466-069-6). HM.

Boyd's Introduction to the Study of Disease. 9th ed. Huntington Sheldon. LC 84-16385. (Illus.). 702p. 1984. text ed. 28.50 o.p. (ISBN 0-8121-0938-4). Lea & Febiger.

Boyhood on the Upper Mississippi: A Reminiscent Letter. Charles A. Lindbergh. LC 75-75804. 50p. 1972. 4.50 o.p. (ISBN 0-87351-069-0). Minn Hist.

Boys & Girls, Girls & Boys. Merrium. 1973. pap. 1.65 o.p. (ISBN 0-03-005716-7). H Holt & Co.

Boys & Sex. rev. ed. Wardell B. Pomeroy. LC 81-65499. 192p. (YA) (gr. 7 up). 1981. 12.95 o.p. (ISBN 0-385-28085-8). Delacorte.

Boys Behind the Bombs. Michael Parfit. 324p. 1983. 15.45i o.p. (ISBN 0-316-69057-0). Little.

Boys! Boys! Boys! Jan Gelman. (Follow Your Heart Romance Ser.). (Orig.). (gr. 5 up). 1983. pap. 1.95 o.p. (ISBN 0-671-52445-3). Archway.

Boys' Fashions Eighteen Eighty-Six to Nineteen-Five. Compiled by Donna H. Felger. (Chronicle for Costume Historians & Doll Costumers Ser.). (Illus.). 113p. (Orig.). 1984. pap. 10.95 o.s.i. (ISBN 0-87588-209-9, 2642). Hobby Hse.

Boys from Brazil. Ira Levin. 1978. pap. 1.95 o.p. (ISBN 0-440-10760-1). Dell.

Boys from Liverpool. Nicholas Schaffner. LC 79-25917. (Illus.). (gr. 6 up). 1980. 11.95 o.p. (ISBN 0-416-30661-6, NO.0176). Routledge Chapman & Hall.

Boys Have Feelings Too. Dale Carlson. LC 80-12895. (Illus.). 160p. (gr. 7 up). 1980. 9.95 o.p. (ISBN 0-689-30770-5, Atheneum). Macmillan.

Boys in the Backroom. Andrew Dallmeyer. 42p. 1983. pap. 5.95 o.p. (ISBN 0-907540-24-4, NO.3988). Routledge Chapman & Hall.

Boy's Life. Horrace Wade. (Illus.). 192p. 1986. 12.95 o.p. (ISBN 0-8059-3016-7). Dorrance.

Braby Commercial Directory, 1983. (ISBN 0-8002-3094-9). Intl Pubns Serv.

Braby's Natal Directory 1981. 79th ed. (Illus.). 1086p. pap. (ISBN 0-8002-2877-4). Intl Pubns Serv.

Braced Frameworks: An Introduction to the Theory of Structures. 2nd ed. E. W. Parkes. LC 74-10556. 1974. 36.00 o.p. (ISBN 0-08-018078-7); pap. 15.25 o.p. (ISBN 0-08-018077-9). Pergamon.

Bradbury's Book of Hallmarks. Rev. ed. Frederick Bradbury. 108p. (Orig.). pap. 5.50 o.p. (ISBN 0-901100-11-0, Pub by JW Northend England). Seven Hills Bk Dists.

Bradbury's Book of Hallmarks. rev. ed. Frederick Bradbury. (Illus.). 108p. (Orig.). 1985. pap. 6.50 o.p. (ISBN 0-911403-30-2, Pub. by J W Northend England). Seven Hills Bk Dists.

Bradford's History of Plymouth Plantation 1606-1646. Ed. by W. T. Davis. (Original Narratives Ser.). 436p. 1959. Repr. of 1908 ed. 21.50x o.p. (ISBN 0-686-63939-1). B&N Imports.

Bradley's Logic. Anthony Manser. LC 82-24407. 230p. 1983. text ed. 29.95x o.p. (ISBN 0-389-20379-3). B&N Imports.

Brady. Jean Fritz. (Illus.). (gr. 4-8). 1960. 7.95 o.p. (ISBN 0-698-20014-4, Coward). Putnam Pub Group.

Brady's Introduction to Medical Terminology. 2nd ed. Carol Lillis. LC 82-20681. (Illus.). 224p. 1983. pap. text ed. 18.50 o.p. (ISBN 0-89303-234-4). Appleton & Lange.

Braeswood Tapestry. Robyn Carr. 1984. 14.95 o.p. (ISBN 0-316-12975-5). Little.

Bragg Apple Cider Vinegar System. 35th, rev. ed. Paul C. Bragg & Patricia Bragg. LC 84-62772. pap. 3.95 o.p. (ISBN 0-87790-016-7). Health Sci.

Bragg Vegetarian Gourmet Recipes. 6th, rev. ed. Paul C. Bragg & Patricia Bragg. LC 74-15983. (Illus.). pap. 5.95 o.p. (ISBN 0-87790-030-2). Health Sci.

Brahms. Walter Niemann. Tr. by Catherine A. Phillips. LC 79-92028. (Illus.). Repr. of 1937 ed. lib. bdg. 25.00x o.p. (ISBN 0-8154-0310-0). Cooper Sq.

Brahms: Variations on a Theme of Haydn. Ed. by Donald M. McCorkle. (Critical Edition Ser.). 1976. pap. 3.95x o.p. (ISBN 0-393-09206-2). Norton.

Brahms's Choral Compositions & His Library of Early Music. Virginia Hancock. Ed. by George J. Buelow. LC 83-18322. (Studies in Musicology: No. 76). 238p. 1983. 42.95 o.p. (ISBN 0-8357-1496-9). UMI Res Pr.

Braided Lives. Marge Piercy. 480p. 1982. 15.95 o.s.i. (ISBN 0-671-43834-4). Summit Bks.

Brain: A User's Manual. The Diagram Group. LC 81-17942. (Illus.). 191p. 1982. 8.95 o.p. (ISBN 0-399-50622-5, Perigee). Putnam Pub Group.

Brain & Activation. Khomskaia. (National Library of Medicine). 380p. 1983. 105.00 o.p. (ISBN 0-08-025993-6). Pergamon.

Brain & Behavior Vol. III: Brain & Gonadal Function. Ed. by Roger A. Gorski & Richard E. Whalen. LC 65-27542. (UCLA Forum in Medical Sciences: No. 3). 1966. 75.00x o.p. (ISBN 0-520-00506-6). U of Cal Pr.

Brain & Behaviour: Proceedings of the 28th International Congress of Physiological Sciences, Budapest, 1980. Ed. by G. Adam et al. LC 80-42186. (Advances in Physiological Sciences Ser.: Vol. 17). (Illus.). 500p. 1981. 87.00 o.p. (ISBN 0-08-027338-6). Pergamon.

Brain & Behaviour: Psychobiology of Everyday Life. Frank Campbell & George Sinaer. (Illus.). 168p. 1980. text ed. 29.00 o.p. (ISBN 0-08-024788-1); pap. text ed. 14.75 o.p. (ISBN 0-08-024787-3). Pergamon.

Brain & Human Behavior. Ed. by A. G. Karczmar & John C. Eccles. LC 78-160592. (Illus.). 1972. 47.00 o.p. (ISBN 0-387-05331-X). Springer-Verlag.

Brain & Intelligence: A Quantitative Study of the Frontal Lobes. Ward C. Halstead. LC 47-2506. (Midway Reprint Ser). xiv, 206p. 1975. pap. text ed. 9.50x o.s.i. (ISBN 0-226-31454-5). U of Chicago Pr.

Brain & Learning: Directions in Early Childhood Education. Marlin Languis et al. LC 80-81273. (Illus.). 72p. (Orig.). 1980. pap. text ed. 2.00 o.p. (ISBN 0-912674-72-5, NAEYC #111). Natl Assn Child Ed.

Brain As a Computer. 2nd ed. F. H. George. 1973. 65.00 o.p. (ISBN 0-08-017022-6). Pergamon.

Brain, Behaviour, & Evolution. Ed. by David A. Oakley & H. C. Plotkin. (Psychology in Progress Ser.). 1979. 12.95x o.p. (ISBN 0-416-71260-6, NO.2350); pap. 14.95x o.p. (ISBN 0-416-71270-3, NO.2349). Routledge Chapman & Hall.

Brain Benders: A Study of the Effects of Isolation. Charles A. Brownfield. 1973. text ed. 6.50 o.p. (ISBN 0-682-47640-4, University); pap. 4.00 o.p. (ISBN 0-682-47643-9). Exposition-Phoenix.

Brain Biochemistry. 2nd ed. H. S. Bachelard. 1981. pap. 8.50 o.p. (ISBN 0-412-23470-X, NO.6490, Pub. by Chapman & Hall). Routledge Chapman & Hall.

Brain Changers: Scientists & the New Mind Control. Maya Pines. LC 73-8721. (Illus.). 1973. 10.00 o.p. (ISBN 0-15-113700-5). HarBraceJ.

Brain Death Criterion of Human Death. D. L. Stickel. (Illus.). 73p. 1982. pap. 23.00 o.p. (ISBN 0-08-025814-X). Pergamon.

Brain Development & Behavior. M. B. Sterman et al. 1971. 85.50 o.p. (ISBN 0-12-666350-5). Acad Pr.

Brain Drain & Income Taxation. Ed. by Jagdish Bhagwati. 1977. pap. text ed. 16.25 o.p. (ISBN 0-08-020600-X). Pergamon.

Brain Drain: Emigration & Return. William A. Glaser. LC 77-30576. (UNITAR Studies). 1978. 65.00 o.p. (ISBN 0-08-022419-9); pap. 80.00 o.p. (ISBN 0-08-022415-6). Pergamon.

Brain Edema. Marinus DeVlieger & Samuel A. DeLange. LC 80-22983. 190p. 1981. 42.95 o.p. (ISBN 0-471-04477-6, Pub. by John Wiley). Krieger.

Brain Edema, Pathophysiology & Therapy, Cerebello Pontine Angle Tumors, Diagnosis & Surgery: Proceedings of the Annual Meeting, 24th, 1973. Annual Meeting on Brain Edema Staff. Ed. by Schuermann et al. LC 73-14237. (Advances in Neurosurgery Ser.: Vol. 1). (Illus.). 400p. 1974. pap. 41.00 o.p. (ISBN 0-387-06486-9). Springer-Verlag.

Brain Electrolytes & Fluid Metabolism. Robert Katzman & Hanna Pappius. LC 72-77322. 419p. 1973. 36.50 o.p. (ISBN 0-683-04522-9, Pub. by W & W). Krieger.

Brain Energy Metabolism. Bo. K. Siesjo. LC 77-2666. 607p. 1978. 159.95 o.p. (ISBN 0-471-99515-0). Wiley.

Brain Function & Macromolecular Synthesis. B. Jakoubek. (Advanced Biochemistry Ser.). 156p. 1974. 16.50x o.p. (ISBN 0-85086-043-1, NO.2916, Pub. by Pion England). Routledge Chapman & Hall.

Brain Function Therapy. Graham E. Powell. 326p. 1981. 24.00x o.p. (ISBN 0-566-00315-5, 04112-2, Pub. by Gower Pub Co England). Lexington Bks.

Brain Games. Will Shortz. 1979. pap. 8.95 o.p. (ISBN 0-671-24719-0, Fireside). S&S.

Brain Games for Kids & Adults Using the Apple II, IIe, & IIc. Softsync, Inc. Staff et al. (Illus.). 256p. 1984. pap. 13.95 o.p. (ISBN 0-89303-362-6); diskette 20.00 o.p. (ISBN 0-89303-366-9). Brady Bks.

Brain Games, No. 2. Will Shortz. (Orig.). 1980. pap. 8.95 o.p. (ISBN 0-671-25073-6, Fireside). S&S.

Brain Hypoxia Pain: Proceedings of the Annual Meeting, Heidelberg, May 1-3, 1975. Annual Meeting of the Deutsche Gesellschaft Fuer Neurochirurgie Staff et al. Ed. by H. Penzholz & M. Brock. (Advances in Neurosurgery: Vol. 3). (Illus.). 480p. 1975. pap. 49.50 o.p. (ISBN 0-387-07466-X). Springer-Verlag.

Brain: In Wisdom, Loving & Hating. Kenneth Artiss. 1985. text ed. 39.50x o.p. (ISBN 0-8290-1362-8). Irvington.

Brain Mechanisms & Behaviour. J. R. Smythies. 1970. 35.00 o.p. (ISBN 0-12-653240-0). Acad Pr.

Brain Mechanisms in Mental Retardation: Based upon a Symposium. Ed. by Nathaniel A. Buchwald & Mary A. Brazier. (UCLA Forum in Medical Sciences Ser.: No. 18). 1975. 37.50 o.p. (ISBN 0-12-139050-0). Acad Pr.

Brain Mechanisms in Sensory Substitution. Ed. by Paul Bach-Y-Rita & C. C. Collins. 1972. 47.50 o.p. (ISBN 0-12-071040-4). Acad Pr.

Brain, Mind, & Behavior. Teyler. Ed. by Linda Chaput & Jim Mauer. 142p. 1984. 25.95 o.p.; study guide for telecourse 9.95 o.p. (ISBN 0-7167-1640-2); study guide 9.95 o.p.; telecourse instr's. manual 3.95 o.p. (ISBN 0-7167-1693-3); instr's manual 3.95 o.p. (ISBN 0-7167-1642-9). W H Freeman.

Brain Tumors in Children. Ed. by C. Di Rocco. (Journal: Child's Brain: Vol. 9, No. 3-4). (Illus.). 176p. 1982. pap. 62.75 o.p. (ISBN 3-8055-3529-5). S Karger.

Brainbooster: Your Guide to Rapid Learning & Remembering. Robert Finkel. (Illus.). 198p. 1983. 13.95 o.p. (ISBN 0-13-080895-4); pap. 6.95 o.p. (ISBN 0-13-080887-3). P-H.

Brainchild. John Saul. 490p. 1986. lib. bdg. 18.95 o.p. (ISBN 0-8161-4099-5, Large Print Bks); pap. 10.95 o.p. (ISBN 0-8161-4100-2, Large Print Bks). G K Hall.

Brainstem Organization of Interacting Behavioral Systems. Ed. by J. Weijnen. (Journal: Brain Behavior & Evolution: Vol. 25, No. 2-3). (Illus.). 94p. 1985. pap. 32.00 o.p. (ISBN 3-8055-4045-0). S Karger.

Brainwashing & the Cults: An Expose on Capturing the Human Mind. Paul A. Verdier. 1977. pap. 3.00 o.p. (ISBN 0-87980-357-6). Wilshire.

Bram Stoker Bedside Companion: Ten Stories by the Author of Dracula. Bram Stoker. Ed. by Charles Osborne. LC 72-7717. 1979. pap. 4.95 o.s.i. (ISBN 0-8008-0964-5). Taplinger.

Bram Stoker Bedside Companion: 10 Stories by the Author of Dracula. Ed. by Charles Osborne. LC 72-7717. 224p. 1973. 7.95 o.s.i. (ISBN 0-8008-0963-7). Taplinger.

Branch of California Redwood. William Oandasan. (Native American Ser.). 62p. 1980. pap. 5.00 o.s.i. (ISBN 0-935626-03-4). U Cal AISC.

Branch Rickey: A Biography. Murray Polner. LC 81-69142. (Illus.). 1982. 14.95 o.p. (ISBN 0-689-11254-8, Atheneum). Macmillan.

Branches. Frank Samperi. 1965. saddlestitched in wrappers 5.00 o.p. (ISBN 0-685-79041-X). Small Pr Dist.

Branchising: Proven Techniques for Rapid Company Expansion. David D. Seltz. LC 79-19549. (Illus.). 288p. 1980. text ed. 31.95 o.p. (ISBN 0-07-056215-6). McGraw.

Brand. Henrik Ibsen. Tr. by Michael Meyer from Norwegian. 112p. 1967. pap. 6.95 o.p. (ISBN 0-413-30900-2, NO.2987). Heinemann Ed.

Brand: A Version for the Stage. rev. 2nd ed. Henrik Ibsen & Geoffrey Hill. LC 81-16055. 160p. 1981. 15.00 o.p. (ISBN 0-8166-1002-9); pap. 8.95x o.p. (ISBN 0-8166-1005-3). U of Minn Pr.

Brand New Kitten. Sally Scott. LC 56-8355. (Illus.). (gr. 1-5). 1956. 4.95 o.p. (ISBN 0-15-211419-X, HJ). HarBraceJ.

Brand of the Damned. Jeffrey M. Wallmann. (Bronc: No. 1). 192p. 1982. pap. 1.95 o.s.i. (ISBN 0-8439-0983-8, Pub. by Leisure Bks CT). Dorchester Pub Co.

Branded Man. Luke Short. 1989. pap. 2.50 o.p. (ISBN 0-440-10785-7). Dell.

Branded Runaway. Zane Spencer & Jay Leech. LC 80-80. (Hiway Bk.: A High Interest-Low Reading Level Bk.). 90p. 1980. 8.95 o.p. (ISBN 0-664-32662-5, Westminster). Westminster John Knox.

Brandis on North Carolina Evidence: With 1986 Supplement, 2 vols. Henry Brandis, Jr. 1232p. 1982. 90.00x o.p. (ISBN 0-87215-447-5); Suppl. 1986. 30.00x o.p. (ISBN 0-87215-782-2). Michie Co.

Brandley's Search. Donna F. Crow. 192p. 1986. pap. 5.95 o.p. (ISBN 0-89693-511-6). Victor Bks.

Brandstetter & Others. Joseph Hansen. LC 84-23217. 235p. 1984. 12.95 o.s.i. (ISBN 0-88150-031-3). Countryman.

Brass Band Robbery. (Tales from Fern Hollow Ser.). (Illus.). 22p. (ps-1). 1985. 1.98 o.p. (ISBN 0-517-42790-7). Outlet Bk Co.

Brass Bed. Alexandra Marshall. LC 85-10172. 288p. 1986. 16.95 o.p. (ISBN 0-385-23294-2). Doubleday.

Brass Dragon. Marion Zimmer Bradley. 1980. pap. 2.25 o.s.i. (ISBN 0-441-07180-5). Ace Bks.

Brass Instruments: Their History & Development. Anthony Baines. 300p. 1981. 25.00 o.p. (ISBN 0-684-15229-0, ScribT); pap. 14.95 o.s.i. (ISBN 0-684-16668-2). Scribner.

Brass Ring. Bill Mauldin. 1972. 7.95 o.p. (ISBN 0-393-07463-3). Norton.
Brassey's Infantry Weapons of the World. 2nd ed. Ed. by J. I. Owen. 488p. 1979. 120.00 o.p. (ISBN 0-08-027013-1). Pergamon.
Brassica Crops & Wild Allies. Ed. by S. Tsunoda et al. 360p. 1980. 38.00x o.p. (ISBN 0-89955-211-0, Pub. by Japan Sci Soc Japan). Intl Spec Bk.
Bratislava Project: Some Cleft Palate Surgical Results. Ed. by Hughlett Morris. LC 77-17633. 192p. 1978. text ed. 17.00 o.p. (ISBN 0-87745-075-7). U of Iowa Pr.
Brauereien und Malzereien in Europa 1980 see Breweries & Malsters in Europe, 1980.
Brave Baby Elephant. Sesyle Joslin & Leonard Weisgard. LC 60-10245. (Illus.). (ps-1). 1960. 4.95 o.p. (ISBN 0-15-211598-6, HJ). HarBraceJ.
Brave Cowboy. Edward Abbey. 320p. 1982. pap. 2.95 o.p. (ISBN 0-380-58966-4, 64386-3). Avon.
Brave Cowboy. Joan W. Anglund. LC 59-5627. (Illus.). (ps-2). 1959. 6.95 o.p. (ISBN 0-15-211956-6, HJ). HarBraceJ.
Brave Little Computer. David Lyon. (Illus.). (ps-5). 1984. 5.95 o.s.i. (ISBN 0-671-52455-0, Little Simon). S&S.
Brave Little Steam Shovel. (gr. k-3). 1951. 0.79 o.p. (ISBN 0-8431-4142-5). Wonder.
Brave Men & Great Captains. R. E. Dupuy & T. N. Dupuy. LC 84-213299. (Illus.). 400p. 1984. Repr. of 1959 ed. text ed. 23.95 o.p. (ISBN 0-915979-03-9). Hero Books.
Brave New World. Aldous Huxley. 48p. (Orig.). 1988. pap. 9.95 o.p. (ISBN 1-55651-079-9); audiocassette tape incl. o.p. (ISBN 1-55651-080-2). Cram Cassettes.
Brave Soldier Janosh. Victor G. Ambrus. LC 66-8387. (gr. k-3). 1967. 5.50 o.p. (ISBN 0-15-211990-6, HJ). HarBraceJ.
Brave the Wild Wind. Johanna Lindsey. 1985. 14.95 o.p. (ISBN 0-317-53060-7, Large Print Bks). G K Hall.
Bravo Burning. Donald Tate. 256p. 1986. 15.95 o.s.i. (ISBN 0-684-18605-5). Scribner.
Bravo Marco. Pauline Priolo. LC 63-10141. (Illus.). 48p. (gr. 3-6). 1963. PLB 6.95 o.p. (ISBN 0-395-27654-3, Pub. by Parnassus). HM.
Brazil. Time-Life Books Editors. (Library of Nations Ser.). (Illus.). 160p. (YA) (gr. 7 up). 1987. 23.93 o.p. (ISBN 0-8094-5316-9). Time-Life.
Brazil. Errol L. Uys. 1986. 18.45 o.p. (ISBN 0-671-46028-5). S&S.
Brazil: An Interim Assessment of Rural Development Programs for the Northeast. 132p. 1983. 5.00 o.p. (ISBN 0-8213-0252-3, BK 0252). World Bank.
Brazil: Education in an Expanding Economy. Augustus F. Faust. LC 77-2635. (U. S. Department of Health, Education, & Welfare, Bulletin 1959: No. 13). 1977. Repr. of 1959 ed. lib. bdg. 35.00x o.p. (ISBN 0-8371-9558-6, FABR). Greenwood.
Brazil: Finance of Primary Education. 88p. 1986. 5.00 o.p. (ISBN 0-317-58515-0, BK 0843). World Bank.
Brazil, Industrial Policies & Manufactured Exports. World Bank Staff & M. Penalver. LC 83-12357. 1983. 15.00 o.p. (ISBN 0-8213-0156-X). World Bank.
Brazil, Portrait of Half a Continent. Thomas L. Smith. LC 73-138183. (Illus.). 466p. 1972. Repr. of 1951 ed. lib. bdg. 35.00x o.p. (ISBN 0-8371-5640-8, SMBR). Greenwood.
Breacadh. T. O'Maille. 146p. 1973. 15.00x o.p. (ISBN 0-7165-2237-3, BBA 02179, Pub. by Irish Academic Pr Ireland). Biblio Dist.
Breach of Faith: Fall of Richard Nixon. Theodore White. LC 74-20350. 1975. 10.95 o.p. (ISBN 0-689-10658-0, Atheneum). Macmillan.
Breach of Faith: The Fall of Richard Nixon. Theodore H. White. 476p. 1986. pap. 2.25 o.p. (ISBN 0-440-30780-5, LE). Dell.
Bread & Breakfast. Linda K. Bristow. LC 85-11416. (Illus.). 144p. (Orig.). 1985. pap. 7.95 o.p. (ISBN 0-89286-246-7, One Hund One Prods). Ortho.
Bread-&-Butter Indian. Anne Colver. (Illus.). (gr. 3-6). 1976. pap. 1.75 o.p. (ISBN 0-380-00699-5, 52092-3, Camelot). Avon.
Bread & Butter Journey. Anne Colver. (Illus.). 132p. (gr. 3-7). 1976. pap. 1.75 o.p. (ISBN 0-380-00708-8, 55715-0, Camelot). Avon.
Bread & Freedom, Man. J. Erskine Richmond. 1978. 4.50 o.p. (ISBN 0-682-49006-7). Exposition-Phoenix.
Bread & Roses. Richard Gambino. 464p. 1982. pap. 3.50 o.p. (ISBN 0-380-59014-X, 59014-X). Avon.
Bread & Water: Welfare & Prison Affluence. Harold S. Austin. 1981. 6.50 o.p. (ISBN 0-682-49140-3). Exposition-Phoenix.
Bread Book. Carolyn Meyer. LC 76-15973. (Illus.). (gr. 3-7). 1976. pap. 1.95 o.p. (ISBN 0-15-614070-5, VoyB). HarBraceJ.
Bread Book: All about Bread & How to Make It. Carolyn Meyer. LC 76-140780. (Illus.). (gr. 4-6). 1971. 6.95 o.p. (ISBN 0-15-212040-8, HJ). HarBraceJ.
Bread Game: Realities of Foundation Fundraising. Rev. ed. 150p. 1981. pap. 9.95 o.p. (ISBN 0-9606198-1-X). Volcano Pr.
Bread of Blessing, Cup of Hope. Michael E. Dixon. Ed. by Herbert H. Lambert. 144p. (Orig.). 1987. pap. 8.95 o.p. (ISBN 0-8272-0217-2). CBP.
Bread of Life. David E. Rosage. (Orig.). 1979. pap. 2.95 o.p. (ISBN 0-89283-067-0). Servant.
Bread of the Oppressed: An American Women's Experiences in War-Disrupted Countries from the Journal & Letters. Frances Berkeley Floore. LC 74-34513. 1975. 10.00 o.p. (ISBN 0-682-48247-1). Exposition-Phoenix.
Bread of Those Early Years. Heinrich Boll. Tr. by Leila Vennewitz from Ger. LC 76-17547. 1976. text ed. 7.95 o.p. (ISBN 0-07-006427-X). McGraw.
Bread, Peace & Liberty. J. Kreitman. 1981. pap. 3.50 o.p. (ISBN 0-87552-857-0). Presby & Reformed.
Bread Winners' Cookbook. Mel London. 1983. pap. 9.95 o.p. (ISBN 0-671-47051-5, Fireside). S&S.
Breads: Breads. Bon Appetit Magazine Editors. LC 85-9860. (Cooking with Bon Appetit Ser.). (Illus.). 144p. 1985. 12.95 o.p. (ISBN 0-89535-168-4). Knapp Pr.
Breads from Many Lands. Lois L. Sumption & Marguerite L. Ashbrook. (Illus.). 256p. 1982. pap. 3.95 o.p. (ISBN 0-486-24327-3). Dover.
Breads, Rolls, & Pastries. Ed. by Georgia Orcutt & Sandra Taylor. LC 81-50147. (Flavor of New England Ser.). (Illus.). 144p. 1981. pap. 8.95 o.p. (ISBN 0-911658-28-9). Yankee Bks.
Break a Leg Betsy Maybe. Lee Kingman. (gr. 7 up). 1976. 7.95 o.p. (ISBN 0-395-24741-1). HM.
Break Dance. Bonnie Nadell & John Small. LC 84-60989. (Illus.). 64p. (Orig.). 1984. lib. bdg. 12.90 o.p. (ISBN 0-89471-290-X); pap. 3.95 o.p. (ISBN 0-89471-288-8). Running Pr.
Break-Even Charts: Their Interpretation & Construction. Learning Systems Ltd. 1968. pap. text ed. 6.00 o.p. (ISBN 0-08-014050-5). Pergamon.
Break of Day. Colette. 1983. 13.00 o.p. (ISBN 0-8446-5981-9). Peter Smith.
Break-up of the Soviet Empire in Eastern Europe. Ghita Ionescu. LC 84-6709. 168p. 1984. Repr. of 1965 ed. lib. bdg. 35.00x o.p. (ISBN 0-313-24524-X, IOBS). Greenwood.
Breakdown & Restoration of Ecosystems. Ed. by M. W. Holdgate & M. J. Woodman. LC 77-18922. (NATO Conference Ser. I, Ecology: Vol. 3). 508p. 1978. 79.50x o.p. (ISBN 0-306-32803-8, Plenum Pr). Plenum Pub.
Breakdown of Capitalism: A History of the Idea in Western Marxism. F. R. Hansen. LC 84-17803. 224p. 1985. 29.95x o.p. (ISBN 0-7102-0015-3). Routledge Chapman & Hall.
Breakdown of Nations. Leopold Kohr. 264p. 1986. pap. 11.95 o.p. (ISBN 0-7102-0889-8). Routledge Chapman & Hall.
Breakfast. Tom Watson & Jenny Watson. LC 82-19944. (What the World Eats Ser.). (Illus.). 64p. (gr. 5 up). 1983. PLB 11.93 o.p. (ISBN 0-516-01856-6). Childrens.
Breakfast & Brunches. Bon Appetit Magazine Editors. LC 82-23308. (Cooking with Bon Appetit Ser.). (Illus.). 144p. 1984. 12.95 o.p. (ISBN 0-89535-115-3). Knapp Pr.
Breakfast by Molly. Ruth Radlauer. (Illus.). (ps-2). 1987. 8.95 o.s.i. (ISBN 0-13-081506-3). S&S.
Breakfast of Champions. Levick. 1986. pap. 5.95 o.p. (ISBN 0-89225-284-7). Gospel Advocate.
Breakfast with My Father. Ron Roy. (Illus.). 32p. (ps-3). 1980. 7.95 o.s.i. (ISBN 0-395-29430-4, Clarion). HM.
Breaking & Schooling Horses. H. Faudel-Phillips. 12.50x o.p. (ISBN 0-87556-237-X). Saifer.
Breaking Bread with the Hungry. Arthur Simon. LC 71-158999. (Venture Ser). (Orig.). 1971. pap. 2.50 o.p. (ISBN 0-8066-9464-5, 10-0857). Augsburg Fortress.
Breaking Communication Barriers with Roleplay. Todd Pinkerton. LC 75-32944. 1976. pap. 5.95 o.p. (ISBN 0-8042-1097-7, John Knox). Westminster John Knox.
Breaking into Prison: A Citizen Guide to Volunteer Action. Marie Buckley. LC 74-206. 192p. 1974. 10.95x o.p. (ISBN 0-8070-0876-1). Beacon Pr.
Breaking into Video. Marjorie Costello & Cynthia Katz. 1985. pap. 7.95 o.p. (ISBN 0-671-50994-2, Pub. by Fireside). S&S.
Breaking Open the Word of God: Resources for Using the Lectionary for Catechists in the RCIA (Cycle C) Ed. by Karen H. Powell & Joseph P. Sinwell. 192p. (Orig.). 1988. pap. 12.95 o.s.i. (ISBN 0-8091-2973-6). Paulist Pr.
Breaking Out: Feminist Consciousness & Feminist Research. Liz Stanley & Sue Wise. 192p. (Orig.). 1983. pap. 10.95x o.p. (ISBN 0-7100-9315-2). Routledge Chapman & Hall.
Breaking String. Date not set. (ISBN 0-8052-0716-3). Random.
Breaking the Bread of Revelation, Vol. 2. Brian K. McCallum. 85p. 1989. pap. text ed. 3.95 o.p. (ISBN 0-9620883-1-5). McCallum Ministries.
Breaking the Deadlock: A CNS Arms Control Proposal. 1987. write for info. o.p. Comm Natl Security.
Breaking the Poverty Cycle: Readings on Income Maintenance. Ed. by Richard L. Edwards. LC 72-6358. (Illus.). 111p. 1972. pap. text ed. 4.75x o.p. (ISBN 0-8422-0216-1). Irvington.
Breaking the Silence. Walter Laqueur & Richard Breitman. (Illus.). 307p. 1986. 17.45 o.p. (ISBN 0-671-54694-5). S&S.
Breaking Through. Bernard M. Bane. 63p. 1984. pap. 5.00 o.s.i. (ISBN 0-930924-18-5). BMB Pub Co.
Breakout in Angola. Major DaSilva. (Mercenary Ser.). 1977. pap. 1.25 o.s.i. (ISBN 0-8439-0437-2, LB437, Pub. by Leisure Bks CT). Dorchester Pub Co.
Breakpoints: Making Career Stages Work for You. Andrew Sherwood. LC 85-20602. 240p. 1986. 16.95 o.s.i. (ISBN 0-385-19952-X). Doubleday.
Breakthrough: From Reading to Writing. John Presley & William Dodd. LC 79-20526. 336p. (Orig.). 1980. pap. text ed. 15.95 o.s.i. (ISBN 0-03-048766-8, HoltC). HR&W.
Breakthroughs: Astonishing Advances in Your Lifetime in Medicine, Science, & Technology. Charles Panati. 1980. 12.95 o.p. (ISBN 0-395-28221-7). HM.
Breakway: Twenty-Eight Steps to a More Reflective Life. Mark Link. LC 67553. 144p. 1980. pap. 3.95 o.p. (ISBN 0-89505-050-1). Tabor Pub.
Breast Cancer. Rose Kushner. LC 75-17688. (Illus.). 400p. 1975. 10.00 o.p. (ISBN 0-15-122569-9). HarBraceJ.
Breast Cancer: A Woman's Handbook. Deborah Dewar. LC 83-70328. 178p. (Orig.). 1983. pap. 8.95 o.p. (ISBN 0-89708-114-5). And Bks.
Breast Cancer: Diagnosis & Treatment, Vol. 1. Ed. by Gianni Bonadonna. (Cancer Investigation & Management Ser.: 1-690). 347p. 1984. text ed. 40.00 o.p. (ISBN 0-471-90193-8, Dist. by A R Liss). Wiley.
Breast Cancer: Epidemiology, Endocrinology, Biochemistry & Pathobiology. Helmuth Vorherr. LC 79-26399. (Illus.). 504p. 1980. text ed. 45.00 o.p. (ISBN 0-8067-2031-X). Urban & S.
Breast Cancer: New Concepts in Etiology & Control. Ed. by Michael J. Brennan et al. 1980. 62.50 o.p. (ISBN 0-12-131150-3). Acad Pr.
Breast Feeding. Date not set. (ISBN 0-8052-3701-1). Random.
Breast Feeding & Food Policy in a Hungry World. Dana Raphael. LC 78-27683. 1979. 19.95 o.p. (ISBN 0-12-580950-6). Acad Pr.
Breast: Its Problems-Benign & Malignant-How to Deal with Them. Oliver Cope. 1978. 8.95 o.p. (ISBN 0-395-25709-3); pap. 3.95 o.p. (ISBN 0-395-27212-2). HM.
Breast: Morphology & Lactation. Helmuth Vorherr. 1974. 68.00 o.p. (ISBN 0-12-728050-2). Acad Pr.
Breast Self Examination & You. P. G. Nama et al. (Illus.). 40p. 1987. pap. 2.00 o.p. (ISBN 0-317-61780-X). Budlong.
Breastfeeding: A Guide for the Medical Profession. 3rd ed. Lawrence. 650p. 1988. 38.95 o.p. (ISBN 0-8016-2903-9). Mosby.
Breastfeeding: A Manual for Health Professionals. Victor A. LaCerva. 1981. pap. text ed. 16.50 o.p. (ISBN 0-87488-169-2). Med Exam.
Breastfeeding: A Problem-Solving Manual. Stephen Saunder. 1987. pap. 8.65 o.p. (ISBN 0-917634-24-1). Creative Infomatics.
Breastfeeding, Child Health & Child Spacing: Cross-Cultural Perspectives. Ed. by Valerie Hull & Mayling Simpson. LC 85-9688. 216p. 1985. 29.00 o.p. (ISBN 0-7099-3312-6, Pub. by Croom Helm Ltd). Routledge Chapman & Hall.
Breastfeeding: The Art of Mothering. Maurice Teitel et al. (Illus.). 48p. 1987. incl. video tape 39.95 o.p. (ISBN 0-9618860-0-5); video 39.95 o.p. (ISBN 0-9618860-2-1); pap. 5.95 o.p. Alive Prodns.
Breath & Name: The Initiation & Foundation Practices of Free Spiritual Life. Da Free John. LC 77-72993. 24.95 o.p. (ISBN 0-913922-29-3); pap. 5.95 o.p. (ISBN 0-913922-31-5). Dawn Horse Pr.
Breath of Clowns & Kings: Shakespeare's Early Comedies & Histories. Theodore Weiss. LC 70-124958. 1971. pap. text ed. 3.25x o.s.i. (ISBN 0-689-70516-6, 207, Atheneum). Macmillan.
Breath of Life. Ann Armstrong. 232p. (Orig.). 1987. pap. 7.95 o.p. (ISBN 0-563-20449-4, Pub. by BBC). Parkwest Pubns.
Breathing Tokens. Carl Sandburg. LC 77-85198. 192p. 1978. 8.95 o.s.i. (ISBN 0-15-114073-1). HarBraceJ.
Breathplay Approach to Whole Life Fitness. Ian Jackson. LC 85-29387. 192p. 1986. pap. 14.95 o.p. (ISBN 0-385-23320-5, Dolp). Doubleday.
Brecht Commentaries. Eric Bentley. 320p. 1981. pap. 9.50 o.p. (ISBN 0-394-17734-7, E743, Ever). Grove.
Brecht Commentaries. Eric Bentley. LC 86-29400. 320p. 1987. pap. 9.95 o.s.i. (ISBN 0-394-62373-8, BC). Grove.
Brecht in Context. John Willett. 1986. pap. 10.95 o.p. (ISBN 0-413-40960-0, 9882). Routledge Chapman & Hall.
Brecht in Exile. Bruce Cook. LC 82-2926. 240p. 1983. 17.95 o.p. (ISBN 0-03-060278-5). H Holt & Co.
Brecht: The Man & His Work. Martin Esslin. 400p. 1974. pap. 4.95 o.p. (ISBN 0-393-00754-5). Norton.
Breed of Horses. Moyra Williams. LC 75-134731. 1971. 55.00 o.p. (ISBN 0-08-007123-6). Pergamon.
Breeder's Guide for 1980. Thoroughbred Owners & Breeders Association Staff. 1981. 57.50 o.p. (ISBN 0-936032-41-3). Blood-Horse.
Breeding a Racehorse. Miles Napier. pap. 4.95 o.p. (ISBN 0-85131-224-1, BL6798, Dist. by Miller). S R Smith Sporting Bks.
Breeding a Racehorse. Miles Napier. (Illus.). 12.50 o.p. (ISBN 0-87556-602-2). Saifer.
Breeding Field Crops. 2nd ed. John M. Poehlman. (Illus.). 1979. 32.95 o.p. (ISBN 0-87055-328-3). AVI.
Breeding for Racing. John Hislop. 1976. 34.95 o.p. (ISBN 0-436-19701-4, Pub. by Secker & Warburg UK). David & Charles.
Breeding Purebred Cats. Anne S. Moore. 112p. (Orig.). 1981. pap. 9.95 o.p. (ISBN 0-939768-00-3). Abraxas Pub WA.
Breeze off the Ocean. Amii Lorin. (Candlelight Ecstasy Ser.: No. 22). 1987. pap. 2.25 o.s.i. (ISBN 0-440-10817-9). Dell.
Brema Brasses. Richard D. Buffum. LC 79-52206. (Illus.). 164p. 1981. 34.95x o.p. (ISBN 0-934542-00-7). Abracadabra Pr.
Brenda Chamberlain: Artist & Writer. Jill Piercey. 240p. 1988. 35.00 o.p. (ISBN 0-907476-89-9, Pub. by Poetry Wales Pr UK). Dufour.
Brendan Behan. Ulick O'Connor. 1973. pap. 1.95 o.p. (ISBN 0-394-17808-4, B372, BC). Grove.
Brendan Behan's New York. Brendan Behan. (Illus.). 1985. 16.45i o.p. (ISBN 0-316-08777-7); pap. 8.70i o.p. (ISBN 0-316-08774-2). Little.
Brent Riley Drawings: Segments I. Sarah Rogers-Lafferty. (Illus.). 1984. pap. 5.00 o.s.i. (ISBN 0-317-06063-5). Contemp Arts.
Breviate of British Diplomatic Blue Books, 1919-1939. Ed. by Robert Vogel. 474p. 1963. 16.50x o.p. (ISBN 0-7735-0005-7, McGill Canada). U of Toronto Pr.
Breviate of Parliamentary Papers 1900-1916. P. Ford & G. A. Ford. 520p. 1969. Repr. of 1957 ed. 45.00x o.p. (ISBN 0-7165-0575-4, Pub. by Irish Academic Pr Ireland). Biblio Dist.
Breviate of Parliamentary Papers 1917-1939. P. Ford & G. A. Ford. 624p. 1969. Repr. of 1951 ed. 45.00x o.p. (ISBN 0-7165-0576-2, Pub. by Irish Academic Pr Ireland). Biblio Dist.
Brevity, a Brilliance & Other Poems. Virginia H. Brunton. 1979. 5.00 o.p. (ISBN 0-682-49493-3). Exposition-Phoenix.
Breweries & Malsters in Europe, 1980. 69th ed. LC 46-33153. Orig. Title: Brauereien und Malzereien in Europa 1980. 610p. (Orig., Eng., Fr. & Ger.). (ISBN 3-8203-0034-1). Intl Pubns Serv.
Brewing Industry. K. H. Hawkins & C. L. Pass. 1979. text ed. 37.00x o.p. (ISBN 0-435-84399-0); pap. text ed. 11.95x o.p. (ISBN 0-435-84400-8). Gower Pub Co.
Brezhia. Terri Belmar. 128p. 1981. 7.00 o.p. (ISBN 0-682-49721-5). Exposition-Phoenix.
Brianna. Linda L. Bartell. 368p. 1986. pap. 3.50 o.p. (ISBN 0-380-75096-1). Avon.
Briargate, Colorado Springs, El Paso County, Colorado. (Panel Advisory Service Report Ser.). 70p. 1980. pap. 10.00 o.p. (ISBN 0-317-06744-3, BO9). Urban Land.
Briarpatch. Ross Thomas. LC 85-5814. 288p. 1984. 15.45 o.p. (ISBN 0-671-53008-9). S&S.
Briarpatch. Ross Thomas. LC 85-5814. (Large Print Books (General Ser.)). 1985. lib. bdg. 17.95 o.p. (ISBN 0-8161-3912-1). G K Hall.
Brice Marden, Marbles, Paintings & Drawings Text. Ed. by William Zimmer. LC 82-18879. (Illus.). 30p. (Orig.). 1982. pap. text ed. 10.50 o.p. (ISBN 0-938608-09-6). Pace Pubns.
Bricker's International Directory of University Executive Programs. 18th ed. LC 73-110249. 405p. 1986. 100.00x o.p. (ISBN 0-87866-553-6). Petersons Guides.
Bricker's International Directory of University Executive Programs. 19th ed. LC 73-110249. 416p. 1987. 110.00x o.p. (ISBN 0-87866-596-X). Petersons Guides.

Bridal Canopy. S. Y. Agnon. Tr. by I. M. Lask from Hebrew. LC 67-14955. 300p. 1967. pap. 8.95 o.p. (ISBN 0-8052-0182-3). Schocken.
Bridal Dress (A Romance from Modern India) Nipla Hasija. 144p. 1986. 8.95 o.p. (ISBN 0-8062-2990-X). Carlton.
Bridal Sweet. Sheila Burns, pseud. (Lythway Ser.). 248p. 1988. lib. bdg. 19.50x o.p. (ISBN 0-7451-0710-9, Pub. by Chivers Pr UK). G K Hall.
Bride. Vonda N. McIntyre. (Orig.). 1985. pap. 2.95 o.p. (ISBN 0-440-10801-2). Dell.
Bride for the Sahib & Other Stories. Khushwant Singh. 168p. 1967. pap. 3.00 o.s.i. (ISBN 0-88253-087-9). Ind-US Inc.
Bride Movie Storybook. Adapted by Jill Wolf. (Collector Sticker Bks.). (Illus.). 22p. (gr. 5-8). 1985. pap. 1.95 o.p. (ISBN 0-89954-384-7). Antioch Pub Co.
Bride of Lowther Fell. Margaret Forster. LC 80-69370. 1981. 11.95 o.p. (ISBN 0-689-11129-0, Atheneum). Macmillan.
Bride of the Machugh. Jan C. Speas. 1978. pap. 1.95 o.p. (ISBN 0-380-01825-X, 36152). Avon.
Bride to Bride Book: A Complete Wedding Planner for the Bride. Pamela A. Piljac. (Illus., Orig.). 1983. pap. 6.95 o.p. (ISBN 0-913339-00-8). Bryce Waterton Pubns.
Bride's Book. Catherine S. Zimmerman. 1985. 25.00 o.p. (ISBN 0-87795-704-5, Arbor Hse). Morrow.
Brideshead Benighted. Auberon Waugh. 1986. 16.95 o.p. (ISBN 0-316-92649-3). Little.
Bridesmaid Wears Track Shoes. Marilyn D. Anderson. 96p. (gr. 5-8). 1985. 2.25 o.s.i. (ISBN 0-87406-008-7). Willowisp Pr.
Bridge. Maggie Hemingway. LC 86-47689. 176p. 1987. 13.95 o.p. (ISBN 0-689-11849-X, Atheneum). Macmillan.
Bridge: A Cross Culture Reading Program, 5 vols. Gary Simpkins et al. LC 76-17216. 1977. Set. pap. text ed. 275.84 o.p. (ISBN 0-395-24917-1). HM.
Bridge: A Reference Guide. William Sachen. LC 84-48058. (Guides to the World We Live in Ser.). 180p. 1984. lib. bdg. 18.00 o.p. (ISBN 0-8240-9094-2). Garland Pub.
Bridge Across. Max Bolliger. (Illus.). 32p. 15.95 o.p. (ISBN 0-905478-72-X, Pub. by Century Hutchinson). David & Charles.
Bridge: An Introduction. Audrey Grant & The American Contract Bridge League Staff. 256p. (Orig.). 1988. pap. 9.95 o.p. (ISBN 0-937359-31-9). HDL Pubs.
Bridge at Arta: And Other Stories. J. I. Stewart. 182p. 1982. 14.95 o.p. (ISBN 0-393-01590-4). Norton.
Bridge at Remagen. Ken Hechler. 1978. pap. 1.95 o.s.i. (ISBN 0-345-27891-7). Ballantine.
Bridge Bearings. (National Cooperative Highway Research Program Synthesis of Highway Practice). 62p. 1977. 4.80 o.p. (ISBN 0-309-02542-7). Transport Res Bd.
Bridge Deck Analysis. A. R. Cusens & R. P. Pama. LC 74-3726. 278p. 1975. 69.95 o.p. (ISBN 0-471-18998-7, Pub. by Wiley-Interscience). Wiley.
Bridge Deck Behavior. Edmund C. Hambley. 1976. 45.00x o.p. (ISBN 0-412-13190-0, NO.6138, Pub. by Chapman & Hall). Routledge Chapman & Hall.
Bridge Decks: Corrosion, Cathodic Protection & Pavement Seals. (Transportation Research Report Ser.). 51p. 1976. 2.80 o.p. Transport Res Bd.
Bridge Design: Six Reports. (Transportation Research Report Ser.). 68p. 1974. 3.40 o.p. (ISBN 0-309-02350-5). Transport Res Bd.
Bridge Design, Testing & Evaluation. (Transportation Research Report Ser.). 83p. 1976. 3.60 o.p. (ISBN 0-309-02582-6). Transport Res Bd.
Bridge Engineering, Vol. 1. (Transportation Research Report Ser.). 270p. 1978. 13.80 o.p. (ISBN 0-309-02696-2). Transport Res Bd.
Bridge Engineering, Vol. 2. (Transportation Research Report Ser.). 260p. 1978. 13.40 o.p. (ISBN 0-309-02697-0). Transport Res Bd.
Bridge Humor. Edwin B. Kantar. 1977. pap. 5.00 o.p. (ISBN 0-87980-342-8). Wilshire.
Bridge of No Return: The Ordeal of the U. S. S. Pueblo. F. Carl Schumacher & George C. Wilson. LC 73-134578. 1971. 7.95 o.p. (ISBN 0-15-113880-X). HarBraceJ.
Bridge of San Luis Rey. Thornton Wilder. 1976. pap. 2.95 o.p. (ISBN 0-380-00589-1, 70010-7, Bard). Avon.
Bridge of Years. May Sarton. LC 76-162709. 1971. 11.95 o.p. (ISBN 0-393-08652-6). Norton.
Bridge of Years. May Sarton. (Large Print Bks (General Ser.)). 350p. 1986. lib. bdg. 16.95x o.p. (ISBN 0-8161-4084-7). G K Hall.
Bridge: The Mind of the Expert. H. W. Kelsey. 192p. 1981. 16.50 o.p. (ISBN 0-571-11710-4). Faber & Faber.
Bridge Through Time: A Memoir. Laila Said. LC 85-8036. 1985. 17.45 o.s.i. (ISBN 0-671-45426-9). Summit Bks.
Bridge to Blue Hill. Margaret L. Tenpas. LC 76-171067. (Illus.). (gr. k-4). 1972. PLB 5.95 o.p. (ISBN 0-87614-030-4). Carolrhoda Bks.
Bridge to Terabithia. Katherine Paterson. (Illus.). 144p. (gr. 10 up). 1979. pap. 2.50 o.p. (ISBN 0-380-43281-1, Camelot). Avon.
Bridge to the Stars: Our Ancient Cosmic Legacy. Luis E. Navia. 1977. 14.95 o.p. (ISBN 0-89529-004-9). Avery Pub.
Bridge Too Far. Cornelius Ryan. 1974. 14.95 o.p. (ISBN 0-671-21792-5). S&S.
Bridged Aromatic Compounds. B. H. Smith. (Organic Chemistry: Vol. 2). 1965. 89.50 o.p. (ISBN 0-12-650350-8). Acad Pr.
Bridges of the Bodymind. Jeanne Achterberg & Frank Lawlis. LC 80-16596. (Illus.). 1980. text ed. 9.75 o.p. (ISBN 0-918296-14-5). Inst Personality & Ability.
Bridges to Employment, Bk. III: Practices for Providing Follow-Through Services to Former Employment & Training Clients. Catherine King-Fitch. 103p. cancelled o.s.i. (ISBN 0-318-22045-8, RD224). Natl Ctr Res Voc Ed.
Bridges to Employment: Practices for Job Development, Placement & Follow-Through of Unemployed Youth for Vocational Education & Manpower Training, Bk. II. Marion T. Johnson et al. 133p. 1980. 8.25 o.p. (ISBN 0-318-22044-X, RD186). Natl Ctr Res Voc Ed.
Bridges to Employment: Recruitment & Counseling Practices for Disadvantaged, Unemployed, Out-of-School Youth in Vocational Programs, Bk. I. Patricia W. Winkfield et al. 61p. 1980. 3.80 o.p. (ISBN 0-318-22046-6, RD185). Natl Ctr Res Voc Ed.
Bridges to Hope. Alvin N. Rogness. LC 74-14182. 88p. (Orig.). 1975. pap. 1.95 o.p. (ISBN 0-8066-1464-1, 10-0875, Augsburg). Augsburg Fortress.
Bridges to Islam: A Christian Perspective on Folk Islam. Phil Parshall. 120p. 1983. pap. 6.95 o.p. (ISBN 0-8010-7081-3). Baker Bk.
Bridgestone Singles & Twins, 50-175cc. Ed. by Clymer Publications. (Illus.). 1967. pap. 3.50 o.p. (ISBN 0-89287-245-4, M301). Clymer Pub.
Bridging Global Barriers: Two New International Orders: NIEO, NWIO. Meheroo Jussawalla. Ed. by Paula Durbin. iii, 24p. (Orig.). 1981. pap. 1.00 o.p. (ISBN 0-86638-000-0). EW Ctr HI.
Bridging the Gap. Amalia Barnea & Aharon Barnea. Tr. by Amir Chava from Hebrew. 1988. 17.95 o.p. (ISBN 0-8021-1006-1). Grove.
Bridging the Gap: College Reading. 2nd ed. Brenda D. Smith. 1985. pap. text ed. (ISBN 0-673-18037-9). Scott F.
Bridging the Gap: Youth & Adults in the Church. Merton P. Strommen. LC 72-90266. (Study of Generations Paperback Ser.). 104p. 1973. pap. 2.95 o.p. (ISBN 0-8066-1313-0, 10-0900, Augsburg). Augsburg Fortress.
Bridging the Generation Gap. Stanley E. Sayers. 6.00 o.p. (ISBN 0-89225-201-4). Gospel Advocate.
Brief Algebra Review Manual: A Program for Self-Instruction. Mildred Reigh et al. (gr. 9 up). 1966. text ed. 25.95 o.p. (ISBN 0-07-051811-4); pap. text ed. 16.95 o.p. (ISBN 0-07-051807-6). McGraw.
Brief & Remarkable Narrative on the Life & Extreme Suffering of Barnabus Downs. facsimile ed. Barnabus Downs. 24p. 1972. pap. 2.95 o.p. (ISBN 0-940160-01-3). Parnassus Imprints.
Brief & True Report of the New Found Land of Virginia. facsimile ed. Thomas Harriot. (Illus.). Repr. of 1590 ed. 10.75 o.p. (ISBN 0-8446-4550-8). Peter Smith.
Brief Calculus & Its Applications. 3rd ed. Larry J. Goldstein et al. (Illus.). 448p. 1984. pap. text ed. (ISBN 0-13-111898-6). P-H.
Brief Course of Higher Mathematics. V. A. Kudryavtsev & B. P. Demidovich. 1981. 16.00 o.p. (ISBN 0-8285-1936-6, Pub. by Mir Pubs USSR). Imported Pubns.
Brief Dictionary of American Superstitions. Vergilius Ferm. 128p. (ISBN 0-8022-0486-4). Philos Lib.
Brief Handbook for Writers. James F. Howell & W. Dean Memering. 416p. 1985. pap. text ed. (ISBN 0-13-082025-3). P-H.
Brief Handbook of English. 2nd ed. Hulon Willis. 292p. 1981. pap. text ed. 8.75 o.p. (ISBN 0-15-505556-9, HC). HarBraceJ.
Brief Handbook of English. Hulon Willis & Enno Klammer. 1975. 8.95 o.p. (ISBN 0-15-505559-3, HC). HarbraceJ.
Brief Handbook of English: With Research Paper. Hulon Willis. LC 75-35324. (Orig.). 1975. pap. text ed. 8.95 o.p. (ISBN 0-15-505561-5, HC). HarBraceJ.
Brief History of Chinese & Japanese Civilizations. Conrad Schirokauer. (Illus.). 662p. (Orig.). 1978. pap. text ed. 21.00 net o.p. (ISBN 0-15-505570-4, HC). HarBraceJ.
Brief History of Psychology. rev. ed. Michael Wertheimer. LC 78-23555. 1979. pap. text ed. 16.95 o.p. (ISBN 0-03-047426-4, HoltC). HR&W.
Brief History of the Presbyterians. 3rd ed. Lefferts A. Loetscher. LC 78-1724. 206p. 1978. pap. 3.95 o.s.i. (ISBN 0-664-24197-2, Westminster). Westminster John Knox.
Brief History of the Western World. 4th ed. Thomas H. Greer. LC 76-29165. (Illus.). 597p. 1982. pap. text ed. 16.75 o.p. (ISBN 0-15-505571-2, HC). HarBraceJ.
Brief History of Western Man, 2 pts. 2nd ed. Thomas H. Greer. 1974. Set. pap. text ed. 16.95 o.p. (ISBN 0-15-505576-3, HC); Vol. 1 Through 1650. pap. text ed. 7.95 o.p. (ISBN 0-15-505577-1); Vol. 2 Since 1500. pap. text ed. 7.95 o.p. (ISBN 0-15-505578-X). HarBraceJ.
Brief History of Western Man. 3rd ed. Thomas H. Greer. 1977. 15.95 o.p. (ISBN 0-15-505581-X). HarbraceJ.
Brief Introduction to Linear Algebra. Stanley I. Grossman. 126p. 1984. pap. text ed. (ISBN 0-534-03495-0). Wadsworth Pub.
Brief Introduction to Speech. Donovan J. Ochs & Anthony C. Winkler. 231p. 1979. pap. text ed. 11.95 o.p. (ISBN 0-15-505583-6, HC). HarBraceJ.
Brief Lives. John Aubrey. 336p. 1979. 24.00 o.p. (ISBN 0-85115-182-5, Pub. by Boydell & Brewer). Longwood Pub Group.
Brief Outline on the Study of Theology. Friedrich Schleiermacher. Tr. by Terrence N. Tice. LC 66-10301. (Orig.). 1966. pap. 4.95 o.p. (ISBN 0-8042-0485-3, John Knox). Westminster John Knox.
Brief Psychotherapy in Medical & Health Practice. Albert Ellis & Eliot R. Abrahms. 224p. 1978. pap. 18.95 o.p. (ISBN 0-8261-2641-3). Springer Pub.
Brief Sketch of the Early History of the Catholic Church on the Island of New York. James R. Bayley. LC 77-359171. (Monograph Ser.: No. 29). 1973. Repr. of 1870 ed. 8.50x o.p. (ISBN 0-930060-09-1). US Cath Hist.
Brief Survey of the Bible. Sara M. Wright. 1958. pap. 5.95 o.p. (ISBN 0-87213-971-9). Loizeaux.
Briefe an Gail, Band 1. Paul Twitchell. Tr. by Eckankar Studiengruppe Munchen. (Illus.). 204p. (Orig., Ger.). 1981. pap. 6.95 o.p. (ISBN 0-914766-41-4, 0554). Illum Way Pub.
Briefe des Sokrates und der Sokratiker. Ioannes Sykoutres. Repr. of 1933 ed. 12.00 o.p. (ISBN 0-384-59300-3). Johnson Repr.
Briefe uber die Wahrscheinlichkeit. A. Renyi. (Science & Civilization Ser.: No. 25). 94p. (Ger.). 1969. 19.95x o.p. (ISBN 0-8176-0307-7). Birkhauser.
Briefing Book: President Reagan's Trip to Asia, Pt. 2. Asian Studies Center. 62p. 1984. pap. 2.00 o.p. (ISBN 0-317-47097-3). Heritage Found.
Briefing for a Descent into Hell. Doris Lessing. 1981. 4.95 o.p. (ISBN 0-394-74662-7). Knopf.
Brier Patch. Sean O'Cene. LC 84-90054. 243p. 1985. 13.95 o.p. (ISBN 0-533-06137-7). Vantage.
Brierfield: Plantation Home of Jefferson Davis. Frank E. Everett. LC 72-156351. 168p. 1979. Repr. of 1971 ed. text ed. 3.95 o.p. (ISBN 0-87805-002-7). U Pr of Miss.
Brigand. Edgar Wallace. 140p. 1985. pap. 6.95 o.p. (ISBN 0-86299-191-9, Pub. by A Sutton Pub England). Academy Chi Pubs.
Brigham Young & Me, Clarissa. Barbara Williams. LC 77-27721. (gr. 3-7). 1978. 6.95 o.p. (ISBN 0-385-14019-3); PLB write for info. o.p. (ISBN 0-385-14020-7). Doubleday.
Brigham Young University Journal of Legal Studies: Summary of Utah Family Law. 1980. 60.00 o.s.i. (ISBN 0-686-40306-1). BYU Clark Law.
Bright Blue Sky. Max Hennessy. LC 82-73019. 250p. 1983. 10.95 o.p. (ISBN 0-689-11352-8, Atheneum). Macmillan.
Bright Days. Madye L. Chastain. LC 52-10063. (Illus.). (gr. 4-7). 1952. 4.50 o.p. (ISBN 0-15-212135-8, HJ). HarBraceJ.
Bright Legacy: Portraits of Ten Outstanding Christian Women. Ann Spangler. 196p. 1985. pap. 6.95 o.p. (ISBN 0-89283-278-9, Pub. by Vine Books). Servant.
Bright Legacy: Portraits of Ten Outstanding Christian Women. Ed. by Ann Spangler. 204p. 1983. 10.95 o.p. (ISBN 0-89283-167-7, Pub. by Vine Bks). Servant.
Bright Lights: A Theatre Life. Marian Seldes. (Illus.). 1978. 9.95 o.p. (ISBN 0-395-26481-2). HM.
Bright Orange for the Shroud. John D. MacDonald. LC 85-17697. (Travis McGee Ser.). 1984. pap. 3.95 o.p. (ISBN 0-449-13358-3, GM). Fawcett.
Bright Orange for the Shroud. John D. MacDonald. 343p. 1985. lib. bdg. 14.95 o.p. (ISBN 0-8161-3979-2, Large Print Bks). G K Hall.
Bright River Trilogy. Annie Greene. 256p. 1985. 14.70 o.p. (ISBN 0-671-49815-0). S&S.
Bright-Shining Place. Cheryl P. Blackwood & Kathryn Slattery. (Epiphany Ser.). 240p. 1983. pap. 2.75 o.s.i. (ISBN 0-345-30698-8). Ballantine.
Brimstone & Treacle. Dennis Potter. 1981. 4.95 o.p. (ISBN 0-413-39470-0, NO.6471). Heinemann Ed.
Brindle Bear Telling the Time. J. Patience. (Illus.). (ps-1). 1985. 1.98 o.s.i. (ISBN 0-517-43880-1). Outlet Bk Co.
Bring Home the Ghost. K. Follis Cheatham. LC 80-7981. 325p. (gr. 7 up). 1980. 8.95 o.p. (ISBN 0-15-212485-3, HJ). HarBraceJ.
Bring Me a Unicorn: Diaries & Letters of Anne Morrow Lindbergh, 1922-1928. Anne M. Lindbergh. LC 71-182329. (Helen & Kurt Wolff Bk). 288p. 1972. 7.95 o.p. (ISBN 0-15-114180-0). HarBraceJ.
Bring on the Empty Horses. David Niven. 1983. pap. 1.95 o.p. (ISBN 0-440-10824-1). Dell.
Bring the Jubilee. Ward Moore. (Science Fiction Rediscovery Ser: Vol. 23). 1976. pap. 2.25 o.p. (ISBN 0-380-00756-8, 30361). Avon.
Bring Your Own Pictures. (Kodak Library of Creative Photography). 1988. 11.95 o.p. (ISBN 0-86706-230-4). Time-Life.
Bringing It Home. John Gehm. LC 84-12075. 304p. 1984. 14.95 o.p. (ISBN 0-914091-48-4). Chicago Review.
Bringing Up a Mentally Handicapped Child. Liz Thompson. 240p. (Orig.). 1987. pap. 9.99 o.p. (ISBN 0-7225-1253-8, Pub. by Thorsons (England)). Sterling.
Bringing up Puppies: A Child's Book of Dog Breeding & Care. Jane W. Levin & Mary M. Steiner. LC 58-9746. (Illus.). (gr. 3-7). 1958. 5.95 o.p. (ISBN 0-15-212493-4, HJ). HarBraceJ.
Brisbane: A Candid Biography. Oliver Carlson. LC 75-98829. Repr. of 1937 ed. lib. bdg. 35.00x o.p. (ISBN 0-8371-2980-X, CABR). Greenwood.
Brisbane Guide. 2nd ed. Sallyanne Atkinson. (Illus.). 126p. 1985. pap. 7.95 o.p. (ISBN 0-7022-1845-6). U of Queensland Pr.
Bristol Channel & Severn Estuary. Ed. by R. S. Glover. 48p. 1984. pap. 6.50 o.p. (ISBN 0-08-031423-6). Pergamon.
Bristol Fighter. J. M. Bruce. (Vintage Warbirds Ser.: No. 4). (Illus.). 64p. (Orig.). 1985. pap. 9.95 o.p. (ISBN 0-85368-704-8, Pub. by Arms & Armour). Sterling.
Bristol Murder see Heinemann Guided Readers.
Bristol Recipe Book: Over 150 Recipes from the Cancer Help Kitchen. Sadhya Rippon. (Illus.). 160p. 1987. pap. 8.95 o.p. (ISBN 0-7126-1518-0, Pub. by Century Hutchinson). David & Charles.
Britain. Nicole Swengle. (Pocket Guides). 1986. pap. 5.95 o.p. (ISBN 0-528-84843-7). Rand McNally.
Britain, a Future That Works. Bernard Nossiter. 1978. 9.95 o.p. (ISBN 0-395-27094-4). HM.
Britain: A World by Itself; Reflections on the Landscape by Eminent British Writers. John Fowles et al. LC 84-81453. (Illus.). 160p. 1984. 27.50 o.p. (ISBN 0-316-91776-1). Little.
Britain & Europe in the Seventeenth Century. James R. Jones. (Foundations of Modern History Ser.). 1966. pap. 3.95x o.p. (ISBN 0-393-09465-0, NortonC). Norton.
Britain & France Between Two Wars: Conflicting Strategies of Peace from Versailles to World War Two. Arnold Wolfers. 1966. pap. 5.95 o.p. (ISBN 0-393-00343-4, Norton Lib). Norton.
Britain & Ireland on Your Own. John Choco & Ronalyn Choco. LC 81-71884. (Illus.). 224p. 1982. 7.95 o.p. (ISBN 0-939596-01-6). Country Rd.
Britain & the EEC. Ed. by Roy Jenkins. 259p. 1984. 29.00x o.p. (ISBN 0-8448-1463-6, Pub. by Crane Russak & Co). Taylor & Francis.
Britain & the United States. W. E. Leuchtenburg et al. LC 80-670039. (Orig.). 1980. pap. text ed. 7.95x o.p. (ISBN 0-435-32527-2). Gower Pub Co.
Britain at Your Leisure. Date not set. (ISBN 0-86145-703-X, Pub. by Auto Assn England). Salem Hse Pubs.
Britain Between East & West: A Concerned Independence. John Burton et al. 172p. 1984. text ed. 32.95 o.p. (ISBN 0-566-00722-3). Gower Pub Co.
Britain by Train: The Complete Travel Guide to Rail Travel for Pleasure. rev. ed. Patrick Golding. (Illus.). 208p. (Orig.). 1987. pap. 8.95 o.p. (ISBN 0-09-948390-4, Pub. by Automobile Assn Brit). Salem Hse Pubs.
Britain Can Take It: The British Cinema in the Second World War. Anthony Aldgate & Jeffrey Richards. 305p. 1986. 34.95x o.p. (ISBN 0-631-13549-9). Basil Blackwell.
Britain: Country Lodging on a Budget. Date not set. (ISBN 1-86995-202-2). Salem Hse Pubs.

Britain, Europe & the World, 1850-1986: Illusions of Grandeur. Bernard Porter. 184p. 1983. 24.95x o.p. (ISBN 0-04-909011-9). Unwin Hyman.
Britain for Free. Date not set. (Pub. by Auto Assn England). Salem Hse Pubs.
Britain in Western Europe: WEU & the Atlantic Alliance. Royal Institute of International Affairs Staff. LC 78-2451. 1978. Repr. of 1956 ed. lib. bdg. 35.00x o.p. (ISBN 0-313-20348-2, RIBW). Greenwood.
Britain since Nineteen Forty-Five: A Political History. David Childs. 320p. 1984. pap. 12.95x o.p. (ISBN 0-416-36480-2, NO. 4058). Routledge Chapman & Hall.
Britain: The Queen, Cricket, Sherlock Holmes, & Other Things Indubitably British. Ed. by Norman Kolpas. (Illus.). 192p. 1987. 22.50 o.p. (ISBN 0-89471-534-8). Running Pr.
Britain Through the Nineteen Eighties. James Morrell. 1980. Vol. I, Framework & Issues, 320p. text ed. 187.25x set (sold as one only) o.p. (ISBN 0-566-02217-6). Vol. II, The Forecaster, 96 p. Gower Pub Co.
Britain's Bilateral Links with Western Europe. William Wallace. (Chatham House Papers). 128p. (Orig.). 1984. pap. 10.95x o.p. (ISBN 0-7102-0298-9). Routledge Chapman & Hall.
Britain's Black Population. Runnymede Trust Staff. 1981. text ed. 28.00x o.p. (ISBN 0-435-82781-2). Gower Pub Co.
Britain's Economic Prospects. Richard E. Caves et al. LC 68-31833. 510p. 1968. 24.95 o.p. (ISBN 0-8157-1322-3). Brookings.
Britain's First Warplanes. J. M. Bruce. (Illus.). 240p. 1988. 24.95 o.p. (ISBN 0-85368-852-4, Pub. by Arms & Armour). Sterling.
Britain's Imperial Air Routes: 1918-1939. Robin Higham. (Illus.). 407p. 1960. 15.00x o.p. (ISBN 0-89745-015-9). Sunflower U Pr.
Britannia, 4 vols. William Camden. (Illus.). Repr. of 1806 ed. Set. cancelled o.s.i. (ISBN 3-487-05492-2). Adlers Foreign Bks.
Britannia Illustrata. Leonard Knyff & Jan Kip. (English Heritage Ser.). (Illus.). 200p. 1987. Repr. of 1707 ed. 49.00 o.p. (ISBN 0-948285-00-1). Archival Facsimiles.
Britannica Atlas. William A. Cleveland. 1988. 89.00 o.p. (ISBN 0-85229-495-6). Ency Brit Ed.
Brite Shade. Martin J. Rosenblum & Steve Nelson-Raney. (Illus.). 40p. 1983. signed & numbered 6.00 o.p. (ISBN 0-89018-012-1). Lion Pub-Roar Rec.
British Academics. A. H. Halsey & M. A. Trow. LC 76-151285. 1971. 34.50x o.s.i. (ISBN 0-674-08210-9). Harvard U Pr.
British Aircraft Carrier. 3rd ed. Paul Beaver. (Illus.). 256p. 1987. 19.95 o.p. (ISBN 0-85059-877-X, Pub. by PSL P Stephens). Sterling.
British & American English since Nineteen Hundred. Eric Partridge & John W. Clark. 1951. (ISBN 0-8022-1277-8). Philos Lib.
British & Irish Architectural History: A Bibliography & Guide to Sources of Information. Ed. by Ruth Kamen. 224p. 1981. 78.50x o.s.i. (ISBN 0-89397-114-6). Nichols Pub.
British & the Grand Tour. Jeremy Black. LC 85-15005. 273p. 1985. 34.50 o.p. (ISBN 0-7099-3257-X, Pub. by Croom Helm Ltd). Routledge Chapman & Hall.
British Antislavery Eighteen Thirty-Three to Eighteen Seventy. Howard Temperley. LC 72-2902. (Illus.). xviii, 302p. 1972. 24.95x o.p. (ISBN 0-87249-268-0). U of SC Pr.
British Architects, Eighteen Forty to Nineteen Seventy-Six: A Guide to Information Sources. Ed. by Lawrence Wodehouse. LC 78-54116. (Art & Architecture Information Guide Ser.: Vol. 8). 376p. 1978. 68.00x o.p. (ISBN 0-8103-1393-6). Gale.
British Army Collar Badges - 1881 to Present. Colin Churchill & Ray Westlake. (Illus.). 68p. 1987. 14.95 o.p. (ISBN 0-85368-895-8, Pub. by Arms & Armour). Sterling.
British Army Fighting Vehicles, Nineteen Forty-Five to the Present. Simon Dunstan. (Tanks Illustrated Ser.: Vol. 12). 1984. pap. 9.95 o.p. (ISBN 0-85368-669-6, Arms & Armour Pr). Sterling.
British Army in Northern Ireland, 1969-Present. Michael Dewar. (Illus.). 272p. 1986. 29.95 o.p. (ISBN 0-85368-716-1, Pub. by Arms & Armour); pap. 9.95 o.p. (ISBN 0-85368-631-9). Sterling.
British Art & Design, Nineteen Hundred-Nineteen Sixty. Carol Hogben. (Illus.). 222p. (Orig.). 1984. pap. 14.95 o.p. (ISBN 0-905209-57-5, Pub. by Victoria & Albert Mus UK). Faber & Faber.
British Atomic Energy Research Establishment, 1946-1951. Harwell. 1952. (ISBN 0-8022-0689-1). Philos Lib.
British Aviation Colours of World War Two: The Official Camouflage, Colours & Markings of RAF Aircraft. (Illus.). 64p. 1987. 19.95 o.p. (ISBN 0-85368-271-2, Pub. by Arms & Armour). Sterling.
British Barbarians. Grant Allen. Ed. by Ian Fletcher & John Stokes. LC 76-20062. (Decadent Consciousness Ser.). 1978. lib. bdg. 46.00 o.p. (ISBN 0-8240-2751-5). Garland Pub.
British Biochemistry: Past & Present. Biochemical Society Symposium, 30th. Ed. by T. W. Goodwin. 1970. 42.50 o.p. (ISBN 0-12-289860-5). Acad Pr.
British Board of Film Censors: Film Censorship in Britain, 1896-1950. James C. Robertson. LC 85-403. 213p. 1985. 29.00 o.p. (ISBN 0-7099-2270-1, Pub. by Croom Helm Ltd). Routledge Chapman & Hall.
British Book Illustration Yesterday & Today, with Commentary. Malcolm C. Salaman. Ed. by Geoffrey Holme. LC 73-175758. (Illus.). viii, 184p. 1974. Repr. of 1923 ed. 51.00x o.p. (ISBN 0-8103-3977-3). Gale.
British Canals. 7th ed. Charles Hadfield. (Canals of the British Isles Ser.). (Illus.). 1985. pap. 20.95 o.p. (ISBN 0-7153-8569-0). David & Charles.
British Cities: An Analysis of Urban Change. Ed. by N. Spence et al. (Illus.). 1982. 53.00 o.p. (ISBN 0-08-028931-2, K120). Pergamon.
British Co-operative Movement in a Socialist Society. George D. Cole. LC 76-22523. 168p. 1976. Repr. of 1951 ed. lib. bdg. 35.00x o.p. (ISBN 0-8371-9002-9, COBCM). Greenwood.
British Columbia. Ed. by J. Lewis Robinson. (Studies in Canadian Geography). 1972. 10.00 o.p. (ISBN 0-8020-1922-6); pap. 6.00x o.p. (ISBN 0-8020-6162-1). U of Toronto Pr.
British Combat Vehicles Today. Simon Dunstan. (Tanks Illustrated Ser.: No. 23). (Illus.). 72p. (Orig.). 1987. pap. 9.95 o.p. (ISBN 0-85368-777-3, Pub. by Arms & Armour). Sterling.
British Computer Industry: Crisis & Development. Tim Kelly. 288p. 1987. 43.00 o.p. (ISBN 0-7099-3123-9, Pub. by Croom Helm UK). Routledge Chapman & Hall.
British Computer Industry: Crisis & Development. Tim Kelly. 288p. 1987. lib. bdg. 55.00x o.p. (ISBN 0-317-64429-7, Pub. by Croom Helm UK). Routledge Chapman & Hall.
British Conservatism, 1832-1914. Robert B. McDowell. LC 74-11987. 191p. 1974. Repr. of 1959 ed. lib. bdg. 22.50 o.p. (ISBN 0-8371-7708-1, MCBC). Greenwood.
British Constitution. Gerald P. Dartford. 1978. pap. text ed. 3.95x o.p. (ISBN 0-88334-107-7). Ind Sch Pr.
British County Maps: A Reference & Price Guide. Yasha Beresiner. (Illus.). 295p. 1983. 69.50 o.p. (ISBN 0-902028-97-9). Antique Collect.
British Cruisers in World War One. R. A. Burt. (Warships Illustrated Ser.: No. 12). (Illus.). 64p. (Orig.). 1988. pap. 9.95 o.p. (ISBN 0-85368-814-1, Pub. by Arms & Armour). Sterling.
British Deportees to America, Pt. 1: 1760-1763. Clifford N. Smith. (British-American Genealogical Research Monograph: No. 1). 97p. (Orig.). 1974. pap. 13.00 o.p. (ISBN 0-915162-25-3). Westland Pubns.
British Destroyers in World War II. R. A. Burt. (Warships Illustrated Ser.: No. 4). (Illus.). 64p. (Orig.). 1986. pap. 9.95 o.p. (ISBN 0-85368-748-X, Pub. by Arms & Armour). Sterling.
British Dissonance: Essays on Ten Contemporary Poets. A. Kingsley Weatherhead. LC 82-13559. 254p. 1983. text ed. 28.00x o.p. (ISBN 0-8262-0391-4). U of Mo Pr.
British Doctors at Home & Abroad. Brian Abel-Smith. 63p. 1964. pap. text ed. 3.75x o.p. (ISBN 0-7199-0929-5, Pub. by Bedford England). Gower Pub Co.
British Documents of the Origin of the War 1898-1914, Vols. 1-11. Great Britain, Foreign Office Staff. Ed. by G. P. Gooch & Harold Temperley. 1926-38. Set. 700.00 o.p. (ISBN 0-384-19770-1); Set. pap. 630.00 o.p. Johnson Repr.
British Dogmatism & French Pragmatism: Central-Local Policy Making in the Welfare State. Douglas E. Ashford. (New Local Government Ser.: No. 22). (Illus.). 432p. 1982. text ed. 49.95 o.p. (ISBN 0-04-352096-0). Unwin Hyman.
British Economic Performance 1880-1980. Ed. by Rex Pope & Bernard Hoyle. LC 84-29217. 214p. 1985. 22.50 o.p. (ISBN 0-7099-2061-X, Pub. by Croom Helm Ltd); pap. 12.00 o.p. (ISBN 0-7099-2077-6, Pub. by Groom Helm Ltd). Routledge Chapman & Hall.
British Elections. Geoffrey Alderman. 1978. 22.95 o.p. (ISBN 0-7134-0196-6, Pub. by Batsford England); pap. 14.95 o.p. David & Charles.
British Family Names. 2nd ed. Henry Barber. LC 68-17914. 304p. 1968. Repr. of 1903 ed. 34.00x o.p. (ISBN 0-8103-3109-8). Gale.
British Film Catalogue, 1895-1970: A Guide to Entertainment Films. Denis Gifford. LC 82-49222. (Cinema Classics Ser.). 900p. 1987. lib. bdg. 138.00 o.p. (ISBN 0-8240-5760-0). Garland Pub.
British Fishery at Newfoundland, 1634-1763. Ralph G. Lounsbury. LC 69-19217. viii, 398p. 1969. Repr. of 1934 ed. 37.50 o.p. (ISBN 0-208-00795-4, Archon). Shoe String.
British Foreign Policy: Some Relevant Documents, January, 1950 - April, 1955. Royal Institute of International Affairs Staff. LC 78-4467. 1978. Repr. of 1955 ed. lib. bdg. 35.00x o.p. (ISBN 0-313-20370-9, RIBF). Greenwood.
British Freshwater Bivalve Mollusca: Keys & Notes for the Identification of the Species. A. E. Ellis. (Volume in the Synopses of the British Fauna Ser.). 1978. pap. 12.00 o.p. (ISBN 0-12-236950-5). Acad Pr.
British Freshwater Rhizopoda & Heliozoa, 5 Vols. J. Cash & J. Hopkinson. 1905-21. Set. 92.00 o.p. (ISBN 0-384-07835-4). Johnson Repr.
British Furniture: 1880-1915. Pauline Agius. (Illus.). 195p. 1977. (ISBN 0-902028-76-6). Antique Collect.
British Further Education. A. J. Peters. 1967. 95.00 o.p. (ISBN 0-08-011893-3). Pergamon.
British Gardeners: A Biographical Dictionary. Ed. by Miles Hadfield et al. (Illus.). 320p. 1986. pap. 37.50 o.p. (ISBN 0-302-00594-3, Pub. by Zwemmer Bks UK). Sotheby Pubns.
British Government & Politics. 2nd ed. R. M. Punnett. 1971. pap. text ed. 5.25x o.p. (ISBN 0-393-09384-0). Norton.
British Graptolites. Gertrude L. Elles & Ethel M. Wood. 1901-1918. Set. pap. 72.00 o.p. (ISBN 0-384-14155-2). Johnson Repr.
British Humanities Index 1979. Library Association, London Staff. LC 63-24940. 744p. 1980. 190.00x o.s.i. (ISBN 0-85365-583-9). Intl Pubns Serv.
British Humanities Index, 1980. 19th ed. Ed. by Library Association, London Staff. LC 63-24940. 886p. 1981. 190.00x o.s.i. (ISBN 0-85365-744-0). Intl Pubns Serv.
British India & Tibet Seventeen Sixty-Six to Nineteen Hundred Ten. Rev. ed. Alastair Lamb. 400p. 1986. lib. bdg. 45.00 o.p. Routledge Chapman & Hall.
British Infantry of the Napoleonic Wars. Philip Haythornthwaite. (Illus.). 88p. 1988. 24.95 o.p. (ISBN 0-85368-890-7, Pub. by Arms & Armour). Sterling.
British Insurance Business 1547-1970: An Introduction & Guide to Historical Records in the United Kingdom. H. A. Cockerell & Edwin Green. 142p. 1976. 16.50 o.p. (ISBN 0-8419-5315-5). Holmes & Meier.
British Isles. 400p. 1987. 29.95 o.p. (ISBN 0-86283-556-9, Pub. by British Tours). Salem Hse Pubs.
British Isles. rev. ed. Vincent Malmstrom & Ruth Malmstrom. LC 77-83908. (World Cultures Ser). (Illus.). 164p. (gr. 6 up). 1978. text ed. 11.20 ea. 1-4 copies o.s.i. (ISBN 0-88296-173-X); text ed. 8.96 ea. 5 or more copies o.s.i.; tchrs'. guide 8.94 o.s.i. (ISBN 0-686-85953-7). Gateway Pr MI.
British Isles & Germany. rev. ed. Vincent H. Malmstrom et al. LC 77-83891. (World Cultures Ser.). (Illus.). 320p. (gr. 6 up). 1978. text ed. 12.43 ea. 1-4 copies o.s.i. (ISBN 0-88296-148-9); text ed. 9.94 ea. 5 or more copies o.s.i.; tchrs'. guide 8.94 o.s.i. (ISBN 0-686-85954-5). Gateway Pr MI.
British Labour & the War: Reconstruction for a New World. Paul U. Kellogg & Arthur Gleason. LC 70-147517. (Library of War & Peace; Labor, Socialism & War). 1972. lib. bdg. 46.00 o.p. (ISBN 0-8240-0306-3). Garland Pub.
British Labour Party: A Functioning Participatory Democracy. Harry B. Cole. 1977. pap. 7.75 o.p. (ISBN 0-08-021811-3). Pergamon.
British Labour Party: A Short History. rev. ed. Carl F. Brand. LC 73-85103. (Publications Ser.: No. 136). 424p. 1974. 13.95x o.p. (ISBN 0-8179-6361-8). Hoover Inst Pr.
British Labourer's Protector & Factory Child's Friend, Nos. 1-31. 1969. Repr. lib. bdg. 13.75x o.p. (ISBN 0-8371-9373-7, BP00). Greenwood.
British Librarianship & Information Science 1971-1975. Ed. by H. A. Whatley. 1977. 30.00 o.p. (ISBN 0-85365-099-3). Nichols Pub.
British Library History, Nineteen Seventy-Three to Nineteen Seventy-Six: A Bibliography. D. Keeling. 1979. 18.00 o.p. (ISBN 0-85365-781-5). Nichols Pub.
British Macroeconomic Policy Since 1940. Jim Tomlinson. LC 85-3748. 236p. 1985. 29.00 o.p. (ISBN 0-7099-2485-2, Pub. by Croom Helm Ltd); pap. 13.50 o.p. (ISBN 0-7099-2497-6, Pub. by Croom Helm Ltd). Routledge Chapman & Hall.
British Manufacturing Investment Overseas: Causes & Consequences. A. Silberston et al. LC 85-124. 192p. 1985. (ISBN 0-416-39490-6, 9554). Routledge Chapman & Hall.
British Mesozoic Fossils. 5th ed. C. P. Castell et al. (Illus.). vi, 207p. 1975. pap. 11.25x o.p. (Pub. by Brit Mus Nat Hist England). Sabbot-Natural Hist Bks.
British Military Administration of Occupied Territories in Africa During the Years of 1941-1947. Francis J. Rennell. 1970. Repr. of 1948 ed. lib. bdg. 35.00x o.p. (ISBN 0-8371-4319-5, REBM). Greenwood.
British Military Helicopters. John Everett-Heath. (Illus.). 224p. 1987. 29.95 o.p. (ISBN 0-85368-805-2, Pub. by Arms & Armour). Sterling.
British Military Longarms Eighteen Fifteen to Eighteen Sixty-Five. D. W. Bailey. (Illus.). 160p. 1987. 19.95 o.p. (ISBN 0-85368-835-4, Pub. by Arms & Armour). Sterling.
British Miniaturists. 1520-1860. Basil Long. (Illus.). 45.00x o.p. (ISBN 0-87556-209-4). Saifer.
British Monetary Experiments, 1650-1710. J. Keith Horsefield. LC 82-48189. (Gold, Money, Inflation & Deflation Ser.). 363p. 1983. lib. bdg. 44.00 o.p. (ISBN 0-8240-5241-2). Garland Pub.
British Moralists. Ed. by L. A. Selby-Bigge. 1986. lib. bdg. 45.00X o.p. (ISBN 0-935005-23-4); pap. text ed. 25.00X o.p. (ISBN 0-935005-24-2). Ibis Pub VA.
British Museum Is Falling Down. David Lodge. 192p. 1981. 25.95 o.p. (ISBN 0-436-25530-8, Pub. by Secker & Warburg UK). David & Charles.
British Museum, London. Lawrence Smith et al. LC 80-82645. (Oriental Ceramics Ser.: Vol. 5). (Illus.). 171p. 1981. 65.00 o.p. (ISBN 0-87011-444-1). Kodansha.
British Museum, London see Oriental Ceramics: The World's Great Collections.
British National Formulary, No. 8. 493p. 1984. pap. 14.00x o.p. (ISBN 0-8002-3873-7, Pub. by British Med Assoc UK). Taylor & Francis.
British Natural History Books from the Beginning to Nineteen Hundred: A Handlist. R. B. Freeman. LC 80-50228. 437p. 1980. 42.50 o.p. (ISBN 0-208-01790-9, Archon). Shoe String.
British Naval Air Power: Nineteen Forty-Five to the Present. Paul Beaver. (Warbirds Illustrated Ser.: No. 33). (Illus.). 68p. (Orig.). 1985. pap. 9.95 o.p. (ISBN 0-85368-710-2, Pub. by Arms & Armour). Sterling.
British New Towns: A Programme Without a Policy. Meryl Aldridge. (International Library of Sociology). (Illus.). 1979. 32.50x o.p. (ISBN 0-7100-0356-0). Routledge Chapman & Hall.
British Newspapers: A History & Guide for Collectors. Brian Lake. (Illus.). 213p. 1984. 21.00 o.s.i. (ISBN 0-900661-33-X, Pub. by Sheppard England). Seven Hills Bk Dists.
British Official Publications. 2nd ed. J. E. Pemberton. LC 73-16231. 328p. 1973. 18.00 o.p. (ISBN 0-08-017797-2). Pergamon.
British Official Publications: Sources of Information. Valerie J. Nurcombe. (Public Administration Ser.: P 1663). 16p. 1985. 2.25 o.p. (ISBN 0-89028-373-7). Vance Biblios.
British Offshore Oil & Gas Policy. Irving Kuczynski. LC 79-53210. (Outstanding Dissertations in Economics Ser.). 280p. 1982. lib. bdg. 36.00 o.p. (ISBN 0-8240-4059-7). Garland Pub.
British Opinions on the Protecting System see Journal of the Proceedings of the Friends of Domestic Industry: In General Convention Met at the City of New York, October 26, 1831.
British Opium Policy in China & India. David E. Owen. LC 68-8024. ix, 399p. 1968. Repr. of 1934 ed. 37.50 o.p. (ISBN 0-208-00676-1, Archon). Shoe String.
British Overseas Trade from 1700 to the 1930's. Werner Schlote. LC 75-40922. 181p. 1976. Repr. of 1952 ed. lib. bdg. 22.50x o.p. (ISBN 0-8371-8692-7, SCBO). Greenwood.
British-Owned Railways in Argentina: Their Effect on the Growth of Economic Nationalism, 1854-1948. Winthrop R. Wright. (Latin American Monographs: No. 34). 319p. 1974. 20.00x o.p. (ISBN 0-292-70710-X). U of Tex Pr.
British Parasitic Copepoda, 2 Vols in 1. T. Scott & A. Scott. Repr. of 1913 ed. 28.00 o.p. (ISBN 0-384-54470-3). Johnson Repr.
British Pharmacopoeia, 2 vols. 2nd ed. Ed. by Pharmaceutical Society of Great Britain Staff. 1980. 165.00 o.p. (ISBN 0-11-320688-7, Pub. by Pharmaceutical). Vol. 1, 540 Pg. Vol. 2, 680 Pg. Rittenhouse.
British Pharmacopoeia: 1982 Addendum. Pharmaceutical Society of Great Britain Staff. 207p. 1982. 26.00 o.p. (ISBN 0-11-320738-7). Rittenhouse.
British Poetry, Eighteen Eighty to Nineteen Twenty: Edwardian Voices. Ed. by Paul L. Wiley & Harold Orel. LC 73-79174. 1969. 39.50x o.p. (ISBN 0-89197-049-5); pap. text ed. 19.95x o.p. (ISBN 0-89197-050-9). Irvington.
British Policy in Palestine: Nineteen Seventeen to Nineteen Twenty-Two. John J. McTague, Jr. 286p. (Orig.). 1983. lib. bdg. 28.50 o.p. (ISBN 0-8191-2933-X); pap. text ed. 14.25 o.p. (ISBN 0-8191-2934-8). U Pr of Amer.

Titles

British Policy Towards Morocco in the Age of Palmerston, 1830-1865. Francis R. Flournoy. LC 74-106835. 1970. Repr. of 1935 ed. 35.00x o.p. (ISBN 0-8371-3457-9, FBP&, Pub. by Negro U Pr). Greenwood.
British Political Sociology Yearbook: Participation in Politics, Vol. 3. Ed. by Colin Crouch. 282p. 1977. 37.00 o.p. (ISBN 0-85664-242-8, Pub. by Croom Helm Ltd). Routledge Chapman & Hall.
British Popular Customs, Present & Past. Thomas F. Thiselton-Dyer. LC 67-23908. (Social History Reference Ser.). (Illus.). 524p. 1968. Repr. of 1876 ed. 34.00x o.p. (ISBN 0-8103-3261-2). Gale.
British Porcelain: An Illustrated Guide. Geoffrey A. Godden. (Illus.). 464p. 39.00 o.p. (ISBN 0-214-66851-7, NO.0221, Pub. by Barrie & Jenkins England). Routledge Chapman & Hall.
British Pottery: An Illustrated Guide. Geoffrey A. Godden. (Illus.). 416p. 1983. 50.00 o.s.i. (ISBN 0-8390-0317-X). Abner Schram Ltd.
British Radicalism & the French Revolution 1789-1815. H. T. Dickinson. (Historical Association Studies). 96p. 1985. pap. 8.95x o.p. (ISBN 0-631-13945-1). Basil Blackwell.
British Rail: The First Twenty-Five Years. Michael R. Bonavia. LC 80-68687. (Illus.). 208p. 1981. 22.95 o.p. (ISBN 0-7153-8002-8). David & Charles.
British Railway Journeys. Date not set. Salem Hse Pubs.
British Railway Wagons. Don Rowland. (Illus.). 160p. 1985. 42.95 o.p. (ISBN 0-7153-8183-0). David & Charles.
British Regional Development since WWI. Christopher M. Law. LC 81-16759. 272p. 1981. pap. 13.95 o.p. (ISBN 0-416-32310-3, NO. 3577). Routledge Chapman & Hall.
British Rifle Man. 386p. 25.00 o.p. (ISBN 0-947898-33-6). Kraus Repr.
British Rigid Airship, Nineteen Hundred Eight to Nineteen Thirty-One: A Study in Weapons Policy. Robin O. Higham. LC 75-26603. (Illus.). 426p. 1975. Repr. of 1961 ed. lib. bdg. 32.50x o.p. (ISBN 0-8371-8247-6, HIBR). Greenwood.
British Rivers. Ed. by John Lewin. (Illus.). 232p. 1983. pap. text ed. 27.95x o.p. (ISBN 0-04-551079-2). Unwin Hyman.
British Scientists. E. J. Holmyard. 1951. (ISBN 0-8022-0739-1). Philos Lib.
British Sculpture in the Twentieth Century. Sandy Nairne & Nicholas Serota. (Illus.). 264p. (Orig.). pap. 20.00 o.p. (ISBN 0-87663-861-2). Universe.
British Seagull Outboards Service-Repair 2-6 hp Handbook. Ed. by Jeff Robinson. (Illus.). pap. 9.00 o.p. (ISBN 0-89287-153-9, B660). Clymer Pub.
British Sign Language. Margaret Deuchar. (Language, Education & Society Ser.). (Illus.). 300p. (Orig.). 1984. 29.95x o.p. (ISBN 0-7100-9643-7). Routledge Chapman & Hall.
British Socialists: The Journey from Fantasy to Politics. Stanley Pierson. LC 78-25820. 1979. 29.50x o.s.i. (ISBN 0-674-08282-6). Harvard U Pr.
British Special Forces, Nineteen Forty-Five to the Present. James G. Shortt. (Uniforms Illustrated Ser.: No. 13). (Illus.). 72p. (Orig.). 1986. pap. 7.95 o.p. (ISBN 0-85368-785-4, Pub. by Arms & Armour). Sterling.
British Submarines in World War II. Paul J. Kemp. (Warships Illustrated Ser.: No. 11). (Illus.). 64p. (Orig.). 1988. pap. 9.95 o.p. (ISBN 0-85368-778-1, Pub. by Arms & Armour). Sterling.
British Technology Index, 1977. Ed. by Library Association, London Staff. LC 63-23735. 1978. 175.00x o.p. (ISBN 0-85365-561-8). Intl Pubns Serv.
British Technology Index, 1978. Ed. by Library Association, London Staff. LC 63-23735. 828p. (ISBN 0-85365-911-7). Intl Pubns Serv.
British Theatre: It's Repertory & Practice, 1100-1900 A.D. Ernest J. Burton. LC 77-22954. (Illus.). 1977. Repr. of 1960 ed. lib. bdg. 22.50x o.s.i. (ISBN 0-8371-9739-2, BUBT). Greenwood.
British Toy Figures 1900 to the Present. Norman Joplin. (Illus.). 68p. 1987. 14.95 o.p. (ISBN 0-85368-781-1, Pub. by Arms & Armour). Sterling.
British Trade & the Opening of China, Eighteen Hundred to Eighteen Forty-Two. Michael Greenberg. LC 78-20465. 1980. Repr. of 1951 ed. 21.45 o.s.i. (ISBN 0-88355-844-0). Hyperion Conn.
British Trade Unionism, 1750-1850: The Formative Years. Ed. by John Rule. 336p. (Orig.). 1988. pap. text ed. 17.95 o.p. (ISBN 0-582-49459-1). Longman.
British Trade Unions & the Problem of Change. Will Paynter. 1970. 6.00 o.p. (ISBN 0-7735-0095-2, McGill Canada). U of Toronto Pr.
British Trade Unions Today. C. Jenkins & J. E. Mortimer. 1965. 18.00 o.p. (ISBN 0-08-011169-6); pap. 35.00 o.p. (ISBN 0-08-011168-8). Pergamon.
British Trotskyism: Theory & Practice. John Callaghan. 250p. 1984. 49.95x o.p. (ISBN 0-85520-742-6). Basil Blackwell.
British Watercolours. rev. ed. Robin Reilly. (Letts Collectors' Guides Ser.). (Illus.). 80p. 1982. 9.95 o.p. (ISBN 0-85097-364-3, Pub. by C Letts Bks UK). Seven Hills Bk Dists.
British Watercolours: A Guide to Current Auction Prices up to 250 Pounds Sterling. Alex Pollock. (Illus.). 216p. 1987. pap. 19.95 o.p. (Pub. by Kevin Francis Pub Ltd England). Seven Hills Bk Dists.
British West Indies at Westminister, 1789-1823. Great Britain, Parliament Staff. LC 70-100306. 1954. 10.75 o.p. (ISBN 0-8371-3235-5, WII&, Pub. by Negro U Pr). Greenwood.
Briton, British, Britisher see Metaphor.
Britons in American Labor. Clifton K. Yearley, Jr. LC 73-13822. (Studies in Historical & Political Science Ser. 75: Ser. 75, No. 1). 332p. 1974. Repr. of 1957 ed. lib. bdg. 22.50x o.p. (ISBN 0-8371-7120-2, YEBA). Greenwood.
Britten's Old Clocks & Watches & Their Makers. 3rd ed. F. W. Britten. (Illus.). 1980. 59.50 o.p. Apollo.
Brittle Diabetes. Pickup. (Illus.). 324p. 1985. 54.95 o.p. (ISBN 0-632-01159-9, B39379). Mosby.
Broad Church. Charles M. Davies. Ed. by Robert L. Wolff. LC 75-1505. (Victorian Fiction Ser.). 1975. Repr. of 1875 ed. lib. bdg. 73.00 o.p. (ISBN 0-8240-1579-7). Garland Pub.
Broadcast-Cable Programming: Strategies & Practices. 2nd ed. Susan T. Eastman et al. 529p. 1985. text ed. (ISBN 0-534-03353-9). Wadsworth Pub.
Broadcast Journalism. Ed. by Marvin Barrett. LC 82-5067. 256p. 1982. 15.95 o.p. (ISBN 0-89696-160-5, Everest House Book). Dodd.
Broadcast News: Radio Journalism & an Introduction to Television. Mitchell Stephens. LC 79-23491. 301p. 1980. text ed. 22.95 o.p. (ISBN 0-03-022066-1, HoltC). HR&W.
Broadcasting & Society, Nineteen Eighteen to Nineteen Thirty-Nine. Mark Pegg. (Illus.). 363p. 1983. 29.25 o.p. (ISBN 0-7099-2039-3, Pub. by Croom Helm Ltd). Routledge Chapman & Hall.
Broadcasting Around the World. William E. McCavitt. 1985. 22.95 o.p. (ISBN 0-8306-9913-9, 1193). TAB Bks.
Broadcasting by Satellite. R. A. Buckland. 220p. 1986. pap. text ed. 190.00x o.p. (ISBN 0-86353-028-1, Pub. by Online). Gower Pub Co.
Broadcasting from Space. (Reports & Papers on Mass Communication: No. 60). 65p. (Orig.). 1970. pap. 5.00 o.p. (ISBN 92-3-100857-9, U60, UNESCO). UNIPUB.
Broadcasting in America. 3rd. ed. Sydney W. Head. LC 75-19534. (Illus.). 704p. 1976. text ed. 20.95 o.p. (ISBN 0-395-20644-8). HM.
Broadcasting in America. 4th ed. Sydney W. Head et al. LC 81-83274. 1982. text ed. 29.95 o.p. (ISBN 0-395-28657-3). HM.
Broadcasting in Mexico. L. A. De Noriega & F. Leach. (Case Studies on Broadcasting Systems). (Orig.). 1979. pap. 17.95x o.p. (ISBN 0-7100-0416-8). Routledge Chapman & Hall.
Broadcasting in the Netherlands. Kees Van Der Haak et al. (Case Studies on Broadcasting Systems). (Orig.). 1978. pap. 17.95x o.p. (ISBN 0-7100-8780-2). Routledge Chapman & Hall.
Broadcasting Pirates. A. Panfilov. 200p. 1981. pap. 4.80 o.p. (ISBN 0-8285-2020-8, Pub. by Progress Pubs USSR). Imported Pubns.
Broadcasting-Vision & Sound. D. Wilson. 1968. pap. text ed. 4.85 o.p. (ISBN 0-08-012849-1). Pergamon.
Broadman Comments. Donald F. Ackland. (Orig.). 1988. pap. 6.95 o.p. (ISBN 0-8054-1567-X). Broadman.
Broadman Comments, April-June 1988. Donald F. Ackland et al. (Orig.). 1988. pap. 2.95 o.p. (ISBN 0-8054-1562-9). Broadman.
Broadman Comments, April-June, 1989. Donald F. Ackland et al. (Orig.). 1989. pap. 3.50 o.p. (ISBN 0-8054-1572-6). Broadman.
Broadman Comments, January-March 1988. Donald F. Ackland et al. (Illus., Orig.). 1987. pap. 2.95 o.p. (ISBN 0-8054-1561-0). Broadman.
Broadman Comments, January-March 1989. Donald F. Ackland et al. (Orig.). 1988. pap. 3.50 o.p. (ISBN 0-8054-1571-8). Broadman.
Broadman Comments, July-September 1988. Donald Ackland et al. (Orig.). 1988. pap. 2.95 o.p. (ISBN 0-8054-1563-7). Broadman.
Broadman Comments, October-December 1988. Donald F. Ackland et al. (Orig.). 1988. pap. 2.95 o.p. (ISBN 0-8054-1564-5). Broadman.
Broadman Comments, 1987-88. Donald F. Ackland. (Orig.). 1987. pap. 5.95 o.p. (ISBN 0-8054-1558-0). Broadman.
Broadsides & Pratfalls. Herbert Kuhner. 1976. pap. 2.50 o.p. (ISBN 0-685-79252-8, Pub. by Menard Pr). Small Pr Dist.
Broadway Musicals: Show by Show. Stanley Green. LC 85-50892. (Illus.). 382p. 1985. 17.95 o.p. (ISBN 0-88188-375-1, Pub. by Leonard Bks). H Leonard Pub Corp.
Broadwood by Appointment: A History. David Wainwright. (Illus.). 360p. 1983. text ed. 30.00x o.p. (ISBN 0-87663-419-6). Universe.
Brocade. Jan Merlin. 400p. 1982. pap. 3.95 o.p. (ISBN 0-380-79939-1, 80408). Avon.
Brock the Balloonist. (Tales from Fern Hollow Ser.). (Illus.). 22p. (ps-1). 1985. 1.98 o.s.i. (ISBN 0-517-42788-5). Outlet Bk Co.
Broderie Anglaise. Violet Trefusis. Tr. by Barbara Bray. LC 85-8524. 144p. 1985. 13.95 o.p. (ISBN 0-15-114240-8). HarBraceJ.
Broken Acres. Joyce P. Beaman. LC 72-156457. (Illus.). 145p. (gr. 5-9). 1976. 2.98 o.p. (ISBN 0-910244-60-X). Blair.
Broken Bough: The Solution to the Riddle of Man. Edward Keating. LC 75-10982. 1975. 12.95 o.p. (ISBN 0-689-10679-3, Aethenum). Macmillan.
Broken Canoe: Conversations & Observations in Micronesia. Ann Nakano. LC 83-5829. (Illus.). 289p. 1984. 25.00x o.p. (ISBN 0-7022-1684-4). U of Queensland Pr.
Broken Family. Elizabeth Christman. 224p. 1982. pap. 2.75 o.p. (ISBN 0-380-59485-4, 59485). Avon.
Broken Heart. John Ford. Ed. by Brian Morris. (New Mermaid Ser.). 1976. pap. 2.95x o.p. (ISBN 0-393-90036-3). Norton.
Broken Place. Michael Shaara. 256p. 1984. pap. 2.95 o.p. (ISBN 0-380-68262-1, 68262). Avon.
Broken Promises: Four Chinese American Plays. David H. Hwang. 272p. 1983. pap. 3.95 o.p. (ISBN 0-380-81844-2, 81844-2, Bard). Avon.
Broken Promises, Mended Dreams: An Alcoholic Woman Fights for Her Life. Richard Meryman. 288p. 1984. 16.95 o.p. (ISBN 0-316-56784-1). Little.
Broken Star-the Warburgs of Altona: Their Life in Germany & Their Death in the Holocaust. Gertrude Wenzel. Orig. Title: Granny. (Illus.). 272p. 1981. 12.50 o.p. (ISBN 0-682-49694-4). Exposition-Phoenix.
Brokers of Morality: Thai Ethnic Adaptation in a Rural Malaysian Setting. Louis Golomb. LC 78-4141. (Asian Studies at Hawaii: No. 23). 1979. pap. text ed. 12.00x o.p. (ISBN 0-8248-0629-8). UH Pr.
Bronchial Hyperactivity. Ed. by John Morley. 1982. 33.00 o.p. (ISBN 0-12-506450-0). Acad Pr.
Bronchogenic Carcinoma. Omar M. Salazar et al. (Onclogic Division of Radiation Oncology Ser.: Vol. 13). (Illus.). 384p. 1981. pap. 135.00 o.p. (ISBN 0-08-027464-1). Pergamon.
Bronte Wilde. Fanny Howe. 1976. pap. 3.25 o.p. (ISBN 0-380-00548-4, 28464). Avon.
Brontes. Brian Wilks. LC 85-26716. (Illustrated Biographies Ser.). (Illus.). 144p. 1986. pap. 9.95 o.p. (ISBN 0-87226-013-5). P Bedrick Bks.
Bronze. Ed. by Tony Curtis. (Illus.). 1978. 2.00 o.p. (ISBN 0-902921-40-1). Apollo.
Bronze & Iron: Ancient Near Eastern Artifacts in the Metropolitan Museum of Art. Oscar W. Muscarella. (Illus.). 512p. 1989. 75.00 o.p. (ISBN 0-87099-525-1). Metro Mus Art.
Brook Farm Book: A Collection of First-Hand Accounts of the Community. Joel Myerson. LC 86-25811. (Garland Reference Library of the Humanities). 368p. 1987. lib. bdg. 49.00 o.p. (ISBN 0-8240-8507-8). Garland Pub.
Brook Kerith. George Moore. LC 74-92700. 1969. 7.95 o.p. (ISBN 0-87140-507-5). Liveright.
Brook to River, River to Sea. Bernice C. Heisler. LC 84-60341. 96p. 1984. 6.95 o.p. (ISBN 0-938232-40-1). Winston-Derek.
Brooklyn Museum Aramaic Papyri: New Documents of the Fifth Century B. C. from the Jewish Colony at Elephantine. Ed. by Emil G. Kraeling. LC 53-7777. (Illus.). 1969. Repr. of 1953 ed. 18.00 o.p. (ISBN 0-405-00873-2). Bklyn Mus.
Brooks Range Passage. David J. Cooper. (Illus.). 208p. 1982. 14.95 o.s.i. (ISBN 0-89886-061-X). Mountaineers.
Broom & Ashes. Beverly Zuckerman. 1979. 5.00 o.p. (ISBN 0-682-49413-5). Exposition-Phoenix.
Brother Artist: A Psychological Study of Thomas Mann's Fiction. James R. McWilliams. LC 82-20243. 428p. (Orig.). 1983. lib. bdg. 35.50 o.p. (ISBN 0-8191-2857-0); pap. text ed. 17.50 o.p. (ISBN 0-8191-2858-9). U Pr of Amer.
Brother Carl. Susan Sontag. LC 72-82949. (Illus.). 176p. 1974. 10.95 o.p. (ISBN 0-374-11700-4). FS&G.
Brother Gander's Rhymes for Adults & Precocious Children. C. J. Hess. 64p. 1987. 6.95 o.p. (ISBN 0-8062-2900-4). Carlton.
Brother Mack, the Frontier Preacher. Andrew J. McNemee. 153p. 1980. 12.00 o.s.i. (ISBN 0-87770-236-5); pap. 9.95 o.s.i. (ISBN 0-87770-253-5). Ye Galleon.
Brother Peter Ferraris. Alvin S. Manni. (Illus.). 1974. pap. 4.95 o.p. (ISBN 0-89944-027-4). Don Bosco Multimedia.
Brother Sunshine-Father Rain. William H. Brown. 64p. 1982. 6.95 o.p. (ISBN 0-682-49816-5). Exposition-Phoenix.
Brother Whale: A Pacific Whalewatcher's Log. Roy Nickerson. LC 76-30828. (Illus.). 160p. 1977. pap. 7.95 o.p. (ISBN 0-87701-423-X). Chronicle Bks.
Brother, Which Drummer. Robert M. Brown. LC 60-7426. 1960. 4.50 o.p. (ISBN 0-15-114423-0). HarBraceJ.
Brotherhood of the Rosy Cross. Arthur E. Waite. 10.00 o.p. (ISBN 0-8216-0169-5, Pub. by Univ Bks). Carol Pub Group.
Brotherly Love. William D. Blankenship. LC 80-70212. 1981. 12.95 o.p. (ISBN 0-87795-301-5, Arbor Hse). Morrow.
Brothers. Dean Hughes. LC 85-31208. 111p. (YA) (gr. 7-12). 1986. 7.95 o.s.i. (ISBN 0-87579-007-0). Deseret Bk.
Brothers & Friends: An Intimate Portrait of C. S. Lewis; the Diaries of Major Warren Hamilton Lewis. Ed. by Clyde S. Kilby & Marjorie L. Mead. LC 80-7756. (Illus.). 1982. 15.39 o.p. (ISBN 0-06-064575-X). HarpR.
Brothers & Keepers. John E. Wideman. LC 84-6582. 288p. 1984. 15.95 o.p. (ISBN 0-03-061754-5). H Holt & Co.
Brothers Ashkenazi. I. J. Singer. LC 80-66017. 1980. 14.95 o.p. (ISBN 0-689-11102-9, Atheneum). Macmillan.
Brothers Bent. C. Currey. 1968. pap. 18.00x o.p. (ISBN 0-424-05700-X, Pub. by Sydney U Pr). Intl Spec Bk.
Brothers by Choice. Elfreida Read. LC 73-21858. 160p. (gr. 7 up). 1974. 6.95 o.p. (ISBN 0-374-30996-5). FS&G.
Brothers Menaechmus see also Menaechmi.
Brothers of the Bible. James A. Auchmuty, Jr. LC 84-17510. 1985. pap. 4.50 o.p. (ISBN 0-8054-2254-4). Broadman.
Brothers Powys. Richard P. Graves. (Illus.). 384p. 1983. 29.50 o.s.i. (ISBN 0-684-17880-X, ScribT). Scribner.
Brothers Reuther & the Story of the U.A.W. A Memoir. Victor G. Reuther. 1976. 16.95 o.p. (ISBN 0-395-24304-1). HM.
Brothers Reuther & the Story of the U.A.W. A Memoir. Victor G. Reuther. 1979. pap. 8.95 o.p. (ISBN 0-395-27515-6). HM.
Brothers System for Liberated Love & Marriage. Joyce Brothers. 1973. pap. 1.50 o.p. (ISBN 0-380-01073-9, 15834). Avon.
Brothers' War: Biafra & Nigeria. John De St. Jorre. 1972. 10.00 o.p. (ISBN 0-395-13934-1). HM.
Brothers Wrong & Wrong Again. Louis Phillips. LC 79-11737. (Illus.). (gr. k-4). 1979. text ed. 9.95 o.p. (ISBN 0-07-049805-9). McGraw.
Brown Bear in a Brown Chair. Irina Hale. LC 82-16244. (Illus.). 32p. (ps-3). 1983. 9.95 o.s.i. (ISBN 0-689-50267-2, M K McElderry). Macmillan.
Brown Rot Fungi of Fruit: Their Biology & Control. R. J. Byrde & H. J. Willetts. 1977. 21.00 o.p. (ISBN 0-08-019740-X). Pergamon.
Brown Sugar & Health. I. I. Brekhman & I. F. Nesterenko. (Illus.). 104p. 1982. 29.00 o.p. (ISBN 0-08-026837-4). Pergamon.
Brownies: Their Book. Palmer Cox. (Illus.). 144p. (gr. 2-6). 1887. pap. 4.95 o.p. (ISBN 0-486-21265-3). Dover.
Browning. Ed. by Patricia Machin. (Pocket Poets Ser.). (Illus.). 52p. 1985. 4.95 o.p. (ISBN 0-86350-048-X). Salem Hse Pubs.
Browning Hi-Power Exotic Weapons System. (Illus.). 72p. (Orig.). 1985. pap. 15.00 o.p. (ISBN 0-87364-316-X). Paladin Pr.
Browning: Plain Texts of the Poets. Robert Browning. 1968. pap. 2.50x o.p. (ISBN 0-7022-0630-X). U of Queensland Pr.
Browns Index to Photocomposition Typography. Bruce Brown. 320p. 1985. 14.95 o.s.i. (ISBN 0-935603-02-6). Rockport Pubs.
Brown's Lawsuit Cookbook: How to Sue & Win. M. H. Brown. 1986. lib. bdg. 79.95 o.p. (ISBN 0-8490-3809-X). Gordon Pr.
Brownsville Raid. John D. Weaver. LC 73-119697. (Illus.). 1970. 7.95 o.p. (ISBN 0-393-05422-5). Norton.
Brownsville Raid. John D. Weaver. 336p. 1973. pap. 2.45 o.p. (ISBN 0-393-00695-6). Norton.
Bruce. Dorothy Wyman. LC 78-23504. (Orion Ser.). 1979. pap. 3.95 o.p. (ISBN 0-8127-0217-4). Review & Herald.
Bruce Davidson: World Champion of Eventing. Bruce Davidson et al. 1980. 25.00 o.p. (ISBN 0-395-29117-8). HM.
Bruce Springsteen: Blinded by the Light. Patrick Humphries & Chris Hunt. LC 85-27183. (Illus.). 176p. 1986. pap. 12.95 o.p. (ISBN 0-03-008532-2, Owl Bks). H Holt & Co.
Bruce! The Ultimate Springsteen Quiz Book. Heather Higgins & Beth Laiderman. LC 85-13033. (Illus.). 96p. (Orig.). 1985. pap. 4.95 o.p. (ISBN 0-87131-465-7). M Evans.

Brucellosis: Distribution in Man, Domestic & Wild Animals. B. M. Thimm. (Sitzungsberichte der Heidelberger Akademie der Wissenschaften Ser., Mathematisch-Naturwissenschaftliche Klasse, 1981; Supplement.). (Illus.). 64p. 1982. 20.00 o.p. (ISBN 0-387-11232-4). Springer-Verlag.

Bruckner-Mahler-Schoenberg. rev. ed. Dika Newlin. 1978. 14.95 o.p. (ISBN 0-393-02203-X). Norton.

Brulebois. Marcel Ayme. 1976. pap. 8.95 o.p. (ISBN 0-686-51910-8). French & Eur.

Bruno Brontosaurus. Nicole Rubel. (Snuggle & Read Story Bks.). 32p. (ps-3). 1983. pap. 2.25 o.p. (ISBN 0-380-83535-5, Camelot). Avon.

Bruno in Venice West & Other Poems. Lawrence Lipton. 8.95 o.p. (ISBN 0-686-32297-5); pap. 4.95 o.p. (ISBN 0-686-32298-3). Ross Erikson.

Bruno le Brontosaure. Nicole Rubel. (Illus.). 32p. (Fr.). (ps-3). 1983. pap. 2.25 o.p. (ISBN 0-380-85084-2, 85084, Camelot). Avon.

Bruno Lier: Ad Topica Carminum Amatorium Symbolae, Repr. Of 1914 Ed. Bruno Lier et al. Ed. by Steele Commager. Bd. with Keith Preston: Studies in the Diction of the Sermo Amatorius in Roman Comedy. Repr. of 1916 ed; Alfons Spies: Militat Omnis Amons. Repr. of 1930 ed. LC 77-70837. (Latin Poetry Ser.). 1978. lib. bdg. 31.00 o.p. (ISBN 0-8240-2973-9). Garland Pub.

Brush up Your Math. B. Woodside. 1982. text ed. 12.95 o.p. (ISBN 0-07-092375-2). McGraw.

Brush with Hate. L. Kovnedhov. 310p. 1979. 7.45 o.p. (ISBN 0-8285-1566-2, Pub. by Progress Pubs USSR). Imported Pubns.

Brussels Travel Guide. Berlitz Editors. (Travel Guides Ser.). 1981. pap. 4.95 o.p. (ISBN 0-317-12099-9, Berlitz). Macmillan.

Bryan Adams. Philip Kamin. (Illus.). 32p. (gr. 3 up). 1985. pap. 4.95 o.p. (ISBN 0-88188-407-3, Pub. by Robus Bks). H Leonard Pub Corp.

Bryan & World Peace. Merle E. Curti. LC 77-147453. (Library of War & Peace; Peace Leaders: Biographies & Memoirs). 1976. lib. bdg. 46.00 o.p. (ISBN 0-8240-0247-4). Garland Pub.

Bryen en Temps Conjuges. Michel Butor. 1975. 25.00 o.p. (ISBN 0-686-51940-X). French & Eur.

BST & the Dairy Industry: A National, Regional & Farm-Level Analysis. Richard Fallert. (Agricultural Economic Report: No. 579). (Illus.). 116p. 1987. pap. 5.50 o.p. (ISBN 0-318-23742-3, S/N 001-019-00561-1). USGPO.

Bubble & Spark Chambers: Principles & Use, 2 vols. Ed. by R. P. Shutt. (Pure & Applied Physics Ser.: Vol. 27). 1967. Vol. 1. 89.00 o.p. (ISBN 0-12-641001-1); Vol. 2. 89.00 o.p. (ISBN 0-12-641002-X). Acad Pr.

Bubble Bubble. Mercer Mayer. LC 80-16777. (Illus.). 48p. (ps-2). 1980. Repr. of 1973 ed. 7.95 o.s.i. (ISBN 0-02-765260-2, Four Winds). Macmillan.

Bubble Reputation. George Pottinger. 256p. 1982. 20.00x o.p. (ISBN 0-7073-0286-2, Pub. by Scot Acad Pr). Longwood Pub Group.

Bubble Trouble. Illus. by Pat Schories. (Splashtime Bks.). (Illus.). 10p. (ps). 1984. vinyl bk. 2.95 o.p. (ISBN 0-448-41225-X, G&D). Putnam Pub Group.

Bubbles. Muriel Rukeyser. LC 66-21607. (Curriculum Related Bks.). (Illus.). (gr. 1-4). 1967. 3.95 o.p. (ISBN 0-15-212830-1, HJ). HarBraceJ.

Buck Alice & the Actor-Robot. Walter Koenig. 256p. (Orig.). 1988. pap. 3.50 o.p. (ISBN 1-55547-240-0). Critics Choice Paper.

Buck Fever Papers. Sherwood Anderson. Ed. by Welford D. Taylor. LC 73-151252. (Illus.). 250p. 1971. 25.00x o.p. (ISBN 0-8139-0322-X). U Pr of Va.

Buckaroo's Code. Wayne D. Overholser. (Orig.). 1980. pap. 1.95 o.p. (ISBN 0-440-11422-5). Dell.

Buckboard Stranger. Stephen W. Meader. LC 54-8574. (Illus.). (gr. 7 up). 1954. 4.95 o.p. (ISBN 0-15-212851-4, HJ). HarBraceJ.

Bucket, or, Murder Near Birmingham Cathedral. R. N. Behar. LC 83-91490. 67p. 1985. 7.95 o.p. (ISBN 0-533-06083-4). Vantage.

Bucket Wheel Excavator: Bulk Materials Handling Ser. Ludwig Rasper. LC 74-77790. (Illus.). 450p. 1975. text ed. 60.00x o.p. (ISBN 0-87849-012-4, Trans Tech Pubns (BRD)). Gower Pub Co.

Buckeyes: A Story of Ohio State Football. Rev. & enl. ed. Wilbur Snypp & Bob Hunter. LC 74-77737. (College Sports Ser.). 1982. 10.95 o.p. (ISBN 0-87397-237-6). Strode.

Buckingham Palace Connection. Ted Willis. 240p. 1980. pap. 2.25 o.p. (ISBN 0-380-48330-0, 48330). Avon.

Buckinghamshire: A Shell Guide. Bruce Watkin. (Illus.). 192p. 1986. pap. 11.95 o.p. (ISBN 0-571-13885-3). Faber & Faber.

Buckle at the Ballet: Selected Ballet Writings. Richard Buckle. LC 80-66015. (Illus.). 1980. 19.95 o.p. (ISBN 0-689-11085-5, Atheneum). Macmillan.

Buckling of Bars, Plates, Shells. Don O. Brush & B. Almroth. (Illus.). 379p. 1974. text ed. 41.95 o.p. (ISBN 0-07-008593-5). McGraw.

Bucks. Peter Chandler. 272p. (Orig.). 1980. pap. 2.50 o.p. (ISBN 0-380-75218-2, 75218). Avon.

Buckskin & Blanket Days: Memoirs of a Friend of the Indians. Thomas H. Tibbles. LC 57-7289. 336p. 1969. pap. 5.95 o.p. (ISBN 0-8032-5199-8, BB 503, Bison). U of Nebr Pr.

Buckskin Rider. W. F. Bragg. 1981. pap. 1.75 o.p. (ISBN 0-8439-0881-5, Pub. by Leisure Bks CT). Dorchester Pub Co.

Bucolic Bull: Fun on a Farm in Australia. Cedric E. Gregory. 160p. 1982. 8.00 o.p. (ISBN 0-682-49892-0). Exposition-Phoenix.

Bucoliques de Virgile. Paul Valery. Bd. with Variations sur les Bucoliques. (Trad. eu vers). pap. 3.95 o.p. (ISBN 0-685-36607-3). French & Eur.

BUC'S Nineteen Eighty Six Used Boat Price Guide, Vol 1 & 2. 49th ed. 1986. Set. 110.00 o.p. (ISBN 0-317-55253-8); Vol. I. 65.00 o.p. (ISBN 0-911778-94-2); Vol. II. 55.00 o.p. (ISBN 0-911778-95-0). Buc Intl.

Bud Hastin's Collector's Price Guide: Avon Bottle Encyclopedia. 9th ed. Bud Hastin. (Illus.). 1982. special price 15.99 o.p. (ISBN 0-89145-152-8). Avons Res.

Buddha & the Gospel of Buddhism. Ananda Coomaraswamy. 10.00 o.p. (ISBN 0-8216-0059-1, Pub. by Univ Bks). Carol Pub Group.

Buddha Uproar. John Tagliabue. (Illus.). 1968. pap. 5.00 o.p. (ISBN 0-87711-030-1). Story Line.

Buddhism. Alexandra David-Neel. 1979. pap. 3.50 o.p. (ISBN 0-380-46185-4, 63594-1, Discus). Avon.

Buddhism & Lamaism of Tibet. Austine Waddell. 1985. text ed. 40.00x o.p. (ISBN 0-86590-615-7, Pub. by Sterling Pubs India). Apt Bks.

Buddhism & Marxism: A Study in Humanism. N. V. Banerjee. 152p. 1978. text ed. 15.00x o.p. (ISBN 0-86131-014-4, Pub. by Orient Longman Ltd India). Apt Bks.

Buddhism & Zen. Ruth S. McCandless & Nyogen Senzaki. 1953. Philos Lib.

Buddhism for Today. Maurice O. Walshe. LC 64-9518. 144p. 1964. (ISBN 0-8022-1802-4). Philos Lib.

Buddhism in the Tibetan Tradition: A Guide. Geshe K. Gyatso. (Illus.). 144p. (Orig.). 1984. pap. 9.95 o.p. (ISBN 0-7102-0242-3). Routledge Chapman & Hall.

Buddhism in Transition. Donald K. Swearer. LC 77-120122. 1970. pap. 2.65 o.s.i. (ISBN 0-664-24896-9, Westminster). Westminster John Knox.

Buddhism: Its Essence & Development. Edward Conze. 1951. (ISBN 0-8022-0290-X). Philos Lib.

Buddhist Civilization in Tibet. Tulko Thondup. LC 87-4493. (Buddhayana Ser.: No. 2). 192p. 1987. pap. 14.95 o.p. (ISBN 0-7102-1087-6, Pub. by Routledge UK). Routledge Chapman & Hall.

Buddhist Himalaya. David Snellgrove. (Illus.). 320p. 1958. (ISBN 0-8022-1605-6). Philos Lib.

Buddhist Praying Wheel. William Simpson. 313p. 1970. 7.95 o.p. (ISBN 0-8216-0060-5, Pub. by Univ Bks). Carol Pub Group.

Buddhist Texts Through the Ages. Edward Conze. 320p. 1954. (ISBN 0-8022-0291-8). Philos Lib.

Buddhist Tradition. World Religions Development Center. (Illus.). 72p. 1978. pap. 6.95 o.p. (ISBN 0-89505-007-2); tchr's. guide 3.75 o.p. Tabor Pub.

Buddhist Yoga. Kanjitsu Iijima. (Illus.). 184p. 1975. pap. 8.95 o.p. (ISBN 0-87040-349-4). Japan Pubns USA.

Buddhists Find Christ: The Spiritual Quest of Thirteen Men & Women in Burma, China, Japan, Korea, Sri Lanka, Thailand, Vietnam. Compiled by Patrick O'Connor. 240p. 1975. pap. 2.25 o.p. (ISBN 0-8048-1146-6). C E Tuttle.

Buddies Tenderfoot. Toby Bluth. (Illus.). 48p. (gr. k-6). 1985. 5.95 o.p. (ISBN 0-8249-8088-3). Ideals.

Budding Wonders: The Flowering Plants. Carl Raab. (Student Scientist Ser.). (Illus.). (YA) (gr. 7-12). 1979. PLB 9.97 o.p. (ISBN 0-8239-0464-4). Rosen Group.

Budgerigars in Color: Their Care & Breeding. rev. ed. A. Rutgers. Ed. by Cyril Rogers. (Illus.). 194p. 1987. 12.95 o.p. (ISBN 0-7137-1855-2, Pub. by Blandford Pr England). Sterling.

Budget & Expenditure Process & Reforms: A Bibliography with Emphasis on Canada. Ontario Ministry of Treasury & Economics Library Staff. (Public Administration Ser.: Bibliography P 1646). 1985. pap. 2.25 o.p. (ISBN 0-89028-336-2). Vance Biblios.

Budget Cuts & Block Grants: Social Needs & the New Federalism. League of Women Voters Education Fund. 1982. pap. 0.75 o.p. Scott F.

Budget Cuts & Block Grants: Social Needs & the New Federalism. League of Women Voters Education Fund Staff. 8p. 1982. pap. text ed. 1.25 o.p. (ISBN 0-89959-325-9, 103). LWV US.

Budget Flying. Dan Ramsey. (McGraw-Hill Series in Aviation). (Illus.). 176p. 1981. text ed. 27.50 o.p. (ISBN 0-07-051202-7). McGraw.

Budget of the United States Government, Fiscal Year 1987. 668p. (Orig.). 1986. pap. 13.00 o.p. (ISBN 0-318-19990-4, S/N 041-001-00299-5). USGPO.

Budget of the United States Government, Fiscal Year 1988. (Illus.). 318p. (Orig.). 1986. pap. 11.00 o.p. (ISBN 0-318-22460-7, S/N 041-001-00315-1). USGPO.

Budget of the United States Government, Fiscal Year 1987, Appendix. 768p. (Orig.). pap. 21.00 o.p. (ISBN 0-318-19989-0, S/N 041-001-00300-2). USGPO.

Budget of the United States Government Fiscal Year 1988, Historical Tables. 328p. (Orig.). 1987. pap. 15.00 o.p. (ISBN 0-318-22459-3, S/N 041-001-00320-7). USGPO.

Budget of the United States Government, Fiscal Year 1988, Supplement. (Illus.). 397p. (Orig.). 1987. pap. 11.00 o.p. (ISBN 0-318-22458-5, S/N 041-001-00322-3). USGPO.

Budget of the United States Government, Fiscal Year 1988, Special Analyses. 381p. (Orig.). 1987. pap. 11.00 o.p. (ISBN 0-318-22486-0, S/N 041-001-00318-5). USGPO.

Budgeting. rev. ed. Reginald Jones & H. George Trentin. 1980. pap. 12.95 o.p. (ISBN 0-8144-7528-0). AMACOM.

Budgeting Basics: A "How to" Guide for Managers. (AMA Reprint Collections Ser). 1975. 8.00 o.p. (ISBN 0-8144-6947-7). AMACOM.

Budgeting for Profit. John C. Camillus. LC 84-1819. (Better Business Ser.). 168p. 1985. 35.00 o.p. (ISBN 0-8019-7552-2). Chilton.

Budgeting for Profit: How to Exploit the Potential of Your Business. John C. Camillus. LC 84-1819. (Alexander Hamilton Institute Bk.). 192p. 1984. pap. 19.95 o.p. (ISBN 0-8019-7523-9). Chilton.

Budgeting Fundamentals for Nonfinancial Executives. Allen Sweeny & John N. Wisener, Jr. LC 75-31915. (Illus.). 152p. 1976. 12.95 o.p. (ISBN 0-8144-5403-8). AMACOM.

Budweiser Cookbook. Anheuser-Busch Brewing Company Staff. (Illus.). 80p. (Orig.). 1983. pap. 4.95 o.p. (ISBN 0-8249-3025-8). Ideals.

Buffalo & Other Stories. Wayne Ude. 1975. pap. 6.00 o.p. (ISBN 0-89924-000-3). Lynx Hse.

Buffalo Bills. James Rothaus. (NFL Today Ser.). (Illus.). 48p. (gr. 4-12). 1986. PLB 8.95 o.p. (ISBN 0-87191-812-9); pap. 4.25 o.p. (ISBN 0-89812-258-9). Creative Ed.

Buffalo Book. David Dary. 448p. 1976. pap. 2.50 o.p. (ISBN 0-380-00475-5, 62786-8, Discus). Avon.

Buffalo Book: The Full Saga of the American Animal. David A. Dary. LC 73-13211. (Illus.). 374p. 1973. 20.00 o.p. (ISBN 0-8040-0653-9, SB); ltd. ed. o.p. 100.00 o.p. (ISBN 0-8040-0717-9). Ohio U Pr.

Buffalo Butte. Will Benton. 1985. 12.95 o.p. (ISBN 0-317-53061-5, Large Print Bks). G K Hall.

Buffalo Hunter. Zane Grey. 1979. pap. 1.75 o.p. (ISBN 0-505-51334-X, Pub. by Tower Bks). Dorchester Pub Co.

Buffalo Jones Adventures on the Plains. Henry Inman. (Illus.). 9.00 o.p. (ISBN 0-8446-0721-5). Peter Smith.

Buffalo Knife. William O. Steele. LC 52-6460. (Illus.). (gr. 4-6). 1968. pap. 2.75 o.p. (ISBN 0-15-614750-5, VoyB). HarBraceJ.

Buffalo Sequence & Other Poems. Mark Pawlak. 64p. (Orig.). 1976. pap. 5.00 o.p. (ISBN 0-914742-19-1). Copper Canyon.

Buffalo Soldiers in Italy: Black Americans in World War II. Hondon B. Hargrove. LC 84-42609. (Illus.). 223p. 1985. lib. bdg. 21.95x o.p. (ISBN 0-89950-116-8). McFarland & Co.

Buffets. Bon Appetit Magazine Editors. LC 84-19402. (Cooking with Bon Appetit Ser.). (Illus.). 1985. 12.95 o.p. (ISBN 0-89535-139-0). Knapp Pr.

Buffo: The Genius of Vulgar Comedy. Anthony Caputi. LC 78-15992. (Illus.). 256p. 1979. 24.95x o.p. (ISBN 0-8143-1606-9). Wayne St U Pr.

Bug-Eyed Monsters. Ed. by Bill Pronzini & Barry Malzberg. LC 79-2771. (Illus.). 1980. pap. 4.95 o.p. (ISBN 0-15-614789-0, Harv). HarBraceJ.

Bugaku Masks. Kyotaro Nishikawa. Tr. by Monica Bethe. LC 77-75971. (Japanese Arts Library: Vol. 5). (Illus.). 1978. 27.95 o.p. (ISBN 0-87011-312-7). Kodansha.

Bugbusters: Getting Rid of Household Pests Without Dangerous Chemicals. Bernice Lifton. 1985. text ed. 15.95 o.p. (ISBN 0-07-037849-5); pap. text ed. 7.95 o.p. (ISBN 0-07-037848-7). McGraw.

Buglar Boy & His Swish Friend. Stanley Eveling. 30p. 1983. pap. 5.95 o.p. (ISBN 0-907540-41-4, NO. 4048, Pub. by Salamander Press). Routledge Chapman & Hall.

Bugles at the Border. Mary Gillett. LC 68-25853. (Illus.). 220p. (gr. 6 up). 1968. PLB 3.98 o.p. (ISBN 0-910244-50-2). Blair.

Bugles in the Afternoon. Colin Morris. LC 78-23273. 1979. pap. 3.95 o.s.i. (ISBN 0-664-24260-X, Westminster). Westminster John Knox.

Bugs & Bytes: Computer for Kids. Carole Marsh. (Tomorrow's Books for Today's Children). (Illus.). 56p. 1983. 7.95 o.p. (ISBN 0-935326-15-4). Gallopade Pub Group.

Bugs in Your Ears. Betty Bates. (gr. 4-6). 1979. pap. 1.95 o.p. (ISBN 0-671-44144-2). Archway.

Buick Century-Regal 1975-85. Chilton Automotives Editorial Staff. LC 84-45479. 256p. (Orig.). 1985. pap. 13.95 o.s.i. (ISBN 0-8019-7570-0). Chilton.

Buick-Olds-Pontiac Full-Size, 1975-87. Chilton Automotives Editorial Staff. LC 86-47785. 336p. 1985. pap. 13.95 o.p. Chilton.

Buick-Olds-Pontiac 1975-85. Chilton Automotives Editorial Staff. LC 84-45490. 324p. (Orig.). 1985. pap. 13.50 o.s.i. (ISBN 0-8019-7560-3). Chilton.

Buick Skylark, 1980. Clymer Publications. 12.95 o.p. (ISBN 0-89287-349-3, A282). Clymer Pub.

Buik of Alexander the Conquerour III. Gilbert Hay. Ed. by John Cartwright. 254p. 1988. text ed. (ISBN 0-08-036999-5, AUP). Pergamon.

Build-a-Bed Book. John Boeschen. (Illus.). 160p. 1982. pap. 10.95 o.p. St Martin.

Build a Personal Earth Station for Worldwide Satellite TV Reception. 2nd ed. Robert J. Traister. (Illus.). 384p. 1985. 21.95 o.p. (ISBN 0-8306-0909-1, 1909); pap. 16.60 o.p. (ISBN 0-8306-1909-7, 1909P). TAB Bks.

Build Beautiful Bulletin Boards. Rosemary W. Edwards. Ed. by Mary E. Wallace. (Illus.). 72p. (Orig.). 1981. pap. 3.95 o.p. (ISBN 0-912315-60-1). Word Aflame.

Build It Together: Twenty-Seven Easy to Make Woodworking Projects for Adults & Children. Katie Hamilton & Gene Hamilton. (Illus.). 192p. 1984. 24.95 o.p. (ISBN 0-684-18125-8, ScribT); pap. 14.95 o.p. (ISBN 0-684-18092-8). Scribner.

Build Your Own Database in a Basic. R. Robertson. 600p. 1989. pap. 32.50 o.p. Ross Bks.

Build Your Own Database in Basic. Raymond Robertson. (Illus.). 580p. 1989. pap. text ed. 37.50 o.p. Ross Bks.

Build Your Own Expert System. Chris Naylor. 1985. pap. 15.95 o.p. (ISBN 0-470-20172-X). Halsted Pr.

Build Your Own Playground: A Sourcebook of Play Sculptures, Designs & Concepts from the Work of Jay Beckwith. Jeremy J. Hewes. LC 74-11206. (San Francisco Ser.). 223p. 1975. 15.00 o.p. (ISBN 0-395-19894-1); pap. 7.95 o.p. (ISBN 0-395-19966-2). HM.

Build Your Own Statue of Liberty. John Harris. (Illus.). 8p. 1984. Hobbies. pap. 7.95 o.s.i. (ISBN 0-385-19622-9, Dolp). Doubleday.

Build Your Own Utopia: An Interdisciplinary Course in Utopian Speculation. rev. ed. Kenneth M. Roemer. LC 80-6248. (Illus.). 121p. 1981. pap. text ed. 10.00 o.p. (ISBN 0-8191-1661-0). U Pr of Amer.

Builders: A Story & Study of Freemasonry. 9th ed. Joseph F. Newton. (Illus.). 345p. 1985. Repr. 13.75 o.p. (ISBN 0-88053-045-6, M 301). Macoy Pub.

Builders Cost of Doing Business Study--Fiscal Year 1984. rev. ed. 84p. 1985. pap. 15.00 o.p. (ISBN 0-86718-240-7). Nat Assn H Build.

Builders Guide to Bathroom Design. Paul Muessig et al. (Illus.). 44p. pap. 5.00 cancelled o.s.i. (ISBN 0-86718-008-0). Nat Assn H Build.

Builders Guide to Home Mortgages. 180p. 1986. pap. 15.00 with plastic spiral o.p. (ISBN 0-86718-245-8). Nat Assn H Build.

Builders Guide to Merchandising. Carol A. Cardella. 55p. 1978. pap. 8.00 o.p. (ISBN 0-86718-012-9). Nat Assn H Build.

Builders: Houses, People, Neighborhoods, Government, Money. Martin Mayer. 1978. 17.50 o.p. (ISBN 0-393-08796-4). Norton.

Builders of the Bay Colony. rev. ed. Samuel E. Morison. (Illus.). 1964. pap. 5.95 o.p. (ISBN 0-395-08381-8, 32, SenEd). HM.

Building a Career in the Business World. Edward J. Fink. 1984. 10.00 o.p. (ISBN 0-533-05968-2). Vantage.

Building a Caring Church. Tom Lovorn & Janie Lovorn. 104p. 1986. pap. 8.95 o.p. (ISBN 0-89693-150-1). Victor Bks.

Building a Christian Marriage. William E. Hulme. LC 65-22192. 1968. pap. 5.95 o.p. (ISBN 0-8066-0813-7, 10-0940, Augsburg). Augsburg Fortress.

Titles

Building a Fortune in Common Stocks. John Ilich. 112p. 1984. 5.95 o.p. (ISBN 0-673-15972-8). Scott F.

Building a Judaica Library Collection: A Resource Guide. Edith Lubetski & Meir Lubetski. LC 83-900. 185p. 1983. lib. bdg. 30.00 o.p. (ISBN 0-87287-375-7). Libs Unl.

Building a Just Society. Patrick Bascio. LC 80-27238. 176p. (Orig.). 1981. pap. 5.95 o.p. (ISBN 0-88344-205-1). Orbis Bks.

Building a Mail Order Business: A Complete Manual for Success. William A. Cohen. LC 81-16071. 442p. 1982. 17.95 o.p. (ISBN 0-471-08803-X, Pub. by Wiley-Interscience). Wiley.

Building a Superior School Band Library. Lawrence Intravaia. (Illus.). 272p. 1972. 10.95 o.p. (ISBN 0-13-087031-5, Parker). P-H.

Building a Teachers' Center. Ed. by Kathleen Devaney. 1979. pap. 9.75x o.p. (ISBN 0-8077-2566-8, Pub. by Teach Ctr Exchange). Tchrs Coll.

Building an Ark: Tools for the Preservation of Natural Diversity Through Land Protection. Phillip M. Hoose. 224p. (Orig.). 1981. pap. 12.00x o.p. (ISBN 0-933280-09-2). Island CA.

Building & Civil Engineering Construction, Vol. 2. Brian W. Boughton. 168p. 1983. pap. text ed. 12.50x o.p. (Pub. by Granada England). Gower Pub Co.

Building & Operating an Effective Board of Directors. Milton C. Lauenstein. (Presidents Association Special Study: No. 70). 1979. pap. 20.00 o.p. (ISBN 0-8144-4070-3). AMACOM.

Building & Protecting the Co-operative Movement: A Brief History of the Co-operative Union of Canada, 1909-1984. Co-operative Union of Canada Staff & Ian MacPherson. 254p. 1984. 5.00 o.s.i. (ISBN 0-318-18137-1, Pub. by Cooperative Union of Canada). NASCO.

Building & Using an Astronomical Observatory. Paul Doherty. (Illus.). 224p. (Orig.). 1987. pap. 12.95 o.p. (ISBN 0-85059-808-7, Pub. by PSL P Stephens England). Sterling.

Building Better Beds. Percy W. Blandford. (Illus.). 304p. 1984. 19.95 o.p. (ISBN 0-8306-0664-5, 1664); pap. 14.50 o.p. (ISBN 0-8306-1664-0). TAB Bks.

Building Birdhouses & Bird-Feeders: Attract Birds to Your Backyard with Birdhouses & Feeders You've Built Yourself. Ed Baldwin & Stevie Baldwin. LC 84-26050. (Family Workshop Bk.). (Illus.). 128p. 1985. 12.95 o.s.i. (ISBN 0-385-19712-8). Doubleday.

Building Christian Community. Catherine Martin. 1.17 o.p. (ISBN 0-8091-9311-6). Paulist Pr.

Building Classroom Discipline: From Models to Practice. 2nd ed. C. M. Charles. 256p. 1984. pap. text ed. 17.45 o.p. (ISBN 0-582-28532-1). Longman.

Building Construction Cost Data, 1986. 44th ed. Means, R. S., Company, Inc. Staff. Ed. by William Mahoney. 480p. 1985. pap. 39.95 o.p. (ISBN 0-87629-000-4). R S Means.

Building Construction Cost Data, 1988. 46th ed. R. S. Means Company, Inc. Staff. (Professional Cost Guides). 1988. pap. 47.95 o.p. (ISBN 0-87629-072-1). R S Means.

Building Construction Cost Data, 1988: Western Edition. R. S. Means Company, Inc. Staff. Ed. by William D. Mahoney. (Illus.). 504p. 1988. pap. 55.95 o.p. (ISBN 0-87629-112-4, 60228). R S Means.

Building Construction Details: Practical Drawings. Hans Banz. 272p. 1982. pap. 18.95 o.p. (ISBN 0-442-21325-5). Van Nos Reinhold.

Building Construction Information Sources. Ed. by Howard B. Bentley. LC 64-16502. (Management Information Guide Ser.: No. 2). 182p. 1964. 68.00x o.p. (ISBN 0-8103-0802-9). Gale.

Building Contracts: A Bibliography. Mary Vance. LC 85-141720. (Architecture Ser.: Bibliography A 1328). 1985. pap. 6.75 o.p. (ISBN 0-89028-278-1). Vance Biblios.

Building Cost Manual 1988. Lisa Andrews. 240p. (Orig.). 1987. pap. 14.00 o.p. (ISBN 0-317-66693-2). Craftsman.

Building Cost Manual, 1988. Ed. by Lisa Andrews. 240p. (Orig.). 1987. pap. 14.00 o.p. (ISBN 0-934041-24-5). Craftsman.

Building Database Application. Frank Sweet. 258p. 1986. pap. 25.00 o.p. (ISBN 0-317-69473-1). Boxes & Arrows.

Building Design Evaluation. 3rd ed. P. A. Stone. 1980. 35.00x o.p. (ISBN 0-419-11720-2, NO.2973, Pub. by E & FN Spon England). Routledge Chapman & Hall.

Building Energy Management--Conventional & Solar Approaches: Proceedings of the International Congress, 12-16 May 1980, Povoa de Varzim, Portugal. Fernandes E. De Oliveira et al. LC 80-40415. 800p. 1981. 220.00 o.p. (ISBN 0-08-026144-2). Pergamon.

Building Entopia. C. A. Doxiadis. (Illus.). 1977. 14.95x o.p. (ISBN 0-393-08362-4). Norton.

Building Estate Maintenance Administration. R. D. Milne. LC 85-10697. 250p. 1985. 25.00x o.p. (ISBN 0-419-13150-7, 9670). Routledge Chapman & Hall.

Building Estimates & Costs: A Bibliography. Mary Vance. LC 85-141665. (Architecture Ser.: Bibliography A 1327). 1985. pap. 4.50 o.p. (ISBN 0-89028-277-3). Vance Biblios.

Building Estimator's Reference Book. 21st ed. William H. Spradlin, Jr. (Illus.). 1270p. 1982. 34.95 o.s.i. (ISBN 0-911592-21-0). F R Walker.

Building Failures: Diagnosis & Avoidance. W. H. Ransom. (Illus.). 176p. 1981. 25.00x o.p. (ISBN 0-419-11750-4, NO.6569, Pub. by E&FN Spon England); pap. 11.95 o.p. (ISBN 0-419-11760-1, NO. 6568). Routledge Chapman & Hall.

Building for Self-Sufficiency. Robin Clarke. LC 76-5093. (Illus.). 302p. 1977. 12.50x o.p. (ISBN 0-87663-230-4); pap. 5.95 o.p. (ISBN 0-87663-945-7). Universe.

Building for the Arts. Architectural Record Magazine Editors. 1978. text ed. 51.00 o.p. (ISBN 0-07-002325-5). McGraw.

Building for the Arts: A Guidebook for the Planning & Design of Cultural Facilities. Catherine R. Brown et al. LC 83-27339. (Illus.). 272p. 1984. pap. 21.95x o.p. (ISBN 0-9611710-1-4). Western States.

Building Free-Form Furniture. Charles M. Durney. (Illus.). 224p. 1982. 15.95 o.p. (ISBN 0-8306-1340-4, 1440); pap. 9.95 o.p. (ISBN 0-8306-1440-0). TAB Bks.

Building Laws: A Bibliography. Mary Vance. LC 85-142972. (Architecture Ser.: Bibliography A-1316). 96p. 1985. pap. 14.25 o.p. (ISBN 0-89028-246-3). Vance Biblios.

Building Maintenance Management. Reginald Lee. 194p. 1976. pap. text ed. 17.50x o.p. (ISBN 0-258-96947-4, Pub. by Granada England). Gower Pub Co.

Building Materials in Developing Countries. Robin Spence & David Cook. LC 82-17434. 360p. 1984. 59.95x o.p. (ISBN 0-471-10235-0). Wiley.

Building Mechanical. 1977. text ed. 45.50 o.p. (ISBN 0-07-001847-2). McGraw.

Building of Boats. Douglas Phillips-Birt. (Illus.). 1980. 29.95 o.p. (ISBN 0-393-03243-4). Norton.

Building of Jalna. Mazo De La Roche. 288p. 1976. pap. 1.50 o.s.i. (ISBN 0-449-23071-6, Crest). Fawcett.

Building of Perry's Fleet on Lake Erie: 1812-1813. Max Rosenberg. LC 50-9593. 72p. (Orig.). 1968. pap. 4.95 o.p. (ISBN 0-911124-49-7). Pa Hist & Mus.

Building on Springs. R. A. Waller. 1969. 29.00 o.p. (ISBN 0-08-006399-3). Pergamon.

Building, Owning & Flying a Composite Homebuilt. Bill Clarke. (Illus.). 176p. 1985. pap. 15.60 o.p. (ISBN 0-8306-2402-3, 2402). Tab Bks.

Building Physics: Acoustics. H. J. Purkis. 1966. 34.00 o.p. (ISBN 0-08-011443-1); pap. 40.00 o.p. (ISBN 0-08-011442-3). Pergamon.

Building Physics: Heat. M. S. Billington. 1967. text ed. 21.00 o.p. (ISBN 0-08-012258-2); pap. 12.50 o.p. (ISBN 0-08-012257-4). Pergamon.

Building Physics: Lighting. W. R. Stevens. 1969. 60.00 o.p. (ISBN 0-08-006370-5); pap. 60.00 o.p. (ISBN 0-08-006369-1). Pergamon.

Building Powerful Nerve Force. 10th ed. Paul C. Bragg & Patricia Bragg. pap. 4.95 o.p. (ISBN 0-87790-003-5). Health Sci.

Building Regulations: A Self Help Guide for the Owner-Builder. Edmund Vitale. (Illus.). 1979. 4.95 o.s.i. (ISBN 0-684-16068-4, ScribT); Encore ed. 4.95 o.s.i. (ISBN 0-684-17691-2). Scribner.

Building Regulations Explained & Illustrated. 5th ed. W. S. Whyte & Vincent Powell-Smith. 299p. 1978. text ed. 24.50 o.p. (ISBN 0-246-11273-5, Pub. by Granada England). Gower Pub Co.

Building Regulations in ECE Countries. pap. 7.00 o.p. (ISBN 0-686-94850-5, E.74.11.E.10). UN.

Building Research Policies. United Nations Economic Commission for Europe. 1978. pap. 51.00 o.p. (ISBN 0-08-022391-5). Pergamon.

Building Science for a Cold Climate. Neil B. Hutcheon & Gustav O. Handegord. 440p. 1984. text ed. 61.95x o.p. (ISBN 0-471-79763-4, Pub. by Wiley-Interscience). Wiley.

Building Self-Esteem. Lilburn S. Barksdale. 42p. 1972. softbound 3.95 o.s.i. (ISBN 0-918588-01-4). Barksdale Foun.

Building Services Design: A Systemic Approach to Decision Making. Thomas N. Maver. 1977. 5.50x o.p. (ISBN 0-900630-16-7, Pub. by RIBA). Intl Spec Bk.

Building Services Integration. P. K. Barton. (Illus.). 1983. 29.95 o.p. (ISBN 0-419-12030-0, NO. 6830, Pub. by E & FN Spon). Routledge Chapman & Hall.

Building Small Groups in the Christian Community. John Mallison. (Abridged Small Group Ser.). (Illus.). 238p. (Orig.). 1978. pap. 9.95 o.p. (ISBN 0-909202-05-2, Pub. by Renewal Pubns). Meyer Stone Bks.

Building Stereo Speakers. Andy J. Wells. (McGraw-Hill VTX Ser.). 208p. 1983. pap. text ed. 9.95 o.p. (ISBN 0-07-069251-3). McGraw.

Building Strong Feet. Rev. ed. Paul C. Bragg & Patricia Bragg. 1986. pap. 4.95 o.p. (ISBN 0-87790-042-6). Health Sci.

Building Successful Quality Circles: A Corporate Facilitator's Guide to Perfectly Operating Quality Circles. Jim Zamagni. 114p. 1985. pap. 5.70 o.p. (ISBN 0-937670-35-9). Quality Circle.

Building Systems: Industrialization & Architecture. Barry Russell. LC 80-41692. 758p. 1981. 118.00 o.p. (ISBN 0-471-27952-8, Pub. by Wiley-Interscience). Wiley.

Building the Earth. Pierre Teilhard De Chardin. 1969. pap. 1.25 o.p. (ISBN 0-380-01075-5, 08938, Discus). Avon.

Building the Timber Frame House. Tedd Benson & James Gruber. (Illus.). 1980. 19.95 o.s.i. (ISBN 0-684-16446-9, ScribT). Scribner.

Building the Word: The Dynamics of Communication & Preaching. J. Randall Nichols. LC 79-3590. 176p. 1981. 10.00 o.p. (ISBN 0-06-066109-7). HarpR.

Building Voluntary Support for the Two-Year College. Ed. by John E. Bennett. 142p. 1981. looseleaf binder 16.50 o.p. (ISBN 0-89964-017-6). Coun Adv & Supp Ed.

Building Wealth: A Layman's Guide to Trust Planning. Adam Starchild. 192p. 1981. 15.95 o.p. (ISBN 0-8144-7594-9). AMACOM.

Building Writing Skills: A Programmed Approach to Sentences & Paragraphs. Alan Casty. 1971. pap. text ed. 10.95 o.p. (ISBN 0-15-505594-1, HC, HC). HarBraceJ.

Building Your Alumni Program. Ed. by Virginia L. Carter & Patricia Alberger. 122p. 1980. 16.50 o.p. (ISBN 0-89964-165-2). Coun Adv & Supp Ed.

Building Your Management Team: A Framework for Public Sector Labor Relations. John Spitz. (IPA Training Manual). 477p. 1976. 10.00 o.p. (ISBN 0-89215-070-X). U Cal LA Indus Rel.

Buildings & Towns in Pastel. Christopher Stones. (Leisure Arts Ser.: No. 22). (Illus.). 32p. 1984. pap. 2.95 o.p. (ISBN 0-89134-086-6). North Light Bks.

Bukhara: A Guide. V. Tiurikov. 79p. 1982. 4.45 o.p. (ISBN 0-8285-2484-X, Pub. by Progress Pubs USSR). Imported Pubns.

Bulb Book: A Photographic Guide to over Eight Hundred Hardy Bulbs. Martyn Rix & Roger Phillips. (Illus.). 192p. (Orig.). 1981. pap. text ed. 15.95x o.p. (ISBN 0-916422-40-2, Pub. by Pan Bks England). Mad River.

Bulbous Plants of Turkey. Brian Mathew & Turhan Baytop. (Illus.). 148p. 1984. 65.00 o.p. (ISBN 0-7134-4517-3, Pub. by Batsford England). David & Charles.

Buld 200 Watt Clear. Date not set. (ISBN 0-07-521256-0). McGraw.

Bulgakov Anthology: From Marxism to Christian Orthodoxy. Sergius Bulgakov. Ed. by Nicolas Zernov & James Pain. LC 76-23245. 220p. 1976. 12.50 o.s.i. (ISBN 0-664-21338-3, Westminster). Westminster John Knox.

Bulgaria & Her Jews: The History of a Dubious Symbiosis. Vicki Tamir. LC 78-62154. (Illus.). 1979. 14.95 o.s.i. (ISBN 0-87203-075-X). Hermon.

Bulgarian-English Dictionary. 2nd ed. T. Atanassova et al. 1050p. (Bulgarian & Eng.). 1980. 55.00x o.p. (ISBN 0-569-08665-5, Pub. by Collets UK). State Mutual Bk.

Bulgarian-English, English-Bulgarian Dictionary (1973-1975, 3 vols. T. Athanassova & M. Roussev. (Bulgarian & Eng.). 1978. 50.00 set o.s.i. (ISBN 0-685-29249-5). E J Brill USA.

Bulgarian Folk Dances. Raina Katzarova-Kukudova & Kiril Djenev. (Illus.). 174p. 1976. pap. 10.95 o.p. (ISBN 0-89357-029-X). Slavica.

Bulgarian Longevity: Clues to a Long Life. Elena B. Craver. 110p. 1982. 6.50 o.p. (ISBN 0-682-49894-7). Exposition-Phoenix.

Bulgarians: From Their Arrival in the Balkans to Modern Times--Thirteen Centuries of History. Christ Anastasoff. (Illus.). 1977. 20.00 o.p. (ISBN 0-682-48899-2, University). Exposition-Phoenix.

Bulimarexia: The Binge-Purge Cycle. Marlene Boskind-White & William C. White, Jr. 1983. 16.45 o.p. (ISBN 0-393-01650-1). Norton.

Bull by the Horns. Elizabeth Johnson House. 1976. 6.50 o.p. (ISBN 0-682-48575-6). Exposition-Phoenix.

Bull in the Forest. Peter Z. Cohen. LC 69-18955. (Illus.). 307p. (gr. 3-7). 1969. PLB 3.07 o.p. (ISBN 0-689-20067-6, Atheneum). Macmillan.

Buller's Birds of New Zealand. Ed. by E. G. Turbott. 280p. 1986. 75.00 o.p. (ISBN 0-7233-0022-4, Pub. by Whitcoulls Nz). Intl Spec Bk.

Bullet Barricade. Leslie Ernenwein. 1975. pap. 0.95 o.p. (ISBN 0-685-59190-5, LB312, Pub. by Leisure Bks CT). Dorchester Pub Co.

Bullet for Georgie. Everett M. Skehan. 1979. 9.95 o.p. (ISBN 0-395-26294-1). HM.

Bullet-Hunting, & Other New Poems. Melville Cane. LC 60-5433. 1960. 3.75 o.p. (ISBN 0-15-114837-6). HarBraceJ.

Bulletin, Vols. 1-13, No. 1. Worker's League for a Revolutionary Party. 1968. Repr. of 1950 ed. lib. bdg. 195.00x o.p. (ISBN 0-8371-9263-3, W100). Greenwood.

Bulletin Board Builders, No. 2. Judy Dorsett. (Illus.). 64p. 1985. 3.95 o.p. (ISBN 0-87239-918-4, 3288). Standard Pub.

Bulletin Board Builders, No. 3. Judy Dorsett. (Illus.). 64p. 1986. 3.95 o.p. (ISBN 0-87403-020-X, 3240). Standard Pub.

Bulletin Boards for the Middle Grades. Doris Ruby & Grant Ruby. 1964. pap. 5.95 o.p. (ISBN 0-8224-1140-7). D S Lake Pubs.

Bulletins: Primier Niveau. Pellissier & Smith. 184p. 1985. pap. text ed. 9.00 o.p. (ISBN 0-88377-283-3). Newbury Hse.

Bullion Flow Between Europe & the East, 1000-1750. Arthur Attman. (Acta Regiae Societas Scientarium et Litterarum Gothoburgensis Humanoria Ser.: No. 20). 149p. (Orig.). 1981. pap. 25.00x o.p. (ISBN 0-317-68034-X, Pub. by Vetenskaps Gothenburg). Coronet Bks.

Bullock Carts & Motor Bikes: Ancient India on a New Road. Beth Roy. LC 72-75281. (gr. 6 up). 1972. 6.95 o.p. (ISBN 0-689-30064-6, Atheneum). Macmillan.

Bullock: The Autobiography of an Artist. Clarence C. Bullock. 1984. 6.95 o.p. (ISBN 0-533-06079-6). Vantage.

Bullring: A Classroom Experiment in Moral Education. A. J. Grainger. 1970. 40.00 o.p. (ISBN 0-08-006973-8); pap. 40.00 o.p. (ISBN 0-08-006972-X). Pergamon.

Bull's Bellow see Needed Words.

Bull's-Eye Crosswords, No. 1. Ed. by Stanley Newman. 96p. 1985. pap. 5.95 spiral-bound o.p. (ISBN 0-89471-374-4). Running Pr.

Bullwhacker. James D. Nichols. (Orig.). 1981. pap. 1.95 o.p. (ISBN 0-505-51629-2, Pub. by Tower Bks). Dorchester Pub Co.

Bultaco Service Repair Handbook: 125-370cc, Through 1977. (Illus.). pap. 13.95 o.s.i. (ISBN 0-89287-174-1, M303). Clymer Pub.

Bulwark Shore: Exploring Thanet & the Cinque Ports. Caroline Hillier. (Illus.). 317p. 1983. pap. 7.95 o.p. (ISBN 0-586-08345-6, Pub. by Granada England). Academy Chi Pubs.

Bumerang. Igor Guberman. (Illus.). 128p. (Rus.). 1982. pap. 6.00 o.p. (ISBN 0-938920-15-4). Hermitage.

Bumf. Alan Coren. LC 84-185786. 160p. 1985. 12.95 o.p. (ISBN 0-88186-026-3). Parkwest Pubns.

Bumper Book of Covers. Private Eye Magazine Staff. (Illus.). 96p. 1984. pap. 6.95 o.p. (ISBN 0-233-97699-X, Pub. by Private Eye UK). David & Charles.

Bumper Book of Things a Boy Can Make. Foulsham, W., & Co. Staff. (Illus.). 1978. pap. 8.95 o.p. (ISBN 0-8306-1090-1, 1090). TAB Bks.

Bumper Tubbs. David McPhail. (Illus.). 48p. (gr. k-3). 1980. 8.95 o.p. (ISBN 0-395-28477-5). HM.

Bun: A Tale from Russia. Marcia Brown. LC 75-167832. (Illus.). 32p. (gr. k-3). 1972. 6.95 o.p. (ISBN 0-15-213450-6, HJ). HarBraceJ.

Bunch of Poems & Verses. Beatrice S. De Regniers. LC 76-28324. (Illus.). 40p. (gr. 1-5). 1979. 7.95 o.p. (ISBN 0-395-28881-9, Clarion). HM.

Bunch of Tagore Poems. 2nd ed. Rabindranath Tagore. Tr. by Monika Varma. (Translated from Bengali). 8.00 o.s.i. (ISBN 0-89253-611-X); flexible cloth 4.80 o.s.i. (ISBN 0-89253-612-8). Ind-US Inc.

Bundling: Its Origin, Progress & Decline in America. Henry R. Stiles. LC 78-167211. 150p. Repr. of 1934 ed. 40.00x o.p. (ISBN 0-8103-3204-3). Gale.

Bunker. Charles Goldstein. 262p. pap. 3.95 o.s.i. (ISBN 0-318-14632-0, 294). JPS Phila.

Bunker. James P. O'Donnell. (Illus.). 1978. 13.95 o.p. (ISBN 0-395-25719-0). HM.

Bunkhouse Logic. Ben Stein. 176p. (Orig.). 1981. pap. 3.95 o.p. (ISBN 0-380-78543-9, 84715-9). Avon.

Bunnechauk: Alaska - Then & Now. Gwenyth B. Goodrich. 128p. 1982. 7.00 o.p. (ISBN 0-682-49821-1). Exposition-Phoenix.

Bunny Tales. rev. ed. Ed. by James A. Kuse. (Illus.). (ps-3). 1979. pap. 2.95 o.p. (ISBN 0-89542-451-7). Ideals.

Bunny: The Real Story of Playboy. Russell Miller. 1985. 16.95 o.p. (ISBN 0-03-063748-1). H Holt & Co.

Buns: A Woman Looks at Men's. Christie Jenkins. (Illus.). 96p. 1980. 71.40 sets of 12 o.p. (ISBN 0-399-50552-0, Perigee); pap. 5.95 o.p. (ISBN 0-399-50500-8). Putnam Pub Group.

Bunyip Aristocracy: The New South Wales Constitution Debate of 1853 & Hereditary Institutions in the British Colonies. Ged Martin. 228p. 1986. 29.00 o.p. (ISBN 0-949614-14-9, Pub. by Croom Helm UK). Routledge Chapman & Hall.
Bunyip Aristocracy: The New South Wales Constitution Debate of 1853 & Hereditary Institutions in the British Colonies. Ged Martin. 288p. 1987. lib. bdg. 37.50x o.p. (ISBN 0-317-64431-9, Pub. by Croom Helm UK). Routledge Chapman & Hall.
Burden. Mary Westmacott. LC 72-97687. 1973. 6.95 o.p. (ISBN 0-87795-057-1, Arbor Hse). Morrow.
Burden. Mary Westmacott, pseud. 1982. 5.95 o.p. (ISBN 0-87795-387-2, Arbor Hse). Morrow.
Burden of the Past & the English Poet. W. Jackson Bate. 1972. 3.95x o.p. (ISBN 0-393-00590-9, Norton Lib). Norton.
Burden-Sharing in NATO. Simon Lunn. (Catham House Papers on Foreign Policy: No. 18). 128p. (Orig.). 1983. pap. 10.95x o.p. (ISBN 0-7100-9233-4). Routledge Chapman & Hall.
Burdick Family Chronology, Vol. 1. Frank P. Mueller. LC 82-72466. (Illus.). 300p. 1986. 30.00 o.p. (ISBN 0-9609100-0-X). Burdick Intl Ancestry.
Bureau: My Thirty Years in Hoover's FBI. William C. Sullivan & Bill Brown. (Illus.). 1979. 14.95 o.p. (ISBN 0-393-01236-0). Norton.
Bureaucratic Corruption in the Third World. David J. Gould. (Policy Studies). 1980. 45.00 o.p. (ISBN 0-08-025084-X); pap. 35.00 (Reproduction on Demand) o.p. Pergamon.
Bureaucratic Politics & Chinese Energy Development. Kenneth Lieberthal & Michel Oksenberg. 417p. (Orig.). 1986. pap. 19.00 o.p. (ISBN 0-318-21330-3, S/N 003-009-00483-7). USGPO.
Bureaucratic Zoo: The Search for the Ultimate Mumble. James H. Boren. LC 76-39967. (Illus.). 1976. 6.95 o.p. (ISBN 0-914440-14-4). EPM Pubns.
Burghers of New Amsterdam & the Freeman of New York, 1675-1866: New York Historical Society Collections 1885. LC 1-13394. 8.00x o.p. (ISBN 0-685-73876-0). U Pr of Va.
Burglar Who Painted Like Mondrian. Lawrence Block. 217p. 1983. 14.50 o.p. (ISBN 0-87795-517-4, Arbor Hse). Morrow.
Burial Chamber of the Treasurer Sobk-Mose from Er-Rizeikat. William C. Hayes. LC 79-168404. (Metropolitan Museum of Art Publications in Reprint). (Illus.). 50p. 1972. Repr. of 1939 ed. 13.00 o.p. Ayer Co Pubs.
Burial of the Sardine. Fernando Arrabal. Tr. by Patrick Bowles from Fr. (Orig.). 1980. pap. 7.95 o.s.i. (ISBN 0-7145-0146-8). Riverrun NY.
Buried. Daniel Helfgott. 288p. 1981. pap. 2.50 o.p. (ISBN 0-380-77644-8, 77644-8). Avon.
Buried City. Howard Moss. LC 74-77853. 1975. 6.95 o.p. (ISBN 0-689-10626-2, Atheneum); pap. 5.95 o.p. (ISBN 0-689-11293-9). Macmillan.
Buried for Pleasure. Edmund Crispin. Ed. by Jacques Barzum & Wendell H. Taylor. LC 75-44967. (Crime Fiction Ser). 1976. Repr. of 1949 ed. lib. bdg. 21.00 o.p. (ISBN 0-8240-2362-5). Garland Pub.
Buried Man. Norman Stahl & D. Horan. 240p. 1985. text ed. 14.95 o.p. (ISBN 0-07-060699-4). McGraw.
Buried Unsung: Louis Tikas & the Ludlow Massacre. Zeese Papanikolas. LC 82-13475. (University of Utah Publications in the American West: Vol. 14). (Illus.). 331p. 1982. 19.95 o.p. (ISBN 0-87480-211-3). U of Utah Pr.
Burkitt's Disease: Immunological Aspects, Vol. 1. Alice Stewart et al. LC 73-16381. 1974. 19.00x o.p. (ISBN 0-8422-7173-2). Irvington.
Burkitt's Disease: Virology & Other Basic Studies, Vol. 2. M. Nonoyama et al. LC 73-16381. 150p. 1974. 19.00x o.p. (ISBN 0-8422-7163-5). Irvington.
Burlesque. John D. Jump. (Critical Idiom Ser.). 1972. pap. 5.50x o.p. (ISBN 0-416-66660-4, NO.2259). Routledge Chapman & Hall.
Burma: A Travel Survival Kit. 3rd ed. Tony Wheeler. (Illus.). 160p. (Orig.). 1985. pap. 7.95 o.p. (ISBN 0-908086-69-5). Lonely Planet.
Burma & Indonesia: Comparative Study of Political Economy & Foreign Policy. Kalyani Bandyopadhyaya. 260p. 1983. text ed. 22.50x o.p. (ISBN 0-391-02931-2). Humanities.
Burn & Scald Accidents to Children: Report of a Working Party of the Child Accident Prevention Trust. 65p. 1985. pap. text ed. 7.90x o.p. (ISBN 0-7199-1160-5). Gower Pub Co.
Burnet County History, 2 vols. Darrell Debo. 1980. 60.00 o.p. (ISBN 0-89015-229-2). Eakin Pr.
Burnie's Hill: A Traditional Rhyme. Illus. by Erik Blegvad. LC 76-28515. (ps-3). 1977. 6.95 o.p. (ISBN 0-689-50070-X, Atheneum). Macmillan.
Burning Barn Mystery. Thomas F. Pursell. LC 77-74011. (Carolrhoda Mini-Mystery Ser.). (Illus.). 32p. (gr. k-4). 1977. PLB 5.95 o.p. (ISBN 0-87614-085-1). Carolrhoda Bks.
Burning Bed. Faith McNulty. LC 79-2764. 320p. 1980. 12.95 o.p. (ISBN 0-15-114981-X). HarBraceJ.
Burning Bush. Stuart Y. Blanch. 1979. pap. 5.95 o.p. (ISBN 0-8192-1260-1). Morehouse Pub.
Burning Daylight. Jack London. (Illus.). 361p. 1987. pap. 7.95 o.s.i. (ISBN 0-932458-34-3). Star Rover.
Burning Down the House: MOVE & the Tragedy of Philadelphia. John Anderson & Hilary Hevenor. (Illus.). 450p. 1987. 18.45 o.p. (ISBN 0-393-02460-1). Norton.
Burning Forest: Essays on Chinese Culture & Politics. Simon Leys. LC 85-5521. 256p. 1986. 16.95 o.p. (ISBN 0-03-005063-4); pap. 9.95 o.p. (ISBN 0-8050-0350-9). H Holt & Co.
Burning Mountain: A Novel of the Invasion of Japan. Alfred Coppel. LC 82-15444. 448p. 1983. 15.95 o.p. (ISBN 0-15-114978-X). HarBraceJ.
Burning Sands. Violet Winspear. (Nightingale Paperbacks Ser.). 1984. pap. 9.95 o.p. (ISBN 0-8161-3564-9, Large Print Bks). G K Hall.
Burning Valley. J. L. Bouma. 1976. pap. 0.95 o.p. (ISBN 0-685-69511-5, LB378NK, Pub. by Leisure Bks CT). Dorchester Pub Co.
Burning Woman. Jessie Ford. (Orig.). 1985. pap. 3.95 o.s.i. (ISBN 0-345-31046-2). Ballantine.
Burnished Sword. J. H. MacLehose. 222p. 1955. (ISBN 0-8022-1031-7). Philos Lib.
Burnout in the Nursing Profession: Causes, Costs & Coping Strategies. Edwina A. McConnell. LC 81-18776. (Illus.). 312p. 1982. pap. text ed. 21.95 o.p. (ISBN 0-8016-3223-4). Mosby.
Burnout: Strategies for Personal & Organizational Life; Speculations on Evolving Paradigms. Michael Lauderdale. LC 81-16298. 334p. 1982. text ed. 16.95 o.p. (ISBN 0-89384-063-7). Univ Assocs.
Burns Book. Paul Day. (Illus.). 92p. pap. 16.95 o.s.i. (ISBN 0-933224-09-5, Pub. by Sound Investments UK). Bold Strummer Ltd.
Burns into English. William K. Seymour. 160p. 1955. (ISBN 0-8022-1538-6). Philos Lib.
Burns of the Upper Extremity. Roger E. Salisbury & Basil A. Pruitt. LC 75-14786. (Major Problems in Clinical Surgery Ser.: Vol. 19). (Illus.). 175p. 1976. text ed. (ISBN 0-7216-7902-1). Saunders.
Burnsite. Shirley Cochrane. LC 79-63170. (Series Four). 44p. 1979. pap. 7.00 o.p. (ISBN 0-931846-11-0). Wash Writers Pub.
Burnt-out Administrator. Carolyn L. Vash. LC 79-14057. 128p. 1980. text ed. 11.95 o.p. (ISBN 0-8261-2910-2). Springer Pub.
Burt. Howard Buten. Ed. by Bobbi Marks. LC 80-11196. 168p. 1981. pap. 5.95 o.p. (ISBN 0-03-057664-4). H Holt & Co.
Burton & Dudley. Marjorie W. Sharmat. (Illus.). (gr. 4-8). 1977. pap. 0.95 o.p. (ISBN 0-380-01732-6, 34215, Camelot). Avon.
Burton Anderson's Guide to Italian Wines. Burton Anderson. 160p. 1985. pap. 8.95 o.s.i. (ISBN 0-671-53022-4). S&S.
Burt's Big Day. Pete Kersten & Rick Kersten. (Kersten Brothers' Critter Tales Stick 'n Play Bks.). 16p. (ps-3). 1986. 6.95 o.p. (ISBN 0-316-49001-6). Little.
Bury Me Not. Harold Gauer. (Orig.). 1981. pap. 2.25 o.s.i. (ISBN 0-505-51605-5, Pub. by Tower Bks). Dorchester Pub Co.
Bus. Paul Kirchner. 1987. pap. 5.95 o.p. (ISBN 0-345-33944-4, Pub. by Ballantine Trade). Ballantine.
Bus & Rural Transit. (Transportation Research Report Ser.). 52p. 1979. 3.00 o.p. (ISBN 0-309-02968-6). Transport Res Bd.
Bus Equipment Guide: Intercity Coaches 1955-1985. Larry Plachno & Richard Wartenberg. Date not set. Transport Res Bd.
Bus of Dreams. Mary Morris. 207p. 1985. 15.45 o.p. (ISBN 0-395-36236-9). HM.
Bus Ride. Terry D. Roehrig. 1985. 11.95 o.p. (ISBN 0-533-06258-6). Vantage.
Bus Stops Here: A Study of School Desegregation in Three Cities. Anna Holden. LC 72-95964. 512p. 1974. 15.00x o.p. Agathon.
Bus Terminals: An Architectural Overview. Coppa & Avery Consultants Staff. (Architecture Ser.: Bibliography A-1308). 1985. pap. 2.00 o.p. (ISBN 0-89028-238-2). Vance Biblios.
Bus Transit Management & Performance. (Transportation Research Report Ser.). 64p. 1980. 5.20 o.p. (ISBN 0-309-03055-2). Transport Res Bd.
Bus Transportation Strategies. (Transportation Research Report Ser.). 59p. 1976. 2.60 o.p. (ISBN 0-309-02579-6). Transport Res Bd.
Bush Blooms Again. Kathleen McArthur. (Orig.). 1987. 16.95 o.p. (ISBN 0-86417-050-5, Pub. by Kangaroo Pr). Intl Spec Bk.
Bush Brother. Graham Jeffery. 1971. 3.95 o.p. (ISBN 0-8192-1129-X). Morehouse Pub.
Bush Is Still Burning. Lloyd J. Ogilvie. 1980. 8.99 o.p. (ISBN 0-8499-3031-6). Word Bks.
Bushbabies. William Stevenson. (Illus.). (gr. 4-6). 1965. 8.95 o.p. (ISBN 0-395-07116-X). HM.
Bushcraft. Date not set. (ISBN 0-8052-0333-8). Random.
Bushwhackers. Lee Floren. (Orig.). 1980. pap. 1.75 o.p. (ISBN 0-505-51531-8, Pub. by Tower Bks). Dorchester Pub Co.
Business. Robert J. Hughes et al. 1980. text ed. 29.50 o.p. (ISBN 0-395-30634-5). HM.
Business: A Novel Approach. Richard N. Farmer. 372p. 1984. pap. 8.95 o.p. (ISBN 0-89815-128-7). Ten Speed Pr.
Business Acquisitions Desk Book. 2nd ed. F. T. Davis. LC 81-6464. 414p. 1981. 65.00 o.p. (ISBN 0-87624-049-X, Inst Busn Plan). P-H.
Business Acquisitions Desk Book, with Checklists & Forms. Frank T. Davis, Jr. LC 77-75863. 264p. 1977. 29.95 o.p. (ISBN 0-87624-050-3, Inst Busn Plan). P-H.
Business Acquisitions: Tax & Legal Guide. Frank L. Brunetti & Stanley J. Yellin. LC 87-9136. 1987. 110.00 o.p. (ISBN 0-916592-69-3). Panel Pubs.
Business Administration: A Textbook for the Computer Age. Roger Carter. LC 83-26177. (Applications of Computer Science Ser.). 1984. pap. text ed. 24.95 o.p. (ISBN 0-88175-008-5, Computer Sci Pr). W H Freeman.
Business Administration & Accounting. 25.00 o.p. Am Consul Eng.
Business Administration & Management. 4th ed. C. Deverell. 1983. pap. 17.95 o.p. (ISBN 0-85258-188-2). Van Nos Reinhold.
Business Administration for the Dental Assistant. 2nd ed. Ann Ehrlich. LC 75-21039. (Illus.). 1983. 13.95 o.p. (ISBN 0-940012-16-2). Colwell Syst.
Business Administration for the Medical Assistant. 2nd ed. Erlich et al. LC 81-67045. (Illus.). 1983. 13.95 o.p. (ISBN 0-940012-01-4). Colwell Syst.
Business: An Introduction. Benjamin M. Compaine & Robert F. Litro. 540p. 1984. text ed. 29.95x o.s.i. (ISBN 0-03-059902-4); study guide 13.95x o.s.i. (ISBN 0-03-063618-3). Dryden Pr.
Business: An Involvement Approach. Herbert G. Hicks et al. 1975. text ed. 41.95 o.p. (ISBN 0-07-028715-5). McGraw.
Business & Commercial Implications see Sharing the Sun.
Business & Economic Research in a World of Risk & Uncertainty. (Auber Proceedings 1983 Ser.: Vol. 4). (Illus.). 205p. 1984. 15.00 o.p. (ISBN 0-86603-017-4). Bur Busn Wis.
Business & Financial Tables Desk Book. Institute for Business Planning Research & Editorial Staff. LC 75-9003. 1975. 25.00 o.p. (ISBN 0-87624-065-1, Inst Busn Plan). P-H.
Business & Government During the Eisenhower Administration: A Study of the Antitrust Policy of the Antitrust Division of the Justice Department. Theodore P. Kovaleff. LC 79-25590. x, 313p. 1980. 19.95x o.p. (ISBN 0-8214-0416-4). Ohio U Pr.
Business & Home Applications for the Macintosh Using Microsoft BASIC. Stan Schat. 224p. 1984. pap. 14.95 o.p. (ISBN 0-89303-403-7). Brady Bks.
Business & Industry Perspectives on U. S. Production: Implications for Vocational Education. Thomas W. Miller. 18p. 1982. 2.50 o.p. (ISBN 0-318-22050-4, OC82). Natl Ctr Res Voc Ed.
Business & Its Legal Environment. Thomas W. Dunfee & Janice Bellace. (Illus.). 688p. 1983. text ed. 35.00 o.p. (ISBN 0-13-101006-9). P-H.
Business & Its Legal Environment: Study Guide & Workbook. Richard L. Coffinberger & Linda B. Samuels. 176p. 1983. (ISBN 0-13-101022-0). P-H.
Business & Law of Music. Joseph Taubman. 111p. 1965. 8.50 o.p. (ISBN 0-87945-009-6). Fed Legal Pubn.
Business & Management Jobs 1985. Ed. by Christopher Billy. (Peterson's Annual Guides-Careers Ser.). 226p. (Orig.). 1985. pap. 12.95 o.p. (ISBN 0-87866-249-9). Petersons Guides.
Business & Management Jobs 1987. 3rd ed. (Peterson's Annual Guides to Jobs Ser). 283p. (Orig.). 1986. pap. 15.95 o.p. (ISBN 0-87866-468-8). Petersons Guides.
Business & Management Jobs 1988. 4th ed. (Peterson's Annual Guides to Jobs Ser.). 291p. (Orig.). 1987. lib. bdg. 22.95 o.p. (ISBN 0-87866-656-7); pap. 17.95 o.p. (ISBN 0-87866-577-3). Petersons Guides.
Business & Management Jobs, 1988. Date not set. Petersons Guides.
Business & Management 1988-89. 7th, rev. ed. LC 73-78578. (Annual Editions Ser.). 224p. 1987. pap. text ed. 9.95x o.p. (ISBN 0-87967-704-X). Dushkin Pub.
Business & Office Education Curriculum. National Center for Research in Vocational Education Staff. 61p. 1984. 4.95 o.p. (ISBN 0-318-22051-2, BB71). Natl Ctr Res Voc Ed.
Business & Office Education: Review & Synthesis of Research. Judith J. Lambrecht et al. 173p. cancelled o.s.i. (ISBN 0-318-22052-0, IN232). Natl Ctr Res Voc Ed.
Business & Politics: Monographs. Mary Vance. (Public Administration Ser.: P 1812). 11p. 1985. 2.00 o.p. (ISBN 0-89028-642-6). Vance Biblios.
Business & Sentiment in a Chinese Market Town. John A. Young. (Asian Folklore & Social Life Monograph: No. 60). 160p. 1974. 14.00x o.p. (ISBN 0-89986-055-9). Oriental Bk Store.
Business & Society: Concepts & Policy Issues. 4th ed. Keith Davis et al. (Management Ser.). (Illus.). 672p. 1980. text ed. 31.95x o.p. (ISBN 0-07-015532-1). McGraw.
Business & Society: Managing Corporate & Social Impact. George Sawyer. LC 78-69570. (Illus.). 1979. text ed. 26.95 o.p. (ISBN 0-395-26541-X). HM.
Business & Technology Videolog. LC 78-74186. 1981. pap. 39.50 o.p. (ISBN 0-88432-070-7, Video-Forum). J Norton Pubs.
Business & the Middle East. Robert A. Kilmarx & Yonah Alexander. (Pergamon Policy Studies). 272p. 1982. 37.00 o.p. (ISBN 0-08-025992-8, K110, L110). Pergamon.
Business Applications for the Apple II & IIe under CP-M. Steven Zimmerman et al. 270p. 1984. 15.95 o.p. (ISBN 0-89303-354-5). Brady Bks.
Business Applications for the IBM Personal Computer. Steven Zimmerman & Leo Conrad. LC 83-3823. (Illus.). 320p. 1983. pap. 19.95 o.p. (ISBN 0-89303-243-3); incl. diskette 49.95 o.p. (ISBN 0-89303-351-0); diskette 30.00 o.p. (ISBN 0-89303-352-9). Brady Bks.
Business Applications of Repertory Grid. V. Stewart & A. Stewart. 256p. 1982. text ed. 26.95 o.p. (ISBN 0-07-084549-2). McGraw.
Business Applications on the BBC Micro. Susan Curran & Margaret Norman. (Illus.). 218p. (Orig.). 1984. pap. 15.95 o.p. (ISBN 0-246-12530-6, Pub. by Granada England). Sheridan.
Business Arbitration: What You Need to Know. 3rd ed. Robert Coulson. 178p. 1987. 10.00 o.p. Am Arbitration.
Business Archives: An Introduction. Edie Hedlin. LC 78-18930. 28p. 1978. pap. 7.00 o.p. (ISBN 0-931828-08-2). Soc Am Archivists.
Business Archives: Studies on International Practices. International Council on Archives, Business Archives Committee. 167p. 1983. pap. text ed. 25.00 o.p. (ISBN 3-598-10516-9). K G Saur.
Business As Usual: Business Cartoons for Business People from the Nationally Syndicated Comic "The Neighborhood" Jerry Van Amerongen. 1986. pap. 5.95 o.p. (ISBN 0-671-60627-1, Fireside). S&S.
Business BASIC. 2nd ed. Robert J. Bent & George C. Sethares. LC 83-19024. (Computer Science Ser.). 240p. 1984. pap. text ed. 21.00 pub net o.p. (ISBN 0-534-03179-X). Brooks-Cole.
Business Borrowers Complete Success Kit. 3rd ed. Tyler G. Hicks. 596p. 1987. pap. 99.50 o.p. (ISBN 0-934311-06-4). Intl Wealth.
Business Building Letters: Ready-to-Use Letters That Build Premiums & Goodwill. Alfred I. Jaffe & Jerome S. Miller. Set. 16.00 o.p. (ISBN 0-686-31036-5, 26627). Rough Notes.
Business Buy-out Agreements. California Continuing Eduacation of the Bar Staff & John O. Hargrove. LC 75-43058. xi, 308p. 1976. 65.00 o.p. (ISBN 0-88124-042-7). Cal Cont Ed Bar.
Business Capital Sources. 3rd ed. Tyler G. Hicks. 150p. 1987. pap. 15.00 o.p. (ISBN 0-934311-09-9). Intl Wealth.
Business Chinese Five Hundred. 1982. incl. 2 tapes 24.95 o.p. (ISBN 0-8351-1383-3). China Bks.
Business Chinese 500. Ed. by Beijing Language Institute & Beijing Institute of Foreign Trade Staff. 309p. (Orig.). 1982. pap. 6.95 o.p. (ISBN 0-8351-1039-7). China Bks.
Business Civilization in Decline. Robert L. Heilbroner. 128p. 1976. 6.95 o.p. (ISBN 0-393-05571-X). Norton.
Business Combinations & Consolidated Financial Statements. Finley E. Belcher & Clyde P. Stickney. 1983. pap. 20.95x o.p. (ISBN 0-256-02788-9). Irwin.
Business Communication. 2nd ed. Richard C. Huseman et al. 656p. 1985. text ed. 30.95 o.s.i. (ISBN 0-03-062512-2). Dryden Pr.
Business Communication. LaJuanna W. Lee et al. LC 81-86019. 1980. text ed. 26.95 o.p. (ISBN 0-395-30657-4). HM.
Business Communication: Getting Results. Paul R. Timm & Christopher G. Jones. 312p. 1983. pap. text ed. (ISBN 0-13-091793-1). P-H.
Business Communication: Theory & Application. 5th ed. Raymond V. Lesikar. 1984. 34.95x o.p. (ISBN 0-256-03157-6). Irwin.

Business Communication: Theory & Practice. Dale A. Level, Jr. & William P. Galle, Jr. 1980. 26.50x o.p. (ISBN 0-256-02203-8). Irwin.

Business Communications. 7th ed. William C. Himstreet & Wayne M. Baty. LC 83-23854. 712p. 1983. text ed. write for info. o.p. (ISBN 0-534-02837-3); instr's. manual avail. o.p. PWS-Kent Pub.

Business Communications: A Problem Solving Approach. Roy W. Poe & Rosemary T. Fruehling. (Illus.). 1978. text ed. 29.90 o.p. (ISBN 0-07-050362-1). McGraw.

Business Communications: Principles & Methods. 6th ed. William C. Himstreet & Wayne M. Baty. 1981. 23.95x o.p. (ISBN 0-534-00908-5). PWS-Kent Pub.

Business Communications: Theory Structure Form. rev. ed. Sheldon F. Katz. 28p. 1977. pap. text ed. 5.00 o.p. (ISBN 0-89917-448-5, Pub. by College Town Pr). Tichenor Pub.

Business Communicator. 2nd ed. Robert E. Swindle & Elizabeth M. Swindle. (Illus.). 464p. 1985. text ed. (ISBN 0-13-091760-5). P-H.

Business Confidential. Boardroom's Experts & Editors. LC 85-17052. 520p. 1985. 50.00 o.p. (ISBN 0-932648-68-1). Boardroom.

Business Correspondence-Thirty. 3rd ed. Rosemary T. Fruehling & Sharon Bouchard. Ed. by Joseph Tinervia. (Illus.). 192p. (gr. 10-12). 1981. text ed. 11.32 o.p. (ISBN 0-07-022513-3). McGraw.

Business Cycles: A Theoretical, Historical & Statistical Analysis of the Capitalist Process, 2 vols. Joseph A. Schumpeter. 1982. Repr. of 1939 ed. Set. lib. bdg. 75.00x o.p. (ISBN 0-87991-807-1). Porcupine Pr.

Business Cycles & National Income. expanded ed. Alvin H. Hansen. 1964. 14.95x o.p. (ISBN 0-393-09726-9, NortonC). Norton.

Business Data Communications: Basic Concepts, Security, & Design. Jerry Fitzgerald. LC 83-14798. (Computers & Information Processing Systems for Business Ser.: 1-661). 502p. 1984. 37.95x o.p. (ISBN 0-471-89549-0). Wiley.

Business Data Processing. 2nd ed. Barbara Burian & Stuart Fink. LC 81-5207. (Illus.). 544p. 1982. text ed. (ISBN 0-13-094045-3). P-H.

Business Data Processing Fundamentals see Accounting Ten-Twelve.

Business Disclosure: Government's Need to Know. H. J. Goldschmid. 1979. text ed. 47.95 o.p. (ISBN 0-07-023670-4). McGraw.

Business English. Roger W. Dow. LC 78-18253. 451p. 1979. pap. 17.50 o.p. (ISBN 0-471-36661-7). tchr's. manual avail. o.p. (ISBN 0-471-05251-5). Wiley.

Business English. Mary E. Guffey. LC 82-21298. 352p. 1983. pap. text ed. write for info. o.p. (ISBN 0-534-01396-1); tchr's. ed. avail. o.p. PWS-Kent Pub.

Business English: A Gregg Text-Kit for Adult Education. 3rd ed. Jeanne Reed. 1978. text ed. 23.85 o.p. (ISBN 0-07-051497-6). McGraw.

Business Enterprise & Economic Change: Essays in Honor of H. F. Williamson. Ed. by Louis Cain & Paul Uselding. LC 72-92365. 350p. 1973. 15.00x o.p. (ISBN 0-87338-134-3). Kent St U Pr.

Business Environment & Public Policy: Implications for Management. Rogene A. Buchholz. (Illus.). 560p. 1982. text ed. (ISBN 0-13-095554-X). P-H.

Business Environment & Public Policy: Implications for Management & Strategy Formulation. 2nd ed. Rogene A. Buchholz. (Illus.). 688p. 1986. text ed. 41.00 o.p. (ISBN 0-13-095571-X). P-H.

Business Ethics. Edward Stevens. LC 79-91409. 248p. (Orig.). 1979. pap. 9.95 o.p. (ISBN 0-8091-2244-8). Paulist Pr.

Business Ethics: Concepts & Cases. Manuel G. Velasquez. 416p. 1982. pap. text ed. (ISBN 0-13-096008-X). P-H.

Business Experience with Value Added Taxation. Michael Schiff. LC 74-75478. 1974. 8.00 o.p. (ISBN 0-910586-09-8). Finan Exec.

Business Financial Management. rev. ed. George N. Engler. 1978. 17.95x o.p. (ISBN 0-256-02076-0); student wkbk. 5.50x o.p. (ISBN 0-686-77074-9). Irwin.

Business Forecasting. Charles W. Gross & Robin T. Peterson. LC 75-31029. (Illus.). 320p. 1976. text ed. 26.95 o.p. (ISBN 0-395-19505-5). HM.

Business Forms Management. William V. Nygren. 1980. 22.95 o.p. (ISBN 0-8144-5524-7). AMACOM.

Business, Government & Society, Vol. 11. Compiled by James W. Dean & Richard Schwindt. 198p. 1985. 14.00 o.p. (ISBN 0-88024-111-X). Eno River Pr.

Business, Government, & the Public. 2nd ed. Murray L. Weidenbaum. 1981. text ed. 31.00 o.p. (ISBN 0-13-099325-5). P-H.

Business Graphics for the IBM PC. Nelson Ford. LC 83-51567. (Illus.). 259p. 1984. pap. 18.95 o.p. (ISBN 0-89588-124-1). SYBEX.

Business Graphics for the Macintosh. Gregory R. Glau. 250p. 1985. pap. 19.95 o.p. (ISBN 0-87094-693-5). Dow Jones-Irwin.

Business Graphics with the IBM PC-XT-AT. Gregory R. Glau. 230p. 1986. pap. 19.95 o.p. (ISBN 0-87094-754-0). Dow Jones-Irwin.

Business Idea: From Birth to Profitable Company. Gilbert N. Dorland & John Van Der Wal. 208p. 1982. pap. 12.95 o.p. (ISBN 0-442-22165-7). Van Nos Reinhold.

Business Idea from Birth to Profitable Company. Gilbert N. Dorland & John Van Der Wal. 1978. 17.95 o.p. (ISBN 0-442-22163-0). Van Nos Reinhold.

Business in Action: An Introduction to Business. Lester R. Bittel. LC 79-9320. 1980. text ed. 29.95 o.p. (ISBN 0-07-079164-3). McGraw.

Business in Society: Consensus & Conflict. Tom Burden & Reg Chapman. 1981. text ed. (ISBN 0-408-10693-X); pap. text ed. (ISBN 0-408-10694-8). Butterworth.

Business in the Age of Information. John Diebold. LC 84-45782. 144p. 1985. 14.95 o.p. (ISBN 0-8144-5792-4). AMACOM.

Business, Industry & Labor Input in Vocational Education Personnel Development. 2nd ed. Catharine P. Warmbrod et al. 199p. 1980. 11.80 o.p. (ISBN 0-318-22053-9, LT59). Natl Ctr Res Voc Ed.

Business Information for Today's Practicing Lawyer, Vol. 338. Practising Law Institute Staff. 631p. 1984. pap. 40.00 o.p. (ISBN 0-317-27414-7, #A4-4098). PLI.

Business Information Guidebook. Oscar Figueroa & Charles Winkler. 256p. 1980. 19.95 o.p. (ISBN 0-8144-5560-3); pap. 9.95 o.p. (ISBN 0-8144-7005-X). AMACOM.

Business Information: Protection & Disclosure, 2 vols. Peter C. Hein. 415p. 1983. Supplements Avail. 130.00 o.p. (ISBN 0-15-100006-9, H42833, Pub. by Law & Business). HarBraceJ.

Business Law. Chaykin C. P. A. Review Staff & Leonard Lakin. LC 84-248737. 440p. 1984. 29.95 o.p. (ISBN 0-8403-3415-X). Kendall-Hunt.

Business Law. Collins et al. 176p. 1986. Appendix. pap. write for info. o.p. (ISBN 0-471-84477-2). Wiley.

Business Law. Albert K. Francisco & Kenneth A. Smith. LC 87-62075. (CPA Examination Review Ser.). 352p. 1988. pap. text ed. 20.95 o.p. (ISBN 0-932276-77-6). Prof Pubns CA.

Business Law. 6th ed. Len Y. Smith et al. (Illus.). 268p. 1985. text ed. 45.25 o.p. (ISBN 0-314-85302-2). West Pub.

Business Law: Alternate Edition. 2nd ed. Rate Howell et al. 931p. 1982. text ed. 33.95x o.s.i. (ISBN 0-03-059742-0); teachers manual 20.00 o.s.i. (ISBN 0-03-061579-8); study guide 12.95x o.s.i. (ISBN 0-03-061581-X). Dryden Pr.

Business Law & the Legal Environment. Jethro K. Lieberman & George J. Siedel. 1334p. 1985. text ed. 32.00 o.p. (ISBN 0-15-505617-4, HC). HarBraceJ.

Business Law & the Regulatory Environment. 6th ed. Michael B. Metzger et al. 1986. 42.95x o.p. (ISBN 0-256-03334-X) (ISBN 0-256-03335-8). Irwin.

Business Law-Florida Edition, Cases & Materials. Alvin Stauber & E. Neil Young. 148p. 1982. pap. text ed. 6.00x o.p. (ISBN 0-89582-089-7). Morton Pub.

Business Law: Instructor's Manual with Test Bank. 4th ed. Jordan L. Paust et al. 351p. 1984. pap. write for info. incl. test bank o.p. (ISBN 0-314-77781-4). West Pub.

Business Law: Legal Environment, Transaction & Regulation. 3rd ed. Cameron & Scaletta. 1989. 43.95 o.p. (ISBN 0-256-07131-4). Irwin.

Business Law: Principles & Cases. Daniel V. Davidson et al. LC 83-23863. 1024p. 1984. text ed. write for info. o.p. (ISBN 0-534-01456-9). PWS-Kent Pub.

Business Law: Principles, Cases & Policy. Mark E. Roszkowski. 1987. text ed. write for info. o.p. (ISBN 0-673-39034-9); write for info., study guide o.p. (ISBN 0-673-39035-7); test bank avail. o.p. (ISBN 0-673-49018-1). Scott F.

Business Law: Selected Questions & Unofficial Answers Indexed to Content Specification Outline. James D. Blum & Mark S. Goldstein. LC 84-189048. 1984. write for info. o.p. Am Inst CPA.

Business Law: Text & Cases. 2nd ed. Rate A. Howell et al. LC 80-65801. 1075p. 1981. text ed. 28.95x o.s.i. (ISBN 0-03-058111-7); study guide 12.95x o.s.i. (ISBN 0-03-058113-3). Dryden Pr.

Business Law: Text & Cases. Henry B. Reiling et al. LC 81-18601. 1216p. 1982. text ed. write for info. o.p. (ISBN 0-534-01132-2). PWS-Kent Pub.

Business Law: Texts & Cases. Purver et al. 1309p. 1983. text ed. 28.75 o.p. (ISBN 0-15-505621-2, HC). HarBraceJ.

Business Laws & Practices of Bahrain. Ed. by Shair Management Services Staff. (Business Laws & Practice Ser.). 120p. 1979. pap. 219.00x o.p. (ISBN 0-86010-903-8). Graham & Trotman.

Business Laws & Practices of Jordan. Ed. by Shair Management Services Staff. 102p. 1979. 219.00x o.p. (ISBN 0-86010-906-2). Graham & Trotman.

Business Letters for Typing. 3rd ed. Harves Rahe. LC 69-19885. (gr. 9-12). 1976. spiral bdg. 5.60 o.p. (ISBN 0-02-830620-1). Glencoe.

Business Loan Workouts, 1983. Practising Law Institute Staff & Albert F. Reisman. LC 83-220288. (Commercial Law & Practice Course Handbook Ser.: No. 309). 536p. 1983. 40.00 o.p. PLI.

Business Management in Girl Scouting. 112p. 1979. pap. 9.00 o.p. (ISBN 0-88441-440-X, 26-169). Girl Scouts USA.

Business Management Laboratory. 3rd ed. Jensen & Cherrington. 1984. 19.95 o.p. (ISBN 0-256-02699-8). Irwin.

Business Management Laboratory: Participants' Manual. rev. ed. Ronald Jensen & David J. Cherrington. 1977. pap. 9.95x o.p. (ISBN 0-256-01953-3). Irwin.

Business Math Basics. Robert E. Swindle. LC 77-28011. 322p. 1979. pap. text ed. 15.95x o.p. (ISBN 0-686-86239-2). PWS-Kent Pub.

Business Math Basics. 2nd ed. Robert E. Swindle. LC 82-20326. 368p. 1983. pap. text ed. write for info. o.p. (ISBN 0-534-01323-6); write for info. tchr's ed. o.p. PWS-Kent Pub.

Business Mathematics. Carl Arendsen. 450p. 1980. (ISBN 0-87150-293-3, 2312, Prindle). PWS-Kent Pub.

Business Mathematics. William Dillon. LC 84-16987. 320p. 1985. spiral bdg. 18.95 o.p. (ISBN 0-8273-2346-8); instr's. guide 11.00 o.p. (ISBN 0-8273-2347-6); 9.95 o.p. business simulation (ISBN 0-8273-2349-2); computerized drill & practice 35.00 o.p. (ISBN 0-8273-2348-4); computerized test 35.00 o.p. (ISBN 0-8273-2344-1). Delmar.

Business Mathematics. Burton S. Kaliski. (Illus.). 466p. 1972. text ed. 13.95 o.p. (ISBN 0-15-505631-X, HC). HarBraceJ.

Business Mathematics. 2nd ed. Burton S. Kaliski. 1977. text ed. 16.95 o.p. (ISBN 0-15-505636-0, HC). HarBraceJ.

Business Mathematics. 3rd ed. Burton S. Kaliski. 402p. 1982. text ed. 22.00 o.p. (ISBN 0-15-505641-7, HC). HarBraceJ.

Business Mathematics. 4th ed. Richard R. McCready. LC 81-19308. 1981. pap. text ed. write for info. o.p. (ISBN 0-534-01075-X); tchr's. ed avail. o.p. PWS-Kent Pub.

Business Mathematics. Jimmy C. McKenzie & J. Roland Kelley. 1980. pap. 33.56 o.p. (ISBN 0-395-30672-8). HM.

Business Mathematics. Robert Ochs & James Gray. 1982. 23.95 o.p. (CBS C). SCP.

Business Mathematics: A Collegiate Approach. 4th ed. Helda Roueche. (Illus.). 640p. 1983. text ed. (ISBN 0-13-105221-7). P-H.

Business Mathematics: A Consumer's Approach. Robert P. Webber. LC 75-26091. (Illus.). 352p. 1976. text ed. 23.50 o.p. (ISBN 0-395-20591-3). HM.

Business Mathematics & Calculating Machines. Bonnie D. Phillips & Dale A. Storey. (Illus.). 224p. 1976. pap. text ed. write for info. o.p. (ISBN 0-02-395280-6). Macmillan.

Business Mediation: What You Need to Know. Robert Coulson. LC 87-70084. 128p. 1987. pap. 8.00 o.p. (ISBN 0-943001-07-2). Am Arbitration.

Business Negotiations with the Japanese. Rosalie L. Tung. LC 82-47965. 250p. 1984. 29.00x o.p. (ISBN 0-669-05724-X). Lexington Bks.

Business of Agriculture. 306p. 1984. 30.00 o.p. (ISBN 0-318-03919-2, 267). PA Bar Inst.

Business of Art. Ed. by Lee E. Caplin. 1982. text ed. 22.95 o.p. (ISBN 0-13-106518-1, Busn); pap. 11.95 o.p. (ISBN 0-13-106500-9). P-H.

Business of Art. Ed. by Lee E. Caplin. 383p. pap. 11.95 o.s.i. (ISBN 0-317-36356-5). Am Council Arts.

Business of Book Publishing. Clive Bingley. LC 71-187175. 1972. text ed. 20.00 o.p. (ISBN 0-08-016844-2). Pergamon.

Business of Business: Managing with Style. Robert Heller. LC 81-47305. 224p. 1981. 14.95 o.p. (ISBN 0-15-114982-8). HarBraceJ.

Business of Filmmaking. Ed. by Eastman Kodak Company Staff. LC 78-55882. (Illus.). 1978. pap. 6.95 o.s.i. (ISBN 0-87985-203-8, H-55). Eastman Kodak.

Business of Mathematics. Margaret Willerding. 1977. write for info. o.p. (ISBN 0-87150-210-0, PWS 1681, Prindle). PWS-Kent Pub.

Business of National Importance. Edwin Green & Michael Moss. 1982. 32.00x o.p. (ISBN 0-416-32220-4, NO. 6729). Routledge Chapman & Hall.

Business Office. Phyllis C. Morrison & J. W. Twing. (Illus.). 1978. text ed. 22.80 o.p. (ISBN 0-07-043231-7). McGraw.

Business Office, Office Career Guide. Phyllis C. Morrison & J. W. Twing. 1978. pap. text ed. 40.96 o.p. (ISBN 0-07-043232-5). McGraw.

Business Officers in Higher Education: A History of NACUBO. Neal O. Hines. Ed. by David W. Jacobson. LC 82-3583. 113p. (Orig.). 1982. pap. 10.00 o.p. (ISBN 0-915164-14-0). NACUBO.

Business-One Thousand Directory, 1984. Ed. by O. A. Battista. LC 80-642221. 504p. 1983. 50.00 o.p. (ISBN 0-915074-10-9). Knowledge Bk Pubs.

Business Opportunities Brokerage: Strategies & Techniques for Real Estate Professionals. Edward I. Bernd. LC 82-25077. 169p. 1983. text ed. 29.95 o.p. (ISBN 0-13-106724-9). P-H.

Business Organization. Ronald R. Pitfield. (Illus.). 256p. 1983. pap. text ed. 16.95x o.p. (ISBN 0-7121-0295-7). Trans-Atl Phila.

Business Organizations, Agencies & Publications Directory, 2 vols. 3rd ed. Ed. by Kay Gill. 2000p. 1986. 290.00X o.p. (ISBN 0-8103-2097-5). Gale.

Business Planning for an Uncertain Future: Scenarios & Strategies. Roy C. Amara & Andrew J. Lipinski. (PPS on Business & Economics Ser.). 200p. 1983. 60.00 o.p. (ISBN 0-08-027545-1). Pergamon.

Business Planning for the Enterpreneur. Edward E. Williams & Salvatore E. Manzo. 208p. 1983. 22.95 o.p. (ISBN 0-442-28970-7). Van Nos Reinhold.

Business Planning with IBM Personal Decision Software. Timothy Berry. 175p. 1986. pap. 25.00 o.p. (ISBN 0-87094-683-8). Dow Jones-Irwin.

Business Policy: A Framework for Analysis. 4th ed. Robert G. Murdick et al. LC 82-24266. 360p. 1984. pap. (ISBN 0-471-84132-3). Wiley.

Business Policy & Strategy. Y. N. Chang & Filemon Campo-Flores. 1980. pap. text ed. 16.30x o.p. (ISBN 0-673-16074-2). Scott F.

Business Policy & Strategy, Vol. 10. Compiled by James W. Dean & Richard Schwindt. 286p. 1985. 14.00 o.p. (ISBN 0-88024-110-1). Eno River Pr.

Business Policy & Strategy: Text & Cases. Y. N. Chang & Filemon Campo-Flores. 1980. text ed. write for info. o.p. (ISBN 0-673-16073-4). Scott F.

Business Power for Your Apple. Gregory R. Glau. 288p. 1984. 37.95 o.p. (ISBN 0-442-22779-5). Van Nos Reinhold.

Business Publications Index & Abstracts: Abstracts 1985 Cumulation. 1500p. 1986. 285.00x o.p. (ISBN 0-8103-1524-6). Gale.

Business Publications Index & Abstracts: Subject-Author Citations 1984 Cumulation. 2263p. 1985. 285.00x o.p. (ISBN 0-8103-1523-8). Gale.

Business Publications Index & Abstracts 1983: Subject-Author Citations Twelve Monthly Issues, Cumulated Quarterly. 1983. pap. 245.00x o.p. (ISBN 0-8103-1520-3). Gale.

Business Realities in the Information Industry. Ed. by Fred S. Rosenau & Leslie Chase. LC 83-80072. 100p. 1983. 30.00 o.p. (ISBN 0-942774-10-8). Info Indus.

Business Report Writing. Carol Baxter. LC 82-21340. 392p. 1983. text ed. write for info. o.p. (ISBN 0-534-01392-9). PWS-Kent Pub.

Business Report Writing. Joel P. Bowman & Bernadine P. Branchaw. 496p. 1984. text ed. 29.95x o.p. (ISBN 0-03-062793-1); instr's. manual w/transparency acetates & masters 19.95 o.p. (ISBN 0-03-062794-X). Dryden Pr.

Business Report Writing. Harry M. Brown. LC 79-55885. 350p. 1980. pap. text ed. 10.95x o.p. PWS-Kent Pub.

Business Research: Concepts & Guides. Robert G. Murdick & Donald Cooper. LC 81-2167. 207p. 1982. pap. 21.50 o.p. (ISBN 0-471-87690-9). Wiley.

Business Research Methods. William G. Zikmund. 624p. 1984. text ed. 32.95 o.p. (ISBN 0-03-045271-6); instr.'s manual 19.95 o.p. (ISBN 0-03-045276-7). Dryden Pr.

Business Segments: A Guide for Managers & Accountants. Adolph G. Lurie. (Illus.). 1979. text ed. 25.95 o.p. (ISBN 0-07-039113-0). McGraw.

Business Side of Medical Practice. 80p. 1986. 12.25 o.p. (ISBN 0-89970-244-9, OP-410-6). AMA.

Business Spelling. Gerald Seligman. (Easy Way Ser.). 144p. 1983. pap. 8.95 o.p. (ISBN 0-8120-2523-7). Barron.

Business Statistics. O. K. Bhatia & Vijay Bhatia. 612p. 1986. pap. text ed. 18.95x o.p. (ISBN 0-7069-2736-2, Pub. by Vikas India). Advent NY.

Business Statistics. R. Lawrence LaForge & Donald W. Kroeber. (Illus.). 1978. write for info. study guide o.p. (ISBN 0-02-428710-5). Macmillan.

Business Statistics: Basic Concepts & Methodology. 2nd ed. Wayne W. Daniel & James C. Terrell. LC 78-69607. (Illus.). 1979. text ed. 25.95 o.p. (ISBN 0-395-26762-5). HM.

Business Statistics: Basic Concepts & Methodology. 3rd ed. Wayne W. Daniel & James C. Terrell. LC 82-83254. 832p. 1982. text ed. 31.95 o.p. (ISBN 0-395-32601-X). HM.

Business Systems Handbook: Analysis, Designs & Documentation Standards. R. Gilmour. 1979. text ed. 39.33 o.p. (ISBN 0-13-107755-4). P-H.

Business Tax Deduction Master Guide. 2nd ed. W. Murray Bradford & Glenn B. Davis. 320p. 1984. 24.95 o.p. (ISBN 0-13-108282-5); 15.95 o.p. (ISBN 0-13-108274-4). P-H.

Business Tax Deduction Master Guide: Strategies for Business & Professional People. 3rd ed. W. Murray Bradford. 1985. pap. 14.95 o.p. (ISBN 0-13-108424-0). P-H.

Business Telecom: Proceedings of the International Conference London, 1983. International Conference London Staff. 350p. (Orig.). 1983. pap. text ed. 123.50x o.p. (Pub. by Online Conferences England). Gower Pub Co.

Business Telecommunications. (Amsterdam Conference, 1977). 142p. (Orig.). 1977. pap. text ed. 26.95x o.p. (ISBN 0-686-44808-1, Pub. by Online Conferences England). Gower Pub Co.

Business Telecoms: The New Regime. 197p. 1981. text ed. 98.00x o.p. (ISBN 0-686-87214-2, Pub. by Online Conferences England). Gower Pub Co.

Business Transaction Forms. 2nd, rev. ed. Stuart J. Faber. 300p. 1983. pap. text ed. 38.50 o.p. (ISBN 0-89074-094-1). Lega Bks.

Business Traveler's City Guide 1987. Ed. by Jean Postlewaite. (Illus.). 440p. 1987. pap. 9.95 o.p. (ISBN 0-528-84238-2). Rand McNally.

Business Traveler's Survival Guide - 1982 Edition: Atlanta. 1981. pap. 8.95 o.p. Watts.

Business Traveler's Survival Guide, 1981 Edition: Atlanta. (Illus.). 1981. pap. 8.95 o.p. Watts.

Business Trends & Forecasting Information Sources. Ed. by James B. Woy. LC 65-28351. (Management Information Guide Ser.: No. 9). 152p. 1965. 68.00x o.p. (ISBN 0-8103-0809-6). Gale.

Business Typewriting. Sylvia F. Parks. (Illus.). 196p. 1983. pap. text ed. 16.95x o.p. (ISBN 0-7121-0294-9, Pub. by Macdonald & Evans). Trans-Atl Phila.

Business: Unsafe at Any Level. S. Mort Zimmerman. 12.50 o.p. (ISBN 0-682-49477-1). Exposition-Phoenix.

Business Writing & Communication. Harry M. Brown & Karen K. Reid. LC 78-62190. 404p. 1979. text ed. 22.95x o.p. (ISBN 0-534-20942-4). PWS-Kent Pub.

Business Writing for Bankers. Reid, James M., Company Staff. 200p. 1984. 55.00 o.s.i. (ISBN 0-318-04572-9); lender's guide 150.00 o.s.i. (ISBN 0-318-04573-7). Robt Morris Assocs.

Business Writing Workshop. rev. ed. Courtland L. Bovee. (Illus.). 225p. 1981. pap. text ed. 17.95x o.p. (ISBN 0-935732-04-7). Roxbury Pub Co.

Busing. Thomas J. Cottle. LC 76-7740. 1976. pap. 4.95x o.p. (ISBN 0-8070-0495-2, BP561). Beacon Pr.

Busman's Honeymoon. Dorothy L. Sayers. 1978. pap. 2.75 o.p. (ISBN 0-380-01076-3, 62489-3). Avon.

Bussy d'Ambois. George Chapman et al. Ed. by Maurice Evans. (New Mermaid Ser.). 1976. pap. 2.95x o.p. (ISBN 0-393-90001-0). Norton.

Busy Bear's Refrigerator: A Book about Colors. Harriet Margolin & Carol Nicklaus. (Busy Bear Bks.). (Illus.). 28p. 4.95 o.p. (ISBN 0-448-30378-7, G&D). Putnam Pub Group.

Busy Body. Donald E. Westlake. 192p. 1987. pap. 3.95 o.p. (ISBN 0-445-40614-3). Mysterious Pr.

Busy Bugs. Ada Graham & Frank Graham. LC 82-22085. (Illus.). 64p. (gr. 5 up). 1983. 10.95 o.p. (ISBN 0-396-08126-6). Putnam Pub Group.

Busy Day. Suzanne Green & Satoru Tsuda. LC 87-6843. (Perlorians Ser.). (Illus.). 32p. (ps-k). 1987. pap. 6.95 o.p. (ISBN 0-385-23507-0). Doubleday.

Busy Times. Fern Hollow. (Fern Hollow Pop-Ups Ser.). (Illus.). (ps-1). 1985. 2.98 o.s.i. (ISBN 0-517-48289-4). Outlet Bk Co.

But As for Me: The Question of Election for God's People Today. Andre Lacocque. LC 78-71042. 1979. 13.00 o.p. (ISBN 0-8042-1172-8, John Knox). Westminster John Knox.

But Do Blondes Prefer Gentlemen? Anthony Burgess. 608p. 1986. text ed. 24.95 o.p. (ISBN 0-07-008977-9). McGraw.

But He Was Already Dead When I Got There. Barbara Paul. 256p. 1986. 13.95 o.s.i. (ISBN 0-684-18615-2). Scribner.

But I'm Only a Social Drinker: A Guide to Coping with Alcohol. Robert Crawford. 132p. 1986. pap. 6.95 o.p. (ISBN 0-7233-0754-7, Pub. by Whitcoulls NZ). Intl Spec Bk.

But in the Fall I'm Leaving. Ann Rinald. 224p. 1986. pap. 2.50 o.p. (ISBN 0-380-70138-3, Flare). Avon.

But Martin! June Counsel. LC 83-25299. (Illus.). 32p. (ps-2). 1984. 7.95 o.p. (ISBN 0-571-13349-5). Faber & Faber.

But Not Forgotten: The Adventure of the University Players. Norris Houghton. LC 79-136071. (Illus.). 1971. Repr. of 1952 ed. lib. bdg. 35.00x o.p. (ISBN 0-8371-5221-6, HONF). Greenwood.

But What About Me. Sandra Love. LC 75-40403. (Illus.). (gr. 3-7). 1976. 8.95 o.p. (ISBN 0-15-249900-8, HJ). HarBraceJ.

But Where Is Love. Marguerite Kloepfer. 1980. pap. 2.25 o.p. (ISBN 0-380-46052-1, 46052). Avon.

Butcher: The Duke of Cumberland & the Suppression of the Forty-Five. W. A. Speck. 240p. 1983. 24.95x o.p. (ISBN 0-631-10501-8); pap. 19.95x o.p. (ISBN 0-631-13287-2). Basil Blackwell.

Butler's Guide: To Clothes Care, Managing the Table, Running the Home & Other Graces. Stanley Ager & Fiona St Aubyn. 1981. pap. 9.50 o.p. (ISBN 0-671-43642-2, Fireside). S&S.

Butter in the Buttercups. Stella Browning. (Illus.). 62p. 1980. 5.50 o.p. (ISBN 0-682-49528-X). Exposition-Phoenix.

Butterflies: If You Throw It. R. C. Winslow. LC 77-83969. 1978. 9.95 o.p. (ISBN 0-916630-07-2). Pr Pacifica.

Butterflies of Georgia. Lucien Harris, Jr. LC 73-160493. (Illus.). 1972. 12.50 o.p. (ISBN 0-8061-0965-3); pap. 9.95 o.p. (ISBN 0-8061-1295-6). U of Okla Pr.

Butterflies of Idaho & the Northern Rockies. Nelson Curtis. LC 84-50760. (Illus.). 472p. (Orig.). 1987. pap. text ed. 24.95 o.p. (ISBN 0-89301-102-9). U of Idaho Pr.

Butterflies of Northern Europe. Bjorn Dal. Ed. by Michael Morris. Tr. by Roger Littleboy. (Illus.). 128p. 1982. 13.00 o.p. (ISBN 0-7099-0810-5, Pub. by Croom Helm Ltd). Routledge Chapman & Hall.

Butterflies of Oregon. Ernst Dornfeld. LC 80-51936. 275p. 1980. pap. 24.95 o.p. (ISBN 0-917304-58-6). Timber.

Butterflies of Scotland: A Natural History. George Thomson. (Illus.). 272p. 1980. 50.00 o.p. (ISBN 0-7099-0383-9, Pub. by Croom Helm Ltd). Routledge Chapman & Hall.

Butterfly & Other Stories. Wang Meng. Tr. by Rui An et al from Chinese. 239p. (Orig.). 1983. pap. 4.95 o.p. (ISBN 0-8351-1021-4). China Bks.

Butterfly Girl. Blossom Elfman. 1980. 7.95 o.p. (ISBN 0-395-28948-3). HM.

Butterfly Hunter. Janwillem Van de Wetering. 1982. 12.45 o.p. (ISBN 0-395-32527-7). HM.

Butterflyfishes of the World. Warren E. Burgess. (Illus.). 1979. 39.95 o.p. (ISBN 0-87666-470-2, H-988). TFH Pubns.

Butter's Going up: A Critical Analysis of Harold Pinter's Work. Steven H. Gale. LC 74-78833. vi, 358p. 1977. 32.00 o.p. (ISBN 0-8223-0339-6). Duke.

Butterscotch Prince. rev. ed. Richard Hall. 164p. 1983. pap. 4.95 o.p. (ISBN 0-932870-29-5). Alyson Pubns.

Button: The Pentagon's Strategic Command & Control System. Daniel F. Ford. 1985. 17.45 o.p. (ISBN 0-671-50068-6). S&S.

Button: The Pentagon's Strategic Command & Control System. Daniel F. Ford. 1986. pap. 8.95 o.p. (ISBN 0-671-62253-6, Touchstone Bks). S&S.

Buydown Agreements. Stephen R. Mettling. (Residential Financing Resource Library). 26p. 1982. pap. 6.50 o.s.i. (ISBN 0-88462-134-0, 1905-14, Real Estate Ed). Longman Finan.

Buyer's Guide to Component TV. Carl Giles & Barbara Giles. (Illus.). 224p. (Orig.). 1985. 19.95 o.p. (ISBN 0-8306-0881-8, 1881); pap. 12.60 o.p. (ISBN 0-8306-1881-3). TAB Bks.

Buyer's Guide to Computer Printers. Sanjiva K. Nath et al. (Illus.). 192p. (Orig.). 1985. 17.95 o.p. (ISBN 0-8306-0872-9, 1872); pap. 12.60 o.p. (ISBN 0-8306-1872-4). TAB Bks.

Buying a Condominium. 3rd ed. Justin W. Heatter. 192p. 1982. 12.95 o.s.i. (ISBN 0-684-17494-4, ScribT). Scribner.

Buying a Heart. George MacBeth. LC 77-76755. 1978. pap. 4.95 o.p. (ISBN 0-689-10816-8, Atheneum). Macmillan.

Buying a New Home: A Step-by-Step Guide, 10 vols. National Association of Home Builders Staff. 24p. 1986. Set. pap. 16.00 o.p. (ISBN 0-86718-258-X). Nat Assn H Build.

Buying & Renovating a House in the City: A Practical Guide. rev. ed. Deidre Stanforth & Marta Stamm. (Illus.). 320p. 1985. pap. 12.95 o.p. (ISBN 0-87052-026-1). Hippocrene Bks.

Buying & Running Your Own Business. 2nd ed. Ian Ford. 210p. 1977. text ed. 21.00x o.p. (ISBN 0-220-66336-X, Pub. by Busn Bks England). Gower Pub Co.

Buying & Selling a Business. Pennsylvania Bar Institute Staff. 94p. 1984. 20.00 o.p. (ISBN 0-318-02195-1, 253). PA Bar Inst.

Buying & Selling a Small Business. Michael M. Coltman. 137p. (Orig.). 1983. pap. 6.95 o.p. ISC Pr.

Buying & Selling Farmland: A Guide to Profitable Investment. Dwight W. Jundt. LC 80-67887. (Illus.). 309p. 1980. 16.95 o.p. (ISBN 0-686-77523-6); pap. text ed. 13.95 o.p. (ISBN 0-932250-10-6). Doane Info Servs.

Buying Guide Issue 1987. Consumer Reports Book Editors. 400p. (Orig.). 1986. pap. 5.95 o.p. (ISBN 0-89043-059-4). Consumer Reports.

Buying Guide Issue, 1988. Rev. ed. Consumer Reports Book Editors. 400p. 1987. pap. 5.95 o.p. (ISBN 0-89043-200-7). Consumer Reports.

Buying the Night Flight. Georgie A. Geyer. 1985. pap. 4.95 o.p. (ISBN 0-440-30922-0, LE). Dell.

Buying Time: An Established Business Fights for Survival. Kim Bartlett. 224p. 1985. 16.95 o.p. (ISBN 0-316-08276-7). Little.

Buying Time in South Africa. Counter Information Services. 56p. 1978. pap. 2.95 o.p. Transaction Pubs.

Buzzbugs. Bruce Carter. 133p. (gr. 5-9). 1979. pap. 1.50 o.p. (ISBN 0-380-43323-0, 43323-0, Camelot). Avon.

By & about Women: An Anthology of Short Fiction. Ed. by Beth K. Schneiderman. 1973. pap. text ed. 8.75 o.p. (ISBN 0-15-505665-4, HC). HarBraceJ.

By Colour of Law: Legal Culture & Constitutional Politics in England, 1660-1689. Howard Nenner. LC 76-25631. 1977. lib. bdg. 20.00x o.s.i. (ISBN 0-226-57275-7). U of Chicago Pr.

By Daylight & in Dream: New & Collected Poems, 1904-1970. John H. Wheelock. 1970. 6.95 o.s.i. (ISBN 0-684-10647-7, ScribT). Scribner.

By George, It's a Dragon! (Danger Mouse Lift-the-Flap Bks.). 32p. (ps-3). 1986. pap. 3.95i o.p. (ISBN 0-316-14708-7). Little.

By Life or By Death: A Practical Commentary on Paul's Letter to the Philippians. H. Leo Eddleman. 176p. (Orig.). 1981. pap. 3.75 o.p. (ISBN 0-682-49700-2, Testament). Exposition-Phoenix.

By Love Alone. Judith E. French. (Avon Romance Ser.). 352p. 1987. pap. 3.95 o.p. (ISBN 0-380-75206-9). Avon.

By Love Possessed. James G. Cozzens. LC 57-10062. 1967. pap. 2.95 o.p. (ISBN 0-15-614870-6, Harv). HarBraceJ.

By Love Renewed. Betty R. Headapohl. 244p. Date not set. pap. 3.50 o.p. (ISBN 0-8423-0348-0). Tyndale.

By One & One. Doreen C. Spitzer. LC 83-13406. (Illus.). 320p. 1984. 20.00 o.p. (ISBN 0-914016-98-9). Phoenix Pub.

By Right of Arms. Robyn Carr. 368p. 1986. 16.95 o.p. (ISBN 0-316-12969-0). Little.

By Special Request: Words of Love. Vivian L. Nelson. 1978. 4.50 o.p. (ISBN 0-682-49245-0). Exposition-Phoenix.

By Still Waters. AE. 52p. 1971. Repr. of 1906 ed. 15.00x o.p. (ISBN 0-7165-1335-8, BBA 02042, Pub. by Cuala Press Ireland). Biblio Dist.

By the Evidence: Memoirs, Nineteen Thirty-Two to Nineteen Fifty-One. L. S. Leakey. LC 76-14846. (Illus.). 1976. pap. 3.95 o.p. (ISBN 0-15-615000-X, Harv). HarBraceJ.

By the River of No Return. Don I. Smith. LC 85-60311. (Illus.). 112p. 1985. pap. 5.95 o.s.i. (ISBN 0-932773-00-1). High Country Bks.

By the Rivers of Babylon. Demille. 1978. 10.00 o.p. (ISBN 0-15-115278-0). HarBraceJ.

By the Sweat of Their Brow: Women Workers at Victorian Coal Mines. Angela V. John. (Illus.). 256p. 1984. pap. 9.95 o.p. (ISBN 0-7102-0142-7). Routledge Chapman & Hall.

By the Waters of Babylon: An Introduction to the History & Theology of the Exile. James D. Newsome, Jr. LC 78-52441. 1979. pap. 3.99 o.p. (ISBN 0-8042-0016-5, John Knox). Westminster John Knox.

By Word of Mouth. Ed. by Anthony Seldon & Joanna Pappworth. LC 83-13405. 258p. 1983. 27.00 o.p. (ISBN 0-416-33020-7, NO. 4039); pap. 12.95 o.p. (ISBN 0-416-36740-2, NO. 4084). Routledge Chapman & Hall.

By Yourself. Sara Gilbert. LC 82-13962. (Illus.). 80p. (gr. 3-6). 1983. PLB 10.88 o.p. (ISBN 0-688-01688-X); pap. 7.50 o.p. (ISBN 0-688-01687-1). Lothrop.

Bypaths see Word Studies in the Greek New Testament, for the English Reader.

Byrne's Standard Book of Pool & Billiards. Robert Byrne. LC 80-25552. (Illus.). 352p. 1978. 17.95 o.p. (ISBN 0-15-115223-3). HarBraceJ.

Byron. Drummond Bone. (Harvester New Readings Ser.). 128p. Date not set. cancelled o.s.i. (ISBN 0-391-03471-5). Humanities.

Byron Exhumed: A Verse Suite. Robert Peters. 1973. 1.00 o.p. (ISBN 0-685-67933-0). Windless Orchard.

Byron's Daughter. Catherine Turney. 1977. pap. 1.75 o.p. (ISBN 0-380-00880-7, 31484). Avon.

Byron's Poetry: A Critical Introduction. Leslie A. Marchand. LC 65-6991. 1965. Repr. of 1965 ed. 18.50x o.s.i. (ISBN 0-674-08950-2). Harvard U Pr.

Byte Book of Pascal. Ed. by W. Liffick Blaise. 1980. text ed. 27.50 o.p. (ISBN 0-07-037823-1, BYTE Bks). McGraw.

Byzantine Art. A. V. Bank. 338p. 1985. 55.00 o.p. (ISBN 0-8285-3050-5, Pub. by Aurora Pubs USSR). Imported Pubns.

Byzantine Coinage. Philip Grierson. (Byzantine Collection Publications Ser.: No. 4). (Illus.). 32p. 1982. pap. 4.50x o.p. (ISBN 0-88402-112-2). Dumbarton Oaks.

Byzantine Empire. Robert Browning. 224p. 1980. 9.95 o.p. (ISBN 0-684-16652-6, ScribT); 9.95 o.p. (ISBN 0-684-17693-9). Scribner.

Byzantine Honeymoon. Philip Glazebrook. LC 78-72965. 1979. 8.95 o.p. (ISBN 0-689-10946-6, Atheneum). Macmillan.

Byzantine Text-Type & New Testament Textual Criticism. Harry A. Sturz. LC 84-11479. 320p. 1984. 18.95 o.p. (ISBN 0-8407-4958-9). Nelson.

C

C: A Reference Manual. Samuel P. Harbison & Guy L. Steele, Jr. (Prentice-Hall Software Ser.). 272p. 1984. text ed. 29.67 o.p. (ISBN 0-13-110016-5); pap. text ed. 22.95 o.p. (ISBN 0-13-110008-4). P-H.

C Algebras & Their Applications of Statistical Mechanics & Quantum Field Theory. Ed. by D. Kastler. (EFS Ser.: Vol. 60). 1987. 90.25 o.p. (ISBN 0-317-65942-1). Elsevier.

C-Algebras & W-Algebras. S. Sakai. LC 75-149121. (Ergebnisse der Mathematik und Ihrer Grenzgehiete: Vol. 60). 1971. 42.00 o.p. (ISBN 0-387-05347-6). Springer-Verlag.

C: An Advanced Introduction. Narain Gehani. LC 84-12145. (Principles of Computer Science Ser.). 332p. 1985. text ed. 34.95 o.p. (ISBN 0-88175-053-0, Computer Sci Pr). W H Freeman.

C Answer Book. Clovis L. Tondo & Scott E. Gimpel. 224p. 1985. pap. text ed. 24.00 o.p. (ISBN 0-13-109877-2). P-H.

C. B. Greenfield: A Little Madness. Lucille Kallen. LC 85-18290. 224p. 1986. 14.95 o.p. (ISBN 0-394-53090-X). Random.

C. B. Greenfield: No Lady in the House. Lucille Kallen. 1982. 12.95 o.s.i. (ISBN 0-671-43240-0, Wyndham Bks). S&S.

C-BIMS: Cassette-Based Information Management System for the PET. Gary Greenberg. (Illus.). 224p. (Orig.). 1983. 16.95 o.p. (ISBN 0-8306-0489-8); pap. 10.95 o.p. (ISBN 0-8306-1489-3, 1489). TAB Bks.

C D B. William Steig. LC 68-25755. (Illus.). 44p. (gr. 1 up). 1979. pap. 3.50 o.s.i. (ISBN 0-671-96030-X). Wanderer Bks.

C. G. in Japan. Ed. by K. Omura. 148p. (Orig.). 1987. pap. 26.95 o.p. (ISBN 4-766-10361-0, Pub. by Graphic Sha Japan). Bks Nippan.

C. G. Jung & the Scientific Attitude. Edmund D. Cohen. (Quality Paperback Ser.: No. 322). 167p. 1976. pap. 4.95 o.p. (ISBN 0-8226-0322-5). Littlefield.

C. G. Jung: His Myth in Our Time. Marie-Louise Von Franz. Tr. by William H. Kennedy. LC 73-77115. 355p. 1975. 15.00 o.p. (ISBN 0-913430-26-9). C G Jung Foun.

C Illustrated, a Guide for Experienced Programmers. J. Perry. (Illus.). pap. write for info. o.s.i. Meghan-Kiffer.

C Language for Programmers. Kenneth Pugh. (Illus.). 208p. 1985. pap. 17.95 o.p. (ISBN 0-673-18034-4). Scott F.

C Language Statement-to-Statement Dictionary. Algo Publishing Staff. 48p. (Orig.). 1987. pap. 14.95 o.p. (ISBN 0-945473-45-1). Algo Pub.

C-Lect Educational & Financial Aid User's Guide. Ed. by Paul Downes. 1987. pap. text ed. 15.75 o.p. (ISBN 1-55631-022-6). Chron Guide.

C-Lect Occupational Module User's Guide. Paul Downes. 1987. pap. text ed. 5.00 o.p. (ISBN 1-55631-021-8). Chron Guide.

C. P. A. Law Review: Under the 1978 Uniform Commercial Code: Text, Previous C. P. A. Law Examination Questions, & the Author's Model Answers. 7th ed. Joseph L. Frascona. LC 84-81123. (Illus.). 1985. 43.95 o.p. (ISBN 0-256-03208-4). Irwin.

C. P. Snow: A Reference Guide. Paul Boytinck. 1980. lib. bdg. 31.50 o.p. (ISBN 0-8161-8357-0, Hall Reference). G K Hall.

C Primer. Leslie Hancock & Morris Krieger. 256p. 1983. pap. text ed. 17.95 o.p. (ISBN 0-07-025981-X, BYTE Bks). McGraw.

C Primer Plus. Waite Group Staff et al. LC 84-50060. 536p. 1984. pap. 22.95 o.p. (ISBN 0-672-22090-3, 22090). Sams.

C Programming Language: Convergent Technologies Edition. Brian W. Kernighan & Dennis M. Ritchie. 240p. 1984. pap. text ed. 13.42 shrinkwrap o.p. (ISBN 0-13-109984-1). P-H.

C Programming Language, Digital Equipment Coporation Edition. Brian W. Kernighan & Dennis M. Ritchie. 240p. 1983. pap. text ed. 19.95 o.p. (ISBN 0-13-109950-7). P-H.

C. S. Lewis: A Biography. Roger L. Green & Walter Hooper. 320p. 1974. 6.95 o.p. (ISBN 0-15-123190-7). HarBraceJ.

C. S. Lewis: A Biography. Roger L. Green & Walter Hooper. LC 75-29425. 320p. 1976. pap. 7.95 o.s.i. (ISBN 0-15-623205-7, Harv). HarBraceJ.

C. S. Lewis & the Church of Rome. Christopher Derrick. LC 80-83049. 225p. (Orig.). 1981. pap. 8.95 o.s.i. (ISBN 0-89870-009-4). Ignatius Pr.

C Self-Study Guide. Jack Purdum. LC 84-62752. 250p. 1985. pap. 16.95 o.p. (ISBN 0-88022-149-6, 176); disk IBMPC Format 39.95 o.p. (ISBN 0-88022-153-4, 284). Que Corp.

C Standard Library. Jack Purdum & Tim Leslie. LC 86-62528. 350p. 1987. pap. 21.95 o.p. (ISBN 0-88022-279-4, 72); disk 39.95 o.p. (ISBN 0-88022-315-4, 275). Que Corp.

C-Thirty-Seven Complete: 1986. IEEE, Inc. Staff. 2000p. 1986. pap. 75.00 o.p. (ISBN 0-471-84563-9). Wiley.

C. Z. Guest's Datebook & Gardener Planner. C. Z. Guest. 1985. 12.95 o.p. (ISBN 0-517-55306-6). Crown.

C-64 Program Factory. George Stewart. (Illus.). 200p. 1984. pap. text ed. 12.95 o.p. (ISBN 0-07-881150-3). Osborne-McGraw.

C-64 Telecommunications. Jonathan Erickson. 180p. 1984. pap. text ed. 16.95 o.p. (ISBN 0-07-881149-X). Osborne-McGraw.

CA 2t Entry Blockers, Adenosine, & Neurohumors. Ed. by Gary F. Merrill & Harvey R. Weiss. LC 82-17591. (Illus.). 345p. 1983. pap. 38.00 o.p. (ISBN 0-8067-1271-6). Urban & S.

Cabal. Norman Carbo. 1979. 10.95 o.p. (ISBN 0-393-08827-8). Norton.

Cabal Seminar, 76-77: Proceedings, Caltech-UCLA Logic Seminar 1976-1977. Ed. by A. S. Kechris & Y. N. Moschovakis. (Lecture Notes in Mathematics Ser.: Vol. 689). 1978. pap. 20.00 o.p. (ISBN 0-387-09086-X). Springer-Verlag.

Cabalist. Amanda Prantera. LC 86-47656. 192p. 1986. 12.95 o.p. (ISBN 0-689-11829-5, Atheneum). Macmillan.

Cabinet Departments with Domestic Reponsibilities: A Working Note & Bibliography, 1933-1981. Matthew Holden, Jr. 81p. 1984. pap. 8.50 o.p. (ISBN 0-318-04155-3). U Va Ctr Pub Serv.

Cabinet-Maker & Upholsterer's Drawing Book. Thomas Sheraton. (Illus.). 18.00 o.p. (ISBN 0-8446-4637-7). Peter Smith.

Cabinetmaking & Millwork. 2nd, rev. ed. John L. Feirer. (Illus.). 1983. 42.50 o.s.i. (ISBN 0-684-17941-5, ScribT). Scribner.

Cabinetmaking, Patternmaking, & Millwork. Gaspar J. Lewis. 438p. Date not set. pap. text ed. 19.95 o.p. (ISBN 0-8273-1816-2); instr's. guide 6.37 o.p. Delmar.

Cabinets & Vanities: A Builder's Handbook. William P. Godley. (Illus.). 160p. (Orig.). 1985. 19.95 o.p. (ISBN 0-8306-0982-2, 1982); pap. 12.95 o.p. (ISBN 0-8306-1982-8). Tab Bks.

Cable Communication. Thomas F. Baldwin & D. Stevens McVoy. (Illus.). 432p. 1983. text ed. (ISBN 0-13-110171-4). P-H.

Cable Harbor. Donald Bowie. LC 81-2700. 336p. 1981. 11.95 o.p. (ISBN 0-87131-347-2). M Evans.

Cable Primer. 10.00 o.p. (ISBN 0-940272-04-0). Natl Cable.

Cable-Stayed Bridges: Theory & Design. M. S. Troitsky. 400p. 1977. text ed. 76.00x o.p. (ISBN 0-258-97034-0, Pub. by Granada England). Gower Pub Co.

Cable-Stayed Bridges: Theory & Design. M. S. Troitsky. 400p. 1977. 60.00x o.p. (ISBN 0-258-97034-0, Pub. by Granada England). Sheridan.

Cable Suspended Roof. McGraw.

Cable-Suspended Roofs. P. Krishna. 1978. text ed. 39.95 o.p. (ISBN 0-07-035504-5). McGraw.

Cable Television & Censorship: A Bibliography. Patrick H. Kellough. (Public Administration Ser.: Bibliography P 1622). 1985. pap. 2.00 o.p. (ISBN 0-89028-292-7). Vance Biblios.

Cable Television: Current Legal Issues. Pennsylvania Bar Institute Staff. 216p. 1983. 25.00 o.p. (ISBN 0-318-02160-9, 220). PA Bar Inst.

Cable Television, 1985: Retrospective & Perspective. Gary L. Christensen. LC 86-102950. (Patents, Copyrights, Trademarks & Literary Property Course Handbook Ser.: NO. 214). (Illus.). 1985. 15.00 o.p. (G43778). PLI.

Cable Television, 1988: Three Years after the Cable Act. (Patents, Copyrights, Trademarks, & Literary Property Ser.). 744p. 1988. 45.00 o.p. (G4-3808). PLI.

Cable '83: International Conferences & Exhibtion on Satellite & Cable TV London - May 10-12, 1983. 400p. (Orig.). 1983. pap. text ed. 171.00x o.p. (ISBN 0-903796-96-1, Pub. by Online Conferences England). Gower Pub Co.

Cable '84: Proceedings of the Second European Conference on Satellite & Cable TV, London, July 1984. 373p. 1984. pap. text ed. 150.00x o.p. (ISBN 0-86353-011-7, Pub. by Online). Gower Pub Co.

Cable '85: Proceedings of the International Conference on Satellite & Cable TV, Brighton, July 1985. 178p. 1985. pap. text ed. 110.00x o.p. (ISBN 0-86353-032-X, Pub. by Online). Gower Pub Co.

Cachar under British Rule in North East India. J. B. Bhattacharjee. 1977. 12.00x o.p. (ISBN 0-8364-0388-6). South Asia Bks.

Cache. Leo Damore. LC 78-73868. 1979. 8.95 o.p. (ISBN 0-87795-222-1, Arbor Hse). Morrow.

Cache Lake Country: Life in the North Woods. John J. Rowlands. (Illus.). 1978. pap. 5.95 o.p. (ISBN 0-393-00908-4). Norton.

Cache of Pearls. Gae'tane. 1977. 4.50 o.p. (ISBN 0-682-48787-2). Exposition-Phoenix.

Cacodylic Acid: Agricultural Uses, Biological Effects, & Environmental Fate. Ronald D. Hood. (VA Monograph). 180p. (Orig.). 1985. pap. 6.00 o.p. (ISBN 0-318-20428-2, S/N 051-000-00177-0). USGPO.

Cacti of the Southwest. W. Hubert Earle. (Illus.). 210p. 1982. 19.00 o.p. (ISBN 0-935810-05-6); pap. 11.75 o.p. (ISBN 0-935810-06-4). Primer Pubs.

Cacti of the Southwest. 7th, rev. ed. W. Hubert Earle. (Illus.). 210p. 1987. 19.00 o.p. (ISBN 0-935810-30-7); pap. 11.75 o.p. (ISBN 0-935810-31-5). Primer Pubs.

Cactus Garden. William Dieter. LC 85-48131. 320p. 1986. 15.95 o.p. (ISBN 0-689-11802-3, Atheneum). Macmillan.

Cactus Pie: Ten Stories. Gerald Green. 1979. 9.95 o.p. (ISBN 0-395-27761-2). HM.

CAD-CAM Databases: Gaining Control. Management Roundtable, Inc. Staff. 350p. 1985. spiral bdg. 295.00 o.p. (ISBN 0-932007-05-8, 0015DB). Mgmt Roundtable.

CAD-CAM: Meeting Today's Productivity Challenge. Ed. by K. S. Taraman. 281p. 1982. 46.00 o.p. (ISBN 0-686-48151-8, 2001). T-C Pubns CA.

CAD-CAM with Personal Computers. Patrick R. Carberry. 189p. 1985. 21.95 o.p. (ISBN 0-8306-0852-4, 1852). TAB Bks.

Cadence--Key to Musical Clarity. Richard McClanahan. 1977. pap. 7.95 o.s.i. (ISBN 0-8008-1136-4, Crescendo). Taplinger.

Cadenza: A Musical Career. Erich Leinsdorf. 1976. 10.95 o.p. (ISBN 0-395-24401-3). HM.

Cadenza for Caruso. Barbara Paul. 230p. 1986. pap. 10.95 o.p. (ISBN 0-8161-3781-1, Large Print Bks). G K Hall.

Cadillac Jack: A Novel. Larry McMurtry. 1985. pap. 8.95 o.s.i. (ISBN 0-671-55541-3). S&S.

Cadillac Nineteen Sixty-Seven to Nineteen Eighty Four: RTUG. Chilton Automotives Editorial Staff. LC 83-45304. 312p. 1984. pap. 13.50 o.s.i. (ISBN 0-8019-7462-3). Chilton.

Cadillac, Standard of the World: The Complete History. 3rd ed. Maurice D. Hendry. LC 72-85846. (Illus.). 480p. 1979. 19.98 o.p. (ISBN 0-915038-10-2). Auto Quarterly.

Cadogan's Crimea. George Cadogan et al. LC 79-88574. (Illus.). 1980. 19.95 o.p. (ISBN 0-689-11022-7, Atheneum). Macmillan.

Cadre School Life: Six Chapters. 2nd ed. Yang Jiang. Tr. by Geremie Barme & Bennett Lee. 90p. 1989. pap. cancelled o.s.i. (ISBN 0-930523-63-6). Readers Intl.

Caesar & Contemporary Roman Society. Erik Wistrand. (Acta Regiae Societatis Scientiarum et Litterarum Goteborg, Humaniora: No. 15). 1979. pap. text ed. 18.50x o.p. Humanities.

Caesar's Gallic War. Olivia Coolidge. (Illus.). (gr. 7 up). 1973. 4.95 o.p. (ISBN 0-395-06716-2). HM.

Cafe du Reve. Marc C. Chamowicz. (Illus.). 200p. 1986. pap. 19.95 o.p. (ISBN 0-500-27392-8). Thames Hudson.

Cage. Roy Brown. LC 77-1586. 160p. (gr. 6 up). 1979. 7.95 o.p. (ISBN 0-395-28892-4, Clarion). HM.

Cage. Susan Cheever. 1982. 11.45 o.p. (ISBN 0-395-32111-5). HM.

Cahiers. Andre Gide. 412p. 1970. 15.95 o.p. (ISBN 0-686-56062-0). Schoenhof.

Cahiers, 29 tomes. Paul Valery. Set. 695.00 o.p. (ISBN 0-685-36608-1). Schoenhof.

Cahiers, 2 vols. Paul Valery. (Pleiade Ser.). 1544p. 1973. Vol. 1. 42.95 o.p. (ISBN 0-686-55110-9); Vol. 2. 46.95 o.p. (ISBN 0-686-55111-7). Schoenhof.

Cahiers du Monde Russe et Sovietique, Numero Special, Vol. 15, Nos. 1-2. 1974. pap. 14.40x o.p. (ISBN 0-686-20913-3). Mouton.

Cahiers Jean Cocteau, Vol. 2. Jean Cocteau. 152p. 1971. 8.95 o.p. (ISBN 0-686-54515-X). French & Eur.

Cain: The Biography of James M. Cain. Roy Hoopes. LC 81-16133. 768p. 1982. 25.00 o.p. (ISBN 0-03-049331-5). H Holt & Co.

Cain's Book. Alexander Trocchi. LC 79-56749. 256p. (Orig.). 1980. pap. 3.50 o.p. (ISBN 0-394-17403-8, B-432, BC). Grove.

Caitlin: Life with Dylan Thomas. Thomas Caitlin & George Tremlett. LC 86-26965. 1987. 17.95 o.p. (ISBN 0-8050-0369-X). H Holt & Co.

Caius Geht Ein Licht Auf see Mystery of the Roman Ransom.

Cajun Boy: The Story of Acadiana. Isadore L. Sonnier. 1980. 6.50 o.p. (ISBN 0-682-49519-0). Exposition-Phoenix.

Cakes. Bon Appetit Magazine Editors. LC 87-3969. (Cooking with Bon Appetit Ser.). 1987. 12.95 o.p. (ISBN 0-89535-180-3). Knapp Pr.

Cakes & Ale: The Ultimate Food Glossary: A Collection of Two Thousand Five Hundred Foods, Techniques, Tools & Cooking Terms. Alice H. Regis. LC 88-70748. (Illus.). 240p. (Orig.). 1988. pap. 11.95 o.p. Axelrod Pub.

Cakes & Custards: Children's Rhymes. Compiled by Brian Alderson. LC 75-24523. (Illus.). 176p. (ps). 1975. PLB 13.88 o.p. (ISBN 0-688-32050-3). Morrow.

Cakes & Pastries. (Step-by-Step Cooking Ser.). (Illus.). 160p. 1985. 10.95 o.p. (ISBN 0-8120-5679-5). Barron.

Calamities of the World. Hubert S. Banner. LC 74-159880. (Tower Bks.). (Illus.). 288p. 1971. Repr. of 1932 ed. 40.00x o.p. (ISBN 0-8103-3918-8). Gale.

Calcareous Nannoplankton. Ed. by Bilal U. Haq. LC 83-4366. (Benchmark Papers in Geology: Vol. 79). 368p. 1983. 46.50 o.p. (ISBN 0-87933-090-2). Van Nos Reinhold.

Calcified Tissue: Proceedings of the European Symposium on Calcified Tissues, 8th, Jerusalem, 1971. European Symposium on Calcified Tissues Staff & Menczel. 1971. 54.00 o.p. (ISBN 0-12-490650-8). Acad Pr.

Calcium & Phosphate Transport Across Biomembranes. Ed. by Felix Bronner & Meindrad Peterlik. LC 81-17617. 1981. 47.50 o.p. (ISBN 0-12-135280-3). Acad Pr.

Calcium & Phosphoros Metabolism. James T. Irving. 1973. 62.00 o.p. (ISBN 0-12-374350-8). Acad Pr.

Calcium & the Heart. Ed. by P. Harris & L. Opie. 198p. 1971. 60.00 o.p. (ISBN 0-12-326950-4). Acad Pr.

Calcium Blockers: Mechanisms of Action & Clinical Applications. Ed. by Stephen Flaim & Robert F. Zelis. LC 82-8548. (Illus.). 313p. 1982. text ed. 44.50 o.p. (ISBN 0-8067-0611-2). Urban & S.

Calcium Chloride in Concrete: Science & Technology. V. S. Ramachandran. (Illus.). 216p. 1976. 55.00 o.p. (ISBN 0-85334-682-8, Pub. by Elsevier Applied Sci England). Elsevier.

Calcium in Drug Action. Ed. by G. B. Weiss. LC 78-8517. 376p. 1978. 65.00x o.p. (ISBN 0-306-40015-4, Plenum Pr). Plenum Pub.

Calcium Ion Antagonists in Cardiovascular Disease: Proceedings of an International Conference, 12-13 October 1979, Toronto, Canada. Ed. by J. Morch. 200p. 1981. pap. 48.00 o.p. (ISBN 0-08-027376-9). Pergamon.

Calcium Movement in Excitable Cells. P. F. Baker & H. Reute. 1975. pap. 35.00 o.p. (ISBN 0-08-018298-4). Pergamon.

Calcium Urolithiasis: Pathogenesis, Diagnosis, & Management. Charles Y. Pak. LC 78-4083. (Topics in Bone & Mineral Disorders Ser.). (Illus.). 174p. 1978. 45.00x o.p. (ISBN 0-306-31110-0, Plenum Med Bk). Plenum Pub.

Calculated Electronic Properties of Metals: Designing Our Career Machines. V. L. Moruzzi et al. LC 79-14183. 1978. 53.00 o.p. (ISBN 0-08-022705-8). Pergamon.

Calculated Risk: A Master Plan for Common Stocks. Robert M. Sharp. 200p. 1986. 19.95 o.p. (ISBN 0-87094-761-3). Dow Jones-Irwin.

Calculating Cook. Jeanne Jones. LC 72-77564. (Illus.). 192p. (Orig.). 1972. pap. 6.95 o.p. (ISBN 0-912238-23-2, One Hund One Prods). Ortho.

Calculation of Drug Dosages: A Workbook. 2nd ed. Ruth K. Radcliff & Sheila J. Ogden. 290p. 1980. pap. text ed. 17.50 o.p. (ISBN 0-8016-4067-9). Mosby.

Calculation of Phase Diagrams & Thermochemistry of Alloy Phases. Y. A. Chang & J. F. Smith. LC 79-87675. 286p. 1979. (Reproduction on Demand - UMI) 30.00 o.p. (ISBN 0-89520-356-1). Minerals Metals.

Calculation of Phase Diagrams & Thermochemistry of Alloy Phases: Proceedings of the TMS-AIME Fall Meeting, Milwaukee, 1979. TMS Staff & AIME Staff. Ed. by Y. A. Chang & J. F. Smith. (TMS Paper Selections). (Illus.). 286p. 30.00 o.p. (ISBN 0-89520-356-1); members 18.00 o.p. (ISBN 0-317-34857-4); student members 10.00 o.p. (ISBN 0-317-34858-2). ASM.

Calculational Methods of Interacting Arrays of Fissile Material. A. F. Thomas & F. Abbey. LC 73-8604. 144p. 1973. 44.00 o.p. (ISBN 0-08-017660-7). Pergamon.

Calculations for Engineering Surveys. John Uren & William F. Price. (Illus.). 309p. 1984. pap. 14.95 o.p. (ISBN 0-442-30583-4). Van Nos Reinhold.

Calculations for the Medical Laboratory. Susan T. Remson & Philip G. Ackermann. 1977. 15.00 o.p. (ISBN 0-316-73999-5). Little.

Calculations in Fundamental Physics, 2 vols. T. Heddle. Incl. Vol. 1. Mechanics & Heat. 1971. pap. text ed. 9.25 (ISBN 0-08-015829-3); Vol. 2. Electricity & Magnetism. 1971. pap. text ed. 9.25 (ISBN 0-08-015831-5). 1971. pap. 7.00 ea. o.p. Pergamon.

Calculations of Chemical Equilbria. A. Kuzanskaya. 326p. 1978. 9.45 o.p. (Pub. by Mir Pubs USSR). Imported Pubns.

Calculations of Chemical Technological Processes. Ed. by I. P. Mukhlyonov. 276p. 1979. 9.00 o.p. (ISBN 0-8285-2116-6, Pub. by Mir Pubs USSR). Imported Pubns.

Calculator Navigation. Mortimer Rogoff. (Illus.). 1980. 29.95 o.p. (ISBN 0-393-03192-6). Norton.

Calculator Programs for Chemical Engineers, Vol. 1. Chemical Engineering Magazine Editors. (Chemical Engineering Ser.). 304p. 1981. text ed. 39.50 o.p. (ISBN 0-07-010793-9). McGraw.

Calculi of Lambda Conversion. Alonzo Church. (Annals of Math). 1941. pap. 15.00 o.p. (ISBN 0-527-02722-7). Kraus Repr.

Calculus. Dennis D. Berkey. LC 83-20046. 1194p. 1984. text ed. 52.75x o.s.i. (ISBN 0-03-059522-3). SCP.

Calculus. Douglas Downing. (Easy Way Ser.). 1982. pap. 8.95 o.p. (ISBN 0-8120-2588-1). Barron.

Calculus. H. Flanders. 1970. text ed. 21.75 o.p. (ISBN 0-12-259640-4); ans. manual 2.50 o.p. (ISBN 0-12-259642-0). Acad Pr.

Calculus. Leonard Gillman & Robert McDowell. 1973. pap. 14.95x o.p. (ISBN 0-393-09350-6). Norton.

Calculus. Stanley I. Grossman. 1977. 26.95 o.p. (ISBN 0-12-304350-6). Acad Pr.

Calculus. 2nd ed. Stanley I. Grossman. 1176p. 1981. 33.00i o.p. (ISBN 0-12-304360-3). Acad Pr.

Calculus. 3rd ed. Stanley I. Grossman. 1984. 35.00 o.p. (ISBN 0-12-304371-9); instr's. manual 9.25 o.p. (ISBN 0-12-304373-5); student manual 10.00 o.p. (ISBN 0-12-304372-7). HarBraceJ.

Calculus: A Tool for Analysis & Decision. Michael L. Kovacic. 1977. text ed. (ISBN 0-87150-233-X, PWS 1871, Prindle). PWS-Kent Pub.

Calculus & Analytic Geometry. C. H. Edwards & David E. Penney. 1120p. 1982. text ed. 45.67 o.p. (ISBN 0-13-111609-6). P-H.

Calculus & Analytic Geometry. Douglas Faires & Barbara Faires. 1026p. 1983. text ed. write for info. o.p. (ISBN 0-87150-323-9, 33L 2571, Prindle). PWS-Kent Pub.

Calculus & Analytic Geometry. 2nd ed. Philip Gillett. 992p. text ed. 38.00 o.p. (ISBN 0-669-06059-3). Heath.

Calculus & Analytic Geometry. 2nd ed. Abe Mizrahi & Michael Sullivan. 1083p. 1986. text ed. write for info. o.p. (ISBN 0-534-05454-4). Wadsworth Pub.

Calculus & Analytic Geometry. 3rd ed. Al Shenk. 1984. text ed. write for info. o.p. (ISBN 0-673-16582-5). Scott F.

Calculus & Analytic Geometry. James E. Shockley. 1212p. 1982. text ed. 39.95x o.s.i. (ISBN 0-03-018886-5). SCP.

Calculus & Analytic Geometry. 2nd ed. Sherman K. Stein. (Illus.). 1977. text ed. 34.95 o.p. (ISBN 0-07-061008-8). McGraw.

Calculus & Computer Science Theory: Proceedings of the Symposium in Rome, March 25-27, 1975. Ed. by C. Boehm. (Lecture Notes in Computer Science: Vol. 37). xiv, 370p. 1975. pap. 20.00 o.p. (ISBN 0-387-07416-3). Springer-Verlag.

Calculus & Its Applications. 3rd ed. LarryJ. Goldstein et al. (Illus.). 656p. 1984. text ed. (ISBN 0-13-111880-3). P-H.

Calculus & Its Applications. Stephen Willard. 1976. write for info. o.p. (ISBN 0-87150-203-8, PWS 1651, Prindle). PWS-Kent Pub.

Calculus & Mathematical Models. Nathaniel A. Friedman. 1979. write for info. o.p. (ISBN 0-87150-265-8, PWS 2151, Prindle). PWS-Kent Pub.

Calculus Blackboard. O'Farrell et al. 64p. 1985. pap. write for info. incl. 2 double-sided disks o.p. (ISBN 0-534-06060-9). Brooks-Cole.
Calculus for Management, Social & Life Sciences. Ray Cannon & Gareth Williams. 576p. text ed. 25.00 sp o.p. (ISBN 0-205-11051-7). Allyn.
Calculus for the Life Sciences: An Introduction. Murray A. Katz. (Biology Textbooks: Vol. 1). 1976. 39.75 o.p. (ISBN 0-8247-6465-X). Dekker.
Calculus for the Management, Life, & Social Sciences. Bernard Kolman. 506p. 1981. 27.00 o.p. (ISBN 0-12-417890-1); student guide 8.00 o.p. (ISBN 0-12-417891-X); instrs.' resource manual 5.00 o.p. (ISBN 0-12-417892-8). Acad Pr.
Calculus for the Practical Worker. 4th ed. J. E. Thompson. 280p. 1982. pap. 8.95 o.p. (ISBN 0-442-28274-5). Van Nos Reinhold.
Calculus: In the First Three Dimensions. Sherman K. Stein. 1967. text ed. 24.00 o.p. (ISBN 0-07-061000-2, C). McGraw.
Calculus: Instructor's Manual. Stanley Grossman. 120p. 1977. 3.00 o.p. (ISBN 0-12-304352-2). Acad Pr.
Calculus Made Easy. Silvanus P. Thompson. LC 86-13377. 320p. 1986. 15.95 o.p. (ISBN 0-89490-149-4). Enslow Pubs.
Calculus of Communicating Systems. R. Milner. (Lecture Notes in Computer Science Ser.: Vol. 92). 260p. 1982. pap. 14.00 o.p. (ISBN 0-387-10235-3). Springer-Verlag.
Calculus of Fractions & Homotopy Theory. Pierre Gabriel & M. Zisman. (Ergebnisse der Mathematik und Ihrer Grenzgebiete: Vol. 35). (Illus.). 1967. 44.00 o.p. (ISBN 0-387-03777-2). Springer-Verlag.
Calculus of One Variable. 2nd ed. Stanley I. Grossman. 1985. text ed. 30.00 o.p. (ISBN 0-12-304390-5). HarBraceJ.
Calculus of One Variable. Kenneth McAloon & Anthony Tromba. (Eagle Mathematics Ser.: Vol. 1BC). (Illus.). 638p. 1972. text ed. 10.95 o.p. (ISBN 0-15-518525-X, HC). HarBraceJ.
Calculus of Several Variables. R. Creighton Buck & Alfred B. Willcox. LC 76-13795. 1971. text ed. 18.50 o.p. (ISBN 0-395-12359-3, 3-07550). HM.
Calculus of Variations. L. E. Elsgolc. 1962. pap. 45.00 o.p. (ISBN 0-08-009554-2). Pergamon.
Calculus of Variations & Optimal Control Theory. Magnus R. Hestenes. LC 79-25451. 418p. 1980. Repr. of 1966 ed. lib. bdg. 28.50 o.p. (ISBN 0-89874-092-4). Krieger.
Calculus: Readings from the Mathematics Teacher. Ed. by Louise Grinstein & Brenda Michaels. LC 77-6615. (Illus.). 230p. 1977. pap. 10.00 o.s.i. (ISBN 0-87353-031-4). NCTM.
Calculus with Analytic Geometry. 2nd ed. Robert Ellis & Denny Gulick. (Illus.). 1027p. 1982. text ed. 32.75 o.p. (ISBN 0-15-505731-6, HC). HarBraceJ.
Calculus with Analytic Geometry. Robert Ellis & Denny Gulick. 1978. 32.95 o.p. (ISBN 0-15-505728-6). HarbraceJ.
Calculus with Analytic Geometry. H. Flanders & J. Price. 1041p. 1978. text ed. 23.50 o.p. (ISBN 0-12-259672-2); instr's. manual 3.50 o.p. (ISBN 0-12-259673-0). Acad Pr.
Calculus with Analytic Geometry. 4th ed. Louis A. Guillou. (Illus.). 368p. 1984. (ISBN 0-13-111824-2). P-H.
Calculus with Analytic Geometry. 4th ed. Edwin J. Purcell & Dale E. Varberg. (Illus.). 896p. 1984. text ed. (ISBN 0-13-111807-2). P-H.
Calculus with Analytic Geometry. 6th ed. E. Johnson Richard et al. 1978. text ed. write for info. o.p. (ISBN 0-205-05917-1, 565917). Wm C Brown.
Calculus with Applications. 3rd ed. Margaret L. Lial & Charles D. Miller. 1985. text ed. write for info. o.p. (ISBN 0-673-15895-0). Scott F.
Calculus with Applications to Business, Economics & Social Science. Richard Bouldin. LC 84-14157. 544p. 1985. text ed. 30.95 o.s.i. (ISBN 0-03-069764-6). SCP.
Calcutta: The City Revealed. Geoffrey Moorhouse. 1985. pap. 9.95 o.p. (ISBN 0-03-004217-8, Owl Bks). H Holt & Co.
Calder Born, Calder Bred. Large Print ed. Janet Dailey. LC 83-18056. 769p. 1984. Repr. of 1983 ed. 16.95 o.p. (ISBN 0-89621-503-2). Thorndike Pr.
Caleb Catlum's America. Vincent McHugh. LC 71-156927. 364p. 1971. Repr. of 1936 ed. 34.00x o.p. (ISBN 0-8103-3717-7). Gale.
Caleb's Colt. Jill Brisco. 1986. pap. 6.95 o.p. (ISBN 0-8249-8112-X). Ideals.
Calendar-Keeper 1987: A Record Keeping System for Child Care Providers Large Edition. 9th ed. Toys 'n Things Press Staff. Ed. by Deb Glander. (Illus.). 60p. (Orig.). 1986. 8.50 o.p. (ISBN 0-934140-34-0). Toys 'n Things.
Calendar-Keeper 1988: A Record Keeping System for Child Care Providers. 10th ed. Toys 'n Things Press Staff. Ed. by Jill Hix. (Illus.). 64p. (Orig.). 1987. pap. text ed. 14.50 o.p. (ISBN 0-934140-40-5); 8.95 o.p. (ISBN 0-934140-39-1). Toys 'n Things.
Calendar of Archival Materials on the Land Patents Issued by the United States Government with Subject, Tract & Name Indexes. Clifford N. Smith. LC 72-3238. (Federal Land Ser.: Vol. 4, Pt. 1, Grants in the Virginia Military District of Ohio). xx, 396p. 1982. 35.00 o.p. (ISBN 0-8389-0364-9). ALA.
Calendar of the Soul. Rudolf Steiner. Tr. by Ruth Pusch & Hans Pusch. 62p. 1982. 7.95 o.p. (ISBN 0-88010-009-5). Anthroposophic.
Calf Love. Joyce Hussey. 144p. 1985. 12.95 o.p. (ISBN 0-88186-051-4). Parkwest Pubns.
Calgary: Canada's Frontier Metropolis. Max Foran & Heather M. Foran. (Illus.). 368p. 1982. 29.95 o.s.i. (ISBN 0-89781-055-4). Windsor Pubns Inc.
Calhoun: Basic Documents. John C. Calhoun. Ed. by John M. Anderson. 330p. 24.95x o.s.i. (ISBN 0-271-00322-7, Pub. by Bald Eagle). Pa St U Pr.
Calhoun County, Alabama, Boy in the 1860s. Glover Moore. Ed. by Glover Moore, Jr. LC 78-15256. (Illus.). 1978. 5.00x o.p. (ISBN 0-87805-081-7). U Pr of Miss.
Calibration & Control Materials for Neonatal Hypothyroid Screening Programs: Proposed Guideline, Vol. 3. National Committee for Clinical Laboratory Standards. 1983. 20.00 o.p. (ISBN 0-318-19402-3, LA8-P). Natl Comm Clin Lab Stds.
California. Peter Andrews et al. (Country Inns of America Ser.). (Illus.). 96p. (Orig.). 1983. 25.00 o.p. (ISBN 0-03-062756-7); pap. 12.95 o.p. (ISBN 0-03-043726-1). H Holt & Co.
California, II. Photos by David Muench. LC 77-77265. (Belding Imprint Ser.). (Illus.). 192p. (Text by Donald Pike). 1977. 29.50 o.s.i. (ISBN 0-912856-32-7). Gr Arts Ctr Pub.
California - A Place, a People, a Dream: A Journey Through California History from Miwok Baskets to Silicon Chips. David Lavender. LC 85-28033. (Illus.). 158p. (Orig.). 1986. pap. 16.95 o.p. (ISBN 0-87701-386-1). Chronicle Bks.
California - Alaska Oil & Gas Review. 1985. 40.00 o.p. (ISBN 0-318-04734-9). Munger Oil.
California: Agency. 8.50 o.p. (ISBN 0-686-90633-0). Am Law Inst.
California-Alaska Oil & Gas Review for 1969. 1970. 40.00 o.p. (ISBN 0-686-28269-8). Munger Oil.
California-Alaska Oil & Gas Review for 1971. 40.00 o.p. (ISBN 0-686-28270-1). Munger Oil.
California-Alaska Oil & Gas Review for 1972. 40.00 o.p. (ISBN 0-686-28271-X). Munger Oil.
California-Alaska Oil & Gas Review for 1973. 1974. 40.00 o.p. (ISBN 0-686-28272-8). Munger Oil.
California-Alaska Oil & Gas Review of 1975. 1976. 40.00 o.p. (ISBN 0-686-28273-6). Munger Oil.
California-Alaska Oil & Gas Review of 1976. 1977. 40.00 o.p. (ISBN 0-686-28274-4). Munger Oil.
California-Alaska Oil & Gas Review of 1978. 1979. 40.00 o.p. (ISBN 0-318-04194-4). Munger Oil.
California-Alaska Oil & Gas Review of 1980. 1981. 40.00 o.p. (ISBN 0-318-04195-2). Munger Oil.
California-Alaska Oil & Gas Review of 1981. 1982. 40.00 o.p. (ISBN 0-318-04196-0). Munger Oil.
California-Alaska Oil & Gas Review of 1982. 1983. 40.00 o.p. (ISBN 0-318-04197-9). Munger Oil.
California-Alaska Oil & Gas Review of 1983. 1984. 40.00 o.p. (ISBN 0-318-04198-7). Munger Oil.
California Almanac: 1986-1987. Ed. by James Fay et al. (Illus.). 696p. 1985. pap. 12.95 o.p. (ISBN 0-89141-244-1). Presidio Pr.
California-American Cookbook: Innovations on American Regional Dishes. Jeannette Ferrary & Louise Fiszer. LC 85-14224. 1985. 16.45 o.s.i. (ISBN 0-671-50503-3). S&S.
California & the Golden West. Carole Chester. (Pocket Guide Ser.). (Illus.). 1983. pap. 5.95 o.p. (ISBN 0-528-84894-1). Rand McNally.
California Angels. rev. ed. Shaw. LC 82-239833. (Baseball Today Ser.). 48p. (gr. 4 up). 1982. PLB 11.45 o.p. (ISBN 0-87191-855-2). Creative Ed.
California Artists Cookbook. Chotsie Blank. LC 82-6798. (Illus.). 216p. 1982. 25.00 o.p. (ISBN 0-89659-246-4). Abbeville Pr.
California Beauty Book: A Total Guide to Health & Beauty. Trisha Yeager. (Illus.). 240p. 1981. pap. 9.95 o.p. (ISBN 0-936602-11-2). Kampmann.
California Bed & Breakfast Book. Kathy Strong. LC 83-49038. (Illus.). 180p. 1984. pap. 7.95 o.p. (ISBN 0-88742-001-X). Globe Pequot.
California Bed & Breakfast Book. rev. ed. Kathy Strong. LC 85-45693. (Illus.). 224p. (Orig.). 1986. pap. 8.95 o.p. (ISBN 0-88742-069-9). Globe Pequot.
California Butterflies. John S. Garth & J. W. Tilden. 1988. pap. 10.95x o.p. (ISBN 0-520-05389-3). U of Cal Pr.
California Civil Discovery Practice. California Continuing Education of the Bar Staff et al. LC 73-620207. (California Practice Bk.: No. 67). (Illus.). xii, 557p. 1975. 65.00 o.p. (ISBN 0-88124-037-0). Cal Cont Ed Bar.
California Civil Writs. California Continuing Education of the Bar Staff. LC 78-630838. 534p. 1970. 65.00 o.p. (ISBN 0-88124-011-7, CP-30260). Cal Cont Ed Bar.
California Coast. 2nd ed. Sunset Magazine & Books Editors. LC 75-58504. (Illus.). 224p. 1978. pap. 12.95 o.p. (ISBN 0-376-05184-1, Sunset Bks.). Sunset-Lane.
California Coastal Access Guide. California Coastal Commission. 250p. (Orig.). 1981. pap. 8.95 o.p. (ISBN 0-520-04576-9). U of Cal Pr.
California Commercial Law, 3 vols. State Bar of California, Committee on Continuing Education of the Bar. LC 65-63004. (California Practice Book: No. 26-28). Date not set. price not set o.p. Cal Cont Ed Bar.
California Community Property Cases & Materials. 4th ed. Harold E. Verrall & Gail B. Bird. LC 83-12459. (American Casebook Ser.). 549p. 1983. text ed. 28.95 o.p. (ISBN 0-314-74112-7). West Pub.
California: Conflict of Laws. 8.50 o.p. (ISBN 0-686-90635-7). Am Law Inst.
California Connection: Politics in the Golden State. Terry Christensen et al. 1984. write for info. o.p. (ISBN 0-673-39427-1). Scott F.
California Construction Defect & Land Subsidence Litigation: 1987 Supplement. Thomas E. Miller. (Trial Practice Library Ser.). 80p. 1987. pap. 30.00 o.p. (ISBN 0-471-62410-1). Wiley.
California Construction Law. 9th ed. Kenneth G. Gibbs & Gordon Hunt. 240p. 1987. pap. 35.00 o.p. (ISBN 0-941161-33-1). PES Inc WI.
California Consumer Health Care Catalog. 260p. 1.00 o.p. (ISBN 0-318-13955-3). Calif Dept CA.
California: Contracts. 8.50 o.p. (ISBN 0-686-90638-1); 6.00 o.p. (ISBN 0-686-90639-X). Am Law Inst.
California Corporation Manual, 3 vols. 2nd ed. Michael H. Dessent. LC 74-26211. 1974. Set. Lawyers Co-Op.
California Crazy. Alan Cartnal. LC 80-27315. 256p. 1981. 9.95 o.p. (ISBN 0-395-28213-6). HM.
California Crimes & Criminal Procedure, 3 vols. B. E. Witkin. LC 63-4033. 172.50 o.p. Lawyers Co-Op.
California Criminal Law Manual. 6th rev. ed. Derald D. Hunt. 288p. 1984. pap. text ed. write for info. o.p. (ISBN 0-8087-4749-5). Burgess MN Intl.
California Cuisine. Carmel B. Reingold. 192p. 1983. pap. 5.95 o.p. (ISBN 0-380-82156-7, 82156-7). Avon.
California Currents: An Exploration of the Ocean's Pleasures, Mysteries & Dilemmas. Marie De Santis. (Illus.). 248p. 1985. 15.95 o.p. (ISBN 0-89141-191-7). Presidio Pr.
California Debt Collection Manual. Victor L. Chuan. LC 77-91934. 858p. 1978. 65.00 o.p. (ISBN 0-88124-053-2, BU-32220). Cal Cont Ed Bar.
California Decedent Estate Administration, Vol. 2. LC 70-635710. 650p. 1975. 65.00 o.p. (ISBN 0-88124-039-7). Cal Cont Ed Bar.
California Discovery Handbook. 3rd ed. Stuart J. Faber. 319p. (Orig.). 1983. pap. text ed. 34.50 o.p. (ISBN 0-89074-082-8). Lega Bks.
California Dreamers. Norman Bogner. 1981. 14.95 o.p. (ISBN 0-671-42877-2, Wyndham Bks). S&S.
California Elections Code: 1988. rev. ed. Thomas Diebolt et al. 570p. 1988. 25.00 o.p. (ISBN 0-9616372-1-8). DFM Assoc.
California Environmental Law Handbook. Ed. by Richard J. Denney, Jr. et al. (State Environmental Law Ser.). 170p. 1987. pap. text ed. 39.00 o.s.i. (ISBN 0-86587-722-X). Gov Insts.
California Environmental Law Handbook. 2nd ed. McCutchen et al. Ed. by Richard J. Denney, Jr. et al. (State Environmental Law Ser.). 176p. 1988. pap. text ed. 44.00 o.p. (ISBN 0-86587-739-4). Gov Insts.
California Fashion Designers: Art & Style. Douglas Bullis. (Illus.). 160p. (Orig.). 1987. pap. 24.95 o.p. (ISBN 0-87905-278-3, Peregrine Smith). Gibbs Smith Pub.
California Ferraris. Alfred S. Cosentino. 80p. 1963. 25.00 o.p. (ISBN 0-929991-01-X). A S Cosentino Bks.
California Ferraris. 2nd ed. Alfred S. Cosentino. 96p. 1964. 25.00 o.p. (ISBN 0-929991-02-8). A S Cosentino Bks.
California Gallery Guide. Camaro Editors. LC 79-18911. 1986. pap. 4.95 o.s.i. (ISBN 0-913290-22-X). Camaro Pub.
California Gas & Oil Exploration: 1963 Annual. 1964. 40.00 o.p. (ISBN 0-686-28263-9). Munger Oil.
California Images of the Landscape. John Fielder. (Illus.). 192p. 1985. 34.95 o.p. (ISBN 0-942394-13-5). Westcliffe Pubs Inc.
California in the Making. Rockwell D. Hunt. LC 73-20904. 325p. 1974. Repr. of 1953 ed. lib. bdg. 25.00x o.p. (ISBN 0-8371-5866-4, HUCM). Greenwood.
California, Inc. Joel Kotkin & Paul Grabowicz. 336p. 1983. pap. 3.95 o.p. (ISBN 0-380-62398-6, 62398-6, Discus). Avon.
California Indians Five: Sagebrush Corner - Opening of California's Northeast. W. N. Davis. (American Indian Ethnohistory Ser: California & Basin - Plateau Indians). (Illus.). 1975. lib. bdg. 51.00 o.p. (ISBN 0-8240-0775-1). Garland Pub.
California: Its Government & Politics. 2nd ed. Michael J. Ross. LC 83-7717. (Political Science Ser.). 200p. 1983. pap. text ed. 11.50 pub net o.p. (ISBN 0-534-03024-6). Brooks-Cole.
California: Judgements. 8.50 o.p. (ISBN 0-686-90640-3). Am Law Inst.
California Juvenile Court Deskbook. 2nd ed. Homer B. Thompson. LC 79-114372. 1978. 50.00 o.p. (ISBN 0-88124-056-7). Cal Cont Ed Bar.
California Legal Secretary Filing Directory. LC 86-216378. Date not set. price not set o.p. (ISBN 0-938065-16-5, Pub. by York Pub). James Pub Santa Ana.
California Manufacturers Register, 1988. 950p. 1988. 137.00 o.p. (ISBN 0-318-22794-0). Manufacturers.
California Marital Termination Settlements. Stuart B. Walzer. 367p. 1971. 60.00 o.p. (ISBN 0-88124-016-8, FA-30340). Cal Cont Ed Bar.
California Marriage & Divorce Law. 9th, rev. ed. Warner et al. LC 80-11750. 175p. 1987. pap. 15.95 o.p. (ISBN 0-87337-055-4). Nolo Pr.
California Mechanics' Liens & Other Remedies. California Continuing Education of the Bar Staff. LC 70-189671. 347p. 1972. 65.00 o.p. (ISBN 0-88124-022-2). Cal Cont Ed Bar.
California Misdemeanor Procedure Benchbook, Revised. California Continuing Education of the Bar Staff et al. LC 75-3641. (Illus.). xiv, 547p. 1975. 50.00 o.p. (ISBN 0-88124-038-9). Cal Cont Ed Bar.
California Museum Directory. Ed. by Kimberly J. Mueller. LC 78-78310. (California Information Guides Ser.). 1980. pap. 15.00x o.p. (ISBN 0-912102-41-1). Cal Inst Public.
California Non-Profit Corporation Book. 4th ed. Anthony Mancuso. LC 80-82465. (Illus.). 288p. 1984. pap. 24.95 o.p. (ISBN 0-917316-70-3). Nolo Pr.
California Notary Law Primer. 6th ed. National Notary Magazine Editors. 1985. pap. 7.95 o.p. (ISBN 0-933134-15-0). Natl Notary.
California Oil & Gas Exploration 1956. 1956. pap. 40.00 o.p. (ISBN 0-686-30734-8). Munger Oil.
California Oil & Gas Exploration 1957. 1957. pap. 40.00 o.p. (ISBN 0-686-30735-6). Munger Oil.
California Oil & Gas Exploration 1959. 1959. pap. 40.00 o.p. (ISBN 0-686-30736-4). Munger Oil.
California Oil & Gas Exploration: 1960 Annual. 1961. 40.00 o.p. (ISBN 0-686-28261-2). Munger Oil.
California Oil & Gas Exploration: 1962 Annual. 1963. 40.00 o.p. (ISBN 0-686-28262-0). Munger Oil.
California Oil & Gas Exploration: 1964 Annual. 1965. 40.00 o.p. (ISBN 0-686-28264-7). Munger Oil.
California Oil & Gas Exploration: 1965 Annual. 1966. 40.00 o.p. (ISBN 0-686-28265-5). Munger Oil.
California Oil & Gas Exploration: 1966 Annual. 1967. 40.00 o.p. (ISBN 0-686-28266-3). Munger Oil.
California Oil & Gas Exploration: 1967 Annual. 1968. 40.00 o.p. (ISBN 0-686-28267-1). Munger Oil.
California Oil & Gas Exploration: 1968 Annual. 1969. 40.00 o.p. (ISBN 0-686-28268-X). Munger Oil.
California Oil & Gas Review, 1977. 1978. 40.00 o.p. (ISBN 0-686-16192-0). Munger Oil.
California Perspectives: Four Leaders Look at the State of the State. Charles Warren et al. LC 77-21485. 1977. pap. 4.50x o.p. (ISBN 0-87772-247-1). UCB IGS.
California: Property, Vols. 3-5. Set. 11.00 o.p. (ISBN 0-686-90643-8). Am Law Inst.
California Real Estate Appraisal: Residential Properties. 2nd ed. George H. Miller et al. LC 77-5121. (Illus.). 1977. text ed. 29.67 o.p. (ISBN 0-13-112599-0). P-H.

Titles

California Real Estate Practice. 2nd ed. Robert J. Bond & Arthur G. Bowman. LC 73-86436. 480p. 1981. text ed. write for info. o.p. (ISBN 0-673-16474-8). Scott F.

California Real Estate Practices. Kathryn J. Haupt et al. (Illus.). 564p. (Orig.). 1987. pap. 29.95 o.p. (ISBN 0-915799-25-1). Natl Real Estate Inst.

California Real Estate Principles. 3rd ed. Arthur G. Bowman & Robert J. Bond. 1982. text ed. write for info. o.p. (ISBN 0-673-16010-6). Scott F.

California Road Atlas & Driver's Guide, 1988. Thomas Bros. Maps Staff. (Illus.). 280p. 1988. pap. 16.95 o.p. (ISBN 0-88130-243-0). Thomas Bros Maps.

California Road Atlas & Recreation Directory. (Illus.). 232p. (Orig.). 1988. pap. 12.95 o.p. (ISBN 0-528-89829-9). Rand McNally.

California Road Atlas & Travel Guide. Thomas Brothers Maps. (Illus.). 272p. 1983. pap. 12.95 o.p. (ISBN 0-88130-057-8). Thomas Bros Maps.

California Road Atlas 1986. Thomas Bros. Maps Staff. (Illus.). 404p. 1986. pap. 14.95 o.p. (ISBN 0-88130-242-2). Thomas Bros Maps.

California Roll. Roger L. Simon. Ed. by Peter Gethers. LC 84-40485. 256p. 1985. 14.45 o.p. (ISBN 0-394-53711-4, Pub. by Villard Bks). Random.

California: Security. 8.50 o.p. (ISBN 0-686-90648-9). Am Law Inst.

California Services Register: 1987. 650p. 1987. 195.00 o.p. (ISBN 0-318-23572-2). Manufacturers.

California (Southern) 1988. 1424p. 1988. 130.00 o.p. Manufacturers.

California State Capitol Restoration, a Pictorial History. Lynn G. Marlowe et al. Ed. by John C. Worsley & Dale E. Dwyer. LC 83-620000. (Illus.). 60p. (Orig.). 1983. pap. 5.00 o.p. (ISBN 0-9611168-0-3). Cal State Leg.

California State Fire Marshal Construction Materials Listing. 112p. 1988. 10.00 o.p. Intl Conf Bldg Off.

California Subdivision Map Act Practice. Daniel J. Curtin & Robert E. Merritt. 300p. 1987. 70.00 o.p. (RE-32350). Cal Cont Ed Bar.

California Superior Court Criminal Trial Judges' Benchbook: 1987 Edition. Ronald M. George. 1042p. 1987. pap. text ed. write for info. o.p. (ISBN 0-314-59198-2). West Pub.

California Superior Court Criminal Trial Judges' Deskbook, 1987. Ronald M. George. 976p. 1987. pap. write for info. o.p. (ISBN 0-314-59199-0). West Pub.

California Superquake, Nineteen Seventy-Five to Nineteen Seventy-Seven: Scientists, Cayce, Psychics Speak. 2nd, enl. & rev. ed. Paul James. 1974. 10.00 o.p. (ISBN 0-682-48041-X). Exposition-Phoenix.

California Taxes. California Continuing Education of the Bar Staff & John O. Hargrove. LC 78-66869. (Illus.). 1978. 65.00 o.p. (ISBN 0-88124-057-5). Cal Cont Ed Bar.

California: Torts, Vol. 3. 9.50 o.p. (ISBN 0-686-90651-9). Am Law Inst.

California: Torts, Vol. 4. 9.50 o.p. (ISBN 0-686-90653-5). Am Law Inst.

California: Trusts. 8.50 o.p. (ISBN 0-686-90655-1). Am Law Inst.

California Two-Thousand Campaign: The Populist Movement with a Meaning for All America. James Stanbery. 1974. 6.00 o.p. (ISBN 0-682-47987-X). Exposition-Phoenix.

California Votes, Nineteen Sixty to Nineteen Seventy-Two: A Review & Analysis of Registration & Voting. new ed. Eugene C. Lee & Bruce E. Keith. LC 74-12271. (Illus.). 172p. 1974. 7.50x o.p. (ISBN 0-87772-201-3); 1974 supplement 1.50x o.p. (ISBN 0-685-51351-3). UCB IGS.

California Water: A Study in Resource Management. Ed. by David Seckler. LC 76-139773. 1971. 48.50x o.p. (ISBN 0-520-01884-2); pap. 7.95 o.p. (ISBN 0-520-02778-7). U of Cal Pr.

California Wills & Probate. 2nd ed. Harry W. Koch. 1987. 8.00 o.p. (ISBN 0-910553-11-4). Ken Bks.

California Wine Label Album. Terry Robards. LC 81-40502. 176p. 1981. looseleaf 16.95 o.p. (ISBN 0-89480-183-X). Workman Pub.

California Wineries: A Photographic Profile, Vol. 1. Vicki Leon. (Ventura, Santa Barbara, San Luis Obispo Ser.). (Illus.). 128p. (Orig.). 1986. pap. 8.95 o.p. (ISBN 0-918303-06-0). Blake Pub.

California Wings: A History of Aviation in the Golden State. William A. Schoneberger & Paul Sonnenburg. (Illus.). 192p. 1984. 24.95 o.s.i. (ISBN 0-89781-078-3). Windsor Pubns Inc.

California: Winter Vacation Guide, 1989. (Illus.). cancelled o.s.i. Wrld Travel.

California's Chumash Indians. Santa Barbara Museum of Natural History Staff. (Illus.). 80p. (Orig.). 1987. pap. 5.95 o.p. (ISBN 0-936784-15-6). J Daniel.

California's Demand for Librarians: Projecting Future Requirements. Michael D. Cooper. LC 78-8919. 1978. pap. 6.50x o.p. (ISBN 0-87772-256-0). UCB IGS.

California's Railroad Era, Eighteen-Fifty to Nineteen-Eleven. Ward McAfee. LC 73-18280. (Illus.). 296p. 14.95 o.s.i. (ISBN 0-87095-048-7). Gldn West Bks.

California's Spanish Place-Names: What They Mean & How They Got There. Barbara Marinacci & Rudy Marinacci. LC 80-11381. (Illus.). 298p. 1980. pap. 9.95 o.p. (ISBN 0-89141-102-X). Presidio Pr.

California's Utopian Colonies. Robert V. Hine. (Illus.). 240p. 1973. pap. 2.45x o.p. (ISBN 0-393-00678-6, Norton Lib). Norton.

Caligula see Malentendu.

Call. Oral Roberts. 1982. pap. 1.25 o.p. (ISBN 0-380-01078-X, 10678). Avon.

Call Back the Dawn. Diane W. Davis. 336p. 1985. pap. 3.25 o.p. (ISBN 0-380-89703-2). Avon.

Call Back Yesterday. James D. Forman. 192p. (gr. 7 up). 1981. 10.95 o.s.i. (ISBN 0-684-17168-6, Pub. by Scribner). Macmillan.

Call for JCS Reform: Crucial Issues. Louis J. Moses. LC 86-600616. (National Security Essays Ser.). 70p. (Orig.). 1985. pap. 1.25 o.p. (ISBN 0-318-19557-7, S/N 008-020-01046-4). USGPO.

Call for the Saint. Leslie Charteris. (Saint Ser.). 224p. 1981. pap. 2.25 o.s.i. (ISBN 0-441-09151-2). Ace Bks.

Call from Hibakusha of Hiroshima & Nagasaki: Proceedings of the International Symposium on the Damage & After-Effects of the Atomic Bombing of Hiroshima & Nagasaki, 21 July - 9 August 1977, Tokyo, Hiroshima & Nagasaki. Japan National Preparatory Committee. (Illus.). 1979. pap. 51.00 o.p. (ISBN 0-08-024306-1). Pergamon.

Call Him a Man: The Story of Hazzard Parks. Amy Lee. LC 72-130777. (Bold Believers Ser). (Orig.). 1970. pap. 0.95 o.p. (ISBN 0-377-84191-9). Friendship Pr.

Call It Accident. Rae Foley. (Illus.). 288p. Date not set. Repr. of 1975 ed. lib. bdg. price not set o.p. (ISBN 0-89621-840-6). Thorndike Pr.

Call It Sleep. Henry Roth. LC 60-13694. Repr. of 1934 ed. 20.00x o.p. (ISBN 0-8154-0198-1). Cooper Sq.

Call Me Angie. Janet Dean. 1976. 5.50 o.p. (ISBN 0-682-48539-X). Exposition-Phoenix.

Call Me Friday the Thirteenth. Betty Bates. LC 83-6146. (Illus.). 112p. (gr. 3-6). 1983. 9.95 o.p. (ISBN 0-8234-0498-6). Holiday.

Call Me Maria. Sel Ander. 1979. 5.00 o.p. (ISBN 0-682-49447-X). Exposition-Phoenix.

Call Me Moose. Molly Cone. LC 78-1026. (Illus.). 160p. (gr. 3-7). 1978. 6.95 o.p. (ISBN 0-395-26457-X). HM.

Call of Silence: Discovering Christian Meditation. Bradley Hanson. LC 80-67794. 144p. (Orig.). 1980. pap. 5.95 o.p. (ISBN 0-8066-1856-6, 10-0962, Augsburg). Augsburg Fortress.

Call of the Dervish. Pir Vilayat Inayat Khan. LC 81-52421. 224p. (Orig.). 1981. pap. 8.95 o.p. (ISBN 0-930872-26-6, 1013P). Omega Pr NY.

Call of the New South: Addresses Delivered at the Southern Sociological Congress. Southern Sociological Congress Staff. Ed. by James E. McCulloch. LC 72-107486. Repr. of 1912 ed. 20.25 o.p. (ISBN 0-8371-3788-8, SONS&, Pub. by Negro U Pr). Greenwood.

Call of the Sea: Lost Sea, Distant Shore, & Sailor's Life. Jan De Hartog. LC 66-16893. (YA) 1966. 6.95 o.p. (ISBN 0-689-10063-9, Atheneum). Macmillan.

Call of the Virgin at San Damiano. Johan Osee. (Illus.). 1977. pap. 6.95 o.p. (ISBN 0-8158-0354-0). Chris Mass.

Call of the Wild. Jack London. Bd. with White Fang. LC 85-60633. (Illus.). 304p. 1985. 12.95 o.p. (ISBN 0-89577-211-6). RD Assn.

Call of the Wild & White Fang. Jack London. (Bantam Classics Ser.). 304p. pap. text ed. 1.95 o.p. (ISBN 0-553-21185-4). Bantam.

Call the Big Hook. Samuel A. Dougherty. (Illus.). 180p. 1984. 21.95 o.p. (ISBN 0-87095-087-8). Gldn West Bks.

Call to Adventure. Hillary Hauser. LC 87-70932. (Illus.). 200p. 1987. price not set o.p. Bookmakers Guild.

Call to Discipleship: A Literary Study of Mark's Gospel. Augustine Stock. LC 82-81396. (Good News Studies: Vol. 1). 1982. pap. 9.95 o.p. (ISBN 0-89453-273-1). M Glazier.

Call to Faith. Rachel Henderlite. LC 55-5552. 224p. 1955. pap. 4.95 o.p. (ISBN 0-8042-3136-2, John Knox). Westminster John Knox.

Call to Greatness. Adlai E. Stevenson. LC 54-6028. 1962. pap. 1.25 o.p. (ISBN 0-689-70188-8, 15, Atheneum). Macmillan.

Call to Islam. M. S. Siddiqui. pap. 2.00 o.p. (ISBN 0-686-63897-2). Kazi Pubns.

Call to Mission. Stephen Neill. LC 77-116460. 1970. 3.95 o.p. (ISBN 0-8006-0217-X, Fortress). Augsburg Fortress.

Call to Remember. Robert E. Hooper. 1978. pap. 5.00 o.p. (ISBN 0-89225-183-2). Gospel Advocate.

Call up the Morning. Clyde M. Brundy. 544p. 1983. pap. 3.95 o.p. (ISBN 0-380-82339-X). Avon.

Callaghan's Michigan Civil Practice Forms: 1968-1983, 10 vols. Harold B. Clark & M. Spencer. LC 67-23959. 1983. Set. 550.00 o.p. (ISBN 0-317-12072-7). Callaghan.

Callaghan's Michigan Digest: 1941, 34 vols. LC 41-3091. 925.00 o.p.; Subscr., 1981. 345.00 o.p.; Subscr., 1982. 292.50 o.p. Callaghan.

Callaghan's Wisconsin Digest: 1950, 28 vols. Callaghan & Company Publisher's Staff. LC 50-2898. Set. 925.00 o.p. (ISBN 0-317-12219-3); Suppl., 1981. 395.00 o.p.; Suppl., 1982. 400.00 o.p. Callaghan.

Callas Legacy. John Ardoin. 1977. 3.95 o.p. (ISBN 0-684-16343-8, ScribT); 5.50 o.p. (ISBN 0-684-15297-5). Scribner.

Callas Legacy: A Biography of a Career. rev. encore ed. John Ardoin. (Illus.). 256p. 1982. 5.50 o.p. (ISBN 0-684-17450-2, ScribT). Scribner.

Called by the Gospel: An Introduction of the Christian Faith. Marc Kolden. LC 82-72651. 112p. 1983. pap. 5.95 o.p. (ISBN 0-8066-1958-9, 10-0967, Augsburg). Augsburg Fortress.

Called to Account: The Public Accounts Committee of the House of Commons. Vilma Flegmann. 328p. 1980. text ed. 39.95x o.p. (ISBN 0-566-00371-6). Gower Pub Co.

Called to Be Saints. Robert G. Gromacki. 1977. pap. 5.95 o.p. (ISBN 0-87227-014-9). Reg Baptist.

Called to Die: The Story of American Linguist Chet Bitterman, Slain by Terrorists. Steve Estes & Verna Estes. 208p. pap. 7.95 o.p. (ISBN 0-310-28381-7, 12197P). Zondervan.

Called to Heal: Releasing the Transforming Power of God. Ralph A. DiOrio. LC 82-45354. (Illus.). 264p. 1984. pap. 7.95 o.s.i. (ISBN 0-385-19704-7, Im). Doubleday.

Called to Holy Worldliness. Richard J. Mouw. Ed. by Mark Gibbs. LC 80-8047. (Laity Exchange). 160p. (Orig.). 1980. pap. 2.95 o.p. (ISBN 0-8006-1397-X, 1-1397, Fortress). Augsburg Fortress.

Called to Splendor. Nelson L. Price. LC 84-17506. 1984. pap. 4.95 o.p. (ISBN 0-8054-5007-6). Broadman.

Calligraphic Alphabets. Arthur Baker. (Illus.). 15.75 o.p. (ISBN 0-8446-5154-0). Peter Smith.

Calligraphic Art of Arthur Baker. Arthur Baker. LC 82-42648. (Illus.). 64p. 1983. 14.95 o.s.i. (ISBN 0-684-17837-0, ScribT). Scribner.

Calligraphic Styles. Tom Gourdie. LC 78-52316. (Illus., Orig.). 1979. pap. 6.95 o.s.i. (ISBN 0-8008-1181-X, Pentalic). Taplinger.

Calligraphy for the Beginner: Giant. Tom Gourdie. LC 78-63439. (Illus.). 1979. pap. 4.50 o.s.i. (ISBN 0-8008-1185-2, Pentalic). Taplinger.

Calligraphy Today. Heather Child. 1976. 12.00 o.s.i. (ISBN 0-8008-1184-4, Pentalic). Taplinger.

Calling. Sterling Watson. 310p. 1986. 13.95 o.p. (ISBN 0-931948-87-8). Peachtree Pubs.

Calling of an Evangelist. Ed. by J. D. Douglas. 1987. pap. 10.00 o.p. (ISBN 0-89066-087-5). World Wide Pubs.

Calling of Bara. Sheila Sullivan. 304p. 1981. pap. 2.50 o.p. (ISBN 0-380-53785-0, 53785). Avon.

Calling the Play: A Beginner's Guide to Amateur Sports Officiating. Edward E. Dolan, Jr. LC 81-66014. (Illus.). 1982. 14.95 o.p. (ISBN 0-689-11183-5, Atheneum). Macmillan.

Calling the Play: A Beginner's Guide to Amateur Sports Officiating. Edward F. Dolan, Jr. LC 81-66014. (Illus.). 256p. 1984. pap. 6.95 o.p. (ISBN 0-689-70676-6, 316, Atheneum). Macmillan.

Calling to Mind: An Account of the First Hundred Years of Steel Brothers & Company Ltd. Ed. by H. E. Braund. (Illus.). 1975. 40.00 o.p. (ISBN 0-08-017415-9). Pergamon.

Callmann Unfair Competition, Trademarks & Monopolies: 1933-1984, 9 vols. 4th ed. Louis Altman. Ed. by Rudolf Callmann. LC 81-7639. 1981-84. 650.00 o.p. (ISBN 0-317-20372-X); Suppl. 1984. 286.00 o.p.; Suppl. 1985. 195.00 o.p. Callaghan.

Calm Horse, Wild Night. Peter Z. Cohen. LC 82-1746. 168p. (gr. 4-8). 1982. 10.95 o.p. (ISBN 0-689-30918-X, Atheneum). Macmillan.

Calmodulin & Intracellular Ca-Plus-Plus Receptors. Ed. by Shiro Kakiuchi et al. LC 82-12326. 486p. 1982. 79.50x o.p. (ISBN 0-306-41109-1, Plenum Pr). Plenum Pub.

Calms of Capricorn. Eugene O'Neill. Ed. by Donald Gallup. LC 82-715. (Illus.). 208p. 1982. 12.95 o.p. (ISBN 0-89919-093-6). Ticknor & Fields.

Calories Don't Count When... Sara Parriott. LC 79-84900. (Illus.). 96p. 1979. pap. 3.95 o.p. (ISBN 0-87477-105-6). J P Tarcher.

Calvary Christ. Gerald O'Collins. LC 76-54973. 1977. softcover 4.95 o.s.i. (ISBN 0-664-24801-2, Westminster). Westminster John Knox.

Calvin & Classical Philosophy 1977. Ed. by Charles Partee. (Studies in the History of Christian Thought: Vol. 14). 30.00 o.p. (ISBN 90-04-04839-1). E J Brill USA.

Calvinisim & the Religious Wars. Franklin C. Palm. LC 78-80579. 1971. Repr. 24.50x o.p. (ISBN 0-86527-020-1). Fertig.

Calvin's Doctrine of the Last Things. Heinrich Quistorp. o.p. (John Knox). Westminster John Knox.

Cambodian Witness: The Autobiography of Someth May. Someth May. LC 86-10108. 256p. 1986. 17.45 o.s.i. (ISBN 0-394-54804-3). Random.

Cambrian Trilobites, 14 vols., pts. 1-14. P. Lake. Repr. of 1946 ed. Set. 120.00 o.p. (ISBN 0-685-13363-X). Johnson Repr.

Cambridge Glass Book. Harold Bennett & Judy Bennett. 1970. pap. 7.95 o.p. (ISBN 0-87069-012-4). Wallace-Homestead.

Cambridge Platonists, a Study. Frederick J. Powicke. 1971. Repr. of 1926 ed. lib. bdg. 35.00x o.p. (ISBN 0-8371-3999-6, POPL). Greenwood.

Cambridge Seven. John Pollack. 1985. pap. 3.95 o.p. (ISBN 0-551-01174-2). OMF Bks.

Cambridge: The Making of a Canadian City. Kenneth McLaughlin. Ed. by Susan Wells. (Illus.). 224p. 1987. 29.95 o.s.i. (ISBN 0-89781-217-4). Windsor Pubns Inc.

Camden Society Publications: Series 1, Vols. 1-105. Camden Society Staff. Repr. of 1838 ed. Set. 2850.00 o.p. (ISBN 0-384-07230-5). Johnson Repr.

Came a Spider. Edward Levy. LC 78-57318. 1978. 8.95 o.p. (ISBN 0-87795-191-8, Arbor Hse). Morrow.

Camel on Wheels. William M. George. 64p. 1986. 6.95 o.p. (ISBN 0-317-60845-2). Carlton.

Camelot Country. Marjorie McEvoy. LC 85-31129. (Starlight Romance Ser.). 192p. 1986. 12.95 o.p. (ISBN 0-385-23578-X). Doubleday.

Camelot Country. Marjorie McEvoy. LC 87-509. (Starlight Romance Ser.). 1987. 17.95 o.s.i. (ISBN 0-385-23988-2, GC Large Print). Doubleday.

Cameo. Wendy Leeds. 320p. (Orig.). 1982. pap. 3.25 o.p. (ISBN 0-8439-1022-4, Pub. by Leisure Bks CT). Dorchester Pub Co.

Cameo. Wendy Leeds. 320p. (Orig.). pap. 3.50 Cancelled o.p. (ISBN 0-8439-2407-1, Pub. by Leisure Bks CT). Dorchester Pub Co.

Cameo of a Champion. Elizabeth Van Steenwyk. LC 77-17060. (Illus.). (gr. 4-8). 1978. text ed. 9.95 o.p. (ISBN 0-07-067167-2). McGraw.

Cameo Proofs. Val J. Webb. (Illus.). 115p. (Orig.). 1984. pap. 14.95 o.p. (ISBN 0-9614430-0-6). Cameo Pub GA.

Cameos. facsimile ed. Cyril Davenport. 16p. pap. 2.95 o.s.i. (ISBN 0-8466-6005-9, U5). Shorey.

Camera Blue Book, 1987. Ed. by Orion Research Corporation Staff. 250p. 1986. 99.50 o.p. (ISBN 0-932089-14-3). Orion Res.

Camera Comparison Charts: 1986 Edition. Harold C. Durbin. 1986. pap. 25.00 o.s.i. (ISBN 0-936786-03-5). Durbin Assoc.

Camera on Africa: The World of an Ethiopian Boy. Victor Englebert. LC 70-128365. (Illus.). (gr. 3 up). 1970. 5.50 o.p. (ISBN 0-15-214068-9, HJ). HarBraceJ.

Camera on the Sahara: The World of Three Young Nomads. new ed. Victor Englebert. LC 70-157874. (Curriculum Related Bks.). (Illus.). 57p. (gr. 8 up). 1971. 5.50 o.p. (ISBN 0-15-214075-1, HJ). HarBraceJ.

Camera Repair Simplified. Jeffrey R. Weber. LC 80-65475. 112p. (Orig.). 1980. pap. text ed. 14.95 o.p. (ISBN 0-9604892-0-7). Weber Systems.

Camerart Photo Trade Directory, 1986. 24th ed. 75.00 o.p. (ISBN 0-8002-3904-0). Intl Pubns Serv.

Cameras: The Facts, a Collector's Guide, 1957-1964. W. D. Emmanuel. Ed. by Andrew Matheson. LC 80-41969. (Illus.). 528p. 1981. 64.95 o.p. (ISBN 0-240-51062-3). Focal Pr.

Cameroons from Mandate to Independence. Victor T. Levine. (Illus.). 1977. Repr. of 1964 ed. lib. bdg. 22.50x o.p. (ISBN 0-8371-8764-8, LECA). Greenwood.

Camillo Sitte: The Birth of Modern City Planning. George R. Collins & Christiane C. Collins. LC 84-42746. (Illus.). 368p. 1984. 45.00 o.p. (ISBN 0-8478-0785-1); pap. 29.95 o.p. (ISBN 0-8478-0556-5). Rizzoli Intl.

Camino see Way.

Camino Hacia el Amor. Donald A Dohr. Orig. Title: Beginning Your Marriage. 92p. (Span.). 1972. pap. 1.15 o.p. (ISBN 0-915388-02-2, Buckley Pubns). ACTA Pubns.

Camomile Lawn. Mary Wesley. LC 83-24255. 297p. 1984. 15.50 o.s.i. (ISBN 0-671-50461-4). Summit Bks.

Camouflage. Guy Hartcup. 1980. 5.95 o.p. (ISBN 0-684-16721-2, ScribT); encore ed 5.95 o.p. (ISBN 0-684-17522-3). Scribner.

Camouflage. Carol Muske. LC 74-26021. (Pitt Poetry Ser). 1975. pap. 6.95 o.p. (ISBN 0-8229-5259-9). U of Pittsburgh Pr.

Camp. Alan Saperstein. LC 82-5811. 256p. 1982. 12.45 o.p. (ISBN 0-89919-094-4). Ticknor & Fields.

Camp Canada. (Illus.). 72p. (Orig.). 1987. pap. 4.95 o.p. (ISBN 0-528-84723-6). Rand McNally.

Camp Interstate Five. (Illus.). 64p. (Orig.). 1987. pap. 2.95 o.p. (ISBN 0-528-84725-2). Rand McNally.

Campaign Eighty-Four: Advertising & Programming Obligations of the Electronic Media. Practising Law Institute Staff & Timothy B. Dyk. LC 83-62217. (Patents, Copyrights, Trademarks, & Literary Property Course Handbook Ser.: No. 165). 512p. 1984. 15.00 o.p. (G43730). PLI.

Campaign Finance Law Eighty-Six: A Summary of State Campaign Finance Laws with Quick Reference Charts. James A. Palmer & Edward D. Feigenbaum. 409p. (Orig.). 1986. pap. 19.00 o.p. (ISBN 0-318-20091-0, S/N 052-006-00035-0). USGPO.

Campaign Speeches of American Presidential Candidates, 1948-1984. rev. ed. Gregory Bush. 400p. 1985. 25.00 o.p. (ISBN 0-8044-1137-9). Ungar.

Campaigning for Fair School Finance: Cases in Point. League of Women Voters Education Fund Staff. 1978. pap. 3.00 o.p. (ISBN 0-89959-300-3, 353). LWV US.

Campaigning for the Poor. Michael McCarthy. 240p. 1986. 39.00 o.p. (ISBN 0-7099-4606-6, Pub. by Croom Helm Ltd); pap. 19.00 o.p. (ISBN 0-7099-3593-5). Routledge Chapman & Hall.

Campaigns Against Hunger. E. C. Stakman et al. LC 67-20882. (Illus.). 1967. 24.50x o.s.i. (ISBN 0-674-09150-7, Belknap Pr). Harvard U Pr.

Campaigns of the Pacific War. U. S. Strategic Bombing Survey Staff. Repr. of 1946 ed. lib. bdg. 38.50x o.p. (ISBN 0-8371-2313-5, CAPA). Greenwood.

Campbell's Microwave Cookbook. Cambells Soup Company Staff. 1988. 9.98 o.p. (ISBN 0-517-65522-5). Crown.

Campbell's Operative Orthopaedics, 2 Vols. 6 ed. A. S. Edmonson & A. H. Crenshaw. LC 80-14731. (Illus.). 2624p. 1980. Set. cloth 199.95 o.p. (ISBN 0-8016-1071-0). Mosby.

Camper Cookery. Richard Bock. 1977. pap. 5.95 o.p. (ISBN 0-89328-008-9). Lorenz Corp.

Campfire Frontier. Ann W. Hafen. 1969. 5.95x o.p. (ISBN 0-933472-43-9). Johnson Bks.

Campground & Trailer Park Guide: U. S. Canada - Mexico. Incl. pap. 10.95 o.p. (ISBN 0-528-84274-9); Eastern Campground & Trailer Parks. pap. 6.95 o.p. (ISBN 0-528-84276-5); Western Campgrounds & Trailer Parks. 1983. pap. 6.95 o.p. (ISBN 0-528-84275-7). 1982. pap. Rand McNally.

Campiello: A Venetian Comedy. Carolo Goldoni. Tr. by Susanna Graham-Jones from Ital. Bill Bryden. (National Theatre Plays Ser.). viii, 64p. (Orig.). 1976. pap. text ed. 6.00x o.p. (ISBN 0-435-23359-9). Heinemann Ed.

Camping & Backpacking: A Guide to Information Sources. Ed. by Cecil F. Clotfelter & Mary L. Clotfelter. LC 79-84659. (Sports, Games, & Pastimes Information Guide Ser.: Vol. 2). 344p. 1979. 68.00x o.p. (ISBN 0-8103-1437-1). Gale.

Camping & Caravaning in Britain, '88. Date not set. (ISBN 0-86145-773-0, Pub. by Auto Assn England). Salem Hse Pubs.

Camping for Fishermen. (Illus., Orig.). 1987. Eastern U. S.-Eastern Canada Edition, 256p. pap. 5.95 o.p. (ISBN 0-528-84719-8); Western U. S.-Western Canada Edition, 208p. pap. 5.95 o.p. (ISBN 0-528-84721-X). Rand McNally.

Camping in Covenant Community. Geneva Giese. (Illus., Orig.). 1967. pap. 3.45 o.p. (ISBN 0-8042-9867-X, John Knox). Westminster John Knox.

Camping-Out: One Hundred & One Ideas & Activities. Bruno Knobel. 1974. pap. 2.00 o.p. (ISBN 0-87980-290-1). Wilshire.

Camping Together As Christians. John Ensign & Ruth S. Ensign. LC 58-6252. 1958. pap. 1.50 o.p. (ISBN 0-8042-1176-0, John Knox). Westminster John Knox.

Campus of the Future: Conference on Information Resources. (OCLC Library, Information, & Computer Science Ser.: No. 6). (Illus.). 160p. 1987. pap. 9.00 o.p. (ISBN 1-55653-010-2). OCLC Online Comp.

Campus Survival Cookbook, No. 2. Jacqueline Wood & Joelyn S. Gilchrist. LC 81-38387. (Illus.). 160p. (Orig.). 1981. pap. 10.95 o.p. (ISBN 0-688-00591-8). Morrow.

Campus Symbolism: Devotions for New Students. David W. Wollenburg. (ISBN 0-911770-52-6). Concordia Schl Grad Studies.

Campus Vacations Directory. 3rd, rev. ed. Joan Beers. 40p. 1988. pap. 10.00 o.p. (ISBN 0-945063-24-5). Campus Vacations.

Can Deterrence Last? Peace Through a Nuclear Strategy. Timothy Garden. 1987. pap. 199.00 o.p. (ISBN 0-907675-32-8, Pub. by Buchan & Enright England). Seven Hills Bk Dists.

Can-Do Tune-up: Pinto & Vega Cars, 1971-74. Advanced Learning, Inc. 1975. pap. 4.95 o.p. (ISBN 0-672-23849-7, Pub. by Audel); pap. 7.95, with cassette tape o.p. (ISBN 0-672-23831-4, 23831). Macmillan.

Can God Survive in Australia. Bruce Wilson. 224p. (Orig.). 1983. pap. 8.95 o.p. (ISBN 0-86760-009-8, Pub. by Albatross Bks). Meyer Stone Bks.

Can I Get There by Candlelight? Jean S. Doty. LC 79-24466. (Illus.). 128p. (gr. 5-9). 1980. 9.95 o.s.i. (ISBN 0-02-732670-5). Macmillan.

Can I Help How I Feel? Carl Morrison & Dorothy V. Morrison. LC 76-4931. (Illus.). (gr. 5-9). 1976. 7.95 o.p. (ISBN 0-689-30542-7, Atheneum). Macmillan.

Can I Make It One More Year? Overcoming the Hazards of the Ministry. Edgar M. Grider. LC 79-87755. 1980. pap. 3.49 o.p. (ISBN 0-8042-1568-5, John Knox). Westminster John Knox.

Can Inflation Be Controlled. Harold G. Moulton. 1958. 10.00 o.p. (ISBN 0-910136-02-5). Anderson Kramer.

Can "IT" Happen Again? Essays on Instability & Finance. Hyman P. Minsky. LC 82-10789. 320p. 1982. 37.50 o.p. (ISBN 0-87332-213-4); pap. 17.95 o.p. (ISBN 0-87332-305-X). M E Sharpe.

Can Man Change the Climate? P. Borisov. 175p. 1973. pap. 3.45 o.p. (ISBN 0-8285-0816-X, Pub. by Progress Pubs USSR). Imported Pubns.

Can Modern Man Survive Modern Government? Joseph Costello. 109p. 1983. 12.95 o.p. (ISBN 0-89803-109-5, Dist. by Kampmann). Green Hill.

Can Organizations Change? Environmental Protection, Citizen Participation, & the Army Corps of Engineers. Daniel A. Mazmanian & Jeanne Nienaber. 220p. 1979. 9.95 o.p. (ISBN 0-8157-5524-4); pap. 9.95 o.p. (ISBN 0-8157-5523-6). Brookings.

Can Supernutrition Make the Difference? Harold Adams. 104p. 1987. 8.95 o.p. (ISBN 0-8062-2840-7). Carlton.

Can the English Language Become Phonetic? Paul Mitrevski. 208p. 1983. 10.00 o.p. (ISBN 0-682-49915-3). Exposition-Phoenix.

Can This Be Love? And Other Quandaries of Love in the Eighties. Bette-Jane Raphael. LC 85-11161. 192p. 1985. 14.95 o.p. (ISBN 0-87795-747-9, Arbor Hse). Morrow.

Can We Change? J. W. Redfearn. 1985. 10.00x o.p. (ISBN 0-317-62004-5, Guild of Pastoral Psych). State Mutual Bk.

Can You Hear Me God? Vic Merrill. 96p. 1981. 6.00 o.p. (ISBN 0-682-49740-1). Exposition-Phoenix.

Can You Prevent Cancer? Realistic Guidelines for Developing Cancer-Preventive Life Habits. Ernest H. Rosenbaum. LC 83-11387. (Illus.). 352p. 1983. pap. 9.95 o.p. (ISBN 0-8016-4198-5). Mosby.

Can You Retire? D. Dixon. 1968. 35.00 o.p. (ISBN 0-08-012725-8). Pergamon.

Can You Speak Venusian? Patrick Moore. 1978. 15.00 o.p. (ISBN 0-86025-802-5, Pub. by Ian Henry Pubns England). State Mutual Bk.

Can You Speak Venusian? A Guide to Independent Thinkers. Patrick Moore. (Illus.). 176p. 1973. 6.95 o.p. (ISBN 0-393-06394-1). Norton.

Can You Talk with Someone Else? Shirley Schwarzrock & C. Gilbert Wrenn. (Coping with Ser.). (Illus.). 36p. (gr. 7-12). 1970. pap. text ed. 3.00 o.p. (ISBN 0-913476-22-6). Am Guidance.

Can You Wait 'til Friday: Psychology of Hope. Ken Olson. 160p. 1975. PLB write for info. o.p. (ISBN 0-89019-050-X); pap. 3.95 o.p. (ISBN 0-89019-047-X). Norwalk Pr.

Canaan. Charlie Smith. 456p. 1985. 17.45 o.s.i. (ISBN 0-671-53295-2). S&S.

Canaan. Charlie Smith. 432p. 1986. pap. 3.95 o.p. (ISBN 0-380-70064-6). Avon.

Canada. rev. ed. Theo L. Hills & Sarah Jane Hills. LC 77-80448. (American Neighbors Ser.). (Illus.). 224p. (gr. 5 up). 1979. text ed. 11.20 1-4 copies, 5 or more copies 8.96 o.s.i. (ISBN 0-88296-090-3); tchrs'. guide o.s.i. 6.96 o.s.i. (ISBN 0-88296-353-8). Gateway Pr MI.

Canada. Nina Nelson. (Illus.). 160p. 1980. 29.95 o.p. (ISBN 0-7134-1841-9, Pub. by Batsford England). David & Charles.

Canada. Time-Life Books Editors. (Library of Nations). (Illus.). 160p. (YA) (gr. 7 up). 1988. lib. bdg. 23.93 o.p. (ISBN 0-8094-5320-7). Time-Life.

Canada-A Travel Survival Kit. 2nd ed. Mark Lightbody. (Illus.). 384p. (Orig.). 1986. pap. 9.95 o.p. (ISBN 0-908086-86-5). Lonely Planet.

Canada & Immigration: Public Policy & Public Concern. Freda Hawkins. (Canadian Public Administration Ser.). 1972. 16.50 o.p. (ISBN 0-7735-0128-2, McGill Canada); pap. 4.95 o.p. (ISBN 0-7735-0160-6). U of Toronto Pr.

Canada & the Far East-Nineteen Forty. Arthur R. Lower. LC 73-3016. 152p. 1973. Repr. of 1941 ed. lib. bdg. 35.00 o.p. (ISBN 0-8371-6831-7, LOCF). Greenwood.

Canada Handbook: The 48th Annual Handbook of Present Conditions & Recent Progress. Statistics Canada Staff. LC 77-642536. (Illus.). 354p. 1980. pap. 9.95x o.p. (ISBN 0-295-95705-0). U of Wash Pr.

Canada, Nineteen Eighty. Steve Birnbaum. (Get 'Em & Go Travel Guides Ser.). 1979. 15.00 o.p. (ISBN 0-395-27774-4); pap. 9.95 o.p. (ISBN 0-395-27775-2). HM.

Canada, Nineteen Eighty-One. Steve Birnbaum. (Get 'em & Go Travel Guide Ser). 1980. pap. 9.95 o.p. (ISBN 0-395-29751-6). HM.

Canada Nineteen Eighty-Seven. Steve Birnbaum. (Illus.). 688p. 1986. pap. 12.70 o.s.i. (ISBN 0-395-42341-4). HM.

Canada, Nineteen Eighty-Two. Steve Birnbaum. (Get 'em & Go Travel Guide Ser.). 608p. 1981. pap. 10.95 o.p. (ISBN 0-395-31532-8). HM.

Canada: Post Report. rev. ed. (Department of State Publication 9175. Department & Foreign Service Ser. 224). (Illus.). 56p. (Orig.). 1985. pap. 2.25 o.p. (ISBN 0-318-19558-5, S/N 044-000-02097-1). USGPO.

Canada Scott's Western Industrial Directory, 1987-88. 700p. 1986. 159.95 o.p. (ISBN 0-318-02850-6). Manufacturers.

Canada, the Commonwealth & the Common Market: Report of the 1962 Summer Institute, Mount Allison University. Ed. by William B. Cunningham. 148p. 1962. pap. 2.95 o.p. (ISBN 0-7735-0016-2, McGill Canada). U of Toronto Pr.

Canada Travel Survival Kit. Mark Lightbody. 1985. pap. 9.95 o.p. (ISBN 0-908086-37-7). Lonely Planet.

Canada Yearbook. Incl. 1975. (Illus.). 1977. 18.50 (SSC17). UNIPUB; 1976-1977. 1977. pap. 23.00 o.p. (ISBN 0-660-00761-4, SSC106). UNIPUB; 1978-1979. 1978. pap. 28.00 o.p. (SSC131). UNIPUB; 1980-1981. 31.50 (SSC169). UNIPUB. SSC). UNIPUB.

Canada Yearbook, 1980-81. 74th ed. (Illus.). 1004p. Intl Pubns Serv.

Canada 1983. Steve Birnbaum. (Get 'em & Go Travel Guide Ser.). 1982. pap. 11.45 o.p. (ISBN 0-395-32868-3). HM.

Canada 1984. Steve Birnbaum. 1983. pap. 11.45 o.p. (ISBN 0-395-34632-0). HM.

Canada, 1985. Steve Birnbaum. (Stephen Birnbaum Travel Guides Ser.). 1984. pap. 11.45 o.p. (ISBN 0-395-36531-7). HM.

Canada's Industrial Space-Economy. David F. Walker. 261p. 1980. 42.95x o.p. (ISBN 0-470-27061-6). Halsted Pr.

Canada's Kids. Sabra Holbrook. LC 83-6355. (Illus.). 192p. (gr. 5 up). 1983. 11.95 o.s.i. (ISBN 0-689-31002-1, Atheneum). Macmillan.

Canada's National Parks: A Visitor's Guide. Marylee Stephenson. (Illus.). 308p. 1984. 19.95 o.p. (ISBN 0-13-113937-1); pap. 11.95 o.p. (ISBN 0-13-113929-0). P-H.

Canadian Academic Relations with the People's Republic of China Since 1970: China Profiles of Canadian Universities-Supplementary Materials, Vol. 2. Martin Singer. (Illus.). 411p. (Orig.). 1986. pap. text ed. 18.00 o.p. (IDRSTS542, Pub. by IDRC). UNIPUB.

Canadian Almanac & Directory, 1981. Ed. by Susan Walters. 1094p. 1981. 39.00x o.p. (ISBN 0-8103-1186-0, Pub. by Copp Clark Pitman). Gale.

Canadian Almanac & Directory 1982. Rev., 135 ed. Susan Bracken. 1122p. 1981. 42.00x o.p. (ISBN 0-8103-1189-5, Pub. by Copp Clark Pitman). Gale.

Canadian Almanac & Directory, 1984. LC 7-24314. 1191p. 60.00 o.p. (ISBN 0-7730-4053-6). Intl Pubns Serv.

Canadian Almanac & Directory 1985. 138th ed. Ed. by Susan Bracken. 1100p. 1985. 64.00x o.p. (ISBN 0-7730-4053-6, Pub. by Copp Clark Pitman). Gale.

Canadian & Provincial Industrial Policies - Strategy Debates since 1970: A Bibliography. Ontario Ministry of Treasury & Economics, Library Services Staff. (Public Administration Ser.: P 1807). 28p. 1985. 4.50 o.p. (ISBN 0-89028-637-X). Vance Biblios.

Canadian Aquatic Resources. Ed. by M. C. Healey & R. R. Wallace. (Canadian Bulletin of Fisheries & Aquatic Sciences Ser.: No. 215). 533p. 1987. pap. 24.00 o.p. (ISBN 0-660-12487-4, Pub. by CEASC). Gower Pub Co.

Canadian Books in Print 1987. Ed. by Marian Butler. Author & Title Index, 1040p. 70.00 o.p. (ISBN 0-8020-4634-7); Subject Index, 642p. 55.00 o.p. (ISBN 0-8020-4635-5). U of Toronto Pr.

Canadian Broadcasting. Stuart McFadyen et al. (Illus.). 277p. 1980. pap. text ed. 15.95x o.p. (ISBN 0-920380-68-9, Pub. by Inst Res Pub Canada). Gower Pub Co.

Canadian Bush Pilot: Ernie Boffa. Florence Whyard. LC 84-6395. (Illus.). 141p. (Orig.). pap. 7.95 o.p. (582). Alaska Northwest.

Canadian CAD-CAM & Robotics: Conference Proceedings. 2nd ed. 200p. 1983. pap. 25.00 o.p. (ISBN 0-87263-119-2). ASME.

Canadian Conference: Proceedings 13th Annual, Oct. 4-8, 1980. Ed. by Mary E. Brennan. 145p. (Orig.). 1981. pap. 11.00 o.p. (ISBN 0-89154-145-4). Intl Found Employ.

Canadian Conference: Proceedings, 15th Annual, 1982. Ed. by Mary E. Brennan. 318p. 1983. pap. text ed. 15.00 o.p. (ISBN 0-89154-204-3). Intl Found Employ.

Canadian Conference, 14th Annual Nov. 23-27, 1981 Proceedings. Ed. by Mary E. Brennan. 280p. (Orig.). 1982. pap. 14.00 o.p. (ISBN 0-89154-177-2). Intl Found Employ.

Canadian Employee Benefit Plans, 1983. Ed. by Mary E. Brennan. LC 77-151688. 302p. (Orig.). 1984. pap. text ed. 15.00 o.p. (ISBN 0-89154-217-5). Intl Found Employ.

Canadian House of Commons: Procedure & Reform. John Stewart. 1977. 20.00x o.p. (ISBN 0-7735-0256-4, McGill Canada). U of Toronto Pr.

Canadian Indian Policy: A Bibliography Supplement. Jim Buchanan. 1986. pap. 6.25 o.p. (ISBN 1-55590-094-1). Vance Biblios.

Canadian Labour in Politics. Gad Horowitz. LC 68-101781. 1968. pap. 6.50c o.p. (ISBN 0-8020-6155-9). U of Toronto Pr.

Canadian Manuscripts in the Boston Public Library: A Descriptive Catalog. Boston Public Library Staff. 1971. lib. bdg. 69.00 o.p. (ISBN 0-8161-0930-3, Hall Library). G K Hall.

Canadian Minerals Year Book, 1983-84. Ed. by Thompson. 1985. pap. text ed. 40.75 o.p. (ISBN 0-660-11816-5, Pub. by Canmet). Gower Pub Co.

Canadian Official Publications. Olga B. Bishop. (Guides to Official Publications Ser.: Vol. 9). 308p. 1980. 59.00 o.p. (ISBN 0-08-024697-4). Pergamon.

Canadian Pacific: A Brief History. J. Lorne Mc Dougall. 212p. 1968. pap. 1.75 o.p. (ISBN 0-7735-9063-3, McGill Canada). U of Toronto Pr.

Canadian Poetry in English. Compiled by Bliss Carman. LC 76-22428. 456p. 1976. Repr. of 1954 ed. lib. bdg. 32.50x o.p. (ISBN 0-8371-9008-8, CACP). Greenwood.

Canadian Population Trends & Public Policy Through the 1980s. Leroy O. Stone & Claude Marceau. 1977. text ed. 8.50x o.p. (ISBN 0-7735-0287-4, McGill Canada); pap. 4.00 o.p. (ISBN 0-7735-0288-2, McGill Canada). U of Toronto Pr.

Canadian Selection: Books & Periodicals for Libraries (Supplement) 1977-79. Isabel McLean & Edith Jarvi. 544p. 1980. 35.00x o.p. (ISBN 0-8020-4593-6). U of Toronto Pr.

Canadian Trailblazer: The New Collective Bargaining Law see Issues in the Public Employee Relations Library: Series 1.

Canadian Who's Who 1988, Vol. XXIII. Ed. by Kieran Simpson. 1988. net 100.00 o.p. (ISBN 0-8020-4644-4). U of Toronto Pr.

Canal Age. Charles Hadfield. LC 80-69343. (Illus.). 240p. 1981. 23.50 o.p. (ISBN 0-7153-8079-6). David & Charles.

Canal & River Craft in Pictures. Hugh McKnight. LC 75-94574. (Illus.). 112p. 1969. 17.95x o.p. (ISBN 0-678-05661-7). Kelley.

Canal Ports: The Urban Achievement of the Canal Age. J. Douglas Porteous. 1977. 66.00 o.p. (ISBN 0-12-561950-2). Acad Pr.

Canal War: Four-Power Conflict in the Middle East. L. L. Whetten. 1974. 42.00x o.p. (ISBN 0-262-23069-0). MIT Pr.

Canalisation & Gene Control. James M. Rendel. LC 67-28421. (Illus.). 1968. 46.00 o.p. (ISBN 0-12-586950-9). Acad Pr.

Canals of South West England. Charles Hadfield. (Illus.). 208p. 1985. 34.95 o.p. (ISBN 0-7153-8645-X). David & Charles.

Canals of the West Midlands. Charles Hadfield. (Illus.). 352p. 1985. 35.95 o.p. (ISBN 0-7153-8644-1). David & Charles.

Canary Island Hopping: The Azores Madeira. Judith Hayter. 1984. pap. 12.95 o.p. (ISBN 0-7221-4496-2). Hippocrene Bks.

Canary Islanders: Their Prehistory, Conquest & Survival. John Mercer. (Illus.). 285p. 1980. 32.50x o.p. (ISBN 0-389-20213-4). B&N Imports.

Canary Islands Travel Guide. Berlitz Editors. (Travel Guides Ser.). 1976. pap. 4.95 o.p. (ISBN 0-317-12100-6, Berlitz). Macmillan.

Canary Murder Case. S. S. Van Dine. 1980. lib. bdg. 11.50 o.p. (ISBN 0-8398-2554-4, Gregg). G K Hall.

Canavan's Trail. Burt Arthur & Budd Arthur. (Gunsmoke Western Ser.). 176p. 1988. text ed. 12.95x o.p. (ISBN 0-85997-850-8, Pub. by Firecrest Pub Ltd). Prescott Pr NH.

Cancer-A Healing Crisis: The Whole-Body Approach to Cancer Therapy. Jack Tropp. 304p. 1980. 15.00 o.p. (ISBN 0-682-49583-2, Banner). Exposition-Phoenix.

Cancer Active Immunotherapy, Immunoprophylaxis & Immunorestoration: An Introduction. G. Mathe. (Recent Results in Cancer Research Ser: Vol. 55). 1976. 37.50 o.p. (ISBN 0-387-07601-8). Springer-Verlag.

Cancer & Chemotheraphy, Vol. 1: Introduction to Neoplasia & Antineoplastic Chemotherapy. Ed. by Stanley T. Crooke & Archie W. Prestayko. 373p. 1980. 72.50 o.p. (ISBN 0-12-197801-X). Acad Pr.

Cancer & Chemotherapy: Antineoplastic Agents, Vol. 3. Ed. by S. T. Crooke & A. W. Prestayko. LC 79-8536. 1981. 72.50 o.p. (ISBN 0-12-197803-6). Acad Pr.

Cancer & Chemotherapy: Introduction to Clinical Oncology, Vol. 2. Stanley T. Crooke & Archie W. Prestayko. LC 79-8536. 1981. 72.50 o.p. (ISBN 0-12-197802-8). Acad Pr.

Cancer & Nutrition: A Ten-Point Plan to Reduce Your Chances of Getting Cancer. C. B. Simone. 260p. 1983. text ed. 15.95 o.p. (ISBN 0-07-057466-9). McGraw.

Cancer & Nutrition: A Ten-Point Plan to Reduce Your Chances of Getting Cancer. C. B. Simone. 256p. 1984. pap. text ed. 7.95 o.p. (ISBN 0-07-057527-4). McGraw.

Cancer As I See It. Henry W. Abelmann. (ISBN 0-8022-0002-8). Philos Lib.

Cancer-Associated Genodermatoses. Henry T. Lynch & Ramon M. Fusaro. 512p. 1982. 46.95 o.p. (ISBN 0-442-22471-0). Van Nos Reinhold.

Cancer Biology Reviews, Vol. 1. Marchalonis. 368p. 1980. 65.00 o.p. (ISBN 0-8247-6856-6). Dekker.

Cancer Cell Organelles: Biochemistry. E. Reid et al. (Methodological Surveys in Biochemistry Ser.: Vol. 2). 415p. 1982. 89.95x o.p. (ISBN 0-470-27244-9). Halsted Pr.

Cancer Cells Three: Growth Factors & Transformation. Ed. by James Feramisco et al. LC 85-3733. (Cancer Cells Ser.: Vol. 3). 450p. (Orig.). 1985. pap. 70.00 o.p. (ISBN 0-87969-178-6). Cold Spring Harbor.

Cancer Cells 2: Oncogenes & Viral Genes. Ed. by G. F. Vande Woude et al. LC 83-26336. (Illus.). 650p. (Orig.). 1984. pap. 65.00x o.p. (ISBN 0-87969-169-7). Cold Spring Harbor.

Cancer Chemotherapy. 3rd ed. Martin J. Cline & Charles M. Haskell. (Illus.). 397p. 1980. text ed. write for info. o.p. (ISBN 0-7216-2609-2). Saunders.

Cancer Connection: And What We Can Do About It. Larry Agran. 1978. 10.95 o.p. (ISBN 0-395-25178-8). HM.

Cancer Control Objectives for the Nation: 1985-2000. (NCI Monographs: No. 2). (Illus.). 121p. 1986. pap. 6.00 o.p. (ISBN 0-318-21676-0, S/N 017-042-00191-9). USGPO.

Cancer Detection. 2nd rev. ed. Commission on Cancer Control, Cancer Detection Committee. (UICC Monograph: Vol. 4). (Illus.). vii, 51p. 1975. pap. 22.00 o.p. (ISBN 0-387-06976-3). Springer-Verlag.

Cancer Epidemiology & Prevention: Current Concepts. Ed. by David Schottenfeld. (Illus.). 592p. 1975. 72.50 o.p. (ISBN 0-398-03173-8). C C Thomas.

Cancer: How & Why It May Be Wiped Out. J. Gordon Roberts. LC 77-70955. 1977. pap. 3.95 o.s.i. (ISBN 0-912760-37-0). Valkyrie Pub Hse.

Cancer Incidence in Five Continents Vol. 1. Ed. by R. Doll et al. 1966. 42.50 o.p. (ISBN 0-387-03475-7). Springer-Verlag.

Cancer Medicine. 2nd ed. Ed. by James F. Holland & Emil Frei, 3rd. LC 81-8382. (Illus.). 2465p. 1982. text ed. 140.00 o.p. (ISBN 0-8121-0603-2). Lea & Febiger.

Cancer Mortality: Environmental & Ethnic Factor. Dorothy G. Wellington et al. LC 79-10560. 1979. 35.00 o.p. (ISBN 0-12-745850-6). Acad Pr.

Cancer Nursing. Ed. by Margaret C. Cahoon. (Recent Advances in Nursing Ser.: Vol. 3). 172p. 1982. pap. text ed. 23.00 o.p. (ISBN 0-443-01935-5). Churchill.

Cancer Nursing, Vol. 1. Ed. by Robert Tiffany. (Medical Ser.). (Illus.). 192p. 1978. 13.95 o.p. (ISBN 0-571-11174-2); pap. 7.95 o.p. (ISBN 0-571-11175-0). Faber & Faber.

Cancer Nursing: A Developmental Approach. Ed. by Sue N. McIntire & Anne L. Cioppa. LC 83-27412. 659p. 1984. text ed. 29.95 o.p. (ISBN 0-471-08290-2, Pub by Wiley Med). Wiley.

Cancer of the Breast. 2nd. ed. William L. Donegan & John S. Spratt, Jr. LC 78-1785. (Major Problems in Clinical Surgery Ser.: Vol. 5). (Illus.). 1979. text ed. write for info. o.p. (ISBN 0-7216-3140-1). Saunders.

Cancer of the Cervix. Stephen G. Brown & Philip J. DiSaisa. (Oncologic Ser.: Vol. 14). (Illus.). 308p. 1981. pap. 135.00 o.p. (ISBN 0-08-027465-X). Pergamon.

Cancer of the Female Reproductive System. Christopher J. Williams & Michael Whitehouse. LC 84-25815. (Cancer Investigation & Management Ser.). 1985. Repr. write for info. o.p. (ISBN 0-471-90470-8, Dist. by A R Liss). Wiley.

Cancer of the Lung. Ed. by B. E. Peterson. LC 76-3894. (Illus.). 296p. 1979. 29.00 o.p. (ISBN 0-88416-118-8). Year Bk Med.

Cancer of the Prostate. Malcolm A. Bagshaw. (OncoLOGIC: 18). (Illus.). 260p. 1984. Vol. 18. pap. 120.00 o.p. (ISBN 0-08-027471-4). Pergamon.

Cancer of the Prostate & Kidney. Ed. by M. Pavone-Macaluso & P. H. Smith. LC 82-16505. (NATO ASI Series A, Life Sciences: Vol. 53). 766p. 1983. 115.00x o.p. (ISBN 0-306-41132-6, Plenum Pr.). Plenum Pub.

Cancer Patient. John W. Dawson. LC 78-52192. (Religion & Medicine Ser.). 1978. pap. 6.95 o.p. (ISBN 0-8066-1662-8, 10-0960, Augsburg). Augsburg Fortress.

Cancer Research Today. I. Berenblum. 1967. 40.00 o.p. (ISBN 0-08-012451-8); pap. 40.00 o.p. (ISBN 0-08-012452-6). Pergamon.

Cancer Risk: Assessing & Reducing the Dangers in Our Society. Office of Technology Assessment, Congress of the United States Staff. (Special Study). 240p. (Orig.). 1982. 24.00x o.p. (ISBN 0-86531-396-2); pap. 12.50x o.p. (ISBN 0-86531-397-0). Westview.

Cancer Surgery. Tadeusz Koszarowski. LC 78-27389. (Illus.). 819p. 1983. text ed. 44.50 o.p. (ISBN 0-8067-1021-7). Urban & S.

Cancer Syndrome. Ralph W. Moss. LC 79-2300. 1980. 12.95 o.s.i. (ISBN 0-394-50859-9, GP828). Grove.

Cancer Syndrome. Ralph W. Moss. LC 79-2300. 320p. 1982. pap. 4.95 o.p. (ISBN 0-394-17655-3, B-468, BC). Grove.

Cancer Syndrome. Ralph W. Moss. LC 79-2300. 320p. 1981. pap. 6.95 o.p. (ISBN 0-394-17896-3, E780, Ever). Grove.

Cancer Today: Origins, Prevention, & Treatment. Leslie Roberts. (Illus.). 144p. 1984. 9.50 o.p. (ISBN 0-309-03436-1). Natl Acad Pr.

Cancer Treatment & Research in Humanistic Perspective. Steven Gross & Solomon Garb. 256p. 1985. text ed. 20.95 o.p. (ISBN 0-8261-4760-7). Springer Pub.

Cancer Treatment: End-Point Evaluation. B. A. Stoll. LC 82-17492. 520p. 1983. 62.00x o.p. (ISBN 0-471-90080-X, 1-666, Dist. by A R Liss). Wiley.

Cancer: Understanding & Fighting It. Sheila L. Burns. Ed. by Madelyn K. Anderson. LC 82-8151. (Illus.). 64p. (gr. 4 up). 1982. lib. bdg. 9.29 o.p. (ISBN 0-671-44250-3). Messner.

Candi. John Benton. (New Hope Bk). 1983. pap. 2.95 o.p. (ISBN 0-8007-8473-1, Spire Bks). Revell.

Candida Albicans: Could Yeast Be Your Problem? Leon Chaitow. 96p. (Orig.). 1985. pap. 4.95 o.p. (ISBN 0-7225-1144-2). Inner Tradit.

Candidates for Maturity. Ed. by Jess Shaver. 328p. 1972. pap. text ed. 9.75x o.p. (ISBN 0-8422-0190-4). Irvington.

Candide; or, All for the Best, 1759 see Prince of Abissinia: A Tale, 1759.

Candido or, Dream Dreamed in Sicily. Leonardo Sciascia. Ed. by Helen Wolff. Tr. by Adrienne Foulke. LC 71-9495. (Helen & Kurt Wolff Bk.). 1979. 7.95 o.p. (ISBN 0-15-115380-9). HarBraceJ.

Candle & the Mirror. Lucinda Mays. LC 81-8115. 192p. (gr. 7 up). 1982. PLB 9.95 o.p. (ISBN 0-689-30885-X, Atheneum). Macmillan.

Candle in the Dark. Lois Henderson. LC 81-70518. (Orig.). (gr. 5-9). 1983. pap. 2.95 o.p. (ISBN 0-89191-504-4, 55046). Cook.

Candle to the Devil. Gail Hamilton. LC 75-9519. (gr. 5-9). 1975. 6.95 o.p. (ISBN 0-689-30478-1, Atheneum). Macmillan.

Candlelight. Aileen Hall. (Illus.). 64p. 1982. 5.00 o.p. (ISBN 0-682-49810-6). Exposition-Phoenix.

Candles of Your Eyes: Stories. James Purdy. LC 86-19087. 160p. 1987. 14.95 o.s.i. (ISBN 1-55584-066-3). Weidenfeld.

Candlewicking from Yesterday for Today. Date not set. pap. 4.98 o.p. (ISBN 0-317-03209-7). Gick.

Candy & Candy Molding. Mildred Brand. (Illus.). 64p. 1982. pap. 3.95 o.p. (ISBN 0-8249-3015-0). Ideals.

Candy Cookbook. Mildred Brand. Ed. by James A. Kuse. (Illus.). 1979. pap. 3.95 o.p. (ISBN 0-89542-615-3). Ideals.

Candy Technology. Justin J. Alikonis. (Illus.). 1979. 45.95 o.p. (ISBN 0-87055-280-5). AVI.

Canek: History & Legend of a Maya Hero. Ermilo A. Gomez. 80p. 1983. pap. 2.50 o.p. (ISBN 0-380-61937-7, 61937-7, Bard). Avon.

Canine & Feline Dermatology: A Systematic Approach. Gene H. Nesbitt. LC 82-12747. (Illus.). 224p. 1983. text ed. 38.50 o.p. (ISBN 0-8121-0859-0). Lea & Febiger.

Canine Terminology. Date not set. (ISBN 0-06-312047-X). Howell Bk.

Cannabis & Health. Ed. by J. D. Graham. 1976. 108.00 o.p. (ISBN 0-12-294650-2). Acad Pr.

Canned Foods: Principles of Thermal Process Control, Acidification & Container Closure Evaluation. 4th, rev. ed. Food Processors Institute Staff. 256p. 1982. pap. 40.00 o.p. (ISBN 0-937774-07-3). Food Processors.

Cannery Kid. Gussie Mills. (gr. 3-7). 1985. 4.95 o.p. (ISBN 0-533-06643-3). Vantage.

Cannibal Cookbook. Joel Rothman. 74p. 1985. pap. 2.95 o.p. (ISBN 0-317-15235-1). Parkwest Pubns.

Cannibal Who Overate. Hugh Pentecost. 1986. 10.95 o.p. (ISBN 0-8161-3998-9, Large Print Bks); pap. 10.95 o.p. G K Hall.

Cannibals. Keefe Braselle. 1971. pap. 1.25 o.p. (ISBN 0-380-01084-4, 08979). Avon.

Cannibals & Missionaries. Mary McCarthy. 1980. pap. 2.75 o.p. (ISBN 0-380-50690-4, 50690-4). Avon.

Cannon Reservoir Human Ecology Project: An Archaeological Study of Cultural Adaptations in the Southern Prairie Peninsula. Ed. by Michael O'Brien et al. (Studies in Archaeology). 1982. 39.95 o.p. (ISBN 0-12-523980-7). Acad Pr.

Canoe: A History of the Craft from Panama to the Arctic. Kenneth G. Roberts & Philip Shackleton. LC 83-48153. (Illus.). 288p. 1983. 24.95 o.p. (ISBN 0-87742-175-7, C200); ltd. ed. o.p. 250.00 o.p. Intl Marine.

Canoe Book. Herbert Gordon. (Illus.). 1978. pap. text ed. 6.95 o.p. (ISBN 0-07-023783-2). McGraw.

Canoe Camping Vermont & New Hampshire Rivers. Roioli Schweiker. Ed. by Catherine J. Baker. LC 76-52884. (Canoeing Ser.). (Illus.). 100p. 1977. pap. 4.95 o.p. (ISBN 0-912274-71-9). Backcountry Pubns.

Canoe Country. Florence P. Jaques. LC 38-27731. (Illus.). 1938. 7.95 o.p. (ISBN 0-8166-0024-4). U of Minn Pr.

Canoe Trails of Northern Wisconsin. 106p. 1984. pap. 9.95 o.s.i. (ISBN 0-915024-26-8). WI Trails.

Canoeing. Boy Scouts of America. (Illus.). 72p. (gr. 6-12). 1977. pap. 1.39x o.p. (ISBN 0-8395-3308-X, 3308). BSA.

Canoeing Ontario's Rivers: Great Canoe Trips in Canada's Northern Wilderness. Ron Reid & Janet Grand. LC 86-60198. (Illus.). 320p. (Orig.). 1986. pap. 10.95 o.s.i. (ISBN 0-87156-760-1). Sierra.

Canon AE1, AT-1, AV-1: Amphoto Pocket Companion. Rick Michaels. (Illus.). 128p. 1981. pap. 4.95 o.p. (ISBN 0-8174-5523-X, Amphoto). Watson-Guptill.

Canon & Authority: Essays in Old Testament Religion & Theology. Ed. by George W. Coats & Burke O. Long. LC 76-62614. 208p. 1977. 7.00 o.p. (ISBN 0-8006-0501-2, 1-501, Fortress). Augsburg Fortress.

Canon SLR Cameras. Carl Shipman. LC 76-50430. (Illus.). pap. 12.95 o.p. (ISBN 0-912656-56-5). Price Stern.

Canones: Values, Crisis, & Survival in a Northern New Mexico Village. Paul Kutsche & John R. Van Ness. LC 80-54562. (Illus.). 260p. 1981. 19.95x o.p. (ISBN 0-8263-0570-9). U of NM Pr.

Canonic Studies. Bernhard Ziehn. Ed. by Ronald Stevenson. 1977. 12.50 o.s.i. (ISBN 0-8008-1232-8, Crescendo). Taplinger.

Cantarow & Trumper Clinical Biochemistry. 7th ed. Albert L. Latner. LC 73-89933. 770p. 1975. text ed. write for info. o.p. (ISBN 0-7216-5637-4). Saunders.

Cantate du Narcisse see Poesies.

Cantatrice Chauve. Eugene Ionesco. (Illus.). 192p. 29.95 o.p. (ISBN 0-686-54186-3). Schoenhof.

Canterbury & Rome, Sister Churches: A Roman Catholic Monk Reflects on Reunion in Diversity. Robert Hale. 7.95 o.p. (ISBN 0-8091-2480-7). Paulist Pr.

Canterbury Tales. Geoffrey Chaucer. 48p. (Orig.). 1988. pap. 9.95 o.p. (ISBN 1-55651-125-6); audiocassette tape incl. o.p. (ISBN 1-55651-126-4). Cram Cassettes.

Canti B Numero Cinquanta. Ottaviano Petrucci. (Monuments of Music & Music Literature in Facsimile: Series I, Vol. 23). (Illus.). 119p. (Lat. & Fr.). 1975. Repr. of 1502 ed. 37.50x o.p. (ISBN 0-8450-2023-4). Broude.

Canticle for Leibowitz. Walter M. Miller, Jr. 336p. 1975. Repr. of 1959 ed. lib. bdg. 15.50 o.p. (ISBN 0-8398-2309-6, Gregg). G K Hall.

Canticle Majesty. Christopher Williams. 1984. 8.95 o.p. (ISBN 0-533-05255-6). Vantage.

Canto for a Gypsy. Martin C. Smith. 176p. 1982. pap. 2.50 o.s.i. (ISBN 0-345-30615-5). Ballantine.

Canto y Grito mi Liberacion: The Liberation of A Chicano Mind. Ricardo Sanchez. LC 72-89676. (Illus.). 159p. 1973. lib. bdg. 25.00 o.p. (ISBN 0-916908-29-1); pap. 5.95 o.p. (ISBN 0-916908-26-7). Place Herons.

Canvas Falcons. Stephen Longstreet. (War Library). 416p. 1983. pap. 3.95 o.s.i. (ISBN 0-345-30891-3). Ballantine.

Canyon. Jack Schaefer. LC 79-2311. (Zia Bks.). 132p. 1980. pap. 5.95 o.p. (ISBN 0-8263-0518-0). U of NM Pr.

Canyon Country. Leonard Lupton. (Gunsmoke Western Ser.). 176p. 1988. text ed. 12.95x o.p. (ISBN 0-85997-857-5, Pub. by Firecrest Pub Ltd). Prescott Pr NH.

Canyon Country Camping. new ed. F. A. Barnes. LC 77-95041. (Illus.). 1978. pap. 2.50 o.p. (ISBN 0-915272-16-4). Wasatch Pubs.

Canyon Passage. Ernest Haycox. 1985. lib. bdg. 14.95 o.p. (ISBN 0-8161-3877-X, Large Print Bks). G K Hall.

Cap & Candle. Dorothy Blatter. (gr. 7-10). 1961. 3.95 o.s.i. (ISBN 0-664-32255-7, Westminster). Westminster John Knox.

Capacitors. Ed. by Steven D'Adolf. 300p. 1987. 95.00 o.p. (ISBN 0-317-57568-6). DATA Busn Pub.

Capacity & Measurement of Effectiveness. (Transportation Research Report Ser.). 61p. 1976. 2.80 o.p. (ISBN 0-309-02591-5). Transport Res Bd.

Capacity & Quality of Service: Seven Reports. (Transportation Research Report Ser.). 75p. 1975. 3.40 o.p. (ISBN 0-309-02389-0). Transport Res Bd.

Capacity of Negroes for Religious & Moral Improvement Considered. Richard Nisbet. LC 73-100295. Repr. of 1789 ed. 35.00x o.p. (ISBN 0-8371-2940-0, NIC&, Pub. by Negro U Pr). Greenwood.

Cape Cod. Henry David Thoreau. Ed. by Dudley C. Lunt. (Masterworks of Literature Ser). (Illus.). 1951. pap. 3.95x o.p. (ISBN 0-8084-0067-3, M5). New Coll U Pr.

Cape Cod & Islands Atlas & Guide Book, Vol. 7. rev. ed. Butterworth Company of Cape Cod, Inc. Staff. (Illus.). 112p. 1986-1987. pap. 10.95 o.s.i. (ISBN 0-937338-03-6). Butterworth of Cape Cod.

Cape Cod Casket. Lockhart Amerman. LC 64-17083. (gr. 7 up). 1964. 5.95 o.p. (ISBN 0-15-214089-1, HJ). HarBraceJ.

Cape Cod: Its People & Their History. 2nd ed. Henry C. Kittredge. LC 68-21055. (Illus.). 1973. 16.95 o.p. (ISBN 0-395-07864-4). HM.

Cape Cod Sampler: A Second Anthology. Twelve O'Clock Scholars Staff. Ed. by Margaret M. Kelly & Eleanor M. Pingree. LC 79-88069. (Illus., Orig.). 1979. pap. 4.50 o.p. (ISBN 0-88492-027-5). W S Sullwold.

Cape of Torments: Slavery & Resistance in South Africa. Robert Ross. (International Library of Anthropology). 176p. 1983. 21.95x o.p. (ISBN 0-7100-9407-8). Routledge Chapman & Hall.

Cape Peninsula Ferns. J. P. Roux. (Illus.). 66p. 1982. pap. 10.00x o.p. (ISBN 0-620-03775-X, Pub. by Timmins S Africa). Intl Spec Bk.

Cape-To-Cairo Dream: A Study in British Imperialism. Lois A. Raphael. 1971. lib. bdg. 34.50x o.p. (ISBN 0-374-96714-8, Octagon). Hippocrene Bks.

Cape Town to Cairo. Lillie B. Douglas. LC 64-15394. (Illus.). 348p. 6.95 o.p. (ISBN 0-87004-035-9). Caxton.

Capetan Konstandis Mavros. Yannis S. Katsoufris. 1981. 7.00 o.p. (ISBN 0-682-49559-X). Exposition-Phoenix.

Capitaine Fracasse. Theophile Gautier. Ed. by Boschot. (Class. Garnier). pap. 9.95 o.p. (ISBN 0-685-34910-1). Schoenhof.

Capitaine Fracasse. Theophile Gautier. Ed. by Boschot. (Coll. Prestige). 27.95 o.p. (ISBN 0-685-34911-X). Schoenhof.

Capital & Politics. Ed. by Roger King. 224p. (Orig.). 1983. pap. 15.95x o.p. (ISBN 0-7100-9445-0). Routledge Chapman & Hall.

Capital Budgeting Handbook. Mike Kaufman. LC 85-70803. 1985. 57.50 o.p. (ISBN 0-87094-522-X). Dow Jones-Irwin.

Capital Corruption: An Assault on American Democracy. Amitai Etzioni. 1984. 16.95 o.p. (ISBN 0-15-115469-4). HarBraceJ.

Capital, Courthouse & City Hall. 6th ed. Robert L. Morlan & David L. Martin. LC 80-82016. (Illus.). 480p. 1981. pap. 21.95 o.p. (ISBN 0-395-29186-0). HM.

Capital Entertaining: Caterers to Call & Places to Party in & Around Washington, D. C. Bunny Polmer & Ann Yonkers. LC 85-13828. (Illus.). 144p. (Orig.). 1985. pap. 6.95 o.p. (ISBN 0-89286-256-4, TX907P595, One Hund One Prods). Ortho.

Capital Flows & Exchange Rate Determination. Ed. by L. R. Klein & W. E. Krelle. (Journal of Economics: Supp. 3). (Illus.). 240p. 1984. pap. 41.10 o.p. (ISBN 0-387-81770-0). Springer Verlag.

Capital Formation 1984: Private & Public Financings. Practising Law Institute Staff & Larry W. Sonsini. LC 82-61810. (Commercial Law & Practice Course Handbook Ser.: No. 335). 1984. 15.00 o.p. (A4-4100). PLI.

Capital Goods Sector in LDCs: A Case for State Intervention. Jayati D. Mitra. (Working Paper Ser.: No. 343). 57p. 1979. 5.00 o.p. (ISBN 0-8213-9218-2, WP 0343). World Bank.

Capital Improvement Programming: A Handbook for Local Government Officials. John Vogt. 90p. 1977. 3.50 o.p. (ISBN 0-686-39437-2). Institute Government.
Capital Investment & Financial Decisions. 2nd ed. Marshall Sarnat. 600p. 1982. text ed. 37.33 o.p. (ISBN 0-13-113589-9). P-H.
Capital, Labour & the Middle Classes. Nicholas Abercrombie & John Urry. (Controversies in Sociology Ser.: No. 15). 176p. (Orig.). 1983. text ed. 29.95x o.p. (ISBN 0-04-301145-4); pap. text ed. 14.95 o.p. (ISBN 0-04-301146-2). Unwin Hyman.
Capital Management for Financial Executives. Richard B. Stockton. LC 84-72636. 150p. 1985. 35.00 o.p. (ISBN 0-8019-7620-0); pap. 19.95 o.p. (ISBN 0-8019-7632-4). Chilton.
Capital Market Imperfections & Economic Development. Vinayak V. Bhatt & Alan R. Roe. (Working Paper: No. 338). 87p. 1979. 5.00 o.p. (ISBN 0-686-36170-9, WP-0338). World Bank.
Capital Markets & Institutions. 4th ed. Herbert E. Dougall & Jack E. Gaumnitz. (Foundations of Finance Ser.). (Illus.). 1980. pap. text ed. 18.00 o.p. (ISBN 0-13-113670-4). P-H.
Capital Punishment-Cruel & Unusual? Ed. by Mark A. Siegel & Nancy R. Jacobs. (Information Aid Ser.). 88p. 1986. pap. text ed. 15.95 o.p. (ISBN 0-936474-53-X). Info Plus TX.
Capital Punishment: The Inevitability of Caprice & Mistake. Charles L. Black, Jr. 96p. 1974. 10.95x o.p. (ISBN 0-393-05546-9); pap. 3.95 o.p. (ISBN 0-393-05550-7). Norton.
Capital, the State, & Regional Development. Michael F. Dunford. (Looking at Society & Space Ser.). (Illus.). 330p. 1987. lib. bdg. 69.50x o.p. (ISBN 0-85086-123-3, Pub. by Pion England). Routledge Chapman & Hall.
Capitalism: A Cooperative Venture. Thomas Katsaros & John Teluk. LC 80-8163. 161p. 1981. lib. bdg. 22.50 o.p. (ISBN 0-8191-1484-7); pap. text ed. 11.00 o.p. (ISBN 0-8191-1485-5). U Pr of Amer.
Capitalism & American Leadership. Oliver C. Cox. 350p. 1962. (ISBN 0-8022-0311-6). Philos Lib.
Capitalism & Colonial Production: Essays on the Rise of Capitalism in Asia. Hamza Alavi et al. (Illus.). 208p. 1982. 28.00 o.p. (ISBN 0-7099-0634-X, Pub. by Croom Helm Ltd). Routledge Chapman & Hall.
Capitalism & Public Policy in the U. K.: A Marxist Approach. Tom Burden & Mike Campbell. LC 85-9995. 69p. 1985. 34.50 o.p. (ISBN 0-7099-0685-4, Pub. by Croom Helm Ltd); pap. 15.95 o.p. (ISBN 0-7099-0686-2, Pub. by Croom Helm Ltd). Routledge Chapman & Hall.
Capitalism: Class Conflict & the New Middle Class. R. Carter. (International Library of Sociology). 200p. 1985. 29.95x o.p. (ISBN 0-7100-9624-0). Routledge Chapman & Hall.
Capitalism in the U. K. A Perspective from Marxist Political Economy. Mike Campbell. (Illus.). 204p. 1981. 28.00 o.p. (ISBN 0-7099-0089-9, Pub. by Croom Helm Ltd); pap. 8.95 o.p. (ISBN 0-7099-0090-2). Routledge Chapman & Hall.
Capitalism, the State & Industrial Relations. Dominic Strinati. 240p. 1983. 32.00 o.p. (ISBN 0-85664-996-1, Pub. by Croom Helm Ltd). Routledge Chapman & Hall.
Capitalism, Yesterday & Today. Maurice Dobb. 64p. 1958. pap. 6.50 o.p. (ISBN 0-8464-0234-3). Beekman Pubs.
Capitalistes et Pouvoir Au Siecle Des Lumieres: Les Fondateurs Des Origines a 1715. Claude-Frederic Levt. 1969. pap. 24.80 o.p. (ISBN 90-2796-421-1). Mouton.
Capitalistic Imperative: The New Biology & the Old Bureaucracy. Howard R. Smith. LC 74-80693. 1975. text ed. 12.50 o.p. (ISBN 0-682-48044-4, University). Exposition-Phoenix.
Capitals for Calligraphy: A Sourcebook of Decorated Letters. Margaret Shepherd. (Illus.). 128p. 1981. 10.95 o.p. (ISBN 0-02-029960-5, Collier). Macmillan.
Capitol, Courthouse & City Hall. 5th ed. Robert L. Morlan. LC 76-13093. (Illus.). 384p. 1977. pap. 11.50 o.p. (ISBN 0-395-24331-9). HM.
Capitol-izing on Computers in Education: Proceedings. Association of Educational Data Systems. Ed. by C. Dianne Martin. LC 84-7084. (Computers in Education Ser.). 1984. 35.95 o.p. (ISBN 0-88175-019-0, Computer Sci Pr). W H Freeman.
Capitol's Concise Dictionary. 1416p. (Eng., Swedish, Dutch, Ger., Ital. & Span.). 1972. 35.95 o.p. (ISBN 84-7183-079-5, S-50438). French & Eur.
Cap'n Smudge. Stephen Cosgrove. (Illus.). 42p. 1967. 1.50 o.p. French & Eur.
Capon on Cooking. Robert F. Capon. (Illus.). 182p. 1983. 14.45 o.p. (ISBN 0-395-34393-3). HM.
Capri Affair. David Hanna. (Orig.). 1980. pap. 1.95 o.p. (ISBN 0-505-51547-4, Pub. by Tower Bks). Dorchester Pub Co.
Capri Nineteen Seventy-Nine to Nineteen Eighty-Two Includes Turbo Shop Manual. Ed. by Eric Jorgensen. (Illus.). pap. text ed. 11.95 o.p. (ISBN 0-89287-336-1). Clymer Pub.
Caprichos: Their Hidden Truth. Oto Bihalji-Merin. Tr. by John E. Woods. LC 81-47300. (Helen & Kurt Wolff Bk.). (Illus.). 192p. 1981. 65.00 o.p. (ISBN 0-15-133463-3). HarBraceJ.
Capricorn Rhyming Dictionary. Ed. by Bessie Redfield. 320p. 1986. pap. 6.95 o.p. (ISBN 0-399-51272-1, Perigee). Putnam Pub Group.
Capricorn Road. Francois Balsan. 256p. 1955. (ISBN 0-8022-0056-7). Philos Lib.
Captain. Jan De Hartog. LC 66-16358. 1966. 5.95 o.p. (ISBN 0-689-10064-7, Atheneum). Macmillan.
Captain America Complex: The Dilemma of Zealous Nationalism. Robert Jewett. LC 73-11489. 288p. 1974. pap. 3.50 o.s.i. (ISBN 0-664-24998-1, Westminster); 10.00 o.s.i. (ISBN 0-664-20987-4, Westminster). Westminster John Knox.
Captain Butcher's Body. Scott Corbett. (Illus.). 144p. (gr. 4-6). 1976. 14.45i o.p. (ISBN 0-316-15727-9, Pub. by Atlantic Monthly Pr). Little.
Captain Dreyfus: The Story of Mass Hysteria. Nicholas Halasz. 1968. pap. 9.95 o.s.i. (ISBN 0-671-20029-1, Touchstone Bks). S&S.
Captain Fraser's Voyages. Thomas G. Fraser. Ed. by Marjory Gee. (Illus.). 1979. 17.50 o.p. (ISBN 0-393-01254-9). Norton.
Captain Gaius Sees a Miracle. Ardith Zook. (Arch Bks.). (gr. k-4). 1980. pap. 1.29 o.p. (ISBN 0-570-06133-4, 59-1251). Concordia.
Captain Mark Phillips on Riding: A Complete Guide for Beginners. Mark Phillips. (Illus.). 128p. 1986. 19.95 o.p. (ISBN 0-13-114521-5). P-H.
Captain Marryat: A Rediscovery. Oliver Warner. LC 78-59050. (Illus.). 1979. Repr. of 1953 ed. 21.50 o.s.i. (ISBN 0-88355-721-5). Hyperion Conn.
Captain Money & the Golden Girl. Donald C. Bauder. LC 85-5512. 266p. 1986. pap. 4.95 o.p. (ISBN 0-15-615397-1, Harv). HarBraceJ.
Captain Money & the Golden Girl: The J. David Affair. Donald C. Bauder. LC 85-5512. (Illus.). 288p. 1985. 15.95 o.p. (ISBN 0-15-115501-1). HarBraceJ.
Captain, My Captain. Deborah Meroff. 208p. (Orig.). 1986. pap. 4.95 o.p. (ISBN 0-310-41551-9, 9158P). Zondervan.
Captain Oates: Soldier & Explorer. Sue Limb & Patrick Cordingley. (Illus.). 176p. 1982. 39.95 o.p. (ISBN 0-7134-2693-4, Pub. by Batsford England). David & Charles.
Captain Sam Grant. Lloyd Lewis. 1950. 19.95 o.p. (ISBN 0-316-52332-1). Little.
Captain Whistler. Leon R. Searles. 1977. 10.00 o.p. (ISBN 0-682-48701-5). Exposition-Phoenix.
Captains. Jack Clary. LC 77-15830. 1978. 7.95 o.p. (ISBN 0-689-10871-0, Atheneum). Macmillan.
Captain's Daughter & Other Tales. Alexander Pushkin. Tr. by Natalie Duddington. 1978. 14.95x o.p. (ISBN 0-460-00898-6, DEL-04049, Evman); pap. 2.95x o.p. (ISBN 0-460-01898-1, DEL-04050, Evman). Biblio Dist.
Captive. Robert Stallman. (Book of the Beast: Vol. 2). (Orig.). 1981. pap. 2.50 o.s.i. (ISBN 0-671-41382-1, Timescape). PB.
Captive Embraces. Fern Michaels. 1983. pap. 4.95 o.p. (ISBN 0-345-31353-4). Ballantine.
Captive Innocence. Fern Michaels. 1982. pap. 4.95 o.p. (ISBN 0-345-30804-2). Ballantine.
Captive of the Heart. Kate Douglas. 1982. pap. 2.75 o.p. (ISBN 0-380-81125-1, 81125-1). Avon.
Captive Soul of Messiah. Date not set. (ISBN 0-8052-3873-5). Random.
Captive Splendors. Fern Michaels. 1983. pap. 2.95 o.p. (ISBN 0-394-31648-7). Ballantine.
Captive Wife: Conflicts of Housebound Mothers. Hannah Gavron. 208p. 1984. pap. 9.95 o.p. (ISBN 0-7102-0035-8). Routledge Chapman & Hall.
Captivity & Behavior: Primates in Breeding Colonies, Laboratories, & Zoos. Joseph Erwin et al. (Primate Behavior & Development Ser.). 1979. 42.95 o.p. (ISBN 0-442-22329-3). Van Nos Reinhold.
Capture, Management & Display of Geological Data: With Special Emphasis on Energy & Mineral Resources. Ed. by D. F. Merriam. LC 76-56893. 1977. pap. 50.00 o.p. (ISBN 0-08-021422-3). Pergamon.
Capture of John Wesley Hardin. Chuck Parsons. LC 78-67552. (Illus.). 121p. 1978. 9.95 o.p. (ISBN 0-932702-00-7). Creative Texas.
Capture the Dream. Helene M. Lehr. 288p. 1984. pap. 2.95 o.p. (ISBN 0-380-88476-3). Avon.
Captured by the Mohawks. Sterling North. (North Star Bks.). (Illus.). (gr. 7-11). 1960. 5.95 o.p. (ISBN 0-395-07248-4). HM.
Captured Images. Laurel Winslow. (Velvet Glove Ser.: No. 2). 176p. 1984. pap. 2.25 o.p. (ISBN 0-380-87700-7, 87700-7). Avon.
Captured Womb: A History of Medical Care of the Pregnant Woman. Ann Oakley. 336p. 1985. 34.95x o.p. (ISBN 0-631-14152-9). Basil Blackwell.
Captured Women. Photos by Jeff Dunas. (Illus.). 96p. pap. 12.95 o.p. (ISBN 0-394-62466-1, Ever). Grove.
Capturing Mood in Watercolor. Phil Austin. LC 84-6004. (Illus.). 192p. 1984. 21.95 o.p. (ISBN 0-89134-069-6, North Light). Writers Digest.
Caqueza: Living Rural Development. H. Zanstra & K. Swanberg. 321p. (Eng. & Span.). 1979. Casebound 15.00 o.p. (ISBN 0-88936-167-3, IDRC107, IDRC). UNIPUB.
Car Buyer's Illustrated Fact & Figure Book 1981. Ed. by Warren E. Benson, Jr. (Illus.). 1981. pap. 5.00 o.p. (ISBN 0-394-17881-5, E761, Ever). Grove.
Car-Free in Boston: The Guide to Public Transit in Greater Boston & New England. 5th ed. Ed. by Gordon Lewin. (Illus.). 160p. 1986. pap. 3.95 o.p. (ISBN 0-945990-00-6). Assn Pub Trans.
Car Industry: Labour Relations & Industrial Adjustment. David Mardsen et al. 240p. 1986. pap. text ed. 13.95 o.p. (ISBN 0-422-79550-X, 9785, Pub. by Tavistock England). Routledge Chapman & Hall.
Car Loan Payment Tables. Financial Publishing Co. Staff. 256p. 1983. pap. 7.75 o.p. (ISBN 0-87600-685-3). Finan Pub.
Car Makers. Phil Drackett. LC 80-51161. (Silver Burdett Careers Ser.). lib. bdg. 12.68 o.p. (ISBN 0-382-06414-3). Silver.
Cara Mia. Joan T. Davis. 1977. 8.00 o.p. (ISBN 0-682-48728-7). Exposition-Phoenix.
Caravan to Xanadu. Edison Marshall. 1977. pap. 1.75 o.p. (ISBN 0-380-00873-4, 31401). Avon.
Carbohydrate Chemistry. Ed. by F. Boschke. (Topics in Current Chemistry: Vol. 14, Pt. 4). (Illus.). 211p. 1970. pap. 55.50 o.p. (ISBN 0-387-04819-7). Springer-Verlag.
Carbohydrate Craver's Diet. Judith J. Wurtman. 214p. 1983. 12.45 o.p. (ISBN 0-395-33160-9). HM.
Carbohydrate Craver's Diet Cookbook. Judith J. Wurtman & Margaret Leibenstein. 230p. 1984. 14.45 o.p. (ISBN 0-395-35424-2). HM.
Carbohydrate Metabolism & Its Disorders, 2 Vols. Ed. by Frank Dickens et al. 1968. Vol. 1. 129.00 o.p. (ISBN 0-12-214901-7); Vol. 2. 66.50 o.p. (ISBN 0-12-214902-5). Acad Pr.
Carbohydrate Metabolism in Pregnancy & the Newborn. 2nd ed. Ed. by Hamish W. Sutherland & John M. Stowers. (Illus.). 237p. 1984. text ed. 55.50 o.p. (ISBN 0-443-02859-1). Churchill.
Carbohydrate Moieties of Immunoglobulin. Ed. by Harold C. Sox, Jr. et al. LC 74-3461. 187p. 1974. text ed. 24.00x o.p. (ISBN 0-8422-7213-5). Irvington.
Carbon Dioxide & Climate: A Second Assessment. Climate Review Panel, Climate Research Committee, National Research Council. 72p. 1982. pap. text ed. 7.25x o.p. (ISBN 0-309-03285-7). Natl Acad Pr.
Carbon Dioxide & Climate: Dedicated to Williard F. Libby & Hans E. Suss. L. M. Libby. (Illus.). 270p. 1980. pap. 48.00 o.p. (ISBN 0-08-026240-6). Pergamon.
Carbon Dioxide, Climate & Society: Proceedings of an IIASA Workshop, Feb. 1978. Ed. by J. Williams. 1978. 65.00 o.p. (ISBN 0-08-023252-3). Pergamon.
Carbon-Fourteen Dating. R. Burleigh. LC 74-183462. (International Monographs on Science in Archaeology). cancelled o.s.i. (ISBN 0-12-785082-1). Acad Pr.
Carbon Monoxide in Organic Synthesis. J. Falbe. Tr. by C. R. Adams. LC 77-108917. (Illus.). 1970. 44.00 o.p. (ISBN 0-387-04814-6). Springer-Verlag.
Carbon Monoxide, Industry & Performance. Ed. by W. H. Walton. 1976. pap. 26.00 o.p. (ISBN 0-08-019966-6). Pergamon.
Carbon Reinforced Epoxy Systems, Pt. 1. Ed. by Carlos J. Hilado. LC 74-83231. (Materials Technology Ser.: Vol. 1). 287p. 1974. pap. 14.95 o.p. (ISBN 0-87762-149-7). Technomic.
Carbon-13 NMR Shift Assignments of Amines & Alkaloids. M. Shamma & D. M. Hindenlang. LC 78-10117. 316p. 1978. 59.50x o.p. (ISBN 0-306-40107-X, Plenum Pr). Plenum Pub.
Carbon-13 NMR Spectral Data: A Living COM-Microfiche Collection of Reference Material. 3rd ed. W. Bremser et al. 1981. 550.00 o.p. (ISBN 3-527-25899-X). VCH Pubs.
Carboniferous Basins of Southeastern New England. Ed. by Barry Cameron. LC 79-51602. 1979. pap. 10.00 o.p. (ISBN 0-913312-14-2). Am Geol.
Carboniferous Lamellibranchiata, Vol. 2. W. Hind. Repr. of 1905 ed. 40.00 o.p. (ISBN 0-384-23280-9). Johnson Repr.
Carbonium Ions, an Introduction. Donald Bethell & V. Gold. 1967. 49.50 o.p. (ISBN 0-12-094250-X). Acad Pr.
Carboranes. Russell N. Grimes. (Organometallic Chemistry Ser). 1970. 85.00 o.p. (ISBN 0-12-303250-4). Acad Pr.
Carcase for Hounds. Meja Mwangi. (African Writers Ser.). 1974. pap. text ed. 6.50 o.p. (ISBN 0-435-90145-1). Heinemann Ed.
Carcinogenesis, Vol. 1. Ed. by Canonico & G. P. Margison. (Illus.). 1979. 85.00 o.p. (ISBN 0-08-024379-7). Pergamon.
Carcinogenesis: Recent Investigations. Fred G. Bock et al. LC 72-6311. (Illus.). 204p. 1972. text ed. 24.50x o.p. (ISBN 0-8422-7017-5). Irvington.
Carcinogenic Hormones. Ed. by C. H. Lingeman. (Recent Results in Cancer Research Ser.: Vol. 66). (Illus.). 1979. 45.10 o.p. (ISBN 0-387-08995-0). Springer-Verlag.
Card-Punch Machine Operation, Bk. 1. P. Pactor & G. Kargilis. 1967. text ed. 16.25 o.p. (ISBN 0-07-048031-1). McGraw.
Card-Punch Machine Operation, Bk. 2. P. Pactor & G. Kargilis. 1973. text ed. 16.25 o.p. (ISBN 0-07-048032-X). McGraw.
Cardboard Carpentry. Jerry DeBruin. 1979. 9.95 o.p. (ISBN 0-916456-39-0). JED.
Cardboard Clock Square. L. Yakhnin. 79p. 1979. 4.95 o.p. (ISBN 0-8285-1578-6, Pub. by Progress Pubs USSR). Imported Pubns.
Cardiac Arrhythmias. Ed. by Arnold Katz. LC 82-19480. (Illus.). 160p. 1983. pap. text ed. 23.50x o.p. (ISBN 0-87893-417-0). Sinauer Assocs.
Cardiac Arrhythmias: Practical Notes on Interpretation & Treatment. David H. Bennett. (Illus.). 176p. 1981. pap. text ed. 20.50 o.p. (ISBN 0-7236-0590-4). Butterworth.
Cardiac Arrythmias: Diagnosis, Prognosis, Therapy-Proceedings. Ed. by M. Schlepper & B. Olsson. (Illus.). 238p. 1983. 20.70 o.p. (ISBN 0-387-12149-8). Springer-Verlag.
Cardiac Catheterization: Diagnostic Interventions. Fred K. Nakhjavan. LC 79-66105. (Illus.). 128p. 1981. text ed. 13.50x o.p. (ISBN 0-89313-015-X). G F Stickley Co.
Cardiac Crises. Ed. by Deborah Lyons & Leah Gabriel. (Nursing Now Ser.). (Illus.). 128p. 1984. text ed. 13.95 o.p. (ISBN 0-916730-79-4). Springhouse Pub.
Cardiac Cycle. Noble. (Illus.). 240p. 1980. 43.50 o.p. (ISBN 0-632-00163-1, B-37104). Mosby.
Cardiac Defibrillation & Cardiopulmonary Resuscitation, Abstracts & Published Papers: Proceedings, 4th Conference. Intro. by W. A. Tacker, Jr. (Medical Instrumentation Ser.: No. 105). (Illus.). 56p. 1983. pap. text ed. 22.00 o.p. (ISBN 0-910275-22-X). Assn Adv Med Instrs.
Cardiac Emergencies. Ed. by Dean T. Mason. LC 77-13996. 280p. Repr. of 1978 ed. 31.50 o.p. (ISBN 0-683-05904-1). Krieger.
Cardiac Function & Aging. Ed. by Jos L. Willems et al. LC 74-11160. 159p. 1974. text ed. 21.00x o.p. (ISBN 0-8422-7245-3). Irvington.
Cardiac Hypertrophy. Norman Alpert. 642p. 1971. 90.00 o.p. (ISBN 0-12-053550-5). Acad Pr.
Cardiac Pacing: Diagnostic & Therapeutic Tools. Ed. by B. Luederitz. (Illus.). 1976. 29.00 o.p. (ISBN 0-387-07711-1). Springer-Verlag.
Cardiac Patient. George W. Paterson. LC 78-52187. (Religion & Medicine Ser.). 1978. pap. 5.95 o.p. (ISBN 0-8066-1661-X, 10-0971, Augsburg). Augsburg Fortress.
Cardiac Physiology for the Clinician. Ed. by Mario Vassale. 1976. 53.00 o.p. (ISBN 0-12-715050-1). Acad Pr.
Cardiac Rhythm Disturbances: A Step by Step Approach. William Fox & Emanuel Stein. LC 82-12727. (Illus.). 287p. 1983. text ed. 34.50 o.p. (ISBN 0-8121-0838-8). Lea & Febiger.
Cardiac Rhythms: A Kit for Instructors. 2nd ed. Raymond E. Phillips. 64p. 1981. write for info. o.p. (ISBN 0-7216-9958-8). Saunders.
Cardiac Surgery & the Conduction System. Saroja Bharati et al. LC 82-17421. 107p. 1983. 65.00 o.p. (ISBN 0-471-08147-7). Wiley.
Cardiac Surgery: Morphology, Diagnostic Criteria, Natural History, Techniques, Results & Indications. John W. Kirklin & Brian G. Barratt-Boyes. LC 85-16938. 1986. 160.00 o.p. (ISBN 0-471-01416-8). Wiley.
Cardiac Surgery: Rob & Smith's Operative Surgery Ser. 4th ed. Jamieson & Shumway. 1986. 118.00 o.p. (ISBN 0-8016-4414-3, C-4414-3). Mosby.
Cardinal D'Espagne. Henry De Montherlant. Ed. by Robert B. Johnson & Patricia J. Johnson. LC 72-177496. (Orig., Fr.). (gr. 10-12). 1972. pap. 7.00 o.p. (ISBN 0-395-12743-2). HM.
Cardinal Federico Borromeo As a Patron & a Critic of the Arts & His Museum of 1625. Arlene Quint Platt. Ed. by S. J. Freedberg. (Outstanding Dissertations in Fine Arts Ser.). (Illus.). 350p. 1985. Repr. of 1974 ed. 55.00 o.p. (ISBN 0-8240-6881-5). Garland Pub.
Cardinal Wyszynski: A Biography. Andrzej Micewski. Tr. by William R. Brand & Katarzyna Mroczkowska-Brand. LC 84-4683. 464p. (Pol.). 1984. 17.95 o.p. (ISBN 0-15-115785-5). HarBraceJ.

Cardioactive Drugs: A Pharmacologic Basis for Practice. Hansjorg Simon & Dennis A. Bloomfield. LC 82-13593. 187p. 1982. pap. 22.50 o.p. (ISBN 0-8067-1851-X). Urban & S.

Cardiology Case Studies. 2nd ed. Nicholas P. DePasquale & Michael S. Bruno. LC 79-91847. 1980. pap. 24.50 o.p. (ISBN 0-87488-001-7). Med Exam.

Cardiology in the U. S. S. R. Ed. by E. I. Chazov. 223p. 1982. pap. 8.95 o.p. (ISBN 0-8285-2748-2, Pub. by Mir Pubs USSR). Imported Pubns.

Cardiology Update, 1983: Reviews for Physicians. E. Rapaport. 360p. 1982. 53.50 o.p. (ISBN 0-444-00763-6, Biomedical Pr). Elsevier.

Cardiopulmonary Physical Therapy. Irwin & Tecklin. 1984. 43.95 o.p. (ISBN 0-8016-2512-2). Mosby.

Cardiopulmonary Technology Examination Review Book, Vol. 2. 2nd ed. Patrick Chun. 1980. pap. 18.00 o.p. (ISBN 0-87488-473-X). Med Exam.

Cardiovascular Disease: Rheumatic Fever, Heart Transplantation & Immunological Aspects. Ed. by J. A. Falk et al. 1977. text ed. 34.00x o.p. (ISBN 0-8422-7280-1). Irvington.

Cardiovascular Diseases, Vol. 28. 2nd ed. Patrick K. Chun. 1984. pap. text ed. 36.75 o.p. (ISBN 0-87488-209-5). Med Exam.

Cardiovascular Nursing: Bodymind Tapestry: American Association of Critical-Care Nurses. Guzzetta & Dossey. 1984. cloth 44.95 o.p. (ISBN 0-8016-2027-9). Mosby.

Cardiovascular Physiology. Lois J. Heller & David E. Mohrman. Ed. by Richard W. Mixter. (Illus.). 176p. 1980. text ed. 16.95 o.p. (ISBN 0-07-027973-X). McGraw.

Cardiovascular Physiology. Ed. by James V. Warren. LC 74-26568. (Benchmark Papers in Human Physiology Ser: No. 4). 1975. 79.00 o.p. (ISBN 0-12-787730-4). Acad Pr.

Cardiovascular Physiology, Heart, Peripheral Circulation & Methodology: Proceedings of the 28th International Congress of Physiological Sciences, Budapest, Hungary, 1980. Ed. by A. G. B. Kovach et al. LC 80-41875. (Advances in Physiological Sciences: Vol. 8). (Illus.). 400p. 1981. 71.00 o.p. (ISBN 0-08-026820-X). Pergamon.

Cardiovascular Physiology, Microcirculation & Capillary Exchange: Proceedings of the 28th International Congress of Physiological Sciences, Budapest, 1980. Ed. by A. G. B. Kovach et al. LC 80-41873. (Advances in Physiological Sciences: Vol. 7). (Illus.). 400p. 1981. 71.00 o.p. (ISBN 0-08-026819-6). Pergamon.

Cardiovascular Physiology-Neural Control Mechanisms: Processings of the 28th International Congress of Physiological Sciences, Budapest, 1980. Ed. by A. G. B. Kovach et al. LC 80-41927. (Advances in Physiological Sciences: Vol. 9). (Illus.). 400p. 1981. 71.00 o.p. (ISBN 0-08-026821-8). Pergamon.

Cardiovascular Problems, Vol. 2. Linda A. Yacone. Ed. by Margaret Van Meter. (RN Nursing Assessment Ser.). 152p. 1983. 15.95 o.p. (ISBN 0-87489-289-9). Med Economics.

Cardiovascular Problems: A Critical Care Nursing Focus. Mary Jackle & Marney Halligan. LC 80-339. (Illus.). 1980. pap. text ed. 14.95 o.p. (ISBN 0-87619-667-9). Appleton & Lange.

Cardiovascular Review 1982. Ed. by Gerald Timmis & Douglas Westveer. LC 80-646560. 1981. 35.00 o.p. (ISBN 0-12-691320-X). Acad Pr.

Cardiovascular Review 1983. Ed. by Gerald C. Timmis et al. (Monograph). 1982. 38.00 o.p. (ISBN 0-12-691340-4). Acad Pr.

Cardiovascular Review: 1984. Gerald C. Timmis et al. 1984. 56.50 o.p. (ISBN 0-12-691346-3). Acad Pr.

Cardiovascular System. 2nd ed. P. P. Turner. LC 84-7606. (Illus.). 245p. pap. 18.00 o.p. (ISBN 0-443-02607-6). Churchill.

Cardiovascular System Dynamics: Models & Measurements. Ed. by T. Kenner et al. LC 81-5856. 686p. 1982. 110.00x o.p. (ISBN 0-306-40727-2, Plenum Pr). Plenum Pub.

Cards on the Table. Agatha Christie. 1980. pap. 2.95 o.p. (ISBN 0-440-11052-1). Dell.

Care & Counseling of the Aging. William M. Clements. Ed. by Howard J. Clinebell & Howard W. Stone. LC 78-54547. (Creative Pastoral Care & Counseling Ser). 96p. 1979. pap. 4.50 o.p. (ISBN 0-8006-0561-6, 1-561, Fortress). Augsburg Fortress.

Care & Counseling of Youth in the Church. Paul B. Irwin. Ed. by Howard J. Clinebell & Howard W. Stone. LC 74-26334. (Creative Pastoral Care & Counseling Ser.). 96p. 1975. pap. 4.50 o.p. (ISBN 0-8006-0552-7, 1-552, Fortress). Augsburg Fortress.

Care & Feeding of New Converts. 1st ed. Ed. by James D. Craig. 12p. 1981. pap. text ed. 0.49 o.p. (ISBN 0-88151-021-1). Lay Leadership.

Care & Feeding of Your Diabetic Child. Sally Vanderpoel. LC 74-12419. 128p. 1974. 9.95 o.p. (ISBN 0-8119-0247-1). Fell.

Care & Handling of Computer Magnetic Storage Media. Sidney B. Geller. (National Bureau of Standards Special Publication 500-101. Computer Science & Technology). 136p. 1983. pap. 5.50 o.p. (ISBN 0-318-20092-9, S/N 003-003-02486-4). USGPO.

Care & Repair of Fishing Tackle. Mel Marshall. LC 76-22569. 1976. 16.95 o.p. (ISBN 0-8329-1831-8, Pub. by Winchester Pr). New Century.

Care & Repair of Glassfibre Yachts: Includes the Detection, Prevention & Treatment of Osmosis. Tony Staton-Bevan. (Illus.). 103p. 1986. pap. 13.95 o.p. (ISBN 0-229-11754-6, Pub. by Adlar Coles). Sheridan.

Care & Repair of Hulls. Michael Verney. (Illus.). 1979. Encore ed. 3.95 o.p. (ISBN 0-684-17524-X, ScribT). Scribner.

Care & Repair of Marine Gasoline Engines. Loris Goring. LC 80-84623. (Illus.). 146p. 1981. 15.00 o.p. (ISBN 0-87742-139-0). Intl Marine.

Care & Repair of Sails. Jeremy Howard-Williams. 1976. 9.95 o.p. (ISBN 0-393-03199-3). Norton.

Care & Repair of Small Marine Diesels. Chris Thompson. LC 81-85261. (Illus.). 130p. 1982. 20.00 o.p. (ISBN 0-87742-159-5). Intl Marine.

Care & Training of the Mentally Handicapped. 6th ed. Hallas et al. 302p. 1978. 19.95 o.p. (ISBN 0-7236-0486-X, Pub. by John Wright UK). Butterworth.

Care Bear Bath Book. Illus. by Pat Sustendal. (Bath & Beach Play Sets). (Illus.). 10p. (ps). 1986. 3.95 o.s.i. (ISBN 0-394-88014-5). Random.

Care Bear Cousins Visit the Woods. Ali Reich. LC 85-60842. (Sniffy Bks.). (Illus.). 24p. (ps-1). 1985. 4.95 o.s.i. (ISBN 0-394-87459-5, BYR). Random.

Care for the Dying. Richard N. Soulen. LC 74-19968. 120p. 1975. pap. 6.95 o.s.i. (ISBN 0-8042-1098-5, John Knox). Westminster John Knox.

Care of Arnold's Corners. Suzanne Newton. LC 73-18063. (gr. 5-7). 1974. 6.95 o.s.i. (ISBN 0-664-32545-9, Westminster). Westminster John Knox.

Care of Souls in the Classic Tradition. Thomas C Oden. LC 83-48912. (Theology & Pastoral Care Ser.). pap. 2.95 o.p. (ISBN 0-8006-1729-0, 1-1729, Fortress). Augsburg Fortress.

Care of the Arthritic Hand. 4th ed. Adrian E. Flatt. LC 82-6428. (Illus.). 320p. 1982. cloth 49.50 o.p. (ISBN 0-8016-1585-2). Mosby.

Care of the Cardiac Surgical Patient. Robert Litwak & Roy Jurado. (Illus.). 635p. 1982. 72.00 o.p. (ISBN 0-8385-1062-0). Appleton & Lange.

Care of the Child Facing Death. Ed. by Lindy Burton. 1974. 19.95x o.p. (ISBN 0-7100-7863-3). Routledge Chapman & Hall.

Care of the Client Receiving Chemotherapy. Joyce Yasko & Barbara Lauffer. 1982. 34.95 o.p. (ISBN 0-8359-0687-6); pap. 29.95 o.p. (ISBN 0-8359-0686-8). Appleton & Lange.

Care of the Client Receiving External Radiation Therapy. Joyce Yasko. 1982. 24.95 o.p. (ISBN 0-8359-0689-2); pap. 19.95 o.p. (ISBN 0-8359-0688-4). Appleton & Lange.

Care of the Earth. Joseph A. Sittler. LC 64-20114. (Orig.). 1964. pap. 0.50 o.p. (ISBN 0-8006-4000-4, Fortress). Augsburg Fortress.

Care of the Elderly Mentally Infirm. Barbara Gray & Bernard Issacs. 1979. 27.00x o.p. (ISBN 0-422-77190-2, NO.6364, Pub. by Tavistock England). Routledge Chapman & Hall.

Care of the Expectant Mother. Josephine Barnes. (Illus.). 280p. 1957. (ISBN 0-8022-0064-8). Philos Lib.

Care of the Patient in Diagnostic Radiography. 6th ed. Chesney & Chesney. 1986. 21.00 o.p. (ISBN 0-8016-1328-0). Mosby.

Care of the Wild: Family First Aid & Care for All Wild Creatures. W. J. Jordan & John Hughes. LC 82-42699. (Illus.). 228p. 1983. 13.95 o.s.i. (ISBN 0-89256-226-9); pap. 8.95 o.s.i. (ISBN 0-89256-240-4). Rawson Assocs.

Care or Custody: Community Homes & the Treatment of Delinquency. Norman Tutt. LC 74-9318. 240p. 1974. 9.00x o.p. (ISBN 0-87586-049-4). Agathon.

Career Accounting Fundamentals. Douglas J. McQuaig. LC 76-15789. (Illus.). 1977. text ed. 16.50 o.p. (ISBN 0-395-18979-9). HM.

Career Adaptive Behavior Inventory Complete Battery. Thomas P. Lombardi. 110p. (Orig.). 1980. pap. text ed. 23.50 o.p. (ISBN 0-87562-065-5). Spec Child.

Career Advancement Guide. Edward L. Adams, Jr. 1975. text ed. 29.95 o.p. (ISBN 0-07-000275-4, P&RB). McGraw.

Career & Occupational Development Objectives. National Assessment of Educational Progress Staff. (First Assessment (1973-74)). 84p. 1971. pap. 1.40 o.p. (ISBN 0-318-13986-3, ED059119, Natl Assessment Ed Progress). Ed Comm States.

Career & Occupational Development Objectives. National Assessment of Educational Progress Staff. (Second Assessment (1975-76)). 100p. 1977. 1.90 o.p. (ISBN 0-318-13987-1, ED143829, Natl Assessment Ed Progress). Ed Comm States.

Career & Vocational Education Programs for Female, Handicapped & Disadvantaged Students. National Center for Research in Vocational Education. 56p. 1984. 4.95 o.p. (ISBN 0-318-22054-7, BB75). Natl Ctr Res Voc Ed.

Career Assessment Instruments. ERIC Clearinghouse on Adult, Career, & Vocational Education Staff. 51p. 1983. 4.95 o.p. (ISBN 0-318-22056-3, BB69). Natl Ctr Res Voc Ed.

Career Blazer Guide to Word Processing. Hal Cornelius & William Lewis. (Career Blazers Guides Ser.). 192p. 1983. pap. 7.95 o.p. (ISBN 0-671-45869-8). Monarch Pr.

Career Counseling & Development Bibliography. 7.50 o.p. (ISBN 0-317-59897-X, 72502C). Am Assn Coun Dev.

Career Criminals. American Society of Criminology Staff & Gordon P. Waldo. LC 83-17855. (Sage Research Progress Series in Criminology: Vol. 30). 142p. 1983. 16.95 o.p. (ISBN 0-8039-2168-3). Sage.

Career Development Education: A Program Approach for Teachers & Counselors. W. Wesley Tennyson & L. Sunny Hansen. 1980. Repr. of 1975 ed. 7.75members o.p. (ISBN 0-911547-09-6, 72213W34); 8.75non-members o.p. Am Assn Coun Dev.

Career Development in the Workplace: A Guide for Program Developers. Susan Imel et al. 50p. 1982. 4.95 o.p. (ISBN 0-318-22058-X, IN247). Natl Ctr Res Voc Ed.

Career Development Needs of Adults. Bert W. Westbrook. 4.15 o.p. (ISBN 1-55620-003-X, 72218C). Am Assn Coun Dev.

Career Development: Needs of Nine Year Olds. Juliet V. Miller. 54p. 1978. pap. text ed. 4.70 o.p. (ISBN 0-911547-10-X, 72215W34). Am Assn Coun Dev.

Career Development Needs of Seventeen-Year Olds. Anita M. Mitchell. 98p. 1978. pap. text ed. 6.40 o.p. (ISBN 0-911547-12-6, 72217W34). Am Assn Coun Dev.

Career Development Needs of Thirteen-Year Olds. Roger F. Aubrey. 82p. 1978. pap. text ed. 5.80 o.p. (ISBN 0-911547-11-8, 72216W34). Am Assn Coun Dev.

Career Directory Series: 1987, 6 vols. 1987. 184.95 o.p. (ISBN 0-934829-23-3); pap. 144.95 o.p. (ISBN 0-934829-22-5). Career Pr Inc.

Career Education: A Proposal for Reform. Sidney P. Marland, Jr. LC 74-11044. 348p. 1974. text ed. 9.95 o.p. (ISBN 0-07-040454-2). McGraw.

Career Education: Collaboration with the Private Sector. Robert D. Bhaerman. 68p. 1982. 5.75 o.p. (ISBN 0-318-22060-1, IN246). Natl Ctr Res Voc Ed.

Career Education for Behaviorally Disordered Students. Ed. by Albert Fink & Charles J. Kokaska. 134p. 1983. pap. 14.95 o.p. (ISBN 0-86586-138-2). Coun Exc Child.

Career Education for the Gifted & Talented. Barbara A. Kerr. 43p. 1981. 3.80 o.p. (ISBN 0-318-22061-X, IN230). Natl Ctr Res Voc Ed.

Career Education Measures: A Compendium of Evaluation Instruments. N. L. McCaslin et al. 354p. 1979. 17.00 o.p. (ISBN 0-318-15406-4, RD 166). Natl Ctr Res Voc Ed.

Career Education: New Approaches to Human Development. Larry J. Bailey & Ronald W. Stadt. 403p. 1974. pap. 16.20 o.p. (ISBN 0-87345-601-7). Glencoe.

Career English: Skill Development for Effective Communication. Phyllis D. Hemphill. (Illus.). 1980. pap. text ed. (ISBN 0-13-114595-9). P-H.

Career Exploration Workshop for Women: Leader's Manual. rev. ed. Ed. by Vivian McCoy & Phyllis Cassell. 126p. 1981. pap. 17.50 spiral bdg. o.p. (ISBN 0-936352-13-2). U of KS Cont Ed.

Career Exploration Workshop for Women: Participant's Personal Portfolio. rev. ed. Ed. by Vivian McCoy & Phyllis Cassell. 96p. 1981. pap. 9.50 o.p. (ISBN 0-936352-14-0). U of KS Cont Ed.

Career Finder: Pathways to over 1500 Entry-Level Jobs. Lester Schwartz & Irv Brechner. LC 82-90224. 352p. 1983. pap. 9.95 o.p. (ISBN 0-345-33679-8). Ballantine.

Career Guidance for a New Age. Henry Borow et al. (Illus.). 336p. 1973. text ed. 21.95 o.p. (ISBN 0-395-14362-4, 3-05191). HM.

Career Guidance Through the Lifespan: Systematic Approaches. 2nd ed. Edwin L. Herr & Stanley H. Cramer. 1984. text ed. write for info. o.p. (ISBN 0-673-39158-2). Scott F.

Career in Speech Pathology. Charles Van Riper. LC 78-9678. 1979. pap. text ed. (ISBN 0-13-114769-2). P-H.

Career Information Service. 4th ed. Willa Norris. 1979. text ed. 29.95 o.p. (ISBN 0-395-30685-X). HM.

Career Issues in Human Resource Management. Ralph Katz. (Applied Management Ser.). (Illus.). 224p. 1982. text ed. 28.67 o.p. (ISBN 0-13-114819-2). P-H.

Career Legal Secretary. Advanced ed. Ed. by National Association of Legal Secretaries (NALS) Staff. LC 82-11174. 1216p. 1982. text ed. 25.95 o.p. (ISBN 0-314-68807-2); tchr's. manual avail. o.p. (ISBN 0-314-70364-0); study guide avail. o.p. (ISBN 0-314-70363-2). West Pub.

Career Planning: A How-to Chart for Your Future. 1976. 7.50 o.p. (ISBN 0-8144-6946-9). AMACOM.

Career Planning: Freedom to Choose. Bruce E. Shertzer. LC 76-12022. (Illus.). 384p. 1977. pap. 9.60 o.p. (ISBN 0-395-19452-0). HM.

Career Planning: Freedom to Choose. 2nd ed. Bruce E. Shertzer. LC 80-81846. (Illus.). 416p. 1980. pap. 14.50 o.p. (ISBN 0-395-29738-9). HM.

Career Planning Practices. James W. Walker & Thomas G. Gutteridge. LC 78-31340. 1979. pap. 13.50 o.p. (ISBN 0-8144-3136-4). AMACOM.

Career Power. R. Rinella & C. Robbins. 1982. pap. 7.95 o.p. (ISBN 0-8144-7586-8). AMACOM.

Career Prep: Electronics Servicing. Kathleen S. Abrams. LC 81-1110. (Jem Bks.). (Illus.). 64p. (Teens reading on a 2-3rd grade level). (gr. 2-3). 1981. lib. bdg. 9.29 o.s.i. (ISBN 0-671-43892-1). Messner.

Career Satisfaction & Success: A Guide to Job Freedom. Bernard Haldane. (AMACOM Executive Bks.). 1978. pap. 4.95 o.p. (ISBN 0-8144-7501-9). AMACOM.

Career Satisfaction & Success: How to Know & Manage Your Strengths. rev. ed. Bernard Haldane. 224p. 1982. 12.95 o.p. (ISBN 0-8144-5709-6). AMACOM.

Career Services Today: A Dynamic College Profession. C Randall Powell & Donald K. Kirts. LC 79-54801. 1980. 11.95 o.p. (ISBN 0-913936-13-8). Coll Placement.

Career-Vocational Education for Handicapped Youth. Sidney R. Miller & Patrick J. Schloss. LC 82-1772. 384p. 1982. text ed. 35.00 o.p. (ISBN 0-89443-683-65-6). Aspen Pub.

Careers & Career Education in the Performing Arts: An Annotated Bibliography. Ed. by William L. Waack. 62p. 1983. pap. text ed. 6.25 o.p. (ISBN 0-8191-3532-1, Co-pub. by Am Theat Assn). U Pr of Amer.

Careers at a Movie Studio. Rivian Bell & Teresa Koenig. LC 82-20865. (Lerner Early Career Bks.). (Illus.). 36p. (gr. 2-5). 1983. PLB 6.95 o.p. (ISBN 0-8225-0347-6). Lerner Pubns.

Careers at a Zoo. Mark Lerner. LC 80-19614. (Lerner Early Career Bks.). (Illus.). (gr. 2-5). 1980. PLB 6.95 o.p. (ISBN 0-8225-0342-5). Lerner Pubns.

Careers for Humanists. Ernest May & D. Blaney. LC 81-15000. 1981. 19.50 o.p. (ISBN 0-12-480620-1). Acad Pr.

Careers in a Bank. Mary Davis. LC 72-7645. (Lerner Early Career Bks.). (Illus.). 36p. (gr. 2-5). 1973. PLB 6.95 o.p. (ISBN 0-8225-0308-5). Lerner Pubns.

Careers in a Department Store. Jennifer B. Dean. LC 72-5411. (Lerner Early Career Bks.). (Illus.). 36p. (gr. 2-5). 1973. PLB 6.95 o.p. (ISBN 0-8225-0301-8). Lerner Pubns.

Careers in a Library. Rebecca Anders. LC 77-90159. (Lerner Early Career Bks.). (Illus.). (gr. 2-5). 1978. PLB 6.95 o.p. (ISBN 0-8225-0334-4). Lerner Pubns.

Careers in a Medical Center. Mary Davis. LC 72-7657. (Lerner Early Career Bks.). (Illus.). 36p. (gr. 2-5). 1973. 6.95 o.p. (ISBN 0-8225-0310-7). Lerner Pubns.

Careers in a Restaurant. Mark Lerner. LC 78-27435. (Lerner Early Career Bks.). (Illus.). (gr. 2-5). 1979. PLB 6.95 o.p. (ISBN 0-8225-0336-0). Lerner Pubns.

Careers in a Supermarket. Mark Lerner. LC 77-72424. (Lerner Early Career Bks.). (Illus.). (gr. 2-5). 1977. PLB 6.95 o.p. (ISBN 0-8225-0332-8). Lerner Pubns.

Careers in Accounting. Gloria L. Gaylord & Glenda E. Ried. LC 83-73709. 225p. 1984. 12.25 o.p. (ISBN 0-87094-433-9); pap. 9.95 o.p. (ISBN 0-87094-547-5). Dow Jones-Irwin.

Careers in Agriculture. Christopher Benson. LC 80-22515. (Lerner Early Career Bks.). (Illus.). 36p. (gr. 2-5). 1974. PLB 6.95 o.p. (ISBN 0-8225-0316-6). Lerner Pubns.

Careers in Animal Care. Christopher Benson. LC 73-22516. (Lerner Early Career Bks.). (Illus.). 36p. (gr. 2-5). 1974. PLB 6.95 o.p. (ISBN 0-8225-0317-4). Lerner Pubns.

Careers in Auto Sales & Service. Christopher Benson. LC 73-22517. (Lerner Early Career Bks.). (Illus.). 36p. (gr. 2-5). 1974. PLB 6.95 o.p. (ISBN 0-8225-0318-2). Lerner Pubns.

Careers in Baseball. Mary Davis. LC 72-7646. (Lerner Early Career Bks.). (Illus.). 36p. (gr. 2-5). 1973. PLB 6.95 o.p. (ISBN 0-8225-0313-1). Lerner Pubns.

Careers in Basketball. Mark Lerner. LC 82-17265. (Lerner Early Career Bks.). (Illus.). 36p. (gr. 2-5). 1983. PLB 6.95 o.p. (ISBN 0-8225-0311-5). Lerner Pubns.

Careers in Beauty & Grooming. Mark Lerner. LC 77-72419. (Lerner Early Career Bks.). (Illus.). (gr. 2-5). 1977. PLB 6.95 o.p. (ISBN 0-8225-0328-X). Lerner Pubns.

Careers in Computers. Texe W. Marrs. 160p. 1984. pap. 8.95 o.p. (ISBN 0-671-50221-2). Monarch Pr.

Careers in Computers. Jo A. Ray. LC 72-7647. (Lerner Early Career Bks.). (Illus.). 36p. (gr. 2-5). 1973. PLB 6.95 o.p. (ISBN 0-8225-0307-7). Lerner Pubns.

Careers in Conservation. Christopher Benson. LC 73-22519. (Lerner Early Career Bks.). (Illus.). 36p. (gr. 2-5). 1974. PLB 6.95 o.p. (ISBN 0-8225-0320-4). Lerner Pubns.

Careers in Construction. Gloria Ramos. LC 74-11903. (Lerner Early Career Bks.). (Illus.). 36p. (gr. 2-5). 1975. PLB 6.95 o.p. (ISBN 0-8225-0323-9). Lerner Pubns.

Careers in Counseling & Guidance. Shelley C. Stone & Bruce E. Shertzer. LC 72-185792. 160p. (Orig.). 1972. pap. 12.50 o.p. (ISBN 0-395-13494-3). HM.

Careers in Dental Care. Joyce K. Kessel. LC 83-25551. (Lerner Early Career Bks.). (Illus.). 36p. (gr. 2-5). 1984. lib. bdg. 6.95 o.p. (ISBN 0-8225-0345-X). Lerner Pubns.

Careers in Education. Christopher Benson. LC 73-22520. (Lerner Early Career Bks.). (Illus.). 36p. (gr. 2-5). 1974. PLB 6.95 o.p. (ISBN 0-8225-0321-2). Lerner Pubns.

Careers in Focus Program Guide. Charles S. Winn. 1975. text ed. 16.90 o.p. (ISBN 0-07-071067-8). McGraw.

Careers in Football. Jo A. Ray. LC 72-7649. (Lerner Early Career Bks.). (Illus.). 36p. (gr. 2-5). 1973. PLB 6.95 o.p. (ISBN 0-8225-0314-X). Lerner Pubns.

Careers in Health Care. Barbara M. Swanson. LC 83-73721. 350p. 1984. 14.95 o.p. (ISBN 0-87094-443-6); pap. 10.50 o.p. (ISBN 0-87094-545-9). Dow Jones-Irwin.

Careers in Health: The Professionals Give You the Inside Picture about Their Jobs. Barbara Zimmermann & David B. Smith. LC 78-53788. 1979. 15.95x o.p. (ISBN 0-8070-2578-X); pap. 4.95 o.p. (ISBN 0-8070-2579-8, BP588). Beacon Pr.

Careers in Hockey. Jo A. Ray. LC 72-7650. (Lerner Early Career Bks.). (Illus.). 36p. (gr. 2-5). 1973. PLB 6.95 o.p. (ISBN 0-8225-0315-8). Lerner Pubns.

Careers in Hotels & Motels. Mark Lerner. LC 78-21171. (Lerner Early Career Bks.). (Illus.). (gr. 2-5). 1979. PLB 6.95 o.p. (ISBN 0-8225-0335-2). Lerner Pubns.

Careers in Industrial Research & Development. J. H. Saunders. 272p. 1974. 45.00 o.p. (ISBN 0-8247-6099-9). Dekker.

Careers in Marketing. David W. Rosenthal & Michael A. Powell. (Illus.). 256p. 1984. text ed. 27.00 o.p. (ISBN 0-13-114935-0); pap. 12.95 o.p. (ISBN 0-13-114927-X). P-H.

Careers in Organizations. Douglas T. Hall. Ed. by Lyman W. Porter. LC 75-13446. (Scott Foresman Series in Management & Organizations). 230p. 1976. pap. text ed. write for info. o.p. (ISBN 0-673-16077-7). Scott F.

Careers in Printing. Mary Davis. LC 72-5416. (Lerner Early Career Bks.). (Illus.). 36p. (gr. 2-5). 1973. PLB 6.95 o.p. (ISBN 0-8225-0306-9). Lerner Pubns.

Careers in Soccer. Arthur Palladian. LC 77-72423. (Lerner Early Career Bks.). (Illus.). (gr. 2-5). 1977. PLB 6.95 o.p. (ISBN 0-8225-0331-X). Lerner Pubns.

Careers in the Air Force. Arthur Palladian. LC 77-90321. (Lerner Early Career Bks.). (Illus.). (gr. 2-5). 1978. PLB 6.95 o.p. (ISBN 0-8225-0333-6). Lerner Pubns.

Careers in the Animal Kingdom. Walter Oleksy. LC 79-20742. (Messner Career Bks.). (Illus.). 256p. (gr. 7 up). 1980. lib. bdg. 8.79 o.s.i. (ISBN 0-671-32939-1). Messner.

Careers in the Army. Arthur Palladian. LC 77-72420. (Lerner Early Career Bks.). (Illus.). (gr. 2-5). 1978. PLB 6.95 o.p. (ISBN 0-8225-0327-1). Lerner Pubns.

Careers in the Navy. Arthur Palladian. LC 77-72421. (Lerner Early Career Bks.). (Illus.). (gr. 2-5). 1977. PLB 5.95 o.p. (ISBN 0-8225-0329-8). Lerner Pubns.

Careers in the Theater. Dennis Babcock & Preston Boyd. LC 74-11907. (Lerner Early Career Bks.). (Illus.). 36p. (gr. 2-5). 1975. PLB 6.95 o.p. (ISBN 0-8225-0324-7). Lerner Pubns.

Careers in the Visual Arts: Talking with Professionals. Dian G. Smith. LC 80-17848. (Messner Career Bks.). (Illus.). 224p. (gr. 7 up). 1980. lib. bdg. 9.79 o.p. (ISBN 0-671-33080-2). Messner.

Careers in Toy Making. Mark Lerner. LC 80-11293. (Lerner Early Career Bks.). (Illus.). (gr. 2-5). 1980. PLB 6.95 o.p. (ISBN 0-8225-0340-9). Lerner Pubns.

Careers in Trucking. Mark Lerner. LC 79-18675. (Lerner Early Career Bks.). (Illus.). (gr. 2-5). 1979. PLB 6.95 o.p. (ISBN 0-8225-0341-7). Lerner Pubns.

Careers, Incorporated. Robert W. Meals. LC 84-90485. 186p. 1985. 11.95 o.p. (ISBN 0-533-06424-4). Vantage.

Careers of Professional Women. Ed. by Rosalie Silverstone & Audrey Ward. 227p. 1980. 30.00 o.p. (ISBN 0-85664-923-6, Pub. by Croom Helm). Routledge Chapman & Hall.

Careers of Social Studies Students. Barbara N. Rodgers. 75p. 1964. pap. text ed. 3.75x o.p. (ISBN 0-686-70843-1, Pub. by Bedford England). Gower Pub Co.

Careers to Explore: Brownie & Junior Leaders' Guide. 16p. 1979. pap. 1.60 o.p. (ISBN 0-88441-325-X, 20-814). Girl Scouts USA.

Careers Tomorrow: The Outlook for Work in a Changing World. Ed. by Edward Cornish. 160p. 1983. pap. 6.95 o.p. Transaction Pubs.

Careers with a Fire Department. Johanna Petersen. LC 74-11904. (Lerner Early Career Bks.). (Illus.). 36p. (gr. 2-5). 1975. PLB 6.95 o.p. (ISBN 0-8225-0309-3). Lerner Pubns.

Careers with a Newspaper. Mark Lerner. LC 77-72422. (Lerner Early Career Bks.). (Illus.). (gr. 2-5). 1977. PLB 6.95 o.p. (ISBN 0-8225-0330-1). Lerner Pubns.

Careers with a Police Department. Jo A. Ray. LC 72-5415. (Lerner Early Career Bks.). (Illus.). 36p. (gr. 2-5). 1973. PLB 6.95 o.p. (ISBN 0-8225-0305-0). Lerner Pubns.

Careers with a Railroad. Chris Meade. LC 74-11906. (Lerner Early Career Bks.). (Illus.). 36p. (gr. 2-5). 1975. PLB 6.95 o.p. (ISBN 0-8225-0325-5). Lerner Pubns.

Careers with a Telephone Company. Mary Davis. LC 72-5412. (Lerner Early Career Bks.). (Illus.). 36p. (gr. 2-5). 1973. PLB 6.95 o.p. (ISBN 0-8225-0302-6). Lerner Pubns.

Careers with a Television Station. Jo A. Ray. LC 72-5414. (Lerner Early Career Bks.). (Illus.). 36p. (gr. 2-5). 1973. PLB 6.95 o.p. (ISBN 0-8225-0304-2). Lerner Pubns.

Careers with an Airline. Jennifer B. Dean. LC 72-5413. (Lerner Early Career Bks.). (Illus.). 36p. (gr. 2-5). 1973. PLB 6.95 o.p. (ISBN 0-8225-0303-4). Lerner Pubns.

Careers with the Circus. Karin Kelly. LC 74-11902. (Lerner Early Career Bks.). (Illus.). 36p. (gr. 2-5). 1975. PLB 6.95 o.p. (ISBN 0-8225-0326-3). Lerner Pubns.

Careers with the City. Christopher Benson. LC 73-22158. (Lerner Early Career Bks.). (Illus.). 36p. (gr. 2-5). 1974. PLB 6.95 o.p. (ISBN 0-8225-0319-0). Lerner Pubns.

Careers with the Postal Service. Johanna Petersen. LC 74-11905. (Lerner Early Career Bks.). (Illus.). 36p. (gr. 2-5). 1975. PLB 6.95 o.p. (ISBN 0-8225-0322-0). Lerner Pubns.

Carefree Getaway Guide for New Yorkers: Day & Weekend Trips Without a Car. Theodore W. Scull. LC 85-840. (Illus.). 199p. (Orig.). 1985. pap. 8.95 o.p. (ISBN 0-916782-68-9). Harvard Common Pr.

Carel Weight. Mervyn Levy. (Royal Academy Painters & Sculptors Ser.). (Illus.). 80p. 1986. 16.95 o.p. (ISBN 0-89733-227-X). Academy Chi Pubs.

Carey's Fortune. Anne Emery. LC 72-82412. (gr. 5-9). 1969. 3.95 o.s.i. (ISBN 0-664-32455-X, Westminster). Westminster John Knox.

Cargo Access Equipment for Merchant Ships. I. L. Buxton et al. LC 78-70528. 366p. 1979. 42.00x o.p. (ISBN 0-87201-099-6). Gulf Pub.

Cargo Handling in a Modern Port. R. B. Oram. 1964. 50.00 o.p. (ISBN 0-08-011306-0); pap. 14.00 o.p. (ISBN 0-08-011305-2). Pergamon.

Cargoes of the East: The Ports, Trade & Culture of the Arabian Seas & Western Indian Ocean. Esmond B. Martin & Chryssee P. Martin. 1979. 34.95 o.p. (ISBN 0-241-89855-2, Pub. by Hamish Hamilton England). David & Charles.

Caribbean, & the Bahamas. Ed. by Kay Shower. (Outdoor Traveler's Guides). (Illus.). 400p. (Orig.). 1989. pap. 16.95 o.p. (ISBN 1-55670-012-1). Stewart Tabori & Chang.

Caribbean Basin Initiative Guidebook. (Illus.). 53p. 1986. pap. 1.75 o.p. (ISBN 0-318-21540-3, S/N 003-009-00492-6). USGPO.

Caribbean Bed & Breakfast Book. Kathy Strong. LC 85-71254. (Illus.). 272p. 1985. pap. 9.95 o.p. (ISBN 0-88742-054-0). Globe Pequot.

Caribbean, Bermuda & the Bahamas, Nineteen Eighty-Two. Steve Birnbaum. (Get 'em & Go Travel Guide Ser.). 672p. 1981. pap. 10.95 o.p. (ISBN 0-395-31533-6). HM.

Caribbean, Bermuda, & the Bahamas, 1980. Steve Birnbaum. (Get 'Em & Go Travel Guides Ser.). 1979. 15.00 o.p. (ISBN 0-395-28418-X); pap. 9.95 o.p. (ISBN 0-395-28413-9). HM.

Caribbean, Bermuda, & the Bahamas 1981. Steve Birnbaum. (Get 'em & Go Travel Guides). 1980. pap. 9.95 o.p. (ISBN 0-395-29749-4). HM.

Caribbean, Bermuda & the Bahamas 1983. Steve Birnbaum. (Get 'em & Go Travel Guide Ser.). 1982. pap. 11.45 o.p. (ISBN 0-395-32869-1). HM.

Caribbean, Bermuda, & the Bahamas 1987. Steve Birnbaum. (Illus.). 688p. 1986. pap. 12.70 o.s.i. (ISBN 0-395-42342-2). HM.

Caribbean Confederation: A Plan for the Union of the Fifteen British West Indian Colonies. Charles S. Salmon. LC 73-89057. 1970. Repr. of 1888 ed. 35.00x o.p. (ISBN 0-8371-1833-6, SAD&, Pub. by Negro U Pr). Greenwood.

Caribbean Gold. George Murray. LC 84-90518. 135p. 1985. 10.95 o.p. (ISBN 0-533-06455-4). Vantage.

Caribbean Integration: The Politics of Regional Negotiations. W. Andrew Axline. 233p. 1979. 32.50 o.p. (ISBN 0-89397-049-2). Nichols Pub.

Caribbean Lands. rev. ed. John P. Augelli. LC 77-84154. (American Neighbors Ser.). (Illus.). (gr. 5 up). 1978. text ed. 11.20 ea. 1-4 copies o.p. (ISBN 0-88296-112-8); text ed. 8.96 ea. 5 or more o.p. Gateway Pr MI.

Caribbean Pilgrims: The Plight of the Haitian Refugees. Daniel Douge. 96p. 1982. 6.00 o.p. (ISBN 0-682-49890-4, University). Exposition-Phoenix.

Caribbean Trip Planner: A New Looseleaf Guide to the Caribbean. Dick Amann & Barbara Amann. (Illus.). 1985. looseleaf 29.95 o.p. (ISBN 0-917194-04-7). Prog Studies.

Caribbean Verse. Ed. by O. R. Dathorne. 1967. pap. text ed. 6.00x o.p. (ISBN 0-435-98220-6). Heinemann Ed.

Caribbean: Winter Vacation Guide, 1989. (Illus.). cancelled o.s.i. Wrld Travel.

Caribou Alphabet. Mary B. Owens. (Illus.). 40p. (gr. k-6). 1988. 13.95 o.p. (ISBN 0-937966-25-8). Dog Ear.

Caricature: The Wit & Humor of a Nation in Picture, Song, & Story. LC 74-14535. (Illus.). 160p. 1976. Repr. of 1903 ed. 53.00x o.p. (ISBN 0-8103-4057-7). Gale.

Caring: A Daughter's Story. Diane Rubin. LC 81-6987. 176p. 1982. 13.45 o.p. (ISBN 0-03-058938-X). H Holt & Co.

Caring & Curing: A Philosophy of Medicine & Social Work. R. S. Downie & Elizabeth Telfer. LC 80-40246. 180p. 1980. 25.00x o.p. (ISBN 0-416-71800-0, NO.2063). Routledge Chapman & Hall.

Caring Enough to Hear & Be Heard: Leader's Guide. Jim Larson. LC 82-403. (Caring Enough Ser.). 1984. pap. 3.95 o.s.i. (ISBN 0-8307-0994-0, 6101948). Regal.

Caring: Experiences of Looking after Severely Disabled Relatives. Ed. by Anna Briggs & Judith Oliver. 160p. (Orig.). 1985. pap. 9.95x o.p. (ISBN 0-7102-0332-2). Routledge Chapman & Hall.

Caring for an Elderly Relative. M. Keith Thompson. (Illus.). 128p. 1986. 14.95 o.p. (ISBN 0-671-61955-1); pap. 8.95 o.p. (ISBN 0-671-61956-X). Arco.

Caring for Kids. Marilyn W. Norris. (Independent Living Ser.). (Illus.). 1977. text ed. 12.00 o.p. (ISBN 0-07-047246-7). McGraw.

Caring for Surgical Patients. Ed. by Jean Robinson & Barbara McVan. LC 81-20269. (Nursing Photobook Ser.). (Illus.). 160p. 1982. text ed. 17.95 o.p. (ISBN 0-916730-43-3). Springhouse Pub.

Caring for the Mentally Handicapped Child. David Wilkin. 223p. 1979. 30.00 o.p. (ISBN 0-85664-648-2, Pub. by Croom Helm Ltd). Routledge Chapman & Hall.

Caring for the Mentally Ill in the Community. Charles A. Butterworth & David Skidmore. (Illus.). 126p. 1981. 21.00 o.p. (ISBN 0-7099-0071-6, Pub. by Croom Helm Ltd); pap. 9.95 o.p. (ISBN 0-7099-0072-4). Routledge Chapman & Hall.

Caring for the Mentally Impaired Elderly: A Family Guide. Florence Safford. 288p. 1987. 19.95 o.p. (ISBN 0-8050-0080-1). H Holt & Co.

Caring for Your Aging Parent. James Kenny & Stephen Spicer. 152p. 1984. pap. 5.95 o.p. (ISBN 0-86716-037-3). St Anthony Mess Pr.

Caring for Your Parents: A Sourcebook of Options & Solutions for Both Generations. Helene MacLean. LC 86-16816. (Illus.). 384p. 1987. pap. 22.50 o.p. (ISBN 0-385-24148-8, Dolp); pap. 13.95 o.p. (ISBN 0-385-23314-0, Dolp). Doubleday.

Caring for Your Sick Child. Patricia H. Rushford. 240p. (Orig.). 1986. pap. 7.95 o.p. (ISBN 0-8007-5211-2). Revell.

Caring Society: The New Deal, the Worker & the Great Depression. Irving Bernstein. LC 84-25129. (History of the American Worker Ser.). 336p. 1985. 22.45 o.s.i. (ISBN 0-395-33116-1). HM.

Carini & Owens' Neurological & Neurosurgical Nursing. 8th ed. Barbara L. Conway-Rutkowski. LC 81-14161. (Illus.). 803p. 1982. text ed. 34.95 o.p. (ISBN 0-8016-1035-4). Mosby.

Carioca Fletch. Gregory McDonald. 528p. 1986. pap. 10.95 o.p. (ISBN 0-8161-3983-0, Large Print Bks). G K Hall.

Carl Larsson. Ed. by Brooklyn Museum. (Illus.). 96p. 1982. 22.50 o.p. (ISBN 0-03-062751-6); pap. 13.95 o.p. (ISBN 0-03-062749-4). H Holt & Co.

Carl Nielsen: Symphonist. Robert Simpson. (Illus.). 260p. 1986. pap. 7.95 o.s.i. (ISBN 0-8008-1261-1). Taplinger.

Carl Orff. Andreas Lless. 184p. Repr. of 1966 ed. lib. bdg. 39.00 o.p. (Pub. by Am Repr Serv). Reprint Servs.

Carleton E. Watkins: Photographer of the American West. Amon Carter Museum Staff & Peter E. Palmquist. LC 82-24824. (Illus.). 252p. 1983. 70.00 o.p. (ISBN 0-8263-0659-4). U of NM Pr.

Carlito's Way. Edwin Torres. 160p. 1982. pap. 2.25 o.p. (ISBN 0-380-60327-6, 60327-6). Avon.

Carlo Mollino. Giovanni Brino. LC 86-43225. (Illus.). 160p. 1987. 40.00 o.p. (ISBN 0-8478-0824-6). Rizzoli Intl.

Carlos P. Romulo: The Barefoot Boy of Diplomacy. Adele De Leeuw. LC 75-35834. (Illus.). (gr. 6 up). 1976. 6.95 o.s.i. (ISBN 0-664-32583-1, Westminster). Westminster John Knox.

Carlotta & the Scientist. 2nd ed. Patricia R. Lenthall. LC 76-20841. (Illus.). 47p. 1976. 5.00 o.p. (ISBN 0-914996-12-6). Lollipop Power.

Carlton Fredericks' Program for Living Longer. Carlton Fredericks. 224p. 1983. pap. 9.50 o.p. (ISBN 0-671-47237-2, Fireside). S&S.

Carmela. Paul Gillette. LC 72-82178. 1972. 7.95 o.p. (ISBN 0-87795-046-6, Arbor Hse). Morrow.

Carmelite Studies II: Carmel & Psychology. John Sullivan. LC 82-1091. 320p. pap. 6.95x o.p. (ISBN 0-935216-00-6). ICS Pubns.

Carmen Miranda Memorial Flagpole. Gerald Rosen. (YA) (gr. 7 up). 1979. pap. 3.95 o.p. (ISBN 0-380-43109-2, 43109-2). Avon.

Carnal Christians: And Other Words That Don't Go Together. Rich Wilkerson. 175p. (Orig.). 1986. pap. 3.95 o.p. (ISBN 0-88368-188-9). Whitaker Hse.

Carnegie Treasures Cookbook. Carnegie Institute, Museum of Art Staff. (Illus.). 292p. 1984. 19.95 o.p. (ISBN 0-689-11428-1, Atheneum). Macmillan.

Carnet De Notes Spiritual. Paul Twitchell. 1978. pap. 3.95 o.p. (ISBN 0-914766-40-6). Illum Way Pub.

Carnet des Dardanelles. Jean Giraudoux. 23.75 o.p. (ISBN 0-685-34178-X). French & Eur.

Carnitine Biosynthesis, Metabolism & Functions. Rene A. Frenkel & J. Denis McGarry. LC 80-11971. 1980. 52.50 o.p. (ISBN 0-12-267060-4). Acad Pr.

Carnival & Theatre: Plebian Culture & the Structure of Authority in Renaissance England. Michael D. Bristol. 350p. 1985. text ed. 33.00 o.p. (ISBN 0-416-35070-4, 9448). Routledge Chapman & Hall.

Carnival in Lights. Helen Greguire. (Illus.). ring bdg. 11.95 o.p. (ISBN 0-686-51509-9). Wallace-Homestead.

Carnival of Demons. William Sno. (Wizards, Warriors & You Ser.: No. 14). 112p. 1986. pap. 2.95 o.p. (ISBN 0-380-75042-2). Avon.

Carnivorous Plants. Randall Schwartz. 1975. pap. 1.25 o.p. (ISBN 0-380-00518-2, 26989). Avon.

Carob Primer. Robin Clute & Sigrid Andersen. (Illus.). 64p. pap. 3.95 o.p. Creative Arts Bk.

Carol Visits Cloud land. Laura Taggart. (Illus.). 32p. (ps-3). 1987. text ed. 6.95 o.p. (ISBN 0-682-40341-5). Exposition-Phoenix.

Carolina Curiosities: Jerry Bledsoe's Outlandish Guide to the Dadblamest Things to See & Do in North Carolina. Jerry Bledsoe. LC 83-49042. 224p. 1984. pap. 8.95 o.p. (ISBN 0-88742-007-9). Globe Pequot.

Caroline: A Biography of Caroline of Brunswick. Thea Holme. LC 79-51398. (Illus.). 1980. 12.95 o.p. (ISBN 0-689-10999-7, Atheneum). Macmillan.

Caroline Drama: A Bibliographic History of Criticism. Ed. by Rachel Fordyce. 1978. lib. bdg. 31.50 o.p. (ISBN 0-8161-7952-2, Hall Reference). G K Hall.

Caroline R. Tim Heald. LC 80-66765. 1980. 11.95 o.p. (ISBN 0-87795-285-X, Arbor Hse). Morrow.

Caroline the Queen. Jean Plaidy. 1986. 17.95 o.p. (ISBN 0-399-13123-X). Putnam Pub Group.

Carol's Side of the Street. Lorraine Beim. LC 51-13195. (Illus.). (gr. 3-6). 1951. 4.95 o.p. (ISBN 0-15-214641-5, HJ). HarBraceJ.

Carol's Story. Chip Ricks. 192p. 1981. pap. 6.95 o.p. (ISBN 0-8423-0208-5). Tyndale.

Carolyn Wells' Book of American Limericks. Carolyn Wells. LC 77-174140. (Tower Bks). (Illus.). viii, 102p. 1972. Repr. of 1925 ed. 40.00x o.p. (ISBN 0-8103-3929-3). Gale.

Carotenoids Chemistry & Biochemistry: Proceedings of the International Symposium on Carotenoids, 6th, Liverpool, U. K., July 26-31, 1981. International Symposium on Carotenoids Staff. Ed. by T. W. Goodwin & G. Britton. (IUPAC Symposium Ser.). (Illus.). 320p. 1982. 135.00 o.p. (ISBN 0-08-026224-4, E115). Pergamon.

Carotenoids-Four: Proceedings. Ed. by Basil Weedon et al. 1977. 70.00 o.p. (ISBN 0-08-020974-2). Pergamon.

Carousel. Theodora Kroeber. LC 77-2003. (gr. 2-5). 1977. 5.95 o.p. (ISBN 0-689-30589-3, Atheneum). Macmillan.

Carpenter. Joy Haney. Ed. by Mary Wallace. LC 85-26498. (Illus.). 96p. (Orig.). 1985. pap. 5.00 o.p. (ISBN 0-912315-97-0). Word Aflame.

Carpenter of the Sun. Nancy Willard. 55p. 1974. 6.95 o.p. (ISBN 0-87140-602-0); pap. 2.50 o.p. (ISBN 0-87140-098-7). Liveright.

Carpenter's Manifesto. Jeffrey Ehrlich & Marc Mannheimer. LC 77-73865. 1977. 12.95 o.p. (ISBN 0-03-016756-6); pap. 9.95 o.p. (ISBN 0-03-016761-2). H Holt & Co.

Carpenter's Monthly Political Magazine, 2 vols, No. 2. 1970. Repr. of 1832 ed. Set. lib. bdg. 23.25x o.p. (ISBN 0-8371-9135-1, CB00). Greenwood.

Carpenter's Wife. B. A. Tompkins. 1977. pap. 1.00 o.p. (ISBN 0-931832-05-5). Fithian Pr.

Carpentry & Building Construction. rev. ed. John L. Feirer & Gilbert R. Hutchings. (Illus.). 1981. 44.50 o.s.i. (ISBN 0-684-16981-9, ScribT). Scribner.

Carpentry in Commercial Construction. 2nd ed. Stanley Badzinski. 1980. text ed. 32.00 o.p. (ISBN 0-13-115220-3). P-H.

Carpet Annual, 1986. 51st ed. 1986. 94.00 o.p. (ISBN 0-86382-032-8). Intl Pubns Serv.

Carpets from Baghdad. Gershon Kranzler. saddle-stitched 5.00 o.p. (ISBN 0-87559-127-2). Shalom.

Carrey Drawings of the Parthenon Sculptures. Ed. by Theodore Bowie & Diether Thimme. LC 77-155287. (Illus.). 112p. 1971. 50.00x o.p. (ISBN 0-253-31320-1). Ind U Pr.

Carrier Communication Over Power Lines. 4th rev. ed. H. K. Podszeck. LC 75-183954. (Illus.). 195p. 1972. 37.80 o.p. (ISBN 0-387-05691-2). Springer-Verlag.

Carrier Strike Force: Pacific Air Combat in World War II. Ernest A. McKay. LC 81-10996. (Illus.). 192p. (gr. 7 up). 1981. lib. bdg. 9.79 o.s.i. (ISBN 0-671-43127-7). Messner.

Carriers of the Dream Wheel. Ed. by Duane Niatum. LC 74-5986. (Contemporary Native American Poetry Ser.). (Illus.). 320p. 1981. pap. 9.95i o.p. (ISBN 0-06-451152-9, CN4021). HarpR.

Carrie's War. Nina Bawden. 1985. 11.95 o.p. (ISBN 0-317-53070-4, Large Print Bks). G K Hall.

Carrie's War: T.V. Ed. Nina Bawden. (Illus.). 1980. pap. 2.95 o.p. (ISBN 0-14-005581-9). Penguin.

Carrot for a Nose: The Form of Folk Sculpture on America's City Streets & Country Roads. M. J. Gladstone. LC 72-11229. (Encore Editions). (Illus.). 72p. (gr. 4-8). 1974. 1.99 o.p. (ISBN 0-684-15833-7, ScribT). Scribner.

Carry It On: A History in Song of Working Men & Women. Pete Seeger & Bob Reiser. 224p. 1985. 18.45 o.p. (ISBN 0-671-49963-7); pap. 10.95 o.p. (ISBN 0-671-60347-7). S&S.

Carry-Out Cuisine. Phyllis Meras & Frances Tenenbaum. 1982. 16.45 o.p. (ISBN 0-395-32212-X); pap. 8.70 o.p. (ISBN 0-395-33010-6). HM.

Carrying Out Special Procedures. Ed. by Patricia R. Urosevich & Barbara McVan. LC 82-25846. (Nursing Photobook Ser.). (Illus.). 160p. 1983. 17.95 o.p. (ISBN 0-916730-45-X). Springhouse Pub.

Carryover: A Maintenance Program for Language Impaired Adolescents. MaryJean Gabler & Lloyd Augustine. 103p. 1984. 3-ring binder, 10 audiocassette tapes 50.00x o.p. (ISBN 0-9610370-6-7). Thinking Pubns.

Cars. (Illus.). 32p. 1985. 4.95 o.p. (ISBN 0-88188-364-6, Robus Books). H Leonard Pub Corp.

Cars & Trucks. (Fact Bks.). 96p. (gr. 4-7). 1987. pap. 3.50 o.p. (ISBN 0-528-87856-5, Checkerboard Pr). Macmillan.

Cars of Pacific Electric: Locomotives, Combination Cars, Etc, Vol. 3. Ira L. Swett. Ed. by Jim Walker. (Special Ser.: No. 37). (Illus.). 1978. pap. 12.00 o.p. (ISBN 0-916374-30-0). Interurban.

Cars That Henry Ford Built. Beverly R. Kimes. LC 78-51029. (Illus.). 136p. 1978. 19.95 o.p. (ISBN 0-915038-08-0). Auto Quarterly.

Carson Kids & the Mystery of the Cove Point Stallion. Jan Pierson. (Carson Kids Ser.). 128p. (Orig.). (gr. 5-10). 1984. pap. 2.95 o.p. (ISBN 0-8423-4661-9). Tyndale.

Carson Kids & the Shipwreck on Grizzly Island. Jan Pierson. (Carson Kids Ser.). 128p. (Orig.). (gr. 3-6). 1986. pap. 3.50 o.p. (ISBN 0-8423-0296-4). Tyndale.

Carson's Conspiracy. Michael Innes. 1985. 13.50 o.p. (ISBN 0-317-53071-2, Large Print Bks). G K Hall.

Cart & Cwidder. Diana W. Jones. LC 76-25198. (gr. 4-6). 1977. 6.95 o.p. (ISBN 0-689-30556-7, Atheneum). Macmillan.

Carte Commentee. Michel Butor. 1974. 59.95 o.p. (ISBN 0-686-51941-8). French & Eur.

Cartels in Action: Case Studies in International Business Diplomacy. George W. Stocking & Myron W. Watkins. LC 46-8321. 1946. 40.00 o.p. (ISBN 0-527-02805-3). Kraus Repr.

Carter Family. Stacy Harris & Robert K. Krishef. LC 77-90154. (Country Music Bks.). (Illus.). (gr. 5 up). 1978. PLB 5.95 o.p. (ISBN 0-8225-1403-6). Lerner Pubns.

Carter, Williams, Boyle, Smith & Mulvihill Families, Vol. 1. Bernard A. Carter, Jr. 72p. 1988. pap. text ed. write for info. o.p. (ISBN 0-933227-88-4). Closson Pr.

Carter's Castle. Wilbur Wright. 288p. 1987. pap. 3.95 o.p. (ISBN 1-55547-136-6). Critics Choice Paper.

Cartesian Meditations: An Introduction to a Phenomenology. Edmund Husserl. 1977. pap. 7.50 o.s.i. (ISBN 9-0247-0068-X). E J Brill USA.

Cartesian Tensors in Engineering Science. L. G. Jaeger. 1966. 35.00 o.p. (ISBN 0-08-011222-6); pap. 35.00 o.p. (ISBN 0-08-011221-8). Pergamon.

Carthage of the Phoenicians: In the Light of Modern Excavation. Mabel Moore. Repr. of 1905 ed. lib. bdg. 40.00 o.p. (ISBN 0-8495-3805-X). Arden Lib.

Carthusian Order in England. E. Margaret Thompson. (Church Historical Society London N. S. Ser.: No. 3). Repr. of 1930 ed. 80.00 o.p. (ISBN 0-8115-3127-9). Kraus Repr.

Cartier: Jewelers Extraordinary. Hans Nadelhoffer. LC 83-26646. (Illus.). 312p. 1984. 50.00 o.s.i. (ISBN 0-8109-0770-4). Abrams.

Cartilaginous Skeleton of the Bronchial Tree. F. Vanpeperstraete. (Advancs in Anatomy, Embryology & Cell Biology: Vol. 48, Pt. 3). (Illus.). 90p. 1974. pap. 33.10 o.p. (ISBN 0-387-06536-9). Springer-Verlag.

Cartographic & Statistical Data Bases & Mapping Software, Vol. 8. Laboratory for Computer Graphics & Spatial Analysis, Harvard University Graduate School of Design Staff. (Harvard Library of Computer Graphics, Mapping Collection). (Illus.). 265p. 1980. pap. 15.95 o.p. (ISBN 0-8122-1188-X). U of Pa Pr.

Cartographic Data Bases & Software, Vol. 13. Laboratory for Computer Graphics & Spatial Analysis, Harvard University Graduate School of Design Staff. (Harvard Library of Computer Graphics, Mapping Collection). (Illus.). 176p. 1981. pap. 15.95 o.p. (ISBN 0-8122-1193-6). U of Pa Pr.

Cartographic Methods. 2nd ed. G. R. Lawrence. (Illus.). xvi, 154p. 1979. 25.00x o.p. (ISBN 0-416-71640-7, NO.2847); pap. 12.00x o.p. (ISBN 0-416-71650-4, NO.2848). Routledge Chapman & Hall.

Cartography & Education, Vol. I: ASPRS-ACSM Annual Convention Technical Papers. American Congress on Surveying & Mapping & American Society for Photogrammetry & Remote Sensing Staff. 306p. 1986. 10.00 o.p. (ISBN 0-317-59916-X, T666). Am Congrs Survey.

Cartoon: Communication to the Quick. Randall P. Harrison. LC 81-5682. (Sage CommText Ser.: Vol. 7). (Illus.). 152p. 1981. 19.95 o.s.i. (ISBN 0-8039-1621-3); pap. 9.95 o.s.i. (ISBN 0-8039-1622-1). Sage.

Cartooning. George F. Horn. LC 65-18202. (Illus.). (YA) (gr. 7-12). 10.95 o.p. (ISBN 0-87192-004-2). Davis Mass.

Cartridges of the World. 5th ed. Frank C. Barnes. LC 65-16729. (Illus.). 416p. (Orig.). 1985. pap. 16.95 o.p. (ISBN 0-910676-95-X). DBI.

Carved in Stone. Paul Quenon. (Illus.). 40p. 1979. pap. 2.50 o.p. (ISBN 0-87793-195-X). Ave Maria.

Carved Wooden Ring. Marjory Hall. LC 76-170114. 176p. (gr. 6 up). 1972. 4.75 o.s.i. (ISBN 0-664-32506-8, Westminster). Westminster John Knox.

Casa de los Espiritus. Isabel Allende. 380p. (Span.). 1984. pap. 10.50 o.s.i. (ISBN 84-01-38011-1, 3027). Ediciones Norte.

Casa Grande. Jude Deveraux. 304p. 1982. pap. 3.50 o.p. (ISBN 0-380-80192-2, 80556-1). Avon.

Casa Grande. Jude Deveraux. (General Ser.). 471p. 1986. lib. bdg. 19.95 o.p. (ISBN 0-8161-4046-4, Large Print Bks). G K Hall.

Casablanca. Ed. by Richard J. Anobile. (Film Classics Library Ser). (Illus.). 256p. 1974. pap. 5.45 o.p. (ISBN 0-380-00086-5, 21097-5, Flare). Avon.

Cascade Alpine Guide: Climbing & High Routes-Stevens Pass to Rainy Pass, Vol. 2. Fred Beckey. LC 77-82368. (Illus.). 1978. flexible plastic 16.95 o.p. (ISBN 0-916890-51-1). Mountaineers.

Casco Deception. Bob Reiss. 228p. 1983. 14.45i o.p. (ISBN 0-316-73965-0). Little.

Case Against Pornography. Ed. by David Holbrook. LC 72-5279. 294p. 1973. 4.95 o.p. (ISBN 0-912050-28-4, Library Pr); 3.95 o.p. (ISBN 0-87548-360-7). Open Court.

Case Against the Sale of Development Rights of Connecticut's Agricultural Land. Aubrey W. Birkelbach, Jr. & Gregory H. Wassall. 1975. pap. text ed. 1.00 o.s.i. (ISBN 0-686-23012-4). Lincoln Inst Land.

Case Concerning Delimitation of the Maritime Boundary in the Gulf of Maine Area: Order of 5 November 1982. International Court of Justice Staff. (Reports of Judgments, Advisory Opinions & Orders Ser.). 5p. 1982. 1.00 o.p. (1CJ 480). UN.

Case Currents Index, 1975-1984. Ed. by Virginia C. Smith & Weslie S. Stubbs. 175p. 1985. pap. 15.00 o.p. (ISBN 0-89964-240-3). Coun Adv & Supp Ed.

Case for a Triangle. John Masterson. 1977. 6.00 o.p. (ISBN 0-682-48688-4). Exposition-Phoenix.

Case for an Auxiliary Priesthood. Raymond Hickey. LC 81-16950. 160p. (Orig.). 1982. pap. 1.99 o.p. (ISBN 0-88344-021-0). Orbis Bks.

Case for Character Education. Frank Goble & B. David Brooks. 170p. (Orig.). 1983. pap. 7.95 o.p. (ISBN 0-89803-129-X, Dist. by Kampmann). Green Hill.

Case for Idealism: International Library of Philosophy. John Foster. 280p. 1982. 25.00x o.p. (ISBN 0-7100-9019-6). Routledge Chapman & Hall.

Case for Jewish Civil Law in the Jewish State. K. Kahana. 6.25x o.p. (ISBN 0-685-01037-6). Bloch.

Case for Jewish Civil Law in the Jewish State. K. Kahana. 120p. 1960. 6.50 o.p. Soncino Pr.

Case for Liberal Socialism. 3rd ed. Burnham P. Beckwith. 1976. text ed. 7.50 o.p. (ISBN 0-682-48487-3, University). Exposition-Phoenix.

Case for Local Government. George Jones & John Stewart. LC 85-15721. (Illus.). 168p. 1984. text ed. 34.95x o.p. (ISBN 0-04-352107-X); pap. text ed. 9.95x o.p. (ISBN 0-04-352108-8). Unwin Hyman.

Case for Local Government. 2nd ed. George Jones & John Stewart. LC 85-15721. (Local Government Briefings Ser.). 164p. 1985. pap. text ed. 14.95x o.p. (ISBN 0-04-352234-3). Unwin Hyman.

Case for Sergeant Beef. Leo Bruce. (Sergeant Beef Mystery Ser.). 1985. 14.95 o.s.i. (ISBN 0-89733-037-4); pap. 4.95 o.s.i. (ISBN 0-89733-036-6). Academy Chi Pubs.

Case for the Central Powers. Maximilian Montgelas. Ed. by Constance Vesey. LC 74-12765. Orig. Title: Lertfaden Zur Kriegsschuldfrage. 255p. 1975. Repr. of 1925 ed. lib. bdg. 35.00x o.p. (ISBN 0-8371-7741-3, MOVV). Greenwood.

Case for the Cruising Trimaran. Jim Brown. LC 78-64789. (Illus.). 1979. 7.50 o.p. (ISBN 0-87742-100-5). Intl Marine.

Case for the Sea Serpent. Rupert T. Gould. LC 72-75791. 303p. 1969. Repr. of 1930 ed. 35.00x o.p. (ISBN 0-8103-3833-5). Gale.

Case Grammar: Development of the Matrix Model (1970-1978). Walter A. Cook. LC 79-11067. 223p. 1979. pap. text ed. 8.95 o.s.i. (ISBN 0-87840-174-1). Georgetown U Pr.

Case Histories in Trade Financing, 1984. (ISBN 0-8002-3162-7). Intl Pubns Serv.

Case Histories of Tentmakers. Ed. by James L. Lowery, Jr. 1976. pap. 3.50 o.p. (ISBN 0-8192-1216-4). Morehouse Pub.

Case History of a Movie. Dore Schary. Ed. by Bruce S. Kupelnick. LC 76-52128. (Classics of Film Literature Ser.). 1978. lib. bdg. 22.00 o.p. (ISBN 0-8240-2893-7). Garland Pub.

Case Membership Directory 1988. 185p. 1988. 100.00 o.p. (ISBN 0-89964-259-4). Coun Adv & Supp Ed.

Case Method in Management Development: Guide for Effective Use. John Reynolds. (Management Development Ser.: No. 17). vi, 264p. 1980. 11.40 o.p. (ISBN 92-2-102363-X). Intl Labour Office.

Case of Mrs. A: The Diagnosis of a Life-Style. 2nd ed. Alfred Adler. Ed. by Bernard Shulman. (Individual Psychology Pamphlets, Medical Pamphlet: No. 1). 1969. pap. 4.00x o.p. (ISBN 0-918560-00-4). A Adler Inst.

Case of the Angry Actress. E. V. Cunningham. 192p. 1984. pap. 2.95 o.p. (ISBN 0-440-11093-9). Dell.

Case of the Bashful Bank Robber. E. W. Hildick. (McGurk Mystery Ser.: No. 10). (Illus.). (gr. 3-5). 1982. pap. 1.95 o.p. (ISBN 0-671-44223-6). Archway.

Case of the Bashful Bank Robber. E. W. Hildick. LC 80-24589. (McGurk Mystery Ser.). (Illus.). 128p. (gr. 3-6). 1981. 9.95 o.p. (ISBN 0-02-743870-8). Macmillan.

Case of the Blonde Bonanza. Erle Stanley Gardner. (Large Print Bks., Nightingale Ser.). 291p. 1987. pap. 11.95x o.p. (ISBN 0-8161-4283-1, Large Print Bks). G K Hall.

Case of the Clever Computer Crooks & Other Mysteries. M. Masters. Ed. by Louise Delagran et al. LC 83-11435. (Can You Solve the Mystery? Ser.: Vol. 5). (Illus.). 108p. (gr. 2-6). 1983. pap. 1.95 o.s.i. (ISBN 0-671-54488-8). Meadowbrook.

Case of the Condemned Cat. E. W. Hildick. (McGurk Mystery Ser.: No. 2). (Illus.). (gr. 3-5). 1978. pap. 1.95 o.p. (ISBN 0-671-44236-8). Archway.

Case of the Counterfeit Racehorse. Elizabeth Levy. (Jody & Jake Mystery Ser.: No.2). (Orig.). (gr. 5-7). 1980. pap. 1.95 o.p. (ISBN 0-671-29965-4). Archway.

Case of the Diamond Eye. Amelia Walden. (gr. 6 up). 1969. 3.95 o.s.i. (ISBN 0-664-32456-8, Westminster). Westminster John Knox.

Case of the Etruscan Treasure. Robert Newman. LC 83-2632. 180p. (gr. 3-7). 1983. 10.95 o.s.i. (ISBN 0-689-30992-9, Atheneum Childrens Bks). Macmillan.

Case of the Famous Chocolate Chip Cookies & Other Mysteries. M. Masters. Ed. by Louise Delagran et al. LC 83-11439. (Can You Solve the Mystery Ser.: Vol. 6). (Illus.). 108p. (gr. 2-6). 1983. pap. 1.95 o.p. (ISBN 0-671-54473-X). Meadowbrook.

Case of the Felon's Fiddle. E. W. Hildick. LC 82-10078. (McGurk Mystery Ser.). (Illus.). 144p. (gr. 3-6). 1982. 9.95 o.s.i. (ISBN 0-02-743900-3). Macmillan.

Case of the Fired-up Gang. Elizabeth Levy. (Jody & Jake Mystery Ser.: No. 3). (gr. 5-7). 1981. pap. 1.95 o.p. (ISBN 0-671-41140-3). Archway.

Case of the Four Flying Fingers. E. W. Hildick. LC 81-2517. (McGurk Mystery Ser.). (Illus.). 128p. (gr. 3-6). 1981. 9.95 o.s.i. (ISBN 0-02-743880-5). Macmillan.

Case of the Frightened Friend. Robert Newman. LC 83-15887. 180p. (gr. 4-8). 1984. 11.95 o.s.i. (ISBN 0-689-31018-8, Atheneum Childrens Bks). Macmillan.

Case of the Frightened Rock Star. Elizabeth Levy. (Jody & Jake Mystery Ser.: No. 1). (Orig.). (gr. 5-7). 1980. pap. 1.95 o.p. (ISBN 0-671-29964-6). Archway.

Case of the Gilded Fly. Edmund Crispin. 1980. pap. 2.95 o.p. (ISBN 0-380-50187-2, 63552-6). Avon.

Case of the Hardboiled Dicks: A Novel. John Blumenthal. 1985. pap. 2.95 o.p. (ISBN 0-671-55538-3, Pub. by Fireside). S&S.

Case of the Invisible Dog. E. W. Hildick. (McGurk Mystery Ser.: No. 5). (Illus.). (gr. 3-5). 1978. pap. 1.95 o.p. (ISBN 0-671-44879-X). Archway.

Case of the Kidnapped Angel. E. V. Cunningham. (Masao Masuto Mystery Ser.: No. 5). 192p. 1983. pap. 2.95 o.p. (ISBN 0-440-11224-9). Dell.

Case of the Missing Bronte: A Perry Trethowan Mystery. Robert Barnard. 192p. 1983. 11.95 o.s.i. (ISBN 0-684-17910-5, ScribT). Scribner.

Case of the Murdered MacKenzie. E. V. Cunningham. (Nightingale Large Print Ser.). 1985. pap. 9.95 o.p. (ISBN 0-8161-3771-4, Large Print Bks). G K Hall.

Case of the Nervous Newsboy. E. W. Hildick. (McGurk Mystery: No. 3). (Illus.). (gr. 3-5). 1978. pap. 1.95 o.p. (ISBN 0-671-46529-5). Archway.

Case of the One-Penny Orange. E. V. Cunningham. LC 81-80704. (Masao Masuto Mystery Ser.). 176p. (Orig.). 1982. pap. 3.50 o.s.i. (ISBN 0-03-059858-3, Owl Bks). H Holt & Co.

Case of the Phantom Frog. E. W. Hildick. (McGurk Mystery Ser.: No. 7). (Illus.). (gr. 3-5). 1980. pap. 1.95 o.p. (ISBN 0-671-43878-6). Archway.

Case of the Phantom Frog. E. W. Hildick. LC 78-10836. (McGurk Mystery Ser.). (Illus.). 112p. (gr. 3-6). 1979. 9.95 o.p. (ISBN 0-02-743840-6). Macmillan.

Case of the Purloined Compass. Mark Taylor. LC 84-21517. (Illus.). 48p. (gr. 3-7). 1985. 11.95 o.s.i. (ISBN 0-689-31104-4, Atheneum Childrens Bks). Macmillan.

Case of the Rolling Bones. Erle Stanley Gardner. (Nightingale Ser.). 350p. 1986. pap. 11.95 o.p. (ISBN 0-8161-4080-4, Large Print Bks). G K Hall.

Case of the Runaway Money. Laura L. Hope. (Bobbsey Twins Ser.). (Illus.). (gr. 2-4). Date not set. pap. 2.95 o.p. (ISBN 0-317-62464-4, Minstrel Bks). S&S.

Case of the Russian Diplomat. E. V. Cunningham. 1982. 3.95 o.p. (ISBN 0-03-022456-X). H Holt & Co.

Case of the Russian Diplomat. E. V. Cunningham. LC 81-80705. (Masao Masuto Mystery Ser.). 176p. 1982. pap. 3.50 o.s.i. (ISBN 0-03-059857-5, Owl Bks). H Holt & Co.

Case of the Secret Scribbler. E. W. Hildick. (McGurk Mystery Ser.: No. 6). (Illus.). (gr. 3-5). 1979. pap. 1.75 o.p. (ISBN 0-671-43293-1). Archway.

Case of the Snowbound Spy. E. W. Hildick. (McGurk Mystery: No. 9). (Illus.). (gr. 3-5). 1981. pap. 1.75 o.p. (ISBN 0-671-41869-6). Archway.

Case of the Snowbound Spy. E. W. Hildick. LC 80-12272. (McGurk Mystery Ser.). (Illus.). 132p. (gr. 3-6). 1980. 9.95 o.s.i. (ISBN 0-02-743860-0). Macmillan.

Case of the Ticklish Tooth. Scott Corbett. (Illus.). (gr. 4-6). 1971. 10.45 o.p. (ISBN 0-316-15720-1, Pub. by Atlantic Monthly Pr.). Little.

Case of the Treetop Treasure. E. W. Hildick. (McGurk Mystery Ser.: No. 8). (gr. 3-5). 1981. pap. 1.95 o.p. (ISBN 0-671-45918-X). Archway.

Case of the Trick Note. Larry Sutton. LC 80-69287. (Carolrhoda Mini-Mysteries Ser.). (Illus.). 32p. (gr. 1-4). 1981. PLB 5.95 o.p. (ISBN 0-87614-134-3). Carolrhoda Bks.

Case of the Vanishing Boy. Alexander Key. (gr. 5-7). 1979. pap. 1.75 o.p. (ISBN 0-671-56006-9). Archway.

Case of the Vanishing Ventriloquist. E. W. Hildick. LC 84-21801. (Illus.). 144p. (gr. 3-7). 1985. 9.95 o.s.i. (ISBN 0-02-743930-5). Macmillan.

Case of the Wild River Ride. Elizabeth Levy. (Jody & Jake Mystery Ser.: No. 4). (gr. 5-7). 1981. pap. 1.95 o.p. (ISBN 0-671-41141-1). Archway.

Case of Valentine Shortis: A True Story of Crime & Politics in Canada. Martin L. Friedland. 1986. 24.95 o.p. (ISBN 0-8020-2606-0). U of Toronto Pr.

Case on Cloud Nine. Lucy Freeman. LC 74-18155. 1975. 6.95 o.p. (ISBN 0-87795-103-9, Arbor Hse). Morrow.

Case Reports in Reading & Learning Disabilities: Psychoeducational Evaluation & Remedial Planning. Joan Raim. (Illus.). 300p. 1982. 36.50 o.p. (ISBN 0-398-04565-8). C C Thomas.

Case Studies & Projects in Communication. Neil McKeown. (Studies in Communication). 224p. 1982. pap. 11.95 o.p. (ISBN 0-416-30740-X, NO. 3744). Routledge Chapman & Hall.

Case Studies from the Ethics of Decision Making. Malcolm W. Eckel. 1968. pap. 0.60 o.p. (ISBN 0-8192-1030-7). Morehouse Pub.

Case Studies in Automation Related to Humanization of Work: Proceedings of the IFAC Symposium, Enschede, The Netherlands, Oct., 1977. IFAC Symposium Staff. Ed. by J. E. Rijnsdorp. 173p. 1979. 55.00 o.p. (ISBN 0-08-022012-6). Pergamon.

Case Studies in Child Development. Beverly Taylor. LC 81-21782. (Psychology Ser.). 256p. 1982. pap. text ed. 14.25 pub net o.p. (ISBN 0-534-01152-7). Brooks-Cole.

Case Studies in Computer Control. Ed. by D. M. Auslander. 87p. 1978. 18.00 o.p. (ISBN 0-685-66791-X, H00117). ASME.

Case Studies in Marketing, Advertising & Public Relations. Colin McIver. (Illus.). 240p. 1984. pap. 30.95 o.p. (ISBN 0-434-91235-2, Pub. by W Heinemann Ltd). David & Charles.

Case Studies in Pollution Control in the Textile Dyeing & Finishing Industries: A Study in Non-Technical Language of Essential Information on the Economics of Control, the Problems & Their Solutions. M. H. Atkins & J. F. Lowe. 1979. 64.00 o.p. (ISBN 0-08-022457-1). Pergamon.

Case Studies in Tourism: A Selected Bibliography. Stephen G. Mann & Paul G. Doherty. (Public Administration Series Bibliography: P 1755). 51p. 1985. pap. 7.50 o.p. (ISBN 0-89028-535-7). Vance Biblios.

Case Study Houses, 1945-1962. 2nd ed. Esther McCoy. LC 77-14499. (Illus.). 1977. 28.50 o.p. (ISBN 0-912158-70-0); pap. 14.95 o.p. (ISBN 0-912158-71-9). Hennessey.

Case Study in Business System Design. Science Research Associates, Data Processing & Curriculum Group Staff. (Illus.). 1970. pap. text ed. 9.95 o.p. (ISBN 0-574-16094-9, 13-0782); instr's guide avail. o.p. (ISBN 0-574-16095-7, 13-0783). SRA.

Case Study Method: Guidelines, Practices & Applications for Vocational Education. Janet E. Spirer. 84p. 1980. 5.50 o.p. (ISBN 0-318-15419-6, RD189). Natl Ctr Res Voc Ed.

Case Study of Mr. Bird: Mind Over Matter or Matter Over Mind. George A. Jackson. 1978. 4.00 o.p. (ISBN 0-682-49087-3). Exposition-Phoenix.

Case Study of Mr. Cage: Toleration Over Assertion or Assertion Over Toleration. George A. Jackson. 1979. 4.00 o.p. (ISBN 0-682-49313-9). Exposition-Phoenix.

Case Study of Mr. Cough: Justification Over Condemnation or Condemnation Over Justification. George A. Jackson. 1980. 5.00 o.p. (ISBN 0-682-49550-6). Exposition-Phoenix.

Case Study of Mr. Paranoid: Victim Over Victimizer or Victimizer Over Victim. George A. Jackson. 64p. 1981. 4.00 o.p. (ISBN 0-682-49692-8). Exposition-Phoenix.

Case Study of the Fairfax County, Virginia, Censorship Controversy. Peter R. Hamlin. (Occasional Papers: No. 95). 23p. 1969. pap. 1.00 o.p. (ISBN 0-317-58874-5). U of Ill Lib Info Sci.

Case Study of the Retarded Prophet: Responses Over Will or Will Over Responses. George A. Jackson. 64p. 1982. 4.00 o.p. (ISBN 0-682-49861-0). Exposition-Phoenix.

CASE: The Potential & the Pitfalls. Chantico Press Staff. 1989. 44.50 o.p. (ISBN 0-89435-285-7). QED Info Sci.

Case Worker. 7th ed. LC 80-18006. 256p. 1980. pap. 8.00 o.p. (ISBN 0-668-04979-0, 4979-0). Arco.

Case Worker. George Konrad. LC 73-15424. (Helen & Kurt Wolff Bk.). 1974. 6.95 o.p. (ISBN 0-15-115790-1). HarBraceJ.

Case Worker. George Konrad. Tr. by Paul Aston. LC 78-6633. 176p. 1978. pap. 4.95 o.p. (ISBN 0-15-615412-9, Harv). HarBraceJ.

Casebook for School Counselors. Lewis B. Morgan. 96p. 1974. 7.50 o.p. (ISBN 0-911547-16-9, 72041W34); members 5.25 o.p. (ISBN 0-686-34284-4). Am Assn Coun Dev.

Casebook in Commercial Banking. Edward W. Reed et al. (Illus.). 1977. pap. text ed. (ISBN 0-13-117473-8). P-H.

Casebook of Management for Nonprofit Organizations: Entrepreneurship & Organizational Change in the Human Services. Dennis R. Young. LC 84-9040. (Monographic Supplement to Administration in Social Work Ser.: Vol. 8). 296p. 1985. text ed. 34.95 o.s.i. (ISBN 0-86656-324-5); pap. text ed. 17.95 o.s.i. (ISBN 0-86656-352-0, B352). Haworth Pr.

Casebook of Social Work with Groups: The Mediating Model. Lawrence Shulman. Date not set. 3.00 o.s.i. (68-340-109). Coun Soc WK Ed.

Casebook on Ethics in Research with Human Participants. American Psychological Association Staff. 1988. pap. price not set o.p. (ISBN 1-55798-016-0, 4290030). Am Psychol.

Casebook on Waiting for Godot. Ed. by Ruby Cohn. (Orig.). (YA) (gr. 9 up). 1967. pap. 4.95 o.p. (ISBN 0-394-17266-3, E441, Ever). Grove.

Casement: The Flawed Hero. Roger Sawyer. 224p. 1984. 25.00x o.p. (ISBN 0-7102-0013-7). Routledge Chapman & Hall.

Cases & Exercises in Personnel & Human Resources Management. 3rd. ed. Ed. by William F. Glueck & George E. Stevens. 1983. pap. 17.95 o.p. (ISBN 0-256-02430-8). Irwin.

Cases & Materials on Equal Employment. 4th ed. Ginsburg. 863p. 1980. 50.00 o.p. (ISBN 0-935165-02-9). GWU Gov Contracts.

Cases & Materials on Family Law. 2nd ed. Caleb Foote et al. 1975. 29.95 o.p. (ISBN 0-316-28850-0); Supplement, 1980. pap. 7.95 o.p. (ISBN 0-316-28852-7); Statutory Appendix. text ed. 5.50 o.p. (ISBN 0-316-28849-7). Little.

Cases & Materials on Federal Labor Standards. 2nd ed. Ginsburg. 502p. 1976. 30.00 o.p. (ISBN 0-935165-03-7). GWU Gov Contracts.

Cases & Materials on Future Interests. Ashbel G. Gulliver. 624p. 1959. 24.95 o.p. (ISBN 0-314-28212-2). West Pub.

Cases & Materials on Judicial Administration & the Administration of Justice. Dorothy W. Nelson. 1032p. 1974. 35.94 o.p. (ISBN 0-314-28276-9). West Pub.

Cases & Materials on Legal Method & Legal System. William T. Fryer & Herman Orentlicher. 1043p. 1967. write for info. o.p. West Pub.

Cases & Materials on Sale of Goods. John Adams. 176p. 1982. pap. 15.50 o.p. (ISBN 0-7099-0509-2, Pub. by Croom Helm Ltd). Routledge Chapman & Hall.

Cases & Materials on Taxation: Individuals, Corporations, Partnerships. 4th ed. Adrian A. Kragen & John K. McNulty. LC 85-8116. (American Casebook Ser.). 1269p. 1985. text ed. 33.95 o.p. (ISBN 0-314-90223-6). West Pub.

Cases & Materials on the English Legal System. 4th ed. Michael Zander. LC 81-147981. (Law in Context Ser.). (Illus.). xxx, 631p. 1984. 32.50x o.p. (ISBN 0-297-78457-9, Pub. by Weidenfeld & Nicolson England). Rothman.

Cases & Materials on Torts & Related Law. Dix W. Noel et al. (Contemporary Legal Education Ser.). 721p. 1981. text ed. 23.00x o.s.i. (ISBN 0-672-84202-5). Michie Co.

Cases & Materials on Torts: 1981 Supplement. Charles O. Gregory et al. 1982. pap. 6.95 o.p. (ISBN 0-316-32782-4). Little.

Cases & Policies in Human Resource Management. 3rd ed. Raymond L. Hilgert et al. LC 77-72903. (Illus.). 1978. pap. 13.95 o.p. (ISBN 0-395-25070-6). HM.

Cases & Policies in Personal-Human Resources Management. 5th ed. Raymond L. Hilgert et al. LC 85-80610. 400p. 1986. pap. 25.96 o.p. (ISBN 0-395-40418-5). HM.

Cases & Policies in Personnel-Human Resources Management. 4th ed. Raymond L. Hilgert et al. LC 81-84466. 1982. pap. 19.50 o.p. (ISBN 0-395-31738-X). HM.

Cases & Problems in Contemporary Retailing. 2nd ed. J. Barry Mason et al. 1987. pap. 17.95 o.p. (ISBN 0-317-61162-3). Irwin.

Cases & Readings for Marketing for Nonprofit Organizations. Philip Kotler et al. (Illus.). 480p. 1983. pap. text ed. (ISBN 0-13-119081-4). P-H.

Cases & Readings in Management Science. 2nd ed. Turban & Loomba. 1982. 22.95 o.p. (ISBN 0-256-02392-1). Irwin.

Cases for Diagnosis. Huntington Sheldon & Simon Braun. (Illus.). 302p. 1983. pap. 24.95x o.p. (ISBN 0-8385-1083-3). Appleton & Lange.

Cases for Discussion. J. R. Lewis. 1965. 14.75 o.p. (ISBN 0-08-011352-4); pap. text ed. 6.25 o.p. (ISBN 0-08-011351-6). Pergamon.

Cases in Civil Liberties. 4th ed. Robert F. Cushman. LC 84-11468. 1985. pap. text ed. (ISBN 0-13-118605-1). P-H.

Cases in Collective Bargaining & Industrial Relations: A Decisional Approach. 5th ed. Sterling H. Schoen & Raymond L. Hilgert. 1985. pap. 20.95 o.p. (ISBN 0-256-03503-2). Irwin.

Cases in Constitutional Law. 6th ed. Robert F. Cushman. 704p. 1984. text ed. (ISBN 0-13-118307-9). P-H.

Cases in Contemporary Business. 3rd ed. James M. Higgins et al. 210p. 1982. pap. text ed. 14.95x o.p. (ISBN 0-03-059768-4); solutions manual 20.00 o.p. (ISBN 0-03-059754-4). Dryden Pr.

Cases in Database Design. Slusky. (Illus.). 176p. 1988. pap. text ed. 14.95 o.p. (ISBN 0-8016-4655-3). Mosby.

Cases in Financial Accounting. 2nd ed. Thomas Dykman & Robert Swieringa. 1988. 17.95 o.p. (ISBN 0-256-06489-X). Irwin.

Cases in Financial Management. Jerry A. Viscione & George A. Aragon. LC 79-87854. 1980. text ed. 25.95 o.p. (ISBN 0-395-26715-3). HM.

Cases in Financial Management. 2nd ed. Jerry A. Viscione & George A. Aragon. LC 83-81685. 608p. 1984. pap. 42.36 o.p. (ISBN 0-395-34267-8); instr's. manual 3.96 o.p. (ISBN 0-395-34268-6). HM.

Cases in Financial Reporting. Charles H. Gibson & Patricia A. Frishkoff. 339p. 1981. pap. text ed. 15.95x o.p. (ISBN 0-534-00972-7). PWS-Kent Pub.

Cases in Health Services Management. Jonathon Rakich et al. (Illus.). 350p. 1983. pap. write for info. o.p. (ISBN 0-7216-7434-8). Saunders.

Cases in Managerial Finance. 5th ed. Eugene F. Brigham et al. 300p. 1982. text ed. 17.95 o.p. (ISBN 0-03-060101-0); instr's. manual 20.00 o.p. (ISBN 0-03-060102-9). Dryden Pr.

Cases in Managerial Finance. Engler & Boquist. 1982. 34.95 o.p. (ISBN 0-256-02784-6). Irwin.

Cases in Marketing Management. rev. ed. Kenneth L. Bernhardt & Thomas C. Kinnear. 1981. 20.95x o.p. (ISBN 0-256-02419-7). Irwin.

Cases in Marketing Management. 3rd ed. Kenneth L. Bernhardt & Thomas C. Kinnear. 1985. 36.95x o.s.i. (ISBN 0-256-03055-3). Irwin.

Cases in Operations Management. Vincent A. Mabert & Michael J. Showalter. 1984. 15.95 o.p. (ISBN 0-256-02898-2). Irwin.

Cases in Organizational & Administrative Behavior. Robert Wegner & Leonard Sayles. LC 71-158913. 1971. pap. text ed. (ISBN 0-13-118562-4). P-H.

Cases in Organizations: Behavior, Structure, Processes. Bernard White et al. 1976. pap. text ed. 7.95x o.p. (ISBN 0-256-01696-8). Irwin.

Cases in Promotional Strategy. rev. ed. James P. Engel & W. Wayne Talarzyk. 1984. pap. 17.50 o.p. (ISBN 0-256-03100-2). Irwin.

Cases in Public Management. 3rd ed. Robert T. Golembiewski & Michael White. 1980. pap. 11.50 o.p. (ISBN 0-395-30807-0). HM.

Cases in Public Policy-Making. 2nd ed. James E. Anderson. 1982. pap. text ed. 16.95 o.p. (ISBN 0-03-058208-3). HR&W.

Cases in Retailing Strategy. Michael J. Etzel & Arch G. Woodside. 304p. 1984. text ed. write for info. o.p. (ISBN 0-02-334380-X); pap. text ed. write for info. o.p. (ISBN 0-02-334370-2). Macmillan.

Cases in Strategic Management. 2nd ed ed. A. J. Strickland & Arthur A. Thompson, Jr. 1985. 23.95x o.s.i. (ISBN 0-256-03172-X). Irwin.

Cases in Strategy & Policy. Strickland & Thompson. 1982. pap. 13.50 o.p. (ISBN 0-256-02753-6). Irwin.

Cases in Structured Systems Design. 2nd ed. James C. Wetherbe. (Illus.). 128p. 1984. pap. text ed. 18.50 o.p. (ISBN 0-314-77860-8). West Pub.

Cases on Agency & Partnership. Warren A. Seavey et al. 599p. 1962. write for info. o.p. West Pub.

Cases on Civil Procedure. Delmar Karlen et al. 923p. 1975. write for info. o.p. West pub.

Cases on Property, 2 vols. Ralph W. Aigler et al. 1339p. 1960. write for info. o.p. West Pub.

Cases on Torts: A Baker's Dozen. 2nd ed. C. M. Hudspeth. 127p. (Orig.). 1976. pap. 9.00x o.p. (ISBN 0-87201-871-7). Gulf Pub.

Casework in Context: A Basis for Practice. Fred Tilbury & Derek Edward. 250p. 1977. 85.00 o.p. (ISBN 0-08-019744-2); pap. text ed. 85.00 o.p. (ISBN 0-08-019743-4). Pergamon.

Cash Application Using MICR Number. Credit Research Foundation. 22p. 1975. 40.00 o.p. (ISBN 0-939050-05-6). Credit Res NYS.

Cash Application Using Remit Card. Credit Research Foundation. 11p. 1975. 40.00 o.p. (ISBN 0-939050-06-4). Credit Res NYS.

Cash Credit Riches Success System. Tyler G. Hicks. 160p. 1987. pap. 100.00 o.p. (ISBN 0-934311-44-7). Intl Wealth.

Cash from Square Foot Gardening. Mel Bartholomew. Date not set. (Garden Way). Storey Comm Inc.

Cash Management: A Practical Guide to Increasing Profits. Edward D. Peterson. (CPA Foundation Ser.). (Illus.). 224p. 1984. 34.95 o.p. (ISBN 0-534-03376-8, Lifetime Learn). Van Nos Reinhold.

Cash: Planning, Forecasting & Control. W. C. Hartley. 210p. 1976. text ed. 31.50x o.p. (ISBN 0-220-66288-6, Pub. by Busn Bks England). Gower Pub Co.

Cashews & Lentils, Apples & Oats. Diana Dalsass. (Illus.). 1981. 14.95 o.p. (ISBN 0-8092-5935-4); pap. 7.95 o.p. (ISBN 0-8092-5934-6). Contemp Bks.

Cashing in. Antonia Gowar. 528p. 1982. 14.95 o.p. (ISBN 0-395-32112-3). HM.

Cashworthiness - Second Impact Litigation 1985: Developments, Trends, & Problems. 861p. 1985. 40.00 o.p. (H4-4981). PLI.

Casilda of the Rising Moon. Elizabeth B. De Trevino. LC 67-10389. 224p. (gr. 7 up). 1967. 3.95 o.p. (ISBN 0-374-31188-9). FS&G.

Casino Games. John Gollehon. LC 86-80200. 176p. 1986. pap. 6.95 o.p. (ISBN 0-914839-12-8). Gollehon Pr.

Casino Royale. Ian Fleming. (James Bond Agent 007 Ser.). pap. 3.50 o.s.i. (ISBN 0-425-08162-1). Jove Pubns.

Casket of Reminiscences. Henry S. Foote. LC 68-58057. Repr. of 1874 ed. 35.00x o.p. (ISBN 0-8371-0421-1, FOR&, Pub. by Negro U Pr). Greenwood.

Caspar Schwenckfeld on the Person & Work of Christ. Paul A. Maier. 115p. 1959. Concordia Schl Grad Studies.

Casper & Richie Rich: Million Dollar Fun. Harvey Comics Staff. 128p. 1982. pap. 1.50 o.s.i. (ISBN 0-448-16988-6, Pub. by Tempo). Ace Bks.

Casper & Wendy. (gr. k-3). 0.79 o.p. (ISBN 0-8431-4117-4, 805-X). Wonder.

Casper Far Out Fables. Harvey Comics Staff. 1981. pap. 1.25 o.s.i. (ISBN 0-448-17251-8, Pub. by Tempo). Ace Bks.

Casper in Fun & Monsters. Harvey Comics Staff. 128p. 1983. pap. 1.95 o.s.i. (ISBN 0-441-09239-X). Ace Bks.

Casper in What's Up. Harvey Comics Staff. 128p. 1985. pap. 1.95 o.p. (ISBN 0-317-31703-2); pap. text ed. 2.25 o.p. (ISBN 0-317-31704-0). Ace Bks.

Casper, No. Four: Casper & Wendy. Harvey Comics Staff. (Illus.). 128p. (Orig.). (gr. 2 up). 1974. pap. 0.95 o.s.i. (ISBN 0-448-14527-8, Pub. by Tempo). Ace Bks.

Casper No. Thirteen: Laughquakes. Harvey Comics Staff. 128p. 1982. pap. 1.50 o.s.i. (ISBN 0-448-16842-1). Ace Bks.

Casper, No. Two: TV Tales. Harvey Comics Staff. 128p. 1983. pap. 1.75 o.s.i. (ISBN 0-441-09232-2). Ace Bks.

Caspian Circle. Donne Raffat. 1978. 10.00 o.p. (ISBN 0-395-25933-9). HM.

Cassadaga: An Inside Look at the South's Oldest Psychic Community with True Experiences of People Who Have Been There. Robert Harrold. (Illus.). 1979. pap. 4.95 o.p. (ISBN 0-916224-49-X). Banyan Bks.

Cassell & the Publishers Association Directory of Publishing 1987. 361p. 1986. pap. 39.00 o.p. (ISBN 0-304-31134-0). Intl Pubns Serv.

Cassell's New Compact French Dictionary: French-English, English-French. Cassells Editors. 672p. (Fr. & Eng.). 1981. pap. 1.25 o.p. (ISBN 0-440-31128-4, LE). Dell.

Cassell's New Compact German Dictionary. Cassells Editors. 560p. (Ger.). 1981. pap. 3.95 o.p. (ISBN 0-440-31100-4, LE). Dell.

Cassell's New Compact Latin Dictionary. Cassells Editors. 384p. (Lat.). 1981. pap. 4.50 o.p. (ISBN 0-440-31101-2, LE). Dell.

Titles

Cassell's New Compact Spanish Dictionary: Spanish-English, English-Spanish. Cassells Editors. 444p. (Span. & Eng.). 1981. pap. 3.95 o.p. (ISBN 0-440-31129-2, LE). Dell.
Casseroles & Vegetables for Foodservice Menu Planning. Eulalia C. Blair. LC 76-29357. (Cahners Foodservice Menu Planning Ser). 288p. 1983. 19.95 o.p. (ISBN 0-8436-2121-4). Van Nos Reinhold.
Cassidy. Morris West. LC 86-8873. 312p. 1986. 17.95 o.s.i. (ISBN 0-385-23403-1). Doubleday.
Cassino: The Hollow Victory-The Battle for Rome, January-June 1944. John Ellis. (Illus.). 624p. 1984. text ed. 19.95 o.p. (ISBN 0-07-019427-0). McGraw.
Cast a Cold Eye. Marjorie Eccles. (Crime Club Ser.). 192p. 1988. pap. 12.95 o.p. (ISBN 0-385-24321-9). Doubleday.
Cast a Long Shadow. Wayne D. Overholser. 1981. pap. 1.95 o.p. (ISBN 0-440-11423-3). Dell.
Cast Iron Wonder: Chevrolet's Fabulous Six, 1929-1953. Doug Bell. Ed. by Clymer Publications. (Illus.). pap. 5.00 o.p. (ISBN 0-89287-267-5, H542). Clymer Pub.
Cast Metals for Structural & Pressure Containment Application: MPC-11. G. V. Smith. 484p. 1979. 50.00 o.p. (ISBN 0-317-33448-4, G00161); members 25.00 o.p. (ISBN 0-317-33449-2). ASME.
Cast of Stars. Allan Prior. LC 82-1029. (William Abrahams Bk.). 444p. 1983. 16.95 o.s.i. (ISBN 0-03-061943-2). H Holt & Co.
Cast Your Bread Upon the Waters. Ruth Y. Nelson & Clarence Nelson. LC 75-22719. 1976. pap. 3.95 o.p. (ISBN 0-8066-1502-8, 10-0973, Augsburg). Augsburg Fortress.
Castaway. James G. Cozzens. LC 67-19207. 1967. uniform ed. 3.50 o.p. (ISBN 0-15-115997-1). HarBraceJ.
Castaway. James G. Cozzens. LC 67-19207. 1968. pap. 1.15 o.p. (ISBN 0-15-615450-1, Harv). HarBraceJ.
Castaway. Lucy Irvine. (General Ser.). 1984. lib. bdg. 18.95 o.p. (ISBN 0-8161-3782-X, Large Print Bks). G K Hall.
Castaway's see Graded Readers for Students of English As a Second Language.
Castaways in Lilliput. Henry Winterfeld. Tr. by Kyrill Schabert. LC 60-8413. (Illus.). (gr. 4-6). 1960. 5.95 o.p. (ISBN 0-15-214820-5, HJ). HarBraceJ.
Castaways on Chimp Island. Sandy Landsman. (gr. 7 up). 1987. 2.50 o.p. (ISBN 0-671-63638-3). Archway.
Castillas Spanish & English Technical Dictionary. 1600p. 1958. (ISBN 0-8022-0221-7). Philos Lib.
Castine. Patricia Chute. LC 86-13586. 288p. 1987. 16.95 o.p. (ISBN 0-385-19820-5). Doubleday.
Casting of Steel. W. C. Newell. 599p. 1957. (ISBN 0-8022-1202-6). Philos Lib.
Casting Techniques. Glynis Beecroft. (Encore Edition). (Illus.). 1979. 4.50 o.p. (ISBN 0-684-17526-6, ScribT). Scribner.
Castle. Franz Kafka. LC 70-3630. 1969. 4.95 o.p. (ISBN 0-394-60388-5). Modern Lib.
Castle Cloud. Elizabeth Norman. 1977. pap. 2.50 o.p. (ISBN 0-380-00889-0, 50062-0). Avon.
Castle D'Or. Arthur Quiller-Couch & Daphne Du Maurier. 274p. 1976. Repr. of 1962 ed. lib. bdg. 17.50x o.p. (ISBN 0-89244-091-0). Queens Hse-Focus Serv.
Castle Explorer's Guide to England, Scotland, & Wales. Frank Bottomley. 1979. pap. 9.95 o.p. (ISBN 0-7182-1219-3, Pub. by Kaye & Ward). David & Charles.
Castle in Medieval England & Wales. Colin Platt. (Illus.). 224p. 1983. 25.00 o.p. (ISBN 0-684-17799-4, ScribT). Scribner.
Castle of Argol. Julien Gracq. Tr. by Louise Varese from Fr. 155p. Date not set. 19.95 o.p. (ISBN 0-932499-61-9); pap. 3.95 o.p. (ISBN 0-932499-62-7). Lapis Pr.
Castle of Bone. Penelope Farmer. LC 78-190553. (gr. 5-9). 1972. 4.95 o.p. (ISBN 0-689-30313-0, Atheneum). Macmillan.
Castle of Crossed Destinies. Italo Calvino. LC 76-27423. (Helen & Kurt Wolff Bk.). (Illus.). 1979. Repr. 10.00 o.p. (ISBN 0-15-115998-X). HarBraceJ.
Castle of Evil. Sandra Abbott. 1974. pap. 0.95 o.p. (ISBN 0-380-01087-9, 18044). Avon.
Castle of Hape. Shirley R. Murphy. 160p. 1981. pap. 1.95 o.p. (ISBN 0-380-54783-X, 54783). Avon.
Castle on the Border. Margot Benary-Isbert. LC 56-5871. 1956. 5.95 o.p. (ISBN 0-15-214999-6, HJ). HarBraceJ.
Castle on the Prairie. Lois S. Harman. (Illus.). 1985. pap. 6.95 o.p. (ISBN 0-682-40217-6). Exposition-Phoenix.
Castledown. Joyce B. Gregorian. LC 76-47627. (Illus.). (gr. 5 up). 1977. 8.95 o.p. (ISBN 0-689-30566-4, Atheneum). Macmillan.
Castlemaker. Nell Harris. LC 85-62997. 350p. (Orig.). 1986. 16.95x o.p. (ISBN 1-55666-015-4); pap. 10.95x o.p. Authors Unltd.
Castlemilk: Family, Community & Unemployment. David Binns & Gerald Mars. 240p. 1987. lib. bdg. 49.95x o.p. (ISBN 0-317-64371-1, Pub. by Croom Helm UK). Routledge Chapman & Hall.
Castlemilk: Family, Community & Unemployment. David Burns & Gerald Mars. 240p. 1987. 39.50 o.p. (ISBN 0-7099-3582-X, Pub. by Croom Helm UK). Routledge Chapman & Hall.
Castles. Neal Travis. 304p. 1982. pap. 4.75 o.p. (ISBN 0-380-79913-8, 80416-6). Avon.
Castles & Historic Places in Wales. rev. ed. Wales Tourist Board Staff. (Illus.). 92p. 1981. pap. 3.95 o.p. (ISBN 0-900784-77-6, Pub. by Automobile Assn Brit). Salem Hse Pubs.
Castles Burning. Arthur Lyons. LC 79-1935. (Rinehart Suspense Novel Ser.). 224p. 1982. pap. 3.95 o.p. (ISBN 0-03-062417-7, Pub. by Owl Bks). H Holt & Co.
Castles in Spain. Orvill E. Ault. 1976. 7.50 o.p. (ISBN 0-682-48496-2). Exposition-Phoenix.
Castles in the Air. Irene Castle. (Illus.). 264p. 1980. pap. 6.95 o.p. (ISBN 0-306-80122-1). Da Capo.
Castles in the Air. Patricia Gallagher. 1976. pap. 2.50 o.p. (ISBN 0-380-00570-0, 83808-7). Avon.
Castles in the Air & Other Tales. Stephen Krensky. LC 78-11836. (Illus.). (gr. 4-6). 1979. 6.95 o.p. (ISBN 0-689-30684-9, Atheneum). Macmillan.
Castles of Ireland. Brian De Breffny. (Illus.). 1986. pap. 12.95 o.s.i. (ISBN 0-500-27398-7). Thames Hudson.
Casual Work & Poverty in Third World Cities. Ed. by Ray Bromley & Chris Gerry. LC 78-11329. 323p. 1979. 78.95 o.p. (ISBN 0-471-99731-5, Pub. by Wiley-Interscience). Wiley.
Casualties of War. Daniel Lang. 1969. pap. text ed. 5.95 o.p. (ISBN 0-07-036235-1). McGraw.
Casualty: A Memoir of Love & War. Corinne Browne. 1981. 12.95 o.p. (ISBN 0-393-01422-3). Norton.
Cat. Helen Chetin. 1977. pap. 1.00 o.p. (ISBN 0-931832-06-3). Fithian Pr.
Cat. Sara B. Stein. LC 84-19146. (Illus.). 32p. (ps-3). 1985. 6.95 o.p. (ISBN 0-15-215150-8, HJ). HarBraceJ.
Cat & Dog. David Lloyd. (First Words Ser.). (Illus.). 32p. (ps-2). 1983. 1.50 o.s.i. (ISBN 0-671-47104-X, Little Simon). S&S.
Cat & Mouse. Gunter Grass. Tr. by Ralph Manheim. 189p. 1963. 10.95 o.p. (ISBN 0-15-116100-3). HarBraceJ.
Cat & the Fiddle. Illus. by Blanche F. Wright. (Real Mother Goose Pop-Ups Ser.). (Illus.). 12p. (ps-1). 1985. 5.95 o.p. (ISBN 0-528-82602-6, Checkerboard Pr). Macmillan.
Cat at Bat. David N. Bruskin. (Story Bus Subseries: School Bus). (Illus.). 10p. (ps-2). 1988. bds. 14.95 o.p. (ISBN 1-55929-012-9). Bound Fun Inc.
Cat Chaser. Elmore Leonard. LC 81-71687. 1982. 13.95 o.p. (ISBN 0-87795-398-8, Arbor Hse). Morrow.
Cat Chaser. Elmore Leonard. (General Ser.). 364p. 1986. lib. bdg. 16.95 o.p. (ISBN 0-8161-3947-4, Large Print Bks). G K Hall.
Cat Country: A Satirical Novel of China in the 1930's. Lao She. Tr. by William A. Lyell, Jr. LC 78-83144. 339p. 1970. 8.00 o.p. (ISBN 0-8142-0013-3). Ohio St U Pr.
Cat from Outer Space. Ted Key. (gr. 5-7). 1978. pap. 1.95 o.p. (ISBN 0-671-43289-3). Archway.
Cat: History, Biology & Behavior. Muriel Beadle. LC 76-53770. 1977. 9.95 o.p. (ISBN 0-671-22451-4). S&S.
Cat in Fairyland & Other Tales. Enid Blyton. (Read for Fun Ser.). (Illus.). 64p. (ps). 1987. 6.95 o.p. (ISBN 0-09-167210-4, Pub. by Century Hutchinson). David & Charles.
Cat Man. Edward Hoagland. 1984. pap. 6.95 o.p. (ISBN 0-87795-601-4, Arbor Hse). Morrow.
C.A.T. No. 1: Tower of Blood. Spike Andrews. (Men of Action Ser.). 224p. (Orig.). 1982. pap. 1.95 o.p. (ISBN 0-446-30182-5). Warner Bks.
Cat Out of Water. David N. Bruskin. (Story Bus Subseries: Camp Bus). (Illus.). 10p. (ps-2). 1988. bds. 14.95 o.p. (ISBN 1-55929-010-2). Bound Fun Inc.
Cat Scan: Three Thousand Years of the Best Things Ever Said about Cats. Robert Byrne & Teressa Skelton. LC 83-45064. 208p. 1983. 11.95 o.s.i. (ISBN 0-689-11390-0, Atheneum). Macmillan.
Cat Walked Through the Casserole: And Other Poems for Children. Pamela Espeland & Marilyn Waniek. LC 84-11381. (Illus.). 40p. (gr. k-4). 1984. PLB 9.95 o.p. (ISBN 0-87614-268-4). Carolrhoda Bks.
Cat Yellow Pages: The Cat Owner's Guide to Goods & Services. Marna S. Fogarty. (Illus.). 224p. 1984. 19.95 o.s.i. (ISBN 0-684-18094-4, ScribT); pap. 12.95 o.s.i. (ISBN 0-684-18158-4). Scribner.
Cataclysm as Catalyst: The Theme of War in William Faulkner's Fiction. T. Nordanberg. (Acta Universitatis Upsaliensis-Studia Anglistica Upsaliensia,). 173p. 1983. pap. text ed. 18.50x o.p. (ISBN 91-554-1451-6). Humanities.
Catacombs: Life & Death in Early Christianity. James Stevenson. 180p. 1985. pap. 8.95 o.p. (ISBN 0-8407-7500-8). Nelson.
Catalan. Eric Schiller. (Illus.). 100p. (Orig.). 1983. pap. 5.50 o.p. (ISBN 0-931462-26-6). Chess Ent Inc.
Catalog. Jasper Tomkins. Date not set. pap. 5.95 o.p. (ISBN 0-310-57021-2, 16102P). Zondervan.
Catalog for the Institute for Contemporary History, 4 pts. Institute for Contemporary History, Munich Staff. Incl. Pt. 1. Alphabetical Catalog, 5 vols. 1970. Set. 420.00 (ISBN 0-8161-0724-6); Pt. 2. Subject Catalog, 2 Vols. 1970. Set. 540.00 (ISBN 0-8161-0176-0); Pt. 3. Regional Catalog, 2 vols. 1970. Set. 145.00 (ISBN 0-8161-0177-9); Pt. 4. Biographical Catalog. 1970. 100.00 (ISBN 0-8161-0178-7). 1970 (Hall Library). G K Hall.
Catalog Marketer Suppliers Guide, 1983. Ed. by Sroge, Maxwell H., Staff. 160p. 1983. perfect bound 29.95 o.p. (ISBN 0-942674-04-9). Sroge M.
Catalog of African Government Documents. 3rd, rev. ed. Boston University Libraries Staff. 1977. lib. bdg. 82.00 o.p. (ISBN 0-8161-0036-5, Hall Library). G K Hall.
Catalog of Architectural Drawings: The Athenaeum of Philadelphia. Athenaeum of Philadelphia Staff. (G. K. Hall Library Catalogs Ser.). 1430p. 1986. lib. bdg. 300.00 o.p. (ISBN 0-8161-0448-4, Hall Library). G K Hall.
Catalog of Books & Manuscripts at the Keats-Shelley Memorial House in Rome. Keats-Shelley Memorial House Staff. 1969. lib. bdg. 78.00 o.s.i. (ISBN 0-8161-0856-0, Hall Library). G K Hall.
Catalog of Brazilian Acquisitions of the Library of Congress, 1964-1974. Library of Congress, Washington, D. C., Staff. 1976. 100.00 o.p. (ISBN 0-8161-0033-0, Hall Library). G K Hall.
Catalog of Broadsides in the Rare Book Division, 4 vols. Library of Congress Staff. 1972. Set. lib. bdg. 445.00 o.p. (ISBN 0-8161-0990-7, Hall Library). G K Hall.
Catalog of Broadsides of American Verse in the Harris Collection of American Poetry & Plays, 5 Vols. John Hay Library, Brown University Staff. (Library Catalogs). 1987. lib. bdg. 900.00 o.p. (ISBN 0-8161-0984-2, Hall Library); 35mm microfilm 5 reels 650.00 o.p. (ISBN 0-8161-1469-2). G K Hall.
Catalog of California Grants Assistance 1987. Ed. by Vera Nicholas. 92p. 1987. pap. 8.95x o.p. (ISBN 0-929722-11-6). CA State Library Fndtn.
Catalog of California State Grants Assistance, 1987. California State Library Staff. 92p. 1987. write for info. o.p. CA State Library Fndtn.
Catalog of Early German Books in the Library of C. Fairfax Murray, 2 Vols. Hugh W. Davies. 240.00x o.p. (ISBN 0-87556-067-9). Saifer.
Catalog of Folklore, Folklife & Folk Songs, 3 vols. 2nd ed. Ed. by Alice N. Loranth. 1978. Set. lib. bdg. 255.00 o.p. (ISBN 0-8161-0249-X, Hall Library). G K Hall.
Catalog of Government Publications, Economics Division, 40 vols. New York Public Library, Research Libraries Staff. 1972. Set. lib. bdg. 3955.00 o.p. (ISBN 0-8161-0781-5, Hall Library). G K Hall.
Catalog of Law Books: Reference Catalogue of Law Books Published Prior to 1894. H. E. Griswold. LC 76-52290. 1977. Repr. of 1894 ed. lib. bdg. 40.00 o.p. (ISBN 0-930342-31-3). W S Hein.
Catalog of Manuscripts & Archives in F. Clark Wood Institute at College of Physicians in Philadelphia. Ed. by Rudolf Hirsch. 250p. 1982. 39.95x o.p. (ISBN 0-8122-7817-8). U of Pa Pr.
Catalog of Manuscripts of the Folger Shakespeare Library, 3 vols. Folger Shakespeare Library Editors, Washington, D. C. (Library Catalogs). 1970 Set. lib. bdg. 270.00 o.p. (ISBN 0-8161-0888-9, Hall Library). G K Hall.
Catalog of Manuscripts of the Massachusetts Historical Society: First Supplement. Massachusetts Historical Society Staff. 1980. lib. bdg. 230.00 o.p. (ISBN 0-8161-0850-1, Hall Library). G K Hall.
Catalog of Maps, Ships' Papers & Logbooks. Mariners Museum Library - Newport News - Virginia Staff. 1964. lib. bdg. 100.00 o.p. (ISBN 0-8161-0686-X, Hall Library). G K Hall.
Catalog of Mass Media College Courses. 3rd ed. Ed. by James Zigerell. 114p. 1983. pap. 20.00 o.p. (ISBN 0-87117-127-9). Am Assn Comm Jr Coll.
Catalog of Operational Transfer Functions. Don Watts. LC 76-25745. (Reference Library of Science & Technology: Vol. 9). (Illus.). 1977. lib. bdg. 32.00 o.p. (ISBN 0-8240-9901-X). Garland Pub.
Catalog of Original & Early Editions of Some of the Poetical & Prose Works from Langland to Prior, 4 Vols. in 1. Grolier Club Staff. 60.00x o.p. (ISBN 0-87556-116-0). Saifer.
Catalog of Periodical Literature in the Social & Behavioral Sciences Section, Library of the Institute for Sex Research, Including Supplement to Monographs, 1973-1975, 4 vols. Indiana University, Institute for Sex Research Staff. 1976. Set. lib. bdg. 395.00 o.p. (ISBN 0-8161-0041-1, Hall Library). G K Hall.
Catalog of Phonorecording of Music & Oral Data Held by the Archives of Traditional Music. Indiana University, Folklore Institute, Archives of Traditional Music Staff. 1977. lib. bdg. 34.50 o.p. (ISBN 0-8161-1120-0, Hall Reference). G K Hall.
Catalog of Printed Books of the Folger Shakespeare Library, 28 vols. Folger Shakespeare Library Editors, Washington, D. C. 1970. Set. lib. bdg. 2340.00 o.p. (ISBN 0-8161-0887-0, Hall Library). G K Hall.
Catalog of Printed Books of the Folger Shakespeare Library, First Supplement. 1976. lib. bdg. 360.00 o.p. (ISBN 0-8161-0949-4, Hall Library). G K Hall.
Catalog of Special & Private Presses in the Rare Book Division, the Research Libraries of the New York Public Library, 2 vols. 1978. Set. lib. bdg. 178.00 o.p. (ISBN 0-8161-0097-7, Hall Library). G K Hall.
Catalog of Teratogenic Agents. 5th ed. Thomas H. Shepard. LC 85-45863. 736p. 1986. text ed. 45.00x o.p. (ISBN 0-8018-3350-7). Johns Hopkins.
Catalog of the Arthur & Elizabeth Schlesinger Library on the History of Women in America: The Manuscript Inventories & the Catalogs of Manuscripts, Books, & Periodicals, 10 vols. 2nd ed. Radcliffe College Editors. 7500p. 1983. lib. bdg. 2080.00 o.p. (ISBN 0-8161-0425-5, Hall Library). G K Hall.
Catalog of the Avery Memorial Architectural Library, 19 Vols. 2nd, enl. ed. Columbia University Editors. 1977. Set. 1590.00 o.p. (ISBN 0-8161-0779-3, Hall Library). G K Hall.
Catalog of the Chinese Collection, 13 Vols. Stanford University, Hoover Institution on War, Revolution & Peace Staff. 1969. Set. 1230.00 o.p. (ISBN 0-8161-0168-X, Hall Library). G K Hall.
Catalog of the Chinese Collection First Supplement, 2 vols. Stanford University, Hoover Institution on War, Revolution & Peace Staff. 1972. Set. lib. bdg. 295.00 o.p. (ISBN 0-8161-1046-8, Hall Library). G K Hall.
Catalog of the Chinese Collection: Second Supplement, 2 vols. Stanford University, Hoover Institution on War, Revolution & Peace Staff. 1977. Set. lib. bdg. 275.00 o.p. (ISBN 0-8161-0039-X, Hall Library). G K Hall.
Catalog of the Communications Library, 3 vols. Ed. by University of Illinois, Communications Library Staff. 1975. Set. lib. bdg. 330.00 o.p. (ISBN 0-8161-1174-X, Hall Library). G K Hall.
Catalog of the Defoe Collection in the Boston Public Library. Boston Public Library Staff. 1970. 69.00 o.p. (ISBN 0-8161-0731-9, Hall Library). G K Hall.
Catalog of the E. Azalia Hackley Memorial Collection of Negro Music, Dance & Drama. Detroit Public Library Staff. 1979. lib. bdg. 100.00 o.p. (ISBN 0-8161-0299-6, Hall Library). G K Hall.
Catalog of the Edgar Fahs Smith Memorial Collection in the History of Chemistry. University of Pennsylvania Staff. 1970. 89.00 o.p. (ISBN 0-8161-0522-7, Hall Library). G K Hall.
Catalog of the Foreign Relations Library, First Supplement. Council on Foreign Relations, Inc. Staff. 1980. lib. bdg. 340.00 o.s.i. (ISBN 0-8161-0306-2, Hall Library). G K Hall.
Catalog of the Foreign Relations Library, 9 Vols. Council on Foreign Relations, Inc., Staff. 1970. Set. lib. bdg. 870.00 o.p. (ISBN 0-8161-0840-4, Hall Library). G K Hall.
Catalog of the Hampton L. Carson Collection Illustrative of the the Growth of the Common Law, 2 Vols. Free Library of Philadelphia Staff. 1970. Set. 200.00 o.p. (ISBN 0-8161-0490-5, Hall Library). G K Hall.
Catalog of the Harvard University Fine Arts Library, 15 vols. Harvard University Staff. 1971. Set. lib. bdg. 1750.00 o.p. (ISBN 0-8161-0919-2, Hall Library); Catalogue of Auction Sales Catalogues 105.00 o.p. (ISBN 0-8161-0105-1). G K Hall.

Catalog of the Hoose Library of Philosophy, 6 Vols. University of Southern California, Los Angeles Staff. 1970. Set. 595.00 o.p. (ISBN 0-8161-0816-1, Hall Library). G K Hall.

Catalog of the Japanese Collection, 7 Vols. Stanford University, Hoover Institution on War, Revolution & Peace Staff. 1970. Set. 695.00 o.p. (ISBN 0-8161-0169-8, Hall Library). G K Hall.

Catalog of the Japanese Collection, First Supplement. Stanford University, Hoover Institution on War, Revolution & Peace Staff. 581p. 1972. lib. bdg. 125.00 o.p. (ISBN 0-8161-1051-4, Hall Library). G K Hall.

Catalog of the Japanese Collection: Second Supplement. Stanford University, Hoover Institution on War, Revolution & Peace Staff. 1977. lib. bdg. 140.00 o.p. (ISBN 0-8161-0040-3, Hall Library). G K Hall.

Catalog of the Latin American Collection of the University of Texas Library, 3 vols, Fourth Suppl. University of Texas at Austin Staff. 1977. lib. bdg. 330.00 o.s.i. (ISBN 0-8161-1156-1, Hall Library). G K Hall.

Catalog of the Latin American Collection of the University of Texas Library: Second Supplement, 3 vols. University of Texas at Austin Staff. 1973. Set. lib. bdg. 340.00 o.p. (ISBN 0-8161-0979-6, Hall Library). G K Hall.

Catalog of the Latin American Collection of the University of Texas Library, Third Supplement, 8 vols. University of Texas at Austin Staff. 1975. Set. lib. bdg. 930.00 o.p. (ISBN 0-8161-1107-3, Hall Library). G K Hall.

Catalog of the Latin American Collection of the University of Texas Library, First Supplement, 5 vols. University of Texas Library, Austin Staff. 1971. 430.00 o.p. (ISBN 0-8161-0889-7, Hall Library). G K Hall.

Catalog of the Latin American Collection of the University of Texas Library, 31 Vols. University of Texas Library, Austin Staff. 1970. Set. lib. bdg. 2960.00 o.p. (ISBN 0-8161-0815-3, Hall Library). G K Hall.

Catalog of the Latin American Library of the Tulane University Library: Third Supplement, 2 vols. Tulane University, New Orleans Staff. 1978. Set. lib. bdg. 275.00 o.p. (ISBN 0-8161-0005-5, Hall Library). G K Hall.

Catalog of the Latin American Library of the Tulane University Library, 9 vols. Tulane University, New Orleans Staff. 1970. Set. lib. bdg. 890.00 o.p. (ISBN 0-8161-0894-3, Hall Library). G K Hall.

Catalog of the Latin American Library of the Tulane University Library, First Supplement, 2 vols. Tulane University, New Orleans Staff. 1973. Set. lib. bdg. 250.00 o.p. (ISBN 0-8161-0914-1, Hall Library). G K Hall.

Catalog of the Latin American Library of the Tulane University Library, Second Supplement. Tulane University, New Orleans Staff. 1975. lib. bdg. 250.00 o.p. (ISBN 0-8161-1052-2, Hall Library). G K Hall.

Catalog of the Library of the Academy of Natural Sciences of Philadelphia, 16 vols. Ed. by Academy of Natural Sciences of Philadelphia Staff. 1972. Set. lib. bdg. 1595.00 o.p. (ISBN 0-8161-0946-X, Hall Library). G K Hall.

Catalog of the Library of the American Hospital Association, Asa S. Bacon Memorial Chicago Library, 5 vols. American Hospital Association Staff. 1976. Set. lib. bdg. 480.00 o.p. (ISBN 0-8161-1210-X, Hall Library). G K Hall.

Catalog of the Library of the Graduate School of Design, Second Supplement, 5 vols. Harvard University, Graduate School of Design Staff. 1974. Set. lib. bdg. 600.00 o.p. (ISBN 0-8161-1173-1, Hall Library). G K Hall.

Catalog of the Library of the Institute for Contemporary History, First Supplement. Institute for Contemporary History, Munich Staff. 1973. lib. bdg. 140.00 alphabetical catalog o.p. (ISBN 0-8161-0920-6, Hall Library); lib. bdg. 255.00 subject catalog (2 vols.) o.p. (ISBN 0-8161-0179-5); lib. bdg. 120.00 biographical catalog & regional catalog o.p. (ISBN 0-8161-1075-1). G K Hall.

Catalog of the Library of the Institute for World Economics, 7 pts. The Institute for World Economics, Kiel, Germany Staff. Incl. Pt. 1. Bibliographical Catalog of Persons, 30 vols. 1970. Set. 2965.00 (ISBN 0-8161-0677-0); Pt. 2. Catalog of Administrative Authorities, 10 vols. 1967. Set. 990.00 (ISBN 0-8161-0189-2); Pt. 3. Catalog of Corporations, 13 vols. 1967. Set. 1285.00 (ISBN 0-8161-0190-6); Pt. 4. Regional Catalog, 52 vols. 1967. Set. 5140.00 (ISBN 0-8161-0191-4); Pt. 5. Subject Catalog, 83 vols. 1968. Set. 7075.00 (ISBN 0-8161-0192-2); Pt. 6. Shelf List of Periodical Holdings, 6 vols. 4734p. 1968. Set. 595.00 (ISBN 0-8161-0193-0); Pt. 7. Title Catalog, 13 vols. 1968. Set. 1285.00 (ISBN 0-8161-0194-9). Hall Library). G K Hall.

Catalog of the Library of the Marine Biological Laboratory & the Woods Hole Oceanographic Institution, 12 vols. Marine Biological Laboratory Staff & Woods Hole Oceanographic Institution, Woods Hole, Massachusetts Staff. 1971. lib. bdg. 1185.00 set o.p. (ISBN 0-8161-0937-0, Hall Library); 55.00 o.p. journal catalog (ISBN 0-8161-0115-9). G K Hall.

Catalog of the Library of the Museum of Modern Art, New York, 14 vols. Ed. by Museum of Modern Art, New York Staff. 1976. Set. lib. bdg. 1190.00 o.p. (ISBN 0-8161-0015-2, Hall Library). G K Hall.

Catalog of the Library of the Royal Entomological Society of London. Royal Entomological Society of London Staff. (Printed Book Catalogs). 1980. lib. bdg. 515.00 o.p. (ISBN 0-8161-0315-1, Hall Library). G K Hall.

Catalog of the Library of the Whitney Museum of American Art, 2 vols. Whitney Museum of American Art Staff. 1979. lib. bdg. 198.00 o.p. (ISBN 0-8161-0288-0, Hall Library). G K Hall.

Catalog of the Manuscript & Archival Collections & Index to the Correspondence of John Torrey. New York Botanical Garden Library Staff. 1973. 68.00 o.p. (ISBN 0-8161-1018-2, Hall Library). G K Hall.

Catalog of the Melville J. Herskovits Library of African Studies, Northwestern University, & Africana in Selected Libraries, Evanston, 8 vols. Northwestern University Staff. 1972. Set. 750.00 o.p. (ISBN 0-8161-0921-4, Hall Library). G K Hall.

Catalog of the Menninger Clinic Library, 4 vols. Menninger Foundation, Topeka, Kansas Staff. 1972. Set. lib. bdg. 395.00 o.p. (ISBN 0-8161-0961-3, Hall Library). G K Hall.

Catalog of the Mosquitoes of the World, Vol. 6. 2nd ed. Kenneth L. Knight & Alan Stone. LC 77-82735. 1977. 20.90 o.p. (ISBN 0-686-04889-X); members 12.50 o.p.; supplement 1978 3.35 o.p. (ISBN 0-686-28524-7); members 2.00 o.p. Entomol Soc.

Catalog of the Mosquitoes of the World see Thomas Say Foundation Publications.

Catalog of the Old Slave Mart Museum & Library. Old Slave Mart Museum & Library Staff. 1978. lib. bdg. 130.00 o.p. (ISBN 0-8161-0073-X, Hall Library). G K Hall.

Catalog of the Oliveira Lima Library, 2 vols. Catholic University of America, Washington, D. C. Staff. 1970. Set. 200.00 o.p. (ISBN 0-8161-0873-0, Hall Library). G K Hall.

Catalog of the Oriental Institute Library, Supplement I, Vol. 1. University of Chicago Staff. 1977. lib. bdg. 110.00 o.p. (ISBN 0-8161-0067-5, Hall Library). G K Hall.

Catalog of the Peace Collection. Swarthmore College Staff. 1982. lib. bdg. 315.00 o.p. (ISBN 0-8161-0377-1, Hall Library). G K Hall.

Catalog of the Police Library of the Los Angeles Public Library, 2 vols. Los Angeles Public Library Staff. 1972. Set. lib. bdg. 200.00 o.p. (ISBN 0-8161-0964-8, Hall Library). G K Hall.

Catalog of the Rare Book Room, 11 vols. Ed. by University of Illinois at Urbana, University Library, Champaign Staff. 1972. Set. 1135.00 o.p. (ISBN 0-8161-0938-9, Hall Library). G K Hall.

Catalog of the Robert Goldwater Library of Primitive Art, 4 vols. Ed. by Metropolitan Museum of Modern Art, New York Staff. 1982. Set. lib. bdg. 415.00 o.s.i. (ISBN 0-8161-0381-X, Hall Library). G K Hall.

Catalog of the Sierra Leone Collection. Fourah Bay College, Library University of Sierra Leone Staff. 1979. lib. bdg. 57.50 o.p. (ISBN 0-8161-8227-2, Hall Reference). G K Hall.

Catalog of the Social & Behavioral Sciences Monograph Section of the Library of the Institute for Sex Research, 4 vols. Indiana University, Institute for Sex Research Staff. 2572p. 1974. Set. lib. bdg. 395.00 o.p. (ISBN 0-8161-1141-3, Hall Library). G K Hall.

Catalog of the Texas Collection in the Barker Texas History Center, 14 vols. University of Texas, Austin Staff. (Library of Texas at Austin). 1979. lib. bdg. 1250.00 o.p. (ISBN 0-8161-0273-2, Hall Library). G K Hall.

Catalog of the Theatre & Drama Collections: First Supplement to Pt. 1, Drama Collection. New York Public Library, Research Libraries Staff. 1973. 110.00 o.p. (ISBN 0-8161-0745-9, Hall Library). G K Hall.

Catalog of the Theatre & Drama Collections, Pt. 3. 30 Vols. Non-book Collection. New York Public Library, Research Libraries Staff. 1976. lib. bdg. 3625.00 o.p. (ISBN 0-8161-1195-2, Hall Library). G K Hall.

Catalog of the Transportation Center Library, Northwestern University. Northwestern University Staff. 1972. Subject Catalog 9 Vols. 890.00 o.p. (ISBN 0-8161-0185-X, Hall Library); Author-title Catalog. 1185.00 o.p. (ISBN 0-8161-0924-9); Set Of 12 Vols. 1185.00 o.p. (ISBN 0-685-01569-6). G K Hall.

Catalog of the United States Geological Survey Library, 25 vols. Ed. by U. S. Department of the Interior, U. S. Geological Survey, Washington, D. C. Staff. 1964. Set. lib. bdg. 2470.00 o.p. (ISBN 0-8161-0712-2, Hall Library). G K Hall.

Catalog of the United States Geological Survey Library: Supplement 1, 11 vols. Ed. by U. S. Department of the Interior, U. S. Geological Survey, Washington, D. C. Staff. 1973. Set. 865.00 o.p. (ISBN 0-8161-0876-5, Hall Library). G K Hall.

Catalog of the United States Geological Survey Library: 2nd Suppl, 4 vols. Ed. by U. S. Department of the Interior, U. S. Geological Survey, Washington, D. C. Staff. 1973. Set. lib. bdg. 430.00 o.p. (ISBN 0-8161-1031-X, Hall Library). G K Hall.

Catalog of the United States Geological Survey 3rd Suppl, 6 vols. Ed. by U. S. Department of the Interior, U. S. Geological Survey, Washington, D. C. Staff. 1976. lib. bdg. 625.00 o.p. (ISBN 0-8161-0051-9, Hall Library). G K Hall.

Catalog of the Warburg Institute Library, 12 Vols. 2nd rev. ed. University of London - Warburg Institute Staff. 1970. Set. 1030.00 o.p. (ISBN 0-8161-0744-0, Hall Library). G K Hall.

Catalog of the Western Language Collections, 63 Vols. Stanford University, Hoover Institution on War, Revolution & Peace Staff. 1970. Set. 6225.00 o.p. (ISBN 0-8161-0859-5, Hall Library). G K Hall.

Catalog of the William Ransom Hogan Jazz Archive, 2 vols. Howard-Tilton Memorial Library Staff. 900p. 1984. Set. lib. bdg. 350.00 o.p. (ISBN 0-8161-0434-4, Hall Reference). G K Hall.

Catalog of the Yale Collection of Western Americana, 4 Vols. Yale University Staff. 1970. Set. 395.00 o.p. (ISBN 0-8161-0585-5, Hall Library). G K Hall.

Catalog to Manuscripts at the National Anthropological Archives, 4 vols. Smithsonian Institution, Washington, D. C. Staff. 1975. Set. lib. bdg. 395.00 o.p. (ISBN 0-8161-1194-4, Hall Library). G K Hall.

Cataloging Legal Literature: A Manual on AACR2 & Library of Congress Subject Headings for Legal Material with Illustrations. Peter Enyingi et al. LC 84-6313. (AALL Publ. Ser.: No. 22). 1984. looseleaf 65.00x o.p. (ISBN 0-8377-0120-1). Rothman.

Cataloging Nonbook Materials: Problems in Theory & Practice. Carolyn O. Frost. Ed. by Arlene T. Dowell. LC 82-18711. 390p. 1983. 28.50 o.p. (ISBN 0-87287-329-3). Libs Unl.

Catalogo de la Biblioteca Nacional de Antropologia y Historia - Catalogs of the National Library of Anthropology & History, 10 vols. National Library of Anthropology & History Staff, Mexico City. 1972. Set. lib. bdg. 875.00 o.p. (ISBN 0-8161-0918-4, Hall Library). G K Hall.

Catalogs of the Asia Library, the University of Michigan, 25 vols. University of Michigan Staff. 1978. Set. 2445.00 o.p. (ISBN 0-8161-0096-9, Hall Library). G K Hall.

Catalogs of the Far Eastern Library, 6 vols. University of Chicago Staff. 1972. Set. lib. bdg. 825.00 o.p. (ISBN 0-8161-1119-7, Hall Library). G K Hall.

Catalogs of the Opera Collections in the Music Libraries: University of California, Berkeley & University of California, Los Angeles. 1983. lib. bdg. 130.00 o.s.i. (ISBN 0-8161-0392-5, Hall Library). G K Hall.

Catalogs of the Scripps Institution of Oceanography Library, First Supplement to Pt. 1: Author-Title Catalog, 3 vols. Ed. by University of California, San Diego Staff. 1973. 245.00 o.p. (ISBN 0-8161-0897-8, Hall Library). G K Hall.

Catalogs of the Western Language Serials & Newspaper Collection, 3 Vols. Stanford University, Hoover Institution on War, Revolution & Peace Staff. 1970. 300.00 o.p. (ISBN 0-8161-0167-1, Hall Library). G K Hall.

Catalogue & Buyer's Guide: Spring & Summer 1895, No. 57. Montgomery Ward & Co. Staff. 20.25 o.p. (ISBN 0-8446-0806-8). Peter Smith.

Catalogue & Reclassification of the Eastern Palearctic Ichneumonidae. Henry Townes et al. (Memoir Ser.: No. 5). 661p. 1965. 45.00x o.p. (ISBN 0-686-00414-0). Am Entom Inst.

Catalogue De Films Sur les Arts Du Spectacle Dans les Pays Arabes et En Asie. 172p. (Fr.). 1976. pap. 7.50 o.p. (ISBN 92-3-201259-6, U66, UNESCO). UNIPUB.

Catalogue de Fonds Speciaux de la Bibliotheque Litteraire Jacques Doucet, (Paris, France) Jacques Doucet. (Fonds Valery). 1972. 100.00 o.p. (ISBN 0-8161-0952-4, Hall Library). G K Hall.

Catalogue de Fonds Speciaux de la Bibliotheque Litteraire Jacques Doucet, (Paris, France) Jacques Doucet. (Fonds Mauriac et Fonds Jouhandeau). 1972. 100.00 o.p. (ISBN 0-8161-0954-0, Hall Library). G K Hall.

Catalogue de Fonds Speciaux de la Bibliotheque Litteraire Jacques Doucet, (Paris, France) Jacques Doucet. (Lettres a Andre Gide). 1972. 100.00 o.p. (ISBN 0-8161-0951-6, Hall Library). G K Hall.

Catalogue de la Section des Russica: Ecrits Sur la Russie en Langues Etrangere, 2 Vols. Bibliotheque Imperiale Publique de St. Petersbourg Staff. LC 72-115679. 1970. Repr. of 1873 ed. Set. lib. bdg. 125.00 o.p. (ISBN 0-306-71933-9). Da Capo.

Catalogue of Artificial Intelligence Tools. Ed. by A. Bundy. (Symbolic Computation, Artificial Intelligence Ser.). (Illus.). xxv, 150p. 1984. pap. 17.00 o.s.i. (ISBN 0-387-13938-9). Springer-Verlag.

Catalogue of Books & Periodicals on Estonia in the British Library Reference Division. Salme Pruuden. 1981. lib. bdg. 61.00 o.p. (ISBN 0-8240-9553-7). Garland Pub.

Catalogue of Books Printed for Private Circulation. Bertram Dobell. LC 66-25693. 244p. 1966. Repr. of 1906 ed. 35.00x o.p. (ISBN 0-8103-3303-1). Gale.

Catalogue of English & American Chap-Books & Broadside Ballads in Harvard College Library. Harvard University Library Staff. LC 67-23932. 188p. 1968. Repr. of 1905 ed. 35.00x o.p. (ISBN 0-8103-3420-8). Gale.

Catalogue of European Printed Books, India Office Library, 10 Vols. Commonwealth Relations Office, Great Britain Staff. 1970. Set. 835.00 o.p. (ISBN 0-8161-0671-1, Hall Library). G K Hall.

Catalogue of Exhibition Catalogues. Victoria & Albert Museum National Art Library, London Staff. 1972. lib. bdg. 125.00 o.p. (ISBN 0-8161-1022-0, Hall Library). G K Hall.

Catalogue of French Paintings: Nineteenth & Twentieth Centuries, Vol. III. Charles Sterling & Margaretta Salinger. LC 41-7098. (Illus.). 272p. 1966. 7.50 o.p. (ISBN 0-87099-061-6); pap. 4.95 o.s.i. (ISBN 0-87099-062-4). Metro Mus Art.

Catalogue of French Paintings: Nineteenth Century. Charles Sterling & Margaretta Salinger. LC 41-7098. (Illus.). 240p. 1966. 7.50 o.p. (ISBN 0-87099-059-4). Metro Mus Art.

Catalogue of Instruments & Models. American Philosophical Society. Ed. by Robert P. Multhauf. LC 61-14630. (Memoirs Ser.: Vol. 53). (Illus.). 1961. 8.00 o.p. (ISBN 0-87169-053-5). Am Philos.

Catalogue of Italian Paintings: Venetian School. Federico Zeri & Elizabeth E. Gardner. LC 73-9831. (Illus.). 244p. 1973. pap. 12.95 o.p. (ISBN 0-87099-080-2). Metro Mus Art.

Catalogue of Mesozoic Mammalia in the Geological Department of the British Museum. George G. Simpson. (Illus.). x, 215p. 1928. 17.50x o.p. (ISBN 0-565-00065-9, Pub. by Brit Mus Nat Hist England). Sabbot-Natural Hist Bks.

Catalogue of Mexican Pamphlets in the Sutro Collection 1623-1888. California State Library Sutro Branch San Francisco. Ed. by P. Radin & A. I. Gans. 1939-1941. 90.00 o.p. (ISBN 0-527-14400-2). Kraus Repr.

Catalogue of Portraits & Other Works of Art. American Philosophical Society Staff. LC 61-14631. (Memoirs Ser.: Vol. 54). (Illus.). 1961. 10.00 o.p. (ISBN 0-87169-054-3). Am Philos.

Catalogue of Printing Presses & Printers' Materials, Lithographic Presses, Stereotyping & Electrotyping Machinery, Binders' Presses & Materials. Hoe, R., & Co. Ed. by John Bidwell. LC 78-74397. (Nineteenth-Century Book Arts & Printing History Ser.: Vol. 11). (Illus.). 1980. lib. bdg. 26.00 o.p. (ISBN 0-8240-3885-1). Garland Pub.

Catalogue of Specimens of Printing Types by English & Scottish Printers & Founders 1665-1830. Turner W. Berry & A. F. Johnson. LC 78-74404. (Nineteenth-Century Book Arts & Printing History Ser.: Vol. 12). 1983. lib. bdg. 46.00 o.p. (ISBN 0-8240-3886-X). Garland Pub.

Catalogue of the American Hesperiidae Indictating the Classification & Nomenclature Adopted in the British Museum (Natural History), Pt. I: Pyrrhopyginae. W. H. Evans. (Illus.). x, 92p. 1951. 16.50x o.p. (ISBN 0-565-00180-9, Pub. by Brit Mus Nat Hist England). Sabbot-Natural Hist Bks.

Catalogue of the American Hesperiidae Indicating the Classification & Nomenclature Adopted in the British Museum (Natural History), Pt. II: Pyrginae, Sect. 1. W. H. Evans. (Illus.). v, 178p. 1952. 26.75x o.p. (ISBN 0-565-00181-7, Pub. by Brit Mus Nat Hist England). Sabbot-Natural Hist Bks.

Catalogue of the American Hesperiidae Indicating the Classification & Nomenclature Adopted in the British Museum (Natural History), Pt. III: Pyrginae, Sect. 2. W. H. Evans. (Illus.). v, 246p. 1953. 30.00x o.p. (ISBN 0-565-00208-2, Pub. by Brit Mus Nat Hist England). Sabbot-Natural Hist Bks.

Catalogue of the American Hesperiidae Indicating the Classification & Nomenclature Adopted in the British Museum (Natural History), Pt. IV: Hesperiinae & Megathyminae, Pt. IV. W. H. Evans. (Illus.). v, 499p. 1955. 34.50x o.p. (ISBN 0-565-00182-5, Pub. by Brit Mus Nat Hist England). Sabbot-Natural Hist Bks.

Catalogue of the Avery Memorial Architectural Library, First Supplement, 4 vols. Columbia University Editors. 3166p. 1978. Set. lib. bdg. 440.00 o.p. (ISBN 0-8161-0780-7, Hall Library). G K Hall.

Catalogue of the Avery Memorial Architectural Library, Second Edition, Fourth Supplement. Columbia University Editors. 1980. lib. bdg. 340.00 o.p. (ISBN 0-8161-0283-X, Hall Library). G K Hall.

Catalogue of the Book Library of the British Film Institute, 3 vols. British Film Institute, London Staff. 1975. Set. lib. bdg. 297.00 o.p. (ISBN 0-8161-0004-7, Hall Library). G K Hall.

Catalogue of the Burney Family Correspondence, 1749-1878. Joyce Hemlow. 488p. 1971. 22.50x o.p. (ISBN 0-7735-0055-3, Pub. by McGill Canada). U of Toronto Pr.

Catalogue of the Cashel Diocesan Library. Cashel Diocesan Library, County Tipperary, Republic of Ireland Staff. 1973. 100.00 o.p. (ISBN 0-8161-1065-4, Hall Library). G K Hall.

Catalogue of the Chess Collection, Including Checkers, 2 Vols. Cleveland Public Library Editors - John G. White Department. (Ser. Seventy). 1970. Set. 130.00 o.p. (ISBN 0-8161-0681-9, Hall Library). G K Hall.

Catalogue of the Colonial Office Library, London, 15 vols. Foreign & Commonwealth Office Editors, London. 1970. Set. 1490.00 o.p. (ISBN 0-8161-0688-6, Hall Library); First Suppl. 1963-67. 140.00 o.p. (ISBN 0-8161-0729-7); Second Suppl. 1972. 2 Vols. 220.00 o.p. (ISBN 0-8161-0843-9). G K Hall.

Catalogue of the Comparative Education Library, 1st Suppl, 3 vols. University of London, Institute of Education Staff. 1974. Set. lib. bdg. 330.00 o.p. (ISBN 0-8161-0988-5, Hall Library). G K Hall.

Catalogue of the Comparative Education Library. University of London, Institute of Education Staff. (Library Catalogs-Bib. Guides). 1971. lib. bdg. 575.00 six reels o.p. (ISBN 0-8161-0923-0, Hall Library). G K Hall.

Catalogue of the Foreign Office Library, 1926-1968, 8 vols. Foreign & Commonwealth Office Editors, London. 6208p. 1973. lib. bdg. 790.00 o.p. (ISBN 0-8161-0998-2, Hall Library). G K Hall.

Catalogue of the Gennadius Library. American School of Classical Studies at Athens, Second Supplement. American School of Classical Studies at Athens Staff. 1981. lib. bdg. 170.00 o.p. (ISBN 0-8161-0011-X, Hall Library). G K Hall.

Catalogue of the Gimo Collection of Italian Manuscript Music in the University of Uppsala. Ake Davidsson. 101p. (Orig.). 1964. pap. text ed. 12.50x o.p. Coronet Bks.

Catalogue of the Greenlee Collection, 2 vols. Newberry Library, Chicago Staff. 1970. Set. 198.00 o.p. (ISBN 0-8161-0903-6, Hall Library). G K Hall.

Catalogue of the Harvard University Fine Arts Library, First Supplement, 3 vols. Harvard University, Fogg Art Museum Staff. 1975. Set. lib. bdg. 400.00 o.p. (ISBN 0-8161-1224-X, Hall Library). G K Hall.

Catalogue of the History of Science: Collections of the University of Oklahoma Libraries, 2 vols. Duane Roller & Marcia M. Goodman. LC 76-381954. 1212p. 1976. Set. 212.00x o.p. (ISBN 0-7201-0452-1). Mansell.

Catalogue of the Imperial College of Tropical Agriculture, 8 vols. University of the West Indies, Imperial College of Tropical Agriculture, Trinidad Staff. 1975. Set. lib. bdg. 750.00 o.p. (ISBN 0-8161-1190-1, Hall Library). G K Hall.

Catalogue of the Library of the Graduate School of Design, 44 Vols. Harvard University - Graduate School of Design Staff. 1968. Set. 3725.00 o.p. (ISBN 0-8161-0812-9, Hall Library). G K Hall.

Catalogue of the Library of the Graduate School of Design, First Supplement, 2 vols. Harvard University - Graduate School of Design Staff. 1970. Set. 240.00 o.p. (ISBN 0-8161-0831-5, Hall Library). G K Hall.

Catalogue of the Library of the Graduate School of Design: Third Supplement. Harvard University Staff. (Library Catalogs). 1979. lib. bdg. 445.00 o.p. (ISBN 0-8161-0284-8, Hall Library). G K Hall.

Catalogue of the Library of the Institute of Advanced Legal Studies, 6 vols. Institute of Advanced Legal Studies, University of London Staff. 1978. lib. bdg. 595.00 o.p. (ISBN 0-8161-0099-3, Hall Library). G K Hall.

Catalogue of the Library of the Museum of Comparative Zoology, 8 Vols. Harvard University Museum of Comparative Zoology Staff. 1970. 760.00 o.p. (ISBN 0-8161-0767-X, Hall Library). G K Hall.

Catalogue of the Library of the National Gallery of Canada. National Gallery of Canada (Ottawa) Staff. 1973. Eight Vols. lib. bdg. 790.00 o.p. (ISBN 0-8161-1043-3, Hall Library). G K Hall.

Catalogue of the Library of the Society for Psychical Research, London, England. Society for Psychical Research, London, England Staff. 1977. lib. bdg. 75.00 o.p. (ISBN 0-8161-0008-X, Hall Library). G K Hall.

Catalogue of the Lichens from India, Nepal, Pakistan & Ceylon. D. D. Awashti. 1965. 24.00x o.p. (ISBN 3-7682-5417-8). Lubrecht & Cramer.

Catalogue of the Manuscript Collections of the American Antiquarian Society, 40 Vols. American Antiquarian Society Staff. 1979. lib. bdg. 390.00 o.s.i. (ISBN 0-8161-0258-9, Hall Library). G K Hall.

Catalogue of the National Map Collection, 16 vols. Public Archives Staff of Canada Ottawa. 1976. Set. lib. bdg. 1490.00 o.p. (ISBN 0-8161-1215-0, Hall Library). G K Hall.

Catalogue of the Pepys Library at Magdalene College Cambridge: Volume 5, Part 2: Modern Manuscripts, Vol. V - Pt. 2. Ed. by Robert Latham. 302p. 1981. 135.00x o.s.i. (ISBN 0-8476-7050-3). Rowman.

Catalogue of the Population Council Library. Population Council Editors. 1979. lib. bdg. 295.00 o.p. (ISBN 0-8161-0278-3, Hall Library). G K Hall.

Catalogue of the Public Archives Library of Canada: Collection of Published Material with a Chronological List of Pamphlets. Public Archives Staff of Canada Ottawa. 1979. lib. bdg. 1250.00 o.p. (ISBN 0-8161-0316-X, Hall Library). G K Hall.

Catalogue of the Singapore-Malaysia Collection. University of Singapore Library Staff. 1970. lib. bdg. 130.00 o.p. (ISBN 0-8161-0818-8, Hall Library). G K Hall.

Catalogue of the Spanish Library, & of the Portuguese Books Bequeathed by George Ticknor to the Boston Public Library. Boston Public Library Staff. 1970. lib. bdg. 78.00 o.p. (ISBN 0-8161-0865-X, Hall Library). G K Hall.

Catalogue of the Tate Gallery's Collection of Modern Art Other Than Works by British Artists. Compiled by Ronald Alley. (Illus.). 822p. 1981. 95.00 o.p. (ISBN 0-85667-102-9). Sotheby Pubns.

Catalogue of the Tavistock Joint Library, 2 vols. Tavistock Joint Library, London Staff. 1975. Set. lib. bdg. 145.00 o.p. (ISBN 0-8161-1167-7, Hall Library). G K Hall.

Catalogue of the Works of Linnaeus Preserved in the Libraries of the British Museum (Natural History) 2nd ed. Basil H. Soulsby. (Illus.). 1933-36. Set. 36.50x o.p. (ISBN 0-686-25779-0, Pub. by Brit Mus Nat Hist England). Catalogue, 1933 (ISBN 0-565-00104-3). Index, 1936 (ISBN 0-565-00066-7). Sabbot-Natural Hist Bks.

Catalogue of Verdi's Operas. Martin Chusid. (Music Indexes & Bibliographies: No. 5). 1974. pap. 17.00 o.p. (ISBN 0-913574-05-8). Eur-Am Music.

Catalogue Raisonne of the Prints of Sir Francis Seymour Haden. Richard S. Schneiderman. (Illus.). 432p. 1985. 150.00 o.s.i. (ISBN 0-8390-0351-X). Abner Schram Ltd.

Catalogues of the Berenson Library, 4 vols. Harvard University Center for Italian Renaissance Studies at Villa I Tatti (Florence, Italy) Staff. 1973. lib. bdg. 435.00 o.p. (ISBN 0-8161-0973-7, Hall Library). G K Hall.

Catalogues of the Canning House Library: Author & Subject Catalogues, 2 pts. Ed. by Canning House Library Editors. Incl. Pt. 1. Hispanic Catalogues, 4 vols. Canning House Library Editors. 1967. 325.00 (ISBN 0-8161-0741-6); First Supplement, 1973. 115.00 (ISBN 0-8161-1125-1); Pt. 2. Luso-Brazilian Catalogues. Canning House Library Editors. 1967. 100.00 (ISBN 0-8161-0126-4); First Supplement, 1973. lib. bdg. 110.00 (ISBN 0-8161-1100-6). Hall Library). G K Hall.

Cataloue of the Avery Memorial Architectural Library, Columbia University, Second Supplement, 4 vols. Columbia University Editors. 1975. Set. lib. bdg. 440.00 o.p. (ISBN 0-8161-1070-0, Hall Library). G K Hall.

Catalysis. Myron L. Bender & Lewis J. Brubacher. (Illus.). 256p. 1983. text ed. 23.95 o.p. (ISBN 0-07-004450-3); pap. text ed. 21.95 o.p. (ISBN 0-07-004451-1). McGraw.

Catalysis by Zeolites: Proceedings. Ed. by B. Imelik et al. (Studies in Surface Science & Catalysis: Vol. 5). 352p. 1980. 116.00 o.p. (ISBN 0-444-41916-0). Elsevier.

Catalysis in Chemistry & Enzymology. William P. Jencks. LC 68-31661. (Advanced Chemistry Ser). (Illus.). 1969. text ed. 45.95 o.p. (ISBN 0-07-032305-4). McGraw.

Catalysis in Organic Synthesis, 1977. Ed. by Gerard V. Smith. 1978. 43.50 o.p. (ISBN 0-12-650550-0). Acad Pr.

Catalysis of Gas Reactions by Metals. A. J. Robertson. (Illus.). 1970. 23.70 o.p. (ISBN 0-387-91031-X). Springer-Verlag.

Catalyst Career Opportunities Series. 1985. 165.00 o.p. (ISBN 0-89584-103-7). Catalyst.

Catalyst Handbook. Agricultural Division Of Imperial Chemical Industries Limited. (Illus.). 1970. 9.90 o.p. (ISBN 0-387-91033-6). Springer-Verlag.

Catalytic Chemistry of Nitrogen Oxides. Ed. by Richard L. Klimisch & John G. Larson. LC 75-22332. (General Motors Research Symposia Ser.). 340p. 1975. 55.00x o.p. (ISBN 0-306-30875-4, Plenum Pr). Plenum Pub.

Catalytic Conversion of Hydrocarbons. J. E. Germain. 1969. 59.50 o.p. (ISBN 0-12-280850-9). Acad Pr.

Catalytic Hydrogenation over Platinum Metals. Paul N. Rylander. 1967. 89.50 o.p. (ISBN 0-12-605350-2). Acad Pr.

Catalytic Processes & Proven Catalysts. Charles L. Thomas. 1970. 83.00 o.p. (ISBN 0-12-687950-8). Acad Pr.

Cataract. Philip Awdry & C. S. Nicholls. LC 84-25884. (Illus.). 250p. (Orig.). 1985. 14.95 o.p. (ISBN 0-571-13478-5); pap. 5.95 o.p. (ISBN 0-571-13425-4). Faber & Faber.

Cataract. Mykhaylo Osadchy. Tr. by Marco Carynnyk from Ukrainian. LC 75-34371. (Helen & Kurt Wolff Bk.). 264p. 1976. 8.95 o.p. (ISBN 0-15-116115-1). HarBraceJ.

Cataract. Mykhaylo Osadchy. Tr. by Marco Carynnyk from Ukrainian. LC 75-34371. (Helen & Kurt Wolff Bk.). 240p. 1976. pap. 3.95 o.p. (ISBN 0-15-615550-8, Harv). HarBraceJ.

Cataracts: The Complete Guide from Diagnosis to Recovery for Patients & Families. Julius Shulman. 256p. 1984. 16.50 o.p. (ISBN 0-671-46917-7). S&S.

Catastrophe in the Caribbean: The Failure of America's Human Rights Policy in Central America. James R. Whelan & Patricia Bozell. LC 85-149603. 1985. 13.95 o.p. (ISBN 0-915463-06-7, Pub. by Jameson Bks). Green Hill.

Catastrophe Theory. Alexander Woodcock & Monte Davis. 1979. pap. 2.75 o.p. (ISBN 0-380-48397-1, 48397). Avon.

Catastrophe Theory for Scientists & Engineers. Robert Gilmore. LC 80-22154. 666p. 1981. 65.00 o.p. (ISBN 0-471-05064-4, Pub. by Wiley-Interscience). Wiley.

Catastrophes in the Earth's History. I. A. Rezanov. Tr. by H. Campbell Creishton. 167p. 1984. pap. 3.95 o.p. (ISBN 0-8285-2815-2, Pub. by Mir Pubs USSR). Imported Pubns.

Catcalendar Cats. B. Kliban. (Illus.). 144p. 1986. pap. 9.95 o.p. (ISBN 0-89480-223-2). Workman Pub.

Catcards for Christmas. Victoria Chess. 1982. pap. 4.95 o.s.i. (ISBN 0-317-56984-8). Macmillan.

Catch a Falling Spy. Len Deighton. LC 76-18248. 1976. 7.95 o.p. (ISBN 0-15-116127-5). HarBraceJ.

Catch a Little Fox. Beatrice S. De Regniers. LC 75-97036. (Illus.). (ps-2). 1979. 7.95 o.p. (ISBN 0-395-28821-5, Clarion). HM.

Catch Me If You Can. Frank W. Abagnale, Jr. 1982. pap. 3.50 o.s.i. (ISBN 0-671-46287-3). PB.

Catch Me: Kill Me. William H. Hallahan. 1978. pap. 1.95 o.p. (ISBN 0-380-37986-4, 37986-4). Avon.

Catch the Saint. Leslie Charteris. (Saint Ser.). 160p. 1979. pap. 1.95 o.p. (ISBN 0-441-09247-0). Ace Bks.

Catch the Wind: A Book of Windmills & Windpower. Landt Dennis. LC 75-45002. (Illus.). 128p. (gr. 7 up). 1976. 8.95 o.s.i. (ISBN 0-02-728680-0, Four Winds). Macmillan.

Catch Twenty-Two. Joseph Heller. 1961. 19.95 o.p. (ISBN 0-671-12805-1). S&S.

Catch 22. Joseph Heller. 48p. (Orig.). 1989. pap. 9.95 o.p. (ISBN 1-55651-131-0); audiocassete tape incl. o.p. (ISBN 1-55651-132-9). Cram Cassettes.

Catcher in the Rye. J. D. Salinger. 48p. (Orig.). 1988. pap. 9.95 o.p. (ISBN 1-55651-127-2); audiocassette tape incl. o.p. (ISBN 1-55651-128-0). Cram Cassettes.

Catcher Was a Lady: The Clem Dreisewerd Story. Edna Dreisewerd. (Illus.). 1978. 7.50 o.p. (ISBN 0-682-49025-3). Exposition-Phoenix.

Catchfire. Graham D. Martin. 192p. (gr. 5-8). 1982. 8.95 o.s.i. (ISBN 0-395-31861-0). HM.

Catching Salmon. Richard Waddington. LC 77-85034. (Illus.). 1978. 22.95 o.p. (ISBN 0-7153-7533-4). David & Charles.

Catchpenny Street. Betty Cavanna. LC 75-2397. (Illus.). 222p. (gr. 6 up). 1975. 7.50 o.s.i. (ISBN 0-664-32574-2, Westminster). Westminster John Knox.

Catechesis - Sow Justice, Reap Peace: 1988 Catechetical Sunday. 48p. (Orig., Eng. & Span.). 1988. pap. 4.95 o.p. (ISBN 1-55586-190-3). US Catholic.

Catechetics from A to Z. Jack W. Murphy & Arlene W. Murphy. LC 82-70787. 160p. (Orig.). 1982. tchrs. guidebook 7.95 o.p. (ISBN 0-87793-250-6). Ave Maria.

Catechism of the Catholic Church. Robert F. Fox. 1979. pap. 5.25 o.p. (ISBN 0-8199-0758-8). Franciscan Her.

Catecholamines & Stress. Ed. by Earl Usdin et al. 644p. 1976. 145.00 o.p. (ISBN 0-08-020588-7). Pergamon.

Catecholamines & the Heart: Recent Advances in Experimental & Clinical Research Symposium Proceedings. Ed. by W. Delius et al. (Illus.). 383p. 1982. pap. 27.60 o.p. (ISBN 0-387-11119-0). Springer-Verlag.

Catecholamines & Their Enzymes in the Neuropathology of Schizophrenia. Steven Matthysse & Seymour S. Kety. LC 75-4093. (Illus.). 382p. 1975. 95.00 o.p. (ISBN 0-08-018242-9). Pergamon.

Catecholamines: Basic & Clinical Frontiers: Proceedings of the Fourth International Catecholamine Symposium; Asilomar Conference Center, Pacific Grove, California; September 17-22, 1978, 2 vols. Ed. by Earl Usdin et al. 1979. 740.00 o.p. (ISBN 0-08-022650-7). Pergamon.

Categorical Framework for the Study of Singular Spaces. William Fulton & Robert MacPherson. LC 81-2246. (Memoirs Ser.: No. 243). 166p. 1981. pap. 12.00 o.p. (ISBN 0-8218-2243-8). Am Math.

Categorical Imperative: A Study in Kant's Moral Philosophy. H. J. Paton. 1971. pap. 12.95x o.p. (ISBN 0-8122-1023-9, Pa Paperbks). U of Pa Pr.

Categories of a Racial Mind. Richard S. Hoehler. 304p. 1986. 14.99 o.p. (ISBN 0-317-53264-2). Noontide.

Categorization & Social Judgment. Ed. by J. R. Eiser & Wolfgang Strobe. (European Monographs in Social Psychology: No. 3). 1973. 36.50 o.p. (ISBN 0-12-235350-1). Acad Pr.

Category Formation & the History of Religions. Robert D. Baird. (Religion & Reason Ser: No. 1). 178p. 1971. text ed. 20.50x o.p. (ISBN 90-2796-889-6). Mouton.

Category Theory Applied to Computation & Control: Proceedings of the International Symposium, 1st, San Francisco, 1974. International Symposium on Category Theory Staff. Ed. by E. G. Manes. LC 74-34481. (Lecture Notes in Computer Science: Vol. 25). x, 245p. 1975. pap. 19.00 o.p. (ISBN 0-387-07142-3). Springer-Verlag.

Category Theory, Homology Theory & Their Applications, 2: Proceedings of the Batelle Memorial Institute Conference, Seattle, 1968. Battelle Memorial Institute Conference Staff. Ed. by Peter J. Hilton. LC 75-75931. (Lecture Notes in Mathematics: Vol. 92). (Orig.). 1969. pap. 18.30 o.p. (ISBN 0-387-04611-9). Springer-Verlag.

Catena of Five Plays: Jerome, Patrick, Melachy, John Scotus, Oliver Plunkett. Peter Kavanagh. 100p. 1963. 100.00 o.p. (ISBN 0-914612-01-8). Kavanagh.

Catenanes, Rotaxanes & Knots. Gottfried Schill. Tr. by J. Boeckmann from Ger. LC 78-127702. (Organic Chemistry Ser.: Vol. 22). 1971. 59.00 o.p. (ISBN 0-12-625450-8). Acad Pr.

Catenary Exchange. Jon Winters. 304p. 1983. pap. 3.95 o.p. (ISBN 0-380-85233-0, 85233). Avon.

Caterina. Eveline Amstutz. 1978. pap. 2.25 o.p. (ISBN 0-8439-0575-1, Pub. by Leisure Bks CT). Dorchester Pub Co.

Catering Services: Creative Suggestion Pages. Alpha Pyramis Research Division Staff. 16p. (Orig.). 1985. pap. text ed. 4.00 o.p o.p. (ISBN 0-913597-89-9, Pub. by Alpha Pyramis). Prosperity & Profits.

Caterpillar & the Polliwog. Jack Kent. (Illus.). 32p. (ps-3). 1982. 10.95 o.s.i. (ISBN 0-13-120469-6). P-H.

Caterpillar & the Polliwog. Jack Kent. (Illus.). 32p. (gr. k-3). 1985. pap. 4.95 o.s.i. (ISBN 0-13-120478-5). P-H.

Caterpillar Cop. James McClure. 1982. pap. 2.95 o.p. (ISBN 0-394-71058-4). Pantheon.

Catfish Cookbook. Wo East. 1982. pap. 5.95 o.p. (ISBN 0-914788-61-2). Globe Pequot.

Catfish Man: A Conjured Life. Jerome Charyn. LC 79-54007. 1980. 10.00 o.p. (ISBN 0-87795-249-3, Arbor Hse). Morrow.

Catfishes for the Advanced Hobbyist. Clifford W. Emmens & Herbert Axelrod. 9.95 o.p. (ISBN 0-87666-018-9, PS-650). TFH Pubns.

Cathedral Book. Maureen Gallagher. LC 82-60592. (gr. 3-6). 1983. pap. 2.95 o.p. (ISBN 0-8091-2485-8). Paulist Pr.

Cathedrals' Crusade. Ian Dunlop. LC 81-14431. (Illus.). 256p. 1982. 20.00 o.s.i. (ISBN 0-8008-1316-2). Taplinger.

Cathedrals of England. Alec Clifton-Taylor. (Illus.). 1980. pap. 8.95 o.p. (ISBN 0-500-20062-9). Thames Hudson.

Catherine Marshall Had a Husband. William J. Petersen. (Living Books Ser.). 240p. (Orig.). 1986. mass 3.95 o.p. (ISBN 0-8423-0204-2). Tyndale.

Catherine Marshall's Story Bible. Catherine Marshall. (Illus.). 197p. (gr. 1-5). 1984. pap. 10.95 o.p. (Chosen Bks). Revell.

Catherine, Royal Mistress. Juliette Benzoni. 1978. pap. 1.95 o.p. (ISBN 0-380-37069-7, 37069). Avon.

Catherine's Quest. Juliette Benzoni. 1978. pap. 1.95 o.p. (ISBN 0-380-37895-7, 37895). Avon.

Catherine's Time for Love. Juliette Benzoni. 1978. pap. 1.95 o.p. (ISBN 0-380-40949-6, 40949). Avon.

Cathodic Protection for Reinforced Concrete Bridge Decks. (National Cooperative Highway Research Program Report). 135p. 1977. 7.00 o.p. (ISBN 0-317-36069-8). Transport Res Bd.

Catholic. David Plante. LC 85-48284. 160p. 1986. 11.95 o.p. (ISBN 0-689-11788-4, Atheneum). Macmillan.

Catholic Almanac, 1986. Ed. by Felician A. Foy & Rose M. Avato. LC 73-64101. 650p. (Orig.). 1985. pap. 5.00 o.p. (ISBN 0-87973-256-3, 256). Our Sunday Visitor.

Catholic Almanac 1987. Ed. by Felician A. Foy & Rose M. Avato. LC 73-64101. 600p. (Orig.). 1986. pap. 13.95 o.p. (ISBN 0-87973-257-1, 257). Our Sunday Visitor.

Catholic Authors: Contemporary Biographical Sketches, 1930-1947. Ed. by Matthew Hoehn. 832p. 1981. Repr. of 1947 ed. 75.00x o.p. (ISBN 0-8103-4314-2). Gale.

Catholic Book of the Mass. William Ogrodowski. LC 84-60752. 168p. 1985. pap. 3.45 o.p. (ISBN 0-87973-600-3, 600). Our Sunday Visitor.

Catholic Church & the Secret Societies in the United States. Fergus Macdonald. LC 46-8049. (Monograph Ser.: No. 22). 1946. 12.50x o.p. (ISBN 0-930060-04-0). US Cath Hist.

Catholic Church in Mexican Political Life. Frederico Muggenburg. (CSIS Significant Issues Ser.). 1989. write for info. o.p. CSI Studies.

Catholic Church in Oregon and the Work of Its Archbishops. John R. Laidlaw. 1980. 5.00 o.p. (ISBN 0-682-49608-1, Testament). Exposition-Phoenix.

Catholic Church of the Future. Ernest L. Ramer. LC 72-94861. 1974. 4.50 o.p. (ISBN 0-682-48078-9). Exposition-Phoenix.

Catholic Education. Robert Bernard. 1982. 15.50 o.s.i. (ISBN 0-03-061123-7). H Holt & Co.

Catholic Education in the Western World. Ed. by James M. Lee. 1967. 17.95x o.p. (ISBN 0-268-00030-1). U of Notre Dame Pr.

Catholic Emancipation: Daniel O'Connell & the Birth of Irish Democracy. F. O'Ferrall. LC 85-14178. 350p. 1985. text ed. 38.50x o.p. (ISBN 0-391-03353-0). Humanities.

Catholic Ethics & Protestant Ethics. Roger Mehl. 1971. 4.95 o.s.i. (ISBN 0-664-20903-3, Westminster). Westminster John Knox.

Catholic Faith in a Process Perspective. Norman Pittenger. LC 81-9615. 160p. (Orig.). 1981. pap. 1.74 o.p. (ISBN 0-88344-091-1). Orbis Bks.

Catholic Footsteps in Old New York: A Chronicle of Catholicity in the City of New York from 1524 to 1808. William H. Bennett. LC 77-359169. (Monograph Ser.: No. 28). 1973. Repr. of 1909 ed. 10.00x o.p. (ISBN 0-930060-08-3). US Cath Hist.

Catholic High School Entrance Examinations. 3rd ed. David R. Turner. LC 78-12582. 1980. pap. 6.95 o.p. (ISBN 0-668-04844-1, 4844-1). Arco.

Catholic Politics in China & Korea. Eric O. Hanson. LC 79-27206. 160p. (Orig.). 1980. pap. 9.95 o.p. (ISBN 0-88344-084-9). Orbis Bks.

Catholic Press Directory. James A. Doyle. 184p. 1985. pap. 25.00 o.p. (ISBN 0-686-30366-0). Cath Pr Assn.

Catholic Press Directory. Regina A. Salzman. 224p. 1987. pap. 25.00 o.p. (ISBN 0-318-23511-0). Cath Pr Assn.

Catholic Press Directory, 1986. Regina A. Salzmann. 208p. 1986. pap. 25.00 o.p. (ISBN 0-318-18711-6). Cath Pr Assn.

Catholic Society in New South Wales 1788-1860. James Waldersee. (Illus.). 348p. 1974. 31.00x o.p. (ISBN 0-424-06460-X, Pub. by Sydney U Pr). Intl Spec Bk.

Catholic Thinkers in the Clear: Giants of Catholic Thought from Augustine to Rahner. William A. Herr. (Basics of Christian Thought Ser.). 276p. 1985. 16.95 o.p. (ISBN 0-88347-179-5). Thomas More.

Catholic Vision. Stephen Happel & David Tracy. LC 83-5687. 196p. 1984. pap. 10.95 o.p. (ISBN 0-8006-1719-3). Augsburg Fortress.

Catholic Why? Book. Andrew Greeley. 167p. 1983. 10.95 o.p. (ISBN 0-88347-154-X). Thomas More.

Catholic Worker, 27 vols. 1971. Repr. of 1961 ed. Set. lib. bdg. 480.00x o.p. (ISBN 0-8371-9137-8, CW00). Greenwood.

Catholicism. John P. Dolan. LC 67-28536. (Orig.). 1968. text ed. 10.00 o.p. (ISBN 0-8120-6013-X); pap. text ed. 6.95 o.p. (ISBN 0-8120-0273-3). Barron.

Catholics: An Unauthorized, Unapproved, Illustrated Guide. Rick Detorie. 1986. pap. 4.95 o.p. (ISBN 0-399-51251-9, Perigee). Putnam Pub Group.

Catholics in Colonial Days. Thomas P. Phelan. LC 74-145706. 320p. Repr. of 1935 ed. 40.00x o.p. (ISBN 0-8103-3685-5). Gale.

Catholics, Jews, & Protestants: A Study of Relationships in the United States & Canada. Claris E. Silcox. LC 78-21101. 1979. Repr. of 1934 ed. lib. bdg. 35.00x o.p. (ISBN 0-313-20882-4, SICJ). Greenwood.

Cathouse Showdown. Dallas Todd. 224p. (Orig.). 1982. pap. 2.25 o.p. (ISBN 0-8439-1029-1, Pub. by Leisure Bks CT). Dorchester Pub Co.

Cation Flux Across Biomembranes. Ed. by Yusuo Mukohata & Lester Packer. 1979. pap. 66.00 o.p. (ISBN 0-12-511050-2). Acad Pr.

Cationic Isomerization: Polymerization of Three-Methyl-One-Butene & Four-Methyl-One-Penene see Polymerization Reactions.

Cationic Polymerization. A. Gandini & H. Cheradame. (Advances in Polymer Science Ser.: Vol. 34, 35). (Illus.). 360p. 1980. 87.00 o.p. (ISBN 0-387-10049-0). Springer-Verlag.

Catone in Utica. Niccolo Piccinni. Ed. by Howard M. Brown. LC 76-20992. (Italian Opera 1640-1770 Ser.: Vol. 50). 1978. lib. bdg. 77.00 o.p. (ISBN 0-8240-2649-7). Garland Pub.

Cats. Wilfrid S. Bronson. LC 50-9467. (Illus.). (gr. 4-6). 1950. 5.50 o.p. (ISBN 0-15-215357-8, HJ). HarBraceJ.

Cats. Nina Leen. LC 79-22137. (Illus.). 80p. (gr. 3-6). 1980. 7.95 o.p. (ISBN 0-03-052331-1). H Holt & Co.

Cats. Joan Phipson. LC 75-43608. 156p. (gr. 5 up). 1976. 6.95 o.p. (ISBN 0-689-50061-0, Atheneum). Macmillan.

Cats & Other People. Paul E. Craft. LC 85-90982. (Illus.). 48p. 1985. pap. 7.50 o.p. (ISBN 0-682-40276-1). Exposition-Phoenix.

Cats of Kilkenny. Nathan Zimelman. LC 72-128817. (Illus.). (gr. 2-5). 1972. PLB 5.95 o.p. (ISBN 0-87614-020-7). Carolrhoda Bks.

Cats of Shambala. Tippi Hedren & Theodore Taylor. (Illus.). 255p. 1985. 18.45 o.p. (ISBN 0-671-53201-4). S&S.

Cat's Pajamas. Ida Chittum. LC 80-10579. (Illus.). 48p. (ps-3). 1980. 5.95 o.s.i. (ISBN 0-686-86560-X); PLB 5.95 o.s.i. (ISBN 0-686-91529-1). Parents.

Cat's Party. Gerte Melle & Rainer Redies. (Illus.). 30p. (ps). 1986. 7.95 o.p. (ISBN 0-8120-5720-1). Barron.

Cat's Paw. Jan Kendrick. 1980. pap. 1.95 o.p. (Pub. by Leisure Bks CT). Dorchester Pub Co.

Cat's Tale. Rikki Cate. LC 81-6997. (Illus.). 48p. (gr. 5-9). 1982. 9.95 o.p. (ISBN 0-15-215538-4, HJ). HarBraceJ.

Catskill Eagle. Robert B. Parker. 1985. 16.95 o.p. (ISBN 0-317-53073-9, Large Print Bks). G K Hall.

Catskill Eagle: A Spenser Novel. Robert B. Parker. LC 84-28617. 288p. 1985. 3.95 o.p. (ISBN 0-385-29385-2, Sey Lawr). Delacorte.

Cattle Towns. Robert R. Dykstra. LC 68-12677. (Illus.). 1970. pap. text ed. 6.95x o.p. (ISBN 0-689-70253-1, 166, Atheneum). Macmillan.

Cattulus. Ed. by Michael MacMillan. (Bolchazy-Carducci Textbook). (Illus.). 121p. (Orig.). pap. text ed. 9.00 o.p. (ISBN 0-86516-002-3). Bolchazy-Carducci.

Catundra. Stephen Cosgrove. Ed. by Mary H. Manoni. (Serendipity Book Cassettes). (Illus.). (gr. 1-3). 1979. pap. text ed. 24.95 o.p. (ISBN 0-89290-069-5). Soc for Visual.

Caucasian Carpets. Erwin Gans-Ruedin. LC 86-42710. (Illus.). 368p. 1986. 95.00 o.p. (ISBN 0-8478-0750-9). Rizzoli Intl.

Caucasian Chalk Circle. Bertolt Brecht. Tr. by Eric Bentley & Maja Apelman. (YA) (gr. 9 up). 1971. pap. 4.95 o.s.i. (ISBN 0-394-17258-2, B312, BC). Grove.

Caughly & Worcester Porcelains, 1775-1800. Geoffrey Godden. (Illus.). 336p. 1981. (ISBN 0-907462-01-4). Antique Collect.

Caught Between. Helen Kromer. (Orig.). 1955. pap. 1.00 o.p. (ISBN 0-377-80521-1). Friendship Pr.

Caught Dead in Philadelphia: A Mystery Introducing Amanda Pepper. Gillian Roberts. 224p. 1987. 16.95 o.s.i. (ISBN 0-684-18809-0). Scribner.

Caught in That Music. Seymore Epstein. 1980. pap. 1.50 o.p. (ISBN 0-380-00077-6, 20305). Avon.

Caught in the Middle. Beverly B. Smith & Patricia De Vorss. Date not set. pap. (75-0355-3). Tyndale.

Caught in the Moving Mountains. Gloria Skurzynski. LC 84-4371. (Illus.). 144p. (gr. 4-8). 1984. 11.00 o.p. (ISBN 0-688-01635-9). Lothrop.

Caul. Edwina Lindsay Travers. 1976. 5.00 o.p. (ISBN 0-682-48395-8). Exposition-Phoenix.

Causal Factors in American Economic Growth in the Nineteenth Century. Peter Temin. (Studies in Economic & Social History). (Orig.). 1975. pap. text ed. 9.95x o.p. (ISBN 0-333-17087-3). Humanities.

Causes & Prevention of Blindness. Ed. by I. C. Michaelson & Elaine R. Berman. 1973. 48.50 o.p. (ISBN 0-12-493650-4). Acad Pr.

Causes of Industrial Disorder: A Comparison of a British & a German Factory. Ian Maitland. (Routledge Direct Edition Ser.). 192p. 1983. pap. 13.95x o.p. (ISBN 0-7100-9207-5). Routledge Chapman & Hall.

Causes of the American Revolution. James Woodburn. pap. 9.00 o.p. (ISBN 0-384-69156-0). Johnson Repr.

Causes of the Industrial Revolution in England. Ed. by Ronald M. Hartwell. 1967. pap. 12.95x o.p. (ISBN 0-416-48000-4, NO.2221). Routledge Chapman & Hall.

Causes of the Present Inflation: An Interdisciplinary Explanation of Inflation in Britain, Germany & the United States. Andrew Tylecote. LC 80-15798. 236p. 1981. text ed. 38.95x o.p. (ISBN 0-470-26953-7). Halsted Pr.

Causses Cevennes. 5th ed. (Green Guides Ser.). 1985. pap. write for info. o.p. (ISBN 2-06-003153-2). Michelin.

Cautionary Tales for Women. Julian Fane. 307p. 1989. 19.95 o.p. (ISBN 0-241-12465-4, Pub. by Hamish Hamilton). David & Charles.

Cavalcade: Negro American Writing from 1760 to the Present. Ed. by Arthur P. Davis & Saunders Redding. LC 70-20257. 1972. text ed. 27.50 o.p. (ISBN 0-395-04345-X). HM.

Cavalier. Leonard J. D'Eon. 256p. 1987. 18.95 o.p. (ISBN 0-399-13227-9, Putnam). Putnam Pub Group.

Cavalleria Rusticana, & Other Stories. Giovanni Verga. Tr. by D. H. Lawrence from Ital. LC 75-9590. 301p. 1975. Repr. of 1928 ed. lib. bdg. 22.50x o.p. (ISBN 0-8371-8105-4, VECR). Greenwood.

Cave Architecture in History: A Selected Bibliography. Bibliographic Research Library Staff. (Architecture Ser.: A 1362). 6p. 1985. 2.00 o.p. (ISBN 0-89028-352-4). Vance Biblios.

Cave Dreamers. Jeanne Williams. 592p. 1984. pap. 4.75 o.p. (ISBN 0-380-86488-6, 86488). Avon.

Cave Notes: First Reflections on Sense & Spirit. Robert E. Meagher. LC 75-13041. 176p. 1975. 1.00 o.p. (ISBN 0-8006-0430-X, Fortress). Augsburg Fortress.

Cavern of the Phantoms. R. L. Stine. (Wizards, Warriors & You Ser.: No. 13). 112p. 1986. pap. 2.95 o.p. (ISBN 0-380-75041-4). Avon.

Cavers, Caves, & Caving. Bruce Sloane. 1977. 30.00 o.p. (ISBN 0-8135-0835-5). Rutgers U Pr.

Caves Du Vatican. Andre Gide. 1956. 18.95 o.p. (ISBN 0-685-11068-0). Schoenhof.

Caves of Colorado. Lloyd Parris. LC 73-188632. (Illus.). 1982. pap. 16.95 o.p. (ISBN 0-87108-589-5). Pruett.

Caves of Fire & Ice. Shirley R. Murphy. LC 80-12887. 180p. (gr. 6 up). 1980. 9.95 o.p. (ISBN 0-689-30784-5, Atheneum). Macmillan.

Caves of Fire & Ice. Shirley R. Murphy. 176p. (YA) (gr. 7 up). 1982. pap. 2.25 o.p. (ISBN 0-380-58081-0, 58081-0, Flare). Avon.

Caviar. Susan R. Friedland. 160p. 1986. 15.95 o.p. (ISBN 0-684-18437-0). Scribner.

Caviar Cruise. Forrest Webb. 1978. pap. 1.75 o.p. (ISBN 0-380-01880-2, 37077). Avon.

Cayuse Courage. Evelyn S. Lampman. LC 76-94333. (gr. 6 up). 1970. 5.50 o.p. (ISBN 0-15-215539-2, HJ). HarBraceJ.

CB Baby. Clark Whelton. 1976. pap. 1.75 o.p. (ISBN 0-380-00856-4, 30999). Avon.

CB Radio. Edward Radlauer. LC 77-20064. (Ready, Get Set, Go Ser.). (Illus.). 32p. (gr. 1-6). 1978. PLB 9.65 o.p. (ISBN 0-516-07468-7, Elk Grove Bks); pap. 2.95 o.p. (ISBN 0-516-47468-5). Childrens.

CBASIC Programming for Business. Harold Highland & Esther Highland. LC 84-25740. 256p. 1985. pap. 19.95 o.p. (ISBN 0-471-80226-3, Pub. by Wiley Pr). Wiley.

CBM Professional Computer Guide. Adam Osborne et al. 514p. 1982. pap. text ed. 17.95 o.p. (ISBN 0-07-931075-3, 75-6). Osborne-McGraw.

CD ROM: The New Papyrus. Ed. by Steve Lambert & Suzanne Ropiequet. LC 86-2369. (CD ROM Ser.). 640p. 1986. 34.95 o.p. (ISBN 0-914845-75-6); pap. 21.95 o.p. (ISBN 0-914845-74-8). Microsoft.

CD-ROMs in Print, 1988: Supplement to Optical Information Systems. 1988. pap. 37.50x o.p. Meckler Corp.

CD-ROMs: The New Generation in Data Storage. Phillip R. Robinson. (Illus.). 208p. (Orig.). 1987. (ISBN 0-8306-0336-0, 2836); pap. Tab Bks.

CDP Examguide 1985-86. 140p. 1985. pap. (ISBN 0-471-81775-9). Wiley.

CDP Review Manual: A Data Processing Handbook. 3rd ed. Kenniston W. Lord, Jr. & James B. Steiner. (Illus.). 495p. 1983. pap. 32.95 o.p. (ISBN 0-442-26087-3). Van Nos Reinhold.

Ce Formidable Bordel. Eugene Ionesco. 4.95 o.p. (ISBN 0-686-54187-1). Schoenhof.

Cebuano Grammar Notes. Maria V. Bunye & Elsa P. Yap. Ed. by Howard P. McKaughan. LC 70-152460. (PALI Language Texts: Philippines). (Orig.). 1971. pap. text ed. 7.50x o.p. (ISBN 0-87022-092-6). UH Pr.

Cecelia's Gerbils. 2nd ed. J. James Hasenau. LC 70-114065. 1970. 4.00 o.p. (ISBN 0-682-47093-7, Banner). Exposition-Phoenix.

Cecil Review of General Internal Medicine. 3rd ed. Lloyd H. Smith & James B. Wyngaarden. (Illus.). 266p. 1985. 34.95 o.p. (ISBN 0-7216-1333-0). Saunders.

Cecily G. & the Nine Monkeys. H. A. Rey. (Illus.). (gr. k-3). 1977. pap. 1.95 o.p. (ISBN 0-395-25380-2). HM.

Cecily Parsley's Nursery Rhymes. Beatrix Potter. (Illus.). (ps-2). 1922. 4.95 o.p. (ISBN 0-7232-0614-7). Warne.

Cedar of Lebanon. Paul Daher. 1957. (ISBN 0-8022-0334-5). Philos Lib.

Cedar's Boy. Stephen W. Meader. 1949. 4.95 o.p. (ISBN 0-15-215715-8, HJ). HarBraceJ.

Cefotetan: A Long-Acting Antibiotic. Ed. by H. Lode et al. LC 84-21462. (Illus.). 296p. 1985. pap. text ed. 79.00 o.p. (ISBN 0-443-03403-6). Churchill.

Celebearties & Other Bears. Phyllis Demong. 128p. 1983. pap. 3.95 o.p. (ISBN 0-380-57034-3, 57034-3). Avon.

Celebrate Friendship. Marion Stroud. (Illus.). 60p. 9.95 o.p. (ISBN 0-85648-814-3). Lion USA.

Celebrate, My Soul. Reginald Johnson. (Spiritual Formation Ser.). 1988. write for info. o.p. Victor Bks.

Celebrate the Future. David W. Romig. (Geneva Press Publication). 1973. pap. 1.65 o.s.i. (ISBN 0-664-71003-4, Westminster). Westminster John Knox.

Celebrate the Golden Years. Marion Stroud. (Illus.). 60p. 9.95 o.p. (ISBN 0-85648-836-4). Lion USA.

Celebrate the Morning. Ella T. Ellis. LC 72-75269. (gr. 5-9). 1972. 7.95 o.p. (ISBN 0-689-30051-4, Atheneum). Macmillan.

Celebrate with Drama: Dramas & Meditations for Six Special Days. W. A. Poovey. LC 74-14172. 88p. (Orig.). 1975. pap. 4.50 o.p. (ISBN 0-8066-1456-0, 10-1010, Augsburg); drama bklet 1.95 o.p. (ISBN 0-8066-1457-9, 10-1011). Augsburg Fortress.

Celebrate with Song. Charles Matonti. LC 81-71237. (Illus.). 144p. (Orig.). 1982. pap. 3.95 o.p. (ISBN 0-87793-245-X). Ave Maria.

Celebrated Jumping Frog of Calaveras County. Samuel L. Clemens. LC 75-91075. (American Humorist Ser.). Repr. of 1867 ed. lib. bdg. 39.00 o.p. (ISBN 0-8398-0267-6). Irvington.

Celebrating Bird: The Triumph of Charlie Parker. Gary Giddins. (Illus.). 128p. 1986. 15.95 o.p. (ISBN 0-688-05950-3, Pub. by Beech Tree Bks). Morrow.

Celebrating Children's Books. Betsy Hearne & Marilyn Kaye. 256p. 1986. pap. 6.95 o.p. (ISBN 0-688-00676-0). Lothrop.

Celebrating Christmas Around the World. Ed. by Herbert H. Wernecke. LC 62-13232. (Illus.). 256p. 1980. pap. 5.95 o.s.i. (ISBN 0-664-24318-5, Westminster). Westminster John Knox.

Celebrating the Medieval Heritage: A Colloquy on the Thought of Aquinas & Bonaventura. David Tracy. 1978. pap. text ed. 8.95x o.s.i. (ISBN 0-226-81125-5). U of Chicago Pr.

Celebrating the Saints. Catholic Church-Sacred Congregation of Divine Worship Staff. Tr. by International Committee on English in the Liturgy, Confraternity of Christian Doctrine for the New American Bible. 1978. pap. 10.00 o.p. (ISBN 0-916134-30-X). Pueblo Pub Co.

Celebration. Ivan Angelo. Tr. by Thomas Colchie. 224p. 1982. pap. 2.95 o.p. (ISBN 0-380-78808-X, 78808-X, Bard). Avon.

Celebration. Harvey Swados. LC 74-23733. 332p. 1975. 8.95 o.p. (ISBN 0-671-21951-0). S&S.

Celebration in Darkness. Yoshioka Minoru. Tr. by Onuma Tadayoshi from Japanese. Bd. with Strangers' Sky. Iijima Koichi. LC 84-23423. (Asian Poetry in Translation Ser: Japan: No. 6). 206p. (Orig.). 1985. pap. 10.95 o.p. (ISBN 0-295-96360-3, Pub. by K T DID Prods). U of Wash Pr.

Celebration in the Bedroom. Charlie Shedd. 1985. pap. 6.95 o.p. (ISBN 0-8499-2974-1, 2974-1). Word Bks.

Celebration of American Family Folklore: Tales & Traditions from the Smithsonian Collection. Steven J. Zeitlin & Amy J. Kotkin. 1982. 19.50 o.s.i. (ISBN 0-394-52095-5); pap. 11.95 o.s.i. (ISBN 0-394-71223-4). Pantheon.

Celebration of Awareness: A Call for Institutional Revolution. Ivan Illich. 190p. pap. 8.95 o.p. (ISBN 0-930588-31-2). Heyday Bks.

Celebration of Cats. Roger A. Caras. (Illus.). 208p. 1986. 16.45 o.s.i. (ISBN 0-671-49287-X). S&S.

Celebration of Demons: Exorcism & the Aesthetics of Healing in Sri Lanka. Bruce Kapferer. LC 81-48677. (Midland Bks: No. 304). (Illus.). 312p. 1983. 32.50x o.p. (ISBN 0-253-31326-0); pap. 18.50x o.p. (ISBN 0-253-20304-X). Ind U Pr.

Celebration of Flowers. Ray Desmond. (Illus.). 208p. 1987. 29.95 o.p. (ISBN 0-600-55075-3). Timber.

Celebration of Life: Our Changing Liturgy. David E. Babin. LC 79-97262. 1969. 4.75 o.p. (ISBN 0-8192-1102-8). Morehouse Pub.

Celebration of Vegetables: Menus for Festive Meat-Free Dining. Robert Ackart. LC 77-76469. (Illus.). 1979. 10.95 o.p. (ISBN 0-689-10805-2, Atheneum); pap. 6.95 o.p. (ISBN 0-689-70581-6, 244). Macmillan.

Celebrations. Michael Cuddihy. 28p. 1980. pap. 8.00 o.p. (ISBN 0-914742-52-3). Copper Canyon.

Celebrations for the Family. Tony Castle. 126p. (Orig.). 1986. pap. 5.95 o.p. (ISBN 0-89283-270-3). Servant.

Celebrations of Life. Rene Dubos. 1981. text ed. 12.95 o.p. (ISBN 0-07-017893-3). McGraw.

Celebrations of Life. Rene Dubos. 276p. 1982. pap. text ed. 5.95 o.p. (ISBN 0-07-017894-1). McGraw.

Celebrities of the Century: Being a Dictionary of Men & Women of the Nineteenth Century. Lloyd C. Sanders. LC 68-27185. 1094p. 1971. Repr. of 1887 ed. 95.00x o.p. (ISBN 0-8103-3774-6). Gale.

Celebrities Sweepsteaks. Elliott Negin. LC 79-17133. (Illus.). 1979. pap. 4.95 o.p. (ISBN 0-416-00161-0, NO.0131). Routledge Chapman & Hall.

Celebrity Cats. Larry Wright. (Illus.). 1982. pap. 3.95 o.s.i. (ISBN 0-03-062418-5, Owl Bks). H Holt & Co.

Celebrity Cookbook. Independent Living Center Staff. 120p. (Orig.). pap. 8.95 o.p. (ISBN 0-87397-256-2). Strode.

Celebrity Doll Price Guide & Annual. John Axe & Glenn A. Mandeville. 88p. (Orig.). 1984. pap. 5.95 o.p. (ISBN 0-87588-225-0, 2861). Hobby Hse.

Celebrity Sex Register: The Private Loves of Public People. Shirley Sealy. 256p. 1982. pap. 9.50 o.p. (ISBN 0-671-44296-1, Fireside). S&S.

Celestial BASIC: Astronomy On Your Computer. Eric Burgess. LC 82-60187. (Illus.). 300p. 1982. pap. 17.95 o.p. (ISBN 0-89588-087-3). SYBEX.

Celestial Bed. Date not set. (ISBN 0-385-29556-1). Delacorte.

Celestial Bed. Irving Wallace. 312p. 1987. 17.95 o.p. (ISBN 0-385-29556-1). Delacorte.

Celestial Chess. Thomas Bontly. 1980. pap. 3.95 o.p. (ISBN 0-345-28678-2). Ballantine.

Celestial Mechanics & Astrodynamics. Ed. by Victor G. Szebehely. (Progress in Astronautics & Aeronautics: Vol. 14). 1967. write for info. o.p. Acad Pr.

Celestial Mechanics Vol. 1: Dynamical Principles & Transformation Theory. Yusuke Hagihara. 1970. 60.00x o.p. (ISBN 0-262-08037-0). MIT Pr.

Celestial Navigation. Mary Blewitt. 64p. 1955. (ISBN 0-8022-0141-5). Philos Lib.

Celestial Omnibus: Collected Tales of Kai Lung. Ernest Bramah. 392p. Date not set. pap. 11.95 o.p. (ISBN 0-317-61295-6). Dufour.

Celestial Song of Creation. Annalee Skarin. 212p. 1962. pap. 5.95 o.p. (ISBN 0-87516-090-5). DeVorss.

Celestial Steam Locomotive. Michael Coney. LC 83-8567. 1983. 13.45 o.p. (ISBN 0-395-34395-X). HM.

Celestina by Fernando de Rojas: An Annotated Bibliography of World Interest 1930-1985. Joseph T. Snow. (Bibliographical Ser.: No. 5). iv, 124p. 1985. 15.00x o.p. (ISBN 0-942260-58-9). Hispanic Seminary.

Celestino Piatti's Animal ABC. Celestino Piatti. (Illus.). (ps-2). 1966. 4.95 o.p. (ISBN 0-689-20335-7, Atheneum). Macmillan.

Celibacy Put to the Gospel Test. Pascal Foresi. 33p. 1969. pap. 1.15 o.p. (ISBN 0-911782-16-8). New City.

Celibataires. Henri De Montherlant. 1958. 7.95 o.p. (ISBN 0-685-11070-2). Schoenhof.

Celibataires. Henry de Montherlant. 256p. 1972. 3.95 o.p. (ISBN 0-686-55511-2). Schoenhof.

Celibataires: Avec: Le Cure de Tours, Pierrette. Honore De Balzac & Anne-Marie Meininger. 1976. pap. 9.95 o.p. (ISBN 0-686-53869-2). French & Eur.

Celibate Passion. Janie Gustafson. LC 77-20439. 1978. 9.95i o.p. (ISBN 0-06-063536-3). HarpR.

Celibates. James Kavanaugh. 432p. 1986. pap. 4.50 o.p. (ISBN 0-380-70129-4). Avon.

Cell. 5th ed. Carl P. Swanson & Peter L. Webster. LC 84-17812. (Illus.). 368p. 1985. text ed. (ISBN 0-13-121799-2). P-H.

Cell Aggregation & Adhesion. Ed. by Nicholas M. Seeds et al. 1976. text ed. 34.50x o.p. (ISBN 0-8290-1930-8). Irvington.

Cell & Molecular Biology. 7th ed. E. D. DeRobertis & E. M. DeRobertis, Jr. 1980. text ed. 40.95x o.p. (CBS C). SCP.

Cell & Tissue Regeneration: A Biochemical Approach. Margery G. Ord & Lloyd A. Stocken. LC 84-3536. (Cell Biology: A Series of Monographs: 1570). 221p. 1984. 57.50 o.p. (ISBN 0-471-86248-7). Wiley.

Cell-Associated Water. Ed. by W. Drost-Hansen. 1979. 72.50 o.p. (ISBN 0-12-222250-4). Acad Pr.

Cell Biology. Seong S. Han. (Illus.). 1979. text ed. 25.00 o.p. (ISBN 0-07-025965-8). McGraw.

Cell Biology. Neal O. Thorpe. LC 83-14785. 752p. 1984. text ed. 41.95 o.p. (ISBN 0-471-08278-3). Wiley.

Cell Biology & Immunology of Leukocyte Function. Ed. by Michael R. Quastel. LC 79-11926. 1979. 72.00 o.p. (ISBN 0-12-569650-7). Acad Pr.

Cell Biology & Physiology. Herbert Levitan. 132p. 1986. pap. text ed. 9.95 o.p. (ISBN 0-8403-4135-0). Kendall Hunt.

Cell Biology of Brain. W. E. Watson. 1976. 55.00x o.p. (ISBN 0-412-11950-1, NO.6312, Pub. by Chapman & Hall England). Routledge Chapman & Hall.

Cell Biology of Breast Cancer. Ed. by Charles M. McGrath et al. LC 80-13804. 1981. 54.50 o.p. (ISBN 0-12-483940-1). Acad Pr.

Cell Biology of Inflammation. G. Weissmann. (Handbook of Inflammation: Vol. 2). 714p. 1980. 133.25 o.p. (ISBN 0-444-80141-3). Elsevier.

Cell Biology of the Eye. Ed. by David McDevitt. (Cell Biology Ser.). 1982. 85.00 o.p. (ISBN 0-12-483180-X). Acad Pr.

Cell Cycle & Cancer. Ed. by Renato Baserga. (Biochemistry of Disease Ser: Vol. 1). 496p. 1971. 89.75 o.p. (ISBN 0-8247-1039-8). Dekker.

Cell Cycle & Cell Differentiation. Ed. by J. Reinert & H. Holtzer. LC 75-8623. (Results & Problems in Cell Differentiation Ser.: Vol. 7). (Illus.). 330p. 1975. text ed. 43.00 o.p. (ISBN 0-387-07069-9). Springer-Verlag.

Cell Cycle Controls. George M. Padilla et al. 1974. 54.50 o.p. (ISBN 0-12-543760-9). Acad Pr.

Cell Cycle: Gene-Enzyme Interactions. George M. Padilla et al. (Cell Biology Ser). 1969. 83.00 o.p. (ISBN 0-12-543750-1). Acad Pr.

Cell Differentiation. J. M. Ashworth. 1973. pap. 6.50x o.p. (ISBN 0-412-11760-6, NO.6013, Pub. by Chapman & Hall). Routledge Chapman & Hall.

Cell Division & Aging. Ed. by Nancy Bucher et al. (Gerontology Ser.). 1977. text ed. 29.50x o.p. (ISBN 0-8422-7251-8). Irvington.

Cell Growth. Ed. by Claudio Nicolini. LC 81-15732. (NATO ASI Series A, Life Sciences: Vol. 38). 838p. 1981. 125.00x o.p. (ISBN 0-306-40815-5, Plenum Pr). Plenum Pub.

Cell Hybrids. N. R. Ringertz & R. E. Savage. 1976. 70.00 o.p. (ISBN 0-12-589150-4). Acad Pr.

Cell in Medical Science, 4 vols. Ed. by Felix Beck & John B. Lloyd. Vol. 1, 1974. 54.50 o.p. (ISBN 0-12-084201-7); Vol. 2, 1975. 71.50 o.p. (ISBN 0-12-084202-5); Vol. 3, 1976. 63.50 o.p. (ISBN 0-12-084203-3); Vol. 4, 1976. 63.50 o.p. (ISBN 0-12-084204-1). Acad Pr.

Cell: Inter & Intra-Relationships. National Science Foundation Staff. Ed. by Warren Kornberg. (Mosaic Reader Ser.). 64p. (Orig.). 1982. pap. text ed. 5.00 o.p. (ISBN 0-89529-171-1). Avery Pub.

Cell Membranes & Viral Envelopes, Vol. 1. H. A. Blough & J. M. Tiffany. LC 79-84537. 1980. 130.50 o.p. (ISBN 0-12-107201-0). Acad Pr.

Cell Membranes & Viral Envelopes, Vol. 2. Ed. by H. A. Blough & J. M. Tiffany. LC 77-84537. 1980. 130.50 o.p. (ISBN 0-12-107202-9). Acad Pr.

Cell Movement & Neoplasia: Proceedings of the Annual Meeting of the Cell Tissue & Organ Culture Study Group, Held at the Janssen Research Foundation, Beerse, Belgium, May 1979. Ed. by M. De Brabander et al. (Illus.). 174p. 1980. 55.00 o.p. (ISBN 0-08-025534-5). Pergamon.

Cell Physiology. Henry Tedeschi. 400p. 1989. text ed. 29.95 o.p. (ISBN 0-89116-324-7). Hemisphere Pub.

Cell Physiology: Molecular Dynamics. Henry Tedeschi. 1974. 23.50 o.p. (ISBN 0-12-685150-6). Acad Pr.

Cell Potassium. Roderick P. Kernan. LC 80-13332. 216p. 1980. 59.50 o.p. (ISBN 0-317-54623-6). Krieger.

Cell Regulation by Intracellular Signal Molecules. Ed. by Stephane Swillens & Jacques E. Dumont. LC 82-483. (NATO ASI Series A, Life Sciences: Vol. 44). 344p. 1982. 62.50x o.p. (ISBN 0-306-40980-1, Plenum Pr). Plenum Pub.

Cell Reproduction: In Honor of Daniel Mazia. Ed. by Ellen R. Dirksen et al. (ICN-UCLA Symposia on Molecular & Cellular Biology, 1978 Ser.: Vol. 12). 1978. 85.00 o.p. (ISBN 0-12-217850-5). Acad Pr.

Cell Surface Alteration As a Result of a Malignant Transformation. Jaro Ankerst et al. LC 72-13690. (Illus.). 237p. 1973. No. 2. text ed. 24.00x o.p. (ISBN 0-8422-7053-1); No. 1. text ed. 25.00x o.p. (ISBN 0-8422-7055-8). Irvington.

Cell Surface Antigens: Studies in Mammals Other Than Man. George D. Snell & W. H. Hildemann. LC 72-13690. (Illus.). 220p. 1973. text ed. 23.00x o.p. (ISBN 0-8422-7100-7). Irvington.

Cell Surface Carbohydrate Chemistry. Ed. by Robert E. Harmon. 1978. 62.50 o.p. (ISBN 0-12-326150-3). Acad Pr.

Cell Surface: Its Molecular Role in Morphogenesis. A. S. Curtis. 1967. 84.50 o.p. (ISBN 0-12-199650-6). Acad Pr.

Cell Surface: Mediator of Developmental Processes, Vol. 38. Society for Developmental Biology Symposium Staff. Ed. by Stephen Subtelny & Norman K. Wessels. 1980. 42.50 o.p. (ISBN 0-12-612984-3). Acad Pr.

Cell Surface Receptors. Ed. by Philip G. Strange. LC 82-23376. (Biochemistry in Medicine & Pharmacology Ser.). 298p. 1983. 89.95x o.p. (ISBN 0-470-27418-2). Wiley.

Cell Synchrony: Studies in Biosynthetic Regulation. Ed. by Ivan L. Cameron & George M. Padilla. 1966. 82.50 o.p. (ISBN 0-12-156950-0). Acad Pr.

Cell Therapy: A New Dimension in Medicine. Franz Schmid. (Illus.). 455p. 79.00 o.s.i. (ISBN 3-7225-6733-5). Medicina Bio.

Cell, Tissue & Organ Cultures in Neurobiology. Ed. by S. Fedoroff & Leif Hertz. 1978. 78.50 o.p. (ISBN 0-12-250450-X). Acad Pr.

Cellist's Guide to the New Approach. Claude Kenneson. LC 73-86546. (Illus.). 1974. 10.00 o.p. (ISBN 0-682-47819-9, University). Exposition-Phoenix.

Cello. Elizabeth Cowling. LC 74-16824. (Illus.). 218p. 1975. 15.00 o.p. (ISBN 0-684-14127-2, ScribT). Scribner.

Cello. rev. ed. Elizabeth Cowling. (Illus.). 240p. 1983. 17.95 o.p. (ISBN 0-684-17870-2, ScribT). Scribner.

Cells & Energy. 2nd ed. Richard A. Goldsby. 1977. pap. text ed. write for info. o.p. (ISBN 0-02-344300-6, 34430). Macmillan.

Cells & Societies. John T. Bonner. LC 55-5002. (Illus.). 1966. pap. 1.95 o.p. (ISBN 0-689-70020-2, 91, Atheneum). Macmillan.

Cells & Tissues by Light & Electron Microscopy. E. B. Sandborn. 1970. Vol. 1. 75.00 o.p. (ISBN 0-12-617901-8); Vol. 2. 75.00 o.p. (ISBN 0-12-617902-6). Acad Pr.

Cells & Tissues in Culture: Methods, Biology, & Physiology, 3 Vols. E. N. Willmer. 1965-1967. Vol. 1. 97.50 o.p. (ISBN 0-12-757601-0); Vol. 2, 1965. 134.00 o.p. (ISBN 0-12-757602-9); Vol. 3, 1967. 134.00 o.p. (ISBN 0-12-757603-7). Acad Pr.

Cells of Immunoglobulin Synthesis. Ed. by Benvenuto Pernis & Henry J. Vogel. LC 78-20000. (P. & S. Biomedical Sciences Symposia Ser.). 1979. 71.50 o.p. (ISBN 0-12-551850-1). Acad Pr.

Cells of Uterine Adenocarcinoma. 2nd rev. ed. J. W. Reagan & A. B. Ng. (Monographs in Clinical Cytology: Vol. 1). (Illus.). 1973. 42.75 o.p. (ISBN 3-8055-1621-5). S Karger.

Cellular Analogues of Conditioning & Neural Plasticity: Proceedings of a Satellite Symposium of the 28th International Congress of Physiological Sciences, Szeged, Hungary, 1980. Ed. by O. Feher & F. Joo. LC 80-41992. (Advances in Physiological Sciences: Vol. 36). (Illus.). 300p. 1981. 57.00 o.p. (ISBN 0-08-027372-6). Pergamon.

Cellular & Mobile Communications International: Proceedings of the Online Conference, London, November 1985. 252p. 1985. pap. text ed. 120.00x o.p. (ISBN 0-86353-037-0, Pub. by Online). Gower Pub Co.

Cellular & Molecular Renewal in the Mammalian Body. Ed. by Ivan L. Cameron & Jack D. Thrasher. LC 76-137622. (Cell Biology Ser). 1971. 82.50 o.p. (ISBN 0-12-156940-3). Acad Pr.

Cellular Antigens. Ed. by A. Nowotny. LC 72-85952. (Illus.). 344p. 1972. 41.00 o.p. (ISBN 0-387-90049-7). Springer-Verlag.

Cellular Basis & Aetiology of Late Somatic Effects of Ionizing Radiations: Proceedings. Ed. by Robert J. Harris. 1961. 57.50 o.p. (ISBN 0-12-327174-6). Acad Pr.

Cellular Basis of Chemical Messengers in the Digestive System. Ed. by Morton I. Grossman et al. LC 81-2318. (UCLA Forum in Medical Sciences Ser.: No. 23). 1981. 37.50 o.p. (ISBN 0-12-304420-0). Acad Pr.

Cellular Basis of Mammalian Reproduction. Jonathan Van Blerkom & Pietro Motta. LC 78-10230. (Illus.). 263p. 1979. text ed. 42.00 o.p. (ISBN 0-8067-2041-7). Urban & S.

Cellular Basis of the Immune Response. 2nd, rev. ed. Edward S. Golub. LC 80-28080. (Illus.). 325p. 1981. pap. text ed. 19.95x o.p. (ISBN 0-87893-212-7). Sinauer Assocs.

Cellular Biology of the Lung. Ed. by Gordon Cumming & Giovanni Bonsignore. LC 81-23407. (Ettore Majorana International Science Ser., Life Sciences: Vol. 10). 496p. 1982. 89.50x o.p. (ISBN 0-306-40910-0, Plenum Pr). Plenum Pub.

Cellular Communications: Proceedings of the Industry Conference, Chicago 1984. 294p. 1984. pap. text ed. 150.00x o.p. (ISBN 0-86353-015-X, Pub. by Online). Gower Pub Co.

Cellular Compartmentalization & Control of Fatty Acid Metabolism. Ed. by F. C. Gran & F. C. Gran. LC 68-31571. (Illus.). 1968. 27.50 o.p. (ISBN 0-12-295050-X). Acad Pr.

Cellular Degradative Processes. R. T. Dean. 1978. pap. 6.95 o.p. (ISBN 0-412-15190-1, NO.6082, Pub. by Chapman Hall). Routledge Chapman & Hall.

Cellular Development. D. R. Garrod. 1973. pap. 8.50 o.p. (ISBN 0-412-11410-0, NO.6117, Pub. by Chapman Hall). Routledge Chapman & Hall.

Cellular Dynamics of the Neuron. International Society for Cell Biology Staff. Ed. by Samuel H. Barondes. (Proceedings: Vol. 8). 1970. 74.50 o.p. (ISBN 0-12-611908-2). Acad Pr.

Cellular Induction. Ed. by Harold C. Slavkin et al. (Mechanism of Cell-Cell Interaction & Communication Ser: Vol. 3). 221p. 1974. text ed. 22.50x o.p. (ISBN 0-8422-7260-7). Irvington.

Cellular Mechanism for Calcium Transfer & Homeostasis. Ed. by George Nichols & R. H. Wasserman. 1971. 65.50 o.p. (ISBN 0-12-518050-0). Acad Pr.

Cellular Membranes in Development. Ed. by Michael Locke & Michael Locke. 1964. 71.00 o.p. (ISBN 0-12-454168-2). Acad Pr.

Cellular Responses to Molecular Modulators. Ed. by Lee Mozes & Julius Schultz. LC 81-12675. (Miami Winter Symposia Ser.: Vol. 18). 1981. 66.00 o.p. (ISBN 0-12-509380-2). Acad Pr.

Cellular Telephone Directory: How to Use Your Cellular Telephone Throughout the U. S. & Canada. Steven S. Brown. (Illus.). 232p. (Orig.). 1987. pap. 14.00 o.s.i. (ISBN 0-945592-00-0). Commns Pub Service.

Cellular Toxicology & Marine Pollution. Ed. by B. L. Bayne. 44p. 1985. pap. 8.25 o.p. (ISBN 0-08-032621-8, Pub by PPL). Pergamon.

Celluloid Literature: Film in the Humanities. 2nd ed. William Jinks. LC 73-7361. (Illus.). 208p. 1974. pap. text ed. write for info. o.p. (ISBN 0-02-474910-9, 47490). Macmillan.

Celluloid Wings. James H. Farmer. (Illus.). 384p. 1984. pap. 15.60 o.p. (ISBN 0-8306-2374-4, 2374). TAB Bks.

Celtic Art in Ancient Europe - Five Protohistoric Centuries: Proceedings. Ed. by Paul-Marie Duval & Christopher Hawkes. 1976. 60.50 o.p. (ISBN 0-12-785180-1). Acad Pr.

Celtic Art Source Book. Courtney Davis. (Illus.). 128p. 1989. 24.95 o.p. (ISBN 0-7137-1982-6, Pub. by Blandford Pr England). Sterling.

Celtic Britain. Lloyd Laing. (Britain Before the Conquest Ser.). 254p. 1983. pap. 9.95 o.p. (ISBN 0-586-08373-1, Pub. by Granada England). Academy Chi Pubs.

Celtic Dawn: A Survey of the Renaissance in Ireland, 1889-1916. Lloyd R. Morris. LC 78-132944. 1971. Repr. of 1917 ed. 22.50x o.p. (ISBN 0-8154-0359-3). Cooper Sq.
Celtic Mysteries: The Ancient Religion. John Sharkey. (Illus.). 1975. pap. 5.95 o.p. (ISBN 0-380-01089-5, 25296, Flare). Avon.
Celtic Warriors: 400 BC - AD 1600. Tim Newark. (Illus.). 160p. 1986. 24.95 o.p. (ISBN 0-7137-1690-8, Pub. by Blandford Pr England). Sterling.
Cement-Aggregate Reactions: Seven Reports. (Transportation Research Report Ser.). 64p. 1974. 3.00 o.p. (ISBN 0-309-02372-6). Transport Res Bd.
Cementing. D. K. Smith. 184p. 1979. 21.00x o.p. (ISBN 0-89520-203-4, 30404). Soc Petrol Engineers.
Cements Research Progress 1975. American Ceramic Society, Inc. Staff. Ed. by J. Francis Young. pap. text ed. 20.00 o.p. (ISBN 0-916094-14-6). Am Ceramic.
Cemetery Inscriptions from Dyer County, Tennessee. Mrs. Quintard Glass. 240p. 1978. 15.00 o.p. (ISBN 0-89308-095-0). Southern Hist Pr.
Cemetery Inscriptions of Ottawa County, Ohio. Ohio Genealogical Society, Ottawa County Chapter Staff. 21.00 o.s.i. (ISBN 0-935057-46-3). OH Genealogical.
Cenelles: A Collection of Poems by Creole Writers of the Early Nineteenth Century. Tr. by Regine Latortue & Gleason R. Adams. 1979. lib. bdg. 25.00 o.p. (ISBN 0-8161-8325-2, Hall Reference). G K Hall.
Censors in the Classroom. Edwin B. Jenkinson. 1982. pap. 3.50 o.p. (ISBN 0-380-59790-X, Discus). Avon.
Censorship Litigation & the Schools. American Library Association, Office for Intellectual Freedom Staff. LC 82-24458. xii, 161p. 1983. pap. text ed. 17.50x o.p. (ISBN 0-8389-3279-7). ALA.
Census Catalog & Guide: 1986. 472p. 1986. 23.00 o.p. (S/N 003-024-06500-2). USGPO.
Census Catalog & Guide: 1987. 42nd ed. (Illus.). 1987. pap. 21.00 o.p. (ISBN 0-318-23542-0, 003-024-06637-8). USGPO.
Census Handbook, 1980: Florida Counties. Ed. by Frances W. Terhune. (Illus.). x, 404p. (Orig.). 1984. pap. 15.00x o.p. (ISBN 0-8130-0807-7). U Presses Fla.
Census of British Newspapers & Periodicals, 1620-1800. R. S. Crane & F. B. Kaye. 20.00x o.p. (ISBN 0-87556-060-1). Saifer.
Census of Manufactures, 1982, Subject Series: Concentration Ratios in Manufacturing. (MC82-S-7). 196p. 1986. pap. 9.50 o.p. (ISBN 0-318-20427-4, S/N 003-024-05630-5). USGPO.
Census Tract Street Directory of the Kalamazoo-Portage Area, 1980: Based on GBF-DIME File of Urbanized Area, with Supplementary Maps. 2nd ed. 1981. 4.95 o.p. W E Upjohn.
Census, U. S. A. Fact Finding for the American People, 1790-1970. Ann H. Scott. LC 68-24734. (Illus.). (YA) (gr. 6 up). 1979. 8.95 o.p. (ISBN 0-395-28924-6, Clarion). HM.
Census Users Handbook. D. Rhind. (Illus.). 1983. 35.00 o.p. (ISBN 0-416-30510-5, NO. 3730); pap. 14.95 o.p. (ISBN 0-416-30520-2). Routledge Chapman & Hall.
Centaur. John Updike. 1983. pap. 4.95 o.p. (ISBN 0-449-20371-9, Crest). Fawcett.
Centenaire du Capital: Exposes et Entretiens Sur le Marxisme. (Nouvelle Serie: No. 10). 1969. pap. 14.00x o.p. (ISBN 90-2796-248-0). Mouton.
Centenaire ou les Deux Beringheld, 2 vols. Honore De Balzac. 468p. 1962. 50.00 ea. o.p. French & Eur.
Centenary at Jalna. Mazo De La Roche. 1978. pap. 1.75 o.p. (ISBN 0-449-23691-9, Crest). Fawcett.
Centennial Treasury of General Electronic Locomotives: Electric-Gas-Turbine-Diesel Electric Locomotives, 2 vols. O. M. Kerr. Ed. by James W. Kerr. (Railroad & Americana Transportation Ser.). (Illus.). 270p. (Orig.). 1986. Set. pap. 90.00 o.p. (ISBN 0-919295-04-5). Delta Pubns VT.
Center Cannot Hold: The Search for a Global Economy of Justice. Marvin M. Ellison. LC 82-23795. 330p. (Orig.). 1983. lib. bdg. 32.75 o.p. (ISBN 0-8191-2963-1); pap. text ed. 16.50 o.p. (ISBN 0-8191-2964-X). U Pr of Amer.
Centerany Book of the University of Sydney Faculty of Medicine. Ed. by J. Young et al. 543p. 1986. 55.00X o.p. (ISBN 0-424-00103-9, Pub. by Sydney U Pr). Intl Spec Bk.
Centered on Christ. Augustine Roberts. LC 79-4036. 1979. 11.95 o.p. (ISBN 0-932506-04-6); pap. 6.95 o.p. (ISBN 0-932506-03-8). St Bedes Pubns.
Centering in Pottery, Poetry, & the Person. Mary C. Richards. LC 64-22372. 1969. pap. 9.95 o.p. (ISBN 0-8195-6011-1). Wesleyan U Pr.
Centerplay: Focusing Your Child's Energy. Holly Y. Huth. (Illus.). 128p. (Orig.). 1984. pap. 7.95 o.p. (ISBN 0-671-50249-2, Fireside). S&S.
Central Administration in Nigeria, Nineteen Fourteen to Nineteen Forty-Eight: The Problem of Polarity. Jeremy J. White. 370p. 1981. 45.00x o.p. (ISBN 0-7165-0057-4, BBA 03050, Pub. by Irish Academic Pr Ireland). Biblio Dist.
Central Adrenaline Neurons: Basic Aspects & Their Role in Cardiovascular Disease: Proceedings of an International Symposium 27-28 August 1979, Wenner-Gren Center, Stockholm. Ed. by Kjell Fuxe et al. (Wenner-Gren Ser.: Vol. 33). (Illus.). 356p. 1980. 81.00 o.p. (ISBN 0-08-025927-8). Pergamon.
Central America & the Caribbean: Today & Tomorrow. Ed. by Barbara A. Lafford. LC 87-9378. 1987. pap. 9.95 o.p. (ISBN 0-87918-068-4). ASU Lat Am St.
Central America: Crisis & Adaptation. Ed. by Steve C. Ropp & James A. Morris. LC 84-2273. (Illus.). 333p. 1984. 22.50x o.p. (ISBN 0-8263-0745-0); pap. 10.95x o.p. (ISBN 0-8263-0746-9). U of NM Pr.
Central America: Current Crisis & Future Prospects. Jorge Dominguez & Marc Lindenberg. LC 85-47807. (Headline Ser.: No. 271). (Illus.). 80p. (Orig.). 1984. pap. 4.00 o.p. (ISBN 0-87124-098-X). Foreign Policy.
Central America Fact Book. Tom Barry & Deb Preusch. LC 85-17179. (Latin America Ser.). 288p. (Orig.). 1986. 19.95 o.s.i. (ISBN 0-394-55011-0). Grove.
Central America Fact Book. Tom Barry & Deb Preusch. LC 85-17179. (Latin America Ser.). 288p. 1986. pap. 10.95 o.p. (ISBN 0-394-62079-8, Ever). Grove.
Central American Refugee Defense Fund Newsletter. free o.p. Natl Lawyers Guild.
Central Analgetics. Daniel Lednicer. LC 82-8567. (Chemistry & Pharmacology of Drugs Monographs). 219p. 1982. 54.95X o.p. (ISBN 0-471-08314-3, Pub. by Wiley-Interscience). Krieger.
Central Appalachian Geology: NE-SE GSA '82 Field Trip Guidebook. Ed. by Peter T. Lyttle. (Illus.). 264p. (Orig.). 1982. pap. 20.00 o.p. Am Geol.
Central Auditory & Language Disorders in Children. Ed. by Robert W. Keith. 210p. 1981. 23.50 o.p. College Hill.
Central Banking in a Planned Economy: The Indian Experiment. C. R. Basu. 1977. 16.00x o.p. (ISBN 0-88386-987-X). South Asia Bks.
Central California Counties Public Schools, 1986. Lillian S. Clancy. (California Public Schools Ser.: How Are They Doing?). 400p. (Orig.). 1985. pap. 24.95 o.p. (ISBN 0-939580-31-4). CA Schl Surveys.
Central California Counties Public Schools, 1987. Lillian S. Clancy. (California Public Schools: How Are They Doing Ser.: Vol. 4). 400p. (Orig.). 1987. pap. 24.95 o.p. (ISBN 0-939580-40-3). CA Schl Surveys.
Central California Counties Public School, 1988, Vol. 4. Lillian S. Clancy. (California Public Schools: How Are They Doing? Ser.). 400p. (Orig.). 1988. pap. 29.95 o.p. (ISBN 0-939580-48-9). CA Schl Surveys.
Central California Counties Public Schools: How Are They Doing? 1985. Lillian S. Clancy. (California Public Schools: How are They Doing? 1985 Ser.: Vol. 4). 390p. 1984. pap. 23.95 o.p. (ISBN 0-939580-22-5). CA Schl Surveys.
Central Coast Women's Yellow Pages. Nancy J. Ward. (Illus.). 88p. (Orig.). 1986. 3.95 o.p. (ISBN 0-934335-00-1). C C W Y P.
Central Heating & Air Conditioning Repair Guide. 2nd ed. William Price & James Price. (Illus.). 320p. 1983. 18.95 o.p. (ISBN 0-8306-0120-1, 1520); pap. 14.60 o.p. (ISBN 0-8306-1520-2). TAB Bks.
Central Interaction Between Respiratory & Cardiovasclar Central Systems. Ed. by H. P. Koepchen et al. (Illus.). 260p. 1980. pap. 27.20 o.p. (ISBN 0-387-09948-4). Springer-Verlag.
Central Message of the New Testament. Joachim Jeremias. LC 81-66890. 96p. 1981. pap. 5.50 o.p. (ISBN 0-8006-1618-9, 1-1618, Fortress). Augsburg Fortress.
Central Nervous Control Mechanisms in Breathing--Physiological & Clinical Aspects of Regular, Periodic & Irregular Breathing in Adults & in the Perinatal Period: Proceedings of the International Symposium Held at the Wenner-Gren Center, Stockholm, Sweden, Sept. 4-6, 1978. Ed. by C. Von Euler & H. Lagercrantz. (Wenne-Gren International Symposium Ser.: Vol. 32). (Illus.). 1979. 130.00 o.p. (ISBN 0-08-024942-6). Pergamon.
Central Nervous Control of Na plus Balance. Ed. by W. Kaufmann & D. Krause. LC 76-28606. (Illus.). 212p. 1976. 25.00 o.p. (ISBN 0-88416-143-9). Year Bk Med.
Central Nervous System & Aging. A. H. Norris et al. LC 73-17289. 222p. 1974. text ed. 23.50x o.p. (ISBN 0-8422-7171-6). Irvington.
Central Nervous System, Studies on Metabolic Regulation & Function. Ed. by E. Genazzani & H. Herken. LC 73-13178. (Illus.). 260p. 1974. 55.00 o.p. (ISBN 0-387-06444-3). Springer-Verlag.
Central North Atlantic Ocean Basin & Continental Margins: Geology, Geophysics, Geochemistry, & Resources, Including the Trans-Atlantic Geotraverse (TAG) Peter A. Rona. (Illus.). 99p. 1981. pap. 45.00 o.p. (ISBN 0-08-026259-7). Pergamon.
Central Power in the Australian Commonwealth: An Examination of the Growth of Commonwealth Power in the Australian Federation. Robert G. Menzies. LC 67-28061. (Virginia Legal Studies). 198p. 1967. 12.95x o.p. (ISBN 0-8139-0177-4). U Pr of Va.
Central Supply Procedure Manual. 3rd ed. Nadean E. Wright. LC 78-26237. 1979. pap. 9.00 o.p. (ISBN 0-87125-046-2). Cath Health.
Central V. I. Lenin Museum. M. Derzhavina. 111p. 1979. 4.95 o.p. (ISBN 0-8285-1790-8, Pub by Progress Pubs USSR). Imported Pubns.
Centralia Conspiracy. facsimile ed. Ralph Chaplin. (Shorey Historical Ser.). 84p. pap. 8.95 o.s.i. (ISBN 0-8466-0183-4, SJS183). Shorey.
Centrality of Administration to Politics. Matthew Holden, Jr. 96p. 1984. pap. 3.50 o.p. (ISBN 0-318-04156-1). U Va Ctr Pub Serv.
Centralized & Decentralized Economic Systems. Wayne A. Leeman. 1977. text ed. 25.50 o.p. (ISBN 0-395-30659-0). HM.
Centralized & Distributed Data Base Systems. Wesley W. Chu & Peter P. Chen. LC 79-89472. (Tutorial Texts Ser.). 662p. 1979. 32.00 o.p. (ISBN 0-8186-0261-9, Q261). IEEE Comp Soc.
Centralized Processing--Recent Trends & Current Status: A Review & Synthesis of the Literature. Mary Hanley. (Occasional Papers: No. 71). 24p. 1964. pap. 1.00 o.p. (ISBN 0-317-58852-4). U of Ill Lib Info Sci.
Centralized Workshops in Singapore. (Asian Programme of Educational Innovation for Development: No. 1). (Illus.). 32p. 1976. pap. 5.00 o.p. (UB1, UB). UNIPUB.
Centre-State Financial Relations in India. H. L. Bhatia. 1979. 11.00x o.p. (ISBN 0-8364-0323-1). South Asia Bks.
Centrifugal Compressors for General Refinery Services. 4th ed. 1979. 13.00 o.p. (ISBN 0-317-33086-1, 822-61700). Am Petroleum.
Centrifugal Pump Clinic. 2nd., rev. & enl. ed. I. J. Karassik. (Mechanical Engineering Ser.: Vol. 6). 680p. 1989. Repr. of 1981 ed. 59.75 o.p. (ISBN 0-8247-1016-9). Dekker.
Centrifugal Pumps & Blowers. Austin H. Church. (Illus.). 320p. 1972. Repr. of 1944 ed. text ed. 22.00 o.p. (ISBN 0-88275-008-9). Krieger.
Centrifugation in Biology & Medical Science. Philip Sheeler. LC 80-21744. 269p. 1981. 59.95 o.p. (ISBN 0-471-05234-5). Wiley.
Cents-Abilities. Cherrie Farnette et al. LC 78-70903. (Kids & Careers Ser.). (Illus.). 108p. (gr. 2-6). 1979. pap. text ed. 6.95 o.p. (ISBN 0-913916-64-1, IP 641). Incentive Pubns.
Centuries of Santa Fe. Paul Horgan. LC 75-14560. (Illus.). 380p. 1976. 20.00x o.p. (ISBN 0-88307-522-9); pap. 14.95 o.p. (ISBN 0-88307-523-7). Gannon.
Centurions II: Barbarian Princess. Damion Hunter. 1982. pap. 3.50 o.s.i. (ISBN 0-345-29826-8). Ballantine.
Centurion's Shadow. George Hunt. 198p. (Orig.). 1984. pap. 4.95 o.p. (ISBN 0-86760-016-0, Pub. by Albatross Bks). Meyer Stone Bks.
Century. Fred M. Steward. (General Ser.). 1984. lib. bdg. 19.95 o.p. (ISBN 0-8161-3635-1, Large Print Bks). G K Hall.
Century of Ballads. John Ashton. LC 67-23925. 378p. 1968. Repr. of 1887 ed. 40.00x o.p. (ISBN 0-8103-3406-2). Gale.
Century of Chair Design. Frank Russell. LC 79-64344. (Illus.). 160p. 1985. 37.50 o.p. (ISBN 0-8478-0232-9); pap. 25.00 o.p. (ISBN 0-8478-0672-3). Rizzoli Intl.
Century of Chinese Revolution, 1851-1949. Wolfgang Franke. Tr. by Stanley Rudman from Ger. LC 72-113808. 202p. 1980. pap. text ed. 11.95x o.p. (ISBN 0-87249-236-2). U of SC Pr.
Century of Commentary on the Works of Washington Irving, 1860-1974. Ed. by Andrew B. Myers. LC 74-7843. (Illus.). 544p. 1976. 20.00 o.p. (ISBN 0-912882-28-X). Sleepy Hollow.
Century of DNA. Franklin H. Portugal & Jack S. Cohen. (Illus.). 400p. 1977. 37.50x o.p. (ISBN 0-262-16067-6); pap. 7.95 o.p. (ISBN 0-262-66046-6). MIT Pr.
Century of Innovation: A History of European & American Theatre & Drama, 1870-1970. O. Brockett & R. Findlay. (Theater & Drama Ser.). 1973. text ed. 51.00 o.p. (ISBN 0-13-122747-5). P-H.
Century of Law at Notre Dame. Philip S. Moore. LC 74-105724. 1970. pap. 2.95x o.p. (ISBN 0-268-00416-1, 114). U of Notre Dame Pr.
Century of Loan Exhibitions, Eighteen Thirteen to Nineteen Twelve, 5 vols. Algernon Graves. 2610p. Set. sewn bdg. 200.00 o.s.i. (ISBN 0-317-54917-0). Apollo.
Century of Model Trains. Allan Levy. (Illus.). 200p. 1984. 39.00 o.s.i. (ISBN 0-904568-00-8, Pub. by New Cavendish England). Schiffer.
Century of Oregon Covered Bridges, 1851-1952. Lee H. Nelson. (Illus.). 116p. 1976. pap. 4.95 o.p. (ISBN 0-87595-011-6). Oregon Hist.
Century of Parody & Imitation. Walter C. Jerrold & R. M. Leonard. LC 68-30585. 448p. 1968. Repr. of 1913 ed. 43.00x o.p. (ISBN 0-8103-3215-9). Gale.
Century of Politics on the Yellowstone. Lawrence F. Small. LC 83-51275. 150p. 1983. pap. 4.95 o.s.i. (ISBN 0-934318-29-8). Falcon Pr Mt.
Century of Psychology in Australia. W. M. O'Neil. 148p. 1987. pap. 17.50 o.p. (ISBN 0-424-00130-6, Pub. by Sydney U Pr). Intl Spec Bk.
Century of Revolution, 1603-1714. Christopher Hill. 1966. pap. 5.95x o.p. (ISBN 0-393-00365-5, Norton Lib). Norton.
Century of Service Eighteen Eighty-Five to Nineteen Eighty-Five at the Firm of Cromwell Truemper Levy Parker & Woodsmall Inc. John J. Truemper, Jr. LC 84-71804. (Illus.). 120p. 1985. 24.95 o.s.i. (ISBN 0-935304-81-9). August Hse.
Century of the Detective. Jurgen Thorwald. LC 64-18296. (Helen & Kurt Wolff Bk). (Illus.). 1965. 12.50 o.p. (ISBN 0-15-116350-2). HarBraceJ.
Century of Ulcer Surgery: Medical & Surgical Therapy Today. Ed. by Hermann Bunte & Peter Langhans. (Illus.). 316p. 1984. 44.50 o.p. (ISBN 0-8067-2391-2). Urban & S.
Century of World Communism: Selective Chronological Outline. rev. ed. G. J. Prpic. LC 71-75835. (gr. 9-12). 1974. 11.25 o.p. (ISBN 0-8120-6075-X); pap. 5.95 o.p. (ISBN 0-8120-0302-0). Barron.
Century Readings in English Literature. 5th ed. Ed. by John W. Cunliffe et al. 1955. 74.50x o.p. (ISBN 0-89197-068-1); pap. text ed. 28.50x o.p. (ISBN 0-89197-694-9). Irvington.
CEO: Corporate Entities & Oddities. 1984. 39.95 o.p. (ISBN 0-8144-5801-7). AMACOM.
Cephalaspids of Great Britain. Erik A. Stensio. (Illus.). 220p. 1932. 26.50x o.p. (ISBN 0-565-00466-2, Pub. by Brit Mus Nat Hist England). Sabbot-Natural Hist Bks.
Ceramic & Graphic Fibers & Whiskers: A Survey of Technology. L. R. McCreight et al. (Refractory Materials Ser., Vol. 1). 1965. 77.00 o.p. (ISBN 0-12-482950-3). Acad Pr.
Ceramic Components for Engines: Proceedings, First International Symposium, Hakone, Japan, October 17-19, 1983. Ed. by S. Somiya & E. Kanai. 812p. 1987. 123.75 o.p. (ISBN 1-85166-078-X, Pub. by Elsevier Applied Sci England). Elsevier.
Ceramic Fuel Elements. Robert B. Holden. LC 66-28066. 244p. 1966. 14.00 o.p. (ISBN 0-685-58271-X, 450002). Am Nuclear Soc.
Ceramic Powder Science. Ed. by G. L. Messing et al. (Advances in Ceramics Ser.: Vol. 21). 840p. 1987. 120.00 o.p. (ISBN 0-916094-83-9). Am Ceramic.
Ceramica Culina. Patsy Adams. (Comunidades y Culturas Peruanas: No. 7). 22p. 1976. pap. 1.65x o.s.i. (ISBN 0-88312-742-3); microfiche 2.00 o.s.i. (ISBN 0-88312-339-8). Summer Inst Ling.
Ceramica Tradicional del Oriente de Guatemala. Italo M. Hidalgo. xiv, 110p. 1980. pap. 13.00x o.s.i. (ISBN 84-8376-001-0). Mus Anthro Mo.
Ceramics for Any Hands. Marty LaVor. LC 82-187599. (Illus.). 104p. 1975. pap. 6.00 o.p. (ISBN 0-686-36023-0). Scott Pubns MI.
Cereals in the United Kingdom. D. K. Britton. 1969. 230.00 o.p. (ISBN 0-08-013896-9). Pergamon.
Cerebellar Cortex: Cytology & Organization. S. L. Palay & V. Chan-Palay. LC 73-77568. (Illus.). 400p. 1974. 96.00 o.p. (ISBN 0-387-06228-9). Springer-Verlag.
Cerebral Angiography in Clinic & Practice. H. Krayenbuehl. (Illus.). 585p. 1982. 94.50 o.p. (ISBN 0-86577-067-0). Thieme Med Pubs.
Cerebral Blood Flow: Clinical & Experimental Results. Ed. by M. Brock et al. LC 71-95562. 1969. 44.50 o.p. (ISBN 0-387-04436-1). Springer-Verlag.
Cerebral Circulation & Metabolism: Proceedings of the 6th International CBF Symposium, June 6-9, 1973. International CBF Symposium Staff et al. Ed. by T. W. Langfitt. LC 74-17491. (Illus.). 530p. 1975. 145.00 o.p. (ISBN 0-387-06645-4). Springer-Verlag.
Cerebral Circulation & Stroke. Ed. by K. J. Zuelch. LC 79-129986. (Illus.). 1971. 29.00 o.p. (ISBN 0-387-05060-4). Springer-Verlag.

Cerebral Control of Eye Movements & Motion Perception: Proceedings of the International Congress on Physiological Sciences, 25th, Munich, 1971. International Congress on Physiological Sciences Staff. Ed. by J. Dichgans & E. Bizzi. (Bibliotheca Ophthalmologica: No. 82). (Illus.). 320p. 1972. 66.75 o.p. (ISBN 3-8055-1359-3). S Karger.

Cerebral Ischemia: Clinical & Experimental Approach. Ed. by Hajime Handa & H. J. Barnett. LC 82-948. (Illus.). 152p. 1982. monograph 38.00 o.p. (ISBN 0-89640-070-0). Igaku-Shoin.

Cerebral Localization: An Otrfied Foerster Symposium. Ed. by K. J. Zuelch et al. (Illus.). 350p. 1975. 54.00 o.p. (ISBN 0-387-07379-5). Springer-Verlag.

Cerebral Magnification Angiography: Physical Basis & Clinical Results. S. Wende et al. LC 73-22648. (Illus.). 160p. 1974. 88.60 o.p. (ISBN 0-387-06651-9). Springer-Verlag.

Cerebral Palsy: Speech, Hearing, & Language Problems. Mariana Newton. LC 76-46053. (Cliffs Speech & Hearing Ser.). 1977. pap. text ed. 4.95 o.p. (ISBN 0-8220-1819-5). Cliffs.

Cerebral Sphingolipidoses: A Symposium on Tay-Sach's Disease & Allied Disorders. Ed. by S. M. Aronson & B. W. Volk. 1962. 91.00 o.p. (ISBN 0-12-064450-9). Acad Pr.

Cerebral Vascular Disease. Ed. by J. S. Meyer et al. LC 75-32669. (Illus.). 242p. 1976. 29.00 o.p. (ISBN 0-88416-134-X). Year Bk Med.

Cerebrospinal Fluid in Diseases of the Nervous System. Robert A. Fishman. LC 79-67304. (Illus.). 384p. 1980. text ed. write for info. o.p. (ISBN 0-7216-3686-1). Saunders.

Ceremonial Magic: A Guide to the Mechanisms of Ritual. Israel Regardie. LC 86-18389. 127p. 1986. lib. bdg. 19.95x o.p. (ISBN 0-8095-7013-0). Borgo Pr.

Ceremonial Order of the Clinic: Parents, Children & Medical Bureaucracies. P. M. Strong. (International Library of Sociology). 1979. 26.95x o.p. (ISBN 0-7100-0379-X). Routledge Chapman & Hall.

Ceremonias del Verano. Marta Traba. 168p. (Span.). 1981. pap. 8.00 o.s.i. (ISBN 84-85859-26-X, 2014). Ediciones Norte.

Ceremonie Pour une Chevre Sur un Nuage. Fernando Arrabal. 24p. 1966. 17.95 o.p. (ISBN 0-686-54450-1). French & Eur.

Ceremony. Robert B. Parker. (Nightingale-Lythway Ser.). 1985. pap. 9.95 o.p. (ISBN 0-8161-3833-8, Large Print Bks). G K Hall.

Ceremony: An Anthropologist's Misadventures in the African Bush. Nigel Barley. 159p. 1986. 15.95 o.p. (ISBN 0-8050-0142-5). H Holt & Co.

Cerissa. Jessica St. Claire. 1979. pap. 2.25 o.p. (ISBN 0-8439-0681-2, Pub. by Leisure Bks CT). Dorchester Pub Co.

Cerro Prieto Geothermal Field: Proceedings of the First Symposium Held at San Diego, California, Sept. 1978. Ed. by E. Barbier. (Illus.). 300p. 1981. pap. 94.00 o.p. (ISBN 0-08-026241-4). Pergamon.

Cerro Prieto Geothermal Field: Proceedings of the Second Symposium, 17-19 October 1979, Mexicali, Mexico-Selected Papers. Ed. by E. Barbier. 144p. 1982. pap. 46.00 o.p. (ISBN 0-08-028746-8). Pergamon.

Certain Life: Contemporary Meditations on the Way of Christ. Herbert O'Driscoll. 96p. (Orig.). 1980. pap. 5.95 o.p. (ISBN 0-8164-2040-8). HarpR.

Certain Noble Plays of Japan. Ernest Fenellosa. Ed. by Ezra Pound. 88p. 1971. Repr. of 1916 ed. 15.00x o.p. (ISBN 0-7165-1350-1, BBA 02051, Pub. by Cuala Press Ireland). Biblio Dist.

Certain Nonprofit Organizations: American Institute of CPAs Audit Guides Ser. 1981. pap. 9.50 o.p. (ISBN 0-686-84274-X). Am Inst CPA.

Certain Rich Girls. Ann Pinchot. LC 77-79537. 1978. 8.95 o.p. (ISBN 0-87795-174-8, Arbor Hse). Morrow.

Certain Sound: Thirty Years of Motor Racing. John Wyer. (Illus.). 260p. 1986. 22.95 o.p. (ISBN 0-85429-478-3, Pub. by Haynes Pubns). Haynes Pubns.

Certain X. Linda Orr. LC 80-21424. 56p. (Orig.). 1980. pap. 4.25 o.p. (ISBN 0-934332-24-X). L'Epervier Pr.

Certainties of Christ's Coming. J. Oswald Sanders. 128p. 1984. pap. 2.95 o.p. (ISBN 0-87788-111-1). Shaw Pubs.

Certificate Book of the Virginia Land Commission, 1779 to 1780: The Register for 1923. Kentucky Historical Society Staff. 416p. 1981. Repr. of 1923 ed. 30.00 o.s.i. (ISBN 0-89308-207-4). Southern Hist Pr.

Certification Model for Professional School Media Personnel. American Association of School Librarians Staff. 40p. 1976. pap. 4.00x o.p. (ISBN 0-8389-3179-0). ALA.

Certified Internal Auditor Examination May 1984: Questions & Suggested Solutions. Institute of Internal Auditors, Inc., Board of Regents Staff. (Thirteen Ser.). (Illus.). 53p. 1984. pap. text ed. 4.75 o.p. (ISBN 0-317-14144-9). Inst Inter Aud.

Certified Internal Auditor Examination, May 1980: Questions & Suggested Solutions, No. 7. AA Board of Regents Staff. (Illus.). 57p. 1980. pap. text ed. 4.75 o.p. (ISBN 0-89413-089-7). Inst Inter Aud.

Certified Internal Auditor Examination: May 1982-Questions & Suggested Solutions, No. 9. Institute of Internal Auditors, Inc., Board of Regents Staff. (Illus.). 51p. 1982. pap. text ed. 4.75 o.p. (ISBN 0-89413-096-X). Inst Inter Aud.

Certified Professional Membership Directory. Healthcare Financial Management Association Staff. 154p. (Orig.). 1982. pap. text ed. 15.00 o.s.i. (ISBN 0-930228-37-5). Healthcare Fin Mgmt Assn.

Cervical & Nasopharyngeal Carcinoma. G. H. Green et al. LC 74-670. 213p. 1974. text ed. 23.50x o.p. (ISBN 0-8422-7206-2). Irvington.

Cervical Pathology & Colposcopy. E. Burghardt et al. LC 77-99150. 160p. 1978. 24.50 o.p. (ISBN 0-88416-241-9). Year Bk Med.

Cesar Chavez: The Rhetoric of Nonviolence. Winthrop Yinger. LC 75-10624. 1975. text ed. 6.50 o.p. (ISBN 0-682-48274-9, University). Exposition-Phoenix.

Cesar Franck. Norman Demuth. (ISBN 0-8022-0379-5). Philos Lib.

Cesar Vallejo: An Anthology of Poetry. Ed. by J. Higgins. 1970. text ed. 24.00 o.p. (ISBN 0-08-015762-9); pap. 50.00 o.p. (ISBN 0-08-015761-0). Pergamon.

C'est de la Prose. Rebecca M. Valette & Robert L. Morgenroth. (Fr). 1968. pap. text ed. 6.50 o.p. (ISBN 0-15-505865-7, HC, HC). HarBraceJ.

C'est La Vie. Paul Pimsleur & Beverly Pimsleur. 1976. 10.95 o.p. (ISBN 0-15-505891-6). HarbraceJ.

C'est la Vie: Lectures d'aujourd'hui. 3rd ed. Paul Pimsleur. (Illus.). 207p. (Fr.). 1982. pap. text ed. 11.25 o.p. (ISBN 0-15-505892-4, HC). HarBraceJ.

CET Exam Book. Dick Glass & Ron Crow. (Illus.). 210p. (Orig.). 1984. 16.95 o.p. (ISBN 0-8306-0670-X); pap. 10.95 o.p. (ISBN 0-8306-1670-5, 1670). TAB Bks.

CETA Training: A National Review & Eleven Case Studies. Ed. by Sar A. Levitan & Garth L. Mangum. LC 81-15981. 932p. (Orig.). 1981. pap. text ed. 22.00 o.p. (ISBN 0-911558-86-1). W E Upjohn.

Cevennes Journal. Robert Louis Stevenson. LC 78-67825. (Illus.). 1979. 11.95 o.s.i. (ISBN 0-8008-1414-2). Taplinger.

Cezanne, the Steins & Their Circle. John Rewald. LC 86-50805. (Walter Neurath Memorial Lecture Ser.). (Illus.). 64p. 1987. 12.95 o.s.i. (ISBN 0-500-55018-2). Thames Hudson.

CH-Acids. O. A. Reutov et al. LC 77-30618. (Illus.). 1979. 63.00 o.p. (ISBN 0-08-021610-2). Pergamon.

Chad & the Elephant Engine. Marjorie F. Stover. LC 74-19312. (Illus.). 80p. (gr. 2-5). 1975. PLB 5.95 o.p. (ISBN 0-689-30458-7, Atheneum). Macmillan.

Chadwick System: Discovering the Perfect Hairstyle for You. John Chadwick & Suzanne Chadwick. LC 82-10461. (Illus.). 250p. 1982. 18.25 o.p. (ISBN 0-671-44016-0). S&S.

Chadwick the Chipmunk & the Sunflower Seeds. Beulah Homan. (gr. 1-2). 1977. 4.00 o.p. (ISBN 0-682-48695-7). Exposition-Phoenix.

Chaga. Will & Nicolas. LC 55-7615. (Illus.). (gr. k-3). 1955. 4.95 o.p. (ISBN 0-15-215894-4, HJ). HarBraceJ.

Chagall. Werner Haftmann. (Master of Art Ser.). 1984. 19.95 o.p. (ISBN 0-8109-0794-1). Abrams.

Chagall Lithographs V: 1974-1979. Charles Sorlier. (Illus.). 250p. 75.00 o.s.i. (ISBN 0-317-54961-8). Apollo.

Chagall's World: Reflections from the Mediterranean. Andre Verdet. LC 84-4056. (Illus.). 128p. 1984. pap. 9.95 o.p. (ISBN 0-385-19324-6, Dial). Doubleday.

Chain of Chance. Stanislaw Lem. LC 77-47668. 192p. 1978. 7.95 o.p. (ISBN 0-15-116589-0). HarBraceJ.

Chain of Reasoning. Clemens Gretter. 1978. 7.50 o.p. (ISBN 0-682-49094-6). Exposition-Phoenix.

Chain Saw Service Manual. 7th ed. Intertec Publishing Staff. 336p. (Orig.). 1985. pap. 12.95 o.s.i. (ISBN 0-87288-001-X, CSS-7). Intertec Pub.

Chairs Through the Ages: A Pictorial Archive of Woodcuts & Engravings. Harold H. Hart. 1983. 14.25 o.p. (ISBN 0-8446-6004-3). Peter Smith.

Chaissac. Barbara Nathan-Neher. (Illus.). 174p. 1988. 50.00 o.p. (ISBN 0-8478-5485-X). Rizzoli Intl.

Chalk Cross. Berthe Amoss. LC 75-4778. 160p. (gr. 6 up). 1979. 6.95 o.p. (ISBN 0-395-28887-8, Clarion). HM.

Challenge, 4 vols, No. 3. Young People's Socialist League Staff. 1970. Repr. of 1946 ed. Set. lib. bdg. 28.00x o.p. (ISBN 0-8371-9139-4, CY00). Greenwood.

Challenge: A Libertarian Weekly, 2 vols, No. 18. 1970. Repr. of 1939 ed. Set. lib. bdg. 72.00x o.p. (ISBN 0-8371-9138-6, CH00). Greenwood.

Challenge & Survival: The History of Canada. H. Herstein et al. 1970. text ed. 30.00 o.p. (ISBN 0-13-125088-4). P-H.

Challenge & the Fun of Teaching. Edward Pulling. 82p. pap. 4.95 o.p. (ISBN 0-88334-174-3). Ind Sch Pr.

Challenge for Angel. Frances Priddy. (gr. 7-10). 1963. 3.25 o.s.i. (ISBN 0-664-32301-4, Westminster). Westminster John Knox.

Challenge for the Comprehensive School: Culture, Curriculum & Community. David H. Hargreaves. 224p. (Orig.). 1982. pap. 10.95x o.p. (ISBN 0-7100-0981-X). Routledge Chapman & Hall.

Challenge: Life of Dominic Savio. Daniel Higgins. (Illus.). (gr. 5-10). 1959. 4.25 o.p. (ISBN 0-89944-025-8). Don Bosco Multimedia.

Challenge of American Foreign Policy. John P. Lovell. 304p. 1985. text ed. write for info. o.p. (ISBN 0-02-371800-5). Macmillan.

Challenge of Black Theology in South Africa. Ed. by Basil Moore. LC 73-16918. 168p. 1974. pap. 5.50 o.p. (ISBN 0-8042-0794-1, John Knox). Westminster John Knox.

Challenge of Change. T. Evans. LC 71-104788. 1970. text ed. 17.25 o.p. (ISBN 0-08-015825-0); pap. text ed. 7.75 o.p. (ISBN 0-08-015824-2). Pergamon.

Challenge of Change: Developing Business Leaders for the 1980s. Denis Boyle & Bill Braddick. 64p. 1981. pap. text ed. 10.00x o.p. (ISBN 0-566-02283-4). Gower Pub Co.

Challenge of Crime in a Free Society. Intro. by I. Silver. 1968. pap. 2.45 o.p. (ISBN 0-380-01090-9, 12633). Avon.

Challenge of Development in the Eighties: Our Response. Ed. by A. Jennings & T. G. Weiss. LC 82-348. 143p. 1982. text ed. 15.95 o.p. (ISBN 0-08-027410-2, K110). Pergamon.

Challenge of Economics: Readings from "Challenge" the Magazine of Economic Affairs. Ed. & intro. by Richard D. Bartel. LC 83-27108. 320p. 1984. pap. 12.95 o.p. (ISBN 0-87332-252-5). M E Sharpe.

Challenge of Education Change: The Content & Organization of Schooling. M. Bloomer & K. E. Shaw. 1979. 43.00 o.p. (ISBN 0-08-022994-8); pap. 21.00 o.p. (ISBN 0-08-022993-X). Pergamon.

Challenge of Interior Design. Walter B. Kleeman. 304p. 1983. 26.95 o.p. (ISBN 0-8436-0133-7). Van Nos Reinhold.

Challenge of Interior Design. Walter B. Kleeman, Jr. 1983. pap. 14.95 o.p. (ISBN 0-442-24745-1). Van Nos Reinhold.

Challenge of Japan's Internationalization: Organization & Culture. Hiroshi Mannari & Harumi Befu. LC 83-83097. (Illus.). 308p. 1985. 14.95 o.p. (ISBN 0-87011-658-4). Kodansha.

Challenge of One Hundred-Sixty (160) Si Dunn. Ed. by Richard C. Force. 54p. 1977. pap. 4.95 o.p. (ISBN 0-88006-003-4, BK 7309). Wayne Green Ent.

Challenge of Partnership: Working with Parents of Children in Foster Care. Ed. by Anthony N. Maluccio & Paula A. Sinanoglu. 225p. (Orig.). 1981. 21.95 o.p. (ISBN 0-87868-198-1, 1981); pap. 16.95 o.p. (ISBN 0-87868-180-9, 1809). Child Welfare.

Challenge of Peace: God's Promise & Our Response. U. S. Catholic Bishops Staff. pap. 1.50 o.p. (ISBN 0-8091-9325-6). Paulist Pr.

Challenge of Pierre Teilhard de Chardin. Catherine Aller. 1967. pap. 2.50 o.p. (ISBN 0-682-45719-1). Exposition-Phoenix.

Challenge of Scandinavia: Norway, Sweden, Denmark, & Finland in Our Time. William L. Shirer. LC 76-49145. 1977. Repr. of 1955 ed. lib. bdg. 24.00x o.p. (ISBN 0-8371-9345-1, SHCS). Greenwood.

Challenge of Science Education. Joseph S. Roucek. 512p. 1959. (ISBN 0-8022-1386-3). Philos Lib.

Challenge of Single Adult Ministry. Douglas W. Johnson. 112p. 1982. pap. 5.95 o.p. (ISBN 0-8170-0939-6). Judson.

Challenge of the Cults. Maurice C. Burrell. (Direction Bks.). 160p. (Orig.). 1982. pap. 3.95 o.p. (ISBN 0-8010-0816-6). Baker Bk.

Challenge of the Land. C. Little. 1969. 18.25 o.p. (ISBN 0-08-006913-4). Pergamon.

Challenge of the Wolf Knight. R. L. Stine. (Wizards, Warriors & You Ser.: No. 7). 96p. (gr. 7 up). 1985. pap. 2.25 o.p. (ISBN 0-380-89944-2). Avon.

Challenge of Violence. Derek Richter. 1973. 13.25 o.p. (ISBN 0-08-017809-X). Pergamon.

Challenge to Democracy in Central America. 82p. (Orig.). 1986. pap. 5.50 o.p. (S/N 008-000-00458-7). USGPO.

Challenge to Medicine: Macrobiotics & the Biological Revolution. William Tara. LC 85-80536. (Illus.). 188p. 1986. pap. 13.95 o.p. (ISBN 0-87040-636-1). Japan Pubns USA.

Challenge '77: Newport & the America's Cup. Theodore A. Jones. (Illus.). 1978. 14.95 o.p. (ISBN 0-393-08811-1). Norton.

Challenged Parenting: A Practical Handbook for Parents of Children with Handicaps. Bonnie Wheeler. LC 82-18144. 224p. 1982. pap. 6.95 o.s.i. (ISBN 0-8307-0835-9, 5416502). Regal.

Challenger Crosswords, No. 4. Harrison. Date not set. pap. 3.95 o.s.i. (ISBN 0-671-44009-8). PB.

Challengers to Capitalism, Marx, Lenin, Stalin & Mao. rev. ed. John G. Gurley. (Illus.). 224p. 1980. 12.95 o.p. (ISBN 0-393-01224-7); pap. 5.95x o.p. (ISBN 0-393-95005-0). Norton.

Challenges in Mental Retardation: Progressive Ideology & Services. Frank J. Menolascino. LC 76-6947. 362p. 1977. text ed. 44.95 o.p. (ISBN 0-87705-295-6). Human Sci Pr.

Challenges in Prayer. Basil Pennington. LC 82-81745. (Ways of Prayer Ser.: Vol. 1). 1982. 8.95 o.p. (ISBN 0-89453-425-4); pap. 4.95 o.p. (ISBN 0-89453-275-8). M Glazier.

Challenges to Astronomy & Astrophysics: Working Documents of the Astronomy Survey Committee. National Research Council, Astronomy Survey Committee. 296p. 1983. pap. text ed. 14.50x o.p. (ISBN 0-309-03335-7). Natl Acad Pr.

Challenges to Inerrancy: A Theological Response. Ed. by Gordon R. Lewis & Bruce Demarest. 458p. (Orig.). 1984. pap. 13.95 o.p. (ISBN 0-8024-0237-2). Moody.

Challenges to Science: Earth Science. Ed. by Robert Heller et al. (Challenges to Science Ser.). (Illus.). 480p. (gr. 8). 1973. text ed. 23.56 o.p. (ISBN 0-07-028045-2). McGraw.

Challenging Heights. Max Hennessy. LC 83-45073. 256p. 1983. 13.95 o.p. (ISBN 0-689-11399-4, Atheneum). Macmillan.

Challenging Problems in Organic Reaction Mechanisms. D. Ranganathan. 1972. 41.50 o.p. (ISBN 0-12-580050-9). Acad Pr.

Chambacu: Black Slum. Manuel Z. Olivella. Tr. by Johnathan Tittler. 1987. Lat Am Lit Rev Pr.

Chamber of Love. G. Boccaccio. 128p. 1958. (ISBN 0-8022-0144-X). Philos Lib.

Chamberlain Cabinet: How the Meetings in 10 Downing Street, 1937-9, Led to the Second World War. Ian Colvin. LC 73-155803. 1971. 8.95 o.s.i. (ISBN 0-8008-1433-9). Taplinger.

Chamberlain-Worcester Porcelain, 1788-1852. Geoffrey A. Godden. (Illus.). 375p. 1982. 140.00 o.p. (ISBN 0-09-145860-9, Pub. by Hutchinson Pub UK). Seven Hills Bk Dists.

Champ of T. V. Wrestling. Scott Siegal & Barbara Siegal. 1986. pap. 2.25 o.p. (ISBN 0-671-61094-5). Archway.

Champagne for One. Rex Stout. (Large Print Bks., Nightinale Ser.). 302p. 1987. pap. 11.95x o.p. (ISBN 0-8161-4282-3, Large Print Bks). G K Hall.

Champion: Joe Louis. Chris Mead. (Illus.). 388p. 1985. 18.95 o.p. (ISBN 0-684-18462-1, ScribT). Scribner.

Champions for God. Jerry Falwell. 132p. 1985. pap. 5.50 o.p. (ISBN 0-89693-534-5). Victor Bks.

Championship Dinghy Sailing. Christopher Caswell & David Ullman. (Illus.). 1978. 8.95 o.p. (ISBN 0-393-03205-1). Norton.

Championship Kenpo. Steve Sanders & Donnie Williams. (Specialties Ser.). (Illus., Orig.). 1983. pap. 6.95 o.p. (ISBN 0-89750-094-6, 429). Ohara Pubns.

Chan Chan: Andean Desert City. Ed. by Michael E. Moseley & Kent C. Day. LC 80-54567. (School of American Research Advanced Seminar Ser.). (Illus.). 395p. 1981. 32.50x o.p. (ISBN 0-8263-0575-X). U of NM Pr.

Chance. Joseph Conrad. 1968. pap. 5.95 o.p. (ISBN 0-393-00456-2, Norton Lib). Norton.

Chance. Joseph Conrad. 352p. 1985. pap. 3.95 o.p. (ISBN 0-553-21177-3). Bantam.

Chance, Cause, Reason: An Inquiry into the Nature of Scientific Evidence. Arthur W. Burks. LC 74-11617. (Illus.). 688p. 1977. lib. bdg. 27.50x o.s.i. (ISBN 0-226-08087-0). U of Chicago Pr.

Chance for Change: Confronting Student under Achievement. John A. Clizbe et al. 1979. 8.00 o.p. (ISBN 0-682-49395-3, University). Exposition-Phoenix.

Chance Meetings. William Saroyan. 1978. 8.95 o.p. (ISBN 0-393-08809-X). Norton.

Chance, No. 10: Bayou Bluff. Clay Tanner. 176p. 1988. pap. 2.75 o.p. (ISBN 0-380-75434-7). Avon.

Chance, No. 3: Dead Man's Hand. Clay Tanner. 176p. 1987. pap. 2.50 o.p. (ISBN 0-380-75162-3). Avon.

Chance, No. 4: Gambler's Revenge. Clay Tanner. 176p. 1987. pap. 2.50 o.p. (ISBN 0-380-75163-1). Avon.

Chance, No. 5: Delta Raiders. Clay Tanner. 176p. 1987. pap. 2.50 o.p. (ISBN 0-380-75164-X). Avon.

Chance, No. 7: Dakota Showdown. Clay Tanner. 176p. (Orig.). 1987. pap. 2.50 o.p. (ISBN 0-380-75392-8). AVon.

Chance, No. 8: Missouri Massacre. Clay Tanner. 176p. 1987. pap. 2.75 o.p. (ISBN 0-380-75391-X). Avon.

Chance, No. 9: Deadly Deal. Clay Tanner. 176p. 1988. pap. 2.75 o.p. (ISBN 0-380-75433-9). Avon.

Chance of Character of Human Existence. John Brill. 1956. (ISBN 0-8022-0178-4). Philos Lib.

Chance: Riverboat Rampage, No. 2. Clay Tanner. 176p. 1986. pap. 2.50 o.p. (ISBN 0-380-75161-5). Avon.

Chance to Change: Women & Men in the Church. Betty Thompson. LC 82-71832. 96p. (Orig.). 1982. pap. 5.50 o.p. (ISBN 0-8006-1645-6, 1-1645, Fortress). Augsburg Fortress.

Chance to Sit Down. Meredith Daneman. 176p. 1981. pap. 2.25 o.p. (ISBN 0-380-54163-7, 54163). Avon.

Chance Vought F4U-Corsair. 2nd, rev. ed. Edward T. Maloney & Uwe Feist. LC 67-16731. (Aero Ser.: Vol. 11). (Illus.). 100p. 1984. pap. 7.95 o.p. (ISBN 0-8168-0541-5, 20541, TAB-Aero). TAB Bks.

Chance Wild Apple. Marian Potter. LC 81-18711. 224p. (gr. 4-6). 1982. 11.75 o.p. (ISBN 0-688-01075-X). Morrow.

Chancel Dramas for Lent. William A. Poovey. LC 69-14181. 1969. pap. 1.95 o.p. (ISBN 0-8066-0902-8, 10-1017, Augsburg). Augsburg Fortress.

Chancelleries of Europe. Alan Palmer. 288p. 1983. Charles II, Royal Politician - see attached. text ed. 34.95x o.p. (ISBN 0-04-940071-1). Unwin Hyman.

Chancellor of Mars. Jay Moon. 1978. 8.00 o.p. (ISBN 0-682-49075-X). Exposition-Phoenix.

Chances in a Mixed Marriage. Harold Billnitzer. 1978. pap. 2.05 o.p. (ISBN 0-933350-11-2). Morse Pr.

Chancing It: Why We Take Risks. Ralph Keyes. 15.95 o.p. (ISBN 0-316-49132-2). Little.

Chandeliers in the Bathroom: Verses & Lyrics from the Seventies. Michael McAllen. 1984. 7.95 o.p. (ISBN 0-533-05802-3). Vantage.

Change Agent. Lee Grossman. LC 74-4744. 180p. 1974. 10.95 o.p. (ISBN 0-8144-5364-3). AMACOM.

Change & Continuity in the 1984 Elections. Paul Abramson et al. 322p. 1986. pap. 12.95 o.p. (ISBN 0-87187-384-2). Congr Quarterly.

Change & Innovation in Education. Jack A. Anderson & J. Wesley Little. LC 74-11415. 116p. 1974. pap. text ed. 9.95x o.p. (ISBN 0-8422-0453-9). Irvington.

Change & Other Plays. Wolfgang Bauer. 237p. 1973. 10.00 o.p. (ISBN 0-8090-3403-4); pap. 3.95 o.p. (ISBN 0-8090-0750-9). Hill & Wang.

Change, Choice & Conflict in Social Policy. Phoebe Hall et al. 1975. text ed. 15.00x o.p. (ISBN 0-435-82670-0); pap. text ed. 11.95x o.p. (ISBN 0-435-82671-9). Gower Pub Co.

Change Factor: The Risks & the Joys. Gary W. Kuhne. 128p. 1986. pap. 6.95 o.p. (ISBN 0-310-27251-3, 12316P). Zondervan.

Change for Heart: Your Family & the Food You Eat. James M. Ferguson & C. Barr Taylor. LC 78-9743. 1978. pap. 5.95 o.p. (ISBN 0-915950-22-7). Bull Pub.

Change in the Church: A Source of Hope. Robert C. Worley. LC 78-126354. 1971. pap. 3.50 o.s.i. (ISBN 0-664-24901-9, Westminster). Westminster John Knox.

Change in the Weather. Fitzhugh Green. (Illus.). 1977. 9.95 o.p. (ISBN 0-393-06429-8). Norton.

Change in the Wind. Phyllis R. Naylor. LC 79-50085. 128p. 1980. pap. 3.95 o.p. (ISBN 0-8066-1752-7, 10-1022, Augsburg). Augsburg Fortress.

Change in View: Principles of Reasoning. Gilbert Harman. 180p. 1986. text ed. 21.95x o.p. (ISBN 0-262-08155-5, Pub by Bradford). MIT pr.

Change Masters: Innovation for Productivity in the American Corporation. Rosabeth Moss Kanter. 1983. 20.45 o.p. (ISBN 0-671-42802-0). S&S.

Change of Air: Climate & Health. William A. Thompson. 1979. 12.50 o.p. (ISBN 0-684-16259-8, ScribT). Scribner.

Change of Face: What You Should Know if You Choose Cosmetic Surgery. Angelo Capozzi. 1985. 13.95 o.p. (ISBN 0-942294-14-9). Kampmann.

Change of Gods. Neal Oxenhandler. LC 62-16727. 1962. 4.50 o.p. (ISBN 0-15-116640-4). HarBraceJ.

Change of Heart. Laura Chapman. 1977. pap. 1.50 o.p. (ISBN 0-380-00977-3, 32540). Avon.

Change of Heart. Sally Mandell. 416p. 1981. pap. 2.95 o.p. (ISBN 0-440-11355-5). Dell.

Change of Name & Law of Names. Edward J. Bander. LC 73-11060. (Legal Almanac Ser.: No. 34). 128p. 1973. lib. bdg. 6.95 o.p. (ISBN 0-379-11088-1). Oceana.

Change-of-Name Guide for Bilalians. Leon H. Rashed. (Illus.). 1979. 4.00 o.p. (ISBN 0-682-49330-9). Exposition-Phoenix.

Change of Scene. Elizabeth Cullinan. 192p. 1982. 10.95 o.p. (ISBN 0-393-01568-8). Norton.

Change Only: Restructuring Steelplants for the Nineties. 344p. 1987. text ed. 56.00x o.p. (Pub. by Inst for Metals). Gower Pub Co.

Change! Seventy-One Glimpses of the Future. Isaac Asimov. 240p. 1981. 10.95 o.p. (ISBN 0-395-31545-X). HM.

Changes. Danielle Steel. (General Ser.). 1984. lib. bdg. 17.95 o.p. (ISBN 0-8161-3630-0, Large Print). G K Hall.

Changes: Becoming the Best You Can Be. Gary R. Collins et al. Ed. by Hank Resnik. (Illus.). 196p. (Orig.). (gr. 6-9). 1985. pap. 7.50 o.p. (ISBN 0-933419-07-4). Quest Intl.

Changes in California Marital Dissolution under the Tax Reform Act of 1984. Ovvie Miller et al. LC 86-231206. 35p. Date not set. price not set o.p. Cal Cont Ed Bar.

Changes in the Structure of Employment with Economic Development. 2nd ed. A. S. Oberai. (WEP Study Ser.). 66p. 1981. pap. 5.25 o.p. (ISBN 92-2-102773-2). Intl Labour Office.

Changes in the U. S. Telecommunications Industry & the Impact on U. S. Telecommunications Trade. 1984. 125.00 o.p. (ISBN 0-317-11985-0). Info Gatekeepers.

Changes of Heart: Reflections of Women's Independence. Liz Heron. 224p. 1986. pap. 8.95 o.p. (ISBN 0-86358-028-9, 80289, Pub. by Routledge UK). Routledge Chapman & Hall.

Changing American School. Ed. by John I. Goodlad. LC 66-2225. (National Society for the Study of Education Yearbooks Ser: No. 65, Pt. 2). 1966. lib. bdg. 7.50x o.s.i. (ISBN 0-226-60083-1). U of Chicago Pr.

Changing Anatomy of Britain. Anthony Sampson. 1984. pap. 8.95 o.p. (ISBN 0-394-72425-9, Vin). Random.

Changing Auditors & the Effect on Earnings, Auditors' Opinions & Stock Prices. Nancy R. Mangold. Ed. by Richard Farmer. LC 87-19128. (Research for Business Decisions: No. 93). 147p. 1987. 49.95 o.p. (ISBN 0-8357-1786-0). UMI Res Pr.

Changing Church. Katharine M. McClinton. 1957. 2.50 o.p. (ISBN 0-8192-1050-1). Morehouse Pub.

Changing Cities: A Challenge to Planning. Ed. by M. Pierre Laconte & Richard D. Lambert. LC 80-66619. (Annals of the American Academy of Political & Social Science Ser.: No. 451). 250p. 1980. pap. 15.00 o.p. (ISBN 0-87761-254-4). Am Acad Pol Soc Sci.

Changing Civil Service. Geoffrey Fry. 144p. 1985. text ed. 20.00x o.p. (ISBN 0-04-350063-3); 34.95 o.p.; pap. text ed. 18.95x o.p. (ISBN 0-04-350064-1). Unwin Hyman.

Changing Climate. Arthur Bloomfield. LC 77-80427. 128p. 1977. pap. 2.95 o.p. (ISBN 0-87123-060-7, 200060). Bethany Hse.

Changing Coastal Oceanography of the Black Sea. D. Tolmazin. (Illus.). 100p. 1985. pap. 44.00 o.p. (ISBN 0-08-033198-X, Pub. by PPL). Pergamon.

Changing Concepts of Educational Evaluation. R. W. Tyler. 114p. 1985. pap. 25.00 o.p. (ISBN 0-08-033663-9, Pub. by PPL). Pergamon.

Changing Concepts of the Nervous Systems: University of Pennsylvania School of Medicine Symposia in Anatomy. Ed. by Adrian R. Morrison & Peter L. Strick. LC 81-15037. 1982. 78.00 o.p. (ISBN 0-12-507750-5). Acad Pr.

Changing Contexts of Our Faith. Ed. by Letty M. Russell. LC 85-4418. 112p. 1985. pap. 1.95 o.p. (ISBN 0-8006-1862-9, 1-1862, Fortress). Augsburg Fortress.

Changing Countryside. Ed. by John Blunden & Nigel Curry. LC 85-5283. (Illus.). 270p. (Orig.). 1985. pap. 20.00 o.p. (ISBN 0-7099-3905-1, Pub. by Croom Helm Ltd). Routledge Chapman & Hall.

Changing Design. Ed. by Barrie Evans et al. LC 81-14682. 379p. 1982. 79.95 o.p. (ISBN 0-471-28045-3). Wiley.

Changing Environment for Library Services in the Metropolitan Area. Ed. by Harold Goldstein. (Allerton Park Institute Ser.: No. 12). 158p. 1966. pap. 4.00x o.p. (ISBN 0-87845-007-6). U of Ill Lib Info Sci.

Changing Environment of Business. Grover Starling. LC 79-26814. 1980. text ed. 24.95x o.p. (ISBN 0-87872-251-3). PWS-Kent Pub.

Changing Face of New England. Betty F. Thomson. LC 77-4476. 1977. pap. 3.95 o.p. (ISBN 0-395-25725-5). HM.

Changing Face of the Suburbs. Ed. by Barry Schwartz. LC 75-7221. 352p. 1976. lib. bdg. 20.00 o.s.i. (ISBN 0-226-74218-0). U of Chicago Pr.

Changing Family: Its Function & Future. 3rd ed. David A. Schulz. (Illus.). 368p. 1982. text ed. (ISBN 0-13-127910-6). P-H.

Changing Flora & Fauna of Britain. Ed. by D. L. Hawksworth. 1974. 109.00 o.p. (ISBN 0-12-333450-0). Acad Pr.

Changing Government of Education. Ed. by Stewart Rauson & John Tomlinson. (Institute of Local Government Studies). 220p. 1986. text ed. 39.95x o.p. (ISBN 0-04-352216-5). Unwin Hyman.

Changing Images: Figurative Painting by Irish Artists since 1970. Sean McCrum. (Illus.). 96p. 1987. 15.95 o.p. (ISBN 0-86327-066-2, Pub. by Wolfhound Pr Ireland); pap. 8.95 o.p. (ISBN 0-86327-065-4, Pub. by Wolfhound Pr Ireland). Irish Bks Media.

Changing Images of Man. Ed. by Center for the Study of Social Policy-SRI International Staff & O. W. Markley. (Systems Science & World Order Library, Explorations of World Order Ser.). (Illus.). 220p. 1981. 65.00 o.p. (ISBN 0-08-024314-2); pap. 58.00 o.p. (ISBN 0-08-024313-4). Pergamon.

Changing Industrial Law. Ed. by Don Rawson & Chris Fisher. 235p. 1985. 24.95 o.p. (ISBN 0-949614-12-2, Pub. by Croom Helm Ltd). Routledge Chapman & Hall.

Changing Law of the Sea. Ed. by Ralph Zacklin. 1974. 40.00 o.s.i. (ISBN 9-0286-0084-1). E J Brill USA.

Changing Life of the Corporate Wife. Maryanne Vandervelde. LC 77-94413. 1979. 10.95 o.p. (ISBN 0-89662-001-8, Atheneum). Macmillan.

Changing Male Roles in Today's World: A Christian Perspective for Men - & the Women Who Care about Them. Richard P. Olson. 160p. 1982. pap. 5.95 o.p. (ISBN 0-8170-0946-9). Judson.

Changing Nature of the Self: A Critical Study of the Autobiographic Discourse. Robert Elbaz. 192p. 1988. lib. bdg. 59.95x o.p. (ISBN 0-7099-5310-0, Pub. by Croom Helm UK). Routledge Chapman & Hall.

Changing New York see New York in the Thirties.

Changing Newspaper: Typographic Trends in Britain & America, 1622-1972. Allen Hutt. (Illus.). 224p. 30.00 o.p. (ISBN 0-913720-34-8, Sandstone). Beil.

Changing of the Guard. John Ehle. 1976. pap. 1.75 o.p. (ISBN 0-380-00858-0, 31252). Avon.

Changing Pattern of Distribution. Nicholas A. Stacey & Wilson Aubrey. 1965. 23.00 o.p. (ISBN 0-08-010654-4); pap. 105.00 o.p. (ISBN 0-08-010653-6). Pergamon.

Changing Patterns in Foreign Trade & Payments. rev. ed. Ed. by Bela Balassa. LC 79-95521. (Problems of Modern Economy Ser). 1970. 5.95 o.p. (ISBN 0-393-05411-X); pap. 2.95x o.p. (ISBN 0-393-09903-2). Norton.

Changing Patterns of Conception & Fertility. Ed. by D. F. Roberts & R. Chester. LC 81-66384. 1981. 37.50 o.p. (ISBN 0-12-589640-9). Acad Pr.

Changing Patterns of Trade in World Industry: An Empirical Study on Revealed Comparative Advantage. United Nations Industrial Development Organization Staff. 203p. 1983. pap. 12.00 o.p. (ISBN 0-686-44044-7, UN82/2B1, UNIDO). UNIPUB.

Changing Perceptions in Economic Policy: Essays in Honour of the Seventieth Birthday of Sir Alec Cairneross. Ed. by Frances Cairneross. 276p. 29.95 o.p. (NO. 3579). Routledge Chapman & Hall.

Changing Performance on the Job. B. Potter. 1984. pap. 9.95 o.p. (ISBN 0-8144-7613-9). AMACOM.

Changing Places: Men & Women in Transitional Occupations. Carol T. Schreiber. 1979. 27.50x o.p. (ISBN 0-262-19177-6); pap. 8.95x o.p. (ISBN 0-262-69075-6). MIT Pr.

Changing Priorities in Teacher Education: An International Survey. Ed. by Richard Goodings & Michael Byram. 240p. 1982. 26.50 o.p. (ISBN 0-89397-141-3). Nichols Pub.

Changing Priorities on the International Agenda: The New International Economic Order. Ed. by Karl P. Sauvant. (Systems Science & World Order Library: Explorations of World Order). (Illus.). 272p. 1981. 69.00 o.p. (ISBN 0-08-023117-9); pap. 40.00 o.p. (ISBN 0-08-026806-4). Pergamon.

Changing Role of Fathers. Graeme Russell. LC 82-20041. (Illus.). 250p. 1985. text ed. 24.50 o.p. (ISBN 0-7022-1942-8); pap. 9.95 o.p. (ISBN 0-7022-1952-5). U of Queensland Pr.

Changing Role of State Library Consultants. Ed. by Guy Garrison. (Monograph: No. 9). 98p. 1968. 4.00x o.p. (ISBN 0-87845-031-9). U of Ill Lib Info Sci.

Changing Role of the Teacher: International Perspectives. (IBE Studies & Surveys in Comparative Education). 234p. (Co-published with Unipub, New York; Ontario Institute for Studies in Education, Toronto). 1977. pap. 14.50 o.p. (ISBN 92-3-101459-5, U768, UNESCO). UNIPUB.

Changing Roles of Debt & Equity in Financing U. S. Capital Formation. Ed. by Benjamin M. Friedman. LC 81-16353. (National Bureau of Economic Research-Project Report). 128p. 1982. lib. bdg. 12.00x o.s.i. (ISBN 0-226-26340-1). U of Chicago Pr.

Changing Roles of Men & Women. Shirley Schwarzrock & C. Gilbert Wrenn. (Coping with Ser.). (Illus.). 31p. (gr. 7-12). 1970. pap. text ed. 3.00 o.p. (ISBN 0-913476-29-3). Am Guidance.

Changing Room. David Storey. Incl. Home; Contractor. 1975. pap. 2.95 o.p. (ISBN 0-380-00301-5, 48116, Bard). Avon.

Changing Schools Through the Arts. J. Remer. 160p. 1982. text ed. 19.95 o.p. (ISBN 0-07-051847-5). McGraw.

Changing Sea-Level along the North Coast of Kuwait Bay. Taiba A. Al-Asfour. 208p. 1982. 50.00x o.p. (ISBN 0-7103-0010-7). Routledge Chapman & Hall.

Changing Special Education. Wilfred K. Brennan. 128p. 1982. 32.00x o.p. (ISBN 0-335-10046-5, Pub. by Open Univ Pr); pap. 15.00x o.p. (ISBN 0-335-10045-7). Taylor & Francis.

Changing Stations. Alicen Adams. (Illus.). 112p. 1983. 7.00 o.p. (ISBN 0-682-40141-2). Exposition-Phoenix.

Changing Stations: The Memoirs of an Air Force Wife. Mary L. Price. 192p. 1984. pap. 10.00 o.p. (ISBN 0-682-40165-X). Exposition-Phoenix.

Changing Structure of Comparative Advantage in American Manufacturing. Keith E. Maskus. Ed. by Fred Bateman. LC 83-9209. (Research in Business Economics & Public Policy Ser.: No. 4). 110p. 1983. 37.95 o.p. (ISBN 0-8357-1443-8). UMI Res Pr.

Changing Structure of the Western Economy. Douglas Copland. (Beatty Memorial Lectures Ser.). 86p. 1963. 2.75 o.p. (ISBN 0-7735-0014-6, McGill Canada). U of Toronto Pr.

Changing Structure of the World Oil Industry. Ed. by David Hawdon. LC 84-23769. 112p. 1985. 26.00 o.p. (ISBN 0-7099-3717-2, Pub. by Croom Helm Ltd). Routledge Chapman & Hall.

Changing Syntheses in Development. Ed. by Meredith N. Runner & Meredith N. Runner. 1971. 57.50 o.p. (ISBN 0-12-612971-1); pap. 43.00 o.p. (ISBN 0-12-612972-X). Acad Pr.

Changing the Word: The Printing Industry in Transition. Alan Marshall. (Comedia Ser.). (Illus.). 160p. 1983. 15.00 o.p. (ISBN 0-906890-10-1, Dist. by Kampmann); pap. 6.95 o.p. (ISBN 0-906890-11-X, Dist. by Kampmann). M Boyars Pubs.

Changing Tide. Iris Bromige. 192p. 1987. 18.95 o.p. (ISBN 0-340-40714-X, Pub. by Hodder & Stoughton UK). David & Charles.

Changing Times. Tim Kennemore. LC 84-13505. 192p. (gr. 6 up). 1984. 14.95 o.p. (ISBN 0-571-13285-5). Faber & Faber.

Changing Times: Changing Libraries. Ed. by George S. Bonn & Sylvia G. Faibisoff. LC 78-1283. (Allerton Park Institutes Ser.: No. 22). 166p. 1978. 8.00x o.p. (ISBN 0-87845-047-5). U of Ill Lib Info Sci.

Changing Urban School. Robert Thornbury. 1978. 27.00x o.p. (ISBN 0-416-55020-7, NO.2545); pap. 12.95x o.p. (ISBN 0-416-55030-4, NO.2546). Routledge Chapman & Hall.

Changing Views About the Principles of Scientific Theory Evaluation. Ed. by G. Buchdahl. 90p. 1981. pap. 20.00 o.p. (ISBN 0-08-027408-0). Pergamon.

Changjiang: The Longest River in China. 1981. 19.95 o.p. (ISBN 0-8351-0818-X); 14.95 o.p. (ISBN 0-8351-0807-4). China Bks.

Channel West & Solent Almanac: A Nautical Almanac for Yachtsmen. Ed. by Goulder. (Illus.). 200p. 1987. spiral bdg. 23.50 o.p. (ISBN 0-229-11727-9, Pub. by Adlard Coles). Sheridan.

Chanoyu: Japanese Tea Ceremony. Hayashiya Seizo. (Illus.). 187p. 1979. pap. 7.50 o.s.i. (ISBN 0-317-34788-8). Japan Soc.

Chanson De Roland. Pierre Le Gentil. Tr. by Frances F. Beer. LC 69-12726. (Illus.). 1969. 13.95x o.p. (ISBN 0-674-10905-8). Harvard U Pr.

Chanson Pour Don Juan. Michel Butor. 1973. 750.00 o.p. (ISBN 0-686-51939-6). French & Eur.

Chant Du Monde: Roman. Jean Giono. (Coll. Soleil). 1963. 14.50 o.p. (ISBN 0-685-11074-5). Schoenhof.

Chant Funebre. Honore De Balzac. 9.95 o.p. (ISBN 0-686-53840-4). French & Eur.

Chants for Children. Mary L. Colgin. LC 81-68685. (Illus.). 75p. (Orig.). (ps-8). 1982. pap. 9.95 o.p. (ISBN 0-9604582-1-2). Colgin Pub.

Chanukah. Howard Greenfeld. LC 76-6527. 1976. 6.95 o.s.i. (ISBN 0-03-015566-5). H Holt & Co.

Chanukah, Passover, Rosh Hashanah, Yom Kippur. Howard Greenfeld. 1982. boxed set 20.00 o.s.i. (ISBN 0-03-057626-1). H Holt & Co.

Titles

Chaos & Context: A Study in William James. Charlene H. Seigfried. LC 77-86346. xiii, 137p. 1978. 15.00x o.p. (ISBN 0-8214-0378-8). Ohio U Pr.

Chaos et la Nuit. Henri De Montherlant. 1963. 13.25 o.p. (ISBN 0-685-11075-3). Schoenhof.

Chaos et la Nuit. Henry de Montherlant. 1973. 3.95 o.p. (ISBN 0-686-55512-0). Schoenhof.

Chapayev. D. Furmanov. 318p. 1974. 3.45 o.p. (ISBN 0-8285-0970-0, Pub. by Progress Pubs USSR). Imported Pubns.

Chapel of Sesostris III at Uronarti. Charles C. Van Siclen, III. 58p. 1982. pap. text ed. 10.00x o.p. (ISBN 0-933175-02-7). Globe Pequot.

Chaplin: His Life & Art. David Robinson. (Illus.). 896p. 1985. text ed. 24.95 o.p. (ISBN 0-07-053181-1). McGraw.

Chapman Piloting, Seamanship, & Small Boat Handling. 57th ed. Elbert S. Maloney. 25.00 o.p. (ISBN 0-688-05890-6). Morrow.

Chapman's Log & Owner's Manual. John Whiting & Tom Bottomley. 192p. 1980. 16.95 o.p. (ISBN 0-87851-801-0); 75.00 o.p. (ISBN 0-686-96737-2). Hearst Bks.

Chapman's Piloting, Seamanship & Small Boat Handling. 56th rev. ed. Charles F. Chapman & Elbert S. Maloney. (Illus.). 624p. 1983. FPT 23.95 o.p. (ISBN 0-87851-814-2, Pub. by Hearst Bks); deluxe ed. 33.95 FPT o.p. (ISBN 0-87851-815-0). Morrow.

Chapter Closed. Dorothy Martin. (Peggy Ser.: No. 8). (gr. 7). 1985. pap. 3.50 o.p. (ISBN 0-8024-8308-9). Moody.

Chapter Eleven: Business Reorganizations. Practising Law Institute Staff & Harold Novikoff. LC 83-62934. (Commercial Law & Practice Course Handbook Ser.: No. 314). (Illus.). 512p. 1983. 40.00 o.p. (A4-4073). PLI.

Chapter of Accidents. Goronwy Rees. LC 73-161407. 271p. 1972. 1.95 o.p. (ISBN 0-912050-08-X, Library Pr). Open Court.

Chapter of Talmud. 1982. 4.50 o.s.i. (ISBN 0-686-76490-0). Feldheim.

Chapter of the Self. Trevor Leggett. (Illus.). 1978. 12.95 o.p. (ISBN 0-7100-8702-0). Routledge Chapman & Hall.

Chapter 13: Federal Plan Repay Debts. 2nd ed. Kosel. 1984. 14.95 o.p. (ISBN 0-917316-84-3). Nolo Pr.

Chapters from the American Experience, Vol. 1. Ed. by Frank Fahey & Marie Fahey. (American History Ser.). (Illus.). 1970. pap. text ed. (ISBN 0-13-128108-9). P-H.

Chapwoman's Guide: Shemanship & Pilot Handling. Anne L. Sirna & Antonia F. Ritchie. LC 86-72289. (Illus.). 99p. (Orig.). 1986. pap. text ed. 7.95 o.p. (ISBN 0-940073-00-5). Anagram Group.

Character Analysis. Wilhelm Reich. 1974. pap. 14.95 o.p. (ISBN 0-671-21779-8, Touchstone Bks). S&S.

Character & Characterization in Shakespeare. Leo Kirschbaum. LC 61-12265. (Waynebooks Ser.: No. 4). 177p. (Orig.). 1962. pap. 8.95x o.p. (ISBN 0-8143-1180-6). Wayne St U Pr.

Character & Conflict in Jane Austen's Novels: A Psychological Approach. Bernard J. Paris. LC 78-13281. 208p. 1979. 21.50x o.p. (ISBN 0-8143-1616-6). Wayne St U Pr.

Character & Opinion in the United States. George Santayana. 1967. pap. 3.45x o.p. (ISBN 0-393-00389-2, Norton Lib). Norton.

Character & Origins of Smog Aerosols: A Digest of Results from the California Aerosol Characterization Experiment (ACHEX, Vol. 9. Ed. by George M. Hidy et al. LC 79-4585. (Advances in Environmental Science & Technology Ser.). 776p. 1980. 100.00 o.p. (ISBN 0-471-04899-2). Wiley.

Character Catalogue. Richard Peterson. 104p. 1984. pap. 6.95x o.p. (ISBN 0-89676-069-3). Drama Bk.

Character Development in College Students, Vol. II: The Curriculum & Longitudinal Results. Janet C. Loxley & John M. Whiteley. 1986. 14.95 o.p. (ISBN 1-55620-004-8, 72151C). Am Assn Coun Dev.

Character Jug Collector's Handbook. Kevin Pearson. (Illus.). 150p. (Orig.). 1988. pap. 15.00 o.p. (ISBN 0-9510768-3-3, Pub. by Kevin Francis Pub Ltd England). Seven Hills Bk Dists.

Character Jug Collectors Handbook. 3rd ed. Kevin Pearson. Ed. by Catherine Braithwrite. (Illus.). 128p. 1987. pap. 15.00 o.p. (ISBN 0-9510768-4-1, Pub. by Kevin Francis Pub Ltd England). Seven Hills Bk Dists.

Character of American History. W. R. Brock. 1960. lib. bdg. 17.50x o.p. (ISBN 0-88307-036-7). Gannon.

Character of the Good Ruler: Puritan Political Ideas in New England, 1630-1730. T. H. Breen. 320p. 1974. pap. 3.95x o.p. (ISBN 0-393-00747-2, Norton Lib.). Norton.

Character, Plot & Thought in Plato's Timaeus-Critias. W. Welliver. (Philosophia Antiqua: No. 32). 1977. pap. text ed. 12.50x o.p. (ISBN 90-04-04870-7). Humanities.

Character Policy: An Emerging Issue. Ed. by Edward A. Wynne. LC 82-40067. (Illus.). 234p. (Orig.). 1982. PLB 36.00 o.p. (ISBN 0-8191-2431-1); pap. text ed. 15.75 o.p. (ISBN 0-8191-2432-X). U Pr of Amer.

Character Recognition. Ed. by A. Holt. 1976. pap. 28.00 o.p. (ISBN 0-08-020715-4). Pergamon.

Character Structure & Impulsiveness. David Kipnis. LC 76-127687. (Personality & Psychopathology Ser.). 1971. 41.00 o.p. (ISBN 0-12-409450-3). Acad Pr.

Characteristics & Identification of Gifted & Talented Students. 2nd ed. Frederick B. Tuttle, Jr. & Laurence A. Becker. 144p. 1980. 8.95 o.p. (ISBN 0-8106-0732-8). NEA.

Characteristics of Mechanical Engineering Systems. Roy Holmes. 1977. text ed. 20.00 o.p. (ISBN 0-08-021033-3); pap. text ed. 8.50 o.p. (ISBN 0-08-021032-5). Pergamon.

Characteristics of Self Aerated Free-Surface Flows. Ed. by N. S. Rao Lakshmana & H. E. Kobus. pap. cancelled o.s.i. (ISBN 3-503-01317-2). Adlers Foreign Bks.

Characteristics of the Population Below the Poverty Level: 1984. (Current Population Reports Series P-60 Consumer Income: No. 152). (Illus.). 164p. 1986. pap. 8.00 o.p. (ISBN 0-318-21366-4, S/N 003-001-91658-4). USGPO.

Characterization of Erythrocyte-Reactive Factors of Panulirus Argus: A Contribution to Immunophylogeny. Peter Weinheimer. LC 72-6280. 110p. 1972. text ed. 27.50x o.p. (ISBN 0-8422-7035-3). Irvington.

Characterization of Materials for Service at Elevated Temperatures, MPC-7. Ed. by G. V. Smith. (Bk. No. G00134). 536p. 1978. 50.00 o.p. (ISBN 0-685-37564-1). ASME.

Characterization of the Polymers in the Solid State I. Ed. by H. H. Kausch & H. G. Zachmann. (Advances in Polymer Science Ser.: Vol. 66). (Illus.). 240p. 1985. 65.00 o.p. (ISBN 0-387-13779-3). Springer-Verlag.

Characterization of the Temporary Radiation Work Force at U. S. Nuclear Power Plants: AIF-NESP-028. Faucett, Jack, Associates Staff & S C & A Inc. Staff. (National Environmental Studies Project: NESP Reports). 1984. 75.00 o.p. (ISBN 0-318-02229-X). US Coun Energy Awareness.

Characters & Commentaries. Giles L. Strachey. LC 78-23722. 1979. Repr. of 1933 ed. lib. bdg. 35.00x o.p. (ISBN 0-313-20763-1, STCCO). Greenwood.

Characters & Kings: A Woman's Workshop on the History of Israel, 2 pts. Carolyn Nystrom. (Woman's Workshop Ser.). 240p. (Orig.). 1985. Part 1. pap. 2.95 o.p. (ISBN 0-310-41881-X, 11279P); Part 2. pap. 2.95 o.p. (ISBN 0-310-41871-2, 11283P). Zondervan.

Characters & Passages from Notebooks. Samuel Butler. 489p. Repr. of 1908 ed. 69.00 o.p. (ISBN 0-403-08911-5). Somerset Pub.

Characters & Their Landscapes. Ronald Blythe. (Helen & Kurt Wolff Bk.). 216p. 1984. pap. 5.95 o.p. (ISBN 0-15-616763-8, Harv). HarBraceJ.

Characters Around the Cross see Were You There.

Characters, Plots & Settings of Calderon's Comedias. Richard W. Tyler & Sergio D. Elizondo. LC 80-53825. 496p. (Orig.). 1981. pap. 35.00 o.p. (ISBN 0-89295-019-6). Society Sp & Sp-Am.

Charade. Peter Stone. 1980. pap. 1.95 o.p. (ISBN 0-380-48520-6, 48520). Avon.

Charco. Dorothy Hamilton. LC 74-153966. (Illus.). 120p. (gr. 4-9). 1971. pap. 3.95 o.p. (ISBN 0-8361-1657-7). Herald Pr.

Charge Transfer Devices. G. S. Hobson. LC 78-40587. (Contemporary Electrical Engineering Ser.). 207p. 1978. 61.95x o.p. (ISBN 0-470-26458-6). Halsted Pr.

Chariot of Fire. E. E. Hales. 1978. pap. 1.75 o.p. (ISBN 0-380-01853-5, 36509). Avon.

Chariot of Israel: Britain, America & the State of Israel. Harold Wilson. (Illus.). 406p. 1982. 24.95 o.p. (ISBN 0-393-01591-2). Norton.

Chariots of God: Biblical Blueprints on Defense. Albion Knight. cancelled o.s.i. (ISBN 0-930462-20-3). Am Bur Eco Res.

Charisma Campaigns. Jack Matthews. LC 71-174511. 1972. 5.95 o.p. (ISBN 0-15-116800-8). HarBraceJ.

Charismata: God's Gift for God's People. John Koenig. LC 77-12700. (Biblical Perspectives on Current Issues). 214p. 1978. softcover 5.95 o.s.i. (ISBN 0-664-24176-X, Westminster). Westminster John Knox.

Charismatic Bureaucrat: A Political Biography of Matsudaira Sadanobu, 1758-1829. Herman Ooms. LC 74-10342. xiv, 226p. 1975. lib. bdg. 15.00x o.s.i. (ISBN 0-226-63031-5). U of Chicago Pr.

Charismatic Christ. A. Michael Ramsey et al. 128p. (Orig.). 1973. pap. 3.95 o.p. (ISBN 0-8192-1141-9). Morehouse Pub.

Charismatic Spiritual Gifts: A Phenomenological Analysis. William J. Sneck. LC 80-8291. 312p. (Orig.). 1981. lib. bdg. 29.25 o.p. (ISBN 0-8191-1765-X); pap. text ed. 15.25 o.p. (ISBN 0-8191-1766-8). U Pr of Amer.

Charisms & Charismatic Renewal: A Biblical & Theological Study. Francis A. Sullivan. 182p. 1982. pap. 8.95 o.p. (ISBN 0-89283-121-9). Servant.

Charity. Emanuel Swedenborg. LC 81-84629. 120p. pap. 1.95 o.s.i. (ISBN 0-87785-168-9). Swedenborg.

Charity, Law & Social Justice. Francis Gladstone. 211p. (Orig.). 1982. pap. text ed. 12.50 Brit. pds. o.p. (ISBN 0-7199-1084-6, Pub. by Bedford England). Gower Pub Co.

Charity Law & Voluntary Organizations. Report of the Goodman Committee. 150p. 1976. pap. text ed. 5.00x o.p. (ISBN 0-7199-0910-4, Pub. by Bedford England). Gower Pub Co.

Charity Never Faileth. Vaughn J. Featherstone. LC 80-10528. 121p. 1980. 8.95 o.s.i. (ISBN 0-87747-806-6). Deseret Bk.

Charlas Sobre la Educacion. Vera Zhukovskaya. 192p. (Span.). 1979. pap. 2.45 o.p. (ISBN 0-8285-1311-2, Pub. by Progress Pubs USSR). Imported Pubns.

Charlatan. William Hamilton. 236p. 1985. 16.45 o.p. (ISBN 0-671-54419-5). S&S.

Charles & Diana. Janice Dunlop. 1981. pap. 2.95 o.p. (ISBN 0-440-11205-2). Dell.

Charles & Diana. Ralph G. Martin. 639p. 1986. lib. bdg. 19.95 o.p. (ISBN 0-8161-4136-3, Large Print Bks). G K Hall.

Charles Atlas Yours in Perfect Manhood. George Butler & Charles Gaines. 192p. 1982. pap. 9.50 o.p. (ISBN 0-671-44574-X, Fireside). S&S.

Charles Baurchfield: Catalogue of Paintings in Public & Private Collections. Munson-Williams-Proctor Institute Staff. (Illus.). 368p. 1970. pap. 14.95 o.p. (ISBN 0-295-96400-6). U of Wash Pr.

Charles Bear & the Mystery of the Forest. Douglas Adamson. LC 77-2805. (Illus.). (gr. 1 up). 1977. 6.95 o.p. (ISBN 0-395-25841-3). HM.

Charles Beard & the Constitution. Robert E. Brown. 1965. pap. 3.25x o.p. (ISBN 0-393-00296-9, Norton Lib). Norton.

Charles Berlitz's World of Strange Phenomena. Charles Berlitz. 288p. 1988. 16.95 o.p. (ISBN 0-8007-7205-9). Wynwood Pr.

Charles Bridgeman: And the English Landscape Garden. Peter Willis. Ed. by John Harris & Alastair Laing. (Studies in Architecture: No. XVII). (Illus.). 233p. 1986. 125.00 o.p. (ISBN 0-302-02777-7, Pub. by Zwemmer Bks UK). Sotheby Pubns.

Charles Brockden Brown: A Reference Guide. Patricia L. Parker. 1980. lib. bdg. 28.00 o.p. (ISBN 0-8161-8450-X, Hall Reference). G K Hall.

Charles Chaplin Film Guide. Timothy J. Lyons. 1978. 36.50 o.p. (ISBN 0-8161-7888-7, Hall Reference). G K Hall.

Charles Darwin. John Chancellor. LC 76-5175. (Illus.). (YA) (gr. 10 up). 13.95 o.s.i. (ISBN 0-8008-1434-7). Taplinger.

Charles Darwin: A Companion. Richard B. Freeman. LC 78-40928. (Illus.). 309p. 1978. 32.50 o.p. (ISBN 0-208-01739-9, Archon). Shoe String.

Charles Darwin: A Man of Enlarged Curiosity. Peter Brent. (Illus.). 560p. 1983. pap. 9.25 o.p. (ISBN 0-393-30109-5). Norton.

Charles Darwin & the Problems of Creation. Neal C. Gillespie. LC 79-11231. 1982. pap. text ed. 7.50x o.s.i. (ISBN 0-226-29375-0). U of Chicago Pr.

Charles de Gaulle: A Biography. Don Cook. 432p. 1985. pap. 10.95 o.p. (ISBN 0-399-51143-1, Perigee). Putnam Pub Group.

Charles Dickens. Jack Lindsay. 1957. (ISBN 0-8022-0977-7). Philos Lib.

Charles Dickens & His World. J. B. Priestley. (Illus.). 1978. 3.95 o.p. (ISBN 0-684-15574-5, ScribT); encore ed. 3.95 o.p. (ISBN 0-684-17252-6). Scribner.

Charles Dickens' Sketches by Boz: End in the Beginning. Virgil Grillo. LC 73-89257. (Illus.). 1974. 17.50x o.p. Univ Pr Colo.

Charles E. Ives: Discography. Compiled by Richard Warren. LC 77-28812. 1978. Repr. of 1972 ed. lib. bdg. 35.00 o.p. (ISBN 0-313-20256-7, WAID). Greenwood.

Charles E. Ives: Memos. Charles E. Ives. Ed. by John E. Kirkpatrick. (Illus.). 1972. 15.00x o.p. (ISBN 0-393-02153-X). Norton.

Charles Eliot Norton: Apostle of Culture in a Democracy. Kermit Vanderbilt. LC 59-10321. (Illus.). 1959. 20.00x o.p. (ISBN 0-674-11025-0, Belknap Pr). Harvard U Pr.

Charles F. Lummis: Crusader in Corduroy. Dudley Gordon. (Illus.). xxii, 344p. 1972. leatherette 20.00 o.p. (ISBN 0-317-11661-4). Dawsons.

Charles F. Lummis: Editor of the Southwest. Edwin R. Bingham. LC 73-15058. (Illus.). 218p. 1973. Repr. of 1955 ed. lib. bdg. 35.00x o.p. (ISBN 0-8371-7149-0, BICL). Greenwood.

Charles First: A Study. Florence M. Higham. LC 78-21342. 1979. Repr. of 1932 ed. lib. bdg. 35.00x o.p. (ISBN 0-8371-6188-6, HICH). Greenwood.

Charles Haddon Spurgeon: A Preachers Progress. Patricia S. Kruppa. Ed. by Peter Stansky & Leslie Hume. LC 81-48362. (Modern British History Ser.). 500p. 1982. lib. bdg. 79.00 o.p. (ISBN 0-8240-5158-0). Garland Pub.

Charles Hartshorhe. new ed. Alan Gragg. Ed. by Bob E. Patterson. LC 70-188063. (Makers of Modern Theological Minds Ser.). 128p. 1973. 8.95 o.p. (ISBN 0-87680-270-6, 80270). Word Bks.

Charles Horton Cooley & the Social Self in American Thought. Marshall J. Cohen. LC 80-8477. (Modern American History Ser.). 278p. 1981. lib. bdg. 43.00 o.p. (ISBN 0-8240-4852-0). Garland Pub.

Charles Hullmandel & James Duffield Harding: The English Art of Drawing on Stone 1800-1850. Christine Swenson. (Illus.). 46p. (Orig.). 1982. pap. text ed. 7.50 o.p. (ISBN 0-87391-031-1). Smith Coll.

Charles Ives & His America. Frank Rossiter. (Illus.). 420p. (Orig.). 1975. 15.00 o.p. (ISBN 0-87140-610-1). Liveright.

Charles Keeping's Book of Classic Ghost Stories. Ed. by Charles Keeping. LC 86-10774. (Illus.). 144p. 1988. pap. 7.95 o.p. (ISBN 0-87226-169-7). P Bedrick Bks.

Charles Lamb's Town & Country Revisited. Wallace Nethery. (Illus.). i, 55p. 1983. 17.50 o.p. (ISBN 0-317-11695-9). Dawsons.

Charles M. Russell. Ed. by Carol Clark. (Illus.). 17p. 1984. 12.50 o.p. (ISBN 0-88360-046-3, Dist by Univ. of Texas Pr). Amon Carter.

Charles M. Russell: Paintings, Drawings & Sculpture in the Amon G. Carter Collection. Frederic G. Renner. LC 74-5114. (Illus.). 296p. 1974. 50.00 o.p. (ISBN 0-8109-0466-7). Abrams.

Charles M. Russell: Paintings, Drawings & Sculpture in the Amon G. Carter Museum. rev. ed. Frederic G. Renner. LC 74-5114. (Illus.). 296p. 1974. 50.00 o.p. (ISBN 0-8109-0466-7, Pub. by Univ. of Texas Pr). Amon Carter.

Charles McCabe Reader: The Best & the Last of Charles McCabe Himself. Charles McCabe. LC 84-17474. 288p. 1984. 14.95 o.p. (ISBN 0-87701-325-X). Chronicle Bks.

Charles Marion Russell. Robert L. Gale. LC 79-53651. (Western Writers Ser.: No. 38). (Illus.). 48p. 1979. pap. 2.95x o.p. (ISBN 0-88430-062-5). Boise St Univ.

Charles Mason Remey & the Baha'i Faith. Francis C. Spataro. 32p. 1987. 6.95 o.p. (ISBN 0-8062-2978-0). Carlton.

Charles Olson: Call Him Ishmael. Paul Christensen. 261p. 1979. text ed. 15.00x o.p. (ISBN 0-292-71046-1). U of Tex Pr.

Charles Olson: Man & Poet. Ed. by George Butterick. LC 85-61156. (Man & Poet Ser.). 480p. (Orig.). 1987. 28.50 o.p. (ISBN 0-915032-65-1); pap. 15.95 o.p. (ISBN 0-915032-66-X). Natl Poet Foun.

Charles Peirce's Empiricism. Justus Buchler. 1966. lib. bdg. 24.00x o.p. (ISBN 0-374-91064-2, Octagon). Hippocrene Bks.

Charles People's River. Max Hall. 1986. 12.95 o.p. (ISBN 0-317-42482-3). Godine.

Charles Pratt: Photographs. Robert Frank & Lisette Model. LC 82-71396. (Illus.). 88p. (Orig.). 1983. pap. 25.00 o.p. (ISBN 0-89381-111-4). Aperture.

Charles Stewart Parnell: The Man & His Family. R. R. Foster. 320p. 1976. pap. 15.00x o.p. (ISBN 0-391-00910-9). Humanities.

Charles Vyse, 1882-1971: Catalogue of an Exhibition Held in 1974. (Illus.). 60p. pap. 12.95 o.s.i. (ISBN 0-317-55034-9). Apollo.

Charles W. Chesnutt: A Reference Guide. Curtis W. Ellison & E. W. Metcalf, Jr. (Reference Publications Ser.). 1980. lib. bdg. 22.00 o.p. (ISBN 0-8161-7825-9, Hall Reference). G K Hall.

Charles W. Moore, North American Architect. Florita Z. De Malave. (Architecture Ser.: Bibliography A 1344). 1985. pap. 2.00 o.p. (ISBN 0-89028-314-1). Vance Biblios.

Charles Wright in Cuba, Eighteen Fifty-Six to Eighteen Sixty-Seven. Richard A. Howard. 102p. 1988. lib. bdg. 95.00x o.p. (ISBN 0-88736-089-0). Meckler Corp.

Charleston & the Kanawha Valley (West Virginia) Otis K. Rice. 136p. 1981. 19.95 o.p. (ISBN 0-89781-046-5). Windsor Pubns Inc.

Charleston Antebellum Architecture & Civic Destiny. Kenneth Stevens. (Illus.). 384p. 1988. 49.95 o.p. (ISBN 0-87049-555-0). U of Tenn Pr.

Charleston Furniture, Seventeen Hundred to Eighteen Twenty-Five. 2nd ed. E. Milby Burton. LC 73-120917. Orig. Title: Contributions from the Charleston Museum: XII. (Illus.). xii, 200p. 1970. lib. bdg. 22.95 o.p. (ISBN 0-87249-198-6). U of SC Pr.
Charleston, the Place & the People. Mrs. St. Julien Ravenel. 1972. pap. 21.50 o.s.i. (ISBN 0-89308-031-4). Southern Hist Pr.
Charleston's Sons of Liberty: A Study of the Artisans, 1763-1789. Richard Walsh. LC 59-15684. (Illus.). xii, 166p. 1968. 15.95x o.p. (ISBN 0-87249-072-6); pap. 2.25x o.p. (ISBN 0-87249-001-7). U of SC Pr.
Charley Dickey & Fred Moses Trout Fishing. Charley Dickey & Fred Moses. LC 47-33540. (Family Guidebooks Ser). (Illus.). 1975. pap. 2.95 o.p. (ISBN 0-8487-0376-6). Oxmoor Hse.
Charley Malarkey & the Belly-Button Machine. William Kennedy & Brendan Kennedy. LC 86-17291. (Illus.). 40p. (ps up). 1986. 10.95 o.p. (ISBN 0-87113-104-8). Atlantic Monthly.
Charley Potata's. Robert M. Wingo & Nancy J. Wingo. (Illus.). 1978. 7.50 o.p. (ISBN 0-682-49013-X, Banner). Exposition-Phoenix.
Charlie. Beverly Haven. 1978. 4.50 o.p. (ISBN 0-682-49055-5). Exposition-Phoenix.
Charlie-Bob's Fan. W. B. Park. LC 80-25166. (Illus.). 32p. (gr. 4-8). 1981. 6.95 o.p. (ISBN 0-15-216221-6, HJ). HarBraceJ.
Charlie Boy. Peter Feiblemen. 1982. pap. 2.95 o.p. (ISBN 0-380-60293-8, 60293). Avon.
Charlie Brown, Snoopy & Me. Charles M. Schulz & R. Smith Kiliper. 128p. 1981. pap. 4.95 o.s.i. (ISBN 0-449-90060-6, Columbine). Fawcett.
Charlie Chan Carries On. Earl D. Biggers. 224p. 1987. pap. 3.95 o.p. (ISBN 0-445-40221-0). Mysterious Pr.
Charlie Dye: One Helluva Western Painter. Paul Weaver. (Illus.). 100p. 1981. 47.50 o.p. (ISBN 0-686-79302-1). Petersen Pub.
Charlie Flowers & the Melody Gardens. Fred Howard. 192p. 1972. 6.95 o.p. (ISBN 0-87140-555-5). Liveright.
Charlie M. Brian Freemantle. 1982. pap. 2.25 o.s.i. (ISBN 0-345-30611-2). Ballantine.
Charlie Meadows. Russell Hoban. LC 84-679. (Illus.). 24p. (gr. k-2). 1984. 4.95 o.p. (ISBN 0-03-069502-3). H Holt & Co.
Charlie Muffin U. S. A. Brian Freemantle. 208p. 1982. pap. 2.50 o.s.i. (ISBN 0-345-29440-8). Ballantine.
Charlie Needs a Cloak. Tomie De Paola. 1973. 12.95x o.s.i. (ISBN 0-13-128355-3). P-H.
Charlie Needs a Cloak. Tomie De Paola. (Illus.). 32p. (ps-2). 1982. pap. 5.95 o.s.i. (ISBN 0-13-128280-8, Pub. by Treehouse). P-H.
Charlie Osburn Story: You Gotta Give It All to Jesus. Charlie Osburn & Fred Lilly. 140p. 1986. pap. 4.95 o.s.i. (ISBN 0-89283-287-8). Servant.
Charlie: The Story of a Baby in the Making. Charlie Reagan. (Illus.). 64p. 1982. 5.00 o.p. (ISBN 0-682-49814-9). Exposition-Phoenix.
Charlie's Tenth Giant Book of Crossword Puzzles. 1983. pap. 5.95 o.s.i. (ISBN 0-671-47003-5). PB.
Charlie's Third Giant Book of Crossword Puzzles. 1979. pap. 3.95 o.s.i. (ISBN 0-671-79108-7). PB.
Charlotte & Emily Bronte: An Annotated Bibliography. Anne Passel. LC 78-68259. (Garland Reference Library of the Humanities: No. 167). 369p. 1979. lib. bdg. 55.00 o.p. (ISBN 0-8240-9770-X). Garland Pub.
Charlotte Bronte: The Self Conceived. Helene Moglen. 1978. 11.95x o.p. (ISBN 0-393-07505-2, Norton Lib); pap. 3.95 o.p. (ISBN 0-393-00888-6). Norton.
Charlotte Mary Yonge, Her Life & Letters. Christabel Coleridge. LC 77-75961. (Library of Lives & Letters). 412p. 1969. Repr. of 1903 ed. 43.00x o.p. (ISBN 0-8103-3891-2). Gale.
Charlotte Mason & the Parents' National Educational Union. Margaret Coombs. 224p. 1987. 34.50 o.p. (ISBN 0-317-52865-3, Pub. by Croom Helm UK). Routledge Chapman & Hall.
Charlotte's Daughter: Or the Three Orphans. Susanna Rowson. LC 72-78812. 1828. Repr. 39.00x o.p. (ISBN 0-403-01983-4). Somerset Pub.
Charlotte's Temple, a Tale of Truth. Susanna Rowson. LC 72-78814. 1794. Repr. 39.00x o.p. (ISBN 0-403-01984-2). Somerset Pub.
Charlotte's Web. E. B. White. 1986. 11.95 o.s.i. (ISBN 0-317-53074-7, Large Print Bks). G K Hall.
Charm of the Bear Claw Necklace: A Story of Stone Age Southeastern Indians. Margaret Z. Searcy. LC 80-27424. (Illus.). 80p. (gr. 4-5). 1981. 9.95 o.s.i. (ISBN 0-8173-0060-0). U of Ala Pr.
Charm of Your Children. Mildred Scott-Washburn. (Illus.). 122p. 1980. 8.00 o.p. (ISBN 0-682-49615-4). Exposition-Phoenix.
Charm: The Career Girls Guide to Business & Personal Success. 2nd ed. Helen Whitcomb & Rosalind Lang. 1971. text ed. 17.75 o.p. (ISBN 0-07-069655-1). McGraw.
Charmed Circle: Gertrude Stein & Company. James R. Mellow. 1976. pap. 3.95 o.p. (ISBN 0-380-00257-4, 61218-6, Discus). Avon.
Charmed Death. Miles Tripp. 192p. 1986. pap. 2.95 o.p. (ISBN 0-931773-84-9). Critics Choice Paper.
Charmed Life. Mary McCarthy. 256p. 1981. pap. 2.95 o.p. (ISBN 0-380-53884-9, 53884-9, Bard). Avon.
Charmes see Poesies.
Charmian Watkins' Clothes Book. Charmian Watkins. 144p. 1986. pap. 9.95 o.p. (ISBN 0-345-31870-6). Ballantine.
Charmstone. Eleanor Hoffman. pap. 4.00 o.p. (ISBN 0-87461-037-0). McNally & Loftin.
Charro en U. S. A. Miguel C. Flores. LC 84-70211. (Illus., Span.). 1984. pap. 10.00 o.p. (ISBN 0-9608806-1-5, 00291). Assoc Pubns.
Chart Your Own Stars. Doris V. Thompson. 286p. 1975. text ed. 15.00 s.p. o.p. (ISBN 0-88053-764-7, A 315). Macoy Pub.
Chart Your Own Way to Career Happiness. James Wellman & Norman Zierold. 1972. pap. 1.50 o.p. (ISBN 0-87516-120-0). DeVorss.
Charted Folk Designs for Cross-Stitch Embroidery. Andreas Foris. LC 75-9175. 1975. lib. bdg. 11.50x o.p. (ISBN 0-88307-591-1). Gannon.
Charter For Progress. Clain-Stefanelli. 14.95 o.p. Acropolis.
Charter of Connecticut: A Study. Albert C. Bates. 72p. 1932. pap. 2.00 o.p. (ISBN 0-940748-03-7). Conn Hist Soc.
Chartering & Shipping Terms: Time-Sheet Supplements. J. Bes. 50.50 ea. o.p. Vol. 2, A-L (ISBN 0-900133-02-3). Vol. 3, M-Z (ISBN 0-900133-03-1). E J Brill USA.
Charting Commodity Market Price Behavior. 2nd ed. L. Dee Belveal. LC 85-70189. 250p. 1985. 40.00 o.p. (ISBN 0-87094-651-X). Dow Jones-Irwin.
Charting the Russian Northern Sea Route: The Arctic Ocean Hydrographic Expedition, 1910-1915. L. M. Starokadomskiy. Tr. by William Barr. (Illus.). 1977. text ed. 18.95x o.p. (ISBN 0-7735-0210-6, McGill Canada). U of Toronto Pr.
Charting Your Way Thru' PMS. Hunter House Staff. Ed. by K. S. Rana & C. Wassil-Grimm. LC 85-80898. (Illus.). 64p. 1985. pap. 2.95 o.s.i. (ISBN 0-89793-034-7). Hunter Hse.
Chartist Circular, 2 vols. 1970. Repr. of 1842 ed. Set. lib. bdg. 72.00x o.p. (ISBN 0-8371-9141-6, CD00). Greenwood.
Chartres Cathedral: Sources & Literary Interpretation, a Critical Bibliography. Jan Van Der Meulen et al. 1080p. 1989. lib. bdg. 75.00x o.s.i. (ISBN 0-8161-8346-5, Hall Reference). G K Hall.
Chartres: The Masons Who Built a Legend. John James. (Illus.). 224p. 1982. 39.95 o.p. (ISBN 0-7100-0886-4). Routledge Chapman & Hall.
Charts & Graphs: Fun, Facts & Activities. Carolyn Arnold. LC 84-7569. (Easy Read Geography Bks.). (Illus.). 32p. (gr. k-4). PLB 10.90 o.p. (ISBN 0-531-04719-9). Watts.
Chase: A Modern Guide to Foxhunting. Michael Clayton. (Illus.). 192p. 1988. 39.95 o.p. (ISBN 0-09-172657-3, Pub. by Century Hutchinson). David & Charles.
Chase Me, Catch Nobody! Erik C. Haugaard. 192p. (gr. 7 up). 1980. 8.95 o.p. (ISBN 0-395-29208-5). HM.
Chase, the Capture: Collecting at the Metropolitan. LC 75-34076. (Illus.). 240p. 1975. pap. 5.95 o.p. (ISBN 0-87099-139-6). Metro Mus Art.
Chase's Annual Events: Special Days, Weeks & Months in 1985. William D. Chase & Helen M. Chase. (Illus.). 224p. (Orig.). 1984. pap. 14.95 o.p. (ISBN 0-8092-5398-4). Contemp Bks.
Chase's Annual Events: Special Days, Weeks & Months in 1986. William D. Chase & Helen M. Chase. (Illus.). 224p. (Orig.). 1985. pap. 14.95 o.p. (ISBN 0-8092-5142-6). Contemp Bks.
Chase's Annual Events: Special Days, Weeks & Months in 1987. William D. Chase & Helen M. Chase. (Illus.). 288p. (Orig.). 1986. pap. 16.95 o.p. (ISBN 0-8092-4846-8). Contemp Bks.
Chase's Annual Events: Special Days, Weeks & Months in 1984. 192p. 1983. pap. 12.95 o.p. (ISBN 0-8092-5464-6). Contemp Bks.
Chasing Fame. Janet K. Clarke. 384p. 1987. pap. price not set o.p. (ISBN 0-345-34206-2). HR&W.
Chasm. Robert Campbell. LC 74-1240. 1974. 5.95 o.p. (ISBN 0-395-18502-5). HM.
Chasms in the Americas. Ed. by Dana S. Green. (Illus., Orig.). 1970. pap. 1.95 o.p. (ISBN 0-377-10251-2). Friendship Pr.
Chastity Morrow. Rosanne Kohake. 368p. 1985. pap. 3.95 o.p. (ISBN 0-380-88542-5). Avon.
Chateau Laurens. Esther J. Neely. (Orig.). 1980. pap. 1.95 o.p. (ISBN 0-505-51515-6, Pub. by Tower Bks). Dorchester Pub Co.
Chateaux & Villas. Intro. by Paige Rense. (World of Architectural Digest Ser.). (Illus.). 160p. 1982. 15.95 o.p. (ISBN 0-89535-101-3). Knapp Pr.
Chateaux of France. Realites Editors. (Illus.). 1979. 45.00 o.p. (ISBN 0-670-21299-7, Co-Pub. with Vendome Pr); pap. 19.95 o.p. (ISBN 0-86565-036-5). Penguin USA.
Chatham House Affairs: International Economic & Monetary Issues, Vol. 1. Ed. by RIIA Staff. (PPS on International Politics). (Illus.). 200p. 1981. 30.00 o.p. (ISBN 0-08-027532-X). Pergamon.
Chattey's Island. James Ehmann. LC 82-5598. (Illus.). 288p. 1982. 14.45 o.p. (ISBN 0-89919-126-6). Ticknor & Fields.
Chatto Book of Modern Poetry: Nineteen Fifteen to Nineteen Fifty-Five. Ed. by Cecil Day-Lewis & John Lehmann. Repr. of 1956 ed. 29.00 o.p. (ISBN 0-403-03067-6). Somerset Pub.
Chaucer. Raymond Preston. (Illus.). 1969. Repr. of 1952 ed. lib. bdg. 24.75x o.p. (ISBN 0-8371-1478-0, PRCH). Greenwood.
Chaucer: An Introduction. 2nd ed. S. S. Hussey. LC 80-41966. 256p. 1981. 25.00 o.p. (ISBN 0-416-72130-3, NO.3471); pap. 10.95 o.p. (ISBN 0-416-72140-0, NO.3470). Routledge Chapman & Hall.
Chaucer & Pagan Antiquity. A. J. Minnis. (Chaucer Studies: No. VIII). 208p. 1982. text ed. 47.50x o.p. (ISBN 0-8476-7195-X). Rowman.
Chaucer & the Imaginary World of Fame. Piero Boitani. LC 84-412. (Chaucer Studies: Vol. X). 264p. 1984. 53.50x o.p. (ISBN 0-389-20476-5, 08036). B&N Imports.
Chaucer & the Making of English Poetry, 2 vols. P. M. Kean. Incl. Vol. 1. Love Vision & Debate. 18.95 o.p. (ISBN 0-7100-7046-2); Vol. 2. The Art of Narrative. 19.95x (ISBN 0-7100-7250-3). (Illus.). 1972. Set. 38.00x o.p. (ISBN 0-7100-7345-3). Routledge Chapman & Hall.
Chaucer & the Making of English Poetry. 2nd ed. P. M. Kean. 1982. pap. 14.95x o.p. (ISBN 0-7100-0898-8). Routledge Chapman & Hall.
Chaucer, Langland & the Creative Imagination. David Aers. 1980. 26.95x o.p. (ISBN 0-7100-0351-X). Routledge Chapman & Hall.
Chaucer Reader: Selections from the Canterbury Tales. Ed. by Charles W. Dunn. 225p. 1952. pap. text ed. 11.00 o.p. (ISBN 0-15-506411-8, HC). HarBraceJ.
Chautauqua. Theodore Morrison. LC 74-75614. 1977. pap. text ed. 6.95x o.s.i. (ISBN 0-226-54063-4, P737, Phoen). U of Chicago Pr.
Chautauqua to Opera: An Autobiography of a Voice Teacher & Daughter of a Chautauqua Pioneer. Frances Perry-Cowen. 1978. 8.00 o.p. (ISBN 0-682-49112-8). Exposition-Phoenix.
Cheap: New Poems & Ballads. Ruth Stone. LC 75-9555. 101p. 1975. 7.95 o.p. (ISBN 0-15-117034-7). HarBraceJ.
Cheap: New Poems & Ballads. Ruth Stone. LC 75-9555. 101p. 1975. pap. 3.95 o.p. (ISBN 0-15-616798-0, HB325, Harv). HarBraceJ.
Cheap Shot. Jay Cronley. LC 83-45499. 256p. 1984. 13.95 o.s.i. (ISBN 0-689-11445-1, Atheneum). Macmillan.
Cheap-Smart Travel: Dependable Alternatives to Travelling Full Fare. Theodore Fischer. 196p. 1986. pap. 6.95 o.p. (ISBN 0-87131-485-1). M Evans.
Cheap Video Cookbook. Don Lancaster. LC 78-51584. 256p. 1978. pap. 8.95 o.p. (ISBN 0-672-21524-1, 21524). Sams.
Cheaper by the Dozen. Frank B. Gilbreth, Jr. & Ernestine G. Carey. (General Ser.). 1984. lib. bdg. 14.95 o.p. (ISBN 0-8161-3736-6, Large Print Bks); pap. 9.95 o.s.i. (ISBN 0-8161-3773-0, Large Print Bks). G K Hall.
Cheats at Work: An Anthology of Workplace Crime. Gerald Mars. (Counterpoint Ser.). 242p. 1983. pap. 7.95 o.p. (ISBN 0-04-301166-7). Unwin Hyman.
Check-List of the Fishes of the North-Eastern Atlantic & the Mediterranean, 2 vols. Ed. by J. C. Hureau & T. Monod. (Illus., Eng. & Fr., 2nd Printing with Suppl. 1979). 1973. Set. pap. 50.50 o.p. (ISBN 92-3-001762-0, U71, UNESCO). Vol. 1, 683p. Vol. 2, 394p. UNIPUB.
Check-List of Works of British Authors Printed Abroad, in Languages Other Than English to 1641. M. A. Shaaber. 168p. 15.00x o.p. (ISBN 0-8139-0938-4). U Pr of Va.
Check Your Commitment: Student. Knofel Staton. 128p. 1985. pap. 2.95 o.p. (ISBN 0-87239-829-3, 39983). Standard Pub.
Check Your Discipleship. Knofel Staton. LC 81-9411. 116p. (Orig., Student's & instructor's ed. bnd. together). 1982. pap. 2.25 student ed. o.p. (ISBN 0-87239-424-7, 39991); instructor's ed. 2.50 o.p. (ISBN 0-87239-423-9, 39990). Standard Pub.
Check Your Homelife. Knofel Staton. LC 82-19600. 176p. (Orig.). 1983. pap. 4.95 o.p. (ISBN 0-87239-649-5, 39973). Standard Pub.
Check Your Life in Christ. Knofel Staton. 160p. pap. 3.95x o.p. (ISBN 0-89900-203-X). College Pr Pub.
Check Your Lifestyle. Knofel Staton. 112p. pap. 3.95 o.p. (ISBN 0-89900-201-3). College Pr Pub.
Check Your Morality. Knofel Staton. LC 83-418. 194p. (Orig.). 1983. pap. 3.95 o.p. (ISBN 0-87239-630-4, 39971). Standard Pub.
Checkerboard Caper. John Morris. 256p. 1975. 7.95 o.p. (ISBN 0-8065-0469-2, Pub. by Citadel Pr). Carol Pub Group.
Checking Back: The Story of NHL Hockey. Neil D. Isaacs. 1977. 9.95 o.p. (ISBN 0-393-08788-3). Norton.
Checklist for Survival: Supplies, Preparations, Investments, Stockpiles, Weapons, Tools, Rural Retreats. T. Lesce & J. Lesce. lib. bdg. cancelled o.s.i. (ISBN 0-8490-3713-1). Gordon Pr.
Checklist of German Emigrant Sources. Arlene H. Eakle. 40p. 1986. pap. 6.00 o.p. (ISBN 0-940764-19-9). Genealog Inst.
Checklist of Government Directories, Lists & Rosters. Richard I. Korman. 1982. pap. 85.00 o.p. (ISBN 0-85964-121-X). Chadwyck-Healey.
Checklist of New London, Connecticut, Imprints 1709-1800. Compiled by Hazel A. Johnson. LC 77-8784. 492p. 1978. 25.00x o.p. (ISBN 0-8139-0703-9). U Pr of Va.
Checklist of the Beetles of North & Central America & the West Indies: Introduction. Ross H. Arnett, Jr. 26p. 1983. with 3-post 4" binder 15.00x o.p. (ISBN 0-916846-29-6). Flora & Fauna.
Checklist of the Beetles of North & Central America & the West Indies, Vol. 10: Bibliography. Ross H. Arnett, Jr. 240p. 1985. pap. 25.00x o.p. (ISBN 0-916846-27-X). Flora & Fauna.
Checklist of the Beetles of North & Central America & the West Indies, 10 vols. Ross H. Arnett, Jr. et al. 2092p. 1983. Set 250.00x o.p. (ISBN 0-916846-26-1). Flora & Fauna.
Checklist of the Beetles of North & Central America & the West Indies: Ground Beetles, Water Beetles, & Related Groups, Vol. 1. Ross H. Arnett, Jr. 135p. 1983. 15.00x o.p. (ISBN 0-916846-12-1). Flora & Fauna.
Checklist of the Beetles of North & Central America & the West Indies: The Rove Beetles & Related Groups, Vol. 2. Ross H. Arnett, Jr. 258p. 1983. looseleaf with binder 28.00x o.p. (ISBN 0-916846-13-X). Flora & Fauna.
Checklist of the Beetles of North & Central America & the West Indies: The Scarab Beetles, Buprestid Beetles, & Related Groups, Vol. 3. Ross H. Arnett, Jr. 254p. 1983. 27.00x o.p. (ISBN 0-916846-14-8). Flora & Fauna.
Checklist of the Beetles of North & Central America & the West Indies: The Click Beetles, Fireflies, Checkered Beetles, & Related Groups, Vol. 4. Ross H. Arnett, Jr. 215p. 1983. 23.00x o.p. (ISBN 0-916846-17-2). Flora & Fauna.
Checklist of the Beetles of North & Central America & the West Indies: The Ladybird Beetles & Related Group, Vol. 5. Ross H. Arnett, Jr. 129p. 1983. 15.00 o.p. (ISBN 0-916846-18-0). Flora & Fauna.
Checklist of the Beetles of North & Central America & the West Indies: The Darkling Beetles, Strepsiptera, & Related Groups, Vol. 6. Ross H. Arnett, Jr. 221p. 1983. 24.00x o.p. (ISBN 0-916846-19-9). Flora & Fauna.
Checklist of the Beetles of North & Central America & the West Indies: The Longhorned Beetles, Vol. 7. John A. Chemsak & E. G. Linsley. 138p. 1982. pap. 18.00x o.p. Flora & Fauna.
Checklist of the Beetles of North & Central America & the West Indies: The Leaf Beetles & the Bean Weevils, Vol. 8. John A. Wilcox & Ross H. Arnett, Jr. 178p. 1983. 20.00x o.p. (ISBN 0-916846-20-2). Flora & Fauna.
Checklist of the Beetles of North & Central America & the West Indies: The Fungus Weevils, Bark Beetles, Weevils & Related Groups, Vol. 9. Ross H. Arnett, Jr. 453p. 1983. 40.00x o.p. (ISBN 0-916846-21-0). Flora & Fauna.
Checklist of United States Trees: Native & Naturalized. Elbert L. Little, Jr. (Agricultural Handbook Ser.: No. 541). 375p. 1979. 13.00 o.p. (ISBN 0-318-22647-2, S/N 001-000-03846-0). USGPO.
Checklist of Vietnamese Holdings of the Wason Collection, Cornell University Libraries, As of June 1971. Giok Po Oey. 337p. 1971. 6.50 o.p. (ISBN 0-87727-084-8, DP 84). Cornell SE Asia.
Checklist of Writings on Eighteenth Century French & Italian Opera (Excluding Mozart) (Music Indexes & Bibliographies: No. 3). pap. 9.00 o.p. (ISBN 0-913574-03-1). Eur-Am Music.

Titles

Checks & Balances in Social Security: Symposium in Honor of Robert J. Myers. Yung-Ping Chen & George F. Rohrlich. (Illus.). 382p. (Orig.). 1986. lib. bdg. 34.00 o.p. (ISBN 0-8191-5424-5); pap. text ed. 18.50 o.p. (ISBN 0-8191-5425-3). U Pr of Amer.

Cheerleader U. S. A. Tryouts to Triumph. Lynda Haller. 60p. (Orig.). 1984. pap. 7.00 spiral bdg. o.p. (ISBN 0-9614174-0-4). Cheertime USA.

Cheerleading. 2nd ed. Newt Loken. LC 81-5999. 100p. 1982. Repr. of 1961 ed. lib. bdg. 9.95 o.p. (ISBN 0-89874-348-6). Krieger.

Cheese. Sunset Editors. LC 86-80866. 96p. 1986. 6.95 o.p. (ISBN 0-376-02262-0, Sunset Bks). Sunset-Lane.

Cheese. Bernard Waber. LC 67-24665. (Illus.). (gr. 5 up). 1967. 1.50 o.p. (ISBN 0-395-07162-3). HM.

Cheese Book. Patricia Haskell & Laurence Senelick. 1985. pap. 8.95 o.p. (ISBN 0-671-53133-6, Pub. by Fireside). S&S.

Cheese Book. Vivienne Marquis & Patricia Haskell. (Illus.). 1969. pap. 7.75 o.p. (ISBN 0-671-20306-1, Fireside). S&S.

Cheese Cookery. Doris M. Townsend. LC 81-80800. (Orig.). 1980. pap. 5.95 o.p. (ISBN 0-89586-039-2). Price Stern.

Cheese Stands Alone. Marjorie M. Prince. (gr. 7-9). 1975. pap. 1.95 o.p. (ISBN 0-671-42449-1). Archway.

Cheese Stands Alone. Marjorie M. Prince. LC 73-6737. (Illus.). 176p. (gr. 5 up). 1973. 7.95 o.p. (ISBN 0-395-17511-9). HM.

Cheeseburgers: The Best of Bob Greene. Bob Greene. LC 85-47602. 320p. 1985. 13.95 o.p. (ISBN 0-689-11611-X, Atheneum). Macmillan.

Cheeseburgers: The Best of Bob Greene. Bob Greene. (Large Print Bks (General Ser.)). 472p. 1986. lib. bdg. 18.95 o.p. (ISBN 0-8161-4097-9). G K Hall.

Cheesemaker Mice & the Giant. Roger Williamson. (Blackbird Bks). (Illus.). 48p. (gr. 5-8). 1984. 5.95 o.p. (ISBN 0-531-03753-3, Macrae). Watts.

Chef - d'Oeuvre Inconnu. Honore De Balzac. (Illus.). 1966. 22.50 o.p. (ISBN 0-686-53842-0). French & Eur.

Chef's Compendium of Professional Recipes. 2nd ed. John Fuller & Edward Renold. LC 84-6004. 1978. 19.95 o.p. (ISBN 0-434-90586-0). AVI.

Chefs' Secrets from Great Restaurants in Georgia. Georgia Hospitality & Travel Association Staff & Susan H. Smith. (Chef's Secrets Cookbooks Ser.). (Illus.). 208p. 1983. pap. 12.95 o.p. (ISBN 0-939944-06-5). Marmac Pub.

Chefs-Secrets from Great Restaurants in Louisiana: 1984 World Exposition Edition. Louisiana Restaurant Association Staff & Susan H. Smith. (Chefs' Secrets Cookbooks Ser.). (Illus.). 240p. 1984. 13.95 o.p. (ISBN 0-939944-25-1, Dist. by Pelican). Marmac Pub.

Cheif Tallon & the S.O.R. John Ball. 196p. 1984. 11.95 o.p. (ISBN 0-396-08307-2). Dodd.

Chekhov: New Perspectives. Rene Wellek & Nonna Wellek. 206p. 1984. 15.95 o.p. (ISBN 0-13-128405-3); pap. 7.95 o.p. (ISBN 0-13-128371-5). P-H.

Chekhov's Art of Writing: A Collection of Critical Essays. Ed. by Paul Debreczeny & Thomas Eekman. iv, 199p. 1977. soft cover 12.95 o.p. (ISBN 0-89357-045-1). Slavica.

Chelation of Heavy Metals. Ed. by W. G. Levine. 1979. 140.00 o.p. (ISBN 0-08-017719-0). Pergamon.

Chelsea Flower Show. Faith Whiten & Geoff Whiten. (Illus.). 128p. 1982. 24.95 o.p. (ISBN 0-241-10744-X, Pub. by Hamish Hamilton England). David & Charles.

Chemehuevi: A Grammar & Lexicon. Margaret L. Press. (UC Publications in Linguistics: Vol. 92). 1980. pap. 21.50x o.p. (ISBN 0-520-09600-2). U of Cal Pr.

Chemical Analysis by Microwave Rotational Spectroscopy. Ravi Varma & Lawrence W. Hrubesh. LC 78-17415. 218p. 1979. text ed. 33.50 o.p. (ISBN 0-471-03916-0, JW). Krieger.

Chemical Analysis of Additives in Plastics. 2nd ed. T. R. Crompton. 1971. text ed. 36.30 o.p. (ISBN 0-08-016627-X). Pergamon.

Chemical Analysis of Organometallic Compounds, 5 vols. T. R. Crompton. (Analysis of Organic Materials Ser). Vol. 1, 1974. 54.00 o.p. (ISBN 0-12-197301-8); Vol. 2, 1975. 43.00 o.p. (ISBN 0-12-197302-6); Vol.3. 45.00 o.p. (ISBN 0-12-197303-4); Vol. 4, 1975. 84.00 o.p. (ISBN 0-12-197304-2); Vol. 5, 1978. 93.50 o.p. (ISBN 0-12-197305-0). Acad Pr.

Chemical & Biological Action of Radiations. Ed. by M. Haissinsky. 1961. Vol. 5. 49.50 o.p. (ISBN 0-12-316505-9). Acad Pr.

Chemical & Biological Aspects of Drug Dependence. S. J. Mule & Henry Brill. LC 72-191695. (Drug Dependence Ser.). 576p. 1972. 55.00 o.p. (ISBN 0-87819-011-2). CRC Pr.

Chemical & Biological Aspects of Pyridoxal Catalysis. Ed. by E. E. Snell et al. 1964. 145.00 o.p. (ISBN 0-08-010423-1). Pergamon.

Chemical & Biological Aspects of Steroid Conjugation. Ed. by Seymour Bernstein & S. Solomon. LC 70-98420. (Illus.). 1970. 63.00 o.p. (ISBN 0-387-05062-0). Springer-Verlag.

Chemical & Biological Basis of Adjuvants. P. Jolles & A. Paraf. (Molecular Biology, Biochemistry & Biophysics Ser.: Vol. 13). (Illus.). 160p. 1973. 36.00 o.p. (ISBN 0-387-06308-0). Springer-Verlag.

Chemical & Molecular Basis of Nerve Activity. 2nd & rev. ed. David Nachmansohn. 1975. 59.50 o.p. (ISBN 0-12-512757-X). Acad Pr.

Chemical & Physical Behavior of Human Hair. Clarence R. Robbins. 1979. 37.95 o.p. (ISBN 0-442-26818-1). Van Nos Reinhold.

Chemical & Process Equipment Design: Vessel Design & Selection. David Azbel. LC 81-70863. 791p. 1982. 64.95 o.p. (ISBN 0-250-40478-8). Butterworth.

Chemical & Process Technology Encyclopedia. Douglas M. Considine. 1184p. 1974. text ed. 99.00 o.p. (ISBN 0-07-012423-X). McGraw.

Chemical Applications of Far Infrared Spectroscopy. A. Finch et al. 1970. 51.00 o.p. (ISBN 0-12-256350-6). Acad Pr.

Chemical Applications of Graph Theory. A. T. Balaban. 1976. 79.50 o.p. (ISBN 0-12-076050-9). Acad Pr.

Chemical Applications of Infrared Spectroscopy. Chintamani N. Rao. 1964. 85.00 o.p. (ISBN 0-12-580250-1). Acad Pr.

Chemical Applications of Mossbauer Spectroscopy. Ed. by V. I. Goldanskii & R. H. Herber. LC 68-18671. (Illus.). 1968. 123.50 o.p. (ISBN 0-12-287350-5). Acad Pr.

Chemical Basis of Life: General, Organic, & Biological Chemistry for the Health Sciences. George H. Schmid. 1982. 27.95 o.p. (ISBN 0-316-77371-9). Little.

Chemical Binding & Structure. J. E. Spice. 1964. 10.00 o.p. (ISBN 0-08-010568-8); pap. 95.00 o.p. (ISBN 0-08-010567-X). Pergamon.

Chemical Biology of Fishes: With a Key to Literature. R. Love. 1970. 96.00 o.p. (ISBN 0-12-455850-X). Acad Pr.

Chemical Bonding in Solids. Ed. by C. K. Jorgensen et al. (Structure & Bonding Ser.: Vol. 19). (Illus.). iv, 165p. 1974. text ed. 44.00 o.p. (ISBN 0-387-06908-9). Springer-Verlag.

Chemical Calculations. George I. Sackheim. (Series B). 1986. 6.80x o.p. (ISBN 0-87563-279-3). Stipes.

Chemical Calculations. rev ed. George I. Sackheim. (Series A). 179p. 1985. pap. text ed. 6.20x o.p. (ISBN 0-87563-262-9). Stipes.

Chemical Carcinogenesis. Ed. by Claudio Nicolini. LC 82-13140. (NATO ASI Series A, Life Sciences: Vol. 52). 510p. 1982. 89.50x o.p. (ISBN 0-306-41111-3, Plenum Pr). Plenum Pub.

Chemical Carcinogenesis, Pt. B. Ed. by P. O. Ts'o. J. A. Di Paolo. (Biochemistry of Disease Ser: Vol. 4). 360p. 1974. 75.00 o.p. (ISBN 0-8247-6170-7). Dekker.

Chemical Carcinogenesis, Pt. A. Ed. by P. O. Ts'o. J. A. Di Paolo. (Biochemistry of Disease Ser.: Vol. 4). 464p. 1974. 75.00 o.p. (ISBN 0-8247-6128-6). Dekker.

Chemical Compounds in the Atmosphere. T. E. Graedel. LC 78-12264. 1979. 59.00 o.p. (ISBN 0-12-294480-1). Acad Pr.

Chemical Directory of Northern Europe: Denmark, Finland, Iceland, Norway, Sweden 1977-79 Ed. 4th ed. 320p. (ISBN 0-8002-0292-9). Intl Pubns Serv.

Chemical Ecology of Insects. Ed. by William T. Bell & Ring T. Carde. LC 83-20212. (Illus.). 550p. 1984. text ed. 45.00x o.p o.p. (ISBN 0-87893-069-8); pap. text ed. 32.50x o.p. (ISBN 0-87893-070-1). Sinauer Assocs.

Chemical Education: Proceedings of an International Symposium, Sao Paulo, Brazil, 1971. Ed. by J. D. Gomez-Ibanez. 56p. 1976. 14.50 o.p. (ISBN 0-08-020734-0). Pergamon.

Chemical Endocrinology. Edward H. Frieden. 1976. 59.00 o.p. (ISBN 0-12-268150-9). Acad Pr.

Chemical Engineering at Supercritical Fluid Conditions. Michael E. Paulaitis & Johan M. L. Penninger. LC 82-71529. (Illus.). 600p. 1983. 52.95 o.p. (ISBN 0-250-40564-4). Butterworth.

Chemical Engineering Education. Institution of Chemical Engineers Staff. 1982. 35.00 o.s.i. (ISBN 0-08-028767-0). Pergamon.

Chemical Engineering Guide to Corrosion in the Process Industries. Chemical Engineering Magazine Editors. 362p. 1986. text ed. 47.50 o.p. (ISBN 0-07-024309-3). McGraw.

Chemical Engineering Guide to Pumps. Kenneth J. McNaughton. 1984. text ed. 42.50 o.p. (ISBN 0-07-024314-X). McGraw.

Chemical Engineering Guide to Valves. R. W. Greene. 250p. 1984. text ed. 42.50 o.p. (ISBN 0-07-024313-1). McGraw.

Chemical Engineering Practice Exam Set. Randall N. Robinson. (Engineering Review Manual Ser.). 112p. 1984. pap. text ed. 14.50 o.p. (ISBN 0-932276-42-3). Prof Pubns CA.

Chemical Engineering to Compressors. R. W. Greene. 250p. 1984. text ed. 39.50 o.p. (ISBN 0-07-024312-3). McGraw.

Chemical Engineers' Handbook. 5th ed. Robert H. Perry & C. H. Chilton. 1973. text ed. 79.50 o.p. (ISBN 0-07-049478-9). McGraw.

Chemical Equilibrium. Robert B. Fischer. 1970. pap. text ed. 18.95 o.p. (ISBN 0-7216-3705-1, CBS C). SCP.

Chemical Equilibrium: A Practical Introduction for the Physical & Life Sciences. William B. Guenther. LC 75-28028. (Illus.). 248p. 1975. 45.00x o.p. (ISBN 0-306-30850-9, Plenum Pr). Plenum Pub.

Chemical Evolution. S. E. Aw. LC 81-70575. 1982. pap. 9.95 o.p. (ISBN 0-89051-082-2). Master Bks.

Chemical Evolution of the Giant Planets. Ed. by Cyril Ponnamperuma. 1976. 39.50 o.p. (ISBN 0-12-561350-4). Acad Pr.

Chemical Experimentation under Extreme Conditions, Vol. 9. Bryant W. Rossiter & A. Weissberger. LC 79-10962. (Techniques of Chemistry Ser.). 369p. 1980. 62.95 o.p. (ISBN 0-471-93269-8). Wiley.

Chemical Foundations of Molecular Biology. Robert F. Steiner. 468p. 1965. 21.50 o.p. (ISBN 0-442-07940-0, Pub. by Van Nos Reinhold). Krieger.

Chemical Hazards in the Workplace. Ronald Scott. (Illus.). 380p. (ISBN 0-87371-059-2). Lewis Pubs Inc.

Chemical Hydrogeology. Ed. by William R. Back & Allan Freeze. LC 81-11853. (Benchmark Papers in Geology Ser.: Vol. 73). 416p. 1983. 54.95 o.p. (ISBN 0-87933-440-1). Van Nos Reinhold.

Chemical Induction of Cancer, Vols. 1 & 2. Joseph C. Arcos et al. Incl. Vol. 1. 1968 (ISBN 0-12-059301-7); Vol. 2A. 1974 (ISBN 0-12-059302-5); Vol. 2B. 1974 (ISBN 0-12-059352-1). LC 66-30118. 100.00 ea. o.p. Acad Pr.

Chemical Kinetics & Reaction Mechanisms. F. Wilkinson. 1980. pap. 24.95 o.p. (ISBN 0-442-30249-5). Van Nos Reinhold.

Chemical Kinetics & Surface & Colloid Chemistry. A. F. Trotman-Dickenson & G. D. Parfitt. (Illus.). 1966. 19.75 o.p. (ISBN 0-08-011257-9); pap. 45.00 o.p. (ISBN 0-08-011256-0). Pergamon.

Chemical Kinetics of Gas Reactions. V. N. Kondratiev. 1964. 205.00 o.p. (ISBN 0-08-010108-9). Pergamon.

Chemical Lasers. K. L. Kompa. Ed. by F. Boschke. LC 51-5497. (Topics in Current Chemistry: Vol. 37). (Illus.). 120p. 1973. pap. 26.70 o.p. (ISBN 0-387-06099-5). Springer-Verlag.

Chemical Mediators in the Acute Inflammatory Reaction. M. Rocha E Silva & J. Garcia Leme. 374p. 1972. 60.00 o.p. (ISBN 0-08-017040-4). Pergamon.

Chemical Metallurgy - A Tribute to Carl Wagner: Proceedings. AIME Annual Meeting, Chicago, 1981. Ed. by Nev A. Gokcen. (Illus.). 506p. 50.00 o.p. (ISBN 0-89520-382-0); members 30.00 o.p. (ISBN 0-317-36234-8); student members 16.00 o.p. (ISBN 0-317-36235-6). ASM.

Chemical Methods of Silicate Analysis: A Handbook. H. Bennett & R. A. Reed. 1972. 66.00 o.p. (ISBN 0-12-088740-1). Acad Pr.

Chemical Microbiology: An Introduction to Microbial Physiology. 3rd ed. Anthony H. Rose. 470p. 1976. 65.00x o.p. (ISBN 0-306-30888-6, Plenum Pr). Plenum Pub.

Chemical Microstructure of Polymer Chains. Jack L. Koenig. LC 80-15165. 414p. 1980. 75.95x o.p. (ISBN 0-471-07725-9, Pub. by Wiley Interscience). Wiley.

Chemical Mutagenesis in Mammals & Man: Proceedings. Ed. by F. Vogel & G. Roehrborn. LC 79-121062. (Illus.). 1970. 98.50 o.p. (ISBN 0-387-05063-9). Springer-Verlag.

Chemical Mutagens: Environmental Effects on Biological Systems. Lawrence Fishbein et al. LC 71-117078. (Environmental Science Ser). 1970. 98.00 o.p. (ISBN 0-12-257150-9). Acad Pr.

Chemical Oxidations with Microorganisms. G. Fonken & R. Johnson. (Oxidation in Organic Chemistry Ser.: Vol. 2). 1972. 85.00 o.p. (ISBN 0-8247-1211-0). Dekker.

Chemical Pharmacology of the Synapse. D. J. Triggle & C. R. Triggle. 1977. 102.00 o.p. (ISBN 0-12-700340-1). Acad Pr.

Chemical Physics of Surfaces. S. Roy Morrison. LC 76-54152. (Illus.). 416p. 1977. 59.50x o.p. (ISBN 0-306-30960-2, Plenum Pr). Plenum Pub.

Chemical Principles. 5th ed. William Masterton & Emil Slowinski. 1981. text ed. 35.95 o.p. (CBS C); Instr's manual 11.95 o.p.; study guide 14.95 o.p.; overhead transparency 400.00 o.p. (ISBN 0-03-059298-4); test bank 100.00 o.p. SCP.

Chemical Principles. 5th ed. William L. Masterton et al. 1980. pap. text ed. 35.95 o.p. (HoltC). HR&W.

Chemical Principles, Using S. I. Units. 5th ed. William Masterton et al. 1981. text ed. 39.95 o.s.i. (ISBN 0-03-057886-8, CBS C). SCP.

Chemical Problem Solving Using Dimensional Analysis. Robert Nakon. (Illus.). 1978. pap. text ed. (ISBN 0-13-128645-5). P-H.

Chemical Process Economics. 2nd rev. & expanded ed. J. Happel & D. Jordan. (Chemical Processing & Engineering Ser: Vol. 1). 528p. 1975. 39.75 o.p. (ISBN 0-8247-6155-3). Dekker.

Chemical Process Hazards, Vol. VII. Institution of Chemical Engineers Staff. 1982. 80.00 o.s.i. (ISBN 0-08-028756-5). Pergamon.

Chemical Process Industries. 4th ed. R. Norris Shreve & Joseph Brink. (Illus.). 1977. text ed. 39.95 o.p. (ISBN 0-07-057145-7). McGraw.

Chemical Reaction Engineering: International Symposium on Chemical Reaction Engineering, Nice, France, March 25-27, 1980, Vol. 1, Contributed Papers. Ed. by J. Villermaux & P. Trambouze. LC 79-41749. 540p. 1980. pap. 94.00 o.p. (ISBN 0-08-024018-6). Pergamon.

Chemical Reaction Engineering: Proceedings of the Fourth International Symposium. Ed. by R. Jottrand. 1971. 115.00 o.p. (ISBN 0-08-013182-4). Pergamon.

Chemical Reaction Engineering: Sixth International Symposium on Chemical Reaction Engineering--Plenary Lectures, Vol. 2. Ed. by J. Villermaux & P. Trambouze. LC 79-41749. (Illus.). 259p. 1980. pap. 48.00 o.p. (ISBN 0-08-026234-1). Pergamon.

Chemical Reactions As a Means of Separation. Billy L. Crynes. (Chemical Processing & Engineering Ser.: Vol. 11). 360p. 1977. 79.75 o.p. (ISBN 0-8247-6374-2). Dekker.

Chemical Reactions in Electrical Discharges. Ed. by Bernard D. Blaustein. LC 70-76951. (Advances in Chemistry Ser: No. 80). 1969. 39.95 o.p. (ISBN 0-8412-0081-5). Am Chemical.

Chemical Reactions in Solvents & Melts. G. Charlot & B. Tremillon. 1969. 130.00 o.p. (ISBN 0-08-012678-2). Pergamon.

Chemical Reactivity & Biological Role of Functional Groups in Enzymes: Proceedings. Biochemical Society Symposium, 31st. Ed. by R. M. Smellie. 1971. 49.00 o.p. (ISBN 0-12-649450-9). Acad Pr.

Chemical Reactor Omnibook Plus. Octave Levenspiel. 1984. 24.00x o.p. (ISBN 0-88246-069-2). Oreg St U Bkstrs.

Chemical Reagents in the Mineral Processing Industry. Intro. by D. Malhortra & W. F. Riggs. LC 86-63354. (Illus.). 312p. (Orig.). 1987. pap. 58.00x o.p. (ISBN 0-87335-062-6). SMM&E Inc.

Chemical Relaxation in Molecular Biology. Ed. by I. Pecht & R. Rigler. (Molecular Biology, Biochemistry & Biophysics Ser.: Vol. 24). 1977. 53.00 o.p. (ISBN 0-387-08173-9). Springer-Verlag.

Chemical Stability of Pharmaceuticals: A Handbook for Pharmacists. Kenneth A. Connors et al. LC 78-1759. 367p. 1979. 42.50x o.p. (ISBN 0-471-02653-0, Pub. by Wiley-Interscience). Wiley.

Chemical Sterilization. Ed. by Paul M. Borick. LC 73-4967. (Benchmark Papers in Microbiology Ser.: Vol. 1). 352p. 1982. 51.95 o.p. (ISBN 0-87933-036-8). Van Nos Reinhold.

Chemical Structure & Bonding. Roger L. DeKock & Harry B. Gray. 1980. 36.95 o.p. (ISBN 0-8053-2310-4). Benjamin-Cummings.

Chemical Synonyms & Trade Names: A Dictionary & Commercial Handbook. 8th ed. William Gardner & Edward I. Cooke. LC 77-85232. 689p. 1981. 75.00x o.p. (ISBN 0-291-39678-X). Intl Pubns Serv.

Chemical Technology. F. A. Henglein. 1969. 215.00 o.p. (ISBN 0-08-011848-8). Pergamon.

Chemical Technology, 2 vols. Ed. by I. Mukhlyonov. 647p. 1979. 13.00 o.p. (ISBN 0-8285-1547-6, Pub. by Mir Pubs USSR). Imported Pubns.

Chemical Theatre. Charles Nicholl. 272p. 1980. 36.95 o.p. (ISBN 0-7100-0515-6). Routledge Chapman & Hall.

Chemical Thermodynamics. M. Karapetyants. 640p. 1978. 15.00 o.p. (ISBN 0-8285-0644-2, Pub. by Mir Pubs USSR). Imported Pubns.

Chemical Thermodynamics - 4: Proceedings. Ed. by J. Rouquerol & R. Sabbah. LC 76-44615. 1977. 32.00 o.p. (ISBN 0-08-021366-9). Pergamon.

Chemical Thermodynamics of Materials. Claude H. Lupis. 608p. 1983. 52.25 o.p. (ISBN 0-444-00713-X, North Holland); pap. 56.00 o.p. (ISBN 0-444-00779-2, North Holland). Elsevier.

Chemical Thermodynamics: Proceedings of an International Conference, Baden Bei Wien, Austria, 1973, Vol. 3. International Union of Pure & Applied Chemistry. 110p. 1976. 35.00 o.p. (ISBN 0-08-020735-9). Pergamon.

Chemical Transmission of Nerve Impulses: A Historical Sketch. Z. M. Bacq. 1975. 42.00 o.p. (ISBN 0-08-020512-7). Pergamon.
Chemical Transport Reactions. Harald Schafer. Tr. by Hans Frankfort. 1964. 47.50 o.p. (ISBN 0-12-621750-5). Acad Pr.
Chemical Vapor Transport Secondary Nucleation & Mass Transfer in Crystal Growth. Ed. by W. R. Wilcox. (Preparation & Properties of Solid State Materials Ser.: Vol. 2). 192p. 1976. 75.00 o.p. (ISBN 0-8247-6330-0). Dekker.
Chemical Warfare, Pyrotechnics & the Fireworks Industry. T. F. Watkins et al. 1968. text ed. 17.75 o.p. (ISBN 0-08-012811-4); pap. text ed. 7.75 o.p. (ISBN 0-08-012810-6). Pergamon.
Chemical Week Pesticides Register. Robert P. Ouellette & John A. King. LC 76-29646. 1977. text ed. 110.00 o.p. (ISBN 0-07-047948-8). McGraw.
Chemical, Work & Cancer. A. Le Serve et al. 1982. pap. 6.95 o.p. (ISBN 0-442-30705-5). Van Nos Reinhold.
Chemically Induced Dynamic Nuclear & Electron Polarizations-Cidnp & Cidep. C. Richard & P. Granger. LC 75-2106. (NMR Basic Principles & Progress: Vol. 8). (Illus.). 127p. 1974. 36.00 o.p. (ISBN 0-387-06618-7). Springer-Verlag.
Chemicals & Cancer. Matthew S. Meselson. 1980. pap. 2.50x o.p. (ISBN 0-87081-081-2). Univ Pr Colo.
Chemicals Controlling Insect Behavior. Ed. by Morton Beroza. (American Chemical Society Symposium). 1970. 49.50 o.p. (ISBN 0-12-093050-1). Acad Pr.
Chemicals for Crop Protection & Pest Control. 2nd ed. Maurice B. Green & T. F. West. LC 77-4881. 1977. text ed. 58.00 o.p. (ISBN 0-08-021174-7); pap. text ed. 20.95 o.p. (ISBN 0-08-019013-8). Pergamon.
Chemicals for the Military. Business Communications Staff. 1989. 2250.00 o.p. (ISBN 0-89336-655-2, C-101). BCC.
Chemie und Hochschule. Heinrich Zollinger. (Poly: No. 11). (Illus.). 163p. (Ger.). 1978. pap. 16.95x o.p. (ISBN 0-8176-1044-8). Birkhauser.
Chemin de la Croix des Ames. Georges Bernanos. 1948. pap. 9.95 o.p. (ISBN 0-686-51932-9). French & Eur.
Chemin des Ecoliers. Marcel Ayme. 1946. pap. 8.95 o.p. (ISBN 0-685-23913-6, 1621). French & Eur.
Chemins de la liberte, 3 tomes. Jean-Paul Sartre. Incl. Tome I. Age de Raison. pap. 13.50 o.p. (ISBN 0-685-35913-1); Tome II. Mort dans l'Ame. pap. 13.95 (ISBN 0-685-35914-X); Tome III. Sursis. pap. 14.95 o.p. (ISBN 0-685-35915-8). (Coll. Soleil). 1960. pap. Schoenhof.
Chemisorption: An Experimental Approach. G. Welder. Tr. by D. Klemperer. 1977. text ed. 24.95 o.p. (ISBN 0-408-10611-5). Butterworth.
Chemisorption & Reactions on Metallic Films, 2 vols. Ed. by J. Anderson. (Physical Chemistry Ser: Vol. 24). 1971. Vol. 1. 133.50 o.p. (ISBN 0-12-058001-2); Vol. 2. 82.50 o.p. (ISBN 0-12-058002-0). Acad Pr.
Chemisorptive Bond: Basic Concepts. Alfred Clark. (Physical Chemistry: A Series of Monographs, Vol. 32). 1974. 68.50 o.p. (ISBN 0-12-175440-5). Acad Pr.
Chemistry. Henry Abrash & Kenneth Hardcastle. 1981. Repr. text ed. write for info. o.p. (ISBN 0-02-471100-4); lab. manual avail. o.p. (ISBN 0-02-471170-5); study guide avail. o.p. (ISBN 0-686-72522-0). Macmillan.
Chemistry. 2nd ed. John C. Bailar, Jr. et al. 1984. 43.20 o.p. (ISBN 0-12-072855-9); instr's. manual 10.00 o.p. (ISBN 0-12-072857-5); student solutions manual 10.00 o.p. (ISBN 0-12-072858-3); study guide 11.00 o.p. (ISBN 0-12-072859-1). Acad Pr.
Chemistry. 2nd ed. Leonard W. Fine. LC 77-12000. 840p. 1978. 22.50 o.p. (ISBN 0-683-03210-0). Krieger.
Chemistry. Claude H. Yoder et al. 1975. text ed. 22.95 o.p. (ISBN 0-15-506465-7, HC). HarBraceJ.
Chemistry. 2nd ed. Claude H. Yoder et al. 876p. 1980. text ed. 30.00 net o.p. (ISBN 0-15-506470-3, HC). HarBraceJ.
Chemistry: A Basic Approach. B. R. Siebring & M. E. Schaff. 1971. text ed. 28.95 o.p. (ISBN 0-07-057349-2). McGraw.
Chemistry: A Life Science Approach. 2nd ed. Stuart J. Baum & Charles W. Scaife. (Illus.). 1980. text ed. write for info. o.p. (ISBN 0-02-306610-5). Macmillan.
Chemistry: A Modern Introduction. 2nd ed. Frank Brescia & Stanley Mehlman. 1978. text ed. 37.95 o.s.i. (ISBN 0-7216-1984-3, CBS C); instr's manual 9.95 o.s.i. (ISBN 0-03-057156-1); study guide 11.95 o.s.i. (ISBN 0-7216-2076-0). SCP.
Chemistry: A Survey of Fundamentals. Lawrence P. Eblin. (Illus.). 1968. text ed. 14.95 o.p. (ISBN 0-15-506485-1, HC). HarBraceJ.
Chemistry: A Survey of Laboratory Techniques & Procedures. Lawrence P. Eblin. (Illus.). 1968. text ed. 6.95 o.p. (ISBN 0-15-506487-8, HC). HarBraceJ.
Chemistry: An Introduction. 2nd ed. Sydney B. Newell. (Illus.). 563p. 1980. text ed. 28.95 o.p. (ISBN 0-316-60454-2); instr's. manual o.p. (ISBN 0-316-60455-0). study guide 10.95 o.p. (ISBN 0-316-60456-9). Little.
Chemistry & Action of Herbicide Antidotes (Symposium) (MS-REPRO) Ed. by Ferenc M. Pallos & John E. Casida. 1978. 41.50 o.p. (ISBN 0-12-544050-2). Acad Pr.
Chemistry & Application of Phenolic Resins. A. Knop & W. Scheib. LC 78-10967. (Polymers: Properties & Applications Vol. 3). (Illus.). 1979. 61.00 o.p. (ISBN 0-387-09051-7). Springer-Verlag.
Chemistry & Biochemistry of Amino Acids, Peptides & Proteins, Vol. 3. Ed. by Boris Weinstein. 336p. 1974. 85.00 o.p. (ISBN 0-8247-6204-5). Dekker.
Chemistry & Biochemistry of Estuaries. Eric Olausson & Ingemar Cato. LC 79-41211. 452p. 1980. 140.00x o.p. (ISBN 0-471-27679-0, Pub. by Wiley-Interscience). Wiley.
Chemistry & Biochemistry of Marine Food Products. Roy E. Martin et al. (Illus.). 1982. 53.95 o.s.i. (ISBN 0-87055-408-5). AVI.
Chemistry & Biochemistry of Plant Pigments, Vol. 1. 2nd ed. Ed. by T. W. Goodwin. 1976. 90.00 o.p. (ISBN 0-12-289901-6). Acad Pr.
Chemistry & Biochemistry of Plant Pigments, Vol. 2. 2nd ed. Ed. by T. W. Goodwin. 1976. 70.00 o.p. (ISBN 0-12-289902-4). Acad Pr.
Chemistry & Biochemistry of Plant Proteins: Proceedings. Phytochemical Society Symposium, No.11, University of Ghent, Belgium, Sept. 1973. Ed. by J. B. Harborne & G. F. Van Sumere. 1975. 65.00 o.p. (ISBN 0-12-324668-7). Acad Pr.
Chemistry & Biochemistry of the Sulfhydryl Group in Amino Acids, Peptides & Proteins. Mendel Friedman. 1973. 150.00 o.p. (ISBN 0-08-016845-0). Pergamon.
Chemistry & Biological Activities of Bacterial Surface Amphiphiles. Ed. by Gerald Shockman & Anthony Wicken. LC 81-15023. 1981. 52.50 o.p. (ISBN 0-12-640380-5). Acad Pr.
Chemistry & Biology of the Starch Granule. N. P. Badenhuizen. (Protoplasmatologia Ser.: Vol. 2B, Pt. 2bs). (Illus.). 1959. pap. 26.00 o.p. (ISBN 0-387-80522-2). Springer-Verlag.
Chemistry & Control of Enzyme Reactions. K. G. Scrimgeour. 1978. 157.00 o.p. (ISBN 0-12-634150-8). Acad Pr.
Chemistry & Cytochemistry of Nucleic Acids & Nuclear Proteins. C. Scholtissek et al. (Protoplasmatologia: Vol. 5, Pt. 3A-D). (Illus.). 1966. pap. 57.90 o.p. (ISBN 0-387-80782-9). Springer-Verlag.
Chemistry & Function of Proteins. 2nd ed. Felix Haurowitz. 455p. 1963. text ed. 21.75 o.p. (ISBN 0-12-332956-6). Acad Pr.
Chemistry & Geochemistry of Solutions at High Temperatures & Pressures: Proceedings of the Royal Swedish Academy of Sciences, Nobel Symposium, Bjorkborns Herrgard, Karlskoga, Sweden, Sept., 1979. Royal Swedish Academy of Sciences Staff. Ed. by David Rickard & Frans E. Wickman. (Physics & Chemistry of the Earth Ser., International Ser. in Earth Sciences: Vols. 13 & 37). (Illus.). 600p. 1982. 205.00 o.p. (ISBN 0-08-026285-6). Pergamon.
Chemistry & Man's Environment. Edward C. Fuller. 464p. 1974. text ed. 25.95 o.p. (ISBN 0-395-17086-9). HM.
Chemistry & Pharmacology of Androgens & Anabolic Agents. Julius A. Vida. 1969. 78.50 o.p. (ISBN 0-12-721850-5). Acad Pr.
Chemistry & Physics of Solid Surfaces. Ed. by Ralf Vanselow & S. Y. Tong. LC 76-49020. (Monotopic Reprint Ser.). 1977. Repr. 28.95 o.p. (ISBN 0-8493-0125-4). CRC Pr.
Chemistry & Physiology of Mitochondria & Microsomes. O. Lindberg & L. Ernster. (Protoplasmatologia: Vol. 3, Pt. 4). (Illus.). 1954. 30.70 o.p. (ISBN 0-387-80346-7). Springer-Verlag.
Chemistry & Physiology of the Human Plasma Proteins: Proceedings of a Conference Sponsored by the Center for Blood Research, Boston, 1978. rev. ed. Ed. by David Bing. LC 79-10742. (Illus.). 416p. 1979. 105.00 o.p. (ISBN 0-08-023860-2). Pergamon.
Chemistry & Reactivity of Collagen. Karl H. Gustavson. 1956. 46.50 o.p. (ISBN 0-12-309950-1). Acad Pr.
Chemistry & Technology of Basic Organic & Petrochemical Synthesis, 2 vols. N. N. Lebedev. 638p. 1984. Set. 16.00 o.p. (ISBN 0-8285-2784-9, Pub. by Mir Pubs USSR). Imported Pubns.
Chemistry & Technology of Leather, 4 vols. Ed. by Fred O'Flaherty et al. LC 76-50622. (ACS Monographs). 1978. Repr. of 1956 ed. Set. 124.75 o.p. (ISBN 0-89874-381-8). Krieger.
Chemistry & Testing of Dairy Products. 4th ed. Henry V. Atherton & John A. Newlander. (Illus.). 1977. pap. 25.95 o.p. (ISBN 0-87055-253-8). AVI.
Chemistry & the Environment. Melvin J. Josephs & Howard J. Sanders. LC 67-30718. 1967. 9.95 o.p. (ISBN 0-8412-0103-X). Am Chemical.
Chemistry & the Living Organism. 3rd ed. Molly M. Bloomfield. LC 83-14788. 688p. 1984. (ISBN 0-471-87627-5). Wiley.
Chemistry, Biochemistry & Pharmacology of Prostanoids. Ed. by S. M. Roberts & F. Scheinmann. 1979. 140.00 o.p. (ISBN 0-08-023799-1). Pergamon.
Chemistry: Definitions, Notions, Terminology. A. I. Busev et al. 295p. 1984. 7.95 o.s.i. (ISBN 0-8285-2817-9, Pub. by Mir Pubs USSR). Imported Pubns.
Chemistry, Energy, & Human Ecology. Frederick Kabbe & Lois Kabbe. LC 75-27126. (Illus.). 464p. 1976. text ed. 24.50 o.p. (ISBN 0-395-19833-X). HM.
Chemistry Explained. Robert L. Wolke. (Illus.). 1980. text ed. (ISBN 0-13-129163-7). P-H.
Chemistry for Changing Times: Student Study Guide. John W. Hill. 102p. (Orig.). 1980. pap. 4.95x student guide o.p. (ISBN 0-8087-3156-4, Feffer & Simons). Burgess MN Intl.
Chemistry for Technologists. G. R. Palin. LC 70-142175. 355p. 1972. 90.00 o.p. (ISBN 0-08-016385-8); pap. 90.00 o.p. (ISBN 0-08-016386-6). Pergamon.
Chemistry for the Future: Proceedings of the 29th IUPAC Congress, Cologne, Federal Republic of Germany, 5-10 June 1983. Ed. by H. Grunewald. LC 83-23825. (IUPAC Symposium Ser.). 268p. 1984. 115.00 o.p. (ISBN 0-08-029249-6). Pergamon.
Chemistry for the Life Sciences. Lee R. Summerlin. Incl. P. S. Associates. 1981. 7.00 o.p. wkbk. (ISBN 0-394-32457-9); William Hendrickson & Juanita Healy. 631p. 1981. text ed. 24.00 o.p. (ISBN 0-394-32215-0, RanC). Random.
Chemistry for Toxicity Testing. C. W. Jameson & Douglas B. Walters. 256p. 1984. text ed. 37.95 o.p. (ISBN 0-250-40547-4). Butterworth.
Chemistry in Evolution & Systematics: Proceedings of an International Symposium, Strasbourg, 1972. Ed. by T. Swain. 326p. 1976. 92.00 o.p. (ISBN 0-08-020737-5). Pergamon.
Chemistry in Space Research. R. A. Lambel et al. 1972. 39.50 o.p. (ISBN 0-444-00118-2). Elsevier.
Chemistry in the Laboratory. George W. Watt et al. (Illus., Orig.). 1964. 15.95x o.p. (ISBN 0-393-09511-8, NortonC); pap. text ed. 9.95x o.p. (ISBN 0-393-09626-2). Norton.
Chemistry, Man & Society. 4th ed. Mark M. Jones et al. 1983. text ed. 32.95 o.p. (ISBN 0-03-063032-0, CBS C); instructor's manual 21.50 o.s.i. (ISBN 0-03-062892-X). SCP.
Chemistry of Acid Derivatives, Supplement B. Ed. by Saul Patai. LC 75-6913. (Chemistry of Functional Groups Ser.). 2226p. 1979. Set. 567.00 o.p. (ISBN 0-471-99609-2); Pt. 1. 191.25 o.p. (ISBN 0-471-99610-6); Pt. 2. 191.25 o.p. (ISBN 0-471-99611-4). Wiley.
Chemistry of Adamantanes: Recent Developments in the Chemistry of Adamantane & Related Polycyclic Hydrocarbons. R. C. Bingham & P. R. Von Schleyer. (Topics in Current Chemistry Ser.: Vol. 18). (Illus.). 1971. pap. 32.50 o.p. (ISBN 0-387-05387-5). Springer-Verlag.
Chemistry of Arsenic, Antimony & Bismuth. J. D. Smith. (Pergamon Texts in Inorganic Chemistry: Vol. 2). 138p. 1975. text ed. 29.00 o.p. (ISBN 0-08-018778-1); pap. text ed. 14.00 o.p. (ISBN 0-08-018777-3). Pergamon.
Chemistry of Boron. N. N. Greenwood. (Pergamon Texts in Inorganic Chemistry: Vol. 8). 328p. 1975. text ed. 54.00 o.p. (ISBN 0-08-018790-0); pap. text ed. 32.00 o.p. (ISBN 0-08-018789-7). Pergamon.
Chemistry of Cements, 2 Vols. Ed. by H. F. Taylor. 1964. Vol. 1. 70.00 o.p. (ISBN 0-12-683901-8); Vol. 2. 70.00 o.p. (ISBN 0-12-683902-6). Acad Pr.
Chemistry of Chlorine, Bromine, Iodine & Astatine. A. J. Downs & C. J. Adams. (Pergamon Texts in Inorganic Chemistry: Vol. 7). 488p. 1975. text ed. 69.00 o.p. (ISBN 0-08-018788-9); pap. text ed. 35.00 o.p. (ISBN 0-08-018787-0). Pergamon.
Chemistry of Chromium, Molybdenum & Tungsten. C. L. Rollinson. (Pergamon Texts in Inorganic Chemistry: Vol. 21). 148p. 1975. text ed. 30.00 o.p. (ISBN 0-08-018868-0); pap. text ed. 14.50 o.p. (ISBN 0-08-018867-2). Pergamon.
Chemistry of Electrode Processes. Ilana Fried. 1974. 55.50 o.p. (ISBN 0-12-267650-5). Acad Pr.
Chemistry of Flotation. M. C. Fuerstenau & J. D. Miller. LC 84-52209. (Illus.). 177p. 1985. 22.00x o.p. (ISBN 0-89520-436-3, 436-3). SMM&E Inc.
Chemistry of Fluorine. T. A. O'Donnell. (Pergamon Texts in Inorganic Chemistry: Vol. 5). 98p. 1975. text ed. 20.00 o.p. (ISBN 0-08-018784-6); pap. text ed. 10.75 o.p. (ISBN 0-08-018783-8). Pergamon.
Chemistry of Fungicidal Action. R. J. Lukens. LC 70-154308. (Molecular Biology, Biochemistry, & Biophysics Ser.: Vol. 10). (Illus.). 1972. 22.00 o.p. (ISBN 0-387-05405-7). Springer-Verlag.
Chemistry of Germanium. Frank Glockling. 1969. 48.50 o.p. (ISBN 0-12-286450-6). Acad Pr.
Chemistry of Germanium, Tin & Lead. E. G. Rochow & E. W. Abel. (Pergamon Texts in Inorganic Chemistry: Vol. 14). 146p. 1975. text ed. 29.00 o.p. (ISBN 0-08-018854-0); pap. text ed. 14.00 o.p. (ISBN 0-08-018853-2). Pergamon.
Chemistry of Glasses. A. Paul. LC 81-16793. (Illus.). 320p. 1982. 55.00 o.p. (ISBN 0-412-23020-8, NO. 6621, Pub. by Chapman & Hall). Routledge Chapman & Hall.
Chemistry of Heterocyclic Compounds. Ed. by R. A. Abramovitch. LC 73-9800. (Series of Monographs Pyridine & Its Derivitives: Vol. 14, Pt. 3). 720p. 1974. 105.00 o.p. (ISBN 0-471-37915-8). Krieger.
Chemistry of Heterocyclic Oxides. A. R. Katritzky & J. J. Lagowski. 1971. 130.50 o.p. (ISBN 0-12-401250-7). Acad Pr.
Chemistry of Iron, Cobalt & Nickel. D. Nicholls. (Pergamon Texts in Inorganic Chemistry: Vol. 24). 184p. 1975. text ed. 34.00 o.p. (ISBN 0-08-018874-5); pap. text ed. 17.50 o.p. (ISBN 0-08-018873-7). Pergamon.
Chemistry of Lignin: Supplementary Volume Covering Literature for 1949-58. Friedrich E. Brauns & Dorothy A. Brauns. 1960. 99.00 o.p. (ISBN 0-12-127861-1). Acad Pr.
Chemistry of Lithium, Sodium, Potassium, Rubidium, Cesium & Francium. W. A. Hart et al. (Pergamon Texts in Inorganic Chemistry: Vol. 13). 200p. 1975. text ed. 30.00 o.p. (ISBN 0-08-018852-4); pap. text ed. 17.50 o.p. (ISBN 0-08-018799-4). Pergamon.
Chemistry of Manganese, Technetium & Rhenium. Ed. by R. Kemmit. R. Peacock. (Pergamon Texts in Inorganic Chemistry: Vol. 22). 208p. 1975. text ed. 30.00 o.p. (ISBN 0-08-018870-2); pap. text ed. 17.50 o.p. (ISBN 0-08-018869-9). Pergamon.
Chemistry of Marine Natural Products. Paul J. Scheuer. 1973. 52.50 o.p. (ISBN 0-12-624050-7). Acad Pr.
Chemistry of Monatomic Gases. A. H. Cockett et al. (Pergamon Texts in Inorganic Chemistry: Vol. 4). 192p. 1975. text ed. 30.00 o.p. (ISBN 0-08-018782-X); pap. text ed. 17.50 o.p. (ISBN 0-08-018781-1). Pergamon.
Chemistry of Natural Protein Fibers. Ed. by R. S. Asquith. LC 76-52636. (Illus.). 418p. 1977. 85.00x o.p. (ISBN 0-306-30898-3, Plenum Pr). Plenum Pub.
Chemistry of Natural Waters. Aly Faust. LC 80-70322. 400p. 1981. text ed. 54.95 o.p. (ISBN 0-250-40387-0). Butterworth.
Chemistry of Nitrogen. K. Jones. (Pergamon Texts in Inorganic Chemistry: Vol. 11). 242p. 1975. text ed. 40.00 o.p. (ISBN 0-08-018796-X); pap. text ed. 22.00 o.p. (ISBN 0-08-018795-1). Pergamon.
Chemistry of Nuclear Power. J. K. Dawson & G. Long. (Illus.). 216p. 1959. (ISBN 0-8022-0364-7). Philos Lib.
Chemistry of Organolithium Compounds. B. J. Wakefield. LC 73-10091. 336p. 1974. 155.00 o.p. (ISBN 0-08-017640-2). Pergamon.
Chemistry of Organophosphorous Compounds, 2. H. Bestmann & R. Zimmermann. (Topics in Current Chemistry: Vol. 20). 1971. 48.40 o.p. (ISBN 0-387-05459-6). Springer-Verlag.
Chemistry of Organophosphorous Compounds, 1. L. Maier & V. Mislow. LC 51-5497. (Topics in Current Chemistry: Vol. 19). (Illus.). 1971. pap. 32.50 o.p. (ISBN 0-387-05458-8). Springer-Verlag.
Chemistry of Organotin Compounds. R. C. Poller. (Organometallic Chemistry Ser). 1970. 82.50 o.p. (ISBN 0-12-560750-4). Acad Pr.
Chemistry of Our Environment. R. A. Horne. LC 77-1156. 869p. 1978. 93.95 o.p. (ISBN 0-471-40944-8, Pub. by Wiley-Interscience). Wiley.
Chemistry of Oxygen. E. A. Ebsworth et al. (Pergamon Texts in Inorganic Chemistry: Vol. 16). 110p. 1975. text ed. 25.00 o.p. (ISBN 0-08-018858-3); pap. text ed. 13.25 o.p. (ISBN 0-08-018857-5). Pergamon.
Chemistry of Peroxides. Ed. by Saul Patai. LC 83-14844. (Chemistry of Functional Groups Ser.: 1-078). 1006p. 1984. text ed. 325.00 o.p. (ISBN 0-471-10218-0, Wiley-Interscience). Wiley.
Chemistry of Phosphorous. A. D. Toy. (Pergamon Texts in Inorganic Chemistry: Vol. 3). 158p. 1975. text ed. 29.00 o.p. (ISBN 0-08-018780-3); pap. text ed. 14.00 o.p. (ISBN 0-08-018779-X). Pergamon.
Chemistry of Plant Processes. C. P. Whittingham. 209p. 1965. (ISBN 0-8022-1874-1). Philos Lib.

Chemistry of Pyrroles. R. A. Jones & G. P. Bean. 1977. 94.50 o.p. (ISBN 0-12-389840-4). Acad Pr.

Chemistry of Ruthenium, Rhodium, Palladium, Osmium, Iridium & Platinum. S. E. Livingstone. (Pergamon Texts in Inorganic Chemistry: Vol. 25). 208p. 1975. text ed. 34.00 o.p. (ISBN 0-08-018876-1); pap. text ed. 17.50 o.p. (ISBN 0-08-018875-3). Pergamon.

Chemistry of Silicon. E. G. Rochow. (Pergamon Texts in Inorganic Chemistry: Vol. 9). 146p. 1975. text ed. 29.00 o.p. (ISBN 0-08-018792-7); pap. text ed. 14.00 o.p. (ISBN 0-08-018791-9). Pergamon.

Chemistry of Soil Solutions. Ed. by Adel M. Elprince. LC 86-7781. (VNR Soil Science Ser.). (Illus.). 416p. 1986. 62.95 o.s.i. (ISBN 0-442-22308-0). Van Nos Reinhold.

Chemistry of Sulphur, Selenium, Tellurium & Polonium. M. Schmidt et al. (Pergamon Texts in Inorganic Chemistry: Vol. 15). 214p. 1975. text ed. 34.00 o.p. (ISBN 0-08-018856-7); pap. text ed. 17.50 o.p. (ISBN 0-08-018855-9). Pergamon.

Chemistry of Synthetic Substances. Emil Dreher. (ISBN 0-8022-0417-1). Philos Lib.

Chemistry of the Actinides. S. Ahrland et al. (Pergamon Texts in Inorganic Chemistry: Vol. 10). 636p. 1975. text ed. 81.00 o.p. (ISBN 0-08-018794-3); pap. text ed. 35.00 o.p. (ISBN 0-08-018793-5). Pergamon.

Chemistry of the Amidines & Imidates. Saul Patai. LC 75-6913. (Chemistry of Functional Groups Ser.). 677p. 1976. 214.00 o.p. (ISBN 0-471-66923-7, Pub by Wiley-Interscience). Wiley.

Chemistry of the Cell Interface, 2 vols. Harry D. Brown. 1971. Vol. 1. 72.00 o.p. (ISBN 0-12-136101-2); Vol. 2. 72.00 o.p. (ISBN 0-12-136102-0); Set. 120.00 o.p. Acad Pr.

Chemistry of the Lanthanides. T. Moeller. (Pergamon Texts in Inorganic Chemistry: Vol. 26). 104p. 1975. text ed. 25.00 o.p. (ISBN 0-08-018878-8); pap. text ed. 13.25 o.p. (ISBN 0-08-018877-X). Pergamon.

Chemistry of the Non-Metallic Elements. E. Sherwin & G. J. Weston. 1966. 50.00 o.p. (ISBN 0-08-011296-X); pap. 50.00 o.p. (ISBN 0-08-011295-1). Pergamon.

Chemistry of the O-Glycosidic Bond: Formation & Cleavage. A. E. Bochkov & G. E. Zaikov. 1979. 65.00 o.p. (ISBN 0-08-022949-2). Pergamon.

Chemistry of Titanium, Zirconium & Hafnium. R. Clark et al. (Pergamon Texts in Inorganic Chemistry: Vol. 19). 136p. 1975. text ed. 29.00 o.p. (ISBN 0-08-018864-8); pap. text ed. 14.00 o.p. (ISBN 0-08-018863-X). Pergamon.

Chemistry of Transuranium Elements. Cornelius Keller. LC 79-173366. (Topical Presentations in Nuclear Chemistry Ser.: Vol. 3). (Illus.). 675p. 1971. 110.60x o.p. (ISBN 3-527-25389-0). VCH Pubs.

Chemistry of Vanadium, Niobium & Tantalum. R. Clark & D. Brown. (Pergamon Texts in Inorganic Chemistry: Vol. 20). 132p. 1975. text ed. 29.00 o.p. (ISBN 0-08-018866-4); pap. text ed. 14.00 o.p. (ISBN 0-08-018865-6). Pergamon.

Chemistry of Vegetable Tannins. E. Haslam. 1966. 16.00 o.p. (ISBN 0-12-330950-6). Acad Pr.

Chemistry of Viruses. C. A. Knight. (Protoplasmatologia: Vol. 4, Pt. 2). (Illus.). 1963. pap. 29.50 o.p. (ISBN 0-387-80652-0). Springer-Verlag.

Chemistry of Viruses. 2nd ed. C. A. Knight. LC 74-11220. (Illus.). x, 336p. 1975. pap. 36.30 o.p. (ISBN 0-387-06772-8). Springer-Verlag.

Chemistry Problems. 2nd ed. Michael J. Sienko. LC 70-151306. (Chemistry Ser). 1972. pap. text ed. 21.95 o.p. (ISBN 0-8053-8808-7). Benjamin-Cummings.

Chemistry: Reactions, Structure, & Properties. 2nd ed. Clyde R. Dillard & David E. Goldberg. (Illus.). 1978. write for info. o.p. (ISBN 0-02-329580-5). Macmillan.

Chemistry: The Central Science. 2nd ed. Theodore L. Brown & H. Eugene LeMay. 832p. 1981. text ed. (ISBN 0-13-128504-1). P-H.

Chemistry: The Central Science. Theodore L. Brown & H. Eugene LeMay, Jr. LC 76-22159. (Illus.). 1977. text ed. (ISBN 0-13-128769-9); lab. exp. 9.95 o.p. (ISBN 0-13-128751-6); solutions 4.95 o.p. (ISBN 0-13-128793-1). P-H.

Chemistry: The Central Science. Theodore L. Brown & H. Eugene LeMay, Jr. (Illus.). 1056p. 1988. text ed. 54.00 o.p. (ISBN 0-13-129792-9). P-H.

Chemistry: The Central Science. 3rd ed. James C. Hill. (Illus.). 30p. 1985. pap. text ed. (ISBN 0-13-127499-6). P-H.

Chemistry: The Central Science, Qualitative Inorganic Analysis. 3rd ed. Theodore L. Brown & H. Eugene LeMay. (Illus.). 160p. 1985. pap. text ed. (ISBN 0-13-127549-6). P-H.

Chemistry: The Easy Way. Joseph A. Mascetta. (Easy Way Ser.). 320p. (gr. 10-12). 1983. pap. 8.95 o.p. (ISBN 0-8120-2624-1). Barron.

Chemistry: The Science & the Scene. Ronald D. Clark & Robert L. Amai. LC 74-22969. 356p. 1975. 23.50 o.p. (ISBN 0-471-15857-7, JW). Krieger.

Chemistry Today: The Portrait of a Science. Alfred Neubauer. (Illus.). 214p. 1983. 12.95 o.p. (ISBN 0-668-05838-2, 5838). Arco.

Chemist's English. Robert Schoenfeld. LC 85-17858. 173p. 1985. lib. bdg. 17.95 o.p. (ISBN 0-89573-436-2). VCH Pubs.

Chemoreception in Marine Organisms. Ed. by P. T. Grant & A. M. Mackie. 1974. 57.00 o.p. (ISBN 0-12-295650-8). Acad Pr.

Chemosurgery. Bennett & Albon. 1987. 85.00 o.p. (ISBN 0-8016-0604-7). Mosby.

Chemotaxis & Inflammation. 2nd ed. Peter C. Wilkinson. (Illus.). 249p. 1982. 37.50 o.p. (ISBN 0-443-02085-X). Churchill.

Chemotherapy & Control of Influenza. Oxford. 1976. pap. 26.50 o.p. (ISBN 0-12-531750-6). Acad Pr.

Chemotherapy of Cancer. 2nd ed. Stephen Carter et al. LC 80-24450. 379p. 1981. 26.00x o.p. (ISBN 0-471-08045-4, Pub. by Wiley Medical). Wiley.

Chemotherapy of Helminthiasis. Ed. by R. Cavier. LC 72-86179. 532p. 1973. 155.00 o.p. (ISBN 0-08-015755-6). Pergamon.

Chemotherapy of Herpes Simplex Virus Infections. Ed. by J. S. Oxford et al. 1977. 30.50 o.p. (ISBN 0-12-531760-3). Acad Pr.

Chemotherapy of Virus Diseases. D. J. Bauer. 1972. 105.00 o.p. (ISBN 0-08-016961-9). Pergamon.

Chendru: The Boy & the Tiger. Astrid B. Sucksdorff. LC 60-3281. (Illus.). (gr. 3 up). 1960. 6.50 o.p. (ISBN 0-15-216431-6, HJ). HarBraceJ.

Chenes qui'on abat. Andre Malraux. (Coll. Soleil). 14.95 o.p. (ISBN 0-685-34269-7). Schoenhof.

Cher. Mark Bego. 1986. pap. 3.50 o.s.i. (ISBN 0-671-62845-3). PB.

Cher. Mary A. Casata. 96p. 1985. 7.95 o.s.i. (ISBN 0-317-40082-7). Sharon Pubns.

Chere Francoise: Revision de la Grammaire Francaise. Jeanette D. Bragger & Robert P. Shupp. 477p. 1983. text ed. 23.95 o.p. (ISBN 0-395-30960-3); Le Monde Francais (Reader) pap. 15.95 o.p. (ISBN 0-395-30962-X). HM.

Cherishable: Love & Marriage. David Augsburger. 1975. pap. (ISBN 0-515-09265-7, PV065). Jove Pubns.

Chernowitz! Fran Arrick. LC 81-7712. 176p. (gr. 7 up). 1981. 9.95 o.s.i. (ISBN 0-02-705720-8). Bradbury Pr.

Cherries & Lemons: The Used-Car Buyer's Handbook. Joe Troise. LC 79-51004. (Illus.). 1979. pap. 4.95 o.s.i. (ISBN 0-89708-005-X). And Bks.

Cherry Blossom Corpse. Robert Barnard. 1987. 14.95 o.p. (ISBN 0-684-18825-2). Scribner.

Cherry Blossom Corpse. Robert Barnhard. (Illus.). 293p. Date not set. Repr. of 1986 ed. lib. bdg. 16.95 o.p. (ISBN 0-89621-844-9). Thorndike Pr.

Cherry Blossoms. Dorothy Fields & Isamitsu Kitakoji. LC 72-93534. (This Beautiful World Ser: Vol. 40). (Illus.). 138p. 1973. pap. 4.95 o.p. (ISBN 0-87011-191-4). Kodansha.

Cherry Delight up Your Ante. Glen Chase. 1976. pap. 1.25 o.p. (ISBN 0-685-72568-5, LB407, Pub. by Leisure Bks CT). Dorchester Pub Co.

Cherry Orchard. Anton Chekhov. 1965. pap. 0.95 o.p. (ISBN 0-380-01093-3, 36848, Bard). Avon.

Cherry Pool. M. Aleveyev. 327p. 1978. pap. 6.45 o.p. (ISBN 0-8285-0938-7, Pub. by Progress Pubs USSR). Imported Pubns.

Cherry Tree Carol. Illus. by Jeanyee Wong. LC 86-61117. (Illus.). 27p. 1986. 5.95 o.p. (ISBN 0-88088-079-1, 880791). Peter Pauper.

Chesapeake in the Seventeenth Century: Essays on Anglo-American Society. Ed. by Thad W. Tate & David L. Ammerman. LC 78-31720. (Institute of Early American History & Culture Ser.). vii, 310p. 1979. 30.00x o.p. (ISBN 0-8078-1360-5). U of NC Pr.

Chesapeake Waters: Pollution, Public Health, & Public Opinion, 1607-1972. John Capper et al. LC 83-40102. 217p. 1983. 19.95 o.p. (ISBN 0-87033-310-0). Tidewater.

Cheshire Cat's Eye. Marcia Muller. (Nightingale Ser.). 278p. 1988. pap. 12.95x o.s.i. (ISBN 0-8161-4396-X, Large Print Bks). G K Hall.

Chess & Computers. David Levy. (Applications of Computer Science Ser.). 145p. 1976. 17.95 o.p. (ISBN 0-914894-03-X, Computer Sci Pr); pap. 12.95 o.p. (ISBN 0-914894-02-1). W H Freeman.

Chess Catechism. Larry Evans. LC 78-101872. 1973. pap. 6.95 o.p. (ISBN 0-671-21531-0, Fireside). S&S.

Chess Computer Book. T. D. Harding. (Pergamon Chess Ser.). (Illus.). 215p. 1981. 19.95 o.p. (ISBN 0-08-026885-4); pap. 10.95 o.p. (ISBN 0-08-026884-6). Pergamon.

Chess: East & West, Past & Present. Charles K. Wilkinson & Jessie McNab. (Illus.). 1988. 16.95 o.p. (ISBN 0-8109-1047-0). Abrams.

Chess Endings: Essential Knowledge. Y. Averbakh. (Pergamon Chess Ser.). (Illus.). 1966. 13.50 o.p. (ISBN 0-08-011823-2); pap. 9.95 o.p. (ISBN 0-08-011822-4). Pergamon.

Chess Endings for the Practical Player. Ludek Pachman. Ed. by John Littlewood. Tr. by Otto Hardy. 196p. 1983. pap. 7.95 o.p. (ISBN 0-7100-9266-0). Routledge Chapman & Hall.

Chess from Morphy to Botwinnik. 2nd ed. Imre Konig. LC 77-72873. 1977. pap. 4.95 o.p. (ISBN 0-486-23503-3). Dover.

Chess Fundamentals. Jose R. Capablanca. LC 22-127. (Illus.). 246p. 1938. 12.95 o.p. (ISBN 0-15-117045-2). HarBraceJ.

Chess in Literature. Ed. by Marcello Truzzi. (Orig.). 1975. pap. 5.45 o.p. (ISBN 0-380-00164-0, 22954-X, Equinox). Avon.

Chess Mysteries of Sherlock Holmes. Raymond Smullyan. LC 79-2101. (Illus.). 1979. 11.95 o.s.i. (ISBN 0-394-50488-7); pap. 8.95 o.p. (ISBN 0-394-73757-1). Knopf.

Chess Player's Handbook. Howard Staunton. (Batsford Chess Classics Ser.). 528p. 1985. 39.95 o.p. (ISBN 0-7134-5056-8, Pub. by Batsford England). David & Charles.

Chess Tactics & Attacking Techniques. Raymond Edwards. (Chess Handbooks: Vol. 5). 1978. pap. 4.95 o.p. (ISBN 0-7100-8821-3). Routledge Chapman & Hall.

Chess Techniques. A. R. B. Thomas. 1975. 15.00 o.p. (ISBN 0-7100-8098-0); pap. 5.95 o.p. (ISBN 0-7100-8099-9). Routledge Chapman & Hall.

Chess: The Records. Ken Whyld. (Illus.). 176p. (Orig.). 1987. pap. 12.95 o.p. (ISBN 0-85112-455-0, Pub. by Guinness Superlative England). Sterling.

Chess Training. Nigel Povah. 176p. 1981. 15.95 o.p. (ISBN 0-571-11604-3); pap. 8.95 o.p. (ISBN 0-571-11608-6). Faber & Faber.

Chessie's King. Kathleen Karr. 224p. 1986. pap. 5.95 o.p. (ISBN 0-310-47451-5, 15591P). Zondervan.

Chessnicdotes I. George Koltanowski. 100p. (Orig.). 1978. pap. 5.00 o.p. (ISBN 0-931462-01-0). Chess Ent Inc.

Chest Injuries. G. Keen. 192p. 1975. 18.50 o.p. (ISBN 0-7236-0413-4, Pub. by John Wright UK). Butterworth.

Chest Radiographic Analysis. Blank. 1988. price not set o.p. (ISBN 0-471-62469-1). Churchill.

Chester County, South Carolina Minutes of the County Court, Seventeen Eighty-Five to Seventeen Ninety-Nine. Brent Holcomb & Elmer O. Parker. 433p. 1979. 30.00 o.s.i. (ISBN 0-89308-148-5). Southern Hist Pr.

Chester Cunningham Sign Design Notebook. (Illus.). 28p. 1982. 16.95 o.p. (ISBN 0-911380-57-4). Signs of Times.

Chester Miracle Plays, Done into Modern English & Arranged for Acting by I. & O. Bolton King. 177p. Repr. of 1930 ed. 29.00x o.p. (ISBN 0-403-04010-8). Somerset Pub.

Chester the Little Black Earth Ant. Andrea Ross. (Illus.). 1980. 5.00 o.p. (ISBN 0-682-49612-X). Exposition-Phoenix.

Chesterfield Bibliography to Eighteen Hundred. Sidney L. Gulick. LC 78-25886. 255p. 1979. 30.00x o.p. U Pr of Va.

Cheval Fou. Jean Giono. 80p. 1974. 4.50 o.p. (ISBN 0-686-53951-6). Schoenhof.

Chevaliers de la Table Ronde see Theatre.

Chevette T-1000 1976-84. Chilton Automotives Editorial Staff. LC 83-45300. 212p. 1984. pap. 14.50 o.s.i. (ISBN 0-8019-7457-7). Chilton.

Chevrolet & GMC Van & Pick-up Maintenance. (A240). Clymer Pub.

Chevrolet Car Tune-up: All Models, 1966-1980. Ed. by Jeff Robinson. (Illus.). pap. text ed. 8.95 o.p. (ISBN 0-89287-191-1, A137). Clymer Pub.

Chevrolet Chevette. (A134). Clymer Pub.

Chevrolet Citation. (A245). Clymer Pub.

Chevrolet Complete Owner's Handbook of Repair & Maintenance: 1929-1955. Clymer Publications. (Illus.). pap. 5.00 o.p. (ISBN 0-89287-268-3, H251). Clymer Pub.

Chevrolet GMC Pick-Ups 1970-84: Repair & Tune-up Guide - Includes Suburban. Chilton Automotives Editorial Staff. LC 83-45306. 312p. 1984. pap. 13.50 o.s.i. (ISBN 0-8019-7464-X). Chilton.

Chevrolet-GMC Vans 1967-84: Repair & Tune-up Guide. Chilton Automotives Editorial Staff. LC 83-45322. 248p. 1985. pap. 13.50 o.s.i. (ISBN 0-8019-7487-9). Chilton.

Chevrolet Performance Guide. Bill Carroll. (Performance Engineering Handbooks Ser.). (Illus., Orig.). (YA) (gr. 7 up). 1971. 7.95 o.p. (ISBN 0-910390-04-5). Auto Bk.

Chevrolet Tune-up & Repair. Ed. by Spence Murray. LC 78-62361. (Tune-up & Repair Ser.). (Illus.). 1978. pap. 4.95 o.p. (ISBN 0-8227-5037-6). Petersen Pub.

Chevrolet 1955. (A251). Clymer Pub.

Chevy-GMC Pickup Repair. Ed. by Spence Murray. LC 78-61768. (Pickups & Vans Ser.). (Illus.). 1978. pap. 4.95 o.p. (ISBN 0-8227-5038-4). Petersen Pub.

Chevy S-Ten--S-Fifteen Blazer, 1982 to 1987. Chilton's Automotives Editorial Staff. 256p. 1987. pap. 13.95 o.p. (ISBN 0-8019-7766-5). Chilton.

Chevy S-10 Blazer, S-15 Jimmy 1982-85. Chilton Automotives Editorial Staff. LC 84-45482. 224p. (Orig.). 1985. pap. 13.50 o.s.i. (ISBN 0-8019-7568-9). Chilton.

Chevy S-10, GMC S15 Pick up 1982-85. Chilton Automotives Editorial Staff. LC 84-45486. 225p. (Orig.). 1985. pap. 13.50 o.s.i. (ISBN 0-8019-7564-6). Chilton.

Cheyenne Captives. Lewis B. Patten. (General Ser.). 263p. 1986. lib. bdg. 14.95x o.p. (ISBN 0-8161-3898-2, Large Print Bks). G K Hall.

Cheyenne Lance. John Legg. (Orig.). 1980. pap. text ed. 1.95 o.p. (ISBN 0-505-51584-9, Pub. by Tower Bks). Dorchester Pub Co.

Cheyenne Lance. John Legg. (Gunsmoke Western Ser.). 176p. 1988. text ed. 12.95x o.p. (ISBN 0-85997-855-9, Pub. by Firecrest Pub Ltd). Prescott Pr NH.

Cheyenne's Woman. Robert E. Mills. (Kansan Ser.: No. 9). 208p. (Orig.). 1982. pap. 2.25 o.s.i. (ISBN 0-8439-1171-9, Pub. by Leisure Bks CT). Dorchester Pub Co.

Chez Francois Cookbook: The Cuisine of Francois R. Haeringer. Jacques E. Haeringer. 1985. pap. 19.95 o.s.i. (ISBN 0-8359-0757-0, Reston). P-H.

Chez les Francais. Lucette R. Kenan. (Illus., Orig., Fr.). 1967. pap. text ed. 8.95 o.p. (ISBN 0-15-506501-7, HC). HarBraceJ.

Ch'i Heavy Sword Coins of the Chou Dynasty, Vol. 5. Arthur B. Coole. LC 72-86801. (Encyclopedia of Chinese Coins Ser.: Vol. 5). (Illus.). 1976. 35.00x o.p. (ISBN 0-88000-014-7). Quarterman.

Chiang Ch'ing: The Emergence of a Revolutionary Political Leader. Dwan L. Tai. LC 74-10618. 1974. 7.50 o.p. (ISBN 0-682-48060-6, University). Exposition-Phoenix.

Chibia, the Dhow Boy. Bronson Potter. (gr. 5-8). 1971. PLB 6.50 o.p. (ISBN 0-689-20685-2, Atheneum). Macmillan.

Chicago. Carl W. Condit. Incl. Nineteen Ten to Nineteen Twenty-Nine - Building, Planning, & Urban Technology. LC 72-94791. 1976. pap. 5.45; pap. 5.45 o.s.i. (ISBN 0-226-11458-9, P693); Nineteen Thirty to Nineteen Seventy - Building, Planning & Urban Technology. LC 73-19996. 0.00 o.s.i. (ISBN 0-226-11459-7, P694). (Illus.). 1976 (Phoen). U of Chicago Pr.

Chicago. Mary J. O'Shea. (Rock 'n Pop Stars Ser.). (Illus.). (gr. 4-12). 1975. PLB 7.95 o.p. (ISBN 0-87191-458-1); pap. 3.95 o.p. (ISBN 0-89812-114-0). Creative Ed.

Chicago Area Business Directory, 1987-88, Vol. 1. rev. ed. American Directory Publishing Co., Inc. 1845p. 1987. pap. 120.00 o.p. (ISBN 0-944316-08-5). Amer Directory.

Chicago Association of Commerce & Industry, Committee of Investigatin or Smoke Abatement: Smoke Papers of the Chicago Association of Commerce Collected 1911-1915 for Preparation of Report Entitled Smoke Abatement & Electrification of Railway Terminals. Ed. by Benjamin Linsky. Repr. of 1915 ed. 218.00 o.s.i. (ISBN 0-08-022302-8). Pergamon.

Chicago at the Turn of the Century in Photographs. Larry A. Viskochil. (Illus.). 16.25 o.p. (ISBN 0-8446-6140-6). Peter Smith.

Chicago Bears. James R. Rothaus. (NFL Today Ser.). (Illus.). 48p. (gr. 4-12). 1981. PLB 10.45 o.p. (ISBN 0-87191-806-4); pap. 4.25 o.p. (ISBN 0-89812-252-X). Creative Ed.

Chicago Bulls. Frank MacDonald. (NBA Today Ser.). (Illus.). 48p. (gr. 4 up). 1984. PLB 10.45 o.p. (ISBN 0-87191-972-9). Creative Ed.

Chicago: Center For Enterprise, 2 vols. Kenan Heise & Michael Edgerton. LC 82-50771. (Illus.). 840p. 1982. 39.95 o.p. (ISBN 0-89781-041-4). Windsor Pubns Inc.

Chicago Ceramics & Glass: An Illustrated History, 1871-1933. Sharon S. Darling. LC 79-91566. (Illus.). 240p. 1980. 25.00 o.s.i. (ISBN 0-226-10414-1). U of Chicago pr.

Chicago, Chicago. Yasuhiro Ishimoto. (Illus.). 160p. 1983. 25.00 o.p. (ISBN 0-87040-553-5). Japan Pubns USA.

Chicago: City on the Make. Nelson Algren. 112p. 1983. pap. text ed. 5.95 o.p. (ISBN 0-07-001012-9). McGraw.

Chicago Cubs. rev. ed. Martin. LC 82-16192. (Baseball Today Ser.). 48p. (gr. 4 up). 1982. PLB 11.45 o.p. (ISBN 0-87191-856-0). Creative Ed.

Chicago Geographic Edition, 1987. 480p. 1986. pap. 65.00 o.p. (ISBN 0-318-02852-2). Manufacturers.

Chicago Girls. Edith Freund. 448p. 1985. 16.45 o.s.i. (ISBN 0-671-50291-3, Pub. by Poseidon). S&S.

Chicago Great Western. 2nd ed. Phil R. Hastings. (Carstens Hobby Bks.: No. C39). 1986. pap. 9.95 o.s.i. (ISBN 0-911868-39-9). Carstens Pubns.
Chicago Guide. 1983. pap. 2.25 o.p. (ISBN 0-528-84435-0). Rand McNally.
Chicago in Your Pocket. (Barron's City in Your Pocket Ser.). 128p. 1982. pap. 2.50 o.p. (ISBN 0-8120-2530-X). Barron.
Chicago in Your Pocket. (City in Your Pocket Ser.). 295p. 1984. pap. 2.95 o.p. (ISBN 0-8120-2974-7). Barron.
Chicago School Architects & Their Critics. Wichit Charernbhak. Ed. by Stephen Foster. LC 83-24299. (Architecture & Urban Design Ser.: No. 1). 228p. 1984. 42.95 o.p. (ISBN 0-8357-1537-X). UMI Res Pr.
Chicago Sculpture: Text & Photographs. James L. Riedy. LC 80-13642. (Illus.). 352p. 1981. 29.95 o.p. (ISBN 0-252-00819-7); pap. 12.50 o.p. (ISBN 0-252-01255-0). U of Ill Pr.
Chicago Sociology, Nineteen Twenty to Nineteen Thirty-Two. Robert E. Faris. LC 76-122368. (Midway Reprints Ser.; Heritage of Sociology Ser.). 1979. pap. text ed. 6.00x o.s.i. (ISBN 0-226-23819-9). U of Chicago Pr.
Chicago: Some Other Traditions. Dennis Adrian & Trent Myers. LC 83-19563. 101p. 1983. 19.95 o.p. (ISBN 0-913883-00-X). Madison Art.
Chicago White Sox. rev. ed. Shaw. LC 82-16197. (Baseball Today Ser.). 48p. (gr. 4 up). 1982. PLB 11.45 o.p. (ISBN 0-87191-857-9). Creative Ed.
Chicagoland Map: Chicago Tribune. 1.95 o.s.i. (ISBN 0-914090-77-1). Chicago Review.
Chicago's Classiest Cuisine. Ann Gerber. (Illus.). 304p. 1983. 25.00 o.p. (ISBN 0-914091-31-X). Chicago Review.
Chicago's Sweet Tooth. Ann Gerber. LC 85-11705. (Illus.). 288p. 1985. 18.95 o.p. (ISBN 0-914091-77-8). Chicago Review.
Chicano Authors: Inquiry by Interview. Bruce-Novoa. (Illus.). 306p. 1980. text ed. 20.00x o.p. (ISBN 0-292-71059-3); pap. text ed. 12.95 o.p. (ISBN 0-292-71062-3). U of Tex Pr.
Chicano Discourse: Socio-Historic Perspectives. Rosaura Sanchez. 192p. 1983. pap. text ed. 17.95 o.p. (ISBN 0-88377-215-9). Newbury Hse.
Chicano, Go Home! The Life of Alfonso Rodriguez. Tomas Lopez. 1976. 8.50 o.p. (ISBN 0-682-48514-4). Exposition-Phoenix.
Chicano Poetry: A Response to Chaos. Bruce-Novoa. 246p. 1982. text ed. 25.00x o.p. (ISBN 0-292-71075-5). U of Tex Pr.
Chicano Workers: Their Utilization & Development. Fred Romero. (Monograph.: No. 8). (Illus.). 160p. (Orig.). 1979. pap. 8.95 o.p. (ISBN 0-89551-011-1). UCLA Chicano Stud.
Chickaree: A Red Squirrel. St. Tamara. LC 79-23933. (Illus.). 48p. (gr. 1-5). 1980. 7.95 o.p. (ISBN 0-15-216612-2, HJ). HarBraceJ.
Chickasaw Gardens. Marie Connors. LC 84-26212. 24p. 1985. 5.00 o.p. (ISBN 0-918518-37-7). Ion Books.
Chicken & Egg: Electronics & Social Change in India. Ward Morehouse & Ravi Chopra. (Illus.). 100p. (Orig.). 1983. pap. 8.00x o.p. LRIS.
Chicken & Other Poultry. (Step-by-Step Cooking Ser.). (Illus.). 160p. 10.95 o.p. (ISBN 0-8120-5681-7). Barron.
Chicken Book. Page Smith & Charles Daniel. LC 75-8684. (Illus.). 448p. 1975. 12.95 o.p. (ISBN 0-316-80151-8). Little.
Chicken Book. Page Smith & Charles Daniel. LC 81-83967. 400p. 1982. pap. 12.00 o.p. (ISBN 0-86547-067-7). N Point Pr.
Chicken Cookbook. Consumer Guide Editors & Sophie Kay. 160p. (Orig.). 1981. pap. 6.95 o.p. (ISBN 0-449-90049-5, Columbine). Fawcett.
Chicken Country Style. Ed. by Annette Gohlke. LC 81-85696. 84p. 1982. pap. 3.95 o.s.i. (ISBN 0-89821-040-2). Reiman Assocs.
Chicken Foot Soup & Other Recipes from the Pine Barrens. Ed. by Arlene M. Ridgway. (Illus., Orig.). 1980. pap. 7.95 o.p. (ISBN 0-8135-0877-0). Rutgers U Pr.
Chicken Soup with Rice: A Book of Months. Maurice Sendak. (Illus.). (gr. k-3). 1970. pap. 1.95 o.p. (ISBN 0-590-02954-1). Scholastic Inc.
Chicken Town. Michele DauNe. 160p. 1985. 10.00 o.p. (ISBN 0-682-40238-9). Exposition-Phoenix.
Chickenbone Special. Dwayne E. Walls. LC 73-4904. 233p. 1973. pap. 2.45 o.p. (ISBN 0-15-616855-3, Harv). HarBraceJ.
Chickpea. Ed. by M. C. Saxena & K. B. Singh. 409p. 1987. 65.00 o.p. (ISBN 0-85198-571-8). CAB Intl.
Chief Executive. 4th ed. Louis W. Koenig. 472p. 1981. pap. text ed. 12.75 o.p. (ISBN 0-15-506673-0, HC). HarBraceJ.
Chief Executive Officers: Contracts & Compensation 1981. R. Steven Nicholson. 56p. (Orig.). 1981. pap. 10.00 o.p. (ISBN 0-87117-118-X). Am Assn Comm Jr Coll.
Chief Executive: Realities of Corporate Leadership. Chester Burger. LC 77-2844. 224p. 1983. 25.95 o.p. (ISBN 0-8436-0747-5). Van Nos Reinhold.
Chief Financial Officer. preliminary ed. Benoit Deschamps & Mehta Dileep. 1987. pap. 19.50 o.p. (ISBN 0-471-85809-9). Wiley.
Chief Joseph's Own Story. facsimile ed. (Shorey Indian Ser.). 34p. pap. 3.95 o.s.i. (ISBN 0-8466-4004-X, 14). Shorey.
Chieftain. George Forty. (Illus.). 1980. encore ed 5.95 o.p. (ISBN 0-684-17527-4, ScribT). Scribner.
Chien Blanc. Romain Gary. (Coll. Soleil). 11.50 o.p. (ISBN 0-685-34123-2). Schoenhof.
Child Abuse & Neglect: A Medical Reference. Norman S. Ellerstein. LC 81-2978. 355p. 1981. 50.00 o.p. (ISBN 0-471-05877-7). Wiley.
Child Abuse & Neglect: How Schools Can Help Combat. 2nd ed. Cynthia C. Tower. LC 83-25071. 112p. 1984. pap. 10.95 o.p.; 19.95 o.p. NEA.
Child Abuse: Guidelines for Intervention. 1985. pap. 4.50 o.s.i. (ISBN 0-317-27066-4). Child Welfare.
Child Abuse-Intervention & Treatment. Ed. by Nancy Ebeling & Deborah Hill. LC 74-82430. 198p. 1975. lib. bdg. 15.00 o.p. (ISBN 0-88416-026-2). Year Bk Med.
Child Abuse: What You Can Do about It. Angela Carl. LC 85-17240. 128p. 1986. pap. 4.95 o.p. (ISBN 0-87403-006-4, 2961). Standard Pub.
Child Abuser: A Study of Child Abusers in Self-Help Group Therapy. Marilyn C. Collins. LC 76-47866. 124p. 1978. pap. 12.00 o.p. (ISBN 0-88416-186-2). Year Bk Med.
Child Adoption in the Modern World. Margaret Kornitzer. 400p. 1952. (ISBN 0-8022-0885-1). Philos Lib.
Child-Adult Differences in Second Language Acquisition. Ed. by Stephen D. Krashen et al. (Issues in Second Language Research Ser.). 240p. 1982. pap. text ed. 19.95 o.p. (ISBN 0-88377-206-X). Newbury Hse.
Child & Health Care: A Bibliography. 75p. 1983. 12.00 o.p. (ISBN 0-318-17769-2); members 8.00 o.p. (ISBN 0-318-17770-6). Assn Care Child.
Child & His Book. 2nd ed. Louise F. Field. LC 67-23937. 368p. 1968. Repr. of 1892 ed. 40.00x o.p. (ISBN 0-8103-3480-1). Gale.
Child & His Image: Self Concept in the Early Years. Ed. by Kaoru Yamamoto. LC 72-163283. (Illus., Orig.). 1972. pap. 18.95 o.p. (ISBN 0-395-12571-5). HM.
Child & Science: Wondering, Exploring, Growing. Ruth Roche. Ed. by Bonnie D. Baron. LC 76-55313. 42p. 1977. 3.50 o.p. (ISBN 0-87173-080-4). ACEI.
Child & Story: The Literary Connection. Ed. by Kay E. Vandergrift & Jane A. Hannigan. LC 80-21996. (Diversity & Direction in Children's Literature Ser.). 340p. (Orig.). 1980. pap. 24.95 o.p. (ISBN 0-317-56212-6). Neal-Schuman.
Child & the Christian Faith. Dorothy B. Fritz. (Illus., Orig.). 1964. pap. 4.50 o.p. (ISBN 0-8042-9402-X, John Knox). Westminster John Knox.
Child & the Serpent: Reflections on Popular Indian Symbols. Jyoti Sahi. (Illus.). 192p. (Orig.). 1980. pap. 12.50 o.p. (ISBN 0-7100-0704-3). Routledge Chapman & Hall.
Child Before Birth. Linda F. Annis. LC 77-3112. (Illus.). 194p. 1978. Paperback Ser. 29.95x o.p. (ISBN 0-8014-1039-8); pap. 8.95x o.p. (ISBN 0-8014-9168-1). Cornell U Pr.
Child Behavior. William C. Sheppard & Robert H. Willoughby. 1975. text ed. 28.95 o.p. (ISBN 0-395-30838-0); pap. 11.50 o.p. (ISBN 0-395-30839-9). HM.
Child Behavior. Grover J. Whitehurst & Ross F. Vasta. LC 76-14009. (Illus.). 1978. text ed. 25.50 o.p. (ISBN 0-395-24446-3). HM.
Child Behavior Modification: A Manual for Teachers, Nurses & Parents. L. S. Watson, Jr. 1973. pap. 40.00 o.p. (ISBN 0-08-017061-7). Pergamon.
Child Care & Mediating Structures. Ed. by Brigitte Berger & Sidney Callahan. 1979. 18.75 o.p. (ISBN 0-8447-2162-X); pap. 9.00 o.p. Am Enterprise.
Child Care & the Family. H. R. Schaffer. 88p. 1968. pap. text ed. 5.00 o.p. (ISBN 0-7135-1511-2, Pub. by Bedford England). Gower Pub Co.
Child Care Issues for Parents & Society: A Guide to Information Sources. Ed. by Andrew Garoogian & Rhoda Garoogian. LC 77-82800. (Social Issues & Social Problems Information Guide Ser.: Vol. 2). 384p. 1977. 68.00x o.p. (ISBN 0-8103-1314-6). Gale.
Child Care: Kith, Kin & Hired Hands. Emmy E. Werner. LC 83-14658. (Illus.). 248p. 1984. pap. 19.00x o.p. (ISBN 0-8391-1805-8, 1231). Pro Ed.
Child Custody: A Study of Families After Divorce. Deborah A. Luepnitz. LC 80-8787. (Illus.). 208p. 1981. 27.00x o.p. (ISBN 0-669-04365-6); pap. 14.00x o.p. (ISBN 0-669-09117-0). Lexington Bks.
Child Custody & Divorce: The Law in Social Context. Susan Maidment. 324p. 1984. 29.95 o.p. (ISBN 0-7099-1737-6, Pub. by Croom Helm Ltd); pap. 15.95 o.p. (ISBN 0-7099-1798-8). Routledge Chapman & Hall.
Child Custody Disputes: A Source Book. Ed. by Gary E. Stollak & Michael Lieberman. 500p. 1985. text ed. 49.50x o.p. (ISBN 0-8290-0966-3). Irvington.
Child Dental Health. 2nd ed. P. J. Holloway & J. N. Swallow. 240p. 1975. pap. text ed. 18.50 o.p. (ISBN 0-7236-0378-2, Pub. by John Wright UK). Butterworth.
Child Development. 4th ed. Sueann R. Ambron & Neil J. Salkind. 1984. text ed. 30.95 o.p. (ISBN 0-03-063302-8). HR&W.
Child Development: An Introduction. Robert F. Biehler. LC 75-31014. 1977. text ed. 19.25 o.p. (ISBN 0-395-20650-2). HM.
Child Development: An Introduction. 2nd ed. Robert F. Biehler. LC 80-82347. (Illus.). 704p. 1981. text ed. 28.95 o.p. (ISBN 0-395-29833-4). HM.
Child Development: Concepts, Issues, & Readings. Richard Hanson & Rebecca Reynolds. 544p. 1980. text ed. 35.50 o.p. (ISBN 0-8299-0336-4). West Pub.
Child: Development from Birth through Adolescence. Robert M. Liebert & Judith R. Harris. (Illus.). 600p. 1984. text ed. (ISBN 0-13-130436-4). P-H.
Child: Development from Birth to Adolescence. Pamela J. Hilligoss & Addison E. Woodward, Jr. (Study Guide with Practice Tests). 176p. 1984. pap. text ed. (ISBN 0-13-130477-1). P-H.
Child Drama. Peter Slade. (Illus.). 370p. 1955. (ISBN 0-8022-1585-8). Philos Lib.
Child, Family, Neighborhood: A Master Plan for Social Service Delivery. June H. Brown et al. 63p. 1982. 10.95 o.s.i. (ISBN 0-87868-209-0, 2090). Child Welfare.
Child Growth & Development. 4th ed. Elizabeth B. Hurlock. (gr. 10-12). 1970. text ed. 30.56 o.p. (ISBN 0-07-031436-5, W). McGraw.
Child Health: A Pediatrician's Guide. Ed. by Barry S. Zuckerman & Pamela M. Zuckerman. (Illus.). 352p. 1986. 22.95 o.p. (ISBN 0-688-05919-8). Hearst Bks.
Child Health: A Textbook for THR DCH. Ed. by David Harvey & Ilya Kovar. LC 84-19954. (Illus.). 374p. 1985. text ed. 49.95 o.p. (ISBN 0-443-02358-1). Churchill.
Child Health & Survival: The UNICEF GOBI-FFF Program. Ed. by Richard Cash et al. 350p. 1986. 43.00 o.p. (ISBN 0-7099-4815-8, Pub. by Croom Helm Ltd); pap. 25.50 o.p. (ISBN 0-7099-4810-7, Pub. by Croom Helm UK). Routledge Chapman & Hall.
Child Health in the Tropics. 5th ed. D. B. Jelliffe. 192p. 1985. pap. 14.95 o.p. (ISBN 0-683-13046-3, Pub. by E Arnold UK). Routledge Chapman & Hall.
Child: His Psychological & Cultural Development, 2 vols. Ed. by Alfred M. Freedman & Harold I. Kaplan. LC 74-178070. (Studies in Human Behavior Ser). 1972. Vol. 1. pap. text ed. 4.95x o.p. (ISBN 0-689-70281-7, HB5, Atheneum); Vol. 2. pap. text ed. 4.95x o.p. (ISBN 0-689-70328-7, HB-6). Macmillan.
Child in Primitive Society. Nathan Miller. LC 76-167074. 314p. 1975. Repr. of 1928 ed. 44.00x o.p. (ISBN 0-8103-3995-1). Gale.
Child in the Family. Maria Montessori. 1976. pap. 3.95 o.p. (ISBN 0-380-01096-8, 67173-5, Discus). Avon.
Child in the Forest. Winifred Foley. LC 85-8455. (Illus.). 192p. 1985. 17.95 o.p. (ISBN 0-03-005857-0). H Holt & Co.
Child Is Born: The Drama of Life Before Birth. Claes Wirsen et al. 160p. 1969. pap. 11.95 o.p. (ISBN 0-440-51214-X, Dell Trade Pbks). Dell.
Child Is Superior to the Man: Children's Experiences with God in the Public School Classroom. Samuel Silverstein. (Illus.). 1980. 6.50 o.p. (ISBN 0-682-49541-7). Exposition-Phoenix.
Child Killer. Edson T. Hamill. (Ryker Ser: No. 5). (Orig.). 1975. pap. 1.25 o.p. (ISBN 0-685-52936-3, LB266ZK, Pub. by Leisure Bks CT). Dorchester Pub Co.
Child Labour: Extract from the Report of the Director-General to the International Labour Conference, 69th Session, 1983. Intro. by Blanchard Francis. iii, 40p. (Orig.). 1983. pap. 7.00 o.p. (ISBN 92-2-105287-7). Intl Labour Office.
Child Maltreatment & Paternal Deprivation: A Manifesto for Research, Prevention, & Treatment. Henry Biller & Richard Solomon. LC 85-45979. 320p. 1986. 23.00x o.p. (ISBN 0-669-12677-2). Lexington Bks.
Child of Fire. Scott O'Dell. LC 74-8718. 224p. (gr. 7 up). 1974. 6.95 o.p. (ISBN 0-395-19496-2). HM.
Child of Mine: Feeding with Love & Good Sense. Ellyn Satter. 432p. (Orig.). 1983. pap. 9.95 o.p. (ISBN 0-915950-54-5). Bull Pub.
Child of the Jago. Arthur Morrison. 208p. 1983. pap. 8.95 o.s.i. (ISBN 0-85115-203-1, Pub. by Boydell & Brewer). Academy Chi Pubs.
Child of the Morning. Barbara Corcoran. LC 81-8057. 132p. (gr. 5-9). 1982. 11.95 o.s.i. (ISBN 0-689-30876-0, Atheneum Childrens Bks). Macmillan.
Child of the Wind. Ethel Bangert. (Silver Bell Ser.). 192p. (Orig.). 1982. pap. 1.95 o.p. (ISBN 0-8439-1128-X, Pub. by Leisure Bks CT). Dorchester Pub Co.
Child of War. Mary Ann Sullivan. LC 84-47832. 144p. (gr. 5 up). 1984. 10.95 o.p. (ISBN 0-8234-0537-0). Holiday.
Child Possessed by Chess. James Howard. 1978. 4.00 o.p. (ISBN 0-682-48587-X). Exposition-Phoenix.
Child Protection Team Handbook. Ed. by Barton D. Schmitt. LC 77-78700. 1979. lib. bdg. 46.00 o.p. (ISBN 0-8240-7000-3, Garland STPM Pr). Garland Pub.
Child Psychiatric Treatment: A Practical Guide. Philip G. Ney & Deanna L. Mulvihill. LC 84-20048. 368p. 1985. 44.00 o.p. (ISBN 0-7099-1823-2, Pub. by Croom Helm Ltd); pap. 22.50 o.p. (ISBN 0-7099-1824-0). Routledge Chapman & Hall.
Child Psychiatry for Students. 3rd ed. Frederick H. Stone & Cyrille Koupernik. LC 84-14972. 124p. 1985. pap. text ed. 16.00 o.p. (ISBN 0-443-02950-4). Churchill.
Child Psychiatry Observed. Elizabeth Gore. Ed. by Jean Nursten. LC 75-6926. 264p. 1976. 34.00 o.p. (ISBN 0-08-017277-6); pap. 18.75 o.p. (ISBN 0-08-017278-4). Pergamon.
Child Psychology. Ed. by Harold W. Stevenson et al. LC 63-24881. (National Society for the Study of Education Yearbks.: No. 62, Pt. 1). x, 556p. 1963. lib. bdg. 8.50x o.s.i. (ISBN 0-226-60068-8). U of Chicago Pr.
Child Psychopathology: Behavior Disorders & Developmental Disabilities. 2nd ed. Marilyn T. Erickson. (Illus.). 368p. 1982. text ed. (ISBN 0-13-131094-1). P-H.
Child Rearing Values: A Cross National Study. Wallace E. Lambert et al. LC 78-19747. 1979. 33.95 o.p. (ISBN 0-03-049086-3). Praeger.
Child-Resistant Packages for Pesticides. Rosalind L. Gross. Ed. by Art Donner & Charles J. Wilbur. (Illus.). 67p. (Orig.). 1985. pap. 1.50 o.p. (ISBN 0-318-18731-0, S/N 055-000-00250-9). USGPO.
Child Savers. Peter Prescott. 1982. pap. 5.75 o.p. (ISBN 0-671-45479-X, Touchstone Bks). S&S.
Child Schooling & the Measurement of Living Standards. Nancy Birdsall. (Working Paper Ser.: No. 14). 97p. 5.00 o.p. (ISBN 0-317-58527-4, BK 0041). World Bank.
Child Sexual Abuse Case in the Courtroom: A Source Book. James Selkin & Peter Schouten. 196p. Date not set. 22.95 o.p. J Selkin.
Child Signs: Understanding Your Child Through Astrology. Dodie Edmands & Allan Edmands. LC 82-45630. (Illus.). 154p. 1983. pap. 8.95 o.p. (ISBN 0-916360-19-9). CRCS Pubns CA.
Child Support & Alimony: 1983: Supplemental Report. Ruth A. Sanders. (Current Population Reports Series P-23, Special Studies, No. 148). (Illus.). 75p. (Orig.). 1986. pap. 3.75 o.p. (ISBN 0-318-21541-1, S/N 803-005-10001-4). USGPO.
Child That Nobody Wanted. Charles V. Bryan. LC 57-12228. 284p. 1957. 4.00 o.p. (ISBN 0-87004-022-7). Caxton.
Child, the Clinic, & the Court. Jane Addams et al. LC 72-137577. 1971. Repr. lib. bdg. 25.00 o.p. (ISBN 0-384-08782-5). Johnson Repr.
Child Welfare & Social Services: A Bibliograhic Review. Alva W. Stewart. (Public Administration Ser.: P 1811). 10p. 1985. 2.00 o.p. (ISBN 0-89028-641-8). Vance Biblios.
Child Welfare League of America Standards for Services to Unmarried Parents. Child Welfare League of America, Committee on Standards. LC 52-4649. 1971. pap. 12.50 o.p. (UM-13). Child Welfare.
Child Without Tomorrow. Anthony M. Graziano. LC 73-3394. 1974. 34.00 o.p. (ISBN 0-08-017085-4). Pergamon.
Child: Your Choice. Jean Shapiro. 192p. 1987. 32.50 o.p. (ISBN 0-86358-073-4, A0812, Pandora Pr); pap. 8.95 o.p. (ISBN 0-86358-195-1, A0816, Pandora Pr). Routledge Chapman & Hall.
Childbirth: Alternatives to Medical Control. Ed. by Shelly Romalis. 262p. 1982. text ed. 22.50x o.p. (ISBN 0-292-71072-0); pap. 10.95 o.p. (ISBN 0-292-71073-9). U of Tex Pr.
Childbirth, Cooperative Style: Family Experience with Prepared Childbirth & Prenatal Classes. Pat Kenschaft. 1977. 6.00 o.p. (ISBN 0-682-48785-6, Banner). Exposition-Phoenix.
Childbirth Wisdom: From the World's Oldest Societies. Judith Goldsmith. (Illus.). 320p. 1985. pap. 18.95 o.p. (ISBN 0-86553-126-9). Congdon & Weed.

Titles

Childcraft: The How & Why Library. Ed. by World Book, Inc. Staff. LC 86-50557. (Illus.). 5000p. (ps-6). 1987. PLB World Bk.
Childcraft: 1988 Edition, 15 vols. Ed. by World Book Editors. LC 87-50086. (How & Why Library). (Illus.). 5000p. (ps-6). Set. lib. bdg. (ISBN 0-7166-0188-5). World Bk.
Childhood & Society. 2nd ed. Erik H. Erikson. 15.75 o.p. (ISBN 0-8446-6205-4). Peter Smith.
Childhood Autism Rating Scale (CARS) For Diagnostic Screening & Classification of Autism. Eric Schopler et al. LC 85-8372. 48p. (Orig.). 1986. pap. text ed. 19.95x incls. rating forms o.p. (ISBN 0-8290-1588-4). Irvington.
Childhood Behavior Disorders: Applied Research & Educational Practice. Bob Algozzine et al. LC 81-4360. 411p. 1981. text ed. 36.00 o.p. (ISBN 0-89443-345-8). Aspen Pub.
Childhood Emotional Pattern: Human Hostility. Leon J. Saul. 1980. 21.95 o.p. (ISBN 0-442-23993-9). Van Nos Reinhold.
Childhood Emotional Pattern: Psycho Therapy. Leon J. Saul. 1980. 29.95 o.p. (ISBN 0-442-26123-3). Van Nos Reinhold.
Childhood Epidemiology. Ed. by E. D. Alberman & C. A. Peckham. (British Medical Bulletin Ser.: Vol. 42, No. 2, April 1986). (Illus.). 102p. (Orig.). 1986. pap. text ed. 51.00 o.p. (ISBN 0-443-03507-5). Churchill.
Childhood in Poetry: A Catalogue, with Biographical & Critical Annotations, of the Books of English & American Poets Comprising the Shaw Childhood in Poetry Collection in the Library of the Florida State University, 5 Vols. Ed. by John M. Shaw. LC 67-28092. (Illus.). 1967. 280.00x o.p. (ISBN 0-8103-0475-9). Gale.
Childhood in Poetry: First Supplement, 3 Vols. Ed. by John M. Shaw. LC 67-28092. (Illus.). 1734p. 1972. Set. 210.00x o.p. (ISBN 0-8103-0476-7). Gale.
Childhood in Poetry: Second Supplement--a Catalogue with Biographical & Critical Annotations, of the Books of English & American Poets Comprising the Shaw Childhood in Poetry Collection in the Library of the Fla. St. U, 2 vols. Ed. by John M. Shaw. LC 67-28092. 1500p. 1976. Set. 180.00x o.p. (ISBN 0-8103-0477-5); Vol. 1. 42.50 o.p.; Vol. 2. index 98.00 o.p. (ISBN 0-8103-0479-1). Gale.
Childhood Is a Time of Innocence. Joan W. Anglund. LC 64-20974. (Illus.). (gr. 3-6). 1964. 2.95 o.p. (ISBN 0-15-216950-4, HJ). HarBraceJ.
Childhood of the Magician. Nancy Willard. (New Writer's Ser). 1973. 5.95 o.p. (ISBN 0-87140-571-7). Liveright.
Childhood Revisited. J. I. Milgram & D. J. Sciarra. 1974. pap. write for info. o.p. (ISBN 0-02-381120-X). Macmillan.
Childkeeper. Sol Stein. LC 75-15823. 211p. 1975. 7.95 o.p. (ISBN 0-15-117233-1). HarBraceJ.
Childless by Choice: Choosing Childlessness in the Eighties. Marion Faux. LC 83-2038. 216p. 1984. 13.95 o.p. (ISBN 0-385-15845-9, Anchor Pr). Doubleday.
Children & Divorce: An Annotated Bibliography & Guide. Evelyn B. Hausslein. LC 81-48420. 140p. 1983. lib. bdg. 20.00 o.p. (ISBN 0-8240-9391-7). Garland Pub.
Children & Gardens. Gertrude Jekyll. (Illus.). 192p. 1982. 29.50 o.s.i. (ISBN 0-907462-27-8). Antique Collect.
Children & Sex: The Parents Speak. Study Group of New York Staff. 382p. 1983. 16.95x o.p. (ISBN 0-87196-603-4). Facts on File.
Children & Sport in the U. S. S. R. M. Kondratyeva & V. Taborko. 172p. 1979. 8.45 o.p. (ISBN 0-8285-1789-4, Pub. by Progress Pubs USSR). Imported Pubns.
Children & the Federal Budget. Children's Defense Fund Staff. 40p. (Orig.). 1981. pap. 2.50 o.p. (ISBN 0-938008-14-5). Children's Defense.
Children & Their Art: Methods for the Elementary School. 2nd ed. Charles D. Gaitskell & Al Hurwitz. 1970. text ed. 16.95 o.p. (ISBN 0-15-507297-8, HC). HarBraceJ.
Children & Their Fathers. Ed. by Hanns Reich. (Illus.). 72p. (ps up). 1960. 4.95 o.p. (ISBN 0-8090-1505-6, Terra Magica). Hill & Wang.
Children & Youth in America: A Documentary History, Vols. 1 & 2. Ed. by Robert H. Bremner et al. LC 74-115473. 1971. Vol. 1. 1600-1865 55.00x o.p. (ISBN 0-674-11610-0); Vol. 2, 2 Bks. 1866-1932 80.00x o.p. (ISBN 0-674-11612-7). Harvard U Pr.
Children Around the World. Jane A. Caballero & Derek Whordley. LC 82-81892. 176p. (Orig.). (ps-4). 1983. pap. 16.95 o.p. (ISBN 0-89334-033-2). Humanics Ltd.
Children As Teachers: Theory & Research on Tutoring. Ed. by Vernon L. Allen. (Educational Psychology Ser.). 1976. 29.95 o.p. (ISBN 0-12-052640-9). Acad Pr.
Children at Risk. Date not set. (ISBN 0-8052-0655-8); (ISBN 0-8052-3675-9). Random.
Children at Risk: The Growing Threat of Bizarre Toys, Fantasy Games, TV, Movies & Illegal Drugs. David Porter. LC 86-72064. 160p. (Orig.). 1987. pap. 7.95 o.p. (ISBN 0-89107-420-1, Crossway Bks). Good News.
Children at Work, Eighteen Thirty to Eighteen Eighty-Five. Elizabeth Longmate & Marjorie Reeves. (Then & There Ser.). (Illus.). 96p. (Orig.). (YA) (gr. 7-12). 1981. pap. text ed. 4.75 o.p. (ISBN 0-582-22294-X). Longman.
Children Discover Music & Dance. Emma D. Sheehy. LC 68-24571. 1968. pap. text ed. 8.95x o.p. (ISBN 0-8077-2150-6). Tchrs Coll.
Children in Adult Jails. Children's Defense Fund Staff. LC 76-55873. 77p. (Orig.). 1978. pap. 4.40 o.s.i. (ISBN 0-938008-24-2). Children's Defense.
Children in an Information Age: Tomorrow's Problems Today: Selected Papers from the International Conference, Varna, Bulgaria, 6-9 May 1985. Ed. by B. Sendov & I. Stanchev. LC 85-28528. 216p. 1986. 55.00 o.p. (ISBN 0-08-033890-9, M110, L110, D135, Pub. by PPL). Pergamon.
Children in & Out of Care. Claire Wendelken. Ed. by Martin Davies. (Community Care Practice Handbook Ser.). viii, 119p. (Orig.). 1983. pap. text ed. 6.50x o.p. (ISBN 0-435-82926-2). Gower Pub Co.
Children in Clinics: A Sociological Analysis of Medical Work with Children. Alan Davis. 300p. 1982. 27.00x o.p. (ISBN 0-422-77370-0, NO. 3715, Pub. by Tavistock). Routledge Chapman & Hall.
Children in English-Canadian Society 1880-1920: Framing the 20th-Century Consensus. Neil Sutherland. LC 76-44228. (Illus.). 1976. 30.00x o.p.; pap. 10.95 o.p. (ISBN 0-8020-6345-4). U of Toronto Pr.
Children in Health Care: Ethical Perspectives. 100p. 12.00 o.p. (ISBN 0-318-17752-8); members 8.00 o.p. (ISBN 0-318-17753-6). Assn Care Child.
Children in Jail. Thomas J. Cottle. LC 75-77440. 1977. 12.50x o.p. (ISBN 0-8070-0492-8); pap. 5.95x o.p. (ISBN 0-8070-0493-6, BP589). Beacon Pr.
Children in Search of Meaning. Violet Madge. (Orig.). 1966. pap. 3.25 o.p. (ISBN 0-8192-1051-X). Morehouse Pub.
Children in Sport. 2nd ed. Ed. by Richard A. Magill et al. LC 82-82668. 327p. 1982. pap. text ed. 11.95x o.p. (ISBN 0-931250-34-X, BMAG0034). Human Kinetics.
Children in the Crossfire: The Tragedy of Parental Kidnapping. Sally Abrahms. LC 82-73030. 320p. 1983. 14.95 o.s.i. (ISBN 0-689-11339-0, Atheneum). Macmillan.
Children in the Crossfire: The Tragedy of Parental Kidnapping. Sally Abrahms. LC 82-73030. 288p. 1984. pap. 7.95 o.p. (ISBN 0-689-70675-8, 315, Atheneum). Macmillan.
Children in the Wind. Bernice Grohskopf. LC 77-4758. (gr. 6-8). 1977. 8.95 o.p. (ISBN 0-689-30583-4, Atheneum). Macmillan.
Children in Turmoil: Tomorrow's Parents. Ed. by L. Hersov. 256p. 1982. pap. 30.00 o.p. (ISBN 0-08-027955-4). Pergamon.
Children in Your Life: A Guide to Child Care & Parenting. Deanna J. Radeloff & Roberta Zechman. LC 80-67826. (Home Economics Ser.). 346p. 1981. pap. 19.95 o.p. (ISBN 0-8273-1748-4); instr's. guide 6.00 o.p. (ISBN 0-8273-1749-2). Delmar.
Children into Pupils: A Study of Language in Early Schooling. Mary J. Willes. (Language, Education, & Society Ser.). 180p. (Orig.). 1983. pap. 10.95x o.p. (ISBN 0-7100-9550-3). Routledge Chapman & Hall.
Children Learn Physical Skills, 1 vol. Liselott Diem. 1978. pap. 8.35x ea. o.p.; Vol. 1. Birth to 3 Years o.p. (ISBN 0-88314-040-3); Vol. 2 o.p. Ages 3-5 8.35x o.p. (ISBN 0-88314-039-X). AAHPERD.
Children Learning. Date not set. (ISBN 0-8052-3745-3). Random.
Children of Aataentsic: A History of the Huron People to 1660, 2 vols. Bruce G. Trigger. (Illus.). 1976. 60.00x set o.p. (ISBN 0-7735-0239-4, McGill Canada). U of Toronto Pr.
Children of Darkness. Ruth Gordon. 400p. 1988. pap. 4.95 o.p. (07-0363-4). Tyndale.
Children of Destiny. Jean M. Burroughs. (Illus.). 1975. pap. 4.95 o.p. (ISBN 0-913270-75-X). Sunstone Pr.
Children of Green Knowe. Lucy M. Boston. LC 55-7608. (Illus.). (gr. 4-6). 1955. 6.95 o.s.i. (ISBN 0-15-217147-9, HJ). HarBraceJ.
Children of Green Knowe. Lucy M. Boston. LC 77-4506. (Illus.). (gr. 4-7). 1977. pap. 3.95 o.p. (ISBN 0-15-616870-7, VoyB). HarBraceJ.
Children of Green Knowe see Adventures at Green Knowe.
Children of Jonestown. Ed. by Kenneth Wooden. (Paperbacks Ser.). 1980. pap. text ed. 5.95 o.p. (ISBN 0-07-071641-2). McGraw.
Children of Naples. Geoffrey Hanks. 1974. pap. text ed. 1.60 o.s.i. (ISBN 0-08-017619-4). Pergamon.
Children of Noah. Ben L. Burman. (gr. 9-12). 5.00 o.s.i. (ISBN 0-685-02658-2). Taplinger.
Children of Privilege: Student Revolt in the Sixties. Cyril Levitt. 288p. 1984. 40.00x o.p. (ISBN 0-8020-5636-9); pap. 15.95 o.p. (ISBN 0-8020-6537-6). U of Toronto Pr.
Children of Promise: The Case for Baptizing Infants. Geoffrey W. Bromiley. LC 79-10346. 1979. pap. 4.95 o.p. (ISBN 0-8028-1797-1). Eerdmans.
Children of Separation & Divorce. Irving Stuart & Lawrence Abt. 352p. 1981. 29.95 o.p. (ISBN 0-442-24431-2). Van Nos Reinhold.
Children of Tender Years. Ted Allbuery. 222p. 1987. pap. 3.50 o.p. (ISBN 1-55547-148-X). Critics Choice Paper.
Children of the Asylum: The Adolescent Perspective on Residential Psychiatric Treatment. 160p. 1979. write for info. o.p. (M-6264). French & Eur.
Children of the Chapel: A Tale. Mary Gordon & Algernon C. Swinburne. Intro. by Robert E. Lougy. LC 82-6436. 1185p. 1982. lib. bdg. 18.95x o.p. (ISBN 0-8214-0631-0). Ohio U Pr.
Children of the Dawn. John M. Alford. 1978. 5.50 o.p. (ISBN 0-682-49003-2). Exposition-Phoenix.
Children of the Devil. William T. Bruner. LC 65-21756. 1966. (ISBN 0-8022-0188-1). Philos Lib.
Children of the Dragon. Frank S. Robinson. 1978. pap. 1.95 o.p. (ISBN 0-380-01819-5, 35774-7). Avon.
Children of the Dream. Bruno Bettelheim. (YA) (gr. 7 up). 1970. pap. 2.25 o.p. (ISBN 0-380-01097-6, 49130-3, Discus). Avon.
Children of the Forest. Elsa Beskow. (Illus.). 1984. bds. 11.95 laminated o.p. (ISBN 0-510-00128-9). Salem Hse Pubs.
Children of the Fox. Jill Paton Walsh. LC 78-8138. (Illus.). 128p. (gr. 3 up). 1978. 9.95 o.p. (ISBN 0-374-31242-7). FS&G.
Children of the Great Depression: Social Change in the Life Experience. Glen H. Elder. LC 73-87301. (Midway Reprint Ser.). xxiv, 400p. 1974. lib. bdg. 10.00 o.s.i. (ISBN 0-226-20262-3). U of Chicago Pr.
Children of the Lion. Peter Danielson. (Children of the Lion Ser.: Bk. 1). 1985. lib. bdg. 12.95 o.p. (ISBN 0-8398-2869-1, Gregg). G K Hall.
Children of the New Testament. (Arch Books Anthology Ser.). (Illus.). 160p. (gr. k-4). 1986. 7.95 o.p. (ISBN 0-570-06206-3, 59-7000). Concordia.
Children of the Night. Michael Kring. (Space Mavericks Ser.: No. 2). 192p. (Orig.). 1981. pap. 1.95 o.p. (ISBN 0-8439-1016-X, Pub. by Leisure Bks CT). Dorchester Pub Co.
Children of the North Pole. Ralph Herrmanns. Tr. by Annabelle MacMillan. LC 64-9895. (Illus.). (gr. 2-5). 1964. 5.50 o.p. (ISBN 0-15-217300-5, HJ). HarBraceJ.
Children of the Old Testament. (Arch Books Anthology Ser.). (Illus.). 152p. (gr. k-4). 1986. 7.95 o.p. (ISBN 0-570-06207-1, 59-7001). Concordia.
Children of the Poor. Jacob A. Riis. 1972. Repr. of 1892 ed. 18.95 o.p. (ISBN 0-8422-8171-1). Irvington.
Children of the Poor. Jacob A. Riis. LC 4-3826. 1971. Repr. of 1892 ed. 29.00 o.p. (ISBN 0-384-50850-2). Johnson Repr.
Children of the Ruins. Thomas Wiseman. 1986. 17.95 o.p. (ISBN 0-316-94857-8). Little.
Children of the Storm: Black Children & American Child Welfare. Andrew Billingsley & Jeanne M. Giovannoni. 263p. 1972. pap. text ed. 11.00 net o.p. (ISBN 0-15-507271-4, HC). HarBraceJ.
Children of the Sun. Jan Carew. (Illus.). 40p. (gr. k up). 1980. 9.95 o.p. (ISBN 0-316-12848-1). Little.
Children of the Sun. Oakley Hall. LC 82-73039. 320p. 1983. 17.95 o.p. (ISBN 0-689-11348-X, Atheneum). Macmillan.
Children of Vietnam. Betty J. Lifton & Thomas C. Fox. LC 72-75274. (Illus.). (gr. 5 up). 1972. 5.95 o.p. (ISBN 0-689-30056-5, Atheneum). Macmillan.
Children on Troublemaker Street. Astrid Lindgren. Tr. by Gerry Bothmer. LC 64-11768. (Illus.). 102p. (gr. 2-4). 1970. 8.95 o.s.i. (ISBN 0-02-759100-X). Macmillan.
Children, Our Greatest Treasure. Inez Elmore. LC 85-91047. 96p. 1986. 10.00 o.p. (ISBN 0-682-40280-X). Exposition-Phoenix.
Children Out of School in America. Children's Defense Fund Staff. LC 74-20229. 366p. (Orig.). 1974. pap. 5.50 o.p. (ISBN 0-938008-25-0). Children's Defense.
Children: To Have or Have Not: A Guide to Making & Living with Your Decision. Diane Elvenstar. 240p. 1982. 13.95 o.p. (ISBN 0-936602-39-2); pap. 9.95 o.p. (ISBN 0-936602-40-6). Kampmann.
Children We See: An Observational Approach to Child Study. Betty Rowen. LC 72-9916. 1973. text ed. 18.95 o.p. (ISBN 0-03-088101-3, HoltC). HR&W.
Children with Asthma: A Manual for Parents. rev. ed. Thomas F. Plaut. LC 83-19444. (Illus.). 156p. 1984. pap. 9.95 o.p. (ISBN 0-914625-02-0). Pedipress.
Children with Exceptional Needs. M. Stephen Lilly. LC 78-26579. 1979. text ed. 29.95 o.p. (ISBN 0-03-021911-6, HoltC). HR&W.
Children with Learning Disabilities. 2nd ed. Janet W. Lerner. LC 75-26085. (Illus.). 448p. 1976. text ed. 19.25 o.p. (ISBN 0-395-20474-7). HM.
Children with Learning Problems: A Handbook for Teachers. Larry A. Faas. LC 79-89741. (Illus.). 1980. text ed. 31.50 o.p. (ISBN 0-395-28352-3). HM.
Children with Special Needs in the Classroom. Lauren Bradway. 1987. 6.95 o.p. (ISBN 0-917634-30-6). Creative Infomatics.
Children Without Health Care. Children's Defense Fund Staff. 32p. (Orig.). 1981. pap. 2.20 o.p. (ISBN 0-938008-26-9). Children's Defense.
Children Without Homes: An Examination of Public Responsibility to Children in Out-of-Home Care. Children's Defense Fund Staff. LC 78-74230. 282p. (Orig.). 1978. pap. 5.50 o.p. (ISBN 0-938008-21-8). Children's Defense.
Children's Authors & Illustrators: A Guide to the Manuscript Collections in United States Research Libraries. Ed. by James R. Fraser & Renee K. Weber. 199p. 1980. lib. bdg. 10.00 o.p. (ISBN 3-598-40504-9). K G Saur.
Children's Bible. Retold by James Bentley. (Illus.). 237p. (gr. k up). 1983. 7.95 o.p. (ISBN 0-531-03592-1). Watts.
Children's Book Illustration Annual 1987: Bologna International Children's Book Fair. (Illus.). 296p. 1987. pap. 24.95 o.p. (ISBN 0-88708-047-2). Picture Bk Studio.
Children's Book of Comic Verse. Compiled by Christopher Logue. (Illus.). 160p. (gr. 3-7). 1980. 18.95 o.p. (ISBN 0-7134-1528-2, Pub. by Batsford England). David & Charles.
Children's Book Review Index Cumulation 1985. Ed. by Barbara Beach & Gary C. Tarbert. 445p. 1986. 85.00x o.p. (ISBN 0-8103-0645-X). Gale.
Children's Books & Reading. Montrose J. Moses. LC 74-23680. 280p. 1975. Repr. of 1907 ed. 37.00x o.p. (ISBN 0-8103-3767-3). Gale.
Children's Books in Print, 1987-88. Ed. by Bowker, R. R., Staff. 1105p. 1987. 75.00 o.p. (ISBN 0-8352-2360-4). Bowker.
Children's Books of Yesterday. Philip James. Ed. by C. Geoffrey Holme. LC 79-174059. (Illus.). 128p. 1976. Repr. of 1933 ed. 46.00x o.p. (ISBN 0-8103-4135-2). Gale.
Children's Books of Yesterday. National Book League Staff. Ed. by Percy H. Muir. LC 76-89280. 224p. 1970. Repr. of 1946 ed. 35.00x o.p. (ISBN 0-8103-3550-6). Gale.
Children's Books, 1983. annual New York Public Library, Office of Children's Services Staff. 1983. pap. 1.50 o.p. (ISBN 0-87104-664-4, Branch Lib). NY Pub Lib.
Children's Books, 1985. Annual Office of Children's Service Staff. 1985. pap. 1.50 o.p. (ISBN 0-87104-676-8, Branch Lib). NY Pub Lib.
Children's Books, 1986. Annual Office of Children's Services Staff. 1986. pap. 1.50 o.p. (ISBN 0-87104-695-4, Branch Libraries). NY Pub Lib.
Children's Books, 1987. Annual Office of Children's Service Staff. 1987. pap. 2.00 o.p. (ISBN 0-87104-692-X, Branch Libraries). NY Pub Lib.
Children's Britannica, 20 vols. (Illus.). 1988. 299.00 set o.p. (ISBN 0-85229-206-6). Ency Brit Ed.
Children's Categorization of Speech Sounds in English. Charles Read. LC 75-26122. (Research Report Ser.: No. 17). 189p. 1975. pap. 6.75 o.p. (ISBN 0-8141-0630-7); pap. 5.00 members o.p. NCTE.
Children's Clothes. Conran Octopus. 1986. pap. 9.95 o.p. (ISBN 0-345-33607-0, Pub. by Ballantine Trade). Ballantine.
Children's Costume in England. P. Cunnington. 1972. text ed. 19.95x o.p. (ISBN 0-7136-0371-2). Humanities.
Children's Crusade. Brenda Thompson & Cynthia Overbeck. LC 76-22469. (Lerner First Fact Bks.). (Illus.). (gr. k-3). 1977. PLB 4.95 o.p. (ISBN 0-8225-1353-6). Lerner Pubns.
Children's Defense Budget FY 1988: An Analysis of Our Nation's Investment in Children. Children's Defense Fund Staff. (Children's Defense Budget Ser.: No. 7). 336p. (Orig.). 1987. pap. 12.95 o.s.i. (ISBN 0-938008-58-7). Children's Defense.
Children's Drawings As Measures of Intellectual Maturity. Dale B. Harris. 367p. 1963. text ed. 24.00 o.p. (ISBN 0-15-507300-1, HC). HarBraceJ.
Children's Experience of Place: A Developmental Study. Roger Hart. (Illus.). 518p. 1979. text ed. 59.50x o.p. (ISBN 0-8290-0865-9). Irvington.

Children's Experience of Place: A Developmental Study. Roger Hart. (Illus.). 518p. 1982. pap. text ed. 29.95x o.p. (ISBN 0-8290-1039-4). Irvington.

Children's Guide to London. Date not set. Salem Hse Pubs.

Children's Guide to...Paris. Irma Kurtz & Clive Unger-Hamilton. LC 85-22994. (Illus.). 96p. (gr. 3 up). 1986. 6.95 o.s.i. (ISBN 0-87226-053-4, Bedrick Blackie). P Bedrick Bks.

Children's History of India. 7th rev. ed. Sheila Dhar. (Illus.). 178p. (gr. 5-7). pap. text ed. 1.50x o.s.i. (ISBN 0-88253-919-1). Ind-US Inc.

Children's Homes. David Berridge. 176p. 1985. 39.95x o.p. (ISBN 0-631-14136-7); pap. 14.95x o.p. (ISBN 0-631-14137-5). Basil Blackwell.

Children's Hospital of Boston: "Built Better Than They Knew" Clement Smith. 284p. 1983. pap. text ed. 21.50 o.p. Little.

Children's Humour. Ed. by Paul E. McGhee & Antony J. Chapman. LC 79-40648. 322p. 1980. 91.95x o.p. (ISBN 0-471-27638-3, Pub. by Wiley-Interscience). Wiley.

Children's Language & Learning. Judith W. Lindfors. (Illus.). 1980. text ed. (ISBN 0-13-131953-1). P-H.

Children's Learning & Attention Problems. Marcel Kinsbourne & Paula Caplan. 1979. 35.00 o.p. (ISBN 0-316-49395-3). Little.

Children's Literature, 6 vols. Ed. by Francelia Butler et al. Bennett Brockman & William E. Sheidley. Incl. Vol. 1. 1972. (ISBN 0-87722-082-4); pap. (ISBN 0-87722-081-6); Vol. 2. 1973. (ISBN 0-87722-080-8); pap. (ISBN 0-87722-079-4); Vol. 3. 1974. (ISBN 0-87722-078-6); pap. (ISBN 0-87722-077-8); Vol. 4. 1975. (ISBN 0-87722-042-5); pap. (ISBN 0-87722-076-X); Vol. 5. 1976. (ISBN 0-87722-069-7); pap. (ISBN 0-87722-070-0); Vol. 6. 1978. (ISBN 0-87722-104-9); pap. (ISBN 0-87722-105-7). LC 75-21550. 17.95 ea. o.p.; pap. 10.95 ea. o.p. Temple U Pr.

Children's Literature Awards & Winners: A Directory of Prizes, Authors, & Illustrators. 1st ed. Ed. by Dolores B. Jones. 1983. 504p. 92.00x, o.p. (ISBN 0-8103-0171-7, Co-pub. by Neal-Schuman); supplement, 136p. 58.00 o.p. (ISBN 0-8103-0173-3). Gale.

Children's Literature in the Elementary School. 3rd rev. ed. Charlotte S. Huck. LC 78-21081. 1979. text ed. 29.95 o.p. (ISBN 0-03-046086-7, HoltC). HR&W.

Children's Mahabharata. Shanto R. Rao. (Illus.). 350p. (gr. 5-7). 1980. pap. text ed. 7.50x o.p. (ISBN 0-86131-266-X, Pub. by Orient Longman Ltd India). Apt Bks.

Children's Massage Workshop, for Kids 10-90. S. Jacob. pap. write for info. o.s.i. Meghan-Kiffer.

Children's Mathematics Calendar: 1989. (Illus.). 28p. (gr. k-8). 1988. pap. 6.95 o.p. (ISBN 0-933174-51-9). Wide World Tetra.

Children's Media Market Place. 2nd ed. Ed. by Carol A. Emmens. LC 82-82058. 353p. 1982. pap. 29.95 o.p. (ISBN 0-918212-33-2). Neal-Schuman.

Children's Museum Activity Book: Ball-Point Pens. Bernie Zubrowski. LC 78-31622. (Children's Museum Bks.). (Illus.). (gr. 5-7). 1979. 6.95g o.p. (ISBN 0-316-98882-0); pap. 6.95 o.p. (ISBN 0-316-98883-9). Little.

Children's Names & Horoscopes. 152p. 1982. 25.00x o.p. (ISBN 0-85223-181-4, Pub. by Ebury Pr England). State Mutual Bk.

Children's Parties. Angela Hollest & Penelope Gaine. (Illus.). 127p. (Orig.). 1985. pap. 5.95 o.p. (ISBN 0-86188-407-8). Haynes Pubns.

Children's Picture Books in German: A Checklist of Titles 1945 -1975. Ed. by Willi Weisman et al. xvi, 488p. 1980. lib. bdg. 100.00 o.p. (ISBN 3-598-10078-7). K G Saur.

Children's Prize Books: An Int'l Listing of 193 Children's Literature Prizes. 2nd rev ed. Ed. by Jesse R. Moransee. (Illus.). xxii, 620p. 1983. 32.00 o.p. (ISBN 3-598-03250-1). K G Saur.

Children's Rights: A Philosophical Study. Colin A. Wringe. (International Library of the Philosophy of Education). 192p. 1981. 27.50x o.p. (ISBN 0-7100-0852-X). Routledge Chapman & Hall.

Children's Rights: A Philosophical Study. Colin A. Wringe. 180p. 1985. pap. 8.95x o.p. (ISBN 0-7102-0534-1). Routledge Chapman & Hall.

Children's Rooms & Play Yards. 3rd ed. Sunset Magazine & Books Editors. LC 79-90336. (Illus.). 96p. 1980. pap. 6.95 o.p. (ISBN 0-376-01055-X, Sunset Bks). Sunset-Lane.

Children's Services of Public Libraries. Ed. by Selma K. Richardson. LC 78-11503. (Allerton Park Institutes Ser.: No. 23). 178p. 1978. 9.00x o.p. (ISBN 0-87845-049-1). U of Ill Lib Info Sci.

Children's Sexual Thinking: A Comparative Study of Children Aged 5 to 15 in Australia, North America, Britain & Sweden. Ronald Goldman & Juliette Goldman. 368p. 1982. 26.95x o.p. (ISBN 0-7100-0883-X). Routledge Chapman & Hall.

Children's Spaces: A Bibliography of Recent Periodical Literature Dealing with Environments for the Child. Carole Cable. (Architecture Ser.: A 1413). 9p. 1985. 2.00 o.p. (ISBN 0-89028-443-1). Vance Biblios.

Children's Theatre: A Philosophy & a Method. Moses Goldberg. LC 73-12954. (P-H Series in Theatre & Drama). (Illus.). 256p. 1974. Reference ed. text ed. 31.00 o.p. (ISBN 0-13-132605-8). P-H.

Children's Travel Guide. James Robison & Darline Robinson. LC 81-68207. (Activities Bk.: Vol. I-Colo., Utah, N.M.). pap. 5.95 o.p. (ISBN 0-89051-079-2). Master Bks.

Children's Views of Themselves. Ira J. Gordon. LC 72-92021. 40p. 1972. pap. 4.00 o.p. (ISBN 0-87173-019-7). ACEI.

Children's Writings: A Bibliography of Works in English. Jane B. Wilson. LC 81-20802. 187p. 1982. lib. bdg. 24.95x o.p. (ISBN 0-89950-043-9). McFarland & Co.

Child's Book of Manners. Fay Maschler & Helen Oxenbury. LC 78-70866. (Illus.). (gr. k-4). 1979. 9.95 o.p. (ISBN 0-689-30701-2, Atheneum). Macmillan.

Child's Book of Old Nursery Rhymes. Joan W. Anglund. LC 73-75429. (Illus.). 32p. (ps up). 1973. 3.95g o.p. (ISBN 0-689-30413-7, Atheneum). Macmillan.

Child's Comfort: Baby & Doll Quilts in American Folk Art. Bruce Johnson. LC 76-24707. (Illus.). 1977. 12.95 o.p. (ISBN 0-15-117184-X). HarBraceJ.

Child's Comfort: Baby & Doll Quilts in American Folk Art. Bruce Johnson. LC 76-24707. (Illus.). 1977. pap. 6.95 o.p. (ISBN 0-15-117185-8, Harv). HarBraceJ.

Child's Concept of Story: Ages Two to Seventeen. Arthur N. Applebee. LC 77-8309. (Illus.). 1980. lib. bdg. 18.00x o.s.i. (ISBN 0-226-02117-3); pap. text ed. 7.00x o.s.i. (ISBN 0-226-02118-1). U of Chicago Pr.

Child's Conception of Number. Jean Piaget. 1965. pap. 5.95 o.p. (ISBN 0-393-00324-8, Norton Lib). Norton.

Child's Dictionary of Jewish Symbols. Alex J. Goldman. (Illus.). (gr. 1-4). 5.00 o.s.i. (ISBN 0-685-09470-7). Feldheim.

Child's Garden of Verses. Robert Louis Stevenson. LC 85-12766. (Illus.). 86p. (ps-3). 1957. 4.95 o.p. (ISBN 0-448-40510-5, G&D); PLB 3.59 o.p. (ISBN 0-448-13052-1, G&D). Putnam Pub Group.

Child's Garden of Verses. Robert Louis Stevenson. LC 77-92195. (Illus.). 1978. ltd. ed printed on arches laid text paper 90.00x o.p. (ISBN 0-915918-04-8). Pr Tuscany.

Child's Garden of Verses to Color. Robert Louis Stevenson. (Color-&-Keep Bks.). (Illus.). 64p. (ps-3). 1985. pap. 2.95 o.s.i. (ISBN 0-394-87275-4, BYR). Random.

Child's Gift of Lullabyes. (Illus.). 1987. book package & audio cassette incl. 12.95 o.s.i. (ISBN 0-88188-477-4). H Leonard Pub Corp.

Child's Journey: Forces That Shape the Lives of Our Young. Julius Segal & Herbert Yahraes. LC 77-17602. 1978. text ed. 25.95 o.p. (ISBN 0-07-056039-0). McGraw.

Child's Story of Past & Present Saints. Zerlina De Santis. (ps up). 1988. plastic bdg. 1.75 o.p. (ISBN 0-317-67469-2, CH0162); pap. 1.00 o.p. (ISBN 0-317-67470-6). Dghtrs St Paul.

Chile: An Attempt at "Historic Compromise" The Real Story of the Allende Years. Jorge Palacios. LC 79-55190. 1979. 12.95 o.s.i. (ISBN 0-916650-10-3); pap. 5.95 o.p. (ISBN 0-916650-11-1). Banner Pr.

Chile-California Mediterranean Scrub Atlas. Ed. by Norman J. Thrower & D. E. Bradbury. (U.S.-T.B.P. Synthesis Ser.: Vol. 2). 1977. 65.50 o.p. (ISBN 0-12-787550-6). Acad Pr.

Chile, CIA, Big Business. F. Sergeyev. 248p. 1981. 6.40 o.p. (ISBN 0-8285-2064-X, Pub. by Progress Pubs USSR). Imported Pubns.

Chile Corvalan Struggle. V. Shragin. 202p. 1980. pap. 4.95 o.p. (ISBN 0-8285-1877-7, Pub. by Progress Pubs USSR). Imported Pubns.

Chile: Legisla el Fascismo. 278p. (Span.). 1980. 8.45 o.p. (ISBN 0-8285-1913-7, Pub. by Progress Pubs USSR). Imported Pubns.

Chile: Politics & Society. Ed. by Arturo Valenzuela & J. Samuel Valenzuela. LC 73-92814. (Third World Ser., CH). 395p. 1976. (ISBN 0-87855-087-9); pap. 5.95x o.p. (ISBN 0-87855-579-X). Transaction Pubs.

Chilean Literature: A Working Bibliography of Secondary Sources. Ed. by David W. Foster. (Reference Publications). 1978. lib. bdg. 35.50 o.p. (ISBN 0-8161-8180-2, Hall Reference). G K Hall.

Chilton Auto Repair Manual 1989. Chilton.

Chilton Import Auto Repair Manual 1989. Chilton.

Chilton's Auto Repair Manual (CARM) 1980-87. Chilton Automotives Editorial Staff. LC 76-648878. 1416p. 1987. 22.95 o.s.i. (ISBN 0-8019-7670-7); slipcase 23.70 o.s.i. (ISBN 0-8019-7671-5). Chilton.

Chilton's Auto Repair Manual 1977-84. Chilton Automotives Editorial Staff. LC 76-648878. 1296p. 1983. 20.95 o.s.i. (ISBN 0-8019-7325-2). Chilton.

Chilton's Auto Repair Manual 1979-86. Chilton Automotives Editorial Staff. LC 80-68280. (Illus.). 1344p. 1985. shrink 21.95 o.s.i. (ISBN 0-8019-7575-1); hollow 22.75 o.s.i. (ISBN 0-8019-7574-3). Chilton.

Chilton's Auto Service Manual Nineteen Eighty-Four to Nineteen Eighty-Eight: Motor-Age Professional Mechanics Edition. Chilton Automotives Editorial Staff. 1856p. 1987. 54.00 o.p. (ISBN 0-8019-7778-9). Chilton.

Chilton's Complete Home Wiring & Lighting Guide. updated ed. L. D. Meyers. LC 80-971. 1980. 14.95 o.p.; pap. 9.95 o.p. (ISBN 0-8019-6791-0). Chilton.

Chilton's Easy Car Care. 2nd, rev. ed. Chilton. LC 78-7152. (Illus.). 544p. 1985. text ed. 14.95 o.p. (ISBN 0-8019-7554-9); pap. 17.95 o.p. (ISBN 0-8019-7553-0). Chilton.

Chilton's Easy Car Care. 2nd, updated ed. Chilton Automotives Editorial Staff. LC 78-7152. (Illus.). 1978. 11.95 o.p. (ISBN 0-8019-6784-8); pap. 8.95 o.p. (ISBN 0-8019-6729-5). Chilton.

Chilton's Ford-Mercury FWD 1981 - 1985. Chilton. 240p. 1985. pap. 13.50 o.p. (ISBN 0-8019-7544-1). Chilton.

Chilton's Ford Vans 1961 - 1986. Chilton Automotives Editorial Staff. LC 85-47964. 356p. (Orig.). 1986. pap. 13.95 o.p. (ISBN 0-8019-7663-4). Chilton.

Chilton's Guide to Brakes, Steering & Suspensions. (Illus.). 348p. 1986. pap. 17.95 o.p. (ISBN 0-8019-7644-8). Chilton.

Chilton's Guide To Electronic Engine Controls 1978-87. Chilton's Automotives Editorial Staff. 576p. 1987. pap. 17.95 o.p. (ISBN 0-8019-7768-1). Chilton.

Chilton's Guide to Major & Small Appliance Repair. LC 86-47609. 272p. 1986. 14.50 o.p. Chilton.

Chilton's Guide to Small Engine Repair: Up to Twenty Horse Power. Chilton Automotives Editorial Staff. LC 83-70013. 250p. 1983. pap. 13.50 o.p. (ISBN 0-8019-7379-1). Chilton.

Chilton's Guide to Small Engine Repair Up to 6HP: Includes Honda, Tanaka, John Deere. Chilton Automotives Editorial Staff. LC 83-45316. 288p. 1984. pap. 11.95 o.p. (ISBN 0-8019-7481-X). Chilton.

Chilton's Guide to Small Engine Repair 6-20HP: Includes Honda, John Deere. Chilton Automotives Editorial Staff. LC 83-45318. 288p. 1984. pap. 11.95 o.p. (ISBN 0-8019-7483-6). Chilton.

Chilton's Import Auto Repair Manual 1977-84. Chilton Automotives Editorial Staff. LC 78-20243. 1488p. 1983. 21.95 o.p. (ISBN 0-8019-7328-7). Chilton.

Chilton's Import Car Repair Manual 1979-86. Chilton Automotives Editorial Staff. LC 78-20243. (Illus.). 1464p. 1985. shrink 21.95 o.s.i. (ISBN 0-8019-7577-8); hollow 22.75 o.s.i. (ISBN 0-8019-7578-6). Chilton.

Chilton's Import Car Repair Manual: 1980-87. Chilton Automotives Editorial Staff. LC 80-68280. 1488p. 1987. 23.95 o.s.i. (ISBN 0-8019-7672-3); slipcase 23.70 o.s.i. (ISBN 0-8019-7673-1). Chilton.

Chilton's Import Car Repair Manual 1985. Chilton Automotives Editorial Staff. LC 78-20243. 1468p. 1984. 21.95 o.s.i. (ISBN 0-8019-7473-9); 21.75 o.s.i. (ISBN 0-8019-7474-7); pap. Chilton.

Chilton's Labor Guide & Parts Manual 1979-85. Chilton Automotives Editorial Staff. LC 83-45332. (Motor Age Professional Mechanics Edition Ser.). 1632p. 1985. text ed. 48.00 o.p. (ISBN 0-8019-7496-8). Chilton.

Chilton's Motor Professional Automotive Service Manual 1981. Chilton Automotives Editorial Staff. LC 54-17274. (Illus.). 1980. 36.00 o.p. (ISBN 0-8019-6976-X). Chilton.

Chilton's Repair & Tune-Up Guide: Chevrolet-GMC S-10, S-15 1982-83. Chilton Automotives Editorial Staff. LC 82-72932. 224p. 1983. pap. 13.95 o.s.i. (ISBN 0-8019-7310-4). Chilton.

Chilton's Repair & Tune-Up Guide: Corvette 1963-84. Chilton Automotives Editorial Staff. LC 83-45315. 288p. 1984. pap. 13.50 o.p. (ISBN 0-8019-7480-1). Chilton.

Chilton's Repair & Tune-up Guide: Ford Bronco 1966-83. Chilton Automotives Editorial Staff. LC 82-72919. 288p. 1983. pap. 13.50 o.p. (ISBN 0-8019-7337-6). Chilton.

Chilton's Repair & Tune-up Guide for Datsun Z & ZX 1970-1984. Chilton Automotives Editorial Staff. LC 83-45308. 224p. 1984. pap. 13.95 o.s.i. (ISBN 0-8019-7466-6). Chilton.

Chilton's Repair & Tune-up Guide for Mazda 1971-1984: RTUG. Chilton Automotives Editorial Staff. LC 83-45321. 226p. 1985. pap. 13.95 o.p. (ISBN 0-8019-7486-0). Chilton.

Chilton's Repair & Tune-up Guide for Opel, 1964-1970. Chilton Automotives Editorial Staff. LC 72-153140. (Illus.). 170p. 1971. pap. 11.95 o.p. (ISBN 0-8019-5792-3). Chilton.

Chilton's Repair & Tune-up Guide for VW Front Wheel Drive 1974-85. Chilton Automotives Editorial Staff. LC 84-45463. 240p. (Orig.). 1986. pap. 13.50 o.s.i. (ISBN 0-8019-7593-X). Chilton.

Chilton's Repair & Tune-up Guide: Toyota Truck 1970-83. Chilton Automotives Editorial Staff. LC 82-72918. 288p. 1983. pap. 13.95 o.p. (ISBN 0-8019-7336-8). Chilton.

Chilton's Repair & Tune-up Guide, Volkswagen Front Wheel Drive, 1974-83. 1985. pap. 12.50 o.p. (ISBN 0-8019-7339-2). Chilton.

Chilton's Small Engines: Repair & Tune-up Guide. 2nd ed. Chilton Automotives Editorial Staff. LC 78-21829. (Repair & Tune-up Guides Ser.). (Illus.). 1979. 11.95 o.p.; pap. 11.95 o.p. (ISBN 0-8019-6811-9). Chilton.

Chilton's Toyota Trucks 1970-86. Chilton Automotives Editorial Staff. LC 85-47962. 288p. (Orig.). 1986. pap. 13.95 o.p. (ISBN 0-8019-7661-8). Chilton.

Chilton's Toyota 1966 - 1970. Chilton Automotives Editorial Staff. LC 73-124092. (Illus.). 175p. 1970. 8.95 o.p. (ISBN 0-8019-5339-1); pap. 13.95 o.p. (ISBN 0-8019-5795-8). Chilton.

Chilton's Truck & Van Manual 1973-1980: Gasoline & Diesel Engines. Chilton Automotives Editorial Staff. (Illus.). 1980. 19.95 o.p. (ISBN 0-8019-6910-7). Chilton.

Chilton's Truck & Van Repair Manual 1977-84. Chilton Automotives Editorial Staff. LC 77-16756. 1464p. 1984. sw 21.95 o.s.i. (ISBN 0-8019-7357-0); hw 21.75 o.s.i. (7460). Chilton.

Chilton's Tune-up Emission Diagnosis & Service Manual, 1988: Motor Age Professional Mechanic's Edition. Chilton Staff. LC 88-43178. (Illus.). 1536p. 1989. text ed. 50.00 o.p. Chilton.

Chime Child: Or, Somerset Singers - Being an Account of Some of Their Songs Collected over Sixty Years. Ruth L. Tongue. LC 68-77292. x, 112p. Repr. of 1968 ed. 35.00x o.s.i. (ISBN 0-8103-5022-X). Gale.

Chime of Words: The Letters of Logan Pearsall Smith. Logan P. Smith. Ed. by Edwin Tribble. LC 83-18010. 240p. 1984. 22.00 o.p. (ISBN 0-89919-232-7). Ticknor & Fields.

Chimeres. Gerard de Nerval. 74p. 1948. 5000.00 o.p. (ISBN 0-686-54812-4). French & Eur.

Chimpanzee: A Series of Volumes on the Chimpanzee, 6 vols. Ed. by G. H. Bourne. Incl. Vol. 1. Anatomy, Behavior, & Diseases of Chimpanzees. 1969. 92.00 (ISBN 3-8055-0721-6); Vol. 2. Physiology, Behavior, Serology, & Diseases of Chimpanzees. 1970. 92.00 (ISBN 3-8055-0722-4); Vol. 3. Immunology, Infections, Hormones, Anatomy, & Behavior. 1970. 92.00 (ISBN 3-8055-0723-2); Vol. 4. Behavior, Growth, & Pathology of Chimpanzees. 1971. 88.00 (ISBN 3-8055-1147-7); Vol. 5. Histology, Reproduction, & Restraint. 1972. 66.75 (ISBN 3-8055-1250-3); Vol. 6. Anatomy & Pathology with General Subject Index & Condensed Bibliographic Index. 1973. 80.75 (ISBN 3-8055-1403-4). (Illus.). Set. 457.50 o.p. (ISBN 3-8055-1631-2). S Karger.

Chin Music. James McManus. LC 86-45514. 208p. 1987. pap. 6.95 o.s.i. (ISBN 0-394-62190-5). Grove.

Chin-Na: The Grappling Art of Self Defense, Vol. II. Willy Lin. Ed. by Todd Henschell. (Series 432). 180p. (Orig.). 1984. pap. 7.50 o.p. (ISBN 0-89750-095-4). Ohara Pubns.

China. (Hildebrand Travel Guides Ser.). 1985. pap. 11.95 o.p. (ISBN 0-87052-036-9). Hippocrene Bks.

China. Jesuit Missionaries Staff. (Illus.). 216p. 150.00 o.p. (ISBN 0-8478-5402-7). Rizzoli Intl.

China. Charles McNulty. (Orig.). (gr. 9-12). 1975. pap. text ed. 8.00 o.p. (ISBN 0-87720-615-5). AMSCO Sch.

China. Harry Schwartz. LC 65-27493. (New York Times Byline Books). 1965. pap. 2.45 o.p. (ISBN 0-689-10244-5, Atheneum). Macmillan.

China. Time-Life Books Editors. (Library of Nations). (Illus.). 160p. (YA) (gr. 7 up). 1984. lib. bdg. 23.95 o.p. Time-Life.

China. Pamela Youdes. (Illus.). 1982. 19.95 o.p. (ISBN 0-393-01653-6). Norton.

China: A Country Study. 3rd ed. Ed. by Frederica M. Bunge & Rinn-Sup Shinn. LC 81-12878. (Area Handbook Ser.: No. 550-60). (Illus.). 622p. 1981. 12.00 o.p. (ISBN 0-318-21934-4, 008-020-00888-5). USGPO.

China: A General Survey. 3rd, rev. ed. Qi Wen. (Illus.). 216p. (Orig.). 1984. pap. 6.95 o.p. (ISBN 0-8351-1353-1). China Bks.

China: A Geographical Survey. Thomas R. Tregear. 372p. 1980. 45.95x o.p. (ISBN 0-470-26925-1); pap. text ed. 39.95x o.p. (ISBN 0-470-26926-X). Halsted Pr.

China: A Statistics Survey in 1985. State Statistical Bureau Staff. 133p. 1985. 24.95x o.p. (ISBN 0-8351-1527-5). China Bks.

China-A Travel Survival Kit. Michael Buckley & Alan Samagalski. (Illus.). 820p. (Orig.). 1986. pap. 14.95 o.p. (ISBN 0-908086-58-X). Lonely Planet.

China ABC. (Illus.). 238p. 1985. pap. 6.95 o.p. (ISBN 0-8351-1393-0). China Bks.

China Adventures. Frederick Fisher. (China Spotlight Ser.). (Illus., Orig.). 1986. pap. 7.95 o.p. (ISBN 0-8351-1661-1). China Bks.

China: An Introduction. Qi Wen. Tr. by Zhou Yicheng from Chinese. (Illus.). 154p. (Orig.). 1984. pap. 4.95 o.p. (ISBN 0-8351-1360-4). China Bks.

China & America: A Bibliography of Interactions, Foreign & Domestic. James M. McCutcheon. LC 74-190449. (East-West Bibliographic Ser.: No. 1). 75p. (Orig.). 1973. pap. text ed. 10.00x o.p. (ISBN 0-8248-0230-6). UH Pr.

China & America: The Story of Their Relations Since 1784. Foster R. Dulles. LC 81-16. vii, 277p. 1981. Repr. of 1946 ed. lib. bdg. 35.00x o.p. (ISBN 0-313-22146-4, DUCA). Greenwood.

China & Inner Asia: From 1368 to the Present Day. Morris Rossabi. LC 74-33174. (Chinese History & Society Ser). (Illus.). 320p. 1975. 20.00x o.p. (ISBN 0-87663-716-0, Pica Pr). Universe.

China & Southeast Asia-The Politics of Survival: A Study of Foreign Policy Interaction. Melvin Gurtov. LC 74-24792. 256p. 1975. pap. 8.95x o.p. (ISBN 0-8018-1683-1). Johns Hopkins.

China & the Search for Happiness: Recurring Themes in Four Thousand Years of Chinese Cultural History. Wolfgang Bauer. Tr. by Michael Shaw from Ger. LC 76-10679. 1976. 22.50 o.p. (ISBN 0-8264-0078-7). Continuum.

China & the West. Wolfgang Franke. Tr. by R. A. Wilson. LC 67-27177. viii, 166p. 1968. 14.95x o.p. (ISBN 0-87249-108-0). U of SC Pr.

China at the Conference: A Report. Westal W. Willoughby. LC 76-144850. 419p. 1972. Repr. of 1922 ed. lib. bdg. 25.00x o.p. (ISBN 0-8371-5978-4, WICH). Greenwood.

China by Rail. William D. Middleton. Ed. by Bill Bradley. (Trans Anglo Bks.). (Illus.). 116p. 1986. pap. 19.95 o.p. (ISBN 0-87046-074-9). Interurban.

China Card. John D. Ehrlichman. LC 85-31791. 523p. 1986. 18.45 o.p. (ISBN 0-671-50716-8). S&S.

China Card. Donald Freed. LC 80-66506. 1980. 12.95 o.p. (ISBN 0-87795-281-7, Arbor Hse). Morrow.

China Clippers. Basil Lubbock. (Century Classic Ser.). 295p. 1988. pap. 11.95 o.s.i. (ISBN 0-7126-0341-7, Pub. by Century Hutchinson). David & Charles.

China Collecting in America. Alice M. Earle. LC 77-99044. 446p. 1970. Repr. of 1892 ed. 40.00x o.p. (ISBN 0-8103-3579-4). Gale.

China Correspondent. Agnes Smedley. 366p. (Orig.). 1984. pap. 9.95 o.p. (ISBN 0-86358-036-X). Routledge Chapman & Hall.

China Country Guide. Berlitz Editors. (Country Guides for English Speakers). 1984. pap. 7.95 o.p. (ISBN 0-02-969960-6, Berlitz). Macmillan.

China: Dilemmas of Modernisation. Ed. by Graham Young. LC 84-23116. 279p. 1985. 34.50 o.p. (ISBN 0-7099-2909-9, Pub. by Croom Helm Ltd). Routledge Chapman & Hall.

China Directory, 1986. 14th ed. Radiopress. 1986. 124.00 o.p. (ISBN 0-8002-3971-7). Intl Pubns Serv.

China Directory: 1987. 15th ed. 700p. 1986. pap. 110.00 o.p. (ISBN 0-8002-4102-9). Intl Pubns Serv.

China Directory, 1988. 1988. 125.00 o.p. (CHD108). China Bks.

China Doll. Margaret Yorke. 1985. 12.95 o.p. (ISBN 0-317-53075-5, Large Print Bks). G K Hall.

China: Enduring Scholarship Selected from the Far Eastern Quarterly, the Journal of Asian Studies 1941-1971. Ed. by John A. Harrison. LC 72-83062. (Thirtieth Anniversary Commemorative Ser: Vol. 2). 230p. 1972. pap. 3.75x o.p. (ISBN 0-8165-0362-1). U of Ariz Pr.

China Enters the Machine Age: A Study of Labor in Chinese War Industry. Ed. by Shih Kuo-Heng & Fei Hsiao-T'Ung. LC 68-23327. 1968. Repr. of 1944 ed. lib. bdg. 35.00x o.p. (ISBN 0-8371-0222-7, SHCL). Greenwood.

China Factor: Sino-American Relations & the Global Scene. Ed. by Richard Soloman. 323p. 1981. 11.95 o.p. (ISBN 0-13-132704-6); 5.95 o.p. (ISBN 0-13-132696-1). P-H.

China Facts & Figures Annual, Vol. 10. Ed. by John L. Scherer. 1987. 69.50 o.p. (ISBN 0-317-62897-6). Academic Intl.

China Facts & Figures Annual, 1978-1984, Vols. 1-10. Ed. by John L. Scherer. (CHIFFA Ser.). 1985. 91.00 ea. o.p. Academic Intl.

China Facts Figures Annual 1987, Vol. 10. J. L. Scheret. 1988. 71.50 o.p. (ISBN 0-317-66678-9); 91.00 o.p. (ISBN 0-317-66679-7). Academic Intl.

China for the West: Chinese Porcelain & Other Decorative Arts for Export Illustrated from the Mottahedeh Collection, 2 vols. David S. Howard & John Ayers. (Illus.). 1978. 225.00 o.p. (ISBN 0-85667-035-9). Sotheby Pubns.

China Guidebook, 1982. Frederic M. Kaplan et al. (Illus.). 752p. (Orig.). 1987. pap. 15.95 o.p. (ISBN 0-395-43090-9). HM.

China Guidebook, 1982-1983. Arne J. DeKeijzer & Fredric M. Kaplan. (Illus.). 1983. pap. 12.95 o.p. (ISBN 0-395-34525-1). HM.

China Guidebook, 1984. Fredric M. Kaplan & Arne J. DeKeijzer. 1984. pap. 12.45 o.p. (ISBN 0-395-35491-9). HM.

China Guidebook 1985. Fredric M. Kaplan et al. 1985. pap. 14.45 o.p. (ISBN 0-395-37762-5). HM.

China Guidebook, 1986. Fredric M. Kaplan et al. 1986. pap. 14.45 o.p. (ISBN 0-395-40797-4). HM.

China Guidebook: 1988 Edition. Fredric M. Kaplan et al. (Illus.). 768p. 1988. pap. 16.95 o.s.i. (ISBN 0-395-46808-6). HM.

China in Convulsion, 2 vols. Arthur H. Smith. (Illus.). 770p. 1972. Repr. of 1901 ed. 75.00x set o.p. (ISBN 0-7165-2040-0, BBA 03057, Pub. by Irish Academic Pr). Biblio Dist.

China in Pictures. Ed. by China Pictorial Staff. (Illus.). 96p. (Orig.). 1984. pap. 9.95 o.p. (ISBN 0-8351-1405-8). China Bks.

China, Iran & the Persian Gulf. A. H. Abidi. 325p. 1982. text ed. 35.00x o.p. (ISBN 0-391-02627-5). Humanities.

China, Japan, & Nineteenth Century Britain. I Nish & D. Steeds. (Government & Society in Nineteenth Century Britain Ser.). 136p. 1977. 30.00x o.p. (ISBN 0-7165-2225-X, BBA 02035, Pub. by Irish Academic Pr Ireland). Biblio Dist.

China Lore, Legends, & Lyrics. R. De Rohan Barondes. (Illus.). 256p. 1960. (ISBN 0-8022-0067-2). Philos Lib.

China Men. Maxine H. Kingston. 288p. 1986. pap. 3.95 o.s.i. (ISBN 0-345-34407-3). Ballantine.

China: One Hundred Years of Revolution. Harrison E. Salisbury. LC 83-264. (Illus.). 1983. 29.45 o.p. (ISBN 0-03-056073-X). H Holt & Co.

China: Pushing Toward the Year Two Thousand. Gil Loescher & Ann D. Loescher. LC 80-8802. (Illus.). 160p. (gr. 7 up). 1981. 11.95 o.p. (ISBN 0-15-217506-7, HJ). HarBraceJ.

China Rose. Marsha Canham. 288p. 1984. pap. 3.50 o.p. (ISBN 0-380-85985-8, 85985). Avon.

China Run. Eric Clark. 288p. 1985. 15.95 o.p. (ISBN 0-316-14491-6). Little.

China Saga. C. Y. Lee. LC 86-24672. 576p. 1987. 22.50 o.s.i. (ISBN 1-55584-056-6). Weidenfeld.

China: Scenes of China. (Illus.). 30.00 o.s.i. (ISBN 0-685-58563-8). E J Brill USA.

China: Science Walks on Two Legs. Science for the People. 1974. pap. 1.75 o.p. (ISBN 0-380-00143-8, 20123, Discus). Avon.

China: Selected Readings. 2nd ed. Hyman Kublin. Ed. by Howard R. Anderson. (World Regional Studies). (gr. 7-12). 1976. pap. 6.60 o.p. (ISBN 0-395-21686-9). HM.

China Since Eighteen Hundred. John A. Harrison. LC 66-28625. (Illus., Orig.). 1967. pap. 4.95 o.p. (ISBN 0-15-616880-4, Harv). HarBraceJ.

China Since Mao. Ed. by Kwan Ha Yim. 220p. 1980. lib. bdg. 24.95 o.p. (ISBN 0-87196-210-1). Facts on File.

China Teapots. Pauline Agius. Ed. by Noel Riley. (Antique Pocket Guides). (Illus.). 64p. (Orig.). 1982. pap. 5.95 o.p. (ISBN 0-7188-2548-9, Pub. by Lutterworth Pr UK). Seven Hills Bk Dists.

China, the Annals of the American Academy of Political & Social Science. Ed. by Thorsten Sellin & Donald Young. LC 80-8830. (China During the Interregnum 1911-1949, The Economy & Society Ser.). 431p. 1982. lib. bdg. 52.00 o.p. (ISBN 0-8240-4685-4). Garland Pub.

China: The History, Diplomacy & Commerce from the Earliest Times to the Present Day. E. H. Parker. LC 78-74314. (Modern Chinese Economy Ser.: Vol. 6). 394p. 1980. lib. bdg. 53.00 o.p. (ISBN 0-8240-4255-7). Garland Pub.

China: The Land & Its People. Photos by John Thomson. (Illus.). 160p. 1980. 13.95 o.p. (ISBN 962-7015-02-4, Pub. by Warner Pubns Hong Kong). Hippocrene Bks.

China: The People's Republic of China & Richard Nixon. C. A. Buss. 118p. 1974. 12.95 o.p. (ISBN 0-317-63475-5). W H Freeman.

China Today: Sin or Virtue? Albert M. Honig. 1978. 7.00 o.p. (ISBN 0-682-49086-5). Exposition-Phoenix.

China Traveler's Phrasebook. Bennett Lee & Geremie Barme. (Chinese.). 1980. pap. 5.95 o.p. (ISBN 0-8351-0729-9). China Bks.

China-U.S. Bilateral Symposium of Polymer Chemistry & Physics: Proceedings. Science Press Staff. 1981. 45.95 o.p. (ISBN 0-442-20073-0). Van Nos Reinhold.

China White. Tony Kenrick. 1986. 16.95 o.p. (ISBN 0-316-48917-4). Little.

Chinaman's Chance. Ross Thomas. 1978. 9.95 o.p. (ISBN 0-671-24070-6). S&S.

China's Ancient Technology. 1983. 8.95 o.p. (ISBN 0-8351-1205-5). China Bks.

China's Banking System: Structure & Reform. Carl Walter. (Occasional Paper of the Northeast Asia-United States Forum on International Policy, Stanford University). 61p. 1983. pap. 6.00 o.p. (ISBN 0-935371-09-5). ISIS.

China's Crafts: The Story of How They're Made & What They Mean. Roberta Stalberg & Ruth Nesi. 1980. 15.95 o.p. (ISBN 0-8351-0755-8); pap. 11.95 o.p. (ISBN 0-8351-0740-X). China Bks.

China's Currency Reform, 1941 see History of China's Internal Loan Issues: Shanghai, 1934.

China's Early Industrialization: Sheng-Hsuan-Huai, 1844-1916 & Mandarin Enterprise. Albert Feuerwerker. LC 58-12967. 1970. pap. text ed. 3.25x o.s.i. (ISBN 0-689-70220-5, 153, Atheneum). Macmillan.

China's Economy & Foreign Trade, 1981-85. 57p. (Orig.). 1984. pap. 2.25 o.p. (ISBN 0-318-18732-9, S/N 003-009-00429-2). USGPO.

China's Economy in Two Thousand. 1987. 14.95 o.p. (ISBN 0-8351-2043-0). China Bks.

China's Foreign Economic Legislation, Vol. 1. 289p. 1982. pap. 7.95 o.p. (ISBN 0-8351-0983-6). China Bks.

China's Foreign Economic Legislation, Vol. 2. 348p. (Orig.). 1987. pap. 9.95 o.p. (ISBN 0-8351-1595-X). China Bks.

China's Foreign Policy in the Arab World 1955-75. H. S. Behbehani. 400p. 1981. 40.00x o.p. (ISBN 0-7103-0008-5). Routledge Chapman & Hall.

China's Foreign Trade Corporations & Organizations. 1986. 7.95 o.p. (ISBN 0-8351-2039-2). China Bks.

China's Livestock Sector. Francis C. Tuan. (Foreign Agricultural Economic Report 226). (Illus.). 86p. 1987. pap. 3.00 o.p. (ISBN 0-317-62838-0, S-N 001-019-00505-0). USGPO.

China's Modernization & Transnational Corporations. N. T. Wang. 224p. 1984. 26.00x o.p. (ISBN 0-669-06266-9). Lexington Bks.

China's Patent Law. Ed. by Su Wenming. (China Today Ser.). 102p. (Orig.). 1987. pap. 2.95 o.p. (ISBN 0-8351-1809-6). China Bks.

China's Provincial Leaders, 1949-1985: Vol. 1, Directory. David S. Goodman. LC 86-20887. 316p. 1986. text ed. 99.00 o.p. (ISBN 0-391-03487-1). Humanities.

China's Socialist Economy: An Outline History, 1949-1984. Ed. by Liu Suinian. 700p. pap. 15.95 o.p. (ISBN 0-8351-1794-4). China Bks.

China's Socialist Modernization. Yu Guangyuan. 775p. 1984. pap. 12.95 o.p. (ISBN 0-8351-1011-7). China Bks.

Chinatown Chance. Tom Cutter. (Tracker Ser.: No. 4). 1983. pap. 2.25 o.p. (ISBN 0-380-84988-7, 84988). Avon.

Chinatown Family. Lin Yutang. 307p. 1980. 6.95x o.p. (ISBN 0-89955-169-6, Pub. by Mei Ya China); pap. 4.95 o.p. (ISBN 0-89955-198-X, Pub. by Mei Ya China). Intl Spec Bk.

Chinatown, the Last Detail, Shampoo: Screenplays. Robert Towne. 352p. (Orig.). 1988. pap. 10.95 o.p. (ISBN 0-87113-213-3). Atlantic Monthly.

Chinese Acrobatics Through the Ages. Fu Qifeng. Tr. by Ouyang Caiwei & Rhoda Stockwell. (Illus.). 125p. (Orig.). 1985. pap. 9.95 o.p. (ISBN 0-8351-1307-8). China Bks.

Chinese Alchemy: Preliminary Studies. Nathan Sivin. LC 67-27093. (Monographs in the History of Science Ser). 1968. 27.00x o.s.i. (ISBN 0-674-12150-3). Harvard U Pr.

Chinese Anarchist Movement. Robert A. Scalapino & George T. Yu. LC 80-23499. (University of California Institute of International Studies, Center for Chinese Studies, Research Ser.). vi, 81p. 1980. Repr. of 1961 ed. lib. bdg. 35.00x o.p. (ISBN 0-313-22586-9, SCCM). Greenwood.

Chinese Archaeological Abstracts. Ed. by Richard C. Rudolph. LC 77-620059. (Monumenta Archaeologica: 6). (Illus.). 611p. 1978. 35.00x o.p. (ISBN 0-917956-05-2). UCLA Arch.

Chinese Architecture: A Bibliography. Lamia Doumato. (Architecture Ser.: A 1514). 10p. 1985. 2.00 o.p. (ISBN 0-89028-664-7). Vance Biblios.

Chinese Architecture in the Straits Settlements & Western Malaya: Temples, Kongsis & Houses. David G. Kohl. (Illus.). xix, 322p. (Orig.). 1984. pap. 20.00 o.p. (ISBN 967-925-066-0). Heinemann Ed.

Chinese Armorial Porcelain. David S. Howard. 1034p. 1974. 199.00 o.p. (ISBN 0-571-09811-8). Faber & Faber.

Chinese Art. Ackerman. LC 76-14077. (Library of the History of Art: Vol.XIV). 1977. lib. bdg. 61.00 o.p. (ISBN 0-8240-2424-9). Garland Pub.

Chinese Astrology. An Nguyen. pap. 8.95 o.p. (ISBN 0-87795-247-7). Morrow.

Chinese Beliefs & Superstitions. 1987. 9.95 o.p. (ISBN 0-8351-1829-0). China Bks.

Chinese Black Chamber: An Adventure in Espionage. Herbert O. Yardley. 1983. 13.45 o.p. (ISBN 0-395-34648-7). HM.

Chinese Book of Table Tennis. Ding Shu De et al. LC 80-65996. 1981. 9.95 o.p. (ISBN 0-689-11082-0, Atheneum). Macmillan.

Chinese Business Dialogues, 2 bks. 1985. Set. incl. 3 tapes 49.95 o.p. (ISBN 962-04-0313-4, CHBUDI). China Bks.

Chinese Calligraphers & Their Art. Ch'En Chih-Mai. 1966. 41.00 o.p. (ISBN 0-522-83559-7, Pub. by Melbourne U Pr). Intl Spec Bk.

Chinese Carpets. E. Gans-Ruedin. LC 81-82719. (Illus.). 198p. 1982. 45.00 o.s.i. Kodansha.

Chinese Catalog: Your Source Book for Things Chinese in America. Ed Laube & Craig Walker. (Illus.). 220p. (Orig.). 1984. pap. 14.95 o.p. (ISBN 0-88254-920-0). Hippocrene Bks.

Chinese Chain & Washer Pumps: Twenty-One Chain & Washer Pumps from the 1958 Peking Agricultural Exhibition. Compiled by Simon Watt. (Illus.). 53p. (Orig.). 1977. pap. 2.75 o.p. (ISBN 0-903031-26-4, Pub. by Intermed Tech England). Intermediate Tech.

Chinese Characteristics. A. H. Smith. (Illus.). 344p. 1972. Repr. of 1900 ed. 32.50x o.p. (ISBN 0-7165-2043-5, BBA 02131, Pub. by Irish Academic Pr Ireland). Biblio Dist.

Chinese Characters Easily Confused. Ed. by Henry C. Fenn. 2.95 o.p. (ISBN 0-88710-013-9). Yale Far Eastern Pubns.

Chinese Communists & Rural Society, Nineteen Twenty-Seven to Nineteen Thirty-Four. Philip Huang et al. LC 78-620018. (China Research Monographs: No. 13). 1978. pap. text ed. 5.00x o.p. (ISBN 0-912966-18-1). IEAS.

Chinese Cookbook, Vol. III. Fu Pei Mei. 1981. 20.00 o.s.i. (ISBN 0-911268-33-2). E J Brill USA.

Chinese Cookbook, Vol. I. Fu Pei Mei. 1969. 20.00 o.s.i. (ISBN 0-911268-14-6). E J Brill USA.

Chinese Cookbook, Vol. II. Fu Pei Mei. 1974. 20.00 o.s.i. (ISBN 0-911268-18-9). E J Brill USA.

Chinese Cookbook. Janet Wilk. (Illus.). 64p. (Orig.). 1981. pap. 3.95 o.p. (ISBN 0-8249-3002-9). Ideals.

Chinese Cooking. rev. ed. (Illus.). 231p. 1987. pap. 12.95 o.p. (ISBN 0-8351-1791-X). China Bks.

Chinese Cooking Secrets. Karen Lee & Alexandra Branyon. LC 80-1724. (Illus.). 384p. 1984. 22.50 o.s.i. (ISBN 0-385-15514-X). Doubleday.

Chinese Cuisine: From the Master Chefs of China. China Pictorial, "The People's Republic of China" Editors. (Illus.). 256p. 1983. 29.95 o.p. (ISBN 0-316-54994-0). Little.

Chinese Design & Pattern in Full Color. Owen Jones. (Illus.). 19.00 o.p. (ISBN 0-8446-5897-9). Peter Smith.

Chinese Divination. James Kao. (Illus.). 144p. 1980. 7.00 o.p. (ISBN 0-682-49590-5). Exposition-Phoenix.

Chinese Dress. Verity Wilson. (Illus.). 136p. 1987. 25.00 o.p. (ISBN 0-948107-18-9, Pub. by Victoria & Albert Mus UK). Faber & Faber.

Chinese Economic Psychology. Richard Wilhelm. Ed. by Ramon H. Myers. LC 80-8825. (China During the Interregnum 1911-1949, the Economy & Society Ser.). 64p. 1982. lib. bdg. 19.00 o.p. (ISBN 0-8240-4680-3). Garland Pub.

Chinese Egg. Catherine Storr. (Illus.). 266p. (gr. 7-10). 1982. pap. 5.95 o.p. (ISBN 0-571-11871-2). Faber & Faber.

Chinese Empire. John A. Harrison. LC 73-178591. (Illus.). 364p. 1972. pap. 5.95 o.s.i. (ISBN 0-15-617093-0, Harv). HarBraceJ.

Chinese-English Dictionary: Taiwan Dialect. K. T. Tan. (Chinese & Eng.). 1978. 65.00x o.p. (ISBN 0-89986-342-6). Oriental Bk Store.

Chinese-English, English-Chinese Dictionary, 2 vols. (Chinese & Eng.). Set. 45.00 o.p. E J Brill USA.

Chinese-English Expressions for Travellers. 1981. pap. 2.95 o.p. (ISBN 0-8351-0843-0). China Bks.

Chinese-English Handbook: Idioms. 1986. 8.95 o.p. (ISBN 962-04-0120-4, CHENHA). China Bks.

Chinese Exclusion Versus the Open Door Policy, 1900-1906: Clashes Over China Policy in the Roosevelt Era. Delber McKee. LC 76-47024. (Illus.). 292p. 1977. 27.50x o.p. (ISBN 0-8143-1565-8). Wayne St U Pr.

Chinese Fairy Tales. (gr. k-6). 1987. 12.95 o.p. (ISBN 0-8249-8159-6). Ideals.

Chinese Family in the Communist Revolution. Ch'ing-k'un Yang. LC 84-4690. x, 246p. 1984. Repr. of 1959 ed. lib. bdg. 38.50 o.p. (ISBN 0-313-24455-3, YACF). Greenwood.

Chinese Farm Economy. John L. Buck. Ed. by Ramon H. Myers. LC 80-8828. (Chinese During the Interregnum 1911-1949, The Economy & Society Ser.). 476p. 1982. lib. bdg. 61.00 o.p. (ISBN 0-8240-4683-8). Garland Pub.

Chinese Fiction from Taiwan: Critical Perspectives. Ed. by Jeannette L. Faurot. LC 80-7490. (Studies in Chinese Literature & Society). 288p. 1980. 20.00x o.p. (ISBN 0-253-12409-3). Ind U Pr.

Chinese Folk Designs: A Collection of 300 Cut-Paper Designs Together with 160 Chinese Art Symbols & Their Meanings. W. M. Hawley. (Illus.). 14.00 o.p. (ISBN 0-8446-0134-9). Peter Smith.

Chinese Folk Toys & Ornaments. 1980. pap. 7.95 o.p. (ISBN 0-8351-0735-3). China Bks.

Chinese Folklore: Belief & Marriage. Nagao Ryuzo. (Asian Folklore & Social Life Monograph: No. 14). (Japanese.). 1938. 14.00x o.p. (ISBN 0-89986-035-4). Oriental Bk Store.

Chinese Games with Dice & Dominoes. Stewart Culin. (Shorey Lost Arts Ser.). (Illus.). 74p. pap. 5.95 o.s.i. (ISBN 0-8466-6017-2, U17). Shorey.

Chinese Gastronomy. Hsiang Ju Lin. LC 76-81570. (Illus.). 1977. pap. 4.95 o.p. (ISBN 0-15-617095-7, Harv). HarBraceJ.

Chinese Herbal Prescriptions: A Practical & Authoritative Self-Help Guide. Stephen Tang & Martin Palmer. (Illus.). 112p. 1987. pap. 15.95 o.p. (ISBN 0-7126-9470-6, Pub. by Century Hutchinson). David & Charles.

Chinese Historiography on the Revolution of 1911: A Critical Survey & a Selected Bibliography. Winston Hsieh. LC 70-152425. (Studies: No. 34). 165p. 1975. 11.95x o.p. (ISBN 0-8179-3341-7). Hoover Inst Pr.

Chinese Ideas of Life & Death. Michael Loewe. 240p. 1982. China Stands Up - see attached. text ed. 30.00x o.p. (ISBN 0-04-180001-X). Unwin Hyman.

Chinese in Sabah, East Malaysia. Han Sin-Fong. (Asian Folklore & Social Life Monographs: No. 67). 260p. 1975. 17.00x o.p. (ISBN 0-89986-062-1). Oriental Bk Store.

Chinese Jade of Five Centuries. Joan M. Hartman. LC 69-12077. (Illus.). 1969. 280.00x o.p. (ISBN 0-8048-0099-5). C E Tuttle.

Chinese Jades in the Avery Brundage Collection. Rene-Yvon L. D'Argence. LC 77-18358. (Illus.). 184p. 1977. pap. 19.95 o.p. (ISBN 0-295-96645-9). U of Wash Pr.

Chinese Letters, Seventeen Forty-One. Jean Baptiste De Boyer Argens. (Flowering of the Novel, 1740-1775 Ser: Vol. 4). 1975. lib. bdg. 61.00 o.p. (ISBN 0-8240-1103-1). Garland Pub.

Chinese Literature for the Nineteen Eighties: The Fourth Congress of Writers & Artists. Tr. by Howard Goldblatt from Chinese. LC 82-744. 195p. 1982. 40.00 o.p. (ISBN 0-87332-208-8). M E Sharpe.

Chinese Menu Cookbook. Joanne Hush & Peter Wong. LC 75-21469. 1976. 9.95 o.p. (ISBN 0-03-014931-2, Owl Bks.); pap. 9.95 o.s.i. (ISBN 0-03-044776-3). H Holt & Co.

Chinese Merchant Families of Iloilo: Commerce & Kin in a Central Philippine City. John T. Omohundro. (Illus.). viii, 206p. 1981. text ed. 19.95x o.p. (ISBN 0-8214-0441-5); pap. text ed. 10.95x o.p. (ISBN 0-8214-0619-1). Ohio U Pr.

Chinese Migration & Settlement in Australia. C. Y. Choi. (Illus.). 144p. 1975. 23.00x o.p. (ISBN 0-424-06810-9, Pub. by Sydney U Pr). Intl Spec Bk.

Chinese Mind. Wang Kung-Hsing. LC 68-23336. 1968. Repr. of 1946 ed. lib. bdg. 35.00x o.p. (ISBN 0-8371-0260-X, WACM). Greenwood.

Chinese Mother Goose Rhymes. Robert Wyndham. (Illus.). 48p. 1982. pap. 4.95 o.p. (ISBN 0-399-20866-6, Philomel). Putnam Pub Group.

Chinese New Year. Hou-Tien Cheng. LC 76-8229. (Illus.). (gr. k-3). 1976. reinforced bdg. 9.95 o.s.i. (ISBN 0-8050-0236-7); pap. 2.95 o.p. (ISBN 0-03-048961-X). H Holt & Co.

Chinese Opera & Painted Face. Pe-Chin Chang. 268p. 1980. 100.00 o.p. (ISBN 0-89955-142-4, Pub. by Mei Ya China). Intl Spec Bk.

Chinese Opium Wars. Jack Beeching. LC 75-16414. (Illus.). 368p. 1976. 14.95 o.p. (ISBN 0-15-117650-7). HarBraceJ.

Chinese Painting. William Cohn. LC 76-6320. (Illus.). 1978. Repr. of 1948 ed. lib. bdg. 60.00 o.p. (ISBN 0-87817-203-3). Hacker.

Chinese Painting: An Expression of a Civilization. Nicole Vandier-Nicolas. (Illus.). 260p. sewn bdg. 45.00 o.p. (ISBN 0-317-54953-7). Apollo.

Chinese Painting & Calligraphy (Chinese-English) Yang Han et al. (Illus.). 167p. 1984. 99.95 o.p. (ISBN 0-8351-1387-6). China Bks.

Chinese Paintings Through the Ages: Paintings of the Palace Museum, Vol. 1. 1979. text ed. 175.00 o.p. (ISBN 0-8351-0638-1). China Bks.

Chinese Popular Literature & the Child. Dorothea H. Scott. LC 80-10412. 192p. 1980. 15.00x o.p. (ISBN 0-8389-0289-8). ALA.

Chinese Pottery & Porcelain. Li Zhiyan & Cheng Wen. Tr. by Ouyang Caiwei from Chinese. (Illus.). 209p. (Orig.). 1984. pap. 12.95 o.p. (ISBN 0-8351-1185-7). China Bks.

Chinese Qigong Therapy. 1985. 14.95 o.p. (ISBN 0-8351-1691-3). China Bks.

Chinese Reader's Manual. William F. Mayers. LC 68-30660. 464p. 1968. Repr. of 1910 ed. 37.00x o.p. (ISBN 0-8103-3335-X). Gale.

Chinese Reading for Beginners. George A. Kennedy. 3.95 o.p. (ISBN 0-88710-019-8). Yale Far Eastern Pubns.

Chinese Revolution: 1900-1950. Ranbir Vohra. (New Perspectives in History Ser). 200p. 1974. pap. 6.75 o.p. (ISBN 0-395-18338-3). HM.

Chinese Rugs Designed for Needlepoint. Maggie Lane. LC 75-5733. (Illus.). 160p. 1975. 12.95 o.s.i. (ISBN 0-684-14195-7, ScribT). Scribner.

Chinese-Russian Phonetic Dictionary. 319p. (Chinese & Rus.). 1957. leatherette 4.95 o.p. (ISBN 0-686-92615-3, M-9126). French & Eur.

Chinese Russian Relations. Michel N. Pavolovsky. (ISBN 0-8022-1291-3). Philos Lib.

Chinese Technique: An Illustrated Guide to the Fundamental Techniques of Chinese Cooking. Ken Hom & Harvey Steiman. (Illus.). 1981. 18.25 o.p. (ISBN 0-671-25347-6). S&S.

Chinese Thought & Institutions. Ed. by John K. Fairbank. LC 57-5272. 1957. lib. bdg. 30.00x o.s.i. (ISBN 0-226-23402-9). U of Chicago Pr.

Chinese Thought & Institutions. Ed. by John K. Fairbank. LC 57-5272. 1967. pap. text ed. 4.50x o.s.i. (ISBN 0-226-23403-7, P270, Phoen). U of Chicago Pr.

Chinese Village Close-Up. Fei H. Tung. (China Studies). (Illus.). 269p. (Orig.). 1983. 8.95 o.p. (ISBN 0-8351-1286-1); pap. 6.95 o.p. (ISBN 0-8351-0959-3). China Bks.

Chinese Way: Life in the People's Republic of China. Gil Loescher & Ann D. Loescher. LC 73-18630. 206p. (gr. 7 up). 1974. 7.95 o.p. (ISBN 0-15-217507-5, HJ). HarBraceJ.

Chinese Way to a Long & Healthy Life. People's Medical Publishing House Staff. (Illus.). 224p. 1984. 14.95 o.p. (ISBN 0-88254-792-5). Hippocrene Bks.

Chinese Women since Mao. Elisabeth Croll. LC 83-16624. 144p. 1984. pap. 12.95 o.p. (ISBN 0-87332-267-3). M E Sharpe.

Chinese Women Speak. Dymphna Cusack. (Century Travellers Ser.). (Illus.). 288p. 1986. pap. 11.95 o.s.i. (ISBN 0-7126-0456-1, Pub. by Century Hutchinson). David & Charles.

Chinese Writing: An Introduction. Diane Wolff. LC 74-20579. (Illus.). 48p. (gr. 5 up). 1975. 7.95 o.p. (ISBN 0-03-013006-9); pap. 2.75 o.p. (ISBN 0-03-048946-6). H Holt & Co.

Chinesische Landwirtschaft. Wilhelm Wagner. LC 78-74338. (Modern Chinese Economy Ser.: Vol. 15). 659p. 1980. lib. bdg. 87.00 o.p. (ISBN 0-8240-4263-8). Garland Pub.

Chinoiseries: A Bibliography. Mary Vance. (Architecture Ser.: A 1405). 6p. 1985. 2.00 o.p. (ISBN 0-89028-435-0). Vance Biblios.

Chinook Indian Language. Franz Boas. (Shorey Indian Ser.). 120p. pap. 9.95 o.s.i. (ISBN 0-8466-4028-7, I28). Shorey.

Chip. Will Baker. LC 79-87510. (gr. 7 up). 1979. 7.95 o.p. (ISBN 0-15-217526-1, HJ). HarBraceJ.

Chip: How Two Americans Invented the Microchip & Launched a Revolution. T. R. Reid. 320p. 1985. 15.45 o.p. (ISBN 0-671-45393-9). S&S.

Chip: How Two Americans Invented the Microchip & Launched a Revolution. T. R. Reid. 1986. pap. 7.95 o.p. (ISBN 0-671-62254-4, Touchstone Bks). S&S.

Chipmunk Christmas. Megan Stine & H. William Stine. LC 85-1840. (Chipmunks Ser.). (Illus.). 32p. (gr. k-3). 1985. 4.95 o.p. (ISBN 0-394-87512-5, BYR). Random.

Chippewa Child Life & Its Cultural Background. Inez Hilger. LC 76-43740. (BAE. Bulletin: 146). Repr. of 1951 ed. 17.50 o.p. (ISBN 0-404-15581-2). AMS Pr.

Chippewa Indians III. Harold Hickerson. Ed. by David A. Horr. (American Indian Ethnohistory Ser.). 1974. lib. bdg. 51.00 o.p. (ISBN 0-8240-0810-3). Garland Pub.

Chiquita Banana Cookbook. Chiquita Banana Cookbook Staff. 1974. pap. 1.25 o.p. (ISBN 0-380-01098-4, 26633). Avon.

Chironomidae-Ecology Systematics Cytology & Physiology: Proceedings of the International Symposium, 7th, Dublin, August, 1979. International Symposium on Chrionomidae Staff. Ed. by D. A. Murray. (Illus.). 380p. 1980. 105.00 o.p. (ISBN 0-08-025889-1). Pergamon.

Chitin. Riccardo A. Muzzarelli. LC 76-52421. 365p. 1977. 80.00 o.p. (ISBN 0-08-020367-1). Pergamon.

Chiy-une. Susan Coon. 320p. (Orig.). 1982. pap. 2.75 o.p. (ISBN 0-380-79301-6, 79301). Avon.

Chloride Electrometallurgy: Proceedings AIME Annual Meeting, Dallas TX, 1982. Ed. by P. D. Parker. (Illus.). 240p. 36.00 o.p. (ISBN 0-89520-454-1); member 24.00 o.p. (ISBN 0-317-36298-4); student members 12.00 o.p. (ISBN 0-317-36299-2). ASM.

Chlorinated Dioxins & Dibenzofurans in the Total Environment. Ed. by G. Choudhary & L. H. Keith. 1984. text ed. 75.00 o.p. (ISBN 0-250-40604-7). Butterworth.

Chlorinated Dioxins & Dibenzofurans in the Total Environment, Vol. II. Keith et al. 540p. 1984. 75.00 o.p. (ISBN 0-250-40646-2). Butterworth.

Chlorinated Dioxins & Related Compounds 1984: Proceedings of the Fourth International Conference held at Ottawa, Canada October 16-18 1984. Ed. by M. J. Boddington et al. (Illus.). 420p. 1985. pap. 51.00 o.p. (ISBN 0-08-032608-0, Pub. by PPL). Pergamon.

Chlorofluorocarbons in the Environment: The Aerosol Controversy. Ed. by T. M. Sugden & T. F. West. 183p. 1980. 84.95 o.p. (ISBN 0-470-26937-5). Halsted Pr.

Chlorophylls: Physical, Chemical & Biological Properties. Leo P. Vernon & G. R. Seely. 1966. 110.00 o.p. (ISBN 0-12-718650-6). Acad Pr.

Chochmo U'Mussar, 3 vols. Salomon Breuer. 1972. Set. 24.00 o.p. (ISBN 0-87306-205-1). Feldheim.

Chocolate, Cocoa & Confectionery: Science & Technology. 2nd ed. Bernard W. Minifie. (Illus.). 1980. 65.95 o.p. (ISBN 0-87055-330-5). AVI.

Chocolate Fads & Fantasies. Date not set. price not set o.p. (Peregrine Smith). Gibbs Smith Pub.

Chocolate Fever. Robert K. Smith. (Illus.). (gr. 2-5). 13.75 o.p. (ISBN 0-8446-6186-4). Peter Smith.

Chocolate Marshmelephant Sundae. Mike Thaler. (Illus.). 1980. pap. 2.25 o.p. (ISBN 0-380-49320-9, 64998-5, Camelot). Avon.

Chocolate Moose for Dinner. Fred Gwynne. LC 80-14150. (Illus.). 48p. (gr. 1-5). 1987. 11.95 o.s.i. (ISBN 0-13-133117-5); pap. 5.95 o.s.i. (ISBN 0-13-133109-4). Prentice Hall Pr.

Chocolate Mouse & Sugar Pig: And How They Ran Away to Escape Being Eaten. Irina Hale. LC 78-6132. (Illus.). 32p. (ps-4). 1979. 8.95 o.p. (ISBN 0-689-50113-7, Atheneum). Macmillan.

Chocolate Spy. David M. Alexander. LC 78-3579. 1978. 342p., 1986 14.95 o.p. (ISBN 0-698-10909-0, Coward). Putnam Pub Group.

Chocolate Thunder: The In-Your-Face, All-Over-the-Place, Death-Defyin', Mesmerizin', Slam-Jam Adventures of Double D. Darryl Dawkins & George Wirt. 224p. 1987. 15.95 o.p. (ISBN 0-8092-4886-7). Contemp Bks.

Choderlos De Laclos, the Man, His Works, & His Critics: An Annotated Bibliography. Colette V. Michael. 1982. lib. bdg. 31.00 o.p. (ISBN 0-8240-9363-1). Garland Pub.

Choephori see also Libation-Bearers.

Choice & Change: The Psychology of Adjustment, Growth, & Creativity. 2nd ed. April O'Connell & Jacqueline Whitmore. (Illus.). 512p. 1985. pap. text ed. (ISBN 0-13-133042-X). P-H.

Choice & Compromise: A Woman's Guide to Balancing Family & Career. Donna N. Douglass. 208p. (Orig.). 1983. 14.95 o.p.; pap. 8.95 o.p. (ISBN 0-8144-7604-X). AMACOM.

Choice & Destiny of Nations. Elizabeth E. Hoyt. LC 78-81813. 1969. (ISBN 0-8022-2292-7). Philos Lib.

Choice Before South Africa. Emil S. Sachs. 220p. 1952. (ISBN 0-8022-1464-9). Philos Lib.

Choice for Survival: The Baby Boomer's Dilemma. Ralph D. Kidder & Edward F. Kelly. LC 85-81362. 224p. (Orig.). 1986. pap. 13.95 o.p. (ISBN 0-87040-660-4). Japan Pubns USA.

Choice Messages from Free Will Baptist Pulpits. Ed. by Van D. Hudson. 1976. pap. 2.50 o.p. (ISBN 0-89265-030-3). Randall Hse.

Choice of Anglo-Saxon Verse. Compiled by & intro. by Richard Hamer. 207p. (Orig.). 1970. pap. text ed. 5.50x o.p. (ISBN 0-571-08765-5). Humanities.

Choice of Catastrophes. Isaac Asimov. 384p. 1981. pap. 6.95 o.s.i. (ISBN 0-449-90048-7, Columbine). Fawcett.

Choice of Catastrophes. Isaac Asimov. 1979. 11.95 o.p. (ISBN 0-671-22701-7). S&S.

Choice of Enemies. George V. Higgins. LC 83-47942. 416p. 1983. 16.45 o.s.i. (ISBN 0-394-52439-X). Knopf.

Choice of Shakespeare's Verse. William Shakespeare. Ed. by Ted Hughes. 212p. 1971. 7.95 o.p. (ISBN 0-571-09426-0); pap. 3.95 o.p. (ISBN 0-571-09427-9). Faber & Faber.

Choice of Technology in Developing Countries. J. Pickett. 1978. pap. 40.00 o.p. (ISBN 0-08-023006-7). Pergamon.

Choice to Be Human: Jesus Alive in the Gospel of Matthew. Eugene C. Kennedy. LC 84-28694. 264p. 1985. 15.95 o.p. (ISBN 0-385-19280-0). Doubleday.

Choices: A Unit on Conflict & Nuclear War. National Education Association Staff & Union of Concerned Scientists. 144p. 1983. 9.95 o.p. (ISBN 0-8106-1425-1). NEA.

Choices & Chances. Linda Vail. (Candlelight Ecstasy Supreme Ser.: No. 96). 1985. pap. 2.75 o.p. Dell.

Choices: In Pursuit of Wholeness. Cecil Paul & Jan Lanham. 88p. 1982. pap. 3.95 o.p. (ISBN 0-8341-0807-0); leader's guide 1.95 o.p. (ISBN 0-8341-0928-X). Beacon Hill.

Choices in Relationships: An Introduction to Marriage & Family. David Knox. (Illus.). 658p. 1985. text ed. 36.75 o.p. (ISBN 0-314-85257-3). West Pub.

Choices in Silviculture for American Forests. American Forestry Association Staff & Wildlife Society Staff. LC 81-51229. (Illus.). 88p. (Orig.). 1981. pap. 4.00 o.s.i. (ISBN 0-939970-09-0). Soc Am Foresters.

Choices of a Growing Woman. Maggie S. Davis. LC 81-1083. 1982. 7.95 o.p. (ISBN 0-87491-418-3); pap. 4.95 o.p. (ISBN 0-87491-525-2). Acropolis.

Choices: Organizing & Teaching a Course in Personal Decision-Making. Joan Kosuth & Sandy Minnesang. (Orig.). 1975. 19.95 o.p. (ISBN 0-913458-28-7). Wright Group.

Choices: Realistic Alternatives in Cancer Treatment. rev. & updated ed. Marion Morra & Eve Potts. LC 79-55572. 800p. 1980. pap. 8.95 o.p. (ISBN 0-380-75291-3). Avon.

Choices...Changes. Joni E. Tada. 240p. 1986. 14.95 o.p. (ISBN 0-310-24010-7, 12018). Zondervan.

Choir Invisible. James L. Allen. 1974. pap. 0.95 o.p. (ISBN 0-380-00035-0, 19570). Avon.

Chokecherry Hunters & Other Poems. Joseph Concha. 31p. 1976. pap. 2.25 o.p. (ISBN 0-913270-57-1). Sunstone Pr.

Cholera Years: The United States in 1832, 1849, & 1866. Charles E. Rosenberg. LC 62-18121. 1968. pap. text ed. 8.00 o.s.i. (ISBN 0-226-72679-7, P320, Phoen). U of Chicago Pr.

Cholinergic Ligand Interactions. Ed. by D. J. Triggle et al. 1971. 48.00 o.p. (ISBN 0-12-700450-5). Acad Pr.

Cholinergic-Monoaminergic Interactions in the Brain. Ed. by Larry L. Butcher. (Behavioral Biology Ser.). 1978. 62.00 o.p. (ISBN 0-12-147850-5). Acad Pr.

Chondroid Bone, Secondary Cartilage & Metaplasia. W. A. Beresford. LC 80-13411. (Illus.). 471p. (Orig.). 1980. text ed. 45.00 o.p. (ISBN 0-8067-0261-3). Urban & S.

Choo-Choo Train. (Chubby Panoramas Ser.). (Illus.). 1983. 2.95 o.s.i. (ISBN 0-671-47663-7, Little Simon). S&S.

Choose-a-Card Series: 9 Bks. 1981. 51.95 o.p. (ISBN 0-86530-009-7, IP09-7). Incentive Pubns.

Choose Life. Marilyn Kunz & Catherine Schell. (Neighborhood Bible Studies). 1973. pap. 2.50 o.p. (ISBN 0-8423-0460-6). Tyndale.

Choose the Sex of Your Baby: A Psychological Approach. Victor B. Dada. 1983. 7.95 o.p. (ISBN 0-533-05256-4). Vantage.

Choosing a Play for Your Amateur Group. Ivan Butler. LC 72-2194. 121p. 1972. 5.95 o.p. (ISBN 0-8008-1499-1); pap. 2.95 o.s.i. (ISBN 0-8008-1500-9). Taplinger.

Choosing Accounting Software for Your Micro. Gary Simon. (Illus.). 160p. 1985. pap. 17.95x o.p. (ISBN 0-00-383006-3, Pub. by Collins England). Sheridan.

Choosing Among Local Impact Models. Marlys Knutson & Lloyd D. Bender. (Rural Development Research Report Ser.: No. 63). (Illus.). 39p. 1986. pap. 2.25 o.p. (ISBN 0-318-21935-2, 001-019-00473-8). USGPO.

Choosing Books for Children. Betsy G. Hearne. 176p. 1982. pap. 2.95 o.s.i. (ISBN 0-440-31576-X, LE). Dell.

Choosing for Health. Robert O'Connor. 1980. pap. text ed. 25.95 o.p. (ISBN 0-03-019921-2, CBS C). SCP.

Choosing Life. Dorothee Soelle. Tr. by Margaret Kohl from Ger. LC 81-43082. 128p. 1981. 9.95 o.p. (ISBN 0-8006-0667-1, 1-667, Fortress). Augsburg Fortress.

Choosing the President. Ed. by James D. Barber. 1974. 7.95 o.p. (ISBN 0-13-133561-8); pap. 3.95 o.p. (ISBN 0-13-133553-7). Am Assembly.

Choosing the President. Date not set. (ISBN 0-8052-0763-5). Random.

Choosing the President: 1980 Edition. League of Women Voters Education Fund Staff. (Illus.). 1980. pap. 1.95 o.p. (ISBN 0-89959-100-0, 420). LWV US.

Choosing the Right School: A Parents' Guide. David Freeman. 246p. (Orig.). 1984. pap. 16.95x o.p. (ISBN 0-7102-0036-6). Routledge Chapman & Hall.

Choosing Your Future: The New York Times Guide to the 101 Best Career Opportunities of Tomorrow. Elizabeth M. Fowler. 352p. 1987. pap. 9.95 o.p. (ISBN 0-317-63090-3). Times Bks.

Chopin. rev. ed. Arthur Hedley. (Master Musicians Ser.: No. M152). (Illus.). 1977. pap. 7.95 o.p. (ISBN 0-8226-0709-3). Littlefield.

Chopin: As Revealed by Extracts from His Diary. S. Tarnowski. Ed. by David Doscher. 1972. pap. 4.50x o.p. (ISBN 0-913000-01-9). Maestro Scope.

Chopin Playing: From the Composer to the Present Day. James Methuen-Campbell. LC 81-8876. 288p. 1981. 14.95 o.s.i. (ISBN 0-8008-1511-4, Crescendo). Taplinger.

Chopped, Minced & Ground Meat Cookbook. Ceil Dyer. LC 75-31070. 1976. 9.95 o.p. (ISBN 0-87795-126-8, Arbor Hse); pap. 3.95 o.p. (ISBN 0-87795-113-6). Morrow.

Chopper Boys: New Zealand's Helicopter Hunters. Rex Forrester. (Illus.). 160p. 1986. pap. 14.95 o.p. (ISBN 0-7233-0706-7, Pub. by Whitcoulls NZ). Intl Spec Bk.

Choral Conducting: A Symposium. Ed. by Harold A. Decker & Julius Herford. LC 72-94347. (Illus.). 320p. 1973. pap. text ed. 38.00 o.p. (ISBN 0-13-133355-0). P-H.

Choral Techniques. 2nd ed. Gordon H. Lamb. 304p. 1979. text ed. write for info. o.p. (ISBN 0-697-03417-8). Wm C Brown.

Choral Tradition. rev. ed. Percy M. Young. (Illus.). 1981. pap. 9.95 o.p. (ISBN 0-393-00058-3, Norton Lib). Norton.

Chorale Harmonization in the Church Modes. Tr. by Hugo Nordon. 1974. pap. 3.75 o.s.i. (ISBN 0-8008-1516-5, Crescendo). Taplinger.

Chorioretinal Heredodegenerations: An Updated Report of La Societe Francaise d'Ophtalmologie. A. Franceschetti et al. (Illus.). 1496p. 1974. 243.75x o.p. (ISBN 0-398-02705-6). C C Thomas.

Chosen. Chaim Potok. 1985. pap. 3.95 o.p. (ISBN 0-449-20962-8, Crest). Fawcett.

Chosen for Children. 3rd ed. Marcus Crouch & Alec Ellis. 1977. 14.50x o.p. (ISBN 0-85365-349-6, Pub by the Library Assn). Nichols Pub.

Chosen Instrument: The Triumph & Tragedy of Pan Am & Its Founder, Juan Trippe. Marylin Bender & Selig Altshul. 544p. 1982. 19.25 o.p. (ISBN 0-671-22464-6). S&S.

Chosen to Serve: The Deacon. Andrew A. Jumper. LC 61-18257. (Orig.). 1961. pap. 3.95 o.p. (ISBN 0-8042-3912-6, John Knox). Westminster John Knox.

Chosen Vessel: The Story of the Very Reverend Harold G. Plume. Elizabeth Kitzman. (Illus.). 208p. 1985. 12.50 o.s.i. (ISBN 0-682-40190-0). Exposition-Phoenix.

Chosen Vessels: Portraits of Ten Outstanding Christian Men. Harry Blamires et al. Ed. by Charles Turner. 224p. (Orig.). 1985. pap. 10.95 o.p. (ISBN 0-89283-226-6, Pub. by Vine Books). Servant.

Choses et Autres. Jacques Prevert. 304p. 1972. 19.95 o.p. (ISBN 0-686-54901-5). Schoenhof.

Chouans. Honore De Balzac. Ed. by Regard. (Class Garnier). pap. 9.95 o.p. (ISBN 0-685-34073-2). Schoenhof.

Chouans. Honore De Balzac. Ed. by Regard. (Coll. Prestige). 27.95 o.p. (ISBN 0-685-34074-0). Schoenhof.

Chrissie, My Own Story. Chris Evert-Lloyd & Neil Amdur. (Illus.). 240p. 1984. pap. 7.75 o.p. (ISBN 0-671-50847-4, Fireside). S&S.

Christ. Maximilian Beyer. (ISBN 0-8022-0123-7). Philos Lib.

Christ. Charles Guignebert. 1966. 10.00 o.p. (ISBN 0-8216-0030-3, Pub. by Univ Bks). Carol Pub Group.

Christ--Present & Coming. Rudolf Schnackenburg. Tr. by Edward Quinn from Ger. LC 77-15246. 80p. 1978. pap. 0.50 o.p. (ISBN 0-8006-1328-7, Fortress). Augsburg Fortress.

Christ & Human Life. Friedrich W. Foerster. 1953. (ISBN 0-8022-0517-8). Philos Lib.

Christ & Humanity. Ed. by Ivar Asheim. LC 73-101426. (Orig.). 1970. pap. 1.00 o.p. (ISBN 0-8006-0186-6, Fortress). Augsburg Fortress.

Christ & Oriental Ideals. 4th ed. Swami Paramananda. 1968. pap. 3.50 o.s.i. (ISBN 0-911564-14-4). Vedanta Ctr.

Christ & Power. Martin Hengel. Tr. by Everett R. Kalin from Ger. LC 76-62608. 96p. (Orig.). 1977. pap. 1.50 o.p. (ISBN 0-8006-1256-6, 1-1256, Fortress). Augsburg Fortress.

Christ & the Judgment of God: Divine Retribution in the New Testament. Stephen H. Travis. 214p. (Orig.). 1987. pap. 10.95 o.p. (ISBN 0-310-55041-6, 19004P). Zondervan.

Christ & the Patriarchs: New Light from Apocryphal Literature & Tradition. Marcus Von Wellnitz. LC 80-83035. 400p. 1980. 9.95 o.p. (ISBN 0-88290-164-8, 2045). Horizon Utah.

Christ & Time: The Primitive Christian Conception of Time & History. rev. ed. Oscar Cullmann. LC 64-2336. 270p. 1964. 11.95 o.s.i. (ISBN 0-664-20488-0, Westminster). Westminster John Knox.

Christ Did Not Perish on the Cross: Christ's Body Buried Alive. Kurt Berna. (Illus.). 1975. 14.50 o.p. (ISBN 0-682-48139-4). Exposition-Phoenix.

Christ in a Pluralistic Age. John B. Cobb, Jr. LC 74-820. 286p. 1975. 12.50 o.s.i. (ISBN 0-664-20861-4, Westminster). Westminster John Knox.

Christ in Context: Divine Purpose & Human Possibility. Eugene TeSelle. LC 74-80426. 192p. 1975. 10.95 o.p. (ISBN 0-8006-0282-X, Fortress). Augsburg Fortress.

Christ in Eclipse: A Clinical Study of the Good Christian. Frank J. Sheed. 158p. 8.95 o.p. (LL9026). Sheed & Ward MO.

Christ in the Light of the Christian-Jewish Dialogue. John T. Pawlikowski. LC 81-83186. (Stimulus Bks.). 208p. (Orig.). 1982. pap. 7.95 o.p. (ISBN 0-8091-2416-5). Paulist Pr.

Christ in You. Carol Eisele. (Aglow Bible Study Basic Ser.: Bk. 10). 64p. 1977. 2.95 o.p. (ISBN 0-930756-22-3, 521010). Aglow Pubns.

Christ Lore: Being the Legends, Traditions, Myths, Symbols, Customs, & Superstitions of the Christian Church. Frederick W. Hackwood. LC 69-16064. (Illus.). 310p. 1971. Repr. of 1902 ed. 34.00x o.p. (ISBN 0-8103-3528-X). Gale.

Christ Nobody Knows: A Sentimental Vision of His Life. Gaspare Pignatelli. (Illus.). 121p. 1987. 117.50 o.p. (ISBN 0-89266-576-9). Am Classical Coll Pr.

Christ of Faith & the Jesus of History: A Critique of Schleiermacher's The Life of Jesus. David F. Strauss. Tr. & intro. by Leander E. Keck. LC 75-37152. (Lives of Jesus Ser.). 288p. 1976. pap. 3.50 o.p. (ISBN 0-8006-1273-6, 1-1273, Fortress). Augsburg Fortress.

Christ of the Antichrist? Orval Smart. 1975. 5.50 o.p. (ISBN 0-682-48369-9). Exposition-Phoenix.

Christ of Vatican Two. Daughters Of St. Paul. (St. Paul Editions). (Illus.). 1968. 2.00 o.p. (ISBN 0-8198-0024-4); pap. 1.00 o.p. (ISBN 0-8198-0025-2). Dghtrs St Paul.

Christ Proclaimed: Christology As Rhetoric. Frans J. Van Beeck. LC 79-66459. 632p. 1979. pap. 9.95 o.p. (ISBN 0-8091-2208-1). Paulist Pr.

Christ the Answer. Peter Sullivan. 272p. 1988. pap. 1.95 o.p. (ISBN 0-317-67487-0, RA0050). Dghtrs St Paul.

Christ: The Fullness of the Godhead, a Study in New Testament Christology. James Gunn. 256p. 1983. pap. 5.50 o.p. (ISBN 0-87213-283-8). Loizeaux.

Christ the Lord: A Study in the Purpose & Theology of Luke-Acts. Eric Franklin. LC 75-28162. 254p. 1976. 10.00 o.s.i. (ISBN 0-664-20809-6, Westminster). Westminster John Knox.

Christ Was an Ad Man: The Amazing New Testament in Advertising. Robert C. Pritikin. (Illus.). 184p. 1980. 10.95 o.p. (ISBN 0-936602-00-7). Kampmann.

Christanus Campoliliensis. Christian Von Lilienfeld. Ed. by G. M. Dreves. 1903. 60.00 o.p. (ISBN 0-384-08940-2). Johnson Repr.

Christbaumschmuck. Eva Stille & Ursula Pfistermeister. (Illus.). 206p. (Ger.). 1983. 19.95 o.s.i. (ISBN 3-418-00456-3, Pub. by Hans Carl Nurnberg W. Germany). Seven Hills Bk Dists.

Christendom. Einar Molland. 424p. 1959. (ISBN 0-8022-1134-8). Philos Lib.

Christendom Divided: The Protestant Reformation. Hans J. Hillerbrand. LC 70-93573. (Theological Resources Ser). 358p. 1971. 9.95 o.s.i. (ISBN 0-664-20912-2, Westminster). Westminster John Knox.

Christgau's Record Guide: Rock Albums of the Seventies. Robert Christgau. LC 81-1977. 480p. 1981. 17.95 o.p. (ISBN 0-89919-025-1); pap. 9.95 o.p. (ISBN 0-89919-026-X). Ticknor & Fields.

Christiaan Barnard's Program for Living with Arthritis. Christiaan Barnard & Peter Evans. (Illus.). 160p. 1984. pap. 9.70 o.p. (ISBN 0-671-47052-3, Fireside). S&S.

Christiad: Latin-English Edition. Marco G. Vida. Ed. by Gertrude C. Drake & Clarence A. Forbes. LC 78-1430. 288p. 1978. 9.85x o.p. (ISBN 0-8093-0814-2). S Ill U Pr.

Christian. Robert Hicks & Richard Bewes. (Understanding Bible Truth Ser.). (Orig.). 1981. pap. 0.95 o.p. (ISBN 0-89840-023-6). Heres Life.

Christian Adulthood 1982. Ed. by Neil A. Parent. 130p. 1982. pap. 5.95 o.p. (ISBN 1-55586-827-4). US Catholic.

Christian & Capital Punishment. John H. Yoder. 24p. 1961. pap. 0.60 o.p. (ISBN 0-87303-113-X). Faith & Life.

Christian & World Affairs. Isabel Rogers. (Orig.). (gr. 11-12). 1964. pap. 1.25 o.p. (ISBN 0-8042-9315-5, John Knox). Westminster John Knox.

Christian Anthropology & Ethics. James M. Childs, Jr. LC 77-78626. 192p. 1978. pap. 3.00 o.p. (ISBN 0-8006-1316-3, 1-1316, Fortress). Augsburg Fortress.

Christian Apologetics. Norman L. Geisler. LC 76-24706. 464p. 1976. 15.95 o.p. (ISBN 0-8010-3704-2). Baker Bk.

Christian Approach to Economics & the Cultural Condition. Douglas Vickers. 1982. 12.50 o.p. (ISBN 0-682-49831-9, University). Exposition-Phoenix.

Christian Approaches to Learning Theory: A Symposium; Major Papers Delivered at the First Annual Conference at Trinity Christian College, November 11-12, 1983. Norman DeJong. 234p. 1985. 26.25 o.p. (ISBN 0-8191-4319-7, Pub. by Trinity Christ Coll). U Pr of Amer.

Christian Approaches to Learning Theory: A Symposium; Major Papers Delivered at the First Annual Conference at Trinity Christian College, November 11-12, 1983. Norman De Jong. 234p. (Orig.). 1985. pap. 13.00 o.p. (ISBN 0-8191-4320-0, Pub. by Trinity Christ Coll). U Pr of Amer.

Christian Approaches to Learning Theory: The Nature of the Learner - Major Papers Delivered at the Second Annual Conference, Trinity Christian College, Palos Heights, Illinois, Nov. 2-3, 1984, Vol. II. Ed. by Norman DeJong. 174p. (Orig.). 1986. lib. bdg. 26.25 o.p. (ISBN 0-8191-5004-5, Pub. by Trinity Christ Coll); pap. text ed. 12.50 o.p. (ISBN 0-8191-5005-3). U Pr of Amer.

Christian Art. Charles R. Morey. (Illus.). 1958. pap. 3.95 o.p. (ISBN 0-393-00103-2, Norton Lib). Norton.

Christian Art in Ancient Ireland, 2 vols. in 1. Adolph R. Mahr. LC 75-11058. 1977. Repr. of 1932 ed. lib. bdg. 50.00 o.p. (ISBN 0-87817-173-8). Hacker.

Christian Art in Asia. W. A. Dyrness. 1979. pap. text ed. 11.50x o.p. (ISBN 0-391-01157-X). Humanities.

Christian Asceticism. Tr. by Walter Mitchell. 1955. (ISBN 0-8022-1126-7). Philos Lib.

Christian Beliefs & Teachings. John C. Meyer. LC 81-40353. 116p. (Orig.). 1981. lib. bdg. 24.75 o.p. (ISBN 0-8191-1757-9); pap. text ed. 10.00 o.p. (ISBN 0-8191-1758-7). U Pr of Amer.

Christian Believing. Robert E. Terwilliger. 128p. (Orig.). 1973. pap. 2.95 o.p. (ISBN 0-8192-1142-7). Morehouse Pub.

Christian Burial: A Case of Murder & the Perversion of Justice. Frank Carrington & Joseph L. Lyle, Jr. 1988. 17.95 o.p. (ISBN 0-89526-565-6). Regnery Gateway.

Christian Care & Counseling: A Practical Guide. Roger F. Hurding. (Illus.). 128p. (Orig.). 1983. pap. 4.95 o.p. (ISBN 0-8192-1321-7). Morehouse Pub.

Christian Celebration of Marriage. 32p. 1987. pap. 3.25 o.p. (ISBN 0-8006-1973-0, 1-1973). Augsburg Fortress.

Christian Church: Biblical Origin, Historical Transformation, & Potential for the Future. Hans Schwarz. LC 81-52286. 368p. 1982. 21.95 o.p. (ISBN 0-8066-1918-X, 10-1105, Augsburg). Augsburg Fortress.

Christian Churches in the United States, 1800-1983. Martin E. Marty. (Illus.). 126p. 1984. 12.95 o.p. (ISBN 0-86683-172-X, 1412). HarpR.

Christian Churches of America. rev. ed. Milton V. Backman, Jr. 288p. 1984. 17.95 o.s.i. (ISBN 0-684-17992-X, P656, ScribT); pap. 12.95 o.s.i. (ISBN 0-684-17995-4). Scribner.

Christian Creeds. Monika Hellwig. 112p. 1973. pap. 1.95 o.p. (ISBN 0-8278-9057-5, Pub. by Pflaum Pr). Pflaum Pr.

Christian Decision in the Nuclear Age. T. R. Milford. Ed. by Franklin Sherman. (Facet Bks). 64p. (Orig.). 1967. pap. 1.00 o.p. (ISBN 0-8006-3038-6, 1-3038, Fortress). Augsburg Fortress.

Christian Deviations. Horton Davies. (Illus.). 130p. 1954. (ISBN 0-8022-0351-5). Philos Lib.

Christian Deviations: The Challenge of the New Spiritual Movements. 3rd, rev. ed. Horton Davies. 1973. pap. 2.75 o.s.i. (ISBN 0-664-24966-3, Westminster). Westminster John Knox.

Christian Devotedness. Norris A. Groves. pap. 1.95 o.p. (ISBN 0-937396-63-X). Walterick Pubs.

Christian Dilemma. W. H. Van de Pol. 1952. (ISBN 0-8022-1761-3). Philos Lib.

Christian Doctrine. John M. Shaw. 390p. 1955. (ISBN 0-8022-1545-9). Philos Lib.

Christian Education in a Secular Society. Ed. by Gustav K. Wiencke. (Yearbooks in Christian Education Two). 1970. pap. 4.95 o.p. (ISBN 0-8006-1043-1, 1-1043, Fortress). Augsburg Fortress.

Christian Education Public Schools: A Teacher's Interpretation. Elizabeth M. Machen. 1978. 5.00 o.p. (ISBN 0-682-48990-5). Exposition-Phoenix.

Christian Entrepreneur. Carl Kreider. LC 80-16836. (Conrad Grebel Lectures Ser.). 214p. 1980. pap. 8.95 o.p. (ISBN 0-8361-1936-3). Herald Pr.

Christian Ethics for Today: An Evangelical Approach. Milton L. Rudnick. LC 79-53924. 1979. pap. 8.95 o.p. (ISBN 0-8010-7738-9). Baker Bk.

Christian Ethics in Secular Society: An Introduction to Christian Ethics. Philip E. Hughes. 240p. 1983. 13.95 o.p. (ISBN 0-8010-4267-4). Baker Bk.

Christian Evolution. Ursula Burton & Janice Dolley. 160p. 1984. pap. 9.95 o.p. (ISBN 0-85500-204-2). Newcastle Pub.

Christian Faith. Henri De Lubac. 1986. pap. 12.95 o.p. (ISBN 0-317-52368-6). HarpR.

Christian Faith. Friedrich Schleiermacher. Ed. by H. R. Mackintosh & J. S. Stewart. LC 76-53313. 772p. 1977. 16.50 o.p. (ISBN 0-8006-0487-3, 1-487, Fortress). Augsburg Fortress.

Christian Faith & Public Choices: The Social Ethics of Barth, Brunner, & Bonhoeffer. Robin W. Lovin. LC 83-48922. 192p. 1984. pap. 1.95 o.p. (ISBN 0-8006-1777-0, 1-1777, Fortress). Augsburg Fortress.

Christian Faith & Public Policy: Thinking & Acting in the Courage of Uncertainty. Richard J. Neuhaus. LC 76-27086. 1977. pap. 8.95 o.p. (ISBN 0-8066-1554-0, 10-1110, Augsburg). Augsburg Fortress.

Christian Faith & the Scientific Attitude. W. A. Whitehouse. 1953. (ISBN 0-8022-1866-0). Philos Lib.

Christian Family Activities for Families with Children. Wayne Rickerson. LC 82-10385. (Illus.). 96p. (Orig.). 1982. pap. 4.95 o.p. (ISBN 0-87239-569-3, 2964). Standard Pub.

Christian Family Activities for Families with Preschoolers. Wayne Rickerson. LC 82-5583. (Illus.). 96p. (Orig.). 1982. pap. 4.95 o.p. (ISBN 0-87239-568-5, 2963). Standard Pub.

Christian Family Activities for Families with Teens. Wayne Rickerson. LC 82-5833. (Illus.). 96p. (Orig.). 1982. pap. 4.95 o.p. (ISBN 0-87239-570-7, 2965). Standard Pub.

Christian Freedom in a Permissive Society. John A. Robinson. LC 75-110149. 256p. 1970. pap. 2.95 o.s.i. (ISBN 0-664-24887-X, Westminster). Westminster John Knox.

Christian Handbook for Defending the Faith. Robert Morey. 1979. pap. 2.75 o.p. (ISBN 0-87552-336-6). Presby & Reformed.

Christian Humanism: A Guide to the Thought of Jacques Maritain. E. L. Allen. Philos Lib.

Christian Humanism & the Reformation: Selected Writings with the Life of Erasmus by Beatus Rhenanus. Erasmus. Ed. by John C. Olin. 11.25 o.p. (ISBN 0-8446-2035-1). Peter Smith.

Christian Imagination: Essays on Literature & the Arts. Ed. by Leland Ryken. LC 80-70154. 344p. (Orig.). 1981. pap. 13.95 o.p. (ISBN 0-8010-7702-8). Baker Bk.

Christian in Today's World: Inner City to World Community. Lewis Smythe. 1974. 6.50 o.p. (ISBN 0-682-48055-X). Exposition-Phoenix.

Christian in Wartime. Frederick H. Lynch. LC 71-147674. (Library of War & Peace; Relig. & Ethical Positions on War). 1972. lib. bdg. 46.00 o.p. (ISBN 0-8240-0431-0). Garland Pub.

Christian Inscriptions. H. V. Nunn. 72p. 1952. (ISBN 0-8022-1235-2). Philos Lib.

Christian Interpretations of the Civil War. William A. Clebsch. Ed. by Richard C. Wolf. LC 76-84556. (Facet Bks.). (Orig.). 1969. pap. 1.00 o.p. (ISBN 0-8006-3054-8, 1-3054, Fortress). Augsburg Fortress.

Christian-Jewish Dialogue: Theological Foundations. Peter Von Der Osten-Sacken. Tr. by Margaret Kohl from Ger. LC 85-45481. 240p. 1986. 24.95 o.p. (ISBN 0-8006-0771-6, 1-771, Fortress). Augsburg Fortress.

Christian Life. Waldo Beach. (Orig.). 1967. pap. 4.95 o.p. (ISBN 0-8042-9070-9, John Knox). Westminster John Knox.

Christian Life Patterns: The Psychological Challenges & Religious Invitations of Adult Life. Evelyn E. Whitehead & James D. Whitehead. LC 81-43442. 288p. 1982. 9.95 o.p. (ISBN 0-385-15130-6). Doubleday.

Christian Lifestyle: Reflections on Romans 12-15. George W. Forell. LC 75-13033. 96p. (Orig.). 1975. pap. 1.00 o.p. (ISBN 0-8006-1200-0, 1-1200, Fortress). Augsburg Fortress.

Christian Look at Secular Society. Gerald H. Slusser. pap. 2.50 o.s.i. (ISBN 0-664-24282-0, Westminster). Westminster John Knox.

Christian-Marxist Dialogue in Eastern Europe. Paul Mojzes. LC 81-76769. 320p. (Orig.). 1981. pap. 16.95 o.p. (ISBN 0-8066-1895-7, 10-1171, Augsburg). Augsburg Fortress.

Christian Maturity & Christian Success. Daniel Jenkins. LC 82-9759. (Laity Exchange Ser.). 144p. 1982. pap. 5.95 o.p. (ISBN 0-8006-1657-X, 1-1657, Fortress). Augsburg Fortress.

Christian Method of Moral Judgment. J. Philip Wogaman. LC 76-40108. 282p. 1977. 12.50 o.s.i. (ISBN 0-664-20763-4, Westminster); pap. 8.95 o.s.i. (ISBN 0-664-24134-4, Westminster). Westminster John Knox.

Christian Mission: The Stewardship of Life in the Kingdom of Death. Douglas John Hall. 1985. 8.95 o.p. (ISBN 0-377-00156-2). Friendship Pr.
Christian Missionary Enterprise in the Niger Delta, 1864-1918. G. O. Tasie. (Studies on Religion in Africa Ser.: No. 3). (Illus.). 1978. text ed. 49.95 o.p. (ISBN 90-04-05243-7). Humanities.
Christian Morality: Biblical Foundations. Raymond F. Collins. LC 85-41020. 256p. 1987. 22.95 o.p. (ISBN 0-268-00758-6). U of Notre Dame Pr.
Christian Mortalism from Tyndale to Milton. Norman T. Burns. LC 72-75406. 224p. 1972. 17.50x o.s.i. (ISBN 0-674-12875-3). Harvard U Pr.
Christian Music in Contemporary Witness: Historical Antecedents & Contemporary Practices. Donald P. Ellsworth. LC 79-52359. 1980. 7.95 o.p. (ISBN 0-8010-3338-1). Baker Bk.
Christian Natural Theology: Based on the Thought of Alfred North Whitehead. John B. Cobb, Jr. LC 65-11612. 1978. softcover 5.95 o.s.i. (ISBN 0-664-24228-6, Westminster); 6.95 o.s.i. (ISBN 0-664-20604-2, Westminster). Westminster John Knox.
Christian Parent Burnout. Edith Lanstrom. LC 12-2979. (Continued Applied Christianity Ser.). 1983. pap. 1.33 o.p. (ISBN 0-570-03897-9). Concordia.
Christian Parenthood. Helen H. Sherrill. (Orig.). 1964. pap. 3.50 o.p. (ISBN 0-8042-9616-2, John Knox). Westminster John Knox.
Christian Pastor. 3rd rev. ed. Wayne E. Oates. LC 63-18553. 1981. pap. 6.95 o.s.i. (ISBN 0-664-24334-7, Westminster). Westminster John Knox.
Christian Planning Calendar. Incl. Sixteen Months Sept-Dec. pap. 3.50 ea. o.p. Morehouse Pub.
Christian Poet in Paradise Lost. William G. Riggs. 1972. 30.00x o.p. (ISBN 0-520-02081-2). U of Cal Pr.
Christian Psychology. Hani R. Abdu. 288p. 1981. 11.00 o.p. (ISBN 0-682-49643-X). Exposition-Phoenix.
Christian Response to the Asian Revolution. M. M. Thomas. 1968. pap. 1.75 o.p. (ISBN 0-377-82701-0). Friendship Pr.
Christian Satisfaction in Aquinas: Towards a Personalist Understanding. Romanus Cessario. LC 81-43836. 390p. (Orig.). 1982. lib. bdg. 33.75 o.p. (ISBN 0-8191-2557-1); pap. text ed. 16.75 o.p. (ISBN 0-8191-2558-X). U Pr of Amer.
Christian Science & Philosophy. H. W. Steiger. (ISBN 0-8022-1637-4). Philos Lib.
Christian Science Today: Power, Policy, Practice. Charles S. Braden. LC 58-11399. (Illus.). 456p. 1969. Repr. of 1958 ed. 19.95x o.p. (ISBN 0-87074-024-5). SMU Press.
Christian Socialism: Moses to Gutierrez. John C. Cort. 26.95 o.p. (ISBN 0-88344-574-3); pap. 13.95 o.p. (ISBN 0-88344-573-5). Orbis Bks.
Christian Sourcebook. Carol Ward. 1986. 14.45 o.s.i. (ISBN 0-345-32248-7, Pub. by Ballantine Epiphany). Ballantine.
Christian Spirituality: A Theological History from the New Testament to Luther & St. John of the Cross. Rowan Williams. LC 80-82190. 193p. 1980. 10.95 o.p. (ISBN 0-8042-0660-0, John Knox); pap. 8.95 o.p. (ISBN 0-8042-0508-6). Westminster John Knox.
Christian Symbols & How to Use Them. Sr. Justina Knapp. LC 74-8172. (Illus.). 176p. 1975. Repr. of 1935 ed. 43.00x o.p. (ISBN 0-8103-4050-X). Gale.
Christian Teaching of Kindergarten Children. Dorothy B. Fritz. (Illus., Orig.). 1964. pap. 2.49 o.p. (ISBN 0-8042-9503-4, John Knox). Westminster John Knox.
Christian Theistic Ethics. Cornelius Van Til. 1975. pap. 7.95 syllabus o.p. (ISBN 0-87552-478-8). Presby & Reformed.
Christian Theology in Plain Language. Bruce L. Shelley. 256p. 1985. 12.95 o.p. (ISBN 0-8499-0381-5, 0381-5). Word Bks.
Christian Theory of Knowledge. Cornelius Van Til. LC 76-76781. 1969. pap. 10.95 o.p. (ISBN 0-87552-480-X). Presby & Reformed.
Christian Tolerance: Paul's Message to the Modern Church. Robert Jewett. LC 82-13480. (Biblical Perspectives on Current Issues Ser.). 168p. 1982. pap. 9.95 o.s.i. (ISBN 0-664-24444-0, Westminster). Westminster John Knox.
Christian Tradition. World Religions Development Center. (Illus.). 192p. 1978. pap. 8.95 o.p. (ISBN 0-89505-013-7). Tabor Pub.
Christian Tradition, Guide. World Religions Development Center. 84p. 1978. pap. 3.75 o.p. (ISBN 0-89505-012-9). Tabor Pub.
Christian Tragic Hero in French & English Literature. G. R. Ridge & B. C. Njoku. 170p. 1983. text ed. 17.50x o.p. (ISBN 0-391-02858-8). Humanities.
Christian Understanding of Atonement. Frederick W. Dillistone. 1968. 7.95 o.s.i. (ISBN 0-664-20827-4, Westminster). Westminster John Knox.
Christian Understanding of the Human Person: Basic Readings. Eugene Lauer & Joel Mlecko. LC 81-8434. 160p. (Orig.). 1982. pap. 7.95 o.p. (ISBN 0-8091-2433-5). Paulist Pr.
Christian Unity & Christian Diversity. John Macquarrie. LC 75-9674. 128p. 1975. softcover 2.85 o.s.i. (ISBN 0-664-24782-2, Westminster). Westminster John Knox.
Christian View of Abortion. J. Klotz. (Contemporary Theology Ser.). 1973. 1.50 o.p. (ISBN 0-570-06721-9, 12RT2560). Concordia.
Christian View of Economics. Marion Loring. 80p. 1983. 5.50 o.p. (ISBN 0-682-49903-X). Exposition-Phoenix.
Christian Vogt: In Camera. Christian Vogt. (Master Collection from Roto-Vision Ser.). (Illus.). 1982. 12.98 o.p. (ISBN 0-393-01933-0). Norton.
Christian Von Schneidau: 1893-1976. Janet B. Dominik. Ed. by Jean Stern. LC 86-60248. (Illus.). 63p. 1986. lib. bdg. 25.00 o.p. (ISBN 0-8227-8046-1, Dist. by Deru's Fine Art). Petersen Pub.
Christian Way. Sydney Cave. (ISBN 0-8022-0225-X). Philos Lib.
Christian Way: A Book of Instructions & Devotions for Members of the Episcopal Church. Frank D. Gifford. (Orig.). pap. 3.25 o.p. (ISBN 0-8192-1033-1). Morehouse Pub.
Christian Wholeness. Thomas A. Langford. LC 78-58011. 1979. pap. 3.50x o.p. (ISBN 0-8358-0383-X). Upper Room.
Christian Wives: Women Behind the Evangelists. James Schaffer & Colleen Todd. LC 87-5291. (Illus.). 168p. 1987. pap. 12.95 o.p. (ISBN 0-385-23581-X, Dolp). Doubleday.
Christian Woman's Planner. Darien B. Cooper. 160p. (Orig.). 1986. pap. 9.95 spiral bdg. o.p. (ISBN 0-310-44621-X, 11742P). Zondervan.
Christian Worker's Manual. Herbert S. Miller. pap. 4.95 o.p. (ISBN 0-87509-065-6). Chr Pubns.
Christian Worship & Its Cultural Setting. Frank C. Senn. LC 82-48587. 160p. 1983. pap. 1.95 o.p. (ISBN 0-8006-1700-2, 1-1700, Fortress). Augsburg Fortress.
Christian Year; Its Purpose & Its History. Walker Gwynne. LC 74-89269. xiv, 306p. 1972. Repr. of 1917 ed. 43.00x o.p. (ISBN 0-8103-3814-9). Gale.
Christianity According to John. D. George Vanderlip. LC 74-34585. 224p. 1975. 10.00 o.s.i. (ISBN 0-664-20737-5, Westminster). Westminster John Knox.
Christianity: An Introduction. Denise L. Carmody & John T. Carmody. 273p. 1983. pap. text ed. (ISBN 0-534-01181-0). Wadsworth Pub.
Christianity: An Introduction. 2nd ed. Denise L. Carmody & John T. Carmody. 252p. 1989. pap. text ed. write for info. o.p. (ISBN 0-534-09474-0). Wadsworth Pub.
Christianity & Anti-Semitism. Nicholas Berdyaev. 64p. 1954. (ISBN 0-8022-0101-6). Philos Lib.
Christianity & Evolution. Pierre Teilhard De Chardin. Tr. by Rene Hague. LC 78-162798. (Helen & Kurt Wolff Bk.). 255p. 1971. 5.95 o.p. (ISBN 0-15-117850-X). HarBraceJ.
Christianity & Real Life. William E. Diehl. LC 76-7860. 128p. 1976. pap. 1.00 o.p. (ISBN 0-8006-1231-0, 1-1231, Fortress). Augsburg Fortress.
Christianity & Society: A Guide to the Thoufht of Reinhold Hiebuhr. E. L. Allen. 1951. Philos Lib.
Christianity & the Narrow Way. Roy C. Jarnagin. 128p. 1982. 7.50 o.p. (ISBN 0-682-49832-7). Exposition-Phoenix.
Christianity, Democracy, & Technology. Zoltan Sztankay. 192p. 1957. (ISBN 0-8022-1683-8). Philos Lib.
Christianity in Conflict: The Struggle for Christian Integrity & Freedom in Secular Culture. Charles Colson et al. Ed. by Peter S. Williamson & Kevin Perrotta. 180p. (Orig.). 1986. pap. 7.95 o.p. (ISBN 0-89283-292-4). Servant.
Christianity in Modern Africa see Tarikh.
Christianity in the People's Republic of China. G. Thompson Brown. LC 82-49018. 240p. 1983. pap. 7.25 o.s.i. (ISBN 0-8042-1484-0, John Knox). Westminster John Knox.
Christianity in the Twentieth Century. John A. Hardon. 1978. 5.95 o.s.i. (ISBN 0-8198-0356-1); pap. 2.95 o.s.i. (ISBN 0-8198-0357-X). Dghtrs St Paul.
Christianity in Tropical Africa: A Selective Annotated Bibliography. Patrick E. Ofori. 461p. 1977. lib. bdg. 48.00 o.p. (ISBN 3-262-00002-7). Kraus Intl.
Christianity Made Simple: Belief, Vol. 1. David Hewetson & David Miller. LC 83-10866. 160p. 1983. pap. 5.95 o.p. (ISBN 0-87784-811-4). Inter-Varsity.
Christianity of Sholem Asch. Chaim Lieberman. 276p. 1953. (ISBN 0-8022-0972-6). Philos Lib.
Christianity Within. Toni Wolff. 1985. 10.00x o.p. (ISBN 0-317-62012-6, Guild of Pastoral Psych). State Mutual Bk.
Christians Alive. Ed. by Cliff Pederson. LC 73-78259. 1973. 4.95 o.p. (ISBN 0-8066-1324-6, 10-1190, Augsburg). Augsburg Fortress.
Christians Alive: Leader's Guide. Cliff Pederson. 1974. pap. 0.50 o.p. (ISBN 0-8066-1417-X, 10-1191, Augsburg). Augsburg Fortress.
Christians & the Many Faces of Marxism. Wayne Stumme. LC 84-10980. 160p. (Orig.). 1984. pap. 10.95 o.p. (ISBN 0-8066-2087-0, 10-1195, Augsburg). Augsburg Fortress.
Christians & the Military: The Early Experience. John Helgeland & Robert J. Daly. Ed. by J. Patout Burns. LC 84-48718. 112p. 1985. pap. 5.95 o.p. (ISBN 0-8006-1836-X, 1-1836, Fortress). Augsburg Fortress.
Christian's Appreciation of Other Faiths. Gilbert Reid. 305p. 1921. 22.95 o.p. (ISBN 0-87548-219-8). Open Court.
Christians, Awake! see How to Witness to a Jehovah's Witness.
Christian's Calling. rev. ed. Donald R. Heiges. LC 84-47923. 112p. 1984. pap. 1.95 o.p. (ISBN 0-8006-1795-9, Fortress). Augsburg Fortress.
Christian's Guide to Pregnancy & Childbirth: Choosing the Best for You & Your Child, from Conception to Delivery. John J. Davis. LC 86-70280. (Orig.). 1986. pap. 7.95 o.p. (ISBN 0-89107-391-4, Crossway Bks). Good News.
Christians in Pain: Perspectives on Suffering. B. W. Woods. 176p. 1982. pap. 4.95 o.p. (ISBN 0-8010-9652-9). Baker Bk.
Christians in the Arab East. Robert B. Betts. LC 78-8674. 1981. 12.50 o.s.i. (ISBN 0-8042-0796-8, John Knox). Westminster John Knox.
Christian's Secret of a Happy Life: Proven Word. Hannah Whitall & Elisabeth E. Smith. 192p. 1985. pap. 5.95 o.p. (ISBN 0-8499-2980-6, 2980-6). Word Bks.
Christians with Secular Power. M. Gibbs. LC 80-8048. (Laity Exchange). 144p. (Orig.). 1981. pap. 2.95 o.p. (ISBN 0-8006-1389-9, 1-1389, Fortress). Augsburg Fortress.
Christie Brinkley's Outdoor Fitness & Beauty Book. Christie Brinkley. 1983. 16.50 o.p. (ISBN 0-671-46190-7). S&S.
Christie's Review of the Season, 1986. 63.00 o.p. (ISBN 0-317-57526-0). Editions Pub.
Christina Rossetti: A Reference Guide. R. W. Crump. (General Ser.). 1976. lib. bdg. 24.00 o.p. (ISBN 0-8161-7847-X, Hall Reference). G K Hall.
Christina's World. Twyla Lubben & Linda L. Hunt. 160p. (Orig.). 1985. pap. 3.95 o.p. (ISBN 0-310-36921-5, 11650P). Zondervan.
Christina's World & Wyeth at Kuerners, 2. Andrew Wyeth & Betsy J. Wyeth. 288p. 1982. Limited ed. 599.00 o.s.i. (ISBN 0-395-32940-X). HM.
Christina's World: Paintings & Prestudies of Andrew Wyeth. Betsy J. Wyeth. 1982. 89.00 o.p. (ISBN 0-395-32221-9). HM.
Christine's Picture Book. Hans Christian Andersen & Grandfather Drewsen. Tr. by Brian Alderson. LC 85-5453. (Illus.). 272p. 1985. 35.00 o.p. (ISBN 0-03-005729-9). H Holt & Co.
Christmas: A Joyful Heritage. Susan A. Madsen. LC 84-72519. (Illus.). 128p. 1984. 6.95 o.p. (ISBN 0-87747-681-0). Deseret Bk.
Christmas & Holiday Cooking. Carol DeMasters. (Illus.). 80p. (Orig.). 1985. pap. 4.95 o.p. (ISBN 0-8249-3051-7). Ideals.
Christmas Angel. Sable Saxon. (Illus.). 51p. (gr. 3-5). 1985. 4.95 o.p. (ISBN 0-533-06135-0). Vantage.
Christmas Angels. Phyllis Meras & Julianna Turkevich. 1979. 12.95 o.p. (ISBN 0-395-27601-2); pap. 6.95 o.p. (ISBN 0-395-28426-0). HM.
Christmas Blessings. 16p. 1984. pap. 1.25 o.p. (ISBN 0-89542-820-2). Ideals.
Christmas Book. Moira Eastman & Wendy Poussard. LC 80-68368. (Illus.). 40p. (gr. k-6). 1980. 5.95 o.p. (ISBN 0-87793-214-X). Ave Maria.
Christmas by Mail: A Series of Letters. Helen Casavant. (Illus.). 27p. (gr. 1-3). 1985. 4.95 o.p. (ISBN 0-533-06324-8). Vantage.
Christmas Carol. Charles Dickens. 240p. 1981. pap. 2.95 o.s.i. (ISBN 0-671-44199-X). WSP.
Christmas Carol Christmas Book. Charles Dickens. 16.95 o.p. (ISBN 0-316-41446-8). Little.
Christmas Carol Sampler. Margaret Cusack. (Illus.). (gr. 4-6). 1983. 10.95 o.p. (ISBN 0-15-217752-3, HJ). HarBraceJ.
Christmas Coat. Ron Jones. LC 79-2605. (Illus.). 1979. pap. 4.00 o.p. (ISBN 0-933280-05-X). Island CA.
Christmas Comes to Blueberry Corners: And Other Christmas Stories for Children. Lois Lenski et al. LC 75-2837. (Illus.). 32p. (ps-4). 1975. 3.95 o.p. (ISBN 0-8066-1483-8, 10-1230, Augsburg). Augsburg Fortress.
Christmas Cookbook. Shona C. Poole. LC 79-63631. 259p. 1981. pap. 6.95 o.p. (ISBN 0-689-70606-5, 267, Atheneum); 1979 10.95, o.p. (ISBN 0-689-11008-1). Macmillan.
Christmas Cookie Tree. Ruth H. Irion. LC 75-26644. (Illus.). 1976. 6.95 o.s.i. (ISBN 0-664-32586-6, Westminster). Westminster John Knox.
Christmas Could-be Tales & Other Verses. M. Rorke. LC 84-61104. 106p. 1984. pap. 5.00 o.p. (ISBN 0-87359-042-2). Northwood Inst Pr.
Christmas Crafts & Customs Around the World. Virginie Fowler. LC 84-9770. (Illus.). 160p. (gr. 5 up). 1984. 11.95 o.s.i. (ISBN 0-13-133661-4). P-H.
Christmas Creatures. Joan Birmingham. 1985. 10.00 o.p. (ISBN 0-317-28883-0). Vantage.
Christmas Customs & Traditions. Frank Muir. LC 77-76504. (Illus.). 1977. 7.95 o.s.i. (ISBN 0-8008-1552-1). Taplinger.
Christmas Cycle. Frederick Kemper. 1982. 6.95 o.p. (ISBN 0-570-03842-1, 12-2945). Concordia.
Christmas Eve at Rancho los Alamitos. Katharine B. Hotchkis. (Illus.). 20p. pap. 1.75 o.p. (ISBN 0-910312-03-6). Calif Hist.
Christmas Fantasy. Carolyn Haywood. LC 71-184244. (Illus.). 32p. (gr. k-3). 1972. 11.75 o.p. (ISBN 0-688-20094-X); 11.88 o.p. (ISBN 0-688-30094-4). Morrow.
Christmas Feasts from History. Lorna J. Sass. Ed. by Jean Atcheson. LC 81-68835. (Great American Cooking Schools Ser.). (Illus.). 84p. 1981. pap. 5.95 o.p. (ISBN 0-941034-01-1). I Chalmers.
Christmas Foundation Meeting of the Anthroposophical Society. Rudolf Steiner. Ed. by R. G. Seddon. 37p. (Orig.). 1980. pap. 3.00 o.p. (ISBN 0-88010-094-X, Pub. by Steinerbooks). Anthroposophic.
Christmas Gifts From The Kitchen Cookbook. 64p. pap. 3.95 o.p. (ISBN 0-89542-635-8). Ideals.
Christmas Greeting. 16p. 1984. pap. 1.25 o.p. (ISBN 0-89542-819-9). Ideals.
Christmas Ideals. Ideals Staff. 1987. pap. 3.95 o.p. (ISBN 0-8249-1056-7). Ideals.
Christmas in All the World. LC 79-50087. (Illus.). 48p. (gr. 1-7). 1979. pap. 4.95 o.p. (ISBN 0-8066-1704-7, 10-1238, Augsburg). Augsburg Fortress.
Christmas in Denmark. Ed. by World Book, Inc. Staff. LC 86-50556. (Round the World Christmas Program Ser.). (Illus.). 80p. 1986. write for info. o.p. (ISBN 0-7166-0886-3). World Bk.
Christmas in Ireland. Ed. by World Book, Inc. Staff. LC 84-51015. (Round the World Christmas Program Ser.). (Illus.). 80p. 1985. write for info. o.p. (ISBN 0-7166-0885-5). World Bk.
Christmas in Las Vegas. Robert Watson. LC 76-162969. 1971. pap. 3.95 o.p. (ISBN 0-689-10469-3, Atheneum). Macmillan.
Christmas in Old New England. Irving Bell. LC 80-69858. 54p. (gr. 3-8). 1981. 8.95 o.p. (ISBN 0-917780-02-7). April Hill.
Christmas in Those Days. Mary Lou Ziegenfuss. Tr. by Durbin Feeling. (Illus.). 21p. (Eng. & Cherokee.). 1981. pap. write for info. o.p. (ISBN 0-940392-01-1). Indian U Pr OK.
Christmas in Washington, D. C. World Book Editors Staff. LC 88-50693. (Around the World Christmas Program Ser.). (Illus.). 80p. (YA) 1988. lib. bdg. (ISBN 0-7166-0888-X). World Bk.
Christmas in Williamsburg. rev. ed. Taylor B. Lewis, Jr. & Joanne B. Young. LC 76-11598. 1976. pap. 5.95 o.p. (ISBN 0-03-089945-1). H Holt & Co.
Christmas Is Here! (ISBN 0-394-87920-1). Random.
Christmas Lover's Handbook. Lasley F. Gober. LC 85-13450. (Illus.). 256p. 1985. pap. 12.95 o.p. (ISBN 0-932620-53-1). Betterway Pubns.
Christmas Owl. Glenn E. Henry. 48p. 1983. 5.00 o.p. (ISBN 0-682-49928-5). Exposition-Phoenix.
Christmas Plays. Barbara Westberg. Ed. by Mary H. Wallace. 40p. (Orig.). 1983. pap. 2.95 o.p. (ISBN 0-912315-62-8). Word Aflame.
Christmas Program Resource Book Two. 48p. 1984. pap. 2.95 o.p. (ISBN 0-8066-2075-7, 23-1501, Augsburg). Augsburg Fortress.
Christmas Programs for the Church, No. 16. Ed. by Judy Sparks. 64p. 1983. pap. 2.95 o.p. (ISBN 0-87239-614-2, 8616). Standard Pub.
Christmas Reflections. Mary B. Christian. (ps-k). 1980. pap. 1.50 o.p. (ISBN 0-570-03494-9, 56-1711). Concordia.
Christmas Sermons. Sterling W. Sill. LC 73-86165. 184p. 1973. 8.95 o.p. (ISBN 0-87747-503-2). Deseret Bk.
Christmas Spy. John Howlett. LC 75-20164. 192p. 1975. 6.95 o.p. (ISBN 0-15-117879-8). HarBraceJ.
Christmas Story. LC 76-47915. (Sunshine Bks.). (Illus.). 1977. pap. 1.00 o.p. (ISBN 0-8006-1579-4, 1-1579, Fortress). Augsburg Fortress.

Titles

Christmas Time. Gail Gibbons. (Illus.). 32p. (gr. k-3). 1985. pap. 5.95 o.p. (ISBN 0-8234-0575-3). Holiday.

Christmas Together-John Denver & the Muppets. 5.95 o.s.i. (ISBN 0-89524-073-4). Cherry Lane.

Christmas Treasury. LC 79-93352. (Illus.). 128p. 1980. 17.50 o.p. (ISBN 0-8066-1777-2, Augsburg). Augsburg Fortress.

Christmas Treasury: Featuring Twas the Night Before Christmas. Ed. by Jean L. Scrocco. (Illus.). 48p. 1984. 8.95 o.p. (ISBN 0-88101-013-8). Unicorn Pub.

Christmas Tree on the Mountain. Carol Fenner. LC 64-6753. (Illus.). (gr. k-3). 1966. 5.95 o.p. (ISBN 0-15-217880-5, HJ). HarBraceJ.

Christmas Truce (The Western Front December 1914) Malcolm Brown & Shirley Seaton. (Illus.). 228p. 1985. 22.50 o.p. (ISBN 0-87052-015-6). Hippocrene Bks.

Christmas Turkey or Prairie Vulture? David R. Harvey. (Illus.). 119p. 1980. pap. text ed. 10.95x o.p. (ISBN 0-920380-66-2, Pub. by Inst Res Pub Canada). Gower Pub Co.

Christmas Twin Pack. Clement Moore & Alice L. Mason. (Illus.). 48p. (ps-2). 1988. pap. 7.95 incl. cassette o.p. (ISBN 0-8249-7258-9). Ideals.

Christmas Window. Laurie F. Manifold. LC 72-155555. (Illus.). (gr. k-3). 1971. 3.95 o.p. (ISBN 0-395-12574-X); Dolphin bdg. 3.57 o.p. (ISBN 0-395-12575-8). HM.

Christmas with Little Women. Illus. by Russ Flint. (Illus.). 48p. (gr. k-5). 1986. 5.95 o.p. (ISBN 0-8249-8150-2). Ideals.

Christological Perspectives. Ed. by Robert F. Berkey & Sarah A. Edwards. 320p. 18.95 o.p. (ISBN 0-8298-0491-9); pap. 10.95 o.p. (ISBN 0-8298-0606-7). Pilgrim NY.

Christology & Myth in the New Testament. Geraint V. Jones. LC 56-4228. 1956. text ed. 6.00xo.p. (ISBN 0-8401-1265-3). A R Allenson.

Christology Beyond Dogma: Matthew's Christ in Process Hermeneutic. Russell Pregeant. Ed. by William A. Beardslee & Dan O. Via, Jr. LC 77-78638. (Semeia Studies). 180p. (Orig.). 1978. pap. 6.95 o.p. (ISBN 0-8006-1507-7, 1-1507, Fortress). Augsburg Fortress.

Christology of Mark's Gospel. Jack D. Kingsbury. LC 83-5576. 224p. 1983. 19.95 o.p. (ISBN 0-8006-0706-6, 1-706, Fortress). Augsburg Fortress.

Christology of the New Testament. rev. ed. Oscar Cullmann. 1964. 9.95 o.s.i. (ISBN 0-664-20564-X, Westminster). Westminster John Knox.

Christopher & His Kind. Christopher Isherwood. 1977. pap. 2.75 o.p. (ISBN 0-380-01795-4, 58685-1, Discus). Avon.

Christopher Brown: The Painted Room. Thomas H. Garver. (Illus.). 1985. 6.95 o.p. (ISBN 0-913883-13-1). Madison Art.

Christopher C. Cat see There's a Skunk in My Trunk.

Christopher Columbus. Gian P. Ceserani. LC 77-86146. (Illus.). (gr. k-3). 1979. 3.95 o.p. (ISBN 0-394-83907-2, BYR); lib. bdg. 4.99 o.p. (ISBN 0-394-93907-7). Random.

Christopher Columbus. Gianni Granzotto. Tr. by Stephen Sartorelli from Ital. LC 85-4387. (Illus.). 336p. 1985. 18.95 o.s.i. (ISBN 0-385-19677-6). Doubleday.

Christopher Dresser, 1834-1904: Catalogue of an Exhibition Held in 1972. (Illus.). 36p. pap. 22.00 o.s.i. (ISBN 0-317-55033-0). Apollo.

Christopher Durang Explains It All for You. Christopher Durang. 240p. 1983. pap. 4.50 o.p. (ISBN 0-380-82636-4, Bard). Avon.

Christopher or Notes of a Father to His Son: The Formative Years. H. G. Freeman. 1977. 9.00 o.p. (ISBN 0-682-48780-5). Exposition-Phoenix.

Christopher Smart: An Annotated Bibliography. Betty Rizzo & Robert Mahoney. LC 82-48498. 550p. 1983. lib. bdg. 76.00 o.p. (ISBN 0-8240-9226-0). Garland Pub.

Christy. Catherine Marshall. 1967. text ed. 14.95 o.p. (ISBN 0-07-040605-7). McGraw.

Christy. Catherine Marshall. 348p. 1968. pap. 4.50 o.p. (ISBN 0-8007-8008-6, Spire Bks). Revell.

Chromans & Tocopherols. Ed. by Gwynn P. Ellis & Ian M. Lockhart. LC 80-16902. (Chemistry of Heterocyclic Compounds: Vol. 36). 1981. 208.95 o.p. (ISBN 0-471-03038-4, Pub. by Wiley-Interscience). Wiley.

Chromatin & Chromosome Structure. Ed. by Hsueh Jei Li. 1977. 59.00 o.p. (ISBN 0-12-450550-3). Acad Pr.

Chromatographic Methods. 3rd ed. R. Stock & C. B. Rice. 1974. pap. 15.95x o.p. (ISBN 0-412-20810-5, NO.6276, Pub. by Chapman & Hall). Routledge Chapman & Hall.

Chromatography: An Adventure in Graduate School. Guy B. Alexander. LC 77-8637. (Chemistry in Action Ser.). 1977. 9.90 o.p. (ISBN 0-8412-0277-X); pap. 5.95 o.p. Am Chemical.

Chromatography of Steroids. I. E. Bush et al. 1962. 76.00 o.p. (ISBN 0-08-009544-5). Pergamon.

Chromium in Nutrition & Metabolism: Proceedings of a Symposium Held in Sherbrooke, Canada, June, 1979. D. Shapcott & J. Hubert. (Developments in Nutrition & Metabolism Ser.: Vol. 2). 1980. 67.50 o.p. (ISBN 0-444-80188-X). Elsevier.

Chromium: Its Physicochemical Behaviour & Petrologic Significance: Proceedings of the Carnegie Institute of Washington Conference, Geophysical Laboratory. Ed. by T. N. Irvine. LC 75-33383. 1976. 75.00 o.p. (ISBN 0-08-019954-2). Pergamon.

Chromosomal Code. Lawrence Watt-Evans. 208p. 1984. pap. 2.50 o.p. (ISBN 0-380-87205-6, 87205, Discus). Avon.

Chromosomal Proteins & Their Role in the Regulation of Gene Expression: Proceedings of the Symposium, University of Florida, Gainsville, March 1975. Symposium, University of Florida, Gainsville Staff. Ed. by Gary S. Stein & Lewis J. Kleinsmith. 1975. 49.50 o.p. (ISBN 0-12-664750-X). Acad Pr.

Chromosome Atlas: Fish, Amphibians, Reptiles & Birds, Vol. 2. Ed. by K. Benirschke & T. C. Hsu. (Illus.). 230p. 1974. 25.00 o.p. (ISBN 0-387-06529-6). Springer-Verlag.

Chromosome Atlas: Fish, Amphibians, Reptiles, & Birds, Vol. 3. Ed. by K. Benirschke et al. LC 73-166079. (Illus.). 240p. 1975. boxed loose-leaf 27.00 o.p. (ISBN 0-387-07207-1). Springer-Verlag.

Chromosome Complement. B. John & K. R. Lewis. (Protoplasmatologia: Vol. 6, Pt. A). (Illus.). 1968. pap. 57.90 o.p. (ISBN 0-387-80881-7). Springer-Verlag.

Chromosome Cycle. B. John & K. R. Lewis. (Protoplasmatologia: Vol. 6, Pt. B). (Illus.). 1969. 42.50 o.p. (ISBN 0-387-80918-X). Springer-Verlag.

Chromosome Damage & Repair. Ed. by Erling Seeberg & Kjell Kleppe. LC 81-19871. (NATO ASI Series A, Life Sciences: Vol. 40). 638p. 1982. 95.00x o.p. (ISBN 0-306-40886-4, Plenum Pr). Plenum Pub.

Chromosome Identification. Ed. by Torbjorn Caspersson & Lore Zech. 1973. 74.50 o.p. (ISBN 0-12-163550-3). Acad Pr.

Chromosome Mutations: Their Potential Relevance to the Genetic Risks in Man. Ed. by H. P. Klinger et al. (Journal: Cytogenetics & Cell Genetics: Vol. 33, No. 1-2). (Illus.). 202p. 1982. pap. 85.50 o.p. (ISBN 3-8055-3569-4). S Karger.

Chromosome Techniques. 3rd ed. Sharma & Sharma. LC 79-41279. 1980. 165.00 o.p. (ISBN 0-408-70942-1). Butterworth.

Chromosomes Today. Ed. by M. D. Bennett et al. (Chromosomes Today Ser.: Vol. VIII). (Illus.). 400p. 1984. text ed. 50.00x o.p. (ISBN 0-04-575023-8). Unwin Hyman.

Chronic Cholecystitis: Its Pathology & the Role of Vascular Factors in Its Pathogenesis. Talya Levine. LC 75-6842. 270p. 1975. 58.95x o.p. (ISBN 0-470-53122-3). Halsted Pr.

Chronic Mental Patient: Problems, Solutions, & Recommendations for a Public Policy, Report of the American Psychiatric Association Conference, January 1979. American Psychiatric Association Conference Staff. Ed. by John A. Talbot. LC 78-73984. 280p. 1979. pap. 11.00x o.p. (ISBN 0-89042-141-2, 42-141-2). Am Psychiatric.

Chronic Pain. Steven F. Brena. LC 77-15888. 1978. 8.95 o.p. (ISBN 0-689-10874-5, Atheneum). Macmillan.

Chronic Ulcers of the Skin. B. Y. Lee. 240p. 1985. text ed. 29.00 o.p. (ISBN 0-07-037297-7). McGraw.

Chronically Ill. Fox. 1957. (ISBN 0-8022-0525-9). Philos Lib.

Chronically Implanted Cardiovascular Instrumentation. Ed. by Ernest P. McCutcheon. (Clinical Engineering Ser). (Based upon a Symposium). 1973. 60.50 o.p. (ISBN 0-12-483150-8). Acad Pr.

Chronicle Agricultural Occupations Guidebook. Chronicle Guidance Publications, Inc., Research Staff. (Illus.). 360p. 1985. 60.50 o.p. (ISBN 0-912578-88-2). Chron Guide.

Chronicle Business Occupations Guidebook. Chronicle Guidance Publications, Inc., Research Staff. (Illus.). 430p. 1985. 83.50 o.p. (ISBN 0-912578-85-8). Chron Guide.

Chronicle Career Index: 1987. Ed. by Paul Downes. 155p. 1987. pap. text ed. 14.25 o.p. (ISBN 1-55631-008-0). Chron Guide.

Chronicle Four-Year College Databook: 1987. Ed. by Paul Downes. 480p. 1987. pap. text ed. 19.00 o.p. (ISBN 1-55631-007-2). Chron Guide.

Chronicle Health Occupations Guidebook. Chronicle Guidance Publications, Inc., Research Staff. (Illus.). 370p. 1985. 60.00 o.p. (ISBN 0-912578-86-6). Chron Guide.

Chronicle Home Economics Occupations Guidebook. Chronicle Guidance Publications, Inc., Research Staff. (Illus.). 290p. 1985. 57.00 o.p. (ISBN 0-912578-84-X). Chron Guide.

Chronicle Industrial Technology Occupations Guidebook. Chronicle Guidance Publications, Inc., Research Staff. (Illus.). 740p. 1985. 111.50 o.p. (ISBN 0-912578-87-4). Chron Guide.

Chronicle Math & Science Occupations Guidebook. Paul Downes. (Illus.). 415p. 1986. text ed. 77.00 o.p. (ISBN 1-55631-000-5). Chron Guide.

Chronicle of England During the Reigns of the Tudors, 2 Vols. Charles W. Wriothesley. Repr. of 1877 ed. 62.00 o.p. (ISBN 0-384-69570-1). Johnson Repr.

Chronicle of Events in the Art World, & a Guide for All Interested in the Progress of Art in America see United States Art Directory & Year-Book.

Chronicle of Jeopardy: Nineteen Forty-Five to Nineteen Fifty-Five. Rexford G. Tugwell. (Midway Reprint Ser). 496p. 1974. pap. text ed. 17.50x o.s.i. (ISBN 0-226-81537-4). U of Chicago Pr.

Chronicle of the Slavs. Helmold Priest Of Bosau. Tr. by Francis J. Tschan. 1967. lib. bdg. 29.00x o.p. (ISBN 0-374-98018-7, Octagon). Hippocrene Bks.

Chronicle of the Twentieth Century. Ed. by Clifton Daniel et al. (Illus.). 1360p. 1987. 49.95 o.p. (ISBN 0-942191-01-3); lib. bdg. Chronicle Pubns.

Chronicle Student Aid Annual: 1987. Ed. by Paul Downes. 416p. 1987. pap. text ed. 19.95 o.p. (ISBN 1-55631-011-0). Chron Guide.

Chronicle Two-Year College Databook: 1987. Ed. by Paul Downes. 399p. 1987. pap. text ed. 16.95 o.p. (ISBN 1-55631-010-2). Chron Guide.

Chronicle Vocational School Manual: 1987. Ed. by Paul Downes. 379p. 1987. pap. text ed. 16.50 o.p. (ISBN 1-55631-009-9). Chron Guide.

Chronicles & Ice Cream. Richard E. Jerin. 1980. 5.00 o.p. (ISBN 0-682-49435-6). Exposition-Phoenix.

Chronicles of Doodah. George L. Walker. LC 85-5220. 246p. 1986. 16.45 o.p. (ISBN 0-395-38174-6). HM.

Chronicles of Fairacre. Miss Read. 1977. 10.95 o.p. (ISBN 0-395-25181-8). HM.

Chronicles of Narnia, 7 vols. C. S. Lewis. (G. K. Hall Large Print Children's Bks.). (gr. 4-8). 1986. lib. bdg. 97.65x o.s.i. (ISBN 0-8161-4188-6). G K Hall.

Chronicles of the Raj: A Study of Literary Reaction to the Imperial Idea Towards the End of the Raj. Shamsul Islam. 130p. 1979. 22.50x o.p. (ISBN 0-8476-6174-1). Rowman.

Chronicles of Yerachmiel. Gaster. Date not set. 35.00 o.p. Ktav.

Chronique see Oeuvre Poetique.

Chronique Latine de Guillaume De Nangis 1113 a 1300, 2 vols. Guillaume De Nangis. Ed. by H. Geraud. Set. 86.00 o.p. (ISBN 0-384-20360-4); Set. pap. 74.00 o.p. (ISBN 0-384-20361-2). Johnson Repr.

Chronological Outlines of English Literature. Frederick Ryland. LC 68-30587. 368p. 1968. Repr. of 1914 ed. 46.00x o.p. (ISBN 0-8103-3223-X). Gale.

Chronology of Business Education in the United States. 1977. pap. 2.50 o.p. (ISBN 0-318-18606-3). Natl Busn Ed Assoc.

Chronology of Leonardo Da Vinci's Architectural Studies after 1500. C. Pedretti. (Illus.). 192p. 1962. text ed. 36.00x o.p. (ISBN 0-317-55913-3, Pub. by Droz Switzerland). Coronet Bks.

Chronology of Modern India for Four Hundred Years From the Close of the Fifteenth Century, A.D. 1494-1894. James Burgess. 490p. 1972. Repr. of 1913 ed. text ed. 37.50x o.p. (ISBN 0-7165-2055-9, Pub. by Irish Academic Pr Ireland). Biblio Dist.

Chronology of Paul's Life. Robert Jewett. LC 78-54553. 176p. 1979. 14.95 o.p. (ISBN 0-8006-0522-5, 1-522, Fortress). Augsburg Fortress.

Chronology of the Origin & Progress of Paper & Paper-Making. Joel Munsell. Ed. by John Bidwell. LC 78-74389. (Nineteenth-Century Book Arts & Printing History Ser.: Vol. 4). 1980. lib. bdg. 33.00 o.p. (ISBN 0-8240-3878-9). Garland Pub.

Chronology of the People's Republic of China 1949-1984. Ed. by Cheng Jin. 99p. (Orig.). 1986. pap. 2.95 o.p. China Bks.

Chronology Out of Time: Dates in the Fiction of H. P. Lovecraft. Peter Cannon. 36p. (Orig.). 1986. pap. 3.95 o.p. (ISBN 0-940884-14-3). Necronomicon.

Chronos. Florence Holland. 1977. 4.00 o.p. (ISBN 0-682-48967-0). Exposition-Phoenix.

Chrysal: Or, the Adventures of a Guinea, 4 vols. Charles Johnstone. Ed. by Ronald Paulson. LC 78-60839. (Novel 1720-1805 Ser.: Vol. 5). 1979. Set. lib. bdg. 150.00 o.p. (ISBN 0-8240-3654-9). Garland Pub.

Chrysalis: A Journey into the New Spiritual America. Mark Allen. (Illus.). 192p. 1978. pap. 4.95 o.s.i. (ISBN 0-89496-011-3). Ross Bks.

Chrysanthemum & the Bat: Baseball Samurai Style. Robert Whiting. 256p. 1983. pap. 3.95 o.p. (ISBN 0-380-63115-6, 63115-6, Discus). Avon.

Chrysanthemums & Other Stories. Feng Jicai. Tr. by Susan W. Chen from Chinese. LC 85-925. 240p. 1985. 19.95 o.p. (ISBN 0-15-117878-X). HarBraceJ.

Chrysler & the UAW. Sam Marcy. 28p. 1981. pap. 0.25 o.p. (ISBN 0-89567-047-X). World View Forum.

Chrysler K-Car & E-Car 1981-1985. Chilton Automotives Editorial Staff. LC 84-45488. 232p. (Orig.). 1985. pap. 13.95 o.p. (ISBN 0-8019-7562-X). Chilton.

Chrysler K-Cars, (1981-1984) Do-It-Yourself Car Care. Larry W. Carley. (Illus.). 352p. (Orig.). 1984. pap. 11.60 o.p. (ISBN 0-8306-2123-7, 2123). TAB Bks.

Chrysler Outboard Service Handbook: 25 to 140 HP, 1966-1983. Ed. by Eric Jorgensen. (Illus.). pap. 9.00 o.p. (ISBN 0-89287-183-0, B657). Clymer Pub.

Chrysler Service-Repair Handbook: 3.5 to 20hp, 1966-1983. (Illus.). pap. text ed. 9.00 o.p. (ISBN 0-89287-221-7, B655). Clymer Pub.

Chu-Shu-Chi-Nien As a Source to the Social History of Ancient China. LC 79-2822. 101p. 1988. Repr. of 1956 ed. 16.00 o.p. Hyperion Conn.

Chucaro, Wild Pony of the Pampa. Francis Kalnay. LC 58-5710. (Illus.). (gr. 4-6). 1958. 5.50 o.p. (ISBN 0-15-218042-7, HJ). HarBraceJ.

Chuckwagon Cookbook, Vol. II. U.S.S. Will Rogers Wive's Staff. Ed. by Kathy A. Bremer. LC 85-72827. 342p. (Orig.). 1985. pap. 10.00 o.p. (ISBN 0-9615766-0-X, 100). Bremer Bks.

Chummy Chipmunk's First Family. Amsel Barton. (gr. k-5). 1976. 5.00 o.p. (ISBN 0-682-48451-2). Exposition-Phoenix.

Chung-Gun & Toi Gye of Tae Kwon Do Hyung. Jhoon Rhee. LC 76-163381. (Ser. 108). (Illus.). 1971. pap. text ed. 8.95x o.p. (ISBN 0-89750-003-2, Dist. by Wehman). Ohara Pubns.

Church. (Papal Teaching Ser.). 700p. 1988. 12.00 o.p. (ISBN 0-317-67501-X, EP0220). Dghtrs St Paul.

Church. William V. Coleman & Patricia R. Coleman. (Daybreak Ser.). (Illus.). 1977. tchrs ed. 9.95x o.p. (ISBN 0-89622-041-9). Twenty-Third.

Church. Robert Hicks & Richard Bewes. (Understanding Bible Truth Ser.). (Orig.). 1981. pap. 0.95 o.p. (ISBN 0-89840-018-X). Heres Life.

Church, a Believing Fellowship. William M. Ramsay & John H. Leith. (Illus., Orig.). (gr. 7-9). 1965. pap. 3.45 o.p. (ISBN 0-8042-9260-4, John Knox). Westminster John Knox.

Church: A Faith Filled People. Mary Jo Tully. 96p. 1982. pap. 3.75 o.p. (ISBN 0-697-01823-7). Wm C Brown.

Church Action in the World. Charles V. Willie. 5.95 o.p. (ISBN 0-8192-1098-6). Morehouse Pub.

Church & Children Under Two. Kathrene M. Tobey. (Orig.). 1964. pap. 1.95 o.p. (ISBN 0-8042-9501-8, John Knox). Westminster John Knox.

Church & Disabled Persons. Ed. by Griff Hogan. 128p. 1983. pap. 8.95 o.p. (ISBN 0-87243-123-1). Templegate.

Church & Freemasonry in Brazil, 1872-1875. Mary C. Thornton. LC 73-2647. 287p. 1973. Repr. of 1948 ed. lib. bdg. 35.00x o.p. (ISBN 0-8371-6816-3, THCF). Greenwood.

Church & Mission in Modern Africa. Adrian Hastings. LC 67-30321. (Orig.). 1967. 25.00 o.p. (ISBN 0-8232-0770-6). Fordham.

Church & Modern Science. Patrick J. McLaughlin. 96p. 1954. (ISBN 0-8022-1019-8). Philos Lib.

Church & Parish: A Guide for Local Historians. J. Bettey. (Illus.). 168p. 1988. 39.95 o.p. (ISBN 0-7134-5101-7, Pub. by Batsford England). David & Charles.

Church & Racial Hostility: A History of Interpretation of Ephesians. William Rader. cancelled o.s.i. (ISBN 3-16-140112-3). Adlers Foreign Bks.

Church & State, Two Vols. Luigi Sturzo. (Vol. 2, O.P.). 1962. Set. pap. 11.90x o.p. (ISBN 0-268-00047-6). U of Notre Dame Pr.

Church & the Churches. T. Watson Street. (Orig.). (gr. 9-12). 1967. pap. 1.25 o.p. (ISBN 0-8042-9374-0, John Knox). Westminster John Knox.

Church & the Liberal Society. Emmet J. Hughes. 1961. pap. 8.95x o.p. (ISBN 0-268-00046-8). U of Notre Dame Pr.

Church & the Nation: The Case for Disestablishment. Peter Cornwell. (Faith & the Future Ser.). 160p. 1984. 24.95x o.p. (ISBN 0-631-13223-6); pap. 14.95x o.p. (ISBN 0-631-13224-4). Basil Blackwell.

Church & the Rural Poor. Ed. by James A. Cogswell. LC 74-7616. 120p. (Orig.). 1975. pap. 1.95 o.p. (ISBN 0-8042-0797-6, John Knox). Westminster John Knox.

Church As a Social Institution. David A. Moberg. 600p. 1984. pap. 18.95 o.p. (ISBN 0-8010-6168-7). Baker Bk.

Church As Evangelist. George E. Sweazey. LC 77-20452. 1978. 11.95i o.p. (ISBN 0-06-067776-7). HarpR.

Church As the Body of Christ. Eduard Schweizer. LC 64-16282. (Orig.). 1964. pap. 2.95 o.p. (ISBN 0-8042-3376-4, John Knox). Westminster John Knox.

Church at Prayer: Part One-The Liturgy. Ed. by A. G. Martimort. 264p. 1969. text ed. 17.50x o.p. (ISBN 0-7165-0511-8, Pub. by Irish Academic Pr Ireland). Biblio Dist.

Church at Prayer Part Two: The Eucharist. Ed. by A. G. Martimort. (Illus.). 250p. 1972. 17.50x o.p. (ISBN 0-7165-1107-X, BBA 01006, Pub. by Irish Academic Pr Ireland). Biblio Dist.

Church Catechism. pap. 0.35x o.p. (ISBN 0-8192-4103-2). Morehouse Pub.

Church Cyclopaedia: A Dictionary of Church Doctrine, History, Organization & Ritual, & Containing Original Articles on Special Topics, Written Expressly for This Work by Bishops, Presbyters, & Laymen. Angelo Ames Benton. LC 74-31499. 810p. 1975. Repr. of 1883 ed. 65.00x o.p. (ISBN 0-8103-4204-9). Gale.

Church Emerging: A U. S. Lutheran Case Study. Ed. by John Reumann. LC 76-62618. 288p. 1977. pap. 5.00 o.p. (ISBN 0-8006-1259-0, 1-1259, Fortress). Augsburg Fortress.

Church, Eucharist & Priesthood: A Theological Commentary on "The Mystery & Worship of the Most Holy Eucharist" Edward J. Kilmartin. LC 81-81343. 112p. (Orig.). 1981. pap. 4.95 o.p. (ISBN 0-8091-2368-1). Paulist Pr.

Church for an Open Future: Biblical Roots & Parish Renewal. Jack W. Lundin. LC 77-78634. 144p. (Orig.). 1977. pap. 1.00 o.p. (ISBN 0-8006-1307-4, 1-1307, Fortress). Augsburg Fortress.

Church Growth & the Whole Gospel: A Biblical Mandate. C. Peter Wagner. LC 81-47433. 224p. 1981. 13.00 o.p. (ISBN 0-06-068942-0). HarpR.

Church Guide for Strengthening Families: Strategies, Models, Programs, & Resources. James Larson. LC 86-7965. 128p. (Orig.). 1984. pap. 9.95 o.p. (ISBN 0-8066-2217-2, 10-1320, Augsburg). Augsburg Fortress.

Church Heritage: A Course in Church History. General Conference, Youth Department Staff. pap. 2.50 o.p. (ISBN 0-686-82636-1). Review & Herald.

Church in France, Eighteen Forty-Eight to Nineteen Hundred Seven. (Church Historical Society London Ser.: No. 19). pap. 60.00 o.p. (ISBN 0-8115-3142-2). Kraus Repr.

Church in France, Seventeen Eighty-Seven to Eighteen Forty-Eight. Charles S. Phillips. (Church Historical Society London Ser.: No. 19A). Repr. of 1934 ed. 40.00 o.p. (ISBN 0-8115-3143-0). Kraus Repr.

Church in History Series, 6 bks. Robert Clouse et al. 1980. pap. 31.95 set o.p. (ISBN 0-570-06277-2, 12-2780). Concordia.

Church in Israel. Reed M. Holmes. (Illus.). 1983. pap. 10.00 o.p. (ISBN 0-8309-0383-6). Herald Hse.

Church in the Bible & the World: An International Study. Ed. by D. A. Carson. 368p. (Orig.). 1988. pap. 19.95 o.p. (ISBN 0-8010-2526-5). Baker Bk.

Church in the Theology of the Reformers. Paul D. Avis. Ed. by Peter Toon & Ralph Martin. LC 80-16186. (New Foundations Theological Library). 256p. 1981. 12.95 o.s.i. (ISBN 0-8042-3708-5, John Knox); pap. 5.95 o.s.i. (ISBN 0-8042-3728-X). Westminster John Knox.

Church Investments, Corporations, & Southern Africa. National Council of Churches Corporate Information Center Staff. 1973. pap. 1.95 o.p. (ISBN 0-377-00020-5). Friendship Pr.

Church Is for All People. Adeline H. Ostwalt. (Illus., Orig.). (gr. 1-2). 1965. pap. 1.95 o.p. (ISBN 0-8042-9432-1, John Knox). Westminster John Knox.

Church: Its Changing Image Through Twenty Centuries. Eric G. Jay. LC 79-92070. 1980. 12.95 o.p. (ISBN 0-8042-0877-8, John Knox); pap. 10.95 o.p. (ISBN 0-8042-0878-6). Westminster John Knox.

Church Kindergarten Resource Book. rev. ed. Josephine Newbury. 1970. pap. 4.49 o.p. (ISBN 0-8042-9505-0, John Knox). Westminster John Knox.

Church, Kingship & Lay Investiture in England, 1089-1135. Norman F. Cantor. 1969. lib. bdg. 26.00x o.p. (ISBN 0-374-91273-4, Octagon). Hippocrene Bks.

Church Lace: Being Eight Ecclesiastical Patterns in Pillow Lace. Ed. by M. E. Milroy. (Illus.). 136p. 1981. Repr. of 1920 ed. 42.00x o.p. (ISBN 0-8103-3014-8). Gale.

Church Leadership & Organization. Flavil Yeakley. pap. 5.95 o.p. (ISBN 0-317-47145-7). Gospel Advocate.

Church: Light of All Mankind. Pope Paul VI. Ed. by Daughters of St. Paul Staff. 1967. 2.00 o.p. (ISBN 0-8198-0027-9). Dghtrs St Paul.

Church Mice & the Moon. Graham Oakley. LC 74-75569. (Illus.). 40p. (gr. k-3). 1974. 10.95 o.s.i. (ISBN 0-689-30437-4, Atheneum Childrens Bks). Macmillan.

Church Militant & Iberian Expansion: 1440-1770. Charles R. Boxer. LC 77-18386. (Johns Hopkins Symposia in Comparative History Ser.: No. 10). (Illus.). 1978. text ed. 17.50x o.p. (ISBN 0-8018-2042-1). Johns Hopkins.

Church Music of William Billings. James M. Barbour. 167p. Repr. of 1960 ed. lib. bdg. 39.00 o.p. (Pub. by Am Repr Serv). Reprint Servs.

Church of England. Jan Baker. 1978. pap. text ed. 3.35 o.s.i. (ISBN 0-08-021408-8). Pergamon.

Church of England. Edward W. Watson. LC 80-22643. (Home University Library of Modern Knowledge: No. 90). 192p. 1981. Repr. of 1961 ed. lib. bdg. 35.00x o.p. (ISBN 0-313-22683-0, WAEN). Greenwood.

Church of Sainta Maria Dei Miracoli in Venice. Ralph E. Lieberman. Ed. by S. J. Freedberg. (Outstanding Dissertations in Fine Arts Ser.). (Illus.). 670p. 1985. Repr. of 1972 ed. 55.00 o.p. (ISBN 0-8240-6861-0). Garland Pub.

Church of the Brethren & the War, 1788-1914. Rufus D. Bowman. LC 75-147667. (Library of War & Peace; Relig. & Ethical Positions on War). 1972. 46.00 o.p. (ISBN 0-8240-0425-6). Garland Pub.

Church on Assignment. W. Eugene Jr. Spears. LC 84-15541. 1985. pap. 3.95 o.p. (ISBN 0-8054-5011-4). Broadman.

Church Organization: A Manual for Effective Local Church Administration. Helmer C. Lundquist & James G. Pendorf. (Illus.). 1977. pap. 4.25 o.p. (ISBN 0-8192-1229-6). Morehouse Pub.

Church-Papal Teachings. 12.00 o.s.i. (ISBN 0-317-46826-X). Dghtrs St Paul.

Church Planting Through Obedience Oriented Teaching. George Patterson. LC 81-285. (Illus.). 64p. (Orig.). 1981. pap. 3.95x o.p. (ISBN 0-87808-910-1). William Carey Lib.

Church Portals: A Bibliography. Mary Vance. (Architecture Ser.: A 1359). 8p. 1985. 2.00 o.p. (ISBN 0-89028-349-4). Vance Biblios.

Church Reforms in Russia, 1905-1918. Alexander Bogolepov. 59p. 1966. pap. 1.95 o.p. (ISBN 0-913836-01-X). St Vladimirs.

Church Roots: Stories of Nine Immigrant Groups That Became the American Lutheran Church. Ed. by Charles P. Lutz. LC 85-1217. 224p. (Orig.). 1985. pap. 10.95 o.p. (ISBN 0-8066-2156-7, 10-1366, Augsburg). Augsburg Fortress.

Church Staff Support: Cultivating & Maintaining Staff Relationships. Frank H. Olsen. (Administration for Churches Ser.). 40p. (Orig.). 1982. pap. 4.95 o.p. (ISBN 0-8066-1964-3, 10-1370, Augsburg). Augsburg Fortress.

Church, State & Nation in Ireland, 1898-1921. David W. Miller. LC 72-95453. 1973. 49.95x o.p. (ISBN 0-8229-1108-6). U of Pittsburgh Pr.

Church-State Relations: An Annotated Bibliography. Albert J. Menendez. LC 75-24894. (Reference Library of Social Science: Vol. 24). 125p. 1976. lib. bdg. 25.00 o.p. (ISBN 0-8240-9956-7). Garland Pub.

Church Teaching Children Grades One Through Six. Mary B. Rudolph. (Orig.). 1964. pap. 4.50 o.p. (ISBN 0-8042-9404-6, John Knox). Westminster John Knox.

Church Universal & the See of Rome: A Study of the Relations Between the Episcopate & the Papacy up to the Schism Between East & West. Henry E. Symonds. (Church Historical Society London N. S. Ser.: No. 36). pap. 60.00 o.p. (ISBN 0-8115-3159-7). Kraus Repr.

Church Ushers' Manual. Willis O. Garrett. 64p. pap. 2.50 o.p. (ISBN 0-8007-8456-1, Spire Bks.). Revell.

Church Wedding Handbook. Kay O. Lewis. 192p. 1981. 9.95 o.p. (ISBN 0-8007-1259-5). Revell.

Churches & Abbeys of Ireland. Brian De Breffny & George Mott. (Illus.). 1976. 14.95 o.p. (ISBN 0-393-04441-6). Norton.

Churches & the American Experience. Thomas A. Askew, Jr. & Peter W. Spellman. 205p. 1984. pap. 9.95 o.p. (ISBN 0-8010-0199-4). Baker Bk.

Churches at the Testing Point: A Study in Rural Michigan. Theodore S. Wilkinson. (World Council of Churches Studies in Mission). 1970. pap. 3.95 o.p. (ISBN 0-377-82021-0). Friendship Pr.

Churches in Cultural Captivity: A History of the Social Attitudes of Southern Baptists. John L. Eighmy. LC 70-111047. 1972. 22.50x o.p. (ISBN 0-87049-115-6). U of Tenn Pr.

Churches of Portugal. Carlos De Azevedo. LC 85-50365. (Illus.). 196p. 1985. 35.00 o.p. (ISBN 0-935748-66-0). Scala Books.

Churchill & DeGaulle. Francois Kersaudy. LC 81-69154. 480p. 1983. 19.95o.p. (ISBN 0-689-11265-3, Atheneum); pap. 11.95 o.p. (ISBN 0-689-70641-3, 290). Macmillan.

Churchill in America: An Affectionate Portrait. Robert H. Pilpel. 1976. 10.00 o.p. (ISBN 0-15-117880-1). HarBraceJ.

Churchill Tank. 140p. 1983. pap. 13.00 o.p. (ISBN 0-11-290404-1). Kraus Intl.

Churchill's Gold. James Follett. 228p. 1981. 9.95 o.p. (ISBN 0-395-30526-8). HM.

Churchill's Private Armies: British Special Forces in Europe, 1939-42. Eric Morris. (Illus.). 286p. 1988. 34.95 o.p. (ISBN 0-09-161920-3, Pub. by Century Hutchinson). David & Charles.

Churchill's "World Crisis" As History. Robin Prior. (Illus.). 339p. 1983. 31.00 o.p. (ISBN 0-7099-2011-3, Pub. by Croom Helm Ltd). Routledge Chapman & Hall.

Church's Worship, Bk. II. Michael DeVito. pap. 3.95 o.p. (ISBN 0-941850-07-2). Liturgical Pubns.

Chute des Anges, un Deluge le Coeur Chef. Jean Giono. 8.95 o.p. (ISBN 0-686-53952-4). French & Eur.

Chute d'un Ange. Alphonse de Lamartine. 250p. 1954. 4.95 o.p. (ISBN 0-686-54275-4). French & Eur.

CIA & the NSA. Consulting Staff. 1985. 395.00 o.p. (ISBN 0-938124-08-0). Rubicon.

CIA & the Third World: A Study in Cryptodiplomacy. Satish Kumar. 210p. 1981. text ed. 22.50x o.p. (ISBN 0-7069-1292-6, Pub by Vikas India). Advent NY.

CIA Contra America Latina. V. Zubenko & K. Tarasov. 333p. 1985. pap. 3.95 o.p. (ISBN 0-8285-2865-9, Pub. by Progress Pubs USSR). Imported Pubns.

CIA Flaps & Seals Manual. 1987. lib. bdg. 79.95 o.p. (ISBN 0-8490-3603-8). Gordon Pr.

CIA Methods for Explosives Preparation. 1986. lib. bdg. 79.95 o.p. (ISBN 0-8490-3547-3). Gordon Pr.

Cibber & the Dunciad see Popeiana.

Cicero & His Influence. John C. Rolfe. LC 63-10281. (Our Debt to Greece & Rome Ser). Repr. of 1930 ed. 18.50x o.p. (ISBN 0-8154-0197-3). Cooper Sq.

Cicero Imperator: Studies in Cicero's Correspondence 51 to 47 B. C. Magnus Wistrand. (Studia Graeca et Latina Gothoburgensia: No. 41). 230p. (Orig.). 1979. text ed. 30.00x o.p. (ISBN 91-7346-063-X). Humanities.

Cicero: Pro Lege Manilia. Ed. by Scottish Classics Group Staff. (Ecce Romani Ser.). (Illus.). 64p. (Lat.). 1980. pap. text ed. 4.00 o.p. (ISBN 0-05-003259-3). Longman.

Cicero's Elegant Style: An Analysis of the Pro Archia. Harold C. Gotoff. LC 79-10245. 266p. 1979. 14.95 o.p. (ISBN 0-252-00730-1). U of Ill Pr.

Cien Anos De Soledad. Gabriel Marquez Garcia. (Span.). 1986. 12.50 o.p. (ISBN 0-8288-2516-5). French & Eur.

Cigarette Sellers of Three Crosses Square. Joseph Ziemian. (YA) (gr. 7-11). 1977. pap. 1.50 o.p. (ISBN 0-380-00967-6, 45682-6). Avon.

Cigarettes. Harry Mathews. LC 87-8174. 288p. 1987. 17.95 o.p. (ISBN 1-55584-092-2). Weidenfeld.

CIH Key to the Groups & Genera of Nematode Parasites of Invertebrates. Ed. by G. O. Poiner, Jr. 43p. 1977. pap. 7.35 o.p. CAB Intl.

CIH Keys to the Nematode Parasites of Vertebrates, No. 1. Ed. by R. C. Anderson et al. 17p. 1974. pap. 7.35 o.p. CAB Intl.

CIH Keys to the Nematode Parasites of Vertebrates, No. 10: Keys to Genera of the Superfamily Trichostrongyloidea (with an Index to Taxa for the Whole Series) Ed. by M. C. Durette-Desset. 86p. 1983. pap. 13.85 o.p. CAB Intl.

CIH Keys to the Nematode Parasites of Vertebrates, No. 3: Keys to Genera of the Order Spirurida, 3 vols, Pts. 1-3. 1976. Set. pap. 22.00 o.p. CAB Intl.

CIH Keys to the Nematode Parasites of Vertebrates, No. 4: Keys to Genera of the Oxyuroidea. Ed. by A. J. Petter & J. C. Quentin. 30p. 1976. pap. 7.35 o.p. CAB Intl.

CIH Keys to the Nematode Parasites of Vertebrates, No. 5: Keys to Genera of the Superfamily Metastrongyloidea. Ed. by R. C. Anderson. 40p. 1978. pap. 7.35 o.p. CAB Intl.

CIH Keys to the Nematode Parasites of Vertebrates, No. 6: Keys to Genera of the Superfamilies Cosmocercoidea, Seuratoidea, Heterakoidea & Subuluroidea. Ed. by A. G. Chabaud. 71p. 1978. pap. 7.35 o.p. CAB Intl.

CIH Keys to the Nematode Parasites of Vertebrates, No. 7: Keys to Genera of the Superfamily Strongyloidea. Ed. by J. R. Lichtenfels. 41p. 1980. pap. 7.35 o.p. CAB Intl.

CIH Keys to the Nematode Parasites of Vertebrates, No. 8: Keys to Genera of the Superfamilies Ancylostomatoidea & Diaphanocephaloidea. Ed. by J. R. Lichtenfels. 26p. 1980. pap. 7.35 o.p. CAB Intl.

CIH Keys to the Nematode Parasites of Vertebrates, No. 9: Keys to Genera of the Superfamilies Rhabditoidea, Dioctophymatoidea, Trichinelloidea & Muspiceoidea. Ed. by R. C. Anderson & O. Bain. 26p. 1982. pap. 7.35 o.p. CAB Intl.

CILA: A New Approach to Problems in the Acquisition of Latin American Library Materials. John S. Clouston. (Occasional Papers: No. 112). 53p. 1974. pap. 2.00 o.p. (ISBN 0-317-58911-3). U of Ill Lib Info Sci.

Cilia & Flagella. Ed. by M. A. Sleigh. 1974. 99.00 o.p. (ISBN 0-12-648150-4). Acad Pr.

Ciliated Protozoa: Characterization, Classification & Guide to the Literature. 2nd ed. John O. Corliss. LC 78-41075. (Illus.). 1979. 120.00 o.p. (ISBN 0-08-018752-8). Pergamon.

Ciliated Protozoa: International Students Edition. 2nd ed. J. O. Corliss. 1981. 120.00 o.p. (ISBN 0-08-028862-6). Pergamon.

Cimabue. Eugenio Battisti. LC 66-25463. (Illus.). 1966. 75.00x o.s.i. (ISBN 0-271-73119-2). Pa St U Pr.

Cimarron. Hank Mitchum. (Nightingale Ser.). 271p. 1988. pap. 12.95x o.p. (ISBN 0-8161-4453-2). G K Hall.

Cimetiere Marin. Paul Valery. Ed. & tr. by Graham D. Martin. (Edinburgh Bilingual Library: No. 1). 107p. 1971. 7.95x o.p. (ISBN 0-292-71005-4); pap. 3.95x o.p. (ISBN 0-292-71003-8). U of Tex Pr.

Cinch. Richard Martins. LC 85-40982. 320p. 1986. 17.45 o.s.i. (ISBN 0-394-55322-5, Pub. by Villard Bks). Random.

Cincinnati & Lake Erie. Jack Keenan. LC 74-23814. (Illus.). 224p. 1975. 24.95 o.p. (ISBN 0-87095-055-X). Gldn West Bks.

Cincinnati Bengals. Julian May. LC 80-17503. (NFL Today Ser.). (gr. 4-8). 1980. PLB 10.45 o.p. (ISBN 0-87191-734-3); pap. 4.25 o.p. (ISBN 0-89812-237-6). Creative Ed.

Cincinnati, Ohio. (Panel Advisory Service Report Ser.). 72p. 1981. pap. 10.00 o.p. (ISBN 0-317-06742-7, C-20). Urban Land.

Cincinnati Reds. rev. ed. Brannon. LC 82-16225. (Baseball Today Ser.). 48p. (gr. 4 up). 1982. PLB 11.45 o.p. (ISBN 0-87191-858-7). Creative Ed.

CINCOM: Courses in Communications - 1987. Communications Library Staff. 90p. (Orig.). 1987. pap. 35.00x o.p. (ISBN 0-934339-93-7). Comm Lib.

Cincom: Courses in Communications, 1985. Communications Library Staff. 60p. (Orig.). 1985. pap. 25.00x o.p. (ISBN 0-934339-92-9). Comm Lib.

Cinderella. Toby Bluth. (Illus.). 48p. (gr. k-5). 1986. 5.95 o.p. (ISBN 0-8249-8152-9). Ideals.

Cinderella. Marcia Brown & Charles Perrault. (Illus.). 32p. (gr. 1-5). 1981. pap. 4.95 o.p. (ISBN 0-689-70484-4, Aladdin). Macmillan.

Cinderella. (Favorite Tale Pop-Up Bks.). (Illus.). (ps-1). 1.98 o.p. (ISBN 0-517-46232-X). Outlet Bk Co.

Cinderella. (Giant 3-D Fairy Tale Bks.). (Illus.). (ps-1). 2.98 o.s.i. (ISBN 0-517-45981-7). Outlet Bk Co.

Cinderella. John Fowles. (Illus.). 32p. (gr. 1-3). 1976. 5.95 o.p. (ISBN 0-316-29101-3). Little.

Cinderella. Ed McBain. LC 85-24766. (Matthew Hope Ser.). 256p. 1986. pap. 14.95 o.p. (ISBN 0-03-004959-8, Owl Bks). H Holt & Co.

Cinderella. Ed McBain. 272p. 1987. pap. 3.95 o.p. (ISBN 0-445-40618-6). Mysterious Pr.

Cinderella Complex: Women's Hidden Fear of Independence. Colette Dowling. 288p. 1981. 15.95 o.s.i. (ISBN 0-671-40052-5). Summit Bks.

Cinderella Dressed in Yella: The First Attempt at a Definitive Study of Australian Children's Play Rhymes. Ed. by Ian Turner. LC 74-172085. 1972. 7.50 o.s.i. (ISBN 0-8008-1585-8). Taplinger.

Cinderella Factor. Barbara Tori. (Orig.). 1972. pap. 1.50 o.p. (ISBN 0-380-01099-2, 11643). Avon.

Cinderella of Europe. Sheila M. O'Callaghan. 1951. (ISBN 0-8022-1237-9). Philos Lib.

Cinderella on Wheels. Demi. LC 82-2996. (Illus.). 12p. (gr. 1-4). 1983. 9.95 o.p. (ISBN 0-03-059473-1). H Holt & Co.

Cinderella Spy. Philip Daniels. 192p. 1986. pap. 2.95 o.p. (ISBN 0-931773-77-6). Critics Choice Paper.

Cindy on Fire. Burt Hirschfeld. 1979. pap. 2.50 o.p. (ISBN 0-380-00267-1, 49270). Avon.

Cinema, 2 vols. Date not set. Vol. 1. (ISBN 0-8052-0735-X); Vol. 2. (ISBN 0-8052-0739-2). Random.

Cinema Borealis: The Art of Ingmar Bergman. Vernon Young. 1972. pap. 5.45 o.p. (ISBN 0-380-01100-X, Equinox). Avon.
Cinema of Carl Dreyer. Tom Milne. LC 78-118772. (International Film Guide Ser). (Illus.). 1970. pap. 4.95 o.s.i. (ISBN 0-498-07711-X). A S Barnes.
Cinema of Satyajit Ray. Chidananda Das Gupta. (Illus.). 88p. 1980. text ed. 32.50x o.p. (ISBN 0-7069-1035-4, Pub. by Vikas India). Advent NY.
Cinema Strikes Back: Radical Filmmaking in the United States, 1930-1942. Russell Campbell. Ed. by Diane Kirkpatrick. LC 82-4819. (Studies in Cinema: No. 20). 398p. 1982. 44.95 o.p. (ISBN 0-8357-1330-X). Univ Microfilms.
Cinemicrography in Cell Biology. Ed. by George G. Rose. 1963. 78.00 o.p. (ISBN 0-12-596850-7). Acad Pr.
CIO & the Democratic Party. Fay Calkins. (Midway Reprint Ser). 1976. pap. text ed. 6.50x o.s.i. (ISBN 0-226-09098-1). U of Chicago Pr.
CIRA Nineteen Seventy-Two. Cospar Committee on the International Reference Atmosphere. 1977. 73.00 o.p. (ISBN 0-08-021997-7). Pergamon.
Circannual Clocks: Annual Biological Rhythms. Eric T. Pengelley. 1974. 65.50 o.p. (ISBN 0-12-550150-1). Acad Pr.
Circle & the Conic Curves. William M. Dawes. 4.95 o.p. (ISBN 0-8283-1620-1). Branden Pub Co.
Circle in the Sea. Steve Senn. LC 81-1397. 264p. (gr. 5-9). 1981. 11.95 o.p. (ISBN 0-689-30861-2, Atheneum). Macmillan.
Circle of Hope: A Child Rescued by Love from a Medical Death Sentence. Sharon Walker. LC 81-9848. 10.95 o.p. (ISBN 0-317-65051-3). M Evans.
Circle of Seasons. Myra C. Livingston. LC 81-20305. (Illus.). 32p. (gr. 1-4). 1988. pap. 5.95 o.p. (ISBN 0-8234-0656-3). Holiday.
Circle of Shadows. Jenny Robertson. LC 76-27079. (gr. 4 up). 1976. pap. 2.25 o.p. (ISBN 0-8066-1555-9, 10-1410, Augsburg). Augsburg Fortress.
Circles. Virginia M. Malterner. (Illus.). (gr. 4-5). 1977. tchrs'. manual 5.75x o.p. (ISBN 0-8192-4079-6); wkbk. 3.95x o.p. (ISBN 0-8192-4080-X); take-home cards packet 2.50x o.p. (ISBN 0-8192-4081-8). Morehouse Pub.
Circles. Doris Mortman. 384p. (Orig.). 1984. pap. text ed. 4.95 o.p. (ISBN 0-553-23983-X). Bantam.
Circles, A Mathematical View. Dan Pedoe. LC 78-73522. (Illus.). 1979. pap. text ed. 4.50 o.p. (ISBN 0-486-63698-4). Dover.
Circles: A Washington Story. Abigail McCarthy. 1978. pap. 1.95 o.p. (ISBN 0-380-39305-0, 39305). Avon.
Circles in a Forest. Dalene Matthee. LC 84-47875. 1984. 14.45 o.s.i. (ISBN 0-394-53911-7). Knopf.
Circuit Design for Electronic Instrumentation: Analog & Digital Devices from Sensor to Display. Darold C. Wobschall. LC 79-9084. (Illus.). 1980. text ed. 51.50 o.p. (ISBN 0-07-071230-1). McGraw.
Circuit Theory & Design. Ed. by G. S. Moschytz & J. Neirynck. 1978. text ed. 84.00x o.p. (ISBN 2-604-00033-4). Gower Pub Co.
Circuit Theory: Foundations & Classical Contributions. Ed. by M. E. Van Valkenburg. LC 74-2475. (Benchmark Papers in Electrical Engineering & Computer Science: Vol. 8). 464p. 1982. 61.95 o.p. (ISBN 0-87933-084-8). Van Nos Reinhold.
Circuit Theory Fundamentals & Applications. Aram Budak. LC 77-22344. (Illus.). 1977. pap. text ed. (ISBN 0-13-133975-3). P-H.
Circuit Theory: The Computational Approach. S. W. Director. LC 75-2016. 679p. 1975. text ed. 51.50 o.p. (ISBN 0-471-21580-5). Wiley.
Circuit Training. Robert P. Sorani. (Physical Education Activities Ser.). 80p. 1966. pap. text ed. (ISBN 0-697-07006-9). Wm C Brown.
Circular Storage Tanks & Silos. A. Ghali. LC 79-12406. 210p. 1979. 45.00x o.p. (ISBN 0-419-11500-5, NO.6121, Pub. by E & FN Spon England). Routledge Chapman & Hall.
Circulating Fluidized Bed Technology: Proceedings of the First International Conference on Circulating Fluidized Beds, Halifax, Canada, 18-20 November 1985. Ed. by P. Basu. (Illus.). 464p. 1986. 85.00 o.s.i. (ISBN 0-08-031868-1, E135, B125, A115, C130, A125, Pub. by PPC). Pergamon.
Circulating Platelet. Ed. by Shirley A. Johnson. 1971. 85.50 o.p. (ISBN 0-12-387550-1). Acad Pr.
Circulation & Interpersonal Networks Linking Rural & Urban Areas: The Case of Roi-et, Northeastern Thailand. Paul Lightfoot & Theodore Fuller. LC 83-5677. (Papers of the East-West Population Institute: No. 84). v, 46p. (Orig.). 1983. pap. text ed. 1.75 o.p. (ISBN 0-86638-007-8). EW Ctr HI.
Circulation in the Extremities. Ed. by David I. Abramson. 1967. 93.50 o.p. (ISBN 0-12-042556-4). Acad Pr.
Circulation in Third World Countries. Ed. by Mansell Prothero & Murray Chapman. 480p. 1985. 59.95x o.p. (ISBN 0-7102-0343-8). Routledge Chapman & Hall.
Circulation of Skeletal Muscle. O. Hudlicka. 1968. 90.00 o.p. (ISBN 0-08-012466-6). Pergamon.
Circulatory & Developmental Aspects of Brain Metabolism. Ed. by M. Spatz et al. LC 80-18746. 450p. 1980. 69.50x o.p. (ISBN 0-306-40542-3, Plenum Pr). Plenum Pub.
Circumcision: An American Health Fallacy. Edward Wallerstein. (Focus on Men Ser.: Vol. 1). 320p. 1980. text ed. 21.95 o.p. (ISBN 0-8261-3240-5); pap. text ed. 22.95 o.p. (ISBN 0-8261-3241-3). Springer Pub.
Circumcision: The Painful Dilemma. Rosemary Romberg. LC 84-24188. 480p. 1985. 39.95 o.s.i. (ISBN 0-89789-073-6); pap. 15.95 o.p. (ISBN 0-89789-074-4). Bergin & Garvey.
Circumnavigators' Handbook. Steve Dashew & Linda Dashew. (Illus.). 1983. 35.00 o.p. (ISBN 0-393-03275-2). Norton.
Circumpolar: A Novel. Richard A. Lupoff. 1984. 15.45 o.s.i. (ISBN 0-671-49941-6). S&S.
Circumpolar North: A Political & Economic Geography of the Arctic & Sub-Artic. Terrence Armstrong et al. 1978. 18.95x o.p. (ISBN 0-416-16930-9, NO.6010); pap. 18.95x o.p. (ISBN 0-416-85430-3, NO.6011). Routledge Chapman & Hall.
Circumpolar Problems: Habitat, Economy & Social Relations in the Arctic. C. Berg. 1973. 70.00 o.p. (ISBN 0-08-017038-2). Pergamon.
Circus ABC. Sue Dreamer. (Illus.). (ps up). 1985. pap. 3.95 o.p. (ISBN 0-316-19196-5). Little.
Circus Animals. Diane Cassidy. (Lift-the-Flap Bks.). (Illus.). (ps up). 1985. pap. 6.95 o.p. (ISBN 0-316-13241-1). Little.
Circus Baby. Illus. by Benton Mahan. (Fast Rolling Books Ser.). (Illus.). 12p. (ps up). 1987. 6.95 o.p. (ISBN 0-448-09881-4, G&D). Putnam Pub Group.
Circus Baggage Stock: A Tribute to the Percheron Horse. Charles P. Fox. LC 82-7631. (Illus.). 250p. 1983. 34.95 o.p. (ISBN 0-87108-625-5). Pruett.
Circus Big & Small: And Now, in the Center Ring, Introducing Circus Opposites! George Karn. (Illus.). 16p. (ps-k). 1986. bds. 3.95i o.p. (ISBN 0-316-30342-9); counter dispay of 12 (six of each title, circus colors & circus big & small) 47.40i o.p. Little.
Circus Boat. John Hooper. (Illus.). 48p. (gr. 1-4). pap. 6.95 o.p. (ISBN 0-89272-179-0, 521). Down East.
Circus Colors: Step Right up & Meet a Rainbow of Colors! George Karn. (Illus.). 16p. (ps-k). 1986. bds. 3.95i o.p. (ISBN 0-316-30343-7); counter display of 12 (six of each title, circus colors & circus big & small) 47.40i o.p. (ISBN 0-316-30344-5). Little.
Circus of Dr. Lao. Charles G. Finney. 1976. pap. 3.95 o.p. (ISBN 0-380-00750-9, 36368). Avon.
Circus People. Diane Cassidy. (Lift-the-Flap Bks.). (Illus.). (ps up). 1985. pap. 6.95 o.p. (ISBN 0-316-13243-8). Little.
Circus Train: This Lovable Locomotive Is a Book & Toy All in One! Sue Dreamer. (Illus.). 16p. (ps-k). 1986. press-out concertina bk. 6.70i o.p. (ISBN 0-316-19200-7). Little.
Circus Trains & Modelling. Ed. by Harold H. Carstens. LC 75-8473. (Rail-Craft Library: C-29). (Illus.). 1975. pap. 3.00 o.p. (ISBN 0-911868-29-1). Carstens Pubns.
Circus Villains: Poems. Richard Frost. LC 65-24647. 55p. 1965. 5.95 o.p. (ISBN 0-8214-0010-X). Ohio U Pr.
Circus World of Willie Sells. Orin C. King. 210p. 1983. 7.95 o.p. Shawnee County Hist.
Cirrhosis. John T. Galambos. LC 78-65970. (Illus.). 1979. text ed. write for info. o.p. (ISBN 0-7216-3987-9). Saunders.
Cis-&-Trans-Decalin. (American Petroleum Institute Monograph Ser.). 55p. 1978. 8.00 o.p. (ISBN 0-317-33088-8, 82270600). Am Petroleum.
CIS-Trans Isomeric Carotenoids, Vitamins A & Arylpolyenes. Laszlo Zechmeister. 1962. 46.00 o.p. (ISBN 0-12-777850-0). Acad Pr.
Cis-Trans Isometric Carotenoids. Vitamins A, - Arylpolyenes. L. Zechmeister. (Illus.). 1962. 24.80 o.p. (ISBN 0-387-80629-6). Springer-Verlag.
Ciskei: Economics & Politics of Dependence in a South African Homeland. Ed. by Nancy Charton. 256p. 1980. 32.50 o.p. (ISBN 0-7099-0332-4, Pub. by Croom Helm Ltd). Routledge Chapman & Hall.
Cisneros: Portrait of a New American. Kemper Diehl & Jan Jarboe. LC 84-72834. (Illus.). 214p. 1985. 16.95 o.p. (ISBN 0-931722-35-7); pap. 7.95 o.p. (ISBN 0-931722-37-3). Corona Pub.
Citadel of the Autarch. Gene Wolfe. (Book of the New Sun Ser.: Vol. 4). 1983. 15.50 o.s.i. (ISBN 0-671-45251-7, Timescape). PB.
Citadelle. Antoine De Saint-Exupery. 1965. 13.95 o.p. (ISBN 0-685-23936-5). Schoenhof.
Cities. George Jonas. (House of Anansi Poetry Ser.: No. 30). 74p. 1974. 2.00 o.p. (ISBN 0-88784-131-7, Pub. by Hse Anansi Pr Canada); pap. 3.95 o.p. (ISBN 0-88784-030-2). U of Toronto Pr.
Cities & Civilizations. Christopher Hibbert. LC 86-10999. (Illus.). 256p. 1986. 24.95 o.p. (ISBN 1-55584-017-5). Weidenfeld.
Cities & Civilizations. Christopher Hibbert. (Illus.). 256p. (Orig.). Date not set. 24.95 o.p. (ISBN 1-55584-017-5). Grove.
Cities & Frontiers in Brazil: Regional Dimensions of Economic Development. Martin T. Katzman. 1977. 18.50x o.s.i. (ISBN 0-674-13280-7). Harvard U Pr.
Cities & Opportunity. Date not set. (ISBN 0-8052-3874-3). Random.
Cities & Planning in the Ancient Near East. Paul Lampl. LC 68-14699. (Planning & Cities Ser). (Illus., Orig.). (YA) (gr. 9-12). 1968. 7.95 o.p. (ISBN 0-8076-0465-8); pap. 4.95 o.p. (ISBN 0-8076-0469-0). Braziller.
Cities & Services: The Geography of Collective Consumption. Steven Pinch. (Illus.). 224p. 1985. 29.95s o.p. (ISBN 0-7102-0054-4); pap. 15.95x o.p. (ISBN 0-7102-0493-0). Routledge Chapman & Hall.
Cities & Urbanism. Ed. by W. Tietze. 104p. 1975. pap. 29.00 o.p. (ISBN 0-08-019666-7). Pergamon.
Cities: Comparisons of Form & Scale. North Carolina State University, School of Design, Students & Richard S. Wurman. 1976. pap. 4.95x o.p. (ISBN 0-262-73035-9). MIT Pr.
Cities for People. Ronald V. Wiedenhoeft. 1981. 32.95 o.p. (ISBN 0-442-29429-8). Van Nos Reinhold.
Cities for Sale. Leonie Sandercock. 1976. text ed. 40.00x o.p. (ISBN 0-435-85980-3). Gower Pub Co.
Cities in Action. E. Van Cleef. LC 79-84197. 1971. 28.00 o.p. (ISBN 0-08-015622-3); pap. 17.00 o.p. (ISBN 0-08-016417-X). Pergamon.
Cities in American Life. Ed. by Richard C. Wade. LC 73-132975. (Life in America Ser). (Illus.). (gr. 9-10). 1971. pap. 8.48 o.p. (ISBN 0-395-11207-9). HM.
Cities in Flight. James Blish. 608p. 1982. pap. 3.95 o.p. (ISBN 0-380-00998-6, 65623-X). Avon.
Cities of the Eastern Roman Provinces. 2nd ed. Arnold H. Jones. Rev. by M. Avi-Yonah et al. (Illus.). 612p. 1971. lib. bdg. 87.50x o.s.i. (ISBN 0-89563-110-5, Pub. by A M Hakkert). Coronet Bks.
Cities of the Red Night. William S. Burroughs. LC 80-13637. 448p. 1981. 14.95 o.p. (ISBN 0-03-053976-5); ltd. ed. 50.00 o.s.i. (ISBN 0-03-058998-3). H Holt & Co.
Cities under Stress. Robert W. Burchell & David Listokin. 766p. 1979. 28.50 o.p. (ISBN 0-88285-064-4). Transaction Pubs.
Cities Without Crisis. Mike Davidow. LC 76-5415. 240p. 1976. 10.00 o.p. (ISBN 0-7178-0448-8); pap. 3.95 o.p. (ISBN 0-7178-0449-6). Intl Pubs Co.
Citizen-Based Indicators of Community Service Performance: The Case of Norman, Oklahoma. Jeffrey L. Brudney & Robert E. England. 50p. 1980. 3.50 o.p. (ISBN 0-686-32060-3). Univ OK Gov Res.
Citizen Bee Guide to American Studies. Close Up Foundation Staff. (Illus.). 228p. 1988. pap. text ed. 12.00x o.p. (ISBN 0-932765-22-X); tchr's. guide avail. o.p.; student's answer key avail. o.p. Close Up Foun.
Citizen Evaluation of the Community Development Block Grant Program in Norman, Oklahoma. Ed. by Deanna H. Greisen. 92p. 1983. 6.00 o.p. (ISBN 0-318-01374-6). Univ OK Gov Res.
Citizen Evaluations of Community Services in Oklahoma. John P. Pelissero. 46p. 1978. 3.00 o.p. (ISBN 0-686-32061-1). Univ OK Gov Res.
Citizen Hughes. Michael Drosnin. 432p. 18.95 o.p. Aviation.
Citizen Hughes: In His Own Words-How Howard Hughes Tried to Buy America. Michael Drosnin. LC 84-25211. 532p. 1985. 18.95 o.s.i. (ISBN 0-03-041846-1). H Holt & Co.
Citizen in the Making. Surendra K. Gupta. LC 75-903605. 1975. 12.75x o.p. (ISBN 0-88386-581-5). South Asia Bks.
Citizen Participation - Alternatives in Municipal Services Delivery: A Bibliography. Mary E. Huls. (Public Administration Ser.: P 1743). 6p. 1985. 2.00 o.p. (ISBN 0-89028-523-3). Vance Biblios.
Citizen Participation in America: Essays on the State of the Art. Ed. by Stuart Langton. LC 78-19913. 1978. 15.00x o.p. (ISBN 0-669-02651-4). Lexington Bks.
Citizen Participation in Local Planning in the U. K. & U. S. A. W. C. Johnson. 74p. 1984. pap. 22.00 o.p. (ISBN 0-08-031720-0). Pergamon.
Citizen Participation: Material Published 1980-1984. Mary Vance. (Public Administration Ser.: P 1701). 47p. 1985. 6.75 o.p. (ISBN 0-89028-451-2). Vance Biblios.
Citizen Tom Paine. 2nd ed. Howard Fast. LC 82-84625. 352p. 1983. pap. 6.95 o.p. (ISBN 0-394-62464-5, E854, Ever). Grove.
Citizen Toussaint. Ralph Korngold. LC 78-21026. 1979. Repr. of 1965 ed. lib. bdg. 24.75x o.p. (ISBN 0-313-20794-1, KOCT). Greenwood.
Citizens As Soldiers: A History of the North Dakota National Guard. Jerry Cooper & Glenn Smith. LC 86-61174. (Illus.). 1986. 9.95 o.p. (ISBN 0-911042-33-4). N Dak Inst.
Citizens Co-Operation for Better Public Schools. Edgar L. Morphet. LC 54-8085. (National Society for the Study of Education Yearbooks Ser: No. 53, Pt. 1). 1954. lib. bdg. 6.50x o.s.i. (ISBN 0-226-60027-0); pap. text ed. 4.50x o.s.i. (ISBN 0-226-60028-9). U of Chicago Pr.
Citizen's Guide to Desegregation: A Study of Social & Legal Change in American Life. Herber Hill & Jack Greenberg. LC 79-564. x, 185p. Repr. of 1955 ed. 35.00x o.p. (ISBN 0-8371-5191-0, HCG&, Pub. by Negro U Pr). Greenwood.
Citizen's Guide to River Conservation. Rolf Diamant et al. LC 84-7799. (Illus.). 113p. (Orig.). 1984. pap. 7.95 o.s.i. (ISBN 0-89164-082-7). Conservation Foun.
Citizens Handbook on Retaining Council-Manager Government: How to Respond to Abandonment Referenda. 132p. 1980. pap. 12.50 o.s.i. (ISBN 0-686-46575-X). Intl City Mgt.
Citizens in Arms: The Army & Militia in American Society to the War of 1812. Lawrence D. Cress. LC 81-15945. (Studies on Armed Forces & Society Ser.). xiv, 238p. 1982. 27.50x o.p. (ISBN 0-8078-1508-X). U of NC Pr.
Citizens in Service: Volunteers in Social Welfare During the Depression, 1929-1941. J. F. Jones & J. M. Herrick. 137p. 1976. 8.75x o.p. (ISBN 0-87013-196-6). Mich St U Pr.
Citizen's Role in Transportation Planning: Four Reports. (Transportation Research Report Ser.). 51p. 1975. 2.40 o.p. (ISBN 0-309-02461-7). Transport Res Bd.
Citizenship Handbook. Barbara Goldin. 128p. (Orig.). 1983. pap. 6.95 o.p. (ISBN 0-671-45331-9). Monarch Pr.
Citizenship in Africa: The Role of Adult Education in the Political Socialization of Tanganyikans, 1891-1961. Joel C. Millonzi. LC 75-30644. (Foreign and Comparative Studies Program, Eastern African Series: No. 19). 119p. 1975. pap. text ed. 5.50x o.p. (ISBN 0-915984-16-4). Syracuse U Foreign Comp.
Citizenship in an Age of Science: A Public Opinion Survey of Young Adults. Jon D. Miller et al. (Pergamon Policy Studies). 1980. 95.00 o.p. (ISBN 0-08-024662-1). Pergamon.
Citizenship in Canada: A Retrospective Bibliography. Meena Nadkarni. (Public Administration Ser.: P 1662). 29p. 1985. pap. 4.50 o.p. (ISBN 0-89028-372-9). Vance Biblios.
Citizenship Objectives. National Assessment of Educational Progress Staff. (First Assessment (1969-70)). 74p. 1969. 1.70 o.p. (ISBN 0-318-13988-X, ED033871, Natl Assessment Ed Progress). Ed Comm States.
Citizenship Objectives. National Assessment of Educational Progress Staff. (Second Assessment (1975-76)). 64p. 1972. 2.00 o.p. (ISBN 0-318-13989-8, ED074010, Natl Assessment Ed Progress). Ed Comm States.
Citizenship-Social Studies Released Exercise Set. National Assessment of Educational Progress Staff. (Exercises or Items). 630p. 1977. Set. 29.00 o.p. (ISBN 0-318-13990-1, Natl Assessment Ed Progress). 5.80, technical appendix o.p. (ISBN 0-318-13991-X). Ed Comm States.
Citrus Fruit. (Commodity Projections: 1985). 41p. 1979. pap. 6.00 o.p. (ISBN 0-686-59424-X, F1616, FAO). UNIPUB.
City. John V. Lindsay. 1970. 5.95 o.p. (ISBN 0-393-05387-3). Norton.
City. Clifford Simak. 320p. 1981. pap. 2.75 o.s.i. (ISBN 0-441-10627-7). Ace Bks.
City & Suburb. Ed. by Benjamin Chinitz. LC 76-1850. 181p. 1976. Repr. of 1965 ed. lib. bdg. 35.00x o.p. (ISBN 0-8371-8679-X, CHCS). Greenwood.
City & Suburb: The Political Fragmentation of Metropolitan Areas, 1850-1970. Jon C. Teaford. LC 78-20519. (Johns Hopkins Studies in Urban Affairs Ser.). 1979. text ed. 18.00x o.p. (ISBN 0-8018-2202-5). Johns Hopkins.
City & the World of Work-A Critical Examination of Life in Los Angeles & Urban America in the Mid-Sixties: Proceedings of the Annual Research Conference, 9th, UCLA, 1966. Annual Research Conference Staff. 2.00 o.p. (ISBN 0-89215-029-7). U Cal LA Indus Rel.

City at Bay. David Thoreau. LC 79-87838. 1979. 9.95 o.p. (ISBN 0-87795-231-0, Arbor Hse). Morrow.
City at War: A Pictorial Memento of Portsmouth, Gosport, Fareham, Havant & Chichester During WWII. Nigel Peake. (Illus.). 160p. 1987. 14.50 o.p. (ISBN 0-903852-93-4, Pub. by Milestone Pubns UK). Seven Hills Bk Dists.
City at World's End. Edmond Hamilton. 1983. pap. 2.75 o.s.i. (ISBN 0-345-30987-1, Del Rey). Ballantine.
City Below the Hill. H. B. Ames. LC 78-163831. (Social History of Canada Ser.). 112p. 1972. pap. 6.00 o.p. (ISBN 0-8020-6142-7). U of Toronto Pr.
City Beneath the Skin. Jonathan Gathorne-Hardy. 224p. 1987. 18.95 o.p. (ISBN 0-241-11868-9, Pub. by Hamish Hamilton England). David & Charles.
City Builder. George Konrad. Tr. by Ivan Sanders. LC 77-73057. (Helen & Kurt Wolff Bks.). 1977. 7.95 o.p. (ISBN 0-15-118009-1). HarBraceJ.
City by the Sea: A History of Corpus Christi, Texas, 1519-1875. Eugenia R. Briscoe. 1985. 15.95 o.p. (ISBN 0-533-06440-6). Vantage.
City Cat: How to Live Healthily & Happily with Your Indoor Pet. Roz Riddle. (Illus.). 176p. 1984. 12.95 o.s.i. (ISBN 0-684-18208-4, ScribT). Scribner.
City College - Jewish Poor. Date not set. (ISBN 0-8052-0712-0). Random.
City-County Index to Eighteen-Fifty Census Schedules. Ed. by J. Carlyle Parker. LC 79-11644. (Genealogy & Local History Ser.: Vol. 6). 240p. 1979. 68.00x o.p. (ISBN 0-8103-1385-5). Gale.
City Development: Studies in Disintegration & Renewal. Lewis Mumford. LC 73-6212. 248p. 1973. Repr. of 1945 ed. lib. bdg. 22.50x o.p. (ISBN 0-8371-6890-2, MUCD). Greenwood.
City Essays. Phyllis A. Tickle. LC 81-5429. (Dixie Flyer Bks.). (Illus.). 52p. (Orig.). 1982. pap. 3.95 o.p. (ISBN 0-918518-19-9, St Luke TN). Peachtree Pubs.
City for Lincoln. John R. Tunis. LC 45-35202. (gr. 7 up). 1945. 4.95 o.p. (ISBN 0-15-218579-8, HJ). HarBraceJ.
City Form & Natural Process: Towards a New Urban Vernacular. Michael Hough. (Illus.). 176p. 1985. 33.95 o.p. (ISBN 0-442-26400-3). Van Nos Reinhold.
City Girl Sees, a City Girl Dreams. Clara Pfister. 56p. 1979. pap. 2.50 o.p. (ISBN 0-914946-14-5). Cleveland St Univ Poetry Ctr.
City in History: Its Origins, Its Transformations, & Its Prospects. Lewis Mumford. LC 61-7689. (Illus.). 1961. 19.95 o.s.i. (ISBN 0-15-118011-3). HarBraceJ.
City in the Ancient World. Mason Hammond. Ed. by Lester Bartson. LC 73-180153. (Studies in Urban History). (Illus.). 640p. 1972. 37.00x o.s.i. (ISBN 0-674-13180-0). Harvard U Pr.
City in West Europe. D. Burtenshaw & G. J. Ashworth. LC 80-41589. 340p. 1981. 67.95 o.p. (ISBN 0-471-27929-3, Pub. by Wiley-Interscience). Wiley.
City Madam. Philip Massinger. (New Mermaids Ser.). 1984. pap. text ed. 5.95x o.p. (ISBN 0-393-90008-8). Norton.
City Map Library. Ed. by Cartographic Editors of Gousha. (Illus.). 64p. (gr. 11-12). 1983. 54.95x o.p. (ISBN 0-88098-014-1, Pub. by Chek-Chart). H M Gousha.
City Moves West: Economic & Industrial Growth in Central West Texas. Robert L. Martin. 200p. 1969. 12.50x o.p. (ISBN 0-292-78412-0). U of Tex Pr.
City of a Million Legends. Jacqueline Lichtenberg. 240p. 1985. pap. 2.75 o.s.i. (ISBN 0-425-07513-3). Berkley Pub.
City of Fading Light. Jon Cleary. LC 85-21422. 352p. 1986. 17.95 o.p. (ISBN 0-688-02660-5). Morrow.
City of Fire: Los Alamos & the Atomic Age, 1943-1945. rev. ed. James W. Kunetka. LC 77-16403. (Illus.). 260p. 1979. pap. 9.95 o.p. (ISBN 0-8263-0515-X). U of NM Pr.
City of Joy. Dominique La Pierre. Tr. by Kathryn Spink from Fr. LC 85-10128. 480p. 1985. 17.95 o.s.i. (ISBN 0-385-18952-4). Doubleday.
City of Joy. Dominique Lapierre. (Special Editions). 712p. 1986. lib. bdg. 20.95 o.p. (ISBN 0-8161-4114-2, Large Print Bks); pap. 11.95 o.p. (ISBN 0-8161-4115-0, Large Print Bks.). G K Hall.
City of Night. John Rechy. 1962. pap. 4.50 o.p. (ISBN 0-394-62169-7, B505, BC). Grove.
City of Night-Access. John Rechy. 1984. pap. 4.50 o.p. (BC). Grove.
City of Sorcery. Marion Zimmer Bradley. 1984. pap. 3.95 o.p. (ISBN 0-88677-122-6). DAW Bks.
City of the Dead. Herbert Lieberman. 1986. pap. 3.95 o.p. (ISBN 0-380-69976-1). Avon.
City of the Gods: A Study in Myth & Mortality. John S. Dunne. LC 78-2588. 1978. Repr. of 1965 ed. text ed. 18.95 o.p. (ISBN 0-268-00725-X). U of Notre Dame Pr.
City on the Bluff. Rebecca Robinson. (Illus.). 45p. 1987. 9.95 o.p. (ISBN 0-918518-54-7, St Luke TN). Peachtree Pubs.
City Planning & Redevelopment Law: Monographs. Mary Vance. (Architecture Ser.: A 1506). 56p. 1985. 8.25 o.p. (ISBN 0-89028-656-6). Vance Biblios.
City Planning in Ancient Times: Digging up the Past. Arthur Segal. LC 75-5294. (Archaeology Ser.). (Illus.). (gr. 5 up). 1977. PLB 8.95 o.p. (ISBN 0-8225-0836-2). Lerner Pubns.
City Primeval. Elmore Leonard. LC 80-66762. 1980. 10.95 o.p. (ISBN 0-87795-282-5, Arbor Hse). Morrow.
City Primeval: High Noon in Detroit. Elmore Leonard. 350p. 1986. lib. bdg. 16.95 o.p. (ISBN 0-8161-3948-2, Large Print Bks). G K Hall.
City Profiles in Periodical Literature: A Checklist, 1974-1984. Dale E. Casper. (Public Administration Ser.: P 1740). 11p. 1985. 2.00 o.p. (ISBN 0-89028-520-9). Vance Biblios.
City Revitalized: The Elderly Lose at Monopoly. Marea Teski et al. LC 83-5786. (Illus.). 214p. 1983. lib. bdg. 27.50 o.p. (ISBN 0-8191-3165-2); pap. text ed. 12.50 o.p. (ISBN 0-8191-3166-0). U Pr of Amer.
City Rose. Ruth Miller. 160p. (gr. 6-8). 1977. text ed. 10.95 o.p. (ISBN 0-07-041950-7). McGraw.
City Shadows: Psychological Interventions in Psychiatry. Arnold Mindell. 224p. 1988. pap. text ed. 12.95 o.p. (ISBN 0-415-00193-5, Pub. by Routledge UK). Routledge Chapman & Hall.
City under the Influence: A Political Autobiography. Joseph J. LaRaia. LC 79-84643. (Illus.). ii, 185p. Date not set. o.p. Nimrod Pr.
City under the Sands. Wallace Henley. (Living Bks.). 320p. (Orig.). 1986. pap. 4.50 o.p. (ISBN 0-8423-0286-7). Tyndale.
City Under the Sea. Kenneth Bulmer. 1979. pap. 2.25 o.p. (ISBN 0-380-48348-3, 48348, Discus). Avon.
Civic & Corporate Heraldry: A Dictionary of Impersonal Arms of England, Wales, & Northern Ireland. Ed. by Geoffrey Briggs. (Illus.). 432p. 1971. 32.00x o.p. (ISBN 0-685-29194-4). Gale.
Civic Center Architecture: A Bibliography. Mary E. Huls. (Architecture Ser.: A 1474). 6p. 1985. 2.00 o.p. (ISBN 0-89028-604-3). Vance Biblios.
Civic Plate & Insignia of the City of Portsmouth. C. Oman. 1965. 41.00x o.p. (ISBN 0-317-43824-7, Pub. by City of Portsmouth). State Mutual Bk.
Civil Aircraft in Colour. Hiroshi Seo. (Illus.). 80p. 1986. 14.95 o.p. (ISBN 0-7106-0346-0). Janes Info Group.
Civil Aircraft of the World. 3rd. ed. John W. Taylor & Gordon Swanborough. LC 77-74718. (Illus.). 1978. Encore ed. 9.95 o.s.i. (ISBN 0-684-15224-X, ScribT). Scribner.
Civil Disobedience in America: A Documentary History. Ed. by David R. Weber. LC 77-90914. 320p. 1978. 32.50x o.p. (ISBN 0-8014-1005-3). Cornell U Pr.
Civil Engineering Drawing. 2nd ed. D. V. Jude. 151p. 1983. pap. text ed. 19.95 o.p. (ISBN 0-246-11752-4, Granada England). Gower Pub Co.
Civil Engineering Hydraulics: Essential Theory with Worked Examples. R. E. Featherstone & C. Nalluri. (Illus.). 384p. 1982. text ed. 23.50x o.p. (ISBN 0-246-11483-5). Sheridan.
Civil Engineering in the Oceans III, 2 vols. 1545p. 1975. Set. pap. 59.00x o.p. (ISBN 0-87262-162-6). Am Soc Civil Eng.
Civil Engineering Procedure. 3rd ed. 112p. 1979. pap. 13.00 o.p. (ISBN 0-7277-0113-4, Pub. by T Telford UK). Am Soc Civil Eng.
Civil Engineering Standard Method of Measurement: Examples. Martin Barnes. 106p. 1977. pap. 6.50x o.p. (ISBN 0-7277-0035-9, Pub. by T Telford UK). Am Soc Civil Eng.
Civil Engineering Standard Method of Measurement in Practice. R. G. McCaffrey et al. 250p. 1983. pap. text ed. 29.95x o.p. (ISBN 0-246-11928-4, Pub. by Granada England). Gower Pub Co.
Civil Environmental Industrial. 10.00 o.p. (ISBN 0-317-65069-6). Am Consul Eng.
Civil Liability for Nuclear Damage: Official Records. International Conference on Civil Liability for Nuclear Damage, Vienna, 1963. (Legal Ser.: No. 2). 522p. (Eng., Fr., Rus. & Span.). 1964. pap. (ISBN 92-0-176064-7, ISP54, IAEA). UNIPUB.
Civil Liberties & American Democracy. John Brigham. LC 84-1869. 300p. 1984. pap. 13.95 o.p. (ISBN 0-87187-303-6). Congr Quarterly.
Civil Liberties & Civil Rights in the United States. Harriet Pollack & Alexander B. Smith. LC 78-5892. 299p. 1978. text ed. 29.75 o.p. (ISBN 0-8299-2003-X). West Pub.
Civil Liberties Today. Donald Parker et al. (Illus.). (gr. 9 up). 1974. pap. 6.72 o.p. (ISBN 0-395-18184-4, 2-43151); pap. 2.48 instr's. manual o.p. (ISBN 0-395-18505-X, 2-43152). HM.
Civil Liberties under the Constitution. rev. ed. M. Glenn Abernathy. LC 85-1052. 618p. 1985. pap. text ed. 22.95x o.p. (ISBN 0-87249-455-1). U of SC Pr.
Civil Liberty in South Africa. Edgar H. Brookes & J. B. Macaulay. LC 72-11232. 175p. 1973. Repr. of 1958 ed. lib. bdg. 22.50x o.p. (ISBN 0-8371-6635-7, BRCL). Greenwood.
Civil Procedure. Kevin M. Clermont. LC 82-2742. (Black Letter Ser.). 308p. 1982. pap. text ed. 13.95 o.p. (ISBN 0-314-65090-3). West Pub.
Civil Procedure, Fifth Edition, Basic Course, 1987 Supplement. Richard H. Field et al. (University Casebook Ser.). 27p. 1987. pap. text ed. (ISBN 0-88277-573-1). Foundation Pr.
Civil RICO 1985. 422p. 1986. 45.00 o.p. (C4-4175). PLI.
Civil Rights. 8th ed. P. M. Bolton. 226p. 1985. 8.95 o.p. (ISBN 0-88908-622-2). ISC Pr.
Civil Rights & Liberties Handbook: Pleadings & Practice. LC 70-24060. 1985. 37.50 o.p. Natl Lawyers Guild.
Civil Rights, Employment, & the Social Status of American Negroes. Harold Sheppard & Herbert Striner. 85p. 1966. pap. 0.50 o.p. (ISBN 0-911558-19-5). W E Upjohn.
Civil Rights in the U. S. Material Published 1980-1984. Mary A. Vance. LC 85-233011. (Public Administration Series-Bibliography). 39p. 1985. 6.00 o.p. (ISBN 0-89028-501-2, P1731). Vance Biblios.
Civil Rights Litigation & Attorney Fees Annual Handbook. 37.50 o.p. Natl Lawyers Guild.
Civil Rights Litigation in Federal Courts. 112p. 1984. 9.00 o.p. (ISBN 0-318-02451-9). ICLE Georgia.
Civil Rights U. S. A. Public Schools, Southern States, 1962, Staff Reports. U. S. Commission on Civil Rights. LC 68-55105. (Illus.). 1968. Repr. of 1962 ed. lib. bdg. 19.75 o.p. (ISBN 0-8371-0692-3, CIR&, Pub. by Negro U Pr). Greenwood.
Civil Service Reform in Brazil: Principles vs. Practice. Lawrence S. Graham. (Latin American Monographs: No. 13). 247p. 1968. 12.50x o.p. (ISBN 0-292-78356-6). U of Tex Pr.
Civil Service Today. Gavin Drewry. 200p. 1984. 45.00x o.p. (ISBN 0-85520-582-2). Basil Blackwell.
Civil Uses of RICO. Pennsylvania Bar Institute Staff. 181p. 1985. 25.00 o.p. (ISBN 0-318-19025-7, 283). PA Bar Inst.
Civil War. Bruce Catton. 1971. write for info. o.p. (ISBN 0-07-010266-X); pap. text ed. 7.95 o.p. (ISBN 0-07-010265-1). McGraw.
Civil War Dictionary. rev. ed. Mark M. Boatner, III. (Illus.). 974p. 1988. write for info. o.p. (ISBN 0-8129-1726-X). Times Bks.
Civil War in France: The Paris Commune. rev. ed. Karl Marx & Vladimir I. Lenin. LC 68-29502. 144p. 1968. 4.95 o.p. (ISBN 0-7178-0247-7); pap. 2.50 o.p. (ISBN 0-7178-0027-X). Intl Pubs Co.
Civil War Military Dictionary. H. L. Scott. Ed. by Martin Rywell. (Illus.). pap. 2.00 o.p. (ISBN 0-913150-08-8). Pioneer Pr.
Civil War Songbook. Richard Crawford. 1986. 14.75 o.p. (ISBN 0-8446-5566-X). Peter Smith.
Civil Wars. June Jordan. LC 80-68164. 216p. 1982. Repr. of 1981 ed. 8.95 o.p. (ISBN 0-8070-3232-8). Beacon Pr.
Civilization & Disease. Henry E. Sigerist. 1962. pap. text ed. 3.95 o.s.i. (ISBN 0-226-75723-4, P511, Phoen). U of Chicago Pr.
Civilization & the Caesars. Chester G. Starr. (Illus.). 1965. pap. 5.95x o.p. (ISBN 0-393-00322-1, Norton Lib). Norton.
Civilization in the Ancient Americas: Essays in Honor of Gordon R. Willey. Ed. by Richard M. Leventhal & Alan L. Kolata. LC 85-25094. (Illus.). 501p. 1983. 39.95x o.p. (ISBN 0-8263-0693-4). U of NM Pr.
Civilization of Ancient Egypt. Paul Johnson. LC 78-3150. 1978. 12.95 o.p. (ISBN 0-689-10921-0, Atheneum). Macmillan.
Civilization of Charlemagne. Jacques Boussard. (World University Library Ser.). (Illus., Orig.). 1968. pap. text ed. 3.95 o.p. (ISBN 0-07-006710-4). McGraw.
Civilization of Christianity. John L. McKenzie. 1986. pap. 10.95 o.p. (ISBN 0-88347-208-2). Thomas More.
Civilization Past & Present: Special Printing. 5th, special ed. T. Walter Wallbank et al. 1983. Single volume edition. text ed. (ISBN 0-673-15624-9). Scott F.
Civilization Primer. Edward M. Anson. 121p. 1984. text ed. 8.00 net spiral bdg. o.p. (ISBN 0-15-507595-0, HC). HarBraceJ.
Civilization That Perished: The Last Years of White Colonial Rule in Haiti. Mederic L. Moreau De Saint-Mery. Abridged by & tr. by Ivor D. Spencer. LC 85-22707. (Illus.). 318p. (Orig.). 1986. lib. bdg. 30.50 o.p. (ISBN 0-8191-5028-2); pap. text ed. 15.00 o.p. (ISBN 0-8191-5029-0). U Pr of Amer.
Civilizations East & West: A Memorial Volume for Benjamin Nelson. Ed. by E. V. Walter et al. 162p. 1985. text ed. 15.00x o.p. (ISBN 0-391-03065-5). Humanities.
Civilizations of the Holy Land. Paul Johnson. LC 78-73358. (Illus.). 1979. 14.95 o.p. (ISBN 0-689-10973-3, Atheneum). Macmillan.
Civilized. Arthur S. Yeranian. 192p. 1980. 9.00 o.p. (ISBN 0-682-49648-0). Exposition-Phoenix.
Civilized vs. Civilization: Primitivism in the Literature of German Pre-Romanticism. Eugene E. Reed. LC 76-56590. 1978. 3.50 o.p. (ISBN 0-89301-039-1). U of Idaho Pr.
Cladding: A Bibliography. Mary E. Huls. (Architecture Ser.: A 1485). 7p. 1985. 2.00 o.p. (ISBN 0-89028-615-9). Vance Biblios.
Claes Oldenburg. (Illus.). 1988. pap. 15.00 o.p. (ISBN 0-918825-79-2, Pub. by Mus Boymans-van Beuingen Holland). Moyer Bell Limited.
Claiming a Right. Muriel Ringstad. 96p. 1972. 1.95 o.p. (ISBN 0-317-35460-4). New Readers.
Claiming God's Promises. Alger Fitch. 144p. (Orig.). 1984. pap. 2.95 o.p. (ISBN 0-87239-750-5, 41028). Standard Pub.
Claims Processing for Benefit Plans, 1983. Ed. by Mary E. Brennan. LC 84-80454. 82p. (Orig.). 1984. pap. 10.00 o.p. (ISBN 0-89154-220-5). Intl Found Employ.
Claims to Territory in International Law & Relations. Norman L. Hill. LC 75-25488. (Illus.). 248p. 1976. Repr. of 1945 ed. lib. bdg. 35.00x o.p. (ISBN 0-8371-8430-4, HICT). Greenwood.
Clam Lake Papers: A Winter in the North Woods. Edward Lueders. LC 77-7845. 1977. 7.95i o.p. (ISBN 0-06-065312-4). HarpR.
Clancy's Coat. Eve Bunting. LC 83-6575. (Illus.). 48p. (gr. 1-5). 1984. 11.95 o.p. (ISBN 0-7232-6252-7). Warne.
Clandestine Collection. Ed. by Roy Godson. (Intelligence Requirements for the Nineteen Eighties Ser.: Vol. 5). 225p. 1982. pap. 8.50 o.p. (ISBN 0-87855-831-4). Transaction Pubs.
Clans of Darkness: Scottish Stories of Fantasy & Horror. Ed. by Peter Haining. LC 74-162964. 1971. 7.50 o.s.i. (ISBN 0-8008-1621-8). Taplinger.
Clapp's Rock. William Rowe. LC 86-16185. 364p. 1987. Repr. of 1986 ed. 18.95 o.p. (ISBN 0-87951-264-4). Overlook Pr.
Clara Schumann: A Dedicated Spirit; A Study of Her Life & Work. Joan Chissell. LC 83-50182. (Illus.). 200p. 1983. 19.95 o.s.i. (ISBN 0-8008-1624-2, Crescendo). Taplinger.
Clara: Thirteen Short Stories & a Novel. Luisa Valenzuela. Tr. by Hortense Carpentier & Jorge Castello. LC 75-42311. 233p. 1976. 12.95 o.p. (ISBN 0-15-118095-4). HarBraceJ.
Clara Tom's Old Fashioned Method of Cantonese Chinese Cooking. Clara T. Tom. LC 77-73326. 1965. soft spiral bdg. 9.95 o.p. (ISBN 0-930492-05-6). Hawaiian Serv.
Clara Weaver Parrish. C. Reynolds Brown. LC 80-82147. (Illus.). 1980. pap. 3.00 o.p. (ISBN 0-89280-016-X). Montgomery Mus.
Clare: The Critical Heritage. Ed. by Mark Storey. (Critical Heritage Ser.). 472p. 1985. pap. 15.00 o.p. (ISBN 0-7102-0512-0). Routledge Chapman & Hall.
Clarendon & Cultural Continuity: A Bibliographical Study. Graham Roebuck. 1980. lib. bdg. 67.00 o.p. (ISBN 0-8240-9769-6). Garland Pub.
Clarendon: Politics, History, & Religion 1640-1660. B. H. Wormald. LC 75-35494. (Midway Reprint Ser.). 1976. pap. text ed. 12.00x o.s.i. (ISBN 0-226-90738-4). U of Chicago Pr.
Clarifying Values Through Subject Matter: Applications for the Classroom. Merrill Harmin et al. 1973. pap. 4.95 o.p. (ISBN 0-03-008241-2, 860). HarpR.
Clarinet. Oskar Kroll. 183p. Repr. of 1968 ed. lib. bdg. 39.00 o.p. (Pub. by Am Repr Serv). Reprint Servs.
Clarinet. F. Geoffrey Rendall. (ISBN 0-8022-1327-8). Philos Lib.
Clarinet & Clarinet Playing. David Pino. (Illus.). 320p. 1983. pap. 9.95 o.s.i. (ISBN 0-684-17831-1, ScribT). Scribner.
Clarinets: A Story of Teenage Friendship & Courage. Franklin S. Myers. 1985. 9.95 o.p. (ISBN 0-533-06683-2). Vantage.
Clarion Cook Book for Boys & Girls. Eva Moore. LC 79-129210. (Illus.). 48p. (gr. 1-4). 1979. 7.95 o.p. (ISBN 0-395-28818-5, Clarion). HM.
Clarise Cumberbatch Want to Go Home. Joan Cambridge. 224p. 1987. 15.45 o.s.i. (ISBN 0-89919-403-6). Ticknor & Fields.
Clark Gable: Legends. James Card. 1986. pap. 14.95 o.p. (ISBN 0-316-50056-9). Little.

Class. Erich Segal. 850p. 1986. lib. bdg. 19.95 o.p. (ISBN 0-8161-4026-X, Large Print Bks). G K Hall.

Class: A Guide Through the American Status System. Paul Fussell. (Illus.). 224p. 1983. 13.50 o.s.i. (ISBN 0-671-44991-5). Summit Bks.

Class Action Litigation. LC 83-70263. (Civil Practice Ser.: No. 4). 232p. 1983. pap. 30.00 o.p. (ISBN 0-941916-09-X). Assn Trial Ed.

Class & Community: The Industrial Revolution in Lynn. Alan Dawley. LC 75-29049. (Harvard Studies in Urban History Ser.). (Illus.). 1979. 27.00x o.s.i. (ISBN 0-674-13390-0); pap. 8.95x o.s.i. (ISBN 0-674-13395-1). Harvard U Pr.

Class & Conformity: A Study in Values. 2nd ed. Melvin L. Kohn. LC 77-85194. 1977. pap. text ed. 11.00x o.s.i. (ISBN 0-226-45030-9). U of Chicago Pr.

Class & Health: Health & Social Mobility. Richard Wilkinson. 300p. 1986. 47.00 o.p. (ISBN 0-422-60360-0, 1016, Pub. by Tavistock England). Routledge Chapman & Hall.

Class & Nation, Historically & in the Current Crisis. Samir Amin. LC 79-3022. 292p. 1980. 15.50 o.p. (ISBN 0-85345-522-8). Monthly Rev.

Class & Nation, Historically & in the Current Crisis. LC 79-3022. 292p. 1981. pap. 6.50 o.s.i. (ISBN 0-85345-523-6). Monthly Rev.

Class, Codes & Control, Vol. 3: Towards a Theory of Educational Transmissions. Basil Bernstein. (Primary Socialization, Language & Education Ser.). 1977. pap. 8.95x o.p. (ISBN 0-7100-8666-0). Routledge Chapman & Hall.

Class, Culture & Community: A Biological Study of Social Change in Mining. Bill Williamson. (Illus.). 288p. (Orig.). 1982. pap. 16.95x o.p. (ISBN 0-7100-0991-7). Routledge Chapman & Hall.

CLASS Directory of Inter Library Loan Policies. 3rd ed. CLASS Cooperative Library for Systems & Services Staff. 100p. 35.00 o.p. (ISBN 0-938098-11-X). CLASS.

Class Inequality & Health Care: The Origins & Impact of the National Health Service. Vivienne Walters. 175p. 1980. 26.00 o.p. (ISBN 0-85664-685-7, Pub. by Croom Helm Ltd). Routledge Chapman & Hall.

Class Kit for Pendul. Date not set. (ISBN 0-07-079758-7). McGraw.

Class Notes. Kate Stimpson. 256p. 1980. pap. 2.25 o.p. (ISBN 0-380-50203-8, 50203). Avon.

Class, Politics & the Economy. Stewart Clegg et al. (International Library of Sociology). 427p. 1986. text ed. 39.95 o.p. (ISBN 0-7102-0452-3). Routledge Chapman & Hall.

Class, Race & Sport in South Africa's Political Economy. Grant Jarvie. 128p. 1985. 39.95x o.p. (ISBN 0-7102-0443-4). Routledge Chapman & Hall.

Class, Sex, & the Woman Worker. Ed. by Milton Cantor & Bruce Laurie. LC 76-15304. (Contributions in Labor History Ser.: No. 1). ix, 253p. 1980. pap. text ed. 9.95 o.p. (ISBN 0-313-22733-0, CSSPB). Greenwood.

Class Structure & Income Determination. Erik O. Wright. (Institute for Research on Poverty Monograph). 1979. 24.50 o.p. (ISBN 0-12-764950-6). Acad Pr.

Class Structure in the Social Consciousness. rev. ed. Stanislaw Ossowski. Tr. by Sheila Patterson from Pol. (International Library of Sociology). 1979. pap. 12.95x o.p. (ISBN 0-7100-0532-6). Routledge Chapman & Hall.

Class Struggle. Karl Kautsky. 1971. pap. 3.95 o.p. (ISBN 0-393-00567-4, Norton Lib). Norton.

Classed Subject Catalog of the Engineering Societies Library, New York City, 9th Supplement. Ed. by Engineering Societies Library Staff. 1973. lib. bdg. 110.00 o.p. (ISBN 0-8161-1050-6, Hall Library). G K Hall.

Classes & Nations. G. Glezerman. 271p. 1979. pap. 2.45 o.p. (ISBN 0-8285-0218-8, Pub. by Progress Pubs USSR). Imported Pubns.

Classes, Conflict & Control: Studies in Criminal Justice Management. Jim L. Munro. (Criminal Justice Tex Ser.). 591p. 1976. pap. text ed. 15.95 o.p. (ISBN 0-87084-590-X). Anderson Pub Co.

Classic American Cooking. Pearl B. Foster. (Illus.). 512p. 1983. 17.45 o.p. (ISBN 0-671-44303-8). S&S.

Classic American Cooking. Pearl B. Foster. 416p. 1984. pap. 9.95 o.p. (ISBN 0-671-53027-5, Fireside). S&S.

Classic Book of Dirty Jokes Anecdota Americana. Frwd. by Al. Goldstein. 1981. 4.98 o.s.i. (ISBN 0-517-33636-7, Bell). Outlet Bk Co.

Classic Chinese Cuisine. Nina Simonds. 1982. 19.45 o.p. (ISBN 0-395-32218-9). HM.

Classic Christian Faith. Edgar M. Carlson. LC 77-84100. 1978. pap. 3.95 o.p. (ISBN 0-8066-1626-1, 10-1440, Augsburg). Augsburg Fortress.

Classic Cinema: Essays in Criticism. Ed. by Stanley J. Solomon. 354p. 1973. pap. text ed. 11.25 o.p. (ISBN 0-15-507629-9, HC). HarBraceJ.

Classic Cooking Made Easy. C. P. Fischer et al. 120p. 1985. 14.95 o.p. (ISBN 0-8120-5663-9). VHS 39.95 o.p. (ISBN 0-8120-7340-1); BETA 39.95 o.p. (ISBN 0-8120-7373-8). Barron.

Classic Country Inns of America, 3 vols. Ed. by Peter Andrews. LC 77-71352. (Illus.). 1978. Set. slip-cased 49.95x o.p. (ISBN 0-03-045556-1). Knapp Pr.

Classic Cuisine of Vietnam. Bach Ngo & Gloria Zimmerman. LC 79-20323. (Illus.). 1979. 21.95 o.p. (ISBN 0-8120-5309-5). Barron.

Classic Diet: The Way to Be Well. Mr. 1047. 1977. 4.00 o.p. (ISBN 0-682-48960-3). Exposition-Phoenix.

Classic Guitar Construction. Irving Sloane. LC 84-8585. (Illus.). 96p. (Orig.). 1985. pap. 9.95 o.p. (ISBN 0-8069-7926-7). Sterling.

Classic in Consumer Behavior. Louis E. Boone. 441p. 1977. pap. text ed. write for info. o.p. (ISBN 0-02-312110-6). Macmillan.

Classic Lives: The Education of a Racehorse. Caroline Silver. LC 72-93148. 1973. 7.50 o.p. (ISBN 0-15-118130-6). HarBraceJ.

Classic Maya Collapse. 2nd ed. Ed. by T. Patrick Culbert. LC 72-94657. (School of American Research Advanced Seminar Ser.). (Illus.). 571p. 1984. pap. 14.95 o.p. (ISBN 0-8263-0724-8). U of NM Pr.

Classic Old Car Value Guide. Quentin Kraft. (Annual Ser.). (Illus.). 200p. (Orig.). 1986. pap. 10.95 o.p. (ISBN 0-911473-10-6, Pub. by Old Car Value Guide). Motorbooks Intl.

Classic Philip Jose Farmer, 1964-1973, No. 2. Philip Jose Farmer. LC 84-7081. (Classics of Modern Science Fiction Ser.). 1984. 8.95 o.p. (ISBN 0-517-55545-X). Crown.

Classic Stories of Crime & Detection. LC 75-44953. (Crime Ficion Ser). 1976. lib. bdg. 21.00 o.p. (ISBN 0-8240-2350-1). Garland Pub.

Classic Theatre: Six French Plays, Vol. 4. Ed. by Eric Bentley. Incl. Misanthrope. Moliere; Cid. Pierre Corneille; Phaedra. Jean Racine; Turcaret. Alain R. Le Sage; False Confessions. Pierre C. Marivaux; Marriage of Figaro. Pierre A. De Beaumarchais. pap. 3.50 o.p. (ISBN 0-385-09872-3, A155D, Anch). Doubleday.

Classic Tradition in Japanese Architecture: Modern Versions of the Sukiya Style. Teiji Itoh. (Illus.). 280p. 80.00 o.s.i. (ISBN 0-317-54982-0). Apollo.

Classic Wicker Furniture. Heywood Brothers & Wakefield Co. Staff. 1983. 14.25 o.p. (ISBN 0-8446-5946-0). Peter Smith.

Classical America IV. Ed. by William A. Coles. (Illus.). 1978. 19.95 o.p. (ISBN 0-393-04497-1). Norton.

Classical & Contemporary Metaphysics: A Source Book. R. T. DeGeorge. 332p. 1962. 22.50 o.p. (ISBN 0-03-011310-5). Krieger.

Classical Banach-Lie Algebras & Banach-Lie Groups of Operators in Hilbert Space. P. De la Harpe. LC 72-88729. (Lecture Notes in Mathematics: Vol. 285). 160p. 1972. pap. 9.00 o.p. (ISBN 0-387-05984-9). Springer-Verlag.

Classical Cooking the Modern Way. Eugen Pauli. LC 78-24208. 640p. 1983. 35.95 o.p. (ISBN 0-8436-2074-9). Van Nos Reinhold.

Classical Dynamics & Its Quantum Analogues. D. A. Park. (Lecture Notes in Physics Ser.: Vol. 110). 339p. 1979. pap. 23.00 o.p. (ISBN 0-387-09565-9). Springer-Verlag.

Classical Evangelical Essays in Old Testament Interpretation. Walter C. Kaiser, Jr. 1972. pap. 9.95 o.p. (ISBN 0-8010-5314-5). Baker Bk.

Classical Guitar. Maurice Summerfield. 312p. (Orig.). 1987. pap. 14.95 o.s.i. (ISBN 0-9506224-7-8, HL 00183146, Pub. by Ashley Mark Pub). H Leonard Pub Corp.

Classical Guitar Design & Construction. McLeod & Welford. (Illus.). 90p. 1979. 12.50 o.p. (ISBN 0-7134-4964-0, Pub. by Batsford England). David & Charles.

Classical Hindu Mythology: A Reader in the Sanskrit Puranas. Ed. by Cornelia Dimmitt. Tr. by J. A. Van Buitenen. LC 77-92643. 388p. 1978. 34.95 o.p. (ISBN 0-87722-117-0); pap. 12.95x o.p. (ISBN 0-87722-122-7). Temple U Pr.

Classical Influence upon the Tribe of Ben. Kathryn A. McEuen. 1968. lib. bdg. 20.50x o.p. (ISBN 0-374-95472-0, Octagon). Hippocrene Bks.

Classical Mechanics. K. M. Khanna. 242p. (Orig.). 1979. pap. 21.50 o.p. (ISBN 0-686-81276-X). Krieger.

Classical Mechanics, Vol. 2. Edward A. Desloge. LC 81-11402. 492p. 1982. 59.95x o.p. (ISBN 0-471-09145-6, Pub. by Wiley-Interscience). Wiley.

Classical Political Economy: Primitive Accumulation & the Social Division of Labor. Michael Perelman. LC 83-13976. 280p. 1984. text ed. 29.50x o.p. (ISBN 0-86598-095-0, Rowman & Allanheld). Rowman.

Classical Speeches. Richard Crosscup. LC 64-16358. 512p. 1965. (ISBN 0-8022-0319-1). Philos Lib.

Classical Subjects 2: Pastoral & Comedy. Ed. by Walter H. Rubsamen. (Ballad Opera Ser.). 1974. lib. bdg. 61.00 o.p. (ISBN 0-8240-0907-X). Garland pub.

Classical Vocal Music in Print. Ed. by Thomas R. Nardone. LC 76-29568. (Music in Print Ser.: Vol. 4). 650p. 1976. lib. bdg. 95.00 o.p. (ISBN 0-88478-008-2). Musicdata.

Classical World Bibliography of Greek & Roman History. Walter Dolan. LC 76-52511. (Library of Humanities Reference Bks.: No. 94). 247p. 1978. lib. bdg. 36.00 o.p. (ISBN 0-8240-9879-X). Garland Pub.

Classical World Bibliography of Roman Drama & Poetry & Ancient Fiction. Intro. by Walter Donlan. LC 76-52516. (Library of Humanities Reference Bks.: No. 97). 1978. lib. bdg. 50.00 o.p. (ISBN 0-8240-9876-5). Garland Pub.

Classical World Bibliography of Vergil. Intro. by Walter Donlan. LC 76-52514. (Library of Humanities Reference Bks.: No. 96). 1978. lib. bdg. 25.00 o.p. (ISBN 0-8240-9877-3). Garland Pub.

Classics in Biology. Zuckerman. 352p. 1960. (ISBN 0-8022-1955-1). Philos Lib.

Classics in Coordination Chemistry: The Selected Papers of Alfred Werner, Pt. 1. Ed. by George B. Kauffman. (Illus.). 9.00 o.p. (ISBN 0-8446-2353-9). Peter Smith.

Classics in Education. Wade Baskin. LC 66-16174. 1966. (ISBN 0-8022-0079-6). Philos Lib.

Classics in Psychology. Thorne Shipley. 1376p. (ISBN 0-8022-1560-2). Philos Lib.

Classics in Scientific Management. Donald Del Mar. Ed. by Roger D. Collons. LC 75-20471. 457p. 1976. 26.75 o.p. (ISBN 0-8173-8701-3). U of Ala Pr.

Classics in Western Civilization. D. C. Somervell. 338p. 1960. (ISBN 0-8022-1608-0). Philos Lib.

Classics of Biology. Pi Suner. 350p. 1955. (ISBN 0-8022-1672-2). Philos Lib.

Classics of Modern Fiction: Ten Short Novels. 2nd ed. Ed. by Irving Howe. 1972. pap. text ed. 11.95 o.p. (ISBN 0-15-507645-0, HC). HarBraceJ.

Classics of Modern Fiction: Ten Short Novels. 3rd ed. Ed. by Irving Howe. 690p. 1980. pap. text ed. 14.50 o.p. (ISBN 0-15-507647-7, HC). HarBraceJ.

Classics of the Foreign Film. Parker Tyler. (Illus.). 1967. pap. 6.95 o.p. (ISBN 0-8065-0182-0, C256, Pub. by Citadel Pr). Carol Pub Group.

Classics of the Silent Screen. Joe Franklin. (Illus.). 1967. pap. 9.95 o.p. (C255, Pub. by Citadel Pr). Carol Pub Group.

Classics of World War Two - The Shadow War: Inside North Pole. Peter Dourlein. Tr. by F. G. Renier & Anne Cliff. 207p. 1988. Repr. of 1953 ed. price not set o.p. (ISBN 0-8094-7262-7); lib. bdg. price not set o.p. (ISBN 0-8094-7263-5). Time-Life.

Classics of World War Two - The Shadow War: Paris-Underground. Etta Shiber et al. 392p. 1988. Repr. of 1943 ed. price not set o.p. (ISBN 0-8094-7258-9); lib. bdg. price not set o.p. (ISBN 0-8094-7259-7). Time-Life.

Classics Reclassified. Richard Armour. (Illus.). 1960. (ISBN 0-07-002256-9); pap. text ed. 3.95 o.p. (ISBN 0-07-002257-7). McGraw.

Classics Revisited. Kenneth Rexroth. 1985. pap. 1.25 o.p. (ISBN 0-380-01101-8, 08920, Discus). Avon.

Classification & Nomenclature of Electroanalytical Techniques. International Union of Pure & Applied Chemistry. 1977. pap. 35.00 o.p. (ISBN 0-08-021226-3). Pergamon.

Classification & Nomenclature of Viruses: Proceedings of the International Committee on Taxonomy of Viruses, 1st Report. International Committee on Taxonomy of Viruses. Ed. by P. Wildy. (Monographs in Virology: Vol. 5). 1971. 18.00 o.p. (ISBN 3-8055-1196-5). S Karger.

Classification & Nomenclature of Viruses: Proceedings of the International Committee on Taxonomy of Viruses, 2nd Report. International Committee on Taxonomy of Viruses. (Intervirology: Vol. 7, No. 1-2). 1976. 10.00 o.p. (ISBN 3-8055-2418-8). S Karger.

Classification Decimale de Dewey et Index, 2 vols. Melvil Dewey. Incl. Vol. 1. Tables Generales. 32.00x (ISBN 0-910608-14-8); Vol. 2. Index. 32.00x (ISBN 0-910608-15-6). 1974. Set. 64.00x o.p. (ISBN 0-910608-31-8). Forest Pr.

Classification of Endogenous Psychoses. Karl Leonhard. Tr. by Russell Berman from Gr. 474p. 1979. text ed. 49.50x o.p. (ISBN 0-8290-0866-7). Irvington.

Classification of Jewish Immigrants & Its Implications: A Survey of Opinion. Nathan Goldberg et al. LC 45-6587. (Yivo English Translation Ser.). 154p. 1945. pap. 2.00 o.p. (ISBN 0-914512-13-7). Yivo Inst.

Classification of Nonbook Materials in Academic Libraries: A Commentary & Bibliography. Donald L. Foster. (Occasional Papers: No. 104). 61p. 1972. pap. 2.00 o.p. (ISBN 0-317-58885-0). U of Ill Lib Info Sci.

Classification Scheme for Illinois State Publications. Yuri Nakata & Michele Strange. (Occasional Papers: No. 116). 38p. 1974. pap. 2.00 o.p. (ISBN 0-317-58923-7). U of Ill Lib Info Sci.

Classification System to Describe Workpieces, Classification System. H. Opitz. Tr. by R. A. Taylor. LC 71-112891. 1970. Set. 80.00 o.p. (ISBN 0-08-015758-0). Pergamon.

Classification Theory of Algebraic Varieties & Compact Complex Spaces. K. Veno. LC 75-1211. (Lecture Notes in Mathematics Ser.: Vol. 439). xix, 278p. 1975. pap. 19.00 o.p. (ISBN 0-387-07138-5). Springer-Verlag.

Classification Theory of Riemannian Manifolds. L. Sario et al. LC 77-22197. (Lecture Notes in Mathematics: Vol. 605). 1977. pap. text ed. 26.00 o.p. (ISBN 0-387-08358-8). Springer-Verlag.

Classification Theory of Semi-Simple Algebraic Groups, Vol. 3. I. Satake. (Lecture Notes in Pure & Applied Mathematics Ser.: Vol. 3). 160p. 1971. 39.75 o.p. (ISBN 0-8247-1607-8). Dekker.

Classified Catalog of the Ecumenical Movement, 2 vols. World Council of Churches, Geneva, Switzerland Staff. 1972. lib. bdg. 185.00 o.p. (ISBN 0-8161-0925-7, Hall Library). G K Hall.

Classified Catalog of the Ecumenical Movement: First Supplement. World Council of Churches, Geneva, Switzerland Staff. 1981. lib. bdg. 105.00 o.p. (ISBN 0-8161-0360-7, Hall Library). G K Hall.

Classified Index of National Labor Relations Board Decisions & Related Court Decisions, December 1985. 428p. (Orig.). 1986. pap. 19.00 o.p. (S/N 831-003-00004-9). USGPO.

Classified Subject Catalog, 42 Vols. John Crerar Library Staff. 1967. incl. subject index 4145.00 o.s.i. (ISBN 0-8161-0195-7, Hall Library); subject index 100.00 o.s.i. (ISBN 0-8161-0196-5). G K Hall.

Classroom Application of Precision Teaching. Ed. by Thomas C. Lovitt & Norris G. Haring. LC 78-52435. 155p. 1979. pap. 8.00x o.p. (ISBN 0-87562-060-4). Spec Child.

Classroom Applications of the Curriculum: A Systems Approach. Charles W. Funkhouser et al. 160p. 1981. pap. text ed. 16.95 o.p. (ISBN 0-8403-2462-6). Kendall-Hunt.

Classroom Centers & Stations in America & Britain. Ed. by Marian P. Franklin. LC 73-10240. 1973. 29.50x o.p. (ISBN 0-8422-5120-0); pap. text ed. 12.50x o.p. (ISBN 0-8422-0327-3). Irvington.

Classroom Collaboration. Phillida Salmon & Hilary Claire. (Routledge Education Bks.). 224p. (Orig.). 1984. pap. 17.95x o.p. (ISBN 0-7100-9957-6). Routledge Chapman & Hall.

Classroom Discipline: Case Studies & Viewpoints. Sylvester Kohut, Jr. & Dale G. Range. 112p. 1979. pap. 8.95 o.p. (ISBN 0-8106-1491-X). NEA.

Classroom Discipline for Effective Teaching & Learning. L. N. Tanner. LC 77-22595. 1978. pap. text ed. 16.95 o.p. (ISBN 0-03-019446-6, HoltC). HR&W.

Classroom Environment. Barry J. Fraser. 240p. 1986. 31.00 o.p. (ISBN 0-7099-1057-6, Pub. by Croom Helm UK). Routledge Chapman & Hall.

Classroom Guide for the Norton Introduction to Literature. 3rd ed. 1982. pap. 2.95x o.p. (ISBN 0-393-95252-5). Norton.

Classroom Guide to Reading Assessment & Instruction. Nicholas J. Silvaroli & Dennis J. Kear. 208p. 1981. text ed. 18.95 o.p. (ISBN 0-8403-2633-5). Kendall-Hunt.

Classroom Management. Johanna K. Lemlech. 316p. 1987. pap. text ed. 12.75 o.p. (ISBN 0-8191-6625-1). U Pr of Amer.

Classroom Management in Business Education. 68p. 1986. 8.00 o.p. (ISBN 0-318-21759-7). Natl Busn Ed Assoc.

Classroom Practices in Teaching English: Activities to Promote Critical Thinking in English, 1986. Committee on Classroom Practices Staff & Jeff Golub. LC 86-21741. 160p. 1986. pap. 10.00 o.p. (ISBN 0-8141-0045-7). NCTE.

Classroom Practices in Teaching English 1978-1979: Activating the Passive Student. Ed. by Gene Stanford. LC 78-11561. 151p. (Orig.). 1978. pap. 8.00 o.p. (ISBN 0-8141-0688-9). NCTE.

Classroom Practices in Teaching English, 1980-1981: Dealing with Differences. Ed. by National Council of Teachers of English Staff & Gene Stanford. (Classroom Practices in Teaching English Ser.). 126p. 1980. 8.00 o.p. (ISBN 0-8141-0690-0). NCTE.

Classroom Psychology. Ruth Fishtein. LC 74-79108. 72p. 1974. pap. 2.95 o.p. (ISBN 0-87594-115-X). Book-Lab.

Classroom Society: The Construction of Educational Experience. Herbert A. Thelen. LC 81-6453. 226p. 1981. 29.95x o.p. (ISBN 0-470-27222-8). Halsted Pr.

Classroom Spaces & Places: Sixty-Five Projects for Improving Your Classroom. Gail Hannah. LC 81-820347. (gr. k-6). 1982. pap. 11.95 o.p. (ISBN 0-8224-1416-3). D S Lake Pubs.

Classroom Teacher's Workbook for Career Education. Joyce S. Mitchell. 1979. pap. 2.75 o.p. (ISBN 0-380-45179-4, 45179). Avon.

Classroom Teaching Skills. Ed. by E. C. Wragg. 220p. 1984. 29.50 o.p. (ISBN 0-89397-186-3); pap. 15.50 o.p. (ISBN 0-89397-187-1). Nichols Pub.

Clauberg Trigger. John Tarrant. LC 78-12455. 1979. 8.95 o.p. (ISBN 0-689-10938-5, Atheneum). Macmillan.

Claude Hanna Retraces Memory's Road. Ed. by Jean E. Bohannan. 1976. 10.00 o.p. (ISBN 0-682-48611-6). Exposition-Phoenix.

Claude Levi-Strauss & His Critics: An International Bibliography (1950-1976) Francois H. Lapointe & Claire C. Lapointe. LC 76-24752. (Reference Library of the Humanities Ser.: Vol. 72). 1977. lib. bdg. 33.00 o.p. (ISBN 0-8240-9925-7). Garland Pub.

Claude Lorrain: Sixteen Hundred to Sixteen Eighty-Two. Diane Russell. LC 82-14250. (Illus.). 480p. 1982. 60.00 o.p. (ISBN 0-8076-1055-0). Braziller.

Claudel's Immortal Heroes: A Choice of Deaths. Harold M. Watson. LC 73-160572. 1971. 40.00 o.p. (ISBN 0-8135-0695-6). Rutgers U Pr.

Claudine. Charlotte R. Miller. 1976. pap. 1.50 o.p. (ISBN 0-380-00564-6, 28761). Avon.

Claudio Monteverdi: Life & Works. Hans F. Redlich. Tr. by Kathleen Dale. 1971. Repr. of 1952 ed. lib. bdg. 35.00x o.p. (ISBN 0-8371-4003-X, REMO). Greenwood.

Claus! Michael C. Witte. (Illus.). 1982. pap. 4.95 o.s.i. (ISBN 0-03-061749-9, Owl BKs). H Holt & Co.

Claverton Outdoor Store: A Voucher System for Business for Chapters 22-29 see College Accounting Fundamentals.

Claw of the Dragon. Bruce Algozin. LC 86-90006. (Endless Quest Bks.: No. 34). 160p. (Orig.). (gr. 3-8). 1986. pap. 2.25 o.p. (ISBN 0-88038-306-2). TSR Inc.

Clay Boats. 2nd ed. Elementary Science Study Staff. 1975. tchr's. guide 9.56 o.p. (ISBN 0-07-018579-4). McGraw.

Clay Courts of Norwich. Stephen Armstrong. (Illus.). 200p. 1984. 12.50 o.p. (ISBN 0-682-40184-6). Exposition-Phoenix.

Clay Pedestal: A Re-examination of the Doctor-Patient Relationship. Thomas A. Preston. 240p. (Orig.). 1986. pap. 9.95 o.p. (ISBN 0-684-18639-X). Scribner.

Clay Pigeons of St Lo. Glover S. Johns, Jr. (Combat Arms Ser.: No. 4). 1979. Repr. of 1958 ed. 17.50 o.p. (ISBN 0-89839-026-5). Battery Pr.

Clay Statements: Australian Contemporary Ceramics. Bruce Anderson & John Hoare. 117p. 1985. pap. 23.95x o.p. (ISBN 0-949414-04-2, Pub. by Darling Downs Inst Pr Australia). Intl Spec Bk.

Cle des Champs. Andre Breton. 15.95 o.p. (ISBN 0-685-37229-4). French & Eur.

Clean Air Act Handbook. 2nd ed. J. Philip Bromberg. LC 83-82074. (Illus.). 328p. 1985. pap. 62.00 o.p. (ISBN 0-86587-039-X). Gov Insts.

Clean & Decent: The History of the Bathroom & the W. C. Lawrence Wright. (Illus.). 224p. 1984. pap. 9.95 o.p. (ISBN 0-7100-4665-0). Routledge Chapman & Hall.

Clean Sweep. Jeffrey M. Wallman. 1978. pap. 1.50 o.p. (ISBN 0-380-01708-3, 33837). Avon.

Clean up the Blood Stream & Live. Lillian Taylor. 45p. 1958. pap. 4.95 o.s.i. (ISBN 0-88697-023-7). Life Science.

Cleaner Breed. Nicholas J. Corea. 1974. pap. 1.25 o.p. (ISBN 0-380-00167-5, 21311). Avon.

Cleaning & Caring for Books. rev. ed. Robert L. Shep. (Illus.). 104p. 1983. 9.00 o.p. (ISBN 0-900661-30-5, Pub. by Sheppard England). Seven Hills Bk Dists.

Cleaning & Caring for Books. Robert L. Shep. (Illus.). 104p. 1987. 9.00 o.p. (ISBN 0-946653-30-5, Pub. by Europa Pubns Ltd England). Seven Hills Bk Dists.

Cleaning House. Nancy Hayfield. 156p. 1980. 10.95 o.p. (ISBN 0-374-12483-3). FS&G.

Cleaning the Bones. William Vernon. 16p. pap. 1.00 o.p. (ISBN 0-317-16905-X). Samisdat.

Cleaning up a Computer Mess. William E. Perry. 272p. 1985. 31.95 o.p. (ISBN 0-442-27491-2). Van Nos Reinhold.

Cleaning up America: An Insider's View of the Environmental Protection Agency. John Quarles, Jr. LC 76-25420. 1976. 8.95 o.p. (ISBN 0-395-24772-1). HM.

Cleaning Up: The Cost of Refinery Pollution Control. CEP Staff & Norris Boothe. Ed. by Mary J. Haley. LC 75-10535. 1975. pap. 25.00 o.p. (ISBN 0-87871-002-7). CEP.

Cleanliness & Godliness. Reginald Reynolds. LC 75-35508. 326p. 1976. pap. 3.95 o.p. (ISBN 0-15-618050-2, Harv). HarBraceJ.

Clear Air Turbulence & Its Detection. Yih-Ho Pao & Arnold Goldburg. LC 73-76507. 542p. 1969. 49.50x o.p. (ISBN 0-306-30397-3, Plenum Pr). Plenum Pub.

Clear & Present Dangers: A Conservative View of America's Government. M. Stanton Evans. 304p. (Orig.). 1975. pap. text ed. 11.95 o.p. (ISBN 0-15-507685-X, HC). HarBraceJ.

Clear for Action. Stephen W. Meader. LC 40-27736. (Illus.). (gr. 7 up). 1940. 4.95 o.p. (ISBN 0-15-218937-8, HJ). HarBraceJ.

Clear Introduction to FORTRAN IV. 2nd ed. Jaffe. LC 77-21300. 1979. pap. text ed. write for info. o.p. (ISBN 0-87872-175-4, Duxbury Pr). PWS-Kent Pub.

Clear Sky, Pure Light: Encounters with Henry David Thoreau. Henry David Thoreau. Ed. by Christopher Childs. LC 78-56627. 1978. 15.00x o.p. (ISBN 0-915778-27-0); deluxe ed. 50.00x o.p. (ISBN 0-915778-26-2). Penmaen Pr.

Clear Technical Reports. William A. Damerst. 1972. 16.95 o.p. (ISBN 0-15-507691-4). HarbraceJ.

Clear Writing: A Business Guide. Marilyn B. Gilbert. LC 82-16043. (Self-Teaching Guides Ser.). 286p. 1983. pap. text ed. 9.95 o.p. (ISBN 0-471-86755-1). Wiley.

Cleared for Takeoff: Flying for Beginners. Gordon Stokes. LC 78-595. (Illus.). 1978. 2.95 o.s.i. (ISBN 0-684-15787-X, ScribT); Encore ed. 2.95 o.p. (ISBN 0-684-16694-1). Scribner.

Cleared to Land. Frank Burnham. LC 75-38050. 1977. 3.95 o.p. (ISBN 0-8168-4500-X, 24500, TAB-Aero). TAB Bks.

Clearing. Wendell Berry. LC 76-27422. 1977. 6.95 o.p. (ISBN 0-15-118150-0). HarBraceJ.

Clearing. Mary Elsie Robertson. LC 81-69164. (Illus.). 192p. 1982. 11.95 o.p. (ISBN 0-689-11275-0, Atheneum). Macmillan.

Cleary & Graham's Handbook of Illinois Evidence: 1986 Supplement. 4th ed. Michael H. Graham. LC 86-82693. 144p. 1986. write for info. o.p. (ISBN 0-316-32303-9). Little.

Cleft Palate & Its Associated Speech Disorders. C. Wells. (Speech Ser.). 1971. text ed. 38.95 o.p. (ISBN 0-07-069243-2). McGraw.

Clemens Brentano. John Fetzer. (World Authors Ser.). 1981. 16.95 o.p. (ISBN 0-8057-6457-7, Twayne). G K Hall.

Clemens' Kingdom. Chris L. Demarest. LC 82-12731. (Illus.). 32p. (gr. k-3). 1983. 11.75 o.p. (ISBN 0-688-01655-3); PLB 11.88 o.p. (ISBN 0-688-01657-X). Lothrop.

Clementine Churchill: The Biography of a Marriage. Mary Soames. 1979. 16.95 o.p. (ISBN 0-395-27597-0). HM.

Cleopatra. Ernle Bradford. LC 73-153683. (Illus.). 1972. 15.00 o.p. (ISBN 0-15-118140-3). HarBraceJ.

CLEP Resource Manual: Introduction to Sociology. Philip A. Cecchettini. 1979. pap. text ed. 13.95 o.p. (ISBN 0-07-010306-2). McGraw.

CLEP Resource Manual: Introduction to Business Management. Philip A. Cecchettini. (Illus.). 1979. pap. text ed. 14.95 o.p. (ISBN 0-07-010308-9). McGraw.

CLEP Resourse Manual: Introduction to General Psychology. Philip A. Cecchettini. 1979. pap. text ed. 16.95 o.p. (ISBN 0-07-010305-4). McGraw.

Clergy Compensation & Financial Planning Workbook. Herbert L. Akin. (Illus.). 100p. 1982. wkbk. 6.95 o.p. (ISBN 0-938736-05-1). Life Enrich.

Clergy Malpractice: An Illegal Legal Theory. rev. ed. Samuel E. Ericsson. (Focus Ser.: No. 2). 45p. (Orig.). pap. text ed. 5.00 o.s.i. (ISBN 0-944561-14-4). Chr Legal.

Clerical Cartoons. 2nd ed. William Armstrong. (Armstrong Cartoon Ser.). (Illus.). 48p. (Orig.). (ps up). 1971. pap. 1.00 o.p. (ISBN 0-913452-02-5). Jesuit Bks.

Cleveland Browns. James R. Rothaus. (NFL Today Ser.). (Illus.). 48p. (gr. 4-12). 1981. PLB 10.45 o.p. (ISBN 0-87191-809-9); pap. 4.25 o.p. Creative Ed.

Cleveland Cavaliers. Frank MacDonlad. (NBA Today Ser.). (Illus.). 48p. (gr. 4 up). 1984. PLB 10.45 o.p. (ISBN 0-87191-973-7). Creative Ed.

Cleveland Era. Henry J. Ford. 1919. 19.50x o.p. (ISBN 0-686-83504-2). Elliots Bks.

Cleveland Indians. rev. ed. Brannon. LC 82-14917. (Baseball Today Ser.). 48p. (gr. 4 up). 1982. PLB 11.45 o.p. (ISBN 0-87191-859-5). Creative Ed.

Cleveland, Ohio: An Evaluation of the Target Area Investment Program for the City of Cleveland, June 5-10, 1983; a Panel Advisory Service Report. Urban Land Institute, Panel Advisory Service Staff. LC 83-241151. (Illus.). 50p. 1983. 10.00 o.p. (C-26). Urban Land.

Clever-Lazy: The Girl Who Invented Herself. Joan Bodger. LC 79-10484. 1979. 8.95 o.p. (ISBN 0-689-30674-1, Atneneum). Macmillan.

Clever Polly & the Stupid Wolf. Catherine Storr. (Illus.). 96p. (gr. k-3). 1979. 8.95 o.p. (ISBN 0-571-18011-6). Faber & Faber.

Click Song. John A. Williams. 1982. 13.95 o.p. (ISBN 0-395-31841-6). HM.

Click's Cookie Cornucopia. Margaret M. Seidenberg. (Illus.). 88p. 1983. pap. 5.95 o.s.i. (ISBN 0-9612920-0-8). Click's Cookbooks.

Client Participation in Human Services: The Prometheus Principle. Ed. by Constance T. Fischer & Stanley L. Brodsky. LC 76-1772. 300p. 1978. 12.95 o.p. (ISBN 0-87855-131-X). Transaction Pubs.

Cliff Castles & Cave Dwellings of Europe. Sabine Baring-Gould. LC 68-17983. (Illus.). 323p. 1968. Repr. of 1911 ed. 35.00x o.p. (ISBN 0-8103-3423-2). Gale.

Clifford at the Circus. Norman Bridwell. (gr. k-3). 1977. pap. 1.50 o.p. (ISBN 0-590-11835-8). Scholastic Inc.

Clifford D. Simak: A Primary & Secondary Bibliography. Muriel R. Becker. 1979. lib. bdg. 22.00 o.p. (ISBN 0-8161-8063-6, Hall Reference). G K Hall.

Clifford Odets: American Playwright. Margaret Brenman-Gibson. LC 80-7927. (Illus.). 1981. 30.00 o.p. (ISBN 0-689-11160-6, Atheneum). Macmillan.

Clifford Takes a Trip. Norman Bridwell. (Illus.). (gr. k-3). 1969. pap. 1.25 o.p. (ISBN 0-590-08029-6). Scholastic Inc.

Clifford the Big Red Dog. Norman Bridwell. (Illus.). (gr. k-3). 1969. pap. 1.25 o.p. (ISBN 0-590-08028-8); pap. 3.95 incl. record o.p. (ISBN 0-590-04385-4). Scholastic Inc.

Clifford, the Small Red Puppy. Norman Bridwell. (Illus.). 32p. (gr. k-3). 1973. pap. 1.95 o.p. (ISBN 0-590-33726-2). Scholastic Inc.

Clifford Va de Viaje. Norman Bridwell. Tr. by Argentina Palacios from Span. (gr. k-3). 1979. pap. 2.95 o.p. Scholastic Inc.

Clifford's Tricks. Norman Bridwell. (Illus.). (gr. k-3). 1971. pap. 1.50 o.p. (ISBN 0-590-33820-X). Scholastic Inc.

Climate & Evolution. Ronald Pearson. 1979. 68.00 o.p. (ISBN 0-12-548250-7). Acad Pr.

Climate & Landforms: A Laboratory Manual in Physical Geography. LaDochy et al. 288p. 1983. pap. 12.95 o.p. (ISBN 0-8403-3784-1, 40378402). Kendall-Hunt.

Climate & Weather. N. Flohn. (Illus.). 256p. (Orig.). 1968. pap. text ed. 3.95 o.p. (ISBN 0-07-021325-9). McGraw.

Climate & Weather in the Tropics. H. Riehl. 1979. 70.50 o.p. (ISBN 0-12-588180-0). Acad Pr.

Climate Canada. 2nd ed. F. K. Hare & M. K. Kenneth-Thomas. 296p. 1980. 34.50 o.p. (ISBN 0-471-08326-7). Wiley.

Climate-Diagram Maps: Of the Individual Continents & the Ecological Climatic Regions of the Earth. H. Walter & E. Harnickell. (Supplement to the Vegetation Monographs). (Illus.). 36p. 1975. cased bdg. 42.50 o.p. (ISBN 0-387-07065-6). Springer-Verlag.

Climate for Creativity. Ed. by C. W. Taylor. 312p. 1972. 36.00 o.p. (ISBN 0-08-016329-7). Pergamon.

Climate in Every Day Life. C. E. Brooks. 1951. (ISBN 0-8022-0184-9). Philos Lib.

Climate in Miniature. Franklin. 160p. 1955. (ISBN 0-8022-0528-3). Philos Lib.

Climate in Review. Geoffrey McBoyle. LC 72-3536. 1973. pap. 14.95 o.p. (ISBN 0-395-16007-3). HM.

Climates of West Africa. Oyediran Ojo. 1977. text ed. 17.50x o.p. (ISBN 0-435-95700-7); pap. text ed. 17.50 o.p. (ISBN 0-435-95701-5). Heinemann Ed.

Climatic Change & World Affairs. C. Tickell. 1978. text ed. 17.25 o.p. (ISBN 0-08-022228-5). Pergamon.

Climatic Change in Deserts. M. Williams. 350p. cancelled o.s.i. (ISBN 0-12-755350-9). Acad Pr.

Climatic Constraints & Human Activities. J. Ausebel & A. K. Biswas. LC 80-41073. (IIASA Proceedings: Vol. 10). (Illus.). 215p. 1980. 46.00 o.p. (ISBN 0-08-026721-1). Pergamon.

Climatic Resources & Economic Activity. J. A. Taylor. LC 74-823. (Illus.). 264p. 1974. 31.95x o.p. (ISBN 0-470-84826-X). Halsted Pr.

Climatology from Satellites. E. C. Barrett. (Illus.). 418p. 1974. 53.00x o.p. (ISBN 0-416-65940-3, NO.2075); pap. 17.00x o.p. (ISBN 0-416-72150-8, NO.2614). Routledge Chapman & Hall.

Climax of Populism: The Election of 1896. Robert F. Durden. LC 81-4137. xii, 190p. 1981. Repr. of 1965 ed. lib. bdg. 35.00x o.p. (ISBN 0-313-22846-9, DUCP). Greenwood.

Climber's Bible: A Complete Basic Guide to Rock & Ice Climbing & an Introduction to Mountaineering. Robin Shaw. LC 78-20097. (Outdoor Bible Ser.). (Illus.). 144p. 1983. pap. 5.95 o.p. (ISBN 0-385-14075-4). Doubleday.

Climbers Guide to Glacier National Park. rev. ed. J. Gordon Edwards. LC 84-14787. 303p. 1984. pap. 9.95 o.s.i. (ISBN 0-87842-177-7). Mountain Pr.

Climber's Guide to North America, Vol. 1: West Coast Rock Climbs. John Harlin, III. (Illus.). 368p. 1984. pap. text ed. 22.00 o.s.i. (ISBN 0-9609452-2-9). Chockstone Pr.

Climber's Guide to the Olympic Mountains. 2nd ed. Olympic Mountain Rescue Staff. LC 70-163356. (Illus.). 240p. (Orig.). 1979. pap. 8.95 o.p. (ISBN 0-916890-83-X). Mountaineers.

Climbing & Hiking in Ecuador. Robert Rachowiecki. (Backpacker's Guide Ser.). (Illus.). 172p. (Orig.). 1984. pap. 10.95 o.p. (ISBN 0-933982-23-2). Bradt Ent.

Climbing Guide to Colorado's Fourteeners. Walter Borneman & Lyndon J. Lampert. LC 78-5947. (Illus.). 1984. pap. 9.95 o.p. (ISBN 0-87108-519-4). Pruett.

Climbing Higher: Reflections on Our Spiritual Journey. David Rosage. 112p. (Orig.). 1983. pap. 5.95 o.p. (ISBN 0-89283-147-2). Servant.

Climbing Jacob's Ladder: The Arrival of Negroes in Southern Politics. Pat Watters & Reese Cleghorn. LC 67-20324. 1970. pap. 2.95 o.p. (ISBN 0-15-618105-3, Harv). HarBraceJ.

Climbing the Corporate Matterhorn. James A. Newman & Roy Alexander. LC 84-15357. 311p. 1985. 16.95 o.p. (ISBN 0-471-80764-8); pap. 9.95 o.p. (ISBN 0-471-85146-9). Wiley.

Climbing the Ladder of Success in High Heels: Backgrounds of Professional Women. Jill A. Steinberg. Ed. by Peter Nathan. LC 83-15921. (Research in Clinical Psychology Ser.: No. 9). 194p. 1984. 37.95 o.p. (ISBN 0-8357-1491-8). UMI Res Pr.

Climbing to the Sun. Jeffrey Carroll. LC 77-8617. 128p. (gr. 6 up). 1979. 6.95 o.p. (ISBN 0-395-28898-3, Clarion). HM.

Clinch River: The Case for Completion. W. B. Behnke, Jr. et al. (Technical & Economic Reports). 1983. 30.00 o.p. (ISBN 0-318-02238-9). US Coun Energy Awareness.

Clinging to the Wreckage: A Part of Life. John Mortimer. LC 82-5728. (Illus.). 224p. 1982. 12.45 o.p. (ISBN 0-89919-133-9). Ticknor & Fields.

Clinic on Library Applications of Data Processing, Proceedings: 1977: Negotiating for Computer Services. Ed. by J. L. Divilbiss. LC 78-13693. 117p. 1978. 9.00x o.p. (ISBN 0-87845-048-3). U of Ill Lib Info Sci.

Clinic on Library Applications of Data Processing, Proceedings, 1979: The Role of the Library in an Electronic Society. Ed. by F. Wilfrid Lancaster. LC 79-19449. 200p. 1980. 9.00x o.p. (ISBN 0-87845-053-X). U of Ill Lib Info Sci.

Clinical Allergy Based on Provocative Testing. Harris Hosen. LC 77-82572. 1978. 10.00 o.p. (ISBN 0-682-48940-9, University). Exposition-Phoenix.

Clinical Anatomy in Action: The Head & Neck, Vol. 2. John Pegington. LC 84-9470. (Illus.). 185p. 1986. pap. text ed. 15.50 o.p. (ISBN 0-443-02869-9). Churchill.

Clinical Anatomy of the Head: Neurocranium, Orbita, Craniocervical Regions. J. Lang. (Illus.). 489p. 1983. 490.00 o.p. (ISBN 0-387-11014-3). Springer-Verlag.

Clinical & Biochemical Aspects of Hemoglobin Abnormalities. Ed. by Winslow Caughey. 1978. 76.50 o.p. (ISBN 0-12-164350-6). Acad Pr.

Clinical & Biochemical Luminescence. Kricka & Carter. (Clinical & Biochemical Analysis Ser.). 280p. 1982. 69.75 o.p. (ISBN 0-8247-1857-7). Dekker.

Clinical & Experimental Neuropsychophysiology. Ed. by Demetrios Papakostopoulos et al. LC 85-21365. 768p. 1985. 78.00 o.p. (ISBN 0-7099-2076-8, Pub. by Croom Helm Ltd). Routledge Chapman & Hall.

Clinical & Laboratory Procedures in the Physician's Office. Mary F. Bodanza. LC 81-11573. 313p. 1982. 21.95 o.p. (ISBN 0-471-06497-1). Wiley.

Clinical & Oral Microbiology. Alexander W. McCracken & Broderick A. Cawson. (Illus.). 1983. text ed. 47.95 o.p. (ISBN 0-07-010296-1). McGraw.

Clinical Anesthesia Procedures of the Massachusetts General Hospital. 2nd ed. Philip W. Lebowitz & Leslie A. Newberg. 1982. pap. text ed. 17.50 o.p. (ISBN 0-316-51867-0). Little.

Clinical Applications of Ribavirin. Robert A. Smith et al. 1984. 30.00 o.p. (ISBN 0-12-652360-6). Acad Pr.

Clinical Applications of Zinc Metabolism. Ed. by Walter J. Pories et al. (Illus.). 320p. 1975. 44.00 o.p. (ISBN 0-398-02968-7). C C Thomas.

Clinical Approaches to High Blood Pressure in the Young. Theodore A. Kotchen & Jane M. Kotchen. 1983. text ed. 36.00 o.p. (ISBN 0-7236-7032-3). Butterworth.

Clinical Aspects of Child Development: An Introductory Synthesis of Developmental Concepts & Clinical Experience. 2nd ed. Melvin Lewis. LC 81-11825. (Illus.). 447p. 1982. text ed. 19.50 o.p. (ISBN 0-8121-0796-9). Lea & Febiger.

Clinical Aspects of the Complement System. Ed. by W. Opferkuch & K. Rother. LC 78-54589. (Illus.). 266p. 1978. 32.50 o.p. (ISBN 0-88416-247-8). Year Bk Med.

Clinical Assisting see Doctors' Administrative Program.

Clinical Atlas of Human Chromosomes. 2nd ed. Jean De Grouchy & Catherine Turleau. LC 83-16839. 487p. 1984. 72.50 o.p. (ISBN 0-471-89205-X). Wiley.

Clinical Bacteriology. P. W. Ross. (Churchill Livingstone Medical Text Ser.). (Illus.). 1980. pap. 10.75 o.p. (ISBN 0-443-01811-1). Churchill.

Clinical Bacteriology. Ed. by John Scimone. (Functional Medical Laboratory Manual). (Illus.). 1978. pap. 17.95 o.s.i. (ISBN 0-87055-267-8). AVI.

Clinical Biochemistry for Medical Technologists. S. H. Kamath. LC 77-155035. 259p. 1972. 13.95 o.p. (ISBN 0-316-48253-6). Little.

Clinical Biochemistry Nearer the Patient. Ed. by V. Marks & K. H. Alberti. (Contemporary Issues in Clinical Biochemistry Ser.). (Illus.). 240p. 1985. text ed. 64.75 o.p. (ISBN 0-443-03159-2). Churchill.

Clinical Biochemistry of Domestic Animals. 3rd ed. Ed. by Jiro J. Kaneko. LC 79-8873. 1980. 79.00 o.p. (ISBN 0-12-396350-8). Acad Pr.

Clinical Biochemistry Reviews, Vol. 2. Ed. by David M. Goldberg. 456p. 1981. 48.00 o.p. (ISBN 0-317-54520-5, Pub. by John Wiley). Krieger.

Clinical Biochemistry Reviews, Vol. 3. Ed. by David M. Goldberg. 504p. 1982. 48.00 o.p. (ISBN 0-317-54522-1, Pub. by John Wiley). Krieger.

Clinical Bladder Cancer. Ed. by L. Denis et al. LC 81-15855. 214p. 1982. 45.00x o.p. (ISBN 0-306-40835-X, Plenum Pr). Plenum Pub.

Clinical Burn Therapy: A Management & Prevention Guide. Robert P. Hummel, Jr. (Illus.). 578p. 1982. 53.00 o.p. (ISBN 0-88416-284-2). Year Bk Med.

Clinical Case Studies in Psychodrama. Marion J. Heisey. LC 81-40109. 212p. (Orig.). 1982. lib. bdg. 29.75 o.p. (ISBN 0-8191-2531-8); pap. text ed. 13.00 o.p. (ISBN 0-8191-2532-6). U Pr of Amer.

Clinical Chemistry: Functional Medical Laboratory Manual. John Scimone & Robert Rothstein. (Illus.). 1978. pap. 15.95 o.p. (ISBN 0-87055-271-6). AVI.

Clinical Chemistry Lab Manual for the Medical Technology Student. V. Michele Chenault. 1979. pap. text ed. 11.95x o.s.i. (ISBN 0-89917-014-5). TIS Inc.

Clinical Computer Tomography Head & Trunk. Ed. by A. Baeft & L. Jeanmart. LC 77-14224. (Illus.). 1977. 49.00 o.p. (ISBN 0-387-08458-4). Springer-Verlag.

Clinical Counseling & Community Psychology: A Student Guide to Graduate Training & Professional Practice, 2 vols. Steven Walfish & Gerry Sumprer. Vol.1. text ed. cancelled o.s.i. (ISBN 0-8290-1059-9); pap. text ed. cancelled o.s.i. (ISBN 0-8290-1075-0). Vol. 2. Irvington.

Clinical Dermatology Illustrated. John Reeves & Howard Maibach. 250p. 1983. text ed. (ISBN 0-86792-010-6, Pub by Adis Pr Australia). Year Bk Med.

Clinical Diagnosis: A Physiologic Approach. 4th ed. Richard D. Judge & George D. Zuidema. 1982. text ed. 36.00 o.p. (ISBN 0-316-47589-0). Little.

Clinical Diagnosis in Pediatric Cardiology. J. R. Zuberbuhler. (Modern Pediatric Cardiology Ser.). (Illus.). 192p. 1981. text ed. 49.95 o.p. (ISBN 0-443-01889-8). Churchill.

Clinical Diagnosis of Mental Disorders: A Handbook. Ed. by Benjamin B. Wolman. LC 78-14969. (Illus.). 910p. 1978. 75.00x o.p. (ISBN 0-306-31141-0, Plenum Pr). Plenum Pub.

Clinical Diagnostic Ultrasound. Barnett & Morley. 1986. 216.00 o.p. (ISBN 0-632-00897-0, B-0482-6). Mosby.

Clinical Disorders of Fluid & Electrolyte Metabolism. 3rd ed. Ed. by Morton H. Maxwell & Charles R. Kleeman. (Illus.). 1980. text ed. 90.00 o.p. (ISBN 0-07-040994-3). McGraw.

Clinical Dysmorphology of Oral-Facial Structures. Ed. by Michael Melnick. Edward D. Shields & Norbert J. Burzynski. (Post Graduate Dental Handbook Ser.: Vol. 12). (Illus.). 544p. 1982. 60.00 o.p. (ISBN 0-88416-169-2). Year Bk Med.

Clinical Echo-Encephalography. W. Schiefer et al. Tr. by M. Klinger. LC 68-56950. 1969. 32.70 o.p. (ISBN 0-387-04323-3). Springer-Verlag.

Clinical Effects of Aging: A Longitudinal Study. J. S. Milne. LC 85-9660. 294p. 1985. 34.50 o.p. (ISBN 0-7099-3529-3, Pub. by Croom Helm Ltd). Routledge Chapman & Hall.

Clinical Electrocardiography. 7th ed. Bernard Lipman. 1984. 62.00 o.p. (ISBN 0-8151-5443-7). Year Bk Med.

Clinical Electrocardiography & Computers: A Symposium Vol. Ed. by C. A. Caceres. 1970. 89.00 o.p. (ISBN 0-12-153840-0). Acad Pr.

Clinical Embryology. R. G. Harrison. (Monographs for Students in Medicine). 1978. pap. 16.00 o.p. (ISBN 0-12-327840-6). Acad Pr.

Clinical Endocrinology. Ed. by Peter O. Kohler & Richard M. Jordan. LC 86-5640. 753p. 1986. 55.00 o.p. (ISBN 0-471-05130-6). Wiley.

Clinical Essays on the Heart, Vols. 1-4. J. Willis Hurst. Incl. Vol. 1. 352p. 1983. text ed. 35.00 o.p. (ISBN 0-07-031494-2); Vol. 2. 400p. 1984. text ed. 35.00 o.p. (ISBN 0-07-031496-9); Vol. 3. 328p. 1984. text ed. 35.00 o.p. (ISBN 0-07-031497-7); Vol. 4. 352p. 1985. text ed. 35.00 o.p. (ISBN 0-07-031498-5). McGraw.

Clinical Essays on the Heart, Vol. 5. J. Willis Hurst. (Illus.). 350p. 1985. text ed. 35.00 o.p. (ISBN 0-07-031499-3). McGraw.

Clinical Evaluation in Breast Cancer. Ed. by J. L. Hayward & R. D. Bulbrook. 1966. 55.00 o.p. (ISBN 0-12-334950-8). Acad Pr.

Clinical Examinations in Neurology. 5th ed. Mayo Clinic Staff. (Illus.). 384p. 1981. write for info. o.p. (ISBN 0-7216-6229-3). Saunders.

Clinical Experience. Paul Atkinson. 148p. 1981. text ed. 34.25x o.p. (ISBN 0-566-00413-5). Gower Pub Co.

Clinical Gastroenterology: A Problem-Oriented Approach. Ed. by Sidney Cohen. LC 82-10926. 464p. 1983. 37.00 o.p. (ISBN 0-471-08071-3). Wiley.

Clinical Guide to Soft Contact Lenses. Michael R. Spinell. LC 78-14621. 1979. 18.50x o.p. (ISBN 0-8019-6786-4); pap. 11.95xo.p. (ISBN 0-8019-6787-2). Chilton.

Clinical Gynaecological Oncology. Shepherd & Monaghan. (Illus.). 436p. 1986. 54.75 o.p. (ISBN 0-632-01127-0, B-4567-0). Mosby.

Clinical Gynecologic Oncology. 2nd ed. Philip J. DiSaia & William T. Creasman. (Illus.). 575p. 1984. cloth 53.50 o.p. (ISBN 0-8016-1315-9). Mosby.

Clinical Haematology. 5th ed. Eastham. 336p. 1977. pap. 15.00 o.p. (ISBN 0-7236-0456-8, Pub. by John Wright UK). Butterworth.

Clinical Handbook of Psychopharmacology. Ed. by Alberto DiMascio & Richard Shader. LC 75-118581. 1970. 30.00x o.p. (ISBN 0-87668-033-3). Aronson.

Clinical Hematology. 8th ed. Maxwell M. Wintrobe et al. LC 81-12395. (Illus.). 2021p. 1981. text ed. 85.00 o.p. (ISBN 0-8121-0718-7). Lea & Febiger.

Clinical Hematology for Blood Bankers: A Case History Approach to Hemolytic Anemia. Denise H. Pottiglio & Lawerence W. Powers. Ed. by Betty Ciesla et al. (S.U.C.C.E.S.S. Program Ser.: No. 1). (Illus.). 64p. (Orig.). 1985. 19.95wkbk o.p. (ISBN 0-943903-00-9). DHP Pub.

Clinical Hypertension & Hypotension. Brunner & Gravas. (Vol. 2). 498p. 1982. 85.00 o.p. (ISBN 0-8247-1279-X). Dekker.

Clinical Immunobiology. Ed. by Fritz H. Bach & Robert A. Good. (Illus.). Vol. 1 1972. 60.50 o.p. (ISBN 0-12-070001-8); Vol. 2 1974. 60.50 o.p. (ISBN 0-12-070002-6); Vol. 3 1976. 77.00 o.p. (ISBN 0-12-070003-4). Acad Pr.

Clinical Immunobiology, Vol. 4. Ed. by Fritz H. Bach. 1980. 39.50 o.p. (ISBN 0-12-070004-2). Acad Pr.

Clinical Immunology of the Kidney. Ed. by John B. Zabriskie et al. E. Lovell Becker. LC 82-4876. (Clinical Immunology Ser.). 453p. 1982. 68.00x o.p. (ISBN 0-471-02675-1, Pub. by Wiley Med). Wiley.

Clinical Immunotheraphy. A. E. Lobuglio. (Immunology Ser.: Vol. 11). 1980. 69.75 o.p. (ISBN 0-8247-6942-2). Dekker.

Clinical Implications of Laboratory Tests. 3rd ed. Sarko M. Tilkian et al. LC 82-18829. (Illus.). 493p. 1983. pap. text ed. 17.95 o.p. (ISBN 0-8016-4960-9). Mosby.

Clinical Laboratory Methods. 9th ed. John D. Bauer & Philip G. Ackermann. LC 81-16820. (Illus.). 1247p. 1982. 47.95 o.p. (ISBN 0-8016-0508-3). Mosby.

Clinical Leprosy. V. N. Sehgal. (Illus.). 1980. text ed. 15.00x o.p. (ISBN 0-7069-0785-X, Pub. by Vikas India). Advent NY.

Clinical Magnetic Resonance Imaging. Margulis & Higgins. 1984. 84.95 o.p. (ISBN 0-8016-3184-X). Mosby.

Clinical Management of Cancer in Children. Ed. by Carl Pochedly. LC 74-82440. 275p. 1975. 12.50 o.p. (ISBN 0-88416-020-3). Year Bk Med.

Clinical Management of Speech Disorders. Donald E. Mowrer & James L. Case. LC 81-19050. 320p. 1982. text ed. 35.00 o.p. (ISBN 0-89443-393-8). Aspen Pub.

Clinical Management of the Osteoporoses. Gilbert S. Gordan & Cynthia Vaughan. LC 75-12022. 200p. 1976. 18.00 o.p. (ISBN 0-88416-102-1). Year Bk Med.

Clinical Management of Voice Disorders. James L. Case. LC 84-2858. 341p. 1984. 37.00 o.p. (ISBN 0-89443-587-6). Aspen Pub.

Clinical Management of Voice Disorders. Donna R. Fox & Mark Blechman. LC 73-91493. (Speech & Hearing Ser.). 82p. (Orig.). 1975. pap. text ed. 4.95 o.p. (ISBN 0-8220-1803-9). Cliffs.

Clinical Manual of Gynecology. Jeffery W. Ellis & Charles R. Beckmann. (Illus.). 608p. 1983. pap. 19.95 o.p. (ISBN 0-8385-1135-X). Appleton & Lange.

Clinical Manual of Health Assessment. 2nd ed. Arden C. Bowers & June M. Thompson. (Illus.). 586p. 1984. pap. text ed. 29.95 o.p. (ISBN 0-8016-4955-2). Mosby.

Clinical Manual of Obstetrics. Jeffrey W. Ellis & Charles R. Beckmann. (Illus.). 800p. 1983. pap. 19.95 o.p. (ISBN 0-8385-1140-6). Appleton & Lange.

Clinical Methods in Pediatric Diagnosis. Balu H. Athreya. 288p. 1980. 37.95 o.p. (ISBN 0-442-23363-9). Van Nos Reinhold.

Clinical Microbiology. Leo R. DiLiello. (Illus.). 1979. pap. 17.95 o.s.i. (ISBN 0-87055-325-9). AVI.

Clinical Microbiology. P. W. Ross & J. F. Peutherer. LC 86-17158. (Illus.). 256p. (Orig.). 1987. pap. text ed. 17.00 o.p. (ISBN 0-443-03333-1). Churchill.

Clinical Microneurosurgery. W. Th. Koos et al. LC 75-16107. (Illus.). 334p. 1976. 39.50 o.p. (ISBN 0-88416-068-8). Year Bk Med.

Clinical Neuroendocrinology. Ed. by Luciano Martini & G. M. Besser. 1978. 75.00 o.p. (ISBN 0-12-475360-4). Acad Pr.

Clinical Neuroimmunology. P. O. Behan & S. Currie. (Major Problems in Neurology: Vol. 8). 1978. text ed. write for info. o.p. (ISBN 0-7216-1672-0). Saunders.

Clinical Neurosonography. Ed. by T. P. Naidich & R. M. Quencer. (Illus.). xi, 276p. 1986. 110.00 o.p. (ISBN 0-387-16923-7). Springer-Verlag.

Clinical Nursing Practice. Ed. by Alison Tierney. LC 85-11715. (Recent Advances in Nursing Ser.: Vol. 14). (Illus.). 241p. (Orig.). 1986. pap. text ed. 20.00 o.p. (ISBN 0-443-02498-7). Churchill.

Clinical Nursing Skills. Sandra F. Smith & Donna Duell. 922p. 1985. pap. 29.95 o.p. (ISBN 0-917010-14-0). Natl Nursing.

Clinical Nutrition. 2nd ed. Victoria Thiele. LC 80-13265. (Illus.). 342p. 1980. pap. text ed. 16.95 o.p. (ISBN 0-8016-4901-3). Mosby.

Clinical Nutrition for Nurses, Dieticians & Other Health Care Professionals. John W. Dickerson & Elizabeth M. Booth. LC 85-4455. 260p. (Orig.). 1985. pap. 17.95 o.p. (ISBN 0-571-13426-2). Faber & Faber.

Clinical Ophthalmology: A Text & Colour Atlas. James L. Bankes. LC 81-68264. (Illus.). 125p. 1983. pap. text ed. 23.95 o.p. (ISBN 0-443-02157-0). Churchill.

Clinical Oral Medicine. 2nd ed. Gayford & Haskell. 298p. 1979. 35.00 o.p. (ISBN 0-7236-0512-2, Pub. by John Wright UK). Butterworth.

Clinical Paediatric Surgery: Diagnosis & Management. Jones & Woodward. 1987. 42.00 o.p. (ISBN 0-8016-2525-4). Mosby.

Clinical Pediatric & Adolescent Endocrinology. Solomon A. Kaplan. (Illus.). 416p. 1982. 60.00 o.p. (ISBN 0-7216-5282-4). Saunders.

Clinical Performance Examination: Development & Implementation. Carrie Lenburg. (Illus.). 334p. 1979. 24.95 o.p. (ISBN 0-8385-1168-6). Appleton & Lange.

Clinical Pharmacology. 6th ed. Date not set. Petersons Guides.

Clinical Pharmacology. Ed. by Louis Lasagna. 1966. Set. 75.00 o.p. (ISBN 0-08-012067-9). Pergamon.

Clinical Pharmacology: A Guide to Training Programs. 6th ed. Ed. by Barbara C. Ready. 153p. (Orig.). 1985. pap. 9.95 o.p. (ISBN 0-87866-385-1). Petersons Guides.

Clinical Pharmacology for Dental Professionals. 2nd ed. S. G. Ciancio & P. C. Bourgaut. (Illus.). 400p. 1984. 29.50 o.p. (ISBN 0-88416-483-7). Year Bk Med.

Clinical Pharmacology in Dental Practice. 3rd ed. Ed. by Sam V. Holroyd. (Illus.). 500p. 1983. pap. text ed. 31.95 o.p. (ISBN 0-8016-2242-5). Mosby.

Clinical Pharmacology of Antieliptic Drugs. (Illus.). 340p. 1976. 73.00 o.p. (ISBN 0-387-06987-9). Springer-Verlag.

Clinical Pharmacology of Psychotherapeutic Drugs. 2nd ed. Leo E. Hollister. (Monographs in Clinical Pharmacology: Vol. 1). (Illus.). 214p. 1983. text ed. 32.00 o.p. (ISBN 0-443-08273-1). Churchill.

Clinical Pharmacology of the B-Adrenoceptor Blocking Agents. 2nd Ed. ed. William H. Frishman. (Illus.). 515p. 1984. 42.50 o.p. (ISBN 0-8385-1155-4). Appleton & Lange.

Clinical Pharmacology: Symposium Proceedings. Ed. by William A. Creasey. 248p. 1975. pap. 60.00 o.p. (ISBN 0-08-018949-0). Pergamon.

Clinical Pharmacy. David H. Lawson & R. Michael Richards. 1982. 49.95 o.p. (ISBN 0-412-22760-6, NO. 6704, Pub. by Chapman & Hall). Routledge Chapman & Hall.

Clinical Pharmacy Sourcebook: Key Articles from the American Journal of Hospital Pharmacy. new ed. American Society of Hospital Pharmacists. LC 75-12030. (Illus.). 1976. 25.00 o.p. (ISBN 0-88416-101-3). Year Bk Med.

Clinical Practice of Blood Transfusion. Ed. by Lawrence D. Petz & Scott N. Swisher. (Illus.). 640p. 1981. text ed. 75.00 o.p. (ISBN 0-443-08067-4). Churchill.

Clinical Practice of Medical-Surgical Nursing. 2nd ed. Marjorie Beyers et al. write for info. o.p. (ISBN 0-673-39383-6). Scott F.

Clinical Practice of the Dental Hygienist. 5th ed. Esther M. Wilkins. LC 82-8966. (Illus.). 913p. 1983. 37.50 o.p. (ISBN 0-8121-0844-2). Lea & Febiger.

Clinical Prediction in Psychotherapy. Leonard Horwitz. LC 74-6949. 348p. 1974. 25.00x o.p. (ISBN 0-87668-149-6). Aronson.

Clinical Preventive Dentistry. Louis P. DiOrio. 352p. 1983. 34.50 o.p. (ISBN 0-8385-1144-9). Appleton & Lange.

Clinical Psychology: A Social Psychological Approach. Peter L. Sheras & Stephen Worchel. 1979. 19.95 o.p. (ISBN 0-442-25208-0). Van Nos Reinhold.

Clinical Psychoneuroendocrinology in Reproduction. Ed. by L. Carenza et al. (Proceedings of the Serono Symposia Ser.). 1979. 91.50 o.p. (ISBN 0-12-159450-5). Acad Pr.

Clinical Radiation Pathology, 2 vols. Phillip Rubin & George W. Casarett. LC 67-17453. Vol. 2. pap. 150.00 o.s.i. Bks Demand UMI.

Clinical Reactions to Food. M. H. Lessof. LC 82-11101. 222p. 1983. 38.00 o.p. (ISBN 0-471-10436-1, Dist. by A R Liss). Wiley.

Clinical Removable Partial Prosthodontics. Kenneth L. Stewart et al. LC 81-22399. (Illus.). 736p. 1982. text ed. 72.00 o.p. (ISBN 0-8016-4813-0). Mosby.

Clinical Respiratory Care of the Adult Patient. Jerome Epstein & John Gaines. LC 82-22628. (Illus.). 448p. 1983. pap. text ed. 24.95 o.p. (ISBN 0-89303-209-3). Appleton & Lange.

Clinical Reviews in Pediatric Infectious Disease. Nelson & McCraken. 1985. 44.00 o.p. (ISBN 0-941158-55-1, D-3683-3). Mosby.

Clinical Scalar Electrocardiography. 6th ed. Bernard S. Lipman et al. (Illus.). 1972. 36.50 o.p. (ISBN 0-8151-5442-9). Year Bk Med.

Clinical Simulations in Neonatal Respiratory Therapy. Robert W. Hirnle. LC 81-13134. 316p. 1982. pap. 19.95 o.p. (ISBN 0-471-08266-X, Pub. by Wiley Medical). Wiley.

Clinical Simulations in Nursing Practice. Nancy A. Corbett & Phyllis Beveridge. LC 78-52724. 332p. 1980. pap. text ed. write for info. o.p. (ISBN 0-7216-2722-6). Saunders.

Clinical Skills & Assisting Techniques for the Medical Assistant. Sharron Zakus. LC 80-27135. (Illus.). 367p. 1981. pap. text ed. 23.95 o.p. (ISBN 0-8016-5672-9). Mosby.

Clinical Social Work Practice with the Elderly: Primary, Secondary, & Tertiary Intervention. Marion L. Beaver & Don Miller. 280p. 1985. pap. text ed. (ISBN 0-534-10991-8). Wadsworth Pub.

Clinical Specialist in Psychiatric Mental Health Nursing: Theory, Research, & Practice. Ed. by Deanne L. Critchley & Judith T. Mauring. LC 84-19509. 545p. 1985. 31.50 o.p. (ISBN 0-471-87506-6). Wiley.

Clinical Studies of Complement. Ed. by Remo Morelli et al. LC 74-7349. (Series on Complement: Vol. 3). 229p. 1974. text ed. 21.50x o.p. (ISBN 0-8422-7231-3). Irvington.

Clinical Supervision. Morris L. Cogan. LC 72-85906. 250p. 1973. text ed. 31.95 o.p. (ISBN 0-395-14027-7). HM.

Clinical Trails in Early Breast Cancer. Ed. by M. Baum & R. Kay. (Experientia Supplementum: Vol. 41). 676p. 1983. text ed. 52.95x o.p. (ISBN 0-8176-1358-7). Birkhauser.

Clinical Trials: A Practical Approach. Stuart J. Pocock. LC 83-1316. 266p. 1984. text ed. 40.00 o.p. (ISBN 0-471-90155-5, Dist. by A R Liss). Wiley.

Clinical Trials in Cancer Medicine: Past Achievement & Future Prospects. Ed. by U. Veronesi & G. Bonadonna. (Bristol Myers Cancer Symposia Ser.). 1985. 71.00 o.p. (ISBN 0-12-718850-9). Acad Pr.

Clinical Ultrasound of the Breast. Ed. by Toshiji Kobayashi. LC 78-1490. (Illus.). 190p. 1978. 39.50x o.p. (ISBN 0-306-31109-7, Plenum Med Bk). Plenum Pub.
Clinical Use of Growth Hormone. Ed. by Z. Laron et al. (Pediatric & Adolescent Endocrinology Ser.: Vol. 16). viii, 284p. 1987. 160.00 o.p. (ISBN 3-8055-4446-4). S Karger.
Clinical Uses for Essential Fatty Acids. Ed. by David F. Horrobin. 214p. 1983. 35.00 o.s.i. (ISBN 0-920792-23-5). Eden Pr.
Clinical Venereology. B. Schwartz. 1966. pap. 40.00 o.p. (ISBN 0-08-011601-9). Pergamon.
Clinician's Handbook: The Psychopathology of Adulthood & Late Adolescence. Robert G. Meyer. 308p. 1983. 47.00 o.p. (ISBN 0-205-07792-7, 797792). Allyn.
Clinico-Pharmacological Models for the Assay of Topical Corticoids. H. Wendt & P. J. Frosch. (Illus.). 62p. (Japanese.). 1982. pap. 22.00 o.p. (ISBN 3-8055-3686-0). S Karger.
Clint: Biography of a Labor Intellectual Clinton S. Golden. Thomas R. Brooks. LC 77-3152. 1978. 14.95 o.p. (ISBN 0-689-10923-7, Atheneum). Macmillan.
Clint's "Be Cheerful" Day. Patricia S. Mahany. (Happy Day Bks.). (Illus.). 24p. (ps-2). 1984. 1.59 o.p. (ISBN 0-87239-731-9, 3701). Standard Pub.
Clio & the Doctors: History, Psycho-History, Quanto History. Jacques Barzun. LC 74-5723. 1976. pap. 3.45 o.s.i. (ISBN 0-226-03850-5, P687, Phoen). U of Chicago Pr.
Clio Brown. Dolores Komo. 1988. write for info. o.p. Crossing Pr.
Clio Was a Woman: Studies in the History of American Women. Ed. by Mabel E. Deutrich & Virginia C. Purdy. LC 79-15336. (National Archives Conference Ser.: Vol. 16). (Illus.). 1980. 19.95 o.s.i. (ISBN 0-88258-077-9). Howard U Pr.
Clipper: A Western Review, 2 vols, No. 9. 1970. Repr. of 1941 ed. Set. lib. bdg. 36.00x o.p. (ISBN 0-8371-9145-9, CP00). Greenwood.
Clipper Ships. A. B. Whipple & Time-Life Books Editors. (Seafarers Ser.). (Illus.). 176p. 1980. 13.95 o.p. (ISBN 0-8094-2677-3). Time-Life.
Clive Bell's Eye. William G. Bywater, Jr. LC 74-23853. (Illus.). 249p. 1975. text ed. 19.95x o.p. (ISBN 0-8143-1534-8). Wayne St U Pr.
Cloak & Dagger. Roger Hall. 1957. 5.50 o.p. (ISBN 0-393-08458-2). Norton.
Clock Book. Wallace Nutting. LC 70-178648. (Illus.). 312p. 1975. Repr. of 1924 ed. 47.00x o.p. (ISBN 0-8103-4145-X). Gale.
Clock Guide Identification, No. 1. rev. ed. Robert W. Miller. 147p. pap. 11.95 o.p. (ISBN 0-87069-360-3). Wallace-Homestead.
Clock Identification & Price Guide, Bk. 1. rev. ed. Roy Ehrhardt & Malvern Rabeneck. (Illus.). 1977. Repr. ring bd. 15.00 o.p. (ISBN 0-913902-23-3). Heart Am Pr.
Clock Is Running. Mobil Corporation Staff. 1983. 14.50 o.p. (ISBN 0-671-43459-4). S&S.
Clock Watcher's Cookbook. Judy Duncan & Allison McCance. LC 82-63133. (Illus.). 128p. (Orig.). 1983. pap. 8.95 o.p. (ISBN 0-89909-013-3). Yankee Bks.
Clockmaker. Thomas C. Haliburton. LC 74-91080. (American Humorists Ser.). 1979. Repr. of 1838 ed. lib. bdg. 46.75 o.p. (ISBN 0-8398-0754-6). Irvington.
Clocks: A Guide to Identification & Prices, Vol. 1. Tran Duy Ly. LC 84-168680. 239p. (Orig.). 1984. pap. 15.00 o.p. (ISBN 0-930163-01-X). Arlington Bk.
Clocks: A Guide to Identification & Prices, Vol. 2. Tran Duy Ly. 240p. 1986. pap. (ISBN 0-930163-02-8). Arlington Bk.
Clocks & Watches, 1344 to 1800. G. H. Baillie. 1981. Repr. of 1981 ed. 50.00 o.p. (ISBN 0-317-03737-4). Saifer.
Clocks: Construction, Maintenance & Repair. Frank W. Coggins. (Illus.). 256p. 1984. 18.95 o.p. (ISBN 0-8306-0269-0, 1569); pap. 13.15 o.p. (ISBN 0-8306-0169-4, 1569P). TAB Bks.
Clocks of Columbus: The Literary Career of James Thurber. Charles S. Holmes. LC 72-78287. (Illus.). 1978. pap. 6.95 o.p. (ISBN 0-689-70574-3, Atheneum, 242). Macmillan.
Clockwork Orange. Anthony Burgess. 1963. 9.95 o.p. (ISBN 0-393-08519-8); pap. 4.95 o.p. (ISBN 0-393-00224-1). Norton.
Cloisonne & Champleve, Fourteen Hundred to Nineteen Hundred. Gunhild G. Avitable. (Illus.). 272p. (Ger.). 1984. 45.00 o.p. (ISBN 0-317-28168-2, Pub. by Kunst & Antiquitaten West Germany). Seven Hills Bk Dists.
Cloisters Apocalypse: A Fourteenth-Century Manuscript in Facsimile. LC 77-162342. (Illus.). 104p. 1971. 125.00 o.p. (ISBN 0-87099-110-8). Metro Mus Art.
Clonal Basis of Development. Ed. by Stephen Subtelny & Ian M. Sussex. (Thirty Sixth Symposia of the Society for Developmental Biology Ser.). 1979. 45.50 o.p. (ISBN 0-12-612982-7). Acad Pr.
Cloning of Man: A Brave New Hope-or Horror? Martin Ebon. (Orig.). 1979. pap. 1.75 o.p. (J8526, Sig). NAL.
Close Connections: Caroline Gordon & the Southern Renaissance. Ann Waldron. (Illus.). 304p. 1987. 22.95 o.p. (ISBN 0-399-13228-7, Putnam). Putnam Pub Group.
Close Encounters. Mike Wallace & Gary P. Gates. LC 84-60844. (Illus.). 416p. 1984. 17.95 o.p. (ISBN 0-688-01116-0). Morrow.
Close Shaves: The Complete Book of Razor Fighting. Bradley Steinor. 1979. pap. 8.00 o.p. (ISBN 0-686-28222-1). Loompanics.
Close to Nature: An Exploration of Nature's Microcosm. Hans Krook. LC 84-7645. 77p. 1984. 14.45 o.p. (ISBN 0-394-54089-1). Pantheon.
Close to the Earth: Living the Social History of the British Isles. Judith Cook. (Illus.). 160p. 1984. 19.95 o.p. (ISBN 0-7100-9634-8). Routledge Chapman & Hall.
Close-up Photography. Ed. by William Owens. LC 74-31880. (Photography How-to Ser.). (Illus.). 80p. 1975. pap. 3.95 o.p. (ISBN 0-8227-0094-8). Petersen Pub.
Close-up Photography in Practice. Axel Bruck. (Illus.). 144p. 1984. 30.95 o.p. (ISBN 0-7153-8403-1). David & Charles.
Close-up Six-Gustav Part 1. LC 75-22942. 6.95 o.s.i. (ISBN 0-914144-06-5). Monogram Aviation.
Close up U. S. A. Teacher's Guide. tchr's. guide 10.00 o.p. (ISBN 0-932765-17-3). Close Up Foun.
Closed: Ninety-Nine Ways to Stop Abortion. Joseph M. Scheidler. LC 85-42646. 350p. (Orig.). 1985. pap. 9.95 o.p. (ISBN 0-89107-346-9, Crossway Bks). Good News.
Closed World of Love. Archie Hill. 1978. pap. 1.75 o.p. (ISBN 0-380-39917-2, 39917). Avon.
Closely Held Corporation Desk Book: Nineteen Eighty-Five Tax Planning Update. rev. ed. Panel Publishers, Inc. Staff. 1985. pap. 39.95 o.s.i. (ISBN 0-916592-53-7). Panel Pubs.
Closely Held Corporation: Tax, Financial & Estate Planning. rev. ed. Ed. by Irving Schreiber. Jonathan Skiba. LC 70-138533. 530p. 1983. 150.00 o.s.i. (ISBN 0-916592-02-2). Panel Pubs.
Closer Look at Comparable Worth: A Study of the Basic Question to Be Addressed in Approaching Pay Equity. 84p. 1984. pap. 15.00 o.p. (ISBN 0-317-61659-5). NFSEP.
Closer Walk with God. David Mains. (Chapel Talks Ser.). 64p. 0.95 o.p. (ISBN 0-89191-264-9, 52647). Cook.
Closing Talks & Techniques. 3.50 o.p. (ISBN 0-686-31041-1, 29023). Rough Notes.
Cloth Dolls: A Guide for Collectors. Phillis A. Rustam. LC 78-69696. (Illus.). 1979. 15.00 o.p. (ISBN 0-498-02284-6). A S Barnes.
Clothes & Your Appearance. Louise A. Liddell. 352p. 1985. 19.40 o.p. (ISBN 0-87006-523-8); activity guide 4.60 o.p. (ISBN 0-87006-524-6); instr's. guide 6.00 o.p. (ISBN 0-87006-525-4); test master 14.00 o.p. (ISBN 0-87006-548-3). Goodheart.
Clothespins & Calendars. Eunice K. Halfmann. LC 85-6368. (Illus.). 112p. 1985. 10.95 o.p. (ISBN 0-914659-11-1). Phoenix Pub.
Clothing Care Handbook. Katherine Robinson. 1985. pap. 7.95 o.s.i. (ISBN 0-449-90150-5, Columbine). Fawcett.
Clothing Construction. 2nd ed. Evelyn A. Mansfield & Ethel G. Lucas. 454p. 1974. text ed. 21.95 o.p. (ISBN 0-395-16728-0). HM.
Clotilde De Lusignan Ou le Beau Juif, 2 vols. facsimile ed. Honore De Balzac. 628p. 1962. 50.00 ea. o.p. French & Eur.
Cloud Book. Tomie DePaola. LC 74-34493. (Illus.). 32p. (gr. k-3). 1984. pap. 5.95 o.p. (ISBN 0-8234-0531-1). Holiday.
Cloud Nine. James M. Cain. (Large Print Books (Nightingale Ser.)). 301p. 1986. pap. 11.95x o.p. (ISBN 0-8161-4117-7). G K Hall.
Clouds of Guilt. John Wainwright. (Nightingale Ser.). 304p. (Orig.). 1985. pap. 9.95 o.p. (ISBN 0-8161-3901-6, Large Print Bks). G K Hall.
Clouds of Witness. Dorothy L. Sayers. 224p. 1976. pap. 2.75 o.p. (ISBN 0-380-01107-7, 64394-4). Avon.
Clouds over Israel. Joseph T. Burrell. 1980. 6.00 o.p. (ISBN 0-682-49490-9). Exposition-Phoenix.
Clown. Heinrich Boll. 1982. pap. 3.95 o.p. (ISBN 0-380-00333-3, 69534, Bard). Avon.
Clown Confessions. Lee Morris. (Illus.). 96p. 1984. 8.00 o.p. (ISBN 0-682-40138-2). Exposition-Phoenix.
Clown: For Circus & Stage. Mark Stolzenberg. LC 80-54337. (Illus.). 160p. (gr. 8 up). 1983. 18.95 o.p. (ISBN 0-8069-7034-0); PLB 17.79 o.p. (ISBN 0-8069-7035-9); pap. 8.95 o.p. (ISBN 0-8069-7740-X). Sterling.
CLU Reference Manual. Barbara Liskov. (Lecture Notes in Computer Science Ser.: Vol. 114). 190p. 1983. pap. 15.00 o.p. (ISBN 0-387-10836-X). Springer-Verlag.
Clubhouse Mystery. Jerry Jenkins. (Bradford Family Adventures Ser.). 128p. (Orig.). (gr. 3-7). 1984. pap. 2.95 o.p. (ISBN 0-87239-793-9, 2943). Standard Pub.
Clubs & Club Life in London with Anecodotes of Its Famous Coffee-Houses, Hostelries, & Taverns from the Seventeenth Century to the Present Time. John Timbs. LC 66-28045. 572p. 1967. Repr. of 1872 ed. 35.00x o.p. (ISBN 0-8103-3262-0). Gale.
Clue in the Embers. Franklin W. Dixon. LC 74-181843. (Hardy Boys Ser.: Vol. 35). (Illus.). 196p. (gr. 5-9). 1956. 4.50 o.p. (ISBN 0-448-08935-1, G&D). Putnam Pub Group.
Clue in the Old Album. Carolyn Keene. (Nancy Drew Ser.: Vol. 24). (gr. 4-7). 1947. 4.50 o.p. (ISBN 0-448-09524-6, G&D); PLB 3.29 o.p. (ISBN 0-448-19524-0, G&D). Putnam Pub Group.
Clue of the Leaning Chimney. Carolyn Keene. (Nancy Drew Ser.: Vol. 26). (gr. 4-7). 1949. 4.50 o.p. (ISBN 0-448-09526-2, G&D); PLB 3.29 o.p. (ISBN 0-448-19526-7, G&D). Putnam Pub Group.
Clue of the Velvet Mask. Carolyn Keene. (Nancy Drew Ser.: Vol. 30). (Illus.). (gr. 4-7). 1953. 4.50 o.p. (ISBN 0-448-09530-0, G&D); PLB 3.29 o.p. (ISBN 0-448-19530-5, G&D). Putnam Pub Group.
Clue of the Whistling Bagpipes. Carolyn Keene. (Nancy Drew Ser.: Vol. 41). (gr. 4-7). 1964. 4.50 o.p. (ISBN 0-448-09541-6, G&D); PLB 3.29 o.p. (ISBN 0-448-19541-0, G&D). Putnam Pub Group.
Clues to America's Past. George Stuart. Ed. by Donald J. Crump. LC 76-688. (Special Publication: Series 11, No. 2). (Illus.). 1976. 7.95 o.p. (ISBN 0-87044-187-6); lib. bdg. 9.50 o.p. (ISBN 0-87044-192-2). Natl Geog.
Clues to Suicide. Ed. by Edwin S. Shneidman & Norman L. Farberow. 1957. pap. text ed. 4.95 o.p. (ISBN 0-07-056981-9). McGraw.
Cluster Analysis: A Survey. Ed. by B. S. Duran & P. L. Odell. (Lecture Notes in Economics & Mathematical Systems Ser.: Vol. 100). vi, 137p. 1974. pap. 8.90 o.p. (ISBN 0-387-06954-2). Springer-Verlag.
Cluster Analysis for Researchers. H. Charles Romesburg. (Research Methods Ser.). (Illus.). 334p. 1984. 44.95 o.p. (ISBN 0-534-03248-6, Lifetime Learn). Van Nos Reinhold.
Cluster Dissection & Analysis Theory FORTRAN Programs Examples. Helmuth Spath. 226p. 1985. 49.95 o.p. (ISBN 0-470-20129-0). Halsted Pr.
Cluster Mystery: Epidemic & the Children of Woburn, Mass. Paula DiPerna. 1985. cloth 13.95 o.p. (ISBN 0-8016-1301-9). Mosby.
CM: Developing, Marketing & Delivering Construction Management Services. Charles B. Thomsen. (Illus.). 192p. 1982. text ed. 45.00 o.p. (ISBN 0-07-064490-X). McGraw.
CMEA: International Significance of Socialist Integration. Ed. by K. I. Mikulsky. 376p. 1982. pap. 6.00 o.p. (ISBN 0-8285-2272-3, Pub. by Progress Pubs USSR). Imported Pubns.
C'mon Doc, You've Gotta Be Kiddin' Pat Patterson. 1978. 5.00 o.p. (ISBN 0-682-49181-0). Exposition-Phoenix.
CMOS Cookbook. Don Lancaster. LC 76-42874. (Illus.). 416p. 1977. pap. 14.95 o.p. (ISBN 0-672-21398-2). Sams.
CMOS, TTL: A User's Guide With Projects. Joseph J. Carr. (Illus.). 336p. 1984. 19.95 o.p. (ISBN 0-8306-0650-5). TAB Bks.
CNCL World Report. 1989. 15.00 o.p. (ISBN 0-918680-38-7, Dist. by Council on Nat'l Literatures). Griffon Hse.
CNS Pharmacology - Neuropeptides: Proceedings of the Eighth International Congress of Pharmacology, Tokyo, Japan,19-24 July, 1981. Ed. by H. Yoshida et al. (Advances in Pharmacology & Therapeutics II: Vol. 1). (Illus.). 300p. 1982. 105.00 o.p. (ISBN 0-08-028021-8). Pergamon.
Co-Op City: A Fantastic Cartoon History. Sam Schwartz. (Illus.). 1979. pap. 4.00 o.p. (ISBN 0-682-49433-X). Exposition-Phoenix.
Co-Op East Law Outlines: Evidence. LC 75-25589. (Orig.). 1975. 6.50 o.p. (ISBN 0-88408-068-4, Sterling Swift). Heath.
Co-Operation & Development in the Energy Sector: The Arab Gulf States & Canada. Ed. by Atif A. Kubursi & Thomas Naylor. LC 85-12840. 128p. 1985. 27.50 o.p. (ISBN 0-7099-1582-9, Pub. by Croom Helm Ltd). Routledge Chapman & Hall.
Co-Operative Bibliography: Supplement No. 1 to Co-operative Information. 1973. 11.40 o.p. (ISBN 92-2-100951-3). Intl Labour Office.
Co-operative Organisation: An Introduction. B. A. Youngjohns. 34p. (Orig.). 1977. pap. 4.00x o.p. (ISBN 0-903031-43-4, Pub. by Intermed Tech England). Intermediate Tech.
Co-Operatives & Community. David H. Wright. 118p. 1979. pap. text ed. 9.75x o.p. (ISBN 0-7199-0952-X, Pub. by Bedford England). Gower Pub Co.
Co-Rec Intramural Sports Handbook. Joseph A. Manjone & Robert T. Bowen. 80p. 1978. pap. text ed. 3.95x o.p. (ISBN 0-918438-10-1, PMAN0010). Leisure Pr.
Coach. Ray Meyer & Ray Sons. (Illus.). 256p. 1987. 17.95 o.p. (ISBN 0-8092-4803-4). Contemp Bks.
Coach (Automobile) Trimming: Part One, 2 vols. Ed. by G. Mortimer et al. (Engineering Craftsmen: No. E3). (Illus.). 1969. Set. spiral bdg. 62.50x set o.p. Trans-Atl Phila.
Coach (Automobile) Trimming: Part Two. Ed. by G. Mortimer et al. (Engineering Craftsmen: No. E23). (Illus.). 1970. spiral bdg. 45.00x o.p. (ISBN 0-85083-124-5). Trans-Atl Phila.
Coach Your Own Football Team: Make It to the Superbowl! Panthers vs. Grizzlies. George Shea & Betty Schwartz. (Coach Your Own Football Team Ser.: No. 1). 128p. 1983. pap. 3.40 o.s.i. (ISBN 0-671-47611-4). Wanderer Bks.
Coaching Football's Attack & Pursuit. Ralph Cummins. 197p. 1985. text ed. 21.95 o.p. (ISBN 0-13-139403-7, Parker). P-H.
Coaching: Ideas & Ideals. Arthur J. Gallon. 400p. 1974. pap. 9.50 o.p. (ISBN 0-395-17624-7). HM.
Coaching: Ideas & Ideals. 2nd ed. Arthur J. Gallon. LC 79-90061. (Illus.). 1980. pap. 27.16 o.p. (ISBN 0-395-28693-X). HM.
Coaching Junior High & Youth League Football. R. Michael Smith. LC 81-86510. (Illus.). 112p. 1984. pap. 9.95 o.p. (ISBN 0-88011-039-2, PSMI0039). Leisure Pr.
Coaching Synchronized Swimming Effectively. Margaret S. Forbes. LC 84-15853. 134p. 1984. pap. text ed. 14.00x o.p. (ISBN 0-931250-80-3, BFOR0080). Human Kinetics.
Coaching Track & Field. William J. Bowerman. 1974. text ed. 29.50 o.p. (ISBN 0-395-17834-7). HM.
Coaching Youth Softball. Robert B. Wenk. LC 83-80784. (Illus.). 368p. (Orig.). 1984. pap. 13.95 o.p. (ISBN 0-88011-196-8, PWENO196). Leisure Pr.
Coagulation Disorders in Obstetrics: Pathobiochemistry-Pathophysiology-Diagnosis-Treatment. H. Graeff & W. Kuhn. Tr. by A. Davis from Ger. LC 79-48020. (Major Problems in Obstetrics & Gynecology Ser.: No. 13). 1980. write for info. o.p. Saunders.
Coal. Audre Lorde. 80p. 1976. 7.95 o.p. (ISBN 0-393-04439-4); pap. 2.95 o.p. (ISBN 0-393-04446-7). Norton.
Coal Age Operating Handbook of Coal Preparation, Vol. III. Coal Age Magazine Editors. (Coal Age Library of Operating Handbooks). 1979. text ed. 33.50 o.p. (ISBN 0-07-011459-5). McGraw.
Coal Age Operating Handbook of Underground Mining, Vol. II. 2nd ed. Coal Age Magazine Editors. (Coal Age Ser.). (Illus.). 430p. 1980. text ed. 32.50 o.p. (ISBN 0-07-011461-7). McGraw.
Coal & Iron Community in the Industrial Revolution. John Addy & Marjorie Reeves. (Then & There Ser.). (Illus.). 108p. (Orig.). (YA) (gr. 7-12). 1980. pap. text ed. 4.95 o.p. (ISBN 0-582-20456-9). Longman.
Coal & the State. Chris Fischer. 350p. 1986. 43.00 o.p. (ISBN 0-949614-25-4, Pub. by Croom Helm UK). Routledge Chapman & Hall.
Coal & the State. Chris Fisher. 352p. 1988. lib. bdg. 55.00x o.p. (ISBN 0-317-64418-1, Pub. by Croom Helm UK). Routledge Chapman & Hall.
Coal: Current Advances in Coal Chemistry & Mining Techniques, Vol. 1. M. A. Nettleton et al. 205p. 1976. text ed. 29.50x o.p. (ISBN 0-8422-7284-4). Irvington.
Coal: Current Advances in Coal Chemistry & Mining Techniques, Vol. 2. M. A. Nettleton et al. 1976. text ed. 28.00x o.p. (ISBN 0-8422-7283-6). Irvington.
Coal Desulfurization Prior to Combustion. Ed. by R. C. Eliot. LC 78-56014. (Chemical Technology Review Ser., Pollution Tech. Rev. 45: No. 113). 113p. 1978. 42.00 o.p. (ISBN 0-8155-0712-7). Noyes.
Coal Exploration: Proceedings of the 2nd International Symposium, Denver, Colorado, Oct. 1978, Vol. 2. International Coal Exploration Symposium Staff. Ed. by George O. Argall, Jr. LC 76-41151. (A World Coal Book). (Illus.). 1979. 35.00 o.p. (ISBN 0-87930-107-4). Miller Freeman.
Coal, Gas & Electricity Industries. D. J. Harris et al. (Reviews of United Kingdom Statistical Sources Ser.: Vol. XI). 1979. 83.00 o.p. (ISBN 0-08-022461-X). Pergamon.
Coal in America: Reserves, Production & Use. R. A. Schmidt. 1979. text ed. 69.95 o.p. (ISBN 0-07-055347-5). McGraw.
Coal in Queensland: The First Fifty Years. R. L. Whitmore. (Illus.). xvii, 185p. 1982. text ed. 34.50x o.p. (ISBN 0-7022-1619-4). U of Queensland Pr.
Coal in Queensland: The Late Nineteenth Century. R. L. Whitmore. LC 84-5268. (Illus.). 338p. 1985. 34.50x o.p. (ISBN 0-7022-1759-X). U of Queensland Pr.

Coal Information Report 1984. IEAD Staff. 421p. (Orig.). 1984. pap. 80.00x o.p. (ISBN 92-64-12642-2). OECD.

Coal Liquid Mixtures: Proceedings of the Second European Conference, London, U. K. 16-18 September 1985, No. 2. Ed. by Institution of Chemical Engineers Staff. (I. Chem. E. Symposium Ser.: Vol. 95). 400p. 1986. 46.00 o.s.i. (ISBN 0-08-031446-5, E135C, B125C, A110C, Pub. by PPL). Pergamon.

Coal Liquid Mixtures: Proceeedings of the European Conference, 1st, Cheltenham, U. K., October 5-6, 1983. Ed. by Institution of Chemical Engineers Staff. (Institution of Chemical Engineers Symposium Ser.: Vol. 83). 250p. 1983. 53.00 o.s.i. (ISBN 0-08-031397-3, 1902, 1903, 1502, 1100). Pergamon.

Coal Mine Structures. Ian. W Farmer. 364p. 1985. 59.95 o.p. (ISBN 0-412-25030-6, NO. 9133, Pub. by Chapman & Hall England). Routledge Chapman & Hall.

Coal Mining. I. C. Statham. (Illus.). 560p. 1956. (ISBN 0-8022-1631-5). Philos Lib.

Coal: Nineteen Eighty-Five & Beyond - A Perspective Study. United Nations Economic Commission for Europe. LC 77-30437. 1978. pap. text ed. 37.00 o.p. (ISBN 0-08-022409-1). Pergamon.

Coal Processing. Ed. by Edward C. Capes et al. LC 74-26744. (Energy Ser.). 1976. text ed. 28.00x o.p. (ISBN 0-8422-7265-8). Irvington.

Coal Utilisation: Technology, Economics & Policy. L. Grainger & J. Gibson. LC 81-7249. 503p. 1982. 59.95 o.p. (ISBN 0-470-27272-4). Halsted Pr.

Coalition & Connection in Games. S. Guiasu & M. Malitza. 1980. 50.00 o.p. (ISBN 0-08-023033-4). Pergamon.

Coalitions & Politics. Barbara Hinckley. 164p. 1981. pap. text ed. 10.95 o.p. (ISBN 0-15-507852-6, HC). HarbraceJ.

Coalport & Coalbrookdale Porcelains. Geoffrey Godden. (Illus.). 310p. 1981. (ISBN 0-907462-02-2). Antique Collect.

Coal's Contribution to U. K. Self-Sufficiency. Louis Turner. (British Institutes Joint Energy Policy Programme - Energy Papers: No. 9). viii, 60p. (Orig.). 1984. pap. text ed. 17.95x o.p. (ISBN 0-435-84340-0). Gower Pub Co.

Coarticulation Assessment in Meaningful Language. Kathryn Kenney & Elizabeth M. Prather. 212p. (Orig.). pap. text ed. 20.00 o.p. (ISBN 0-88450-898-6, 7206-B). Communication Skill.

Coast of Trees. A. R. Ammons. 1981. 12.95 o.p. (ISBN 0-393-01447-9); pap. 4.95 o.p. (ISBN 0-393-00051-6). Norton.

Coastal & Offshore Environmental Inventory: Cape Hatteras to Nantucket Shoals. Ed. by Saul B. Saila. LC 72-619712. (Marine Publications Ser.). 1973. No. 2. pap. 10.00 o.p. (ISBN 0-938412-04-3); No. 3. pap. 5.00, complementary vol. o.p. (ISBN 0-938412-20-5). Sea Grant Pubns.

Coastal Aquaculture: Development Perspectives in Africa & Case Studies from Other Regions. Ed. by Andre G. Coche. (Commission for Inland Fisheries of Africa (CIFA): Technical Papers: No. 9). 264p. (Eng. & Fr.). 1983. pap. text ed. 18.00 o.p. (ISBN 92-5-001300-0, F2422, FAO). UNIPUB.

Coastal Changes. William W. Williams. LC 75-3873. (Illus.). 220p. 1975. Repr. of 1960 ed. lib. bdg. 35.00 o.p. (ISBN 0-8371-8088-0, WICOC). Greenwood.

Coastal Conservation: Essays on Experiments in Governance. Ed. by Stanley Scott. LC 79-25504. 56p. 1981. pap. text ed. 5.50x o.s.i. (ISBN 0-87772-270-6). UCB IGS.

Coastal Daytrips in New England. Harriet Webster. LC 83-51248. (Magazine Guidebook Ser.). (Illus.). 176p. 1984. pap. 8.95 o.p. (ISBN 0-89909-032-X). Yankee Bks.

Coastal Ghosts: Haunted Places from Wilmington to Savannah. Nancy Rhyne. LC 85-71258. (Illus.). 192p. 1985. 12.95 o.p. (ISBN 0-88742-057-5). Globe Pequot.

Coastal Upwelling Ecosystems Analysis Program. Ed. by Francis A. Richards. 1977. pap. 23.00 o.p. (ISBN 0-08-021375-8). Pergamon.

Coastal Vegetation. 2nd ed. V. J. Chapman. 1976. 75.00 o.p. (ISBN 0-08-020896-7); pap. 75.00 o.p. (ISBN 0-08-019687-X). Pergamon.

Coastal Wetlands. H. H. Prince & F. M. D'Itri. LC 85-19914. (Illus.). 325p. 1985. 34.95 o.p. (ISBN 0-87371-052-5). Lewis Pubs Inc.

Coastal Zone Management: Monographs. Mary Vance. (Public Administration Series: Bibliography P 1759). 1985. pap. 9.75 o.p. (ISBN 0-89028-559-4). Vance Biblios.

Coat & Skirt Making: Skirts, Trousers, Jackets & Coats. 6th ed. Samuel Heath. (Illus.). 192p. 1981. text ed. 19.00 o.p. (ISBN 0-246-11500-9, Pub. by Granada England). Gower Pub Co.

Coat Hanger Christmas Tree. Eleanor Estes. LC 73-75433. (Illus.). 96p. (gr. 4-7). 1973. 8.95 o.p. (ISBN 0-689-30416-1, Atheneum). Macmillan.

Coat of Blue & a Coat of Gray. Helen H. Bannister. (Illus.). 64p. 1984. 7.50 o.p. (ISBN 0-682-40192-7). Exposition-Phoenix.

Coated Particle Fuels. 573p. 1977. 40.00 o.p. (ISBN 0-317-32990-1, 120020). Am Nuclear Soc.

Coatings & Bimetallics for Aggressive Environments. Ed. by R. D. Sisson, Jr. 236p. 1985. 66.00 o.p. (ISBN 0-87170-210-X). ASM.

Coats Book of Modern European Embroidery. Jean Kinmond. (Illus.). 104p. 1980. 34.95 o.p. (ISBN 0-7134-3305-1, Pub. by Batsford England). David & Charles.

Cobalt: A Retrospective of the Life & Art of Dorothy Sturm. Dorothy Sturm. Ed. by Karen B. Carrier & Donna Leatherman. LC 88-1969. (Illus.). 1988. ltd. ed. 300.00 o.p. (ISBN 0-918518-67-9, St Luke TN). Peachtree Pubs.

Cobalt in Biology & Biochemistry. Roland Young. 1979. 58.00 o.p. (ISBN 0-12-772750-7). Acad Pr.

Cobbett's Political Register, Vols. 1-89. Incl. Vol. 1. lib. bdg. 39.00 (ISBN 0-313-21872-2, PR01); Vol. 2. lib. bdg. 50.00 (ISBN 0-313-21873-0, PR02); Vol. 3. lib. bdg. 72.00 (ISBN 0-313-21874-9, PR03); Vol. 4. lib. bdg. 61.00 (ISBN 0-313-21875-7, PR04); Vol. 5. lib. bdg. 33.00 (ISBN 0-313-21876-5, PR05); Vol. 6. lib. bdg. 33.00 (ISBN 0-313-21877-3, PR06); Vol. 7. lib. bdg. 33.00 (ISBN 0-313-21878-1, PR07); Vol. 8. lib. bdg. 50.00 (ISBN 0-313-21879-X, PR08); Vol. 9. lib. bdg. 33.00 (ISBN 0-313-21880-3, PR09); Vol. 10. lib. bdg. 33.00 (ISBN 0-313-21881-1, PR10); Vol. 11. lib. bdg. 33.00 (ISBN 0-313-21882-X, PR11); Vol. 12. lib. bdg. 33.00 (ISBN 0-313-21883-8, PR12); Vol. 13. lib. bdg. 33.00 (ISBN 0-313-21884-6, PR13); Vol. 14. lib. bdg. 33.00 (ISBN 0-313-21885-4, PR14); Vol. 15. lib. bdg. 33.00 (ISBN 0-313-21886-2, PR15); Vol. 16. lib. bdg. 33.00 (ISBN 0-313-21887-0, PR16); Vol. 17. lib. bdg. 33.00 (ISBN 0-313-21888-9, PR17); Vol. 18. lib. bdg. 39.00 (ISBN 0-313-21889-7, PR18); Vol. 19. lib. bdg. 39.00 (ISBN 0-313-21890-0, PR19); Vol. 20. lib. bdg. 33.00 (ISBN 0-313-21891-9, PR20); Vols. 21 & 22. lib. bdg. 50.00 (ISBN 0-313-21892-7, PR21); Vols. 23 & 24. lib. bdg. 50.00 (ISBN 0-313-21893-5, PR22); Vols. 25 & 26. lib. bdg. 50.00 (ISBN 0-313-21894-3, PR23); Vols. 27-29. lib. bdg. 50.00 (ISBN 0-313-21895-1, PR24); Vols. 30 & 31. lib. bdg. 50.00 (ISBN 0-313-21896-X, PR25); Vol. 32. lib. bdg. 33.00 (ISBN 0-313-21897-8, PR26); Vols. 33 & 34. lib. bdg. 50.00 (ISBN 0-313-21898-6, PR27); Vol. 35. lib. bdg. 33.00 (ISBN 0-313-21899-4, PR28); Vol. 36. lib. bdg. 39.00 (ISBN 0-313-21900-1, PR29). 1971. Repr. Set. lib. bdg. 2145.00x o.p. (ISBN 0-8371-9375-3, PR00). Greenwood.

Cobblestone Architecture of the Great Lake Region: An Annotated Bibliography. Melvin W. Johnson. (Architecture Ser.: A 1416). 46p. 1985. 6.75 o.p. (ISBN 0-89028-446-6). Vance Biblios.

COBOL. George Jackson. (Illus.). 300p. 1982. 16.95 o.p. (ISBN 0-8306-0051-5, 1398); pap. 9.95 o.p. (ISBN 0-8306-1398-6). TAB Bks.

COBOL: A Vehicle for Information Systems. Robert G. Grauer. 1981. text ed. (ISBN 0-13-139709-5). P-H.

COBOL: Elements of Programming Style. William M. Fuori. 450p. 1986. pap. 24.95 o.p. Sams.

COBOL for Beginners. Christopher Lampton. (Computer Literacy Skills Ser.). 96p. 1984. lib. bdg. 11.90 o.p. (ISBN 0-531-04746-6). Watts.

COBOL for Beginners. Thomas Worth. (Illus.). 1976. pap. text ed. (ISBN 0-13-139378-2). P-H.

COBOL for Medium & Small Sized Computers. Asad Khailany & Claude Duplissey. LC 75-23647. (Illus.). 400p. 1976. pap. 19.50 o.p. (ISBN 0-395-18921-7). HM.

COBOL for Students. 2nd ed. Andrew Parkin. 212p. 1983. pap. text ed. 14.95 o.p. (ISBN 0-7131-3477-1, Pub. by E Arnold UK). Routledge Chapman & Hall.

COBOL Logic & Programming. 5th ed. Fritz A. McCameron. LC 84-18730. (Information & Decision Sciences Ser.). 451p. 1985. pap. text ed. 25.95x o.p. (ISBN 0-256-03210-6). Irwin.

COBOL Programmer's Book of Rules. George Ledin, Jr. et al. LC 83-81672. 221p. 1983. pap. 19.95 o.p. Van Nos Reinhold.

COBOL Reference Summary. National Computing Centre, Ltd. Staff. 100p. (Orig.). 1981. pap. 17.50x o.s.i. (ISBN 0-85012-318-6). Intl Pubns Serv.

Cobol Self Teaching, 3 vols. Ashley et al. Set. 29.85 o.p. (ISBN 0-471-08947-8). Wiley.

COBOL with Style: Programming Proverbs. Henry F. Ledgard & Louis J. Chmura, Jr. (Computer Programming Ser.). 1976. pap. text ed. 10.95 o.p. (ISBN 0-8104-5781-4). Sams.

Cobwebs & Crystal: Colorado's Grand Old Hotels. Betty Hull. LC 81-20966. (Illus.). 100p. (Orig.). 1982. pap. 6.95 o.p. (ISBN 0-87108-611-5). Pruett.

Cocaine: The Mystique & the Reality. Joel Phillips & Ronald D. Wynne. 1980. pap. 3.95 o.p. (ISBN 0-380-48678-4, 58248-1, Discus). Avon.

Cocaine Use in America: Epidemiological & Clinical Perspectives. Nicholas J. Rozel & Edgar H. Adams. (National Institute on Drug Abuse Monograph: No. 61). (Illus.). 240p. (Orig.). 1985. pap. 5.00 o.p. (ISBN 0-318-18734-5, S/N 017-024-01258-1). USGPO.

Coccidian Parasites of Carnivores. Norman D. Levine & Virginia Ivens. LC 80-25205. (Illinois Biological Monographs: No. 51). (Illus.). 205p. 1981. 15.95 o.p. (ISBN 0-252-00856-1). U of Ill Pr.

Cockfighter. Charles Willeford. 1974. pap. 1.50 o.p. (ISBN 0-380-00120-9, 20495). Avon.

Cockleburr Quarters. Charlotte Baker. (Illus.). (gr. 3-7). 1981. pap. 1.25 o.p. (ISBN 0-380-01108-5, 35857, Camelot). Avon.

Cockpit. Jerzy Kosinski. LC 75-4619. 272p. 1975. 8.95 o.p. (ISBN 0-395-20671-5). HM.

Cockpit Computers & Navigation Avionics. P. Garrison. 256p. 1982. text ed. 31.50 o.p. (ISBN 0-07-022893-0). McGraw.

Cockpit Navigation Guide. Don Downie. 1962. 8.95 o.p. (ISBN 0-8306-9939-2); pap. 4.95 o.p. (ISBN 0-8306-2208-X, 2208). TAB Bks.

Cockroach Combat Manual. Austin M. Frishman & Arthur P. Schwartz. LC 80-288. (Illus.). 1980. 8.95 o.p. (ISBN 0-688-03613-9). Morrow.

Cocktail Book. Michael Walker. LC 80-81668. (Orig.). 1980. pap. 7.95 o.p. (ISBN 0-89586-069-4). Price Stern.

Cocktail of Poems. Eugene Grundt. 64p. 1980. 5.00 o.p. (ISBN 0-682-49656-1). Exposition-Phoenix.

Cocoa. (Commodity Projections: 1985). 1979. pap. 7.50 o.p. (ISBN 0-686-59426-6, F1614, FAO). UNIPUB.

Cocoanut Grove. Edward Keyes. LC 83-45080. 320p. 1984. 14.95 o.p. (ISBN 0-689-11406-0, Atheneum). Macmillan.

Coconut Book. Richard Maynard. 176p. 1986. Repr. of 1985 ed. 15.95 o.s.i. (ISBN 0-394-55300-4). Grove.

Coconut Kiss: A Novel. Dee Phillips. 1983. 14.00 o.p. (ISBN 0-393-01679-X). Norton.

Coconuts: Production, Processing, Products. 2nd ed. J. G. Woodroof. (Illus.). 1979. 37.95 o.p. (ISBN 0-87055-276-7). AVI.

Cocurricular Activity Programs in Secondary Schools. Ronald E. Gholson & Robert L. Buser. 24p. 1983. pap. 5.00 o.p. (ISBN 0-88210-145-5). Natl Assn Principals.

Codbangers. Hervey Benham. (Illus.). 207p. 1979. 14.00 o.p. (ISBN 0-9505944-1-5, Pub. by Boydell & Brewer). Longwood Pub Group.

Code Cases Book: Boilers & Pressure Vessels. (Boiler & Pressure Vessel Code Ser.). 1980. pap. 100.00 loose-leaf o.p. (ISBN 0-686-70009-0, V00120). ASME.

Code Cases Book: Boilers & Pressure Vessels. (Boiler & Pressure Vessel Code Ser.). 1977. pap. 70.00 loose-leaf o.p. (ISBN 0-685-76835-X, W00120). ASME.

Code Cases Book: Nuclear Components. (Boilers & Pressure Vessel Code Ser.). 1980. pap. 140.00 loose-leaf o.p. (ISBN 0-686-70377-4, V0012N). ASME.

Code Directory, 1983. 1983. 7.00 o.p. (ISBN 0-686-43030-1). AAU Pubns.

Code Enforcement Handbook for Municipal Officials. David W. Tees & Jay G. Stanford. 86p. 1973. 6.50 o.p. (ISBN 0-936440-37-6). Inst Urban Studies.

Code Ezra. Gay Courter. LC 85-27339. 607p. 1986. 18.45 o.p. (ISBN 0-395-36438-8). HM.

Code for Cataloging Non Book Media. Anthony Croghan. (Orig.). 1972. pap. 8.50 o.p. (ISBN 0-9501212-4-X). J Norton Pubs.

Code Name Nimrod. James Leasor. 1981. 10.95 o.p. (ISBN 0-395-30228-5). HM.

Code of Federal Regulations Index, 1988, 3 vols. 1988. 399.00 o.p. (ISBN 0-8352-2439-2). Bowker.

Code of Honor. John A. Dramesi. 271p. 1975. 7.95 o.p. (ISBN 0-393-05533-7). Norton.

Code of Life. Alvin Silverstein & Virginia Silverstein. LC 77-175558. (Illus.). (gr. 5-9). 1972. 6.95 o.p. (ISBN 0-689-30038-7, Atheneum). Macmillan.

Code of Safe Practice for Bulk Cargoes. (Illus.). 137p. 1977. 15.25 o.p. (ISBN 0-686-70783-4, IMCO9, IMO). UNIPUB.

Code of Terpsichore. Carlo Blasis. LC 75-9166. (Illus.). 560p. 1975. pap. 20.95 o.p. (ISBN 0-87127-055-2, Pub. by Dance Horiz). Princeton Bk Co.

Code of Virginia. 2nd ed. Virginia. Laws, Statutes Staff. LC 78-109365. xxiii, 1022p. 1970. Repr. of 1860 ed. 39.00 o.p. (ISBN 0-8371-3870-1, CVI&, Pub. by Negro U Pr). Greenwood.

Codebreakers. David Kahn. (RL 7). 1973. pap. 4.95 o.p. (ISBN 0-451-12651-3, AE2651, Sig). NAL.

Codes, Ciphers, & Computers: An Introduction to Information Security. Bruce Bosworth. 1982. pap. 16.50 o.p. (5149). Sams.

Codeword: Catherine. Jodie Collins. 240p. (Orig.). 1984. pap. 6.95 o.p. (ISBN 0-8423-0301-4). Tyndale.

Codex Alimentarius Commission Reports. Incl. Vol. 31. Methods of Analysis for Processed Fruits & Vegetables. 14p. 1980. pap. 4.50 (ISBN 92-5-100813-2, F1886). UNIPUB; Recommended International Standards for Canned Tropical Fruit Salad. 14p. 1980. pap. 4.50 (ISBN 92-5-100809-4, F1884). UNIPUB; Recommended International Standard for Quick Frozen Leeks. 12p. 1980. pap. 3.00 (ISBN 92-5-100808-6, F1885). UNIPUB; Recommended International Code of Hygenic Practice for Egg Products: Section 5 - End Product Specification; Annex 2 - Microbiologic Specifications for Pastuerized Egg Products. 35p. pap. 7.50 (ISBN 92-5-100818-3, F1891). UNIPUB. 1979 (FAO). UNIPUB.

Codex Benedictus. (Illus.). 262p. 6000.00 o.p. (ISBN 0-8115-0904-4). Kraus Repr.

Codification of Presidential Proclamations & Executive Orders, Jan. 20, 1961-Jan. 20, 1985. Intro. by John E. Byrne. 975p. (Orig.). 1985. pap. 20.00 o.p. (ISBN 0-318-18735-3, S/N 022-002-00110-1). USGPO.

Coding & Complexity. Ed. by G. Longo. (International Centre for Mechanical Sciences Ser.: No. 216). (Illus.). 1977. soft cover 34.00 o.p. (ISBN 0-387-81341-1). Springer-Verlag.

Coding for Markov Sources: Proceedings of the CISM, Department of Automation & Information University of Trieste, 1971. CISM (International Center for Mechanical Sciences), Department of Automation & Information Staff. Ed. by G. Longo. (CISM Publicaions: No. 110). (Illus.). 99p. 1973. pap. 13.90 o.p. (ISBN 0-387-81154-0). Springer-Verlag.

Coding the Therapeutic Process: Emblems of Encounter. Murray Cox. LC 77-30463. 1978. 27.00 o.s.i. (ISBN 0-08-021454-1); pap. text ed. 10.00 o.s.i. (ISBN 0-08-021453-3). Pergamon.

Coding Theorems of Information Theory. 3rd ed. Jacob Wolfowitz. (Ergebnisse der Mathematik und Ihrer Grenzgebiete: Vol. 31). 1978. 36.00 o.p. (ISBN 0-387-08548-3). Springer-Verlag.

Coding Theory. 2nd rev. ed. J. H. Van Lint. (Lecture Notes in Mathematics: Vol. 201). viii, 136p. 1973. pap. 9.20 o.p. (ISBN 0-387-06363-3). Springer-Verlag.

Coeliac Disease. W. T. Cooke & G. K. Holmes. (Illus.). 281p. 1984. text ed. 64.75 o.p. (ISBN 0-443-02827-3). Churchill.

Coercive Persuasion. Edgar H. Schein et al. 1971. pap. 2.45 o.p. (ISBN 0-393-00613-1, Norton Lib). Norton.

Coercive Social Worker: British Lessons for American Social Services. Joel F. Handler. 1973. 14.50 o.p. (ISBN 0-12-322850-6). Acad Pr.

Coeur a Cuivre. Jacques Audiberti. 288p. 1950. 9.95 o.p. (ISBN 0-686-54483-8). French & Eur.

Coffee: A Guide to Buying, Brewing & Enjoying. 3rd., rev. ed. Kenneth Davids. LC 87-7658. (Illus.). 204p. (Orig.). 1987. pap. 8.95 o.p. (ISBN 0-89286-275-0, One Hund One Prods). Ortho.

Coffee: A Revised Guide to Buying, Brewing & Enjoying. rev. ed. Kenneth Davids & M. L. Duniec. LC 80-27222. (Illus.). 192p. 1981. pap. 7.95 o.p. (ISBN 0-89286-186-X, One Hund One Prods). Ortho.

Coffee & Capitalism in the Venezuelan Andes. William Roseberry. (Latin American Monographs: No. 59). 271p. 1983. text ed. 22.50x o.p. (ISBN 0-292-71535-8). U of Tex Pr.

Coffee & Conflict in Colombia, 1886-1910. Charles W. Bergquist. 1978. 23.25 o.p. (ISBN 0-8223-0418-X). Duke.

Coffee: Botany, Biochemistry & Production of Beans & Beverage. Ed. by M. N. Clifford & K. C. Willson. 1985. 59.95 o.p. (ISBN 0-87055-491-3). AVI.

Coffee Talk: Sharing Christ Through Friendly Gatherings. Barbara Ball. LC 79-53980. 80p. 1980. pap. 4.95 o.p. (ISBN 0-934396-08-6). Churches Alive.

Coffin Nails & Corporate Strategies. Robert H. Miles. (Illus.). 320p. 1982. text ed. 27.67 o.p. (ISBN 0-13-139816-4); pap. text ed. (ISBN 0-13-139808-3). P-H.

Cog Railway to Pike's Peak. Morris W. Abbott. LC 73-9520. (Illus.). 48p. pap. 2.95 o.s.i. (ISBN 0-87095-052-5). Gldn West Bks.

Cogeneration & Resource Recovery: Current Prospects & Future Opportunities. 5th ed. Ed. by Michael J. Zimmer. 178p. 1985. 65.00 o.p. Gov Insts.

Cogeneration: Current Prospects & Future Opportunities. 3rd. ed. Ed. by Michael Zimmer. 310p. 1983. Wkbk. 48.00 o.p. (ISBN 0-86587-112-4). Gov Insts.

Cogeneration: Current Prospects & Future Opportunities. 4th ed. Ed. by Michael J. Zimmer. (Illus.). 216p. 1984. 3-ring binder 56.00 o.p. (ISBN 0-86587-069-1). Gov Insts.

Cogeneration District Heating Applications. Ed. by I. Oliker. 52p. 1978. 7.00 o.p. (ISBN 0-685-66792-8, H00128). ASME.

Cogeneration in California. Ed. by Michael J. Zimmer & Martin L. Heavner. (Illus.). 304p. 1983. 3-ring binder 68.00 o.p. (ISBN 0-86587-116-7). Gov Insts.

Cogeneration in California, 1984. 2nd ed. Ed. by Government Institutes Staff. 200p. 1984. 3-ring binder 69.00 o.p. (ISBN 0-86587-071-3). Gov Insts.

Cogiter's Treasury. Sam Goodman. LC 61-12619. 416p. 1962. (ISBN 0-8022-0607-7). Philos Lib.

Cognates: Vocabulary Enrichment for Bilinguals. Ed. by Joe R. Gonzalez & David L. Zufelt. (Span. & Eng.). 1973. pap. text ed. 9.95x o.p. (ISBN 0-8422-0311-7). Irvington.

Cognition: Theory & Applications. Stephen K. Reed. LC 81-3829. 448p. 1981. text ed. 22.50 pub net o.p. (ISBN 0-8185-0462-5). Brooks-Cole.

Cognitive Behavior Modification: An Integrative Approach. Donald Meichenbaum. LC 77-5847. (Plenum Behavior Therapy Ser.). (Illus.). 306p. 1977. 24.50x o.p. (ISBN 0-306-31013-9, Plenum Pr). Plenum Pub.

Cognitive Behavior Therapy: Research & Application. John P. Foreyt & Diana P. Rathjen. LC 78-15948. (Illus.). 280p. 1978. 32.50x o.p. (ISBN 0-306-31145-3, Plenum Pr). Plenum Pub.

Cognitive Development: An Information-Processing View. David Klahr & J. F. Wallace. LC 76-13901. 244p. 1976. 16.50 o.p. (ISBN 0-470-15128-5, Pub. by Wiley). Krieger.

Cognitive Development & Education. Johanna Turner. Ed. by Peter Herriot. LC 83-17355. (New Essential Psycholgy Ser.). 192p. 1984. pap. 6.50 o.p. (ISBN 0-416-33670-1, NO. 4044). Routledge Chapman & Hall.

Cognitive Psychology. Robert L. Solso. 499p. 1979. text ed. 26.00 o.p. (ISBN 0-15-507870-4, HC). HarBraceJ.

Cognitive Psychology: New Directions. Ed. by Guy Claxton. (International Library of Psychology). 1980. 35.00x o.p. (ISBN 0-7100-0485-0); pap. 17.50x o.p. (ISBN 0-7100-0486-9). Routledge Chapman & Hall.

Cognitive Psychology: The Study of Knowing, Learning & Thinking. Barry F. Anderson. 1975. 16.95 o.p. (ISBN 0-12-057850-6). Acad Pr.

Cognitive Strategies & Mathematics for the Learning Disabled. Ed. by John F. Cawley et al. 265p. 1985. 36.00 o.p. (ISBN 0-87189-120-4). Aspen Pub.

Cognitive Style, Learning Style & Transfer Skill Acquisition. Patricia Kirby. 113p. 1979. 7.25 o.p. (ISBN 0-318-15433-1, IN195). Natl Ctr Res Voc Ed.

Cognitive Theories in Social Psychology: Papers from Advances in Experimental Social Psychology. Ed. by Leonard Berkowitz. 1978. 27.00 o.p. (ISBN 0-12-091850-1). Acad Pr.

Cohabiting with Computers: A Computer Science Convocation at Columbia University. Ed. by Joseph F. Traub. 128p. 1985. 15.00 o.p. (ISBN 0-86576-079-9). W Kaufmann.

Coherence & Quantum Optics III. Ed. by L. Mandel & E. Wolf. LC 73-76700. 914p. 1973. 125.00x o.p. (ISBN 0-306-30731-6, Plenum Pr). Plenum Pub.

Coherence & Quantum Optics IV. Ed. by L. Mandel & E. Wolf. LC 78-15470. 1028p. 1978. 145.00x o.p. (ISBN 0-306-40038-3, Plenum Pr). Plenum Pub.

Coherent Non-Linear Interaction of Waves in Plasmas. J. C. Weiland & H. Wilhelmsson. 1977. 90.00 o.p. (ISBN 0-08-020964-5). Pergamon.

Coherent Raman Spectroscopy. G. L. Eesley. (Illus.). 150p. 1981. 57.00 o.p. (ISBN 0-08-025058-0). Pergamon.

Cohesion: The Human Element in Combat. William D. Henderson. LC 84-601104. (Illus.). 219p. (Orig.). 1985. pap. 6.00 o.p. (ISBN 0-318-21937-9, 008-020-01005-7). USGPO.

Cohomology Theories for Compact Abelian Groups. K. H. Hofmann & P. S. Mostert. 200p. 1974. 39.00 o.p. (ISBN 0-387-05730-7). Springer-Verlag.

Coil Spring Making. 2nd ed. Ed. by E. T. Gross et al. (Engineering Craftsmen: No. H6). (Illus.). 1974. spiral bdg. 45.00x o.p. (ISBN 0-85083-172-5). Trans-Atl Phila.

Coiled Pottery: Traditional & Contemporary Ways. Betty Blandino. LC 84-21470. 112p. 1985. pap. 12.95 o.p. (ISBN 0-8019-7601-4). Chilton.

Coin Collector's Price Guide. Robert Obojski. LC 86-14462. (Illus.). 128p. (Orig.). 1987. o. p. 10.95 o.p.; pap. 5.95 o.p. (ISBN 0-8069-4746-2). Sterling.

Coin Yearbook, 1984. 1983. (ISBN 0-901265-19-5). Intl Pubns Serv.

Coins of Gold. Paul Twitchell. 1972. 8.95 o.p. (ISBN 0-914766-02-3). Illum Way Pub.

Coins of the Ancient World. Ya'akov Meshorer. Ed. by Richard L. Currier. LC 72-10795. (Lerner Archaeology Ser.). (Illus.). 96p. (gr. 5 up). 1975. PLB 8.95 o.p. (ISBN 0-8225-0835-4). Lerner Pubns.

Cointelpro: The FBI's Secret War on Political Freedom. 3rd ed. Nelson Blackstock et al. Ed. by Cathy Perkus. LC 75-34818. (Illus.). 160p. 1976. 16.00 o.p. (ISBN 0-913460-41-9, Dist. by Path Pr NY); pap. 7.95 o.p. Anchor Found.

Coke & Other Solid Fuel Derivatives from Coal. Ed. by Clifford K. Gordon. LC 74-26747. 1976. text ed. 29.50x o.p. (ISBN 0-685-55477-5). Irvington.

Col Frontier Book Pk, No. 10. (Our Nations Heritage Ser.). Date not set. (ISBN 0-07-375416-1). McGraw.

C.O.L.A.R. Alfred Slote. 148p. (gr. 2-5). 1983. pap. 2.25 o.p. (ISBN 0-380-63982-3, Camelot). Avon.

Cold & Freezer Storage Manual. 2nd ed. Elliott R. Hallowell. (Illus.). 1980. 43.95 o.s.i. (ISBN 0-87055-366-6). AVI.

Cold & Frost Injuries: Rewarming Damages. H. Killian. (Disaster Medicine: Vol. 3). (Illus.). 260p. 1981. pap. 65.70 o.p. (ISBN 0-387-08991-8). Springer-Verlag.

Cold Chills. Robert Bloch. 1978. pap. 1.75 o.p. (ISBN 0-8439-0542-5, Pub. by Leisure Bks CT). Dorchester Pub Co.

Cold Cuisine. (Illus.). 256p. 1986. 22.95 o.p. (ISBN 0-8249-3058-4). Ideals.

Cold Cuisine. Helen Hecht. LC 80-69374. 1981. 12.95 o.s.i. (ISBN 0-689-11130-4, Athenem). Macmillan.

Cold Cuisine. Helen Hecht. 320p. 1985. pap. 8.95 o.p. (ISBN 0-689-70644-8, 293, Atheneum). Macmillan.

Cold Enamelling. Ursula Kuehnemann. LC 72-2181. (Illus.). 65p. 1973. 4.95 o.s.i. (ISBN 0-8008-1684-6); pap. 2.95 o.p. (ISBN 0-8008-1685-4). Taplinger.

Cold Hands. Joseph Pintauro. 1979. 10.95 o.p. (ISBN 0-671-24726-3). S&S.

Cold Heaven. Brian Moore. 1983. 14.95 o.p. (ISBN 0-03-063257-9). H Holt & Co.

Cold Heaven: Irish Religious Poetry of Faith & Doubt. Ed. by John F. Deane. 224p. (Orig.). 1988. pap. 16.95 o.p. (ISBN 0-86327-144-8, Pub. by Wolfhound Pr Ireland). Irish Bks Media.

Cold Is the Sea. Edward L. Beach. LC 77-18841. 1978. 9.95 o.p. (ISBN 0-03-013916-3). H Holt & Co.

Cold Judgement. Joanne Fluke. (Orig.). 1985. pap. 3.50 o.p. (ISBN 0-440-11311-3). Dell.

Cold Moon over Babylon. Michael McDowell. 1980. pap. 2.50 o.p. (ISBN 0-380-48660-1, 48660-1). Avon.

Cold Print. Ramsey Campbell. (Illus.). 248p. 1985. lib. bdg. 17.50 o.p. (ISBN 0-910489-13-0). Scream Pr.

Cold Rain on the Water. Rose Blue. (gr. 7 up). 1979. text ed. 7.95 o.p. (ISBN 0-07-006168-8). McGraw.

Cold Sea Rising. Richard Moran. 1985. 16.95 o.p. (ISBN 0-87795-755-X, Arbor Hse). Morrow.

Cold Sea Rising. Richard Moran. 1986. 16.95 o.p. (ISBN 0-87795-687-1). Morrow.

Cold Spring Harbor. Date not set. pap. (ISBN 0-385-29596-0). Delacorte.

Cold Spring Harbor. Richard Yates. 192p. 1987. pap. 9.95 o.p. (ISBN 0-385-29596-0, Delta). Delacorte.

Cold Tolerant Microbes in Spoilage & the Environment. Ed. by A. D. Russell & R. Fuller. 1979. 46.00 o.p. (ISBN 0-12-603750-7). Acad Pr.

Cold War. David Brierly. 192p. 1984. 9.50 o.s.i. (ISBN 0-671-47753-6). Summit Bks.

Cold War & Detente: The American Foreign Policy Process since 1945. Paul Y. Hammond. 370p. (Orig.). 1975. pap. text ed. 13.00 net o.p. (ISBN 0-15-507881-X, HC). HarBraceJ.

Cold War, Cold Peace: The United States & Russia since 1945. Bernard A. Weisberger. (American Heritage Bks.). (Illus.). 342p. 1984. 17.45 o.p. (ISBN 0-8281-1163-4). HM.

Cold War to Detente. 2nd ed. Colin Bown & Peter Mooney. 1981. pap. 12.00x o.p. (ISBN 0-435-32132-3). Heinemann Ed.

Cold Weather Flying. Jeff W. Griffin. (Modern Aviation Ser.). 1980. 9.95 o.p. (ISBN 0-8306-9711-X); pap. 5.95 o.p. (ISBN 0-8306-2273-X, 2273). TAB Bks.

Cold Wild Wind. Frances C. Kerns. 1975. pap. 1.95 o.p. (ISBN 0-380-00550-6, 36715-7). Avon.

Colder, the Better. David Wilson. LC 79-63793. 1980. 9.95 o.p. (ISBN 0-689-10873-7, Atheneum). Macmillan.

Coldest War: Russia's Game in China. C. L. Sulzberger. LC 74-1466. 113p. 1975. pap. 2.45 o.p. (ISBN 0-15-618500-8, Harv). HarBraceJ.

Coldest War: The Russian Game in China. C. L. Sulzberger. LC 74-1466. 1974. 5.95 o.p. (ISBN 0-15-118979-X). HarBraceJ.

Colditz Story. Patrick R. Reid. LC 77-28513. (Illus.). 1978. Repr. of 1953 ed. lib. bdg. 25.75x o.p. (ISBN 0-313-20245-1, RECS). Greenwood.

Coleco Adam User's Handbook. Weber Systems, Inc. Staff. (Orig.). 1984. 9.95 o.p. (ISBN 0-345-31839-0). Ballantine.

Colectividad y la Educacion De la Personalidad. Anton Makarenko. 312p. (Span.). 1977. 5.45 o.p. (ISBN 0-8285-1312-0, Pub. by Progress Pubs USSR). Imported Pubns.

Coleridge. Henry D. Traill. LC 67-23874. 232p. 1968. Repr. of 1884 ed. 40.00x o.p. (ISBN 0-8103-3052-0). Gale.

Coleridge in Memoriam: A Poetry Anthology to Samuel Taylor Coleridge (1834-1984) Ed. by John H. Morgan. 346p. (Orig.). 1988. pap. 12.95x o.p. (ISBN 1-55605-060-7). Wyndham Hall.

Coleridge, Opium & Kubla Khan. Elisabeth Schneider. 1966. lib. bdg. 27.50x o.p. (ISBN 0-88254-846-8, Octagon). Hippocrene Bks.

Coleridge: The Critical Heritage. Ed. by J. R. Jackson. 1970. 40.00x o.p. (ISBN 0-7100-6594-9). Routledge Chapman & Hall.

Coleridge's Variety: Bicentenary Studies. Ed. by John Beer. LC 74-2051. 1974. 27.95x o.p. (ISBN 0-8229-1114-0). U of Pittsburgh Pr.

Colette. Jean Cocteau. 113p. 1955. 8.95 o.p. (ISBN 0-686-54517-6). French & Eur.

Colette. Elaine Marks. LC 81-13246. 256p. 1982. Repr. of 1960 ed. lib. bdg. 35.00x o.p. (ISBN 0-313-23258-X, MART). Greenwood.

Colette: A Biography. Michele Sarde. Tr. by Richard Miller from Fr. LC 79-24978. (Illus.). 1980. 12.95 o.p. (ISBN 0-688-03601-5). Morrow.

Colette: A Taste for Life. Yvonne Mitchell. LC 77-3517. (Illus.). 240p. 1977. pap. 7.95 o.p. (ISBN 0-15-618550-4, Harv). HarBraceJ.

Collaboration in Experiential Education: A Profile of Participant Expectations. Louise E. Wasson & Richard J. Miguel. 73p. 1979. 5.10 o.p. (ISBN 0-318-15943-0, RD198). Natl Ctr Res Voc Ed.

Collaboration with Communist Countries in Managing Global Problems: An Examination of the Options. Chihiro Hosoya et al. (Triangle Papers: No. 13). 1977. 15.00 o.s.i. (ISBN 0-318-02790-9); pap. 6.00 o.s.i. (ISBN 0-318-02791-7). Trilateral Comm.

Collaboration with Communist Countries in Managing Global Problems: Am Examination of the Options see Trilateral Commission Task Force Reports.

Collaborations for Literacy: Tutor's Handbook. Michelle M. Staryos & Laura Winig. 161p. (Orig.). 1985. pap. text ed. 6.00 o.p. (ISBN 0-917754-25-5). Inst Responsive.

Collaborative Consultation. Lorna Idol-Maestas et al. 256p. 1986. 33.00 o.p. (ISBN 0-87189-371-1). Aspen Pub.

Collaborative Learning. Edwin Mason. LC 72-166549. 1972. 7.95x o.p. (ISBN 0-87586-028-1). Agathon.

Collage of Dreams: The Writings of Anais Nin. Sharon Spence. LC 80-25143. 240p. 1981. pap. 5.95 o.p. (ISBN 0-15-618581-4, Harv). HarBraceJ.

Colleagues or Competitors. Margaret Martin. 103p. 1969. pap. text ed. 5.00x o.p. (ISBN 0-7135-1538-4, Pub. by Bedford England). Gower Pub Co.

Collect Canada Covers. Edward A. Richardson. 1978. 8.00 o.p. (ISBN 0-686-24136-3). Am Philatelic Society.

Collected Earlier Poems: Before Nineteen Forty. William Carlos Williams. LC 51-8849. 1951. 22.50 o.p. (ISBN 0-8112-0426-X). New Directions.

Collected Editorials. Dave Moursund. (ICCE Monograph Ser.). 1985. 12.00 o.p. (ISBN 0-924667-26-5). Intl Council Comp.

Collected Essays, 4 Vols. Virginia Woolf. LC 67-20327. 1967. Vol. 1. 7.50 o.s.i. (ISBN 0-15-118550-6); Vol. 2. 7.50 o.s.i. (ISBN 0-15-118551-4); Vol. 3. 6.95 o.s.i. (ISBN 0-15-118552-2); Vol. 4. 6.95 o.s.i. (ISBN 0-15-118553-0). HarBraceJ.

Collected Essays, Journalism, & Letters of George Orwell, 4 vols. George Orwell. Ed. by Ian Angus. Incl. Vol. 1. Age Like This: Nineteen Twenty to Nineteen Forty. 574p. 1971. pap. 8.95 (ISBN 0-15-618620-9); Vol. II. My Country Right or Left: Nineteen Forty to Nineteen Forty-Three. 477p. 1971. pap. 6.95 (ISBN 0-15-618621-7); Vol. III. As I Please: Nineteen Forty-Three to Nineteen Forty-Five. 435p. 1971. pap. 6.95 (ISBN 0-15-618622-5); Vol. IV. In Front of Your Nose: Nineteen Forty-Five to Nineteen Fifty. 555p. 1971. pap. 8.95 (ISBN 0-15-618623-3). 1971. Set. pap. 29.95 o.p. (ISBN 0-15-618624-1, Harv). HarBraceJ.

Collected Essays, Journalism, & Letters of George Orwell, 4 vols. Ed. by George Orwell & Ian Angus. 1969. Set. 67.80 o.p. (ISBN 0-15-118545-X). HarBraceJ.

Collected Essays of Asa Briggs. Asa Briggs. 1988. pap. 14.95 ea. o.p. Vol. I: Words, Numbers, Places, People (ISBN 0-252-06004-0). Vol. II: Images, Problems, Standpoints, Forecasts (ISBN 0-252-06005-9). U of Ill Pr.

Collected Letters Eighteen Seventy-Four to Eighteen Ninety-Seven. George Bernard Shaw. (Illus.). 1965. 12.50 o.p. (ISBN 0-396-05226-6). Dodd.

Collected Papers of Kenneth E. Boulding, Vol. 1. Ed. by Fred. R. Glahe. LC 77-135288. 1971. 19.50x o.p. (ISBN 0-87081-011-1). Univ Pr Colo.

Collected Papers of Kenneth E. Boulding, Vol. 2. Ed. by Fred R. Glahe. LC 77-135288. 1971. 27.50x o.p. (ISBN 0-87081-012-X). Univ Pr Colo.

Collected Papers of Kenneth E. Boulding: Towards the Twenty First Century, Vol. 6. Ed. by Larry D. Singell. LC 77-135288. 1985. 29.95x o.p. (ISBN 0-87081-139-8). Univ Pr Colo.

Collected Papers of Kenneth E. Boulding, Vol. 3: Political Economy. Kenneth E. Boulding. Ed. by Larry D. Singell. LC 77-135288. 465p. 1973. text ed. 27.50x o.p. (ISBN 0-87081-046-4). Univ Pr Colo.

Collected Papers of Kenneth E. Boulding, Vol. 4: Toward a General Social Science. Kenneth E. Boulding. Ed. by Larry D. Singell. LC 77-135288. 1974. 22.50x o.p. (ISBN 0-87081-053-7). Univ Pr Colo.

Collected Papers of Kenneth E. Boulding, Vol. 5: International Systems. Kenneth E. Boulding. Ed. by Larry D. Singell. LC 77-135288. 500p. 1975. 27.50x o.p. (ISBN 0-87081-062-6). Univ Pr Colo.

Collected Papers of Neville Coghill: Shakespearian & Medievalist. Neville Coghill. 288p. 1987. 27.50 o.p. (ISBN 0-389-20739-X). B&N Imports.

Collected Papers of P. L. Kapitza, 2 vols. P. L. Kapitza. Ed. by D. Ter Haar. 1965. Vol. 1. 1965. 125.00 o.p. (ISBN 0-08-010744-3); Vol. 2. 1965. 120.00 o.p. (ISBN 0-08-010973-X). Pergamon.

Collected Plays with Their Prefaces: Definitive Edition in Seven Volumes. George Bernard Shaw. 1975. 20.00 ea. o.p.; Vol. 1. (ISBN 0-396-07125-2); Vol. 2. (ISBN 0-396-07126-0); Vol. 3. (ISBN 0-396-07127-9); Vol. 4. (ISBN 0-396-07128-7). Vol. 5 (ISBN 0-396-07129-5). Vol. 6 (ISBN 0-396-07130-9). Vol. 7 (ISBN 0-396-07131-7). Dodd.

Collected Poems. e. e. Cummings. LC 63-37949. 1938. 12.95 o.s.i. (ISBN 0-15-118563-8). HarBraceJ.

Collected Poems. Leslie Konnyu. Tr. by Joseph Gross. LC 68-8832. 1968. pap. 3.00 o.p. (ISBN 0-911862-08-0). Hungarian Rev.

Collected Poems. Thomas MacGreevy. (Belacqua Ser.). 77p. 1983. 12.95 o.p. (ISBN 0-906897-64-5). Dufour.

Collected Poems. Edward Thomas. 190p. 1974. 7.95x o.p. (ISBN 0-393-04383-5); pap. 2.45 o.p. (ISBN 0-393-00713-8). Norton.

Collected Poems. Gilbert Thomas. LC 70-382760. 1969. 8.95 o.s.i. (ISBN 0-8008-1690-0). Taplinger.

Collected Poems, Vol. 1. Michael Hartnett. LC 84-72523. 168p. 1985. 17.95 o.p. (ISBN 0-906897-74-2, Pub. by Raven Arts Pr); pap. 13.95 o.p. (ISBN 0-906897-72-6, Pub. by Raven Arts Pr). Dufour.

Collected Poems & Plays. Wyndham Lewis. Ed. by Alan Munton. 229p. 1981. pap. 7.95 o.p. (ISBN 0-89255-054-6). Persea Bks.

Collected Poems in English & French. Samuel Beckett. 1977. pap. 3.95 o.p. (ISBN 0-394-17013-X, E700, Ever). Grove.

Collected Poems, Nineteen Fifty-Eight to Nineteen Seventy. George MacBeth. LC 78-183613. 1972. 7.50 o.p. (ISBN 0-689-10448-0, Atheneum). Macmillan.

Collected Poems of Howard Nemerov. Howard Nemerov. LC 77-544. (Illus.). 1977. 20.00 o.s.i. (ISBN 0-226-57258-7). U of Chicago Pr.

Collected Poems of Muriel Rukeyser. Muriel Rukeyser. 1982. pap. text ed. 9.95 o.p. (ISBN 0-07-054271-6). Mcgraw.

Collected Poems of Wendell Berry, 1957-1982. Wendell Berry. LC 84-62305. 288p. Date not set. pap. 8.50 o.p. (ISBN 0-317-62328-1). N Point Pr.

Collected Poems, 1938-1983. Sheila Wingfield. 208p. 1983. 17.50 o.p. (ISBN 0-8090-3535-9); pap. 9.95 o.p. (ISBN 0-8090-1500-5). Hill & Wang.

Collected Poems: 1970-1983. Donald Davie. LC 83-50745. 176p. 1984. text ed. 16.95 o.s.i. (ISBN 0-268-00745-4). U of Notre Dame Pr.

Collected Poetry of Robinson Jeffers, Vol. 1: 1920-1928. Robinson Jeffers. Ed. by Tim Hunt. 552p. Date not set. 60.00 o.p. Stanford U Pr.

Collected Problems in Physics. S. Kozel et al. 182p. 1986. pap. 4.95 o.p. (ISBN 0-8285-3215-X, Pub. by Mir Pubs USSR). Imported Pubns.

Collected Short Stories. Carson McCullers. Bd. with Ballad of the Sad Cafe. 1973. 9.95 o.p. (ISBN 0-395-07982-9). HM.
Collected Shorter Plays of Samuel Beckett. Samuel Beckett. LC 83-49371. 320p. (Orig.). 1984. pap. 11.95 o.p. (ISBN 0-394-62098-4, E907, Ever). Grove.
Collected Stories. Caroline Gordon. 352p. 1981. 17.95 o.p. (ISBN 0-374-12630-5); pap. 9.95 o.p. (ISBN 0-374-51675-8). FS&G.
Collected Stories. Frank Tuohy. 352p. 1984. 19.95 o.p. (ISBN 0-03-057648-2). H Holt & Co.
Collected Stories of Hortense Calisher. Hortense Calisher. LC 75-11148. 1975. 15.00 o.p. (ISBN 0-87795-115-2, Arbor Hse); pap. 6.95 o.p. (ISBN 0-87795-166-7). Morrow.
Collected Stories of Jack Schaefer. Jack Schaefer. 1985. 7.95 o.p. (ISBN 0-87795-712-6, Arbor Hse). Morrow.
Collected Stories of John O'Hara. Ed. by Frank MacShane. (General Ser.). 806p. 1986. lib. bdg. 19.95 o.p. (ISBN 0-8161-4019-7, Large Print Bks). G K Hall.
Collected Stories of Katherine Anne Porter. Katherine A. Porter. LC 65-19706. 1965. 12.50 o.p. (ISBN 0-15-118992-7). HarBraceJ.
Collected Works of Billy the Kid. Michael Ondaatje. 112p. 1974. 9.95 o.p. (ISBN 0-393-08702-6). Norton.
Collected Works of Samuel Beckett, 29 vols. Samuel Beckett. LC 74-28586. 1981. Set. 175.00 o.s.i. (ISBN 0-394-49789-9, 29V). Grove.
Collected Writings of Dougal Graham, Skellat Bellman of Glasgow, 2 vols. Dougal Graham. LC 69-16478. 586p. 1968. Repr. of 1883 ed. Set. 40.00x o.p. (ISBN 0-8103-3535-2). Gale.
Collectible Sonja Henie. John Axe. (Illus.). 48p. pap. 2.95 o.p. (ISBN 0-87588-146-7, 417). Hobby Hse.
Collecting & Identifying Old Clocks. Henry G. Harris. LC 76-21577. (Illus.). 1977. 15.95 o.p. (ISBN 0-87523-187-X). Emerson.
Collecting & Using Classic Cameras. Ivor Matantle. (Illus.). 1986. 35.00 o.p. (ISBN 0-500-01365-9). Thames Hudson.
Collecting Antique Jewelry. Mona Curran. (Illus.). 12.95 o.s.i. (ISBN 0-87523-149-7). Emerson.
Collecting Antique Toys: A Practical Guide. Joseph Doucette & Charles Collins. (Illus.). 146p. 1981. 17.95 o.p. (ISBN 0-02-533010-1). Macmillan.
Collecting Art Nouveau, Identification & Values. Don Fredgant. (Illus.). 362p. (Orig.). 1982. pap. 10.95 o.p. (ISBN 0-89689-036-8, 1406). Bks Americana.
Collecting Bottles for Fun & Profit. William Ketchum, Jr. LC 84-62579. (Illus.). 96p. pap. 7.95 o.p. (ISBN 0-89586-251-4). Price Stern.
Collecting Comic Books. Marcia Leiter. (Illus.). 128p. 1983. pap. 8.70i o.p. (ISBN 0-316-52030-6). Little.
Collecting Costume: The Care & Display of Clothes & Accessories. Naomi Tarrant. (Illus.). 160p. 1983. 24.95 o.p. (ISBN 0-04-746017-2). Unwin Hyman.
Collecting Irish Silver. Douglas Bennett. (Illus.). 228p. 1985. 28.95 o.s.i. (ISBN 0-285-62622-1, Pub. by Souvenir Pr Ltd UK). Seven Hills Bk Dists.
Collecting Miniatures. Daphne Foskett. (Illus.). 500p. 1980. 62.50 o.p. (ISBN 0-902028-79-0). Antique Collect.
Collecting Rhinestone Jewelry. Maryanne Dolan. (Illus.). 236p. (Orig.). 1984. pap. 10.95 o.p. (ISBN 0-89689-049-X, 1532). Bks Americana.
Collecting the Animals. Peter Everwine. LC 72-94240. 1970. pap. 3.95 o.p. (ISBN 0-689-10542-8, Atheneum). Atheneum.
Collecting Toys: A Collectors Identification & Value Guide. 3rd ed. Richard O'Brien. (Illus.). 590p. 1982. pap. 9.95 o.p. (ISBN 0-89689-031-7). Bks Americana.
Collecting World Coins: A Century of Monetary Issues. Ed. by Colin Bruce. LC 86-82722. (Illus.). 592p. pap. 13.95 o.s.i. (ISBN 0-87341-100-5). Krause Pubns.
Collection & Enforcement of Judgments. Pennsylvania Bar Institute Staff. 146p. 1985. 30.00 o.p. (ISBN 0-318-19026-5, 292). PA Bar Inst.
Collection Development Policies: Clip Note 2-81. 131p. 1981. 12.00 o.p. (ISBN 0-8389-6738-8). Assn Coll & Res Libs.
Collection Development: The Selection of Materials for Libraries. William A. Katz. LC 79-19861. 352p. 1980. text ed. 26.95 o.p. (ISBN 0-03-050266-7, HoltC). HR&W.
Collection of College Words & Phrases. Benjamin H. Hall. LC 68-17995. 516p. 1968. Repr. of 1856 ed. 48.00x o.p. (ISBN 0-8103-3282-5). Gale.
Collection of Employer Contributions Institute, Las Vegas, Nevada, June 15 to 18, 1980: Proceedings. Ed. by Elizabeth A. Hieb. 77p. (Orig.). 1980. pap. 8.00 o.p. (ISBN 0-89154-138-1). Intl Found Employ.
Collection of Employer Contributions Institute: Proceedings. June 28-July 1, 1981, Lake Tahoe, Nevada. 72p. (Orig.). 1982. pap. text ed. 8.50 o.p. (ISBN 0-89154-168-3). Intl Found Employ.
Collection of Employer Contributions: Institute Proceedings, May 10-13, 1982, Las Vegas. Becky A. Wright. 103p. (Orig.). 1982. pap. 10.00 o.p. (ISBN 0-89154-196-9). Intl Found Employ.
Collection of Great Science Fiction Films. rev. ed. A. W. Strickland & Forrest J Ackerman. 200p. 1984. write for info. cancelled o.p. (ISBN 0-89917-321-7). TIS Inc.
Collection of Nagasaki Colour Prints & Paintings: Showing the Influence of Chinese & European Art on That of Japan. N. H. Mody. LC 69-11088. (Illus.). 1979. 72.50 o.p. (ISBN 0-8048-0111-8). C E Tuttle.
Collection of Problems in Physical Chemistry. Jiri Bares et al. 1962. text ed. 29.00 o.p. (ISBN 0-08-009577-1). Pergamon.
Collection of Problems on the Equations of Mathematical Physics. A. V. Bitsadze & D. F. Kalinichenko. 1980. 9.45 o.p. (ISBN 0-8285-1779-7, Pub. by Mir Pubs USSR). Imported Pubns.
Collection of Several Pieces, 2 vols. John Toland. Ed. by Rene Wellek. LC 75-11258. (British Philosophers & Theologians of the 17th & 18th Centuries: Vol. 57). 1976. Repr. of 1726 ed. Set. lib. bdg. 101.00 o.p. (ISBN 0-8240-1808-7). Garland Pub.
Collection of TradeMarks & Logotypes in Japan 1984-85. Ed. by S. Hasegawa. (Illus.). 450p. 1988. pap. 42.95 o.p. (ISBN 4-766-10407-2, Pub. by Graphic Sha Japan). Bks Nippan.
Collection of Trademarks & Logotypes in Japan, 1982-83. Ed. by Sumio Hasegawa & Shigeji Kobayashi. (Illus.). 480p. 1986. pap. 30.00 o.p. (ISBN 0-8161-8806-8, Pub. by Graphic-Sha Pub Co Ltd Japan). G K Hall.
Collection Program in Elementary & Middle Schools: Concepts, Practices, & Information Sources. Phyllis J. Van Orden. LC 82-15325. (Library Science Text Ser.). (Illus.). 301p. 1982. text ed. 18.50 o.p. (ISBN 0-87287-335-8). Libs Unl.
Collection, Use, & Care of Historical Photographs. Robert A. Weinstein & Larry Booth. LC 76-27755. (Illus.). 222p. 1977. cloth 20.00 o.s.i. (ISBN 0-910050-21-X). AASLH Pr.
Collections: A North Carolina Law Practice System. Marion G. Follin, III & Norman B. Smith. (Law Practice Systems Ser.). 436p. 1984. looseleaf 75.00x o.p. (ISBN 0-87215-760-1). Michie Co.
Collective Bargaining. 2nd ed. Neil W. Chamberlain & J. W. Kuhn. 1965. text ed. 34.95 o.p. (ISBN 0-07-010437-9). McGraw.
Collective Bargaining & Civil Service in Public Employment: Conflict & Accommodation. Paul Prasow. (IPA Training Manual Ser.). 344p. 1976. 10.00 o.p. (ISBN 0-89215-068-8). U Cal LA Indus Rel.
Collective Bargaining & Labor Relations. E. Edward Herman. (Illus.). 576p. 1981. pap. text ed. 36.33 o.p. (ISBN 0-13-140558-6). P-H.
Collective Bargaining & Public Administration see Issues in the Public Employee Relations Library: Series 4.
Collective Bargaining: How It Works & Why: A Manual of Theory & Practice. Thomas R. Colosi & Arthur E. Berkeley. LC 85-72636. 187p. 1986. pap. 14.95 o.p. (ISBN 0-943001-03-X). Am Arbitration.
Collective Bargaining in Industrialised Market Economies. International Labour Office Staff. vi, 415p. (Orig.). 1981. write for info. o.p. (ISBN 92-2-101065-1); pap. 24.50 o.p. (ISBN 92-2-101050-3). Intl Labour Office.
Collective Bargaining in Industrialised Market Economies: A Comparative Study of Methods & Practices. Ed. by John P. Windmuller. vi, 415p. (5th Impression 1985). 1977. cloth 24.50 o.p. (ILO84, ILO). UNIPUB.
Collective Bargaining in Libraries. Ed. by Frederick L. Schlipf. LC 75-25240. (Allerton Park Institute Ser.: No. 20). 179p. 1975. 8.00x o.p. (ISBN 0-87845-042-4). U of Ill Lib Info Sci.
Collective Bargaining in Public Employment. Michael H. Moskow et al. LC 81-40795. 352p. 1981. pap. text ed. 14.50 o.p. (ISBN 0-8191-1803-6). U Pr of Amer.
Collective Bargaining in the Federal Civil Service. Wilson R. Hart. LC 73-1143. 302p. 1974. Repr. of 1961 ed. lib. bdg. 22.50x o.p. (ISBN 0-8371-7062-1, HACB). Greenwood.
Collective Bargaining in the Public Sector: A Selected Periodical Guide, 1974-1984. Joseph C. Santora. (Public Administration Ser.: P 1800). 19p. 1985. 3.00 o.p. (ISBN 0-89028-630-2). Vance Biblios.
Collective Behavior. 2nd ed. Ralph H. Turner & Lewis Killian. (Illus.). 480p. 1972. text ed. (ISBN 0-13-140657-4). P-H.
Collective Behavior: A Bibliography. Denton E. Morrison & Kenneth E. Hornback. LC 75-24098. (Reference Library of Social Science: Vol. 15). 534p. 1976. lib. bdg. 67.00 o.p. (ISBN 0-8240-9975-3). Garland Pub.
Collective Goods Approach to Understanding Transnational Action. Harvey Starr & Charles W. Ostrom. (CISE Learning Package Ser.: No. 18). (Illus.). 67p. (Orig.). 1976. pap. text ed. 3.50x o.p. (ISBN 0-936876-31-X). LRIS.
Collective Management: The Reform of Global Economic Organizations. Miriam Camps & Catherine Gwin. 371p. 1982. text ed. 23.95 o.p. (ISBN 0-07-009708-9); pap. 10.95 o.p. (ISBN 0-07-009709-7). McGraw.
Collective Models of the Nucleus. John P. Davidson. LC 68-18665. 1968. 75.50 o.p. (ISBN 0-12-205250-1). Acad Pr.
Collective Properties of Physical Systems: Proceedings. Ed. by Bengt Lundqvist & Stig Lundqvist. 1974. 81.50 o.p. (ISBN 0-12-460350-5). Acad Pr.
Collective Public Employee Relations in Australia see Issues in the Public Employee Relations Library: Series 3.
Collective Public Employee Relations Abroad: Some Foreign Answers to American Questions see Issues in the Public Employee Relations Library: Series 4.
Collective Unconscience of Odd Bodkins. Dan O'Neill. LC 73-88368. (Illus.). 108p. 1973. pap. 4.95 o.p. (ISBN 0-912078-33-2). Volcano Pr.
Collectivization, Convergence & Capitalism: Political Economy in a Divided World. Michael Ellman. 1984. 79.00 o.p. (ISBN 0-12-237520-3). Acad Pr.
Collector Prints Old & New: An Identification & Value Guide. Carl F. Luckey. (Illus.). 350p. (Orig.). 1982. pap. 14.95 o.p. (ISBN 0-89689-025-2, 1313). Bks Americana.
Collector Prints Old & New: An Identification & Value Guide. Carl F. Luckey. (Illus.). 350p. pap. 20.00 o.p. (ISBN 0-317-54923-5). Apollo.
Collectors. Philippe Julian. LC 71-94033. (Illus.). 1970. 3.50 o.p. (ISBN 0-8048-0112-6). C E Tuttle.
Collectors. Intro. by Paige Rense. (World of Architectural Digest Ser.). (Illus.). 160p. 15.95 o.p. (ISBN 0-89535-103-X). Knapp Pr.
Collector's Beethoven. John Briggs. LC 77-28258. (Keystone Books in English Ser.). 1978. Repr. of 1962 ed. lib. bdg. 35.00x o.p. (ISBN 0-313-20243-5, BRBE). Greenwood.
Collector's Cabinet. Ruth Berges. LC 77-84560. (Illus.). 1980. 20.00 o.p. (ISBN 0-498-02117-3). A S Barnes.
Collectors Catalogue. Jose Wilson & Arthur Leaman. LC 78-10168. (Illus.). 1979. 12.95 o.p. (ISBN 0-03-042756-8); pap. 8.95 o.p. (ISBN 0-03-042751-7). H Holt & Co.
Collector's Encyclopedia of Depression Glass. Gene Florence. 1981. 17.95 o.p. (ISBN 0-89145-180-3). Collector Bks.
Collectors' Encyclopedia of Depression Glass. Gene Florence. 1983. 17.95 o.p. (ISBN 0-89145-240-0). Collector Bks.
Collector's Encyclopedia of Shells. 2nd ed. S. Peter Dance. 1977. pap. text ed. 24.95 o.p. (ISBN 0-07-015292-6). McGraw.
Collector's Guide to Japanese Cameras. Ed. by Koich Sugiyama et al. LC 85-40113. (Illus.). 328p. 1985. 85.00 o.s.i. (ISBN 0-87011-743-2). Kodansha.
Collector's Guide to Nineteenth Century Jugs. Kathy Hughes. (Illus.). 96p. 1985. 34.50 o.p. (ISBN 0-7102-0302-0). Routledge Chapman & Hall.
Collector's Guide to Staffordshire Pottery Figures. H. A. Turner. (Illus.). 1971. 19.95 o.s.i. (ISBN 0-87523-175-6). Emerson.
Collector's Haydn. Cornelius G. Burke. LC 77-28259. (Keystone Books in English Ser.: No. KB 7). (Addendum by Arthur Cohn). 1978. Repr. of 1959 ed. lib. bdg. 35.00x o.p. (ISBN 0-313-20239-7, BUCH). Greenwood.
Collectors' History of English Pottery. 3rd ed. Griselda Lewis. (Illus.). 360p. 1985. 59.50 o.p. (ISBN 1-85149-000-0). Antique Collect.
Collector's Illustrated Price Guide to Russel Wright Dinnerware. Benjamin Klein. (Illus.). 1981. 11.95 o.p. (ISBN 0-682-49745-2). Exposition-Phoenix.
College: A Smith Mosaic. Jacqueline Van Voris. LC 75-312689. 1975. 7.00 o.p. (ISBN 0-87391-000-1). Smith Coll.
College Accounting Fundamentals. Douglas J. McQuaig. LC 76-15788. (Illus.). 1977. text ed. 21.50 o.p. (ISBN 0-395-18986-1); instr. man(1-15) o.p. 5.25 o.p. HM.
College Accounting Fundamentals. 2nd ed. Douglas J. McQuaig. Incl. Westside Lanes: A Sole-Proprietorship Service Business for Chapters 1-10. 1981. pap. 14.76 Practice Set I (ISBN 0-395-29412-6); Driscoe's Rugs: A Sole-Proprietorship Merchandising Business for Chapters 1-15. 1981. Practice set II. pap. 14.76 (ISBN 0-395-29413-4); Claverton Outdoor Store: A Voucher System for Business for Chapters 22-29. 1981. Practice set III. pap. 14.76 (ISBN 0-395-29414-2); Denton Appliance. 1982. 15.96 (ISBN 0-395-32030-5); CW Hale. 1982. 2.36 (ISBN 0-395-32819-5); Accounting Stationery. 1981; Transparencies for Problem Solutions. 1981; Instructor's Annotated Ed., Accounting Stationery. 1981; Mt. Chandler Legal Practice Set. 1982. 15.96 (ISBN 0-395-32029-1); CW Hale Medical Practice Set. 12.95; Computer-Assisted Practice Set (Denton Appliance & Air Conditioning) 1982. wkbk. 15.96 (ISBN 0-395-32031-3); sol. manual 2.36 (ISBN 0-395-32068-2); 14.36 (ISBN 0-395-32824-1); Achievement Tests. (Series A). 1981; Achievement Tests. (Series B). 1981; Answer Key for Achievement Tests. (Series A-B). 1981. Chapters 1-29. 3.16 o.p. (ISBN 0-395-29425-8). 1981. Chapters 1-29. text ed. 28.95 o.p. (ISBN 0-395-29408-8); Chapters 1-15. text ed. 21.95 o.p. (ISBN 0-395-29409-6); Chapters 1-10. text ed. 18.95 o.p. (ISBN 0-395-29410-X). HM.
College Ahead! A Guide for High School Students & Their Parents. rev. ed. Eugene S. Wilson & Charles A. Bucher. LC 60-12727. 1964. pap. 1.65 o.p. (ISBN 0-15-619117-2, HB80, Harv). HarBraceJ.
College Algebra. William G. Ambrose. (Illus.). 320p. 1976. text ed. write for info. o.p. (ISBN 0-02-302520-4, 30252). Macmillan.
College Algebra. 2nd ed. Raymond A. Barnett. (Illus.). 1979. text ed. 26.95 o.p. (ISBN 0-07-003778-7). McGraw.
College Algebra. 3rd, rev. ed. Raymond A. Barnett. (Illus.). 544p. 1984. text ed. 39.95 o.p. (ISBN 0-07-003861-9). McGraw.
College Algebra. Robert Ellis & Denny Gulick. 514p. 1981. text ed. 22.50 o.p. (ISBN 0-15-507905-0, HC). HarBraceJ.
College Algebra. 2nd ed. Walter Fleming & Dale E. Varberg. (Illus.). 496p. 1984. text ed. (ISBN 0-13-141630-8). P-H.
College Algebra. 2nd ed. Jimmie Gilbert et al. 420p. 1986. text ed. (ISBN 0-534-05298-3). Wadsworth Pub.
College Algebra. Vivian S. Groza. 1980. text ed. 27.95 o.s.i. (ISBN 0-03-040376-6, CBS C). SCP.
College Algebra. 2nd ed. Bernard Kolman & Arnold Shapiro. 1984. text ed. 24.00 o.p. (ISBN 0-12-417897-9). Acad Pr.
College Algebra. 4th ed. Margaret L. Lial & Charles D. Miller. 1985. text ed. write for info. o.p. (ISBN 0-673-18024-7); write for info. study guide o.p. (ISBN 0-673-18025-5); write for info. solutions manual o.p. (ISBN 0-673-18123-5). Scott F.
College Algebra. 8th, rev. ed. Paul K. Rees et al. (Illus.). 560p. 1981. text ed. 37.95 o.p. (ISBN 0-07-051733-9). McGraw.
College Algebra. 2nd ed. Bernard J. Rice & Jerry D. Strange. 1980. 24.50 o.p. (ISBN 0-87150-288-7, 2261, Prindle). PWS-Kent Pub.
College Algebra. 5th ed. Joseph B. Rosenbach et al. 656p. 1988. Repr. of 1971 ed. price not set o.p. (ISBN 0-89464-274-X). Krieger.
College Algebra. Richard B. Thompson. 1978. pap. text ed. write for info. o.p. (ISBN 0-87150-229-1, PWS 1832, Prindle). PWS-Kent Pub.
College Algebra & College Algebra Trigonometry. Chris Vancil. 550p. 1983. text ed. write for info. o.p. (ISBN 0-02-422420-0). Macmillan.
College Algebra & Trigonometry. Robert Ellis & Denny Gulick. 661p. 1981. text ed. 20.75 o.p. (ISBN 0-15-507907-7, HC). HarBraceJ.
College Algebra & Trigonometry. Linda Gilbert & Jimmie Gilbert. 566p. 1986. text ed. (ISBN 0-534-06120-6). Wadsworth Pub.
College Algebra & Trigonometry. Bernard Kolman & Arnold Shapiro. 1981. 32.40i o.p. (ISBN 0-12-417840-5). Acad Pr.
College Algebra & Trigonometry. 2nd ed. Bernard Kolman & Arnold Shapiro. 1986. text ed. 24.00 o.p. (ISBN 0-12-417905-3). Acad Pr.
College Algebra with Applications. Jose Barros-Neto. (Illus.). 526p. 1985. text ed. 36.25 o.p. (ISBN 0-314-85217-4). West Pub.
College Algebra with Calculators. Marshall D. Hestenes & Richard O. Hill. (Illus.). 416p. 1982. text ed. (ISBN 0-13-140806-2). P-H.
College & Career: Adjusting to College & Selecting an Occupation. Nancy G. Cattell & Shirley I. Sharp. LC 78-111101. (Orig.). 1970. pap. text ed. 12.95x o.p. (ISBN 0-89197-085-1). Irvington.
College & University Personnel Policy Models. 129p. 15.00 o.p. (ISBN 0-910402-61-2); 10.00 o.p. Coll & U Personnel.

College Bible. Ed. by Norman Foerster & M. Willard Lampe. 1938. 29.50x o.p. (ISBN 0-89197-086-X); pap. text ed. 14.95x o.p. (ISBN 0-89197-087-8). Irvington.

College Board Achievement Test Biology. Research & Education Association Staff. (Illus.). 288p. 1987. pap. text ed. 12.95 o.p. (ISBN 0-317-60145-8). Res & Educ.

College Bound Digest, 1985-1986. 1985. pap. 1.50 o.p. (ISBN 0-915130-97-1). Educ Comm.

College Business Law. 5th ed. R. Robert Rosenberg et al. Ed. by Edward E. Byers. 1978. text ed. 31.60 o.p. (ISBN 0-07-053885-9). McGraw.

College Chemistry: A Laboratory Manual. Clark E. Bricker. (Orig.). 1967. pap. text ed. 10.95 o.p. (ISBN 0-15-507925-5, HC). HarBraceJ.

College Comes Sooner Than You Think! Jill Reilly & Bonnie Featherstone. (Illus.). 176p. (Orig.). 1987. pap. 9.95 o.p. (ISBN 0-934829-24-1). Career Pr Inc.

College Cost Book 1983-84. 4th ed. The College Scholarship Service of the College Board. 240p. (Orig.). 1983. pap. 9.95 o.p. (ISBN 0-87447-160-5, 001605). College Bd.

College Cost Book, 1984-85. 5th ed. College Board, College Scholarship Service. 220p. (Orig.). 1984. pap. 10.95 o.p. (ISBN 0-87447-187-7, 001877). College Bd.

College Cost Book, 1987-88. College Board College Scholarship Service Staff. 280p. (Orig.). 1987. pap. 10.95 o.p. (ISBN 0-87447-288-1). College Bd.

College Detective Stories Bibliography. John E. Kramer, Jr. & John E. Kramer, III. LC 82-48291. 300p. 1983. lib. bdg. 40.00 o.p. (ISBN 0-8240-9237-6). Garland Pub.

College Dictation for Transcription. Louis A. Leslie et al. (Diamond Jubilee Ser.). 384p. 1975. text ed. 27.50 o.p. (ISBN 0-07-037430-9). McGraw.

College Dropout & the Utilization of Talent. Ed. by Lawrence A. Pervin et al. 1966. 28.50x o.p. (ISBN 0-691-09310-5). Princeton U Pr.

College English & Communication. 3rd ed. Marie M. Stewart et al. (Illus.). 544p. 1975. text ed. 29.60 o.p. (ISBN 0-07-061401-6). McGraw.

College English: The First Year. 6th ed. Alton C. Morris et al. 1973. text ed. 15.50 o.p. (ISBN 0-15-508199-3, HC). HarBraceJ.

College English: The First Year. 7th ed. Alton C. Morris et al. LC 77-92321. (Illus.). 845p. 1978. text ed. 19.95 o.p. (ISBN 0-15-508202-7, HC). HarBraceJ.

College Graduate's Career Guide. Robert J. Ginn, Jr. 224p. 1981. 14.95 o.s.i. (ISBN 0-684-17155-4, ScribT). Scribner.

College Grants from Uncle Sam: Am I Eligible & for How Much?, 1988-89. 7th ed. Anna Leider. 28p. 1987. pap. text ed. 2.25 o.p. (ISBN 0-317-60092-3). Octameron Assocs.

College Handbook: Foreign Student Supplement, 1987-88. 245p. (Orig.). 1987. pap. 10.95 o.p. (ISBN 0-87447-290-3). College Bd.

College Handbook, 1983-1984. 1760p. (Orig.). (gr. 11-12). 1983. pap. 13.95 o.p. (ISBN 0-87447-158-3). College Bd.

College Handbook, 1984-85. 22nd ed. College Entrance Examination Board. LC 41-12971. 1850p. 1984. pap. 14.95 o.p. (ISBN 0-87447-185-0, 001850). College Bd.

College Handbook: 1985-86. 24th ed. 1900p. (Orig.). 1986. pap. 15.95 o.p. (ISBN 0-87447-254-7). College Bd.

College Handbook, 1987-88. 25th ed. Ed. by Maureen Matheson. 2025p. (Orig.). 1987. pap. 16.95 o.p. (ISBN 0-87447-286-5). College Bd.

College Housing: A Critique of the Federal College Housing Loan Program. John J. Agria. 1972. pap. 5.25 o.p. (ISBN 0-8447-3074-2). Am Enterprise.

College Instruction in Photography. 8th ed. C. William Horrell. Ed. by Eastman Kodak Co. (KODAK Publication Ser.: No. T-17). 96p. 1983. pap. 4.95 o.p. (ISBN 0-87985-344-1). Eastman Kodak.

College Is Only the Beginning: A Student Guide to Higher Education. Ed. by John N. Gardner & A. Jerome Jewler. 335p. 1985. pap. text ed. (ISBN 0-534-04275-9). Wadsworth Pub.

College Learning Anytime, Anywhere. Ewald B. Nyquist et al. 1977. pap. 7.95 o.p. (ISBN 0-15-119139-5). HarBraceJ.

College Level Examinations in Mathematics: Algebra, Algebra-Trigonometry, Trigonometry. Arco Editorial Board. LC 77-21106. (Illus.). 1978. pap. text ed. 5.95 o.p. (ISBN 0-668-04339-3, 4339). Arco.

College Library Management. G. L. Trehan. 426p. 1986. text ed. 45.00x o.p. (ISBN 81-207-0114-3, Pub. by Sterling Pubs India). Apt Bks.

College Math. John Bryant & Chris Lacher. 500p. 1982. text ed. write for info. o.p. (33L 2551). PWS-Kent Pub.

College Mathematics for Business & Workbook to Accompany: College Mathematics Ser. Don Busche & Flora M. Locke. 1985. 24.95 o.p. (ISBN 0-471-84690-2). Wiley.

College Money Handbook. Karen C. Hegener. 487p. 1983. pap. 9.95 o.p. (ISBN 0-87866-251-0). Petersons Guides.

College Money Handbook 1987: The Complete Guide to Expenses, Scholarships, Loans, Jobs & Special Aid Programs at Four-Year Colleges. 4th ed. (Peterson's Annual Guides Ser). 568p. (Orig.). 1986. pap. 15.95 o.p. (ISBN 0-87866-526-9). Petersons Guides.

College Money Handbook 1988: The Only Complete Guide to Scholarships, College Costs, & Financial Aid. 5th ed. (Peterson's Annual Guides Ser.). 599p. (Orig.). 1987. lib. bdg. 22.95 o.p. (ISBN 0-87866-649-4); pap. 17.95 o.p. (ISBN 0-87866-571-4). Petersons Guides.

College of Trivial Knowledge. Robert A. Nowlan. LC 83-1012. 160p. 1983. 14.95 o.p. Morrow.

College of Trivial Knowledge. Robert A. Nowlan. 160p. 1983. pap. 6.45 o.p. (ISBN 0-688-02072-0, QUill NY). Morrow.

College Physics. 3rd ed. Franklin Miller. (Illus.). 749p. 1972. text ed. 17.95 o.p. (ISBN 0-15-511732-7, HC). HarBraceJ.

College Physics. 5th ed. Franklin Miller, Jr. 892p. 1982. text ed. 26.50 o.p. (ISBN 0-15-511737-8, HC). HarBraceJ.

College Physics. 4th ed. Franklin Miller, Jr. 1977. 23.95 o.p. (ISBN 0-15-511734-3). HarbraceJ.

College Physics. 2nd ed. John J. O'Dwyer. 808p. 1984. text ed. (ISBN 0-534-02950-7). Wadsworth Pub.

College Planning-Search Book. rev., 12th ed. American College Testing Program Staff. (Illus.). 312p. (gr. 9-12). 1986. pap. text ed. 6.00 o.p. (ISBN 0-937734-09-8). Am Coll Testing.

College Planning Search Book. rev., 13th ed. The American College Testing Program Staff. (Illus.). 312p. (YA) (gr. 9-12). 1987. pap. text ed. 6.00 o.p. (ISBN 0-937734-60-8). Am Coll Testing.

College Presidency Nineteen Hundred to Nineteen Sixty: An Annotated Bibliography. United States Office of Education, Division of Higher Education Staff. Ed. by Walter C. Eells. LC 78-12207. 1979. Repr. of 1961 ed. lib. bdg. 35.00 o.p. (ISBN 0-313-20680-5, EECP). Greenwood.

College Programs for Paraprofessionals: A Directory of Degree-Granting Programs in the Human Services. Ed. by Alan Gartner. LC 74-12066. 135p. 1975. text ed. 24.95 o.p. (ISBN 0-87705-229-8). Human Sci Pr.

College Reading, Bk. 2. 2nd ed. Janet Maker & Minnette Lenier. 399p. 1986. pap. text ed. (ISBN 0-534-05838-8). Wadsworth Pub.

College Reading & Study Skills. 3rd ed. Kathleen T. McWhorter. 1986. pap. text ed. write for info. o.p. (ISBN 0-673-39280-5). Scott F.

College Recruitment. William J. McBurney, Jr. 256p. 1982. 34.95 o.p. (ISBN 0-8144-5679-0). AMACOM.

College Student Development Revisited: Programs, Issues & Practices. rev. ed. Ed. by Roy F. Giroux & Donald A. Biggs. 364p. 1979. 9.75 o.p. (ISBN 0-911547-18-5, 72104W34); members 7.25 o.p. Am Assn Coun Dev.

College Study Skills. James F. Shepherd. LC 78-69533. (Illus.). 1979. pap. 10.50 o.p. (ISBN 0-395-26261-5). HM.

College Study Skills. 2nd ed. James F. Shepherd. 1983. pap. 17.95 o.p. (ISBN 0-395-32582-X). HM.

College Survey of English Literature. rev. ed. Ed. by Alexander M. Witherspoon. 1951. text ed. 13.95 o.p. (ISBN 0-15-510249-4, HC). HarBraceJ.

College Trigonometry. Linda Gilbert & Jimmie Gilbert. 372p. 1985. text ed. (ISBN 0-534-03647-3). Wadsworth Pub.

College Vocabulary Builder. Charles I. Freundlich. 256p. (Orig.). 1981. pap. 7.95 o.p. (ISBN 0-671-41337-6). Monarch Pr.

College Vocabulary Skills. James F. Shepherd. LC 78-69548. (Illus.). 1979. pap. 11.50 o.p. (ISBN 0-395-26851-6). HM.

College Vocabulary Skills. 2d ed. James F. Shepherd. 1983. pap. 16.95 o.p. (ISBN 0-395-32811-X). HM.

College Writer's Handbook. 2nd ed. Suzanne Jacobs & Roderick A. Jacobs. 288p. 1976. pap. text ed. write for info. o.p. (ISBN 0-673-15683-4). Scott F.

College Writing Basics: A Progressive Approach. Thomas E. Tyner. 422p. 1987. pap. text ed. write for info. o.p. (ISBN 0-534-06888-X). Wadsworth Pub.

College 101. Date not set. Petersons Guides.

College 101. Ronald T. Farrar. LC 84-9534. 187p. (Orig.). 1984. pap. 6.95 o.p. (ISBN 0-87866-269-3). Petersons Guides.

Collegiate Programs for Older Adults: A Summary Report on a 1976 Survey. Carol Florio. LC 78-51940. (Academy Occasional Papers: No. 7). 52p. (Orig.). 1978. pap. 3.00 o.p. (ISBN 0-89492-003-0). Acad Educ Dev.

Collegium Internationale Neuro-Psychopharmacologicum, 10th Congress: Proceedings, 2 vols. Ed. by P. Deniker. 1978. Set. 425.00 o.p. (ISBN 0-08-021506-8). Pergamon.

Colliery Spoil Tips: After Aberfan. 64p. 1972. 10.00x o.p. (ISBN 0-901948-59-4). Am Soc Civil Eng.

Colline. Jean Giono. 192p. 1960. 3.95 o.p. (ISBN 0-686-53953-2). Schoenhof.

Colline. Jean Giono. (Illus.). deluxe ed. 45.40 o.p. (ISBN 0-685-34172-0). Schoenhof.

Colline: Roman. Jean Giono. (Coll. Soleil). 1960. 11.50 o.p. (ISBN 0-685-11091-5). Schoenhof.

Collins: Correctional Law 1987. William C. Collins. 123p. 1988. 25.00 o.p. Am Correctional.

Collins French-English Dictionary. Collins Staff. 512p. (Orig., Fr. & Eng.). 1985. pap. 3.50 o.s.i. (ISBN 0-425-08295-4). Berkley Pub.

Collins Guide to Dog Nutrition. Date not set. (ISBN 0-87605-418-1). Howell Bk.

Collins Pocket Guide to British Birds. Fitter & Richardson. 1966. 26.95 o.s.i. (ISBN 0-00-219174-1, Collins Pub England). Greene.

Collision. Jack Pulman. LC 78-11450. 1979. 9.95 o.p. (ISBN 0-689-10941-5, Atheneum). Macmillan.

Collision Course: How to Handle Your Own Automobile Damage Claim Without Getting Ripped Off. Fred Utz. LC 84-60086. (Illus.). 128p. (Orig.). 1984. pap. 7.50 o.p. (ISBN 0-935834-34-6). Rainbow Books.

Collision in Brussels: The Common Market Crisis of 30 June 1965. John Newhouse. LC 67-26064. (Orig.). 1967. pap. 3.95x o.p. (ISBN 0-393-09779-X, NortonC). Norton.

Collocation Methods for Parabolic Equations in a Single Space Variable: Based on C to the First Power-Piecewise-Polynomial Spaces. J. Douglas, Jr. & T. Dupont. (Lecture Notes in Mathematics: Vol. 385). v, 147p. 1974. pap. text ed. 12.00 o.p. (ISBN 0-387-06747-7). Springer-Verlag.

Colloid Chemistry. 2nd ed. S. Voyutsky. 559p. 1978. 9.45 o.p. (ISBN 0-8285-5202-9, Pub. by Mir Pubs USSR). Imported Pubns.

Colloquial Hungarian. 2nd ed. Arthur H. Whitney. (Trubner's Colloquial Manuals). (Illus.). 1977. pap. 7.95 o.p. (ISBN 0-7100-8550-8). Routledge Chapman & Hall.

Colloquial Japanese. Noboru Inamoto. LC 71-133865. 1972. 21.95 o.p. (ISBN 0-8048-0741-8). C E Tuttle.

Colloquial Language in Literature see Needed Words.

Colloquial Vietnamese. rev ed. Nguyen Dinh-Hoa. LC 74-5132. 398p. 1974. text ed. 14.95x o.p. (ISBN 0-8093-0685-9); pap. text ed. 15.95x o.p. (ISBN 0-8093-0686-7). S Ill U Pr.

Colloquies of Erasmus. Desiderius Erasmus. Tr. by Craig R. Thompson. LC 64-22246. 1965. lib. bdg. 45.00x o.s.i. (ISBN 0-226-21481-8). U of Chicago Pr.

Colloquium on Crime: Eleven Reowned Mystery Writers Discuss Their Work. Ed. by Robin W. Winks. 256p. 1986. 15.95 o.p. (ISBN 0-684-18428-1). Scribner.

Colmillo Del Tigre. Paul Twitchell. Tr. by Lottie Gilpatrick et al. 180p. (Orig., Span.). 1980. pap. 3.95 o.p. (ISBN 0-914766-52-X, 0906). Illum Way Pub.

Colombia: An Export Market Profile. Christine H. Bolling. (Foreign Agricultural Economic Reports: No. 225). (Illus.). 67p. 1987. pap. 3.25 o.p. (ISBN 0-318-22881-5, S/N 001-019-00491-6). USGPO.

Colon Cancer Genetics. Henry T. Lynch et al. 1984. 51.95 o.p. (ISBN 0-442-24918-7). Van Nos Reinhold.

Colonel Aaron Burr, the American Phoenix. Samuel E. Burr, Jr. 1963. 10.00 o.p. (ISBN 0-682-42019-0). Exposition-Phoenix.

Colonel Grunt. Jenny Partridge. LC 81-7067. (Oakapple Wood Stories Ser.). (Illus.). 32p. (gr. k-2). 1982. 4.95 o.p. (ISBN 0-03-061511-9). H Holt & Co.

Colonel Joe, the Last of the Rough Riders: Recollections of a Centenarian. Claudia J. Brownlee. 1977. 8.00 o.p. (ISBN 0-682-48988-3, Lochinvar). Exposition-Phoenix.

Colonel Sager, Practitioner. Floyd C. Sager & Milton C. Toby. (Illus.). 150p. 1980. 10.75 o.p. (ISBN 0-936032-35-9). Blood-Horse.

Colonel Stephens Railways. John Scott-Morgan. LC 77-91737. 1978. 16.95 o.p. (ISBN 0-7153-7544-X). David & Charles.

Colonial Africa. A. J. Christopher. 240p. 1984. 28.50x o.p. (ISBN 0-389-20452-8, 08013). B&N Imports.

Colonial America. rev. ed. Margaret Fisher et al. LC 78-74045. (American History & Culture Ser). (Illus.). 148p. (gr. 4 up). 1979. text ed. 8.70, 5 or more copies 6.96 ea. o.p. (ISBN 0-88296-038-5). Gateway Pr MI.

Colonial America. Jerome R. Reich. (Illus.). 320p. 1984. pap. text ed. (ISBN 0-13-151167-X). P-H.

Colonial Doll Family. rev. ed. Designed by Sandy Williams. (Illus.). 32p. 1985. pap. 3.95 o.p. (ISBN 0-87588-240-4, 433). Hobby Hse.

Colonial Frontier. (Our Nations Heritage Ser.). Date not set. (ISBN 0-07-375395-5). McGraw.

Colonial Frontiers: Art & Life in Spanish New Mexico, the Fred Harvey Collection. Ed. by Christine Mather. LC 83-70073. (Museum of International Folk Art Ser.). (Illus.). 120p. 1983. 24.95 o.p. (ISBN 0-941270-16-5); pap. 12.95 o.p. (ISBN 0-941270-15-7). Ancient City Pr.

Colonial History of Hartford: Bicentennial Edition. William D. Love. (Illus.). 369p. 1974. Repr. of 1914 ed. 15.00x o.p. (ISBN 0-686-26742-7). Conn Hist Soc.

Colonial House Then & Now: A Picture Study of the Early American House Adapted to Modern Living. Francis Underwood. LC 75-28720. 1975. 17.50 o.p. (ISBN 0-8048-1150-4). C E Tuttle.

Colonial Immigrants in a British City: A Class Analysis. John Rex et al. 356p. 1984. pap. 12.95x o.p. (ISBN 0-7102-0019-6). Routledge Chapman & Hall.

Colonial Manila: The Context of Hispanic Urbanism & Process of Morphogenesis. Robert R. Reed. (UC Publications in Geography: Vol. 22). 1978. pap. 21.50x o.p. (ISBN 0-520-09579-0). U of Cal Pr.

Colonial Mobile. Peter J. Hamilton. Ed. by Charles G. Summersell. LC 75-19291. (Southern Historical Series: No. 20). 896p. 1976. Repr. of 1910 ed. 27.50 o.s.i. (ISBN 0-8173-5228-7). U of Ala Pr.

Colonial Organs & Organ Builders. E. N. Matthews. 1969. 35.00x o.p. (ISBN 0-522-83906-1, Pub by Melbourne U Pr). Intl Spec Bk.

Colonial Parson of New England. Frank S. Child. LC 74-19532. 230p. 1974. Repr. of 1896 ed. 35.00x o.p. (ISBN 0-8103-3667-7). Gale.

Colonial Period of American History: The Settlements, 3 vols. Charles M. Andrews. Vol. 1 1934. 55.00x o.p. (ISBN 0-300-00269-6); Vol. 2 1936. 50.00 o.p. (ISBN 0-300-00271-8); Vol. 3 1937. 50.00x o.p. (ISBN 0-300-00272-6); Vol. 4 1938. 50.00 o.p. (ISBN 0-300-00273-4). Yale U Pr.

Colonial Revival in America. Ed. by Alan Axelrod. (Winterthur Bk.). (Illus.). 377p. 1985. 29.45 o.p. (ISBN 0-393-01942-X). Norton.

Colonial Sunset: Australia & Papua New Guinea 1970-74. L. W. Johnson. LC 82-21875. (Illus.). 271p. 1984. 34.50x o.p. (ISBN 0-7022-1823-5). U of Queensland Pr.

Colonial Transformation of Kenya: The Kamba, Kikuyu, & Maasai from 1900-1939. R. Tignor. 1975. 45.50x o.p. (ISBN 0-691-03103-7). Princeton U Pr.

Colonial Virginia: Its People & Customs. Mary N. Stanard. LC 78-99055. (Social History Reference Ser.). (Illus.). 384p. 1970. Repr. of 1917 ed. 50.00x o.p. (ISBN 0-8103-0161-X). Gale.

Colonialism & Foreign Ownership of Capital: A Trade Theorist's View. Bharat R. Hazari. 108p. 1982. 24.00 o.p. (ISBN 0-7099-1241-2, Pub. by Croom Helm). Routledge Chapman & Hall.

Colonies in Space: The Next Giant Step. Frederic Golden. LC 76-46784. (Illus.). (gr. 7 up). 1977. 8.95 o.p. (ISBN 0-15-219400-2, HJ). HarBraceJ.

Colonists. William S. Long. (Australians Ser.: Vol. VI). 1984. lib. bdg. 12.95 o.p. (ISBN 0-8398-2829-2, Gregg). G K Hall.

Colonists in Bondage: White Servitude & Convict Labor in America, 1607-1776. Abbot E. Smith. 1971. pap. 5.95x o.p. (ISBN 0-393-00592-5, Norton Lib). Norton.

Colonization & Christianity: A Popular History of the Treatment of the Natives by the Europeans in All Their Colonies. William Howitt. LC 70-76856. 1970. Repr. of 1838 ed. 35.00 o.p. (ISBN 0-8371-1162-5, HOC&, Pub. by Negro U Pr). Greenwood.

Colonization of Australia (1829-42) The Wakefield Experiment in Empire Building. Richard C. Mills. xx, 364p. 1975. 27.00x o.p. (ISBN 0-424-00004-0, Pub. by Sydney U Pr). Intl Spec Bk.

Color Aerial Photography in the Pl Sc & Related Fields: Seventh Biennial Workshop. Intro. by William M. Ciesla. 255p. 1979. pap. 12.00 (7.00 member) o.p. (ISBN 0-937294-11-X). ASP & RS.

Color & Constitution of Organic Molecules. J. Griffiths. 1977. 55.00 o.p. (ISBN 0-12-303550-3). Acad Pr.

Color & Human Nature: Negro Personality Development in a Northern City. William L. Warner. LC 78-106844. 1970. Repr. of 1941 ed. 35.00x o.p. (ISBN 0-8371-3466-8, WCH/, Pub. by Negro U Pr). Greenwood.

Color & Personality. Audrey Kargere. (ISBN 0-8022-0825-8). Philos Lib.

Color & Shape in American Indian Art. Zena P. Mathews. Ed. by Margaret Aspinwall & Amy Horbar. LC 83-787. (Illus.). 24p. (Orig.). 1983. pap. 1.95 o.p. (ISBN 0-87099-334-8). Metro Mus Art.

Color Atlas of Colposcopy. Hanskurt Bauer. LC 78-62047. (Illus.). 1979. 45.00 o.p. (ISBN 0-89640-031-X). Igaku-Shoin.

Color Atlas of Geriatric Medicine. Asif Kamal & J. C. Brocklehurst. 176p. 1984. casebound 69.95 o.s.i. (ISBN 0-87489-366-6). Med Economics.

Color Atlas of Gynecological Surgery, Vol. 2: Abdominal Operations for Benign Conditions. David Lees & Albert Singer. 1978. 111.00 o.p. (ISBN 0-8151-5352-X). Year Bk Med.

Color Atlas of Gynecological Surgery, Vol. 5: Infertility Surgery. David H. Lees & Albert Singer. (Illus.). 400p. 1981. 111.00 o.p. (ISBN 0-8151-5355-4). Year Bk Med.

Color Atlas of Hematological Cytology. 2nd ed. F. G. Hayhoe & R. J. Flemans. LC 81-71285. 240p. 1982. 85.00 o.p. (ISBN 0-471-86868-X, Pub. by Res Stud Pr). Wiley.

Color Atlas of Insect Tissues Via the Flea. Miriam R. Schlein & Susuu Ito. (Illus.). 184p. 1986. text ed. 79.95 o.p. (ISBN 0-7234-0891-2, 1011, Pub. by Chapman & Hall England). Routledge Chapman & Hall.

Color Atlas of Surgical Diagnosis. Rainer F. Lick. LC 78-54518. (Illus.). 530p. 1980. text ed. write for info. o.p. (ISBN 0-7216-5767-2). Saunders.

Color by Quant: Your Complete Personal Guide to Beauty & Fashion. Mary Quant. (Illus.). 144p. 1985. text ed. 17.95 o.p. (ISBN 0-07-051019-9). McGraw.

Color Computer Fun House. Richard Ramella. pap. incl. disk o.p. (ISBN 0-88006-077-8, CC7412). Wayne Green Ent.

Color Creations in Buttercream. Richard V. Snyder. LC 75-46425. (Illus.). 1976. 11.50 o.p. (ISBN 0-682-48458-X, Banner). Exposition-Phoenix.

Color Encyclopedia of Gemstones. Joel E. Arem. (Illus.). 1977. 44.95 o.p. (ISBN 0-442-20333-0). Van Nos Reinhold.

Color for Profit. Louis Cheskin. (Illus.). 1951. 6.95x o.p. (ISBN 0-87140-964-X). Liveright.

Color for the Hand Papermaker. Elaine Koretsky. LC 83-62415. (Illus.). 180p. 1983. special ed. 200.00x o.p. (ISBN 0-9612216-3-1); pap. text ed. 35.00x o.p. (ISBN 0-9612216-0-7). Carriage Hse Pr.

Color for the Watercolor Painter. rev. & enl. ed. Tom Hill. (Illus.). 160p. 1982. 24.95 o.p. (ISBN 0-8230-0734-0). Watson-Guptill.

Color Historic Atlanta. James J. Duffy. Ed. by Phyllis Mueller. (Color America Ser.). (Illus.). 32p. (ps-6). 1986. pap. 2.50 o.p. (ISBN 0-932419-08-9). Susan Hunter.

Color Historic Florida. James J. Duffy. (Illus.). 32p. 1987. pap. 2.50 o.p. (ISBN 0-932419-09-7). Susan Hunter.

Color Historic Georgia. James J. Duffy. Ed. by Phyllis Mueller. (Color America Ser.). (Illus.). 32p. (Orig.). (ps-6). 1986. pap. 2.50 o.p. (ISBN 0-932419-07-0). Susan Hunter.

Color Me Christian. Daisy Hepburn. LC 83-24624. (Life with Spice Bible Study Ser.). 1984. 2.95 o.s.i. (ISBN 0-8307-0949-5, 6101867). Regal.

Color Me Macho. Carl Franz. (Illus.). 112p. 1985. pap. 6.95 o.p. (ISBN 0-912528-46-X). John Muir.

Color Me White: The Autobiography of a Black Dancer Who Turned White. Arthur Wright. (Illus.). 1980. 12.50 o.p. (ISBN 0-682-49557-3). Exposition-Phoenix.

Color New York. Roxie Munro. pap. 8.95 o.p. (ISBN 0-87795-698-7). Morrow.

Color of Greed. Gary Valcour. 176p. 1984. pap. 3.50 o.p. (ISBN 0-380-87726-0, 87726-0). Avon.

Color of Minerals. G. Rapp. (Earth Science Curriculum Project Pamphlet Ser). 1971. pap. 4.60 o.p. (ISBN 0-395-02620-2). HM.

Color of the Night: Reflections on the Book of Job. Gerhard E. Frost. LC 77-72458. 1977. pap. 6.95 o.p. (ISBN 0-8066-1583-4, 10-1520, Augsburg). Augsburg Fortress.

Color Orange: A Supper Bowl Season with the Denver Broncos. Russell Martin. (Illus.). 336p. 1987. 18.95 o.p. (ISBN 0-8050-0562-5). H Holt & Co.

Color Photographic Standards for Surface Preparation (SSPC-Vis 1) rev. ed. Steel Structures Painting Council Staff et al. (Illus.). 48p. (Eng., Swedish, Ger., Span., Fr. & Rus.). 1982. spiral bound 90.00 o.s.i. (ISBN 0-938477-04-8). SSPC.

Color Photography Simplified. Jerry Yulsman. (Modern Photo Guide Ser.). (Illus.). 1977. 10.95 o.p. (ISBN 0-8174-2425-3, Amphoto); pap. 5.95 o.p. (ISBN 0-8174-0176-8). Watson-Guptill.

Color Printers. International Resource Development, Inc. Staff. 190p. 1984. 1650.00x o.p. (ISBN 0-88694-597-6). Intl Res Dev.

Color Printing. Bob Mitchell. LC 75-8142. (Photography How-to Ser.). (Illus.). 1975. pap. 4.95 o.p. (ISBN 0-8227-0101-4). Petersen Pub.

Color Purple: A Language Perspective. Patricia A. Geuder. 32p. 1986. 6.95 o.p. (ISBN 0-8062-2946-2). Carlton.

Color Related Decorating Textiles. Tonya S. Rhodes. LC 76-24006. (Shuttle Craft Guild Monograph: No. 14). (Illus.). 35p. 1965. pap. 7.95 o.s.i. (ISBN 0-916658-14-7). Shuttle Craft.

Color Separation Scanner Comparison Charts: 1985 Edition. Harold Durbin. 1985. write for info. o.s.i. (ISBN 0-936786-10-8). Durbin Assoc.

Color Separation Scanner Comparison Charts: 1988 Edition. Harold Durbin. 1986. pap. 25.00 o.p. (ISBN 0-936786-10-8). Durbin Assoc.

Color Television: Reception & Decoding Techniques. B. W. Osborne. (Illus.). 168p. 1968. 26.00 o.p. (ISBN 0-85334-030-7, Pub. by Elsevier Applied Sci England). Elsevier.

Color Television Servicing. 2nd ed. Gordon J. King. 18.95 o.p. (ISBN 0-408-00137-2, NB 34, Pub. by Newnes-Butterworth). Sams.

Color TV Case Histories Illustrated: Photo Guide to Troubles & Cures. Robert Goodman. LC 74-33619. (Illus.). 238p. 1975. 8.95 o.p. (ISBN 0-8306-5746-0); pap. 7.95 o.p. TAB Bks.

Color Your Hair. Peter Waters. 1984. pap. 9.95 o.p. (ISBN 0-03-070504-5). H Holt & Co.

Color Your Hair Like A Pro. Vincent Nardi & Fred Nardi. (Illus.). 144p. 1986. pap. 10.95 o.p. (ISBN 0-399-51187-3). Putnam Pub Group.

Color Your Self Beautiful. Eadeth Daum. 1979. 5.00 o.p. (ISBN 0-682-49328-7). Exposition-Phoenix.

Colorado. Photos by David Muench. LC 78-51219. (Belding Imprint Ser.). (Illus.). 192p. (Text by David Sumner). 1978. 29.50 o.s.i. (ISBN 0-912856-42-4). Gr Arts Ctr Pub.

Colorado Accommodations Guide. D. O'Neill. LC 85-91091. 1986. pap. 7.95 o.s.i. (ISBN 0-934318-81-6). Falcon Pr MT.

Colorado: Agency. 8.50 o.p. (ISBN 0-686-90658-6). Am Law Inst.

Colorado & Utah Industrial Minerals. 1974. 15.50 o.p. (ISBN 0-942218-01-9). Minobras.

Colorado Books in Print: 1984 Supplement. Compiled by Jene-Hagan Bookcorp Staff & Eleanor Ayer. 64p. (Orig.). 1984. pap. 8.95 o.p. (ISBN 0-939650-41-X). R H Pub.

Colorado Business Directory, 1987-88. American Directory Publishing Co., Inc. Staff. 1379p. (Orig.). 1987. pap. 85.00 o.p. (ISBN 0-944316-02-6). Amer Directory.

Colorado: Conflict of Laws. 8.50 o.p. (ISBN 0-686-90435-4). Am Law Inst.

Colorado Front Range: A Landscape Divided. Gleaves Whitney. LC 83-81113. (Illus.). 176p. (Orig.). 1983. pap. 8.95 o.p. (ISBN 0-933472-71-4). Johnson Bks.

Colorado Gun. W. Edwin Booth. (Orig.). 1981. pap. 1.75 o.p. (ISBN 0-505-51614-4, Pub. by Tower Bks). Dorchester Pub Co.

Colorado High Country. Margaret Lamb. LC 64-9814. (Illus., Orig.). 1965. pap. 1.75 o.p. (ISBN 0-8040-0053-0, SB). Ohio U Pr.

Colorado History. 5th ed. Carl Ubbelohde et al. LC 81-15812. 400p. 1982. 18.95 o.p. (ISBN 0-87108-240-3); pap. 13.50 o.p. (ISBN 0-87108-241-1). Pruett.

Colorado, Images of the Alpine Landscape. John Fielder. (Illus.). 192p. 1985. 34.95 o.p. (ISBN 0-942394-10-0). Westcliffe Pubs Inc.

Colorado in the Great Depression. James F. Wickens. Ed. by Frank Freidel. LC 78-62518. (Modern American History Ser.: Vol. 20). 1979. lib. bdg. 36.00 o.p. (ISBN 0-8240-3643-3). Garland Pub.

Colorado Jury Instructions: Civil. 2nd ed. Supreme Court Committee on Civil Jury Instructions. 75.00 o.p.; Suppl.1987. 23.00 o.p.; Suppl. 1988. 27.00 o.p. Lawyers Co-Op.

Colorado Kid: Memoirs of a Life Nurtured by Faith. Russell Happey. 1978. 5.00 o.p. (ISBN 0-682-49155-1). Exposition-Phoenix.

Colorado Reader. rev. ed. Ed. by Carl Ubbelohde et al. LC 82-457. 300p. 1982. 14.95 o.p. (ISBN 0-87108-238-1); pap. 10.95 o.p. (ISBN 0-87108-239-X). Pruett.

Colorado Scenic Guide: Southern Region. Lee Gregory. LC 84-80536. (Illus.). 208p. (Orig.). 1984. pap. 9.95 o.p. (ISBN 0-933472-83-8). Johnson Bks.

Colorado Technological Center, Louisville, Colorado. (Panel Advisory Service Report Ser.). 63p. 1982. pap. 10.00 o.p. (ISBN 0-317-06729-X, C-22). Urban Land.

Colorado Trivia. Rex Burger. LC 85-63181. (Illus.). 205p. 1986. pap. 7.95 o.s.i. (ISBN 0-933341-31-8). Quinlan Pr.

Colorado: Trusts. 8.50 o.p. (ISBN 0-686-90663-2). Am Law Inst.

Colorado's Government. 3rd ed. Robert S. Lorch. LC 83-71695. 1983. 12.50x o.p. (ISBN 0-87081-148-7); pap. 7.95x o.p. (ISBN 0-87081-141-X). Univ Pr Colo.

Colorado's Loneliest Railroad: The San Luis Southern. P. R. Griswold. LC 82-3714. (Illus.). 200p. 1980. 32.50 o.p. (ISBN 0-87108-554-2). Pruett.

Colorectal Cancer. William Duncan. (Recents Results in Cancer Research Ser.: Vol. 83). (Illus.). 156p. 1982. 46.00 o.p. (ISBN 0-387-11395-9). Springer-Verlag.

Colorectal Surgery. Edward Hughes et al. (Illus.). 433p. 1983. text ed. 89.00 o.p. (ISBN 0-443-02726-9). Churchill.

Colored American Magazine, Vols. 1-17, No. 5. Incl. Vol. 1-2. 85.00 (ISBN 0-8371-1576-0, CF1&); Vol. 3-4. 110.00 (ISBN 0-8371-1577-9, CF2&); Vol. 5. 55.00 (ISBN 0-8371-1578-7, CF3&); Vol. 6. 55.00 (ISBN 0-8371-1579-5, CF4&); Vol. 7. 55.00 (ISBN 0-8371-1580-9, CF5&); Vol. 8-9. 110.00 (ISBN 0-8371-1581-7, CF6&); Vol. 10-11. 110.00 (ISBN 0-8371-1582-5, CF7&); Vol. 12-13. 110.00 (ISBN 0-8371-1583-3, CF8&); Vol. 14. 55.00 (ISBN 0-8371-1584-1, CF9&); Vol. 15-17. 140.00 (ISBN 0-8371-1585-X, CG0&). 1970. Repr. of 1909 ed. Set. 845.00x o.p. (ISBN 0-8371-9108-4, CAM&, Pub. by Negro U Pr). Greenwood.

Colored Symmetry. A. V. Shubnikov & N. V. Belov. 1964. 75.00 o.p. (ISBN 0-08-010505-X); pap. 75.00 o.p. (ISBN 0-08-013790-3). Pergamon.

Colorimetric Determination of Nonmetals. 2nd ed. David F. Boltz & James A. Howell. LC 77-12398. (Chemical Analysis Ser.: Vol. 8). 543p. 1978. 92.00 o.p. (ISBN 0-471-08750-5, Pub by Wiley-Interscience). Wiley.

Colorimetric Methods of Analysis: Inorganic Determinations Including Photometric Methods. Foster D. Snell et al. Incl. LC 48-5959. (IIA). 804p. 1972. Repr. of 1959 ed. 41.50 (ISBN 0-88275-051-8, VAN NOSTRAND); 3rd ed. (Vol. III). 614p. 1974. Repr. of 1953 ed. 35.50 (ISBN 0-88275-160-3, VAN NOSTRAND); 3rd ed. (Vol. IV). 684p. 1976. Repr. of 1954 ed. 38.50 (ISBN 0-88275-201-4, VAN NOSTRAND); (Vol. IIIA). 586p. 1973. Repr. of 1961 ed. 32.50 (ISBN 0-88275-095-X, Van Nostrand). (Organic Compounds Ser.). Krieger.

Coloring Cookbook for Children. Annie Meyer & Mary Lynn Munro. 64p. (Orig.). (gr. 1-6). 1974. pap. 3.95 o.p. (ISBN 0-89716-061-4). Peanut Butter.

Coloring Review of Neuroscience. D. Michael McKeough. 114p. 1982. pap. text ed. 12.00 o.p. Little.

Colormetric & Fluorimetric Analysis of Steroids. J. Bartos & M. Pesez. 1977. 76.00 o.p. (ISBN 0-12-080150-7). Acad Pr.

Colors. Leo Lionni. LC 84-10092. (To Talk About Ser.). (Illus.). 12p. (ps). 1985. 3.95 o.p. (ISBN 0-394-87003-4, Pant Bks Young). Pantheon.

Colors. Jan Pienkowski. (Concept Bks.). (Illus.). 32p. (ps-k). 1981. 3.95 o.s.i. (ISBN 0-671-44453-0, Little Simon). S&S.

Colors. Peter Seymore. (Turn & Learn Bks.). (Illus.). 8p. (ps-1). 1984. 5.95 o.s.i. (ISBN 0-02-782080-7). Macmillan.

Colors. Illus. by Tony Tallarico. (Preschool See & Say Bks.). (Illus.). 12p. (ps). 1986. bds. 2.95 o.p. (ISBN 0-89828-259-4). Tuffy Bks.

Colors of My Rainbow Activity Book. Joe Wayman. (gr. k-8). 1979. 6.95 o.p. (ISBN 0-916456-38-2, GA103). Good Apple.

Colors of Space. rev. ed. Marion Zimmer Bradley. Ed. by Hank Stine. LC 82-5008. (Illus.). 146p. 1983. pap. 5.95 o.p. (ISBN 0-89865-191-3, AACR2, Starblaze). Donning Co.

Colossal Fossils: Dinosaur Riddles. Ed. by Charles Keller. LC 86-22656. 64p. (gr. 3-7). 1987. 10.95 o.s.i. (ISBN 0-13-151184-X). P-H.

Colossal Hamilton of Texas. John L. Waller. 164p. 1968. 8.00 o.p. (ISBN 0-87404-012-4). Tex Western.

Colossal Sculpture of the Cinquecento. Virginia Bush. LC 75-23785. (Outstanding Dissertations in the Fine Arts - 16th Century). (Illus.). 1976. lib. bdg. 58.00 o.p. (ISBN 0-8240-1981-4). Garland Pub.

Colossians, Philippians & Philemon. Wesley R. Willis. (Personal Growth Bible Studies). 1988. write for info. o.p. Victor Bks.

Colour Chemistry. R. Allen. 1971. pap. 29.95 o.p. (ISBN 0-442-30669-5). Van Nos Reinhold.

Colour for the Artist. Hans Schwarz. LC 79-56605. (Start to Paint Ser.). (Illus.). 104p. 1980. pap. 3.95 o.s.i. (ISBN 0-8008-1726-5, Pentalic). Taplinger.

Colour: Its Measurement, Computation & Application. C. J. Chamberlin & D. J. Chamberlin. (International Topics in Science Ser.). 148p. 1980. 48.95 o.p. (ISBN 0-471-25625-0). Wiley.

Colour London Streetfinder. Date not set. Salem Hse Pubs.

Colour Printing & Colour Printers. Robert M. Burch. LC 78-74393. (Nineteenth Century Book Arts & Printing History Ser.: Vol. 8). 1982. lib. bdg. 40.00 o.p. (ISBN 0-8240-3882-7). Garland Pub.

Colour Scheme. Ngaio Marsh. 1984. pap. 2.95 o.s.i. (Medallion). Berkley Pub.

Colour Scheme. Ngaio Marsh. (Nagaio Marsh Mystery Ser.). 288p. 1984. pap. 3.50 o.s.i. (ISBN 0-515-07881-6). Jove Pubns.

Colour since Matisse. Ed. by Henry-Claude Cousseau. (Illus.). 166p. 1987. 29.95 o.s.i. (ISBN 0-8008-1727-3). Taplinger.

Coloured Key to the Wildfowl of the World. rev. ed. P. Scott. (Illus.). 1972. 15.00 o.s.i. E J Brill USA.

Coloured Type & Song Canaries. G. B. Walker. (Illus.). 368p. 1987. 29.95 o.p. (ISBN 0-7137-1620-7, Pub. by Blandford Pr England). Sterling.

Colourful Lady Lebanon. Thelma Penwarden. 1978. 4.00 o.p. (ISBN 0-682-49242-6). Exposition-Phoenix.

Colours Aloft. Alexander Kent. 272p. 19.95 o.p. (ISBN 0-09-164400-3, Pub. by Century Hutchinson). David & Charles.

Colposcopie Pratique. R. Cartier. (Illus., Fr.). 1977. 153.50 o.p. (ISBN 3-8055-2820-5). S Karger.

Colposcopy. Santiago Dexeus, Jr. et al. Tr. by Karl L. Austin from Span. LC 74-177752. (Major Problems in Obstetrics & Gynecology: Vol. 10). (Illus.). 1977. text ed. write for info. o.p. (ISBN 0-7216-3050-2). Saunders.

Coltrane Saga: Love & Dreams, Vol. 6. Patricia Hagan. 1988. pap. 3.95 o.p. Avon.

Columbia Encyclopedia of Nutrition. Institute of Human Nutrition, Columbia University College of Physicians & Surgeons. Ed. by Myron Winick. 352p. 1988. 22.95 o.p. (ISBN 0-399-13298-8, Putnam). Putnam Pub Group.

Columbia University College of Physicians & Surgeons Complete Home Medical Guide. Columbia University College of Physicians & Surgeons Staff. (Illus.). 950p. 1985. 39.95 o.p. (ISBN 0-517-55842-4). Crown.

Columbus & His Discovery of America. Herbert B. Adams & Henry Wood. (Works of Herbert B. Adams). 88p. Repr. of 1892 ed. lib. bdg. 49.00 o.p. (ISBN 0-318-03808-0, Pub. by Am Repr Serv). Reprint Servs.

Columbus' Cabin Boy. Lee Templeton. (Illus.). 192p. (gr. 4-7). 1983. 8.95 o.p. (ISBN 0-89015-372-8). Eakin Pr.

Columbus Picture Analysis of Growth Towards Maturity: A Series of 24 Pictures & a Manual. 2nd ed. M. J. Langeveld. 76p. 1976. 47.50 o.p. (ISBN 3-8055-2329-7). S Karger.

Comanche Barrier to South Plains Settlement. Rupert N. Richardson. LC 73-9712. 424p. 1973. Repr. of 1933 ed. 52.00 o.p. (ISBN 0-527-75230-4). Kraus Repr.

Comanche Revenge. Jeanne Sommers. (American Indians Ser.: No. 1). 368p. (Orig.). 1981. pap. 2.75 o.p. (ISBN 0-440-01525-1, Standish). Dell.

Comanches & Other Indians of Texas. Marian T. Place. LC 79-103829. (Curriculum Related Bks.). (gr. 7 up). 1970. 5.50 o.p. (ISBN 0-15-219451-7, HJ). HarBraceJ.

Combat Aircraft Prototypes Since 1945. Arco.

Combat Aircraft Prototypes Since 1945. P-H.

Combat Films: American Realism. Steven J. Rubin. LC 80-17022. (Illus.). 245p. 1981. lib. bdg. 18.95x o.p. (ISBN 0-89950-013-7); pap. 11.95x o.p. (ISBN 0-89950-014-5). McFarland & Co.

Combat Handgunnery. Jack Lewis & Jack Mitchell. LC 83-72347. (Illus.). 288p. (Orig.). 1983. pap. 12.95 o.p. (ISBN 0-910676-62-3). DBI.

Combat Handguns. George C. Nonte. LC 79-21398. (Illus.). 352p. 1980. 19.95 o.p. (ISBN 0-8117-0409-2). Stackpole.

Combat Ready, Bk. 1: The Victor. Fred L. Brown. LC 87-71208. (Illus.). 165p. (Orig.). 1989. pap. 10.95 o.p. (ISBN 0-942551-02-8). Combat Ready.

Combat Skills of the Fighting Soldier. (Illus.). 256p. 1985. pap. 14.95 o.p. (ISBN 0-87364-336-4). Paladin Pr.

Combat Tracker & Tracker Dog Training & Employment: FM 7-42. (Illus.). 88p. 1986. pap. 10.00 o.p. (ISBN 0-87364-413-1). Paladin Pr.

Combat Without Weapons. (Illus.). 48p. 1975. pap. 5.00 o.p. (ISBN 0-87364-060-8). Paladin Pr.

Combat World War II, 2 vols. Ed. by Don Congdon. Incl. European Theater of Operations. 608p. 24.95 (ISBN 0-87795-457-7); Pacific Theater of Operations. 24.95 (ISBN 0-87795-458-5). (Illus.). 1983 (Arbor Hse). Morrow.

Combat WW II: Pacific. Don Congdon. pap. 12.95 o.p. (ISBN 0-87795-659-6). Morrow.

Combating the Number One Killer: The Science Report on Heart Research. Jean L. Marx & Gina B. Kolata. LC 78-3626. (Illus.). 205p. 1978. casebound 10.00 o.p. (ISBN 0-87168-219-2, 80-08S); pap. 7.50 o.p. (ISBN 0-87168-235-4). AAAS.

Combatting Cardiovascular Diseases Skilfully. 2nd ed. Ed. by Susan R. Williams & Barbara McVan. LC 84-563. (New Nursing Skillbook). (Illus.). 192p. 1984. 14.95 o.p. (ISBN 0-916730-66-2). Springhouse Pub.

Combatting Poverty Through Adult Education: National Development Strategies. Ed. by Chris Duke. LC 84-23777. (Series in International Adult Education). 256p. 1985. 31.00 o.p. (ISBN 0-7099-0861-X, Pub. by Croom Helm). Routledge Chapman & Hall.

Combinatorial Identities. John Riordan. LC 78-26915. 270p. 1979. Repr. of 1968 ed. 23.50 o.p. (ISBN 0-88275-829-2). Krieger.

Combinatorial Methods. J. K. Percus. LC 78-152001. (Applied Mathematical Sciences Ser.: Vol. 4). (Illus.). 208p. 1971. pap. 27.00 o.p. (ISBN 0-387-90027-6). Springer-Verlag.

Combinatorial Problems & Exercises. L. Lovasz. LC 78-12133. 450p. 1979. pap. 52.75 o.p. (ISBN 0-444-85242-5, North Holland); 110.75 o.p. (ISBN 0-444-85219-0, North Holland). Elsevier.

Combinatorial Search Problems. CISM (International Center for Mechanical Sciences) Deartment of Automation & Information Staff. Ed. by G. Katona. (CISM Pubns. Ser: No. 145). 57p. 1973. pap. 8.60 o.p. (ISBN 0-387-81169-9). Springer-Verlag.

Combinatorial Set Theory. N. H. Williams. (Studies in Logic: Vol. 91). 028p. 1977. 63.25 o.p. (ISBN 0-7204-0722-2, North-Holland). Elsevier.

Combinatorial Surveys: Proceedings of British Combinatorial Conference, Sixth. British Combinatorial Conference Staff. Ed. by Peter Cameron. 1977. 51.50 o.p. (ISBN 0-12-157150-5). Acad Pr.

Combinatorial Theory. M. Aigner. (Grundlehren der Mathemtischen Wissenschaften Ser.: Vol. 234). (Illus.). 1979. 64.90 o.p. (ISBN 0-387-90376-3). Springer-Verlag.

Combinatorics Graphs & Algebra. Centre de Mathematique Sociale Ecole des Hautes Etudes En Sciences Sociales Staff. (Methods & Models in the Social Sciences: No. 5). (Illus., Orig.). 1976. text ed. 16.80x o.p. (ISBN 90-2797-511-6). Mouton.

Combinatorics: Room Squares, Sum-Free Sets, Hadamard Matrices. W. D. Wallis et al. LC 72-90443. (Lecture Notes in Mathematics Ser.: Vol. 292). 508p. 1972. pap. 23.00 o.p. (ISBN 0-387-06035-9). Springer-Verlag.

Combined Cumulative Index to Obstetrics & Gynecology: 1985 Supplement. 1986. 65.00 o.s.i. (ISBN 0-88471-049-1, SUB. 267). Numarc Bk Corp.

Combined Cumulative Index to Obstetrics & Gynecology: 1986 Supplement. 1987. 65.00 o.s.i. (ISBN 0-88471-056-4, SUB. 267). Numarc Bk Corp.

Combined Forces. Jack Smithers. 1987. 14.50 o.p. (ISBN 0-907675-10-7, Pub. by Buchan & Enright England). Seven Hills Bk Dists.

Combined Heat, Ice & Water Balance at Selected Glacier Basins, 2 Pts. Incl. Pt. 2. Specifications, Standards & Data Exchange. 32p. pap. 5.00 (ISBN 92-3-101050-6, U738). UNIPUB. (Technical Papers in Hydrology Ser.: No. 5). (Co-published with IAHS). 1973. pap. (UNESCO). UNIPUB.

Combined Immunodeficiency Disease & Adenosine Deaminase Deficiency: A Molecular Defect-Proceedings. Ed. by Hilaire J. Meuwissen et al. 1975. 63.50 o.p. (ISBN 0-12-492750-5). Acad Pr.

Combined Membership List, 1985-1986. 400p. 1985. Repr. of 1987 ed. 34.00 o.p. (ISBN 0-8218-0085-X). Am Math.

Combined Nonlinear & Linear (Micro & Macro) Fracture Mechanics: Applications to Modern Engineering Structures - Selected Papers, U.S.-Japan Seminar. Ed. by H. Liebowitz. 1976. pap. 56.00 o.p. (ISBN 0-08-019982-8). Pergamon.

Combined Production of Electric Power & Heat: Proceedings of a Seminar Organized by the Committee on Electric Power of the United Nations Economic Commission for Europe, Hamburg, FR Germany, 6-9 November 1978. United Nations Economic Commission for Europe. LC 80-755. (Illus.). 150p. 1980. 46.00 o.p. (ISBN 0-08-025677-5). Pergamon.

Combined Textbook of Obstetrics & Gynecology. 9th ed. J. Walker et al. LC 76-8406. (Illus.). 1976. 98.00 o.p. (ISBN 0-443-01072-2). Churchill.

Combing the Coast - San Francisco to San Luis Obispo: A Lively Guide to Beaches, Backroads, Parks, Historic Sites & Towns. Ruth A. Jackson. LC 85-7687. (Illus.). 216p. (Orig.). 1985. pap. 10.95 o.p. (ISBN 0-87701-285-7). Chronicle Bks.

Combing the Coast II: Santa Cruz to Carmel. Ruth A. Jackson. LC 82-4327. (Illus.). 120p. 1982. pap. 6.95 o.p. (ISBN 0-87701-236-9). Chronicle Bks.

Combustion & Heat Transfer in Gas Turbine Systems. E. R. Norster. (Cranfield International Symposium Ser: Vol. 11). (Illus.). 1971. 120.00 o.p. (ISBN 0-08-016524-9). Pergamon.

Combustion & Mass Transfer. D. B. Spalding. 1979. 105.00 o.p. (ISBN 0-08-022105-X); pap. 105.00 o.p. (ISBN 0-08-022106-8). Pergamon.

Combustion, Flames, & Explosions of Gases. 2nd ed. Bernard Lewis & Guenther Von Elbe. 1961. 109.00 o.p. (ISBN 0-12-446750-4). Acad Pr.

Combustion in Advanced Gas Turbine Systems. I. E. Smith. 1969. 34.10 o.p. (ISBN 0-08-013275-8). Pergamon.

Combustion Processes in the Spark Ignition Engine. D. Hodgetts. 1966. 50.00 o.p. (ISBN 0-08-011909-3). Pergamon.

Come & Get It: Reading for Information, Made Easy Through Recipes. Leola G. Hayes. (Illus.). 1976. 4.00 o.p. (ISBN 0-682-48472-5, University); pap. 2.00 o.p. (ISBN 0-682-48473-3). Exposition-Phoenix.

Come by Here. Olivia Coolidge. LC 72-115451. (Illus.). (gr. 5 up). 1970. 9.95 o.p. (ISBN 0-395-10912-4). HM.

Come Care with Me. Lottie R. Crim. LC 82-73369. (Illus.). 1983. pap. 4.50 o.p. (ISBN 0-8054-5431-4). Broadman.

Come Celebrate: A Daily Devotional. Aglow Editors. 266p. 1984. pap. 6.95 o.p. (ISBN 0-930756-78-9, 531018). Aglow Pubns.

Come Children Sing! Mary E. Pinzino. (Illus.). pap. 11.00 spiral bdg. o.p. (ISBN 0-918812-34-8). MMB Music.

Come, Follow Me. Philip Michaels. 336p. 1983. pap. 3.50 o.p. (ISBN 0-380-83006-X, 83006). Avon.

Come Follow Me, Vol. III. Bhagwan Shree Rajneesh. Ed. by Swami Deva Paritosh. LC 80-8343. (Jesus Ser.). (Illus.). 272p. (Orig.). 1976. 9.95 o.p. (ISBN 0-88050-036-0). Chidvilas Inc.

Come Holy Spirit. A. Michael Ramsey et al. 128p. (Orig.). 1976. pap. 3.95 o.p. (ISBN 0-8192-1186-9). Morehouse Pub.

Come Holy Spirit-I Need Thee. Grace E. Gresk. 48p. 1985. 5.95 o.p. (ISBN 0-533-06177-6). Vantage.

Come Home to Love. Amii Lorin. 288p. 1984. pap. 2.95 o.s.i. (ISBN 0-8439-2076-9, Leisure NY). Dorchester Pub Co.

Come Home to Love. Paula Roberts. (Orig.). 1980. pap. 2.25 o.p. (ISBN 0-505-51484-2, Pub. by Tower Bks). Dorchester Pub Co.

Come Home, Wilma. Mitchell Sharmat. Ed. by Kathleen Tucker. LC 80-18991. (Albert Whitman Concept Bks.). (Illus.). 32p. (ps-2). 1980. PLB 10.75 o.p. (ISBN 0-8075-1278-8). A Whitman.

Come in & Find Your World. Joshua H. Garrett. 96p. 1986. 7.95 o.p. (ISBN 0-8062-2903-9). Carlton.

Come Like the Benediction: A Tribute to Tuskegee Institute & Other Essays. Clyde O. Jackson. (Illus.). 1981. 7.00 o.p. (ISBN 0-682-49723-1). Exposition-Phoenix.

Come, Lord Jesus. Rolf E. Aaseng. LC 74-77675. (Illus.). 144p. 1974. pap. 3.95 o.p. (ISBN 0-8066-1423-4, 10-1550, Augsburg). Augsburg Fortress.

Come Lord Jesus! Come Quickly! Constance F. Parvey. LC 75-13044. 96p. 1976. pap. 1.50x o.p. (ISBN 0-8006-1212-4, Fortress). Augsburg Fortress.

Come on Down!!! The TV Game Show Book. Jefferson Graham. (Illus.). 216p. 1988. pap. 16.95 o.p. (ISBN 0-89659-794-6). Abbeville Pr.

Come on into My House. Judy Segraves. Ed. by Mary Wallace. (Illus.). 90p. (Orig.). 1985. pap. 4.95 o.p. (ISBN 0-912315-87-3). Word Aflame.

Come on Seabiscuit. Ralph Moody. (Illus.). (gr. 6-9). 1973. 6.95 o.p. (ISBN 0-395-06947-5). HM.

Come Out & Play, Little Mouse. Robert Kraus. LC 85-30198. (Illus.). 32p. (ps-1). 1987. 11.95 o.p. (ISBN 0-688-05837-X); PLB 11.88 o.p. (ISBN 0-688-05838-8). Greenwillow.

Come Over to My House. Lora L. Parrott. 1984. pap. 9.95 o.p. (ISBN 0-87162-403-6, D3067). Warner Pr.

Come Pour the Wine. Cynthia Freeman. LC 80-66501. 1980. 12.95 o.p. (ISBN 0-87795-276-0, Arbor Hse). Morrow.

Come Ride "The Rails " with Me: All over the United States & Norway, England & Wales. Essye P. Flaten. (Illus.). 1985. 5.50 o.p. (ISBN 0-682-40214-1). Exposition-Phoenix.

Come Run with Me. Peter Strudwick. 1979. 9.95 o.p. (ISBN 0-682-49423-2, Banner). Exposition-Phoenix.

Come, Search with Me. Glenice M. Emery. LC 84-90035. 92p. 1984. 7.95 o.p. (ISBN 0-533-06123-7). Vantage.

Come! Sit! Stay! Joan M. Lexau. LC 83-16808. (Easy-Read Story Bks.). (Illus.). 32p. (gr. 1-3). 1984. lib. bdg. 10.40 o.p. (ISBN 0-531-04715-6). Watts.

Come Spring. Kathryn O. Galbraith. LC 79-12311. 216p. (gr. 4-7). 1979. 8.95 o.s.i. (ISBN 0-689-50142-0, M K McElderry). Macmillan.

Come Spring. Charlotte Hinger. 352p. 1986. 18.45 o.s.i. (ISBN 0-671-55429-8). S&S.

Come Through Dayton. James Walter. 1984. pap. text ed. 10.95x o.s.i. (ISBN 0-89917-422-1). Tichenor Pub.

Come to Africa & Save Your Marriage: And Other Stories. Maria Thomas. 235p. 14.95 o.p. (ISBN 0-317-64589-7). SoHo Press.

Come to be Killed. E. X. Ferrars. LC 86-32783. (Crime Club Ser.). 192p. 1987. 12.95 o.s.i. (ISBN 0-385-24199-2). Doubleday.

Come to Me in Silence. Rod McKuen. 1973. 8.95 o.p. (ISBN 0-671-21633-3). S&S.

Come to Me Warmly. Gerry Paul Little. 1977. 4.00 o.p. (ISBN 0-682-48707-4). Exposition-Phoenix.

Come to My House, No. 7236. Florence Temko. Ed. by Leslie Lawrence & Ronald Weingartner. (Bright Beginnings Ser.: II). (Illus.). 32p. (gr. k-4). 1982. pap. 1.39 cancelled o.s.i. (ISBN 0-88049-003-9, 7232). Milton Bradley Co.

Come to My Place: Meet My Island Family. Compiled by Esiteri Kamikamica. (gr. 3-6). 1982. pap. 4.95 o.p. (ISBN 0-377-00121-X). Friendship Pr.

Come to the Edge. Julia Cunningham. (Illus.). 88p. (gr. 7 up). 1985. pap. 1.25 o.p. (ISBN 0-380-40337-4, 60517-1, Camelot). Avon.

Come to the Waters. Diane Head. 96p. 1985. pap. 4.95 o.p. (ISBN 0-310-25941-X, 9586P). Zondervan.

Come to Think of It, Lord: Personal & Prayerful Reflections. Ron Fernandes. 1977. 5.00 o.p. (ISBN 0-682-48851-8). Exposition-Phoenix.

Come with Me: Poems for the Young. Edith Segal. pap. 1.25 o.p. (ISBN 0-8065-0179-0, Pub. by Citadel Pr). Carol Pub Group.

Comeback. Ryne Duren & Robert F. Drury. 1978. 7.95 o.p. (ISBN 0-89328-014-3). Lorenz Corp.

Comeback: Building the Resurgence of American Business. Ezra Vogel. 1986. pap. 8.95 o.p. (ISBN 0-671-61772-9, Touchstone Bks). S&S.

Comeback: Capturing the Future for America. Azra Vogel. 320p. 1985. 17.45 o.p. (ISBN 0-671-46079-X). S&S.

Comeback Guy. C. H. Frick. LC 61-6115. (gr. 7 up). 1961. 5.50 o.p. (ISBN 0-15-219474-6, HJ). HarBraceJ.

Comeback Guy. C. H. Frick. LC 61-6115. (gr. 7 up). 1965. pap. 1.45 o.s.i. (ISBN 0-15-619450-3, VoyB). HarBraceJ.

Comeback Kids: The Philadelphia Phillies & the 1980 World Series. Bob Ibach & Tim Panaccio. (Illus.). 1981. pap. 2.95 o.s.i. (ISBN 0-939188-00-7). Chapter & Cask.

Comeback Year. Lawrence A. Keating. (gr. 7-10). 1966. 4.25 o.s.i. (ISBN 0-664-32380-4, Westminster). Westminster John Knox.

Comedians. Trevor Griffiths. LC 76-16727. 1976. pap. 3.95 o.p. (ISBN 0-394-17913-7, E677, Ever). Grove.

Comedians of Country Music. Stacy Harris. LC 77-90150. (Country Music Bks.). (gr. 5 up). 1978. PLB 5.95 o.p. (ISBN 0-8225-1409-5). Lerner Pubns.

Comedies of Terence. Terence. Ed. by Frank O. Copley. 1967. pap. text ed. write for info. o.p. (ISBN 0-02-325270-7). Macmillan.

Comedy. Moelwyn Merchant. (Critical Idiom Ser.). 1972. pap. 5.50x o.p. (ISBN 0-416-75050-8, NO. 2315). Routledge Chapman & Hall.

Comedy of Errors. William Shakespeare. Ed. by Louis B. Wright & Virginia LaMar. 208p. pap. 2.95 o.p. (ISBN 0-671-46717-4). WSP.

Comedy of Manners. David L. Hirst. (Critical Idiom Ser.). 1979. 14.95x o.p. (ISBN 0-416-85590-3, NO.2757); pap. 5.50x o.p. (ISBN 0-416-85570-9, NO.2758). Routledge Chapman & Hall.

Comedy of Neil Simon. Neil Simon. 1986. pap. 5.95 o.p. (ISBN 0-380-00789-4, 53827-X). Avon.

Comedy: Plays, Theory & Criticism. Ed. by Marvin Felheim. 1962. pap. text ed. 8.95 o.p. (ISBN 0-15-512280-0, HC). HarBraceJ.

Comenius & Contemporary Education. pap. 5.00 o.p. (U76, UNESCO). UNIPUB.

Comes the Revolution. Edward W. Lewis. LC 78-139298. 1971. 6.50 o.p. (ISBN 0-87795-013-X, Arbor Hse). Morrow.

Comet Fever. Donald Gropman & Kenneth Mirvis. 1985. pap. 7.95 o.p. (ISBN 0-671-60307-8, Fireside). S&S.

Comet! The Story Behind Halley's Comet. Greg Walz-Chojnacki. Ed. by Nancy Mack. LC 85-15632. (Illus.). 64p. (gr. 4-10). 1985. 5.75 o.p. (ISBN 0-913135-03-8); PLB 12.95 o.p. (ISBN 0-89831-51-2). Kalmbach.

Comfort My People: A Guide to Isaiah 40-66. E. John Hamlin. LC 79-27587. (Illus.). 230p. 1980. pap. 5.95 o.p. (ISBN 0-8042-0127-7, John Knox). Westminster John Knox.

Comfort: Prayers & Promises for Times of Sorrow. John M. Robertson. 1977. pap. 2.95 o.p. (ISBN 0-8423-0432-0). Tyndale.

Comfort Zones: A Practical Guide for Retirement Planning. Elwood N. Chapman. 1985. 12.50 o.p. (4019). Am Assn Comm Jr Coll.

Comforting Food. Judith Olney. LC 79-63845. 1979. 12.95 o.p. (ISBN 0-689-11007-3, Atheneum). Macmillan.

Comforting Those Who Grieve. Cecil Murphey. LC 78-71052. 64p. 1979. pap. 1.95 o.s.i. (ISBN 0-8042-1099-3, John Knox). Westminster John Knox.

Comforting Those Who Grieve: A Guide for Helping Others. Doug Manning. LC 84-48226. 112p. 1985. 10.45 o.p. (ISBN 0-06-065418-X). HarpR.

Comic Art of Laurence Sterne: Convention & Innovation in "Tristram Shandy" & "A Sentimental Journey" John M. Stedmond. LC 67-1995. 1967. 25.00 o.p. (ISBN 0-8020-7056-6). U of Toronto Pr.

Comic Book Price Guide, No. 9. rev. ed. Robert M. Overstreet. (Illus.). 1979. pap. 8.95 o.p. (ISBN 0-517-53696-X, Harmony). Crown.

Comic Book Price Guide, No. 10. Robert M. Overstreet. (Illus.). 600p. 1980. pap. 9.95 o.p. (ISBN 0-517-54021-5, Harmony). Crown.

Comic Book Price Guide, No. 12. Robert M. Overstreet. (Illus.). 600p. 1982. pap. 9.95 o.p. (ISBN 0-517-54349-4, Harmony). Crown.

Comic Book Price Guide, No. 13. Robert M. Overstreet. 1983. pap. 9.95 o.p. (ISBN 0-517-54915-8, Harmony). Crown.

Comic Book Price Guide, No. 14. Robert M. Overstreet. pap. 9.95 o.p. (ISBN 0-517-55296-5, Harmony). Crown.

Comic Book Price Guide, No. 15. Robert M. Overstreet. 1985. pap. 10.95 o.p. (ISBN 0-517-55680-4). Crown.

Comic Book Price Guide, No. 11. Robert M. Overstreet. 1981. pap. 9.95 o.p. (ISBN 0-517-54268-4, Harmony). Crown.

Comic in Theory & Practice. Ed. by John J. Enck et al. (Orig.). 1960. pap. text ed. o.p. (ISBN 0-13-152561-1). P-H.

Comic Theatre: A Comedy in Three Acts. Carlo Goldoni. Tr. by John W. Miller. LC 69-14867. xxii, 94p. 1969. 10.95x o.p. (ISBN 0-8032-0056-0). U of Nebr Pr.

Coming Age of Solar Energy. D. S. Halacy, Jr. 1975. pap. 2.25 o.p. (ISBN 0-380-00233-7, 38034). Avon.

Coming Alive from Nine to Five: The Career Search Handbook. 2nd ed. Betty N. Michelozzi. 276p. 1984. pap. 10.95 o.p. (ISBN 0-87484-594-7). Mayfield Pub.

Coming Back: A Guide to Recovering from Heart Attack & Living Confidently with Coronary Disease. Keith Cohn et al. 1979. 10.95 o.p.; pap. 7.95 o.p. (ISBN 0-201-04561-3). Addison-Wesley.

Coming Back: The Community Experiences of Deinstitutionalized Mentally Retarded People. Elinor Gollay et al. LC 78-68165. 1978. text ed. 30.00 o.p. (ISBN 0-89011-512-5). Abt Bks.

Coming Back Up. Suzanne Lipsett. LC 85-47605. 256p. 1985. 14.95 o.p. (ISBN 0-689-11602-0, Atheneum). Macmillan.

Coming Boom. Herman Kahn. 1982. 16.50 o.p. (ISBN 0-671-44262-7). S&S.

Coming Boom: Economic, Political & Social. Herman Kahn. 240p. 1983. pap. 7.75 o.p. (ISBN 0-671-49265-9, Touchstone). S&S.

Coming Crisis of Western Sociology. Alvin W. Gouldner. 1971. pap. 5.45 o.p. (ISBN 0-380-01109-3, Equinox). Avon.

Coming Decade in Counseling Psychology. John M. Whiteley et al. 1984. 16.95 o.p. (ISBN 1-55620-005-6, 71009C). Am Assn Coun Dev.

Coming down Again. John Balaban. LC 84-25302. 256p. 1985. 15.95 o.p. (ISBN 0-15-119519-6). HarBraceJ.

Coming Fury. Bruce Catton. LC 61-12502. (Centennial History of the Civil War Ser.: Vol. 1). 1961. pap. 17.95 o.p. (ISBN 0-385-09813-8). Doubleday.

Coming Home: A Guide to Home Care for the Terminally Ill. rev. ed. Deborah Duda. (Illus.). 275p. (Orig.). 1984. pap. 8.95 o.p. (ISBN 0-912528-39-7). John Muir.

Coming Home From Camp. Lonny Kaneko. 1986. 17.50 o.p. (ISBN 0-918116-35-X); pap. 8.50 o.p. (ISBN 0-918116-36-8). Brooding Heron Pr.

Coming Home-To China. Creighton Lacy. LC 78-5404. 156p. 1978. pap. 4.95 o.s.i. (ISBN 0-664-24201-4, Westminster). Westminster John Knox.

Coming Late to Motherhood: Twenty Women Tell Their Stories. Joan Michelson & Sue Gee. 272p. 1985. pap. 8.95 o.p. (ISBN 0-7225-0893-X). Newcastle Pub.

Coming of Age in Shakespeare. Marjorie Garber. LC 80-41920. 320p. 1981. 35.00x o.p. (ISBN 0-416-30350-1, NO.2127). Routledge Chapman & Hall.

Coming of Seth see How to Develop Your ESP Power.

Coming of the Maori. Te R. Hiro. 574p. 1986. 19.95 o.p. (ISBN 0-7233-0408-4, Pub. by Whitcoulls NZ). Intl Spec Bk.

Titles

Coming of the Pilgrims. E. Brooks Smith & Robert Meredith. (gr. 1-4). 1976. 11.45 o.p. (ISBN 0-316-80048-1). Little.

Coming of the Preachers: A Tale of the Rise of Methodism, 1901 see Minder: The Story of the Courtship, Call & Conflicts of John Ledger, Minder & Minister, 1900.

Coming on Center: English Education in Evolution. James Moffett. LC 81-10041. 192p. (Orig.). 1981. pap. text ed. 12.50x o.p. (ISBN 0-86709-005-7). Boynton Cook Pub.

Coming Race. Edward G. Bulwer-Lytton. (Banquo Bks.). 1979. pap. 7.95 o.p. (ISBN 0-912800-68-2). Woodbridge Pr.

Coming Through School. Richard A. Hawley. (gr. 9-11). 1982. pap. 7.50x o.p. (ISBN 0-88334-155-7). Ind Sch Pr.

Coming to Terms: From Alpha to X-Ray, a Lexicon for the Science-Watcher. Wayne Biddle. 128p. 1982. pap. 4.95 o.p. (ISBN 0-380-61093-0, 61093-0). Avon.

Comings of God: Meditations for the Advent Season. Richard S. Hanson. LC 81-65645. 128p. (Orig.). 1981. pap. 6.95 o.p. (ISBN 0-8066-1881-7, 10-1590, Augsburg). Augsburg Fortress.

Comintern & the East: Strategy & Tactics. A. Reznikov. 294p. 1985. 7.95 o.p. (ISBN 0-8285-2924-8, Pub. by Progress Pubs USSR). Imported Pubns.

Command Performance: AppleWorks. Charles Rubin. LC 85-31954. (Command Performance Ser.). 416p. 1986. pap. 18.95 o.p. (ISBN 0-914845-72-1). Microsoft.

Command Performance: dBASE III. Douglas Hergert. (Command Performance Ser.). 504p. (Orig.). 1985. pap. 22.95 o.p. (ISBN 0-914845-63-2). Microsoft.

Command Performance: Microsoft Word. Nancy Andrews. LC 86-33125. (Command Performance Ser.). 352p. (Orig.). 1987. pap. 19.95 o.p. (ISBN 1-55615-017-2). Microsoft.

Command Structure for Theater Warfare: The Quest for Unity of Command. Thomas A. Cardwell. LC 84-71218. (Illus.). 106p. (Orig.). 1984. pap. 4.50 o.p. (ISBN 0-318-20096-1, S/N 008-070-00520-4). USGPO.

Commander Amanda. George Revelli. LC 68-29443. 224p. 1986. pap. 3.95 o.s.i. (ISBN 0-394-62134-4, BC). Grove.

Commanding MultiMate Advantage II: A Comprehensive User's Guide. William W. Pitts. (Illus.). 304p. 1988. pap. 17.95 o.p. (ISBN 0-8306-9343-2, 3043P). TAB Bks.

Commandments & Promises of God. Bernard P. Brockbank. LC 82-23629. 667p. 1983. 15.95 o.p. (ISBN 0-87747-889-9). Deseret Bk.

Commandos. Elliot Arnold. 304p. 1982. pap. 2.75 o.p. (ISBN 0-505-51859-7, Pub. by Tower Bks). Dorchester Pub Co.

Commandos in Action. Graeme Cook. LC 73-13016. (Illus.). 176p. 1974. 6.95 o.s.i. (ISBN 0-8008-1749-4). Taplinger.

Commands of Christ for Christian Living: An Exposition of the Bible's Second Set of Commandments. Robert C. Brock. 1977. 7.50 o.p. (ISBN 0-682-48951-4, Testament). Exposition-Phoenix.

Commedia. Marcella Evaristi. 39p. 1983. pap. 5.95 o.p. (ISBN 0-907540-34-1, NO.3986). Routledge Chapman & Hall.

Commemorative Medal: Its Appreciation & Collection. Howard A. Linecar. LC 72-12989. (Illus.). 158p. 1974. 35.00x o.p. (ISBN 0-8103-2012-6). Gale.

Commentar Zu Kants Kritik der Reinen Vernunft, 2 vols. Hans Vaihinger. Ed. by Lewis W. Beck. Incl. Vol. 1. Stuttgart 1881; Vol. 2. Stuttgart & Berlin 1892. LC 75-32048. (Philosophy of Immanual Kant Ser.: Vol. 8). 1976. Repr. of 1892 ed. Set. lib. bdg. 80.00 o.p. (ISBN 0-8240-2332-3). Garland Pub.

Commentaries in Plant Science. Ed. by Harry Smith. LC 76-7531. 272p. 1976. 71.00 o.p. (ISBN 0-08-019759-0). Pergamon.

Commentaries in Plant Science, Vol. 2. Ed. by H. Smith. LC 80-41007. (Illus.). 250p. 1981. 77.00 o.p. (ISBN 0-08-025898-0). Pergamon.

Commentaries in the Neurosciences. A. D. Smith et al. (Illus.). 702p. 1980. 105.00 o.p. (ISBN 0-08-025501-9). Pergamon.

Commentaries in the Neurosciences: International Student Edition. H. Smith. 1981. 44.00 o.p. (ISBN 0-08-028861-8). Pergamon.

Commentaries on European Affairs, 1870-1914. Ed. by D. G. Rohr. 225p. 1970. pap. text ed. 9.50x o.p. (ISBN 0-8290-1110-2). Irvington.

Commentaries on the Constitution of the Empire of Japan. 2nd ed. Hirobumi Ito. Tr. by Miyoji Ito from Japanese. LC 74-15166. 310p. 1978. Repr. of 1906 ed. lib. bdg. 24.25x o.p. (ISBN 0-8371-7810-X, ITEG). Greenwood.

Commentaries on the Law in Shakespeare. Edward J. White. xviii, 524p. 1987. Repr. of 1911 ed. lib. bdg. 35.00 o.p. (ISBN 0-89941-572-5, 305250). W S Hein.

Commentaries on the Law of Suretyship, & the Rights & Obligations of Parties Thereto. William Burge. Ed. by R. H. Helmholz & Bernard D. Reams, Jr. LC 80-84858. (Historical Writings in Law & Jurisprudence Ser.: No. 18, Bk. 26). 616p. 1981. Repr. of 1847 ed. lib. bdg. 45.00 o.p. (ISBN 0-89941-078-2). W S HEIN.

Commentaries on the New Testament Books: Colossians & Philemon. Charles R. Erdman. 1966. pap. 4.95 o.p. (ISBN 0-664-24720-2, Westminster). Westminster John Knox.

Commentaries on the New Testament Books: Corinthians I & II, 2 vols. Charles R. Erdman. 1966. pap. 4.95 ea. o.p. (Westminster). Vol. 1 (ISBN 0-664-24715-6). Vol. 2 (ISBN 0-664-24716-4). Westminster John Knox.

Commentaries on the New Testament Books: Acts. Charles R. Erdman. 1966. pap. 4.95 o.p. (ISBN 0-664-24713-X, Westminster). Westminster John Knox.

Commentaries on the New Testament Books, 17 Vols. Charles R. Erdman. 1966. Set. pap. 79.00 o.p. (ISBN 0-664-24726-1, Westminster). Westminster John Knox.

Commentaries on the New Testament Books: Ephesians. Charles R. Erdman. 1966. pap. 4.95 o.p. (ISBN 0-664-24718-0, Westminster). Westminster John Knox.

Commentaries on the New Testament Books: Galatians. Charles R. Erdman. 1966. pap. 4.95 o.p. (ISBN 0-664-24717-2, Westminster). Westminster John Knox.

Commentaries on the New Testament Books: Hebrews. Charles R. Erdman. 1966. pap. 4.95 o.p. (ISBN 0-664-24723-7, Westminster). Westminster John Knox.

Commentaries on the New Testament Books: John. Charles R. Erdman. 1966. pap. 4.95 o.p. (ISBN 0-664-24712-1, Westminster). Westminster John Knox.

Commentaries on the New Testament Books: Luke. Charles R. Erdman. 1966. pap. 4.95 o.p. (ISBN 0-664-24711-3, Westminster). Westminster John Knox.

Commentaries on the New Testament Books: Mark. Charles R. Erdman. 1966. pap. 4.95 o.p. (ISBN 0-664-24710-5, Westminster). Westminster John Knox.

Commentaries on the New Testament Books: Matthew. Charles R. Erdman. 1966. pap. 4.95 o.p. (ISBN 0-664-24709-1, Westminster). Westminster John Knox.

Commentaries on the New Testament Books: Romans. Charles R. Erdman. 1966. pap. 4.95 o.p. (ISBN 0-664-24714-8, Westminster). Westminster John Knox.

Commentaries on the New Testament Books: Philippians. Charles R. Erdman. 1966. pap. 4.95 o.p. (ISBN 0-664-24719-9, Westminster). Westminster John Knox.

Commentaries on the New Testament Books: Pastoral Epistles of Paul: Timothy 1 & 2, Titus. Charles R. Erdman. 1966. pap. 4.95 o.p. (ISBN 0-664-24722-9, Westminster). Westminster John Knox.

Commentaries on the New Testament Books: Revelation of John. Charles R. Erdman. 1966. pap. 4.95 o.p. (ISBN 0-664-24725-3, Westminster). Westminster John Knox.

Commentaries on the New Testament Books: Thessalonians. Charles R. Erdman. 1966. pap. 4.95 o.p. (ISBN 0-664-24721-0, Westminster). Westminster John Knox.

Commentaries on the New Testament Books: The General Epistles: James, Peter 1 & 2, John 1 & 2 & 3, Jude. Charles R. Erdman. 1966. pap. 4.95 o.p. (ISBN 0-664-24724-5, Westminster). Westminster John Knox.

Commentarius Cantabrigiensis in Epistolas Pauli e Schola Petri Abaelardi, 3 vols. Arthur Landgraf. Incl. Vol. 1. In Epistolam Ad Romanos. 223p. 1937. 17.95 (ISBN 0-268-00133-2); Vol. 2. In Epistolam Ad Corinthios Iam et Iiam, Ad Galatas et Ad Ephesios. 1223p. 1960. 17.95 (ISBN 0-268-00134-0); Vol. 3. In Epistolam ad Philippenses, ad Colossenses, ad Thessalonicenses Primam et Secundam, ed Timotheam Primam et Secundam, ad Titum et Philemonem. 447p. 1944. 17.95 (ISBN 0-268-00132-4). (Mediaeval Studies Ser.: No. 2). U of Notre Dame Pr.

Commentary of Wordsworth's "Prelude, Bks. I-V. Ted Holt & John Gilroy. LC 83-10897. 124p. (Orig.). 1984. pap. text ed. 8.95x o.p. (ISBN 0-7100-9569-4). Routledge Chapman & Hall.

Commentary on Catulus, Oxford, Eighteen Eighty-Nine. 2nd ed. Ellis Robinson. Ed. by Steele Commager. LC 77-70812. (Latin Poetry-Editions, Commentations Critical Works). 1978. lib. bdg. 67.00 o.p. (ISBN 0-8240-2953-4). Garland Pub.

Commentary on First Peter. Robert Leighton. LC 74-165058. 512p. 1975. 16.95 o.p. (ISBN 0-8254-3103-4). Kregel.

Commentary on Kant's Critick of Pure Reason. Kuno Fischer. Ed. by Lewis W. Beck. LC 75-32039. (Philosophy of Immanuel Kant Ser.: Vol. 3). 1976. Repr. of 1866 ed. lib. bdg. 32.00 o.p. (ISBN 0-8240-2327-7). Garland Pub.

Commentary on Luke. 3rd ed. Frederic L. Godet. LC 81-18614. (Kregel Reprint Library). 586p. 1981. Repr. of 1887 ed. 24.95 o.p. (ISBN 0-8254-2720-7). Kregel.

Commentary on Revelation. Ethelbert W. Bullinger. LC 83-24917. 768p. 1984. 22.95 o.p. (ISBN 0-8254-2239-6). Kregel.

Commentary on Romans: A Classic Commentary from the Reformed Perspective. William G. Shedd. (Thornapple Commentaries Ser.). 1980. pap. 8.95 o.p. (ISBN 0-8010-8175-0). Baker Bk.

Commentary on the Chymical Wedding of Christian Rosenkreutz, with the Text of the Foxcroft Translation Revised & Modernized. Ed. by Deirdre Green & Adam Mclean. Tr. by Ezechiel Foxcroft & Donald Mclean. (Magnum Opus Hermetic Sourceworks Ser.: No. 18). (Illus.). 127p. (Orig.). 1987. pap. 15.00 o.p. (ISBN 0-933999-08-9). Phanes Pr.

Commentary on the Confession of Nineteen Sixty-Seven & an Introduction to the Book of Confessions. Edward A. Dowey, Jr. 1968. pap. 2.65 o.s.i. (ISBN 0-664-24829-2, Westminster). Westminster John Knox.

Commentary on the Epistle to the Galatians. Martin Luther. Tr. by P. S. Watson from Ger. 573p. 1978. Repr. of 1972 ed. 29.50 o.p. (ISBN 0-227-67437-5). Attic Pr.

Commentary on the Mutus Liber. Commentary by Adam Mclean. (Magnum Opus Hermetic Sourceworks Ser.: No. 11). (Illus.). 65p. (Orig.). 1987. pap. 15.00 o.p. (ISBN 0-933999-06-2). Phanes Pr.

Commentary on the Whole Bible, 6 vols. Matthew Henry. 7100p. 89.95 o.p. (ISBN 0-8007-0196-8); reference lib. ed. 74.95 o.p. (ISBN 0-8007-0968-3). Revell.

Commentary to Commercial Law. Robert L. Jordan & William D. Warren. (University Casebook). 346p. 1983. pap. text ed. (ISBN 0-88277-138-8). Foundation Pr.

Commentary to Kant's Critique of Pure Reason. 2nd ed. Norman Kemp-Smith. 1962. text ed. 45.00x o.p. (ISBN 0-391-00457-3). Humanities.

Commerce & Culture: The Maritime Communities of Colonial Massachusetts, 1690-1750. Christine L. Heyrman. LC 83-8175. (Illus.). 432p. 1984. 24.50 o.p. (ISBN 0-393-01781-8). Norton.

Commerce Defended. James Mill. LC 65-19652. 154p. Repr. of 1808 ed. 27.50x o.s.i. (ISBN 0-678-00088-3). Kelley.

Commerce Department Speaks on Import Administration & Export Administration, 2 vols. (Corporate Law & Practice Ser.: 1984-85). 1491p. 1984. Set. 15.00 o.p. (ISBN 0-317-15174-6, B46801). PLI.

Commerce Department Speaks, 1987, 2 vols. (Corporate Law & Practice Ser.). 1332p. 1987. 45.00 o.p. (B4-6801). PLI.

Commerce International en 1982-83. 227p. (Fr.). 1983. pap. text ed. 18.50 o.p. (ISBN 92-870-2009-4, G159, Gatt). UNIPUB.

Commercial & Consumer Law Teaching Materials. 3rd ed. Richard E. Speidel et al. LC 81-2984. (American Casebook Ser.). 1490p. 1981. text ed. 34.95 o.p. (ISBN 0-314-58801-9). West Pub.

Commercial & Debtor-Creditor Law: Selected Statutes. Theodore Eisenberg et al. 1435p. 1984. pap. text ed. 30.00 o.p. (ISBN 0-88277-188-4). Foundation Pr.

Commercial & Industrial Condominiums. John C. Melaniphy, Jr. LC 76-27171. (Illus.). 73p. 1976. pap. 19.00 o.p. (ISBN 0-87420-572-7). Urban Land.

Commercial & Shopping Center Management. (Journal of Property Management Reprints). (Illus., Orig.). 1984. pap. 8.95 o.p. (ISBN 0-317-02672-0, NO. 903). Inst Real Estate.

Commercial Applications of Wind Power. Paul N. Vosburgh. 272p. 1983. 29.95 o.p. (ISBN 0-442-29036-5). Van Nos Reinhold.

Commercial Banking. Oliver G. Wood, Jr. LC 78-420. 376p. 1978. text ed. 21.95x o.p. (ISBN 0-442-29535-9). PWS-Kent Pub.

Commercial Banking & Interstate Expansion: Issues, Prospects, & Strategies. Larry A. Frieder. Ed. by Richard Farmer. LC 84-28109. (Research for Business Decisions Ser.: No. 74). 206p. 1985. 44.95 o.p. (ISBN 0-8357-1621-X). UMI Res Pr.

Commercial Diving Manual. Richard Larn & Rex Whistler. (Illus.). 484p. 1983. 45.00 o.s.i. (ISBN 0-7153-8414-7). David & Charles.

Commercial FCC License Handbook. 4th ed. Harvey F. Swearer & Joseph J. Carr. 1985. 17.95 o.p. (ISBN 0-8306-0053-1, 1482); pap. 15.95 o.p. (ISBN 0-8306-1482-6). TAB Bks.

Commercial Food Patents, U. S. Nineteen Seventy-Nine. Hallie B. North. (Illus.). 1980. lib. bdg. 30.00 o.p. (ISBN 0-87055-358-5). AVI.

Commercial Foods Exposed! Gaye Horsley. 1975. 7.95 o.p. (ISBN 0-89036-043-X); pap. 5.95 o.p. (ISBN 0-89036-131-2). Hawkes Pub Inc.

Commercial Information. D. E. Davinson. 1965. text ed. 8.25 o.p. (ISBN 0-08-010870-9). Pergamon.

Commercial Language Systems. Bates. (Infotech Computer State of the Art Reports). 555p. 1974. 61.00x o.p. (ISBN 0-08-028537-6). Pergamon.

Commercial Law. Robert L. Jordan & William D. Warren. LC 83-1623. (University Casebook). 1015p. 1983. text ed. 29.50 o.p. (ISBN 0-88277-119-1). Foundation Pr.

Commercial Law for the CPA Candidate. Mark Roszkowski. 500p. 1984. pap. text ed. 19.40 o.p. (ISBN 0-87563-263-7). Stipes.

Commercial Law Information Sources. Julius J. Marke & Edward J. Bander. LC 73-120909. (Management Information Guide Ser.: No. 17). 226p. 1970. 68.00x o.p. (ISBN 0-8103-0817-7). Gale.

Commercial Law, 1986 Bankruptcy Supplement to., Robert L. Jordan & William D. Warren. (University Casebook Ser.). 167p. 1985. pap. text ed. 6.95 o.p. (ISBN 0-88277-316-X). Foundation Pr.

Commercial Lending by Thrift Institutions. 2nd ed. Charles S. Dickerson. 52p. 1987. pap. text ed. 35.00 o.s.i. Robt Morris Assocs.

Commercial Loan Documentation. William C. Hillman. 345p. 1986. text ed. 65.00 o.p. (ISBN 0-686-95387-8, AL-1288). PLI.

Commercial Loan Documentation. Practising Law Institute Staff & William C. Hillman. LC 82-60959. (Illus.). xiii, 357p. 1982. 40.00 o.p. PLI.

Commercial Newsgathering from Space: A Technical Memorandum. LC 87-619818. (OTA-TM-ISC: No. 40). (Illus.). 61p. (Orig.). 1987. pap. 3.00 o.p. (ISBN 0-318-22882-3, S/N 052-003-01066-6). USGPO.

Commercial Nuclear Power: Prospects for the United States & the World. (Illus.). 154p. 1986. pap. 8.00 o.p. (S/N 061-003-00491-1). USGPO.

Commercial Opportunities in Electrochemistry. Business Communications Staff. 231p. 1986. 1950.00 o.p. (ISBN 0-89336-351-0, C-044). BCC.

Commercial Paper. Robert L. Jordan & William D. Warren. LC 83-80652. (University Casebook Ser.). 481p. 1983. text ed. 20.00 o.p. (ISBN 0-88277-129-9). Foundation Pr.

Commercial Pilot-Airplane Written Test Guide. rev. ed. Federal Aviation Administration Staff. 141p. 1979. pap. text ed. 5.50 o.p. (ISBN 0-939158-14-0). Flightshops.

Commercial Pilot-Practical Test Standards-ASMEL. rev. ed. Federal Aviation Administration Staff. 70p. 1975. pap. text ed. 3.95 o.p. (ISBN 0-939158-10-8). Flightshops.

Commercial Pilot Question Book. (FAA-T-8080-2A Ser.). (Illus.). 163p. 1986. pap. 6.50 o.p. (ISBN 0-318-19982-3, S/N 050-007-00731-1). USGPO.

Commercial Radio Operator's Question & Answer License Guide, Element 4. Martin Schwartz. LC 72-88407. 1981. pap. 2.25 o.p. (ISBN 0-912146-06-0). AMECO.

Commercial Real Estate Desk Book. Milt Tanzer. LC 81-1190. (Illus.). 414p. 1981. 69.50 o.p. (ISBN 0-87624-090-2, Inst Busn Plan). P-H.

Commercial Real Estate from Purchase & Sale to Closing. Massachusetts Continuing Legal Education, Inc. Staff. LC 83-63413. (Illus.). 356p. 1984. write for info. o.p. Mass CLE.

Commercial Real Estate Loans. Massachusetts Continuing Legal Education, Inc. Staff. LC 84-61764. (Illus.). write for info. o.p. Mass CLE.

Commercial Software Engineering: For Productive Program Design. James Janossy. LC 84-25695. 472p. 1985. 31.95 o.p. (ISBN 0-471-81576-4). Wiley.

Commercial Storage of Fruits, Vegetables & Florist & Nursery Stocks. Robert E. Hardenburg et al. (Agriculture Handbook 66 Ser.). 130p. 1986. pap. 6.00 o.p. (ISBN 0-318-21608-6, S/N 001-000-04478-8). USGPO.

Commercial Transactions Desk Book. Arnold S. Goldstein. LC 77-79601. 1977. 39.50 o.p. (ISBN 0-87624-095-3, Inst Busn Plan). P-H.

Commercial Vegetable Processing. B. S. Luh & J. G. Woodroof. (Illus.). 1975. 55.95 o.p. (ISBN 0-87055-186-8). AVI.

Commerical Handbook of China, 2 vols. Julean Arnold & Ramon H. Myers. LC 78-24800. (Modern Chinese Economy Ser.: Vol. 16). (Illus.). 1979. Set. lib. bdg. 133.00 o.p. (ISBN 0-8240-4264-6). Garland Pub.

Comming Information Age: An Overview of Technology, Economics, & Politics. 2nd ed. W. P. Dizard. LC 84-12625. 224p. 1984. pap. text ed. 14.95x o.p. (ISBN 0-582-28522-4). Longman.

Commissar's Report. Martyn Burke. 320p. 1984. 14.45 o.p. (ISBN 0-395-35490-0). HM.

Commissioner Lin & the Opium War. Hsin-Pao Chang. 1970. pap. 5.95 o.p. (ISBN 0-393-00521-6, Norton Lib). Norton.

Commissioning Procedures for Nuclear Plants: A Safety Guide. (Safety Ser.: No. 50-SG-04). 58p. pap. 15.00 o.p. (ISBN 0-686-69439-2, ISP574, IAEA). UNIPUB.

Commissions Are Bigger! the Bonuses Are Higher! Milton M. Harris. LC 80-70924. 130p. 1981. 14.95 o.p. (ISBN 0-87094-263-8). Dow Jones-Irwin.

Commitment to the Committed: Treatment As Interaction in a Forensic Mental Hospital. J. T. Feldbrugge. 292p. (Orig.). 1986. pap. 24.00 o.p. (ISBN 9-02650-678-3). CJ Hogrefe Pubs.

Commitment Without Ideology. C. Daniel Batson et al. LC 72-13000. 1973. 6.95 o.p. (ISBN 0-8298-0245-2). Pilgrim NY.

Committee. Donald Seaman. LC 77-12358. 1978. 6.95 o.p. (ISBN 0-689-10838-9, Atheneum). Macmillan.

Committee: The Extraordinary Career of the House Committee on Un-American Activities. Walter Goodman. LC 68-13010. (Illus.). 564p. 1968. 15.00 o.p. (ISBN 0-374-12688-7). FS&G.

Commodities Trading: The Essential Primer. Russell R. Wasendorf. LC 82-73636. 300p. 35.00 o.p. (ISBN 0-87094-292-1). Dow Jones-Irwin.

Commodity Coding: Its Effects on Data Recording & Transfer. Ed. by National Computing Centre, Ltd. Staff. LC 70-365720. 135p. (Orig.). 1970. pap. 10.00x o.s.i. (ISBN 0-85012-005-5). Intl Pubns Serv.

Commodity Futures: An Expanding Regulatory World. Practising Law Institute Staff & Stephen F. Selig. LC 84-144176. (Corporate Law & Practice Course Handbook Ser.). 40.00 o.p. PLI.

Commodity Futures Game: Who Wins? Who Loses? Why? 2nd ed. Richard J. Teweles et al. LC 77-1853. 1977. pap. text ed. 7.95 o.p. (ISBN 0-07-063727-X). McGraw.

Commodity Futures Game: Who Wins? Who Loses? Why? Richard J. Teweles et al. (Illus.). 544p. 1974. text ed. 52.00 o.p. (ISBN 0-07-063726-1). McGraw.

Commodity Futures Trading Commission: Current Issues. Practising Law Institute Staff & Susan M. Phillips. LC 85-233215. (Corporate Law & Practice Course Handbook Ser.: No. 500). (Illus.). 320p. 1985. 40.00 o.p. PLI.

Commodity Market Controls. Carmine Nappi. LC 78-24715. (Illus.). 224p. 1979. 30.00x o.p. (ISBN 0-669-02812-6). Lexington Bks.

Commodore BASIC Manual. Lynne Mass & Thomas M. Kemnitz. LC 85-436. (Kids Working with Computers Ser.). (Illus.). 48p. (gr. 2 up). 1985. lib. bdg. 11.27 o.p. (ISBN 0-516-08425-9). Childrens.

Commodore LOGO Manual. Lynne Mass & Thomas M. Kemnitz. LC 85-5274. (Kids Working with Computers Ser.). (Illus.). 48p. (gr. 2 up). 1985. lib. bdg. 11.27 o.p. (ISBN 0-516-08433-X). Childrens.

Commodore Moore & the Texas Navy. Tom H. Wells. 1960. o.p. (ISBN 0-292-73194-9); pap. write for info. o.p. (ISBN 0-292-70103-9). U of Tex Pr.

Commodore Sixty-Four, MicroMasion: Using Your Computer to Have a Safer, More Convenient Home. David B. Bonynge. (Illus.). 176p. (Orig.). 1985. pap. 11.95 o.p. (ISBN 0-8306-1936-4, 1936). TAB Bks.

Commodore 64 Assembly Language. W. Douglas Maurer. LC 84-16981. 415p. 1985. pap. 24.95 o.p. (ISBN 0-88175-040-9, Computer Sci Pr); diskette 27.95 o.p. (ISBN 0-7167-8074-7). W H Freeman.

Commodore 64 Assembly Language Arcade Game Programming. Steve Bress. pap. 14.60 o.p. (ISBN 0-8306-1919-4, 1919). TAB Bks.

Commodore 64 BASIC Programming & Applications. Larry J. Goldstein & F. Mosher. LC 83-25705. (Illus.). 320p. 1984. 15.95 o.p. (ISBN 0-89303-381-2). Brady Bks.

Commodore 64 Connection. James W. Coffron. LC 84-51242. 250p. 1984. pap. 12.95 o.p. (ISBN 0-89588-192-6). SYBEX.

Commodore 64 Fun & Games. Ronald Jeffries et al. 192p. (Orig.). 1983. pap. text ed. 12.95 o.p. (ISBN 0-07-881116-3). Osborne-McGraw.

Commodore 64 Graphics. Nick Hampshire. 1983. pap. 14.95 o.p. (ISBN 0-317-04693-4). Sams.

Commodore 64 Illustrated. Bob Nadler. 176p. pap. 10.95 o.p. (6453). Sams.

Commodore 64 in Wonderland. Fred D'Ignazio. 144p. pap. 9.95 o.p. (6308); cassette & documentation 29.95 o.p. (7602). Sams.

Commodore 64 Music Master. Scrimshaw & Vogel. write for info. o.p. Sams.

Commodore 64 Playground. Fred D'Ignazio. 130p. pap. 9.95 o.p. (6307); cassette & documentation 29.95 o.p. (7601). Sams.

Commodore 64 Programmer's Library. Robert W. Baker. (Orig.). 1984. pap. spiral bdg. o.p. (ISBN 0-88006-087-5, CC7414). Wayne Green Ent.

Commodore 64 Starter Book. Jonathan A. Titus et al. LC 83-51228. 1984. pap. 17.95 o.p. (ISBN 0-672-22293-0). Sams.

Commodore 64: Step by Step Programming Guides. Phil Cornes. 64p. 1984. Bk. 1. 9.95 o.p. (ISBN 0-13-152141-1); 19.95 o.p. (ISBN 0-13-152117-9); 9.95 o.p. (ISBN 0-13-152158-6). P-H.

Commodore 64 Tutor for Home & School: How to Program in LOGO, PILOT, & BASIC. Julie Knott & Dave Prochnow. 210p. 1985. pap. 9.95 o.p. (ISBN 0-673-18074-3). Scott F.

Commodore 64 User's Handbook. Weber Systems Inc. Staff. (WSI's How to Use Your Personal Computer Ser.). 320p. (Orig.). 1983. pap. 14.95 o.p. (ISBN 0-938862-50-2). Weber Systems.

Commodore's Handbook of Simons' BASIC. Jane G. Reh. (Illus.). 224p. 1985. pap. 12.95 o.p. (ISBN 0-89303-419-3). Brady Bks.

Commom Pediatric Problems. Lifshitz. (Perspectives in Pediatric Ser.). 464p. 1984. 89.75 o.p. (ISBN 0-8247-7212-1). Dekker.

Common Afghan Street Games. Nico J. Van Oudenhoven. 78p. 1980. pap. 19.00 o.p. (ISBN 90-265-0293-1, Pub. by Swets Pub Serv Holland). Swets North Am.

Common Agenda for History Museums: Conference Proceedings. Ed. by Lonn W. Taylor. 64p. 1987. pap. 8.75 o.p. (ISBN 0-910050-89-9). AASLH Pr.

Common Agricultural Policy. Brian Hill. LC 84-4556. (EEC Ser.). 336p. 1984. text ed. 27.00 o.p. (ISBN 0-416-32180-1, 3919); pap. text ed. 12.95 o.p. (ISBN 0-416-32190-9, 3920). Routledge Chapman & Hall.

Common Agricultural Policy: Prospects for Change. Joan Pearce. (Chatham House Papers: No. 13). 122p. 1982. pap. 10.95x o.p. (ISBN 0-7100-9069-2). Routledge Chapman & Hall.

Common Algorithms in Pascal with Programs for Reading. David V. Moffat. (Software Ser.). 192p. 1984. pap. text ed. 19.00 o.p. (ISBN 0-13-152637-5). P-H.

Common Background of Greek & Hebrew Civilizations. Cyrus H. Gordon. (Illus.). 1965. pap. 7.95 o.p. (ISBN 0-393-00293-4, Norton Lib). Norton.

Common Cents: The Complete Money Management Workbook. Judy Lawrence. 85p. 1985. pap. 10.95 o.p. Dow Jones-Irwin.

Common Cents: The Complete Money Management Workbook. Judy M. Lawrence. 84p. (Orig.). 1986. pap. 9.95 o.p. (ISBN 0-87094-694-3). Dow Jones-Irwin.

Common Clinical Perplexities. Carl Lyle & Raymond Bianchi. LC 78-71347. 1979. spiral 14.50 o.p. (ISBN 0-87488-958-8). Med Exam.

Common Courtesy: In Which Miss Manners Solves the Problem That Baffled Jefferson. Judith Martin. LC 85-47608. (Illus.). 96p. 1985. 10.95 o.p. (ISBN 0-689-11652-7, Atheneum). Macmillan.

Common Denominators in Art & Science. Ed. by M. Pollock. 220p. 1983. 28.50 o.p. (ISBN 0-08-028457-4). Humanities.

Common Disorders of the Temporomandibular Joint. H. D. Ogus. (Dental Practitioner Handbook Ser.: No. 26). (Illus.). 120p. 1981. pap. text ed. 20.50 o.p. (ISBN 0-7236-0574-2). Butterworth.

Common Edible & Useful Plants of the East & Midwest. Muriel Sweet. LC 75-8914. (Illus.). 79p. 1975. 10.95 o.p. (ISBN 0-87961-035-2); pap. 4.95 o.p. (ISBN 0-87961-034-4). Naturegraph.

Common Facial Dermatoses. Marks. 154p. 1976. 24.50 o.p. (ISBN 0-7236-0379-0, Pub. by John Wright UK). Butterworth.

Common Fisheries Policy of the European Community. M. Wise. (EEC Ser.). 332p. (Orig.). 1984. 33.00 o.p. (ISBN 0-416-32390-1, 3917); pap. 14.95 o.p. (ISBN 0-416-32400-2). Routledge Chapman & Hall.

Common Gastroenterological Problems. Salter. 120p. 1977. pap. 11.00 o.p. (ISBN 0-7236-0470-3, Pub. by John Wright UK). Butterworth.

Common Grace & the Gospel. Cornelius Van Til. LC 73-190462. 1972. pap. 8.95 o.p. (ISBN 0-87552-482-6). Presby & Reformed.

Common Ground: Shared Interests in ESP & Communication Studies. Ed. by J. Kirkman et al. LC 83-13440. (English Language Teaching Documents: Vol. 117). (Illus.). 192p. 1984. pap. text ed. 7.50 o.s.i. (ISBN 0-08-031055-9, Dist. by Alemany Pr). Pergamon.

Common Knowledge: Controlling Your Destiny. Beverly B. Shippy. 437p. 1978. 5.00 o.p. (ISBN 0-682-48998-0). Exposition-Phoenix.

Common Law of the Shop see Issues in the Public Employee Relations Library: Series 3.

Common Man Through the Centuries: A Book of Costume Drawings. Max Barsis. LC 68-31447. (Illus.). 380p. 1973. 35.00 o.p. (ISBN 0-8044-1075-5). Ungar.

Common Market & How It Works. A. J. Kerr. (Illus.). 270p. 1983. text ed. 32.00 o.p. (ISBN 0-08-030230-0); pap. text ed. 17.50 o.p. (ISBN 0-08-030207-6). Pergamon.

Common Muse. Pinto & Rodway. 484p. 1957. (ISBN 0-8022-1979-9). Philos Lib.

Common Names of Insects & Related Organisms. Floyd G. Werner. 1982. pap. 15.00 o.p. (ISBN 0-938522-18-3); members 9.95 o.p. Entomol Soc.

Common Pediatric Disorders: Metabolism, Heart Disease, Allergies, Substance Abuse & Trauma. Ed. by Fima Lifshitz. (Clinical Pediatrics Ser.: Vol. 1). (Illus.). 464p. 1984. 89.75 o.p. Dekker.

Common Reader: First Series. annotated, rev. ed. Virginia Woolf. 1955. pap. 3.95 o.p. (ISBN 0-15-619805-3, Harv). HarBraceJ.

Common Sense & Testing in English. National Council of Teachers of English Task Force on Measurement & Evaluation in the Study of English Staff & Alan Purves. 33p. 1975. pap. 3.75 o.p. (ISBN 0-8141-0773-7). NCTE.

Common Sense & the Gospel: A Study of the Wisdom Books. D. P. McGeachy, 3rd. (Illus., Orig.). 1970. pap. 1.50 o.p. (ISBN 0-8042-9025-3, Westminster). Westminster John Knox.

Common-Sense English Grammar. Clarabelle D. Decker. 1980. Index. 5.00 o.p. (ISBN 0-682-49578-6). Exposition-Phoenix.

Common Sense Etiquette: For Business Women, Wives, Mistresses. L. Elizabeth De Feldy. (Illus.). 119p. 1983. pap. 18.00x o.p. (ISBN 0-935402-15-2). IBMI Irvine.

Common Sense in Piano Study. Victor Seroff. 1977. pap. 1.95 o.s.i. (ISBN 0-8008-1753-2, Crescendo). Taplinger.

Common Sense in United States-Soviet Trade. 173p. 5.00 o.p. (ISBN 0-318-13321-0). Am Comm US Soviet.

Common Sense Medical Guide & Outdoor Reference. Newell D. Breyfogle. (Illus.). 365p. 1981. text ed. 16.00 o.p. (ISBN 0-07-007672-3); pap. text ed. 9.95 o.p. (ISBN 0-07-007673-1). McGraw.

Common Sense Safety Guide to Applied Recreational Diving. Dan Orr. 1987. pap. text ed. 13.95x o.s.i. (ISBN 0-89917-499-X, College Town Press). TIS Inc.

Common Stocks for Common Sense Investors. William E. Mitchell & Thomas R. Ireland. 241p. 19.95 o.p. (ISBN 0-471-82057-1). Wiley.

Common Symptom Guide. John Wasson et al. 368p. (Orig.). 1975. text ed. 13.95 o.p. (ISBN 0-07-068435-9). McGraw.

Common S,mptoms of Disease in Children. 8th ed. Illingworth. (Illus.). 392p. 1984. 19.95 o.p. (ISBN 0-632-01279-X, B-2369-3). Mosby.

Common Treatment Problems in Depression. Alan F. Schatzberg. LC 85-3896. (Clinical Insights Monograph). 128p. 1985. pap. text ed. 12.00x o.p. (ISBN 0-88048-091-2, 48-091-2). Am Psychiatric.

Common Vertebral Joint Problems. Ed. by Gregory P. Grieve. (Illus.). 500p. 1981. text ed. 98.00 o.p. (ISBN 0-443-02106-6). Churchill.

Common Weeds of the United States. U. S. Department of Agriculture, Agricultural Research Service Staff. (Illus.). 16.50 o.p. (ISBN 0-8446-0066-0). Peter Smith.

Commonalities in Substance Abuse & Habitual Behavior. Ed. by Peter K. Levison & Dean R. Gerstein. LC 82-48537. 384p. 1983. 39.00x o.p. (ISBN 0-669-06293-6). Lexington Bks.

Commonsense Architecture. John S. Taylor. (Illus.). 1983. 12.95 o.p. (ISBN 0-393-01647-1). Norton.

Commonsense Cataloging: A Cataloger's Manual. 3rd ed. Rosalind Miller & Jane Terwillegar. LC 83-1306. 166p. 1983. 32.00 o.p. (ISBN 0-8242-0689-4). Wilson.

Commonsense Guide to Birth & Babies. Time-Life Books Editors. 1985. pap. 12.95 o.s.i. (ISBN 0-03-004424-3, Owl Bks). H Holt & Co.

Commonsense Guide to Birth & Babies. Time-Life Books Editors. 19.95 o.p. (ISBN 0-03-004413-8). H Holt & Co.

Commonwealth: A Study of the Role of Government in the American Economy, Massachusetts, 1774-1861. rev. ed. Oscar Handlin & Mary F. Handlin. LC 69-18032. 1969. 21.00x o.p. (ISBN 0-674-14690-5, Belknap Pr). Harvard U Pr.

Commonwealth & the Nation. S. R. Mehrotra. 1978. 8.95x o.p. (ISBN 0-7069-0673-X, Pub. by Vikas India). Advent NY.

Commonwealth at Work. D. Ingram. 1969. text ed. 13.25 o.p. (ISBN 0-08-013869-1); pap. 4.75 o.p. (ISBN 0-08-013868-3). Pergamon.

Commonwealth Caribbean. Stephen H. Fisher. LC 79-53429. (World Education Ser.). (Illus.). 256p. (Orig.). 1979. pap. text ed. 6.00 o.p. (ISBN 0-910054-55-X). Am Assn Coll Registrars.

Commonwealth Literature Periodicals: A Bibliography, Including Periodicals of Former Commonwealth Countries, with Locations in the United Kingdom. Compiled by Ronald Warwick. 172p. 1979. 53.00x o.p. (ISBN 0-7201-0800-4). Mansell.

Commonwealth of Man: An Inquiry into Power Politics & World Government. Frederick L. Schuman. LC 76-30305. 1977. Repr. of 1972 ed. lib. bdg. 35.00x o.p. (ISBN 0-8371-9372-9, SCCO). Greenwood.

Commonwealth Short Stories. Ed. by Anna Rutherford & Donald Hannah. 245p. 1980. 19.50 o.s.i. (ISBN 0-8419-5074-1); pap. text ed. 9.50x o.s.i. (ISBN 0-686-96739-9). Holmes & Meier.

Commonwealth Universities Yearbook, 1984, 4 vols. 60th ed. LC 59-24175. 2650p. 1984. boxed set 170.00x o.p. (ISBN 0-85143-088-0). Intl Pubns Serv.

Commonwealth Universities Yearbook 1986, 4 vols. 62nd ed. Ed. by Anastasios Christodolou & Tom Craig. 2800p. 1987. 185.00x o.p. (ISBN 0-85143-100-3, Pub. by Assn. of Commonwealth Univs). Gale.

Communal Organizations, a Study of Local Societies. George A. Hillery, Jr. LC 68-16696. 1968. lib. bdg. 26.00x o.s.i. (ISBN 0-226-33965-3). U of Chicago Pr.

Communal Violence in India. P. R. Rajgopal. 1987. 29.95 o.p. Asia Bk Corp.

Communale. Jean L'Hote. Ed. by Robert W. Torrens & James B. Sanders. LC 59-7033. (Illus., Fr.). 1959. 17.95x o.p. (ISBN 0-8290-2359-3); pap. text ed. 6.95x o.p. (ISBN 0-89197-092-4). Irvington.

Communes: Historical & Contemporary. Ed. by Ruth S. Cavan & Man S. Das. 1979. text ed. 30.00x o.p. (ISBN 0-7069-0786-8, Pub. by Vikas India). Advent NY.

Communicado con Palabras. Paula Kane & Patricia Short. 108p. (Span.). 1984. pap. text ed. 21.00 o.p. (ISBN 0-88377-360-0). Newbury Hse.

Communicards, I. Catharine S. Bush. (Expressive Language Ser.). 46p. (Orig.). 1981. pap. text ed. 24.95 o.p. (ISBN 0-88450-739-4, 3133-B). Communication Skill.

Communicards II: Synonyms & Concepts Set. Catharine S. Bush. 1983. pap. 24.95incl. four card decks o.p. (ISBN 0-88450-843-9, 4615-B). Communication Skill.

Communicate. John C. Souter. 80p. (YA) (gr. 7 up). 1988. pap. 4.95 o.p. (ISBN 0-8423-5406-9). Tyndale.

Communicate in Writing: A Functional Approach to Writing Through Reading Comprehension. Keith Johnson. (English As a Second Language Bk.). 1981. pap. text ed. 7.95 o.p. (ISBN 0-582-74811-9). Longman.

Communicating. 4th ed. Anita Taylor et al. (Illus.). 412p. 1986. pap. text ed. (ISBN 0-13-153396-7). P-H.

Communicating: A Social & Career Focus. 2nd ed. Roy M. Berko & Andrew D. Wolvin. (Illus.). 432p. 1981. pap. 17.50 o.p. (ISBN 0-395-29170-4). HM.

Communicating Effectively. (AMA Reprint Collections Ser). 1975. 7.50 o.p. (ISBN 0-8144-6943-4). AMACOM.

Communicating in Business. 2nd ed. Norman B. Sigband & David N. Bateman. 1985. text ed. (ISBN 0-673-15906-X). Scott F.

Communicating in Spanish, Level I. Enrique E. Lamadrid et al. 800p. (Span.). 1978. text ed. 27.95 o.p. (ISBN 0-395-27062-6). HM.

Communicating Online: All about Data Communications Software. 16.95 o.p. (ISBN 0-8104-6779-8). Sams.

Communicating Personality: A Theory of Interpersonal Communication & Human Relationships. Charles M. Rossiter, Jr. & W. Barnett Pearce. 286p. 1975. pap. text ed. write for info. o.p. (ISBN 0-02-403930-6). Macmillan.

Communicating to Make Friends: A Program for the Classroom Teacher. C. Lynn Fox. (Creative Teaching Ser.). (Illus.). 130p. (Orig.). (gr. k-6). 1980. pap. 9.95x o.p. (ISBN 0-935266-04-6). Jalmar Pr.

Communicating with Display Terminals. R. K. Debry. 256p. 1985. text ed. 43.50 o.p. (ISBN 0-07-016185-2). McGraw.

Communicating with Graphics: A Series from Industrial Engineering. Richard D. Filley & Kathryn Szoka. 1982. pap. text ed. 19.50 o.p. (ISBN 0-89806-036-2, 627). Inst Indus Eng.

Communication. 3rd ed. Larry L. Barker. (Illus.). 464p. 1984. pap. text ed. (ISBN 0-13-153718-0). P-H.

Communication: A Book for Students. C. Deverell. 1983. pap. 14.95 o.p. (ISBN 0-85258-169-6). Van Nos Reinhold.

Communication Alert Series. Incl. Non-Parents & Schools: Creating a New Team (ISBN 0-87545-022-9, 411-13303); School Labor Strife: Rebuilding the Team (ISBN 0-87545-023-7, 411-13305); New Voices on the Right: Impact on Schools (415-14403). 29.95 set o.p. (ISBN 0-317-35250-4); 10.95 ea. o.p. Natl Sch PR.

Communication & Affect-a Comparative Approach. Ed. by Thomas Alloway. 1972. 36.50 o.p. (ISBN 0-12-053050-3). Acad Pr.

Communication & Communication Barriers in Sociology. Ed. by G. Boalt et al. LC 75-44623. 163p. 1976. 45.95x o.p. (ISBN 0-470-15016-5). Halsted Pr.

Communication & Consensus: An Introduction to Rhetorical Discourse. Howard H. Martin & C. William Colburn. 293p. 1972. text ed. 12.95 o.p. (ISBN 0-15-512296-7, HC). HarBraceJ.

Communication & Culture: A Reading-Writing Text. 2nd ed. Joan Y. Gregg. 316p. 1985. pap. text ed. (ISBN 0-534-04626-6). Wadsworth Pub.

Communication & Human Relationships: The Study of Interpersonal Communication. Gerald M. Phillips & Julia T. Wood. 304p. 1983. pap. text ed. write for info. o.p. (ISBN 0-02-395240-7). Macmillan.

Communication & Imperial Control in China: Evolution of the Palace Memorial System, 1693-1735. Silas H. Wu. LC 73-119078. (East Asian Ser: No. 51). 1970. 16.00x o.s.i. (ISBN 0-674-14801-0). Harvard U Pr.

Communication & the Schools. C. W. Bending. LC 71-103930. 1970. 34.00 o.p. (ISBN 0-08-015663-0); pap. 80.00 o.p. (ISBN 0-08-015662-2). Pergamon.

Communication at Work: Writing & Speaking. Roger Wilcox. LC 76-14651. (Illus.). 1977. text ed. 23.95 o.p. (ISBN 0-395-24372-6). HM.

Communication Channels: Characterization & Behavior. Ed. by Bernard Goldberg. LC 75-23596. 776p. cancelled o.s.i. (ISBN 0-87942-058-8, PP00638). Inst Electrical.

Communication: Concepts & Perspectives. Ed. by Lee Thayer. (Illus.). 1967. 16.10 o.p. (ISBN 0-685-45852-0, 0-8104-9138). Sams.

Communication: Concepts & Processes. 3rd ed. Joseph A. DeVito. (Illus.). 320p. 1981. pap. text ed. (ISBN 0-13-153411-4). P-H.

Communication Cord. Brian Friel. 72p. (Orig.). 1983. pap. 7.95 o.p. (ISBN 0-571-13092-5). Faber & Faber.

Communication Economics & Development: Proceedings of an East-West Communication Institute Workshop, Honolulu, Hawaii, June 1980. Ed. by Meheroo Jussawalla & D. M. Lamberton. LC 81-13826. (Pergamon Policy Studies on International Development). 356p. 1982. 46.00 o.p. (ISBN 0-08-027520-6). Pergamon.

Communication, Family & Marriage. Ed. by Don D. Jackson. LC 68-21576. (Human Communication Ser.: Vol. 1). (Orig.). 1968. pap. 6.95x o.p. (ISBN 0-8314-0015-3). Sci & Behavior.

Communication for Business & the Professions. 3rd ed. Treece. 608p. 1986. text ed. 40.00 o.p. (ISBN 0-205-08566-0). Allyn.

Communication for Dental Auxilliaries. Cheryl Wiles & William Ryan. 1982. text ed. 24.95 o.p. (ISBN 0-8359-0897-6); pap. text ed. 18.95 o.p. (ISBN 0-8359-0896-8). Appleton & Lange.

Communication for Management & Business. 4th ed. Norman B. Sigband & Arthur H. Bell. 1986. text ed. (ISBN 0-673-18268-1). Scott F.

Communication for Managers. Paul Preston. 1979. text ed. 27.67 o.p. (ISBN 0-13-153957-4). P-H.

Communication: From Cave Writing to Television. Julie F. Batchelor. LC 53-7860. (gr. 4-6). 1953. 4.95 o.p. (ISBN 0-15-219832-6, HJ). HarBraceJ.

Communication History. John D. Stevens & Hazel D. Garcia. LC 80-11132. (Sage Commtext Ser.: No. 2). (Illus.). 159p. 1980. 19.95 o.p. (ISBN 0-8039-1256-0); pap. 9.95 o.p. (ISBN 0-8039-1257-9). Sage.

Communication in Action. Dorothy G. Hennings. 1978. pap. 19.95 o.p. (ISBN 0-395-30624-8); Instr's. manual 1.00 o.p. (ISBN 0-686-97262-7). HM.

Communication in Action: Teaching the Language Arts. 2nd ed. Dorothy G. Hennings. 1981. text ed. 27.95 o.p. (ISBN 0-395-31702-9). HM.

Communication in Business & Industry. William M. Schutte & Erwin R. Steinberg. LC 74-13262. 414p. 1977. Repr. of 1960 ed. 9.25 o.p. (ISBN 0-88275-199-9). Krieger.

Communication in Development: Proceedings of the Society for the Study of Developmental Biology, 28th Symposium, 1969. Society for the Study of Developmental Biology Staff. Ed. by Anton Lang. (Journal of Developmental Biology: Suppl. 3). 1970. 59.50 o.p. (ISBN 0-12-612968-1); pap. 39.00 o.p. (ISBN 0-12-612969-X). Acad Pr.

Communication in Organizations: An Annotated Bibliography & Sourcebook. Ed. by Robert M. Carter. LC 73-161194. (Management Information Guide Ser.: No. 25). 1972. 65.00x o.p. (ISBN 0-8103-0825-8). Gale.

Communication in Pharmacy Practice: A Practical Guide for Students & Practitioners. Ed. by William N. Tindall et al. LC 83-19887. (Illus.). 182p. 1984. pap. 11.50 o.p. (ISBN 0-8121-0923-6). Lea & Febiger.

Communication in Pulpit & Parish. Merrill R. Abbey. 1973. 8.95 o.p. (ISBN 0-664-20967-X, Westminster). Westminster John Knox.

Communication in Pulpit & Parish. Merrill R. Abbey. LC 72-14329. 238p. 1980. pap. 8.50 o.s.i. (ISBN 0-664-24312-6, Westminster). Westminster John Knox.

Communication in Social Work. Peter R. Day. LC 72-8466. 128p. 1972. text ed. 20.00 o.p. (ISBN 0-08-017064-1); pap. text ed. 9.25 o.p. (ISBN 0-08-017065-X). Pergamon.

Communication in the Classroom. Larry L. Barker. 208p. 1982. text ed. (ISBN 0-13-153551-X). P-H.

Communication in the Courtroom: How to Tell, Explain & Persuade. Sonya B. Hamlin. 1983. 55.00 o.p. (ISBN 0-15-100012-3, H42922, Pub. by Law & Business). HarBraceJ.

Communication in Writing. E. F. Pardoe. 1965. 11.25 o.p. (ISBN 0-08-011136-X); pap. 35.00 o.p. (ISBN 0-08-011135-1). Pergamon.

Communication: Key to Your Marriage, Manual. H. Norman Wright. (Illus.). 64p. 1979. 12.95 o.s.i. (ISBN 0-8307-0718-2, 5202507). Regal.

Communication: Logic & Command. W. John Weilgart. (Illus.). pap. 2.00 o.p. (ISBN 0-912038-20-9). Cosmic Comm.

Communication Matrix: Ways of Winning with Words. Georgette F. McGregor & Joseph A. Robinson. 208p. 1981. 19.95 o.p. (ISBN 0-8144-5649-9). AMACOM.

Communication Nil! Rosalind E. Dickenson. 1979. 5.00 o.p. (ISBN 0-682-49346-5). Exposition-Phoenix.

Communication One Hundred One Course Manual. Applegate & Waldhart. 72p. 1984. pap. text ed. 8.50 o.p. (ISBN 0-8403-3425-7). Kendall-Hunt.

Communication Planning Processes in the MUDA Agricultural Development Authority (MADA). Ramli Mohamed. (Institute of Culture & Communication Case Studies:: No. 7). xi, 106p. (Orig.). 1984. pap. text ed. 5.00 o.p. (ISBN 0-86638-039-6). EW Ctr HI.

Communication Policies in Peru. Carlos Ortega & Carlos Romera. (Communication Policy Studies). (Illus.). 68p. 1977. pap. 6.00 o.p. (ISBN 92-3-101366-1, U85, UNESCO). UNIPUB.

Communication Policies in Sri Lanka: A Study Carried Out by a Committee Appointed by the Secretary to the Ministry of Education, Sri Lanka. M. A. De Silva & Reggie Siriwardenc. (Communication Policy Studies). 59p. 1977. pap. 5.00 o.p. (ISBN 92-3-101416-1, U86, UNESCO). UNIPUB.

Communication Policy & Planning: A Case Study of the American Cancer Society Public Education Program. Gerald E. Klonglan & Chun Nan Lo. (Institute of Culture & Communication Case Studies: No. 8). xii, 61p. (Orig.). 1984. pap. text ed. 5.00 o.p. (ISBN 0-86638-044-2). EW Ctr HI.

Communication Policy in Developed Countries. Patricia Edgar & Syed A. Rahim. 297p. (Orig.). 1984. pap. 17.95x o.p. (ISBN 0-7103-0060-3, Kegan Paul). Routledge Chapman & Hall.

Communication Processes & Relationship. Robyn Penman. 1980. 46.00 o.p. (ISBN 0-12-550380-6). Acad Pr.

Communication Revolution in Politics, Vol. 34. 4th ed. LC 82-72550. 1982. 6.95 o.p. (ISBN 0-318-23653-2). Acad Poli Sci.

Communication Satellites. Ed. by L. J. Carter. 1963. 39.50 o.p. (ISBN 0-12-161650-9). Acad Pr.

Communication Skills for Business: A Handbook. 281p. 1986. pap. 11.00 o.p. (ISBN 0-912857-31-5). Inst Finan Educ.

Communication Skills for Exceptional Learners. Margaret S. Webber. LC 80-28094. 275p. 1981. text ed. 33.00 o.p. (ISBN 0-89443-343-1). Aspen Pub.

Communication Skills for Ministry. John Lawyer & Neil Katz. 176p. 1983. pap. text ed. 17.95 o.p. (ISBN 0-8403-2987-3, 40371201). Kendall-Hunt.

Communication Skills in the Organization. Gary T. Hunt. (Illus.). 1980. text ed. (ISBN 0-13-153296-0). P-H.

Communication Strategies: A Guide for Agricultural Change Agents. Herbert F. Lionberger & Paul Gwin. 239p. 1982. pap. text ed. 11.95x o.p. (ISBN 0-8134-2236-1). Inter Print Pubs.

Communication Strategy: A Guide to Speech Preparation. Roselyn L. Schiff et al. 1981. pap. text ed. write for info. o.p. (ISBN 0-673-15437-8). Scott F.

Communication: The Social Matrix of Psychiatry. Jurgen Ruesch & Gregory Bateson. 1968. pap. 5.95 o.p. (ISBN 0-393-00114-8, Norton Lib). Norton.

Communication: The Study of Human Interaction. C. David Mortensen. 480p. 1972. text ed. 34.95 o.p. (ISBN 0-07-043395-X). McGraw.

Communication Theory. Ernest Bormann. LC 79-24333. 264p. 1980. pap. text ed. 25.95 o.p. (ISBN 0-03-019086-X, HoltC). HR&W.

Communication Through Optics: Proceedings of the SPIE Seminar, France, 1979. (SPIE Seminar Proceedings: Vol. 213). 78p. 17.00 o.p. (ISBN 0-89252-241-0); members 10.00 o.p. (ISBN 0-317-34609-1). SPIE.

Communication Training & Consulting in Business, Industry, & Government. Ed. by William J. Buchholz. 290p. 1983. pap. text ed. 9.95 o.p. (ISBN 0-931874-14-9). Assn Busn Comm.

Communication Training Through Amplification: Audiologic Management of Adults. Carl A. Binnie. (Orig.). 1988. pap. text ed. 27.50 o.p. (ISBN 0-316-09517-6, 095176). College-Hill.

Communication, Vol. 3 (incl. 1985-1987 Supplements) Ed. by Eleanor C. Goldstein. 1987. 45.00 o.p. (ISBN 0-89777-083-8). Soc Issues.

Communication Works. Michael Gamble & Teri K. Gamble. 1984. pap. text ed. 14.00 o.p. (ISBN 0-394-32804-3, RanC). Random.

Communication Yearbook, Vol. 1. Ed. by Brent D. Ruben. LC 76-45943. 656p. 1977. text ed. 29.95 o.s.i. (ISBN 0-87855-206-5). Transaction Pubs.

Communications & National Integration in Communist China. Alan P. Liu. (Center for Chinese Studies, Univ. of Michigan: No. 1). 1971. 34.50x o.p. (ISBN 0-520-01882-6); pap. 11.95x o.p. (ISBN 0-520-02901-1). U of Cal Pr.

Communications for the Safety Professional. Robert B. Konikow & Frank E. McElroy. LC 75-11315. (Illus.). 518p. 1975. text ed. 33.45 o.p. (ISBN 0-87912-089-4, 151.14). Natl Safety Coun.

Communications in Business. 3rd ed. Walter Wells. 553p. 1981. text ed. 27.95x o.p. (ISBN 0-534-00943-3). PWS-Kent Pub.

Communications in Interviews. Lamar Reinsch & Michael Stano. 256p. 1982. pap. text ed. (ISBN 0-13-153502-1). P-H.

Communications Institute Proceedings, July 11-14, 1982, Hershey, Pa. Ed. by Becky A. Wright. 84p. (Orig.). 1982. pap. 8.00 o.p. (ISBN 0-89154-194-2). Intl Found Employ.

Communications Law 1984, 2 vols. (Patents, Copyrights, Trademarks, & Literary Property Ser.). 1871p. 1984. Set. 15.00 o.p. (ISBN 0-686-80167-9, G4-3754). PLI.

Communications Networks. (European Computing Conference on Communications Networks Held in London, 1975). 530p. 1975. text ed. 26.95x o.p. (ISBN 0-903796-05-8, Pub. by Online Conferences England). Gower Pub Co.

Communications Policy for National Development: A Comparative Perspective. Ed. by Majid Teharanian et al. 1977. 31.95x o.p. (ISBN 0-7100-8597-4). Routledge Chapman & Hall.

Communications Standard Dictionary. Martin H. Weik. 928p. 1982. 45.95 o.p. (ISBN 0-442-21933-4). Van Nos Reinhold.

Communications System Engineering Handbook. Ed. by Donald H. Hamsher. 1967. text ed. 105.50 o.p. (ISBN 0-07-025960-7). McGraw.

Communications Technologies: Their Effect on Adult, Career, & Vocational Education. Christopher J. Dede et al. Ed. by Norman M. Singer. 42p. 1982. 4.25 o.p. (ISBN 0-318-22063-6, IN244). Natl Ctr Res Voc Ed.

Communicative Disorders Related to Cleft Lip & Palate. 2nd ed. Kenneth Bzoch. 1979. 26.00 o.s.i. (ISBN 0-316-11936-9). Little.

Communicative Performance of Literature. Carolyn A. Gilbert. (Illus.). 1977. pap. write for info. o.p. (ISBN 0-02-342900-3). Macmillan.

Communicative Reading. 4th ed. Elbert R. Bowen et al. (Illus.). 1978. write for info. o.p. (ISBN 0-02-313000-8). Macmillan.

Communicators & Society. D. Wilson. 1968. pap. 4.70 o.p. (ISBN 0-08-012977-3). Pergamon.

Communicator's Commentary: Corinthians First; Second, Vol. 7. Kenneth L. Chafin & Lloyd J. Ogilvie. 1983. 18.99 o.p. (ISBN 0-8499-0347-5). Word Bks.

Communicator's Guide to Marketing. Ed. by Clara Degen. (Illus.). 226p. 1987. 34.95 o.p. (ISBN 0-582-28645-X). Longman.

Communion of the Christian with God. Wilhelm Herrmann. Ed. by Robert T. Voelkel & Leander E. Keck. Tr. by J. Sandys Stanyon from Ger. LC 78-154491. (Lives of Jesus Ser). 440p. 1971. pap. 2.50 o.p. (ISBN 0-8006-1270-1, 1-1270, Fortress). Augsburg Fortress.

Communism & Agrarian Reform in Iraq. Rony Gabbay. 240p. 1978. 32.00 o.p. (ISBN 0-85664-567-2, Pub. by Croom Helm). Routledge Chapman & Hall.

Communism & China: Ideology in Flux. Benjamin I. Schwartz. LC 68-28696. 1970. pap. text ed. 3.95x o.s.i. (ISBN 0-689-70251-5, 164, Atheneum). Macmillan.

Communism & Cultural Heritage. Ed. by Eleazar Baller. 267p. 1984. 7.95 o.p. (ISBN 0-8285-2809-8, Pub. by Progress Pubns USSR). Imported Pubns.

Communism & Development. Robert Bideleux. 320p. 1985. 39.95 o.p. (ISBN 0-416-73410-3, 4028). Routledge Chapman & Hall.

Communism as a Social Formation. P. Lopata. 183p. 1983. pap. 1.45 o.p. (ISBN 0-8285-2370-3, Pub. by Progress Pubs USSR). Imported Pubns.

Communism in Africa. Ed. by David E. Albright. LC 78-13813. 288p. 1980. 15.00x o.p. (ISBN 0-253-12814-5). Ind U Pr.

Communism in Hungary from Kun to Kadar. Bennett Kovrig. Ed. by Richard F. Staar. LC 78-59863. (Publications Ser.: No. 211). (Illus.). 1979. pap. 10.95x o.p. (ISBN 0-8179-7112-2). Hoover Inst Pr.

Communism in Japan. Paul F. Langer. LC 73-152426. (Studies: No. 30). 112p. 1972. 7.95x o.p. (ISBN 0-8179-3301-8). Hoover Inst Pr.

Communism in Mexico. Karl M. Schmitt. 302p. 1965. 13.50x o.p. (ISBN 0-292-73195-7). U of Tex Pr.

Communism on the Decline. George C. Guins. 1957. (ISBN 0-8022-0644-1). Philos Lib.

Communist China: The Politics of Student Opposition. Tr. by Dennis J. Doolin. LC 64-16879. (Studies Ser.: No. 2). 1964. pap. 4.50x o.p. (ISBN 0-8179-3022-1). Hoover Inst Pr.

Communist Controversy in Washington: From the New Deal to McCarthy. Earl Latham. LC 66-14447. (Orig.). 1969. pap. text ed. 4.25x o.p. (ISBN 0-689-70121-7, 149, Atheneum). Macmillan.

Communist Manifesto. Karl Marx & Friedrich Engels. LC 85-5627. (YA) (gr. 9 up). 1968. pap. 2.25 o.p. (ISBN 0-14-020915-8, Pelican). Penguin.

Communist Movement: From Comintern to Cominform, 2 vols. Fernando Claudin. Tr. by Brian Pearce from Fr. LC 74-25015. 739p. 1976. Set. 27.00 o.p. (ISBN 0-85345-366-7). Monthly Rev.

Communist Movement in China. Kung-Po Ch'en. 1966. lib. bdg. 19.00x o.p. (ISBN 0-374-91464-8, Octagon). Hippocrene Bks.

Communist Organization in Singapore: Its Techniques of Manpower Mobilization & Management, 1948-1966. Lee T. Hui. 151p. (Orig.). 1976. pap. text ed. 11.50x o.p. (ISBN 0-566-04001-8, Pub. by Inst Southeast Asian Stud). Gower Pub Co.

Communist Party of Venezuela. Robert J. Alexander. LC 77-77320. (Studies Ser.: No. 24). 246p. 1969. 11.95x o.p. (ISBN 0-8179-3241-0); pap. 7.95x o.p. (ISBN 0-8179-3242-9). Hoover Inst Pr.

Communist Regimes in Eastern Europe. 4th ed. Richard F. Staar. LC 81-84232. (Publication Ser.: No. 269). (Illus.). 392p. 1982. pap. text ed. 9.95x o.p. (ISBN 0-8179-7692-2). Hoover Inst Pr.

Communist Resistance in Nazi Germany. A. Merson. 382p. 1986. text ed. 39.95 o.p. (ISBN 0-391-03366-2). Humanities.

Communist: Series 1 & 2. Communist Labor Party of America Staff. 1971. Repr. of 1921 ed. lib. bdg. 83.00x o.p. (ISBN 0-8371-9147-5, CC00). Greenwood.

Communists & Chinese Peasant Rebellions: A Study in the Rewriting of Chinese History. James P. Harrison. LC 68-16867. 1971. pap. text ed. 3.45x o.s.i. (ISBN 0-689-70269-8, 176, Atheneum). Macmillan.

Communities Left Behind: Alternatives for Development. facsimile ed. North Central Regional Center for Rural Development Staff. (Illus.). 152p. 1974. pap. 8.20x o.p. (ISBN 0-8138-2365-X). Iowa St U Pr.

Communities of the Past. Jane Gray & William Berry. LC 81-4069. 623p. 1982. 55.95 o.p. (ISBN 0-87933-362-6). Van Nos Reinhold.

Community Action & Local Government. Sean Baine. 96p. 1975. pap. text ed. 8.75 o.p. (Pub. by Bedford England). Gower Pub Co.

Community Action for Change. Ray Lees & Marjorie Mayo. 250p. (Orig.). 1984. pap. 13.95x o.p. (ISBN 0-7100-9743-3). Routledge Chapman & Hall.

Community Against Government: The British Community Development Project 1968-78. Martin Looney. (Illus.). 221p. 1983. text ed. 28.50 o.p. (ISBN 0-435-82545-3); pap. text ed. 11.85 o.p. (ISBN 0-435-82546-1). Heinemann Ed.

Community & Communications. Seymour J. Mandelbaum. 160p. 1972. 5.95x o.p. (ISBN 0-393-01001-5). Norton.

Community & Environment. E. A. Gutkind. 1954. (ISBN 0-8022-0650-6). Philos Lib.

Community & Message of Isaiah Fifty Six-Sixty Six: A Theological Commentary. Elizabeth Achtemeier. LC 81-52284. 160p. (Orig.). 1982. pap. 10.95 o.p. (ISBN 0-8066-1916-3, 10-1610, Augsburg). Augsburg Fortress.

Community & Revolution in Modern Vietnam. Alexander B. Woodside. LC 75-18429. (Illus.). 418p. 1976. text ed. 24.95 o.p. (ISBN 0-395-20367-8). HM.

Community & Social Service Education in the Community College: Issues & Characteristics. Edward A. Brawley & Ruben Schindler. Date not set. 3.00 o.s.i. (72-650-15). Coun Soc WK Ed.

Community Associations & Centres: A Comparative Study. A. C. Twelvetrees. 146p. 1976. 40.00 o.p. (ISBN 0-08-019938-0); pap. 40.00 o.p. (ISBN 0-08-019937-2). Pergamon.

Community Based Corrections. John O. Smykla. 1981. text ed. write for info. o.p. (ISBN 0-02-477790-0). Macmillan.

Community-Based Social Care: The Avon Experience. Ed. by Wally Harbert & Pat Rogers. (NCVO Occasional Paper: No. 4). 87p. (Orig.). 1983. pap. text ed. 12.25x o.p. (ISBN 0-7199-1101-X, Pub. by Bedford England). Gower Pub Co.

Community Called Church. Juan L. Segundo. Tr. by John Drury from Span. LC 72-85795. (Theology for Artisans of a New Humanity Ser., Vol. 1). Orig. Title: Esa communidad Lleamasha Iglesia. 181p. 1973. 7.95x o.p. (ISBN 0-88344-481-X); pap. 4.95x o.p. (ISBN 0-88344-487-9). Orbis Bks.

Community Care & the Mentally Handicapped: Services for Mothers & Their Mentally Handicapped Children. Sam Ayer & Andy Alaszewski. LC 84-45289. 262p. 1984. 25.00 o.p. (ISBN 0-7099-0533-5, Pub. by Croom Helm Ltd). Routledge Chapman & Hall.

Community Careering Gamebook. Ira M. Bank. 59p. (gr. 3-6). 1983. wkbk. 2.00 o.p. (ISBN 0-912578-15-7). Chron Guide.

Community Careering Guidebook. new ed. Ira M. Bank. 16p. 1974. pap. 3.00 o.p. (ISBN 0-912578-14-9). Chron Guide.

Community Centers: An Architectural Guide. Coppa & Avery Consultants Staff. (Architecture Ser.: A 1369). 11p. 1985. 2.00 o.p. (ISBN 0-89028-359-1). Vance Biblios.

Community Clinical Psychology. Ed. by Hugh Koch. 226p. 1986. 39.00 o.p. (ISBN 0-7099-1579-9, Pub. by Croom Helm Ltd). Routledge Chapman & Hall.

Community College Centers for Contracted Programs. James R. Mahoney. 70p. 1982. pap. 6.00 o.p. (ISBN 0-87117-122-8). Am Assn Comm Jr Coll.

Community College Conflict: Chicano Under Fire. Y. Arturo Cabrera & Jose A. Perea. LC 78-56755. (Illus.). 1979. pap. 3.95x o.p. (ISBN 0-932848-03-6). Sierra Pubns CA.

Community College Foundation. Ed. by W. Harvey Sharron, Jr. 1982. 19.50 o.p. (4020). Am Assn Comm Jr Coll.

Community College in America: A Short History. rev. ed. George B. Vaughan. 44p. 1982. pap. 6.00 o.p. (ISBN 0-87117-141-4); pap. 5.00 ea. 10 or more copies o.p. Am Assn Comm Jr Coll.

Community Colleges & Their Share of Student Financial Assistance. Susan Nelson. 69p. 1980. 4.00 o.p. (ISBN 0-317-33973-7, 218911). College Bd.

Community Colleges of Tennessee: The Founding & Early Years. Ed. by Roy S. Nicks. (Tennessee Ser.: No.2). (Illus.). (gr. 9-12). 1989. 12.95x o.p. (ISBN 0-87870-054-4). Memphis St Univ.

Community Colleges: The Untold American Story. Arthur S. Flemming. 1986. 7.50 o.p. (1067). Am Assn Comm Jr Coll.

Community Corrections. American Correctional Association Staff. (Series 1: No. 5). 83p. (Orig.). 1981. pap. 5.00 o.p. (ISBN 0-942974-20-4). Am Correctional.

Community Dentistry: A Problem-Oriented Approach. Stephen L. Silberman & Ames F. Tryon. (Illus.). 350p. 1980. 36.00 o.p. (ISBN 0-88416-157-9). Year Bk Med.

Community Development - Planning & Action: Recent Writings, 1980-1984. Dale E. Casper. (Public Administration Ser.: P 1714). 12p. 1985. 2.00 o.p. (ISBN 0-89028-464-4). Vance Biblios.

Community Development: Learning & Action. Hayden Roberts. LC 78-12986. 1979. 17.50x o.p. (ISBN 0-8020-5437-4); pap. 9.95c o.p. (ISBN 0-8020-6351-9). U of Toronto Pr.

Community Development Paraprofessionals in Bolivia: NCDS Promoters in the Field. Margaret M. Savino. (Special Series on Paraprofessionals). 60p. Date not set. pap. 00.00 o.p. (ISBN 0-86731-057-X). Cornell CIS RDC.

Community Education. Ed. by Christian O. Arndt. LC 59-751. (National Society for the Study of Education Yearbooks Ser: No. 58, Pt. 1). 1959. lib. bdg. 7.00x o.s.i. (ISBN 0-226-60048-3); pap. text ed. 4.50x o.s.i. (ISBN 0-226-60049-1). U of Chicago Pr.

Community, Educational & Social Impact Perspectives. Ed. by Donna H. Schoeny & Larry E. Decker. 230p. (Orig.). 1984. lib. bdg. 30.00 o.p. (ISBN 0-8191-3537-2, Co-pub. by Atlantic Ctr Comm); pap. text ed. 12.25 o.p. (ISBN 0-8191-3538-0). U Pr of Amer.

Community Experiences of Immigrant Minorities: A Selected Bibliography. Dale E. Casper. (Public Administration Series Bibliography: P-1610). 10p. 1985. pap. 2.00 o.p. (ISBN 0-89028-260-9). Vance Biblios.

Community Health. Ed. by June Clark & Jill Henderson. LC 82-22038. (Illus.). 317p. 1983. pap. text ed. 17.25 o.p. (ISBN 0-443-02000-0). Churchill.

Community Health: An Epidemiological Approach. Bryan C. Smith. (Illus.). 1979. text ed. write for info. o.p. (ISBN 0-02-412570-9). Macmillan.

Community Health Nursing: Process & Practice for Promoting Health. Marcia Stanhope & Jeannette Lancaster. (Illus.). 950p. 1984. text ed. 36.95 o.p. (ISBN 0-8016-4760-6). Mosby.

Community Health Nursing: Skills & Strategies. Carolyn Elkins. LC 83-9934. (Illus.). 432p. 1983. text ed. 21.95 o.p. (ISBN 0-89303-264-6). Appleton & Lange.

Community in America. 3rd ed. Roland L. Warren. 1978. text ed. 27.50 o.p. (ISBN 0-395-30765-1). HM.

Community in Urban Society. Larry Lyon. 276p. 1987. pap. text ed. (ISBN 0-534-10684-6). Wadsworth Pub.

Community Influence on Local Planning Policy. A. G. Smith et al. 84p. 1985. pap. 24.00 o.p. (ISBN 0-08-033680-9, Pub. by PPI). Pergamon.

Community Kitchens' Complete Guide to Gourmet Coffee. Community Kitchens Staff. 240p. 1986. pap. 9.95 o.s.i. (ISBN 0-671-55870-6). S&S.

Community Leaders of the World: First Commemorative Issue. Ed. by J. M. Evans. LC 83-72168. 500p. 1985. 65.00 o.p. (ISBN 0-934544-31-X). Am Biog Inst.

Community Manpower Services for the Disadvantaged. Frank C. Pierson. 86p. 1971. pap. 1.25 o.p. (ISBN 0-911558-06-3). W E Upjohn.

Community Medicine: A Textbook for Nurses & Health Visitors. W. E. Waters & K. S. Cliff. (Illus.). 146p. 1983. pap. 13.50 o.p. (ISBN 0-7099-2751-7, Pub. by Croom Helm Ltd). Routledge Chapman & Hall.

Community Medicine in the United Kingdom: Medical Education & an Emerging Specialty Within the Reorganized National Health Service. William S. Jordan, Jr. LC 78-4226. (Health Care & Society Ser.: Vol. 3). 1978. text ed. 23.95 o.p. (ISBN 0-8261-2410-0). Springer Pub.

Community Mental Health & the Criminal Justice System. Ed. by John Monahan. 350p. 1976. pap. 17.00 o.p. (ISBN 0-08-018758-7). Pergamon.

Community Mental Health Nursing: New Directions in Theory & Practice. Dixie Koldjeski. LC 83-14768. 328p. 1984. 25.00 o.p. (ISBN 0-471-04442-3, Pub. by Wiley Med.). Wiley.

Community of Character: Toward a Constructive Christian Social Ethic. Stanley Hauerwas. LC 80-53072. 320p. 1981. text ed. 24.95 o.s.i. (ISBN 0-268-00733-0). U of Notre Dame Pr.

Community of God. Marcella Bush. (Illus.). (gr. 6-7). 1975. pap. 3.75x o.p. (ISBN 0-8192-4057-5); tchr's guide 4.95x o.p. (ISBN 0-8192-4056-7). Morehouse Pub.

Community of Knowledge. Michael Welbourne. LC 86-17326. (Scots Philosophical Monographs: No. 9). 120p. 1986. text ed. 29.95x o.p. (ISBN 0-391-03395-6); pap. text ed. 15.00x o.p. (ISBN 0-391-03396-4). Humanities.

Community of the Future. Vindling Kruse. 1952. (ISBN 0-8022-0898-3). Philos Lib.

Community of the Mind. J. L. Dixon. LC 66-26964. 176p. 1967. (ISBN 0-8022-0405-8). Philos Lib.

Community of the New Age: Studies in Mark's Gospel. Howard C. Kee. LC 76-49484. 1977. 13.95 o.s.i. (ISBN 0-664-20770-7, Westminster). Westminster John Knox.

Community of the Spirit. Richard Reichert. 120p. 1982. pap. 3.60 o.p. (ISBN 0-697-01796-6); tchr's manual o.p. 4.00 o.p. (ISBN 0-697-01797-4); spirit masters 10.95 o.p. (ISBN 0-697-01798-2). Wm C Brown.

Community of Women & Men in the Church: A Study Program. Advisory Committee. (Orig.). 1978. pap. 1.95 o.p. (ISBN 0-377-00092-2). Friendship Pr.

Community of Women & Men in the Church. Ed. by Constance F. Parvey. LC 82-71831. 288p. (Orig.). 1982. pap. 14.95 o.p. (ISBN 0-8006-1644-8, 1-1644, Fortress). Augsburg Fortress.

Community Organization & Social Planning. Robert Perlman & Arnold Gurin. LC 71-177887. (Community Organization Ser.). 292p. 1972. write for info. o.p. (ISBN 0-02-393450-6). Macmillan.

Community Organization Efforts, Political & Institutional Change, & Diffusion of Change Produced by Community Action Programs. James J. Vanecko et al. (Report Ser: No. 122). 1970. 3.00x o.p. (ISBN 0-932132-14-6). NORC.

Community-Oriented Primary Care: From Principle to Practice. Paul Nutting. (HHS Publication HRSA HRS-A-PE: No. 86-1). (Illus.). 567p. 1987. pap. 16.00 o.p. (ISBN 0-317-62840-2, S-N 017-026-00107-7). USGPO.

Community Planning & Conceptions of Change: Dilemmas of Inner City Planning. Peter Marris. 208p. 1983. 21.95x o.p. (ISBN 0-7100-9349-7). Routledge Chapman & Hall.

Community Policing. Evelyn B. Schaffer. 145p. 1980. 25.00 o.p. (ISBN 0-85664-939-2, Pub. by Croom Helm Ltd). Routledge Chapman & Hall.

Community Problem Solving: The Delinquency Example. Irving Spergel. 1969. lib. bdg. 10.00x o.s.i. (ISBN 0-226-76930-5). U of Chicago Pr.

Community Property in a Nutshell. Robert L. Mennell. LC 82-11163. (Nutshell Ser.). 447p. 1982. pap. text ed. 10.95 o.p. (ISBN 0-314-66185-9). West Pub.

Community Psychiatric Nursing. P. J. Carr et al. (Illus.). 1980. pap. text ed. 15.75 o.p. (ISBN 0-443-01550-3). Churchill.

Community Psychology. M. P. Bender. (Essential Psychology Ser.). 1976. pap. 4.50x o.p. (ISBN 0-416-82330-0, NO.2611). Routledge Chapman & Hall.

Community Relations Kit. 134p. 1980. 15.00 o.p. (ISBN 0-318-14775-0). Lit Vol Am.

Community Research. Robert J. Havighurst & Anton J. Jansen. (Current Sociology. la Sociologie Contemporaine: No. 15, Pt. 2). pap. 9.20x o.p. (ISBN 90-2796-573-0). Mouton.

Community Response to Alcohol-Related Problems: World Health Organization Project Monograph. Irving Rootman & Joy Moser. (DHHS Publication ADM 85-1371). 186p. 1984. pap. 7.00 o.p. (ISBN 0-318-22485-2, S/N 017-024-01262-9). USGPO.

Community School. Maurice F. Seay. LC 53-1815. (National Society for the Study of Education Yearbooks Ser: No. 52, Pt. 2). 1953. lib. bdg. 6.50x o.s.i. (ISBN 0-226-60025-4). U of Chicago Pr.

Community Self-Help Housing Manual: Partnership in Action. rev. ed. Ed. by Robert W. Stevens & Ted Swisher. (Illus.). 120p. (Orig.). 1986. pap. 6.00x o.p. (ISBN 0-942850-05-X, Pub. by Intermed Tech England). Intermediate Tech.

Community Surveys with Local Talent: A Handbook. Eve Weinberg. (Report Ser: No. 123). 1971. 5.00x o.s.i. (ISBN 0-932132-15-4). NORC.

Community, Technical, & Junior College Directory. 1985. 25.00 o.p. (ISBN 0-317-40577-2). Am Assn Comm Jr Coll.

Community Versus Crime. Colin Moore & John Brown. (Illus.). 150p. 1981. text ed. 22.00x o.p. (ISBN 0-7199-1059-5, Pub. by Bedford England); pap. 12.95 o.p. Gower Pub Co.

Community Work & Racism. Ashok Ohri et al. (Community Work Ser.: No. 7). 168p. (Orig.). 1982. pap. 11.50x o.p. (ISBN 0-7100-9032-3). Routledge Chapman & Hall.

Community Work & the State: Towards a Radical Practice-Community Work Eight. Ed. by Gary Craig & Nick Derricourt. (Community Work Ser.). 176p. (Orig.). 1982. pap. 9.95x o.p. (ISBN 0-7100-9305-5). Routledge Chapman & Hall.

Community Work: One. David Jones & Marjorie Mayo. 1974. 18.95x o.p. (ISBN 0-7100-7709-2). Routledge Chapman & Hall.

Commutative Matrices. Dmitri A. Suprunenko & R. I. Tyshkevich. LC 68-18683. (Orig.). 1968. 37.50 o.p. (ISBN 0-12-677049-2); pap. 23.50 o.p. (ISBN 0-12-677050-6). Acad Pr.

Commuter Airlines: A Study of the History & Operational Requirements. James L. De Looff. 1979. 10.00 o.p. (ISBN 0-682-49315-5, University). Exposition-Phoenix.

Como Mantener Tu Volkswagen Vivo. rev. ed. John Muir. Tr. by Virginia Holt from Eng. LC 75-21414. (Illus., Orig.). 1980. pap. 10.00 o.p. (ISBN 0-912528-21-4). John Muir.

Como Se Desarrolla la Sociedad. E. Plimak & A. Volodin. 166p. 1985. pap. 1.45 o.p. (ISBN 0-317-47695-5, Pub. by Progress Pubs USSR). Imported Pubns.

Comp-Lab Exercises: Self-Teaching Exercises for Basic Writing. Mary Epes et al. 1980. pap. text ed. (ISBN 0-13-153601-X). P-H.

Compact Audio Disc: Understanding the New Digital Technology. Heitaro Nakajima & Hiroshi Ogawa. (Illus.). 240p. 1988. 22.95 o.p. (ISBN 0-8306-0149-X); pap. 14.95 o.p. (ISBN 0-8306-2949-1). TAB Bks.

Compact Bible Atlas with Gazetteer. (Illus.). 1979. pap. 4.95 o.p. (ISBN 0-8010-2432-3). Baker Bk.

Compact Guide to Colleges. 4th ed. Samuel C. Brownstein & Mitchel Weiner. 1984. pap. 3.95 o.p. (ISBN 0-8120-2826-0). Barron.

Compact Heat Exchangers. 2nd ed. William M. Kays & A. L. London. (Mechanical Engineering Ser.). 1964. text ed. 42.50 o.p. (ISBN 0-07-033391-2). McGraw.

Compact Heat Exchangers: HTD-Vol. 10. Ed. by R Shah. 200p. 1980. 30.00 o.p. (ISBN 0-317-33456-5, G00183); 15.00 o.p. (ISBN 0-317-33457-3). ASME.

Compact History of Civil War. rep. ed. R. E. Dupuy & T. N. Dupuy. (Illus.). 446p. pap. 13.95 o.p. (ISBN 0-915979-13-6). Hero Books.

Compact House Book: Thirty-Three Prize Winning Designs one thousand square feet or less. Ed. by Don Metz. (Illus.). 200p. (Orig.). 1988. pap. 14.95 o.p. (ISBN 0-88266-323-2, Garden Way Pub); 27.95 o.p. (ISBN 0-88266-351-8). Storey Comm Inc.

Compact Semitopological Semigroups & Weakly Almost Periodic Functions. J. F. Berglund & K. H. Hoffmann. (Lecture Notes in Mathematics: Vol. 42). (Orig.). 1967. pap. 10.90 o.p. (ISBN 0-387-03913-9). Springer-Verlag.

Compaction Technology. (Conference Proceedings Ser.). 177p. 1988. 54.00 o.p. (ISBN 0-7277-1338-8). Am Soc Civil Eng.

Companion Guide to London. David Piper. (Illus.). 520p. 1983. 16.95 o.p. (ISBN 0-13-154542-6); pap. 12.95 o.p. (ISBN 0-13-154534-5). P-H.

Companion Guide to New York. Michael Leapman. (Illus.). 337p. 1983. 15.95 o.p. (ISBN 0-13-154682-1); pap. 7.95 o.p. (ISBN 0-13-154674-0). P-H.

Companion to Chinese History. Hugh B. O'Neill. LC 83-11685. 397p. 1987. 24.95 o.p. (ISBN 0-87196-841-X); pap. write for info. o.p. Facts on File.

Companion to Narnia, a Complete Illustrated Guide to the Themes, Characters & Events of C. S. Lewis Imaginary World. Paul F. Ford. LC 80-7734. (Illus.). 304p. 1980. 14.95i o.p. (ISBN 0-06-250340-5). HarpR.

Companion to the Roots of Modern English. 2nd ed. Richard L. Hoffman & L. M. Myers. 1979. pap. 16.50 o.p. (ISBN 0-316-36836-9). Scott F.

Companion to the Summa, 4 vols. Walter Farrell. 1985. Set. pap. 65.00 o.p. (ISBN 0-87061-117-8). Chr Classics.

Companions along the Way. Ruth Montgomery. 256p. 1986. pap. 3.50 o.p. (ISBN 0-449-20671-8, Crest). Fawcett.

Companions of the Unseen. Paul Tabori. LC 68-18756. (Illus.). 220p. 1968. 5.95 o.p. (ISBN 0-8216-0062-1, Pub. by Univ Bks). Carol Pub Group.

Company. Samuel Beckett. LC 80-995. 64p. 1981. pap. 8.95 o.p. (ISBN 0-394-17928-5, E-781, Ever). Grove.

Company Accounts. 2nd ed. J. O. Magee. 386p. 1978. pap. 22.00x o.p. (ISBN 0-7121-0384-8, Pub. by Macdonald & Evans England). Trans-Atl Phila.

Company Accounts. 3rd ed. J. O. Magee. 441p. 1984. pap. 22.00x o.p. (ISBN 0-7121-0470-4). Trans-Atl Phila.

Company Auditing U. K. 2nd ed. Lee. 1982. pap. 23.95 o.p. (ISBN 0-85258-221-8). Van Nos Reinhold.

Company Commander. rev. ed. Charles B. Macdonald. 15.95 o.p. (ISBN 0-89201-059-2). Zenger Pub.

Company K. William March. LC 57-9761. (Library of Contemporary Americana). 192p. 1984. pap. 6.95 o.p. (ISBN 0-87795-647-2, Arbor Hse). Morrow.

Company Law Study Book. T. Martyn. 1983. pap. 12.95 o.p. (ISBN 0-85258-174-2). Van Nos Reinhold.

Company Manners: An Insider Tells How to Succeed in the Real World of Corporate Protocol & Power Politics. Lois Wyse. 304p. 1986. text ed. 16.95 o.p. (ISBN 0-07-072193-9). McGraw.

Company She Keeps. Mary McCarthy. 224p. 1981. pap. 3.50 o.p. (ISBN 0-380-55509-3, 55509-3, Bard). Avon.

Company She Keeps. Mary McCarthy. LC 60-3858. 1960. 7.50 o.p. (ISBN 0-15-120357-1). HarBraceJ.

Company Shops: The Town Built by a Railroad. Durward T. Stokes. LC 81-18167. 169p. 1981. 4.98 o.p. (ISBN 0-89587-016-9). Blair.

Company Tax Systems in OECD Member Countries. Organization for Economic Cooperation & Development Staff. 142p. 1973. 5.00x o.p. (ISBN 92-64-11125-5). OECD.

Company Wide Quality Control: Questions & Answers. Robert G. Tate, Jr. (Illus.). 18p. 1984. pap. 4.25 o.p. (ISBN 0-937670-32-4). Quality Circle.

Compaq Portable Computer: Use, Applications & BASIC. William Arnold. LC 84-19219. 1985. pap. text ed. 18.45 o.p. (ISBN 0-03-064119-5). HR&W.
Compaq Portable Computer User's Guide. Larry J. Goldstein & Joseph K. Rensin. LC 83-17140. (Illus.). 400p. 1983. pap. 18.95 o.p. (ISBN 0-89303-389-8). Brady Bks.
Compaq Users Handbook. Louis E. Fregel, Jr. & Louis E. Fregel. LC 84-50647. 1984. pap. 15.95 o.p. (ISBN 0-672-22037-7). Sams.
Compaq User's Handbook. Weber Systems, Inc. Staff. LC 84-2255. (WSI's How to Use Your Personal Computer Ser.). 350p. (gr. 9-12). 1983. pap. 15.95 o.p. (ISBN 0-938862-11-1). Weber Systems.
Comparability of Degrees & Diplomas in International Law: A Study of the Structural & Functional Aspects. Rene J. Dupuy & Gregory Tunkin. (Studies on the Evaluation of Qualifications at the Higher Education Level). 75p. (Orig.). 1973. pap. 5.00 o.p. (ISBN 92-3-101057-3, U94, UNESCO). UNIPUB.
Comparable Work & Equal Pay: A Bibliography. Anthony G. White. (Public Administration Ser.: Bibliography P 1650). 1985. pap. 2.25 o.p. (ISBN 0-89028-340-0). Vance Biblios.
Comparable Worth & Public Policy: The Case of Pennsylvania. Suzanne M. Perrin. LC 85-51721. (Labor Relations & Public Policy Ser.). 123p. 1985. pap. 15.00 o.p. (ISBN 0-89546-058-0). Indus Res Unit-Wharton.
Comparative Analysis of Traffic Assignment Techniques with Actual Highway Use. (National Cooperative Highway Research Program Report). 85p. 1968. 3.60 o.p. (ISBN 0-317-36070-1, 1712). Transport Res Bd.
Comparative Anatomy of Domestic Animals: A Guide. Bonnie Beaver. (Illus.). 210p. 1980. pap. 13.50x o.p. (ISBN 0-8138-1545-2). Iowa St U Pr.
Comparative Anatomy of the Vertebrates. 5th ed. George C. Kent. LC 82-2078. (Illus.). 604p. 1982. 33.95 o.p. (ISBN 0-8016-2651-X). Mosby.
Comparative Biochemistry & Physiology of Enzymatic Digestion. Ed. by Hubertus J. Vonk & Richard H. Western. 1984. 124.00 o.p. (ISBN 0-12-727850-8). Acad Pr.
Comparative Biochemistry of Flavonoids. Ed. by Jeffrey B. Harborne. 1967. 65.00 o.p. (ISBN 0-12-324650-4). Acad Pr.
Comparative Biochemistry of Nitrogen Metabolism, Vols. 1 & 2. Ed. by J. W. Campbell. 1970. Vol. 1. 77.50 o.p. (ISBN 0-12-157901-8); Vol. 2. 64.50 o.p. (ISBN 0-12-157902-6). Acad Pr.
Comparative Biochemistry of Parasites. Ed. by Van Den Bossche. 1972. 74.50 o.p. (ISBN 0-12-711050-X). Acad Pr.
Comparative Biochemistry of Photoreactive Systems. Ed. by Mary B. Allen. 1960. 79.00 o.p. (ISBN 0-12-051750-7). Acad Pr.
Comparative Communist Political Leadership. Carl Beck et al. LC 72-75454. (Comparative Studies of Political Life Ser.). 1973. text ed. 14.95x o.p. (ISBN 0-679-30031-7, Pub. by MacKay). Longman.
Comparative Cranial Myology of North American Natricine Snakes. Alexander Varkey. (Publications in Biology & Geology Ser.: No. 4). 76p. 1979. 7.50 o.p. (ISBN 0-89326-035-5). Milwaukee Pub Mus.
Comparative Cultural Analysis: An Introduction to Anthropology. 2nd ed. Keith Otterbein. LC 76-47694. 1977. text ed. 15.95 o.p. (ISBN 0-03-089991-5, HoltC). HR&W.
Comparative Diagnosis of Viral Diseases: Human & Related Viruses, Vol. 1 A. E. Kurstak & Christine Kurstak. 1978. 117.00 o.p. (ISBN 0-12-429701-3). Acad Pr.
Comparative Diagnosis of Viral Diseases, Vol. 2 B. E. Kurstak & Christine Kurstak. 1977. 84.00 o.p. (ISBN 0-12-429702-1). Acad Pr.
Comparative Diagnosis of Viral Diseases, Vol. 3: Vertebrate Animal & Related Viruses, DNA Viruses, Vol. 3 Part A. Ed. by E. Kurstak & C. Kurstak. LC 81-7951. 1981. 78.00 o.p. (ISBN 0-12-429703-X) (ISBN 0-686-85518-3). Acad Pr.
Comparative Diagnosis of Viral Diseases, Vol. 4: Vertebrate Animal & Related Viruses, Part B-BNA Viruses, Vol. 4, Part B. Ed. by E. Kurstak & C. Kurstak. LC 81-7951. 1981. 103.50 o.p. (ISBN 0-12-429704-8). Acad Pr.
Comparative Dismissal Law. Ed. by B. W. Napier et al. 175p. 1982. 27.00 o.p. (ISBN 0-7099-1808-9, Pub. by Croom Helm Ltd). Routledge Chapman & Hall.
Comparative Document on the Legislation in Force in the American States in Regard to Family Law. Inter-American Commission of Women Assembly. LC 82-134100. 68p. 1976. write for info. o.p. OAS.
Comparative Ecology & Behaviour of Primates. Ed. by Richard P. Michael & John H. Crook. 1973. 138.00 o.p. (ISBN 0-12-493450-1). Acad Pr.
Comparative Ecology of Two Colubrid Snakes, Masticophis T. Taeniatus & Pituophis Melanolucus Deserticola in Northern Utah. William S. Parker & William S. Brown. (Publications in Biology & Geology Ser.: No. 7). 104p. 1980. 9.95 o.p. (ISBN 0-89326-058-4). Milwaukee Pub Mus.
Comparative Economic Systems. 2nd ed. John E. Elliott. 495p. 1985. text ed. (ISBN 0-534-01313-9). Wadsworth Pub.
Comparative Economic Systems. Paul R. Gregory & Robert C. Stuart. LC 79-87859. 1980. text ed. 29.50 o.p. (ISBN 0-395-28183-0). HM.
Comparative Economic Systems. 2nd ed. Paul R. Gregory & Robert C. Stuart. LC 84-80474. 450p. 1985. text ed. 41.16 o.p. (ISBN 0-395-34241-4). HM.
Comparative Economic Systems: Competing Ways to Stability, Growth & Welfare. 2nd ed. Allan G. Gruchy. LC 76-10899. (Illus.). 1977. text ed. 43.96 o.p. (ISBN 0-395-18606-4). HM.
Comparative Economic Systems: Models & Cases. 5th ed. Ed. by Morris Bornstein. 1985. 29.95x o.p. (ISBN 0-256-03215-7). Irwin.
Comparative Education. Phillip G. Altbach et al. 1982. text ed. write for info. o.p. (ISBN 0-02-301920-4). Macmillan.
Comparative Endocrinology of Prolactin. D. M. Ensor. 1978. 53.00 o.p. (ISBN 0-412-12720-2, NO.6103, Pub. by Chapman & Hall). Routledge Chapman & Hall.
Comparative Enzyme Histochemical Observations on Submammalian Brains. K. F. Baker-Cohen. Incl. Pt. 1: Striatal Structures in Reptiles & Birds; Pt. 2: Basal Structures of the Brainstem in Reptiles & Birds. (Advances in Anatomy: Vol. 40, Pt. 6). (Illus.). 70p. 1968. pap. 18.90 o.p. (ISBN 0-387-04090-0). Springer-Verlag.
Comparative Higher Education: Research Trends & Bibliography. Philip G. Altbach. 218p. 1979. 31.00x o.p. (ISBN 0-7201-0825-X). Mansell.
Comparative Historical Analysis of Three Associations of Professional Schools. Donald G. Davis, Jr. (Occasional Papers: No. 115). 39p. 1974. pap. 2.00 o.p. (ISBN 0-317-58918-0). U of Ill Lib Info Sci.
Comparative History of Metrology. Ed. by H. J. Griffin. 1983. 30.00 o.p. Mansell.
Comparative Legal Cultures. Henry W. Ehrmann. 176p. 1976. pap. text ed. (ISBN 0-13-153858-6). P-H.
Comparative Literature: Method & Perspective. rev. ed. Ed. by Newton P. Stallknecht & Horst Frenz. LC 71-83780. 384p. 1971. 7.95x o.p. (ISBN 0-8093-0046-X). S Ill U Pr.
Comparative Methods in the Social Science. Neil J. Smelser. LC 75-42020. (Illus.). 272p. 1976. pap. text ed. (ISBN 0-13-154138-2). P-H.
Comparative Morphology & Biology of the Fungi, Mycetozoa, & Bacteria. Anton De Bary. Ed. by I. B. Balfour. Tr. by E. H. Garnsey. Repr. of 1887 ed. 50.00 o.p. (ISBN 0-384-11145-9). Johnson Repr.
Comparative Negligence Defense Tactics. James G. McConnell. LC 84-28423. 242p. 1985. Annual supplements avail. 75.00 o.p. (ISBN 0-471-89165-7). Wiley.
Comparative Nutrition of Man & Domestic Animals, Vol. 2. Harold H. Mitchell. 1964. 63.50 o.p. (ISBN 0-12-499602-7). Acad Pr.
Comparative Organellography of the Cytoplasm. A. Frey-Wyssling. (Protoplasmatologia: Vol. 3g). (Illus.). vii, 106p. 1973. 31.30 o.p. (ISBN 0-387-81139-7). Springer-Verlag.
Comparative Physiology of Desert Animals: Proceedings of the Zoological Society of London Symposium, 31st. Zoological Society of London Symposium Staff. Ed. by C. M. O. Maloiy & W. V. MacFarlane. 1973. 88.00 o.p. (ISBN 0-12-613331-X). Acad Pr.
Comparative Physiology of Osmoregulation in Animals, Vol. I. Ed. by G. M. Maloiy. 1979. 134.00 o.p. (ISBN 0-12-467001-6). Acad Pr.
Comparative Physiology of Osmoregulation in Animals, Vol. 2. Ed. by G. W. Maloiy. LC 77-93492. 1980. 69.00 o.p. (ISBN 0-12-467002-4). Acad Pr.
Comparative Physiology of Thermoregulation. Ed. by G. Causey Whittow. LC 79-107580. Vol.1. 1970. 71.50 o.p. (ISBN 0-12-747601-6); Vol.2. 1971. 72.50 o.p. (ISBN 0-12-747602-4); Vol. 3. 1973. 57.50 o.p. (ISBN 0-12-747603-2). Acad Pr.
Comparative Planetology. Ed. by Cyril Ponnamperuma. 1978. 41.00 o.p. (ISBN 0-12-561340-7). Acad Pr.
Comparative Politics: System, Process, & Policy. 2nd ed. Gabriel A. Almond & G. Bingham Powell, Jr. (Little, Brown Series in Comparative Politics). 435p. 1978. pap. text ed. 18.75 o.p. Scott F.
Comparative Politics 1988-89. 6th, rev. ed. Ed. by Christian Soe. LC 83-647654. (Annual Editions Ser.). (Illus.). 288p. 1988. pap. text ed. 9.95x o.p. (ISBN 0-87967-735-X). Dushkin Pub.
Comparative Psychology in the Twentieth Century. Donald Dewsbury. 1983. 39.95 o.p. (ISBN 0-87933-108-9). Van Nos Reinhold.
Comparative Public Policy & Citizen Participation: Energy, Education, Health & Local Governance in the U. S. A. & Germany. Ed. by Charles R. Foster. (Pergamon Policy Studies). 1980. 53.00 o.p. (ISBN 0-08-024624-9). Pergamon.
Comparative Regional Systems: West & East Europe, North America, the Middle East & Developing Countries. Ed. by Werner Feld & Gavin Boyd. (Pergamon Policy Studies). 1980. 78.00 o.p. (ISBN 0-08-023358-9); pap. 135.00 o.p. (ISBN 0-08-023357-0). Pergamon.
Comparative Religious Ethics. David Little & Sumner B. Twiss, Jr. LC 76-10003. (Illus.). 1978. 10.95ixi o.p. (ISBN 0-06-065254-3). HarpR.
Comparative Religious Scripture. J. Stern. Date not set. 9.95 o.p. Ktav.
Comparative Research on Education: Overview, Strategy & Applications in Eastern & Western Europe. Ed. by M. Niessen & J. Peschar. (Vienna Century Ser.). 281p. 1982. 75.00 o.p. (ISBN 0-08-027934-1). Pergamon.
Comparative Sociology. Marsh. 1967. text ed. 15.95 o.p. (ISBN 0-15-512401-3, HC). HarBraceJ.
Comparative Spermatology. Ed. by Baccio Baccetti. 1971. 104.00 o.p. (ISBN 0-12-069950-8). Acad Pr.
Comparative Statutory Sources. 2nd ed. J. S. Schultz. LC 78-60176. xxxv, 68p. 1978. lib. bdg. 30.00 o.p. (ISBN 0-930342-62-3). W S Hein.
Comparative Structure & Function of Muscle. Henry Huddart. 1975. 85.00 o.p. (ISBN 0-08-017845-6). Pergamon.
Comparative Studies in Community Property Law. Ed. by Jan P. Charmatz & Harriet S. Daggett. LC 77-1740. ix, 190p. 1977. Repr. of 1955 ed. lib. bdg. 35.00x o.p. (ISBN 0-8371-9523-3, CHCST). Greenwood.
Comparative Studies in Folklore: Asia, Europe, America. Archer Taylor. (Asian Folklore & Social Life Monograph: No. 41). 454p. 1972. 22.00x o.p. (ISBN 0-89986-040-0). Oriental Bk Store.
Comparative Studies of Blacks & Whites in the United States. Ed. by Kent S. Miller & Ralph M. Dreger. LC 72-82126. (Quantitative Studies in Social Relations Ser). 1973. 65.50 o.p. (ISBN 0-12-785526-2). Acad Pr.
Comparative Study of Politics. David Roth & Frank L. Wilson. LC 75-31002. (Illus.). 512p. 1976. text ed. 18.50 o.p. (ISBN 0-395-20103-9). HM.
Comparative Study of Politics. 2nd ed. David Roth & Frank L. Wilson. (Illus.). 1980. text ed. (ISBN 0-13-154237-0). P-H.
Comparative Study of the Management & Organization of Irrigation Projects. Anthony F. Bottrall. (Working Paper Ser.: No. 458). 274p. 15.00 o.p. (ISBN 0-8213-9317-0, WP 0458). World Bank.
Comparative View of the Roles of Women & Men. Barbar Miller et al. (Illus.). 265p. (Orig.). (gr. 6-12). 1982. pap. 16.95 o.p. (ISBN 0-943804-14-0). U of Denver Teach.
Comparative Virology. Ed. by Karl Maramorosch & E. Kurstak. 552p. 1971. 92.00 o.p. (ISBN 0-12-470260-0). Acad Pr.
Comparative World Issues for Grades One to Twelve. Steven L. Lamy et al. (Illus.). 189p. (Orig.). 1981. pap. 16.95 o.p. (ISBN 0-686-48250-6). U of Denver Teach.
Comparing Strategies for Reducing Traffic Related Problems: The Potential for Road Pricing. Thomas Higgins. 40p. (Orig.). 1978. pap. text ed. 6.00x o.p. (ISBN 0-87766-227-4). Urban Inst.
Comparison Between Counselling & Analysis. Joan Mance. 1985. 10.00x o.p. (ISBN 0-317-62016-9, Guild of Pastoral Psych). State Mutual Bk.
Comparison of Box-Jenkins & Bonn Monetary Prediction Performance. M. N. Bhattacharyya. (Lecture Notes in Economics & Mathematical Systems Ser.: Vol. 178). (Illus.). 146p. 1980. pap. 18.00 o.p. (ISBN 0-387-10011-3). Springer-Verlag.
Comparison of Panizzi's 91 Rules & the AACR of 1967. Donald J. Lehnus. (Occasional Papers: No. 105). 39p. 1972. pap. 2.00 o.p. (ISBN 0-317-58887-7). U of Ill Lib Info Sci.
Comparison of the Experimental Housing Allowance Program & Great Britain's Rent Allowance Program. John Trutko et al. 52p. 1978. pap. 10.00x o.p. (ISBN 0-87766-222-3, 22500). Urban Inst.
Comparison of the Reading Interests of Kankakee Senior High School Students with Those Revealed in Nationwide Surveys. J. F. Borowski. (Occasional Papers: No. 92). 29p. 1968. pap. 1.00 o.p. (ISBN 0-317-58869-9). U of Ill Lib Info Sci.
Compass of Irony. D. C. Muecke. 276p. 1983. 49.95 o.p. (ISBN 0-416-74360-9, NO. 2670). Routledge Chapman & Hall.
Compass Rose. Ursula K. Le Guin. 288p. pap. 3.50 o.s.i. (ISBN 0-553-23512-5). Bantam.
Compass Stone. Fernando Arrabal. Tr. by Andrew Hurley from Span. LC 87-12120. 192p. 1987. 16.95 o.s.i. (ISBN 0-8021-0002-3). Grove.
Compassion & Self-Hate. Theodore I. Rubin. 228p. 1976. pap. 2.75 o.p. (ISBN 0-345-29475-0). Ballantine.
Compassion: Life Maps. Chuck Swindoll. 64p. 1984. 5.95 o.p. (ISBN 0-8499-0443-9, 0443-9). Word Bks.
Compassionate Peace: A Future for the Middle East. American Friends Service Committee. (Illus.). 242p. 1982. 13.95 o.p. (ISBN 0-8090-3575-8); pap. 6.95 o.p. (ISBN 0-8090-1399-1). Hill & Wang.
Compelling Selling. Philip R. Lund. (Executive Bks.). 238p. 1978. pap. 9.95 o.p. (ISBN 0-8144-7506-X). AMACOM.
Compelling Selling: A Framework for Persuasion. 1979 ed. Philip R. Lund. 234p. text ed. 38.95x o.p. Gower Pub Co.
Compendium - Questions & Suggested Solutions: Certified Internal Auditor Examinations 1980 Through 1983. Institute of Internal Auditors Inc., Board of Regents Staff. (Illus.). 364p. 1984. pap. text ed. 21.50 o.p. (ISBN 0-89413-127-3). Inst Inter Aud.
Compendium of Communication & Broadcast Satellites 1958-1980. Ed. by Martin P. Jr. Brown. LC 81-81858. 392p. cancelled o.s.i. (ISBN 0-87942-153-3, PC01461). Inst Electrical.
Compendium of Design Features to Reduce Occupational Radiaton Exposure at Nuclear Power Plants. Paul J. Pettit. (National Environmental Studies Project: NESP Reports). 61p. 1981. 20.00 o.p. (ISBN 0-318-13563-9, AIF-NESP-020); NESP sponsors 10.00 o.p. (ISBN 0-318-13564-7). US Coun Energy Awareness.
Compendium of Immunology, 3 Vols. Schwartz. 1984. Set. 129.95 o.p. (ISBN 0-442-28054-8). Van Nos Reinhold.
Compendium of Immunology, Vol. II. 2nd ed. Schwartz. 1981. 52.95 o.p. (ISBN 0-442-26708-8). Van Nos Reinhold.
Compendium of Immunology, Vol. III. Ed. by Lazar M. Schwartz. (Illus.). 688p. 1983. 57.95 o.p. (ISBN 0-442-28107-2). Van Nos Reinhold.
Compendium of Immunology, Vol.1. 2nd ed. Lazar M. Schwartz. 515p. 1979. 44.95 o.p. (ISBN 0-442-27472-6). Van Nos Reinhold.
Compendium of Placement-Related Literature. David Vandergoot & Pamela B. Avellani. LC 78-62048. 352p. 1978. 9.25 o.p. (ISBN 0-686-43001-8). Human Res Ctr.
Compensating Auto Accident Victims: A Follow-Up Report on No-Fault Auto Insurance Experiences. (DOT-P-30-84-20 Ser.). (Illus.). 166p. (Orig.). 1985. pap. 6.50 o.p. (ISBN 0-318-11764-9, S/N 050-000-00507-1). USGPO.
Compensation. Rev. ed. Robert E. Sibson. 288p. 1981. 18.95 o.p. (ISBN 0-8144-5654-5). AMACOM.
Compensation Administration. reference ed. David W. Belcher. (Industrial Relations & Personnel Ser.). (Illus.). 576p. 1974. pap. text ed. 36.33 o.p. (ISBN 0-13-154161-7). P-H.
Compensation Eighty-Four: Annual Report on Local Government Executive Salaries & Fringe Benefits. International City Management Association Staff. (Illus.). 298p. 1984. 100.00 o.p. (ISBN 0-87326-990-X). Intl City Mgt.
Compensation for Librarians: A Checklist of Materials. Donna H. Chen. (Public Administration Ser.: P 1681). 7p. 1985. 2.00 o.p. (ISBN 0-89028-411-3). Vance Biblios.
Compensation Report on Hospital-Based Physicians, 1984-85. Zabka, John R., Associates Inc. Staff. (Annual Report Ser.). 105.00 o.p. (ISBN 0-939326-15-9). Hosp Compensation.
Compensations of War: The Diary of an Ambulance Driver during the Great War. Guy E. Bowerman, Jr. Ed. by Mark C. Carnes. LC 82-23846. (Illus.). 200p. 1983. 12.50 o.p. (ISBN 0-292-71074-7). U of Tex Pr.
Compensatory Renal Hypertrophy. Ed. by W. W. Nowinski & R. J. Goss. 1970. 64.00 o.p. (ISBN 0-12-522750-7). Acad Pr.
Compete: A Dynamic Marketing Simulation. 3rd ed. A. J. Faria et al. 1984. 18.95 o.p. (ISBN 0-256-03060-X). Irwin.
Compete: A Dynamic Marketing Simulation. rev. ed. Anthony J. Faria et al. 1979. pap. 8.50x o.p. (ISBN 0-256-02077-9). Irwin.
Competence: A Continuum. P. Willes. 1971. pap. text ed. 8.95x o.p. (ISBN 0-8422-0143-2). Irvington.
Competence: Inquiries into Its Meaning & Acquisition in Educational Settings. Ed. by Edmund C. Short. 192p. (Orig.). 1984. lib. bdg. 24.50 o.p. (ISBN 0-8191-3995-5); pap. text ed. 12.00 o.p. (ISBN 0-8191-3996-3). U Pr of Amer.

Competency Based Education Sourcebook. 2nd ed. Oregon Competencies Program Northwest Regional Educ. Lab. Staff. 752p. 1978. 28.50 o.p. (ISBN 0-89354-104-4). Northwest Regional.

Competency Based Learning: Management, Technology, & Design. Ivor K. Davies. Orig. Title: Management of Learning. 254p. 1973. text ed. 40.95 o.p. (ISBN 0-07-084420-8). McGraw.

Competition & Collaboration in Renewable Energy. 1983. 27.50 o.p. (ISBN 0-905347-48-X). C I D E.

Competition & Human Behavior. Chester R. Wasson et al. LC 68-16463. (Illus., Orig.). 1968. pap. text ed. 4.95x o.p. (ISBN 0-89197-100-9). Irvington.

Competition & Industrial Policy in the European Economic Community. Dennis Swann. LC 83-13061. (Methuen's EEC Ser.). (Illus.). 200p. 1983. 25.00 o.p. (ISBN 0-416-32410-X, NO. 3915); pap. 11.95 o.p. (ISBN 0-416-32420-7, NO. 3916). Routledge Chapman & Hall.

Competition Between Legumes & Grasses. (Agricultural Research Reports: No. 687). 1966. pap. 4.00 o.p. (PDC166, PUDOC). UNIPUB.

Competition Course in Speech. Roger A. Emmert. LC 73-91095. 1974. 3.50 o.p. (ISBN 0-682-47850-4, University). Exposition-Phoenix.

Competition in Australian Bookselling: Resale Price Maintenance & After. J. P. Nieuwenhuysen. (Illus.). 96p. 1975. pap. 8.50x o.p. (ISBN 0-522-84081-7, Pub. by Melbourne U Pr). Intl Spec Bk.

Competition in the General-Freight Motor-Carrier Industry. Annette M. LaMond. LC 79-3048. 128p. 1980. 25.00x o.p. (ISBN 0-669-03308-1). Lexington Bks.

Competition in the Local Exchange Telephone Service Market. Alfred Lee & Timothy Sloan. (NTIA Report 87-210). (Illus.). 57p. (Orig.). 1987. pap. 3.00 o.p. (ISBN 0-318-22646-4, S/N 003-000-00647-6). USGPO.

Competition Rules for Athletics. 1988. 8.00 o.p. Athletics Cong.

Competition Rules for Athletics: 1988. 8.00 o.p. Athletics Cong.

Competitive Assessment of the United States Ball & Roller Bearings Industry. (Competitive Assessment Ser.). (Illus.). 88p. (Orig.). 1985. pap. 3.25 o.p. (ISBN 0-318-22456-9, S/N 003-009-00453-5). USGPO.

Competitive Assessment of the United States Computer-Aided Design & Manufacturing Systems Industry. (Competitive Assessment Ser.). 69p. (Orig.). 1987. pap. 3.50 o.p. (ISBN 0-318-22645-6, S/N 003-009-00498-5). USGPO.

Competitive Assessment of the United States Disk Storage Industry. (Illus.). 67p. (Orig.). 1985. pap. 2.50 o.p. (ISBN 0-318-18737-X, S/N 003-009-00461-6). USGPO.

Competitive Assessment of the United States Flexible Manufacturing Systems Industry. (Competitive Assessment Ser.). (Illus.). 136p. (Orig.). 1985. pap. 4.75 o.p. (ISBN 0-318-18736-1, S/N 003-009-00464-1). USGPO.

Competitive Assessment of the United States General Aviation Aircraft Industry. (Competitive Assessment Ser.). (Illus.). 89p. pap. 4.25 o.p. (ISBN 0-318-21365-6, S/N 003-009-00484-5). USGPO.

Competitive Assessment of the United States Manufacturing Automation Equipment Industries. (Illus.). 111p. (Orig.). 1984. pap. 4.50 o.p. (ISBN 0-318-21939-5, 003-009-00432-2). USGPO.

Competitive Assessment of the United States Nitrogen Fertilizer Industry. (Competitive Assessment Ser.). (Illus.). 107p. (Orig.). 1986. pap. 5.00 o.p. (S/N 003-009-00493-4). USGPO.

Competitive Assessment of the United States Robotics Industry. (Competitive Assessment Ser.). 99p. (Orig.). 1987. pap. 4.75 o.p. (ISBN 0-318-22755-X, S/N 003-009-00499-3). USGPO.

Competitive Challenges Facing the Mortgage Banking Industry in the 80's. 1983. 20.00 o.p. (ISBN 0-318-03603-7). Mortgage Bankers.

Competitive Employment: New Horizons for Severely Disabled Individuals. Paul Wehman. LC 80-24926. (Illus.). 276p. (Orig.). 1981. pap. text ed. 18.50 o.p. (ISBN 0-933716-12-5, 125). P H Brookes.

Competitive Fitness: Featuring the Officially Licensed Fitness Program of the XIV Olympic Winter Games. Blair Walliser. (Orig.). 1984. pap. 7.70 o.p. (ISBN 0-671-49800-2). S&S.

Competitive Marketing Strategies: An Alexander Hamilton Book. James W. Taylor. LC 85-21263. (Better Business Ser.). 190p. 1986. 35.00 o.p. (ISBN 0-8019-7697-9); pap. 19.95 o.p. (ISBN 0-8019-7698-7). Chilton.

Competitive Status of the U. S. Ferrous Metals Industry. 1983. pap. 9.95 o.p. Natl Acad Pr.

Competitive Strategy for Health Care Organizations. Alan Sheldon & Susan R. Windham. LC 83-73089. 200p. 1984. 35.00 o.p. (ISBN 0-87094-501-7). Dow Jones-Irwin.

Competitive Strength of European, Japanese, & U. S. Suppliers on Asian Markets. Ulrich Hiemenz et al. iv, 160p. 1988. 55.00x o.p. (ISBN 3-16-345284-1, Pub. by J C B Mohr BRD). Coronet Bks.

Competitive Structure of the International Banking Industry. Seung H. Kim & Stephen W. Miller. Ed. by Alfred F. Miossi. LC 81-47970. 256p. 1983. 32.00x o.p. (ISBN 0-669-05189-6). Lexington Bks.

Competitive Swimming for New Champions. Don Van Rossen & Barbara Woodrich. (Illus.). (gr. 6 up). 1978. text ed. 8.95 o.p. (ISBN 0-07-067150-8). McGraw.

Competitive Tendering for Engineering Contracts. M. Horgan. LC 83-14494. 250p. 1984. 35.00x o.p. (ISBN 0-419-11630-3, NO. 6841). Routledge Chapman & Hall.

Compilation & Analysis of Data on Occupational Radiation Exposure Experienced at Operating Nuclear Power Plants (AIF NESP-005) SAI Services, Inc. (National Environmental Studies Project: NESP Reports). 105p. 1975. 7.00 o.p. (ISBN 0-318-13565-5); to NESP sponsors 7.00 o.p. (ISBN 0-318-13566-3). US Coun Energy Awareness.

Compiler Design & Construction. Arthur B. Pyster. (Electrical-Computer Science & Engineering Ser.). 384p. 1980. 28.95 o.p. (ISBN 0-442-24394-4). Van Nos Reinhold.

Compiler Design & Construction. Arthur B. Pyster. 357p. 1983. pap. text ed. write for info. o.p. (ISBN 0-87150-428-6, 8060). PWS-Kent Pub.

COMPINT 85: Computer Aided Technologies, Proceedings. LC 84-62804. 820p. 1985. 70.00 o.p. (ISBN 0-8186-0621-5, Q621); microfiche 70.00 o.p. (ISBN 0-8186-4621-7). IEEE Comp Soc.

Compleat Angler. Isaak Walton. 1986. 29.75X o.p. (Pub. by Harrap Ltd England). State Mutual Bk.

Compleat Angler's Catalog: A Sourcebook for Fly Fishermen. Scott Roederer. LC 85-80407. (Illus.). 360p. (Orig.). 1985. pap. 14.95 o.p. (ISBN 0-933472-93-5). Johnson Bks.

Compleat Enchanter. L. Sprague De Camp & Fletcher Pratt. 416p. (Orig.). 1984. pap. 2.95 o.s.i. (ISBN 0-345-31435-2). Ballantine.

Compleat Horseman. Gervase Markham. Ed. by Dan Lucid. LC 75-8544. 1975. 6.95 o.p. (ISBN 0-395-21499-8). HM.

Compleat Mana. McGraw.

Compleat Strategyst. rev. ed. John D. Williams. 1965. text ed. 22.95 o.p. (ISBN 0-07-070396-5). McGraw.

Compleat Violinist. Yehudi Menuhin. 1986. 15.45 o.s.i. (ISBN 0-671-61294-8). Summit Bks.

Complementary Definitions of Programming Language Semantics. J. E. Donahue. (Lecture Notes in Computer Science Ser.: Vol. 42). 1976. pap. 11.00 o.p. (ISBN 0-387-07628-X). Springer-Verlag.

Complete Acolyte. W. Ellwood Post. 1978. 1.95 o.p. (ISBN 0-8192-1241-5). Morehouse Pub.

Complete & Easy Guide to Social Security & Medicare. rev. ed. Faustin F. Jehle. 175p. (Orig.). 1985. pap. 7.95 o.p. (ISBN 0-930045-00-9). Fraser Inc.

Complete & Easy Guide to Social Security & Medicare. rev. ed. Faustin F. Jehle. 178p. (Orig.). 1986. pap. 8.95 o.p. (ISBN 0-930045-01-7). Fraser Inc.

Complete Art of Breaking. Richard Bryne. Ed. by Mike Lee. (Specialties Ser.). 128p. 1984. pap. 7.95 o.p. (ISBN 0-89750-099-7, 434). Ohara Pubns.

Complete Backyard Planner. L. Donald Meyers. LC 84-14147. (Illus.). 288p. 1985. 17.50 o.p. (ISBN 0-684-18117-7, ScribT). Scribner.

Complete Bible: An American Translation. John M. Smith. Ed. by Edgar J. Goodspeed. xviii, 1332p. 1939. 25.00 o.s.i. (ISBN 0-226-76353-6). U of Chicago Pr.

Complete Birds of the World. Michael Walters. LC 79-56434. 256p. 1980. 39.95 o.p. (ISBN 0-7153-7666-7). David & Charles.

Complete Book of Adult Toys. David Lachenbruch & Craig Norback. LC 82-47663. (Illus.). 168p. 1983. pap. 12.95 o.p. (ISBN 0-15-620946-2, Harv). HarBraceJ.

Complete Book of Bathrooms. Judy Ramsey et al. (Illus.). 368p. 1986. 24.95 o.p. (ISBN 0-8306-0408-1, NO. 2708); pap. 15.60 o.p. (ISBN 0-8306-2708-1). TAB Bks.

Complete Book of Bible Trivia. J. Stephen Lang. Date not set. pap. price not set o.p. (75-0421-5). Tyndale.

Complete Book of Bonds: How to Buy & Sell Profitably. Robert L. Holt. LC 81-47307. 224p. 1981. 13.95 o.p. (ISBN 0-15-120642-2). HarBraceJ.

Complete Book of Breads. Bernard Clayton, Jr. 1974. 19.95 o.s.i. (ISBN 0-671-21548-5). S&S.

Complete Book of Breastfeeding. Sally W. Olds & Marvin S. Eiger. LC 76-25090. (Illus.). 224p. 1976. 8.95 o.p. (ISBN 0-89480-010-8, 121); pap. 4.95 o.p. (ISBN 0-911104-88-7). Workman Pub.

Complete Book of British Birds. Date not set. (ISBN 0-86145-663-7, Pub. by Auto Assn England). Salem Hse Pubs.

Complete Book of Buddy "L" Toys: A Greenberg Guide. Albert McCollough. (Illus.). 160p. 1982. 40.00 o.p. (ISBN 0-89778-009-4). Greenberg Pub Co.

Complete Book of Budgerigars. John Scoble. (Illus.). 144p. 1987. pap. 14.95 o.p. (ISBN 0-7137-1871-4, Pub. by Blandford Pr England). Sterling.

Complete Book of Car Maintenance & Repair. John D. Hirsch. LC 77-3252. (Illus.). 1977. encore ed. 5.95 o.p. (ISBN 0-684-16901-0, ScribT). Scribner.

Complete Book of Cat Care. rev. ed. Leon F. Whitney & George D. Whitney. LC 79-7216. (Illus.). 288p. 1985. pap. 8.95 o.p. (ISBN 0-385-23296-9). Doubleday.

Complete Book of Cat Health. Animal Medical Center Editors & William J. Kay. (Illus.). 288p. 1985. 19.95 o.p. (ISBN 0-02-502350-0). Macmillan.

Complete Book of Closing Sales. Sal T. Massimino. LC 80-69684. 160p. 1981. 14.95 o.p. (ISBN 0-8144-5592-1). AMACOM.

Complete Book of Cooking Equipment. 2nd ed. Jule Wilkinson. 336p. 1983. 33.95 o.s.i. (ISBN 0-8436-2186-9). Van Nos Reinhold.

Complete Book of Cosmetic Facial Surgery: A Step-by-Step Guide to the Physical & Psychological Process. Dennis P. Cirillo & Mark Rubenstein. LC 84-1397. (Illus.). 176p. 1984. 16.45 o.p. (ISBN 0-671-47743-9). S&S.

Complete Book of Drink. T. E. Carling. 208p. 1952. (ISBN 0-8022-0213-6). Philos Lib.

Complete Book of Fences. Dan Ramsey. LC 82-19343. (Illus.). 256p. 1983. 19.95 o.p. (ISBN 0-8306-0508-8); pap. 13.60 o.p. (ISBN 0-8306-1508-3, 1508). TAB Bks.

Complete Book of Furniture Repair & Refinishing. rev. ed. Ralph P. Kinney. (Illus.). 256p. 1983. 12.95 o.s.i. (ISBN 0-684-18029-4, ScribT). Scribner.

Complete Book of Herbs & Herb Growing. Roy Genders. LC 79-93206. (Illus.). 160p. 1980. 16.95 o.p. (ISBN 0-8069-3928-1); pap. 9.95 o.p. (ISBN 0-8069-3930-3). Sterling.

Complete Book of Herbs & Spices. Claire Loewenfeld & Philippa Back. (Illus.). 319p. 1980. 30.95 o.p. (ISBN 0-7153-7656-X). David & Charles.

Complete Book of Herbs & Spices. Claire Loewenfeld & Philippa Back. 1976. pap. 9.70i o.p. (ISBN 0-316-53070-0). Little.

Complete Book of Home Remodeling. Robert Scharff. 1975. text ed. 37.95 o.p. (ISBN 0-07-055167-7). McGraw.

Complete Book of Illustrated Learning Aids, Games & Activities. Hal Malehorn. 256p. 1982. text ed. 16.95 o.p. (ISBN 0-13-157362-4). P-H.

Complete Book of Major U. S. Show Business Awards. Mike Kaplan. (Reference Library of the Humanities). 600p. 1984. pap. 15.95 o.p. Garland Pub.

Complete Book of Manufacturing Management. Steven A. Wassermann. 384p. 1982. pap. 85.00 o.p. (ISBN 0-8144-1126-6). AMACOM.

Complete Book of Minerals for Health. rev. ed. Prevention Magazine Editors & Sharon Faelten. 1981. 19.95 o.p. (ISBN 0-87857-360-7). Rodale Pr Inc.

Complete Book of Office Mispractice. Paul Smith. (Illus.). 192p. (Orig.). 1985. pap. 10.95 o.p. (ISBN 0-7102-0434-5). Routledge Chapman & Hall.

Complete Book of Outrageous & Atrocious Practical Jokes. Justin Geste. LC 85-4451. (Illus.). 144p. 1985. pap. 5.95 o.p. (ISBN 0-385-23044-3, Dolp). Doubleday.

Complete Book of Pasta. Enrica Jarratt & Vernon Jarrat. 1983. 15.50 o.p. (ISBN 0-8446-5940-1). Peter Smith.

Complete Book of Pastry: Sweet & Savory. Bernard Clayton, Jr. (Illus.). 1981. 17.95 o.p. (ISBN 0-671-24276-8). S&S.

Complete Book of Platform Tennis. Dick Squires. (Houghton Mifflin Paperbacks). 1974. 9.95 o.p. (ISBN 0-395-19445-8); pap. 5.95 o.p. (ISBN 0-395-25858-8). HM.

Complete Book of Plymouth, Dodge, Chrysler. 2nd ed. Ed. by Spence Murray. LC 73-83693. (Tune-up & Repair Ser.). (Illus.). 160p. 1977. pap. 3.95 o.p. (ISBN 0-8227-5008-2). Petersen Pub.

Complete Book of Sandwiches for the Professional Chef. Terence Janericco. (Illus.). 144p. 1983. 24.95 o.p. (ISBN 0-8436-2270-9). Van Nos Reinhold.

Complete Book of Soups & Stews. Bernard Clayton, Jr. (Illus.). 416p. 1984. 18.45 o.p. (ISBN 0-671-43863-8). S&S.

Complete Book of Stenciling: Furniture Decoration & Restoration. Pat Midkiff. LC 83-24150. (Illus.). 160p. 1984. 15.95 o.p. (ISBN 0-8069-5516-3); pap. 6.95 o.p. (ISBN 0-8069-7822-8). Sterling.

Complete Book of Stuffedwork. Toni Scott. 1978. 14.95 o.p. (ISBN 0-395-25769-7). HM.

Complete Book of Swedish Massage. Armand Maanum & Herb Montgomery. 96p. (Orig.). 1985. pap. 6.95 o.p. (ISBN 0-86683-864-3). HarpR.

Complete Book of Symphony Macros. Lighthouse Publishing Staff et al. 160p. (Orig.). 1985. pap. text ed. 16.95 o.p. (ISBN 0-07-881204-6). Osborne-McGraw.

Complete Book of Taekwon Do Forms. Keith D. Yates. (Illus.). 168p. 1982. pap. 14.95 o.p. (ISBN 0-87364-244-9). Paladin Pr.

Complete Book of the Bow & Arrow. rev., 3rd ed. G. Howard Gillelan. LC 76-30484. (Illus.). 204p. 1981. pap. 12.95 o.p. (ISBN 0-8117-2118-3). Stackpole.

Complete Book of the Dog. David MacDonald et al. 224p. 1985. 18.95 o.p. (ISBN 0-03-006019-2). H Holt & Co.

Complete Book of the Porsche. Consumer Guide Staff. 1988. 15.95 o.p. (ISBN 0-517-66188-8). Crown.

Complete Book of the Wild Turkey. rev. ed. Roger M. Latham. LC 76-7079. (Illus.). 224p. 1976. 14.95 o.p. (ISBN 0-8117-0414-9). Stackpole.

Complete Book of Traditional Knitting. Rae Compton. LC 82-62119. (Illus.). 240p. 1983. 22.50 o.s.i. (ISBN 0-684-17866-4, ScribT). Scribner.

Complete Book of Turkish Cooking. Ayla E. Algar. (Illus.). 250p. 1985. 29.95 o.p. (ISBN 0-7103-0101-4, Kegan Paul). Routledge Chapman & Hall.

Complete Book of Vitamins. Prevention Magazine Editors. Ed. by William Gootlieb. 848p. 1984. 21.95 o.p. (ISBN 0-87857-495-6, 05-195-2); deluxe ed. 29.95 o.p. (ISBN 0-87857-503-0, 05-195-4). Rodale Pr Inc.

Complete Book of Water Polo. Ed. by U. S. Olympic Water Polo Team Staff & Ralph W. Hale. 1986. pap. 12.95 o.p. (ISBN 0-671-55563-4, Fireside). S&S.

Complete Book of Wills & Trusts. Albert M. Lehrman. LC 78-61133. (Estate Planning & Administration Ser.). 592p. 59.50 o.p. (ISBN 0-87624-100-3, Inst Busn Plan). P-H.

Complete Book of Wood Finishing. 2nd ed. Robert Scharff. (Illus.). 384p. 1974. text ed. 41.50 o.p. (ISBN 0-07-055166-9). McGraw.

Complete Boxer. 3rd ed. Milo G. Denlinger. LC 69-19392. (Complete Breed Book Ser.). (Illus.). 304p. 1969. 15.95 o.p. (ISBN 0-87605-060-7). Howell Bk.

Complete Brittany Spaniel. Maxwell Riddle. LC 72-88976. (Complete Breed Book Ser.). (Illus.). 288p. 1984. 15.95 o.p. (ISBN 0-87605-065-8). Howell Bk.

Complete CAD-CAE Electronics Marketplace Directory. Management Roundtable, Inc. Staff. (Illus., Orig.). 1987. perfect bdg. 79.00 o.p. (ISBN 0-932007-12-0, B55). Mgmt Roundtable.

Complete Cairn Terrier. Date not set. (ISBN 0-87605-072-0). Howell Bk.

Complete Calligrapher. Frederick Wong. (Illus.). 184p. 1980. 27.50 o.p. (ISBN 0-8230-0778-2). Watson-Guptill.

Complete Canoeist's Guide. Raymond Bridge. LC 77-27865. (Encore Edition). (Illus.). 1978. 3.95 o.p. (ISBN 0-684-17176-7, ScribT). Scribner.

Complete Chart Hits of 1984. 232p. 1985. pap. 9.95 o.p. (ISBN 0-88188-374-3). H Leonard Pub Corp.

Complete Chihuahua. 4th ed. William Denlinger et al. LC 63-21874. (Complete Breed Book Ser.). (Illus.). 256p. 1963. 16.95 o.p. (ISBN 0-87605-100-X). Howell Bk.

Complete Communications Handbook. John C. Sans, Jr. (Illus.). 164p. (Orig.). 1985. pap. 12.95 o.p. (ISBN 0-915381-79-6). Wordware Pub.

Complete Consultants Library. Bly. 1987. pap. 38.85 o.p. (ISBN 0-471-63509-X). Wiley.

Complete Consumer's Guide to the Latest Telephones. Benedict A. Leerburger. (Illus.). 160p. 1985. pap. 5.95 o.p. (ISBN 0-396-08506-7). Dodd.

Complete Course in Canning, Vols. 1 & 2. 11th, rev. ed. Intro. by Anthony Lopez. LC 46-19487. (Illus., Orig.). 1981. Set. text ed. 75.00x o.p. (ISBN 0-930027-00-0); Set. pap. text ed. 40.00x o.p. (ISBN 0-930027-03-5). CTI Pubns.

Complete Course in Short-Cut Mathematics. B. A. Slade. 144p. 1953. 15.95 o.s.i. (ISBN 0-911012-11-7). Nelson-Hall.

Complete Course in Super Ju Jitsu. Nelson Hall. 180p. 1958. pap. 16.95 o.s.i. (ISBN 0-911012-38-9). Nelson-Hall.

Complete Course of Lithography. Alois Senefelder. LC 68-27721. (Graphic Art Ser.). (Illus.). 1968. Repr. of 1819 ed. lib. bdg. 35.00 o.p. (ISBN 0-306-71155-9). Da Capo.

Complete CPA Examination Review. Belverd E. Needles & Doyle Z. Williams. 1985. Study Aids & Self-Examinations, Vol. I, 1024p. pap. 33.95 ea. o.p. (ISBN 0-395-35703-9); Questions, Problems, & Solutions Vol. II, 1108p. pap. 33.95 o.p. (ISBN 0-395-39097-4). HM.

Complete CPA Examination Review. 4th ed. Belverd E. Needles, Jr. & Dayle Z. Williams. LC 83-80084. 1984. Vol. I, Study guides & Self-Examinations. pap. 31.50 o.p. (ISBN 0-395-34541-3); Vol. II, Questions, Problems & Solutions. pap. 31.50 o.p. (ISBN 0-395-34542-1). HM.

Complete CPA Examination Review. 5th ed. Belverd E. Needles, Jr. & Dayle Z. Williams. 1985. Vol. I, Study Guides & Self-Examination. pap. 31.95 o.p. (ISBN 0-395-36336-5); Vol. II, Questions, Problems, & Solutions Auditing. pap. 31.95 o.p. (ISBN 0-395-36337-3). HM.

Complete Defence to 1P-K4: A Study of Petroff's Defence. 2nd ed. Cafferty. 151p. 1979. 19.00 o.p. (ISBN 0-08-024089-5); pap. 9.95 o.p. (ISBN 0-08-024088-7). Pergamon.

Complete Directory of Large Print Books & Serials, 1988. Ed. by Bowker, R. R., Staff. 228p. 1988. pap. 69.95 o.p. (ISBN 0-8352-2322-1). Bowker.

Complete Disciple. Paul W. Powell. 120p. 1982. pap. 5.50 o.p. (ISBN 0-88207-307-9). Victor Bks.

Complete Dog Book: The Official Publication of the American Kennel Club. 16th ed. American Kennel Club. LC 79-1490. (Illus.). 1979. 13.95 o.p. (ISBN 0-87605-462-9). Howell Bk.

Complete, Easy to Read, Medical Handbook. Ed. by William J. McGuire & Joseph D. Scrocco, Jr. (Health Watch Ser.). (Illus.). 400p. (Orig.). 1983. pap. 4.95 o.s.i. (ISBN 0-88101-006-5). Unicorn Pub.

Complete Electrical Estimating Course, 4 vols. E. R. Belt. 1976. Vol. 1: Electrical Estimating. (ISBN 0-07-004454-6); Vol. 2: Electrical Pricing Units & Procedures. (ISBN 0-07-004455-4); Vol. 3: Pricing Forms. (ISBN 0-07-004456-2); Vol. 4: Take-Off Forms. (ISBN 0-07-004457-0); Complete Course. text ed. 65.00 o.p. (ISBN 0-07-095030-X). McGraw.

Complete Fairy Tales of George MacDonald. Date not set. (ISBN 0-8052-3700-3). Random.

Complete Family Guide to Living with High Blood Pressure. Michael K. Rees. LC 80-18767. 1980. 9.95 o.p. (ISBN 0-13-160432-5). P-H.

Complete Family Nature Guide. Jean R. Worthley. (Illus.). 1977. pap. 2.25 o.p. (ISBN 0-380-01651-6, 33092). Avon.

Complete Food Handbook. Rodger P. Doyle & James L. Redding. LC 79-52123. (Illus.). 320p. (Revised & Updated ed.). 1980. pap. 3.50 o.p. (ISBN 0-394-17398-8, B431, BC). Grove.

Complete Ford Owner's Handbook of Repair & Maintenance: 1932-1955. Clymer Publications. (Illus.). 1955. pap. 5.00 o.p. (ISBN 0-89287-270-5, A252). Clymer Pub.

Complete German Shepherd Dog. 4th ed. Jane G. Bennett et al. LC 78-94493. (Complete Breed Book Ser.). (Illus.). 1970. 15.95 o.p. (ISBN 0-87605-150-6). Howell Bk.

Complete German Shepherd Dog. Nem Elliot & Percy Elliot. (Illus.). 304p. 1983. 25.95 o.p. (ISBN 0-7182-2350-0, Pub. by Kaye & Ward). David & Charles.

Complete Guide to Aerobic Dancing. Consumer Guide Editors & Beth A. Kuntzleman. (Orig.). 1981. pap. 2.50 o.p. (ISBN 0-449-80001-6, Columbine). Fawcett.

Complete Guide to Affordable In-Home Childcare. Roth Elliott & Jim Savage. 1988. pap. 9.95 o.p. (ISBN 0-13-690728-8). Prentice Hall Pr.

Complete Guide to American Pocket Watches: Pocket Watches from 1809-1950. Cooksey Shugart. Ed. by Peter Schrieber. 1981. pap. 8.95 o.p. (ISBN 0-517-54378-8, Harmony). Crown.

Complete Guide to Anti-Aging Nutrients. Sheldon S. Hendler. 362p. 1985. 16.45 o.p. (ISBN 0-671-50615-3). S&S.

Complete Guide to Appraising Condominiums & Cooperatives. Ed. by Samuel T. Barash. LC 81-4441. 288p. 1981. text ed. 34.50 o.p. (ISBN 0-13-159822-8, Busn). P-H.

Complete Guide to Automotive Refinishing. Harry T. Chudy. (Illus.). 464p. 1982. Reference ed. pap. text ed. 32.00 o.p. (ISBN 0-13-160440-6). P-H.

Complete Guide to Aviation Photography. Peter M. Bowers. (Modern Aviation Ser.). (Illus.). 240p. 1980. 12.95 o.p. (ISBN 0-8306-9727-6); pap. 6.95 o.p. (ISBN 0-8306-2281-0, 2281). TAB Bks.

Complete Guide to Bed & Breakfast Inns. Pamela Valdez. 1984. pap. 9.95 o.p. (ISBN 0-912528-35-4). John Muir.

Complete Guide to Bed & Breakfasts, Inns & Guesthouses. 3rd, rev ed. Pamela Lanier. (Illus.). 576p. 1986. pap. 11.95 o.p. (ISBN 0-912528-53-2). John Muir.

Complete Guide to Bed & Breakfasts, Inns & Guesthouses in the U. S. & Canada. rev. 5th ed. Pamela Lanier. (Illus.). 625p. 1988. pap. 13.95 o.p. (ISBN 0-912528-82-6). John Muir.

Complete Guide to Bed & Breakfasts: 1987-88 Edition. 4th., rev. ed. Pamela Lanier. (Illus.). 672p. 1987. pap. 12.95 o.p. (ISBN 0-912528-61-3). John Muir.

Complete Guide to Better Golf. Bob Toski. (Illus.). 1977. 12.95 o.p. (ISBN 0-689-10722-6, Atheneum). Macmillan.

Complete Guide to Car Stereo Systems. Van Waterford. (Illus.). 144p. 1982. pap. 7.95 o.p. (ISBN 0-8306-1121-5, 1121). TAB Bks.

Complete Guide to Children's Literature - Jewish. Date not set. (ISBN 0-8052-3760-7). Random.

Complete Guide to Coaching Women's Basketball. Dorothy A. Guiliani. 1982. text ed. 18.95 o.p. (ISBN 0-13-160465-1, Parker). P-H.

Complete Guide to Effective Dictation. Jean Gonzalez. 1980. pap. text ed. 13.95x o.p. (ISBN 0-534-00811-9). PWS-Kent Pub.

Complete Guide to Employee Benefit Plans. rev. ed. Ned A. Miller. LC 79-88343. 1985. 39.95 o.p. (ISBN 0-87863-149-6, Farnsworth Pub Co). Longman Finan.

Complete Guide to Fiduciary Accounting. J. G. Denhard & John D. Grider. LC 80-28061. 218p. 1981. text ed. 39.95 o.p. (ISBN 0-13-160572-0, Busn). P-H.

Complete Guide to Fighting Folders. Russell Maynard. LC 87-50244. 200p. (Orig.). pap. cancelled o.s.i. (ISBN 0-86568-092-2). Unique Pubns.

Complete Guide to Finance & Accounting for Non-Financial Managers. Steven A. Finkler. (Illus.). 222p. 1983. 22.95 o.p. (ISBN 0-13-160531-3); pap. 10.95 o.p. (ISBN 0-13-160523-2). P-H.

Complete Guide to Framing. Jenny Rodwell & George Short. (Illus.). 144p. 1986. 16.95 o.p. (ISBN 0-89134-129-3). North Light Bks.

Complete Guide to Game Care & Cookery. Sam Fadala. (Illus.). 288p. (Orig.). pap. 12.95 o.p. (ISBN 0-910676-32-1). DBI.

Complete Guide to Gun Shows. Thomas W. Thielen. 1980. pap. 6.95 o.p. (ISBN 0-686-30707-0). Loompanics.

Complete Guide to Home Video Programming. Pamela Levine et al. 1984. pap. 10.95 o.p. (ISBN 0-03-071082-0, Owl Bks). H Holt & Co.

Complete Guide to Homebuilt Rotorcraft. Kas Thomas & Jack Lambie. (Illus.). 128p. 1982. pap. 8.70 o.p. (ISBN 0-8306-2335-3, 2335P). TAB Bks.

Complete Guide to Instrumental Jazz Instruction. John Kuzmich, Jr. & Lee Bash. LC 83-21141. 263p. 1984. text ed. 22.95x o.p. (ISBN 0-13-160565-8, Parker). P-H.

Complete Guide to Kayaking. Raymond Bridge. LC 77-3230. (Encore Edition). (Illus.). 1978. 4.95 o.p. (ISBN 0-684-17696-3, ScribT); pap. 6.95 o.p. (ISBN 0-684-15041-7, ScribT). Scribner.

Complete Guide to Lower Phone Costs. Center for the Study of Services Staff. 1985. 6.95 o.p. (ISBN 0-317-12263-0). Ctr Study Serv.

Complete Guide to Making Home Video Movies. Martin Porter. 128p. 1984. pap. 8.95 o.p. (ISBN 0-671-50854-7, Fireside). S&S.

Complete Guide to Micromounts. Milton J. Speckels. 96p. pap. 2.00 o.p. (ISBN 0-910652-04-X). Gembooks.

Complete Guide to Oriental Manual Therapy. Ron Teeguarden. LC 87-82006. (Illus.). 256p. 1988. pap. 15.95 o.p. (ISBN 0-87040-695-7). Japan Pubns USA.

Complete Guide to Planned Giving: Everything You Need to Know to Compete for Major Gifts in the 1980's. Debra Ashton. (Nonprofit Tech Assistance Ser.: Vol. 2). 1987. pap. 35.00 o.p. (ISBN 0-940374-13-7). JLA Pubns.

Complete Guide to Prescription & Non-Prescription Drugs. H. Winter Griffith. LC 83-82397. 1983. pap. 12.95 o.p. (ISBN 0-89586-275-1). Price Stern.

Complete Guide to Real Estate Financing. Jack Cummings. (Illus.). 1977. 29.95 o.p. (ISBN 0-13-160481-3, Busn). P-H.

Complete Guide to Running a Business. 2nd Rev. ed. John R. Klug. LC 83-3697. 336p. 1983. 50.00 o.p. (ISBN 0-932648-41-X). Boardroom.

Complete Guide to Security. Martin Clifford. LC 82-50656. 336p. 1982. pap. 13.95 o.p. (ISBN 0-672-21955-7). Sams.

Complete Guide to Self-Publishing: Everything You Need to Know to Write, Publish, Promote & Sell Your Own Book. Tom Ross & Marilyn Ross. (Illus.). 400p. (Orig.). 1985. 19.95 o.p. (ISBN 0-89879-167-7). Writers Digest.

Complete Guide to Snakes of Florida. William E. Haast & Robert Anderson. LC 81-80463. (Illus.). 139p. 1981. pap. 9.95 o.s.i. (ISBN 0-916224-68-6). Banyan Bks.

Complete Guide to Software Testing. William Hetzel. LC 83-83116. (Illus.). 255p. 1984. pap. 34.50x o.p. (ISBN 0-89435-110-9, HG1109). QED Info Sci.

Complete Guide to Specialty Cars. Curt Scott. Ed. by Judy Scott. (Illus.). 1986. pap. 121.00 o.p. (ISBN 0-9614882-1-2). Crown Pub CA.

Complete Guide to Specialty Cars. Curt Scott. Ed. by Judy Scott. (Illus.). 1987. pap. 12.95 o.p. (ISBN 0-9614882-2-0, Dist. by Motorbooks Intl). Crown Pub CA.

Complete Guide to Specialty Cars. Curt Scott. Ed. by Judy Scott. (Illus.). 128p. 1988. pap. 12.00 o.p. (ISBN 0-9614882-3-9). Crown Pub CA.

Complete Guide to Success with the IBM PCjr. Norman Sondak et al. (Illus.). 416p. 1984. pap. text ed. 14.95 o.p. (ISBN 0-8016-4671-5). Mosby.

Complete Guide to the Christian's Budget. new ed. Michael L. Speer. LC 74-80341. 160p. 1975. pap. 3.25 o.p. (ISBN 0-8054-5227-3). Broadman.

Complete Guide to the Golden Gate National Recreation Area. Karen Liberatore. LC 82-4241. (Illus.). 120p. 1982. pap. 7.95 o.p. (ISBN 0-87701-259-8). Chronicle Bks.

Complete Guide to the Marital Deduction in Estate Planning. J. Erdman. LC 78-54860. (Estate Planning & Administration Ser.). 1978. 19.95 o.p. (ISBN 0-87624-104-6, Inst Busn Plan). P-H.

Complete Guide to Total Fitness. Jan Percival et al. LC 77-9867. (Illus.). 1977. pap. text ed. 7.95 o.p. (ISBN 0-416-00371-0, NO.0005). Routledge Chapman & Hall.

Complete Guide to Travel Agency Automation. Nadine Godwin. LC 81-83505. (Travel Management Library). (Illus.). 160p. 1982. 12.95 o.p. (ISBN 0-916032-13-2). Delmar.

Complete Guide to U. S. Civil Service Jobs. 8th ed. David R. Turner. LC 81-65360. 176p. (Orig.). 1981. pap. 5.00 o.p. (ISBN 0-668-05245-7, 5245). Arco.

Complete Guide to Video. Martin Clifford. LC 83-60165. 342p. 1983. pap. text ed. 15.95 o.p. (ISBN 0-672-21912-3). Sams.

Complete Guide to Windsurfing. Jeremy Evans. (Illus.). 192p. 1983. 15.95x o.p. (ISBN 0-87196-137-7); pap. 9.95x o.p. (ISBN 0-87196-248-9). Facts on File.

Complete Guide to Winning Slot-I Football. Ken Lyons. 240p. 1981. text ed. 15.95 o.p. (ISBN 0-13-160697-2, Parker). P-H.

Complete Guide to Writing Software User Manuals. Brad M. McGehee. 300p. (Orig.). 1984. pap. 14.95 o.p. (ISBN 0-89879-138-3). Writers Digest.

Complete Guide to Your Child's Emotional Health: From Early Infancy to Early Adulthood. Barbara Powell. 240p. 1984. 15.95 o.p. (ISBN 0-531-09753-6). Watts.

Complete Hair Book: The Ultimate Guide to Your Hairs Health & Beauty. Philip Kingsley. (A Fred Jordan Book Ser.). (Illus.). 1982. pap. 10.95 o.p. (ISBN 0-394-17981-1, Ever). Grove.

Complete Handbook of Activities & Recreational Programs for Nursing Homes. Linda E. Hastings. LC 81-2852. 246p. 1981. text ed. 44.95x o.p. (ISBN 0-13-160911-4, Busn). P-H.

Complete Handbook of Business English. William Repp. 1982. 29.50 o.p. (ISBN 0-13-160960-2, Busn). P-H.

Complete Handbook of Children's Reading Disorders: A Critical Evaluation of Their Clinical, Educational & Social Dimensions, 2 vols. Hilda L. Mosse. LC 81-132. 714p. 1982. Set. 80.00 o.p. (ISBN 0-89885-077-0); Vol. I. 44.95 o.p. (ISBN 0-89885-021-5); Vol. II. 44.95 o.p. (ISBN 0-89885-026-6). Human Sci Pr.

Complete Handbook of Inflation Accounting. Thomas A. Ratcliffe & Paul H. Munter. LC 80-29378. 225p. 1981. text ed. 34.95 o.p. (ISBN 0-13-160952-1). P-H.

Complete Handbook of Kindergarten Music Lesson Plans & Activities. Marcelle Vernazza. LC 80-39724. 240p. 1981. text ed. 16.50x o.p. (ISBN 0-13-161190-9, Parker). P-H.

Complete Handbook of Nutrition. Gary Null & Steve Null. 1973. pap. 1.25 o.p. (ISBN 0-440-11613-9). Dell.

Complete Handbook of Operational & Management Auditing. William T. Thornhill. 288p. 1981. text ed. 49.95 o.p. (ISBN 0-13-161141-0). P-H.

Complete Handbook of Pregnancy. George B. Feldman & Anne Felshman. (Illus.). 1985. 17.95 o.p. (ISBN 0-399-12957-X). Putnam Pub Group.

Complete Handbook of Sewing Machine Repair. Howard Hutchison. (Illus.). 1980. 14.95 o.p. (ISBN 0-8306-9731-4); pap. 10.60 o.p. (ISBN 0-8306-1163-0, 1163). TAB Bks.

Complete Handbook of Woodworking Tools & Hardware. Charles R. Self. (Illus.). 400p. 1983. 21.95 o.p. (ISBN 0-8306-0484-7, 1484); pap. 14.95 o.p. (ISBN 0-8306-1484-2). TAB Bks.

Complete Health Club Handbook. John Dietrich & Susan Waggoner. (Orig.). 1983. pap. 9.50 o.p. (ISBN 0-671-47027-2). S&S.

Complete History of Algiers. John Morgan. LC 76-109343. 1970. Repr. of 1731 ed. lib. bdg. 39.00x o.p. (ISBN 0-8371-3613-X, MHA&, Pub. by Negro U Pr). Greenwood.

Complete History of Guam. Paul Carano & Pedro C. Sanchez. LC 64-21619. (Illus.). 1964. 20.50 o.p. (ISBN 0-8048-0114-2). C E Tuttle.

Complete House Kit. Frank Coffee. (Orig.). 1979. pap. 10.95 o.s.i. (ISBN 0-671-79037-4, Wallaby). PB.

Complete Humorous Sketches & Tales of Mark Twain. Ed. by Charles Weider. LC 61-6503. 1961. 15.95 o.s.i. (ISBN 0-385-01094-X). Doubleday.

Complete Index to Astounding-Analog. Michael Ashley & Terry Jeeves. LC 86-2285. 253p. 1986. Repr. of 1981 ed. lib. bdg. 29.95x o.p. (ISBN 0-89370-079-7). Borgo Pr.

Complete Intravenous Nutrition: Proceedings of the Europen Nutritionists, 10th Meeting, Saltsjoebaden, 1971. European Nutritionists Staff. Ed. by A. Wretlind. (Nutrition & Metabolism Ser.: Vol. 14, Suppl.). (Illus.). 300p. 1972. pap. 21.75 o.p. (ISBN 3-8055-1450-6). S Karger.

Complete Introductory Lectures on Psychoanalysis. Sigmund Freud. Ed. & tr. by James Strachey. (Standard ed.). 1966. 27.95 o.p. (ISBN 0-393-01077-5). Norton.

Complete Irish Wolfhound. 3rd ed. Alma J. Starbuck. LC 79-76834. (Complete Breed Book Ser.). (Illus.). 1969. 16.95 o.p. (ISBN 0-87605-170-0). Howell Bk.

Complete Job Search Handbook. Howard Figler. LC 79-4153. 348p. 1980. 11.95 o.s.i. (ISBN 0-03-044121-8, Owl Bks.); pap. 7.95 o.s.i. (ISBN 0-03-044126-9, Owl Bks). H Holt & Co.

Complete Jogger. Jack Batten. LC 76-55527. (Illus.). 1977. pap. 4.95 o.p. (ISBN 0-15-120699-6, Harv). HarBraceJ.

Complete Junk Food Book. Michael Lasky. LC 77-9367. 1977. 10.95 o.p. (ISBN 0-07-036501-6); pap. text ed. 7.95 o.p. (ISBN 0-07-036502-4). McGraw.

Complete Keeshond. Date not set. (ISBN 0-87605-174-3). Howell Bk.

Complete Kindergarten Handbook. Terry L. Romer. (Illus.). 1979. text ed. 15.50x o.p. (ISBN 0-13-161331-6, Parker). P-H.

Complete Labrador Retriever. 2nd ed. Helen Warwick. LC 65-24487. (Complete Breed Book Ser.). (Illus.). 304p. 1983. 15.95 o.p. (ISBN 0-87605-205-7). Howell Bk.

Complete Lurcher. D. Brian Plummer. (Illus.). 182p. 1980. 22.00 o.p. (ISBN 0-85115-118-3, Pub. by Boydell & Brewer). Longwood Pub Group.

Complete Magnus Ridolph. Jack Vance. 256p. 1984. 15.95 o.p. (ISBN 0-934438-98-6). Underwood-Miller.

Complete Make It Now Bake It Later. Barbara Goodfellow. 224p. 1985. pap. 8.95 o.p. (ISBN 0-671-45082-4, Fireside). S&S.

Complete Mary Poppins, 4 vols. P. L. Travers. 1976. pap. 17.25 o.p. (ISBN 0-15-619810-X, VoyB). HarBraceJ.

Complete Medical Examination. I. Rosenfeld. 1979. pap. 6.95 o.p. (ISBN 0-380-46391-1, 65581-1). Avon.

Complete Medical Guide. 4th rev. ed. Benjamin F. Miller & Lawrence Galton. 1978. 24.95 o.p. (ISBN 0-671-24107-9). S&S.

Complete Method for Voice & Guitar: Instruction Manual in Accompaniment Playing & Singing. Oscar J. Lehrer. 1941. with cassette 12.00 2.00 o.p. (ISBN 0-913650-26-9). CPP Belwin.

Complete Microcomputer Systems Handbook. Edward L. Safford, Jr. (Illus.). 1980. 14.95 o.p. (ISBN 0-8306-9715-2); pap. 9.95 o.p. (ISBN 0-8306-1201-7, 1201). TAB Bks.

Complete Middle East Cookbook. Tess Mallos. LC 79-19349. (Illus.). 400p. 1979. text ed. 29.95 o.p. (ISBN 0-07-039810-0). McGraw.

Complete Miniature Schnauzer. Date not set. (ISBN 0-87605-215-4). Howell Bk.

Complete Moving Planner. David Feruson. 96p. (Orig.). 1985. pap. 4.50 o.p. (ISBN 0-440-51218-2, Dell Trade Pbks). Dell.

Complete Nutrition Guide for You & Your Baby: From Pregnancy Through the First Three Years. Alice White. (Orig.). 1983. pap. 2.95 o.s.i. (ISBN 0-345-29718-0). Ballantine.

Complete Operas of Mozart. Charles Osborne. LC 78-55623. 1978. 14.95 o.p. (ISBN 0-689-10886-9, Atheneum). Macmillan.

Complete Operas of Puccini: A Critical Guide. Charles Osborne. LC 81-69141. 1982. 15.95 o.s.i. (ISBN 0-689-11184-3, Atheneum). Macmillan.

Complete Outdoorsman's Guide to Birds of Eastern North America. John P. MacKenzie. (Houghton Mifflin Paperbacks). 1977. pap. 4.95 o.p. (ISBN 0-395-25774-3). HM.

Complete Outdoorsman's Guide to Edible Wild Plants. Berndt Berglund & Clare E. Bolsby. LC 77-82243. (Illus.). 1978. pap. 4.95 o.p. (ISBN 0-684-15481-1). Scribner.

Complete Outfitting & Source Book for Bicycle Touring. Gail Heilman. LC 79-55215. (Illus.). 216p. (Orig.). 1980. 14.95 o.p. (ISBN 0-03-056851-X); pap. 7.95 o.p. (ISBN 0-03-056849-8). H Holt & Co.

Complete Parent's Guide to Soccer. Gerald Fecht. (Illus.). 1979. pap. 9.95 o.p. (ISBN 0-673-16184-6). Scott F.

Complete Partnership Manual & Guide with Tax, Financial & Managerial Strategies. Daniel L. McKnight, Jr. LC 82-5799. 304p. 1982. text ed. 39.50 o.p. (ISBN 0-13-162230-7, Busn). P-H.

Complete Passive Solar Home Book. Brad Schepp & Stephen M. Hastie. (Illus.). 320p. (Orig.). 1985. 24.95 o.p. (ISBN 0-8306-0657-2, 1657); pap. 16.60 o.p. (ISBN 0-8306-1657-8). TAB Bks.

Complete Patient History. Maurice Kraytman. 320p. 1979. text ed. 21.95 o.p. (ISBN 0-07-035421-9). McGraw.

Complete Peterkin Papers. Lucretia P. Hale. (Illus.). 302p. (gr. 5-7). 1960. 8.95 o.p. (ISBN 0-395-06792-8). HM.

Complete PFS Book. Ralph Mylius. LC 84-26924. (Illus.). 192p. (Orig.). 1985. pap. 15.95 o.p. (ISBN 0-915381-70-2). Wordware Pub.

Complete Photobook. Ron Spillman. (Illus.). 208p. 17.95 o.p. (ISBN 0-86343-010-4, Pub. by Fountain Pr UK). Seven Hills Bk Dists.

Complete Piano Works for Four Hands. Johannes Brahms. Ed. by Eusebius Mandyczewski. 12.00 o.p. (ISBN 0-8446-5458-2). Peter Smith.

Complete Picture Guide to Newport, R. I. John T. Hopf. (Illus.). 64p. (Orig.). 1981. pap. 3.95 o.s.i. (ISBN 0-917012-74-7). RI Pubns Soc.

Complete Plays of T. S. Eliot. T. S. Eliot. LC 50-14646. 1969. 12.95 o.s.i. (ISBN 0-15-120755-0). HarBraceJ.

Complete Plays of William Wycherley. William Wycherley. Ed. by Gerald Weales. 1972. pap. 5.95x o.p. (ISBN 0-393-00440-6, Norton Lib). Norton.

Complete Plays with Prefaces, Vols. 2 & 5-6. George Bernard Shaw. LC 62-13608. 1962. 7.50 ea. o.p. Vol. 2 (ISBN 0-396-04650-9). Vol. 5 (ISBN 0-396-04653-3). Vol. 6 (ISBN 0-396-04654-1). Dodd.

Complete Poems. John Donne. 1976. 9.95x o.p. (ISBN 0-460-00867-6, Evman); pap. 3.50x o.p. (ISBN 0-460-01867-1). Biblio Dist.

Complete Poems - Quasimodo. Date not set. pap. (ISBN 0-8052-0757-0). Random.

Complete Poems & Selected Letters: Keats. Ed. by Clarence D. Thorpe. 719p. 1935. pap. text ed. write for info. o.p. (ISBN 0-02-420760-8). Macmillan.

Complete Poems of Cavafy. Expanded ed. C. P. Cavafy. Tr. by Rae Dalven. LC 76-22804. 311p. 1961. 6.75 o.p. (ISBN 0-15-121047-0). HarBraceJ.

Complete Poems of Ray Bradbury. Ray Bradbury. 288p. 1982. pap. 2.95 o.s.i. (ISBN 0-345-30556-6, Del Rey). Ballantine.

Complete Poems: 1927-1979. Elizabeth Bishop. 298p. 1983. 17.50 o.p. (ISBN 0-374-12747-6); pap. 8.95 o.p. (ISBN 0-374-51817-3). FS&G.

Complete Poetical Works. John Dryden. Ed. by George R. Noyes. (Cambridge Editions Ser.). 12.50 o.p. (ISBN 0-395-07484-3). HM.

Complete Poetical Works. Oliver Goldsmith. Repr. of 1911 ed. 49.00x o.p. (ISBN 0-403-08925-5). Somerset Pub.

Complete Poetical Works of Amy Lowell. Amy Lowell. (Cambridge Editions Ser.). 1978. 15.00 o.p. (ISBN 0-395-07489-4). HM.

Complete Poetry & Prose of Geoffrey Chaucer. Geoffrey Chaucer. Ed. by John H. Fisher. LC 76-44011. 1977. text ed. 39.00 o.p. (ISBN 0-03-080273-3, HoltC). HR&W.

Complete Poetry of Ben Jonson. Ben Jonson. Ed. by William B. Hunter, Jr. (Seventeenth Century Ser). (Illus.). 1968. pap. 5.95x o.p. (ISBN 0-393-00436-8, N436, Norton Lib). Norton.

Complete Poetry of Robert Herrick. Robert Herrick. Ed. by J. Max Patrick. (Seventeenth-Century Ser). 1968. pap. 2.95 o.p. (ISBN 0-393-00435-X, Norton Lib). Norton.

Complete Pre-GED Basic Skills Program. Trafalgar House Publishing, Inc. Staff. Ed. by Thomas J. Dembofsky. (Paperbacks Ser.). 384p. 1985. pap. 7.95 o.p. (ISBN 0-07-065107-8). McGraw.

Complete Pregnancy Exercise Program. Diana Simkin. LC 82-36712. (Mosby Medical Library). (Illus.). 176p. 1982. pap. 5.95 o.p. (ISBN 0-8016-4622-7). Mosby.

Complete Preparation for High School Entrance Examination for Special Private & Parochial High Schools. Jacqueline Robinson & Dennis M. Robinson. LC 80-22278. 538p. 1981. lib. bdg. 12.00 o.p. (ISBN 0-668-05149-3); pap. 7.95 o.p. (ISBN 0-668-05155-8). Arco.

Complete Preparation for the MCAT, 2 vols. James L. Flowers et al. 1985. Set. pap. text ed. 35.00 o.p. (ISBN 0-941406-08-3). Betz Pub Co Inc.

Complete Preparation for the Multi-State Bar Examination. Richard A. Lord. LC 81-13029. (Illus.). 336p. 1982. 14.95 o.p. (ISBN 0-668-05158-2); pap. 7.95 o.p. (ISBN 0-668-05160-4). Arco.

Complete Puli. Date not set. (ISBN 0-87605-270-7). Howell Bk.

Complete Pun Book. Art Moger. (Illus.). 1978. 9.95 o.s.i. (ISBN 0-8065-0664-4, Pub. by Citadel Pr). Carol Pub Group.

Complete Real Estate Exchange & Acquisition Handbook. Joseph E. Kearsley. LC 82-496. 234p. 1982. text ed. 34.95 o.p. (ISBN 0-13-162420-2, Busn). P-H.

Complete Real Estate Math Book. Margie Sussex & John F. Stapleton. (Illus.). 320p. 1982. pap. text ed. 21.33 o.p. (ISBN 0-13-162388-5). P-H.

Complete Resume Guide. Marian Faux. LC 79-12208. (Orig.). 1979. pap. 6.95 o.p. (ISBN 0-671-18393-1). Monarch Pr.

Complete Runner. Runner's World Magazine Editors. 1978. pap. 6.95 o.p. (ISBN 0-380-01885-3, 59196-0). Avon.

Complete St. Bernard. Date not set. (ISBN 0-87605-271-5). Howell Bk.

Complete Samoyed. Date not set. (ISBN 0-87605-273-1). Howell Bk.

Complete Sexenders Program: The Celibacy Movement That's Cooling off All America. Cathy Hiller & Robert Hofler. (Illus.). 1983. pap. 4.95 o.p. (ISBN 0-87795-537-9, Arbor Hse). Morrow.

Complete Shade Gardener. George Schenk. (Illus.). 288p. 1984. 24.45 o.p. (ISBN 0-395-35397-1). HM.

Complete Shooter. Sam Fadala. LC 84-71763. (Illus.). 448p. (Orig.). 1984. pap. 18.95 o.p. (ISBN 0-910676-65-8). DBI.

Complete Short Stories of Mark Twain. Ed. by Charles Weider. LC 57-5536. 1957. 15.95 o.p. (ISBN 0-385-01502-X). Doubleday.

Complete Siamese Cat. Date not set. (ISBN 0-87605-811-X). Howell Bk.

Complete Ski Cross-Country. Michael Brady. LC 81-15131. 288p. 1982. 24.95 o.p. (ISBN 0-385-27450-5, Dial); pap. 12.95 o.p. (ISBN 0-385-27677-X, Dial). Doubleday.

Complete Skin & Hair Care Program for the Active Man. Joe Saffon & Charles Fancisco. LC 86-8517. 1986. 12.95 o.p. (ISBN 0-8329-0420-1). New Century.

Complete Solutions Manual to Accompany Swokowski's Calculus: Alternate Ed. Stephen Rodi. 750p. 1982. pap. text ed. write for info. o.p. (ISBN 0-87150-342-5, 2733, Prindle). PWS-Kent Pub.

Complete Song Cycles: From the Breitkopf & Hartel Complete Works Edition. Franz Schubert. Tr. by Henry S. Drinker. 10.25 o.p. (ISBN 0-8446-0249-3). Peter Smith.

Complete Songs for Solos Voice & Piano, Series IV. Johannes Brahms. Ed. by Eusebius Mandyczewski. Tr. by Stanley Appelbaum from Ger. 224p. 1980. pap. 8.50 o.p. (ISBN 0-486-23823-7). Dover.

Complete Spanish-English Reference Guide. Joseph F. Simeone. 1984. 11.95 o.p. (ISBN 0-533-05530-X). Vantage.

Complete String Quartets & Grosse Fuge: From the Breitkopf & Hartel Complete Works Edition. Ludwig Van Beethoven. 10.00 o.p. (ISBN 0-8446-0028-8). Peter Smith.

Complete Survival Guide. Mark Thiffault. LC 83-70141. (Illus.). 256p. (Orig.). 1983. pap. 11.95 o.p. (ISBN 0-910676-53-4). DBI.

Complete Transposition of the Great Arteries. Reda M. Shaher. 1973. 96.00 o.p. (ISBN 0-12-638150-X). Acad Pr.

Complete Treasury of Stories for Public Speakers. Morris Mandel. LC 73-8433. 1973. 12.50 o.p. (ISBN 0-8246-0160-2). Jonathan David.

Complete Vegetable Gardner's Sourcebook. Duane Newcomb. 304p. (Orig.). 1980. pap. 9.95 o.p. (ISBN 0-380-75333-2, 75333-2). Avon.

Complete VLF-TR Metal Detector Handbook: All about Ground Cancelling Metal Detectors. Roy Lagal & Charles Garrett. Ed. by Bettye Nelson. LC 78-60309. (Illus.). 200p. (Orig.). 1980. pap. 8.95 o.p. (ISBN 0-915920-32-8). Ram Pub.

Complete Word Game Dictionary. Ed. by Tom Pulliam & Gorton Carruth. 648p. 19.95 o.p. (ISBN 0-87196-112-1). Facts on File.

Complete Works of Horace. Horace. Tr. by Charles E. Passage from Gr. LC 81-70126. 500p. 1983. 35.00x o.p. (ISBN 0-8044-2404-7). Ungar.

Complete Works of Oscar Wilde. Intro. by John Gilbert. 956p. 1988. 14.95 o.p. (ISBN 0-600-39372-0, Pub. by Hamlyn Pub Group England). Hippocrene Bks.

Complete Works of Thomas Lodge: 1580-1623, 4 Vols. Thomas Lodge. Repr. of 1883 ed. Set. 150.00 o.p. (ISBN 0-384-33350-8). Johnson Repr.

Complete Works of Washington Irving, Journals & Notebooks: 1803-1806, Vol. I. Ed. by Nathalia Wright. (Critical Editions Program Ser.). 1969. lib. bdg. 33.50 o.p. (ISBN 0-8057-8500-0, Twayne). G K Hall.

Complete 1980 CB Handbook. Jethro K. Lieberman & Neil S. Rhodes. 1976. pap. 1.75 o.p. (ISBN 0-380-00712-6, 29553-9). Avon.

Completely Civil Servant. G. Arthur Sage. (Illus.). 118p. (Orig.). 1985. pap. 9.95 o.p. (ISBN 0-920792-48-0, Dist. by University Toronto Press). Eden Pr.

Completing Berkeley's Project: Classical vs. Modern Philosophy. Theodore A. Young. LC 85-17762. 226p. 1986. lib. bdg. 28.75 o.p. (ISBN 0-8191-4945-4); pap. text ed. 12.50 o.p. (ISBN 0-8191-4946-2). U Pr of Amer.

Complex Analysis. Ed. by H. L. Resnikoff & R. O. Wells, Jr. (Rice University Studies: Vol. 54, No. 4). 84p. 1968. pap. 10.00x o.p. (ISBN 0-89263-198-8). Rice Univ.

Complex Analysis: The Argument Principle in Analysis & Topology. A. F. Beardon. LC 78-8540. 239p. 1979. 91.95x o.p. (ISBN 0-471-99671-8, Pub. by Wiley-Interscience). Wiley.

Complex Analysis Trieste: Proceedings, 1981. Ed. by J. Eells. (Lecture Notes in Mathematics Ser.: Vol. 950). 428p. 1982. pap. 29.70 o.p. (ISBN 0-387-11596-X). Springer-Verlag.

Complex Analysis, 1969. Ed. by H. L. Resnikoff & R. O. Wells, Jr. (Rice University Studies: Vol. 56, No. 2). 222p. 1970. pap. 10.00x o.p. (ISBN 0-89263-204-6). Rice Univ.

Complex Analysis, 1972, Vol. 1: Geometry of Singularities. Ed. by H. L. Resnikoff & R. O. Wells, Jr. (Rice University Studies: Vol. 59, No. 1). 162p. 1973. pap. 10.00x o.p. (ISBN 0-89263-215-1). Rice Univ.

Complex Analysis, 1972, Vol. 2: Analysis on Singularities. Ed. by H. L. Resnikoff & R. O. Wells, Jr. (Rice University Studies: Vol. 59, No. 2). 163p. 1973. pap. 10.00x o.p. (ISBN 0-89263-216-X). Rice Univ.

Complex Analytic Geometry. G. Fischer. (Lecture Notes in Mathematics Ser.: Vol. 538). 1976. soft cover 16.00 o.p. (ISBN 0-387-07857-6). Springer-Verlag.

Complex Analytic Manifolds. L. Schwartz. (Tata Institute of Fundamental Research Lectures: Vol. 4). iv, 186p. 1987. pap. 12.60 o.p. (ISBN 0-387-12877-8). Springer-Verlag.

Complex Digital Control Systems. Guthikonda V. Rao. 300p. 1979. 52.95 o.p. (ISBN 0-442-20110-9). Van Nos Reinhold.

Complex Function Theory. Maurice Heins. (Pure & Applied Mathematics Ser.: Vol. 28). 1968. text ed. 25.00 o.p. (ISBN 0-12-337950-4). Acad Pr.

Complex Sulfides: Processing of Ores, Concentrates & By-Products. Ed. by A. D. Zunkel et al. LC 85-18962. (Illus.). 938p. 1985. 87.00 o.p. (ISBN 0-87339-006-7). Minerals Metals.

Complex Variables. Herb Silverman. 1975. text ed. 26.50 o.p. (ISBN 0-395-18582-3). HM.

Complex Variables & Applications. 3rd ed. Ruel V. Churchill & James W. Brown. (Illus.). 352p. 1974. text ed. 42.95 o.p. (ISBN 0-07-010855-2). McGraw.

Complex Variables for Scientists & Engineers. John D. Paliouras. (Illus.). 416p. 1975. text ed. write for info. o.p. (ISBN 0-02-390550-6). Macmillan.

Complex Variables Problem Solver. Research & Education Association Staff. (Illus.). 928p. 1988. pap. text ed. 28.85 o.p. (ISBN 0-87891-604-0). Res & Educ.

Complex Vision: A Collection of Short Stories. Ray Kytle & Annette P. Kytle. 307p. 1972. pap. text ed. 7.95 o.p. (ISBN 0-15-512615-6, HC). HarBraceJ.

Complexity of Legal & Ethical Experience: Studies in the Method of Normative Subjects. Filmer S. Northrop. LC 78-790. (Illus.). 331p. 1978. Repr. of 1959 ed. lib. bdg. 27.75x o.p. (ISBN 0-313-20286-9, NOCL). Greenwood.

Compliance in Health Care. Brian Haynes et al. LC 78-20527. 1979. text ed. 55.00x o.p. (ISBN 0-8018-2162-2). Johns Hopkins.

Complications of Hand Surgery. S. H. Norris. (Complications in Surgery Ser.). (Illus.). 240p. 1986. (ISBN 0-7020-1143-6). Saunders.

Complot Contre la Vie. Rene Bel. Date not set. price not set o.p. (ISBN 0-913631-02-7). Anastasia VA.

Complying with Consumer Credit: A Creditor's Guide. 2nd ed. Lawrence J. Bugge et al. 358p. 1987. 65.00 o.p. (ISBN 0-941161-07-2). PES Inc WI.

Complying with Consumer Credit Regulations: A Creditor's Guide. 2nd. ed. Professional Education Systems Staff. 358p. 1986. 65.00 o.p. (ISBN 0-317-60067-2). PES Inc WI.

Component & Modular Techniques: A Builder's Handbook. 2nd ed. R. J. Lytle & R. C. Reschke. 1981. text ed. 32.50 o.p. (ISBN 0-07-039274-9). McGraw.

Component Element Method in Dynamics. Samuel Levy & John P. Wilkinson. 1976. text ed. 53.50 o.p. (ISBN 0-07-037398-1). McGraw.

Component Support Snubbers: Design, Application & Testing. Ed. by D. D. Reiff. (PVP: No. 42). 130p. 1980. 10.00 o.p. (ISBN 0-686-69844-4, H00169). ASME.

Component Testers. Don Grayson et al. Ed. by Sandy Cole. (Seventy-Three Test Equipment Library: Vol. 1). 104p. 1976. pap. text ed. 4.95 o.p. (ISBN 0-88006-010-7, LB 7359). Wayne Green Ent.

Components & Instruments for Distributed Computer Control Systems: Proceedings of the IFAC Symposium, Paris, France, Dec. 1982. IFAC Symposium Staff. Ed. by Z. Binder & R. Perret. LC 83-11448. (IFAC Proceedings). 178p. 1983. 80.00 o.p. (ISBN 0-08-029991-1). Pergamon.

Components & Structural Dynamics, Vol II. Ed. by G. J. Bohm et al. 812p. 1972. 35.00 o.p. (ISBN 0-317-33458-1, G00020); members 17.50 o.p. (ISBN 0-317-33459-X). ASME.

Components of Computers (1977) F. F. Mazda. 65.00 o.s.i. (ISBN 0-685-86891-5). E J Brill USA.

Components Quality Reliability Handbook. Intel Staff. 308p. (Orig.). 1986. pap. 20.00 o.p. (ISBN 1-55512-006-7, 210997-001). Intel Corp.

Composer Between Man & Music. Ed. by H. Sabbe. 138p. 1981. pap. text ed. 15.25 o.p. (ISBN 90-265-0371-7, Pub. by Swets Pub Serv Holland). Swets North Am.

Composer Society: Le Compositeur dans la Societe - Komponist und Gesellschaft. Ed. by H. Sabbe. xii, 64p. 1983. pap. 16.95 o.p. (ISBN 0-318-02039-4, Pub. by Swets Pub Serv Holland). Swets North Am.

Composing with Confidence. Alan Meyers. 1987. pap. text ed. write for info. o.p. (ISBN 0-673-18178-2). Scott F.

Composing with Wordstar. Rosalie Hewitt. 80p. 1986. pap. text ed. 6.95 o.p. (ISBN 0-8403-4106-7). Kendall Hunt.

Composing Your Paintings. Bernard Dunstan. LC 79-84661. (Start to Paint Ser.). (Illus.). 1979. pap. 3.95 o.s.i. (ISBN 0-8008-1803-2, Pentalic). Taplinger.

Composite Art of Acting. Jerry Blunt. 1966. text ed. write for info. o.p. (ISBN 0-02-311150-X, 31115). Macmillan.

Composite Engineering Laminates. Ed. by Albert G. Dietz. 1969. 45.00x o.p. (ISBN 0-262-04017-4). MIT Pr.

Composite Materials in the Automobile Industry. S. V. Kulkarni et al. 216p. 1978. 30.00 o.p. (ISBN 0-685-66793-6). ASME.

Composite Structures of Steel & Concrete, Vol. 11: Bridges with a Commentary on BS 5400, Pt. 5. R. P. Johnson & R. J. Buckby. 524p. 1979. text ed. 76.00x o.p. (ISBN 0-258-97104-5, Pub. by Granada England). Gower Pub Co.

Composites: Computer-Generated Portraits. Nancy Burson et al. (Illus.). 96p. 1986. 19.95 o.p. (ISBN 0-688-02601-X, Pub. by Beech Tree Bks). Morrow.

Composition: A Media Approach. Frederick B. Tuttle, Jr. 96p. 1978. pap. 7.75 o.p. (ISBN 0-8106-1499-5, 1499-5-06). NEA.

Composition & Function of Body Fluids. 3rd ed. Shirley R. Burke. LC 80-17952. (Illus.). 221p. 1980. pap. text ed. 15.95 o.p. (ISBN 0-8016-0903-8). Mosby.

Composition in Art. Henry R. Poore. 14.25 o.p. (ISBN 0-8446-5603-8). Peter Smith.

Composition of Wax & Oil in Green Coffee Beans. (Agricultural Research Reports Ser.: No. 854). 1979. pap. 5.50 o.p. (ISBN 90-220-0613-1, PDC145, PUDOC). UNIPUB.

Composition: Skills & Models. 2nd ed. Sidney T. Stovall et al. LC 77-77681. (Illus.). 1978. pap. 18.95 o.p. (ISBN 0-395-25749-2). HM.

Composition Steps. Vivian Horn. LC 76-57147. 1977. pap. text ed. 12.95 o.p. (ISBN 0-88377-069-5); tchr's. manual 3.50 o.p. (ISBN 0-88377-085-7). Newbury Hse.

Compound Interest & Annuity Tables. Frederick C. Kent & Maude E. Kent. 1963. pap. text ed. 4.95 o.p. (ISBN 0-07-034121-4). McGraw.

Compound Verb in Hindi. Peter Edwin Hook. LC 74-82629. (Michigan Papers in South & Southeast Asian Languages & Linguistics Ser.: No. 1). xxv, 318p. (Orig.). 1974. pap. 11.95 o.p. (ISBN 0-89148-051-X). Ctr S&SE Asian.

Compounds Containing AS-N Bonds. Ed. by Larry K. Krannich. LC 76-11783. (Benchmark Papers in Inorganic Chemistry: Vol. 5). 1976. 82.50 o.p. (ISBN 0-12-786869-0). Acad Pr.

Compounds Containing Phosphorus-Phosphorus Bonds. Ed. by Alan H. Cowley. LC 72-90631. (Benchmark Papers in Inorganic Chemistry: Vol. 3). 322p. 1982. 62.95 o.p. (ISBN 0-87933-017-1). Van Nos Reinhold.

Compounds of the Transition Elements Involving Metal-Metal Bonds. D. L. Kepert & K. Vrieze. (Pergamon Texts in Inorganic Chemistry: Vol. 27). 158p. 1975. text ed. 30.00 o.p. (ISBN 0-08-018880-X); pap. text ed. 17.50 o.p. (ISBN 0-08-018879-6). Pergamon.

Comprador. David R. Cudlip. 432p. 1985. pap. 3.95 o.p. (ISBN 0-380-69908-7). Avon.

Comprehension & Learning: A Conceptual Framework for Teachers. Frank Smith. LC 75-2041. 1975. pap. text ed. 17.95 o.p. (ISBN 0-03-011011-4, HoltC). HR&W.

Comprehension Corral. Imogene Forte. (Skills Stretchers Ser.). (Illus.). 32p. (gr. 2-5). 1981. pap. 3.95 o.p. (ISBN 0-86530-032-1, IP 32-1). Incentive Pubns.

Comprehension Master Level 1. Barbara W. Levy. (Comprehension Master Ser.). (Illus.). 48p. (ps-2). 1985. wkbk. 5.95 o.p. (ISBN 0-86653-294-3). Good Apple.

Comprehension Master Level 2. Barbara W. Levy. (Comprehension Master Ser.). (Illus.). 48p. (gr. 1-3). 1985. wkbk. 5.95 o.p. (ISBN 0-86653-295-1). Good Apple.

Comprehension Master Level 3. Barbara W. Levy. (Comprehension Master Ser.). (Illus.). 48p. (gr. 2-5). 1985. wkbk. 5.95 o.p. (ISBN 0-86653-297-8). Good Apple.

Comprehension Master Level 4. Barbara W. Levy. (Comprehension Master Ser.). (Illus.). 48p. (gr. 5-7). 1985. wkbk. 5.95 o.p. (ISBN 0-86653-319-2). Good Apple.

Comprehensive Administration of Special Education. Richard S. Podemski et al. LC 84-6369. 363p. 1984. 38.00 o.p. (ISBN 0-89443-590-6). Aspen Pub.

Comprehensive Analytical Chemistry: Analysis of Complex Hydrocarbon Mixtures, 2 pts, Vol.13A. Ed. by G. Svehla & C. Wilson. 1982. Pt. A: Separation Methods. 144.75 o.s.i. (ISBN 0-444-99736-9); Pt. B: Group Analysis & Detailed Analysis. 144.75 o.s.i. (ISBN 0-444-99735-0). Elsevier.

Comprehensive Bibliography of Music for Film & Television. Steven D. Wescott. LC 85-27184. (Detroit Studies in Music Bibliography: No. 54). 1986. 60.00 o.p. (ISBN 0-89990-027-5). Harmonie Pk Pr.

Comprehensive Bibliography on Foster Families. 1985. pap. 4.50 o.s.i. (ISBN 0-317-27071-0). Child Welfare.

Comprehensive Cardiac Care: A Text for Nurses, Physicians & Other Health Practitioners. 5th ed. Kathleen G. Andreoli et al. LC 82-12570. (Illus.). 556p. 1983. pap. text ed. 22.95 o.p. (ISBN 0-8016-0265-3). Mosby.

Comprehensive Cardiac Rehabilitation Program. Archbishop Bergan Mercy Hospital Staff. LC 80-13599. 62p. 1980. pap. 8.00 o.p. (ISBN 0-87125-063-2). Cath Health.

Comprehensive Care in Dentistry, Vol. 3. Ed. by Clifton E. Crandell. LC 78-16967. (Postgraduate Dental Handbook Ser.). 170p. 1979. 22.00 o.p. (ISBN 0-88416-164-1). Year Bk Med.

Comprehensive Classroom Management: Creating Positive Learning Environments & Solving Problems. Lewis & Clark College Staff & Beaverton School District Staff. 350p. 1981. write for info. o.p. (ISBN 0-205-07270-4, 247270). Allyn.

Comprehensive Crime Control Act of 1984, Vol. 136. Practising Law Institute Staff. 752p. 1985. pap. 40.00 o.p. (ISBN 0-317-27645-X, #C4-4171). PLI.

Comprehensive Dental Hygiene Care. 2nd ed. Irene R. Woodall et al. LC 80-15145. (Illus.). 800p. 1985. text ed. 41.95 casebound o.p. (ISBN 0-8016-5700-8). Mosby.

Comprehensive Dictionary of Psychological & Psychoanalytical Terms. Horace B. English & Ava C. English. LC 57-10524. 1958. pap. text ed. 17.95 o.p. (ISBN 0-679-30033-3, Pub. by MacKay). Longman.

Comprehensive Dissertation Index, 1974: Supplement, 1975, 5 vols. Incl. Sciences, 2 pts. Vol. 1, (Pt. 1 (ISBN 0-8357-0070-4). Vol. 2 (Pt. 2 (ISBN 0-8357-0071-2); Social Sciences & Humanities, 2 pts. Vol. 3, (Pt. 1 (ISBN 0-8357-0072-0). Vol. 4, (Pt. 2 (ISBN 0-8357-0073-9); Author Index. Vol. 5 (ISBN 0-8357-0074-7). write for info. o.p. (Pub. by Dissertations). Univ Microfilms.

Comprehensive Dissertation Index, 1983: Supplement 1984, 5 vols. write for info. o.p. (Pub. by Dissertations). Sciences: Pt. 1 (ISBN 0-8357-0629-X). Univ Microfilms.

Comprehensive Employment & Training Act of 1973: A Selected & Annotated Bibliography. Carolyn Woods. (Public Administration Ser.: Bibliography P 1629). 1985. pap. 6.75 o.p. (ISBN 0-89028-299-4). Vance Biblios.

Comprehensive Examination Review in Radiography. William L. Leonard & William F. Toeppe. 1983. pap. text ed. 19.50 o.p. (ISBN 0-87488-444-6). Med Exam.

Comprehensive History of Texas, 2 vols. Dudley G. Wooten. 1808p. Repr. Limited to 500 sets. 115.00 o.p. (ISBN 0-87611-020-0). Tex St Hist Assn.

Comprehensive Institutional Planning in Two-Year Colleges: An Overview & Conceptual Framework, Vol. 1. Steven Van Ausdle. 53p. 1980. 4.50 o.p. (ISBN 0-318-15429-3, SN26). Natl Ctr Res Voc Ed.

Comprehensive Institutional Planning in Two-Year Colleges: A Planning Process & Case Study, Vol. 2. Stephen Van Ausdle. 79p. 1980. 6.25 o.p. (ISBN 0-318-15428-5, SN27). Natl Ctr Res Voc Ed.

Comprehensive Intervention with Hearing - Impaired Infants & Preschool Children. M. Suzanne Hasenstab & John S. Horner. LC 81-14989. 528p. 1982. text ed. 35.00 o.p. (ISBN 0-89443-384-9). Aspen Pub.

Comprehensive Maintenance & Repair Program: Guidelines & Standards for the Maintenance & Repair of State-Owned Facilities. rev ed. 192p. 15.50 o.p. (ISBN 0-317-33654-1); members 10.00 o.p. (ISBN 0-913359-04-1). Assn Phys Plant Admin.

Comprehensive Medical Assisting: Administrative & Clinical Procedures. Mary A. Frew & David R. Frew. LC 81-9820. 756p. 1983. 26.95x o.p. (ISBN 0-8036-3858-2); wkbk. 10.95 o.p. Davis Co.

Comprehensive Respiratory Care. Eubanks. 1985. cloth 38.95 o.p. (ISBN 0-8016-1652-2). Mosby.

Comprehensive Review for the Radiologic Technologist. Stevens. (Illus.). 262p. 1982. pap. text ed. 19.95 o.p. (ISBN 0-8016-4790-8). Mosby.

Comprehensive Russian-English Agricultural Dictionary. B. N. Ussovsky & W. Linnard. (Rus. & Eng.). 1967. 120.00 o.p. (ISBN 0-08-010898-9). Pergamon.

Comprehensive School: Guidelines for the Reorganization of Secondary Education. rev ed. E. Halsall. LC 72-10107. 248p. 1974. pap. 65.00 o.p. (ISBN 0-08-018231-3). Pergamon.

Comprehensive Split Dollar. Ronald G. Floridis. 180p. (Orig.). 1983. pap. 19.00 o.p. (ISBN 0-87218-424-2). Natl Underwriter.

Comprehensive Structured COBOL. Gary S. Popkin. LC 83-25596. 560p. 1984. write for info. o.s.i. (ISBN 0-534-03112-9). PWS-Kent Pub.

Comprehensive Textbook of Classical Mathematics: A Contemporary Interpretation. H. B. Griffiths & P. J. Hilton. 1978. pap. 29.50 o.p. (ISBN 0-387-90342-9). Springer-Verlag.

Comprehensive Treatise on Inorganic & Theoretical Chemistry. J. W. Mellor & G. D. Parkes. Incl. Vol. 1. 1922. o.p. (ISBN 0-471-59295-1); Vol. 3. 1922. o.p. (ISBN 0-471-59297-8); Vol. 4. 1923. o.p. (ISBN 0-471-59298-6); Vol. 5. 1924. o.p. (ISBN 0-471-59303-6); Vol. 6. 1929. o.p. (ISBN 0-471-59304-4); Vol. 7. 1930. o.p. (ISBN 0-471-59305-?); Vol. 8. 1930. o.p. (ISBN 0-471-59306-0); Vol. 10. 1930. o.p. (ISBN 0-471-59308-7); Vol. 11. A Comprehensive Treatise on Inorganic & Theoretical Chemistry. Joseph W. Mellor. 1962. 99.95 o.p. (ISBN 0-471-59309-5); Vol. 12. 1932. o.p. (ISBN 0-471-59310-9); Vol. 13. 1934. o.p. (ISBN 0-471-59311-7); Vol. 14. 1935. o.p. (ISBN 0-471-59312-5); Vol. 15. 1936. o.p. (ISBN 0-471-59313-3); Vol. 16. 1937. o.p. (ISBN 0-471-59314-1). Halsted Pr.

Comprehensive View of Career Development. Ed. by Garry Walz et al. 104p. 1974. pap. 8.50 o.p. (ISBN 0-911547-19-3, 72047W34); pap. 6.00 o.p. (ISBN 0-686-34286-0). Am Assn Coun Dev.

Comprehensive Virology, Vol. 11: Genetics of Plant Viruses. Ed. by Heinz Fraenkel-Conrat & Robert R. Wagner. LC 77-7908. (Illus.). 364p. 1977. 59.50x o.p. (ISBN 0-306-35151-X, Plenum Pr). Plenum Pub.

Comprehensive Virology, Vol. 12: Newly Characterized Protist & Invertebrate Viruses. Ed. by Heinz Fraenkel-Conrat & Robert R. Wagner. LC 77-27552. (Illus.). 360p. 1978. 59.50x o.p. (ISBN 0-306-35152-8, Plenum Pr). Plenum Pub.

Compressible Flow Theory & Engineering Applications, Vol. 8. 1988. 195.00 o.p. (ISBN 0-87201-542-4). Gulf Pub.

Compromise of Principle: Congressional Republicans & Reconstruction 1863-1869. Michael L. Benedict. (Illus.). 1975. 18.95x o.p. (ISBN 0-393-05524-8). Norton.

COMPSAC 85: The IEEE Computer Society's Ninth International Computer Software & Applications Conference. LC 83-640060. 528p. 1985. 54.00 o.p. (ISBN 0-8186-0643-6, Q643); microfiche 54.00 o.p. (ISBN 0-8186-4643-8). IEEE Comp Soc.

Compton Scattering: A Tool for the Investigation of Electron Momentum Distribution. Brian G. Williams. LC 76-42261. (Illus.). 1977. text ed. 70.95x o.p. (ISBN 0-07-070360-4). McGraw.

Compton's Encyclopedia, 26 vols. (gr. 5-10). 1988. Set. 539.00 o.p. (ISBN 0-85229-474-3). Ency Brit Ed.

Compulsion. Meyer Levin. LC 56-9911. (Arbor House Library of Contemporary Americana). 506p. 1984. pap. 9.95 o.p. (ISBN 0-87795-650-2, Arbor Hse). Morrow.

Compulsory Arbitration in Public Employment see Issues in the Public Employee Relations Library: Series 5.

Computability & Decidability. J. Loeckx. LC 72-82761. (Lecture Notes in Economics & Mathematical Systems: Vol. 68). (Illus.). 82p. 1972. pap. 6.30 o.p. (ISBN 0-387-05869-9). Springer-Verlag.

Computable Analysis. Oliver Aberth. (Illus.). 208p. 1980. text ed. 46.50 o.p. (ISBN 0-07-000079-4). McGraw.

Computation, Calculators & Computers: Tools of Engineering Problem Solving-Including FORTRAN. George C. Beakley & Robert E. Lovell. 368p. 1983. pap. text ed. write for info. o.p. (ISBN 0-02-307150-8). Macmillan.

Computation of Fixed Points & Applications. M. J. Todd. (Lecture Notes in Economics & Mathematical Systems Ser.: Vol. 124). 1976. pap. 11.00 o.p. (ISBN 0-387-07685-9). Springer-Verlag.

Computational Analysis with the HP-25 Pocket Calculator. Peter Henrici. LC 77-1182. 280p. 1977. pap. 26.50 o.p. (ISBN 0-471-02938-6, Pub. by Wiley-Interscience). Wiley.

Computational Arithmetic. Llewellyn R. Snyder. LC 67-26174. 1968. text ed. 28.95 o.p. (ISBN 0-07-059552-6). McGraw.

Computational Fluid Mechanics & Heat Transfer. D. A. Anderson et al. LC 83-18614. (Series in Computational Methods in Mechanics & Thermal Sciences). 624p. 1984. text ed. 50.95 o.p. (ISBN 0-07-050328-1). McGraw.

Computational Light Scattering. P. W. Barber & S. C. Hill. 500p. 1989. 68.00 o.p. (ISBN 9971-50-813-3); pap. 34.00 o.p. (ISBN 9971-50-832-X). World Scientific Pub.

Computational Mechanics: Lectures in Computational Methods in Nonlinear Mechanics. Ed. by J. T. Oden. (Lecturenotes in Mathematics Ser.: Vol. 461). vii, 328p. (Orig.). 1975. 20.00 o.p. (ISBN 0-387-07169-5). Springer-Verlag.

Computational Method in Plasma Physics. F. Bauer et al. LC 78-8982. (Springer Ser. in Computational Physics). (Illus.). 1978. 25.00 o.p. (ISBN 0-387-08833-4). Springer-Verlag.

Computational Methods & Experimental Measurements, Washington, D.C. 1982: Proceedings. Ed. by George A. Keramidas & C. A. Brebbia. 838p. 1982. 78.20 o.p. (ISBN 0-387-11648-6). Springer-Verlag.

Computational Methods in Nonlinear Mechanics Structures. J. T. Oden & E. B. Becker. 1981. pap. 56.00 o.p. (ISBN 0-08-026153-1). Pergamon.

Computational Methods in Nonlinear Mechanics: Selected Papers of the 2nd Conference, Univ. of Texas at Austin. International Conference on Computational Methods in Nonlinear Mechanics Staff. Ed. by J. T. Oden. 160p. 1980. pap. 50.00 o.p. (ISBN 0-08-025068-8). Pergamon.

Computational Methods in Optimal Control Problems. I. H. Mufti. LC 77-121990. (Lecture Notes in Operations Research & Mathematical Systems: Vol. 27). 1970. pap. 10.70 o.p. (ISBN 0-387-04951-7). Springer-Verlag.

Computational Probability. Ed. by P. M. Kahn. LC 80-15014. 1980. 39.50 o.p. (ISBN 0-12-394680-8). Acad Pr.

Computational Problems in Abstract Algebra. J. Leech. 1970. 105.00 o.p. (ISBN 0-08-012975-7). Pergamon.

Computational Problems, Methods, & Results in Algebraic Number Theory. H. G. Zimmer. LC 72-78191. (Lecture Notes in Mathematics Ser.: Vol. 262). 108p. 1972. pap. 9.00 o.p. (ISBN 0-387-05822-2). Springer-Verlag.

Computational Skills for College Students. Calman Goozner. 1976. pap. text ed. 11.50 o.p. (ISBN 0-87720-976-6). AMSCO Sch.

Computational Techniques for Interface Problems, Vol. 30. Ed. by K. C. Park & D. K. Gartling. 192p. 1978. 24.00 o.p. (ISBN 0-685-66794-4, H00113). ASME.

Compute Arabia. 2nd ed. pap. write for info. o.s.i. Meghan-Kiffer.

Computed Brain & Orbital Tomography: Technique & Interpretation. Carlos F. Gonzalez et al. LC 76-28530. (Diagnostic & Therapeutic Radiology Ser.). 276p. 1976. 70.00x o.p. (ISBN 0-471-01692-6, Pub. by Wiley-Med). Krieger.

Computed Tomography of the Abdomen. Haaga & Alfidi. 1984. cloth 79.00 o.p. (ISBN 0-8016-2028-7). Mosby.

Computed Tomography of the Brain, Head & Neck. Haaga & Alfidi. 1984. cloth 79.00 o.p. (ISBN 0-8016-2029-5). Mosby.

Computed Tomography of the Brain in Axial, Coronal, & Sagittal Planes. George A. Binder et al. 1979. 59.95 o.p. (ISBN 0-316-09507-9). Little.

Computed Tomography of the Head & Spine: A Photographic Atlas of CT, Gross & Microscopic Anatomy. H. Norman Schnitzlein et al. LC 82-13515. (Illus.). 126p. 1982. text ed. 65.00 o.p. (ISBN 0-8067-1771-8). Urban & S.

Computed Tomography of the Spine. Haughton & Williams. 1982. cloth 55.95 o.p. (ISBN 0-8016-2118-6). Mosby.

Computed Tomography of the Whole Body, 2 vols. Ed. by John R. Haaga & Ralph J. Alfidi. LC 82-22868. (Illus.). 1184p. 1983. text ed. 147.00 o.p. (ISBN 0-8016-2047-3). Mosby.

Computed Tomography: Techniques & Procedures. Cleary et al. (Illus.). 450p. 1989. 39.95 o.p. (ISBN 0-8016-1173-3). Mosby.

Computer Aided Analysis & Optimization of Mechanical System Dynamics. Ed. by E. J. Haug. (NATO ASI Ser., Series F - Computer & Systems Sciences: Vol. 9). xxii, 700p. 1984. 58.00 o.p. (ISBN 0-387-12887-5). Springer-Verlag.

Computer-Aided Circuit Design: Simulation & Optimization. Ed. by S. W. Director. LC 73-16060. (Benchmark Papers in Electrical Engineering & Computer Science: Vol. 5). 380p. 1982. 56.95 o.p. (ISBN 0-87933-068-6). Van Nos Reinhold.

Computer-Aided Control System Design. H. H. Rosenbrock. 1975. 68.00 o.p. (ISBN 0-12-597450-7). Acad Pr.

Computer-Aided Design & Drafting for Design Professionals. 70p. 1983. 15.00 o.p. (96); 10.00_members o.p. Am Consul Eng.

Computer Aided Design Modelling, Systems Engineering, CAD Systems. J. Encarnacao. (Lecture Notes in Computer Science Ser.: Vol. 89). 459p. 1980. pap. 29.00 o.p. (ISBN 0-387-10242-6). Springer-Verlag.

Computer Aided Design of Control Systems: Proceedings of the IFAC Symposium, Zurich,Switzerland, Aug. 29-31, 1979. IFAC Symposium, Zurich, Switzerland, 29-31 Aug. 1979. Ed. by M. A. Cuenod. LC 79-42655. (IFAC Proceedings Ser.). (Illus.). 702p. 1980. 175.00 o.p. (ISBN 0-08-024488-2). Pergamon.

Computer Aided Design of Pipe & Pipe Supports. Ed. by E. Van Stijgeren. (PVP Ser.: Vol. 54). 86p. 1981. 18.00 o.p. (ISBN 0-686-34514-2, H00190). ASME.

Computer Aided Drafting, Programming & Plotting Using the Tektronix 4051. Donald G. Crist et al. LC 86-22727. (Illus.). 160p. (Orig.). 1987. pap. text ed. 13.20 o.p. (ISBN 0-87006-626-9). Goodheart.

Computer Aided Engineering. (IEE Conference Publication: No. 243). 177p. 1984. pap. 70.00 o.s.i. (ISBN 0-85296-303-3). Inst Elect Eng.

Computer-Aided Experimentation: Interfacing to Mini-Computers. Jules Finkel. LC 74-22060. 422p. 1975. 30.50 o.p. (ISBN 0-471-25884-9). Krieger.

Computer-Aided Part Programming for Numerical Control: An Industry Study. John D. McCarroll. (Illus.). 152p. 1976. 12.00 o.p. (ISBN 0-938654-02-0, CAPP). Indus Dev Inst Sci.

Computer Aided Power System Operation & Analysis. R. N. Dhar. (Illus.). 320p. 1983. text ed. 32.50 o.p. (ISBN 0-07-451580-2). McGraw.

Computer-Aided Processes In Instruction & Research. George C. Beakley. 1985. 33.00 o.p. (ISBN 0-12-083520-7); pap. 27.50 o.p. (ISBN 0-12-083521-5). Acad Pr.

Computer Algebra. Ed. by J. A. Van Hulzen. (Lecture Notes in Computer Science Ser.: Vol. 162). 305p. 1984. pap. 17.00 o.p. (ISBN 0-387-12868-9). Springer Verlag.

Computer Alphabet Book. Elizabeth S. Wall. (Illus.). 64p. (ps-3). 1984. pap. 2.25 o.p. (ISBN 0-380-87106-8, 87106-8, Camelot). Avon.

Computer Analysis of Large-Scale Structures. Ed. by K. C. Park & R. F. Jones, Jr. (AMD Ser.: Vol. 49). 102p. 1981. 24.00 o.p. (ISBN 0-686-34481-2, H00196). ASME.

Computer Analysis of Neuronal Structures. Ed. by Robert Lindsay. LC 76-50605. (Illus.). 226p. 1977. 49.50x o.p. (ISBN 0-306-30964-5, Plenum Pr). Plenum Pub.

Computer Analysis of Skeletal Structures. C. T. Ross & T. Johns. 1981. 32.00 o.p. (ISBN 0-419-11970-1, NO.6597, Pub. by E & FN Spon England). Routledge Chapman & Hall.

Computer & Business Equipment Market Book. CBEMA, Inc. Staff. 1985. 75.00 o.p. (ISBN 0-8104-6349-0). Sams.

Computer & Property Management. (Journal of Property Management Reprints). (Illus., Orig.). 1984. pap. 8.95 o.p. (ISBN 0-317-02671-2, 904). Inst Real Estate.

Computer Animation Primer. David Fox & Mitchell Waite. (Illus.). 208p. 1984. pap. text ed. 24.95 o.p. (ISBN 0-07-021742-4, BYTE Bks). McGraw.

Computer Anxiety & the Use of Microcomputers in Management. Geoffrey S. Howard. Ed. by Richard Farmer. LC 86-6904. (Research for Business Decisions Ser.: No. 92). 149p. 1986. 39.95 o.p. (ISBN 0-8357-1759-3). UMI Res Pr.

Computer Applications in Architecture. Ed. by John S. Gero. (Illus.). x, 413p. 1977. 86.00 o.p. (ISBN 0-85334-737-9, Pub. by Elsevier Applied Sci England). Elsevier.

Computer Applications in Chemical Engineering: Proceedings of the 12th Symposium of the European Federation of Chemical Engineering, Montreaux, April 1979. Ed. by D. W. Rippin & R. R. Hughes. 639p. 1981. pap. 160.00 o.p. (ISBN 0-08-025022-X). Pergamon.

Computer Applications in Counseling: Bibliography. 7.50 o.p. (ISBN 0-317-59902-X, 72120C). Am Assn Coun Dev.

Computer Applications in Manufacturing. Thomas G. Gunn, Jr. LC 81-6544. (Illus.). 204p. 1981. 32.95x o.p. (ISBN 0-8311-1087-2). Indus Pr.

Computer Applications in Personnel & Human Resources Management: A Bibliography. Mary E. Huls. (Public Administration Ser.: P 1747). 9p. 1985. 2.00 o.p. (ISBN 0-89028-527-6). Vance Biblios.

Computer Applications in Property Management Accounting. Ed. by Kenneth Anderson. 55p. 1984. pap. 16.95 o.p. (ISBN 0-912104-81-3, 990). Inst Real Estate.

Computer Applications in Property Management Accounting. rev. ed. IREM Research Department Staff. 55p. 1988. pap. 16.95 o.p. (ISBN 0-944298-06-0, 990). Inst Real Estate.

Computer Applications in Reading. 2nd ed. George E. Mason et al. 215p. (Orig.). 1983. pap. 8.00 o.p. (ISBN 0-87207-936-8, 936). Intl Reading.

Computer Applications in the Automation of Shipyard Operation & Ship Design, Vol. 4. Ed. by D. F. Rogers. (Computer Applications in Shipping & Shipbuilding: Vol. 9). 356p. 1982. 73.75 o.p. (ISBN 0-444-86408-3, I-300-82, North-Holland). Elsevier.

Computer Applications in the Earth Sciences: An International Symposium. Ed. by D. F. Merriam. LC 76-102212. 282p. 1969. 45.00x o.p. (ISBN 0-306-30445-7, Plenum Pr). Plenum Pub.

Computer Applications in the Earth Sciences: An Update of the Seventies. Ed. by D. F. Merriam. LC 81-10707. (Computer Applications in the Earth Sciences Ser.). 400p. 1981. 69.50x o.p. (ISBN 0-306-40809-0, Plenum Pr). Plenum Pub.

Computer Applications of Educational Measurement Concepts. Harold M. Kanter. 160p. 1985. text ed. write for info. o.p. (ISBN 0-02-362700-X). Macmillan.

Computer Appreciation for the Majority. Ed. by National Computing Centre, Ltd. Staff. LC 72-97128. 220p. 1973. pap. 2750.00x o.s.i. (ISBN 0-85012-153-1). Intl Pubns Serv.

Computer Architecture. 2nd ed. Caxton C. Foster. 1976. 26.50 o.p. (ISBN 0-442-22434-6). Van Nos Reinhold.

Computer Arithmetic. F. H. George. 1966. text ed. 18.50 o.p. (ISBN 0-08-011464-4); pap. 7.75 o.p. (ISBN 0-08-011463-6). Pergamon.

Computer Assigned Credit Line Program. 13p. 1981. 40.00 o.p. (ISBN 0-939050-08-0). Credit Res NYS.

Computer Assistance in the Analysis of High-Resolution NMR Spectra. P. Diehl et al. (NMR Basic Principles & Progress Ser.: Vol. 6). (Illus.). 100p. 1972. 27.00 o.p. (ISBN 0-387-05532-0). Springer-Verlag.

Computer Assisted Indexing in the Central State University Library. George L. Gardiner. (Occasional Papers: No. 120). 24p. 1975. pap. 2.00 o.p. (ISBN 0-317-58939-3). U of Ill Lib Info Sci.

Computer-Assisted Instruction at Stanford, 1966-68. Patrick Suppes & Mona Morningstar. 1972. 19.95 o.p. (ISBN 0-12-676856-0). Acad Pr.

Computer Assisted Instruction in Geology: Proceedings of the 4th Geochautauqua, Syracuse University, 1975. Ed. by D. F. Merriam. 1976. pap. 50.00 o.p. (ISBN 0-08-021040-6). Pergamon.

Computer-Assisted Instruction: Stanford's 1965-66 Arithmetic Program. Patrick C. Suppes et al. (Illus.). 1968. 19.95 o.p. (ISBN 0-12-676850-1). Acad Pr.

Computer Assisted Learning in Physics Education. Ed. by A. Bork. LC 80-41129. (Illus.). 80p. 1980. 44.00 o.p. (ISBN 0-08-025812-3). Pergamon.

Computer Assisted Learning in Science Education. Ed. by G. Beech. LC 78-40566. 1979. pap. text ed. 55.00 o.p. (ISBN 0-08-023010-5). Pergamon.

Computer-Assisted Medical Record Systems: An Examination of Case Studies. Ed. by American Hospital Association Clearinghouse for Hospital Management Engineering Staff. 148p. 1982. pap. 18.75 o.p. (ISBN 0-87258-375-9, AHA-148200). Am Hospital.

Computer Assisted Research in the Humanities: A Directory of Scholars Active, 1966-1972. Joseph Raben. LC 75-16447. 1977. text ed. 75.00 o.p. (ISBN 0-08-019870-8). Pergamon.

Computer Basics. Time-Life Book Editors. (Understanding Somputers Ser.). 128p. 1985. 19.93 o.p.; lib. bdg. 23.93 o.p. Time-Life.

Computer Basics: A Guide for Business Application. Joseph M. Vles. LC 81-66220. 192p. 1983. pap. 6.95 o.p. (ISBN 0-8144-7599-X). AMACOM.

Computer Blue Book, 1985. 290p. 1985. 49.50 o.p. (ISBN 0-932089-04-6). Orion Res.

Computer Blue Book, 1986. 300p. Date not set. 99.50 o.p. (ISBN 0-932089-11-9). Orion Res.

Computer Blue Book, 1987. Ed. by Orion Research Corporation Staff. 350p. 1986. 99.50 o.p. (ISBN 0-932089-16-X). Orion Res.

Computer Bridge. Thomas Throop. 160p. 1983. pap. 10.95 o.p. (ISBN 0-317-00356-9). Sams.

Computer Briefing: Using the Trends for Better Managerial Decisions. Lynn M. Salerno. LC 85-17966. (Problem Solving, Decision Making & Strategic Thinking Ser.). 224p. 1986. 19.95 o.p. (ISBN 0-471-89609-8). Wiley.

Computer Buyer's Guide. 250p. 1985. 19.50 o.p. (ISBN 0-932090-02-8). Orion Res.

Computer Buyer's Guide, 1985. Orion Research Staff. Ed. by Roger Rohrs. 200p. (Orig.). 1984. pap. 20.00 o.p. (ISBN 0-318-03744-0). Busn Comp CO.

Computer Buyer's Pocket Notebook. Richard H. Montgomery. (Illus.). 64p. (Orig.). 1984. pap. 3.50 o.p. (ISBN 0-915991-03-9). R H Mont Assocs.

Computer Buyer's Survival Manual. C. Amos Johnson. (Illus.). 224p. (Orig.). 1984. 15.95 o.p. (ISBN 0-8306-0767-6); pap. 9.70 o.p. (ISBN 0-8306-1767-1, 1767). TAB Bks.

Computer Capacity: A Production Control Approach. Melvin J. Strauss. 288p. 1984. 32.95 o.p. (ISBN 0-442-26243-4); pap. 21.95 o.p. (ISBN 0-442-28050-5). Van Nos Reinhold.

Computer Careers: Planning, Prerequisites, Potential. John Maniotes & James Quasney. (Illus.). 192p. 1974. pap. 7.50 o.p. (ISBN 0-8104-5913-2). Sams.

Computer Carnival. Richard Ramella. (Illus.). 218p. (Orig.). 1982. spiral 16.95 o.p. (ISBN 0-88006-055-7, BK7389). Wayne Green Ent.

Computer Carnival-Carnival Companion. Richard Ramella. (Illus.). 218p. (Orig.). 1982. spiralbound incl. software 24.95 o.p. (ISBN 0-88006-074-3, CC7389). Wayne Green Ent.

Computer Chess. Ludek Pachman & Vas I. Kuhnmund. (Illus.). 176p. 1986. pap. 9.95 o.p. (ISBN 0-7100-9785-9, 98659). Routledge Chapman & Hall.

Computer Communication Techniques. E. G. Brooner & Phil Wells. LC 83-60166. 144p. 1983. pap. text ed. 15.95 o.p. (ISBN 0-672-21998-0). Sams.

Computer Communications: Architectures, Protocols, & Standards. Ed. by William Stallings. LC 85-60383. (Tutorial Text Ser.). 485p. (Orig.). 1985. 39.00 o.p. (ISBN 0-8186-0604-5, Q604); microfiche 39.00 o.p. (ISBN 0-8186-4604-7). IEEE Comp Soc.

Computer Communications Asia '85: Proceedings of the Conference Held in Singapore, December 1985. 415p. 1985. pap. text ed. 120.00x o.p. (ISBN 0-86353-042-7, Pub. by Online). Gower Pub Co.

Computer Companion for the Apple II-Apple IIe. Robert P. Haviland. 128p. 1983. pap. 9.95 o.p. (ISBN 0-8306-1603-9, 1603). TAB Bks.

Computer Compilation of Molecular Weights & Percentage Compositions for Organic Compounds. M. J. Dewar & R. Jones. 1969. 125.00 o.p. (ISBN 0-08-012707-X). Pergamon.

Computer Concordance to the Novum Testamentum Graece of Nestle-Aland, 26th Edition & to the Greek New Testament, 3rd Edition. 2nd ed. Ed. by The Institute for New Testament Textural Research & The Computer Center of Muenster University with Collaboration of H. Bachmann & W. A. Slaby. x, 1018p. 1985. 72.00 o.p. (ISBN 3-11-010528-4). De Gruyter.

Computer Connection. Benedict. Date not set. 5.00 o.p. (ISBN 0-318-23314-2). Quill & Scroll.

Computer Connections. Ed. by Jean Nazzaro. 192p. 1981. 16.65 o.p. (ISBN 0-86586-119-6). Coun Exc Child.

Computer Courses for Adults: Anxious Human Meets Computer (A Resource Book for Instructors) Tony J. Allen. (Monograph). 108p. 1985. 10.00 o.p. (ISBN 0-924667-19-2). Intl Council Comp.

Computer Crazy. Daniel Le Noury. LC 84-50034. (Illus.). 96p. (Orig.). 1984. pap. 5.95 o.p. (ISBN 0-89588-173-X). SYBEX.

Computer Crime: Computer Security Techniques. 231p. 1982. pap. 7.50 o.p. (ISBN 0-318-11768-1, S/N 027-000-01169-1). USGPO.

Computer Data & Database Source Book. Matthew Lesko. 768p. 1984. pap. 14.95 o.p. (ISBN 0-380-86942-X). Avon.

Computer Data Structures. John Pfaltz. (Illus.). 1977. text ed. 47.95 o.p. (ISBN 0-07-049743-5). McGraw.

Computer Design. Boon. (Infotech Computer State of the Art Reports). 666p. 1974. 85.00 o.p. (ISBN 0-08-028496-5). Pergamon.

Computer Design Development: Principal Papers. Earl E. Swartzlander. 320p. 1975. 14.95x o.p. (ISBN 0-8104-5988-4). Sams.

Computer Dictionary. 4th ed. Charles J. Sippl. LC 84-51436. 576p. 1985. pap. 24.95 o.p. (ISBN 0-672-22205-1). Sams.

Computer Dictionary. 2nd ed. Donald D. Spencer. LC 78-31738. 1979. 11.95 o.p. (ISBN 0-89218-037-4); pap. 6.95 o.p. (ISBN 0-89218-038-2). Camelot Pub.

Computer Dictionary for Everyone. Donald D. Spencer. 1981. pap. 5.95 o.s.i. (ISBN 0-684-16946-0, ScribT). Scribner.

Computer Dictionary for Everyone. rev. ed. Donald D. Spencer. 1980. 11.95 o.s.i. (ISBN 0-684-16305-5, ScribT). Scribner.

Computer-Ease: A Guide to Selecting Your Personal Computer. Gordon Morrell. LC 83-62229. (Illus.). 98p. (Orig.). 1983. pap. 6.95 o.p. (ISBN 0-912528-34-6). John Muir.

Computer Education: A Catalog of Projects Sponsored by the United States Department of Education, 1983. 315p. 1984. pap. 9.00 o.p. (ISBN 0-318-11766-5, S/N 065-000-00202-7). USGPO.

Computer Education for Developing Nations. Dennis O. Harper. (Monograph Ser.). 46p. 1985. 10.00 o.p. (ISBN 0-924667-20-6). Intl Council Comp.

Computer Environments for Children: A Reflection of Theories of Learning & Education. Cynthia Solomon. (Illus.). 228p. 1986. text ed. 22.50x o.p. (ISBN 0-262-19249-7). MIT Pr.

Computer Establishment. K. D. Fishman. 480p. 1982. pap. text ed. 7.95 o.p. (ISBN 0-07-021127-2). McGraw.

Computer Fitness. Pinchot Publications Staff. incl. disk 60.00 o.p. (ISBN 0-8359-0816-X, Reston). P-H.

Computer Fraud & Countermeasures. Leonard I. Krauss & Aileen MacGahar. (Illus.). 1979. Reference ed. text ed. 60.67 o.p. (ISBN 0-13-164772-5). P-H.

Computer Frontiers. Ed. by Thomas Massam. (Illus.). 1977. 32.50x o.p. (ISBN 2-604-00024-5). Gower Pub Co.

Computer Fundamentals for Nonspecialists. Joseph M. Vles. LC 81-662201. 192p. 1981. 15.95 o.p. (ISBN 0-8144-5664-2). AMACOM.

Computer FX 'Eighty-Four: Computer Animation & Digital Effects. 213p. 1984. pap. text ed. 100.00x o.p. (ISBN 0-86353-013-3, Pub. by Online). Gower Pub Co.

Computer Game Playing. Ed. by Hans Berliner. 63p. 1988. pap. text ed. 20.00x o.p. (ISBN 0-929280-04-0). Amer Artificial.

Computer Gardening. Pinchot Publications Staff. incl. disk 60.00 o.p. (ISBN 0-8359-0817-8, Reston). P-H.

Computer-Generated Time Standards: A Methodology. Wilbert Steffy & Daniel R. Darby. (Illus.). 78p. 1980. 12.00 o.p. (ISBN 0-938654-13-6, CGTS). Indus Dev Inst Sci.

Computer Glossary, It's Not Just a Glossary. Alan Freedman. 86p. 1981. pap. (ISBN 0-941878-00-7). Computer Lang.

Computer Glossary: It's Not Just a Glossary. 3rd ed. Alan Freedman. (Illus.). 324p. 1983. 14.95 o.p. (ISBN 0-941878-02-3). Computer Lang.

Computer Graphics: A Powerful New Tool for the Prestressed Concrete Industry. (PCI Journal Reprints Ser.). 13p. pap. 5.00 o.p. (ISBN 0-686-40141-7, JR237). P-PCI.

Computer Graphics & Reporting Financial Data. Irwin M. Jarett. LC 82-23765. 360p. 1983. 55.00x o.p. (ISBN 0-471-86761-6, Pub by Ronald Pr). Wiley.

Computer Graphics Eighty-One: Proceedings of the International Conference. 545p. 1981. pap. 98.00x o.p. (ISBN 0-686-97779-3, Pub. by Online Conferences England). Gower Pub Co.

Computer Graphics for Artists. C. Hudson. pap. write for info. o.s.i. Meghan-Kiffer.

Computer Graphics Glossary. Stuart Hubbard. LC 83-82558. (Illus.). 112p. 1984. pap. 17.95 o.p. (ISBN 0-442-23618-2). Van Nos Reinhold.

Computer Graphics Hardware, Vol. 9. Laboratory for Computer Graphics & Spatial Analysis, Harvard University Graduate School of Design Staff. (Harvard Library of Computer Graphics, Mapping Collection). (Illus.). 80p. 1980. pap. 15.95 o.p. (ISBN 0-8122-1189-8). U of Pa Pr.

Computer Graphics Hardware, Vol. 14. Laboratory for Computer Graphics & Spatial Analysis, Harvard University Graduate School of Design Staff. (Harvard Library of Computer Graphics, Mapping Collection). (Illus.). 79p. 1981. pap. 15.95 o.p. (ISBN 0-8122-1194-4). U of Pa Pr.

Computer Graphics in Energy Exploration & Production. Allan Schmidt. 1985. 395.00 o.p. (P1971). PennWell Bks.

Computer Graphics in Engineering Education. Ed. by D. F. Rogers. 136p. 1982. 45.00 o.p. (ISBN 0-08-028949-5). Pergamon.

Computer Graphics Programming. G. Enderle. (Symbolic Computation Ser.). 450p. 1984. 54.00 o.p. (ISBN 0-387-11525-0). Springer-Verlag.

Computer Graphics: Techniques & Applications. R. D. Parslow et al. LC 74-31472. 234p. 1969. 39.50x o.p. (ISBN 0-306-30393-0, Plenum Pr); pap. 14.95x o.p. (ISBN 0-306-20016-3). Plenum Pub.

Computer Graphics User's Guide. Andrew S. Glassner. LC 83-50378. 240p. 1984. pap. 19.95 o.p. (ISBN 0-672-22064-4, 22064). Sams.

Computer Graphics with Twenty-Nine Ready-to-Run Programs. David W. Chance. 280p. 1981. 15.95 o.p. (ISBN 0-8306-9636-9); pap. 9.95 o.p. (ISBN 0-8306-1276-9, 1276). TAB Bks.

Computer Images. Time-Life Books Editors. (Understanding Computers Ser.). 128p. 1986. 19.93 o.p.; lib. bdg. 23.93 o.p. Time-Life.

Computer Interfacing & On-Line Operation. John C. Cluley. LC 74-16952. (Computer Systems Engineering Ser.). (Illus.). 181p. 1975. 19.50x o.p. (ISBN 0-8448-0567-X, Pub. by Crane Russak & Co). Taylor & Francis.

Computer Is Down. 2nd ed. Evangelina Vigil. LC 83-72576. 64p. (Orig.). 1984. pap. 5.00 o.p. (ISBN 0-934770-32-8). Arte Publico.

Computer Laboratory Manual for Number Theory. Donald G. Malm. 256p. 1980. pap. text ed. 9.95x o.p. (ISBN 0-933694-13-X). COMPress.

Computer Languages. P. C. Sanderson. 1970. (ISBN 0-8022-2330-3). Philos Lib.

Computer Law: Buying & Selling Computer Hardware & Software. Pennsylvania Bar Institute Staff. 221p. 1983. 30.00 o.p. (ISBN 0-318-02159-5, 239). PA Bar Inst.

Computer Law Forms Handbook: A Legal Guide to Drafting & Negotiating. Lauren R. Schwartz. LC 86-207904. 512p. 1986. pap. 55.00 o.p. (ISBN 0-87632-514-2). Clark Boardman.

Computer Law Institue 1985. Daniel T. Brooks. 1016p. 1985. 15.00 o.p. (G4-3775). PLI.

Computer Law Institute 1983-84. rev. ed. Daniel T. Brooks. (Commercial Law & Practices Course Handbook Ser.). 775p. 1983. pap. text ed. 45.00 o.p. (ISBN 0-317-02424-8, G4-3736). PLI.

Computer Law 1986: Cumulative Supplement. Scott. 1986. pap. 45.00 o.p. (ISBN 0-471-84593-0). Wiley.

Computer Leasing. Henry S. Beers, Jr. 320p. 1983. 35.95 o.p. Van Nos Reinhold.

Computer Literacy. Levi Reiss. 526p. 1984. pap. text ed. 21.00 o.p. (ISBN 0-87150-693-9, 8100). PWS-Kent Pub.

Computer Literacy: Definition & Survey Items for Assessment in Schools. Marlaine E. Lockheed. 219p. 1983. pap. 7.00 o.p. (ISBN 0-318-11767-3, S/N 065-000-00196-9). USGPO.

Computer Literacy for School Administrators. Stephen Radin & Harold M. Greenberg. LC 82-48597. 288p. 1983. 35.00x o.p. (ISBN 0-669-06330-4). Lexington Bks.

Computer Litigation 1984, Resolving Computer Related Disputes & Protecting Proprietary Rights. William A. Fenwick & Practising Law Institute. LC 82-63160. (Litigation & Administrative Practice Ser.: No. 216). (Illus.). 1002p. 1984. 15.00 o.p. (H4-4933). PLI.

Computer Logic, Testing & Verification. J. Paul Roth. LC 79-27230. (Digital System Design Ser.). (Illus.). 176p. 1980. text ed. 42.95 o.p. (ISBN 0-914894-62-5, Computer Sci Pr). W H Freeman.

Computer Mapped Flora: A Study of the County of Warwickshire. Ed. by J. G. Hawkes et al. 1972. 69.00 o.p. (ISBN 0-12-333360-1). Acad Pr.

Computer Mapping Applications in Urban, State, & Federal Government: Plus Computer Graphics & Education, Vol. 16. Laboratory for Computer Graphics & Spatial Analysis, Harvard University Graduate School of Design Staff. (Harvard Library of Computer Graphics, Mapping Collection). (Illus.). 140p. 1981. pap. 14.50 o.p. (ISBN 0-8122-1196-0). U of Pa Pr.

Computer Mapping in Education, Research, & Medicine, Vol. 5. Laboratory for Computer Graphics & Spatial Analysis, Harvard University Graduate School of Design Staff. (Harvard Library of Computer Graphics, Mapping Collection). (Illus.). 112p. 1979. pap. 14.50 o.p. (ISBN 0-8122-1185-5). U of Pa Pr.

Titles

Computer Mapping in Natural Resources & Environment: Including Applications of Satellite-Derived Data, Vol. 4. Laboratory for Computer Graphics & Spatial Analysis, Harvard University Graduate School of Design Staff. (Harvard Library of Computer Graphics, Mapping Collection). (Illus.). 138p. 1979. pap. 15.95 o.p. (ISBN 0-8122-1184-7). U of Pa Pr.

Computer Mapping of Natural Resources & the Environment: Including Applications of Satellite-Derived Data, Vol. 10. Laboratory for Computer Graphics & Spatial Analysis, Harvard University Graduate School of Design Staff. (Harvard Library of Computer Graphics, Mapping Collection). (Illus.). 131p. 1980. pap. 15.95 o.p. (ISBN 0-8122-1190-1). U of Pa Pr.

Computer Mapping of Natural Resources & the Environment: Plus Satellite-Derived Data Applications, Vol. 15. Laboratory for Computer Graphics & Spatial Analysis, Harvard University Graduate School of Design Staff. (Harvard Library of Computer Graphics, Mapping Collection). (Illus.). 180p. 1981. pap. 15.95 o.p. (ISBN 0-8122-1195-2). U of Pa Pr.

Computer Mathematics. Clifford L. Conrad et al. 1975. 12.90x o.p. (ISBN 0-8104-5095-X); solutions manual 2.10x o.p. (ISBN 0-8104-5779-2). Sams.

Computer Metaphors: Approaches to Computer Literacy. Howard Peelle. 48p. 1984. 6.00 o.p. (ISBN 0-924667-03-6). Intl Council Comp.

Computer Methods for Civil Engineering. R. Cope & F. Sawko. 336p. 1982. text ed. 19.00 o.p. (ISBN 0-07-084129-2). McGraw.

Computer Methods for Nonlinear Solids & Structural Mechanics. Ed. by Satya Atluri & Nicholas Perrone. 264p. 1983. pap. text ed. 50.00 o.p. (ISBN 0-317-02562-7, G00224). ASME.

Computer Methods for Partial Differential Equations: Elliptical Equations & the Finite Element Method, Vol. 1. Robert Vichenevetsky. (Illus.). 400p. 1981. text ed. 56.67 o.p. (ISBN 0-13-165233-8). P-H.

Computer Networks. Andrew S. Tanenbaum. (Illus.). 544p. 1981. text ed. 57.00 o.p. (ISBN 0-13-165183-8). P-H.

Computer Operator Tests. Jonathan Hodgson. 176p. Date not set. pap. 10.00 o.p. (ISBN 0-668-05906-0). Arco.

Computer Photography. Pinchot Publications Staff. 60.00 o.p. (ISBN 0-8359-0821-6, Reston). P-H.

Computer Pioneers: The Making of the Modern Computer. David Ritchie. 256p. 1986. 17.45 o.p. (ISBN 0-671-52397-X). S&S.

Computer Power for Your Accounting Firm. James Morgan. LC 84-51244. 222p. 1984. pap. 17.95 o.p. (ISBN 0-89588-164-0). SYBEX.

Computer Principles of Modeling & Simulation. Theodore G. Lewis & Brian J. Smith. LC 78-69604. (Illus.). 1979. text ed. 40.50 o.p. (ISBN 0-395-27143-6). HM.

Computer Processing of Dynamic Images from an Anger Scintillation Camera. Ed. by Kenneth B. Larson & Jerome R. Cox, Jr. LC 73-90924. (Illus.). 226p. 1974. lib. bdg. 15.00 o.p. (ISBN 0-88416-037-8). Year Bk Med.

Computer Product & Service Directory. Real Estate Institute of Canada Staff. 1983. 29.95 o.p. (ISBN 0-317-12272-X). Inst Real Estate.

Computer Programming: FORTRAN IV. Decima M. Anderson. (Illus., Orig.). 1966. pap. text ed. (ISBN 0-13-164822-5). P-H.

Computer Programming Tests. Jonathan Hodgson. 176p. Date not set. pap. 10.00 o.p. (ISBN 0-668-05908-7). Arco.

Computer Programs for Chemistry, Vol. 4. Ed. by Delos F. Detar. 1972. 75.00 o.p. (ISBN 0-12-151504-4). Acad Pr.

Computer Programs for Elementary Decision Analysis. Robert Schlaifer. LC 75-151633. (Illus.). 247p. 1971. 24.95x o.p. (ISBN 0-87584-091-4, Dist. by Harper & Row Pubs., Inc.). Harvard Busn.

Computer Programs for Spelling Correction. J. L. Petersen. (Lecture Notes in Computer Science Ser.: Vol. 96). 213p. 1980. pap. 17.00 o.p. (ISBN 0-387-10259-0). Springer-Verlag.

Computer Programs for the Kitchen. Terence F. Dicker. (Illus.). 304p. 1984. 18.95 o.p. (ISBN 0-8306-0707-2, 1707); pap. 13.15 o.p. (ISBN 0-8306-1707-8). TAB Bks.

Computer Ratio Analysis: An Aid to Decision Making. Wilbert Steffy et al. (Illus.). 63p. 12.00 o.p. (ISBN 0-938654-14-4, CRA). Indus Dev Inst Sci.

Computer Representation & Manipulation of Chemical Information. Ed. by W. Todd Wipke et al. LC 80-11684. 336p. 1981. Repr. of 1974 ed. lib. bdg. 29.50 o.p. (ISBN 0-89874-142-4). Krieger.

Computer Security & Protection Structures. B. J. Walker & Ian F. Blake. 1982. 35.95 o.p. (ISBN 0-87933-247-6). Van Nos Reinhold.

Computer Semantics: Studies of Algorithms Processors & Languages. John A. Lee. LC 77-7263. 416p. 1978. Repr. of 1972 ed. 28.00 o.p. (ISBN 0-88275-546-3). Krieger.

Computer Simulation of Classical Substitution: Cryptographics Systems. Rudolph F. Lauer. 1981. lib. bdg. 32.80 o.p. (ISBN 0-89412-081-6); pap. 24.80 o.p. (ISBN 0-89412-050-6). Aegean Park Pr.

Computer Simulation of Competitive Market Response. Arnold E. Amstutz. (Illus.). 1967. pap. 12.50x o.p. (ISBN 0-262-51009-X). MIT Pr.

Computer Simulation of Physiological Systems. Ed. by Thomas G. Coleman. 40p. pap. 10.00 o.p. (ISBN 0-686-36684-0). Soc Computer Sim.

Computer Simulation of Solids. Ed. by C. R. Catlow & W. C. Mackrodt. (Lecture Notes in Physics Ser.: Vol. 166). 320p. 1982. pap. 21.00 o.p. (ISBN 0-387-11588-9). Springer-Verlag.

Computer Simulation, 1951-1976: An Index to the Literature. Per Holst. 454p. 1979. 60.00x o.p. (ISBN 0-7201-0734-2). Mansell.

Computer Software & Chips: Protection & Marketing 1985, 2 vols. 1745p. 1985. 15.00 o.p. (G4-3769). PLI.

Computer Software for the Geosciences: Proceedings of the Geochautauqua, 5th, 1976. Ed. by D. F. Merriam. LC 77-30468. 1977. pap. 50.00 o.p. (ISBN 0-08-022090-8). Pergamon.

Computer Software: Protection & Marketing, 1984. 1984. 15.00 o.p. (G4-3751). PLI.

Computer Solution of Large Sparse Positive Definite. Alan George & Joseph W. Liu. (Illus.). 256p. 1981. text ed. 56.67 o.p. (ISBN 0-13-165274-5). P-H.

Computer Solution: Strategies for Success in the Information Age. Eugene F. Bedell. LC 84-71130. 300p. 1984. 35.00 o.p. (ISBN 0-87094-474-6). Dow Jones-Irwin.

Computer Studies: Computers in Education. Stephen Taffee. 288p. 1985. pap. 8.95 o.p. (ISBN 0-87967-559-4). Dushkin Pub.

Computer Studies: Computers in Society. Kathryn Schellenberg. 256p. 1986. pap. 8.95 o.p. (ISBN 0-87967-616-7). Dushkin Pub.

Computer System for Checking Proofs. Scott D. Johnson. Ed. by Harold Stone. LC 82-6990. (Computer Science: Artificial Intelligence Ser.: No. 12). 280p. 1983. 49.95 o.p. (ISBN 0-8357-1343-1). UMI Res Pr.

Computer Systems for Human Systems. A. Demb. LC 77-30730. (Illus.). 186p. 1979. 63.00 o.p. (ISBN 0-08-023029-6). Pergamon.

Computer Systems Measurement. Bunyan. (Infotech Computer State of the Art Reports). 701p. 1974. 310.00x o.p. (ISBN 0-08-028551-1). Pergamon.

Computer Systems Requirements. Kenneth L. Thurber. LC 80-83088. (Tutorial Texts Ser.). 356p. 1980. 25.00 o.p. (ISBN 0-8186-0313-5, Q313). IEEE Comp Soc.

Computer Talk. Melvin Berger. LC 83-22120. (Illus.). 96p. (gr. 4 up). 1984. lib. bdg. 9.29 o.p. (ISBN 0-671-47342-5). Messner.

Computer Tape Atlas of Mass Spectral Data. Einar Stenhagen et al. 1000.00 o.p. (ISBN 0-471-16708-8). Wiley.

Computer Techniques for Electromagnetics. Ed. by R. A. Mittra. 416p. 1973. 130.00 o.p. (ISBN 0-08-016888-4). Pergamon.

Computer Techniques in Image Processing. Harry C. Andrews. 1970. 52.50 o.p. (ISBN 0-12-058550-2). Acad Pr.

Computer Techniques in Shielding & Dosimetry. Ed. by Walter R. Nelson & T. M. Jenkins. LC 79-20872. (Ettore Majorana International Science Ser., Physical Sciences: Vol. 3). 534p. 1980. 89.50x o.p. (ISBN 0-306-40307-2, Plenum Pr). Plenum Pub.

Computer Technology for the Handicapped in Special Education & Rehabilitation: A Resource Guide, 2 vols, Vols. 1 & 2. Phillip Browning & Jeri Carter. Vol. 1. 7.00 o.p. (ISBN 0-924667-04-4); Vol. 2. 10.00 o.p. (ISBN 0-924667-23-0); Set. 15.00 o.p. Intl Council Comp.

Computer Technology in Fusion Energy Research: PVP-PB-31. Ed. by J. E. Akin & W. H. Gray. 117p. 1978. 18.00 o.p. (ISBN 0-317-33466-2, H00136); members 9.00 o.p. (ISBN 0-317-33467-0). ASME.

Computer Technology: Simplified. Frank L. Bouquet. (Illus.). 75p. (Orig.). 1988. lib. bdg. 75.00x o.p. (ISBN 0-317-67821-3); text ed. 60.00x o.p. (ISBN 0-317-67822-1); pap. text ed. 40.00x o.p. (ISBN 0-317-67823-X). Systems Co.

Computer Tools for Ancient Texts: Proceedings of the 1980 Ann Arbor Symposium on Biblical Studies & the Computer. Ed. by H. Van Dyke Parunak. 1987. text ed. price not set o.p. (ISBN 0-931464-32-3). Eisenbrauns.

Computer User's Guide to Electronics. Art Margolis. (Illus.). 320p. (Orig.). 1985. 24.95 o.p. (ISBN 0-8306-0899-0, 1899); pap. 15.95 o.p. (ISBN 0-8306-1899-6, 1899P). TAB Bks.

Computer User's Legal Guide. R. Lee Hagelshaw. LC 84-45690. 232p. (Orig.). 1985. pap. 17.95 o.p. (ISBN 0-8019-7550-6). Chilton.

Computer Workout. Software Lab East Staff. 64p. (gr. 3-5). 1984. 2.95 o.p. (ISBN 0-8104-6314-8). Sams.

Computercise: Your 21-Day Personalized Body Shaping Program. Lucille Roberts. 192p. 1984. 16.50 o.p. (ISBN 0-671-46773-5). S&S.

Computerist's Handy Databook-Dictionary. Clayton Hallmark. (Illus.). 1979. pap. 4.95 o.p. (ISBN 0-8306-1069-3, 1069). TAB Bks.

Computerized Accounting Methods & Controls. 2nd ed. Michael R. Tyran. (Illus.). 250p. 1978. text ed. 39.95 o.p. (ISBN 0-13-165761-5, Busn). P-H.

Computerized Axial Tomography. J. Gambarelli et al. 1977. 144.00 o.p. (ISBN 0-387-07961-0). Springer-Verlag.

Computerized Bookkeeping & Tax Form Preparation: A Simple Guide to an Integrated Spreadsheet System. Phil Philcox. LC 85-47834. 262p. 1985. pap. 19.95 o.p. (ISBN 0-8019-7607-3). Chilton.

Computerized Career Information System. ERIC Clearinghouse on Adult, Career, & Vocational Education Staff. 44p. 1983. 4.95 o.p. (ISBN 0-318-22064-4, BB64). Natl Ctr Res Voc Ed.

Computerized Financial Forecasting & Performance Reporting. Michael R. Tyran. 384p. 1980. text ed. 50.00 o.p. (ISBN 0-13-166173-6). P-H.

Computerized Knitting. Thom Thiele. 80p. 1986. 7.95 o.p. (ISBN 0-8062-2811-3). Carlton.

Computerized Systems in Library & Information Services: Proceedings of a Conference of the Aslib Biological & Agricultural Sciences Group, London, 1982. 76p. 1983. pap. 16.00 o.p. (ISBN 0-85142-169-5). Learned Info.

Computerized Tomography: Proceedings. Ed. by J. M. Caille & G. Salomon. (Illus.). 310p. 1980. pap. 54.00 o.p. (ISBN 0-387-09808-9). Springer Verlag.

Computerizing Your Accounting: All about Integrated Accounting Software. 1985. 19.95 o.p. (ISBN 0-8104-6782-8). Sams.

Computerizing Your Medical Office: A Guide for Physicians & Their Staffs. Dot Sellars. 228p. 1983. pap. 24.95 o.p. (ISBN 0-87489-305-4). Med Economics.

Computers. Daniel Cohen. Ed. by Wendy Barish. (Question & Answer Bk.). (Illus.). 128p. (gr. 5-6). 1983. 6.75 o.s.i. (ISBN 0-671-49340-X). Wanderer Bks.

Computers: An Introduction. Donald D. Spencer. LC 85-63151. 348p. 1986. pap. 23.00 o.s.i. (ISBN 0-89218-172-9, NO. 2012). Camelot Pub.

Computers & Composing: How the New Technologies are Changing Writing. Jeanne W. Halpern & Sarah Liggett. 144p. 1984. 10.95 o.p. (ISBN 0-317-37084-7). NCTE.

Computers & Crafts: A Practical Guide. Mark Goldring. 120p. 7.95 o.s.i. (ISBN 0-9614141-0-3). Am Council Arts.

Computers & Data Processing. Marvin R. Gore & John W. Stubbe. (Illus.). 1979. text ed. 33.95 o.p. (ISBN 0-07-023787-5, C). McGraw.

Computers & Data Processing Information Sources. Chester Morrill, Jr. LC 70-85486. (Management Information Guide Ser.: No. 15). 282p. 1969. 68.00x o.p. (ISBN 0-8103-0815-0). Gale.

Computers & Data Processing Today. 2nd ed. Steven L. Mandell. (Illus.). 472p. 1985. pap. text ed. 34.25 o.p. (ISBN 0-314-93200-3). West Pub.

Computers & Embryos: Models in Developmental Biology. R. J. Ransom. 224p. 1981. 54.95 o.p. (ISBN 0-471-09972-4, Pub. by Wiley-Interscience). Wiley.

Computers & End-User Software: With BASIC. Thomas H. Athey et al. 1987. pap. text ed. write for info. o.p. (ISBN 0-673-18618-0). Scott F.

Computers & End User Software Without Basic. Thomas H. Athey et al. 1987. pap. text ed. write for info. o.p. (ISBN 0-673-18619-9). Scott F.

Computers & Executives. Rubicon Consulting Staff. 1985. 295.00 o.p. (ISBN 0-938124-04-8). Rubicon.

Computers & Indivdualized Instruction Moving to Alternative Learning Environments. Richard J. Robbat. 56p. (Orig.). 1985. pap. text ed. 6.00 o.p. (ISBN 0-924667-27-3). Intl Council Comp.

Computers & Information Processing. Fuori & Lawrence J. Aufiero. 220p. 1986. text ed. 35.00 o.p. (ISBN 0-13-165515-9). P-H.

Computers & Information Processing. 2nd ed. James A. O'Brien. 1986. pap. 31.95x o.p. (ISBN 0-256-03337-4); study guide 11.95x o.p. (ISBN 0-256-03338-2). Irwin.

Computers & Information Processing: An Introduction. Robert Behling. 680p. 1986. text ed. 24.50 o.p. (ISBN 0-534-03999-5). PWS-Kent Pub.

Computers & Information Processing with Business Applications. T. J. O'Leary & B. K. Williams. 1985. text ed. 35.95 o.p. (ISBN 0-8053-6920-1); study guide by James Adair 8.95 o.p. (ISBN 0-8053-6922-8); instr's. guide 5.95 o.p. (ISBN 0-8053-6921-X); test bank 5.95 o.p. (ISBN 0-8053-6923-6); transparency masters 40.00 o.p. (ISBN 0-8053-6925-2); lab manual 14.95 o.p. (ISBN 0-8053-6926-0). Benjamin-Cummings.

Computers & Information Systems. George J. Brabb. 1976. text ed. 17.50 o.p. (ISBN 0-395-20657-X). HM.

Computers & Information Systems in Business. 2nd ed. George J. Brabb. LC 79-88716. (Illus.). 1980. text ed. 27.50 o.p. (ISBN 0-395-28671-9). HM.

Computers & Litigation Support. Stephen L. Haynes. 791p. 1981. 75.00 o.p. (ISBN 0-15-100014-X, H39980, Pub. by Law & Business). HarBraceJ.

Computers & Mathematics with Applications: A Memorial Dedicated to Cornelius Lanczos. E. Y. Rodin. 1976. pap. 100.00 o.p. (ISBN 0-08-020521-6). Pergamon.

Computers & Microprocessors: Components & Systems. A. C. Downton. 1984. 27.95 o.p. (ISBN 0-442-30571-0); pap. 14.95 o.p. (ISBN 0-442-30572-9). Van Nos Reinhold.

Computers & Operations Research: Environmental Applications. Ed. by Ellison S. Raff. 1977. pap. 42.00 o.p. (ISBN 0-08-021348-0). Pergamon.

Computers & Problem Solving: A Workshop for Educators. David Moursund. 96p. (Orig.). 1986. pap. 8.00 o.p. (ISBN 0-924667-34-6). Intl Council Comp.

Computers & Programming: A System 360-370 Assembler Language Approach. Reino Hannula. 400p. 1974. text ed. 25.95 o.p. (ISBN 0-395-16796-5). HM.

Computers & Remote Computing Services. Doris G. Duncan & S. David Aviel. LC 82-20094. (Illus.). 258p. (Orig.). 1983. lib. bdg. 30.00 o.p. (ISBN 0-8191-2881-3); pap. text ed. 14.00 o.p. (ISBN 0-8191-2882-1). U Pr of Amer.

Computers & Social Controversy. Thomas Logsdon. LC 79-24611. (Computer Software Engineering Ser.). (Illus.). 400p. 1980. text ed. 27.95 o.p. (ISBN 0-914894-14-5, Computer Sci Pr); wkbk. 9.95 o.p. (ISBN 0-914894-68-4). W H Freeman.

Computers & Society with BASIC & Pascal. Michael A. Gallo & Robert B. Nenno. 1985. pap. text ed. 22.50 o.p. (ISBN 0-87150-852-4, 37L8700). PWS-Kent Pub.

Computers & Teacher Training: A Practical Guide. Ed. by Dennis M. Adams. LC 85-16392. (Monographic Supplement to Computers in the Schools Ser.: Vol. 2). 163p. 1986. text ed. 22.95 o.s.i. (ISBN 0-86656-312-1, B312); 19.95 o.s.i. (ISBN 0-86656-378-4). Haworth Pr.

Computers & the Cybernetic Society. 2nd ed. Michael Arbib. 1984. 20.00 o.p. (ISBN 0-12-059046-8); pap. text ed. 15.00 o.p. (ISBN 0-12-059049-2); instr's. manual 10.00 o.p. (ISBN 0-12-059047-6). Acad Pr.

Computers & the General Practitioner: Proceedings of the GP-Info Symposium, London March, 13-15, 1980. GP-Info Symposium Staff. Ed. by A. Malcolm & J. Poyser. (Illus.). 142p. 1981. 29.00 o.p. (ISBN 0-08-026865-X). Pergamon.

Computers & the Law: A Selected Bibliography. Joseph J. Galin. (Public Administration Ser.: Bibliography P 1627). 1985. pap. 2.00 o.p. (ISBN 0-89028-297-8). Vance Biblios.

Computers & the Life Sciences. Theodor D. Sterling & Seymour V. Pollack. LC 65-27765. (Illus.). 362p. 1965. 52.00x o.p. (ISBN 0-231-02744-3). Columbia U Pr.

Computers & Your Child. Ray Hammond. LC 83-9205. (Illus.). 264p. 1984. 15.45 o.p. (ISBN 0-89919-210-6); pap. 7.70 o.p. (ISBN 0-89919-211-4). Ticknor & Fields.

Computers, Chess & Long-Range Planning. M. M. Botvinnik. Tr. by A. Brown. LC 75-85203. (Heidelberg Science Library: Vol. 11). (Illus.). 1970. pap. 6.50 o.p. (ISBN 0-387-90012-8). Springer-Verlag.

Computers: Concepts & Uses. Mary Sumner. 640p. 1985. pap. text ed. 31.00 o.p. (ISBN 0-13-163718-5). P-H.

Computers for Business: A Book of Readings. 2nd ed. Hugh H. Watson & Archie B. Carroll. 1984. 17.95 o.p. (ISBN 0-256-03135-5). Irwin.

Computers for Business: A Book of Readings. Ed. by Hugh J. Watson & Archie B. Carroll. 1980. pap. 10.50x o.p. (ISBN 0-256-02289-5). Irwin.

Computers for Business: A Managerial Emphasis. rev. ed. Hugh J. Watson & Archie B. Carroll. 1980. text ed. 25.95x o.p. (ISBN 0-256-02288-7). Irwin.

Computers for Everybody. Jerry Willis & Merl Miller. LC 80-70784. 145p. 1979. pap. 7.95 o.p. (ISBN 0-918398-49-5). Dilithium Pr.

Computers for Grocery Stores & Supermarkets. Peter Luedtke. (Computer Selection Ser.). 1985. pap. 19.95 o.p. (ISBN 0-15-600299-X). HarBraceJ.

Computers for Insurance Agencies: Computer Selection Ser. Peter Luedtke. 1985. pap. 19.95 o.p. (ISBN 0-15-600301-5). HarBraceJ.

Computers for Law Offices. Peter Luedtke & Rainer Luedtke. LC 84-4488. (Computer Selection Books for Professionals Ser.). 1984. pap. 19.95 o.p. (ISBN 0-15-600288-4, BFP). HarBraceJ.

Computers for Medical Office & Patient Management. Ed. by Stacey B. Day & Jan F. Brandejs. 224p. 1982. 27.95 o.p. (ISBN 0-442-21316-6). Van Nos Reinhold.

Computers for Membership Organizations. Peter Luedtke. (Computer Selection Ser.). 1985. pap. 19.95 o.p. (ISBN 0-15-600293-0). HarBraceJ.

Computers for Retailers: Computer Selection Ser. Peter Luedtke. 1985. pap. 19.95 o.p. (ISBN 0-15-600309-0). HarBraceJ.

Computers for Spectroscopists. Carrington. LC 74-12526. 275p. 1975. 59.95x o.p. (ISBN 0-470-13581-6). Halsted Pr.

Computers in Aerodynamics: Proceedings of the Symposium, Polytechnic Institute of New York, Aerodynamics Laboratories, 1979. Computers in Aerodynamics Symposium Staff. Ed. by S. G. Rubin & M. H. Bloom. 130p. 1980. pap. 46.00 o.p. (ISBN 0-08-025426-8). Pergamon.

Computers in Biomedical Research, 4 vols. Ralph W. Stacy & Bruce Waxman. 1965-1964. Vol. 1, 1965. 89.00 o.p. (ISBN 0-12-662301-5); Vol. 2, 1965. 81.00 o.p. (ISBN 0-12-662302-3); Vol. 3, 1969. 81.00 o.p. (ISBN 0-12-662303-1); Vol. 4. 1974. 75.50 o.p. (ISBN 0-12-662304-X). Acad Pr.

Computers in Business & Industry. Laura Greene. (Computer Applications Book Ser.). 128p. (YA) (gr. 7 up). 1984. 11.90 o.p. (ISBN 0-531-04842-X). Watts.

Computers in Chemical & Biochemical Research, Vol. 1. Ed. by Charles E. Klopfenstein & Charles L. Wilkins. 1972. 71.50 o.p. (ISBN 0-12-151301-7). Acad Pr.

Computers in Chemical Education & Research. Ed. by E. V. Ludena et al. LC 77-9473. 488p. 1977. 65.00x o.p. (ISBN 0-306-31071-6, Plenum Pr). Plenum Pub.

Computers in Civil Engineering Design. Ed. by National Computing Centre, Ltd. Staff. 160p. 1972. pap. 40.00x o.s.i. (ISBN 0-85012-105-1). Intl Pubns Serv.

Computers in Criminal Justice: A Selective Bibliography. Mary E. Huls. LC 86-109591. (Public Administration Ser.: P1673). 7p. 1985. 2.00 o.p. (ISBN 0-89028-383-4). Vance Biblios.

Computers in Critical & Pulmonary Medicine, Vol. 3. Ed. by Sreedhar Nair. LC 83-4077. 342p. 1983. 65.00x o.p. (ISBN 0-306-41187-3, Plenum Pr). Plenum Pub.

Computers in Government & the Military. Richard B. Lyttle. (Computer Applications Book Ser.). 112p. (gr. 7 up). 1984. 11.90 o.p. (ISBN 0-531-04844-6). Watts.

Computers in Laboratory Medicine. Ed. by Derek Enlander. 1975. 52.00 o.p. (ISBN 0-12-239950-1). Acad Pr.

Computers in Nonassociative Rings & Algebras. R. E. Beck & B. Kolman. 1977. 49.50 o.p. (ISBN 0-12-083850-8). Acad Pr.

Computers in Nutrition. Chalda Maloff & Russell Zears. LC 79-4339. 350p. 1979. 20.00 o.p. (ISBN 0-89006-077-0). Artech Hse.

Computers in Our World, Today & Tomorrow. Martin Hintz & Sandra Hintz. (Computer Awareness First Book Ser.). (Illus.). 96p. (gr. 5 up). PLB 10.40 o.p. (ISBN 0-531-04639-7). Watts.

Computers in Police Work: A Selective Bibliography. Mary E. Huls. (Public Administration Ser.: Bibliography P 1628). 1985. pap. 2.00 o.p. (ISBN 0-89028-298-6). Vance Biblios.

Computers in Public Administration: An International Perspective. Ed. by Samuel J. Bernstein. 450p. 1976. 71.00 o.p. (ISBN 0-08-017869-3). Pergamon.

Computers in School Psychology: An Overview. C. Sue McCullough. 60p. (Orig.). 1985. pap. text ed. 10.00 o.p. (ISBN 0-924667-24-9). Intl Council Comp.

Computers in the Creative Arts: A Studyguide. National Computing Centre, Ltd. Staff. Ed. by J. D. Lomax. LC 74-159449. (Illus.). 69p. 1973. pap. 10.50x o.s.i. (ISBN 0-85012-097-7). Intl Pubns Serv.

Computers in the English Classroom: A Primer for Teachers. Sally N. Standiford et al. 56p. 1983. pap. 7.00 o.p. (ISBN 0-8141-0818-0). NCTE.

Computers in the Life Sciences: Applications in Research & Education. Ed. by R. Lewis. 123p. 1979. 25.00 o.p. (ISBN 0-85664-863-9, Pub. by Croom Helm Ltd). Routledge Chapman & Hall.

Computers in the Practice of Medicine: Survey of Medical Computing, Vol. 3. Covvey et al. 1987. 23.95 o.p. (ISBN 0-8016-3198-X). Mosby.

Computers in the Service of Society. Ed. by Robert L. Chartrand. LC 73-112401. 256p. 1972. 42.00 o.p. (ISBN 0-08-016332-7). Pergamon.

Computers in the Social Sciences: A Study Guide. National Computing Centre, Ltd. Staff. Ed. by G. Penney. LC 74-164433. (Computers & People Ser.). 48p. 1973. pap. 10.00x o.s.i. (ISBN 0-85012-095-0). Intl Pubns Serv.

Computers in Today's World: Microcomputer Study Guide. Stair. 1986. Apple 11.95x o.p. (ISBN 0-256-03562-8); 11.95 o.p. (ISBN 0-256-03563-6). Irwin.

Computers, Language Reform, & Lexicography in China. Ed. by Jim Mathias & Thomas L. Kennedy. vii, 76p. (Orig.). 1980. pap. 8.00 o.p. (ISBN 0-87422-015-7). Wash St U Pr.

Computers on the Battlefield: Can They Survive? Richard J. DeBastiani. (National Security Affairs Monograph Ser. 83-5). (Illus.). 111p. 1983. pap. 4.50 o.p. (ISBN 0-318-20100-3, S/N 008-020-00954-7). USGPO.

Computers Security. Time-Life Books Editors. (Understanding Computer Ser.). 128p. (YA) (gr. 7 up). 1986. 19.93 o.p.; lib. bdg. 23.93 o.p. Time-Life.

Computers: The User Perspective. Stallings & Hutchinson. (Illus.). 784p. 1987. 32.95 o.p. (ISBN 0-8016-4752-5). Mosby.

Computers: Their Impact & Use-BASIC Language. Robert E. Lynch & John A. Rice. LC 74-9773. 410p. 1975. pap. text ed. 18.95 o.p. (ISBN 0-03-088526-4, HoltC). HR&W.

Computerspace: Home Office Strategies That Work for Computers. James Wagenvoord. LC 83-22111. (Illus.). 128p. 1984. pap. 9.95 o.p. (ISBN 0-399-51020-6, Perigee). Putnam Pub Group.

Compute's Atari ST Artist. Selby Bateman & Lee Noel, Jr. 1986. 18.95 o.p. (ISBN 0-87455-070-X); disk 15.95 o.p. (70XBDSK); bk-disk combination 29.95 o.p. (ISBN 0-87455-071-8). Compute Pubns.

Compute's Data File Handler for the Commodore 64. Blaine D. Standage et al. Ed. by Compute! Magazine Staff. 271p. (Orig.). 1985. pap. 12.95 o.p. (ISBN 0-942386-86-8). Compute Pubns.

Compute's First Book of Atari Games. Ed. by Compute! Magazine Staff. 232p. (Orig.). 1983. pap. 12.95 o.p. (ISBN 0-942386-14-0). Compute Pubns.

Compute's First Book of PET-CBM. Ed. by Compute! Magazine Staff. (Illus.). 244p. (Orig.). 1981. pap. 12.95 o.p. (ISBN 0-942386-01-9). Compute Pubns.

Compute's First Book of TI Games. Ed. by Compute! Magazine Staff & C. Regena. 211p. (Orig.). 1983. pap. 12.95 o.p. (ISBN 0-942386-17-5). Compute Pubns.

Compute's Guide to TI-99-4A Sound & Graphics. Raymond Herold. 224p. (Orig.). 1984. pap. 12.95 o.p. (ISBN 0-942386-46-9). Compute Pubns.

Compute's Second Book of Atari. Ed. by Compute! Magazine Staff. (Illus.). 250p. (Orig.). 1983. pap. 12.95 o.p. (ISBN 0-942386-06-X). Compute Pubns.

Compute's Telecomputing on the IBM. Arlan R. Levitan & Sheldon Leemon. Ed. by Compute! Magazine Staff. 274p. (Orig.). 1985. pap. 14.95 o.p. (ISBN 0-942386-96-5). Compute Pubns.

Compute's VIC-20 Collection. Ed. by Compute! Magazine Staff. 338p. (Orig.). 1985. pap. 12.95 o.p. (ISBN 0-87455-007-6). Compute Pubns.

Computing: A Problem-Solving Approach Using FORTRAN 77. T. Ray Nanney. (Illus.). 432p. 1981. text ed. (ISBN 0-13-165209-5). P-H.

Computing Economics. Hugo. (Infotech Computer State of the Art Reports). 600p. 1973. 85.00 o.p. (ISBN 0-08-028497-3). Pergamon.

Computing for Engineers & Scientists with FORTRAN 77. Daniel D. McCracken. LC 83-23473. 361p. 1984. (ISBN 0-471-09701-2). Wiley.

Computing for Executives. John W. Chadwick. (Illus.). 240p. (Orig.). 1984. 19.95 o.p. (ISBN 0-8306-0796-X); pap. 12.60 o.p. (ISBN 0-8306-1796-5, 1796). TAB Bks.

Computing in the Humanities. Ed. by Peter C. Patton & Renee A. Holoien. LC 79-3185. 416p. 1981. 33.00x o.p. (ISBN 0-669-03397-9). Lexington Bks.

Computing in the Social Studies Classroom. Allen Glenn & Don Rawitsch. 48p. 1984. 3.50 o.p. (ISBN 0-924667-06-0). Intl Council Comp.

Computing Marketplace: A Directory of Computing Services & Software Supplies for Word Processors, Micros, Minis, & Mainframes. 2nd ed. BIS-PEDDER Associates, Ltd. Staff. (Computing Services for the Eighties Ser.). 472p. (Orig.). 1983. pap. text ed. 69.50x o.p. (ISBN 0-566-03476-X). Gower Pub Co.

Computing Methods in Applied Sciences & Engineering, 1977, I: Proceedings of the International Symposium, 3rd, December 5-9, 1977. Ed. by R. Glowinski & J. L. Lions. (Lecture Notes in Mathematics Ser.: Vol. 704). 1979. pap. 22.00 o.p. (ISBN 0-387-09123-8). Springer-Verlag.

Computing Methods in Applied Sciences & Engineering, 1977, II: Proceedings of the International Symposium, 3rd, December 5-9, 1977. Ed. by R. Glowinski & J. L. Lions. (Lecture Notes in Physics Ser.: Vol. 91). 1979. pap. 22.00 o.s.i. (ISBN 0-387-09119-X). Springer-Verlag.

Computing Methods in Geophysical Mechanics-AMD, Vol. 25. Ed. by Richard P. Shaw. 208p. 1977. pap. text ed. 22.00 o.p. (ISBN 0-685-86858-3, I00113). ASME.

Computing Methods in Optimization Problems Two. Ed. by L. A. Zadeh et al. 1969. 71.50 o.p. (ISBN 0-12-775250-1). Acad Pr.

Computing Methods in Optimization Problems: Proceedings. Ed. by A. V. Balakrishna & Lucien W. Neustadt. 1964. 60.50 o.p. (ISBN 0-12-076950-6). Acad Pr.

Computing Practice: Security Aspects. National Computing Centre, Ltd. Staff. 53p. (Orig.). 1979. pap. 25.00x o.s.i. (ISBN 0-85012-215-5). Intl Pubns Serv.

Computing Strategies in Small Universities & Colleges. Patrick J. Coughlin. LC 86-70008. (Monograph Ser.). 144p. (Orig.). 1986. pap. CAUSE.

Computing Techniques for Robots. Ed. by Igor Aleksander. 276p. 1985. 39.50 o.p. (ISBN 0-412-01091-7, 9660). Routledge Chapman & Hall.

Computing Today: Microcomputer Concepts & Applications. David R. Sullivan et al. LC 84-81936. 448p. 1985. pap. 33.56 o.p. (ISBN 0-395-37011-6). HM.

COMSEARCH: Special Topics. rev. ed. 1985. write for info. o.p. Foundation Ctr.

COMSEARCH: Subjects. 1986. pap. 17.50 o.p. (ISBN 0-87954-129-6). Foundation Ctr.

COMSEARCH: Subjects. The Foundation Center Staff. (Annual Ser.). (Orig.). 1989. pap. 25.00 o.p. (ISBN 0-87954-304-3); microfiche 9.00 o.p. (ISBN 0-87954-305-1). Foundation Ctr.

COMSEARCH: 1987 Special Topics. 1987. pap. 28.00 o.p. (ISBN 0-87954-229-2). Foundation Ctr.

COMSEARCH: 1987 Subjects. 1987. pap. 17.50 o.p. (ISBN 0-87954-227-6); microfiche 6.00 o.p. (ISBN 0-317-66538-3). Foundation Ctr.

Comtesse de Noailles: Oui et Non. Jean Cocteau. (Illus.). 296p. 1963. 13.50 o.p. (ISBN 0-686-54518-4). French & Eur.

Comunicando: A First Course in Spanish. David M. Stillman & Ronni L. Gordon. 1979. text ed. 26.50 o.p. (ISBN 0-669-01359-5). Heath.

Con Man. Ed McBain. 296p. 1986. pap. 10.95 o.p. (ISBN 0-8161-3982-2, Large Print Bks). G K Hall.

Con Mucho Gusto: Lengua y Cultura del Mundo Hispanico. 2nd ed. Jean-Paul Valette et al. (Span.). 1984. text ed. 29.95 o.p. (ISBN 0-03-063893-3); tchr's. ed. 25.95 o.p. (ISBN 0-03-063894-1); wkbk. 13.95 o.p. (ISBN 0-03-063897-6); lab manual 11.95 o.p. (ISBN 0-03-063896-8); tapes avail. o.p. (ISBN 0-03-063898-4). HR&W.

Conceived in Conflict: The Politics of the Women's Movement & the Crusade for the ERA. Elisabeth Griffithe. LC 87-43235. (Illus.). 288p. 1989. 18.45 o.p. (ISBN 0-394-55253-9). Random.

Concentration Functions. Walter Hengartner & Rado Theodorescu. 1973. 49.50 o.p. (ISBN 0-12-341050-9). Acad Pr.

Concept & Composition: The Basis of Successful Art. Fritz Henning. LC 83-2319. 208p. 1983. 24.95o.p. (ISBN 0-89134-059-9); pap. 16.95 o.p. (ISBN 0-89134-060-2). North Light Bks.

Concept & Logic of Classical Thermodynamics As a Theory of Heat Engines. Rigorously Constructed Upon Foundations Laid by S. Carnot & F. Reech. C. Truesdell & S. Bharatha. LC 76-48115. (Texts & Monographs in Physics). (Illus.). 1977. 41.00 o.p. (ISBN 0-387-07971-8). Springer-Verlag.

Concept & Quality: A World Hypothesis. Stephen C. Pepper. LC 66-19679. (Paul Carus Lecture Ser). 666p. 1966. 19.95 o.p. (ISBN 0-87548-095-0). Open Court.

Concept de Litterarite: Essai sur les Possibilities Theoriques d'une Science de la Litterature. Mircea Marghescour. (De Proprietatibus Litterarum, Ser. Minor: No. 23). 119p. (Fr.). 1975. pap. text ed. 8.80x o.p. (ISBN 90-2793-372-3). Mouton.

Concept Formation in Social Science. William Outhwaite. (International Library of Sociology). 240p. 1983. 31.95x o.p. (ISBN 0-7100-9195-8). Routledge Chapman & Hall.

Concept of Corporate Strategy. 3rd ed. Kenneth R. Andrews. 160p. 1986. 25.00 o.p. (ISBN 0-87094-983-7). Dow Jones-Irwin.

Concept of Education. Ed. by R. S. Peters. 226p. 1970. pap. 8.95x o.p. (ISBN 0-7100-7658-4). Routledge CHapman & Hall.

Concept of Energy Simply Explained. Morton Mott-Smith. LC 63-19496. 1964. lib. bdg. 10.50x o.p. (ISBN 0-88307-626-8). Gannon.

Concept of Heat & Its Workings. Morton Mott-Smith. Orig. Title: Heat & Its Workings. 1933. pap. 3.95 o.p. (ISBN 0-486-20978-4). Dover.

Concept of Irony. Soren Kierkegaard. Tr. by Lee M. Capel. 442p. 1983. Repr. of 1966 ed. lib. bdg. 40.00 o.p. (ISBN 0-88254-867-0, Octagon). Hippocrene Bks.

Concept of Schizophrenia. W. F. McAuley. 145p. 1954. (ISBN 0-8022-1007-4). Philos Lib.

Concept of the Avant-Garde. John Weightman. 323p. 1974. 8.95 o.p. (ISBN 0-912050-40-3, Library Pr). Open Court.

Conception of Immortality. Josiah Royce. 1968. Repr. of 1900 ed. lib. bdg. 22.50x o.p. (ISBN 0-8371-0207-3, ROCI). Greenwood.

Concepts for Eighteen-Thirty GHZ Satellite Communications System Study. Exec. Summary. 20.00 o.p. (ISBN 0-686-33009-9); Final Report. 100.00 o.p. (ISBN 0-686-33010-2). Info Gatekeepers.

Concepts in Adoption. Pat Holmes. 128p. Date not set. 9.95 o.p. (ISBN 0-317-62066-5). Our Child Pr.

Concepts in Architectural Acoustics. M. David Egan. (Illus.). 192p. 1972. text ed. 53.50 o.p. (ISBN 0-07-019053-4). McGraw.

Concepts in Biology. 4th ed. Eldon D. Enger et al. 560p. 1985. pap. text ed. write for info. o.p. (ISBN 0-697-05023-8); lab manual avail. o.p. (ISBN 0-697-04799-7); instr's. manual avail. o.p. (ISBN 0-697-05101-3); transparencies avail. o.p. (ISBN 0-697-05102-1). Wm C Brown.

Concepts in Chemistry. 3rd ed. Arthur W. Greenstone & Sydney P. Harris. 644p. (gr. 10-12). 1975. text ed. 23.70 o.p. (ISBN 0-15-362426-4, HC). HarBraceJ.

Concepts in Coaching Wrestling. Bill Dotson et al. LC 83-25635. (Illus.). 160p. 1984. pap. 10.95 o.p. (ISBN 0-88011-188-7, PDOT0188). Leisure Pr.

Concepts in Geostatistics. Ed. by R. B. McCammon. LC 74-23669. (Illus.). xvi, 184p. 1975. pap. 20.00 o.p. (ISBN 0-387-06892-9). Springer-Verlag.

Concepts in Hadron Physics: Proceedings of the International University Courses on Nuclear Physics, 10th, Schladming, Austria, 1971. International University Courses on Nuclear Physics Staff. (Acta Physica Austriaca: Suppl. 8). (Illus.). xvi, 424p. 1971. 63.80 o.p. (ISBN 0-387-81032-3). Springer-Verlag.

Concepts in Physics. Robert Adair. 1969. 27.25i o.p. (ISBN 0-12-044050-4). Acad Pr.

Concepts in Quantum Mechanics. F. A. Kaempffer. (Pure & Applied Physics: Vol. 18). 1964. 43.50 o.p. (ISBN 0-12-394150-4). Acad Pr.

Concepts of Actuarial Soundness in Pension Plans. Dorrance C. Bronson. 1957. 10.95 o.p. (ISBN 0-256-00641-5). Irwin.

Concepts of Algebra & Trigonometry. Howard E. Campbell. 656p. 1982. text ed. write for info. o.p. (ISBN 0-87150-332-8, 2651, Prindle). PWS-Kent Pub.

Concepts of Calculus with Applications to Business & Economics. David G. Crowdis et al. 1975. text ed. write for info. o.p. (ISBN 0-02-473010-6); tchr's. manual avail. o.p. (ISBN 0-02-473020-3). Macmillan.

Concepts of Chemistry. William M. Porterfield. (Illus.). 1972. text ed. 18.95x o.p. (ISBN 0-393-09385-9). Norton.

Concepts of College Algebra. Howard E. Campbell. 480p. 1982. text ed. write for info. o.p. (ISBN 0-87150-325-5, 33L 2591, Prindle). PWS-Kent Pub.

Concepts of Communication: Reading, Ideas Module, Inferences Module. Mary L. Conlin. LC 77-78895. (Illus.). 1978. pap. 23.56 o.p. (ISBN 0-395-25492-2). HM.

Concepts of Communication: Reading Vocabulary Module. Mary Lou Conlin. LC 77-78866. (Illus.). 1978. pap. 10.95 o.p. (ISBN 0-395-25494-9). HM.

Concepts of Communication: Writing, 5 units. Mary Lou Conlin. 1975. Units 1-3. pap. text ed. 10.25 o.p. (ISBN 0-395-19223-4). HM.

Concepts of Communication: Writing Skills Module. 2nd ed. Mary L. Conlin. LC 79-49830. 1980. pap. 19.95 o.p. (ISBN 0-395-28484-8); 1.10 o.p. HM.

Concepts of Communication: Writing: Summary, Paragraph, Essay-Test, Theme Module. 2nd ed. Mary L. Conlin. LC 79-49830. 1980. pap. 22.76 o.p. (ISBN 0-395-28735-9). HM.

Concepts of Contemporary Astronomy. 2nd ed. Paul W. Hodge. 1979. text ed. 36.95 o.p. (ISBN 0-07-029147-0). McGraw.

Concepts of Government Auditing: A Book of Readings from the Internal Auditor. Ed. by Mortimer A. Dittenhofer. 1977. pap. text ed. 10.00 o.p. (ISBN 0-89413-059-5). Inst Inter Aud.

Concepts of International Politics: A Global Perspective. 3rd ed. Abdul A. Said & Charles Lerche. 1979. text ed. 32.00 o.p. (ISBN 0-13-166033-0). P-H.

Concepts of Leisure. 2nd ed. James F. Murphy. (Illus.). 192p. 1981. text ed. (ISBN 0-13-166512-X). P-H.

Concepts of Political & Social Authority: A Selected Bibliography. Robert Goehlert. (Public Administration Ser.: Bibliography P 1655). 1985. pap. 2.25 o.p. (ISBN 0-89028-345-1). Vance Biblios.

Concepts of Reality. Raphael F. Rammairone. 64p. 1986. 6.95 o.p. (ISBN 0-8062-2991-8). Carlton.

Concepts of Space: The History of Theories of Space in Physics. 2nd ed. Max Jammer. LC 69-18034. 1969. 17.50x o.s.i. (ISBN 0-674-15771-0). Harvard U Pr.

Concepts of Trigonometry. Howard E. Campbell. LC 80-22168. 249p. 1981. text ed. write for info. o.p. (ISBN 0-87150-299-2, 2351, Prindle). PWS-Kent Pub.

Conceptual Analysis & Method in Psychology: Essays in Honour of W. M. O'Neil. J. P. Sutcliffe. 1978. 22.00x o.p. (ISBN 0-424-00055-5, Pub. by Sydney U Pr). Intl Spec Bk.

Conceptual Approach to Teaching about Pennsylvania. Pennsylvania Department of Education, Social Studies Division Staff. LC 72-90894. 1973. pap. 6.50 o.s.i. (ISBN 0-931992-13-3). Penns Valley.

Conceptual Approaches to Human Ecology. A Terry Rambo. LC 83-16460. (East-West Environment & Policy Institute Research Report: No. 14). (Orig.). 1983. pap. text ed. 3.00 o.p. (ISBN 0-86638-049-3). EW Ctr HI.

Conceptual Blockbusting: A Guide to Better Ideas. 2nd ed. James L. Adams. (Illus.). 160p. 1980. 10.95 o.p. (ISBN 0-393-01223-9); pap. text ed. 5.95x o.p. (ISBN 0-393-95016-6). Norton.

Conceptual Foundation of Genetics: Selected Readings. Harry O. Corwin & John B. Jenkins. LC 75-26092. (Illus.). 448p. 1976. pap. 19.50 o.p. (ISBN 0-395-24064-6). HM.

Conceptual Frameworks Used in Baccalaureate & Master's Degree Curricula. Dolores Santora. (League Exchange Ser.: No. 126). 49p. 1980. 7.95 o.p. (ISBN 0-88737-177-9, 15-1828). Natl League Nurse.

Conceptual Issues in Psychology. E. R. Valentine. 213p. 1982. text ed. 39.95x o.p. (ISBN 0-04-150079-2); pap. text ed. 14.95 o.p. (ISBN 0-04-150080-6). Unwin Hyman.

Conceptual Nervous System. Henry A. Buchtel. LC 82-16509. (Foundations & Philosophy of Science & Technology Ser.). (Illus.). 196p. 1982. 44.00 o.p. (ISBN 0-08-027418-8). Pergamon.

Conceptual Physics. 5th ed. Paul G. Hewitt. 1985. pap. text ed. write for info. o.p. (ISBN 0-673-39541-3); tchr's. ed. avail. o.p. (ISBN 0-316-35975-0); test bank avail. o.p. (ISBN 0-316-35976-9). Scott F.

Conceptual Programming Using BASIC. Allen Baker & Kathy Hamrick. (Illus.). 224p. 1984. pap. text ed. (ISBN 0-13-166678-9). P-H.

Concerning Heretics. Roland H. Bainton. 1965. Repr. lib. bdg. 27.50x o.p. (ISBN 0-374-90323-9, Octagon). Hippocrene Bks.

Concerning Relations of Great Britain, Spain, & Portugal, to Each Other, & to the Common Enemy, at This Crisis; & Specifically as Affected by the Convention of Cintra: The Whole Brought to the Test of Those Principles, by Which Alone the Independence & Freedom of Nations Can Be Preserved or Recovered. William Wordsworth. (Illus.). 230p. 1983. pap. 6.95 o.p. (ISBN 0-8425-2140-2). Brigham.

Concerning the Biosynthesis of Vitamin B12. A. I. Scott. 1976. pap. 15.50 o.p. (ISBN 0-08-020478-3). Pergamon.

Concerns for Applied Sociology: A Bibliography. Jessica L. Kohout. (Public Administration Ser.: Bibliography P 1652). 1985. pap. 6.00 o.p. (ISBN 0-89028-342-7). Vance Biblios.

Concilation in Industrial Disputes: A Practical Guide. 4th ed. viii, 133p. 1985. 11.40 o.p. (ISBN 92-2-101007-4). Intl Labour Office.

Conciliation & Arbitration of Industrial Disputes in English-Speaking Countries of Africa. (Labour-Management Relations Ser: No. 37). 208p. 1970. 2.80 o.p. (ISBN 92-2-100063-X, LMR37). Intl Labour Office.

Conciliation in Separation & Divorce: Finding Common Ground. Lisa Parkinson. 192p. 1986. 22.50 o.p. (ISBN 0-7099-4047-5, Pub. by Croom Helm Ltd); pap. 15.50 o.p. (ISBN 0-7099-4053-X). Routledge Chapman & Hall.

Conciliation Services: Structures, Functions & Techniques. International Labour Office Staff et al. Intro. by Efren Cordova. (Labour-Management Relations Ser.: No. 62). iii, 141p. 1983. pap. 10.00 o.p. (ISBN 92-2-103236-1). Intl Labour Office.

Concise American Heritage Dictionary. American Heritage Dictionary Editors. LC 76-4047. 1976. 7.70 o.s.i. (ISBN 0-395-24522-2). HM.

Concise Bibliography of Northern Chad & Fezzan in Southern Libya. Mohamed A. Alawar. 229p. 1985. lib. bdg. 30.00x o.p. Lynne Rienner.

Concise Dictionary of American Grammar & Usage. Whitford & Foster. 176p. 1955. (ISBN 0-8022-1865-2). Philos Lib.

Concise Dictionary of English Slang. William Freeman. 288p. 1956. (ISBN 0-8022-0534-8). Philos Lib.

Concise Dictionary of Greek & Roman Mythology. Michael Stapleton. LC 85-15101. (Orig.). 1986. pap. 4.95 o.s.i. (ISBN 0-87226-006-2). P Bedrick Bks.

Concise Dictionary of Medieval History. Harry Wedeck. LC 63-18058. 384p. 1964. (ISBN 0-8022-1830-X). Philos Lib.

Concise Dictionary of Physics. Ed. by J. Thewlis. 376p. 1973. 27.50 o.p. (ISBN 0-08-016900-7). Pergamon.

Concise Encyclopedia of Atomic Energy. Frank Gaynor. (ISBN 0-8022-0571-2). Philos Lib.

Concise Encyclopedia of Biochemistry. Ed. by Thomas Scott & Mary Brewer. LC 82-22148. (Illus.). vi, 519p. 1983. 34.95 o.p. (ISBN 3-11-007860-0). De Gruyter.

Concise Encyclopedia of Jewish Music. o.s.i 9.95 o.s.i. (ISBN 0-686-76494-3). Feldheim.

Concise Encyclopedia of the Sciences. Ed. by John-David Yule. 590p. 1982. pap. 22.95 o.p. (ISBN 0-442-29208-2). Van Nos Reinhold.

Concise Encyclopedia of World Timbers. F. H. Titmuss. (Illus.). 264p. 1959. (ISBN 0-8022-1725-7). Philos Lib.

Concise Encyclopedic Guide to Shakespeare. Michael R. Martin & Richard A. Harrier. 1975. pap. 2.65 o.p. (ISBN 0-380-00238-8, 16832, Discus). Avon.

Concise English Handbook. 4th ed. Hans P. Guth. 1977. (ISBN 0-534-00480-6). Wadsworth Pub.

Concise History of Astronomy. Peter Doig. 1951. (ISBN 0-8022-0409-0). Philos Lib.

Concise History of Catholicism. Marian McKenna. (Quality Paperback: No. 143). 285p. 1962. pap. 2.95 o.p. (ISBN 0-8226-0143-5). Littlefield.

Concise History of Mathematics. Dirk J. Struik. LC 66-28622. 1967. lib. bdg. 12.50x o.p. (ISBN 0-88307-615-2). Gannon.

Concise Index to English. Eugene Ehrlich & Daniel Murphy. 1974. pap. text ed. 3.95 o.p. (ISBN 0-07-019101-8). McGraw.

Concise Introduction to Organic Chemistry. Albert Zlatkis et al. 624p. 1973. text ed. 41.95 o.p. (ISBN 0-07-072850-X). McGraw.

Concise Polish-English, English-Polish Concise Dictionary. Iwo Pogonowski. 436p. (Orig., Pol. & Eng.). 1983. pap. 4.95 o.p. (ISBN 0-88254-799-2). Hippocrene Bks.

Concise Survey of Computer Methods. Peter Naur. 397p. (Orig.). 1974. pap. text ed. 35.50x o.p. (ISBN 0-317-02800-6, Pub. by Chartwell-Bratt England). Gower Pub Co.

Concise Survey of French Literature. Germaine Mason. 328p. 1959. Philos Lib.

Concise Swedish-English Glossary of Legal Terms. Torild Backe et al. 164p. (Swedish & Eng.). 1973. text ed. 13.50x o.p. (ISBN 0-8377-0305-0). Rothman.

Concise Textbook of Gastroenterology. 2nd ed. M. J. Langman. (Illus.). 212p. 1982. pap. text ed. 13.95 o.p. (ISBN 0-443-02055-8). Churchill.

Concise Textbook of Hematology. 6th ed. Thompson & Proctor. 528p. 1984. pap. 19.50 o.s.i. (ISBN 0-8067-1926-5). Urban & S.

Concise Textbook of Organic Chemistry. C. G. Lyons et al. 1965. text ed. 14.50 o.p. (ISBN 0-08-010657-9); pap. text ed. 6.25 o.p. (ISBN 0-08-010656-0). Pergamon.

Concise Usage & Abusage. Eric Partridge. 1954. (ISBN 0-8022-1278-6). Philos Lib.

Concise World History. Ben Finger, Jr. 832p. 1960. (ISBN 0-8022-0501-1). Philos Lib.

Concord & Liberty. Jose Ortega Y Gasset. 1963. pap. 2.45 o.p. (ISBN 0-393-00124-5, Norton Lib). Norton.

Concord Desk Encyclopedia. Ed. by Robert A. Rosenbaum et al. LC 81-71378. (Illus.). 1312p. (Orig.). 1982. pap. 8.95 o.p. (ISBN 0-940994-01-1). Concord Ref Bks.

Concord Hymn. Gabriel N. Seymour. LC 75-35512. (Illus.). 64p. 1976. 9.95 o.p. (ISBN 0-915998-00-9); pap. text ed. 4.95 o.p. (ISBN 0-915998-01-7). Lime Rock Pr.

Concordance of Walt Whitman's Leaves of Grass & Selected Prose Writings. Edwin H. Eby. LC 76-90500. 1970. Repr. of 1955 ed. lib. bdg. 55.00 o.p. (ISBN 0-8371-2122-1, EBCW). Greenwood.

Concordance to Andre Gide's "La Symphonie Pastorale" Joyce I. Cunningham & W. D. Wilson. LC 78-19620. (Reference Library of the Humanities: Vol. 124). 1978. lib. bdg. 48.00 o.p. (ISBN 0-8240-9754-8). Garland Pub.

Concordance to Beowulf. Albert S. Cook. LC 68-23146. 440p. 1968. Repr. of 1911 ed. 40.00x o.p. (ISBN 0-8103-3169-1). Gale.

Concordance to Conrad's "Almayer's Folly" Sue M. Briggum & Todd K. Bender. LC 77-83408. (Reference Library in the Humanities: Vol. 101). 160p. 1978. lib. bdg. 48.00 o.p. (ISBN 0-8240-9843-9). Garland Pub.

Concordance to Conrad's Lord Jim. Todd K. Bender et al. LC 75-34972. (Reference Library in the Humanities: Vol. 10). 1976. lib. bdg. 73.00 o.p. (ISBN 0-8240-9995-8). Garland Pub.

Concordance to Conrad's Secret Agent. Todd K. Bender. LC 78-68258. (Reference Library of Humanities Ser.). 1979. lib. bdg. 73.00 o.p. (ISBN 0-8240-9810-2). Garland Pub.

Concordance to Conrad's the Arrow of Gold. Bender & Gaston. 1981. lib. bdg. 73.00 o.p. (ISBN 0-8240-9370-4). Garland Pub.

Concordance to Conrad's Victory. Todd K. Bender et al. LC 78-68275. (Reference Library of Humanities Ser.). 1979. lib. bdg. 121.00 o.p. (ISBN 0-8240-9808-0). Garland Pub.

Concordance to Ezra Pound's Cantos. Robert J. Dilligan et al. LC 77-83375. (Garland Reference Library of the Humanities: No. 106). 1981. lib. bdg. 121.00 o.p. (ISBN 0-8240-9837-4). Garland Pub.

Concordance to F. Scott Fitzgerald's the Great Gatsby. Compiled by Andrew Crosland. LC 74-11607. (Bruccoli Clark Book). (Illus.). 425p. 1975. 80.00x o.p. (ISBN 0-8103-1005-8). Gale.

Concordance to Flaubert's Bouvard et Pecuchet. Charles Carlut. LC 79-7915. 1021p. 1980. lib. bdg. 121.00 o.p. (ISBN 0-8240-9518-9). Garland Pub.

Concordance to Flaubert's La Tentation de Saint Antoine. Charles Carlut et al. LC 79-7914. (Garland Reference Library of the Humanities: No. 180). 1979. lib. bdg. 73.00 o.p. (ISBN 0-8240-9547-2). Garland Pub.

Concordance to Flaubert's L'Education Sentimentale, 2 vols. Charles Carlut et al. LC 78-68262. (Reference Library of the Humanities: Vol. 125). 1978. Set. lib. bdg. 169.00 o.p. (ISBN 0-8240-9795-5). Garland Pub.

Concordance to Flaubert's "Madame Bovary, 2 vols. Charles Carlut. LC 77-83409. (Library of Humanities Reference Bks.: No. 109). 1185p. 1978. Set. lib. bdg. 145.00 o.p. (ISBN 0-8240-9832-3). Garland Pub.

Concordance to Flaubert's Salammbo, 2 vols. Charles Carlut et al. LC 78-68268. (Garland Reference Library of the Humanities: No. 148). 1979. Set. lib. bdg. 121.00 o.p. (ISBN 0-8240-9794-7). Garland Pub.

Concordance to Flaubert's Trois Contes. Charles Carlut et al. LC 79-17347. (Garland Reference Library of the Humaities: No. 178). 1980. lib. bdg. 73.00 o.p. (ISBN 0-8240-9548-0). Garland Pub.

Concordance to Ford Madox Ford's The Good Soldier. C. Ruth Sabol & Todd K. Bender. 1981. lib. bdg. 61.00 o.p. (ISBN 0-8240-9371-2). Garland Pub.

Concordance to Night & Day By Virginia Woolf. Ed. by J. M. Haule. vi, 24p. 1986. 100.00 o.s.i. (ISBN 0-08-033539-X, K150); 10.00 o.s.i. (ISBN 0-08-033540-3). Pergamon.

Concordance to Pascal's "Les Provinciales" Pierre H. Dube & Hugh M. Davidson. LC 79-54323. (Garland Reference Library of the Humanities). 1000p. 1980. lib. bdg. 121.00 o.p. (ISBN 0-8240-9536-7). Garland Pub.

Concordance to the Five Novels of Nathaniel Hawthorne. John R. Byers, Jr. & James J. Owen. LC 79-7910. 951p. 1980. lib. bdg. 152.00 o.p. (ISBN 0-8240-9545-6). Garland Pub.

Concordance to the Gospel of Sri Ramakrishna. Katherine Whitmarsh. LC 85-50340. 640p. (Orig.). 1985. pap. text ed. 59.95x o.p. (ISBN 0-87481-042-6). Vedanta Pr.

Concordance to the Oeuvres Completes of Arthur Rimbaud. Ed. by William C. Carter & Robert F. Vines. LC 75-36985. xiv, 810p. 1978. 45.00x o.p. (ISBN 0-8214-0216-1). Ohio U Pr.

Concordance to the Poems & Fragments of Wilfred Owen. Donald A. Heneghan. 1979. lib. bdg. 37.00 o.p. (ISBN 0-8161-8371-6, Hall Reference). G K Hall.

Concordance to the Poems of Ben Jonson. Steven L. Bates & Sidney D. Orr. LC 76-25613. xiv, 878p. 1978. 48.00x o.p. (ISBN 0-8214-0359-1). Ohio U Pr.

Concordance to the Poetry of George Meredith. Lewis Sawin. 1982. lib. bdg. 182.00 o.p. (ISBN 0-8240-9521-9). Garland Pub.

Concordance to the Works of John Webster, Vol. 1 Pt. 2. Richard Corballis & J. M. Harding. (Salzburg Studies in English Literature, Jacobean Drama: No. 70-1). (Orig.). 1980. pap. text ed. 25.00x o.p. (ISBN 0-391-01316-5). Humanities.

Concordance to the Writings of William Blake, 2 Vols. Ed. by David V. Erdman. (Concordances Ser.). 2317p. 1968. 99.50x o.p. (ISBN 0-8014-0120-8). Cornell U Pr.

Concordances to Conrad's Tales of Unrest, Tales of Hearsay. Todd K. Bender. LC 81-43332. 242p. 1981. lib. bdg. 73.00 o.p. (ISBN 0-8240-9297-X). Garland Pub.

Concordances to Conrad's the Shadow Line & Youth. Todd K. Bender. LC 79-8416. 150p. 1980. lib. bdg. 48.00 o.p. (ISBN 0-8240-9520-0). Garland Pub.

Concorde Diplomacy: The Ambassador's Role in the World Today. Geoffrey Jackson. 254p. 1982. 24.95 o.p. (ISBN 0-241-10524-2, Pub. by Hamish Hamilton England). David & Charles.

Concordia Bible Dictionary. 176p. 1963. text ed. 5.50 o.p. (ISBN 0-570-03186-9, 12-2213). Concordia.

Concrete, Aggregates, Marking Materials, Corrosion & Joint Seals. (Transportation Research Report Ser.). 64p. 1977. 4.00 o.p. (ISBN 0-317-36071-X). Transport Res Bd.

Concrete & Concrete Masonry. rev. ed. Donald L. Ahrens et al. (Illus.). 1976. pap. text ed. 6.75x o.p. (ISBN 0-913163-09-0, 176). Hobar Pubns.

Concrete & Masonry Cost Data, 1986. 4th ed. Means, R. S., Company, Inc. Staff. Ed. by Arthur Thornely. (Illus.). 350p. 1985. pap. 40.95 o.p. (ISBN 0-87629-009-8). R S Means.

Concrete & Steel Bridges: Eight Reports. (Transportation Research Report Ser.). 72p. 1975. 3.40 o.p. (ISBN 0-309-02452-8). Transport Res Bd.

Concrete Boot. Kenneth Royce. 1973. pap. 0.95 o.p. (ISBN 0-380-01110-7, 14720). Avon.

Concrete Construction Handbook. 2nd ed. Ed. by Joseph J. Waddell. LC 73-17385. 960p. 1974. text ed. 82.00 o.p. (ISBN 0-07-067654-2). McGraw.

Concrete Construction Standards. Mary Vance. (Architecture Ser.: Bibliography A 1355). 1985. pap. 2.00 o.p. (ISBN 0-89028-325-7). Vance Biblios.

Concrete Fit for People. P. Ritter. 1981. 48.00 o.p. (ISBN 0-08-024671-0). Pergamon.

Concrete in Highway Engineering. D. R. Sharp. LC 77-118319. 1970. text ed. 21.00 o.p. (ISBN 0-08-015845-5). Pergamon.

Concrete Making Materials. Popovics. 370p. 1979. 51.00 o.p. (ISBN 0-89116-502-9). Hemisphere Pub.

Concrete Making Materials. Sandor Popovics. LC 78-1111. (Illus.). 1979. text ed. 46.95 o.p. (ISBN 0-07-050505-5). McGraw.

Concrete Mama: Prison Profiles from Walla Walla. John Hoffman. LC 81-4482. (Illus.). 240p. 1981. text ed. 27.95 o.p. (ISBN 0-8262-0340-X). U of Mo Pr.

Concrete Pavement Construction & Joints & Loader-Truck Production Studies: Eight Reports. (Transportation Research Report Ser.). 96p. 1975. 4.20 o.p. (ISBN 0-309-02386-6). Transport Res Bd.

Concrete Placing: A Bibliography. Mary Vance. (Architecture Ser.: Bibliography A 1356). 1985. pap. 2.00 o.p. (ISBN 0-89028-326-5). Vance Biblios.

Concrete Walkways Projects. Jack King. (Mini Guide Ser.). 96p. 1974. pap. 0.99 o.p. (ISBN 0-672-23804-7, Pub. by Audel). Macmillan.

Concurring Beasts. Stephen Dobyns. LC 70-182377. 1972. pap. 3.95 o.p. (ISBN 0-689-10489-8, Atheneum). Macmillan.

Concurring Opinion: The Privileges or Immunities Clause of the Fourteenth Amendment. 2nd ed. Arnold J. Lien. LC 75-28665. (Washington Univ. Studies). 150p. 1975. Repr. of 1957 ed. lib. bdg. 22.50x o.p. (ISBN 0-8371-8481-9, LIC00). Greenwood.

Condemnation Appraisal Practice, Vol. II. 717p. (Reprints from the Appraisal Journal, 1961-1971). 12.50 o.p. (ISBN 0-318-15176-6, 21-1010). Natl Assoc Realtors.

Condemned of Altona. Jean-Paul Sartre. Tr. by Sylvia Leeson & George Leeson. 1978. pap. 2.95 o.p. (ISBN 0-393-00889-4, Norton Lib). Norton.

Condemned to Die: Life Under Sentence of Death. R. Johnson. 190p. 1981. pap. 22.00 o.p. (ISBN 0-444-99089-5). Elsevier.

Condensation in Buildings. Ed. by D. J. Croome & A. F. Sherratt. (Illus.). x, 271p. 1972. 52.00 o.p. (ISBN 0-85334-548-1, Pub. by Elsevier Applied Sci England). Elsevier.

Condensed Chemical Dictionary. 10th ed. Gessner Hawley. 1150p. 1981. 46.75 o.p. (ISBN 0-442-23244-6). Van Nos Reinhold.

Condensed Pyrazines, Vol. 35. Ed. by G. W. Chesseman & R. F. Cookson. LC 78-17533. (Chemistry of Heterocyclic Compounds Ser.). 835p. 1979. 330.00 o.p. (ISBN 0-471-38204-3). Wiley.

Condensed Pyridazines Including Cinnolines & Phthaiazines, Vol. 27. Ed. by Raymond N. Castle. LC 72-6304. (Heterocyclic Compounds Ser.). 1124p. 1973. 124.00 o.p. (ISBN 0-471-38211-6, Pub. by Wiley). Krieger.

Condensers: Theory & Practice. Institution of Chemical Engineers. 1983. 70.00 o.s.i. (ISBN 0-08-028772-7). Pergamon.

Condiment Cookbook. Heinz Foods Editors. 1974. pap. 1.25 o.p. (ISBN 0-380-01111-5, 19612). Avon.

Condiminium Home. Date not set. pap. Longman.

Condition Humaine. Andre Malraux. 1972. 3.95 o.p. (ISBN 0-686-56320-4). Schoenhof.

Condition of Education, 1986: A Statistical Report. Ed. by Joyce D. Stern & Mary F. Williams. (Education Department Publication CS-404). (Illus.). 275p. 1987. pap. 13.00 o.p. (ISBN 0-318-22455-0, S/N 065-000-00276-1). USGPO.

Condition of Education, 1987: A Statistical Report. Ed. by Joyce D. Stern & Marjorie O. Chandler. (Education Department Publication Ser.: 87-365). (Illus.). 257p. 1987. pap. 12.00 o.p. (ISBN 0-318-23546-3, 065-000-00309-1). USGPO.

Condition of the Working Class in England. Frederick Engels. 351p. 1973. text ed. 19.95 o.p. (ISBN 0-8464-1329-9). Beekman Pubs.

Conditioning & Physical Fitness: Current Answers to Relevant Questions. Philip E. Allsen. 304p. 1978. pap. text ed. write for info. o.p. (ISBN 0-697-07148-0). Wm C Brown.

Conditioning: Representation of Involved Neural Functions. Ed. by Charles D. Woody. LC 82-9857. (Advances in Behavioral Biology Ser.: Vol. 26). 762p. 1982. 95.00x o.p. (ISBN 0-306-41028-1, Plenum Pr). Plenum Pub.

Conditions Affecting Vocational Education Planning: Implications for Administration & Research. Harold Starr & Harold Merz. 60p. 1981. 4.50 o.p. (ISBN 0-318-15432-3, RD204). Natl Ctr Res Voc Ed.

Conditions of Contract. 5th ed. 52p. 1973. 5.25 o.p. (ISBN 0-7277-0074-X, Pub. by T Telford UK). Am Soc Civil Eng.

Condominium & Cooperative Apartment Buyer's & Seller's Guide. David W. Kennedy. LC 83-6586. 314p. 1983. pap. 14.95x o.p. (ISBN 0-471-09617-2, Pub. by Wiley-Interscience). Wiley.

Condominium Home: A Special Marketing Challenge. Janet Scavo. Ed. by Patricia Allen. LC 80-54757. (Illus.). 265p. (Orig.). 1981. pap. 11.95 prof. o.s.i. (ISBN 0-913652-22-9, 140). Realtors Natl.

Condominium Management. Jack R. Holeman. (Illus.). 1980. text ed. 35.00 o.p. (ISBN 0-13-167155-3). P-H.

Condominium Management Agreement A. 1974. 9.95 o.p. (ISBN 0-686-46411-7). Inst Real Estate.

Condominium Management Agreement B. 1978. 9.95 o.p. (ISBN 0-686-46412-5). Inst Real Estate.

Condorcet: From Natural Philosophy to Social Mathematics. Keith M. Baker. LC 74-5725. xiv, 538p. 1975. lib. bdg. 27.50x o.s.i. (ISBN 0-226-03532-8). U of Chicago Pr.

Condos & Co-Ops-Multi-Use Structures: Techniques. Practising Law Institute Staff et al. LC 83-62452. (Real Estate Law & Practice Course Handbook Ser.: No. 233-234). (Illus.). 1983. 40.00 o.p. PLI.

Conduct & Accountability: A Report to the President. 162p. (Orig.). 1986. pap. 8.50 o.p. (S/N 040-000-00497-1). USGPO.

Conduct Expected: The Unwritten Rules for a Successful Business Career. William Lareau. LC 84-27280. 256p. 1985. 12.95 o.p. (ISBN 0-8329-0388-4). New Century.

Conduct Unbecoming. Rupert Croft-Cooke. 1985. 11.95 o.p. (ISBN 0-317-53079-8, Large Print Bks). G K Hall.

Conducting Bodies. Claude Simon. 1987. pap. 7.95 o.s.i. (ISBN 0-394-62289-8). Grove.

Conducting Educational Research. Bruce W. Tuckman. (Illus.). 402p. 1972. text ed. 14.95 o.p. (ISBN 0-15-512980-5, HC). HarBraceJ.

Conducting Educational Research. 2nd ed. Bruce W. Tuckman. (Illus.). 479p. 1978. text ed. 25.00 o.p. (ISBN 0-15-512981-3, HC). HarBraceJ.

Conducting Surveys in Developing Countries: Practical Problems & Experiences in Brazil, Malaysia & the Philippines. Christopher Scott et al. (LSMS Working Paper Ser.: No. 5). 126p. 5.00 o.p. (ISBN 0-317-58542-8, BK 0032). World Bank.

Conductive Education: A System for Overcoming Motor Disorder. Ed. by Philippa J. Cottam & Andrew Sutton. 200p. 1985. 34.50 o.p. (ISBN 0-7099-2290-6, Pub. by Croom Helm Ltd); pap. 17.00 o.p. (ISBN 0-7099-4201-X). Routledge Chapman & Hall.

Conductors: A New Generation. Philip Hart. (Illus.). 1979. encore ed. 5.95 o.p. (ISBN 0-684-16389-6, ScribT). Scribner.

Conductors: A New Generation. Philip Hart. (Illus.). 344p. 1983. pap. 10.95 o.p. (ISBN 0-684-18019-7, ScribT). Scribner.

Conductor's Art. Henry W. Braithwaite. (Illus.). 1978. Repr. of 1952 ed. lib. bdg. 35.00x o.p. (ISBN 0-313-20058-0, BRCAR). Greenwood.

Cones, Matrices & Mathematical Programming. A. Berman. LC 72-96725. (Lecture Notes in Economics & Mathematical Systems: Vol. 79). 96p. 1973. pap. 12.00 o.p. (ISBN 0-387-06123-1). Springer-Verlag.

Confederacy of Dunces. John K. Toole. LC 80-8922. 416p. 1982. pap. 4.50 o.s.i. (ISBN 0-394-17969-2, B-474, BC). Grove.

Confederate Postal History. Ed. by Francis J. Crown, Jr. LC 75-39499. (Illus.). 1976. 30.00x o.p. (ISBN 0-88000-077-5). Quarterman.

Conference of the Birds: A Sufi Fable. Farid Ud-Din Attar. Tr. by C. S. Nott. (Clear Light Ser). (Illus.). 147p. (Orig.). 1974. pap. 6.95 o.p. (ISBN 0-87773-031-8, 73001-1). Shambhala Pubns.

Conference on Aircraft Structures & Materials Application: Meeting Held September 9-11, 1969, Seattle, Washington. (National SAMPE Technical Conference Ser.: Vol. 1). 563p. 1983. 10.00 o.p. (ISBN 0-938994-00-X). SAMPE.

Conference on Fish Behavior in Relation to Fishing Techniques & Tactics: Proceedings, Bergen, Norway, 1968-69, Vols. 1 & 3. (Fisheries Reports: No. 62). pap. 7.50 o.p. (ISBN 0-686-92921-7, F1674, FAO); Vol. 3, 427p. pap. 25.50 o.p. (ISBN 0-686-98784-5). UNIPUB.

Conference on Harmonic Analysis in Honor of Antoni Zygmund. Ed. by William Beckner et al. LC 82-11172. (Mathematics Ser.: Vols. I & II). 837p. 1983. write for info. o.p. (ISBN 0-534-98043-0). Brooks-Cole.

Conference on Materials & Processes - In Service Performance: Meeting Held October 4-6, 1977, Atlanta, Georgia. (National SAMPE Technical Conference Ser.: Vol. 9). 562p. 1983. 20.00 o.p. (ISBN 0-938994-04-2). SAMPE.

Conference on New Horizons - Materials & Processes for the Eighties: Meeting Held November 13-15, 1979, Boston, Massachusetts. (National SAMPE Technical Conference Ser.: Vol. 11). 1051p. 1983. 50.00 o.p. (ISBN 0-938994-05-0). SAMPE.

Conference on Petroleum Hydrocarbons & Organic, 1987: Proceedings. LC 87-1623. 1987. 43.75 o.p. (ISBN 0-318-23043-7). Natl Water Well.

Conference on the State & Economic Growth, New York, 1956. Ed. by Hugh G. Aitken. LC 59-9954. 30.00 o.p. (ISBN 0-527-03306-5). Kraus Repr.

Conference Package. 88p. 2.50 o.p. (ISBN 0-318-15177-4, 111-224); 4 or more copies 2.00 ea. o.p. Natl Assoc Realtors.

Conferences on Canadian-U. S. Economic Relations. Institute for Research on Public Policy, Canada & Brookings. 94p. 1978. pap. text ed. 3.00x o.p. (ISBN 0-920380-09-3, Pub. by Inst Res Pub Canada). Gower Pub Co.

Conferencing Parents of Exceptional Children. Richard L. Simpson. LC 82-1770. 396p. 1982. 35.50 o.p. (ISBN 0-89443-694-5). Aspen Pub.

Confessing One Faith: A Joint Commentary on the Augsburg Confession by Lutheran & Catholic Theologians. George W. Forell & James F. McCue. LC 80-65557. 368p. 1981. pap. 16.95 o.p. (ISBN 0-8066-1802-7, 10-1637, Augsburg). Augsburg Fortress.

Confession d'un Enfant du Siecle. Alfred De Musset. Ed. by Allem. (Coll. Prestige). 27.95 o.p. (ISBN 0-685-34951-9). Schoenhof.

Confession d'un Enfant du Siecle. Alfred de Musset & Gerard Barrier. 1973. 9.95 o.p. (ISBN 0-686-55544-9). Schoenhof.

Confession of a Catholic. Michael Novak. LC 82-484236. 240p. 1983. 12.45i o.p. (ISBN 0-06-066319-7). HarpR.

Confession of a Prime Minister. Sam Spiller. 1980. 6.00 o.p. (ISBN 0-682-49531-X). Exposition-Phoenix.

Confession: Studies in Deviance & Religion. Bryan S. Turner & Mike Hepworth. 200p. 1982. 23.95x o.p. (ISBN 0-7100-9198-2). Routledge Chapman & Hall.

Confession: The Road to Forgiveness. Andrew Murray. Orig. Title: Have Mercy Upon Me. 160p. 1983. pap. text ed. 2.95 o.p. (ISBN 0-88368-134-X). Whitaker Hse.

Confessions & Interrogations after Miranda: A Comprehensive Guideline of the Law-1982 Supplement. 6th, rev. ed. James Zagel. 1982. 2.00 o.p. (ISBN 0-318-18687-X). Natl Coll DA.

Confessions of a Conservative Evangelical. Jack Rogers. LC 74-12249. 1974. pap. 2.65 o.s.i. (ISBN 0-664-24996-5, Westminster). Westminster John Knox.

Confessions of a Ladykiller. George Stade. 1979. 10.95 o.p. (ISBN 0-393-08837-5). Norton.

Confessions of a Moonlight Writer: A Freelancer's Guide to the Church Market. James H. Cox. LC 80-70315. 97p. (Orig.). 1982. pap. 5.95 o.p. (ISBN 0-939298-00-7). J M Prods.

Confessions of a Poet. Paul Verlaine. (ISBN 0-8022-1773-7). Philos Lib.

Confessions of a Pregnant Father. Dan Greenburg. 256p. 1986. 16.95 o.p. (ISBN 0-02-545450-1). Macmillan.

Confessions of a Prime Time Kid. Mark J. Harris. 144p. (gr. 5 up). 1986. pap. 2.50 o.p. (ISBN 0-380-70101-4, Flare). Avon.

Confessions of a Promiscuous Counterfeiter. Robert Baudin. LC 78-22243. 1979. 9.95 o.p. (ISBN 0-15-121853-6). HarBraceJ.

Confessions of a Reformer. Frederic C. Howe. 10.00 o.p. (ISBN 0-8446-2276-1). Peter Smith.

Confessions of a Scilly Birdman. David Hunt. LC 85-7847. (Illus.). 176p. (Orig.). 1985. pap. 14.75 o.p. (ISBN 0-7099-3724-5, Pub. by Croom Helm Ltd). Routledge Chapman & Hall.

Confessions of a Single Father. Jim Covington. LC 82-13232. 192p. 1982. 13.95 o.p. (ISBN 0-8298-0412-9). Pilgrim NY.

Confessions of a Socialist. Cartoon Archetypical Slogan Theatre Staff. 32p. 1981. pap. 3.95 o.p. (ISBN 0-86104-200-X, NO. 4121). Routledge Chapman & Hall.

Confessions of a Spent Youth. Vance Bourjaily. 1986. pap. 8.95 o.p. (ISBN 0-87795-775-4). Morrow.

Confessions of a Young Man, by George Moore: An Annotated Critical Edition. Ed. by Susan M. Dick. 1972. 17.50 o.p. (ISBN 0-7735-0097-9, McGill Canada). U of Toronto Pr.

Confessions of Aleister Crowley: An Autobiography. Ed. by John Symonds & Kenneth Grant. 1979. 37.00 o.p. (ISBN 0-7100-0175-4). Routledge Chapman & Hall.

Confessions of an Actor: An Autobiography. Laurence Olivier. (Illus.). 330p. 1982. 17.25 o.p. (ISBN 0-671-41701-0). S&S.

Confessions of an Advertising Man. David Ogilvy. LC 63-17855. 1963. 10.00 o.p. (ISBN 0-689-10215-1, Atheneum). Macmillan.

Confessions of an Infomaniac. Elizabeth M. Ferrarini. LC 84-50357. 202p. 1984. 12.95 o.p. (ISBN 0-89588-221-3); pap. 6.95 o.p. (ISBN 0-89588-186-1). SYBEX.

Confessions of Augustine. 2nd ed. John Gibb & William Montgomery. LC 78-66639. (Ancient Philosophy Ser.). 554p. 1980. lib. bdg. 67.00 o.p. (ISBN 0-8240-9597-9). Garland Pub.

Confessions of Augustine in Modern English. Sherwood E. Wirt. 144p. 1986. pap. 5.95 o.p. (ISBN 0-310-34641-X, 10807P). Zondervan.

Confessions of Jeremiah in Context: Scenes of Prophetic Drams. A. R. Diamond. (JSOT Supplement Ser.: No. 45). 250p. pap. text ed. 14.95x o.s.i. (Pub. by JSOT Pr England). Eisenbrauns.

Confessions of St. Augustine. Tr. & frwd. by F. J. Sheed. 208p. 1988. pap. 9.95 o.p. Sheed & Ward MO.

Confessions of the Old Wizard. Hjalmar H. Schacht. LC 74-15559. (Illus.). 484p. 1975. Repr. of 1956 ed. lib. bdg. 27.50x o.p. (ISBN 0-8371-7827-4, SCOW). Greenwood.

Confessions of Victor X. Donald Rayfield. LC 84-73544. 160p. 1985. 17.50 o.p. (ISBN 0-394-54630-X, E-990, Ever); pap. 6.95 o.p. (ISBN 0-394-62055-0). Grove.

Confetti. Madeline C. Barich. 64p. 1983. 5.50 o.p. (ISBN 0-682-49981-1). Exposition-Phoenix.

Confetti Generation: American Social Character in the Age of the New Electronic Communications. William J. Donnelly. 256p. 1986. 18.95 o.p. (ISBN 0-8050-0095-X). H Holt & Co.

Confidence in Communication: A Guide to Assertive & Social Skills. Ronald B. Adler. LC 76-58530. 334p. 1977. pap. text ed. 19.95x o.p. (ISBN 0-03-016696-9, HoltC). HR&W.

Confidence in Fact. William J. Cook. 1969. pap. 3.95 o.p. (ISBN 0-89137-700-X). Quality Pubns.

Confident Collector: How to Recognize an Authentic Antique. John Bly. (Illus.). 224p. 1986. 19.95 o.p. (ISBN 0-13-167487-0). P-H.

Confident Parent. Bob Pedrick. 1979. pap. 3.95 o.p. (ISBN 0-89191-167-7). Cook.

Confident Woman. Joanne Wallace. (Illus.). 192p. (Orig.). 1984. pap. 12.95 o.p. (ISBN 0-8007-1229-3). Revell.

Confident Writer: A Norton Handbook. Constance Gefvert. 1985. text ed. 13.95x o.p. (ISBN 0-393-95411-0). Norton.

Confidential Clerk. T. S. Eliot. LC 54-5253. 1954. 9.95 o.p. (ISBN 0-15-122013-1). HarBraceJ.

Confidential Memos of I. M. Vested: An Expose of Corporate Mismanagement by a Senior Executive of a Major American Company. I. M. Vested. LC 81-47558. 192p. 1981. 10.95 o.p. (ISBN 0-15-193072-4). HarBraceJ.

Confirmation: A Workbook. Carl G. Carlozzi. (Orig.). (gr. 6). 1969. pap. text ed. 2.50x o.p. (ISBN 0-8192-4101-6); tchr's ed. 4.25x o.p. (ISBN 0-8192-4102-4). Morehouse Pub.

Confirmation & Education. Ed. by W. Kent Gilbert. LC 72-4725. (Yearbooks in Christian Education). 224p. (Orig.). 1969. pap. 4.50 o.p. (ISBN 0-8006-1041-5, 1-1041, Fortress). Augsburg Fortress.

Confirmation & Morphology. (Advances in Polymer Science Ser.: Vol. 26). (Illus.). 1978. 49.00 o.p. (ISBN 0-387-08677-3). Springer-Verlag.

Confirmation & the Charismata. Theodore R. Jungkuntz. LC 83-10450. 126p. (Orig.). 1983. lib. bdg. 25.25 o.p. (ISBN 0-8191-3344-2); pap. text ed. 9.25 o.p. (ISBN 0-8191-3345-0). U Pr of Amer.

Conflict & Bargaining. Ed. by Sanjaya Lall. 1976. pap. 19.75 o.p. (ISBN 0-08-021060-0). Pergamon.

Conflict & Coal: A Case Study of Industrial Relations in the Open-Cut Coal Mining Industry of Queensland. Kevin Hince. LC 81-11464. (Illus.). 1982. text ed. 39.50x o.p. (ISBN 0-7022-1632-1). U of Queensland Pr.

Conflict & Compromise: Class Formation in English Society, 1830-1914, with Particular Reference to Education, Industry & Politics in Birmingham & Sheffield. Dennis Smith. 1982. 39,95x o.p. (ISBN 0-7100-0969-0). Routledge Chapman & Hall.

Conflict & Conflict Resolution. Jack N. Porter. LC 81-43345. 200p. 1982. lib. bdg. 29.00 o.p. (ISBN 0-8240-9287-2). Garland Pub.

Conflict & Control in an African Trade Union: A Study of the Nigerian Coal Miner's Union. David R. Smock. LC 75-76971. (Studies Ser.: No. 23). 170p. 1969. 11.95x o.p. (ISBN 0-8179-3231-3); pap. 5.95x o.p. (ISBN 0-8179-3232-1). Hoover Inst Pr.

Conflict & Order: An Introduction to International Relations. Forest L. Grieves. LC 76-10901. (Illus.). 1977. text ed. 33.56 o.p. (ISBN 0-395-24332-7). HM.

Conflict & Stability in Europe. Ed. by Clive Emsley. 384p. 1979. 35.00 o.p. (ISBN 0-7099-0154-2, Pub. by Croom Helm Ltd); pap. 9.00 o.p. (ISBN 0-7099-0155-0). Routledge Chapman & Hall.

Conflict & Understanding in Marriage. Paul Plattner. 1970. 3.45 o.p. (ISBN 0-8042-1093-4, John Knox). Westminster John Knox.

Conflict Between Energy & Urban Environment: Consolidated Edison Versus the City of New York. Regina Axelrod. LC 80-67179. 214p. (Orig.). 1982. lib. bdg. 27.50 o.p. (ISBN 0-8191-2376-5); pap. text ed. 13.25 o.p. (ISBN 0-8191-2377-3). U Pr of Amer.

Conflict in American Foreign Policy: The Issues Debated. Don L. Mansfield & Gary J. Buckley. 400p. 1985. pap. text ed. (ISBN 0-13-166844-7). P-H.

Conflict in Northwest Africa: The Western Sahara Dispute. John Damis. (Publication Ser.: 278). (Illus.). 245p. 1983. 19.95x o.p. (ISBN 0-8179-7781-3); pap. text ed. 9.95x o.p. (ISBN 0-8179-7782-1). Hoover Inst Pr.

Conflict in the Shadows. James E. Cross. LC 75-17468. 180p. 1975. Repr. of 1963 ed. lib. bdg. 22.50x o.p. (ISBN 0-8371-8305-7, CRCS). Greenwood.

Conflict of Generations in Ancient Greece & Rome. Ed. by Stephen Bertman. 1976. text ed. 32.50x o.p. (ISBN 90-6032-033-6). Humanities.

Conflict of Interests. Clive Egleton. LC 83-45068. 256p. 1983. 13.95 o.p. (ISBN 0-689-11394-3, Atheneum). Macmillan.

Conflict of Laws, Cases, Comments, Questions. 3rd ed. Roger C. Cramton et al. LC 81-7405. (American Casebook Ser.). 1026p. 1981. text ed. 32.95 o.p. (ISBN 0-314-59493-0). West Pub.

Conflict of the Ages: The Mystery of Lawlessness, Its Origin, Historic Development & Coming Defeat. XRev ed. Arno C. Gaebelein. 1983. pap. 4.95 o.p. (ISBN 0-87213-206-4). Loizeaux.

Conflict of Values. Melville Chaning-Pearce. 1985. 10.00x o.p. (ISBN 0-317-62019-3, Guild of Pastoral Psych). State Mutual Bk.

Conflict, Retrenchment, & Reappraisal: The Administration of Higher Education. Clark Kerr et al. LC 78-74239. 172p. 1979. 16.95 o.p. (ISBN 0-252-00773-5). U of Ill Pr.

Conflict: The Separation of the Church & State. Clayton L. Nuttall. LC 80-21267. 126p. 1980. pap. 4.95 o.p. (ISBN 0-87227-076-9, RBP5088). Reg Baptist.

Conflicting Interests: Corporate-Governance Controversies. Fred D. Baldwin et al. LC 83-48400. 224p. 1984. 26.00x o.p. (ISBN 0-669-07123-4). Lexington Bks.

Conflicts of Interest in the Proxy Voting System. James E. Heard & Howard D. Sherman. 100p. (Orig.). 1987. pap. 75.00 o.p. (ISBN 0-931035-18-X). IRRC Inc DC.

Conformation in Fibrous Protein & Related Synthetic Polypeptides. R. D. Fraser & T. P. MacRae. (Molecular Biology: An International Series of Monographs & Textbooks). 1973. 123.50 o.p. (ISBN 0-12-266850-2). Acad Pr.

Conformation of Biological Molecules & Polymers. Ed. by E. D. Bergman & Bernard Pullman. 1973. 99.00 o.p. (ISBN 0-12-091065-9). Acad Pr.

Conformation Theory. Michael Hanack. Tr. by H. C. Newmann. (Organic Chemistry Ser.: Vol. 3). 1965. 98.00 o.p. (ISBN 0-12-322550-7). Acad Pr.

Conformational Analysis: Proceedings of an International Symposium, Brussels, 1969. Ed. by G. Chiurdoglu. 208p. 1976. 24.00 o.p. (ISBN 0-08-020747-2). Pergamon.

Conformational Analysis: Scope & Present Limitations. Ed. by G. Chiurdoglu. (Organic Chemistry Ser.: Vol. 21). 1971. 74.50 o.p. (ISBN 0-12-173050-6). Acad Pr.

Conformational States & Biological Activity of Cyclic Peptides. Yu A. Ovchinniko & V. T. Ivanov. Ed. by Derek Barton. 1976. pap. 15.50 o.p. (ISBN 0-08-020426-0). Pergamon.

Conforming Constitutions to the New Code. Joseph F. Gallen. 58p. 1984. pap. 2.00 o.p. (ISBN 0-317-18638-8). Dghtrs St Paul.

Conformity's Children: An Approach to the Superfluous Man in Russian Literature. Ellen B. Chances. iv, 210p. 1978. pap. 11.95 o.p. (ISBN 0-89357-051-6). Slavica.

Confound & Destroy: One Hundred Group & the Bomber Support Campaign. Martin Streetly. (Illus.). 280p. 1986. pap. 24.95 o.p. (ISBN 0-7106-0356-8). Janes Info Group.

Confrontation in Central Europe: Weimar Germany & Czechoslovakia. F. Gregory Campbell. LC 74-11618. (Midway Reprint). 1978. pap. text ed. 14.00x o.s.i. (ISBN 0-226-09252-6). U of Chicago Pr.

Confrontation of Co-Operation? Twelfth World Conference of the Society for International Development Proceedings. Ed. by Pushpa N. Schwartz. 1976. pap. 23.00 o.p. (ISBN 0-08-020491-0). Pergamon.

Confrontations with Prophets. Hans W. Wolff. LC 82-48585. 80p. 1983. pap. 1.00 o.p. (ISBN 0-8006-1702-9, Fortress). Augsburg Fortress.

Confronted by Christ. Cecil Culverhouse. (Orig., For leaders of gr. 9-12). 1969. pap. 2.95 o.p. (ISBN 0-8042-9880-7, John Knox). Westminster John Knox.

Confronting Christianity: Adults & Authority. Richard Reichert. LC 78-53634. 44p. 1978. pap. 9.95 o.p. (ISBN 0-88489-102-X). St Marys.

Confronting Nonpromotability: How to Manage a Stalled Career. Edward Roseman. LC 77-8013. (Illus.). 1977. 14.95 o.p. (ISBN 0-8144-5441-0). AMACOM.

Confronting Utilization Variations: The Maine Approach. 1986. pap. 12.00 o.p. (ISBN 0-89970-246-5, OP-007). AMA.

Confronting War: An Examination of Humanity's Most Pressing Problem. Ronald J. Glossop. LC 82-23950. 304p. 1983. pap. 19.95x o.p. (ISBN 0-89950-073-0). McFarland & Co.

Confronting Youth Unemployment in the Nineteen Eighties: Rhetoric Versus Reality. Ed. by Ray C. Rist. LC 80-19730. (Pergamon Policy Studies on Social Issues). 236p. 1980. pap. 60.00 o.p. (ISBN 0-08-026077-2). Pergamon.

Confucian Analects, the Great Learning & the Doctrine of the Mean. Confucius. Tr. by James Legge. 15.50 o.p. (ISBN 0-8446-0067-9). Peter Smith.

Confucius & Christ. L. Sherley Price. 1952. (ISBN 0-8022-1552-1). Philos Lib.

Confucius, His Life & Time. Wu-chi Liu. 1956. (ISBN 0-8022-1937-3). Philos Lib.

Confusion & Hope: Clergy, Laity, & the Church in Transition. Ed. by Glenn R. Bucher & Patricia R. Hill. LC 74-76923. 144p. (Orig.). 1974. pap. 0.50 o.p. (ISBN 0-8006-1303-1, Fortress). Augsburg Fortress.

Congenital Abnormalities of the Optic Nerve & Related Forebrain. Thomas E. Acers. LC 82-24962. (Illus.). 75p. 1983. 14.50. o.p. (ISBN 0-8121-0889-2). Lea & Febiger.

Congenital Anomalies of the Heart. Naomasa Okamoto. LC 79-89192. (Illus.). 1980. 51.00 o.p. (ISBN 0-89640-036-0). Igaku-Shoin.

Congenital Arteriovenous Aneurysms of the Carotid & Vertebral Arterial Systems. H. Olivecrona & J. Ladenheim. (Illus.). 1957. 69.70 o.p. (ISBN 0-387-02204-X). Springer-Verlag.

Congenital Deafness: A New Approach to Early Detection of Deafness Through a High Risk Register. F. O. Black et al. LC 76-135285. 1971. 15.00x o.p. (ISBN 0-87081-005-7). Univ Pr Colo.

Congenital Defects: New Directions in Research. Ed. by Dwight T. Janerich et al. 1974. 54.50 o.p. (ISBN 0-12-380350-0). Acad Pr.

Congenital Heart Disease. Ed. by William J. Rashkind. LC 81-6979. (Benchmark Papers in Human Physiology: Vol. 16). 416p. 1982. 59.95 o.p. (ISBN 0-87933-414-2). Van Nos Reinhold.

Congenital Heart Disease: Morphologic Echocardiographic Correlations. Elma J. Gussenhoven & Anton E. Becker. LC 82-4474. (Modern Pediatric Cardiology Ser.). (Illus.). 220p. 1983. text ed. 83.25 o.p. (ISBN 0-443-02262-3). Churchill.

Congenital Malformations: Case Studies in Developmental Anatomy. Martha E. Sucheston & M. Samuel Cannon. (Illus.). 271p. 1973. pap. text ed. 11.00x o.p. (ISBN 0-8036-8210-7). Davis Co.

Conglomeroid Cocktail Party. Robert Silverberg. 1984. 14.95 o.p. (ISBN 0-87795-577-8, Arbor Hse). Morrow.

Congo. Michael Crichton. 1981. pap. 3.95 o.p. (ISBN 0-380-56176-X, 69682-7). Avon.

Congratulations - God Believes in You. Lloyd Ogilvie. 128p. 1980. 6.99 o.p. (ISBN 0-8499-2994-6). Word Bks.

Congratulations, America. Maria Aschwanden. 184p. 1982. 8.50 o.p. (ISBN 0-682-49800-9). Exposition-Phoenix.

Congratulations! You're Going to Be a Grandmother. Lanie Carter. LC 80-1345. 80p. 1980. PLB 5.95 o.s.i. (ISBN 0-916392-48-1); pap. 3.95 o.s.i. (ISBN 0-916392-53-8). Oak Tree Pubns.

Congregate Housing for Older People: A Solution for the 1980's. Ed. by Robert D. Chellis et al. LC 81-47983. 240p. 1982. 35.00x o.p. (ISBN 0-669-05210-8). Lexington Bks.

Congregational House Churches. T. Ed Barlow. (Orig.). 1978. pap. 1.50 o.p. (ISBN 0-8309-0214-7). Herald Hse.

Congregational Outreach & Care: A Manual for Mini-Parish Leadership. Daniel Fuelling & Audrey Rothmaler. 40p. (Orig.). 1982. pap. 3.50 o.p. (ISBN 0-8066-1967-8, 10-1643, Augsburg). Augsburg Fortress.

Congress. Randall B. Ripley. (Illus.). 352p. 1975. 9.95x o.p. (ISBN 0-393-09250-X). Norton.

Congress & Money: Budgeting, Spending & Taxing. Allen Schick. LC 80-53322. 604p. 1980. 28.90 o.p. (ISBN 0-87766-278-9); pap. 15.25x o.p. (ISBN 0-87766-294-0). Urban Inst.

Congress & the Administrative State. Lawrence C. Dodd & Richard L. Schott. LC 79-14347. (Viewpoints on American Politics Ser.). 364p. 1979. pap. text ed. write for info. o.p. (ISBN 0-02-330690-4). Macmillan.

Congress & the American People. 2nd ed. William J. Keefe. (Illus.). 256p. 1984. pap. text ed. (ISBN 0-13-167635-0). P-H.

Congress & the Budget. Joel Havemann. LC 78-1851. 256p. 1978. 18.95x o.p. (ISBN 0-253-31406-2). Ind U Pr.

Congress & the Court. Walter F. Murphy. LC 62-9739. 1965. pap. text ed. 3.95x o.s.i. (ISBN 0-226-55185-7, P196, Phoen). U of Chicago Pr.

Congress & the Munitions Merchants: The Secret Committee of Trade During the American Revolution, 1775-1777. Elizabeth M. Nuxoll. Ed. by Stuart Bruchey. LC 84-48313. (American Economic History Ser.). 552p. 1985. lib. bdg. 70.00 o.p. (ISBN 0-8240-6661-8). Garland Pub.

Congress & the Nation, Vol. I. 1983. (ISBN 0-87187-294-3). Congr Quarterly.

Congress & the Nation, 5 Vols. 1983. (ISBN 0-87187-302-8). Congr Quarterly.

Congress & the Public Trust: Report of the Association of the Bar of the City of New York - Special Committee on Congressional Ethics. James C. Kirby et al. LC 78-108830. 1971. pap. text ed. 3.45x o.p. (ISBN 0-689-70273-6, 179, Atheneum). Macmillan.

Congress Dances. Susan M. Alsop. 1985. pap. 3.95 o.s.i. (ISBN 0-317-56895-7). PB.

Congress of the International Council of the Aeronautical Sciences, 15th, London, England, 7-12 September, 1986: Proceedings, 2 vols. International Council of Aeronautical Sciences Staff. 1200p. 1987. Set. pap. 89.50 o.p. (ISBN 0-930403-16-9). AIAA.

Congress: Perspectives on Representation in American Government. Close Up Foundation Staff. (Illus.). 34p. 1987. pap. text ed. 6.00x o.p. (ISBN 0-932765-10-6); tchr's. guide avail. o.p. Close Up Foun.

Congress: The First Branch of Government. Ed. by Alfred de Grazia. 515p. 1966. pap. 17.25 o.p. (ISBN 0-8447-3053-X). Am Enterprise.

Congressional Action on R & D in FY 1987 Budget. Albert Teich et al. 52p. 1986. pap. 7.50 o.p. (ISBN 0-87168-288-5). AAAS.

Congressional Action on Research & Development in the FY 1983 Budget. Intersociety Working Group Staff. 38p. 1983. pap. 4.00 o.p. (ISBN 0-87168-262-1). AAAS.

Congressional District Data Book, 98th Congress. Ed. by Bureau of Census Staff. (Congressional District Data Book PHC80-4 Ser.). 1983. three-ring binder 60.00x o.p. (ISBN 0-527-67325-0). Kraus Intl.

Congressional Elections. Barbara Hinckley. LC 81-2413. 173p. 1981. pap. 9.95 o.p. (ISBN 0-87187-171-8). Congr Quarterly.

Congressional Leadership: Seeking a New Role. Richard Cohen. (Washington Papers: Vol. VIII, No. 79). 88p. (Orig.). 1980. pap. text ed. 7.95 o.p. (ISBN 0-8191-6023-7, Pub. by CSIS). U Pr of Amer.

Congressional Medal of Honor Library: Vietnam - The Names, The Deeds. 1987. pap. 3.95 o.p. (ISBN 0-440-11453-5). Dell.

Congressional Medal of Honor Library: World War II The Names, The Deeds (A-L) 1987. pap. 3.95 o.p. (ISBN 0-440-11454-3). Dell.

Congressional Oversight Investigations, Vol. 134. Practising Law Institute Staff. 139p. 1984. pap. 40.00 o.p. (ISBN 0-317-27632-8, #C4-4168). PLI.

Congressional Pictorial Directory, 100th Congress, February 1987. (Illus.). 210p. 1987. fabricoid 12.00 o.p. (ISBN 0-318-22884-X, S/N 052-070-06230-4). USGPO.

Congressional Power: Congress & Social Change. Gary Orfield. 339p. (Orig.). 1975. pap. text ed. 7.95 o.p. (ISBN 0-15-513081-1, HC). HarBraceJ.

Congressional Publications: A Research Guide to Legislation, Budgets & Treaties. Jerrold Zwirn. LC 82-18652. 195p. 1983. lib. bdg. 25.00 o.p. (ISBN 0-87287-358-7). Libs Unl.

Congressional Roll Call, 1977. Congressional Quarterly Inc. Staff. LC 72-77849. 1977. pap. text ed. 12.00 o.p. (ISBN 0-87187-121-1). Congr Quarterly.

Congressional Roll Call 1979. Congressional Quarterly Inc. Staff. (Roll Call Ser.). 1980. pap. text ed. 12.00 o.p. (ISBN 0-87187-191-2). Congr Quarterly.

Conjugates of Steroid Hormones. H. E. Hadd & R. T. Blickenstaff. 1969. 54.00 o.p. (ISBN 0-12-312850-1). Acad Pr.

Connaitre et Se Connaitre. 2nd ed. Gilbert A. Jarvis et al. (Fr.). 1980. text ed. 15.95 o.p. (ISBN 0-03-050596-8). HR&W.

Connally-Hicks Debate on Divorce & Remarriage. Andrew M. Connally & Olan Hicks. 1979. pap. 13.00 o.p. (ISBN 0-934916-31-4). Natl Christian Pr.

Connecticut Clockmakers of the Eighteenth Century. 2nd ed. Penrose R. Hoopes. (Illus.). 11.25 o.p. (ISBN 0-8446-5046-3). Peter Smith.

Connecticut: Contracts. 9.50 o.p. (ISBN 0-686-90665-9). Am Law Inst.

Connecticut Low. Bruce Boehm & Janet Winn. (gr. 7 up). 1980. 6.95 o.p. (ISBN 0-395-29518-1). HM.

Connecticut Place Names. Arthur H. Hughes & Morse S. Allen. 907p. 1976. 25.00x o.p. (ISBN 0-940748-06-1). Conn Hist Soc.

Connecticut Railroads: An Illustrated History. Gregg M. Turner & Melancthon W. Jacobus. Ed. & frwd. by Oliver O. Jensen. (Illus.). 336p. 1986. 39.95 o.p. (ISBN 0-940748-89-4); pap. 25.95 o.p. (ISBN 0-940748-90-8). Conn Hist Soc.

Connecticut-Rhode Island Directory of Manufacturers, 1987-88. 350p. 1987. pap. 62.50 o.p. (ISBN 0-318-02856-5). Manufacturers.

Connecticut River: New England's Historic Waterway. Edmund Delaney. LC 83-80635. (Illus.). 182p. 1983. pap. 9.95 o.p. (ISBN 0-87106-980-6). Globe Pequot.

Connecticut State Industrial Directory, 1988. 460p. 1988. 85.00 o.p. (ISBN 0-318-22817-3, Pub. by Mac Ral's). Manufacturers.

Connecticut Supplement for Modern Real Estate Practice. 3rd ed. University of Connecticut, Center for Real Estate & Urban Economic Studies Staff & Michael L. Galonska. LC 84-6806. 192p. (Orig.). 1984. pap. text ed. 10.95 o.p. (ISBN 0-88462-483-8, 1510-27, Real Estate Ed). Longman Finan.

Connecticut: Trusts. 8.50 o.p. (ISBN 0-686-90668-3). Am Law Inst.

Connecticut Yankee in King Arthur's Court. Mark Twain. LC 84-60184. (Illus.). 336p. 1984. 12.95 o.p. (ISBN 0-89577-185-3). RD Assn.

Connecting: A Handbook for Housewives Returning to Paid Work. Sally Ashley. 224p. 1982. pap. 5.95 o.p. (ISBN 0-380-79251-6, 79251-6). Avon.

Connection. Jack Gelber. 1960. pap. 3.95 o.p. (ISBN 0-394-17222-1, E223, Ever). Grove.

Connections Between Old English & Medieval Celtic Literature: Three Essays by Daniel Frederick Melia, Joseph Falaky Nagy, & Sarah Lynn Higley. Ed. by Patrick K. Ford & Karen G. Borst. (Old English Colloquium Ser.: No. 2). 76p. 1985. pap. text ed. 8.00 o.p. (ISBN 0-8191-4511-4). U Pr of Amer.

Connections: Bridges-Ladders-Ramps-Staircases-Tunnels. Hal Foster & Janet Kardon. (Illus.). 72p. 1982. 10.00 o.p. (ISBN 0-317-57675-5). U of Pa Contemp Art.

Connections: Ideas for Writing. Sheila Hancock & Edward Hancock. (Illus.). 288p. (Orig.). 1974. pap. text ed. 10.95 o.p. (ISBN 0-15-513254-7, HC). HarBraceJ.

Connections: Nutrition, Contraception, Women, Eating. Janet Schwartz et al. 75p. (Orig.). 1981. pap. text ed. 7.00 o.p. (ISBN 0-940050-01-3). Sun Rose.

Connections: Nutrition, Contraception, Women, Eating. rev. ed. Janet Schwartz et al. (Illus.). 100p. (Orig.). 1985. pap. 7.95 o.p. (ISBN 0-940050-03-X). Sun Rose.

Connective Tissue in Health & Disease. Asboe-Hansen. 1957. Philos Lib.

Connective Tissue: Macromolecular Structure & Evolution. M. B. Mathews. (Molecular Biology Biochemistry & Biophysics Ser.: Vol. 19). (Illus.). xii, 318p. 1975. 46.00 o.p. (ISBN 0-387-07068-0). Springer-Verlag.

Connie. Anne Alexander. LC 76-4477. (Illus.). 208p. (gr. 5-8). 1976. 6.95 o.p. (ISBN 0-689-30534-6, Atheneum). Macmillan.

Connie Hagar: The Life History of a Texas Birdwatcher. Karen H. McCracken. LC 85-40748. 312p. 1986. 18.95 o.p. (ISBN 0-89096-248-0). Tex A&M Univ Pr.

Connoisseur's Book of Cigar. Zino Davidoff. (Illus.). 96p. 1969. text ed. 12.95 o.p. (ISBN 0-07-015460-0). McGraw.

Connoisseur's Guide to Beer. 4th ed. James Robertson. 288p. 1985. pap. 11.95 o.p. (ISBN 0-915463-05-9, Pub. by Jameson Bks, Dist. by Kampmann). Green Hill.

Connoisseur's Guide to Beer: 1984. rev. ed. James Robertson. (Illus.). 288p. (Orig.). 1983. pap. 11.95 o.p. (ISBN 0-89803-136-2, Dist. by Kampmann). Green Hill.

Connoisseur's Guide to the Movies. James Monaco. (Illus.). 320p. 16.95 o.p. (ISBN 0-87196-964-5); pap. 9.95 o.p. (ISBN 0-87196-963-7). Facts on File.

Connoisseurs' Handbook of California Wines. 2nd, rev. ed. Charles Olken et al. LC 81-48103. (Illus.). 1982. pap. 6.95 o.p. (ISBN 0-394-72710-X). Knopf.

Connoisseurs Handbook of Marijuana. William Drake. (Illus.). 320p. 1987. 14.95 o.p. (ISBN 0-914171-14-3). Ronin Pub.

Conquer: The Story of the Ninth Army 1943-1945. LC 80-65182. (Combat Arms Ser.: No. 5). (Illus.). 1980. Repr. of 1947 ed. 25.00 o.p. (ISBN 0-89839-027-3). Battery Pr.

Conquering Cancer. Robert W. Bermudes. 1983. 5.50 o.p. (ISBN 0-89536-619-3, 0388). CSS of Ohio.

Conquering Disease the Natural Way: Confessions of a Hypoglycemic Victim. Patricia J. Huggins. LC 85-90984. 1985. 6.00 o.p. (ISBN 0-682-40218-4). Exposition-Phoenix.

Conquering Government Regulation: A Business Guide. M. Stokes. 288p. 1982. text ed. 32.50 o.p. (ISBN 0-07-061640-X). McGraw.

Conquering the Kill-Joys: Positive Living in a Negative World. Bill Weber. 160p. 1986. 12.95 o.p. (ISBN 0-8499-0439-0, 0439-0). Word Bks.

Conquering the Night Season. Aaron I. Jones. LC 84-17515. 1985. pap. 4.95 o.p. (ISBN 0-8054-2255-2). Broadman.

Conquering Your Agoraphobia. Mona Woodford. 128p. (Orig.). 1987. pap. 6.95 o.p. (ISBN 0-7137-1788-2, Pub. by Javelin England). Sterling.

Conquerors. Andre Malraux. Tr. by Stephen Becker from Fr. LC 77-77883. 1977. pap. 3.95 o.s.i. (ISBN 0-394-17023-7, E701, Ever). Grove.

Conquerors & Rulers: Social Forces in Medieval China. 2nd rev. ed. W. Eberhard. 1970. 35.00 o.p. (ISBN 0-88431-200-3). E J Brill USA.

Conquest & Colonization of Honduras, 1502-1550. Robert S. Chamberlain. 1967. lib. bdg. 20.00x o.p. (ISBN 0-374-91368-4, Octagon). Hippocrene Bks.

Conquest of a Bacteria. Frank S. Taylor. (ISBN 0-8022-1697-8). Philos Lib.

Conquest of Copper Mountain. Forbes Wilson. LC 80-69369. 1981. 20.00 o.p. (ISBN 0-689-11153-3, Atheneum). Macmillan.

Conquest of the Antarctic. Norman Kemp. (Illus.). 160p. 1957. (ISBN 0-8022-0842-8). Philos Lib.

Conquest of the Barbarians. M. Stine & H. William Stine. (Wizards, Warriors & You Ser.: No. 17). 1986. pap. 2.95 o.p. (ISBN 0-380-75046-5). Avon.

Conquest of the Incas. John Hemming. LC 74-117593. 1970. 15.00 o.p. (ISBN 0-15-122560-5). HarBraceJ.

Conquest of the Sky: Childcraft Annual, 1985. Ed. by World Book, Inc. Staff. LC 65-25105. (Childcraft--The How & Why Library). (Illus.). 304p. (gr. 3-7). 1985. write for info. o.p. (ISBN 0-7166-0685-2). World Bk.

Conquest of the Time Master. R. L. Stine. (Wizards, Warriors & You Ser.: No. 8). 96p. (gr. 7 up). 1985. pap. 2.25 o.p. (ISBN 0-380-89945-0). Avon.

Conquest of Violence: The Gandhian Philosophy of Conflict. rev. ed. Joan V. Bondurant. LC 65-23153. (gr. 9 up). 1965. 25.00x o.p. (ISBN 0-520-00143-5); pap. 10.95x o.p. (ISBN 0-520-00145-1). U of Cal Pr.

Conquest of Virginia. Conway W. Sams. Incl. The Forest Primeval. LC 73-677. (Illus.). 526p. Repr. of 1916 ed. 20.00 o.s.i. (ISBN 0-87152-122-9); The First Attempt, 1584-1602. LC 73-668. (Illus.). 872p. Repr. of 1924 ed. o.p. (ISBN 0-87152-123-7); The Second Attempt, 1606-1610. LC 73-676. (Illus.). 1232p. Repr. of 1929 ed. 30.00 o.s.i. (ISBN 0-87152-124-5); The Third Attempt, 1610-1624. LC 73-675. (Illus.). 842p. Repr. of 1939 ed. 25.00 o.s.i. (ISBN 0-87152-125-3). 1973. Reprint.

Conquistador. Peter Lappin. LC 69-19398. 1970. 6.95 o.p. (ISBN 0-89944-040-1). Don Bosco Multimedia.

Conquistadora. rev. ed. Pedro R. Ortega. LC 83-18292. (Illus.). 32p. (Orig., Eng. & Span.). 1985. pap. 4.95 o.p. (ISBN 0-913270-72-5). Sunstone Pr.

Conrad: The Critical Heritage. Ed. by Norman Sherry. (Critical Heritage Ser.). 1973. 34.00x o.p. (ISBN 0-7100-7388-7). Routledge Chapman & Hall.

Conscience. new ed. Ed. by John Donnelly & Leonard Lyons. LC 72-6720. 249p. (Orig.). 1973. pap. 4.95 o.p. (ISBN 0-8189-0259-0). Alba.

Conscience. Jung Institute, Curatorium Staff. Tr. by R. F. Hull & Ruth Horine. (Studies in Jungian Thought). 1970. 13.95 o.s.i. (ISBN 0-8101-0297-8). Northwestern U Pr.

Conscience: A Structural Theory. Michael Kroy. 244p. 1974. casebound 17.95x o.p. (ISBN 0-87855-202-2). Transaction Pubs.

Conscience & Caring. Geoffrey Peterson. LC 82-7401. (Creative Pastoral Care & Counseling Ser.). 96p. 1982. pap. 4.50 o.p. (ISBN 0-8006-0570-5, 1-570, Fortress). Augsburg Fortress.

Conscience & Society: A Study of the Psychological Prerequisites of Law & Order. Ranyard West. LC 77-138192. 261p. 1972. Repr. of 1945 ed. lib. bdg. 35.00x o.p. (ISBN 0-8371-5649-1, WESO). Greenwood.

Conscience & the King: A Study of Hamlet. Bertram L. Joseph. Repr. of 1953 ed. 29.00x o.p. (ISBN 0-403-08615-9). Somerset Pub.

Conscience & the State. Julien Cornell. Bd. with Conscientious Objector & the Law. Julien Cornell. LC 70-147636. (Library of War & Peace; Conscrip. & Cons. Object.). 1973. lib. bdg. 46.00 o.p. (ISBN 0-8240-0412-4). Garland Pub.

Conscience: Development & Self-Transcendence. Walter E. Conn. LC 80-24043. 230p. (Orig.). 1981. pap. 12.95 o.p. (ISBN 0-89135-025-X). Religious Educ.

Conscience in Conflict: The Life of St. George Jackson Mivart. Jacob W. Gruber. LC 79-17545. (Illus.). 1980. Repr. of 1960 ed. lib. bdg. 35.00x o.p. (ISBN 0-313-22041-7, GRCC). Greenwood.

Conscience of a Nation. James T. Draper. LC 82-73420. 1983. pap. 7.95 o.p. (ISBN 0-8054-1530-0). Broadman.

Conscience Plays. Claire W. Durstewitz. 1982. pap. 4.95 o.p. (ISBN 0-89536-527-8, 0340). CSS of Ohio.

Conscience: The Search for Truth. P. D. Ouspensky. 1979. pap. 7.95 o.p. (ISBN 0-7100-0397-8). Routledge Chapman & Hall.

Conscience: The Search for Truth. P. D. Ouspensky. (Illus.). 168p. 1988. pap. text ed. 10.95 o.p. (ISBN 1-85063-102-6). Routledge Chapman & Hall.

Conscientious Objector & the Law see Conscience & the State.

Conscientization & Deschooling: Freire's & Illich's Proposals for Reshaping Society. John L. Elias. LC 76-20618. 1976. 12.95 o.s.i. (ISBN 0-664-20787-1, Westminster). Westminster John Knox.

Conscious & Unconscious Expressive Art: Theories, Methodology & Pathographies - Proceedings of the. Annual Meeting of the American Society of Psychopathology, 4th, Belmont, Mass., October 1969. Ed. by Irene Jakab. (Psychiatry & Art: Vol. 3). (Illus.). 1971. 38.75 o.p. (ISBN 3-8055-1190-6). S Karger.

Consciousness & Cure. Gerhard Adler. 1985. 10.00x o.p. (ISBN 0-317-62020-7, Guild of Pastoral Bk). State Mutual Bk.

Consciousness Industry: On Literature Politics & the Media. Hans M. Enzensberger. LC 73-17873. 1974. 6.95 o.p. (ISBN 0-8264-0082-5). Continuum.

Consciousness of Wealth: Creating a Money Magnet. John-Roger. LC 76-16594. 1976. pap. 5.00 o.p. (ISBN 0-914829-06-8). Mandeville LA.

Consecutive Numbers, No. 1. (Orig.). 1983. pap. 14.95 o.p. (ISBN 0-87280-048-2, Asher-Gallant). Caddylak Systs.

Consensual Democracies? The Government & Politics of the Scandinavian States. Neil Elder & Alastair H. Thomas. (Illus.). 256p. 1984. 45.00x o.p. (ISBN 0-85520-423-0). Basil Blackwell.

Consensual Democracies? The Government & Politics of the Scandinavian States. Neil Elder & Alastair H. Thomas. (Illus.). 256p. 1987. pap. 16.95x o.p. (ISBN 0-85520-716-7). Basil Blackwell.

Consensus & Confrontation: The United States & the Law of the Sea Convention, W7, Law of the Sea Workshop, No. 7. Ed. by Jon M. Van Dyke. 576p. 1985. 29.50 o.s.i. (ISBN 0-911189-11-4). Law Sea Inst.

Conservation & Agriculture. Ed. by John Davidson & Richard Lloyd. LC 77-697. 252p. 1978. 71.95x o.p. (ISBN 0-471-99502-9, Pub. by Wiley-Interscience). Wiley.

Conservation & the Gospel of Efficiency: The Progressive Conservation Movement, 1890-1920. Samuel P. Hays. LC 59-9274. 1969. pap. text ed. 4.95x o.p. (ISBN 0-689-70091-1, 139, Atheneum). Macmillan.

Conservation & the Gospel of Efficiency: The Progressive Conservation Movement, 1890-1920. Samuel P. Hays. LC 59-9274. (Historical Monographs Ser: No. 40). 1959. 22.50x o.p. (ISBN 0-674-16500-4). Harvard U Pr.

Conservation Archaeology: A Guide for Cultural Resources Management Studies. Ed. by M. B. Schiffer & G. J. Gumerman. 1977. 39.95 o.p. (ISBN 0-12-624160-0). Acad Pr.

Conservation Directory, 1988. 33rd, rev. ed. Ed. by Rue Gordon. 1987. pap. 15.00 o.p. (ISBN 0-912186-87-9). Natl Wildlife.

Conservation for People: Alternatives for the Future. Ed. by David Pitt. 192p. 1988. lib. bdg. 65.00 o.p. (ISBN 0-415-00455-1). Routledge Chapman & Hall.

Conservation in the Production of Petroleum. Erich W. Zimmermann. LC 76-15231. (Illus.). 1976. Repr. of 1957 ed. lib. bdg. 31.50x o.p. (ISBN 0-8371-8618-8, ZICP). Greenwood.

Conservation Law of Illinois. Gould Editorial Staff. 350p. looseleaf 16.95 o.p. Gould.

Conservation of Orbital Symmetry. R. B. Woodward & R. Hoffmann. LC 79-103636. (Illus.). 178p. 1970. pap. 17.95x o.p. (ISBN 0-89573-109-6). VCH Pubs.

Conservation Policy for Research Libraries. Carolyn C. Morrow. (Occasional Papers: No. 139). 23p. 1979. pap. 2.00 o.p. (ISBN 0-317-58982-2). U of Ill Lib Info Sci.

Conservation Treatment Procedures: A Manual of Step-by-Step Procedures for the Maintenance & Repair of Library Materials. Carolyn C. Morrow. LC 82-181. 191p. 1982. pap. text ed. 19.50 o.p. (ISBN 0-87287-294-7). Libs Unl.

Conservation with Equity: Strategies for Sustainable Development. (Illus.). 466p. (Orig.). 1987. pap. text ed. 21.00 o.p. (ISBN 2-88032-926-4, IUCN207, IUCN). UNIPUB.

Conservative Economic Policy: 1979-1984. Grahame Thompson. 240p. 1986. 31.00 o.p. (ISBN 0-7099-2480-1, Pub. by Croom Helm Ltd); pap. 13.50 o.p. (ISBN 0-7099-2484-4, Pub. by Croom Helm Ltd). Routledge Chapman & Hall.

Conservative Government: 1979-1984. Ed. by David S. Bell. LC 85-16642. 217p. 1985. 27.50 o.p. (ISBN 0-7099-3258-8, Pub. by Croom Helm Ltd). Routledge Chapman & Hall.

Conservative Mind. 6th rev. ed. Kirk Russell. LC 71-189058. 16.95 o.p.; pap. 8.95 o.p. Regnery Gateway.

Conservative Reformation & Its Theology. Charles P. Krauth. 1963. 18.50 o.p. (ISBN 0-8066-0315-1, 10-1665, Augsburg). Augsburg Fortress.

Conservatories, Greenhouses & Garden Rooms. Alexander Bartholomew. 1985. 22.95 o.p. (ISBN 0-03-002992-9). H Holt & Co.

Conservators. Elliott Roosevelt. 456p. 1983. 17.95 o.p. (ISBN 0-87795-456-9, Arbor Hse). Morrow.

Considerations on France. Joseph De Maistre. Ed. & tr. by Richard A. Lebrun. 220p. 1974. 15.00x o.p. (ISBN 0-7735-0182-7, McGill Canada). U of Toronto Pr.

Consignments to El Dorado: A Record of the Voyage of the Sutton by Thomas Whaley. Ed. by June A. Reading. LC 70-186487. 1972. 10.00 o.p. (ISBN 0-682-47444-4, Lochinvar). Exposition-Phoenix.

Consistency in Cognitive Social Behavior: An Introduction to Social Psychology. C. J. White. (Introductions to Modern Psychology Ser.). 201p. 1982. 25.00x o.p. (ISBN 0-7100-9028-5); pap. 12.95x o.p. (ISBN 0-7100-9029-3). Routledge Chapman & Hall.

Consistency Measurement & Control. (Bibliographic Ser.: No. S10). 51p. 1966. 8.00 o.p. (ISBN 0-317-34355-6). Inst Paper Chem.

Consistent Force Field. S. R. Niketic. (Lecture Notes in Chemistry: Vol. 3). 1977. 21.00 o.p. (ISBN 0-387-08344-8). Springer-Verlag.

Consolidated Approach to Activated Sludge Process Design. S. H. Jenkins. 1975. pap. 55.00x flexi-cover o.p. (ISBN 0-08-019835-X). Pergamon.

Consolidated Bargaining in California Construction: An Appraisal of Twenty-Five Years' Experience. Gordon W. Bertram. (Monograph Ser.: No. 12). 259p. 1966. 6.00 o.p. (ISBN 0-89215-013-0). U Cal LA Indus Rel.

Consolidated Grants: A Means of Maintaining Fiscal Responsibility. George C. Benson & Harold F. McClleIland. 41p. 1961. pap. 3.75 o.p. (ISBN 0-8447-3030-0). Am Enterprise.

Consolidated Index to Minnesota History 1930-1967, Vols. 11-40. Ed. by Helen T. Katz. LC 15-11185. 274p. 1983. lib. bdg. 35.00 o.p. (ISBN 0-87351-163-8). Minn Hist.

Consolidated Index to Minnesota History, Volumes 11-40 (1930-67) LC 15-11185. 274p. 1983. 35.00 o.p. Minn Hist.

Consolidated Schedule of Tariff Concessions, 5 Vols. (avail. as set only). pap. 15.00 set o.p. (G20, GATT). UNIPUB.

Consolidated Standards Manual: 1987 Edition. LC 86-81891. 243p. 1986. pap. 40.00 o.s.i. (ISBN 0-86688-105-0). Joint Comm Hlthcare.

Consolidated Tax Returns 1985. 129p. 1985. 45.00 o.p. (J4-3576). PLI.

Consolidation of the Socialist Countries' Unity. A. P. Butenko. 268p. 1981. pap. 3.20 o.p. (ISBN 0-8285-2034-8, Pub. by Progress Pubs USSR). Imported Pubns.

Consolidation of the South China Frontier. George V. Moseley, 3rd. (Center for Chinese Studies, UC Berkeley). 1973. 40.00x o.p. (ISBN 0-520-02102-9). U of Cal Pr.

Consolidation: The Second Poets Anthology. Ed. by Thomas Shapcott. 265p. 1983. text ed. 25.00 o.p. (ISBN 0-7022-1677-1); pap. 10.95 o.p. (ISBN 0-7022-1676-3). U of Queensland Pr.

Conspiracy & Civil Liberties. Robert Hazell. 128p. 1974. pap. text ed. 6.25x o.p. (ISBN 0-7135-1909-6, Pub. by Bedford England). Gower Pub Co.

Conspiracy of Angels. Frank A. Ross. LC 86-47695. 320p. 1987. 18.95 o.p. (ISBN 0-689-11853-8, Atheneum). Macmillan.

Conspiracy of Knaves. Dee Brown. LC 86-14845. 320p. 1987. 17.95 o.p. (ISBN 0-8050-0075-5). H Holt & Co.

Constable's England. Graham Reynolds. LC 83-2469. (Illus.). 184p. 1983. 29.95 o.p. (ISBN 0-8076-1083-6). Braziller.

Constable's England. Graham Reynolds. Ed. by Mary Laing. (Illus.). 184p. 1983. 7.95 o.p. (Copub. by George Braziller Inc.); pap. 3.95 o.p. (ISBN 0-87099-335-6). Metro Mus Art.

Constantinople: The Forgotten Empire. Isaac Asimov. LC 78-122907. (Illus.). (gr. 7 up). 1970. 4.75 o.p. (ISBN 0-395-10908-6). HM.

Constipation Control: An Exercise Program to Achieve Regularity. Richard R. Fuller. 64p. 1981. 5.00 o.p. (ISBN 0-682-49690-1). Exposition-Phoenix.

Constitution. Sam Fink. 1987. pap. 15.95 o.p. (ISBN 0-394-75336-4). Random.

Constitution & Biosynthesis of Lignin. K. Freudenberg & A. C. Neish. (Molecular Biology, Biochemistry & Biophysics: Vol. 2). 1968. 20.40 o.p. (ISBN 0-387-04274-1). Springer-Verlag.

Constitution of People's Republic of China. 79p. 1987. 5.95 o.p. (ISBN 0-8351-1982-3). China Bks.

Constitution on the Church: De Ecclesia. Gregory Baum. LC 65-17864. 192p. 1965. pap. 2.95 o.p. (ISBN 0-8091-1528-X). Paulist Pr.

Constitution Will Hang by a Thread. Larry Wilcox. 1975. pap. 1.95 o.p. (ISBN 0-89036-057-X). Hawkes Pub Inc.

Constitutional & Political Aspects of the Legislative Veto. Karen F. Harrell. (Public Administration Ser.: Bibliography P 1620). 1985. pap. 2.00 o.p. (ISBN 0-89028-290-0). Vance Biblios.

Constitutional Convention: How Well Would It Work? Paul Bator et al. 41p. 1979. 3.75 o.p. (ISBN 0-8447-2164-6). Am Enterprise.

Constitutional Government in Arizona. Bruce B. Mason & Heinz R. Hink. Ed. by Broderick H. Johnson. LC 70-189658. (Illus.). 1972. pap. 5.50 o.p. (ISBN 0-912586-17-6, Pub by Arizona State U). Navajo Coll Pr.

Constitutional Issues of Growth Management. David R. Godschalk & David J. Brower. LC 78-71241. 476p. 1979. pap. 20.95 o.s.i. (ISBN 0-918286-16-6). Planners Pr.

Constitutional Issues of Growth Management. rev. ed. David R. Godschalk & David J Brower. 476p. 1979. pap. 18.95 o.p. (ISBN 0-318-12953-1); pap. 16.95 members o.p. (ISBN 0-318-12954-X). Am Plan Assn.

Constitutional Law. Jerome Barron & Thomas Dienes. LC 83-12554. (Black Letter Ser.). 310p. 1983. pap. text ed. 13.95 o.p. (ISBN 0-314-74263-8). West Pub.

Constitutional Law, American Constitution, Cases & Material on Constitutional Rights & Liberties Cases, Comments, Questions: 1984 Supplement. 5th ed. William B. Lockhart et al. (American Casebook Ser.). 326p. pap. 8.95 o.p. (ISBN 0-314-85071-6). West Pub.

Constitutional Law: Cases & Other Problems, 2 vols. 3rd ed. Paul A. Freund et al. Incl. Vol. 1. 911p. 12.50 o.p. (ISBN 0-316-29331-8); Vol. 2. 1287p. 14.50 o.p. (ISBN 0-316-29332-6). 1967. 1975 suppl. 6.95 o.p. (ISBN 0-685-24273-0). Little.

Constitutional Law: Cases-Comments-Questions. 5th ed. William B. Lockhart et al. LC 80-21518. (American Casebook Ser.). 1705p. 1980. text ed. 28.95 o.p. (ISBN 0-8299-2110-9); 1982 supplement avail. o.p. (ISBN 0-314-69854-X). West Pub.

Constitutional Law, Civil Liberty & Individual Rights: 1985 Supplement. 2nd ed. William Cohen & John Kaplan. (University Casebook Ser.). 66p. 1985. pap. text ed. 3.95 o.p. (ISBN 0-88277-313-5). Foundation Pr.

Constitutional Law, the American Constitution, Constitutional Rights & Liberties: 1986 Supplement. 6th ed. William B. Lockhart & Yale Kamisar. (American Casebook Ser.). 85p. 1986. pap. text ed. 5.95 o.p. (ISBN 0-314-28598-9). West Pub.

Constitutional Law: 1982 Pocket Part. John E. Nowak et al. (Hornbook Ser.). 261p. 1982. supplement 7.95 o.p. (ISBN 0-314-65638-3). West Pub.

Constitutional Law: 1986 Case Supplement to 11th Edition. Gerald Gunther & Fred Schauer. Bd. with Individual Rights in Constitutional Law: 1986 Supplement 4th Edition. (University Casebook Ser.). 185p. 1986. pap. text ed. 7.95 o.p. (ISBN 0-88277-524-3). Foundation Pr.

Constitutional Officers, Agencies, Boards & Commissions in California State Government: 1849-1975. Elizabeth A. Capell. (Research Report: 77-1). 1977. pap. 3.50x o.p. (ISBN 0-685-87444-3). UCB IGS.

Constitutional Polity: Essays on the Founding Principles of American Politics. Sidney A. Pearson, Jr. LC 82-15953. 364p. (Orig.). 1983. lib. bdg. 32.25 o.p. (ISBN 0-8191-2744-2); pap. text ed. 15.00 o.p. (ISBN 0-8191-2745-0). U Pr of Amer.

Constitutional Psychophysiology: Research in Review (Monograph) Mihcael Myrtek. Tr. by Mark Greenlee from Ger. LC 82-18396. 1983. 52.50 o.p. (ISBN 0-12-512480-5). Acad Pr.

Constitutional Rights & Liberties Cases & Materials. 5th ed. William B. Lockhart et al. LC 80-54541. (American Casebook Ser.). 1290p. 1981. text ed. 21.95 o.p. (ISBN 0-8299-2135-4). West Pub.

Constitutional Rights & Student Life: Value Conflict in Law & Education; Cases & Materials. Frank R. Kemerer & Kenneth L. Deutsch. LC 79-13935. 735p. 1979. text ed. 34.25 o.p. (ISBN 0-8299-2051-X). West Pub.

Constitutional Uniformity & Equality in State Taxation, 2 vols. 2nd ed. Wade J. Newhouse. LC 84-82004. 153p. 1984. Set. lib. bdg. 115.00 o.p. (ISBN 0-89941-376-5, 303490). W S Hein.

Constitutions of the Communist Party-States. Ed. by Jan F. Triska. LC 67-29975. (Publications Ser.: No. 70). 1968. 19.00x o.p. (ISBN 0-8179-1701-2). Hoover Inst Pr.

Constitutive Equations for Engineering Materials: Elasticity & Modeling, Vol. 1. Wai-Fah Chen & Atef F. Saleeb. LC 81-16433. 580p. 1982. 78.95x o.p. (ISBN 0-471-09149-9). Wiley.

Constitutive Equations in Viscoplasticity: Phenomenological & Physical Aspects AMD, Vol. 21. Ed. by K. C. Valanis. 80p. 1976. pap. text ed. 14.00 o.p. (ISBN 0-685-75517-7, I00107). ASME.

Constrained Extrema: Introduction to the Differentiable Case with Economic Applications. M. A. El-Hodiri. LC 72-177567. (Lecture Notes in Economics Ser.: Vol. 56). 130p. 1971. 10.70 o.p. (ISBN 0-387-05637-8). Springer-Verlag.

Constraint Directed Reasoning. Rina Dechter & Mark Fox. (Illus.). 75p. 1988. pap. text ed. 12.00x o.p. (ISBN 0-929280-18-0). Amer Artificial.

Constructing Achievement Tests. 3rd ed. Norman E. Gronlund. (Illus.). 176p. 1982. Reference ed. pap. text ed. (ISBN 0-13-169151-1). P-H.

Constructing & Manufacturing Wood Products. Wayne H. Zook. (Illus.). 434p. (YA) (gr. 9-12). 1974. 19.96 o.p. (ISBN 0-87345-048-5). Glencoe.

Constructing Social Theories. Arthur L. Stinchcombe. 303p. (Orig.). 1968. pap. text ed. 16.95 o.p. (ISBN 0-15-513455-8, HC). HarBraceJ.

Construction & Documentation. John A. Ricchini. 1986. 35.00 o.p. PES Inc WI.

Construction & Principle Use of Mathematical Instruments, 1758. M. Bion. Tr. by Edmund Stone from Lat. (Illus.). 90.00 o.p. (ISBN 0-87556-159-4). Saifer.

Construction & Quality Control of Pavements & Structures. (Transportation Research Report Ser.). 80p. 1977. 5.00 o.p. (ISBN 0-309-02681-4). Transport Res Bd.
Construction & Reconstruction of Democratic Societies. Ed. by David M. Muchnick & Martin Weinstein. 1980. text ed. 1.00 o.p. (ISBN 0-87855-299-5). Transaction Pubs.
Construction & the Related Professions. M. C. Fleming. (Illus.). 1980. 210.00 o.p. (ISBN 0-08-024034-8). Pergamon.
Construction & Use of Atomic & Molecular Models. H. Bassow. 1968. text ed. 21.00 o.p. (ISBN 0-08-012925-0); pap. text ed. 9.75 o.p. (ISBN 0-08-012924-2). Pergamon.
Construction Claims. Katz et al. 466p. 1984. pap. 40.00 o.p. (ISBN 0-941161-34-X). Pes Inc WI.
Construction Claims Workshop, 1983. Practising Law Institute Staff & Luther P. Cochrane. LC 84-115189. (Real Estate Law & Practice Course Handbooks: No. 231). 1983. PLI.
Construction Contract Changes, Changed Conditions & Equitable Adjustments. 2nd ed. (Monographs: No. 3). 56p. 1975. 6.00 o.p. (ISBN 0-935165-10-X). GWU Gov Contracts.
Construction Contract Dictionary. Leonard Fletcher et al. LC 81-16935. 128p. 1981. 25.00x o.p. (ISBN 0-902132-65-2, 6632, Pub. by E & Fn. Spon England). Routledge Chapman & Hall.
Construction Cost Control. rev. ed. National Association of Home Builders Staff. (Illus.). 64p. 1982. pap. 13.00 o.p. (ISBN 0-86718-153-2). Nat Assn H Build.
Construction Cost Estimates. Charles R. Tumblin. LC 79-16376. (Ser. of Practical Construction Guides). 406p. 1980. 41.50x o.p. (ISBN 0-471-05699-5, Pub. by Wiley-Interscience). Wiley.
Construction Costs & Price Indices: Description & Use. B. A. Tysoe. 1981. 28.00x o.p. (ISBN 0-419-11930-2, NO.6492, Pub. by E & FN Spon). Routledge Chapman & Hall.
Construction Design for Landscape Architects. Albe E. Munson. (Illus.). 212p. 1975. text ed. 62.50 o.p. (ISBN 0-07-044046-8). McGraw.
Construction Detail Banking: Systematic Storage & Retrieval. Philip M. Bennett. LC 83-14490. 174p. 1984. 39.95x o.p. (ISBN 0-471-88621-1). Wiley.
Construction Engineer's Form Book. Edward R. Fisk. LC 80-22395. 624p. 1981. 62.95 o.p. (ISBN 0-471-06307-X). Wiley.
Construction Equipment: Monographs. Mary Vance. (Architecture Ser.: A 1379). 22p. 1985. 3.00 o.p. (ISBN 0-89028-389-3). Vance Biblios.
Construction Industry Handbook. 2nd ed. R. A. Burgess. 1983. 33.95 o.p. (ISBN 0-8436-0119-1). Van Nos Reinhold.
Construction Industry in Developing Countries: Alternative Strategies for Development. Jill Wells. 208p. 1986. 43.00 o.p. (ISBN 0-7099-3626-5, Pub. by Croom Helm Ltd). Routledge Chapman & Hall.
Construction Industry Labor Relations, 1982. Practising Law Institute Staff et al. LC 82-61507. (Litigation & Administrative Practice Ser.). 302p. 1982. 35.00 o.p. PLI.
Construction Industry: OSHA Safety & Health Standards (29 CFR 1926/1910) rev. ed. (OSHA Ser.: No. 2207). (Illus.). 528p. 1987. pap. 16.00 o.p. (ISBN 0-318-22756-8, S/N 029-015-00071-6). USGPO.
Construction Inspection Handbook. 2nd ed. James O'Brien. 684p. 1983. 53.95 o.p. (ISBN 0-442-25741-4). Van Nos Reinhold.
Construction Litigation: Representing the Contractor, 1986 Cumulative Supplement. Ed. by Robert F. Cushman et al. (Trial Practice Library). 104p. 1987. pap. 28.00 o.p. (ISBN 0-471-85646-0). Wiley.
Construction Management & Contracting. Alonzo Wass. 1972. text ed. 39.00 o.p. (ISBN 0-13-168708-5). P-H.
Construction Materials II. Resource Systems International Staff. 1982. pap. text ed. 15.00 o.p. (ISBN 0-8359-0941-7, Reston). P-H.
Construction Measurements. B. Austin Barry. LC 72-13073. (Practical Construction Guides). 304p. 1973. 46.95 o.p. (ISBN 0-471-05428-3, Pub. by Wiley-Interscience). Wiley.
Construction Methods & Management. Stephens W. Nunnally. (Illus.). 1980. text ed. 39.33 o.p. (ISBN 0-13-168807-3). P-H.
Construction of an Astronomical Telescope. G. Mathewson. 1957. (ISBN 0-8022-1086-4). Philos Lib.
Construction of Buildings, 4 Vol. Set. R. Barry. (Illus.). 478p. 1988. pap. 49.95 o.p. (ISBN 0-8464-1307-8). Beekman Pubs.
Construction of Buildings: Foundations, Walls, Floors & Roofs. R. Barry. Incl. Vol. I. 3rd ed. 1969. pap. text ed. 12.50x (ISBN 0-258-96765-X); Vol. II. 2nd ed. 140p. 1970. pap. text ed. 13.50x (ISBN 0-258-96798-6); Vol. III. 2nd ed. 101p. 1972. pap. text ed. 13.50x (ISBN 0-258-96844-3); Vol. IV. 2nd ed. 120p. 1971. pap. text ed. 13.50x (ISBN 0-258-96829-X); Vol. V. 108p. 1978. pap. text ed. 13.50x (ISBN 0-258-97077-4). pap. Gower Pub Co.
Construction of Cranes & Machinery, Circa 1850. Joseph Glynn. (Illus.). 12.50 o.p. (ISBN 0-87556-102-0). Saifer.
Construction of Madness: Emerging Conceptions & Interventions into Psychotic Process. Peter A. Magaro. 240p. 1976. 34.00 o.p. (ISBN 0-08-019904-6); pap. 16.00 o.p. (ISBN 0-08-019903-8). Pergamon.
Construction of Nuclear Power Plants. V. B. Dubrovsky. 279p. 1981. 11.00 o.p. (ISBN 0-8285-2023-2, Pub. by Mir Pubs USSR). Imported Pubns.
Construction of Personality. Sarah E. Hampson. (Introductions to Modern Psychology Ser.). 250p. 1982. 27.95x o.p. (ISBN 0-7100-0872-4); pap. 11.95x o.p. (ISBN 0-7100-0873-2). Routledge Chapman & Hall.
Construction of the International Labour Organisation & Standing Orders of the International Labour Conference, 1980 Edition. International Labour Office Staff. 84p. (Eng., Fr. & Span.). 1980. pap. 5.70 o.p. (ISBN 92-2-002471-3). Intl Labour Office.
Construction of Trail Suspended Bridges in Nepal: An Application of Traditional Technology. 20p. 1981. pap. 5.00 o.p. (ISBN 92-808-0251-8, TUNU157, UNU). UNIPUB.
Construction Planning, Equipment & Methods. 3rd ed. Robert L. Peurifoy. (Illus.). 1979. text ed. 39.95 o.p. (ISBN 0-07-049760-5). McGraw.
Construction Plant: Management & Investment Decisions. Frank Harris & Ronald McCaffer. 256p. 1982. pap. text ed. 29.50 o.p. (ISBN 0-246-11240-9, Granada England). Gower Pub Co.
Construction Project Administration. 2nd ed. Edward R. Fisk. LC 81-15932. 434p. 1982. (ISBN 0-471-09186-3). Wiley.
Construction Safety, Security, & Loss Prevention. James B. Fullman. LC 84-5077. (Wiley Practical Construction Guides Ser.: 1-344). 286p. 1984. text ed. 42.95x o.p. (ISBN 0-471-86821-3, Pub. by Wiley Interscience). Wiley.
Construction Specifications Handbook. 3rd ed. Hans W. Meier. LC 83-16018. 1983. text ed. 75.00 o.p. (ISBN 0-13-168831-6). P-H.
Construction Technology, Vol. 1. J. T. Grundy. (Illus.). 1977. pap. 19.95x o.p. (ISBN 0-7131-3387-2). Trans-Atl Phila.
Construction Technology, Vol. 2. J. T. Grundy. (Illus.). 200p. 1979. pap. 19.95x o.p. (ISBN 0-7131-3403-8). Trans-Atl Phila.
Construction Technology, Vol. 3. J. T. Grundy. (Illus.). 208p. 1981. pap. 19.95x o.p. (ISBN 0-7131-3419-4). Trans-Atl Phila.
Constructional Mathematics, Vol. 1. Peter Horrobin. 1970. pap. text ed. 7.00 o.p. (ISBN 0-08-006890-1). Pergamon.
Constructional Steelwork. Oscar Faber. (Illus.). 400p. 1955. (ISBN 0-8022-0464-3). Philos Lib.
Constructions of Deviance in Sociological Theory: The Problem of Commensurability. Charles Wright. LC 84-7501. 224p. (Orig.). 1984. lib. bdg. 26.25 o.p. (ISBN 0-8191-3993-9); pap. text ed. 13.50 o.p. (ISBN 0-8191-3994-7). U Pr of Amer.
Constructive Approaches to Mathematical Models. C. V. Coffman & G. J. Fix. LC 79-51673. 1979. 82.50 o.p. (ISBN 0-12-178150-X). Acad Pr.
Constructive Methods for Elliptic Equations. R. P. Gilbert. LC 73-21280. (Lectures Notes in Mathematics: Vol. 365). vii, 397p. 1974. pap. 18.00 o.p. (ISBN 0-387-06690-X). Springer-Verlag.
Constructive Revolutionary: John Calvin & His Socio-Economic Impact. W. Fred Graham. LC 72-107321. 1978. pap. 5.95 o.p. (ISBN 0-8042-0881-6, John Knox). Westminster John Knox.
Constructive Uses of Atomic Energy: Proceedings, American Nuclear Society Conference, Washington DC, November 10-15, 1968. 400p. 28.00 o.p. (ISBN 0-317-33027-6, 700002). Am Nuclear Soc.
Constructivism in Poland. Ed. by Hilary Gresty & Jeremy Lewison. (Illus.). 88p. (Orig.). 1984. pap. 12.50 o.p. (ISBN 0-87663-585-0). Universe.
Constructs of Sociability & Individuality. Ed. by P. Stringer & D. Bannister. 1980. 82.00 o.p. (ISBN 0-12-673750-9). Acad Pr.
Consul of God. Jeffrey Richards. 1980. 27.95x o.p. (ISBN 0-7100-0346-3). Routledge Chapman & Hall.
Consul's Daughter. Ann Schlee. LC 72-175562. (gr. 5-8). 1972. 4.50 o.p. (ISBN 0-689-30065-4, Atheneum). Macmillan.
Consultant Design: The History & Practice of the Designer in Industry. Penny Sparke. (Pembridge History of Design Ser.). 98p. 1983. 17.50 o.p. (ISBN 0-86206-007-9, Pub. by Pembridge Pr UK). Shoe String.
Consultants & Consulting Organizations Directory, 2 vols. 7th ed. Ed. by Janice McLean. 1750p. 1986. Set. 365.00x o.p. (ISBN 0-8103-0482-1). Gale.
Consultants & Consulting Organizations Directory. 8th ed. Ed. by Janice McLean. 2000p. 1987. 380.00x o.p. (ISBN 0-8103-2526-8). Gale.
Consultant's Edge: Using the Computer As a Marketing Tool. Herman Holtz. LC 85-5117. 364p. 1985. 24.95 o.p. (ISBN 0-471-81190-4). Wiley.
Consultants: Selecting, Using & Evaluating Business Consultants. Henry O. Golightly. 256p. 1985. 16.95 o.p. (ISBN 0-531-09591-6). Watts.
Consultation with a Divorce Lawyer: Everything You Must Know to Protect Your Rights. Bernard Clair & Anthony Daniele. 224p. 1982. pap. 9.95 o.p. (ISBN 0-671-44192-2, Fireside). S&S.
Consulting Engineer. Charles K. Coe. (Getting the Most from Professional Services Ser.). 38p. (Orig.). 1979. pap. 4.00 o.p. (ISBN 0-89854-046-1). U of GA Inst Govt.
Consulting Engineering: A Guide for the Engagement of Engineering Services. Compiled by American Society of Civil Engineers Staff. (Manual & Report on Engineering Practice Ser.: No. 45). 96p. 1981. pap. 8.00x o.p. (ISBN 0-87262-276-2). Am Soc Civil Eng.
Consulting Engineering: A Guide to the Engagement of Engineering Services. Compiled by American Society of Civil Engineers Staff. (Manual & Report on Engineering Practice Ser.: No. 45). 96p. 1972. pap. text ed. 3.00 o.p. (ISBN 0-87262-220-7). Am Soc Civil Eng.
Consulting Engineering: Practice Manual. 195p. 1981. member 20.00 o.p. (ISBN 0-686-48380-4); non-member 24.95 o.p. (ISBN 0-686-48381-2). Am Consul Eng.
Consumer Adviser: An Action Guide to Your Rights. Reader's Digest Editors. LC 84-2044. 416p. 1984. 21.99 o.p. (ISBN 0-89577-180-2). RD Assn.
Consumer Advocate Versus the Consumer. Ralph K. Winter, Jr. 16p. 1972. pap. 3.75 o.p. (ISBN 0-8447-1070-9). Am Enterprise.
Consumer & Corporate Accountability. Ed. by Ralph Nader. 1973. pap. text ed. 10.95 o.p. (ISBN 0-15-513461-2, HC). HarBraceJ.
Consumer & Small Business Bankruptcy: A Complete Working Guide. William A. Chatterton. LC 82-12040. 258p. 1982. text ed. 89.50 o.p. (ISBN 0-87624-101-1, Inst Busn Plan). P-H.
Consumer Bankruptcy Law & Practice: 1982 & 1984 Supplement. National Consumer Law Center. LC 85-71785. 523p. 1985. pap. 57.00 o.p. (ISBN 0-943116-38-4). Nat Consumer Law.
Consumer Bankruptcy Law & Practice: 1985 & 1987 Supplement. 2nd ed. National Consumer Law Center Staff. (Consumer Credit & Sales Legal Practice Ser.). (Orig.). 1985. pap. 57.00 o.p. Nat Consumer Law.
Consumer Behavior. 4th ed. James F. Engel & Roger D. Blackwell. 700p. 1982. text ed. 35.95x o.p. (ISBN 0-03-059242-9); instr's. manual 20.00 o.p. (ISBN 0-03-059243-7). Dryden Pr.
Consumer Behavior. 3rd ed. Hawkins et al. 1986. 38.95 o.p. (ISBN 0-256-03414-1). Irwin.
Consumer Behavior. Fred D. Reynolds & William D. Wells. (Marketing Ser.). (Illus.). 1976. text ed. 34.95 o.p. (ISBN 0-07-052031-3). McGraw.
Consumer Behavior. 2nd ed. Leon G. Schiffman & Leslie L. Kanuk. 592p. 1983. pap. text ed. (ISBN 0-13-168880-4). P-H.
Consumer Behavior & Marketing Action. Henry Assael. 641p. 1981. text ed. 27.95x o.p. (ISBN 0-534-00958-1). PWS-Kent Pub.
Consumer Behavior & Marketing Management. James H. Myers & William H. Reynolds. LC 68-1942. (Illus., Orig.). 1967. pap. 12.50 o.p. (ISBN 0-395-04987-3). HM.
Consumer Behavior: Concepts & Applications. David L. Loudon. (Marketing). (Illus.). 1979. text ed. 32.95 o.p. (ISBN 0-07-038753-2, C). McGraw.
Consumer Behavior: Implications for Marketing Strategy. 2nd ed. Delbert I. Hawkins et al. 1983. 27.95 o.p. (ISBN 0-256-02871-0). Irwin.
Consumer Behavior: Theory & Applications. Barbara J. Redman. (Illus.). 1979. pap. 17.95 o.p. (ISBN 0-87055-324-0). AVI.
Consumer Behaviour & Economic Growth in the Modern Economy. Ed. by Henri Baudet & Henk Van Der Meulen. (Illus.). 283p. 1982. 27.50 o.p. (ISBN 0-7099-0646-3, Pub. by Croom Helm Ltd). Routledge Chapman & Hall.
Consumer Beware! Beatrice T. Hunter. 1972. pap. 8.70 o.p. (ISBN 0-671-21232-X, Touchstone Bks). S&S.
Consumer Book of Hints & Tips. Richard Trubo. LC 76-26125. (Illus.). 1978. 12.50 o.p. (ISBN 0-8246-0212-9). Jonathan David.
Consumer Choice: The Economics of Personal Living. Andrew J. Allentuck & Gordon E. Bivens. 510p. 1977. text ed. 19.95 o.p. (ISBN 0-15-513456-6, HC). HarBraceJ.
Consumer Class Actions: Legislative Analysis. 33p. 1977. 3.75 o.p. (ISBN 0-8447-0190-4). Am Enterprise.
Consumer Cooperation: The Heritage & the Dream. Consumers Cooperative Publishing Association Staff et al. 214p. 1980. 6.00 o.p. (ISBN 0-318-15063-8). NASCO.
Consumer Credit 1985. 997p. 1985. 15.00 o.p. (A4-4120). PLI.
Consumer Economics. Daniel A. McGowan. 1980. text ed. 24.95 o.p. (ISBN 0-395-30668-X). HM.
Consumer Economics & Personal Money Management. Francis M. Albin. (Illus.). 496p. 1982. text ed. (ISBN 0-13-169490-1). P-H.
Consumer Europe. 5th ed. 420p. 1985. 335.00x o.p. (ISBN 0-86338-045-X, Pub. by Euromonitor Pubns). Gale.
Consumer Expenditure Survey: Diary Survey, 1982-83. (Bureau of Labor Statistics Bulletin: No. 2245). 76p. 1986. pap. 2.75 o.p. (ISBN 0-318-20101-1, S/N 029-001-02890-3). USGPO.
Consumer Expenditure Survey: Interview Survey, 1982-83. (Labor Statistics Bureau Bulletin: No. 2246). 199p. 1986. pap. 7.00 o.p. (ISBN 0-318-20102-X, S/N 029-001-02888-1). USGPO.
Consumer Expenditure Survey: Interview Survey, 1984. annual ed. (Bureau of Labor Statistics Bulletin 2267 Ser.). (Illus.). 95p. 1986. pap. 4.50 o.p. (ISBN 0-318-21598-5, S/N 029-001-02905-5). USGPO.
Consumer Finance. Edward Burda. (Illus.). 1975. text ed. 14.95 o.p. (ISBN 0-15-513466-3, HC). HarBraceJ.
Consumer Handbook of Solar Energy for the United States & Canada. John H. Keyes. LC 78-65084. 273p. 1979. 19.95 o.s.i. (ISBN 0-87100-156-X, 2149); pap. 10.95 o.p. (ISBN 0-87100-149-7). Morgan.
Consumer Health: A Guide to Intelligent Decisions. 3rd ed. Harold J. Cornacchia & Stephen Barrett. 352p. 1984. pap. text ed. 26.95 o.p. (ISBN 0-8016-1122-9). Mosby.
Consumer in the Marketplace. 2nd ed. Leon Levy et al. LC 74-34004. text ed. cancelled o.s.i. (ISBN 0-8224-2105-4); cancelled o.s.i. (ISBN 0-8224-2106-2); cancelled o.s.i. (ISBN 0-8224-2107-0). Glencoe.
Consumer Legal Kit: General Contracts. Jeffrey A. Isaac. 1985. pap. 6.95 o.p. (ISBN 0-671-55765-3). S&S.
Consumer Legal Kit: Setting up a Delaware Corporation. Jeffrey A. Isaac. 1985. pap. 6.95 o.p. (ISBN 0-671-55767-X). S&S.
Consumer Legal Kit: Starting a Small Business. Jeffrey A. Isaac. 1985. pap. 6.95 o.p. (ISBN 0-671-55766-1). S&S.
Consumer Legislation in Belgium & Luxemburg. Fontaine & Bourgoignie. 1982. 42.50 o.p. (ISBN 0-442-30418-8). Van Nos Reinhold.
Consumer Legislation in Denmark. B. Dahl. 1981. 42.50 o.p. (ISBN 0-442-30425-0). Van Nos Reinhold.
Consumer Legislation in France. Aloy J. Calais. 1982. 42.50 o.p. (ISBN 0-442-30415-3). Van Nos Reinhold.
Consumer Legislation in Italy. Gustavo Ghidini. 1980. 42.50 o.p. (ISBN 0-442-30426-9). Van Nos Reinhold.
Consumer Legislation in the E. C. Countries. N. Reich. 1980. 42.50 o.p. (ISBN 0-442-30409-9). Van Nos Reinhold.
Consumer Legislation in the Federal Republic of Germany. N. Reich. 1981. 42.50 o.p. (ISBN 0-442-30421-8). Van Nos Reinhold.
Consumer Legislation in the Netherlands. E. Hondius. 1980. 42.50 o.p. (ISBN 0-442-30424-2). Van Nos Reinhold.
Consumer Legislation in U. K. & Ireland. Michael Whincup. 1980. 42.50 o.p. (ISBN 0-442-30427-7). Van Nos Reinhold.
Consumer Lending Guide. 110p. 1981. 50.00 o.s.i. (ISBN 0-929097-05-X, 13433). US League Savi Inst.
Consumer Market Developments. 9th ed. Fairchild Marketing Research Division Staff. (Fairchild Fact Files Ser.). (Illus.). 55p. 1986. pap. 20.00 o.p. (ISBN 0-87005-530-5). Fairchild.
Consumer Market Developments, 1986. 2nd ed. Fairchild Market Research Division Staff. (Fairchild Fact Files Ser.). (Illus.). 50p. 1987. pap. 20.00 o.p. (ISBN 0-87005-560-7). Fairchild.
Consumer Math Series, 7 bks. David H. Knowles. 1972. pap. 9.00 ea. o.p. (ISBN 0-8449-0200-4). Carroll CA.

Consumer Mathematics. Linda L. Thompson. LC 76-4003. 470p. 1978. text ed. 15.68 o.p. (ISBN 0-02-479280-2). Glencoe.
Consumer Product Safety Law. J. J. McGillan et al. LC 76-52772. 235p. 1977. pap. 25.00 o.p. (ISBN 0-86587-079-9). Gov Insts.
Consumer Products: Government Regulation & Product Liability. Practising Law Institute Staff & Kenneth Ross. LC 84-62194. (Litigation & Administrative Practice Ser.). 1984. 40.00 o.p. (ISBN 0-317-27344-2). PLI.
Consumer Regulation Needed Protection or Too Much Bureaucracy? Rev. ed. Ed. by Mark A. Siegel & Nancy R. Jacobs. (Instructional Aides Ser.). 80p. 1982. pap. text ed. 13.95 o.p. (ISBN 0-936474-23-8). Info Plus TX.
Consumer Reports Buying Guide 1983. Consumer Union. 400p. 1982. pap. 3.50 o.p. (ISBN 0-385-18349-6). Doubleday.
Consumer Reports Buying Guide, 1985. Consumer's Union. 1984. pap. 4.95 o.p. (ISBN 0-385-19643-1). Doubleday.
Consumer Reports Buying Guide 1988. Ed. by Consumer Reports Editors. 1988. pap. Consumer Reports.
Consumer Research Study on Reading & Book Purchasing, 1978. Yankelovich, Skelly & White, Inc. Staff. (Research Report: No. 6). (Illus.). 333p. 1978. (ISBN 0-940016-06-0); pap. pap. 50.00 additional copies members o.p. (ISBN 0-317-33886-2); pap. 50.00 to non-voting members o.p. (ISBN 0-317-33887-0). Bk Indus Study.
Consumer Sourcebook: Supplement. 4th ed. Ed. by Paul Wasserman & Gita Siegman. 200p. 1987. pap. text ed. 85.00x o.p. (ISBN 0-8103-0371-X). Gale.
Consumer Tactics Manual: How to Get Action on Your Complaints. John Dorfman. LC 80-65987. 1980. 9.95 o.p. (ISBN 0-689-11105-3, Atheneum); pap. 6.95 o.p. (ISBN 0-689-11115-0). Macmillan.
Consumer Telephone Equipment. 177p. 1984. 1650.00x o.p. (ISBN 0-88694-632-8). Intl Res Dev.
Consumer Transactions: Cases & Materials. David A. Rice. 1000p. 1975. 25.00 o.p. (ISBN 0-316-74317-8). Little.
Consumer Usury & Credit Overcharges: 1982 & 1986 Supplement. National Consumer Law Center Staff. LC 82-60505. 203p. 1982. pap. 53.00 o.p. (ISBN 0-943116-08-2). Nat Consumer Law.
Consumerism, Vol. 3, (Incl. 1987 Supplement) Ed. by E. Goldstein. 1988. 15.00 o.p. (ISBN 0-89777-089-7). Soc Issues.
Consumer's Book of Health: Advice on Stretching Your Health Care Dollar. Jordan Braverman. 1981. 11.95 o.p. (ISBN 0-03-059079-5); pap. 7.95 o.p. (ISBN 0-03-059078-7). H Holt & Co.
Consumer's Catalog of Economy & Ecology. Jeanne Bendick & Robert Bendick. LC 74-8081. 160p. (gr. 9-12). 1974. pap. text ed. 5.95 o.p. (ISBN 0-07-004511-9). McGraw.
Consumers, Commissions, & Congresses: Law, Theory, & the Federal Trade Commission, 1968-1985. Bernice Rothman Hasin. LC 86-7023. (ISBN 0-88738-118-9). Transaction Pubs.
Consumers Confidential. Boardroom's Experts & Editors. LC 86-6166. 590p. 1986. 50.00 o.p. (ISBN 0-932648-69-X). Boardroom.
Consumer's Dictionary of Cosmetic Ingredients. new rev. ed. Ruth Winter. 1976. 7.95 o.p. (ISBN 0-517-52736-7); pap. 5.95 o.p. (ISBN 0-517-52737-5). Crown.
Consumer's Dictionary of Food Additives. Ruth Winter. 1978. 8.95 o.p. (ISBN 0-517-53160-7); pap. 4.95 o.p. (ISBN 0-517-53161-5). Crown.
Consumer's Guide to Menswear. Donald Dolce & Jean-Paul Devellard. (Illus.). 1983. pap. 9.95 o.p. (ISBN 0-89696-188-5). Dodd.
Consumer's Guide to Package Travel Around the World. Frederick Pratson. LC 83-49219. (Illus.). 272p. (Orig.). 1984. pap. 10.95 o.p. (ISBN 0-87106-935-0). Globe Pequot.
Consumer's Guide to Poison Protection. Harold M. Silverman. 288p. 1984. pap. 8.95 o.p. (ISBN 0-380-88682-0). Avon.
Consumers Union Report on Life Insurance: A Guide to Planning & Buying the Protection You Need. Consumer Reports Book Editors. 384p. 1981. 16.95 o.p. (ISBN 0-03-059109-0); pap. 8.95 o.p. (ISBN 0-03-059108-2). H Holt & Co.
Consuming Fire: Encounters with Elie Wiesel & the Holocaust. John K. Roth. LC 78-52442. 1979. 8.95 o.p. (ISBN 0-8042-0812-3, John Knox). Westminster John Knox.
Consuming Passions: The Anthropology of Eating. Peter Farb & George Armelagos. 1980. 12.95 o.p. (ISBN 0-395-29448-7). HM.
Consumption Patterns in Eastern & Western Europe. Vera Cao-Pinna & Stanislav S. Shatalin. 1979. 57.00 o.p. (ISBN 0-08-021808-3). Pergamon.
Consumptive Use of Water & Irrigation Water Requirements. Compiled by American Society of Civil Engineers Staff. 227p. 1974. pap. 11.00x o.p. (ISBN 0-87262-068-9). Am Soc Civil Eng.
Contact. Date not set. (ISBN 0-8052-3879-4). Random.
Contact. Carl Sagan. 320p. 1985. 18.45 o.p. (ISBN 0-671-43400-4). S&S.
Contact: A Guide to Writing Skills. Robert T. Mundhenk & William R. Siebenschuh. LC 77-73468. (Illus.). 1978. pap. 21.50 o.p. (ISBN 0-395-25110-9). HM.
Contact at Sea. Peter Schroeder. LC 67-16336. (Illus.). 1967. lib. bdg. 19.00x o.p. (ISBN 0-8398-1851-3). Irvington.
Contact Dermatitis. Etain Cronin. (Illus.). 960p. 1980. text ed. 83.00 o.p. (ISBN 0-443-02014-0). Churchill.
Contact Inhibition. D. E. Steward. LC 85-71446. 144p. (Orig.). 1985. pap. 8.95 o.p. (ISBN 0-932238-29-7, Pub. by Avant Bks). Slawson Comm.
Contact Lens Practice. 3rd ed. Robert B. Mandell. (Illus.). 932p. 1981. 49.25x o.p. (ISBN 0-398-04494-5). C C Thomas.
Contact Manifold in Riemannian Geometry. D. E. Blair. (Lecture Notes in Mathematics Ser.: Vol. 509). 1976. pap. 13.00 o.p. (ISBN 0-387-07626-3). Springer-Verlag.
Contact, Negotiation, & Conflict: An Ethnohistory of the Eastern Dakota, 1819-1839. John S. Wozniak. LC 78-62248. 1978. pap. text ed. 11.50 o.p. (ISBN 0-8191-0569-4). U Pr of Amer.
Contact Print, Nineteen Forty-Six to Nineteen Eighty-Two. James Alinder. LC 82-83985. (Untitled Ser.: No. 30). (Illus.). 52p. 1982. pap. 15.00 o.p. (ISBN 0-933286-32-5). Friends Photography.
Contact U. S. A. An ESL Reading & Vocabulary Textbook. Paul Abraham & Joan Mackey. 200p. 1982. pap. text ed. (ISBN 0-13-169599-1). P-H.
Contacts Between High Energy Physics & Other Fields of Physics: Proceedings. Ed. by P. Urban. (Acta Physica Austriaca: Suppl. 18). (Illus.). 1979. 122.80 o.p. (ISBN 0-387-81454-X). Springer-Verlag.
Contacts: Langue et Culture Francaises. Jean-Paul Valette & Rebecca Valette. LC 75-32873. 1976. text ed. 17.35 o.p. (ISBN 0-395-20690-1). HM.
Contacts: Langue et Culture Francaises. 2nd ed. Jean-Paul Valette & Rebecca Valette. (Illus.). 528p. 1982. text ed. 27.95 o.p. (ISBN 0-395-29328-6). HM.
Container Costs. K. Lidgren & J. Butlin. 1984. 72.95 o.p. (ISBN 0-442-30534-6). Van Nos Reinhold.
Container Gardening. Peter McHoy. (Blandford Hardening Handbooks Ser.). (Illus.). 128p. 1986. 14.95 o.p. (Pub. by Blandford Pr England); pap. 9.95 o.p. (ISBN 0-7137-1579-0, Pub. by Blandford Pr England). Sterling.
Containerisation International Yearbook, 1987. Ed. by Ebury Press. 522p. 1986. 495.00x o.p. (ISBN 0-85223-195-4, Pub. by Ebury Pr England). State Mutual Bk.
Containing Corporate Health Care Costs, 1983. Ed. by Mary E. Brennan. 47p. (Orig.). 1983. pap. 10.00 o.p. (ISBN 0-89154-234-5). Intl Found Employ.
Containment: Concept & Policy, Vol. 1. Ed. by Terry L. Diebel & John L. Gaddis. LC 86-23582. 299p. (Orig.). 1986. pap. 9.00 o.p. (ISBN 0-318-22638-3, S/N 008-020-01080-4). USGPO.
Containment: Concept & Policy, Vol. 2. Ed. by Terry L. Diebel & John L. Gaddis. LC 86-23582. 471p. (Orig.). 1986. pap. 13.00 o.p. (ISBN 0-318-22636-7, S/N 008-020-01104-5). USGPO.
Containment of Organized Crime. Herbert Edelhertz et al. LC 82-48633. (Battelle Human Affairs Research Center Ser.). 128p. 1984. 25.00x o.p. (ISBN 0-669-06364-9). Lexington Bks.
Contamination of Groundwater & Groundwater Treatment: Part of the Proceedings of the Specialized Conference of the IWSA Held in Berlin, FRG, 22-28 April 1985. Ed. by R. Urbistondo. LC 83-13344. (Illus.). 234p. 1985. pap. 73.00 o.p. (ISBN 0-08-033230-7, Pub. by PPL). Pergamon.
Contemplating Music. Joseph Kerman. 7.95 o.p. Harvard U Pr.
Contemplation in a World of Action. Thomas Merton. 400p. 1973. pap. 5.50 o.p. (ISBN 0-385-02550-5, Im). Doubleday.
Contemporaries of Marco Polo. Ed. by Manuel Komroff. (Black & Gold Lib). 1937. 6.95 o.p. (ISBN 0-87140-899-6). Liveright.
Contemporary Adulthood. 2nd ed. Jeffrey S. Turner & Donald B. Helms. LC 81-13505. (Illus.). 1982. text ed. 29.95 o.p. (ISBN 0-03-060143-6). HR&W.
Contemporary Adulthood. 3rd ed. Jeffrey S. Turner & Donald B. Helms. 480p. 1986. text ed. 30.95 o.p. (ISBN 0-03-071743-4, HoltC). HR&W.
Contemporary Advertising. 2nd ed. Courtland L. Bovee & William F. Arens. 1986. 40.95x o.p. (ISBN 0-256-03302-1); o.p. (ISBN 0-256-02779-X). Irwin.
Contemporary Africa: Continent in Transition. rev. ed ed. T. W. Wallbank. (Anvil Ser.). 191p. 1964. pap. 7.50 o.p. (ISBN 0-442-00015-4, Pub. by Van Nos Reinhold). Krieger.
Contemporary American & Australian Poetry. Ed. by Thomas Shapcott. 1976. text ed. 19.95x o.p. (ISBN 0-7022-1201-6); pap. text ed. 12.95x o.p. (ISBN 0-7022-1211-3). U of Queensland Pr.
Contemporary American Photography, Pt. 1. Intro. by Mark Johnstone. (Min Gallery Series of Contemporary American & Japanese Photography). (Illus.). 144p. 1989. pap. 35.00 o.p. (ISBN 4-906265-01-4). Aperture.
Contemporary American Poetry. 2nd ed. A. Poulin, Jr. 1975. pap. 9.95 o.p. (ISBN 0-395-18618-8). HM.
Contemporary American Poetry. 3rd ed. A. Poulin, Jr. LC 79-91632. (Illus.). 1980. pap. 18.50 o.p. (ISBN 0-395-28635-2). HM.
Contemporary American Society: An Introduction to Social Science. Willard Sloshberg & William C. Nessmith. (Illus.). 600p. pap. text ed. 28.25 o.p. (ISBN 0-314-69671-7); 11.00 o.p. (ISBN 0-314-71126-0). West Pub.
Contemporary American Speeches. 5th ed. Wil A. Linkugel et al. LC 77-20387. 1983. pap. text ed. 12.95 o.p. (ISBN 0-8403-3267-X, 40326702). Kendall-Hunt.
Contemporary Analytic Geometry. Thomas L. Wade & Howard E. Taylor. LC 79-22955. 338p. 1980. Repr. of 1969 ed. lib. bdg. 23.50 o.p. (ISBN 0-89874-034-7). Krieger.
Contemporary Apartments. Ed. & intro. by Paige Rense. (World of Architectural Digest Ser.). 160p. 1982. 15.95 o.p. (ISBN 0-89535-104-8). Knapp Pr.
Contemporary Applied Management. 2nd ed ed. DuBrin. 1985. 21.95 o.p. (ISBN 0-256-03258-0). Irwin.
Contemporary Appliqued Beadwork. Annabel W. Woodsmall et al. Ed. by Virginia I. Harvey & Vicki Adams. LC 79-92788. (Threads in Action, Monograph II). (Illus.). 40p. 1979. pap. write for info. o.s.i. (ISBN 0-916658-35-X). Shuttle Craft.
Contemporary Astrology. Jerry J. Williams. (Illus.). 360p. 1981. pap. 8.95 o.p. (ISBN 0-914918-31-1). Whitford Pr.
Contemporary Basketry. Sharon Robinson. Ed. by George Horn & Sarita Rainey. LC 77-921193. (Illus.). 1978. 18.95 o.p. (ISBN 0-87192-097-2). Davis Mass.
Contemporary Benefit Issues & Administration Answer to the Questions on: Subject Matter, CEBS Course, 10. 7th ed. (Orig.). 1985. pap. text ed. 15.00 o.p. Intl Found Employ.
Contemporary Benefit Issues & Administration: Learning Guide, CEBS Course 10. 6th ed. (Orig.). Spiral bdg. 18.00 o.p. (ISBN 0-89154-260-4). Intl Found Employ.
Contemporary Benefit Issues & Administration: Learning Guide, CEBS Course, No. 10. 7th ed. (Orig.). 1985. 18.00 o.p. Intl Found Employ.
Contemporary Biology. 2nd ed. Mary E. Clark. 1979. text ed. 32.95 o.p. (ISBN 0-7216-2598-3, CBS C). SCP.
Contemporary Britain. Ed. by Angus Stewart. 220p. (Orig.). 1983. pap. 12.95x o.p. (ISBN 0-7100-9406-X). Routledge Chapman & Hall.
Contemporary Business. 4th ed. Louis E. Boone & David L. Kurtz. 720p. 1985. text ed. 28.95 o.p. (ISBN 0-03-071413-3); study guide 13.95 o.p. (ISBN 0-03-071414-1). Dryden Pr.
Contemporary Cases in Sales Management. Charles M. Futrell. LC 80-65797. 288p. 1981. pap. text ed. 15.95x o.s.i. (ISBN 0-03-054736-9); instr's. manual 10.00 o.s.i. (ISBN 0-03-054741-5). Dryden Pr.
Contemporary Catholic Theology: An Introduction. John T. Carmody & Denise L. Carmody. LC 80-7743. 256p. (Orig.). 1980. pap. text ed. 14.95x o.p. (ISBN 0-06-061317-3, RD340). HarpR.
Contemporary Ceramic Techniques. John W. Conrad. 1979. text ed. 38.00 o.p. (ISBN 0-13-169540-1). P-H.
Contemporary Children's Theater. Betty J. Lifton. 1974. pap. 6.45 o.p. (ISBN 0-380-00145-4, 20677). Avon.
Contemporary China: A Research Guide. Peter Berton & Eugene Wu. LC 67-14235. (Bibliographical Ser.: No. 31). 695p. 1967. 25.00x o.p. (ISBN 0-8179-2311-X). Hoover Inst Pr.
Contemporary Chinese Photographs. Ma Xiaoqing et al. (Illus.). 98p. (Orig.). 1985. pap. 19.95 o.p. (ISBN 0-8351-1680-8). China Bks.
Contemporary Chinese Politics: An Introduction. 2nd ed. James C. Wang. (Illus.). 336p. 1985. pap. text ed. 28.00 o.p. (ISBN 0-13-169996-2). P-H.
Contemporary Chinese Short Stories. Zhang Xianliang et al. 274p. (Orig.). 1983. pap. 5.95 o.p. (ISBN 0-8351-1076-1). China Bks.
Contemporary Chinese Theatre. Roger Howard. 1978. text ed. 16.50x o.p. (ISBN 0-435-18456-3); pap. text ed. 9.00x o.p. (ISBN 0-686-65264-9, 00119). Heinemann Ed.
Contemporary Christian Music: Where It Came from, Where It Is, Where It Is Going. rev. ed. Paul Baker. 1985. pap. 9.95 o.p. (ISBN 0-89107-343-4, Crossway Bks). Good News.
Contemporary Class Piano. 2nd ed. Elyse Mach. 307p. (Orig.). 1982. 16.50 o.p. (ISBN 0-15-513480-9, HC). HarBraceJ.
Contemporary Classics: Furniture of the Masters. Charles D. Gandy & Susan Zimmerman-Stidham. LC 80-17283. (Illus.). 192p. 1982. text ed. 38.50 o.p. (ISBN 0-07-022760-8); pap. text ed. 7.95 o.p. (ISBN 0-07-022762-4). McGraw.
Contemporary Cooking: Lessons & Recipes from the School of Contemporary Cooking. Sherri Zitron & Charles G. Powell. LC 81-13261. 320p. 1982. 19.95 o.p. (ISBN 0-395-31843-2). HM.
Contemporary Cultural Anthropology. 2nd ed. Michael Howard & Patrick C. McKim. 1986. pap. text ed. write for info. o.p. (ISBN 0-673-39006-3). Scott F.
Contemporary Devil's Dictionary. Gary Brodsky. 128p. (Orig.). 1988. pap. 2.95 o.p. (ISBN 1-55547-255-9). Critics Choice Paper.
Contemporary Dramatists. 4th ed. Ed. by D. L. Kirkpatrick. 750p. 1988. 85.00x o.s.i. (St James). Gale.
Contemporary East European Marxism, Vol. II. Edward D'Angelo et al. (Praxis: Vol. 7). 275p. 1982. pap. text ed. 27.75x o.p. (ISBN 0-391-02788-3). Humanities.
Contemporary East European Marxism, Vol. I. Edward D'Angelo et al. (Praxis - Philosophical & Scientific Reprints Ser.: Vol. 6). 302p. 1982. pap. text ed. 28.50x o.p. (ISBN 0-391-02651-8). Humanities.
Contemporary Economic Analysis: Papers Presented at the Conference of the Association of University Teachers of Economics April 1977. Ed. by Michael J. Artis & A. R. Nobay. 448p. 1978. 29.00 o.p. (ISBN 0-85664-802-7, Pub. by Croom Helm). Routledge Chapman & Hall.
Contemporary Economic Issues & Answers. Ed. by James F. Anderson. 181p. 1978. text ed. 19.00x o.p. (ISBN 0-8422-5275-4). Irvington.
Contemporary Education Policy. Ed. by John Ahier & Michael Flude. (Illus.). 288p. 1983. pap. 19.50 o.p. (ISBN 0-7099-0512-2, Pub. by Croom Helm Ltd). Routledge Chapman & Hall.
Contemporary Educational Administration. William G. Monahan & Herbert R. Hengst. 1982. text ed. write for info. o.p. (ISBN 0-02-381930-8). Macmillan.
Contemporary England: 1914-1964. W. N. Medlicott. LC 67-26796. (Social & Economic History of England Ser.). 1976. pap. text ed. 14.95x o.p. (ISBN 0-582-48487-1). Longman.
Contemporary Ethical Theories. Luther J. Binkley. LC 61-10605. 203p. 1961. (ISBN 0-8022-0129-6). Philos Lib.
Contemporary Europe: A History. 5th ed. H. Stuart Hughes. (Illus.). 656p. 1981. text ed. (ISBN 0-13-170027-8). P-H.
Contemporary Financial Management. 3rd ed. Charles R. Moyer et al. LC 86-15945. (Illus.). 775p. 1986. text ed. 45.25 o.p. (ISBN 0-314-25863-9); study guide 13.00 o.p. (ISBN 0-314-34514-0). West Pub.
Contemporary Financial Management (International Edition) 2nd ed. Charles Moyer et al. 650p. 1983. 17.00 o.p. (ISBN 0-939426-01-3). West Pub.
Contemporary French Poetry. Joseph Chiari. 1952. (ISBN 0-8022-0238-1). Philos Lib.
Contemporary French Theater. Bettina L. Knapp. 1979. pap. 5.50 o.p. (ISBN 0-380-01116-6, 16840). Avon.
Contemporary Games: A Directory & Bibliography Describing Play Situations or Simulations, Vol. 1: Directory. Ed. by Jean Belch. LC 72-6353. 574p. 1973. 110.00x o.p. (ISBN 0-8103-0968-8). Gale.
Contemporary Games: A Directory & Bibliography Describing Play Situations or Simulations, Vol. 2. Ed. by Jean Belch. LC 72-6353. 576p. 1974. 98.00x o.p. (ISBN 0-8103-0969-6). Gale.
Contemporary German Theater. Ed. by Michael Roloff. (Orig.). 1972. pap. 5.45 o.p. (ISBN 0-380-01117-4, 13664-3). Avon.
Contemporary Government & Business Relations. Martin Schnitzer. 1978. text ed. 23.50 o.p. (ISBN 0-395-30727-9). HM.
Contemporary Government & Business Relations. 2d ed. Martin Schnitzer. 608p. 1982. text ed. 30.75 o.p. (ISBN 0-395-31764-9). HM.

Contemporary Group Work. Charles D. Garvin. (P-H Ser. in Social Work Practice). (Illus.). 304p. 1981. text ed. (ISBN 0-13-170233-5). P-H.

Contemporary Homes of the Pacific Northwest. Harry Martin. LC 80-208. (Illus.). 224p. 1980. 30.00 o.p. (ISBN 0-914842-31-5). Madrona Pubs.

Contemporary Indian Short Stories, 2 vols. Ed. by Bhabani Bhattacharya. 1967. Vol. 1. 3.50 o.s.i. (ISBN 0-88253-409-2); Vol. 2. 3.50 o.s.i. (ISBN 0-88253-327-4). Ind-US Inc.

Contemporary Indian Short Stories. Ed. by Ka N. Subramanyam. 1982. 12.50 o.p. (ISBN 0-7069-0684-5, Pub. by Vikas India); pap. 3.95 o.p. (ISBN 0-7069-1624-7). Advent NY.

Contemporary Influences in Early Childhood Education. 2nd ed. Ellis D. Evans. LC 74-16007. 1975. text ed. 22.95 o.p. (ISBN 0-03-089584-7, HoltC). HR&W.

Contemporary Instrumental Techniques. Gardner Read. LC 75-27455. (Illus.). 1976. 23.95 o.s.i. (ISBN 0-02-872100-4). Schirmer Bks.

Contemporary Introduction to Logic with Applications. Codell K. Carter. 1977. text ed. write for info. o.p. (ISBN 0-02-471500-X). Macmillan.

Contemporary Irish Poetry: An Anthology. Ed. by Anthony Bradley. LC 76-50244. 1980. 25.00x o.p. (ISBN 0-520-03389-2). U of Cal Pr.

Contemporary Issues & Practices in Marketing. Hoel. 310p. 1987. pap. text ed. 17.00 o.p. (ISBN 0-205-10545-9); write for info. tchr's. manual o.p. (ISBN 0-205-10647-1). Allyn.

Contemporary Issues in Bioethics. 2nd ed. Ed. by Tom L. Beauchamp & LeRoy Walters. 614p. 1982. text ed. (ISBN 0-534-01102-0). Wadsworth Pub.

Contemporary Issues in Civil Rights & Liberties. Ed. by Harrison W. Fox, Jr. 319p. 1972. pap. text ed. 9.75x o.p. (ISBN 0-8422-0191-2). Irvington.

Contemporary Issues in Comparative Education. Ed. by Keith Watson & Raymond Wilson. LC 84-21402. 228p. 1985. 27.50 o.p. (ISBN 0-7099-3607-9, Pub. by Croom Helm Ltd). Routledge Chapman & Hall.

Contemporary Issues in Cost & Managerial Accounting: A Discipline in Transition. 3rd ed. Hector R. Anton et al. LC 77-74383. (Illus.). 1978. text ed. 29.95 o.p. (ISBN 0-395-25435-3). HM.

Contemporary Issues in Special Education. Rex E. Schmid et al. (Special Education Ser.). (Illus.). 1976. text ed. 18.95 o.p. (ISBN 0-07-055330-0, C). McGraw.

Contemporary Japan: A Teaching Workbook. 2nd ed. Ed. by Roberta Martin & Amy V. Heinrich. (East Asian Curriculum Project Ser.). 710p. 1985. looseleaf bound 45.00 o.p. (ISBN 0-913418-00-5). Columbia U E Asian Inst.

Contemporary Japanese Architecture: Its Development & Challenge. Botond Bognar. (Illus.). 304p. 1985. 43.95x o.p. (ISBN 0-442-21174-0). Van Nos Reinhold.

Contemporary Lamps. Wallace W. Holbrook. (gr. 9 up). 1968. text ed. 15.28 o.p. (ISBN 0-87345-029-9). Glencoe.

Contemporary Literary Criticism. Robert C. Davis. (English & Humanities Ser.). 511p. 1986. text ed. 25.95 cased o.p. (ISBN 0-582-28569-0). Longman.

Contemporary Managerial Accounting: A Casebook. John K. Shank. (Illus.). 352p. 1981. pap. text ed. (ISBN 0-13-170357-9). P-H.

Contemporary Marketing. 4th ed. Louis E. Boone & David L. Kurtz. 656p. 1983. text ed. 32.95x o.p. (ISBN 0-03-062638-2); instr's. manual 20.00 o.p. (ISBN 0-03-062639-0); study guide 13.95 o.p. (ISBN 0-03-062641-2); transparencies 250.00 o.p. (ISBN 0-03-062644-7); test bank 100.00 o.p. (ISBN 0-03-062643-9). Dryden Pr.

Contemporary Mathematics. 3rd ed. Bruce E. Meserve & Max A. Sobel. (Illus.). 688p. 1981. pap. text ed. (ISBN 0-13-170076-6). P-H.

Contemporary Mexican Painting in a Time of Change. Shifra M. Goldman. LC 80-17107. (Texas Pan American Ser.). (Illus.). 255p. 1981. text ed. 35.00x o.p. (ISBN 0-292-71061-5). U of Tex Pr.

Contemporary Models of the Atomic Nucleus. P. E. Nemirovskii. 1963. 53.00 o.p. (ISBN 0-08-009840-1); pap. 75.00 o.p. (ISBN 0-08-013582-X). Pergamon.

Contemporary Music Education. Michael L. Mark. LC 77-80230. 1979. text ed. 16.95 o.p. (ISBN 0-02-871640-X). Schirmer Bks.

Contemporary Newspaper Design: A Structural Approach. Mario R. Garcia. (Illus.). 240p. 1981. pap. text ed. (ISBN 0-13-170381-1); pap. text ed. (ISBN 0-13-170373-0). P-H.

Contemporary Novel in German: A Symposium. Ed. by Robert R. Heitner. (Dept of Germanic Languages Sers.). 147p. 1967. 10.95x o.p. (ISBN 0-292-73670-3). U of Tex Pr.

Contemporary Nursing Management: Issues & Practice. Ann Marriner. LC 81-14165. (Illus.). 403p. 1982. pap. text ed. 19.95 o.p. (ISBN 0-8016-3168-8). Mosby.

Contemporary Organic Chemistry. M. O'Leary. 1975. text ed. 34.95 o.p. (ISBN 0-07-047694-2). McGraw.

Contemporary Personal Finance. Daniel A. McGowan. 1981. text ed. 42.36 o.p. (ISBN 0-395-30823-2). HM.

Contemporary Perspectives in Consumer Research. Richard J. Lutz. LC 80-27890. 466p. 1981. pap. text ed. 17.25 o.p. (ISBN 0-534-00942-5). PWS-Kent Pub.

Contemporary Perspectives in International Business. Harold W. Berkman & Ivan R. Vernan. 1979. pap. 29.56 o.p. (ISBN 0-395-30562-4). HM.

Contemporary Perspectives in Organizational Behavior. Donald D. White. 500p. 1981. 26.00 o.s.i. (ISBN 0-205-07350-6, 087350); instr's. manual avail. o.s.i. (ISBN 0-205-07351-4). Allyn.

Contemporary Perspectives on Adulthood & Aging. Alicia S. Cook. 384p. 1983. text ed. write for info. o.p. (ISBN 0-02-324600-6). Macmillan.

Contemporary Perspectives on Strategic Market Planning. Kerin et al. 1989. 25.95 o.p. (ISBN 0-256-06155-6). Irwin.

Contemporary Physical Geography. John G. Navarra. (Illus.). 544p. 1981. text ed. 33.95 o.s.i. (ISBN 0-03-057859-0, CBS C); instr's. manual 10.95 o.s.i. (ISBN 0-03-058243-1); overhead transparencies 400.00 o.s.i. (ISBN 0-03-059358-1). SCP.

Contemporary Physical Science: Our Impact on Our World. Robert C. Belloli. (Illus.). 1978. write for info. o.p. (ISBN 0-02-308070-1). Macmillan.

Contemporary Physics. David Park. LC 64-23458. (Illus., Orig.). 1964. pap. 2.45 o.p. (ISBN 0-15-622566-2, Harv). HarBraceJ.

Contemporary Pied-a-Terre: A Bibliography of Recent Periodical Literature. Carole Cable. (Architecture Ser.: A 1442). 4p. 1985. 2.00 o.p. (ISBN 0-89028-512-8). Vance Biblios.

Contemporary Poetry. Date not set. (ISBN 0-8052-3577-9). Random.

Contemporary Polish Graphic Art. Irena Jakimowicz. (Illus.). 1977. 35.00 o.p. E J Brill USA.

Contemporary Polish Paintings. J. Zanozinski. (Illus.). 1975. 25.00 o.s.i. E J Brill USA.

Contemporary Polish Stage Design. Z. Strzelecki. Tr. by Jerzy A. Baldyga from Pol. (Illus.). 1985. 45.00 o.p. (ISBN 83-213-3020-7). E J Brill USA.

Contemporary Polish Theatre (1977) Witold Filler. (Illus.). pap. 6.00 o.s.i. (ISBN 0-685-86892-3). E J Brill USA.

Contemporary Political Ideologies: Movements & Regimes. 3rd ed. Roy C. Macridis. 1986. pap. text ed. write for info. o.p. (ISBN 0-673-39462-X). Scott F.

Contemporary Political Thinkers. Bhikhu Parekh. LC 82-7212. 232p. 1983. text ed. 26.00x o.p. (ISBN 0-8018-2886-4). Johns Hopkins.

Contemporary Politics: Europe. Alexander J. Groth et al. 1976. text ed. 22.00 o.p. (ISBN 0-316-52498-0). Little.

Contemporary Problems of Economic Policy: Essays from the Clare Group. Ed. by R. C. Matthews & J. R. Sargent. 160p. 1983. pap. 9.95 o.p. (ISBN 0-416-34820-3, NO. 3846). Routledge Chapman & Hall.

Contemporary Psychotherapies. Gary S. Belkin. 1980. pap. 20.95 o.p. (ISBN 0-395-30781-3). HM.

Contemporary Public Budgeting. Ed. by Thomas Lynch. LC 79-67062. 224p. 1981. pap. text ed. 7.95x o.p. (ISBN 0-87855-722-9). Transaction Pubs.

Contemporary Quilting. Sharon Robinson. LC 81-66572. (Illus.). 120p. 1982. 18.95 o.p. (ISBN 0-87192-134-0). Davis Mass.

Contemporary Quilts: Original Patterns Based on the Drawings of M. C. Escher. Kay Parker. LC 81-9720. (Illus.). 128p. 1981. 24.95 o.p. (ISBN 0-89594-045-0). Crossing Pr.

Contemporary Radiology: An Introduction to Imaging. Harry J. Griffiths & Robert C. Sarno. LC 78-64711. (Illus.). 356p. 1979. text ed. write for info. o.p. (ISBN 0-7216-4282-9). Saunders.

Contemporary Readings for General Biology. Ed. by John W. Crane. 154p. 1987. pap. text ed. (ISBN 0-534-06931-2). Wadsworth Pub.

Contemporary Readings in American Government. Byron W. Daynes & Raymond Tatalovich. (Orig.). 1980. pap. text ed. 13.00 o.p. (ISBN 0-669-01163-0). Heath.

Contemporary Readings in Biology. Ed. by Julius S. Greenstein. 1972. 34.00x o.p. (ISBN 0-8422-5013-1). Irvington.

Contemporary Readings in Child Psychology. Mavis E. Hetherington & Ross D. Parke. 1977. text ed. 21.95 o.p. (ISBN 0-07-028425-3). McGraw.

Contemporary Readings in Psychopathology. 2nd ed. John M. Neale et al. LC 77-27636. 463p. 1978. pap. 21.50 o.p. (ISBN 0-471-03943-8). Wiley.

Contemporary Real Estate: Theory & Practice. Gaylon E. Greer & Michael D. Farrell. 480p. 1983. text ed. 35.95x o.p. (ISBN 0-03-056682-7); instr's manual 20.00 o.p. (ISBN 0-03-056683-5). Dryden Pr.

Contemporary Research in Behavioral Pharmacology. Ed. by D. E. Blackman & D. J. Sanger. LC 77-16206. (Illus.). 520p. 1978. 69.50x o.p. (ISBN 0-306-31061-9, Plenum Pr). Plenum Pub.

Contemporary Research in the Sociology of Education. Ed. by John Eggleston. 1974. pap. 13.95x o.p. (ISBN 0-416-78790-8, NO.2177). Routledge Chapman & Hall.

Contemporary Research Topics in Nuclear Physics. Ed. by Da Hsuan Feng et al. LC 82-3677. 602p. 1982. 95.00x o.p. (ISBN 0-306-40986-0, Plenum Pr). Plenum Pub.

Contemporary Retailing. 2nd ed. William H. Bolen. 528p. 1982. pap. text ed. (ISBN 0-13-170266-1). P-H.

Contemporary Rhetoric. 2nd ed. Maxine C. Hairston. LC 77-78916. (Illus.). 1978. text ed. 13.95 o.p. (ISBN 0-395-25450-7). HM.

Contemporary Rhetoric. 3rd ed. Maxine C. Hairston. LC 81-83233. 1981. text ed. 18.95 o.p. (ISBN 0-395-31494-1). HM.

Contemporary Rural Architecture of Soviet Estonia. V. Viirmaa. 151p. 1985. 8.95 o.p. (ISBN 0-8285-3128-5, Pub. by Perioodika Tallinn). Imported Pubns.

Contemporary School Psychology: Readings from Psychology in the Schools. 2nd ed. Ed. by James L. Carroll. 1981. pap. text ed. 12.95 o.p. (ISBN 0-88422-014-1). Clinical Psych.

Contemporary Selling. Richard Cummings. 1980. text ed. 28.95 o.p. (ISBN 0-395-30584-5). HM.

Contemporary Social Problems. 3rd ed. Ed. by Robert K. Merton & Robert A. Nisbet. 1971. text ed. 16.95 o.p. (ISBN 0-15-513790-5, HC). HarBraceJ.

Contemporary Sociological Theory. George Ritzer. 349p. 1983. pap. text ed. 15.00 o.p. (ISBN 0-394-32816-7, KnopfC). Knopf.

Contemporary Sociology. Joseph S. Roucek. 120p. 1958. 20.00 o.p. (ISBN 0-8022-1957-8). Philos Lib.

Contemporary Sociology in the United States. Singh M. Das. 329p. 1983. text ed. 35.00x o.p. (ISBN 0-7069-2104-6, Pub. by Vikas India). Advent NY.

Contemporary Soviet Politics: An Introduction. reference ed. Donald Barry & Carol Barner-Barry. 464p. 1982. pap. text ed. 24.00 o.p. (ISBN 0-13-170191-6). P-H.

Contemporary Spanish Economy: A Historical Perspective. Sima Lieberman. (Illus.). 392p. 1982. text ed. 39.95 o.p. (ISBN 0-04-339026-9). Unwin Hyman.

Contemporary Spanish Theatre: Seven One-Act Plays. Ed. by Patricia W. O'Connor & Anthony M. Pasquariello. LC 79-26859. pap. text ed. 8.95 o.p. (ISBN 0-684-16500-7, ScribC). Scribner.

Contemporary Stained Glass. Joel Russ & Lou Lynn. LC 85-7029. 192p. 1986. 40.00 o.p. (ISBN 0-385-23338-8). Doubleday.

Contemporary Studies in Mexican History (Investigaciones contemporaneas sobre historia de Mexico) Reunion de Historiadores Mexicanos y Norteamericanos Staff. (Institute of Latin American Studies Special Publication Ser.). 755p. (Eng. & Span.). 1971. 22.50x o.p. (ISBN 0-292-70125-X). U of Tex Pr.

Contemporary Suburban America. Peter O. Muller. (Illus.). 240p. 1981. pap. text ed. (ISBN 0-13-170647-0). P-H.

Contemporary Theory in International Relations. Ed. by Stanley Hoffman. LC 77-24275. (Illus.). 1977. Repr. of 1960 ed. lib. bdg. 23.50x o.p. (ISBN 0-8371-9750-3, HOCT). Greenwood.

Contemporary Topics in Analytical & Clinical Chemistry. Ed. by D. M. Hercules et al. LC 77-8099. (Illus.). Vol. 1, 1977, 328p. 55.00x o.p. (ISBN 0-306-33521-2, Plenum Pr); Vol. 2, 1978, 296p. 55.00x o.p. (ISBN 0-306-33522-0, Plenum Pr). Plenum Pub.

Contemporary Topics in Polymer Science, Vol. 2. Ed. by E. M. Pearce & J. R. Schaefgen. LC 77-21311. 324p. 1977. 59.50x o.p. (ISBN 0-306-36262-7, Plenum Pr). Plenum Pub.

Contemporary Topics in Polymer Science, Vol. 3. Ed. by Mitchell Shen. LC 79-641014. 352p. 1979. 59.50x o.p. (ISBN 0-306-40283-1, Plenum Pr). Plenum Pub.

Contemporary Topics in Polymer Science, Vol. 4. Ed. by William J. Bailey & Teiji Tsuruta. LC 79-641014. 1030p. 1983. 150.00x o.p. (ISBN 0-306-41248-9, Plenum Pr). Plenum Pub.

Contemporary Topics in Polymer Science, Vol. 1: Macromolecular Science - Retrospect & Prospect. Ed. by R. D. Ulrich. LC 78-6116. 290p. 1978. 57.50x o.p. (ISBN 0-306-36261-9, Plenum Pr). Plenum Pub.

Contemporary Topics in the Study of Diabetes & Metabolic Endocrinology. Ed. by E. Shafrir. (Based upon a symposium). 1976. 61.00 o.p. (ISBN 0-12-638060-0). Acad Pr.

Contemporary Transportation. 2nd ed. Donald F. Wood & James C. Johnson. 768p. 1983. text ed. write for info. o.p. (ISBN 0-02-360980-X). Macmillan.

Contemporary Travis Picking: Solo Style. Mark D. Hanson. (Orig.). 1987. pap. 16.95 o.p. (ISBN 0-936799-03-X). Accent Music.

Contemporary World Poets. Ed. by Donald Junkins. 1976. pap. text ed. 11.00 o.p. (ISBN 0-15-513817-0, HC). HarBraceJ.

Contemporary Writing from the Continents. Ed. by Rainer Schulte. LC 82-177955. xviii, 431p. 1982. lib. bdg. 21.95x o.p. (ISBN 0-8214-0656-6, 82-84267); pap. 14.95x o.p. (ISBN 0-8214-0657-4, 82-84275). Ohio U Pr.

Contending Approaches to International Politics. Ed. by Klaus Knorr & James N. Rosenau. LC 68-27404. (Center of International Studies Ser.). 1969. 34.00x o.p. (ISBN 0-691-05638-2); pap. 9.95x o.p. (ISBN 0-691-02164-3). Princeton U Pr.

Contending Forces: A Novel. Pauline E. Hopkins. LC 77-18724. (Lost American Fiction Ser.). (Illus.). 414p. 1978. Repr. of 1900 ed. 9.95 o.p. (ISBN 0-8093-0874-6). S Ill U Pr.

Content Addressable Parallel Processors. Caxton C. Foster. (Computer Science Ser.). 233p. 1976. 22.95 o.p. (ISBN 0-442-22433-8). Van Nos Reinhold.

Content & Structure: Readings for College Writers. Hulon Willis. 430p. 1976. pap. text ed. 10.95 o.p. (ISBN 0-15-513902-9, HC). HarBraceJ.

Content Reading: A Diagnostic Prescriptive Approach. Betty L. Criscoe & Thomas C. Gee. (Illus.). 384p. 1984. text ed. (ISBN 0-13-171389-2). P-H.

Contented Amish: An Inside View. Harold Graham. LC 84-90033. 1984. 7.95 o.p. (ISBN 0-533-06120-2). Vantage.

Contentious Community: Constructive Conflict in the Church. John M. Miller. LC 78-3682. 108p. 1978. pap. 4.95 o.s.i. (ISBN 0-664-24198-0, Westminster). Westminster John Knox.

Contes Africains. Ed. by Mildred P. Mortimer. LC 71-168855. (Illus., Orig.). 1903. pap. 15.96 o.p. (ISBN 0-395-12078-0). HM.

Contes Choisis. Guy De Maupassant. Ed. by W. R. Price. 1930. 3.50 o.p. (ISBN 0-672-73238-6). Odyssey Pr.

Contes Choisis. Guy De De Maupassant. Ed. by William R. Price. 200p. (Fr.). pap. text ed. 3.50x o.p. (ISBN 0-8290-0551-X). Irvington.

Contes de Jacques Tournebroche, Histoire Contemporaine see **Romans et Contes.**

Contest Cookbook. Bill Zachary. 170p. 1979. pap. 5.95 o.p. (ISBN 0-88006-002-6, BK 7308). Wayne Green Ent.

Contest for Educational Resources: Equity & Reform in a Meritocratic Society. W. Timothy Weaver. LC 81-47332. (Illus.). 208p. 1981. 29.00x o.p. (ISBN 0-669-04586-1). Lexington Bks.

Contest for the South China Sea. Marwyn S. Samuels. LC 81-18868. (Illus.). 250p. 1982. 33.00x o.p. (ISBN 0-416-33140-8, NO. 3614). Routledge Chapman & Hall.

Contest Over Japan: The Soviet Bid for Power in the Far East, 1945-1952. Herbert Feis. 1968. pap. 1.85x o.p. (ISBN 0-393-00466-X, Norton Lib). Norton.

Contestable Markets & the Theory of Industry Structure. William J. Baumol & John C. Panzar. 510p. 1982. text ed. 32.00 o.p. (ISBN 0-15-513910-X, HC). HarBraceJ.

Contesting Deportability: Tactics & Issues in Deportation Hearings. L.A. Immigration Committee. 30.00 o.p. Natl Lawyers Guild.

Context of Contemporary Theology: Essays in Honor of Paul Lehmann. Ed. by Alexander J. McKelway & E. David Willis. LC 73-16916. 288p. 1974. 12.50 o.p. (ISBN 0-8042-0513-2, John Knox). Westminster John Knox.

Context of National Information Systems in Developing Countries: India & China in a Comparative Perspective. Erik Baark. (Lund Research Policy Institute Ser.). 212p. (Orig.). 1986. pap. text ed. 36.50x o.p. (ISBN 91-86002-58-9). Coronet Bks.

Context of Public Policy. William J. Ruckstuhl et al. 137p. 1969. pap. text ed. 6.95x o.p. (ISBN 0-8422-0043-6). Irvington.

Contexts for Learning: The Major Sectors of American Higher Education. Intro. by Zelda Gamson. 101p. 1985. pap. 3.75 o.p. (ISBN 0-318-19979-3, S/N 065-000-00239-6). USGPO.

Contexts of Canadian Criticism. Eli Mandel. LC 78-143280. 1971. pap. text ed. 3.45 o.s.i. (PLC9). U of Chicago Pr.

Contexts of Criticism. Harry Levin. LC 57-7613. 1963. pap. 1.65 o.p. (ISBN 0-689-70123-3, 29, Atheneum). Macmillan.

Contexts of the Drama. Richard A. Goldstone. LC 68-13092. (Illus.). 1968. text ed. 28.95 o.p. (ISBN 0-07-023662-3). McGraw.

Contexts: Strategies for Vocabulary Enrichment. I. K. Kankashian. 205p. (gr. 11-12). 1987. pap. text ed. 8.50 o.p. (ISBN 0-13-171455-4, 20634). Prentice ESL.
Contextual Architecture: Responding to Existing Styles. Architectural Record Magazine Editors. Ed. by Keith Ray. (Architecture Ser.). (Illus.). 1981. text ed. 41.95 o.p. (ISBN 0-07-002332-8). McGraw.
Contextualization of Theology: An Evangelical Assessment. Bruce C. E. Fleming. LC 80-174. 147p. 1980. pap. 5.95 o.p. (ISBN 0-87808-431-2). William Carey Lib.
Conti Commodity Futures Handbook. Martin J. Pring. 720p. 1985. text ed. 52.00 o.p. (ISBN 0-07-050881-X). McGraw.
Continent of Lies: A Novel. James Morrow. 1984. 15.95 o.s.i. (ISBN 0-03-062861-X). H Holt & Co.
Continental Congress. Edmund C. Burnett. LC 75-25252. 757p. 1976. Repr. of 1941 ed. lib. bdg. 43.25x o.p. (ISBN 0-8371-8386-3, BUCC). Greenwood.
Continental Drift. Ed. by S. K. Runcorn. (International Geophysics Ser: Vol. 3). 1962. 24.95 o.p. (ISBN 0-12-602450-2). Acad Pr.
Continental Endogenous Regimes. V. V. Beloussov. 295p. 1981. 10.00 o.p. (ISBN 0-8285-2281-2, Pub. by Mir Pubs USSR). Imported Pubns.
Continental Handbook, 1981. (ISBN 0-317-11977-X). Intl Pubns Serv.
Continental Margins: Geological & Geophysical Research Needs. National Research Council, Ocean Sciences Board Staff. 1979. pap. 17.75 o.p. (ISBN 0-309-02793-4). Natl Acad Pr.
Continental Porcelain. Rev. ed. John Cushion. (Letts Collectors' Guides). (Illus.). 79p. 1982. 9.95 o.p. (ISBN 0-85097-354-6, Pub by C Letts Bks UK). Seven Hills Bk Dists.
Continents in Collision. Russell Miller. (Planet Earth Ser.). (Illus.). 176p. (YA) (gr. 7 up). 1983. 18.60 o.p. (ISBN 0-8094-4326-0); lib. bdg. 22.60 o.p. Time-Life.
Continents in Collision: Documents. Robert A. Hecht. LC 82-45064. 152p. (Orig.). 1982. lib. bdg. 26.25 o.p. (ISBN 0-8191-2374-9); pap. text ed. 10.25 o.p. (ISBN 0-8191-2375-7). U Pr of Amer.
Contingencies of Reinforcement: A Theoretical Analysis. B. F. Skinner. 1972. pap. text ed. 32.00 o.p. (ISBN 0-13-171728-6). P-H.
Contingency Approach to Management Readings. John W. Newstrom et al. (Illus.). 592p. 1974. text ed. 33.95 o.p. (ISBN 0-07-046415-4). McGraw.
Contingency Measures & Fiscal Limitations: The Real World Significance of Some Recent State Budget Innovations. (Legislative Finance Papers Ser.). 23p. 1984. 6.25 o.s.i. (ISBN 1-55516-043-3). Natl Conf State Legis.
Contingency Planning & Management: A Bibliographical Guide. Goppa & Avery Consultants Staff. (Public Administration Ser.: Bibliography P 1647). 1985. pap. 2.00 o.p. (ISBN 0-89028-337-0). Vance Biblios.
Continual Burnt Offering: Daily Meditations on the Word of God. H. A. Ironside. 370p. 1981. pap. 4.95 o.s.i. (ISBN 0-87213-353-2). Loizeaux.
Continuation De L'Histoire Genealogique et Chronologique De la Maison Royale De France Du Pere Anselme, 3 Vols. Pol Potier De Courcy. (Fr). 1969. Repr. of 1868 ed. Set. 315.00 o.p. (ISBN 0-384-47374-1). Johnson Repr.
Continuation Methods. Ed. by Hansjorg Wacker. 1978. 49.50 o.p. (ISBN 0-12-729250-0). Acad Pr.
Continuing Care of Terminal Cancer Patients: Proceedings of an International Seminar on Continuing Care of Terminal Cancer Patients, 19-20 October 1979, Milan, Italy. R. G. Twycross & V. Ventafridda. 300p. 1980. 63.00 o.p. (ISBN 0-08-024943-4). Pergamon.
Continuing Care Retirement Communities: An Empirical, Financial, & Legal Analysis. Howard E. Winklevoss & Alwyn V. Powell. 1984. 25.95x o.p. (ISBN 0-256-03125-8). Irwin.
Continuing Education. Samuel F. Pickering, Jr. LC 85-40492. 176p. 1988. pap. 8.95 o.p. U Pr of New Eng.
Continuing Education as a National Capital Investment. Herbert Striner. 118p. 1972. pap. 1.25 o.p. (ISBN 0-911558-08-X). W E Upjohn.
Continuing Education for Real Estate Brokers & Salespersons. Gaines & Coleman. 1986. (ISBN 0-88462-587-7, 1610-08, Real Estate Ed). Longman Finan.
Continuing Education for Real Estate Brokers & Salespersons: 1987 Edition. George Gaines, Jr. & David S. Coleman. 144p. 1985. pap. text ed. 6.95 o.p. (ISBN 0-88462-532-X, 1610-08, Pub. by Real Estate Ed). Longman Finan.
Continuing Medical Education Syllabus. American Psychiatric Association Staff. 320p. 1986. pap. text ed. 15.00 o.p. (ISBN 0-89042-086-6, 42-0866). Am Psychiatric.
Continuing Professional Education in Librarianship & Other Fields: A Classified & Annotated Bibliography, 1965-1974. Mary E. Michael. LC 75-8998. (Reference Library of Humanities: Vol. 16). 224p. 1975. lib. bdg. 31.00 o.p. (ISBN 0-8240-1085-X). Garland Pub.
Continuing Quest: Large Scale Ocean Science for the Future. National Research Council, Ocean Sciences Board Staff. (Orig.). 1979. pap. text ed. 8.75x o.p. (ISBN 0-309-02798-5). Natl Acad Pr.
Continuity & Change in Marxism. Ed. by N. Fischer & N. Georgopoulos. 249p. 1982. text ed. 19.95x o.p. (ISBN 0-391-02564-3). Humanities.
Continuity & Support Following Residential Treatment. Delores A. Taylor & Stuart W. Alpert. LC 72-92327. 52p. 1973. pap. 6.30 o.p. (ISBN 0-87868-098-5, 0985). Child Welfare.
Continuity of Music: A History of Influence. Irving Kolodin. 366p. Repr. of 1969 ed. lib. bdg. 49.00 o.p. (Pub. by Am Repr Serv). Reprint Servs.
Continuous Casting, Vol. 1. A. McLean & L. Heaslip. 160p. 1983. nonmember 40.00 o.p. Da Capo.
Continuous Casting of Small Cross Sections. Ed. by Y. V. Murty & F. R. Mollard. LC 81-85418. (Illus.). 203p. 1981. 10.00 o.p. (ISBN 0-317-56530-3). Minerals Metals.
Continuous Casting of Small Cross Sections: Proceedings TMS Fall Meeting, Pittsburgh, 1980. Ed. by Y. V. Murty & F. R. Mollard. (Illus.). 224p. 40.00 o.p. (ISBN 0-89520-384-7); members 24.00 o.p. (ISBN 0-317-36236-4); student members 12.00 o.p. (ISBN 0-317-36237-2). ASM.
Continuous Cultivation of Microorganisms: Proceedings. Ed. by Ivan Malek & Zdenek Fencl. 1970. 96.50 o.p. (ISBN 0-12-466260-9). Acad Pr.
Continuous Flows in the Plane. A. Beck et al. LC 73-11952. (Grundlehren der Mathematischen Wissenschaften Ser.: Vol. 201). (Illus.). 480p. 1975. 66.00 o.p. (ISBN 0-387-06157-6). Springer-Verlag.
Continuously Under Review. Rosemary Stewart. 70p. 1967. pap. text ed. 5.00x o.p. (ISBN 0-686-70844-X, Pub. by Bedford England). Gower Pub Co.
Continuum Theory of Inhomogeneities in Simple Bodies: A Reprint of Six Memoirs. W. Noll et al. LC 68-56948. 1968. 25.00 o.p. (ISBN 0-387-04069-2). Springer-Verlag.
Contours of Public Policy, Nineteen Thirty-Nine to Nineteen Forty-Five. Richard N. Chapman. Ed. by Frank Freidel. LC 80-8460. (Modern American History Ser.). 319p. 1981. lib. bdg. 43.00 o.p. (ISBN 0-8240-4851-2). Garland Pub.
Contra Adimantum see De Utilitate Credendi.
Contra Costa Country Public Schools, 1986. Lillian S. Clancy. (California Public Schools Ser.: How Are They Doing). 70p. (Orig.). 1985. pap. 12.95 o.p. (ISBN 0-939580-35-7). CA Schl Surveys.
Contra Costa County Public Schools: How Are They Doing? Lillian S. Clancy. 312p. (Orig.). 1981. pap. 9.95 o.p. (ISBN 0-939580-00-4). CA Schl Surveys.
Contra Costa County Public Schools: How Are They Doing? (1984) Lillian S. Clancy. (How Are They Doing Ser.). 65p. (Orig.). 1984. pap. 8.95 o.p. (ISBN 0-939580-04-7). CA Schl Surveys.
Contra Costa County Public Schools: How Are They Doing? 1985. Lillian S. Clancy. (California Public Schools Ser.). 61p. (Orig.). 1984. pap. 12.95 o.p. (ISBN 0-939580-26-8). CA Schl Surveys.
Contra Costa County Street Atlas 1985. Thomas Bros. Maps Staff. (Illus.). 132p. pap. 9.95 o.p. (ISBN 0-88130-115-9). Thomas Bros Maps.
Contra Costa County Street Atlas: 1987. rev. ed. Thomas Bros. Maps Staff. (Illus.). 132p. 1986. pap. 11.95 o.p. Thomas Bros Maps.
Contra Costa County Street Guide & Directory, 1988. Thomas Bros. Maps Staff. (Illus.). 142p. 1987. pap. 11.95 o.p. (ISBN 0-88130-268-6). Thomas Bros Maps.
Contra Costa-Solano Counties Street Atlas & Directory, 1988. rev. ed. Thomas Bros. Maps Staff. (Illus.). 208p. 1988. pap. 18.95 o.p. Thomas Bros Maps.
Contra Costa-Solano Counties Street Guide & Directory, 1988. Thomas Bros. Maps Staff. (Illus.). 214p. (Orig.). 1988. pap. 18.95 o.p. (ISBN 0-88130-269-4). Thomas Bros Maps.
Contra Costa Street Guide & Directory, 1988. Thomas Bros. Maps Staff. (Illus.). 136p. Date not set. pap. 11.95 o.p. (ISBN 0-88130-206-6). Thomas Bros Maps.
Contra Fortunatem see De Utilitate Credendi.
Contra Viento y Marea. Mario V. Llosa. 464p. (Span.). 1983. pap. 9.50 o.s.i. (ISBN 84-322-7010-5, 3009). Ediciones Norte.
Contraception. Ed. by L. L. Langley. LC 73-4256. (Benchmark Papers in Human Physiology: Vol. 2). 500p. 1982. 61.95 o.p. (ISBN 0-87933-025-2). Van Nos Reinhold.
Contract. Joe Poyer. LC 78-55610. 1978. 10.95 o.p. (ISBN 0-689-10907-5, Atheneum). Macmillan.
Contract. J. W. Rhoads. LC 85-24908. 1986. 12.95 o.p. (ISBN 0-03-008082-7). H Holt & Co.
Contract. J. W. Rhoads. 120p. 1988. pap. 3.50 o.p. (ISBN 0-380-70396-3). Avon.
Contract Administration for Architects & Quantity Surveyors. 5th ed. AQUA Group Staff. 87p. 1979. pap. text ed. 17.25x o.p. (ISBN 0-258-97139-8, Pub. by Granada England). Gower Pub Co.
Contract Farming & Economic Integration. Ewell P. Roy. LC 70-134471. (Illus.). 661p. 1972. 11.95 o.p. (ISBN 0-8134-1425-3, 1425); pap. text ed. 8.95x o.p. Inter Print Pubs.
Contract for Life. Robert Anastas & Kalia Lulow. 1986. pap. 4.95 o.s.i. (ISBN 0-671-61874-1). PB.
Contract in England: A Select Bibliography on the Forms of Contracts for Building Work Since 1980. Valerie J. Nurcombe. LC 85-233044. (Architecture Bibliography Ser.). 1985. 3.75 o.p. (ISBN 0-89028-556-X). Vance Biblios.
Contract Negotiation Handbook. P. D. Marsh. 416p. 1974. text ed. 78.95x o.p. Gower Pub Co.
Contract on Cherry Street. Philip Rosenberg. 1976. pap. 1.75 o.p. (ISBN 0-380-00591-3, 28704). Avon.
Contract with the World. Jane Rule. LC 80-7939. 324p. 1980. 12.95 o.p. (ISBN 0-15-122578-8). HarBraceJ.
Contract Writing & Engineering - Pipeline Hydraulics - Offshore Structure Technology: A Workbook for Engineers. Ed. by T. Kozic. 132p. 1983. pap. text ed. 30.00 o.p. (ISBN 0-317-02565-1, I00160). ASME.
Contractile Vacuoles of Protozoa; Food Vacuoles: Food Vacuoles see Vacuome de la Cellule Vegetale: Morphologie.
Contracting for Atoms. Harold Orlans. LC 80-58. (Illus.). xvii, 242p. 1980. Repr. of 1967 ed. lib. bdg. 35.00x o.p. (ISBN 0-313-22287-8, ORCA). Greenwood.
Contracting-Out - Alternatives in Municipal Services Delivery: A Bibliography. Mary E. Huls. (Public Administration Ser.: P 1744). 8p. 1985. 2.00 o.p. (ISBN 0-89028-524-1). Vance Biblios.
Contracting with the Federal Government. Frank M. Alston et al. LC 83-17008. 525p. 1984. 60.00x o.p. (ISBN 0-471-87078-1). Wiley.
Contractor see Changing Room.
Contractors of Chartres, 2 Vols. John James. 1982. 96.00 set o.p. (ISBN 0-7099-1414-8, Pub. by Croom Helm Ltd). Routledge Chapman & Hall.
Contractors of Chartres, Vol. 1. John James. (Illus.). 292p. 1982. 60.00 o.p. (ISBN 0-7099-0180-1, Pub. by Croom Helm UK). Routledge Chapman & Hall.
Contracts Management Deskbook. W. Hirsch. 1983. 29.95 o.p. (ISBN 0-317-31405-X). AMACOM.
Contradictions of Control: School Structure & School Knowledge. Linda M. McNeil. (Critical Social Thought Ser.). 208p. 1986. 29.95 o.p. (ISBN 0-7102-0246-6, 02466, Pub. by Routledge UK). Routledge Chapman & Hall.
Contradictions of Foreign Aid. Desmond McNeill. (Illus.). 114p. 1981. 27.50 o.p. (ISBN 0-7099-1713-9, Pub. by Croom Helm Ltd). Routledge Chapman & Hall.
Contrast & Connection: Bicentennial Essays in Anglo-American History. Ed. by H. C. Allen & Roger Thompson. LC 76-7095. x, 373p. 1976. 20.00x o.p. (ISBN 0-8214-0355-9). Ohio U Pr.
Contrasting Decades: The Nineteen Twenties & Nineteen Thirties. D. Duane Cummins & William G. White. (Inquiries into American History Ser.). (gr. 11-12). 1980. pap. 6.00 o.p. (ISBN 0-02-652900-9, 64135). Glencoe.
Contrasting Styles: A Catalogue of the Exhibition of Netsuke & Kizeruzutsu from Private English Collections. London Netsuke Committee. (Illus.). 79p. (Orig.). 1980. pap. 12.00 o.p. (ISBN 0-903697-09-2, Pub. by R G Swagers UK). C E Tuttle.
Contre Sainte-Beuve & Pastiches et Melanges see Oeuvres.
Contre Sainte-Beuve: Avec: Nouveaux Melanges 1954. Marcel Proust. 448p. 1954. 6.95 o.p. (ISBN 0-686-54646-6). Schoenhof.
Contribution Eight in Research Reports in Archaeology: The Snyders Mound & Five Other Mound Groups in Calhoun County, Illinois. David P. Braun & James B. Griffin. (Technical Report Ser: No. 13). (Illus.). 178p. (Orig.). 1982. pap. 7.50x o.p. (ISBN 0-932206-90-5). U Mich Mus Anthro.
Contribution of Chemistry to Food Supplies: Proceedings of a Symposium, Hamburg, 1973. Ed. by I. Morton & D. N. Rhodes. 448p. 1976. 110.00 o.p. (ISBN 0-08-020748-0). Pergamon.
Contribution to Our Knowledge of Seedlings, 2 vols. Sir John Lubbock. LC 78-51429. (Landmark Reprints in Plant Science Ser.). 1978. Repr. of 1892 ed. Vol. 1. text ed. 29.50x o.s.i. (ISBN 0-86598-008-X, Pub. by Allanheld); Vol. 2. text ed. 29.50 o.s.i. (ISBN 0-86598-025-X). Rowman.
Contribution to the Functional Morphology of Articular Surfaces. Bernhard Tillmann. Ed. by Wolfgang Bargmann & Wilhelm Doerr. Tr. by G. Konorza from Ger. LC 78-54588. (Normal & Pathologic Anatomy Ser.). (Illus.). 60p. 1978. pap. 20.00 o.p. (ISBN 0-88416-248-6). Year Bk Med.
Contribution to the Knowledge of the Desmids of the State of Sao Paulo. Carlos M. Bicudo. (Illus.). 1969. 15.00x o.p. (ISBN 3-7682-0653-X). Lubrecht & Cramer.
Contribution to the Somatology of Periodic Catatonia. Lieve Gjessing. Tr. by H. Marshall. 1976. 120.00 o.p. (ISBN 0-08-015650-9). Pergamon.
Contributions from the Charleston Museum: XII see Charleston Furniture, Seventeen Hundred to Eighteen Twenty-Five.
Contributions of a Chemistry to Health, Vol. 2. Ed. by H. Machleidt. 600p. 1987. pap. text ed. 85.00 o.p. (ISBN 0-89573-621-7). VCH Pubs.
Contributions of Chemistry to Health: Perspectives & Recommendations Compiled at the Fifth CHEMRAWN Conference Heidelberg, 1986, Vol. 1. Ed. by H. Machleidt et al. 54p. 1987. pap. 16.00 o.p. (ISBN 0-89573-655-1). VCH Pubs.
Contributions of Faraday & Maxwell to Electrical Science. R. A. Tricker. 1966. 75.00 o.p. (ISBN 0-08-011977-8); pap. 15.25 o.p. (ISBN 0-08-011976-X). Pergamon.
Contributions of Joseph Ives to Connecticut Clock Technology, 1810-1862. Kenneth D. Roberts. LC 77-118414. 1970. 25.00 o.p. (ISBN 0-913602-00-0). K Roberts.
Contributions of Voice Research to Singing. Ed. by John Large. LC 79-57539. (Illus.). 432p. pap. 52.00 o.s.i. College-Hill.
Contributions of Women: Aviation. Ann Genett. LC 74-19004. (Contributions of Women Ser.). (Illus.). 116p. (gr. 6 up). 1975. PLB 8.95 o.p. (ISBN 0-87518-089-2). Dillon.
Contributions of Women: Labor. Marcia M. Biddle. LC 78-23303. (Contributions of Women Ser.). (Illus.). 128p. (gr. 6 up). 1979. PLB 8.95 o.p. (ISBN 0-87518-167-8). Dillon.
Contributions of Women: Medicine. Demerris C. Ranahan. LC 81-7793. (Contributions of Women Ser.). (Illus.). 120p. (gr. 6 up). 1981. PLB 8.95 o.p. (ISBN 0-87518-213-5). Dillon.
Contributions of Women: Music. Catherine Scheader. LC 85-6808. (Contributions of Women Ser.). (Illus.). 136p. (gr. 6 up). 1985. PLB 8.95 o.p. (ISBN 0-87518-274-7). Dillon.
Contributions on the Biology of the Gulf of Mexico. Ed. by Willis E. Pequegnat & Fenner A. Chace, Jr. LC 71-135998. (Texas A&M University Oceanographic Studies: Vol. 1). 270p. 1970. 35.00x o.p. (ISBN 0-87201-346-4). Gulf Pub.
Contributions on the Geological & Geophysical Oceanography of the Gulf of Mexico. Ed. by Richard Rezak & Vernon J. Henry. LC 73-149761. (Texas A&M University Oceanographic Studies on the Gulf of Mexico: Vol. 3). 303p. 1972. 35.00x o.p. (ISBN 0-87201-348-0). Gulf Pub.
Contributions on the Physical Oceanography of the Gulf of Mexico. Ed. by L. R. Capurro & Joseph L. Reid. LC 71-135998. (Texas A&M University Oceanographic Studies on the Gulf of Mexico: Vol. 2). 288p. 1972. 35.00x o.p. (ISBN 0-87201-347-2). Gulf Pub.
Contributions to Algebra: A Collection of Papers Dedicated to Ellis Kolchin. Ed. by Hyman Bass et al. LC 76-45980. 1977. 82.50 o.p. (ISBN 0-12-080550-2). Acad Pr.
Contributions to Analysis: A Collection of Papers Dedicated to Lipman Bers. Ed. by Lars V. Ahlfors et al. 1974. 91.00 o.p. (ISBN 0-12-044850-5). Acad Pr.
Contributions to Econometrics & Statistics Today. Ed. by H. Schneeweiss & H. Strecker. (Illus.). ix, 311p. 1986. 43.10 o.p. (ISBN 0-387-15058-7). Springer-Verlag.
Contributions to English Syntax & Philology. C. L. Barber et al. 223p. (Orig.). 1962. pap. text ed. 28.50x o.p. Coronet Bks.
Contributions to Input-Output Analysis, 2 vols. Ed. by A. Carter & A. Brody. 1970. Vol. 1: Techniques Geneva 1968. 87.50 o.p. (ISBN 0-444-10044-X, North-Holland); Vol. 2: Applications to Input Output Analysis. 70.25 o.p. (ISBN 0-444-10029-6). Elsevier.
Contributions to Mechanics. Ed. by David Abir. 1969. 115.00 o.p. (ISBN 0-08-012822-X). Pergamon.

Contributions to Medical Psychology, Vol. 2. Ed. by S. Rachman. (Illus.). 352p. 1980. 85.00 o.p. (ISBN 0-08-024684-2). Pergamon.

Contributions to Mycology: A Tribute to Professor C. T. Ingold on His Eightieth Birthday. Ed. by W. M. Dick et al. 375p. (Orig.). 1987. pap. 43.50 o.p. (ISBN 0-12-214860-6). Acad Pr.

Contributions to Nonlinear Functional Analysis: Proceedings of the MRC Symposium, 1971. MRC Symposium Staff. Ed. by Eduardo H. Zarantonello. 1971. 44.50 o.p. (ISBN 0-12-775850-X). Acad Pr.

Contributions to Probability: A Collection of Papers Dedicated to Eugene Lukacs. Ed. by J. Gani & V. K. Rohatgi. LC 80-768. 1981. 69.50 o.p. (ISBN 0-12-274460-8). Acad Pr.

Contributions to Sensory Psychology, Vol. 7. William D. Neff. 240p. 1982. 63.50 o.p. (ISBN 0-12-151807-8). Acad Pr.

Contributions to Statistics. William G. Cochran. LC 81-13077. (Probability & Mathematical Statistics Ser.). 1835p. 1982. 98.95x o.p. (ISBN 0-471-09786-1, Pub. by Wiley-Interscience). Wiley.

Contributions to Survey Sampling & Applied Statistics: Papers in Honor of H. O. Hartley. Ed. by H. A. David. 1978. 29.95 o.p. (ISBN 0-12-204750-8). Acad Pr.

Contributions to the Founding of the Theory of Transfinite Numbers. Georg Cantor. Tr. by P. E. Jourdain. 220p. 1952. 21.95 o.p. (ISBN 0-87548-157-4). Open Court.

Contributions to the Prehistory of Nubia. Ed. by Fred Wendorf. LC 65-5730. (No. 1). (Illus.). 210p. 1965. pap. 15.95x o.p. (ISBN 0-87074-124-1). SMU Press.

Contributions to the Theory of Games. Harold W. Kuhn. Ed. by A. W. Tucker. (Annals of Mathematics Studies: Nos. 24). (Orig.). 1950. Vol. 1. 35.00 o.p. (ISBN 0-691-07934-X); Vol. 2. 47.00 o.p. (ISBN 0-691-07935-8); Vol. 3. pap. 15.00 o.p. (ISBN 0-691-07936-6). Princeton U Pr.

Contributions to the Von Neumann Growth Model. Ed. by G. Bruckmann. LC 71-155280. (Illus.). xv, 116p. 1971. 55.00 o.p. (ISBN 0-387-81011-0). Springer-Verlag.

Contributions to Thermal Physiology: Proceedings of a Satellite Symposium of the 28th International Congress of Physiological Sciences, Budapest, 1980. Z Szelenyi & M. Szekely. LC 80-41854. (Advances in Physiological Sciences Ser.: Vol. 32). (Illus.). 560p. 1981. 87.00 o.p. (ISBN 0-08-027354-8). Pergamon.

Control see Distributed Parameter Systems Theory.

Control Applications of Non-Linear Programming & Optimization: Proceedings of the IFAC Workshop, Capri, Italy, 11-14 June 1985. G. Di Pillo. (IFAC Publication). (Illus.). 210p. 1986. 75.00 o.p. (ISBN 0-08-031665-4, Pub. by PPL). Pergamon.

Control Aspects of Prosthetics & Orthotics: Proceedings of the IFAC Symposium, Columbus, Ohio, May, 1982. IFAC Symposium Staff & R. M. Campbell. (Illus.). 240p. 1983. 80.00 o.p. (ISBN 0-08-029350-6). Pergamon.

Control Frontiers in Knowledge Based & Man-Machine Systems. Ed. by A. P. Sage. 180p. 1984. pap. 38.00 o.p. (ISBN 0-08-031153-9). Pergamon.

Control in Electroplating. 92p. 1959. 13.00 o.p. (ISBN 0-318-12524-2). Am Electro Surface.

Control in Power Electronics & Electrical Drives: Proceedings of the IFAC Symposium, 2nd, Dusseldorf, Brd, Oct. 1977. IFAC Symposium Staff. Ed. by W. Leonhard. 1038p. 1978. 290.00 o.p. (ISBN 0-08-022014-2). Pergamon.

Control Materials in Clinical Chemistry: Tentative Guideline, Vol. 2. National Committee for Clinical Laboratory Standards. 1982. 15.00 o.p. (ISBN 0-318-19378-7, C23-T). Natl Comm Clin Lab Stds.

Control Mechanisms in Developmental Processes. Ed. by Michael Locke & Michael Locke. 1968. 57.50 o.p. (ISBN 0-12-612950-9). Acad Pr.

Control Mechanisms in the Expression of Cellular Phenotypes. International Society for Cell Biology Staff. Ed. by Helen A. Padyluka. (Proceedings: Vol. 9). 1970. 74.50 o.p. (ISBN 0-12-611909-0). Acad Pr.

Control of Aggression & Violence. Ed. by Jerome L. Singer. (Personality & Psychopathology Ser: Vol. 10). 1971. 43.50 o.p. (ISBN 0-12-646650-5). Acad Pr.

Control of Air Emissions from Coke Plants: Proceedings of the Air Pollution Control Association, Technical Conference, Pittsburgh, PA, 1979. Air Pollution Control Association. 192p. 1979. 12.50 o.p. (ISBN 0-318-12247-2, VIP-1); members 10.00 o.p. (ISBN 0-318-12248-0). Air & Waste.

Control of Breast Cancer Through Mass Screening. Philip Strax. LC 77-99144. (Illus.). 246p. 1979. 26.00 o.p. (ISBN 0-88416-197-8). Year Bk Med.

Control of Cell Growth & Proliferation. Carlo M. Veneziale. 1984. 49.95 o.p. (ISBN 0-442-28829-8). Van Nos Reinhold.

Control of Commercial Fraud. L. H. Leigh. xii, 339p. 1982. text ed. 39.00 o.p. (ISBN 0-435-82519-4). Gower Pub Co.

Control of Distortion & Residual Stress in Weldments. 1977. 22.00 o.p. (ISBN 0-87170-046-8). ASM.

Control of DP Production. National Computing Centre, Ltd. Staff. Ed. by G. S. Walker. LC 80-483613. (Illus.). 121p. 1980. 27.50x o.s.i. (ISBN 0-85012-227-9). Intl Pubns Serv.

Control of Electrostatic Discharge. Tarak N. Bhar & Edward J. McMahon. 244p. 1986. 24.95 o.p. (ISBN 0-8104-5689-3). Sams.

Control of Energy. R. Bruce Lindsay. (Benchmark Papers in Energy: Vol. 6). 1977. 69.50 o.p. (ISBN 0-12-786962-X). Acad Pr.

Control of Energy Metabolism. Ed. by Britton Chance et al. 1966. 77.00 o.p. (ISBN 0-12-167850-4). Acad Pr.

Control of Engineering Projects. Ed. by S. H. Wearne. (Illus.). 1974. pap. 23.50x o.p. (ISBN 0-7131-3330-9). Trans-Atl Phila.

Control of Enzyme Activity. 2nd ed. Philip Cohen. (Outlines Studies in Biology). 1983. pap. 8.50 o.p. (ISBN 0-412-25560-X, 6870, Pub. by Chapman & Hall). Routledge Chapman & Hall.

Control of Fertility. Ed. by Gregory Pincus. 1965. 58.00 o.p. (ISBN 0-12-557056-2). Acad Pr.

Control of Flow Separation: Energy Conservation, Operational Efficiency & Safety. Paul K. Chang. (McGraw-Hill Series in Thermal & Fluids Engineering). (Illus.). 1976. text ed. 67.95x o.p. (ISBN 0-07-010513-8). McGraw.

Control of Fluid Power: Analysis & Design. 2nd rev. ed. D. McCloy. LC 80-40027. (Ellis Horwood Series in Engineering Science). 505p. 1980. 106.95x o.p. (ISBN 0-470-27012-8). Halsted Pr.

Control of Foreign Relations in Modern Nations. Ed. by Philip W. Buck & Martin B. Travis, Jr. 1957. 13.95x o.p. (ISBN 0-393-09528-2, NortonC). Norton.

Control of Gene Expression. N. Maclean. 1976. 61.00 o.p. (ISBN 0-12-464950-5). Acad Pr.

Control of Human Fertility: A Text for Health Professionals. Porter. 1987. pap. 16.00 o.p. (ISBN 0-8016-3981-6). Mosby.

Control of Human Reproduction. R. L. Holmes & C. A. Fox. (Monographs for Students of Medicine). 1979. 19.50 o.p. (ISBN 0-12-353450-X). Acad Pr.

Control of Indoor Climate. T. C. Angus. 1968. 35.00 o.p. (ISBN 0-08-012729-0). Pergamon.

Control of Large Wind Turbine Generators Connected to Utility Networks. E. N. Hinrichsen. 96p. 1984. pap. 22.00 o.p. (ISBN 0-88016-033-0). Windbks.

Control of Migraine. John B. Brainard. 1977. 10.95 o.p. (ISBN 0-393-06421-2). Norton.

Control of Mycotoxins: Proceedings of a Symposium, Goteborg, Sweden, 1972. Ed. by P. Krogh. 116p. 1976. 35.00 o.p. (ISBN 0-08-020749-9). Pergamon.

Control of Natural Monopolies. Richard Schmalensee. LC 78-6061. 1979. 29.00x o.p. (ISBN 0-669-02322-1). Lexington Bks.

Control of Ovulation. Ed. by C. A. Villee. 1961. pap. 49.00 o.p. (ISBN 0-08-013650-8). Pergamon.

Control of Specific (Toxic) Pollutants: Proceedings, Air Pollution Control Association Specialty Conference, Gainesville FL, 1979. 514p. 1979. 18.75 o.p. (ISBN 0-318-12267-7, SP-30); members 15.00 o.p. (ISBN 0-318-12268-5). Air & Waste.

Control of Sulphur & Other Gaseous Emissions. Institution of Chemical Engineers. 1982. 57.00 o.s.i. (ISBN 0-08-028755-7). Pergamon.

Control of the Sea-Bed: An Updated Report. Evan Luard. LC 76-11050. 320p. 1976. 16.50 o.s.i. (ISBN 0-8008-1811-3). Taplinger.

Control of Water Resource Systems: Proceedings of a IIASA Workshop, October, 1979. Ed. by E. F. Wood & A. Szollosi-Nagy. (IIASA Proceedings Ser: Vol. 8). 1980. 85.00 o.p. (ISBN 0-08-024486-6). Pergamon.

Control Processes in Neoplasia. Ed. by Myron A. Mehlman & Richard W. Hanson. (Symposia on Metabolic Regulation Ser.). 1974. 43.50 o.p. (ISBN 0-12-487860-1). Acad Pr.

Control System Design by Pole-Zero Assignment. Ed. by F. Fallside. 1978. 48.50 o.p. (ISBN 0-12-248250-6). Acad Pr.

Control Systems Engineering. 2nd ed. I. J. Nagrath & M. Gopal. LC 81-7470. 525p. 1982. 29.95x o.p. (ISBN 0-470-27148-5). Halsted Pr.

Control Systems for Heating, Ventilating & Air Conditioning. 3rd ed. Roger W. Haines. (Engineering Ser.). 320p. 1983. 31.95 o.p. (ISBN 0-442-23649-2). Van Nos Reinhold.

Control Systems Functions & Programming Approaches, 2 Vols. Dimitrius N. Chorafas. (Mathematics in Science & Engineering: Vol. 27A & B). 1966. Vol. A. 84.00 o.p. (ISBN 0-12-174061-7); Vol. B. 69.50 o.p. (ISBN 0-12-174062-5). Acad Pr.

Control Theory & the Calculus of Variations. Ed. by A. V. Balakrishna. LC 74-91431. 1969. 66.00 o.p. (ISBN 0-12-076953-0). Acad Pr.

Control Theory of Systems Governed by Partial Differential Equations. Ed. by A. K. Aziz et al. 1977. 49.50 o.p. (ISBN 0-12-068640-6). Acad Pr.

Control Your Blood Pressure Without Drugs. Cleaves M. Bennett & Charles Cameron. LC 83-45022. 1984. 15.95 o.p. (ISBN 0-385-18927-3). Doubleday.

Control Your Future: Find Your Fortune in the Financial Services Revolution. Robert W. MacDonald. LC 85-63885. 162p. (Orig.). 1986. pap. 12.00 o.p. (ISBN 0-87218-047-6). Natl Underwriter.

Controlled & Conditioned Invariance: Proceedings of the CISM, Department of Automation & Information, University of Geneva, 1971. CISM (International Center for Mechanical Sciences), Department of Automation & Information Staff. Ed. by G. Basile. (CISM Publications: No. 109). (Illus.). 51p. 1973. pap. 7.50 o.p. (ISBN 0-387-81132-X). Springer-Verlag.

Controlled Atmospheres for Heat Treatment. R. Nemenyi. (Illus.). 225p. 1983. 65.00 o.p. (ISBN 0-08-019883-X); pap. 65.00 o.p. (ISBN 0-08-029997-0). Pergamon.

Controlled Fusion & Plasma Physics: Invited Papers from the Eleventh European Conference of the European Physical Society Plasma Physics Division, 5-9 September 1983, Aachen, Federal Republic of Germany. Ed. by A. Gibson. 276p. 1984. pap. 26.00 o.p. (ISBN 0-08-030286-6). Pergamon.

Controlled Nuclear Fusion: Current Research & Potential Progress. National Research Council. 1978. pap. text ed. 5.25x o.p. (ISBN 0-309-02863-9). Natl Acad Pr.

Controlled Painting. Frank Covino. LC 81-22583. 176p. 1981. 22.50 o.p. (ISBN 0-89134-042-4); pap. 14.95 o.p. (ISBN 0-89134-044-0). North Light Bks.

Controlled Release of Pesticides & Pharmaceuticals. Ed. by D. H. Lewis. LC 81-7336. 350p. 1981. 69.50x o.p. (ISBN 0-306-40743-4, Plenum Pr). Plenum Pub.

Controller Involvement in Management. Vijay Sathe. (Illus.). 192p. 1982. text ed. 42.00 o.p. (ISBN 0-13-171660-3). P-H.

Controlling Airborne Effluents from Fuel Cycle Plants: Proceedings, American Nuclear Society Topical Meeting, Sun Valley, August 5-8. 560p. softcover 19.00 o.p. (ISBN 0-317-33031-4, 700016). Am Nuclear Soc.

Controlling & Analyzing Costs in Food Service Operations. James R. Keiser & Elmer Kallio. LC 73-20156. 291p. 1974. text ed. write for info. o.p. (ISBN 0-02-362670-4). Macmillan.

Controlling Assets & Transactions in Hospitals: How to Improve Internal Accounting Control. Rev. ed. Touche Ross & Co. Staff. (Illus.). 108p. 1982. pap. 9.95 o.s.i. (ISBN 0-930228-17-0). Healthcare Fin Man Assn.

Controlling Corrosion in Process Industry. Kenneth J. McNaughton et al. (Chemical Engineering Book Ser.). 288p. 1980. text ed. 36.50 o.p. (ISBN 0-07-010691-6). McGraw.

Controlling Infection. Ed. by Jean Robinson & Barbara McVan. LC 81-6601. (Nursing Photobook Ser.). (Illus.). 160p. 1981. text ed. 16.95 o.p. (ISBN 0-916730-35-2). Springhouse Pub.

Controlling Public Pensions. Mary E. Stakes. 40p. (Orig.). 1982. pap. 5.50 o.p. (ISBN 0-89854-083-6). U of GA Inst Govt.

Controlling the Money Supply. rev. ed. David Gowland. 244p. 1984. pap. 13.95 o.p. (ISBN 0-7099-1170-X, Pub. by Croom Helm Ltd). Routledge Chapman & Hall.

Controlling the Offenders in the Community: Reforming the Community Supervision Function. Todd R. Clear & Vincent O'Leary. LC 81-47444. 208p. 1982. 37.00x o.p. (ISBN 0-669-04633-7). Lexington Bks.

Controlling Women: The Normal & the Deviant. Ed. by Bridget Hutter & Gillian Williams. (Illus.). 207p. 1981. 23.00 o.p. (ISBN 0-7099-0469-X, Pub. by Croom Helm Ltd); pap. 13.95 o.p. (ISBN 0-7099-1218-8). Routledge Chapman & Hall.

Controlling Your Cash Flow with Jazz & the Macintosh. Gregory R. Glau. 230p. 1986. pap. 19.95 o.p. (ISBN 0-87094-703-6). Dow Jones-Irwin.

Controlling Your Cash Flow with 1-2-3 or Symphony. Gregory Glau. 230p. 1986. pap. 19.95 o.p. (ISBN 0-87094-702-8). Dow Jones-Irwin.

Controversial Coyote. Laurence Pringle. LC 76-46789. (Illus.). (gr. 7 up). 1977. 5.95 o.p. (ISBN 0-15-219930-6, HJ). HarBraceJ.

Controversial Horse. R. S. Summerhays & Stella A. Walker. (Illus.). 8.75 o.p. (ISBN 0-85131-075-3, Pub. by J A Allen U K). S R Smith Sporting Bks.

Controversies in Anesthesiology. James E. Eckenhoff. (Illus.). 312p. 1979. write for info. o.p. (ISBN 0-7216-3322-6). Saunders.

Controversies in Child Health & Pediatrics. David H. Smith & Robert A. Hokelman. (Illus.). 480p. 1981. text ed. 32.00 o.p. (ISBN 0-07-058510-5). McGraw.

Controversies in Dermatology. Ervin Epstein. (Illus.). 512p. 1984. write for info. o.p. (ISBN 0-7216-3398-6). Saunders.

Controversies in Orthopaedic Surgery. Robert E. Leach & Franklin T. Hoaglund. (Illus.). 516p. 1982. write for info. o.p. (ISBN 0-7216-5657-9). Saunders.

Controversies in Surgery, Two. Ed. by John P. Delaney & Richard L. Varco. (Illus.). 464p. 1983. (ISBN 0-7216-3038-3). Saunders.

Controversy in Ophthalmology. Ed. by Robert J. Brockhurst et al. LC 75-40634. (Illus.). 1977. text ed. write for info. o.p. (ISBN 0-7216-1989-4). Saunders.

Controversy over German Industrialization, 1890-1902. Kenneth Barkin. LC 78-101359. 1970. lib. bdg. 25.00x o.s.i. (ISBN 0-226-03712-6). U of Chicago Pr.

Controversy: Roots of the Creation-Evolution Conflict. Donald E. Chittick. LC 84-22670. (Critical Concern Ser.). 1984. 13.95 o.p. (ISBN 0-88070-019-X); pap. 9.95 o.p. Multnomah.

Conundrum. Jan Morris. LC 74-525. (Helen & Kurt Wolff Bk.). 1974. 6.95 o.p. (ISBN 0-15-122563-X). HarBraceJ.

Convection Cookery. Caroline Kriz. LC 80-19915. (Illus.). 152p. (Orig.). 1980. pap. 5.95 o.s.i. (ISBN 0-89286-181-9, One Hund One Prods). Ortho.

Convective Transport & Instability Phenomena. Ed. by Juergen Zierep & Herbert Oertel, Jr. (Illus.). 577p. 1982. text ed. 65.00x o.p. (ISBN 3-7650-1114-2). Sheridan.

Convention. Richard Reeves. Ed. by Daniel Okrent. LC 76-27426. 1977. 10.00 o.p. (ISBN 0-15-122582-6). HarBraceJ.

Convention & Recommendation Concerning the Protection of Workers Against Ionising Radiations see Manual of Industrial Radiation Protection.

Convention at Washington-on-the-Brazos, Vol. 13: January 15 Through March 17, 1836. LC 73-78014. (Illus.). 792p. 1987. lib. bdg. 40.00 o.p. (ISBN 0-932408-13-3). UTA Pr.

Convention Girls. Ellen Evans. 224p. 1982. pap. 2.50 o.p. (ISBN 0-505-51850-3, Pub. by Tower Bks). Dorchester Pub Co.

Convention on the Privileges & Immunities of the United Nations Adopted by the General Assembly of the United Nations on 13 February 1946. (Eng., Chinese, Fr., Rus. & Span.). pap. 2.00 o.p. (ISBN 0-686-94997-8, UN75/10/1, UN). UNIPUB.

Convention Sales & Services. Milton T. Astroff & James R. Abbey. 464p. 1978. pap. write for info. o.p. (ISBN 0-697-08408-6). Wm C Brown.

Convergence. Jack Fuller. 1984. pap. 3.50 o.s.i. (ISBN 0-345-31181-7). Ballantine.

Convergence Seventy-Four: Automotive Electronic Technology. 170p. 1975. pap. 25.00 o.p. (ISBN 0-89883-031-1, P-57). Soc Auto Engineers.

Convergent Evolution in Chile & California: Mediterranean Climate Ecosystems. Ed. by Harold A. Mooney. (US-IBP Synthesis Ser.: Vol. 5). 1977. 49.50 o.p. (ISBN 0-12-787080-6). Acad Pr.

Conversacion con Jose Luis Gonzalez. Arcadio Diaz. (Norte Ser.). 160p. 1977. pap. 4.95 o.p. (ISBN 0-940238-11-X). Ediciones Huracan.

Conversar Sin Parar. George Rooks et al. 144p. 1982. pap. text ed. 9.00 o.p. (ISBN 0-88377-222-1). Newbury Hse.

Conversation Book: English in Everyday Life, Bk. 1. Tina K. Carver & S. Douglas Fotinos. (Illus.). 1977. pap. text ed. (ISBN 0-13-172239-5). P-H.

Conversation Book: English in Everyday Life, Bk. 2. Tina K. Carver & S. Douglas Fotinos. (Illus.). 1977. pap. text ed. 11.67 o.p. (ISBN 0-13-172247-6). P-H.

Conversation in French: Points of Departure. 4th ed. Peter Bonnel & Frank Sedwick. 128p. 1985. pap. text ed. 16.75 o.p. (ISBN 0-8384-1274-2). Heinle & Heinle.

Conversation in German: Points of Departure. 4th ed. Peter Bonnell & Frank Sedwick. 128p. 1985. pap. text ed. 16.75 o.p. (ISBN 0-8384-1275-0). Heinle & Heinle.

Conversation in Spanish: Points of Departure. 4th ed. Frank Sedwick. 128p. 1985. pap. text ed. 16.75 o.p. (ISBN 0-8384-1273-4). Heinle & Heinle.

Conversation on Counseling Between a Doctor & a Priest. 2nd ed. Ed. by Marcus Lefebure. 128p. pap. 6.95 o.p. (ISBN 0-317-31445-9, Fortress) (ISBN 0-317-31446-7). Augsburg Fortress.

Conversational Hindi. Narayan Prasad Jain. (Illus.). 286p. 1978. pap. 3.95 o.s.i. (ISBN 0-88253-298-7). Ind-US Inc.

Conversational Statistics with IDA. 2nd ed. Harry V. Roberts & Robert F. Ling. (Data Analysis Ser.). 592p. 1982. text ed. 26.95x o.p. (ISBN 0-07-053137-4). McGraw.

Conversationally Speaking: Tested New Ways to Increase Your Personal & Social Effectiveness. Alan Garner. 164p. (Orig.). 1981. pap. text ed. 5.95 o.p. (ISBN 0-07-022885-X). McGraw.

Conversations. Virginia Bonnici. (Illus.). 80p. 1985. 10.00 o.p. (ISBN 0-682-40245-1). Exposition-Phoenix.

Conversations in Japan: Modernization, Politics, & Culture. David Riesman & Evelyn T. Riesman. (Midway Reprint Ser.). 1976. pap. text ed. 13.00x o.s.i. (ISBN 0-226-71739-9). U of Chicago Pr.

Conversations sans Fin. George Rooks. 136p. 1983. pap. text ed. 8.25 o.p. (ISBN 0-88377-278-7). Newbury Hse.

Conversations with American Writers. Charles Ruas. LC 84-47848. (Illus.). 1985. 17.45 o.s.i. (ISBN 0-394-52787-9). Knopf.

Conversations with Casals. Pablo Casals. 240p. Repr. of 1957 ed. lib. bdg. 39.00 o.p. (Pub. by Am Repr Serv). Reprint Servs.

Conversations with Igor Stravinsky. Igor F. Stravinsky. 162p. Repr. of 1959 ed. lib. bdg. 39.00 o.p. (Pub. by Am Repr Serv). Reprint Servs.

Conversations with Isaac Bashevis Singer. Isaac Bashevis Singer & Richard Burgin. LC 85-1490. 192p. 1985. 15.95 o.p. (ISBN 0-385-17999-5). Doubleday.

Conversations with Jazz Musicians. Ed. by Matthew J. Bruccoli et al. LC 77-9143. (Conversations Ser.: Vol. 2). 296p. 1977. 50.00x o.p. (ISBN 0-8103-0944-0, A Bruccoli Clark Book). Gale.

Conversations with Jean Piaget. Jean-Claude Bringuier. Tr. by Basia Gulati. LC 79-15669. 1982. pap. 6.95 o.s.i. (ISBN 0-226-07504-4). U of Chicago Pr.

Conversations with Kennedy. Benjamin C. Bradlee. (Illus.). 251p. 1975. 7.95 o.p. (ISBN 0-393-08722-0). Norton.

Conversations with Klemperer. rev. ed. Peter Heyworth. LC 84-24740. (Illus.). 160p. 1985. pap. 10.95 o.p. (ISBN 0-571-13561-7). Faber & Faber.

Conversations with Lord Byron on Perversion, 163 Years after His Lordship's Death. Amanda Prantera. LC 87-17354. 174p. 1987. 16.95 o.p. (ISBN 0-689-11882-1, Atheneum). Macmillan.

Conversations with Losey. Michel Ciment. 320p. 1985. 39.95 o.p. (ISBN 0-416-40470-7, 9601); pap. 16.95 o.p. (ISBN 0-416-40120-1, 9602). Routledge Chapman & Hall.

Conversations with Stalin. Milovan Djilas. Tr. by Michael B. Petrovich. LC 62-14470. 1962. 9.95 o.s.i. (ISBN 0-15-122590-7). HarBraceJ.

Conversion. Erik Routley. LC 77-20298. 64p. 1978. pap. 0.50 o.p. (ISBN 0-8006-1327-9, 1-1327, Fortress). Augsburg Fortress.

Conversion of Computer Software. John R. Wolberg. (Illus.). 240p. 1983. text ed. 41.00 o.p. (ISBN 0-13-172148-8). P-H.

Conversion of Constantine. Ed. by John W. Eadie. LC 76-25480. (European American Studies). 118p. 1977. pap. text ed. 6.50 o.p. (ISBN 0-88275-453-X). Krieger.

Conversion of Tropical Moist Forests. 1980. 13.95x o.p. (ISBN 0-309-02945-7). Natl Acad Pr.

Conversion vs. Preservation - America's Farmland: A Bibliography. Mary E. Huls. (Public Administration Ser.: P 1708). 10p. 1985. 2.00 o.p. (ISBN 0-89028-458-X). Vance Biblios.

Converter's Guide to High Profits from Condo & Time Sharing Conversion. Milt Tanzer. LC 81-20262. 278p. 1982. 65.00 o.p. (ISBN 0-87624-103-8, Inst Busn Plan). P-H.

Convertibility, Multilateralism & Freedom: World Economic Policy in the Seventies. Essays in Honour of Reinhard Kamitz. Ed. by W. Schmitz. LC 76-186940. 400p. 1972. 37.80 o.p. (ISBN 0-387-81056-0). Springer-Verlag.

Convertibles: The Complete Story. John G. Gunnell. (Illus.). 224p. 20.15 o.p. (ISBN 0-8306-2110-5, 2110). TAB Bks.

Converting New York State Utilities to Coal: A Study of the Costs & Environmental Impacts of Conversion. James S. Cannon. 37p. 1982. pap. 10.00x o.p. (ISBN 0-918780-26-8). INFORM.

Converting to Phacoemulsification: A Manual for the Surgeon in Transition. Paul S. Koch. LC 87-4625. 96p. 1987. pap. 24.95 o.p. (ISBN 1-55642-017-X). Slack Inc.

Converting to Timex-Sinclair BASIC. Stuart L. Bird. 206p. 1983. spiral binding 14.95 o.p. (ISBN 0-88006-063-8, BK7396). Wayne Green Ent.

Convex Function. A. Wayne Roberts & Dale E. Varberg. (Pure & Applied Mathematics Ser.). 1973. 69.50 o.p. (ISBN 0-12-589740-5). Acad Pr.

Conveyancer's Guide to Local & Public Authorities: A Desk-Top Companion. Waterlow. (Waterlow Publications Ser.). 224p. 1988. pap. 23.00 o.p. (ISBN 0-08-033102-5). Pergamon.

Conveyor Terms & Definitions. 4th ed. American National Standards Institute Staff. (CEMA Standards: No. 102). (Illus.). 93p. 1982. 7.00 o.p. (ISBN 0-318-13804-2). Conveyor Equip Mfrs.

Convict. James L. Burke. LC 85-11332. 145p. 1985. text ed. 15.95 o.p. (ISBN 0-8071-1273-9); pap. 9.95 o.p. (ISBN 0-8071-1275-5). La State U Pr.

Conviction: The Determination of Guilt or Innocence Without Trial. Donald J. Newman. 1966. pap. 7.95 o.p. (ISBN 0-316-60483-6). Little.

Convictions: A Novel of the Sixties. Taffy Cannon. Ed. by Laurie Lister. LC 84-29468. 384p. 1985. 18.95 o.p. (ISBN 0-688-04343-7). Morrow.

Convocation of the Clergy: A Study of Antecedents & Its Rise, with Special Emphasis upon Its Growth & Activities in the Thirteenth & Fourteenth Centuries. Dorothy B. Weske. (Church Historical Society London N. S. Ser.: No. 23). Repr. of 1937 ed. 60.00 o.p. (ISBN 0-8115-3147-3). Kraus Repr.

Coo-My-Dove, My Dear. Joseph Jacobs. LC 76-4467. (Illus.). 32p. (gr. k-3). 1976. 5.95 o.p. (ISBN 0-689-30543-5, Atheneum). Macmillan.

Cook Ahead. Ed. by Veronica Sperling & Sonya Mills. (Step-by-Step Cooking Ser.). 160p. 1986. 10.95 o.p. (ISBN 0-8120-5685-X). Barron.

Cook & Company: Illustrated Catalogue of Carriages & Special Business Advertiser. (Illus.). 17.00 o.p. (ISBN 0-8446-0552-2). Peter Smith.

Cook & Serve Book. Sunbeam Staff. Ed. by Marilyn Kostick. LC 80-68016. (Illus.). 160p. 1980. 8.95 o.p. (ISBN 0-916752-43-7). Longman Trade.

Cook Is the Captain. Neil Hollander & Harald Mertes. (Illus.). 1979. 14.95 o.p. (ISBN 0-393-03234-5). Norton.

Cook Japanese. Masaru Doi. LC 65-10171. (Illus.). 129p. 1964. 15.95 o.p. (ISBN 0-87011-121-3). Kodansha.

Cook Now, Dine Later. rev. ed. Catherine Althaus & Peter F. French-Hodges. LC 84-26083. 243p. 1985. pap. 8.95 o.p. (ISBN 0-571-13559-5). Faber & Faber.

Cookbook - Chiyaan iitini Binaaltsoos. Regina H. Lynch. LC 86-62125. 34p. Date not set. price not set o.s.i. (ISBN 0-936008-26-1). Navajo Curr.

Cookbook for Diabetics. Ed. by Gaynor Maddox. LC 66-25572. pap. 3.95 o.p. (ISBN 0-8008-1825-3). Taplinger.

Cookery Encyclopedia. Philip Harben. (Illus.). 480p. 1956. (ISBN 0-8022-0678-6). Philos Lib.

Cookery for One or Two. Barbara Swain. 1981. pap. 3.95 o.s.i. (ISBN 0-440-11431-4). Dell.

Cookie Book. Eva Moore. LC 76-190381. 64p. (gr. 1-4). 1979. 9.95 o.p. (ISBN 0-395-28866-5, Clarion). HM.

Cookie Craft: No-Bake Designs for Edible Party Decorations. Barbara Williams & Rosemary Williams. LC 77-3184. (Illus.). (gr. 6 up). 1977. 7.95 o.p. (ISBN 0-03-020451-8); pap. 3.50 o.p. (ISBN 0-03-048971-7). H Holt & Co.

Cookin' for Kids. Ed. by Ann Kaiser. LC 83-60709. 64p. 1983. pap. 3.95 o.s.i. Reiman Assocs.

Cooking Adventures for Kids. Sharon Cadwallader. LC 74-9544. (San Francisco Ser.). 101p. 1974. 8.95 o.p. (ISBN 0-395-19976-X); pap. 6.95 o.p. (ISBN 0-395-19980-8). HM.

Cooking Amid Chaos. Bow Ross. 1983. pap. 7.95 o.p. (ISBN 0-89272-168-5). Down East.

Cooking As Therapy. Louis Parrish. LC 75-11150. (Priam Ser.). 1979. pap. 4.95 o.p. (ISBN 0-87795-243-4, Arbor Hse). Morrow.

Cooking As Therapy. Louis Parrish. LC 75-1146. 1975. 8.95 o.p. (ISBN 0-87795-117-9, Arbor Hse). Morrow.

Cooking, Basic & Advanced, for Pathfinders: A Youth Enrichment Skill. Lou Gattis. (Illus., Orig.). 1987. pap. 4.95 o.p. (ISBN 0-317-61539-4). Cheetah Pub.

Cooking Bibliography. School of Salerno Staff. 1983. 50.00 o.p. (ISBN 0-87556-668-5). Saifer.

Cooking Craft. 6th ed. S. Elizabeth Nash. 416p. 1975. 17.95x o.p. (ISBN 0-8464-0287-4). Beekman Pubs.

Cooking Fish & Wild Game. Francine Dufresne. LC 75-25760. (Illus.). 144p. 1975. 4.95 o.s.i. (ISBN 0-912238-75-5, One Hund One Prods). Ortho.

Cooking for All It's Worth: Making the Most of Every Morsel of Food You Buy. Jay Jacobs. 1983. text ed. 14.95 o.p. (ISBN 0-07-032155-8). McGraw.

Cooking for Giving. Bert Greene & Phillip S. Schulz. (Great American Cooking Schools Ser.). (Illus.). 84p. (Orig.). 1984. pap. 5.95 o.p. (ISBN 0-941034-22-4). I Chalmers.

Cooking for Life. Michel Abehsera. 384p. 1985. pap. 3.95 o.p. (ISBN 0-380-00777-0, 35188). Avon.

Cooking for Men Only. Caroline Kriz. LC 84-5179. (Illus.). 192p. 1984. 14.95 o.p. (ISBN 0-89286-227-0, One Hund One Prods); pap. 7.95 o.p. (ISBN 0-89286-230-0). Ortho.

Cooking for One or Two or More. Amy G. Ireson & Shirley F. Lipscomb. LC 77-75156. (Illus.). 1978. pap. 15.95 lab manual spiral bdg. o.p. (ISBN 0-395-25823-5). HM.

Cooking for Regeneration: Macrobiotic Relief from Cancer, AIDS, & Degenerative Diseases. Cecile T. Levin. LC 87-80496. (Illus.). 288p. 1987. pap. 15.95 o.p. (ISBN 0-87040-692-2). Japan Pubns USA.

Cooking for Special Occasions. (Step-by-Step Cooking Ser.). (Illus.). 160p. 1985. 10.95 o.p. (ISBN 0-8120-5678-7). Barron.

Cooking for Two. Evelyn M. Fett. 1980. 6.00 o.p. (ISBN 0-682-49472-0). Exposition-Phoenix.

Cooking from a Country Kitchen. Suzanne Taylor. Ed. by Jean Atcheson. LC 83-71031. (Great American Cooking Schools Ser.). (Illus.). 84p. (Orig.). 1983. pap. 5.95 o.p. (ISBN 0-941034-17-8). I Chalmers.

Cooking from an Italian Garden: Classic Meatless Recipes from Antipasti to Dessert. Paola Scaravelli & Jon Cohen. 344p. 1984. 18.95 o.p. (ISBN 0-03-063312-5). H Holt & Co.

Cooking from the Caucasus. Sonia Uvezian. LC 78-6191. Orig. Title: Best Foods of Russia. 1978. pap. 3.95 o.p. (ISBN 0-15-622594-8, Harv). HarBraceJ.

Cooking in Ten Minutes. Edouard De Pomaine. LC 84-28774. 144p. 1985. pap. 6.95 o.p. (ISBN 0-571-13599-4). Faber & Faber.

Cooking in the Nude: For Playful Gourmets. Stephen Cornwell & Debbra Cornwell. (Illus.). 64p. 1982. pap. 4.95 o.p. (ISBN 0-943678-00-5). Wellton Enter.

Cooking is an Act of Love. Katherine Gottsegen. (Illus.). 165p. 7.95 o.p. (ISBN 0-9610094-0-3). Berkshire Traveller.

Cooking Light 1986. LC 85-7844. (Illus.). 256p. 19.95 o.p. (ISBN 0-8487-0677-3). Oxmoor Hse.

Cooking Metric Is Fun. Julia C. McCleary. (Illus.). (gr. 3-7). 1979. spiral bdg 8.95 o.p. (ISBN 0-15-219961-6, HJ). HarBraceJ.

Cooking of South-West France: A Collection of Traditional & New Recipes. Paula Wolfert. LC 83-2091. (Illus.). 368p. 1983. 24.95 o.s.i. (ISBN 0-385-27463-7, Dial). Doubleday.

Cooking of the South. Nathalie Dupree. Ed. by Richard Atcheson. LC 81-70443. (Great American Cooking Schools Ser.). (Illus.). 84p. 1982. pap. 5.95 o.p. (ISBN 0-941034-11-9). I Chalmers.

Cooking on the Go. rev. ed. Janet Groene. (Illus.). 1981. 13.95 o.p. (ISBN 0-393-03259-0). Norton.

Cooking Out-of-Doors: For Juniors, Brownies, Cadettes, Seniors & Leaders. Girl Scouts of the U. S. A. Staff. (Illus.). 216p. (gr. 1-12). 1960. 7.00 o.p. (ISBN 0-88441-128-1, 19-984). Girl Scouts USA.

Cooking the Dutch Oven Way. Leroy L. Woodruff. (Illus.). 144p. 1980. pap. 10.95 o.p. (ISBN 0-934802-01-7). ICS Bks.

Cooking the Nouvelle Cuisine in America. Michele Urvater & David Liedermann. LC 79-64785. (Illus.). 480p. 1982. 14.95 o.p. (ISBN 0-89480-111-2); pap. 12.95 o.p. (ISBN 0-89480-215-1, 452). Workman Pub.

Cooking the Professional Way. rev. ed. Kenneth C. Wolfe. 352p. 1982. 16.95 o.p. (ISBN 0-442-23887-8). Van Nos Reinhold.

Cooking the Wild Harvest. J. Wayne Fears. LC 84-9142. (Illus.). 275p. (Orig.). 1984. pap. 12.95 o.p. (ISBN 0-934802-14-9). ICS Bks.

Cooking under Pressure. Helen Cox. 10.50 o.p. (ISBN 0-571-10825-3); pap. 6.50 o.p. (ISBN 0-571-11103-3). Faber & Faber.

Cooking Vessels from Minoan Kommos: A Preliminary Report. Philip Betancourt. (Occasional Paper: 7). (Illus.). 15p. 1980. 3.00x o.p. (ISBN 0-917956-16-8). UCLA Arch.

Cooking What Comes Naturally see One Pinch of Sunshine, One-Half Cup of Rain.

Cooking Wild Game. Zack Hanle. 1974. 12.95 o.p. (ISBN 0-87140-595-4). Liveright.

Cooking with a Harvard Accent: A Collection of International Recipes from the Harvard Community. Melanie Marcus. 1979. 9.95 o.p. (ISBN 0-395-27783-3). HM.

Cooking with Antoine at Le Perigord. Antoine Bouterin & Elizabeth Crossman. (Illus.). 258p. 1986. 24.95 o.p. (ISBN 0-399-13135-3). Putnam Pub Group.

Cooking with Bon Appetit: American Regional Favorites. Bon Appetit Magazine Editors. LC 85-14647. (Illus.). 144p. 1985. 12.95 o.p. (ISBN 0-89535-169-2). Knapp Pr.

Cooking with Bon Appetit: Make-Ahead Meals. Bon Appetit Magazine Editors. (Illus.). 144p. 1984. 12.95 o.p. (ISBN 0-89535-106-4). Knapp Pr.

Cooking with Country. Claudia Burgess. LC 77-15810. (Illus., Orig.). 1978. pap. 6.95 o.p. (ISBN 0-689-70570-0, Atheneum). Macmillan.

Cooking with Craig Claiborne & Pierre Franey. Craig Claiborne & Pierre Franey. LC 83-45038. 512p. 1983. 17.45 o.s.i. (ISBN 0-8129-1078-8). Times Bks.

Cooking with Exotic Fruits & Vegetables. Jane Grigson & Charlotte Knox. LC 86-18288. 1987. 17.95 o.p. (ISBN 0-8050-0205-7). H Holt & Co.

Cooking With Herbs. Susan Belsinger & Carolyn Dille. (Illus.). 240p. 1983. 19.95 o.p. (ISBN 0-8436-2225-3); pap. 18.95 o.p. (ISBN 0-8436-2226-1). Van Nos Reinhold.

Cooking with Herbs & Spices. Felicity Jackson & Miren Lopategui. (Step-by-Step Cooking Ser.). 160p. 1986. 10.95 o.p. (ISBN 0-8120-5682-5). Barron.

Cooking with Katherine Wise. Fisher Broadcasting Staff. Ed. by Katherine Wise. 310p. (Orig.). 1984. pap. 9.95 o.p. (ISBN 0-89716-133-5). Peanut Butter.

Cooking with Madame Wu & Yang Recipes for Health & Longevity. S. Wu. 304p. 1983. text ed. 17.95 o.p. (ISBN 0-07-072110-6). McGraw.

Cooking with Michael Field. Michael Field. Ed. by Joan Scobey. LC 78-752. (Illus.). 1978. 14.95 o.p. (ISBN 0-03-018501-7). H Holt & Co.

Cooking with Mushrooms. Kay S. Nelson. 11.25 o.p. (ISBN 0-8446-5599-6). Peter Smith.

Cooking with Pride. Peter Van Kleek. 114p. 1974. pap. text ed. 4.75 o.p. (ISBN 0-8422-0391-5). Irvington.

Cooking with Spirits. Beverly Barbour. LC 76-6838. (Illus.). 192p. (Orig.). 1976. 7.95 o.s.i. (ISBN 0-912238-83-6, One Hund One Prods); pap. 4.95 o.s.i. (ISBN 0-912238-82-8). Ortho.

Cooking with Style. Chicago Cutlery Staff. 148p. 1984. 8.95 o.p. (ISBN 0-914091-44-1). Chicago Review.

Cooking with the Cuisinart Food Processor. Roy A. De Groot. LC 76-46586. 1977. text ed. 14.95 o.p. (ISBN 0-07-016273-5). McGraw.

Cooking with the Danes. 2nd ed. Astrid Slebsager. 78p. (Orig., Danish.). 1988. text ed. 15.00x o.p. (ISBN 87-14-28385-9, D-760). Vanous.

Cooking with the Santa Fe Opera. Santa Fe Opera Guild Staff. LC 83-621. (Illus.). 160p. (Orig.). 1983. 19.95 o.p. (ISBN 0-86534-027-7). Sunstone Pr.

Cooking with Wild Plants: How to Recognize & Prepare Edible Wilderness Plants of the Rocky Mountains. Alan Briscoe. LC 78-52405. (Illus.). 1979. pap. 2.95 o.p. (ISBN 0-88290-091-9). Horizon Utah.

Cooking Your Own Mushrooms. Jo Mueller. LC 76-20638. (Illus.). 180p. 1976. 8.95 o.p. (ISBN 0-88266-090-X, Garden Way Pub); pap. 6.95 o.p. (ISBN 0-88266-089-6). Storey Comm Inc.

Cooks & Bakers. Robert A. Anderson. 192p. 1984. pap. 2.95 o.p. (ISBN 0-380-79590-6, 87429-6). Avon.

Cook's Book. H. Hillman. (Illus.). 1981. pap. 8.95 o.p. (ISBN 0-380-76794-5, 76794-5). Avon.

Cook's Collage: Favorite Fare of the Junior League of Tulsa. Junior League of Tulsa, Inc. Staff. 352p. 1978. 9.95 o.p. (ISBN 0-9604368-0-4). Jr League Tulsa.

Cook's Garden. Jan Mahnken. LC 85-397. 256p. 1985. pap. 12.95 o.s.i. (ISBN 0-88150-036-4). Countryman.

Cook's Magazine Cookbook. Ed. by Judith Hill & Michael Hill. 1985. 18.45 o.s.i. (ISBN 0-671-55481-6). S&S.

Cook's Marketplace New York: A Culinary Sourcebook. Irene Sax. (Cook's Marketplace Ser.). 276p. (Orig.). 1984. pap. 8.95 o.p. (ISBN 0-89286-228-9, One Hund One Prods). Ortho.

Cooks' Marketplace: San Francisco Bay Area Sourcebook. Sherry Virbila. LC 82-7839. (Illus.). 276p. (Orig.). pap. 8.95 o.s.i. (ISBN 0-89286-198-3, One Hund One Prods). Ortho.

Cool Entertaining. Irma Rhode. LC 75-41420. 1976. 8.95 o.p. (ISBN 0-689-10710-2, Atheneum). Macmillan.

Cool Fire: How to Make It in Television. Bob Shanks. (Illus.). 318p. 1976. 9.95 o.p. (ISBN 0-393-08363-2). Norton.

Cool It Now: The Authorized Biography of New Edition. Nelson George. (Illus.). 128p. (Orig.). 1986. pap. 6.95 o.p. (ISBN 0-8092-5004-7). Contemp Bks.

Cool Pool. Paul White. (Jungle Doctor Picture Fable Ser.). 21p. (gr. k-5). 1986. pap. 26.50 o.p. (ISBN 0-85364-373-3, Pub. by Paternoster UK). Attic Pr.

Cool Repentance: A Jemima Shore Mystery. Antonia Fraser. 1983. 12.95 o.p. (ISBN 0-393-01625-0). Norton.

Cool Shades. Amy Ephron. 93p. (Orig.). 1984. pap. 2.95 o.p. (ISBN 0-440-11434-9). Dell.

Cool Web: The Pattern of Children's Reading. Margaret Meek et al. LC 77-3852. 1978. 14.95 o.p. (ISBN 0-689-10834-6, Atheneum). Macmillan.

Coolant Boundary Integrity Considerations in Breeder Reactor Design, PVP-PB-027. Ed. by R. H. Mallett & B. R. Nair. (Pressure Vessel & Piping Division: Bk. No. G00135). 133p. 1978. 14.00 o.p. (ISBN 0-685-37567-6). ASME.

Coolbroth Family. G. T. Ridlon. (Saco Valley Settlements Ser). 1970. pap. 2.75 o.p. (ISBN 0-8048-0753-1). C E Tuttle.

Cooling Tower Plume Modeling & Drift Measurement: A Review of the State-of-the-Art. (ASME Pubns.: No. H00088). 170p. 1975. pap. text ed. 25.00 o.p. (ISBN 0-685-61212-0). ASME.

Cooper Industries, 1833-1983. David N. Keller. LC 83-60527. (Illus.). xii, 387p. 1983. text ed. 20.00x o.p. (ISBN 0-8214-0751-1). Ohio U Pr.

Cooper Rollow's Chicago Bears Football Book. rev. ed. Cooper Rollow. (Illus.). 224p. 1985. pap. 5.95 o.p. (ISBN 0-915463-29-6, Pub. by Jameson Bks, Dist. by Kampmann). Green Hill.

Cooperation Between the Sexes: Writings on Women, Love, Marriage & Its Disorders. Alfred Adler. LC 76-23804. 480p. 1980. Repr. of 1978 ed. 25.00x o.s.i. (ISBN 0-87668-443-6). Aronson.

Cooperation Between Types of Libraries: The Beginnings of a State Plan for Library Services in Illinois. Ed. by Cora E. Thomassen. LC 72-625423. (Allerton Park Institute Ser.: No. 15). 100p. 1969. 5.00x o.p. (ISBN 0-87845-010-6). U of Ill Lib Info Sci.

Cooperative & Non-Cooperative Many Players Differential Games. CISM (International Center for Mechanical Sciences) Dept. of Automation & Information, 1973. Ed. by G. Lietmann. (CISM International Centre for Mechanical Sciences Ser.: No. 190). (Illus.). 77p. 1974. pap. 9.20 o.p. (ISBN 0-387-81275-X). Springer-Verlag.

Cooperative Business Enterprise. M. A. Abrahamsen. 1976. text ed. 31.95 o.p. (ISBN 0-07-000151-0). McGraw.

Cooperative Hybrid Maize Tests in Europe & Mediterranean Countries: 1952. (Agricultural Development Papers: No. 42). pap. 6.00 o.p. (F105, FAO). UNIPUB.

Cooperative Learning: Student Teams. Robert E. Slavin. (What Research Says to the Teacher Ser.). 36p. 1983. 2.50 o.p. (ISBN 0-8106-1055-8). NEA.

Cooperative Movement & Some of Its Problems. P. H. Casselman. 1952. (ISBN 0-8022-0218-7). Philos Lib.

Cooperative Phenomena in Biology. Ed. by George Karreman. LC 78-16572. 1980. 74.00 o.p. (ISBN 0-08-023186-1). Pergamon.

Cooperative Programs for Transition from School to Work. Duncan Ballantyne. 141p. 1985. pap. 5.00 o.p. (ISBN 0-318-18739-6, S/N 065-000-00237-0). USGPO.

Cooperative Sports & Games Book: Challenge Without Competition. Terry Orlick. LC 77-88771. 1978. 10.00 o.p. (ISBN 0-394-42215-5); pap. 9.95 o.p. (ISBN 0-394-73494-7). Pantheon.

Cooper's Journal; or Unfettered Thinker & Plain Speaker for Truth, Freedom & Progress, Nos. 1-30. 1970. Repr. of 1850 ed. Set. lib. bdg. 26.00x o.p. (ISBN 0-8371-9155-6, CJ00). Greenwood.

Cooperstown: Where Baseball Legends Live Forever. Sporting News Editors. 1986. 12.98 o.p. (ISBN 0-517-60739-5). Crown.

Coordinate-Free Approach to Gauss-Markov Estimation. H. Drygas. LC 78-147405. (Lecture Notes in Operations Research & Mathematical Systems: Vol. 40). 1970. pap. 10.70 o.p. (ISBN 0-387-05326-3). Springer-Verlag.

Coordinated Work Measurement. B. Piercy & R. Jandrell. (Illus.). 1975. 27.50x o.p. (ISBN 0-7131-3345-7). Trans-Atl Phila.

Coordinating Australian University Development: A Study of the Australian Universities Commission, 1959-1970. A. P. Gallagher. LC 82-1973. (Scholars Library). 244p. 1983. text ed. 37.50x o.p. (ISBN 0-7022-1657-7). U of Queensland Pr.

Coordinating Community Services for the Elderly: The Triage Experience. Joan Quinn et al. 144p. 1982. 33.00 o.p. (ISBN 0-8261-3300-2). Springer Pub.

Coordination in Vocational Education Planning: Barriers & Facilitators. Harold Starr et al. 52p. 1980. 3.80 o.p. (ISBN 0-318-15435-8, RD 187). Natl Ctr Res Voc Ed.

Coordinative Interactions. Ed. by J. D. Dunitz et al. Incl. Metal Complexes of Chelating Olefin-Group V Ligands. R. J. Williams et al; Structural Radii, Electron-Cloud Radii, Ionic Radii & Solvation. E. C. Baughan; Quantitative Evaluation & Prediction of Donor-Acceptor Interactions. R. S. Drago; Redox Properties: Changes Affected by Coordination. V. Gutmann; Thermodynamics of the Stepwise Formation of Metal-Ion Complexes in Aqueous Solution. S. Ahrland. (Structure & Bonding Ser.: Vol. 15). (Illus.). 189p. 1973. pap. 40.00 o.p. (ISBN 0-387-06410-9). Springer-Verlag.

Coordinators: A New Focus in Parish Religious Education. Joseph C. Neiman. (Illus.). 328p. (Orig.). 1971. 4.80 o.p. (ISBN 0-88489-019-8). St Marys.

Coordinators of Children's & Young Adult Services in Public Library Systems Service of at Least 100,000 People. 62p. 1984. 7.50x o.p. (ISBN 0-8389-6774-4). ALA.

Cop World: Policing the Streets of San Diego. James McClure. LC 84-25431. 1985. 16.45 o.s.i. (ISBN 0-394-51007-0). Pantheon.

Copains. Jules Romains. (Coll. Soleil). 1957. 9.95 o.p. (ISBN 0-685-11106-7). Schoenhof.

Copenhagen Connection. Elizabeth Peters. 320p. 1985. pap. 3.50 o.p. (ISBN 0-931773-11-3). Critics Choice Paper.

Copenhagen Travel Guide. (Travel Guides Ser.). (Illus.). 1982. pap. 4.95 o.p. (ISBN 0-02-969070-6, Berlitz). Macmillan.

Coping: Issues of Emotional Living in an Age of Stress for Clergy & Religious. Ed. by Bernard J. Bush. LC 76-362761. 83p. 1976. pap. 2.95 o.p. (ISBN 0-89571-000-5). Affirmation.

Coping with a Miscarriage. Hank Pizer & Christine O. Palinski. LC 81-11112. (Mosby Medical Library). 192p. 1982. pap. 4.95 o.p. (ISBN 0-8016-3945-X). Mosby.

Coping with America. 2nd ed. Peter Trudgill. (Illus.). 176p. 1985. 29.95x o.p. (ISBN 0-631-14324-6). Basil Blackwell.

Coping with Anger. Paul J. Gelinas. (YA) (gr. 7-12). 1979. PLB 12.95 o.p. (ISBN 0-8239-0473-3). Rosen Group.

Coping with Being Handicapped. Gillian R. Holzhauser. 224p. 1984. 15.95 o.p. (ISBN 0-8119-0700-7). Fell.

Coping with Capitalism: The Economic Transformation of the United States 1776-1980. Roger L. Ransom. (Illus.). 224p. 1981. pap. text ed. (ISBN 0-13-172288-3). P-H.

Coping with Changing Values. Robert B. Nordberg. (Personal Adjustment Ser.). 136p. (gr. 7-12). 1983. lib. bdg. 12.95 o.p. (ISBN 0-8239-0596-9). Rosen Group.

Coping with Cliques. Shirley Schwarzrock & C. Gilbert Wrenn. (Coping with Ser.). (Illus.). 31p. (gr. 7-12). 1971. pap. text ed. 3.00 o.p. (ISBN 0-913476-30-7). Am Guidance.

Coping with Diabetes. Othniel J. Seiden. (Illus.). 96p. (Orig.). 1984. pap. 6.70 o.p. (ISBN 0-8306-1814-7, 1814). TAB Bks.

Coping with Difficult People. Robert N. Bramson. 176p. 1987. pap. 3.50 o.s.i. (ISBN 0-345-35294-7). Ballantine.

Coping with Divorce. Jim Greteman. LC 81-65334. (Illus.). 80p. 1981. spiralbound 4.95 o.p. (ISBN 0-87793-226-3). Ave Maria.

Coping with Illness. 2nd ed. Karen A. Noonan. LC 80-67825. (Practical Nursing Ser.). (Illus.). 288p. 1981. pap. text ed. 13.95 o.p. (ISBN 0-8273-1438-8); instr's. guide 5.00 o.p. (ISBN 0-8273-1922-3). Delmar.

Coping with Imprisonment. Ed. by Nicolette Parisi. (Perspectives in Criminal Justice: Vol. 3). (Illus.). 168p. 1982. 25.00 o.p. (ISBN 0-8039-1785-6); pap. 12.95 o.p. (ISBN 0-8039-1786-4). Sage.

Coping with Infertility. Judith A. Stigger. LC 82-72649. 112p. (Orig.). 1983. pap. 5.95 o.p. (ISBN 0-8066-1956-2, 10-1692, Augsburg). Augsburg Fortress.

Coping with Life after High School. Michael Dumond. (Personal Adjustment Ser.). 1983. lib. bdg. 12.95 o.p. (ISBN 0-8239-0606-X). Rosen Group.

Coping with Neurologic Disorders. Ed. by Jean Robinson & Barbara McVan. LC 81-13364. (Nursing Photobook Ser.). (Illus.). 160p. 1981. text ed. 16.95 o.p. (ISBN 0-916730-42-5). Springhouse Pub.

Coping with Neurologic Problems Proficiently. 2nd ed. Ed. by Susan Williams & Barbara McVan. LC 83-20067. (New Nursing Skillbook Ser.: Vol. 4). (Illus.). 208p. 1984. text ed. 14.95 o.p. (ISBN 0-916730-64-6). Springhouse Pub.

Coping with Special Needs: A Guide for New Teachers. Geof Sewell. 192p. (Orig.). 1986. 29.00 o.p. (ISBN 0-7099-3378-9, Pub. by Croom Helm Ltd); pap. 12.00 o.p. (ISBN 0-7099-3390-8, Pub. by Croom Helm Ltd). Routledge Chapman & Hall.

Coping with Stress. Roger Bauer. 1981. pap. 4.50 o.p. (ISBN 0-8309-0313-5). Herald Hse.

Coping with Stress: RN's Survival Sourcebook. Donnelly. 226p. 1983. pap. 18.95 o.p. (ISBN 0-87489-299-6). Med Economics.

Coping With the Corporate Jungle: Ten Keys to Success. Jacob W. Spatz. 32p. 1982. pap. text ed. 3.00 o.p. (ISBN 0-938033-03-4). Alert Pubs.

Coping with the Dating Game. rev ed. Michael Dumond. (Coping Ser.). 115p. (gr. 7-12). 1988. 12.95 o.p. (ISBN 0-8239-0806-2). Rosen Group.

Coping with Your Allergies. Natalie Golos et al. 1979. 18.25 o.p. (ISBN 0-671-24078-1). S&S.

Coping with Your Husband's Retirement. Roslyn Friedman & Annette Nussbaum. 240p. 1986. pap. 6.95 o.s.i. (ISBN 0-671-54719-4, Fireside). S&S.

Copper & Copper-Base Powder Alloys. 464p. 1976. 48.50 o.p. (ISBN 0-317-34847-7); members 39.50 o.p. (ISBN 0-317-34848-5). Metal Powder.

Copper & Its Alloys. E. G. West. (Ellis Harwood Series in Industrial Metals). 241p. 1982. 74.95 o.p. (ISBN 0-470-27533-2). Halsted Pr.

Copper & Nickel Converters: Proceedings AIME Annual Meeting, New Orleans, LA., 1979. (Illus.). 395p. 36.00 o.p. (ISBN 0-89520-137-2); members 20.00 o.p. (ISBN 0-317-34859-0); student members 11.00 o.p. (ISBN 0-317-34860-4). ASM.

Copper: Its Mining & Use by the Aborigines of the Lake Superior Region. George A. West. 1970. Repr. of 1929 ed. lib. bdg. 22.50x o.p. (ISBN 0-8371-4634-8, WECO). Greenwood.

Copper Mill Tailings, Incinerator Residue, Low-Quality Aggregate Characteristics, & Energy Savings in Construction. (Transportation Research Report Ser.). 53p. 1979. 3.40 o.p. (ISBN 0-309-02989-9). Transport Res Bd.

Copper Smelting - An Update: Proceedings AIME Annual Meeting, Dallas, TX, 1982. Ed. by David B. George & John C. Taylor. (Illus.). 345p. 30.00 o.p. (ISBN 0-89520-387-1). ASM.

Copper Spike. Lone E. Janson. LC 75-16446. (Illus.). 175p. 1975. pap. 9.95 o.s.i. (ISBN 0-88240-066-5). Alaska Northwest.

Copperbritches: Your ForeBear. Carole Marsh. (Illus.). 50p. (Orig.). 1986. pap. 9.95 o.p. (ISBN 0-935326-55-3). Gallopade Pub Group.

Cops & Dollars: The Economics of Criminal Law & Justice. Helen Reynolds. (Illus.). 280p. 1981. spiral bdg. 33.50 o.p. (ISBN 0-398-04115-6). C C Thomas.

Cops & Kidnappers. C. Monty Ritchie. LC 83-91016. 202p. 1984. 12.95 o.p. (ISBN 0-533-06009-5). Vantage.

Cops: Their Lives in Their Own Words. Mark Baker. 320p. 1985. 18.45 o.p. (ISBN 0-671-49970-X). S&S.

Copts in Egyptian Politics 1918 - 1952. Barbara L. Carter. 256p. 1985. 43.00 o.p. (ISBN 0-7099-3417-3, Pub. by Croom Helm Ltd). Routledge Chapman & Hall.

Copy, Combine, & Compose: Controlling Composition. Roseann D. Gonzalez et al. 314p. 1983. pap. text ed. (ISBN 0-534-01341-4). Wadsworth Pub.

Copycat. Barbara Samuels. 64p. (Orig.). 1982. pap. 3.95 o.p. (ISBN 0-380-57018-1, 57018-1). Avon.

Copyright & Antitrust. Joseph Taubman. (Illus.). 217p. 1960. 10.00 o.p. (ISBN 0-87945-004-5). Fed Legal Pubn.

Copyright Book: A Practical Guide. 2nd ed. William S. Strong. 224p. 1984. 14.95 o.p. (ISBN 0-262-19234-9). MIT Pr.

Copyright in Congress, Seventeen Hundred Eighty-Nine to Nineteen Hundred Four. U. S. Copyright Office. Ed. by Thorvald Solberg. LC 75-35377. (U. S. Government Documents Program Ser.). 468p. 1976. Repr. of 1905 ed. lib. bdg. 24.00x o.p. (ISBN 0-8371-8597-1, USCC). Greenwood.

Copyright Law: A Practitioners Guide. Harry G. Henn. LC 79-83833. 785p. 1988. text ed. 50.00 o.p. (ISBN 0-685-94306-2, GI-0652). PLI.

Copyright Laws & Treaties of the World. UNESCO Staff. 1984. 23 suppls. 1957-1983 595.00, o.p. (ISBN 0-686-88611-9); 1981-1983 suppl. only loose-leaf 150.00, o.p. (ISBN 0-686-88612-7). BNA.

Copyright Litigation. (Patents, Copyrights, Trademarks, & Literary Property Course Handbook Ser.: Vol. 167). 534p. 1983. 15.00 o.p. (ISBN 0-317-11427-1, G4-3732). PLI.

Copyright: Practical Guide to Microcomputer Licenses. Stephen Strauss. 135p. (Orig.). 1986. pap. 13.95x o.p. (ISBN 0-317-44658-4). Copyright Info.

Copyright Registration Forms PA & SR: How to Prepare Applications to Register Songs, Movies, Performing Arts Works & Sound Recordings with the U. S. Copyright Office. Walter E. Hurst. Ed. by Matthew Gentry. (Entertainment Industry Ser.: Vol. 16). (Orig.). 1979. 15.00 o.s.i. (ISBN 0-911370-33-1); pap. 10.00 o.s.i. (ISBN 0-911370-34-X). Seven Arts.

Coquette. Hannah W. Foster. LC 72-78707. 1797. Repr. 39.00x o.p. (ISBN 0-403-01949-4). Somerset Pub.

Cora Fry. Rosellen Brown. 1977. 9.95 o.p. (ISBN 0-393-04455-6); pap. 2.95 o.p. (ISBN 0-393-04461-0). Norton.

Cora Ravenwing. Gina Wilson. LC 79-23259. 168p. (gr. 5-9). 1980. 8.95 o.p. (ISBN 0-689-50170-6, Atheneum). Macmillan.

Cora the Crow, a Spring Story. Mirabel Cecil. LC 79-22538. (New Series of Nature Bks.). (Illus.). (gr. k-3). 1980. text ed. 3.95 o.p. (ISBN 0-07-010320-8). McGraw.

Corbaccio. Giovanni Boccaccio. Ed. & tr. by Anthony K. Cassell. LC 75-9844. (Illus.). 216p. 1975. 19.95 o.p. (ISBN 0-252-00479-5). U of Ill Pr.

Cord, Hunt the Man Down. Owen Rountree. 1984. pap. 2.25 o.s.i. (ISBN 0-345-31019-5). Ballantine.

Cord of Three Strands. Linda R. Wright. 256p. 1987. 10.95 o.p. (ISBN 0-8007-1523-3). Revell.

Cord, the Nevada War. Owen Rountree. 1982. pap. 1.95 o.s.i. (ISBN 0-345-29590-0). Ballantine.

Corded Shell: Reflections on Musical Expression. Peter Kivy. LC 80-7539. (Princeton Essays on the Arts: No. 9). 176p. 1980. 23.50x o.p. (ISBN 0-691-07258-2); pap. 6.95 o.p. (ISBN 0-691-02014-0). Princeton U Pr.

Cordelia? Garson Kanin. LC 81-71687. 1982. 13.95 o.p. (ISBN 0-87795-397-X, Arbor Hse). Morrow.

Cordial Cookery. Marjorie White. LC 82-938. (Illus.). 160p. 1982. pap. 8.95 o.p. (ISBN 0-8437-3389-6). Hammond Inc.

Cordon Ombilical. Jean Cocteau. 96p. 1962. 8.95 o.p. (ISBN 0-686-54519-2). French & Eur.

Cordon Vert: Fifty-Two Vegetarian Gourmet Dinner Party Menus. Colin Spencer. (Illus.). 208p. 1987. 17.95 o.p. (ISBN 0-8092-4728-3). Contemp Bks.

Core Concepts in Health. 4th ed. Paul M. Insel & Walton T. Roth. LC 81-84690. (Illus.). 555p. 1985. pap. text ed. 23.95 o.p. (ISBN 0-87484-675-7); avail. instructors manual o.p. (ISBN 0-87484-726-5). Mayfield Pub.

Core Curriculum. Gordon Kirk. (Changing Perspectives in Education Ser.: Vol. 1). 128p. (Orig.). 1986. pap. text ed. 14.95 o.s.i. (ISBN 0-340-39516-8). Princeton Bk Co.

Corey Lane. Norman Zollinger. LC 81-5670. (Joan Kahn Bk.). 408p. 1981. 13.95 o.p. (ISBN 0-89919-048-0). Ticknor & Fields.

Corinthians, Vol. VII. Beacon Bible Expositions Staff. 6.95 o.p. (ISBN 0-8010-0681-3). Baker Bk.

Coriolanus see also Tragedy of Coriolanus.

Coriolanus. William Shakespeare. Ed. by Louis B. Wright & Virginia A. LaMar. (Folger Lib. Ser). 352p. (gr. 12). pap. text ed. 3.95 o.p. (ISBN 0-671-49966-1). WSP.

Corispero. Alessandro Stradella. Ed. by Howard M. Brown. LC 76-20990. (Italian Opera 1640-1770 Ser.: Vol. 10). 1979. lib. bdg. 83.00 o.p. Garland Pub.

Corkscrew. Ted Wood. (Reid Bennett Mystery Ser.). 240p. 1987. 14.95 o.s.i. (ISBN 0-684-18853-8). Scribner.

Cornelius. David C. Phipps. 116p. 1984. pap. 5.95 o.p. (ISBN 0-89505-182-6). Tabor Pub.

Corneo-Plastic Surgery. Ed. by P. V. Rycroft. LC 68-58885. 1969. 160.00 o.p. (ISBN 0-08-013013-5). Pergamon.

Cornerstones Book. (Our Nations Heritage Ser.). Date not set. (ISBN 0-07-375418-8). McGraw.

Cornflakes. Lois H. Johnson. (Illus.). 64p. 1981. 6.00 o.p. (ISBN 0-682-49695-2). Exposition-Phoenix.

Cornkister Days. David K. Cameron. (Illus.). 272p. 1984. 24.95 o.p. (ISBN 0-575-03492-0, Pub. by Gollancz England). David & Charles.

Cornshuck Crafts. Marguerite C. Crawford & Marietta C. Fuller. 1967. 6.00 o.p. (ISBN 0-682-45705-1, Banner). Exposition-Phoenix.

Cornucopia. Robert Oliver. LC 77-24655. (Illus.). (gr. 4-6). 1978. 5.95 o.p. (ISBN 0-689-30626-1, Atheneum). Macmillan.

Cornwall. Rita Pope. (Visitor's Guides Ser.). (Illus.). 192p. 1986. pap. 8.95 o.p. (ISBN 0-935161-26-0). Hunter Pub NY.

Cornwall: AA-OS Leisure Guide. Date not set. (Pub. by Auto Assn England). Salem Hse Pubs.

Corona. Greg Bear. (Gregg Fiction Star Trek Ser.). 1985. lib. bdg. 11.95 o.p. (ISBN 0-8398-2889-6, Gregg). G K Hall.

Coronal Holes & High Speed Wind Streams. Ed. by Jack B. Zirker. LC 77-84528. (Skylab Solar Workshop Ser.: No. 1). (Illus.). 1977. 29.95x o.p. (ISBN 0-87081-109-6). Univ Pr Colo.

Coronary Angiography. Guillermo Pujadas. (Illus.). 1980. text ed. 45.00 o.p. (ISBN 0-07-050912-3). McGraw.

Coronary Angiography & Angina Pectoris. P. R. Lichtlen. LC 76-9263. (Illus.). 402p. 1976. 34.00 o.p. (ISBN 0-88416-086-6). Year Bk Med.

Coronary Arterial Variations in the Normal Heart & in Congenital Heart Disease. Zeev Vlodaver et al. 1975. 45.50 o.p. (ISBN 0-12-722450-5). Acad Pr.

Coronary Artery Disease: Etiology, Hemodynamic Consequences, Drug Therapy & Clinical Implications. Ed. by William P. Santamore & Alfred A. Bove. LC 81-19731. 308p. 1982. 39.50 o.p. (ISBN 0-8067-1761-0). Urban & S.

Coronary Bypass Surgery: Who Needs It? Siegfried Kra. LC 85-7093. 1986. 16.45 o.p. (ISBN 0-393-01988-8). Norton.

Coronary Care. Ed. by Joel Karliner & Gabriel Gregoratos. 1000p. 1981. text ed. 62.00 o.p. (ISBN 0-443-08061-5). Churchill.

Coronary Disease. (Landmark Ser.). 1979. 34.50x o.p. (ISBN 0-8422-4111-6). Irvington.

Coronary Heart Disease. Robert M. Davidson. (Contemporary Patient Managment Ser.: Vol. 2). 1985. text ed. 41.75 o.p. (ISBN 0-87488-874-3). Med Exam.

Coronation Street. Richard Dyer et al. (Television Monograph: No. 13). (Illus.). 108p. 1981. pap. 8.95 o.p. (ISBN 0-85170-110-8, Pub. by British Film Inst England). U of Ill Pr.

Coroner. Thomas T. Noguchi & Joseph DiMona. 1983. 15.45 o.p. (ISBN 0-671-46772-7). S&S.

Coroner at Large. Thomas T. Noguchi. 1985. 16.45 o.s.i. (ISBN 0-671-54462-4). S&S.

Coroner's Autopsy: A Guide to Non-Criminal Autopsies for the General Pathologist. Bernard Knight. LC 82-20689. (Illus.). 299p. 1983. 27.75 o.p. (ISBN 0-443-02374-3). Churchill.

Corporate Advertising: The What, the Why, & the How. Thomas Garbett. (Illus.). 224p. 1981. text ed. 41.50 o.p. (ISBN 0-07-022787-X). McGraw.

Corporate America: A Historical Bibliography. LC 83-11232. (ABC-Clio Research Guides Ser.: No. 5). 341p. 1984. lib. bdg. 34.00 o.p. (ISBN 0-87436-362-4). ABC-Clio.

Corporate & Industrial Security. A. Lewis Russell. LC 80-15789. 276p. 1980. 21.00x o.p. (ISBN 0-87201-796-6). Gulf Pub.

Corporate & Personal Taxation in the Arab World: 1978. Arab World & Iran Business Guides. 1978. pap. 12.50 o.p. (ISBN 0-931000-05-X). Suburban Pub CT.

Corporate Anti-Takeover Defenses: The Posion Pill Device. Paul W. Richter. 1987. pap. 3.00 o.p. (ISBN 0-87632-540-1). Clark Boardman.

Corporate Aviation. R. J. Whempner. 1982. text ed. 26.95 o.p. (ISBN 0-07-069529-6). McGraw.

Corporate Bestiary. William G. Zikmund. (Illus.). 1985. pap. 4.95 o.p. (ISBN 0-03-002998-8, Owl Bks). H Holt & Co.

Corporate Bond Financing. Ray Garrett & Thomas Arthur. (Corporate Practice Ser.: No. 13). 1979. 92.00 o.p. (ISBN 0-317-55270-8). BNA.

Corporate Cash Management Including Electronic Funds Transfer. Alfred L. Hunt. LC 78-16648. 1978. 19.95 o.p. (ISBN 0-8144-5464-X). AMACOM.

Corporate Cash Management: Techniques & Analysis. Ed. by Frank Fabozzi & Leslie N. Masonson. LC 84-71295. 385p. 1984. 55.00 o.p. (ISBN 0-87094-477-0). Dow Jones-Irwin.

Corporate Collections in Montgomery. Ed. by Diane J. Gingold. LC 76-15913. (Illus.). 1976. pap. 3.00 o.p. (ISBN 0-89280-002-X). Montgomery Mus.

Corporate Counsel Law Institute. 139p. 1983. 7.50 o.p. (ISBN 0-318-02385-7). ICLE Georgia.

Corporate Counsellor's Desk Book. Ed. by Dennis J. Block et al. 297p. 1982. 50.00 o.p. (ISBN 0-15-100015-8, H42817, Pub. by Law & Business). HarBraceJ.

Corporate Couple: Living the Corporate Game. Peggy Berry. 320p. 1985. 16.95 o.p. (ISBN 0-531-09592-4). Watts.

Corporate Crime in the Pharmaceutical Industry. John Braithwaite. 500p. 1986. pap. 14.95 o.p. (ISBN 0-7102-0860-X). Routledge Chapman & Hall.

Corporate Director. Little Inc. et al. LC 75-4838. 160p. 1983. 22.95 o.p. (ISBN 0-8436-0739-4). Van Nos Reinhold.

Corporate Divestment. Gordon Bing. LC 77-86528. 166p. 1978. 25.00x o.p. (ISBN 0-87201-141-0). Gulf Pub.

Corporate Finance. Ross & Westerfield. (Illus.). 864p. 1987. text ed. 45.95 o.p. (ISBN 0-8016-4211-6). Mosby.

Corporate Finance Bluebook. National Register Publishing Co. Staff. LC 85-642719. 1987. 350.00 o.p. (ISBN 0-87217-932-X). Natl Register.

Corporate Finance, Cases & Materials: 1984 Supplement. 2nd ed. Victor Brudney & Marvin A. Chirelstein. (University Casebook Ser.). 235p. 1984. pap. text ed. 5.95 o.p. (ISBN 0-88277-202-3). Foundation Pr.

Corporate Finance Law: A Guide for the Executive. Bruce Wasserstein. 1978. text ed. 38.50 o.p. (ISBN 0-07-068423-5). McGraw.

Corporate Finance Sourcebook. National Register Publishing Co. Staff. LC 86-642719. 1987. 269.00 o.p. (ISBN 0-87217-925-7). Natl Register.

Corporate Financial Analysis. Harrington & Wilson. 1983. pap. 17.95 o.p. (ISBN 0-256-02931-8). Irwin.

Corporate Financial Analysis. 2nd ed. Harrington & Wilson. 1986. 18.95 o.p. (ISBN 0-256-03413-3). Irwin.

Corporate Foundation Profiles. 4th ed. LC 80-69622. 593p. 1985. pap. 55.00 o.p. (ISBN 0-87954-135-0). Foundation Ctr.

Corporate Giving: Policy & Practice. Frank Koch. (President's Association Special Studies: No. 67). 1978. 20.00 o.p. (ISBN 0-8144-4067-3). AMACOM.

Corporate Governance & Institutional Ethics. Ed. by Michael W. Hoffman et al. LC 84-47818. 336p. 1984. 38.00 o.p. (ISBN 0-669-08259-7). Lexington Bks.

Corporate Human Resource Development. Leonard Nadler. (American Society for Training & Development Ser.). 224p. 1980. 18.95 o.p. (ISBN 0-442-25624-8). Van Nos Reinhold.

Corporate Information Systems Management: Text & Cases. James I. Cash, Jr. et al. 1983. text ed. 39.95x o.p. (ISBN 0-256-02912-1). Irwin.

Corporate Information Systems Management: The Issues Facing Senior Executives. F. Warren McFarlan & James L. McKenney. LC 82-73926. 180p. 1982. 29.95 o.p. (ISBN 0-87094-347-2). Dow Jones-Irwin.

Corporate Insolvency. P. Totty & M. Crystal. 1983. text ed. 24.95 o.p. (ISBN 0-07-084582-4). McGraw.

Corporate Manager's Guide to Better Communication. W. Charles Redding. (PROCOM Ser.). 176p. 1984. pap. 9.95 o.p. (ISBN 0-673-15564-1). Scott F.

Corporate, Partnership, Estate & Gift Taxation, 1988. James W. Pratt et al. 1988. 41.95 o.p. (ISBN 0-256-06470-9). Irwin.

Corporate, Partnership, Estate & Gift Taxation, 1989 Edition. James Pratt et al. 1988. 46.00 o.p. (ISBN 0-256-06730-9); study guide 13.50 o.p. Irwin.

Corporate Personality in Ancient Israel. H. Wheeler Robinson. LC 79-8887. 64p. 1980. pap. 2.95 o.p. (ISBN 0-8006-1380-5, 1-1380, Fortress). Augsburg Fortress.

Corporate Planning & Procurement. Ed. by David H. Farmer & Bernard Taylor. LC 74-19369. 272p. 1975. 21.50 o.p. (ISBN 0-470-25499-8). Krieger.

Corporate Planning: Techniques & Applications. Malcom W. Pennington & Robert J. Allio. LC 78-25803. (Illus.). 1979. 26.95 o.p. (ISBN 0-8144-5497-6). AMACOM.

Corporate Policy: A Casebook. Jules J. Schwartz. (Illus.). 1978. text ed. (ISBN 0-13-174813-0). P-H.

Corporate Promotables. Sexton Adams & Don Fyffe. LC 76-101144. 212p. 1969. 19.00x o.p. (ISBN 0-87201-150-X). Gulf Pub.

Corporate Reader: Work & Family Life in the 1980's. Children's Defense Fund Staff. LC 83-70745. 160p. 1983. pap. 7.50 o.s.i. (ISBN 0-938008-04-8). Children's Defense.

Corporate Secretary's Complete Forms Handbook. Miklos Nicholson. 864p. 1980. text ed. 79.00 o.p. (ISBN 0-13-175448-3). P-H.

Corporate Showcase Five: Illustration, Photography & Graphic Design. Compiled by American Showcase Staff, Inc. Staff. (Illus.). 303p. 1986. 32.50 o.p. (ISBN 0-8230-0950-5). Watson-Guptill.

Corporate Showcase 7. Date not set. price not set o.p. Am Showcase.

Corporate Social Responsibility: Contemporary Viewpoints. Suzanne R. Ontiveros. LC 86-3416. (Dynamic Orgnization Ser.). 229p. 1986. lib. bdg. 39.00 o.p. (ISBN 0-87436-469-8). ABC-Clio.

Corporate Strategic Planning: The Political Dimension. Dan Haendel. (Washington Papers: Vol. IX, No. 86). 88p. (Orig.). 1981. pap. text ed. 7.95 o.p. (ISBN 0-8191-6030-X, Pub. by CSIS). U Pr of Amer.

Corporate Tax Caper. William C. Marks. 80p. 1981. 5.50 o.p. (ISBN 0-682-49788-6). Exposition-Phoenix.

Corporate TrendTrac: Issues 7-88 Through 6-89. Ed. by A. Dale Timpe. 200p. 1988. pap. 174.00x o.p. (ISBN 0-8103-4257-X). Gale.

Corporate Tuition Aid Programs: A Directory of College Financial Aid for Employees at America's Largest Corporations. Joseph P. O'Neill. 200p. (Orig.). 1985. pap. 12.95 o.s.i. (ISBN 0-87866-338-X). Petersons Guides.

Corporate Turnaround: How Managers Turn Losers into Winners. Donald Bibeault. 416p. 1982. text ed. 39.95 o.p. (ISBN 0-07-005190-9). McGraw.

Corporate Use of Research Libraries. Systems & Procedures Exchange Center Staff. (SPEC Kit & Flyer Ser.: No. 88). 101p. 1982. 20.00 o.p. (ISBN 0-318-03467-0). Assn Res Lib.

Corporate Warriors. Douglas K. Ramsey. 256p. 1987. 17.45 o.s.i. (ISBN 0-395-35487-0). HM.

Corporate Wives Corporate Casualties: Why Women are Challenging American Business. Robert Seidenberg. LC 73-77954. 192p. 1980. pap. 5.95 o.p. (ISBN 0-8144-7525-6). Amacom.

Corporation As a Creative Environment. Don Fabun. 1972. pap. text ed. write for info. o.p. (ISBN 0-02-475240-1, 47524). Macmillan.

Corporation Ethics: The Quest for Moral Authority. rev. ed. Ed. by George W. Forell & William H. Lazareth. LC 79-8899. (Justice Bks.). 1980. pap. 1.50 o.p. (ISBN 0-8006-1556-5, 1-1556, Fortress). Augsburg Fortress.

Corporation in Modern Society. Ed. by Edward S. Mason. LC 60-5392. 1966. pap. text ed. 4.95x o.s.i. (ISBN 0-689-70136-5, 86, Atheneum). Macmillan.

Corporation Income Tax in India. V. G. Rao. 240p. 1980. text ed. 15.00x o.p. (ISBN 0-391-02133-8). Humanities.

Corporation Tax U. K. Rankin. 1985. pap. 30.95 o.p. (ISBN 0-85258-242-0). Van Nos Reinhold.

Corporations. Robert W. Hamilton. LC 82-1893. (Black Letter Ser.). 415p. 1982. pap. text ed. 14.95 o.p. (ISBN 0-314-65091-1). West Pub.

Corporations & the Environment: How Should Decisions Be Made? Committee for Corporate Responsibility, Stanford University. LC 81-9761. 136p. 1981. 14.95 o.p. (ISBN 0-86576-020-9); pap. 8.95 o.p. (ISBN 0-86576-019-5). W Kaufmann.

Corporations & the First Amendment. Herbert Schmertz. LC 78-26099. 1978. pap. 10.00 o.p. (ISBN 0-8144-2230-6). AMACOM.

Corporations As Criminals. Ellen Hochstedler & Academy of Criminal Justice Sciences Staff. LC 83-19093. (Perspectives in Criminal Justice Ser.: No. 6). 1984. 25.00 o.p. (ISBN 0-8039-2158-6); pap. 12.95 o.p. (ISBN 0-8039-2159-4). Sage.

Corporations, Cases & Materials on: 1986 Supplement. 5th ed. William L. Cary & Melvin Eisenberg. (University Casebook Ser.). 398p. 1986. 10.95 o.p. (ISBN 0-88277-347-X). Foundation Pr.

Corporations Formation with Forms: Missouri. Bowman & McQueen. 34.95 o.p. Lawyers Co-Op.

Corporations: Including Partnership & Limited Partnerships-Cases & Materials, 2nd ed. 1985 Supplement. 2nd ed. Robert W. Hamilton. (American Casebook Ser.). 142p. 1985. pap. text ed. 6.95 o.p. (ISBN 0-314-90414-X). West Pub.

Corporations Law & Policy. Lewis D. Solomon et al. LC 82-11128. (American Casebook Ser.). 1161p. 1982. text ed. 34.95 o.p. (ISBN 0-314-65583-2); tchr's. manual avail. o.p. (ISBN 0-314-71638-6). West Pub.

Corporations-Law & Policy Materials & Problems 1984: Supplement to Solomon, Stevenson & Schwartz's. Lewis D. Solomon et al. (American Casebook Ser.). 213p. 1984. pap. 7.95 o.p. (ISBN 0-314-86344-3). West Pub.

Corpse & Mirror. John Yau. LC 82-15544. (National Poetry Ser.). 96p. 1983. pap. 7.95 o.p. (ISBN 0-03-063041-X). H Holt & Co.

Corpse Cargo. Grant Stockbridge. (Spider Ser.: No. 2). 192p. 1984. pap. 2.95 o.p. (ISBN 0-89300-010-8). Blazing Pubns.

Corpse for a Candidate. Michael Geller. (Bud Dugan Ser.: No. 2). 1980. pap. text ed. 1.75 o.p. (ISBN 0-505-51478-8, Pub. by Tower Bks). Dorchester Pub Co.

Corpse in a Gilded Cage. Robert Barnard. (Nightingale Paperbacks Ser.). 1985. pap. 10.95 o.p. (ISBN 0-8161-3874-5, Large Print Bks). G K Hall.

Corpse on the Dike. Janwillem Van de Wetering. 1976. 6.95 o.p. (ISBN 0-395-24675-X). HM.

Corpus of Joe Bailey. Oakley Hall. LC 52-14032. (Library of Contemprary Americana). 480p. 1984. pap. 8.95 o.p. (ISBN 0-87795-653-7, Arbor Hse). Morrow.

Corpuscles: Atlas of Red Blood Cell Shapes. M. Bessis. LC 73-77351. (Illus.). xvi, 140p. 1974. 56.00 o.p. (ISBN 0-387-06375-7). Springer-Verlag.

Corragio Chiesa! see Courage, Church! Essays in Ecclesial Spirituality.

Correct Language, Tojolabal: A Grammar with Ethnographic Notes. Louanna Furbee-Losee. LC 75-25115. (American Indian Linguistics Ser.). 1976. lib. bdg. 51.00 o.p. (ISBN 0-8240-1966-0). Garland Pub.

Correct Sadist. Terence Sellers. LC 84-180950. 180p. 1985. pap. 6.95 o.s.i. (ISBN 0-394-62016-X, E-982, Ever). Grove.

Correct Writing, Form Two. 2nd ed. Eugenia Butler et al. 1978. pap. text ed. 15.00 o.p. (ISBN 0-669-01627-6); answer key 1.95 o.p. (ISBN 0-669-01629-2). Heath.

Correction. Thomas Bernhard. LC 83-48034. (Library of Contemporary World Literature). 288p. 1983. pap. 7.95 o.p. (ISBN 0-394-72210-8, Vin). Random.

Correctional Law: An Updated Bibliography of Selected Books & Articles. Rev. ed. American Correctional Association Staff. 44p. 1987. pap. 10.00 o.p. (ISBN 0-942974-15-8). Am Correctional.

Correctional Management. American Correctional Association Staff. (Series 1: No. 2). 40p. (Orig.). 1981. pap. 5.00 o.p. (ISBN 0-686-37661-7). Am Correctional.

Correctional Psychology. R. M. Lindner. (ISBN 0-8022-0976-9). Philos Lib.

Correctional Standards Supplement. 89p. 1986. pap. 12.50 o.p. (ISBN 0-942974-72-7). Am Correctional.

Corrections & Additions to the Dictionary of National Biography Cumulated from the Bulletin of the Institute of Historical Research Covering the Years 1923-1963. University of London, Institute of Historical Research Staff. 1970. lib. bdg. 79.00 o.p. (ISBN 0-8161-0723-8, Hall Library). G K Hall.

Corrections & Public Awareness. American Correctional Association Staff. (Series 2: No. 1). 25p. (Orig.). 1981. pap. 3.50 o.p. (ISBN 0-942974-22-0). Am Correctional.

Corrections at the Crossroads: Designing Policy. Ed. by Sherwood E. Zimmerman & Harold D. Miller. LC 80-28847. (Perspectives in Criminal Justice Ser.: Vol. 1). 176p. 1981. 25.00 o.p. (ISBN 0-8039-1579-9); pap. 12.95 o.p. (ISBN 0-8039-1580-2). Sage.

Corrections: Organization & Administration. Henry Burns. (Criminal Justice Ser.). 1975. text ed. 33.50 o.p. (ISBN 0-314-28369-2); instr's. manual avail. o.p. West Pub.

Corrections: Problems & Prospects. 2nd ed. David M. Peterson & Charles W. Thomas. (Criminal Justice Ser.). 1980. pap. text ed. 36.00 o.p. (ISBN 0-13-178350-5). P-H.

Corrective & Remedial Teaching. 3rd ed. Wayne Otto & Richard J. Smith. LC 79-89740. (Illus.). 1980. text ed. 28.95 o.p. (ISBN 0-395-28355-8). HM.

Corrective & Remedial Teaching. 2nd ed. Wayne Otto et al. LC 72-4799. 500p. 1973. text ed. 16.95 o.p. (ISBN 0-395-12662-2, 3-42395). HM.

Correlation Tables for the Structural Determination of Organic Compounds by Ultraviolet Light Absorptiometry. M. Pestemer. 163p. 1975. 57.70x o.p. (ISBN 3-527-25531-1). VCH Pubs.

Correlations & Entropy in Classical Statistical Mechanics. J. Yvon. 1969. 42.00 o.p. (ISBN 0-08-012755-X). Pergamon.

Correlative Neuroradiology: Intracranial Radiographic Analysis with Computed Tomography, Angiography & Magnetic Resonance Imaging. 2nd ed. Ronald G. Quisling & Preston R. Lotz. LC 84-20896. 422p. 1985. pap. 68.00 o.p. (ISBN 0-471-89587-3). Wiley.

Correlative Physiology of the Nervous System. H. J. Campbell. 1966. 48.00 o.p. (ISBN 0-12-157650-7). Acad Pr.

Correspondance avec Zulma Carraud. Honore De Balzac. 312p. 1951. 9.95 o.p. (ISBN 0-686-53860-9). French & Eur.

Correspondance 1786-1830. Benjamin Constant & R. de Constant. 8.95 o.p. (ISBN 0-686-54606-7). French & Eur.

Correspondance 1818-1822. Benjamin Constant & Charles L. Goyet de la Sarthe. 1973. 75.00 o.p. (ISBN 0-686-54607-5). French & Eur.

Correspondence, 3 vols. Thomas Gray. Repr. of 1935 ed. 75.00 o.p. (ISBN 0-403-04017-5). Somerset Pub.

Correspondence see Doctors' Administrative Program.

Correspondence of Boris Pasternak & Olga Freidenberg: Russian Edition. Ed. by Elliot Mossman. LC 79-3852. (Illus.). 464p. 1981. pap. 15.00 o.p. (ISBN 0-15-622598-0, Harv). HarBraceJ.

Correspondence of Boris Pasternak & Olga Friedenberg, 1910-1954. Compiled by Elliot Mossman. Tr. by Margaret Wettlin. (Helen & Kurt Wolff Bk.). (Illus.). 416p. 1982. 19.95 o.p. (ISBN 0-15-122630-X). HarBraceJ.

Correspondence of Henry Oldenburg, 2 Vols, Vol. 12 & 13. Ed. by A. Hall & M. B. Hall. 1986. 81.00 ea. o.p. Vol. 12, The Correspondence of Henry Oldenburg between October 1675 & July 1676. Vol. 13, Contains Essential Additions & Corrections to Earlier Volumes. Taylor & Francis.

Correspondence of Henry Oldenburg: May 1674 - Sept. 1675, Vol. 11. A. Rupert Hall & Marie B. Hall. 567p. 1977. 64.00x o.p. (ISBN 0-7201-0630-3). Mansell.

Correspondence of John Adams & Thomas Jefferson. John Adams. LC 25-20253. Repr. of 1925 ed. 30.00 o.p. (ISBN 0-527-00460-X). Kraus Repr.

Correspondence of Pope Gregory VII. Pope Gregory Seventh. Tr. by E. Emerton. (Columbia University Records of Civilization Ser.). 1969. pap. 5.95x o.p. (ISBN 0-393-09859-1). Norton.

Corresponding English & Chinese Proverbs & Phrases. John D. Chinnery & Cui Mingqui. 258p. 1984. pap. 4.95 o.p. (ISBN 0-8351-0951-8). China Bks.

Corrigan. Cameron Judd. 1980. pap. 1.75 o.p. (ISBN 0-8439-0853-X, Pub. by Leisure Bks CT). Dorchester Pub Co.

Corroboree. Graham Masterton. LC 85-21813. 510p. 1986. 17.95 o.p. (ISBN 0-688-04974-5). Morrow.

Corrosion & Corrosion Protection: Six Reports. (Transportation Research Report Ser.). 50p. 1974. 2.20 o.p. (ISBN 0-309-02290-8). Transport Res Bd.

Corrosion, Concrete Quality Control & Paint Beads: Eleven Reports. (Transportation Research Report Ser.). 112p. 1975. 4.80 o.p. (ISBN 0-309-02390-4). Transport Res Bd.

Corrosion Data Survey - Metals Section. 6th ed. 283p. 160.00 o.p. Natl Corrosion Eng.

Corrosion-Erosion Behavior of Materials: Proceedings TMS-AIME Fall Meeting, St. Louis, MO., 1978. (Illus.). 314p. 32.00 o.p. ASM.

Corrosion Inhibitors: Developments since 1980. Ed. by M. J. Collie. LC 83-13055. (Chemical Technology Review No. 223). 379p. 1984. 48.00 o.p. (ISBN 0-8155-0957-X). Noyes.

Corrosion of Metal Processed by Directed Energy Beams: Proceedings TMS-AIME Fall Meeting, Louisville, KY, 1981. Ed. by C. R. Clayton & C. M. Preece. (Illus.). 163p. 36.00 o.p. student 12.00 o.p. (ISBN 0-317-36301-8). ASM.

Corrosion of Metals in Concrete. T. Rose & R. Rider. (Technical Report Ser.: No. 58). 142p. 1977. 2.00 o.p. (ISBN 0-938412-28-0, P629). Sea Grant Pubns.

Corrosion of Reactor Materials, 2 Vols. (Proceedings Ser.). 1962. Vol. 1. pap. 16.50 o.p. (ISBN 92-0-050562-7, ISP59-1, IAEA); Vol. 2. pap. 18.00 o.p. (ISBN 92-0-050662-3, ISP59-2). UNIPUB.

Corrosion of Steel & Aluminum Scuba Tanks. F. C. Cichy & H. V. Schenck. (Technical Report Ser.: No. 62). 769p. 1978. 3.50 o.p. (ISBN 0-938412-05-1, P769). Sea Grant Pubns.

Corsican. Bill S. Ballinger. 356p. 1986. pap. 3.95 o.p. (ISBN 0-931773-61-X). Critics Choice Paper.

Corsican. William Heffernan. 448p. 1983. 16.50 o.p. (ISBN 0-671-44909-5). S&S.

Cortes Letter. Michael Gillette. 240p. 1983. pap. 2.75 o.p. (ISBN 0-380-83881-8, 83881-8). Avon.

Cortez & Montezuma. Maurice Collis. 1978. pap. 3.95 o.p. (ISBN 0-380-40402-8, 60178-8, Discus). Avon.

Cortical Projections of the Medial Geniculate Body in the Cat. A. Sousa-Pinto. LC 73-13493. (Advances in Anatomy, Embryology & Cell Biology: Vol. 48, Pt. 2). (Illus.). 1973. pap. 18.90 o.p. (ISBN 0-387-06477-X). Springer-Verlag.

Corticospinal Neurones: Their Role in Movement. Ed. by C. G. Phillips. (Monographs of the Physiological Society). 1978. 99.00 o.p. (ISBN 0-12-553950-9). Acad Pr.

Cortisone. Edward C. Kendall. LC 72-123853. 1971. 7.95 o.s.i. (ISBN 0-684-31062-7, ScribT). Scribner.

Corvair Owners Handbook of Maintenance & Repair: 1960-1965. Ed. by Clymer Publications. (Illus.). pap. 7.95 o.p. (ISBN 0-89287-246-2, A140). Clymer Pub.

Corvette, 1953 to 1962. LC 70-154690. (Illus.). 144p. 1976. pap. 13.95 o.p. (ISBN 0-8019-6576-4). Chilton.

Corvette, 1955-62: Complete Owner's Handbook. Clymer Publications Staff. (Illus.). pap. 7.95 o.p. (ISBN 0-89287-247-0, A141). Clymer Pub.

Corvettes for the Road. Ed. by Henry Rasmussen. LC 84-11497. (Survivors Ser.). (Illus.). 128p. 12.98 o.p. (ISBN 0-87938-182-5). Motorbooks Intl.

Corwin & Peltason's Understanding the Constitution. 9th ed. J. W. Peltason. 1982. pap. text ed. 18.95 o.p. (ISBN 0-03-060126-6). HR&W.

Cosby Wit: His Life & Humor. Bill Adler. (Illus.). 1986. 10.95 o.p. (ISBN 0-88184-299-0). Carroll & Graf.

Coshiri. Marjorie Watson. (Illus.). 16p. (gr. k-4). 1980. pap. text ed. 4.45 o.p. CEF Press.

Cosima Wagner's Diaries: 1869 to 1877, Vol. 1. Cosima Wagner. Ed. by Martin Gregor-Dellin & Dietrich Mack. Tr. by Geoffrey Skelton. LC 78-53919. (Helen & Kurt Wolff Bks.). 1978. 29.95 o.p. (ISBN 0-15-122635-0). HarBraceJ.

Cosima Wagner's Diaries: 1878 to 1883, Vol. 2. Cosima Wagner. Tr. by Geoffrey Skelton. LC 78-53919. (Helen & Kurt Wolff Bk.). (Illus.). 1216p. 1980. Repr. of 1977 ed. 35.00 o.s.i. (ISBN 0-15-122636-9). HarBraceJ.

Cosmep. Frwd. by James A. Michener. 200p. 7.95 o.p. (ISBN 0-317-43321-0); microfiche 11.95 o.p. (ISBN 0-317-43322-9). COSMEP.

Cosmetology: The Keystone Guide to Beauty Culture. rev. ed. Anthony B. Colletti. 1981. text ed. 10.00 o.p. (1248-00); pap. text ed. 7.14 o.p. (ISBN 0-912126-60-4, 1249-00). Keystone Pubns.

Cosmic Carnival of Stanislaw Lem: An Anthology of Entertaining Stories by the Modern Master of Science Fiction. Stanislaw Lem. Ed. by Michael Kandel. 256p. (Orig.). 1981. pap. 7.95 o.p. (ISBN 0-8264-0043-4). Continuum.

Cosmic Christ. Holmes Rolston, 3rd. (gr. 11-12). 1967. pap. 1.25 o.p. (ISBN 0-8042-9375-9, John Knox). Westminster John Knox.

Cosmic Christmas. Ken Sobol. (gr. k). 1979. pap. 2.95 o.p. (ISBN 0-380-45930-2, 45930-2, Camelot). Avon.

Cosmic Code: Quantum Physics As the Law of Nature. Heinz Pagels. 1982. 16.95 o.p. (ISBN 0-671-24802-2). S&S.

Cosmic Dawn: The Origins of Matter & Life. Eric Chaisson. (Illus.). 320p. 1981. 18.45i o.p. (ISBN 0-316-13590-9, An Atlantic Little, Brown Book). Little.

Cosmic Evolution: An Indroduction to Astronomy. George Field et al. LC 77-76420. (Illus.). 1978. text ed. 24.50 o.p. (ISBN 0-395-25321-7). HM.

Cosmic History of the Biogenic Elements & Compounds. John A. Wood & Sherwood Chang. (NASA SP Ser.: No. 476). (Illus.). 88p. 1985. pap. 3.50 o.p. (ISBN 0-318-22333-3, S/N 033-000-00948-8). USGPO.

Cosmic Joy & Local Pain: Musings of a Mystic Scientist. Harold J. Morowitz. 1987. 18.95 o.p. (ISBN 0-684-18443-5). Scribner.

Cosmic Rays. Arnold W. Wolfendale. 192p. 1962. (ISBN 0-8022-1918-7). Philos Lib.

Cosmic Rays in the Heliosphere. Ed. by A. J. Somogyi. (Advances in Space Research: Vol. 1, No. 3). (Illus.). 177p. 1981. pap. 25.00 o.p. (ISBN 0-08-027159-6). Pergamon.

Cosmic Rays, Solar Particles & Space Research. Ed. by B. Peters. (Italian Physical Society: Vol. 19). 1964. 77.00 o.p. (ISBN 0-12-368819-1). Acad Pr.

Cosmic Science of the Ancient Masters. 2nd ed. Hilton Hotema. 32p. 1960. pap. 8.95 o.s.i. (ISBN 0-88697-031-8). Life Science.

Cosmic Society: Essays on the Social Concepts of Prout. 2nd ed. Shyam Sundar. 55p. 1981. pap. 2.75 o.s.i. (ISBN 0-686-95466-1). Ananda Marga.

Cosmic Symphony. H. R. Banderbyll. 1958. (ISBN 0-8022-1765-6). Philos Lib.

Cosmo Report: An In-Depth Landmark Work Revealing "the Sexual Behavior of 106,000 'Cosmopolitan' Readers" Linda Wolfe. LC 80-70226. 256p. 1981. 15.75 o.p. (ISBN 0-87795-315-5, Arbor Hse). Morrow.

Cosmochemistry. Ed. by F. Boschke. LC 51-5479. (Topics in Current Chemistry: Vol. 44). (Illus.). 200p. 1974. 31.00 o.p. (ISBN 0-387-06457-5). Springer-Verlag.

Cosmographia of Ptolemy. 268p. 7500.00 o.p. (ISBN 0-8115-0903-6). Kraus Repr.

Cosmography. Sebastian Munster. (Science & Medicine Ser.). 1969. Repr. of 1550 ed. lib. bdg. 200.00 o.p. (ISBN 0-306-71816-2). Da Capo.

Cosmology & Gravitation: Spin, Torsion, Rotation, & Supergravity. Ed. by Peter G. Bergmann & Venzo De Sabbath. LC 80-23742. (NATO ASI Series B, Physics: Vol. 58). 520p. 1980. 85.00x o.p. (ISBN 0-306-40478-8, Plenum Pr). Plenum Pub.

Cosmology, Fusion & Other Matters: A Memorial to George Gamow. Ed. by Frederick Reines. LC 77-159018. (Illus.). 336p. 1972. 25.00x o.p. (ISBN 0-87081-025-1). Univ Pr Colo.

Cosmology Now. Ed. by Laurie John. LC 76-15091. 1976. 10.95 o.s.i. (ISBN 0-8008-1925-X). Taplinger.

Cosmology: Theories of the Universe. Jean Charon. Tr. by Patrick Moore from Fr. LC 73-77023. (Illus., Orig.). 1970. text ed. 4.95 o.p. (ISBN 0-07-010657-6); pap. 3.95 o.p. (ISBN 0-07-010656-8). McGraw.

Cosmopolitan's Super Diets & Exercise Guide. Marcia Seligson. 1982. pap. 2.95 o.p. (ISBN 0-380-00004-0, 60111-7). Avon.

Cossack Chief. (Guild Books Classics Illustrated Ser.). (Illus.). pap. 0.59 o.p. (ISBN 0-685-74107-9, 164). Guild Bks.

Cossack Fairy Tales & Folk-Tales. Ed. by Robert N. Bain. LC 76-9882. (Children's Literature Reprint Ser.). (Illus.). (gr. 4-6). 1976. 18.75x o.p. (ISBN 0-8486-0200-5). Roth Pub Inc.

Cost Accountability for Hospital Social Work. American Hospital Association, Society for Hospital Social Work Directors. LC 80-12334. 48p. (Orig.). 1980. pap. 12.50 o.p. (ISBN 0-87258-277-9, AHA-187123). AHPI.

Cost Accounting. Black. (Plaid Ser.). 1978. pap. 10.95 o.p. (ISBN 0-256-01280-6). Dow Jones-Irwin.

Cost Accounting: A Managerial Emphasis. 5th ed. Charles T. Horngren. (Illus.). 928p. 1982. pap. text ed. 42.67 o.p. (ISBN 0-13-179671-2). P-H.

Cost Accounting: A Multidimensional Emphasis. Ahmed Belkaoui. 656p. 1983. text ed. 37.95x o.s.i. (ISBN 0-03-061121-0); solutions manual 21.95 o.s.i. (ISBN 0-03-061122-9). Dryden Pr.

Cost Accounting: Accounting Data for Management's Decisions. 2nd ed. 1974. 26.95 o.p. (ISBN 0-15-514198-8). HarbraceJ.

Cost Accounting: Accounting Data for Management's Decisions. 3rd ed. Nicholas Dopuch et al. 726p. 1982. text ed. 36.00 net o.p. (ISBN 0-15-514201-1, HC). HarBraceJ.

Cost Accounting: Accumulation, Analysis & Use. Maurice L. Hirsch, Jr. & Joseph G. Louderback. LC 81-19288. 960p. 1982. text ed. write for info. o.s.i. (ISBN 0-534-01026-1). PWS-Kent Pub.

Cost Accounting: Concepts & Techniques for Management. Larry Killough & Wayne Leininger. 334p. 1984. revised instr's. manual with test bank o.p. (ISBN 0-314-86991-3). West Pub.

Cost Accounting Concepts for Nonfinancial Executives. new ed. Joseph P. Simini. LC 76-9851. (Illus.). 176p. 1976. 12.95 o.p. (ISBN 0-8144-5421-6). AMACOM.

Cost Accounting Concepts for Nonfinancial Executives & Managers. Joseph P. Simini. 1978. pap. text ed. 3.95 o.p. (ISBN 0-07-057324-7). McGraw.

Cost Accounting Handbook for Colleges & Universities. James A. Hyatt. Ed. by David W. Jacobson. LC 82-18840. 149p. (Orig.). 1983. pap. 25.00 o.p. (ISBN 0-915164-16-7). NACUBO.

Cost Accounting: Principles & Managerial Applications. 4th ed. Gerald Crowningshield & Kenneth A. Gorman. LC 78-69551. (Illus.). 1979. text ed. 32.50 o.p. (ISBN 0-395-26797-8). HM.

Cost-Benefit Analysis: A Bibliography. Coppa & Avery Consultants Staff. (Public Administration Ser.: P 1798). 12p. 1985. 2.00 o.p. (ISBN 0-89028-628-0). Vance Biblios.

Cost-Benefit Analysis & the Adult Educator: A Literature Review. Sara Steele. 128p. 1971. 3.00 o.p. (ISBN 0-88379-002-5). A A A C E.

Cost-Benefit Analysis & Water Pollution Policy. Henry M. Peskin & Eugene P. Seskin. 370p. 1975. 16.50 o.p. (ISBN 0-87766-119-7); pap. 11.00 o.p. (ISBN 0-87766-120-0). Urban Inst.

Cost-Benefit Analysis for Collections Managers. 8p. 1979. 40.00 o.p. (ISBN 0-939050-10-2). Credit Res NYS.

Cost-Benefit Evaluation of LDC Industrial Sectors Which Have Foreign Ownership. Garry G. Pursell. (Working Paper: No. 465). 45p. 1981. pap. 3.50 o.p. (ISBN 0-686-39750-9, WP-0465). World Bank.

Cost Control & Information Systems: A Complete Guide to Effective Design & Implementation. Pravin Shah. (Illus.). 608p. 1981. text ed. 35.95 o.p. (ISBN 0-07-056369-1). McGraw.

Cost Control for Hospitality Industry. M. Coltman. 1986. pap. (ISBN 0-442-21792-7). Van Nos Reinhold.

Cost Control for the Hospitality Industry. Michael M. Coltman. 1983. 24.95 o.p. (ISBN 0-8436-2193-1). Van Nos Reinhold.

Cost Control in Design & Construction. Sol A. Ward & Thorndike Litchfield. (Illus.). 1980. text ed. 39.50 o.p. (ISBN 0-07-068139-2). McGraw.

Cost Effective Contract Food Service: An Institutional Guide. Herman Zaccarelli & Jack Ninemeier. LC 81-20566. 320p. 1982. text ed. 85.00 o.p. (ISBN 0-89443-399-7). Aspen Pub.

Cost-Effective Energy Management. Bajaj & Singh. LC 82-4243. (Illus.). 200p. 1982. 24.95 o.p. (ISBN 0-912524-22-7). Busn News.

Cost-Effective Maintenance Management: Productivity Improvement & Downtime Reduction. Frank Herbaty. LC 83-13072. 260p. 1984. 28.00 o.p. (ISBN 0-8155-0953-7). Noyes.

Cost-Effectiveness-Benefit Analysis of Postsecondary Vocational Programs. Indiana University Staff. 70p. 1979. 10.00 o.p. (ISBN 0-318-22067-9, SN23). Natl Ctr Res Voc Ed.

Cost Effectiveness in Training & Instruction. Alberto Pena & Ruth de Blick. 1980. 6.95 o.p. (ISBN 0-931816-01-7). Transaction Pubs.

Cost Factors in Dimensional Co-ordination. P. Goodacre et al. 85p. 1982. pap. 9.95 o.p. (ISBN 0-902132-66-0, NO. 6723, Pub. by E & FN Spon England). Routledge Chapman & Hall.

Cost Finding & Rate Setting for Hospitals. 103p. 1968. 9.25 o.p. (ISBN 0-686-68591-1, 1365). Healthcare Fin Man Assn.

Cost Management for Profit Centers. Carole B. Cheatham. LC 81-6944. 247p. 1981. 69.50 o.p. (ISBN 0-87624-106-2, Inst Busn Plan). P-H.

Cost of Authority: Manipulation & Freedom in the New Testament. Graham Shaw. LC 82-48545. 320p. 1983. pap. 16.95 o.p. (ISBN 0-8006-1707-X, Fortress). Augsburg Fortress.

Cost of Doing Business for the Single-Family Home Builder, 1986. 7th ed. National Association of Home Builders Staff. 74p. 1987. pap. (ISBN 0-86718-280-6). Nat Assn H Build.

Cost of Educational Media: Guidelines for Planning & Evaluation. Dean T. Jamison et al. LC 77-17782. (People & Communication Ser.: Vol. 3). 255p. 1978. 24.00 o.p. (ISBN 0-8039-0747-8); pap. 16.95 o.p. (ISBN 0-8039-0748-6). Sage.

Cost of Energy & a Clean Environment. Ed. by Russell G. Thompson et al. LC 77-71491. (Illus.). 550p. 1978. 39.00x o.p. (ISBN 0-87201-260-3). Gulf Pub.

Cost of Good Intentions: New York & the Liberal Experiment. C. R. Morris. (McGraw-Hill Paperback Ser.). 1981. pap. text ed. 6.95 o.p. (ISBN 0-07-043280-5). McGraw.

Cost of Good Intentions: New York City & the Liberal Experiment. Charles R. Morris. 1980. 14.95 o.p. (ISBN 0-393-01339-1). Norton.

Cost of Living Studies, No. 5, How Mexicans Earn & Live. University of California, Heller Committee for Research in Social Economics. 1933. pap. 9.00 o.p. (ISBN 0-685-13463-6). Johnson Repr.

Cost of Nursing Education: A Manual for Analysis of Expenditures. Ed. by Lucille Knopf. Incl. Pt. I. Method, Directions, & Examples: Baccalaureate Program. 66p. 35.00 (ISBN 0-88737-081-0, 19-1909); Pt. I. Methods, Directions, & Examples: Associate Degree Program. 74p. 35.00 (ISBN 0-88737-082-9, 19-1910); Pt. I. Method, Directions, & Examples: Diploma Program. 59p. 35.00 (ISBN 0-88737-083-7, 19-1911); Pt. II. Data-Gathering Instruments. 49p. 15.00 (ISBN 0-88737-084-5, 19-1912). 1982. Natl League Nurse.

Cost-of-Risk Survey 1985. Ed. by James D. Blinn. Michael R. Levin. (Illus.). 80p. 1986. pap. 70.00 o.s.i. (ISBN 0-937802-23-9). Risk Management.

Cost Planning of Buildings. 4th ed. Douglas J. Ferry. 258p. 1972. 29.50x o.p. (ISBN 0-258-96865-6, Pub. by Granada England). Gower Pub Co.

Cost Planning of Buildings. 4th ed. Douglas J. Ferry & Peter S. Brandon. 385p. 1980. pap. text ed. 17.00x o.p. (ISBN 0-246-11337-5, Pub. by Granada England). Gower Pub Co.

Cost Reduction & Profit Inprovement Handbook. Harry E. Figgie. LC 84-29166. 1985. 25.95 o.p. (ISBN 0-442-22584-9). Van Nos Reinhold.

Cost Reduction in Product Design. William Chow. 1978. 37.95x o.p. (ISBN 0-442-21540-1). Van Nos Reinhold.

Cost Savings in Distillation. Institution of Chemical Engineers. 1982. 46.50 o.s.i. (ISBN 0-08-028759-X). Pergamon.

Costa Blanca Travel Guide. (Travel Guides Ser.). (Illus.). 1982. pap. 4.95 o.p. (ISBN 0-02-969100-1, Berlitz). Macmillan.

Costa Mesa, California. (Panel Advisory Service Report Ser.). 48p. 1983. pap. 10.00 o.p. (ISBN 0-317-06734-6, C-25). Urban Land.

Costa Rica: Post Report. Rev ed. (State Department Publication: No. 9363). (Illus.). 20p. (Orig.). 1986. pap. 1.25 o.p. (ISBN 0-317-53839-X, S/N 044-000-02145-5). USGPO.

Costa Ricans. reference ed. Richard Biesanz et al. (Illus.). 304p. 1982. pap. text ed. (ISBN 0-13-179606-2). P-H.

Costing Matters for Managers. E. G. Wood. 199p. 1974. text ed. 29.00x o.p. (ISBN 0-220-66243-6, Pub. by Busn Bks England). Gower Pub Co.

Costing Open Learning in Further Education. Derek W. Birch & Robert E. Cuthbert. (Orig.). 1981. pap. text ed. 22.00x o.p. (ISBN 0-318-21728-7). Trans Atl Phila.

Costing Union Demands. W. D. Heisel & Gordon S. Skinner. (Public Employee Relations Library: No. 55). 73p. 1976. pap. 14.00 o.p. (ISBN 0-686-81161-5). Intl Personnel Mgmt.

Costs & Scale of Bus Services. A. A. Walters. (Working Paper: No. 325). iv, 49p. 1979. 3.50 o.p. (ISBN 0-686-36225-X, WP-0325). World Bank.

Costs of Caring: Families with Disabled Children. Sally Baldwin. (International Library of Social Policy). 224p. 1985. 34.95x o.p. (ISBN 0-7100-9882-0). Routledge Chapman & Hall.

Costs of Children. Lawrence Olson. LC 82-48173. 176p. 1982. 24.00x o.p. (ISBN 0-669-06040-2). Lexington Bks.

Costs of Contracting & the Decline of Tenancy in the South, 1930-1960. Ed. by Lee J. Alston & Stuart Bruchey. LC 84-48302. (American Economic History Ser.). 109p. 1985. lib. bdg. 25.00 o.p. (ISBN 0-8240-6650-2). Garland Pub.
Costs of Financing of Adult Education & Training. Richard E. Anderson & Elizabeth Kasl. LC 81-47276. (Illus.). 352p. 1982. 35.00x o.p. (ISBN 0-669-04570-5). Lexington Bks.
Costs of the Common Agricultural Policy. Allan Buckwell et al. 208p. 1982. 28.50 o.p. (ISBN 0-7099-0671-4, Pub. by Croom Helm Ltd). Routledge Chapman & Hall.
Costs, Returns & Repayment Experience of Ujamaa Villages in Tanzania, 1973-1976. Jean M. Due. LC 80-490. 167p. 1980. text ed. 26.25 o.p. (ISBN 0-8191-1019-1); pap. text ed. 12.00 o.p. (ISBN 0-8191-1020-5). U Pr of Amer.
Costume of the Classical World. Marion Sichel. (Illus.). 72p. 1980. 22.95 o.s.i. (ISBN 0-7134-1511-8, Pub. by Batsford England). David & Charles.
Costume Party. W. B. Park. LC 83-8000. (Illus.). 32p. (gr. 1-3). 1983. PLB 10.45i o.p. (ISBN 0-316-69077-5). Little.
Costume Patterns & Designs. Max Tilke. (Illus.). 240p. 1986. 70.00 o.p. (ISBN 0-302-00266-9, Pub. by Zwemmer Bks UK). Sotheby Pubns.
Costume Reference, No. 1: Roman Britain & the Middle Ages. Marion Sichel. (Costume Reference Ser.). (Illus.). 72p. 1977. 12.00 o.p. (ISBN 0-8238-0211-6). Plays.
Costume Reference, No. 4: The Eighteenth Century. Marion Sichel. (Costume Reference Ser.). (Illus.). 1977. 12.00 o.p. (ISBN 0-8238-0216-7). Plays.
Costume Reference, No. 6: The Victorians. Marion Sichel. (Costume Reference Ser). (Illus.). 1978. 12.00 o.p. (ISBN 0-8238-0218-3). Plays.
Costume Through the Ages. Ed. by James Laver. (Orig.). (YA) (gr. 7-12). 1967. pap. 8.50 o.p. (ISBN 0-671-16521-6, Touchstone Bks). S&S.
Costumes for Nursery Tale Characters. Jean Greenhowe. LC 75-23444. (Illus.). 87p. 1976. 10.95 o.p. (ISBN 0-8238-0199-3). Plays.
Costumes for Plays & Playing. Gail E. Haley. LC 78-16155. (Illus.). (gr. 3 up). 1978. 9.95 o.p. (ISBN 0-416-30581-4, NO.0063). Routledge Chapman & Hall.
Cote de Guermantes: A la Recherche Du Temps Perdu. Avec: Sodome et Gomorrhe, Vol. 4. Marcel Proust. 504p. 1969. 52.50 o.p. (ISBN 0-686-54654-7). Schoenhof.
Coterminal Characteristics of Political Units & Economic Regions in China. Robert F. Dernberger & Robert M. Hartwell. xi, 199p. 1983. pap. 10.00 o.p. (ISBN 0-89264-054-5). U of Mich Ctr Chinese.
Cotswolds. (AA Ordinance Survey Leisure Guides Ser.). (Illus.). 120p. 1986. pap. 18.95 o.p. (ISBN 0-86145-349-2, Pub. by Automobile Assn Brit); 22.95 o.p. (ISBN 0-86145-270-4, Pub. by Automobile Assn Brit). Salem Hse Pubs.
Cotswolds. Richard Sale. (Vistor's Guides Ser.). (Illus.). 192p. (Orig.). 1986. pap. 8.95 o.p. (ISBN 0-935161-62-7). Hunter Pub NY.
Cottage Industries & Handicrafts: Some Guidelines for Employment Promotion. M. Allal & E. Chuta. 202p. 1984. 14.00 o.p. (ISBN 92-2-103029-6). Intl Labour Office.
Cotton Is King & Pro-Slavery Arguments. Ed. by E. N. Elliott. LC 68-55884. 1969. Repr. of 1850 ed. lib. bdg. 35.00x o.p. (ISBN 0-8371-4847-2, ELC/, Pub. by Negro U Pr). Greenwood.
Cotton Manufacture of Great Britain Systematically Investigated, 2 Vols. Andrew Ure. LC 73-136749. Repr. of 1836 ed. Set. 80.00 o.p. (ISBN 0-384-63350-1). Johnson Repr.
Cotton Patch Version of Hebrews & the General Epistles. Clarence Jordan. LC 73-14856. (Cotton Patch Translations of the Bible Ser.). 1973. pap. 4.95 o.s.i. (ISBN 0-8329-1879-2, Assn Pr). New Century.
Cotton Patch Version of Luke & Acts. Clarence Jordan. LC 69-18840. 1969. pap. 4.95 o.s.i. (ISBN 0-8329-1173-9, Assn Pr). New Century.
Cotton Patch Version of Matthew & John. Clarence Jordan. LC 83-61334. 1970. pap. 4.95 o.s.i. (ISBN 0-8329-1062-7, Assn Pr). New Century.
Cotton Patch Version of Paul's Epistles. Clarence Jordan. LC 68-11487. 1968. pap. 4.95 o.s.i. (ISBN 0-8329-1041-4, Assn Pr). New Century.
Cotton Planter's Manual. J. A. Turner. LC 74-90138. 1970. Repr. of 1857 ed. 35.00x o.p. (ISBN 0-8371-1996-0, TUC&, Pub. by Negro U Pr). Greenwood.
Couch Potato Guide to Life. Jack Mingo et al. 112p. 1985. pap. 4.95 o.p. (ISBN 0-380-89556-0). Avon.
Coulomb Excitation: A Collection of Reprints. Ed. by Kurt Alder & Aage Winther. (Perspectives in Physics Ser). 1966. 54.50 o.p. (ISBN 0-12-049250-4); pap. 10.00 o.p. Acad Pr.
Coulometry in Analytical Chemistry. G. W. Milner & G. Phillips. 1968. 31.00 o.p. (ISBN 0-08-012439-9); pap. 15.25 o.p. (ISBN 0-08-012438-0). Pergamon.
Council of Trent, the Spiritual Exercises & the Catholic Reform. Robert E. McNally. Ed. by Charles S. Anderson. LC 70-96863. (Facet Bks). 64p. 1970. pap. 1.00 o.p. (ISBN 0-8006-3056-4, 1-3056, Fortress). Augsburg Fortress.
Counseling. Shelagh Brumfitt. 73p. 1987. pap. text ed. 9.95 o.p. (ISBN 0-88450-985-0, 7433). Communication Skill.
Counseling. John J. Pietrofesa et al. 1978. text ed. 24.50 o.p. (ISBN 0-395-30698-1). HM.
Counseling: A Problem Solving Approach. D. N. Dixon & J. A. Glover. 239p. 1984. write for info. o.p. (ISBN 0-02-330180-5). Macmillan.
Counseling Adults: Bibliography. 7.50 o.p. (ISBN 0-317-59903-8, 72121C). Am Assn Coun Dev.
Counseling Adults: Life Cycle Perspectives. Dan Jones. Ed. by Sandra S. Moore. 145p. (Orig.). 1985. pap. text ed. 22.50 o.p. (ISBN 0-936352-20-5). U of KS Cont Ed.
Counseling & Accountability: Methods & Critique. H. D. Burck et al. 224p. 1974. 75.00 o.p. (ISBN 0-08-017029-3); pap. 75.00 o.p. (ISBN 0-08-017684-4). Pergamon.
Counseling & Psychotherapy. Carl R. Rogers. LC 42-24693. 1942. text ed. 18.95 o.p. (ISBN 0-395-05321-8). HM.
Counseling & Psychotherapy: Skills, Theories & Practices. Allen E. Ivey. (Illus.). 1980. pap. text ed. (ISBN 0-13-183152-6). P-H.
Counseling & the Five Points of Calvinism. Jay E. Adams. 1981. pap. 0.75 o.p. (ISBN 0-87552-072-3). Presby & Reformed.
Counseling Children & Adolescents. Ed. by AACD Library Staff. 25p. 1985. pap. text ed. 7.50 o.p. (ISBN 0-911547-91-6, 72513W34). Am Assn Coun Dev.
Counseling Clients in the Entertainment Industry 1985, Vol. 197. Practising Law Institute Staff. 399p. 1985. pap. 50.00 o.p. (ISBN 0-317-27500-3, G4-3762). PLI.
Counseling Employees see Issues in the Public Employee Relations Library: Series 1.
Counseling for Careers. Ed. by Stephen G. Weinrach. 1973. 29.50x o.p. (ISBN 0-8422-5114-6). Irvington.
Counseling for Careers in the Nineteen Eighties. S. Norman Feingold. LC 78-74700. (Illus.). 186p. 1979. pap. 6.95 o.p. (ISBN 0-912048-09-3). Garrett Pk.
Counseling for Liberation. Charlotte H. Clinebell. Ed. by Howard J. Clineball & Howard W. Stone. LC 75-36447. (Creative Pastoral Care & Counseling Ser). 96p. (Orig.). 1976. pap. 4.50 o.p. (ISBN 0-8006-0555-1, 1-555, Fortress). Augsburg Fortress.
Counseling Girls & Women. 1985. pap. text ed. 7.50 o.p. (ISBN 0-911547-88-6, 72510W34). Am Assn Coun Dev.
Counseling Men. Thomas M. Skovholt et al. 1980. 7.25 o.p. (ISBN 1-55620-006-4, 71006C). Am Assn Coun Dev.
Counseling Practices & Programs K-12. Ed. by AACD Library Staff. 48p. 1985. pap. text ed. 7.50 o.p. (ISBN 0-911547-90-8, 7251ZW34). Am Assn Coun Dev.
Counseling Process. 2nd ed. Sheldon Eisenberg & Daniel J. Delaney. 1977. pap. 13.50 o.p. (ISBN 0-395-30796-1). HM.
Counseling Process & Procedures. James C. Hansen. (Illus.). 1978. pap. write for info. o.p. (ISBN 0-02-350030-1). Macmillan.
Counseling Psychology: A Historical Perspective. John M. Whiteley. 1984. 14.95 o.p. (ISBN 0-317-59904-6, 71010C). Am Assn Coun Dev.
Counseling Relationship: A Study of the Client's Experience. Susan Oldfield. 240p. (Orig.). 1983. pap. 11.95x o.p. (ISBN 0-7100-9422-1). Routledge Chapman & Hall.
Counseling Small Businesses. Pennsylvania Bar Institute Staff. 270p. 1985. 35.00 o.p. (296). PA Bar Inst.
Counseling Techniques & Theories: Bibliography. 7.50 o.p. (ISBN 0-317-59905-4, 72119C). Am Assn Coun Dev.
Counseling the Aged, with Index: A Training Syllabus for Educators. Ed. by Mary Ganikos. 320p. 1979. pap. text ed. 18.75 o.p. (ISBN 0-911547-27-4, 72106W34). Am Assn Coun Dev.
Counseling the Aging. Ed. by AACD Library Staff. 28p. 1985. pap. text ed. 7.50 o.p. (ISBN 0-317-04372-2, 72501W34). Am Assn Coun Dev.
Counseling the College Student. H. D. Bragdon. pap. 19.00 o.p. (ISBN 0-384-05490-0). Johnson Repr.
Counseling the Handicapped. Ed. by AACD Library Staff. (Shell Bibliographies Ser.). 35p. (Orig.). 1983. pap. text ed. 7.50 o.p. (ISBN 0-911547-83-5, 72505W34). Am Assn Coun Dev.
Counseling the Nursing Mother. Childbirth Education Association of Greater Philadelphia, Inc. Staff. (Childbirth Reference Ser.). 528p. 1983. loose leaf 26.95 o.p. (ISBN 0-89529-206-8). Avery Pub.
Counseling the Older Adult: A Training Manual. Patricia Alpaugh & Margaret Haney. LC 77-99241. 1978. 19.95 o.p. (ISBN 0-88474-043-9, 05727-4). Lexington Bks.
Counseling: With the Pastor & CPE Student in Mind. Calvin C. Green. 1984. 12.95 o.p. (ISBN 0-533-05923-2). Vantage.
Counseling Women. National Association for Women Deans, Administrators & Counselors. 1974. pap. 6.00 o.p. (ISBN 0-686-09583-9). Natl Assn Women.
Counseling Youth. new ed. Clyde M. Narramore. 128p. (Orig.). 1974. pap. 5.95 o.p. (ISBN 0-310-29891-1, 12229P). Zondervan.
Counselling at Work. A. G. Watts. 92p. 1977. text ed. 4.40x o.p. (ISBN 0-7199-0925-2, Pub. by Bedford England); pap. text ed. 7.25x o.p. (ISBN 0-7199-0924-4, Pub. by Bedford England). Gower Pub Co.
Counselling in Rehabilitation. William Stewart. LC 85-18992. 320p. (Orig.). 1985. pap. 18.00 o.p. (ISBN 0-7099-4310-5, Pub. by Croom Helm Ltd). Routledge Chapman & Hall.
Counselling Young People. Ellen Noonan. 192p. 1983. 25.00 o.p. (ISBN 0-416-36210-9, NO. 4032); pap. 10.95 o.p. (ISBN 0-416-36220-6, NO. 4033). Routledge Chapman & Hall.
Counselor. Goland Ziran. LC 82-72058. 1982. 14.95 o.p. (ISBN 0-87795-420-8, Arbor Hse). Morrow.
Counselor As an Applied Behavioral Scientist. Ed. by J. Leonard Steinberg. 190p. 1974. text ed. 29.00x o.p. (ISBN 0-8422-5168-5); pap. text ed. 9.95x o.p. (ISBN 0-8422-0381-8). Irvington.
Counselor Licensure Action Packet. Ed. by John McFadden & David K. Brooks, Jr. 126p. 1983. pap. text ed. 10.00 o.p. (ISBN 0-911547-29-0, 72129W34). Am Assn Coun Dev.
Counselor Preparation & Supervision. Ed. by AACD Library Staff. 23p. (Orig.). 1985. pap. text ed. 7.50 o.p. (ISBN 0-911547-81-9, 72503W34). Am Assn Coun Dev.
Counselor Preparation Personnel, 1983-85: Programs, Personel, Trends. 5th ed. Joseph W. Hollis & Richard Wantz. (Orig.). 1983. pap. 25.95 o.p. (ISBN 0-915202-40-9). Accel Devel.
Counselor Supervision: Approaches, Preparation, Practices. John Boyd et al. LC 78-53069. (Illus.). 552p. 1978. pap. text ed. 15.45x o.p. (ISBN 0-915202-15-8). Accel Devel.
Counselor's Guide to Vocational Guidance Instruments. Jerome Kapes & Marjorie Mastie. 254p. 1982. pap. text ed. 13.50 o.p. (ISBN 0-911547-32-0, 72188W34). Am Assn Coun Dev.
Count It All Joy. Grady Wilson. LC 84-4934. (Illus.). 368p. 1984. 10.95 o.p. (ISBN 0-8054-7214-2). Broadman.
Count Me among the Living: The Story of My Wheelchair Liberation. Victoria M. Ballardo. 145p. 1983. 8.50 o.p. (ISBN 0-682-49945-5). Exposition-Phoenix.
Count of Coucy. 1980. 6.95 o.p. (ISBN 0-686-76500-1). Feldheim.
Count Unico Wilhelm van Wassenaer 1692-1766: A Master Unmasked or The Pergolesi-Ricciotti Puzzle Solved. A. Dunning. (Illus.). 1980. 75.00 o.p. (ISBN 9-06027-400-8). E J Brill USA.
Count Witte: Scenes from His Life & Times, 1902-1915. Vladimir Brenner. LC 78-74647. 186p. 1979. 7.50 o.p. (ISBN 0-682-49293-0). Exposition-Phoenix.
Count Your Calories Cookbook. 2nd ed. Jenifer Wright. 136p. 1986. pap. 12.95 spiral bound o.p. (ISBN 0-7233-0742-3, Pub. by Whitcoulls NZ). Intl Spec Bk.
Count Your Change: A Woman's Guide to Sudden Financial Change. Bonnie Siverd. LC 83-70466. 180p. 1983. pap. 6.95 o.p. (ISBN 0-87795-460-7, Arbor Hse). Morrow.
Countdown on SALT II: The Case for Preserving SALT II Limits on U. S. & Soviet Srategic Forces. 68p. 1985. 3.00 o.p. (ISBN 0-317-47274-7). Arms Control.
Countdown WW III, No. 4: Operation Persian Gulf. Strategic Operations Group Staff & W. X. Davies. 240p. 1984. pap. 2.95 o.s.i. (ISBN 0-425-07388-2). Berkley Pub.
Countdown WW III: Operation North Africa. Strategic Operations Group Staff & W. X. Davies. 240p. 1984. pap. 2.95 o.s.i. (ISBN 0-425-06563-4). Berkley Pub.
Counted Cross-Stitch Designs for All Seasons. Jana H. Lindberg. (Illus.). 96p. 1983. 17.95 o.p. (ISBN 0-684-17883-4, ScribT). Scribner.
Counted Cross-Stitch Designs for the Home. Jana H. Lindberg. (Illus.). 96p. 1985. 17.95 o.p. (ISBN 0-684-18364-1, ScribT). Scribner.
Counter-Coup. Michael Bradford. 337p. 1986. pap. 3.50 o.p. (ISBN 0-931773-75-X). Critics Choice Paper.
Counter Current Extraction. S. Hartland. LC 69-17867. 1970. 50.00 o.p. (ISBN 0-08-012976-5). Pergamon.
Counter-Insurgency in Rhodesia. J. K. Cilliers. LC 84-45702. 266p. 1985. 29.00 o.p. (ISBN 0-7099-3412-2, Pub. by Croom Helm Ltd). Routledge Chapman & Hall.
Counter Monuments: Krzysztof Wodiczko's Public Projections. Katy Kline & Ewa Lajer-Burcharth. LC 86-63518. (Illus.). 50p. (Orig.). 1987. pap. 7.50 o.p. (ISBN 0-938437-18-6). MIT List Visual Arts.
Counter-Renaissance. Hiram C. Haydn. LC 50-3937. 1967. pap. 3.95 o.p. (ISBN 0-15-622680-4, Harv). HarBraceJ.
Counterattack: Taking Back Ground Lost to Sin. Jay Carty. 1988. price not set o.p. Multnomah.
Counterblast. Marshall McLuhan. LC 73-85015. (Illus.). 1969. 8.95 o.p. (ISBN 0-15-122675-X). HarBraceJ.
Counterblast. Marshall McLuhan. LC 73-85015. (Illus.). 1970. pap. 1.95 o.p. (ISBN 0-15-622670-7, HB186, Harv). HarBraceJ.
Countercoup: The Struggle for the Control of Iran. Kermit Roosevelt. (McGraw-Hill Paperback Ser.). 1981. pap. text ed. 5.95 o.p. (ISBN 0-07-053593-0). McGraw.
Counterexamples in Topological Vector Spaces. S. M. Khaleolulla. (Lecture Notes in Mathematics Ser.: Vol. 936). 179p. 1982. pap. 13.00 o.p. (ISBN 0-387-11565-X). Springer-Verlag.
Counterfeit Lady. Jude Deveraux. 1985. lib. bdg. 17.95 o.p. (ISBN 0-8161-3826-5, Large Print Bks). G K Hall.
Counterfeit or Genuine? Ed. by David O. Fuller. LC 74-82807. 232p. 1975. pap. 7.95 o.p. (ISBN 0-8254-2615-4). Kregel.
Counterforce Syndrome: A Guide to United States Nuclear Weapons & Strategic Doctrine. Robert C. Aldridge. 76p. 1978. pap. 2.50 o.p. Transaction Pubs.
Counterinsurgency As Terrorism: Human Rights Violations in Guatemala. 1983. 4.50 o.p. Natl Lawyers Guild.
Counterintelligence. Ed. by Roy Godson. (Intelligence Requirements for the Nineteen Eighties Ser.: Vol. 3). 384p. 1981. pap. 7.95 o.p. (ISBN 0-87855-829-2). Transaction Pubs.
Counterparts: Form & Emotion in Photographs. Weston J. Naef. (Illus.). 148p. 1982. 4.95 o.p. (ISBN 0-317-59764-7). Metro Mus Art.
Counterpoint. 2nd reference ed. Kent Kennan. LC 73-168625. (Illus.). 1972. pap. text ed. (ISBN 0-13-184291-9). P-H.
Counterpoint in Composition: The Study of Voice Leading. F. Salzer & C. Schacheter. (Music Ser.). 1969. text ed. 62.95 o.p. (ISBN 0-07-054497-2). McGraw.
Counterpoint in Maori Culture. F. A. Hanson & Louise Hanson. LC 83-9462. (International Library of Anthropology Ser.). (Illus.). 232p. 1983. 35.00x o.p. (ISBN 0-7100-9546-5). Routledge Chapman & Hall.
Counterpoint: The Polyphonic Vocal Style of the Sixteenth Century. reference ed. Knud Jeppesen. Tr. by G. Haydon. 1939. text ed. 40.00 o.p. (ISBN 0-13-183608-0). P-H.
Countess Below Stairs. Eva Ibbotson. 288p. 1982. pap. 2.95 o.p. (ISBN 0-380-61374-3, 61374-3). Avon.
Countess from Minneapolis. Barbara Guest. (Burning Deck Poetry Ser.). 1976. 15.00 o.p. (ISBN 0-930900-05-7); pap. 4.00 o.p. (ISBN 0-930900-06-5). Burning Deck.
Counting-Out Rhymes of Children. Henry C. Bolton. LC 68-23139. 133p. 1969. Repr. of 1888 ed. 30.00x o.p. (ISBN 0-8103-3475-5). Gale.
Counting People: The Census in History. Hyman Alterman. LC 74-82635. (Illus.). 1969. 7.50 o.p. (ISBN 0-15-220170-X, HJ). HarBraceJ.
Counting Rhymes. (gr. k-3). 1986. pap. 0.79 o.p. (ISBN 0-8431-4103-4). Wonder.
Counting the Eons. Isaac Asimov. 224p. 1984. pap. 3.95 o.p. (ISBN 0-380-67090-9, 67090, Discus). Avon.
Counting the People in 1980: An Appraisal of Census Plans. National Research Council. 1978. pap. text ed. 10.95x o.p. (ISBN 0-309-02797-7). Natl Acad Pr.
Countries. Anne Waldman. LC 80-10777. (Illus., Orig.). 1980. signed 20.00 o.p. (ISBN 0-915124-35-1, Pub. by Toothpaste); pap. 4.00 o.p. (ISBN 0-915124-36-X). Coffee Hse.
Countries & Concepts: An Introduction to Comparative Politics. 2nd ed. Michael G. Roskin. (Illus.). 416p. 1986. text ed. (ISBN 0-13-184250-1). P-H.
Countries of the World & Their Leaders Yearbook: 1987. Frank Bair. 1500p. 1986. 120.00x o.p. (ISBN 0-8103-2116-5). Gale.
Countries of the World & Their Leaders Yearbook 1986, 2 vols. 1986 ed. Ed. by Frank E. Bair. 1060p. 1985. 110.00x o.p. (ISBN 0-8103-2117-3). Gale.
Countries of the World & Their Leaders Yearbook 1988, 2 vols. (Illus.). 1600p. 1987. 130.00x o.p. (ISBN 0-8103-2343-5). Gale.

Titles

Countries of the World & their Leaders Yearbook, 1987: Supplement. Ed. by Frank E. Bair. 400p. 1987. pap. text ed. 65.00 o.p. (ISBN 0-8103-2199-8). Gale.

Countries of the World & Their Leaders Yearbook, 1988: Supplement. Ed. by Frank E. Bair. 400p. 1988. pap. text ed. 65.00x o.p. (ISBN 0-8103-2344-3). Gale.

Country & Calling. William K. Hancock. LC 78-6026. 1978. Repr. of 1954 ed. lib. bdg. 35.00x o.p. (ISBN 0-313-20447-0, HACAC). Greenwood.

Country Animal Doctor. Arthur Ingram. (Album Ser.: No. 40). (Illus.). 32p. (Orig.). 1979. pap. 2.95 o.p. (ISBN 0-85263-462-5, Pub. by Shire Pubns England). Seven Hills Bk Dists.

Country Antiques & Collectibles: How to Find Them--Where to Buy Them--How to Decorate with Them. Ed. by Carter Smith. LC 81-80140. (Illus.). 224p. 1981. 29.95 o.p. (ISBN 0-8487-0529-7). Oxmoor Hse.

Country Boy Grown Old: His Story of Earlier Days. E. Hoyt Palmer. 1985. 13.95 o.p. (ISBN 0-533-06600-X). Vantage.

Country Bread Cookbook. 64p. pap. 3.95 o.p. (ISBN 0-89542-608-0). Ideals.

Country Camera, Eighteen Forty-Four to Nineteen Fourteen: Rural Life As Depicted in Photographs from the Early Days of Photography to the Outbreak of the First World War. Gordon Winter. LC 76-148407. (Illus.). 120p. 1971. Repr. of 1966 ed. 35.00x o.p. (ISBN 0-8103-3399-6). Gale.

Country Catalog of Memories: A Childhood on a German-American Farm in the Late 1920s & Early 1930s. Helen E. Ouimette. LC 86-9498. (Illus.). 230p. (Orig.). 1986. pap. 14.95 o.p. (ISBN 0-9617116-0-4). H Ouimette.

Country Chaff. Jerry Easterling. 168p. 1983. pap. 5.95 o.p. (ISBN 0-8323-0419-0). Binford-Metropolitan.

Country Christmas Cookbook. Ideals Staff. (Illus.). 64p. (Orig.). 1984. pap. 3.95 o.p. (ISBN 0-8249-3032-0). Ideals.

Country Christmas Entertaining. Ed. by Jill Nickerson. LC 83-62128. 64p. 1983. pap. 5.95 o.s.i. (ISBN 0-89821-055-0). Reiman Assocs.

Country Cookery of Many Lands. Coralie Castle & Margaret Gin. LC 75-21504. (Illus.). 192p. (Orig.). 1975. pap. 4.95 o.s.i. (ISBN 0-912238-70-4, One Hund One Prods). Ortho.

Country Cousin. Louis Auchincloss. 1978. 8.95 o.p. (ISBN 0-395-26687-4). HM.

Country Cousins. Michael Brownstein. LC 74-79059. 256p. 1974. 7.95 o.p. (ISBN 0-8076-0749-5, Venture Bks.). Braziller.

Country Diary Cookery Notes. Edith Holden & Alison Harding. 1984. 9.95 o.p. (ISBN 0-03-000748-8). H Holt & Co.

Country Enterprise: Pleasure & Profit from Home Produce. Jonathan Ffrench & Heather Ffrench. (Illus.). 215p. 1983. 17.50 o.p. (ISBN 0-7099-1034-7, Pub. by Croom Helm Ltd). Routledge Chapman & Hall.

Country Folk Ain't So Bad: Recollections of the Old South. Thelma S. Sessions. 72p. 1983. 5.50 o.p. (ISBN 0-682-49956-0). Exposition-Phoenix.

Country Handcrafts Christmas Collection. Sandra L. Wright. 34p. 1985. pap. 5.95 o.s.i. (ISBN 0-89821-069-0). Reiman Assocs.

Country Handcrafts Doll & Toy Collection. Sandra L. Wright. 34p. 1985. pap. 5.95 o.s.i. (ISBN 0-89821-068-2). Reiman Assocs.

Country Homes. Intro. by Paige Rense. (World of Architectural Digest Ser.). (Illus.). 160p. 1982. 15.95 o.p. (ISBN 0-89535-102-1). Knapp Pr.

Country House Guide to England Scotland & Wales. Robin Fedden & John Kenworthy-Browne. (Illus.). 1979. 24.95 o.p. (ISBN 0-393-01259-X). Norton.

Country House Remembered: Recollections of Life Between the Wars. Merlin Waterson. (Illus.). 192p. 1985. 25.00 o.p. (ISBN 0-7102-0376-4). Routledge Chapman & Hall.

Country Inns: A Selection of Maine's Distinctive Accommodations. Barbara Feller-Roth. (Maine Geographic Ser.). (Illus.). 48p. 1983. pap. 2.95 o.p. (ISBN 0-89933-063-0). DeLorme Map.

Country Inns & Back Roads Cookbook. Ed. by Norman T. Simpson. LC 79-52080. 176p. (Orig.). 1980. pap. 8.95 o.p. (ISBN 0-912944-56-0). Berkshire Traveller.

Country Inns & Back Roads: North America. 18th ed. Norman T. Simpson. LC 70-615664. (Illus.). 486p. (Orig.). 1983. pap. 8.95 o.p. (ISBN 0-912944-75-7). Berkshire Traveller.

Country Inns Britain 86-87. Emily Oreilly. 1986. pap. 7.95 o.p. (ISBN 0-89102-325-9). B Franklin.

Country Inns California. Anthony Hitchcock. 1984. pap. 6.95 o.p. (ISBN 0-89102-297-X). B Franklin.

Country Inns Cookery: The Best of American Regional Cooking. Coralie Castle & Jacqueline Killeen. LC 82-61102. (Illus.). 160p. 1982. pap. 6.95 o.p. (ISBN 0-89286-202-5, One Hund One Prods). Ortho.

Country Inns: Lodges & Historic Hotels, New England States, 1988-89. Anthony Hitchcock. 1988. pap. 8.95 o.p. (ISBN 0-89102-373-9). B Franklin.

Country Inns of America, 3 vols. Ed. by Peter Andrews. Incl. Vol. I. New England & the Maritimes. o.s.i (ISBN 0-03-042836-X); Vol. II. The Mid Atlantic & the South. o.p. (ISBN 0-03-042841-6); Vol. III. The Pacific Coast & the Southwest. o.p. (ISBN 0-03-042846-7). LC 77-71352. (Illus.). 1978. 16.00 ea. o.s.i. H Holt & Co.

Country Inns of America, California. rev. ed ed. pap. 12.95 o.p. (ISBN 0-8050-0215-4). H Holt & Co.

Country Inns of America Cookbook. Ed. by Robert Reid. (Illus.). 180p. 1982. 24.95 o.p. (ISBN 0-03-062174-7). H Holt & Co.

Country Inns of America: Lower New England. Roberta Gardner et al. 1985. pap. 10.95 o.p. (ISBN 0-03-003319-5, Owl Bks). H Holt & Co.

Country Inns of America: New York & Mid-Atlantic. rev. ed. Roberta H. Gardner. (Illus.). 1986. pap. 11.95 o.p. (ISBN 0-03-008517-9, Owl Bks). H Holt & Co.

Country Inns of America: Pacific Northwest. Fred Busk & Peter Andrews. LC 81-1617. (Illus.). 96p. 1981. pap. 9.95 o.s.i. (ISBN 0-03-059181-3, Owl Bks). H Holt & Co.

Country Inns of California. Ed. by Peter Andrews. LC 79-22906. (Country Inns Guides Ser.). (Illus.). 1980. pap. 6.95 o.p. (ISBN 0-03-043726-1). Knapp Pr.

Country Inns of New England. Pat Brooks & Fran J. Garvan. (Country Inns Ser.). (Illus.). 200p. 1984. pap. 7.95 o.p. (ISBN 0-89286-229-7, One Hund One Prods). Ortho.

Country Inns of the Far West: A Guide to the Inns of California, Oregon, Washington & British Columbia. rev. enl. ed. Jacqueline Killeen et al. LC 81-86322. (Illus.). 280p. 1982. pap. 6.95 o.p. (ISBN 0-89286-196-7, One Hund One Prods). Ortho.

Country Inns of the Far West: California. rev. ed. Jacqueline Killeen. LC 84-2318. (Country Inns Ser.). (Illus.). 276p. 1984. pap. 7.95 o.p. (ISBN 0-89286-231-9, One Hund One Prods). Ortho.

Country Inns of the Far West: California. rev. ed. Jacqueline Killeen. LC 86-21735. (Country Inns Ser.). (Illus.). 246p. 1987. pap. 8.95 o.p. (ISBN 0-89286-268-8, One Hund One Prods). Ortho.

Country Inns of the Far West: Pacific NW. rev. ed. Rachel Bard. LC 84-3611. (Country Inns Ser.). (Illus.). 228p. 1984. pap. 7.95 o.p. (ISBN 0-89286-232-7, One Hund One Prods). Ortho.

Country Inns of the Great Lakes. 2nd, rev. ed. Robert Morris. (Country Inns Ser.). (Illus.). 160p. (Orig.). 1988. pap. (ISBN 0-89286-272-6, One Hund One Prods). Ortho.

Country Inns of the Great Lakes: A Guide to Inns, Lodges, & Historic Hostelries of the Upper Midwest. Robert Morris. LC 81-3962. 180p. (Orig.). 1981. pap. 4.95 o.p. (ISBN 0-89286-165-7, One Hund One Prods). Ortho.

Country Inns of the Old South. Robert Tolf. 8.95 o.s.i. (ISBN 0-89286-208-4). Trend Bk Div.

Country Inns of the Old South. Robert W. Tolf. LC 78-11262. (Illus.). 1978. pap. 4.95 o.p. (ISBN 0-89286-144-4, One Hund One Prods). Ortho.

Country Inns of the Old South. Robert W. Tolf. LC 78-11262. (Country Inns Ser.). (Illus.). 300p. (Orig.). 1983. pap. 7.95 o.s.i. (ISBN 0-89286-208-4, One Hund One Prods). Ortho.

Country Journal New England Weather Book. David M. Ludlum. 1976. 10.95 o.p. (ISBN 0-395-24299-1); pap. 7.95 o.p. (ISBN 0-395-24402-1). HM.

Country Journal Woodburner's Cookbook. Janet B. Chadwick. (Illus.). 1981. 14.95 o.p. (ISBN 0-393-01503-3); pap. 9.95 o.p. (ISBN 0-393-00076-1). Norton.

Country Journal Woodlot Primer: The Right Way to Manage Your Woodland. Richard M. Brett. (Illus.). 144p. (Orig.). 1983. pap. 9.95 o.p. (ISBN 0-918678-04-8). Cowles Mags.

Country Kitchen Cookbook. Wes Bauman et al. 1981. pap. 9.95 o.p. (ISBN 0-8423-0448-7). Tyndale.

Country Kitchen Cookbook. Darlene Kronschnabel. Ed. by James K. Kuse. (Illus.). 1979. pap. 3.95 o.p. (ISBN 0-89542-633-1). Ideals.

Country Life of J. B. Rabbit. Doris S. Smith. (Illus.). (ps-4). 1983. 5.95 o.p. (ISBN 0-448-16586-4, G&D). Putnam Pub Group.

Country Life Picture Book of Britain. Gordon Winter. (Illus.). 1983. 19.45 o.p. (ISBN 0-393-01735-4). Norton.

Country Life Picture Book of Devon & Cornwall. Paul Pettit. (Illus.). 1982. 19.95 o.p. (ISBN 0-393-01626-9). Norton.

Country Life Picture Book of Royal London. Gordon Winter. (Illus.). 1983. 19.45 o.p. (ISBN 0-393-01747-8). Norton.

Country Life Picture Book of the Thames. Gordon Winter. (Illus.). 1982. 19.95 o.p. (ISBN 0-393-01628-5). Norton.

Country Life Picture Book of Wales. Roger Thomas. (Illus.). 1982. 19.95 o.p. (ISBN 0-393-01526-2). Norton.

Country Life Picture Book: Scotland. Lord Tweedsmuir. (Illus.). 1983. 19.45 o.p. (ISBN 0-393-01734-6). Norton.

Country: Living Legends & Dying Metaphors in America's Biggest Music. rev. ed. Nick Tosches. (Illus.). 296p. 1985. 22.50 o.p. (ISBN 0-684-18346-3, ScribT); pap. 9.95 o.p. (ISBN 0-684-18345-5). Scribner.

Country Music: A Look at the Men Who've Made It. Cynthia Farah & Marina Nickerson. LC 81-70858. (Illus.). 88p. pap. 8.95 o.p. (ISBN 0-9607514-0-8). C M Pub.

Country Music Book. Ed. by Michael Mason. (Illus.). 384p. 1985. 24.95 o.p. (ISBN 0-684-18013-8, ScribT); pap. 14.95 o.p. (ISBN 0-684-18046-4). Scribner.

Country Musicians: The Carter Family, Charlie Daniels, Waylon Jennings, Bill Monroe, Willie Nelson, Ricky Skaggs, Merle Travis, & 27 Other Great American Artists-Their Music & How they Made It. Ed. by Judie Eremo & Guitar Player & Frets Magazine Staff. (Illus.). 160p. 1987. 24.95 o.s.i. (ISBN 0-8021-0008-2); pap. 14.95 o.s.i. (ISBN 0-8021-3003-8, Ever). Grove.

Country of Resemblances. Beth Bentley. LC 75-14549. 78p. 1976. 8.95 o.p. (ISBN 0-8214-0196-3, 82-82006); pap. 5.95 o.p. (ISBN 0-8214-0210-2). Ohio U Pr.

Country of the Heart. Barbara Wersba. LC 75-6947. 128p. (gr. 7 up). 1975. 6.95 o.p. (ISBN 0-689-30469-2, Atheneum). Macmillan.

Country of the Pointed Firs. Sarah O. Jewett. 1977. pap. 1.75 o.p. (ISBN 0-380-00879-3, 31476). Avon.

Country of the Risen King: Anthology of Christian Poetry. Merle Meeter. LC 77-87993. 1978. 12.95 o.p. (ISBN 0-8010-6042-7). Baker Bk.

Country Operas, One: Romantic Intrigue & Deception with Southwark Fair, the Village Opera, the Chamber Maid, the Gentleman Gardiner, the Country Coquet, an Opera Called Westmeon Village. Ed. by Walter H. Rubsamen. (Ballad Opera Ser.). 1974. lib. bdg. 61.00 o.p. (ISBN 0-8240-0914-2). Garland Pub.

Country Operas, Three: Sentimental & Moral Comedies with Sylvia, the Jovial Crew, Lucinda, the Reapers. Ed. by Walter H. Rubsamen. (Ballad Opera Ser.). 1974. lib. bdg. 61.00 o.p. (ISBN 0-8240-0916-9). Garland Pub.

Country Operas, Two: Farcial Humor & Stratagem With Country Wedding, the Wedding (Hawker), Flora, a Sequel to Flora, the Livery Rake, the Whim, the Deceit, the Country-Wedding. Ed. by Walter H. Rubsamen. (Ballad Opera Ser.). 1975. lib. bdg. 61.00 o.p. (ISBN 0-8240-0915-0). Garland Pub.

Country Railroad Station in America. H. Roger Grant & Charles Bohi. LC 78-15135. (Illus.). 183p. 1978. 24.95 o.p. (ISBN 0-87108-523-2). Pruett.

Country Reports on Human Rights Practices for 1987. 1368p. (Orig.). 1988. pap. 31.00 o.p. (052-070-06410-2). USGPO.

Country Risk. 2nd ed. P. J. Nagy. 195p. 1984. pap. 120.00 o.p. (ISBN 0-317-57432-9). Intl Pubns Serv.

Country Squash. Ed. by Annette Gohlke. LC 83-61948. 64p. 1983. pap. 3.95 o.s.i. (ISBN 0-89821-054-2). Reiman Assocs.

Country Store. Elspeth. 1975. pap. 1.50 o.p. (ISBN 0-87588-243-9, 476). Hobby Hse.

Country Store Candy Cookbook. Ed. by Jill Nickerson. LC 84-61390. 66p. 1984. pap. 3.95 o.s.i. (ISBN 0-89821-063-1). Reiman Assocs.

Country Such as This. James Webb. 576p. 1985. pap. 4.95 o.s.i. (ISBN 0-553-24734-4). Bantam.

Country Teacher Tells It. Leo Gentry. 1979. 5.00 o.p. (ISBN 0-682-49489-5). Exposition-Phoenix.

Country Vet. Denis Farrier. LC 72-6615. 1973. 6.95 o.s.i. (ISBN 0-8008-1950-0). Taplinger.

Country Walks in Connecticut. Susan D. Cooley. (Country Walks Ser.). (Illus.). 224p. 1982. pap. 8.95 o.p. (ISBN 0-910146-41-1). AMC Books.

Country Walks Near Baltimore. Alan Fisher. (Country Walks Ser.). (Illus.). 232p. 1982. pap. 7.95 o.p. (ISBN 0-910146-36-5). AMC Books.

Country Walks Near New York. William G. Scheller. (Illus.). 200p. (Orig.). 1980. pap. 6.95 o.p. (ISBN 0-910146-29-2); members 5.95 o.p. AMC Books.

Country with a Government & a Flag: The Rif War in Morocco, 1921-1926. C. R. Pennell. 260p. 1986. lib. bdg. 35.00x o.p. (ISBN 0-906559-23-5). Lynne Rienner.

County & City Data Book, 1983: A Statistcal Abstract Supplement, States; Counties; Places of 25,000 or More; Places of 2,500 or More. 10th ed. (Illus.). 1060p. 1983. 24.00 o.p. (ISBN 0-318-04548-6, S/N 003-024-05833-2). USGPO.

County Business Patterns, Nineteen Eighty-Five: United States, Employment & Payrolls, Number & Employment Size of Establishments by Detailed Industry. (CBP Ser.: 85-1). 121p. (Orig.). 1987. pap. 6.00 o.p. (S/N 003-024-06519-3). USGPO.

County Business Patterns, 1984: United States Employment & Payrolls, Number & Employment Size of Establishments by Detailed Industry. annual ed. (CBP 84-1 Ser.). (Illus.). 123p. 1986. pap. 5.50 o.p. (ISBN 0-318-21618-3, S/N 003-024-06376-0). USGPO.

County Government in North Carolina. 2nd. ed. Ed. by Joseph S. Ferrell. 417p. 1979. 15.00 o.p. (ISBN 0-686-39428-3). Institute Government.

County Salaries in North Carolina. Compiled by Carol Burgess. 57p. 1987. 7.00 o.p. (ISBN 0-686-39429-1). Institute Government.

Coup d'Etat. John Harvey. LC 84-45046. 480p. 1985. 16.95 o.p. (ISBN 0-689-11484-2, Atheneum). Macmillan.

Coup D'Etat: A Practical Manual. Gregor Ferguson. LC 87-673322. (Illus.). 208p. 1987. 24.95 o.p. (ISBN 0-85368-761-7, Pub. by Arms & Armour). Sterling.

Couples with Children. Virginia DeLuca & Randy Wolfson. LC 81-3268. 190p. 1981. 12.95 o.p. (ISBN 0-934878-07-2). Dembner Bks.

Coups & Cocaine: Journeys in South America. Anthony Daniels. LC 86-18054. (Illus.). 240p. 1987. Repr. of 1986 ed. 17.95 o.p. (ISBN 0-87951-263-6). Overlook Pr.

Courage. John Shannon. 232p. 1975. 6.95 o.p. (ISBN 0-393-08711-5). Norton.

Courage, Church! Essays in Ecclesial Spirituality. Walbert Buhlmann. Tr. by Mary Smith from Ital. LC 78-1381. Orig. Title: Corragio Chiesa! 149p. (Orig.). 1978. pap. 2.98 o.p. (ISBN 0-88344-068-7). Orbis Bks.

Courage for Dialogue: Ecumenical Issues in Inter-Religious Relationships. S. J. Samartha. LC 81-16936. 172p. (Orig.). 1982. pap. 4.48 o.p. (ISBN 0-88344-094-6). Orbis Bks.

Courage of a Conservative. James Watt & Doug Wead. 211p. 1985. 15.45 o.s.i. (ISBN 0-671-52835-1). S&S.

Courage to Be Imperfect: The Life & Work of Rudolf Dreikurs. Janet Terner & W. L. Pew. LC 75-220. (Illus.). 412p. 1978. text ed. 16.50 o.p. (ISBN 0-89116-182-1). Hemisphere Pub.

Courage to Change: From Insight to Self-Innovation. Edrita Fried. 256p. (Orig.). 1981. pap. 7.95 o.p. (ISBN 0-394-17935-8, E786, Ever). Grove.

Courage to Change: Hope & Help for Alcoholics & Their Families. Dennis Wholey. 1984. 15.45 o.s.i. (ISBN 0-395-35977-5). HM.

Courage to Change: Personal Conversations about Alcoholism. Dennis Wholey. 478p. 1985. lib. bdg. 17.95 o.p. (ISBN 0-8161-3959-8, Large Print Bks). G K Hall.

Courage to Create. Rollo May. 143p. 1975. 13.95 o.p. (ISBN 0-393-01119-4). Norton.

Courage to Love. William S. Coffin, Jr. LC 81-48386. 128p. 1982. pap. 5.95 o.p. (ISBN 0-06-061508-7, RD515). HarpR.

Courageous & the Proud. Samuel Vance. LC 69-14710. 1970. 4.95 o.p. (ISBN 0-393-07444-7). Norton.

Courageous Heart. B. Lavranyov. 28p. 1978. pap. 1.99 o.p. (ISBN 0-8285-1127-6, Pub. by Progress Pubs USSR). Imported Pubns.

Courageous Turk. Thomas Goffe. Ed. by Susan G. O'Malley & Stephen Orgel. LC 78-66772. (Renaissance Drama Ser.). 1979. lib. bdg. 40.00 o.p. (ISBN 0-8240-9737-8). Garland Pub.

Courier from Warsaw. Jan Nowak. LC 82-8599. (Illus.). 480p. 1982. 24.95x o.p. (ISBN 0-8143-1725-1). Wayne St U Pr.

Courier Job. James Pattinson. 189p. 1986. pap. 2.95 o.p. (ISBN 1-55547-104-8). Critics Choice Paper.

Courrier Sud. Antoine De Saint-Exupery. (Coll. Soleil). 1956. 12.95 o.p. (ISBN 0-685-11118-0). Schoenhof.

Cours Superieur. W. F. Whitmarsh. 1952. pap. 5.95x o.p. (ISBN 0-679-30044-9, Pub. by MacKay). Longman.

Course in Analytical Chemistry, 2 vols. Yaroslarisev & Kreshkov. 738p. 1977. Set. 11.25 o.p. (ISBN 0-8285-0645-0, Pub. by Mir Pubs USSR). Imported Pubns.

Course in Computational Probability & Statistics. W. Freiberger & U. Grenander. LC 76-176272. (Applied Mathematical Sciences: Vol. 6). 168p. 1977. pap. 21.95 o.p. (ISBN 0-387-90029-2). Springer-Verlag.

Course in Cryptanalysis. S I Course, 2 vols. 1981. lib. bdg. 26.80 ea. o.p.; Vol. I, 72p. lib. bdg. (ISBN 0-89412-082-4); Vol. II, 69p. lib. bdg. (ISBN 0-89412-083-2); pap. 18.80 ea. o.p.; Vol. I. pap. (ISBN 0-89412-052-2); Vol. II. pap. (ISBN 0-89412-053-0). Aegean Park Pr.

Course in Descriptive Geometry. V. O. Gordon. 1980. 10.00 o.p. (ISBN 0-8285-1870-X, Pub. by Mir Pubs USSR). Imported Pubns.

Course in Diagnostics for Fusion Experiments: Proceedings of the Commission of the European Communities, Varenna, Italy, 1978. Ed. by C. Wharton & E. Sindoni. (Commission of the European Communities, EUR, 6123). (Illus.). 1979. pap. 170.00 o.p. (ISBN 0-08-023429-1). Pergamon.

Course in General Linguistics. Ferdinand De Saussure. 1959. (ISBN 0-8022-1493-2). Philos Lib.

Course in Linear Algebra. David B. Damiano & John B. Little. 114p. 1988. pap. text ed. 30.00 o.p.; instr's. manual 1.50 o.p. (ISBN 0-15-515135-5). HarBraceJ.

Course in Modern Linguistics. Charles F. Hockett. (Illus.). 1958. text ed. write for info. o.p. (ISBN 0-02-355090-2). Macmillan.

Course in Phonetics. Peter Ladefoged. 1975. 14.95 o.p. (ISBN 0-15-515180-0). HarbraceJ.

Course in Theoretical Physics, 2 vols. A. Kompaneyets. 986p. 1978. Set. 26.00 o.p. (ISBN 0-8285-0774-0, Pub. by Mir Pubs USSR). Imported Pubns.

Course in Thermodynamics, 2 Vols. J. Kestin. 1979. Vol. 1. 38.50 o.p. (ISBN 0-07-034281-4); Vol. 2. 38.50 o.p. (ISBN 0-07-034282-2). McGraw.

Course of Alcoholism: Four Years After Treatment. J. Michael Polich & David J. Armor. Ed. by Harriet B. Braiker. LC 80-24316. (Personality Processes Ser.). 334p. 1981. 39.95x o.p. (ISBN 0-471-08682-7, Pub. by Wiley-Interscience). Wiley.

Course of Applied Functional Analysis. Arthur Wouk. LC 78-15026. (Pure & Applied Mathematics Ser.). 443p. 1979. 53.50x o.p. (ISBN 0-471-96238-4, Pub. by Wiley-Interscience). Wiley.

Course on Instabilities & Confinement in Toroidal Plasmas. International School of Plasma Physics, Varenna (Como), Italy, 1971. 1975. pap. 120.00 o.p. (ISBN 0-08-020452-X). Pergamon.

Course on Optimization & Best Approximation. R. B. Holmes. (Lecture Notes in Mathematics: Vol. 257). 233p. 1972. pap. 7.50 o.p. (ISBN 0-387-05764-1). Springer-Verlag.

Course on Plasma Diagnostics & Data Acquisition Systems. new ed. Ed. by H. Eubank & E. Sindoni. (Commission of the European Communities). (Illus.). 1979. pap. 140.00 o.p. (ISBN 0-08-024462-9). Pergamon.

Course on Stationary & Quasi-Stationary Toroidal Reactors. International School of Fusion Reactor Technology, Erice (Trapani), Italy, Sept. 4-15, 1972. 1975. pap. 120.00 o.p. (ISBN 0-08-020455-4). Pergamon.

Course on Words. Waldo E. Sweet & Glenn M. Knudsvig. 353p. 1982. pap. text ed. 11.00 net o.p. (ISBN 0-15-515183-5, HC). HarBraceJ.

Courses for Horses. new ed. C. Coldrey. 1978. 12.95 o.p. (ISBN 0-85131-305-1, BL2331, Pub. by J A Allen U K). S R Smith Sporting Bks.

Courses in Lambents. Wesli Court. (Illus.). (YA) (gr. 7-12). 1977. 15.00 o.s.i. (ISBN 0-930000-00-5); PLB 8.95 o.s.i. (ISBN 0-930000-01-3); pap. 3.95 o.s.i. (ISBN 0-930000-02-1). Mathom.

Court & the Country: The Beginning of the English Revolution. Perez Zagorin. LC 72-104129. 1971. pap. text ed. 3.25x o.p. (ISBN 0-689-70275-2, 181, Atheneum). Macmillan.

Court Awarded Attorney Fees: Report 3. Matthew Bender Publishers Staff. 1983. write for info. o.p. Bender.

Court, Church & Castle. Margaret W. Labarge. (Illus.). 112p. 1972. pap. 3.25 o.p. (ISBN 0-88884-431-X, 56310-3, Pub. by Natl Mus Canada). U of Chicago Pr.

Court Decisions Relating to the National Labor Relations Act V 30: January 1, 1977 Through August 31, 1978. 1333p. 1983. 28.00 o.p. (ISBN 0-318-23098-4, 031-000-00242-7). USGPO.

Court Intrigue & Scandal, One: With Calista, Vanelia, the Humours of the Court, the Intriguing Courtiers. Ed. by Walter H. Rubsamen. (Ballad Opera Ser.). 1974. lib. bdg. 61.00 o.p. (ISBN 0-8240-0917-7). Garland Pub.

Court Intrigue & Scandal, Two: With the Fox Uncased, the Court Legacy, the Court Medley, the Fortunate Prince, the Wedding. Ed. by Walter A. Rubsamen. (Ballad Opera Ser.). 1974. lib. bdg. 61.00 o.p. (ISBN 0-8240-0918-5). Garland Pub.

Court Martial of George Armstrong Custer. Douglas C. Jones. 304p. 1984. pap. 8.95 o.s.i. (ISBN 0-684-18255-6, ScribT). Scribner.

Court of Domestic Revelation. Charles De Spelder. 1976. 7.50 o.p. (ISBN 0-682-48464-4). Exposition-Phoenix.

Court of Flora. J. J. Grandville. LC 80-70276. Orig. Title: Fleurs Animees. (Illus.). 120p. 1981. 30.00 o.p. (ISBN 0-8076-1014-3); pap. 12.95 o.p. (ISBN 0-8076-1006-2). Braziller.

Court of the Stone Children. Eleanor Cameron. (gr. 5-10). 1976. pap. 1.25 o.p. (ISBN 0-380-00681-2, 48942). Avon.

Court Officer. 5th ed. Arco Editorial Board. LC 71-99892. 1974. lib. bdg. 7.50 o.p. (ISBN 0-668-01534-9); pap. 9.00 o.p. (ISBN 0-668-00519-X). Arco.

Court Organization & Administration: A Bibliography. Dorothy C. Tompkins. LC 73-17209. 200p. (Orig.). 1973. 8.00x o.p. (ISBN 0-87772-193-9). UCB IGS.

Courtesans & Cuckolds: A Glossary of Renaissance Dramatic Bawdy (Exclusive of Shakespeare) James T. Henke. LC 79-7918. 367p. 1979. lib. bdg. 55.06 o.p. (ISBN 0-8240-9546-4). Garland Pub.

Courting Pandemonium. Frederick Barton. 350p. 1986. 14.95 o.p. (ISBN 0-931948-98-3). Peachtree Pubs.

Courtly Cats. William Shakespeare. (Illus.). 48p. 1986. 9.95 o.p. (ISBN 0-8050-0156-5). H Holt & Co.

Courtroom Jungle. Robert C. Van Auken. 135p. (Orig.). 1986. pap. 12.95 o.p. (ISBN 0-317-40362-1). Linch Pub.

Courts & Politics: The Federal Judicial System. Howard Ball. 1980. pap. text ed. (ISBN 0-13-184655-8). P-H.

Courtship, Marriage, & the Family. 2nd ed. Robert K. Kelley. (Illus.). 629p. 1974. text ed. 17.95 o.p. (ISBN 0-15-515335-8, HC). HarBraceJ.

Courtship, Marriage, & the Family. 3rd ed. Robert K. Kelley. 650p. 1979. text ed. 16.00 o.p. (ISBN 0-15-515338-2, HC). HarBraceJ.

Courtship Rite. Donald Kingsbury. 1982. 16.95 o.s.i. (ISBN 0-671-44033-0, Timescape); pap. 8.50 o.s.i. (ISBN 0-671-45224-X). PB.

Cousins & Circuses. Lucy Sypher. LC 73-84837. (Illus.). 256p. (gr. 4-6). 1974. 6.95 o.p. (ISBN 0-689-30148-0, Atheneum). Macmillan.

Covalent Bond. H. S. Pickering. LC 78-50008. (Wykeham Science Ser.: No. 47). 101p. 1978. 19.50x o.p. (ISBN 0-8448-1310-9, Pub. by Crane Russak & Co). Taylor & Francis.

Coven of Women. Jean Brody. LC 86-47948. 224p. 1987. 16.95 o.p. (ISBN 0-689-11863-5, Atheneum). Macmillan.

Covenant & Creation: A Theology of Old Testament Covenants. W. J. Dumbrell. 220p. 1986. pap. 8.95 o.p. (ISBN 0-8407-3053-5). Nelson.

Covenant at Coldwater. John Osier. LC 83-19264. 224p. (Orig.). 1984. pap. 7.95 o.p. (ISBN 0-918518-28-8, St Luke TN). Peachtree Pubs.

Covenant Connection. Ed. by John Kincaid & Daniel J. Elazar. LC 87-72627. 260p. Date not set. lib. bdg. (ISBN 0-89089-327-6). Carolina Acad Pr.

Covenant of Peace: A Liberation Prayer Book. John P. Brown & Richard L. York. 1971. pap. 4.50 o.p. (ISBN 0-8192-1115-X). Morehouse Pub.

Covenant of the Crown. Howard Weinstein. (Star Trek Ser.). 1985. lib. bdg. 11.95 o.p. (ISBN 0-8398-2886-1, Gregg). G K Hall.

Covenanted People: The Religious Tradition & the Origins of American Constitutionalism. Donald S. Lutz & Jack D. Warren. (Illus.). 104p. 1987. pap. 30.00 o.p. (ISBN 0-317-61643-9); suppl. 10.00 o.p. (ISBN 0-317-61644-7). J C Brown.

Covent Garden Album: Two Hundred Fifty Years of Theatre, Opera & Ballet. Lord Drogheda et al. 1982. 35.00 o.p. (ISBN 0-7100-0880-5); pap. 16.95 o.p. (ISBN 0-7100-9336-5). Routledge Chapman & Hall.

Cover Her Face. P. D. James. Ed. by J. Barzun & W. H. Taylor. LC 81-47380. (Crime Fiction 1950-1975 Ser.). 254p. 1982. lib. bdg. 18.00 o.p. (ISBN 0-8240-4983-7). Garland Pub.

Covered Wagon Boy. Kermit Shelby. LC 83-63459. 1984. pap. 3.95 o.p. (ISBN 0-89051-096-2). Master Bks.

Covering All the Bases: A Comprehensive Research Guide to Sports Law. Gary A. Uberstine. (Legal Research Guides Ser.: Vol. 2). xiv, 224p. 1985. lib. bdg. 27.50 o.p. (ISBN 0-89941-431-1). W S Hein.

Covering the Desegregation Story. Center for Equal Education Staff. LC 76-45286. 1976. 3.00 o.s.i. (ISBN 0-912008-12-1). Equity & Excel.

Coversationes sobre la fe see Faith: Conversations with Contemporary Theologians.

Covert Action. Ed. by Roy Godson. (Intelligence Requirements for the Nineteen Eighties Ser.: Vol. 4). 200p. 1981. pap. 7.50 o.p. (ISBN 0-87855-830-6). Transaction Pubs.

Covert Conditioning: A Review & Evaluation. Ed. by H. J. Eysenck & S. Rachman. (Advances in Behaviour Research & Therapy Ser.: Vol. 2, No. 2). 1979. pap. 23.00 o.p. (ISBN 0-08-024271-5). Pergamon.

Cow & the Coronary: Diary of Discovery, Nineteen Forty-Eight to Nineteen Seventy-Eight. C. Austin. (Illus.). 1979. 10.00 o.p. (ISBN 0-682-49327-9). Exposition-Phoenix.

Cow in the Kitchen. Evelyne Johnson. LC 82-23987. (Illus.). (gr. 3up). 1983. lib. bdg. 8.79 o.s.i. (ISBN 0-671-46004-8). Messner.

Cowboy. Aaron Fletcher. (Orig.). 1977. pap. 1.50 o.p. (ISBN 0-505-51152-5, BT51152, Pub. by Tower Bks). Dorchester Pub Co.

Cowboy. Don Hedgpeth. (Illus.). 84p. 1979. pap. 12.95 o.p. (ISBN 0-8032-6304-X, Buffalo Bill Hist. Ctr.). U of Nebr Pr.

Cowboy & His Friend. Joan W. Anglund. LC 61-6110. (Illus.). (ps-2). 1961. 3.95 o.p. (ISBN 0-15-220369-9, HJ). HarBraceJ.

Cowboy & His Friend. Joan W. Anglund. LC 61-6110. (Illus.). (gr. k-2). 1976. pap. 1.95 o.p. (ISBN 0-15-622715-0, VoyB). HarBraceJ.

Cowboy Artists of America: Twenty-Second Annual Exhibition Catalog. 64p. 1987. pap. 16.00 o.p. (ISBN 0-87358-459-7); ltd. ed. 150.00 o.p. (ISBN 0-87358-460-0). Northland.

Cowboy Artists of America: Twenty-Third Annual Exhibition Catalog. LC 88-62539. (Illus.). 64p. 1988. limited ed. 150.00 o.p. (ISBN 0-87358-478-3); pap. 16.00 o.p. (ISBN 0-87358-477-5). Northland.

Cowboy Conspiracy. Larry D. Names. LC 86-32951. (Double D Western Ser.). 192p. 1987. 12.95 o.s.i. (ISBN 0-385-23233-0). Doubleday.

Cowboy Culture. David Dary. 1982. pap. 7.95 o.p. (ISBN 0-380-60632-1, 60632-1). Avon.

Cowboy-English, English-Cowboy Dictionary. Bill Dana. 96p. (Orig.). 1982. pap. 1.95 o.s.i. (ISBN 0-345-30155-2). Ballantine.

Cowboy, Game Warden & Longhorns. Melba Steele. 104p. 1981. 6.95 o.p. (ISBN 0-686-72645-6). Dorrance.

Cowboy Joe of the Circle S. Helen Rushmore. LC 50-9425. (Illus.). (gr. 4-6). 1966. pap. 3.95 o.p. (ISBN 0-15-622720-7, VoyB). HarBraceJ.

Cowboy Life on the Texas Plains: The Photographs of Ray Rector. Ed. by Margaret Rector. LC 82-40316. (Centennial Series of the Association of Former Students: No. 12). (Illus.). 124p. 1982. 19.95 o.p. (ISBN 0-89096-131-X); special limited edition 50.00x o.p. (ISBN 0-89096-139-5). Tex A&M Univ Pr.

Cowboy Wally Show. Kyle Baker. LC 87-19858. (Illus.). 1988. pap. 8.95 o.p. (ISBN 0-385-24122-4, Dolp). Doubleday.

Cowboys. Kristin Helberg. (Illus.). 32p. (Orig.). (gr. k-8). 1982. pap. 3.95 o.p. (ISBN 0-8431-4082-8). Troubador Pr.

Cowboys & Computers: Life on a Modern Ranch. Margaret G. Malone. LC 82-3492. (Illus.). 64p. (gr. 4 up). 1982. lib. bdg. 9.29 o.s.i. (ISBN 0-671-33047-0). Messner.

Cowboy's Christmas. Joan W. Anglund. LC 70-190551. (Illus.). (ps-2). 1972. 2.95 o.p. (ISBN 0-689-30301-7, Atheneum). Macmillan.

Cowboy's Secret Life. Joan W. Anglund. LC 63-16029. (Illus.). (ps-2). 1963. 3.95 o.p. (ISBN 0-15-220565-9, HJ). HarBraceJ.

Cowdry's Care of the Geriatric Patient. 6th ed. Ed. by Franz U. Steinberg. LC 75-37566. (Illus.). 532p. 1982. 57.00 o.p. (ISBN 0-8016-4775-4). Mosby.

Coweta County, Georgia: Chronicles. Mary G. Jones & Lily Reynolds. (Illus.). 888p. 1976. Repr. of 1928 ed. 40.00 o.p. (ISBN 0-89308-016-0). Southern Hist Pr.

Cowman's Vengeance. Will Brennan. 1986. 13.50 o.p. (ISBN 0-317-53082-8, Large Print Bks). G K Hall.

Coxarthrosis: Surgical & Conservative Treatment. August Rutt. LC 75-44531. (Illus.). 180p. 1976. lib. bdg. 20.00 o.p. (ISBN 0-88416-061-0). Year Bk Med.

Coyote: Confessions of an Illegal Alien Smuggler. Ray Monroe. 48p. 1987. 6.95 o.p. (ISBN 0-8062-2899-7). Carlton.

Coyote Cried Twice. Austin Bay. 1985. 14.95 o.p. (ISBN 0-87795-728-2). Morrow.

Coyote Stories of the Navajo People. Robert A. Roessel. 118p. Date not set. price not set o.s.i. (ISBN 0-89019-005-4). Navajo Curr.

Coyotes. Wilfrid S. Bronson. LC 46-6355. (Illus.). (gr. 1-5). 1946. 5.50 o.p. (ISBN 0-15-220727-9, HJ). HarBraceJ.

CP-M & the Personal Computer: Popular. Thomas A. Dwyer & Margot Critchfield. LC 82-20703. (Microcomputer Bks.). 280p. 1983. pap. 19.95 o.p. (ISBN 0-201-10355-9). Addison-Wesley.

CP-M Diskguide. 1983. pap. text ed. 4.00 o.p. (ISBN 0-07-931097-4). McGraw.

CP-M Handbook with MP-M. Rodnay Zaks. LC 80-51415. (Illus.). 320p. 1980. pap. 17.95 o.p. (ISBN 0-89588-048-2, C300). SYBEX.

CP-M Plus Handbook. Alan R. Miller. LC 84-50033. 248p. 1984. pap. 14.95 o.p. (ISBN 0-89588-158-6). SYBEX.

CP-M Primer. Stephen M. Murtha & Mitchell Waite. LC 80-53271. 1980. pap. 14.95 o.p. (ISBN 0-672-21791-0, 21791). Sams.

CP-M Revealed. Jack Dennon. 1983. pap. 15.95 o.p. (ISBN 0-8104-5204-9, 5204). Sams.

CP-M User's Guide. Thom Hogan. LC 81-3948. 350p. (Orig.). 1981. pap. 15.95 o.p. (ISBN 0-931988-44-6). Osborne-McGraw.

CP-M Users Guide Microsoft. (ISBN 0-07-931081-8). McGraw.

CPA Exam Booklet: Intermediate Accounting. Sidney Davidson et al. 112p. 1984. pap. 10.95x o.s.i. (ISBN 0-03-071937-2). Dryden Pr.

CPA Exam Questions on Auditing. Albert K. Francisco & Kenneth A. Smith. LC 87-62329. (CPA Examination Review Ser.). 160p. 1988. pap. text ed. 14.95 o.p. (ISBN 0-932276-82-2). Prof Pubns CA.

CPA Examination Official Questions: Nineteen Seventy-Eight to Nineteen Eighty-Three, 3 vols. o.p. 8.50 ea. o.p. Am Inst CPA.

CPA Examination Review: Auditing. 1987 ed. Patrick R. Delaney & Irvin N. Gleim. 1986. pap. 34.95 o.p. (ISBN 0-471-84936-7). Wiley.

CPA Examination Review: Auditing, Business Law & Theory & Practice. 1987 ed. Patrick R. Delaney & Irvin N. Gleim. 1986. pap. 84.85 o.p. (ISBN 0-471-84937-5). Wiley.

CPA Examination Review: Business Law. 1987 ed. Patrick R. Delaney & Irvin N. Gleim. 1986. pap. 24.95 o.p. (ISBN 0-471-84934-0). Wiley.

CPA Examination Review: Business Law. Edwin W. Tucker. 512p. (Orig.). 1984. pap. 14.95 o.p. (ISBN 0-668-05429-8, 5429-8). Arco.

CPA Examination Review: Outlines & Study Guides, Vol. 1. 13th ed. Irvin N. Gleim & Patrick R. Delancy. 1300p. 1986. pap. 34.95 o.p. (ISBN 0-471-83931-0). Wiley.

CPA Examination Review: Problems & Solutions, Vol. 2. 13th ed. Irvin N. Gleim & Patrick R. Delancy. 1130p. 1986. pap. 34.95 o.p. (ISBN 0-471-83930-2). Wiley.

CPA Examination Review: Theory & Practice. 1987 ed. Patrick R. Delaney & Irvin N. Gleim. 1986. pap. 34.95 o.p. (ISBN 0-471-84935-9). Wiley.

CPA Examination Review 1984 Edition: Theory & Practice, Vol. 1. Patrick R. Delaney & Irvin N. Gleim. 1368p. 1984. pap. 31.95x o.p. (ISBN 0-471-88221-6); Set. pap. (ISBN 0-471-88220-8). Wiley.

CPA Examination Unofficial Answers: 1978-1983, 3 vols. 8.50 ea. o.p. Am Inst CPA.

CPA Review Manual. A. N. Mosich & E. John Larsen. (Illus.). 1978. text ed. 42.95 o.p. (ISBN 0-07-043435-2). McGraw.

CPA Review: Theory, Practice, & Auditing, Vol. 1. David F. Fetyko et al. (Business Ser.). 960p. 1981. text ed. 23.95 o.p. (ISBN 0-534-00966-2). PWS-Kent Pub.

CPA Review, 1981-82: Volume II: Problems & Solutions. David F. Fetyko et al. (Business Ser.). 1088p. 1981. text ed. 23.95x o.p. (ISBN 0-534-00967-0). PWS-Kent Pub.

CPM Profile, 1986. Institute of Real Estate Management Staff. 36p. 1986. pap. 15.50 o.p. (ISBN 0-317-53459-9). Inst Real Estate.

CPSU: Ideological, Political & Organizational Principles. I. Shvets & I. Yudin. 368p. 1985. pap. 4.95 o.p. (ISBN 0-8285-3401-2, Pub. by Progress pubs USSR). Imported Pubns.

CPT-Dermatogolgy, Plastic & Reconstructive Surgery. American Medical Association Staff. (Orig.). 1987. pap. 30.00 o.p. (ISBN 0-89970-297-X, OP-341/8F). AMA.

CPT-General Surgery. American Medical Association Staff. (Orig.). 1987. pap. 30.00 o.p. (ISBN 0-89970-295-3, OP-341/8G). AMA.

CPT-Gynecology, Obstetrics & Urology. American Medical Association Staff. (Orig.). 1987. pap. 30.00 o.p. (ISBN 0-89970-299-6, OP-341/8D). AMA.

CPT-Head & Neck Surgery, Otorhinolaryngology & Opthalmology. American Medical Association Staff. (Orig.). 1987. pap. 30.00 o.p. (ISBN 0-89970-298-8, OP-341/8H). AMA.

CPT-Hospital Outpatient Surgery. American Medical Association Staff. (Orig.). 1987. pap. 30.00 o.p. (ISBN 0-89970-303-8, OP-341/8I). AMA.

CPT-Medical Specialties. American Medical Association Staff. (Orig.). 1987. pap. 30.00 o.p. (ISBN 0-89970-294-5, OP-341/8A). AMA.

CPT-Neurological & Orthopaedic Surgery. American Medical Association Staff. (Orig.). 1987. pap. 30.00 o.p. (ISBN 0-89970-296-1, OP-341/8E). AMA.

CPT-Pathology & Laboratory. American Medical Association Staff. (Orig.). 1987. pap. 30.00 o.p. (ISBN 0-89970-301-1, OP-341/8C). AMA.

CPT, Radiology, Nineteen Eighty-Eight. American Medical Association Staff. (Orig.). 1987. pap. 30.00 o.p. (ISBN 0-89970-300-3, OP-341/8B). AMA.

CPT 1988: Physician's Current Procedural Terminology. 4th ed. American Medical Association Staff. (Orig.). 1987. 30.00 o.p. (ISBN 0-89970-293-7, OP-341/8). AMA.

Crab Book. Cy Liberman & Pat Liberman. (Illus.). 128p. pap. 4.95 o.p. (ISBN 0-317-66674-6). Mid Atlantic.

Crabbe. Arthur Pollard. (Critical Heritage Ser.). 514p. 1985. pap. 15.00 o.p. (ISBN 0-7102-0597-X). Routledge Chapman & Hall.

Crabbe's Arabesque: Social Drama in the Poetry of George Crabbe. Ronald B. Hatch. 1976. text ed. 14.00x o.p. (ISBN 0-7735-0250-5, McGill Canada). U of Toronto Pr.

Crabtree & Evelyn Cookbook. Christopher Baker. Date not set. price not set o.p. Stewart Tabori & Chang.

Crack in the Teacup: Britain in the Twentieth Century. Marina Warner. LC 78-27423. (Illus.). 160p. (gr. 6 up). 1979. 10.95 o.p. (ISBN 0-395-28972-6, Clarion). HM.

Crack in Time. Miesje Jolley. (Illus.). 48p. (Orig.). 1980. pap. 3.00 o.p. (ISBN 0-931122-20-1). West End.

Cracking the Code. LeRoy Lawson. LC 76-57045. 1977. pap. 2.25 o.p. (ISBN 0-87239-125-6, 40042). Standard Pub.

Crackle Weave. Mary E. Snyder. 1986. 5.00 o.p. (ISBN 0-318-19570-4). Robin & Russ.

Crackpot: The Obsessions of John Waters. John Waters. LC 86-5324. 192p. 1986. 14.95 o.p. (ISBN 0-02-624440-3). Macmillan.

Cracks in the Melting Pot. 2nd ed. M. Steinfield. 1973. pap. o.p. (ISBN 0-02-478670-5, 47867). Macmillan.

Crackup. Len Morgan. LC 68-22399. 64p. 1981. pap. 7.95 o.p. (ISBN 0-8168-4513-1, 24513, TAB-Aero). TAB Bks.

Craft & Its Symbols. 5th printing ed. Allen E. Roberts. LC 73-89493. (Illus.). 92p. 1985. Repr. text ed. 8.75 o.p. (ISBN 0-88053-058-8, M 321). Macoy Pub.

Craft Architects. Margaret Richardson. (Illus.). 160p. 1983. 25.00 o.p. (ISBN 0-8478-0483-6); pap. 19.95 o.p. (ISBN 0-8478-0482-8). Rizzoli Intl.

Craft Business Encyclopedia. Michael Scott. LC 76-54209. (Illus.). 1977. 10.00 o.p. (ISBN 0-15-122752-7). HarBraceJ.

Craft New Zealand: The Art of the Craftsman. Doreen Blumhardt & Brian Brake. (Illus.). 300p. 1981. text ed. 100.00x o.p. (ISBN 0-87663-374-2). Universe.

Craft of Calligraphy. Dorothy Mahoney. LC 81-23235. (Illus.). 128p. 1982. pap. 9.95 o.s.i. (ISBN 0-8008-1970-5, Pentalic). Taplinger.

Craft of Comedy Writing. Sol Saks. 231p. 1985. 14.95 o.p. (ISBN 0-89879-192-8). Writers Digest.

Craft of Crewel Embroidery. Erica Wilson. LC 62-9637. (Illus.). 1971. pap. 5.95 o.s.i. (ISBN 0-684-12501-3, SL211, ScribT). Scribner.

Craft of Literary Biography. Ed. by Jeffrey Meyers. LC 84-5614. 300p. 1985. 23.00x o.s.i. (ISBN 0-8052-3943-X). Schocken.

Craft of Macrame. Helene Bress. 1977. pap. 3.95 o.s.i. (ISBN 0-684-14723-8, ScribT). Scribner.

Craft of Social Anthropology. Ed. by A. L. Epstein. 1979. 70.00 o.p. (ISBN 0-08-023693-6). Pergamon.

Craft of Teaching: A Guide to Mastering the Professor's Art. Kenneth E. Eble. LC 76-11894. (Higher Education Ser.). 1976. 21.95x o.p. (ISBN 0-87589-284-1). Jossey-Bass.

Craft of the Ancient Historian: Essays in Honor of Chester G. Starr. Ed. by John W. Eadie & Josiah Ober. (Orig.). 1985. lib. bdg. 38.00 o.p. (ISBN 0-8191-4789-3, Assn Ancient Historians); pap. text ed. 20.75 o.p. (ISBN 0-8191-4790-7). U Pr of Amer.

Craft of the Essay. Ed. by Halsey P. Taylor & Victor N. Okada. LC 76-45937. 408p. 1977. pap. text ed. 8.00 o.p. (ISBN 0-15-515624-1, HC). HarBraceJ.

Craft of the Gunsmith. G. W. Spearing. (Illus.). 144p. 1987. 14.95 o.p. (ISBN 0-7137-1730-0, Pub. by Blandford Pr England). Sterling.

Craft of the Screenwriter. John Brady. 1981. 19.50 o.p. (ISBN 0-671-25229-1). S&S.

Craft of the Weaver. Ann Sutton et al. LC 82-24942. (Illus.). 152p. (Orig.). 1982. 18.50 o.p. (ISBN 0-937274-09-7); pap. 12.95 o.p. (ISBN 0-937274-10-0). Lark Bks.

Craft of Writing. William Sloane. Ed. by Julia Sloane. LC 78-24551. (Illus.). 1979. 10.95 o.p. (ISBN 0-393-04471-8). Norton.

Craft Sources: The Ultimate Catalog for Craftspeople. Deborah Lippman & Paul Colin. LC 75-12543. (Illus.). 240p. 1975. 12.50 o.p.; pap. 5.95 o.p. (ISBN 0-87131-184-4). M Evans.

Craft Sources: The Ultimate Catalogue for Crafts People. Paul Colin & Deborah Lippman. LC 75-12543. 240p. (YA) (gr. 7 up). pap. 5.95 o.p. (ISBN 0-317-65058-0). M Evans.

Crafts: A Career Alternative. Carol S. Kushner. LC 81-11132. (Illus.). 160p. (gr. 7 up). 1981. lib. bdg. 9.79 o.s.i. (ISBN 0-671-42035-6). Messner.

Crafts & Craftsmen. Ed. by Bruce Alexander. (Illus.). 216p. 1975. 9.95 o.s.i. (ISBN 0-8008-1980-2). Taplinger.

Crafts for Christmas. Katherine N. Cutler & Kate C. Bogle. (Illus.). 96p. (gr. 3 up). 1975. pap. 1.95 o.p. (ISBN 0-688-46663-X). Lothrop.

Crafts for Your Leisure Years. Cora Bodkin et al. 1976. 14.95 o.p. (ISBN 0-395-24767-5); pap. 7.95 o.p. (ISBN 0-395-24837-X). HM.

Craftsman Builder. Boericke & Shapiro. 1979. pap. 7.95 o.p. (ISBN 0-671-25192-9, Fireside). S&S.

Craftsman in Engineering. Muriel Venning & Owen Frith. (Illus.). 107p. 1980. 44.95x o.p. (ISBN 0-85083-506-2). Trans-Atl Phila.

Craftsman Manual Set, Vols. 1 & 2. F. J. Christopher & Rosemary B. Christopher. (Illus.). 384p. 1958. (ISBN 0-8022-0247-0). Philos Lib.

Craftsman's Handbook. C. D'Andrea Cennini. Tr. by D. V. Thompson, Jr. 14.00 o.p. (ISBN 0-8446-0542-5). Peter Smith.

Craftsman's Handbook: Henry Lapp. Henry Lapp. LC 75-5212. (Illus.). 104p. 1975. pap. 6.95 o.p. (ISBN 0-87633-019-7). Phila Mus Art.

Craftsmen of the Word: Three Poets of Modern Russia Gumilyov, Akhmatova, Mandelstam. Leonid I. Strakhovsky. LC 79-91774. (Illus.). 114p. 1949. Repr. lib. bdg. 35.00x o.p. (ISBN 0-8371-2784-X, STCW). Greenwood.

Crag Mollusca, 2 Pts in 4 Nos. S. V. Wood. Repr. of 1855 ed. Set. 100.00 o.p. (ISBN 0-384-69151-X). Johnson Repr.

Cragg Commentaries. Ernest E. Cragg. LC 79-50349. 1979. 9.95 o.s.i. (ISBN 0-87863-176-3, Farnsworth Pub Co). Longman Finan.

Craig Brucke's Great American Authors Series - Ernest Hemingway Set. Contrib. by Craig Brucke. 1989. bookends 59.95 o.p. (ISBN 0-929264-54-1). Longstreet Pr Inc.

Craig Brucke's Great American Humorists Series - Mark Twain Individual. Ed. by Craig Brucke. 1989. statuette 35.00 o.p. (ISBN 0-929264-53-3). Longstreet Pr Inc.

Craig Claiborne's Gourmet Diet. Craig Claiborne. 1988. pap. 3.95 o.p. (ISBN 0-345-00623-2). Ballantine.

Craig's Care of the Newly Born Infant. 7th ed. A. J. Keay & D. M. Morgan. (Illus.). 528p. 1982. pap. 28.75 o.p. (ISBN 0-443-02344-1). Churchill.

Cram Course for the GRE. Ronald G. Vlk. (Cram Courses Ser.). (Illus.). 128p. (Orig.). pap. 0.00 o.s.i. Monarch Pr.

Cram Course for the LSAT. Ronald G. Vlk. (Cram Courses Ser.). (Illus.). 128p. (Orig.). pap. 0.00 o.s.i. Monarch Pr.

Crampton Hodnet. Barbara Pym. 345p. 1986. lib. bdg. 14.95 o.p. (ISBN 0-8161-3968-7, Large Print Bks). G K Hall.

Cranberry Book. Elizabeth Gemming. LC 82-19797. (Illus.). (ps-3). 1983. 9.95 o.p. (ISBN 0-698-20568-5, Coward). Putnam Pub Group.

Crane Safety & Operation. Ed. by Signs of the Times Staff. (Illus.). 1971. pap. 2.95 o.p. (ISBN 0-685-51821-3). Signs of Times.

Cranes at Dusk. Hisako Matsubara. Tr. by Leila Vennewitz from Ger. LC 84-7031. 264p. 1985. 15.95 o.s.i. (ISBN 0-385-27858-6, Dial). Doubleday.

Crane's Bill: Zen Poems of China & Japan. Tr. by Lucien Stryk et al from Chinese & Japanese. LC 80-8949. 208p. 1981. pap. 4.95 o.p. (ISBN 0-394-17912-9, B458, BC). Grove.

Cranford. Elizabeth Gaskell. 1973. pap. 3.95x o.p. (ISBN 0-460-01083-2, Evman). Biblio Dist.

Cranial Computed Tomography. Seungho H. Lee & Krishna C. Rao. (Illus.). 704p. 1983. text ed. 105.00 o.p. (ISBN 0-07-037399-X). McGraw.

Cranial Osteology of the Hylid Frog: Smilisca Baudini. Linda Trueb. (Museum Ser.: Vol. 18, No. 2). 25p. 1968. 1.50 o.p. (ISBN 0-317-04895-3). U of KS Mus Nat Hist.

Craniofacial Growth in Man. R. E. Moyers & W. M. Krogman. 1971. 95.00 o.p. (ISBN 0-08-016331-9). Pergamon.

Craniotomography: An Atlas & Guide. K. Reisner & J. Gosepath. Tr. by L. S. Michaelis from Ger. LC 75-16102. (Illus.). 208p. 1977. 54.50 o.p. (ISBN 0-88416-244-3). Year Bk Med.

Craniovertebral Region in Chronic Inflammatory Rheumatic Diseases. Y. Dirheimer. LC 77-5884. 1977. 62.00 o.p. (ISBN 0-387-08160-7). Springer-Verlag.

Cranmer & the Reformation under Edward VI. Charles H. Smyth. 1970. Repr. of 1926 ed. lib. bdg. 22.50x o.p. (ISBN 0-8371-4025-0, SMCR). Greenwood.

Crash. Rob Elder & Sarah Elder. 1977. 8.95 o.p. (ISBN 0-689-10758-7, Atheneum). Macmillan.

Crash Course on Kleinian Groups: Proceedings of the American Mathematical Society, Special Session, San Francisco, Jan., 1974. American Mathematical Society Staff. Ed. by L. Bers & I. Kra. (Lecture Notes in Mathematics Ser.: Vol. 400). vii, 130p. 1974. pap. 13.00 o.p. (ISBN 0-387-06840-6). Springer-Verlag.

Crash Go the Chariots. rev. ed. Clifford Wilson. LC 76-20176. 1976. pap. 2.95 o.p. (ISBN 0-89051-023-7). Master Bks.

Crash of Seventy-Nine. Paul E. Erdman. 1976. 9.95 o.p. (ISBN 0-671-22365-8). S&S.

Crashworthiness - Second Impact Litigation: Prosecution, Evaluation, & Defense. 669p. 1985. 45.00 o.p. (H4-4981). PLI.

Crater. Richard Slotkin. LC 80-65988. 1980. 17.95 o.p. (ISBN 0-689-11107-X, Atheneum). Macmillan.

Crater: Or, Vulcan's Peak. James Fenimore Cooper. (John Harvard Library, Belknap Press). 501p. 1962. text ed. 20.00x o.p. (ISBN 0-674-17550-6). Harvard U Pr.

Craters of the Moon: An Observational Approach. Patrick Moore & Peter J. Cattermole. LC 68-10883. (Illus.). 1967. 5.95 o.p. (ISBN 0-393-06355-0). Norton.

Craving. Emily Arnold. 1986. pap. 4.50 o.p. (ISBN 0-440-31699-5, LE). Dell.

Crayfish. 2nd ed. Elementary Science Study Staff. 1975. tchr's. guide 17.12 o.p. (ISBN 0-07-018580-8). McGraw.

Crazy Animal Stories. Dalmais. 1983. text ed. 9.95 o.p. (ISBN 0-07-015198-9). McGraw.

Crazy Charlie's Crew. Rocky Whitely. (Illus.). 1977. 6.00 o.p. (ISBN 0-682-48820-8). Exposition-Phoenix.

Crazy Creature Number Puzzles. Studio D Staff. LC 86-5981. (Illus.). 96p. (gr. 4 up). 1987. 13.95 o.p. (ISBN 0-8069-4750-0); PLB 12.49 o.p. (ISBN 0-8069-4751-9); pap. 4.95 o.p. (ISBN 0-8069-4752-7). Sterling.

Crazy Creature Picture Puzzles. Studio D Staff. LC 85-27622. (Illus.). 96p. (Orig.). (gr. 2 up). 1986. 10.95 o.p. (ISBN 0-8069-4716-0); PLB 13.29 o.p. (ISBN 0-8069-4717-9); pap. 4.95 o.p. (ISBN 0-8069-6226-7). Sterling.

Crazy Crocheting. Ferne G. Cone. LC 81-1275. (Illus.). 192p. (gr. 5-7). 1981. 12.95 o.s.i. (ISBN 0-689-30867-1, Atheneum Childrens Bks). Macmillan.

Crazy Games for Your Commodore 64. Hal Renko & Sam Edwards. (Illus.). 144p. 1984. pap. (ISBN 0-201-16483-3). Addison-Wesley.

Crazy Judah: Father of the Transcontinental Railroad. Helen Hinckley. (Illus.). 208p. pap. 7.95 o.s.i. (ISBN 0-87095-083-5). Gldn West Bks.

Crazy Kill. Chester Himes. 160p. 1973. Repr. of 1959 ed. 7.95x o.p. (ISBN 0-911860-32-0). Chatham Bkseller.

Crazy Lady. Constance B. Schnurr. LC 69-11601. (Illus.). (gr. 3-6). 1969. 4.50 o.p. (ISBN 0-15-220864-X, HJ); 4.50 o.p. (ISBN 0-15-220865-8). HarBraceJ.

Crazy Mary. Molly Cone. (Illus.). 144p. (gr. 7-9). 1966. 4.50 o.p. (ISBN 0-395-06701-4). HM.

Crazy Minnie. Margaret Poynter. (Challenge Bks.). (Illus.). 56p. (gr. 4 up). 1979. PLB 8.95 o.p. (ISBN 0-87191-680-0). Creative Ed.

Crazy Pete. Dan Gillis. 1977. 4.00 o.p. (ISBN 0-682-48682-5). Exposition-Phoenix.

Crazy Quilt. Jocelyn Riley. LC 84-1017. (gr. 7-9). 1983. 11.50 o.p. (ISBN 0-688-03873-5, Morrow Junior Books). Morrow.

Crazy to Fly. Martha O. Conn. LC 77-23871. (Illus.). (gr. 4-8). 1978. 8.95 o.p. (ISBN 0-689-30616-4, Atheneum). Macmillan.

Crazy Town. Dona V. Smoak & Isaacsen-Bright. LC 84-52559. (Predictable Reading Book Ser.). (Illus.). 24p. (gr. k-3). 1985. 7.95 o.s.i. Willowisp Pr.

Crazy Town. Dona V. Smoak & Isaacsen-Bright. (Predictable Reading Book Ser.). (Illus.). 24p. (gr. k-2). 1985. 1.50 o.s.i. (ISBN 0-317-60969-6). Willowisp Pr.

Crazy Town. Smoke & Isaacsen-Bright. Ed. by Margaret Holland. (ps-1). 1985. 7.95 o.p. (ISBN 0-87406-000-1). Sterling.

Crazy Years: Paris in the Twenties. William Wiser. (Nonfiction Ser.). 1985. pap. 9.95 o.p. (ISBN 0-8398-2859-4). G K Hall.

CRC Handbook of Biochemistry & Molecular Biology: Cumulative Index. 3rd ed. Ed. by Gerald D. Fasman. 295p. 1977. 68.00 o.p. (ISBN 0-8493-0511-X). CRC Pr.

CRC Handbook of Chemistry & Physics. 67th ed. Ed. by Robert C. Weast. 2424p. 69.95 o.p. (ISBN 0-317-57988-6). CRC Pr.

Creaciones y Creadores: A Basic Literary Reader. William F. Ratliff. 128p. 1981. pap. text ed. 8.00 o.p. (ISBN 0-394-32654-7, RanC). Random.

Create: A New Model for Career Change - Participants Manual. Ed. by Vivian R. McCoy et al. 163p. (Orig.). 1979. pap. 12.00 spiral bdg. o.p. (ISBN 0-936352-08-6). U of KS Cont Ed.

Create: A New Model for Career Change - Trainers Manual. Ed. by Vivian R. McCoy et al. 163p. (Orig.). pap. 17.50 spiral bdg. o.p. (ISBN 0-936352-09-4). U of KS Cont Ed.

Creating a Climate of Confidence. O. Bykov. 80p. 1986. pap. 2.95 o.p. (ISBN 0-8285-3210-9, Pub. by Progress Pubs USSR). Imported Pubns.

Creating a Community Association: The Developer's Role in Condominium & Homeowner Associations. C. James Dowden. LC 76-56982. 78p. 1977. 28.00 o.p. (ISBN 0-87420-574-3). Urban Land.

Creating a Database: Undersea Adventure. Steve Rodgers. (Write Your Own Program Ser.). (Illus.). 48p. (gr. 3-12). 1985. PLB 12.40 o.p. (ISBN 0-531-03490-9). Watts.

Creating a New Garden. Faith Whiten & Geoff Whiten. 1986. 22.00 o.p. (ISBN 0-393-02350-8). Norton.

Creating a Successful Christian Marriage. Cleveland McDonald. LC 74-20202. 1975. 10.95 o.p. (ISBN 0-87227-038-6). Reg Baptist.

Creating an Information Service. Sylvia P. Webb. 101p. 1985. pap. 19.00 o.p. (ISBN 0-85142-186-5). Learned Info.

Creating & Planning the Corporate Data Base System Project. Leo J. Cohen. LC 81-52903. 324p. 1981. Repr. of 1981 ed. 29.50 o.p. QED Info Sci.

Creating & Using Learning Games. Craig Pearson & Joseph Marfuggi. LC 75-12461. (Learning Handbooks Ser.). 1975. pap. 5.95 o.p. (ISBN 0-8224-1624-7). D S Lake Pubs.

Creating Arcade Games on the Timex-Sinclair. Seth McEvoy. 192p. (Orig.). 1984. 12.95 o.p. (ISBN 0-942386-26-4). Compute Pubns.

Creating Change in Mental Health Organizations. George W. Fairweather et al. 200p. 1974. 25.00 o.p. (ISBN 0-08-017833-2); pap. 14.25 o.p. (ISBN 0-08-017832-4). Pergamon.

Creating Common Wealth. Ian Hore-Lacy. 103p. (Orig.). 1985. pap. 5.95 o.p. (ISBN 0-86760-024-1, Pub. by Albatross Bks). Meyer Stone Bks.

Creating Community Acceptance for Handicapped People. Roberta Nelson. (Illus.). 240p. 1978. 30.00 o.p. (ISBN 0-398-03788-4). C C Thomas.

Creating Compositions. 3rd ed. Harvey S. Wiener. Ed. by Phillip A. Butcher. (Illus.). 448p. 1980. text ed. 18.95x o.p. (ISBN 0-07-070160-1). McGraw.

Creating Efficient Industrial Management. Arthur W. Stinchcombe. 1974. 38.00 o.p. (ISBN 0-12-785805-9). Acad Pr.

Creating Facts: Israel, Palestinians & the West Bank. Geoffrey Aronson. LC 87-3341. 334p. 1987. 24.95 o.p. Inst Palestine.

Creating Family Life Education Programs in the Public Schools: A Guide for State Education Policymakers. 32p. 1985. 4.00 o.p. (ISBN 0-318-18975-5). NASBE.

Creating Food & Fellowship. Date not set. price not set o.p. (ISBN 0-918403-06-5). Agape Ministries.

Creating Interiors for Unusual Spaces. Mirko Mejetta & Simonetta Spada. (Illus.). 128p. 1984. 32.50 o.p. (ISBN 0-8230-7131-6, Whitney Lib). Watson-Guptill.

Creating Original Programming for Cable TV. Ed. by Wm. D. Shaffer & Richard Wheelwright. LC 83-127126. 161p. (Orig.). 1983. pap. 21.95x o.p. (ISBN 0-89461-036-8). Broadcasting Pubns.

Creating Political Order: The Party-States of West Africa. Aristide R. Zolberg. LC 84-2751. (Midway Reprint Ser.). viii, 168p. 1984. pap. text ed. 9.00x o.s.i. (ISBN 0-226-98901-1). U of Chicago Pr.

Creating Rural Employment. Bill Kinsey. 192p. 1986. 39.50 o.p. (ISBN 0-7099-1557-8, Pub. by Croom Helm UK). Routledge Chapman & Hall.

Creating Strategic Vision: Long-Range Planning for National Security. Perry Smith et al. LC 87-14000. (Illus.). 151p. 1987. pap. 3.75 o.p. (ISBN 0-318-23452-1, S/N 008-020-01108-8). USGPO.

Creating Success: A Master Plan. Roger Fritz. 224p. 1984. 15.95 o.p. (ISBN 0-8119-0701-5). Fell.

Creating the Technical Report. Steven Schmidt. (Illus.). 160p. 1983. text ed. 30.00 o.p. (ISBN 0-13-189027-1). P-H.

Creating Wealth. Robert G. Allen. 1983. 17.45 o.p. (ISBN 0-671-44281-3). S&S.

Creating Your Own Soft Furnishing: How to Decorate with Fabric. Angela Fishburn. LC 85-11210. 112p. 1986. 22.95 o.p. (ISBN 0-03-008513-6, Owl Bks); pap. 10.95 o.p. (ISBN 0-03-006312-4, Owl Bks). H Holt & Co.

Creation. LC 76-11268. (Sunshine Bks.). (Illus.). 20p. 1976. pap. 1.00 o.p. (ISBN 0-8006-1575-1, 1-1575, Fortress). Augsburg Fortress.

Creation. (Illus.). 180p. 1988. pap. 19.95 o.p. (ISBN 0-8230-5811-5). Watson-Guptill.

Creation. Claus Westermann. Tr. by John J. Scullion from Ger. LC 74-75730. 136p. (Orig.). 1974. pap. 4.95 o.p. (ISBN 0-8006-1072-5, 1-1072, Fortress). Augsburg Fortress.

Creation & Annihilation Operators. Author's Guild Inc. Staff. 1977. text ed. 44.95 o.p. (ISBN 0-07-002504-5). McGraw.

Creation & Detection of the Excited State, Vol. 2. Ed. by William R. Ware. 240p. 1974. 95.00 o.p. (ISBN 0-8247-6113-8). Dekker.

Creation & Detection of the Excited State, Vol. 3. Ed. by William R. Ware. 208p. 1974. 95.00 o.p. (ISBN 0-8247-6114-6). Dekker.

Creation & Detection of the Excited State, Vol. 4. Ed. by William R. Ware. 336p. 1976. 95.00 o.p. (ISBN 0-8247-6451-X). Dekker.

Creation & Its Critics. H. Morris. LC 82-84483. 32p. 1982. pkg of 5 5.00 o.p. (ISBN 0-89051-091-1). Master Bks.

Creation Controversy: Science or Scripture in the Schools? Dorothy Nelkin. LC 83-45954. 242p. 1984. pap. 9.95x o.p. (ISBN 0-8070-3155-0, BP 675). Beacon Pr.

Creation, Fall & Flood. Terence E. Fretheim. LC 69-14184. (Tower Bk.). 1969. pap. 4.50 o.p. (ISBN 0-8066-9359-2, 10-1706, Augsburg). Augsburg Fortress.

Creation: For Kids & Other People Too. Judy Stonecipher. LC 82-62362. (Accent Discoveries Ser.). (Illus.). 64p. (Orig.). (gr. 1-8). 1982. gift book 4.50 o.p. (ISBN 0-89636-095-4). Accent Bks.

Creation of Elizabethville, Nineteen Ten to Nineteen Forty. Bruce Fetter. (Publication Ser.: No. 154). 1976. 10.95x o.p. (ISBN 0-8179-6541-6). Hoover Inst Pr.

Creation of the Roman Frontier. Stephen L. Dyson. Ed. by S. Barb. LC 84-42881. 324p. 1985. 39.50x o.p. (ISBN 0-691-03577-6). Princeton U Pr.

Creation of the Sun & the Moon. B. Traven. (Illus.). 72p. pap. 4.95 o.p. (ISBN 0-88208-087-3). Creative Arts Bk.

Creation: The Cutting Edge-Acts, Facts, Impacts, Vol. 5. Ed. by Henry M. Morris et al. LC 82-83646. 240p. 1982. pap. 7.95 o.p. (ISBN 0-89051-088-1). Master Bks.

Creation: The Facts of Life. Gary E. Parker. LC 80-66536. (Illus.). 195p. 1980. pap. 8.95 o.p. (ISBN 0-89051-064-4). Master Bks.

Creative Advertising of France Three. Ed. by RotoVision Staff. (Illus.). 496p. 1987. 79.50 o.p. (ISBN 0-8230-5792-5). Watson-Guptill.

Creative American Quilting Inspired by the Bible. Suzzy C. Payne & Susan A. Murwin. (Illus.). 192p. 1982. 18.95 o.p. (ISBN 0-8007-1402-4). Revell.

Creative & Critical Thinking. Wilbert E. Moore. LC 67-7864. 1983. text ed. 26.50 o.p. (ISBN 0-395-04939-3); instr's. manual o.p. 2.15 o.p. HM.

Creative Approach to Music Fundamentals. 2nd ed. William Duckworth. 339p. 1985. pap. text ed. (ISBN 0-534-03753-4). Wadsworth Pub.

Creative Approaches in Casework with the Aging. Edna Wasser. LC 66-30763. 98p. 1966. pap. 6.50 o.p. (ISBN 0-87304-090-2). Family Serv.

Creative Black Book Portfolio Edition: 1986. Marty Goldstein & Stuart Waldman. (Illus.). 1000p. 1986. 60.00 o.s.i. (ISBN 0-916098-21-4). Creat Black Bk.

Creative Black Book Portfolio Edition: 1987. Marty Goldstein & Stuart Waldman. 1987. 65.00 o.p. (ISBN 0-916098-24-9). Creat Black Bk.

Creative Black Book Producer's Volume: 1987. Marty Goldstein & Stuart Waldman. 1987. write for info. o.p. (ISBN 0-916098-25-7). Creat Black Bk.

Creative Black Book: 1987, 2 vols. Marty Goldstein & Stuart Waldman. 1987. 100.00 o.p. (ISBN 0-916098-26-5). Creat Black Bk.

Creative Black Book: 1987, Vol. I. Marty Goldstein & Stuart Waldman. 1987. write for info. o.p. (ISBN 0-916098-27-3). Creat Black Bk.

Creative Black Book: 1987, Vol. II. Marty Goldstein & Stuart Waldman. 1987. write for info. o.p. (ISBN 0-916098-28-1). Creat Black Bk.

Creative Bookbinding. Pauline Johnson. LC 63-10798. (Illus.). 275p. 1973. pap. 17.50 o.p. (ISBN 0-295-95267-9). U of Wash Pr.

Creative Brain. Ned Herrmann. LC 87-72980. (Illus.). 456p. 1988. 34.95 o.p. (ISBN 0-944850-00-6). Brain Bks.

Creative Children of God. Ed. by James J. Davidson. 1984. 6.95 o.p. (ISBN 0-533-05967-4). Vantage.

Creative Color for the Oil Painter. rev. ed. Wendon Blake. (Illus.). 160p. 1983. 27.50 o.p. (ISBN 0-8230-1036-8). Watson-Guptill.

Creative Color Photography. Roger W. Hicks. LC 87-8952. (Illus.). 1987. 14.98 o.p. (ISBN 0-517-64129-1). Crown.

Creative Computer-Video. Carolyn Cooper. LC 85-5393. (Computer Awareness Ser.). (Illus.). 59p. (gr. 4-6). 1985. PLB 9.90 o.p. (ISBN 0-531-10037-5). Watts.

Creative Conflict. Richard Krebs. LC 82-7945. 112p. 1982. pap. 5.50 o.p. (ISBN 0-8066-1920-1, 10-1712, Augsburg). Augsburg Fortress.

Creative Cooking Course. Ed. by Charlotte Turgeon. 1975. 24.95 o.p. Exposition-Phoenix.

Creative Cooking Sugar Free. Caroline Weiss et al. (Illus.). 1985. pap. 2.99 o.p. (ISBN 0-686-65551-6). Budlong.

Creative Cooking with Soup Cookbook. Campbells Soup Company Staff. 1989. pap. 5.98 o.p. (ISBN 0-517-67557-9). Crown.

Creative Customizing. Ed. by Spence Murray. LC 78-50827. (Illus.). 176p. (Orig.). 1978. pap. 6.95 o.p. (ISBN 0-8227-5026-0). Petersen Pub.

Creative Dance for Schools. See Leese & Moira Packer. LC 81-123. (Illus.). 96p. 1981. pap. 7.95 o.p. (ISBN 0-8238-0251-5). Plays.

Creative Darkroom Techniques. PhotoGraphic Magazine Editors & Kalton C. Lahue. LC 73-82536. (Photography How-to Ser.). (Illus.). 80p. 1973. pap. 4.95 o.p. (ISBN 0-8227-0018-2). Petersen Pub.

Creative Drama & Improvised Movement for Children. Janet Goodridge. LC 70-131937. Orig. Title: Drama in the Primary School. 1970. 10.00 o.p. (ISBN 0-8238-0120-9). Plays.

Creative Drama for the Classroom Teacher. 2nd ed. Ruth B. Heinig & Lyda Stillwell. LC 80-21275. (Illus.). 352p. 1981. text ed. (ISBN 0-13-189415-3). P-H.

Creative Drama in Religious Education. Isabel B. Burger. 1977. pap. 6.95 o.p. (ISBN 0-8192-1223-7). Morehouse Pub.

Creative Dramatics for All Children. Emily Gillies. Ed. by Patricia M. Markun & Monroe D. Cohen. LC 72-97349. (Illus.). 64p. 1976. Repr. of 1973 ed. 5.20x o.p. (ISBN 0-87173-020-0). ACEI.

Creative Editing & Writing Workbook. Ed. by Emily P. Flint. 279p. 1979. 40.00 o.p. (ISBN 0-89964-038-9). Coun Adv & Supp Ed.

Creative Expression. Stanley Rosner & Lawrence E. Abt. LC 75-37977. (Illus.). 384p. 1976. 18.00 o.p. (ISBN 0-88427-015-7). North River.

Creative Feltmaking. Kay Donald. 84p. (Orig.). 1985. pap. 4.95 o.p. (ISBN 0-949924-35-0, Pub. by Kangaroo Pr). Intl Spec Bk.

Creative Financing in the 1980's. Peter H. Darrow & Ricardo A. Mestres. LC 83-62925. (Corporate Law & Practice Course Handbook Series: No. 432). 1983. 45.00 o.p. PLI.

Creative Financing of Real Estate. James A. Misko. LC 81-6329. 202p. 1981. 49.50 o.p. (ISBN 0-87624-108-9, Inst Busn Plan). P-H.

Creative Flower Arrangement. Jean Taylor. (Illus.). 388p. 1987. pap. 19.95 o.p. (ISBN 0-09-113631-8, Pub. by Century Hutchinson). David & Charles.

Creative Food Experiences for Children. rev. ed. Mary T. Goodwin & Gerry Pollen. (Illus.). 256p. 1980. text ed. 12.95 o.p. (ISBN 0-89329-028-9). Ctr Sci Public.

Creative Games for Learning: Parent, Teacher Made Games. Ed. by Merle B. Karnes. 1977. pap. text ed. 8.50 o.p. (ISBN 0-86586-016-5). Coun Exc Child.

Creative Games for Teaching English: Fun & Wonderful Sourcebook of Knowledge, Vocabulary & Grammar Games to Supplement Your English Lessons for Gifted Elementary, English As a Second Language & Jr. High Through Jr. College Level Students. Beatrice Levin. Ed. by Frank Alaxander. (Illus.). 98p. (Orig.). pap. 7.95 o.s.i. (ISBN 0-915256-15-0). Front Row.

Creative Gardener's Cookbook. (Illus.). 384p. 1986. 22.95 o.p. (ISBN 0-8249-3057-6). Ideals.

Creative Gift Wrapping. Philippa Kirby. Date not set. 19.95 o.s.i. (ISBN 0-317-66505-7); pap. 13.95 o.s.i. (ISBN 0-317-66506-5). Grove.

Creative Gift Wrapping: The Complete Guide to Techniques & Ideas. Philippa Kirby. LC 87-13368. (Illus.). 128p. 1987. 19.95 o.s.i. (ISBN 1-55584-086-8); pap. 12.95 o.s.i. (ISBN 1-55584-087-6). Weidenfeld.

Creative Growth Games. Eugene Raudsepp & George P. Hough. LC 77-2522. (Illus.). 1977. pap. 3.95 o.p. (ISBN 0-15-622735-5, Harv). HarBraceJ.

Creative Ideas for Small Group in the Christian Community. John Mallison. (Abridged Small Group Ser.). 250p. (Orig.). 1978. pap. 9.95 o.p. (ISBN 0-909202-06-0, Pub. by Renewal Pubns). Meyer Stone Bks.

Creative Insomnia. Douglas Colligan. 1979. pap. text ed. 3.95 o.p. (ISBN 0-07-011797-7). McGraw.

Creative Jewelry. Patti Clarke. LC 77-90127. 1978. 13.95 o.s.i. (ISBN 0-8008-1995-0). Taplinger.

Creative Kid Books, No. 1. Marlene LeFever & Kathy Weyna. (gr. 3-7). 1984. pap. 2.50 o.p. (ISBN 0-89191-935-X, 59352). Cook.

Creative Kid Books, No. 2. Marlene LeFever & Kathy Weyna. (gr. 3-7). 1984. pap. 2.50 o.p. (ISBN 0-89191-936-8, 59360). Cook.

Creative Kid's Guide to Home Computers. Fred D'Ignazio. LC 79-6860. (Illus.). 144p. (gr. 6). 1981. 10.95 o.p. (ISBN 0-385-15313-9); PLB o.p. (ISBN 0-385-15314-7). Doubleday.

Creative Kind of Killer. Jack Early. 1984. 12.95 o.p. (ISBN 0-531-09835-4). Watts.

Creative Kitchen Poultry Cookbook. Reader's Digest Editors. (Illus.). 148p. 1985. 9.95 o.p. (ISBN 0-88850-134-X, Pub. by RD Assn). Random.

Creative Knitting: Complete Sourcebook to Patternmaking & Design. Mary A. Erickson & Eve Cohen. 176p. (Orig.). 1986. pap. 12.95 o.p. Bantam.

Creative Land Development: Bridge to the Future. Robert A. Lemire. 1979. 8.95 o.p. (ISBN 0-395-28590-9). HM.

Creative Lettering. Michael Harvey. LC 84-26907. 64p. (Orig.). 1985. pap. 7.95 o.p. (ISBN 0-8008-1997-7). Taplinger.

Creative Living. National Federation of Community Assoc. 76p. 1974. pap. text ed. 3.75x o.p. (ISBN 0-7199-0896-5, Pub. by Bedford England). Gower Pub Co.

Creative Living: Memories, Reflections & Dreams. Dorothy Henderson. 91p. 1980. 6.50 o.p. (ISBN 0-682-49597-2). Exposition-Phoenix.

Creative Loneliness. William E. Hulme. LC 76-27083. 112p. 1977. pap. 5.95 o.p. (ISBN 0-8066-1556-7, 10-1715, Augsburg). Augsburg Fortress.

Creative Long-Term Care Administration. George K. Gordon & Ruth Stryker. (Illus.). 406p. 1983. 38.00x o.p. (ISBN 0-398-04822-3). C C Thomas.

Creative Marriage. Mel Krantzler. 1981. text ed. 12.95 o.p. (ISBN 0-07-035398-0). McGraw.

Creative Mathematics. H. S. Wall. 201p. 1963. pap. 6.95x o.p. (ISBN 0-292-71039-9). U of Tex Pr.

Creative Mind. Henri Bergson. 256p. (ISBN 0-8022-0106-7). Philos Lib.

Creative Needlepoint Borders. Maggie Wall. LC 76-46366. (Encore Edition). (Illus.). 1977. 5.95 o.p. (ISBN 0-684-16204-0, ScribT). Scribner.

Creative Ordeal: The Story of Raytheon. Otto J. Scott. LC 74-77859. (Illus.). 448p. 1974. 12.95 o.p. (ISBN 0-689-10633-5, Atheneum). Macmillan.

Creative Painting from Photographs. Rudy De Reyna. (Illus.). 160p. 1986. pap. 16.95 o.p. (ISBN 0-8230-1093-7). Watson-Guptill.

Creative Painting of Everyday Subjects. Ted Smuskiewicz. (Illus.). 144p. 1986. 24.95 o.p. (ISBN 0-8230-1094-5). Watson-Guptill.

Creative Pattern Practice: A New Approach to Writing. 2nd ed. Mary E. Whitten. 349p. 1975. pap. text ed. 9.50 o.p. (ISBN 0-15-515808-2, HC). HarBraceJ.

Creative Piano: A Modular Approach for Adult Beginners. Lily Owyang & Linda Ostrander. LC 77-78909. (Illus.). 1978. pap. 17.50 spiral bdg. o.p. (ISBN 0-395-25569-4). HM.

Creative Pinhole Photography. 3.95 o.p. (ISBN 0-89816-084-7). Embee Pr.

Creative Power of Mind. Ed. by Willis H. Kinnear. 368p. 1966. pap. 8.95 o.p. (ISBN 0-911336-01-X). Sci of Mind.

Creative Problem Solving: The Door to Progress & Change. Thomas Dombroski. 1979. 8.00 o.p. (ISBN 0-682-49160-8). Exposition-Phoenix.

Creative Puzzles of the World. Pieter Van Delft & Jack Botermans. LC 77-80234. (Illus.). 1978. 19.95 o.p. (ISBN 0-8109-0765-8). Abrams.

Creative Real Estate Financing 1986, Vol. 279. Practising Law Institute Staff. 1063p. 1986. pap. 45.00 o.p. (ISBN 0-317-27695-6, N4-4458). PLI.

Creative Relaxation: Turning Your Stress into Positive Energy. Deborah Bright. LC 79-1815. 1979. 8.95 o.p. (ISBN 0-15-122802-7). HarBraceJ.

Creative Singlehood & Pastoral Care. John R. Landgraf. LC 82-7439. 96p. 1982. pap. 4.50 o.p. (ISBN 0-8006-0569-1, 1-569, Fortress). Augsburg Fortress.

Creative Source: Seventh Annual. Ed. by Peter Cordy. (Illus.). 480p. 1985. 51.50 o.p. (ISBN 0-317-19811-4, Pub. by Rotovision). R Silver.

Creative Speech Communication. James W. Gibson & Clifton Cornwell. 1978. pap. text ed. write for info. o.p. (ISBN 0-02-341720-X). Macmillan.

Creative Stitches. Edith John. (Illus.). 10.75 o.p. (ISBN 0-8446-5050-1). Peter Smith.

Creative Strategy in Advertising. 2nd ed. A. Jerome Jewler. 304p. 1985. pap. text ed. (ISBN 0-534-03879-4). Wadsworth Pub.

Creative Suffering. Paul Tournier. LC 82-48939. 160p. 1983. 10.53 o.p. (ISBN 0-06-068296-5). HarpR.

Creative Supervision. Karen R. Gillespie. 399p. 1981. pap. text ed. 13.00 net o.p. (ISBN 0-15-515822-8, HC). HarBraceJ.

Creative Teaching in Health. 3rd ed. Donald A. Read & Walter H. Greene. (Illus.). 1980. text ed. write for info. o.p. (ISBN 0-02-398700-6). Macmillan.

Creative Techniques in Animal Photography. Christian Payne & Paddy Cutts. (Illus.). 168p. 1983. 35.95 o.p. (ISBN 0-7134-3899-1, Pub. by Batsford England). David & Charles.

Creative Techniques in Marine & Seascape Photography. Jonathan Eastland. (Illus.). 116p. 1983. 39.95 o.p. (ISBN 0-7134-4170-4, Pub. by Batsford England). David & Charles.

Creative Techniques in Stage & Theatrical Photography. Paddy Cutts & Rosemary Curr. (Illus.). 168p. 1983. text ed. 12.50 o.p. (ISBN 0-7134-0667-4). Drama Bk.

Creative Techniques in Underwater Photography. Derek Berwin & David Barber. (Illus.). 144p. 1983. 39.95 o.p. (ISBN 0-7134-4035-X, Pub. by Batsford England). David & Charles.

Creative Urban Youth Ministries. Glandion Carney. 74p. 1984. pap. 6.95 o.p. (ISBN 0-89191-846-9). Cook.

Creative Watercolour Techniques. John Blockley. (Leisure Arts Ser.: Bk. 7). (Illus.). 32p. 1984. pap. 2.95 o.p. (ISBN 0-89134-083-1, Pub. by North Light). Writers Digest.

Creative Wellsprings for Science Teaching. Alfred De Vito. LC 84-70142. (Illus.). 260p. (Orig.). (gr. 3-8). 1984. pap. 14.95 o.p. (ISBN 0-942034-02-3). Creat Ventures IN.

Creative Wheat Cookery: Three Hundred Easy Tips, Tasty Recipes & Low Cost Ideas for Using Wheat & Gluten in the Home. Evelyn C. Ethington. LC 75-5321. (Illus.). 94p. 1975. pap. 5.95 o.p. (ISBN 0-88290-046-3). Horizon Utah.

Creative Woman's Guide to Success in Real Estate. Patti Runco. 112p. 1981. pap. text ed. 17.95 o.p. (ISBN 0-8403-2584-3). Kendall-Hunt.

Creative World of Beethoven. Ed. by Paul H. Lang. 1971. pap. 4.95 o.p. (ISBN 0-393-00605-0, Norton Lib.). Norton.

Creative Writing see Disney Practice Workbooks.

Creative Writing: A Review of the Study at the College Level. Roger W. Berry. (Illus.). 1984. 12.95 o.p. (ISBN 0-533-06025-7). Vantage.

Creative Writing in Action. Elizabeth Marten & Nina Crosby. (gr. 3-8). 1981. 6.95 o.p. (ISBN 0-86653-004-5, GA 232). Good Apple.

Creativity & Openness: Essays in Honor of James S. Fulton. Ed. by Konstantin Kolenda et al. (Rice University Studies: Vol. 61, No. 3). 107p. 1976. pap. 10.00x o.p. (ISBN 0-89263-225-9). Rice Univ.

Creativity for Kids Through Word Play. Bob Stanish. (Illus.). 64p. (gr. 1-6). 1983. wkbk. 6.95 o.p. (ISBN 0-86653-112-2, GA 484). Good Apple.

Creativity in the Classroom. (What Research Says to the Teacher Ser.). 2.95 o.p. (ISBN 0-8106-1003-5). NEA.

Creativity in the Life Cycle, 2 vols. A. R. Arasteh. Incl. Vol. 1. Annotated Bibliography; Vol. 2. Interpretative Account of Creativity in Childhood, Adolescence & Adulthood. 1968. Set. 75.00 o.p. (ISBN 90-04-00103-4). E J Brill USA.

Creator, Creation, & Faith. Norman Young. LC 76-10324. 1976. 8.50 o.s.i. (ISBN 0-664-21334-0, Westminster). Westminster John Knox.

Creator's World. Robert C. Carver & Susan Thiess. (gr. k-3). 1978. 4.95x o.p. (ISBN 0-8192-4082-6); parent pupil packet 4.95x o.p. (ISBN 0-8192-4083-4). Morehouse Pub.

Creature! A Chrestomathy of "Monstery" Bill Pronzini. LC 80-70221. 304p. 1981. 12.95 o.p. (ISBN 0-87795-310-4, Arbor Hse); pap. 5.95 o.p. (ISBN 0-87795-321-X). Morrow.

Creature Comforts. Charles Addams. (Illus.). 96p. 1983. pap. 9.50 o.p. (ISBN 0-671-43963-4, Fireside). S&S.

Creatures of the Dark. R. G. Austin. (Which Way Bks.: No. 9). (Illus., Orig.). (gr. 3-6). 1982. pap. 1.95 o.p. (ISBN 0-671-52449-6). Archway.

Crecimiento Del Militarismo y la Explotacion Fiscal De los Trabajadores En EE. UU. N. Vetrova & R. Lipkin. 159p. (Span.). 1978. pap. 2.95 o.p. (ISBN 0-8285-1413-5, Pub. by Progress Pubs USSR). Imported Pubns.

Credit & Collection Principles & Practice. 7th ed. Chapin & Hassett. 1960. text ed. 40.95 o.p. (ISBN 0-07-010538-3). McGraw.

Credit & Collections for Small Business: An Easy-to-Read Guide to Effective Collections. Donald R. Kitzing. (Illus.). 174p. 1981. text ed. 27.95 o.p. (ISBN 0-07-034915-0). McGraw.

Credit by Examination Comes of Age: Implications of AP & CLEP for Colleges, Schools, & Students. LC 79-54968. (Illus.). 168p. (Orig.). 1980. pap. 10.95 o.p. (ISBN 0-87447-122-2, 001222). College Bd.

Credit: Get It, Use It, Stretch It, Save It. Bert Johnson. 180p. 1981. pap. 9.95 o.p. (ISBN 0-936602-25-2). Kampmann.

Credit Management: How to Manage Credit Effectively. R. M. Bass. 352p. 1979. text ed. 36.75x o.p. (ISBN 0-220-67026-9, Pub. by Busn Bks England); pap. text ed. 14.75x o.p. (ISBN 0-220-67029-3). Gower Pub Co.

Credit Marketing & Consumer Protection. Terence G. Ison. 522p. 1979. 65.00 o.p. (ISBN 0-85664-728-4, Pub. by Croom Helm Ltd). Routledge Chapman & Hall.

Credit System in France, Great Britain & the United States. Henry C. Carey. LC 73-18238. 1974. Repr. of 1848 ed. 25.00x o.s.i. (ISBN 0-678-01024-2). Kelley.

Credit Where Credit Is Due. Glen Walker. LC 79-4201. 208p. 1979. 10.95 o.p. (ISBN 0-03-042356-2); pap. 4.95 o.p. (ISBN 0-03-042351-1). H Holt & Co.

Creditor Rights & Bankruptcy in State. National Business Institute Staff. LC 87-241583. (Illus.). 1987. 30.00 o.s.i. Natl Busn Inst.

Creditors' Remedies: Pennsylvania Legal Practice Course Materials. Pennsylvania Bar Institute Staff. 68p. 1985. 25.00 o.p. (ISBN 0-318-02158-7, PLP-85). PA Bar Inst.

Credits & Collections. 5th ed. Richard P. Ettinger & D. E. Golieb. 1962. text ed. (ISBN 0-13-192641-1). P-H.

Credo of Maimonides. Carol Klein. 1958. (ISBN 0-8022-0868-1). Philos Lib.

Credo: The Christian View of Faith & Life. Gustaf Wingren. Tr. by Edgar M. Carlson. LC 80-67807. 192p. (Orig.). 1981. pap. 10.95 o.p. (ISBN 0-8066-1870-1, 10-1717, Augsburg). Augsburg Fortress.

Credulities Past & Present. William Jones. LC 67-24355. 576p. 1968. Repr. of 1880 ed. 46.00x o.p. (ISBN 0-8103-3447-X). Gale.

Creed & Personal Identity: The Meaning of the Apostles' Creed. David B. Harned. LC 80-8056. 120p. 1981. 7.95 o.p. (ISBN 0-8006-0645-0, 1-645, Fortress). Augsburg Fortress.

Creeds in the Making: A Short Introduction to the History of Christian Doctrine. Alan Richardson. LC 81-43073. 128p. 1981. pap. 5.95 o.p. (ISBN 0-8006-1609-X, 1-1609, Fortress). Augsburg Fortress.

Creeds of the Churches: A Reader in Christian Doctrine from the Bible to the Present. rev. ed. Ed. by John H. Leith. LC 73-5346. 608p. 1973. pap. 5.95 o.p. (ISBN 0-8042-0515-9, John Knox). Westminster John Knox.

Creeds to Love & Live by. Ed. by Sandpiper Studios Staff. LC 77-93902. (Illus.). 1978. pap. 4.95 o.p. (ISBN 0-88396-027-3). Blue Mtn Pr CO.

Creek. Victor Depta. LC 72-85541. 64p. 1973. 7.95 o.p. (ISBN 0-8214-0121-1). Ohio U Pr.

Creek Rifles. David Moltke-Hansen. (American Indian Ser.: No. 5). (Orig.). 1982. pap. 2.75 o.p. (ISBN 0-440-01215-5). Dell.

Creep-Fatigue-Environment Interactions: Proceedings TMS-AIME Fall Meeting, Milwaukee, WI, 1979. Ed. by R. Pelloux & N. Stoloff. (Illus.). 179p. 26.00 o.p. ASM.

Creep in Structures: Proceedings of the International Union of Theoretical & Applied Mechanics Symposium, Stanford University, 1960. International Union of Theoretical & Applied Mechanics Staff. Ed. by N. J. Hoff. (Illus.). 1962. 74.40 o.p. (ISBN 0-387-02796-3). Springer-Verlag.

Creep Transition in Cylinders. CISM (International Center for Mechanical Sciences), Department for Mechanics of Deformable Bodies Staff. Ed. by B. R. Seth. (CISM Pubnlications: No. 149). 29p. 1973. pap. 5.90 o.p. (ISBN 0-387-81170-2). Springer-Verlag.

Creepy Thing. Fernando Krahn. (Illus.). 32p. 1982. 8.95 o.p. (ISBN 0-89919-099-5). HM.

Cremation. Paul E. Irion. LC 68-10291. 160p. 1968. pap. 3.95x o.p. (ISBN 0-8006-1067-9, 1-1067, Fortress). Augsburg Fortress.

Creosote Bush. Ed. by T. J. Mabry et al. LC 76-58381. (US-IBP Synthesis Ser.). 1977. 66.00 o.p. (ISBN 0-12-787010-5). Acad Pr.

Crescas' Critique of Aristotle: Problems of Aristotle's Physics in Jewish & Arabic Philosophy. Harry A. Wolfson. (Semitic Ser: No. 6). xviii, 759p. 1971. Repr. of 1929 ed. 42.00x o.s.i. (ISBN 0-674-17575-1). Harvard U Pr.

Crescendo. Laura Kalpakian. LC 86-13964. 339p. 1987. 17.45 o.s.i. (ISBN 0-394-55852-9). Random.

Crescent & Green. Toynbee et al. 176p. 1956. (ISBN 0-8022-1734-6). Philos Lib.

Crescent & the Rose: Islam & England During the Renaissance. Samuel C. Chew. 1965. lib. bdg. 37.50x o.p. (ISBN 0-374-91501-6, Octagon). Hippocrene Bks.

Crescent in the East. Ed. by Raphael Israeli. 200p. 1980. text ed. 15.00 o.p. (ISBN 0-391-02099-4). Humanities.

Crescent Moon & Other Stories. Lao She. Tr. by Don J Cohn & Sidney Shapiro. 324p. (Orig.). 1985. pap. 7.95 o.p. (ISBN 0-8351-1334-5). China Bks.

Crest of the Summer. N. Voronov. 1980. 7.95 o.p. (ISBN 0-8285-1875-0, Pub. by Progress Pubs USSR). Imported Pubns.

Crete Nineteen Forty-One: The Battle at Sea. David A. Thomas. (Illus.). 1980. pap. 7.50 o.p. (ISBN 0-686-91772-3). E J Brill USA.

CRI Directory of Expert Systems. Ed. by Computer Resources International Staff. 1986. 75.00 o.p. (ISBN 0-904933-51-2). Learned Info.

Crib Death: Scourge of Infants, Shame of Society. Richard H. Raring. LC 74-84431. 1975. 7.50 o.p. (ISBN 0-682-48122-X, Banner). Exposition-Phoenix.

Cricket in Times Square. Chuck Jones. (Illus.). 48p. (gr. k-8). 1984. 5.95 o.p. (ISBN 0-8249-8074-3). Ideals.

Cricket Songs: Japanese Haiku. Tr. by Harry Behn. LC 64-11489. (Illus.). (gr. 4 up). 1964. 6.95 o.p. (ISBN 0-15-220890-9, HJ). HarBraceJ.

Crickets & Bullfrogs & Whispers of Thunder: Poems & Pictures by Harry Behn. Harry Behn. Ed. by Lee B. Hopkins. LC 83-18347. (Illus.). 96p. (ps-3). 1984. 11.95 o.s.i. (ISBN 0-15-220885-2, HJ). HarBraceJ.

Crickets & Frogs: A Fable in Spanish & English. Gabriela Mistral. Tr. by Doris Dana from Span. LC 72-77131. (Illus.). 32p. (gr. 1-5). 1972. 5.95 o.p. (ISBN 0-689-30303-3, Atheneum). Macmillan.

Cricklewood Diet. Alan Coren. LC 83-61287. 176p. 1984. 9.95 o.p. (ISBN 0-88186-050-6). Parkwest Pubns.

Cries & Itinerant Trades: A Bibliography. Ed. by Karen F. Beall. 1976. 235.00x o.p. (ISBN 0-8103-4352-5, Pub. by Dr. E. Hauswedell). Gale.

Cries of Swimmers. Maura Stanton. LC 84-2227. (Poetry Ser.). 72p. (Orig.). 1984. pap. 7.95 o.p. (ISBN 0-87480-232-6). U of Utah Pr.

Crime & Conflict. Harold E. Pepinsky. 1976. 41.00 o.p. (ISBN 0-12-550050-5). Acad Pr.

Crime & Criminal Justice. Ed. by David W. Patterson. LC 74-4155. 149p. 1974. pap. text ed. 6.95x o.p. (ISBN 0-8422-0396-6). Irvington.

Crime & Criminalization. 2nd ed. Clayton A. Hartjen. LC 76-51075. 270p. 1978. lib. bdg. 16.50 o.p. (ISBN 0-88275-722-9, Pub. by John Wiley). Krieger.

Crime & Criminology. 3rd ed. Sue T. Reid. 1982. text ed. 27.95 o.p. (ISBN 0-03-059248-8). HR&W.

Crime & Criminology. 4th ed. Sue T. Reid. LC 84-25176. 720p. 1985. 32.95x o.p. (ISBN 0-03-070752-8). HR&W.

Crime & Delinquency. 3rd ed. Martin R. Haskell & Lewis Yablonsky. 1978. text ed. 27.95 o.p. (ISBN 0-395-30616-7). HM.

Crime & Human Nature. James Q. Wilson & Richard J. Herrnstein. 559p. 1985. 23.45 o.p. (ISBN 0-671-54130-7). S&S.

Crime & Insanity. Richard Nice. 288p. 1958. (ISBN 0-8022-1213-1). Philos Lib.

Crime & Justice in America. Ed. by John T. O'Brien. LC 79-182. (Pergamon Policy Studies). (Illus.). 1979. 95.00 o.p. (ISBN 0-08-023857-2). Pergamon.

Crime & Justice in America: Seventeen Seventy-Six to Nineteen Seventy-Six. Ed. by Graeme R. Newman. LC 75-36472. (Annals of the American Academy of Political Science Ser.: No. 423). pap. 8.95 o.p. (ISBN 0-87761-197-1). Am Acad Pol Soc Sci.

Crime & Punishment. Fyodor Dostoyevsky. Tr. by Constance Garnett. 1977. 11.95x o.p. (ISBN 0-460-00501-4, Evman); pap. 3.75x o.p. (ISBN 0-460-01501-X, DEL-04072). Biblio Dist.

Crime & Punishment. rev. ed. Fyodor Dostoyevsky. Ed. by George Gibian. (Critical Editions Ser). (gr. 9-12). 1975. pap. 9.95x o.p. (ISBN 0-393-09292-5, NortonC); pap. text ed. 2.95x o.p. (ISBN 0-393-09633-5). Norton.

Crime & Punishment. Fyodor Dostoyevsky. 48p. (Orig.). 1988. pap. 9.95 o.p. (ISBN 1-55651-129-9); audiocassete tape incl. o.p. (ISBN 1-55651-130-2). Cram Cassettes.

Crime & Punishment: Changing Attitudes in America. Arthur L. Stinchcombe et al. LC 80-8004. (Social & Behavioral Science Ser.). 1980. text ed. 29.95x o.p. (ISBN 0-87589-472-0). Jossey-Bass.

Crime & Punishment in America: A Historical Bibliography. LC 83-12248. (ABC-Clio Research Guides Ser.: No. 6). 346p. 1984. 34.00 o.p. (ISBN 0-87436-363-2). ABC-Clio.

Crime & Responses to Crime: Discussion Paper, Topic 1. United Nations Congress on the Prevention of Crime & the Treatment of Offenders Staff & Alvar Nelson. LC 82-144978. 65p. Date not set. price not set o.p. UN.

Crime & Science: The New Frontier in Criminology. Jurgen Thorwald. LC 67-20323. 1969. pap. 5.95 o.p. (ISBN 0-15-623050-X, HB159, Harv). HarBraceJ.

Crime & the Mind, an Outline of Psychiatric Criminology. Walter Bromberg. LC 77-170192. 219p. 1972. Repr. of 1948 ed. lib. bdg. 79.50x o.p. (ISBN 0-8371-6249-1, BRCM). Greenwood.

Crime, Corruption, Conviction. John H. Orr. LC 85-90188. 131p. 1985. 10.00 o.p. (ISBN 0-533-06688-3). Vantage.

Crime de Sylvestre Bonnard see Romans et Contes.

Crime, Delinquency, & Criminal Justice Within the Rural Context: A Bibliography. David P. Van Buren. (Public Administration Ser.: Bibliography P 1626). 1985. pap. 9.00 o.p. (ISBN 0-89028-296-X). Vance Biblios.

Crime Dictionary. Ralph De Sola. LC 80-23348. 240p. 1982. 24.95x o.p. (ISBN 0-87196-443-0); pap. 10.95x o.p. (ISBN 0-8160-1102-8). Facts on File.

Crime Free. Michael Castleman. 1984. 16.45 o.p. (ISBN 0-671-45172-3). S&S.

Crime Free. Michael Castleman. 240p. 1986. pap. 7.95 o.p. (ISBN 0-671-60279-9, Fireside). S&S.

Crime in Society. Ed. by Leonard D. Savitz & Norman Johnston. LC 78-806. 963p. 1978. pap. text ed. write for info. o.p. (ISBN 0-02-406430-0). Macmillan.

Crime, Justice & Public Order in Old Regime France: The Senechaussee of Libourne, 1696-1789. Julius R. Ruff. 212p. 1984. 29.95 o.p. (ISBN 0-7099-2256-6, Pub. by Croom Helm Ltd). Routledge Chapman & Hall.

Crime Lab. George E. Stanley. (Illus.). 96p. (Orig.). (gr. 3-7). 1985. pap. 2.50 o.p. (ISBN 0-380-87122-X, Camelot). Avon.

Crime, Law & Social Science. Jerome Michael & Mortimer J. Adler. (Social Science Classics Ser.). 440p. 19.95 o.p. (ISBN 0-87855-362-2); text ed. 19.95 o.p. (ISBN 0-686-68056-1); pap. (ISBN 0-87855-786-5). Transaction Pubs.

Crime of Dorothy Sheridan. Leo Damore. LC 77-93047. 1978. 9.95 o.p. (ISBN 0-87795-189-6, Arbor Hse). Morrow.

Crime of Imprisonment. G. B. Shaw. 1946. (ISBN 0-8022-1543-2). Philos Lib.

Crime Prevention: Monographs. Mary Vance. (Public Administration Ser.: P 1752). 35p. 1985. 5.25 o.p. (ISBN 0-89028-532-2). Vance Biblios.

Crime, Protest, Community, & Police in Nineteenth Century Britain. David Jones. 288p. 1982. 32.00x o.p. (ISBN 0-7100-9008-0). Routledge Chapman & Hall.

Crime, Race & Culture: A Study in a Developing Country. Howard Jones. LC 80-42064. 200p. 1981. 51.95 o.p. (ISBN 0-471-27996-X). Wiley.

Crime Scene & Evidence Collection Handbook. rev. ed. Intro. by John M. Walker, Jr. Orig. Title: Forensic Handbook. (Illus.). 1985. pap. 4.50 o.p. (ISBN 0-318-19978-5, S/N 048-012-00080-9). USGPO.

Crime, the Police & Criminal Statistics: An Analysis of Official Statistics for England & Wales Using Economic Methods. Roy Carr-Hill & Nicholas Stern. (Quantitative Studies in Social Relations). 1979. 65.00 o.p. (ISBN 0-12-160350-4). Acad Pr.

Crimean War: Pro & Con. Incl. The Soldier That Went Not to Sebastopol; The Letter of John Bright, Esq., M. P., on the War. John Bright; The Conduct of the War. Sidney Herbert; War with Russia. John A. Langford; The War, Its Origin & Its Consequences. Horatio Southgate; Some Observations on the War in the Crimea. Duke Of Wellington; The Close of the War. LC 78-147701. (Library of War & Peace; Histories of the Organized Peace Movement). 1973. lib. bdg. 46.00 o.p. (ISBN 0-8240-0230-X). Garland Pub.

Crimes of the Heart. Beth Henley. 1982. pap. 4.95 o.p. (ISBN 0-14-048173-7). Penguin.

Crimes Without Punishment & Other Tales. Culver Sherrill. 1977. 6.00 o.p. (ISBN 0-682-48931-X). Exposition-Phoenix.

Criminal Behavior: A Psychosocial Approach. Curt R. Bartol. (Criminal Justice Ser.). (Illus.). 1980. text ed. 32.00 o.p. (ISBN 0-13-193169-5). P-H.

Criminal Behavior: An Introduction to Criminology & the Penal System. 2nd ed. Herschel Prins. 320p. 1982. 29.95 o.p. (ISBN 0-422-77680-7, NO. 3713, Pub. by Tavistock); pap. 11.95 o.p. (ISBN 0-422-77690-4, NO. 3714). Routledge Chapman & Hall.

Criminal Behavior & Social Systems. 2nd ed. Anthony L. Guenther. 1976. pap. 19.50 o.p. (ISBN 0-395-30612-4). HM.

Criminal Code. Martin Flavin. 1956. 4.95 o.p. (ISBN 0-87140-797-3). Liveright.

Criminal Corrections: Ideals & Realities. Jameson W. Doig. LC 81-48633. (Policy Studies Organization Bk.). 240p. 1982. 30.00x o.p. (ISBN 0-669-05467-4). Lexington Bks.

Criminal Evidence: Principles, Cases & Readings. Thomas J. Gardner. (Criminal Justice Ser.). (Illus.). 694p. 1978. text ed. 35.50 o.p. (ISBN 0-8299-0148-5); instr's. manual avail. o.p. (ISBN 0-8299-0589-8). West Pub.

Criminal Investigation. Jerry L. Dowling. (HBJ Criminal Justice Ser.). 219p. 1979. pap. text ed. 10.95 o.p. (ISBN 0-15-516090-7, HC). HarBraceJ.

Criminal Investigation. Southwestern Law Enforcement Institute Staff. 144p. 1962. 15.95x o.p. (ISBN 0-398-01813-8). C C Thomas.

Criminal Investigation Digest. W. E. Renoud. 230p. 1981. 31.50x o.p. (ISBN 0-398-04489-9). C C Thomas.

Criminal Investigation Techniques. Donald O. Schultz. LC 77-99265. 220p. 1978. 19.00x o.p. (ISBN 0-87201-164-X). Gulf Pub.

Criminal Justice: A Public Policy Approach. James P. Levine et al. 591p. 1980. text ed. 27.00 net o.p. (ISBN 0-15-516094-X, HC). HarBraceJ.

Criminal Justice Adminstration: Cases & Materials. 2nd ed. Frank W. Miller et al. LC 82-7273. (University Casebook Ser.). 1078p. 1982. text ed. 25.00 o.p. (ISBN 0-88277-051-9). Foundation Pr.

Criminal Justice: An Overview. 2nd ed. Alexander B. Smith & Pollack Harriet. LC 78-27645. 252p. 1979. pap. text ed. 16.95 o.s.i. (ISBN 0-03-046586-9, HoltC). HR&W.

Criminal Justice & the Social Sciences. Burton Wright & Vernon Fox. LC 77-78576. (Illus.). 1978. text ed. 18.95 o.p. (ISBN 0-7216-9610-4). HR&W.

Criminal Justice & the Victim. Ed. by William F. McDonald. LC 75-42754. (Sage Criminal Justice System Annuals Ser.: Vol. 6). 288p. 1976. 29.95 o.p. (ISBN 0-8039-0508-4); pap. 14.95 o.p. (ISBN 0-8039-0509-2). Sage.

Criminal Justice in America: A Sociological Approach. Randall G. Sheldon. 1982. text ed. 29.75 o.p. (ISBN 0-316-78372-2). Little.

Criminal Justice: Introductory Cases & Materials. 3rd ed. John Kaplan & Jerome H. Skolnick. LC 81-17480. 642p. 1981. text ed. 21.00 o.p. (ISBN 0-88277-053-5). Foundation Pr.

Criminal Justice: Law & Politics. 4th ed. George F. Cole. LC 83-7501. 1983. pap. text ed. 13.75 pub net o.p. (ISBN 0-534-02767-9). Brooks-Cole.

Criminal Justice, Leading Constitutional Cases. 1986 ed. Lloyd L. Weinreb. 1290p. 1986. pap. text ed. 19.95 o.p. (ISBN 0-88277-341-0). Foundation Pr.

Criminal Justice Reform - Determinate Sentencing: A Bibliography. Mary E. Huls. (Public Administration Ser.: Bibliography P 1624). 1985. pap. 2.00 o.p. (ISBN 0-89028-294-3). Vance Biblios.

Criminal Justice System. Ed. by Bruce D. Sales. LC 77-7369. (Perspectives in Law & Psychology Ser: Vol. 1). (Illus.). 280p. 1977. 42.50x o.p. (ISBN 0-306-33561-1, Plenum Pr). Plenum Pub.

Criminal Justice System: An Introduction. 2nd ed. Ronald J. Waldron et al. LC 79-65288. (Illus.). 1980. text ed. 23.95 o.p. (ISBN 0-395-28669-7). HM.

Criminal Justice System: An Introduction. 3rd ed. Ronald J. Waldron et al. LC 83-81944. 544p. 1984. text ed. 27.50 o.p. (ISBN 0-395-34269-4). HM.

Criminal Justice System: An Introduction. Ronald J. Waldron et al. LC 75-26098. (Illus.). 480p. 1976. text ed. 16.50 o.p. (ISBN 0-395-18592-0). HM.

Criminal Justice System & Its Psychology. Alfred Cohn & Roy Udolf. 1979. 29.95 o.p. (ISBN 0-442-28882-4). Van Nos Reinhold.

Criminal Justice: 1984 Annual. Ed. by Bruno Leone et al. (Opposing Viewpoints SOURCES Ser.). 110p. pap. text ed. 9.95 o.p. (ISBN 0-89908-517-2). Greenhaven.

Criminal Justice, 1985 Annual. Ed. by Bruno Leone et al. (Opposing Viewpoints SOURCES Ser.). 100p. 1985. pap. text ed. 9.95 o.p. (ISBN 0-89908-512-1). Greenhaven.

Criminal Justice, 1986 Annual. Ed. by Bruno Leone et al. (Opposing Viewpoints SOURCES Ser.). 100p. 1985. pap. text ed. 9.95 o.p. (ISBN 0-89908-522-9). Greenhaven.

Criminal Justice 1988-89. 12th, rev. ed. Ed. by John Sullivan & Joseph Victor. LC 77-640116. (Annual Editions Ser.). (Illus.). 288p. 1988. pap. text ed. 9.95 o.p. (ISBN 0-87967-712-0). Dushkin Pub.

Criminal Law. Wayne R. LaFave & Austin Scott. (Hornbook Ser.). 763p. 1972. 20.95 o.p. (ISBN 0-317-00019-5). West Pub.

Criminal Law. Alan Wells. LC 77-17489. 1978. text ed. 20.00 o.p. (ISBN 0-394-33367-5, RanC). Random.

Criminal Law & Its Adminstration, 1986 Supplement to. Fred E. Inbau et al. 211p. 1986. (ISBN 0-88277-285-6). Foundation Pr.

Criminal Law & Procedure, Cases & Materials: 1985 Supplement. 2nd ed. James Vorenberg. 119p. 1984. pap. text ed. 7.95 o.p. (ISBN 0-314-88260-X). West Pub.

Criminal Law & the Criminal Procedure Law of China. Tr. by Jerome A. Cohen et al from Chinese. 298p. (Orig.). 1984. pap. 7.95 o.p. (ISBN 0-8351-1015-X). China Bks.

Criminal Law, Cases & Comments. 3rd ed. Fred E. Inbau et al. LC 83-8858. (University Casebook Ser.). 968p. 1983. text ed. 27.00 o.p. (ISBN 0-88277-122-1). Foundation Pr.

Criminal Law Cases & Materials. 2nd ed. George E. Dix & M. Michael Sharlot. LC 79-16929. (American Casebook Ser.). 764p. 1979. text ed. 24.95 o.p. (ISBN 0-8299-2056-0). West Pub.

Criminal Law: Cases & Materials. Peter W. Low et al. LC 82-7468. (University Casebook Ser.). 1116p. 1982. text ed. 27.00 o.p. (ISBN 0-88277-050-0). Foundation Pr.

Criminal Law: Cases & Materials, 1983 Supplement. Peter W. Low et al. (University Casebook Ser.). 161p. 1983. pap. text ed. 5.75 o.p. (ISBN 0-88277-153-1). Foundation Pr.

Criminal Law: Cases, Comment & Questions. 3rd ed. Lloyd L. Weinreb. LC 80-14620. (University Casebook Ser.). 855p. 1980. text ed. 20.50 o.p. (ISBN 0-88277-008-X). Foundation Pr.

Criminal Law Defenses: 1986 Pocket Parts, 2 vols. J. Grall Robinson. (Criminal Practice Ser.). 150p. 1986. Set. write for info. o.p. (ISBN 0-314-98556-5). West Pub.

Criminal Law for Police Officers. 3rd ed. Ed. by Neil C. Chamelin & Marcello Truzzi. (Criminal Justice Ser.). 352p. 1981. pap. text ed. 33.00 o.p. (ISBN 0-13-193821-5). P-H.

Criminal Law: New York Questions & Answers. 250p. 1981. 6.95 o.p. (ISBN 0-87526-203-1). Gould.

Criminal Law of Kentucky Annotated, 1986. 1020p. Date not set. pap. 73.00 o.p. (ISBN 0-8322-0179-0). Banks-Baldwin.

Criminal Law Review 1986. Ed. by James G. Carr. (Criminal Law Ser.). 1986. 62.50 o.p. (ISBN 0-87632-508-8). Clark Boardman.

Criminal Law Symposium, 2 vols. Pennsylvania Bar Institute Staff. 169p. 1988. Set. 65.00 o.p. (ISBN 0-318-19073-7, 439). PA Bar Inst.

Criminal Laws of California. 500p. (Supplemented annually). looseleaf 12.95 o.p. Gould.

Criminal Laws of Florida. Gould Editorial Staff. (Annual). text ed. 12.95x o.p. Gould.

Criminal Laws of Massachusetts. Gould Editorial Staff. 400p. (Supplemented annually). looseleaf 17.00 o.p. (ISBN 0-87526-135-3). Gould.

Criminal Procedure: An Analysis of Constitutional Cases & Concepts. Charles H. Whitebread. LC 80-14619. (University Textbook Ser.). 622p. 1980. text ed. 18.50 o.p. (ISBN 0-88277-006-3). Foundation Pr.

Criminal Procedure & Evidence. Rolando Del Carmen. (HBJ Criminal Justice Ser.). 190p. 1979. pap. text ed. 10.95 o.p. (ISBN 0-15-516100-8, HC). HarBraceJ.

Criminal Procedure, Cases & Comments On: 1986 Supplement. 2nd ed. Fred E. Inbau et al. (University Casebook Ser.). 416p. 1986. pap. text ed. 12.95 o.p. (ISBN 0-88277-526-X). Foundation Pr.

Criminal Procedure in a Nutshell. 3rd ed. Jerold H. Israel & Wayne R. LaFave. LC 80-23164. (Nutshell Ser.). 438p. 1980. pap. text ed. 10.95 o.p. (ISBN 0-8299-2107-9). West Pub.

Criminal Procedure in New York, 1971-1982, Part Two: Criminal Evidence. rev. ed. Carlton Brownwell. LC 82-9425. 85.00 o.p. (ISBN 0-317-12199-5); Suppl., 1982. 62.50 o.p.; Suppl., 1983. 20.00 o.p. Callaghan.

Criminal Procedure: The Supreme Court's View Cases. Peter W. Lewis. (Criminal Justice Ser.). (Illus.). 690p. 1979. pap. text ed. 33.75 o.p. (ISBN 0-8299-0236-8); resource manual avail. o.p. (ISBN 0-8299-0597-9). West Pub.

Criminal Procedure, 1984 Supplement. Charles H. Whitebread. (University Textbook Ser.). 195p. 1984. pap. text ed. 5.95 o.p. (ISBN 0-88277-193-0). Foundation Pr.

Criminal Procedure, 1986 Pocket Part. Wayne R. LaFave & Jerold Israel. (Hornbook Ser.). 80p. 1986. 7.95 o.p. (ISBN 0-314-32558-1). West Pub.

Criminal Procedures: Cases & Comments. 2nd ed. Fred E. Inbau et al. LC 80-17843. (University Casebooks Ser.). 1564p. 1980. text ed. 27.00 o.p. (ISBN 0-88277-011-X). Foundation Pr.

Criminal Process: Cases, Comments, Questions, 1985 Supplement to. 3rd ed. Lloyd L. Weinreb. (University Casebook Ser.). 402p. 1985. pap. 11.95 o.p. (ISBN 0-88277-272-4). Foundation Pr.

Criminal Sociology. Enrico Ferri. LC 67-20717. 624p. 1967. Repr. of 1917 ed. 40.00x o.p. (ISBN 0-87586-004-4). Agathon.

Criminalistics: An Introduction to Forensic Science. 2nd ed. Richard Saferstein. (Criminal Justice Ser.). 1981. pap. text ed. 36.00 o.p. (ISBN 0-13-193300-0). P-H.

Criminological Research Trends in Western Germany: German Reports. International Congress on Criminology, 6th, Madrid, 1970. Ed. by G. Kaiser & T. Wuertenberger. 1972. pap. 30.70 o.p. (ISBN 0-387-05754-4). Springer-Verlag.

Criminologist. Ed. by Nigel Morland. LC 72-4369. (Illus.). 331p. 1972. 12.95 o.p. (ISBN 0-912050-27-6, Library Pr). Open Court.

Criminology. 2nd ed. Martin R. Haskell & Lewis Yablonsky. pap. 16.95 o.p. (ISBN 0-395-30620-5). HM.

Criminology. 2nd ed. Larry J. Siegel. LC 85-20351. (Illus.). 627p. 1986. text ed. 44.25 o.p. (ISBN 0-314-93511-8). West Pub.

Criminology: Crime & Criminality. 3rd ed. Martin R. Haskell & Lewis Yablonsky. LC 82-81586. 560p. 1983. pap. 24.50 o.p. (ISBN 0-395-32574-9). HM.

Criminology of Deviant Women. Freda Adler & Rita J. Simon. LC 78-69555. (Illus.). 1979. pap. 17.50 o.p. (ISBN 0-395-26719-6). HM.

Crimson Ramblers of the World, Farewell. Jessamyn West. LC 72-117578. 1970. 5.95 o.p. (ISBN 0-15-123086-2). HarBraceJ.

Crimson Sea. Gary Gygax & Flint Dille. (Sagard the Barbarian Gamebooks: No. 3). (YA) (gr. 7 up). pap. 2.25 o.p. (ISBN 0-671-55489-1). Archway.

Crimson Tide: Alabama Football. Clyde Bolton. (College Sports Ser.: Football). 1982. 10.95 o.p. Strode.

Crimson Web of Terror. Robert D. Chapman. 170p. 1980. 16.95 o.p. (ISBN 0-87364-187-6). Paladin Pr.

Crimson Wind. Max Hennessy. LC 84-45623. 256p. 1985. 13.95 o.p. (ISBN 0-689-11530-X, Atheneum). Macmillan.

Crimsoned Prairie. S. L. Marshall. LC 72-4947. (Illus.). 320p. 1972. 20.00 o.s.i. (ISBN 0-684-13089-0, ScribT). Scribner.

Crippled Tree. Han Suyin. 1985. pap. 6.95 o.p. (ISBN 0-89733-291-1, Pub. by Granada England). Academy Chi Pubs.

Crises & Growth: Making the Most of Hard Times. Anita L. Spencer. 1988. pap. 8.95 o.p. Paulist Pr.

Crisis, A Record of the Darker Races, Vols. 1-47. National Association for the Advancement of Colored People. Incl. Vols. 1 & 2. 33.00 (ISBN 0-8371-1186-2, C30&); Vols. 3 & 4. 33.00 (ISBN 0-8371-1187-0, C31&); Vols. 5 & 6. 33.00 (ISBN 0-8371-1188-9, C32&); Vols. 7 & 8. 33.00 (ISBN 0-8371-1189-7, C33&); Vols. 9 & 10. 33.00 (ISBN 0-8371-1190-0, C34&); Vols. 11 & 12. 33.00 (ISBN 0-8371-1191-9, C35&); Vols. 13 & 14. 33.00 (ISBN 0-8371-1192-7, C36&); Vols. 15 & 16. 33.00 (ISBN 0-8371-1193-5, C37&); Vols. 17 & 18. 33.00 (ISBN 0-8371-1194-3, C38&); Vol. 19. 33.00 (ISBN 0-8371-1195-1, C39&); Vols. 20 & 21. 33.00 (ISBN 0-8371-1196-X, C40&); Vols. 22 & 23. 33.00 (ISBN 0-8371-1197-8, C41&); Vols. 24 & 25. 33.00 (ISBN 0-8371-1198-6, C42&); Vols. 26 & 27. 33.00 (ISBN 0-8371-1199-4, C43&); Vols. 28 & 29. 33.00 (ISBN 0-8371-1200-1, C44&); Vols. 30 & 31. 33.00 (ISBN 0-8371-1201-X, C45&); Vols. 32 & 33. 33.00 (ISBN 0-8371-1202-8, C46&); Vol. 34. 33.00 (ISBN 0-8371-1203-6, C47&); Vol. 35. 33.00 (ISBN 0-8371-1204-4, C48&); Vol. 36. 33.00 (ISBN 0-8371-1205-2, C49&); Vol. 37. 33.00 (ISBN 0-8371-1206-0, C50&); Vol. 38. 33.00 (ISBN 0-8371-1207-9, C51&); Vol. 39. 33.00 (ISBN 0-8371-1208-7, C52&); Vol. 40. 33.00 (ISBN 0-8371-1209-5, C53&); Vol. 41. 33.00 (ISBN 0-8371-1210-9, C54&); Vol. 42. 33.00 (ISBN 0-8371-1211-7, C55&); Vol. 43. 33.00 (ISBN 0-8371-1212-5, C56&); Vol. 44. 33.00 (ISBN 0-8371-1213-3, C57&); Vol. 45. 33.00 (ISBN 0-8371-1214-1, C58&); Vol. 46. 33.00 (ISBN 0-8371-1215-X, C59&); Vol. 47. 33.00 (ISBN 0-8371-1216-8, C60&). 1910-1940. Repr. Set. 745.00x o.p. (ISBN 0-8371-9113-0, CRR&, Pub. by Negro U Pr). Greenwood.

Crisis & Decline: The Viceroyalty of Peru in the Seventeenth Century. Kenneth J. Andrien. LC 84-23436. (Illus.). 298p. 1985. 27.50x o.p. (ISBN 0-8263-0791-4). U of NM Pr.

Crisis at the Bar: The Unethical Ethics of Lawyers (and What to Do About It) Jethro K. Lieberman. 1978. 14.95x o.p. (ISBN 0-393-05644-9). Norton.

Crisis Del Sistema Monetario Del Capitalismo. A. Stadnichenko. 277p. (Span.). 1975. 5.45 o.p. (ISBN 0-8285-1414-3, Pub. by Progress Pubs USSR). Imported Pubns.

Crisis: Heterosexual Behavior in the Age of AIDS. William H. Masters et al. 1988. 14.95 o.p. (ISBN 0-317-66212-0). Grove.

Crisis in American Institutions. 6th ed. Jerome H. Skolnick & Elliott Currie. 1985. pap. text ed. write for info. o.p. (ISBN 0-673-39598-7). Scott F.

Crisis in Economic Relations between North & South. Ed. by Norman Schofield. 456p. 1984. 41.00 o.p. (ISBN 0-566-00479-8). Gower Pub Co.

Crisis in Europe, Fifteen Sixty to Sixteen Sixty: Essays from "Past & Present" Ed. by Trevor Aston. 376p. 1983. pap. 9.95X o.p. (ISBN 0-7100-6889-1). Routledge Chapman & Hall.

Crisis in Freedom: The Alien & Sedition Acts. John C. Miller. 1964. pap. 6.95 o.p. (ISBN 0-316-57233-0, Pub. by Atlantic Monthly Pr). Little.

Crisis in Historical Materialism: Class, Politics & Culture in Marxist Theory. Stanley Aronowitz. 376p. 1981. 34.95x o.s.i. (ISBN 0-03-059031-0); pap. 16.95 o.s.i. (ISBN 0-03-062026-0). Bergin & Garvey.

Crisis in Indian Judiciary. K. S. Hegde. 1973. 6.00x o.p. (ISBN 0-88386-546-7). South Asia Bks.

Crisis in Marriage. Ed. by George W. Forell & William H. Lazareth. LC 77-20538. (Justice Bks). 64p. (Orig.). 1978. pap. 1.50 o.p. (ISBN 0-8006-1552-2, 1-1552, Fortress). Augsburg Fortress.

Crisis in Power. cancelled o.s.i. (ISBN 0-8002-3811-7). Taylor & Francis.

Crisis in the Curriculum. Ed. by E. C. Cuff & G. C. Payne. LC 84-29202. 248p. 1985. 31.00 o.p. (ISBN 0-7099-3421-1, Pub. by Croom Helm Ltd). Routledge Chapman & Hall.

Crisis in the Health Service: The Politics of Management. Stuart Haywood & Andy Alaszewski. 208p. 1980. 30.00 o.p. (ISBN 0-7099-0013-9, Pub. by Croom Helm Ltd). Routledge Chapman & Hall.

Crisis in the Nationalised Industries. Henry Parris. 256p. 1985. 43.00 o.p. (ISBN 0-7099-2078-4, Pub. by Croom Helm Ltd). Routledge Chapman & Hall.

Crisis in the Public Sector--Challenge to the Public Health: American Public Health Association 1980 Meeting in Detroit, Michigan. Ed. by O. Gish. 48p. 1982. pap. 18.25 o.p. (ISBN 0-08-028948-7). Pergamon.

Crisis in Urban Government. Georgetown Law Journal Association Staff. 15.00 o.p. Anderson Pub Co.

Crisis in Urban Schools. Ed. by Thomas E. Glass. LC 73-4330. 1973. pap. text ed. 8.50x o.p. (ISBN 0-8422-0298-6). Irvington.

Crisis Intervention: Case Histories. J. K. Morrice. Ed. by J. H. Kahn. 117p. 1976. 23.00 o.p. (ISBN 0-08-019742-6); pap. 10.25 o.p. (ISBN 0-08-019741-8). Pergamon.

Crisis of Capitalism & the Condition of the Working People. G. Chernikov. 252p. 1980. 7.45 o.p. (ISBN 0-8285-1775-4, Pub. by Progress Pubs USSR). Imported Pubns.

Crisis of German Ideology: Intellectual Origins of the Third Reich. George L. Mosse. LC 78-19126. viii, 373p. 1981. Repr. of 1964 ed. 40.00x o.p. (ISBN 0-86527-036-8). Fertig.

Crisis of International Cooperation. Francois Duchene et al. (Triangle Papers: No. 2). 1974. pap. 6.00 o.p. Trilateral Comm.

Crisis of Parliamentary Democracy. Carl Schmitt. Tr. by Ellen Kennedy from Ger. (Studies in Contemporary German Social Thought). 224p. 1985. text ed. 19.00 o.p. (ISBN 0-262-19240-3). MIT Pr.

Crisis of the Constitution. Margaret A. Judson. 1964. lib. bdg. 27.50x o.p. (ISBN 0-374-94465-2, Octagon). Hippocrene Bks.

Crisis of the Negro Intellectual. Harold Cruse. 1967. pap. 10.95 o.p. (ISBN 0-688-25224-9). Morrow.

Crisis of the Sugar Colonies: Or, an Enquiry into the Objects & Probable Effects of the French Expedition to the West Indies. James Stephen. LC 70-88418. 1970. Repr. of 1802 ed. 35.00x o.p. (ISBN 0-8371-1832-8, STC&, Pub. by Negro U Pr). Greenwood.

Crisis of the University. Peter Scott. 277p. 1984. 28.00 o.p. (ISBN 0-7099-3303-7, Pub. by Croom Helm Ltd); pap. 15.95 o.p. (ISBN 0-7099-3310-X). Routledge Chapman & Hall.

Crisis of the Working Mother: Resolving the Conflict Between Family & Work. Barbara J. Berg. 1986. 16.45 o.s.i. (ISBN 0-671-49956-4). S&S.

Crisis on Conshelf Ten. Monica Hughes. LC 76-25204. (gr. 5-8). 1977. 5.95 o.p. (ISBN 0-689-30555-9, Atheneum). Macmillan.

Crisis Theory: A Critical Overview. Rae S. Lindsay. (Illus.). 1976. pap. 7.50x o.p. (ISBN 0-85564-116-9, Pub. by U of W Austral Pr). Intl Spec Bk.

Crispan Magicker. Mark M. Lowenthal. 1979. pap. 1.95 o.p. (ISBN 0-380-42333-2, 42333). Avon.

Crisscross Shadow. rev. ed. Franklin W. Dixon. (Hardy Boys Ser: Vol. 32). (gr. 5-9). 1953. 4.50 o.p. (ISBN 0-448-08932-7, G&D); PLB 3.29 o.p. (ISBN 0-448-18932-1, G&D). Putnam Pub Group.

Cristina Ferrare's Style: How to Have It in Every Part of Your Life. Cristina F. DeLorean & Sherry S. Cohen. 1984. 16.45 o.p. (ISBN 0-671-46849-9). S&S.

Cristini-Puricelli Nature Set. Ermanno Cristini & Luigi Puricelli. (Illus.). (ps up). 1985. pap. 12.95 o.p. (ISBN 0-88708-010-3). Picture Bk Studio.

Criteria (Dose Effect Relationships) for Organichlorine Pesticides: Report of a Working Group of Experts Prepared for the Commission of the European Communities. Ed. by M. Mercier. 400p. 1981. pap. 81.00 o.p. (ISBN 0-08-023441-0). Pergamon.

Criteria for a Recommended Standard: Occupational Exposure to Hot Environments, Revised Criteria 1986. (DHHS Publication (NIOSH) Ser.: No. 86-113). 152p. 1986. pap. 8.00 o.p. (S/N 017-033-00423-4). USGPO.

Criteria for Awarding School Leaving Certificates, an International Discussion: Proceedings of the International Association for Education Assessment of the 3rd Annual Conference, Narrobi, May 23, 1977. International Association for Educational Assessment Staff. Ed. by Frances M. Ottobre. 1979. 46.00 o.p. (ISBN 0-08-024685-0). Pergamon.

Criteria for Evaluating Advancement Programs. Warren Heemann. 25p. (Orig.). 1985. pap. text ed. 10.00 o.p. (ISBN 0-89964-241-1). Coun Adv & Supp Ed.

Criteria for Nuclear Safety Related Piping & Component Support Snubbers. M. H. Bressler et al. (PVP: No. 45). 40p. 1980. 6.00 o.p. (ISBN 0-686-69846-0, H00172). ASME.

Criteria for Selecting Appropriate Technologies Under Different Cultural, Technical & Social Conditions: Proceedings of the IFAC Symposium, Bari, Italy, May, 1979. IFAC Symposium Staff. Ed. by A. De Giorgio & C. Roveda. (IFAC Proceedings Ser.). (Illus.). 320p. 1980. 80.00 o.p. (ISBN 0-08-024455-6). Pergamon.

Criteria for Underground Heat Distribution Systems. Building Research Advisory Board. LC 74-32581. 1975. pap. 6.25x o.p. (ISBN 0-309-02320-3). Natl Acad Pr.

Criteria-Standards-Indicators. rev. ed. 16p. 1982. pap. 7.50 pkg. of ten o.p. (ISBN 0-88441-435-3, 26-176-010). Girl Scouts USA.

Critic As Scientist: The Modernist Poetics of Ezra Pound. Ian F. Bell. LC 80-41826. 302p. 1981. 37.00 o.p. (ISBN 0-416-31350-7, NO. 3451). Routledge Chapman & Hall.

Critical Approach to Children's Literature. Ed. by Sara I. Fenwick. LC 60-2341. (Midway Reprint Ser.). 1976. pap. text ed. 6.00x o.s.i. (ISBN 0-226-24162-9). U of Chicago Pr.

Critical Bibliography of Building Conservation: Historic Towns, Buildings, Their Furnishings & Fittings. Compiled by John F. Smith. 234p. 1978. lib. bdg. 43.00x o.p. (ISBN 0-7201-0707-5). Mansell.

Critical Care. 4th ed. Lenette O. Burrell & Zeb L. Burrell, Jr. LC 81-9544. (Illus.). 622p. 1981. text ed. 34.95 o.p. (ISBN 0-8016-0906-2). Mosby.

Critical-Care: Care Plans. Nancy M. Holloway. Date not set. price not set o.p. Springhouse Pub.

Critical Care Nursing of the Multi-Injured Patient. American Association of Critical Care Nurses Staff. Ed. by James K. Mann & Annalee R Oakes. LC 79-67787. (Illus.). 168p. 1980. pap. (ISBN 0-7216-1002-1). Saunders.

Critical Care Nursing Review & Self-Test. Billie Meador. 320p. 1983. pap. 23.95 o.s.i. (ISBN 0-87489-300-3). Med Economics.

Critical Dictionary of English Literature & British & American Authors, 3 Vols. S. Austin Allibone. LC 67-295. 3163p. 1965. Repr. of 1872 ed. Set. 210.00x o.p. (ISBN 0-8103-3017-2). Gale.

Critical Difference: Essays in the Contemporary Rhetoric of Reading. Barbara Johnson. LC 80-21533. 168p. 1981. text ed. 19.50x o.p. (ISBN 0-8018-2458-3). Johns Hopkins.

Critical Dissertation on the Nature, Measure & Causes of Value. Samuel Bailey. LC 65-26359. 1967. Repr. of 1821 ed. 50.00x o.s.i. (ISBN 0-678-00223-1). Kelley.

Critical Edge: Controversy in Recent American Architecture. Ed. by Tod A. Marder. (Illus.). 200p. 1985. 25.00 o.p. (ISBN 0-262-13207-9). MIT Pr.

Critical Elections & the Mainsprings of American Politics. Walter D. Burnham. (Illus.). 1971. pap. 5.95x o.p. (ISBN 0-393-09397-2). Norton.

Critical Essays on Ambrose Bierce. Cathy N. Davidson. (Critical Essays on American Literature Ser.). 1982. 33.00 o.s.i. (ISBN 0-8161-8393-7, Twayne). G K Hall.

Critical Essays on Cervantes. Ruth E. Saffar. (Critical Essays on World Literature Ser.). 240p. 1986. lib. bdg. 35.00x o.s.i. (ISBN 0-8161-8825-4). G K Hall.

Critical Essays on Charles Brockden Brown. Bernard Rosenthal. (Critical Essays on American Literature Ser.). 1981. lib. bdg. 29.00 o.s.i. (ISBN 0-8161-8255-8, Twayne). G K Hall.

Critical Essays on E. M. Forster. Alan Wilde. (British Literature Ser.). 192p. 1985. lib. bdg. 35.00 o.p. (ISBN 0-8161-8754-1). G K Hall.

Critical Essays on F. Scott Fitzgerald's Tender is the Night. Milton R. Stern. (Critical Essays on American Literature Ser.). 280p. 1986. lib. bdg. 35.00x o.s.i. (ISBN 0-8161-8444-5). G K Hall.

Critical Essays on Gabriel Miro. Ed. by Ricardo Landeira. LC 79-64045. 1979. pap. 20.00 o.p. Society Sp & Sp-Am.

Critical Essays on Henry Adams. Earl N. Harbert. (Critical Essays on American Literature Ser.). 1981. 29.00 o.s.i. (ISBN 0-8161-8280-9, Twayne). G K Hall.

Titles

Critical Essays on Herman Melville's "Pierre; or "the Ambiguities" Brian Higgins & Hershel Parker. (Critical Essays on American Literature Ser.). 312p. 1983. lib. bdg. 40.50 o.s.i. (ISBN 0-8161-8319-8). G K Hall.

Critical Essays on Jonathan Edwards. William J. Scheick. (Critical Essay on American Literature Ser.). 1979. lib. bdg. 29.00 o.s.i. (ISBN 0-8161-8304-X). G K Hall.

Critical Essays on Margaret Fuller. Ed. by Joel Myerson. (Critical Essay on American Literature Ser.). 281p. 1980. lib. bdg. 29.00 o.p. (ISBN 0-8161-8283-3). G K Hall.

Critical Essays on Psychoanalysis. S. Rachman. 1963. text ed. 19.25 o.p. (ISBN 0-08-010181-X). Pergamon.

Critical Essays on Randall Jarrell. Suzanne Ferguson. (Critical Essays on American Literature Ser.). 1983. lib. bdg. 40.50 o.s.i. (ISBN 0-8161-8486-0). G K Hall.

Critical Essays on Richard Wright. Yoshinobu Hakutani. (Critical Essays on American Literature Ser.). 1982. 32.00 o.p. (ISBN 0-8161-8425-9, Twayne). G K Hall.

Critical Essays on Sinclair Lewis. Martin Bucco. (Critical Essays on American Literature Ser.). 248p. 1986. lib. bdg. 37.50x o.p. G K Hall.

Critical Essays on Thomas Pynchon. Richard Pearce. (Critical Essays on American Literature Ser.). 1981. 29.00 o.s.i. (ISBN 0-8161-8320-1, Twayne). G K Hall.

Critical Essays on Toni Morrison. Nellie Y. McKay. (Critical Essays Ser.). 216p. 1988. 37.50 o.s.i. (ISBN 0-8161-8884-X). G K Hall.

Critical Essays on W. B. Yeats. Richard J. Finneran. (Critical Essays on British Literature Ser.). 264p. 1986. lib. bdg. 35.00x o.s.i. (ISBN 0-8161-8758-4). G K Hall.

Critical Essays on William Styron. Ed. by Arthur D. Casciato & James L. West, III. (Critical Essays on American Literature Ser.). 1982. lib. bdg. 37.00 o.s.i. (ISBN 0-8161-8261-2). G K Hall.

Critical Evaluation of Contemporary "New Left" Sociology. Daniel De Sousa. 1979. pap. 6.50 o.p. (ISBN 0-682-49247-7, University). Exposition-Phoenix.

Critical Faith: A Case for Religion. Gerd Theissen. Tr. by John Bowden from Ger. LC 79-7393. 112p. 1979. pap. 4.95 o.p. (ISBN 0-8006-1373-2, 1-1373, Fortress). Augsburg Fortress.

Critical Food Issues of the Nineteen Eighties. Marylin Chou & David P. Harmon, Jr. LC 79-14718. (Pergamon Policy Studies). (Illus.). 1979. 72.00 o.p. (ISBN 0-08-024611-7); pap. 13.75 o.p. (ISBN 0-08-024639-7). Pergamon.

Critical Incidents in Management. 5th ed. John M. Champion & John H. James. 1985. pap. 19.95x o.p. (ISBN 0-256-03225-4). Irwin.

Critical Issues in Coal Transportation Systems. Maritime Transportation Research Board Staff & National Research Council Staff. 1979. pap. text ed. 10.25 o.p. (ISBN 0-309-02869-8). Natl Acad Pr.

Critical Issues in Competency Based Education. LC 79-14355. (Pergamon General Psychology Ser.). 1980. 46.00 o.p. (ISBN 0-08-024623-0). Pergamon.

Critical Issues in Medical Technology. Ernest G. Cravalho. Ed. by Barbara J. McNeil. 432p. 1982. 28.00 o.p. (ISBN 0-86569-070-7). Auburn Hse.

Critical Materials Problems in Energy Production. Ed. by Charles Stein. 1976. 83.00 o.p. (ISBN 0-12-665050-0). Acad Pr.

Critical Moment: How Personal Crisis Can Enrich a Woman's Life. Margaret Wold. LC 77-84090. 1978. pap. 4.50 o.p. (ISBN 0-8066-1615-6, 10-1720, Augsburg). Augsburg Fortress.

Critical Needs of the Child with Long Term Orthopaedic Impairment: Conference Report. Ed. by Newton C. McCullough, III. 182p. 1985. 15.00 o.p. (ISBN 0-89203-005-4). Amer Acad Ortho Surg.

Critical Observations. Julian Symons. LC 81-8904. (Joan Kahn Bk.). 216p. 1981. 12.95 o.p. (ISBN 0-89919-055-3). Ticknor & Fields.

Critical Path: Construction & Analysis. L. W. Morris. 1967. 33.00 o.p. (ISBN 0-08-012472-0); pap. 17.00 o.p. (ISBN 0-08-012471-2). Pergamon.

Critical Period in American Religion 1875-1900. Arthur M. Schlesinger, Sr. Ed. by Richard C. Wolf. LC 67-24338. (Facet Bks.). 1967. pap. 0.50 o.p. (ISBN 0-8006-3044-0, 1-3044, Fortress). Augsburg Fortress.

Critical Periods. Ed. by J. P. Scott. LC 78-632. (Benchmark Papers in Animal Behavior: Vol. 12). 381p. 1982. 55.95 o.p. (ISBN 0-87933-119-4). Van Nos Reinhold.

Critical Perspectives on Calderon de la Barca. Ed. by Frederick De Armas et al. LC 80-53823. 150p. (Orig.). 1981. pap. 25.00 o.p. (ISBN 0-89295-004-8). Society Sp & Sp-Am.

Critical Perspectives on Gabriel Garcia Marquez. Ed. by Nora Vera & Bradley Shaw. LC 83-51008. 159p. 1986. pap. 20.00 o.p. Society Sp & Sp-Am.

Critical Perspectives on Imperialism & Social Class in the Third World. James Petras. LC 78-13915. 314p. 1979. pap. 7.50 o.s.i. (ISBN 0-85345-529-5). Monthly Rev.

Critical Phenomena. Ed. by J. Brey & R. B. Jones. (Lecture Notes in Physics: Vol. 54). 1976. 14.60 o.p. (ISBN 0-387-07862-2). Springer-Verlag.

Critical Philosophy of Immanuel Kant, 2 Vols, Vol. 1. Edward Caird. LC 4-196. 1968. Repr. of 1889 ed. Set. 58.00 o.p. (ISBN 0-527-14100-3). Kraus Repr.

Critical Reputation of Tennessee Williams: A Reference Guide. John S. McCann. 474p. 1983. lib. bdg. 69.00 o.p. (ISBN 0-8161-8635-9, Hall Reference). G K Hall.

Critical Review of the Effects of Synthetic Detergents on Aquatic Life. R. Marchese. (GFCM Studies & Reviews: No. 26). 34p. (Eng. & Fr.). 1965. pap. 7.50 o.p. (ISBN 92-5-101944-4, F1787, FAO). UNIPUB.

Critical Social Policy, Vol. 1, No. 1. Collective Editorial Staff. 136p. 1981. journal 4.95 o.p. (ISBN 0-86104-480-0, Pub by Pluto Pr). Longwood Pub Group.

Critical Social Policy, Vol. 1, No. 2. 1981. journal 4.95 o.p. (ISBN 0-86104-481-9, Pub by Pluto Pr). Longwood Pub Group.

Critical Social Psychology. Philip Wexler. (Critical Social Thought Ser.). 176p. 1983. 19.95x o.p. (ISBN 0-7100-9194-X). Routledge Chapman & Hall.

Critical Sociology. Ed. by J. W. Freiberg. 418p. 1979. 39.50x o.p. (ISBN 0-8290-0862-4). Irvington.

Critical Strategies: German Fiction in the Twentieth Century. Elizabeth Boa & J. H. Reid. 224p. 1972. 15.00x o.p. (ISBN 0-7735-0174-6, McGill Canada); pap. 5.00 o.p. (ISBN 0-7735-0175-4, McGill Canada). U of Toronto Pr.

Critical Studies in American Jewish History, 3 vols. Jacob R. Marcus. 1971. 35.00x o.s.i. Ktav.

Critical Studies in Organization & Bureaucracy. Ed. by Frank Fischer & Carmen Sirianni. 520p. 1984. lib. bdg. 34.95 o.p. (ISBN 0-87722-343-2); pap. text ed. 12.95 o.p. (ISBN 0-87722-344-0). Temple U Pr.

Critical Study of Freud's Concept of Unconscious Mental Processes with Special Reference to Gestalt Psychology. Allan R. Strauss, Jr. (Illus.). 160p. 1980. 15.00 o.p. (ISBN 0-682-49602-2, University). Exposition-Phoenix.

Critical Surgical Illness. 2nd ed. James D. Hardy. (Illus.). 750p. 1980. text ed. write for info. o.p. (ISBN 0-7216-4511-9). Saunders.

Critical Theory & Education. Rex Gibson. (Studies in Teaching & Learning). 192p. (Orig.). 1986. pap. text ed. 22.95 o.s.i. (ISBN 0-340-39515-X). Princeton Bk Co.

Critical Thinking: Evaluating Claims & Arguments in Everyday Life. Brooke Moore & Richard Parker. 403p. 1986. pap. text ed. 19.95 o.p. (ISBN 0-87484-734-6); instr's. manual avail. o.p. (ISBN 0-87484-766-4). Mayfield Pub.

Critical Thinking: Reading Across the Curriculum. Ed. by Anne B. Grinols. LC 83-73116. 292p. 1984. 10.95x o.p. (ISBN 0-8014-9281-5). Cornell U Pr.

Critical Twilight: Explorations in the Ideology of Anglo-American Literary Theory from Eliot to McLuhan. John Fekete. (International Library of Phenomenology & Moral Sciences). 1978. 24.95x o.p. (ISBN 0-7100-8618-0). Routledge Chapman & Hall.

Critical Views on Vicente Aleixandre's Poetry. Ed. by Vicente Cabrera & Harriet Boyer. LC 79-65008. 1979. pap. 18.00 o.p. (ISBN 0-89295-006-4). Society Sp & Sp-Am.

Critical Vision: A History of Social & Political Art in the U. S. Paul Von Blum. 250p. 1982. 25.00 o.p. (ISBN 0-89608-172-9); pap. 9.50 o.p. (ISBN 0-89608-171-0). South End Pr.

Critically Ill, Vol. 7. Billie C. Meador. (RN Assessment Ser.). 176p. 1985. pap. 15.95 o.p. (ISBN 0-87489-292-9). Med Economics.

Critically Safety in Storage of Fissile Material Proceedings. 409p. 1985. 45.00 o.p. (ISBN 0-89448-119-3). Am Nuclear Soc.

Criticism, Cynicism, & a Bit of Witticism. Louis A. Wilhelm. 144p. 1987. 6.75 o.p. (ISBN 0-8062-2880-6). Carlton.

Criticism in Society. Imre Salusinszky. (New Accents Ser.). 250p. 1987. 19.95 o.p. (ISBN 0-416-92270-8, 1100); pap. (ISBN 0-416-92280-5). Routledge Chapman & Hall.

Criticism of Traditional Postsecondary School Admissions Criteria: A Search for Alternatives. Carlos M. Haro. (Occasional Papers: No. 1). (Illus.). 58p. (Orig.). 1978. pap. 3.50 o.p. (ISBN 0-89551-019-7). Ucla Chicano Stud.

Critics & Composers: Lectures & Radio Talks. Stewart H. Edwards. (Illus.). 1984. 10.00 o.p. (ISBN 0-533-06022-2). Vantage.

Critic's Credentials. Stanley Edgar Hyman. LC 77-88902. 1978. 12.95 o.p. (ISBN 0-689-10847-8, Atheneum). Macmillan.

Critique of Practical Reason & Other Writings in Moral Philosophy. Immanuel Kant. Tr. by Lewis W. Beck. LC 75-32038. (Philosophy of Immanuel Kant Ser.: Vol. 1). 1976. Repr. of 1949 ed. lib. bdg. 43.00 o.p. (ISBN 0-8240-2325-0). Garland Pub.

Critique of Pure English see Fate of French-E in English: The Plural of Nouns Ending in-th.

Critique of Pure Reason. 2nd ed. Immanuel Kant. 1978. Repr. of 1934 ed. 8.95x o.p. (ISBN 0-460-00909-5, Evman); pap. 4.95x o.p. (ISBN 0-460-01909-0, Evman). Biblio Dist.

Critique of Radiometric Dating. Harold S. Slusher. LC 81-802593. (ICR Technical Monograph: No. 2). (Illus.). 58p. 1973. pap. 5.95 o.p. (ISBN 0-932766-04-8). Master Bks.

Critique of Relativity. Jonas Sepetys. LC 73-88709. 1974. (ISBN 0-8022-2262-5). Philos Lib.

Critique of the Empiricist Explanation of Morality: Is There a Natural Equivalent of Categorical Morality? C. W. Maris. 500p. 1981. cancelled 72.00 o.p. (ISBN 90-654-4011-9, Pub. by Kluwer Law Netherlands). Kluwer Academic.

Critiques Litteraires, Vol. 1. Jean-Paul Sartre. 416p. 1975. 4.95 o.p. (ISBN 0-686-54976-7). Schoenhof.

Critters' Kitchen. Michele Reynolds. LC 79-12115. (Illus.). 1979. 6.95 o.p. (ISBN 0-689-30723-3, Atheneum); pap. 2.95 o.p. (ISBN 0-689-11023-5). Macmillan.

Croatian Serbian-English Dictionary. 5th ed. M. Drvodelic. 849p. 1982. 27.50x o.s.i. (ISBN 0-89918-672-6, Y-672). Vanous.

Crochet for the Home. Ondori Publishing Company Staff. LC 80-84415. (Illus.). 1981. pap. 8.95 o.p. (ISBN 0-87040-495-4). Japan Pubns USA.

Crochet Stitches & Edgings. Coats, J & P Staff. LC 78-50728. (Illus.). 1978. pap. 2.25 o.s.i. (ISBN 0-684-15642-3, SL796, ScribT). Scribner.

Crock Marches On. Bill Rechin & Don Wilder. (Crock Ser.: No. 10). 128p. 1985. pap. 2.25 o.s.i. (ISBN 0-449-12959-4, GM). Fawcett.

Crockett: Brand of Fear. Brad Lang. 1976. pap. 1.25 o.p. (ISBN 0-685-69159-4, LB367ZK, Pub. by Leisure Bks CT). Dorchester Pub Co.

Crockett on the Loose. Brad Lang. (Crockett Ser). (Orig.). 1975. pap. 1.25 o.p. (ISBN 0-685-53900-8, LB283ZK, Pub. by Leisure Bks CT). Dorchester Pub Co.

Crocodile & the Dumper Truck. Ray Marshall & Paul Korky. (Illus.). 1982. PLB 10.95 o.p. (ISBN 0-689-20703-4, Atheneum). Macmillan.

Crocodile Blood. George Mandel. 1985. 17.95 o.p. (ISBN 0-87795-742-8, Arbor Hse). Morrow.

Crocodile, Crocodile. Peter Nickl. Tr. by M. E. Cutler from Ger. (Tundra Collection of Children's Books As Works of Art). Orig. Title: Krokodil, Krokodil. (Illus.). (gr. 4 up). 1976. 6.95 o.p. (ISBN 0-88776-073-2). Tundra Bks.

Crocodile Man: A Case of Brain Chemistry & Criminal Violence. Andre Mayer & Michael Wheeler. 224p. 1982. 12.95 o.p. (ISBN 0-395-31840-8). HM.

Croesus Conspiracy. Benjamin Stein. 1978. 9.95 o.p. (ISBN 0-671-22870-6). S&S.

Croissance et Ajustement: Les Problemes de L'Afrique de L'Ouest. Ed. by Patrick Guillaumont. 248p. (Fr.). 1985. 10.00 o.s.i. (ISBN 2-7178-0947-3). Intl Monetary.

Cromwell's Boy. Erik C. Haugaard. 224p. (gr. 7 up). 1978. 7.95 o.p. (ISBN 0-395-27203-3). HM.

Cronistoria, 5 vols. Ed. by Giselda Capetti. LC 80-68484. 400p. (Orig.). 1980. Set. pap. 40.00 o.p. (ISBN 0-89944-043-6); Vol. 1. pap. (ISBN 0-89944-044-4); Vol. 2. pap. (ISBN 0-89944-045-2); Vol. 3. pap. (ISBN 0-89944-046-0); Vol. 4. pap. (ISBN 0-89944-047-9); Vol. 5. pap. (ISBN 0-89944-048-7). Don Bosco Multimedia.

Cronopios & Famas. Julio Cortazar. Tr. by Paul Blackburn from Span. LC 69-15477. (Illus.). 1978. pap. 2.00 o.p. (ISBN 0-394-73616-8). Pantheon.

Crooked & Narrow Streets of the Town of Boston, 1630-1822. Annie H. Thwing. LC 74-129974. (Illus.). 302p. 1970. Repr. of 1920 ed. 40.00x o.p. (ISBN 0-8103-3538-7). Gale.

Crooked Flight. Basil Jackson. 208p. 1986. pap. 2.95 o.p. (ISBN 0-931773-87-3). Critics Choice Paper.

Crooked House. large type ed. Agatha Christie. (Popular Author Ser.). 300p. 1988. lib. bdg. 16.95 o.s.i. (ISBN 0-8161-4463-X, Large Print Bks); pap. 10.95 o.s.i. (ISBN 0-8161-4502-4). G K Hall.

Crooked Shall Be Made Straight. Rosalie Griesse. LC 78-52446. 1979. 10.00 o.p. (ISBN 0-8042-1101-9, John Knox). Westminster John Knox.

Crooked Trail. Fred Donaldson. 208p. (Orig.). 1982. pap. 2.25 o.p. (ISBN 0-8439-1134-4, Pub. by Leisure Bks CT). Dorchester Pub Co.

Crop Insurance for Developing Countries. Produced by United Nations Conference on Trade & Development Staff. 19p. 1981. pap. 2.50 o.p. (E.81.11.D.2). UN.

Crop Loss Assessment Methods. Ed. by L. Chiarappa. 276p. 1971. pap. 22.00 looseleaf o.p. CAB Intl.

Crop Loss Assessment Methods: Complete Work Manual. Ed. by L. Chiarappa. 561p. 1971. Set. pap. 48.50 looseleaf incl. 3 supplements o.p. CAB Intl.

Crop Loss Assessment Methods: Supplement, No. 1. 94p. 1973. pap. 7.35 looseleaf o.p. (ISBN 0-85198-287-5). CAB Intl.

Crop Loss Assessment Methods: Supplement, No. 2. 68p. 1977. pap. 7.35 looseleaf o.p. (ISBN 0-85198-487-8). CAB Intl.

Crop Management Economics. Alan N. Rae. (Illus.). 544p. (Orig.). 1982. pap. text ed. 29.50 o.p. (ISBN 0-246-11808-3, Pub. by Granada England). Gower Pub Co.

Crop Pests in Tanzania & Their Control. 2nd rev. ed. E. Bohlen. (Illus.). 142p. 1978. lib. bdg. 34.00 o.p. (ISBN 3-489-65126-X). Parey Sci Pubs.

Crop Production: Cereals & Legumes. Brian F. Bland. 1971. 73.50 o.p. (ISBN 0-12-104050-X). Acad Pr.

Crop Production Equipment: A Practical Guide for Farmers, Operators, & Trainees. H. T. Lovegrove. 406p. (Orig.). 1981. pap. text ed. 16.95x o.p. (ISBN 0-09-085391-1, Hutchinson & Co). Gower Pub Co.

Crop Protection. C. J. Rose. 1955. (ISBN 0-8022-1372-3). Philos Lib.

Crop Protection Chemicals Reference. 3rd ed. Chemical & Pharmaceutical Press Staff. 2000p. 1987. (ISBN 0-471-85368-2). Wiley.

Crop Responses to Water at Different Stages of Growth. Ed. by P. J. Salter & J. E. Goode. 246p. 1967. 11.00 o.p. CAB Intl.

Cross. Nancy Peelman. (Illus.). 40p. (Orig.). 1976. pap. 3.25 o.p. (ISBN 0-8192-1212-1). Morehouse Pub.

Cross Age & Peer Tutoring: Help for Children with Learning Problems. Joseph R. Jenkins & Linda M. Jenkins. LC 80-68283. 93p. 1981. pap. 6.00 o.p. (ISBN 0-86586-110-2). Coun Exc Child.

Cross & Sword: The Political Role of Christian Missions in the Belgian Congo, 1908-1960. Marvin D. Markowitz. LC 75-170209. (Publications Ser.: No. 114). 1973. 13.50x o.p. (ISBN 0-8179-1141-3). Hoover Inst Pr.

Cross & the Shroud: A Medical Examiner Investigates the Crucifixion. Frederick T. Zugibe. (Illus.). 1982. 12.00 o.s.i. (ISBN 0-682-49859-9). Exposition-Phoenix.

Cross-Country. Herbert Kastle. 352p. 1984. pap. 1.95 o.p. (ISBN 0-440-14585-6). Dell.

Cross-Country Ski Trails of Washington's Cascades & Olympics. Tom Kirkendall & Vicky Spring. (Illus.). 208p. (Orig.). 1983. pap. 9.95 o.p. (ISBN 0-89886-062-8). Mountaineers.

Cross-Country Skier's Handbook: A Complete Guide to Technique, Equipment, Competition Clubs, & Trails. Samuel P. Osborne. (Illus.). 240p. 1985. 17.95 o.p. (ISBN 0-684-18441-9). Scribner.

Cross-Country Skiing. 2nd ed. Ned Gillette & John Dostal. LC 79-19415. (Illus.). 240p. 1983. pap. 10.95 o.p. (ISBN 0-89886-079-2). Mountaineers.

Cross-Country Skiing. Illus. by Laszlo Konkor. (Sports & Hobbies Ser.). (Illus.). 48p. (gr. 3 up). 1979. PLB 10.60 o.p. (ISBN 0-516-04371-4); pap. 2.95 o.p. (ISBN 0-516-44371-2). Childrens.

Cross-Country Skiing: The Complete Beginner's Book. George Sullivan. LC 80-19798. (Illus.). 128p. (gr. 5 up). 1980. lib. bdg. 9.79 o.s.i. (ISBN 0-671-33098-5). Messner.

Cross Creek. Marjorie K. Rawlings. 384p. 1984. pap. 7.95 o.s.i. (ISBN 0-684-18070-7, ScribT). Scribner.

Cross-Cultural Psychiatry. Ed. by Albert Gaw. 384p. 1982. text ed. 41.00 o.p. (ISBN 0-88416-338-5). Year Bk Med.

Cross-Cultural Research: The Role of Culture in Understanding Human Behavior. Richard W. Brislin & Marshall H. Segall. (CISE Learning Package Ser.: No.16). 95p. (Orig.). 1975. pap. text ed. 4.00x o.p. (ISBN 0-936876-29-8). LRIS.

Cross Currents, No. 2. Ed. by Ladislav Matejka & Benjamin A. Stolz. (Michigan Slavic Materials Ser.: No. 23). 1983. pap. 15.00 o.p. (ISBN 0-930042-53-0). Mich Slavic Pubns.

Cross Currents, No. 4. Ed. by Ladislav Matejka. (Michigan Slavic Materials Ser.: No. 25). 1985. 15.00 o.p. (ISBN 0-930042-61-1). Mich Slavic Pubns.

Cross Currents, No. 5. Ed. by Ladislav Matejka. (Michigan Slavic Materials Ser.: No. 26). 1986. 15.00 o.p. (ISBN 0-930042-62-X). Mich Slavic Pubns.

Cross-Eyed Cat. Mimi G. Carpenter. (Illus.). 24p. (Orig.). (gr. k-6). 1985. pap. 4.95 o.p. (ISBN 0-9614628-1-7). Beachcomber Pr.

Cross Fork Tales: True Stories from the Pennsylvania Black Forest & Ole Bull's Lost Colony. Inez Bull. (Illus.). 1970. 3.50 o.p. (ISBN 0-686-67699-8). Exposition-Phoenix.

Cross Fox. Jane Scott. LC 80-13515. 144p. (gr. 4-7). 1980. 7.95 o.p. (ISBN 0-689-50183-8, Atheneum). Macmillan.

Cross in Faith & Conduct. Gordon Watt. 1965. pap. 1.50 o.p. (ISBN 0-87508-964-X). Chr Lit.

Cross-Index, Defense Acquisition Regulation to Federal Acquisition Regulation & Department of Defense Federal Acquistion Regulation Supplement. 358p. 1984. looseleaf 8.50 o.p. (ISBN 0-318-11773-8, S/N 008-000-00406-4). USGPO.

Cross-National Comparative Survey Research: Theory & Practice - Papers & Proceedings of a Round Table Conference, Budapest, 1972. Ed. by A. Szalai & R. Petrelia. LC 76-8272. 1977. 71.00 o.p. (ISBN 0-08-020979-3). Pergamon.

Cross-National Data Analysis. Arthur S. Banks. (CISE Learning Package Ser.: No. 3). (Illus.). 99p. (Orig.). 1974. pap. text ed. 4.00x o.p. (ISBN 0-936876-21-2). LRIS.

Cross National Study of Health Systems by Countries & World Region, & Special Problems: A Guide to Information Sources. Ed. by Ray H. Elling. LC 79-26099. (Health Affairs Information Guide Ser.: Vol. 3). 312p. 1980. 68.00x o.p. (ISBN 0-8103-1453-3). Gale.

Cross Prefigured & Fulfilled. Josiah B. Lowe. 251p. 1986. 8.95 o.p. (ISBN 0-8254-3126-3). Kregel.

Cross-Section Data for Nuclear Reactor Analyses. Ed. by S. Pearlstein. (Illus.). 216p. 1984. pap. 88.00 o.p. (ISBN 0-08-031686-7). Pergamon.

Cross Sectional Story of Early Career Development. David B. Teideman et al. 8.75 o.p. (ISBN 1-55620-011-0, 72219C). Am Assn Coun Dev.

Cross Stitch & Sampler Book. Jan Eaton & Liz Mundie. (Illus.). 176p. 19.95 o.p. (ISBN 0-8069-5542-2). Sterling.

Cross Words: Sermons & Dramas for Lent. W. A. Poovey. LC 68-13421. 1968. pap. 4.50 o.p. (ISBN 0-8066-0800-5, 10-1759, Augsburg). Augsburg Fortress.

Cross Your Heart. Bruce Hart & Carol Hart. (gr. 7 up). 1988. 2.95 o.p. Morrow.

Crosscuts Through History. Dagobert D. Runes. 1965. (ISBN 0-8022-1427-4). Philos Lib.

Crossexion. Clell Edgar Bowman. 1976. 8.00 o.p. (ISBN 0-682-48518-7). Exposition-Phoenix.

Crossfacts. Len Fellows. 64p. 1983. pap. 6.75 spiral bound o.p. (ISBN 0-671-46874-X, Fireside). S&S.

Crossfire. Tom Lord. (Ash Tallman Ser.: No. 2). 176p. 1984. pap. 2.25 o.p. (ISBN 0-380-86926-8, 86926). Avon.

Crossfire. Nigel Slater. LC 77-15543. 1978. 6.95 o.p. (ISBN 0-689-10844-3, Atheneum). Macmillan.

Crossfire in Professional Education. Bruno A. Boley. LC 76-47033. 1977. 21.00 o.p. (ISBN 0-08-021429-0). Pergamon.

Crossing. Christopher Keane. LC 77-93004. 1978. 8.95 o.p. (ISBN 0-87795-187-X, Arbor Hse). Morrow.

Crossing Cocytus & Other Poems. Paul Mariani. LC 81-48539. (Grove Press Poetry Ser.). 94p. 1982. 12.50 o.p. (ISBN 0-394-52829-8, GP853). Grove.

Crossing Cocytus & Other Poems. Paul Mariani. LC 81-48539. (Poetry Ser.). 94p. 1982. pap. 5.95 o.p. (ISBN 0-394-17978-1, E801, Ever). Grove.

Crossing the Delaware: The Story of the Delaware Memorial Bridge, the Longest Twin Suspension Bridge in the World. William J. Miller, Jr. Ed. by Kathy K. Demerast. LC 83-71879. (Illus.). 114p. 1983. 9.95 o.p. (ISBN 0-911293-02-7); pap. 5.95 o.p. (ISBN 0-911293-01-9). Delapeake Pub Co.

Crossing's Guide to Dartmoor. 2nd ed. William Crossing. (Illus.). 529p. 1965. 14.50 o.p. (ISBN 0-7153-4017-4, Pub. by Batsford, England); pap. 4.95 o.p. (ISBN 0-7153-4034-4). David & Charles.

Crossover. Wayne Karlin. 210p. 1984. 13.95 o.p. (ISBN 0-15-123152-4). HarBraceJ.

Crosstown Sabbath: Autobiography. Frederick Morton. 128p. 1987. 15.95 o.p. (ISBN 0-394-56070-1). Grove.

Crosswinds. Nancy Moulton. 416p. 1985. pap. 2.95 o.p. (ISBN 0-380-89591-9). Avon.

Crossword Adventures. George Carlson. LC 76-43215. (Busyback Bks). (Illus.). (gr. 2-6). 1977. pap. 1.95 o.p. (ISBN 0-448-48005-0, G&D). Putnam Pub Group.

Crossword Puzzle Book, No 128. Eugene T. Maleska & Margaret P. Farrar. 96p. 1982. pap. 5.95 o.s.i. (ISBN 0-671-44392-5, Fireside). S&S.

Crossword Puzzle Book, No 129. Margaret P. Farrar & Eugene Maleska. 64p. 1982. pap. 5.95 o.s.i. (ISBN 0-671-44393-3, Fireside). S&S.

Crossword Puzzle Book, No. 100. Ed. by Margaret P. Farrar. 1970. pap. 5.95 o.s.i. (ISBN 0-671-20743-1, Fireside). S&S.

Crossword Puzzle Book, No. 110. Ed. by Margaret P. Farrar. 1975. pap. 4.95 spiral bound o.s.i. (ISBN 0-671-22171-X, Fireside). S&S.

Crossword Puzzle Book, No. 111. Ed. by Margaret P. Farrar. 1976. pap. 2.95 o.s.i. (ISBN 0-671-22265-1, Fireside). S&S.

Crossword Puzzle Book, No. 112. Ed. by Margaret P. Farrar. 1976. pap. 5.70 o.s.i. (ISBN 0-671-22430-1, Fireside). S&S.

Crossword Puzzles for Texas: The Land & Its People. Gay Bunch. 30p. 1982. pap. 6.95x o.p. (ISBN 0-937460-08-7). Hendrick Long.

Crosswords Club, The Third Year. Will Weng. (Orig.). 1986. pap. 7.95 o.p. (Dell Trade Pbks). Dell.

Crosswords for the Connoisseur, No. 21. Ed. by Charles Preston. pap. 2.95 o.p. (ISBN 0-448-01561-7, G&D). Putnam Pub Group.

Crosswords from the Daily Times, No. 25. Ed. by Margaret Farrar. 1972. pap. 4.95 o.s.i. (ISBN 0-671-21353-9). PB.

Crosswords from the Times (Daily) Margaret P. Farrar. 96p. 1982. pap. 5.75 o.p. (ISBN 0-671-45874-4, Fireside). S&S.

Crosswords from the Times (Daliy, No 42. Margaret P. Farrar. 96p. 1982. pap. 5.75 o.p. (ISBN 0-671-44772-6, Fireside). S&S.

Crosswords from the Times, No. 32. Ed. by Margaret P. Farrar. 1977. pap. 4.95 spiral bound o.s.i. (ISBN 0-671-22761-0, Fireside). S&S.

Crostics Omnibus, No 12. Thomas H. Middleton. 96p. 1983. pap. 6.95 o.s.i. (ISBN 0-671-45876-0, Fireside). S&S.

Crostics 88. Thomas H. Middleton. 64p. 1982. pap. 6.95 o.s.i. (ISBN 0-671-45873-6, Fireside). S&S.

Crow Indians. Incl. The Crow Tribe of Indians. Norman B. Plummer; Findings of Fact, & Opinion. Indian Claims Commission. (American Indian Ethnohistory Ser: Plains Indians). (Illus.). 1974. lib. bdg. 51.00 o.p. (ISBN 0-8240-0756-5). Garland Pub.

Crow Warriors. Bill Hotchkiss. (Indian Ser.: No. 3). (Orig.). 1981. pap. 2.75 o.p. (ISBN 0-440-01588-X, Banbury). Dell.

Crowd Action in Revolutionary Massachusetts, 1765-1780. Dirk Hoerder. 1977. 33.00 o.p. (ISBN 0-12-351650-1). Acad Pr.

Crowded Earth: People & the Politics of Population. Pranay Gupte. LC 84-6145. 352p. 1984. 17.45 o.p. (ISBN 0-393-01927-6). Norton.

Crowding Behavior & the Future. Bernard G. Rosenthal & John E. Mayer. 109p. 1983. text ed. 22.50x o.p. (ISBN 0-8290-1027-0); pap. text ed. 9.95x o.p. (ISBN 0-8290-1434-9). Irvington.

Crowding: Theoretical & Research Implications for Population - Environment Psychology. Ed. by Larry Severy. LC 78-61527. 94p. 1979. pap. 12.95 o.p. (ISBN 0-87705-376-6). Human Sci Pr.

Crown & Nobility, 1450-1509. J. R. Lander. 350p. 1976. lib. bdg. 25.00x o.p. (ISBN 0-7735-0269-6, McGill Canada). U of Toronto Pr.

Crown of India. Samuel Fuller. 252p. 1986. pap. 3.50 o.p. (ISBN 1-55547-120-X). Critics Choice Paper.

Crown of Jewels. Cora M. Groff. 144p. 1985. pap. 6.00 o.p. (ISBN 0-682-40210-9). Exposition-Phoenix.

Crown of Life: Essays in Interpretation of Shakespeare's Final Plays. G. Wilson Knight. 1965. pap. 14.95x o.p. (ISBN 0-416-68770-9, NO.2273). Routledge Chapman & Hall.

Crown of Passion. Jocelyn Carew. 416p. 1980. pap. 2.75 o.p. (ISBN 0-380-76414-8, 76414-8). Avon.

Crown Prince: A Novel. John Barchilon. 1984. 15.45 o.p. (ISBN 0-393-01765-6). Norton.

Crowned in a Far Country: Portraits of Eight Royal Brides. HRH Princess Michael of Kent. LC 86-13156. (Illus.). 208p. 1986. 20.00 o.s.i. (ISBN 1-55584-011-6). Weidenfeld.

Crowned with Glory & Honor: The Life of Rev. Lacey Kirk Williams. Ed. by L. Venchael Booth. 1978. 8.00 o.p. (ISBN 0-682-48939-5). Exposition-Phoenix.

Crowning Fifty Years. Abilene Christian University Lectureship Staff. Ed. by J. D. Thomas. LC 68-21004. 1968. 9.95 o.p. (ISBN 0-89112-030-0). Abilene Christ U.

Crows of War. Steven Rayson. LC 74-19355. Orig. Title: Mai-Dun. 272p. (gr. 7 up). 1975. PLB 7.50 o.p. (ISBN 0-689-30455-2, Atheneum). Macmillan.

CRT Controller Handbook. Gerry Kane. 224p. (Orig.). 1980. pap. text ed. 9.95 o.p. (ISBN 0-07-931045-1). Osborne-McGraw.

Crucial American Elections. Arthur S. Link et al. LC 73-79577. (Memoirs Ser.: Vol. 99). 1973. 5.00 o.p. (ISBN 0-87169-099-3). Am Philos.

Crucial Conversations. May Sarton. 156p. 1975. 12.95 o.p. (ISBN 0-393-08725-5). Norton.

Crucial Issues in Education. 7th ed. Henry J. Ehlers. 1981. pap. text ed. 18.95 o.p. (ISBN 0-03-058089-7, HoltC). HR&W.

Crucial Moments of the Civil War. Willard Webb. (Illus.). 350p. Repr. cancelled o.s.i. (ISBN 0-685-41737-9). Irvington.

Crucible. Arthur Miller. 48p. (Orig.). 1989. pap. 9.95 o.p. (ISBN 1-55651-133-7); audiocassette tape incl. o.p. (ISBN 1-55651-134-5). Cram Cassettes.

Crucible of Evil. Lyda B. Long. 1974. pap. 0.95 o.p. (ISBN 0-380-00063-6, 19646). Avon.

Crucible Year. Norma Johnston. LC 78-12173. (gr. 7 up). 1979. 7.95 o.p. (ISBN 0-689-30683-0, Atheneum). Macmillan.

Crucified Messiah. Nils A. Dahl. LC 74-14189. 192p. (Orig.). 1975. pap. 3.95 o.p. (ISBN 0-8066-1469-2, 10-1775, Augsburg). Augsburg Fortress.

Crucifixion by Power: Essays on Guatemalan National Social Structure, 1944-1966. Richard N. Adams. 567p. 1970. 25.00x o.p. (ISBN 0-292-70035-0). U of Tex Pr.

Cruel Choice: A New Concept in the Theory of Development. Denis Goulet. LC 73-145632. 1971. pap. text ed. 4.95x o.p. (ISBN 0-689-70341-4, 197, Atheneum). Macmillan.

Cruel Madness. Colin Thubron. Ed. by Joyce Johnson. LC 85-47784. 168p. 1985. 13.95 o.p. (ISBN 0-87113-023-8). Atlantic Monthly.

Cruelty. Ai. 1973. 4.95 o.p. (ISBN 0-395-17720-0); pap. 2.95 o.s.i. (ISBN 0-395-17714-6). HM.

Cruelty to Children. Eustace Chesser. 1952. (ISBN 0-8022-0236-5). Philos Lib.

Cruise Answer Book: A Comprehensive Guide to the Ships & Ports of North America. Charlanne F. Herring. LC 86-33181. (Illus.). 272p. (Orig.). 1987. pap. 9.95 o.p. (ISBN 0-938179-03-9). Mills Sanderson.

Cruise of the Antarctic. Henric Bull. (Antarctic Classics Ser.). (Illus.). 288p. 1987. Repr. of 1896 ed. 40.00 o.s.i. (ISBN 0-9506104-4-5). Archival Facsimiles.

Cruising: A Manual for the Small Sailing Boat Owner. J. D. Sleightholme. (Illus.). 238p. 1977. 21.95x o.p. (ISBN 0-8464-0305-6). Beekman Pubs.

Cruising Designs from the Board of Thomas E. Colvin. Thomas E. Colvin. (Illus.). 112p. 1977. 14.95 o.p. (ISBN 0-915160-17-X). Seven Seas.

Cruising Guide to the Lesser Antilles. rev. ed. Donald M. Street. (Illus.). 320p. 1974. 23.95 o.p. (ISBN 0-393-03154-3). Norton.

Cruising in a Nutshell: The Art & Science of Enjoyable Coastwise Voyaging in Small Auxiliary Yachts. Tony Gibbs. LC 83-42664. (Illus.). 285p. 1984. 19.45 o.p. (ISBN 0-393-03289-2). Norton.

Cruising San Juan Islands. Date not set. 24.95 o.p. (ISBN 0-393-60000-9). Norton.

Cruising: The Boats & the Places. Bill Robinson. (Illus.). 1981. 17.95 o.p. (ISBN 0-393-03258-2). Norton.

Cruising the Pacific Coast: Acapulco to Skyway. Carolyn West & Jack West. 10.95 o.p. (ISBN 0-393-60022-X). Norton.

Cruising World Best of People & Food Cookbook. Ed. by Barbara Davis. LC 83-9523. (Illus.). 384p. 1983. 22.50 o.p. (ISBN 0-915160-56-0). Seven Seas.

Crunch. Pat Toomay. (Illus.). 203p. 1975. 7.95 o.p. (ISBN 0-393-08726-3). Norton.

Crusade for Civic Democracy: The Story of the Tuskegee Civic Association, 1941-1970. Jessie P. Guzman. 1984. 11.95 o.p. (ISBN 0-533-05700-0). Vantage.

Crusade: Historiography & Bibliography. Aziz S. Atiya. LC 75-22640. 1976. lib. bdg. 35.00x o.p. (ISBN 0-8371-8364-2, ATTC). Greenwood.

Crusade: The Presidential Election of Nineteen Fifty-Two. John R. Greene. (Illus.). 354p. (Orig.). 1986. lib. bdg. 32.25 o.p. (ISBN 0-8191-4931-4); pap. text ed. 16.75 o.p. (ISBN 0-8191-4932-2). U Pr of Amer.

Crusader Conspiracy. Lois Parker. Ed. by Gerald Wheeler. (Banner Bks.). (Illus.). 128p. (Orig.). (gr. 5 up). 1984. pap. 6.95 o.p. (ISBN 0-8280-0166-9). Review & Herald.

Crusader No. 2: The Passionate Princess. John Cleve. 1974. pap. 1.50 o.p. (ISBN 0-685-47911-0, D6039 314, BC). Grove.

Crusader No. 3: Julanar the Lioness. John Cleve. 1975. pap. 1.50 o.p. (ISBN 0-685-56547-5, D4731, BC). Grove.

Crusaders & Pragmatists: Movers of Modern American Foreign Policy. John G. Stoessinger. 1979. 19.95 o.p. (ISBN 0-393-01284-0); pap. text ed. 5.95x o.p. (ISBN 0-393-95063-8). Norton.

Crusaders, Criminals, Crazies: Terror & Terrorism in Our Time. Frederick J. Hacker. 1977. 9.95 o.p. (ISBN 0-393-01127-5). Norton.

Crush. Jane Futcher. 256p. 1984. pap. 2.25 o.p. (ISBN 0-380-67462-9, 67462, Flare). Avon.

Crushed for Better Wine. Sara Robbins. (ISBN 0-8022-1356-1). Philos Lib.

Crusoe: Poems Selected & New. Eli Mandel. LC 73-75842. (House of Anansi Poetry Ser.: No. 25). 107p. 1973. 2.00 o.p. (ISBN 0-88784-127-9, Pub. by Hse Anansi Pr Canada). U of Toronto Pr.

Crusoe's Daughter. Jane Gardam. LC 85-19952. 224p. 1986. 12.95 o.p. (ISBN 0-689-11792-2, Atheneum). Macmillan.

Cruz das Almas, a Brazilian Village. Donald Pierson. LC 75-118766. (Illus.). 226p. 1973. Repr. of 1951 ed. lib. bdg. 22.50x o.p. (ISBN 0-8371-5083-3, SMIM). Greenwood.

Cry for Help: For Families of Alcohol & Other Drug-Dependent Persons. Sharon A. Nale. 96p. 1982. pap. 3.70 o.p. (ISBN 0-686-82063-0, 1-1953, Fortress). Augsburg Fortress.

Cry for the World. Lucille Oliver. 1981. pap. 3.00 o.p. (ISBN 0-8309-0307-0). Herald Hse.

Cry from The Abyss. Henry Suld. LC 86-913950. 192p. 1986. text ed. 15.00 o.p. (ISBN 0-682-40318-0). Exposition-Phoenix.

Cry Hungary! Reg Gadney. LC 86-47669. (Illus.). 192p. 1986. 16.95 o.p. (ISBN 0-689-11838-4, Atheneum). Macmillan.

Cry in Echo Canyon. Zig Ziglar. (Zig Ziglar Ser.: No. 1). 48p. 1987. pap. 2.50 o.p. (ISBN 0-8423-0494-0). Tyndale.

Cry of Angels. Jeff Fields. LC 73-91623. 1974. 8.95 o.p. (ISBN 0-689-10593-2, Atheneum). Macmillan.

Cry of My People. Esther Arias & Mortimer Arias. (Orig.). 1980. pap. 2.95 o.p. Friendship Pr.

Cry of Players. William Gibson. LC 69-15505. 1969. 4.95 o.p. (ISBN 0-689-10093-0, Atheneum). Macmillan.

Cry of the Environment: Rebuilding the Christian Creation Tradition. Ed. by Philip N. Joranson & Ken Butigan. LC 84-72254. (Illus.). 476p. (Orig.). 1984. pap. 14.95 o.s.i. (ISBN 0-939680-17-3). Bear & Co.

Cry of the Kalahari. Mark Owens & Delia Owens. 1984. 19.45 o.p. (ISBN 0-395-32214-6). HM.

Cry of the Kalahari. Mark Owens & Delia Owens. (Illus.). 590p. 1986. lib. bdg. 19.95 o.p. (ISBN 0-8161-3972-5, Large Print Bks). G K Hall.

Cry of the Wolf. Zane Spencer & Jay Leech. LC 76-56450. 144p. (gr. 6-9). 1977. 7.95 o.s.i. (ISBN 0-664-32611-0, Westminster). Westminster John Knox.

Cry Sorrow, Cry Joy: Selections from Contemporary African Writers. Ed. by Jane A. Moore. (Orig.). 1971. pap. 1.95 o.p. (ISBN 0-377-11011-6). Friendship Pr.

Cry, the Beloved Country. Alan Paton. 304p. 1982. pap. 4.95 rack size o.s.i. (ISBN 0-684-17473-1, ScribT). Scribner.

Cry Tough. Irving Shulman. 232p. 1986. pap. 2.95 o.p. (ISBN 0-931773-90-3). Critics Choice Paper.

Cry Wolf. Wilbur Smith. 1978. pap. 2.25 o.p. (ISBN 0-440-11495-0). Dell.

Crybabies: Coping with Colic, What to Do When Baby Won't Stop Crying. Marc Weissbluth. 160p. 1984. pap. 4.95 o.p. (ISBN 0-87795-611-1, Arbor Hse). Morrow.

Crying & Babies: Helping Families Cope. John Kirkland. LC 84-4319. 212p. 1985. 29.00 o.p. (ISBN 0-7099-1564-0, Pub. by Croom Helm Ltd); pap. 15.50 o.p. (ISBN 0-7099-1565-9). Routledge Chapman & Hall.

Crying Heart Tattoo. David Martin. LC 81-6956. 352p. 1982. 14.45 o.p. (ISBN 0-03-060488-5). H Holt & Co.

Cryobiochemistry: An Introduction. P. Douzou. 1977. 76.00 o.p. (ISBN 0-12-221050-6). Acad Pr.

Cryptanalysis of an Enciphered Code Problem: Where an "Additive" Method of Encipherement Has Been Used. Wayne G. Barker. (Cryptographic Ser.). (Orig.). 1979. lib. bdg. 31.80 o.p. (ISBN 0-89412-086-7); pap. 23.80 o.p. (ISBN 0-89412-037-9). Aegean Park Pr.

Cryptography. rev. ed. Andre Langie. 1984. lib. bdg. 28.80 o.p. (ISBN 0-89412-091-3); pap. text ed. 20.80 o.p. (ISBN 0-89412-061-1). Aegean Park Pr.

Cryptorchidism. F. Hadziselimovic. (Advances in Anatomy, Embryology & Cell Biology: Vol. 53, Pt. 3). (Illus.). 1977. 26.00 o.p. (ISBN 0-387-08361-8). Springer-Verlag.

Cryptorchidism: Proceedings. International Symposium on Crytorchidism Staff. LC 79-40947. (Serono Symposia). 1980. 98.00 o.p. (ISBN 0-12-097450-9). Acad Pr.

Crystal & the Way of Light: Meditation, Contemplation & Self Liberation. Namkhai Norbu. Ed. by John Shane. (Illus.). 224p. 1986. pap. 14.95 o.p. (ISBN 0-7102-0833-2, 08332). Routledge Chapman & Hall.

Crystal Cat: A Novel of Suspense. Velda Johnston. LC 85-6999. 192p. 1985. 14.95 o.p. (ISBN 0-396-08731-0). Dodd.

Crystal Chemistry & Semiconduction in Transition Metal Binary Compounds. J. P. Suchet. 1971. 89.00 o.p. (ISBN 0-12-675650-3). Acad Pr.

Crystal Clouds. Robert E. Vardeman. (Jade Demons Ser.: No. 3). 1985. pap. 2.95 o.p. (ISBN 0-380-89800-4). Avon.

Crystal Crown. B. W. Clough. 208p. 1984. pap. 3.50 o.p. (ISBN 0-87997-922-4). DAW Bks.

Crystal Dove. Mollie Hardwick. (Nightingale Ser.). 412p. 1987. pap. 12.95 o.p. (ISBN 0-8161-4213-0, Large Print Bks.). G K Hall.

Crystal Flower & the Sun. Faridah Fardjam. LC 71-128814. (Illus.). (gr. k-5). 1972. PLB 4.95 o.p. (ISBN 0-87614-017-7). Carolrhoda Bks.

Crystal Form & Structure. Ed. by C. J. Schneer. (Benchmark Papers in Geology: Vol. 34). 1977. 78.00 o.p. (ISBN 0-12-787425-9). Acad Pr.

Crystal Growth. 2nd ed. Brian Pamplin. 1980. 67.00 o.p. (ISBN 0-08-026489-1). Pergamon.

Crystal Growth. Brian R. Pamplin. LC 73-21909. 1976. 82.00 o.p. (ISBN 0-08-017003-X); pap. 37.00 o.p. (ISBN 0-08-021310-3). Pergamon.

Crystal Growth: A Tutorial Approach. Ed. by W. Bardsley et al. (North Holland Series in Crystal Growth: Vol. 2). 408p. 1979. 105.25 o.p. (ISBN 0-444-85371-5, North Holland). Elsevier.

Crystal Growth & Characterization of Polytype Structures, Vol. 7/1-4. Ed. by P. Krishna. (Illus.). 512p. 1983. 155.00 o.p. (ISBN 0-08-031010-9). Pergamon.

Crystal Growth & Characterization: Proceedings of the International Spring School on Crystal Growth, 2nd, Japan, 1974. International Spring School on Crystal Growth Staff. Ed. by R. Ueda & J. B. Mullin. 420p. 1976. 74.50 o.p. (ISBN 0-444-11061-5, North-Holland). Elsevier.

Crystal Growth from High Temperature Solutions. D. Elwell & H. J. Scheel. 1975. 104.00 o.p. (ISBN 0-12-237550-5). Acad Pr.

Crystal Memory. Stephen Leigh. 256p. (Orig.). 1987. pap. 3.50 o.p. (ISBN 0-380-89960-4). Avon.

Crystal Mirror, Vol. III. Ed. by Tarthang Tulku. (Illus.). 1974. pap. 9.95 o.p. (ISBN 0-913546-05-4). Dharma Pub.

Crystal Nights. Michele Murray. LC 72-93807. 320p. (gr. 6 up). 1979. 9.95 o.s.i. (ISBN 0-395-28920-3, Clarion). HM.

Crystal Oscillator Design & Temperature Compensation. Marvin E. Frerking. 1978. 28.95 o.p. (ISBN 0-442-22459-1). Van Nos Reinhold.

Crystal Physics. G. S. Zhdanov. 1966. 84.00 o.p. (ISBN 0-12-779650-9). Acad Pr.

Crystal Spirit. Date not set. (ISBN 0-8052-0755-4). Random.

Crystal Structures: The Structure of Benzene Derivatives, Vol. 6, Pt. 1. 2nd ed. R. W. Wyckoff. LC 63-22897. 455p. 1969. 49.50 o.p. (ISBN 0-471-96869-2, Pub. by Wiley). Krieger.

Crystalline Electric Field Effects in f-Electron Magnetism. Ed. by Robert P. Guertin & Wojciech Suski. LC 82-5267. 604p. 1982. 95.00x o.p. (ISBN 0-306-41004-4, Plenum Pr). Plenum Pub.

Crystallizing Public Opinion. rev. ed. Edward L. Bernays. 1961. 5.95x o.p. (ISBN 0-87140-975-5). Liveright.

Crystallography & Crystal Chemistry. F. D. Bloss. LC 77-136774. 1971. text ed. 40.95 o.p. (ISBN 0-03-085155-6, HoltC). HR&W.

Crystallometry. P. Terpstra & L. W. Codd. 1961. 85.00 o.p. (ISBN 0-12-685250-2). Acad Pr.

Crystals. Janet Rodney. 1979. pap. 3.95 o.p. (ISBN 0-913028-60-6). North Atlantic.

Crystals & Compounds: Molecular Structure & Composition in Nineteenth-Century French Science. Seymour Mauskopf. LC 76-3197. (Transactions Ser.: Vol. 66, Pt. 3). (Illus.). 1976. pap. 10.00 o.p. (ISBN 0-87169-663-0). Am Philos.

Crystals & Joint Disease. P. Dieppe & P. Calvert. LC 83-23445. (Illus.). 180p. 1983. 55.00x o.p. (ISBN 0-412-22150-0, NO. 6782, Pub by Chapman & Hall). Routledge Chapman & Hall.

Crystals Associated to Barsotti-Tate Groups: With Applications to Abelian Schemes. W. Messing. LC 72-79007. (Lecture Notes in Mathematics: Vol. 264). 193p. 1972. pap. 10.00 o.p. (ISBN 0-387-05840-0). Springer-Verlag.

Crystals for Magnetic Applications. Ed. by C. J. Rooijmans. (Crystals - Growth, Properties, & Applications: Vol. 1). (Illus.). 1978. 36.00 o.p. (ISBN 0-387-09002-9). Springer-Verlag.

CS Amphibians. Date not set. (ISBN 0-07-102593-6). McGraw.

CS Birds. Date not set. (ISBN 0-07-102595-2). McGraw.

CS Digestion. Date not set. (ISBN 0-07-102512-X). McGraw.

CS Fish. Date not set. (ISBN 0-07-102592-8). McGraw.

CS Insects. Date not set. (ISBN 0-07-102591-X). McGraw.

CS Mammals. Date not set. (ISBN 0-07-102596-0). McGraw.

CS Reptiles. Date not set. (ISBN 0-07-102594-4). McGraw.

CS Set Speaking. 1974. text ed. 19.95 o.p. (ISBN 0-07-079428-6). McGraw.

CS Severe Bleeding. Date not set. (ISBN 0-07-102847-1). McGraw.

Cuaderno Espiritual. Paul Twitchell. Tr. by Mario Proano & Maria A. De Mercado. 256p. (Orig., Span.). 1979. pap. 4.95 o.p. (ISBN 0-914766-48-1, 0928). Illum Way Pub.

Cub Scout Family Book. Boy Scouts of America. (Illus.). 32p. (YA) (gr. 6-12). pap. cancelled o.s.i. (ISBN 0-8395-3846-4, 3846). BSA.

Cuba. Edmund Lindon. LC 79-24010. (gr. 4 up). 1980. PLB 9.40 o.p. (ISBN 0-531-04101-8). Watts.

Cuba, Castro, & the United States. Philip W. Bonsal. LC 72-151505. (Pitt Latin American Ser.). 1971. 32.95x o.p. (ISBN 0-8229-3225-3). U of Pittsburgh Pr.

Cuba: Dictatorship or Democracy? Marta Harnecker. LC 78-24775. 288p. 1980. 15.95 o.s.i. (ISBN 0-88208-100-4); pap. 8.95 o.s.i. (ISBN 0-88208-101-2). Chicago Review.

Cuba Today. Lee Chadwick. LC 75-43185. (Illus.). 224p. 1976. 7.95 o.s.i. (ISBN 0-88208-065-2); pap. 5.95 o.s.i. (ISBN 0-88208-066-0). Chicago Review.

Cuban Communism. 3rd ed. Ed. by Irving L. Horowitz. LC 76-3214. 1977. pap. text ed. 8.95x o.p. (ISBN 0-87855-618-4). Transaction Pubs.

Cuban Communism. Ed. by Irving L. Horowitz. 143p. 1972. pap. 3.95 o.p. (ISBN 0-87855-046-1). Transaction Pubs.

Cuban Communism. Ed. by Irving L. Horowitz. 143p. 1970. (ISBN 0-87855-009-7). Transaction Pubs.

Cuban Communism. 2nd ed. Ed. by Irving L. Horowitz. 328p. 1972. pap. 3.95x o.p. (ISBN 0-87855-539-0). Transaction Pubs.

Cuban Revolution, National Liberation & the Soviet Union: Two Speeches by Fidel Castro. Fidel Castro. 40p. 1974. pap. 0.70 o.s.i. (ISBN 0-87898-109-8). New Outlook.

Cube Games. Don Taylor & Leanne Rylands. (Illus.). 64p. pap. 3.95 o.p. (ISBN 0-03-061524-0, Owl Bks). H Holt & Co.

Cubs: The Complete Record of Chicago Cubs Baseball. MacMillan Editorial Staff. (Illus.). 550p. 1986. pap. 10.95 o.p. (ISBN 0-02-029420-4, Collier). Macmillan.

Cucina Italiana. 1986. 14.98 o.p. (ISBN 0-517-61037-X). Crown.

Cuckolds, Clerics & Countrymen: Medieval French Fabliaux. Tr. by John DuVal. LC 81-14731. 192p. 1982. text ed. 17.00x o.p. (ISBN 0-938626-06-X). U of Ark Pr.

Cuckoo Clocks, a Guide to Repair, Identification & Prices. Tran Duy Ly. (Illus.). 240p. (Orig.). 1986. (ISBN 0-930163-31-1); pap. Arlington Bk.

Cuckoo Sister. Vivien Alcock. (Lythway Ser.). 256p. (gr. 3-7). 1987. PLB 14.95x o.p. (ISBN 0-7451-0586-6, Pub. by Chivers Pr UK). G K Hall.

Cucumbers in a Flowerpot. rev. ed. Alice Skelsey. LC 83-40551. (Illus.). 144p. 1984. pap. 4.95 o.p. (ISBN 0-89480-729-3, 729). Workman Pub.

Cudmore & the America's Cup. Malcolm McKeag. (Illus.). 177p. 1988. 29.95 o.p. (ISBN 0-434-98120-6, Pub. by W Heinemann Ltd). David & Charles.

Cuentistas de Hoy. Mario B. Rodriguez. LC 52-14409. (Span). 1952. pap. 18.76 o.p. (ISBN 0-395-05317-X). HM.

Cuentistas Hispanoamericanos del Siglo Veinte. Luis Leal. 256p. 1972. pap. text ed. 8.00 o.p. (ISBN 0-394-31669-X, RanC). Random.

Cuento de la Mujer del Mar. Manuel Ramos. 120p. 1979. pap. 4.95 o.p. (ISBN 0-940238-12-8). Ediciones Huracan.

Cuento de la Princesita Muerta y los Siete Paladines. Aleksandr Pushkin. 37p. (Span.). 1973. pap. 2.95 o.p. (ISBN 0-8285-1288-4, Pub. by Progress Pubs USSR). Imported Pubns.

Cuentos Contemporaneos. Ed. by Doris K. Arjona & Edith F. Helman. (Orig., Span.). 1935. pap. 6.95x o.p. (ISBN 0-393-09432-4, NortonC). Norton.

Cuentos de Juan Bobo. Rosario Ferre. LC 81-69787. (Illus.). 32p. (gr. 7). 1982. pap. 4.50 o.p. (ISBN 0-940238-62-4). Ediciones Hura.

Cuentos del Hombre Cacataibo (Cashibo) II. Compiled by Gregorio Estrella & Olive Shell. (Comunidades y Cultura Peruanas: No. 11). 90p. 1977. pap. 4.25x o.s.i. (ISBN 0-88312-340-1); microfiche 2.00 o.s.i. (ISBN 0-88312-745-8). Summer Inst Ling.

Cuentos Escogido H Quiroga. Franco. Ed. by Jean Franco. 1968. pap. text ed. 7.25 o.s.i. (ISBN 0-08-012791-6). Pergamon.

Cuentos Espanoles Concertados. Ed. by Gonzalo Sobejano & Gary D. Keller. 305p. (Orig., Span.). 1975. pap. text ed. 10.95 o.p. (ISBN 0-15-516682-4, HC). HarBraceJ.

Cugel's Saga. Jack Vance. 334p. 1983. 14.50 o.s.i. (ISBN 0-671-49450-3, Timescape). PB.

Cuisine for All Seasons: A Menu Cookbook. Helen Hecht. LC 82-73033. 320p. 1983. 16.95 o.p. (ISBN 0-689-11351-X, Atheneum). Macmillan.

Cuisine of California. California Restaurant Association Staff. 116p. 1984. pap. 9.95 o.p. (ISBN 0-939944-40-5, Dist. by Pelican). Marmac Pub.

Cuisine of Hungary. G. Lang. 495p. 1985. pap. 40.00x o.p. (ISBN 0-317-40734-1, Pub. by Collets UK). State Mutual Bk.

Cuisine of Jacques Maximin. Jacques Maximin. (Illus.). 365p. 1986. 19.95 o.p. (ISBN 0-87795-810-6). Morrow.

Cuisine of Normandy: French Regional Cooking with Princess Marie-Blanche de Broglie. Marie-Blanche De Broglie & Harriet Zukas. LC 84-9020. 1984. 18.45 o.p. (ISBN 0-395-36552-X). HM.

Culinary Art of Modern Taiwan. Benita M. Wong. (East Asian Folklore & Social Life Monographs: Vol. 104). 24p. 1981. 14.00x o.p. (ISBN 0-89986-335-3). Oriental Bk Store.

Culinary Arts Institute Encyclopedic Cookbook. Ed. by Ruth Berolzheimer. 1980. pap. 13.95 o.s.i. (ISBN 0-671-41408-9, Fireside). S&S.

Culinary Arts Institute French Cookbook. Culinary Arts Institute Staff. (Illus.). 192p. 1983. pap. 7.75 spiral binding o.p. (ISBN 0-671-47238-0, Fireside). S&S.

Culinary Arts Institute Italian Cookbook. 192p. 1982. pap. 7.75 o.p. (ISBN 0-671-45081-6, Fireside). S&S.

Culinary Arts Institute Polish Cookbook. 192p. 1982. pap. 7.95 o.p. (ISBN 0-671-45080-8, Fireside). S&S.

Culinary Craft. Judy Gorman. Ed. by Sandra J. Taylor. LC 84-50427. (Illus.). 416p. 1984. 17.95 o.p. (ISBN 0-89909-038-9). Yankee Bks.

Culpeper's Complete Herbal & English Physician. enl. ed. Nicholas Culpeper. (Illus.). 420p. 1987. Repr. of 1814 ed. 25.00 o.p. (ISBN 0-916638-38-3). Meyerbooks.

Cult Controversies: The Societal Response to the New Religious Movements. James A. Beckford. 336p. 1985. 39.95 o.p. (ISBN 0-422-79630-1, 9592, Pub. by Tavistock England); pap. 13.95 o.p. (ISBN 0-422-79640-9, 9593, Pub. by Tavistock England). Routledge Chapman & Hall.

Cult Movies: The Classics, the Sleepers, the Weird & the Wonderful. Danny Peary. 400p. (Orig.). 1981. pap. 14.95 o.p. (ISBN 0-440-51631-5, Dell Trade Pbks). Dell.

Cult of the Atom: The Secret Papers of the Atomic Energy Commission. Daniel F. Ford. 1984. pap. 6.70 o.p. (ISBN 0-671-25302-6). S&S.

Cult of the Black Virgin. Ean Begg. (Illus.). 288p. (Orig.). 1985. pap. 11.95 o.p. (ISBN 1-85063-022-4, Ark Paperbks). Routledge Chapman & Hall.

Cult of the Sun: Myth & Magic in Ancient Egypt. Rosalie David. (Illus.). 208p. 1980. 24.50x o.p. (ISBN 0-460-04284-X, BKA 03250, Pub. by J. M. Dent England). Biblio Dist.

Culte d'Horus a Edfou: Au Temps des Ptolemees, 2 Vols, Pt. 2. Maurice Alliot. (Arabic & Fr.). 1979. 75.00 o.p. (ISBN 0-86685-335-9). Intl Bk Ctr.

Cultism to Charisma: My Seven Years with Jeane Dixon. Alice Braemer & Dolores Hayford. 1977. 4.00 o.p. (ISBN 0-682-48755-4). Exposition-Phoenix.

Cultivating Religious Growth Groups. Charles M. Olsen. LC 83-27328. (The Pastor's Handbook Ser.: Vol. 3). 118p. (Orig.). 1984. pap. 7.95 o.s.i. (ISBN 0-664-24617-6, Westminster). Westminster John Knox.

Cultivation of Christmas Trees. T. S. Eliot. 1956. 2.00 o.p. (ISBN 0-374-13304-2). FS&G.

Cults & Creeds in Graeco-Roman Egypt. H. Idris Bell. 128p. 1954. (ISBN 0-8022-0096-6). Philos Lib.

Cults in America: Programmed for Paradise. Willa Appel. LC 82-15538. 228p. 1983. 15.95 o.p. (ISBN 0-03-054836-5, Owl Bks.); pap. 7.95 o.p. H Holt & Co.

Cultura y Historia. V. Mezhuev. 279p. (Span.). 1980. 5.95 o.p. (ISBN 0-8285-1800-9, Pub. by Progress Pubs USSR). Imported Pubns.

Cultural Analysis: The Work of Peter L. Berger, Mary Douglas, Michel Foucault, & Jurgen Habermas. Robert Wuthnow et al. 224p. 1984. 26.95x o.p. (ISBN 0-7100-9894-4); pap. 10.95 o.p. (ISBN 0-7100-9994-0). Routledge Chapman & Hall.

Cultural & Economic Reproduction in Education. Ed. by Michael W. Apple. (Routledge Educaton Bks.). 350p. 1982. 27.95x o.p. (ISBN 0-7100-0845-7); pap. 12.95x o.p. (ISBN 0-7100-0846-5). Routledge Chapman & Hall.

Cultural & Social Anthropology: An Overture. 2nd ed. Robert F. Murphy. (Illus.). 256p. 1986. pap. text ed. (ISBN 0-13-195470-9). P-H.

Cultural Anthropology. 4th ed. Carol R. Ember & Melvin Ember. (Illus.). 432p. 1985. pap. text ed. (ISBN 0-13-195421-0). P-H.

Cultural Anthropology. 4th ed. William A. Haviland. LC 83-4404. 1983. pap. 24.95 o.p. (ISBN 0-03-062921-7, HoltC). HR&W.

Cultural Anthropology: A Christian Perspective. Stephen A. Grunlan & Marvin K. Mayers. 1979. 10.95 o.p. (ISBN 0-310-36321-7, 11280P). Zondervan.

Cultural Anthropology: Study Guide & Workbook. 4th ed. Dennis Werner. 128p. 1985. pap. text ed. (ISBN 0-13-195322-2). P-H.

Cultural Boundaries & the Cohesion of Canada. Raymond Breton et al. (Illus.). 422p. 1980. pap. text ed. 18.95x o.p. (ISBN 0-920380-37-9, Pub. by Inst Res Pub Canada). Gower Pub Co.

Cultural Checklist: A Technique for Selecting Reading Materials for Foreign Students. Walter P. Allen. 1973. pap. 9.95 o.p. (ISBN 0-87789-072-2). ELS Educ Servs.

Cultural Dialogue: An Introduction to Intercultural Communication. Michael H. Prosser. LC 77-89049. (Illus.). 1978. text ed. 18.95 o.p. (ISBN 0-395-24448-X). HM.

Cultural Factors in Inter-American Relations. Samuel Shapiro. 1968. 18.95 o.p. (ISBN 0-268-00066-2); pap. 3.45x o.p. (ISBN 0-268-00309-2). U of Notre Dame Pr.

Cultural Foundations of Industrial Civilization. John U. Nef. LC 73-13743. xvi, 164p. 1974. Repr. of 1958 ed. 18.00 o.p. (ISBN 0-208-01406-3, Archon). Shoe String.

Cultural Geography of the Modern Tarascan Area. Robert C. West. LC 77-118761. (Illus.). 77p. 1973. Repr. of 1948 ed. lib. bdg. 35.00x o.p. (ISBN 0-8371-5078-7, SMIH). Greenwood.

Cultural Heritage of Ancient India. S. K. Maity. 120p. 1982. text ed. 12.50x o.p. (ISBN 0-391-02809-X). Humanities.

Cultural Pluralism in Education: Theoretical Foundations, IE. Nicholas Appleton & Nicole Benevento. LC 82-12741. (Illus.). 288p. (Orig.). 1983. pap. text ed. 16.95 o.p. (ISBN 0-582-29009-0). Longman.

Cultural Policy in Yugoslavia: Self-Management & Culture. Stevan Majstorovic. (Studies & Documents on Cultural Policies). (Illus.). 96p. 1980. pap. 5.00 o.p. (ISBN 92-3-101829-9, U1141, UNESCO). UNIPUB.

Cultural Relations in the Plateau of Northwestern America. Verne F. Ray. (Illus.). 1964. Repr. of 1939 ed. 5.00 o.p. (ISBN 0-916561-18-6). Southwest Mus.

Cultural Resource Development: A Planning Survey & Analysis. New York State Commission on Cultural Resources. LC 75-19790. (Special Studies). (Illus.). 300p. 1976. 19.95 o.p. (ISBN 0-275-55640-9). Praeger.

Cultural Resource Reconnissance of the Tennessee National Wildlife Refuge with Archaeological Survey of Selected Areas, 2 vols. William O. Autry, Jr. & Jane S. Hinshaw. (T.A.R.A. Report: No. 1). (Illus.). viii, 268p. (Orig.). 1981. Vol. 1. pap. 10.00x o.s.i. (ISBN 0-940148-00-5); Vol. 2. pap. 20.00x o.p. (ISBN 0-940148-01-3); Set. pap. 30.00x o.p. (ISBN 0-940148-02-1). Anthro Research.

Cultural Resources Directory, 1987-88. Cultural Alliance of Greater Hampton Roads. 160p. (Orig.). pap. 5.00 o.p. (ISBN 0-943133-00-9). Cultural Alliance.

Cultural Revolution in China: An Annotated Bibliography. James C. Wang. LC 75-24099. (Reference Library of Social Science: Vol. 16). 246p. 1976. lib. bdg. 34.00 o.p. (ISBN 0-8240-9973-7). Garland Pub.

Cultural Revolution: 1967 in Review. Michel Oksenberg et al. (Michigan Monographs in Chinese Studies: No. 2). (Illus.). 125p. 1968. pap. 2.50 o.p. (ISBN 0-89264-002-2). U of Mich Ctr Chinese.

Cultural Subversion of the Biblical Faith: Life in the 20th Century under the Sign of the Cross. James D. Smart. LC 77-22063. 126p. 1977. pap. 5.95 o.s.i. (ISBN 0-664-24148-4, Westminster). Westminster John Knox.

Culture & Civilization of the U. S. S. R. Shankar Basu. 126p. 1984. text ed. 20.00x o.p. (ISBN 0-86590-269-0, Pub. by Sterling Pubs India). Apt Bks.

Culture & Cognition: Readings in Cross-Cultural Psychology. J. W. Berry & P. R. Dasen. (Illus.). 525p. 1974. pap. 12.95x o.p. (ISBN 0-416-75180-6, NO.2086). Routledge Chapman & Hall.

Culture & Commitment (1929-1945) Ed. by Warren Susman. LC 77-188361. (American Culture Ser). (Illus.). 386p. 1973. 8.95 o.p. (ISBN 0-8076-0631-6); pap. 6.95 o.p. (ISBN 0-8076-0630-8). Braziller.

Culture & Curing: Anthropological Perspectives on Traditional Medical Beliefs & Practices. Ed. by Peter Morley & Roy Wallis. LC 78-62194. (Contemporary Community Health Ser.). (Illus.). 1980. 14.95 o.p. (ISBN 0-8229-1136-1); pap. 9.95x o.p. (ISBN 0-8229-5325-0). U of Pittsburgh Pr.

Culture & Evaluation. Ed. by Michael Q. Patton. LC 84-82376. (Program Evaluation Ser.: No. 25). (Orig.). 1985. pap. text ed. 12.95x o.p. (ISBN 0-87589-763-0). Jossey-Bass.

Culture & Immorality As Forces Capable to Create & Destroy Nations & the Position of the United States in the Conflict. Seymour Smythe. (Illus.). 117p. 1987. 127.45 o.p. (ISBN 0-89266-593-9). Am Classical Coll Pr.

Culture & Personality. John J. Honigmann. (Illus.). 499p. 1973. Repr. of 1954 ed. lib. bdg. 27.50x o.p. (ISBN 0-8371-6641-1, HOCP). Greenwood.

Culture & Personality. Ed. by S. Stansfeld Sargent & Marion Smith. LC 73-76142. (Illus.). 219p. 1975. Repr. of 1949 ed. lib. bdg. 22.50x o.p. (ISBN 0-8154-0488-3). Cooper Sq.

Culture & Practical Reason. Marshall Sahlins. LC 75-27899. (Illus.). 1977. lib. bdg. 17.50x o.s.i. (ISBN 0-226-73359-9). U of Chicago Pr.

Culture & Related Corporate Realities. Vijay V. Sathe. 1985. pap. 29.95x o.p. (ISBN 0-256-03142-8). Irwin.

Culture & Revolution. Raymond Williams. 240p. 1988. 42.50 o.p. (ISBN 0-86091-229-9, Pub. by Verso); pap. 14.95 o.p. (ISBN 0-86091-943-9, Pub. by Verso). Routledge Chapman & Hall.

Culture & Self: Asian & Western Perspectives. Ed. by Anthony J. Marsella et al. 264p. 1985. 25.00 o.p. (ISBN 0-422-79130-X, 9232, Pub. by Tavistock England); pap. 11.95 o.p. (ISBN 0-422-79140-7, 9233, Pub. by Tavistock England). Routledge Chapman & Hall.

Culture in Conflict: Skilled Workers & Industrial Capitalism in Hamilton, Ontario 1860-1914. Bryan D. Palmer. 1979. 25.00x o.p. (ISBN 0-7735-0346-3, McGill Canada); pap. 10.95 o.p. (ISBN 0-7735-0347-1, McGill Canada). U of Toronto Pr.

Culture in Retrospect. S. J. Knudson. 1978. text ed. 28.95 o.p. (ISBN 0-395-30647-7). HM.

Culture, Language & Society. 2nd ed. Ward H. Goodenough. 1981. pap. text ed. 13.95 o.p. (ISBN 0-8053-3341-X). Benjamin-Cummings.

Culture of Bureaucracy. Charles Peters & Michael Nelson. LC 78-11051. 1979. pap. text ed. 13.95 o.p. (ISBN 0-03-044216-8, HoltC). HR&W.

Culture of Contemporary Rural Communities, 6 vols. in 1. United States Department of Agriculture, Bureau of Agricultural Economics Staff. LC 78-24169. 1979. Repr. of 1943 ed. lib. bdg. 55.00x o.p. (ISBN 0-313-20686-4, USRL). Greenwood.

Culture of Early Charleston. Frederick P. Bowes. LC 78-897. (Illus.). 1978. Repr. of 1942 ed. lib. bdg. 35.00x o.p. (ISBN 0-313-20278-8, BOCE). Greenwood.

Culture of Narcissism: American Life in an Age of Diminishing Expectations. Christopher Lasch. 1979. 14.95 o.p. (ISBN 0-393-01177-1). Norton.

Culture of Time & Space, Eighteen Eighty to Nineteen Eighteen. Stephen Kern. (Illus.). 384p. 1983. text ed. 27.00 o.p. (ISBN 0-674-17972-2). Harvard U Pr.

Cumberland & Pennsylvania. Krause & Kramer. (Carsten's Hobby Bks.: No. C-42). 1981. pap. 8.50 o.p. (ISBN 0-911868-42-9). Carstens Pubns.

Cumberland Station: Poems. Dave Smith. LC 76-13582. 112p. 1976. 7.95 o.p. (ISBN 0-252-00581-3); pap. 8.95 o.p. (ISBN 0-252-00582-1). U of Ill Pr.

Cumulated Citations: 1973 see Hearing, Speech & Communication Disorders.

Cumulated Citations: 1974 see Hearing, Speech & Communication Disorders.

Cumulated Dramatic Index. 1909-1949, 2 vols. Faxon, F. W. Co. Staff. 1965. lib. bdg. 615.00 o.p. (ISBN 0-8161-0402-6, Hall Library). G K Hall.

Cumulated Subject Index to Psychological Abstracts, 1927-1960, 2 Vols. Compiled by Hall, G. K. & Co. Staff. 1973. 745.00 o.p. (ISBN 0-8161-0570-7, Pub. byHall Library); first suppl. 1961-1965 310.00 o.p. (ISBN 0-8161-0730-0); second suppl. 1966-1968 410.00 o.p. (ISBN 0-8161-0776-9). G K Hall.

Cumulation of the Library Catalog Supplements of Martin P. Catherwood Library of the New York State School of Industrial & Labor Relations, 9 vols. Cornell University, New York State School of Industrial & Labor Relations Staff. 1977. Set. lib. bdg. 1285.00 o.p. (ISBN 0-8161-0022-5, Hall Library). G K Hall.

Cumulative Author Index to Psychological Index, 1894 to 1935, & Psychological Abstracts, 1927 to 1958, 5 vols. Columbia University, New York Staff. 1970. Set. 460.00 o.p. (ISBN 0-8161-0470-0, Hall Library); first supplement (1959-1963) 110.00 o.p. (ISBN 0-8161-0598-7); second supplement (1964-1968) 2 vols. 290.00 o.p. (ISBN 0-8161-0749-1). G K Hall.

Cumulative Bibliography of African Studies, International African Institute, London Author Catalog, 2 vols. International African Institute Staff. 1973. Set. lib. bdg. 200.00 o.p. (ISBN 0-8161-1045-X, Hall Library). G K Hall.

Cumulative Bibliography of African Studies, International African Institute, London Classified Catalog, 3 vols. International African Institute Staff. 1975. Set. lib. bdg. 300.00 o.p. (ISBN 0-8161-1076-X, Hall Library). G K Hall.

Cumulative Bibliography of Asian Studies, 1941-1965, Author Bibliography, 4 Vols. Association for Asian Studies Editors. 1970. Set. 405.00 o.p. (ISBN 0-8161-0805-6, Hall Library). G K Hall.

Cumulative Bibliography of Asian Studies, 1941-1965, Subject Bibliography, 4 Vols. Ed. by Association For Asian Studies. 1970. Set. 415.00 o.p. (ISBN 0-8161-0127-2, Hall Library). G K Hall.

Cumulative Book List: Annual Volume, 1986. Ed. by Whitaker, J. & Sons Ltd. 1300p. 1987. 75.00 o.p. (ISBN 0-85021-174-3, Pub. by J Whitaker UK). Bowker.

Cumulative Index of SAE Technical Papers, 1965-1985. 8th ed. Society of Automotive Engineers Staff. 1985. 115.00 o.p. (ISBN 0-89883-652-2). Soc Auto Engineers.

Cumulative Index to Clinical Obstetrics & Genecology, Vols. 1-17 (1958-1974) new ed. LC 75-45525. 1976. lib. bdg. 45.00 o.s.i. (ISBN 0-88471-035-1, SUB. 267). Numarc Bk Corp.

Cumulative Index to Obstetrics & Gynecology: 1978-1982, Vols. 51-60. 1983. 62.50 o.s.i. (ISBN 0-88471-045-9, SUB. 267). Numarc Bk Corp.

Cumulative Index to the American Journal of Public Health, Vols. 60-69: 1970-1979. 1981. lib. bdg. 48.50 o.s.i. (ISBN 0-88471-042-4, SUB. 268). Numarc Bk Corp.

Cuna Indian Art: The Culture & Craft of Panama's San Blas Islanders. Clyde E. Keeler. LC 68-24875. 1969. 25.00 o.p. (ISBN 0-682-46815-0, University). Exposition-Phoenix.

Cuna Song: Cancion de los Cunas. Adapted by Harriet Rohmer. Jesus G. Rea. LC 76-29122. (Fifth World Tales Ser.). (Illus., Eng. & Span.). (gr. k-6). 1976. pap. 5.95 o.p. (ISBN 0-89239-008-5, Imprenta de Libros Infantiles). Childrens Book Pr.

Cunning of History: The Holocaust & the American Future. Richard Rubenstein. 14.75 o.p. (ISBN 0-8446-5860-X). Peter Smith.

Cup. Jean Carlson. LC 81-86002. 1982. 2.50 o.p. (ISBN 0-8323-0401-8). Binford-Metropolitan.

Cup & Bowl. Sue Tarsky. (Look & Say Ser.). (Illus.). 32p. 1983. 1.50 o.s.i. (ISBN 0-671-47658-0, Little Simon). S&S.

Cup of Butterflies & Birdsongs. MAC Staff. LC 76-55450. (Illus.). 1976. pap. 4.95 o.p. (ISBN 0-89638-005-X). CompCare.

Cup of News: The Life of Thomas Nashe. Charles Nicholl. (Illus.). 352p. 1984. 29.95x o.p. (ISBN 0-7100-9517-1). Routledge Chapman & Hall.

Cup of Sun: A Book of Poems. Joan W. Anglund. LC 67-24870. (Illus.). 63p. 1967. 6.95 o.p. (ISBN 0-15-123390-X). HarBraceJ.

Cupid & Psyche. Walter Pater. (Illus.). 48p. 1977. 9.95 o.p. (ISBN 0-571-11115-7). Faber & Faber.

Curation in the Small Museum: Human Bones. Sarah Gehlert. (Miscellaneous Publications in Anthropology Ser.: No. 8). ii, 12p. 1980. pap. 0.80 o.p. (ISBN 0-913134-81-3). Mus Anthro Mo.

Cure for Anxiety. William M. Elliott, Jr. LC 64-18326. (Orig.). 1964. pap. 2.45 o.p. (ISBN 0-8042-3388-8, John Knox). Westminster John Knox.

Cure Is in the Cause: A Humane Approach to Child Discipline. Wallace D. Labenne. LC 74-163002. 87p. 1971. pap. text ed. 5.00 o.p. (ISBN 0-89039-002-9). Ann Arbor Pubs.

Cures: The Story of Cures That Failed. James J. Walsh. LC 70-137343. 304p. 1971. Repr. of 1923 ed. 43.00x o.p. (ISBN 0-8103-3773-8). Gale.

Curieux, le glorieux et la sagesse du monde dans la premiere moitie du XVIe siecle: L'exemple de Panurge. Gerard Defaux. LC 81-71430. (French Forum Monographs: No. 34). 196p. (Orig.). 1982. pap. 15.95x o.p. (ISBN 0-917058-33-X). French Forum.

Curiosities of Civilization. Andrew Wynter. LC 67-23949. (Social History Reference Ser.: No. 11). 546p. 1968. Repr. of 1860 ed. 35.00x o.p. (ISBN 0-8103-3264-7). Gale.

Curiosities of Clocks & Watches from the Earliest Times. Edward J. Wood. LC 70-174149. (Illus.). x, 456p. 1974. Repr. of 1866 ed. 43.00x o.p. (ISBN 0-8103-3984-6). Gale.

Curiosities of Indo-European Tradition & Folk-Lore. Walter K. Kelly. LC 68-22032. 320p. 1969. Repr. of 1863 ed. 40.00x o.p. (ISBN 0-8103-3837-8). Gale.

Curiosities of London. rev. ed. John Timbs. LC 68-22056. 886p. 1968. Repr. of 1867 ed. 51.00x o.p. (ISBN 0-8103-3497-6). Gale.

Curiosities of Medical Experience. J. G. Millingen. LC 72-83373. 582p. 1969. Repr. of 1839 ed. 43.00x o.p. (ISBN 0-8103-3487-9). Gale.

Curiosities of the Search-Room. Julia Byrne. LC 70-78117. 424p. 1969. Repr. of 1880 ed. 40.00x o.p. (ISBN 0-8103-3573-5). Gale.

Curious Art of Autobiography. H. H. Wethered. 238p. 1956. (ISBN 0-8022-1854-7). Philos Lib.

Curious Boating Inventions. Joachim Schult. LC 74-1525. (Illus.). 150p. 1974. 14.95 o.s.i. (ISBN 0-8008-2103-3). Taplinger.

Curious Case of Sidd Finch. George Plimpton. 1987. 14.95 o.p. (ISBN 0-02-597650-8). Macmillan.

Curious Creatures. E. Pinner. 1954. (ISBN 0-8022-1978-0). Philos Lib.

Curious Creatures in Zoology. John Ashton. LC 68-57297. 362p. 1968. Repr. of 1890 ed. 43.00x o.p. (ISBN 0-8103-3525-5). Gale.

Curious Facts. John May et al. LC 80-12123. 336p. 1981. 14.95 o.p. (ISBN 0-03-046776-4, Owl Bks); pap. 7.95 o.p. (ISBN 0-03-046771-3). H Holt & Co.

Curious Missie. Virginia Sorensen. LC 53-7872. (Illus.). (gr. 3-6). 1953. 5.50 o.p. (ISBN 0-15-221085-7, HJ). HarBraceJ.

Curious Street. Desmond Hogan. 194p. 1984. 12.95 o.p. (ISBN 0-8076-1099-2). Braziller.

Curious Yachting Inventions. Joachim Schult. LC 74-1526. (Illus.). 139p. 1974. 14.95 o.s.i. (ISBN 0-8008-2104-1). Taplinger.

Curley Cat Baby-Sits. Pauline Watson. LC 77-1589. (Let Me Read Ser.). (Illus.). 32p. (gr. k-2). 1977. 5.95 o.p. (ISBN 0-15-221110-1, HJ). HarBraceJ.

Curley Cat Baby-Sits. Pauline Watson. LC 77-1589. (Let Me Read Ser.). (Illus.). 32p. (gr. 1-4). 1977. pap. 2.95 o.p. (ISBN 0-15-622700-2, VoyB). HarBraceJ.

Currency Lass. Margaret Reeson. 272p. (Orig.). 1985. pap. 10.95 o.p. (ISBN 0-86760-018-7, Pub. by Albatross Bks). Meyer Stone Bks.

Currency Risk. Boris Antl. 194p. 1980. 120.00 o.p. (ISBN 0-8002-3417-0). Intl Pubns Serv.

Current Algebras & Their Applications. B. Renner. 1968. 51.00 o.p. (ISBN 0-08-012504-2). Pergamon.

Current Aspects of Biochemical Energetics. Ed. by Nathan O. Kaplan & Eugene P. Kennedy. 1967. 79.00 o.p. (ISBN 0-12-397350-3). Acad Pr.

Current British Directories. 10th ed. CBD Research Staff. 1985. 135.00 o.p. (ISBN 0-8002-3554-1). Intl Pubns Serv.

Current Concepts in Erythropoiesis. Ed. by C. D. Dunn. 415p. 1983. 60.00 o.p. (ISBN 0-471-90033-8, Pub. by Wiley Med). Wiley.

Current Concepts in Hand Surgery. Ed. by John A. Boswick, Jr. LC 82-24897. (Illus.). 287p. 1983. text ed. 37.50 o.p. (ISBN 0-8121-0881-7). Lea & Febiger.

Current Concepts in Occupational Education. Ed. by James A. Lahren & Albert J. Pautler. LC 72-12560. 93p. 1973. pap. text ed. 3.50x o.p. (ISBN 0-8290-1406-3). Irvington.

Current Concepts in the Management of Lymphoma & Leukemia. Ed. by J. E. Ultmann et al. LC 71-146232. (Recent Results in Cancer Research: Vol. 36). (Illus.). 1971. 31.00 o.p. (ISBN 0-387-05309-3). Springer-Verlag.

Current Contents of Academic Journals in Japan, 1970. Compiled by Kokusai B. Shinkokai. 208p. 1971. 10.00x o.p. (ISBN 0-86008-056-0, Pub. by Japan Sci Soc Japan). Intl Spec Bk.

Current Crises of Psychology. Gordon Westland. 1978. text ed. 29.50x o.p. (ISBN 0-435-82943-2); pap. text ed. 9.50x o.p. (ISBN 0-435-82944-0). Gower Pub Co.

Current Development of the World Economy. 74p. 1980. pap. 5.00 o.p. (ISBN 92-808-0150-3, TUNU096, UNU). UNIPUB.

Current Developments in Bankruptcy & Reorganization 1985: Vols. 344 & 345, 2 vols. Practising Law Institute Staff. 1407p. 1985. pap. 40.00 o.p. (ISBN 0-317-27433-3, #A4-4109). PLI.

Current Developments in Patent Law, 1984. (Patents, Copyrights, Trademarks, & Literary Property Course Handbook Ser.). 452p. 1984. 15.00 o.p. (ISBN 0-686-79964-X, G4-3742). PLI.

Current Developments in Patent Law 1985. 389p. 1985. 15.00 o.p. (G4-3779). PLI.

Current Developments in Trademark Law 1986. (Patents, Copyrights, Trademarks, & Literary Property Course Handbook Ser.). 354p. 1986. 45.00 o.p. (ISBN 0-686-79968-2, G4-3794). PLI.

Current Employment Law Issues. Wake Forest University School of Law Staff. 125.00cancelled o.s.i. (ISBN 0-318-19519-4). Wake Forest Law.

Current Estimates from the National Health Interview Survey, United States 1984. Peter W. Ries. LC 86-17926. (DHHS Publication PHS 86-1584; Data from the National Health Survey Series 10, No. 156). 195p. 1986. pap. 9.50 o.p. (S/N 017-022-00966-8). USGPO.

Current European Anaesthesiology, 1986: The Yearbook of the European Academy of Anaesthesiology, Vol. 2. Ed. by R. M. Jones. 1986. 48.00 o.p. (ISBN 0-471-91112-7, Dist. by A R Liss). Wiley.

Current History Encyclopedia of Developing Nations. Ed. by Carol L. Thompson et al. (Illus.). 384p. 1982. text ed. 65.50 o.p. (ISBN 0-07-064387-3). McGraw.

Current Issues in Energy. C. Starr. 1979. 44.00 o.p. (ISBN 0-08-023243-4); pap. 17.00 o.p. (ISBN 0-08-023244-2). Pergamon.

Current Issues in Financial Accounting for Lawyers. Samuel P. Gunther. LC 83-61992. 1983. 45.00 o.p. (ISBN 0-317-04101-0). PLI.

Current Issues in Marriage & the Family. 3rd ed. J. Gipson Wells. 1983. pap. text ed. write for info. o.p. (ISBN 0-02-425480-0). Macmillan.

Current Issues in Public-Utility Economics: Essays in Honor of James C. Bonbright. Ed. by Albert L. Danielson & David R. Kamerschen. LC 81-48612. 352p. 1983. 40.00x o.p. (ISBN 0-669-05440-2). Lexington Bks.

Current Issues in Secondary Education. Ed. by John R. Shaffer. 191p. 1969. pap. text ed. 8.95x o.p. (ISBN 0-686-80319-1). Irvington.

Current Law of California Real Estate, 5 vols. in 6 bks. Harry B. Miller & Marvin M. Starr. LC 67-5714. 390.00 o.p.; Suppl. 1987. 61.50 o.p.; Suppl. 1986. 53.00 o.p. Lawyers Co-Op.

Current Literature on Communication in Personnel Management, 1980-1984. Jacqueline Mundell. (Public Administration Ser.: P 1746). 10p. 1985. 2.00 o.p. (ISBN 0-89028-526-8). Vance Biblios.

Current Medical Diagnosis & Treatment. 26th ed. Marcus A. Krupp et al. 1176p. 1987. pap. 32.50 o.p. (ISBN 0-8385-1413-8, Dist. by Prentice-Hall). Appleton & Lange.

Current Medical Terminology. Vera Pyle. LC 85-62411. 204p. 1985. 17.00 o.p. (ISBN 0-934385-00-9). Prima Vera Pubns.

Current Municpal Defaults & Bankruptcy 1983. Practicing Law Institute Staff & James E. Spiotto. LC 83-235797. (Real Estate Law & Practice Course Handbook Ser.: NO. 238). 1983. 45.00 o.p. (N44415). PLI.

Current National Bibliographies. U. S. Library of Congress, General Reference & Bibliography Division Staff. LC 68-55128. (Illus.). 1968. Repr. of 1955 ed. lib. bdg. 35.00x o.p. (ISBN 0-8371-0716-4, CUNB). Greenwood.

Current Paratransit & Ride-Sharing Activities. (Transportation Research Report Ser.). 57p. 1979. 3.40 o.p. (ISBN 0-309-02974-0). Transport Res Bd.

Current Perspectives in Allergy. Ed. by Edward J. Goetzl & A. B. Kay. LC 82-9494. (Contemporary Issues in Clinical Immunology & Allergy Ser.: Vol. 1). (Illus.). 185p. 1982. pap. text ed. 37.00 o.p. (ISBN 0-443-02503-7). Churchill.

Current Problems in Elementary Particle & Mathematical Physics. Ed. by P. Urban. (Acta Physica Austriaca: Supplementum 15). (Illus.). 1976. 87.40 o.p. (ISBN 0-387-81401-9). Springer-Verlag.

Current Problems in Federal Civil Practice, 1986. Practising Law Institute Staff & Barry H. Garfinkel. LC 83-226001. (Litigation & Administration Practice Ser.: No. 318-319). 1803p. 1986. 45.00 o.p. (H4-5007). PLI.

Current Problems in Religion. Hermon F. Bell. 640p. 1956. (ISBN 0-8022-0093-1). Philos Lib.

Current Problems of Contemporary Capitalism. M. Bunkina. 206p. 1982. pap. 2.95 o.p. (ISBN 0-8285-2508-0, Pub. by Progress Pubs USSR). Imported Pubns.

Current Procedures in Clinical Bacteriology. Paul D. Ellner. (Illus.). 240p. 1978. 31.50x o.p. (ISBN 0-398-03759-0). C C Thomas.

Current Protocols in Molecular Biology. Ed. by Frederick Ausubel et al. 672p. 1987. 165.00 o.p. (ISBN 0-471-62594-9). Wiley.

Current Psychotherapies. 3rd ed. Ed. by Raymond J. Corsini. LC 83-61991. 570p. 1984. pap. text ed. 24.95 o.p. (ISBN 0-87581-298-8). Peacock Pubs.

Current Research in Marijuana. Ed. by M. F. Lewis. 1972. 41.00 o.p. (ISBN 0-12-447050-5). Acad Pr.

Current Research in Oncology. Ed. by C. B. Anfinsen et al. 1973. pap. 44.00 o.p. (ISBN 0-12-058752-1). Acad Pr.

Current Research in Ophthalmic Electron Microscopy, Vol. 2. Ed. by M. Spitznas. (Illus.). 1979. pap. 28.40 o.p. (ISBN 0-387-09160-2). Springer-Verlag.

Current Research in Ophthalmic Electron Microscopy: Transactions of the 5th Annual Meeting of the European Club for Opthalmic Fine Structure in Zuerich, March 25 & 26, 1977. Ed. by M. Spitznas. (Illus.). 1977. pap. 28.40 o.p. (ISBN 0-387-08508-4). Springer-Verlag.

Current Research in Ophthalmic Electron Microscopy, 3. Ed. by W. R. Lee. (Illus.). 160p. 1980. 29.10 o.p. (ISBN 0-387-09953-0). Springer-Verlag.

Current Research in Petroleum Fuels, I. R. D. McCoy et al. (Energy & Environmental Studies: Petroleum Research). 1976. text ed. 30.00x o.p. (ISBN 0-8422-7293-3). Irvington.

Current Research in Petroleum Fuels, II. Herman Taylor, Jr. et al. (Energy & Environmental Studies: Petroleum Research). 1976. text ed. 32.00x o.p. (ISBN 0-8422-7294-1). Irvington.

Current Research Inventory (Spring 1982) Pref. by Wayne A. Cornelius. (Research Inventory Ser.: Vol. 1). 77p. (Orig.). 1982. pap. 3.00 o.p. (ISBN 0-935391-55-X, RI-01). Ctr Mex Studies.

Current Research on Scientific & Technical Information Transfer. National Science Foundation, Division of Science Information Staff. LC 77-9216. (Micropapers Editions Ser). 1977. 12.95x o.p. (ISBN 0-88432-007-3). J Norton Pubs.

Current Research on the Consequences of Maternal Drug Abuse. Ed. by Theodore Pinkert. (National Institute on Drug Abuse Research Monograph). 118p. (Orig.). 1985. pap. 2.50 o.p. (ISBN 0-318-18741-8, S/N 017-024-01249-1). USGPO.

Current Solutions to Hydrogen Problems in Steels. Ed. by C. G. Interrante & G. M. Pressouyre. 1982. 68.00 o.p. (ISBN 0-87170-148-0). ASM.

Current Soviet Policies I: The Documentary Record of the 19th Communist Party Congress & the Reorganization after Stalin's Death. Leo Gruliow. Tr. by Current Digest of the Soviet Press Staff. 268p. 1953. 31.00 o.p. (ISBN 0-913601-21-7); pap. 25.00 o.p. (ISBN 0-913601-01-2). Current Digest.

Current Soviet Policies: The Documentary Record of the Extraordinary Twenty-First Communist Party Congress, Vol. III. Ed. by Leo Gruliow & Mark Neuweld. Tr. by The Current Digest of the Soviet Press Staff. 230p. (Orig.). 1960. 31.00 o.p. (ISBN 0-913601-23-3); pap. 25.00 o.p. (ISBN 0-913601-03-9). Current Digest.

Current Soviet Policies: The Documentary Record of the Twentieth Communist Party Congress & Its Aftermath, Vol. II. Ed. by Leo Gruliow. Tr. by The Current Digest of the Soviet Press Staff. 247p. (Orig.). 1957. 30.00 o.p. (ISBN 0-913601-22-5); pap. 25.00 o.p. (ISBN 0-913601-02-0). Current Digest.

Current Soviet Policies: The Documentary Record of the Twenty-Second Congress of the Communist Party of the Soviet Union, Vol. IV. Ed. by Charlotte Saikowski et al. Tr. by The Current Digest of the Soviet Press Staff. 248p. (Orig.). 1962. 31.00 o.p. (ISBN 0-913601-24-1); pap. 25.00 o.p. (ISBN 0-913601-04-7). Current Digest.

Current State of Social Studies: A Report of Project SPAN. Project SPAN Staff. (Project SPAN Reports Ser.). 326p. (Orig.). 1982. pap. 21.95 o.p. (ISBN 0-89994-272-5). Soc Sci Ed.

Current Status of Some Major Problems in Developmental Biology: Proceedings of the Soceity for the Study of Developmental Biology, 25th Symposium. Society for the Study of Developmental Biology Staff. Ed. by Michael Locke. 1967. 71.00 o.p. (ISBN 0-12-454162-3). Acad Pr.

Current Studies on Thyrotropin, I. B. J. Ormston et al. 168p. 1974. text ed. 29.50x o.p. (ISBN 0-8422-7128-7). Irvington.

Current Studies on Thyrotropin, II. Charles Gual et al. 233p. 1974. text ed. 32.50x o.p. (ISBN 0-8422-7162-7). Irvington.

Current Surgical Management of Neurologic Disease. Charles B. Wilson & Julian T. Hoff. (Illus.). 355p. 1980. text ed. 48.00 o.p. (ISBN 0-443-08042-9). Churchill.

Current Surgical Therapy 1984-1985. John L. Cameron. 616p. 1984. 59.50 o.p. (ISBN 0-941158-20-9, D-1161-X). Mosby.

Current Therapy in Allergy Immunology & Rheumatology 1985-1986. Lawrence M. Lichtenstein & Anthony S. Fauci. 337p. 1985. 48.00 o.p. (ISBN 0-941158-48-9, D3003-7). Mosby.

Current Therapy in Cardiovascular Disease 1984-1985. Nicholas J. Fortuin. (Illus.). 392p. 1984. 48.00 o.p. (ISBN 0-941158-27-6, D1651-4). Mosby.

Current Therapy in Dermatology 1985-1986. Thomas T. Provost & Evan R. Farmer. 400p. 1984. 44.00 o.p. (ISBN 0-941158-32-2, D-4050-4). Mosby.

Current Therapy in Endocrinology 1985-1986. Ed. by Dorothy T. Krieger & C. Wayne Bardin. 420p. 1985. 49.50 o.p. (ISBN 0-941158-47-0, D-2757-5). Mosby.

Current Therapy in Gastroenterology & Liver Disease 1984-1985. Bayless. 538p. (Orig.). 1983. 58.00 o.p. (ISBN 0-941158-26-8, D-0460-5). Mosby.

Current Therapy In Hematology-Oncology 1985-1986. Brain & Carbone. (Illus.). 318p. 1985. 44.00 o.p. (ISBN 0-941158-38-1, D-0741-8). Mosby.

Current Therapy in Infectious Disease: 1983 to 1984. Edward H. Kass & Richard Platt. 400p. 1983. text ed. 44.00 o.p. (ISBN 0-941158-06-3, D2621-8). Mosby.

Current Therapy in Nephrology & Hypertension 1984-1985. Richard J. Glassock. 400p. 1984. text ed. 56.00 o.p. (ISBN 0-941158-30-6, D-1862-2). Mosby.

Current Therapy in Neurological Surgery, 1985-1986. Long. 1985. 48.00 o.p. (ISBN 0-941158-49-7, D-3151-3). Mosby.

Current Therapy in Otolaryngology: Head & Neck Surgery 1984-1985. George A. Gates. (Illus.). 450p. 1984. text ed. 59.50 o.p. (ISBN 0-941158-23-3, D-1758-8). Mosby.

Current Therapy in Respiratory Disease, 1986-87, Vol. 2. 2nd ed. Cherniack. 300p. 1986. 47.50 o.p. (ISBN 0-941158-71-3, D-1068-0). Mosby.

Current Therapy in Respiratory Medicine 1984-1985. Reuben M. Cherniack. (Illus.). 360p. 1984. 44.00 o.p. (ISBN 0-941158-24-1, D1174-1). Mosby.

Current Therapy of Infertility: Nineteen Eighty-Four to Nineteen Eighty-Five, No. 2. Celso-Ramon Garcia. 280p. 1984. text ed. 44.00 o.p. (ISBN 0-941158-22-5, D1737-5). Mosby.

Current Therapy of Trauma, Vol. 1. Ed. by Donald D. Trunkey & Frank R. Lewis, Jr. 300p. 1983. text ed. 28.00 o.p. (ISBN 0-941158-12-8, D5152-2). Mosby.

Current Topics in Biochemistry. Ed. by C. B. Anfinsen & Alan N. Schechter. 1974. 44.00 o.p. (ISBN 0-12-058751-3). Acad Pr.

Current Topics in Biochemistry: National Institute of Health Lectures in Biomedical Sciences. C. B. Anfinsen et al. 1972. pap. 49.50 o.p. (ISBN 0-12-058750-5). Acad Pr.

Current Topics in Bioenergetics, 8 vols. Ed. by D. Rao Sanadi. Vol. 1, 1966. 79.50 o.p. (ISBN 0-12-152501-5); Vol. 2, 1967. 79.50 o.p. (ISBN 0-12-152502-3); Vol. 3, 1969. 79.50 o.p. (ISBN 0-12-152503-1); Vol. 4, 1971. 79.50 o.p. (ISBN 0-12-152504-X); Vol. 5, 1973. 79.50 o.p. (ISBN 0-12-152505-8); Vol. 6, 1977. 84.50 o.p. (ISBN 0-12-152506-6); Vol. 7, 1978. 79.50 o.p. (ISBN 0-12-152507-4); Vol. 8, 1978. 79.50 o.p. (ISBN 0-12-152508-2). Acad Pr.

Current Topics in Clinical & Community Psychology. Ed. by C. D. Spielberger. Vol. 1, 1969. 61.50 o.p. (ISBN 0-12-153501-0); Vol. 2, 1970. 61.50 o.p. (ISBN 0-12-153502-9); Vol. 3, 1971. 61.50 o.p. (ISBN 0-12-153503-7). Acad Pr.

Current Topics in Coagulation. Ed. by Gottfried Schmer & Paul E. Strandjord. 1973. 42.00 o.p. (ISBN 0-12-626250-0). Acad Pr.

Current Topics in Comparative Pathobiology, 2 vols. Ed. by Thomas Cheng. 1971-73. Vol. 1. 77.00 o.p. (ISBN 0-12-153401-4); Vol. 2. 89.00 o.p. (ISBN 0-12-153402-2). Acad Pr.

Current Topics in Elementary Particle Physics. Ed. by K. H. Mutter & K. Schilling. LC 81-10652. (NATO ASI Series B, Physics: Vol. 70). 352p. 1981. 59.50x o.p. (ISBN 0-306-40801-5, Plenum Pr). Plenum Pub.

Current Topics in Extrapyramidal Disorders. Ed. by A. Carlsson et al. (Journal of Neural Transmission Supplementum: No. 16). (Illus.). 240p. 1980. 57.90 o.p. (ISBN 0-387-81570-8). Springer-Verlag.

Current Topics in Microbiology & Immunology, Vol. 105. E. G. Strauss & J. H. Strauss. (Illus.). 220p. 1983. 46.50 o.p. (ISBN 0-387-12492-6). Springer-Verlag.

Current Topics in Microbiology & Immunology, Vol. 114. (Illus.). 245p. 1985. 49.00 o.p. (ISBN 0-387-15103-6). Springer-Verlag.

Current Topics in Microbiology & Immunology, Vol. 62. Ed. by W. Arber et al. LC 73-17985. (Illus.). 170p. 1973. 49.00 o.p. (ISBN 0-387-06598-9). Springer-Verlag.

Current Topics in Microbiology & Immunology, Vol. 68. P. S. Sarma et al. LC 75-12910. (Illus.). 180p. 1975. 46.00 o.p. (ISBN 0-387-07074-5). Springer-Verlag.

Current Topics in Microbiology & Immunology, Vol. 69. A. C. Frazer et al. (Illus.). 200p. 1975. 46.00 o.p. (ISBN 0-387-07195-4). Springer-Verlag.

Current Topics in Microbiology & Immunology, Vol. 99. Ed. by M. Cooper et al. (Illus.). 200p. 1982. 46.00 o.p. (ISBN 0-387-11419-X). Springer-Verlag.

Current Topics in Pathology, Vol. 58. Ed. by Altmann et al. LC 56-49162. (Illus.). 190p. 1973. 70.80 o.p. (ISBN 0-387-06405-2). Springer-Verlag.

Current Topics in Pathology, Vol. 59. Ed. by E. Grundmann & W. H. Kirsten. 270p. 1974. 87.40 o.p. (ISBN 0-387-06737-X). Springer-Verlag.

Current Topics in Sports Medicine. Norbort Bachl et al. 1159p. (Orig.). 1984. pap. 59.00 o.p. (ISBN 0-317-65595-7). Urban & S.

Current Topics in Thyroid Research. Ed. by C. Cassano & M. Andreoli. 1966. 104.00 o.p. (ISBN 0-12-163750-6). Acad Pr.

Current Treaty Index. Igor I. Kavass & Adolf Sprudzs. ix, 429p. 1987. pap. 49.50 o.p. (ISBN 0-89941-636-5). W S Hein.

Current Trends in Dynamic Personality Theory: Problems of Normal & Disturbed Development. Ed. by Harold B. Davis & Sybil Gottlieb. LC 72-8722. 340p. 1972. text ed. 29.00x o.p. (ISBN 0-8422-5068-9). Irvington.

Current Trends in Indian Environment. Desh Bandhu & Eklavya Chauhan. 240p. 1977. 10.00 o.p. (ISBN 0-88065-080-X, Pub. by Messers Today & Tomorrow Printers & Publishers). Scholarly Pubns.

Current Trends in Optics. F. T. Arecchi & F. R. Aussenegg. LC 81-7046. 190p. 1981. pap. 42.95x o.p. (ISBN 0-470-27278-3). Halsted Pr.

Current Trends in Organic Synthesis: Proceedings of the Fourth International Conference on Organic Synthesis, Tokyo, Japan, August 22-27, 1982. Ed. by H. Nozaki. LC 82-22445. (IUPAC Symposium Ser.). (Illus.). 442p. 1983. 110.00 o.p. (ISBN 0-08-029217-8). Pergamon.

Current Trends in Scientific Research. Pierre Auger. 1961. 5.00 o.p. (ISBN 92-3-100470-0, U146, UNESCO). UNIPUB.

Current Trends in the Biochemistry of Lipids: Proceedings. Ed. by J. Ganguly & R. M. Smellie. 1973. 117.00 o.p. (ISBN 0-12-274250-8). Acad Pr.

Currents: 1983-1984. 1984. 11.00 o.p. (ISBN 0-317-19105-5). ICA Inc.

Curricular Challenges. Ed. by Lois V. Edinger et al. (Education in the Eighties Ser.). 192p. 1981. cloth 18.95 o.p. (ISBN 0-8106-3170-9); pap. 12.95 o.p. (ISBN 0-8106-3169-5). NEA.

Curriculm Development. Donald E. Orlosky & B. Othanel Smith. 1978. pap. 22.95 o.p. (ISBN 0-395-30687-6). HM.

Curriculum & Instruction in Nursing. Virginia C. Conley. 1973. 22.50 o.p. (ISBN 0-316-15307-9). Little.

Curriculum & Instruction in the Elementary School. Frederick A. Rodgers. (Illus.). 320p. 1975. text ed. write for info. o.p. (ISBN 0-02-402610-7). Macmillan.

Curriculum Beyond School. Geoffrey Squires. (Studies in Teaching & Learning Ser.). 192p. (Orig.). 1987. pap. text ed. 26.95 o.s.i. (ISBN 0-340-39701-2). Princeton Bk Co.

Curriculum Building in Nursing. 3rd ed. Em O. Bevis. LC 81-18888. (Illus.). 282p. 1982. pap. text ed. 22.95 o.p. (ISBN 0-8016-0667-5). Mosby.

Curriculum Careering Gamebook. Ira M. Bank. (Illus.). 60p. (gr. 4-6). 1978. Repr. 2.00 o.p. (ISBN 0-912578-16-5). Chron Guide.

Curriculum Careering Guidebook. Ira M. Bank. 31p. (Orig.). (gr. 4-6). 1974. pap. 3.00 o.p. (ISBN 0-912578-17-3). Chron Guide.

Curriculum Development for the Gifted. C. June Maker. LC 81-14985. 404p. 1981. text ed. 36.50 o.p. (ISBN 0-89443-347-4). Aspen Pub.

Curriculum Development in Vocational & Technical Education: Planning Content, & Implementation. 2nd ed. Curtis R. Finch & John R. Crunkilton. 352p. 1984. pap. text ed. 36.95 o.p. (ISBN 0-205-08116-9, 238116, Pub. by Longwood Div). Allyn.

Curriculum Development: Theory & Practice. Hilda Taba. 1962. text ed. 20.95 o.p. (ISBN 0-15-516740-5, HC). HarBraceJ.

Curriculum for the Modern Elementary School. Walter T. Petty. 1976. text ed. 26.95 o.p. (ISBN 0-395-30695-7). HM.

Curriculum Guide to The Constitution: Perspectives in Contemporary American Democracy. curriculum guide 6.00 o.p. (ISBN 0-932765-18-1). Close Up Foun.

Curriculum Guides for Undergraduate Field Instruction Programs. write for info. o.p. Coun Soc Wk Ed.

Curriculum in Graduate Education in Nursing: Part II - Components in the Curriculum Development Process. Joan C. Hoexter & Janice E. Hayes. 64p. 1976. 5.95 o.p. (ISBN 0-88737-189-2, 15-1632). Natl League Nurse.

Curriculum Integration & Lifelong Education. J. B. Ingram. (Advances in Lifelong Education: Vol 6). 1979. text ed. 16.25 o.p. (ISBN 0-08-024301-0); pap. text ed. 9.75 o.p. (ISBN 0-08-024300-2). Pergamon.

Curriculum Priorities in Australian Higher Education. Anthony J. Fielding & Darol M. Cavanagh. 200p. 1983. 19.95 o.p. (ISBN 0-949614-03-3, Pub. by Croom Helm Ltd). Routledge Chapman & Hall.

Curriculum Process for Developing or Revising Baccalaureate Nursing Programs. Helen Yura & Arlyne Friesner. 65p. 1978. 8.95 o.p. (ISBN 0-88737-186-8, 15-1700). Natl League Nurse.

Curriculum Process in Nursing: A Guide to Curriculum Development. Gertrude Torres & Marjorie Stanton. (Illus.). 208p. 1982. 24.95 o.p. (ISBN 0-13-196261-2). Appleton & Lange.

Curriculum: Quest for Relevance. 2nd ed. William Van Til. LC 79-144319. 400p. 1974. pap. 21.50 o.p. (ISBN 0-395-17787-1). HM.

Curriculum, Retrospect & Prospect. Ed. by Robert M. McClure. LC 6-16938. (National Society for the Study of Education Yearbooks Ser: No. 70, Pt. 1). 1974. pap. text ed. 4.50x o.s.i. (ISBN 0-226-60106-4). U of Chicago Pr.

Curriculum Studies & Educational Planning. Denis Lawton. (Studies in Teaching & Learning). 161p. (Orig.). 1983. pap. text ed. 18.95 o.s.i. (ISBN 0-340-33281-6). Princeton Bk Co.

Curriculum Workshop: An Introduction to Whole Curriculum Planning. Maurice Holt. (Education Bks.). 200p. (Orig.). 1983. pap. 13.95x o.p. (ISBN 0-7100-9512-0). Routledge Chapman & Hall.

Currier & Ives Chronicles America. J. Lowell Pratt. 1985. 12.98 o.p. (ISBN 0-517-48970-8). Crown.

Curry Every Sunday: An Asian Cookbook for Western Palates. Lawrence M. Prescott & Ellen G. Prescott. LC 83-21530. (Illus.). 192p. 1984. pap. 8.95 o.p. (ISBN 0-932620-33-7). Betterway Pubns.

Curry Primer: A Grammar of Spice Cookery. Juel Andersen. LC 84-45102. 64p. (Orig.). 1984. pap. 4.50 o.p. (ISBN 0-916870-79-0). Creative Arts Bk.

Curse of the Moonraker. Eth Clifford. LC 77-24431. 192p. (gr. 5-9). 1977. 6.95 o.p. (ISBN 0-395-25837-5). HM.

Curse of the Pharoahs. Philipp Vandenberg. 1976. pap. 1.75 o.s.i. (ISBN 0-671-80810-9). PB.

Curse of the Two-Headed Bull. Lee Falk. (Phantom Ser.: No. 15). 1975. pap. 0.95 o.p. (ISBN 0-380-00381-3, 24729). Avon.

Curse of the Werewolf. Chris Martindale. LC 86-91525. (Advanced Dungeons & Dragons Adventure Gamebook Ser.: No. 12). 192p. 1987. pap. 2.95 o.p. (ISBN 0-88038-432-8). TSR Inc.

Curso Basico de Ciencias Sociales: Con especial interes para Puerto Rico. Jose J. Santa Pinter. LC 79-15841. (Illus.). 500p. (Span.). 1984. pap. text ed. 12.00 o.p. (ISBN 0-8477-2449-2). U of PR Pr.

Curso de Algebra Superior. A. G. Kurosch. 442p. (Span.). 1977. 7.95 o.p. (ISBN 0-8285-1683-9, Pub. by Mir Pubs USSR). Imported Pubns.

Curtain of Green & Other Stories. Eudora Welty. 1947. 7.95 o.p. (ISBN 0-15-123669-0). HarBraceJ.

Curtain of Time. Paul R. Cagle, Jr. & Mary H. Wallace. (Illus., Orig.). 1984. pap. 6.95 o.p. (ISBN 0-912315-76-8). Word Aflame.

Curtis Park. Don Etter. LC 78-73982. 1980. 19.50 o.p. (ISBN 0-87081-077-4). Univ Pr Colo.

Curtiss P-40. Aero Publishers, Inc., Aeronautical Staff et al. LC 65-24307. (Aero Ser: Vol. 3). 1965. pap. 5.95 o.p. (ISBN 0-8168-0508-3, 20508, TAB-Aero). TAB Bks.

Curtiss Standard JN-4D Military Tractor (Aircraft) Handbook. Curtiss Aeroplane & Motor Corp. Ed. by M. S. Rice. (Illus.). 1976. pap. 6.95 o.p. (ISBN 0-87994-013-1). Aviat Pub.

Curvature & Characteristic Classes. J. L. Dupont. (Lecture Notes in Mathematics: Vol. 640). 1978. pap. 13.00 o.p. (ISBN 0-387-08663-3). Springer-Verlag.

Curves of Pursuit. Thomas Farber. 192p. 1985. pap. 3.50 o.p. (ISBN 0-380-69838-2, Bard). Avon.

Curzon in India, 2 vols. David Dilks. Incl. Vol. 1. Achievement (ISBN 0-8008-2106-8); Vol. 2. Frustration (ISBN 0-8008-2107-6). LC 70-88619. 10.00 ea. o.s.i. Taplinger.

Custer Died for Your Sins. Vine Deloria, Jr. (YA) (gr. 7 up). 1981. pap. 3.50 o.p. (ISBN 0-380-00250-7, 64477-0). Avon.

Custody. Irma Walker. 1984. pap. 2.75 o.s.i. (ISBN 0-345-31284-8). Ballantine.

Custody: A True Story. Elizabeth Morgan. 16.95 o.p. (ISBN 0-316-58294-8). Little.

Custody Cases & Expert Witnesses: A Manual for Attorneys. Melvin G. Goldzband. 216p. 1980. 35.00 o.p. (ISBN 0-15-100016-6, H39840, Pub. by Law & Business). HarBraceJ.

Custody Handbook: A Woman's Guide to Child Custody Disputes. Women's Legal Defense Fund Staff. 74p. (Orig.). 1984. pap. 7.00 o.p. (ISBN 0-932689-00-0). Women's Legal Defense.

Custom & Government in the Lower Congo. Wyatt MacGaffey. LC 70-85415. (Illus.). 1970. 38.50x o.p. (ISBN 0-520-01614-9). U of Cal Pr.

Custom Cars. Kirk L. Ready. LC 82-7757. (Superwheels & Thrill Sports Bks.). (Illus.). 48p. (gr. 4 up). 1982. PLB 9.95 o.p. (ISBN 0-8225-0508-8). Lerner Pubns.

Custom Vans. Mark Rich. LC 80-25792. (On the Move Ser.). (Illus.). 48p. (gr. 3-6). 1981. PLB 10.60 o.p. (ISBN 0-516-03885-0); pap. 2.95 o.p. (ISBN 0-516-43885-9). Childrens.

Custom, Work & Market Capitalism: The Forest of Dean Colliers, 1788-1888. Chris Fisher. (Illus.). 203p. 1981. 27.00 o.p. (ISBN 0-7099-1001-0, Pub. by Croom helm). Routledge Chapman & Hall.

Customer Deductions: Evaluation & Resolution. Credit Research Foundation. 22p. 1977. 40.00 o.p. (ISBN 0-939050-16-1). Credit Res NYS.

Customer Deductions Impact on Receivables. Credit Research Foundation. 12p. 1982. 40.00 o.p. (ISBN 0-939050-17-X). Credit Res NYS.

Customizing Your Van. 2nd, rev. ed. Allan Girdler. Rev. by Carl Caiati. (Illus.). 256p. 1983. 16.95 o.p. (ISBN 0-8306-0212-7); pap. 11.60 o.p. (ISBN 0-8306-0112-0, 212). TAB Bks.

Customs & Cultures: Anthropology for Christian Missions. 2nd ed. Eugene A. Nida. LC 54-8976. (Applied Cultural Anthropology Ser.). 306p. 1975. Repr. of 1954 ed. 7.95x o.p. (ISBN 0-87808-723-0). William Carey Lib.

Customs Law Handbook (Titles 18, 19 U.S.C. & Related Statutes) Gould Editorial Staff. 1100p. looseleaf 18.00 o.p. Gould.

Customs Union Issue. Jacob Viner. 1950. 20.00 o.p. (ISBN 0-910136-01-7). Anderson Kramer.

Cut & Sew: Working with Machine Knitted Fabrics. Pam Turbett. (Illus.). 120p. 1986. pap. 14.95 o.s.i. (ISBN 0-7134-4410-X, Pub. by Batsford England). David & Charles.

Cut & Shoot: Texas. Robin N. Montgomery. 160p. 1984. 11.95 o.p.; pap. 8.95 o.p. (ISBN 0-89015-429-5). Eakin Pr.

Cut-Outs: Native American Art. James H. Howard. (Contributions in Anthology & History Ser.: No. 2). (Illus.). 32p. 1982. 4.95 o.p. (ISBN 0-89326-089-4). Milwaukee Pub Mus.

Cut Your Own Taxes & Save, 1988. Robert Metz & Sidney Kess. (Illus.). 96p. 1987. pap. 3.95 o.p. (ISBN 0-88687-339-8, World Almanac). Pharos Bks NY.

Cutaneous Laser Therapy: Principles & Methods. Ed. by K. A. Arndt et al. 241p. 1983. 55.00x o.p. (ISBN 0-471-90075-3, Dist. by A R Liss). Wiley.

Cute Guys. Fran Pelzman & Martha Thomases. 1984. pap. 6.95 o.p. (ISBN 0-03-062905-5). H Holt & Co.

Cutlass Nineteen Seventy to Nineteen Eighty-Two. LC 81-70246. (Illus.). 288p. 1982. pap. 13.50 o.s.i. (ISBN 0-8019-7190-X). Chilton.

Cuts from a San Francisco Rock Journal. Debora Hill. LC 81-68393. (Illus.). 370p. (Orig.). 1981. pap. 9.95 o.p. (ISBN 0-89708-079-3). And Bks.

Cuttin' a Rug. John Byrne. (Paisley Patterns Trilogy). 40p. 1983. pap. 5.95 o.p. (ISBN 0-907540-21-X, NO.3985). Routledge Chapman & Hall.

Cutting: Arc. Resource Systems International Staff. 1982. pap. text ed. 15.00 o.p. (ISBN 0-8359-1206-X, Reston). P-H.

Cutting Edge. Dennis Etchison. LC 86-8854. 312p. 1986. 16.95 o.s.i. (ISBN 0-385-23430-9). Doubleday.

Cutting Health Care Costs. Paul B. Grant & Joseph G. Kozlowski. 290p. 1987. 79.95 o.p. (ISBN 0-85013-158-8); write for info. wkbk. o.p. Dartnell Corp.

Cutting Lisa. Percival Everett. 228p. 1986. 14.45 o.s.i. (ISBN 0-89919-412-5). Ticknor & Fields.

Cutting: Oxyfuel I. Resource Systems International Staff. 1982. pap. text ed. 15.00 o.p. (ISBN 0-8359-1204-3, Reston). P-H.

Cutting: Oxyfuel II. Resource Systems International Staff. 1982. pap. text ed. 15.00 o.p. (ISBN 0-8359-1205-1, Reston). P-H.

Cutting Through Spiritual Material. Chogyam Trungpa. 1980. pap. 8.95 o.p. (ISBN 0-394-73023-2). Random.

CV: Carrier Aviation. rev. ed. Peter Garrison. (Airpower Bk.). (Illus.). 110p. 1984. pap. 12.95 o.p. Presidio Pr.

CWLA Directory of Member Agencies, 1986. 10.00 o.p. (ISBN 0-87868-255-4, D-10, 2554). Child Welfare.

CWLA Standards for Adoption Service. rev ed. LC 78-73022. 101p. 1978. pap. 12.50 o.p. (ISBN 0-87868-013-6, 0136). Child Welfare.

CWLA Standards for Child Protective Service. rev ed. LC 73-79082. 85p. 1973. pap. 12.50 o.p. (ISBN 0-87868-113-2, 1132). Child Welfare.

CWLA Standards for Services for Unmarried Parents. rev. ed. 89p. 7.50 o.p. Child Welfare.

CWLA Statement on Child Advocacy. 21p. 1981. pap. text ed. 5.00 o.p. (ISBN 0-87868-199-X, 1990). Child Welfare.

CWLA's Foster Parenting an Adolescent. cancelled o.s.i. (TP2-01). Child Welfare.

Cyberiad: Fables for the Cybernetic Age. Stanislaw Lem. 240p. 1976. pap. 2.50 o.p. (ISBN 0-380-00517-4, 51557-1, Bard). Avon.

Cybernetic Approach to Stock Market Analysis: Versus Efficient Market Theory. Jerry Felsen. LC 74-34512. (Illus.). 1975. 20.00 o.p. (ISBN 0-682-48224-2, University). Exposition-Phoenix.

Cybernetic Music. Jaxitron. LC 85-17305. (Illus.). 352p. (Orig.). 1985. 26.95 o.p. (ISBN 0-8306-0856-7, 1856); pap. 18.60 o.p. (ISBN 0-8306-1856-2). Tab Bks.

Cybernetic Samurai. Victor Milan. Ed. by Robert Silverberg. 298p. 1985. 16.95 o.p. (ISBN 0-87795-642-1, Arbor Hse). Morrow.

Cybernetic Society. R. Parkman. 402p. 1974. 100.00 o.p. (ISBN 0-08-016949-X); pap. text ed. 71.00 o.p. (ISBN 0-08-017185-0). Pergamon.

Cyborg. Martin Caidin. LC 73-183758. 1972. 7.95 o.p. (ISBN 0-87795-025-3, A4159, Arbor Hse). Morrow.

Cyborg Four. Martin Caidin. LC 74-80703. 1975. 7.95 o.p. (ISBN 0-87795-085-7, Arbor Hse). Morrow.

Cyborg Nine, Vol. 2. (Big Little Bks.: No. 87). (Illus.). 350p. 1984. 6.95 o.p. (ISBN 0-318-02718-6). Bks Nippan.

Cyborg Nine (Movie) (Big Little Bks.: No. 74). (Illus.). 350p. 1984. 6.95 o.p. (ISBN 0-318-02711-9). Bks Nippan.

Cycle of Chinese Festivities. C. S. Wong. (Illus.). 1967. 20.00 o.s.i. (ISBN 0-685-25494-1). E J Brill USA.

Cycle of Fire. Hal Clement. 192p. 1981. pap. 2.25 o.s.i. (ISBN 0-345-29172-7, Del Rey). Ballantine.

Cycles of Essential Elements. Ed. by Lawrence R. Pomeroy. LC 74-4252. (Benchmark Papers in Ecology Ser: Vol. 1). 384p. 1982. 53.95 o.p. (ISBN 0-87933-129-1). Van Nos Reinhold.

Cycles of Heaven. Guy L. Playfair & Scott Hill. 1979. pap. 2.75 o.p. (ISBN 0-380-45419-X, 45419). Avon.

Cycles: What They Are, What They Mean, How to Profit by Them. Dick Stoken. (Illus.). 1978. text ed. 38.95 o.p. (ISBN 0-07-061632-9). McGraw.

Cyclic AMP. G. Alan Robison. 528p. 1971. 85.00 o.p. (ISBN 0-12-590450-9). Acad Pr.

Cyclic-Amp-Dependent Protein Kinase. (Landmark Ser.). 1979. 22.50x o.p. (ISBN 0-8422-4117-5). Irvington.

Cyclic & Event Stratification. Ed. by G. Einsele & A. Soilacher. (Illus.). 550p. 1982. pap. 32.00 o.p. (ISBN 0-387-11373-8). Springer-Verlag.

Cyclic Compounds. T. Eicher et al. LC 75-11665. (Topics in Current Chemistry Ser.: Vol. 57). 160p. 1975. 37.00 o.p. (ISBN 0-387-07290-X). Springer-Verlag.

Cyclic Difference Sets. L. Baumert. LC 73-153466. (Lecture Notes in Mathematics: Vol. 182). 1971. pap. 11.00 o.p. (ISBN 0-387-05368-9). Springer-Verlag.

Cyclic Nucleotides & Protein Phosphorylation in Cell Regulation: Proceedings of the 12th FEBS Meeting, Dresden, 1978. Ed. by E. G. Krause et al. (Federation of European Biochemical Society. Symposia: Vol. 54). (Illus.). 1979. 93.00 o.p. (ISBN 0-08-023178-0). Pergamon.

Cyclic Phenomena in Marine Plants & Animals. Ed. by E. Naylor & E. G. Hartnoll. 1979. 105.00 o.p. (ISBN 0-08-023217-5). Pergamon.

Cyclist Training Diary. Illus. by Cor Vos. 192p. 1987. 8.95 o.p. (ISBN 0-941950-12-3). Vitesse Pr.

Cyclist's Guide to Overnight Stops: Western States. Seymour Levine. 1982. pap. 3.95 o.s.i. (ISBN 0-345-30117-X). Ballantine.

Cyclist's Training Diary. rev. ed. Photos by Michael Chritton. (Illus.). 192p. 1985. 7.95 o.p. (ISBN 0-941950-08-5). Vitesse Pr.

Cyclist's Training Diary. Illus. by Tom Moran. (Illus.). 176p. 1983. 7.95 o.p. (ISBN 0-318-00246-9). Vitesse Pr.

Cyclitols & Phosphoinositides. Ed. by William W. Wells & Frank Eisenberg, Jr. (National Institute of Arthritis, Metabolism, & Digestive Diseases). 1978. 71.50 o.p. (ISBN 0-12-741750-8). Acad Pr.

Cycloaddition Reactions of Heterocumulenses. Henri Ulrich. (Organic Chemistry Ser.: Vol. 9). 1967. 82.50 o.p. (ISBN 0-12-708250-6). Acad Pr.

Cycloaddition Reactions: Proceedings of a Symposium, Munich, 1970. Ed. by R. Gompper. 116p. 1976. 28.00 o.p. (ISBN 0-08-020757-X). Pergamon.

Cyclobutadiene & Related Compounds. Michael P. Cava & M. J. Mitchell. (Organic Chemistry Ser.: Vol. 10). 1967. 98.50 o.p. (ISBN 0-12-164450-2). Acad Pr.

Cyclone. O. Gonchar. 322p. 1972. pap. 3.95 o.p. (ISBN 0-8285-0974-3, Pub. by Progress Pubs USSR). Imported Pubns.

Cyclopaedia of Fraternities. 2nd rev. ed. Albert C. Stevens. LC 66-20332. 470p. 1966. Repr. of 1907 ed. 43.00x o.p. (ISBN 0-8103-3084-9). Gale.

Cyclopaedia of Literary & Scientific Anecdote: Illustrative of the Characters, Habits, & Conversation of Men of Letters & Science. Ed. by William Keddie. LC 74-156925. 456p. 1971. Repr. of 1859 ed. 51.00x o.p. (ISBN 0-8103-3730-4). Gale.

Cyclopedia of Anecdotes of Literature. Kazlitt Arvine. LC 67-14020. 722p. 1967. Repr. of 1851 ed. 46.00x o.p. (ISBN 0-8103-3296-5). Gale.

Cyclops. Clive Cussler. 1986. 18.45 o.p. (ISBN 0-671-50374-X). S&S.

Cyclotomic Fields. S. Lang. (Graduate Texts in Mathematics: Vol. 59). 1978. 35.00 o.p. (ISBN 0-387-90307-0). Springer-Verlag.

Cyclotron Waves in Plasma. D. G. Lominadze. Ed. by S. M. Hamberger. Tr. by A. N. Dellis. (International Series of Natural Philosophy: Vol. 102). (Illus.). 220p. 1981. 48.00 o.p. (ISBN 0-08-021680-3). Pergamon.

Cylinder Theory in Dynamic Exhibitional Charts Depicting the Traumatic Extremes of the Stock Market: The Excesses of the National Economy & the Dangerous Extravagances of History from Which New Nations Are Born & Old Nations Die. Carlo M. De Flumiani. 1977. 137.75 o.p. (ISBN 0-89266-064-3). Am Classical Coll Pr.

Cylindric Algebras, Pt. I. Leon Henkin et al. (Studies in Logic: Vol. 64). 1971. 59.00 o.p. (ISBN 0-7204-2043-1, North Holland). Elsevier.

Cymbeline see also Tragedy of Cymbeline.

Cynara. Janis Flores. 1979. pap. 10.95 o.p. (ISBN 0-441-51040-X). Ace Bks.

Cyndi Lauper. Chris Crocker. (In the Spotlight Ser.). (Illus.). 64p. (gr. 3-7). 1985. lib. bdg. 9.29 o.p. (ISBN 0-671-55478-6). Messner.

Cynical Americans: Living & Working in an Age of Discontent & Disillusion. Donald L. Kanter & Philip H. Mirvis. LC 88-46087. (Management Ser.). 1989. text ed. 22.95x o.p. (ISBN 1-55542-150-4). Jossey-Bass.

Cynthia Freeman: A World Full of Strangers, the Days of Winter, Portraits, & Come Pour the Wine. Cynthia Freeman. 1981. boxed set 50.00 o.p. (ISBN 0-87795-353-8, Arbor Hse). Morrow.

Cynthia's Great Paint Adventure. Mary H. Manoni. Ed. by Susan Mahoney. (Raggedy Ann's & Raggedy Andy's Friends Book Cassettes). (Illus.). 16p. (gr. k-3). pap. text ed. cancelled o.s.i. (ISBN 0-89290-067-9). Soc for Visual.

Cypress & Other Writings of a German Pioneer in Texas. Hermann Seele. Tr. by Edward C. Breitenkamp from Ger. LC 79-11769. (Elma Dill Russell Spencer Foundation Ser.: No. 9). (Illus.). 231p. 1979. 14.95 o.p. (ISBN 0-292-79014-7). U of Tex Pr.

Cyprus. Michael Lee & Hanka Lee. (Islands Ser.). 1974. 18.95 o.p. (ISBN 0-7153-5980-0). David & Charles.

Cyprus Passion Cycle. August C. Mahr. (Mediaeval Studies Ser.: No. 9). (Illus.). 1947. 25.00 o.p. (ISBN 0-268-00401-3); pap. 14.95 o.p. (ISBN 0-268-00069-7). U of Notre Dame Pr.

Cyprus, the Sweet Land. 2nd, rev., enl. ed. P. Stavrou. (Illus.). 25.00 o.s.i. (ISBN 0-685-79119-X). E J Brill USA.

Cyriacus of Ancona's Journeys in the Propontis & the Northern Aegean: 1444-1445. Edward W. Bodnar & Charles Mitchell. LC 75-35466. (Memoirs Ser.: Vol. 112). 1976. pap. 10.00 o.p. (ISBN 0-87169-112-4). Am Philos.

Cyril Connolly: Journal & Memoir. David Pryce-Jones. LC 83-24282. 304p. 1984. 19.45 o.p. (ISBN 0-89919-280-7). Ticknor & Fields.

Cyrock. Claude D. McBride. (Illus.). 1978. 5.50 o.p. (ISBN 0-682-49147-0). Exposition-Phoenix.

Cysteine Proteinases. G. Lowe. 1976. pap. 15.50 o.p. (ISBN 0-08-020471-6). Pergamon.

Cystitis. Peter Evans. 1979. 12.95 o.p. (ISBN 0-8464-0053-7). Beekman Pubs.

Cytochromes: Current Research, I. Yoshiyuki Ichikawa et al. LC 72-6247. 223p. 1972. text ed. 22.50x o.p. (ISBN 0-8422-7014-0). Irvington.

Cytochromes: Current Research, II. Richard A. Morton et al. LC 72-6247. 220p. 1972. 28.50x o.p. (ISBN 0-8422-7033-7). Irvington.

Cytodifferentiation & Macromolecular Synthesis: Proceedings. Society for the Study of Developmental Biology Staff. Ed. by Michael Locke. 1963. 56.50 o.p. (ISBN 0-12-454156-9). Acad Pr.

Cytogenetics. Ronald L. Phillips & Charles R. Burnham. (Benchmark Papers in Genetics: Vol. 6). 1977. 84.50 o.p. (ISBN 0-12-787225-6). Acad Pr.

Cytogenetics of Cells in Culture. International Society for Cell Biology Staff. Ed. by R. J. Harris. (Proceedings: Vol. 3). 1964. 74.50 o.p. (ISBN 0-12-611903-1). Acad Pr.

Cytogenetics of Livestock. Franklin E. Eldridge. (Illus.). 1985. 53.95 o.s.i. (ISBN 0-87055-483-2). AVI.

Cytogenetics of Man & Other Animals. A. McDermott. (Outline Studies in Biology). 1975. pap. 8.50 o.p. (ISBN 0-412-13910-3, NO.6197, Pub. by Chapman & Hall). Routledge Chapman & Hall.

Cytological Technique. J. R. Baker. 1966. pap. 7.95x o.p. (ISBN 0-412-20300-6, NO.6580, Pub. by Chapman & Hall). Routledge Chapman & Hall.

Cytology of Female Genital Tract Tumours. C. Riotton & William Christopherson. (World Health Organization: International Histological Classification of Tumours Ser.: No. 8). (Illus.). 1977. books & slides 168.50 o.p. (ISBN 0-89189-109-9, 70-1-008-00). Am Soc Clinical.

Cytology of Non-Gynaecological Sites. G. Riotton & W. M. Christopherson. (World Health Organization: International Histological Classification of Tumours Ser.: No. 17). (Illus.). 1977. text ed. 69.50 o.p. (ISBN 92-4-176017-6, 70-1-017-20). Am Soc Clinical.

Cytopathology in Viral Diseases. N. F. Cheville. Ed. by J. L. Melnick. (Monographs in Virology: Vol. 10). (Illus.). xii, 236p. 1975. 84.75 o.p. (ISBN 3-8055-2203-7). S Karger.

Cytoplasm of Hepatocytes During Carcinogenesis: Electron & Lightmicroscopial Investigations of the Nitrosomorphiline-Intoxicated Rat Liver. P. Bannasch. LC 69-18017. (Recent Results in Cancer Research: Vol. 19). (Illus.). 1969. 29.00 o.p. (ISBN 0-387-04308-X). Springer-Verlag.

Cytoplasmic Genes & Organelles. Ruth Sager. 1972. 41.00 o.p. (ISBN 0-12-614650-0). Acad Pr.

Cytotoxic Estrogens in Hormone Receptive Tumors. Ed. by J. Raus et al. 1980. 58.50 o.p. (ISBN 0-12-583050-5). Acad Pr.

CZ Service-Repair Handbook: Single Exhaust Models-Through 1978. Ed. by Jeff Robinson. (Illus.). pap. text ed. 10.95 o.p. (ISBN 0-89287-102-4, M425). Clymer Pub.

CZ 250 Twins '74-'78. Pete Shoemark. (Owners Workshop Manual Ser.). 13.50 o.p. (ISBN 0-85696-329-1, 329). Haynes Pubns.

Czech-English-Czech Dictionary. 6th ed. J. Poldauf. 1971. text ed. 20.00x o.s.i. (ISBN 0-89918-253-4, C253). Vanous.

Czech-English, English-Czech Concise Technical Dictionary. Ed. by Z. Jouklova. (Czech. & Eng.). 17.50 o.s.i. (ISBN 0-685-58550-6). E J Brill USA.

Czech-English, English-Czech Dictionary of Electrical Engineering & Electronics. Ed. by Libuse Malinova. 1982. 40.00 o.p. (ISBN 0-318-00245-0). E J Brill USA.

Czech-English Technical Dictionary. 2nd, rev. & enl. ed. Ed. by B. Kloudova & V. Stakeova. (Czech. & Eng.). 1971-72. 35.00 o.s.i. (ISBN 0-685-47298-1). E J Brill USA.

Czech Literature. Arne Novak. Ed. by W. E. Harkins. (Joint Committee on Eastern Europe Publication Ser.: No. 4). 1976. 15.00 o.p. (ISBN 0-930042-20-4). Mich Slavic Pubns.

Czech-Say It in Czech: English-Czech Phrase Book with Pronunciation. A. Krusina. 1963. 8.50 o.s.i. (ISBN 0-686-77980-0). E J Brill USA.

Czechoslovak-Polish Relations 1918-1939: A Selected & Annotated Bibliography. C. M. Nowak. LC 75-39562. (Bibliographical Ser.: No. 55). 218p. 1976. 12.95x o.p. (ISBN 0-8179-2551-1). Hoover Inst Pr.

Czechoslovakia. Ed. by Ludvik Uhlir & Frantisek Miklos. (Illus.). 320p. 1980. 55.00 o.p. (ISBN 0-318-00244-2). E J Brill USA.

Czechoslovakia Nineteen Sixty-Eight - Nineteen Sixty-Nine: Annotation, Bibliography, Chronology. Zdenek Hejzlar & Vladimir Kusin. LC 74-17178. (Reference Library of Social Science: No. 4). 316p. 1975. lib. bdg. 46.00 o.p. (ISBN 0-8240-1055-8). Garland Pub.

CZ125, 175, & 175 Trail '69 - '76. Mervyn Bleach. (Owners Workshop Manuals Ser.: No. 185). 1979. 13.50 o.p. (ISBN 0-85696-185-X). Haynes Pubns.

D

D. B. Cooper: What Really Happened. Max Gunther. (Illus.). 224p. 1986. pap. 6.95 o.p. (ISBN 0-8092-4854-9). Contemp Bks.

D-Day Tank Battles: Beachhead to Breakout, No. 10. George Balin. (Tanks Illustrated Ser.). (Illus.). 64p. 1984. pap. 7.95 o.p. (ISBN 0-85368-633-5, Pub. by Arms & Armour Pr). Sterling.

Titles

D-Day to Bastogne: A Paratrooper Recalls World War II. Robert J. Houston. (Illus.). 1980. 10.00 o.p. (ISBN 0-682-49560-3). Exposition-Phoenix.

D. H. Lawrence Album. George Hardy & Nathaniel Harris. 1986. 15.95 o.p. (ISBN 0-531-15013-5). Watts.

D. H. Lawrence & America. Armin Arnold. 256p. 1959. (ISBN 0-8022-0039-7). Philos Lib.

D. H. Lawrence in Italy. Leo Hamalian. LC 81-502261. 224p. 1982. 12.95 o.s.i. (ISBN 0-8008-4572-2). Taplinger.

D. H. Lawrence: Son of Woman. John M. Murry. Repr. of 1954 ed. 24.00 o.p. (ISBN 0-527-65950-9). Kraus Repr.

D. W. Griffith: An American Life. Richard Schickel. LC 83-20151. (Illus.). 672p. 1984. 24.00 o.p. (ISBN 0-671-22596-0). S&S.

Da Capo: A Review Grammar. Graziana Lazzarino. (Ital.). 1979. text ed. 22.95 o.p. (ISBN 0-03-043846-2); tapes avail. o.p. (ISBN 0-03-043851-9). HR&W.

DAC-Easy Accounting & Payroll Made Easy. Gary West & William R. Mills. (Illus.). 272p. 1987. pap. 16.95 o.p. (ISBN 0-8306-2914-9, 2914). Tab Bks.

DAC Easy Made Easy. Bud E. Smith. 192p. 1987. pap. 19.95 o.p. (ISBN 0-87094-931-4). Dow Jones-Irwin.

Dacia: An Outline of the Early Civilizations of the Carpatho-Danubian Countries. Vasile Parvan. Tr. by I. L. Evans & M. P. Charlesworth. LC 78-26364. (Illus.). 1979. Repr. of 1928 ed. lib. bdg. 35.00x o.p. (ISBN 0-313-20798-4, PADA). Greenwood.

Dada: Performance, Poetry & Art. John Erickson. (World Authors Ser.: No. 703). 171p. 1984. lib. bdg. 19.95 o.p. (ISBN 0-8057-6550-6, Twayne). G K Hall.

Daddy & Ben Together. Miriam B. Stecher. LC 81-4425. (Illus.). (ps-2). 1981. 11.75 o.p. (ISBN 0-688-00735-X); PLB 11.88 o.p. (ISBN 0-688-00736-8). Lothrop.

Daddy, but No Mama. Carolyn Phillips. 96p. 1986. 7.95 o.p. (ISBN 0-8062-2972-1). Carlton.

Daddy King. Martin Luther King, Sr. & Clayton Riley. (General Ser.). 1981. lib. bdg. 13.95 o.p. (ISBN 0-8161-3157-0, Large Print Bks). G K Hall.

Daddy: The Diary of an Expectant Father. Dennis Danziger. LC 86-71873. 252p. 1987. 14.95 o.p. (ISBN 0-89586-526-2). Price Stern.

Daddy's Girl. Charlotte V. Allen. 1980. 10.95 o.s.i. (ISBN 0-671-61024-4, Wyndham). S&S.

Daddy's Girl. J. D. Landis. LC 83-18966. 208p. (gr. 7 up). 1984. 10.25 o.p. (ISBN 0-688-02763-6). Morrow.

Daddy's Girl. J. D. Landis. (Nancy Drew Files Ser.). (YA) (gr. 8 up). pap. 2.50 o.p. (ISBN 0-671-55823-4). Archway.

Daddy's Gonna Buy Me a Diamond Ring. Christopher C. Brown. 112p. (gr. 5-8). 1985. 1.95 o.s.i. (ISBN 0-87406-055-9). Willowisp Pr.

Dads Are Special, Too. J. David Purdy. 96p. 1985. pap. 3.95 o.p. (ISBN 0-8423-0503-3). Tyndale.

Daedalus & Icarus. Penelope Farmer. LC 71-96319. (Illus.). 47p. (gr. 3-6). 1971. 4.95 o.p. (ISBN 0-15-221212-4, HJ). HarBraceJ.

Daggerspell. Katharine Kerr. LC 86-2123. 432p. 1986. 16.95 o.s.i. (ISBN 0-385-23108-3). Doubleday.

Dahl's Russian Dictionary, 4 vols. Vladimir I. Dahl. LC 79-40161. (Illus.). 3000p. (Rus.). 1981. Set. 290.00 o.p. (ISBN 0-08-023573-5). Pergamon.

Dahl's Russian Dictionary, Vol. 1. V. I. Dahl. 1979. 83.00 o.p. (ISBN 0-08-023590-5, PBL). Pergamon.

Dahl's Russian Dictionary, Vol. 2. V. I. Dahl. LC 80-40989. 1980. 83.00 o.p. (ISBN 0-08-023591-3, PBL). Pergamon.

Dahl's Russian Dictionary, Vol. 3. V. I. Dahl. LC 80-41732. 1980. 83.00 o.p. (ISBN 0-08-023592-1, PBL). Pergamon.

Dahl's Russian Dictionary, Vol. 4. V. I. Dahl. LC 80-41733. 1981. 83.00 o.p. (ISBN 0-08-023593-X, PBL). Pergamon.

Dai-Sho. Marc Olden. 480p. 1983. 15.95 o.p. (ISBN 0-87795-501-8, Arbor Hse). Morrow.

Daily Assignment Problems in First Year Chemistry. Walter W. Hanneman. No. 1, 1957. write for info. o.p. (ISBN 0-8087-0807-4). Burgess MN Intl.

Daily Bread Cookbook. LC 82-83956. 1975. pap. 6.95 o.p. (ISBN 0-916035-00-X, BE-141). Evangel Indiana.

Daily Bread Nineteen Eighty-Eight. Ed. by Richard Brown. 1987p. pap. 8.00 o.p. (ISBN 0-8309-0475-1). Herald Hse.

Daily Bread, Nineteen Eighty-Six. Ed. by Imogene Goodyear. 1985. pap. 7.50 o.p. (ISBN 0-8309-0407-7). Herald Hse.

Daily Bread, 1987. Ed. by Imogene Goodyear. 1986. pap. 8.00 o.p. (ISBN 0-8309-0435-2). Herald Hse.

Daily Crosswords, No. 1. Robert Gillespie. 128p. 1981. pap. 1.75 o.s.i. (ISBN 0-441-13541-2). Ace Bks.

Daily Devotional Bible Commentary, 4 vols. LC 76-46492. 1982. Repr. of 1974 ed. 39.95 o.p. (ISBN 0-8054-1228-X). Broadman.

Daily Devotional Bible Commentary: Genesis--Job, Vol. 1. LC 79-46492. 1982. Repr. of 1974 ed. 10.95 o.p. (ISBN 0-8054-1224-7). Broadman.

Daily Devotional Bible Commentary: Matthew--Acts, Vol. 3. LC 76-46441. 1982. Repr. of 1974 ed. 10.95 o.p. (ISBN 0-8054-1226-3). Broadman.

Daily Devotional Bible Commentary: Psalms--Malachi, Vol. 2. LC 76-46493. 1982. Repr. of 1974 ed. 10.95 o.p. (ISBN 0-8054-1225-5). Broadman.

Daily Devotional Bible Commentary: Romans--Revelation, Vol. 4. LC 76-46442. 1982. Repr. of 1974 ed. 10.95 o.p. (ISBN 0-8054-1227-1). Broadman.

Daily He Leads Me: Inspirational Devotions for Every Day of the Year. Hannah W. Smith. Ed. by Ann Spangler. 232p. (Orig.). 1985. pap. 6.95 o.p. (ISBN 0-89283-228-2, Pub. by Vine Books). Servant.

Daily Help. Charles H. Spurgeon. 1959. 4.95 o.p. (ISBN 0-399-12825-5, G&D). Putnam Pub Group.

Daily Life of the Christian. John Murray. 128p. 1955. (ISBN 0-8022-1180-1). Philos Lib.

Daily Light. deluxe ed. 384p. 1985. 12.95 o.p. (ISBN 0-8407-5480-9). Nelson.

Daily Light on the Daily Path. large print ed. 384p. 1975. kivar 10.95 o.p. (ISBN 0-310-23067-5, 18011L). Zondervan.

Daily Living Skills. Charlotte Goldman & David Pozzi-Johnson. LC 79-73907. (Illus.). 1979. pap. text ed. 159.00 o.s.i. (ISBN 0-89290-151-9, A584-SATC). Soc for Visual.

Daily Living with a Handicapped Child. Diana M. Millard. 104p. (Orig.). 1984. pap. 15.95 o.p. (ISBN 0-7099-1701-5, Pub. by Croom Helm Ltd). Routledge Chapman & Hall.

Daily News Fifteen Dollars Restaurant Guide. Daniel Young. (Illus.). 142p. 1989. 8.95 o.p. Wynwood Pr.

Daily Planet Almanac, 1985. Ed. by Terry Reim. 224p. 1984. pap. 3.95 o.p. (ISBN 0-380-88344-9, 88344). Avon.

Daily Planet Almanac, 1987. Terry Reim & Kim Long. (Illus.). 1986. lib. bdg. 12.90 o.p. (ISBN 0-89471-455-4); pap. 3.95 o.p. (ISBN 0-89471-454-6). Running Pr.

Daily Power Thoughts. Robert Schuller. 384p. 1982. pap. 3.95 o.p. (ISBN 0-515-08164-7). Ace Bks.

Daily Prayer & Praise. George Appleton. LC 78-10551. 1979. soft cover 3.95 o.s.i. (ISBN 0-664-24251-0, Westminster). Westminster John Knox.

Daily Prayer Poems & Words of Wisdom. Gilbert Gervais. 1984. 5.95 o.p. (ISBN 0-533-05772-8). Vantage.

Daily Promises. Herbert Lockyer. 9.95 o.p. (ISBN 0-8407-5434-5). Nelson.

Daily Telegram Quick Crosswords. Alan Cash. 1980. pap. 2.95 o.p. (ISBN 0-14-005089-2). PB.

Daily Thoughts for Disciples. Oswald Chambers. 251p. 1976. 12.95 o.p. (ISBN 0-87508-141-X). Chr Lit.

Daily Training Bulletin of the Los Angeles Police Department: Consisting of Bulletins 1-173. Los Angeles Police Department Staff. Ed. by W. H. Parker. (Illus.). 284p. 1963. 28.75x o.p. (ISBN 0-398-04345-0). C C Thomas.

Daily Training Bulletin of the Los Angeles Police Department: Consisting of Bulletins from Vols. II, III, IV. Los Angeles Police Department Staff. Ed. by W. H. Parker. (Illus.). 304p. 1958. 30.50x o.p. (ISBN 0-398-04346-9). C C Thomas.

Dairy Cattle Judging Techniques. 3rd ed. George W. Trimberger & William M. Etgen. (Illus.). 384p. 1983. pap. text ed. 36.33 o.p. (ISBN 0-13-196352-X). P-H.

Dairy Hollow House Cookbook: Over 400 Delectable Recipes from America's Famed"Nouveau "Zarks" Cuisine. Crescent Dragonwagon & Jan Brown. (Illus.). 400p. 1986. 19.95 o.p. (ISBN 0-02-533440-9). Macmillan.

Dairy Industry & Dairy Packaging. Business Communications Staff. 184p. 1985. 1500.00 o.p. (ISBN 0-89336-410-X, GA-048R). BCC.

Dairy Science Handbook see International Stockman's School Handbooks, 1984.

Dairy Science Handbook: International Stockmen's School Handbooks, Vol. 15. Ed. by Frank H. Baker. 500p. text ed. 50.00 o.p. (ISBN 0-86531-508-6). Westview.

Daisy. Fritzi Ketcher. 1977. 4.00 o.p. (ISBN 0-682-48806-2). Exposition-Phoenix.

Daisy Girl Scouts Leaders' Guide. (Illus.). 128p. (Orig.). 1983. pap. 3.00 o.p. Girl Scouts USA.

Dakota Feud. Cyril Donson. (Lythway Ser.). 168p. 1988. lib. bdg. 17.50x o.s.i. (ISBN 0-7451-0682-X, Pub. by Chivers Pr UK). G K Hall.

Dakota Skies. Joyce S. Whitcomb. LC 85-91014. (Illus.). 80p. 1985. 8.50 o.p. (ISBN 0-682-40242-7). Exposition-Phoenix.

Dakota Twilight: The Standing Rock Sioux, 1874-1890. Edward A. Milligan. 1976. 8.50 o.p. (ISBN 0-682-48421-0, Lochinvar). Exposition-Phoenix.

Dale Loves Sophie to Death. Robb F. Dew. 217p. 1981. 11.95 o.p. (ISBN 0-374-13450-2). FS&G.

Dalhousie in India: 1848-1856. Suresh C. Ghosh. LC 75-904110. 1975. 9.50x o.p. (ISBN 0-88386-577-7). South Asia Bks.

Dali. Max Gerard. LC 68-28386. (Illus.). 1968. 60.00 o.p. (ISBN 0-8109-0063-7). Abrams.

Dali. David Larkin. 1980. pap. 10.95 o.s.i. (ISBN 0-345-29541-2). Ballantine.

Dallas. Lee Raintree. LC 88-883. 28p. 1980. pap. 2.25 o.p. (ISBN 0-440-11752-6). Dell.

Dallas. Laura Van Wormer. LC 84-28693. (Illus.). 224p. 1985. pap. 14.95 o.p. (ISBN 0-385-23058-3, Dolp). Doubleday.

Dallas Cowboys Bluebook V. Steve Perkins & Greg Aiello. (Bluebook Ser.). (Illus.). 112p. 1984. 11.95 o.p. (ISBN 0-87833-451-3). Taylor Pub.

Dallas Doctors' Diet: A Revolutionary Way to Eat Yourself Thin. Sandra Breithaupt & H. Wayne Agnew. 240p. 1984. pap. text ed. 6.95 o.p. (ISBN 0-07-007448-8). McGraw.

Dallas Mavericks. Jim Moore. (NBA Today Ser.). (Illus.). 48p. (gr. 4 up). 1984. PLB 10.45 o.p. (ISBN 0-87191-974-5). Creative Ed.

Dallas Restaurants: One Hundred Fifty of the Best Places to Eat in Dallas-Fort Worth. The Dallas Morning News Staff. LC 86-6063. 200p. (Orig.). 1986. pap. 7.95 o.p. (ISBN 0-87701-384-5). Chronicle Bks.

Dam. Robert Byrne. LC 80-22109. 1981. 12.95 o.p. (ISBN 0-689-11123-1, Atheneum). Macmillan.

Dam-Burst of Dreams. Christopher Nolan. LC 81-9669. xvi, 128p. 1982. 11.95 o.p. (ISBN 0-8214-0658-2). Ohio U Pr.

Damaged Parents: An Anatomy of Child Neglect. Norman A. Polansky et al. LC 80-22793. (Illus.). xii, 272p. 1981. 15.00x o.s.i. (ISBN 0-226-67221-2). U of Chicago Pr.

Damages. Helena H. Worthen. 1986. 15.95 o.p. (ISBN 0-87795-805-X). Morrow.

Damian. Melissa Mather. 288p. 1986. 16.95 o.p. (ISBN 0-531-15005-4). Watts.

Damien & the Island of Sickness: A Story About Damien. new ed. Kenneth Christopher. (Stories About Christian Heroes Ser.). (Illus.). (gr. 1-3). 1979. pap. 1.95 o.p. (ISBN 0-86683-768-X). HarpR.

Damn the School System Full Speed Ahead. Vearl G. McBride. LC 73-77585. 1973. 6.00 o.p. (ISBN 0-682-47695-1, University). Exposition-Phoenix.

Damn Yankee. Bunny Banks. 1978. 4.00 o.p. (ISBN 0-682-48814-3). Exposition-Phoenix.

Damnation Game. Clive Barker. 1984. 14.95 o.p. Weidenfeld.

Damned Art. Ed. by Sydney Anglo. 258p. 1985. pap. 9.95 o.p. (ISBN 0-7102-0684-4). Routledge Chapman & Hall.

Damned Englishman: A Study of Erskine Childers (1870-1922) Tom Cox. LC 73-86542. 1975. 10.00 o.p. (ISBN 0-682-47821-0, University). Exposition-Phoenix.

Damned in Paradise: A Life of John Barrymore. John Kobler. LC 77-76752. (Illus.). 1977. 12.95 o.p. (ISBN 0-689-10814-1, Atheneum). Macmillan.

Damned Old Crank: A Self-Portrait of E. W. Scripps Drawn from His Unpublished Writings. Edward W. Scripps. Ed. by Charles R. McCabe. (Illus.). 1971. Repr. of 1951 ed. lib. bdg. 35.00x o.p. (ISBN 0-8371-6159-2, SCDO). Greenwood.

Damping Applications for Vibration Control. Ed. by P. J. Torvik. (AMD: Vol. 38). 164p. 1980. 24.00 o.p. (ISBN 0-686-69848-7, G00171). ASME.

Dampness in Buildings. Alan C. Oliver. 221p. 1988. 39.50 o.p. (999). Inst Real Estate.

Dams. S. Leliavsky. (Design Textbooks in Civil Engineering Ser.: Vol. 6). (Illus.). 250p. 1982. 45.00x o.p. (ISBN 0-412-22550-6, NO.6596, Pub. by Chapman & Hall England). Routledge Chapman & Hall.

Dams, People & Development: The Aswan High Dam Case. Hussein M. Fahim. LC 80-23929. (Pergamon Policy Studies on International Development). 208p. 1981. 50.00 o.p. (ISBN 0-08-026307-0). Pergamon.

Damselfishes. Gerald R. Allen. (Illus.). 240p. 1975. 24.95 o.p. (ISBN 0-87666-034-0, H-950). TFH Pubns.

Dan de Lion. Thomas M. Disch. (Illus.). 32p. 9.95 o.p. (ISBN 0-317-46118-4); deluxe ed. 35.00 o.p. Coffee Hse.

Dan Marino - Joe Montana. John Holmstrom. (Avon Superstars Ser.). 1985. pap. 60.00 o.s.i. (ISBN 0-380-75079-1, Camelot). Avon.

Dan Moves Up. Paul J. Deegan. LC 74-17069. (Dan Murphy Sports Ser.). (Illus.). 40p. (gr. 4 up). 1975. PLB 7.95 o.p. (ISBN 0-87191-406-9). Creative Ed.

Dance: A Very Social History. Carol M. Wallace et al. LC 86-28580. (Illus.). 128p. 1987. 25.00 o.p. (ISBN 0-8478-0819-X). Rizzoli Intl.

Dance a White Horse to Sleep: And Other Stories. Antonio Enriquez. (Asian & Pacific Writings Ser). 1977. 18.95x o.p. (ISBN 0-7022-1471-X); pap. 10.50x o.p. (ISBN 0-7022-1472-8). U of Queensland Pr.

Dance As Education. Charles B. Fowler. 1977. pap. text ed. 5.20x o.p. (ISBN 0-88314-051-9). AAHPERD.

Dance As Life. Franklin Stevens. (YA) (gr. 7 up). 1977. pap. 2.95 o.p. (ISBN 0-380-01711-3, 53587-4, Discus). Avon.

Dance Card. John R. Feegel. 320p. 1982. pap. 3.50 o.p. (ISBN 0-380-58040-3, 60053-6). Avon.

Dance for a Diamond. Christopher Murphy. 272p. 1987. pap. 3.95 o.p. (ISBN 0-380-70377-7). Avon.

Dance for Two. Kit Daley. (Candlelight Ecstasy Ser.: No. 205). (Orig.). 1984. pap. 1.95 o.p. (ISBN 0-440-11662-7). Dell.

Dance Genghis Cohn. Date not set. (ISBN 0-8052-0693-0). Random.

Dance Hall of the Dead. Tony Hillerman. (YA) (gr. 9 up). 1982. pap. 2.95 o.p. (ISBN 0-380-00217-5, 60093-5). Avon.

Dance in the Dust. Denise Robins. 360p. 1986. pap. 10.95x o.p. (ISBN 0-8161-3978-4, Large Print Bks). G K Hall.

Dance Jamaica: Cultural Definition & Artistic Discovery, the National Dance Theatre Company of Jamaica 1962-1983. Rex Nettleford. LC 84-48415. 320p. 1985. 29.95 o.s.i. (ISBN 0-394-54316-5, GP-956). Grove.

Dance of Change: An Eco-Spiritual Approach to Transformation. Michael Lindfield. 192p. 1986. pap. 12.95 o.p. (ISBN 1-85063-035-6, 30356). Routledge Chapman & Hall.

Dance of the Wolves. Roger Peters. 1985. text ed. 16.95 o.p. (ISBN 0-07-049580-7). McGraw.

Dance Therapy. American Alliance for Health Physical Education Recreation, & Dance Staff. (Focus on Dance: VII). 80p. 1974. 8.65 o.p. (ISBN 0-88314-072-1, 243-25570). AAHPERD.

Dance Workshop: A Guide to the Fundamentals of Movement. Robert Cohan. 192p. 1986. 17.45 o.s.i. (ISBN 0-671-61281-6). S&S.

Dance Writings of Carl Van Vechten. Carl Van Vechten. Ed. by Paul Padgette. LC 79-57139. (Illus.). 182p. 1980. pap. 14.95 o.s.i. (ISBN 0-87127-114-1, Pub. by Dance Horiz). Princeton Bk Co.

Dancer's Book of Health. Larry M. Vincent. LC 78-7523. (Illus.). 1978. pap. 5.95 o.p. (ISBN 0-8362-2402-7). Andrews & McMeel.

Dancer's Death. Phil Davis. 176p. 1981. pap. 2.25 o.p. (ISBN 0-380-76612-4, 76612-4). Avon.

Dancers! Horizons in American Dance. Ellen A. Switzer. LC 82-1701. (Illus.). 288p. (gr. 7 up). 1982. 16.95 o.s.i. (ISBN 0-689-30943-0, Atheneum Childrens Bks). Macmillan.

Dancers Land. Elizabeth Kidd. (Avon Romance Ser.). 352p. (Orig.). 1984. pap. 2.95 o.p. (ISBN 0-380-89219-7). Avon.

Dances of Death. Michael Sidnell. (Illus.). 368p. 1984. 40.00 o.p. (ISBN 0-571-13321-5). Faber & Faber.

Dancing: A Handbook of the Terpsichorean Arts in Diverse Places & Times, Savage & Civilized. Lilly Grove. LC 76-76138. (Illus.). xviii, 482p. 1969. Repr. of 1895 ed. 40.00x o.p. (ISBN 0-8103-3469-0). Gale.

Dancing All the Dances, Singing All the Songs. Conrad Weiser. LC 74-80419. (Center Bks). (Illus.). 128p. 1975. pap. 0.50x o.p. (ISBN 0-8006-5079-4, Fortress). Augsburg Fortress.

Dancing Back Strong the Nation. Maurice Kenny. 1981. 2.50 o.p. (ISBN 0-934834-28-8). White Pine.

Dancing Bees: An Account of the Life & Senses of the Honey Bee. Karl Frisch. LC 66-17713. (Illus.). 1967. 6.95 o.p. (ISBN 0-15-123808-1). HarBraceJ.

Dancing Bees: An Account of the Life & Senses of the Honey Bee. Karl Von Frisch. Tr. by Dora Ilse. LC 66-17713. (Illus.). 1961. pap. 5.95 o.p. (ISBN 0-15-623807-1, Harv). HarBraceJ.

Dancing Doll. Janet L. Roberts. 1987. pap. 2.95 o.p. (ISBN 0-440-11715-1). Dell.

Dancing Games for Children of All Ages. Esther L. Nelson. LC 83-18147. 72p. (gr. k-5). 1984. 13.95 o.p.; PLB 16.79 o.p.; pap. 9.95 o.p. (ISBN 0-8069-7818-X). Sterling.

Dancing Girls: And Other Stories. Margaret Atwood. 1982. 14.50 o.p. (ISBN 0-671-24249-0). S&S.

Dancing Girls & Other Stories. Margaret Atwood. 1985. pap. 6.95 o.p. (ISBN 0-553-34115-4). Bantam.

Dancing in Prints: A Portfolio Assembled from the Archives of the Dance Collection, 1634-1870. Marian Eames. (Illus.). 1964. 25.00 o.p. (ISBN 0-87104-060-3). NY Pub Lib.

Dancing in the Dark. Joan Barfoot. 192p. 1984. pap. 2.95 o.p. (ISBN 0-380-67058-5, 67447-5). Avon.

Dancing in the Moon: Counting Rhymes. Fritz Eichenberg. LC 55-8674. (Illus.). (gr. k-3). 1955. 12.95 o.p. (ISBN 0-15-221443-7, HJ). HarBraceJ.

Dancing Man. Ruth Bornstein. LC 77-29124. (Illus.). 32p. (ps-3). 1979. 6.95 o.p. (ISBN 0-395-28770-7, Clarion). HM.

Dancing Men. Duncan Kyle. LC 85-27275. 256p. 1986. 16.95 o.p. (ISBN 0-03-008507-1). H Holt & Co.

Dancing Princess. Jean Bothwell. LC 65-18726. (gr. 7 up). 1965. 4.50 o.p. (ISBN 0-15-221637-5, HJ). HarBraceJ.

Dancing Season. Carla Neggers. (Finding Mr. Right Ser.). 208p. 1983. pap. 2.75 o.p. (ISBN 0-380-82602-X, 82602X). Avon.

Dancing Turtle. Maggie Duff. LC 80-24683. (Illus.). 32p. (gr. k-3). 1981. PLB 8.95 o.s.i. (ISBN 0-02-733010-9). Macmillan.

Dandelion on the Ball. Ralph E. Fernbaugh. 1977. 7.50 o.p. (ISBN 0-682-48902-6). Exposition-Phoenix.

Dandelions, Fireflies, & Rhubarb Pie: The Adventures of Grandma Bagley & Her Friends. Ethel Marbach & Mary Lu Walker. LC 83-51403. (Illus.). 64p. (gr. 1-7). 1984. bk. & cassette 8.00 o.p. (ISBN 0-8358-0489-5). Upper Room.

Dandylions Never Roar Book. Gary Grimm & Don Mitchell. (gr. k-8). 1976. 6.95 o.p. (ISBN 0-916456-03-X, GA53). Good Apple.

Danebury: Anatomy of an Iron Age Hillfort. Barry Cunliffe. 192p. 1985. 29.95 o.p. (ISBN 0-7134-0998-3, NO. 9351). Routledge Chapman & Hall.

Daneshvar's Playhouse - (Five Stories) Simin Daneshvar. Tr. & intro. by Maryam Mafi. 144p. (Orig.). 1989. 20.00 o.p. (ISBN 0-89410-578-7); pap. 10.00 o.p. (ISBN 0-89410-579-5). Three Continents.

Daneshvar's Playhouse: Five Stories. Tr. by Maryam Mafi. 144p. 1989. 20.00 o.p.; pap. 10.00 o.p. Three Continents.

Danger at the Golden Dragon. Carole Smith. Ed. by Ann Fay. LC 83-1278. (High-Low Mysteries Ser.). (Illus.). 128p. (gr. 3-8). 1983. PLB 8.95 o.p. (ISBN 0-8075-1449-7). A Whitman.

Danger at Your Door. Gordon McLean. LC 83-70954. 183p. 1984. pap. 5.95 o.p. (ISBN 0-89107-296-9). Good News.

Danger by the Nile. Barbara Cartland. 1967. pap. 1.25 o.p. (ISBN 0-380-00314-7, 23325). Avon.

Danger, Disaster, & Horrid Deeds. Ed. by Clarissa M. Silitch. LC 74-83983. (Illus.). 288p. 1974. 12.95 o.p. (ISBN 0-911658-62-9); pap. 14.95 o.p. (ISBN 0-911658-92-0). Yankee Bks.

Danger in Paradise. Kit Daley. (Supreme Ser.: No. 156). (Orig.). 1987. pap. 2.75 o.p. (ISBN 0-440-11714-3). Dell.

Danger in Sagebrush Country. Dorothy Y. Croman. (Outlands Adventure Ser.). 144p. (gr. 4-7). 1984. 2.95 o.p. (ISBN 0-8423-0514-9). Tyndale.

Danger in the Air. O. Stewart. (Illus.). 198p. 1958. (ISBN 0-8022-1646-3). Philos Lib.

Danger Light & Other Stories. Brian Harrison. (Readers Ser.: Stage 4). 1978. pap. text ed. 7.95 o.p. (ISBN 0-88377-090-3). Newbury Hse.

Danger Mouse File. (Danger Mouse Lift-the-Flap Bks.). 16p. (ps-3). 5.70i o.p. (ISBN 0-316-14709-5). Little.

Danger Mouse: Lift the Flap Books. 16p. (ps-3). 1986. 119.00 set o.p. (ISBN 0-316-14728-1). Little.

Danger Mouse Saves the World--Again. (Danger Mouse Ser.). 32p. (Orig.). 1986. pap. 3.70i o.p. (ISBN 0-316-14717-6). Little.

Danger, Second-Hand. Bruce Algozin. LC 87-50415. (Lazer Tag Adventure Ser.: No. 2). 128p. (Orig.). (gr. 4 up). 1987. pap. 2.95 o.p. (ISBN 0-88038-515-4). TSR Inc.

Danger Spot of Europe. Alan H. Brodrick. 1952. (ISBN 0-8022-0181-4). Philos Lib.

Danger Tree. Olivia Manning. LC 77-2435. 1977. 8.95 o.p. (ISBN 0-689-10802-8, Atheneum). Macmillan.

Danger We All Face: Suppressed Truth about Radiation. Raymond Bernard. 62p. pap. 7.95 o.s.i. (ISBN 0-88697-045-8). Life Science.

Dangerfield Newby Moves Uptown. Richard D. Waters. 1968. pap. 0.95 o.p. (ISBN 0-377-80001-5). Friendship Pr.

Dangerous Acquaintances. Choderlos De Laclos. Tr. by Richard Aldington from Fr. (Open University Set Text Ser.). (Orig.). 1979. pap. 7.95 o.p. (ISBN 0-7100-8858-2). Routledge Chapman & Hall.

Dangerous & the Endangered. John P. Conrad. LC 78-405. (Dangerous Offender Project Ser.). 176p. 1985. 23.00 o.p. (ISBN 0-669-02184-9). Lexington Bks.

Dangerous Aquatic Animals of the World: A Color Guide. Bruce W. Halstead. LC 84-70417. (Illus.). 288p. 1989. 39.95 o.p. (ISBN 0-87850-045-6). Darwin Pr.

Dangerous Deceptions. Arabella Seymour. 352p. 1987. 18.95 o.p. (ISBN 0-399-13199-X, Putnam). Putnam Pub Group.

Dangerous Edge: A Novel. Robert Daley. 1983. 16.50 o.p. (ISBN 0-671-47057-4). S&S.

Dangerous Enchantment. Jean Hager. (Velvet Glove Ser.: No. 4). 176p. 1984. pap. 2.25 o.p. (ISBN 0-380-88252-3, 88252-3). Avon.

Dangerous Games. Shana Alexander. 1988. 19.95 o.p. Weidenfeld.

Dangerous Games. Louis A. Schreiber. 384p. 1986. pap. 3.95 o.p. (ISBN 1-55547-128-5). Critics Choice Paper.

Dangerous Hideaway Assignment. Allan Stewart. 1983. pap. 2.95 o.p. Tyndale.

Dangerous Highway. Kit Daley. (Candlelight Supreme Ser.: No. 172). (Orig.). 1987. pap. 2.75 o.p. (ISBN 0-440-11678-3). Dell.

Dangerous Journey. Laszlo Hamori. Tr. by Annabelle MacMillian. LC 62-8742. (Illus.). (gr. 5 up). 1962. 5.95 o.p. (ISBN 0-15-221790-8, HJ). HarBraceJ.

Dangerous Journey. Laszlo Hamori. Tr. by Annabelle MacMillan. LC 62-8742. (Illus.). (gr. 4-6). 1966. pap. 1.75 o.p. (ISBN 0-15-623821-7, VoyB). HarBraceJ.

Dangerous Journey see Heinemann Guided Readers.

Dangerous Lady. Barbara Hazard. 224p. (Orig.). 1980. pap. 1.75 o.p. (ISBN 0-449-50120-5, Coventry). Fawcett.

Dangerous Men: The Sociology of Parole. Richard McCleary. LC 78-19859. (Sage Library of Social Research: Vol. 71). 1979 27.50 o.p. (ISBN 0-8039-1094-0); pap. 12.50 1978 o.p. (ISBN 0-8039-1095-9). Sage.

Dangerous Patriots: Canada's Unknown Prisoners of War. William Repka & Kathleen Repka. 249p. 1982. lib. bdg. 17.00 o.p. (ISBN 0-919573-06-1); pap. 7.95 o.p. (ISBN 0-919573-07-X). Left Bank.

Dangerous Properties of Industrial Materials. 6th ed. N. Irving Sax & Benjamin Feiner. 3136p. 1984. 259.95 o.p. (ISBN 0-442-28304-0). Van Nos Reinhold.

Dangerous Secrets: Maladaptive Responses to Stress. Michael Weissberg. 256p. 1983. 16.00 o.p. (ISBN 0-393-01732-X). Norton.

Dangerous to Man. Roger A. Caras. (Illus.). 432p. pap. 7.95 o.p. (ISBN 0-88317-034-5). Stoeger Pub Co.

Dangerous Waters. Larry S. Landgraf. LC 86-91173. (Illus.). 80p. 1986. 8.50 o.p. (ISBN 0-682-40296-6). Exposition-Phoenix.

Dangerous Years. Max Hennessy. 1979. 8.95 o.p. (ISBN 0-689-10945-8, Atheneum). Macmillan.

Dangers. Heather McHugh. 1977. 5.95 o.p.; pap. 4.50 o.p. (ISBN 0-395-25175-3). HM.

Dangers of Deterrence: Philosophers on Nuclear Strategy. Ed. by Nigel Blake & Kay Pole. 169p. (Orig.). 1984. pap. 9.95x o.p. (ISBN 0-7100-9885-5). Routledge Chapman & Hall.

Dangling Man. Saul Bellow. 1984. pap. 1.65 o.p. (ISBN 0-380-00332-5, 50849-4). Avon.

Dani Trap. Elizabeth Levy. 112p. (YA) (gr. 7 up). 1986. pap. 2.50 o.p. (ISBN 0-380-69995-8, Flare). Avon.

Daniel, a Commentary. Norman W. Porteous. LC 65-21071. (Old Testament Library). 174p. 1965. 14.95 o.s.i. (ISBN 0-664-20663-8, Westminster). Westminster John Knox.

Daniel Boone's Echo. William O. Steele. LC 57-9741. (Illus.). (gr. k-3). 1957. 5.95 o.p. (ISBN 0-15-221980-3, HJ). HarBraceJ.

Daniel Defoe: A Critical Study. James Sutherland. LC 70-159532. 1971. pap. 5.75 o.p. (ISBN 0-395-11253-2, 3-54595, RivSl). HM.

Daniel Defoe & the Status of Women. Shirlene Mason. LC 78-59369. 1978. 12.95 o.p. (ISBN 0-88831-025-0). Eden Pr.

Daniel Deronda. George Eliot. 11.50 o.p. (ISBN 0-8446-2028-9). Peter Smith.

Daniel Hewett's List of Newspapers & Periodicals in the United States in 1828. Daniel Hewett. 32p. 1935. pap. 3.00x o.p. (ISBN 0-912296-22-4, Dist. by U Pr of Va). Am Antiquarian.

Daniel O'Connell & His World. Dudley Edwards. LC 77-77380. (Illus.). 1977. 10.95 o.p. (ISBN 0-684-15302-5, ScribT). Scribner.

Daniel Webster. Irving H. Bartlett. (Illus.). 1978. 14.95x o.p. (ISBN 0-393-07524-9). Norton.

Danielle Steel. Incl. Passion's Promise; Now & Forever; Seasons of Passion. 1983. pap. 12.60 boxed set o.p. (ISBN 0-440-11652-X). Dell.

Daniel's Big Decision. Jerry B. Jenkins. (Bradford Family Adventures Ser.). (Illus.). 128p. (gr. 3-6). 1986. 2.95 o.p. (ISBN 0-87403-093-5, 2923). Standard Pub.

Daniel's Big Surprise. Jerry Jenkins. (Bradford Family Adventures Ser.). 128p. (gr. 3-7). 1984. pap. 2.95 o.p. (ISBN 0-87239-791-2, 2941). Standard Pub.

Danish Cooperative Movement. 3rd ed. Ed. by Clemens Pedersen. (Danish Information Handbooks). 154p. 1977. 7.95x o.p. (ISBN 87-7429-029-0, Pub. by Det Danske Selskab Denmark). Nordic Bks.

Danish Design. Ed. by Svend E. Moller et al. Tr. by Mogens Kay-Larsen from Danish. (Denmark in Print & Pictures). (Illus.). 164p. 1974. 8.95 o.p. (ISBN 87-7429-016-9, Pub. by Det Danske Selskab Denmark). Nordic Bks.

Danish: Laer at Talk. A. Salling. 200p. 1984. pap. text ed. 20.00x o.p. (ISBN 87-429-9032-7, D775). Vanous.

Danish Made Easy for the Tourist. 13th, rev. ed. P. Host. 1984. pap. 6.00x o.p. (ISBN 87-14-63184-9, D732). Vanous.

Danish Pocket Dictionary. 6th ed. Host. (Eng. & Danish.). 1978. pap. text ed. 10.00x o.p. (ISBN 87-146-1178-3, D711). Vanous.

Dankmar Adler, Eighteen Forty-Four to Nineteen Hundred. Lamia Doumato. (Architecture Ser.: A 1450). 14p. 1985. 2.25 o.p. (ISBN 0-89028-540-3). Vance Biblios.

Danny: Champion of the World. (ISBN 0-679-80085-9). Random.

Danny Dunn & the Universal Glue. Jay Williams & Raymond Abrashkin. (Danny Dunn Ser.: No. 4). (Illus.). (gr. 4-6). 1979. pap. 1.95 o.p. (ISBN 0-671-43877-8). Archway.

Danny Dunn & the Universal Glue. Jay Williams & Raymond Abrashkin. LC 77-78764. (Illus.). (gr. 4-6). 1977. text ed. 9.95 o.p. (ISBN 0-07-070550-X). McGraw.

Danny Dunn & the Voice from Space. Jay Williams & Raymond Abrashkin. LC 67-22974. (Danny Dunn Ser.: No. 12). (Illus.). (gr. 4-6). 1979. pap. 1.95 o.s.i. (ISBN 0-671-42684-2); pap. 2.25 o.p. (ISBN 0-671-47235-6). Archway.

Danny Dunn, Scientific Detective. Jay Williams & Raymond Abrashkin. (Danny Dunn Ser.: No. 3). (Illus.). (gr. 4-6). 1981. pap. 1.95 o.s.i. (ISBN 0-671-44382-8). Archway.

Danny Dunn Universe. McGraw.

Danny White: The Kicking Quarterback. Ray Buck. (Sports Stars Ser.). (Illus.). 48p. (gr. 2-8). 1983. PLB 11.27 o.p. (ISBN 0-516-04335-8). Childrens.

Danny's Orange Christmas Camel. Edith Eckblad. LC 72-121962. 32p. (gr. k-3). 1970. pap. 1.25 o.p. (ISBN 0-8066-1011-5, 10-1815, Augsburg). Augsburg Fortress.

Danse de Gengis Cohn. Romain Gary. 280p. 1965. 10.95 o.p. (ISBN 0-686-55892-8). Schoenhof.

Danseur: The Male in Ballet. Richard Philp & Mary Whitney. (Illus.). 1977. pap. text ed. 8.95 o.p. (ISBN 0-07-049812-1). McGraw.

Dante into English: A Study of the Translation of the Divine Comedy in Britain & America. William J. De Sua. Repr. of 1964 ed. 18.00 o.p. (ISBN 0-384-11523-3). Johnson Repr.

Dante's Comedy As Self-Analysis & Integration. C. G. Hardie. 1985. 10.00x o.p. (ISBN 0-317-62028-2, Guild of Pastoral Psych). State Mutual Bk.

Dante's Daughter. Heather X. Graham. (Candlelight Supreme Ser.: No. 109). (Orig.). 1986. pap. 2.75 o.s.i. (ISBN 0-440-11653-8). Dell.

Dante's Infernal Guide to Your School. Frank Behrens. LC 75-154091. 1971. pap. 3.95 o.p. (ISBN 0-671-20975-2, Fireside). S&S.

Danubian Region. Ed. by L. Kadar & Z. Borsy. 100p. 1975. pap. 24.00 o.p. (ISBN 0-08-019669-1). Pergamon.

Danzig Trilogy of Gunter Grass: A Study of The Tin Drum, Cat & Mouse, & Dog Years. John Reddick. 1975. 13.50 o.p. (ISBN 0-15-123815-4). HarBraceJ.

Daoist Health Preservation Exercise. Bian Zhizhong. Tr. by Liu Zongren from Chinese. (Illus.). 135p. (Orig.). 1987. pap. 4.95 o.p. (ISBN 0-8351-1830-4). China Bks.

Daoud's Aviation Dictionary. Hesham O. Daoud. 1972. pap. 9.95 o.p. (ISBN 0-911720-55-3, Pub. by Daouds). Aviation.

Daphne. Marion Chesney. 280p. 1986. pap. 9.95x o.p. (ISBN 0-8161-3910-5, Large Print Bks). G K Hall.

Dar. Vladimir Nabokov. (Rus.). 1979. pap. 9.95 o.p. (ISBN 0-88233-195-7). Ardis Pubs.

Dara. Patrick Besson. 202p. 1987. 15.95 o.p. (ISBN 0-531-15056-9). Watts.

DARAD Plus. rev. ed. Eric A. Seiden. Ed. by DAR Systems International Staff. 75p. 1984. 49.95 o.p. (ISBN 0-916163-45-8); program disk, technical ref. manual & self-teaching manual incl. o.p. Dar Syst.

Dardanelles: A Midshipman's Diary. H. M. Denham. (Illus.). 200p. 1986. 19.95 o.p. (ISBN 0-88186-078-6). Parkwest Pubns.

Darden Technique For Weight Loss, Body Shaping & Slenderizing. Ellington Darden. 256p. 1986. pap. 10.95 o.s.i. (ISBN 0-671-44228-7, Fireside). S&S.

Dare. Philip Jose Farmer. 1980. lib. bdg. 12.50 o.p. (ISBN 0-8398-2621-4, Gregg). G K Hall.

Dare. Gloria G. Morrell. (gr. 1-3). 1986. pap. 3.95 o.p. (ISBN 0-8054-4336-3). Broadman.

Dare the Devil, No. 499. Elaine R. Chase. (Candlelight Ecstasy Ser.). (Orig.). 1984. pap. 1.95 o.p. (ISBN 0-440-11759-3). Dell.

Dare to Care Like Jesus. Leslie B. Flynn. LC 81-51949. 119p. 1982. pap. 4.95 o.p. (ISBN 0-88207-348-6). Victor Bks.

Dare to Discipline. James Dobson. 1977. pap. 3.50 mass o.p. (ISBN 0-8423-0635-8). Tyndale.

Dare to Live Free. Hoyt E. Stone. 132p. 1984. pap. 4.95 o.p. (ISBN 0-88207-617-5). Victor Bks.

Dare to Love Again. Rose M. Ferris. (Candlelight Ecstasy Ser.: No. 434). (Orig.). 1986. pap. 2.25 o.s.i. (ISBN 0-440-11698-8). Dell.

Daredevil & Kingpin in the King Takes a Dare. James M. Ward. LC 86-91770. (One-On-One Adventure Gamebook Ser.: No. 9). 160p. 1987. pap. 7.95 o.p. (ISBN 0-88038-459-X). TSR Inc.

Daring Dairy Recipes. H. P. Hood. LC 85-963148. (Illus.). 144p. 1985. 7.95 o.p. (ISBN 0-317-38045-1). Dorison Hse.

Daring Prayer. David Willis. LC 76-44975. 1977. 6.95 o.p. (ISBN 0-8042-2249-5, John Knox). Westminster John Knox.

Daring Rascals: True Tales of the Outrageous. Ed. by David A. Boehm. (Illus.). 128p. (Orig.). 1986. pap. 6.95 o.p. (ISBN 0-8069-6370-0). Sterling.

Daring to Dream: Eighteen Thirty-Six to Nineteen Nineteen. Ed. by Carol F. Kessler. 256p. (Orig.). 1984. pap. 8.95 o.p. (ISBN 0-86358-013-0, Pandora Pr). Routledge Chapman & Hall.

Dario Fo: People's Court Jester. Tony Mitchell. 80p. 1984. pap. 8.95 o.p. (ISBN 0-413-52910-X). Heinemann Ed.

Dark Ages. Isaac Asimov. LC 68-28051. (Maps). (gr. 7 up). 1968. 9.95 o.p. (ISBN 0-395-06565-8). HM.

Dark Ages & the Age of Gold. Russell Fraser. LC 70-29786. 472p. 1973. 45.50x o.p. (ISBN 0-691-06216-1). Princeton U Pr.

Dark & Dashing Horsemen. Stan Steiner. LC 81-47420. (Illus.). 192p. 1981. 12.98i o.p. (ISBN 0-06-250850-4). HarpR.

Dark & Lonely Hiding Place. Edith Begner. 1977. pap. 1.95 o.p. (ISBN 0-380-01742-3, 34546). Avon.

Dark Angel. V. C. Andrews. 1987. pap. 4.95 o.s.i. (ISBN 0-671-52543-3). PB.

Dark Caves, Bright Visions: Life in Ice Age Europe. Randall White. (Illus.). 1986. 34.50 o.p. (ISBN 0-393-02410-5). Norton.

Dark Changeline. Marianne Lamont. 1973. pap. 0.95 o.p. (ISBN 0-380-01130-1, 17509). Avon.

Dark City. Max A. Collins. 1987. pap. 3.50 o.p. (ISBN 0-553-26539-3). Bantam.

Dark Comet. Elaine Kimmelman. 1983. pap. 4.95 o.p. (ISBN 0-380-81828-0, 81828-0, Bard). Avon.

Dark Didn't Catch Me. Crystal Thrasher. LC 74-18193. 192p. (gr. 4-8). 1975. 7.95 o.p. (ISBN 0-689-50025-4, Atheneum). Macmillan.

Dark Flight. John Rossiter. LC 80-69380. 1981. 9.95 o.p. (ISBN 0-689-11139-8, Atheneum). Macmillan.

Dark Green Tunnel. Allan W. Eckert. LC 83-12078. (Illus.). 256p. (gr. 7up). 1984. 13.45i o.p. (ISBN 0-316-20881-7). Little.

Dark Horseman. Marianne Harvey. 1981. pap. 2.50 o.p. (ISBN 0-440-11758-5). Dell.

Dark Is Rising. Susan Cooper. (YA) (gr. 7 up). 1976. pap. 3.95 o.s.i. (ISBN 0-689-70420-8, Aladdin). Macmillan.

Dark Is the Forest. Betty Swinford. (Illus.). 184p. (YA) (gr. 11-12). 1963. 2.95 o.p. (ISBN 0-88243-705-4, 02-0705). Gospel Pub.

Dark Journey Home. Patricia Hagan. 160p. 1976. pap. 2.50 o.p. (ISBN 0-380-01131-X, 85258-6). Avon.

Dark Journey Home. Patricia Hagan. (Nightingale Paperbacks Ser.). 280p. 1987. pap. 10.95 o.p. (ISBN 0-8161-4310-2, Large Print Bks). G K Hall.

Dark Lady. Louis Auchincloss. 1977. 8.95 o.s.i. (ISBN 0-395-25402-7). HM.

Dark Laughter. Sherwood Anderson. LC 60-53556. 1970. pap. 3.45 o.p. (ISBN 0-87140-205-X). Liveright.

Dark Moon. J. H. Brennan. LC 80-20034. 264p. 1981. 13.95 o.p. (ISBN 0-03-058013-7). H Holt & Co.

Dark Nebulae, Globules, & Protostars. Ed. by Beverly T. Lynds. LC 73-152040. (Illus.). 150p. 1971. 12.50x o.p. (ISBN 0-8165-0300-1). U of Ariz Pr.

Dark Page. Samuel Fuller. 256p. 1983. pap. 2.95 o.p. (ISBN 0-380-62117-7, 62117-7). Avon.

Dark Palazzo. Virginia Coffman. LC 72-94015. 1973. 6.95 o.p. (ISBN 0-87795-051-2, Arbor Hse). Morrow.

Dark Paradise. Jackie Black. (Candlelight Supreme Ser.: No. 157). (Orig.). 1987. pap. 2.75 o.p. (ISBN 0-440-11744-5). Dell.

Dark Peninsula: Logging History, Upper Peninsula, Mich. 3rd ed. LC 75-42923. (Illus.). 4.95 o.p. (ISBN 0-932212-04-2). Avery Color.

Dark Side. Doug Hornig. 256p. 1987. pap. 3.95 o.p. (ISBN 0-445-40635-6). Mysterious Pr.

Dark Side of the Millennium: The Problem of Evil in Revelation 20: 1-10. Arthur H. Lewis. 96p. (Orig.). 1980. pap. 3.95 o.p. (ISBN 0-8010-5596-2). Baker Bk.

Dark Side of the Sun. Terry Practchett. 158p. 1976. 13.95 o.p. (ISBN 0-901072-20-6, Pub. by Colin Smythe Ltd Britain). Dufour.

Dark Soldier. Katherine Myers. (Avon Romance Ser.). 304p. 1983. pap. 2.95 o.p. (ISBN 0-380-82214-8, 82214-8). Avon.

Dark Streaks & Empty Places: A Dan Roman Mystery. Edward Mathis. 240p. 1986. 13.95 o.s.i. (ISBN 0-684-18678-0). Scribner.

Dark Sunshine. Dorothy Lyons. LC 51-11741. 1965. pap. 1.95 o.p. (ISBN 0-15-623936-1, VoyB). HarBraceJ.

Dark Surrender. Diana Blayne. (Candlelight Ecstasy Ser.: No. 184). 192p. (Orig.). 1983. pap. 1.95 o.p. (ISBN 0-440-11833-6). Dell.

Dark Thirty. Terry Kay. 351p. 1984. 16.45 o.s.i. (ISBN 0-671-49932-7, Pub. by Poseidon). S&S.

Dark Tide. Joyce Christmas. 256p. 1983. pap. 2.95 o.p. (ISBN 0-380-83667-X, 83667). Avon.

Dark Tower & Other Stories. C. S. Lewis. Ed. by Walter Hooper. LC 76-55027. 1977. 6.95 o.p. (ISBN 0-15-123902-9). HarBraceJ.

Dark Wind. Tony Hillerman. 224p. 1983. pap. 3.50 o.p. (ISBN 0-380-63321-3). Avon.

Dark Winds. Virginia Coffman. 1985. 16.95 o.p. (ISBN 0-87795-631-6, Arbor Hse). Morrow.

Dark Wing. Katherine MacLean & Carl West. LC 78-10837. 1979. 8.95 o.p. (ISBN 0-689-30688-1, Atheneum). Macmillan.

Darken Fruits. Orah I. Juengst. 1978. 4.00 o.p. (ISBN 0-682-49187-X). Exposition-Phoenix.

Darker Than Amber. John D. MacDonald. 192p. 1984. pap. 3.50 o.p. (ISBN 0-449-12752-4, GM). Fawcett.

Darkness & Day. Ivy Compton-Burnett. 248p. 1951. 22.95 o.p. (ISBN 0-575-03477-7, Pub. by Gollancz England). David & Charles.

Darkness & Daylight: Or, Lights & Shadows of New York Life: A Pictorial Record of Personal Experiences by Day & Night in the Great Metropolis with Hundreds of Thrilling Anecdotes & Incidents. Helen Campbell. LC 76-81511. 744p. 1969. Repr. of 1895 ed. 48.00x o.p. (ISBN 0-8103-3566-2). Gale.

Darkness at Sethanon: The Finale of the Riftwar Saga. Raymond E. Feist. LC 84-28715. 432p. 1986. 17.95 o.p. (ISBN 0-385-19215-0). Doubleday.

Darkness over the Valley. Wendelgard Von Staden. Tr. by Mollie C. Peters from Ger. LC 80-15579. Orig. Title: Nacht Uber dem Tal. 176p. 1981. 9.95 o.p. (ISBN 0-89919-009-X). Ticknor & Fields.

Darkness Where Light Fails to Shine: Open Fields Where the Wisdom of Men Seldom Probes. Robert Van Dyke Small. 1976. 4.50 o.p. (ISBN 0-682-48457-1). Exposition-Phoenix.

Darkover Landfall. Marion Zimmer Bradley. (Darkover Ser.). 1978. lib. bdg. 10.95 o.p. (ISBN 0-8398-2404-1, Gregg). G K Hall.

Darkroom Guide. Kalton C. Lahue. (Petersen's Photographic Library: Vol. 1). (Illus.). 160p. 1980. pap. 8.95 o.p. (ISBN 0-8227-4039-7). Petersen Pub.

Darlene. Eloise Greenfield. (Illus.). 32p. (ps). 1980. 8.95 o.p. (ISBN 0-416-30701-9, NO.0201). Routledge Chapman & Hall.

Darlin' Bill. Jerome Charyn. LC 80-66763. 1980. 11.95 o.p. (ISBN 0-87795-283-3, Arbor Hse). Morrow.

Darling. Harriet Daimler, pseud. LC 82-84624. 176p. (Orig.). 1983. pap. 3.50 o.p. (ISBN 0-394-62458-0, B489, BC). Grove.

Darrians, Alien Module Eight. Marc W. Miller et al. (Traveller Ser.). 49p. (Orig.). 1987. pap. 7.00 o.s.i. (ISBN 0-943580-40-4). Game Designers.

DART: Test A-4. MCP Test & Research Bureau Staff et al. (Diagnostic & Achievement Reading Tests Ser.). (gr. 1). 1977. 5.88 o.p. (ISBN 0-87895-144-X). Modern Curr.

DART: Test B-1. MCP Test & Research Bureau Staff et al. (Diagnostic & Achievement Reading Tests Ser.). (gr. 2). 1977. 5.88 o.p. (ISBN 0-87895-231-4). Modern Curr.

DART: Test B-2. MCP Test & Research Bureau Staff et al. (Diagnostic & Achievement Reading Test Ser.). (gr. 2). 1977. 4.44 o.p. (ISBN 0-87895-232-2). Modern Curr.

DART: Test B-3. MCP Test & Research Bureau Staff et al. (Diagnostic & Achievement Reading Test Ser.). (gr. 2). 1977. 4.44 o.p. (ISBN 0-87895-233-0). Modern Curr.

DART: Test C-1. MCP Test & Research Bureau Staff et al. (Diagnostic & Achievement Reading Tests Ser.). (gr. 3). 1977. 5.88 o.p. (ISBN 0-87895-331-0). Modern Curr.

DART: Test C-2. MCP Test & Research Bureau Staff et al. (Diagnostic & Achievement Reading Tests Ser.). (gr. 3). 1977. 4.44 o.p. (ISBN 0-87895-332-9). Modern Curr.

DART: Test C-3. MCP Test & Research Bureau Staff et al. (Diagnostic & Achievement Reading Tests Ser.). (gr. 3). 1977. 4.44 o.p. (ISBN 0-87895-333-7). Modern Curr.

Dartmoor: A New Study. Crispin Gill. 1978. 26.00 o.p. (ISBN 0-7153-5041-2); pap. 17.95 o.p. (ISBN 0-7153-8581-X). David & Charles.

Dartmouth Bible. 2nd ed. Roy B. Chamberlin & Herman Feldman. (Illus.). 1961. 20.00 o.p. (ISBN 0-395-07519-X). HM.

Dartmouth Bible. rev. ed. Ed. by Roy B. Chamberlin & Herman Feldman. (Illus.). 1974. pap. 10.95 o.p. (ISBN 0-395-08394-X, 45, SenEd). HM.

Darts. Ivan L. Brackin & William Fitzgerald. 176p. 1984. pap. 5.95 o.p. (ISBN 0-671-53239-1, Fireside). S&S.

Darts. Leighton Rees & Dave Lanning. LC 79-4896. (Illus.). 1980. 9.95 o.p. (ISBN 0-689-11017-0, Atheneum). Macmillan.

Darwin. Ed. by Philip Appleman. (Critical Editions). (Annotated with critical essays). 1970. pap. text ed. 5.95x o.p. (ISBN 0-393-09901-6). Norton.

Darwin & His Flowers: The Key to Natural Selection. Mea Allan. LC 77-77261. (Illus.). 1977. 14.50 o.s.i. (ISBN 0-8008-2113-0). Taplinger.

Darwin & the Mysterious Mr. X: New Light on the Evolutionists. Loren Eiseley. LC 80-24833. 304p. 1981. pap. 6.95 o.p. (ISBN 0-15-623949-3, Harv). HarBraceJ.

Darwinism Comes to America: 1859-1900. Bert J. Loewenberg. Ed. by Richard C. Wolf. LC 79-84546. (Facet Bks.). (Orig.). 1969. pap. 1.00 o.p. (ISBN 0-8006-3055-6, 1-3055, Fortress). Augsburg Fortress.

Darwin's Enigma. Luther Sunderland. LC 84-62231. 178p. 1984. pap. 6.95 o.p. (ISBN 0-89051-108-X). Master Bks.

Darwin's Universe: Origins & Crises in the History of Life. Charles R. Pellegrino & Jesse A. Stoff. (Illus.). 256p. 1982. 24.95 o.p. (ISBN 0-442-27526-9). Van Nos Reinhold.

Data & Voice Multiplexers. International Resource Development, Inc. Staff. 164p. 1983. 985.00x o.p. (ISBN 0-88694-578-X). Intl Res Dev.

Data Base & Computer Systems Security. John M. Carroll. Ed. by Robert M. Curtice. (Data Base Monograph: No. 4). 1976. pap. 15.00x o.s.i. (ISBN 0-89435-002-1). QED Info Sci.

Data Base Design Technique I: Requirements & Logical Structures New York 1978: Proceedings. Ed. by S. B. Yao et al. (Lecture Notes in Computer Sciences Ser.: Vol. 132). 227p. 1982. pap. 16.00 o.p. (ISBN 0-387-11214-6). Springer-Verlag.

Data Base Design Techniques II: Physical Structures & Applications Tokyo 1979: Proceedings. Ed. by S. B. Yao & T. L. Kunii. (Lecture Notes in Computer Sciences: Vol. 133). 170p. 1982. pap. 14.00 o.p. (ISBN 0-387-11215-4). Springer-Verlag.

Data Base Directions, Information Resource Management: Making It Work. Ed. by Elizabeth N. Fong & Alan H. Goldfine. (National Bureau of Standards Special Publication 500-139. Computer Science & Technology Ser.). (Illus.). 185p. 1986. pap. 9.00 o.p. (ISBN 0-318-21280-3, S/N 003-003-02738-3). USGPO.

Data Base in Perspective. National Computing Centre, Ltd. Staff. Ed. by Brian Davis. 110p. (Orig.). 1980. 27.50x o.p. (ISBN 0-85012-219-8). Intl Pubns Serv.

Data Base Management Systems: A Guide to Microcomputer Software. David Kruglinski. 260p. (Orig.). 1983. pap. text ed. 16.95 o.p. (ISBN 0-07-931084-2). Osborne-McGraw.

Data Base: Structured Techniques for Design, Performance & Management: With Case Studies. Shakuntala Atre. LC 80-14808. (Business Data Processing Ser.). 442p. 1980. 39.95x o.p. (ISBN 0-471-05267-1). Wiley.

Data Base Systems. Bunyan. (Infotech Computer State of the Art Reports). 722p. 1975. 310.00x o.p. (ISBN 0-08-028549-X). Pergamon.

Data Base Systems. Ed. by H. Hasselmeier & W. C. Spruth. (Lecture Notes in Computer Science: Vol. 39). 390p. 1976. pap. 16.80 o.p. (ISBN 0-387-07612-3). Springer-Verlag.

Data Base Techniques for Pictorial Applications. Ed. by A. Blaser. (Lecture Notes in Computer Sciences: Vol. 81). 599p. 1980. pap. 39.00 o.p. (ISBN 0-387-09763-5). Springer-Verlag.

Data Bases for Beginners. Elayne E. Schulman. LC 86-9248. (Computer Literacy Skills Ser.). (Illus.). 112p. (YA) (gr. 7-12). 1987. PLB 11.90 o.p. (ISBN 0-531-10230-0). Watts.

Data Book for Welfare-Employment Programs. Demetra S. Nightingale & John J. Mitchell. 187p. 1978. pap. 9.50 o.p. (ISBN 0-87766-239-8). Urban Inst.

Data Center Disaster Consultant. 2nd ed. Kenniston W. Lord. (Q.E.D. Information Services, Inc. Ser.). 224p. 1983. text ed. 56.00 o.p. (ISBN 0-13-196239-6). P-H.

Data Center Operations: A Guide to Effective Planning, Processing & Performance. Howard Schaeffer. 1981. text ed. 53.33 o.p. (ISBN 0-13-196360-0). P-H.

Data Communications: A Comprehensive Approach. Gilbert Held & Ray Sarch. (Data Communications Bk.). 441p. 1984. text ed. 49.95 o.p. (ISBN 0-07-027974-8). McGraw.

Data Communications & Local Area Networking Handbook. Britt Rorabaugh. (Illus.). 240p. 1985. 24.00 o.p. (ISBN 0-8306-0603-3, NO.2603). Tab Bks.

Data Communications & Teleprocessing Systems. Trevor Housley. (P-H Data Processing Management Ser.). (Illus.). 1979. text ed. 41.67 o.p. (ISBN 0-13-197368-1). P-H.

Data Communications Dictionary. Charles Sippl. 545p. 1980. pap. 14.95 o.p. (ISBN 0-442-21931-8). Van Nos Reinhold.

Data Communications for Business. Lientz & Rea. 352p. 1987. 40.95 o.p. (ISBN 0-8016-3013-4). Mosby.

Data Communications Procurement Manual. Gilbert Held. LC 79-18075. (Illus.). 150p. 1980. text ed. 44.95 o.p. (ISBN 0-07-027952-7). McGraw.

Data Communications Symposium, Ninth, 1985. 212p. 1985. 40.00 o.p. (ISBN 0-89791-164-4, 85-60169). IEEE Comp Soc.

Data Communications Techniques & Technology. Zendex Corporation Staff & Joel Effron. 225p. 1984. 37.95 o.s.i. (ISBN 0-534-03270-2). Van Nos Reinhold.

Data Dictionaries & Data Administration: Concepts & Practices for Data Resource Management. Ronald G. Ross. 384p. 1981. 29.95 o.p. (ISBN 0-8144-5596-4). AMACOM.

Data Distributions. Ronald Christensen. (Entropy Minimax Sourcebook Ser.: Vol. VIII). (Illus.). x, 299p. 1984. lib. bdg. 36.95 o.p. (ISBN 0-938876-17-1). Entropy Ltd.

Data Entry Without Keypunching: Improved Preparation for Social-Data Analysis. Martin D. Sorin. LC 78-24637. 288p. 1982. 23.00x o.p. (ISBN 0-669-02803-7). Lexington Bks.

Data File Handling for the IBM PC & XT. Howard White. 192p. 1985. pap. 16.95 o.p. (ISBN 0-89303-402-9). Brady Bks.

Data File Programming on Your IBM PC. Alan Simpson. LC 84-50366. 219p. (Orig.). 1984. 18.95 o.p. (ISBN 0-89588-146-2). SYBEX.

Data Handling Utilities in C. Robert A. Radcliffe & Thomas J. Raab. LC 86-61061. 519p. (Orig.). 1986. pap. 22.95 o.p. (ISBN 0-89588-304-X). Sybex.

Data in Modern Biology: Selected Papers from the 9th International CODATA Conference, Jerusalem, Israel, June 1984. Ed. by CODATA Staff. (Illus.). 63p. 1985. pap. 11.00 o.p. (ISBN 0-08-032483-5). Pergamon.

Data Management for On-Line Systems. David Lefkovitz. (Illus.). 300p. 1974. 14.95x o.p. (ISBN 0-8104-5100-X). Sams.

Data Management for Professionals. Bryan Lewis. 153p. 1983. pap. 15.95 o.p. (ISBN 0-912677-04-X). Tate Pub.

Data Management in Cost Containment & Quality Review Strategies: QRB Special Edition. 104p. 1983. 20.00 o.p. Joint Comm Hlthcare.

Data Network Design Strategies. Ray Sarch. (Data Communications Bk.). 288p. 1984. text ed. 31.95 o.p. (ISBN 0-07-054725-4). McGraw.

Data on Blindness & Visual Impairment in the U. S. A. A Resource Manual on Characteristics, Education, Employment & Service Delivery. Corinne Kirchner. LC 85-11117. (Illus.). 320p. 1985. pap. 15.00 o.p. (ISBN 0-89128-116-9, PIR116). Am Foun Blind.

Data Processing. Melvin Berger. LC 83-6879. (Computer Awareness First Bk.). (Illus.). 96p. (gr. 5 up). PLB 9.90 o.p. (ISBN 0-531-04640-0). Watts.

Data Processing: An Introduction. James M. Adams. LC 81-66793. (Data Processing Ser.). (Illus.). 253p. 1982. text ed. 18.95 o.p. (ISBN 0-8273-1616-X); tchr's. guide 9.00 o.p. (ISBN 0-8273-1617-8). Delmar.

Data Processing Contracts: Structure, Contents, & Negotiations. 2nd ed. Dick H. Brandon et al. LC 83-5842. 1983. 48.95 o.p. (ISBN 0-442-21034-5). Van Nos Reinhold.

Data Processing Cost Reduction & Control. Dick H. Brandon. (Computer Science Ser.). (Illus.). 234p. 1978. 29.95 o.p. (ISBN 0-442-21032-9). Van Nos Reinhold.

Data Processing for Builders. National Association of Home Builders Staff. 55p. 1984. pap. 15.00 o.p. (ISBN 0-86718-227-X). Nat Assn H Build.

Data Processing for Business. 3rd ed. Gerald A. Silver & Joan B. Silver. 622p. 1981. text ed. 19.00 o.p. (ISBN 0-15-516814-2, HC). HarBraceJ.

Data Processing for Business. Gerald A. Silver & Joan B. Silver. (Illus., Orig.). 1973. text ed. 15.95 o.p. (ISBN 0-15-516804-5, HC); pap. 4.95 student guide o.p. (ISBN 0-685-34876-8). HarBraceJ.

Data Processing for Business. 2nd ed. Gerald A. Silver & Joan B. Silver. (Illus.). 1977. text ed. 20.95 o.p. (ISBN 0-15-516809-6, HC). HarBraceJ.

Data Processing Forms. (Easy-to-Make Photocopier Bks.). (Orig.). 1983. pap. 14.95 o.p. (ISBN 0-87280-047-4, Asher-Gallant). Caddylak Systs.

Data Processing in Australia: A Profile & Forward Perspective of Skills & Usage. Roy Kriegler et al. 120p. 1986. pap. text ed. 19.95x o.p. (ISBN 0-86861-655-9). Unwin Hyman.

Data Processing: The Fundamentals. Wilson T. Price. 185p. 1982. pap. text ed. 16.95 o.p. (ISBN 0-03-059744-7). HR&W.

Data Quality of Criminal History Records. Robert R. Belair. (Criminal Justice Information Policy). 127p. (Orig.). 1985. pap. 4.75 o.p. (ISBN 0-318-18742-6, S/N 027-000-01239-6). USGPO.

Data Sharing with 1-2-3 & Symphony; Including MainFrame Links. Dick Andersen. LC 86-61341. 262p. 1985. pap. 22.95 o.p. (ISBN 0-89588-283-3). SYBEX.

Data Structures & Program Design. Robert L. Kruse. (Software Engineering Ser.). (Illus.). 496p. 1984. pap. text ed. 42.67 o.p. (ISBN 0-13-196253-1). P-H.

Data Structures & Their Implementation. Robert J. Baron & Linda G. Shapiro. (University Computer Science Ser.). 416p. 1980. 28.95 o.p. (ISBN 0-442-20586-4). Van Nos Reinhold.

Data Structures & Their Implementation. Robert J. Baron & Linda G. Shapiro. 469p. pap. text ed. write for info o.p. (ISBN 0-87150-429-4, 8070). PWS Kent Pub.

Data Structures for Personal Computers. Yedidyah Langsam et al. LC 84-3326. (Illus.). 576p. 1985. text ed. 48.00 o.p. (ISBN 0-13-196221-3). P-H.

Data Structures Using Pascal. Moshe Augenstein & Aaron M. Tenenbaum. (Illus.). 528p. 1981. text ed. 39.33 o.p. (ISBN 0-13-196501-8). P-H.

Data, Text & Voice Encryption Worldwide Markets. International Resource Development, Inc. Staff. 185p. 1987. 2100.00x o.p. (ISBN 0-88694-727-8). Intl Res Dev.

Data Types & Structures. reference ed. C. C. Gotlieb & Leo R. Gotlieb. (Illus.). 1978. text ed. (ISBN 0-13-197095-X). P-H.

Database: A Bibliography, Vol. 1. Yahiko Kambayashi. LC 80-26672. (Digital Systems Design Ser.). 499p. 1981. text ed. 45.00x o.p. (ISBN 0-914894-64-1, Computer Sci Pr). W H Freeman.

Database Design. Gio Wiederhold. (Computer Science Ser.). 1977. text ed. 36.95 o.p. (ISBN 0-07-070130-X, C). McGraw.

Database Directory. Ed. by Knowledge Industry Publications Staff & American Society for Information & Science Staff. 750p. 1987. pap. 195.00 o.p. (ISBN 0-86729-214-8). Knowledge Indus.

Database Directory, Nineteen Eighty-Seven to Eighty-Eight. Knowledge Industry Publications Staff. Ed. by American Society for Information & Science Staff. 750p. 1986. pap. 95.00 o.p. (ISBN 0-86729-199-0). Knowledge Indus.

Database Directory: Nineteen Eighty-Seven to Eighty-Eight. Ed. by Knowledge Industry Publications Staff. (ASIS Ser.). 750p. 1986-87. pap. 95.00 o.p. (ISBN 0-86729-212-1). Knowledge Indus.

Database Illustrated: A Professional Guide to Local Design. M. E. Ragel. (Illus.). pap. write for info. o.s.i. Meghan-Kiffer.

Database Management Systems. R. A. Frost. 288p. 1984. text ed. 38.95 o.p. (ISBN 0-07-022564-8). McGraw.

Database Management Systems for the Eighties. Shaku Atre. LC 83-60769. 600p. 1984. 48.00 o.s.i. (ISBN 0-89435-118-4). QED Info Sci.

Databases & Clearinghouses: Information Resources for Education. 5th ed. Compiled by Ruth Gordon. 121p. 1983. 8.75 o.p. (ISBN 0-318-22072-5, IN248). Natl Ctr Res Voc Ed.

Dateline America. Charles Kuralt. LC 78-22262. (Illus.). 224p. 1982. pap. 7.95 o.p. (ISBN 0-15-623962-0, Harv). HarBraceJ.

Dateline Chicago: A Veteran Newsman Recalls Its Heyday. William T. Moore. LC 72-6614. (Illus.). 1973. 7.95 o.s.i. (ISBN 0-8008-2114-9). Taplinger.

Dating & Relating. Cherie Scalf & Kenneth Waters. 160p. 1982. pap. 7.95 o.p. (ISBN 0-8499-2890-7). Word Bks.

Dating & Waiting: A Christian View of Love, Sex, & Dating. Les Christie. LC 83-1232. (Illus.). 80p. (Orig.). 1983. pap. 2.95 o.p. (ISBN 0-87239-643-6, 39972). Standard Pub.

Dating Games. Tina Sunshine. 1986. pap. 2.50 o.p. (ISBN 0-380-89767-9, Flare). Avon.

Dating Methods in Archaeology. Joseph W. Michels. LC 72-84274. (Studies in Archaeology Ser). 1973. 29.95 o.p. (ISBN 0-12-785520-3). Acad Pr.

Dating Tips. Nathanael Pugh. Ed. by Mary H. Wallace. (Illus.). 120p. 1983. pap. 4.95 o.p. (ISBN 0-912315-00-8). Word Aflame.

Datsun F10 & 310: 1976-1981 Shop Manual. Alan Ahlstrand. (Illus.). pap. text ed. 12.95 o.p. (ISBN 0-89287-318-3, A202). Clymer Pub.

Datsun Sports Car Handbook: 1600 & 2000cc. Ed. by Clymer Publications. (Illus.). 1970. pap. 11.00 o.p. (ISBN 0-89287-248-9, A150). Clymer Pub.

Datsun 1200, 210 & Nissan Sentra 1973-84: RTUG. Chilton Automotives Editorial Staff. LC 83-45325. 212p. 1984. pap. 13.95 o.p. (ISBN 0-8019-7490-9). Chilton.

Datsun 200 SX, 510, 610, 710, 810, 1973-84: RTUG. Chilton Automotives Editorial Staff. LC 83-45313. 212p. 1984. pap. 12.50 o.p. (ISBN 0-8019-7478-X). Chilton.

Datsun 4-Wheel Drive Pickups: 1980-1983 Shop Manual. Alan Ahlstrand. Ed. by Sydnie A. Wauson. (Illus., Orig.). 1981. pap. 12.95 o.p. (ISBN 0-89287-344-2, A207). Clymer Pub.

Datsun 510 1978-1979 Shop Manual. (Illus.). pap. text ed. 13.95 o.p. (ISBN 0-89287-244-6, A201). Clymer Pub.

Datsun 810 1977-1980 Shop Manual. Ed. by Eric Jorgensen. (Illus.). pap. text ed. 12.95 o.p. (ISBN 0-89287-334-5, A204). Clymer Pub.

Daughter of a Revolutionary: Natalie Herzen & the Bakunin-Nechayev Circle. Michael Confino. LC 73-86555. 416p. 1974. 12.95 o.p. (ISBN 0-912050-15-2, Library Pr). Open Court.

Daughter of Fire: A Portrait of Iceland. Katharine Scherman. (Illus.). 1976. 16.95 o.p. (ISBN 0-316-77325-5). Little.

Daughter of the Nobility. Natasha Borovsky. LC 84-22453. 512p. 1985. 16.40 o.p. (ISBN 0-03-003294-6). H Holt & Co.

Daughter of the Swan. Joan J. Buck. 352p. 1987. 17.95 o.p. (ISBN 1-55584-118-X). Weidenfeld.

Daughter of the Waves: Memories of Growing up in Pre-War Palestine. Ruth Jordan. LC 80-39526. (Illus.). 224p. 1983. 12.95 o.s.i. (ISBN 0-8008-2120-3). Taplinger.

Daughter's a Daughter. Mary Westmacott. LC 70-184884. 192p. 1972. 5.95 o.p. (ISBN 0-87795-030-X, Arbor Hse). Morrow.

Daughter's a Daughter. Mary Westmacott. 1982. pap. 2.95 o.p. (ISBN 0-440-11674-0). Dell.

Daughter's a Daughter. Mary Westmacott, pseud. 1982. 5.95 o.p. (ISBN 0-87795-388-0, Arbor Hse). Morrow.

Daughters of Change: Growing up Female in America. Janet Chase. 1981. 11.95 o.p. (ISBN 0-316-13820-7). Little.

Daughters of Danaus. Mona Caird. 540p. 1989. 29.95 o.p. (ISBN 1-55861-014-6); pap. 11.95 o.p. (ISBN 1-55861-015-4). Feminist Pr.

Daughters of Jerusalem. Roger Cleeve. LC 85-15007. 304p. 1986. 15.95 o.p. (ISBN 0-917561-02-3). Adler & Adler.

Daughters of Karl Marx: Family Correspondence 1866-98. Tr. by Jenny Marx et al. Ed. by Faith Evans. LC 81-47302. (Illus.). 384p. 1982. 19.95 o.p. (ISBN 0-15-123971-1). HarBraceJ.

Daumier. Robert Rey. (Library of Great Painters). (Illus.). 160p. 40.00 o.p. (ISBN 0-8109-1058-6). Abrams.

Daumier's Clowns: Les Saltimbanques et Les Parades, New Biographical & Political Functions for a Nineteenth Century Myth. Paula H. Harper. LC 79-6173. (Outstanding Dissertations in the Fine Arts Ser.: No.5). 290p. 1981. lib. bdg. 46.00 o.p. (ISBN 0-8240-3949-1). Garland Pub.

Dave Durant & the Mystery of the Stone House. Gloria Repp. (Windrider Ser.). 192p. (Orig.). (gr. 4-6). 1986. pap. 3.95 o.p. (ISBN 0-8423-0519-X). Tyndale.

Dave Given Rock 'n' Roll Star's Handbook. Dave F. Given. 1980. 15.00 o.p. (ISBN 0-682-49577-8, Banner). Exposition-Phoenix.

Dave Peck's World Championship Racquetball: Learning to Play by the Numbers. Dave Peck & Jerry Day. (Illus.). 128p. 1985. pap. 8.95 o.p. (ISBN 0-671-49434-1, Fireside). S&S.

Dave Whitlock's Guide to Aquatic Trout Foods. Dave Whitlock. (Illus.). 224p. 1982. 27.95 o.p. (ISBN 0-8329-3770-3). Lyons & Burford.

David. Nancy Roberts. LC 74-3710. (Illus.). 72p. 1974. pap. 3.95 o.p. (ISBN 0-8042-2031-X, John Knox). Westminster John Knox.

David. Marie Rothenberg & Mel White. (Illus.). 200p. 1984. 12.95 o.p. (ISBN 0-8007-1226-9); pap. 3.95 o.p. (ISBN 0-8007-8589-4). Revell.

David. Marie Rothenberg & Mel White. 1985. 12.95x o.p. (ISBN 0-8007-6240-1). Phoenix Soc.

David Ahl's BASIC Computer Adventures: Ten Treks & Travels Through Time & Space. David Ahl. 272p. (Orig.). 1986. pap. 9.95 o.s.i. (ISBN 0-914845-92-6). MicroSoft.

David & Goliath. Ruth F. Brin. (Old Testament Bible Stories). (Illus.). 32p. (gr. k-5). 1977. PLB 6.95 o.p. (ISBN 0-8225-0365-4). Lerner Pubns.

David & Goliath: The U. S. War Against Nicaragua. Kent Norsworthy & William Robinson. (MR-CENSA Series on the Americas). 320p. 1987. 27.00 o.s.i. (ISBN 0-85345-721-2); pap. 11.00 o.s.i. (ISBN 0-85345-720-4). Monthly Rev.

David Bowie. Kevin Cann. LC 83-25411. (Illus.). 239p. 1984. pap. 8.70 o.p. (ISBN 0-671-50537-8, Fireside). S&S.

David Bowie: An Illustrated Record. Roy Carr & Charles S. Murray. 120p. 1981. pap. 12.95 o.p. (ISBN 0-380-77966-8). Avon.

David Bowie's Serious Moonlight: The World Tour. Chet Flippo. LC 83-40140. (Illus.). 256p. 1984. 35.00 o.p. (ISBN 0-385-19265-7, Dolp); pap. 16.95 o.p. (ISBN 0-385-19266-5). Doubleday.

David Claypool Johnston: American Graphic Humorist, 1798-1865. Malcolm Johnson. 1970. pap. 2.00x o.p. (ISBN 0-912296-23-2, Dist. by U Pr of Va). Am Antiquarian.

David Copperfield. abr. ed. Charles Dickens. Ed. by Edmund Fuller. 416p. 1958. pap. 2.50 o.p. (ISBN 0-440-31675-8, LE). Dell.

David Copperfield. Charles Dickens. LC 85-62342. (Illus.). 736p. (gr. 7-12). 1986. 12.95 o.p. (ISBN 0-89577-223-X). RD Assn.

David Copperfield. Charles Dickens. 48p. (Orig.). 1988. pap. 9.95 o.p. (ISBN 1-55651-177-9); audiocassette tape incl. o.p. (ISBN 1-55651-178-7). Cram Cassettes.

David Harum. Edward N. Westcott. 1974. pap. 1.50 o.p. (ISBN 0-380-00107-1, 20156). Avon.

David Hicks Garden Design. David Hicks. (Illus.). 200p. 1982. 32.50 o.p. (ISBN 0-7100-9228-8). Routledge Chapman & Hall.

David Hockney. Marco Livingston. LC 81-81028. (Illus.). 252p. 1981. 19.95 o.s.i. (ISBN 0-03-059861-3, Owl Bks); pap. 10.95 o.s.i. (ISBN 0-03-059859-1). H Holt & Co.

David Hockney Faces. Marco Livingstone. LC 86-83167. (Illus.). 96p. 1987. pap. 19.95 o.s.i. (ISBN 0-500-27464-9). Thames Hudson.

David Hume: Common Sense Moralist, Sceptical Metaphysician. David F. Norton. LC 81-47937. 300p. 1984. pap. 14.50x o.p. (ISBN 0-691-02032-9). Princeton U Pr.

David Hume: Writings on Economics. Ed. by Eugene Rotwein. LC 55-12064. 336p. 1970. pap. 7.95x o.p. (ISBN 0-299-01324-3). U of Wis Pr.

David Hurn: Photographs 1956-76. Intro. by Tom Hopkinson. (Illus.). 64p. 1980. 20.00 o.p. (ISBN 0-7287-0202-9); pap. 10.00 o.p. (ISBN 0-7287-0203-7). Eastview.

David II: The Shepherd King. W. Phillip Keller. 224p. 1986. 11.95 o.p. (ISBN 0-8499-0559-1). Word Bks.

David Ingram's Investment Guide. David Ingram. 204p. (Orig.). 1985. pap. text ed. 9.95 o.p. (ISBN 0-88839-111-0). Hancock House.

David Jones: An Annotated Bibliography & Guide to Research. Samuel Rees. LC 76-24748. (Reference Library of the Humanities Ser.: Vol. 68). 1977. lib. bdg. 24.00 o.p. (ISBN 0-8240-9929-X). Garland Pub.

David Kimhi: The Man & the Commentaries. Frank E. Talmage. LC 75-1747. (Harvard Judaic Monographs: No. 1). 224p. 1976. text ed. 17.50x o.p. (ISBN 0-674-19340-7). Harvard U Pr.

David Kopay Story. David Kopay & Perry D. Young. LC 76-29229. 1980. pap. 5.95 o.p. (ISBN 0-87795-290-6, Arbor Hse). Morrow.

David Kopay Story. David Kopay & Perry D. Young. LC 76-29229. 1977. 8.95 o.p. (ISBN 0-87795-145-4, Arbor Hse). Morrow.

David Lange: Prime Minister. Vernon Wright. (Illus.). 146p. 1985. pap. text ed. 14.95x o.p. Unwin Hyman.

David Lean: A Guide to References & Resources. Louis Castelli & Caryn L. Cleeland. 1980. lib. bdg. 23.00 o.s.i. (ISBN 0-8161-7933-6, Hall Reference). G K Hall.

David Lee Roth. Philip Kamin. (Illus.). 32p. (gr. 8 up). 1985. pap. 4.95 o.p. (ISBN 0-88188-391-3, Robus Bks). H Leonard Pub Corp.

David McCheever's Twenty-Nine Dogs. Margaret Holt. (Read-by-Yourself Bks.). (Illus.). (gr. 1-2). 1980. reinforced bdg. 6.95 o.p. (ISBN 0-395-18777-X); pap. 2.95 o.p. (ISBN 0-395-29928-4). HM.

David, My Jewish Friend. Alice L. Goddard. (gr. 3-6). 1968. pap. 1.95 o.p. (ISBN 0-377-07701-1). Friendship Pr.

David Parrish. Mitchell D. Kahan. LC 81-81735. (Illus.). 24p. 1981. pap. 3.50 o.p. (ISBN 0-89280-017-8). Montgomery Mus.

David, the Chosen King: A Traditio-Historical Approach to the 2nd Book of Samuel. R. A. Carlson. 304p. (Orig.). 1964. pap. text ed. 23.50x o.p. Coronet Bks.

David Thompson's Narrative of His Explorations in Western America, 1784-1812. David Thompson. Ed. by J. B. Tyrrell. LC 68-28603. 1969. Repr. of 1916 ed. lib. bdg. 50.00x o.p. (ISBN 0-8371-3879-5, THNE). Greenwood.

David, Young Chief of the Quileutes: An American Indian Today. Ruth Kirk. LC 67-10206. (Illus.). (gr. 3-5). 1967. 5.95 o.p. (ISBN 0-15-222498-X, HJ). HarBraceJ.

David's First Day at School. Nigel Snell. (Illus.). 32p. (ps-1). 1981. 7.95 o.p. (ISBN 0-241-10641-9, Pub. by Hamish Hamilton England). David & Charles.

David's Real World. Ruth R. Stornetta. (Illus.). 87p. 1981. 6.00 o.p. (ISBN 0-682-49624-3). Exposition-Phoenix.

David's Seder. Norman Geller. (Illus.). 16p. (gr. 1-4). 1983. pap. 4.95 o.p. (ISBN 0-915753-01-4). N Geller Pub.

Davidson County Marriage Record Book I: 1789-1837. Silas E. Lucas, Jr. 166p. 1979. 22.50 o.p. (ISBN 0-89308-187-6, TN 21). Southern Hist Pr.

Davidson File. Stuart Jackman. LC 82-13443. 128p. 1983. pap. 7.95 o.s.i. (ISBN 0-664-24459-9, Westminster). Westminster John Knox.

Davidson's Principles & Practice of Medicine. 15th ed. Ed. by John MacLeod. (Illus.). 1987. text ed. 46.00 o.p. (ISBN 0-443-03003-0); pap. text ed. 32.00 o.p. (ISBN 0-443-03002-2). Churchill.

Davis H. Waite: The Ideology of a Western Populist. John R. Morris. LC 82-40106. (Illus.). 240p. (Orig.). 1982. PLB 30.50 o.p. (ISBN 0-8191-2445-1); pap. text ed. 13.25 o.p. (ISBN 0-8191-2446-X). U Pr of Amer.

Davison's Textile Blue Book. 123rd ed. 675p. 1989. 90.00 o.p. Davison.

Davita's Harp. Chaim Potok. (Large Print Books (General Ser.)). 548p. 1985. lib. bdg. 18.95 o.p. (ISBN 0-8161-3951-2). G K Hall.

Davor: Ein Stuck in 13 Szenen. Gunter Grass. Ed. by Victor Lange & Frances Lange. 182p. 1973. pap. text ed. 4.00 o.p. (ISBN 0-15-516963-7, HC). HarBraceJ.

Davy Crockett. Constance Rourke. LC 34-4692. (Illus.). (gr. 7 up). 1934. 5.50 o.p. (ISBN 0-15-222517-X, HJ). HarBraceJ.

Davy Crockett: The Untold Story. Frank Driskill. 1981. 6.95 o.p. (ISBN 0-89015-298-5). Eakin Pr.

Davy Crockett's Earthquake. William O. Steele. LC 56-6920. (Illus.). (gr. k-3). 1956. 5.95 o.p. (ISBN 0-15-222696-6, HJ). HarBraceJ.

Dawn. Elie Wiesel. 1981. pap. 1.95 o.p. (ISBN 0-380-01132-8, 52779, Bard). Avon.

Dawn at Red Mountain. Grover C. Hunter, Jr. 1985. 7.95 o.p. (ISBN 0-533-06529-1). Vantage.

Dawn Horse Testament. Da Free John. LC 85-20536. 1985. 45.00 o.s.i. (ISBN 0-913922-95-1); pap. 24.95 o.s.i. (ISBN 0-913922-90-0). Dawn Horse Pr.

Dawn Is Golden. Anne Hampson. (Silhouette Romances Ser.). 1984. lib. bdg. 8.95 o.p. (ISBN 0-8398-2806-3, Gregg). G K Hall.

Dawn of African Women. John E. Njoku. 1977. 5.00 o.p. (ISBN 0-682-48862-3). Exposition-Phoenix.

Dawn of Apocalyptic: The Historical & Sociological Roots of Jewish Apocalyptic Eschatology. rev. ed. Paul D. Hanson. LC 79-17099. 464p. 1979. 16.95 o.p. (ISBN 0-8006-0285-4, 1-1809); pap. 12.95 o.p. (ISBN 0-8006-1809-2, Fortress). Augsburg Fortress.

Dawn of Christianity. Robert H. Bogue. 1985. 15.00 o.p. (ISBN 0-533-06545-3). Vantage.

Dawn of Italian Painting, 1250-1400. Alastair Smart. LC 77-78657. (Illus.). 288p. 1978. 47.50x o.p. (ISBN 0-8014-1124-6); pap. 16.95x cancelled o.p. (ISBN 0-8014-9172-X). Cornell U Pr.

Dawn of Modern Geography, 2 vols. Charles R. Beazley. (Illus.). Vols. 1 & 2 with map. each 20.00 o.p. (ISBN 0-8446-1063-1). Peter Smith.

Dawn of Modern Science: From the Arabs to Leonardo Da Vinci. Thomas Goldstein. 1980. 12.95 o.p. (ISBN 0-395-26298-4). HM.

Dawn of Modern Science: From the Arabs to Leonardo da Vinci. Thomas Goldstein. 1982. pap. 7.70 o.s.i. (ISBN 0-395-32132-8). HM.

Dawn of the Nineteenth Century in England. John Ashton. LC 67-23941. (Social History Reference Ser.). 504p. 1968. Repr. of 1886 ed. 34.00x o.p. (ISBN 0-8103-3247-7). Gale.

Dawn of the Post-Modern Era. E. J. Trueblood. 1954. (ISBN 0-8022-1738-9). Philos Lib.

Dawn Wind. Christina Savage. (Orig.). 1980. pap. 3.95 o.p. (ISBN 0-440-11824-7). Dell.

Dawning. Lawrence Ray. 64p. 1982. 5.00 o.p. (ISBN 0-682-49749-5). Exposition-Phoenix.

Dawns Are Quiet Here. B. Vassilyev. 287p. 1975. 5.45 o.p. (ISBN 0-8285-1950-1, Pub. by Progress Pubs USSR). Imported Pubns.

Dawn's Early Light. Walter Lord. (Illus.). 384p. 1972. 12.95 o.p. (ISBN 0-393-05452-7). Norton.

Day by Day with C. H. Spurgeon. Bryant. 1985. Repr. 7.95 o.p. (ISBN 0-317-27135-0). Word Bks.

Day by Day with God. Francoise Darey-Bembe & John P. Bembe. 1982. 4.95 o.p. (ISBN 0-8215-9908-9). Sadlier.

Day by Day With Pope John Paul II. Pope John Paul II. 1982. pap. 6.95 o.p. (ISBN 0-8091-2458-0). Paulist Pr.

Day Camp Program Book. Virginia Musselman. LC 79-23754. 336p. 1980. pap. 12.95 o.p. (ISBN 0-8329-1339-1). New Century.

Day Care: Investing in Ohio's Children. CDF Staff. LC 84-73513. 103p. (Orig.). 1985. pap. 4.50 o.p. (ISBN 0-938008-41-2). Children's Defense.

Day for Knights. Bluth Brothers Staff. (Buddies Ser.). (Illus.). 48p. (gr. k-6). 1984. 5.95 o.p. (ISBN 0-8249-8062-X). Ideals.

Day in Shadow. Nayantara Sahgal. 236p. 1972. 6.95 o.p. (ISBN 0-393-08433-7). Norton.

Day in the Life of a Director of Religious Education. 36p. 1977. 3.60 o.p. Natl Cath Educ.

Day in the Life of Australia. (Illus.). 288p. 1982. 45.00 o.p. (ISBN 0-8109-1801-3). Collins SF.

Day in the Life of Hawaii. Rick Smolan & David Cohen. LC 84-7224. (Illus.). 224p. 1984. 40.00 o.p. (ISBN 0-89480-760-9, 760). Workman Pub.

Day in the Life of Petronella Pig. Tatjana Hauptmann. LC 80-82138. (Illus.). 28p. (gr. k-2). 1982. 12.95 o.p. (ISBN 0-03-057794-2). H Holt & Co.

Day Is Short: An Autobiography. Morris B. Abram. LC 80-8738. (Illus.). 288p. 1982. 14.95 o.p. (ISBN 0-15-123982-7). HarBraceJ.

Day Nazi Germany Died. Beate Wilder-Smith. LC 82-71148. 1982. pap. 2.95 o.p. (ISBN 0-89051-083-0). Master Bks.

Day-Night Circus Clowns. Sharon H. Fischel. (gr. 1-3). 1986. 4.95 o.p. (ISBN 0-533-07105-4). Vantage.

Day of Benediction. Ellen G. White. (Newsprint Ser.). 172p. 1982. pap. 0.30 o.p. (ISBN 0-8163-0493-9). Pacific Pr Pub Assn.

Day of Chaminuka. William Rayner. LC 76-41329. 1977. 7.95 o.p. (ISBN 0-689-10778-1, Atheneum). Macmillan.

Day of Infamy. Walter Lord. (Illus.). (gr. 9 up). 1957. 9.95 o.p. (ISBN 0-03-027620-9). H Holt & Co.

Day of Judgement. Jack Higgins. LC 78-15043. 1979. 8.95 o.p. (ISBN 0-03-046171-5). H Holt & Co.

Day of Judgment. Salvatore Satta. write for info. o.p. FS&G.

Day of Small Things: Abolitionism in the Midst of Slavery, Berea, Kentucky, 1854-1864. Richard D. Sears. LC 85-22781. 474p. (Orig.). 1986. lib. bdg. 36.75 o.p. (ISBN 0-8191-5043-6); pap. text ed. 24.75 o.p. (ISBN 0-8191-5044-4). U Pr of Amer.

Day of the Bomb: Countdown to Hiroshima. Dan Kurzman. 1985. text ed. 19.95 o.p. (ISBN 0-07-035683-1). McGraw.

Day of the Cobra. Jeffrey St. John. LC 84-4780. (Illus.). 192p. 1984. 11.95 o.p. (ISBN 0-8407-5381-0). Nelson.

Day of the Drag Race. Philip Harkins. LC 60-11707. (gr. 7 up). 1960. 11.75 o.p. (ISBN 0-688-21223-9, Morrow Junior Books). Morrow.

Day of Trinity. Lansing Lamont. LC 84-45635. (Illus.). 352p. 1985. pap. 11.95 o.p. (ISBN 0-689-70686-3, 326, Atheneum). Macmillan.

Day on Fire. James R. Ullman. 1978. pap. 2.50 o.p. (ISBN 0-380-38430-2, 38430). Avon.

Day One: Before Hiroshima & After. Peter Wyden. 409p. 1984. 19.45 o.p. (ISBN 0-671-46142-7). S&S.

Day the Circus Came to Lone Tree. Glen Rounds. LC 73-78458. (Illus.). 40p. (gr. k-3). 1973. reinforced bdg. 10.95 o.p. (ISBN 0-8234-0232-0). Holiday.

Day the Cow Sneezed. James Flora. LC 57-9740. (Illus.). (ps-3). 1957. 6.95 o.p. (ISBN 0-15-222875-6, HJ). HarBraceJ.

Day the Cow Sneezed. James Flora. LC 75-8746. (Illus.). 42p. (gr. k-1). 1975. pap. 1.95 o.p. (ISBN 0-15-624213-3, VoyB). HarBraceJ.

Day the Gods Came. George King. (Illus.). 72p. 1965. 11.00 o.p. (ISBN 0-937249-05-X). Aetherius Soc.

Day the River. Cornelis Vleeskens. LC 84-11961. 77p. 1985. 9.95 o.p. (ISBN 0-7022-1944-4). U of Queensland Pr.

Day the Sun Split. Cynthia Cahn. pap. 3.00 o.p. (ISBN 0-938078-14-3). Anhinga Pr.

Day They Gave Babies Away. Dale Eunson. LC 72-84484. (Illus.). 64p. 1970. 6.95 o.p. (ISBN 0-374-31760-7). FS&G.

Day-to-Day Union-Management Relationships see Issues in the Public Employee Relations Library: Series 4.

Day to Remember. Bernard Stone. (Illus.). 32p. (gr. k-3). 1981. 10.95 o.s.i. (ISBN 0-02-708910-X, Four Winds). Macmillan.

Titles

Day Trips Out of Charleston - A Guide to Low Country Adventures. William P. Baldwin. (Illus.). 192p. (Orig.). 1988. pap. text ed. write for info. o.p. (ISBN 0-933101-07-4). Legacy Pubns.

Day Velvet Disappeared. Louise Kantenwein. (Illus.). 64p. 1980. 5.00 o.p. (ISBN 0-682-49649-9). Exposition-Phoenix.

Day Without Sunshine. Les Whitten. LC 84-45634. 320p. 1985. 16.95 o.p. (ISBN 0-689-11529-6, Atheneum). Macmillan.

Daybook: The Journal of an Artist. Anne Truitt. 1982. 14.45 o.p. (ISBN 0-394-52398-9). Pantheon.

Daybreakers. Jane L. Curry. LC 72-94332. (gr. 4-6). 1970. 5.95 o.p. (ISBN 0-15-222853-5, HJ). HarBraceJ.

Daylight in Architecture. Benjamin Evans. LC 80-26066. (Illus.). 204p. 1981. text ed. 47.50 o.p. (ISBN 0-07-019768-7). McGraw.

Daylighting. R. G. Hopkinson et al. 584p. 1966. 29.95 o.p. (ISBN 0-434-90763-4, Pub. by W Heinemann Ltd). David & Charles.

Daynight Lamp. Tr. by Max Knight. 1974. 5.95 o.p. (ISBN 0-685-31470-7); pap. 3.95 o.p. (ISBN 0-395-19778-3). HM.

Days at the Factories: Manufacturing in the Nineteenth Century. George Dodd. (Illus.). 408p. 1975. Repr. of 1843 ed. 26.95x o.p. (ISBN 0-8464-0313-7). Beekman Pubs.

Days Before Christmas: How Your Family Can Prepare for the Coming of Jesus. W. A. Poovey. LC 75-2835. (Illus.). 112p. (Orig.). 1975. pap. 5.50 o.p. (ISBN 0-8066-1480-3, 10-1825, Augsburg). Augsburg Fortress.

Days Before Easter. W. A. Poovey. LC 76-27074. 1977. pap. 4.50 o.p. (ISBN 0-8066-1557-5, 10-1835, Augsburg). Augsburg Fortress.

Days Between Stations: A Novel. Steve Erickson. 1985. 15.45 o.s.i. (ISBN 0-671-53275-8, Poseidon). S&S.

Days Grow Short: The Life & Music of Kurt Weill. Ronald Sanders. LC 79-17331. (Illus.). 480p. 1980. 16.95 o.p. (ISBN 0-03-019411-3). H Holt & Co.

Days of Courage. Niels Jensen. Tr. by Oliver Stallybrass. LC 73-5241. (gr. 4-6). 1973. 5.75 o.p. (ISBN 0-15-222880-2, HJ). HarBraceJ.

Days of Dimitrov: As I Witnessed & Recorded Them. Nedelcho Ganchovski. Tr. by Svelta Maneva. 603p. 1979. 12.95 o.p. (ISBN 0-8285-2709-1, Pub. by Sofia Bulgaria). Imported Pubns.

Days of Holly Hobbie. (Platt & Munk Cricket Bks.). (Illus.). 24p. (ps-3). 1978. PLB 3.99 o.p. (ISBN 0-448-13053-X, G&D). Putnam Pub Group.

Days of Lorne: Impressions of a Governor-General. William S. MacNutt. LC 77-16170. (Illus.). 1978. Repr. of 1955 ed. lib. bdg. 35.00x o.p. (ISBN 0-313-20021-1, MADL). Greenwood.

Days of My Life. Danny C. Dunston. 32p. 1986. 6.95 o.p. (ISBN 0-8062-3031-2). Carlton.

Days of Pentecost: Devotions, Customs, & Summertime Activities to Celebrate the Season of the Spirit. W. A. Poovey. LC 78-66953. 1979. pap. 3.50 o.p. (ISBN 0-8066-1678-4, 10-1844, Augsburg). Augsburg Fortress.

Days of the French Revolution. Christopher Hibbert. LC 81-9666. (Illus.). 384p. 1981. Repr. 12.95 o.p. (ISBN 0-688-03704-6). Morrow.

Days of the Year. Joyce McLellan. (gr. 2-6). 1971. 3.15 o.p. (ISBN 0-08-006799-9). Pergamon.

Days of Winter. Cynthia Freeman. LC 77-79533. 1978. 9.95 o.p. (ISBN 0-87795-171-3, Arbor Hse). Morrow.

Days Remembered. Alma Barkman. (Illus.). 96p. 1983. pap. 8.95 o.p. (ISBN 0-8024-0188-0). Moody.

Days That Were. Gerald W. Brace. 1976. 10.95 o.p. (ISBN 0-393-07509-5). Norton.

Days to Remember. Date not set. (ISBN 0-8052-0687-6). Random.

Days to Remember. Date not set. (ISBN 0-8052-0686-8). Random.

Daystar. Lucye Walker. 1978. 4.00 o.p. (ISBN 0-682-49009-1). Exposition-Phoenix.

Daytime. Sue Porter. (Baby Book Ser.). (Illus.). 12p. (ps). 1985. bds. 3.95 o.p. (ISBN 0-911745-98-X, Bedrick Blackie). P Bedrick Bks.

Daytime Star. Simon Mitton. (Illus.). 208p. 1983. pap. 6.95 o.s.i. (ISBN 0-684-17829-X, ScribT). Scribner.

Daytrips, Getaway Weekends, & Budget Vacations in the Mid-Atlantic States. Patricia Foulke & Robert Foulke. LC 86-7627. (Illus.). 480p. (Orig.). 1986. pap. 11.95 o.p. (ISBN 0-87106-894-X). Globe Pequot.

Daytrips in Germany: Fifty One Day Adventures by Rail or Car. Earl Steinbicker. (Illus.). 1984. 9.95 o.p. (ISBN 0-8038-1584-0). Hastings.

Dayworld. Philip Jose Farmer. 336p. 1985. 16.95 o.p. (ISBN 0-399-12967-7, Putnam). Putnam Pub Group.

DBASE II for Every Business. R. A. Byers. 1985. pap. text ed. 19.95 o.p. (ISBN 0-07-912603-0). McGraw.

DBASE II for the First-Time User. Alan Freedman. 1985. pap. text ed. 19.95 o.p. (ISBN 0-07-912608-1). McGraw.

DBASE II for the First-Time User: A Visual Guide. Alan Freedman. 1984. 19.95 o.p. (ISBN 0-8359-1244-2, Reston). P-H.

DBASE II Guide for Small Business. Robert J. Schadewald & William Dickey. 350p. 1984. pap. 24.95 o.p. (ISBN 0-912677-07-4). Tate Pub.

DBASE III. (Workbook Ser.). 1985. Introduction to dBASE III, Level One Course. pap. write for info. o.p. (ISBN 0-912677-61-9). Using dBASE III, Level Two Course (ISBN 0-912677-64-3). Programming with dBASE III, Level Three Course (ISBN 0-912677-67-8). Tate Pub.

DBASE III for Every Business. R. A. Byers. 1985. pap. text ed. 19.95 o.p. (ISBN 0-07-912632-4). McGraw.

dBASE III for Every Business. R. A. Byers. 1987. pap. text ed. 19.95 o.p. (ISBN 0-07-912707-X). McGraw.

DBASE III for Every Business. Robert A. Byers. 300p. 1985. pap. 19.95 o.p. (ISBN 0-912677-32-5). Tate Pub.

DBASE III for Sales Professionals. Bill Dickey. 300p. 1985. pap. 29.95 incl. disk o.p. (ISBN 0-912677-46-5). Tate Pub.

DBASE III PLUS: Advanced Applications for Non-Programmers. Richard H. Baker. 1987. 27.95 o.p. (ISBN 0-8306-2508-9, 2808); pap. 19.60 o.p. (ISBN 0-8306-2808-8). Tab Bks.

DBASE III Plus & Total Area Network: A Managers Guide. William Bates & Andres Fortino. 350p. (Orig.). 1986. pap. 24.95 o.p. (ISBN 0-912677-80-5). Tate Pub.

DBASE III Plus Power Tools: Communications, Debugging & File Integration. Robert Krumm. (MIS: Press Ser.). 402p. (Orig.). 1986. pap. 21.95 o.s.i. (ISBN 0-943518-66-0). MIS Press.

DBASE III Plus Programmer's Reference Guide. Alan Simpson. (Ready Reference Ser.). 1035p. (Orig.). 1987. 29.95 o.p. (ISBN 0-89588-382-1); pap. 26.95 o.p. (ISBN 0-89588-508-5). Sybex.

DBASE III Plus Trail Guide. H. Dickler. 1986. pap. text ed. 29.95 o.p. (ISBN 0-07-912709-6). McGraw.

DBASE III Trail Guide. Howard Dickler. 350p. 1985. pap. 29.95 incl. disk o.p. (ISBN 0-912677-56-2). Tate Pub.

dBASE Language Handbook. Ed. by David M. Kalman. (Lance A. Leventhal Data Base Advisor Ser.). Date not set. price not set o.p. Slawson Comm.

DC-AC Laboratory Manual. Thomas C. Power. Ed. by Irving L. Kosow. (Electronic Technology Ser.). 1969. pap. text ed. 25.00 o.p. (ISBN 0-13-197129-8). P-H.

DC Motors, Speed Controls, Servo Systems: An Engineering Handbook. 3rd exp. ed. Electro-Craft Corp. Staff. LC 76-56647. 504p. 1977. 135.00 o.p. (ISBN 0-08-021714-1); pap. 135.00 o.p. (ISBN 0-08-021715-X). Pergamon.

De Basil's Ballets Russes. Katherine S. Walker. LC 82-16339. 317p. 1983. 19.95 o.s.i. (ISBN 0-689-11365-X, Atheneum). Macmillan.

De Baumugne. Jean Giono. (Coll. Soleil). 1957. 12.25 o.p. (ISBN 0-685-11608-5). French & Eur.

De Baumugnes: Livre des Conduite du Metteur en Scene (Indications et Dialogues) Jean Giono. (Illus.). 172p. 1961. 30.00 o.p. (ISBN 0-686-53954-0). French & Eur.

De Canibus: Dog & Hound in Antiquity. R. H. Merlen. (Illus.). 5.95 o.p. (ISBN 0-85131-054-0, NL51, Pub. by J A Allen U K). S R Smith Sporting Bks.

De Cive or the Citizen. Thomas Hobbes. Ed. by Sterling P. Lamprecht. LC 82-11829. 211p. 1982. Repr. of 1949 ed. lib. bdg. 35.00x o.p. (ISBN 0-313-23659-3, HODE). Greenwood.

De Duabus Animabus see De Utilitate Credendi.

De Instructione Puerorum of William of Tournai. Ed. by James A. Corbett. (Text & Studies Ser). pap. 8.00x o.p. (ISBN 0-268-00075-1). U of Notre Dame Pr.

De la Perfectibilite de l'Espece Humaine. Benjamin Constant. 1967. 7.95 o.p. (ISBN 0-686-54608-3). French & Eur.

De L'Allegorie see Versuch einer Allegorie.

De Minimis Concentrations of Radionuclides in Solid Wastes (AIF-NESP-016) Nuclear Safety Associates Staff. (National Environmental Studies Project: NESP Reports). 92p. 1978. 45.00 o.p. (ISBN 0-318-13567-1); NESP sponsors 15.00 o.p. (ISBN 0-318-13568-X). US Coun Energy Awareness.

De Perfectione Ivstitiae Hominis, De Gestis Pelagii, De Gratia Christi et De Peccato Originali Liber Duo. Aurelius Augustinus. (Corpus Scriptorum Ecclesiasticorum Latinorum Ser: Vol. 42). Repr. of 1902 ed. 50.00 o.p. (ISBN 0-384-02495-5). Johnson Repr.

De Profundis. Oscar Wilde. 1976. pap. 1.95 o.p. (ISBN 0-380-00701-0, 29793, Bard). Avon.

De Profundis. Oscar Wilde. 1960. Philos Lib.

De Re Aedificatoria. Leon B. Alberti. (Documents of Art & Architectural History Series 2: Vol. 1). 420p. (Lat.). Date not set. 45.00x o.s.i. (ISBN 0-89371-201-9). Broude Intl Edns.

De Republica Anglorum: A Discourse on the Commonwealth of England. Thomas Smith. (Development of Industrial Society Ser.). 264p. 1972. Repr. of 1906 ed. 27.50x o.p. (ISBN 0-7165-1795-7, BBA 03068, Pub. by Irish Academic Pr). Biblio Dist.

De Sade's Quantitative Moral Universe: Of Irony, Rhetoric & Boredom. Roberta J. Hackel. (De Proprietatibus Litterarum Series Practica: No. 95). 101p. (Orig.). 1976. pap. text ed. 13.20x o.p. (ISBN 90-2793-294-8). Mouton.

De Utilitate Credendi, Pt. 1. Aurelius Augustinus. Bd. with De Duabus Animabus; Contra Fortunatem; Contra Adimantum. (Corpus Scriptorum Ecclesiasticorum Latinorum Ser: Vol. 25). Repr. of 1891 ed. 50.00 o.p. (ISBN 0-384-02364-9). Johnson Repr.

De Witt's War. Hans Koning. (International Crime Ser.). 1984. pap. 2.95 o.p. (ISBN 0-394-72278-7). Pantheon.

Deacon in the Church. Edward P. Echlin. LC 75-158571. 1971. 4.95 o.p. (ISBN 0-8189-0213-2). Alba.

Dead Are Discreet. Arthur Lyons. LC 83-103. 224p. 1983. pap. 3.95 o.p. (ISBN 0-03-060393-5). H Holt & Co.

Dead Cert. Dick Francis. Ed. by J. Barzun & W. H. Taylor. LC 81-47383. (Crime Fiction 1950-1975 Ser.). 220p. 1983. lib. bdg. 18.00 o.p. (ISBN 0-8240-4991-8). Garland Pub.

Dead Cities & Forgotten Tribes. Gordon Cooper. 1952. (ISBN 0-8022-0297-7). Philos Lib.

Dead Faces Laughing. David Delman. LC 86-29282. (Crime Club Ser.). 192p. 1987. 12.95 o.p. (ISBN 0-385-24200-X). Doubleday.

Dead for a Ducat. Laurence Payne. LC 85-29312. (Crime Club Ser.). 192p. 1986. 12.95 o.p. (ISBN 0-385-23499-6). Doubleday.

Dead Giveaway. Simon Brett. (Charles Paris Mystery Ser.). 169p. 1986. 13.95 o.p. (ISBN 0-684-18517-2, ScribT). Scribner.

Dead Giveaway. Simon Brett. (Nightingale Ser.). 237p. 1987. pap. 10.95x o.p. (ISBN 0-8161-4218-1, Large Print Bks). G K Hall.

Dead Languages: Selected Poems, 1946-1984. Tamura Ryuichi. Tr. by Christopher Drake from Japanese. LC 84-12621. (Asian Poetry in Translation: Japan: No. 5). 308p. (Orig.). 1984. pap. 14.95 o.p. (ISBN 0-295-96359-X). U of Wash Pr.

Dead Liberty. Catherine Aird. LC 86-16753. (Crime Club Ser.). 192p. 1987. 12.95 o.s.i. (ISBN 0-385-23554-2). Doubleday.

Dead Low Tide. John D. MacDonald. Ed. by J. Barzun & W. H. Taylor. LC 81-47338. (Crime Fiction 1950-1975 Ser.). 160p. 1983. lib. bdg. 18.00 o.p. (ISBN 0-8240-4986-1). Garland Pub.

Dead Man's Cache. M. Paul White. 304p. 1984. pap. 2.95 o.p. (ISBN 0-380-86017-1, 86017). Avon.

Dead Man's Flower. Constance Christopher. 1988. pap. 3.50 o.p. (ISBN 0-7701-0957-8). PaperJacks US.

Dead Man's Mooring. Bill Knox. LC 87-17777. (Crime Club Ser.). 192p. 1988. pap. 12.95 o.p. (ISBN 0-385-24320-0). Doubleday.

Dead Man's Ransom. Ellis Peters. Ed. by Jennifer Williams. LC 84-22668. 224p. 1985. Repr. of 1984 ed. 13.95 o.p. (ISBN 0-688-04194-9). Morrow.

Dead Meat: A Brady Coyne Mystery. William G. Tapply. 1987. 14.95 o.p. (ISBN 0-684-18682-9). Scribner.

Dead of Winter. William H. Hallahan. 1977. pap. 1.75 o.p. (ISBN 0-380-01692-3, 24216-8). Avon.

Dead on Arrival: An Inspector Luker Thanet Mystery. Dorothy Simpson. 208p. 1987. 14.95 o.p. (ISBN 0-684-18732-9). Scribner.

Dead Reckoning. C. Northcote Parkinson. 1978. 10.95 o.p. (ISBN 0-395-27115-0). HM.

Dead Ringer. Arthur Lyons. LC 83-104. 240p. 1983. pap. 3.95 o.p. (ISBN 0-03-060396-X). H Holt & Co.

Dead Ringer. Roger Ormerod. 192p. 1986. 13.95 o.s.i. (ISBN 0-684-18587-3). Scribner.

Dead Romantic. Simon Brett. 176p. 1986. 13.95 o.s.i. (ISBN 0-684-18466-4). Scribner.

Dead Romantic. Simon Brett. (Nightingale Ser.). 289p. 1986. pap. 11.95 o.p. (ISBN 0-8161-4135-5, Large Print Bks). G K Hall.

Dead Runner. Frank Ross. LC 76-44499. 1977. 8.95 o.p. (ISBN 0-689-10774-9, Atheneum). Macmillan.

Dead Skip. Joe Gores. 1981. pap. 2.25 o.s.i. (ISBN 0-345-29206-5). Ballantine.

Dead Solid Perfect. Dan Jenkins. LC 74-81235. 320p. 1974. 7.95 o.p. (ISBN 0-689-10620-3, Atheneum). Macmillan.

Dead to Rights. Kenn Davis. 224p. 1981. pap. 2.25 o.p. (ISBN 0-380-78295-2, 78295). Avon.

Dead Towns & Living Men. Woolley. (Illus.). 220p. 1956. (ISBN 0-8022-1933-0). Philos Lib.

Deadlier Odds. Ed. by Richard Peyton. (Lythway Ser.). 296p. 1988. lib. bdg. 19.50x o.p. (ISBN 0-7451-0688-9, Pub. by Chivers Pr UK). G K Hall.

Deadline at Dawn. Cornell Woolrich. 224p. 1983. pap. 2.25 o.s.i. (ISBN 0-345-30653-8). Ballantine.

Deadline for a Critic, No. 9. William X. Kienzle. 288p. 1987. 14.95 o.p. (ISBN 0-8362-6123-2). Andrews & McMeel.

Deadly Arts. Marcia Muller & Bill Pronzini. 308p. 1985. 15.95 o.p. (ISBN 0-87795-688-X, Arbor Hse). Morrow.

Deadly Business: Sam Cummings, Interarms, & the Arms Trade. Patrick Brogan & Albert Zarca. LC 83-4044. 384p. 1983. 17.45 o.p. (ISBN 0-393-01766-4). Norton.

Deadly Communion. Owen Brookes. LC 83-22832. 272p. 1984. 14.95 o.p. (ISBN 0-03-062366-9). H Holt & Co.

Deadly Design. Linda A. Cooney. (Moonstone Novels Ser.: No. 1). 160p. (Orig.). (gr. 5 up). 1985. pap. 2.25 o.p. (ISBN 0-671-50782-6). Archway.

Deadly Dilemma. John A. Saginario. 187p. 1984. 10.95 o.p. (ISBN 0-533-05589-X). Vantage.

Deadly Dream. Theodore S. Drachman. 224p. 1982. 9.95 o.p. (ISBN 0-8397-1900-0). Eriksson.

Deadly Inheritance. Fionnuala Reeves. 224p. 1983. pap. 3.50 o.p. (ISBN 0-380-84129-0, 84129-0). Avon.

Deadly Litter. James White. 1981. pap. 2.25 o.s.i. (ISBN 0-345-29640-0, Del Rey). Ballantine.

Deadly Medicine: Doctors & True Crime. Arthur Kent. LC 74-20210. Orig. Title: Death Doctors. 237p. 1975. 8.50 o.s.i. (ISBN 0-8008-2129-7). Taplinger.

Deadly Messiah. David Hill & Albert Hill. 1977. pap. 1.95 o.p. (ISBN 0-380-00969-2, 32466). Avon.

Deadly Messiah. David C. Hill & Albert F. Hill. LC 76-15036. 1976. 8.95 o.p. (ISBN 0-689-10746-3, Atheneum). Macmillan.

Deadly Nightshade: Seventeen Strange Tales of the Dark. Ed. by Peter Haining. LC 77-92767. 1978. 8.50 o.s.i. (ISBN 0-8008-2123-8). Taplinger.

Deadly Odds: Crime & Mystery Stories of The Turf. (Lythway Ser.). 1987. lib. bdg. 17.50x o.p. (ISBN 0-7451-0593-9, Pub. by Chivers Pr UK). G K Hall.

Deadly Prey. Ralph Hayes. (Hunter Ser). (Orig.). 1975. pap. 1.25 o.p. (ISBN 0-685-53130-9, LB277ZK, Pub. by Leisure Bks CT). Dorchester Pub Co.

Deadly Sickness. John Penn. (Inspector Thorne-Sergeant Abbot Mystery Ser.). 196p. 1985. 13.95 o.s.i. (ISBN 0-684-18464-8, ScribT). Scribner.

Deaf Adult Speaks Out. 2nd, rev. ed. Leo M. Jacobs. LC 80-83505. xiv, 200p. 1981. 10.95 o.p. (ISBN 0-913580-63-5); pap. 9.50 o.p. (ISBN 0-913580-71-6). Gallaudet Univ Pr.

Deaf & Their Problems. Kenneth W. Hodgson. 384p. 1954. (ISBN 0-8022-0732-4). Philos Lib.

Deaf-Blind Baby: A Programme of Care. P. Freeman. (Illus.). 1985. pap. 20.00x o.p. (ISBN 0-317-40537-3). E J Brill USA.

Deaf-Blind Children & Their Education: Proceedings of the International Conference, St. Michielsgestel, The Netherlands, Aug. 25-29, 1968. Intro. by J. Van Eijndhover. (Modern Approaches to the Diagnosis & Instruction of Multi-Handicapped Children Ser.: Vol. 2). 150p. 1971. text ed. 16.00 o.p. (ISBN 90-237-4102-1, Pub. by Swets & Zeitlinger Netherlands). CJ Hogrefe Pubs.

Deaf Like Me. James P. Spradley & Thomas S. Spradley. 1978. 16.45 o.p. (ISBN 0-394-42825-0). Random.

Deafness. 4th ed. John Ballantyne. LC 77-3104. (Illus.). 1984. pap. text ed. 20.00 o.p. (ISBN 0-443-02930-X). Churchill.

Deafness & Public Responsibility. Peter Gregory. 56p. 1964. pap. text ed. 3.75x o.p. (ISBN 0-686-70845-8, Pub. by Bedford England). Gower Pub Co.

Deafness in the Adult: What a Hearing Loss Means & What Can Be Done to Help. Winifred Brinson. 192p. (Orig.). 1986. pap. 8.99 o.p. (ISBN 0-7225-1251-1, Pub. by Thorsons (England)). Sterling.

Deafness, Mutism, & Mental Deficiency in Children. Minski. 96p. 1958. (ISBN 0-8022-1124-0). Philos Lib.

Dealer Take All. Cole Richard. (Lythway Ser.). 1987. lib. bdg. 16.50x o.p. (ISBN 0-7451-0611-0, Pub. by Chivers Pr UK). G K Hall.

Dealer's Choice. Adrienne Palmer. 1978. pap. 1.75 o.p. (ISBN 0-505-51323-4, Pub. by Tower Bks). Dorchester Pub Co.

Dealers, Critics, & Collectors or Modern Painting: Aspects of the Parisian Art Market Between 1910 & 1930. Malcolm Gee. LC 79-57508. (Outstanding Dissertations in the Fine Arts Ser.: No.5). 570p. 1981. lib. bdg. 67.00 o.p. (ISBN 0-8240-3931-9). Garland Pub.

Dealers in Books: A Directory of Dealers in Secondhand & Antiquarian Books in the British Isles, 1984-1986. 11th ed. Compiled by Sheppard Press, Ltd. Staff. 474p. 1984. 21.00 o.p. (ISBN 0-900661-32-1, Pub. by Sheppard England). Seven Hills Bk Dists.

Dealing with Data. A. J. Lyon. LC 76-92111. 1970. text ed. 105.00 o.p. (ISBN 0-08-006398-5); pap. text ed. 17.00 o.p. (ISBN 0-08-006397-7). Pergamon.

Dealing with Doublemindedness. William E. Hulme. LC 82-47745. 128p. (Orig.). 1982. pap. 5.72i o.p. (ISBN 0-06-064079-0, RD/412). HarpR.

Dealing with Emergencies. Ed. by Jean Robinson & Barbara McVan. LC 80-11450. (Nursing Photobook). (Illus.). 160p. 1980. text ed. 17.95 o.p. (ISBN 0-916730-20-4). Springhouse Pub.

Dean Acheson. Gaddis Smith. Ed. by Robert H. Ferrel. LC 62-20139. (American Secretaries of State & Their Diplomacy Ser.). (Illus.). xvi, 473p. 1972. lib. bdg. 25.00x o.p. (ISBN 0-8154-0414-X). Cooper Sq.

Dean's Big Book of Fairy Stories. (Illus.). (ps-1). 6.98 o.s.i. (ISBN 0-517-43884-4). Outlet Bk Co.

Dean's Pop-up Book of Animals. (Pop-Ups Bks.). (Illus.). (ps-1). 1.98 o.s.i. (ISBN 0-517-43890-9). Outlet Bk Co.

Dear Cherry: Questions & Answers on Eating Disorders. Cherry B. O'Neill. LC 85-4127. 162p. 1985. 11.95 o.p. (ISBN 0-8264-0357-3). Continuum.

Dear Daughter. Denise George. LC 85-15145. 1985. 6.95 o.p. (ISBN 0-8054-5663-5). Broadman.

Dear, Dear Brenda: The Love Letters of Henry Miller to Brenda Venus. Brenda Venus & Henry Miller. Ed. by Gerald S. Sindell. LC 85-15424. (Illus.). 192p. 1986. 15.95 o.p. (ISBN 0-688-02816-0). Morrow.

Dear Diary. Jeanne Betancourt. (Illus.). 100p. (gr. 6-8). 1983. pap. 1.95 o.p. (ISBN 0-380-82057-9, 89501-3, Flare). Avon.

Dear Dragon: And Other Useful Letter Forms for Young Ladies & Gentlemen Engaged in Everyday Correspondence. Sesyle Joslin & Irene Haas. LC 62-17041. (Illus.). (gr. k up). 1962. 4.50 o.p. (ISBN 0-15-223052-1, HJ). HarBraceJ.

Dear Father in Heaven. rev. ed. R. Schlesselman & L. Ahrens. (Illus.). (gr. 10-12). 1977. pap. 1.25 o.p. (ISBN 0-570-03469-8, 56-1301). Concordia.

Dear Friend: Heart-to-Heart Talks with God. Julie A. Stine. LC 78-52199. 1978. pap. 3.95 o.p. (ISBN 0-8066-1669-5, 10-1845, Augsburg). Augsburg Fortress.

Dear George: Advice & Answers from America's Leading Expert on Everything from A to B. George Burns. (General Ser.). 221p. 1986. lib. bdg. 13.95 o.p. (ISBN 0-8161-4072-3, Large Print Bks). G K Hall.

Dear George: Advice & Answers from America's Leading Expert on Everything from A to B. George Burns. (Illus.). 1986. pap. 5.95 o.p. (ISBN 0-399-51274-8, Perigee). Putnam Pub Group.

Dear God, Pourquoi? Why Did You Born Me in Texas. John H. Hill. LC 84-91310. 167p. 1985. 10.95 o.p. (ISBN 0-533-06400-7). Vantage.

Dear Grace: A Romance of History. Margaret Gillett. (Illus.). 224p. 1986. 24.95 o.p. (ISBN 0-920792-58-8). Eden Pr.

Dear Heavenly Father: Letters from an Adopted Son. T. T. Martin. 1978. 4.50 o.p. (ISBN 0-682-49049-0). Exposition-Phoenix.

Dear Hildegarde. Bernard Waber. (Illus.). (gr. 3 up). 1980. 4.95 o.p. (ISBN 0-395-29745-1). HM.

Dear Miss Liberty. Ed. by Lynne Bundesen. 96p. (Orig.). 1986. pap. 7.95 o.p. (ISBN 0-87905-258-9, Peregrine Smith). Gibbs Smith Pub.

Dear Mr. Capote. Gordon Lish. LC 82-15543. 264p. 1983. 15.95 o.s.i. (ISBN 0-03-061477-5). H Holt & Co.

Dear Mr. Capote. Gordon Lish. (Signature Editions Ser.). 256p. 1986. pap. 5.95 o.p. (ISBN 0-684-18675-6). Scribner.

Dear Mr. Fantasy: Diary of a Decade. Ethan A. Russell. 1986. pap. 14.45 o.p. (ISBN 0-395-39585-2). HM.

Dear Mr. Fantasy: Diary of a Decade, Our Time & Rock & Roll. Ethan A. Russell. LC 85-10890. (Illus.). 256p. 1985. 29.45 o.p. (ISBN 0-395-34421-2). HM.

Dear Mr. President. J. C. Weithaus. 1977. 4.50 o.p. (ISBN 0-682-48945-X). Exposition-Phoenix.

Dear Mom & Dad: Parents & the Preschooler. Barbara J. Taylor. LC 78-5121. (Illus.). 1978. pap. 7.95 o.p. (ISBN 0-8425-1231-4). Brigham.

Dear Peter Pan. Catherine Haill. (Illus.). 64p. 1984. 7.95 o.p. (ISBN 0-905209-51-6, Pub. by Victoria & Albert Mus UK). Faber & Faber.

Dear Phoebe. Sue Alexander. LC 83-23856. (Illus.). 32p. (ps-3). 1984. 12.95 o.p. (ISBN 0-316-03132-1). Little.

Dear Rat. Julia Cunningham. (Illus.). 130p. (gr. 2-5). 1977. pap. 1.95 o.p. (ISBN 0-380-00908-0, 58644-4, Camelot). Avon.

Dear Sixty Minutes. CBS, Inc. Staff & Kathleen Fury. 256p. (Orig.). 1985. pap. 4.95 o.s.i. (ISBN 0-671-50753-2, Fireside). S&S.

Dear Worried Brown Eyes. Rosemary Ratcliff. 1969. 10.75 o.p. (ISBN 0-08-007041-8). Pergamon.

Dearest Debbie. Dale E. Rogers. 1966. pap. 2.95 o.s.i. (ISBN 0-515-09028-X). Jove Pubns.

Dearest Madame: Handmade, Inexpensive Ways to Make a House a Home. Irma Hunt. 1978. text ed. 12.95 o.p. (ISBN 0-07-031306-7). McGraw.

Dearest Prickles: The Story of a Hedgehog Family. Walter Poduschka & Christl Poduschka. LC 72-2182. (Illus.). 128p. 1972. 6.50 o.s.i. (ISBN 0-8008-2124-6). Taplinger.

Dearly Beloved: A Theme & Variations. Anne M. Lindbergh. LC 62-13520. (Helen & Kurt Wolff Bk.). 1962. 7.95 o.s.i. (ISBN 0-15-124070-1). HarBraceJ.

Death among Strangers. Deidre S. Laiken. 288p. 1987. 17.95 o.p. (ISBN 0-02-567400-5). Macmillan.

Death & Dying, Vol. 3 (Incl. 1987 Supplement) Ed. by E. Goldstein. 1988. 15.00 o.p. (ISBN 0-89777-091-9). Soc Issues.

Death & Dying: Attitudes of Patient & Doctor, Vol. 5. Group for the Advancement of Psychiatry Staff. LC 65-28440. (Symposium: No. 11). 1965. pap. 7.50 o.p. (ISBN 0-87630-366-1, Pub. by GAP). Brunner-Mazel.

Death & Dying: The Tibetan Tradition. Glen H. Mullin. 288p. 1986. pap. 12.95 o.p. (ISBN 1-85063-024-0). Routledge Chapman & Hall.

Death & Life. Jinni E. Davis. 64p. 1986. (ISBN 0-8062-2585-8). Carlton.

Death & Life in the New Testament: The Teaching of Jesus & Paul. Xavier Leon-Dufour. Tr. by Terrance Prendergast. LC 82-47749. 288p. 1984. 16.30 o.p. (ISBN 0-06-065241-1). HarpR.

Death & Society: A Book of Readings & Sources. Ed. by James P. Carse & Arlene B. Dallery. 1977. pap. text ed. 8.75 o.p. (ISBN 0-15-517211-5, HC). HarBraceJ.

Death & the Dutiful Daughter. Anne Morice. 265p. 1986. pap. 10.95x o.p. (ISBN 0-8161-3866-4, Large Print Bks). G K Hall.

Death & the Good Life. Richard Hugo. 224p. 1982. pap. 2.50 o.p. (ISBN 0-380-59840-X, 59840-X). Avon.

Death & the King's Horseman: A Play. Wole Soyinka. 1976. 6.95x o.p. (ISBN 0-393-04422-X); pap. 4.95 o.p. (ISBN 0-393-04429-7). Norton.

Death & the Magician. Raymund FitzSimons. LC 80-21071. 1981. 10.95 o.p. (ISBN 0-689-11122-3, Atheneum). Macmillan.

Death & the Princess. Robert Barnard. 192p. 1982. 10.95 o.s.i. (ISBN 0-684-17759-5, ScribT). Scribner.

Death & the Supreme Court. Barrett Prettyman, Jr. LC 61-12348. 1968. pap. 2.95 o.p. (ISBN 0-15-625235-X, Harv). HarBraceJ.

Death As a Fact of Life. David Hendin. 1973. 16.95 o.p. (ISBN 0-393-08540-6). Norton.

Death at an Early Age: The Destruction of the Hearts & Minds of Negro Children in the Boston Public Schools. Jonathan Kozol. 1967. 9.95 o.p. (ISBN 0-395-07868-7). HM.

Death at Buffalo Creek. Tom Nugent. (Illus.). 192p. 1973. 5.95 o.p. (ISBN 0-393-05482-9). Norton.

Death at Yew Corner. Richard Forrest. (Suspense Novel Ser.). 228p. 1981. 10.95 o.s.i. (ISBN 0-03-053386-4). H Holt & Co.

Death Be Not Proud. John Gunther. LC 53-5344. 1953. 5.95 o.s.i. (ISBN 0-394-60469-5). Modern Lib.

Death Before Dishonor. Kevin D. Randle. 1987. pap. 3.50 o.p. (ISBN 0-380-75282-4). Avon.

Death Blade. Peg Case. 1988. pap. 3.95 o.p. (ISBN 0-7701-0900-4). PaperJacks US.

Death, Burial & the Individual in Early Modern England. Clare Gittings. 224p. 1984. 34.50 o.p. (ISBN 0-7099-1167-X, Pub. by Croom Helm Ltd). Routledge Chapman & Hall.

Death by Analysis. Gillian Slovo. LC 87-26129. 192p. 1988. pap. 12.95 o.p. (ISBN 0-385-24327-8). Doubleday.

Death by Bread Alone: Texts & Reflections on Religious Experience. Dorothee Soelle. Tr. by David L. Scheidt from Ger. LC 77-78643. 168p. 1978. 2.00 o.p. (ISBN 0-8006-0514-4, 1-514, Fortress). Augsburg Fortress.

Death by Decision: The Medical, Moral, & Legal Dilemmas of Euthanasia. Jerry B. Wilson. LC 74-34482. 1975. 7.50 o.s.i. (ISBN 0-664-20729-4, Westminster). Westminster John Knox.

Death by Hoax. Lionel Black. 1978. pap. 1.75 o.p. (ISBN 0-380-41376-0, 41376-0). Avon.

Death by Sheer Torture. Robert Barnard. 192p. 1982. 10.95 o.s.i. (ISBN 0-684-17437-5, ScribT). Scribner.

Death Can Be Beautiful. Alfred Hitchcock. 1982. pap. 2.95 o.p. (ISBN 0-440-11755-0). Dell.

Death Chants. Craig K. Strete. LC 87-33143. (Science Fiction Ser.). 192p. 1988. 12.95 o.p. (ISBN 0-385-23353-1). Doubleday.

Death Comes Dancing: Celebrating Life with Bhagwan Shree Rajneesh. Ma Satya Bharti. 200p. 1981. pap. 9.95 o.p. (ISBN 0-7100-0705-1). Routledge Chapman & Hall.

Death Comes Home. Simon Stephens. 116p. (Orig.). 1973. pap. 2.50 o.p. (ISBN 0-8192-1137-0). Morehouse Pub.

Death Dance. Peter McCurtin. (Sundance Ser.: No. 27). 1979. pap. 1.75 o.p. (ISBN 0-8439-0669-3, Pub. by Leisure Bks CT). Dorchester Pub Co.

Death Doctors see Deadly Medicine: Doctors & True Crime.

Death Drop. B. M. Gill. 240p. 1980. 8.95 o.s.i. (ISBN 0-684-16464-7, ScribT). Scribner.

Death, Dying, & the Biological Revolution: Our Last Quest for Responsibility. Robert M. Veatch. LC 75-43337. 1976. 32.00x o.p. (ISBN 0-300-01949-1); pap. 11.95x o.p. (ISBN 0-300-02290-5). Yale U Pr.

Death-Dying, 1985 Annual. Ed. by Bruno Leone et al. (Opposing Viewpoints SOURCES Ser.). 115p. 1985. pap. text ed. 9.95 o.p. (ISBN 0-89908-511-3). Greenhaven.

Death-Dying, 1986 Annual. Ed. by Bruno Leone et al. (Opposing Viewpoints SOURCES Ser.). 100p. 1986. pap. text ed. 9.95 o.p. (ISBN 0-89908-520-2). Greenhaven.

Death Education. James M. Eddy & Wesley F. Alles. LC 82-2122. (Illus.). 383p. 1982. pap. text ed. 21.95 o.p. (ISBN 0-8016-1497-X). Mosby.

Death Education: A Concern for the Living. A. Barbara Gibson et al. LC 81-86311. (Fastback Ser.: No. 173). 50p. (Orig.). 1982. pap. 0.90 o.p. (ISBN 0-87367-173-2). Phi Delta Kappa.

Death Education: An Annotated Resource Guide. Hannelore Wass et al. LC 79-27707. (Death Education, Aging, & Health Care Ser.). 303p. 1980. text ed. 34.95 o.p. (ISBN 0-89116-170-8). Hemisphere Pub.

Death "En Voyage" Richard Grayson. 296p. 1988. lib. bdg. 22.95x o.s.i. (ISBN 0-7451-0782-6, Pub. by Chivers Pr UK). G K Hall.

Death Games. Dinah Brooke. LC 75-37524. 180p. 1976. 6.95 o.p. (ISBN 0-15-124093-0). HarBraceJ.

Death Has Deep Roots. Michael Gilbert. (Black Dagger Crime Ser.). 256p. 1987. text ed. 14.95x o.p. (ISBN 0-86220-705-3, Pub. by Firecrest Pub Ltd). Prescott Pr Nh.

Death in a Bowl. Raoul Whitfield. LC 85-19237. (Quill Mysterious Classic Ser.). 288p. 1986. pap. 3.95 o.p. (ISBN 0-688-02864-0, Quill). Morrow.

Death in Autumn: A Florentine Mystery. Magdalen Nabb. (Marshal Guarnaccia Mysteries Ser.). 160p. 1985. 12.95 o.s.i. (ISBN 0-684-18337-4, ScribT). Scribner.

Death in California. Joan Barthel. 1982. pap. 3.95 o.p. (ISBN 0-440-12038-1). Dell.

Death in Camera. Michael Underwood. (Nightingale-Lythway Ser.). 1985. pap. 10.95 o.p. (ISBN 0-8161-3811-7, Large Print Bks). G K Hall.

Death in China. William D. Montalbano & Carl Hiaasen. LC 83-45496. 320p. 1984. 14.95 o.p. (ISBN 0-689-11448-6, Atheneum). Macmillan.

Death in Delhi: Modern Hindi Short Stories. Ed. & tr. by Gordon Roadarmel. LC 74-187871. (Center for South & Southeast Asia Studies). 1973. 27.50x o.p. (ISBN 0-520-02220-3). U of Cal Pr.

Death in Fashion. Marion Babson. (Nightingale Ser.). 269p. 1987. pap. 12.95x o.p. (ISBN 0-8161-4214-9, Large Print Bks). G K Hall.

Death in Literature. Val S. Ferretti & David L. Scott. (Patterns in Literary Art Ser). (gr. 10-12). 1977. text ed. 9.80 o.p. (ISBN 0-07-020633-3). McGraw.

Death in Springtime: A Florentine Mystery. Magdalen Nabb. 168p. 1984. 11.95 o.s.i. (ISBN 0-684-18133-9, ScribT). Scribner.

Death in the Afternoon: America's Newspaper Giants Struggle for Survival. Peter Benjaminson. LC 84-14499. 200p. 1984. 14.95 o.p. (ISBN 0-8362-7955-7). Andrews & McMeel.

Death in the Family: A Self-Help Guide to Coping with Grief. McCarthy. 1988. pap. 8.95 o.s.i. (ISBN 0-88908-671-0, 9560). TAB Bks.

Death in the Life. Dorothy S. Davis. 208p. 1977. pap. 1.75 o.p. (ISBN 0-380-01747-4, 57372). Avon.

Death in the Morning. Sheila Radley. 1980. pap. 3.50 o.p. (ISBN 0-440-11785-2). Dell.

Death in Washington: The Murder of Orlando Letelier. Donald Freed & Fred S. Landis. LC 80-52434. 274p. 1980. 12.95 o.p. (ISBN 0-88208-123-3); pap. 7.95 o.p. (ISBN 0-88208-124-1). Chicago Review.

Death Is a Good Solution: The Convict Experience in Early Australia. A. W. Baker. LC 83-23556. (Scholar's Library). 223p. 1985. text ed. 37.50 o.p. (ISBN 0-7022-1685-2). U Of Queensland Pr.

Death Is a Red Rose. Dorothy Eden. (Black Dagger Crime Ser.). 200p. 1987. text ed. 13.95x o.p. (ISBN 0-86220-704-5, Pub. by Firecrest Pub Ltd). Prescott Pr Nh.

Death Is Relative. Edward Phillips. 224p. 1985. pap. 2.95 o.p. (ISBN 0-380-69867-6). Avon.

Death March: The Survivors of Bataan. Donald Knox. LC 81-47555. (Illus.). 412p. 1981. 19.95 o.s.i. (ISBN 0-15-124094-9). HarBraceJ.

Death Merchant: The Rise & Fall of Edwin P. Wilson. Joseph C. Goulden & Alexander W. Raffio. LC 84-5547. 453p. 1984. 17.45 o.p. (ISBN 0-671-49341-8). S&S.

Death Notebooks. Anne Sexton. LC 73-17311. 1974. 8.95 o.p. (ISBN 0-395-18281-6); pap. 3.45 o.p. (ISBN 0-395-18462-2). HM.

Death Notes. Ruth Rendell. 1981. 9.95 o.p. (ISBN 0-394-52078-5). Pantheon.

Death of a Christian: The Rite of Funerals. Richard Rutherford. (Studies in the Reformed Rites of the Catholic Church: Vol. 7). 1980. pap. 9.95 o.p. (ISBN 0-916134-40-7). Pueblo Pub Co.

Death of a Dancing Lady: A Sargent Bragg-Constable Morton Mystery. Ray Harrison. 256p. 1986. 13.95 o.s.i. (ISBN 0-684-18581-4). Scribner.

Death of a Hawker. Janwillem Van de Wetering. 1977. 6.95 o.p. (ISBN 0-395-25171-0). HM.

Death of a Hero. Jiri Frel. (Illus.). 80p. 1984. 16.00 o.p. (ISBN 0-89236-055-0); pap. 9.00 o.p. (ISBN 0-89236-056-9). J P Getty Trust.

Death of a Man. Lael T. Wertenbaker. LC 73-16889. 192p. 1974. pap. 8.95x o.p. (ISBN 0-8070-2763-4, BP482). Beacon Pr.

Death of a Marriage. Martin Ford. 128p. 1986. 8.75 o.p. (ISBN 0-8062-2708-7). Carlton.

Death of a Minor Poet. William Krasner. 192p. 1984. 12.95 o.s.i. (ISBN 0-684-18121-5, ScribT). Scribner.

Death of a President. William Manchester. 720p. 1985. pap. 10.95 o.p. (ISBN 0-87795-758-4, Arbor Hse). Morrow.

Death of a Revolutionary: The Last Days of Che Guevara. Richard L. Harris. LC 79-77405. (Illus.). 1970. 6.95 o.p. (ISBN 0-393-07445-5). Norton.

Death of a Salesman. Arthur Miller. 48p. (Orig.). 1988. pap. 9.95 o.p. (ISBN 1-55651-175-2); audiocassette tape incl. o.p. (ISBN 1-55651-176-0). Cram Cassettes.

Death of a Schoolboy. Hans Koning. LC 73-15430. (Helen & Kurt Wolff Bk). 1974. 6.95 o.p. (ISBN 0-15-124155-4). HarBraceJ.

Death of a Soldier see Heinemann Guided Readers.

Death of an Englishman. Magdalen Nabb. 176p. 1982. 10.95 o.s.i. (ISBN 0-684-17757-9, ScribT). Scribner.

Death of an Honourable Member. Ray Harrison. 160p. 1985. 11.95 o.p. (ISBN 0-684-18245-9). Scribner.

Death of Anton Weber. Hans Moldenhauer. LC 61-10610. (Illus.). 128p. 1962. (ISBN 0-8022-1133-X). Philos Lib.

Death of Dialogue & Beyond. Sanford Seltzer & Max L. Stackhouse. (Illus.). 1969. pap. 2.25 o.p. (ISBN 0-377-39021-6). Friendship Pr.

Death of God. Gabriel Vahanian. LC 61-9962. 1961. 6.95 o.p. (ISBN 0-8076-0144-6); pap. 2.95 o.p. (ISBN 0-8076-0360-0). Braziller.

Death of James Dean. Warren N. Beath. (Illus.). 224p. 1986. Repr. of 1986 ed. 15.95 o.s.i. (ISBN 0-394-55758-1). Grove.

Death of Man. J. Langmead Casserly. 1.00 o.p. (ISBN 0-8192-1014-5). Morehouse Pub.

Death of Men. Allan Massie. 256p. 1982. 10.95 o.p. (ISBN 0-395-31854-8). HM.

Death of the Detective. Mark Smith. 640p. 1977. pap. 2.25 o.p. (ISBN 0-380-00549-2, 58016-2, Bard). Avon.

Death of the Heart. Elizabeth Bowen. 320p. 1985. pap. 5.95 o.p. (ISBN 0-14-001690-2). Penguin.

Death of the Mayfly. LC 86-50151. (Amazing Stories Ser.: Bk. 6). 221p. (Orig.). 1986. pap. 2.95 o.p. (ISBN 0-88038-263-5). TSR Inc.

Death of the Prophet. Jason Leen. LC 79-18719. (Illus.). 1979. 11.95 o.p. (ISBN 0-87961-094-8); pap. 5.95 o.p. (ISBN 0-87961-093-X). Naturegraph.

Death of the Soul. William E. Barrett. LC 82-45317. 192p. 1986. 16.95 o.s.i. (ISBN 0-385-15965-X, Anchor Pr). Doubleday.

Death of Tragedy. George Steiner. 376p. 1963. 13.95 o.p. (ISBN 0-571-05467-6); pap. 8.95 o.p. (ISBN 0-571-05658-X). Faber & Faber.

Death on an Aisle. Richard Lockridge & Frances Lockridge. 1986. pap. 9.95 o.p. (ISBN 0-553-06512-2). Bantam.

Death On Call. Sandra Wilkinson. 256p. 1984. 12.95 o.p. (ISBN 0-396-08334-X). Dodd.

Death on Call. Sandra Wilkinson. 256p. 1985. pap. 2.95 o.p. (ISBN 0-931773-30-X). Critics Choice Paper.

Death on the Rocks: A Jacob Lomax Mystery. Michael Allegretto. 1987. 15.95 o.p. (ISBN 0-684-18758-2). Scribner.

Death Overcome: Towards a Convergence of Eastern & Western Views. Jung Y. Lee. LC 82-20192. 98p. (Orig.). 1983. lib. bdg. 23.00 o.p. (ISBN 0-8191-2901-1); pap. text ed. 9.00 o.p. (ISBN 0-8191-2902-X). U Pr of Amer.

Death Plays a Duet. Arthur L. Davies. 1977. 6.50 o.p. (ISBN 0-682-48810-0). Exposition-Phoenix.

Death Race. Barbara Siegel & Scott Siegel. (Orig.). 1986. pap. 2.50 o.p. (ISBN 0-345-33389-6, Pub. by Ballantine Trade). Ballantine.

Death Sails the Bay. John R. Feegel. 1978. pap. 1.95 o.p. (ISBN 0-380-01972-8, 38570). Avon.

Death Speaks Softly. Anthea Fraser. LC 86-32887. (Crime Club Ser.). 192p. 1987. 12.95 o.s.i. (ISBN 0-385-24147-X). Doubleday.

Death Sty: A Pig's Tale. Raymond Cousse. 1980. 9.50 o.p. (ISBN 0-394-50867-X, GP829). Grove.

Death Sty: A Pig's Tale. Raymond Cousse. LC 79-2349. Orig. Title: Strategie Pour Deux Jambons. 1980. pap. 5.95 o.p. (ISBN 0-394-17573-5, E747, Ever). Grove.

Death: The Riddle & the Mystery. Eberhard Jungel. LC 74-28021. 1975. 6.95 o.s.i. (ISBN 0-664-20821-5, Westminster). Westminster John Knox.

Death Turns Right. Joseph Mathewson. 176p. (Orig.). 1982. pap. 2.25 o.p. (ISBN 0-380-79210-9, 79210-9). Avon.

Death Under Par. Janice Law. 1981. 9.95 o.p. (ISBN 0-395-30227-7). HM.

Death Valley & the Amargosa. Richard E. Lingenfelter. 1988. pap. 16.95x o.p. (ISBN 0-520-06356-2). U of Cal Pr.

Death Valley: The Story Behind the Scenery. rev. ed. William D. Clark. LC 79-91050. (Illus.). 48p. 1980. 8.95 o.p. (ISBN 0-916122-37-9); pap. 4.50 o.p. (ISBN 0-916122-12-3). KC Pubns.

Death Wears a Red Hat. William X. Kienzle. 288p. 1981. pap. 3.50 o.p. (ISBN 0-553-26524-5). Bantam.

Death Whispers. Winston L. Foster. 304p. 1987. 14.95 o.p. (ISBN 0-8062-2919-5). Carlton.

Death Wish. Iceberg Slim. 1988. pap. 2.95 o.p. (ISBN 0-87067-824-8). Holloway.

Deathbringer. Dana Reed. 400p. (Orig.). 1985. pap. 3.75 o.p. (ISBN 0-8439-2246-X, Pub. by Leisure Bks CT). Dorchester Pub Co.

Deathgame. Franklin W. Dixon. (Hardy Boys Casefiles Ser.: No. 7). 160p. (Orig.). (YA) (gr. 7 up). 1987. pap. 2.75 o.p. (ISBN 0-671-62648-5). Archway.

Deathless Trumpeter & Other Stories about Young Heroes. A. Gaidar. 165p. 1975. 3.95 o.p. (ISBN 0-8285-1130-6, Pub. by Progress Pubs. USSR). Imported Pubns.

Death's Clenched Fist. James Sherburne. 204p. 1982. 10.95 o.p. (ISBN 0-395-31835-1). HM.

Death's Gray Angel. James Sherburne. 216p. 1981. 10.95 o.p. (ISBN 0-395-31265-5). HM.

Death's Midwives. Margareta Ekstrom. Tr. by Eva Claeson. LC 85-18774. (Ontario Review Press Translation Ser.). 149p. 1985. 17.95 o.p. (ISBN 0-86538-046-5); pap. 8.95 o.p. (ISBN 0-86538-047-3). Ontario Rev NJ.

Death's Pale Horse. James Sherburne. 1980. 8.95 o.p. (ISBN 0-395-29087-2). HM.

Deathstalk. Bruce Clark. 1981. pap. 1.75 o.p. (ISBN 0-8439-0897-1, Pub. by Leisure Bks CT). Dorchester Pub Co.

Debate about the Bible: Inerrancy Vs. Infallibility. Stephen T. Davis. LC 77-3457. 148p. 1977. pap. 6.95 o.s.i. (ISBN 0-664-24119-0, Westminster). Westminster John Knox.

Debate on Disarmament. Ed. by Michael Clarke & Marjorie Mowlam. 192p. (Orig.). 1982. pap. 8.95x o.p. (ISBN 0-7100-9269-5). Routledge Chapman & Hall.

Debates in the House of Commons in 1625. Great Britain, House of Commons Staff. Ed. by Samuel R. Gardiner. 1873. 27.00 o.p. (ISBN 0-384-19810-4). Johnson Repr.

Debates with Historians. Pieter Geyl. 250p. 1956. (ISBN 0-8022-0577-1). Philos Lib.

Debating American Government. Peter Woll. 1986. pap. text ed. write for info. o.p. (ISBN 0-673-39499-9). Scott F.

Debating: Applied Rhetorical Theory. Theodore F. Scheckels, Jr. LC 83-22172. (College Composition & Communication Ser.). 1984. text ed. 20.95 o.p. (ISBN 0-582-28387-6). Longman.

Debrett's Handbook of Australia & New Zealand. 2nd ed. 997p. 1984. 85.00 o.s.i. (ISBN 0-949137-00-6). Marquis.

Debrett's Peerage & Baronetage, 1985. 2800p. 1985. 125.00 o.s.i. (ISBN 0-333-37824-5, 030472). Marquis.

Debrett's Stately Homes of Britian. Sibylla J. Flower. 1985. pap. 14.95 o.s.i. (ISBN 0-03-002843-4, Owl Bks). H Holt & Co.

Debrett's Stately Homes of Great Britain. Compiled by Sybilla J. Flower. (Illus.). 240p. 1982. 24.95 o.s.i. (ISBN 0-03-061993-9). H Holt & Co.

Debrett's Texas Peerage. Hugh Best. (Illus.). 352p. 1983. 25.00 o.p. (ISBN 0-698-11244-X, Coward). Putnam Pub Group.

Debriefing. Robert Littell. 1981. pap. 2.75 o.p. (ISBN 0-440-11873-5). Dell.

Debs Magazine, Vols. 1-2. 1970. Repr. lib. bdg. 36.00x o.p. (ISBN 0-8371-9378-8, DM00). Greenwood.

Debschitz School: A Selectively Annotated Bibliography. Beate Ziegert. (Architecture Ser.: A 1492). 13p. 1985. 2.00 o.p. (ISBN 0-89028-622-1). Vance Biblios.

Debt & Danger: The World Financial Crisis. Harold Lever & Christopher Huhne. LC 86-70573. 1986. 16.95 o.p. (ISBN 0-87113-067-X). Atlantic Monthly.

Debt & Development in Latin America. Ed. by Kwan Kim & David Ruccio. LC 85-40598. 256p. 1985. text ed. 24.95x o.p. (ISBN 0-268-00855-8, 85-08558, Dist. by Har-Row). U of Notre Dame Pr.

Debt Collection Harassment: 1982 & 1986 Supplement. National Consumer Law Center Staff. LC 82-81235. 143p. 1982. pap. 53.00 o.p. (ISBN 0-943116-02-3). Nat Consumer Law.

Debt Collection Letters in Ten Languages. John Butterworth. LC 79-65006. 1979. 35.00 o.p. (ISBN 0-8144-5577-8). AMACOM.

Debtor-Creditor Law in a Nutshell. 2nd ed. David G. Epstein. LC 79-25091. (Nutshell Ser.). 324p. 1980. pap. text ed. 8.95 o.p. (ISBN 0-8299-2072-2). West Pub.

Debtors & Creditors Cases & Materials. 2nd ed. David G. Epstein & Jonathan M. Landers. LC 82-7088. (American Casebook Ser.). 725p. 1982. 21.95 o.p. (ISBN 0-314-66044-5); 1983 tchr's. manual avail. o.p. (ISBN 0-314-73913-0). West Pub.

Debugging C. Robert Ward. LC 86-61152. 350p. (Orig.). 1986. pap. 19.95 o.p. (ISBN 0-88022-261-1, 60). Que Corp.

Debunking the Genocide Myth. Paul Rassinier. LC 78-53090. 441p. 1978. 15.50o.p. (ISBN 0-911038-24-8, Dist by Inst Hist Rev); pap. 8.00 o.p. (ISBN 0-911038-58-2). Noontide.

Debut. Anita Brookner. 1981. 11.95 o.p. (ISBN 0-671-42626-5, Linden). S&S.

Debutantes. June F. Singer. 1983. pap. 4.75 o.p. (ISBN 0-380-83402-2, 83402-2). Avon.

DEC Microcomputer Directory: Hardware, Software & Peripherals. Kelly-Grimes Corporation Staff. LC 84-19523. (Kelly-Grimes Buyers Guide Ser.: 1-702). 351p. 1985. pap. 26.95 o.p. (ISBN 0-471-87822-7, Pub. by Wiley Pr). Wiley.

Decade of Creation: Acts-Facts-Impacts, Vol. 4. Morris & Rohrer. LC 80-67426. 320p. 1981. pap. 7.95 o.p. (ISBN 0-89051-069-5). Master Bks.

Decade of Decision. Michael Harrington. 1981. pap. 7.50 o.p. (ISBN 0-671-42808-X, Touchstone). S&S.

Decade of Dreams. Mary C. Evans. LC 82-83875. (Illus.). 160p. 1982. 12.95 o.s.i. (ISBN 0-87833-325-8); pap. 7.95 o.p. (ISBN 0-686-46034-0). Taylor Pub.

Decade of Reform: England in the Eighteen Thirties. Geoffrey Finlayson. LC 79-102943. 1970. pap. 3.95x o.p. (ISBN 0-393-09915-6). Norton.

Decade of Shocks: From Dallas to Watergate, 1963-1974. Tom Shachtman. 352p. 1983. 16.50 o.s.i. (ISBN 0-671-44252-X, Poseidon). PB.

Decadence (A Philosophical Inquiry) C. E. Joad. (ISBN 0-8022-0802-9). Philos Lib.

Decadent Imagination, Eighteen Eighty to Nineteen Hundred. Jean Pierrot. Tr. by Derek Coltman from Fr. LC 81-4828. viii, 310p. 1984. pap. text ed. 12.50 o.s.i. (ISBN 0-226-66823-1). U of Chicago Pr.

Decadents. Juzo Suzuki & Isaburo Oka. Tr. by John Bester. LC 69-16370. (Masterworks of Ukiyo-e Ser.). (Illus.). 1969. pap. 13.50 o.p. (ISBN 0-87011-098-5). Kodansha.

Decameron, 2 vols. in 1. Giovanni Boccaccio. 1953. 16.95x o.p. (ISBN 0-460-10845-X, Evman). Biblio Dist.

Decapitated Chicken & Other Stories. Horacio Quiroga. Tr. by Margaret S. Peden from Span. (Texas Pan American Ser). (Illus.). 213p. 1976. pap. 14.95 o.p. (ISBN 0-292-77514-8). U of Tex Pr.

Deceived Majority. Gordon Fellman. 350p. 1972. 9.95 o.p. (ISBN 0-87855-043-7). Transaction Pubs.

Deceived with Kindness: A Bloomsbury Childhood. Angelica Garnett. LC 84-19281. (Illus.). 192p. 1985. 14.95 o.p. (ISBN 0-15-124185-6). HarBraceJ.

Deceivers. Joanna Barnes. LC 74-122642. 1970. 6.95 o.p. (ISBN 0-87795-007-5, Arbor Hse). Morrow.

December Ultimatum. Michael Nicholson. LC 84-62279. 240p. 1985. 14.95 o.p. (ISBN 0-88186-075-1). Parkwest Pubns.

Decennial Census Data for Selected Health Occupations, United States, 1980. G. Gloria Kapantais. (DHHS Publication Ser.: No. PHS 86-1826). 59p. (Orig.). 1985. pap. 2.25 o.p. (ISBN 0-318-19976-9, S/N 017-022-00901-3). USGPO.

Decennial Cumulative Index 1941-1950 to United States Government Publications Monthly Catalog, 2 Vols. United States Superintendent of Documents. LC 77-84611. 1862p. 1972. Repr. of 1953 ed. 95.00x o.p. (ISBN 0-8103-3361-9). Gale.

Decentered Universe of Finnegans Wake: A Structuralist Analysis. Margot C. Norris. LC 76-25507. 160p. 1977. 12.00x o.p. (ISBN 0-8018-1820-6); pap. text ed. 5.95x o.p. (ISBN 0-8018-2148-7). Johns Hopkins.

Decentralization & Self-Government in Russia, 1830-1870. S. Frederick Starr. LC 73-173761. 424p. 1972. 42.00x o.p. (ISBN 0-691-03090-1); pap. 20.00 L.P.E. o.p. (ISBN 0-691-10008-X). Princeton U Pr.

Decentralization of Municipal Services: A Selected Bibliography. Jamie W. Coniglio. (Public Administration Ser.: P 1773). 5p. 1985. 2.00 o.p. (ISBN 0-89028-573-X). Vance Biblios.

Decentralized Company: Making the Most of Entrepreneurial Management. Robert E. Levinson. 192p. 1983. 16.95 o.p. (ISBN 0-8144-5674-X). AMACOM.

Decepticon Hijack. Marvel. (New Transformers Storybooks Ser.). 1985. pap. 1.95 o.p. (ISBN 0-517-55957-9). Crown.

Deception & Desire. Suzannah Davis. (Candlelight Ecstasy: No. 513). (Orig.). 1987. pap. 2.25 o.p. (ISBN 0-440-11754-2). Dell.

Deception Patrol. (Transformers Coloring & Activity Bks.). (Illus.). 48p. 1985. 0.99 o.p. (ISBN 0-517-55642-1). Crown.

Deception Poison. Judith B. Stamper. (Transformers Find Your Fate Junior Ser.: No. 6). (Orig.). (gr. 4 up). 1986. pap. 2.50 o.p. (ISBN 0-345-33073-0). Ballantine.

Deceptions. Judith Michaels. 500p. 1982. 15.95 o.s.i. (ISBN 0-671-42491-2, Poseidon). PB.

Decidable Theories: Buechi's Monadic Second Order Successor Arithmetic. D. Siefkes. LC 70-111900. (Lecture Notes in Mathematics Ser.: Vol. 120). 1970. pap. 10.70 o.p. (ISBN 0-387-04909-6). Springer-Verlag.

Deciding to Forego Life-Sustaining Treatment: A Report on the Ethical, Medical, & Legal Issues in Treatment Decisions. LC 83-600503. 568p. 1983. pap. 8.00 o.p. (ISBN 0-318-11774-6, S/N 040-000-00470-0). USGPO.

Deciduous Fruit Tree Cultivars for Tropical & Sub-Tropical Regions. Ed. by H. C. Ruck. 91p. 1975. pap. 9.70 o.p. (ISBN 0-85198-341-3). CAB Intl.

Decimation. Ranbir S. Sodhi. 192p. 1984. pap. 5.95 o.p. (ISBN 0-682-40206-0). Exposition-Phoenix.

Deciphering the Senses: The Expanding World of Human Perception. Robert Rivlin & Karen Gravelle. 320p. 1984. 15.50 o.p. (ISBN 0-671-49206-3). S&S.

Decision Analysis in Litigation. Thomas M. Stanton & W. Stuart Parsons. (Illus.). 89p. 1988. manual 35.00 o.p. (80663-1). PES Inc WI.

Decision & Estimation Theory. James L. Melsa & Davis L. Cohn. (Illus.). 1978. text ed. 47.95 o.p. (ISBN 0-07-041468-8). McGraw.

Decision at Burlington. Steve Dolan. 1978. 6.95 o.p. (ISBN 0-87839-034-0). North Star.

Decision Information. Ed. by Chris P. Tsokos & Robert M. Thrall. 1979. 63.50 o.p. (ISBN 0-12-702250-3). Acad Pr.

Decision-Making for Schools & Colleges. Dean F. Juniper. 324p. 1976. 53.00 o.p. (ISBN 0-08-019885-6); pap. 25.00 o.p. (ISBN 0-08-019884-8). Pergamon.

Decision Making in Administration: Text, Critical Incidents & Cases. Jim Gatza et al. 1979. pap. text ed. 13.95 o.p. (ISBN 0-7216-4056-7). SCP.

Decision Making in an Era of Fiscal Instability. Daniel L. Duke. LC 84-61198. (Fastback Ser.: No. 212). 50p. 1984. pap. 0.90 o.p. (ISBN 0-87367-212-7). Phi Delta Kappa.

Decision Making in Otolaryngology: Head & Neck Surgery. G. Richard Holt et al. 256p. 1983. 44.00 o.p. (ISBN 0-941158-09-8, D2250-6). Mosby.

Decision Making in the Church: A Biblical Model. Luke T. Johnson. LC 82-17675. 112p. 1983. pap. 1.95 o.p. (ISBN 0-8006-1694-4, Fortress). Augsburg Fortress.

Decision Making under Time Pressure: An Experimental Study of Stress Behavior in Business Management. Rolf Bronner. LC 81-47626. 208p. 1982. 25.00x o.p. (ISBN 0-669-04696-5). Lexington Bks.

Decision Modeling. Enabling Technologies Staff. (Decision Maker Series for Frame Work II). (Orig.). 1985. pap. 69.95 o.p. (ISBN 0-912677-76-7). Tate Pub.

Decision Models for Industrial Systems Engineers & Managers. Ed. by P. Adulbhan & M. T. Tabucanon. (Illus.). 467p. 1981. 115.00 o.p. (ISBN 0-08-027612-1). Pergamon.

Decision Models in Academic Administration. Ed. by Albert C. Heinlein. LC 74-11585. 135p. 1975. 9.50x o.p. (ISBN 0-87338-167-X, Pub. by Comp. Adm. Research Inst.). Kent St U Pr.

Decision Networks. N. A. Hastings & J. M. Mello. 196p. 1978. 76.00 o.p. (ISBN 0-471-99531-2, Pub. by Wiley-Interscience). Wiley.

Decision Processes in Visual Perception. D. Vickers. (Cognition & Perception Ser.). 1979. 76.00 o.p. (ISBN 0-12-721550-6). Acad Pr.

Decision Styles & Organizational Effectiveness. B. L. Maheshwari. 240p. 1980. text ed. 22.50x o.p. (ISBN 0-7069-1032-X, Pub. by Vikas India). Advent NY.

Decision Support Systems: A Bibliography, 1980-1894. Christine E. Thompson. (Public Administration Series Bibliography: P 1745). 1985. pap. 2.00 o.p. (ISBN 0-89028-525-X). Vance Biblios.

Decision to Divide Germany: American Foreign Policy in Transition. John H. Backer. LC 77-84614. x, 212p. 1978. 22.50 o.p. (ISBN 0-8223-0391-4). Duke.

Decision to Go to the Moon: Project Apollo & the National Interest. John M. Logsdon. LC 75-27414. xii, 188p. 1976. pap. text ed. 3.95x o.s.i. (ISBN 0-226-49175-7, P673, Phoen). U of Chicago Pr.

Decisions & Orders of the National Labor Relations Board: August 5, 1983 Through October 13, 1983, Vol. 267. 1380p. 1984. 25.00 o.p. (ISBN 0-318-21940-9, S/N 031-000-00249-4). USGPO.

Decisions & Orders of the National Labor Relations Board: December 29, 1982 Through August 4, 1983, Vol. 266. 1262p. 1984. 23.00 o.p. (ISBN 0-318-22762-2, S/N 031-000-00247-8). USGPO.

Decisions & Orders of the National Labor Relations Board, V 268: October 14, 1983 Through March 5, 1984. 1528p. 1985. 25.00 o.p. (ISBN 0-318-23099-2, S/N 031-000-00250-8). USGPO.

Decisions! Decisions! George A. Chauncey. LC 73-161841. (Christian Ethics for Modern Man Ser.). (Illus.). 128p. (Orig.). 1972. pap. 1.95 o.p. (ISBN 0-8042-9090-3, John Knox). Westminster John Knox.

Decisions, Decisions: Game Theory & You. Robert Bell & John Coplans. (Illus.). 160p. 1976. 7.95 o.p. (ISBN 0-393-01121-6). Norton.

Decisions, Decisions: Style in Writing. Mary E. Whitten. (Illus.). 1971. pap. text ed. 10.95 o.p. (ISBN 0-15-517260-3, HC). HarBraceJ.

Decisions in Marketing. Lawrence J. Ring et al. 1984. 36.95 o.p. (ISBN 0-256-02777-3). Irwin.

Decisions of the Federal Labor Relations Authority: April-August 1983, Vol. 12. 889p. 1984. 23.00 o.p. (ISBN 0-318-23101-8, 063-000-00023-0). USGPO.

Decisions of the Federal Labor Relations Authority: February 1 - May 31, 1984, Vol. 14. 964p. 1985. 23.00 o.p. (ISBN 0-318-23102-6, 063-000-00025-6). USGPO.

Decisions of the Federal Labor Relations Authority: January-March 1983, Vol. 11. 840p. 1984. 22.00 o.p. (ISBN 0-318-23100-X, 063-000-00022-1). USGPO.

Decisions of the Federal Labor Relations Authority: September 1, 1983 - January 31, 1984, Vol. 13. 856p. 1985. 22.00 o.p. (ISBN 0-318-23097-6, 063-000-00024-8). USGPO.

Decisive Battle. Nathaniel Harris. (Day that Made History Ser.). (gr. 6 up). 1988. 16.95 o.p. (ISBN 0-317-69586-X, Pub. by Batsford England). David & Charles.

Decisive Battles of the Civil War. Joseph B. Mitchell. 1981. pap. 2.50 o.p. (ISBN 0-449-30836-7, Prem). Fawcett.

Decker's Patterns of Exposition, No. 9. Randall E. Decker & Robert A. Schwegler. 1984. write for info. o.p. (ISBN 0-673-39206-6). Scott F.

Decker's Patterns of Exposition, No. 10. Randall E. Decker & Robert A. Schwegler. 1986. pap. text ed. write for info. o.p. (ISBN 0-673-39207-4). Scott F.

Declassified Documents Reference System: 1975-1985 Annual Collections. year 500.00 ea. o.p. (ISBN 0-8408-0328-1). Res Pubns CT.

Decline & Fail: The Ailing Nuclear Power Industry. Peter Stoler. (Illus.). 256p. 1985. 16.95 o.p. (ISBN 0-396-08527-X). Dodd.

Decline & Fall of the Roman Empire. Edward Gibbon. Abridged by Frank C. Bourne. 735p. 1963. pap. 4.25 o.p. (ISBN 0-440-31879-3, LE). Dell.

Decline & Rise of Europe: A Study in Recent History with Particular Emphasis on the Development of a European Consciousness. John A. Lukacs. LC 75-41503. 1977. Repr. of 1965 ed. lib. bdg. 22.50x o.p. (ISBN 0-8371-8702-8, LUDR). Greenwood.

Decline of Agrarian Democracy. Grant McConnell. LC 53-9387. 1969. pap. text ed. 4.95x o.s.i. (ISBN 0-689-70140-3, 150, Atheneum). Macmillan.

Decline of American Liberalism. Arthur A. Ekirch, Jr. LC 67-13171. 1967. pap. text ed. 5.95x o.p. (ISBN 0-689-70069-5, 111, Atheneum). Macmillan.

Decline of Arab Oil Revenues. Ed. by Abdel M. Farid. 224p. 1986. 39.00 o.p. (ISBN 0-7099-0589-0, Pub. by Croom Helm Ltd). Routledge Chapman & Hall.

Decline of Mechanism see Rise of the New Physics: Its Mathematical & Physical Theories.

Decline of Serfdom in Medieval England. R. H. Hilton. (Studies in Economic & Social History). 1969. pap. text ed. 9.95x o.p. (ISBN 0-333-10117-0). Humanities.

Decline of the British Motor Industry: The Effects of Government Policy, 1945-1979. Peter J. Dunnett. 208p. 1980. 28.50 o.p. (ISBN 0-7099-0012-0, Pub. by Croom Helm Ltd). Routledge Chapman & Hall.

Decline of the New. Irving Howe. LC 78-95876. 1970. 7.50 o.p. (ISBN 0-15-124510-X). HarBraceJ.

Decline of the West. Oswald Spengler. Ed. by Helmut Werner. LC 65-1578. 1965. 7.95 o.s.i. (ISBN 0-394-60488-1). Modern Lib.

Decline of the West. Oswald Spengler. Date not set. 18.50 ea. o.p.; Set. 36.00 o.p. (ISBN 0-317-53255-3). Noontide.

Decline of U. S. Power & What We Can Do about It. Business Week Magazine Staff. 1980. 9.95 o.p. (ISBN 0-395-29248-4). HM.

Decline of Western Hill. Graham Jackson. LC 83-5533. 164p. 1984. text ed. 16.95 o.p. (ISBN 0-7022-1793-X); pap. 7.95 o.p. (ISBN 0-7022-1803-0). U of Queensland Pr.

Decline of Wisdom. Gabriel Marcel. 64p. 1955. (ISBN 0-8022-1053-8). Philos Lib.

Declining Enrollments: A New Dilemma for Educators. William F. Keough, Jr. LC 78-61320. (Fastback Ser.: No. 116). 1978. pap. 0.90 o.p. (ISBN 0-87367-116-3). Phi Delta Kappa.

Decoding Inventory. Lyndon W. Searfoss & H. Donald Jacobs. (Kendall-Hunt Reading Ser.). 1979. pap. text ed. 8.95 o.p. (ISBN 0-8403-8008-9). Kendall-Hunt.

Decomposition of Superpositions of Density Functions & Discrete Distributions. Pal Medgyessy. LC 75-46231. 308p. 1977. 57.95x o.p. (ISBN 0-470-15017-3). Halsted Pr.

Decorate Your Home with Love. Mary C. Crowley. 1985. 16.95 o.p. (ISBN 0-8007-1454-7). Revell.

Decorated Tile: An Illustrated History of English Tile-Making & Design. Jill Austwick & Brian Austwick. (Illus.). 1981. encore ed. 7.95 o.p. (ISBN 0-684-16761-1, ScribT); pap. 10.95 o.p. (ScribT). Scribner.

Decorating Cakes for Children's Parties. Polly Pinder. 1985. 15.95 o.p. (ISBN 0-03-003667-4). H Holt & Co.

Decorating Cakes for Fun & Profit. Richard V. Snyder. (Illus.). 1953. 8.50 o.s.i. (ISBN 0-682-40088-2, Banner). Exposition-Phoenix.

Decorating with Crochet. Anne Halliday. LC 75-15893. (Illus.). 176p. 1975. 16.95 o.p. (ISBN 0-395-20992-7). HM.

Decorating with Fabric. Judy Lindahl. LC 82-60392. 1977. 10.95 o.s.i. (ISBN 0-8329-0198-9). New Century.

Decorating with Plants. Sunset Magazine & Books Editors. LC 79-90333. (Illus.). 80p. 1980. pap. 4.95 o.p. (ISBN 0-376-03342-8, Sunset Bks). Sunset-Lane.

Decorations from Nature: Growing, Preserving, & Arranging Naturals. Linda L. Lindgren. LC 86-47614. (Arts, Craft & Hobby Ser.). 1986. pap. 12.95 o.p. (ISBN 0-8019-7696-0). Chilton.

Decorative & Ornamental Brickwork. James Stokoe. 1983. 14.00 o.p. (ISBN 0-8446-5932-0). Peter Smith.

Decorative Antique Ironwork: A Pictorial Treasury. Henry R. D'Allemagne. (Illus.). 19.00 o.p. (ISBN 0-8446-1939-6). Peter Smith.

Decorative Art of Leon Bakst. Leon Bakst. Tr. by Harry Melvill. (Illus.). 13.25 o.p. (ISBN 0-8446-4620-2). Peter Smith.

Decorative Art of New Guinea. Albert B. Lewis. (Illus.). 10.25 o.p. (ISBN 0-8446-5111-7). Peter Smith.

Decorative Arts in Dane County. (Illus.). 59p. 1982. 8.95 o.p. (ISBN 0-913883-03-4). Madison Art.

Decorative Arts in Europe Seventeen Ninety to Eighteen Fifty. Leon De Groer. LC 85-42864. (Illus.). 360p. 1986. 90.00 o.p. (ISBN 0-8478-0621-9). Rizzoli Intl.

Decorative Dressmaking. (Illus.). 160p. 1985. 21.95 o.p. (ISBN 0-87857-579-0); pap. 12.95 o.p. (ISBN 0-87857-580-4). Rodale Pr Inc.

Decorative Home Embroidery. One Hundred Idees Staff. 1987. pap. 9.95 o.p. (ISBN 0-345-34718-8). Ballantine.

Decorative Home Sewing. (Cent Idees Ser.). 1987. pap. 9.95 o.p. (ISBN 0-345-34418-9). Ballantine.

Decorative Techniques. Ed. by Time-Life Books Staff. LC 75-29597. (Art of Sewing Ser.). (Illus.). (gr. 6 up). 1976. PLB 11.97 o.p. (ISBN 0-8094-1763-4, Pub. by Time-Life). Silver.

Decorative Work of John la Farge. H. Barbara Weinberg. LC 76-23654. (Outstanding Dissertations in the Fine Arts - 2nd Series - American). (Illus.). 1977. Repr. of 1972 ed. lib. bdg. 101.00 o.p. (ISBN 0-8240-2736-1). Garland Pub.

Decouvert et Creation. 3rd ed. Gerard Jian & Ralph Hester. 1981. text ed. 28.95 o.p. (ISBN 0-395-30987-5). HM.

Decouverte de l'Essai. Ed. by Sarah Lawall et al. 249p. (Orig., Fr.). 1975. pap. text ed. 7.25 o.p. (ISBN 0-15-517285-9, HC). HarBraceJ.

Decoys of the Atlantic Flyway. George R. Starr, Jr. LC 74-78699. 1974. 24.95 o.s.i. (ISBN 0-8329-1416-9, Pub. by Winchester Pr). New Century.

Decree & Destiny. Shaykh F. Haeri. 200p. cancelled o.s.i. (ISBN 0-7103-0270-3, A0837, Pub. by Routledge UK). Routledge Chapman & Hall.

Dedicating & Reserving Land to Provide Access to North Carolina Beaches. Richard D. Ducker et al. LC 83-622902. 175p. 1983. Institute Government.

Dedication of Books to Patron & Friend. Henry B. Wheatley. LC 68-30615. 268p. 1968. Repr. of 1887 ed. 35.00x o.p. (ISBN 0-8103-3316-3). Gale.

Deduct This Book: How Not to Pay Taxes While Ronald Reagan Is President. J. Peter Segall. LC 83-48404. 156p. 1983. pap. 6.95 o.s.i. (ISBN 0-394-62009-7, E884, Ever). Grove.

Deeds of Frederick Barbarossa. Otto of Freising. Tr. by Christopher Mierow. 1966. pap. 7.45x o.p. (ISBN 0-393-09697-1, NortonC). Norton.

Deep Between the Rocks. Joan S. Sidney. LC 85-1253. 20p. (Orig.). 1985. pap. 4.00 o.p. (ISBN 0-916897-03-6). Andrew Mtn Pr.

Deep Blue Good-by. John D. MacDonald. (Travis McGee Ser.). 1984. pap. 3.50 o.p. (ISBN 0-449-12673-0, GM). Fawcett.

Deep Blue Good-by. John D. MacDonald. (General Ser.). 1984. lib. bdg. 12.95 o.p. (ISBN 0-8161-3626-2, Large Print Bks); pap. 8.95 o.s.i. (ISBN 0-8161-3740-4). G K Hall.

Deep Dyslexia. Ed. by Max Coltheart et al. (International Library of Psychology). 1980. 50.00x o.p. (ISBN 0-7100-0456-7). Routledge Chapman & Hall.

Deep Dyslexia. Ed. by Max Coltheart et al. (International Library of Psychology). 456p. 1986. pap. 16.95 o.p. (ISBN 0-7102-0834-0). Routledge Chapman & Hall.

Deep End. Frederic Brown. LC 84-60846. (Quill Mysterious Classic Ser.). 256p. 1984. pap. 3.50 o.p. (ISBN 0-688-03919-7, Quill). Morrow.

Deep Forest Award. Jean B. Mosley. LC 84-72003. (Illus.). 224p. (ps-3). 1985. pap. 5.95 o.p. (ISBN 0-89107-342-6, Crossway Bks). Good News.

Deep Freeze & Other Stories. Marcello Maestro. 1977. 5.50 o.p. (ISBN 0-682-48866-6). Exposition-Phoenix.

Deep in the Heart. Wyatt Wyatt. LC 80-65986. 1980. 12.95 o.p. (ISBN 0-689-11084-7, Atheneum). Macmillan.

Deep Inelastic & Fusion Reactions with Heavy Ions. Ed. by W. Von Oertzen. (Lecture Notes in Physics Ser.: Vol. 117). 410p. 1980. pap. 33.00 o.p. (ISBN 0-387-09965-4). Springer-Verlag.

Deep Lie: A Novel. Stuart Woods. LC 85-15334. 344p. 1986. 15.45 o.p. (ISBN 0-393-02272-2). Norton.

Deep Ocean Mining. Ed. by J. E. Flipse. (OED: Vol. 8). 80p. 1975. 8.00 o.p. (ISBN 0-317-33470-0, G00162); members 4.00 o.p. (ISBN 0-317-33471-9). ASME.

Deep Pools. John F. Beeson. 1978. 4.00 o.p. (ISBN 0-682-49223-X). Exposition-Phoenix.

Deep Range. Arthur C. Clarke. LC 57-6214. 1957. 6.95 o.s.i. (ISBN 0-15-124635-1). HarBraceJ.

Deep Sea Drilling Project, Legs 1-25. American Geological Institute Staff. (AGI Reprint Ser.: No. 1). 1975. 10.00 o.p. (ISBN 0-913312-16-9). Am Geol.

Deep Sea Drilling Project, Legs 26-44. American Geological Institute Staff. (AGI Reprint Ser.: No. 2). 1976. 10.00 o.p. (ISBN 0-913312-17-7). Am Geol.

Deep Sea Drilling Project, Legs 45-62. American Geological Institute Staff. LC 78-74943. (AGI Reprint Ser.: No. 4). 1979. pap. 10.00 o.p. (ISBN 0-913312-12-6). Am Geol.

Deep-Sea Photography. Ed. by John B. Hersey. LC 66-16038. (Oceanographic Studies: No. 3). (Illus.). 368p. 1968. 39.50x o.p. (ISBN 0-8018-0270-9). Johns Hopkins.

Deep Six. Clive Cussler. 432p. 1984. 18.45 o.p. (ISBN 0-671-50373-1). S&S.

Deep South: Memory & Observation. Erskine Caldwell. LC 80-16013. (Brown Thrasher Bks.). 270p. 1980. pap. 6.95 o.p. (ISBN 0-8203-0525-1). U of Ga Pr.

Deep Test of Articulation: Picture. Eugene T. McDonald. 52p. (Orig.). 1964. pap. text ed. 19.95 o.p. (ISBN 0-88450-911-7, 7242-B). Communication Skill.

Deepwater Mooring & Drilling. Ed. by Y. K. Lou. (OED: Vol.7). 212p. 1979. 30.00 o.p. (ISBN 0-317-33472-7, G00163); members 15.00 o.p. (ISBN 0-317-33473-5). ASME.

Deer & the Tiger: A Study of Wildlife in India. George B. Schaller. LC 66-23697. (Illus.). 1967. lib. bdg. 14.00x o.s.i. (ISBN 0-226-73633-4). U of Chicago Pr.

Deer at the River. Joseph Caldwell. 228p. 1984. 15.45i o.p. (ISBN 0-316-12438-9). Little.

Deer Hunter's Bible. rev. ed. George Laycock. LC 76-50875. 1971. pap. 6.95 o.p. (ISBN 0-385-12896-7). Doubleday.

Deer Park. Norman Mailer. LC 79-20163. 375p. 1980. Repr. of 1955 ed. 35.00x o.p. (ISBN 0-86527-235-2). Fertig.

Deer Range: Improvement & Management. 2nd ed. William Dasmann. LC 80-28280. (Illus.). 176p. 1981. lib. bdg. 18.95x o.p. (ISBN 0-89950-027-7). McFarland & Co.

Deer Wars: The Story of Deer in New Zealand. Graeme Caughley. (Illus.). 187p. 1983. 15.00x o.p. (ISBN 0-86863-389-5, Pub. by Heinemann Pub New Zealand). Intl Spec Bk.

Deer Watch. Richard Prior. (Illus.). 200p. 1987. 29.95 o.p. (ISBN 0-7153-8804-5). David & Charles.

Deerslayer. James Fenimore Cooper. (Great Illustrated Classics Ser.). (YA) (gr. 9 up). 1979. 10.95 o.s.i. (ISBN 0-396-07746-3). Dodd.

Def Leppard. (Metal Mania Ser.). (Illus.). 48p. (gr. 4-12). 1984. 6.95 o.p. (ISBN 0-317-16150-4, Robus Books). H Leonard Pub Corp.

Default & Rescheduling: Corporate & Sovereign Borrowers, 1984. D. Suratgar. 163p. 1984. 120.00 o.p. (ISBN 0-8002-3163-5). Intl Pubns Serv.

Defaulted Bonds & Bankruptcy: The Problems of Indenture Trustees & Bondholders. Practising Law Institute Staff. 350p. 1985. pap. 15.00 o.p. (ISBN 0-317-27418-X, N44451). PLI.

Defeat of Distance: Qantas 1919-1939. John Gunn. LC 84-11978. (Illus.). 400p. 1985. 25.00x o.p. (ISBN 0-7022-1707-7). U of Queensland Pr.

Defects in Insulating Crystals: Riga 1981: Proceedings. Ed. by V. M. Tuchkevich & K. K. Shvarts. (Illus.). 774p. 1982. 49.00 o.p. (ISBN 0-387-10782-7). Springer-Verlag.

Defence. Charles Freeman. (Today's World Ser.). (Illus.). 72p. (gr. 7-12). 1983. 17.95 o.p. (ISBN 0-7134-0969-X, Pub. by Batsford England). David & Charles.

Defence of Dramatick Poetry. Elkanah Settle. Incl. Farther Defence of Dramatick Poetry. LC 79-170450. (English Stage Ser.: Vol. 25). 1973. lib. bdg. 61.00 o.p. (ISBN 0-8240-0608-9). Garland Pub.

Defence of the Realm in the 1980's. Dan Smith. 272p. 1980. 38.00 o.p. (ISBN 0-85664-873-6, Pub. by Croom Helm Ltd); pap. 11.50 o.p. (ISBN 0-7099-2332-5). Routledge Chapman & Hall.

Defend Yourself: Scientific Personal Defense. Armond Seidler. LC 77-79405. (Illus.). 1978. pap. 17.50 o.p. (ISBN 0-395-25822-7). HM.

Defenders of Pakistan. Mohamed Amin et al. 1988. 39.95 o.p. Avery Pub.

Defending "A Christian Country" Churchmen & Society in New South Wales in the 1880's & After. Walter Phillips. (Illus.). 332p. 1982. text ed. 39.95 o.p. (ISBN 0-7022-1539-2). U of Queensland Pr.

Defending Civilization. Philip F. O'Connor. LC 87-34038. 1988. 18.95 o.p. (ISBN 1-55584-124-4). Weidenfeld.

Defending the Galaxy: The Complete Handbook of VideoGaming. Ed. by Michael Rubin. (Illus.). 224p. (Orig.). (gr. 6-12). pap. 4.95 o.p. (ISBN 0-937404-17-9). Triad Pub FL.

Defending Traffic Cases. Pennsylvania Bar Institute Staff. 196p. 1985. 35.00 o.p. (ISBN 0-318-19032-X, 285). PA BAr Inst.

Defense, Vol. 3 (Incl. 1987 Supplement) Ed. by E. Goldstein. (Social Issues Resources Ser.). 1988. write for info. o.p. (ISBN 0-89777-088-9). Soc Issues.

Defense Choices: Greater Security with Fewer Dollars. Jo L. Husbands. (Military Budget Study Ser.). (Illus.). 37p. (Orig.). 1986. pap. text ed. 4.50 o.p. (ISBN 0-937115-02-9). Comm Natl Security.

Defense Department Annual Report, Fiscal Year 1987. (Illus.). 336p. (Orig.). 1986. pap. 14.00 o.p. (ISBN 0-318-19975-0, S/N 008-000-00446-3). USGPO.

Defense Management, Interim Report to the President. Ed. by M. David Packard. 30p. 1985. pap. 1.75 o.p. (ISBN 0-318-19974-2, S/N 040-000-00493-9). USGPO.

Defense of Biblical Infallibility. Clark Pinnock. pap. 2.50 o.p. (ISBN 0-8010-6863-0). Baker Bk.

Defense of Liberty Against Tyrants. Philppe Mornay. Ed. by Harold Laski. 12.00 o.p. (ISBN 0-8446-1316-9). Peter Smith.

Defense of the Homeland & the End of the War: Japanese Military Studies 1937-1949. Ed. by Donald S. Detwiler & Charles B. Burdick. (War in Asia & the Pacific Ser., 1937 to 1949: Vol. 12). 1980. lib. bdg. 74.00 o.p. (ISBN 0-8240-3296-9). Garland Pub.

Defense of the Supreme God. H. M. Cummings. 1952. Philos Lib.

Defense of Western Europe. Ed. by Lewis H. Gann. 320p. 1986. 45.00 o.p. (ISBN 0-7099-1194-7, Pub. by Croom Helm UK). Routledge Chapman & Hall.

Defense Planning in Less-Industrialized States: The Middle East & South Asia. Stephanie G. Neuman. LC 81-48632. 336p. 1984. 37.00x o.p. (ISBN 0-669-05468-2). Lexington Bks.

Defense Priorities & Allocations Systems. 72p. (Orig.). 1987. pap. 2.25 o.p. (ISBN 0-318-22891-2, S/N 003-009-00508-6). USGPO.

Defense, Science & Public Policy. Ed. by Edwin Mansfield. (Problems of the Modern Economy Series). 1968. pap. 4.95x o.p. (ISBN 0-393-09794-3, NortonC). Norton.

Defense Technology Base: Introduction & Overview, a Special Report of OTA's Assessment on Maintaining the Defense Technology Base. LC 88-600517. 122p. (Orig.). 1988. pap. 5.00 o.p. (S/N 052-003-01099-2). USGPO.

Defensible Programs for the Gifted: Critical Issues in Gifted Education, Vol. I. Ed. by C. June Maker. 384p. 1986. 34.95 o.p. (ISBN 0-87189-377-0). Aspen Pub.

Defensive Football. Nick Buoniconti & Dick Anderson. Ed. by Bill Bondurant. LC 73-80752. (Illus.). 1973. 7.95 o.p. (ISBN 0-689-10573-8, Atheneum). Macmillan.

Defiant Bride. Jean Bothwell. LC 69-13771. (gr. 7 up). 1969. 5.95 o.p. (ISBN 0-15-223090-4, HJ). HarBraceJ.

Defiant Destiny. Nancy Moulton. 368p. 1982. pap. 2.95 o.p. (ISBN 0-380-81430-7, 81430-7). Avon.

Defiant Dreams. Cheri Michaels. (Dawn of Love Ser.: No. 5). (YA) (gr. 7 up). pap. 2.25 o.p. (ISBN 0-671-54430-6). Archway.

Defining America: A Christian Critique of the American Dream. Robert Benne & Philip Hefner. LC 73-89062. 160p. 1974. pap. 1.00 o.p. (ISBN 0-8006-1075-X, 1-1075, Fortress). Augsburg Fortress.

Defining Death: A Report on the Medical, Legal, & Ethical Issues in the Determination of Death. (Illus.). 176p. 1981. 6.50 o.p. (ISBN 0-318-23082-8, S/N 040-000-00451-3). USGPO.

Defining Females: The Nature of Women in Society. Ed. by Shirley Ardener. LC 78-16867. 227p. 1978. 31.95x o.p. (ISBN 0-470-26465-9). Halsted Pr.

Defining the Manager's Job. rev. ed. Max Wortman & Joann Sperling. 1980. pap. 9.95 o.p. (ISBN 0-8144-7526-4). AMACOM.

Definition of Programming Languages. A. Ollengren. 1975. 76.00 o.p. (ISBN 0-12-525750-3). Acad Pr.

Definition of Psychology. 2nd ed. Fred S. Keller. LC 72-94282. 128p. 1973. text ed. 15.00 o.p. (ISBN 0-13-197616-8). P-H.

Defoe. Pat Rogers. (Critical Heritage Ser.). 242p. 1985. pap. 15.00 o.p. (ISBN 0-7102-0595-3). Routledge Chapman & Hall.

Defoe: The Critical Heritage. Ed. by Pat Rogers. (Critical Heritage Ser.). 1972. 29.95x o.p. (ISBN 0-7100-7259-7). Routledge Chapman & Hall.

Deformation & Deposition Between a Foreland Uplift & an Impinging Thrust Belt: Hoback Basin, Wyoming. John A. Dorr, Jr. et al. LC 77-70022. (Special Paper Ser.: No. 177). (Illus.). 1977. pap. 10.00 o.p. (ISBN 0-8137-2177-6). Geol Soc.

Deformation & Fracture of High Polymers. Ed. by H. Henning Kausch et al. LC 73-19857. 644p. 1973. 69.50x o.p. (ISBN 0-306-30772-3, Plenum Pr). Plenum Pub.

Deformation & Fracture of Solids. Robert M. Caddell. (Illus.). 1980. pap. text ed. 49.00 o.p. (ISBN 0-13-198309-1). P-H.

Deformation Geometry for Material Scientists. C. N. Reid. LC 73-4716. 220p. 1974. 55.00 o.p. (ISBN 0-08-017237-7); pap. 55.00 o.p. (ISBN 0-08-017745-X). Pergamon.

Deformation, Processing & Structure. 524p. 1984. 121.00 o.p. (6103L). ASM.

Defy the Thunder. Virginia Brown. (Avon Romance Ser.). 416p. 1984. pap. 2.95 o.p. (ISBN 0-380-89537-4). Avon.

Degas: Form & Space. Ed. by Maurice Guillaud & Jacqueline Guillaud. (Illus.). 492p. 1985. 50.00 o.p. (ISBN 0-8478-5407-8). Rizzoli Intl.

Degas in Motion. Norton Simon Museum Staff. (Illus.). 18p. (Orig.). 1982. pap. 9.95 o.p. (ISBN 0-295-96122-8, Norton Simon Museum). U of Wash Pr.

Degas: In the Art Institute of Chicago. Richard R. Brettell & Suzanne F. McCullagh. (Illus.). 200p. 1984. 37.50 o.p. Abrams.

Degas Monotypes: Essay, Catalogue & Checklist see Exhibition Catalogues from the Fogg Art Museum.

Degas: The Dancers. George T. Shackelford. LC 84-20585. (Illus.). 1985. 24.50 o.p. (ISBN 0-393-01975-6). Norton.

Dehumanization of Art, & Other Essays on Art, Culture & Literature. rev. ed. Jose Ortega Y Gasset. 1968. 16.50x o.p. (ISBN 0-691-07147-0); pap. 8.95x o.p. (ISBN 0-691-01961-4). Princeton U Pr.

Dehumanization of Man. Ashley Montagu & Floyd Matson. 1983. text ed. 14.95 o.p. (ISBN 0-07-042845-X). McGraw.

Deidre of the Sorrows: And the Tinker's Wedding & the Shadow of the Glen. John Millington Synge. (Unwin Bk.). 1967. pap. 3.95 o.p. (ISBN 0-04-822023-X). Unwin Hyman.

Deinking of Paper. 2nd ed. (Bibliographic Ser.: No. 151-2). 113p. 1951. photocopies 10.00 o.p. (ISBN 0-317-34362-9); Suppl. 1, 1961. photocopies 12.00 o.p. (ISBN 0-317-34363-7); Suppl. 2, 1967. 8.00 o.p. (ISBN 0-317-34364-5). Inst Paper Chem.

Deinstitutionalization & Institutional Reform. R. C. Scheerenberger. (Illus.). 272p. 1976. 34.50 o.p. (ISBN 0-398-03552-0). C C Thomas.

Deirdre & Desire. Marion Chesney. (Nightingale Paperbacks). 1985. pap. 10.95 o.p. (ISBN 0-8161-3824-9, Large Print Bks). G K Hall.

Deist's Manual; or a Rational Enquiry into the Christian Religion. Charles Gildon. Ed. by Rene Wellek. LC 75-11220. (British Philosophers & Theologians of the 17th & 18th Centuries Ser.: Vol. 23). 1976. Repr. of 1705 ed. lib. bdg. 51.00 o.p. (ISBN 0-8240-1774-9). Garland Pub.

Deity & Morality-with Regard to the Naturalistic Fallacy. Burton F. Porter. LC 68-16017. 1968. text ed. 7.95x o.p. (ISBN 0-04-100012-9). Humanities.

Del Corso's Gallery. Philip Caputo. LC 83-156. 374p. 1983. 15.95 o.p. (ISBN 0-03-058277-6). H Holt & Co.

Delacroix & Raphael. Sara Lichtenstein. Ed. by Sydney J. Freedberg. LC 78-74970. (Outstanding Dissertations in the Fine Arts Ser.). (Illus.). 1979. lib. bdg. 53.00 o.p. (ISBN 0-8240-3972-6). Garland Pub.

DeLange Syndrome. J. M. Berg et al. LC 72-124065. 1970. 35.00 o.p. (ISBN 0-08-016125-1). Pergamon.

Delaware Advance Annotation Service. Michie Company Editorial Staff. 1985. 45.00 o.p. (ISBN 0-87215-520-X). Michie Co.

Delaware Corporation: Legal Aspects of Organization & Operation. David A. Drexler & A. Gilchrist Sparks, III. (Corporation Practice Ser.: No. 1). 1978. 92.00 o.p. (ISBN 0-317-55273-2). BNA.

Delaware Directory of Commerce & Industry, 1987-88. 310p. 1986. pap. 53.00 o.p. (ISBN 0-318-02857-3). Manufacturers.

Delaware General Corporation Law: A Commentary & Analysis. Ernest L. Folk, III. 1972. 60.00 o.p. (ISBN 0-316-28780-6). Little.

Delaware Indian Symposium. Ed. by Herbert C. Kraft. LC 75-623195. (Pennsylvania Historical & Museum Comm. Anthropological Ser., No. 4). (Illus.). 160p. 1974. 9.95 o.p. (ISBN 0-911124-77-2); pap. 6.95 o.p. (ISBN 0-911124-76-4). Pa Hist & Mus.

Delaware Law for Corporate Lawyers: Recent Developments, Vol. 483. Practising Law Institute Staff. 440p. 1985. pap. 45.00 o.p. (ISBN 0-317-27490-2, #B4-6717). PLI.

Delaware: Trusts. 8.50 o.p. (ISBN 0-686-90672-1). Am Law Inst.

Delay & Functional Differential Equations & Their Applications. Ed. by Klaus Schmitt. 1972. 85.50 o.p. (ISBN 0-12-627250-6). Acad Pr.

Delegation in General Practice: A Study of Doctors & Nurses. Ann Bowling. 250p. 1981. 23.00x o.p. (ISBN 0-422-77490-1, NO.3474, Pub. by Tavistock). Routledge Chapman & Hall.

Delfia cada tarde. Edgardo Sanabria. 100p. 1978. pap. 3.95 o.p. (ISBN 0-940238-13-6). Ediciones Huracan.

Delftware: Falence Production of the Delft. (Illus.). 201p. 75.00 o.p. (ISBN 0-686-47032-X). Apollo.

Delhi: The City of Future. Shiv C. Gupta. x, 163p. 1987. text ed. 27.50x o.p. (ISBN 0-7069-3723-6, Pub. by Vikas India). Advent NY.

Delicate Balance. Edward Albee. LC 66-28773. 1966. 5.00 o.p. (ISBN 0-689-10005-1, Atheneum). Macmillan.

Delicate Dependency: A Novel of Vampire Life. Michael Talbot. 368p. 1982. pap. 3.50 o.p. (ISBN 0-380-77982-X, 77982-X). Avon.

Delicious Quick-Trim Diet. Samm S. Baker & Sylvia Schur. 352p. 1985. pap. 3.95 o.s.i. (ISBN 0-345-30832-8). Ballantine.

Delicious Sex: A Book for Women & the Men Who Want to Love Them Better. Gael Greene. (Illus.). 224p. 1986. 15.95 o.p. (ISBN 0-13-075953-8). P-H.

Delilah. Carole Hart. (Illus.). 64p. (gr. 2-5). 1983. pap. 1.95 o.p. (ISBN 0-380-62729-9, 62729-9, Camelot). Avon.

Delinquency & Adolescent Psychopathology. Ed. by Scott W. Henggeler. LC 81-22027. 272p. 1982. text ed. 28.00 o.p. (ISBN 0-7236-7041-2). Butterworth.

Delinquents & Nondelinquents in Perspective. Sheldon Glueck & Eleanor T. Glueck. LC 68-25609. 1968. 19.50x o.s.i. (ISBN 0-674-19600-7). Harvard U Pr.

Deliquency & Drift. D. Matza. LC 64-18135. 199p. 1970. pap. text ed. write for info. o.p. (ISBN 0-02-377350-2). Macmillan.

Delirium. Barbara Alberti. Tr. by Lawrence Venuti from Ital. 256p. 1980. 12.95 o.p. (ISBN 0-374-13744-7). FS&G.

Delius. Lionel Carley & Robert Threlfall. (Illus.). 103p. 1984. pap. 9.95 o.p. (ISBN 0-87663-856-6). Universe.

Deliverance in Shanghai. Jerome Agel & Eugene Boe. LC 83-7349. 362p. 1983. 14.95 o.p. (ISBN 0-934878-32-3). Dembner Bks.

Delivering In-Home Services to the Aged & Disabled: The Wisconsin Experiment. Frederick Seidl et al. LC 81-48068. (Illus.). 224p. 1983. 32.00x o.p. (ISBN 0-669-05243-4). Lexington Bks.

Delivery. Georges Simenon. Ed. by Eileen Ellenbogen. LC 80-8759. (Helen & Kurt Wolff Bk.). 1981. 10.95 o.p. (ISBN 0-15-124655-6). HarBraceJ.

Dell Book of Quizzes & Puzzles for Literature Lovers. Maggie Lane & Nigel Bartlett. 1986. pap. 6.95 o.p. (ISBN 0-440-54709-1, Pub. by Dell Trade Pbks). Dell.

Della Difesa della Comedia di Dante see On the Defense of the Comedy of Dante: Introduction & Summary.

Delmore Schwartz: The Life of an American Poet. James Atlas. 418p. 1977. 15.00 o.p. (ISBN 0-374-13761-7). FS&G.

Delocalized Phosphorus-Carbon Double Bonds: Phosphamethin-Cyanines Lambda to the Third Power - Phosphorins & Lambda to the Fifth Power - Phosphorins. K. Dimroth. LC 51-5497. (Topics in Current Chemistry: Vol. 38). (Illus.). 170p. 1973. pap. 31.60 o.p. (ISBN 0-387-06164-9). Springer-Verlag.

DeLorean. John DeLorean. 304p. 1985. 9.95 o.p. (ISBN 0-310-37940-7, 12800). Zondervan.

Delphine. Mel Arrighi. LC 77-15828. 1978. 10.95 o.p. (ISBN 0-689-10862-1, Atheneum). Macmillan.

Delphiniums. Colin Edwards. (Illus.). 192p. 1981. 22.95x o.p. (ISBN 0-460-04423-0, Pub. by J. M. Dent England). Biblio Dist.

Delta Blood. Barbara F. Johnson. 1977. pap. 3.50 o.p. (ISBN 0-380-00989-7, 63867-3). Avon.

Delta Force. Charlie A. Beckwith & Donald Knox. (Illus.). 320p. 1983. 14.95 o.p. (ISBN 0-15-124657-2). HarBraceJ.

Delta Mystery. Leon Ware. LC 74-6441. 224p. (gr. 6-9). 1974. 5.50 o.s.i. (ISBN 0-664-32553-X, Westminster). Westminster John Knox.

Delta of Venus: Erotica. Anais Nin. LC 76-54856. 1977. 10.00 o.p. (ISBN 0-15-124656-4). HarBraceJ.

Delta of Venus: Erotica. Anais Nin. 276p. 1986. pap. 5.95 o.p. (ISBN 0-15-625277-5, Harv). HarBraceJ.

Delta Wedding. Eudora Welty. LC 46-3217. 1946. 7.95 o.p. (ISBN 0-15-124773-0). HarBraceJ.

Deluxe Illustrated Petroleum Reference Dictionary. 3rd ed. Robert Langenkamp. LC 78-71326. 696p. 1985. 59.95 o.p. (ISBN 0-87814-272-X, P-4392). Pennwell Bks.

Deluxe Littlest Angel. Charles Tazewell. (Illus.). 48p. (gr. k-6). 1984. 6.95 o.p. (ISBN 0-8249-8071-9). Ideals.

Deluxe Story of Christmas. Date not set. 5.95 o.p. Ideals.

Demand for Telecommunications Services in the U. S. 1980-2000. 200.00 o.p. (ISBN 0-686-32972-4). Info Gatekeepers.

Demented: The World of the Opera Diva. Ethan Mordden. (Illus.). 320p. 1984. 16.95 o.p. (ISBN 0-531-09754-4). Watts.

Dementia: A Clinical Approach. Pearce. (Illus.). 188p. 1984. 29.00 o.p. (ISBN 0-632-00878-4, B-38550). Mosby.

Dementia Praecox & Paraphrenia: With Historical Introduction. Emil Kraepelin. LC 73-154542. 356p. 1971. Repr. of 1919 ed. 27.50 o.p. (ISBN 0-88275-035-6). Krieger.

Demeter's Daughters: The Women Who Founded America (1587-1792) Selma R. Williams. LC 75-13773. (Illus.). 352p. (gr. 12 up). 1976. 9.95 o.p. (ISBN 0-689-30494-3, Atheneum). Macmillan.

Demetrius & the Golden Goblet. Eve Bunting. LC 79-14865. (Illus.). (gr. k-4). 1980. pap. 3.95 o.p. (ISBN 0-15-625282-1, VoyB). HarBraceJ.

Deming Management Method. Mary Walton. 1986. pap. 9.95 o.p. (ISBN 0-396-08895-3). Dodd.

Demise of the Professional Corporation? Seminar Materials. New Jersey Institute for Continuing Legal Education Staff et al. LC 83-185939. 67p. 0.00 o.p. NJ Inst CLE.

Demo Pk Micro TSP 4. 1985. 30.00 o.p. (ISBN 0-07-852153-X). McGraw.

Democracy. Joan Didion. 1984. 13.50 o.p. (ISBN 0-671-41977-3). S&S.

Democracy & Dictatorship in Venezuela, 1945-1958. Glen L. Kolb. LC 73-17111. (Connecticut College Monograph Ser.: No. 10). viii, 228p. 1974. 22.50 o.p. (ISBN 0-208-01416-0, Archon). Shoe String.

Democracy & the Ethical Life: A Philosophy of Politics & Community. Claes G. Ryn. LC 77-9505. x, 208p. 1978. 25.00 o.p. (ISBN 0-8071-0352-7). La State U Pr.

Democracy & the Quaker Method. Francis E. Pollard et al. 1950. Philos Lib.

Democracy at Its Best: America's Hope - the People's Branch of Government. Albert H. Ahr. 1979. 5.00 o.p. (ISBN 0-682-49401-1). Exposition-Phoenix.

Democracy, Bureaucracy & Hypocrisy. Dwight Waldo. LC 77-3606. 1977. pap. 2.50x o.p. (ISBN 0-87772-225-0). UCB IGS.

Democracy in America, Vol. 2. Alexis De Tocqueville. LC 61-16651. (YA) (gr. 9 up). 1961. pap. 2.95 o.p. (ISBN 0-8052-0014-2). Schocken.

Democracy in Nicaragua: An Investigation of Political Pluralism. NLG Delegation. 1985. 2.00 o.p. Natl Lawyers Guild.

Democracy in Trade Unions: Studies in Membership Participation & Control. Mary Dickenson. LC 82-2065. (Policy, Politics, & Administration Ser.). (Illus.). 249p. 1983. text ed. 37.50x o.p. (ISBN 0-7022-1666-6). U of Queensland Pr.

Democracy: Panacea or Pandemonium? Wallace R. Wirths. 1985. 7.95 o.p. (ISBN 0-533-06619-0). Vantage.

Democracy Thwarted. Richard Cloward & Frances Piven. LC 87-43012. 208p. 1987. 19.95 o.p. (ISBN 0-394-55396-9); pap. 8.95 o.p. (ISBN 0-394-75549-9). Pantheon.

Democracy Under Pressure. 3rd ed. Milton C. Cummings. (Illus.). 1977. text ed. 19.95 o.p. (ISBN 0-15-517340-5, HC). HarBraceJ.

Democracy Under Pressure: An Introduction to the American Political System. 2nd ed. Milton C. Cummings, Jr. & David Wise. (Illus.). 704p. 1974. text ed. 15.95 o.p. (ISBN 0-15-517338-3, HC). HarBraceJ.

Democracy under Pressure: An Introduction to the American Political System. 4th ed. Milton C. Cummings, Jr. & David Wise. 689p. 1981. text ed. 25.95 o.p. (ISBN 0-15-517343-X, HC); tests o.p. HarBraceJ.

Democracy vs. Capitalism. Robert Laurence, pseud. 96p. 1963. (ISBN 0-8022-0936-X). Philos Lib.

Democratic Defence. Peter Tatchell. 224p. 1982. pap. 7.50 o.p. (ISBN 0-946097-16-X, Pub. by GMP England). Alyson Pubns.

Democratic Policeman. George Berkley. LC 73-84791. 256p. 1969. pap. 6.95x o.p. (ISBN 0-8070-0887-7, BP470). Beacon Pr.

Democratic Republic of Congo, (Zaire), Malagasy Republic, Malawi, Mauritius & Zambia see Surveys of African Economies.

Democratic Socialism & the Cost of Defence: The Report & Papers of the Labour Party Defence Study Group. Ed. by Mary Kaldor et al. 578p. 1979. 35.00 o.p. (ISBN 0-85664-886-8, Pub. by Croom Helm Ltd). Routledge Chapman & Hall.

Democratic South. Dewey W. Grantham. 1965. pap. 1.45x o.p. (ISBN 0-393-00299-3, Norton Lib). Norton.

Democrats of Oregon: The Pattern of Minority Politics, 1900-1956. Robert E. Burton. LC 70-20919. 1970. 7.50 o.p. (ISBN 0-87114-051-9). U of Oreg Bks.

Demographic Genetics. Ed. by K. M. Weiss & P. A. Ballonoff. LC 75-31580. (Benchmark Papers in Genetics: Vol. 3). 414p. 1975. 68.00 o.p. (ISBN 0-12-787745-2). Acad Pr.

Demographic Year Book. rev. annually ed. United Nations Staff. 1976 45.00 o.p. (ISBN 0-685-20771-4, E-F 77, XIII, 1); 1979 50.00 o.p. (E-F. 80, XIII, 1). UN.

Demographic Year Book 1980. United Nations Staff. 65.00 o.p. (ISBN 0-686-84891-8, E/F.81.XIII.1). UN.

Demographic Yearbook: General Tables, 1978, Vol. 1. 30th ed. United Nations Staff. LC 50-641. (Illus.). 463p. 1979. 36.00x o.p. (ISBN 0-8002-1051-4, E.79.XIII.1). UN.

Demographic Yearbook, 1980. 32nd ed. United Nations Staff. LC 50-641. (Illus.). 973p. 1982. 65.00x o.p. (ISBN 0-8002-3062-0, E.81.XIII.1). UN.

Demographic Yearbook, 1982. 34th ed. LC 50-641. 1043p. 1984. 85.00 o.p. (ISBN 0-8002-3461-8); pap. 75.00 o.p. (ISBN 0-8002-3469-3). Intl Pubns Serv.

Demography of Immigrants & Minority Groups in the United Kingdom. Ed. by D. A. Coleman. 1983. pap. 50.50 o.p. (ISBN 0-12-179780-5). Acad Pr.

Demolition of Buildings: A Bibliography. Edward H. Teague. (Architecture Ser.: A 1472). 5p. 1985. 2.00 o.p. (ISBN 0-89028-602-7). Vance Biblios.

Demolition of Skid Row. Ronald J. Miller. LC 81-47182. 160p. 1981. 22.00x o.p. (ISBN 0-669-04563-2). Lexington Bks.

Demon & the Dove: Personality Growth Through Literature. Adrian Van Kamm & Kathleen Healy. LC 82-20173. 308p. 1983. pap. text ed. 14.00 o.p. (ISBN 0-8191-2897-X). U Pr of Amer.

Demon du Bien. Henry de Montherlant. 256p. 1972. 3.95 o.p. (ISBN 0-686-55514-7). Schoenhof.

Demon from under the Earth. (Real Ghostbuster Storybooks). (gr. 1-5). 1987. pap. 2.25 o.s.i. (ISBN 0-671-64570-6). Wanderer Bks.

Demon Kind. Roger Ellwood. 1973. pap. 0.75 o.p. (ISBN 0-380-01135-2, 14886). Avon.

Demon Possession. John L. Nevius. LC 68-27729. 368p. 1986. pap. 11.95 o.p. (ISBN 0-8254-3316-9). Kregel.

Demon Possession & the Christian. C. Fred Dickason. (Orig.). 1987. pap. 10.95 o.p. (ISBN 0-8024-2125-3). Moody.

Demon State. Jake Page. 1985. 14.45 o.p. (ISBN 0-393-02245-5). Norton.

Demonic: A Selected Theological Study: An Examination into the Theology of Edwin Lewis, Karl Barth, & Paul Tillich. Vernon Mallow. LC 83-1143. 192p. (Orig.). 1983. lib. bdg. 27.50 o.p. (ISBN 0-8191-3069-9); pap. text ed. 12.25 o.p. (ISBN 0-8191-3070-2). U Pr of Amer.

Demons at My Door. Barbara Morgenroth. LC 80-12053. 168p. (gr. 5-10). 1980. 8.95 o.p. (ISBN 0-689-30781-0, Atheneum). Macmillan.

Demons Within: And Other Disturbing Tales. Ed. by Helen Hoke. LC 77-76473. 1977. 8.95 o.s.i. (ISBN 0-8008-2156-4). Taplinger.

Demonstrations of Physical Signs on Clinical Surgery. 16th ed. Clain. 624p. 1980. 37.00 o.p. (ISBN 0-7236-0518-1, Pub. by John Wright UK). Butterworth.

Demos. George Gissing. 1983. pap. 8.95 o.p. (ISBN 0-901759-20-1, NO. 3876). Routledge Chapman & Hall.

Demosthenes Im Urteile Des Altertums. Engelbert Drerup. 1923. pap. 19.00 o.p. (ISBN 0-384-12805-X). Johnson Repr.

Demotic Mathematical Papyri. Richard A. Parker. LC 77-177501. (Brown Egyptological Studies: No. 7). (Illus.). 100p. 1972. 40.00x o.p. (ISBN 0-87057-132-X). U Pr of New Eng.

Demystifying Homosexuality: A Teaching Guide about Lesbians & Gay Men. Human Rights Foundation Staff. 150p. 1983. pap. 14.95 o.s.i. (ISBN 0-8290-1273-7). Irvington.

Den: Neverwhere. 2nd ed. Richard Corben. (Den Ser.). (Illus.). 120p. (Orig.). 1984. pap. 10.95 o.p. (ISBN 0-87416-003-0). Catalan Communs.

Denial of Death. Ernest Becker. 1975. pap. 8.95 o.p. (ISBN 0-02-902310-6). Macmillan.

Denim, Lace, & Bandanas. Willadeene. 1976. pap. 3.95 o.p. (ISBN 0-682-48595-0). Exposition-Phoenix.

Dennis Adams: Building Against Image 1979-1987. Alternative Museum Staff. LC 86-72924. (Illus., Orig.). 1987. pap. 5.00 o.p. (ISBN 0-932075-13-4). Alternative Mus.

Dennis Nechvatal Painting & Drawings: The Landscape of Anxiety. Thomas H. Garver. (Illus.). 1982. 0.50 o.p. (ISBN 0-913883-09-3). Madison Art.

Dennis the Menace: Five Years at the Same Location. Hank Ketcham. (Illus.). 80p. 1987. pap. 4.95 o.p. (ISBN 0-399-51389-2, Perigee Bks). Putnam Pub Group.

Dennis the Menace: Good Intenshuns. Hank Ketcham. 128p. 1981. pap. 1.50 o.p. (ISBN 0-449-14395-3, GM). Fawcett.

Dennis the Menace: One More Time! Hank Ketcham. 128p. 1981. pap. 1.50 o.s.i. (ISBN 0-449-14423-2, GM). Fawcett.

Denny Davis & the Drooping Ears. R. Antzak. (ps up). 1988. 1.75 o.p. (ISBN 0-317-67471-4, CH0190). Dghtrs St Paul.

Denny Laine: How to Play the Guitar. Denny Laine. (Illus.). 110p. 1980. 10.95 o.p. (ISBN 0-517-54207-2, Harmony); pap. 19.95 o.p. (ISBN 0-517-54208-0, Harmony). Crown.

Densa Quiz: The Official & Complete DQ Test of the International Densa Society. Stephen Price & J. Webster Shields. 64p. 1983. pap. 2.95 o.p. (ISBN 0-380-85563-1, 85563). Avon.

Density Standards for Field Compaction of Granular Bases & Subbases. (National Cooperative Highway Research Program Report Ser.). 73p. 1976. 4.80 o.p. (ISBN 0-309-02513-3). Transport Res Bd.

Dental Analgesia. Ed. by Gerald D. Allen et al. LC 78-55278. (Illus.). 258p. 1979. casebound 31.00 o.p. (ISBN 0-88416-153-6). Year Bk Med.

Dental Anatomy: Its Correlation with Dental Health Service. 3rd ed. Ed. by Julian B. Woelfel. LC 84-754. (Illus.). 289p. 1984. pap. 29.50 o.p. (ISBN 0-8121-0915-5). Lea & Febiger.

Dental Assistant. 4th rev. ed. Pauline Anderson & Martha Burkard. (Dental Assisting Ser.). (Illus.). 400p. 1982. pap. text ed. 18.95 o.p. (ISBN 0-8273-1436-1); instr's. guide 7.50 o.p. (ISBN 0-8273-1915-0). Delmar.

Dental Assistant. 3rd ed. Pauline C. Anderson. 372p. 1981. 19.95 o.p. (ISBN 0-442-21873-7). Van Nos Reinhold.

Dental Assistant. 5th ed. Richard E. Richardson & Roger E. Barton. (Illus.). 1978. text ed. 38.00 o.p. (ISBN 0-07-052301-0). McGraw.

Dental Elevators: Principles for Safe Usage. G. Stacey. 1968. 18.00x o.p. (ISBN 0-424-05730-1, Pub. by Sydney U Pr). Intl Spec Bk.

Dental Health Education. 5th ed. Frances A. Stoll. LC 76-28768. (Illus.). 235p. 1977. text ed. 11.00 o.p. (ISBN 0-8121-0579-6). Lea & Febiger.

Dental Hygiene Examination Review, Vol. 1. 4th ed. Theodore E. Bolden et al. 1982. 21.00 o.p. (ISBN 0-87488-461-6). Med Exam.

Dental Instruments. Loretta M. Carter & Peter Yaman. LC 80-28707. (Illus.). 202p. 1981. pap. text ed. 15.95 o.p. (ISBN 0-8016-0980-1). Mosby.

Dental Jurisprudence: A Handbook of Practical Law. Ed. by Oliver C. Schroeder, Jr. LC 78-551279. 240p. 1980. 28.00 o.p. (ISBN 0-88416-158-7). Year Bk Med.

Dental Litigation. 2nd ed. William O. Morris. 1977. 30.00x o.p. (ISBN 0-87215-198-0). Michie Co.

Dental Management of the Handicapped: Approaches for Dental Auxiliaries. Brian M. Lange & Beverly M. Entwistle. LC 82-23939. (Illus.). 169p. 1983. pap. 9.50 o.p. (ISBN 0-8121-0884-1). Lea & Febiger.

Dental Management of the Medically Compromised Patient. 2nd ed. James W. Little & Donald A. Falace. LC 80-15164. (Illus.). 300p. 1984. pap. text ed. 27.95 o.p. (ISBN 0-8016-3035-5). Mosby.

Dental Office: A Pictorial History. Richard A. Glenner. LC 83-63457. (Illus.). 152p. 1984. pap. 9.95 o.p. (ISBN 0-933126-42-5). Pictorial Hist.

Dental Public Health & Community Dentistry. Anthony Jong. LC 80-28708. (Illus.). 304p. 1981. pap. text ed. 25.95 o.p. (ISBN 0-8016-2575-0). Mosby.

Dental Radiology. 5th ed. Arthur H. Wuehrmann & Lincoln R. Manson-Hing. LC 81-2040. (Illus.). 508p. 1981. text ed. 41.95 o.p. (ISBN 0-8016-5643-5). Mosby.

Dental Specialties for the Dental Hygienist. 2nd ed. Ed. by Pauline F. Steele. LC 77-13396. (Illus.). 376p. 1978. text ed. 16.00 o.p. (ISBN 0-8121-0623-7). Lea & Febiger.

Dental Specialties in General Practice. Ed. by Alvin L. Morris. Harry M. Bohannan. LC 68-23689. (Illus.). 1969. write for info. o.p. (ISBN 0-7216-6560-8). Saunders.

Dental Students Dictionary. rev. 2nd ed. J. E. Fairpo & C. G. Fairpo. (Illus.). 1985. pap. 17.95x o.p. (ISBN 0-433-10702-2). E J Brill USA.

Dentist & the Empress: The Adventures of Dr. Tom Evans in Gaslight Paris. Gerald Carson. 1983. 15.45 o.p. (ISBN 0-395-33122-6). HM.

Dentistry for the Child & Adolescent. 4th ed. Ralph E. McDonald & David R. Avery. LC 82-14195. (Illus.). 720p. 1983. 42.95 o.p. (ISBN 0-8016-3277-3). Mosby.

Dentistry in Cerebral Palsy & Related Handicapping Conditions. Solomon N. Rosenstein. (Illus.). 184p. 1978. 22.75 o.p. (ISBN 0-398-03710-8). C C Thomas.

Dentition of Living Primates. Daris Swindler. 1976. 65.00 o.p. (ISBN 0-12-679250-X). Acad Pr.

Denumerable Markov Chains. 2nd ed. J. G. Kemeny et al. LC 76-3535. (Graduate Texts in Mathematics Ser.: Vol. 40). 1976. Repr. 25.50 o.p. (ISBN 0-387-90177-9). Springer-Verlag.

Denver: A Photographic Survey of the Metropolitan Area. Robert Adams. LC 76-44035. (Illus.). 1977. 22.50 o.p. (ISBN 0-87081-101-0); pap. 12.50 o.p. (ISBN 0-87081-102-9). Univ Pr Colo.

Denver: America's Mile High Center of Enterprise. Jerry Richmond. LC 83-16710. (Illus.). 256p. 1983. 29.95 o.p. (ISBN 0-89781-082-1). Windsor Pubns Inc.

Denver Broncos. Julian May. (NFL Today Ser.). (gr. 4-8). 1980. lib. bdg. 10.45 o.p. (ISBN 0-87191-732-7); pap. 4.25 o.p. (ISBN 0-89812-235-X). Creative Ed.

Denver Delicious. rev. ed. Katie Stapleton. (Illus.). 238p. (Orig.). 1981. pap. 4.95 o.p. (ISBN 0-933472-59-5). Johnson Bks.

Denver Nuggets. Pam Banks. (NBA Today Ser.). (Illus.). 48p. (gr. 4 up). 1984. PLB 10.45 o.p. (ISBN 0-87191-975-3). Creative Ed.

Denver's Lively Past. Caroline Bancroft. 48p. 1959. pap. 3.00 o.p. (ISBN 0-933472-17-X). Johnson Bks.

Departing As Air. Allen Wier. 224p. 1983. 14.50 o.p. (ISBN 0-671-43307-5). S&S.

Department of Defense Atlas: State Data Abstract for the United States Fiscal Year 1985. (LC3 Ser.). (Illus.). 151p. 1985. pap. 6.00 o.p. (ISBN 0-318-19973-4, S/N 008-000-00440-4). USGPO.

Department of Defense Dictionary of Military & Associated Terms, 1986. (Joint Chiefs of Staff Publication Ser.: No. 1). 407p. (Orig.). 1986. pap. 15.00 o.p. (ISBN 0-318-11775-4, S/N 008-004-00024-2). USGPO.

Department of Defense Dictionary of Military & Associated Terms. (JCS Pub. Ser.: No. 1). 414p. 1987. pap. 21.00 o.p. (ISBN 0-318-23549-8, S/N 008-004-00026-9). USGPO.

Department of Nursing Staff Education Manual. Massachusetts General Hospital Department of Nursing Staff. Ed. by Cheryl B. Stetler et al. 1981. text ed. 37.50 o.p. (ISBN 0-8359-4251-1, Reston). P-H.

Department of War, Seventeen Eighty-One to Seventeen Ninety-Five. Harry M. Ward. LC 80-28410. xi, 287p. 1981. Repr. of 1962 ed. lib. bdg. 35.00x o.p. (ISBN 0-313-22895-7, WADW). Greenwood.

Department Store Sale, 1986. 10th ed. Fairchild Market Research Division Staff. (Fact Files Ser.). 50p. 1987. pap. 20.00 o.p. (ISBN 0-87005-559-3). Fairchild.

Department Store Sales, 1985. Fairchild Market Research Division Staff. (Fairchild Fact Files). (Illus.). 55p. 1986. pap. 17.50 o.p. (ISBN 0-87005-529-1). Fairchild.

Departs: An Introductory (French) Course. Barbara Lyons et al. LC 77-12971. 1978. text ed. 27.95 o.p. (ISBN 0-03-023071-3, HoltC). HR&W.

Departure. Janet Stevenson. LC 84-25231. 352p. 1985. 17.95 o.p. (ISBN 0-15-125195-9). HarBraceJ.

Dependence. Albert Memmi. Tr. by Philip A. Facey from Fr. LC 83-70652. 192p. 1985. 17.95x o.p. (ISBN 0-8070-4300-1); pap. 7.95 o.p. (ISBN 0-8070-4301-X, BP691). Beacon Pr.

Dependence & Interdependence in Education: International Perspectives. Ed. by Keith Watson. LC 84-14298. 222p. 1984. 34.50 o.p. (ISBN 0-7099-3619-2, Pub. by Croom Helm Ltd). Routledge Chapman & Hall.

Dependent Commonwealth: Utah's Economy from Statehood to the Great Depression. Leonard J. Arrington & Thomas G. Alexander. Intro. by Dean May. (Charles Redd Monographs in Western History: No. 4). (Illus.). 112p. 1974. pap. 4.75 o.p. (ISBN 0-8425-1013-3, Dist. by Signature Bks). C Redd Ctr.

Dependent Development in United Kingdom Regions with Particular Reference to Wales. Cooke. (Progress in Planning Ser.: Vol. 15, Part 1). 90p. 1980. pap. 16.25 o.p. (ISBN 0-08-026809-9). Pergamon.

Depositions, Expert Witnesses & Demonstrative Evidence in Personal Injury Cases. Practising Law Institute Staff & David G. Miller. LC 85-212826. (Litigation & Administrative Practice Ser.). 1985. 15.00 o.p. (H4-4977). PLI.

Depreciating Assets. W. Baxter. 1981. pap. 17.95 o.p. (ISBN 0-85258-204-8). Van Nos Reinhold.

Depreciation Desk Book. Rolf Auster. 1979. 59.50 o.p. (ISBN 0-87624-111-9, Inst Busn Plan). P-H.

Depreciation Practices for Small Telephone Utilities. 61p. 1972. 7.50 o.p. (ISBN 0-318-14985-0). NARUC.

Depressed Woman: A Study of Social Relationships. Myrna M. Weissman & Eugene S. Paykel. LC 73-90944. 289p. 1974. 8.50 o.s.i. (ISBN 0-226-89160-7). U of Chicago Pr.

Depression & Masochism: An Account of Mechanisms. Nathan Leites. 1979. 19.95x o.p. (ISBN 0-393-01247-6). Norton.

Depression & Protectionism: Britain Between the Wars. Forrest Capie. 192p. 1983. text ed. 37.95x o.p. (ISBN 0-04-330338-2). Unwin Hyman.

Depression: Era Glassware. Carl F. Lucky. (Identification & Value Guide Ser.). (Illus.). 200p. 1983. pap. 9.95 o.p. (ISBN 0-89689-040-6). Bks Americana.

Depression, Fragmentation, & the Void. James Park. (Existential Freedom Ser.: No. 9). 1976. pap. 5.00x o.p. (ISBN 0-89231-009-X). Existential Bks.

Depression in the Elderly: A Behavioral Treatment Manual. Ed. by Dolores Gallagher & Larry W. Thompson. LC 81-66766. 159p. 1981. pap. 17.00x o.p. (ISBN 0-88474-125-7, 05734-7). Lexington Bks.

Depression in the Elderly: A Selected Bibliography. Ed. by Dolores Gallagher. Margaret Kronauer. LC 81-4326. (Technical Bibliographies on Aging Ser.). 58p. 1981. pap. 4.00x o.p. (ISBN 0-88474-099-4, 05756-8). Lexington Bks.

Depression: Its Causes & How to Overcome Them. Carolyn Shreeve. (Illus.). 128p. (Orig.). 1985. pap. 7.99 o.p. (ISBN 0-85500-198-4, Pub. by Turnstone Pr England). Sterling.

Depression Politics in Michigan, 1929-1933. Richard T. Ortquist. LC 80-8472. (Modern American History Ser.). 290p. 1982. lib. bdg. 43.00 o.p. (ISBN 0-8240-4864-4). Garland Pub.

Depression Years: As Photographed by Arthur Rothstein. Arthur Rothstein. 16.50 o.p. (ISBN 0-8446-5669-0). Peter Smith.

Deprived, the Disabled & the Fullness of Life. Ed. by Flavian Dougherty. LC 84-81242. 1984. pap. 4.95 o.p. (ISBN 0-89453-442-4). M Glazier.

Depth Psychology & Modern Man. Ira Progoff. 1983. 12.50 o.p. (ISBN 0-8446-6058-2). Peter Smith.

Deputy. Rolf Hochhuth. Tr. by Richard Winston & Clara Winston. 1963. pap. 7.95 o.s.i. (ISBN 0-394-17125-X, B154, BC). Grove.

Deputy Dan & the Bank Robbers. Joseph Rosenbloom. (Step into Reading Book & Cassette Library). 48p. (gr. 2-3). 1986. pap. 5.95 book & cassette o.s.i. (ISBN 0-394-88336-5, BYR). Random.

Der? Die? Das? The Gender of German. G. A. Medges. LC 74-34516. 1975. text ed. 6.00 o.p. (ISBN 0-682-48189-0, University). Exposition-Phoenix.

Der Mythos des 20. Jahrhunderts see Myth of the Twentieth Century.

Deranged Memory: A Psychonomic Study of the Amnesic Syndrome. George A. Talland. 1965. 65.50 o.p. (ISBN 0-12-683150-5). Acad Pr.

Derby Porcelain. John Twitchett. (Illus.). 319p. 1980. 60.00 o.p. (ISBN 0-214-20507-X, Pub. by Hutchinson Pub UK). Seven Hills Bk Dists.

Deregulating Wall Street: Commercial Bank Penetration of the Corporate Securities Market. Ingo Walter. LC 85-5321. (Professional Banking & Finance Ser.). 315p. 1985. 39.95 o.p. (ISBN 0-471-81713-9). Wiley.

Deregulation of Bus Services. Ian Savage. 200p. 1985. text ed. 32.50 o.p. (ISBN 0-566-05051-X). Gower Pub Co.

Deregulation of International Telecommunications. Ronald S. Eward. 425p. 1985. text ed. 55.00 o.p. (ISBN 0-89006-158-0). Artech Hse.

Derek Walcott. Robert D. Hamner. (World Authors Ser.). 1981. lib. bdg. 17.95 o.s.i. (ISBN 0-8057-6442-9, Twayne). G K Hall.

Derivatives of Hydrazine & Other Hydronitogens Having N-N Bonds. P. A. Smith. 1983. text ed. 59.95 o.p. (ISBN 0-8053-8902-4). Benjamin-Cummings.

Dermatoglyphics in Medical Disorders. B. Schaumann & M. Alter. LC 75-37772. 1976. 47.00 o.p. (ISBN 0-387-07555-0). Springer-Verlag.

Dermatologic Disorders in Black Children & Adolescents. Theresita Laude & Raymond M. Russo. 1983. text ed. 44.75 o.p. (ISBN 0-87488-409-8). Med Exam.

Dermatology & Skin Care. John A. Parrish. (Illus.). 320p. 1975. text ed. 26.00 o.p. (ISBN 0-07-048508-9). McGraw.

Dermatology in General Medicine. 2nd ed. Thomas B. Fitzpatrick et al. LC 78-9850. (Illus.). 1979. text ed. 115.00 o.p. (ISBN 0-07-021196-5). McGraw.

Dermatology in General Medicine: Update One. Thomas B. Fitzpatrick et al. (Illus.). 320p. 1983. text ed. 54.00 o.p. (ISBN 0-07-021198-1). McGraw.

Dermatomyositis & Polymyositis. Ed. by Walter F. Lever et al. LC 73-16450. 162p. 1974. text ed. 19.00x o.p. (ISBN 0-8422-7174-0). Irvington.

Dermatophilus Infection in Animals & Man. Ed. by D. H. Lloyd & K. C. Sellers. 1976. 55.00 o.p. (ISBN 0-12-453750-2). Acad Pr.

Dermatotoxicology. 2nd ed. Ed. by Francis N. Marzulli & Howard I. Maibach. LC 82-9234. (Illus.). 605p. 1983. text ed. 89.95 o.p. (ISBN 0-89116-250-X). Hemisphere Pub.

DES Daughter: The Joyce Bichler Story. Joyce Bichler. 192p. 1981. pap. 2.25 o.p. (ISBN 0-380-78147-6). Avon.

Desarme: Quien esta en Contra. U. S. S. R. Ministry of Defense Staff. 68p. 1984. pap. 0.95 o.p. (ISBN 0-8285-9096-6, Pub. by Military Pubs USSR). Imported Pubns.

Desarme y La Economia. R. Faramazian. 208p. (Span.). 1982. 4.95 o.p. (ISBN 0-8285-2499-8, Pub. by Progress Pubs USSR). Imported Pubns.

Descendants of Gottfried & Wilhelmine Griepp & Their Hintz & Rathke Kinships. Frank R. Griepp & Muriel H. Griepp. (Illus.). 1980. 25.00 o.p. (ISBN 0-682-49596-4). Exposition-Phoenix.

Descendants of Star. Thomas C. Bailey. 96p. 1980. 5.50 o.p. (ISBN 0-682-49601-4). Exposition-Phoenix.

Descent from the Cross: Its Relation to the Extra-Liturgical Depositio Drama. Elizabeth C. Parker. LC 77-94713. (Outstanding Dissertations in the Fine Arts Ser.). 1978. lib. bdg. 41.00 o.p. (ISBN 0-8240-3245-4). Garland Pub.

Descent from Xanadu. Harold Robbins. 384p. 1984. 15.45 o.p. (ISBN 0-671-41633-2). S&S.

Descent of Pierre-Saint-Martin. N. Casteret. (Illus.). 160p. 1956. (ISBN 0-8022-0220-9). Philos Lib.

Descent of the Dove. Charles W. Williams. 1965. pap. 7.95 o.p. (ISBN 0-8028-1225-2). Eerdmans.

Descent to Suez: Foreign Office Diaries 1951-1956. Evelyn Shuckburgh. Ed. by John Charmley. (Illus.). 1987. 24.45 o.p. (ISBN 0-393-02414-8). Norton.

Description & Analysis of Medicare Prospective Price Setting Including Changes for Year Three. Healthcare Financial Management Association Staff. (Orig.). 1985. pap. 6.00 o.s.i. (ISBN 0-930228-45-6). Healthcare Fin Mgmt Assn.

Description & History of the Pianoforte. Alfred J. Hipkins. LC 74-75891. (Detroit Reprints in Music Ser.). 164p. 1975. Repr. of 1929 ed. 8.50 o.p. (ISBN 0-911772-72-3). Harmonie Pk Pr.

Description de San Marco. Michel Butor. pap. 7.50 o.p. (ISBN 0-685-37244-8). Schoenhof.

Descriptions of New & Rare Diatoms. R. K. Greville. (Trans. Microscop. Soc. Ser.). (Illus.). 1968. 44.00x o.p. (ISBN 3-7682-0570-3). Lubrecht & Cramer.

Descriptive & Inferential Statics: An Introduction. 2nd ed. Loether & McTavish. 1985. 40.00 o.p. (ISBN 0-205-06905-3, 816905); wkbk. avail. o.p. (ISBN 0-205-06907-X, 816907). Allyn.

Descriptive Map of the United Nations. pap. 1.75 o.p. (UN80/1/13, UN). UNIPUB.

Desde los Pobres de la Tierra see Religious Life & the Poor: Liberation Theology Perspectives.

Desert Flight. Jim Razzi. (Transformers Find Your Fate Junior Ser.: No. 5). (Orig.). (gr. 4 up). 1986. pap. 2.50 o.p. (ISBN 0-345-33072-2). Ballantine.

Desert Hiking. David Ganci. LC 83-51474. (Illus.). 192p. 1984. pap. 9.95 o.p. Wilderness Pr.

Desert Images: An American Landscape. Edward Abbey & David Muench. LC 78-4889. 1979. 100.00 o.p. (ISBN 0-15-125302-1). HarBraceJ.

Desert Men. Roger A. Hall. (Illus.). 25p. (Director's Production Script). 1973. pap. 6.50 o.p. (ISBN 0-88680-037-4). I E Clark.

Desert My Dwelling Place. David L. Owen. (Special Forces Library). (Illus.). 272p. 1987. 24.95 o.p. (ISBN 0-85368-754-4, Pub. by Arms & Armour). Sterling.

Desert Passages: Encounters with the American Deserts. Patricia Nelson Limerick. LC 84-28032. 222p. 1985. 22.50x o.p. (ISBN 0-8263-0794-9); pap. 12.95 o.p. (ISBN 0-8263-0808-2). U of NM Pr.

Desert Road Racer. Margaret Ogan & George Ogan. LC 75-110725. (Hiway Bks.: A High Interest-Low Reading Level Book). (gr. 7-10). 1970. 3.95 o.s.i. (ISBN 0-664-32474-6, Westminster). Westminster John Knox.

Desert Rose: A Novel. Larry McMurtry. 254p. 1983. 75.00 o.s.i. (ISBN 0-671-49423-6); 14.50 o.s.i. (ISBN 0-671-46143-5). S&S.

Desert Splendor. Samantha Hughes. (Candlelight Ecstasy Ser.: No. 179). 192p. (Orig.). 1983. pap. 1.95 o.p. (ISBN 0-440-11800-X). Dell.

Desert: The American Southwest. Ruth Kirk. (Naturalist's America Ser.: Vol. 3). (Illus.). 1973. 10.00 o.p. (ISBN 0-395-17209-8). HM.

Desert Walkabout. Vincent Serventy. 1976. 9.95 o.s.i. (ISBN 0-8008-2169-6). Taplinger.

Deserteur et Autres Recits. Jean Giono. 288p. 1973. 17.50 o.p. (ISBN 0-686-53958-3). Schoenhof.

Desertification & Deforestation: A Selected Bibliography of English Language Sources. Earleen H. Cook. (Public Administration Ser.: Bibliography P 1641). 1985. pap. 3.75 o.p. (ISBN 0-89028-331-1). Vance Biblios.

Desertification: Its Causes & Consequences. United Nations, Secretariat. Conference on Desertification, Nairobi 1977. LC 77-81423. 1977. 130.00 o.p. (ISBN 0-08-022023-1); pap. 110.00 o.p. (ISBN 0-08-022395-8). Pergamon.

Deserts. Darrell Vodopich & Randy Moore. 64p. (YA) (gr. 6-12). 1989. lib. bdg. 12.95 o.p. (ISBN 0-89490-182-6). Enslow Pubs.

Deserts of the World. M. P. Petrov. LC 75-12921. 447p. 1977. 128.95 o.p. (ISBN 0-470-68447-X). Halsted Pr.

Design & Analysis of Time-Series Experiments. Ed. by Gene V. Glass et al. LC 74-84779. (Illus.). 200p. 1975. text ed. 19.50x o.p. (ISBN 0-87081-063-4). Univ Pr Colo.

Design & Control of Concrete Mixtures. 12th ed. 140p. 1979. pap. 8.25 o.p. (ISBN 0-89312-044-8, EB001T). Portland Cement.

Design & Drafting of Printed Circuits. Bishop Graphics, Inc. Staff. 1979. text ed. 49.50 o.p. (ISBN 0-07-005430-4). McGraw.

Design & Drafting of Printed Circuits. 2nd ed. Darry Lindsey. (Illus.). 400p. 1983. text ed. 64.00 o.p. (ISBN 0-07-037844-4). McGraw.

Design & Installation of Communication Circuits. Ed. by Andrew L. Mular & Gerald V. Jergensen, III. LC 82-71992. (Illus.). 1022p. 1982. 40.00x o.p. (ISBN 0-89520-401-0). SMM&E Inc.

Design & Installation of Concentration & Dewatering Circuits. Intro. by A. L. Mular & M. A. Anderson. LC 85-63667. (Illus.). 842p. 1986. 83.50x o.p. (ISBN 0-87335-052-9). SMM&E Inc.

Design & Makeup of the Newspaper. Albert A. Sutton. LC 71-110838. (Illus.). 1971. Repr. of 1948 ed. lib. bdg. 32.50x o.p. (ISBN 0-8371-2510-3, SUDM). Greenwood.

Design & Manufacture of Plastic Parts. R. L. Brown. (Illus.). 204p. 1980. 65.00 o.p. (ISBN 0-686-48177-1, 0802). T-C Pubns CA.

Design & Meaning in Japanese Gardens. Mitchell Bring & Josse Wayembergh. (Illus.). 1981. text ed. 49.50 o.p. (ISBN 0-07-007825-4). McGraw.

Design & Operation of Small Sewage Works. D. Barnes & F. Wilson. 180p. 1976. 35.00x o.p. (ISBN 0-419-10980-3, NO.6024, Pub. by E & FN Spon England). Routledge Chapman & Hall.

Design & Performance of Gas Turbine Power Plants. Ed. by William R. Hawthorne & W. T. Olson. (High Speed Aerodynamics & Jet Propulsion, Vol. 11). 1960. 63.00x o.p. (ISBN 0-691-07942-0). Princeton U Pr.

Design & Use of Computer Simulation Models. James R. Emshoff & Roger L. Sisson. (Illus.). 1970. write for info. o.p. (ISBN 0-02-333720-6, 33372). Macmillan.

Design Arts Two. Municipal Art Society of New York Staff. 112p. 1981. 7.50 o.p. (ISBN 0-317-14548-7, D30). Urban Land.

Design Calculations in Wastewater Treatment. F. Wilson. 1980. 43.00x o.p. (ISBN 0-419-11690-7, NO. 6535, Pub. by E & FN Spon); pap. 15.95x o.p. (ISBN 0-419-11700-8, NO. 6534). Routledge Chapman & Hall.

Design Competitions. Paul D. Spreiregen. 1979. text ed. 44.50 o.p. (ISBN 0-07-060381-2). McGraw.

Design Concepts for Information Systems. Rev. ed. Gerald Nadler et al. 1983. 13.00 o.p. (ISBN 0-89806-015-X, 107). Inst Indus Eng.

Design Connection: Energy & Technology in Architecture. Ed. by Ralph W. Crump. Martin J. Harms. (Preston Thomas Memorial Series in Architecture). 144p. 1981. 28.95 o.p. (ISBN 0-442-23125-3). Van Nos Reinhold.

Design Cost Analysis for Architects & Engineers. Herbert Swinburne. (Illus.). 1980. text ed. 39.00 o.p. (ISBN 0-07-062635-9). McGraw.

Design Criteria for Decommissioning of Nuclear Fuel Reprocessing Plants (ANSI N300) 15p. 1975. pap. 9.50 o.p. (ISBN 0-8169-0006-X, A-22). Am Inst Chem Eng.

Design, Drafting, & Construction Practices for Electronics. Cortland C. Doan. LC 77-6064. 1985. pap. text ed. 24.00 o.p. (ISBN 0-534-04722-X, PWS-Kent Ser Tech). PWS-Kent Pub.

Design Drawing. rev ed. William K. Lockard. 290p. 1983. 38.95 o.p. (ISBN 0-442-26007-5). Van Nos Reinhold.

Design Education: The Foundation Years. Richard Kimbell. (Routledge Education Bks.). (Illus.). 196p. (Orig.). 1982. pap. 15.95x o.p. (ISBN 0-7100-9018-8). Routledge Chapman & Hall.

Design Eighty-Two: Proceedings of the Symposium Organised by the Institution of Chemical Engineers at the University of Aston in Birmingham, U. K., September 22-23, 1982. Institution of Chemical Engineers Staff. (Institution of Chemical Engineers Symposium Ser.: No. 76). 425p. 1983. 69.00 o.s.i. (ISBN 0-08-028773-5). Pergamon.

Design for Accessibility. Robert J. Sorensen. LC 78-11801. (Illus.). 1979. text ed. 37.50 o.p. (ISBN 0-07-059680-8). McGraw.

Design for Arid Regions. Gideon S. Golany. 400p. 1982. 45.95 o.p. (ISBN 0-442-22924-0). Van Nos Reinhold.

Design for Assembly. M. Myrup Andreasen et al. 189p. 1983. 46.00 o.p. (ISBN 0-317-18026-6). Robot Inst Am.

Design for Crash Survival of Automobile Occupants: Five Reports. (Transportation Research Report Ser.). 58p. 1976. 2.60 o.p. (ISBN 0-309-02550-8). Transport Res Bd.

Design for Flying. David B. Thurston. (Illus.). 1976. text ed. 27.95 o.p. (ISBN 0-07-064553-1). McGraw.

Design for Good Acoustics & Noise Control. J. E. Moore. 1988. text ed. 17.50x o.p. (Pub. by Macmillan England); pap. 25.00x o.p. (ISBN 0-333-24293-9, Pub. by Macmillan England). Scholium Intl.

Design for Need. Ed. by J. Bicknell & L. McQuiston. 1977. 40.00 o.p. (ISBN 0-08-021500-9). Pergamon.

Design for the Real World: Human Ecology & Social Change. Victor Papanek. LC 70-154020. 1971. 8.95 o.p. (ISBN 0-394-47036-2). Pantheon.

Design for the Real World: Human Ecology & Social Change. 2nd, rev., New Academy Chicago ed. Victor Papanek. (Illus.). 405p. 1985. pap. 10.95 o.p. (ISBN 0-89733-153-2, Pub. by Granada England). Academy Chi Pubs.

Design for Tourism: An I.C.S.I.D. Interdesign Report. Ed. by Michael Gorman & Frank Height. 64p. 1977. 22.00 o.p. (ISBN 0-08-021481-9). Pergamon.

Design for Writing Workbook. Janet F. Egleson. 1970. pap. text ed. write for info. o.p. (ISBN 0-02-474140-X, 47414). Macmillan.

Design Fundamentals. Robert G. Scott. LC 79-28515. 216p. 1980. Repr. of 1951 ed. lib. bdg. 16.50 o.p. (ISBN 0-89874-040-1). Krieger.

Design Graphics. 12.00 o.p. (ISBN 0-317-65067-X). Am Consul Eng.

Design Graphs for Brick-Block Double Skin Panel Walls. C. B. Wilby. LC 81-6257. 132p. 1981. 29.95x o.p. (ISBN 0-470-27193-0). Halsted Pr.

Design in Architecture & the Human Sciences. Geoffrey Broadbent. LC 71-39233. 504p. 1978. pap. 41.95x o.p. (ISBN 0-471-99527-4). Wiley.

Design in Civil Architecture. A. E. Richardson & Hector O. Corfiato. (Illus.). 744p. 1956. Philos Lib.

Design in General Education. Ed. by John Harahan. 104p. 1978. pap. 14.50x o.p. (ISBN 0-435-86541-2, Pub. by Design Council England). Intl Spec Bk.

Design Interface: How Man & Machine Communicate: Olivetti Design Research. Gianni Barbacetto. (Project to Product Ser.). (Illus.). 128p. 45.00 o.s.i. (ISBN 0-317-66853-6). Princeton Arch.

Design: Libraries for Schools & University. Peters. 1972. pap. 10.95 o.p. (ISBN 0-442-26658-8). Van Nos Reinhold.

Design Manual for Cabinet Furniture. Furniture Development Council. 1959. pap. text ed. 3.90 o.p. (ISBN 0-08-013679-6). Pergamon.

Design Manual for High Temperature Hot Water & Steam Systems. Roger E. Cofield, Jr. LC 83-1135. 340p. 1984. 46.50x o.p. (ISBN 0-471-89363-3, Pub. by Wiley-Interscience). Wiley.

Design Methods for Digital Systems. J. Chinal. Tr. by A. Preston from Fr. LC 72-86277. (Illus.). 506p. 1973. 60.00 o.p. (ISBN 0-387-05871-0). Springer-Verlag.

Design Methods: Seeds of Human Futures - 1980 Edition - A Review of New Topics. J. Christopher Jones. LC 80-41757. 448p. 1981. pap. 41.95x o.p. (ISBN 0-471-27958-7, Pub. by Wiley Interscience). Wiley.

Design Mix Manual for Concrete Construction. Leslie Long et al. Ed. by Patricia Allen-Browne. LC 81-2363. 384p. 1982. text ed. 68.00 o.p. (ISBN 0-07-038683-8). McGraw.

Design Objectives for Highly Radioactive Solid Material Handling & Storage Facilities in a Reprocessing Plant (ANSI N305) 16p. 1975. pap. 9.50 o.p. (ISBN 0-8169-0005-1, A-21). Am Inst Chem Eng.

Design of an Interactive Manipulator Programming Environment. Ron Goldman. Ed. by Harold Stone. LC 84-28091. (Computer Science: Artificial Intelligence Ser.: No. 16). 158p. 1985. 44.95 o.p. (ISBN 0-8357-1616-3). UMI Res Pr.

Design of Biopharmaceutical Properties Through Prodrugs & Analogs. Ed. by Edward B. Roche. LC 77-81663. 455p. 1977. 30.00 o.p. (ISBN 0-917330-16-1); members 20.00 o.p. Am Pharm Assn.

Design of Building Frames. J. S. Gero & H. J. Cowan. (Illus.). 450p. 1976. 80.00 o.p. (ISBN 0-85334-644-5, Pub. by Elsevier Applied Sci England). Elsevier.

Design of Chemical Plants. Coppa & Avery Consultants Staff. (Architecture Ser.: A 1512). 10p. 1985. 2.00 o.p. (ISBN 0-89028-662-0). Vance Biblios.

Design of Computer Data Files. Owen Hanson. LC 78-31090. 358p. 1982. 32.95 o.p. (ISBN 0-914894-17-X, Computer Sci Pr). W H Freeman.

Design of Digital Computers. 2nd. ed. H. W. Gschwind & E. J. McCluskey. (Texts & Monographs in Computer Science Ser.). 1976. 26.00 o.p. (ISBN 0-387-06915-1). Springer-Verlag.

Design of Drama: An Introduction. Lloyd Hubenka & Reloy Garcia. LC 72-5455. 1973. pap. text ed. 8.95x o.p. (ISBN 0-679-30052-X). Longman.

Design of Electrical Services for Buildings. 2nd ed. F. Porges. 320p. 1982. 39.95 o.p. (ISBN 0-419-12360-1, NO. 6682, Pub. by E & FN Spon). Routledge Chapman & Hall.

Design of Energy-Responsive Commercial Buildings. Ed. by Solar Energy Research Institute Staff. LC 84-11864. 370p. 1985. text ed. 44.95 o.p. (ISBN 0-471-80463-0, Pub by Wiley-Interscience). Wiley.

Design of Equilibrium Stage Processes. Buford D. Smith. (Chemical Engineering Ser.). 1963. text ed. 62.50 o.p. (ISBN 0-07-058637-3). McGraw.

Design of Exhibition Facilities: A Focus on Architecture Contributions to Visitor Experience in Zoos, Aquariums, & Related Facilities. Jon A. Sanford & J. Scott Taylor. (Architecture Ser.: A 1463). 21p. 1985. 3.00 o.p. (ISBN 0-89028-553-5). Vance Biblios.

Design of Fire Resisting Structures. H. L. Melhotra. 1982. 49.95x o.p. (ISBN 0-412-00121-7, NO. 5019, Pub. by Chapman & Hall). Routledge Chapman & Hall.

Design of Global System Models & Their Limitations see Towards a Plan of Actions for Mankind.

Design of Long-Term Care Facilities. Laszlo Aranyi & Larry L. Goldman. 240p. 1980. 44.95 o.p. (ISBN 0-442-26120-9). Van Nos Reinhold.

Design of Microprocessor Systems. John H. Carson. LC 79-89495. (Tutorial Texts Ser.). 262p. 1979. 18.00 o.p. (ISBN 0-8186-0260-0, Q260). IEEE Comp Soc.

Design of Models for Testing Cancer Therapeutic Agents. Isiah Fidler & Richard White. (Litton Bionetics Workshop Ser.). 278p. 1981. 42.95 o.p. (ISBN 0-442-23897-5). Van Nos Reinhold.

Design of Nuclear Reactors. Coppa & Avery Consultants Staff. (Architecture Ser.: A 1412). 10p. 1985. 2.00 o.p. (ISBN 0-89028-442-3). Vance Biblios.

Design of Organizations. Pradip N. Khandwalla. 713p. 1977. text ed. 25.95 o.p. (ISBN 0-15-517366-9, HC). HarBraceJ.

Design of Organizations for Rural Development Projects: A Progress Report. William E. Smith et al. (Working Paper Ser.: No. 375). 48p. 1980. 5.00 o.p. (ISBN 0-8213-9240-9, WP 0375). World Bank.

Design of Petroleum Offshore Drilling Structures. Coppa & Avery Consultants Staff. (Architecture Ser.: A 1410). 12p. 1985. 2.00 o.p. (ISBN 0-89028-440-7). Vance Biblios.

Design of Piled Foundations. Thomas Whitaker. LC 70-99995. 1975. text ed. 29.00 o.p. (ISBN 0-08-019706-X); pap. text ed. 14.50 o.p. (ISBN 0-08-019705-1). Pergamon.

Design of Rehabilitation Services in Psychiatric Hospital Settings. Gail S. Fidler. LC 84-60474. 144p. 1984. pap. text ed. 26.00 o.p. (ISBN 0-943596-05-X, RAMSCO 00900). Ramsco Pub.

Design of Reinforced Concrete Elements. Patrick Morrell. 214p. 1977. pap. text ed. 23.00x o.p. (ISBN 0-258-97018-9, Pub. by Granada England). Gower Pub Co.

Design of Reinforced Concrete in Accordance with the Metric SAA Concrete Structures Code. Henry J. Cowan. (Illus.). 240p. 1975. 26.00x o.p. (ISBN 0-424-00000-8, Pub by Sydney U Pr). Intl Spec Bk.

Design of Reinforced Concrete Structures. Henry J. Cowan. (Illus.). 304p. 1982. text ed. 48.00 o.p. (ISBN 0-13-201376-2). P-H.

Design of Reinforced Concrete Structures. M. Nadim Hassoun. 1985. text ed. write for info. o.p. (ISBN 0-534-03759-3, 21R2400, Pub. by PWS Engineering). PWS-Kent Pub.

Design of Sailing Yachts. Pierre Gutelle. LC 83-82851. (Illus.). 210p. 1984. 6.70 o.p. (ISBN 0-87742-183-8, D340). Intl Marine.

Design of Sewage Disposal Plants: A Bibliography. Coppa & Avery Consultants Staff. (Architecture Ser.: Bibliography A 1320). 1985. pap. 2.00 o.p. (ISBN 0-89028-270-6). Vance Biblios.

Design of Storage Facilities for Radioactive Substances. Coppa & Avery Consultants Staff. (Architecture Ser.: A 1411). 11p. 1985. 2.00 o.p. (ISBN 0-89028-441-5). Vance Biblios.

Design of Systems & Circuits for Maximum Reliability or Maximum Production Yield. Peter W. Becker & Finn Jensen. (Illus.). 1977. text ed. 44.00 o.p. (ISBN 0-07-004230-6). McGraw.

Design of User-Friendly Programs for Small Computers. Henry K. Simpson. 256p. 1985. pap. text ed. 19.95 o.p. (ISBN 0-07-057300-X). McGraw.

Design of Wood Structures. Donald E. Breyer & John A. Ank. (Illus.). 1980. text ed. 54.50 o.p. (ISBN 0-07-007671-5). McGraw.

Design-Operation Interactions at Large Waste Water Treatment Plants. S. H. Jenkins. 1978. pap. 55.00 flexi-cover o.p. (ISBN 0-08-020901-7). Pergamon.

Design: Purpose, Form, & Meaning. John F. Pile. (Illus.). 1982. pap. 11.95 o.p. (ISBN 0-393-95106-5). Norton.

Design Techniques for Electronics Engineers. Electronics Magazine Editors. 1978. text ed. 43.50 o.p. (ISBN 0-07-019158-1). McGraw.

Design Through Discovery. 4th ed. Marjorie E. Bevlin. LC 83-18387. 426p. 1984. pap. text ed. 22.95 o.p. (ISBN 0-03-062148-8, HoltC). HR&W.

Design: Without a Designer? Elvera Johnson. LC 84-90001. 91p. 1985. 8.95 o.p. (ISBN 0-533-06095-8). Vantage.

Design Your Own. Linda Harrison. (Illus.). 80p. (gr. 2-6). 1984. pap. text ed. 6.95 o.p. (ISBN 0-86530-075-5, IP 75-5). Incentive Pubns.

Designated Hitter. Walter Wager. LC 81-71678. 1982. 13.95 o.p. (ISBN 0-87795-385-6, Arbor Hse). Morrow.

Designed to Win. Roger Marshall. (Illus.). 1981. 28.50 o.p. (ISBN 0-393-03229-9). Norton.

Designer Textiles: Stitching for Interiors. Emroiderers' Guild. (Illus.). 128p. 1988. 19.95 o.p. (ISBN 0-7153-9040-6, Pub. by David & Charles Pub England). Sterling.

Designer's Choice: The Best Products, Graphics & Environments of 1980. Industrial Design Magazine Staff. Ed. by George Finley. 120p. 1980. pap. text ed. 7.95 o.p. (ISBN 0-07-031710-0). McGraw.

Designer's Guide to OSHA: A Practical Design Guide to the Occupational Safety & Health Act for Architects, Engineers, & Builders. 2nd ed. Peter S. Hopf. (Illus.). 1982. text ed. 53.50 o.p. (ISBN 0-07-030317-7). McGraw.

Designer's Handbook of Pressure Sensing Devices. Jerry L. Lyons. 304p. 1980. 32.95 o.p. (ISBN 0-442-24964-0). Van Nos Reinhold.

Designing Academic Program Reviews. Ed. by Richard F. Wilson. LC 81-48479. (Higher Education Ser.: No. 37). 1982. text ed. 11.95x o.p. (ISBN 0-87589-895-5). Jossey-Bass.

Designing an Effective Sales Compensation Program. John K. Moynahan. (Illus.). 256p. 1980. 16.95 o.p. (ISBN 0-8144-5591-3). AMACOM.

Designing & Building a Solar House. rev. & expanded ed. Donald Watson. LC 84-73329. (Illus.). 248p. 1985. 25.00 o.p. (ISBN 0-88266-086-1, Garden Way Pub); pap. 15.95 o.p. (ISBN 0-88266-401-8). Storey Comm Inc.

Designing & Building a Solar House: Your Place in the Sun. Donald Watson. LC 76-53830. (Illus.). 288p. 1977. 14.95 o.p. (ISBN 0-88266-086-1, Garden Way Pub); pap. 10.95 o.p. (ISBN 0-88266-085-3). Storey Comm Inc.

Designing & Building Special Cars. Andre Jute. (Illus.). 168p. 1985. 34.95 o.p. (ISBN 0-7134-0778-6, Pub. by Batsford England). David & Charles.

Designing & Building Your Own Professional Office. Murray Schwartz. 336p. 1981. casebound 33.95 o.p. (ISBN 0-87489-228-7). Med Economics.

Designing & Conducting Behavioral Research. C. J. Drew & M. L. Hardman. (Pergamon General Psychology Ser.: No. 134). 311p. 1986. pap. (ISBN 0-08-033988-3). Pergamon.

Designing & Making Handwoven Rugs: Techniques for Creating European, Oriental & American Rugs & Household Fabrics. Osma G. Tod & Josephine C. Del Deo. 14.00 o.p. (ISBN 0-8446-5616-X). Peter Smith.

Designing & Making Handwrought Jewelry. Joseph F. Shoenfelt. (Illus.). 1960. pap. text ed. 3.50 o.p. (ISBN 0-07-057004-3). McGraw.

Designing & Managing Organizations. Stephen L. Fink et al. 1983. 35.95x o.p. (ISBN 0-256-02628-9). Irwin.

Designing & Programming Modern Computers & Systems. Svetland Kartashev & Steven Kartashev. (LSI Modular Computer Systems Ser.: Vol. I). (Illus.). 736p. 1982. text ed. 68.00 o.p. (ISBN 0-13-201343-6). P-H.

Designing & Using Feedback Forms. Geraldine Markel & Daniel Wolter. (Michigan Learning Modules Ser.: No. 22). 1978. pap. 3.50x o.p. (ISBN 0-914004-25-5). Ulrich.

Designing, Building & Selling Energy Conserving Homes. National Association of Home Builders Staff. 131p. 1978. pap. 6.25 o.p. (ISBN 0-86718-021-8). Nat Assn H Build.

Designing For Building Utilisation. Ed. by James A. Powell & Ian Cooper. 400p. 1985. 52.00 o.p. (ISBN 0-419-13470-0, NO. 9337, Pub. by E & FN Spon England). Routledge Chapman & Hall.

Designing for Fire Safety. E. G. Butcher & A. C. Parnell. 372p. 1983. 73.95 o.p. (ISBN 0-471-10239-3). Wiley.

Designing for Human Behavior: Architecture & the Behavioral Sciences. Ed. by J. Lang et al. LC 73-22208. (Community Development Ser.: Vol. 6). 353p. 1982. pap. 28.95 o.p. (ISBN 0-87933-217-4). Van Nos Reinhold.

Designing for Industry. F. C. Ashford. 232p. 1955. (ISBN 0-8022-0041-9). Philos Lib.

Designing for Printed Textiles: A Guide to Studio & Freelance Work. Carol Joyce. (Illus.). 132p. 1982. 18.95 o.p. (ISBN 0-13-201327-4); 9.95 o.p. (ISBN 0-13-201319-3). P-H.

Designing from Nature: A Source Book for Artists & Craftsmen. Esther W. Dendel. LC 77-92756. 1978. 10.95 o.s.i. (ISBN 0-8008-2173-4); pap. 5.95 o.s.i. (ISBN 0-8008-2174-2). Taplinger.

Designing Interior Environment. Mary J. Alexander. (Illus.). 236p. 1972. text ed. 16.95 o.p. (ISBN 0-15-517372-3, HC). HarBraceJ.

Designing Jewelery. James Warwick. (ISBN 0-684-17705-6). Scribner.

Designing Pictures with String. Robert Sharpton. 1987. pap. 15.95 o.s.i. (ISBN 0-317-65142-0). Emerson.

Designing Staircases. Willibald Mannes. 144p. 1982. 27.95 o.p. (ISBN 0-442-22578-4). Van Nos Reinhold.

Designing Today's Manufactured Products. John R. Lindbeck. LC 72-79110. 225p. (gr. 10-12). 1972. text ed. 21.28 o.p. (ISBN 0-87345-440-5). Glencoe.

Designing with Light: An Introduction to Stage Lighting. J. Michael Gillette. LC 78-51945. (Illus.). 195p. 1978. pap. text ed. 13.95 o.p. (ISBN 0-87484-420-7). Mayfield Pub.

Designing with Linear Integrated Circuits. Ed. by Jerry Eimbinder. LC 68-56161. 301p. 1969. 21.50 o.p. (ISBN 0-471-23455-9, Pub. by Wiley). Krieger.

Designing with the Wool see Working with the Wool: How to Weave a Navajo Rug.

Designing with TTL Integrated Circuits. Texas Instruments, Inc. Staff. 1971. text ed. 59.95 o.p. (ISBN 0-07-063745-8). McGraw.

Designs & Patterns for Embroiderers & Craftsmen: 512 Motifs from the Wm. Briggs & Co. "Album of Transfer Patterns" Briggs, Wm. & Co.Staff. Ed. by Marion Nichols. 15.25 o.p. (ISBN 0-8446-5164-8). Peter Smith.

Designs for Casual Living. Barbara Taylor Bradford. (Illus.). 1977. 16.95 o.p. (ISBN 0-671-21969-3). S&S.

Designs for Fund-Raising: Principles, Patterns, Techniques. Harold J. Seymour. 1966. text ed. 42.50 o.p. (ISBN 0-07-056354-3). McGraw.

Designs for Wood: How to Plan & Create Your Own Furniture. Alonzo W. Kettless. LC 77-87177. (Illus.). 1978. 4.95 o.p. (ISBN 0-684-15541-9, ScribT); encore ed. 4.95 o.p. (ISBN 0-684-17533-9). Scribner.

Designs from Pre-Columbian Mexico. Jorge Encisco. (Illus.). 14.50 o.p. (ISBN 0-8446-0088-1). Peter Smith.

Designs from the Ancient Mimbrenos With Hopi Interpretation. Fred Kabotie. LC 82-80587. (Illus.). 100p. 1982. 40.00 o.p. (ISBN 0-87358-308-6); ltd. ed. o.p. 125.00 o.p. (ISBN 0-686-97963-X). Northland.

Designsource Nineteen Eighty-Six. Patricia M. Schilling. 400p. 1985. 30.00 o.p. (ISBN 0-914999-02-8). Turnbull & Co.

Desirable Characteristics of Student Library Media Personnel & The Concept of the Future As It Is Presented in Children's Books Today. Peggy A. Sullivan. (Occasional Papers: No. 119). 21p. 1975. pap. 2.00 o.p. (ISBN 0-317-58936-9). U of Ill Lib Info Sci.

Desirable Husband. Frances Vernon. 232p. 1988. 19.95 o.p. (ISBN 0-7181-2658-0, Pub. by Michael Joseph). David & Charles.

Desire. Anne Hampson. (Silhouette Romances Ser.). 1984. lib. bdg. 8.95 o.p. (ISBN 0-8398-2808-X, Gregg). G K Hall.

Desire (A Play) Pablo Picasso. (ISBN 0-8022-1970-5). Philos Lib.

Desire & Conquer. Diane Dunaway. (Candlelight Ecstasy Ser.: No. 158). (Orig.). 1983. pap. 1.95 o.p. (ISBN 0-440-11779-8). Dell.

Desire & Denial: Celibacy & the Church. Gordon Thomas. 1986. 19.95 o.p. (ISBN 0-316-84097-1). Little.

Desire & Dream. Kaye Dobkin. 352p. 1984. pap. 3.50 o.p. (ISBN 0-380-89342-8, 89342-8). Avon.

Desire & Surrender. Katherine Sutcliffe. 400p. 1986. pap. 3.75 o.p. (ISBN 0-380-75067-8). Avon.

Desires. John L'Heureux. LC 80-20228. 1981. 12.95 o.p. (ISBN 0-03-058902-9). H Holt & Co.

Desk Book for Setting up the Closely-Held Corporation. Robert P. Hess. LC 79-19309. 1979. 59.50 o.p. (ISBN 0-87624-113-5, Inst Busn Plan). P-H.

Desk Reference for Neuroanatomy: A Guide to Essential Terms. L. Lockard. LC 77-21707. 1977. 29.95 o.p. (ISBN 0-387-90278-3). Springer-Verlag.

Deskbook of Business Management Terms. Leon A. Wortman. LC 78-23257. 1979. 24.95 o.p. (ISBN 0-8144-5470-4). AMACOM.

Deskbook of Math Formulas & Tables. Joanne B. Auth. 208p. 1984. 19.95 o.p. (ISBN 0-442-20813-8); pap. 17.95 o.p. (ISBN 0-442-21106-6). Van Nos Reinhold.

Desktop Publishing Systems. Harold C. Durbin. 1988. 25.00 o.p. (ISBN 0-936786-14-0). Durbin Assoc.

Desktop Publishing with Microsoft WORD on the Macintosh. Tim Ericson & William Finzer. 400p. (Orig.). 1987. pap. 22.95 o.p. (ISBN 0-89588-447-X). Sybex.

Desktop Publishing with WordPerfect Version 5. Clifford Philip. Date not set. pap. 18.95 o.s.i. (ISBN 0-673-38360-1). Scott F.

Desktop Publishing with Your IBM PC & Compatible. Jerry Willis. LC 87-3697. 320p. 1987. pap. 15.95 o.p. (ISBN 0-89586-586-6). Price Stern.

Desmidieen aus dem Suedosten der Vereinigten Staaten von Amerika. K. Foerster. (Illus.). 132p. 1972. pap. text ed. 24.00x o.p. (ISBN 3-7682-0874-5). Lubrecht & Cramer.

Desperadoes. Ron Hansen. 288p. 1984. pap. 3.50 o.s.i. (ISBN 0-345-32500-1). Ballantine.

Desperate Adversaries. Jack Hoffenberg. 1976. pap. 1.95 o.p. (ISBN 0-380-00702-9, 29801). Avon.

Desperate Remedies: The Tragedy of Santa Maria, CA. Les Conrad. (Illus., Orig.). 1987. pap. 5.95 o.p. (ISBN 0-9619042-0-8). Atlas Signs.

Desperate Rider see Texan Came Riding.

Despotism. Dagobert D. Runes. LC 62-22269. (Illus.). 288p. 1963. (ISBN 0-8022-1428-2). Philos Lib.

Desserts with Spirit! Robert Carmack & Gino Cofacci. LC 84-45056. 244p. 1985. 15.95 o.p. (ISBN 0-689-11473-7, Atheneum). Macmillan.

Destination. Peter Caruso. LC 72-118307. 1970. 12.95 o.p. (ISBN 0-8022-2342-7). Philos Lib.

Destined for the Cross. Paul E. Billheimer. 1982. pap. 4.95 o.p. (ISBN 0-8423-0604-8). Tyndale.

Destinies. Charlotte V. Allen. 384p. 1986. pap. 3.95 o.s.i. (ISBN 0-425-07444-7). Berkley Pub.

Destiny at Dawn. Alex Ely. Orig. Title: Erich's Sunrise. 161p. 1981. 7.50 o.p. (ISBN 0-682-49709-6). Exposition-Phoenix.

Destiny of Our Monetary & Economic World. Julian B. Shealy. LC 72-90069. 1972. 7.50 o.p. (ISBN 0-682-47588-2). Exposition-Phoenix.

Destiny of the Warrior. Georges Dumezil. Tr. by Alf Hiltebeitel. LC 75-113254. 184p. 1971. lib. bdg. 15.00x o.s.i. (ISBN 0-226-16970-7); pap. write for info. o.s.i. (ISBN 0-226-16971-5). U of Chicago Pr.

Destiny of the World: The Socialist Shape of Things to Come. G. Shakhnazarov. 334p. 1979. 6.45 o.p. (ISBN 0-8285-1611-1, Pub. by Progress Pubs USSR). Imported Pubns.

Destiny Stone. Robert E. Vardeman & Victor Milan. LC 80-82223. (War of Powers Ser.: Bk. 3). 224p. (Orig.). 1980. pap. 2.50 o.s.i. (ISBN 0-86721-085-0). Berkley Pub.

Destiny's Calendar. Gary Metras. 66p. 1985. 5.00 o.p. (ISBN 0-317-17703-6). Samisdat.

Destiny's Lady. (Candlelight Ecstasy Ser.: No. 494). (Orig.). 1987. pap. 2.25 o.p. (ISBN 0-440-11810-7). Dell.

Destiny's Pawn. Mary R. Daheim. 432p. 1984. pap. 3.95 o.p. (ISBN 0-380-86884-9, 86884). Avon.

Destiny's Plan: The Story of a Combination Family. A. Mac Gant. LC 81-90504. (Illus.). 196p. 1982. 8.95 o.p. (ISBN 0-533-05115-0). Vantage.

Destroy, She Said. Marguerite Duras. Tr. by Barbara Bray from Fr. 144p. 1986. pap. 6.95 o.p. (ISBN 0-394-62326-6, Ever). Grove.

Destruction of a Continent: Africa & International Aid. Karl Borgin & Kathleen Corbett. LC 82-47677. 216p. 1982. 14.95 o.p. (ISBN 0-15-125308-0). HarBraceJ.

Destruction of Death. Nelson L. Price. LC 82-72464. 1983. 4.50 o.p. (ISBN 0-8054-1528-9). Broadman.

Destruction of Nature in the Soviet Union. Boris Komarov. Tr. by Michel Vale & Joe Hollander. LC 80-5452. Orig. Title: Unichtozhenie Prioroda Obostrenie Ekologicheskogo Krizisa V SSSR. 132p. 1980. 30.00 o.p. (ISBN 0-87332-157-X). M E Sharpe.

Destructive David. Franklin Straus. (gr. k-5). 1980. pap. 3.95 o.p. (ISBN 0-570-03483-3, 56-1704). Concordia.

Desulfurization of Iron & Steel & Sulfide Shape Control. 161p. 1980. 40.00 o.p. (ISBN 0-89520-151-8). Iron & Steel.

Detachable Man. Donald Finkel. LC 83-45521. 96p. 1984. 14.95 o.p. (ISBN 0-689-11458-3, Atheneum); pap. 7.95 o.p. (ISBN 0-689-11459-1, Atheneum). Macmillan.

Detail & Pattern: Essays for Composition. 3rd rev. ed. Robert A. Baylor. (Illus.). 224p. 1976. text ed. 22.95 o.p. (ISBN 0-07-004145-8). McGraw.

Detailed Account of the Major Famous Audacities Associated with Leading Characters of History. W. Trowbridge. (Illus.). 317p. 1988. Repr. of 1909 ed. 198.75 o.p. (ISBN 0-89266-615-3). Am Classical Coll Pr.

Detailed Diagnosis & Procedures for Patients Discharged from Short-Stay Hospitals: United States, 1985. Robert Pokras. (Vital & Health Statistics Data from the National Health Series 13: No. 90). 294p. 1987. pap. 14.00 o.p. (ISBN 0-318-22893-9, S/N 017-022-00994-3). USGPO.

Detailed Land Classification. Land Study Bureau, Univ. of Hawaii Staff. Incl. Island of Hawaii. (No. 6). 763p. 1965. pap. 38.00 o.p. (ISBN 0-8248-0311-6); Island of Kauai. (No. 9). 151p. 1967. pap. 9.00x o.p. (ISBN 0-8248-0309-4); Island of Lanai. (No. 8). (Illus.). 60p. 1967. pap. 3.00x (ISBN 0-8248-0310-8); Island of Maui. (No. 7). (Illus.). 167p. 1967. pap. 9.50x (ISBN 0-8248-0312-4); Island of Molokai. (No. 10). (Illus.). 95p. 1968. pap. 5.00x (ISBN 0-8248-0308-6); Island of Oahu. rev. ed. (No. 11). 320p. 1973. pap. 17.00x o. p. o.p. (ISBN 0-8248-0320-5). (Land Study Bureau Bulletin Ser.). pap. UH Pr.

Detailing for Building Construction: A Designer's Manual of Over 350 Standard Details. Greater London Council Department of Architecture & Civic Design Staff. (Illus.). 500p. 1980. 52.50x o.p. (ISBN 0-85139-233-4); pap. 37.75x o.p. (ISBN 0-85139-234-2). Nichols Pub.

Detecting Sequences of Events-Level A: Developing Reading Comprehension. Lynda F. Kest. 56p. 1978. o.p. (ISBN 0-379-20270-0). Oceana.

Detection of Fish. D. H. Cushing. 220p. 1973. 65.00 o.p. (ISBN 0-08-017123-0). Pergamon.

Detection of Ischaemic Myocardium with Exercise: Symposium. Ed. by F. Loogen & L. Seipel. (Illus.). 191p. 1982. pap. 28.50 o.p. (ISBN 0-387-11237-5). Springer-Verlag.

Detection of New Adverse Drug Reactions. M. B. Stephens. LC 85-2834. 260p. 1985. 80.00x o.p. (ISBN 0-943818-33-8, Stockton Pr). Groves Dict Music.

Detection Theory. Iuan Selin. (Rand Corporation Research Studies). 1965. 34.00x o.p. (ISBN 0-691-07944-7). Princeton U Pr.

Detectionary. Otto Pensler et al. 1980. pap. 2.95 o.s.i. (ISBN 0-345-29086-0). Ballantine.

Detectionary. Mill Roseman. Ed. by Otto Fenzler et al. LC 75-27326. (Illus.). 320p. 1980. 22.95 o.p. (ISBN 0-87951-041-2); pap. 12.95 o.p. (ISBN 0-87951-114-1). Overlook Pr.

Detective Mole. Robert Quackenbush. LC 75-25806. (Lothrop Fun-to-Read Bks.). (Illus.). 64p. (gr. 1-4). 1976. 10.00 o.p. (ISBN 0-688-41726-4); PLB 10.88 o.p. (ISBN 0-688-51726-9). Lothrop.

Detective of London. Robert Kraus & Bruce Kraus. LC 72-24450. (Illus.). 28p. (gr. 3 up). 1979. 6.95 o.s.i. (ISBN 0-671-96169-1). Windmill Bks.

Detectives in Togas. Henry Winterfeld. LC 56-6922. (Illus.). (gr. 4-6). 1966. pap. 2.25 o.p. (ISBN 0-15-625315-1, VoyB). HarBraceJ.

Detector Owner's Field Manual. rev. ed. Roy Lagal. Ed. by Bettye Nelson. LC 75-44706. (Illus.). 236p. (Orig.). 1982. pap. 8.95 o.p. (ISBN 0-915920-43-3). Ram Pub.

Detente. Ed. by G. R. Urban. LC 75-33483. 1976. 25.00x o.p. (ISBN 0-87663-271-1). Universe.

Detente: Prospects for Democracy & Dictatorship. 2nd ed. Aleksandr Solzhenitsyn. 134p. 1980. text ed. 9.95x o.p. (ISBN 0-87855-352-5); pap. text ed. 9.95x o.s.i. (ISBN 0-87855-750-4). Transaction Pubs.

Detergent Analysis: A Handbook for Cost-Effective Quality Control. B. M. Milwidsky & D. M. Gabriel. LC 81-19840. 291p. 1982. 75.95 o.p. (ISBN 0-470-27257-0). Halsted Pr.

Deterioration of the English Language. John M. Adamiak. 1974. 4.00 o.p. (ISBN 0-682-48132-7). Exposition-Phoenix.

Determinants of Behavioral Development: Proceedings of the International Society for the Study of Behavioral Development, University of Nijmegen, the Netherlands, July 1971. International Society for the Study of Behavioral Development Symposium Staff. Ed. by F. J. Monks et al. 1972. 84.00 o.p. (ISBN 0-12-504750-9). Acad Pr.

Determinants of Fertility in Developing Countries. Rodolfo A. Bulatao & Ronald D. Lee. LC 83-17135. (Studies Population Ser.). 1983. Vol. 1: Supply & Demand for Children. 45.50 o.p. (ISBN 0-12-140501-X); Vol. 2: Fertility Regulation & Institutional Influences. 51.00 o.p. (ISBN 0-12-140502-8). Acad Pr.

Determinants of Free Will: A Psychological Analysis of Responsible, Adjustive Behavior. James Easterbrook. (Personality & Psychopathology Ser.). 1978. 33.00 o.p. (ISBN 0-12-227550-0). Acad Pr.

Determinants of Health Levels in Developing Countries. G. E. Cumper. LC 83-13906. (Tropical Medicine Research Studies Ser.: 1-520). 150p. 1984. 54.95x o.p. (ISBN 0-471-90268-3, Pub by Res Stud Pr). Wiley.

Determinants of Spatial Organization: Symposium of the Society for Developmental Biology, 37th. Ed. by Stephen Subtelny & Irwin R. Konigsberg. LC 78-23508. 1979. 43.50 o.p. (ISBN 0-12-612983-5). Acad Pr.

Determination of Carboxylic Functional Groups. R. D. Tiwari & J. P. Sharma. LC 73-104121. 1970. 35.00 o.p. (ISBN 0-08-015516-2). Pergamon.

Determination of Epoxide Groups. B. Dobinson et al. 1969. 35.00 o.p. (ISBN 0-08-012788-6). Pergamon.

Determination of Hydrazine-Hydrazide Groups. H. E. Malone. 1970. 100.00 o.p. (ISBN 0-08-015871-4). Pergamon.

Determination of Impurities in Nuclear Grade Sodium Metal & Related Sodium Compounds. Louis Silverman. 156p. 1971. 40.00 o.p. (ISBN 0-08-016165-0). Pergamon.

Determination of Liquid Water Structure, Coordination Numbers for Ions & Solvation for Biological Molecules. E. Clementi. (Lecture Notes in Chemistry: Vol. 2). 1976. soft cover 13.00 o.p. (ISBN 0-387-07870-3). Springer-Verlag.

Determination of Organic Compounds with N-Bromosuccinimide & Allied Reagents. N. K. Mathur & C. K. Narang. (Analysis of Organic Materials Ser.). 1975. 43.00 o.p. (ISBN 0-12-479750-4). Acad Pr.

Determination of Organic Peroxides. R. M. Johnson & I. W. Siddiqi. LC 75-104884. 1970. 35.00 o.p. (ISBN 0-08-015586-3). Pergamon.

Determination of Sulphur-Containing Groups. M. R. Ashworth. (Analysis of Organic Materials & International Series of Monographs, No. 2). Vol. 1 1973. 76.00 o.p. (ISBN 0-12-065001-0); Vol. 2 1976. 76.00 o.p. (ISBN 0-12-065002-9); Vol. 3 1977. 76.00 o.p. (ISBN 0-12-065003-7). Acad Pr.

Determination of Tissue Oxygen Pressure in Patients. Ed. by A. M. Ehrly. (Illus.). 112p. 1983. 24.00 o.p. (ISBN 0-08-029785-4). Pergamon.

Determinative Team. Andrew P. Swanson. 1979. pap. 6.00 o.p. (ISBN 0-682-49248-5). Exposition-Phoenix.

Determining Compensation in the Public Sector: A Bibliography. Mary E. Huls. (Public Administration Ser.: P 1721). 9p. 1985. 2.00 o.p. (ISBN 0-89028-491-1). Vance Biblios.

Determining Effectiveness of Teaching Home Economics. H. Chadderdon. LC 74-78396. 1971. pap. 2.50 o.p. (ISBN 0-686-00147-8, 261-08408). Home Econ Educ.

Determining Pavement Skid Resistance Requirements at Intersections & Braking Sections. (National Cooperative Highway Research Project Report). 64p. 1974. 4.40 o.p. (ISBN 0-309-02306-8). Transport Res Bd.

Deterrence & Incapacitation: Estimating the Effects of Criminal Sanctions on Crime Rates. Assembly of Behavioral & Social Sciences. 1978. pap. 16.75x o.p. (ISBN 0-309-02649-0). Natl Acad Pr.

Detling Secret. Julian Symons. 1982. (ISBN 0-89919-096-0, Kahn Bks). Ticknor & Fields.

Detoxication of Hazardous Waste. Ed. by Jurgen H. Exner. LC 82-70696. (Illus.). 362p. 1982. 42.95 o.p. (ISBN 0-250-40521-0). Butterworth.

Detroit Lions. James R. Rothaus. (NFL Today Ser.). (Illus.). 48p. (gr. 4-12). 1982. PLB 10.45 o.p. (ISBN 0-87191-811-0); pap. 4.25 o.p. (ISBN 0-89812-257-0). Creative Ed.

Detroit Pistons. Jim Moore. (NBA Today Ser.). (Illus.). 48p. (gr. 4 up). 1984. PLB 10.45 o.p. (ISBN 0-87191-976-1). Creative Ed.

Detroit Tigers. Martin. LC 82-16183. (Baseball Today Ser.). 48p. (gr. 4 up). 1982. PLB 11.45 o.p. (ISBN 0-87191-860-9). Creative Ed.

Deuce & Don'ts of Tennis. Bil Keane. LC 75-14107. 80p. 1975. pap. 4.95 o.p. (ISBN 0-89019-045-3). Norwalk Pr.

Deuteromycotina & Selected Ascomycotina from Wood & Wood Products. Elwin L. Stewart et al. (Contributions from the University of Minnesota Plant Pathology Department Ser.: No. 1). 283p. (Orig.). 1988. 20.00 o.p. (ISBN 0-8087-6983-9). Burgess MN Intl.

Deuteronomistic History. 2nd ed. Martin Noth. (Journal for the Study of the Old Testament, Supplement Ser.: No. 15). pap. text ed. 16.50x o.s.i. (ISBN 0-905774-25-6, Pub. by JSOT Pr England). Eisenbrauns.

Deuteronomy, Jeremiah. Elizabeth Achtemeier. Ed. by Foster R. McCurley. LC 77-15226. (Proclamation Commentaries: the Old Testament Witnesses for Preaching Ser.). 96p. (Orig.). 1978. pap. 3.95 o.p. (ISBN 0-8006-0590-X, 1-590, Fortress). Augsburg Fortress.

Deutsch fur Alle: Beginning College German: a Comprehensive Approach Workbook. 2nd ed. Werner Haas & Gustave B. Mathieu. LC 82-17637. 336p. 1983. text ed. (ISBN 0-471-86406-4). text ed. 27.50 o.p. (ISBN 0-471-86407-2). Wiley.

Deutsch Heute: Grundstufe. 2nd ed. Jack R. Moeller & Helmut Liedloff. LC 78-52718. (Illus.). 1979. text ed. 27.95 o.p. (ISBN 0-395-27175-4). HM.

Deutsch-Vietnamesisches Woerterbuch. 7th ed. D. Ho-gia-Huong et al. 365p. (Ger. & Vietnamese.). 1980. 65.00 o.p. (ISBN 0-8288-1088-5, F 65650). French & Eur.

Deutsch X 3. Incl. Gespraechsbuch II "Meine Meinung" (Illus.). 1978. pap. text ed. 4.30x (ISBN 3-468-49656-7); Glossar III, Einsprachig Deutsch. pap. text ed. 2.10x (ISBN 3-468-49711-3); Lehrerheft III. pap. text ed. 2.10x (ISBN 3-468-49706-7); Leseheft III, "Aktuell und interessant" Die wichtigsten Staedte in den deutsch sprachigen Laendern. (Illus.). pap. text ed. 3.75x (ISBN 3-468-49761-X); Loesungsheft III. pap. text ed. 2.10x (ISBN 3-468-49741-5); Sprachlabor-Cassetten II mit Sprechuebungen. price not set cassettes (ISBN 0-685-60100-5); Sprachlabor-Tonbaender II mit Sprechuebungen. price not set tapes (ISBN 0-685-60101-3); Sprechuebungen II. pap. text ed. price not set (ISBN 3-468-49646-X); Text-Cassette II mit ausgewaehlten Lektionstexten. cassette 10.90x (ISBN 3-468-84741-6); Uebungsbuch III. pap. text ed. 3.20x (ISBN 3-468-49751-2). 1978. M S Rosenberg.

Deutsch X 3. Heinz Griesbach. Incl. Gespraechsbuch I mit Uebungen, "Unterwegs" (Illus.). 1975. pap. text ed. 4.30x (ISBN 3-468-49556-0); Glossary I, German-English. 1974. pap. text ed. 2.10x (ISBN 3-468-49511-0); Glossary II, German-English. 1976. pap. text ed. 2.65x (ISBN 3-468-49611-7); Lehrerheft I. (Illus.). 1974. pap. text ed. 2.10x (ISBN 3-468-49506-4); Lehrerheft II. 1976. pap. text ed. 2.10x (ISBN 3-468-49606-0); Lernbuch I. Illus. by Herbert Horn. 1974. pap. text ed. 4.85x (ISBN 3-468-49501-3); Lernbuch II. Illus. by Herbert Horn. 1975. pap. text ed. 4.85x (ISBN 3-468-49601-X); Lernbuch III. (Illus.). 1977. pap. text ed. 4.85x (ISBN 3-468-49701-6); Leseheft I mit Uebungen, "Aktuell und interessant" (Illus.). 1975. pap. text ed. 3.75x (ISBN 3-468-49561-7); Leseheft II mit Uebungen, "Aktuell und interessant" Die Laender der Bundesrepublik Deutschland. (Illus.). 1977. pap. text ed. 3.75x (ISBN 3-468-49661-3); Loesungsheft I. 1974. pap. text ed. 2.10x (ISBN 3-468-49541-2); Loesungsheft II. 1976. pap. text ed. 2.65x (ISBN 3-468-49641-9); Sprachlabor-Cassetten, Saemtliche Sprechuebungen, Doppelspur Mitnachsprechpausen, 10 Casetten. 1974. pap. text ed. 136.80x (ISBN 3-468-84722-X); Sprachlabor-Tonbaender saemtliche Sprechuebungen, Vollspur mit Nachsprechpausen, 10 Tonbaender. 1974. pap. text ed. 239.40x (ISBN 3-468-84726-2); Sprechuebungem I - Textheft. 1974. pap. text ed. 3.75x (ISBN 3-468-49546-3). pap. M S Rosenberg.

Deutsche Blatter Leben, Kunst Wissenschaft: Herausgegeben Von Karl Gutzkow see Deutsche Revue: Herausgegeben Von Karl Gutzkow & Ludolf Weinbarg.

Deutsche Drama, Vol. 2. Ed. by Harry Steinhauer. 1939. 6.95x o.p. (ISBN 0-393-09435-9, NortonC). Norton.

Deutsche Drama von Kleist bis Hauptmann. Ed. by A. Peter Foulkes & Edgar Lohner. LC 76-185793. 680p. 1973. text ed. 27.50 o.p. (ISBN 0-395-12742-4). HM.

Deutsche Kulturgeschichte. Pauline Reinkraut-Freidjung. 1968. text ed. 7.50 o.p. (ISBN 0-682-45727-2, University). Exposition-Phoenix.

Deutsche Literatur Von Heute: An Intermediate German Course. Agnes K. Domandi & D. S. Guilloton. 1974. text ed. 20.00 o.p. (ISBN 0-03-005626-8, HoltC). HR&W.

Deutsche Lyrik. Ed. by Konrad Schaum. (Orig., Ger.). 1963. pap. 2.95x o.p. (ISBN 0-393-09612-2, NortonC). Norton.

Deutsche Novelle, 1880-1950. expanded ed. Ed. by Harry Steinhauer. 1958. 7.50x o.p. (ISBN 0-393-09515-0, NortonC). Norton.

Deutsche Novellen Von Tieck Bis Hauptmann. Ed. by A. Peter Foulkes & Edgar Lohner. (Ger). 1969. text ed. 16.50 o.p. (ISBN 0-395-04809-5). HM.

Deutsche Revue: Herausgegeben Von Karl Gutzkow & Ludolf Weinbarg, No. 1. Bd. with Nos. 1 & 2. Deutsche Blatter Leben, Kunst Wissenschaft: Herausgegeben Von Karl Gutzkow. (Unpublished). Repr. of 1835 ed. (Unpublished). 1973. Repr. of 1835 ed. 23.00 o.p. (ISBN 0-384-11535-7); unbound 14.50 o.p. (ISBN 0-685-30624-0). Johnson Repr.

Deutsche Texte und Wortschatzuebungen. M. Skilton. LC 76-93127. 1969. 4.60 o.p. (ISBN 0-08-006462-0); pap. 3.20 o.p. (ISBN 0-08-006461-2). Pergamon.

Deutschen: Vergangenheit und Gegenwart. 2nd ed. Wulf Koepke. 1980. text ed. 15.95 o.p. (ISBN 0-03-048696-3, HoltC). HR&W.

Deutschland und Amerika: Unter der Lupe. Mark Rectanus et al. (Ger.). 1984. pap. text ed. 9.00 o.p. (ISBN 0-88377-345-7). Newbury Hse.

Deux Cavaliers de l'Orage. Jean Giono. 13.50 o.p. (ISBN 0-685-34166-6). Schoenhof.

Develop Your Potential: How to Use Applied Psychology to Accomplish Your Purpose. John Tzanetakis. 1977. 7.50 o.p. (ISBN 0-682-48861-5). Exposition-Phoenix.

Developed Socialist Society: Basic Features & Place in History. F. Gelbuch & P. Lopata. 123p. 1980. pap. 3.95 o.p. (ISBN 0-8285-1816-5, Pub. by Progress Pubs USSR). Imported Pubns.

Developing a Competency-Based Instructional Supervisory System: A School Management Development Program. John H. Bolden. LC 74-80671. 1974. 5.00 o.p. (ISBN 0-682-48033-9, University). Exposition-Phoenix.

Developing a Data Dictionary System. Julia Van Duyn. (Illus.). 208p. 1982. text ed. 40.33 o.p. (ISBN 0-13-204289-4). P-H.

Developing a Respect for Work. Philadelphia Suburban School Study Council Staff. 37p. 1963. pap. text ed. 1.25x o.p. (ISBN 0-8134-0147-X, 147). Inter Print Pubs.

Developing & Administering a Child Care Center. Dorothy J. Sciarra & Anne G. Dorsey. LC 78-69564. (Illus.). 1979. text ed. 37.56 o.p. (ISBN 0-395-26263-1). HM.

Developing & Administering an Industrial Training Program. John R. Dowling. LC 79-10713. (Illus.). 200p. 1983. pap. 16.95 o.p. (ISBN 0-8436-0777-7). Van Nos Reinhold.

Developing Areas: A Classed Bibliography of the Joint Bank-Fund Library, World Bank Group & International Monetary Fund, 3 vols. Joint Bank-Fund Library (Washington, D. C.) Staff. Incl. Vol. 1. Latin America & the Caribbean. lib. bdg. 100.00 (ISBN 0-8161-0023-3); Vol. 2. Africa & the Middle East. lib. bdg. 100.00 (ISBN 0-8161-0024-1); Vol. 3. Asia & Oceania. lib. bdg. 100.00 (ISBN 0-8161-0025-X). 1977. Set. lib. bdg. 300.00 o.p. (ISBN 0-8161-0003-9, Hall Library). G K Hall.

Developing Basic Writing Skills in English As a Second Language. Marie H. Eichler. LC 81-3068. (Pitt Series in English As a Second Language). 174p. (Orig.). 1981. pap. 5.95x o.p. (ISBN 0-8229-8211-0). U of Pittsburgh Pr.

Developing Brain & its Disorders. Ed. by Masataka Arima et al. 316p. 1985. 96.00x o.p. (ISBN 3-8055-4010-8). Transaction Pubs.

Developing Business Strategies. David A. Aaker. LC 83-21906. (Marketing Management Ser.: 1-372). 391p. 1984. 27.95 o.p. (ISBN 0-471-87179-6). Wiley.

Developing Children - Their Changing Movement: A Guide for Teachers. Mary Ann Roberton & Lolas E. Halverson. LC 83-17513. 158p. 1984. pap. 8.50 o.p. (ISBN 0-8121-0919-8). Lea & Febiger.

Developing College Reading. 2nd ed. Lee A. Jacobus. 343p. 1979. pap. text ed. 13.95 o.p. (ISBN 0-15-517602-1, HC). HarBraceJ.

Developing College Reading. Lee A. Jacobus. 1970. pap. text ed. 10.95 o.p. (ISBN 0-15-517600-5, HC). HarBraceJ.

Developing Communicative Competence: RolePlays in English as a Second Language. Christina B. Paulston et al. (Pitt Series in English as A Second Language). 1975. pap. text ed. 3.95x o.p. (ISBN 0-8229-8205-6). U of Pittsburgh Pr.

Developing Competence in Teaching Reading: Instructional Modules in Reading Education. Colden Garland. 500p. 1978. write for info. plastic comb o.p. (ISBN 0-697-06015-2). Wm C Brown.

Developing Corporate Character: How to Successfully Change an Organization Without Destroying It. Alan L. Wilkins. LC 88-26698. (Management Ser.). 256p. 1989. text ed. 20.95x o.p. (ISBN 1-55542-133-4). Jossey-Bass.

Developing Cost Volumes. Larry J. Newman et al. cancelled o.s.i. (ISBN 0-933427-29-8). Shipley.

Developing Countries & the World Economic Order. Lars Anell & Birgitta Nygren. 208p. 1980. pap. 10.95x o.p. (ISBN 0-416-74630-6, NO.2002). Routledge Chapman & Hall.

Developing Country Debt. Lawrence G. Franko & Marilyn J. Seiber. 1979. 80.00 o.p. (ISBN 0-08-023864-5). Pergamon.

Developing Economies & the Environment: The Southeast Asia Experience. C. MacAndrews & L. S. Chia. 1979. text ed. 13.00 o.p. (ISBN 0-07-099458-7). McGraw.

Developing Effective Telephone Skills. 2nd ed. Robert A. Lapp. 56p. 1987. manual 15.00 o.p. (ISBN 0-941161-20-X, 00164). PES Inc WI.

Developing Faith: Lesson Plans for Senior High Religion Classes. Kieran Sawyer. LC 78-72942. (Illus.). 152p. 1978. pap. text ed. 5.95 o.p. (ISBN 0-87793-164-X). Ave Maria.

Developing Global New Products: Challenges to U.S. Competitiveness. Dean G. Van Nest. Ed. by Richard Farmer. LC 87-5844. (Research for Business Decisions Ser.: No. 134). 372p. 1987. 49.95 o.p. (ISBN 0-8357-1793-3). UMI Res Pr.

Developing High Technology Industries: The Case of Massachusetts. Michael Stevenson. (Public Administration Ser.: P 1692). 12p. 1985. 2.00 o.p. (ISBN 0-89028-422-9). Vance Biblios.

Developing Human. 3rd ed. Keith L. Moore. (Illus.). 496p. 1982. 34.95 o.p. (ISBN 0-7216-6472-5). Saunders.

Developing Interviewing Skills in Education. Colin Riches. 224p. 1987. 29.00 o.p. (ISBN 0-7099-2239-6, Pub. by Croom Helm UK). Routledge Chapman & Hall.

Developing Jail Mental Health Services: Practices & Principles. Henry J. Steadman et al. (DHHS Publication ADM Ser.: No. 86-1458). 158p. 1986. pap. 4.50 o.p. (ISBN 0-318-21671-X, S/N 017-024-01312-9). USGPO.

Developing Labor Law Third Supplement, 1982-86. Ed. by Stuart Linnick et al. 750p. 1988. pap. text ed. 50.00 o.p. (ISBN 0-87179-566-3, 0566). BNA.

Developing Law of Business Errors & Omissions Insurance. Practising Law Institute Staff & Dennis R. Yaeger. LC 82-63159. (Litigation Course & Administrative Practice Handbook Ser.: No. 217). (Illus.). 2224p. 1982. 40.00 o.p. PLI.

Developing Lifelong Readers. Ed. by Leila Christenbury. 111p. 4.00 o.p. (ISBN 0-8141-1091-6). NCTE.

Developing Microcomputer-Based Business Systems. Chris Edwards. (Illus.). 224p. 1983. pap. 26.95 o.p. (ISBN 0-13-204545-1). P-H.

Developing Nations: A Guide to Information Sources. Ed. by Eloise ReQua & Jane Statham. LC 65-17576. (Management Information Guide Ser.: No. 5). 340p. 1965. 68.00x o.p. (ISBN 0-8103-0805-3). Gale.

Developing Nations: Challenges Involving Women. Ed. by Barbara J. Stoecker & Evelyn T. Montgomery. 251p. 1982. 10.00 o.s.i. (ISBN 0-318-17668-8, 82-1). Intl Ctr Arid & Semi-Arid.

Developing New Products & Repositing Mature Brands: A Risk-Reduction System That Produces Investment Alternatives. Eugene J. Cafarelli. LC 80-13112. (Ronald Series on Marketing Management). 253p. 1980. 41.95 o.p. (ISBN 0-471-04634-5, Pub by Ronald Pr). Wiley.

Developing Observation Skills. Carol A. Cartwright & G. Phillip Cartwright. (Illus.). 180p. 1974. text ed. 18.95 o.p. (ISBN 0-07-010184-1, C). McGraw.

Developing Performance Excellence in Catholic Educational Policymaking: A Handbook of Training Programs. Mary-Angela Harper. 82p. 1982. 6.00 o.p. (ISBN 0-686-39917-X). Natl Cath Educ.

Developing Priorities & A Style: Selected Readings in Education for Teachers & Parents. 2nd ed. Ed. by Richard D. Kellough. 208p. 1974. text ed. 29.00x o.p. (ISBN 0-8422-5147-2); pap. text ed. 12.95x o.p. (ISBN 0-8422-0374-5). Irvington.

Developing Reading Skills for Business & Industry. Richard P. Santeusanio. LC 80-23463. 330p. 1983. pap. 15.95 o.p. (ISBN 0-8436-0792-0). Van Nos Reinhold.

Developing Reading Skills for the High School Equivalency Examination (Ged) in Social Studies, Science, & Literature: In 26 Lessons. Eugene J. Farley & Alice R. Farley. LC 72-84413. 1972. pap. text ed. 6.95 o.p. (ISBN 0-8120-0487-6). Barron.

Developing Second Language Skills: Theory to Practice. 2nd ed. Kenneth Chastain. 1976. pap. 27.95 o.p. (ISBN 0-395-31008-3). HM.

Developing Support Groups: A Manual for Facilitators & Participants. Howard Kirschenbaum & Barbara Glaser. LC 78-60280. 82p. 1978. pap. 10.50 o.p. (ISBN 0-88390-145-5). Univ Assocs.

Developing Teacher Competencies. Ed. by James E. Weigand. LC 70-149972. (Illus.). 1971. pap. text ed. (ISBN 0-13-205278-4). P-H.

Developing Teaching Skills in Physical Education. Daryl Siedentop. LC 75-26084. (Illus.). 352p. 1976. pap. 14.25 o.p. (ISBN 0-395-20616-2). HM.

Developing Thinking: Approaches to Children's Cognitive Development. Ed. by Sara Meadows. (Psychology in Progress Ser.). 212p. 1983. 29.00 o.p. (ISBN 0-416-33030-4, NO. 3977); pap. 12.95 o.p. (ISBN 0-416-33040-1, NO. 3978). Routledge Chapman & Hall.

Developing Through Relationships: A Reader. Compiled by Vivian Rogers et al. 159p. (Orig.). 1982. pap. text ed. 17.50 o.p. (ISBN 0-936352-15-9). U of KS Cont Ed.

Developing Training Competencies for Career Guidance Personnel. Linda Phillips-Jones & Brian G. Jones. 82p. 1981. pap. text ed. 4.75 o.p. (ISBN 0-911547-34-7, 72192W34). Am Assn Coun Dev.

Developing Women Managers: What Needs to Be Done? Martha G. Burrow. LC 78-10334. 1978. pap. 13.50 o.p. (ISBN 0-8144-3135-6). AMACOM.

Developing Writer: A Guide to Basic Skills. 2nd ed. Martin M. McKoski & Lynne C. Hahn. 1984. pap. text ed. write for info. o.p. (ISBN 0-673-15867-5). Scott F.

Developing Your Chemistry Fundamentals. Lawrence Rocks. 564p. 1979. 23.95 o.p. (ISBN 0-87814-041-7, P-4390). Pennwell Bks.

Development & Aging in the Nervous System. Ed. by Morris Rockstein & Marvin L. Sussman. 1973. 41.50 o.p. (ISBN 0-12-591650-7). Acad Pr.

Development & Dependence in Lesotho the Enclave of South Africa. Gabriele W. Strom. (Scandinavian Institute of African Studies, Uppsala). (Illus.). 1978. pap. 12.95 o.p. (ISBN 0-226-77228-4); pap. text ed. 9.75x o.p. (ISBN 0-8419-9727-6). Holmes & Meier.

Development & Diffusion of Improved Hybrid Silkworms in Japan: The First Filial Generation. 56p. 1982. pap. 5.00 o.p. (ISBN 92-808-0253-4, TUNU177, UNU). UNIPUB.

Development & Environment in Peninsular Malaysia. S. R. Aiken & C. H. Leigh. 1983. text ed. 34.50 o.p. (ISBN 0-07-099204-5). McGraw.

Development & Evaluation of A Pre-School Curriculum For Severely Disabled Children. Marie Meier. 44p. 1970. 1.50 o.p. (ISBN 0-686-38802-X). Human Res Ctr.

Development & Evolution of Brain Size: Behavioral Implications. Ed. by Martin E. Hahn et al. LC 79-23145. 1979. 44.00 o.p. (ISBN 0-12-314650-X). Acad Pr.

Development & Practice of Electronic Music. Ed. by Jon H. Appleton & Ronald C. Perera. LC 74-12478. (Illus.). 288p. 1975. pap. text ed. 39.00 o.p. (ISBN 0-13-207605-5). P-H.

Development & Stress in Navajo Religion. Guy H. Cooper. 126p. (Orig.). 1984. pap. text ed. 20.00x o.p. (ISBN 91-7146-337-2). Coronet Bks.

Development & Structure of the English School System. Keith Evans. (Studies in Teaching & Learning). 275p. (Orig.). 1985. pap. text ed. 24.95 o.s.i. (ISBN 0-340-35905-6). Princeton Bk Co.

Development & Structure of the Furniture Industry. J. L. Oliver. 1966. 50.00 o.p. (ISBN 0-08-011460-1). Pergamon.

Development Co-operation with Women: The Experience & Future Directions of the Fund: Summary Findings, Conclusions & Future Operational Features of the Fund. United Nations Development Fund for Women Staff. 195p. 1985. 19.50 o.p. (ISBN 92-1-127001-4, E.85.III.C.2). UN.

Development Economics Reading Lists, Vol. 5. Compiled by Edward Tower. 200p. 1985. 14.00 o.p. (ISBN 0-88024-205-1). Eno River Pr.

Development Finance Companies: Aspects of Policy & Operation. (Sector Policy Paper). 68p. 1976. 5.00 o.p. (ISBN 0-686-36180-6, JN-1066). World Bank.

Development Finance Companies, State & Privately Owned: A Review. David L. Gordon. (Working Paper Ser.: No. 578). 84p. 1983. 5.00 o.p. (ISBN 0-8213-0226-4, WP 0578). World Bank.

Development from Kant to Hegel, with Chapters on the Philosophy of Religion. Andrew Seth. Ed. by Lewis W. Beck. LC 75-32044. (Philosophy of Immanuel Kant Ser.: Vol. 7). 1976. Repr. of 1882 ed. lib. bdg. 24.00 o.p. (ISBN 0-8240-2331-5). Garland Pub.

Development Gaps: A Spatial Analysis of World Poverty & Inequality. J. P. Cole. LC 80-40284. 454p. 1981. 79.95x o.p. (ISBN 0-471-27796-7, Pub. by Wiley-Interscience). Wiley.

Development in & Through Reading. Ed. by Paul A. Witty. LC 61-1837. (National Society for the Study of Education Yearbooks Ser.: No. 60, Pt. 1). 1961. lib. bdg. 7.00x o.s.i. (ISBN 0-226-60059-9). U of Chicago Pr.

Development in Flowering Plants. John G. Torrey. (Orig.). 1967. pap. text ed. write for info. o.p. (ISBN 0-02-420960-0). Macmillan.

Development in Malaysia: Poverty, Wealth & Trusteeship. Ozay Mehmet. 1986. 34.50 o.p. (ISBN 0-7099-3525-0, Pub. by Croom Helm UK). Routledge Chapman & Hall.

Development of Aesthetic Experience. M. Ross. LC 82-3742. (Curriculum Issues in Arts Education: Vol. 3). 222p. 1982. 26.00 o.p. (ISBN 0-08-028908-8). Pergamon.

Development of Air Doctrine in the Army Air Arm: 1917 Through 1941. Thomas H. Greer. LC 85-21378. (Special Studies, United States Air Force, Office of Air Force History). (Illus.). 162p. (Orig.). 1985. pap. 6.00 o.p. (S/N 008-070-00567-1). USGPO.

Development of Aircraft Engines & Fuels. R. Schlaifer & S. D. Heron. 1950. Repr. of 1950 ed. 125.00 o.p. (ISBN 0-08-018740-4). Pergamon.

Development of American Citizenship, 1608-1870. James H. Kettner. LC 78-954. (Institute of Early American History & Culture Ser.). xii, 391p. 1978. 32.50x o.p. (ISBN 0-8078-1326-5). U of NC Pr.

Development of American Literary Criticism. Ed. by Floyd Stovall. LC 80-12269. ix, 262p. 1980. Repr. of 1955 ed. lib. bdg. 35.00x o.p. (ISBN 0-313-22440-4, STDE). Greenwood.

Development of American Political Science: From Burgess to Behavioralism. enl. ed. Albert Somit & Joseph Tanenhaus. 1982. 29.50x o.s.i. (ISBN 0-8290-0122-0); pap. text ed. 12.95x o.s.i. (ISBN 0-8290-0123-9). Irvington.

Development of Angiography & Cardiovascular Catheterization. T. Doby. LC 76-4678. (Illus.). 220p. 1976. 20.00 o.p. (ISBN 0-88416-139-0). Year Bk Med.

Development of Arthurian Romance. Roger S. Loomis. (Norton Library). 1970. pap. 4.25x o.p. (ISBN 0-393-00518-6, Norton Lib.). Norton.

Development of Behavior: A Synthesis of Developmental & Comparative Psychology. Bill M. Seay & Nathan Gottfried. LC 78-50639. (Illus.). 1978. text ed. 39.56 o.p. (ISBN 0-395-24747-0). HM.

Development of British Immigration Law. Vaughan Bevan. 512p. 1986. 50.00 o.p. (ISBN 0-7099-0663-3, Pub. by Croom Helm Ltd). Routledge Chapman & Hall.

Development of Economic Analysis. 4th ed. I. H. Rima. 1986. 37.95 o.p. (ISBN 0-256-03350-1). Irwin.

Development of Education in Ecuador. Jacques M. Wilson. LC 76-122289. (Hispanic-American Studies Ser.: No. 24). 1970. 8.95x o.p. (ISBN 0-87024-164-8). U of Miami Pr.

Development of Educational Teams. Mitchell Schwartz & Richard A. Schmuck. 1976. 3.00 o.p. (ISBN 0-936276-03-7). Ctr Educ Policy Mgmt.

Development of European Society: 1770-1870. John R. Gillis. LC 76-10891. (Illus.). 1977. text ed. 18.95 o.p. (ISBN 0-395-24482-X). HM.

Development of Flexible Automation Systems. (IEE Conference Publications: No. 237). 123p. 1984. pap. 58.00 o.s.i. (ISBN 0-85296-294-0, IC237). Inst Elect Eng.

Development of Hearing. Sybil Yeates. 238p. 1980. text ed. 17.50 o.p. (ISBN 0-88416-378-4). Year Bk Med.

Development of Information Requirements & Transmission Techniques for Highway Users. (National Cooperative Highway Research Program Report). 239p. 1971. 9.60 o.p. (ISBN 0-309-02003-4). Transport Res Bd.

Development of Life Insurance Values in the U. S. 1973. 9.95 o.p. (ISBN 0-256-04483-X). Irwin.

Development of Magnetic B-Ray Spectroscopy. M. Mladjenovic. (Lecture Notes in Physics Ser.: Vol. 52). 1976. 17.00 o.p. (ISBN 0-387-07851-7). Springer-Verlag.

Development of Mammalian Absorptive Processes. Ciba Foundation Staff. (Ciba Symposium Ser.: Vol. 70). 1980. 59.00 o.p. (ISBN 0-444-90101-9). Elsevier.

Development of Management Capability. (National Cooperative Highway Research Program Synthesis of Highway Practice). 50p. 1972. 3.20 o.p. (ISBN 0-309-02014-X). Transport Res Bd.

Development of Modal Reasoning: Genesis of Necessity & Probability Notions. Gilbert Pieraut-Le Bonniec. LC 79-24969. (Developmental Psychology Ser.). 1980. 19.95 o.p. (ISBN 0-12-554650-5). Acad Pr.

Development of Psycho-Motor Competence: Selected Readings. Linda Blane. LC 74-31488. 201p. 1975. 20.00x o.p. (ISBN 0-8422-5219-3); pap. text ed. 6.95x o.p. (ISBN 0-8422-0443-1). Irvington.

Development of Rainfed Agriculture under Arid & Semiarid Conditions: Proceedings of the Sixth Agriculture Sector Symposium. Ed. by Ted J. Davis. 424p. 1986. 20.00 o.p. (BK0817). World Bank.

Development of Shakespeare's Imagery. 2nd ed. Wolfgang H. Clemen. 237p. 1977. 42.00x o.p. (ISBN 0-416-85740-X, NO.2764); pap. 15.95x o.p. (ISBN 0-416-85730-2, NO.2765). Routledge Chapman & Hall.

Development of Spiritual Healing. 3rd ed. Hazrat Inayat Khan. LC 78-65080. 112p. pap. 4.95 o.s.i. (ISBN 0-900217-15-4, Pub. by Sufi Pub Co England). Hunter Hse.

Development of the Autonomic Nervous System: Symposium No. 83. CIBA Foundation Symposium. 400p. 1986. 47.50 o.p. (ISBN 0-471-91052-X). Wiley.

Development of the Clinical Nephrology Practitioner: A Focus on Independent Learning. Elaine Larson et al. LC 81-14169. (Illus.). 328p. 1982. pap. text ed. 29.95 o.p. (ISBN 0-8016-2868-7). Mosby.

Development of the Detective Novel. Murch. 1958. (ISBN 0-8022-1174-7). Philos Lib.

Development of the English Playhouse. Richard Leacroft. LC 72-6713. (Illus.). 354p. 1973. 72.50x o.p. (ISBN 0-8014-0750-8). Cornell U Pr.

Development of the Film: An Interpretive History. Alan Casty. 1973. pap. text ed. 12.95 o.p. (ISBN 0-15-517622-6, HC). HarBraceJ.

Development of the Idea of History in Antiquity. Gerald A. Press. (McGill-Queens Studies in the History of Ideas). 172p. 1982. 25.00x o.p. (ISBN 0-7735-1002-8, Pub. by McGill Canada). U of Toronto Pr.

Development of the Infant: The First Year of Life in Photographs. M. Van Blankenstein & U. R. Welbergen. (Illus.). 1975. pap. 15.00 o.p. (ISBN 0-433-03235-9). E J Brill USA.

Development of the Labour Process in Capitalist Societies. Craig R. Littler. x, 226p. 1982. text ed. 32.90 o.p. (ISBN 0-435-82540-2). Gower Pub Co.

Development of the Lymphatic System in Man. S. C. Van Der Putte. (Advances in Anatomy, Embryology & Cell Biology: Vol. 51, Pt. 1). (Illus.). 60p. 1975. pap. 22.50 o.p. (ISBN 0-387-07204-7). Springer-Verlag.

Development of the Marxian Dialectic. Dick Howard. LC 75-181984. 222p. 1972. 9.95x o.p. (ISBN 0-8093-0559-3). S Ill U Pr.

Development of the Muscles of Mastication in the Rat. John Rayne & G. Cullen Crawford. LC 73-172110. (Advances in Anatomy, Embryology & Cell Biology: Vol. 44, Pt. 5). (Illus.). 1971. pap. 23.10 o.p. (ISBN 0-387-05525-8). Springer-Verlag.

Development of the Negro Religion. Ruby F. Johnston. (Illus.). 1954. Philos Lib.

Development of the Secondary Curriculum. Ed. by Michael H. Price. 160p. 1986. 35.00 o.p. (ISBN 0-7099-4006-8, Pub. by Croom Helm UK). Routledge Chapman & Hall.

Development of Volitional Competence: Selected Readings. P. Conway. 1975. text ed. 19.50x o.p. (ISBN 0-8290-1077-7); pap. text ed. 6.00x o.p. (ISBN 0-8422-0424-5). Irvington.

Development of Welfare Services for Elderly People. Robin Means & Randall Smith. LC 84-23234. 379p. 1985. 31.00 o.p. (ISBN 0-7099-3531-5, Pub. by Croom Helm Ltd). Routledge Chapman & Hall.

Development Perspectives & Population Change. Ozzie G. Simmons. LC 83-8886. (Papers of the East-West Population Institute Ser.: No. 85). v, 41p. (Orig.). 1983. pap. text ed. 1.50 o.p. (ISBN 0-86638-006-X). EW Ctr HI.

Development Perspectives for the 1980s. S. C. Dube. 127p. 1983. text ed. 9.95x o.p. (ISBN 0-391-02947-9). Humanities.

Development Potential of Dimension Stone. pap. 8.50 o.p. (ISBN 0-686-94782-7, UN76/2A4, UN). UNIPUB.

Development Potential of Precambrian Mineral Deposits. Natural Resources & Energy Division, U. N. Dept. of Technical Co-Operation for Development. (Illus.). 435p. 1982. 90.00 o.p. (ISBN 0-08-027193-6). Pergamon.

Development Problems of Mineral Exporting Countries. Gobindram T. Nankani. (Working Paper: No. 354). xii, 106p. 1979. 5.00 o.p. (ISBN 0-686-36095-8, WP-0354). World Bank.

Development Puzzle. Nance L. Fyson. 192p. (Orig.). 1985. pap. text ed. 19.95 o.s.i. (ISBN 0-340-34940-9). Princeton Bk Co.

Development Strategies in Semi-Industrial Economies. Bela Balassa & Associates. LC 81-15558. (World Bank Publication). 408p. 1982. pap. 39.95x o.p. (ISBN 0-8018-2569-5). Johns Hopkins.

Development Strategy of Bangladesh. Nural Islam. 1978. text ed. 20.00 o.p. (ISBN 0-08-021840-7). Pergamon.

Development Systems Handbook. rev. ed. Intel Staff. 752p. 1986. pap. 18.00 o.p. (ISBN 1-55512-005-9, 210940). Intel Corp.

Development Technology. H. J. Duller. (International Library of Anthropology). 192p. (Orig.). 1982. pap. 14.95x o.p. (ISBN 0-7100-0990-9). Routledge Chapman & Hall.

Development Without Aid: Growth, Poverty & Government. Melvyn B. Krauss. LC 84-21017. 220p. 1985. pap. text ed. 10.75 o.p. (ISBN 0-8191-4248-4). U Pr of Amer.

Development Without Dependence. Pierre Uri. LC 75-19829. (Praeger Special Studies). 186p. 1976. text ed. 16.95 o.p. (ISBN 0-275-55830-4); pap. text ed. 18.95x o.p. (ISBN 0-275-91469-0, B1469). Praeger.

Developmental & Cellular Skeletal Biology. Brian K. Hall. 1978. 56.50 o.p. (ISBN 0-12-318950-0). Acad Pr.

Developmental & Cognitive Aspects of Learning to Spell: A Reflection of Word Knowledge. Ed. by Edmund Henderson & James Beers. 152p. (Orig.). 1980. pap. text ed. 11.00 o.p. (ISBN 0-87207-941-4). Intl Reading.

Developmental Aspects of Antibody Formation & Structure: Proceedings, Vols. 1 & 2. Ed. by J. Sterzl & I. Riha. 1971. Vol. 1. 89.50 o.p. (ISBN 0-12-667901-0); Vol. 2. 89.50 o.p. (ISBN 0-12-667902-9). Acad Pr.

Developmental Aspects of Oral Biology. Ed. by Harold C. Slavkin & Lucien A. Bavetta. 1972. 90.50 o.p. (ISBN 0-12-648350-7). Acad Pr.

Developmental Aspects of the Cell Cycle. Ed. by Ivan L. Cameron & George M. Padilla. (Cell Biology Ser.). 1971. 74.50 o.p. (ISBN 0-12-156960-8). Acad Pr.

Developmental Biology. Scott F. Gilbert. LC 84-10658. (Illus.). 600p. 1985. text ed. 37.95x o.p. (ISBN 0-87893-246-1). Sinauer Assocs.

Developmental Biology: Patterns, Problems & Principles. John W. Saunders. 736p. 1982. text ed. write for info. o.p. (ISBN 0-02-406370-3). Macmillan.

Developmental Counseling & Teaching. V. Lois Erickson & John M. Whiteley. 1980. 9.50 o.p. (ISBN 1-55620-012-9, 71004C). Am Assn Coun Dev.

Developmental Deficiencies, Vol. 1: A Comparative Approach. new ed. Ed. by John H. Hollis. LC 72-13480. (Illus.). 1973. text ed. 26.50x o.p. (ISBN 0-8422-5077-8); pap. text ed. 14.50x o.p. (ISBN 0-8422-0279-X). Irvington.

Developmental Deficiencies, Vol. 2: An Interdisciplinary Approach. Ed. by John H. Hollis. 1973. 36.50x o.p. (ISBN 0-8422-5118-9); pap. text ed. 14.50x o.p. (ISBN 0-8422-0314-1). Irvington.

Developmental Disabilities: Management Through Diet & Medication. Eric Denhoff & Steven A. Feldman. (Pediatric Habilitation Ser.: Vol. 2). (Illus.). 280p. 1981. 39.75 o.p. (ISBN 0-8247-1565-9). Dekker.

Developmental Education & Guidance of Talented Learners. Philip Perrone & Robert A. Male. LC 81-3463. 264p. 1981. text ed. 34.50 o.p. (ISBN 0-89443-359-8). Aspen Pub.

Developmental Games for Physically Handicapped Children. Bryant J. Cratty. 1969. pap. text ed. 3.95 o.p. (ISBN 0-917962-17-6). T H Peek.

Developmental Immunology: Clinical Problems & Aging. Edwin Cooper & Mary Brazier. LC 82-4035. (UCLA Forum in Medical Sciences Ser.: No. 25). 1982. 46.00 o.p. (ISBN 0-12-188040-0). Acad Pr.

Developmental Language Intervention: Psycholinguistic Application. Kenneth F. Ruder. Ed. by Michael D. Smith. LC 83-23426. (Illus.). 320p. 1984. text ed. 24.00x o.p. (ISBN 0-8391-1632-2, 1321). Pro Ed.

Developmental Neurobiology of Vision. Ed. by R. D. Freeman. LC 79-19389. (NATO ASI Series A, Life Sciences: Vol. 27). 460p. 1979. 79.50x o.p. (ISBN 0-306-40306-4, Plenum Pr). Plenum Pub.

Developmental Neuropathology. R. L. Friede. (Illus.). 550p. 1976. 71.00 o.p. (ISBN 0-387-81325-X). Springer-Verlag.

Developmental Neuropsychology of Sensory Deprivation. Austin H. Riesen. 1975. 52.50 o.p. (ISBN 0-12-588550-4). Acad Pr.

Developmental Psychology: A Life-Span Approach. James E. Birren et al. LC 80-82839. (Illus.). 736p. 1981. text ed. 39.96 o.p. (ISBN 0-395-29717-6). HM.

Developmental Reading. Daniel Hittleman. 1980. text ed. 22.95 o.p. (ISBN 0-395-30629-9). HM.

Developmental Reading in Middle & Secondary Schools. Lawrence E. Hafner. (Illus.). 1977. text ed. write for info. o.p. (ISBN 0-02-348820-4). Macmillan.

Developmental Reading, K-8: Teaching from a Psycholinguistic Perspective. 2d ed. Daniel Hittleman. LC 82-83378. 480p. 1983. text ed. 30.95 o.p. (ISBN 0-395-32770-9). HM.

Developmental Screening in Early Childhood: A Guide. Samuel J. Meisels. LC 78-70706. 60p. 1985. pap. text ed. 3.50 o.p. (ISBN 0-912674-63-6, NAEYC #121). Natl Assn Child Ed.

Developmental Stages in the Rhesus Monkey (Macaca Mulatta) A. A. Gribnau & L. G. Geijsberts. (Advances in Anatomy, Embryology & Cell Biology Ser.: Vol. 68). (Illus.). 86p. 1982. pap. 22.40 o.p. (ISBN 0-387-10469-0). Springer-Verlag.

Developmental Teaching of Mathematics for the Learning Disabled. Ed. by John F. Cawley. LC 84-6247. 329p. 1984. 36.50 o.p. (ISBN 0-89443-581-7). Aspen Pub.

Developmental Therapy Sourcebook, Vol. 1. Mary M. Wood. LC 80-18320. 208p. (Orig.). 1981. pap. 19.00x o.p. (ISBN 0-8391-1600-4, 1208). Pro-Ed.

Developmental Therapy Sourcebook, Vol. 2. Mary M. Wood. LC 80-18320. 256p. (Orig.). 1981. pap. 19.00x o.p. (ISBN 0-8391-1601-2, 1207). Pro-Ed.

Developmentally Disabled Child: A Manual for Primary Physicians. Doman K. Keele. (Illus.). 250p. 1983. text ed. 29.95 casebound o.p. (ISBN 0-87489-271-6). Med Economics.

Developments & Borderlines of Nuclear Physics. H. Morinaga. (Italian Physical Society Course: No. 53). 1974. 66.00 o.p. (ISBN 0-12-368853-1). Acad Pr.

Developments in Chemical Engineering: A Festschrift for P. V. Danckwerts. Ed. by J. Bridgwater. (Illus.). 190p. 1983. pap. 39.00 o.p. (ISBN 0-08-030251-3). Pergamon.

Developments in Clinical Immunology. Ed. by M. Ricci et al. 1978. 54.50 o.p. (ISBN 0-12-587180-5). Acad Pr.

Developments in Corporate Tax Accounting, Vol. 218. Practising Law Institute Staff. 318p. 1985. pap. 45.00 o.p. (ISBN 0-317-27524-0, #J4-3562). PLI.

Developments in Electron Microscopy & Analysis. J. A. Venables. 1976. 99.00 o.p. (ISBN 0-12-716950-4). Acad Pr.

Developments in High-Energy Physics: Italian Physical Society. Ed. by R. Gatto. (Course 54). 1973. 90.50 o.p. (ISBN 0-12-368854-X). Acad Pr.

Developments in High Energy Physics: Proceedings. International University Courses on Nuclear Physics, 9th, Schladming, Austria, 1970. LC 77-133409. (Acta Physica Austriaca: Suppl. 7). (Illus.). 1970. 75.60 o.p. (ISBN 0-387-80974-0). Springer-Verlag.

Developments in Labour Market Analysis. Caroline Joll & Chris McKenna. (Illus.). 40p. 1983. text ed. 39.95x o.p. (ISBN 0-04-331089-3); pap. text ed. 19.95x o.p. (ISBN 0-04-331090-7). Unwin Hyman.

Developments in Mammals, 3 vols. Ed. by M. Johnson. Vol. 1, 1977. 68.50 o.p. (ISBN 0-7204-0631-5, Biomedical Pr); Vol. 2, 1977. 62.75 o.p. (ISBN 0-7204-0646-3); Vol. 3, 1978. 122.75 o.p. (ISBN 0-7204-0663-3). Elsevier.

Developments in Meat Science, 2 vols. R. Lawrie. (Illus.). 1980-81. Vol. 1. 77.50 o.p. (ISBN 0-85334-866-9, Pub. by Elsevier Applied Sci England); Vol. 2. 83.00 o.p. (ISBN 0-85334-986-X). Elsevier.

Developments in Power System Protection. (Conference Publications: No. 249). 226p. 1985. pap. 85.00 o.s.i. (ISBN 0-85296-305-X, IC249). Inst Elect Eng.

Developments in Robotics. Ed. by Brian Rooks. 265p. 1983. 47.00 o.p. (ISBN 0-317-18030-4). Robot Inst Am.

Developments in Soft Drinks Technology, Vols. 1 & 2. Ed. by L. F. Green. H. W. Houghton. (Illus.). 1984. Vol. 1, 1978. 77.50 o.p. (ISBN 0-85334-767-0, Pub. by Elsevier Applied Sci England); Vol. 2, 1984. 52.00 o.p.; Vol. 3, 1984. 48.25 o.p. Elsevier.

Developments in Soil Information Systems: Proceedings of ISSS Working Group Meeting on Soil Information, Varna-Sofia, Bulgaria, May 30-June 4, 1977. ISSS Working Group Staff. Ed. by A. D. Sadovsky & S. W. Bie. 119p. 1978. pap. 7.50 o.p. (ISBN 0-686-93147-5, PDC107, Pudoc). UNIPUB.

Developments in Theoretical & Applied Mechanics, Vols. 2-4. 1970. Vol. 2. 1965. 160.00 o.p. (ISBN 0-08-011024-X); Vol. 3. 1968. 195.00 o.p. (ISBN 0-08-012211-6); Vol. 4. 1970. 115.00 o.p. (ISBN 0-08-006513-9). Pergamon.

Developments in Transport Theory. Ed. by E. Inonu & P. F. Zweifel. 1967. 66.00 o.p. (ISBN 0-12-372350-7). Acad Pr.

Developments in Treatment for Parkinson's Disease. Ed. by George Cotzias & Fletcher McDowell. LC 73-2629. 91p. 1971. pap. 9.95 o.p. (ISBN 0-685-90281-1, Pub. by W & W). Krieger.

Developments with Thermosetting Plastics. Ed. by A. Whelan & J. A. Brydson. LC 74-34013. 198p. 1975. 49.95 o.p. (ISBN 0-470-93772-6). Halsted Pr.

Devere Allen & a Radical Approach to War. Charles Chatfield. LC 75-147691. (Library of War & Peace; Documentary Anthologies). 1976. lib. bdg. 46.00 o.p. (ISBN 0-8240-0447-7). Garland Pub.

Devi Mahatmya. Thomas Coburn. 1985. 22.00x o.p. (ISBN 0-686-42973-7). South Asia Bks.

Deviance & Control. A. Cohen. 1966. pap. text ed. 16.00 o.p. (ISBN 0-13-208389-2). P-H.

Deviance & Moral Boundaries: Witchcraft, the Occult, Science Fiction, Deviant Sciences & Scientists. Nachman Ben-Yehuda. LC 85-1167. x, 260p. 1985. 25.00x o.s.i. (ISBN 0-226-04335-5). U of Chicago Pr.

Deviancy: The Psychology of Being Different. Jonathan N. Freedman & Anthony Doob. LC 68-14666. (Social Psychology Ser). 1968. 22.00 o.p. (ISBN 0-12-266550-3). Acad Pr.

Deviant Behavior. Alex Thio. LC 77-90439. (Illus.). 1978. text ed. 21.95 o.p. (ISBN 0-395-25323-3). HM.

Deviant Behavior. 2nd ed. Alex Thio. LC 82-82647. 480p. 1983. text ed. 29.50 o.p. (ISBN 0-395-32584-6). HM.

Deviant Behavior in Sweden. Louis Bultena. 1971. 7.50 o.p. (ISBN 0-682-47339-1, University); pap. 4.00 o.p. (ISBN 0-682-47340-5). Exposition-Phoenix.

Deviant Life-Styles. Ed. by James M. Henslin. LC 76-1765. 380p. 1977. 12.95 o.p. (ISBN 0-87855-101-8); pap. (ISBN 0-87855-595-1). Transaction Pubs.

Deviants & Deviance. Edward Sagarin. 458p. 1975. pap. text ed. 17.95 o.p. (ISBN 0-275-64360-3). HR&W.

Device Good Manufacturing Practices Manual. Andrew Lowery & Richard J. Rivera. LC 87-4179. (DHHS Publication FDA Ser.). 370p. 1987. pap. 18.00 o.p. (ISBN 0-318-23744-X, 017-012-00330-3). USGPO.

Devil & Daniel Mouse. Ken Sobol. (gr. k). 1979. pap. 2.95 o.p. (ISBN 0-380-45864-0, 45864-0, Camelot). Avon.

Devil & Daniel Webster & Other Stories. Stephen V. Benet. (gr. 7-9). 1972. pap. 1.75 o.p. Archway.

Devil & I. Olive R. Thompson. (Illus.). 272p. 1960. (ISBN 0-8022-1716-8). Philos Lib.

Devil & the Deep Blue Sea. Michael Behrens. Date not set. pap. (Flare). Avon.

Devil at the Reins. Henry Sharp. 1980. pap. 1.75 o.p. (ISBN 0-440-11789-5). Dell.

Devil by the Sea. Nina Bawden. 1978. pap. 1.50 o.p. (ISBN 0-380-01922-1, 57695). Avon.

Devil Drives: A Life of Sir Richard Burton. Fawn M. Brodie. (Illus.). 1967. 15.95 o.p. (ISBN 0-393-07374-2). Norton.

Devil in God's Old Man. Sue M. Newhall. (Illus.). 1969. 5.95 o.p. (ISBN 0-393-07378-5). Norton.

Devil of a State. Anthony Burgess. 288p. 1975. pap. 3.95 o.p. (ISBN 0-393-00778-2, Norton Lib). Norton.

Devil Rides with Me, Six Fantastic Stories. Al Slote. LC 79-23092. (gr. 4-9). 1980. 8.95 o.p. (ISBN 0-416-30141-X, NO.0139). Routledge Chapman & Hall.

Devil Tree. Jerzy Kosinski. LC 72-88804. 1973. 6.95 o.p. (ISBN 0-15-125328-5). HarBraceJ.

Devils & Canon Barham: Essays on Poets, Novelists & Monsters. Edmund Wilson. LC 72-93789. 232p. 1973. 7.95 o.p. (ISBN 0-374-13843-5). FS&G.

Devils & Demons. Ed. by Marvin Kaye. LC 87-6772. 576p. 1987. 15.95 o.p. (ISBN 0-385-18563-4). Doubleday.

Devil's Birthday: The Bridges to Arnhem 1944. Geoffrey Powell. 320p. 1985. 18.95 o.p. (ISBN 0-531-09791-9). Watts.

Devil's Butcher Shop: The New Mexico Prison Uprising. Roger Morris. 288p. 1983. 17.95 o.p. (ISBN 0-531-09807-9). Watts.

Devil's Children: Tales of Demons & Exorcists. Ed. by Michel Parry. LC 74-21721. 212p. 1975. 7.95 o.s.i. (ISBN 0-8008-2188-2). Taplinger.

Devil's Church & Other Stories. Joaquim M. Machado de Assis. Tr. by Jack Schmitt & Lorie Ishimatsu. LC 76-53828. (Texas Pan American Ser). 166p. 1977. pap. 10.95 o.p. (ISBN 0-292-77535-0). U of Tex Pr.

Devil's Elixirs. E. T. Hoffmann. Tr. by Ronald Taylor from Ger. 1980. pap. 10.95 o.s.i. (ISBN 0-7145-0194-8). Riverrun NY.

Devil's Gold. Jess Cody. (Gunsmoke Western Ser.). 176p. 1988. text ed. 12.95 o.p. (ISBN 0-85997-860-5, Pub. by Firecrest Pub Ltd). Prescott Pr NH.

Devil's Horsemen. James Chambers. LC 78-22055. 1979. 11.95 o.p. (ISBN 0-689-10942-3, Atheneum). Macmillan.

Devil's Horsemen: The Mongol Invasion of Europe. James Chambers. LC 78-22055. (Illus.). 208p. 1985. pap. 7.95 o.p. (ISBN 0-689-70693-6, 330, Atheneum). Macmillan.

Devil's Imp. Evangelist Charlotte Reynolds. 1978. 9.50 o.p. (ISBN 0-682-48959-X). Exposition-Phoenix.

Devil's Island. Brian Peachment. 1974. pap. text ed. 1.60 o.s.i. (ISBN 0-08-017613-5). Pergamon.

Devil's Island: Revelations of the French Penal Settlements in Guiana. William Allison-Booth. LC 71-162504. (Illus.). 248p. 1971. Repr. of 1931 ed. 40.00x o.p. (ISBN 0-8103-3761-4). Gale.

Devils-Jewish Style. Louis Stricker. 1975. 7.00 o.p. (ISBN 0-682-48222-6). Exposition-Phoenix.

Devil's Music: A History of the Blues. Giles Oakley. LC 78-6161. (Illus.). 1978. pap. 6.95 o.p. (ISBN 0-15-625586-3, Harv). HarBraceJ.

Devil's Stocking: A Last Interview by W. J. Weatherby. Nelson Algren. 1983. 16.95 o.p. (ISBN 0-87795-547-6, Arbor Hse); pap. 9.95 o.p. (ISBN 0-87795-548-4). Morrow.

Devils Tower. (National Park Service Handbook Ser.: No. 3). (Illus.). 81p. 1981. pap. 3.50 o.p. (ISBN 0-318-21942-5, S/N 024-005-00899-3). USGPO.

Devil's Voyage. Jack Chalker. 224p. 1985. pap. 3.75 o.p. (ISBN 0-931773-38-5). Critics Choice Paper.

Devil's Wager: A Faustian Drama of the Second Fall & a Second Redemption. Frederick L. Santee. 1979. 10.00 o.p. (ISBN 0-682-49210-8). Exposition-Phoenix.

Deviner et Appendre. Shirley S. Price. 77p. (gr. 9-12). 1983. pap. text ed. 18.25 o.p. (ISBN 0-88377-280-9). Newbury Hse.

Devon. (AA-OS Leisure Guides). (Illus.). 120p. 1988. pap. 19.95 o.p. (ISBN 0-86145-655-6, Pub. by British Tour). Salem Hse Pubs.

Devon Pillow Lace: Its History & How to Make It. Ed. by Penderel Moody. (Illus.). 160p. 1981. Repr. of 1907 ed. 42.00x o.p. (ISBN 0-8103-3031-8). Gale.

Devon's Way: The Quicksilver Solution. Rod Pennington. 224p. 1988. pap. 2.95 o.p. (ISBN 1-55547-222-2). Critics Choice Paper.

Devonshire Flavour: A Devonshire Treasury of Recipes & Personal Notes. Elizabeth Lothian. LC 74-76189. 1974. 12.95 o.p. (ISBN 0-7153-7271-8). David & Charles.

Devoted Friends. Joe Poyer. LC 81-69139. (Illus.). 384p. 1982. 15.95 o.p. (ISBN 0-689-11251-3, Atheneum). Macmillan.

Devotional Dramas for Easter. Sarah W. Miller. (Orig.). 1967. pap. 1.95 o.p. (ISBN 0-8054-9715-3). Broadman.

Devotional Dramas for the Christian Life. Sarah W. Miller. (Orig.). 1968. pap. 1.95 o.p. (ISBN 0-8054-9717-X). Broadman.

Devotional Guide to the Gospels: Three Hundred Sixty-Six Meditations. John Killinger. 588p. 1984. Repr. 14.95 o.p. (ISBN 0-8499-3008-1, 3008-1). Word Bks.

Devotionals for Nurses. Rhonda S. Lapp. (Ultra Bks.). 4.95 o.p. (ISBN 0-8010-5539-3). Baker Bk.

Devotions for Boys & Girls. Compiled by Hester Monsma. (Devotions for Daily Living Ser.). 30p. 1982. pap. 1.50 o.p. (ISBN 0-8010-2924-4). Baker Bk.

Devotions for Dieters. Charlie Shedd. 1983. 8.95 o.p. (ISBN 0-8499-0330-0). Word Bks.

Devotions for the Children's Hour. Kenneth N. Taylor. (gr. 2-7). 4.95 o.p. (ISBN 0-8024-2211-X); pap. 3.95 o.p. (ISBN 0-8024-0061-2). Moody.

Dewain Valentine: Double Pyramid. Trent Myers. (Illus.). 1983. 0.50 o.p. (ISBN 0-913883-06-9). Madison Art.

Dewey Decimal Classification & Relative Index. 10th abridged ed. Melvil Dewey. LC 70-164427. 1971. 18.00x o.p. (ISBN 0-910608-13-X). Forest Pr.

Dewey Decimal Classification & Relative Index, 3 vols. 18th ed. Melvil Dewey. Incl. Vol. 1. Introduction & Tables. 20.00x (ISBN 0-910608-10-5); Vol. 2. Schedules. 20.00x; Vol. 3. Index. 20.00x (ISBN 0-910608-11-3). LC 78-140002. (Illus.). 2692p. 1971. Set. 60.00x o.p. (ISBN 0-685-26876-4). Forest Pr.

Dewey Decimal Classification & Relative Index, 3 vols. 19th ed. Melvil Dewey. LC 77-27967. 1979. Set. 120.00x o.p. (ISBN 0-910608-23-7); Vol 1, Introduction & Tables. 42.00x o.p. (ISBN 0-910608-19-9); Vol. 2, Schedules. 42.00x o.p. (ISBN 0-910608-20-2); Vol. 3, Index. 42.00x o.p. (ISBN 0-910608-21-0). Forest Pr.

Dewey Decimal Classification: Manual on the Use of the DDC: Edition 19. John P. Comaromi & Margaret J. Warren. LC 82-1516. 551p. 1982. pap. text ed. 10.00 o.p. (ISBN 0-910608-32-6). Forest Pr.

Dewey Decimal Classification: 004-006 Data Processing & Computer Science, & Changes in Related Disciplines. Melvil Dewey. Ed. by Julianne Beall et al. LC 85-1667. 66p. 1985. pap. text ed. 10.00x o.p. (ISBN 0-910608-36-9). Forest Pr.

Dewi. William J. Constandse. 168p. 1982. pap. 9.00 o.s.i. (Pub. by Graham Brash Singapore). Three Continents.

Dharani Sutra. Commentary by Tripitaka Master Hua. Tr. by Buddhist Text Translation Society Staff. (Illus.). 352p. (Orig.). 1976. pap. 50.00 o.p. (ISBN 0-917512-13-8). Buddhist Text.

Dharma in Hindu Ethics. Austin Creel. 1978. 11.00x o.p. (ISBN 0-88386-999-3). South Asia Bks.

Diabetes: Controlling It the Easy Way. Stanley Mirsky & Joan R. Hellman. LC 81-6047. 224p. 1982. 13.00 o.p. (ISBN 0-394-51148-4); pap. text ed. 8.95 o.p. Random.

Diabetes Mellitus: Diagnosis & Treatment. 2nd ed. Mayer B. Davidson. 589p. 1986. 25.00 o.p. (ISBN 0-471-83016-X). Wiley.

Diabetes, Obesity & Hyperlipidemias. Ed. by G. Crepaldi et al. 1979. 99.00 o.p. (ISBN 0-12-197035-3). Acad Pr.

Diabetes: Reach for Health & Freedom. Dorothea F. Sims. LC 80-16065. (Illus.). 92p. 1984. pap. 9.95 o.p. (ISBN 0-8016-0163-0). Mosby.

Diabetes: The Comprehensive Self-Management Handbook. large print ed. Diabetes Education Center, Nassau Hospital Staff et al. LC 82-45392. (Illus.). 408p. 1984. 19.95 o.p. (ISBN 0-385-18292-9). Doubleday.

Diabetes Treatment with Implantable Insulin Infusion Systems. Karl Irsigler et al. 326p. (Orig.). 1983. pap. 39.50 o.p. (ISBN 0-317-65607-4). Urban & S.

Diabetes Without Fear. Joseph I. Goodman & W. Watts Biggers. LC 77-90663. 1980. pap. 5.95 o.p. (ISBN 0-87795-294-9, Arbor Hse). Morrow.

Diabetes Without Fear. Joseph I. Goodman & W. Watts Biggers. LC 77-90663. 1978. 8.95 o.p. (ISBN 0-87795-181-0, Arbor Hse). Morrow.

Diabetic & Health Care. Dorothy Blevins. (Illus.). 1979. text ed. 31.95 o.p. (ISBN 0-07-005902-0). McGraw.

Diabetic Breakfast & Brunch Cookbook. Mary J. Finsand. LC 86-28506. 160p. 1987. 16.95 o.p.; pap. 19.95 o.p. (ISBN 0-8069-6498-7). Sterling.

Diabetic Child & Young Adult. Mimi Belmonte. 150p. 1983. pap. 8.95 o.s.i. (ISBN 0-920792-17-0). Eden Pr.

Diabetic Foot. 3rd ed. Marvin E. Levin & Lawrence W. O'Neal. LC 82-3456. (Illus.). 336p. 1982. text ed. 55.00 o.p. (ISBN 0-8016-2991-8). Mosby.

Diabetic's Brand-Name Food Exchange Handbook: Food Exchanges for Over 3,000 Supermarket, Grocery Store & Fast-Food Products. Andrea Barrett. LC 84-2105. 176p. 1984. 17.95 o.p. (ISBN 0-89471-256-X). Running Pr.

Diabetics' Diet Book. Oxford Dietetic Group Staff & Jim Mann. LC 81-22875. (Illus.). 123p. 1983. 12.95 o.p. (ISBN 0-668-05325-9, 5325). Arco.

Diable et le Bon Dieu. Jean-Paul Sartre. (Coll. Soleil). 1958. 13.95 o.p. (ISBN 0-685-11135-0). Schoenhof.

Diable et le Bon Dieu. Jean-Paul Sartre. 288p. 1951. 10.95 o.p. (ISBN 0-686-54977-5). Schoenhof.

Diagenesis of Sandstone: Cement-Porosity Relationships. Ed. by Earle F. McBride. (Reprint Ser.: No.9). 233p. 1979. 13.00 o.p. (ISBN 0-918985-35-8, 9). SEPM.

Diaghilev. Richard Buckle. LC 78-73084. 1979. 22.50 o.p. (ISBN 0-689-10952-0, Atheneum). Macmillan.

Diagnosing Mental Illness: Evaluation in Psychiatry & Psychology. Ed. by Alfred M. Freedman & Harold I. Kaplan. LC 78-178071. (Studies in Human Behavior Ser). 1972. pap. 4.95x o.p. (ISBN 0-689-70282-5, HB1, Atheneum). Macmillan.

Diagnosis & Correction in Reading Instruction. Dorothy Rubin. 1982. text ed. 28.95 o.p. (ISBN 0-03-059292-5). HR&W.

Diagnosis & Genetics of Defective Color Vision. Hans Kalmus. 1965. 37.00 o.p. (ISBN 0-08-011119-X). Pergamon.

Diagnosis & Management of Acute Poisoning. A. T. Proudfoot. (Illus.). 246p. 1982. pap. text ed. 18.25 o.p. (ISBN 0-632-00584-X, B 4058-X). Mosby.

Diagnosis & Management of Depression. Aaron T. Beck. LC 73-83290. 160p. 1973. 15.95x o.p. (ISBN 0-8122-7674-4). U of Pa Pr.

Diagnosis & Management of Diabetes Mellitus: A Clinical Manual for Medical Students, Residents, & Primary Care Physicians. Charles Olson. LC 80-27025. 294p. 1981. pap. 18.50 o.p. (ISBN 0-8121-0790-X). Lea & Febiger.

Diagnosis & Management of Endocrine Diseases Including Diabetes Mellitus. A. D. Toft et al. (Illus.). 412p. 1982. pap. text ed. 26.75 o.p. (ISBN 0-632-00553-X, B 4998-6). Mosby.

Diagnosis & Management of Ocular Motility Disorders. Mein & Harcourt. 1986. 75.95 o.p. (ISBN 0-8016-2083-X). Mosby.

Diagnosis & the Difference It Makes. Paul Pruyser. LC 77-73153. 1977. 20.00x o.p. (ISBN 0-87668-321-9). Aronson.

Diagnosis & Therapy of Porphyrias & Lead Toxication. Ed. by M. Doss. (International Symposium Clinical Biochemistry). (Illus.). 1978. pap. 43.00 o.p. (ISBN 0-387-08863-6). Springer-Verlag.

Diagnosis & Treatment in Child Psychiatry. Group for the Advancement of Psychiatry. LC 73-17782. 192p. 1974. 17.50x o.p. (ISBN 0-87668-129-1). Aronson.

Diagnosis & Treatment in Prosthodontics. Ed. by William R. Laney et al. LC 82-15171. (Illus.). 561p. 1983. text ed. 60.00 o.p. (ISBN 0-8121-0275-4). Lea & Febiger.

Diagnosis & Treatment of Cardiac Arrhythmias: Proceedings of the International Symposium on Diagnosis & Treatment of Cardiac Arrhythmias, Barcelona, Spain, Oct 5-8, 1977. International Symposium on Diagnosis & Treatment of Cardiac Arrhythmias Staff. Ed. by A. J. Bayes De Luna. (Illus.). 1980. 315.00 o.p. (ISBN 0-08-024426-2). Pergamon.

Diagnosis & Treatment of Chronic Pain. Ed. by Nelson H. Hendler et al. LC 82-4733. (Illus.). 272p. 1982. 27.50 o.p. (ISBN 0-7236-7011-0). Butterworth.

Diagnosis & Treatment of Fetal Disorders: Proceedings. International Symposium on Diagnosis & Treatment of Disorders Affecting the Intrauterine Patient, Dorado, Puerto Rico, 1967. Ed. by K. Adamsons. (Illus.). 1969. 38.30 o.p. (ISBN 0-387-04451-5). Springer-Verlag.

Diagnosis Before First Aid. 2nd ed. Neville Marsden. LC 84-21419. (Illus.). 225p. 1985. pap. text ed. 13.85 o.p. (ISBN 0-443-02837-0). Churchill.

Diagnostic & Criterion Referenced Reading Tests: Review & Evaluation. Ed. by Leo Schell. 91p. (Orig.). 1981. pap. 6.00 o.p. (ISBN 0-87207-731-4). Intl Reading.

Diagnostic & Laboratory Cards for Clinical Use. Marie Jaffe & Linda Skidmore. 288p. 1984. cards 17.50 o.p. (ISBN 0-89303-400-2). Appleton & Lange.

Diagnostic Criteria of Syphilis, Yaws & Treponarid (Treponematoses) & of Some Other Diseases in Dry Bones (for Use in Osteo-Archaeology) C. J. Hackett. (Illus.). 1976. pap. 50.80 o.p. (ISBN 0-387-07967-X). Springer-Verlag.

Diagnostic Electrocardiography & Vectorcardiography. 2nd ed. H. Harold Friedman. (Illus.). 1976. text ed. 45.00 o.p. (ISBN 0-07-022424-2). McGraw.

Diagnostic Electron Microscopy. Jan V. Johannessen. 210p. 1983. text ed. 38.00 o.p. (ISBN 0-07-032543-X). McGraw.

Diagnostic Electron Microscopy, Vol. 1. B. F. Trump & R. T. Jones. LC 77-12817. 346p. 1978. 70.00 o.p. (ISBN 0-471-89195-9). Wiley.

Diagnostic Electron Microscopy, Vol. 2. B. F. Trump & R. T. Jones. LC 77-12817. (Diagnostic Electron Microscopy Ser.). 401p. 1979. text ed. 70.00 o.p. (ISBN 0-471-89196-7, Pub. by Wiley Med). Wiley.

Diagnostic Electron Microscopy, Vol. 3. B. F. Trump & R. T. Jones. LC 76-18952. (Diagnostic Electron Microscopy Ser.). 536p. 1980. 82.00x o.p. (ISBN 0-471-05150-0, Pub. by Wiley-Interscience). Wiley.

Diagnostic Electron Microscopy, Vol. 4. Ed. by Benjamin F. Trump & Raymond T. Jones. LC 77-12817. (Diagnostic Electron Microscopy Ser.). 544p. 1983. 70.00 o.p. (ISBN 0-471-05149-7, Pub. by Wiley Med). Wiley.

Diagnostic Methods in Clinical Virology. 3rd ed. Grist & Urquhart. (Illus.). 240p. 1979. 24.00 o.p. (ISBN 0-632-00152-6, B-2007-4). Mosby.

Diagnostic Prescriptive Reading Program. Incl. Management System for Personalizing Reading Instruction. Lloyd J. Eldredge. pap. 7.95 o.p. (ISBN 0-89036-800-7); assessment inventory pads 0.60 ea., specimen set 4.95, complete set 47.95 o.p. (ISBN 0-685-46922-0); retrieval chart pads 0.65ea, set 4.95 o.p. (ISBN 0-685-46923-9); Reading Prescriptions: Phonics Skills, Vol.1. Lloyd J. Eldredge. pap. 9.95 o.p. (ISBN 0-89036-806-6); student worksheets & reponse cards 3.95 o.p. (ISBN 0-685-46924-7); Word Discoveries. Charles Pearce & Rhoda Coyte. 1973. pap. 9.95 o.p. (ISBN 0-89036-808-2); tchr's. guide 1.50 o.p. (ISBN 0-89036-809-0); word hunt file cards 4.95 o.p. (ISBN 0-685-46925-5). 1973. pap. Hawkes Pub Inc.

Diagnostic Procedures: A Reference for Health Practitioners & a Guide for Patient Counseling. Barbara Skydell & Anne S. Crowder. 300p. 1975. pap. 10.50 o.p. (ISBN 0-316-79733-2). Little.

Diagnostic Procedures for Viral, Rickettsial & Chlamydial Infections. 5th ed. Ed. by Edwin H. Lennette & Nathalie J. Schmidt. 1138p. 1979. 40.00 o.p. (ISBN 0-87553-087-7, 017). Am Pub Health.

Diagnostic Procedures in Nursing Practice. Jane V. Corbett. 186p. (Orig.). 1983. pap. 17.95 o.p. (ISBN 0-8385-1597-5). Appleton & Lange.

Diagnostic Radiology of the Dog & Cat. J. Kevin Kealy. LC 78-54517. (Illus.). 1979. text ed. (ISBN 0-7216-5306-5). Saunders.

Diagnostic Radiology, 1984. Margulis & Gooding. 1984. 89.50 o.p. (ISBN 0-8016-3183-1). Mosby.

Diagnostic Significance of Enzymes & Proteins in Urine. Ed. by U. C. Dubach & U. Schmidt. CJ Hogrefe Pubs.

Diagnostic Testing in the Emergency Department. Ed. by Neal Flomenbaum & Lewis Goldfrank. 340p. 1984. 43.50 o.p. (ISBN 0-89443-592-2). Aspen Pub.

Diagnostic Ultrasonics: Principles & Use of Instruments. 2nd ed. W. N. McDicken. LC 80-20750. 381p. 1981. 46.00 o.p. (ISBN 0-471-05740-1). Wiley.

Diagnostic Use of Rorschach with Children. Jesse Francis-Williams. 1969. 45.00 o.p. (ISBN 0-08-013057-7); pap. 45.00 o.p. (ISBN 0-08-013056-9). Pergamon.

Diagnostico Enzimatico en las Enfermedades de Corazon, Higado y Pancreas. L. Adolph & Rita Lorenz. (Illus.). 126p. 1980. pap. 12.00 o.p. (ISBN 3-8055-0506-X). S Karger.

Diagnostics for Fusion Reactor Conditions: Proceedings of the Course & Workshop, Varenna, 6-17 September 1982, 3 vols. Ed. by P. E. Stott et al. 1228p. 1984. Set. pap. 105.00 o.p. (ISBN 0-08-031161-X). Pergamon.

Diahann. Diahann Carroll & Ross Firestone. 1986. 16.95 o.p. (ISBN 0-316-13019-2). Little.

Dial-a-Skill: A Manual of Procedures for Team Members of Special Education & Related Services. Betty D. Harrison. LC 77-16371. (Illus.). 1978. pap. 9.95x o.p. (ISBN 0-8425-0907-0). Brigham.

Dial-a-Word from the Bible. Gordon DeYoung. (Quiz & Puzzle Bks). 1977. pap. 0.95 o.p. (ISBN 0-8010-2862-0). Baker Bk.

Dialectic. Robert Palmer Saalbach. 1974. 3.50 o.p. (ISBN 0-682-48051-7). Exposition-Phoenix.

Dialectic & Difference. J. Taminiaux. Tr. by J. Decker & R. Crease. (Contemporary Studies in Philosophy & the Human Sciences). 177p. 1986. text ed. 19.95x o.p. (ISBN 0-391-03113-9). Humanities.

Dialectic of Action: A Philosophical Interpretation of History & the Humanities. Frederick A. Olafson. LC 79-10316. 1979. lib. bdg. 22.00x o.s.i. (ISBN 0-226-62564-8). U of Chicago Pr.

Dialectic of Illusion. Ann Warner. 64p. 1986. 6.75 o.p. (ISBN 0-8062-2776-1). Carlton.

Dialectical Phenomenology: Marx's Method. Roslyn W. Bologh. (International Library of Phenomenology & Moral Sciences). 1979. 25.00x o.p. (ISBN 0-7100-0335-8). Routledge Chapman & Hall.

Dialectical Psychology. Allan R. Buss. 222p. 1979. 24.50x o.p. (ISBN 0-8290-0856-X). Irvington.

Dialectics, 9 vols. 1970. Repr. of 1939 ed. Set. lib. bdg. 16.50x o.p. (ISBN 0-8371-9157-2, DI00). Greenwood.

Dialectics of Nature. Frederick Engels. 399p. 1940. 7.50 o.p. (ISBN 0-7178-0049-0); pap. 3.50 o.p. (ISBN 0-7178-0048-2). Intl Pubs Co.

Dialogue Mit Dem Meister. Paul Twitchell. Tr. by Steve DeWitt et al. 320p. (Orig., Ger.). 1980. pap. 6.95 o.p. (ISBN 0-914766-99-6). Illum Way Pub.

Dialogue & Discourse: A Socio-Linguistic Approach to Modern Drama Dialogue & Naturally-Occurring Conversation. Deirdre Burton. 220p. 1980. 31.95x o.p. (ISBN 0-7100-0560-1). Routledge Chapman & Hall.

Dialogue & Discourse: A Sociolinguistic Approach to Modern Drama, Dialogue, & Naturally Occuring Conversation. Deirdre Burton. 222p. 1984. pap. 13.95x o.p. (ISBN 0-7102-0386-1). Routledge Chapman & Hall.

Dialogue avec Trente Trais Variations de Ludwig van Beethoven sur une Valse de Diabelli. Michel Butor. (Coll. le Chemin). pap. 8.95 o.p. (ISBN 0-685-37245-6). Schoenhof.

Dialogue Between a Philosopher & a Student of the Common Laws of England. Thomas Hobbes. Ed. by Joseph Cropsey. LC 76-120008. 1971. lib. bdg. 16.00x o.s.i. (ISBN 0-226-34540-8). U of Chicago Pr.

Dialogue Between Theology & Psychology. Ed. by Peter Homans. LC 68-16698. (Essays in Divinity Ser: Vol. 3). 1968. lib. bdg. 25.00x o.s.i. (ISBN 0-226-35110-6). U of Chicago Pr.

Dialogue Des Carmelites. Georges Bernanos. 1960. 24.95 o.p. (ISBN 0-685-11136-9). French & Eur.

Dialogue in the Pedagogical Praxis of Paulo Freire. (Project on Goals, Processes & Indicators of Development). 37p. 1981. pap. 5.00 o.p. (ISBN 92-808-0329-8, TUNU162, UNU). UNIPUB.

Dialogue on the Subject Catalogue--J. M. Perreault, "A Representative of the New Left in American Subject Cataloging"--A Review Essay on Sanford Berman's The Joy of Cataloging, with Response by Sanford Berman. (Occasional Papers: No. 161). 64p. 1983. pap. 3.00 o.p. (ISBN 0-317-59008-1). U of Ill Lib Info Sci.

Dialogues de Betes. Colette. 1975. pap. 3.95 o.p. (ISBN 0-686-54572-9). Schoenhof.

Dialogues of Lewis & Clark: A Narrative Poem. Robert E. Lee. LC 78-67631. 1979. 12.50 o.p. (ISBN 0-87081-124-X). Univ Pr Colo.

Dialogues of Plato. Plato. Ed. by William C. Greene. Tr. by B. Jowett. 1954. 7.95x o.p. (ISBN 0-87140-858-9). Liveright.

Dialogues on "MAC" Management Organization. Elliott Carlisle. (New Press Ser.). 144p. 1983. text ed. 10.95 o.p. (ISBN 0-07-009843-3). McGraw.

Dialogues with God: Sonnet Psalms on the Significance of Being Human. Benito F. Reyes. LC 78-244706. 139p. 1969. pap. 10.00 o.p. (ISBN 0-939375-37-0). World Univ Amer.

Diamond: A Biography. Alan Grossman et al. (Illus.). 256p. 1987. 16.95 o.p. (ISBN 0-8092-4825-5). Contemp Bks.

Diamond in the Rough. Patrick Finley. LC 86-3629. 200p. 14.95 o.p. (ISBN 0-914091-90-5). Chicago Review.

Diamond People. Murray Schumach. (Illus.). 1981. 12.95 o.p. (ISBN 0-393-01404-5). Norton.

Diamond Thin Film: The Threshold of Commercialization. Int'l Resource Development Inc. 123p. 1987. 985.00x o.p. (ISBN 0-88694-733-2). Intl Res Dev.

Diamonds Are Forever. Ian Fleming. 224p. 1980. pap. 3.50 o.s.i. (ISBN 0-425-08986-X). Jove Pubns.

Diamonds at the Bottom of the Sea & Other Stories. Desmond Hogan. 1980. 8.95 o.p. (ISBN 0-8076-0934-X). Braziller.

Diamonds From Daniel. William G. Heslop. LC 76-12082. (W. G. Heslop Bible Study Aids Ser.). 184p. 1976. pap. text ed. 4.50 o.p. (ISBN 0-8254-2833-5). Kregel.

Diamonds in the Sky. Samantha Hughes. (Candlelight Ecstasy Supreme Ser.: No. 29). 288p. (Orig.). 1984. pap. 2.50 o.p. (ISBN 0-440-11899-9). Dell.

Diamond's Japan Business Directory, 1986. 20th ed. 470.00 o.p. (ISBN 0-8002-3985-7). Intl Pubns Serv.

Diamonds Wild. Alan Caillou. 1979. pap. 1.95 o.p. (ISBN 0-380-43588-8, 43588). Avon.

Diana. J. Randy Tarraborrelli & Reggie Wilson. LC 82-45976. (Illus.). 256p. 1985. 29.95 o.p. (ISBN 0-385-18762-9, Dolp); pap. 14.95 o.p. (ISBN 0-385-18763-7). Doubleday.

Diana & Nikon: Essays on the Aesthetic of Photography. Janet Malcolm. LC 78-74547. (Illus.). 176p. 1981. 17.95 o.s.i. (ISBN 0-87923-273-0); pap. 8.95 o.s.i. (ISBN 0-87923-387-7). Godine.

Diana of the Crossways. George Meredith. 432p. 1973. pap. 3.95 o.p. (ISBN 0-393-00700-6). Norton.

Diana, Princess of Wales. Nicholas Courtney. LC 82-83165. 96p. 1983. pap. 7.95 o.s.i. (ISBN 0-03-063229-3, Owl Bks). H Holt & Co.

Diana, Princess of Wales. Penny Junor. Ed. by Charles R. Woods. (Illus.). 272p. 1984. pap. 7.95 o.p. (ISBN 0-671-50851-2, Fireside). S&S.

Diana: The Fairy Tale Princess. Lucy Butler. LC 83-5109. (gr. 2-4). 1983. 6.95 o.s.i. (ISBN 0-671-47301-8). Summit Bks.

Diana: The Fashion Princess. Davina Hanmer. 1984. pap. 8.95 o.p. (ISBN 0-03-072068-0, Owl Bks). H Holt & Co.

Diana the Huntress. Marion Chesney. 1986. pap. 2.50 o.s.i. (ISBN 0-449-20584-3, Crest). Fawcett.

Diana the Huntress. Ed. by Marion Chesney. 295p. 1986. pap. 10.95 o.p. (ISBN 0-8161-3997-0, Large Print Bks). G K Hall.

Diane Arbus: Magazine Work Essay. Ed. by Thomas W. Southall. LC 84-70444. (Illus.). 176p. 1986. pap. 19.95 o.p. (ISBN 0-89381-233-1). Aperture.

Dianetics: The Modern Science of Mental Health. rev. ed. L. Ron Hubbard. 640p. 1985. pap. 4.95 o.p. (ISBN 0-88404-219-7). Bridge Pubns Inc.

Diaper Days of Dallas. Ted Dealey. LC 75-11544. (Illus.). 192p. 1975. Repr. of 1966 ed. 12.50 o.p. (ISBN 0-87074-140-3). SMU Press.

Diaphragm Walls & Anchorages. Ed. by Institution of Civil Engineers Staff. 231p. 1975. 55.50x o.p. (ISBN 0-7277-0005-7, Pub. by T Telford UK). Am Soc Civil Eng.

Diaries & Letters of American Women: An Annotated Bibliography. Joyce D. Goodfriend. LC 87-17908. 187p. 1987. lib. bdg. 30.00x o.s.i. (ISBN 0-8161-8778-9, Hall Reference). G K Hall.

Diaries & Letters of Harold Nicolson, Vol. 2, The War Years: 1939-1945. Ed. by Nigel Nicolson. (Illus.). 1967. 8.50 o.p. (ISBN 0-689-10210-0, Atheneum). Macmillan.

Diaries & Letters of Harold Nicolson, Vol. 3, The Later Years, 1945-1962. Harold G. Nicolson. Ed. by Nigel Nicolson. (Illus.). 1968. 8.50 o.p. (ISBN 0-689-10211-9, Atheneum). Macmillan.

Diaries of Auberon Waugh: A Turbulent Decade 1976-1985. Private Eye Magazine Staff. (Illus.). 192p. 1985. pap. 12.95 o.p. (ISBN 0-233-97811-9, Pub. by Private Eye UK). David & Charles.

Diaries of Evelyn Waugh. Ed. by Michael Davie. 1977. 19.95 o.p. (ISBN 0-316-17450-5). Little.

Diaries of John Bright. J. Bright. Ed. by R. Walling. Repr. of 1931 ed. 24.00 o.p. (ISBN 0-527-10900-2). Kraus Repr.

Diaries of Judith Malina 1947-1957. Ed. by Judith Malina. LC 83-48293. 548p. 1984. 27.50 o.p. (ISBN 0-394-53132-9, GP-867). Grove.

Diarrhoeal Disease & Malnutrition: A Clinical Update. Ed. by Michael Gracey. LC 84-21412. (Illus.). 230p. 1985. text ed. 45.00 o.p. (ISBN 0-443-02892-3). Churchill.

Diary & Autobiography of John Adams, 4 vols. Ed. by Lyman H. Butterfield et al. LC 60-5387. (Adams Paper Ser). (Illus.). 1964. pap. 2.65 ea. o.p. (Atheneum); pap. o.p. (ISBN 0-689-70035-0); Vol. 1. pap. (ISBN 0-689-70031-8, TAP 1); Vol. 2. pap. (ISBN 0-689-70032-6, TAP 2); Vol. 3. pap. (ISBN 0-689-70033-4, TAP 3). Vol. 4 (ISBN 0-689-70034-2, TAP 4). Macmillan.

Diary by Dickie Doyle. Dickie Doyle. pap. 8.95 o.p. (ISBN 0-317-02545-7). Faber & Faber.

Diary by E. B. B. Ed. by Philip Kelley & Ronald Hudson. LC 68-18390. (Illus.). 358p. 1969. 17.50x o.p. (ISBN 0-8214-0047-9, Dist. by Wedgestone). Ohio U Pr.

Diary for Teachers of Young Children. Freda Cliff & Philip Cliff. pap. 1.95x o.p. (ISBN 0-8192-4036-2). Morehouse Pub.

Diary of a Dark Horse: The 1980 Anderson Presidential Campaign. Mark Bisnow. LC 83-329. (Illus.). 352p. 1983. 24.95 o.p. (ISBN 0-8093-1114-3). S Ill U Pr.

Diary of a Hunter. D. Brian Plummer. (Illus.). 114p. 1981. 24.00 o.p. (ISBN 0-85115-153-1, Pub. by Boydell & Brewer). Longwood Pub Group.

Diary of a Lover of Marilyn Monroe. Hans J. Lembourn. LC 78-73861. 1979. 8.95 o.p. (ISBN 0-87795-216-7, Arbor Hse). Morrow.

Diary of a Mad Iranian. Teymoor Tajeri. LC 84-90123. 239p. 1985. 12.95 o.p. (ISBN 0-533-06208-X). Vantage.

Diary of a Spy Pilot. Tobias R. Funt. 144p. 1987. 9.50 o.p. (ISBN 0-8062-2929-2). Carlton.

Diary of a Woman in White. Andre Soubiran. 1974. pap. 1.50 o.p. (ISBN 0-380-00075-X, 20180). Avon.

Diary of a Writer. Fyodor Dostoyevsky. Tr. by Boris Brasol from Rus. LC 78-32010. 1100p. 1985. pap. 15.95 o.p. (ISBN 0-87905-046-2, Peregrine Smith). Gibbs Smith Pub.

Diary of a Yuppie. Louis Auchincloss. 215p. 1986. 16.45 o.s.i. (ISBN 0-395-41649-3). HM.

Diary of an Artist. Rachel Sheen. 33p. 1985. 5.95 o.p. (ISBN 0-533-05932-1). Vantage.

Diary of an OD Man. Robert R. Blake & Jane S. Mouton. LC 75-18202. 356p. 1976. 25.00x o.p. (ISBN 0-87201-169-0). Gulf Pub.

Diary of Anais Nin, 7 vols. Anais Nin. 1978. Set. pap. 22.50 o.p. (ISBN 0-15-626034-4, Harv). HarBraceJ.

Diary of Anais Nin, Vols. 1-4. Anais Nin. Ed. by Gunther Stuhlmann. Incl. Vol. 1. 1931-34. (Illus.). 384p. 1969. 9.50 o.p. (ISBN 0-15-125588-1); pap. 9.95 (ISBN 0-15-626025-5); Vol. 2. 1934-39. (Illus.). 357p. 1970. 11.95 o.p. (ISBN 0-15-125589-X); pap. 9.95 (ISBN 0-15-626026-3); Vol. 3. 1939-44. (Illus.). 327p. 1971. 9.50 o.p. (ISBN 0-15-125591-1); pap. 9.95 (ISBN 0-15-626027-1); Vol. 4. 1944-47. (Illus.). 235p. 1972. 9.50 o.p. (ISBN 0-15-125592-X); pap. 9.95 (ISBN 0-15-626028-X). LC 66-12917. 1966. HarBraceJ.

Diary of Anais Nin, 1947-1955, Vol. 5. Anais Nin. LC 66-12917. 1974. 7.95 o.p. (ISBN 0-15-125593-8). HarBraceJ.

Diary of Anais Nin: 1955-1966, Vol. 6. Anais Nin. Ed. by Gunther Stuhlmann. LC 66-12917. (Illus.). 464p. 1976. 12.95 o.p. (ISBN 0-15-125594-6). HarBraceJ.

Diary of Anais Nin: 1966-1974, Vol. 7. Anais Nin. LC 66-12917. (Illus.). 432p. 1980. 14.95 o.p. (ISBN 0-15-125596-2). HarBraceJ.

Diary of Anna Green Winslow, a Boston Schoolgirl of 1771. Anna G. Winslow. Ed. by Allic M. Earle. LC 71-124586. (Illus.). 142p. 1970. Repr. of 1894 ed. 30.00x o.p. (ISBN 0-8103-3586-7). Gale.

Diary of Anne Frank. Adapted by Linda A. Cadrain. (Contemporary Motivators Ser.). (Illus.). 32p. (Orig.). (YA) (gr. 4-12). 1979. pap. text ed. 2.25 o.p. (ISBN 0-88301-308-8). Pendulum Pr.

Diary of Baron Waldstein: A Traveller in Elizabethan England. Baron Waldstein. Tr. by G. W. Groos. (Illus.). 184p. 1981. 18.95 o.s.i. (ISBN 0-500-01254-7). Thames Hudson.

Diary of Charles Francis Adams: January 1820-September 1829, 2 vols. Ed. by Lyman H. Butterfield et al. LC 64-20588. (Adams Papers Ser). (Illus.). 1967. pap. 3.95 ea. o.p. (Atheneum); Vol. 1. pap. (ISBN 0-689-70038-5, TAP 7); Vol. 2. pap. (ISBN 0-689-70039-3, TAP 8). Macmillan.

Diary of James A. Garfield: Vol. I, 1848-1871, Vol. II, 1872-1874, 2 vols. Ed. by Harry J. Brown & Frederick D. Williams. 1967. Set. 30.00x o.p. (ISBN 0-87013-111-7). Mich St U Pr.

Diary of James C. Hagerty: Eisenhower in Mid-Course, 1954-1955. Ed. by Robert H. Ferrell. LC 82-48477. (Illus.). 288p. 1983. 19.50x o.p. (ISBN 0-253-11625-2). Ind U Pr.

Diary of Prayer: Daily Meditations on the Parables of Jesus. J. Barrie Shepherd. LC 80-27037. 132p. 1981. pap. 5.95 o.s.i. (ISBN 0-664-24352-5, Westminster). Westminster John Knox.

Diary of Prayers-Personal & Public. John B. Coburn. LC 75-12824. 1975. 7.50 o.s.i. (ISBN 0-664-20823-1, Westminster); softcover 3.50 o.s.i. (ISBN 0-664-24764-4, Westminster). Westminster John Knox.

Diary of Selma Lagerloef. Selma O. Lagerloef. Tr. by Velma S. Howard. LC 36-30959. 1975. Repr. of 1936 ed. 35.00 o.p. (ISBN 0-527-54000-5). Kraus Repr.

Diary of the Strawbridge Place. Helen P. Jacob. LC 77-22713. (gr. 4-6). 1978. 8.95 o.p. (ISBN 0-689-30619-9, Atheneum). Macmillan.

Diary of the Twentieth Congress of the Communist Party of the Soviet Union. Vittorio Vidali. Tr. by Nell A. Cattonar & A. M. Elliot. LC 82-12053. 216p. (Orig.). 1984. pap. 8.95 o.p. (ISBN 0-88208-134-9). Chicago Review.

Diary of the Voyage of H. M. S. Beagle. Charles Darwin. Ed. by Nora Barlow. LC 34-6168. 1969. Repr. of 1933 ed. 25.00 o.p. (ISBN 0-527-21600-3). Kraus Repr.

Diary of the Voyage of H. M. S. Rattlesnake. Thomas H. Huxley & Julian S. Huxley. Repr. of 1936 ed. 35.00 o.p. (ISBN 0-527-43860-X). Kraus Repr.

Diary of Virginia Woolf, Vol. 2: 1920-1924. Virginia Woolf. Ed. & pref. by Anne O. Bell. LC 78-53907. 1978. 12.95 o.s.i. (ISBN 0-15-125598-9). HarBraceJ.

Diary of Virginia Woolf: Vol. 3, 1925-1930. Virginia Woolf. Ed. by Anne O. Bell & Andrew McNeillie. LC 77-73111. 416p. 1980. 15.95 o.s.i. (ISBN 0-15-125599-7). HarBraceJ.

Diary of Virginia Woolf, Vol. 4: 1931-1935. Virginia Woolf. Ed. by Anne O. Bell. LC 77-73111. 416p. 1982. 19.95 o.s.i. (ISBN 0-15-125602-0). HarBraceJ.

Diaspora: The Post-Biblical History of the Jews. Werner Keller. LC 68-24393. 1971. pap. 4.95 o.p. (ISBN 0-15-626033-6, HB217, Harv). HarBraceJ.

Diatomees Marines de la France, 2 vols. H. Peragallo & M. Peragallo. (Illus.). 1965. 110.00x o.p. (ISBN 90-6123-212-0). Lubrecht & Cramer.

Diatomic Interaction Potential Theory, 2 vols. Jerry Goodisman. Incl. Vol. 1. Fundamentals. 1973. 73.50 (ISBN 0-12-290201-7); Vol. 2. Applications. 1973. 78.00 (ISBN 0-12-290202-5). (Physical Chemistry Ser.). Acad Pr.

Dibs: In Search of Self. Virginia M. Axline. 1965. 8.95 o.p. (ISBN 0-395-07371-5). HM.

Diccionario De las Religiones Prerromanas De Hispania. Jose M. Blazquez. 192p. (Span.). 1975. pap. 9.95 o.p. (ISBN 84-7090-071-4, S-50058). French & Eur.

Diccionario Actualizado de la Lengua Espanola. 3rd ed. Juan Capdevila Font. 392p. (Span.). 1976. 10.50 o.p. (ISBN 84-85117-06-9, S-50266); pap. 9.25 o.p. (ISBN 84-85117-28-X, S-50265). French & Eur.

Diccionario Actualizado De Sinonimos y Contrarios De la Lengua Espanola. 2nd ed. Juan Capdevila Font. 513p. (Span.). 1978. pap. 13.95 o.p. (ISBN 84-7176-301-X, S-50267). French & Eur.

Diccionario Aleman-Espanol, Espanol-Aleman de Medicina. 2nd ed. Francisco Ruiz Torres. 860p. (Ger. & Span.). 1971. pap. 41.25 o.p. (ISBN 84-205-0010-0, S-50089). French & Eur.

Diccionario Auxiliar del Crucigramista. 3rd ed. Fausto Turell Baldovi. (Span.). 1978. pap. 8.75 o.p. (ISBN 84-02-00817-8, S-50154). French & Eur.

Diccionario Basico De Seguros. Julio Castelo Matran. 312p. (Span.). 1978. pap. 18.50 o.p. (ISBN 84-7100-049-0, S-50036). French & Eur.

Diccionario Basico Escolar de la Lengua Espanola. 2nd ed. Juan Capdevilla Font. 398p. (Span.). 1975. 6.75 o.p. (ISBN 84-85117-17-4, S-50254). French & Eur.

Diccionario Biografico De Autores De Todos los Tiempos y Paises, 3 vols. 3050p. (Span.). 1973. Set. 150.00 o.p. (ISBN 84-274-0507-3, S-12327). French & Eur.

Diccionario de Americanismos. Marcos A. Morinigo. (Span.). 35.00 o.p. (ISBN 0-686-56690-4, S-12121). French & Eur.

Diccionario de Ciencias. Chapman Ubarov. 226p. (Span.). 1970. 12.25 o.p. (ISBN 84-237-0299-5, S-50245). French & Eur.

Diccionario de Ciencias Sociales, 2 vols. UNESCO Staff. 2370p. (Span.). 1975. Set. pap. 60.00 o.p. (ISBN 84-259-0434-X, S-50061). French & Eur.

Diccionario de Citas. Juan Capdevila Font. 132p. (Span.). 1977. pap. 13.95 o.p. (ISBN 84-85117-43-3, S-50580). French & Eur.

Titles

Diccionario de Computadores. Anthony Chandor. 402p. (Span.). 1975. leather 28.50 o.p. (ISBN 84-335-6411-0, S-31859). French & Eur.
Diccionario de Crucigramas. Litero. 435p. (Span.). 1974. pap. 7.50 o.p. (ISBN 84-252-0783-5, S-50276). French & Eur.
Diccionario de Demonologia. 3rd ed. Frederick Koning. (Span.). 1978. pap. 2.95 o.p. (ISBN 0-686-57362-5, S-50155). French & Eur.
Diccionario de Economia Politica. 2nd ed. Borisov et al. 256p. (Span.). 1977. pap. 6.95 o.p. (ISBN 84-253-0610-8, S-50074). French & Eur.
Diccionario de Economia Politica. Borisov et al. 264p. (Span.). 1975. pap. 6.95 o.p. (ISBN 84-7339-060-1, S-50150). French & Eur.
Diccionario De Electronica. S. Handel. 470p. (Span.). 1976. 39.75 o.p. (ISBN 84-335-6408-0, S-50070). French & Eur.
Diccionario de Especialidades Farmaceuticas. 33rd, Mexican ed. Ed. by E. Rosenstein. (Span.). 1987. pap. 60.00x o.p. (ISBN 968-460-064-X). Drug Intell Pubns.
Diccionario de Especialidades Farmaceuticas. 34th, Mexican ed. Ed. by E. Rosenstein. (Span.). 1988. pap. 60.00x o.p. (ISBN 2-85091-064-3). Drug Intell Pubns.
Diccionario de Filosofia, 2 vols. Mora Ferrater. (Span.). 95.00 set o.p. (ISBN 0-686-56658-0, S-31443). French & Eur.
Diccionario De Filosofia. 2nd ed. Dagobert D. Runes. 400p. (Span.). 1977. 15.75 o.p. (ISBN 84-253-0127-0, S-13007). French & Eur.
Diccionario de Grupos, Fuerzas, y Partidos Politicos Espanoles. Gerardo Duelo. 128p. (Span.). 1977. pap. 5.25 o.p. (ISBN 84-7080-940-7, S-50175). French & Eur.
Diccionario de Historia de Espana, 3 vols. German Bleiberg. 3776p. (Span.). 1979. Set. pap. 70.00 o.p. (ISBN 84-206-5997-5, S-50374). French & Eur.
Diccionario de Incorreciones, Dudas y Normas Gramaticales. 655p. (Span.). 1975. pap. 17.50 o.p. (ISBN 84-02-04591-X, S-50156). French & Eur.
Diccionario de la Politica. 2nd ed. Jean-Noel Aquistapace. 344p. (Span.). 1969. pap. 7.95 o.p. (ISBN 84-265-7047-X, S-21237). French & Eur.
Diccionario de las Matematicas Modernas. 2nd ed. Lucien Chambadal. 264p. (Span.). 1976. pap. 5.25 o.p. (ISBN 84-01-90307-6, S-12248). French & Eur.
Diccionario de Leyes y Efectos Cientificos En Quimica-Fisica Matematicas. D. W. Ballentyne & L. E. Walker. 216p. (Span.). 14.95 o.p. (ISBN 0-686-56711-0, S-33054). French & Eur.
Diccionario de Medicina, Farmacia Veterinaria y Quimica. Castulo Carrasco Martinez. 1040p. (Span.). 1978. pap. 49.95 o.p. (ISBN 84-7391-013-3, S-50123). French & Eur.
Diccionario de Mitologia. Homero Lelama. 364p. (Span.). 1974. 44.95 o.p. (ISBN 0-686-56670-X, S-33075). French & Eur.
Diccionario de Modismos Ingleses. Pablo Caldwell. 496p. (Eng. & Span.). 1973. 17.50 o.p. (ISBN 0-686-56672-6, S-33065). French & Eur.
Diccionario de Musica. Arthur Jacobs. 392p. (Span.). 1966. 15.95 o.p. (ISBN 0-686-56715-3, S-33050). French & Eur.
Diccionario de Palabras Anticuadas y en Desuso. 2nd ed. Anita Luft. 308p. (Span.). 1974. pap. 17.50 o.p. (ISBN 84-359-0071-1, S-12060). French & Eur.
Diccionario de Philosofia. 2nd ed. M. Rosental. (Span.). 1977. pap. 9.95 o.p. (ISBN 84-7339-107-1, S-50149). French & Eur.
Diccionario de Siglas Relacionadas con la Informatica. IBM Staff. 200p. (Span.). 1974. pap. 9.95 o.p. (ISBN 84-360-2250-5, S-50370). French & Eur.
Diccionario de Sinonimos. S. D. Gili Gaya. (Span.). 1958. 8.50x o.s.i. (ISBN 0-686-00854-5). Colton Bk.
Diccionario de Temas Regionalistas En la Poesia Puertorriquena. Salvador Arana Soto. (Span.). 12.50 o.p. (ISBN 0-686-56649-1, S-5220). French & Eur.
Diccionario de Terminos Electrorales y Parlamentarios. Jose M. Gil-Robles. 268p. (Span.). 1977. pap. 15.25 o.p. (ISBN 84-306-3039-2, S-50001). French & Eur.
Diccionario del Comunismo. Jorge Sole Tura. 96p. (Span.). 1977. pap. 2.25 o.p. (ISBN 84-7235-299-4, S-50082). French & Eur.
Diccionario del Jefe de Empresa. Jean Romeuf & Jean P. Guinot. 644p. (Span.). 1966. 44.95 o.p. (ISBN 84-335-6524-9, S-14191). French & Eur.
Diccionario del Trabajo Social. Ezequiel Ander Egg. 424p. (Span.). 1977. pap. 12.25 o.p. (ISBN 84-280-0606-7, S-50011). French & Eur.
Diccionario Enciclopedico Danae, 12 vols. 7220p. (Span.). 1977. Set. leather 600.00 o.p. (ISBN 84-7060-457-0, S-50521). French & Eur.
Diccionario Enciclopedico de la Masoneria. (Span.). 40.95 o.p. (ISBN 0-686-56654-8, S-14860). French & Eur.
Diccionario Enciclopedico Distein 2, 2 vols. Juan Capdevila Font. 992p. (Span.). 1976. Set. leather 29.50 o.p. (ISBN 84-85117-24-7, S-50450). French & Eur.
Diccionario Enciclopedico Ilustrado, 8 vols. 6th ed. 3920p. (Span.). 1977. Set. leather 345.00 o.p. (ISBN 84-01-60122-3, S-50519). French & Eur.
Diccionario Enciclopedico Ilustrado, 4 vols. 2nd ed. 2000p. (Span.). 1977. Set. leather 180.00 o.p. (ISBN 84-01-60135-5, S-50520). French & Eur.
Diccionario Enciclopedico y Critico De los Hombres De Espana. Enrique Esperabe De Artega. 530p. (Span.). 1956. pap. 6.95 o.p. (ISBN 84-290-0972-8, S-50137). French & Eur.
Diccionario Erotico de El y Ella. 640p. (Span.). 1977. pap. 37.50 o.p. (ISBN 84-85265-17-3, S-50128). French & Eur.
Diccionario Escolar De Sinonimos y Contrarios De la Lengua Espanola. Juan Capdevila Font. 499p. (Span.). 1978. 12.25 o.p. (ISBN 84-7176-302-8, S-50268). French & Eur.
Diccionario Escolar Roble. 5th ed. Francisco Gordo Guarinos. 712p. (Span.). 1975. pap. 4.50 o.p. (ISBN 84-346-0191-5, S-50046). French & Eur.
Diccionario Grafico de Arte y Oficios Artisticos, 4 vols. J. Lapoulide. 1600p. (Span.). 1963. Set. 125.00 o.p. (ISBN 84-7186-037-6, S-12333). French & Eur.
Diccionario Ideologico Manual de la Lengua Espanola. Juan Capdevila Font. 900p. (Span.). 1976. 18.75 o.p. (ISBN 84-85117-22-0, S-50264). French & Eur.
Diccionario Ilustrado De Fotografia. 212p. (Span.). 1974. pap. 22.50 o.p. (ISBN 84-342-0117-8, S-50014). French & Eur.
Diccionario Ilustrado De Frases Celebres y Citas Literarias. Vincente Vega. 939p. (Span.). 1973. pap. 20.50 o.p. (ISBN 84-252-0128-4, S-50280). French & Eur.
Diccionario Ilustrado de la Muerte. Robert Sabatier. 612p. (Span.). 1970. pap. 24.75 o.p. (ISBN 84-252-0351-1, S-50581). French & Eur.
Diccionario Infantil Ilustrado, 7 vols. 968p. (Span.). 1977. Set. 140.00 o.p. (ISBN 84-01-70210-0, S-50043). French & Eur.
Diccionario Infantil Ilustrado Bruguera. Consuelo Guisset Poch & Prado Castellanos Alentorn. 96p. (Span.). 1977. pap. 9.95 o.p. (ISBN 84-02-05211-8, S-50160). French & Eur.
Diccionario Ingles-Espanol, Espanol-Ingles Forja. 17th ed. Eleesbaan Serrano Mesa. 488p. (Eng. & Span.). 1977. 4.50 o.p. (ISBN 84-7105-098-6, S-50352). French & Eur.
Diccionario Ingles-Espanol, Spanish-English. Mauricio Bohigas Rosell. 1370p. (Eng. & Span.). 1974. 7.95 o.p. (ISBN 84-7183-007-8, S-12385). French & Eur.
Diccionario Internacional Abreviado De Siglas Contracciones y Abreviaturas. Donato Millan Contreras. 224p. (Span.). 1974. pap. 9.95 o.p. (ISBN 0-686-57355-2, S-50239). French & Eur.
Diccionario Lunfardo Ilustrado. Jose Gobello. (Span.). 55.00 o.p. (ISBN 0-686-56669-6, S-33076). French & Eur.
Diccionario Para Pobres. Francisco Umbral Perez. 240p. (Span.). 1977. 9.95 o.p. (ISBN 84-7454-002-X, S-50099). French & Eur.
Diccionario Porrua de Historia, Biografia y Geografia de Mexico, 2 vols. (Span.). 150.00 set o.p. (ISBN 0-686-56692-0, S-12279). French & Eur.
Diccionario Practico Escolar de la Lengua Espanola. Juan Capdevila Font. 500p. (Span.). 1976. pap. 3.25 o.p. (ISBN 84-85117-38-7, S-50256). French & Eur.
Diccionario Ruso-Espanol de la Ciencia y la Tecnica. 2nd ed. Patronato J. De la Cierva. 700p. (Span.). 1972. 50.00 o.p. (ISBN 84-237-0407-6, S-50249). French & Eur.
Diccionario Secreto, 3 vols. 2nd ed. Camilo J. Cela Trulock. 1184p. (Span.). 1975. Set. pap. 20.95 o.p. (ISBN 84-206-1997-3, S-29231). French & Eur.
Diccionario Simultaneo en 21 Idiomas. Juan Capdevilla Font. 416p. (Span., Eng., Fr., Ger., Ital., Port., Catalan., Czech., Danish., Esperanto., Finnish., Gr., Dutch., Hungarian., Malay., Pol., Romanian., Rus., Swedish. & Turkish.). 1977. pap. 18.75 o.p. (ISBN 0-686-57350-1, S-31466). French & Eur.
Diccionario Simultaneo en 6 Idiomas. Juan Capdevila Font. 192p. (Span., Eng., Fr., Ital., Ger. & Port.). 1975. pap. 6.75 o.p. (ISBN 84-85117-14-X, S-31467). French & Eur.
Diccionario Tecnico de la Industria del Petroleo y Derivados. Ed. by Mendez. 588p. (Span.). 1980. 44.95 o.p. (ISBN 84-283-1097-1, S-37582). French & Eur.
Diccionario Terminologia Medica Explicada. Juan Prada Becares. 128p. (Span.). 1977. pap. 9.95 o.p. (ISBN 84-400-3894-1, S-50111). French & Eur.
Diccionario Vasco-Castellano, Castellano-Vasco De Voces Comunes a Dos O Mas Dialectos Del Euskera. 2nd ed. Buenaventura de Oyeregui. 372p. 1978. pap. 7.50 o.p. (ISBN 0-686-57354-4, S-50454). French & Eur.
Diccionario Visual Del Sexo. 328p. (Span.). 1979. 53.95 o.p. (ISBN 84-278-0556-X, S-50031). French & Eur.
Dice Cup: Selected Prose Poems. Max Jacob. Ed. by Michael Brownstein. Tr. by John Ashbery et al. LC 79-26610. (Illus.). 122p. (Orig.). 1980. pap. 8.00 o.p. (ISBN 0-915342-32-4). SUN.
Dicey's Song. Cynthia Voigt. 1984. pap. 2.25 o.p. (ISBN 0-449-70071-2). Fawcett.
Dickens at Work. John Butt & Kathleen Tillotson. (Library Reprints Ser.). 1982. 44.00x o.p. (ISBN 0-416-34030-X, NO. 3704). Routledge Chapman & Hall.
Dickens Companion. Date not set. (ISBN 0-8052-3883-2). Random.
Dickens, Dali, & Others. George Orwell. LC 63-22950. 1946. 5.95 o.s.i. (ISBN 0-15-125601-2). HarBraceJ.
Dicken's Doctors. David Smithers. 1979. 24.00 o.p. (ISBN 0-08-023386-4). Pergamon.
Dickens Dramatized. H. Philip Bolton. 400p. 1986. 100.00 o.p. (ISBN 0-7201-1804-2). Mansell.
Dickens: Interviews & Recollections, 2 vols. Ed. by Philip Collins. (Illus.). 1981. 28.50x ea. o.p. Vol. 1, 210 1 Pgs (ISBN 0-389-20042-5). Vol. 2, 200 Pgs (ISBN 0-389-20043-3). B&N Imports.
Dickens on America & the Americans. Charles Dickens. Ed. by Michael Slater. (Illus.). 260p. 1978. 20.00 o.p. (ISBN 0-292-71517-X). U of Tex Pr.
Dicky: A True Story of a California Valley Quail. Edward B. Cassina & Shirley E. Cassina. LC 84-90003. (Illus.). (gr. 1 up). 1985. 7.95 o.p. (ISBN 0-533-06099-0). Vantage.
Dictation for Transcription. Louis A. Leslie & Charles E. Zoubek. (Diamond Jubilee Ser). 1963. text ed. 24.35 o.p. (ISBN 0-07-037315-9). McGraw.
Dictation of the Law. Carol A. Fulton. 64p. 1986. 6.50 o.p. (ISBN 0-8062-2660-9). Carlton.
Dictatorships & Double Standards: Rationalism & Reason in Politics. Jeane J. Kirkpatrick. 270p. 1982. 14.50 o.p. (ISBN 0-671-43836-0). S&S.
Dictatorships & Double Standards: Rationalism & Reason in Politics. Jeane J. Kirkpatrick. 270p. 1983. pap. 8.95 o.p. (ISBN 0-671-49266-7, Touchstone). S&S.
Diction Harry's Magical, Marvelous, Motivational Dictionary Kit. Elaine Prizzi & Jeanne Hoffman. (gr. 4-8). 1982. pap. 10.95 o.p. (ISBN 0-8224-2252-2). D S Lake Pubs.
Dictionaries & Their Users. Ed. by R. R. Hartmann. (Papers from the 1978 Seminar on Lexicography). 1979. pap. 18.00 o.p. E J Brill USA.
Dictionaries of British & America. James R. Hulbert. 128p. 1955. Philos Lib.
Dictionary & Picture Postcards in Britain 1894-1939. A. W. Coysh. (Illus.). 1984. 49.50 o.p. (ISBN 1-85149-015-9). Antique Collect.
Dictionary Catalog & Shelf List of the Spencer Collection of Illustrated Books & Manuscripts & Fine Bindings, 2 vols. New York Public Library, Research Libraries Staff. 1970. Set. lib. bdg. 198.00 o.p. (ISBN 0-8161-0862-5, Hall Library). G K Hall.
Dictionary Catalog of Jewish Collection, 14 Vols. New York Public Library, Research Libraries Staff. 1970. Set. 1240.00 o.p. (ISBN 0-8161-0409-3, Pub. by Hall Library). G K Hall.
Dictionary Catalog of Materials on New York City. New York Public Library, Research Libraries Staff. 1977. lib. bdg. 300.00 o.p. (ISBN 0-8161-0079-9, Hall Library). G K Hall.
Dictionary Catalog of Printed Books, 38 Vols. Mitchell Library, Sydney, Australia Staff. 1970. Set. lib. bdg. 3735.00 o.p. (ISBN 0-8161-0790-4, Hall Library); lib. bdg. 135.00 1st suppl. o.p. (ISBN 0-8161-0848-X). G K Hall.
Dictionary Catalog of the American Indian Collection. Huntington Free Library, Reading Room Staff. 1977. lib. bdg. 395.00 o.p. (ISBN 0-8161-0065-9, Hall Library). G K Hall.
Dictionary Catalog of the Art & Architecture Division, Supplement 1974. New York Public Library, Research Libraries Staff. 1976. lib. bdg. 85.00 o.p. (ISBN 0-8161-0061-6, Hall Library). G K Hall.
Dictionary Catalog of the Art & Architecture Division, The Research Libraries of The New York Public Library, 30 vols. New York Public Library, Research Libraries Staff. 1975. Set. lib. bdg. 3070.00 o.p. (ISBN 0-8161-1157-X, Hall Library). G K Hall.
Dictionary Catalog of the Dance Collection, Performing Arts Research Center, 10 vols. New York Public Library, Research Libraries Staff. 1974. Set. lib. bdg. 855.00 o.p. (ISBN 0-8161-1124-3, Hall Library). G K Hall.
Dictionary Catalog of the Department Library, 37 Vols. Ed. by U. S. Department of the Interior, Washington, D. C. Staff. 1967. Set. 3655.00 o.p. (ISBN 0-8161-0715-7, Hall Library). G K Hall.
Dictionary Catalog of the Department Library, Fourth Suppl, 8 vols. Ed. by U. S. Department of the Interior, Washington, D. C. Staff. 1975. Set. lib. bdg. 825.00 o.p. (ISBN 0-8161-0016-0, Hall Library). G K Hall.
Dictionary Catalog of the Edward E. Ayer Collection of Americana & American Indians, First Supplement, 3 vol. Newberry Library, Chicago Staff. 1970. Set. lib. bdg. 330.00 o.p. (ISBN 0-8161-0810-2, Hall Library). G K Hall.
Dictionary Catalog of the Edward E. Ayer Collection of Americana & American Indians, 16 Vols. Newberry Library, Chicago Staff. 1970. Set. 1165.00 o.p. (ISBN 0-8161-0586-3, Hall Library). G K Hall.
Dictionary Catalog of the G. Robert Vincent Library. Michigan State University, East Lansing Staff. 1974. 78.00 o.p. (ISBN 0-8161-1149-9, Hall Library). G K Hall.
Dictionary Catalog of the Giannini Foundation of Agricultural Economics Library, 12 vols. Ed. by University of California, Berkeley Staff. 1971. 1185.00 o.p. (ISBN 0-8161-0908-7, Hall Library). G K Hall.
Dictionary Catalog of the Henry W. & Albert A. Berg Collection of English & American Literature, 5 Vols. New York Public Library, Research Libraries Staff. 1970. Set. lib. bdg. 485.00 o.p. (ISBN 0-8161-0870-6, Hall Library). G K Hall.
Dictionary Catalog of the History of the Americas Collection, 28 Vols. New York Public Library, Research Libraries Staff. 1970. Set. lib. bdg. 2290.00 o.p. (ISBN 0-8161-0540-5, Hall Library). G K Hall.
Dictionary Catalog of the History of the Americas Collection, First Supplement, 9 vols. New York Public Library, Research Libraries Staff. 1974. Set. lib. bdg. 985.00 o.p. (ISBN 0-8161-0771-8, Hall Library). G K Hall.
Dictionary Catalog of the J. Lloyd Eaton Collection of Science Fiction & Fantasy Literature, 3 vols. 1982. Set. lib. bdg. 300.00 o.p. (ISBN 0-8161-0379-8, Hall Library). G K Hall.
Dictionary Catalog of the Jewish Collection, First Supplement, 8 vols. New York Public Library, Research Libraries Staff. 5424p. 1975. Set. lib. bdg. 875.00 o.p. (ISBN 0-8161-0773-4, Hall Library). G K Hall.
Dictionary Catalog of the Library of the Bernice P. Bishop Museum, 9 vols. Bishop, Bernice P., Museum Editors. 1964. Set. lib. bdg. 890.00 o.p. (ISBN 0-8161-0679-7, Hall Library); lib. bdg. 120.00 1st suppl. 1967 o.p. (ISBN 0-8161-0722-X); lib. bdg. 110.00 2nd suppl. 1970 o.p. (ISBN 0-8161-0834-X). G K Hall.
Dictionary Catalog of the Library of the Center for Applied Linguistics, Washington, D. C, 4 vols. Center for Applied Linguistics, Washington, D. C. Staff. 1974. Set. lib. bdg. 370.00 o.p. (ISBN 0-8161-1114-6, Hall Library). G K Hall.
Dictionary Catalog of the Library of the Freer Gallery of Art, 6 Vols. Smithsonian Institution, Washington, D. C. Staff. 1970. Set. lib. bdg. 555.00 o.p. (ISBN 0-8161-0799-8, Hall Library). G K Hall.
Dictionary Catalog of the Library of the Massachusetts Horticultural Society, 3 Vols. Massachusetts Horticultural Society, Boston Staff. 1970. Set. lib. bdg. 260.00 o.p. (ISBN 0-8161-0648-7, Hall Library). G K Hall.
Dictionary Catalog of the Library of the Massachusetts Horticultural Society, First Supplement. Massachusetts Horticultural Society, Boston Staff. 1972. lib. bdg. 110.00 o.p. (ISBN 0-8161-1038-7, Hall Library). G K Hall.
Dictionary Catalog of the Library of the Mariners Museum, 9 Vols. Mariners Museum Library - Newport News - Virginia Staff. 1970. Set. lib. bdg. 890.00 o.p. (ISBN 0-8161-0674-6, Hall Library). G K Hall.
Dictionary Catalog of the Library of the Pontifical Institute of Medieval Studies: First Supplement. Pontifical Institute of Medieval Studies, Toronto Staff. 1979. lib. bdg. 130.00 o.p. (ISBN 0-8161-1061-1, Hall Library). G K Hall.
Dictionary Catalog of the Local History & Genealogy Division, 20 vols. New York Public Library, Research Libraries Staff. 1974. Set. lib. bdg. 1600.00 o.p. (ISBN 0-8161-0784-X, Hall Library). G K Hall.

Dictionary Catalog of the Manuscript Division, 2 Vols. New York Public Library, Research Libraries Staff. 1970. Set. lib. bdg. 156.00 o.p. (ISBN 0-8161-0750-5, Hall Library). G K Hall.
Dictionary Catalog of the Map Division, 10 vols. New York Public Library, Research Libraries Staff. 1971. Set. lib. bdg. 990.00 o.p. (ISBN 0-8161-0783-1, Hall Library). G K Hall.
Dictionary Catalog of the Music Collection, Boston Public Library, 20 vols. Boston Public Library Staff. 15617p. 1975. Set. lib. bdg. 1976.00 o.p. (ISBN 0-8161-0956-7, Hall Library); lib. bdg. 440.00 1st suppl., 4 vols. 1976 o.p. (ISBN 0-8161-1014-X). G K Hall.
Dictionary Catalog of the Music Collection, 33 Vols. New York Public Library, Research Libraries Staff. 1974. Set. lib. bdg. 3260.00 o.p. (ISBN 0-8161-0709-2, Hall Library). G K Hall.
Dictionary Catalog of the Music Collection. 2nd ed. New York Public Library, Research Libraries Staff. 1983. lib. bdg. 6240.00 o.p. (ISBN 0-8161-0374-7, Hall Library). G K Hall.
Dictionary Catalog of the National Agricultural Library, 1862-1965, 73 Vols. 56500p. Set. 1460.00x o.p. (ISBN 0-87471-001-4). Rowman.
Dictionary Catalog of the Negro Collection of the Fisk University Library, 6 vols. Fisk University Library Editors, Nashville. 1974. Set. lib. bdg. 510.00 o.p. (ISBN 0-8161-1055-7, Hall Library). G K Hall.
Dictionary Catalog of the Oriental Collection: First Supplement, 8 vols. New York Public Library, Research Libraries Staff. 1976. Set. lib. bdg. 1000.00 o.p. (ISBN 0-8161-0775-0, Hall Library). G K Hall.
Dictionary Catalog of the Oriental Collection, 16 Vols. New York Public Library, Research Libraries Staff. 1970. Set. lib. bdg. 1200.00 o.p. (ISBN 0-8161-0410-7, Hall Library). G K Hall.
Dictionary Catalog of the Princeton University Plasma Physics Laboratory Library, 4 vols. Princeton University Staff. 1970. Set. lib. bdg. 395.00 o.p. (ISBN 0-8161-0881-1, Hall Library). G K Hall.
Dictionary Catalog of the Princeton University Plasma Physics Laboratory Library, First Supplement. Princeton University Staff. 1973. lib. bdg. 160.00 o.p. (ISBN 0-8161-1032-8, Hall Library). G K Hall.
Dictionary Catalog of the Prints Division, 5 vols. New York Public Library, Research Libraries Staff. 1975. Set. lib. bdg. 495.00 o.p. (ISBN 0-8161-1148-0, Hall Library). G K Hall.
Dictionary Catalog of the Rare Book Division: First Supplement. New York Public Library, Research Libraries Staff. 1973. 115.00 o.p. (ISBN 0-8161-1089-1, Hall Library). G K Hall.
Dictionary Catalog of the Rare Book Division, 21 vols. New York Public Library, Research Libraries Staff. 1971. Set. 2075.00 o.p. (ISBN 0-8161-0782-3, Hall Library). G K Hall.
Dictionary Catalog of the Rodgers & Hammerstein Archives of Recorded Sound, 15 vols. 1981. Set. lib. bdg. 1535.00 o.p. (ISBN 0-8161-0359-3, Hall Library). G K Hall.
Dictionary Catalog of the Schomburg Collection of Negro Literature & History, 9 vols. New York Public Library, Research Libraries Staff. LC 66-1573. 1973. Set. 830.00 o.p. (ISBN 0-8161-0632-0, Hall Library); 1st suppl. 1970, 2 vols. 120.00 o.p. (ISBN 0-8161-0735-1); 2nd suppl., 1972, 4 vols. 440.00 o.p. (ISBN 0-8161-0820-X). G K Hall.
Dictionary Catalog of the Slavonic Collection, 44 vols. 2nd, rev. ed. New York Public Library, Research Libraries Staff. 1974. Set. lib. bdg. 3952.00 o.p. (ISBN 0-8161-0777-7, Hall Library). G K Hall.
Dictionary Catalog of the Stefansson Collection on the Polar Regions, 8 Vols. Dartmouth College Library, Hanover, N. H. Staff. 1970. Set. lib. bdg. 720.00 o.p. (ISBN 0-8161-0676-2, Hall Library). G K Hall.
Dictionary Catalog of the United States Department of Housing & Urban Development Library & Information Division, 19 vols. Ed. by U. S. Department of Housing & Urban Development, Washington, D. C. Staff. 1972. Set. lib. bdg. 1880.00 o.p. (ISBN 0-8161-1007-7, Hall Library). G K Hall.
Dictionary Catalog of the United States Department of Housing & Urban Development Library & Information Division, First Supplement, 2 vols. Ed. by U. S. Department of Housing & Urban Development, Washington, D. C. Staff. 1974. Set. lib. bdg. 220.00 o.p. (ISBN 0-8161-1135-9, Hall Library). G K Hall.
Dictionary Catalog of the Vivian G. Harsh Collection of Afro-American History & Literature: Chicago Public Library, 4 vols. 1978. Set. lib. bdg. 367.00 o.p. (ISBN 0-8161-0252-X, Hall Library). G K Hall.
Dictionary Catalog of the Water Resources Center Archives, 5 vols. Ed. by University of California, Berkeley Staff. 1970. lib. bdg. 495.00 o.p. (ISBN 0-8161-0884-6, Hall Library); first suppl. (1971) 115.00 o.p. (ISBN 0-8161-0895-1); second suppl. (1972 115.00 o.p. (ISBN 0-8161-0983-4). G K Hall.
Dictionary Catalog of the Water Resources Center Archives, Fourth Suppl. Ed. by University of California, Berkeley Staff. 942p. 1975. lib. bdg. 115.00 o.p. (ISBN 0-8161-0002-0, Hall Library). G K Hall.
Dictionary Catalog of the Water Resources Center Archives: Sixth Supplement, 2 vols. Ed. by University of California, Berkeley Staff. 1978. Set. lib. bdg. 260.00 o.p. (ISBN 0-8161-0244-9, Hall Library). G K Hall.
Dictionary Catalog of William Andrews Clark Memorial Library, 15 vols. Clark, William Andrews, Memorial Library, Los Angeles Staff. 1974. Set. 1405.00 o.p. (ISBN 0-8161-1049-2, Hall Library). G K Hall.
Dictionary Catalog on Deafness & the Deaf, 2 vols. Gallaudet College Library Editors, Washington, D. C. 1970. Set. lib. bdg. 170.00 o.p. (ISBN 0-8161-0877-3, Hall Library). G K Hall.
Dictionary Catalogue of the Blacker - Wood Library of Zoology & Ornithology, 9 vols. McGill University, Blacker - Wood Library of Zoology & Ornithology Staff. 6300p. 1977. Set. lib. bdg. 845.00 o.p. (ISBN 0-8161-0719-X, Hall Library). G K Hall.
Dictionary Catalogue of the Byzantine Collection of the Dumbarton Oaks Research Library, 12 vols. Harvard University Dumbarton Oaks Research Library Staff. 1975. Set. lib. bdg. 1390.00 o.p. (ISBN 0-8161-1150-2, Hall Library). G K Hall.
Dictionary Catalogue of the Columbia University Law Library, 28 Vols. Columbia University Law Library Staff. 1970. Set. lib. bdg. 2860.00 o.p. (ISBN 0-8161-0800-5, Hall Library). G K Hall.
Dictionary Catalogue of the Columbia University Law Library, First Supplement, 7 vols. Columbia University Law Library, New York Staff. 1978. Set. lib. bdg. 940.00 o.p. (ISBN 0-8161-0802-1, Hall Library). G K Hall.
Dictionary Catalogue of the Harris Collection of American Poetry & Plays, Brown University, 13 vols. Brown University Staff. 1975. Set. lib. bdg. 1690.00 o.p. (ISBN 0-8161-0974-5, Hall Library). G K Hall.
Dictionary Catalogue of the History of Printing from the John M. Wing Foundation, Second Supplement. John M. Wing Foundation, Newberry Library Staff. 1981. lib. bdg. 455.00 o.p. (ISBN 0-8161-0326-7, Hall Library). G K Hall.
Dictionary Catalogue of the History of Printing from the John M. Wing Foundation, 6 Vols. Newberry Library, Chicago Staff. 1970. Set. lib. bdg. 595.00 o.p. (ISBN 0-8161-0587-1, Hall Library). G K Hall.
Dictionary Catalogue of the History of Printing from the John M. Wing Foundation, First Supplement, 3 vols. Newberry Library, Chicago Staff. 1970. Set. lib. bdg. 330.00 o.p. (ISBN 0-8161-0809-9, Hall Library). G K Hall.
Dictionary Catalogue of the Library of Sports in the Racquet & Tennis Club with Special Collections on Tennis, Lawn Tennis, & Early American Sports, 2 vols. Racquet & Tennis Club, New York Staff. 1971. Set. lib. bdg. 200.00 o.p. (ISBN 0-8161-0916-8, Hall Library). G K Hall.
Dictionary Catalogue of the Library of the Provincial Archives of British Columbia, 8 vols. Provincial Archives Staff & Victoria, British Columbia. 1971. Set. lib. bdg. 790.00 o.p. (ISBN 0-8161-0912-5, Hall Library). G K Hall.
Dictionary Catalogue of the Library of the Pontifical Institute of Medieval Studies, 5 vols. Pontifical Institute of Medieval Studies, Ontario Staff. 1973. Set. lib. bdg. 505.00 o.p. (ISBN 0-8161-0970-2, Hall Library). G K Hall.
Dictionary Catalogue of the Teachers College Library, 36 vols. Columbia University Editors. 1979. Set. lib. bdg. 3900.00 o.p. (ISBN 0-8161-0855-2, Hall Library). G K Hall.
Dictionary Catalogue of the Teachers College Library, Columbia University Third Supplement. Columbia University, Teachers College Library Staff. 1977. lib. bdg. 1095.00 o.p. (ISBN 0-8161-0017-9, Hall Library). G K Hall.
Dictionary Catalogue of the Teachers College Library, First Supplement, 5 vols. Columbia University Editors. 1971. Set. lib. bdg. 550.00 o.p. (ISBN 0-8161-0958-3, Hall Library). G K Hall.
Dictionary Catalogue of the Teachers College Library, Second Supplement, 2 vols. Columbia University Editors. 1973. Set. lib. bdg. 270.00 o.p. (ISBN 0-8161-1039-5, Hall Library). G K Hall.
Dictionary Catalogue of the Yale Forestry Library, 12 Vols. Yale University - Henry S. Graves Memorial Library Staff. 1970. Set. lib. bdg. 1185.00 o.p. (ISBN 0-8161-0631-2, Hall Library). G K Hall.
Dictionary Dynamite. Imogene Forte & Joy MacKenzie. (Choose-A-Card Ser.). (gr. 2-6). 1979. pap. text ed. 6.95 o.p. (ISBN 0-913916-85-4, IP85-4). Incentive Pubns.
Dictionary for the Glass Industry: Fachwoerterbuch fuer die Glasindustrie, 2 Pts. E. Hoffmann. (Pt, 1, Ger-Eng, Pt, 2, Eng-Ger). 1963. 26.60 o.p. (ISBN 0-387-03007-7). Springer-Verlag.
Dictionary of Advertising & Marketing. Clemens Gruber. (Eng. & Ger.). pap. cancelled o.s.i. Adlers Foreign Bks.
Dictionary of American Authors. 5th ed. Oscar F. Adams. LC 68-2175. 598p. 1969. Repr. of 1904 ed. 42.00x o.p. (ISBN 0-8103-3148-9). Gale.
Dictionary of American Folklore. Marjorie Tallman. 336p. 1959. (ISBN 0-8022-1688-9). Philos Lib.
Dictionary of American Food & Drink. John F. Mariani. LC 83-4977. 512p. 1983. 19.45 o.p. (ISBN 0-89919-199-1). Ticknor & Fields.
Dictionary of American Food & Drink. John F. Mariani. LC 83-4977. 478p. 1985. pap. 11.70 o.s.i. (ISBN 0-89919-359-5). Ticknor & Fields.
Dictionary of American History. Solomon Holt. LC 63-15623. 380p. 1963. (ISBN 0-379-00193-4). Oceana.
Dictionary of American Idioms. rev. ed. Maxine Boatner & John E. Gates. Ed. by Adam Makkai. LC 75-42110. 1976. 14.95 o.p. (ISBN 0-8120-5102-5); pap. 9.95 o.p. (ISBN 0-8120-0612-7). Barron.
Dictionary of American Naval Fighting Ships, 8 vols, Vols. 1-8. James L. Mooney. 1981. 142.00 o.p. (ISBN 0-318-04549-4, S/N 608-046-00105-1). USGPO.
Dictionary of American Proverbs. David Kin. 296p. 1955. (ISBN 0-8022-0863-0). Philos Lib.
Dictionary of American Social Reform. Louis Filler. LC 62-12824. 860p. 1963. (ISBN 0-8022-0499-6). Philos Lib.
Dictionary of American Wines. Ralph Hutchinson et al. LC 85-70575. (Illus.). 224p. 1985. 19.95 o.p. (ISBN 0-688-02833-0, Pub by Beech Tree Bks). Morrow.
Dictionary of Anagrams. Samuel D. Hunter. 160p. 1982. 15.00 o.p. (ISBN 0-7100-9006-4). Routledge Chapman & Hall.
Dictionary of Anthropology. Charles Winick. 592p. 1956. (ISBN 0-8022-1900-4). Philos Lib.
Dictionary of Antiques & the Decorative Arts. rev. ed. Louise A. Boger & H. Batterson Boger. (Illus.). 1979. 35.00 o.p. (ISBN 0-684-10030-4, ScribT). Scribner.
Dictionary of Applied Geology. A. Nelson & K. D. Nelson. (Illus.). 480p. 1968. (ISBN 0-8022-1188-7). Philos Lib.
Dictionary of Architectural Science. Henry J. Cowan. LC 73-15839. (Illus.). 354p. 1973. pap. 24.95x o.p. (ISBN 0-470-18070-6). Halsted Pr.
Dictionary of Architecture. Ware. (ISBN 0-8022-1809-1). Philos Lib.
Dictionary of Archival Terminology: With Equivalents in Dutch, German, Italian, Russian & Spanish. Peter Walne. (ICA Handbook Ser.). 226p. 1984. pap. text ed. 30.00 o.p. (ISBN 3-598-20275-X). K G Saur.
Dictionary of Artists: London Exhibitions 1760-1893. 3rd rev. ed. Algernon Graves. 25.00 o.s.i. (ISBN 0-912729-04-X). Newbury Bks.
Dictionary of Astrology. Fred Gettings. 320p. 1985. 38.50 o.p. (ISBN 0-7100-9672-0); pap. 19.95 o.p. (ISBN 0-7102-0650-X). Routledge Chapman & Hall.
Dictionary of Astronomy & Astronautics. A. Spitz. (Illus.). 448p. 1959. (ISBN 0-8022-1624-2). Philos Lib.
Dictionary of Audio-Visual Terms. Bernard Happe. 1983. text ed. 37.95 o.p. Butterworth.
Dictionary of Australian Colloquialisms. 2nd ed. G. A. Wilkes. 470p. 1985. 35.00 o.p. (ISBN 0-424-00113-6, Pub. by Sydney U Pr). Intl Spec Bk.
Dictionary of Australian History. B. Murphy. 340p. 1982. text ed. 19.00 o.p. (ISBN 0-07-072946-8). McGraw.
Dictionary of Bad Manners. London Ganning. 1982. 16.45 o.p. (ISBN 0-395-32509-9); pap. 8.70 o.p. (ISBN 0-395-33012-2). HM.
Dictionary of Banking. 2nd ed. F. E. Perry. 378p. 1983. pap. 23.95x o.p. (ISBN 0-7121-0437-2, Pub. by Macdonald & Evans England). Trans-Atl Phila.
Dictionary of Basic Bible Truths. Lawrence O. Richards. 528p. 1987. pap. 14.95 o.p. (ISBN 0-310-43521-8, 18164P). Zondervan.
Dictionary of Basic Military Terms: A Soviet View. (Soviet Military Thought: No. 9). 256p. (Orig.). 1976. pap. 6.50 o.p. (ISBN 0-318-21943-3, S/N 008-070-00360-1). USGPO.
Dictionary of Battles. Thomas B. Harbottle. LC 66-22672. 304p. 1966. Repr. of 1905 ed. 33.00x o.p. (ISBN 0-8103-3004-0). Gale.
Dictionary of Biochemistry. Malisoff. Philos Lib.
Dictionary of Biochemistry. K. Theilman. 742p. 1980. 90.00x o.p. (ISBN 0-686-44721-2, Pub. by Collets UK). State Mutual Bk.
Dictionary of Biographies of Authors Represented in the Authors Digest Series: With a Supplemental List of Later Titles & a Supplementary Biographical Section. Ed. by Rossiter Johnson. LC 71-167011. 476p. 1974. Repr. of 1927 ed. 53.00x o.p. (ISBN 0-8103-3876-9). Gale.
Dictionary of Biography. George T. Kurian. 560p. (Orig.). 1980. pap. 3.75 o.s.i. (ISBN 0-440-31889-0, LE). Dell.
Dictionary of Biomedical Acronyms & Abbreviations. Jaques Dupayrat. 131p. 1985. pap. 14.50 o.p. (ISBN 0-471-90582-8, Dist. by A R Liss). Wiley.
Dictionary of Boilermaker Items. Resource Systems International Staff. 1982. pap. text ed. 10.00 o.p. (ISBN 0-8359-1283-3, Reston). P-H.
Dictionary of Book Publishing: German-English. Ed. by Ulrich Stiehl. 538p. 1977. lib. bdg. 36.00 o.p. (ISBN 3-7940-4147-X). K G Saur.
Dictionary of Botany. R. John Little & C. Eugene Jones. 400p. 1983. pap. 14.95 o.p. (ISBN 0-442-26019-9). Van Nos Reinhold.
Dictionary of British Folk-Tales. Katherine M. Briggs. 2633p. 1986. Repr. of 1970 ed. lib. bdg. 395.00 o.p. (ISBN 0-7100-0207-6). Routledge Chapman & Hall.
Dictionary of British Marine Painters. Arnold Wilson. (Illus.). 90p. sewn bdg. 60.00 o.p. (ISBN 0-317-54915-4). Apollo.
Dictionary of British Surnames. 2nd ed. P. H. Reaney. 1976. 42.00 o.p. (ISBN 0-7100-8106-5). Routledge Chapman & Hall.
Dictionary of British Watercolour Artists Up to 1920: Vol. 1, The Text. H. L. Mallalieu. 298p. 1976. 44.50 o.p. (ISBN 0-902028-48-0). Antique Collect.
Dictionary of Buddhism. T. O. Ling. LC 72-37231. 244p. 1972. 7.95 o.s.i. (ISBN 0-684-12763-6, ScribT). Scribner.
Dictionary of Business & Science. 3rd ed. Compiled by David F. Tver. LC 74-7838. 632p. 1974. 29.00x o.p. (ISBN 0-87201-172-0). Gulf Pub.
Dictionary of Caribbean Biography, Vol. 1. 1969. 15.00x o.p. (ISBN 0-686-26225-5). Biblio Dist.
Dictionary of Ceramics. A. E. Dodd. LC 64-7431. (Illus.). 332p. 1964. (ISBN 0-8022-0407-4). Philos Lib.
Dictionary of Chemical Names. W. E. Flood. 238p. 1963. (ISBN 0-8022-0516-X). Philos Lib.
Dictionary of Chemistry. Oxford University Press Editors. 320p. 1986. pap. 7.95 o.p. (ISBN 0-446-38203-5). Warner Bks.
Dictionary of Chinese Symbols: Hidden Symbols in Chinese Life & Thought. Wolfram Eberhard. (Illus.). 384p. 1986. lib. bdg. 21.95 o.p. (ISBN 0-7102-0191-5). Routledge Chapman & Hall.
Dictionary of Christian Ethics. Ed. by John Macquarrie. LC 67-17412. 378p. 1967. 18.95 o.s.i. (ISBN 0-664-20646-8, Westminster). Westminster John Knox.
Dictionary of Christian Theology. Ed. by Alan Richardson. LC 69-19153. 376p. 1969. 13.95 o.s.i. (ISBN 0-664-20860-6, Westminster). Westminster John Knox.
Dictionary of Church Music. G. W. Stubbings. (ISBN 0-8022-1667-6). Philos Lib.
Dictionary of Civil Defense. Carlton Wallace. 1952. (ISBN 0-8022-1799-0). Philos Lib.
Dictionary of Civil Engineering. Rolt Hammond. 256p. 1965. (ISBN 0-8022-0667-0). Philos Lib.
Dictionary of Classical Mythology. Robert E. Bell. 1982. pap. ABC-CLIO.
Dictionary of Collective Nouns & Group Terms. 2nd ed. Ed. by Ivan G. Sparkes. 286p. 1985. 65.00x o.p. (ISBN 0-8103-2188-2). Gale.
Dictionary of Collectors Terms. Michael Goodman. (Illus.). 317p. 1968. (ISBN 0-8022-0606-9). Philos Lib.
Dictionary of Composers. Ed. by Charles Osborne. LC 78-58291. (Illus.). 1978. 14.95 o.s.i. (ISBN 0-8008-2194-7, Crescendo). Taplinger.
Dictionary of Composers & Their Music. Eric Gilder. 592p. 1986. 21.95 o.s.i. (ISBN 0-03-007177-1). H Holt & Co.
Dictionary of Computers, Data Processing & Telecommunications. Jerry M. Rosenberg. LC 83-12359. 614p. 1984. 39.95 o.p. (ISBN 0-471-87638-0); pap. 18.95 o.p. (ISBN 0-471-88582-7). Wiley.
Dictionary of Computing: Data Communications, Hardware & Software Basics, Digital Electronics. Ed. by Frank J. Galland. 330p. 1982. 51.95x o.p. (ISBN 0-471-10468-X, Pub. by Wiley-Interscience); pap. 31.95x o.p. (ISBN 0-471-10469-8). Wiley.
Dictionary of Contemporary English. Givi Zvidadze. 400p. 1983. text ed. 35.00x o.p. (ISBN 0-391-02592-9). Humanities.

Titles

Titles

Dictionary of Contemporary Politics of South America. Phil Gunson et al. 288p. 1988. text ed. 39.95 o.p. (ISBN 0-415-02808-6). Routledge Chapman & Hall.
Dictionary of Contemporary Politics of Southern Africa. Gwyneth Williams & Brian Hackland. 288p. 1988. text ed. 39.95 o.p. (ISBN 0-415-00245-1). Routledge Chapman & Hall.
Dictionary of Criminology. Richard Nice. LC 65-10995. 216p. (ISBN 0-8022-1215-8). Philos Lib.
Dictionary of Criminology. Dermot Walsh & Adrian Poole. LC 83-4611. 1983. 24.95x o.p. (ISBN 0-7100-9549-X); pap. 12.95x o.p. (ISBN 0-7100-9556-2). Routledge Chapman & Hall.
Dictionary of Cryptic Crossword Clues. Adrian Room. 288p. 1983. 19.95 o.p. (ISBN 0-7100-9415-9). Routledge Chapman & Hall.
Dictionary of Cryptic Crossword Clues. Adrian Room. 288p. 1984. pap. 10.95 o.p. (ISBN 0-7102-0384-5). Routledge Chapman & Hall.
Dictionary of Data Processing, Including Applications in Industry. 5th ed. A. Wittman & J. Klos. 1987. 156.00 o.p. (ISBN 0-444-99628-1). Elsevier.
Dictionary of Dates & Anniversaries. Robert Collison. LC 62-20868. 438p. 1962. (ISBN 0-8022-0283-7). Philos Lib.
Dictionary of Demography. Ed. by Roland Pressat & Christopher Wilson. (Reference Bks.). 253p. 1985. 60.00x o.p. (ISBN 0-631-12746-1). Basil Blackwell.
Dictionary of Dietetics. Rhoda Ellis. 160p. 1956. (ISBN 0-8022-0449-X). Philos Lib.
Dictionary of Early English. Joseph T. Shipley. 768p. 1955. (ISBN 0-8022-1555-6). Philos Lib.
Dictionary of Ecclesiastical Terms: Being a History & Explanation of Certain Terms Used in Architecture, Ecclesiology, Liturgiology, Music, Ritual, Cathedral, Constitution, Etc. John S. Bumpus. LC 68-30653. 327p. 1969. Repr. of 1910 ed. 35.00x o.p. (ISBN 0-8103-3321-X). Gale.
Dictionary of Economics & Commerce. Hanson. 401p. 1965. (ISBN 0-8022-0675-1). Philos Lib.
Dictionary of Education. Ed. by P. J. Hills. (Routledge Education Bks.). 300p. 1984. pap. 13.95x o.p. (ISBN 0-7102-0388-8). Routledge Chapman & Hall.
Dictionary of Electrical Circuits. 203p. (Eng. & Chinese.). 1975. pap. 3.95 o.p. (ISBN 0-686-92288-3, M-9572). French & Eur.
Dictionary of Electronic Organ Stops. Stevens Irwin. 1969. pap. 9.95 o.s.i. (ISBN 0-02-871120-3). Schirmer Bks.
Dictionary of Energy. Martin Counihan. (Illus.). 200p. 1981. 16.95x o.p. (ISBN 0-7100-0847-3). Routledge Chapman & Hall.
Dictionary of Energy. Date not set. (ISBN 0-8052-3816-6). Random.
Dictionary of English Authors: Biographical & Bibliographical. Ed. by R. Farquharson Sharp. LC 75-35577. 376p. 1978. Repr. of 1904 ed. 45.00x o.p. (ISBN 0-8103-4281-2). Gale.
Dictionary of English Domestic Architecture. A. L. Osborne. (Illus.). 112p. 1956. (ISBN 0-8022-1250-6). Philos Lib.
Dictionary of English Word-Roots. Robert W. Smith. 373p. 1966. 9.00x o.s.i. (ISBN 0-87471-238-6). Rowman.
Dictionary of English Word-Roots: English-Roots & Roots-English with Examples & Exercises. Robert W. Smith. (Quality Paperback: No. 98). 384p. (Orig.). 1980. pap. 9.95 o.p. (ISBN 0-8226-0098-6). Littlefield.
Dictionary of Erotic Literature. Harry E. Wedeck. LC 62-12827. (Illus.). 576p. 1963. (ISBN 0-8022-1831-8). Philos Lib.
Dictionary of Essential Quotations. Compiled by Kevin Goldstein-Jackson. (Helix Bks.). 188p. 1984. pap. 6.95 o.s.i. (ISBN 0-8226-0389-6, Rowman & Allanheld). Rowman.
Dictionary of Etiquette. Nancy Loughridge. 200p. 1955. (ISBN 0-8022-0998-X). Philos Lib.
Dictionary of European History. William S. Roeder. 1954. (ISBN 0-8022-1364-2). Philos Lib.
Dictionary of European Literature, Designed As a Companion to English Studies. rev. ed. Laurie Magnus. LC 74-6269. xii, 618p. 1975. Repr. of 1927 ed. 56.00x o.p. (ISBN 0-8103-4014-3). Gale.
Dictionary of Existentialism. Ralph B. Winn. 128p. 1960. (ISBN 0-8022-1390-1). Philos Lib.
Dictionary of Factual & Fictional Riders & Their Horses. John G. Fetros. 1979. 10.00 o.p. (ISBN 0-682-49417-8). Exposition-Phoenix.
Dictionary of Foreign Quotations. Robert Collison & Mary Collison. LC 81-22090. 416p. 1982. pap. 11.95 o.p. (ISBN 0-89696-158-3, Everest House Book). Dodd.
Dictionary of Fuel Technology. Gilpin. 350p. 1970. (ISBN 0-8022-2315-X). Philos Lib.
Dictionary of Gambling. John S. Salak. LC 62-15034. 1963. Philos Lib.
Dictionary of Games. J. B. Pick. 1953. (ISBN 0-8022-1973-X). Philos Lib.
Dictionary of Gemmology. Peter G. Read. 1982. text ed. 45.00 o.p. (ISBN 0-408-00571-8). Butterworth.
Dictionary of Ghost Lore. Peter Haining. (Illus.). 270p. 1984. 16.95 o.p. (ISBN 0-13-210485-7); pap. 8.95 o.p. (ISBN 0-13-210477-6). P-H.
Dictionary of Historical Allusions. Thomas B. Harbottle. LC 68-23163. 306p. 1968. Repr. of 1904 ed. 40.00x o.p. (ISBN 0-8103-3088-1). Gale.
Dictionary of Human Geography. R. J. Johnston. (Illus.). 350p. 1981. text ed. 40.00 o.p. (ISBN 0-02-903550-3, 91651). Free Pr.
Dictionary of Hypnosis. Ralph B. Winn. LC 65-10663. 124p. 1965. (ISBN 0-8022-1902-0). Philos Lib.
Dictionary of Indian Biography. Charles E. Buckland. LC 68-23140. 512p. 1968. Repr. of 1906 ed. 65.00x o.p. (ISBN 0-8103-3156-X). Gale.
Dictionary of Industrial Technology: English-French-German-Portuguese-Spanish. Ed. by Michel Feutry et al. 90.00 o.s.i. (ISBN 2-85608-000-6). E J Brill USA.
Dictionary of Information Technology. Ed. by Dennis Longley & Michael Shain. 379p. 1983. 55.00x o.p. (ISBN 0-471-89574-1, Pub. by Wiley-Interscience). Assn Inform & Image Mgmt.
Dictionary of Insurance. 6th, rev. ed. Lewis E. Davids. LC 83-16091. (Helix Bks.: No. 381). 338p. 1984. 24.95x o.s.i. (ISBN 0-8476-7340-5, Rowman & Allanheld); pap. 14.95 o.s.i. (ISBN 0-8226-0381-0). Rowman.
Dictionary of International Biography 1982. 17th ed. Ed. by Ernest Kay. LC 64-1109. 885p. 1982. 107.00x o.p. (ISBN 0-900332-57-3). Intl Pubns Serv.
Dictionary of Inventions & Discoveries. E. F. Carter. 20p. 1967. (ISBN 0-8022-0215-2). Philos Lib.
Dictionary of Irish Artists, 2 vols. Walter G. Strickland. (Illus.). 1358p. 1969. Repr. of 1913 ed. 150.00x set o.p. (ISBN 0-7165-0602-5, BBA 02188, Pub. by Irish Academic Pr Ireland). Biblio Dist.
Dictionary of Last Words. Edward Le Comte. 1955. (ISBN 0-8022-0947-5). Philos Lib.
Dictionary of Latin Literature. James Mantinband. 303p. 1956. Philos Lib.
Dictionary of Life Sciences. 2nd rev. ed. E. A. Martin. LC 83-13253. (Illus.). 416p. 1984. 25.00x o.p. (ISBN 0-87663-740-3, Pica Pr). Universe.
Dictionary of Linguistics. Mario Pei & Frank Gaynor. (Quality Paperback: No. 177). 1980. pap. 9.95 o.p. (ISBN 0-8226-0177-X). Littlefield.
Dictionary of Literary Terms. Harry Shaw. LC 72-179884. 418p. 1972. text ed. 32.50 o.p. (ISBN 0-07-056490-6). McGraw.
Dictionary of Lowland Scotch. Charles Mackay. LC 68-17998. 432p. 1968. Repr. of 1888 ed. 51.00x o.p. (ISBN 0-8103-3284-1). Gale.
Dictionary of Magic. Harry E. Wedeck. 1956. (ISBN 0-8022-1829-6). Philos Lib.
Dictionary of Mechanical Engineering Terms. 9th rev. & enl. ed. J. G. Horner. Ed. by G. K. Grahame-White. 32.50 o.s.i. (ISBN 0-685-29250-9). E J Brill USA.
Dictionary of Mechanical Engineering Terms. J. G. Horner. 422p. 1967. 32.50 o.s.i. (ISBN 0-291-39357-8, Pub. by Technical Press UK). E J Brill USA.
Dictionary of Mechanical Engineering Terms. J. G. Horner. 420p. 1955. Philos Lib.
Dictionary of Medical Ethics & Practice. Thomson. 272p. 1977. 27.95 o.p. (ISBN 0-7236-0454-1, Pub. by John Wright UK). Butterworth.
Dictionary of Metallurgy. D. Birchon. (Illus.). 410p. 1965. (ISBN 0-8022-0131-8). Philos Lib.
Dictionary of Microbiology. Paul Singleton & Diana Sainsbury. LC 78-4532. 481p. 1978. 97.95x o.p. (ISBN 0-471-99658-0, Pub. by Wiley-Interscience). Wiley.
Dictionary of Military Terms. F. Krollman. 800p. (Ger. & Eng.). 1958. (ISBN 0-8022-0897-5). Philos Lib.
Dictionary of Mining. A. Nelson. 523p. 1965. (ISBN 0-8022-1187-9). Philos Lib.
Dictionary of Modern Chess. Byrne J. Horton. (ISBN 0-8022-0746-4). Philos Lib.
Dictionary of Modern Culture. Ed. by Justin Wintle. (Ark Paperback Reprint Ser.). 1984. pap. 9.95 o.p. (ISBN 0-7448-0007-2). Routledge Chapman & Hall.
Dictionary of Modern Engineering, Vol. 1. 3rd ed. Alfred Oppermann. (Eng. & Ger.). 1971. 113.00 o.p. (ISBN 3-7940-6001-6, M-7109). French & Eur.
Dictionary of Modern Engineering, Vol. 2. 3rd ed. Alfred Oppermann. (Ger. & Eng.). 1974. 113.00 o.p. (ISBN 3-7940-6002-4, M-7108). French & Eur.
Dictionary of Modern Engineering: English-German-German-English, 2 Vols. 4th ed. Ed. by Alfred Oppermann. 1864p. 1982. lib. bdg. 110.00 o.p. (ISBN 3-598-10471-5). K G Saur.
Dictionary of Modern French Idioms, 2 vols. Barbara L. Gerber & Gerald H. Storzer. LC 76-24743. (Reference Library of the Humanities Ser.: Vol. 63). (Fr. & Eng.). 1977. Set. lib. bdg. 133.00 o.p. (ISBN 0-8240-9935-4). Garland Pub.
Dictionary of Modern History. Alan W. Palmer. (Reference Ser.). (Orig.). (YA) (gr. 11 up). 1964. pap. 5.95 o.p. (ISBN 0-14-051026-5). Penguin.
Dictionary of Mottoes. L. G. Pine. 150p. 1983. 19.95 o.p. (ISBN 0-7100-9339-X). Routledge Chapman & Hall.
Dictionary of Mountaineering. R. G. Collomb. (Illus.). 180p. 1958. (ISBN 0-8022-0285-3). Philos Lib.
Dictionary of Musical Terms in Seven Languages: English-German-French-Italian-Spanish-Hungarian-Russian. 2nd ed. Ed. by H. Leuchtmann. (Illus., Eng., Ger., Fr., Ital., Span., Rus. & Hungarian.). 1980. 120.00 o.s.i. (ISBN 3-7618-0553-5). E J Brill USA.
Dictionary of Mysticism. Frank Gaynor. 1953. (ISBN 0-8022-0572-0). Philos Lib.
Dictionary of Named Effects & Laws in Chemistry, Physics & Mathematics. 4th ed. D. W. Ballentyne & D. R. Lovett. 1980. 19.95x o.p. (ISBN 0-412-22390-2, NO. 6780, Pub. by Chapman & Hall England). Routledge Chapman & Hall.
Dictionary of Nautical Terms. A. G. Course. 216p. 1963. (ISBN 0-8022-0309-4). Philos Lib.
Dictionary of New Words & Meanings in Russian. E. A. Levashov. 806p. 1984. 18.95 o.p. (ISBN 0-8285-2781-4, Pub. by Rus Lang Pubs USSR). Imported Pubns.
Dictionary of Ngizim. Russell G. Schuh. (UC Publications in Linguistics: Vol. 99). 256p. 1981. pap. 15.50x o.p. (ISBN 0-520-09636-3). U of Cal Pr.
Dictionary of Non-Christian Religions. Geoffrey Parrinder. LC 73-4781. (Illus.). 320p. 1973. 10.95 o.s.i. (ISBN 0-664-20981-5, Westminster). Westminster John Knox.
Dictionary of North American Authors Deceased Before 1950. William S. Wallace. LC 68-19955. 536p. 1968. Repr. of 1951 ed. 46.00x o.p. (ISBN 0-8103-3153-5). Gale.
Dictionary of Obsolete English. Trench. 288p. 1958. (ISBN 0-8022-1736-2). Philos Lib.
Dictionary of Occult, Hermetic & Alchemical Sigils. Fred Gettings. 1981. 40.00 o.p. (ISBN 0-7100-0095-2). Routledge Chapman & Hall.
Dictionary of Onomatopoeic Sounds, Tones, & Noises in English & Spanish. Donald R. Kloe. LC 77-2627. (Eng. & Span.). 1977. 25.50 o.p. (ISBN 0-87917-059-X). Ethridge.
Dictionary of Oriental Quotations. Claud H. Field. LC 68-23157. 360p. 1969. Repr. of 1911 ed. 38.00x o.p. (ISBN 0-8103-3183-7). Gale.
Dictionary of Orthodox Theology. George H. Demetrakopoulos. LC 63-13346. 204p. 1964. (ISBN 0-8022-0376-0). Philos Lib.
Dictionary of Pali Proper Names, 2 vols. Compiled by G. P. Malalasekera. 1938. Set. 115.00x o.p. (ISBN 0-7100-7945-1). Routledge Chapman & Hall.
Dictionary of Pastoral Psychology. Vergilius Ferm. 1955. (ISBN 0-8022-0492-9). Philos Lib.
Dictionary of Pharmacology. Bowman. 1986. 11.50 o.p. (ISBN 0-8016-0628-4). Mosby.
Dictionary of Philosophy. A. R. Lacey. 1976. 21.95x o.p. (ISBN 0-7100-8361-0). Routledge Chapman & Hall.
Dictionary of Philosophy & Religion: Eastern & Western Thought. William L. Reese. text ed. 29.95x 648p. 1980 o.p. (ISBN 0-391-00688-6); pap. text ed. 19.95x 644p. 1981 o.p. (ISBN 0-391-00941-9). Humanities.
Dictionary of Photographic Terms. A. Page. (Illus.). 1966. 25.00 o.p. E J Brill USA.
Dictionary of Photography. L. M. Sowerby. 702p. 1956. (ISBN 0-8022-1613-7). Philos Lib.
Dictionary of Poisions. Ibert Mellan & Eleanor Mellan. 160p. 1956. Philos Lib.
Dictionary of Political Economy, 3 vols. Robert H. Palgrave. LC 74-31358. 2588p. 1976. Repr. of 1910 ed. Set. 230.00x o.p. (ISBN 0-8103-4210-3). Gale.
Dictionary of Political Phrases & Allusions with a Short Bibliography. Hugh Montgomery. LC 68-28333. 416p. 1968. Repr. of 1906 ed. 40.00x o.p. (ISBN 0-8103-3092-X). Gale.
Dictionary of Professional Business Terms: English-Arabic. Middle East Economic Digest Staff. 550p. 1987. pap. 50.00x o.p. (ISBN 0-946510-14-8). Lynne Rienner.
Dictionary of Psychoanalysis. Sigmund Freud. 224p. 1958. Philos Lib.
Dictionary of Publishing. David M. Brownstone & Irene M. Franck. 304p. 1982. 25.95 o.p. (ISBN 0-442-25874-7). Van Nos Reinhold.
Dictionary of Quotable Definitions. Eugene E. Brussell. 640p. 1984. pap. 15.95 o.p. (ISBN 0-13-210626-4). P-H.
Dictionary of Races or Peoples. United States Immigration Commission. LC 68-30665. 157p. 1969. Repr. of 1911 ed. 35.00x o.p. (ISBN 0-8103-3364-3). Gale.
Dictionary of Radio & Television. W. E. Pannett. 352p. 1967. (ISBN 0-8022-1262-X). Philos Lib.
Dictionary of Religion & Ethics. Ed. by Shailer Mathews & Gerald B. Smith. LC 70-145713. 528p. 1971. Repr. of 1921 ed. 54.00x o.p. (ISBN 0-8103-3196-9). Gale.
Dictionary of Reprography: German with Definitions in English, French, & Spanish. Ed. by Gesellschaft fur Information und Dokumentation Staff. 353p. 1982. pap. 20.00 o.p. (ISBN 3-598-10444-8). K G Saur.
Dictionary of Rogues. William R. Hunt. LC 74-10328. 156p. 1970. Philos Lib.
Dictionary of Russian Literature. William E. Harkins. 1956, (ISBN 0-8022-0679-4). Philos Lib.
Dictionary of Satanism. Wade Baskin. LC 75-155971. (Illus.). 351p. 1972. (ISBN 0-8022-2056-8). Philos Lib.
Dictionary of Science. rev. ed. E. B. Uvarov et al. (Reference Ser.). (Orig.). (YA) (gr. 7 up). 1950. pap. 6.95 o.p. (ISBN 0-14-051001-X). Penguin.
Dictionary of Science & Technology. Maxim Newmark. (ISBN 0-8022-1207-7). Philos Lib.
Dictionary of Scottish Business Bioghraphy, 2 vols. Ed. by A Slaven & S. G. Checkland. 900p. 1986. Vol. 1 The Staple Industries. price 64.00 set o.s.i. (ISBN 0-08-032421-5, Pub. by AUP). Pergamon.
Dictionary of Sects, Heresies, Ecclesiastical Parties & Schools of Religious Thought. John H. Blunt. LC 74-9653. 660p. 1974. Repr. of 1874 ed. 75.00x o.p. (ISBN 0-8103-3751-7). Gale.
Dictionary of Selected Synonyms in the Principal Indo-European Languages. Carl D. Buck. LC 49-11769. 1949. lib. bdg. 100.00x o.s.i. (ISBN 0-226-07932-5). U of Chicago Pr.
Dictionary of Slang & Its Analogues, 2 Vols. John S. Farmer & W. E. Henley. 1965. Vol. 1. (ISBN 0-8216-0068-0, Pub. by Univ Bks); 15.00 o.p. (ISBN 0-685-20856-7); Vol. 8. 10.00 o.p. (ISBN 0-685-20857-5). Carol Pub Group.
Dictionary of Soccer. rev. ed. Rick Braithwaite. (Illus.). 32p. (gr. 4 up). 1986. pap. 3.95 o.p. (ISBN 0-940893-01-0). Cool Change Pub.
Dictionary of Social Science Methods. P. M. Miller & M. J. Wilson. 124p. 1983. 54.95x o.p. (ISBN 0-471-90035-4); pap. 27.00x o.p. (ISBN 0-471-90036-2). Wiley.
Dictionary of Social Services: Policy & Practice. Joan Clegg. 147p. 1977. text ed. 14.50x o.p. (ISBN 0-7199-0932-5, Pub. by Bedford England). Gower Pub Co.
Dictionary of Sociology. Henry P. Fairchild. (ISBN 0-8022-0467-8). Philos Lib.
Dictionary of Soldier Talk. John R. Elting et al. LC 82-42642. 383p. 1984. 35.00 o.p. (ISBN 0-684-17862-1, ScribT). Scribner.
Dictionary of Spanish Literature. Maxim Newmark. (Quality Paperback: No. 149). 352p. 1970. pap. 1.50 o.p. (ISBN 0-8226-0149-4). Littlefield.
Dictionary of Spanish Literature. Maxim Newmark. 360p. 1956. (ISBN 0-8022-1208-5). Philos Lib.
Dictionary of Symbols & Imagery. 2nd. rev. ed. A. De Vries. 516p. 1976. 89.50 o.p. (ISBN 0-444-10607-3, North-Holland). Elsevier.
Dictionary of Terms & Concepts in Reading. 2nd ed. Delwyn G. Schubert. 392p. 1969. 46.00 o.p. (ISBN 0-398-01688-7). C C Thomas.
Dictionary of Terms & Techniques in Archaeology. Sara Champion. (Illus.). 144p. 1982. pap. 7.95 o.p. (ISBN 0-89696-162-1, An Everest House Book). Dodd.
Dictionary of Terms in Art. Ed. by Frederick W. Fairholt. LC 68-30630. (Illus.). 480p. 1969. Repr. of 1854 ed. 37.00x o.p. (ISBN 0-8103-3071-7). Gale.
Dictionary of Terms in Mechanical Engineering. J. G. Horner. 420p. 1955. (ISBN 0-8022-0744-8). Philos Lib.
Dictionary of Terms in Music: English-German, German-English. Ed. by Horst Leuchtmann. 560p. 1981. lib. bdg. 28.00 o.p. (ISBN 3-598-10338-7). K G Saur.
Dictionary of Terms Used in the Safety Profession. Ed. by William E. Tarrants. 80p. 1988. Repr. of 1980 ed. 25.00 o.p.; members 19.00 o.p. ASSE.
Dictionary of the American Indian. John L. Stoutenbergh, Jr. 462p. 1960. (ISBN 0-8022-1659-5). Philos Lib.
Dictionary of the Arts. Martin L. Wolf. 1951. (ISBN 0-8022-1915-2). Philos Lib.
Dictionary of the Characters & Proper Names in the Works of Shakespeare. Francis G. Stokes. Repr. of 1960 ed. 49.00x o.p. (ISBN 0-403-04029-9). Somerset Pub.

Dictionary of the Characters in George Meredith's Fiction. Maurice McCullen & Lewis Sawin. LC 75-42886. (Reference Library of the Humanities Ser.: Vol. 48). 1977. lib. bdg. 30.00 o.p. (ISBN 0-8240-9952-4). Garland Pub.

Dictionary of the European Communities. Geoffrey Parker & Brenda Parker. 90p. 1981. pap. text ed. 14.95 o.p. (ISBN 0-408-10732-4). Butterworth.

Dictionary of the New Testament. Xavier Leon-Dufour. Tr. by Terrence Prendergast. LC 79-3004. (Illus.). 448p. (Fr.). 1980. 21.95i o.p. (ISBN 0-06-062100-1). HarpR.

Dictionary of the Nisqually Indian Language of Western Washington. George Gibbs. (Shorey Indian Ser.). 82p. pap. 9.95 o.s.i. (ISBN 0-8466-4022-8, I22). Shorey.

Dictionary of the Opera. Charles Osborne. 384p. 1983. 22.25 o.p. (ISBN 0-671-49218-7). S&S.

Dictionary of the Opera. Charles Osborne. (Illus.). 384p. 1986. pap. 10.95 o.s.i. (ISBN 0-671-62801-1, Fireside). S&S.

Dictionary of Thought. Dagobert D. Runes. LC 64-22817. 128p. 1965. (ISBN 0-8022-1432-0). Philos Lib.

Dictionary of Tools Used in the Woodworking & Allied Trades c. 1700-1970. R. A. Salaman. LC 75-35059. 1976. 60.00 o.s.i. (ISBN 0-684-14535-9, ScribT). Scribner.

Dictionary of Tourism. 2nd ed. Charles J. Metelka. LC 85-62566. 122p. 1986. pap. 12.00x o.p. (ISBN 0-916032-26-4). Delmar.

Dictionary of Tourism. 2nd ed. Ed. by Charles J. Metelka. LC 80-83526. (Travel Management Library). 91p. 1986. 12.00 o.p. (ISBN 0-916032-10-8). Delmar.

Dictionary of True Etymologies. Adrian Room. 193p. 1986. lib. bdg. 22.50 o.p. (ISBN 0-7102-0340-3). Routledge Chapman & Hall.

Dictionary of United States History: Alphabetical, Chronological, Statistical. rev. ed. J. Franklin Jameson. Ed. by Albert E. McKinley. LC 68-30658. (Illus.). 888p. 1971. Repr. of 1931 ed. 65.00x o.p. (ISBN 0-8103-3332-5). Gale.

Dictionary of Wedgwood. Robin Reilly & George Savage. (Illus.). 414p. 1980. 69.50 o.s.i. (ISBN 0-902028-85-5). Antique Collect.

Dictionary of Wedgwood. Rielly & Savage. (Illus.). 1980. 69.50 o.s.i. (ISBN 0-902028-85-5). Apollo.

Dictionary of Women in Church History. Mary L. Hammack. LC 84-14710. 1984. 12.95 o.p. (ISBN 0-8024-0332-8). Moody.

Dictionary of Word Processing & Printers. Philip E. Burton. LC 84-10348. 264p. 1984. 25.00 o.p. (ISBN 0-8240-7289-8); pap. 18.00 o.p. (ISBN 0-8240-7291-X). Garland Pub.

Dictionary of World Cultures. George Wilson & Joyce Moss. 350p. text ed. cancelled o.s.i. (ISBN 0-87436-487-6). ABC Clio.

Dictionary of World Literature. Joseph T. Shipley. (ISBN 0-8022-1556-4). Philos Lib.

Dictionary of World Pottery & Porcelain. Louise Boger. LC 72-123829. (Encore Edition). (Illus.). 1971. 9.95 o.p. (ISBN 0-684-14962-1, ScribT). Scribner.

Dictionary Real Estate Terms. Paul T. O'Donnell. 87p. 1975. 10.95 o.p. (ISBN 0-7216-6915-8). Dryden Pr.

Dictionary, Schmictionary. Paul Hoffman & Matt Freedman. LC 83-3050. (Illus.). 160p. (Orig.). 1983. pap. 6.70 o.p. (ISBN 0-688-02162-X, Quill NY). Morrow.

Dictionary with Description & Prices of the Famous Bernal Collection of Pottery, Porcelain & Other Works of Art As It Was Disposed at the End of the Last Century. Henry G. Bohn. (Illus.). 491p. 1988. 127.45 o.p. (ISBN 0-86650-258-0). Gloucester Art.

Dictionary Yakan-Filipino-English. Janet Pack & Dietlinde Brehrens. 20p. 1973. pap. 1.00 o.p. (ISBN 0-88312-753-9). Summer Inst Ling.

Dictionnaire Alphabetique et Analogique de la Langue Francaise, 9 vols. Robert. (Illus., Fr.). Set. 995.00 o.p. (ISBN 0-685-11140-7). French & Eur.

Dictionnaire Anglais-Francais des Sciences Medicales et Paramedicales. W. J. Gladstone. 1154p. (Fr.). 1978. 175.00 o.p. (ISBN 0-686-56787-0, M-6583, Pub. by Maloine). French & Eur.

Dictionnaire Arabe-Francais-Anglais, 2, Pts. 13-24. Regis Blachere & Moustafa Chouemi. (Arabic, Fr. & Eng.). 1970. 350.00 o.p. (ISBN 0-686-56919-9, M-6035). French & Eur.

Dictionnaire Armenien-Francais, 2 vols. Ambroise Calfa. 1038p. (Armenian & Fr.). 1973. Set. pap. 49.95 o.p. (ISBN 0-686-56934-2, M-6056). French & Eur.

Dictionnaire Basque Francais. Pierre Lhande. 1117p. (Basque & Fr.). 1938. 79.95 o.p. (ISBN 0-686-57020-0, M-6377). French & Eur.

Dictionnaire Classique de la Langue Chinoise. F. S. Couvveur. 1080p. (Fr & Chinese.). 1966. 35.00 o.p. (ISBN 0-686-56810-9, M-6588). French & Eur.

Dictionnaire de Droit, 2 vols. 2nd ed. (Fr.). 1966. Set. 17.50 o.p. (ISBN 0-686-57096-0, M-6120). French & Eur.

Dictionnaire de la Biologie--B.L.V. 496p. (Eng., Ger., Fr. & Span.). 1976. 95.00 o.p. (ISBN 0-686-57097-9, M-6121). French & Eur.

Dictionnaire de la Chasse. Tony Burnand. 250p. (Fr.). 1970. pap. 7.50 o.p. (ISBN 0-686-56817-6, M-6595, Pub. by Larousse). French & Eur.

Dictionnaire de la Contradiction. Maurice Toesca. 234p. (Fr.). 1969. pap. 10.95 o.p. (ISBN 0-686-56825-7, M-6603). French & Eur.

Dictionnaire de la Langue Francaise. Littre. Ed. by Beaujean & Geraud-Venzac. (Fr.). 24.95 o.p. (ISBN 0-685-36652-9). French & Eur.

Dictionnaire de La Langue Francaise, 7 tomes. Emile Littre. (Fr.). 21.95 o.p. (ISBN 0-685-11141-5); Set. 245.00 o.p. (ISBN 0-685-11142-3). French & Eur.

Dictionnaire de la Musique, Vol. 1. Ed. by Marc Honegger. 1232p. (Fr.). 1970. 65.00 o.p. (ISBN 0-686-56821-4, M-6599). French & Eur.

Dictionnaire de la Revolution Francaise, 2 vols. Decembre-Alonnier. (Fr.). Repr. of 1868 ed. 285.00 o.p. (ISBN 0-8115-3523-1). Kraus Repr.

Dictionnaire de Litterature Francais Contemporaine. Claude Bonnefoy et al. 411p. (Fr.). 1977. 39.95 o.p. (ISBN 0-686-56924-5, M-6042). French & Eur.

Dictionnaire De Musique. Jean-Jacques Rousseau. (Fr). Repr. of 1768 ed. 50.00 o.p. (ISBN 0-384-52200-9). Johnson Repr.

Dictionnaire de Theologie Catholigue. E. Amanne. (Fr.). Set. pap. 1995.00 o.p. (ISBN 0-686-56893-1, M-6003). French & Eur.

Dictionnaire d'Electronique et Tele-Communication: Anglais-Francais. G. J. Proulx. 582p. (Fr. & Eng.). 1979. 15.95 o.p. (ISBN 0-686-57089-8, M-6469). French & Eur.

Dictionnaire Des Artistes, Dont Nous Avons Des Estampes, Avec une Notice Detailee De Leurs Ouvrages Graves, 4 vols. Karl H. Von Heinecken. LC 4-7666. (Fr) 1970. Repr. of 1790 ed. Set. 280.00 o.p. (ISBN 0-384-22089-4). Johnson Repr.

Dictionnaire des Arts du Spectacle: Theatre, Cinema, Cirque, Danse, Radio... Cecile Giteau. 456p. (Fr., Eng & Ger.). 1970. 52.50 o.p. (ISBN 0-686-57302-1, M-6276). French & Eur.

Dictionnaire des Canalisations a Grande Distance: Anglais-Francais-Allemand. H. Bucksch & A. Altemeyer. 288p. (Eng., Fr. & Ger.). 1969. 120.00 o.p. (ISBN 0-686-56931-8, M-6052). French & Eur.

Dictionnaire des Communes de France (Guide to French Townships) Michelin Guides & Maps. (Fr.). 1979. 45.00 o.p. (ISBN 2-06-007500-9). Michelin.

Dictionnaire des Herbes et des Epices. Colin Clair. 259p. (Fr.). 1963. pap. 6.95 o.p. (ISBN 0-686-56842-7, M-6621). French & Eur.

Dictionnaire des Hommes. Anne-Marie Carriere. 252p. (Fr.). 1962. 8.95 o.p. (ISBN 0-686-56845-1, M-6623). French & Eur.

Dictionnaire Des Horlogers Francais (Dictionary of Clock & Watchmakers in France, 2 vols. in 1. Tardy & Paul Brateau. (Illus.). 760p. (Orig., Fr.). 1972. pap. 110.00 o.p. (ISBN 0-911403-02-7, 2390149, Pub. by Tardy FR). Seven Hills Bk Dists.

Dictionnaire des Science de la Gestion. Henri Tezenas du Montcel. 332p. (Fr.). 1972. pap. 19.95 o.p. (ISBN 0-686-57230-0, M-6531). French & Eur.

Dictionnaire des Types et Charateres Litteraires. C. Aziza & C. Olivieri. 208p. (Fr.). 1978. pap. 29.95 o.p. (ISBN 0-686-56866-4, M-6644). French & Eur.

Dictionnaire du Francais Contemporain. J. Dubois. 1263p. (Fr.). 1980. 19.95 o.p. (ISBN 2-03-320101-5, M-9357). French & Eur.

Dictionnaire du Scrabble. Annie Carillon & Beatrice de Goutel. 215p. (Fr.). 1976. pap. 12.95 o.p. (ISBN 0-686-56872-9, M-6650). French & Eur.

Dictionnaire Illustre de l'Automobile "Kluwer," en 6 Langues. C. Blok & W. Jezewski. 504p. (Fr., Eng., Ger., Ital., Rus. & Dutch.). 1979. 145.00 o.p. (ISBN 0-686-56923-7, M-6039). French & Eur.

Dictionnaire International de Metallurgie, Mineralogie, Geologie et Industries Extractives, 2 vols. Angelo Cagnacci-Schwicker. 1530p. (Fr.). 1969. Set. 95.00 o.p. (ISBN 0-686-56933-4, M-6054). French & Eur.

Dictionnaire Italien-Francais, Francais-Italien de la Langue d'Aujourd'hui. Ghiotti et al. (Fr. & Ital.). 1976. 27.50 o.p. (ISBN 0-686-57196-7, M-6270). French & Eur.

Dictionnaire Memento D'electronique. 3rd ed. Raymond Brosset & Pierre Fondaneche. 512p. (Fr.). 1969. 39.95 o.p. (ISBN 0-686-56929-6, M-6047). French & Eur.

Dictionnaire Raisonne De Mathematiques. Andre Warusfel. (Fr.). 1966. pap. 27.95 o.p. (ISBN 0-686-57257-2, M-6567). French & Eur.

Dictionnaire Technique De la Construction Electrique. P. Sizaire. 172p. (Fr.). 1968. 29.95 o.p. (ISBN 0-686-57222-X, M-6520). French & Eur.

Dictyostelium Discoideum: A Developmental System. William F. Loomis. 1975. 53.50 o.p. (ISBN 0-12-456150-0). Acad Pr.

Did Adam Name the Vinegarroon? X. J. Kennedy. LC 80-83964. (Illus.). 64p. (gr. 2-5). 1984. 11.95 o.s.i. (ISBN 0-87923-357-5). Godine.

Did Christ Rule Out Women Priests? J. N. Wijngaards. 96p. 1977. pap. 1.95 o.p. (ISBN 0-85597-204-1). Attic Pr.

Did Dorit Die in Vain? E. Hoigjelle. 1986. 8.95 o.p. (ISBN 0-533-06862-2). Vantage.

Did Jesus Exist? G. A. Wells. (Skeptic's Bookshelf Ser.). 250p. 1986. 24.95 o.p.; pap. 15.95 o.p. Prometheus Bks.

Didane the Koala. Grahame L. Walsh. LC 85-8572. (Illus.). 42p. (gr. 1-7). 1986. 15.95 o.p. (ISBN 0-7022-1889-8). U of Queensland Pr.

Diderot & Descartes: A Study of Scientific Naturalism in the Enlightment. Aram Vartanian. LC 75-18406. (History of Ideas Series: No. 6). 336p. 1975. Repr. of 1953 ed. lib. bdg. 22.50x o.p. (ISBN 0-8371-8337-5, VADD). Greenwood.

Diderot: Reason & Resonance. Elisabeth De Fontenay. Tr. by Jeffrey Mehlman from Fr. LC 82-9649. 274p. 1982. 14.95 o.p. (ISBN 0-8076-1035-6). Braziller.

Didman. John Speicher. 1973. pap. 1.25 o.p. (ISBN 0-380-01139-5, 15248). Avon.

Didone Abbandonata. Leonardo Da Vinci. LC 76-20964. (Italian Opera, 1640-1770 Ser. No.1: Vol. 29). 1977. lib. bdg. 77.00 o.p. (ISBN 0-8240-2628-4). Garland Pub.

Die & Mould Making. Ed. by L. R. Brazier et al. (Engineering Craftsmen: No. H22). (Illus.). 1970. spiral bdg. 42.50x o.p. (ISBN 0-85083-126-1). Trans-Atl Phila.

Die of Gold. Chet Cunningham. 1980. pap. 1.50 o.p. (ISBN 0-505-51471-0, Pub. by Tower Bks). Dorchester Pub Co.

Die Song: A Journey into the Mind of a Mass Murderer. Donald T. Lunde & Jefferson Morgan. 1980. 14.95 o.p. (ISBN 0-393-01315-4). Norton.

Diego Rivera: The Cubist Years. Phoenix Art Museum Staff. (Illus.). 190p. (Orig.). 1984. pap. 30.00 o.p. (ISBN 0-87663-860-4). Universe.

Dielectric Materials Measurements & Applications. (IEE Conference Publications: No. 239). 313p. 1984. pap. 90.00 o.s.i. (ISBN 0-85296-296-7, IC239). Inst Elect Eng.

Dielectric Properties of Binary Solutions: A Data Handbook. Ya Y. Akhadov. 400p. 1981. 165.00 o.p. (ISBN 0-08-023600-6). Pergamon.

Diesel Engine Principles & Practice. C. C. Pounder. (Illus.). 848p. 1955. (ISBN 0-8022-2006-1). Philos Lib.

Diesel Engine Repair. John F. Dagel. LC 81-615. 586p. 1982. (ISBN 0-471-03542-4). Wiley.

Diesel Engines Noise Conference: Proceedings. LC 79-83912. 370p. 1979. Thirty papers. 45.00 o.p. (ISBN 0-89883-050-8, P80). Soc Auto Engineers.

Diesel Fuels: Performance & Characteristics. 1986. 35.00 o.p. (ISBN 0-89883-946-7, SP 675). Soc Auto Engineers.

Diesel Technology. National Research Council Diesel Impact Study Committee. 1982. pap. text ed. 18.95x o.p. (ISBN 0-309-03243-1). Natl Acad Pr.

Diesel: The Man & the Engine. Morton Grosser. LC 78-6196. (Illus.). 224p. (YA) 1978. 8.95 o.p. (ISBN 0-689-30652-0, ATheneum). Macmillan.

Diesel Years. Robert Olmsted. LC 75-17721. (Illus.). 170p. 1975. 22.95 o.p. (ISBN 0-87095-054-1). Gldn West Bks.

Diet Against Disease: A New Plan for Safe & Healthy Eating. Alice A. Martin & Frances Tenenbaum. 1980. 11.95 o.p. (ISBN 0-395-29451-7). HM.

Diet & Health in Modern Britain. Ed. by Derek J. Oddy & Derek S. Miller. 326p. 1985. 38.00 o.p. (ISBN 0-7099-1922-0, Pub. by Croom Helm Ltd). Routledge Chapman & Hall.

Diet Center Cookbook. Sybil Ferguson. 320p. 1986. 17.45 o.s.i. (ISBN 0-671-60445-7). S&S.

Diet for a Happy Heart. Jeanne Jones. LC 75-6713. (Illus.). 192p. 1975. pap. 5.95 o.p. (ISBN 0-912238-57-7, One Hund One Prods). Ortho.

Diet for a Happy Heart: A Low-Cholesterol, Low-Saturated Fat, Low Calorie Cookbook. rev. ed. Jeanne Jones. LC 80-25796. (Illus.). 192p. 1981. pap. 7.95 o.p. (ISBN 0-89286-183-5, One Hund One Prods). Ortho.

Diet in Workhouses & Prisons: Eighteen Thirty-Five to Eighteen Ninety-Five. Valerie J. Johnston. Ed. by Peter Mathias & Stuart Bruchey. LC 84-46004. (British Economic History Ser.). 340p. 1985. lib. bdg. 39.00 o.p. (ISBN 0-8240-6684-7). Garland Pub.

Diet Management for Ulcerative Colitis: Menus, Recipes & Methods of Food Preparation for Anti-Inflammatory Treatment. Map Hanson. 80p. 1971. spiral 17.00x o.p. (ISBN 0-398-02307-7). C C Thomas.

Diet to Lose & Win. Merilyn L. Cummings. 33p. 1986. pap. 19.95 o.p. (ISBN 0-9617195-5-9); pap. 24.95 o.p. (ISBN 0-9617195-6-7); cassette incl. o.p.; cassette 19.95 o.p. (ISBN 0-9617195-7-5). Abrahamson Pub.

Diet to Lose & Win: Self-Help System. Merilyn L. Cummings. (Illus.). (Orig.). 1987. pap. (ISBN 0-9617195-3-2). Abrahamson Pub.

Dietary Guidelines. Ed. by Evelyn J. Lorenzen. LC 78-53194. 192p. 1978. 14.00x o.p. (ISBN 0-87201-176-3). Gulf Pub.

Dietary Policy & Procedure Manual. Rose G. Downs. LC 79-16595. 1979. pap. 10.00 o.p. (ISBN 0-87125-058-6). Cath Health.

Dietary Reconstruction at Chalcatzingo, a Formative Period Site in Morelos, Mexico. Margaret J. Schoeninger. (Technical Reports Ser.: No. 9). (Illus., Orig., Contribution 2 in contributions in human biology). 1979. pap. 3.50x o.p. (ISBN 0-932206-78-6). U Mich Mus Anthro.

Dieter's Gourmet Cookbook. Francine Prince. 1986. pap. 8.95 o.s.i. (ISBN 0-671-62021-5, Fireside). S&S.

Dieter's Guide to Weight Loss after Sex. Richard Smith. LC 79-56531. 144p. 1980. pap. 3.50 o.p. (ISBN 0-89480-081-7, 403). Workman Pub.

Dieter's Stress Guide: A Weight-Loss Guide for Professional Eaters. Richard Smith. 160p. (Orig.). 1984. pap. 4.95 o.p. (ISBN 0-380-86108-9, 86108). Avon.

Dieting Makes You Fat: A Guide to Energy, Food, Fitness & Health. Geoffrey Cannon & Hetty Einzig. 363p. 1985. 15.45 o.p. (ISBN 0-671-53072-0). S&S.

Dietrich Bonhoeffer. Dallas M. Roark. Ed. by Bob E. Patterson. LC 72-76439. (Makers of the Modern Theological Mind Ser.). 140p. 1972. 8.95 o.p. (ISBN 0-87680-253-6, 80253). Word Bks.

Dietrich Bonhoeffer. Edwin H. Robertson. LC 66-15514. (Makers of Contemporary Theology Ser.). (Orig.). 1966. pap. 3.95 o.p. (ISBN 0-8042-0535-3, John Knox). Westminster John Knox.

Dieux Ont Soif see Romans et Contes.

Diez Dias Que Estremecieron el Mundo. J. Reed. 419p. (Span.). 1977. 8.95 o.p. (ISBN 0-8285-1676-6, Pub. by Progress Pubs USSR). Imported Pubns.

Diez Talentos Libro de Cocinar: Una Buena Cocinera. (Span.). 1987. write for info. o.p. (ISBN 0-9603532-5-9). Ten Talents.

Difference Equations. Ronald E. Mickens. LC 86-10990. (Professional Books Ser.). (Illus.). 288p. 1987. 41.95 o.p. (ISBN 0-442-26076-8). Van Nos Reinhold.

Difference in Being a Christian Today. John A. Robinson. LC 75-188532. 92p. 1972. pap. 1.50 o.s.i. (ISBN 0-664-24954-X, Westminster). Westminster John Knox.

Differences & Similarities Between the Public & Private Sectors: A Bibliography. J. Norman Baldwin. (Public Administration Ser.: P 1670). 16p. 1985. 2.25 o.p. (ISBN 0-89028-380-X). Vance Biblios.

Differences in Income, Nutrition, & Poverty Within Brazil. Vinod Thomas. (World Bank Staff Working Paper: No. 505). 91p. 1982. pap. 5.00 o.p. (ISBN 0-686-39729-0, WP-0505). World Bank.

Different Drum: Community Making & Peace. M. Scott Peck. 1987. 16.45 o.s.i. (ISBN 0-671-60192-X). S&S.

Different Drummer Notes. Nathan Garner. 64p. (Orig.). 1973. pap. text ed. 3.95 o.p. (ISBN 0-8220-0389-9). Cliffs.

Different Drummer: The Story of E. J. Banfield, the Beachcomber of Dunk Island. Michael Noonan. LC 86-16027. (Illus.). 237p. 1987. pap. 9.95 o.p. (ISBN 0-7022-2027-2). U of Queensland Pr.

Different Drummers. Nell Dunn. LC 76-27413. 1977. 10.00 o.p. (ISBN 0-15-152928-0). HarBraceJ.

Different Kind of Gentleman: Parish Clergy As Professional Men in Early & Mid-Victorian England. Brian Heeney. LC 76-17329. (Studies in British History & Culture: Vol. 5). (Illus.). xii, 169p. 1976. 21.50 o.p. (ISBN 0-208-01605-8, Archon). Shoe String.

Different Kind of Love. Michael Borich. LC 84-22492. 176p. (gr. 6-9). 1985. 11.95 o.s.i. (ISBN 0-03-003249-0). H Holt & Co.

Different Kind of Love. Michael Borich. LC 84-22492. (YA) (gr. 7 up). 11.45 o.p. HR&W.

Different Kind of Rain. Dewitt S. Copp. 1978. 8.95 o.p. (ISBN 0-393-08818-9). Norton.

Titles

Different Music. Mary Milo. 1979. pap. 2.25 o.p. (ISBN 0-380-43596-9, 43596). Avon.

Different Woman. Jane Howard. 1978. pap. 1.95 o.p. (ISBN 0-380-00079-2, 39263). Avon.

Differentiable Periodic Maps. 2nd ed. P. E. Conner. (Lecture Notes in Mathematics: Vol. 738). 1979. pap. 14.00 o.p. (ISBN 0-387-09535-7). Springer-Verlag.

Differential & Combinatorial Topology: A Symposium in Honor of Marston Morse. Ed. by S. S. Cairns. (Princeton Mathematical Ser.: No. 27). 1965. 34.00 o.p. (ISBN 0-691-07945-5). Princeton U Pr.

Differential & Integral Calculus. Ya S. Bugrov & S. M. Nikolsky. 464p. 1982. 8.95 o.p. (ISBN 0-8285-2306-1, Pub. by Mir Pubs USSR). Imported Pubns.

Differential & Integral Calculus U. K. Wallis. 1984. 34.95 o.p. (ISBN 0-442-30578-8). Van Nos Reinhold.

Differential Calculus. P. J. Hilton. (Library of Mathematics). 1968. pap. 5.00 o.p. (ISBN 0-7100-4341-4). Routledge Chapman & Hall.

Differential Calculus in Locally Convex Spaces. H. H. Keller. LC 74-20715. (Lectures Notes in Mathematics Ser.: Vol. 417). xvi, 131p. 1974. pap. 13.00 o.p. (ISBN 0-387-06962-3). Springer-Verlag.

Differential Calculus in Topological Linear Spaces. S. Yamamuro. LC 73-21376. (Lecture Notes in Mathematics: Vol. 374). iv, 179p. 1974. pap. 13.00 o.p. (ISBN 0-387-06709-4). Springer-Verlag.

Differential Diagnosis in Clinical Psychiatry. Paul Hoch. LC 72-76812. 1972. 40.00x o.p. (ISBN 0-87668-053-8). Aronson.

Differential Diagnosis in Neurology. Bernard H. Smith. LC 78-31117. (Illus.). 312p. 1979. pap. 18.95 o.p. (ISBN 0-668-04033-5). Appleton & Lange.

Differential Diagnosis of Internal Diseases, 2 vols. A. Vinogradov. 1136p. 1982. 20.95 o.p. (ISBN 0-8285-2315-0, Pub. by Mir Pubs USSR). Imported Pubns.

Differential Equations. Martin M. Guterman & Zbigniew H. Nitecki. 1984. text ed. 42.00 o.s.i. (ISBN 0-03-062502-5, CBS C); study manual 15.75 o.s.i. (ISBN 0-03-062503-3). SCP.

Differential Fertility in Brazil. J. V. Saunders. LC 58-13205. (Illus.). 1958. 4.95 o.p. (ISBN 0-8130-0201-X). U Presses Fla.

Differential Fertility in Central India. Edwin D. Driver. 1963. 22.00x o.p. (ISBN 0-691-09314-8). Princeton U Pr.

Differential Games & Applications: Proceedings of a Workshop, Enschede, Netherlands, March 16-25,1977. Ed. by P. Hagedorn et al. (Lecture Notes in Control & Information Sciences: Vol. 3). 1977. pap. text ed. 19.00 o.p. (ISBN 0-387-08407-X). Springer-Verlag.

Differential Geometrical Methods in Mathematical Physics. Ed. by K. Bleuler & A. Reetz. LC 76-30859. (Lecture Notes in Mathematics Ser.: Vol. 570). 1977. pap. 24.60 o.p. (ISBN 0-387-08068-6). Springer-Verlag.

Differential Geometrical Methods in Mathematical Physics II: Proceedings, University of Bonn, July 13-16, 1977. Ed. by K. Bleuler et al. (Lecture Notes in Mathematics Ser.: Vol. 676). 1978. pap. 37.00 o.p. (ISBN 0-387-08935-7). Springer-Verlag.

Differential-Geometrical Methods in Statistics. S. Amari. (Lecture Notes in Statistics Ser.: Vol. 28). (Illus.). v, 290p. 1985. pap. 19.60 o.p. (ISBN 0-387-96056-2). Springer-Verlag.

Differential Geometry: An Integrated Approach. N. Prakash. 1981. text ed. 8.80 o.p. (ISBN 0-07-096560-9). McGraw.

Differential Oral Diagnosis of Systemic Diseases. Gardner. 316p. 1970. 18.50 o.p. (ISBN 0-7236-0254-9, Pub. by John Wright UK). Butterworth.

Differential Psychology. 3rd ed. Anne Anastasi. (Illus.). 1958. text ed. (ISBN 0-02-302800-9, 30280). Macmillan.

Differential Thermal Analysis: Application & Results in Mineralogy. W. Smykatz-Kloss. LC 74-17490. (Minerals & Rocks Ser.: Vol. 11). (Illus.). xiv, 185p. 1974. 34.00 o.p. (ISBN 0-387-06906-2). Springer-Verlag.

Differential Thermal Analysis, Vol. 1: Fundamental Aspects. R. C. MacKenzie. 1970. 137.00 o.p. (ISBN 0-12-464401-5). Acad Pr.

Differential Topology: An Introduction. Gauld. (Texts & Monographs in Pure & Applied Mathematics). 312p. 1982. 45.00 o.p. (ISBN 0-8247-1709-0). Dekker.

Differential Topology: First Steps. Andrew Wallace. 1968. pap. write for info. o.p. (ISBN 0-8053-9485-0, Adv Bk Prog MSP). Addison-Wesley.

Differentiated Staffing for Urban Schools. Bobby F. Gentry. LC 85-80146. (Illus.). 64p. 1985. pap. 5.00 o.p. (ISBN 0-682-40216-8). Exposition-Phoenix.

Differentiation & Development: Miami Winter Symposia, Vol. 15. Ed. by F. Ahmad et al. 1978. 91.50 o.p. (ISBN 0-12-045450-5). Acad Pr.

Differentiation & Growth of Cells in Vertebrate Tissues. Ed. by G. Goldspink. 1974. 55.00x o.p. (ISBN 0-412-11390-2, NO.6128, Pub. by Chapman & Hall). Routledge Chapman & Hall.

Differentiation & Immunology. International Society for Cell Biology Staff. Ed. by Katherine B. Warren. (Proceedings: Vol. 7). 1969. 74.50 o.p. (ISBN 0-12-611907-4). Acad Pr.

Differentiation & Neoplasia. Ed. by R. G. McKinnell. (Results & Problems in Cell Differentiation: Vol. 11). (Illus.). 350p. 1980. 83.00 o.p. (ISBN 0-387-10177-2). Springer-Verlag.

Difficult Child. Joseph Roucek. 304p. 1964. Philos Lib.

Difficult Decision. Janet Dailey. (Nightingale Ser.). 228p. 1986. pap. 10.95 o.p. (ISBN 0-8161-4014-6, Large Print Bks). G K Hall.

Difficult Loves. Italo Calvino. Tr. by William Weaver et al. LC 84-685. (Helen & Kurt Wolff Bk.). (Ital.). 1984. 14.95 o.p. (ISBN 0-15-125610-1). HarbraceJ.

Difficult Problems in Hand Surgery. James W. Strickland & James B. Steichen. LC 82-2230. (Illus.). 348p. 1982. text ed. 58.00 o.p. (ISBN 0-8016-4851-3). Mosby.

Difficult Role of a Father. Spartaco Lucarini. Tr. by Hugh Moran from Ital. LC 79-84940. (Education in the Family Ser.). 75p. 1979. pap. 2.95 o.p. (ISBN 0-911782-32-X). New City.

Difficult Role of a Mother. Anne M. Zanzucchi. Ed. by Gerry Bartram. Tr. by Lenny Szczesniak from Ital. LC 79-84941. (Education in the Family Ser.). 90p. 1979. pap. 2.95 o.p. (ISBN 0-911782-33-8). New City.

Difficult Sayings of Jesus. William Neil. 1977. pap. 3.95 o.p. (ISBN 0-8028-1668-1). Eerdmans.

Difficult Years of Survival. Fouad Guirguis. LC 83-90921. 89p. 1985. 7.95 o.p. (ISBN 0-533-05937-2). Vantage.

Difficulties in Christian Belief. MacIntyre. 128p. 1960. (ISBN 0-8022-1030-9). Philos Lib.

Diffraction of Light by Ultrasound. Michael V. Berry. 1967. 33.00 o.p. (ISBN 0-12-093350-0). Acad Pr.

Diffraction Theory & Antennas. R. H. Clarke & John Brown. LC 80-40388. (Ellis Horwood Series in Electrical & Electronic Engineering). 292p. 1980. 108.95x o.p. (ISBN 0-470-27003-9). Halsted Pr.

Diffusion & Sorption in the Fibers & Films: An Introduction with Particular Reference to Dyes, Vol. 1. R. McGregor. 1974. 49.50 o.p. (ISBN 0-12-484101-5). Acad Pr.

Diffusion Problems & Partial Differential Equations. S. R. Varadhan. (Tata Institute Lectures on Mathematics Ser.). 315p. 1980. pap. 13.00 o.p. (ISBN 0-387-08773-7). Springer-Verlag.

Diffusion Processes & Their Sample Paths. K. Ito & H. P. McKean, Jr. (Grundlehren der Mathematischen Wissenschaften: Vol. 125). 1965. 45.00 o.p. (ISBN 0-387-03302-5). Springer-Verlag.

Dig: A Journey under the Earth's Crust. John Hubley & Faith Hubley. LC 72-88169. 1973. 5.95 o.p. (ISBN 0-15-223490-X, HJ). HarBraceJ.

Digest of Education Statistics, 1987. Thomas D. Snyder. (Education - Department Publication CS: No. 87-345). (Illus.). 386p. 1987. pap. 18.00 o.p. (ISBN 0-317-62842-9, S-N 065-000-00293-1). USGPO.

Digest of Job Descriptions for Medical Group Administrators. 73p. 1978. 15.00 o.p. (ISBN 0-317-34826-4, 13-0000-903); members 8.00 o.p. (ISBN 0-317-34827-2). Med Group Mgmt.

Digest of Legal Activities of International Organizations & Other Institutions. 5th ed. International Institute for the Unification of Private Law Staff. LC 74-19327. 1982. 85.00 o.p.; suppplement 1977 o.p. 15.00 o.p. (ISBN 0-686-96816-6). Oceana.

Digest of Legal Activities of International Organizations & Other Institutions. 7th ed. International Institute for the Unification of Private Law Staff. LC 74-19327. 1985. 1 bdr. looseleaf 100.00 o.p. (ISBN 0-379-00525-5). Oceana.

Digest of Legal Activities of International Organizations: Other Institutions. 6th ed. International Institute for Unification of Private Law Staff. 1984. o.p. Oceana.

Digest of Medical Group Employment Contracts & Income Distribution Plans. 179p. 1978. 30.00 o.p. (ISBN 0-317-34828-0, 100003). Med Group Mgmt.

Digest of Official Actions, Nineteen Eighty-Five to Nineteen Eighty-Six. American Medical Association Staff. (Orig.). 1988. pap. (ISBN 0-89970-318-6). AMA.

Digest of Official Actions, 1983-84. (ISBN 0-89970-233-3). AMA.

Digest of Papers from the SPIE International Optical Computing Conference, Italy, 1976. 158p. 16.00 o.p. (ISBN 0-317-34624-5); members 12.00 o.p. (ISBN 0-317-34625-3). SPIE.

Digestibility for Veal Calves of Fish Protein Concentrates. (Agricultural Research Reports: No. 819). 1974. pap. 5.00 o.p. (ISBN 90-220-0515-1, PDC194, PUDOC). UNIPUB.

Digestive Physiology & Metabolism in Ruminants. Y. Ruckebusch & P. Thivend. (Illus.). 1980. 65.95 o.p. (ISBN 0-87055-359-3). AVI.

Digging Up Bones: The Excavation, Treatment & Study of Human Skeletal Remains. 2nd ed. Don R. Brothwell. (Illus.). 1972. pap. 6.75 o.p. (ISBN 0-565-00704-1, Pub. by Brit Mus Nat Hist England). Sabbot-Natural Hist Bks.

Digital Bipolar Integrated Circuits. Mohamed I. Elmasry. LC 82-21868. (Illus.). 322p. 1983. 47.50 o.p. (ISBN 0-471-05571-9). Wiley.

Digital Circuits & Logic Design. Samuel C. Lee. (Illus.). 1976. text ed. (ISBN 0-13-212225-1). P-H.

Digital Circuits for Binary Arithmetic. R. M. Oberman. LC 78-31460. 340p. 1979. 64.95x o.p. (ISBN 0-470-26373-3). Halsted Pr.

Digital Computation & Numerical Methods. R. Southworth & S. De Leeuw. 1965. text ed. 46.95 o.p. (ISBN 0-07-059799-5). McGraw.

Digital-Computer-Controlled Traffic Signal System for a Small City. (National Cooperative Highway Research Program Report). 82p. 1966. 4.00 o.p. (ISBN 0-317-36075-2, 1474). Transport Res Bd.

Digital Computer Design: Its Logic, Circuitry, & Synthesis. Edward L. Braun. 1963. 93.50 o.p. (ISBN 0-12-127250-8). Acad Pr.

Digital Computers in Analytical Chemistry, 2 pts. Ed. by J. B. Justice & T. L. Isenhour. LC 81-2933. (Benchmark Papers in Analytical Chemistry: Vol. 3). 1983. Set. 124.95 o.p. (ISBN 0-87933-095-3); Pt. 1, 1950-1968. 67.95 o.p. (ISBN 0-87933-061-9); Pt. 2, 1970-1978. 67.95 o.p. (ISBN 0-87933-062-7). Van Nos Reinhold.

Digital Computer's Memory Technology. 2nd ed. D. Dutta Majumdar & J. Das. 533p. 1984. 33.95x o.p. (ISBN 0-470-27419-0). Halsted Pr.

Digital Concepts Using Standard Integrated Circuits. Richard Sandige. (Illus.). 1978. text ed. 42.95 o.p. (ISBN 0-07-054653-3). McGraw.

Digital Counter Handbook. Louis E. Frenzel. 1981. pap. 10.95 o.p. (ISBN 0-672-21758-9). Sams.

Digital Electronic Watch. Tom M. Hyltin. 1978. 24.95 o.p. (ISBN 0-442-22596-2). Van Nos Reinhold.

Digital Electronics. James Bignell & Robert Donovan. LC 84-23853. 300p. 1985. text ed. 31.95 o.p. (ISBN 0-8273-2307-7). Delmar.

Digital Electronics. David Casasent. (Illus.). 276p. 1982. pap. text ed. 31.00 o.p. (ISBN 0-13-212340-1). P-H.

Digital Electronics. Roger L. Tokheim. Ed. by Charles A. Schuler. (Basic Skills in Electricity & Electronics Ser). (Illus.). 1979. text ed. 31.96 o.p. (ISBN 0-07-064954-5). McGraw.

Digital Electronics: A Hands-on Learning Approach. George Young. (gr. 12). 1980. pap. 9.95 o.p. (ISBN 0-8104-5668-0). Sams.

Digital Electronics & Laboratory Computer Experiments. Charles L. Wilkins et al. LC 75-11570. (Illus.). 284p. 1975. 35.00x o.p. (ISBN 0-306-30822-3, Plenum Pr). Plenum Pub.

Digital Experiments. Richard E. Gasperini. (Illus.). 1976. pap. 9.95 o.p. (ISBN 0-8104-5713-X). Sams.

Digital Filters. Richard W. Hamming. (Illus.). 304p. 1983. text ed. 52.00 o.p. (ISBN 0-13-212506-4). P-H.

Digital Filters & the Fast Fourier Transform. Ed. by Bede Liu. LC 75-9533. (Benchmark Papers in Electrical Engineering & Computer Science Ser.: Vol. 12). 423p. 1975. 51.00 o.p. (ISBN 0-12-786980-8). Acad Pr.

Digital Hardware Design. John B. Peatman. 1980. text ed. 49.95 o.p. (ISBN 0-07-049132-1). McGraw.

Digital Harmony: On the Complementarity of Music & Visual Art. John Whitney. (Illus.). 200p. 1981. text ed. 25.95 o.p. (ISBN 0-07-070015-X, BYTE Bks). McGraw.

Digital Image Processing: A Systems Approach. William B. Green. (Van Nostrand Reinhold Electrical-Computer Science & Engineering Ser.). (Illus.). 204p. 1982. 38.95 o.p. (ISBN 0-442-28801-8). Van Nos Reinhold.

Digital Instrumentation. A. J. Bouwens. 1984. text ed. 44.95 o.p. (ISBN 0-07-006712-0). McGraw.

Digital Integrated Circuits for Electronics Technicians. Edward J. Pasahow. (Illus.). 1979. text ed. 33.95 o.p. (ISBN 0-07-048710-3). McGraw.

Digital Logic Circuits: Tests & Analysis. Robert G. Middleton. LC 81-86555. 224p. 1983. pap. 16.95 o.p. (ISBN 0-672-21799-6). Sams.

Digital Logic Techniques. T. J. Stonham. 1984. pap. 15.95 o.p. (ISBN 0-442-30595-8). Van Nos Reinhold.

Digital Microwave Radio Markets. (Reports Ser.: No. 533). 154p. 1983. 985.00x o.p. (ISBN 0-88694-533-X). Intl Res Dev.

Digital Modulation Techniques in an Interference Environment. Kamilo Feher. Ed. by Donald R. White. LC 76-52508. (Illus.). 182p. 1977. text ed. 42.00 o.p. (ISBN 0-932263-18-6). White Consult.

Digital Picture Analysis. Ed. by A. Rosenfeld. (Topics in Applied Physics Ser: Vol. 11). 1976. 46.00 o.p. (ISBN 0-387-07579-8). Springer-Verlag.

Digital PLL Frequency Synthesizers: Theory & Design. Ulrich L. Rohde. (Illus.). 608p. 1983. text ed. 57.33 o.p. (ISBN 0-13-214239-2). P-H.

Digital Processing of Signals. Bernard Gold & Charles M. Rader. LC 82-14072. 282p. 1983. Repr. of 1969 ed. lib. bdg. 23.50 o.p. (ISBN 0-89874-548-9). Krieger.

Digital Signal Analysis. Sam D. Stearns. 288p. 1975. text ed. 31.95 o.p. (ISBN 0-8104-5828-4). Sams.

Digital Signal Processing & Control & Estimation Theory: Points of Tangency, Areas of Intersection, & Parallel Directions. Alan S. Willsky. 1979. 37.50x o.p. (ISBN 0-262-23091-7). MIT Pr.

Digital Simulation in Electrochemistry. B. Britz. (Lecture Notes in Chemistry Ser.: Vol. 23). 120p. 1981. pap. 16.50 o.p. (ISBN 0-387-10564-6). Springer-Verlag.

Digital System Design with LSI Bit-Slice Logic. Glenford J. Myers. LC 79-26258. 338p. 1980. 51.95x o.p. (ISBN 0-471-05376-7, Pub. by Wiley-Interscience). Wiley.

Digital System Fundamentals. John M. Motil. Ed. by John G. Truxal & R. A. Rohrer. (Electronic Systems Ser.). (Illus.). 416p. 1972. text ed. 46.95 o.p. (ISBN 0-07-043515-4). McGraw.

Digital Systems: Principles & Applications. 3rd ed. Ronald J. Tocci. (Illus.). 496p. 1985. text ed. 44.00 o.p. (ISBN 0-13-212374-6). P-H.

Digital Transmission & Its Potential. 50.00 o.p. (ISBN 0-686-32967-8). Info Gatekeepers.

Digital Troubleshooting: Practical Digital Theory & Troubleshooting Tips. Richard E. Gasperini. 1976. pap. 11.95 o.p. (ISBN 0-8104-5708-3). Sams.

Dignity of Labour? A Study of Childbearing & Induction. Ann Cartwright. 1979. 29.95x o.p. (ISBN 0-422-76690-9, NO.2039, Pub by Tavistock England). Routledge Chapman & Hall.

Dignity of the Human Person. Edward Cronan. 1955. (ISBN 0-8022-0317-5). Philos Lib.

Digs. Bette Pesetsky. LC 84-47850. 304p. 1984. 14.45 o.s.i. (ISBN 0-394-53932-X). Knopf.

Dilemma of Daniel. Fred M. Wood. LC 83-71065. 1985. pap. 6.95 o.p. (ISBN 0-8054-1231-X). Broadman.

Dilemma of Democratic Socialism: Edward Bernstein's Challenge to Marx. Peter Gay. 1979. Repr. of 1952 ed. lib. bdg. 24.50x o.p. (ISBN 0-374-93017-1, Octagon). Hippocrene Bks.

Dilemma of Mexico's Development: The Roles of the Private & Public Sectors. Raymond Vernon. LC 63-17214. (Center for International Affairs Ser). 1963. 16.00x o.s.i. (ISBN 0-674-20650-9). Harvard U Pr.

Dilemma of Our Society: A Proposal for Moral Maturity. Errol A. Gibbs & Marjorie G. Lindo. (Illus.). 311p. 1980. 15.00 o.p. (ISBN 0-682-49650-2). Exposition-Phoenix.

Dilemma of Prison Reform. Thomas O. Murton. 285p. 1982. pap. text ed. 14.95x o.p. (ISBN 0-8290-1012-2). Irvington.

Dilemma of Reform in the Soviet Union. Timothy J. Colton. 128p. 1984. pap. 6.95 cancelled o.p. (ISBN 0-87609-002-1). Coun Foreign.

Dilemma of the Horn of Africa. Raman Bhardwaj. (Illus.). 1980. text ed. 15.00x o.p. (ISBN 0-391-01028-X). Humanities.

Dilemmas of Administrative Behavior. John D. Aram. 144p. 1976. Ref. Ed. pap. text ed. 23.00 o.p. (ISBN 0-13-214247-3). P-H.

Dilemmas of Democracy: Readings in American Government. Ed. by Peter Collier. 385p. (Orig.). 1976. pap. text ed. 10.95 o.p. (ISBN 0-15-517650-1, HC). HarBraceJ.

Dilemmas of Liberal Democracies: Studies in Fred Hirsch's Social Limits to Growth. Adrian Ellis & Krishan Kumar. LC 83-13207. (Tavistock Studies in Sociology). 212p. 1984. 29.95x o.p. (ISBN 0-422-78460-5, 4002); pap. 13.95x o.p. (ISBN 0-422-78470-2, 4001). Routledge Chapman & Hall.

Dilemmas of Masculinity: A Study of College Youth. Mirra Komarovsky. 250p. 1976. 9.95x o.p. (ISBN 0-393-01125-9). Norton.

Dilemmas of Masculinity: A Study of College Youth. Mirra Komarovsky. 1976. pap. 8.95x o.p. (ISBN 0-393-09169-4). Norton.

Dilemmas of Political Development. 3rd ed. Monte Palmer. LC 85-61764. 335p. 1985. pap. text ed. 19.95 o.p. (ISBN 0-87581-314-3). Peacock Pubs.

Dilemmas of Schooling. Ann Berlak & Harold Berlak. 309p. 1981. 21.00x o.p. (ISBN 0-416-74140-1, NO.3566); pap. 11.95 o.p. (ISBN 0-416-74110-X, NO.3565). Routledge Chapman & Hall.

Dilemmas of Urban America. Robert C. Weaver. LC 65-22056. 1967. pap. text ed. 1.95x o.s.i. (ISBN 0-689-70201-9, 105, Atheneum). Macmillan.

Dillen. Ron Hutchinson. (Royal Shakespeare Company Playtext Ser.). 48p. 1983. pap. 3.95 o.p. (ISBN 0-413-53330-1, NO. 3901). Heinemann Ed.

DIM Definitions: German-English with an English-German Vocabulary. 2nd rev. ed. Compiled by Henry G. Freeman. (Ger. & Eng.). 80.00 o.s.i. (ISBN 3-4101-0804-1). E J Brill USA.

Dim Sum & Chinese One Dish Meals. Jean Yueh. Ed. by Anne Becker & Irene Rich. LC 81-68834. (Great American Cooking Schools Ser.). (Illus.). 84p. 1981. pap. 5.95 o.p. (ISBN 0-941034-05-4). I Chalmers.

Dimanche de la Vie. Raymond Queneau. 308p. 1952. 9.95 o.p. (ISBN 0-686-54668-7). Schoenhof.

Dimension in Health Research: Search for the Medicines of Tomorrow. Herbert Weissbach & Robert Kunz. 1978. 36.50 o.p. (ISBN 0-12-744260-X). Acad Pr.

Dimensional Analysis & Group Theory in Astrophysics. Rudolf Kurth. 249p. 1972. 80.00 o.p. (ISBN 0-08-016616-4). Pergamon.

Dimensional Structure of Time. Morgenstern. LC 60-13653. 1960. (ISBN 0-8022-1148-8). Philos Lib.

Dimensionality of Signs, Tools & Models: An Introduction. James H. Bunn. LC 80-8151. (Advances in Semiotics Ser.). (Illus.). 224p. 1981. 17.50 o.p. (ISBN 0-253-16916-X). Ind U Pr.

Dimensionless Parameters: Theory & Methodology. H. A. Becker. LC 76-1570. 128p. 1976. 39.95x o.p. (ISBN 0-470-15048-3). Halsted Pr.

Dimensions in Abnormal Psychology. 2nd ed. Glenn D. Shean. 1976. pap. 25.50 o.p. (ISBN 0-395-30837-2). HM.

Dimensions in Modern Management. 2nd ed. Patrick E. Connor. LC 77-75692. (Illus.). 1978. pap. 13.95 o.p. (ISBN 0-395-25515-5). HM.

Dimensions Interwoven. Yana I. Alcamo. LC 84-91338. 102p. 1985. 7.95 o.p. (ISBN 0-533-06436-8). Vantage.

Dimensions of Change. Don Fabun. 1971. text ed. write for info. o.p. (ISBN 0-02-475500-1, 47550). Macmillan.

Dimensions of Community Health. Dean F. Miller. 416p. 1985. pap. write for info o.p. (ISBN 0-697-00145-8). Wm C Brown.

Dimensions of Evil & Transcendence: A Sociological Perspective. Natalia R. Moehle. LC 78-59124. 1978. pap. text ed. 14.00 o.p. (ISBN 0-8191-0550-3). U Pr of Amer.

Dimensions of Faith. James A. Mohler. LC 69-13120. (Orig.). 1969. pap. 2.80 o.p. (ISBN 0-8294-0100-8). Loyola.

Dimensions of Hospitality Management: An Industry Performance in Seven Acts, 2 vols. Ed. by Lothar A. Kreck & John W. McCracken. LC 75-15701. 838p. 1983. Vol. 1. 21.95 o.p. (ISBN 0-8436-2075-7); Vol. 2. 21.95 o.p. (ISBN 0-8436-2085-4). Van Nos Reinhold.

Dimensions of Liberty. Oscar Handlin & Mary Handlin. LC 61-16694. 1966. pap. text ed. 1.75x o.s.i. (ISBN 0-689-70087-3, 84, Atheneum). Macmillan.

Dimensions of Midnight: Poetry & Prose. Cecil Hemley. Ed. by Elaine Gottlieb. LC 66-25957. xv, 233p. 1966. 12.00 o.p. (ISBN 0-8214-0023-1). Ohio U Pr.

Dimensions of Organizational Behavior. 2nd ed. Theodore T. Herbert. 513p. 1981. text ed. write for info. o.p. (ISBN 0-02-353670-5). Macmillan.

Dimensions of Privacy: A National Opinion Research Survey of Attitudes Toward Privacy. Harris, Louis, & Associates Staff & Alan F. Westin. LC 80-9010. (Louis Harris Publications Ser.: Refrence Lib. of Social Science, Vol. 98). 1981. lib. bdg. 24.00 o.p. (ISBN 0-8240-9372-0). Garland Pub.

Dimensions of Psychology. G. Morris. 1971. pap. text ed. 6.00x o.p. (ISBN 0-8422-0174-2). Irvington.

Dimensions of Reading Difficulties. A. T. Ravenette. 1968. 14.50 o.p. (ISBN 0-08-012956-0); pap. 35.00 o.p. (ISBN 0-08-012955-2). Pergamon.

Dimensions of the Priesthood. new ed. Ed. by Daughters of St. Paul. 1973. 5.75 o.s.i. (ISBN 0-8198-0253-0); pap. 4.50 o.s.i. (ISBN 0-8198-0254-9). Dghtrs St Paul.

Dimitrov of Bulgaria. Charles Moser. 14.95 o.p. (Dist. by Kampmann). Green Hill.

Dimly Burning Wicks: Reflections on the Gospel after a Time Away. John W. Vannorsdall. LC 81-70661. 112p. 1982. pap. 6.95 o.p. (ISBN 0-8006-1622-7, 1-1622, Fortress). Augsburg Fortress.

Dinah Faire. Virginia Coffman. LC 78-73863. 1979. 9.95 o.p. (ISBN 0-87795-218-3, Arbor Hse). Morrow.

Dinah Shore Cookbook. Dinah Shore. LC 80-2436. (Illus.). 400p. 1983. 19.95 o.s.i. (ISBN 0-385-15928-5). Doubleday.

Diners. John Baeder. LC 77-13203. (Illus.). 1978. pap. 14.95 o.p. (ISBN 0-8109-2078-6). Abrams.

Dingley Falls. Michael Malone. LC 79-3529. 540p. 1980. 12.95 o.p. (ISBN 0-15-125673-X). HarBraceJ.

Dingo. Charles Wood. 1969. pap. 1.95 o.p. (ISBN 0-394-17377-5, E519, Ever). Grove.

Dining by Design. Ed. by Edie L. Cohen & Sherman R. Emery. (Illus.). 224p. 1984. 49.95 o.p. (ISBN 0-943370-04-3). Van Nos Reinhold.

Dining In - Boston. Rev. ed. Steven Raichlen. (Dining In Ser.). 194p. 1987. pap. 8.95 o.p. (ISBN 0-89716-124-6). Peanut Butter.

Dining In - Chicago, Vol. III. Barbara Grunes. (Dining In Ser.). 192p. 1983. pap. 8.95 o.s.i. (ISBN 0-89716-125-4). Peanut Butter.

Dining In - Chicago, Vol. 2. Barbara Grunes. (Dining In Ser.). 200p. (Orig.). 1982. pap. 8.95 o.s.i. (ISBN 0-89716-108-4). Peanut Butter.

Dining In - Cleveland. Stephen Michaelides & Michael Deluca. (Dining in Ser.). 176p. (Orig.). 1982. pap. 8.95 o.s.i. (ISBN 0-89716-034-7). Peanut Butter.

Dining In - Dallas. Rev. ed. Marilyn W. Ingram & Lois J. Folse. (Dining In Ser.). 200p. 1982. pap. 8.95 o.s.i. (ISBN 0-89716-113-0). Peanut Butter.

Dining In - Denver. Jaydee Boat. (Dining in Ser.). 185p. (Orig.). 1981. pap. 7.95 o.p. (ISBN 0-89716-036-3). Peanut Butter.

Dining In - Hampton Road. John Gounaris et al. Ed. by Elaine Lotzgar. (Dining in Ser.). (Illus., Orig.). 1984. pap. 8.95 o.s.i. (ISBN 0-89716-136-X). Peanut Butter.

Dining In - Hawaii. Maxine Saltonstall. (Dining In Ser.). 200p. (Orig.). 1981. pap. 8.95 o.s.i. (ISBN 0-89716-066-5). Peanut Butter.

Dining In - Houston, Vol. II. Ann Criswell. (Dining in Ser.). 200p. 1980. pap. 7.95 o.p. (ISBN 0-89716-065-7). Peanut Butter.

Dining In - Kansas City. Rev. ed. James Rieger & Boots Mathews. (Dining In Ser.). 188p. 1983. pap. 8.95 o.s.i. (ISBN 0-89716-127-0). Peanut Butter.

Dining In - Los Angeles. Rev. ed. Laurie B. Grad. (Dining In Ser.). (Illus.). 190p. 1982. pap. 8.95 o.p. (ISBN 0-89716-121-1). Peanut Butter.

Dining In - Minneapolis-St. Paul, Vol. II. Carla Waldemar. (Dining In Ser.). 210p. 1982. pap. 8.95 o.p. (ISBN 0-89716-120-3). Peanut Butter.

Dining In - Monterey Peninsula. Regina Hicks et al. (Dining in Ser.). 190p. (Orig.). 1979. pap. 7.95 o.p. (ISBN 0-89716-033-9). Peanut Butter.

Dining In - New Orleans, Vol. I. Phyllis Dennery. 190p. (Orig.). 1985. pap. 8.95 o.s.i. (ISBN 0-89716-020-7). Peanut Butter.

Dining In - New Orleans, Vol. II. Phyllis Dennery. 201p. 1987. pap. 8.95 o.p. Peanut Butter.

Dining In - Philadelphia. Pearl Nipon. (Dining In Ser.). 200p. (Orig.). 1982. pap. 8.95 o.p. (ISBN 0-89716-039-8). Peanut Butter.

Dining In - Phoenix. Renee Eager. (Dining In Ser.). 200p. (Orig.). 1982. pap. 8.95 o.p. (ISBN 0-89716-035-5). Peanut Butter.

Dining In - Pittsburgh. rev. ed. Barbara Klein & Judith Roscow. (Dining in Ser.). 192p. 1981. pap. 7.95 o.p. (ISBN 0-89716-103-3). Peanut Butter.

Dining In - Portland. Muriel B. Logan & Emily Crumpacker. (Dining in Ser.). 189p. (Orig.). 1979. pap. 7.95 o.p. (ISBN 0-89716-043-6). Peanut Butter.

Dining In - St. Louis. J. A. Baer & Cecile K. Lowenhaupt. 187p. (Orig.). 1979. pap. 7.95 o.p. (ISBN 0-89716-045-2). Peanut Butter.

Dining In - Salt Lake City. Larry Gerlock & Carol Von Schmidt. 219p. 1985. pap. 8.95 o.p. (ISBN 0-89716-139-4). Peanut Butter.

Dining In - Sun Valley. Joan Hemingway & Russ Armstrong. (Dining In Ser.). 130p. (Orig.). 1982. pap. 7.95 o.p. (ISBN 0-89716-078-9). Peanut Butter.

Dining In - Vancouver, B.C. Virginia J. Johns. (Dining in Ser.). 175p. (Orig.). 1982. pap. 8.95 o.p. (ISBN 0-89716-084-3). Peanut Butter.

Dining in Atlanta. Anne Byrn. Ed. by Shiela Hosner. (Dining in Ser.). (Orig.). 1987. pap. 8.95 o.p. (ISBN 0-89716-166-1). Peanut Butter.

Dining in Philadelphia. Marilynn Marter. Ed. by Sheila Hosner. (Dining in Ser.). 200p. (Orig.). 1988. pap. 8.95 o.p. (ISBN 0-89716-202-1). Peanut Butter.

Dining In: Restaurant Guide. Elliott Wolf. Ed. by Sheila Hosner. (Orig.). 1987. pap. 5.95 o.p. (ISBN 0-89716-168-8). Peanut Butter.

Dining with William Shakespeare. Madge Lorwin. 1976. 14.95 o.p. (ISBN 0-689-10731-5, Atheneum). Macmillan.

Dinky Toys & Modelled Miniatures. Mike Richardson & Sue Richardson. (Illus.). 312p. 1983. 39.95 o.s.i. (ISBN 0-904568-33-4, Pub. by New Cavendish England). Schiffer.

Dinner Against the Clock. Madeleine Kamman. LC 72-94248. 1973. 10.00 o.p. (ISBN 0-689-10545-2, Atheneum). Macmillan.

Dinner in the Clouds. Glenn Howe. 1985. text ed. 17.95 o.p. (ISBN 0-918376-03-3, Pub. by Trans-Anglo). Interurban.

Dinner Party. Gretchen Finletter. LC 81-3517. 236p. 1981. pap. 6.95 o.p. (ISBN 0-689-70611-1, 270, Atheneum). Macmillan.

Dinner Party Menus. 1985. (ISBN 0-8249-3048-7). Ideals.

Dinny & the Witches: Two Plays. William Gibson. Bd. with Miracle Worker. LC 60-7778. 1960. 4.50 o.p. (ISBN 0-689-10095-7, Atheneum). Macmillan.

Dinobots Strike Back. Todd Casey. (Transformers Find Your Fate Junior Ser.: No. 1). 80p. (Orig.). (gr. 4 up). 1985. pap. 1.95 o.p. (ISBN 0-345-32669-5). Ballantine.

Dinobots Strike Back. Todd Casey. (Transformers Find Your Fate Junior Ser.: No. 1). 80p. (Orig.). (gr. 4 up). 1986. pap. 2.50 o.p. (ISBN 0-345-34150-3). Ballantine.

Dinosaur & Co. Studies in the Corporate Evolution. Tom Lloyd. 224p. 1984. 19.95x o.p. (ISBN 0-7100-9933-9). Routledge Chapman & Hall.

Dinosaur Days. David C. Knight. LC 77-7917. (Illus.). (ps-3). 1977. text ed. 10.95 o.p. (ISBN 0-07-035101-5). McGraw.

Dinosaur Hunt. George O. Whitaker & Joan Meyers. LC 65-12614. (Illus.). (gr. 5 up). 1965. 5.95 o.p. (ISBN 0-15-223501-9, HJ). HarBraceJ.

Dinosaur World. (Fact Bks). (Illus.). 96p. (gr. 4-7). 1987. pap. 3.50 o.p. (ISBN 0-02-688788-6, Checkerboard Pr). Macmillan.

Dinosaurs. Holsaert. 1979. pap. 3.00 o.s.i. (ISBN 0-03-048956-3). H Holt & Co.

Dinosaurs. 5th ed. W. E. Swinton. (Illus.). 1974. pap. text ed. 2.00x o.p. (ISBN 0-565-00542-1, Pub. by Brit Mus Nat Hist England). Sabbot-Natural Hist Bks.

Dinosaurs. Peter Zallinger. LC 76-24178. (Pictureback Library Editions). (ps-2). 1978. lib. bdg. 5.99 o.s.i. (ISBN 0-394-93485-7, BYR). Random.

Dinosaurs & More Dinosaurs. 2nd ed. M. Jean Craig. LC 68-27276. (Illus.). 96p. (gr. 3-6). 1968. 9.95 o.s.i. (ISBN 0-02-724900-X, Four Winds). Macmillan.

Dinosaurs & Other Prehistoric Animals. Darlene Geis. (Illus.). (gr. 4-6). 1959. 8.95 o.p. (ISBN 0-448-02881-6, G&D). Putnam Pub Group.

Dinosaurs & People: Fossils, Facts & Fantasies. Laurence Pringle. LC 78-52810. (Illus.). (gr. 4-6). 1978. 7.95 o.p. (ISBN 0-15-260501-0, HJ). HarBraceJ.

Dinosaurs & Their World. Laurence Pringle. LC 68-11506. (Illus.). (gr. 4-6). 1968. 8.95 o.p. (ISBN 0-15-223520-5, HJ). HarBraceJ.

Dinosaurs of North Carolina. C. D. Huneycutt. (Illus.). 80p. (Orig.). 1986. pap. 4.80x o.p. (ISBN 0-915153-20-3). Gold Star Pr.

Dinosaurs of the Colorado Plateau, Vol. 54, No. 2 & 3. Edwin Colbert. 48p. 1983. pap. 5.00 o.p. (ISBN 0-686-46250-5). Mus Northern Ariz.

Diode Discontinued Devices. 1987. 70.00 o.p. DATA Busn Pub.

Diodes, Transistors, & Integrated Circuits for Switching Systems. Robert Lyon-Caen. (Electrical Science Ser.). 1968. 93.50 o.p. (ISBN 0-12-460550-8). Acad Pr.

Dion Boucicault, the Shaughraun, Vol. 1. Sven E. Molin & Robin Goodefellowe. 1979. 11.00x o.p. (ISBN 0-912262-62-1); pap. 3.95x o.p. (ISBN 0-912262-63-X). Proscenium.

Dionne: A Novel. Celeste Moll. LC 84-91349. 295p. 1985. 13.95 o.p. (ISBN 0-533-06446-5). Vantage.

Dionne Years: A Thirties Melodrama. Pierre Berton. (Illus.). 1978. 14.95 o.p. (ISBN 0-393-07529-X). Norton.

Diophantine Approximation & Its Applications. Ed. by Charles F. Osgood. 1973. 60.50 o.p. (ISBN 0-12-528650-3). Acad Pr.

Diophantine Equations. L. J. Mordell. (Pure & Applied Mathematics Ser.: Vol. 30). 1969. 82.50 o.p. (ISBN 0-12-506250-8). Acad Pr.

Diphyllobothriasis in Man. Bertel Von Bonsdorff. 1978. 45.50 o.p. (ISBN 0-12-724050-0). Acad Pr.

Diplomacy in a Democracy. Henry M. Wriston. LC 74-7541. 115p. 1974. Repr. of 1956 ed. lib. bdg. 35.00 o.p. (ISBN 0-8371-7580-1, WRDD). Greenwood.

Diplomacy of Economic Development. Eugene R. Black. LC 60-15888. 1963. pap. 1.25 o.p. (ISBN 0-689-70015-6, 34, Atheneum). Macmillan.

Diplomacy of Frustration: The Manchurian Crisis of 1931-1933 As Revealed in the Papers of Stanley K. Hornbeck. Compiled by Justus D. Doenecke. (Publication Ser.: No. 231). 1981. 22.95x o.p. (ISBN 0-8179-7311-7). Hoover Inst Pr.

Diplomacy of the Dollar, 1919-1932. Herbert Feis. 1966. pap. 1.45 o.p. (ISBN 0-393-00333-7, Norton Lib). Norton.

Diplomat World Atlas. Ed. by Hammond Staff. (Illus.). 272p. 24.95 o.p. (ISBN 0-8437-1260-0). Hammond Inc.

Diplomatic History of the Southern Confederacy. James M. Callahan. LC 69-13849. Repr. of 1901 ed. lib. bdg. 35.00x o.p. (ISBN 0-8371-0336-3, CADH). Greenwood.

Diplomatic Practices. Paul M. Kattenburg. (CISE Learning Package Ser.: No. 8). (Illus.). 47p. (Orig.). 1980. pap. text ed. 3.00x o.p. (ISBN 0-936876-24-7). LRIS.

Diplomats & Bureaucrats: The First Institutional Responses to Twentieth-Century Diplomacy in France & Germany. Paul G. Lauren. LC 75-29785. (Publications Ser.: No. 153). (Illus.). 300p. 1976. 13.95x o.p. (ISBN 0-8179-6531-9). Hoover Inst Pr.

Diplomats, Nineteen Nineteen to Nineteen Thirty-Nine, 2 vols. Ed. by Gordon A. Craig & Felix Gilbert. LC 53-6378. 1963. Vol. 1. pap. text ed. 3.45x o.p. (ISBN 0-689-70054-7, 41A, Atheneum); Vol. 2. pap. text ed. 4.95x o.p. (ISBN 0-689-70055-5, 41B). Macmillan.

Diplopia. Robert A. Crone. 488p. 1974. 202.75 o.p. (ISBN 0-444-16000-0, Excerpta Medica). Elsevier.

Dirdir. Jack Vance. 240p. 1983. lib. bdg. 15.95 o.p. (ISBN 0-934438-24-2). Underwood-Miller.

Dire Straits. Philip Kamin. (Robus Bks.). (Illus.). 32p. (Orig.). (gr. 3 up). 1985. pap. 4.95 o.p. (ISBN 0-88188-453-7, HL00183205). H Leonard Pub Corp.

Direccion: Moncloa: An Intermediate Cultural Reader. Jerald R. Green. 1977. pap. 16.50 o.p. (ISBN 0-395-30980-8). HM.

Direct & Alternating Currents. 2nd ed. S. L. Oppenheimer & Borchers. 1973. text ed. 45.95 o.p. (ISBN 0-07-047665-9). McGraw.

Direct Current Circuit Analysis Through Experimentation. 4th ed. Kenneth Fiske & James H. Harter. 240p. 1982. pap. 9.50x o.p. Tech Ed Pr.

Direct Generation of Electricity. Ed. by Kenneth H. Spring. 1966. 76.00 o.p. (ISBN 0-12-659550-X). Acad Pr.

Direct Investment in the United Kingdom by Smaller European Firms. Peter J. Buckley et al. 251p. 1984. 33.00x o.p. (ISBN 0-8448-1457-1, Pub. by Crane Russak & Co). Taylor & Francis.

Direct Mail. Garfield. 1988. 25.90 o.p. (ISBN 0-471-61585-4). Wiley.

Direct Mail Advertising & Selling for Retailers. 19.75 o.p. (ISBN 0-87102-063-7, 60-8664). Natl Ret Merch.

Direct Mail Databook. 4th ed. J. Durlacher. 300p. (Orig.). 1983. pap. text ed. 68.50x o.p. (ISBN 0-566-02386-5). Gower Pub Co.

Direct Marketing: Strategy, Planning, Execution. Edward L. Nash. 1982. text ed. 32.50 o.p. (ISBN 0-07-046019-1). McGraw.

Direct Metal Sculpture: Creative Techniques & Appreciation. Dona Z. Meilach & Donald Seiden. (Arts & Crafts Ser.). (Illus.). 1969. 12.95 o.p. (ISBN 0-517-02448-9). Crown.

Direct Method for Sparse Matrices. O. Osterby & Z. Zlatev. (Lecture Notes in Computer Science Ser.: Vol. 157). 127p. 1983. pap. 11.00 o.p. (ISBN 0-387-12676-7). Springer Verlag.

Direct Payment for Services. Alan A. Richter. 64p. 1984. pap. 5.50 o.p. (ISBN 0-682-40205-2). Exposition-Phoenix.

Direct Reduced Iron: Technology & Economics of Production & Use. 243p. 1980. 62.00 o.p. (ISBN 0-89520-150-X). Iron & Steel.

Direct Teaching Tactics for Exceptional Children: A Practice & Supervision Guide. Joseph J. Stowitschek et al. LC 84-11025. 173p. 1984. 38.00 o.p. (ISBN 0-89443-595-7). Aspen Pub.

Direct Work with Children: Social Work Practice in Family Service Units. Sheila Martel. 95p. 1981. pap. 8.75x o.p. (ISBN 0-7199-1065-X, Pub. by Bedford England). Gower Pub Co.

Directing the Work of Others. (Illus.). 20p. 1972. pap. 1.50 package of ten o.p. (ISBN 0-88441-023-4, 19-981-010). Girl Scouts USA.

Direction: Tacuba: An Introductory Conversational Reader. Jerald R. Green. pap. 10.50 o.p. (ISBN 0-395-30981-6). HM.

Directions. Carla Foehn. (Illus.). (gr. 2-5). 1978. pap. text ed. 6.95 o.p. (ISBN 0-918932-56-4). Activity Resources.

Directions. Jeff MacNelly. (Illus.). 180p. 1984. pap. 6.95 o.p. (ISBN 0-8362-1220-7). Andrews & McMeel.

Directions: A Guide to Career Planning. Thomas D. Bachhuber & Richard K. Harwood. LC 77-78015. (Illus.). 1978. pap. 14.50 o.p. (ISBN 0-395-25385-3). HM.

Directions: A Look at the Paths of Life. Walter R. Scragg. LC 77-78101. (Horizon Ser.). 1977. pap. 5.95 o.p. (ISBN 0-8127-0136-4). Review & Herald.

Directions for World Trade in the Nineteen-Seventies. Guido C. Di Paliano et al. (Triangle Papers: No. 4). 1974. pap. 6.00 o.p. Trilateral Comm.

Directions in Healthcare 1985 to 1987. Healthcare Financial Management Association Staff. 48p. (Orig.). 1985. pap. 15.00 o.p. (ISBN 0-930228-43-X). Healthcare Fin Mgmt Assn.

Directives to Lay Apostles: Eighty-Six Pronouncements. Pope Pius Twelfth. Ed. by Monks of Solesmes Staff. 1964. 4.00 o.s.i. (ISBN 0-8198-0035-X); pap. 3.00 o.s.i. (ISBN 0-8198-0036-8). Dghtrs St Paul.

Director. Henry Denker. 1976. pap. 1.95 o.p. (ISBN 0-380-00669-3, 29355). Avon.

Directories for Small-Scale Hydropower Development. Frederick Frankena. (Public Administration Ser.: P 1693). 11p. 1985. 2.00 o.p. (ISBN 0-89028-423-7). Vance Biblios.

Directorio Turisto-Tourist Directory. rev. ed. OAS, General Secretariat. 50p. (Eng. & Span.). 1980. pap. 3.00 o.p. (ISBN 0-8270-1316-7). OAS.

Directors' & Officers' Liability Insurance 1987. Dan L. Goldwasser et al. (Course Handbook Ser.: No. 3). 422p. 1987. pap. 45.00 o.p. (A4-4187). PLI.

Director's Lawyer & the Company Secretary's Legal Guide. 4th ed. Ewan Mitchell. 645p. 1978. text ed. 51.00x o.p. (ISBN 0-220-66346-7, Pub. by Busn Bks England). Gower Pub Co.

Directors: Myth & Reality. Myles L. Mace. LC 79-168849. (Harvard Business School Publications). 207p. 1971. text ed. 15.95x o.p. (ISBN 0-87584-094-9). Harvard Busn.

Directory. annual 409p. 1980. annual 10.00 o.p. (ISBN 0-309-03066-8). Transport Res Bd.

Directory - American Society of Journalists & Authors, 1987. rev. ed. Ed. by Publications Committee, ASJA Staff. 80p. 1986. pap. 50.00 o.p. (ISBN 0-9612200-4-X). Am Soc Jrnl & Auth.

Directory, American Society of Journalists & Authors. 1986. 1985. pap. 50.00 o.p. (ISBN 0-9612200-3-1). Am Soc Jrnl & Auth.

Directory American Society of Journalist & Authors, 1985: A Listing of Professional Free Lance Writers. 80p. 1984. pap. 50.00 o.p. (ISBN 0-9612200-1-5). Am Soc Jrnl & Auth.

Directory for Exceptional Children. 10th ed. Ed. by Porter Sargent Staff. LC 54-4975. (Special Education Ser.). (Illus.). 1440p. 1984. 40.00 o.s.i. (ISBN 0-87558-110-2). Porter Sargent.

Directory for the Environment: Organisations in Britain & Ireland, 1984-85. Michael J. Barker. 296p. (Orig.). 1984. pap. 19.95x o.p. (ISBN 0-7102-0227-X). Routledge Chapman & Hall.

Directory Information Service. 5th ed. Ed. by Cecilia A. Marlow. 200p. 1988. pap. text ed. 135.00x o.p. (ISBN 0-8103-2510-1). Gale.

Directory of Administrators of Community, Technical & Junior Colleges, 1984. Ed. by Holly Jellison. 1984. pap. 30.00 o.p. (ISBN 0-87117-133-3). Am Assn Comm Jr Coll.

Directory of Agricultural Education & Training Institutions in the Near East Region. 1976. pap. 37.50 o.p. (ISBN 0-685-74968-1, F752, FAO). UNIPUB.

Directory of American Business in Austria, 1977. 7th ed. (Eng. & Ger.). 1978. pap. 30.00 o.s.i. (ISBN 0-685-85948-7). E J Brill USA.

Directory of American Business in Germany. 6th ed. P. G. Baudler. 1976. pap. 36.00 o.s.i. (ISBN 0-685-70788-1). E J Brill USA.

Directory of American Preservation Commissions. National Trust for Historic Preservation Staff. Ed. by Stephen N. Dennis. 132p. (Orig.). 1981. pap. 6.95 o.p. (ISBN 0-89133-100-X). Preservation Pr.

Directory of American Research & Technology, 1988. 22nd ed. Ed. by Bowker, R. R., Staff. 763p. 1987. 199.95 o.p. (ISBN 0-8352-2417-1). Bowker.

Directory of Aquaculturists in the Northeast. Marine Aquaculture Association Staff & Northeast Regional Coastal Information Center Staff. 56p. 1980. pap. 1.00 o.p. (ISBN 0-938412-22-1, P856). Sea Grant Pubns.

Directory of Atomic, Molecular & Optical Scientists. National Research Council. 182p. 1986. pap. text ed. 19.95x o.p. (ISBN 0-309-03696-8). Natl Acad Pr.

Directory of Biomedical & Health Care Grants. Oryx Press Staff. LC 83-5330. 280p. 1985. pap. 74.50 o.p. (ISBN 0-89774-208-7). Oryx Pr.

Directory of British Associations & Associations in Ireland. 8th ed. 1986. 180.00 o.p. (ISBN 0-8002-3573-8). Intl Pubns Serv.

Directory of British Associations & Associations in Ireland. 8th ed. Ed. by G. P. Henderson & S. P. Henderson. 500p. 1986. 140.00x o.p. (ISBN 0-900246-45-6, Pub. by CBD Research Ltd). Gale.

Directory of British Fossiliferous Localities. Palaeontographical Society Staff. Repr. of 1954 ed. 18.00 o.p. (ISBN 0-384-44550-0). Johnson Repr.

Directory of British Official Publications: A Guide to Sources. 2nd ed. Stephen Richard. LC 84-12559. 468p. 1984. 60.00x o.p. (ISBN 0-7201-1706-2). Mansell.

Directory of Building Research, Information & Development Organizations. 4th ed. International Council for Building Research Studies & Documentation Staff. 215p. 1981. pap. 42.00x o.p. (ISBN 0-419-12550-7, NO.6637, Pub by E&FN Spon England). Routledge Chapman & Hall.

Directory of Catholic Charities, 1986-1987: Agencies and Institutions. 110p. 1987. 10.00 o.p. (ISBN 0-318-15956-2). Catholic Charities.

Directory of Colleges & Universities Granting Degrees in Microbiology, 1980. American Society for Microbiology, Education & Training Board Staff. 1980. 5.00 o.p. (ISBN 0-686-95711-3). Am Soc Microbio.

Directory of Convenience Stores 1985. rev ed. LC 82-640890. (Illus.). 125.00 o.p. (ISBN 0-911790-46-2). Prog Grocers Trade.

Directory of Corporate Affiliations. National Register Publishing Co. Staff. LC 67-22770. 1300p. 1985. 528.00 o.p. (ISBN 0-87217-051-9). Natl Register.

Directory of Day Schools in the United States & Canada. (Illus.). 7.00 o.p. (ISBN 0-317-53893-4). Torah Umesorah.

Directory of Directories. 5th ed. Ed. by Cecilia A. Marlow. 2200p. 1987. 195.00x o.p. (ISBN 0-8103-2508-X). Gale.

Directory of Distinguished Americans. 3rd ed. Ed. by J. M. Evans. LC 81-71699. 500p. 1985. 55.00 o.p. (ISBN 0-934544-36-0). Am Biog Inst.

Directory of Editorial Resources, 1987-88. Ed. by Betsy Colgan & Eleanor Johnson. 1987. pap. 9.50 o.p. (ISBN 0-935012-09-5). Edit Experts.

Directory of Educational Documentation & Information Services. 76p. 1979. pap. 5.00 o.p. (U1245, UNESCO). UNIPUB.

Directory of Educational Software in Nursing, 1987. Christine Bolwell. 330p. (Orig.). 1987. pap. 29.95 o.p. (ISBN 0-88737-358-5, 41-2167). Natl League Nurse.

Directory of Engineering Firms Engaged in Resource Recovery & Solid Waste Management. 55p. 1979. 5.00 o.p. (ISBN 0-317-32500-0). Am Consul Eng.

Directory of Engineering Societies & Related Organizations. 12th ed. Gordon Davis. 300p. (Orig.). 1987. pap. 105.00 o.p. (ISBN 0-87615-004-0). AAES.

Directory of European Associations: National Industrial, Trade & Professional Associations, Pt. 1, Vol. 1. 3rd ed. Ed. by I. G. Anderson. 500p. 1981. 195.00x o.p. (ISBN 0-900246-35-9, Pub. by CBD Research Ltd.). Gale.

Directory of European Associations: National Learned, Scientific & Technical Societies, Pt. 2. 3nd ed. Ed. by I. G. Anderson. LC 76-11697. 1979. 135.00x o.p. (Pub. by CBD Research). Gale.

Directory of Executive Recruiters. 16th ed. Ed. by James H. Kennedy. LC 73-642226. 1985. pap. 21.00 o.p. (ISBN 0-916654-38-9). Consultants News.

Directory of Expert Witnesses in Technology. 500p. 1985. 95.00 o.p. (ISBN 0-89235-085-7). Res Pubns CT.

Directory of Financing Sources for Buyouts & Acquisitions. 5th ed. 390p. 1988. 95.00 o.p. Venture Econ Inc.

Directory of Florida Industries, 1986-87. Date not set. 49.95 o.s.i. (ISBN 0-318-22289-2). Trend Bk Div.

Directory of Geoscience Departments. 25th ed. Ed. by Nicholas H. Claudy. 240p. (Orig.). 1986. pap. 18.95 o.p. (ISBN 0-913312-86-X). Am Geol.

Directory of Geoscience Departments. 26th ed. Ed. by Nicholas H. Claudy. 240p. (Orig.). 1987. pap. 18.95 o.p. (ISBN 0-913312-90-8). Am Geol.

Directory of Government Document Collections & Librarians. Ed. by Nancy Klein & Jaia Heymann. 544p. 1978. 22.50 o.p. (ISBN 0-912380-49-7); members 17.50x o.p. ALA.

Directory of Graduate Medical Education Programs. 679p. 1987. pap. 30.00 o.p. (ISBN 0-89970-237-6, OP-167-7). AMA.

Directory of Graduate Physical Education Programs 1982. 80p. 3.95 o.p. (ISBN 0-88314-058-6). AAHPERD.

Directory of Hospital Psychosocial Policies & Programs. 110p. 1982. 12.00 o.p. (ISBN 0-318-17756-0); members 8.00 o.p. (ISBN 0-318-17757-9). Assn Care Child.

Directory of Hydrogen Energy Products & Services, 1980-1981. IAHO Staff. 32p. 1981. pap. 12.00 o.p. (ISBN 0-08-027326-2). Pergamon.

Directory of Independent Workers' Clinics. Laurence M. Naviasky. 36p. 1986. pap. 4.95x o.p. (ISBN 0-918780-33-0). INFORM.

Directory of Institutions & Individuals Active in Environmentally-Sound & Appropriate Technologies. United Nations Environment Programme Staff. 1979. 36.00 o.p. (ISBN 0-08-025658-9). Pergamon.

Directory of Institutions in the Federal Republic of Germany Co-operating with Developing Countries in Science & Technology. Ed. by Gottstein Research Unit Staff & Planck, Max, Society Staff. 340p. 1987. lib. bdg. 20.00 o.p. (ISBN 3-598-10626-2). K G Saur.

Directory of International Consumer Goods Industries-1986. Ministry of Light Industry, Scientific & Technical Information Institute Staff. 306p. (Orig.). 1986. pap. text ed. 24.95 o.p. (ISBN 0-8351-1752-9). China Bks.

Directory of Leading Private Companies. National Register Publishing Co. Staff. 1986. 327.00 o.p. (ISBN 0-87217-073-X). Natl Register.

Directory of Legislative Leaders, 1987-88. The National Conference of State Legislatures Staff. 112p. 1987. pap. 10.00 o.p. (ISBN 1-55516-724-1). Natl Conf State Legis.

Directory of Library & Information Professionals Vol. 1 Listings Vol. 2 Indexes. 1988. lib. bdg. 345.00 o.p. (ISBN 0-89235-125-X). Res Pubns CT.

Directory of Literary Magazines, 1987. Coordinating Council of Literary Magazines Staff. 128p. 1987. pap. 6.95 o.p. (ISBN 0-942332-10-5, Dist. by Kampmann & Co.). Moyer Bell Limited.

Directory of Manufacturers of Vacuum Plant, Components & Associated Equipment in the U. K., 1982. Ed. by J. S. Colligon. 56p. 1982. pap. 14.50 o.p. (ISBN 0-08-029323-9, C145, A145). Pergamon.

Directory of Medical Schools Worldwide. 3rd ed. Ed. by Stanley Alperin. LC 77-93356. 1982. text ed. 24.95 o.p. (ISBN 0-916524-17-5). US Direct Serv.

Directory of Medical Specialists, 3 vols. 22nd, rev. ed. 5000p. 1985. Set. 265.00x o.s.i. (ISBN 0-8379-0522-2). Marquis.

Directory of Multihospital Systems, 1985. 100p. (Orig.). 1985. 49.95 o.p. (ISBN 0-939450-42-9, 103155). Am Hospital.

Directory of Music Companies: United States & Foreign. J. W. Worrel. pap. 4.95 o.p. (ISBN 0-686-15898-9). Instrumental Co.

Directory of National Institutions of Educational Planning & Administration in Asia & the Pacific. UNESCO, Regional Office for Education in Asia & the Pacific Staff. 72p. 1985. pap. 7.50 o.p. (UB175 5111, UNESCO). UNIPUB.

Directory of Nature Centers & Related Environmental Education Facilities, 1979. Ed. by Oki Kitazono. (Illus.). 1979. pap. 6.95 o.p. (ISBN 0-930698-08-8). Natl Audubon.

Directory of NCTM Individual Members, 1987. National Council of Teachers of Mathematics Staff. 434p. (Orig.). 1987. pap. 25.00 o.p. (ISBN 0-87353-248-1). NCTM.

Directory of North American Fisheries Scientists. Ed. by Mary J. Lewis. 450p. 1984. pap. 30.00 o.p. (ISBN 0-913235-18-0); members 25.00 o.p. Am Fisheries Soc.

Directory of Nuclear Power Reactors. Incl. Vol. 1. Power Reactors. (Superseded by Vol. 4, ISP397-1). UNIPUB; Vol. 2. Research, Test & Experimental Reactors. pap. 11.25 (ISBN 92-0-152159-6, ISP397-2). UNIPUB; Vol. 3. Research, Test & Experimental Reactors. pap. 13.00 (ISP397-3); pap. 13.75 (ISBN 92-0-152060-3, ISP379-3SUPP). UNIPUB; Vol. 4. Power Reactors. (Replaces Vol. 1). pap. 13.75 (ISBN 92-0-152062-X, ISP397-4). UNIPUB; Vol. 5. Research, Test & Experimental Reactors. pap. 16.00 (ISBN 92-0-152064-6, ISP397-5). UNIPUB; Vol. 6. Research, Test & Experimental Reactors. pap. 13.50 o.p. (ISBN 92-0-152066-2, ISP397-6). UNIPUB; Vol. 7. Power Reactors. pap. 21.00 (ISBN 92-0-152067-0, ISP397-7). UNIPUB; Vol. 8. Research, Test & Experimental Reactors. pap. 17.75 (ISBN 92-0-152170-7, ISP397-8). UNIPUB; Vol. 9. Power Reactors. pap. 17.75 (ISBN 92-0-152171-5, ISP397-9). UNIPUB; Vol. 10. Power & Research Reactors. 402p. 1976. pap. 41.75 (ISBN 92-0-152076-X, ISP397-10). UNIPUB. IAEA). UNIPUB.

Directory of Overseas Summer Jobs 1985. Ed. by David Woodworth. 176p. 1984. pap. 8.95 o.p. (ISBN 0-907638-30-9, 3034, Pub. by Vacation Work Pub). Writers Digest.

Directory of Overseas Summer Jobs 1987. Ed. by David Woodworth. 192p. (Orig.). 1987. pap. 8.95 o.p. (ISBN 0-907638-65-1, Pub. by Vacation-Work England). Writers Digest.

Directory of Overseas Summer Jobs 1988. Ed. by David Woodworth. 192p. (Orig.). 1987. pap. 9.95 o.p. (ISBN 0-907638-79-1, Pub. by Vacation-Work England). Writers Digest.

Directory of Periodicals Online: Indexed, Abstracted & Full-Text News, Law & Business, Vol. 1. 524p. 1986. softcover 125.00 o.p. (ISBN 0-317-52868-8, Pub. by Federal Document Retrieval, Inc.). Learned Info.

Directory of Personal Image Consultants 1986-1987. 6th rev. ed. Ed. by Jacqueline Thompson & Image Industry Publications Staff. 160p. pap. 25.00 biennial o.p. (ISBN 0-318-14465-4). Image Industry.

Directory of Postsecondary Institutions, 1986: Four-Year & Two-Year, Vol. 1. Martin M. Franket. (Education Department Publication CS 87-314-1). 284p. 1987. pap. 13.00 o.p. (ISBN 0-318-22634-0, S/N 065-000-00280-9). USGPO.

Directory of Professional Workers in State Agriculture Experiment Stations & Other Cooperating State Institutions, 1986-1987. (Agriculture Handbook Ser.: No. 305). 247p. 1987. pap. 12.00 o.p. (ISBN 0-318-22631-6, S/N 001-000-04490-7). USGPO.

Directory of Public High Technology & Medical Corporations, 1988, 2 vols. 5th ed. Ed. by Ronald P. Smolin. 1100p. (Orig.). 1988. pap. text ed. 195.00x o.p. (ISBN 0-89563-815-0). Trans-Atl Phila.

Directory of Radio Collectors & Suppliers: Including Phonograph & TV Collectors. 8th ed. ARS Enterprises Editors. (Orig.). 1982. pap. 4.00 o.p. (ISBN 0-938630-02-4, P-1). ARS Enterprises.

Directory of Religious Bodies in the United States. James G. Melton & James V. Geisendorfer. (Reference Library of the Humanities: Vol. 91). (LC 76-052700). 1977. lib. bdg. 40.00 o.p. (ISBN 0-8240-9882-X). Garland Pub.

Directory of Research Grants 1986. Ed. by Oryx Press Staff. LC 76-47074. 760p. 1985. pap. 95.00 o.p. (ISBN 0-89774-207-9). Oryx Pr.

Directory of Scientific Directories: A World Guide to Scientific Directories Including Medicine, Agriculture, Engineering, Manufacturing, & Industrial Directories. 4th ed. Ed. by J. Burkett. LC 79-40288. 650p. 115.00x o.s.i. (ISBN 0-582-90151-0, Pub. by Longman). Gale.

Directory of Security Personnel in Financial Institutions 1984. 143p. 1987. 36.00 o.p. (ISBN 0-317-36470-7, 2314). Bank Admin Inst.

Directory of Selected Scientific Institutions in Mainland China. Ed. by Ralph J. Watkins. LC 76-138410. (Publications Ser.: No. 96). 1971. 19.50x o.p. (ISBN 0-8179-1961-9). Hoover Inst Pr.

Directory of Software Publishers: How & Where to Sell Your Program. Eric Balkan. 320p. 1983. 29.95 o.p. (ISBN 0-442-21429-4). Van Nos Reinhold.

Directory of Special Libraries & Information Centers, 2 pts. 11th ed. Ed. by Brigitte T. Darnay. 1987. Special Libraries & Information Centers in the United States & Canada. Vol. 1, 1850 pgs 350.00x o.p.; Geographic & Personnel Indexes. Vol. II, 950pgs 290.00x o.p. Gale.

Directory of Special Libraries & Information Centers, 2 vols. 11th ed. Ed. by Brigitte T. Darnay. 1968p. 1987. Vol. 1: Special Libraries & Information Centers in the United States & Canada, 2 pts., 1850 pgs. 350.00x o.p. (ISBN 0-8103-2696-5); Vol. 2: Geographical & Regional Indexes, 950 pgs. 290.00x o.p. (ISBN 0-8103-2697-3). Gale.

Directory of State & Local Judges. National College of the State Judiciary Staff. (Series 175). 1975. 7.50 o.p. (ISBN 0-686-00406-X). Natl Judicial Coll.

Directory of the Cornell Southeast Asia Program: 1951-1976. Ed. by Frank H. Golay & Peggy Lush. 88p. 1976. 3.00 o.p. (ISBN 0-87727-103-8, DP 103). Cornell SE Asia.

Directory of the Geologic Division, U. S. Geological Survey. American Geological Institute Staff. (Illus.). 144p. 1980. pap. 10.00 o.p. (ISBN 0-913312-45-2). Am Geol.

Directory of the Professional Organizations Set Up at Community Level. 818p. pap. 100.00 o.p. (ISBN 2-8029-0025-0, ED14, ED). UNIPUB.

Directory of the World's Capital Ships. Paul H. Silverstone. (Illus.). 496p. 1985. 70.00 o.p. (ISBN 0-88254-979-0). Hippocrene Bks.

Directory of Tourism Education Programs: Guide to Programs in Aviation, Hospitality & Tourism. Ed. by Lloyd E. Hudman. 116p. (Orig.). 1981. pap. 6.50 o.p. (ISBN 0-916032-11-6). Delmar.

Directory of Undergraduate Internships in the Humanities. Washington Center Staff. 138p. 1984. pap. 12.50x o.p. (ISBN 0-87352-137-4). Modern Lang.

Directory of Unit Trust Management. Ed. by Desmond Corner. 1986. 75.00 o.p. (ISBN 0-912289-56-2). St James Pr.

Directory of United States Adult & Continuing Postsecondary Education. J. M. De La Croix & Carole Copeland. (Illus.). 146p. 1987. pap. 30.00 o.p. (ISBN 0-939893-08-8). Elite Assocs.

Directory of U. S. College & University Programs in Environmental Studies & Natural Resources Management. Rev. ed. Ed. by Sierra Club International Earthcare Center Staff. 154p. 1983. pap. text ed. 24.95 o.p. (ISBN 0-89059-027-3, UPB125, UPB). UNIPUB.

Directory of U. S. Labor Organizations, 1986-87. Courtney D. Gifford. 1986. pap. text ed. 17.50 o.p. (ISBN 0-87179-531-0, 0531). BNA.

Directory of United States Postsecondary Education: Directory of American Colleges & Universities Legally Empowered to Grant Academic Degrees (The Best & Worst American Colleges & Universities) J. M. De La Croix & Carole Copeland. 136p. 1987. pap. 28.00 o.p. (ISBN 0-939893-06-1). Elite Assocs.

Directory of Urban Forestry Professionals. 2.50 o.p. (ISBN 0-317-59266-1). Am Forestry.

Directory of Vocational Education Personnel (1985-1986) Compiled by Wesley Budke. 195p. cancelled o.s.i. (ISBN 0-318-22077-6, SN43). Natl Ctr Res Voc Ed.

Directory of Western European Specialists in North American Libraries. 20p. 1984. 5.00 o.p. (ISBN 0-8389-6762-0). Assn Coll & Res Libs.

Directory of Women Religious in the United States. Ed. by Magdalen O'Hara. LC 85-47752. 1985. 65.00 o.p. (ISBN 0-89453-528-5). M Glazier.

Directory of Workers' Education Institutions & Programmes in Developing Countries. International Labour Office. 142p. (Orig.). pap. 19.25 o.p. (ISBN 92-2-002208-7). Intl Labour Office.

Directory: State Library Agencies, Consultants, & Adminstrative Staff 1985. Compiled by Association of Specialized & Cooperative Library Agencies, Headquaters Staff. 32p. 1985. pap. 5.00x o.p. (ISBN 0-8389-6919-4). ALA.

Dirk's Wooden Shoes. Ilona Fennema & Georgette Apol. LC 75-11785. (Illus.). (gr. k-3). 1970. 4.95 o.p. (ISBN 0-15-223567-1, HJ). HarBraceJ.

Dirt Bike Racing. D. J. Herda. Ed. by Madelyn K. Anderson. LC 82-60637. (Illus.). 96p. (gr. 4-6). 1982. lib. bdg. 9.29 o.p. (ISBN 0-671-44249-X). Messner.

Dirty Boy. Bob Kavet. LC 74-128820. (Illus.). (gr. k-3). 1971. pap. 3.95g o.p. (ISBN 0-87614-023-1). Carolrhoda Bks.

Dirty Feet. Steven Kroll. LC 80-17570. (Illus.). 48p. (ps-3). 1981. 5.95 o.s.i. (ISBN 0-8193-1035-2); PLB 5.95 o.s.i. (ISBN 0-8193-1036-0). Parents.

Dirty Hand: The Literary Notebooks of Winfield Townley Scott. Winfield T. Scott. 175p. 1969. 11.95x o.p. (ISBN 0-292-78416-3). U of Tex Pr.

Dirty Money: The Global Financiers of Violence, Revolution, & Crime. Larry Gurwin. 320p. 1988. 19.45 o.p. (ISBN 0-8129-1590-9). Times Bks.

Dirty Tricks: Or Nick Noxin's Natural Nobility. John Seelye. 152p. 1974. 5.95 o.p. (ISBN 0-87140-577-6). Liveright.

Dis Others Picpkt G1. Cherrholmes. Date not set. (ISBN 0-07-011918-X). McGraw.

Disability & the Labor Market: Economic Problems, Policies & Programs. Ed. by Monroe Berkowitz & M. Anne Hill. 336p. 1986. 34.00 o.p. (ISBN 0-87546-125-5). ILR Pr.

Disability in Adolescence. Elizabeth M. Anderson & Lynda Clarke. 400p. 1982. 35.00 o.p. (ISBN 0-416-72730-1, 3766); pap. 14.95 o.p. (ISBN 0-416-72740-9, 3767). Routledge Chapman & Hall.

Disability Income & Health Insurance. Ed. by Price Gaines. 255p. 1987. pap. 20.50 o.p. (ISBN 0-87218-056-5). Natl Underwriter.

Disability Income Insurance: The Unique Risks. Charles E. Soule. LC 83-72623. 238p. 1984. 25.00 o.p. (ISBN 0-87094-473-8). Dow Jones-Irwin.

Disability Insurance: In the Business Buy-Out Agreement. William Harmelin. 18.00 o.p. (ISBN 0-686-31054-3, 29350). Rough Notes.

Disability Separation. (DA Pam Ser.: No. 360-506). 36p. (Orig.). 1987. pap. 1.75 o.p. (S/N 008-001-00151-7). USGPO.

Disability, Theatre & Education. Richard Tomlinson. LC 83-49406. (Human Horizons Ser.). (Illus.). 200p. (Orig.). 1984. 17.50x o.p. (ISBN 0-253-31779-7); pap. 8.95x o.p. (ISBN 0-253-21254-5). Ind U Pr.

Disabled Child in the Library. Linda Lucas & Marilyn H. Karrenbrock. LC 83-1035. 288p. 1983. lib. bdg. 22.50 o.p. (ISBN 0-87287-355-2). Libs Unl.

Disabled Schoolchild: A Study of Integration in Primary Schools. Elizabeth M. Anderson. 377p. 1973. pap. 14.95x o.p. (ISBN 0-416-78190-X, NO.2062). Routledge Chapman & Hall.

Disabled We Stand. Allan T. Sutherland. LC 83-49408. 160p. 1984. 12.95x o.p. (ISBN 0-253-31780-0); pap. 6.95x o.p. (ISBN 0-253-21255-3). Ind U Pr.

Disadvantaged Child: Issues & Innovations. 2nd ed. Joe L. Frost & Glenn R. Hawkes. LC 70-16422. (Illus., Orig.). 1972. pap. 20.95 o.p. (ISBN 0-395-04475-8). HM.

Disadvantaged Children: Health, Nutrition, & School Failure. Herbert G. Birch & Joan D. Gussow. LC 78-102443. 1970. 10.00 o.p. (ISBN 0-15-125725-6). HarBraceJ.

Disadvantaged Early Adolescent. Helen F. Storen. 1968. pap. text ed. 4.95 o.p. (ISBN 0-07-061750-3). McGraw.

Disaffection from School. Ken Reid. 230p. 1986. 29.95 o.p. (ISBN 0-423-51540-3, 9996). Routledge Chapman & Hall.

Disaggregated Farm Income by Type of Farm, 1959-82. Agapi Somwaru. (Agricultural Economic Report 558). (Illus.). 117p. (Orig.). 1986. pap. 5.50 o.p. (ISBN 0-318-21616-7, S/N 001-019-00469-0). USGPO.

Disappearance of Odile. Georges Simenon. LC 72-75422. (Helen & Kurt Wolff Bk.). 1972. 6.95 o.p. (ISBN 0-15-125720-5). HarBraceJ.

Disappearances. William Wiser. LC 79-55616. 1980. 11.95 o.p. (ISBN 0-689-11062-6, Atheneum). Macmillan.

Disarmament. L. Henkin. LC 63-19588. (Hammarskjold Forum: No. 4). 112p. 1964. pap. 10.00 o.p. (ISBN 0-379-11804-1). Oceana.

Disarmament: A Periodic Review by the United Nations, Vol. V, No. 1. United Nations Staff. 1982. 5.00 o.p. (ISBN 0-686-84895-0, E.82.IX.5). UN.

Disarmament: A World View. Jerome Davis. (Orig.). 1964. 3.95 o.p. (ISBN 0-8065-0171-5, Pub. by Citadel Pr). Carol Pub Group.

Disarmament & Colonial Freedom. Nikita S. Khrushchev. LC 74-31868. (Illus.). 299p. 1975. Repr. of 1960 ed. lib. bdg. 35.00x o.p. (ISBN 0-8371-7945-9, KHDI). Greenwood.

Disarmament & Development: Declaration by the Panel of Eminent Personalities, New York April 16-18, 1986. 11p. 1986. pap. 3.00 o.p. (ISBN 92-1-142119-5, E.86.IX.5). UN.

Disarmament & the Economy. R. Farmazyan. 172p. 1981. 5.80 o.p. (ISBN 0-8285-2098-4, Pub. by Progress Pubs USSR). Imported Pubns.

Disarmament & World Development. Ed. by Richard Jolly. 1978. text ed. 31.00 o.p. (ISBN 0-08-023019-9); pap. text ed. 10.25 o.p. (ISBN 0-08-023018-0). Pergamon.

Disarmament: The Human Factor: Proceedings of a Colloquim on the Societal Context for Diasarmament. Ed. by Ervin Laszlo & Donald Keys. 200p. 1981. 34.00 o.p. (ISBN 0-08-024703-2); pap. 17.25 o.p. (ISBN 0-08-028129-X). Pergamon.

Disarmament: Who's Against? 63p. 1983. pap. 1.50 o.p. (ISBN 0-8285-3056-4, Pub. by Military Pubs USSR). Imported Pubns.

Disaster & Deliverance. Larry Armstrong. LC 79-88400. 1979. pap. 3.75 o.p. (ISBN 0-933350-22-8). Morse Pr.

Disaster at Sea. J. Marriott. (Illus.). 176p. 1987. 25.00 o.s.i. (ISBN 0-87052-450-X). Hippocrene Bks.

Disaster Beliefs & Emergency Planning. Charles E. Faupel et al. 259p. 1985. pap. text ed. 12.95x o.p. (ISBN 0-8290-1530-2). Irvington.

Disaster Detectives. Louis Wolfe. LC 81-4939. (Illus.). 160p. (gr. 7 up). 1981. lib. bdg. 9.79 o.s.i. (ISBN 0-671-34042-5). Messner.

Disaster Planning for Local Government. Roger E. Herman. LC 81-16178. 1982. 20.00x o.p. (ISBN 0-87663-378-5, Pica Spec Stud). Universe.

Disaster Preparedness: A Family Protection Handbook. J. R. Christiansen et al. LC 84-81385. 184p. 1985. 13.95 o.p. (ISBN 0-88290-254-7). Horizon Utah.

Disaster Survival Handbook. Alton L. Thygerson. LC 79-4242. (Illus.). 1979. pap. 1.00 o.p. (ISBN 0-8425-1629-8). Brigham.

Disasters & the Small Dwelling. Ed. by I. Davis. 220p. 1981. 42.00 o.p. (ISBN 0-08-024753-9). Pergamon.

Disasters: Hospital Planning. P. E. Savage. 1979. 40.00 o.p. (ISBN 0-08-024914-0); pap. 50.00 o.p. (ISBN 0-08-024913-2). Pergamon.

Disasters: Medical Organization. Ed. by Jan De Boer & Thomas W. Baillie. (Illus.). 112p. 1980. 24.00 o.p. (ISBN 0-08-025491-8). Pergamon.

Disastrous Hurricanes & Tornadoes. Max Alth & Charlotte Alth. LC 81-7544. (First Bks.). (Illus.). 72p. (gr. 4 up). 1981. lib. bdg. 10.40 o.p. (ISBN 0-531-04327-4). Watts.

Disastrous Volcanoes. Melvin Berger. LC 81-2995. (First Bks.). (Illus.). 72p. (gr. 4 up). 1981. lib. bdg. 10.40 o.p. (ISBN 0-531-04329-0). Watts.

Discernment E politica see Spiritual Discernment & Politics: Guidelines for Religious Communities.

Discernment of Spirits: According to the Life & Teachings of St. Ignatius Loyola van Heel. Piet Penning De Vries. LC 72-90063. 1973. 8.00 o.p. (ISBN 0-682-47592-0). Exposition-Phoenix.

Discharge of Selected Rivers of the World. Incl. Vol. 1. General & Regime Characteristics of Stations Selected. 70p. 1969. pap. 9.25 (ISBN 92-3-001164-9, U165). UNIPUB; Vol. 2. Monthly & Annual Discharges Recorded at Various Selected Stations (From Start of Observations up to 1964) 194p. 1971. pap. 12.50 (ISBN 92-3-000847-8, U166). UNIPUB; Vol. 3, Pt. 1. Mean Monthly & Extreme Discharges (1965-1969) 98p. 1971. pap. o.p. (ISBN 92-3-000919-9, U167). UNIPUB; Vol. 3, Pt. 2. Mean Monthly & Extreme Discharges (1969-1972) 214p. 1974. pap. 13.25 (ISBN 92-3-001178-9, U168). UNIPUB; Vol. 3, Pt. 3. Mean Monthly & Extreme Discharges (1972-1975) 123p. 1979. pap. 9.25 (ISBN 92-3-001569-5, U916). UNIPUB. (Studies & Reports in Hydrology: No. 5). (Orig., Eng., Fr., Span. & Rus., UNESCO). UNIPUB.

Discharges in Electronegative Gases. Ed. by K. G. Emelus & G. A. Woolsey. 162p. cancelled o.s.i. (ISBN 0-85066-035-1). Taylor & Francis.

Disciple's Profile of Jesus. William R. Cannon. LC 75-2956. 1975. 2.95x o.p. (ISBN 0-8358-0322-8). Upper Room.

Discipleship in the New Testament. Ed. by Fernando F. Segovia. LC 85-47730. 240p. 1985. pap. 16.95 o.p. (ISBN 0-8006-1873-4, 1-1873, Fortress). Augsburg Fortress.

Discipleship: The Price & the Prize. Jack Mayhall. 156p. 1984. pap. 6.50 o.p. (ISBN 0-88207-110-6). Victor Bks.

Disciplinary Policies & Practices see Issues in the Public Employee Relations Library: Series 5.

Discipline. Mary Brunton. (Mothers of the Nove Reprint Ser.). 470p. 1986. pap. 8.95 o.p. (ISBN 0-86358-105-6, 81056, Pandora Pr). Routledge Chapman & Hall.

Discipline & Behavioral Management: A Handbook of Tactics, Strategies & Programs. David Sabatino & Lester Mann. LC 82-24427. 394p. 1983. 35.00 o.p. (ISBN 0-89443-933-2). Aspen Pub.

Discipline & Classroom Management. D. Keith Osborn & Janie D. Osborn. LC 77-76198. (Illus.). 1977. pap. 4.95 o.p. (ISBN 0-918772-03-6); pap. text ed. write for info. o.p. (ISBN 0-918772-02-8). Daye Pr.

Discipline or Disaster: Management's Only Choice. Paul M. Magoon & John B. Richards. 1966. 12.50 o.s.i. (ISBN 0-682-44029-9, Banner). Exposition-Phoenix.

Discipline: Policies & Procedures. James R. Redeker. 280p. 1983. text ed. 30.00 o.p. (ISBN 0-87179-394-6, 0394); pap. text ed. 20.00 o.p. (ISBN 0-87179-399-7, 0399). BNA.

Discipline That Can't Fail. Arnold H. Burron. 1986. pap. 4.95 o.p. (ISBN 0-8010-0940-5). Baker Bk.

Disciplines of the Beautiful Woman. Gift ed. Anne Ortland. 131p. 1986. Repr. 9.95 o.p. (ISBN 0-8499-0551-6). Word Bks.

Disciplines of War: Memories of the War of 1914-18. J. E. Levyns. 1984. 12.95 o.p. (ISBN 0-533-06021-4). Vantage.

Discipling for Jesus. Lawrence Wiseman. LC 83-70959. 1983. pap. 4.95 o.s.i. (ISBN 0-89900-199-8). College Pr Pub.

Discjockies Good Dance Guide. Willie Mann. 64p. pap. 3.95 o.p. (ISBN 0-682-40204-4). Exposition-Phoenix.

Disclosing the Past: An Autobiography. Mary Leakey. LC 84-10189. 256p. 1984. 15.95 o.p. (ISBN 0-385-18961-3). Doubleday.

Disclosing the Past: An Autobiography. Mary Leakey. (Large Print Books (General Ser.)). 1985. lib. bdg. 18.95 o.p. (ISBN 0-8161-3913-X). G K Hall.

Disclosures of Inflation Accounting Information. (Financial Report Survey Ser.: No. 23). 1982. pap. 30.00 o.p. (ISBN 0-686-84295-2). Am Inst CPA.

Disco Dancing. Joetta Cherry & Gwynne Tomlin. LC 79-51213. (Illus.). (gr. 2 up). 1979. PLB 3.79 o.p. (ISBN 0-448-13613-9, G&D); pap. 3.95 o.p. (ISBN 0-448-16562-7). Putnam Pub Group.

Discontented Mother. Ben Shecter. LC 80-14435. (Illus.). 32p. (gr. k-3). 1980. 6.95 o.p. (ISBN 0-15-223574-4, HJ). HarBraceJ.

Discord, Dialogue, & Concord: Studies in the Lutheran Reformation's Formula of Concord. Ed. by Lewis W. Spitz & Wenzel Lohff. LC 77-78644. 224p. 1977. 5.00 o.p. (ISBN 0-8006-0511-X, 1-511, Fortress). Augsburg Fortress.

Discord in the Pacific: Challenges to the Japanese-American Alliance. Ed. by Henry Rosovsky. LC 72-93017. pap. 3.00 o.p. (ISBN 0-910416-16-8). Am Assembly.

Discounted Cash Flow. Learning Systems Ltd. 1967. pap. 8.50 flexi-cover o.p. (ISBN 0-08-014026-2). Pergamon.

Discounting Hospital Services: Some Arithmetic. Daniel B. Hill. 20p. 1985. pap. 5.00 tchr's. ed. o.p. (ISBN 0-930228-42-1). Healthcare Fin Mgmt Assn.

Discours de la Religion des Anciens Romains Illustre. Guillaume Du Choul. LC 75-27851. (Renaissance & the Gods Ser.: Vol. 9). (Illus.). 1976. Repr. of 1556 ed. lib. bdg. 88.00 o.p. (ISBN 0-8240-2058-8). Garland Pub.

Discourse Analysis in Second Language Research. Ed. by Diane Larsen-Freeman. 200p. (Orig.). 1980. pap. text ed. 16.00 o.p. (ISBN 0-88377-163-2). Newbury Hse.

Discourse & Learning. Ed. by Philip Riley & C. N. Candlin. 389p. (Orig.). 1986. pap. 14.95x o.p. (ISBN 0-582-55374-1). Longman.

Discourse on Method: Meditations on a First Philosophy, & Principles of Philosophy. Rene Descartes. 1975. 14.95x o.p. (ISBN 0-460-00570-7, Evman); pap. 3.50x o.p. (ISBN 0-460-01570-2, Evman). Biblio Dist.

Discourse on the Grounds & Reasons of the Christian Religion. Anthony Collins. Ed. by Rene Wellek. LC 75-11212. (British Philosophers & Theologians of the 17th & 18th Centuries: Vol. 15). 1976. Repr. of 1724 ed. lib. bdg. 51.00 o.p. (ISBN 0-8240-1766-8). Garland Pub.

Discourses, 2 vols. Niccolo Machiavelli. Tr. by Leslie J. Walker. 1975. Set. 45.00x o.p. (ISBN 0-7100-8076-X); 24.50x ea. o.p. Routledge Chapman & Hall.

Discourses on War. William E. Channing. LC 77-149545. (Library of War & Peace; Relig. & Ethical Positions on War). 1972. lib. bdg. 46.00 o.p. (ISBN 0-8240-0508-2). Garland Pub.

Discover Brunch: A New Way of Entertaining. Ruth Macpherson. LC 76-30683. (Illus.). 160p. 1977. spiral bdg. 8.95 o.p. (ISBN 0-8437-2110-3). Hammond Inc.

Discover Dayton. (Everything Bks.). 128p. 1983. pap. 2.98 o.p. (ISBN 0-913428-77-9). Landfall Pr.

Discover FORTH: Learning & Programming the FORTH Language. Thom Hogan. 146p. 1982. pap. text ed. 19.95 o.p. (ISBN 0-07-931079-6, 79-9). Osborne McGraw.

Discover France: A Travellers' Guide. British Automobile Association Staff. 144p. (Orig.). 1984. pap. 14.95 o.p. (ISBN 0-86145-176-7, Pub. by Automobile Assn Brit). Salem Hse Pubs.

Discover Self-Love. Robert H. Schuller. (Orig.). 1978. pap. 1.25 o.p. (ISBN 0-89081-134-2). Harvest Hse.

Discover the Wines You Don't Know. 1988. 2.00 o.p. (111). Am Bartenders.

Discover Your Fountain of Health. N. W. Walker. 60p. 1979. pap. 0.95 o.p. (ISBN 0-89019-070-4). Norwalk Pr.

Discover Your High-Tech Talents. Barry Gale & Linda Gale. 1984. 16.45 o.p. (ISBN 0-671-49968-8); pap. 8.70 o.p. (ISBN 0-671-50740-0). S&S.

Discoverers. LC 79-11548. (Living Past Ser.). (Illus.). 64p. (gr. 4 up). 1979. 7.95 o.p. (ISBN 0-668-04784-4, 4784-4). Arco.

Discoverers of the Universe. N. Mellersh. 1970. 4.05 o.p. (ISBN 0-08-008741-8). Pergamon.

Discoveries. Dan Harless. 1982. pap. 4.95 o.p. (ISBN 0-89225-207-3). Gospel Advocate.

Discoveries in Physics for Scientists & Engineers. 2nd ed. Leonard H. Greenberg. 1975. pap. text ed. 20.95 o.p. (CBS C). SCP.

Discoveries of Christ & the Destinies of Mankind. Adrian C. Whittemore. (Illus.). 154p. 1988. 117.50 o.p. (ISBN 0-89266-627-7). Am Classical Coll Pr.

Discoveries of the Hidden Things of God. Erma Mestinsek & Minnie G. Mestinsek. 64p. 1980. 12.50 o.p. (ISBN 0-682-49635-9). Exposition-Phoenix.

Discovering an Evangelical Heritage. Donald W. Dayton. LC 75-36750. (Illus.). 160p. 1976. pap. 6.68i o.p. (ISBN 0-06-061780-2, RD 142). HarpR.

Discovering Art History. Gerald F. Brommer. LC 79-57018. (Illus.). 384p. 1981. 26.95 o.p. (ISBN 0-87192-121-9); teachers guide 8.95 o.p. (ISBN 0-87192-137-5). Davis Mass.

Discovering Astronomy: With Discovery Kit. William H. Jefferys & R. Robert Robbins. LC 80-22558. 466p. 1981. 37.95 o.p. (ISBN 0-471-44125-2). Wiley.

Discovering Backgammon. R. C. Bell. (Discovering Ser.: No. 201). (Illus.). 64p. (Orig.). 1979. pap. 2.95 o.p. (ISBN 0-85263-474-9, Pub. by Shire Pubns England). Seven Hills Bk Dists.

Discovering BASIC: A Problem Solving Approach. Robert E. Smith. (Illus.). (gr. 10 up). 1970. pap. 8.95 o.p. (ISBN 0-8104-5783-0). Sams.

Discovering BASIC with Wozzy: For the Apple II Plus, IIe, & IIc. Carton & Dimon. 1985. 9.95 o.p. (ISBN 0-8104-6302-4). Sams.

Discovering BBC Micro Machine: How to Get More Speed & Power. A P. Stephenson. (Illus.). 160p. (Orig.). 1983. pap. 13.95 o.p. (ISBN 0-246-12160-2, Pub. by Granada England). Sheridan.

Discovering Biology. 2nd. ed. J. A. Jackson et al. (Illus.). 1979. lab manual 6.95 o.p. (ISBN 0-89459-035-9). Hunter Textbks.

Discovering Career Satisfaction. Vincent W. Kafka. 79p. 1986. pap. 19.95 cancelled o.p. (ISBN 0-913261-14-9). Effect Learn Sys.

Discovering Chemistry. Elizabeth K. Cooper. LC 59-7281. (Illus.). (gr. 7 up). 1959. 5.50 o.p. (ISBN 0-15-223591-4, HJ). HarBraceJ.

Discovering Chess. R. C. Bell. (Discovering Bks: No. 221). (Illus.). 48p. (Orig.). 1983. pap. 2.75 o.p. (ISBN 0-85263-478-1, Pub. by Shire Pubns England). Seven Hills Bk Dists.

Discovering Cinque Ports. C. E. Whitney. (Discovering Ser.: No. 237). (Illus.). 63p. (Orig.). 1983. pap. 2.95 o.p. (ISBN 0-85263-416-1, Pub. by Shire Pubns England). Seven Hills Bk Dists.

Discovering Corn Dollies. M. Lambeth. (Discovering Ser.: No. 199). (Illus.). 48p. 1985. pap. 3.50 o.p. (ISBN 0-85263-283-5, Pub. by Shire Pubns England). Seven Hills Bk Dists.

Discovering Country Crafts. Rev. ed. D. J. Smith. (Discovering Ser.: No. 230). (Illus.). 64p. (Orig.). 1980. pap. 2.75 o.p. (ISBN 0-85263-487-0, Pub. by Shire Pubns England). Seven Hills Bk Dists.

Discovering Country Winemaking. Daphne More. (Discovering Ser.: No. 249). (Illus.). 33p. (Orig.). 1986. pap. 3.50 o.p. (ISBN 0-85263-480-3, 3381209, Pub. by Shire Pubns England). Seven Hills Bk Dists.

Discovering DNA. Nancy A. Tiley. LC 82-4771. 304p. 1982. 25.95 o.p. (ISBN 0-442-26260-4). Van Nos Reinhold.

Discovering Ecology. Patrick H. Armstrong. (Discovering Ser.: No. 154). (Illus.). 72p. 1983. pap. 2.95 o.p. (ISBN 0-85263-413-7, Pub. by Shire Pubns England). Seven Hills Bk Dists.

Discovering Epitaphs. Geoffrey Wright. (Discovering Ser.: No. 144). (Illus.). 63p. (Orig.). 1983. pap. 2.75 o.p. (ISBN 0-85263-170-7, 3381449, Pub. by Shire Pubns England). Seven Hills Bk Dists.

Discovering Farm Livestock. Nigel Harvey. (Discovering Ser.: No. 246). (Illus.). 64p. (Orig.). 1983. pap. 2.75 o.p. (ISBN 0-85263-465-X, 3382069, Pub. by Shire Pubns England). Seven Hills Bk Dists.

Discovering Geology. Patrick Armstrong. (Discovering Ser.: No. 189). (Illus., Orig.). 1983. pap. 3.95 o.p. (ISBN 0-85263-409-9, Pub. by Shire Pubns England). Seven Hills Bk Dists.

Discovering Hampshire & the New Forest. R. Jowitt & D. Jowitt. (Discovering Ser.: No. 60). (Illus.). 59p. pap. (ISBN 0-85263-296-7, 3380809, Pub. by Shire Pubns England). Seven Hills Bk Dists.

Discovering Horse-Drawn Transport of the British Army. D. J. Smith. (Discovering Ser.: No. 233). (Illus.). 64p. (Orig.). 1983. pap. 2.95 o.p. (ISBN 0-85263-403-X, 3381899, Pub. by Shire Pubns England). Seven Hills Bk Dists.

Discovering Hydroponic Gardening: Beginner's Guide to the Pleasures of Soil-Less Gardening. Alexandra Dickerman & John Dickerman. LC 75-17274. (Illus.). 160p. (Orig.). 1975. pap. 5.95 o.p. (ISBN 0-912800-19-4). Woodbridge Pr.

Discovering Ideas: An Anthology for Writers. Ed. by Jean Wyrick. 1982. pap. text ed. 15.95 o.p. (ISBN 0-03-056158-2). HR&W.

Discovering Jesus. Gordon Moyes. (Illus.). 160p. (Orig.). 1984. pap. 9.95 o.p. (ISBN 0-86760-005-5, Pub. by Albatross Bks). Meyer Stone Bks.

Discovering London's Villages. John Wittich. (Discovering Ser.: 215). (Illus.). 64p. 1979. pap. 1.95 o.p. (ISBN 0-85263-451-X, 3382389, Pub. by Shire Pubns England). Seven Hills Bk Dists.

Discovering Maritime Museums & Historic Ships. M. K. Stammers. (Discovering Ser.: No. 228). 1983. pap. 2.95 o.p. (ISBN 0-85263-369-6, Pub. by Shire Pubns England). Seven Hills Bk Dists.

Discovering Military Traditions. Arthur Taylor. (Discovering Ser.: No. 67). (Illus.). 72p. 1983. pap. 2.95 o.p. (ISBN 0-85263-171-5, Pub. by Shire Pubns England). Seven Hills Bk Dists.

Discovering Mormon Trails. Stanley B. Kimball. LC 79-53092. (Illus.). 1979. pap. 4.95 o.p. (ISBN 0-87747-756-6). Deseret Bk.

Discovering Music: Developing Music Curriculum in Secondary Schools. Keith Swanwick & Dorothy Taylor. (Illus.). 144p. 1982. 19.95 o.p. (ISBN 0-7134-4065-1, Pub. by Batsford England). David & Charles.

Discovering Music with Young Children. E. Bailey. (Illus.). 128p. 1958. (ISBN 0-8022-0050-8). Philos Lib.

Discovering Oil Lamps. Cecil A. Meadows. (Discovering Ser.: No. 145). (Illus.). 55p. (Orig.). 1983. pap. 2.95 o.p. (ISBN 0-85263-288-6, 3380189, Pub. by Shire Pubns England). Seven Hills Bk Dists.

Discovering Pantomime. Gyles Brandreth. (Discovering Ser.: NO. 177). (Illus.). 63p. 1983. pap. 2.95 o.p. (ISBN 0-85263-230-4, 3381499, Pub. by Shire Pubns England). Seven Hills Bk Dists.

Discovering Past Landscapes. Ed. by Michael Reed. 320p. 1984. 34.50 o.p. (ISBN 0-7099-2265-5, Pub. by Croom Helm Ltd). Routledge Chapman & Hall.

Discovering Process. Stephen Lewis & Cecile Forte. 350p. 1985. text ed. write for info. o.p. (ISBN 0-02-370500-0). Macmillan.

Discovering Science. John W. Harrington. LC 80-80721. (Illus.). 144p. 1980. text ed. 16.95 o.p. (ISBN 0-395-25527-9). HM.

Discovering Science on Your ADAM, with 25 Programs. Talcott Mountain Science Center Staff. (Illus.). 176p. (Orig.). 1984. 15.95 o.p. (ISBN 0-8306-0780-3); pap. 9.70 o.p. (ISBN 0-8306-1780-9, 1780). TAB Bks.

Discovering Space & Astronomy. Ian Ridpath. (Discovering Ser.: No. 126). (Illus.). 63p. (Orig.). 1983. pap. 2.95 o.p. (ISBN 0-85263-139-1, 3381269, Pub. by Shire Pubns England). Seven Hills Bk Dists.

Discovering Stained Glass. John Harries. (Discovering Ser.: No. 43). (Illus., Orig.). 1983. pap. 2.75 o.p. (ISBN 0-85263-508-7, 3381329, Pub. by Shire Pubns England). Seven Hills Bk Dists.

Discovering Suffolk. J. Rotheroe. (Discovering Ser.: No. 125). (Illus.). 1983. pap. 2.75 o.p. (ISBN 0-85263-372-6, Pub. by Shire Pubns England). Seven Hills Bk Dists.

Discovering the American Stork. Jack D. Scott. LC 75-41393. (Illus.). (gr. 1 up). 1976. 6.50 o.p. (ISBN 0-15-223580-9, HJ). HarBraceJ.

Discovering the Folklore of Plants. 2nd ed. Margaret Baker. (Discovering Ser.: No. 74). (Illus.). 64p. (Orig.). 1980. pap. 2.75 o.p. (ISBN 0-85263-491-9, Pub. by Shire Pubns England). Seven Hills Bk Dists.

Discovering the Individual. Jean Hamburger. 1978. 7.95 o.p. (ISBN 0-393-06433-6). Norton.

Discovering the Mysterious Egret. Jack D. Scott. LC 77-88967. (Illus.). (gr. 1 up). 1978. 7.95 o.p. (ISBN 0-15-223593-0, HJ). HarBraceJ.

Discovering the North Downs Way. D. J. Allen & P. R. Imrie. (Discovering Ser.: No. 252). (Illus., Orig.). 1983. pap. 2.95 o.p. (ISBN 0-85263-512-5, 3381439, Pub. by Shire Pubns England). Seven Hills Bk Dists.

Discovering the Real Self. E. F. McDaniel. 1958. (ISBN 0-8022-1013-9). Philos Lib.

Discovering Tutankhamen's Tomb. Ed. by Shirley Glubok. LC 68-12069. (Illus.). 144p. (gr. 5 up). 1968. 14.95 o.s.i. (ISBN 0-02-736030-X). Macmillan.

Discovering What Gerbils Do. Seymour Simon. (Illus.). (gr. 2-6). 1971. text ed. 7.95 o.p. (ISBN 0-07-057434-0). McGraw.

Discovering Women's History: A Practical Handbook. Deirdre Beddoe. (Illus.). 229p. (Orig.). 1983. pap. 7.95 o.p. (ISBN 0-86358-008-4, Pandora Pr). Routledge Chapman & Hall.

Discovering You. Charles S. Winn & C. Healy. (Careers in Focus Ser.). 1975. text ed. 14.88 o.p. (ISBN 0-07-071051-1). McGraw.

Discovery. Rev. ed. James R. Jenner. LC 80-623514. (California Criminal Law Practice Ser.). (Illus.). xi, 150p. 1980. 30.00 o.p. (ISBN 0-88124-071-0). Cal Cont Ed Bar.

Discovery: A Resource Book for Use with Persons Who Have Learning Difficulties. Ed. by Rosemary K. Roorbach. LC 72-133176. (Exploring Life Ser). (Illus.). 1971. pap. 2.95 set of 4 pupil bks. o.s.i. (ISBN 0-664-29751-X, Westminster); tchrs. guide 3.75 o.s.i. (ISBN 0-664-24875-6, Westminster). Westminster John Knox.

Discovery & Conquest of Mexico. Bernal Diaz Del Castillo. 478p. 1956. pap. 11.95 o.p. (ISBN 0-374-50384-2). FS&G.

Discovery Book of Size. Judith Conaway. LC 76-46471. (Discovery Ser.). (Illus.). (gr. k-3). 1977. PLB 13.31 o.p. (ISBN 0-8172-0252-8). Raintree Pubs.

Discovery Book of up & Down. Judith Conaway. LC 76-46470. (Discovery Ser.). (Illus.). (gr. k-3). 1977. PLB 13.31 o.s.i. (ISBN 0-8172-0251-X). Raintree Pubs.

Discovery in Medical Malpractice, Products Liability, & Personal Injury Cases, Vol. 281. Practising Law Institute Staff. 157p. 1985. pap. 15.00 o.p. (ISBN 0-317-27598-4, #H4-4967). PLI.

Discovery of Animal Behavior. John Sparks. 1982. 24.95 o.p. (ISBN 0-316-80492-4). Little.

Discovery of Australia: The Charts & Maps of the Navigators & Explorers. T. M. Perry. (Illus.). 160p. 1983. 125.00 o.p. (ISBN 0-241-10863-2, Pub. by Hamish Hamilton England). David & Charles.

Discovery of Insulin. Michael Bliss. (Illus.). 304p. 1982. 25.00x o.s.i. (ISBN 0-226-05897-2). U of Chicago Pr.

Discovery of King Arthur. Debretts Peerage Editors & Geoffrey Ashe. LC 83-45168. (Illus.). 240p. 1985. 18.95 o.p. (ISBN 0-385-19032-8, Anchor Pr). Doubleday.

Discovery of the Century. G. Sviridov. 192p. 1978. 4.10 o.p. (ISBN 0-8285-1050-4, Pub. by Progress Pubs USSR). Imported Pubns.

Discovery: The Search for the DNA's Secrets. Mahlon B. Hoagland. (Illus.). 224p. 1981. 10.95 o.p. (ISBN 0-395-30510-1). HM.

Discovery: The Story of the Second Byrd Antarctic Expedition. Richard E. Byrd. LC 76-159906. (Tower Bks). (Illus.). 430p. 1971. Repr. of 1935 ed. 47.00x o.p. (ISBN 0-8103-3904-8). Gale.

Discovery to Discourse: The Composing Process. Becky Wendling & Becky Kirschner. 300p. 1983. pap. text ed. write for info. o.p. (ISBN 0-02-364480-X). Macmillan.

Discreet Art of Luis Bunuel. Gwynne Edwards. (Illus.). 288p. 1985. pap. 12.95 o.p. (ISBN 0-7145-2832-3, Dist. by Kampmann). M Boyars Pubs.

Discrete & Switching Functions. Marc Davio et al. 1978. text ed. 127.95x o.p. (ISBN 0-07-015509-7). McGraw.

Discrete Choice Models in Regional Science. Ed. by D. Pitfield. (London Papers in Regional Science: No. 14). 202p. 1984. pap. text ed. 15.95 o.p. (ISBN 0-85086-113-6, 9120). Routledge Chapman & Hall.

Discrete Computational Structures. Robert R. Korfhage. 1974. 38.50 o.p. (ISBN 0-12-420850-9). Acad Pr.

Discrete Field Analysis of Structural Systems. D. L. Dean. (International Centre for Mechanical Sciences Ser.: No. 203). 1977. 23.00 o.p. (ISBN 0-387-81377-2). Springer-Verlag.

Discrete Groups & Automorphic Functions. Ed. by W. J. Harvey. 1978. 99.00 o.p. (ISBN 0-12-329950-0). Acad Pr.

Discrete Mathematical Structures for Computer Science. Bernard Kolman & Robert C. Busby. (Illus.). 512p. 1984. pap. text ed. (ISBN 0-13-215418-8). P-H.

Discrete Probability. R. A. Gangolli & Donald Ylvisaker. (Harbrace College Mathematics Ser.). (Orig.). 1967. pap. text ed. 12.95 o.p. (ISBN 0-15-517690-0, HC). HarBraceJ.

Discrete Transforms & Their Applications. Ed. by K. Ramamohan Rao. (Benchmark Papers in Electrical Engineering & Computer Science). (Illus.). 368p. 1985. 60.95 o.p. (ISBN 0-442-27669-9). Van Nos Reinhold.

Discrete Variable Methods in Ordinary Differential Equations. Peter Henrici. LC 61-17359. 407p. 1962. 45.50x o.p. (ISBN 0-471-37224-2, Pub. by Wiley-Interscience). Wiley.

Discretion & Valour: Religious Conditions in Russia & Eastern Europe. Rev. ed. Trevor Beeson. LC 81-70664. 416p. 1982. pap. 15.95 o.p. (ISBN 0-8006-1621-9, 1-1621, Fortress). Augsburg Fortress.

Discretus Calculus. Herbert S. Ingham. LC 63-20078. 224p. 1964. (ISBN 0-8022-0776-6). Philos Lib.

Discrimination of Genera of Euplectini of North & Central America: Coleoptera; Pselaphidae. Albert A. Grigarick & Robert O. Schuster. (UC Publications in Entomology: Vol. 87). 1980. pap. 25.50x o.p. (ISBN 0-520-09609-6). U of Cal Pr.

Discrimination, Personality & Achievement: A Survey of Northern Negroes. Robert L. Crain & Carlos S. Weisman. LC 72-10104. (Quantitative Studies in Social Relations Er). 1972. 46.50 o.p. (ISBN 0-12-785142-9). Acad Pr.

Discrimination Process & Development. B. J. Fellows. 1968. 60.00 o.p. (ISBN 0-08-012521-2). Pergamon.

Discrimination: What Does It Mean? Richard E. Biddle. 1973. 4.50 o.p. (ISBN 0-685-47832-7). Intl Personnel Mgmt.

Discussions on Philosophy & Literature. William Hamilton. 1986. Repr. of 1858 ed. lib. bdg. 40.00x o.p. (ISBN 0-935005-39-0). Ibis Pub VA.

Disease & the Environment: Proceedings of the Inaugural Conference of the Society for Environmental Therapy, Held in Oxford, 21-23March 1981. Ed. by A. R. Rees & H. J. Purcell. 224p. 1982. 52.50 o.p. (ISBN 0-471-10203-2, Pub. by Wiley Med). Wiley.

Disease, Pain & Sacrifice: Toward a Psychology of Suffering. David Bakan. 1971. pap. 5.95x o.p. (ISBN 0-8070-2971-8, BP394). Beacon Pr.

Diseases in Free Living Wild Animals: Proceedings of the Zoological Society of London Symposium, 24th. Zoological Society of London Symposium Staff. Ed. by McDiarmid. 1969. 72.00 o.p. (ISBN 0-12-613324-7). Acad Pr.

Diseases of Budgerigais. Cessa Feyerabend. 7.95 o.p. (ISBN 0-87666-953-4, PS-671). TFH Pubns.

Diseases of Children & Their Remedies. Nicholas R. Von Rosenstein. (Nutrition Foundation Reprint Ser.). 1982. 43.00 o.p. (ISBN 0-12-727550-9). Acad Pr.

Diseases of Dogs. 2nd ed. H. J. Christoph. LC 71-163386. 279p. 1980. 125.00 o.p. (ISBN 0-08-025940-5). Pergamon.

Diseases of Fish: Proceedings of the Zoological Society of London Symposium, 30th. Zoological Society of London Symposium Staff. Ed. by Lionel E. Mawdesley-Thomas. 1972. 79.50 o.p. (ISBN 0-12-613330-1). Acad Pr.

Diseases of Latent & Slow Growth Viruses. Robert W. Leader et al. (Illus.). 220p. 1973. text ed. 21.00x o.p. (ISBN 0-8422-7092-2). Irvington.

Diseases of Medical Progress, a Study of Iatrogenic Disease: A Contemporary Analysis of Illness Produced by Drugs & Other Therapeutic Procedures. 3rd ed. Robert H. Moser. 976p. 1969. 118.00x o.p. (ISBN 0-398-01356-X). C C Thomas.

Diseases of Occupations. 6th ed. Donald Hunter. 1978. pap. 99.00 o.p. (ISBN 0-316-38260-4). Little.

Diseases of the Gastrointestinal Tract & Liver. Ed. by David J. Shearman & Niall D. Finlayson. (Illus.). 974p. 1982. 111.00 o.p. (ISBN 0-443-01498-1). Churchill.

Diseases of the Nose, Throat & Ear. 12th ed. Ian S. Hall & Bernard H. Colman. (Illus.). 1981. pap. text ed. 16.50 o.p. (ISBN 0-443-02355-7). Churchill.

Diseases of the Skin in Children & Adolescents. 3rd. ed. G. W. Korting et al. LC 77-24000. (Illus.). 1979. text ed. write for info. o.p. (ISBN 0-7216-5491-6). Saunders.

Diseases of the Tempormandibular Apparatus: A Multidisciplinary Approach. 2nd ed. Douglas H. Morgan et al. LC 81-16819. (Illus.). 659p. 1982. 72.00 o.p. (ISBN 0-8016-3492-X). Mosby.

Diseases, Pests & Weeds in Tropical Crops. Ed. by J. Kranz et al. LC 78-6212. 666p. 1978. 134.95 o.p. (ISBN 0-471-99667-X, Pub. by Wiley-Interscience). Wiley.

Disent les Imbeciles. Nathalie Sarraute. 192p. 1976. 12.95 o.p. (ISBN 0-686-54961-9), Schoenhof.

Disguised. Pat Moore & Paul Conn. 160p. 1985. 10.95 o.p. (ISBN 0-8499-0516-8, 0516-8). Word Bks.

Disinherited: The Lost Birthright of the American Indian. Dale Van Every. (YA) (gr. 7 up). 1976. pap. 2.95 o.p. (ISBN 0-380-01141-7, 51326-9, Discus). Avon.

Disjecta. Samuel Beckett. Ed. by Ruby Cohn. LC 83-48308. 176p. 1984. pap. 5.95 o.p. (ISBN 0-394-62489-0, E868, Ever). Grove.

Disk Systems for the BBC Micro. Ian Sinclair. (Illus.). 115p. (Orig.). 1984. pap. 13.95 o.p. (ISBN 0-246-12325-7, Pub. by Granada England). Sheridan.

Disks, Files, & Printers for the Apple II. Brian D. Blackwood & George H. Blackwood. LC 83-61068. 264p. 1983. pap. text ed. 15.95 o.p. (ISBN 0-672-22163-2, 22163). Sams.

Dislocations & Plastic Deformations. T. Kovacs & L. Zsoldos. LC 73-6995. 364p. 1974. 36.00 o.p. (ISBN 0-08-017062-5). Pergamon.

Dismal Thing to Do. Alisa Craig. LC 85-16194. (Crime Club Ser.). 192p. 1986. 12.95 o.p. (ISBN 0-385-23263-2). Doubleday.

Dismantling America: The Rush to Deregulate. Susan J. Tolchin & Martin Tolchin. 1983. 16.45 o.p. (ISBN 0-395-34427-1). HM.

Dismantling the Universe: The Nature of Scientific Discovery. Richard B. Morris. 224p. 1983. 14.50 o.s.i. (ISBN 0-671-45239-8). S&S.

Disney Animation. Date not set. Abbeville Pr.

Disney Animation: The Illusion of Life. Frank Thomas & Ollie Johnston. LC 81-12699. (Illus.). 576p. 1981. text ed. 75.00 o.p. (ISBN 0-89659-232-4); collector's edition 125.00 o.p. (ISBN 0-89659-233-2). Abbeville Pr.

Disney Flash Ahead with ABC's. Walt Disney. (Disney Flash-Ahead Ser.). (Illus.). 32p. (ps-2). 1983. pap. 4.95 spiral o.s.i. (ISBN 0-671-44561-8, Little Simon). S&S.

Disney Flash Ahead with Numbers. Walt Disney. (Disney Flash-Ahead Ser.). (Illus.). 32p. (ps-2). 1983. pap. 4.95 spiral o.s.i. (ISBN 0-671-44559-6, Little Simon). S&S.

Disney Flash Ahead with Phonics. Walt Disney. (Disney Flash-Ahead Ser.). (Illus.). 32p. (ps-2). 1983. pap. 4.95 spiral o.s.i. (ISBN 0-671-44562-6, Little Simon). S&S.

Disney Flash Ahead with Time Telling. Walt Disney. (Disney Flash-Ahead Ser.). (Illus.). 32p. (ps-2). 1983. pap. 4.95 spiral o.s.i. (ISBN 0-671-44560-X, Little Simon). S&S.

Disney Practice Workbooks. Incl. Phonics (ISBN 0-448-16120-6); Spelling & Dictionary Skills (ISBN 0-448-16121-4); Creative Writing (ISBN 0-448-16122-2); Reading Comprehension (ISBN 0-448-16123-0); Numbers: Addition & Subtraction (ISBN 0-448-16124-9); Number: Multiplication (ISBN 0-448-16125-7). (Mickey's Practice Workbooks Ser.). (Illus.). (gr. k-3). 1978. pap. 1.25 ea. o.p. (G&D). Putnam Pub Group.

Disney Version. Richard Schickel. 1981. pap. 1.25 o.p. (ISBN 0-380-01142-5, 08953, Bard). Avon.

Disneyland Nineteen Eighty-Seven. Steve Birnbaum. (Illus.). 160p. 1986. pap. 6.95 o.s.i. (ISBN 0-395-42721-5). HM.

Disneyland 1983. Steve Birnbaum. 1982. pap. 4.95 o.p. (ISBN 0-395-32924-8). HM.

Disneyland 1984. Steve Birnbaum. 1983. pap. 5.95 o.p. (ISBN 0-395-34893-5). HM.

Disneyland, 1985. Steve Birnbaum. (Stephen Birnbaum Travel Guide Ser.). (Orig.). 1984. pap. 5.95 o.p. (ISBN 0-395-36526-0). HM.

Disorders of Auditory Function, II. Ed. by S. D. Stephens. 1977. 86.00 o.p. (ISBN 0-12-665750-5). Acad Pr.

Disorders of Cardiac Function. Csapo Roskamm. (Basic & Clinical Cardiology Ser.: Vol. 1). 376p. 1982. 65.00 o.p. (ISBN 0-8247-1684-1). Dekker.

Disorders of Esophageal Motility. Alfred L. Hurwitz et al. (Major Problems in Internal Medicine Ser.: Vol. 16). (Illus.). 179p. 1979. write for info. o.p. (ISBN 0-7216-4876-2). Saunders.

Disorders of Posture & Gait. Ed. by W. Bles & T. Brandt. 358p. 1986. 138.00 o.p. (ISBN 0-444-80756-X). Elsevier.

Disorders of Renal-Electrolytes & Mineral Metabolism. Chan. (Perspectives in Nephrology & Hypertension Ser.). 1988. price not set o.p. (ISBN 0-471-05511-5). Churchill.

Disorders of Space Exploration & Cognition. Ennio De Renzi. LC 80-42313. 265p. 1982. 49.95 o.p. (ISBN 0-471-28024-0). Wiley.

Disorganized Crime. Richard Hall. 27.50 o.p. (ISBN 0-7022-1955-X). U of Queensland Pr.

Dispersal & Migration. Ed. by W. Z. Lidicker, Jr. & R. L. Caldwell. LC 82-9326. (Benchmark Papers in Ecology: Vol. 11). 311p. 1982. 47.95 o.p. (ISBN 0-87933-435-5). Van Nos Reinhold.

Dispersion Forces. Ed. by J. Mahanty & B. W. Ninham. 1977. 66.00 o.p. (ISBN 0-12-465050-3). Acad Pr.

Dispersion Fuel Elements. A. N. Holden. LC 67-29666. 255p. 1967. 13.00 o.p. (ISBN 0-685-58274-4, 450017). Am Nuclear Soc.

Dispersion Modeling from Complex Sources: Proceedings, St. Louis, Mo., April 1981. Air Pollution Control Association Specialty Conference. 344p. 1981. 17.00 o.p. (ISBN 0-318-12249-5, SP-41); members 13.00 o.p. (ISBN 0-318-12250-2). Air & Waste.

Dispersion Relations & Their Connection with Causality. Ed. by Eugene P. Wigner. (Italian Physical Society Ser.: Course 29). 1964. 82.50 o.p. (ISBN 0-12-368829-9). Acad Pr.

Dispersions of Materials. R. Hammond. (Illus.). 224p. 1958. (ISBN 0-8022-0668-9). Philos Lib.

Displaced Homemakers: Organizing for a New Life. Laurie Shields. (McGraw-Hill Paperback Ser.). 256p. (Orig.). 1980. pap. text ed. 5.95 o.p. (ISBN 0-07-056802-2). McGraw.

Displaced Homemakers: Programs & Policies, an Interim Report. Intro. by John H. Gibbons. LC 85-600606. 43p. (Orig.). 1985. pap. 1.75 o.p. (ISBN 0-318-18745-0, S/N 052-003-01011-9). USGPO.

Display & Commercial Space Design, Vol. 14. Ed. by Rikuyo-Sha Staff. (Illus.). 380p. 1986. text ed. 65.00 o.s.i. (ISBN 4-897-37057-4, Pub. by Rikuyo-Sha Japan). Bks Nippan.

Display & Commercial Space Design, No. 15. Ed. by Rikuyo-sha. 380p. 1988. 65.00 o.p. (ISBN 4-897-37066-3). Bks Nippan.

Disposable Medical Supplies. (Reports Ser.: No. 531). 225p. 1983. 985.00x o.p. (ISBN 0-88694-531-3). Intl Res Dev.

Disposable People. Marshall Goldberg & Kenneth Kay. (Orig.). 1980. pap. text ed. 2.25 o.p. (ISBN 0-505-51574-1, Pub. by Tower Bks). Dorchester Pub Co.

Disposal Bag Package. Date not set. (ISBN 0-07-521089-4). McGraw.

Disposal of Chemical Munitions & Agents. National Research Council. 216p. 1984. pap. text ed. 16.40x o.p. (ISBN 0-309-03527-9). Natl Acad Pr.

Disposal of Chemical Waste in the Marine Environment: Implications of International Dumping Conventions: Proceedings of the International Symposium, Rotterdam, Sept 11-12, 1980. Ed. by E. H. Hueck-Van Der Plas. 216p. 1981. pap. 19.25 o.p. (ISBN 0-08-026289-9). Pergamon.

Disposal of Dredged Material in Rhode Island: An Evaluation of Past Practices & Future Options. George R. Seavey & S. D. Pratt. (Marine Technical Report Ser.: No. 72). 5.00 o.p. (ISBN 0-938412-06-X). Sea Grant Pubns.

Disposal of the Dead. Polson et al. 322p. 1953. (ISBN 0-8022-2001-0). Philos Lib.

Disposition of Toxic Drugs & Chemicals in Man. 2nd ed. Randall C. Baselt. LC 81-66543. (Illus.). 800p. 1982. text ed. 65.00 o.p. (ISBN 0-931890-08-X, Biomed Pubns). Year Bk Med.

Disposition of Toxic Drugs & Chemicals in Man: Centrally-Acting Drugs, Vol. 1. Randall C. Baselt. LC 77-93428. (Illus.). 1978. text ed. 25.00 o.p. (ISBN 0-931890-01-2, Biomed Pubns). Year Bk Med.

Disposition of Toxic Drugs & Chemicals in Man: Peripherally-Acting Drugs & Common Toxic Chemicals, Vol. 2. Randall C. Baselt. LC 77-93428. (Illus.). 1978. text ed. 25.00 o.p. (ISBN 0-931890-02-0, Biomed Pubns). Year Bk Med.

Dispositional Properties. David Weissman. LC 65-11655. (Philosophical Explorations Ser). 231p. 1965. 8.95x o.p. (ISBN 0-8093-0163-6). S Ill U Pr.

Disproportionate Share & Uncompensated Care. HFMA Staff. 20p. pap. text ed. 5.00 o.p. (ISBN 0-317-66617-7). Healthcare Fin Mgmt Assn.

Dispute & Conflict Resolution in Plymouth County, Massachusetts, 1725-1825. William E. Nelson. LC 80-17403. (Studies in Legal History). xiii, 212p. 1981. 22.00x o.p. (ISBN 0-8078-1454-7). U of NC Pr.

Dispute Resolution Training: The State of the Art. American Arbitration Association Staff & Thomas R. Colosi. Ed. by Charlotte Gold & Ruth Lyons. LC 78-51451. 104p. 1978. pap. 2.50 o.p. (ISBN 0-943001-14-5). Am Arbitration.

Dispute Resolution Under Fact-Finding & Arbitration: An Empirical Analysis. Thomas A. Kochan et al. 240p. 12.00 o.p. (ISBN 0-318-12377-0); members 9.00 o.p. (ISBN 0-318-12378-9). Am Arbitration.

Disputed Crown. Valerie Anand. 320p. 1982. 14.95 o.s.i. (ISBN 0-684-17629-7, ScribT). Scribner.

Disquisitions Relating Matter & Spirit, 2 vols. in 1. Joseph Priestley. Ed. by Rene Wellek. Bd. with Doctrine of Philosophical Necessity Illustrated: Being an Appendix to the Disquestions Relating to Matter & Spirit. LC 75-11248. (British Philosophers & Theologians of the 17th & 18th Centuries: Vol. 47). 1976. Repr. of 1777 ed. lib. bdg. 51.00 o.p. (ISBN 0-8240-1799-4). Garland Pub.

Disregard of the Corporate Fiction & Allied Corporation Problems. I. Maurice Wormser. xxi, 199p. 1981. Repr. of 1927 ed. lib. bdg. 22.00x o.p. (ISBN 0-8377-1315-3). Rothman.

Dissection of a Principal. Thomas D. Williams. Ed. by Jon Rapport. LC 86-71931. 120p. (Orig.). 1986. pap. 6.95 o.p. (ISBN 1-55666-007-3). Authors Unltd.

Dissemination. Jacques Derrida. Tr. by Barbara Johnson. LC 81-3359. 400p. 1981. lib. bdg. 26.00x o.s.i. (ISBN 0-226-14327-9). U of Chicago Pr.

Dissemination of Information. T. D. Wilson & J. Stephenson. 80p. 1966. (ISBN 0-8022-1896-2). Philos Lib.

Dissemination of Scientific & Technical Information: Toward a Paperless System. F. Wilfrid Lancaster. (Occasional Papers: No. 127). 27p. 1977. pap. 2.00 o.p. (ISBN 0-317-58968-7). U of Ill Lib Info Sci.

Dissent in Three American Wars. Samuel E. Morison et al. LC 74-105373. (Illus.). 1970. 10.00x o.s.i. (ISBN 0-674-21278-9); pap. 3.95x o.s.i. (ISBN 0-674-21279-7). Harvard U Pr.

Dissent on Bonhoeffer. David H. Hopper. LC 75-22120. 192p. 1975. 8.50 o.s.i. (ISBN 0-664-20802-9, Westminster). Westminster John Knox.

Dissent on Development: Studies & Debates in Development Economics. P. T. Bauer. LC 70-189158. 550p. 1972. 30.00x o.p. (ISBN 0-674-21281-9); pap. 9.95x o.p. (ISBN 0-674-21282-7). Harvard U Pr.

Dissenters: Voices from Contemporary America. John L. Gwaltney. LC 85-28113. (Illus.). 384p. 1986. 19.45 o.s.i. (ISBN 0-394-52725-9). Random.

Dissenting Tradition: Essays for Leland H. Carlson. Ed. by C. Robert Cole & Michael E. Moody. LC 74-27706. xxiii, 272p. 1975. 17.00x o.p. (ISBN 0-8214-0176-9). Ohio U Pr.

Dissertation on Miracles, Containing an Examination of the Principles Advanced by David Hume, Esq. in an Essay on Miracles. George Campbell. LC 82-48331. (Philosophy of David Hume Ser.). 300p. 1983. lib. bdg. 39.00 o.p. (ISBN 0-8240-5403-2). Garland Pub.

Dissertation on Natural Phonology. David Stampe. Ed. by Jorge Hankamer. LC 78-66538. (Outstanding Dissertations in Linguistics Ser.). 1985. lib. bdg. 21.00 o.p. (ISBN 0-8240-9674-6). Garland Pub.

Dissertations Concerning the Fundamental Principle & Immediate Criterion of Virtue see Essay on the Origin of Evil.

Dissertations in History: An Index to Dissertations Completed in History Departments of United States & Canadian Universities 1970 - June 1980. Warren F. Kuehl. LC 84-18452. 466p. 1985. lib. bdg. 61.00 o.p. (ISBN 0-87436-356-X). ABC-Clio.

Dissertations in Philosophy Accepted in American Universities, 1861-1975. Thomas C. Bechtle & Mary F. Riley. (Reference Library of the Humanities: Vol. 112). (LC 77-083392). 1978. lib. bdg. 73.00 o.p. (ISBN 0-8240-9835-8). Garland Pub.

Dissertations on Pennsylvania History, 1886-1976: A Bibliography. Ed. by Roland M. Baumann. LC 79-622900. 80p. 1978. pap. 2.95 o.p. (ISBN 0-911124-93-4). Pa Hist & Mus.

Dissociation Constants of Organic Bases in Aqueous Solution. D. D. Perrin. 1976. 55.00 o.p. (ISBN 0-08-020826-6). Pergamon.

Dissociation Constants of Organic Bases in Aqueous Solution, Vol. 12. D. D. Perrin. 524p. 1976. 300.00 o.p. (ISBN 0-08-020827-4). Pergamon.

Distance Geometry & Conformational Calculations. G. M. Crippen. LC 80-42044. (Chemometrics Research Studies Ser.). 58p. 1981. 49.95 o.p. (ISBN 0-471-27991-9). Wiley.

Distancers. William Gibson. 1986. write for info. o.p. (ISBN 0-87795-689-8). Morrow.

Distant Eden. Donna Grundman. (Orig.). 1982. pap. 3.50 o.p. (ISBN 0-440-12136-1). Dell.

Distant Encounters: The Exploration of Jupiter & Saturn. Mark Washburn. LC 82-47659. (Illus.). 288p. 1983. 19.95 o.p. (ISBN 0-15-125744-2). HarBraceJ.

Distant Encounters: The Exploration of Jupiter & Saturn. Mark Washburn. LC 82-15709. (Illus.). 288p. 1983. pap. 12.95 o.p. (ISBN 0-15-626108-1, Harv). HarBraceJ.

Distant Stations. Jonathan Schwartz. 320p. 1980. pap. 2.50 o.p. (ISBN 0-380-50583-5, 50583). Avon.

Distant Summer. Sarah Patterson. (gr. 7-9). 1977. pap. 1.95 o.p. (ISBN 0-671-44232-5). Archway.

Distant Water: The Fate of the North Atlantic Fisherman. William W. Warner. (Illus.). 352p. 1983. 17.45i o.p. (ISBN 0-316-92328-1, Pub. by Atlantic Monthly Pr). Little.

Distillation - 1979, 2 vols. Institution of Chemical Engineers. 1982. 99.00 o.s.i. (ISBN 0-08-028754-9). Pergamon.

Distorted Image: Changing Conceptions of the American Character Since Turner. Thomas L. Hartshorne. LC 79-28120. xiv, 226p. 1980. Repr. of 1968 ed. lib. bdg. 35.00x o.p. (ISBN 0-313-22220-7, HADS). Greenwood.

Distortion in Art: The Eye & the Mind. J. B. Deregowski. (International Library of Psychology). (Illus.). 256p. 1984. 50.00x o.p. (ISBN 0-7100-9516-3). Routledge Chapman & Hall.

Distributed Control. 2nd ed. Robert E. Larson et al. LC 82-83404. (Tutorial Texts Ser.). 381p. 1982. 36.00 o.p. (ISBN 0-8186-0451-4, Q451). IEEE Comp Soc.

Distributed Data Base Management. Philip A. Bernstein et al. LC 78-70844. (Tutorial Texts Ser.). 195p. 1978. 20.00 o.p. (ISBN 0-8186-0212-0, Q212). IEEE Comp Soc.

Distributed Database Technology. National Computing Centre, Ltd. Staff. (Illus.). 149p. (Orig.). 1980. pap. 20.00x o.s.i. (ISBN 0-85012-226-0). Intl Pubns Serv.

Distributed Parameter Systems Theory, 2 pts. Ed. by Peter Stavroulakis. Incl. Pt. 1. Control. (Vol. 26). 1983. 51.95 o.p. (ISBN 0-87933-071-6); Pt. 2. Estimation. (Vol. 27). 1983. 51.95 o.p. (ISBN 0-87933-072-4). LC 82-21218. (Benchmark Papers in Electrical Engineering & Computer Science). 832p. 1983. Set. 92.95 o.p. (ISBN 0-87933-103-8). Van Nos Reinhold.

Distributed Processing. 3rd rev. ed. Burt H. Liebowitz & John H. Carson. LC 80-85249. (Tutorial Texts Ser.). 640p. 1981. 32.00 o.p. (ISBN 0-8186-0363-1, Q363). IEEE Comp Soc.

Distributed Processor Communication Architecture. Kenneth J. Thurber. LC 79-89474. (Tutorial Texts Ser.). 517p. 1979. 30.00 o.p. (ISBN 0-8186-0258-9, Q258). IEEE Comp Soc.

Distributed Processor Communication Architecture. Kenneth J. Thurber & G. M. Masson. LC 79-1563. (Illus.). 288p. 1979. 32.00x o.p. (ISBN 0-669-02914-9). Lexington Bks.

Distributed System Design. Michael P. Mariani & David F. Palmer. LC 79-89494. (Tutorial Texts Ser.). 409p. 1979. 27.00 o.p. (ISBN 0-8186-0267-8, Q267). IEEE Comp Soc.

Distribution, Allocation, Social Structure & Spatial Form: Elements of Planning Theory. Portugali. (Progress in Planning Ser.: Vol. 14, Part 3). (Illus.). 83p. 1980. pap. 16.25 o.p. (ISBN 0-08-026808-0). Pergamon.

Distribution & Marketing: The New Antitrust Environment. 838p. 1986. 15.00 o.p. (B4-6742). PLI.

Distribution & Redistribution of Incomes. David Piachaud. 140p. 1982. pap. text ed. 11.00x o.p. (ISBN 0-7199-1086-2, Pub. by Bedford England). Gower Pub Co.

Distribution & Transportation Handbook. Harry J. Bruce. LC 76-132669. (Illus.). 416p. 1983. 25.95 o.p. (ISBN 0-8436-1400-5). Van Nos Reinhold.

Distribution Channel Strategy for Export Marketing: The Case of Hong Kong Firms. T. S. Chan. Ed. by Richard N. Farmer. LC 83-18158. (Research for Business Decisions Ser.: No. 67). 140p. 1984. 37.95 o.p. (ISBN 0-8357-1494-2). UMI Res Pr.

Distribution Channels: Behavioral Dimensions. Ed. by Louis W. Stern. LC 71-2882. (Illus., Orig.). 1969. pap. 11.95 o.p. (ISBN 0-395-05431-1). HM.

Distribution of the Aboriginal Population of Michigan. W. B. Hinsdale. (Occasional Contributions Ser.: No. 2). (Illus.). 1968. Repr. of 1932 ed. pap. 1.00x o.p. (ISBN 0-932206-74-3). U Mich Mus Anthro.

Distributions & Fourier Transforms. William F. Donoghue. (Pure & Applied Mathematics Ser.: Vol. 32). 1969. 69.50 o.p. (ISBN 0-12-220650-9). Acad Pr.

Distributive System. S. R. Hill. 1966. text ed. 16.25 o.p. (ISBN 0-08-011738-4); pap. text ed. 7.00 o.p. (ISBN 0-08-011737-6). Pergamon.

District Heating. Robert W. Lockerby. (Architecture Ser.: A 1415). 17p. 1985. 2.25 o.p. (ISBN 0-89028-445-8). Vance Biblios.

District Heating Thermal Generation & Distribution. MacKenzie. 1979. 55.00 o.p. (ISBN 0-08-022711-2). Pergamon.

District Nursing: The Nurse, the Patients & the Work. Molly Antrobus. LC 85-5226. (Illus.). 250p. (Orig.). 1985. pap. 9.95 o.p. (ISBN 0-571-13651-6). Faber & Faber.

Disturbances of Amino Acid Metabolism: Clinical Chemistry & Diagnosis. Hans J. Bremer et al. LC 78-31995. (Illus.). 536p. 1980. text ed. 57.00 o.p. (ISBN 0-8067-0251-6). Urban & S.

Disturbed Communication. Jurgen Ruesch. 1972. pap. 4.95 o.p. (ISBN 0-393-00634-4, Norton Lib). Norton.

Disturbed Peace: Selected Writings of an Irish Catholic Homosexual. Brian R. McNaught. LC 81-67627. 125p. (Orig.). 1981. pap. 5.95 o.p. (ISBN 0-940680-00-9). Dignity Inc.

Disturbing, Disordered, or Disturbed? Perspectives on the Definition of Problem Behavior in Educational Settings. Ed. by Frank H. Wood & K. Charlie Lakin. 94p. 1982. pap. 7.00 o.p. (ISBN 0-86586-123-4). Coun Exc Child.

Disturbing the Peace. Date not set. pap. (ISBN 0-385-29332-1). Delacorte.

Disturbing the Peace. Richard Yates. 288p. 1984. pap. 7.95 o.p. (ISBN 0-385-29332-1, Delta). Dell.

Ditty Bag Book. Frank Rosenow. (Illus.). 1977. 7.95 o.p. (ISBN 0-393-03200-0). Norton.

Diuretics. George De Stevens. (Medicinal Chemistry Ser.: Vol. 1). 1963. 55.00 o.p. (ISBN 0-12-212156-2). Acad Pr.

Diva. Delacorta, pseud. Tr. by Lowell Bair from Fr. 1983. 9.50 o.s.i. (ISBN 0-671-47056-6). Summit Bks.

Divan & Other Writings. Federico Garcia Lorca. Tr. by Edwin Honig. LC 74-75120. (Illus.). 1977. pap. 4.50 o.p. (ISBN 0-914278-14-2). Copper Beech.

Dive for the Sun. Sandra Love. 224p. (gr. 7 up). 1982. 10.95 o.s.i. (ISBN 0-395-32864-0). HM.

Dive to Adventure see Sharks, Wrecks, & Movie Stars: The Adventures of an Underwater Photographer.

Divers Guide to Underwater America. rev. ed. John Shobe & Kate Kelley. (Illus.). 360p. 1987. casebound 12.95 o.p. (ISBN 0-89732-059-X). Menasha Ridge.

Diversifications: Poems. A. R. Ammons. 98p. 1975. 6.95 o.p. (ISBN 0-393-04414-9). Norton.

Diversions of Pleasure: Luis Bunuel & the Crises of Desire. Paul Sandro. LC 86-31192. (Illus.). 184p. 1987. 20.00 o.p. (ISBN 0-8142-0433-3). Ohio St U Pr.

Diversity. Ed. by Ruth Patrick. LC 83-4365. (Benchmark Papers in Ecology: Vol. 13). 432p. 1983. 47.95 o.p. (ISBN 0-87933-420-7). Van Nos Reinhold.

Diversity & Development in Southeast Asia. Guy J. Pauker et al. LC 77-23441. (Nineteen Eighties Project, Council on Foreign Relations Ser.). 1977. text ed. (ISBN 0-07-048917-3); pap. text ed. 5.95 o.p. (ISBN 0-07-048918-1). McGraw.

Diversity in Unity: The Development & Expansion of the Cherubim & Seraphim Church in Nigeria. Akin Omoyajowo. LC 83-21706. 126p. (Orig.). 1984. lib. bdg. 23.25 o.p. (ISBN 0-8191-3655-7); pap. text ed. 9.50 o.p. (ISBN 0-8191-3656-5). U Pr of Amer.

Diversity of Scripture: Trajectories in the Confessional Heritage. Paul D. Hanson. LC 81-43079. (Overtures to Biblical Theology Ser.: No. 11). 1982. pap. 8.95 o.p. (ISBN 0-8006-1535-2, 1-1535, Fortress). Augsburg Fortress.

Diversity of Worlds. Raymond Aron & August Heckscher. LC 72-12631. 178p. 1973. Repr. of 1957 ed. lib. bdg. 35.00x o.p. (ISBN 0-8371-6686-1, ARDW). Greenwood.

Diverting Adventures of Tom Thumb. Barry Wilkinson. LC 74-140867. (Illus.). (gr. 3-6). 1969. 4.95 o.p. (ISBN 0-15-201620-1, HJ). HarBraceJ.

Divided Children: A Legal Guide for Divorcing Parents. Michael Wheeler. 1980. 10.95 o.p. (ISBN 0-393-01310-3). Norton.

Divided Mind: Studies in Defoe & Richardson. Sudesh Vaid. 1980. text ed. 15.00x o.p. (ISBN 0-391-01729-2). Humanities.

Divided Soul. David Ritz. 1986. pap. 4.95 o.p. (ISBN 0-7701-0423-1). PaperJacks US.

Divided Soul: The Life of Marvin Gaye. David Ritz. 416p. 1985. text ed. 16.95 o.p. (ISBN 0-07-052929-9). McGraw.

Divided Working Class: Worker Migration in Australia. Constance Lever-Tracy & Michael Quinlan. 352p. 1988. text ed. 65.00 o.p. (ISBN 0-7102-0814-6, Pub. by Routledge UK); pap. text ed. (ISBN 0-7102-1393-X, Pub. by Routledge UK). Routledge Chapman & Hall.

Divina Comedia. Dante Alighieri. (Biblioteca De Cultura Basica Ser.). pap. 4.00 o.p. (ISBN 0-8477-0703-2). U of PR Pr.

Divine Assassin. Rob Reiss. 224p. 1985. 15.95 o.p. (ISBN 0-316-73969-3). Little.

Divine Communication: Word & Sacrament in Biblical, Historical & Contemporary Perspective. Hans Schwarz. LC 84-48732. 176p. 1985. pap. 1.50 o.p. (ISBN 0-8006-1846-7, 1-1846, Fortress). Augsburg Fortress.

Divine Courtship: A History of Our Salvation. Jeffrey Mirus. 183p. 1977. 7.95 o.p. (ISBN 0-931888-13-1). Christendom Coll Pr.

Divine Direction or Chaos: A Layman Looks at Philosophy, Natural Science, & Devine Metaphysics. Charles H. Lee. 1952. Philos Lib.

Divine Guidance: That Voice Behind You. Charles G. Coleman. LC 77-6796. 1977. pap. 2.50 o.s.i. (ISBN 0-87213-087-8). Loizeaux.

Divine Healing Today. Richard Mayhue. 1983. pap. 6.95 o.p. (ISBN 0-8024-0453-7). Moody.

Divine Inspiration. Louis Gaussen. LC 75-155249. (Kregel Reprint Library). 382p. 1971. lib. bdg. 14.95 o.p. (ISBN 0-8254-2707-X). Kregel.

Divine Origin of the Craft of the Herbalist. E. Wallis Budge. LC 78-174013. (Illus.). 107p. 1971. Repr. of 1928 ed. 40.00x o.p. (ISBN 0-8103-3794-0). Gale.

Divine Physical Healing, Past & Present. 272p. pap. 2.50 o.p. (ISBN 0-686-29107-7). Faith Pub Hse.

Divine Quest in Music. Mendl. 240p. 1957. (ISBN 0-8022-1102-X). Philos Lib.

Divine Rebel: The Life of Anne Marbury Hutchinson. Selma R. Williams. LC 80-20109. 256p. 1981. 14.95 o.p. (ISBN 0-03-055846-8). H Holt & Co.

Divine Struggle for Human Salvation: Biblical Convictions in Their Historical Settings. Andrew C Tunyogi. LC 78-65852. 1979. pap. text ed. 20.75 o.p. (ISBN 0-8191-0676-3). U Pr of Amer.

Diving. Sammy Lee & Steve Lehrman. LC 78-55522. (Illus.). 1983. pap. 5.95 o.p. (ISBN 0-689-70660-X, 303, Atheneum). Macmillan.

Diving Complete. George W. Rackham. (Illus.). 232p. (Orig.). 1975. pap. 5.95 o.p. (ISBN 0-571-10940-3). Faber & Faber.

Diving for Science: The Story of the Deep Submersible. Edward H. Shenton. LC 74-90990. (Illus.). 1972. 8.95 o.p. (ISBN 0-393-06380-1). Norton.

Divinity of the Roman Emperor, Middletown, 1931. Lily Ross Taylor. (Latin Poetry Ser.). 1978. 40.00 o.p. (ISBN 0-8240-2980-1). Garland Pub.

Division. Reusable ed. K. Wehrli. (Michigan Arithmetic Program Ser.). (gr. 4). 1976. 6.00 o.p. (ISBN 0-89039-180-7). Ann Arbor Pubs.

Division Bell Mystery. Ellen Wilkinson. LC 75-46006. (Crime Fiction). 1976. Repr. of 1932 ed. lib. bdg. 21.00 o.p. (ISBN 0-8240-2398-6). Garland Pub.

Division in the Protestant House: The Basic Reasons Behind Intra-Church Conflicts. Dean R. Hoge. 1976. pap. 3.95 o.s.i. (ISBN 0-664-24793-8, Westminster). Westminster John Knox.

Division of Labor in Cells. 2nd ed. Geoffrey Bourne. 287p. 1970. pap. text ed. 8.50 o.p. (ISBN 0-12-119259-8). Acad Pr.

Division of the World, Nineteen Forty-One to Nineteen Fifty-Five. Wilfried Loth. Tr. by Clare Krojzlova from Ger. 256p. 1988. lib. bdg. 59.95 o.p. (ISBN 0-415-00364-4). Routledge Chapman & Hall.

Division One: Appendices. (Boiler & Pressure Vessel Code Ser.: Sec. 3). 1980. 100.00 o.p. (ISBN 0-686-70369-3, P0003A); pap. 125.00 loose-leaf o.p. (ISBN 0-686-70370-7, V0003A). ASME.

Division One-Nuclear Power Plant Components: General Requirements. (Boiler & Pressure Vessel Code Ser.: Sec. 3). 1980. 55.00 o.p. (ISBN 0-686-70367-7, P0003R); pap. 80.00 loose-leaf o.p. (ISBN 0-686-70368-5, V0003R). ASME.

Division One: Subsection NB-Class 1 Components. (Boiler & Pressure Vessel Code Ser.: Sec. 3). 1980. 70.00 o.p. (ISBN 0-686-70371-5, P0003B); pap. 100.00 loose-leaf o.p. (ISBN 0-686-70372-3, V0003B). ASME.

Division One: Subsection NC-Class 2 Components. (Boiler & Pressure Vessel Code Ser.: Sec. 3). 1980. 70.00 o.p. (ISBN 0-686-70373-1, P0003C); loose-leaf 100.00 o.p. (ISBN 0-686-70374-X, V0003C). ASME.

Division One: Subsection ND-Class 3 Components. (Boiler & Pressure Vessel Code Ser.: Sec. 3). 1980. 70.00 o.p. (ISBN 0-686-70378-2, P0003D); pap. 100.00 loose-leaf o.p. (ISBN 0-686-70379-0, V0003D). ASME.

Division One: Subsection NE Class MC Components. (Boiler & Pressure Vessel Code Ser.: Sec. 3). 1980. bound edition 70.00 o.p. (ISBN 0-686-70380-4, P0003E); pap. 100.00 loose-leaf o.p. (ISBN 0-686-70381-2, V0003E). ASME.

Division One: Subsection NF-Component Supports. (Boiler & Pressure Vessel Code Ser.: Sec. 3). 1980. 55.00 o.p. (ISBN 0-686-70382-0, P0003F); pap. 65.00 loose-leaf o.p. (ISBN 0-686-70383-9, V0003F). ASME.

Division Street: America. Studs Terkel. 1981. pap. 2.50 o.p. (ISBN 0-380-00279-5, 55723, Discus). Avon.

Division Two-Code for Concrete Reactor Vessels & Containments. (Boiler & Pressure Vessel Code Ser.: Sec. 3). 1980. 90.00 o.p. (ISBN 0-686-70386-3, P00032); pap. 125.00 loose-leaf o.p. (ISBN 0-686-70387-1, V00032). ASME.

Divisional Performance. David Solomons. 1965. 14.00 o.p. (ISBN 0-317-20197-2). Finan Exec.

Divorce Experience of Working & Middle Class Women. Toni L'Hommedieu. Ed. by Peter Nathan. LC 83-17967. (Research in Clinical Psychology Ser.: No. 8). 178p. 1984. 37.95 o.p. (ISBN 0-8357-1478-0). UMI Res Pr.

Divorce Guide for British Columbia. 12th ed. Wayne Powell. 74p. 1987. 9.95 o.p. (ISBN 0-88908-252-9). ISC Pr.

Divorce Guide for Ontario: A Step-by-Step Guide to Obtaining Your Own Divorce. 6th ed. Gloria Epstein. 137p. 1986. 12.95 o.p. (ISBN 0-88908-352-5). ISC Pr.

Divorce Guide for Washington: Step-by-Step Guide for Obtaining Your Own Divorce. 4th ed. M. Pattersen. 256p. 1987. pap. text ed. 14.95 o.p. (ISBN 0-88908-731-8). ISC Pr.

Divorce in the United States, Canada & Great Britain: A Guide to Information Sources. Ed. by Kenneth D. Sell & Betty Sell. LC 78-15894. (Social Issues & Social Problems Information Guide Ser.: Vol. 1). 320p. 1978. 68.00x o.p. (ISBN 0-8103-1396-0). Gale.

Divorce Is a Grown up Problem. Janet Sinberg. (YA) 1978. pap. 4.95 o.p. (ISBN 0-380-01901-9, 84418-4). Avon.

Divorce Judgements & Post Divorce Problems. Massachusetts Continuing Legal Education Staff. LC 84-61784. 262p. write for info. o.p. Mass CLE.

Divorce, Support & Community Property. Earleen H. Cook. 41p. 1985. pap. 6.00 o.p. (ISBN 0-89028-681-7). Vance Biblios.

Divorce Taxation Guide. Mark A. Vogel. LC 83-16869. 374p. 1984. 75.00 o.p. (ISBN 0-471-87079-X); Supp. 1985. pap. 30.00 o.p. (ISBN 0-471-82939-0). Wiley.

Divorce Without Victims: Helping Children Through Divorce with a Minimum of Pain & Trauma. Stuart M. Berger. 200p. 1983. 12.45 o.p. (ISBN 0-395-33115-3). HM.

Divorce Won't Help. Edmund Bergler. 1979. 12.95 o.p. (ISBN 0-87140-635-7); pap. 5.95 o.p. (ISBN 0-87140-124-X). Liveright.

Divorced. B. J. Smith & Irene B. Harrell. 175p. 1983. pap. 6.00 o.p. (ISBN 0-8423-0605-6). Tyndale.

Divorced Kids: Children of Divorce Speak Out & Give Advice to Mothers, Fathers, Lovers, Stepparents, Brothers & Sisters, Boyfriends & Girlfriends, Each Other. Warner Troyer. LC 79-3531. 180p. 1980. Repr. of 1979 ed. 8.95 o.p. (ISBN 0-15-125748-5). HarBraceJ.

Divorced Woman's Guide to Meeting New Men: Where to Go & What to Do to Find Your Man. Eric Weber. Ed. by Pat Golbitz. LC 83-742. 192p. 1984. 11.95 o.p. (ISBN 0-688-01841-6). Morrow.

Divorcee's Kitchen Give You Servings from One to Six. Robert Canino. 1986. 11.95 o.p. (ISBN 0-533-06508-9). Vantage.

Divry's New Spanish-English & English-Spanish Handy Dictionary. Ed. by J. M. Douglas & A. Lomo. (Span. & Eng.). 1965. pocket size, flexible 4.00 o.p. (ISBN 0-685-09033-7); thumb indexed 7.00 o.p. (ISBN 0-685-09034-5). Divry.

Diwan Abu Tammam. Tr. by Arthur Wormhoudt. (Arab Translation Ser.: No. 11). 184p. 1974. pap. 6.50x o.p. (ISBN 0-916358-61-5). Wormhoudt.

Diwan Al Sanaubari. Tr. by Arthur Wormhoudt from Arabic. (Arab Translation Ser.: No. 23). 1976. pap. 6.50x o.p. (ISBN 0-916358-73-9). Wormhoudt.

Diwan Ibn Al Nabih Al Misri. (Arab Translation Ser.: No. 13). 1974. pap. 6.50x o.p. (ISBN 0-916358-63-1). Wormhoudt.

Diwan Ibn Al Rumi,'Ali Ibn Al' Abbas. Tr. by Arthur Wormhoudt from Arabic. (Arab Translation Ser.: No. 26). 1977. pap. 6.50x o.p. (ISBN 0-916358-76-3). Wormhoudt.

Diwan Imru Al Qais. Tr. by Arthur Wormhoudt. (Arab Translation Ser.: No. 15). 1974. pap. 6.50x o.p. (ISBN 0-916358-65-8). Wormhoudt.

Diwan Ka'b ibn Zuhair & Akhbar Majnun. Tr. by Arthur Wormhoudt from Arabic. (Arab Translation Ser.: No. 18). 1975. pap. 6.50x o.p. (ISBN 0-916358-68-2). Wormhoudt.

Diwan 'Umar Ibn Abu Rabi'a Al Makhzumi. Tr. by Arthur Wormhoudt from Arabic. (Arab Translation Ser.: No. 28). 1977. pap. 6.50x o.p. (ISBN 0-916358-78-X). Wormhoudt.

Diwan Zuhair Ibn Abu Sulma & Diwan Al Hallaj. Tr. by Arthur Wormhoudt. (Arab Translation Ser.: No. 20). 1975. pap. 6.50x o.p. (ISBN 0-916358-70-4). Wormhoudt.

Dixcionario de Filosofia. Eduardo Pallares. 652p. (Span.). 17.50 o.p. (ISBN 0-686-56706-4, S-21915). French & Eur.

Dixie Association. Donald Hays. 352p. 1984. 16.45 o.p. (ISBN 0-671-47564-9). S&S.

Dixie's Forgotten People: The South's Poor Whites. J. Wayne Flynt. LC 78-20613. (Minorities in Modern America: Midland Bks: NO. 244). (Illus.). 224p. 1979. 15.00x o.p. (ISBN 0-253-19765-1); pap. 6.95x o.p. (ISBN 0-253-20244-2). Ind U Pr.

Dizionario Tecnico Inglese-Italiano: Elettronica, Elettrotecnica. Ed. by Henry Piraux. 534p. (Ital.). 1981. 26.00x o.p. (ISBN 0-913298-73-5). S F Vanni.

Djanggawul. Ronald M. Berndt. (Illus.). 344p. 1953. (ISBN 0-8022-0113-X). Philos Lib.

Django Reinhardt. Charles Delaunay. 300p. (Orig.). 1987. pap. 14.95 o.s.i. (ISBN 0-9506224-6-X, HL 00183208, Pub. by Ashley Mark Pub). H Leonard Pub Corp.

Djinn. Alain Robbe-Grillet. Tr. by Yvonne Lenard & Walter Wells. LC 81-86393. Orig. Title: Rendez-Vous. 1982. 10.95 o.p. (ISBN 0-394-52569-8, GP-852); pap. 4.95 o.p. (ISBN 0-394-17983-8). Grove.

Djinn: Text Edition. Alain Robbe-Grillet. 144p. pap. 9.95 o.p. (ISBN 0-394-62460-2, E850, Ever). Grove.

Dmitry: A Young Soviet Immigrant. Joanne E. Bernstein. (Illus.). 80p. (gr. 4-7). 1981. 10.95 o.s.i. (ISBN 0-89919-034-0, Clarion). HM.

DNA in Human Tumors: A Cytophotometric Study see Aortic Alterations in Rabbits Following Sheathing with Silastic & Polyethylene Tubes.

DNA: Protein Interactions & Gene Regulation. Ed. by E. Brad Thompson & John Papaconstantinou. (Medical Branch Ser. in Biomedical Science). (Illus.). 304p. 1987. text ed. 32.50x o.p. (ISBN 0-292-71552-8). U of Tex Pr.

DNA: Recombination, Interactions & Repair. FEBS Symposium on DNA, Liblice, 24-29 September, 1979. Ed. by S. Zadrazil & J. Sponar. (Vol. 63). (Illus.). 600p. 1980. 145.00 o.p. (ISBN 0-08-025494-2). Pergamon.

DNA Replication & Biosynthesis. Ed. by Reed B. Wickner. LC 74-77107. (Methods in Molecular Biology Ser.: Vol. 7). 320p. 1974. 79.75 o.p. (ISBN 0-8247-6202-9). Dekker.

DNA: The Ladder of Life. 2nd ed. Edward Frankel. (Illus.). (gr. 7 up). 1979. text ed. 10.95 o.p. (ISBN 0-07-021883-8). McGraw.

DNA: The Master Molecule. National Science Foundation Staff. Ed. by Warren Kornberg. (Mosaic Reader Ser.). 64p. (Orig.). 1982. pap. text ed. 5.00 o.p. (ISBN 0-89529-172-X). Avery Pub.

D'Nealian Manuscript: A Continuous Stroke Approach to Handwriting. Donald N. Thurber. 80p. 1984. pap. text ed. 8.00 o.p. (ISBN 0-87879-445-X). Acad Therapy.

Do Decimals First. Verda Holmberg. (Illus., Orig.). (gr. 3-8). 1976. tchr's. ed. 6.95 o.p. (ISBN 0-918932-08-4); wkbk. 1.95 o.p. (ISBN 0-918932-09-2). Activity Resources.

Do Diapers Give You Leprosy? What Every Parent Should Know about Bringing Up Babies. Ira Alterman. 96p. 1984. pap. 3.95 o.p. (ISBN 0-8092-5365-8). Contemp Bks.

Do Evil Cheerfully. Sarah Bird. 192p. 1983. pap. 2.95 o.p. (ISBN 0-380-84137-1, 84137-1). Avon.

Do Evil in Return. Margaret Millar. 1974. pap. 0.95 o.p. (ISBN 0-380-00033-4, 19398). Avon.

Do I Know the "Me" Others See? Shirley Schwarzrock & C. Gilbert Wrenn. (Coping With Ser.). (Illus.). 55p. (gr. 7-12). 1973. pap. text ed. 3.00 o.p. (ISBN 0-913476-27-7). Am Guidance.

Do-It-Better Book. Shari Lewis. LC 79-3839. (Kids-Only Club Bks.). (Illus.). 96p. (Orig.). (gr. 3-6). 1981. 6.95 o.p. (ISBN 0-03-049721-3); pap. 3.95 o.p. (ISBN 0-03-049726-4). H Holt & Co.

Do It in the Dark. Tom Burk. LC 74-82516. (Illus.). 200p. 1975. pap. 7.95 o.p. (ISBN 0-912656-28-X). Price Stern.

Do It Yourself. Dovie Arnold & Kayte Lee Posey. 1971. pap. 2.25x o.p. (ISBN 0-88323-007-0, 187). Pendergrass Pub.

Do-It-Yourself Designer Furniture. Richard Entwistle. (Illus.). 160p. (Orig.). 1986. pap. 12.95 o.p. (ISBN 0-8069-6344-1). Sterling.

Do-It-Yourself Marketing for Small-Volume Builders: How to Beat the Competition on a Shoestring. Charles Clark & David Parker. 1987. write for info. o.p. (ISBN 0-86718-286-5). Nat Assn H Build.

Do-It-Yourself Marketing Research. 2nd ed. George E. Breen & A. B. Blankenship. 1982. text ed. 37.50 o.p. (ISBN 0-07-007446-1). McGraw.

Do-it-Yourself Mutual Fund Book. Frank L. Bouquet. (Illus.). 63p. (Orig.). 1986. text ed. 50.00 o.p. (ISBN 0-937041-12-2); pap. text ed. 30.00 o.p. (ISBN 0-937041-13-0). Systems Co.

Do-It-Yourself Show Book of Home Improvements. Robert Roskind. 1985. write for info. o.p. (ISBN 0-201-06573-8); pap. write for info. o.p. (ISBN 0-201-06574-6). Addison-Wesley.

Do Renshaw Cells Exist? Ed. by W. Riss. (Brain, Behavior & Evolution: Vol. 4, No. 1). 1971. pap. 11.00 o.p. (ISBN 3-8055-1195-7). S Karger.

Do Russian People Stand for War. Wilton J. Brown. 70p. 1985. 20.00x o.p. (ISBN 0-317-42761-X, Pub by Collets (UK)). State Mutual Bk.

Do This in Memory of Me. Thomas A. Dunne. LC 81-67927. (Illus.). 237p. (Orig.). (gr. 10-12). 1981. pap. text ed. 4.95x o.p. (ISBN 0-89944-056-8); tchr's manual 2.95x o.p. (ISBN 0-89944-057-6). Don Bosco Multimedia.

Do What You Love, the Money Will Follow: Discovering Your Right Livelihood. Marsha Sinetar. 208p. 1987. pap. 7.95 o.p. (ISBN 0-8091-2874-8). Paulist Pr.

Do You Know How the Sun Laughs? V. Beshlyage et al. 262p. 1976. 3.95 o.p. (ISBN 0-8285-0948-4, Pub. by Progress Pubs USSR). Imported Pubns.

Do You Know What Anything Is? Da Free John. LC 84-70215. 1984. pap. 12.95 o.s.i. (ISBN 0-913922-87-0). Dawn Horse Pr.

Do You Read Me? Practical Approaches to Teaching Reading Comprehension. Arnold A. Griese. LC 76-9913. (Illus.). 1977. pap. 12.95 o.p. (ISBN 0-673-16354-7); 13.95 o.p. (ISBN 0-673-16353-9). Scott F.

Do You Really Need a Home Computer? The Book to Read Before You Byte. Derek Rowntree. (Illus.). 120p. 1985. pap. 6.95 o.p. (ISBN 0-684-18182-7). Scribner.

Do You Want Me to Do All That & Plow Too? Dan P. Logan, Sr. 1978. 7.50 o.p. (ISBN 0-682-49146-2). Exposition-Phoenix.

Do Your Own Car Body Repairs. 2nd ed. Paul Revere. (Illus.). 96p. 1982. 11.95x o.p. (ISBN 0-572-01182-2). Trans-Atl Phila.

Do Your Own Public Relations. Philip Benoit & Carl Hausman. (Illus.). 256p. 1983. pap. 13.15 o.p. (ISBN 0-8306-1595-4, 1595P). TAB Bks.

DOA: I Came Back. Michael J. Veldhuis. LC 84-60866. 1984. pap. 3.95 o.p. (ISBN 0-89051-101-2). Master Bks.

Doc Flighty. John A. Norcross & Joseph P. Tracy. LC 65-14327. (Illus.). 1965. 1.95 o.p. (ISBN 0-8168-5200-6, TAB-Aero); pap. 1.00 o.p. (ISBN 0-8168-5203-0). TAB Bks.

Doc: The Story of Dennis Littky & His Fight for a Better School. Susan Kammeraad-Campbell. (Illus.). (YA) 17.95 o.s.i. (ISBN 0-8092-4611-2). Contemp Bks.

Doccionari De L'utillatage Quimic. Salvador Alegret Sanroma. 64p. (Catalan.). 1977. pap. 8.75 o.p. (ISBN 84-7283-013-6, S-50061). French & Eur.

Dr. & Mrs. Fix-It: The Story of Frank & Bessie Beck. Natalie Barber. LC 79-130776. (Bold Believers Ser). (Orig.). 1969. pap. 0.95 o.p. (ISBN 0-377-84181-1). Friendship Pr.

Doctor & the Damned. Albert Haas. 336p. 1985. pap. 3.95 o.p. (ISBN 0-380-69935-4, Discus). Avon.

Doctor & the Soul: From Psychotherapy to Logotherapy. Viktor E. Frankl. LC 85-40681. 336p. 1986. pap. 6.95 o.p. (ISBN 0-394-74317-2, Vin). Random.

Dr. Andy Answers Your Everyday Medical Questions. Andrew P. Morley, Jr. LC 86-16337. 320p. 1986. 15.95 o.p. (ISBN 0-8407-9070-8). Oliver-Nelson.

Dr. Anne. Gloria Swanson & Viginia Ott. LC 79-50083. 1979. pap. 3.95 o.p. (ISBN 0-8066-1705-5, 10-1925, Augsburg). Augsburg Fortress.

Doctor as Judge of Who Shall Live & Who Shall Die. Helmut Thielicke. Tr. by Edward A. Cooperrider from Ger. LC 75-42836. 48p. (Orig.). 1976. pap. 0.50 o.p. (ISBN 0-8006-1228-0, 1-1228, Fortress). Augsburg Fortress.

Doctor at Sea. Patrick R. Allanson. 1980. 8.50 o.p. (ISBN 0-682-49510-7). Exposition-Phoenix.

Dr. Berger's Immune Power Diet. Stuart M. Berger. 1988. 3.98 o.p. (ISBN 0-517-64260-3). Crown.

Doctor Bey's Bedside Bug Book. Derek Pell. LC 78-6574. (Illus.). 1978. pap. 3.95 o.p. (ISBN 0-15-626115-4, Harv). HarBraceJ.

Dr. Bob Shipp's Guide to the Fishes of the Gulf of Mexico. 2nd ed. Bob Shipp. LC 86-71419. (Illus.). 256p. Date not set. spiral bdg. 15.95 o.p. (ISBN 0-938917-03-X); text ed. 26.95 o.p. (ISBN 0-938917-01-3); pap. text ed. 16.95 o.p. (ISBN 0-938917-02-1). Marine Environ.

Dr. Booboo's Baby & Child Repair. John Buskin & Alfred Gingold. 96p. (Orig.). 1985. pap. 6.95 o.p. (ISBN 0-380-89509-9). Avon.

Dr. Burns' Prescription for Happiness. George Burns. (Illus.). 170p. 1986. lib. bdg. 13.95 o.p. (ISBN 0-8161-3942-3, Large Print Bks). G K Hall.

Dr. C. Wacko Presents Atari BASIC & the Whiz-Bang Miracle Machine. David Heller & John Johnson. 1245p. 1984. pap. (ISBN 0-201-11491-7). Addison-Wesley.

Dr. C. Wacko's Miracle Guide to Designing & Programming Your Own Atari Computer Arcade Games. David Heller et al. 1983. pap. 12.95 o.p. (ISBN 0-201-11488-7); write for info. book & software o.p. (ISBN 0-201-11490-9). Addison-Wesley.

Doctor Copernicus. John Banville. 1977. 8.95 o.p. (ISBN 0-393-08757-3). Norton.

Dr. Dan's Prescriptions. Dan Kiley. 256p. 1985. pap. 3.95 o.p. (ISBN 0-380-69928-1). Avon.

Dr. David Livingstone & Henry Morton Stanley: An Annotated Bibliography with Commentary. James A. Casada. LC 75-24101. (Reference Library of Social Science: Vol. 21). 225p. 1976. lib. bdg. 31.00 o.p. (ISBN 0-8240-9967-2). Garland Pub.

Doctor Discusses a Man's Sexual Health. Robert E. Dunbar. (Illus.). 1984. pap. 2.99 o.p. (ISBN 0-685-64313-1). Budlong.

Doctor Discusses Cancer. Tom Maher & Malcolm Schwartz. (Illus.). 1981. pap. 2.99 o.p. (ISBN 0-686-69338-8). Budlong.

Doctor Discusses Care of the Back. Paul Neimark & Gerald Berkowitz. 1987. pap. 2.99 o.p. (ISBN 0-910304-04-1). Budlong.

Doctor Discusses Female Surgery. Paul Neimark & Samuel Matlin. (Illus.). 1986. pap. 2.99 o.p. (ISBN 0-686-65550-8). Budlong.

Doctor Discusses Learning to Cope with Arthritis Rheumatism & Gout. Robert E. Dunbar. (Illus., Orig.). 1986. pap. 2.99 o.p. (ISBN 0-685-35675-2). Budlong.

Doctor Discusses Learning to Live with Heart Trouble. Arthur J. Snider & I. J. Adatto. (Illus.). 1985. pap. 2.99 o.p. (ISBN 0-685-35677-9). Budlong.

Doctor Discusses Nutrition During Pregnancy & Breast Feeding. Bonnie Worthington & Lynda Taylor. (Illus.). 1986. pap. 2.99 o.p. (ISBN 0-686-70167-4). Budlong.

Doctor Discusses Pregnancy. William G. Birch & Dona Z. Meilach. (Illus.). 1987. pap. 2.99 o.p. (ISBN 0-910304-00-9). Budlong.

Doctor Discusses Prepared Childbirth. Lou Joseph & Ulisse Cucco. 1986. pap. 2.99 o.p. (ISBN 0-910304-21-1). Budlong.

Doctor Discusses Talking with Your Child About Sex. Arlene Uslander & Lee D. Weiss. (Illus.). 1986. pap. 2.99 o.p. (ISBN 0-685-46343-5). Budlong.

Dr. Dobb's Journal of Computer Calisthenics & Orthodontia: For Users of Small Computer Systems, Vol. 4. 1982. pap. 27.75 o.p. (ISBN 0-8104-5491-2). M&T Pub Inc.

Dr. Drummond's Spirited Guide to Health Care in a Dying Empire. Hugh Drummond. LC 80-994. 352p. 1980. pap. 3.95 o.s.i. (ISBN 0-394-17674-X, B447, BC). Grove.

Doctor: Father Figure or Plumber? James McCormick. 168p. 1979. 20.00 o.p. (ISBN 0-85664-593-1, Pub. by Croom Helm Ltd). Routledge Chapman & Hall.

Doctor Faustus. Christopher Marlowe. 48p. (Orig.). 1989. pap. 9.95 o.p. (ISBN 1-55651-179-5); audiocassette tape incl. o.p. (ISBN 1-55651-180-9). Cram Cassettes.

Doctor Faustus: Text & Major Criticism, Marlowe. Ed. by Irving Ribner. 216p. 1966. pap. text ed. (ISBN 0-02-399720-6). Macmillan.

Dr. Fegg's Encyclopedia of All World Knowledge. Terry Jones & Michael Palin. LC 84-24479. (Illus.). 96p. 1985. pap. 7.99 o.p. (ISBN 0-87226-005-4). P Bedrick Bks.

Dr. Fischer of Geneva or the Bomb Party. Graham Greene. 144p. 1981. pap. 2.50 o.p. (ISBN 0-380-55202-7, 55202-7). Avon.

Dr. Gardner's Modern Fairy Tales. Richard A. Gardner. LC 76-53252. (Illus.). 106p. (ps-2). 1977. PLB 8.95 o.p. (ISBN 0-89313-002-8). G F Stickley Co.

Doctor Gardner's Stories About the Real World. Richard A. Gardner. 1976. pap. 1.50 o.p. (ISBN 0-380-00625-1, 29025). Avon.

Dr. Gruber's Daughter. Janice Elliot. 159p. 1988. 18.95 o.p. (ISBN 0-340-39762-4, Pub. by Hodder & Stoughton UK). David & Charles.

Dr. Heimlich's Home Guide to Emergency Medical Situations. Henry J. Heimlich & Lawrence Galton. 1980. 10.95 o.p. (ISBN 0-671-24947-9, 24947). S&S.

Dr. Heimlich's Home Guide to Emergency Medical Situations. Henry J. Heimlich & Lawrence Galton. 352p. 1984. pap. 5.95 o.p. (ISBN 0-671-53075-5, Fireside). S&S.

Dr. Ida: Passing on the Torch of Life. Dorothy C. Wilson. 1976. pap. 3.50 o.p. (ISBN 0-377-84221-4). Friendship Pr.

Doctor in Rags. Louise A. Vernon. LC 75-5367. (Illus.). 160p. (gr. 4-9). 1973. 5.95 o.p. (ISBN 0-8361-1697-6); pap. 3.95 o.p. (ISBN 0-8361-1698-4). Herald Pr.

Dr. Jekyll & Mr. Hyde: An Anthology of Commentary, Including the Text. Harry M. Geduld. LC 82-48271. 175p. 1983. lib. bdg. 28.00 o.p. (ISBN 0-8240-9469-7). Garland Pub.

Dr. Jesus Christ & the Sick World. Money Alian Kirby. 1980. 4.50 o.p. (ISBN 0-682-49101-2). Exposition-Phoenix.

Dr. Jim's Elementary Math Prescriptions. James Overholt. LC 78-2031. (Illus.). 1978. 13.95 o.p. (ISBN 0-673-16355-5); pap. 12.95 o.p. (ISBN 0-673-16356-3). Scott F.

Dr. Johnson's "Dear Mistress" Winifred Carter. 1950. (ISBN 0-8022-0216-0). Philos Lib.

Dr. Kilgore's Feel Good Parenting Book. James D. Kilgore. 1986. 9.95 o.p. (ISBN 0-8007-1508-X). Revell.

Dr. Kritsick's Tender Loving Cat Care. Stephen M. Kritsick. 320p. 1986. 16.45 o.p. (ISBN 0-671-46725-5, Linden Pr). S&S.

Dr. Lendon Smith's Diet Plan for Teenagers. Lendon Smith. 288p. 1986. text ed. 16.95 o.p. (ISBN 0-07-058700-0). McGraw.

Dr. Lendon Smith's Low-Stress Diet. Lendon Smith. 192p. 1985. text ed. 14.95 o.p. (ISBN 0-07-058500-8). McGraw.

Dr. Mandell's Allergy-Free Cookbook. Fran G. Mandell. 1983. pap. 3.50 o.s.i. (ISBN 0-671-49562-3). PB.

Dr. Michael Fox's Massage Program for Cats & Dogs see Healing Touch.

Doctor Migration & World Health. Oscar Gish. 151p. 1971. pap. text ed. 6.75x o.p. (ISBN 0-7135-1611-9, Pub. by Bedford England). Gower Pub Co.

Dr. Miriam Stoppard's Book of Baby Care. Miriam Stoppard. LC 77-76668. (Illus.). 1977. 10.95 o.p. (ISBN 0-689-10810-9, Atheneum). Macmillan.

Dr. Mom: A Guide to Baby & Child Care. Marianne Neifert & Anne Price. LC 85-25748. 448p. 1986. 19.95 o.p. (ISBN 0-399-13124-8). Putnam Pub Group.

Dr. Moore's Legacy. Agatha Young. 1975. pap. 1.50 o.p. (ISBN 0-380-00297-3, 23275). Avon.

Doctor No. Ian Fleming. 240p. 1980. pap. 3.50 o.s.i. (ISBN 0-425-08679-8). Jove Pubns.

Doctor of Desire: A Novel. Allen Wheelis. 1987. 14.45 o.p. (ISBN 0-393-02425-3). Norton.

Doctor Rat. William Kotzwinkle. 224p. 1983. pap. 3.95 o.p. (ISBN 0-380-63990-4, Bard). Avon.

Dr. Robinson's Voice in the Wilderness, 3 vols, No. 2. 1970. Repr. of 1920 ed. Set. lib. bdg. 22.00x o.p. (ISBN 0-8371-9159-9, DR00). Greenwood.

Dr. Rubin, Please Make Me Happy. Theodore I. Rubin. LC 73-90111. 1982. pap. 7.95 o.p. (ISBN 0-87795-427-5, Arbor Hse). Morrow.

Doctor Ruth's Guide to Good Sex. Ruth Westheimer. (Large Print Series). 576p. 1986. lib. bdg. 19.95 o.p. (ISBN 0-8161-4075-8, Large Print Bks); pap. 12.95 o.p. (ISBN 0-8161-4076-6). G K Hall.

Doctor Sax. Jack Kerouac. 1959. pap. 5.95 o.p. (ISBN 0-394-17278-7, B394, BC). Grove.

Dr. Sheehan on Fitness. George A. Sheehan. (Illus.). 256p. 1983. 13.50 o.p. (ISBN 0-671-45478-1). S&S.

Doctor Talks to Five to Eight Year Olds. Dona Z. Meilach & Elias Mandel. (Illus.). 1985. pap. 2.99 o.p. (ISBN 0-910304-14-9). Budlong.

Doctor Talks to Nine to Twelve Year Olds. Caroline Weiss & Arlene Uslander. (Illus.). 1986. pap. 2.99 o.p. (ISBN 0-910304-03-3). Budlong.

Doctor Tree: Developmental Stages in the Growth of Physicians. Ralph N. Zabarenko & Lucy M. Zabarenko. LC 77-18340. (Contemporary Community Health Ser.). 1978. 17.95x o.p. (ISBN 0-8229-3370-5). U of Pittsburgh Pr.

Doctor Was a Guest. Claire Vernon. (Lythway Ser.). 200p. 1988. lib. bdg. 18.50x o.p. (ISBN 0-7451-0689-7, Pub. by Chivers Pr UK). G K Hall.

Dr. Webb of Colorado Springs. Helen Clapesattle. LC 84-70852. 1984. 19.95 o.p. (ISBN 0-87081-050-2); pap. 9.95 o.p. (ISBN 0-87081-164-9). Univ Pr Colo.

Doctor! What You Should Know About Health Care Before You Call a Physician. T. C. Johnson. 432p. 1975. text ed. 8.95 o.p. (ISBN 0-07-032664-9). McGraw.

Dr. Who Special Effects. Mat Irvine. (Illus.). 96p. (YA) (gr. 8 up). 1987. 22.95 o.p. (ISBN 0-09-167920-6, Pub. by Century Hutchinson). David & Charles.

Dr. Wright's Guide to Healing with Nutrition. Ed. by Jonathan V. Wright & Carol Baldwin. (Illus.). 624p. 1984. 19.95 o.p. (ISBN 0-87857-485-9, 05-0440). Rodale Pr Inc.

Dr. Zizmor's Skin Care Book. Jonathan Zizmor & John Foreman. LC 76-29920. 1977. 8.95 o.p. (ISBN 0-03-017846-0); pap. 5.95 o.p. (ISBN 0-03-021471-8). H Holt & Co.

Doctoral Research on Russia & the Soviet Union: 1960-1975. Jesse J. Dossick. LC 75-5115. (Reference Library of Social Science: Vol. 7). 200p. 1975. lib. bdg. 47.00 o.p. (ISBN 0-8240-1079-5). Garland Pub.

Doctoral Scientists in Oceanography. National Research Council, Ocean Sciences Board Staff. 1981. pap. text ed. 9.25x o.p. (ISBN 0-309-03133-8). Natl Acad Pr.

Doctors' Administrative Program, 8 vols. Avis Ziegler. Incl. Dap 1. Patient Contact & Public Relations (ISBN 0-87489-150-7); Dap 2. Bookkeeping & Tax Reports (ISBN 0-87489-151-5); Dap 3. Insurance & Third-Party-Payable Claims (ISBN 0-87489-152-3); Dap 4. Correspondence (ISBN 0-87489-153-1); Dap 5. Billing & Collections; Dap 7. Clinical Assisting (ISBN 0-87489-156-6). 1979-82. Set. 155.00 o.p. (ISBN 0-87489-158-2); 19.95 ea. o.p. Med Economics.

Doctors & Medicine in Medieval England, 1340-1530. Robert S. Gottfried. (Illus.). 328p. 1986. text ed. 45.00x o.p. (ISBN 0-691-05481-9). Princeton U Pr.

Doctors & Nurses. T. K. Oommen. 1978. 14.00x o.p. (ISBN 0-8364-0258-8). South Asia Bks.

Doctors & Society: Three Asian Case Studies. T. N. Madan et al. 1980. text ed. 25.00x o.p. (ISBN 0-7069-C814-7, Pub. by Vikas India). Advent NY.

Doctors & Wives. Ann Pinchot. LC 79-87839. 1980. 10.95 o.p. (ISBN 0-87795-236-1, Arbor Hse). Morrow.

Doctor's Anti-Breast Cancer Diet: How the Right Foods Can Reduce Your Risk of Breast Cancer. Sherwood L. Gorbach & David R. Zimmerman. 1984. 15.45 o.p. (ISBN 0-671-49552-6). S&S.

Doctor's Boy. Karin Anckarsvard. Tr. by Annabelle MacMillan. LC 65-12330. (Illus.). (gr. 4-7). 1965. 5.50 o.p. (ISBN 0-15-223925-1, HJ). HarBraceJ.

Doctor's Casebook in the Light of the Bible. Paul Tournier. LC 60-8140. 1976. pap. 5.95i o.p. (ISBN 0-06-068311-2, RD 318). HarpR.

Doctors' Computer Handbook. Peter J. Fell & William D. Skees. (Management Ser.). (Illus.). 290p. 1984. 34.95 o.p. (ISBN 0-534-02724-5, Lifetime Learn). Van Nos Reinhold.

Doctor's Life. Nicholas S. Assali. LC 79-1808. 1979. 12.95 o.p. (ISBN 0-15-126161-X). HarBraceJ.

Doctors' Metabolic Diet. William F. Kremer & Laura Kremer. 1976. pap. 1.75 o.p. (ISBN 0-380-00726-6, 29991). Avon.

Doctor's Odyssey. J. M. Sanchez-Perez. 1973. 7.50 o.p. (ISBN 0-682-47649-8). Exposition-Phoenix.

Doctors, Patients & Pathology. Hilarly Rose. 79p. 1972. pap. text ed. 5.00x o.p. (ISBN 0-7135-1741-7, Pub. by Bedford England). Gower Pub Co.

Doctor's Prescription for Gourmet Cooking. Reba M. Hill. 274p. (Orig.). 1984. pap. 9.95 o.s.i. (ISBN 0-89716-135-1). Peanut Butter.

Doctor's Quartet & More. Lionel A. Canaan. 1980. 8.95 o.p. (ISBN 0-533-04693-9). Vantage.

Doctor's Quick Inches-off Diet. Irwin M. Stillman & Samm S. Baker. 1983. pap. 3.95 o.p. (ISBN 0-440-12043-8). Dell.

Doctor's Quick Weight Loss Diet. Irwin M. Stillman & Samm S. Baker. 1987. pap. 3.95 o.p. (ISBN 0-440-12045-4). Dell.

Doctor's Sensible Approach to Dieting & Weight Control. Eugene Scheimann & Paul Neimark. (Illus.). 1986. pap. 2.99 o.p. (ISBN 0-910304-19-X). Budlong.

Doctor's Sex Guide for Patients. Bernard S. Greenblatt. (Illus.). 1986. pap. 2.99 o.p. (ISBN 0-685-07679-2). Budlong.

Doctor's Soliloquy. Joseph Krimsky. Philos Lib.

Doctor's Tax Manual. Bender's Editorial Staff & Peter Reiss. 1981. Updates avail. pap. 35.00 o.p. (ISBN 0-317-37791-4, 196); pap. 25.00, 1983 o.p. (ISBN 0-317-37792-2); pap. 30.00, 1984 o.p. (ISBN 0-317-37793-0). Bender.

Doctor's Wife. Brian Moore. 277p. 1976. 8.95 o.p. (ISBN 0-374-14096-0). FS&G.

Doctrinal Theology of the Evangelical Lutheran Church. Heinrich Schmid. LC 66-13052. 1961. 27.95 o.p. (ISBN 0-8066-0107-8, 10-1930, Augsburg). Augsburg Fortress.

Doctrine & Covenants & Pearl of Great Price Digest. John D. Hawkes. 1977. pap. text ed. 4.95 o.p. (ISBN 0-89036-100-2). Hawkes Pub Inc.

Doctrine & Covenants: Our Modern Scripture. rev. ed. Richard O. Cowan. LC 78-19190. (Illus.). 1978. pap. 7.95 o.p. (ISBN 0-8425-1316-7). Brigham.

Doctrine & Word. Mark Ellingsen. LC 82-21311. 192p. 1983. pap. 9.95 o.p. (ISBN 0-8042-0533-7, John Knox). Westminster John Knox.

Doctrine of Jehovah's Witnesses. R. D. Quidam. 128p. 1958. (ISBN 0-8022-2023-1). Philos Lib.

Doctrine of Philosophical Necessity Illustrated: Being an Appendix to the Disquestions Relating to Matter & Spirit see Disquisitions Relating Matter & Spirit.

Doctrine of Scripture. Cornelius Van Til. 1967. pap. 5.50 syllabus o.p. (ISBN 0-87552-484-2). Presby & Reformed.

Document Mark (BLIP) Used in Image Mark Retrieval Systems: ANSI-AIIM MS8-1979. Rev. ed. Association for Information & Image Management Staff. (Standards & Recommended Practices). 1980. 10.00 o.p. (ISBN 0-89258-060-7, MS08). Assn Inform & Image Mgmt.

Document Organization, Management & Production. Sandra J. Breslauer et al. 176p. 1988. manual 30.00 o.p. (00369). PES Inc WI.

Document Retrieval: Sources & Services, (the Only Directory of Public & Private Document Retrieval Suppliers) 3rd ed. 1983. 60.00 o.p. (ISBN 0-317-00239-2). Learned Info.

Documentary History of American Economic Policy Since 1789. enl. & rev. ed. Ed. by William Letwin. 1972. pap. 4.45x o.p. (ISBN 0-393-00442-2, Norton Lib). Norton.

Documentary History of Communism: Volume 1, Communism in Russia. updated, rev. ed. Ed. by Robert V. Daniels. LC 88-5580. 480p. 1988. 14.95x o.p. (ISBN 0-87451-459-2). U Pr of New Eng.

Documentary History of Reconstruction: Political, Military, Social, Religious, Educational & Industrial, 2 vols. in 1. Walter L. Fleming. 26.00 o.p. (ISBN 0-8446-1184-0). Peter Smith.

Documentary Report of the Ann Arbor Symposium: Applications of Psychology to the Teaching & Learning of Music, Sessions I & II. Music Educators National Conference Staff. 372p. 1981. 18.75 o.p. (ISBN 0-940796-24-4, 1010). Music Ed Natl.

Documentary Report of the Ann Arbor Symposium. Music Educators National Conference. 372p. 1981. 18.75 o.p. Music Ed Natl.

Documentary Report of the Tanglewood Symposium. Ed. by Robert A. Choate. LC 68-57058. 160p. (Orig.). 1968. pap. 12.50 o.p. (ISBN 0-940796-02-3, 1011). Music Ed Natl.

Documentary Study of Hendrik De Man, Socialist Critic of Marxism. Ed. by Peter Dodge. LC 78-70288. 1979. 40.00x o.p. (ISBN 0-691-03123-1). Princeton U Pr.

Documenting Systems (the User's View) Ed. by National Computing Centre, Ltd. Staff. (Computers & the Professional Ser). 130p. 1972. pap. 23.00x o.s.i. (ISBN 0-85012-057-8). Intl Pubns Serv.

Documents for Drama & Revolution. Ed. by Bernard F. Dukore. LC 76-137988. 1971. pap. text ed. 10.95x o.p. (ISBN 0-03-083651-4). Irvington.

Documents in the Case. Dorothy L. Sayers. 1971. pap. 1.75 o.p. (ISBN 0-380-01143-3, 58263-5). Avon.

Documents of German History. Ed. by Louis L. Snyder. LC 75-32435. 619p. 1975. Repr. of 1958 ed. lib. bdg. 33.00x o.p. (ISBN 0-8371-8493-2, SNDG). Greenwood.

Documents of Modern Literary Realism. Ed. by George J. Becker. 1963. 32.50x o.p. (ISBN 0-691-06026-6); pap. 18.95x o.p. (ISBN 0-691-01258-X). Princeton U Pr.

Documents of the Arab-Israel Conflict: The Resolutions of the United Nations Organization, 2 vols. Ed. by Wilhelm Wengler & Josef Tittel. Vol. 1. cancelled o.s.i. (ISBN 3-87061-012-3); cancelled o.s.i. (ISBN 3-87061-163-4). Adlers Foreign Bks.

Documents on Disarmament. Compiled by R. William Nary. (Arms Control & Disarmament Agency Publication Ser.: No. 126). 970p. (Orig.). 1986. pap. 27.50 o.p. (S/N 002-000-00091-1). USGPO.

Documents on Fundamental Human Rights, the Anglo-American Tradition, 2 Vols. Ed. by Zechariah Chafee, Jr. LC 53-205. 1963. pap. 1.95 ea. o.p. (Atheneum). Vol. 1 (ISBN 0-689-70043-1, 20A). Vol. 2 (ISBN 0-689-70045-8, 20B). Macmillan.

Documents on Major European Governments. Ed. by Randolph L. Braham. 11.25 o.p. (ISBN 0-8446-1723-7). Peter Smith.

Documents on the History of the Russian-American Company. Ed. by Richard A. Pierce. Tr. by Marina Ramsay. (Alaska History Ser.: No. 7). (Illus.). 220p. 1976. 16.50 o.p. (ISBN 0-919642-08-X). Limestone Pr.

Documents Relating to Indian Affairs, May 21, 1750-August 7, 1754. Ed. by William L. McDowell, Jr. LC 70-627805. (Colonial Records of South Carolina Ser.: No. 2). 1958. 39.95x o.p. (ISBN 0-87249-911-1). U of SC Pr.

Documents Relating to Ireland, 1795-1804. John T. Gilbert. 282p. 1969. Repr. of 1893 ed. text ed. 32.50x o.p. (ISBN 0-7165-0048-5, BBA 02164, Pub. by Irish Academic Pr. Ireland). Biblio Dist.

Documents Relating to the Proceedings Against William Prynne, in 1634 & 1637. Ed. by Samuel R. Gardiner. Repr. of 1877 ed. 31.00 o.p. (ISBN 0-384-17635-6). Johnson Repr.

Dodge - Plymouth Vans 1967-84: RTUG. Chilton Automotives Editorial Staff. LC 83-45307. 264p. 1984. pap. 13.50 o.p. (ISBN 0-8019-7465-8). Chilton.

Dodge & Plymouth 4-Wheel Drive Tune-Up: 4-Wheel Drive Maintenance, 1965-1982. Ed. by Eric Jorgensen. pap. 9.95 o.p. (ISBN 0-89287-289-6, A231). Clymer Pub.

Dodge Aspen: 1976-1979 Shop Manual. Ed. by Eric Jorgensen. (Illus.). pap. text ed. 11.95 o.p. (ISBN 0-89287-311-6, A199). Clymer Pub.

Dodge Assemblies Cost Data, 1987. Dodge Cost Information Systems Staff. 220p. 1987. text ed. 69.50 o.p. (ISBN 0-07-017554-3). McGraw.

Dodge Car Tune-up & Maintenance, 1968-1982. Ed. by Jeff Robinson. (Illus.). pap. 9.95 o.p. (ISBN 0-89287-143-1, A-153). Clymer Pub.

Dodge Colt & Challenger Nineteen Seventy-one to Nineteen Eighty-One. Chilton Automotives Editorial Staff. LC 80-70346. (Illus.). 242p. 1980. pap. 11.95 o.p. (ISBN 0-8019-7037-7). Chilton.

Dodge Construction Systems Costs, 1985. Dodge Cost Information Systems Staff. 1985. pap. text ed. 60.50 o.p. (ISBN 0-07-017416-4). McGraw.

Dodge Guide to Public Works & Heavy Construction. Dodge Cost Information Systems Staff. 1985. pap. text ed. 48.50 o.p. (ISBN 0-07-017417-2). McGraw.

Dodge Heavy Construction Cost Data, 1988. Dodge Cost Information Systems Staff. 228p. 1988. text ed. 59.00 o.p. (ISBN 0-07-017594-2). McGraw.

Dodge Heavy Construction Costs, 1987. Dodge Cost Information Systems Staff. 250p. 1987. text ed. 59.50 o.p. (ISBN 0-07-017553-5). McGraw.

Dodge Man Build Con. 1986. text ed. 48.50 o.p. (ISBN 0-07-017544-6). McGraw.

Dodge Manual for Building Construction Pricing & Scheduling. Dodge Cost Information Systems Staff. 1984. pap. text ed. 45.50 o.p. (ISBN 0-07-017418-0). McGraw.

Dodge Manual for Building Construction Pricing & Scheduling, 1979. Dodge Building Cost Services Staff. 1978. text ed. 24.80 o.p. (ISBN 0-07-017321-4). McGraw.

Dodge Pickup Repair. Ed. by Spence Murray. LC 79-53094. (Pickups & Vans Ser.). (Illus.). 1979. pap. 4.95 o.p. (ISBN 0-8227-5043-0). Petersen Pub.

Dodge Plymouth Tune-up Maintenance: Vans & Pickups, 1965-1978. Mike Bishop. Ed. by Eric Jorgensen. (Illus.). 1978. pap. 7.00 o.p. (ISBN 0-89287-239-X, A241). Clymer Pub.

Dodge-Plymouth Vans, Nineteen Sixty-Seven to Nineteen Eighty-Two. Chilton Automotives Editorial Staff. 1982. pap. 13.50 o.p. (ISBN 0-8019-7168-3). Chilton.

Dodge Remodeling & Retrofit Cost Data, 1987. Dodge Cost Information Systems Staff. 270p. 1987. text ed. 45.00 o.p. (ISBN 0-07-017551-9). McGraw.

Dodge Remodeling & Retrofit Cost Data, 1988. Dodge Cost Information Systems Staff. 400p. 1988. text ed. 37.00 o.p. (ISBN 0-07-017595-0). McGraw.

Dodge Trucks Nineteen Sixty-Seven through Eighty-Four: RTUG - Includes Pick-Ups, Ramcharger, Trailduster. Chilton Automotives Editorial Staff. LC 83-45302. 288p. 1984. pap. 13.50 o.p. (ISBN 0-8019-7459-3). Chilton.

Dodge Unit Cost Data, 1987. Dodge Cost Information Systems Staff. 260p. 1987. text ed. 55.00 o.p. (ISBN 0-07-017552-7). McGraw.

Dodgem. Bernard Ashley. (gr. 7 up). 1982. lib. bdg. 9.90 o.p. (ISBN 0-531-04363-0, MacRae). Watts.

Dodgers: The Complete Record of Dodger Baseball. MacMillan Editorial Staff. (Illus.). 384p. 1986. pap. 9.95 o.p. (ISBN 0-02-028380-6). Macmillan.

Dodges: The Auto Family Fortune & Misfortune. Jean M. Pitrone & Joan P. Elwart. (Illus.). 352p. 1981. 18.95 o.s.i. (ISBN 0-89651-150-2). B L Pub.

Dod's Parlimentary Companion, 1986, 154th Yr. 100.00 o.p. Intl Pubns Serv.

Dodsworth. Sinclair Lewis. 1939. (ISBN 0-15-126192-X). HarBraceJ.

Doers & Dreamers: Social Reformers of the 19th Century. Lynne Deur. LC 79-128808. (Pull Ahead Bks.). (gr. 5-11). 1972. PLB 5.95 o.p. (ISBN 0-8225-0462-6). Lerner Pubns.

Does God Give Interviews? Carolyn Hall. 56p. 1985. 7.95 o.p. (ISBN 0-533-06644-1). Vantage.

Does Khaki Become You? The Militarization of Women's Lives. Cynthia Enloe. 224p. 1983. 20.00 o.p. (ISBN 0-89608-184-2); pap. 8.00 o.p. (ISBN 0-89608-183-4). South End Pr.

Does Prayer Make a Difference? Dan D. Whitsett. (Prayers in My Life Ser.: Ser. I). 1974. pap. 1.25x o.p. (ISBN 0-8358-0312-0). Upper Room.

Does This Mean My Kid's a Genius. L. P. Moore. 224p. 1981. text ed. 11.95 o.p. (ISBN 0-07-042960-X). McGraw.

Does Your Small Business Need a Computer? Martha Eischen. (Illus.). 168p. 1983. 18.95 o.p. (ISBN 0-8306-0224-0, 1624); pap. 10.95 o.p. (ISBN 0-8306-0624-6). TAB Bks.

Dog-Access. (Access Guides Ser.). pap. 2.50 o.p. (ISBN 0-671-60378-7). S&S.

Dog & Cat Nutrition: A Handbook for Students, Veterinarians, Breeders & Owners. Ed. by A. T. Edney. (Illus.). 124p. 1982. text ed. 35.00 o.p. (ISBN 0-08-028891-X); pap. text ed. 16.25 o.p. (ISBN 0-08-028890-1). Pergamon.

Dog at My Heel. Veronica Heath. 1987. 18.00 o.p. (ISBN 0-85115-482-4, Pub. by Boydell & Brewer). Longwood Pub Group.

Dog Behavior: The Genetic Basis. Ed. by John P. Scott & John L. Fuller. LC 64-23429. 1974. pap. text ed. 12.50x o.s.i. (ISBN 0-226-74338-1). U of Chicago Pr.

Dog Book. Ed. by Jerrold Mundis. (Illus.). 356p. 1983. 19.95 o.p. (ISBN 0-87795-461-5, Arbor Hse). Morrow.

Dog Breeding. Ernest H. Hart. (Illus.). text ed. 12.95 o.p. (ISBN 0-87666-654-3, H-958). TFH Pubns.

Dog Judge's Handbook. Sari B. Tietjen. LC 80-36820. (Illus.). 224p. 1980. 12.95 o.p. (ISBN 0-87605-512-9). Howell Bk.

Dog Named Sam. Melvin T. Chambers. 1978. 6.00 o.p. (ISBN 0-682-49064-4). Exposition-Phoenix.

Dog People Are Crazy. Date not set. (ISBN 0-87605-536-6). Howell Bk.

Dog Soldiers. Robert Stone. 352p. 1981. 11.95 o.p. (ISBN 0-395-18481-9); pap. 6.70 o.p. (ISBN 0-395-31665-0). HM.

Dog Team Transportation: Basic Field Manual. facs. ed. U. S. Department of War Staff. (Shorey Lost Arts Ser.). 84p. pap. 6.95 o.s.i. (ISBN 0-8466-6048-2, U48). Shorey.

Dog That Was Barking Yesterday. Patricia Goedicke. (Orig.). 1979. pap. 5.00 o.p. (ISBN 0-89924-022-4). Lynx Hse.

Dog Training for Kids. Carol L. Benjamin. LC 76-14019. (Illus.). 96p. (gr. 8-12). 1976. 9.95 o.p. (ISBN 0-87605-516-1). Howell Bk.

Dog Who Thought He Was a Boy. Cora Annett. (Illus.). 48p. (gr. k-3). 1965. PLB 8.95 o.p. (ISBN 0-395-18471-1); pap. 0.95 o.p. (ISBN 0-395-18564-5). HM.

Dog Years. Gunter Grass. Tr. by Ralph Manheim. 570p. 1965. 6.95 o.p. (ISBN 0-15-126222-5). HarBraceJ.

Dogalypse. Andrei Voznesensky. LC 79-189356. (Pocket Poets Ser.: No. 29). 1972. pap. 2.00 o.p. (ISBN 0-87286-070-1). City Lights.

Dogancay. Roy Moyer et al. LC 86-359. (Illus.). 252p. 1986. 75.00 o.p. (ISBN 0-933920-61-X, Dist. by Rizzoli). Hudson Hills.

Dogen Kigen - Mystical Realist. rev. ed. Hee-Jin Kim. LC 74-33725. (Association for Asian Studies Monograph: No. 29). 384p. 1975. pap. 8.95x o.p. (ISBN 0-8165-0513-6). U of Ariz Pr.

Dogen's Formative Years in China: Historical Study & Annotated Translation of the Hokyo-ki. Tr. by Takashi J. Kodera from Japanese. LC 79-12848. (Illus.). 1980. write for info. o.p. (ISBN 0-87773-710-X, Prajna). Shambhala Pubns.

Dogma of Christ, & Other Essays on Religion, Psychology, & Culture. Erich Fromm. 1963. pap. 3.95 o.p. (ISBN 0-03-018421-5). H Holt & Co.

Dogmatic & Mystical Theology of John Donne. Husain Itrat. (Church Historical Society London, New Ser.: No. 30). Repr. of 1938 ed. 40.00 o.p. (ISBN 0-8115-3154-6). Kraus Repr.

Dogmatics in Outline. Karl Barth. (ISBN 0-8022-0073-7). Philos Lib.

Dogs. Henry Morgan & George Booth. 1977. pap. 1.95 o.p. (ISBN 0-395-25169-9). HM.

Dogs & Other Large Mammals in Aging Research, Vol. 1. A. C. Andersen et al. LC 74-8039. 168p. 1974. text ed. 21.50x o.p. (ISBN 0-8422-7226-7). Irvington.

Dogs & Other Large Mammals in Aging Research, Vol. 2. James W. Buchanan et al. LC 74-8039. 194p. 1974. text ed. 29.50x o.p. (ISBN 0-8422-7227-5). Irvington.

Dogs & Puppies. Jane Rockwell. (Illus.). (gr. 4-6). 1979. pap. 1.75 o.p. (ISBN 0-671-43134-X). Archway.

Dogs: Best Breeds for Young People. Wilfrid S. Bronson. LC 69-11594. (Illus.). (gr. 5-8). 1969. 6.50 o.p. (ISBN 0-15-223935-9, HJ). HarBraceJ.

Dogs: How to Train & Show Them. Hilary Harmar. (Illus.). 192p. 1984. 24.95 o.p. (ISBN 0-7153-8323-X). David & Charles.

Dog's Life. Ed. by Lee B. Hopkins. LC 82-974. (Illus.). 48p. (gr. 3 up). 1983. 9.95 o.p. (ISBN 0-15-223937-5, HJ). HarBraceJ.

Dog's Medical Dictionary. A. J. Sewell. 1952. (ISBN 0-8022-1537-8). Philos Lib.

Dogs: Records, Stars, Feats, & Facts. Roger Caras & Pamela C. Graham. LC 79-87511. (Handy Bks.). (Illus.). (gr. 4-7). 1979. 2.95 o.p. (ISBN 0-15-223939-1, HJ). HarBraceJ.

Dogwatch. Ted Jones. (Illus.). 1981. 14.95 o.p. (ISBN 0-393-03252-3). Norton.

Doing & Deserving: Essays in the Theory of Responsibility. Joel Feinberg. 1970. 21.50 o.p. (ISBN 0-691-07170-5); pap. 10.50 o.p. (ISBN 0-691-01981-9). Princeton U Pr.

Doing Art Together: The Remarkable Parent-Child Workshop of the Metropolitan Museum of Art. Muriel Silberstein-Storfer & Mablen Jones. (Illus.). 1982. 17.25 o.s.i. (ISBN 0-671-24109-5). S&S.

Doing Business Abroad: Everything the Businessman Needs to Know for Successful Negotiation, Barter, Trade & Business Entertaining Around the World. Gavin Kennedy. 210p. 1985. 18.45 o.p. (ISBN 0-671-55484-0). S&S.

Doing Business with Pascal. Richard Hergert & Douglas Hergert. LC 82-62361. (Illus.). 371p. 1983. pap. text ed. 14.95 o.p. (ISBN 0-89588-091-1). SYBEX.

Doing It Now: A Twelve-Step Program for Curing Procrastination & Achieving Your Goals. Edwin C. Bliss. (Illus.). 192p. 1983. 12.95 o.s.i. (ISBN 0-684-18001-4, ScribT). Scribner.

Doing the Ethnography of Schooling: Educational Anthropology in Action. George D. Spindler. 1982. text ed. 38.95 o.p. (ISBN 0-03-059039-6). HR&W.

Doing the Eucharist: A Guide to Trial Use. David E. Babin. (Orig.). pap. 2.75 o.p. (ISBN 0-8192-1125-7). Morehouse Pub.

Doings of Raffles Haw. 256p. 1986. 15.00 o.p. (ISBN 0-947898-37-9). Kraus Repr.

Doll & Drum. Sue Tarsky. (Look & Say Ser.). (Illus.). 32p. 1983. 1.50 o.s.i. (ISBN 0-671-47659-9, Little Simon). S&S.

Doll Baby. Burt Hirschfeld, pseud. 384p. (Orig.). 1985. pap. 2.95 o.p. (ISBN 0-440-02125-1, Emerald). Dell.

Doll Collecting for Fun & Profit. Mildred Seeley & Colleen Seeley. LC 82-84016. (Illus.). 144p. 1983. 14.95 o.p. (ISBN 0-89586-207-7). Price Stern.

Doll Collector's Manual. 160p. 1983. 12.95 o.p. (ISBN 0-87588-194-7, 598). Hobby Hse.

Doll Costuming. Mildred Seeley & Colleen Seeley. LC 84-80056. (Illus.). 144p. 1983. 14.95 o.p. (ISBN 0-89586-299-9). Price Stern.

Doll Directory & Buying Guide, 1986. 4th ed. Nancie A. Lutz. (Illus.). 223p. 1986. lib. bdg. 29.00 o.p. (ISBN 0-940070-28-6); pap. 12.50 o.p. (ISBN 0-940070-27-8). Doll Works.

Doll Named Moses. Arch Crawford. 424p. 1982. 15.00 o.p. (ISBN 0-682-49729-0). Exposition-Phoenix.

Doll Without Hands. Jimmie N. Morgan. LC 85-91023. 152p. 1986. 10.00 o.p. (ISBN 0-682-40277-X). Exposition-Phoenix.

Dollar Covenant. Michael Sinclair. 208p. 1973. 5.95 o.p. (ISBN 0-393-08369-1). Norton.

"Dollar Drain" & American Forces in Germany: Managing the Political Economics of Alliance. Gregory F. Treverton. LC 76-51689. xvi, 226p. 1978. 14.00x o.p. (ISBN 0-8214-0368-0). Ohio U Pr.

Dollar Sign on the Muscle. Kevin Kerrane. 352p. 1985. pap. 3.95 o.p. (ISBN 0-380-69934-6). Avon.

Dollar-Wise Guide to England & Scotland: 1983-84. pap. 7.95 o.p. (ISBN 0-671-44791-2, 10800). Prentice Hall Pr.

Dollar-Wise Guide to France, 1983-84. pap. 8.95 o.p. (ISBN 0-671-44790-4, 10801). Prentice Hall Pr.

Dollar-Wise Guide to Italy: 1983-84 Edition. pap. 7.95 o.p. (ISBN 0-671-44917-6, 10802). Prentice Hall Pr.

Dollars & Dictators: A Guide to Central America. Tom Barry et al. LC 83-81370. 288p. 1983. pap. 6.95 o.p. (ISBN 0-394-62485-8, E864, Ever). Grove.

Dollars & Percents of Development Finance, 3rd Quarter to the 4th Quarter 1985. Cecil Sears & Jane Buckwalter. (Dollars & Percents of Development Finance Ser.). 64p. 1986. pap. 60.00 o.p. Urban Land.

Dollars & Sense: Introduction to Economics. 4th ed. Marilu McCarty. 1985. pap. text ed. write for info. o.p. (ISBN 0-673-18118-9). Scott F.

Dollars, Dependents, & Dogma: Overseas Chinese Remittances to Communist China. Chun-hsi Wu. LC 67-24368. (Publications Ser.: No. 55). 1967. 13.95x o.p. (ISBN 0-8179-1551-6). Hoover Inst Pr.

Dollars for Scholars Student Aid Catalog: Minnesota Edition. Marlys C. Johnson & Linda J. Thompson. Ed. by Citizen's Scholarship Foundation of America Staff. LC 81-23503. (Dollars for Scholars Aid Catalogs Ser.). 216p. (Orig.). 1982. pap. 7.95 o.p. (ISBN 0-87866-194-8). Petersons Guides.

Dollars for Scholars Student Aid Catalog: New Hampshire Edition. Linda J. Thompson & Marlys C. Johnson. Ed. by Citizen's Scholarship Foundation of America Staff. LC 81-23502. (Dollars for Scholars Student Aid Catalogs Ser.). 174p. (Orig.). 1982. pap. 5.95 o.p. (ISBN 0-87866-193-X). Petersons Guides.

Dollars from Washington: An Individual's Share, 1930-81. Charles F. Lasure. 64p. 1980. 5.00 o.p. (ISBN 0-682-49647-2). Exposition-Phoenix.

Dollars on Your Doorstep: The Complete Guide to Home-Based Businesses. Gregory F. Kishel & Patricia G. Kishel. LC 83-21890. (Small Business Ser.: 1-382). 183p. (Orig.). 1984. pap. 8.95 o.p. (ISBN 0-471-88452-9). Wiley.

Dollarwise Guide to Austria & Hungary, 1985-1986. Darwin Porter. 408p. 1984. pap. 10.95 o.p. (ISBN 0-671-50943-8). Prentice Hall Pr.

Dollarwise Guide to Bermuda & the Bahamas. Darwin Porter. 264p. 1985. pap. 10.95 o.p. (ISBN 0-671-55627-4). S&S.

Dollarwise Guide to California & Las Vegas. Nancy McGrath. 304p. 1985. pap. 9.95 o.p. (ISBN 0-671-52651-0). Prentice Hall Pr.

Dollarwise Guide to California & Las Vegas, 1983-84. 312p. pap. 7.95 o.p. (ISBN 0-671-45111-1). Prentice Hall Pr.

Dollarwise Guide to Canada. John Godwin et al. 672p. 1986. pap. 12.95 o.p. (ISBN 0-671-55629-0). S&S.

Dollarwise Guide to Canada, 1984-85. 688p. 1984. 10.95 o.p. (ISBN 0-671-46793-X). Prentice Hall Pr.

Dollarwise Guide to Cruises from the United States, 1985-1986. Marylyn Springer & Don A. Schultz. 456p. 1984. pap. 10.95 o.p. (ISBN 0-671-49904-1). Prentice Hall Pr.

Dollarwise Guide to Egypt. Nancy McGrath. 264p. 1985. pap. 11.95 o.p. (ISBN 0-671-55597-9). S&S.

Dollarwise Guide to Egypt, 1984-1985. pap. 9.95 o.p. (ISBN 0-671-47599-1). Prentice Hall Pr.

Dollarwise Guide to England & Scotland. Darwin Porter. 640p. 1985. pap. 10.95 o.p. (ISBN 0-671-52442-9). Prentice Hall Pr.

Dollarwise Guide to Florida. Marilyn Springer. 398p. 1985. pap. 10.95 o.p. (ISBN 0-671-55596-0). S&S.

Dollarwise Guide to Florida, 1984-85. 384p. 1983. 9.95 o.p. (ISBN 0-671-47291-7). Prentice Hall Pr.

Dollarwise Guide to France. Darwin Porter. 512p. 1985. pap. 10.95 o.p. (ISBN 0-671-52441-0). Prentice Hall Pr.

Dollarwise Guide to Germany, 1984-85. 352p. 1984. 9.95 o.p. (ISBN 0-671-46791-3). Prentice Hall Pr.

Dollarwise Guide to Italy. Darwin Porter. 448p. 1985. pap. 10.95 o.p. (ISBN 0-671-52440-2). Prentice Hall Pr.

Dollarwise Guide to New England, 1984-85. 400p. 1984. 9.95 o.p. (ISBN 0-671-46794-8). Prentice Hall Pr.

Dollarwise Guide to Portugal Including Madeira & the Azores. Darwin Porter. 312p. 1986. pap. 11.95 o.p. (ISBN 0-671-55616-9). S&S.

Dollarwise Guide to Portugal, Madeira & the Azores, 1984-85. 1984. pap. 9.95 o.p. (ISBN 0-671-46792-1). Prentice Hall Pr.

Dollarwise Guide to Skiing U. S. A. East. I. William Berry. 242p. 1985. pap. 10.95 o.p. (ISBN 0-671-55415-8). Prentice Hall Pr.

Dollarwise Guide to Skiing U. S. A. West. Lois Friedland. 372p. 1985. pap. 10.95 o.p. (ISBN 0-671-55507-3). S&S.

Dollarwise Guide to the Carribean. Darwin Porter. 612p. 1985. pap. 12.95 o.p. (ISBN 0-671-54720-8). S&S.

Dollarwise Guide to the Carribean, 1984-1985 Including Bermuda & the Bahamas. 672p. 1983. pap. 10.95 o.p. (ISBN 0-671-46790-5). Prentice Hall Pr.

Dollarwise Guide to the Northwest. Marylyn Springer & Don A. Schultz. 456p. 1985. pap. 10.95 o.p. (ISBN 0-671-49905-X). Prentice Hall Pr.

Dollarwise Guide to the Southeast & New Orleans, 1984-85. 384p. 1983. 9.95 o.p. (ISBN 0-671-46795-6). Prentice Hall Pr.

Dollarwise Guide to the Southwest. Roy Bongartz. 456p. 1985. pap. 10.95 o.p. (ISBN 0-671-50620-X). Prentice Hall Pr.

Dollhouse Kit & Dining Room Accessories. Glick Baggett. 30p. pap. 0.99 o.p. (ISBN 0-87588-150-5, 655). Hobby Hse.

Dollhouse Lamps & Chandeliers. Glick Baggett. 30p. pap. 0.99 o.p. (ISBN 0-87588-149-1, 656). Hobby Hse.

Dolls. Edwina Lindsay Travers. 1977. 5.50 o.p. (ISBN 0-682-48976-X). Exposition-Phoenix.

Doll's House. Henrik Ibsen. Tr. by Michael Meyer. (Student Editions Ser.). 144p. (Orig.). 1985. pap. text ed. 3.95 o.p. (ISBN 0-413-54470-2, 9346). Heinemann Ed.

Doll's Houses in America. Flora G. Jacobs. 1983. 30.00 o.s.i. (ISBN 0-684-13583-3). Scribner.

Dolls' Houses in America: Historic Preservation in Miniature. Flora G. Jacobs. LC 73-1100. (Encore Edition Ser.). (Illus.). 1978. pap. 6.95 o.p. (ISBN 0-684-16905-3). Scribner.

Dolly & Her Dresses. 1980. pap. 2.75 o.p. (ISBN 0-87588-159-9, 710). Hobby Hse.

Dolly Madison. Maud W. Goodwin. LC 67-30157. 1967. Repr. of 1896 ed. 20.00 o.s.i. (ISBN 0-87152-039-7). Reprint.

Dolphin Guide to Hawaii. Tom Horton & Karen Horton. LC 85-4495. (Illus.). 464p. 1985. pap. 8.95 o.p. (ISBN 0-385-19929-5, Dolp). Doubleday.

Dolphins & Porpoises: A Comprehensive, Annotated Bibliography of the Smaller Cetacea. Ed. by Deborah Truitt. LC 73-19803. 594p. 1974. 98.00x o.p. (ISBN 0-8103-0966-1). Gale.

Dombroff on Demonstrative Evidence: 1987 Cumulative Supplement. Dombroff. (Trial Practice Library). 1986. pap. 27.00 o.p. (ISBN 0-471-85724-6). Wiley.

Dombroff on Unfair Tactics: 1987 Cumulative Supplement, No. 1. Mark A. Dombroff. (Trial Practice Library). 208p. 1987. pap. 30.00 o.p. (ISBN 0-471-62549-3). Wiley.

Dome People. Ruth Howell. LC 73-84829. (Illus.). 64p. (gr. 4-6). 1974. 5.25 o.p. (ISBN 0-689-30139-1, Atheneum). Macmillan.

Domes: A Bibliography. Mary Vance. (Architecture Ser.: A 1361). 15p. 1985. 2.25 o.p. (ISBN 0-89028-351-6). Vance Biblios.

Domesday Book: England's Heritage Then & Now. Thomas Hinde. LC 85-12796. 352p. 1985. 19.95 o.p. (ISBN 0-517-55868-8). Crown.

Domesday of Saint Paul of the Year Twelve Twenty-Two. London - St. Paul's Cathedral Staff. Repr. of 1858 ed. 37.00 o.p. (ISBN 0-384-33475-X). Johnson Repr.

Domestic Adjustment & International Trade. Gary C. Hufbauer & Howard F. Rosen. c, 300p. (Orig.). 1988. write for info. o.p. (ISBN 0-88132-029-3). Inst Intl Eco.

Domestic Affairs. Miriam Finkelstein. 180p. 1982. 10.95 o.p. (ISBN 0-395-31822-X). HM.

Domestic American Textiles: A Bibliographic Sourcebook. Beverly Gordon. 217p. pap. 14.95 o.s.i. (ISBN 0-318-13870-0); pap. 12.95 members o.s.i. (ISBN 0-318-13871-9). Ctr Hist Am Needle.

Domestic Consumption Trends: 1972-82, & Forecasts to 1993 for Major Metals. LC 86-600154. (Mines Bureau Information Circular: No. 9101). (Illus.). 38p. 1986. pap. 2.00 o.p. (ISBN 0-318-21944-1, S/N 024-004-02170-5). USGPO.

Domestic Interests & International Obligations. Irving B. Kravis. LC 74-25537. 448p. 1975. Repr. of 1963 ed. lib. bdg. 27.75x o.p. (ISBN 0-8371-7870-3, KRDI). Greenwood.

Domestic Potential of Solar & Other Renewable Energy Sources. National Research Council. 1979. pap. 8.50x o.p. (ISBN 0-309-02927-9). Natl Acad Pr.

Domestic Relations, Cases & Other Materials: Successor Edition, 1985 Supplement. Walter Wadlington. (University Casebook Ser.). 1985. pap. 6.95 o.p. (ISBN 0-88277-250-3). Foundation Pr.

Domestic Resource Mobilization in Pakistan: Selected Issues. World Bank Staff et al. LC 84-2304. (World Bank Staff Working Papers: No. 632). 1984. 8.00 o.p. (ISBN 0-8213-0335-X, WP 0632). World Bank.

Domestic Service. C. V. Butler. LC 79-56953. (English Working Class Ser.). 1980. lib. bdg. 20.00 o.p. (ISBN 0-8240-0107-9). Garland Pub.

Domestic Student Exchange Programs: Coordinators Handbook. 1984. 6.00 o.p. (ISBN 0-88210-069-6). Natl Assn Principals.

Domestic Transportation: Practice, Theory, & Policy. 4th ed. Roy J. Sampson & Martin T. Farris. LC 79-69576. (Illus.). 1979. text ed. 30.95 o.p. (ISBN 0-395-26793-5). HM.

Domestic Violence--No Longer Behind the Curtain. Instructional Aides, Inc. (Instructional Aides Ser.). 92p. 1983. pap. 13.95 o.p. (ISBN 0-936474-27-0). Info Plus TX.

Domestic Violence: No Longer Behind the Curtains. Ed. by Mark A. Siegel et al. (Information Plus Ser.). 136p. 1987. pap. 16.95 o.p. (ISBN 0-936474-68-8). Info Plus TX.

Domestic Water Treatment. Jay H. Lehr et al. (Illus.). 1979. text ed. 30.00 o.p. (ISBN 0-07-037068-0). McGraw.

Domiciliary Services for the Elderly. Liam Clarke. 190p. 1984. 24.00 o.p. (ISBN 0-7099-0756-7, Pub. by Croom Helm Ltd). Routledge Chapman & Hall.

Dominance Relations: An Ethological View of Human Conflict & Social Interactions. Donald Omark et al. LC 79-14352. 528p. 1980. lib. bdg. 63.00 o.p. (ISBN 0-8240-7048-8). Garland Pub.

Dominant Firm: A Study of Market Power. Alice P. White. Ed. by Fred Bateman. LC 83-5001. (Research in Business Economics & Public Policy Ser.: No. 5). 160p. 1983. 42.95 o.p. (ISBN 0-8357-1444-6). Univ Microfilms.

Domination in 2545 Endgame Studies. G. M. Kasparyan. 542p. 1981. 10.00 o.s.i. (ISBN 0-8285-2161-1, Pub. by Progress Pubs USSR). Imported Pubns.

Dominican Republic Crisis, 1965. Aaron J. Thomas & Ann Thomas. Ed. by John Carey. LC 67-14395. (Hammarskjold Fourm Ser.: No. 9). 164p. 1967. pap. 3.45 o.p. (ISBN 0-379-11809-2). Oceana.

Dominion. Pamela Ferguson. LC 77-15829. 1978. 10.95 o.p. (ISBN 0-689-10870-2, Atheneum). Macmillan.

Dominique. Eugene Fromentin. Ed. by Hoog. (Bibliotheque de Cluny Ser.). pap. 6.95 o.p. (ISBN 0-685-34908-X). French & Eur.

Dominique & the Dragon. Jurgen Tamchina. LC 68-59618. (Illus.). (gr. 3-6). 1969. 6.50 o.p. (ISBN 0-15-223972-3, HJ). HarBraceJ.

Dominoes: Sixty-Seven Games & Tricks. Malcolm A. Bryan. pap. 6.95 o.p. (ISBN 0-8306-1308-0, 1308). TAB Bks.

Dominus: A Woman Looks at Men's Lives. Natalie Gittelson. LC 78-23725. 1979. pap. 3.95 o.p. (ISBN 0-15-626118-9, Harv). HarBraceJ.

Don Bosco's Lay Religious: Essays on the Salesian Brother, Pt. 1. Enzo Bianco. Tr. by Peter Swain. LC 84-72160. 75p. pap. 3.00 o.p. (ISBN 0-89944-078-9). Don Bosco Multimedia.

Don Bosco's Lay Religious: Profiles in Courage, Pt. 2. Enzo Bianco. Tr. by Peter Swain. 101p. pap. 3.00 o.p. (ISBN 0-89944-079-7). Don Bosco Multimedia.

Don Bueno. Zulfikar Ghose. 243p. 1984. 16.95 o.p. (ISBN 0-03-069398-5). H Holt & Co.

Don Coyote: The Good & Bad Times of a Maligned American Original. Dayton O. Hyde. 222p. 1986. 16.95 o.p. (ISBN 0-87795-783-5). Morrow.

Don Francisco De Paula Marin: A Biography with Letters & Journal. Ross H. Gast & Agnes C. Conrad. LC 77-188980. (Illus.). 354p. 1973. 12.95x o.p. (ISBN 0-8248-0220-9). UH Pr.

Don Giovanni. Wolfgang A. Mozart. Tr. & Ellen H. Bleiler. (Dover Opera Guide & Libretto Ser.). 11.75 o.p. (ISBN 0-8446-2625-2). Peter Smith.

Don Juan. Henry De Montherlant. pap. 3.95 o.p. (ISBN 0-685-36977-3). Schoenhof.

Don Juan. Henry De Montherlant. (Illus.). deluxe ed. 481.25 o.p. (ISBN 0-685-36995-1). Schoenhof.

Don Juan. Moliere. Tr. & intro. by Wallace Fowlie. (gr. 10 up). 1965. pap. text ed. 1.95 o.p. (ISBN 0-8120-0056-0). Barron.

Don Juan. Moliere, pseud. (Illus.). 1964. pap. 2.95 o.p. (ISBN 0-685-11149-0). Schoenhof.

Don Juan, Mescalito & Modern Magic: The Mythology of Inner Space. Nevill Drury. 256p. 1985. pap. 8.95 o.p. (ISBN 1-85063-015-1, Ark Paperbks). Routledge Chapman & Hall.

Don Quijote De la Mancha, Pt. 1. Adapted by Jose U. Selma. (gr. 12 up). 1971. pap. 3.95 o.p. (ISBN 0-88345-137-9); 16 filmstrips, 8 cassettes 145.00 o.p. (ISBN 0-685-65049-9). Prentice ESL.

Don Quijote De la Mancha, Pt. 2. Miguel De Cervantes Saavedra. (Illus., Span.). (gr. 11-12). 1971. pap. 3.95 o.p. (ISBN 0-88345-138-7); manual, filmstrips, & cassettes o.p. 145.00 o.p. (ISBN 0-685-69627-8). Prentice ESL.

Don Quixote see also Adventures of Don Quixote.

Don Quixote see also Don Quixote de la Mancha.

Don Quixote. Kathy Acker. 208p. 1986. pap. 7.95 o.p. (ISBN 0-394-62085-2, Ever). Grove.

Don Quixote. Kathy Acker. 208p. (Orig.). Date not set. pap. 8.95 o.s.i. (ISBN 0-8021-3040-2). Grove.

Don Quixote. Miguel De Cervantes. 48p. (Orig.). 1989. pap. 9.95 o.p. (ISBN 1-55651-181-7); audiocassette tape incl. o.p. (ISBN 1-55651-182-5). Cram Cassettes.

Don Quixote de la Mancha see also Don Quixote.

Don Quixote Rides Again: Or the Truth of the Story as Told by Sancho Panza. Earl M. Swan. 160p. 1983. 8.00 o.p. (ISBN 0-682-49921-8). Exposition-Phoenix.

Dona Flor & Her Two Husbands. Jorge Amado. 1977. pap. 4.95 o.p. (ISBN 0-380-01796-2, 60044-7, Bard). Avon.

Donald Barthelme. Maurice Couturier & Regis Durand. (Contemporary Writers Ser.). 96p. 1982. pap. 5.95x o.p. (ISBN 0-416-31870-3, NO. 3557). Routledge Chapman & Hall.

Donald Barthelme. Lois Gordon. (United States Author Ser.). 1981. lib. bdg. 14.50 o.p. (ISBN 0-8057-7347-9, Twayne). G K Hall.

Donald Duck. Carl Barks. LC 78-14844. (Walt Disney Best Comics Ser.). (Illus.). 196p. 1978. 15.95 o.s.i. (ISBN 0-89659-006-2). Abbeville Pr.

Donald Duck & His Nephews. LC 81-20603. (Walt Disney Best Comics Ser.). (Illus.). 190p. (YA) (gr. 7 up). 1984. 25.00 o.p. (ISBN 0-89659-511-0). Abbeville Pr.

Donald Writes No More. Eddie Stone. (Orig.). 1977. pap. 2.25 o.p. (ISBN 0-87067-017-4, BH017). Holloway.

Donald Zolan's Oil Paintings of Early Childhood. rev. ed. John D. Hugunin. (Illus.). 164p. 1988. 24.95 o.p. (ISBN 0-9613070-1-3). Pemberton Oakes.

Donatello E I Suoi. 287p. 1986. pap. 22.00 o.s.i. (ISBN 0-89558-121-3). Detroit Inst Arts.

Donavan's Dusters. Margaret Ogan & George Ogan. LC 75-17760. (Hiway Book: A High Interest-Low Reading Level Book). 152p. (gr. 5-9). 1975. 6.50 o.s.i. (ISBN 0-664-32576-9, Westminster). Westminster John Knox.

Done This Day: The European Idea in Action. Oliver Crawford. LC 74-102067. 1970. 13.50 o.s.i. (ISBN 0-8008-2266-8). Taplinger.

Donkey Head. Lisl Weil. LC 77-2865. (ps-3). 1977. 8.95 o.p. (ISBN 0-689-30600-8, Atheneum). Macmillan.

Donkey Wisdom. Paul White. (Jungle Doctor Picture Fable Ser.). 21p. (gr. k-5). 1986. pap. 26.50 o.p. (ISBN 0-85364-369-5, Pub. by Paternoster UK). Attic Pr.

Donkey's Tale. Margaret Gray. (Illus.). 32p. 1984. pap. 3.95 casebound o.s.i. (ISBN 0-8307-0963-0, 5111209). Regal.

Donnager's Cat. Edwin E. Kania. 176p. 1986. 9.95 o.p. (ISBN 0-8062-2994-2). Carlton.

Donne: Concordance to the Poems. John Donne. Ed. by Homer C. Combs & Z. R. Sullins. Date not set. price not set o.p. (ISBN 0-87532-036-8). Hendricks House.

Donner Party. George Keithley. LC 75-183185. 1972. 6.50 o.p. (ISBN 0-8076-0638-3). Braziller.

Donnie's Dangers. Aleda Renken. (Haley Adventures Bks.). (gr. 3-9). 1981. pap. 1.00 o.p. (ISBN 0-570-07235-2, 39-1070). Concordia.

Donny & Marie. Patricia M. Eldred. (Rock 'n Pop Stars Ser.). (Illus.). (gr. 4-12). 1978. PLB 6.95 o.p. (ISBN 0-87191-618-5); pap. 2.75 o.p. (ISBN 0-89812-121-3). Creative Ed.

Donovan, a Novel, 1882. Ada E. Bayley. Ed. by Robert L. Wolff. LC 75-1529. (Victorian Fiction Series). 1977. lib. bdg. 73.00 o.p. (ISBN 0-8240-1601-7). Garland Pub.

Don't Ask Miranda. Lila Perl. LC 78-23835. 164p. (gr. 6 up). 1979. 10.45 o.p. (ISBN 0-395-28961-0, Clarion). HM.

Don't Be a Puppet on a String. Bob Donahue & Marilyn Donahue. 1983. pap. 3.95 o.p. (ISBN 0-8423-0610-2). Tyndale.

Don't Be Afraid...Recovery from Alcoholism. S. A. S. 1978. 6.50 o.p. (ISBN 0-682-49061-X). Exposition-Phoenix.

Don't Be Scared Book: Scares, Remedies & Pictures. Isle-Margret Vogel. LC 64-19564. (Illus.). 48p. (ps-1). 1972. pap. 2.95 o.s.i. (ISBN 0-689-70307-4, Aladdin). Macmillan.

Don't Blame the Kids: The Trouble with America's Public Schools. Gene I. Maeroff. 224p. 1982. text ed. 17.95 o.p. (ISBN 0-07-039465-2); pap. text ed. 6.95 o.p. (ISBN 0-07-039466-0). McGraw.

Don't Call Me Orphan! Michael Leach. LC 78-26928. 96p. 1979. 8.95 o.s.i. (ISBN 0-664-32645-5, Westminster). Westminster John Knox.

Don't Die on Me, Billie Jean. Stanton Forbes. LC 86-29292. (Crime Club Ser.). 192p. 1987. 12.95 o.p. (ISBN 0-385-19771-3). Doubleday.

Don't Ever Retire but Do It Early & Often. Joseph Schwartz. LC 79-53374. 1979. 9.95 o.p. (ISBN 0-87863-196-8, Farnsworth Pub Co). Longman Finan.

Don't Get Hit by a Cocoanut. Caimite. (Illus.). 1979. 10.00 o.p. (ISBN 0-682-49246-9). Exposition-Phoenix.

Don't Get Taken! A Preventive Legal Guide to Protect Your Home, Money, Family & Job. S. M. Sack. 382p. 1984. text ed. 15.95 o.p. (ISBN 0-07-054398-4). McGraw.

Don't Get Taken Every Time: The Insider's Guide to Buying Your Next Car. Remar Sutton. 382p. 1983. pap. 6.95 o.p. (ISBN 0-14-046597-9). Penguin.

Don't Give up, Charlie Brown: Selected from Vol. 2 of "You've Had It, Charlie Brown" Charles M. Schulz. (Peanuts Ser.). (Illus.). 1982. pap. 1.95 o.p. (ISBN 0-449-20006-X, Crest). Fawcett.

Don't Laugh, You're Next. Skip Morrow. 96p. 1983. pap. 3.95 o.p. (ISBN 0-03-059361-1). H Holt & Co.

Don't Let Them Kiss You: A Cat's Guide to Choosing & Training People. Thomas Felidae & H. M Davenport. (Illus.). 1984. pap. 3.95 o.p. (ISBN 0-87795-575-1, Arbor Hse). Morrow.

Don't Lie to Me. Tucker Coe. 1979. pap. 1.95 o.p. (ISBN 0-441-15835-8). Ace Bks.

Don't Look a Gift Shark in the Mouth. Ed. by Alfred Hitchcock. 1976. pap. 1.25 o.p. (ISBN 0-440-13620-2). Dell.

Don't Look & It Won't Hurt. Richard Peck. (YA) (gr. 7 up). 1979. pap. 2.25 o.p. (ISBN 0-380-00781-9, 60102-8, Flare). Avon.

Don't Look Now. Linda A. Cooney. (Moonstone Novels Ser.: No. 4). (Orig.). (gr. 5 up). 1984. pap. o.p. (ISBN 0-671-50784-2). Archway.

Don't Make Fun! Bernard Wiseman. LC 82-6240. (Illus.). 32p. (gr. k-3). 1982. 8.70 o.p. (ISBN 0-395-32086-0). HM.

Don't Miss the Present Moment. Patricia Herrington. Ed. by Helen Graves. LC 86-40288. 140p. 1987. 8.95 o.p. (ISBN 0-938232-99-1). Winston-Derek.

Don't (or How to Care for Your Computer) Rodnay Zaks. LC 81-51129. 213p. 1981. 13.95 o.p. (ISBN 0-89588-065-2). SYBEX.

Don't (or How to Care for Your New Computer) Rodnay Zaks. 11.95 o.p. (ISBN 0-317-06039-2). Wayne Green Ent.

Don't Put Your Cart Before the Race Horse. Thomas Van Aarle. (Illus.). 48p. (gr. k-3). 1980. PLB 8.95 o.p. (ISBN 0-395-29095-3). HM.

Don't Shoot the Dog! Karen Pryor. 192p. 1984. 14.70 o.p. (ISBN 0-671-43842-5). S&S.

Don't Shrink to Fit! A Confrontation with Dehumanization in Psychiatry & Psychology. Eileen Walkenstein. LC 76-17473. 1976. pap. 3.95 o.p. (ISBN 0-394-17004-0, E689, Ever). Grove.

Don't Slam the Door When You Go. Barbara Corcoran. LC 72-75267. (gr. 5-9). 1972. 7.95 o.p. (ISBN 0-689-30049-2, Atheneum). Macmillan.

Don't Smile Until Christmas: Accounts of the First Year of Teaching. Ed. by Kevin Ryan. LC 72-103428. 1970. lib. bdg. 20.00 o.s.i. (ISBN 0-226-73230-4). U of Chicago Pr.

Don't Stop Now, You're Killing Me: The Sadomasochism Game in Everyday Life & How Not to Play It. David Brandt. LC 86-5103. 235p. 1986. 15.45 o.s.i. (ISBN 0-671-52795-9, Poseidon). PB.

Don't Talk to Strangers. Pamela A. Grau. (Illus.). (gr. k-1). 1985. 4.95 o.p. (ISBN 0-533-06542-9). Vantage.

Don't Tell Me a Ghost Story. Phyllis R. Eisenberg. (Illus.). 48p. (ps-3). 1982. 8.95 o.p. (ISBN 0-15-224029-2, HJ). HarBraceJ.

Don't Tickle the Elephant Tree: Sensitive Plants. Philip Barnard. LC 81-16834. (Illus.). 64p. (gr. 4-6). 1982. lib. bdg. 8.97 o.s.i. (ISBN 0-671-41625-1). Messner.

Don't You Belong to Me? Monk of New Clairvaux. LC 79-88985. 180p. 1979. pap. 7.95 o.p. (ISBN 0-8091-2217-0). Paulist Pr.

Don't You Dare Shoot That Bear! A Story of Theodore Roosevelt. Robert Quackenbush. LC 84-4693. (Illus.). 40p. (gr. 1-5). 1984. 9.95 o.s.i. (ISBN 0-13-218496-6). P-H.

Doodling As an Art. Alex Hossu. 1979. 7.50 o.p. (ISBN 0-682-49200-0). Exposition-Phoenix.

Doom Wind. Max Gunther. 352p. 1986. 17.95 o.p. (ISBN 0-8092-5043-8). Contemp Bks.

Doomsday Canyon. Ray Hogan. (Large Print Book (General Ser.)). 1985. lib. bdg. 13.95 o.p. (ISBN 0-8161-3836-2). G K Hall.

Doomsday Device, 2 bks. James M. Ward. LC 86-90229. (One-On-One(TM) Adventure Gamebook Ser.: No. 8). 320p. (Orig.). 1986. pap. 5.95 o.p. (ISBN 0-88038-305-4). TSR Inc.

Doomsday Trail. Ray Hogan. (General Ser.). 1984. lib. bdg. 12.95 o.p. (ISBN 0-8161-3722-6, Large Print Bks). G K Hall.

Doonesbury Desk Diary 1988. G. B. Trudeau. (Illus.). 96p. 1987. spiral bd. 9.95 o.p. (ISBN 0-8050-0452-1). H Holt & Co.

Door Ajar. Benton. 4.45 o.p. Pilgrim NY.

Door in the Hedge. Robin McKinley. 224p. 1984. pap. 2.75 o.s.i. (ISBN 0-441-15313-5). Ace Bks.

Door into Fire. Diane Duane. 288p. 1984. pap. 7.95 o.p. (ISBN 0-312-94107-2). Bluejay Bks.
Door into Ocean. Joan Slonczewski. 353p. 1986. 17.95 o.p. (ISBN 0-87795-763-0, Arbor Hse). Morrow.
Door Through Space. Marion Zimmer Bradley. Ed. by James P. Baen. 1979. pap. 1.95 o.s.i. (ISBN 0-441-15935-4). Ace Bks.
Door to Chinese Festivals, Feasts, Fortunes. Anita W. Jones. 126p. 1971. 13.45 o.p. (ISBN 0-89955-155-6, Pub. by Mei Ya China). Intl Spec Bk.
Doorless Door. John Tagliabue. 1970. 10.00 o.p. (ISBN 0-685-78978-0, Pub. by Mushinsha Bks). Small Pr Dist.
Doors: Excellence in International Design. Gretl Hoffmann. (Illus.). 1977. 55.00x o.p. (ISBN 0-8230-7135-9). Trans-Atl Phila.
Doors of Perception. Harry Duncan. 1983. 150.00x o.p. W T Taylor.
Doorway Papers: The Virgin Birth & the Incarnation, Vol. 5. Arthur C. Custance. 400p. 1985. pap. text ed. 10.95 o.p. (ISBN 0-310-22991-X, 10663P). Zondervan.
Doorway to a New Age: A Study of Paul's Letter to the Romans. James D. Smart. LC 74-8559. 208p. 1975. pap. 2.95 o.s.i. (ISBN 0-664-24997-3, Westminster). Westminster John Knox.
Doppler Echocardiography: A Practical Manual. Pravin M. Shah et al. LC 84-21883. 143p. 1985. 22.95 o.p. (ISBN 0-471-80914-4). Wiley.
Doppler Effect: An Introduction to the Theory of the Effect. T. P. Gill. 1965. 28.50 o.p. (ISBN 0-12-283350-3). Acad Pr.
Dora Russell Reader: Fifty Seven Years of Writing & Journalism, 1925-1982. Dora Russell. 242p. (Orig.). 1985. pap. 7.95 o.p. (ISBN 0-86358-020-3, Pandora Pr). Routledge Chapman & Hall.
Dorchester Boy. David Viscott. LC 73-82182. 1973. 7.95 o.p. (ISBN 0-87795-070-9, Arbor Hse). Morrow.
Dori: The Life & Times of Theodor Herzl in Budapest, 1860-1878. Andrew Handler. LC 82-8509. (Judaic Studies). (Illus.). 176p. 1983. text ed. 16.95 o.s.i. (ISBN 0-8173-0125-9). U of Ala Pr.
Doris Diamond-Private Eye. Andy Martin & Joseph Greene. Ed. by Joanne Dresner. (Photo Stories Ser.). (Illus.). 48p. (Orig.). 1985. pap. text ed. 4.95 o.p. (ISBN 0-582-79810-8). Longman.
Doris Fein: Dead Heat at Long Beach. T. Ernesto Bethancourt. LC 82-48754. (Doris Fein Ser.). 160p. (YA) (gr. 9 up). 1983. 10.95 o.p. (ISBN 0-8234-0485-4). Holiday.
Doris Fein: Quartz Boyar. T. Ernesto Bethancourt. LC 80-15920. 160p. (YA) (gr. 7 up). 1980. 10.95 o.p. (ISBN 0-8234-0378-5). Holiday.
Doris Lessing. Lorna Sage. LC 82-20846. (Contemporary Writers Ser.). 96p. 1983. pap. 5.95x o.p. (ISBN 0-416-31730-8, NO. 3783). Routledge Chapman & Hall.
Doris Ulmann: American Portraits. David Featherstone. LC 84-15208. (Illus.). 238p. 1985. 60.00 o.p. (ISBN 0-8263-0783-3); pap. 29.95 o.p. (ISBN 0-8263-0804-X). U of NM Pr.
Dorland's Illustrated Medical Dictionary. 26th ed. (Illus.). 1800p. 1981. text ed. write for info. o.p. (ISBN 0-7216-3150-9); Indexed. 39.95 o.p. (ISBN 0-7216-3151-7); Indexed. deluxe ed. 60.00 o.p. (ISBN 0-7216-3145-2). Saunders.
Dorland's Medical Dictionary. Ed. by Franz J. Ingelfinger. 1982. 17.95 o.p. (ISBN 0-03-056744-0). H Holt & Co.
Dorland's Pocket Medical Dictionary. LC 76-19604. (Illus.). 1983. thumb-indexed 13.95 o.p. (ISBN 0-7216-3162-2); write for info. plain o.p. (ISBN 0-7216-3163-0). Saunders.
Dormancy & Developmental Arrest: Experimental Analysis in Plants & Animals. Ed. by Mary E. Clutter. 1978. 56.00 o.p. (ISBN 0-12-177050-8). Acad Pr.
Dornier 335. J. Richard Smith & Eddie J. Creek. LC 83-61696. (Monogram Close-Up 21 Ser.). (Illus.). 32p. 1984. 6.95 o.s.i. (ISBN 0-914144-21-9). Monogram Aviation.
Dorothy & the Wizard in Oz. L. Frank Baum. LC 79-88479. 1985. pap. 2.25 o.s.i. (ISBN 0-345-28226-4); 2.25 o.s.i. (ISBN 0-345-31948-6). Ballantine.
Dorothy L. Sayers. James Brabazon. 344p. 1982. pap. 3.95 o.p. (ISBN 0-380-58990-7, 58990-7, Discus). Avon.
Dorothy L. Sayers. Sr. Mary B. Durkin. (English Authors Ser.: No. 281). 1980. lib. bdg. 13.50 o.p. (ISBN 0-8057-6778-9, Twayne). G K Hall.
Dorothy L. Sayers: A Biography. James Brabazon. (Illus.). 320p. 1981. Encore 4.50 o.p. (ISBN 0-684-16864-2, ScribT). Scribner.
Dorothy L. Sayers: A Pilgrim Soul. Nancy M. Tischler. LC 79-87739. 1980. 4.49 o.p. (ISBN 0-8042-0882-4, John Knox). Westminster John Knox.
Dorothy Parker. Arthur F. Kinney. (United States Authors Ser.: No. 315). 1978. 13.50 o.s.i. (ISBN 0-8057-7241-3, Twayne). G K Hall.
Dorothy Richardson: The Genius They Forgot. John Rosenberg. 1979. pap. 10.95x o.p. (ISBN 0-7156-0655-7, Pub. by Duckworth England). Biblio Dist.
Dorp Dead. Julia Cunningham. (Illus.). 92p. (gr. 3-7). 1980. pap. 1.95 o.p. (ISBN 0-380-00709-6, 65953-0, Camelot). Avon.
Do's & Don'ts of Yesterday. Eric Sloane. (Illus.). 1975. pap. 3.45 o.p. (ISBN 0-380-00429-1, 25841). Avon.
Dos Passos & the Fiction of Despair. Iain Colley. 170p. 1978. 27.50x o.p. (ISBN 0-8476-6020-6). Rowman.
DOS-VSE JCL: Instructor's Guide. Steve Eckols. LC 85-61545. 252p. 1985. 3-ring binder 75.00 o.p. (ISBN 0-911625-26-7). M Murach & Assoc.
Dosage Calculation: Method & Workbook. 2nd ed. Ann Aurigemma & Barbara Bohny. 165p. 1984. pap. text ed. 12.95 o.p. (ISBN 0-88737-116-7, 20-1966). Natl League Nurse.
Dosage Calculations. Gloria D. Pickar. LC 82-71146. (Illus.). 128p. 1982. pap. text ed. 10.95 o.p. (ISBN 0-8273-2090-6); software 149.95 o.p. Delmar.
Dossier Agences '87. Ed. by RotoVision Staff. 900p. 1987. pap. 79.50 o.p. (ISBN 0-8230-5793-3). Watson-Guptill.
Dossier Agences 88, 2 vols. 920p. 1988. Set. pap. 79.95 o.p. (ISBN 0-8230-5810-7). Watson-Guptill.
Dosso & Battista Dossi: Court Painters at Ferrara. Felton Gibbons. LC 68-11441. (Monographs in Art & Archaeology: No. 39). (Illus.). 1968. 73.50 o.p. (ISBN 0-691-03850-3). Princeton U Pr.
DOStalk Scrapbook. Tom Weishaar & Burt Kersey. (Illus.). 280p. (Orig.). 1985. 21.95 o.p. (ISBN 0-8306-0415-4, 2615); pap. 14.60 o.p. (ISBN 0-8306-0315-8). Tab Bks.
Dostoevsky & the Novel: The Wages of Biography. Michael Holquist. 1977. 26.50x o.s.i. (ISBN 0-691-06342-7). Princeton U Pr.
Dostoevsky: New Perspectives. Robert L. Jackson. 269p. 1984. 15.95 o.p. (ISBN 0-13-218586-5); pap. 5.95 o.p. (ISBN 0-13-218578-4). P-H.
Dostoevsky: Reminiscences. Anna Dostoevesky. Tr. by Beatrice Stillman from Rus. 1977. pap. 5.95 o.p. (ISBN 0-87140-117-7). Liveright.
Dostoievesky. Andre Gide. (Coll. Idees Ser.). pap. 3.95 o.p. (ISBN 0-685-34144-5). Schoenhof.
Dostoyevsky: Reminiscences. Anna Dostoyevsky. Ed. & tr. by Beatrice Stillman. (Illus.). 448p. 1975. 12.50 o.p. (ISBN 0-87140-592-X). Liveright.
Double-Agent Fugitive. Max Ross. 1978. 10.00 o.p. (ISBN 0-682-48972-7). Exposition-Phoenix.
Double Bed. Eve Merriam. LC 73-179083. 144p. 1972. 5.95 o.p. (ISBN 0-87131-044-9). M Evans.
Double Bill. Alec McCowen. LC 80-66018. 1980. 10.95 o.p. (ISBN 0-689-11070-7, Atheneum). Macmillan.
Double Contrast Examination of the Colon: Experiences with the Welin Modification. S. Welin & G. Welin. LC 75-37198. (Illus.). 120p. 1976. 23.00 o.p. (ISBN 0-88416-088-2). Year Bk Med.
Double Contrast Gastrointestinal Radiology: With Endoscopic Correlation. Igor Laufer. LC 78-64716. (Illus.). 1979. text ed. write for info. o.p. (ISBN 0-7216-5734-6). Saunders.
Double Contrast Radiography of the Stomach. H. Ichikawa. 130p. 1974. pap. 36.00x o.p. (ISBN 0-89955-340-0, Pub. by Japan Sci Soc Japan). Intl Spec Bk.
Double Counterpoint & Canon. Ebenezer Prout. Repr. of 1893 ed. lib. bdg. 35.00x o.p. (ISBN 0-8371-2265-1, PRDC). Greenwood.
Double Cross: Messages on the Seven Deadly Sins & the Seven "Deadly" Virtues. Stephen O. Swanson. LC 79-54110. 94p. 1979. text ed. 4.50 o.p. (ISBN 0-8066-1754-3, 10-1950, Augsburg). Augsburg Fortress.
Double-Crostics by Fans, No. 5. Ed. by Thomas H. Middleton. 1969. pap. 4.80 o.s.i. (ISBN 0-671-20405-X). S&S.
Double-Crostics by Fans, No. 6. Ed. by Thomas H. Middleton. 1971. pap. 4.80 o.s.i. (ISBN 0-671-21087-4). S&S.
Double Dare. Edward Keyes. 348p. 1981. text ed. 12.95 o.p. (ISBN 0-07-034450-7). McGraw.
Double Dare. Edward Keyes. 352p. 1986. pap. 3.95 o.s.i. (ISBN 0-394-62246-4, BC). Grove.
Double Dealing. M. Arthur Bogen. 160p. 1983. pap. 2.25 o.p. (ISBN 0-380-83394-8, 83394-8, Flare). Avon.
Double Discovery. Jessamyn West. LC 80-7948. 256p. 1980. 11.95 o.p. (ISBN 0-15-126402-3). HarBraceJ.
Double, Double. Ellery Queen. 1983. pap. 2.25 o.s.i. (ISBN 0-345-31364-X). Ballantine.
Double Double. Jose Yglesias. 1974. 29.50 o.p. (ISBN 0-670-28051-8); pap. 8.95 o.p. (ISBN 0-89197-737-6). Irvington.
Double Dutch-Double Fun Rulebook. (Illus.). 12p. 1981. pap. 1.10 o.p. (ISBN 0-88441-445-0, 26-640). Girl Scouts USA.
Double Dutch Treat. Elmore Leonard. 1986. 17.95 o.p. (ISBN 0-87795-804-1). Morrow.
Double Eagle. Mr. X Staff. (Espionage-Intelligence Library). 288p. 1982. pap. 2.95 o.s.i. (ISBN 0-345-30192-7). Ballantine.
Double Entry: A Spirited Tale. Bert Kopperl. 1980. 6.00 o.p. (ISBN 0-682-49537-9). Exposition-Phoenix.
Double Exposure. Jim Stinson. (Stoney Winston Mystery Ser.). 224p. 1985. 13.95 o.s.i. (ISBN 0-684-18458-3, ScribT). Scribner.
Double Flowers: A Scientific Study. J. Reynolds & J. Tampion. 184p. 1983. 29.95 o.p. (ISBN 0-442-27844-6). Van Nos Reinhold.
Double Image. Helen MacInnes. LC 66-12370. 1966. 7.50 o.s.i. (ISBN 0-15-126411-2). HarBraceJ.
Double Indemnity. James M. Cain. (Nightingale-Lythway Ser.). 1985. pap. 9.95 o.p. (ISBN 0-8161-3830-3, Large Print Bks). G K Hall.
Double King's Pawn, 1982. Ed. by David Levy et al. (Illus.). 1982. 19.95 o.s.i. (ISBN 0-907352-14-6, Capablanca). Imprint Edns.
Double Life: The Autobiography of Miklos Rozsa. Miklos Rozsa. (Illus.). 1982. 22.50 o.p. (ISBN 0-88254-683-X). Hippocrene Bks.
Double Occupancy. Elaine R. Chase. (Candlelight Ecstasy Ser.: No. 56). (Orig.). 1982. pap. 2.25 o.p. (ISBN 0-440-11732-1). Dell.
Double or Nothing. Lynn Patrick. (Candlelight Supreme Ser.: No. 87). 1985. pap. 2.75 o.p. (ISBN 0-440-12123-X). Dell.
Double Redaction of the Deuteronomistic History. Richard D. Nelson. (Journal for the Study of the Old Testament, Supplement Ser.: No. 18). 185p. pap. text ed. 14.95x o.s.i. (Pub. by JSOT Pr England). Eisenbrauns.
Double Star. Robert A. Heinlein. 1980. lib. bdg. 10.50 o.p. (ISBN 0-8398-2446-7, Gregg). G K Hall.
Double Take. Gregory Dowling. 191p. 1986. pap. 2.95 o.p. (ISBN 1-55547-101-3). Critics Choice Paper.
Double Tree: Selected Poems 1942-1976. Judith Wright. (New Poetry Ser.). 1978. 9.95 o.p. (ISBN 0-395-26480-4); pap. 5.95 o.p. (ISBN 0-395-26466-9). HM.
Double Trouble. Doreen Tovey. (Illus.). 144p. 1972. 5.95 o.p. (ISBN 0-393-08547-3). Norton.
Double Vision. Linsey Abrams. LC 84-45058. 352p. 1984. 14.95 o.p. (ISBN 0-689-11470-2, Atheneum). Macmillan.
Double Witness: Poems, Nineteen Seventy to Nineteen Seventy-Six. Ben Belitt. LC 77-2534. (Princeton Series of Contemporary Poets). 1977. 16.00x o.p. (ISBN 0-691-06346-X); pap. 7.95 o.p. (ISBN 0-691-01341-1). Princeton U Pr.
Double Your Reading Speed. The Reading Laboratory Staff. 1979. pap. 1.95 o.p. (ISBN 0-449-30856-1, Prem). Fawcett.
Doubleday Book of Interior Decorating & Encyclopedia of Styles. Albert Kornfeld. LC 65-16142. 1965. pap. 16.95 o.p. (ISBN 0-385-03711-2). Doubleday.
Doubleday Roget's Thesaurus in Dictionary Form. Ed. by Sidney I. Landau & Ronald Bogus. LC 76-7696. 564p. 1977. 11.95 o.p. (ISBN 0-385-01236-5); thumb-indexed 12.95 o.p. (ISBN 0-385-12379-5). Doubleday.
Doublefields. Elizabeth Enright. LC 66-23806. 1966. 4.75 o.p. (ISBN 0-15-126408-2). HarBraceJ.
Doubleman. C. J. Koch. 336p. 1986. text ed. 15.95 o.p. (ISBN 0-07-035221-6). McGraw.
Doubleman. C. J. Koch. 336p. 1987. pap. 4.50 o.p. (ISBN 0-380-70310-6). Avon.
Doubling Over. Larry E. Marnes. 64p. 1987. 8.75 o.p. (ISBN 0-8062-3057-6). Carlton.
Doubly Stochastic Poisson Processes. J. Grandell. (Lecture Notes in Mathematics Ser.: Vol. 529). 1976. soft cover 17.00 o.p. (ISBN 0-387-07795-2). Springer-Verlag.
Doubting Castle. Date not set. (ISBN 0-8052-3899-9). Random.
Doubting Thomas Today. Russell D. Davies. 1953. (ISBN 0-8022-0353-1). Philos Lib.
Doug Flutie. Scott Siegel & Barbara Siegel. (Avon Supertars Ser.). 1985. pap. 2.50 o.p. (ISBN 0-380-75040-6, Camelot). Avon.
Doughty Scot: An Autobiographical Fragment. George W. Donalson. Ed. by Frank R. Ford, Jr. 146p. 1986. 8.95 o.p. (ISBN 0-8062-2727-3). Carlton.
Douglas Cobb's 1-2-3 Handbook: The Complete Guide for Power Users. Douglas Cobb et al. Ed. by Marjorie Phifer & Linda Baughman. LC 86-72580. (Illus.). 700p. (Orig.). 1986. pap. 22.95 o.s.i. (ISBN 0-936767-03-0). Cobb Group.
Douglass' Monthly Magazines, Vols. 1-5. 1858-1863. Repr. Set. 165.00x o.p. (ISBN 0-8371-9110-6, DOM&, Pub. by Negro U Pr); Vol. 1-3. 88.00 o.p. (ISBN 0-8371-1586-8, D01&); Vol. 4-5. 88.00 o.p. (ISBN 0-8371-1587-6, D04&). Greenwood.
Doulton Burslem Wares. Desmond Eyles. (Illus.). 191p. 1980. 62.50 o.p. (ISBN 0-09-138260-2, Pub. by Barrie & Jenkins England). Seven Hills Bk Dists.
Doulton Lambeth Wares. Desmond Eyles. (Illus.). 179p. 1975. 62.50 o.p. (ISBN 0-09-124240-1, Pub. by Barrie & Jenkins England). Seven Hills Bk Dists.
Dover New York Walking Guide: Greenwich Village. Mary J. Shapiro. (New York City Ser.). 64p. 1985. pap. 2.50 o.p. (ISBN 0-486-24858-5). Dover.
Dow Jones Averages 1885-1985. rev. ed. Ed. by Phyllis Pierce. 410p. 1986. 60.00 o.p. (ISBN 0-87094-921-7). Dow Jones-Irwin.
Dow Jones Crosswords for the Serious, Bk. 32. Charles Preston. (Crosswords Ser.). 48p. 1985. pap. 4.50 o.p. (ISBN 0-87094-699-4). Dow Jones-Irwin.
Dow Jones Industrial Average: History & Role in an Investment Strategy. Richard J. Stillman. 200p. 1986. 24.95 o.p. (ISBN 0-87094-586-6). Dow Jones-Irwin.
Dow Jones Investor's Handbook, 1984. Phyllis Pierce. LC 66-17630. 132p. 1984. 12.95 o.s.i. (ISBN 0-87094-483-5); pap. 7.95 o.s.i. (ISBN 0-87094-548-3). Dow Jones-Irwin.
Dow Jones Investor's Handbook, 1987. Ed. by Phyllis Pierce. 132p. 1987. pap. 11.95 o.p. (ISBN 0-87094-995-0). Dow Jones-Irwin.
Dow Jones Investors Handbook, 1988. Ed. by Phyllis Pierce. 160p. (Orig.). 1988. pap. 13.95 o.p. (ISBN 1-55623-100-8). Dow Jones-Irwin.
Dow Jones-Irwin Business & Investment Almanac, 1986. rev. ed. Sumner N. Levine. 720p. 1986. pap. 24.95 o.p. (ISBN 0-87094-697-8). Dow Jones-Irwin.
Dow Jones-Irwin Business & Investment Almanac, 1987. Ed. by Sumner N. Levine. 637p. 1986. pap. 29.95 o.p. (ISBN 0-87094-915-2). Dow Jones-Irwin.
Dow Jones-Irwin Business & Investment Almanac, 1988. Ed. by Sumner N. Levine. 637p. 1988. pap. 29.95 o.p. (ISBN 1-55623-047-8). Dow Jones-Irwin.
Dow Jones-Irwin Crosswords for the Serious. Charles Preston. 1980. pap. 4.50 ea. o.p. Bk. I (ISBN 0-87128-585-1). Bk. 2 (ISBN 0-87128-586-X). Dow Jones-Irwin.
Dow Jones-Irwin Crosswords for the Serious, Bk. 3. Charles Preston. 64p. 1981. pap. 4.50 o.p. (ISBN 0-87094-238-7). Dow Jones-Irwin.
Dow Jones-Irwin Crosswords for the Serious, Bk. 4. Charles Preston. 64p. 1981. pap. 4.50 o.p. (ISBN 0-87094-239-5). Dow Jones-Irwin.
Dow Jones-Irwin Crosswords for the Serious, Bk. 6. Charles Preston. 60p. (Orig.). 1981. pap. 4.50 o.p. (ISBN 0-87094-254-9). Dow Jones-Irwin.
Dow Jones-Irwin Crosswords for the Serious, Bk. 7. Charles Preston. 60p. (Orig.). 1982. pap. 5.50 o.p. (ISBN 0-87094-295-6). Dow Jones-Irwin.
Dow Jones-Irwin Guide to Buying & Selling Treasury Securities. Howard M. Berlin. LC 83-72199. 210p. 1984. 25.00 o.p. (ISBN 0-87094-464-9). Dow Jones-Irwin.
Dow Jones-Irwin Guide to Fine Gems & Jewelry. David Marcum. LC 85-71432. (Illus.). 250p. 1985. 25.00 o.p. (ISBN 0-87094-687-0). Dow Jones-Irwin.
Dow Jones-Irwin Guide to High Tech Investing: Picking Tomorrow's Winners Today. James Powell. 1985. 45.00 o.p. (ISBN 0-87094-596-3). Dow Jones-Irwin.
Dow Jones-Irwin Guide to Interest. rev. ed. Lawrence R. Rosen. LC 81-67119. 1981. 30.00 o.p. (ISBN 0-87094-260-3). Dow Jones-Irwin.
Dow Jones-Irwin Guide to Laptop Computers. Josef Bernard. 200p. 1986. pap. 19.95 o.p. (ISBN 0-87094-780-X). Dow Jones-Irwin.
Dow Jones-Irwin Guide to Mutual Funds. rev. ed. Donald D. Rugg & Norman B. Hale. LC 82-71381. 1982. 25.00 o.p. (ISBN 0-87094-352-9). Dow Jones-Irwin.
Dow Jones-Irwin Guide to Property Ownership: How to Understand, Control & Protect Your Assets. Margaret B. Schulman. 250p. 1986. 25.00 o.p. (ISBN 0-87094-662-5). Dow Jones-Irwin.
Dow Jones-Irwin Guide to Real Estate Investing. rev. ed. Chris Mader & John Bortz. LC 82-73928. 1983. 30.00 o.p. (ISBN 0-87094-214-X). Dow Jones-Irwin.
Dow Jones-Irwin Guide to Retirement Planning. Ray Vicker. LC 85-70566. 250p. 1985. 19.95 o.p. (ISBN 0-87094-658-7). Dow Jones-Irwin.
Dow Jones-Irwin Guide to Using the Wall Street Journal. Michael B. Lehmann. LC 83-70874. 227p. 1984. 19.95 o.p. (ISBN 0-87094-309-X). Dow Jones-Irwin.

Titles

Down among the Dead Men. Brian Peachment. 1974. pap. text ed. 1.60 o.s.i. (ISBN 0-08-017615-1). Pergamon.

Down by the Old Blood Stream. Alfred Hitchcock. 1981. pap. 2.95 o.p. (ISBN 0-440-12127-2). Dell.

Down East Murders. J. S. Borthwick. 296p. 1986. pap. 3.50 o.s.i. (ISBN 0-931773-58-X). Critics Choice Paper.

Down East Printmaker: Carroll Thayer Berry. Elwyn Dearborn. (Illus.). 1983. limited ed. 60.00 o.p. (ISBN 0-89272-169-3); trade ed. 29.95 o.p. (ISBN 0-89272-164-2). Down East.

Down for the Count. Stuart M. Kaminsky. (Large Print Bks (Nightingale Ser.)). 307p. 1986. pap. 11.95x o.p. (ISBN 0-8161-4000-6). G K Hall.

Down Home Southern Cooking. LaMont Burns. LC 86-11448. (Illus.). 192p. 1987. pap. 17.95 o.p. (ISBN 0-385-19748-9). Doubleday.

Down in Tennessee, Back by Way of Richmond. James R. Gilmore. LC 76-107515. 1970. Repr. of 1864 ed. lib. bdg. 22.50x o.p. (ISBN 0-8371-3762-4, GDT&, Pub. by Negro U Pr). Greenwood.

Down Into the Water. Nancy Fitzgerald. 52p. 1984. 1.95 o.p. (ISBN 0-89900-143-2). College Pr Pub.

Down the Nineteenth Fairway. Peter Dobereiner. LC 82-73279. (Illus.). 256p. 1983. 13.95 o.p. (ISBN 0-689-11380-3, Atheneum). Macmillan.

Down the Rabbit Hole: Adventures & Misadventures in the Realm of Children's Literature. Selma Lanes. LC 73-135575. (Illus.). 1976. pap. text ed. 4.95x o.p. (ISBN 0-689-70533-6, 222, Atheneum). Macmillan.

Down There on a Visit. Christopher Isherwood. 1978. pap. 2.50 o.p. (ISBN 0-380-01883-7, 50369-7, Bard). Avon.

Down to a Sunless Sea. David Graham. 1981. 13.95 o.p. (ISBN 0-671-41217-5). S&S.

Down to Earth. Robin Place. (Illus.). 128p. 1955. Philos Lib.

Down to Earth: An Insider's View of a Frank Lloyd Wright Prairie House. Maya Moran. (Illus.). 128p. 1989. 29.95 o.s.i. (ISBN 0-8093-1559-9); pap. 18.95 o.s.i. (ISBN 0-8093-1560-2). S Ill U Pr.

Down to Earth at Walden. Marilynne K. Roach. (Illus.). 96p. (gr. 5 up). 1980. 7.95 o.p. (ISBN 0-395-29647-1). HM.

Down to Earth: Environment & Human Needs. Erik P. Eckholm. 220p. 1982. 14.95 o.p. (ISBN 0-393-01600-5). Norton.

Down to Earth: Studies in Christianity & Culture. 2nd ed. John R. Stott & Robert Coote. (Orig.). 1980. pap. 9.95 o.p. (ISBN 0-8028-1827-7). Eerdmans.

Down to the Bay. Dora M. Bostwick. 104p. 1986. 8.75 o.p. (ISBN 0-8062-2786-9). Carlton.

Down Town. Viido Polikarpus & Tappan King. (Illus.). 280p. 1985. 16.95 o.p. (ISBN 0-87795-673-1, Arbor Hse). Morrow.

Downfall of Cartesianism, Sixteen Seventy-Three to Seventeen Twelve. Richard A. Watson. (International Studies in the History of Ideas). (ISBN 0-89690-006-1). Austin Hill Pr.

Downhill Flats. Mary H. Sayler. LC 81-67373. (gr. 5-9). 1982. pap. 6.95 o.p. (ISBN 0-8054-4805-5, 4248-05). Broadman.

Downstate Illinois Business Directory, 1987-88, Vol. 2. rev. ed. American Directory Publishing Co., Inc. 1234p. 1987. pap. 85.00 o.p. (ISBN 0-944316-07-7). Amer Directory.

Downtown Express: A Selection of Poems. J. B. Miller. 29p. 1987. pap. 3.50 o.p. (ISBN 0-9615997-9-0). QED Pr Ann Arbor.

Downtown Improvement Manual. Emanuel Berk. (APA Planners Press Ser.). 780p. 1976. pap. 32.95 o.s.i. Planners Pr.

Downtown Improvement Manual. Emanuel Berk. 780p. 1976. pap. 19.00 o.p. (ISBN 0-318-12962-0); pap. 16.00 members o.p. (ISBN 0-318-12963-9). Am Plan Assn.

Downtown Mall & Peter Pond Hotel, Fort McMurray, Alberta. (Panel Advisory Service Report Ser.). 84p. 1982. pap. 10.00 o.p. (ISBN 0-317-06740-0, F-06). Urban Land.

Downtown Mall Annual & Urban Design Report, Vol. 4. Ed. by Laurence A. Alexander. LC 75-646900. (Design Ser.). (Illus.). 1978. pap. 9.50 o.p. (ISBN 0-915910-11-X). Downtown Res.

Downtown Office Growth & the Role of Public Transit. J. Thomas Black & Michael Morina. LC 82-50921. (Illus.). 128p. (Orig.). 1982. 29.00 o.p. (ISBN 0-87420-615-4, D31). Urban Land.

Downtown Planning & Development Annual, 1977, Vol. 1. Ed. by Laurence Alexander. LC 77-641768. (Planning & Development Ser.). 1977. pap. 9.50 o.p. (ISBN 0-915910-08-X). Downtown Res.

Downward Ascent. Edna Hong. LC 78-66942. 1979. pap. 5.95 o.p. (ISBN 0-8066-1679-2, 10-1955, Augsburg). Augsburg Fortress.

Dozens of Ways to Make Money. Yvonne Horn. LC 76-39930. (gr. 7 up). 1977. 5.95 o.p. (ISBN 0-15-224184-1, HJ). HarBraceJ.

Dozens of Ways to Make Money. Yvonne M. Horn. LC 76-39930. (gr. 7 up). 1977. pap. 2.95 o.p. (ISBN 0-15-224185-X, VoyB). HarBraceJ.

Dracula. Bram Stoker. LC 83-5471. 1932. 6.95 o.s.i. (ISBN 0-394-60447-4). Modern Lib.

Dracula see New Method Supplementary Readers: Bestseller Pack.

Dracula Archives. Raymond Rudorff. LC 73-183380. 204p. 1972. 5.95 o.p. (ISBN 0-87795-027-X, A4316, Arbor Hse). Morrow.

Dracula Murders. Philip Daniels. 190p. 1986. pap. 2.95 o.p. (ISBN 0-931773-81-4). Critics Choice Paper.

Dracula was a Woman. R. T. McNally. 1983. text ed. 14.95 o.p. (ISBN 0-07-045671-2). McGraw.

Draft Counseling Packet. 1983. 3.00 o.p. Natl Lawyers Guild.

Draft: Gay Question, Serious Answers. 2nd ed. Joseph Schuman. 1984. 0.40 o.p. Natl Lawyers Guild.

Draft Registration & the Law. 2nd ed. R. Charles Johnson. Ed. by Charles E. Sherman. (Illus.). 256p. 1985. pap. 9.95 o.p. (ISBN 0-87337-006-6). Nolo Pr.

Drafting California Irrevocable Inter Vivos Trusts. Ed. by John R. Cohan. LC 73-623473. (California Practice Book Ser.: No. 63). xiii, 490p. 1973. 60.00 o.p. (ISBN 0-88124-025-7). Cal Cont Ed Bar.

Drafting Documents in Plain Language 1981. (Commercial Law & Practice Ser.). 312p. 1981. 15.00 o.p. (ISBN 0-686-80121-0, A4-3093). PLI.

Drafting of the Covenant, 2 Vols. David H. Miller. 1969. Repr. of 1928 ed. Set. 110.00 o.p. (ISBN 0-384-38920-1). Johnson Repr.

Drafting: Technology & Practice. William P. Spence. 1981. 32.50 o.p. (ISBN 0-684-16772-7). Scribner.

Drafting the Public Sector Labor Agreement see Issues in the Public Employee Relations Library: Series 2.

Drafting Wills & Trust Agreements: A Systems Approach. 125.00 o.p. Shepards-McGraw.

Drafting Wills & Trusts. Pennsylvania Bar Institute Staff. 192p. 1983. 20.00 o.p. (ISBN 0-318-02171-4, 231). PA Bar Inst.

Dragon. Alfred Coppel. LC 76-54584. 1977. 10.00 o.p. (ISBN 0-15-126500-3). HarBraceJ.

Dragon Bound: Revelation Speaks to Our Times. Ernest L. Stoffel. 120p. (Orig.). 1981. pap. 5.25 o.s.i. (ISBN 0-8042-0227-3, John Knox). Westminster John Knox.

Dragon by the Tail: American, British, Japanese, & Russian Ecounters with China & One Another. John P. Davies, Jr. (Illus.). 1972. 10.00x o.p. (ISBN 0-393-05455-1). Norton.

Dragon in Class Four. June Counsel. (Illus.). 96p. (gr. 1-4). 1984. 11.95 o.p. (ISBN 0-571-13249-9). Faber & Faber.

Dragon Kite. Nancy Luenn. LC 81-11709. (Illus.). 32p. (ps-3). 1982. 12.95 o.p. (ISBN 0-15-224196-5, HJ). HarBraceJ.

Dragon Kite. Nancy Luenn. LC 81-11709. (Illus.). 12p. (ps-3). 1983. pap. 5.95 o.p. (ISBN 0-15-224197-3, VoyB). HarBraceJ.

Dragon Lady of the Ninja. Ashida Kim. (Illus.). 112p. (Orig.). 1984. pap. 10.00 o.p. (ISBN 0-87364-302-X). Paladin Pr.

Dragon Mountain. Lee Daniel. LC 84-90278. 161p. 1985. 11.95 o.p. (ISBN 0-533-06317-5). Vantage.

Dragon Night & Other Lullabies. Jane Yolen. (Illus.). 32p. (ps-3). 1980. 8.95 o.p. (ISBN 0-416-30711-6, NO.0202). Routledge Chapman & Hall.

Dragon Queen's Revenge. Eric Affabee. (Wizards, Warriors & You Ser.: No. 9). 1986. pap. 2.50 o.p. (ISBN 0-380-89946-9). Avon.

Dragon Robe. Charles C. Vance. 240p. 1985. pap. 2.95 o.p. (ISBN 0-380-89630-3). Avon.

Dragon Waiting: A Masque of History. John M. Ford. 368p. 1983. 15.50 o.s.i. (ISBN 0-671-47552-5, Timescape). PB.

Dragon Who Lived Downstairs. Burr Tillstrom. LC 83-17285. (Illus.). 48p. (gr. 1up). 1984. 12.00 o.p. (ISBN 0-688-02734-2); PLB 11.88 o.p. (ISBN 0-688-02735-0). Morrow.

Dragon Wore Pink. Christopher Hope. LC 85-7964. (Illus.). 32p. (gr. 2). 1985. 12.95 o.s.i. (ISBN 0-689-31175-3, Atheneum Childrens Bks). Macmillan.

Dragons. Barbara Hayes. LC 86-17754. (Enchanted World of...Ser.). (Illus.). (ps-3). Date not set. PLB 8.95 o.p. (ISBN 0-86592-318-3). Rourke Corp.

Dragon's Claw. Peter O'Donnell. 1979. 10.50 o.p. (ISBN 0-285-62381-8, Pub. by Souvenir Pr). Intl Spec Bk.

Dragons of Mist & Torrent. Teo Savory. LC 74-76907. 1974. 6.00 o.p. (ISBN 0-87775-042-4). Unicorn Pr.

Dragons of Rizvania. Carol Handy. (Illus.). 64p. 1984. 9.95 o.s.i. (ISBN 0-85398-192-2). G Ronald Pub.

Dragons on the Road. Patricia L. Gauch. (YA) (gr. 7-10). pap. 2.50 o.p. (ISBN 0-671-61775-3). Archway.

Dragonsword of Lankhmar. James M. Ward. LC 85-52202. (One-on-One, Advanced Dungeons & Dragons Adventure Gamebooks Ser.). 1986. pap. 5.95 o.p. (ISBN 0-88038-289-9). TSR Inc.

Dragonwand of Krynn: A Dragonlance Adventure, 2 bks. Greg Fahlgren & Nancy Fahlgren. LC 87-90080. (One-On-One Adventure Gamebooks). 320p. (Orig.). 1987. Set. pap. 5.95 o.p. (ISBN 0-88038-460-3). TSR Inc.

Dragonwyck. Anya Seton. 1968. 9.95 o.p. (ISBN 0-395-08175-0). HM.

Drainage Basin Morphology. Ed. by Stanley A. Schumm. LC 77-7365. (Benchmark Papers in Geology: Vol. 41). 1977. 69.50 o.p. (ISBN 0-12-787438-0). Acad Pr.

Drakov Memoranda. Jon Winters. 1979. pap. 2.25 o.p. (ISBN 0-380-47563-4, 47563). Avon.

Drama A to Z: A Handbook. Jack A. Vaughn. LC 78-4298. 1978. 11.95x o.p. (ISBN 0-8044-2937-5); pap. 8.95 o.p. (ISBN 0-8044-6946-6). Ungar.

Drama & Society in the Age of Jonson. Lionel C. Knights. 1968. pap. 2.25x o.p. (ISBN 0-393-00451-1, Norton Lib). Norton.

Drama & the Dramatic. S. W. Dawson. (Critical Idiom Ser.). 1970. pap. 5.50 o.p. (ISBN 0-416-17280-6, NO.2160). Routledge Chapman & Hall.

Drama in English Teaching. Tricia Evans. LC 84-12753. 192p. 1984. 26.00 o.p. (ISBN 0-7099-0923-3, Pub. by Croom Helm Ltd). Routledge Chapman & Hall.

Drama in the Church: Planning & Staging Dramatic Productions. Bev Johnson. 80p. 1983. pap. 9.95 o.p. (ISBN 0-8066-2027-7, 10-1976, Augsburg). Augsburg Fortress.

Drama in the Primary School see Creative Drama & Improvised Movement for Children.

Drama in the Western World, Fifteen Plays with Essays. Ed. by Samuel A. Weiss. Incl. Oedipus the King. Sophocles; The Bacchae. Euripides; Lysistrata. Aristophanes; The Misanthrope. Moliere; Phaedra. Jean Racine; The Prince of Homburg. Friedrich Von Kleist; Ghosts. Henrik Ibsen; A Dream Play. August Strindberg; Caesar & Cleopatra. George Bernard Shaw; Uncle Vanya. Anton Chekhov; Six Characters in Search of an Author. Luigi Pirandello; Desire Under the Elms. Eugene O'Neill; The Caucasian Chalk Circle. Bertolt Brecht; The Glass Menagerie. Tennessee Williams; All That Fall. Samuel Beckett. pap. text ed. 11.95x o.p. (ISBN 0-669-46649-2). Heath.

Drama of Discrimination in Henry James. Susan R. Moore. LC 82-11111. (Scholars' Library). 127p. 1983. text ed. 37.50 o.p. (ISBN 0-7022-1668-2). U of Queensland Pr.

Drama of Nommo: Black Theater in the African Continuum. Paul C. Harrison. LC 72-3711. 1972. pap. 2.45 o.p. (ISBN 0-394-17777-0, E603, Ever). Grove.

Drama of Thought: An Inquiry into the Place of Philosophy in Human Experience. David A. Sprintzen. LC 78-64821. 1978. pap. text ed. 12.00 o.p. (ISBN 0-8191-0640-2). U Pr of Amer.

Drama Through Performance. Mark Auburn & Katherine Burkman. LC 76-19458. (Illus.). 1977. pap. 19.50 o.p. (ISBN 0-395-24548-6). HM.

Dramas. LC 10-5248. 72p. 1980. pap. 2.95 o.p. (ISBN 0-8066-1764-0, Augsburg). Augsburg Fortress.

Dramas of Life: Lazarus & His Beloved & the Blind. Kahlil Gibran. Ed. by Jean Gibran. LC 81-19810. 104p. 1982. 8.95 o.s.i. (ISBN 0-664-21387-1, Westminster). Westminster John Knox.

Drama's Patrons: A Study of the Eighteenth-Century London Audience. Leo Hughes. 219p. 1971. 12.95x o.p. (ISBN 0-292-70091-1). U of Tex Pr.

Dramatherapy & Psychiatry. Dorothy M. Langley & Gordon E. Langley. (Illus.). 224p. 1983. pap. 14.95 o.p. (ISBN 0-7099-1624-8, Pub. by Croom Helm Ltd). Routledge Chapman & Hall.

Dramatic Compositions Copyrighted in the United States, 1870-1916, 2 Vols. U. S. Copyright Office Staff. Repr. of 1918 ed. Set. 220.00 o.p. (ISBN 0-384-62950-4). Johnson Repr.

Dramatic Construction of Balzac's Novels. Ray P. Bowen. 1940. pap. 1.00 o.p. (ISBN 0-87114-000-4). U of Oreg Bks.

Dramatic Idyls. Robert Browning. (Illus.). 101p. 1981. Repr. of 1879 ed. 117.75 o.p. (ISBN 0-89901-368-6). Found Class Reprints.

Dramatic Monologue Preaching. Alton H. McEachern. LC 82-82953. 1984. pap. 4.50 o.p. (ISBN 0-8054-2111-4). Broadman.

Dramatic Portfolio of the Greatest Art Masterpieces of the Dutch Genius. Ed. by Anthony E. Peterman. (Illus.). 89p. 1985. 137.75 o.p. (ISBN 0-86650-153-3). Gloucester Art.

Dramatic Romance: Plays, Theory, Criticism. Howard M. Felperin. 1973. pap. text ed. 7.95 o.p. (ISBN 0-15-518362-1, HC). HarBraceJ.

Dramatic Tax Savings Through Real Estate Transactions. Vernon Hoven & Harold H. Holen. 208p. 1982. 29.95 o.p. (ISBN 0-13-219071-0). P-H.

Dramatists Sourcebook 1987-88. 1987. pap. 11.95 o.p. (ISBN 0-930452-65-8). Theatre Comm.

Dramatized Classics for Radio-Style Reading. Lewy Olfson. (YA) (gr. 7-12). 1964. Vol. 1. 10.95 o.p. (ISBN 0-8238-0056-3); Vol. 2. 10.95 o.p. (ISBN 0-8238-0057-1). Plays.

Dramocles: An Intergalactic Soap Opera. Robert Sheckley. 228p. 1983. 15.95 o.p. (ISBN 0-03-059037-X). H Holt & Co.

Draughtsmanship: Architectural & Building Graphics. 3rd ed. Fraser Reekie. (Illus.). 248p. 1976. pap. 22.00x o.p. (ISBN 0-7131-3368-6). Trans-Atl Phila.

Draw a Dozen with Basic Shapes. Ethel J. Rossi. (Makemaster Book Ser.). 1980. pap. 5.95 o.p. (ISBN 0-8224-2350-2). D S Lake Pubs.

Draw Birds. David Brown. LC 79-64251. (Learn to Draw Ser.). (Illus.). 1980. pap. 2.25 o.s.i. (ISBN 0-8008-2276-5, Pentalic). Taplinger.

Draw Boats & Harbours. Peter Caldwell. LC 78-14071. (Learn to Draw Ser.). (Illus.). 1980. pap. 2.25 o.s.i. (ISBN 0-8008-4578-1, Pentalic). Taplinger.

Draw Buildings & Cityscapes. Hans Schwarz. LC 79-64252. (Learn to Draw Ser.). (Illus.). 1980. pap. 2.25 o.s.i. (ISBN 0-8008-2277-3, Pentalic). Taplinger.

Draw Dogs. Jeremy Morgan. LC 78-14059. (Learn to Draw Ser.). (Illus.). 48p. (Orig.). 1981. pap. 2.25 o.s.i. (ISBN 0-8008-4577-3, Pentalic). Taplinger.

Draw Flowers & Plants. Mary Seymour. LC 78-14070. (Learn to Draw Ser.). (Illus.). 1980. pap. 2.25 o.s.i. (ISBN 0-8008-4581-1, Pentalic). Taplinger.

Draw Horses. David Brown. LC 79-87588. (Learn to Draw Ser.). (Illus.). 48p. (Orig.). 1981. pap. 2.25 o.s.i. (ISBN 0-8008-2280-3, Pentalic). Taplinger.

Draw Horses with Sam Savitt. Sam Savitt. 1985. 4.98 o.p. (ISBN 0-517-46789-5). Crown.

Draw in Pencil, Charcoal, Crayon & Other Media. Hans Schwarz. LC 78-14069. (Learn to Draw Ser.). (Illus.). 1980. pap. 2.25 o.s.i. (ISBN 0-8008-4582-X, Pentalic). Taplinger.

Draw Landscapes. Norman Battershill. LC 78-14063. (Learn to Draw Ser.). (Illus.). 1980. pap. 2.25 o.s.i. (ISBN 0-8008-4583-8, Pentalic). Taplinger.

Draw Portraits. Benedict Rubbra. LC 78-14066. (Learn to Draw Ser.). (Illus.). 1980. pap. 2.25 o.s.i. (ISBN 0-8008-4586-2, Pentalic). Taplinger.

Draw Still Life. Moira Huntly. LC 79-64258. (Learn to Draw Ser.). (Illus.). 48p. (Orig.). 1981. pap. 2.25 o.s.i. (ISBN 0-8008-2286-2, Pentalic). Taplinger.

Draw Trees. Norman Battershill. LC 78-14062. (Learn to Draw Ser.). (Illus.). 1980. pap. 2.25 o.s.i. (ISBN 0-8008-4588-9, Pentalic). Taplinger.

Drawing: A Contemporary Approach. Claudia W. Betti & Teel Sale. LC 79-26976. 276p. (Orig.). 1980. pap. text ed. 25.95 o.p. (ISBN 0-03-045976-1, HoltC). HR&W.

Drawing & Materials. 2nd ed. V. E. Boxall. (Illus.). 1975. pap. 26.50x o.p. (ISBN 0-7131-3320-1). Trans-Atl Phila.

Drawing & Modelmaking: A Primer for Students of Architecture & Design. Alexander Ratensky. (Illus.). 160p. 1983. 22.95 o.p. (ISBN 0-8230-7369-6, Whitney Lib). Watson-Guptill.

Drawing & Painting Animals. Fritz Henning. LC 81-3995. 192p. 1981. 19.95 o.p. (ISBN 0-89134-037-8); pap. 14.95 o.p. (ISBN 0-89134-039-4). North Light Bks.

Drawing & Painting Buildings: Reggie Stanton's Guide to Architectural Rendering. Reggie Stanton. LC 78-11890. 144p. 1979. 19.95 o.p. (ISBN 0-89134-015-7). North Light Bks.

Drawing Animals. Norman Adams & Joe Singer. (Illus.). 160p. 1979. 22.50 o.p. (ISBN 0-8230-1361-8). Watson-Guptill.

Drawing Animals & Birds. Don Davy. LC 77-91048. 1978. pap. 4.95 o.s.i. (ISBN 0-8008-2268-4, Pentalic). Taplinger.

Drawing As a Means to Architecture. William K. Lockard. 1982. 33.95 o.p. (ISBN 0-442-26009-1). Van Nos Reinhold.

Drawing Boats & Water. Don Davy. LC 80-50085. (Illus.). 96p. 1980. pap. 4.95 o.s.i. (ISBN 0-8008-2269-2, Pentalic). Taplinger.

Drawing Book. Jeffery Camp. (Illus.). 256p. 1981. 24.95 o.p. (ISBN 0-03-059888-5). H Holt & Co.

Drawing Buildings. Don Davy. LC 81-50606. (Illus.). 66p. 1981. pap. 4.95 o.s.i. (ISBN 0-8008-2267-6, Pentalic). Taplinger.

Drawing File for Architects, Illustrators, & Designers. Marc Szabo. (Illus.). 256p. 1976. pap. 19.95 o.p. (ISBN 0-442-27878-0). Van Nos Reinhold.

Titles

Drawing: History of an Art. Genevieve Monnier & Bernice Rose. LC 79-64709. (Illus.). 280p. 1979. 35.00 o.p. (ISBN 0-8478-0239-6). Rizzoli Intl.

Drawing: Ideas, Materials, Techniques. rev. ed. Gerald Brommer. Ed. by George F. Horn. LC 78-59861. (Illus.). 1978. text ed. 14.95 o.p. (ISBN 0-87192-099-9). Davis Mass.

Drawing in the Italian Renaissance Workshop. Francis Ames-Lewis & Joanne Wright. (Illus.). 328p. (Orig.). pap. 15.95 o.p. (ISBN 0-905209-31-1, Pub. by Victoria & Albert Mus UK). Faber & Faber.

Drawing Interior Architecture: A Guide to Rendering & Presentation. Norman Diekman & John Pile. 176p. 1983. 32.50 o.p. (ISBN 0-8230-7159-6, Whitney Lib). Watson-Guptill.

Drawing on the Artist Within. Betty Edwards. LC 85-27688. (Illus.). 224p. 1986. 18.45 o.s.i. (ISBN 0-671-49386-8). S&S.

Drawing Out: Second Language Acquisition Through Student-Created Images. Sharron Bassano & Mary A. Christison. Ed. by Roger E. Olsen. 136p. 1982. pap. text ed. 12.95 o.p. (ISBN 0-88084-006-4). Alemany Pr.

Drawing Pets. Carol Nicklaus. LC 80-11847. (gr. 1-3). 1980. PLB 9.40 o.p. (ISBN 0-531-04138-7). Watts.

Drawing Sharp Focus Still Lifes. Robert Zappalorti. (Illus.). 192p. 1981. 22.50 o.p. (ISBN 0-8230-1435-5). Watson-Guptill.

Drawing: The Creative Process. Seymour Simmons & Marc S. Winer. (Illus.). 1977. 22.95 o.p. (ISBN 0-13-219378-7, Spec); pap. 10.95 o.p. (ISBN 0-13-219360-4, Spec). P-H.

Drawing the Line: The Origin of the American Containment Policy in South Asia. Robert Blum. 1982. 22.95 o.p. (ISBN 0-393-01565-3). Norton.

Drawings by Japanese Contemporary Architects. Graphic-Sha Editorial Staff. Ed. by Peter Cook. (Illus.). 168p. 28.95 o.p. (ISBN 4-766-10263-0, Pub. by Graphic Sha Japan). Bks Nippan.

Drawings: Eighty-First Exhibition by Artists of Chicago & Vicinity. Ed. by Lyn Delliquadri. 32p. (Orig.). 1985. pap. 6.95 o.p. (ISBN 0-86559-071-0). Art Inst Chi.

Drawings of Antonio Canaletto in the Collection of Her Majesty the Queen at Windsor Castle. K. T. Parker. Repr. of 1948 ed. write for info. o.p. (ISBN 0-384-44796-1). Johnson Repr.

Drawings of Ciro Ferri. Bruce Davis. Ed. by S. J. Freedberg. (Outstanding Dissertations in Fine Arts Ser.). (Illus.). 430p. 1985. Repr. of 1982 ed. 55.00 o.p. (ISBN 0-8240-6854-8). Garland Pub.

Drawings of Henri Matisse. John Elderfield. LC 84-50423. (Illus.). 312p. 1987. pap. 14.95 o.p. (ISBN 0-500-27394-4). Thames Hudson.

Drawings of Henri Matisse. John Golding & John Elderfield. LC 84-50423. (Illus.). 1984. 29.95f o.p. (ISBN 0-500-23401-9). Thames Hudson.

Drawings of Maynard Dixon. LC 85-71042. (Illus.). 64p. (Orig.). 1985. pap. 9.95 o.p. (ISBN 0-88401-046-5). Fine Arts Mus.

Drawings of Milton Avery. Burt Chernow. LC 83-9245. (Illus.). 131p. 1984. 17.95 o.s.i. (ISBN 0-8008-2298-6); pap. 11.95 o.s.i. (ISBN 0-8008-2299-4). Taplinger.

Drawings of Rosso Fiorentino, 2 vols. Eugene A. Carroll. LC 75-23786. (Outstanding Dissertations in the Fine Arts - 16th Century). (Illus.). 1976. Set. lib. bdg. 146.00 o.p. (ISBN 0-8240-1982-2). Garland Pub.

Drawings of William Blake: Ninety-two Pencil Studies. William Blake. Intro. by Geoffrey Keynes. (Illus.). 17.00 o.p. (ISBN 0-8446-0033-4). Peter Smith.

Drawings: The Pluralist Decade. Nancy Foote et al. LC 80-83653. (Illus.). 1979. pap. 14.00 o.p. (ISBN 0-88454-057-X). U of Pa Contemp Art.

Drawn & Quartered. E. M. Cioran. Tr. by Richard Howard from Fr. LC 81-2872. 192p. 1983. 17.95 o.s.i. (ISBN 0-394-51811-X); pap. 9.95 o.s.i. (ISBN 0-394-17841-6). Seaver Bks.

Drawn & Quartered: The Best Political Cartoons of Paul Conrad. Ed. by Richard C. Bergholtz. (Illus.). 176p. 1985. 24.95 o.p. (ISBN 0-8109-1291-0). Abrams.

Drawn by Cincinnati: Architectural Drawings in the Collection of the Cincinnati Historical Society. Jayne Merkel & William J. Rudd. (Illus., Orig.). 1980. pap. 5.00 o.s.i. (ISBN 0-917562-12-7). Contemp Arts.

Drawn from New England: A Portrait in Words & Pictures. Bethany Tudor. LC 79-14230. (Illus.). 1979. 17.95 o.p. (ISBN 0-399-20835-6, Philomel). Putnam Pub Group.

DRE Reader: A Sourcebook in Education & Ministry. Ed. by Maria Harris. LC 80-52059. 192p. (Orig.). 1980. pap. 6.95 o.p. (ISBN 0-88489-124-0). St Marys.

Dreadful Lemon Sky. John D. MacDonald. (Travis McGee Ser.). 272p. 1985. pap. 3.50 o.p. (ISBN 0-449-12964-0, GM). Fawcett.

Dream. Keith Miller. 128p. 1985. 8.95 o.p. (ISBN 0-8499-0462-5, 0462-5). Word Bks.

Dream & the Deal: The Federal Writers Project. Jerre Mangione. 1974. pap. 4.45 o.p. (ISBN 0-380-00026-1, 18283-1). Avon.

Dream Babies. James Fritzhand. 1978. pap. 2.25 o.p. (ISBN 0-380-01818-7, 35758). Avon.

Dream Buyers. Myrick Land. 1980. 9.95 o.p. (ISBN 0-393-01393-6). Norton.

Dream Cars. Jean Rodolphe-Piccard. (Illus.). 1981. 49.95 o.p. (ISBN 2-88001-087-X). Norton.

Dream Carver. Sonya Massie. (Orig.). 1989. pap. 4.50 o.p. Pinnacle MO.

Dream Chaser. Norma Seely. LC 86-29213. (Starlight Romance Ser.). 192p. 1987. 12.95 o.p. (ISBN 0-385-23568-2). Doubleday.

Dream Collector. Arthur Tress & John Minahan. (Illus.). 1973. pap. 4.45 o.p. (ISBN 0-380-01149-2, 16535X). Avon.

Dream Compels Us: Voices of Salvadoran Women. Ed. by D. Loeb et al. (Illus.). 214p. 1989. pap. 10.00 o.p. (ISBN 0-942638-13-1). New Amer Pr.

Dream Cycles. Dusty Bunker. 229p. (Orig.). 1981. pap. 9.95 o.p. (ISBN 0-914918-30-3). Whitford Pr.

Dream Days. Kenneth Grahame. (Illus.). 1975. pap. 4.95 o.p. (ISBN 0-380-00288-4, 23994, Equinox). Avon.

Dream Days. Kenneth Grahame. (Orig.). 1987. pap. 7.95 o.p. (ISBN 0-86228-059-1, Pub. by Paul Harris Pub London). Riverrun NY.

Dream Fishing the World's Greatest Waters. Trevor Housby. (Illus.). 192p. 1987. pap. 29.95 o.p. (ISBN 0-7137-1654-1, Pub. by Blandford Pr England). Sterling.

Dream Houses: The Edwardian Ideal. Roderick Gradidge. LC 80-17866. 272p. 30.00 o.p. (ISBN 0-8076-0988-9). Braziller.

Dream Lake. Marietta D. Moskin. LC 80-18999. 156p. (gr. 5-9). 1981. PLB 8.95 o.p. (ISBN 0-689-30821-3, Atheneum). Macmillan.

Dream Mates. Leonhard Frank. (ISBN 0-8022-0527-5). Philos Lib.

Dream Museum. Seymour Epstein. 1973. pap. 1.25 o.p. (ISBN 0-380-01150-6, 15222). Avon.

Dream of Chaucer: Representation & Reflection in the Early Narratives. Robert R. Edwards. 224p. 1989. lib. bdg. 32.50 o.p. (ISBN 0-8223-0871-1). Duke.

Dream of Debs, Together with An Account of the San Francisco Cooks & Waiters Strike. Jack London. (Revolutionary Classics Ser.). 64p. lib. bdg. cancelled o.s.i. (ISBN 0-88286-148-4); pap. cancelled o.s.i. (ISBN 0-88286-123-9). C H Kerr.

Dream of Descartes. Jacquest Maritain. (ISBN 0-8022-1058-9). Philos Lib.

Dream of Islands. Gavan Daws. (Illus.). 1980. 14.95 o.p. (ISBN 0-393-01293-X). Norton.

Dream of Lhasa: The Life of Nikolay Przhevalsky (1839-88), Explorer of Central Asia. Donald Rayfield. LC 70-20326. (Illus.). xii, 221p. 1976. 18.00x o.p. (ISBN 0-8214-0369-9). Ohio U Pr.

Dream of Naked Women. rev. ed. Bryan Carson. (Illus., Orig.). 1975. pap. 4.50 o.p. (ISBN 0-317-67946-5). Left Bank.

Dream of Orchids. Phyllis A. Whitney. 1985. lib. bdg. 19.95 o.p. (ISBN 0-8161-3857-5, Large Print Bks). G K Hall.

Dream of the Highway. Tom James et al. 1979. pap. 1.50 o.p. (ISBN 0-931122-32-5). West End.

Dream of the Little Elephant. Ruth Bornstein. LC 76-27748. (Illus.). 32p. (ps-3). 1979. 6.95 o.p. (ISBN 0-395-28771-5, Clarion). HM.

Dream Play. August Strindberg. Ed. by Jacques Chwat. 1974. pap. 0.75 o.p. (ISBN 0-380-00090-3, 18655, Bard). Avon.

Dream Poet. Richard M. Jones. 192p. 1979. pap. text ed. 11.25x o.p. (ISBN 0-87073-903-4). Schenkman Bks Inc.

Dream Recurring. (Arlen House - Maxwell House Winners Ser.). 112p. pap. 4.95 o.p. (ISBN 0-905223-23-3, Dist. by Kampmann). M Boyars Pubs.

Dream Sharing. Robin Shohet. 160p. 1985. pap. 9.99 o.p. (ISBN 0-85500-180-1, Pub. by Turnstone Pr England). Sterling.

Dream Turf Ravers. David G. Fowler. (Illus.). 32p. (Orig.). 1979. lib. bdg. 25.00 o.p. (ISBN 0-916908-34-8); pap. 3.00 o.p. (ISBN 0-916908-13-5). Place Herons.

Dream Voyages. John-Roger. LC 79-88974. 1979. pap. 8.00 o.s.i. (ISBN 0-914829-08-4). Mandeville LA.

Dream Watcher. Barbara Wersba. LC 68-28750. (gr. 6 up). 1968. PLB 6.95 o.p. (ISBN 0-689-20621-6, Atheneum). Macmillan.

Dream Weaver. Martin Brooks. LC 77-94412. 1978. 10.95 o.p. (ISBN 0-89662-000-X, Atheneum). Macmillan.

Dream with No Stump Roots in It: Stories. David Huddle. LC 74-22229. (Breakthrough Bks). 128p. 1975. 9.95 o.p. (ISBN 0-8262-0174-1). U of Mo Pr.

Dream Workbook. Jill Morris. 224p. 1985. 16.95 o.p. (ISBN 0-316-58404-5). Little.

Dreamboats & Milestones: Cars of the '50s. Halla. 232p. 1981. 18.95 o.p. (ISBN 0-8306-9625-3); pap. 11.95 o.p. (ISBN 0-8306-2065-6, 2065). TAB Bks.

Dreamed Life. Tr. by Ulla Printz-Pahlson from Swedish. LC 82-2196. Orig. Title: Dromen om ett liv. vi, 201p. 1983. 16.95 o.p. (ISBN 0-8214-0710-4); pap. 8.95 o.p. (ISBN 0-8214-0711-2, 82-84804). Ohio U Pr.

Dreamer of the Vine: A Novel About Nostradamus. Liz Greene. 1981. 12.95 o.p. (ISBN 0-393-01434-7). Norton.

Dreamers Are Thinkers. Rayvond Gaines. 1981. 5.00 o.p. (ISBN 0-682-49538-7). Exposition-Phoenix.

Dreaming Jungles. Michel Rio & William Carlson. LC 86-22560. 144p. 1987. 10.45 o.p. (ISBN 0-394-55661-5); pap. 6.95 o.p. (ISBN 0-394-75035-7). Pantheon.

Dreaming Pool. Paula Christopher. (Orig.). 1987. pap. 3.50 o.p. (ISBN 0-440-11950-2). Dell.

Dreaming Swimmer. Elisabeth Ogilvie. 1978. pap. 1.75 o.p. (ISBN 0-380-01878-0, 37051). Avon.

Dreaming the Dark: Magic, Sex, & Politics. Starhawk. LC 81-70485. 256p. 1982. 15.95x o.p. (ISBN 0-8070-1000-6); pap. 9.95 o.p. (ISBN 0-8070-1001-4, BP633). Beacon Pr.

Dreamland. Newton Thornburg. 1983. 14.95 o.p. (ISBN 0-87795-444-5, Arbor Hse). Morrow.

Dreamland. Newton Thornburg. 272p. 1984. pap. 3.75 o.p. (ISBN 0-380-68510-8, 68510-8). Avon.

Dreams & Reality. Brone Martin. 1979. 10.00 o.p. (ISBN 0-682-49321-X). Exposition-Phoenix.

Dreams & the Growth of Personality: Expanding Awareness in Psychotherapy. Ernest L. Rossi. 232p. 1972. 60.00 o.p. (ISBN 0-08-016787-X). Pergamon.

Dreams Are Not Enough. Jacqueline Briskin. 480p. 1986. 17.95 o.p. (ISBN 0-399-13162-0, Perigee). Putnam Pub Group.

Dreams Are Not Enough. Jacqueline Briskin. 672p. 1987. 20.95 o.p. (ISBN 0-8161-4335-8). G K Hall.

Dreams Come Due: Government & Economists As If Freedom Really Mattered. John Galt. 1986. 17.45 o.s.i. (ISBN 0-671-61159-3). S&S.

Dreams, "Evolution," & Value Fulfillment: A Seth Book, Vol. II. Jane Roberts. 288p. 1986. 15.95 o.p. (ISBN 0-13-219460-0). P-H.

Dreams, "Evolution" & Value Fulfillment. Jane Roberts. (Seth Book Ser.: Vol. I). 464p. 1986. 15.95 o.p. (ISBN 0-13-219452-X). P-H.

Dreams: Hidden Meanings & Secrets. 288p. (Orig.). 1983. pap. 6.95 o.p. (ISBN 0-668-05777-7, 5777). Arco.

Dreams of a Young Girl. David Hamilton & Alain Robbe-Grillet. 1971. 22.50 o.p. (ISBN 0-688-01482-8). Morrow.

Dreams of Allon. Steven W. Newell. 224p. 1987. 9.95 o.p. (ISBN 0-8062-2872-5). Carlton.

Dreams of Roses & Fire. Eyvind Johnson. Ed. by Erik J. Friis. LC 83-26690. (Library of Nordic Literature). 384p. 1984. 14.95 o.p. (ISBN 0-88254-897-2). Hippocrene Bks.

Dreams of the Kalahari. Carolyn Slaughter. 1987. 19.95 o.p. (ISBN 0-684-18765-5). Scribner.

Dreams: Visions of the Night. David Coxhead & Susan Hiller. 1976. pap. 5.95 o.p. (ISBN 0-380-01151-4, 27862). Avon.

Dreamsnake. Vonda N. McIntyre. 324p. 1978. 11.95 o.p. (ISBN 0-395-26470-7). HM.

Dred Scott's Case. rev. ed. Vincent C. Hopkins. LC 51-13327. 1967. pap. text ed. 4.95x o.p. (ISBN 0-689-70099-7, 110, Atheneum). Macmillan.

Dress Blues & Tears. Sgt. Gregory L. Rice. 1977. 7.50 o.p. (ISBN 0-682-48818-6). Exposition-Phoenix.

Dress Fitting. 2nd ed. Natalie Bray. (Illus.). 120p. 1982. pap. text ed. 17.00 o.p. (Granada England). Gower Pub Co.

Dress Fitting: Basic Principles & Practice. Natalie Bray. 128p. 1970. 17.95x o.p. (ISBN 0-8464-0342-0). Beekman Pubs.

Dress Her in Indigo. John D. MacDonald. (Travis McGee Ser.). 1985. pap. 3.50 o.p. (ISBN 0-449-12984-5, GM). Fawcett.

Dress Her in Indigo. John D. MacDonald. 1985. pap. 9.95 o.p. (ISBN 0-8161-3820-6, Large Print Bks). G K Hall.

Dress Pattern Designing: The Basic Principles of the Cut & Fit. 4th ed. Natalie Bray. (Illus.). 144p. 1982. pap. text ed. 14.50 o.p. (ISBN 0-246-11716-8, Granada England). Gower Pub Co.

Dress with Style. Joanne Wallace. (Illus.). 256p. 1982. pap. 12.95 o.p. (ISBN 0-8007-1313-3). Revell.

Dresses & Related Apparel: (Women's Misses & Juniors) 7th ed. Fairchild Market Research Division Staff. (Fact File Ser.). 45p. 1988. pap. 20.00 o.p. (ISBN 0-87005-644-1). Fairchild.

Dresses & Related Apparel: Women's, Misses', Juniors' 5th ed. Fairchild Market Research Division Staff. (Fact Files Ser.). (Illus.). 50p. 1986. pap. 20.00 o.p. (ISBN 0-87005-558-5). Fairchild.

Dressing Sexy. Molly Cochran. (Orig.). 1981. pap. 6.95 o.p. (ISBN 0-671-41529-8, Fireside). S&S.

Dressing Thin: How to Look up to 35 Pounds Thinner Without Losing an Ounce. Dale Goday & Molly Cochran. 128p. 1981. pap. 6.95 o.p. (ISBN 0-671-43826-3, Fireside). S&S.

Dressmaking Simplified. 3rd ed. Valerie Cock. (Illus.). 239p. 1982. text ed. 12.00 o.p. (ISBN 0-246-11501-7, Granada England). Gower Pub Co.

Dreyfus Affair: A National Scandal. Betty Schechter. (Illus.). 256p. (gr. 7 up). 1965. 9.95 o.p. (ISBN 0-395-07092-9). HM.

DRI Report on U. S. Manufacturing Industries. O. Eckstein et al. 208p. 1984. text ed. 27.50 o.p. (ISBN 0-07-018969-2). McGraw.

Drift. Date not set. (ISBN 0-385-29446-8). Delacorte.

Drift. William Mayne. LC 85-20567. 168p. (gr. 4-6). 1986. 14.95 o.p. (ISBN 0-385-29446-8). Delacorte.

Drifters. James A. Michener. 1983. pap. 4.95 o.p. (ISBN 0-449-20522-3, Crest). Fawcett.

Drilling. J. A. Short. 600p. 1983. 69.95 o.p. (ISBN 0-87814-242-8, P-43277). Pennwell Bks.

Drilling Rig Task Details & Performance Standards, 5 vols. Canadian Association of Oilwell Drilling Contractors Staff. (Orig.). 1982. Set. 59.00x o.s.i. (ISBN 0-87201-927-6). Rig Manager (ISBN 0-87201-929-2). Driller (ISBN 0-87201-930-6). Derrickhand (ISBN 0-87201-931-4). Motorhand (ISBN 0-87201-932-2). Floorhand (ISBN 0-87201-933-0). Gulf Pub.

Drilling Technology. S. F. Krar & Oswald. LC 73-13486. 1977. pap. text ed. 12.20 o.p. (ISBN 0-8273-0210-X). Delmar.

Drink from the Deeper Wells. Stanley E. Sayers. 7.50 o.p. (ISBN 0-89225-079-8). Gospel Advocate.

Drink to Yesterday. Manning Coles. (Seagull Library of Mystery & Suspense). 1967. Repr. 4.50 o.p. (ISBN 0-393-08550-3). Norton.

Drinking. Jack B. Weiner. 1976. 11.95 o.p. (ISBN 0-393-08749-2). Norton.

Drinking: Alcohol in American Society - Issues & Current Research. Ed. by John A. Ewing & Beatrice A. Rouse. LC 76-47522. 456p. 1978. 26.95x o.s.i. (ISBN 0-88229-129-7); pap. text ed. 13.95x o.s.i. (ISBN 0-88229-569-1). Nelson-Hall.

Drinking & Driving: What to Do if Your'e Caught. 1st ed. Donald J. Purich. 133p. 1978. 4.50 o.p. (ISBN 0-88908-043-7). ISC Pr.

Drinking Behavior: Oral Stimulation, Reinforcement, & Preference. Ed. by J. A. Weijnen & J. Mendelson. LC 77-8299. (Illus.). 438p. 1977. 55.00x o.p. (ISBN 0-306-31003-1, Plenum Pr). Plenum Pub.

Drinking Careers: Occupations, Drinking Habits, & Drinking Problems. Martin A. Plant. (Illus.). 1979. 34.00x o.p. (ISBN 0-422-76590-2, NO.2366, Pub. by Tavistock England). Routledge Chapman & Hall.

Drinking Water: A Community Issue. Ed. by Susan Boyd et al. 30p. (Orig.). 1986. pap. text ed. 3.00 o.p. (ISBN 0-937345-03-2). Concern.

Drinks of the World. James Mew & John Ashton. LC 70-78207. (Illus.). 368p. 1971. Repr. of 1892 ed. 43.00x o.p. (ISBN 0-8103-3772-X). Gale.

Drippings from a Cracked Churn: The Foibles & Follies of Our Educational Bureaucracy. James W. Wafer. (Illus.). 256p. 1983. 11.50 o.p. (ISBN 0-682-49926-9, Banner). Exposition-Phoenix.

Driscoe's Rugs: A Sole-Proprietorship Merchandising Business for Chapters 1-15 see College Accounting Fundamentals.

Drive Across Africa. Ferenc J. Bodo. 1977. 17.50 o.p. (ISBN 0-682-48660-4). Exposition-Phoenix.

Drive It Till It Drops: Keep Your Car Running Forever. Joe Troise. LC 80-123393. (Illus.). 120p. 1980. pap. 4.95 o.s.i. (ISBN 0-89708-024-6). And Bks.

Driven to Murder. Alan D. Burke. Ed. by C. Michael Curtis. LC 85-22897. 232p. 1986. 15.95 o.p. (ISBN 0-87113-033-5). Atlantic Monthly.

Driver & Home Safety Manual. 64p. 1982. 4.80 o.p. (ISBN 0-87912-128-9, 330.59). Natl Safety Coun.

Driver Performance, Passenger Safety Devices, & the Bicyclist. (Transportation Research Report Ser.). 50p. 1979. 3.00 o.p. (ISBN 0-309-02995-3). Transport Res Bd.

Driving Ambition. Alan Jones & Keith Botsford. LC 82-45166. 184p. 1982. 12.95 o.p. (ISBN 0-689-11308-0, Atheneum). Macmillan.

Driving Forces in History. Halvdan Koht. Tr. by Einar Haugen. LC 64-16065. 1968. pap. text ed. 2.25x o.p. (ISBN 0-689-70119-5, 121, Atheneum). Macmillan.

Drogen unter uns. 4th ed. D. Ladewig & V. Hobi. Ed. by H. Dubacher & V. Faust. (Illus.). viii, 100p. 1983. pap. 8.00 o.p. (ISBN 3-8055-3608-9). S Karger.

Droll Stories. Honore De Balzac. Ed. by Ernest Boyd. (Black & Gold Lib). 1944. 7.95 o.p. (ISBN 0-87140-984-4, Co-Pub with Tudor). Liveright.

Dromen om ett liv see Dreamed Life.

Droodles Storybook of Proverbs. Ray Cioni & Sally Cioni. (gr. k-5). 8.95 o.p. (ISBN 0-89191-472-2, 54726). Cook.

Drop Hammer. Emanuel Fried. 1978. pap. 2.50 o.p. (ISBN 0-931122-05-8). West End.

Drop into Hell. Gene Olson. (gr. 8 up). 1969. 3.75 o.s.i. (ISBN 0-664-32436-3, Westminster). Westminster John Knox.

Drop Too Many. John Frost. (Illus.). 1987. 19.95 o.p. (ISBN 0-317-66072-1, Pub. by Buchan & Enright UK). Seven Hills Bk Dists.

Dropping Ashes on the Buddha: The Teaching of Zen Master Seung Sahn. Seung Sahn. Tr. by Stephen Mitchell. 1976. pap. 6.95 o.s.i. (ISBN 0-394-17910-2, E675, Ever). Grove.

Dropping Your Guard. Charles A. Swindoll. 1986. deluxe ed. 9.95 o.p. (ISBN 0-8499-3850-3). Word Bks.

Drowned Ammet. Diana W. Jones. LC 77-21108. (gr. 5 up). 1978. 7.95 o.p. (ISBN 0-689-30620-2, Atheneum). Macmillan.

Drowning Pool. Ross MacDonald. Ed. by Jacques Barzun & Wendell H. Taylor. LC 75-44990. (Crime Fiction Ser.). 1976. Repr. of 1950 ed. lib. bdg. 21.00 o.p. (ISBN 0-8240-2382-X). Garland Pub.

Drug Abuse & Drug Counseling. Thomas Weisman. LC 73-17748. 1974. Repr. 20.00x o.s.i. (ISBN 0-87668-125-9). Aronson.

Drug Abuse in the Modern World: A Perspective for the Eighties: Proceedings of a Symposium Held at the College of Physicians & Surgeons of Columbia University, New York, N.Y. Ed. by Gabriel G. Nahas & Henry C. Frick, II. (Illus.). 320p. 1981. 58.00 o.p. (ISBN 0-08-026300-3); pap. text ed. 13.75 o.p. (ISBN 0-08-027550-8). Pergamon.

Drug Abuse: The Truth about Today's Drug Scene. Tony Blaze-Gosden. (Take Control Ser.). (Illus.). 144p. (Orig.). 1988. pap. 9.95 o.p. (ISBN 0-7153-9038-4, Pub. by David & Charles Pub England). Sterling.

Drug Abuse Treatment Client Characteristics & Pretreatment Behaviors. Robert L. Hubbard et al. (Treatment Research Monograph). 86p. 1986. pap. 4.25 o.p. (ISBN 0-318-21672-8, S/N 017-024-01310-2). USGPO.

Drug Analysis: Keynote & Plenary Papers from the First International Symposium, June 1983, Brussels, Belgium. Ed. by A. F. Fell. 200p. 1984. pap. 22.00 o.p. (ISBN 0-08-031441-4). Pergamon.

Drug & Alcohol Abuse: A Clinical Guide to Diagnosis & Treatment. 2nd ed. Marc A. Schuckit. LC 83-13815. (Critical Issues in Psychiatry Ser.). 288p. 1984. 25.00x o.p. (ISBN 0-306-41457-0, Plenum Pr). Plenum Pub.

Drug & Alcohol Problems: Exploring Biology, Behavior, & Public Health. 150p. 1988. 24.95 o.p. (ISBN 0-309-03931-2); pap. 14.95 o.p. (ISBN 0-309-03849-9). Natl Acad Pr.

Drug Awareness: Key Documents on LSD, Marijuana & the Drug Culture. Ed. by Richard E. Horman & Allan M. Fox. (Orig.). 1970. pap. 1.45 o.p. (ISBN 0-380-01152-2, 11064, Discus). Avon.

Drug Consultant 1985-86: The Pocket Clinical Guide to Drugs & Their Usefulness. Ed. by Rhoda M. Michaels & G. R. Brown. 383p. 1985. pap. text ed. 18.95 o.p. (ISBN 0-471-80894-6, Pub. by Wiley Med). Wiley.

Drug Delivery Systems. Business Communications Staff. 221p. 1984. 1500.00 o.p. (ISBN 0-89336-388-X, C-050). BCC.

Drug Delivery Systems: A Technology Survey. Technical Insights, Inc. Staff. LC 84-50989. 288p. 1984. 710.00 o.p. (ISBN 0-914993-03-8). Tech Insights.

Drug Dependence & Alcoholism, Vol. 1: Biomedical Issues. Ed. by Arnold J. Schecter. LC 79-24558. 1370p. 1981. 95.00x o.p. (ISBN 0-306-40323-4, Plenum Pr). Plenum Pub.

Drug Dependence & Alcoholism, Vol. 2: Social & Behavioral Issues. Ed. by Arnold J. Schecter. LC 79-24558. 1064p. 1981. 95.00x o.p. (ISBN 0-306-40324-2, Plenum Pr). Plenum Pub.

Drug Dependence: Aspects of Ego Functions. Henry Krystal & Herbert A. Raskin. LC 76-121920. 120p. 1970. text ed. 15.95x o.p. (ISBN 0-8143-1419-8). Wayne St U Pr.

Drug Design & Adverse Reactions. Hans Bundgaard et al. 1977. 82.50 o.p. (ISBN 0-12-141150-8). Acad Pr.

Drug Discrimination & State Dependent Learning. Ed. by B. T. Ho et al. 1978. 67.50 o.p. (ISBN 0-12-350250-0). Acad Pr.

Drug Dosage in Laboratory Animals: A Handbook. 2nd rev. & enl. ed. C. D. Barnes & L. G. Eltherington. LC 64-21066. 1973. 48.00x o.p. (ISBN 0-520-02273-4). U of Cal Pr.

Drug Hang-up: America's Fifty Year Folly. Rufus King. 398p. 1974. spiral 21.75x o.p. (ISBN 0-398-03071-5). C C Thomas.

Drug Identification Guide from PDR. 6th ed. Medical Economics Company Staff. 1980. pap. 10.95 o.p. (ISBN 0-87489-241-4). Med Economics.

Drug-Inactivating Enzymes & Other Problems of Resistance to Antibacterial Drugs: Proceedings. Symposium on Antibiotics Resistance, 2nd, Smolenice Castle, Czechoslovakia, Jun 5-8, 1974. Ed. by S. Mitsuhashi et al. 450p. 1976. 61.00 o.p. (ISBN 0-387-07113-X). Springer-Verlag.

Drug: Induced Blood Disorders. De Gruchy. (Illus.). 212p. 1975. 36.00 o.p. (ISBN 0-632-00027-9, B-1241-1). Mosby.

Drug-Induced Ocular Side Effects & Drug Interactions. 2nd ed. F. T. Fraunfelder. LC 82-146. 544p. 1982. text ed. 30.00 o.p. (ISBN 0-8121-0850-7). Lea & Febiger.

Drug Information for the Consumer. Consumer Reports Editors. 1224p. (Orig.). 1987. pap. 25.00 o.p. (ISBN 0-89043-084-5). Consumer Reports.

Drug Information for the Consumer, 1988 Edition. Rev. ed. U. S. Pharmacopeial Convention, Incorporated Staff. 1344p. 1988. pap. 25.00 o.p. (ISBN 0-89043-210-4). Consumer Reports.

Drug Interactions. 5th ed. Philip D. Hansten. LC 84-19397. 460p. 1985. pap. 22.50 o.p. (ISBN 0-8121-0944-9). Lea & Febiger.

Drug Interactions. Ed. by Susan R. Williams & Barbara McVan. LC 84-5639. (Nursing Now Ser.). (Illus.). 136p. 1984. text ed. 13.95 o.p. (ISBN 0-916730-78-6). Springhouse Pub.

Drug Interactions: Basic Principles & Clinical Problems. Joseph Albanese & Thomas Bond. (Illus.). 1978. text ed. 19.95 o.p. (ISBN 0-07-000940-6). McGraw.

Drug Interactions Index. F. Lerman & R. Weinbert. 304p. 1982. 21.95 o.p. (ISBN 0-87489-266-X). Med Economics.

Drug Monitoring. Ed. by F. H. Gross & W. H. Inman. 1978. 84.00 o.p. (ISBN 0-12-304550-9). Acad Pr.

Drug Monitoring Data Pocket Guide. Ed. by Gordon Ireland. 125p. 1980. pap. 5.00 Discounts avail. on bulk orders for educ. purposes o.p. (ISBN 0-317-17658-7, 504). Am Assn Clinical Chem.

Drug Receptor Interactions in Antimicrobial Chemotherapy: Proceedings. Symposium, Vienna, Sept. 4-6, 1974. Ed. by J. Drews & F. E. Hahn. (Topics in Infectious Diseases Ser.: Vol. 1). (Illus.). 340p. 1975. pap. 27.00 o.p. (ISBN 0-387-81311-X). Springer-Verlag.

Drug Resistance & Selectivity: Biochemical & Cellular Basis. Ed. by Enrico Mihich. 1973. 95.50 o.p. (ISBN 0-12-495765-X). Acad Pr.

Drug Resistance of Microorganisms. Robert J. Schnitzer & Emanuel Grunberg. 1957. 57.50 o.p. (ISBN 0-12-628450-4). Acad Pr.

Drug Therapy in Obstetrics & Gynecology. 2nd ed. William F. Rayburn & Frederick P. Zuspan. 528p. 1986. 54.00 o.p. (ISBN 0-8385-1809-5). Appleton & Lange.

Drug Therapy in the Elderly. Ed. by R. E. Vestal. 300p. 1982. text ed. 44.00 o.p. (ISBN 0-86792-008-4, Pub by Adis Pr Australia). Year Bk Med.

Drug Transport Across the Blood-Brain Barrier. Ed. by I. P. Bates & N. G. Burnet. (Ellis Horwood Health Science Ser.). 1987. lib. bdg. (ISBN 0-89573-574-1). VCH Pubs.

Drug Treatment in Obstetrics: A Handbook of Prescribing. R. S. Ledward & D. F. Hawkins. (Illus.). 272p. 1983. 29.00 o.p. (ISBN 0-412-24770-4, NO. 6789); pap. 13.95 o.p. (ISBN 0-412-15020-4, NO. 6790). Routledge Chapman & Hall.

Drug Treatment in Psychiatry. 3rd ed. Trevor Silverstone & Paul Turner. (Social & Psychological Aspects of Medical Practices Ser.). 1982. pap. 19.95x o.p. (ISBN 0-7100-9050-1). Routledge Chapman & Hall.

Drug Use & Abuse: A Guide to Research Findings, 2 vols. Gregory A. Austin et al. LC 84-3015. 1984. Vol. 1: Adults, 443p. lib. bdg. 55.00 o.p. (ISBN 0-87436-412-4); Vol. 2: Adolescents, 510p. lib. bdg. 65.00 o.p. (ISBN 0-87436-413-2); Set. lib. bdg. 110.00 o.p. (ISBN 0-87436-414-0). ABC-Clio.

Drug Use in Pregnancy. Leo Stern. 300p. 1983. 36.00 o.p. (ISBN 0-86792-011-4, Pub by Adis Pr Australia). Year Bk Med.

Drug Use in Renal Disease. Craig Brater. (Illus.). 250p. 1982. text ed. 27.50 o.p. (ISBN 0-86792-005-X, Pub by Adis Pr Australia). Year Bk Med.

Drug Warning: Illustrated Guide for Parents & Teachers. David Stockley. (Illus.). 160p. 1986. 28.50x o.p. (ISBN 0-356-12423-1, Pub. by MacD & Co). Trans-Atl Phila.

Drugs. 2nd ed. Ed. by Larry N. Gever et al. LC 84-1333. (Nurse's Reference Library). (Illus.). 1159p. 1984. text ed. 25.95 o.p. (ISBN 0-916730-87-5). Springhouse Pub.

Drugs, Vol. 4 (incl. 1985-1987 supplements) Ed. by Eleanor C. Goldstein. (Social Issues Resources Ser.). 1987. 45.00 o.p. (ISBN 0-89777-120-6). Soc Issues.

Drugs: A Factual Account. 3rd ed. Dorothy Dusek-Girdano. 352p. 1980. pap. text ed. 11.25 o.p. (ISBN 0-394-34875-3, RanC). Random.

Drugs & Hormones in Brain Development. Ed. by Margret Schlumph & Walter Lichtensteiger. 252p. 1983. 98.95x o.p. (ISBN 3-8055-3514-7). Transaction Pubs.

Drugs & Nursing Implications. 4th ed. Laura E. Govoni & Janice E. Hayes. (Illus.). 1155p. 1982. 24.50x o.p. (ISBN 0-8385-1786-2). Appleton & Lange.

Drugs & Ocular Tissues: Proceedings of the International Society for Eye Research, 2nd Meeeting, Jerusalem, Sept. 12-17, 1976. International Society for Eye Research Staff. Ed. by S. Dikstein. 1977. 49.50 o.p. (ISBN 3-8055-2637-7). S Karger.

Drugs & People: Medications, Their History & Origins, & the Way They Act. rev. ed. Alfred Burger. LC 88-12218. x, 176p. 1988. 17.50x o.p. (ISBN 0-8139-1101-X). U Pr of Va.

Drugs & Pharmacology for Nurses. 9th ed. S. J. Hopkins. LC 85-19509. (Student Nurse Ser.). (Illus.). 459p. (Orig.). 1986. pap. 19.00 o.p. (ISBN 0-443-03556-3). Churchill.

Drugs & Social Policy. Ed. by Lenore Kupperstein et al. LC 74-84800. (Annals Ser: No. 417). 250p. 1975. pap. 15.00 o.p. (ISBN 0-87761-184-X). Am Acad Pol Soc Sci.

Drugs & Society: A Biological Perspective. Patricia Witters-Jones & Weldon Witters. LC 82-21738. 400p. 1983. pap. text ed. 22.50 o.p. (ISBN 0-86720-367-6). Jones & Bartlett.

Drugs & the Aged. William D. Poe & Donald A. Holloway. 295p. 1980. text ed. 17.50 o.p. (ISBN 0-07-050330-3). McGraw.

Drugs & the Cell Cycle. Ed. by A. M. Zimmerman et al. (Cell Biology Ser.). 1973. 74.50 o.p. (ISBN 0-12-781260-1). Acad Pr.

Drugs & the Elderly. rev. ed. Ed. by Ronald C. Kayne. LC 78-52886. 1978. 10.00x o.p. (ISBN 0-88474-045-5, 05738-X). Lexington Bks.

Drugs & the Inheritance of Behavior: A Survey of Comparative Psychopharmacogenetics. Ed. by P. L. Broadhurst. LC 78-3617. (Illus.). 214p. 1978. 39.50x o.p. (ISBN 0-306-31105-4, Plenum Pr). Plenum Pub.

Drugs & Youth. Robert Coles et al. LC 72-114383. 1971. 8.95x o.p. (ISBN 0-87140-501-6, 1970); pap. 3.95 o.p. (ISBN 0-87140-239-4). Liveright.

Drugs & Youth: The Challenge of Today. Ed. by E. Harms. 1973. 60.00 o.p. (ISBN 0-08-017063-3). Pergamon.

Drugs-Crime Connection. Ed. by James A. Inciardi. LC 81-5328. (Sage Annual Reviews of Drug & Alcohol Abuse Ser.: Vol. 5). (Illus.). 271p. 1981. 29.95 o.s.i. (ISBN 0-8039-1634-5); pap. 14.95 o.s.i. (ISBN 0-8039-1635-3). Sage.

Drugs, Diet & You. Robert J. Benowicz. 640p. 1984. pap. 9.50 o.p. (ISBN 0-671-46174-5, Fireside). S&S.

Drugs, Drinking, & Adolescents. Donald Ian Macdonald & Miller Newton. 200p. 1984. 24.00 o.p. (ISBN 0-8151-5810-6). Year Bk Med.

Drugs During Pregnancy. R. W. Karim. 152p. 1981. 17.00 o.p. (ISBN 0-89313-050-8). G F Stickley Co.

Drugs for Young People: Their Use & Misuse. 2nd ed. Kenneth Leech & Brenda Jordan. 1974. 3.85 o.p. (ISBN 0-08-017938-X). Pergamon.

Drugs in Litigation: Damage Awards Involving Prescription & Nonprescription Drugs. 1987 ed. Ed. by Michie Company Staff. 712p. 45.00x o.p. (ISBN 0-87473-290-5). Michie Co.

Drugs in Relation to the Drug User. Ed. by Stanley Einstein. 1980. 70.00 o.p. (ISBN 0-08-019596-2). Pergamon.

Drugs, Society & Behavior 1988-89. 3rd, rev. ed. Ed. by William B. Rucker & Marion E. Rucker. (Annual Editions Ser.). (Illus.). 256p. 1988. pap. text ed. 9.95 o.p. (ISBN 0-87967-721-X). Dushkin Pub.

Drugs, Society & Human Behavior. 3rd ed. Oakley Ray. LC 82-8203. (Illus.). 512p. 1982. pap. text ed. 19.95 o.p. (ISBN 0-8016-4092-X). Mosby.

Drugs Studies in CVD & PVD: Proceedings of the International Symposium, Geneva, May 25-26, 1981. Ed. by Scientific Research Staff. (Illus.). 250p. 1983. 55.00 o.p. (ISBN 0-08-027084-0). Pergamon.

Druid. Leonard Mosley. LC 80-69367. 1981. 12.95 o.p. (ISBN 0-689-11106-1, Atheneum). Macmillan.

Drum, Hammer & Cross. Vern Rossman. (gr. 9 up). 1967. pap. 0.75 o.p. (ISBN 0-377-80021-X). Friendship Pr.

Drummer Hoff. Barbara Emberley. (Illus.). (ps-1). 1972. 12.95x o.s.i. (ISBN 0-13-220822-9, Pub. by Treehouse); pap. 5.95 o.s.i. (ISBN 0-13-220855-5). P-H.

Drummer in the Dark. Francis Clifford. LC 75-34223. 204p. 1976. 7.95 o.p. (ISBN 0-15-126580-1). HarBraceJ.

Drums & Trumpets: The House of Stuart. Kristy McLeod. LC 77-1496. (gr. 6 up). 1979. 8.95 o.p. (ISBN 0-395-28918-1, Clarion). HM.

Drums of Darkness (Leo) Marion Zimmer Bradley. (Zodiac Ser.). (Orig.). 1976. pap. 1.25 o.p. (ISBN 0-345-25108-3). Ballantine.

Drums of ECK. Paul Twitchell. 1970. pap. 3.95 o.p. (ISBN 0-914766-04-X). Illum Way Pub.

Drums Speak: The Story of Kofi, a Boy of West Africa. Marc Bernheim & Evelyne Bernheim. LC 70-137761. (Illus.). 48p. (gr. 3 up). 1972. 6.50 o.p. (ISBN 0-15-224233-3, HJ). HarBraceJ.

Drunk in Madrid. Joyce Elbert. LC 72-80329. 216p. 1972. 6.95 o.p. (ISBN 0-87795-037-7, Arbor Hse). Morrow.

Drunk on the Divine: An Account of Life in Ashram of Bhagwan. Ma Satya Bharti. LC 79-6168. 1981. 6.95 o.p. (ISBN 0-394-17656-1, E754, Ever). Grove.

Dry & Save. Dora D. Flack. LC 77-72665. (Illus., Orig.). 1977. pap. 4.95 o.p. (ISBN 0-912800-41-0). Woodbridge Pr.

Dry Biological Systems. Ed. by John H. Crowe & James S. Clegg. 1978. 58.00 o.p. (ISBN 0-12-198080-4). Acad Pr.

Dry Your Smile. Robin Morgan. LC 86-32972. 480p. 1987. 18.95 o.p. (ISBN 0-385-23226-8). Doubleday.

Dryden. George E. Saintsbury. LC 67-23875. 208p. 1968. Repr. of 1881 ed. 43.00x o.p. (ISBN 0-8103-3053-9). Gale.

Dryden: A Selection. Ed. by John Conaghan. 1978. 19.50 o.p. (ISBN 0-416-80160-9, NO.2622); pap. 19.50x o.p. (ISBN 0-416-80170-6, NO.2623). Routledge Chapman & Hall.

Drying Cereal Grains. Donald B. Brooker et al. (Illus.). 1974. pap. 25.95 o.p. (ISBN 0-87055-303-8). AVI.

Drying Eighty: Developments in Drying, Vol. 1. Ed. by Arun S. Mujumdar. LC 80-10432. (Illus.). 518p. 1980. text ed. 74.50 o.p. (ISBN 0-89116-200-3). Hemisphere Pub.

Drying: Principles & Practice. R. B. Keey. 1973. 95.00 o.p. (ISBN 0-08-016903-1). Pergamon.

Drylongso: A Self-Portrait of Black American. John L. Gwaltney. LC 79-5558. 1980. 12.95 o.p. (ISBN 0-394-51017-8). Random.

DSM III Case Book: A Learning Companion to the Diagnostic & Statistical Manual of Mental Disorders. Third Edition ed. Robert L. Spitzer et al. LC 81-65970. 392p. (Orig.). 1981. 29.95x o.p. (ISBN 0-89042-050-5, 42-050-5); pap. 19.50x o.p. (ISBN 0-89042-051-3). Am Psychiatric.

DSO As a Management Tool. Credit Research Foundation. 30p. 1978. 40.00 o.p. (ISBN 0-939050-20-X). Credit Res NYS.

DTV Woerterbuch der Medizin, Vol. 3. 5th ed. Herbert Von Schaldach. (Ger.). 1973. pap. 7.95 o.p. (ISBN 3-423-03030-5, M-7344, Pub. by DTV Deutscher Taschenbuch Vlg.). French & Eur.

Dual Ether Universe: Introducing a New Unified Field Theory. Leonid Sokolow. LC 76-56036. 1977. 12.50 o.p. (ISBN 0-682-48721-X, University). Exposition-Phoenix.

Dual Heritage: Immigrants from the Atlas Mountains in an Israeli Village. Moshe Shokeid. 270p. 1985. text ed. 32.95x o.p. (ISBN 0-88738-028-X). Transaction Pubs.

Dual-Mode Transportation. (Special Report). 158p. 1976. 6.40 o.p. (ISBN 0-309-02552-4). Transport Res Bd.

Dual Theory. Ed. by M. Jacob. LC 74-83266. (Physics Reports Reprint Book Ser.: Vol. 1). 399p. 1975. 37.00 o.p. (ISBN 0-444-10743-6, North-Holland). Elsevier.

Duality of Human Existence: Isolation & Communion in Western Man. David Bakan. (Illus.). 1971. pap. 6.95x o.p. (ISBN 0-8070-2969-6, BP395). Beacon Pr.

Dubin's Lives. Bernard Malamud. 432p. 1980. pap. 2.50 o.p. (ISBN 0-380-48413-7, 48413-7). Avon.

Dublin. Peter Somerville-Large. (Illus.). 319p. 1979. 30.95 o.p. (ISBN 0-241-10111-5, Pub. by Hamish Hamilton England). David & Charles.

Dublin Pawn. John Keckhut. 1977. 8.95 o.p. (ISBN 0-393-08761-1). Norton.

Dubliners: A Facsimile of Drafts & Manuscripts. James Joyce. Ed. by Michael Groden. LC 78-16029. (The James Joyce Archive Ser.). 1978. lib. bdg. 89.00 o.p. (ISBN 0-8240-2803-1). Garland Pub.

Dubliners: A Facsimile of Proofs for the 1910 Edition. James Joyce. Ed. by Michael Groden. LC 77-22832. (James Joyce Archive Ser.). 1977. lib. bdg. 89.00 o.p. (ISBN 0-8240-2804-X). Garland Pub.

Dubliners: A Facsimile of Proofs for the 1914 Edition. James Joyce. Ed. by Michael Groden. LC 77-22835. (James Joyce Archive Ser.). 1977. lib. bdg. 89.00 o.p. (ISBN 0-8240-2805-8). Garland Pub.

Dubrovnik Travel Guide. (Travel Guides Ser.). (Illus.). 1982. pap. 4.95 o.p. (ISBN 0-02-969180-X, Berlitz). Macmillan.

Duchess of Kneedeep. Atanielle A. Noel. 170p. 1986. pap. 2.95 o.p. (ISBN 0-380-89917-5). Avon.

Duck Hunter's Handbook. rev. ed. Bob Hinman. LC 85-21714. 288p. 1985. 15.95 o.s.i. (ISBN 0-8329-0404-X, Pub. by Winchester Pr). New Century.

Duck-Huntingest Gentleman. Keith C. Russell. LC 80-17607. (Illus.). 312p. 1980. 17.95 o.p. (ISBN 0-8329-3281-7, Pub. by Winchester Pr). New Century.

Duck Says Quack. John P. Miller. (Bathtime Bks). (Illus.). 10p. (ps). 1984. 2.95 o.s.i. (ISBN 0-394-86813-7, Pub. by BYR). Random.

Duckling Sees. Illus. by Hargrave Hands. (First Look Nature Bks.). (Illus.). 10p. (gr. k). 1985. 2.95 o.p. (ISBN 0-448-10579-9, G&D). Putnam Pub Group.

Ducks at Third Avenue. Judy Hale. 32p. 1987. 6.75 o.p. (ISBN 0-8062-3030-4). Carlton.

Ductility & Toughness Considerations in Elevated Temperature Service: MPC-8. Ed. by G. V. Smith. 416p. 1978. 46.00 o.p. (ISBN 0-317-33484-0, H00132). ASME.

Dudley & the Monster. Judy Taylor. LC 85-30743. (Dudley Dormouse Bks.). (Illus.). 24p. (ps-1). 1986. 4.95 o.p. (ISBN 0-399-21329-5, Putnam). Putnam Pub Group.

Dudley & the Strawberry Shake. Judy Taylor. (Dudley Dormouse Bk.). (Illus.). (ps-1). 1987. 4.95 o.p. (ISBN 0-399-21330-9, Putnam). Putnam Pub Group.

Dudley Goes Flying. Judy Taylor. LC 85-31181. (Dudley Dormouse Bks.). (Illus.). 24p. (ps-1). 1986. 4.95 o.p. (ISBN 0-399-21328-7, Putnam). Putnam Pub Group.

Dudley in a Jam. Judy Taylor. (Dudley Dormouse Bk.). (Illus.). (ps-1). 1987. 4.95 o.p. (ISBN 0-317-52818-1, Putnam). Putnam Pub Group.

Dudley's Dog Days: Joining Faith to Life. Harley G. Rusch. LC 81-43074. 80p. 1981. pap. 4.95 o.p. (ISBN 0-8006-1610-3, 19-1610, Fortress). Augsburg Fortress.

Due Sense of Differences: An Evaluative Approach to Canadian Literature. Wilfred Cude. LC 80-67244. 237p. lib. bdg. 25.25 o.p. (ISBN 0-8191-1206-2); pap. text ed. 13.00 o.p. (ISBN 0-8191-1207-0). U Pr of Amer.

Duel for the Samurai Sword. J. J. Fortune et al. (Illus.). 160p. (Orig.). (YA) (gr. 7-12). 1984. pap. 2.25 o.s.i. (ISBN 0-440-92172-4, LFL). Dell.

Duel for the Sky. Christopher Shores. LC 85-4380. (Illus.). 208p. 1985. pap. 9.95 o.p. (ISBN 0-385-19917-1). Doubleday.

Duel of Desire. Charlotte Lamb. (Nightingale Ser.). 290p. 1987. pap. 11.95x o.p. (ISBN 0-8161-4191-6, Large Print Bks.). G K Hall.

Duel to the Death: Eyewitness Accounts of Great Battles at Sea. Ed. by John Slinkman & Navy Times Editors. LC 69-13779. (Illus.). (gr. 4-7). 1969. 5.50 o.p. (ISBN 0-15-224290-2, HJ). HarBraceJ.

Dueltrack. LC 86-91550. (Car Wars Adventure Gamebook Ser.: No. 3). 192p. (Orig.). 1987. pap. 2.95 o.p. (ISBN 0-88038-443-3). TSR Inc.

Duesenberg. Louis W. Steinwedel & J. Herbert Newport. (Automobile Ser.). (Illus.). 1983. 15.45 o.p. (ISBN 0-393-01589-0). Norton.

Duet. Wendy Susans. 1981. pap. 2.75 o.p. (ISBN 0-8439-0914-5, Pub. by Leisure Bks CT). Dorchester Pub Co.

Dufay to Sweelinck, Netherlands Masters of Music. Edna R. Sollitt. 1970. Repr. of 1933 ed. lib. bdg. 35.00x o.p. (ISBN 0-8371-4028-5, SODS). Greenwood.

Duke Decides. John R. Tunis. LC 39-27882. (Illus.). (gr. 7 up). 1941. 4.95 o.p. (ISBN 0-15-224307-0, HJ). HarBraceJ.

Duke-Elder's Practice of Refraction. 9th ed. J. D. Abrams. (Illus.). 1978. text ed. 40.00 o.p. (ISBN 0-443-01478-7). Churchill.

Duke Ellington in Person: An Intimate Memoir. Mercer Ellington & Stanley Dance. 1978. 10.95 o.p. (ISBN 0-395-25711-5). HM.

Duke's Mistress. F. W. Kenyon. 1978. pap. 1.95 o.p. (ISBN 0-505-51299-8, Pub. by Tower Bks). Dorchester Pub Co.

Duluth: An Illustrated History of the Zenith City. Glenn N. Sandvik. LC 82-50190. (Illus.). 128p. 1983. 24.95 o.p. (ISBN 0-89781-059-7). Windsor Pubns Inc.

Duluth Superior: World's Largest Inland Seaport. 3rd ed. (Illus.). 1977. 3.95 o.s.i. (ISBN 0-932212-06-9). Avery Color.

Dumbarton Oaks Bibliographies Based on "Byzantinische Zeitschrift" Ed. by Jelisaveta S. Allen. LC 72-81538. (Ser. 1, Literature on Byzantine Art: Vol. 1, Parts 1 & 2, by Location). 1095p. 1973. Set. 72.00 o.p. (ISBN 0-7201-0217-0). Mansell.

Dumbarton Oaks Bibliographies Based on "Byzantinische Zeitschrift" Literature on Byzantine Art 1892-1967, Vol. 2, by Categories. Ed. by Jelisaveta S. Allen. 614p. 1976. 64.00 o.p. (ISBN 0-7201-0218-9). Mansell.

Dumbarton Oaks Papers, Nos. 1-19. Harvard University, Dumbarton Oaks Research Library and Collection, Washington, D.C. Staff. 1941-1966. 665.00 o.p. (ISBN 0-384-21640-4). Johnson Repr.

Duncan Phillips: Centennial Exhibition. Intro. by Laughlin Phillips. LC 86-12368. 50p. 1986. pap. 6.00 o.p. (ISBN 0-943044-08-1). Phillips Coll.

Dunciad see Popeiana.

Dunciad & Other Matters see Popeiana.

Dunciad, One see Popeiana.

Dunciad, Three see Popeiana.

Dunciad, Two see Popeiana.

Dune Coloring & Activity Book. (Dune Ser.). (Illus.). 48p. (gr. 2-5). 1984. pap. 1.95 o.p. (ISBN 0-448-23354-1, G&D). Putnam Pub Group.

Dune Cut-out Activity Book. (Illus.). 32p. (Orig.). (gr. 2-5). 1984. pap. 3.95 o.p. (ISBN 0-448-23352-5, G&D). Putnam Pub Group.

Dune Shadow. Nancy Stone. 176p. 1980. 7.95 o.p. (ISBN 0-395-29744-3). HM.

Dune Witch. Evelyn Minshull. LC 76-164510. (gr. 4-6). 1972. 4.95 o.s.i. (ISBN 0-664-32505-X, Westminster). Westminster John Knox.

Dungeon Master: The Disappearance of James Dallas Egbert, III. William Dear. 1984. 16.45 o.p. (ISBN 0-395-35536-2). HM.

Dungeons & Dragons: Basic Rule Book. Gary Gygax et al. (Adult Fantasy Role-Playing Game Ser.). (Also avail. with bk., 1 game, 1 module, 4 minigames, 1 calendar & 1 advanced module). 1981. 6.00 o.p. (ISBN 0-394-52199-4); indiv. components o.p. 12.00 o.p. (ISBN 0-394-51834-9). Random.

Dunnell Minnesota Digest. rev., 2nd ser. ed. Butterworth Editorial Staff. (42 vols in course of publication). 1350.00 o.p. (ISBN 0-86678-002-5). Butterworth MN.

Dunnybrook. Gladys H. Carroll. (Illus.). 1978. 11.95 o.p. (ISBN 0-393-08822-7). Norton.

Duodenitis. R. Cheli & H. Aste. LC 75-16096. (Illus.). 106p. 1976. 15.00 o.p. (ISBN 0-88416-125-0). Year Bk Med.

Dupe. Liza Cody. 252p. 1981. 10.95 o.s.i. (ISBN 0-684-17153-8, ScribT). Scribner.

Duplex Stainless Steels. Ed. by R. A. Lula. 1983. 91.00 o.p. (ISBN 0-87170-166-9). ASM.

Durability of Concrete Bridge Decks. (National Cooperative Highway Research Program Synthesis of Highway Practice). 60p. 1979. 6.00 o.p. (ISBN 0-309-02906-6). Transport Res Bd.

Duran Duran. Duran Duran. Ed. by Charmain Lammers. (Easy Guitar Ser.). 64p. (gr. 7 up). 1984. pap. 6.95, perfect bdg. o.p. (ISBN 0-88188-466-9, HLOO699707). H Leonard Pub Corp.

Duran Duran: Arena. Duran Duran. (Piano-Vocal-Guitar Ser.). (Illus.). 56p. 1985. pap. 8.95 o.p. (ISBN 0-88188-367-0). H Leonard Pub Corp.

Duran Duran "Arena" (Illus.). 48p. (Orig.). (gr. 3 up). 1986. pap. 9.95 o.p. (ISBN 0-9510118-1-2, HL 00183232, Pub. by Tritec Pubns). H Leonard Pub Corp.

Duran Duran: The Book of Words. Ed. by De Graaf Garrett. 96p. (gr. 10 up). 1984. Perfect bound 12.95 o.p. (ISBN 0-88188-322-0). H Leonard Pub Corp.

Duration of Unemployment Benefits. Merrill G. Murray. 80p. 1974. pap. 3.95 o.p. (ISBN 0-911558-25-X). W E Upjohn.

Durations: The Encyclopedia of How Long Things Take. Stuart Sandow. (YA) (gr. 7 up). 1978. pap. 2.25 o.p. (ISBN 0-380-39859-1, 39859). Avon.

Durer. Michael Levey. (Illus.). 1964. 5.95 o.p. (ISBN 0-393-04235-9). Norton.

Durer - Kunst und Geometrie. Eberhard Schroder. (Wissenschaft & Kultur Ser.: Bd. 37). 96p. (Ger.). 1980. 15.95x o.p. (ISBN 0-8176-1182-7). Birkhauser.

Durer's Cities: Nuremberg & Venice. Clifton Olds et al. (Illus.). 63p. 1971. pap. 3.50 o.p. (ISBN 0-912303-04-2). Michigan Mus.

During My Conversion. large print ed. Pearl Brians. 44p. 1984. pap. 8.00 o.p. (ISBN 0-914009-11-7). VHI Library.

During Sleep. Robert Crookall. LC 33-78746. 1974. 5.95 o.p. (ISBN 0-8216-0170-9, Pub. by Univ Bks). Carol Pub Group.

Durkee Spice & Herb Cookbook. Durkee Staff. (Illus.). 64p. (Orig.). 1983. pap. 3.95 o.p. (ISBN 0-8249-3020-7). Ideals.

Durkheim: Essays on Morals & Education. Ed. by W. S. Pickering. Tr. by H. L. Sutcliffe from Fr. 1979. 29.95x o.p. (ISBN 0-7100-0321-8). Routledge Chapman & Hall.

Durkheim's "Suicide" A Classic Analyzed. Whitney Pope. LC 75-27890. (Midway Reprint Ser.). 248p. 1982. pap. text ed. 10.00x o.s.i. (ISBN 0-226-67540-8). U of Chicago Pr.

Durrell in Russia. Gerald Durrell & Lee Durrell. 1986. 19.45 o.p. (ISBN 0-671-61298-0). S&S.

Durrenmatt: A Study in Plays, Prose, Theory. Timo Tiusanen. LC 76-45915. (Illus.). 1977. 47.00x o.p. (ISBN 0-691-06332-X). Princeton U Pr.

Dust Bowl: Men, Dirt, & Depression. Paul Bonnifield. LC 78-55706. (Illus.). 243p. 1980. Repr. of 1979 ed. 14.95 o.p. (ISBN 0-8263-0485-0). U of NM Pr.

Dust Bunnies. Frank Douglas. (Illus.). 32p. (gr. k-5). 1986. 6.95 o.p. (ISBN 0-86679-026-8, Pub. by Oak Tree). Oak Tree Pubns.

Dust Bunnies & the Rescue of Buttons the Bear. Frank Douglas. (Illus.). 32p. (ps-2). 1986. 6.95 o.p. (ISBN 0-86679-037-3). Oak Tree Pubns.

Dust Control & Air Cleaning. R. G. Dorman. LC 73-6969. 628p. 1974. text ed. 155.00 o.p. (ISBN 0-08-016750-0). Pergamon.

Dust for the Dancer. Dean & Carrell. (Illus.). 228p. 1957. Philos Lib.

Dust in Space & Comets: Proceedings of the Topical Meeting of the COSPAR Interdisciplinary Scientific Commission B (Meetings B1 & B2) of the COSPAR 25th Plenary Meeting, Graz, Austria, 25 June-7 July 1984. Ed. by G. E. Morfill. (Illus.). 324p. 1985. pap. 54.00 o.p. (ISBN 0-08-032745-1, Pub. by PPL). Pergamon.

Dusti Bonge: The Life of an Artist. Dusti Bonge. Ed. by Nancy Longnecker. LC 82-4804. (Mississippi Art Ser.). (Illus.). 128p. (Orig.). 1982. pap. 1.00 o.p. (ISBN 0-87805-160-0). U Pr of Miss.

Dustman to Ashes. Rosemonde Peltz. LC 86-29220. (Crime Club Ser.). 192p. 1987. 12.95 o.p. (ISBN 0-385-23552-6). Doubleday.

Dusty Answer. Rosamond Lehmann. LC 74-17031. 375p. 1975. pap. 3.95 o.p. (ISBN 0-15-626290-8, Harv). HarBraceJ.

Dutch Americans: A Guide to Information Sources. Ed. by Linda P. Doezema. LC 79-13030. (Ethnic Studies Information Guide Ser.: Vol. 3). 344p. 1979. 68.00x o.p. (ISBN 0-8103-1407-X). Gale.

Dutch & Flemish Etchings, Engravings & Woodcuts: 1450 to 1700, Vols. 1-29. Ed. by F. W. Hollstein. (Illus.). write for info. o.p. E J Brill USA.

Dutch Blue Error. William G. Tapply. 240p. 1985. 12.95 o.s.i. (ISBN 0-684-18213-0, ScribT). Scribner.

Dutch Calvinism in Modern America: A History of a Conservative Subculture. James D. Bratt. (Illus.). 368p. (Orig.). 1984. pap. 14.95 o.p. (ISBN 0-8028-0009-2). Eerdmans.

Dutch Contributions to the Sixth International Congress of Slavicists, Prague, 1968. Ed. by A. G. Van Holk. (Slavistic Printings & Reprintings Ser.). 1968. 35.00x o.p. (ISBN 0-686-21261-4). Mouton.

Dutch Costumes. A. Groen. (Illus.). pap. 12.50 o.p. (ISBN 90-612-0094-6). E J Brill USA.

Dutch Costumes. E. M. Valeton. (Illus.). 15.00 o.s.i. (ISBN 0-685-47296-5). E J Brill USA.

Dutch Design Nineteen Fourty-Five to Nineteen Eighty-Seven. Ed. by Gert Staal & Hester Wolters. (Illus.). 296p. Date not set. pap. 50.00 o.p. (Pub. by Mus Boymans-van Beuningen Holland). Moyer Bell Limited.

Dutch: Een Goed Begin, a Contemporary Dutch Reader, 2 vols. 2nd ed. R. B. Bird & W. Z. Shetter. 1978. Set. pap. 12.50 o.p. (ISBN 9-0247-2073-7). Vol. 1 (ISBN 9-0247-2071-0). Vol. 2. E J Brill USA.

Dutch-English Dictionary. Berlitz Editors. 1979. pap. 5.95 o.p. (ISBN 0-02-964540-9, Berlitz). Macmillan.

Dutch-English, English-Dutch. pap. 10.00 o.p. E J Brill USA.

Dutch Influence on English Vocabulary see Persian Words in English.

Dutch Masters. Horace Shipp. (Illus.). 132p. 1953. (ISBN 0-8022-1561-0). Philos Lib.

Dutch Pictures from the Royal Collection. Ed. by Oliver Millar. LC 79-172996. (Illus.). 104p. 14.95x o.s.i. (ISBN 0-271-01109-2). Pa St U Pr.

Dutch Shea, Jr. John G. Dunne. 1982. 16.50 o.p. (ISBN 0-671-41292-2). S&S.

Dutch Uncle. Marilyn Durham. LC 73-6601. 1973. 7.50 o.p. (ISBN 0-15-126930-0, HC). HarBraceJ.

Duties of the Ruling Elder. rev. ed. Paul S. Wright. LC 72-181899. 86p. 1972. pap. 4.50 o.s.i. (ISBN 0-664-24952-3, Westminster). Westminster John Knox.

Dutton's Navigation & Piloting. 13th ed. Albert S. Maloney. LC 77-87943. (Illus.). 960p. 1978. 26.95 o.p. (ISBN 0-87021-164-1). Naval Inst Pr.

Dutton's Point. Stephen J. Pyne. LC 81-82546. (Illus.). 64p. (Orig.). 1983. pap. 10.00 o.p. (ISBN 0-938216-19-8). GCNHA.

Duty & Hypocrisy in Hegel's Phenomonology of Mind. Jonathan Robinson. 1977. 20.00x o.p. (ISBN 0-8020-5380-7). U of Toronto Pr.

Dvorak. John Clapham. (Illus.). 1979. 19.95x o.p. (ISBN 0-393-01204-2). Norton.

Dvorak. Alec Robertson. (Master Musicians Ser.: No. M157). (Illus.). 1977. pap. 7.95 o.p. (ISBN 0-8226-0710-7). Littlefield.

Dwarf Cichlids. Date not set. 9.95 o.p. (ISBN 0-86622-895-0, KW-155). TFH Pubns.

Dwarf Rapes Nun, Flees in UFO. Arnold Sawislak. 1987. pap. 3.50 o.p. (ISBN 0-440-12191-4). Dell.

Dwarf Shrubs for the Midwest. Rebecca M. Keith & Floyd A. Giles. LC 80-12867. (Illus.). 179p. 1980. 20.00 o.p. (ISBN 0-252-00817-0). U of Ill Pr.

Dwarks Meet Skunk Momma. (Skylark Choose Your Own Adventure Ser.). (Orig.). 1984. pap. text ed. 1.95 o.s.i. (ISBN 0-553-15216-5). Bantam.

Dwight Gooden & Dale Murphy. Jordon Deutsh. (Avon Superstar Ser.). 64p. 1986. pap. 2.50 o.p. (ISBN 0-380-75115-1, Camelot). Avon.

Dyadic Communication. 2nd ed. Date not set. (ISBN 0-394-34995-4). Random.

Dybbuk: A Play. S. Ansky. 1972. pap. 3.95 o.p. (ISBN 0-87140-262-9). Liveright.

Dyed for Death. Warrick W. Rider. (Orig.). 1980. pap. 1.95 o.p. (ISBN 0-505-51497-4, Pub. by Tower Bks). Dorchester Pub Co.

Dying. Wass. 426p. 1979. 37.00 o.p. (ISBN 0-89116-517-7); pap. 14.95 o.p. (ISBN 0-89116-518-5). Hemisphere Pub.

Dying at Home with Hospice. Deborah Chase. 1985. cloth 15.95 o.p. (ISBN 0-8016-0959-3). Mosby.

Dying Child. Jo-Eileen Gyulay. 1977. text ed. 22.95 o.p. (ISBN 0-07-025360-9). McGraw.

Dying: Facing the Facts. Hennelore Wass. (Illus.). 1979. text ed. 38.95 o.p. (ISBN 0-07-068438-3); pap. text ed. (ISBN 0-07-068437-5). McGraw.

Dying for a Drink: What You Should Know about Alcoholism. Anderson Spickard & Barbara R. Thompson. 192p. 1985. 11.95 o.p. (ISBN 0-8499-0467-6, 0467-6). Word Bks.

Dying for Enlightenment: Living Bhagwan Shree Rajneesh. Bernard Gunther. LC 78-15841. (Illus., Orig.). 1979. pap. 6.95i o.p. (ISBN 0-06-063527-4, RD 226). HarpR.

Dying Patient: A Supportive Approach. Rita E. Caughill. LC 75-30280. 1976. pap. text ed. 11.00 o.p. (ISBN 0-316-13216-0). Little.

Dying to Smoke. Robert Osborn & Fred W. Benton. (Illus.). 1972. 6.95 o.p. (ISBN 0-395-08058-4). HM.

Dylan. Rolling Stone Press Staff & Jonathan Cott. LC 84-4049. (Illus.). 256p. 1984. 35.00 o.p. (ISBN 0-385-19161-8). Doubleday.

Dylan. Rolling Stone Press Staff & Jonathan Cott. LC 84-4049. (Illus.). 256p. 1985. pap. 15.95 o.p. (ISBN 0-385-19162-6, Dolp). Doubleday.

Dylan Thomas. Jacob Korg. (English Authors Ser.). 1965. lib. bdg. 13.50 o.p. (ISBN 0-8057-1548-7, Twayne). G K Hall.

Dynagraph Analysis of Sucker Rod Pumping. J. C. Slonneger. LC 60-53496. 216p. 1961. 38.00x o.p. (ISBN 0-87201-216-6). Gulf Pub.

Dynamic Approach to Counseling. Michael J. Plezbert. 94p. 1984. 7.00 o.p. (ISBN 0-682-40158-7). Exposition-Phoenix.

Dynamic Art of Breaking. Pu Gill Gwon. LC 77-89191. (Ser. 128). 1977. pap. 8.95x o.p. (ISBN 0-89750-023-7, Dist. by Wehman). Ohara Pubns.

Dynamic Aspects of Host Parasite Relationships, Vol.1. Ed. by Avivah Zuckerman & David W. Weiss. 1973. 47.50 o.p. (ISBN 0-12-782001-9). Acad Pr.

Dynamic Aspects of Host-Parasite Relationships, Vol. 2. Ed. by A. Zuckerman. LC 70-189940. 225p. 1976. 57.95x o.p. (ISBN 0-470-98430-9). Halsted Pr.

Dynamic Astronomy. 4th ed. Robert T. Dixon. (Illus.). 544p. 1984. pap. text ed. (ISBN 0-13-221333-8). P-H.

Dynamic Body Tissues. William S. Bullough. 1983. 41.95 o.p. (ISBN 0-442-21315-8). Van Nos Reinhold.

Dynamic Business Strategy: The Art of Planning for Success. Theodore A. Smith. (Illus.). 1977. text ed. 24.95 o.p. (ISBN 0-07-059090-7). McGraw.

Dynamic Chemistry. Ed. by F. Boschke. LC 51-5497. (Topics in Current Chemistry: Vol. 45). (Illus.). 250p. 1974. 38.00 o.p. (ISBN 0-387-06471-0). Springer-Verlag.

Dynamic Closing Arguments. Mark A. Dombroff. LC 85-9335. 1985. text ed. 69.50 o.p. (ISBN 0-13-221391-5). P-H.

Dynamic Compression Plate (DCP) M. Allgoewer. LC 73-13494. (Illus.). 1978. pap. 19.00 o.p. (ISBN 0-387-06466-4). Springer-Verlag.

Dynamic Discipleship. Kenneth C. Kinghorn. 160p. 1975. pap. 4.95 o.p. (ISBN 0-8010-5357-9). Baker Bk.

Dynamic Earth. Scientific American Editors. (Scientific American Reader Series: September '83 Issue). 128p. 1983. pap. text ed. 13.95 o.p. (ISBN 0-7167-1611-9). W H Freeman.

Dynamic Electrocardiography. Ed. by R. W. Campbell & A. Murray. (Illus.). 135p. 1985. text ed. 55.50 o.p. (ISBN 0-443-02407-3). Churchill.

Dynamic Judaism. Date not set. (ISBN 0-8052-3997-9). Random.

Dynamic Laws of Prosperity: Forces That Bring Riches to You. Catherine Ponder. 1962. pap. 9.95 o.p. (ISBN 0-13-221341-9, Reward). P-H.

Dynamic Mass Spectrometry, Vol. 1. Ed. by D. Price & J. E. Williams. 254p. 1970. 128.00 o.p. (ISBN 0-471-25961-6, Pub. by Wiley Heyden). Wiley.

Dynamic Mass Spectrometry, Vol. 6. Ed. by D. Price & J. F. Todd. 384p. 1982. 153.00 o.p. (ISBN 0-471-26191-2). Wiley.

Dynamic Modelling & Control of National Economies, 1983: Proceedings of the IFAC-IFORS Symposium, 4th, Washington, DC, June 1983. T. Basar. Ed. by F. L. Pau. 550p. 1984. 160.00 o.p. (ISBN 0-08-030557-1). Pergamon.

Dynamic NMR Spectroscopy. rev. ed. H. W. Spiess & A. Steigel. (NMR - Basic Principles & Progress: Vol. 15). (Illus.). 1978. 61.30 o.p. (ISBN 0-387-08784-2). Springer-Verlag.

Dynamic Optimization & Economic Applications. Ronald E. Miller. (Illus.). 1979. text ed. 40.95 o.p. (ISBN 0-07-042180-3). McGraw.

Dynamic Plasticity of Metals. CISM (International Center for Mechanical Sciences), Dept. for Mechanics of Deformable Bodies, 1970. Ed. by J. D. Campbell. (CISM Pubns. Ser.: No. 46). (Illus.). 92p. 1973. pap. 11.50 o.p. (ISBN 0-387-81149-4). Springer-Verlag.

Dynamic Positioning of Vessels at Sea: Proceedings of the CISM, Department of Experimental Methods in Mechanics, 1971. CISM (International Center for Mechanical Sciences), Department of Experimental Methods in Mechanics Staff. Ed. by J. Pinkster. (CISM International Centre for Mechanical Sciences Ser.: No. 105). (Illus.). 36p. 1974. pap. 6.70 o.p. (ISBN 0-387-81221-0). Springer-Verlag.

Dynamic Praying for Exciting Results. Russ Johnston & Maureen Rank. 1982. pap. 3.95 o.p. (ISBN 0-8423-0611-0). Tyndale.

Dynamic Programming & Its Application. Ed. by Martin L. Puterman. LC 78-21621. 1979. 48.50 o.p. (ISBN 0-12-568150-X). Acad Pr.

Dynamic Programming & Its Applications to Optimal Control. R. Boudarel et al. (Mathematics in Science & Engineering Ser.: Vol. 81). 1971. 77.00 o.p. (ISBN 0-12-118950-3). Acad Pr.

Dynamic Programming-Code. R. Bellman. (Rand Corporation Research Studies). 1957. 47.50x o.p. (ISBN 0-691-07951-X). Princeton U Pr.

Dynamic Programming in Chemical Engineering & Process Control. Sanford M. Roberts. (Mathematics in Science & Engineering Ser.: Vol. 12). 1964. 83.00 o.p. (ISBN 0-12-589450-3). Acad Pr.

Dynamic Programming of Human Systems: A Social & Historical Analysis. John Wilkinson et al. 53p. 1974. pap. text ed. 2.95x o.p. (ISBN 0-8422-8300-5). Irvington.

Dynamic Properties of Glia Cells: An Interdisciplinary Approach to Their Study in the Central & Peripheral Nervous System. Ed. by E. Schoffeniels et al. LC 78-40218. 1978. 105.00 o.p. (ISBN 0-08-021555-6). Pergamon.

Dynamic Psychiatry in Theory & Practice. Edwin R. Wallace. LC 82-14880. 407p. 1983. text ed. 30.00 o.p. (ISBN 0-8121-0856-6). Lea & Febiger.

Dynamic Psychology of Early Buddhism. Rune Johansson. (Scandinavian Institute of Asian Studies Monographs: No. 37). (Illus.). 1979. pap. text ed. 15.00x o.p. (ISBN 0-7007-0114-1). Humanities.

Dynamic Religious Movements: Case Studies of Rapidly Growing Religious Movement Around the World. Ed. by David J. Hesselgrave. 1978. 9.95 o.p. (ISBN 0-8010-4130-9). Baker Bk.

Dynamic Response of Structures. Ed. by G. Herrmann & N. Perrone. 1973. 95.00 o.p. (ISBN 0-08-016850-7). Pergamon.

Dynamic Semiconductor RAM Structures. A. Cardon & L. Fransen. (European Patent Office Ser.: Vol. 1). (Illus.). 488p. 1984. 125.00 o.p. (ISBN 0-08-030578-4). Pergamon.

Dynamic Simulation Model of the World Jute Economy. Jock Anderson. (Working Paper: No. 391). 39p. 1980. pap. 3.50 o.p. (ISBN 0-686-39658-8, WP-0391). World Bank.

Dynamic Stability of Bodies Containing Fluid. N. N. Moiseyev & V. V. Rumyantsev. LC 68-22688. (Applied Physics & Engineering Ser.: Vol. 6). (Illus.). 1969. 59.00 o.p. (ISBN 0-387-04052-8). Springer-Verlag.

Dynamic Stability: The Soviet Economy Today. Ellen Perlo & Victor Perlo. LC 80-18105. (Illus.). 344p. (Orig.). 1982. pap. 4.75 o.p. (ISBN 0-7178-0577-8). Intl Pubs Co.

Dynamic Stereochemistry. Ed. by F. Boschke. LC 51-5497. (Topics in Current Chemistry: Vol. 15, No. 3). (Illus.). 1970. pap. 43.70 o.p. (ISBN 0-387-05101-5). Springer-Verlag.

Dynamic Structure of Cell Membranes: Proceedings. Gesellschaft Fuer Biologische Chemie, 22nd Colloquium, Mossbach Baden, 1971. Ed. by D. F. Wallach & H. Fischer. (Illus.). 240p. 1972. 26.00 o.p. (ISBN 0-387-05669-6). Springer-Verlag.

Dynamic Topology. G. Whyburn & E. Duda. (Undergraduate Texts in Mathematics). (Illus.). 1979. 16.00 o.p. (ISBN 0-387-90358-5). Springer-Verlag.

Dynamic Transcendence: The Correlation of Confessional Heritage & Contemporory Experience in a Biblical Model of Divine Activity. Paul D. Hanson. LC 78-54552. 112p. 1978. pap. 4.95 o.p. (ISBN 0-8006-1338-4, 1-1338, Fortress). Augsburg Fortress.

Dynamic Universe: An Introduction to Astronomy. 2nd ed. Theodore P. Snow, Jr. (Illus.). 598p. 1985. text ed. 41.00 o.p. (ISBN 0-314-88512-9). West Pub.

Dynamical Behaviour of Structures. 2nd ed. Ed. by Geoffrey B. Warburton. 1976. 90.00 o.p. (ISBN 0-08-020364-7); pap. 90.00 o.p. (ISBN 0-08-020363-9). Pergamon.

Dynamical Systems. Ed. by A. R. Bednarek & L. Cesari. 1977. 65.50 o.p. (ISBN 0-12-083750-1). Acad Pr.

Dynamical Systems. Ed. by M. M. Peixoto. 1973. 112.00 o.p. (ISBN 0-12-550350-4). Acad Pr.

Dynamical Systems: An International Symposium, Vol. I. Lamberto Cesari et al. 1976. 91.00 o.p. (ISBN 0-12-164901-6). Acad Pr.

Dynamical Systems: An International Symposium, Vol. 2. Ed. by Lamberto Cesari et al. 1976. 89.50 o.p. (ISBN 0-12-164902-4). Acad Pr.

Dynamical Systems & Chaos: Proceedings, Sitges, Barcelona, Spain, 1982. Ed. by L. Garrido. (Lecture Notes in Physics: Vol. 179). 298p. 1983. pap. 21.00 o.p. (ISBN 0-387-12276-1). Springer-Verlag.

Dynamical Systems & Microphysics. Ed. by A. Blaquiere et al. (CISM - International Centre for Mechanical Sciences Courses & Lectures: Vol. 261). (Illus.). ix, 412p. 1980. pap. 48.00 o.p. (ISBN 0-387-81533-3). Springer-Verlag.

Dynamical Systems & Microphysics. Ed. by Austin Blaquriere & George Leitmann. 1984. 35.00 o.p. (ISBN 0-12-104365-7). Acad Pr.

Dynamical Systems in the Plane. Otomar Hajek. 1968. 45.00 o.p. (ISBN 0-12-317240-3). Acad Pr.

Dynamical Systems: Stability Theory & Applications. N. P. Bhatia & G. P. Szegoe. (Lecture Notes in Mathematics: Vol. 35). (Illus., Orig.). 1967. pap. 21.90 o.p. (ISBN 0-387-03906-6). Springer-Verlag.

Dynamical Systems, Theory & Applications. J. Moser. LC 75-14488. (Lecture Notes in Physics Ser.). vi, 624p. 1975. pap. 23.90 o.p. (ISBN 0-387-07171-7). Springer-Verlag.

Dynamics & Control of Continuous Distillation Units. O. Rademaker et al. LC 74-83315. 726p. 1975. 179.00 o.p. (ISBN 0-444-41234-4). Elsevier.

Dynamics & Modeling of Reactive Systems. Ed. by Warren E. Stewart et al. LC 80-19714. (Mathematics Research Center Ser.). 1980. 35.50 o.p. (ISBN 0-12-669550-4). Acad Pr.

Dynamics of a Labor Market: A Study of the Impact of Employment Changes on Labor Mobility, Job Satisfactions, & Company & Union Policies. Charles A. Myers & George P. Schultz. LC 75-36100. 219p. 1976. Repr. of 1951 ed. lib. bdg. 35.00x o.p. (ISBN 0-8371-8620-X, MYLM). Greenwood.

Dynamics of Achievement. Hans D. Siebel. pap. text ed. 3.95x o.p. (ISBN 0-8290-0329-0). Irvington.

Dynamics of Apocalypse: A Systems Simulation of the Classic Maya Collapse. John W. Lowe. LC 84-19503. (Illus.). 232p. 1985. 22.50x o.p. (ISBN 0-8263-0765-5). U of NM Pr.

Dynamics of Brain Edema: Proceedings of Dynamic Aspects of Cebral Edema International Workshops, 3rd, Montreal, June 25-29, 1976. Dynamic Aspects of Cerebral Edema International Workshop Staff. Ed. by H. M. Pappius et al. (Illus.). 1977. pap. 28.00 o.p. (ISBN 0-387-08009-0). Springer-Verlag.

Dynamics of Church Growth. Ron Jenson & Jim Stevens. 280p. 1981. pap. 8.95 o.p. (ISBN 0-8010-5161-4). Baker Bk.

Dynamics of Comprehension: How to Learn from a College Textbook. Marion H. Klein. 1970. pap. 3.95 o.p. (ISBN 0-89197-130-0). Irvington.

Dynamics of Creation. Anthony Storr. LC 85-47639. 264p. 1985. pap. 8.95 o.p. (ISBN 0-689-70700-2, 334, Atheneum). Macmillan.

Dynamics of dBASE III. Aiala Reizer et al. 300p. 1985. 19.95 o.p. (ISBN 0-87094-654-4). Dow Jones-Irwin.

Dynamics of Degeneration & Growth in Neurons. Ed. by K. Fuxe et al. 1974. 185.00 o.p. (ISBN 0-08-017917-7). Pergamon.

Dynamics of Detente. Arthur M. Cox. 1976. 8.95 o.p. (ISBN 0-393-05592-2). Norton.

Dynamics of Development: Experiments & Inferences. Paul A. Weiss. LC 68-23476. (Illus.). 1968. 54.50 o.p. (ISBN 0-12-742850-X). Acad Pr.

Dynamics of Faith & Confession. Charles Capps. 288p. (Orig.). 1983. pap. 6.95 o.s.i. (ISBN 0-914307-05-3, Dist. by Harrison Hse). R Tilton Ministries.

Dynamics of Fluid-Structure Systems in the Energy Industry. Ed. by M. K. Au-Yang et al. (PVP-39). (Orig.). 1979. 30.00 o.p. (ISBN 0-685-96305-5, H00153). ASME.

Dynamics of Fluids & Plasmas: Proceedings. Dynamics of Fluids & Plasmas Symposium Staff. Ed. by S. I. Pai. 1967. 92.50 o.p. (ISBN 0-12-544250-5). Acad Pr.

Dynamics of Framework. Nelson T. Dinerstein. 200p. 1985. pap. 19.95 o.p. (ISBN 0-87094-671-4). Dow Jones-Irwin.

Dynamics of Gas-Surface Scattering. Frank O Goodman & Harold Y. Wachman. 1976. 90.50 o.p. (ISBN 0-12-290450-8). Acad Pr.

Dynamics of Geomagnetically Trapped Radiation. J. G. Roederer. LC 73-109668. (Physics & Chemistry in Space: Vol. 2). (Illus.). 1970. 26.00 o.p. (ISBN 0-387-04987-8). Springer-Verlag.

Dynamics of Group Psychotherapy. S. R. Slavson & Mortimer Schiffer. LC 78-68010. 830p. 1979. 40.00x o.p. (ISBN 0-87668-372-3). Aronson.

Dynamics of Host Defence. John A. Bailey & Brian J. Deverall. LC 83-70713. 233p. 1983. 39.50 o.p. (ISBN 0-12-073460-5). Acad Pr.

Dynamics of Housing Rehabilitation: Macro & Micro Analyses. David Listokin. 240p. 1973. (ISBN 0-87855-083-6). Transaction Pubs.

Dynamics of International Law. Georg Schwarzenberger. xii, 139p. 1976. text ed. 15.00x o.p. (ISBN 0-903486-19-9); pap. 8.00 o.p. (ISBN 0-903486-18-0). Rothman.

Dynamics of Interviewing: Theory, Technique, & Cases. Robert L. Kahn & Charles F. Cannell. LC 82-9892. 378p. 1983. Repr. of 1957 ed. lib. bdg. 29.50 o.p. (ISBN 0-89874-493-8). Krieger.

Dynamics of Large Mammal Populations. Charles W. Fowler & Tim D. Smith. LC 81-115. 477p. 1981. 49.95x o.p. (ISBN 0-471-05160-8, Oub. by Wiley-Interscience). Wiley.

Dynamics of Law. James L. Houghteling, Jr. (Orig.). 1968. pap. text ed. 9.95 o.p. (ISBN 0-15-518512-8, HC). HarBraceJ.

Dynamics of Literary Response. Norman N. Holland. 400p. 1975. pap. 6.95 o.p. (ISBN 0-393-00790-1, N790, Norton Lib). Norton.

Dynamics of Offshore Structures. Ed. by James F. Wilson. LC 83-19862. (Ocean Engineering: A Wiley Ser.: 1-194). 546p. 1984. 59.95x o.p. (ISBN 0-471-87568-6, Pub. by Wiley-Interscience). Wiley.

Dynamics of Oncology Nursing. Ed. by Pamela K. Burkhalter & Diana Donley. (Illus.). 1978. text ed. 30.00 o.p. (ISBN 0-07-009052-1). McGraw.

Dynamics of Personal Financial Planning. Russ Von Hoelscher & George Sterne. 414p. 1984. 14.95 o.p. (ISBN 0-940398-10-9). Profit Ideas.

Dynamics of Petroleum Reservoirs Under Gas Injection. Rafael Sandrea & Ralph Nielsen. LC 74-4829. 180p. 1974. 25.00x o.s.i. (ISBN 0-87201-219-0). Gulf Pub.

Dynamics of Planned Change: A Comparative Study of Principles & Techniques. Ronald Lippitt et al. 1958. text ed. 18.95 o.p. (ISBN 0-15-518514-4, HC). HarBraceJ.

Dynamics of Planning. E. P. Ward. 1970. 33.00 o.p. (ISBN 0-08-015512-X); pap. 17.00 o.p. (ISBN 0-08-015513-8). Pergamon.

Dynamics of Police Administration. 2nd ed. John Truitt. 120p. 1978. pap. write for info. o.p. (ISBN 0-87084-853-4). Anderson Pub C.

Dynamics of Prostar. Jane Davis. 300p. 1985. pap. 19.95 o.p. (ISBN 0-87094-669-2). Dow Jones-Irwin.

Dynamics of Reflex. Trish McClelland. 250p. 1987. pap. 21.95 o.p. (ISBN 0-87094-948-9). Dow Jones-Irwin.

Dynamics of Religion: Meaning & Change in Religious Traditions. Peter Slater. LC 78-4426. 1978. pap. 6.95x o.p. (ISBN 0-685-53934-2, RD 280). HarpR.

Dynamics of Rotors: Selected Papers. Indian Society of Theoretical & Applied Mechanics, 20th Congress, India, 1975. Ed. by J. S. Rao. 1977. pap. 29.00 o.p. (ISBN 0-08-022124-6). Pergamon.

Dynamics of Rotors: Stability & System Identification. Ed. by O Mahrenholtz. (CISM International Centre for Mechanical Sciences: Vol. 273). (Illus.). vi, 511p. 1985. pap. 37.40 o.p. (ISBN 0-387-81846-4). Springer-Verlag.

Dynamics of Satellites: Proceedings, May 20-24, 1969. COSPAR-IAU-IAG-IUGG-IUTAM Staff. Ed. by B. Morando. (Illus.). vii, 312p. (Eng. & Fr.). 1970. 82.10 o.p. (ISBN 0-387-04792-1). Springer-Verlag.

Dynamics of Stellar Systems. K. F. Ogorodnikov. 1965. 71.00 o.p. (ISBN 0-08-010163-1); pap. 37.00 o.p. (ISBN 0-08-013772-5). Pergamon.

Dynamics of Symphony. Kenniston W. Lord, Jr. & Delbert S. Jones. 1986. 19.95 o.p. (ISBN 0-87094-644-7). Dow Jones-Irwin.

Dynamics of Symphony Macros. Steven Armbrust & Janice L. Deringer. 250p. pap. cancelled o.s.i. (ISBN 0-87094-958-6). Dow Jones-Irwin.

Dynamics of Teaching Secondary Mathematics. Thomas J. Cooney et al. 1975. text ed. 23.50 o.p. (ISBN 0-395-18617-X). HM.

Dynamics of the Female Labour Force: Patterns of Demographic & Socio-Economic Change in Argentina. (Women in a World Perspective Ser.). 98p. 1983. pap. text ed. 6.50 o.p. (ISBN 92-3-101996-1, U1326, UNESCO). UNIPUB.

Dynamics of Utilization Management. Melody Drew Connor et al. LC 84-21571. (Illus.). 304p. (Orig.). 1984. pap. 49.95 o.p. (ISBN 0-939450-49-6, 001113). AHPI.

Dynamics of Vehicles on Roads Tracks: Proceedings of the Ninth IAVSD Symposium Held at the Linkoping University, Linoping, Sweden, June 24-29, 1985. Ed. by O. Nordstrom. 663p. (Orig.). 1986. pap. 45.00 o.p. (ISBN 9-02650-710-0). CJ Hogrefe Pubs.

Dynamics of VisiCalc. Barry D. Bayer & Joseph J. Sobel. LC 82-73621. 225p. 1983. 19.95 o.p. (ISBN 0-87094-391-X). Dow Jones-Irwin.

Dynamics of War & Revolution. Lawrence Dennis. 296p. 1980. pap. 10.00 o.p. Inst Hist Rev.

Dynamics of War & Revolution. 2nd ed. Lawrence Dennis & James J. Martin. 259p. 1941. pap. 10.00 o.p. (Inst Hist Rev). Noontide.

Dynamics of Wordperfect. Trish McClelland. (Dynamics Ser.). 300p. 1985. pap. 19.95 o.p. (ISBN 0-87094-655-2). Dow Jones-Irwin.

Dynamics of World Power, 5 vols. Ed. & intro. by Arthur M. Schlesinger, Jr. Incl. Vol. 1. Western Europe. 1974. text ed. 48.50 o.p. (ISBN 0-07-055322-X); Vol. 2. Eastern Europe & the Soviet Union. 1975. text ed. 48.50 o.p. (ISBN 0-07-055323-8); Vol. 3. Latin America. 44.50 o.p. (ISBN 0-07-055324-6); Vol. 4. Far East. 1975. text ed. 48.50 o.p. (ISBN 0-07-055325-4); Vol. 5. United Nations, Middle East, Subsaharan Africa. 1975. text ed. 48.50 o.p. (ISBN 0-07-055326-2). LC 78-150208. 4500p. 1973. Set. text ed. 239.00 o.p. (ISBN 0-07-079729-3). McGraw.

Dynamite in the Middle East. Totah. 60p. 1955. (ISBN 0-8022-1731-1). Philos Lib.

Dynamo & the Tree: My Twins & I Journeying in a Technate in the Year of 1981. William G. Brown. 1977. 12.00 o.p. (ISBN 0-682-48722-8). Exposition-Phoenix.

Dynamo Davis: A Memoir of a Multi-Faceted Life. George F. Davis, Sr. (Illus.). 264p. 1986. text ed. 20.00 o.p. (ISBN 0-682-40294-X). Exposition-Phoenix.

Dynamo Jim Stiles, Pioneer of Progress. Edward Uhlan. 1959. 6.00 o.p. (ISBN 0-682-45900-3, Banner). Exposition-Phoenix.

Dynasty of Air. Jack Ansell. LC 74-187807. 1974. 6.95 o.p. (ISBN 0-87795-094-6, Arbor Hse). Morrow.

Dynasty of Power. David Thoreau. LC 81-71677. 1982. 14.50 o.p. (ISBN 0-87795-383-X, Arbor Hse). Morrow.

Dynasty of Raghu. Kalidasa. Tr. by Robert Antoine from Sanskrit. (Writers Workshop Saffronbird Book Ser.). 217p. 1975. 15.00 o.s.i. (ISBN 0-88253-532-3); pap. text ed. 6.75 o.s.i. (ISBN 0-88253-531-5). Ind-US Inc.

Dynasty of Spies. Dan Sherman. LC 79-54012. 1980. 11.95 o.p. (ISBN 0-87795-255-8, Arbor Hse). Morrow.

Dyserythropoiesis. S. M. Lewis & R. Verwilghen. 1978. 90.00 o.p. (ISBN 0-12-446840-3). Acad Pr.

Dysfunctional Alliance: Emotion & Reason in Justice Administration. Ed. by Daniel B. Kennedy. LC 77-73529. 271p. 1977. pap. text ed. 10.95 o.p. (ISBN 0-87084-483-0). Anderson Pub Co.

Dziga Vertov: A Guide to References & Resources. Seth R. Feldman. 1979. lib. bdg. 36.50 o.p. (ISBN 0-8161-8085-7, Hall Reference). G K Hall.

E

E. A. T. Eating Awareness Training. Molly Groger. 224p. 1983. 12.50 o.s.i. (ISBN 0-671-46887-1). Summit Bks.

E. C. T. A Clinical Guide. Morris Fraser. LC 82-2666. 150p. 1982. 20.00x o.p. (ISBN 0-471-10416-7, Dist. by A R Liss). Wiley.

E D P Institute, Las Vegas, Oct. 12-15, 1980: Proceedings. Ed. by Mary E. Brennan. 63p. (Orig.). 1981. pap. 8.00 o.p. (ISBN 0-89154-144-6). Intl Found Employ.

E. E. Cummings: A Reference Guide. Guy L. Rotella. 1979. lib. bdg. 30.50 o.p. (ISBN 0-8161-8079-2, Hall Reference). G K Hall.

Titles

E. J. Bellocq: Storyville Portraits. John Szarkowski. 1970. pap. 9.95 o.p. Museum Mod Art.

E. L. Doctorow. Paul Levine. 128p. 1985. pap. text ed. 5.95 o.p. (ISBN 0-416-34840-8, 9470). Routledge Chapman & Hall.

E. L. Godkin & American Foreign Policy: 1865-1900. William M. Armstrong. LC 77-9534. 1977. Repr. of 1957 ed. lib. bdg. 35.00x o.p. (ISBN 0-8371-9711-2, ARGA). Greenwood.

E. L. Kirchner: Drawings & Pastels. Ed. by Roman N. Ketterer. (Illus.). 315p. 50.00 o.p. (ISBN 0-317-54966-9). Apollo.

E. M. Forster: A Life. P. N. Furbank. LC 78-53882. (Illus.). 621p. 1978. 19.95 o.s.i. (ISBN 0-15-128759-7). HarBraceJ.

E. M. Forster: A Tribute with Selections from His Writings on India. Ed. by K. Natwar-Singh. LC 64-11526. 145p. 1964. 9.95 o.p. (ISBN 0-15-128760-0). HarBraceJ.

E. M. Forster As Critic. Rukun Advani. LC 84-45981. 256p. 1984. 29.00 o.p. (ISBN 0-7099-0545-9, Pub. by Croom Helm Ltd). Routledge Chapman & Hall.

E. M. Forster: Centenary Revaluations. Ed. by Judith S. Herz & Robert K. Martin. 288p. 1982. 25.00x o.p. (ISBN 0-8020-2454-8). U of Toronto Pr.

E. M. Forster: The Critical Heritage. Ed. by Philip Gardner. (Critical Heritage Ser.). 1984. pap. 15.00 o.p. (ISBN 0-7102-0392-6). Routledge Chapman & Hall.

E. M. Forster: The Personal Voice. John Colmer. 256p. 1975. 21.00x o.p. (ISBN 0-7100-8209-6). Routledge Chapman & Hall.

E. M. Forster: The Personal Voice. John Colmer. 1983. pap. 8.95 o.p. (ISBN 0-7100-9496-5). Routledge Chapman & Hall.

E-MJ Operating Handbook of Mineral Processing, Vol. II. 2nd ed. Engineering & Mining Journal Editors. 500p. 1980. text ed. 33.50 o.p. (ISBN 0-07-019527-7). McGraw.

E. P. Papanoutsos. G. P. Henderson. (World Authors Ser.). 1983. lib. bdg. 28.95 o.s.i. (ISBN 0-8057-6526-3, Twayne). G K Hall.

E. S. Paxson, Frontier Artist. William E. Paxson, Jr. LC 84-4771. (Illus.). 176p. 1984. 24.95 o.p. (ISBN 0-87108-663-8); deluxe ed. 200.00 o.p. (ISBN 0-87108-680-8). Pruett.

E. T. Barnette: The Strange Story of the Man Who Founded Fairbanks. Terrence Cole. LC 81-3452. (Illus.). 176p. 1981. pap. 7.95 o.p. (ISBN 0-88240-269-2). Alaska Northwest.

E. T. Counting. Lawrence Henry. Ed. by Kate Klimo. (Learn with E.T. Ser.). (Illus.). 24p. 1983. pap. 1.90 o.s.i. (ISBN 0-671-46440-X, Little). S&S.

Eads Bridge: Photographic Essay. Quinta Scott. LC 78-19640. (Illus.). 144p. 1979. text ed. 27.00x o.s.i. (ISBN 0-8262-0266-7). U of Mo Pr.

Eager Reader. Kathleen D. Stearns. 170p. 1985. pap. text ed. 10.00 o.p. (ISBN 0-88450-914-1, 7222-B). Communication Skill.

Eagle & the Dove: Reassessing John Donne. Ed. by Claude Summers & Ted-Larry Pebworth. LC 85-20874. 256p. 1986. text ed. 24.00 o.p. (ISBN 0-8262-0489-9). U of Mo Pr.

Eagle & the Fort: The Story of John McLoughlin. Dorothy N. Morrison. LC 78-12911. (Illus.). (gr. 5-9). 1979. 7.95 o.p. (ISBN 0-689-30691-1, Atheneum). Macmillan.

Eagle & the Rising Sun: Americans & the New Religions of Japan. Robert S. Ellwood, Jr. LC 74-7317. 1974. 7.95 o.s.i. (ISBN 0-664-20707-3, Westminster). Westminster John Knox.

Eagle Butte, U. S. A. Rachel Dunning. LC 85-42731. (Illus.). 108p. (Orig.). 1985. pap. 7.95 o.s.i. (ISBN 0-317-54431-4). Harpswell Pr.

Eagle Claw Fish Cookbook. Kenneth N. Anderson. LC 77-89549. (Illus.). 1978. 9.95 o.p. (ISBN 0-916752-17-8). Longman Trade.

Eagle Eye. Hortense Calisher. LC 73-82181. 1973. 7.50 o.p. (ISBN 0-87795-062-8, Arbor Hse). Morrow.

Eagle in the Sky. Wilbur Smith. 1981. pap. 1.95 o.p. (ISBN 0-440-14592-9). Dell.

Eagle Mask: A West Coast Indian Tale. James Houston. LC 66-10074. (Illus.). (gr. 2-6). 1966. 5.50 o.p. (ISBN 0-15-224444-1, HJ). HarBraceJ.

Eagle Song. James Houston. (Illus.). 300p. 1983. 15.95 o.p. (ISBN 0-15-127117-8). HarBraceJ.

Eagle to the Wind. Mel Ellis. LC 77-10930. 1978. 6.95 o.p. (ISBN 0-03-022766-6). H Holt & Co.

Eagles. Lewis Orde. 1983. 15.95 o.p. (ISBN 0-87795-520-4, Arbor Hse). Morrow.

Eagle's Gift. Carlos Castaneda. 1981. 14.95 o.s.i. (ISBN 0-671-23087-5). S&S.

Eagles of Savoy: The House of Savoy in Thirteenth Century Europe. Eugene L. Cox. LC 73-16966. 484p. 1974. 50.50 o.p. (ISBN 0-691-05216-6). Princeton U Pr.

Eagles, Urns, & Columns: Decorative Arts in the Federal Period. Ed. by Robert Doty & Melvin Watts. LC 79-54956. (Illus.). 1986. 11.95 o.s.i. (ISBN 0-87923-303-6); pap. 11.95 o.s.i. Godine.

Eakins Watercolors. Donelson F. Hoopes. (Illus.). 88p. 1985. pap. 16.95 o.p. (ISBN 0-8230-1591-2). Watson-Guptill.

Ear. 4th ed. Ballantyne & Morrison. (Rob & Smith's Operative Surgery Ser.). 1986. 79.95 o.p. (ISBN 0-8016-4412-7, C-4412-7). Mosby.

Ear Acupressure. Pedro Chan. 1977. pap. 6.95 o.p. Borden.

Ear, Nose & Throat. Maurice Hawthorne & Richard Num. 223p. 1985. 19.50 o.p. (ISBN 0-471-83803-9). Wiley.

Ear, Nose, & Throat Disorders. Gordon W. Hickish. LC 84-21440. (Illus.). 226p. 1985. pap. text ed. 29.00 o.p. (ISBN 0-443-02977-6). Churchill.

Ear on Washington: A Chrestomathy of Scandal, Rumor & Gossip among the Capital's Elite. Diana McLellan. LC 81-71683. 1982. 14.95 o.p. (ISBN 0-87795-394-5, Arbor Hse). Morrow.

Earl & the Heiress. Barbara Metzger. 192p. 1983. pap. 2.50 o.p. (ISBN 0-380-65516-0, 65516). Avon.

Earl Campbell. Rothaus et al. (Sports Superstars Ser.). (Illus.). 32p. Date not set. PLB 8.95 o.p. (ISBN 0-87191-758-0). Creative Ed.

Earl Campbell: The Texas Tornado, Sports Stars. Hal Lundgren. LC 81-6137. (Illus.). 48p. (gr. 2-8). 1981. PLB 10.33 o.p. (ISBN 0-516-04316-1); pap. 2.95 o.p. (ISBN 0-516-44316-X). Childrens.

Earl Covey Story. 2nd ed. Frances A. Covey. (Illus.). 164p. 1979. 10.00 o.p. (ISBN 0-682-49443-7). Exposition-Phoenix.

Earlier History of English Bookselling. William Roberts. LC 66-28043. 1967. Repr. of 1889 ed. 35.00x o.p. (ISBN 0-8103-3314-7). Gale.

Earliest Round Coins of China. Arthur B. Coole. LC 80-54408. (Encyclopedia of Chinese Coins Ser.: Vol. 7). 325p. 1981. lib. bdg. 40.00x o.p. (ISBN 0-88000-122-4). Quarterman.

Earlihee the Turtle. Bruce Stringer. (Illus.). pap. 4.95 o.s.i. (ISBN 0-932298-06-0). Tri-State Pr Corp.

Early African Christianity see Tarikh.

Early America & the Polynesians. Paul R. Cheesman. 8.95 o.p. (ISBN 0-686-21716-0). Eagle Mktg Corp.

Early American Antique Country Furnishings: Northeastern America, 1650-1800. G. C. Neumann. (Illus.). 368p. 1984. text ed. 27.95 o.p. (ISBN 0-07-046311-5). McGraw.

Early American Books & Printing. John T. Winterich. (Illus.). 288p. 1981. pap. 5.95 o.p. (ISBN 0-486-24171-8). Dover.

Early American Brides. E. Haines. 150p. 1982. pap. 7.95 o.p. (ISBN 0-87588-176-9, 832). Hobby Hse.

Early American Cinema. Anthony Slide. LC 77-119639. (International Film Guide Ser). 1970. pap. 4.95 o.p. (ISBN 0-498-07717-9). A S Barnes.

Early American Furniture. James M. O'Neill. (gr. 7 up). 1963. text ed. 16.64 o.p. (ISBN 0-87345-045-0). Glencoe.

Early American Gardens: For "Meate & Medicine" Ann Leighton. (Illus.). 1973. 14.95 o.p. (ISBN 0-395-07907-1). HM.

Early American Metal Projects. Joseph W. Daniele. LC 75-130495. 16.64 o.p. (ISBN 0-87345-142-2). Glencoe.

Early American Plays, 1714-1830. rev. 2nd ed. Oscar Wegelin. 1968. 16.00 o.p. (ISBN 0-384-66440-7). Johnson Repr.

Early American Pottery & China. John Spargo. LC 74-78148. (Illus.). 1974. 12.50 o.p. (ISBN 0-8048-1135-0). C E Tuttle.

Early American Stencils on Walls & Furniture. Janet Waring. (Illus.). 18.00 o.p. (ISBN 0-8446-3138-8). Peter Smith.

Early American Weaving & Dyeing: The Domestic Manufacturer's Assistant & Family Directory in the Arts of Weaving & Dyeing. J. Bronson & R. Bronson. 14.00 o.p. (ISBN 0-8446-5560-0). Peter Smith.

Early American Woodcarving. Erwin Christensen. (Illus.). 11.25 o.p. (ISBN 0-8446-4722-5). Peter Smith.

Early American Wooden Ware. Mary E. Gould. LC 69-13499. (Illus.). 1962. 15.00 o.p. (ISBN 0-8048-0153-3). C E Tuttle.

Early Anthropology in the Sixteenth & Seventeenth Centuries. Margaret T. Hodgen. LC 62-11265. (Illus.). 1971. pap. text ed. 15.95x o.p. (ISBN 0-8122-1014-X, Pa Paperbks). U of Pa Pr.

Early Archaic Chinese: A Descriptive Grammar. W. A. Dobson. LC 63-1488. 1962. 30.00x o.p. (ISBN 0-8020-5106-5). U of Toronto Pr.

Early Arianism: A View of Salvation. Robert C. Gregg & Dennis E. Groh. LC 79-7379. 224p. 1981. 5.00 o.p. (ISBN 0-8006-0576-4, 1-576, Fortress). Augsburg Fortress.

Early Astronomy from Babylonia to Copernicus. W. M. O'Neil. 213p. 1986. 27.50 o.p. (ISBN 0-424-00117-9, Pub. by Sydney U Pr). Intl Spec Bk.

Early Ballads, Illustrative of History, Traditions, & Customs. Ed. by Robert Bell. LC 67-23928. 408p. 1968. Repr. of 1877 ed. 43.00x o.p. (ISBN 0-8103-3408-9). Gale.

Early Behavior: Comparative & Developmental Approach. Ed. by Harold W. Stevenson et al. LC 75-5858. 316p. 1975. Repr. of 1967 ed. text ed. 21.50 o.p. (ISBN 0-88275-307-X). Krieger.

Early Care of the Stroke Patient: A Positive Approach. rev. ed. Janet Carr & Roberta Shepherd. (Illus.). 1979. pap. 17.50 o.s.i. (ISBN 0-433-30140-6). E J Brill USA.

Early Care of the Stroke Patient: A Positive Approach. Janet H. Carr & Roberta B. Shepherd. 55p. 1979. 9.95 o.p. (ISBN 0-89443-812-3). Aspen Pub.

Early Celtic Art, 2 vols. Paul Jacobstabal. LC 45-5693. 1944. Repr. 59.00 o.p. (ISBN 0-403-04033-7). Somerset Pub.

Early Chevrolet History: 1912-1945. Doug Bell. Ed. by Clymer Publications. (Illus.). pap. 5.00 o.p. (ISBN 0-89287-269-1, H544). Clymer Pub.

Early Child Day Care. Peter Neubauer et al. LC 74-9268. 128p. 1974. Repr. 15.00x o.p. (ISBN 0-87668-186-0). Aronson.

Early Childhood Education. Ed. by Ira J. Gordon. LC 6-16938. (National Society for the Study of Education Yearbooks Ser: No. 71, Pt. 2). (Illus.). xvi, 400p. 1975. pap. text ed. 6.00x o.s.i. (ISBN 0-226-60110-2). U of Chicago Pr.

Early Childhood Education. Bernard Spodek. (Viewpoint & Alternatives Ser.). (Illus.). 288p. 1973. pap. text ed. (ISBN 0-13-222414-3). P-H.

Early Childhood Education: An International Perspective. G. R. Austin. (Educational Psychology Ser.). 1976. 49.50 o.p. (ISBN 0-12-068550-7). Acad Pr.

Early Childhood Education: An Introduction to the Profession. 2nd ed. James L. Hymes, Jr. LC 75-3791. (Illus.). 71p. 1975. pap. text ed. 1.00 o.p. (ISBN 0-912674-47-4, NAEYC #300). Natl Assn Child Ed.

Early Childhood Education at Work. Millie Almy. 276p. 1975. pap. text ed. 19.95 o.p. (ISBN 0-07-001125-7); pap. text ed. 3.25 o.p. (ISBN 0-07-001126-5). McGraw.

Early Childhood Education in Historical Perspective. D. Keith Osborn. LC 75-30492. 1977. pap. 4.95 o.p. (ISBN 0-918772-01-X). Daye Pr.

Early Childhood Education: Special Environmental, Policy & Legal Considerations. Ed. by Elizabeth M. Goetz & K. Eileen Allen. LC 83-9950. 354p. 1983. 34.00 o.p. (ISBN 0-89443-879-4). Aspen Pub.

Early Childhood Education: Special Problems, Special Solutions. K. Eileen Allen & Elizabeth M. Goetz. LC 82-4029. 368p. 1982. 36.00 o.p. (ISBN 0-89443-657-0). Aspen Pub.

Early Childhood Education 1988-89. 9th, rev. ed. Ed. by Judy S. McKee & Karen M. Paciorek. LC 77-640114. (Annual Editions Ser.). (Illus.). 256p. 1987. pap. text ed. 9.95 o.p. (ISBN 0-87967-705-8). Dushkin Pub.

Early Childhood Musical Development: A Bibliography of Research Abstracts, 1960-1975. Gene M. Simons. 136p. 1978. 3.75 o.p. (ISBN 0-686-37913-6, 1012). Music Ed Natl.

Early Childhood: The Development of Self-Regulatory Mechanisms. Ed. by Dwain N. Walcher & Donald L. Peters. 1971. 52.50 o.p. (ISBN 0-12-731750-3). Acad Pr.

Early China & the Wall. Peter Nancarrow. LC 80-7446. (Cambridge Topic Bks.). (Illus.). (gr. 5-10). 1980. PLB 8.95 o.p. (ISBN 0-8225-1218-1). Lerner Pubns.

Early Christian & Byzantine Architecture. Richard Krautheimer. (Pelican History of Art Ser.). (Illus.). 1975. pap. 18.95 o.p. (ISBN 0-14-056124-2, Pelican). Penguin.

Early Christian & Byzantine Political Philosophy: Origins & Background, 2 vols. Francis Dvornik. LC 67-4089. (Dumbarton Oaks Studies: Vol. 9). 975p. 1966. 50.00x o.p. (ISBN 0-88402-016-9). Dumbarton Oaks.

Early Christian Church. John G. Davies. LC 75-3989. (Illus.). 314p. 1976. Repr. of 1965 ed. lib. bdg. 24.00x o.p. (ISBN 0-8371-7696-4, DAECC). Greenwood.

Early Christian Worship. Oscar Cullmann. LC 78-6636. 126p. 1978. pap. 6.95 o.s.i. (ISBN 0-664-24220-0, Westminster). Westminster John Knox.

Early Christians of the Twenty-First Century. Chad Walsh. LC 78-138136. 188p. 1972. Repr. of 1950 ed. lib. bdg. 35.00x o.p. (ISBN 0-8371-5709-9, WACH). Greenwood.

Early Coins of the Chou Dynasty. Arthur B. Coole. LC 72-86804. (Encyclopedia of Chinese Coins Ser.: Vol. 2). (Illus.). 550p. 1973. 35.00x o.p. (ISBN 0-88000-010-4). Quarterman.

Early Community at Bedford Park: The Pursuit of "Corporate Happiness" in the First Garden Suburb. Margaret J. Bolsterli. LC 76-8299. (Illus.). xii, 133p. 1977. 14.00x o.p. (ISBN 0-8214-0224-2). Ohio U Pr.

Early Criticism, Seventeen Eleven to Seventeen Sixteen see Popeiana.

Early Cycladic Art in North American Collections. Pat Getz-Preziosi. (Illus.). 368p. 1987. 55.00 o.p. (ISBN 0-295-96552-5); pap. 29.95 o.p. (ISBN 0-295-96553-3). U of Wash Pr.

Early Dark. Reynolds Price. LC 77-3189. 1977. 7.95 o.p. (ISBN 0-689-10799-4, Atheneum). Macmillan.

Early Days in Detroit: Papers Written by General Friend Palmer, of Detroit, Being His Personal Reminiscences of Important Events & Descriptions of the City for Over Eighty Years. Friend Palmer. LC 74-13871. (Illus.). 1038p. 1979. Repr. of 1906 ed. 55.00x o.p. (ISBN 0-8103-4068-2). Gale.

Early Days: Photographer George A. Grant & the Western National Parks. Mark Sawyer. LC 85-63417. (Illus.). 144p. (Orig.). 1986. pap. 19.95 o.s.i. (ISBN 0-87358-397-3). Northland.

Early Detection of Breast Cancer. Ed. by S. Brunner et al. (Recent Results in Cancer Research Ser.: Vol. 90). (Illus.). 240p. 1984. 46.00 o.p. (ISBN 0-387-12348-2). Springer-Verlag.

Early Diagnosis of Pancreatic Cancer. Keiichi Kawai. LC 80-81619. (Illus.). 290p. 1980. 42.50 o.p. (ISBN 0-89640-042-5). Igaku-Shoin.

Early Diary of Anais Nin: Vol. IV, 1927-1931. Anais Nin. 528p. 1985. 29.95 o.p. (ISBN 0-15-127185-2). HarBraceJ.

Early Diary of Anais Nin: 1920 to 1923, Vol. II. Anais Nin. (Illus.). 576p. 1982. 19.95 o.p. (ISBN 0-15-127183-6). HarBraceJ.

Early Diary of Anais Nin: 1923-27, Vol. III. Anais Nin. 320p. 1983. 17.95 o.p. (ISBN 0-15-127184-4). HarBraceJ.

Early Disorder. Rebecca Josephs. LC 79-27269. 192p. 1980. 10.95 o.p. (ISBN 0-374-14579-2). FS&G.

Early Drawings of Charles Edouard Jeanneret le Corbusier 1902-1908. Mary P. Sekler. LC 76-23726. (Outstanding Dissertations in the Fine Arts Ser.). 1977. lib. bdg. 97.00 o.p. (ISBN 0-8240-2728-0). Garland Pub.

Early Editions of Arthur Hugh Clough. Patrick G. Scott. LC 76-24761. (Reference Library of the Humanities Ser.: Vol. 47). (Illus.). 1977. lib. bdg. 28.00 o.p. (ISBN 0-8240-9916-8). Garland Pub.

Early Electrodynamics. R. A. Tricker. 1965. 19.75 o.p. (ISBN 0-08-010794-X); pap. 10.50 o.p. (ISBN 0-08-010793-1). Pergamon.

Early English & French Voyages, Fifteen Thirty-Four to Sixteen Eight, Chiefly from Hakluyt. Ed. by Henry S. Burrage. (Original Narratives). 453p. 1967. Repr. of 1906 ed. 21.50x o.p. (ISBN 0-06-480120-9, 06376). B&N Imports.

Early English Chamber Music: From the Middle Ages to Purcell. Ernst H. Meyer. Ed. by Diane Poulton. LC 82-1161. (Illus.). 363p. 1983. 30.00 o.p. (ISBN 0-7145-2777-7, Dist. by Kampmann). M Boyars Pubs.

Early Florentine Woodcuts. Paul Kristeller. 1897. 45.00x o.p. (ISBN 0-87556-141-1). Saifer.

Early Graves. Joseph Hansen. LC 87-42701. 208p. 1987. 15.95 o.p. (ISBN 0-89296-249-6). Mysterious Pr.

Early Greece: The Bronze & Archaic Ages. M. I. Finley. LC 78-95884. (Ancient Culture & Society Ser). 1970. pap. 4.95 o.p. (ISBN 0-393-00541-0, Norton Lib). Norton.

Early Greek Concept of the Soul. Jan Bremmer. LC 82-47583. 190p. 1983. 35.00 o.p. (ISBN 0-691-03131-2). Princeton U Pr.

Early Greek Poetry & Philosophy. Hermann Frankel. Tr. by Moses Hadas & James Willis. LC 74-10724. (Helen & Kurt Wolff Bk.). 576p. 1975. 25.00 o.p. (ISBN 0-15-127190-9). HarBraceJ.

Early Greek Thinking. Martin Heidegger. Tr. by David Krell & Frank Capuzzi. LC 74-6767. 160p. 1975. 7.95 o.p. (ISBN 0-06-063858-3, CN 4111). HarpR.

Early Hanoverian Age 1714-1760: Commentaries of an Era. A. F. Scott. (Illus.). 175p. 1980. 20.00 o.p. (ISBN 0-7099-0145-3, Pub. by Croom Helm Ltd). Routledge Chapman & Hall.

Early Histological Diagnosis of Cervical Cancer. Erich Burghardt. LC 79-176203. (Major Problem in Obstetrics & Gynecology Ser.: Vol. 6). (Illus.). 1973. text ed. write for info. o.p. (ISBN 0-7216-2175-9). Saunders.

Early History of Cuba, 1492-1586. Irene A. Wright. LC 71-120682. 1970. Repr. lib. bdg. 27.50x o.p. (ISBN 0-374-98773-4, Octagon). Hippocrene Bks.

Early History of Motley County. Harry H. Campbell. 1968. 6.95 o.p. (ISBN 0-685-48802-0). Eakin Pr.

Early History of Upson County, Georgia. Carolyn W. Nottingham & Evelyn Hannah. 1969. Repr. of 1930 ed. 40.00 o.p. (ISBN 0-89308-029-2). Southern Hist Pr.

Early Irish Church: From the Beginnings to the Two Doves. Paul R. Lonigan. LC 84-73489. (Illus.). 151p. (Orig.). 1985. pap. 15.99x o.p. (ISBN 0-9614753-0-7). Celt Heritage Pr.
Early Irish Church: From the Beginnings to the Two Doves. 2nd ed. Paul R. Lonigan. (Illus.). 100p. 1986. pap. 15.99x o.p. (ISBN 0-9614753-1-5). Celt Heritage Pr.
Early Irish Literature. Myles Dillon. LC 48-6027. 1948. lib. bdg. 13.00x o.s.i. (ISBN 0-226-14918-8). U of Chicago Pr.
Early Japan. Jonathan N. Leonard. (Great Ages of Man Ser.). (Illus.). 1968. 13.95 o.p. (ISBN 0-8094-0360-9). Time-Life.
Early Jews of New Orleans. Berton W. Korn. 1970. 15.00x o.p. (Pub. by Am Jewish Hist Soc). Ktav.
Early Language: Acquisition & Intervention. Ed. by Richard L. Schiefelbusch & Dianne D. Bricker. LC 81-4569. (Illus.). 616p. 1981. text ed. 29.00x o.p. (ISBN 0-8391-1618-7, 1324). Pro Ed.
Early Life History of Fish. J. H. Blaxter. LC 74-4895. (Illus.). 660p. 1974. 52.80 o.p. (ISBN 0-387-06719-1). Springer-Verlag.
Early Life of Robert Southey. William Haller. 1967. lib. bdg. 24.00x o.p. (ISBN 0-374-93382-0, Octagon). Hippocrene Bks.
Early Man in North-West India. Ed. by S. R. Chopra. 1979. 10.00x o.p. (ISBN 0-8364-0451-3). South Asia Bks.
Early Maps. Tony Campbell. LC 80-24787. (Illus.). 148p. 1981. 55.00 o.p. (ISBN 0-89659-191-3). Abbeville Pr.
Early Maps of North America. Robert M. Lunny. (Illus.). 48p. 1961. pap. 6.95 o.p. (ISBN 0-686-81821-0). NJ Hist Soc.
Early Methodist People. Leslie Church. (ISBN 0-8022-0249-7). Philos Lib.
Early Mid & Late Georgian Houses, 3 vols. 2nd. ed. Christopher Hussey et al. 288p. 1985. 195.00 o.p. (ISBN 0-907462-68-5). Apollo.
Early Missionary Preaching: A Study of Luke's Report in Acts 13. C. A. Joachim Pillai. 1979. 8.00 o.p. (ISBN 0-682-49403-8, University). Exposition-Phoenix.
Early Modern Town in Scotland. Ed. by Michael Lynch. 1987. 47.50 o.p. (ISBN 0-7099-1677-9, Pub. by Croom Helm UK). Routledge Chapman & Hall.
Early Moon. Carl Sandburg. LC 30-28479. (Illus.). (gr. 7-9). 1930. 9.95 o.p. (ISBN 0-15-224486-7, HJ). HarBraceJ.
Early Narratives of the Northwest, 1634-1699. Ed. by Louise P. Kellogg. (Original Narratives). 384p. 1967. Repr. of 1917 ed. 21.50x o.p. (ISBN 0-06-480455-0). B&N Imports.
Early New England Catechisms. Wilberforce Eames. LC 68-31081. 112p. 1969. Repr. of 1898 ed. 35.00x o.p. (ISBN 0-8103-3478-X). Gale.
Early Nonconformity, Fifteen Sixty-Six to Eighteen Hundred: A Catalogue of Books in Dr. Williams' Library, London, 3 pts. Ed. by Dr. Williams' Library, London Staff. Incl. Pt. 1. Author Catalogue, 5 vols. Set. 495.00 (ISBN 0-8161-0797-1); Pt. 2. Subject Catalogue, 5 vols. Set. 495.00 (ISBN 0-8161-0174-4); Pt. 3. Chronological Catalogue, 2 vols. Set. 198.00 (ISBN 0-8161-0173-6). 1968 (Hall Library). G K Hall.
Early North American Dollmaking. Iris Jones. LC 76-44413. (Illus.). 1976. 8.95 o.s.i. (ISBN 0-89286-107-X, One Hund One Prods); pap. 4.95 o.s.i. (ISBN 0-89286-108-8). Ortho.
Early One-Design Sailboats. Diana Esterly. (Illus.). 1979. encore ed 3.95 o.p. (ISBN 0-684-17536-3, ScribT). Scribner.
Early Painters & Engravers in Canada. J. Russell Harper. 1981. 75.00 o.p. (ISBN 0-686-43128-6). Apollo.
Early Phonics Crossword Puzzle Book see Phonics Crossword Puzzles Series.
Early Postglacial Settlement of Northern Europe: An Ecological Perspective. Ed. by Paul Mellars. LC 78-63264. (Illus.). 1979. 39.95x o.p. (ISBN 0-8229-1137-X). U of Pittsburgh Pr.
Early Printed Maps of the British Isles, 1477-1650. Rev. ed. R. W. Shirley. (Illus.). 225p. 1980. 45.00 o.p. (ISBN 0-87556-670-7). Saifer.
Early Reading Acquisition: Six Psycholinguistic Case Studies. Fernando Mino-Garces. 126p. (Orig.). 1981. pap. 6.95 o.p. (ISBN 0-87840-190-3). Georgetown U Pr.
Early Reading Experiences for Young Children: A Book of Selected Readings for Students, Interns & Teachers. Ed. by Heath W. Lowry. 1974. 29.50x o.p. (ISBN 0-8422-5148-0); pap. text ed. 9.75x o.p. (ISBN 0-8422-0366-4). Irvington.
Early Reminiscences, 1834-1864. Sabine Baring-Gould. LC 67-23868. 378p. 1967. Repr. of 1923 ed. 35.00x o.p. (ISBN 0-8103-3049-0). Gale.
Early Retirement on Medical Grounds. 2nd ed. Peter Jewell & Barbara Spiers. 51p. (Orig.). 1982. pap. text ed. 6.95 o.p. (ISBN 0-7199-1112-5, Pub. by Bedford England). Gower Pub Co.
Early Ripening: American Women's Poetry Now. Marge Piercy. 222p. 1987. 29.95 o.p. (ISBN 0-86358-108-0, Pandora Pr); pap. 9.95 o.p. (ISBN 0-86358-141-2, Pandora Pr). Routledge Chapman & Hall.
Early Schooling in England & Israel. Norma D. Feshback et al. (IDEA Reports on Schooling). 224p. 1973. text ed. 3.50 o.p. (ISBN 0-07-020635-X). McGraw.
Early Sea Charts. Robert Putman. LC 83-8746. (Illus.). 144p. 1983. 45.00 o.p. (ISBN 0-89659-392-4). Abbeville Pr.
Early Selected Y Mas: Collected Poems, 1949-1966. Paul Blackburn. Ed. by Robert Kelly. LC 72-10359. 130p. (Orig.). 1977. pap. 5.00 o.p. (ISBN 0-87685-120-0). Black Sparrow.
Early Settlers of Barbour Co., Ala, Vols. 1 & 2. Marie H. Godfrey. 376p. 1979. 30.00 o.s.i. (ISBN 0-89308-160-4). Southern Hist Pr.
Early Settlers of Terry County. Ed. by Mrs. R. L. Bowers. (Illus.). 1985. Repr. 15.00 o.p. (ISBN 0-933512-02-3). Pioneer Bk Tx.
Early Solar Physics. A. J. Meadows. LC 74-103021. 1970. 80.00 o.p. (ISBN 0-08-006653-4); pap. text ed. 12.75 o.p. (ISBN 0-08-006654-2). Pergamon.
Early Soviet Photographers. Daniela Mrazkova & Vladimir Remes. Ed. by John Hoole. (Illus.). 88p. 1985. pap. 12.50 o.p. (ISBN 0-87663-866-3). Universe.
Early Texas Homes. Dorothy K. Bracken & Maurine W. Redway. LC 56-12565. (Illus.). 204p. 1982. Repr. of 1956 ed. 19.95 o.p. (ISBN 0-87074-023-7). SMU Press.
Early Therapeutic, Social, & Vocational Problems in the Rehabilitation of Persons with Spinal Cord Injuries. Ed. by Marian Weiss. LC 77-79008. 392p. 1977. 65.00x o.p. (ISBN 0-306-31075-9, Plenum Pr). Plenum Pub.
Early V-Eight Ford Service Manual: 1932-1950. Victor W. Page. Ed. by Clymer Publications. (Illus.). pap. 12.00 o.p. (ISBN 0-89287-266-7, H527). Clymer Pub.
Early View of the Land-Grant Colleges. Convention of Friends of Agricultural Education, Chicago Staff. LC 67-20999. 162p. 1967. 15.95 o.p. (ISBN 0-252-72463-1). U of Ill Pr.
Early Warning Health Guide. V. McVerry. 1977. pap. 4.95 o.p. (ISBN 0-89019-058-5). Norwalk Pr.
Early Window: Effects of Television on Children & Youth. 2nd ed. Robert M. Liebert et al. LC 82-5327. (Pergamon General Psychology Ser.: No. 34). (Illus.). 280p. 1982. text ed. 35.00 o.p. (ISBN 0-08-027548-6, J125); pap. text ed. 12.95 o.p. (ISBN 0-08-027547-8). Pergamon.
Early Work of Signorelli: 1465-1490. Gloria Kury. LC 77-94701. (Outstanding Dissertations in the Fine Arts Ser.). (Illus.). 1978. lib. bdg. 55.00 o.p. (ISBN 0-8240-3233-0). Garland Pub.
Early Works of Charles E. Burchfield, 1915-1921. John I. Baur & Richard Wootten. Ed. by Norma Roberts. (Illus.). 64p. pap. 8.00 o.p. (ISBN 0-918881-19-6). Columbus Mus Art.
Early Years in Childhood Education. Betty L. Broman. 1980. text ed. 20.95 o.p. (ISBN 0-395-30565-9). HM.
Early Years in Childhood Education. 2nd ed. Betty L. Broman. LC 81-82557. 1982. text ed. 36.36 o.p. (ISBN 0-395-31803-3). HM.
Earn & Learn: Cooperative Education Opportunities Offered by the Federal Government, 1988-89. 9th, rev. ed. Joseph M. Re. 28p. 1987. pap. 2.75 o.p. (ISBN 0-317-60093-1). Octameron Assocs.
Earned International Reserve Units: The Catalyst of Two Complementary World Problems - Monetary & Development. Chris Economides. 24p. 1976. pap. 35.00 o.p. (ISBN 0-08-021178-X). Pergamon.
Earning, Saving, Investing... & Planning. A. Wade Blankenship. 134p. (Orig.). 1983. software diskette & book pkg 49.95 o.s.i. (ISBN 0-9613038-0-8). Blankenship & Co.
Earnings in Nineteen Eighty-Three of Married-Couple Families, by Characteristics of Husbands & Wives. 2nd ed. (Current Population Reports Ser. P-60; Consumer Income, No. 153). 37p. 1986. pap. 2.25 o.p. (ISBN 0-318-20371-5, S/N 003-001-91659-2). USGPO.
Ears Near to the Lips of God. Lonnell E. Johnson. LC 84-90175. 53p. 1985. 6.95 o.p. (ISBN 0-533-06229-2). Vantage.
Earth: A Topical Geography. 2nd ed. Harm J. De Blij. LC 79-18051. 472p. 1980. (ISBN 0-471-05169-1). Wiley.
Earth Abides. George R. Stewart. 1983. pap. 3.50 o.p. (ISBN 0-449-20390-5, Crest). Fawcett.
Earth Afire! Volcanoes & Their Activity. Ronald V. Fodor. LC 81-3984. (Morrow Junior Bks.). (Illus.). 96p. (gr. 4-6). 1981. 11.75 o.p. (ISBN 0-688-00706-6); PLB 11.88 o.p. (ISBN 0-688-00707-4). Morrow.
Earth & Cosmos. Robert S. Kandel. (Illus.). 1980. 55.00 o.p. (ISBN 0-08-025016-5); pap. 21.00 o.p. (ISBN 0-08-023086-5). Pergamon.
Earth & Human Evolution see Geographical Introduction to History.
Earth Ascending: An Illustrated Treatise on the Law Governing Whole Systems. Jose Arguelles. LC 83-20052. (Illus.). 150p. 1984. pap. 12.95 o.p. (ISBN 0-87773-263-9, 72330-9). Shambhala Pubns.
Earth Beneath the Continents. Ed. by J. S. Steinhart & T. J. Smith. (Geophysical Monograph Ser.: Vol. 10). 663p. 1966. 21.00 o.p. (ISBN 0-87590-010-0). Am Geophysical.
Earth Beneath the Sea. rev. ed. Francis P. Shepard. LC 67-12522. (Illus.). 1968. pap. text ed. 3.95x o.s.i. (ISBN 0-689-70180-2, 56, Atheneum). Macmillan.
Earth for Sam. rev. ed. W. Maxwell Reed. Ed. by Paul F. Brandwein. LC 59-12825. (Illus.). (gr. 7 up). 1960. 7.95 o.p. (ISBN 0-15-224665-7, HJ). HarBraceJ.
Earth in Motion: The Concept of Plate Tectonics. Ronald V. Fodor. LC 77-12568. (Illus.). (gr. 3-7). 1978. 10.25 o.p. (ISBN 0-688-22135-1); PLB 10.88 o.p. (ISBN 0-688-32135-6). Morrow.
Earth Is Sore: Native Americans on Nature. Aline Amon. LC 80-36854. (Illus.). 96p. (gr. 5 up). 1981. PLB 9.95 o.p. (ISBN 0-689-30798-5, Atheneum). Macmillan.
Earth Is the Lord's. Mary J. McFadyen. (Illus., Orig.). 1967. pap. 3.95 o.p. (ISBN 0-8042-9864-5, John Knox). Westminster John Knox.
Earth Manual. Malcolm Margolin. LC 75-1324. (San Francisco Ser.). 208p. 1975. 10.00 o.p. (ISBN 0-395-20425-9). HM.
Earth Movers. Mark Rich. LC 79-23494. (On the Move Ser.). (Illus.). 48p. (gr. 3-6). 1980. PLB 10.60 o.p. (ISBN 0-516-03884-2); pap. 2.95 o.p. (ISBN 0-516-43884-0). Childrens.
Earth Observation & Remote Sensing by Satellites: Proceedings of the Symposium on Earth Observation & Remote Sensing by Satellites, Hannover, West Germany, 21 May 1982. Ed. by R. E. Lo. 56p. 1984. pap. 45.00 o.p. (ISBN 0-08-031152-0). Pergamon.
Earth One: The Upper Atmosphere, Ionisphere & Magnetosphere. C. W. Gordon & V. Canuto. (Handbook of Astronomy, Astrophysics & Geophysics Ser.: Vol. I). 420p. 1978. 140.00 o.p. Gordon & Breach.
Earth Reinforcement. Compiled by American Society of Civil Engineers Staff. 910p. 1979. pap. 40.00x o.p. (ISBN 0-87262-144-8). Am Soc Civil Eng.
Earth Rites: Fertility Practices in Pre-Industrial Britain. Janet Bord & Colin Bord. (Illus.). 288p. pap. 7.95 o.p. (ISBN 0-586-08452-5, Pub. by Granada England). Academy Chi Pubs.
Earth Science: An Individualized Approach. 3rd ed. Joseph C. Gould & Charles J. Mott. (Illus.). 250p. 1982. pap. text ed. 13.95x o.p. (ISBN 0-89459-185-1). Hunter Textbks.
Earth Science Curriculum Project Pamphlet Series, 10 Vols. 1971. Set. pap. 44.96 o.p. (ISBN 0-395-12066-7). HM.
Earth, Sea & Sky: The Work of Edmond Halley. Linda W. Girard. (Albert Whitman Biography Ser.). (Illus.). 64p. (gr. 3 up). 1985. 9.75 o.p. (ISBN 0-8075-1868-9). A Whitman.
Earth Sheltered Community Design: Energy-Efficient Residential Development. Underground Space Center Staff. 270p. 1981. 31.95 o.p. (ISBN 0-442-28557-4); pap. 19.95 o.p. (ISBN 0-442-28558-2). Van Nos Reinhold.
Earth-Sheltered Habitat: History, Architecture & Urban Design. Gideon Golany. 192p. 1982. 29.95 o.p. (ISBN 0-442-22992-5); pap. 19.95 o.p. (ISBN 0-442-22993-3). Van Nos Reinhold.
Earth Sheltered Housing: Code, Zoning, & Financing Issues. Underground Space Center Staff. 144p. 1982. 21.95 o.p. (ISBN 0-442-28689-9); pap. 15.95 o.p. (ISBN 0-442-28688-0). Van Nos Reinhold.
Earth Shine. Anne M. Lindbergh. LC 77-84877. (Helen & Kurt Wolff Bk.). 1969. 6.95 o.s.i. (ISBN 0-15-127236-0). HarBraceJ.
Earth Shine: Shine. Anne M. Lindbergh. LC 77-84877. (Illus.). 1970. pap. 2.95 o.p. (ISBN 0-15-627400-0, HB192, Harv). HarBraceJ.
Earth Song. Joel Trejo. (Illus.). 1978. 4.00 o.p. (ISBN 0-682-49043-1). Exposition-Phoenix.
Earth Spirit: Its Ways, Shrines & Mysteries. John Mitchell. 1976. pap. 5.95 o.p. (ISBN 0-380-01514-9, 26880). Avon.
Earth Through Time. 2nd ed. Harold Levin. 1983. text ed. 35.95 o.s.i. (ISBN 0-03-058354-3, CBS C). SCP.
Earth, Time & Life: An Introduction to Geology. Charles W. Barnes. LC 79-17236. 583p. 1980. (ISBN 0-471-05616-2). Wiley.
Earth Voyager. (First Adventures Ser.). (ps-5). 1984. 5.70 o.s.i. (ISBN 0-671-50764-8, Little Simon). S&S.
Earth Watch. Roger M. Borsheim. 168p. 1980. 8.00 o.p. (ISBN 0-682-49634-0). Exposition-Phoenix.
Earthlight. Arthur C. Clarke. LC 72-188459. 1972. 5.95 o.s.i. (ISBN 0-15-127225-5). HarBraceJ.
Earthly Paradise & the Renaissance Epic. A. Bartlett Giamatti. 1966. 23.00x o.p. (ISBN 0-691-06030-4); pap. 11.95 o.p. (ISBN 0-691-01292-X). Princeton U Pr.
Earthly Pleasures: Tales from a Biologist's Garden. Roger B. Swain. (Illus.). 192p. 1981. 10.95 o.s.i. (ISBN 0-684-16657-7, ScribT). Scribner.
Earthly Powers. Anthony Burgess. 720p. 1981. pap. 3.95 o.p. (ISBN 0-380-56903-5, 56903-5). Avon.
Earthquake. Matt Christopher. (Illus.). 128p. (gr. 4-6). 1975. 11.45 o.p. (ISBN 0-316-13968-8). Little.
Earthquake. Ann Matthews. (Transformers Find Your Fate Junior Ser.: No. 4). (Orig.). (gr. 4 up). 1986. pap. 2.50 o.p. (ISBN 0-345-33071-4). Ballantine.
Earthquake. Harold Richards. LC 79-13559. (Flame Ser.). 1979. pap. 1.25 o.p. (ISBN 0-8127-0240-9). Review & Herald.
Earthquake Behavior & Safety of Oil & Gas Storage Facilities, Buried Pipelines & Equipment, Vol. 77. Ed. by T. Ariman. 478p. 1983. pap. text ed. 70.00 o.p. (ISBN 0-317-02615-1, H00263). ASME.
Earthquake-Induced Dynamic Response of Bridges & Bridge Measurements: Nine Reports. (Transportation Research Report Ser.). 103p. 1976. 4.80 o.p. (ISBN 0-309-02493-5). Transport Res Bd.
Earthquake Protection of Essential Building Equipment: Design, Engineering, & Installation. Gary L. McGavin. LC 80-23067. 464p. 1981. 58.95x o.p. (ISBN 0-471-06270-7, Pub. by Wiley-Interscience). Wiley.
Earthquakes & Buildings: A Revision of A-521. Mary Vance. (Architecture Ser.: A 1500). 100p. 1985. 15.00 o.p. (ISBN 0-89028-650-7). Vance Biblios.
Earth's Amazing Animals. Thomas B. Allen et al. Ed. by Cecilia I. Parker. LC 83-17324. (Illus.). 208p. 1983. 18.95 o.p. (ISBN 0-912186-48-8). Natl Wildlife.
Earth's Core. J. A. Jacobs. (International Geophysics Ser.). 1976. 60.00 o.p. (ISBN 0-12-378950-8). Acad Pr.
Earth's Core & Geomagnetism. J. A. Jacobs. 1963. 40.00 o.p. (ISBN 0-08-010340-5); pap. 40.00 o.p. (ISBN 0-08-010339-1). Pergamon.
Earth's Crust & Upper Mantle. Ed. by P. J. Hart. LC 75-600572. (Geophysical Monograph Ser.: Vol. 13). (Illus.). 735p. 1969. pap. 10.00 o.p. (ISBN 0-87590-013-5). Am Geophysical.
Earth's Crust: Its Nature & Physical Properties. Ed. by John Heacock. LC 77-83153. (Geophysical Monograph Ser.: Vol. 20). (Illus.). 754p. 1977. 45.00 o.p. (ISBN 0-87590-020-8). Am Geophysical.
Earth's Density. K. E. Bullen. 1975. 49.95 o.p. (ISBN 0-412-10860-7, NO.6045, Pub. by Chapman & Hall). Routledge Chapman & Hall.
Earth's Energy & Mineral Resources. 196p. Date not set. pap. 9.95 o.p. (ISBN 0-913232-90-4). W Kaufmann.
Earth's Greatest Day. E. L. Austin. 96p. (Orig.). 1980. pap. 3.95 o.p. (ISBN 0-8010-0163-3). Baker Bk.
Earth's Moon. (Wonders of Learning Kits Ser.). (gr. 3-6). 1981. incl. cass. & tchr's. guide 28.95 o.p. (ISBN 0-686-73887-X, 04920). Natl Geog.
Earth's Shape & Gravity. G. D. Garland. 1965. text ed. 23.00 o.p. (ISBN 0-08-010823-7); pap. text ed. 9.75 o.p. (ISBN 0-08-010822-9). Pergamon.
Earth's Surface Studied from Space: Proceedings of Workshop II of the COSPAR Twenty-Fifth Plenary Meeting Held in Graz, Austria, 25 June-7 July 1984. S. G. Ungar. (Illus.). 124p. 1985. pap. 54.00 o.p. (ISBN 0-08-033194-7, Pub. by PPL). Pergamon.
Earthscape. John O. Simonds. (Illus.). 352p. 1977. text ed. 41.50 o.p. (ISBN 0-07-057395-6). McGraw.
Earthwatch: Space-Time Investigations with a Globe. Julius Schwartz. (Illus.). 64p. (gr. 7-9). 1977. text ed. 9.95 o.p. (ISBN 0-07-055685-7). McGraw.
Earthworks. 2nd ed. P. C. Horner. 54p. 1981. pap. 8.00 o.p. (ISBN 0-7277-0091-X, Pub. by T Telford UK). Am Soc Civil Eng.
Earthworks: Land Reclamation as Sculpture. Seattle Art Museum Staff. (Illus.). 72p. pap. 5.95 o.p. (ISBN 0-295-95869-3). U of Wash Pr.
Easier Way: Handbook for the Elderly & Handicapped. Jean V. Sargent. LC 81-19785. (Illus.). 220p. 1981. pap. 10.50 o.p. (ISBN 0-8138-0870-7). Iowa St U Pr.

Titles

Easing into the Year Two Thousand: One-Liners for a Cartoonist's Pen. R. W. North. 48p. 1983. pap. 4.00 o.p. (ISBN 0-682-49982-X). Exposition-Phoenix.

Easing the Scene. Shirley Schwarzrock & C. Gilbert Wrenn. (Coping with Ser.). (Illus.). (gr. 7-12). 1970. pap. text ed. 3.00 o.p. (ISBN 0-913476-23-4). Am Guidance.

East Africa. Time-Life Books Editors. (Library of Nations). (Illus.). 160p. (YA) (gr. 7 up). 1987. lib. bdg. 23.93 o.p. (ISBN 0-8094-5319-3). Time-Life.

East Africa with Malawi & Zambia. Joe Yogerst. (Illus.). 196p. (Orig.). 1984. pap. 12.95 o.p. (ISBN 0-933982-81-X). Bradt Ent.

East African Culture History. Ed. by Joseph Gallagher. LC 76-50927. (Foreign & Comparative Studies Program, Eastern Africa Ser.: No. 25). 93p. 1976. pap. text ed. 5.50x o.p. (ISBN 0-915984-22-9). Syracuse U Foreign Comp.

East & West. Mary B. Messner. (ISBN 0-8022-1106-2). Philos Lib.

East Asia: A Survey of Holdings at the Hoover Institution on War, Revolution & Peace. John T. Ma. LC 74-142948. (Library Survey Ser.: No. 2). 24p. 1971. pap. 2.00x o.p. (ISBN 0-8179-5022-2). Hoover Inst Pr.

East Asian Economies: A Guide to Information Sources. Ed. by Molly K. Lee. LC 78-13114. (Economics Information Guide Ser.: Vol. 1). 336p. 1979. 68.00x o.p. (ISBN 0-8103-1427-4). Gale.

East Asiatic Library, 2 pts. University of California - Berkeley Staff. Incl. Pt. 1. Author-Title Catalog, 13 vols. Set. lib. bdg. 1285.00 (ISBN 0-8161-0801-3); Pt. 2. Subject Catalog, 6 vols. Set. lib. bdg. 595.00 (ISBN 0-8161-0128-0). 1970 (Hall Library). G K Hall.

East Asiatic Library. University of California, Berkeley Staff. Incl. Author Catalog, First Supplement, 2 Vols. 240.00 (ISBN 0-8161-0842-0); Subject Catalog, First Supplement, 2 vols. lib. bdg. 240.00 (ISBN 0-8161-0129-9). 1973 (Hall Library). G K Hall.

East Broad Top Railroad. Frank Kyper & Lee Rainey. (Illus.). 224p. 36.95 o.p. (ISBN 0-87095-078-9). Gldn West Bks.

East Came West. Peter J. Huxley-Blythe. 225p. Date not set. pap. 5.00 o.p. (ISBN 0-317-53237-5). Noontide.

East Central Europe: Yesterday, Today, Tomorrow. Ed. by Milorad Drachkovitch. (Publication Ser.: No. 240). 417p. 1982. 25.95x o.p. (ISBN 0-8179-1601-6). Hoover Inst Pr.

East Coast Bed & Breakfast Guide: New England & the Mid-Atlantic. Roberta Gardner. (Illus.). 160p. 1986. pap. 12.95 o.p. (ISBN 0-671-62947-6). P-H.

East European Economic Handbook. 300p. 1985. 80.00x o.p. (ISBN 0-86338-029-8, Pub. by Euromonitor Pubns). Gale.

East European Integration & East-West Trade. Ed. by Paul Marer & John M. Montias. LC 79-3181. 416p. 1980. 32.50x o.p. (ISBN 0-253-16865-1). Ind U Pr.

East European Peasantries: Social Relations: An Annotated Bibliography of Periodical Articles, Vol. II. Irwin T. Sanders & Walter C. Bisselle. 1981. lib. bdg. 19.00 o.p. (ISBN 0-8161-8488-7, Hall Reference). G K Hall.

East European Peasantries: Social Relations; an Annotated Index of Periodical Articles. Irwin T. Sanders & Roger Whittaker. 1976. lib. bdg. 16.00 o.p. (ISBN 0-8161-7860-7, Hall Reference). G K Hall.

East Hampton's Heritage: An Illustrated Architectural Record. Clay Lancaster et al. (Illus.). 1982. 25.00 o.p. (ISBN 0-393-01572-6); pap. 12.95 o.p. (ISBN 0-393-30058-7). Norton.

East India Slavery. George Saintsbury. 52p. 1972. Repr. of 1929 ed. 20.00x o.p. (ISBN 0-7165-1816-3, BBA 02130, Pub. by Irish Academic Pr Ireland). Biblio Dist.

East Indiamen. Time-Life Books Editors & Russell Miller. (Seafarers Ser.). (Illus.). 176p. 1981. 13.95 o.p. (ISBN 0-8094-2689-7). Time-Life.

East Indian Art Styles: A Study in Parallel Trends. B. N. Mukherjee. (Illus.). 66p. 1981. text ed. 22.50x o.p. (ISBN 0-391-02500-7). Humanities.

East Midlands from AD 1000: A Regional History of England. Beckett. (Illus.). 448p. 1988. text ed. 39.95 o.p. (ISBN 0-582-49269-6). Longman.

East of the Sun & West of the Moon. Kathleen Hague & Michael Hague. LC 80-13499. (Illus.). 48p. (gr. 1-5). 1980. 9.95 o.s.i. (ISBN 0-15-224702-5, HJ). HarBraceJ.

East River. Sholem Asch. 541p. 1986. pap. 4.50 o.p. (ISBN 1-55547-122-6). Critics Choice Paper.

East Shore & Suburban Railway. Erle C. Hanson. LC 77-11120. (Illus.). 34p. 1978. pap. 4.95 o.s.i. (ISBN 0-87095-073-8). Gldn West Bks.

East Timor, Nationalism & Colonialism. Jill Joliffe. (Illus.). 1978. 27.50x o.p. (ISBN 0-7022-1480-9); pap. 12.95x o.p. (ISBN 0-7022-1481-7). U of Queensland Pr.

East-West Business Directory: A Guide to Commercial Contacts with Eastern European Countries in OECD States. Intro. by Carl H. McMillan. 450p. 1986. text ed. 99.00x looseleaf o.p. (ISBN 0-910129-31-2). Wiener Pub Inc.

East-West Strategic Balance. T. B. Millar. 200p. 1981. text ed. 28.50x o.p. (ISBN 0-04-355015-0); pap. text ed. 14.95x o.p. (ISBN 0-04-355017-7). Unwin Hyman.

East-West Strategic Trade, COCOM & the Atlantic Alliance. Gary K. Bertsch. (Atlantic Papers: No. 49). (Illus.). 52p. 1983. pap. 7.00x o.p. (ISBN 0-86598-143-4, Rowman & Allanheld). Rowman.

East-West Trade 1975: International Yearbook. Ed. by Z. Zeman & J. Zoubek. 170p. 1975. pap. 225.00 o.p. (ISBN 0-08-019504-0). Pergamon.

East Wind. Julie Ellis. 1983. 15.95 o.p. (ISBN 0-87795-498-4, Arbor Hse). Morrow.

East Wind. Maria Z Linke & Ruth Hunt. 1978. pap. 2.50 o.p. (ISBN 0-310-27852-X). Zondervan.

East Wind, Rain. Richard Nash. LC 76-40433. 1977. 9.95 o.p. (ISBN 0-689-10773-0, Atheneum). Macmillan.

Easter. Howard G. Hageman & J. C. Beker. LC 73-88346. (Proclamation 1: Aids for Interpreting the Lessons of the Church Year, Ser. B). 64p. 1974. pap. 2.95 o.p. (ISBN 0-8006-4055-1, 1-4055, Fortress). Augsburg Fortress.

Easter. F. Wellford Hobbie. LC 84-18756. (Proclamation Three C Ser.). 64p. 1986. pap. 3.75 o.p. (ISBN 0-8006-4129-9, 1-4129, Fortress). Augsburg Fortress.

Easter. Edgar Krentz. LC 84-18756. (Proclamation 3, Ser. B). 64p. 1985. pap. 3.75 o.p. (ISBN 0-8006-4105-1, 1-4105, Fortress). Augsburg Fortress.

Easter. Edgar Krentz & Arthur A. Vogel. Ed. by Elizabeth Achtemeier et al. LC 79-7377. (Proclamation 2: Aids for Interpreting the Lessons of the Church Year, Ser. C). 64p. 1980. pap. 3.75 o.p. (ISBN 0-8006-4080-2, 1-4080, Fortress). Augsburg Fortress.

Easter. George W. MacRae & Charles P. Price. LC 79-7377. 64p. 1982. pap. 3.75 o.p. (ISBN 0-8006-4087-X, 1-4087, Fortress). Augsburg Fortress.

Easter. Charles Rice & J. Louis Martyn. LC 74-24958. (Proclamation 1: Aids for Interpreting the Lessons of the Church Year, Ser. B). 64p. 1975. pap. 2.95 o.p. (ISBN 0-8006-4075-6, 1-4075, Fortress). Augsburg Fortress.

Easter. John H. Snow & Victor P. Furnish. LC 74-76927. (Proclamation 1: Aids for Interpreting the Lessons of the Church Year, Ser. A). 64p. 1975. pap. 2.95 o.p. (ISBN 0-8006-4065-9, 1-4065, Fortress). Augsburg Fortress.

Easter. Bruce Vawter & William J. Carl, III. LC 79-7377. (Proclamation 2: Aids for Interpreting the Lessons of the Church Year, Ser. A). 64p. (Orig.). 1981. pap. 3.75 o.p. (ISBN 0-8006-4095-0, 1-4095, Fortress). Augsburg Fortress.

Easter. James Wharton. LC 84-18756. (Proclamation 3A). 64p. 1987. pap. 3.75 o.p. (ISBN 0-8006-4121-3, 1-4121). Augsburg Fortress.

Easter Bear. John Barrett. (Illus.). 32p. (gr. k-6). 1981. 3.95 o.p. (ISBN 0-8249-8007-7). Ideals.

Easter Buds Are Springing: Poems for Easter. Ed. by Lee B. Hopkins. LC 78-10888. (Illus.). (gr. 1-5). 1979. 10.95 o.p. (ISBN 0-15-224705-X, HJ). HarBraceJ.

Easter Bunny That Overslept. Priscilla Friedrich & Otto Friedrich. LC 82-13013. (Illus.). 40p. (gr. k-3). 1983. 11.95 o.p. (ISBN 0-688-01540-9); PLB 11.88 o.p. (ISBN 0-688-01541-7). Lothrop.

Easter Enigma: Are the Resurrection Accounts in Conflict? John Wenham. 176p. 1984. pap. 6.95 o.p. (ISBN 0-310-29861-X, 12448P). Zondervan.

Easter Gospels: The Resurrection of Jesus According to the Four Evangelists. Robert H. Smith. LC 83-70518. 272p. (Orig.). 1983. pap. 15.95 o.p. (ISBN 0-8066-2024-2, 10-1988, Augsburg). Augsburg Fortress.

Easter Ideals. Date not set. pap. 3.95 o.p. (ISBN 0-8249-1060-5). Ideals.

Easter Parade. Date not set. pap. (ISBN 0-385-29283-X). Delacorte.

Easter Parade. Richard Yates. 240p. 1983. pap. 8.95 o.p. (ISBN 0-385-29283-X, Delta). Dell.

Easter Rising & Irish Independence. E. G. Power. Ed. by Marjorie Reeves. (Then & There Ser.). (Illus.). 96p. (Orig.). (gr. 7-12). 1979. pap. text ed. 4.95 o.p. (ISBN 0-582-22120-X). Longman.

Easter Rising in Song & Ballad. C. Desmond Greaves. 88p. 1980. 10.00 o.p. (Pub. by Stanmore Pr England); pap. 5.95 o.p. Facsimile Bk.

Eastern & Central England. Allan Straw & Keith Clayton. (Geomorphology of the British Isles Ser.). 248p. 1979. 35.00x o.p. (ISBN 0-416-84660-2, NO.2855). Routledge Chapman & Hall.

Eastern & Southern Africa: Past Trends & Future Prospects. Ravi Gulhati. (Working Paper: No. 413). 24p. 1980. pap. 3.50 o.p. (ISBN 0-686-39673-1, WP-0413). World Bank.

Eastern Campground & Trailer Parks see Campground & Trailer Park Guide: U. S. Canada - Mexico.

Eastern Canada. (Rand McNally Pocket Guide Ser.). (Illus., Orig.). 1987. pap. 5.95 o.p. (ISBN 0-528-84408-3). Rand McNally.

Eastern Churches Review, Vols. I-X, 1966-1978. Ed. by Barbara Fry et al. LC 66-9909. 2000p. 1985. pap. text ed. 90.00x o.p. (ISBN 0-89370-095-9). Borgo Pr.

Eastern Europe. Time-Life Books Editors. (Library of Nations). (Illus.). 160p. (YA) (gr. 7 up). 1987. lib. bdg. 23.93 o.p. Time-Life.

Eastern Europe & Russia-Soviet Union: A Handbook of West European Archival & Library Resources. Richard C. Lewanski. 317p. 1981. lib. bdg. 50.00 o.p. (ISBN 3-598-08012-3). K G Saur.

Eastern Intellectuals & Western Solutions: Follower Syndrome in Asia. Doh Joon-Chien. 160p. 1980. text ed. 15.95x o.p. (ISBN 0-7069-0968-2, Pub. by Vikas India). Advent NY.

Eastern Left, Western Left: Totalitarianism, Freedom & Democracy. Ferenc Feher & Agnes Heller. LC 86-20045. 300p. 1987. text ed. 39.95 o.p. (ISBN 0-391-03492-8). Humanities.

Eastern Way of Love. Mary E. Jones. LC 76-50636. 1977. 14.95 o.s.i. (ISBN 0-671-22448-4). S&S.

Eastern-Western Regional Conference on Ground Water Management, 1983: Proceedings. 1984. 43.75 o.p. (ISBN 0-318-23028-3). Natl Water Well.

Eastern Winds: The Imprint of Japan on Nineteenth- & Early Twentieth-Century Western Graphics. Rafael Fernandez. (Illus.). 32p. (Orig.). 1982. pap. 3.50 o.p. (ISBN 0-931102-08-1). S & F Clark Art.

Eastman's Expectant Motherhood Seventh Edition Revisied. Keith P. Russell. (Illus.). 1970. 6.95 o.p. (ISBN 0-316-20395-5). Little.

Eastward to Empire: Exploration & Conquest on the Russian Open Frontier, to 1750. George V. Lantzeff & Richard A. Pierce. (Illus.). 240p. 1973. 17.50x o.p. (ISBN 0-7735-0133-9, McGill Canada). U of Toronto Pr.

Easy As One-Two-Three. Constance F. McCarthy & Ann D. Sheehy. 20p. 1982. 9.95 o.p. (ISBN 0-88450-830-7, 4612-B). Communication Skill.

Easy BASIC Programs for the IBM PC & PCjr. Brian Flynn. 359p. (Orig.). 1984. pap. 14.95 o.p. (ISBN 0-942386-58-2). Compute Pubns.

Easy Bazaar Crafts. Better Homes & Gardens Editors. (Illus.). 96p. 1981. 6.95 o.p. (ISBN 0-696-00665-0). BH&G.

Easy Cake Decorating. Mildred Brand. (Illus., Orig.). 1980. pap. 3.95 o.p. (ISBN 0-89542-622-6). Ideals.

Easy Connection. Lynn Z. Bloom. 491p. 1984. pap. text ed. 12.00 o.p. (ISBN 0-669-04476-8). Heath.

Easy Embroidery. Lis Paludan. LC 75-10065. (Illus.). 128p. 1975. 9.95 o.s.i. (ISBN 0-8008-2358-3). Taplinger.

Easy Entrees. Bon Appetit Magazine Editors. LC 87-3738. (Cooking with Bon Appetit Ser.). 1987. 12.95 o.p. (ISBN 0-89535-183-8). Knapp Pr.

Easy Favors. Neil Clareman. 208p. 1987. pap. 3.95 o.p. (ISBN 1-55547-129-3). Critics Choice Paper.

Easy Find Ref Card, Labenski. 1983. 2.95 o.p. (ISBN 0-07-035720-X). McGraw.

Easy Going: A Comprehensive Guide to Grant, Iowa & Lafayette Counties. James C. Stewart & Shirley L. Stewart. LC 76-2413. (Easy Going Ser). (Illus.). 150p. 1976. pap. 5.00 o.p. (ISBN 0-915024-05-5). WI Trails.

Easy Going: A Comprehensive Guide to Sauk & Columbia Counties. Charles F. Church. LC 75-11855. (Easy Going Ser). (Illus.). 144p. 1976. pap. 5.00 o.p. (ISBN 0-915024-03-9). WI Trails.

Easy Going: Madison & Dane County. Sara Rath & Rick Smith. LC 77-8058. (Easy Going Ser.). (Illus.). 1977. pap. 7.50 o.p. (ISBN 0-915024-13-6). WI Trails.

Easy Going: Vilas & Oneida Counties. Michael Dunn, III. LC 78-908. (Easy Going Ser.). (Illus., Orig.). 1978. pap. 5.00 o.p. (ISBN 0-915024-16-0). WI Trails.

Easy History of the Prophet of Islam. Nadvi. pap. 3.95 o.p. (ISBN 0-686-18309-6). Kazi Pubns.

Easy Introduction to the Slide Rule. Isaac Asimov. (Illus.). (gr. 7 up). 1973. 6.95 o.p. (ISBN 0-395-06575-5). HM.

Easy Lace. Nihon Vogue Staff. (Illus.). 50p. (Orig.). 1985. pap. 6.95 o.p. (ISBN 0-87040-644-2). Japan Pubns USA.

Easy Money. Arthur Mather. 1982. pap. 3.50 o.p. (ISBN 0-440-12211-2). Dell.

Easy Reading: Book Series & Periodicals for Less Able Readers. Michael Graves et al. (IRA Reading Aids Ser.). (Orig.). 1979. pap. text ed. 4.50 o.p. (ISBN 0-87207-224-X). Intl Reading.

Easy Reading Selections in English. rev. ed. Robert J. Dixson. (Illus., Orig., Sequel to Elementary Reader in English). (gr. 7-9). 1971. pap. text ed. 3.75 o.p. (ISBN 0-88345-043-7, 17976); cassettes 40.00 o.p. (ISBN 0-685-19788-3, 58211) (ISBN 0-685-19789-1). Prentice ESL.

Easy Steps to Playing Guitar, Vol. II. Victor J. Lawrence. 1954. 2.95 o.p. (ISBN 0-913650-28-5). CPP Belwin.

Easy Steps to Playing Guitar, Vol. III. Victor J. Lawrence. 1954. 3.95 o.p. (ISBN 0-913650-29-3). CPP Belwin.

Easy-to-Make Children's Furniture. David Stiles. (Illus.). 1980. pap. 7.95 o.p. (ISBN 0-394-73871-3). Pantheon.

Easy-to-Make Water Toys That Really Work. Mary Blocksma & Dewey Blocksma. (Illus., Orig.). (gr. 2-6). 1988. 5.95 o.s.i. (ISBN 0-13-223207-3). S&S.

Easy-to-Read Books for the Teenage. New York Public Library, Office of Young Adult Services Staff. 1988. pap. 1.50 o.p. (ISBN 0-87104-693-8, Dist. by Branch Lib). NY Pub Lib.

Easy-to-Read California Driver's Handbook. Gail P. Venable & Jerry Stemach. 1978. pap. text ed. 4.00x o.p. (ISBN 0-87879-173-6); tests with answering key 6.00 o.p. (173-6-C). Acad Therapy.

Easy-to-Understand Guide to Home Computers. Consumer Guide Editors. 95p. 1984. pap. 1.00 o.p. (ISBN 0-517-42584-X, Pub. by Beekman Hse). Outlet Bk Co.

Easy Way of Doing Things. Glenn F. Daly. 1978. pap. 4.00 o.p. (ISBN 0-682-49177-2). Exposition-Phoenix.

EasyWriter Simplified for the IBM Personal Computer. Don Cassel. 208p. 1984. text ed. 23.33 o.p. (ISBN 0-13-222449-6); pap. 12.95 o.p. (ISBN 0-13-222431-3). P-H.

Eat Cheaper! Brock Junkin & Elizabeth Junkin. 80p. 1982. 5.50 o.p. (ISBN 0-682-49787-8). Exposition-Phoenix.

Eat 'Em up, Cougars, Houston Football. Rev. & enl. ed. Jerry Wizig. LC 77-79555. (College Sports Ser.). 1981. 10.95 o.p. (ISBN 0-87397-122-1). Strode.

Eat to Win: Sports Nutrition Book. Robert Haas. 1988. 4.98 o.p. (ISBN 0-517-49035-8). Crown.

Eat Well, Get Well, Stay Well. Carlton Fredericks. LC 79-91618. 1981. 9.95 o.p. (ISBN 0-448-12258-8, G&D); pap. 19.81 o.s.i. (ISBN 0-448-12023-2, G&D). Putnam Pub Group.

Eat Your Way to a Better Relationship. Cathy Guisewite. LC 82-72420. 60p. (Orig.). 1983. pap. 2.95 o.p. (ISBN 0-8362-1987-2). Andrews & McMeel.

Eating & Drinking with Jesus: An Ethical & Biblical Inquiry. Arthur C. Cochrane. LC 73-22364. 208p. 1974. 9.00 o.s.i. (ISBN 0-664-20865-7, Westminster). Westminster John Knox.

Eating Cheap. Ragnar Benson. 120p. 1982. pap. 8.00 o.p. (ISBN 0-87364-252-X). Paladin Pr.

Eating Dangerously: The Hazards of Hidden Allergies. Richard Mackarness. 1976. 6.95 o.p. (ISBN 0-15-127265-4). HarBraceJ.

Eating for the Eighties. Janie C. Hartbarger & Neil J. Hartbarger. LC 80-53187. 256p. 1981. 14.95 o.p. (ISBN 0-03-059077-9); pap. 6.95 o.p. (ISBN 0-03-059076-0). H Holt & Co.

Eating for Two. Laurie Bohlke. 32p. (Orig.). 1985. write for info. o.p. (ISBN 0-940050-05-6). Sun Rose.

Eating Gorilla Comes in Peace. abridged ed. John Da Free. 180p. 1984. pap. 3.95 o.p. (ISBN 0-913922-76-5). Dawn Horse Pr.

Eating the Oregon Way. Elsie Palmer & Jody Oeltjen. LC 82-73683. (Illus.). 180p. (Orig.). pap. 8.95 o.p. (ISBN 0-9609912-0-4). Berry Patch.

Eating Well! Living Well! The Over-50 Cookbook. Jane W. Wilson. LC 85-40525. (Illus.). 320p. 1986. 19.95 o.p. (ISBN 0-89480-944-X); pap. 12.95 o.p. (ISBN 0-89480-943-1). Workman Pub.

Eating What Grows Naturally. Martin Gay & Kathlyn Gay. LC 80-70278. (Illus.). 140p. 1980. pap. 5.95 o.s.i. (ISBN 0-89708-031-9). And Bks.

Eau Vive: Rondeurs des Jours, Vol. 1. Jean Giono. 1973. 9.95 o.p. (ISBN 0-686-53961-3). French & Eur.

Ebony Ark: Black Africa's Battle to Save Its Wild Life. Eric Robins. LC 70-125931. (Illus.). 1970. 6.50 o.s.i. (ISBN 0-8008-2360-5). Taplinger.

Ebony Cross. (Nick Carter Ser.). 1978. pap. 1.75 o.p. (ISBN 0-441-18270-4). Ace Bks.

Ecce Romani: Versiculi: A Companion in Verse. Ed. by Scottish Classics Group Staff. 1976. pap. text ed. 3.75 o.p. (ISBN 0-05-002897-9); tchr's notes 2.95 o.p. (ISBN 0-05-002898-7). Longman.

Eccentric Lives & Peculiar Notions. John Michell. LC 84-4543. (Illus.). 240p. 1984. 15.95 o.p. (ISBN 0-15-127358-8). HarBraceJ.

Ecclesia Militans: The Inquisition. Miroslav Hroch & Anna Skybova. (Illus.). 264p. 1989. 30.00 o.s.i. (ISBN 0-88029-129-X). Hippocrene Bks.

Ecclesial Man: A Social Phenomenology of Faith & Reality. Edward Farley. LC 73-88359. 304p. 1975. 12.95 o.p. (ISBN 0-8006-0272-2, 1-272, Fortress). Augsburg Fortress.

Ecclesial Reflection: An Anatomy of Theological Method. Edward Farley. LC 81-43088. 1982. 29.95 o.p. (ISBN 0-8006-0670-1, Fortress). Augsburg Fortress.

Ecclesiastes in A. S. L. - Chapter Three, Verses 1-4: Written in Sutton Sign Writing. David McKee & Nancy E. Woo. pap. 3.00x o.p. (ISBN 0-317-56109-X). Ctr Sutton Movement.

Ecclesiastes Speaks to Us Today. Lawrence Bottoms. LC 78-71053. (Bible Speaks to Us Today). 1979. pap. 1.99 o.p. (ISBN 0-8042-0104-8, John Knox). Westminster John Knox.

Ecclesiastical Cartoons. 2nd ed. Wm. Armstrong. (Armstrong Cartoon Ser.). (Illus.). 48p. (Orig.). 1972. pap. 1.00 o.p. (ISBN 0-913452-08-4). Jesuit Bks.

Ecclesiology of Vatican II. Bonaventure Kloppenburg. 1974. 6.95 o.p. (ISBN 0-8199-0484-8). Franciscan Herald.

ECG - an Introductory Course. M. J. Halhuber et al. (Illus.). 1979. pap. 19.50 o.p. (ISBN 0-387-09326-5). Springer-Verlag.

ECG: A Pocket Guide. Sylvia Talkington. LC 82-71576. (Critical Care Nursing Ser.). (Illus.). 99p. (Orig.). 1982. pap. text ed. 8.95 o.p. (ISBN 0-471-88807-9). Wiley.

ECG Case Studies, Vol. 3. Julian Frieden & Ira L. Rubin. 1984. pap. text ed. 22.00 o.p. (ISBN 0-87488-217-6). Med Exam.

Echanges. Raymond F. Comeau & Normand J. Lamoureux. (Fr.). 1982. text ed. 27.95 o.p. (ISBN 0-03-043596-X); instr's manual 19.95 o.p. (ISBN 0-03-058078-1); wkbk.-lab manual 11.95 o.p. (ISBN 0-03-043601-X); tapes 350.00 o.p. (ISBN 0-03-043606-0). HR&W.

Echidnas. M. Griffiths. LC 68-21385. 1968. 60.00 o.p. (ISBN 0-08-012650-2). Pergamon.

Echinoderm Biology: Proceedings of the Zoological Society of London Symposium, 20th. Zoological Society of London Symposium Staff. Ed. by N. Millot. 1968. 61.00 o.p. (ISBN 0-12-613320-4). Acad Pr.

Echo. Ed. by Mei Ting. (Beginning Science Ser.). (Illus.). 38p. (gr. 2). 1987. 4.95 o.p. (ISBN 0-8351-1197-0); pap. 2.95 o.p. (ISBN 0-8351-1347-7). China Bks.

Echo Time-Word His Te. Ostrowksi. Date not set. (ISBN 0-07-047931-3). McGraw.

Echo Viruses. H. A. Wenner et al. Bd. with Reoviruses. L. Rosen. (Virology Monographs: Vol. 1). (Illus.). iv, 107p. 1968. 19.50 o.p. (ISBN 0-387-80889-2). Springer-Verlag.

Echocardiography: Techniques & Interpretation. 2nd. ed. Sonia Chang. LC 81-2200. (Illus.). 362p. 1981. text ed. 22.50 o.p. (ISBN 0-8121-0784-5). Lea & Febiger.

Echoes. Frances Noel. LC 85-91008. 128p. 1985. 8.00 o.s.i. (ISBN 0-682-40261-3). Exposition-Phoenix.

Echoes & Embers. Patricia Gallagher. 1983. pap. 3.50 o.p. (ISBN 0-380-80929-X, 80929-X). Avon.

Echoes from Old Calcutta. H. E. Busteed. (Illus.). 454p. 1972. Repr. of 1908 ed. 47.50x o.p. (ISBN 0-7165-2115-6, Pub. by Irish Academic Pr Ireland). Biblio Dist.

Echoes from the South. Edward A. Pollard. LC 79-107521. 1970. Repr. of 1866 ed. lib. bdg. 22.50x o.p. (ISBN 0-8371-3768-3, PES&, Pub. by Negro U Pr). Greenwood.

Echoes in an Empty Room: And Other Supernatural Tales. Carolyn Lane. LC 80-20278. (gr. 4-7). 1981. 7.95 o.p. (ISBN 0-03-057477-3). H Holt & Co.

Echoes: Memoirs of Andre Kostelanetz. Andre Kostelanetz & Gloria Hammond. LC 80-8751. (Illus.). 288p. 1981. 14.95 o.p. (ISBN 0-15-127392-8). HarBraceJ.

Echoes of Our Being. Tahlequah Indian Writer's Group Staff. Ed. by Robert J. Conley. (Illus.). 76p. 1982. pap. 5.00x o.p. (ISBN 0-940392-00-3). Indian U Pr OK.

Echoing Grove. Rosamond Lehmann. LC 53-5646. 1953. 4.50 o.s.i. (ISBN 0-15-127395-2). HarBraceJ.

Eck-Vidya: Ancienne Science de Prophetie. Paul Twitchell. Tr. by L. Marchand et al from Fr. 272p. (Orig.). 1980. pap. 3.95 o.p. (ISBN 0-914766-44-9, 0330). Illum Way Pub.

Eck Vidya, die Uralte Wissenschaft der Propheseiuns. Paul Twitchell. (Ger.). 1983. pap. 6.95 o.p. (ISBN 0-914766-62-7). Illum Way Pub.

Eckankar: Der Schlussel Zu Geheim Welten. Paul Twitchell. 1977. pap. 5.95 o.p. (ISBN 0-88155-016-7). Illum Way Pub.

Eckankar: La Clave de los Mondos Secretos. Paul Twitchell. 1978. pap. 5.95 o.p. (ISBN 0-88155-029-9). Illum Way Pub.

Eckankar: La Cle des Mondes Secrets. Paul Twitchell. 288p. 1973. pap. 3.95 o.p. (ISBN 0-914766-27-9). Illum Way Pub.

Eckerd. Jack Eckerd & Charles P. Conn. (Illus.). 1987. 12.95 o.p. (ISBN 0-8007-1532-2). Revell.

Eclipse. William Stevenson. LC 85-7038. 384p. 1986. 17.95 o.p. (ISBN 0-385-23209-8). Doubleday.

Eclipse of Symbolism. Peter Fingesten. LC 77-86194. (Illus.). 1970. 22.95x o.p. (ISBN 0-87249-172-2). U of SC Pr.

Eclipse Phenomena in Astronomy. F. Link. LC 68-56208. (Illus.). 1969. 50.70 o.p. (ISBN 0-387-04646-1). Springer-Verlag.

Eclogues & Georgics. Virgil. Tr. by T. S. Royds. 1965. Repr. of 1946 ed. 11.95x o.p. (ISBN 0-460-00222-8, Evman). Biblio Dist.

Ecodefense: A Field Guide to Monkeywrenching. Ed. by Dave Foreman. (Illus.). 184p. (Orig.). 1985. pap. 10.00 o.p. (ISBN 0-933285-01-9). Ned Ludd Bks.

Ecogeographic Analysis of the Herpetofauna of the Yucatan Peninsula. Julian C. Lee. (Miscellaneous Publications: No. 67). 75p. 1980. 4.00 o.p. (ISBN 0-317-04867-8). U of KS Mus Nat Hist.

Ecole des Femmes: Avec Robert, Genevieve, le Promethee Mal Enchaine. Andre Gide. 299p. 1970. 18.95 o.p. (ISBN 0-686-56068-X). Schoenhof.

Ecologic Atlas of Benthic Foraminifera of the Gulf of Mexico. C. Wylie Poag. LC 81-3720. 192p. 1982. 34.95 o.p. (ISBN 0-87933-900-4). Van Nos Reinhold.

Ecological Adaptation & Population Change: Semang Foragers & Temuan Horticulturists in West Malaysia. Alberto G. Gomes. LC 82-18286. (East-West Environment & Policy Institute Research Report: No. 12). vii, 51p. (Orig.). 1982. pap. text ed. 3.00 o.p. (ISBN 0-86638-034-5). EW Ctr HI.

Ecological Approach to Visual Perception. James J. Gibson. LC 78-69585. (Illus.). 1979. text ed. 41.50 o.p. (ISBN 0-395-27049-9). HM.

Ecological Approaches to Clinical & Community Psychology. Ed. by William A. O'Connor & Bernard Lubin. LC 83-23420. (Personality Processes Ser.: 1-341). 404p. 1984. 47.95x o.p. (ISBN 0-471-87669-0, Pub. by Wiley-Interscience). Wiley.

Ecological Aspects of Development in the Humid Tropics. Assembly of Life Sciences, National Research Council. 1982. pap. text ed. 16.50x o.p. (ISBN 0-309-03235-0). Natl Acad Pr.

Ecological Aspects of Used Water Treatment, Vol. 3. Ed. by C. R. Curds & H. A. Hawkes. 1983. 99.00 ea. o.p. (ISBN 0-12-199503-8). Acad Pr.

Ecological Assessment of Child Problem Behavior. Robert G. Wahler et al. 1976. pap. 9.75 o.p. (ISBN 0-08-019586-5). Pergamon.

Ecological Characteristics of Rocky Mountain Montane & Subalpine Wetlands. John T. Windell et al. (Interior Department Biological Report Ser.: No. 86(11)). (Illus.). 320p. 1986. pap. 15.00 o.p. (ISBN 0-318-21946-8, S/N 024-010-00672-2). USGPO.

Ecological Crisis: Readings for Survival. Glen A. Love & Rhoda M. Love. (Illus.). 1970. pap. text ed. 10.95 o.p. (ISBN 0-15-518778-3, HC). HarBraceJ.

Ecological Diversity. E. C. Pielou. LC 75-9663. 176p. 1975. 29.95 o.p. (ISBN 0-317-54716-X). Krieger.

Ecological Energetics. Ed. by Richard G. Wiegert. LC 75-30762. (Benchmark Papers in Ecology: Vol. 4). 448p. 1976. 69.50 o.p. (ISBN 0-12-787763-0). Acad Pr.

Ecological Energetics of Homeotherms. James A. Gessaman. LC 72-80316. 155p. 1973. pap. 7.50 o.p. (ISBN 0-87421-053-4). Utah St U Pr.

Ecological Ethics & Politics. H. J. McCloskey. LC 82-3840. (Philosophy & Society Ser.). 176p. 1983. text ed. 30.95x o.p. (ISBN 0-8476-7111-9). Rowman.

Ecological Genetics. 4th ed. E. B. Ford. 1979. 29.95x o.p. (ISBN 0-412-16130-3, NO.6110, Pub. by Chapman & Hall). Routledge Chapman & Hall.

Ecological Interactions in the Soil Environment. Ed. by A. H. Fitter. (Illus.). 400p. 1985. pap. text ed. 57.00x o.p. (ISBN 0-632-01386-9). Blackwell Sci.

Ecological Principles for Economic Development. Raymond F. Dasmann et al. LC 72-8597. 252p. 1973. pap. 38.95 o.p. (ISBN 0-471-19606-1, Pub. by Wiley-Interscience). Wiley.

Ecological Processes in Coastal & Marine Systems. Ed. by R. J. Livingston. LC 79-12388. (Marine Science Ser.: Vol. 10). 560p. 1979. 89.50x o.p. (ISBN 0-306-40318-8, Plenum Pr). Plenum Pub.

Ecological Processes in Coastal Environments: Nineteenth Symposium of the British Ecological Society. Ed. by R. L. Jefferies & A. J. Davy. 684p. 1979. 121.95 o.p. (ISBN 0-470-26741-0). Halsted Pr.

Ecological Renewal. Paul E. Lutz & H. Paul Santmire. LC 76-179633. (Confrontation Bks.). 175p. 1972. pap. 0.50x o.p. (ISBN 0-8006-1450-X, Fortress). Augsburg Fortress.

Ecological Succession. Ed. by Frank B. Golley. LC 76-52930. (Benchmark Papers in Ecology Ser.: Vol. 5). 1982. 48.95 o.p. (ISBN 0-87933-256-5). Van Nos Reinhold.

Ecological Systems & the Environment. Theodore C. Foin, Jr. LC 75-25010. (Illus.). 640p. 1976. text ed. 25.95 o.p. (ISBN 0-395-20666-9). HM.

Ecological Transition. John W. Bennett. 1976. text ed. 29.00 o.p. (ISBN 0-08-017867-7); pap. text ed. 16.00 o.p. (ISBN 0-08-017868-5). Pergamon.

Ecology & Change: Rural Modernization in an American Community. C. Gregory Knight. 1974. 24.95 o.p. (ISBN 0-12-785435-5). Acad Pr.

Ecology & Coal Resource Development: Proceedings of the International Congress for Energy & the Ecosystem, University of North Dakota, June 12-16, 1978, 2 Vols. International Congress for Energy & the Ecosystem Staff. Ed. by Mohan K. Wali. LC 78-26238. 1980. 275.00 o.p. (ISBN 0-08-023863-7). Pergamon.

Ecology & Environmental Planning. J. M. Edington & M. A. Edington. 1977. 33.00 o.p. (ISBN 0-412-13300-8, NO.6095, Pub. by Chapman & Hall). Routledge Chapman & Hall.

Ecology & Evolutionary Biology: A Round Table on Research. Ed. by George W. Salt. LC 83-24088. (Illus.). vi, 130p. 1984. pap. text ed. 7.95x o.s.i. (ISBN 0-226-73443-9). U of Chicago Pr.

Ecology & Human Need. Thomas S. Derr. 1975. pap. 3.45 o.s.i. (ISBN 0-664-24806-3, Westminster). Westminster John Knox.

Ecology & Management of the World's Savannas. Ed. by J. C. Tothill & J. J. Mott. 384p. 1985. pap. text ed. 49.95 o.p. (ISBN 0-85198-535-1). CAB Intl.

Ecology & Phytogeography of High Altitude Plants of the Northwest Himalayas. M. S. Mani. 1979. 41.95x o.p. (ISBN 0-412-15710-1, NO.6186, Pub. by Chapman & Hall). Routledge Chapman & Hall.

Ecology in the Antarctic. Ed. by W. N. Bonner & R. J. Berry. (Linnean Society of London). 1981. 29.50 o.p. (ISBN 0-12-114950-1). Acad Pr.

Ecology of Animals. 3rd ed. C. S. Elton. 1977. pap. 7.95 o.p. (ISBN 0-412-20390-1, NO. 6099, Pub. by Chapman & Hall). Routledge Chapman & Hall.

Ecology of Faith. Joseph Sittler. LC 61-10278. 112p. 1970. pap. 0.50 o.p. (ISBN 0-8006-1882-3, 1-1882, Fortress). Augsburg Fortress.

Ecology of Fossils: An Illustrated Guide. Ed. by W. Stuart McKerrow. (Illus.). 1978. text ed. 37.50x o.p. (ISBN 0-262-13144-7); pap. 12.50 o.p. (ISBN 0-262-63086-9). MIT Pr.

Ecology of Fresh Waters. Brian Moss. LC 80-11259. 332p. 1980. pap. 41.95 o.p. (ISBN 0-470-26942-1). Halsted Pr.

Ecology of Halophytes. Robert J. Reimold & William H. Queen. 1974. 70.50 o.p. (ISBN 0-12-586450-7). Acad Pr.

Ecology of Insect Populations in Theory & Practice. L. R. Clark et al. 1974. pap. 13.95 o.p. (ISBN 0-412-21170-X, NO.6059, Pub. by Chapman & Hall). Routledge Chapman & Hall.

Ecology of Lake St. Clair Wetlands: A Community Profile. Charles E. Herdendorf et al. LC 86-600404. (Biological Report Ser.: No. 85(7-7)). (Illus.). 203p. 1986. pap. 10.00 o.p. (ISBN 0-318-22374-0, S/N 024-010-00673-1). USGPO.

Ecology of Pools 19 & 20, Upper Mississippi River: A Community Profile. Larry A. Jahn & Richard V. Anderson. LC 86-600373. (Interior Department Biological Report: No. 85(7.6)). (Illus.). 154p. 1986. pap. 8.00 o.p. (ISBN 0-318-22448-8, S/N 024-010-00674-9). USGPO.

Ecology of Populations. 2nd ed. Arthur S. Boughey. (Illus.). 192p. 1973. pap. text ed. write for info. o.p. (ISBN 0-02-312730-9, 31273). Macmillan.

Ecology of Public Administration & Management in Africa. African Association for Public Administration & Management Staff. 303p. 1986. text ed. 45.00x o.p. (ISBN 0-7069-2867-9, Pub. by Vikas India). Advent NY.

Ecology of Resource Degradation & Renewal. M. J. Chadwick & G. T. Goodman. LC 75-5776. (British Ecological Society Symposia Ser.). 480p. 1976. 69.95x o.p. (ISBN 0-470-14295-2). Halsted Pr.

Ecology of Salt Marshes & Sand Dunes. D. S. Ranwell. (Illus.). 1972. 39.95 o.p. (ISBN 0-412-10500-4, NO.6305, Pub. by Chapman & Hall). Routledge Chapman & Hall.

Ecology of Small Mammals. Ed. by D. M. Stoddart. 386p. 1979. 49.95 o.p. (ISBN 0-412-14790-4, NO.6277, Pub. by Chapman & Hall England). Routledge Chapman & Hall.

Ecology of Soil Fungi. D. M. Griffin. LC 72-247. (Illus.). 208p. 1972. text ed. 19.95x o.p. (ISBN 0-8156-5035-3). Syracuse U Pr.

Ecology of Steak & Eggs: A Homo Sapiens' Viewpoint. Rod Collier. LC 73-82084. 1972. 4.00 o.p. (ISBN 0-682-47384-7). Exposition-Phoenix.

Ecology of Sumatra. Anthony J. Whitten et al. (Illus.). xiv, 587p. 1987. 45.00x o.p. (ISBN 0-317-65222-2); pap. 22.00x o.p. (ISBN 0-317-65223-0). Sinauer Assocs.

Ecology of Vertebrate Olfaction. D. M. Stoddart. 240p. 1980. 45.00x o.p. (ISBN 0-412-21820-8, NO.2884, Pub. by Chapman & Hall England). Routledge Chapman & Hall.

Ecology, Pollution & Environment. Amos Turk et al. 1972. pap. text ed. 16.95 o.p. (ISBN 0-7216-8925-6, CBS C). SCP.

ECONOCALC (TM) Project & Venture Economics & Analysis. Mack Atcheson & John Mills. LC 85-7648. 200p. 1985. incl. floppy disk 550.00x o.p. (ISBN 0-87201-239-5). Gulf Pub.

Econometric Estimation of Cost Functions for the Regulated Transportation Industries. Richard H. Spady. LC 78-75058. (Outstanding Dissertations in Economics Ser.). 1979. lib. bdg. 31.00 o.p. (ISBN 0-8240-4135-6). Garland Pub.

Econometric Model of Income Distribution. C. E. Metcalf. 1972. 21.50 o.p. (ISBN 0-12-492450-6). Acad Pr.

Econometric Studies of Japan. Ed. by Richard Kosobud & Ryishin Minami. LC 76-30360. 512p. 1977. 32.95 o.p. (ISBN 0-252-00255-5). U of Ill Pr.

Econometrics of Investment. J. C. Rowley & P. K. Trivedi. LC 74-32176. (Monographs in Applied Econometrics). 205p. 1975. 73.95 o.p. (ISBN 0-471-74361-5). Wiley.

Economia de los Paises Latinoamericanos. Ed. by L. Klochkovski. 504p. (Span.). 1978. 9.45 o.p. (ISBN 0-8285-1418-6, Pub. by Progress Pubs USSR). Imported Pubns.

Economic Analysis of an Urban Housing Market. John F. McDonald. LC 79-20969. (Studies in Urban Economics). 1979. 34.50 o.p. (ISBN 0-12-483360-8). Acad Pr.

Economic Analysis of Forestry Projects: Case Studies. Hans Gregerson & Arnoldo H. Contreras. (Forestry Papers: No. 17). 208p. (Eng., Fr. & Span., 2nd Printing 1981). 1979. pap. 14.00 o.p. (ISBN 92-5-100827-2, F1907, FAO). UNIPUB.

Economic Analysis of Pressing Social Problems. 2nd ed. Uad Phillips & H. L. Yotey. 1977. pap. 14.95 o.p. (ISBN 0-395-30696-5). HM.

Economic & Demographic Change in Preindustrial Japan, 1600-1868. Susan B. Hanley & Kozo Yamamura. LC 77-71983. 1978. 48.50x o.p. (ISBN 0-691-03111-8); pap. 19.50x o.p. (ISBN 0-691-10055-1). Princeton U Pr.

Economic & Financial Analysis of Capital Investments. G. T. Stevens, Jr. LC 78-27851. 386p. 1979. 52.50 o.p. (ISBN 0-471-04851-8). Wiley.

Economic & Monetary Union in Europe: The Economic Implications of Monetary Integration. Geoffrey Denton. LC 74-18622. 118p. 1975. 29.95x o.p. (ISBN 0-470-20940-2). Halsted Pr.

Economic & Social Analysis of Projects & of Price Policy: The Morocco Fourth Agricultural Credit Project. Kevin M. Cleaver. (Working Paper: No. 369). 59p. 1980. pap. 3.50 o.p. (ISBN 0-686-39650-2, WP-0369). World Bank.

Economic & Social Aspects of Transportation. (Transportation Research Report Ser.). 64p. 1980. 8.20 o.p. (ISBN 0-309-03056-0). Transport Res Bd.

Economic & Social Development of Merseyside. Sheila Marriner. (Illus.). 176p. 1982. 28.00 o.p. (ISBN 0-7099-0260-3, Pub. by Croom Helm Ltd). Routledge Chapman & Hall.

Economic & Social History of Britain, 1760-1970. Trevor May. LC 86-143. (Illus.). 360p. 1987. text ed. 24.95 o.p. (ISBN 0-582-35281-9); pap. text ed. 14.95 o.p. (ISBN 0-582-35280-0). Longman.

Economic & Social Problems of the Machine Age. Arthur B. Anthony. LC 30-24166. 79p. 1984. Repr. of 1930 ed. lib. bdg. 19.95x o.p. (ISBN 0-89370-860-7). Borgo Pr.

Economic & Social Survey of Asia & the Pacific. United Nations Staff. 80p. 1979. pap. 14.00 o.p. (ISBN 0-685-20776-5, 80.II.F.1). UN.

Economic & Social Survey of Asia & the Pacific. new ed. United Nations Staff. 1980. pap. 11.00 o.p. (ISBN 0-686-84897-7, 81.11.F.1.). UN.

Economic & Social Survey of Asia & the Pacific, 1979. 33rd ed. LC 76-643956. (Illus.). 161p. (Orig.). 1982. pap. 14.00x o.p. (ISBN 0-8002-3009-4). Intl Pubns Serv.

Economic & Social Survey of Asia & the Pacific, 1976. 30th annual ed. United Nations Staff. LC 76-643956. 1978. 9.50x o.p. (ISBN 0-8002-1056-5, E.77.11.F.1). UN.

Economic & Social Survey of Asia & the Pacific, 1977. 31st ed. United Nations Staff. LC 76-643956. (Illus.). 104p. (Orig.). 1982. pap. 8.00x o.p. (ISBN 0-8002-1057-3, E.78.11.F.1). UN.

Economic & Social Survey of Asia & the Pacific, 1978. 32nd ed. United Nations Staff. LC 76-643956. (Illus.). 167p. (Orig.). 1982. pap. 12.00x o.p. (ISBN 0-8002-1058-1, E.79.11.F.1). UN.

Economic & Social Survey of Asia & the Pacific, 1980. 34th ed. United Nations Staff. LC 76-643956. (Illus.). 143p. (Orig.). 1983. pap. 11.00x o.p. (ISBN 0-8002-3111-2, E.81.11.F.1). UN.

Economic & Social Survey of Chamber of Commerce Japan, Asia & Pacific. United Nations Staff. 1982. 19.00x o.s.i. (ISBN 0-317-27017-6). Intl Pubns Serv.

Economic & Social Transformation in Rural Kenya. John Carlsen. (Centre for Development Research Ser.: No. 4). (Illus.). 230p. 1983. pap. 12.50 o.p. (ISBN 0-8419-9759-4, Africana). Holmes & Meier.

Economic Anxiety & Christian Faith. Larry L. Rasmussen. LC 80-67795. 96p. (Orig.). 1981. pap. 5.95 o.p. (ISBN 0-8066-1857-4, 10-1994, Augsburg). Augsburg Fortress.

Economic Appraisal of Rural Roads: Simplified Operational Procedures for Screening & Appraisal. H. L. Beenhakker & A. M. Lago. (Working Paper Ser.: No. 610). 236p. 1983. 12.95 o.p. (ISBN 0-8213-0250-7, WP 0610). World Bank.

Economic Aspects of Natural Hazards. Alan L. Sorkin. LC 79-48027. (Illus.). 1982. 35.00x o.p. (ISBN 0-669-03639-0). Lexington Bks.

Economic Atlas of Ontario: Atlas Economique de l'Ontario. Ed. by W. G. Dean. LC 73-653512. (Illus.). 1969. 100.00x o.p. (ISBN 0-8020-3235-4). U of Toronto Pr.

Economic Botany. 2nd ed. Albert F. Hill. (Botanical Sciences Ser.). (Illus.). 1952. text ed. 47.95 o.p. (ISBN 0-07-028789-9). McGraw.

Economic Bulletin for Africa, Vol. 12, No. 1. United Nations Staff. pap. 7.00 o.p. (ISBN 92-1-125039-0, 76.II.K.6). UN.

Economic Bulletin for Asia & the Pacific. United Nations Staff. Vol. 29, No. 2. pap. 12.50 o.p. (ISBN 0-685-20773-0, E.79.II.F.9); Vol. 30, No. 2. pap. 10.00 o.p. (ISBN 0-686-66557-0, E, 81.II.F.5); Vol. 30, No. 2. 10.00 o.p. (ISBN 0-686-86823-4, E, 81.II.F.5); Vol. 31, No. 1. 10.00 o.p. (E.81.II.F.12). UN.

Economic Bulletin for Europe, Vol. 34/2. UNECE Staff. 1982. pap. 28.00 o.p. (ISBN 0-08-027946-5). Pergamon.

Economic Change in Rural China. Luo Hanxian. (China Studies). (Illus.). 217p. 1985. text ed. 9.95 o.p. (ISBN 0-8351-1640-9); pap. 6.95 o.p. (ISBN 0-8351-1525-9). China Bks.

Economic Co-operation in the Commonwealth. G. Arnold. 1967. 34.00 o.p. (ISBN 0-08-012449-6); pap. 50.00 o.p. (ISBN 0-08-012448-8). Pergamon.

Economic Concentration & the Monopoly Problem. Edward S. Mason. LC 57-6351. 1964. 1.95 o.p. (ISBN 0-689-70137-3, 47, Atheneum). Macmillan.

Economic Concentration: Structure, Behavior & Public Policy. John M. Blair. (Harbrace Business & Economics Ser.). (Illus.). 832p. 1972. text ed. 20.95 o.p. (ISBN 0-15-518781-3, HC). HarBraceJ.

Economic Consequences & Future Implications of Population Growth in China. Robert F. Dernberger. LC 81-15119. (Papers of the East-West Population Institute Ser.: No. 76). v, 32p. (Orig.). 1981. pap. text ed. 1.00 o.p. (ISBN 0-86638-015-9). EW Ctr HI.

Economic Crisis & American Society. Manuel Castells. LC 79-3194. (Illus.). 285p. 1980. 29.50 o.p. (ISBN 0-691-04220-9); pap. 10.50x o.p. (ISBN 0-691-00361-0). Princeton U Pr.

Economic Crisis, Trade Unions & the State. Ed. by Otto Jacobi et al. LC 85-28055. 304p. 1986. 34.50 o.p. (ISBN 0-7099-1447-4, Pub. by Croom Helm Ltd). Routledge Chapman & Hall.

Economic Cycle: Postwar Developments. S. Menshikov. 390p. 1975. 5.45 o.p. (ISBN 0-8285-0355-9, Pub. by Progress Pubs USSR). Imported Pubns.

Economic Decision-Making Structures & Processes in Hungary: The Dilemmas of Decentralization. Peter Knight. LC 84-11955. (World Bank Staff Working Papers: No. 648). 1985. 5.00 o.p. (ISBN 0-8213-0375-9). World Bank.

Economic Development. John Kenneth Galbraith. LC 64-18762. 1964. 9.95x o.s.i. (ISBN 0-674-22701-8). Harvard U Pr.

Economic Development. rev. ed. Benjamin Higgins. (Illus.). 1968. 17.95x o.p. (ISBN 0-393-09714-5, NortonC). Norton.

Economic Development. Llewellyn M. Mullings & James Fenner. 157p. 1971. pap. text ed. 6.95x o.p. (ISBN 0-8422-0132-7). Irvington.

Economic Development & Regional Cooperation: Kuwait. Ragaei El Mallakh. LC 68-20512. (Publications of the Center for Middle Eastern Studies Ser.). 1968. lib. bdg. 11.50x o.s.i. (ISBN 0-226-20157-0). U of Chicago Pr.

Economic Development & the Use of Energy Resources in Communist China. Yuan-li Wu. LC 63-15122. (Publications Ser.: No. 30). 275p. 1963. 12.95x o.p. (ISBN 0-8179-1301-7). Hoover Inst Pr.

Economic Development in Namibia: Toward Acceptable Development Strategies for Independent Namibia. Wolfgang H. Thomas. 368p. 1984. pap. text ed. 16.95x o.p. (ISBN 3-7867-0714-6). Transaction Pubs.

Economic Development in the Soviet Union. Stanley H. Cohn. LC 74-114433. (Illus.). 1970. 29.00x o.p. (ISBN 0-8290-1387-3). Irvington.

Economic Development in the Third World. 3rd ed. Michael P. Todaro. LC 84-9722. Orig. Title: Economic Development in the Third World Second Ed. 672p. 1985. text ed. 29.95 o.p. (ISBN 0-582-28500-3). Longman.

Economic Development in the Third World Second Ed. see Economic Development in the Third World.

Economic Development in the Tropics. 3rd ed. B. W. Hodder. 255p. 1980. 11.95x o.p. (ISBN 0-416-74250-5, NO.2013); pap. 9.95x o.p. (ISBN 0-416-74260-2, NO.2012). Routledge Chapman & Hall.

Economic Development of Communist Yugoslavia, 1947-1964. Joseph T. Bombelles. LC 68-28098. (Publications Ser.: No. 73). (Illus., Orig.). 1968. 9.95x o.p. (ISBN 0-8179-1731-4); pap. 6.95x o.p. (ISBN 0-8179-1732-2). Hoover Inst Pr.

Economic Development of Libya. Ed. by Bichara Khader & Bashir El-Wifati. 288p. 1986. 39.00 o.p. (ISBN 0-7099-3111-5, Pub. by Croom Helm Ltd). Routledge Chapman & Hall.

Economic Development of Medieval Europe. Robert-Henri Bautier. Ed. by Geoffrey Barraclough. LC 73-74198. (History of European Civilization Library). (Illus.). 286p. 1971. pap. text ed. 8.00 o.p. (ISBN 0-15-518780-5, HC). HarBraceJ.

Economic Development of Syria. E. Kanovasky. 181p. 1977. pap. 4.95x o.p. (ISBN 0-87855-669-9). Transaction Pubs.

Economic Development of Western Civilization see European Economic History.

Economic Development Planning in Ghana. Kodwo Ewusi. LC 73-82085. 1973. 6.00 o.p. (ISBN 0-682-47750-8, University). Exposition-Phoenix.

Economic Development Projects in the Arab World & Iran: 1978. Arab World & Iran Business Guides. 1978. pap. 20.00 o.p. (ISBN 0-931000-02-5). Suburban Pub CT.

Economic Doctrines of Knut Wicksell. Carl G. Uhr. (Institute of Business & Economic Research UC Berkeley). 1960. 48.50x o.p. (ISBN 0-520-01290-9). U of Cal Pr.

Economic Dynamics. 3rd ed. William J. Baumol. (Illus.). 1970. text ed. write for info. o.p. (ISBN 0-02-306660-1, 30666). Macmillan.

Economic Education: A Guide to Information Sources. Ed. by Catherine A. Hughes. LC 73-17576. (Economics Information Guide Ser.: Vol. 6). 280p. 1977. 68.00x o.p. (ISBN 0-8103-1290-5). Gale.

Economic Efficiency & Air Pollution Control. Anthony C. Fisher. LC 81-17464. (East-West Environment & Policy Institute Research Report: No. 8). v, 74p. (Orig.). 1981. pap. text ed. 3.00 o.p. (ISBN 0-86638-030-2). EW Ctr HI.

Economic Evaluation of Soviet Socialism. Alan Abouchar. (Pergamon Policy Studies). 1979. 40.00 o.p. (ISBN 0-08-023870-X). Pergamon.

Economic Facts, 4 Vols. National Research Council Staff. LC 78-74325. (Modern Chinese Economy Ser.: Vol. 11). 1980. Set. lib. bdg. 200.00 o.p. (ISBN 0-8240-4260-3). Garland Pub.

Economic Fictions. Paul K. Crosser. 320p. 1957. (ISBN 0-8022-0320-5). Philos Lib.

Economic Forecasts: Election Years & the Media. Media Institute Staff. LC 84-62181. (Media Research Ser.). (Illus.). 54p. (Orig.). 1984. pap. 10.00 o.p. (ISBN 0-937790-25-7). Media Inst.

Economic Geography. 2nd ed. John W. Alexander & L. Gibson. 1978. text ed. (ISBN 0-13-225151-5). P-H.

Economic Geography of the World. Ed. by V. Maksakovsky. (Illus.). 1978. 10.00 o.p. (ISBN 0-8285-0002-9, Pub. by Progress Pubs USSR). Imported Pubns.

Economic Geography: Theory & Methods. Y. G. Saushkin. 312p. 1980. 8.95 o.p. (ISBN 0-8285-1721-5, Pub. by Progress Pubs USSR). Imported Pubns.

Economic Geology & Geotectonics. Ed. by D. H. Tarling. LC 81-673. 213p. 1981. 58.95x o.p. (ISBN 0-470-27145-0). Halsted Pr.

Economic Growth & Environmental Decay: The Solution Becomes the Problem. Paul W. Barkley & David Seckler. 193p. 1972. pap. text ed. 10.00 o.p. (ISBN 0-15-518795-3, HC). HarBraceJ.

Economic Growth & Residential Patterns: A Methodological Investigation. James W. Hughes. 216p. 1972. pap. 8.00x o.p. (ISBN 0-87855-555-2). Transaction Pubs.

Economic Growth & Stability: An Analysis of Economic Change & Policies. Gottfried Haberler. (Principles of Freedom Ser.). 319p. 1980. text ed. 10.50x o.p. (ISBN 0-8402-1337-9). Humanities.

Economic Growth & Structure. Simon Kuznets. 1965. 13.95x o.p. (ISBN 0-393-09475-8, NortonC). Norton.

Economic Growth & the Generation of Waterborne Wastes. (Marine Technical Report: No. 12). 1973. pap. 1.00 o.p. (ISBN 0-686-23174-0). Sea Grant Pubns.

Economic Growth Debate. E. J. Mishan. 1977. pap. text ed. 11.95 o.p. (ISBN 0-04-330281-5). Unwin Hyman.

Economic Growth in China & India, 1952-70. Subramanian Swamy. 1973. 10.00X o.s.i. (ISBN 0-226-78315-4). U of Chicago Pr.

Economic Growth in Japan & the U. S. S. R. Angus Maddison. LC 70-78065. 1969. pap. text ed. 4.95x o.p. (ISBN 0-393-09870-2, NortonC). Norton.

Economic Guidelines for Justifying Capital Purchases: With Numerical Control Emphasis. Wilbert Steffy et al. (Illus.). 149p. 1977. 12.00 o.p. (ISBN 0-938654-15-2, ECO G). Indus Dev Inst Sci.

Economic Handbook of the World: 1981. Arthur S. Banks et al. 608p. 1981. text ed. 49.95 o.p. (ISBN 0-07-003691-8). McGraw.

Economic Healing. rev. ed. A. R. E. New York Members Staff. 29p. 1974. pap. 1.50 o.p. (ISBN 0-87604-074-1). ARE Pr.

Economic History of Canada: A Guide to Information Sources. Trevor J. Dick. LC 73-17571. (Economics Information Guide Ser.: Vol. 9). 192p. 1978. 68.00x o.p. (ISBN 0-8103-1292-1). Gale.

Economic History of England: The Eighteenth Century. Thomas S. Ashton. 270p. 1972. pap. 13.95x o.p. (ISBN 0-416-57360-6, NO.2065). Routledge Chapman & Hall.

Economic History of the British Building History: 1815-1979. C. G. Powell. LC 81-16830. 1982. pap. 10.95x o.p. (ISBN 0-416-32010-4, NO. 3593). Routledge Chapman & Hall.

Economic History of the Middle East: A Book of Readings. Ed. by Charles Issawi. LC 66-11883. (Midway Reprints Ser). 1976. pap. text ed. 22.00x o.s.i. (ISBN 0-226-38609-0). U of Chicago Pr.

Economic Illusion: False Choices Between Prosperity & Social Justice. Robert Kuttner. 300p. 1984. 19.45 o.p. (ISBN 0-395-35347-5). HM.

Economic Incentives for Clean Air: Proceedings, San Francisco, Ca., Jan, 1981. Air Pollution Control Association Specialty Conference. 288p. 1981. 17.00 o.p. (ISBN 0-318-12251-0, SP-41); members 13.00 o.p. (ISBN 0-318-12252-9). Air & Waste.

Economic Inquiries & Studies, 2 Vols. Robert Giffen. (Development of Industrial Society Ser.). 942p. 1971. Repr. of 1904 ed. 67.50x o.p. (ISBN 0-7165-1758-2, BBA 03545, Pub. by Irish Academic Pr). Biblio Dist.

Economic Integration among Unequal Partners: The Case of the Andean Group. Alicia Puyana De Palacios. (Pergamon Policy Studies on International Development). (Illus.). 300p. 1982. 105.00 o.p. (ISBN 0-08-028822-7). Pergamon.

Economic Issues & Policies: Readings in Introductory Economics. 3rd ed. John E. Elliott & Arthur Grey. 1975. pap. 17.95 o.p. (ISBN 0-395-19824-0). HM.

Economic Library of Jacob H. Hollander. Jacob H. Hollander. Ed. by Elsie A. Marsh. LC 67-14032. 340p. 1966. Repr. of 1937 ed. 40.00x o.p. (ISBN 0-8103-3103-9). Gale.

Economic Life of the Ancient World. Jean-Phillippe Levy. Ed. by John G. Biram. LC 67-20575. 1967. lib. bdg. 10.00x o.s.i. (ISBN 0-226-47641-3). U of Chicago Pr.

Economic Man in Sha Tin: Vegetable Gardeners in a Hong Kong Valley. Goran Aijmer. (Scandanavian Institute of Asian Studies Monograph: No. 43). (Orig.). 1980. pap. text ed. 12.50x o.p. (ISBN 0-7007-0135-4). Humanities.

Economic Models: An Exposition. E. F. Beach. LC 57-10800. 227p. 1957. text ed. 14.50 o.p. (ISBN 0-471-06072-0, Pub. by Wiley). Krieger.

Economic Models, Estimation & Risk Programming: Essays in Honor of Gerhard Tintner. Ed. by K. A. Fox et al. LC 72-98260. (Lecture Notes in Operations Research & Mathematical Economics: Vol. 15). 1969. pap. 21.90 o.p. (ISBN 0-387-04638-0). Springer-Verlag.

Economic Modernization of France Seventeen Thirty to Eighteen Eighty. Roger Price. LC 75-14447. 235p. 1975. 19.50 o.p. (ISBN 0-470-69722-9, Pub. by Wiley). Krieger.

Economic Neocolonialism. L. L. Kolchkovsky. 309p. 1975. 5.45 o.p. (ISBN 0-8285-0358-3, Pub. by Progress Pubs USSR). Imported Pubns.

Economic Opportunity & Crime. Marvin Ross. 1977. pap. text ed. 12.20x o.p. (ISBN 0-685-87412-5). Gower Pub Co.

Economic Policy & Industrial Growth in Pakistan. Stephen R. Lewis, Jr. 1969. 25.00x o.p. (ISBN 0-262-12031-3). MIT Pr.

Economic Policy & Planning in India. Ed. by A. K. Singh et al. 488p. 1985. text ed. 60.00x o.p. (ISBN 0-86590-339-5, Pub. by Sterling Pubs India). Apt Bks.

Economic Policy Beyond the Headlines. George P. Shultz & Kenneth W. Dam. (Illus.). 240p. 1980. pap. 4.95 o.p. (ISBN 0-393-00988-2). Norton.

Economic Policy in an Interdependent World. Richard N. Cooper. (Illus.). 352p. 1985. text ed. 30.00x o.p. (ISBN 0-262-03113-2). MIT Pr.

Economic Policy Reform in Mexico: A Case Study for Developing Countries. Leopoldo Solis. LC 80-26937. (Pergamon Press Series on International Development). 240p. 1981. 60.00 o.p. (ISBN 0-08-026330-5). Pergamon.

Economic Problem. 6th ed. Robert L. Heilbroner & L. Thurow. 1981. pap. text ed. (ISBN 0-13-233304-X). P-H.

Economic Problem. 7th ed. Robert L. Heilbroner & Lester C. Thurow. (Illus.). 704p. 1984. text ed. (ISBN 0-13-233221-3); pap. text ed. (ISBN 0-13-233214-0). P-H.

Economic Problem: (Third CPCU Edition) 6th ed. Robert L. Heilbroner & Lester C. Thurow. LC 83-9556. 670p. 1984. Repr. of 1981 ed. text ed. 30.00 o.p. (ISBN 0-13-233198-5). Am Inst Property.

Economic Problems of Latin America. John M. Hunter & James W. Foley. 1975. text ed. 26.95 o.p. (ISBN 0-395-18941-1). HM.

Economic Recovery Tax Act of Nineteen Eighty-One: Supplement to Accompany the 1982 Annual Edition of West's Federal Taxation. William H. Hoffman. 72p. 1981. 32.75 o.p. (ISBN 0-314-64025-8). West Pub.

Economic Reform & Income Distribution. Henryk Flakierski. LC 85-26048. 224p. 1986. 35.00 o.p. (ISBN 0-87332-371-8). M E Sharpe.

Economic Reforms in Eastern Europe & Prospects for the 1980s: NATO Colloquium, Brussels, 1980. NATO Staff. (Illus.). 325p. 1981. 115.00 o.p. (ISBN 0-08-026801-3). Pergamon.

Economic Relations Between West Asia & Southeast Asia. Ed. by Lee Soo Ann. 256p. 1978. pap. text ed. 30.00 o.p. (ISBN 0-566-04003-4, Pub. by Inst Southeast Asian Stud). Gower Pub Co.

Economic Report of the President, 1986. 382p. pap. 8.50 o.p. (ISBN 0-318-19972-6, S/N 040-000-00492-1). USGPO.

Economic Report of the President, 1987. (Illus.). 372p. (Orig.). 1987. pap. 10.00 o.p. (ISBN 0-318-22375-9, S/N 040-000-00507-2). USGPO.

Economic Sanctions: Ideals & Experience. M. S. Daoudi & M. S. Dajani. (International Library of Economics). 244p. 1983. 26.95x o.p. (ISBN 0-7100-9583-X). Routledge Chapman & Hall.

Economic Stabilization in Latin America: Political Dimensions. Ed. by Alejandro Foxley & Laurence Whitehead. 120p. 1980. pap. 20.00 o.p. (ISBN 0-08-026788-2). Pergamon.

Economic Studies: Contributions to the Critique of Economic Theory. David P. Levine. 1977. 35.00x o.p. (ISBN 0-7100-8573-7). Routledge Chapman & Hall.

Economic Study of Chinese Agriculture. Chi-Yu Tang. LC 78-74306. (Modern Chinese Economy Ser.: Vol. 14). 514p. 1980. lib. bdg. 67.00 o.p. (ISBN 0-8240-4262-X). Garland Pub.

Economic Study of Roadway Lighting. (National Cooperative Highway Research Program Report). 77p. 1966. 3.20 o.p. (ISBN 0-317-36076-0, 1219). Transport Res Bd.

Economic Survey of Europe. 1982. 27.00x o.p. (ISBN 0-8002-3899-0, United Nations). Intl Pubns Serv.

Economic Survey of Europe. United Nations Staff. 1979. pap. 17.00 o.p. (ISBN 0-685-20777-3, E.80.II.E.1). UN.

Economic Survey of Europe. United Nations Staff. 1980. pap. 17.00 o.p. (ISBN 0-686-84901-9, E.81.II.E.1). UN.

Economic Survey of Europe in 1979. 32nd ed. United Nations Staff. LC 48-10193. (Illus.). 227p. (Orig.). 1982. pap. 17.00x o.p. (ISBN 0-8002-1062-X, E.80.11.E.1). UN.

Economic Survey of Europe in 1980. 33rd ed. United Nations Staff. LC 48-10193. (Illus.). 241p. (Orig.). 1982. pap. 17.00x o.p. (ISBN 0-8002-1063-8, E.81.11.E.1). UN.

Economic Survey of Latin America & the Caribbean, 1982, Vol. II. 186p. 1984. 13.00 o.p. (ISBN 92-1-121079-8, E.84.11.G.1). UN.

Economic Survey of Latin America 1977. United Nations Staff. LC 50-3616. 462p. 1977. pap. 22.00x o.p. (ISBN 0-8002-1066-2, E.79.11.G.1). UN.

Economic Survey of Latin America 1979. United Nations Staff. LC 50-3616. (Illus.). 534p. (Orig.). 1981. pap. 29.00x o.p. (ISBN 0-8002-1069-7, E.81.11.G.1). UN.

Economic Survey of Latin America, 1980. United Nations Staff. LC 50-3616. (Illus.). 585p. (Orig.). 1982. 29.00x o.p. (ISBN 0-8002-1070-0, E.82.11.G.1). UN.

Economic Theory & the Cities. J. V. Henderson. 1978. 34.50 o.p. (ISBN 0-12-340350-2). Acad Pr.

Economic Theory & the Core. Lester G. Telser. LC 77-21151. (Illus.). 1978. lib. bdg. 36.00x o.s.i. (ISBN 0-226-79191-2). U of Chicago Pr.

Economic Theory of Business Strategy: An Essay in Dynamics. Scott J. Moss. LC 81-6751. 300p. 1981. 37.95x o.p. (ISBN 0-470-27264-3). Halsted Pr.

Economic Theory of Price Indices: Two Essays on the Effects of Taste, Quality & Technological Change. Franklin M. Fisher & Karl Shell. (Economic Theory & Mathematical Economics Ser). 1972. 14.95 o.p. (ISBN 0-12-257750-7). Acad Pr.

Economic Theory: The Elementary Relations of Economic Life. David P. Levine. 1978. 35.00x o.p. (ISBN 0-7100-8837-X). Routledge Chapman & Hall.

Economic Theory: The System of Economic Relations As a Whole, Vol. II. David Levine. 320p. 1981. 35.00x o.p. (ISBN 0-7100-0948-8). Routledge Chapman & Hall.

Economic Transformation of America. Robert L. Heilbroner & Aaron Singer. LC 76-24990. (Illus.). 276p. (Orig.). 1977. pap. text ed. 10.95 o.p. (ISBN 0-15-518800-3, HC). HarBraceJ.

Economic Transformation of American Cities. Thierry J. Noyelle & Thomas M. Stanback, Jr. LC 83-21292. (Conservation of Human Resources Ser.: Vol. 19). 298p. 1984. 32.95x o.s.i. (ISBN 0-86598-144-2, Rowman & Allanheld). Rowman.

Economic Transformation of Cuba. Edward Boorstein. LC 68-13652. 306p. 1969. pap. 5.95 o.p. (ISBN 0-85345-095-1). Monthly Rev.

Economic Trends & Problems in the Early Republican Period: 1931. Institute of Pacific Relations Staff. LC 78-74312. (Modern Chinese Economy Ser.: Vol. 25). 537p. 1980. lib. bdg. 67.00 o.p. (ISBN 0-8240-4273-5). Garland Pub.

Economic Trends in the Republic of China, 1912-1949. Albert Feuerwerker. (Michigan Monographs in Chinese Studies: No. 31). 1977. pap. 6.00 o.s.i. (ISBN 0-89264-031-6). U of Mich Ctr Chinese.

Economic Viability of the Nuclear Industry: Proceedings, American Nuclear Society Executive Conference. 392p. 45.00 o.p. (ISBN 0-89448-304-8, 650007). Am Nuclear Soc.

Economic Workbooks & Data. D. I. Trotman-Dickenson. 1969. 26.00 o.p. (ISBN 0-08-012958-7); pap. 10.25 o.p. (ISBN 0-08-012957-9). Pergamon.

Economical Construction of Concrete Dams. Compiled by American Society of Civil Engineers Staff. 566p. 1972. pap. 20.00x o.p. (ISBN 0-87262-043-3). Am Soc Civil Eng.

Economical Economy. Jay Carlton. 64p. 1984. 6.00 o.p. (ISBN 0-682-40203-6). Exposition-Phoenix.

Economically Important Members of the Genus Liriomyza Mik: A Selected Bibliography. M. P. Parrella & K. L. Robb. (Miscellaneous Publications of the E.S.A. Ser.: No. 59). 32p. 1985. 7.50 o.p. (ISBN 0-318-04408-0). Entomol Soc.

Economics. Herman Berliner & Dominick Salvatore. (College Outlines Ser.). 1972. pap. 4.95 o.s.i. (ISBN 0-671-08029-6, 08029). Monarch Pr.

Economics. Martin Bronfenbrenner et al. Incl. Macroeconomics. LC 83-82353. 400p. 1983. pap. 22.95 o.p. (ISBN 0-395-34228-7); Microeconomics. LC 83-82354. 496p. 1983. pap. 22.95 o.p. (ISBN 0-395-34229-5). LC 83-82341. 848p. 1984. text ed. 38.95 o.p. (ISBN 0-395-34227-9). HM.

Economics. 3rd ed. Ralph T. Byrns & Gerald W. Stone. 1987. text ed. write for info. o.p. (ISBN 0-673-16675-9). Scott F.

Economics. 4th ed. Edwin G. Dolan. 944p. 1986. text ed. 33.95 o.s.i. (ISBN 0-03-005447-8); wkbk. 13.95 o.s.i. (ISBN 0-03-005449-4). Dryden Pr.

Economics. Robert B. Ekelund & Robert D. Tollison. 1986. text ed. (ISBN 0-673-39121-3); (ISBN 0-673-39122-1). Little.

Economics. Belton M. Fleisher & Thomas J. Kniesner. 528p. 1985. 26.00 o.s.i. (ISBN 0-205-11493-8, H1493-9); study guide 27.00 o.p. (ISBN 0-205-11494-6, H1494-7); instr's. manual avail. o.p. (ISBN 0-205-11495-4, H1495-4); transparencies avail. o.p. (ISBN 0-205-11496-2, H1496-2). Allyn.

Economics. Arnold Heertje et al. 480p. 1983. pap. text ed. 23.95 o.p. (ISBN 0-03-059336-0); study guide 11.95 o.p. (ISBN 0-03-062798-2). Dryden Pr.

Economics. Hyman. (Illus.). 1104p. 1989. 42.95 o.p. (ISBN 0-8016-2420-7); International ed. 24.95 o.p. (ISBN 0-8016-2839-3). Mosby.

Economics. 9th ed. Paul A. Samuelson. (Illus.). 928p. 1973. text ed. 32.95 o.p. (ISBN 0-07-054561-8, C). McGraw.

Economics. Lila F. Truett & Dale B. Truett. (Illus.). 848p. 1982. text ed. 34.00 o.p. (ISBN 0-314-63298-0). West Pub.

Economics see **How a Market Economy Works.**

Economics: A Student's Guide. John Beardshaw. (Illus.). 698p. 1984. pap. text ed. 34.00x o.p. (ISBN 0-7121-0598-0). Trans-Atl Phila.

Economics Abstracts International Online User Manual. 1983. 30.00 o.p. (ISBN 0-317-01044-1). Learned Info.

Economics, Accounting, & Property Theory. David P. Ellerman. LC 82-47648. 224p. 1982. 29.50x o.p. (ISBN 0-669-05552-2). Lexington Bks.

Economics: An Application of Logic. Barron. 1986. pap. 24.95 o.p. (ISBN 0-8016-3060-6); pap. 10.95 study guide o.p. (ISBN 0-8016-0426-5). Mosby.

Economics: An Introduction to Analysis & Policy. 10th ed. George L. Bach. (Illus.). 1980. text ed. 23.95 o.p. (ISBN 0-13-227231-8). P-H.

Economics & Ethics: A Christian Inquiry. J. P. Wogaman. LC 85-45478. 160p. 1986. pap. 9.95 o.p. (ISBN 0-8006-1904-8, 1-1904, Fortress). Augsburg Fortress.

Economics & Finance: Index to Periodical Articles, 1947-1971, 4 vols. Joint Bank-Fund Library (Washington, D. C.) Staff. 1972. Set. lib. bdg. 505.00 o.p. (ISBN 0-8161-0977-X, Hall Library). G K Hall.

Economics & Finance: Index to Periodical Articles, 1975-1976-1977. Joint Bank-Fund Library (Washington, D. C.) Staff. 1979. lib. bdg. 100.00 o.p. (ISBN 0-8161-0302-X, Hall Library). G K Hall.

Economics & Financial Management of Research Libraries: A Report on an Exploratory Meeting Sponsored by the Association of Research Libraries & the Research Libraries Group, Inc., October 14, 1981, Washington, D.C. 5.00 o.p. (ISBN 0-318-03473-5). Assn Res Lib.

Economics & Management of Food Processing. W. Smith Greig. (Illus.). 1984. 62.95 o.s.i. (ISBN 0-87055-449-2). AVI.

Economics & Operational Research. M. H. Beilby. 1976. 41.00 o.p. (ISBN 0-12-085750-2). Acad Pr.

Economics & Quantitative Economics. Ed. by David F. Hendry & Kenneth F. Wallis. 320p. 1985. 49.95x o.p. (ISBN 0-631-13797-1). Basil Blackwell.

Economics & Social Choice. 2nd ed. Jack W. Nickson, Jr. (Illus.). 352p. 1974. text ed. 22.95 o.p. (ISBN 0-07-046523-1). McGraw.

Economics & Social Problems. Max E. Fletcher. LC 78-69590. (Illus.). 1979. text ed. 29.56 o.p. (ISBN 0-395-26508-8). HM.

Economics & the Art of Controversy. John Kenneth Galbraith. 111p. 1980. Repr. of 1955 ed. lib. bdg. 16.50x o.p. (ISBN 0-374-92972-6, Octagon). Hippocrene Bks.

Economics & the Politics of Protection: Some Case Studies of Industries. Vincent Cable. (Staff Working Paper: No. 569). 80p. 1983. 5.00 o.p. (ISBN 0-8213-0199-3, WP 0569). World Bank.

Economics & the Private Interest: An Introduction to Microeconomics. 2nd ed. Richard T. Gill. LC 75-22754. 288p. 1976. pap. text ed. write for info. o.p. (ISBN 0-673-16161-7); write for info. o.p. Scott F.

Economics & the Public Purpose. John Kenneth Galbraith. 1973. 18.95 o.p. (ISBN 0-395-17206-3). HM.

Economics: Applications to Agriculture & Agribusiness. 3rd ed. Ewell P. Roy et al. 569p. 1981. 22.60 o.p. (ISBN 0-8134-2113-6, 2113); text ed. 16.95x o.p. Inter Print Pubs.

Economics: Concepts, Applications, Analysis. Roy J. Sampson & Thomas W. Calmus. 425p. 1974. text ed. 28.50 o.p. (ISBN 0-395-17812-6). HM.

Economics Explained. Robert L. Heilbroner & Lester Thurow. LC 81-20975. 256p. 1982. 12.95 o.p. (ISBN 0-13-229708-6); pap. 8.95 o.p. (ISBN 0-13-229690-X). P-H.

Economics Explained. Robert L. Heilbroner & Lester Thurow. 256p. 1986. pap. 8.95 o.s.i. (ISBN 0-671-62236-6, Touchstone Bks). S&S.

Economics for 'A' Level. D. J. Browne. (Illus.). 328p. 1983. pap. text ed. 17.95x o.p. (ISBN 0-7131-0866-5). Trans-Atl Phila.

Economics for Eastern Africa. 2nd ed. Ian Livingstone & H. W. Ord. (Orig.). 1981. pap. text ed. 22.50x o.p. (ISBN 0-435-97400-9). Heinemann Ed.

Economics for Professional Studies. 2nd ed. Henry Toch. (Illus.). 240p. 1977. pap. 18.95x o.p. (ISBN 0-7121-0568-9, Pub. by Macdonald & Evans England). Trans-Atl Phila.

Economics for the Profitable Mining & Marketing of Gold, Silver, Copper, Lead & Zinc Ores. Rodger D. Carlson. LC 81-40818. (Illus.). 88p. (Orig.). 1982. lib. bdg. 24.50 o.p. (ISBN 0-8191-2021-9); pap. text ed. 8.00 o.p. (ISBN 0-8191-2022-7). U Pr of Amer.

Economics in Canadian Society: Principles & Applications. 1985. 28.95 o.p. (ISBN 0-471-79778-2). Wiley.

Economics in One Lesson. Henry Hazlitt. 218p. 1982. pap. 6.95 o.p. (ISBN 0-517-54823-2, Arlington Hse). Crown.

Economics in the Real World: How Political Decisions Affect the Economy. Leonard Silk. 384p. 1985. 16.45 o.p. (ISBN 0-671-25030-2). S&S.

Economics of Abundance: A Primer of Economic Law. Francis L. Maus. LC 67-20668. (Orig.). 1967. pap. 1.75 o.p. (ISBN 0-87004-100-2). Caxton.

Economics of Adam Smith. Samuel Hollander. LC 72-185717. (Studies in Classical Political Economy Ser.). 320p. 1973. 30.00x o.p. (ISBN 0-8020-1811-4); pap. 9.95c o.p. (ISBN 0-8020-6302-0). U of Toronto Pr.

Economics of Aging. 3rd ed. James H. Shultz. 224p. 1985. 32.95 o.s.i. (ISBN 0-442-28132-3). Van Nos Reinhold.

Economics of Aging: The Future of Retirement. Ed. by Malcolm H. Morrison. 304p. 1981. 29.95 o.p. (ISBN 0-442-25553-5). Van Nos Reinhold.

Economics of Agricultural Policy. 2nd ed. Graham Hallett. LC 81-1192. 365p. 1981. 52.95x o.p. (ISBN 0-470-27157-4). Halsted Pr.

Economics of American Negro Slavery see **Time on the Cross: The Economics of Negro Slavery.**

Economics of Atomic Energy. M. S. Goldring. (Illus.). 192p. 1958. (ISBN 0-8022-0604-2). Philos Lib.

Economics of Common Currencies. Harry G. Johnson & Alexander K. Swoboda. LC 73-76382. 302p. 1973. text ed. 25.00x o.p. (ISBN 0-674-23226-7). Harvard U Pr.

Economics of Cyprus: A Survey to 1914. Diamond Jenness. (Illus.). 232p. 1962. 10.50x o.p. (ISBN 0-7735-0003-0, McGill Canada). U of Toronto Pr.

Economics of Development. Malcolm Gillis et al. 650p. 1983. text ed. 26.95x o.p. (ISBN 0-393-95253-3). Norton.

Economics of Development in Small Countries with Special Reference to the Caribbean. William G. Demas. (Keith Callard Lecture Ser). 1965. pap. 4.00 o.p. (ISBN 0-7735-0044-8, McGill Canada). U of Toronto Pr.

Economics of Disability: International Perspectives. Ed. by Susan Hammerman & Stephen Maikowski. LC 81-4397. (Illus.). 238p. (Orig.). 1981. pap. 15.00 o.p. (ISBN 0-9605554-0-4, UN). UNIPUB.

Economics of Engineering & Social Systems. Ed. by Morley J. English. 332p. 1972. 24.95 o.p. (ISBN 0-471-24180-6, Pub. by Wiley). Krieger.

Economics of Environmental Improvement. Donald T. Savage et al. 256p. 1974. pap. 9.95 o.p. (ISBN 0-395-18146-1). HM.

Economics of Fibre Markets: Interdependence Between Man-Made Fibres, Wool, & Cotton. C. A. Tisdell & P. W. McDonald. 1979. 69.00 o.p. (ISBN 0-08-022468-7). Pergamon.

Economics of Governmental Activity. David N. Hyman. LC 72-80260. 333p. 1973. text ed. 16.95x o.p. (ISBN 0-03-085617-5). Dryden Pr.

Economics of High-Rise Apartment Buildings of Alternate Design Configuration. Compiled by American Society of Civil Engineers Staff & Richard D. Steyert. 187p. 1972. pap. 6.00x o.p. (ISBN 0-87262-038-7). Am Soc Civil Eng.

Economics of Housing Policy. D. C. Stafford. 163p. 1978. 22.00 o.p. (ISBN 0-85664-159-6, Pub. by Croom Helm Ltd); pap. 10.95 o.p. (ISBN 0-85664-604-0). ROutledge Chapman & Hall.

Economics of Information. Samuel A. Wolpert & Joyce F. Wolpert. (Illus.). 192p. 1986. 39.95 o.s.i. (ISBN 0-442-29371-2). Van Nos Reinhold.

Economics of Involuntary Transfers: A Unified Approach to Pollution & Congestion Externalities. T. Page. LC 73-82363. (Lecture Notes in Economics & Mathematical Systems: Vol. 85). xi, 159p. 1973. pap. 12.00 o.p. (ISBN 0-387-06348-X). Springer-Verlag.

Economics of Israel. D. Horowitz. 1967. 34.00 o.p. (ISBN 0-08-013450-5); pap. 15.25 o.p. (ISBN 0-08-012206-X). Pergamon.

Economics of Library Automation: Proceedings of the Clinic on Library Applications of Data Processing, 1976. Clinic on Library Applications of Data Processing Staff. Ed. by J. L. Divilbiss. LC 77-75153. 163p. 1977. 8.00x o.p. (ISBN 0-87845-046-7). U of Ill Lib Info Sci.

Economics of Machine Tool Procurement. Wilbert Steffy. LC 77-90986. (Manufacturing Data Ser.). 1978. 12.75 o.p. (ISBN 0-87263-041-2). SME.

Economics of Mass Migration in the Twentieth Century. Sidney Klein. LC 86-16945. 179p. 1987. 22.95 o.p. (ISBN 0-88702-212-X); pap. 10.95 o.p. (ISBN 0-88702-213-8). Washington Inst Pr.

Economics of Medical Care. Joseph P. Newhouse. 116p. 1978. 4.95 o.p. (ISBN 0-201-08369-8, 1150). Healthcare Fin Mgmt Assn.

Economics of Minorities: A Guide to Information Sources. Kenneth Gagala. LC 73-17573. (Economics Information Guide Ser.: Vol. 2). 222p. 1976. 68.00x o.p. (ISBN 0-8103-1294-8). Gale.

Economics of Non-Wage Labour Costs. Robert Hart. (Illus.). 192p. 1984. text ed. 34.95x o.p. (ISBN 0-04-331096-6). Unwin Hyman.

Economics of Nuclear Energy. L. G. Brookes & H. Motamen. LC 83-14281. 420p. 1984. 69.95x o.p. (ISBN 0-412-24350-4, NO. 6872). Routledge Chapman & Hall.

Economics of Pollution Control in the Non-Ferrous Metals Industry. M. H. Atkins & J. F. Lowe. (Illus.). 1979. 69.00 o.p. (ISBN 0-08-022458-X). Pergamon.

Economics of Poverty & Discrimination. 4th ed. Bradley R. Schiller. (Illus.). 256p. 1984. pap. text ed. (ISBN 0-13-232034-7). P-H.

Economics of Production & Innovation: An Industrial Perspective. Gerhard Rosegger. (Illus.). 1980. text ed. 35.60 o.p. (ISBN 0-08-024047-X); pap. text ed. 17.00 o.p. (ISBN 0-08-024046-1). Pergamon.

Economics of Public Education. 3rd ed. Charles S. Benson. LC 77-77670. (Illus.). 1978. text ed. 35.95 o.p. (ISBN 0-395-18619-6). HM.

Economics of Recurrent Education & Training. Vladimir Stoikov. (WEP Study Ser.). viii, 115p. 1975. pap. 17.50 o.p. (ILO770, ILO). UNIPUB.

Economics of Social Issues. 5th ed. Richard H. Leftwich & Ansel M. Sharp. 1982. pap. text ed. 9.95x o.p. (ISBN 0-256-02310-7); wkbk. & student guide 4.95x o.p. (ISBN 0-256-02355-7). Irwin.

Economics of Social Issues. 6th ed. Richard H. Leftwich & Ansel M. Sharp. 1984. 14.95 o.p. (ISBN 0-256-03115-0); study guide 8.25 o.p. (ISBN 0-256-03116-9). Irwin.

Economics of Social Issues. 7th ed. Sharp & Register. 1988. 19.95 o.p.; study guide 11.95 o.p. (ISBN 0-256-06307-9). Irwin.

Economics of Soviet Planning. Abram Bergson. LC 80-13737. (Studies in Comparative Economics: No. 5). (Illus.). xxii, 394p. 1980. Repr. of 1964 ed. lib. bdg. 37.50x o.p. (ISBN 0-313-22413-7, BEES). Greenwood.

Economics of Supplemental Feeding of Malnourished Children: Leakages, Costs, & Benefits. Odin K. Knudsen. (Working Paper: No. 451). iv, 76p. 1981. 5.00 o.p. (ISBN 0-686-36190-3, WP-0451). World Bank.

Economics of Technological Change. Edwin Mansfield. (Orig.). 1968. 8.50x o.p. (ISBN 0-393-09810-9, NortonC). Norton.

Economics of the Canadian Corporate Bond Market. J. Ross Peters. 256p. 1971. 8.25 o.p. (ISBN 0-7735-0065-0, McGill Canada). U of Toronto Pr.

Economics of the Consumer. Marc Rosenblum. LC 72-84425. (Real World of Economics Ser.). (Illus.). (gr. 5-11). 1970. PLB 4.95 o.p. (ISBN 0-8225-0622-X). Lerner Pubns.

Economics of the Corporate Economy. James B. Herendeen. 278p. 1975. text ed. 27.50x o.p. (ISBN 0-8290-1579-5). Irvington.

Economics of the Environment: Selected Readings. Robert Dorfman & Nancy S. Dorfman. (Illus.). 426p. (Orig.). 1972. pap. text ed. 5.95x o.p. (ISBN 0-393-09403-0). Norton.

Economics of the Firm: Theory & Practice. 4th ed. Arthur A. Thompson, Jr. (Illus.). 624p. 1985. text ed. (ISBN 0-13-231499-1). P-H.

Economics of the Minerals Industries. 3rd ed. LC 72-86920. 1976. 30.00x o.p. (ISBN 0-89520-033-3). SMM&E Inc.

Economics of the Postal System: Alternatives & Reform. Alan Sorkin. LC 78-19228. 224p. 1980. 28.00x o.p. (ISBN 0-669-02460-0). Lexington Bks.

Economics of the Shadow Economy. Ed. by W. Gaertner & A. Wenig. (Studies in Contemporary Economics: Vol. 15). xiv, 401p. 1985. pap. 32.50 o.p. (ISBN 0-387-15095-1). Springer-Verlag.

Economics of the Tax Revolt: A Reader. Arthur B. Laffer & Jan P. Seymour. 138p. 1979. pap. text ed. 9.00 o.p. (ISBN 0-15-518920-4, HC). HarBraceJ.

Economics of Time. C. Sharp. LC 81-11565. 231p. 1981. 34.95x o.p. (ISBN 0-470-27263-5, EK00 05). Halsted Pr.

Economics of Town & Country Planning. K. G. Willis. 281p. 1980. text ed. 30.00x o.p. (ISBN 0-246-11342-1, Pub. by Granada England). Gower Pub Co.

Economics of Underdeveloped Countries. Michael Belshaw. LC 74-84420. (Real World of Economics Ser.). (Illus.). (gr. 5-11). 1970. PLB 4.95 o.p. (ISBN 0-8225-0617-3). Lerner Pubns.

Economics of Underdeveloped Countries. Jagdish Bhagwati. (Illus., Orig.). 1966. pap. text ed. 3.95 o.p. (ISBN 0-07-005150-X). McGraw.

Economics of Urban Problems. 2nd ed. Arthur F. Schreiber et al. LC 75-31004. (Illus.). 480p. 1976. text ed. 22.95 o.p. (ISBN 0-395-20619-7). HM.

Economics of VAT: Preserving Efficiency, Capitalism & Social Progress. Richard W. Lindholm. LC 80-8428. 208p. 1980. 24.50x o.p. (ISBN 0-669-04111-4). Lexington Bks.

Economics, Peace & Laughter. John Kenneth Galbraith. 1971. 7.95 o.s.i. (ISBN 0-395-12095-0). HM.

Economics: Principles & Issues. Snider. Irwin.

Economics: Principles & Policy. 2nd ed. William J. Baumol & Alan S. Blinder. 836p. 1982. text ed. 22.50 o.p. (ISBN 0-15-518835-6, HC); pap. 9.95 o.p. (ISBN 0-15-518836-4). HarBraceJ.

Economics: Principles & Policy. 3rd ed. William J. Baumol & Alan S. Blinder. 893p. 1985. text ed. 30.00 net o.p. (ISBN 0-15-518841-0, HC). HarBraceJ.

Economics: Principles of Political Economy. 2nd ed. Daniel R. Fusfeld. 1985. text ed. (ISBN 0-673-18116-2). Scott F.

Economics: Principles, Problems, Decisions. 3rd ed. Edwin Mansfield. 1980. text ed. 20.95x o.p. (ISBN 0-393-95118-9). Norton.

Economics: Principles, Problems, Decisions. 2nd ed. Edwin Mansfield. (Illus.). 1977. text ed. 17.95x o.p. (ISBN 0-393-09112-0); pap. 6.95x study guide o.p. (ISBN 0-393-09117-1). Norton.

Economics: Private & Public Choice. James D. Gwartney & Richard Stroup. 1980. 28.00 o.p. (ISBN 0-12-311040-8). Acad Pr.

Economics Problems: Concepts, Essays, Tests, Workbook. Edwin Mansfield. 1974. pap. 3.95x o.p. (ISBN 0-393-09262-3). Norton.

Economics: Reality Through Theory. William C. Blanchfield & Jacob Oser. 1973. pap. text ed. 13.95 o.p. (ISBN 0-15-518802-X, HC). HarBraceJ.

Economics: The Science of Choice. Lloyd C. Atkinson. (Student Guide by Dennis Sullivan). 1982. 31.95x o.p. (ISBN 0-256-02486-3); student guide 12.50x o.p. (ISBN 0-256-02487-1). Irwin.

Economics: The Way We Choose. Paul W. Barkley. 1977. text ed. 19.95 o.p. (ISBN 0-15-518812-7, HC). HarBraceJ.

Economics: Theory & Practice. Patrick J. Welch & Gerry F. Welch. 480p. 1982. pap. text ed. 23.95x o.p. (ISBN 0-03-055626-0); study guide 11.95 o.p. (ISBN 0-03-060144-4). Dryden Pr.

Economics Two. Barron & Lynch. (Illus.). 528p. 1988. pap. 26.95 o.p. Mosby.

Economics Without Equilibrium. Nicholas Kaldor. LC 85-1875. 96p. 1985. 12.50 o.p. (ISBN 0-87332-336-X). M E Sharpe.

Economics 1988-89. 17th, rev. ed. Ed. by Don Cole. LC 78-942037. (Annual Editions Ser.). (Illus.). 288p. 1988. pap. text ed. 9.95 o.p. (ISBN 0-87967-729-5). Dushkin Pub.

Economie Rurale et la Vie Des Campagnes Dans l'Occident Medieval see Rural Economy & Country Life in the Medieval West.

Economies of East Africa. Anthony Killick. 1978. lib. bdg. 18.00 o.p. (ISBN 0-8161-7916-6, Hall Reference). G K Hall.

Economies of the Arabian Gulf: A Statistical Source Book. Atif Kubursi. 206p. 1984. 75.00 o.p. (ISBN 0-7099-1543-8, Pub. by Croom Helm Ltd). Routledge Chapman & Hall.

Economies of the World Today: Their Organization, Development & Performance. 3rd ed. Clair Wilcox et al. (Illus.). 180p. 1976. pap. text ed. 9.95 o.p. (ISBN 0-15-519717-7, HC). HarBraceJ.

Economist: A Periodical Paper - Explanatory of the New System of Society Projected by Robert Owen, Nos. 1-5, Vol. 2. 1969. Repr. of 1822 ed. Set. lib. bdg. 39.00x o.p. (ISBN 0-8371-9164-5, EP00). Greenwood.

Economist-Business Professional As Expert Witness: A Bibliography. Frederick Frankena. (Public Administration Ser.: P 1826). 9p. 1985. 2.00 o.p. (ISBN 0-89028-676-0). Vance Biblios.

Economists. Leonard Silk. 1978. pap. 3.50 o.p. (ISBN 0-380-01835-7, 61309-3, Discus). Avon.

Economist's Handbook: A Manual of Statistical Sources. Gerlof Verwey. LC 74-157492. 470p. 1971. Repr. of 1934 ed. 65.00x o.p. (ISBN 0-8103-3728-2). Gale.

Economists of Modern Britain: An Introduction to Macroeconomics. 3rd ed. John Black. 281p. 1982. 39.95x o.p. (ISBN 0-631-13908-7); pap. 19.95x o.p. (ISBN 0-631-13909-5). Basil Blackwell.

Economizing of Ecology: Why Big Rare Whales Still Die. 130p. 4.00 o.s.i. (ISBN 0-318-13864-6). Ctr Action Endangered.

Economy & Ecological Equilibrium. P Muller. 100p. 1975. pap. 23.00 o.p. (ISBN 0-08-019681-0). Pergamon.

Economy & Society: A Study in the Integration of Economic & Social Theory. Talcott Parsons & Neil J. Smelser. 362p. 1984. pap. 17.95x o.p. (ISBN 0-7102-0383-7). Routledge Chapman & Hall.

Economy & Society in Early Colonial Maryland. Russell R. Menard. Ed. by Stuart Bruchey. LC 84-48312. (American Economic History Ser.). 527p. 1985. lib. bdg. 70.00 o.p. (ISBN 0-8240-6660-X). Garland Pub.

Economy Motel Guide. Meadowbrook Reference Group. Ed. by Louise Delagran. LC 82-23953. (Orig.). 1983. pap. 5.95 o.p. (ISBN 0-915658-56-9). Meadowbrook.

Economy of Death. Richard J. Barnet. LC 72-97133. 1969. pap. text ed. 3.45x o.p. (ISBN 0-689-70264-7, 171, Atheneum). Macmillan.

Economy: Old Myths & New Realities. Walter W. Heller. 1976. 8.95 o.p. (ISBN 0-393-05595-7); pap. 4.95x o.p. (ISBN 0-393-09151-1). Norton.

Economy, Society & Culture in Contemporary Yemen. Ed. by B. R. Pridham. LC 84-23102. 257p. 1985. 34.50 o.p. (ISBN 0-7099-2093-8, Pub. by Croom Helm Ltd). Routledge Chapman & Hall.

Ecophysiology of Tropical Crops. Ed. by Paulo De T. Alvim. 1977. 49.95 o.p. (ISBN 0-12-055650-2). Acad Pr.

ECOSOC: Options for Reform. (Policy & Efficacy Studies: No. 4). 33p. 1981. pap. 5.00 o.p. (ISBN 0-686-97556-1, UN81/15PE4, UNITAR). UNIPUB.

Ecosystem of the "Sick" Child: Implications for Classification & Intervention for Disturbed & Mentally Retarded Children. Ed. by Suzanne Salzinger et al. 1980. 38.50 o.p. (ISBN 0-12-617250-1). Acad Pr.

Ecotoxicology: The Study of Pollutants in Exosystems. Ed. by F. Moriarty. 1983. 38.50 o.p. (ISBN 0-12-506760-7). Acad Pr.

Ecrire Pour Quoi? Pour Qui. Roland Barthes et al. 1974. 9.95 o.p. (ISBN 0-686-53932-X). French & Eur.

Ecrits et Discours Politiques, 2 vols. Benjamin Constant. (Illus.). 256p. Set. 29.95 o.p. (ISBN 0-686-54610-5). French & Eur.

Ecrits sur l'Art, 2 vols. Charles Baudelaire. 1971. Set. pap. 19.95 o.p. (ISBN 0-686-51926-4). French & Eur.

Ecstasy: A Study of Some Secular & Religious Experiences. Marghanita Laski. LC 68-55635. (Illus.). 1969. Repr. of 1962 ed. lib. bdg. 27.50x o.p. (ISBN 0-8371-0529-3, LAEC). Greenwood.

Ecstasy of Victory & the Agony of Defeat. Jesse C. Mitchell. 128p. 1987. 9.95 o.p. (ISBN 0-8062-3075-4). Carlton.

Ecstasy: The MDMA Story. Bruce Eisner. Date not set. price not set o.p. Ronin Pub.

Ecstasy's Captive. Nelle McFather. 416p. 1982. pap. 3.50 o.p. (ISBN 0-505-51861-9, Pub. by Tower Bks). Dorchester Pub Co.

Ectomycorrhizae: Their Ecology & Physiology. Ed. by G. C. Marks & T. T. Kozlowski. (Physiological Ecology Ser.). 1973. 91.50 o.p. (ISBN 0-12-472850-2). Acad Pr.

Ecuador. (Let's Visit Places & Peoples - - Nations, Dependencies, & Sovereignties of the World Ser.). (Illus.). (gr. 5 up). 1988. 12.95 o.p. Chelsea Hse.

Ecuador & the Galapagos Islands-A Travel Survival Kit. Rob Rachowiecki. (Illus.). 240p. (Orig.). 1989. pap. 7.95 o.p. (ISBN 0-908086-79-2). Lonely Planet.

Ecuador: Development Problems & Prospects. Alexander G. Nowicki. xvii, 643p. 1979. pap. 20.00 o.p. (ISBN 0-686-36105-9, RC-7908). World Bank.

Ecumenical Advance: A History of the Ecumenical Movement, Vol. 2, 1948-1968. Ed. by Harold E. Fey. 1970. 10.00 o.s.i. (ISBN 0-664-20875-4, Westminster). Westminster John KNox.

Ecumenical Testimony: The Concern for Christian Unity Within the Reformed & Presbyterian Churches. John T. McNeill & James H. Nichols. LC 74-977. 320p. 1974. 10.00 o.s.i. (ISBN 0-664-20998-X, Westminster). Westminster John Knox.

Ecumenism: A Movement Toward Church Unity. William G. Rusch. LC 84-48707. 96p. 1985. pap. 1.95 o.p. (ISBN 0-8006-1847-5, 1-1847, Fortress). Augsburg Fortress.

Ecumenopolis: The Inevitable City of the Future. C. A. Doxiadis & J. G. Papaioannou. (Illus.). 1976. 15.95x o.p. (ISBN 0-393-08730-1). Norton.

Ed Emberley Little Drawing Book of Birds. Ed Emberley. (gr. 1 up). 1973. pap. 1.00 o.p. (ISBN 0-316-23602-0). Little.

Ed Emberley Little Drawing Book of Farms. Ed Emberley. (gr. 1 up). 1973. pap. 1.00 o.p. (ISBN 0-316-23603-9). Little.

Ed Emberley Little Drawing Book of Trains. Ed Emberley. (gr. 1 up). 1973. pap. 1.00 o.p. (ISBN 0-316-23604-7). Little.

Ed Emberley Little Drawing Book of Weirdoes. Ed Emberley. (gr. 1 up). 1973. pap. 1.00 o.p. (ISBN 0-316-23605-5). Little.

Ed Emberley Little Drawing Books. Ed Emberley. (gr. 1 up). 1978. 4.00 o.p. (ISBN 0-316-23614-4). Little.

Eddie. Hugh Delano. LC 75-38345. (YA) (gr. 9 up). 1976. 8.95 o.p. (ISBN 0-689-10715-3, Atheneum). Macmillan.

Eden of America: Rhode Island Landscapes, 1820-1920. Robert Workman et al. LC 85-63665. (Illus.). 96p. (Orig.). 1986. pap. 18.95 o.p. (ISBN 0-911517-10-3). Mus of Art RI.

Eden on the Marsh: An Illustrated History of Savannah. Edward Chan Sieg. 216p. 1985. 24.95 o.p. (ISBN 0-89781-115-1). Windsor Pubns Inc.

Eden Phillpotts (Eighteen Sixty-Two to Nineteen Sixty) Selected Letters. Ed. by James Y. Dayananda. LC 83-26125. (Illus.). 334p. 1984. lib. bdg. 30.25 o.p. (ISBN 0-8191-3827-4); pap. text ed. 16.75 o.p. (ISBN 0-8191-3828-2). U Pr of Amer.

Eden Seekers: The Settlement of Oregon, 1818-1862. Malcolm Clark, Jr. 320p. 1981. 15.00 o.p. (ISBN 0-395-27622-5). HM.

Edgar Allan Poe: Inner Patterns. David M. Rein. 132p. 1960. (ISBN 0-8022-1320-0). Philos Lib.

Edgar Award-Winning Mysteries. William L. DeAndrea et al. 1981. pap. 7.80 Boxed Set o.p. (ISBN 0-380-55962-5, 55962). Avon.

Edgar Cayce's Massage, Hydrotherapy & Oils. Joseph B. Duggan & Sandra Duggan. (Illus.). 160p. (Orig.). 1989. pap. 12.95 o.p. (ISBN 0-917483-12-X). InnerVision.

Edgar Poe: Seer & Craftsman. 2nd ed. Stuart Levine. LC 75-89576. 1973. lib. bdg. 25.00 o.p. (ISBN 0-912112-14-X). Everett-Edwards.

Edgar Rice Burroughs: The Man Who Created Tarzan. Irwin Porges. LC 75-15980. (Illus.). 820p. 1975. 19.95 o.p. (ISBN 0-8425-0079-0). Brigham.

Edgard Varese. Fernand Ouellette. 270p. Repr. of 1968 ed. lib. bdg. 39.00 o.p. (Pub. by Am Repr Serv). Reprint Servs.

Edge. John V. Lindsay. 240p. 1976. 7.95 o.p. (ISBN 0-393-08732-8). Norton.

Edge of Nowhere. Lucy J. Sypher. LC 72-75285. (Illus.). (gr. 4-6). 1972. 6.95 o.p. (ISBN 0-689-30069-7, Atheneum). Macmillan.

Edge of Reckoning. Marianne Joyce. (Velvet Glove Ser.: No. 24). 208p. 1985. pap. 2.50 o.p. (ISBN 0-380-89790-3). Avon.

Edge of the Sea. Rachel Carson. 1955. 7.95 o.p. (ISBN 0-395-07505-X). HM.

Edge of the Sea. Russell Sackett. (Planet Earth Ser.). (Illus.). 176p. (YA) (gr. 7 up). 1983. 18.60 o.p. (ISBN 0-8094-4334-1); lib. bdg. 22.60 o.p. Time-Life.

Edge: Organized Crime, Business & Labor Unions: Report to the President & the Attorney General Appendix. 356p. (Orig.). 1985. pap. 10.00 o.p. (S/N 040-000-00483-1). USGPO.

Edible & Useful Wildplants of the Urban West. Alan MacPherson & Sue MacPherson. LC 79-20899. (Illus.). 1979. pap. 9.95 o.p. (ISBN 0-87108-533-X). Pruett.

Edible Landscaping. Margaret McAvin. (Architecture Ser.: A 1509). 11p. 1985. 2.00 o.p. (ISBN 0-89028-659-0). Vance Biblios.

Edible Oils & Fats: Developments since 1978. Ed. by S. Torrey. LC 82-19091. (Food Technology Review: No. 57). (Illus.). 402p. 1983. 44.00 o.p. (ISBN 0-8155-0923-5). Noyes.

Edible Ornamental Garden. John Bryan & Coralie Castle. LC 73-91941. (Illus.). 192p. (Orig.). 1974. pap. 4.95 o.s.i. (ISBN 0-686-76998-8, One Hund One Prods). Ortho.

Edie on the Warpath. Elizabeth C. Spykman. LC 66-14797. 191p. (gr. 4-6). 1970. pap. 2.50 o.p. (ISBN 0-15-627650-X, VoyB). HarBraceJ.

Edinburgh Guide. Date not set. Salem Hse Pubs.

Edinburgh LCF: A Mechanised Logic of Computation. M. Gordon et al. (Lecture Notes in Computer Sciences Ser.: Vol. 78). 159p. 1980. pap. 15.00 o.p. (ISBN 0-387-09724-4). Springer-Verlag.

Edith Pechey-Phipson, M.D. The Story of England's Foremost Pioneering Woman Doctor. Edythe Lutzker. LC 72-90066. 1973. 7.50 o.p. (ISBN 0-682-47597-1, Banner). Exposition-Phoenix.

Edith Wharton Omnibus. Edith Wharton. (Encore Edition). 1978. 4.95 o.p. (ISBN 0-684-16933-9, ScribT). Scribner.

Editing. R. Thomas Berner. 1982. text ed. 25.95 o.p. (ISBN 0-03-057469-2). HR&W.

Editing British & American Literature: 1880-1920. Ed. by Eric Domville. LC 76-7323. (Conference on Editorial Problems Ser.). 1976. lib. bdg. 22.00 o.p. (ISBN 0-8240-2409-5). Garland Pub.

Editing Canadian Texts. Ed. by Francess G. Halpenny. (Conference on Editorial Problems Ser.). 1976. lib. bdg. 22.00 o.p. (ISBN 0-8240-2407-9). Garland Pub.

Editing Correspondence: Papers Given at the Fourteenth Annual Conference on Editorial Problems, University of Toronto, 3-4 November 1978. J. A. Dainard. LC 80-22003. (Conferences on Editorial Problems Ser.). 143p. 1980. lib. bdg. 22.00 o.p. (ISBN 0-8240-2429-X). Garland Pub.

Editing Eighteenth-Century Novels. Ed. by G. E. Bently, Jr. (Conference on Editorial Problems Ser.). 1976. lib. bdg. 22.00 o.p. (ISBN 0-8240-2408-7). Garland Pub.

Editing Eighteenth-Century Texts. Ed. by D. I. Smith. (Conference on Editorial Problems Ser.). 1976. lib. bdg. 22.00 o.p. (ISBN 0-8240-2402-8). Garland Pub.

Editing Illustrated Books: Papers Given at the Fifteenth Annual Conference on Editorial Problems, University of Toronto, 2-3 November 1979. William Blissett. LC 80-22003. (Conferences on Editorial Problems Ser.). 133p. 1981. lib. bdg. 22.00 o.p. (ISBN 0-8240-2430-3). Garland Pub.

Editing Medieval Texts: English, French & Latin Written in England. Papers Given at the 12th Annual Conference on Editorial Problems, University of Toronto, 5-6 November 1976. Ed. by A. G. Rigg. LC 76-52722. (Conference on Editorial Problems Ser.). 128p. 1977. lib. bdg. 22.00 o.p. (ISBN 0-8240-2426-5). Garland Pub.

Editing Nineteenth-Century Fiction, Vol. 13. Ed. by Jane Millgate. LC 78-3393. (Conference on Editorial Problems Ser.). 1978. lib. bdg. 22.00 o.p. (ISBN 0-8240-2428-1). Garland Pub.

Editing Nineteenth-Century Texts. Ed. by John M. Robson. (Conference on Editorial Problems Ser.). 1976. lib. bdg. 22.00 o.p. (ISBN 0-8240-2401-X). Garland Pub.

Editing of Renaissance Dramatic Texts: English, Italian, & Spanish. Ed. by Anne Lancashire. LC 76-7324. (Conference on Editorial Problems Ser.: No. 11). 1976. lib. bdg. 22.00 o.p. (ISBN 0-8240-2410-9). Garland Pub.

Editing Seventeenth-Century Prose. Ed. by D. I. Smith. (Conference on Editorial Problems Ser.). 1976. lib. bdg. 22.00 o.p. (ISBN 0-8240-2405-2). Garland Pub.

Editing Sixteenth-Century Texts. Ed. by R. J. Schoeck. (Conference on Editorial Problems Ser). 1976. lib. bdg. 22.00 o.p. (ISBN 0-8240-2400-1). Garland Pub.

Editing Texts of the Romantic Period. Ed. by John D. Baird. (Conference on Editorial Problems Ser.). 1976. lib. bdg. 22.00 o.p. (ISBN 0-8240-2406-0). Garland Pub.

Editing Twentieth Century Texts. Ed. by Francess G. Halpenny. (Conference on Editorial Problems Ser.). 1976. lib. bdg. 22.00 o.p. (ISBN 0-8240-2404-4). Garland Pub.

Editing Your Newsletter: A Guide to Writing, Design & Production. 2nd ed. Mark Beach. LC 81-70670. 128p. 1982. pap. 9.95 o.p. (ISBN 0-9602664-6-1). Coast to Coast.

Editing Your Newsletter: How to Produce an Effective Publication using Traditional Tool & Computers. 3rd ed. Mark Beach. (Illus.). 144p. 1988. write for info. o.p. (ISBN 0-943381-00-2); pap. text ed. 18.50 o.p. (ISBN 0-943381-01-0). Coast to Coast.

Edition of Anthony Munday's John a Kent & John a Cumber. Arthur Pennell. LC 79-54356. (Renaissance Drama Ser.). 150p. 1980. lib. bdg. 24.00 o.p. (ISBN 0-8240-4473-8). Garland Pub.

Edition of Robert Wilson's Three Ladies of London & Three Lords & Three Ladies of London. Ed. by Stephen Orgel. (Renaissance Imagination Ser.). 365p. 1987. lib. bdg. 55.00 o.p. (ISBN 0-8240-8416-0). Garland Pub.

Editor at Large see Travel Editor's Diary.

Editor to Author: The Letters of Maxwell E. Perkins. Maxwell E. Perkins. (Illus.). 1979. 12.50 o.p. (ISBN 0-684-16173-7, ScribT); encore ed. 2.95 o.p. (ISBN 0-684-16917-7). Scribner.

Editorial Page. Washington Post Writers Group. 1977. pap. 13.95 o.p. (ISBN 0-395-24015-8). HM.

Editorially Speaking. O. W. Polen. 1975. pap. 2.25 o.p. (ISBN 0-87148-300-9). Pathway Pr.

Editors, Publishers & Newpaper Ethics. Philip Meyer. 105p. 1983. pap. 2.00 o.p. (ISBN 0-943086-02-7). Am Soc News.

Edmond. David Mamet. LC 82-24178. 112p. 1983. 15.00 o.s.i. (ISBN 0-394-53104-3, GP864). Grove.

Edmond. David Mamet. LC 82-24178. 96p. 1983. pap. 6.95 o.p. (ISBN 0-394-62445-9, E848, Ever). Grove.

Edmund Burke. George Fasel. (English Authors Ser.: No. 286). 169p. 1983. lib. bdg. 13.50 o.p. (ISBN 0-8057-6861-0, Twayne). G K Hall.

Edmund Gosse: A Literary Landscape, 1849-1928. Ann Thwaite. LC 83-18076. (Illus.). 592p. 1984. 25.00x o.s.i. (ISBN 0-226-80136-5). U of Chicago Pr.

Edmund Husserl & His Logical Investigations: Cambridge, Mass., 1949. 2nd ed. A. D. Osborn. Ed. by Maurice Natanson. (Phenomenology). 1980. 20.00 o.p. (ISBN 0-8240-9561-8). Garland Pub.

Edmund Husserl's Phenomenological Psychology. Joseph J. Kockelmans. (Psychology Ser.: No. 4). 1978. Repr. of 1967 ed. text ed. 17.50x o.p. (ISBN 0-391-00875-7). Humanities.

Edmund Husserl's The Origin of Geometry: An Introduction. Jacques Derrida. Tr. by John P. Leavey from Fr. LC 77-13723. 1977. 12.95 o.p. (ISBN 0-89254-006-0). Nicolas-Hays.

Edmund Ludlow: A Voyce from the Watch Tower 1660-1662, Pt. 5. Edmund Ludlow. Ed. by A. B. Worden. (Camden Fourth Ser.: Vol. 21). 370p. 1978. 27.00 o.p. (ISBN 0-901050-43-1, Pub. by Boydell & Brewer). Longwood Pub Group.

Edmund Ruffin: A Biography. Betty L. Mitchell. LC 80-8381. 320p. 1981. 22.50x o.p. (ISBN 0-253-30876-3). Ind U Pr.

Edmund Spenser's Poetry. Edmund Spenser. Ed. by Hugh Maclean. (Norton Crical Editions). 1969. pap. 8.95x o.p. (ISBN 0-393-09569-X, NortonC). Norton.

Edmund Wilson. David Castronovo. (Literature & Life Ser.). 208p. (Orig.). 1987. pap. 9.95 o.p. (ISBN 0-8044-6108-2). Ungar.

Edmund Wilson. Leonard Kriegel. LC 74-156783. (Crosscurrents-Modern Critiques Ser.). 158p. 1971. 6.95x o.p. (ISBN 0-8093-0523-2). S Ill U Pr.

Edmund's Economy Car Buying Guide. 1987. pap. 3.50 o.p. (ISBN 0-440-02154-5). Dell.

Edmund's Foreign Car Prices. 1987. pap. 3.50 o.p. (ISBN 0-440-02155-3). Dell.

Edmund's New Car Prices. 1987. pap. 3.50 o.p. (ISBN 0-440-02129-4). Dell.

Edmund's Nineteen Eighty-Seven Car Price Buyer's Guide. 1987. pap. 3.50 o.p. (ISBN 0-440-02148-0). Dell.

Edmund's Used Car Prices, 1986. 1986. pap. 3.50 o.p. (ISBN 0-440-02174-X). Dell.

Edna St. Vincent Millay: A Reference Guide. Ed. by Judith Nierman. 1977. lib. bdg. 20.00 o.p. (ISBN 0-8161-7950-6, Hall Reference). G K Hall.

EDP: Applications for Employee Benefit Plans. Ed. by June M. Lehman. 55p. (Orig.). 1985. pap. text ed. 10.00 o.p. (ISBN 0-89154-276-0). Intl Found Employ.

EDP: Applications for Employee Benefit Plans. Ed. by June M. Lehman. 55p. 1985. avail. o.p. Intl Found Employ.

EDP: Applications for Employee Benefit Plans, 1983. Ed. by Becky A. Wright. 109p. (Orig.). 1983. pap. 14.00 o.p. (ISBN 0-89154-218-3). Intl Found Employ.

EDP: Controls & Auditing. 2nd ed. W. Thomas Porter, Jr. & William Perry. 1977. pap. (ISBN 0-534-00534-9). PWS Kent Pub.

EDP: Controls & Auditing. 3rd ed. W. Thomas Porter, Jr. & William E. Perry. 312p. 1981. pap. text ed. (ISBN 0-534-00933-6). PWS-Kent Pub.

EDP Institute, Dec. 1-4, 1982, Miami, Florida: Proceedings. Ed. by Becky A. Wright. 136p. (Orig.). 1983. 14.00 o.p. (ISBN 0-89154-205-1). Intl Found Employ.

EDP Physical Security Briefing & Checklist. 1977. pap. 5.00 o.p. (ISBN 0-918734-13-4). Reymont.

Eduardo Mallea: Todo verdor perecera. Ed. by D. L. Shaw. 1968. 8.30 o.p. (ISBN 0-08-012868-8); pap. 5.75 o.p. (ISBN 0-08-012867-X). Pergamon.

Educate, Agitate, Organize: One Hundred Years of Fabian Socialism. Patricia Pugh. (Illus.). 344p. 1985. 38.00 o.p. (ISBN 0-416-39080-3, 9323). Routledge Chapman & Hall.

Educated American Women: Life-Styles & Self-Portraits. Eli Ginzberg & Alice M. Yohalem. LC 66-28964. 198p. 1966. 28.00x o.p. (ISBN 0-231-03027-4); pap. 14.00x o.p. (ISBN 0-231-03604-3). Columbia U Pr.

Educated Child. Philadelphia Suburban School Study Council, Group E Staff. LC 65-29050. 1965. pap. text ed. 1.50x o.p. (ISBN 0-8134-6856-6, 6856). Inter Print Pubs.

Educated Palate. Blake School Parent Association Cookbook Staff. Ed. by Lois Nordstrom. (Illus.). 120p. (Orig.). 1985. pap. 10.00 o.p. (ISBN 0-933023-00-6). Blake School.

Educating. D. Bob Gowin. LC 81-66646. 216p. 1981. 24.50x o.p. (ISBN 0-8014-1418-0). Cornell U Pr.

Educating Act: A Phenomenological View. J. Gordon Chamberlin. LC 80-6076. 202p. 1981. lib. bdg. 26.75 o.p. (ISBN 0-8191-1449-9); pap. text ed. 11.50 o.p. (ISBN 0-8191-1450-2). U Pr of Amer.

Educating Adolescents with Learning & Behavior Problems. Bruno J. D'Alonzo. LC 82-16363. 564p. 38.00 o.p. (ISBN 0-89443-847-6). Aspen Pub.

Educating Exceptional Children. 3rd ed. Samuel A. Kirk & James J. Gallagher. LC 78-69609. (Illus.). 1980. text ed. 22.95 o.p. (ISBN 0-395-26526-6). HM.

Educating Exceptional Children. 4th ed. Samuel A. Kirk & James J. Gallagher. 560p. 1983. text ed. 28.95 o.p. (ISBN 0-395-32772-5). HM.

Educating Exceptional Children 1988-89. 4th, rev. ed. Ed. by Karen Frieberg. LC 76-644171. (Annual Editions Ser.). (Illus.). 256p. 1987. pap. 9.95x o.p. (ISBN 0-87967-706-6). Dushkin Pub.

Educating for a Computer Age. P. J. Hills. (New Information Technology Ser.). 200p. 1986. 29.00 o.p. (ISBN 0-7099-4705-4, Pub. by Croom Helm UK). Routledge Chapman & Hall.

Educating for the Future in Family Life. Elizabeth J. Simpson. 36p. 1981. 3.25 o.p. (ISBN 0-318-22081-4, IN228). Natl Ctr Res Voc Ed.

Educating for the Professions. Ed. by G. Lester Anderson. LC 66-19134. (National Society for the Study of Education Yearbooks Ser: No. 61, Pt. 2). 1962. lib. bdg. 6.50x o.s.i. (ISBN 0-226-60064-5). U. of Chicago Pr.

Educating Gifted & Talented Learners. Don Sellin & Jack Birch. LC 80-19565. 359p. 1981. text ed. 35.00 o.p. (ISBN 0-89443-295-8). Aspen Pub.

Educating Handicapped Infants: Issues in Development & Intervention. S. Gray Garwood & Rebecca R. Fewell. LC 82-16274. 554p. 1982. 38.00 o.p. (ISBN 0-89443-836-0). Aspen Pub.

Educating Spastic Children. F. Eleanor Schonell. (Illus.). 256p. 1956. (ISBN 0-8022-1511-4). Philos Lib.

Educating Special Learners. 2nd ed. G. Phillip Cartwright et al. 499p. 1985. text ed. (ISBN 0-534-03675-9). Wadsworth Pub.

Educating the Chronically Ill Child. Susan B. Kleinberg. LC 81-20560. 335p. 1982. text ed. 34.00 o.p. (ISBN 0-89443-652-X). Aspen Pub.

Educating the Deaf: Psychology, Principles & Practices. Donald F. Moores. LC 77-72896. (Illus.). 1978. text ed. 22.95 o.p. (ISBN 0-395-24486-2). HM.

Educating the Deaf: Psychology, Principles, & Practices. 2nd ed. Donald F. Moores. 1982. text ed. 32.95 o.p. (ISBN 0-395-31707-X). HM.

Educating the Inner-City Child: Readings in Psychology. Ed. by M. Hart. 1971. pap. text ed. 7.25x o.p. (ISBN 0-8422-0169-6). Irvington.

Educating the Learning Disabled. Ernest Siegel & Ruth Gold. 1982. text ed. write for info. o.p. (ISBN 0-02-410400-0). Macmillan.

Educating the User. I. Malley. 1979. 12.00 o.p. (ISBN 0-85365-761-0). Nichols Pub.

Education. Ed. by Monks of Solesmes Staff. 1960. 8.50 o.s.i. (ISBN 0-8198-2300-7). Dghtrs St Paul.

Education: A Beginning. 2nd ed. William Van Til. 624p. 1974. text ed. 36.76 o.p. (ISBN 0-395-17576-3); instr's. manual 1.96 o.p. (ISBN 0-395-17850-9). HM.

Education: A Journal of Reputation, Vols. 1-2, No. 4. 1970. Repr. 59.50x o.p. (ISBN 0-8371-9379-6, EDU&, Pub. by Negro U Pr). Greenwood.

Education & American Civilization. George S. Counts. LC 73-19569. 491p. 1974. Repr. of 1952 ed. lib. bdg. 26.00x o.p. (ISBN 0-8371-7293-4, COEA). Greenwood.

Education & Anthropology: An Annotated Bibliography. Annette Rosenstiel. LC 75-24100. (Reference Library of Social Science: Vol. 20). 1977. lib. bdg. 75.00 o.p. (ISBN 0-8240-9969-9). Garland Pub.

Education & Anthropology: Other Cultures & the Teacher. Frank Musgrove. 193p. 1982. text ed. 48.95x o.p. (ISBN 0-471-10143-5). Wiley.

Education & Day Care for Young Children in Need: The American Experience. Tessa Blackstone. LC 74-169306. (Doughty Street Papers: No. 1). 72p. 1973. pap. 5.00x o.p. Intl Pubns Serv.

Education & Day Care for Young Children in Need: The American Experience. Tessa Blackstone. 72p. 1973. pap. text ed. 1.90x o.p. (ISBN 0-7199-0875-2, Pub. by Bedford England). Gower Pub Co.

Education & Employment: A Critical Appraisal. Martin Carnoy. (Fundamentals of Educational Planning: No. 26). 91p. 1977. pap. 5.00 o.p. (ISBN 92-803-1078-X, U779, UNESCO, IIEP). UNIPUB.

Education & Human Motivation. Harry Giles. (ISBN 0-8022-0592-5). Philos Lib.

Education & Income. Ed. by Timothy King. (Working Paper: No. 402). viii, 315p. 1980. 5.00 o.p. (ISBN 0-686-36035-4, WP-0402). World Bank.

Education & Income Distribution in Asia: A Study Prepared for the International Labour Office Within the Framework of the World Employment Programme. P. Richards & M. Leonor. (ILO-WEP Study). 190p. 1981. 35.50 o.p. (ISBN 0-7099-2201-9, Pub. by Croom Helm Ltd). Routledge Chapman & Hall.

Education & Inquiry. John Anderson. Ed. by D. Z. Phillips. (Values & Philosophical Inquiry Ser.). 228p. 1980. 28.50x o.p. (ISBN 0-389-20075-1, 06847). B&N Imports.

Education & Knowledge: The Structured Misrepresentation of Reality. Kevin Harris. 1979. 26.95x o.p. (ISBN 0-7100-0137-1); pap. 10.95x o.p. (ISBN 0-7100-0140-1). Routledge Chapman & Hall.

Education & Political Development. Ed. by James S. Coleman. (Studies in Political Development: No. 4). 1965. 48.50x o.p. (ISBN 0-691-07506-9); pap. 9.95 o.p. (ISBN 0-691-02154-6). Princeton U Pr.

Education & Politics in Africa: The Tanzanian Case. David R. Morrison. 304p. 1976. 22.00x o.p. (ISBN 0-7735-0258-0, McGill Canada). U of Toronto Pr.

Education & Schooling. W. Kenneth Richmond. 211p. 1975. pap. 8.95x o.p. (ISBN 0-416-78770-3, NO.2407). Routledge Chapman & Hall.

Education & Schooling in America. Gerald L. Gutek. (Illus.). 416p. 1983. pap. text ed. 26.95 o.p. (ISBN 0-13-240523-7, Busn). P-H.

Education & Social Awakening in Iran, 1850-1968. rev. & enl. ed. A. R. Arasteh. 1969. 40.00 o.p. (ISBN 90-04-00104-2). E J Brill USA.

Education & Social Change. Ed. by Len Barton & Stephen Walker. LC 85-19020. 288p. 1985. 34.50 o.p. (ISBN 0-7099-3904-3, Pub. by Croom Helm Ltd). Routledge Chapman & Hall.

Education & Society. Joseph Scimecca. LC 79-17991. 306p. 1980. pap. text ed. 27.95 o.p. (ISBN 0-275-85800-6, HoltC). HR&W.

Education & Technological Innovations: Academic Performance & Economical Advantages. Hadj Benyahia. 163p. (Orig.). 1983. pap. text ed. 19.95 o.p. (ISBN 0-317-02590-2). Gower Pub Co.

Education & the American Indian: The Road to Self-Determination since 1928. 2nd ed. Margaret C. Szasz. LC 77-11742. (Illus.). 271p. 1974. pap. 10.95x o.p. (ISBN 0-8263-0468-0). U of NM Pr.

Education & the City: Theory, History & Contemporary Practice. Ed. by Gerald Grace. 350p. (Orig.). 1984. pap. 16.95x o.p. (ISBN 0-7100-9918-5). Routledge Chapman & Hall.

Education & the Common Good: A Moral Philosophy of the Curriculum. Philip H. Phenix. LC 77-22594. 1977. Repr. of 1961 ed. lib. bdg. 22.50x o.p. (ISBN 0-8371-9728-7, PHEC). Greenwood.

Education & the Cultural Process: Toward an Anthropology or Education. George D. Spindler. LC 74-1347. 561p. 1974. pap. text ed. 22.95 o.p. (ISBN 0-03-085180-7, HoltC). HR&W.

Education & the Employment Problem in Developing Countries. 4th ed. Mark Blaug. 1981. 6.85 o.p. (ISBN 92-2-101005-8). Intl Labour Office.

Education & the Good Life. new ed. Bertrand Russell. LC 73-114378. 1970. pap. 5.95 o.p. (ISBN 0-87140-212-2). Liveright.

Education & the National Economy. J. R. Hough. 250p. 1987. 29.00 o.p. (ISBN 0-7099-3735-0, Pub. by Croom Helm UK). Routledge Chapman & Hall.

Education & the Natonal Economy. J. R. Hough. 320p. 1987. lib. bdg. 55.00x o.p. (ISBN 0-317-64365-7, Pub. by Croom Helm UK). Routledge Chapman & Hall.

Education & the Nature of Knowledge. R. J. Brownhill. (New Patterns of Learning Ser.). 135p. 1983. 27.25 o.p. (ISBN 0-7099-0654-4, Pub. by Croom Helm Ltd). Routledge Chapman & Hall.

Education & the Social Condition. Harold Silver. 1981. 23.00x o.p. (ISBN 0-416-74020-0, NO.2055); pap. 10.95x o.p. (ISBN 0-416-74030-8, NO.2054). Routledge Chapman & Hall.

Education & the Taming of Power. Sidney Hook. LC 72-98117. 310p. 1973. 9.95 o.p. (ISBN 0-87548-083-7). Open Court.

Education & the World View. Cyrus R. Vance et al. LC 80-68195. 72p. 1981. pap. 6.95 o.p. (ISBN 0-915390-27-2, Pub. by Change Mag). Transaction Pubs.

Education & Training in Contemporary Cartography. D. R. Taylor. LC 85-3160. (Progress in Contemporary Cartography Ser.). 1985. 64.95 o.p. (ISBN 0-471-90305-1). Wiley.

Education & Training of Industrial Manpower in Japan. Ken Inoue. (Working Paper Ser.: No. 729). 85p. 1985. 5.00 o.p. (ISBN 0-8213-0552-2, WP 0729). World Bank.

Education & Western Civilization-the Long View: An Attempt to Gain Perspective. Mowat G. Fraser. LC 73-91097. 1974. 9.00 o.p. (ISBN 0-682-47867-9, University); pap. 3.50 o.p. (ISBN 0-682-47868-7). Exposition-Phoenix.

Education as an Art. Rudolf Steiner et al. Intro. by Paul M. Allen. LC 73-130816. 128p. 1988. pap. 7.50 o.p. (ISBN 0-317-68205-9). Garber Comm.

Education: Can Success Be Measured? Instructional Aides, Inc. 1981. pap. 11.95 o.p. (ISBN 0-936474-13-0). Info Plus TX.

Education, Class Language & Ideology. Noelle Bisseret. 1979. 21.95x o.p. (ISBN 0-7100-0118-5). Routledge Chapman & Hall.

Education, Culture & Politics in Modern France. W. D. Halls. 1976. 13.75 o.p. (ISBN 0-08-018961-X); text ed. 28.00 o.p. (ISBN 0-08-018962-8). Pergamon.

Education Directory: Colleges & Universities, 1985-86. Susan G. Broyles et al. (Education Department Publication CS-36-309). 315p. 1986. pap. 15.00 o.p. (ISBN 0-318-21691-4, S/N 065-000-00268-0). USGPO.

Education Directory 1987: A Guide to Decisionmakers in the Federal Government, the States & Education Associations. Ed. by Leslie A. Ratzlaff. 97p. (Orig.). 1986. pap. 45.00 o.s.i. (ISBN 0-937925-04-7). Capitol VA.

Education, Employment & Leisure. M. P. Carter. 1963. text ed. 8.55 o.p. (ISBN 0-08-010322-7); pap. text ed. 4.40 o.p. (ISBN 0-08-010321-9). Pergamon.

Education Europeenne. Romain Gary. 1956. pap. 13.50 o.p. (ISBN 0-685-11154-7). Schoenhof.

Education for a Culture in Crisis. William L. Griffen & J. D. Marciano. LC 72-86266. 177p. 1972. pap. text ed. 6.95x o.p. (ISBN 0-8422-0219-6). Irvington.

Education for Administrative Careers in Government Service. Stephen B. Sweeney et al. LC 72-7831. 366p. 1973. Repr. of 1958 ed. lib. bdg. 35.00x o.p. (ISBN 0-8371-6535-0, SWAC). Greenwood.

Education for Childbirth & Parenthood. Elizabeth R. Perkins. 180p. 1980. 27.50 o.p. (ISBN 0-7099-0273-5, Pub. by Croom Helm Ltd). Routledge Chapman & Hall.

Education for Clinical Social Work Practice: Continuity & Change. Ed. by L. S. Bandler. (Social Work Ser.). 178p. 1983. 40.00 o.p. (ISBN 0-08-030184-3); pap. 12.00 o.p. (ISBN 0-08-030185-1). Pergamon.

Education for Communism: School & State in the People's Republic of Albania. John I. Thomas. LC 69-17329. (Studies: No. 22). 131p. 1969. 8.95x o.p. (ISBN 0-8179-3221-6); pap. 5.95x o.p. (ISBN 0-8179-3222-4). Hoover Inst Pr.

Education for International Understanding: Examples & Suggestions for Classroom Use. (Orig.). 1964. pap. 5.00 o.p. (ISBN 92-3-100437-9, U189, UNESCO). UNIPUB.

Education for Leadership: The International Administrative Staff Colleges, 1948-1984. A. T. Cornwall-Jones. (Illus.). 272p. 1985. 29.95x o.p. (ISBN 0-7102-0464-7). Routledge Chapman & Hall.

Education for Librarianship: The Design of the Curriculum of Library Schools. Ed. by Herbert Goldhor. LC 78-633332. (Monograph: No. 11). 195p. 1971. 5.00x o.p. (ISBN 0-87845-033-5). U of Ill Lib Info Sci.

Education for Living: A Common-Sense Program for Grades K-6. Eileen Harrington. 1978. pap. 5.50 o.p. (ISBN 0-682-49098-9). Exposition-Phoenix.

Education for Participation: Development Guide for Secondary School Programs in Law & Public Affairs. (Program Guides). 69p. 3.00 o.p. (ISBN 0-318-13790-9). Constitutional Rights Found.

Education for Personal Autonomy. H. J. Blackham. 211p. 1978. pap. text ed. 9.70x o.p. (ISBN 0-7199-0936-8, Pub. by Bedford England). Gower Pub Co.

Education for Rare Book Librarianship: A Reexamination of Trends & Problems. Lawrence J. McCrank. (Occasional Paper: no.144). 1980. 3.00 o.p. U of Ill Lib Info Sci.

Titles

Education for Sexuality: Concepts & Programs for Teaching. 3rd ed. John J. Burt & Linda B. Meeks. 1985. text ed. 22.95 o.p. HR&W.

Education for the Future: The Case for Radical Change. P. A. Coggin. 170p. 1979. 35.00 o.p. (ISBN 0-08-023729-0). Pergamon.

Education for the Real World. Henry M. Morris. LC 77-78017. 1977. pap. 8.95 o.s.i. (ISBN 0-89051-093-8). Master Bks.

Education for Urban Design. Ed. by Institute for Urban Design Staff. LC 81-86580. 183p. 1982. pap. 24.95 o.p. (ISBN 0-87933-433-9). Van Nos Reinhold.

Education for World Peace. Benito F. Reyes. 112p. 1971. pap. 7.50 o.p. (ISBN 0-939375-12-5). World Univ Amer.

Education for World Understanding. J. L. Henderson. 1968. 16.00 o.p. (ISBN 0-08-013217-0); pap. 7.75 o.p. (ISBN 0-08-013216-2). Pergamon.

Education from Before Birth to Maturity. 3rd ed. Hazrat Inayat Khan. LC 78-65081. 128p. 1979. pap. 5.95 o.p. (ISBN 0-900217-06-5, Pub. by Sufi Pub Co England). Hunter Hse.

Education in a Free Society: An American History. 4th ed. Alexander S. Rippa. LC 83-17561. 480p. 1983. pap. text ed. 19.95 o.p. (ISBN 0-582-28505-4). Longman.

Education in Egypt. Judith Cochran. LC 85-28017. 176p. 1986. 31.00 o.p. (ISBN 0-7099-3447-5, Pub. by Croom Helm Ltd). Routledge Chapman & Hall.

Education in Latin America: A Bibliography. Ludwig Lauerhass, Jr. & Vera L. Haugse. 1981. lib. bdg. 63.50 o.p. (ISBN 0-8161-8516-6, Hall Reference). G K Hall.

Education in Nineteenth-Century Britain. Ed. by Gillian R. Sutherland et al. (Government & Society in Nineteenth Century Britain Ser.). 246p. 1977. 30.00x o.p. (ISBN 0-7165-2211-X, BBA 02034, Pub. by Irish Academic Pr Ireland). Biblio Dist.

Education in Rural Communities. Ruth Strang. LC 52-7759. (National Society for the Study of Education Yearbooks Ser: No. 51, Pt. 2). 1952. lib. bdg. 6.50x o.s.i. (ISBN 0-226-60020-3); pap. text ed. 4.50x o.s.i. (ISBN 0-226-60021-1). U of Chicago Pr.

Education in the Eighteenth Century. Ed. by John Browning. LC 79-18182. (McMaster Eighteenth Century Studies). 145p. 1979. lib. bdg. 31.00 o.p. (ISBN 0-8240-4006-6). Garland Pub.

Education in the Eighties: English. R. Baird Shuman. 168p. 1981. 15.95 o.p. (ISBN 0-8106-3152-0); pap. 9.95 o.p. (ISBN 0-8106-3151-2). NEA.

Education in the Eighties: Health Education. Robert D. Russell. 128p. 1981. 15.95 o.p. (ISBN 0-8106-3154-7); pap. 9.95 o.p. (ISBN 0-8106-3153-9). NEA.

Education in the One Hundredth Congress: A Guide to Committees. Eileen O'Brien & Leslie Ratzlaff. 71p. (Orig.). 1987. pap. 45.00 o.s.i. (ISBN 0-937925-25-X). Capitol VA.

Education in the Soviet Union: Policies & Institutions since Stalin. Mervyn Mathews. 240p. 1982. text ed. 31.95x o.p. (ISBN 0-04-370114-0). Unwin Hyman.

Education in the Third World. Ed. by Keith Watson. (Illus.). 242p. 1982. 29.95 o.p. (ISBN 0-7099-2749-5, Pub. by Croom Helm Ltd). Routledge Chapman & Hall.

Education in the Truth. Norman DeJong. 1969. pap. 7.95 o.p. (ISBN 0-87552-252-1). Presby & Reformed.

Education in the U. S. A. Kenneth Richmond. 200p. 1956. (ISBN 0-8022-1340-5). Philos Lib.

Education in the U. S. S. R. Joseph I. Zajda. (International Studies in Education & Social Change). (Illus.). 200p. 1980. 70.00 o.p. (ISBN 0-08-025807-7); pap. text ed. 63.00 o.p. (ISBN 0-08-025806-9). Pergamon.

Education in West Germany: A Quest for Excellence. Hans G. Lingens & Barbara Lingens. LC 79-93116. (Fastback Ser.: No. 140). (Orig.). 1980. pap. 0.90 o.p. (ISBN 0-87367-140-6). Phi Delta Kappa.

Education in Western Culture. Robert Ulich. (Professional Education for Teachers Ser.). (Orig.). 1965. pap. text ed. 9.95 o.p. (ISBN 0-15-520895-0, HC). HarBraceJ.

Education Literature, Nineteen Hundred Seven to Nineteen Thirty-Two, Vol. II. Ed. by Malcolm C. Hamilton. (Education Literature Ser.). 1979. 40.00 o.p. (ISBN 0-8240-3701-4). Garland Pub.

Education Literature, Nineteen Hundred Seven to Nineteeh Thirty-Two, Vol. IV. Ed. by Malcolm C. Hamilton. (Education Literature Ser.). 1979. 40.00 o.p. (ISBN 0-8240-3703-0). Garland Pub.

Education Literature, Nineteen Hundred Seven to Nineteen Thirty-Two, Vol. IX. Ed. by Malcolm C. Hamilton. (Education Literature Ser.). 1979. 40.00 o.p. (ISBN 0-8240-3708-1). Garland Pub.

Education Literature Nineteen Hundred Seven to Nineteen Thirty-Two, Vol. 1. Ed. by Malcolm C. Hamilton. 1979. lib. bdg. 40.00 o.p. (ISBN 0-8240-3700-6). Garland Pub.

Education Literature, Nineteen Hundred Seven to Nineteen Thirty-Two, Vol. 8. Ed. by Malcolm C. Hamilton. 1979. lib. bdg. 40.00 o.p. (ISBN 0-8240-3707-3). Garland Pub.

Education Literature, Nineteen Hundred Seven to Nineteen Thirty-Two, Vol. 10. Ed. by Malcolm C. Hamilton. 1979. lib. bdg. 40.00 o.p. (ISBN 0-8240-3709-X). Garland Pub.

Education Literature, Nineteen Hundred Seven to Nineteen Thirty-Two, Vol. 11. Ed. by Malcolm C. Hamilton. 1979. lib. bdg. 40.00 o.p. (ISBN 0-8240-3710-3). Garland Pub.

Education of a Golfer. Sam Snead & Al Stump. 1962. 5.95 o.p. (ISBN 0-671-21945-6). S&S.

Education of Adults: A World Perspective. 2nd, Rev. ed. John Lour. 233p. (Co-published with OISE Press, Toronto). 1982. pap. 8.00 o.p. (ISBN 92-3-102055-2, U1256, UNESCO). UNIPUB.

Education of an Ordinary Woman. Lois M. Stalvey. LC 81-66039. 1982. 14.95 o.p. (ISBN 0-689-11143-6, Atheneum). Macmillan.

Education of Black People: Ten Critiques, 1906-1960. W. E. B. Du Bois. Ed. by Herbert Aptheker. LC 72-90495. 184p. 1973. 17.50x o.p. (ISBN 0-87023-130-8). U of Mass Pr.

Education of Children with Severe Learning Difficulties: Bridging the Gap Between Theory & Practice. Ed. by Judith D. Coupe & Jill Porter. 384p. 1986. 34.50 o.p. (ISBN 0-7099-3445-9, Pub. by Croom Helm Ltd); pap. 17.00 o.p. (ISBN 0-7099-3446-7). Routledge Chapman & Hall.

Education of Exceptional Learners. 3rd ed. Frank M. Hewett & Steven R. Forness. 1983. text ed. 35.00 o.s.i. (ISBN 0-205-08102-9, 248102); write for info. instr's. manual o.s.i. (ISBN 0-205-08103-7). Allyn.

Education of Hyman Kaplan. Leonard Q. Ross. LC 38-6588. (Modern Classics Ser.). 1949. 3.95 o.p. (ISBN 0-15-127809-1). HarBraceJ.

Education of Koko. Francine Patterson & Eugene Linden. LC 81-1325. (Illus.). 240p. 1981. 15.95 o.p. (ISBN 0-03-046101-4); pap. 7.95 o.p. (ISBN 0-03-063551-9). H Holt & Co.

Education of le Corbusier. Paul V. Turner. LC 76-23658. (Outstanding Dissertations in the Fine Arts - Twentieth Century). (Illus.). 1977. Repr. of 1971 ed. lib. bdg. 58.00 o.p. (ISBN 0-8240-2732-9). Garland Pub.

Education of Living. Jacob S. List. LC 61-9317. 128p. 1961. (ISBN 0-8022-0982-3). Philos Lib.

Education of Man. Heinrich Pestalozzi. (ISBN 0-8022-1962-4). Philos Lib.

Education of Mrs. Henry Adams. Eugenia Kaledin. LC 81-9431. (American Civilization Ser.). (Illus.). 306p. 1982. 29.95 o.p. (ISBN 0-87722-230-4). Temple U Pr.

Education of Patrick Silver. Jerome Charyn. LC 76-8633. 1976. 7.95 o.p. (ISBN 0-87795-142-X, Arbor Hse). Morrow.

Education of Patrick Silver. Jerome Charyn. 208p. 1977. pap. 2.75 o.p. (ISBN 0-380-01698-2, 53603-X, Bard). Avon.

Education of Primary & Secondary School Teachers. Jose B. Gimeno & M. Ibanez. (Studies on the Evaluation of Qualifications at the Higher Education Level). (Illus.). 271p. 1981. pap. 11.00 o.p. (ISBN 92-3-101750-0, U1142, UNESCO). UNIPUB.

Education of T. C. Mits. Hugh G. Lieber & Lillian R. Lieber. (Illus.). 1978. 7.95 o.p. (ISBN 0-393-06278-3); pap. 5.95 o.p. (ISBN 0-393-00906-8). Norton.

Education of the Gifted - A Challenge & a Promise: Special Issue of Exceptional Children, October 1981. Ed. by M. Angele Thomas. 96p. 1981. pap. 5.00 o.p. (ISBN 0-86586-129-3). Coun Exc Child.

Education of the Gifted & Talented. Gary A. Davis & Sylvia Rimm. (Illus.). 416p. 1985. text ed. 27.95 o.p. (ISBN 0-13-236597-9). P-H.

Education of the Individual. A. Adler. 160p. 1958. (ISBN 0-8022-0007-9). Philos Lib.

Education of the Mexican Nation. George F. Kneller. LC 73-1817. 258p. 1973. Repr. lib. bdg. 19.50x o.p. (ISBN 0-374-94595-0, Octagon). Hippocrene Bks.

Education of the Public. Malcolm L. Warford. 1981. pap. 2.95 o.p. (ISBN 0-8298-0418-8). Pilgrim NY.

Education of the Sub Normal Child. Frances Lloyd. 1954. (ISBN 0-8022-0984-X). Philos Lib.

Education of Tom Webber. T. R. Peters, Sr. LC 76-50832. 1977. 5.50 o.p. (ISBN 0-682-48720-1, Banner). Exposition-Phoenix.

Education of Winnie D. Wendy Owen. LC 78-27167. 1979. 8.95 o.s.i. (ISBN 0-8008-2365-6). Taplinger.

Education of Young Children. D. E. M. Gardiner. 120p. 1957. (ISBN 0-8022-0563-1). Philos Lib.

Education Programs & Projects: Analytical Techniques, Case Studies, & Exercises. rev. ed. Irving A. Sirken. ix, 287p. 1979. pap. 6.00 o.p. (ISBN 0-686-36036-2). World Bank.

Education: Reflecting Our Society. Rev. ed. Ed. by Mark A. Siegel & Nancy R. Jacobs. (Information Plus Ser.). 120p. 1986. pap. 15.95 o.p. (ISBN 0-936474-55-6). Info Plus TX.

Education, State & Crisis: A Marxist Perspective. Madan Sarup. (Routledge Education Bks.). 120p. 1982. 21.95x o.p. (ISBN 0-7100-0956-9); pap. 9.95x o.p. (ISBN 0-7100-0959-3). Routledge Chapman & Hall.

Education 1988-89. 15th, rev. ed. Ed. by Fred Schultz. LC 73-78580. (Annual Editions Ser.). (Illus.). 256p. 1988. pap. text ed. 9.95 o.p. (ISBN 0-87967-714-7). Dushkin Pub.

Educational Achievement: Explanation & Implications of Recent Trends. (Illus.). 123p. 1987. pap. 5.00 o.p. (ISBN 0-318-23551-X, S/N 052-070-06360-2). USGPO.

Educational & Economic Effects of Promotion & Repetition Practices. Wadi D. Daddad. (Working Paper: No. 319). 52p. 1979. 5.00 o.p. (ISBN 0-686-36054-0, WP-0319). World Bank.

Educational & Psychological Measurement: Selected Readings. L. Masih. 1969. pap. text ed. 8.50x o.p. (ISBN 0-8290-1107-2). Irvington.

Educational & the Development of Reason, 3 pts. R. F. Dearden et al. Incl. Pt. 1. Critique of Current Educationl Aims. pap. 9.95x (ISBN 0-7100-8084-0); Pt. 2. Reason. pap. 9.95x (ISBN 0-7100-8101-4); Pt. 3. Education & Reason. pap. 9.95x (ISBN 0-7100-8102-2). 1975. pap. Routledge Chapman & Hall.

Educational Audiology. Ivan Tucker & Michael Nolan. LC 84-45286. 300p. 1984. 43.00 o.p. (ISBN 0-7099-2430-5, Pub. by Croom Helm Ltd); pap. 24.00 o.p. (ISBN 0-7099-2464-X). Routledge Chapman & Hall.

Educational Conflict & the Law. David Milman. 256p. 1986. 29.00 o.p. (ISBN 0-7099-3521-8, Pub. by Croom Helm Ltd). Routledge Chapman & Hall.

Educational Crisis. Arieta E. Mobiley. LC 85-91006. (Illus.). 192p. 1985. 15.00 o.p. (ISBN 0-682-40234-6). Exposition-Phoenix.

Educational Development Through Consultancy. David Bond & Rod McDonald. 54p. 1981. pap. 14.00 o.p. (ISBN 0-900868-81-3, Open Univ Pr). Taylor & Francis.

Educational Developmental Program, Kit 2: The Preacademic Instructional Program. Wretha Petersen. 1975. 725.00 o.p. (ISBN 0-87562-034-5). Spec Child.

Educational Diagnosis & Prescriptive Teaching: A Practical Approach to Special Education in the Least Restrictive Environment. Douglas Prillaman & John Abbott. 1982. pap. 22.50 o.p. (ISBN 0-8224-1960-2). D S Lake Pubs.

Educational Diagnosis: Nat'l Society for the Study of Education 34th Yearbook. Leo J. Brueckner. 1975. pap. text ed. 4.50x o.s.i. (ISBN 0-226-59964-7). U of Chicago Pr.

Educational Differences. Arthur R. Jensen. 1973. 42.00x o.p. (ISBN 0-416-75980-7, NO.2251). Routledge Chapman & Hall.

Educational Displays & Exhibits. Preston J. Lockridge. (Bridges for Ideas Handbook Ser.). 1966. pap. text ed. 6.00x o.p. (ISBN 0-913648-07-8). U Tex Austin Film Lib.

Educational Evaluation. W. James Popham. 1975. pap. text ed. (ISBN 0-13-240515-6). P-H.

Educational Evaluation in the Netherlands. Ed. by B. Creemers & N. Verloop. 100p. 1985. pap. 33.00 o.p. (ISBN 0-08-032340-5). Pergamon.

Educational Evaluation: New Roles, New Means. Ed. by Ralph W. Tyler. (National Society for the Study of Education Yearbooks: No. 68, Pt. 2). 1976. pap. text ed. 6.00x o.s.i. (ISBN 0-226-60099-8). U of Chicago Pr.

Educational Finance & Resources. W. F. Dennison. 288p. 1984. 27.50 o.p. (ISBN 0-7099-0842-3, Pub. by Croom Helm Ltd). Routledge Chapman & Hall.

Educational Futures. P. J. Hills. (New Patterns of Learning Ser.). 200p. 1987. 29.00 o.p. (ISBN 0-7099-4706-2, Pub. by Croom Helm UK). Routledge Chapman & Hall.

Educational Futures. P. J. Hills. (New Patterns of Learning Ser.). 208p. 1987. lib. bdg. 35.00x o.p. (ISBN 0-317-64366-5, Pub. by Croom Helm UK). Routledge Chapman & Hall.

Educational Games & Simulations. National Education Association Staff & William R. Heitzmann. LC 74-16182. (What Research Says to the Teacher Ser.). 1983. pap. 2.50 o.p. (ISBN 0-8106-1030-2). NEA.

Educational Governance & Administration. Thomas J. Sergrovanni et al. 1980. text ed. (ISBN 0-13-236653-3). P-H.

Educational Gymnastics. Inner London Council Staff. 1973. 2.95 o.p. (ISBN 0-8238-0164-0). Plays.

Educational Imagery: Strategies to Personalize Classroom Instruction. Glenn E. Richardson. (Illus.). 208p. 1982. 31.50 o.p. (ISBN 0-398-04639-5). C C Thomas.

Educational Issues of the Seventies: Foundations of Education. Ed. by Richard Kraft. 1973. 32.50x o.p. (ISBN 0-8422-5108-1). Irvington.

Educational Law. Marvin Rosenberg & Martin Schiff. 1980. pap. 13.95 o.s.i. (ISBN 0-89529-077-4). Avery Pub.

Educational Materials for Obstetrics & Gynecology. 5.00 o.p. (ISBN 0-686-24122-3). Am Coll Obstetric.

Educational Measurement & Evaluation. 2nd ed. Jim C. Nunnally. (Illus.). 480p. 1972. text ed. 47.95 o.p. (ISBN 0-07-047553-9). McGraw.

Educational Planning in a Decentralized System: The Papua New Guinean Experience. Mark Bray. (Illus.). 159p. (Orig.). 1985. pap. text ed. 10.00 o.p. (ISBN 0-424-00109-8, Pub. by Sydney U Pr). Intl Spec Bk.

Educational Policy-Making: A Study of Interest Groups & Parliament. Maurice Kogan. LC 75-17014. 262p. 1975. 26.00 o.p. (ISBN 0-208-01562-0, Linnet). Shoe String.

Educational Problems in Turkey, 1920-1940. Ilhan Basgoz & H. E. Wilson. LC 67-65317. (Uralic & Altaic Ser: Vol. 86). 268p. 1968. pap. text ed. 8.00x o.p. (ISBN 0-87750-077-0). Res Ctr Lang Semiotic.

Educational Process in Critical Care Nursing. JoAnn G. Alspach. LC 82-2090. (Illus.). 432p. 1982. text ed. 31.95 o.p. (ISBN 0-8016-0141-X). Mosby.

Educational Psychology. 2nd ed. Lee J. Cronbach. 1963. text ed. 15.95 o.p. (ISBN 0-15-520878-0, HC). HarBraceJ.

Educational Psychology. 3rd ed. Lee J. Cronbach. 875p. 1977. text ed. 22.00 o.p. (ISBN 0-15-520883-7, HC). HarBraceJ.

Educational Psychology. 2nd ed. Nathaniel L. Gage & David C. Berliner. 1980. pap. 23.95 o.p. (ISBN 0-395-30802-X). HM.

Educational Psychology. 3rd ed. Nathaniel L. Gage & David C. Berliner. LC 83-82704. 752p. 1984. pap. 35.96 o.p. (ISBN 0-395-32762-8). HM.

Educational Psychology. 2nd ed. Thomas L. Good & Jere E. Brophy. 1980. text ed. 26.95 o.p. (ISBN 0-03-053191-8, HoltC). HR&W.

Educational Psychology. reference ed. David W. Johnson. (Illus.). 1979. pap. text ed. (ISBN 0-13-236760-2). P-H.

Educational Psychology. 4th, rev. ed. C. L. Kundu & D. N. Tutoo. 576p. 1985. text ed. 50.00x o.p. (ISBN 0-86590-540-1, Pub. by Sterling Pubs India). Apt Bks.

Educational Psychology & Children. Lovell. 272p. 1959. (ISBN 0-8022-1000-7). Philos Lib.

Educational Psychology & Its Classroom Applications. 2nd ed. M. Daniel Smith. 1978. pap. text ed. 35.00 o.p. (ISBN 0-205-06025-0, 246025); student guide avail. o.p. (ISBN 0-205-06028-5, 246028); instr's. manual avail. o.p. (ISBN 0-205-06026-9, 246028); tests avail. o.p. (ISBN 0-205-06027-7). Allyn.

Educational Psychology for Teachers. 2nd ed. Anita E. Woolfolk & Lorraine Nicolich. (Illus.). 640p. 1984. pap. text ed. (ISBN 0-13-240465-6). P-H.

Educational Psychology of the Gifted. Joe Khatena. LC 81-11452. 480p. 1978. text ed. write for info. o.p. (ISBN 0-02-363080-9). Macmillan.

Educational Psychology: Theory into Practice. Robert E. Slavin. 704p. 1986. pap. text ed. 27.95 o.p. (ISBN 0-13-236803-X, Busn). P-H.

Educational Psychology, 1987-88. 3rd ed. Fredric Linder & James McMillan. LC 82-640517. (Annual Editions Ser.). (Illus.). 256p. 1987. pap. text ed. 9.95 o.p. (ISBN 0-87967-663-9). Dushkin Pub.

Educational Reform & Social Studies: Implications of Six Reports. Fred M. Newmann. LC 84-22231. 37p. (Orig.). 1984. pap. 5.95 o.p. (ISBN 0-89994-299-7). Soc Sci Ed.

Educational Research. 4th ed. Walter S. Borg & Meredith D. Gall. LC 82-20849. (Illus.). 768p. 1983. text ed. 32.95 o.p. (ISBN 0-582-28246-2). Longman.

Educational Research in Europe: A New Look at the Relationship Between School Education & Work: Second All-European Conference for Directors of Educational Research Institutions, Madrid, Sept. 11-13, 1979. H. A. Becker & H. Dueuzeide. Compiled by M. Dino Carelli. (International Studies in Education: No. 37). 164p. 1980. pap. write for info. o.p. (U1364, UNESCO). UNIPUB.

Educational Research: Readings in Focus. 2nd ed. Irvin J. Lehmann & William A. Mehrens. LC 78-27136. 1979. pap. text ed. 17.95 o.p. (ISBN 0-03-043016-X, HoltC). HR&W.

Educational Staff Development. Alex Main. LC 84-29384. (New Patterns of Learning Ser.). 129p. 1985. 27.50 o.p. (ISBN 0-7099-1760-0, Pub. by Croom Helm). Routledge Chapman & Hall.

Educational Systems of Africa. Martena Sasnett & Inez Sepmeyer. LC 66-27654. 1966. 90.00x o.p. (ISBN 0-520-01122-8). U of Cal Pr.

Educator in an Era of Social Change - Evolutionist or Revolutionist? National Associations of Women Deans & Counselors. 1970. pap. 3.00 o.p. (ISBN 0-686-14983-1). Natl Assn Women.

Educator's Cry. Roberta S. Gunchuck. 1985. 6.95 o.p. (ISBN 0-533-06475-9). Vantage.

Educators Grade Guide to Free Teaching Aids. 33rd ed. 1987. 43.50 o.p. (ISBN 0-87708-188-3). Ed Prog.

Educators Grade Guide to Free Teaching Aids. 34th ed. 1988. 43.75 o.p. (ISBN 0-87708-200-6). Ed Prog.

Educators Guide to Free Audio & Video Materials. 34th ed. 1987. 22.25 o.p. (ISBN 0-87708-182-4). Ed Prog.

Educators Guide to Free Audio & Video Materials. 35th ed. 1988. 22.25 o.p. (ISBN 0-87708-194-8). Ed Prog.

Educators Guide to Free Films. 47th ed. 1987. 27.00 o.p. (ISBN 0-87708-179-4). Ed Prog.

Educators Guide to Free Films. 48th ed. 1988. 27.50 o.p. (ISBN 0-87708-191-3). Ed Prog.

Educators Guide to Free Filmstrips & Slides. 40th ed. 1988. 20.00 o.p. (ISBN 0-87708-192-1). Ed Prog.

Educators Guide to Free Guidance Materials. 27th ed. 1988. 25.25 o.p. (ISBN 0-87708-197-2). Ed Prog.

Educators Guide to Free Guidance Materials. 26th ed. Ed. by Mary H. Saterstrom. 1987. 25.25 o.p. (ISBN 0-87708-185-9). Ed Prog.

Educators Guide to Free Health, Physical Education & Recreation Materials. 21st ed. 1988. 26.25 o.p. (ISBN 0-87708-198-0). Ed Prog.

Educators Guide to Free Health, Physical Education & Recreation Materials. 20th ed. Patricia Horkheimer. 1987. 25.75 o.p. (ISBN 0-87708-186-7). Ed Prog.

Educators Guide to Free Home Economics Materials. 4th ed. 1987. 22.50 o.p. (ISBN 0-87708-187-5). Ed Prog.

Educators Guide to Free Home Economics Materials. 5th ed. 1988. 22.75 o.p. (ISBN 0-87708-199-9). Ed Prog.

Educators Guide to Free Science Materials. 28th ed. 1987. 24.75 o.p. (ISBN 0-87708-183-2). Ed Prog.

Educators Guide to Free Science Materials. 29th ed. 1988. 25.75 o.p. (ISBN 0-87708-195-6). Ed Prog.

Educators Guide to Free Social Studies Materials. 27th ed. 1987. 26.75 o.p. (ISBN 0-87708-184-0). Ed Prog.

Educators Guide to Free Social Studies Materials. 28th ed. 1988. 27.00 o.p. (ISBN 0-87708-196-4). Ed Prog.

Educators Index of Free Materials. 96th ed. 1987. 45.50 o.p. (ISBN 0-87708-178-6). Ed Prog.

Educators Index of Free Materials. 97th ed. 1988. 45.75 o.p. (ISBN 0-87708-190-5). Ed Prog.

Educators, Parents & Micros: How to Help Your School Get & Use Computer Power. Robert W. Howell et al. LC 83-80469. 232p. 1983. pap. text ed. 15.95x o.p. (ISBN 0-918452-42-2). Learning Pubns.

Educators Present Arms: The Use of the Schools & Colleges As Agents of War Propaganda, 1914-1918 see Propaganda & Myth in Time of War.

Educreation: Education for Creation, Growth & Change. 2nd ed. Paul Ritter. 1979. 81.00 o.p. (ISBN 0-08-021475-4); pap. 35.00 o.p. (ISBN 0-08-021476-2). Pergamon.

Edward Albee: A Playwright in Protest. Michael E. Rutenberg. pap. 1.65 o.p. (ISBN 0-380-01155-7, 11916, Bard). Avon.

Edward & the Horse. Ann Rand & Olle Eksell. LC 61-6121. (Illus.). (gr. k-2). 1961. 3.25 o.p. (ISBN 0-15-225202-9, HJ). HarBraceJ.

Edward Bond. David Hirst. Ed. by Bruce King & Adele King. LC 85-47544. (Modern Dramatists Ser.). 172p. 1986. pap. 11.95 o.p. (ISBN 0-394-62067-4, Ever). Grove.

Edward F. Beale & the American West. Gerald Thompson. LC 83-1323. (Illus.). 321p. 1983. 24.95x o.p. (ISBN 0-8263-0663-2). U of NM Pr.

Edward Hicks, Painter of the Peaceable Kingdom. Alice E. Ford. LC 52-13392. (Illus.). 1973. Repr. of 1952 ed. 63.00 o.p. (ISBN 0-527-30400-X). Kraus Repr.

Edward Hopper: The Art & the Artist. Gail Levin. (Illus.). 1981. 49.50 o.p. (ISBN 0-393-01374-X). Norton.

Edward Hyde, Earl of Clarendon. George E. Miller. (English Authors Ser.). 1983. lib. bdg. 21.95 o.s.i. (ISBN 0-8057-6823-8, Twayne). G K Hall.

Edward Kennedy & the Camelot Legacy. James M. Burns. (Illus.). 384p. 1976. 11.95 o.p. (ISBN 0-393-07501-X). Norton.

Edward Kennedy: The Myth of Leadership. Murray B. Levin & T. A. Repak. 1980. 10.95 o.p. (ISBN 0-395-29249-2). HM.

Edward Lear. Ina R. Hark. (English Authors Ser.). 1982. lib. bdg. 14.50 o.s.i. (ISBN 0-8057-6822-X, Twayne). G K Hall.

Edward Lear & His World. John Lehmann. LC 77-73133. (Encore Edition). (Illus.). 1977. 3.95 o.p. (ISBN 0-684-16548-1, ScribT). Scribner.

Edward Lear: Eighteen Twelve to Eighteen Eighty-Eight. Vivian Noakes. (Illus.). 216p. 35.00 o.p. (ISBN 0-8109-1262-7). Abrams.

Edward Marshall. Edward Marshall. (Collected Poems Ser.). 255p. (Orig.). 1989. write for info. o.p. (ISBN 0-915032-90-2); pap. write for info. o.p. (ISBN 0-915032-91-0). Natl Poet Foun.

Edward Munch. N. Stang. (Illus.). 1972. pap. 22.50 o.s.i. (ISBN 0-685-36168-3). E J Brill USA.

Edward Randolph & the American Colonies, 1676-1703. Michael G. Hall. (Institute of Early American History & Culture Ser.). xi, 241p. 1960. 25.00x o.p. (ISBN 0-8078-0798-2). U of NC Pr.

Edward S. Curtis: The Life & Times of a Shadow Catcher. Barbara Davis. LC 85-9715. (Illus.). 256p. 1985. 45.00 o.p. (ISBN 0-87701-346-2). Chronicle Bks.

Edward Seventh, Prince & King. Giles St. Aubyn. LC 78-63294. (Illus.). 1979. 19.95 o.p. (ISBN 0-689-10937-7, Atheneum). Macmillan.

Edward the Rake: An Unwholesome Biography of Edward the Seventh. John Pearson. LC 75-14500. (Illus.). 192p. 1975. 8.95 o.p. (ISBN 0-15-127965-9). HarBraceJ.

Edward the Second. Christopher Marlowe. Ed. by Jacques Chwat. 1974. pap. 0.75 o.p. (ISBN 0-380-01158-1, 18648, Bard). Avon.

Edward Weston in Mexico: Nineteen Twenty-Three to Nineteen Twenty-Six. Amy Conger. LC 85-5877. (Illus.). 147p. 1983. 25.00 o.p. (ISBN 0-8263-0665-9); pap. 15.95 o.p. (ISBN 0-8263-0666-7). U of NM Pr.

Edward Weston Omnibus. Ed. by Beaumont Newhall & Amy Conger. (Illus.). 208p. 1984. pap. 16.95 o.p. (ISBN 0-87905-131-0, Peregrine Smith). Gibbs Smith Pub.

Edwardian Age: Conflict & Stability, 1900-1914. Ed. by Alan O'Day. LC 79-11809. 199p. 1979. 22.50 o.p. (ISBN 0-208-01823-9, Archon). Shoe String.

Edwardian Lady. Ina Taylor. (Illus.). 208p. 1980. 18.95 o.s.i. (ISBN 0-03-057454-4). H Holt & Co.

Edwardian Season. John S. Goodall. LC 79-89497. (Illus.). 64p. (ps up). 1980. 7.95 o.p. (ISBN 0-689-50155-2, Atheneum). Macmillan.

Edwardian Summer. John S. Goodall. LC 76-336. (Illus.). 72p. (ps up). 1976. 6.95 o.p. (ISBN 0-689-50062-9, Atheneum). Macmillan.

Edwardian Turn of Mind. Samuel Hynes. LC 68-12929. (Illus.). 1968. 44.50x o.p. (ISBN 0-691-06031-2); pap. 11.50x o.p. (ISBN 0-691-01302-0). Princeton U Pr.

Edwardians. Vita Sackville-West. 224p. 1976. pap. 3.95 o.p. (ISBN 0-380-00326-0, 65870-4, Bard). Avon.

Edwardians: Costume Cut-out Book. Sue Shields. 24p. (gr. 5-8). 1988. pap. 9.95 o.p. (ISBN 0-434-96315-1, Pub. by W Heinemann Ltd). David & Charles.

Edwin Diller Starbuck: Pioneer in the Psychology of Religion. Howard J. Booth. LC 80-5731. 304p. 1981. lib. bdg. 29.75 o.p. (ISBN 0-8191-1702-1); pap. text ed. 16.50 o.p. (ISBN 0-8191-1703-X). U Pr of Amer.

Edwin Muir: Uncollected Scottish Criticism. Ed. by Andrew Noble. (Barnes & Noble Critical Studies). 270p. 1982. 28.50x o.p. (ISBN 0-389-20202-9). B&N Imports.

Edwin Romanzo Elmer: Eighteen Fifty to Nineteen Twenty-Three. Betsy B. Jones. LC 83-51554. (Illus.). 170p. (Orig.). 1983. pap. 17.50 o.p. (ISBN 0-87391-033-8). Smith Coll.

Edwina: Countess Mountbatten of Burma. Richard Hough. LC 83-62979. (Illus.). 288p. 1984. 15.95 o.p. (ISBN 0-688-03766-6). Morrow.

EEC & the Third World. Ed. by K. B. Lall & H. S. Chopra. 500p. 1980. text ed. 35.00x o.p. (ISBN 0-391-02004-8). Humanities.

EEG Informatics: A Didactic Review of Methods & Applications of EEG Data Processing. Ed. by A. Remond. 426p. 1977. 98.00 o.p. (ISBN 0-444-80005-0, Biomedical Pr). Elsevier.

Eel: Biology & Management of Anguillid Eels. F. W. Tesch. Tr. by Jennifer Greenwood. 1977. 55.00 o.p. (ISBN 0-412-14370-4, NO.6286, Pub. by Chapman & Hall). Routledge Chapman & Hall.

Eells Family History in America: Sixteen Thirty-Three to Nineteen Fifty-Two. Ernest E. Eells. 600p. 1985. Repr. of 1969 ed. 25.00x o.p. (ISBN 0-932334-72-5). Heart of the Lakes.

EEO: Avoiding Compliance Headaches. 1976. 8.00 o.p. (ISBN 0-8144-6952-3). AMACOM.

Effect of a Study of Transformational Grammar on the Writing of Ninth & Tenth Graders. Donald Bateman & Frank Zidonis. 1966. pap. 3.25 o.p. (ISBN 0-8141-1295-1). NCTE.

Effect of Air Pollution Regulations on Highway Construction & Maintenance. (National Cooperative Highway Research Program Report). 81p. 1978. 7.00 o.p. (ISBN 0-317-36077-9). Transport Res Bd.

Effect of Constant & Cycling Temperature on Ectotherms: Proceedings of Conference at Trinity College, Dublin, 1-2 July 1981. Ed. by J. N. Grainger. (Illus.). 248p. 1981. pap. 43.00 o.p. (ISBN 0-08-028005-6, H145). Pergamon.

Effect of Control Devices on Traffic Operations. (National Cooperative Highway Research Program Report). 83p. 1967. 3.60 o.p. (ISBN 0-317-36078-7, 1545). Transport Res Bd.

Effect of Creativity, Response Mode & Subject Matter Familiarity on Achievement from Programmed Instruction. S. Tobias. 1968. pap. text ed. 9.50x o.p. (ISBN 0-8290-1114-5). Irvington.

Effect of Curb Geometry & Location on Vehicle Behavior. (National Cooperative Highway Research Program Report). 88p. 1974. 4.80 o.p. (ISBN 0-309-02301-7). Transport Res Bd.

Effect of Hydrogen on Behavior of Materials: Proceedings of Symposium, Jackson Lake, Wyoming, 1975. Ed. by Anthony W. Thompson & I. M. Bernstein. (Illus.). 710p. pap. 35.50 o.p. (ISBN 0-318-14805-6). Minerals Metals.

Effect of Modern Agriculture on Rural Developement. Ed. by Gyorgy Enyedi & Ivan Volgyes. LC 80-25232. (Pergamon Policy Studies on International Developement Comparative Rural Transformations Ser.). (Illus.). 256p. 1982. 49.00 o.p. (ISBN 0-08-027179-0). Pergamon.

Effect of Repeated Electroshock on Learning in Depressives. J. C. Brengelmann. (Monographien Aus Dem Gesamtgebiete der Neurologie: Vol. 84). (Illus.). 1959. 12.40 o.p. (ISBN 0-387-02447-6). Springer-Verlag.

Effect of Research & Development on U. S. Market Structure. Edward M. Scahill. Ed. by Fred Bateman. LC 85-14118. (Research in Business Economics & Public Policy Ser.: No. 9). 103p. 1985. 39.95 o.p. (ISBN 0-8357-1691-0). UMI Res Pr.

Effect of Roadway Geometrics on Traffic Operations: Six Reports. (Transportation Research Report Ser.). 55p. 1975. 2.60 o.p. (ISBN 0-309-02394-7). Transport Res Bd.

Effect of Seasoning on Pitch Troubles in Hardwood Sulfite Pulping. (Bibliographic Ser.: No. S16). 62p. 1967. 8.00 o.p. (ISBN 0-317-34372-6). Inst Paper Chem.

Effect of Stress on Freeze-Thaw Durability of Concrete Bridge Decks. (National Cooperative Highway Research Program Report). 70p. 1970. 3.60 o.p. (ISBN 0-309-01889-7). Transport Res Bd.

Effect of Vehicle Characteristics on Road Accidents. I. S. Jones. 200p. 1976. 55.00 o.p. (ISBN 0-08-018963-6). Pergamon.

Effect of Weldments on the Fatigue Strength of Steel Beams. (National Cooperative Highway Research Project Report). 114p. 1970. 5.40 o.p. (ISBN 0-309-01890-0). Transport Res Bd.

Effective & Selective Use of the Marital Deduction. Practising Law Institute Staff & Linda B. Hirschson. LC 86-60314. (Tax Law & Estate Planning Ser.). (Illus.). 622p. 1986. 45.00 o.p. (D4-5185). PLI.

Effective Approaches to Faculty Development. Ed. by William C. Nelsen & Michael E. Siegel. 149p. (Orig.). 1980. pap. 6.50 o.s.i. (ISBN 0-911696-00-8). Assn Am Coll.

Effective Bank Director. 263p. 1985. 54.00 o.p. (ISBN 0-318-04780-2, 359). Bank Admin Inst.

Effective Behavior in Organizations: Learning from the Interplay of Cases, Concepts & Student Experiences. 4th ed. Allan R. Cohen et al. 1988. 37.95x o.p.; tchr's. manual avail. o.p. Irwin.

Effective Bible Study. Howard F. Vos. (Contemporary Evangelical Perspectives Ser.). 1956. kivar 8.95 o.p. (ISBN 0-310-33851-4, 10966P). Zondervan.

Effective Body Building: Biblical Steps to Spiritual Growth. Peter C. Wagner. LC 81-86297. 160p. 1982. pap. 5.95 o.p. (ISBN 0-89840-029-5). Heres Life.

Effective Business Communications. Bonnie D. Phillips. LC 76-41086. (Technical Communications Ser.). 200p. 1977. pap. text ed. 12.39 o.p. (ISBN 0-8273-1405-1); instr's. guide 5.50 o.p. (ISBN 0-8273-1407-8). Delmar.

Effective Business Writing. Lawrence J. Starzyk & John B. Jewell. 320p. 1983. text ed. write for info. o.p. (ISBN 0-02-415800-3). Macmillan.

Effective Chemical Marketing, Advertising & Promotion: A Practical Guide for the Chemical Marketing Professional. J. Roger Hart. LC 83-12179. (Illus.). 121p. 1984. 24.00 o.p. (ISBN 0-8155-0954-5, Noyes Pubns). Noyes.

Effective Classroom Control. John Robertson. (Studies in Teaching & Learning). 117p. (Orig.). 1981. pap. text ed. 14.95 o.s.i. Princeton Bk Co.

Effective Coaching & Tipping. George L. Germain. LC 74-32536. (Effective Series Training Program for Supervisors). (Illus.). 37p. 1975. Incl. transparency masters. 3-ring binder 57.50 o.p. (ISBN 0-88061-024-7). Inst Pub ILCI.

Effective Collection of Employer Contributions 1983. Ed. by Becky A. Wright. 97p. (Orig.). 1983. pap. 10.00 o.p. (ISBN 0-89154-230-2). Intl Found Employ.

Effective Committees & Groups in the Church. Ernest G. Bormann & Nancy Bormann. LC 73-78263. 1973. 4.50 o.p. (ISBN 0-8066-1328-9, 10-2025, Augsburg). Augsburg Fortress.

Effective Communication. Learning Systems Ltd. 1968. pap. text ed. 4.20 o.p. (ISBN 0-08-014048-3). Pergamon.

Effective Communication in Nursing: Theory & Practice. Joseph F. Ceccio & Cathy M. Ceccio. LC 81-15999. 315p. 1982. pap. 16.95 o.p. (ISBN 0-471-07911-1, Pub. by Wiley Med). Wiley.

Effective Communication on the Job. 3rd ed. Ed. by William K. Fallon. 320p. 1981. 17.95 o.p. (ISBN 0-8144-5698-7). AMACOM.

Effective Compensatory Eduction Sourcebook, Vol. 3: Project Profiles. Dorothy L. Alexander. 168p. 1987. pap. 8.00 o.p. (ISBN 0-318-23454-8, S/N 065-000-00294-9). USGPO.

Effective Direct & Cross-Examination. William A. Brockett & John W. Keker. 375p. 1986. text ed. 65.00 o.p. (ISBN 0-88124-143-1). Cal Cont Ed Bar.

Effective EDP Manager. Michael R. Frank. 288p. 1981. 17.95 o.p. (ISBN 0-8144-5635-9). AMACOM.

Effective Employee Assistance: A Comprehensive Guide for the Employer. Joseph A. Muldoon & Mitchell Berdie. 1980. 49.95 o.p. (Illus.). (ISBN 0-89638-048-3). CompCare.

Effective Feature Writing. A. Clay Schoenfeld & Karen S. Diegmueller. 1982. text ed. 26.95 o.p. (ISBN 0-03-057788-8). HR&W.

Effective Health Care Supervisor. Charles R. McConnell. LC 81-19058. 317p. 1982. text ed. 37.50 o.p. (ISBN 0-89443-390-3). Aspen Pub.

Effective Human Relations in Business. Barry L. Reece & Rhonda O. Brandt. 1981. text ed. 24.95 o.p. (ISBN 0-395-30701-5). HM.

Effective Human Relations in Organizations. 2nd ed. Barry L. Reece & Rhonda Brandt. LC 83-80586. 480p. 1984. text ed. 33.25 o.p. (ISBN 0-395-34292-9). HM.

Effective Information Management. R. I. Tricker. 204p. 1984. 28.95 o.p. (ISBN 0-442-28307-5). Van Nos Reinhold.

Effective Intervention with the Language Impaired Child. Martha L. Cole & Jack T. Cole. LC 80-28037. 336p. 1981. text ed. 34.00 o.p. (ISBN 0-89443-344-X). Aspen Pub.

Effective Job Instruction. George L. Germain. LC 77-77275. (Effective Series Training Program for Supervisors). (Illus.). 38p. 1977. 3-ring binder 57.50 o.p. (ISBN 0-88061-022-0). Inst Pub ILCI.

Effective Laboratory Supervisor. Umiker. 304p. 1982. pap. 23.95 o.p. (ISBN 0-87489-406-9). Med Economics.

Effective Letters in Business. 2nd ed. Robert L. Shurter. 1954. text ed. 9.50 o.p. (ISBN 0-07-057339-5); pap. 5.95 o.p. (ISBN 0-07-057340-9). McGraw.

Effective Litigation of Employment Discrimination Cases. 136p. 1983. 6.00 o.p. (ISBN 0-318-02413-6). ICLE Georgia.

Effective Management by Objectives: The 3-D Method of MBO. W. J. Reddin. 1970. text ed. 34.50 o.p. (ISBN 0-07-051360-0). McGraw.

Effective Managerial Leadership. James J. Cribbin. (AMACOM Executive Books). 1978. pap. 4.95 o.p. (ISBN 0-8144-7504-3). AMACOM.

Effective Meal Planning & Food Preparation for the Mentally Retarded-Developmentally Disabled: Comprehensive & Innovative Teaching Methods. Issam B. Amary. (Illus.). 232p. 1979. 26.50x o.p. (ISBN 0-398-03882-1). C C Thomas.

Effective Meetings for Busy People: Let's Decide It & Go Home. William T. Carnes. 1980. text ed. 22.95 o.p. (ISBN 0-07-010117-5). McGraw.

Effective Meetings for Busy People: Let's Decide It & Go Home. William T. Carnes. 368p. 1983. pap. text ed. 11.50 o.p. (ISBN 0-07-010118-3). McGraw.

Effective Methods of EDP Quality Assurance. William E. Perry. (Q. E. D. Information Sciences Ser.). (Illus.). 400p. 1983. text ed. 50.67 o.p. (ISBN 0-13-244336-8). P-H.

Effective Mormon Families. William G. Dyer & Phillip R. Kunz. LC 86-71891. xii, 174p. 1986. 9.95 o.p. (ISBN 0-87579-062-3). Deseret Bk.

Effective Nurse: Leader & Manager. 2nd ed. Laura M. Douglass. LC 83-6796. (Illus.). 295p. 1983. pap. text ed. 19.95 o.p. (ISBN 0-8016-1449-X). Mosby.

Effective Operator Training-Lift Trucks. Raymond L. Kuhlman. LC 78-56971. (Effective Series Training Program for Supervisors). (Illus.). 87p. 1978. Incl. transparency masters. 3-ring binder 57.50 o.p. (ISBN 0-88061-026-3). Inst Pub ILCI.

Effective Operator Training: Motorized Equipment. Raymond L. Kuhlman. (Effective Series Training Program for Supervisors). (Illus.). 71p. 1978. Incl. transparency masters. 3-ring binder 57.50 o.p. (ISBN 0-88061-027-1). Inst Pub ILCI.

Effective Participation in Government: A Policy Skills Manual. William D. Coplin & Michael K. O'Leary. 230p. (Orig.). (YA) (gr. 10 up). 1986. text ed. 18.50x o.p. (ISBN 0-936826-23-1); pap. text ed. 12.50x o.p. (ISBN 0-936826-22-3). PS Assocs Croton.

Effective Phrases for Performance Appraisals: A Guide to Successful Evaluations. 4th ed. James E. Neal, Jr. LC 85-90517. 113p. 1986. spiral bdg. 6.95 o.p. (ISBN 0-9609006-4-0). Neal Pubns Inc.

Effective Police Manager. P. Whisenand. 1981. pap. text ed. 35.00 o.p. (ISBN 0-13-244509-3). P-H.

Effective Principal, Effective School. James Lipham. Ed. by Thomas Koerner. (Orig.). 1981. pap. text ed. 5.75 o.p. (ISBN 0-88210-119-6). Natl Assn Principals.

Effective Protection, Domestic Resource Costs & Shadow Prices: A General Equilibrium Perspective. Edward Tower. (Working Paper Ser.: No. 664). 202p. 1984. 10.00 o.p. (ISBN 0-8213-0404-6, WP 0664). World Bank.

Effective Psychotherapy: A Handbook of Research. Alan S. Gurman & Andrew M Razin. LC 76-23300. 1977. 150.00 o.p. (ISBN 0-08-019508-3). Pergamon.

Effective Psychotherapy: The Silent Dialog. Robert J. Decker. 76p. 1982. softcover 5.95 o.p. (ISBN 0-932930-51-4). Pilgrimage Inc.

Effective Publications for Colleges & Universities. Kelvin J. Arden & William J. Whalen. 180p. 1978. 16.50 o.p. (ISBN 0-89964-034-6). Coun Adv & Supp Ed.

Effective Remedies for Common Ailments. Ben Tawshunsky. 1977. 4.00 o.p. (ISBN 0-682-49018-0). Exposition-Phoenix.

Effective Research Report Writing in Government. J. Monroe. 1980. text ed. 29.95 o.p. (ISBN 0-07-042784-4). McGraw.

Effective Retailing. Lawrence G. Golden & Donald A. Zimmerman. 1980. text ed. 28.95 o.p. (ISBN 0-395-30609-4). HM.

Effective Safe Behavior Reinforcement. George L. Germain. (Effective Series Training Program for Supervisors). (Illus.). 37p. 1975. 3-ring binder 57.50 o.s.i. (ISBN 0-88061-025-5). Inst Pub ILCI.

Effective Safety Talk Technique. George L. Germain. LC 74-32536. (Effective Series Training Program for Supervisors). (Illus.). 49p. 1975. Incl. transparency masters. 3-ring binder 57.50 o.s.i. (ISBN 0-88061-023-9). Inst Pub ILCI.

Effective Sales Incentive Compensation. John W. Barry & Porter J. Henry. (Illus.). 192p. 1981. text ed. 23.95 o.p. (ISBN 0-07-003860-0). McGraw.

Effective School Board Member. Lloyd W. Ashby. LC 68-9492. (Illus.). 120p. 1968. pap. text ed. 3.50x o.p. (ISBN 0-8134-1053-3, 1053). Inter Print Pubs.

Effective Selling: A Short Course for Professionals. William J. Crissy et al. LC 76-45818. 338p. 1977. 24.95 o.p. (ISBN 0-471-01924-0). Krieger.

Effective Series Training Program for Supervisors, 6 manuals. George L. Germain & Raymond L. Kuhlman. 3-ring binder 345.00 o.s.i. (ISBN 0-88061-021-2). Inst Pub ILCI.

Effective Settlement Strategy. 296p. 1984. 25.00 o.p. (ISBN 0-88129-137-4). Wash Bar CLE.

Effective Small Business Management. James F. Moreau. 1980. text ed. 35.16 o.p. (ISBN 0-395-30676-0). HM.

Effective Speaker. Edward S. Strother & Alan W. Huckleberry. LC 68-7238. (Illus.). 1968. text ed. 19.95 o.p. (ISBN 0-395-05441-9). HM.

Effective Supervisor's Handbook. 2nd ed. Louis V. Imundo. LC 79-54838. 256p. 1984. pap. 8.95 o.p. (ISBN 0-8144-7621-X). AMACOM.

Effective Supervisory Practices. International City Management Association Staff. LC 77-28712. (Municipal Management Ser.). (Orig.). 1978. pap. text ed. 24.00 o.s.i. (ISBN 0-87326-019-8). Intl City Mgt.

Effective Supervisory Safety Salesmanship. H. Greg Adams. LC 81-86317. (Illus.). 40p. 1982. Incl. transparency masters & slides. 3-ring binder 37.50 o.p. (ISBN 0-88061-028-X). Inst Pub ILCI.

Effective Systems Integration & Optical Design I: Proceedings. Society of Photo-Optical Instrumentation Engineers Staff. (SPIE Seminar Proceedings: Vol. 54). 176p. 1975. 11.00 o.p. (ISBN 0-89252-066-3). SPIE.

Effective Teacher. Bennie E. Goodwin, II. LC 84-28869. 48p. 1985. pap. 1.95 o.p. (ISBN 0-87784-333-3). Inter-Varsity.

Effective Technical Speeches & Sessions: A Guide for Speakers & Program Chairmen. Howard H. Manko. LC 69-18731. (Illus.). 1969. text ed. 29.95 o.p. (ISBN 0-07-039896-8). McGraw.

Effective Use of Advertising Media. Martyn Davis. 322p. 1981. text ed. 36.75x o.p. (ISBN 0-09-142970-6, Pub. by Busn Bks England); pap. text ed. 18.25 o.p. (ISBN 0-09-142971-4, Pub. by Busn Bks England). Gower Pub Co.

Effective Washington Representation. Ed. by Stanley J. Marcuss. 350p. 1983. 65.00 o.p. (ISBN 0-15-100018-2, H42876, Pub. by Law & Business). HarBraceJ.

Effective Weight Manager. Fred Kummer. 160p. 1986. 12.95 o.p. (ISBN 0-8264-0365-4). Continuum.

Effective Writing. Christopher Turk & John Kirkman. 1982. 23.00x o.p. (ISBN 0-419-11670-2, NO. 6636, Pub. by E & FN Spon); pap. 9.95 o.p. (ISBN 0-419-11680-X, NO. 6635). Routledge Chapman & Hall.

Effectiveness of Antitrust Policy Towards Horizontal Mergers. David B. Audretsch. Ed. by Fred Bateman. LC 83-6985. (Research in Business Economics & Public Policy Ser.: No. 1). 164p. 1983. 42.95 o.p. (ISBN 0-8357-1434-9). UMI Res Pr.

Effectiveness of Bail Systems: An Analysis of Failure to Appear in Court & Rearrest while on Bail. Stevens H. Clarke et al. (Illus.). 37p. 1976. pap. 3.00 o.p. (ISBN 0-318-00251-5). Institute Government.

Effectiveness of Chapter One Services. Mary M. Kennedy. (Education Department Publication OR 87-501). (Illus.). 187p. 1987. pap. 9.00 o.p. (ISBN 0-318-22629-4, S/N 065-000-00283-3). USGPO.

Effectiveness of the Annual Reports. David Hawkins & Barbara Brown. 24p. 1986. write for info. o.p. Finan Exec.

Effects & Dose Response Relationships of Toxic Metals. G. F. Nordberg. 56p. 1976. 209.00 o.p. (ISBN 0-444-41370-7, Biomedical Pr). Elsevier.

Effects of Changes in United States Agricultural Production on Demand for Farm Inputs. Robbin Shoemaker. (Agriculture Department Technical Bulletin Ser.: No. 1722). 19p. 1986. pap. 1.25 o.p. (ISBN 0-318-22376-7, S/N 001-019-00478-9). USGPO.

Effects of DDT on Man & Other Mammals II. Gary L. Henderson et al. LC 73-289. 1973. 32.50x o.p. (ISBN 0-8422-7111-2). Irvington.

Effects of DDT on Man & Other Mammals I. Thomas H. Jukes et al. LC 73-289. (Illus.). 220p. 1973. text ed. 36.50x o.p. (ISBN 0-8422-7110-4). Irvington.

Effects of Deicing Salts on Plant Biota & Soils: Experimental Phase. (National Cooperative Highway Research Program Report). 88p. 1976. 5.60 o.p. (ISBN 0-309-02511-7). Transport Res Bd.

Effects of Deicing Salts on Water Quality & Biota: Literature Review & Recommended Research. (National Cooperative Highway Research Project Report). 70p. 1970. 3.20 o.p. (ISBN 0-309-01878-1). Transport Res Bd.

Effects of Different Methods of Stockpiling & Handling Aggregates. (National Cooperative Highway Research Program Report). 102p. 1967. 4.60 o.p. (ISBN 0-317-36079-5, 1580). Transport Res Bd.

Effects of Drugs on the Cell Nucleus: Bristol-Meyers Cancer Symposia. Ed. by Harris Busch et al. LC 79-51690. 1979. 71.00 o.p. (ISBN 0-12-147654-5). Acad Pr.

Effects of Extending the Mandatory Retirement Age. Henry M. Wallfesh. LC 78-14430. 1978. pap. 7.50 o.p. (ISBN 0-8144-2225-X). AMACOM.

Effects of Federal Policies on Extracorporeal Shock Wave Lithotripsy. LC 85-600554. (Health Case Technology Study 36 OTA-HCS-36). 118p. (Orig.). 1986. pap. 5.50 o.p. (ISBN 0-318-21332-X, S/N 052-003-01041-1). USGPO.

Effects of Fluorides in Animals. National Research Council Staff. LC 74-4061. (Illus.). 76p. 1974. pap. 5.75x o.p. (ISBN 0-309-02219-3). Natl Acad Pr.

Effects of Government Deficits: A Comparative Analysis of Crowding Out, No. 158. Charles E. Dumas. LC 85-19423. (Essays in International Finance Ser.). 1985. pap. text ed. 6.50x o.p. (ISBN 0-88165-065-X). Princeton U Int Finan Econ.

Effects of Hormones on Immunity, Vol. 2. Maria S. De Sousa et al. LC 72-13691. (Illus.). 220p. 1973. text ed. 30.00x o.p. (ISBN 0-8422-7098-1). Irvington.

Effects of Hormones on Immunity, Vol. 1. James Watson et al. 1973. 30.00x o.p. (ISBN 0-8422-7113-9). Irvington.

Effects of Induced Abortion on Subsequent Reproductive Function & Pregnancy Outcome: Hawaii. Chin S. Chung & Patricia G. Steinhoff. LC 83-11536. (Papers of the East-West Population Institute: No. 86). xii, 144p. 1983. pap. text ed. 3.00 o.p. (ISBN 0-86638-046-9). EW Ctr HI.

Effects of Ionizing Radiation on DNA: Physical, Chemical & Biological Aspects. Ed. by A. J. Bertinchamps et al. LC 77-25857. (Molecular, Biology, Biochemistry & Biophysics: Vol 27). (Illus.). 1978. 56.00 o.p. (ISBN 0-387-08542-4). Springer-Verlag.

Effects of Melting & Processing Variables on Mechanical Properties of Steels, Series MPC-6. Ed. by G. V. Smith. 1977. pap. text ed. 35.00 o.p. (ISBN 0-685-86861-3, G00126). ASME.

Effects of Negative Conditioning on Children. Rolland M. Lim. 72p. 1986. 7.95 o.p. (ISBN 0-8062-2937-3). Carlton.

Effects of Nuclear War. LC 79-600080. (Office of Technology Assessment NS 89 Ser.). 151p. (Orig.). 1979. pap. 6.50 o.p. (ISBN 0-318-11780-0, S/N 052-003-00668-5). USGPO.

Effects of Petroleum on Arctic & Subarctic Marine Environments & Organisms: Biological Effects, Vols. 1 &2. Ed. by Donald C. Malins. 1977. Vol. 1. 46.50 o.p. (ISBN 0-12-466901-8); Vol. 2. 44.50 o.p. (ISBN 0-12-466902-6). Acad Pr.

Effects of Piping Restraints on Piping Integrity: PVP, Vol. 40. Ed. by R. H. Mallet et al. 320p. 1980. 40.00 o.p. (ISBN 0-317-33492-1, H00167); members 20.00 o.p. (ISBN 0-317-33493-X). ASME.

Effects of Poisonous Plants on Livestock. Ed. by Richard F. Keeler et al. 1978. 39.95 o.p. (ISBN 0-12-403250-8). Acad Pr.

Effects of Psychological Therapy. 2nd, enl. ed. S. J. Rachman & G. T. Wilson. (FEBS Ser.: Vol. 24). 400p. 1980. 37.00 o.p. (ISBN 0-08-024675-3); pap. 22.00 o.p. (ISBN 0-08-024674-5). Pergamon.

Effects of Psychotherapy. 2nd ed. S. Rachman. 196p. 1971. text ed. 25.00 o.p. (ISBN 0-08-016805-1); pap. text ed. 12.75 o.p. (ISBN 0-08-016807-8). Pergamon.

Effects of Radiation on Materials & Components. John F. Kircher & Richard E. Bowman. LC 64-16977. 702p. (Orig.). 1964. 41.00 o.p. (ISBN 0-686-81277-8, VN). Krieger.

Effects of the Space Environment on Materials Symposium: Proceedings, St. Louis MO, 19-21 April 1967. (Science of Advanced Materials & Process Engineering Ser., Vol. 11). 20.00 o.p. (ISBN 0-938994-11-5). SAMPE.

Effects of Various Diseases on the Development of Atherosclerosis. Anatolii M. Vikhert & Valentin S. Zhdanov. Ed. by James E. Muller. LC 80-13069. 220p. 1981. 40.00 o.p. (ISBN 0-08-025555-8). Pergamon.

Effects of Weapons on Ecosystems. J. P. Robinson. LC 79-41226. (Illus.). 76p. 1979. 12.25 o.p. (ISBN 0-08-025656-2); pap. 8.00 o.p. (ISBN 0-08-025657-0). Pergamon.

Efferent Organization & the Integration of Behavior. Ed. by Jack D. Maser. 1973. 65.50 o.p. (ISBN 0-12-476950-0). Acad Pr.

Efficiency & Empire. Arnold White. Ed. by G. R. Searle. LC 70-131993. (Society & Victorians Ser.: No. 15). 315p. 1973. Repr. of 1901 ed. text ed. 17.50x o.p. (ISBN 0-901759-42-2). Humanities.

Efficiency & Limits of Radiologic Examination of the Pancreas. Anacker. LC 75-18931. (Illus.). 290p. 1975. lib. bdg. 18.50 o.p. (ISBN 0-88416-054-8). Year Bk Med.

Efficiency Measurement for Local Government Services: Some Initial Suggestions. Harry Hatry et al. 204p. 1979. pap. text ed. 8.50 o.p. (ISBN 0-87766-266-5). Urban Inst.

Efficiency of Human Movement. 4th ed. Marion R. Broer & Ronald F. Zernicke. (Illus.). 453p. 1973. 28.95 o.p. (ISBN 0-7216-2088-4). HR&W.

Efficiency of Manufacturing Systems. Ed. by B. Wilson et al. (NATO Conference Series II, Systems Science: Vol. 14). 346p. 1983. 59.50x o.p. (ISBN 0-306-41256-X, Plenum Pr). Plenum Pub.

Efficient Patterns for Adequate Library Service in a Large City: A Survey of Boston. Leonard Grundt. (Monograph: No. 6). 121p. 1968. pap. 4.00x o.p. (ISBN 0-87845-028-9). U of Ill Lib Info Sci.

Efficient Port. R. B. Oram & C. C. Baker. 1971. text ed. 22.00 o.p. (ISBN 0-08-016396-3). Pergamon.

Efficient Use of Systems with Many Processors. Robert J. Chansler, Jr. Ed. by Harold Stone. LC 86-6962. (Computer Science: Computer Architecture & Design Ser.: No. 6). 138p. 1986. 39.95 o.p. (ISBN 0-8357-1749-6). UMI Res Pr.

Effluent Variability from Waste Water Treatment Processes & Its Control. W. W. Eckenfelder & A. J. Englander. 1976. pap. 55.00 o.p. (ISBN 0-08-019843-0). Pergamon.

Egg at Easter: A Folklore Study. Venetia Newall. (Illus.). 423p. 1985. 25.00 o.p. (ISBN 0-7100-6845-X). Routledge Chapman & Hall.

Egg Cookery. Lou S. Pappas. LC 76-13015. (Illus.). 168p. (Orig.). 1976. pap. 5.95 o.p. (ISBN 0-912238-80-1, One Hund One Prods). Ortho.

Egg Recipes by the Dozen. Ed. by Annette Gohlke. LC 83-63229. 66p. 1984. pap. 3.95 o.s.i. (ISBN 0-89821-057-7). Reiman Assocs.

Eggbeater Book: The First & Last Word about Man's Greatest Invention. Don Thorton. (Illus.). 1983. 16.95 o.p. (ISBN 0-87795-557-3, Arbor Hse). Morrow.

Egghead & I. Lenna Gauss. 1977. 6.50 o.p. (ISBN 0-682-48816-X). Exposition-Phoenix.

Eggplant & Squash. Sheryl London. 1976. 12.95 o.p. (ISBN 0-689-10709-9, Atheneum). Macmillan.

Eggs As Usual Breakfast...Etc. Nidra Poller. (Illus.). 26p. (gr. 2 up). 1980. PLB 10.00 stiched binding o.p. (ISBN 0-686-68704-3). Chicago Review.

Eggshells to Objects: A New Approach to Eggcraft. Susan Arnold. LC 79-4328. (Illus.). 128p. (gr. 6 up). 1979. 7.95 o.p. (ISBN 0-03-043981-7). H Holt & Co.

Ego & Its Own. Max Stirner. Tr. by Steven Byington from Ger. (Illus.). 366p. 1982. pap. 11.00 o.s.i. (ISBN 0-946061-00-9). Left Bank.

Ego & the Centaur: Poems. Jean Garrigue. LC 76-138236. 126p. 1972. Repr. of 1947 ed. lib. bdg. 35.00x o.p. (ISBN 0-8371-5593-2, GAEC). Greenwood.

Ego Psychology & Communication: Theory for the Interview. Norman A. Polansky. LC 74-116533. 1971. 29.95x o.p. (ISBN 0-202-26052-6). Aldine de Gruyter.

Ego: Revealer-Concealer, a Key to Yoga. Frank R. Podgorski. (Illus.). 306p. 1985. lib. bdg. 29.00 o.p. (ISBN 0-8191-4345-6); pap. text ed. 15.25 o.p. (ISBN 0-8191-4346-4). U Pr of Amer.

Egoist: A Play from the Novel by George Meredith. George Meredith & Alfred Sutro. Ed. by Lewis Sawin. LC 80-28494. 145p. 1981. text ed. 15.00x o.p. (ISBN 0-8214-0552-7). Ohio U Pr.

Egon Eiermann, Architect. Florita Z. Louis de Malave. (Architecture Ser.: Bibliography A-1305). 5p. 1985. pap. 2.00 o.p. (ISBN 0-89028-235-8). Vance Biblios.

Egon Ronay's Eat Out on a Budget. Date not set. (ISBN 0-86145-783-8, Pub. by Auto Assn England). Salem Hse Pubs.

Egon Ronay's Guide to Best Pubs in Britain. Date not set. (ISBN 0-86145-782-X, Pub. by Auto Assn England). Salem Hse Pubs.

Egon Ronay's Guide to Hotels & Restaurants in Britain. Date not set. (ISBN 0-86145-781-1, Pub. by Auto Assn England). Salem Hse Pubs.

Egon Ronay's Lucas Guide to Hotels, Restaurants & Inns in Great Britain & Ireland, 1983. Egon Ronay. LC 74-644899. (Illus.). 862p. 1983. pap. 13.95 o.s.i. (ISBN 0-03-063331-1). H Holt & Co.

Egon Ronay's Taste of Europe. Date not set. (ISBN 0-86145-784-6, Pub. by Auto Assn England). Salem Hse Pubs.

Egon Schiele. Ed. by Serge Sabarsky. (Illus.). 124p. 1979. pap. 14.00 o.p. (ISBN 0-918825-46-6, Dist. by Kampmann & Co.). Moyer Bell Limited.

Egon Schiele. Ed. by Serge Sabarsky. (Illus.). 208p. (Ger.). 1982. pap. 14.00 o.p. (ISBN 0-918825-47-4, Dist. by Kampmann & Co). Moyer Bell Limited.

Egotistical Sublime: A History of Wordsworth's Imagination. Henry J. Jones. LC 78-2460. ix, 212p. 1978. Repr. of 1954 ed. lib. bdg. 24.75x o.p. (ISBN 0-313-20307-5, JOES). Greenwood.

Egypt & the East Mediterranean World: 2200-1900 B.C. William Ward. 160p. 1971. text ed. 24.95x o.p. (ISBN 0-8156-6038-3, Am U Beirut). Syracuse U Pr.

Egypt: Burdens of the Past, Options for the Future. John Waterbury. LC 78-3248. (Illus.). 336p. 1978. 15.00x o.p. (ISBN 0-253-28092-3). Ind U Pr.

Egyptian Carpets. Sidna Rachid & Luanne Brown. 1986. pap. 21.50 o.p. (ISBN 977-424-057-X, Pub. by Am Univ Cairo Pr). Columbia U Pr.

Egyptian Magic. E. Wallis Budge. (Illus.). 1979. pap. 6.95 o.p. (ISBN 0-7100-0135-5). Routledge Chapman & Hall.

Egyptian Magic. Wallis Budge. 1974. 5.95 o.p. (ISBN 0-8216-0176-8, Pub. by Univ Bks). Carol Pub Group.

Egyptian Mummy: Secrets & Science. Stuart Fleming & Bernard Fishman. LC 80-20555. (University of Pennsylvania Museum). (Illus.). 94p. 1986. pap. 17.95 o.p. (ISBN 0-8122-0951-6). U of Pa Pr.

Egyptian Mysteries. Arthur Versluis. 192p. 1988. pap. 11.95 o.p. (ISBN 1-85063-087-9). Routledge Chapman & Hall.

Egyptian Policy in the Arab World: Intervention in Yemen, 1962-1967 Case Study. Ali A. Rahmy. LC 82-23812. (Illus.). 412p. (Orig.). 1983. lib. bdg. 33.75 o.p. (ISBN 0-8191-2997-6); pap. text ed. 18.75 o.p. (ISBN 0-8191-2998-4). U Pr of Amer.
Egyptian Religion. E. Wallis Budge. (Illus.). 1979. pap. 6.95 o.p. (ISBN 0-7100-0134-7). Routledge Chapman & Hall.
Egyptian Religion. E. Wallis Budge. 1974. 5.95 o.p. (ISBN 0-8216-0177-6, Pub. by Univ Bks). Carol Pub Group.
Egyptian Religion. E. Wallis Budge. 200p. 1987. pap. 11.95 o.p. (ISBN 1-85063-084-4, Pub. by Routledge UK). Routledge Chapman & Hall.
Egyptians. Isaac Asimov. LC 67-20371. 288p. (YA) (gr. 7 up). 1967. 11.45 o.p. (ISBN 0-395-06572-0). HM.
Egypt's Economic Potential. Roberto Aliboni et al. 256p. 1984. 29.95 o.p. (ISBN 0-7099-1319-2, Pub. by Croom Helm Ltd). Routledge Chapman & Hall.
Egypt's Young Rebels: "Young Egypt", 1933-1952. James P. Jankowski. LC 75-8654. (Publications Ser.: No.145). 1975. 9.95x o.p. (ISBN 0-8179-6451-7). Hoover Inst Pr.
Eider Down. Marjorie K. Lawrence. 1975. 4.50 o.p. (ISBN 0-682-48392-3). Exposition-Phoenix.
Eight A. M. Shadows. Patricia Hubbell. LC 65-21718. (Illus.). (gr. 2-7). 1965. 2.95 o.p. (ISBN 0-689-20184-2, Atheneum). Macmillan.
Eight American Authors. rev. ed. Ed. by James Woodress et al. 416p. 1972. pap. 3.95x o.p. (ISBN 0-393-00651-4, Norton Lib). Norton.
Eight American Writers. Ed. by Norman Foerster et al. 1963. 19.95x o.p. (ISBN 0-393-09524-X, NortonC). Norton.
Eight Black Horses. Ed McBain. 1985. 15.95 o.p. (ISBN 0-87795-681-2, Arbor Hse). Morrow.
Eight Black Horses. Ed McBain. 350p. 1986. lib. bdg. 15.95 o.p. (ISBN 0-8161-4022-7, Large Print Bks). G K Hall.
Eight Boyle Lectures on Atheism. Richard Bentley. Ed. by Rene Wellek. LC 75-11196. (British Philosophers & Theologians of the 17th & 18th Centuries Ser.: Vol. 3). 1976. Repr. of 1692 ed. lib. bdg. 51.00 o.p. (ISBN 0-8240-1752-8). Garland Pub.
Eight Favorite Anthems. Evan Stephens. 1972. pap. 1.95 o.p. (ISBN 0-87747-350-1). Deseret Bk.
Eight Idaho Poets: An Anthology. Ed. by Ronald E. McFarland. LC 78-68559. 170p. 1979. 5.95 o.p. (ISBN 0-89301-060-X). U of Idaho Pr.
Eight Keys to Communicate Better. Andre Bustanoby. LC 85-14199. 64p. (Orig.). 1985. pap. 2.95 o.p. (ISBN 0-310-46242-8, 9266P). Zondervan.
Eight Million Ways to Die. Lawrence Block. LC 81-71689. 1982. 12.95 o.p. (ISBN 0-87795-405-4, Arbor Hse). Morrow.
Eight Years in Another World. Harding Lemay. LC 80-69363. 1981. 10.95 o.p. (ISBN 0-689-11149-5, Atheneum). Macmillan.
Eighteen-Forty Citizens of Texas: Land Grants, Vol. I. Gifford White. LC 83-83045. 290p. 1983. 27.00 o.s.i. (ISBN 0-911317-25-2); pap. 20.00 o.p. (ISBN 0-911317-24-4). Ericson Bks.
Eighteen Hundred Seven Land Lottery of Georgia. Silas E. Lucas, Jr. (Illus.). 1968. 25.00 o.p. (ISBN 0-89308-020-9). Southern Hist Pr.
Eighteen Hundred Woodcuts by Thomas Bewick & His School. Thomas Bewick. Ed. by Blanche Cirker. (Illus.). 15.75 o.p. (ISBN 0-8446-0490-9). Peter Smith.
Eighteen Ninety-Eight: The Story of the Spanish American War & the Philippine Insurrection Told with Pictures. Irving Werstein. LC 65-21406. (Illus., Orig.). 1966. 18.50x o.p. (ISBN 0-8154-0251-1); pap. 4.95x o.p. (ISBN 0-8154-0250-3). Cooper Sq.
Eighteen Ninety-Seven Watches. Benjamin, Allen & Co. Staff & Green, William Brothers Staff. 1968. pap. 5.50 o.p. (ISBN 0-915706-11-3). Am Reprints.
Eighteen Short Songs of the Bitter Motherland. Yannis Ritsos. Ed. by Theofanis G. Stavrou. Tr. by Amy Mims from Gr. (Modern Greek History & Culture Ser.). (Illus.). 1974. 15.00 o.p. (ISBN 0-317-18642-6). Nostos Bks.
Eighteen Sixty-One to Eighteen Sixty-Five: The Adventure of the Civil War Told with Pictures. Irving Werstein. LC 60-4840. (Illus., Orig.). 18.50x o.p. (ISBN 0-8154-0249-X); pap. 4.95x o.p. (ISBN 0-8154-0248-1). Cooper Sq.
Eighteen Songs of a Nomad Flute: The Story of Lady Wen-Chi. Tr. by Robert A. Rorex & Wen Fong. LC 74-11140. (Illus.). 1974. 18.50 o.p. (ISBN 0-87099-095-0). Metro Mus Art.
Eighteen Thirty Citizens of Texas. Gifford White. 1982. 24.95 o.p. (ISBN 0-89015-343-4). Eakin Pr.
Eighteen Twenty-Seven Land Lottery of Georgia. Martha L. Houston. (Illus.). 1976. Repr. of 1929 ed. 30.00 o.p. (ISBN 0-89308-015-2). Southern Hist Pr.
Eighteen Twenty-Six Journal of John James Audubon. 2nd rev. ed. John J. Audubon. Ed. by Alice Ford. LC 86-28813. (Illus.). 448p. 1987. Repr. of 1966 ed. 29.95 o.p. (ISBN 0-89659-689-3). Abbeville Pr.
Eighteenth Annual Immigration & Naturalization Institute. 735p. 1985. 40.00 o.p. (H4-4980). PLI.
Eighteenth Century Child's Bedroom. 1976. pap. 1.50 o.p. (ISBN 0-87588-127-0, 858). Hobby Hse.
Eighteenth Century English Furniture: The Norman Adams Collection, Whittington. C. Claxton Stevens. (Illus.). 490p. 1985. 89.50 o.p. (ISBN 0-902028-88-X). Apollo.
Eighteenth Century English Literature. Date not set. (ISBN 0-8052-3882-4). Random.
Eighteenth-Century French Life-Drawing. James H. Rubin & Pierre Rosenberg. LC 76-56719. (Publication of the Art Museum of Princeton University Ser.). (Illus.). 104p. 1977. 44.50x o.p. (ISBN 0-691-03926-7). Princeton U Pr.
Eighteenth Century Gothic Novel: An Annotated Bibliography of Criticism & Selected Texts. Dan J. McNutt. LC 74-22490. (Reference Library of Humanities: No. 4). 353p. 1975. lib. bdg. 51.00 o.p. (ISBN 0-8240-1058-2). Garland Pub.
Eighteenth-Century Musical Tour in Central Europe & the Netherlands. Charles Burney. 268p. Repr. of 1959 ed. lib. bdg. 39.00 o.p. (Pub. by Am Repr Serv). Reprint Servs.
Eighteenth-Century Musical Tour in France & Italy. Charles Burney. 328p. Repr. of 1959 ed. lib. bdg. 49.00 o.p. (Pub. by Am Repr Serv). Reprint Servs.
Eighteenth Century Novel: The Idea of the Gentleman. Homai J. Shroff. 1978. text ed. 15.00 o.p. (ISBN 0-391-01067-0). Humanities.
Eighteenth Century Woman. Paul M. Ettesvold. Ed. by Poly Cone et al. (Illus.). 64p. (Orig.). 1982. pap. 2.50 o.p. (ISBN 0-87099-296-1). Metro Mus Art.
Eighteenth Emergency. Betsy Byars. (gr. 4-6). 1980. pap. 1.50 o.p. (ISBN 0-380-00099-7, 51367, Camelot). Avon.
Eighteenth Journees Nationales de Neonatologie, 1988. Ed. by J. P. Relier. (Progres en Neonatologie Ser.: Vol. 8). (Illus.). vi, 328p. 1988. 100.00 o.p. (ISBN 3-8055-4861-3). S Karger.
Eighth & Ninth Symphonies in Full Orchestral Score. Ludwig van Beethoven. 392p. 1976. pap. 10.95 o.p. (ISBN 0-486-23380-4). Dover.
Eighth Annual Institute for Corporate Counsel: Corporate Financial Transactions. 741p. 1985. 15.00 o.p. (B4-6728). PLI.
Eighth Biennial Workshop on Color Aerial Photography in the Plant Sciences & Related Fields. American Society of Photogrammetry Staff. 167p. pap. 16.00 (17.00 member) o.p. (ISBN 0-937294-34-9). ASP & RS.
Eighth Century Prophets: Amos, Hosea, Isaiah, Micah. Bernhard W. Anderson. Ed. by Foster R. McCurley. LC 78-54545. (Proclamation Commentatries: the Old Testament Witnesses for Preaching). 128p. 1978. pap. 5.95 o.p. (ISBN 0-8006-0595-0, 1-595, Fortress). Augsburg Fortress.
Eighth Commandment. Lawrence Sanders. 1986. 18.95 o.p. (ISBN 0-399-13125-6). Putnam Pub Group.
Eighth Day. Thornton Wilder. 1976. pap. 2.25 o.p. (ISBN 0-380-00639-1, 44149-7, Bard). Avon.
Eighth Dwarf. Ross Thomas. 1979. 9.95 o.p. (ISBN 0-671-24653-4). S&S.
Eighth Ground Water Quality Symposium: Proceedings. LC 75-602296. 1974. 43.75 o.p. (ISBN 0-318-23002-X). Natl Water Well.
Eighth Moon. Sansan. As told to Bette B. Lord. 224p. 1983. pap. 2.95 o.p. (ISBN 0-380-63677-8, 63677-8). Avon.
Eighty: An American Souvenir. Eric Sloane. LC 84-18678. (Illus.). 96p. 1985. ltd. signed ed 60.00 o.p. (ISBN 0-396-08641-1); 29.95 o.p. (ISBN 0-396-08569-5). Dodd.
Eighty Appalachian Folk Songs. Ed. by Maud Karpeles & Cecil J. Sharp. LC 82-24252. 112p. 1983. pap. 6.95 o.p. (ISBN 0-571-10049-X). Faber & Faber.
Eighty-Eight Apple LOGO Programs. Don Martin & Jennifer Martin. LC 84-50181. 19.95 o.p. (ISBN 0-672-22343-0). Sams.
Eighty Eighty-Eight Assembler Language Programming: The IBM-PC. David C. Willen & Jeffrey I. Krantz. LC 83-60163. 192p. 1983. pap. 15.95 o.p. (ISBN 0-672-22024-5, 22024). Sams.
Eighty Eighty, Eighty Eighty-Five Microprocessor Book. Intel Marketing Communications Staff. LC 78-16936. (Intel Ser.: No. 1-402). 603p. 1980. 34.95x o.p. (ISBN 0-471-03568-8, Pub. by Wiley-Interscience). Wiley.
Eighty Eighty-Six & Eighty Eighty-Eight Primer. 10.95 o.p. (ISBN 0-317-06046-5). Wayne Green Ent.
Eighty-Four, Charing Cross Road. Helene Hanff. (Portway Ser.). 136p. 1988. lib. bdg. 14.50x o.s.i. (ISBN 0-7451-7115-X, Pub. by Chivers Pr UK). G K Hall.
Eighty Micro's Review Guide. Eighty Micro Editors. 480p. 1983. softcover 7.95 o.p. (ISBN 0-913531-00-6). Wayne Green Ent.
Eighty-Three to Eighty-Seven in the Saudan, with an Account of Sir William Hewett's Mission to King John of Abyssinia, 2 vols. Augustus B. Wylde. LC 72-82088. (Illus.). 1970. Repr. of 1888 ed. lib. bdg. 28.00x o.p. (ISBN 0-8371-9957-3, WYS&, Pub. by Negro U Pr); Vol. 1. lib. bdg. 16.50 o.p. (ISBN 0-8371-1525-6, WYT&); Vol. 2. lib. bdg. 16.50 o.p. (ISBN 0-8371-1526-4, WYU&). Greenwood.
Eileen Goudge's Swept Away Number Four: Star Struck. Fran Lantz. (Young Adults Ser.). 208p. 1987. pap. 2.50 o.p. (ISBN 0-380-75131-3, Flare). Avon.
Eileen Goudge's Swept Away Number One: Gone with the Wish. Eileen Goudge. (Young Adults Ser.). 1986. pap. 2.50 o.p. (ISBN 0-380-75129-1, Flare). Avon.
Eileen Goudges Swept Away, Number Six: Once Upon a Kiss. Mar Garrido. 1987. pap. 2.50 o.p. (ISBN 0-380-75133-X). Avon.
Eiler Collection...Now. Trent Myers. 16p. 1983. pap. 2.95 o.p. (ISBN 0-913883-01-8). Madison Art.
Einfuehrung in das SAS. rev. ed. SAS Institute, Inc. Staff. (Ger.). pap. 9.95 o.p. (ISBN 0-917382-70-6). SAS Inst.
Einfuehrung in die Freie Geometrie Ebener Kurven. L. Locher-Ernst. (Elemente der Mathematik Vom Hoeheren Standpunkt Aus: Vol. 1). 85p. (Ger.). 1952. pap. 13.95x o.p. (ISBN 0-8176-0252-6). Birkhauser.
Einfuehrung in die Statistische Qualitatskontrolle. A. G. Hopper. Tr. by W. Berchtold from Eng. (Lehr- und Handbucher der Ingenierwissenschaften Ser.: No. 30). 194p. (Ger.). 1971. 35.95 o.p. (ISBN 0-8176-0528-2). Birkhauser.
Einstein & Modern French Drama: An Analogy. Kenneth S. White. LC 82-21789. 132p. (Orig.). 1983. lib. bdg. 23.50 o.p. (ISBN 0-8191-2942-9); pap. text ed. 9.25 o.p. (ISBN 0-8191-2943-7). U Pr of Amer.
Einstein & Newton: A Comparison of the Two Greatest Scientists. Aaron B. Lerner. LC 72-7653. (Books for Adults & Young Adults). (Illus.). (gr. 7 up). 1973. PLB 10.95 o.p. (ISBN 0-8225-0752-8). Lerner Pubns.
Einstein Spaces. A. A. Petrov. 1969. 110.00 o.p. (ISBN 0-08-012315-5). Pergamon.
Einstein Syndrome: Corporate Anti-Semitism in America Today. Stephen L. Slavin & Mary A. Pradt. LC 81-43767. (Illus., Orig.). 1982. lib. bdg. 27.75 o.p. (ISBN 0-8191-2370-6); pap. text ed. 12.00 o.p. (ISBN 0-8191-2371-4). U Pr of Amer.
Einstein's Legacy. Julian Schwinger. LC 85-19665. (Scientific American Library). (Illus.). 256p. 1985. (ISBN 0-7167-5011-2, Dist. by W H Freeman). Sci Am Bks.
Einstein's Space & Van Gogh's Sky: Physical Reality & Beyond. Lawrence LeShan & Henry Margenau. 255p. 1982. 14.95 o.p. (ISBN 0-02-570460-5). Macmillan.
EISCAT Science: Results from the First Year's Operation of the European Incoherent Scatter Radar: Papers from the EISCAT Workshop, Aussois, France, 5-8 September 1983. Ed. by H. Rishbeth. 184p. 1984. pap. 73.00 o.p. (ISBN 0-08-031440-6). Pergamon.
Eisenhower Deception. Clive Egleton. LC 80-69372. 1981. 10.95 o.p. (ISBN 0-689-11127-4, Atheneum). Macmillan.
Eisenhower, Kennedy, & Foreign Aid. W. W. Rostow. (Ideas & Action Ser.: No. 5). 358p. 1985. 30.00x o.p. (ISBN 0-292-74018-2). U of Tex Pr.
Eisenhower, Vol. I: Soldier, General of the Army, President-Elect 1890-1952. Stephen E. Ambrose. 640p. 1983. 23.00 o.s.i. (ISBN 0-671-44069-1). S&S.
Eisenhower, Vol. 2: The President. Stephen E. Ambrose. LC 83-9892. (Illus.). 752p. 1984. 24.45 o.s.i. (ISBN 0-671-49901-7). S&S.
EISS Yearbook, Nineteen Seventy-Eight to Nineteen Eighty: The Retirement Age in Europe, Pt. I. European Institute of Social Security Staff. 224p. 1982. pap. 24.00 cancelled o.p. (ISBN 90-3120-134-0, Pub. by Kluwer Law Netherlands). Kluwer Academic.
Either-Or, 2 Vols. Soren Kierkegaard. Tr. by W. Lowrie. 1944. Vol. 1. 33.00 o.p. (ISBN 0-691-07177-2); Vol. 2. 22.50 o.p. (ISBN 0-691-07178-0); Vol 1. pap. 9.95 o.p. (ISBN 0-691-01976-2); Vol. 2. pap. 9.95x o.p. (ISBN 0-691-01977-0). Princeton U Pr.
Either Way, I Win: A Guide for Growth in the Power of Prayer. Lois W. Johnson. LC 79-50078. 1979. pap. 4.95 o.p. (ISBN 0-8066-1706-3, 10-2040, Augsburg). Augsburg Fortress.
Ejercicios de espanol. J. G. Bruton. (gr. 9 up). 1968. 5.15 o.p. (ISBN 0-08-012838-6); pap. 4.30 o.p. (ISBN 0-08-012837-8). Pergamon.
El Cholo Feeling Passes. Fredrick Barton. LC 85-61975. 461p. 1985. 14.95 o.p. (ISBN 0-931948-78-9). Peachtree Pubs.
El Dorado Trail: The Story of the Gold Rush Routes Across Mexico. Ferol Egan. LC 75-95799. (Illus.). 1970. text ed. 9.95 o.p. (ISBN 0-07-019057-7). McGraw.
El-Hi Textbooks & Serials in Print, 1988. Ed. by Bowker, R. R., Staff. 1135p. 1988. 85.00 o.p. (ISBN 0-8352-2448-1). Bowker.
El Salvador. Tsuyoshi Nakagawa. LC 74-78596. (This Beautiful World Ser.: Vol. 54). (Illus.). 1975. pap. 4.95 o.p. (ISBN 0-87011-236-8). Kodansha.
El Salvador & Economic Integration in Central America: An Econometric Study. Gabriel Siri. LC 82-47649. (Wharton Econometric Studies). 240p. 1984. 35.00x o.p. (ISBN 0-669-05551-4). Lexington Bks.
El Salvador: Central America in the New Cold War. Ed. by Marvin E. Gettleman et al. 412p. pap. 9.95 o.p. (ISBN 0-394-17956-0, Ever). Grove.
El Salvador: Demographic Issues & Prospects. Farid Dhanji. ii, 69p. 1979. pap. 20.00 o.p. (ISBN 0-686-36106-7, RC-7910). World Bank.
Elan. Yvone Lenard. (Fr.). (YA) (gr. 7 up). 1979. text ed. 27.95 o.p. (ISBN 0-03-045961-3). HR&W.
Elastic Constants of Crystals. Hillard B. Huntington. (Solid State Reprint Ser.). (Illus.). 1964. 24.00 o.p. (ISBN 0-12-608456-4). Acad Pr.
Elastic-Plastic Fracture Mechanics. V. Parton. 233p. 1978. 10.00 o.p. (ISBN 0-8285-0678-7, Pub. by Mir Pubs USSR). Imported Pubns.
Elastic Waves & Non-Destructive Testing of Materials: AMD, Vol. 29. Ed. by Y. H. Pao. 112p. 1978. 24.00 o.p. (ISBN 0-685-66796-0, H00112). ASME.
Elasticidades Poeticas. Maria D. Alcorn. 1978. 5.50 o.p. (ISBN 0-682-49126-8). Exposition-Phoenix.
Elastin & Elastic Tissue. Ed. by L. B. Sandberg et al. LC 77-1467. (Advances in Experimental Medicine & Biology Ser.: Vol. 79). 798p. 1977. 95.00x o.p. (ISBN 0-306-39079-5, Plenum Pr). Plenum Pub.
Elasto-Hydrodynamics Lubrication: SI Edition. 2nd ed. Duncan Dowson & Gordon R. Higginson. 1977. 60.00 o.p. (ISBN 0-08-021303-0); pap. 60.00 o.p. (ISBN 0-08-021302-2). Pergamon.
Elastomeric Bearing Research. (National Cooperative Highway Research Program Report). 53p. 1970. 3.00 o.p. (ISBN 0-309-01897-8). Transport Res Bd.
Elastomers & Rubber Technology: Proceedings of the 32nd Sagamore Conference held July 22-26, 1985, Lake Luzerne, New York. Ed. by Robert E. Singler & Catherine A. Byrne. LC 86-600600. (National Bureau of Standards Special Publication: No. 709). (Illus.). 602p. 1987. 28.00 o.p. (ISBN 0-318-22754-1, S/N 008-000-00465-0). USGPO.
Elbow Room. Oliver Gogarty. 48p. 1971. Repr. of 1939 ed. 15.00x o.p. (ISBN 0-7165-1388-9, BBA 02053, Pub. by Cuala Press Ireland). Biblio Dist.
Elbow Room: Stories. James A. McPherson. 1977. 14.45i o.p. (ISBN 0-316-56328-5, Atlantic-Little, Brown). Little.
Elder Brother: A Bibliography of Charles Webster Leadheater. Gregory Tillet. 320p. 1982. 26.95 o.p. (ISBN 0-7100-0926-7). Routledge Chapman & Hall.
Elder Statesman. T. S. Eliot. 134p. 1959. 4.95 o.p. (ISBN 0-374-14676-4). FS&G.
Elder Tastes. Mary G. Falzone. LC 81-9024. 41p. 1986. 5.95 o.p. (ISBN 0-533-05094-4). Vantage.
Elder's Public Prayers. 2nd rev., enl. ed. Toyozo W. Nakarai. 1979. 7.50 o.p. (ISBN 0-682-49351-1). Exposition-Phoenix.
Eldership of the Churches of Christ. H. Leo Boles. 1978. pap. 1.50 o.p. (ISBN 0-89225-179-4). Gospel Advocate.
Eldorado Network. Derek Robinson. 1980. 10.95 o.p. (ISBN 0-393-01322-7). Norton.
Eleanor: A Novel. Rhoda Lerman. LC 78-15140. 304p. 1980. 10.00 o.p. (ISBN 0-03-021066-6); pap. 4.95 o.p. (ISBN 0-03-057643-1). H Holt & Co.
Eleanor Roosevelt, an Eager Spirit: The Letters of Dorothy Dow, 1933-45. Dorothy Dow. Ed. by Ruth K. McClure. (Illus.). 1984. 16.45 o.p. (ISBN 0-393-01879-2). Norton.
Elect. William J. McDonald. 1977. 10.00 o.p. (ISBN 0-682-48870-4). Exposition-Phoenix.
Elected Officials Handbooks, 2 vols. 2nd ed. 1983. pap. 45.00 o.p. (ISBN 0-686-46566-0). Intl City Mgt.
Election of Nineteen Eighty-Four: Reports & Interpretations. Gerald M. Pomper et al. LC 85-4223. 208p. 1985. 20.00 o.p. (ISBN 0-934540-42-X); pap. 11.95x o.p. (ISBN 0-934540-41-1). Chatham Hse Pubs.

Election Special. (Electing the President Ser.). 48p. (gr. 9 up). 1983. pap. text ed. 8.95 tchr's ed o.p. (ISBN 0-88102-014-1). Janus Bks.

Elections in Developing Countries. T. E. Smith. LC 73-9130. 278p. 1974. Repr. of 1960 ed. lib. bdg. 22.50x o.p. (ISBN 0-8371-6987-9, SMED). Greenwood.

Elections in Israel: Nineteen Seventy-Seven. Asher Arian. 290p. 1980. pap. 24.95 o.p. (ISBN 0-87855-996-5). Transaction Pubs.

Elections Without Choice. Ed. by Guy Hermet et al. LC 77-16116. 256p. 1978. 34.95x o.p. (ISBN 0-470-99292-1). Halsted Pr.

Electoral College Abolition or Reform: Views of the U. S. Congress. Harold F. Nufer. LC 85-90923. (Illus.). 128p. 1985. 20.00 o.p. (ISBN 0-682-40266-4). Exposition-Phoenix.

Electric Children: Roots & Branches of Modern Folkrock. Jacques Vassal. Tr. by Paul Barnett from Fr. LC 75-8198. (Illus.). 320p. 1976. pap. 5.95 o.s.i. (ISBN 0-8008-2383-4). Taplinger.

Electric Circuit Problems with Solutions: SI-Version. 2nd ed. F. A. Benson. 1975. pap. 12.95x o.p. (ISBN 0-412-21260-9, NO.6035, Pub. by Chapman & Hall). Routledge Chapman & Hall.

Electric Circuit Theory. R. Yorke. LC 80-41323. (Applied Electricity & Electronics Ser.). (Illus.). 272p. 1981. text ed. 39.00 o.p. (ISBN 0-08-026133-7); pap. text ed. 21.00 o.p. (ISBN 0-08-026132-9). Pergamon.

Electric Circuits. Joseph A. Edminister. (Schaum's Outline Ser). (Orig.). 1965. pap. 7.95 o.p. (ISBN 0-07-018974-9, SP). McGraw.

Electric Clocks: A Guide to Repair, Identification & Prices. Tran Duy Ly. (Illus.). 300p. (Orig.). 1986. pap. (ISBN 0-930163-28-1). Arlington Bk.

Electric Contacts: Theory & Application. 4th ed. Ragnar Holm & Else Holm. (Illus.). 1967. 74.00 o.p. (ISBN 0-387-03875-2). Springer-Verlag.

Electric Controls for Refrigeration & Air Conditioning. Billy C. Langley. 1973. 31.95 o.p. (ISBN 0-13-247072-1); Reference ed. pap. text ed. 30.00 o.p. (ISBN 0-13-247064-0). P-H.

Electric Motor Control. 2nd ed. Walter Alerich. LC 73-13484. 236p. 1975. pap. 16.95 o.p. (ISBN 0-8273-1157-5); lab. manual 7.28 o.p. (ISBN 0-8273-1159-1); instr's. guide 4.18 o.p. (ISBN 0-8273-1158-3). Delmar.

Electric Motor Control. 3rd, rev ed. Walter Alerich. 1983. 19.95 o.p. (ISBN 0-442-20862-6). Van Nos Reinhold.

Electric Motor Repair. 2nd ed. Robert Rosenberg. LC 73-93476. 750p. 1970. 45.25 o.p. (ISBN 0-03-079090-5, HoltC). HR&W.

Electric Motor Test & Repair. 3rd ed. Jack Beater. 14.95 o.p. (ISBN 0-8306-0059-0, 1321); pap. 8.95 o.p. (ISBN 0-8306-1321-8). TAB Bks.

Electric Music: A Practical Manual. John Jenkins & Jon Smith. LC 75-18233. (Midland Bks.: No. 195). (Illus.). 176p. 1976. 12.95x o.p. (ISBN 0-253-31944-7); pap. 3.50x o.p. (ISBN 0-253-20195-0). Ind U Pr.

Electric Power Business. 2nd ed. Edwin Vennard. 1970. text ed. 41.50 o.p. (ISBN 0-07-067399-3). McGraw.

Electric Power Systems. 3rd ed. B. M. Weedy. LC 79-40081. 524p. 1979. 54.95x o.p. (ISBN 0-471-27584-0, Pub. by Wiley-Interscience). Wiley.

Electric Probes in Stationary & Flowing Plasmas: Theory & Application. P. M. Chung et al. LC 74-8844. (Applied Physics & Engineering Ser.: Vol. 11). (Illus.). 152p. 1975. 34.00 o.p. (ISBN 0-387-06800-7). Springer-Verlag.

Electric Railroads of Kentucky & Tennessee. Elmer G. Sulzer. Date not set. pap. Transport Res Bd.

Electric Railway Era in Northwest Washington, 1890-1930. Turbeville. (Occasional Papers: No. 12). pap. WWU CPNS.

Electric Utility Financial & Operating Performance Review. 229p. 1984. 25.00 o.p. NARUC.

Electric Vehicle Development: Proceedings of the International Electric Vehicle Development Group Conference, 1st, London, 1977. Society of Automotive Engineers Staff. (PPL Conference Publication Ser.: No. 21). 108p. 1977. pap. 18.95 o.p. (ISBN 0-901223-63-8, PPL 14, SAE Warrendale, Pa.). Inst Elect Eng.

Electrical & Electronics Drawing. 4th ed. Charles J. Baer & John R. Ottaway. LC 79-15837. (Illus.). 1980. text ed. 31.50 o.p. (ISBN 0-07-003010-3). McGraw.

Electrical & Electronics Trades Directory. 620p. 1986. 98.00 o.p. (ISBN 0-86341-051-0, BBO86). Inst Elect Eng.

Electrical & Electronics Trades Directory. 640p. 1988. 98.00 o.p. (ISBN 0-86341-122-3, 88088). Inst Elect Eng.

Electrical Assembly & Wiring. Ed. by E. Bethell et al. (Engineering Craftsmen: No. G4). (Illus.). 1969. spiral bdg. 39.95x o.p. (ISBN 0-85083-031-1). Trans-Atl Phila.

Electrical Conduction in Solid Materials: Physico-Chemical Bases & Possible Applications. J. P. Suchet. 204p. 1975. 50.00 o.p. (ISBN 0-08-018052-3). Pergamon.

Electrical Conductivity in Ceramics & Glass, Pt. B. Ed. by N. M. Tallan. (Ceramics & Glass: Science & Technology Ser.: Vol. 4). 304p. 1974. 85.00 o.p. (ISBN 0-8247-6088-3). Dekker.

Electrical Control for Machines. 2nd ed. Kenneth Rexford. 384p. 1983. pap. text ed. 25.50 o.p. (ISBN 0-8273-2175-9); instr's. guide 8.00 o.p. (ISBN 0-8273-2176-7); lab manual 7.50 o.p. (ISBN 0-8273-2177-5). Delmar.

Electrical Double Layer. M. J. Sparnaay. 427p. 1972. 105.00 o.p. (ISBN 0-08-016852-3). Pergamon.

Electrical Electronic. 8.00 o.p. (ISBN 0-317-65073-4). Am Consul Eng.

Electrical Energy: Its Generation, Transmission & Use. L. Laithwaite & T. Freris. 365p. 1980. text ed. 20.95 o.p. (ISBN 0-07-084109-8). McGraw.

Electrical Engineering. 2nd ed. Seymour B. Hammond & D. K. Gehmlich. 1971. text ed. 49.95 o.p. (ISBN 0-07-025901-1). McGraw.

Electrical Engineering Programmed Instruction Library. (Siemens Programmed Instructions "pi" Self Study Bks.: No. 01-16). 1981. 78.95x o.p. (ISBN 0-471-25986-1, Pub. by Wiley Heyden). Wiley.

Electrical Experiments see Electrostatic Experiments: Encyclopedic Description of 417 Classical Experiments from the Golden Age of Electrostatics.

Electrical Fitting, Vol. 1. Ed. by R. T. Anderson et al. (Engineering Craftsmen: No. G3). (Illus.). 1968. spiral bdg. 39.95x o.p. Trans-Atl Phila.

Electrical Fitting, Vol. 2. Ed. by J. R. Bisby et al. (Engineering Craftsmen: No. G23). (Illus.). 1969. spiral bdg. 47.50x o.p. (ISBN 0-89563-002-8). Trans-Atl Phila.

Electrical Inspection. Ed. by R. Davey et al. (Engineering Craftsmen: No. G24). (Illus.). 1969. spiral bdg. 47.50x o.p. (ISBN 0-85083-066-4). Trans-Atl Phila.

Electrical Installation Calculations, Vol. 1. 3rd ed. A. J. Watkins. 112p. 1981. pap. text ed. 15.95x o.p. (ISBN 0-7131-3422-4). Trans-Atl Phila.

Electrical Installation Calculations, Vol. 2. 3rd ed. A. J. Watkins. (Illus.). 100p. 1983. pap. text ed. 15.95x o.p. (ISBN 0-7131-3488-7). Trans-Atl Phila.

Electrical Installation Calculations, Vol. 3. A. J. Watkins. (Illus.). 154p. 1982. pap. text ed. 15.95x o.p. (ISBN 0-7131-3224-8). Trans-Atl Phila.

Electrical Installation Theory & Practice. M. Neidle. 1984. text ed. 9.95 o.p. (ISBN 0-07-084668-5). McGraw.

Electrical Installations Technology. I. C. Whitfield. 1968. 95.00 o.p. (ISBN 0-08-012704-5); pap. 95.00 o.p. (ISBN 0-08-012703-7). Pergamon.

Electrical Interference. A. P. Hale. 1956. (ISBN 0-8022-0656-5). Philos Lib.

Electrical Load-Curve Coverage: Proceedings of the Symposium, Rome, Oct. 1977. Load-Curve Coverage in Future Electrical Power Generating Systems Symposium Staff. Ed. by United Nations Economic Commission for Europe. LC 78-40342. (Illus.). 1979. 170.00 o.p. (ISBN 0-08-022422-9). Pergamon.

Electrical Machine Analysis. Richard T. Smith. LC 81-4541. (Illus.). 240p. 1982. 60.00 o.p. (ISBN 0-08-027174-X). Pergamon.

Electrical Machines & Their Applications. J. Hindmarsh. LC 79-20595. (Illus.). 800p. (Arabic.). 1981. pap. text ed. 22.00 o.s.i. (ISBN 0-08-026158-2). Pergamon.

Electrical Machines: Design & Applications. (IEE Conference Publication Ser.: No. 213). 272p. 1982. pap. 66.00 o.s.i. (ISBN 0-85296-260-6, IC 213). Inst Elect Eng.

Electrical Maintenance & Installation: Part One. 2nd ed. Ed. by F. Butcher et al. (Engineering Craftsmen: No. J2). (Illus.). 1975. spiral bdg 42.50x o.p. (ISBN 0-89563-003-6). Trans-Atl Phila.

Electrical Maintenance & Installation, Pt. 2. (Illus.). 1976. 42.50x o.p. (ISBN 0-85083-329-9). Trans-Atl Phila.

Electrical Noise & EMI Specifications. Donald R. White. LC 72-138444. (Electromagnetic Interference & Compatibility Ser.: Vol. 1). (Illus.). 482p. 1971. text ed. 58.00 o.p. (ISBN 0-932263-00-3). White Consult.

Electrical Principles & Practices. 2nd ed. James E. Adams. 1973. text ed. 28.70 o.p. (ISBN 0-07-000281-9). McGraw.

Electrical Principles for Electronics. rev ed. Angelo C. Gilli, Sr. LC 77-4676. (Illus.). 1977. text ed. 32.00 o.p. (ISBN 0-07-023293-8). McGraw.

Electrical Principles for Technicians, Vol. 1. G. Watersworth. 264p. 1981. pap. text ed. 19.95x o.p. (ISBN 0-7131-3421-6). Trans-Atl Phila.

Electrical Principles for Technicians, Vol. 2. K. G. Waterworth & R. P. Phillips. (Illus.). 256p. 1982. pap. text ed. 19.95x o.p. (ISBN 0-7131-3443-7). Trans-Atl Phila.

Electrical Project Management. Sam Meland. (Illus.). 320p. 1984. text ed. 44.50 o.p. (ISBN 0-07-041338-X). McGraw.

Electrical Properties of Wood & Line Design. M. Darveniza. (Illus.). 197p. (Orig.). 1980. pap. text ed. 37.50x o.p. (ISBN 0-7022-1523-6). U of Queensland Pr.

Electrical Safety. Swann. 1959. (ISBN 0-8022-1681-1). Philos Lib.

Electrical Shocks-Safety & Related Criteria: Symposium on Safety-Related Criteria for Electrical Shocks, Toronto, Canada, Sept. 7-9, 1983. Ed. by M. Vainberg. (Illus.). 350p. 1985. 95.00 o.p. (ISBN 0-08-025399-7). Pergamon.

Electrical Stimulation of Bone Growth & Repair. Ed. by F. Burny et al. 1978. pap. 18.00 o.p. (ISBN 0-387-08505-X). Springer-Verlag.

Electrical Wiring-Commercial. 4th, rev. ed. Ray C. Mullin & Robert L. Smith. LC 80-65467. (Electrical Trades Ser.). (Illus.). 236p. 1981. pap. text ed. 17.95 o.p. (ISBN 0-8273-1953-3); instr's. guide 6.00 o.p. (ISBN 0-8273-1954-1). Delmar.

Electrical Wiring: Commercial. 4th ed. Ray C. Mullin & Robert L. Smith. 240p. 1982. 14.95 o.p. (ISBN 0-442-26592-1). Van Nos Reinhold.

Electrical Wiring-Commercial. 5th ed. Raymond Mullin & Robert Smith. 240p. 1984. pap. text ed. 17.95 o.p. (ISBN 0-8273-2262-3); instr's. guide 6.00 o.p. (ISBN 0-8273-2263-1). Delmar.

Electrical Wiring: Industrial. 4th ed. Robert L. Smith. LC 81-71831. (Illus.). 160p. 1982. pap. text ed. 15.95 o.p. (ISBN 0-8273-1947-9); instr's. guide 5.00 o.p. (ISBN 0-8273-1948-7). Delmar.

Electrical Wiring-Industrial. 4th ed. Robert L. Smith. 135p. 1982. 21.95 o.p. (ISBN 0-442-28159-5). Van Nos Reinhold.

Electrical Wiring-Industrial. 5th ed. Robert L. Smith. LC 83-26307. 160p. 1984. pap. text ed. 15.95 o.p. (ISBN 0-8273-2265-8); instr's. guide 5.00 o.p. (ISBN 0-8273-2266-6). Delmar.

Electrical Wiring-Residential. 7th ed. Ray C. Mullin. LC 80-75458. 1981. pap. 17.95 o.p. (ISBN 0-8273-1951-7); instr's. guide 7.00 o.p. (ISBN 0-8273-1952-5). Delmar.

Electrical Wiring-Residential. 8th ed. Ray C. Mullin. LC 83-72062. 288p. 1984. pap. text ed. 19.95 o.p. (ISBN 0-8273-2260-7); instr's. guide 7.00 o.p. (ISBN 0-8273-2261-5). Delmar.

Electrical Wiring: Residential-Utility-Buildings-Service-Areas. (Illus.). 184p. 1985. softbound 13.00 o.p. (ISBN 0-89606-030-6, 305); tchr's guide 14.00 o.p. (ISBN 0-89606-103-5, 305TG); student wkbk. 7.00 o.p. (ISBN 0-89606-061-6, 305SW); a-v 290.00 o.p. (ISBN 0-318-12432-7, AV305). Am Assn Voc Materials.

Electricity. H. H. Gerrish. 120p. 1983. 7.20 o.p. (ISBN 0-87006-412-6). Goodheart.

Electricity & Basic Electronics. Stephen R. Matt. LC 81-20008. (Illus.). 1982. text ed. 18.00 o.p. (ISBN 0-87006-401-0). Goodheart.

Electricity & Electronic Fundamentals, 3 vols. S. L. Bacharach et al. (Illus.). 1971. Set. loseleaf 195.00x o.p. (ISBN 0-87683-316-4); Vol. 1. 79.50x o.p. (ISBN 0-87683-317-2); Vol. 2; lab. manual; 270p. looseleaf 79.50x o.p. (ISBN 0-87683-318-0); Vol. 3; solutions manual; 270p. losseleaf 79.50x o.p. (ISBN 0-87683-319-9); Lesson Plans; 320p. looseleaf 595.00x o.p. (ISBN 0-87683-321-0). GP Pub.

Electricity & Electronics. Howard H. Gerrish & William E. Dugger, Jr. LC 79-6345. (Illus.). 1980. text ed. 17.60 o.p. (ISBN 0-87006-284-0); lab manual 6.00 o.p. (ISBN 0-87006-310-3); instr's. guide 1.00 o.p. (ISBN 0-87006-377-4). Goodheart.

Electricity & Magnetism. J. Newton. (Illus.). 620p. 1956. (ISBN 0-8022-1212-3). Philos Lib.

Electricity Applied to Marine Engineering. 4th ed. W. Laws. Rev. by R. Tyrell. 454p. 1966. pap. 12.00x o.p. (ISBN 0-900976-31-4, Pub. by Inst Marine Eng). Intl Spec Bk.

Electricity, Electronics, & Electromagnetics: Principles & Applications. 2nd ed. Robert L. Boylestad & Louis Nashelsky. (Illus.). 544p. 1983. text ed. 45.00 o.p. (ISBN 0-13-248146-4). P-H.

Electricity-Electronics Fundamentals: A Text-Lab Manual. 2nd ed. Electronic Industries Association Staff & Paul B. Zbar. (Illus.). 1977. pap. text ed. 20.95 o.p. (ISBN 0-07-072748-1). McGraw.

Electricity for Refrigeration, Heating, & Air Conditioning. 2nd ed. Russell E. Smith. Date not set. 31.95 o.p. (ISBN 0-8273-2623-8). Delmar.

Electricity from Sunlight: The Future of Photovoltaics. Christopher Flavin. LC 82-62631. (Worldwatch Papers). 1982. pap. 4.00 o.p. (ISBN 0-916468-50-X). Worldwatch Inst.

Electro- & Thermo-Transport in Metals & Alloys: Proceedings of the TMS-AIME Fall Meeting, Niagara Falls, NY, 1976. (Illus.). 159p. pap. 15.00 o.p. (ISBN 0-317-34865-5). ASM.

Electro-Optical Devices. Y. Yakushenkov. 399p. 1983. 9.95 o.p. (ISBN 0-8285-2690-7, Pub. by Mir Pubs USSR). Imported Pubns.

Electro-Slag Refining. Walter E. Duckworth & G. Hoyle. 1969. 30.00 o.p. (ISBN 0-412-09670-6, NO.6091, Pub. by Chapman & Hall). Routledge Chapman & Hall.

Electroanesthesia: Biomedical & Biophysical Studies. Anthony Sances, Jr. & Sanford J. Larson. (Clinical Engineering Ser.). 1975. 82.50 o.p. (ISBN 0-12-617750-3). Acad Pr.

Electrocardiography for Nurses: Physiological Correlates. Jeanette G. Kernicki & Kathi M. Weiler. LC 80-28705. 262p. 1981. pap. 28.50 o.p. (ISBN 0-471-05752-5). Wiley.

Electrocardiography: Practical Applications with Vectorial Principles. 3rd ed. Edward K. Chung. (Illus.). 784p. 1985. 89.00 o.p. (ISBN 0-8385-2167-3). Appleton & Lange.

Electrocardiography: The Monitoring Lead. Richard Wiederhold. 319p. 1988. pap. text ed. 18.00 o.p. (ISBN 0-15-520953-1, HC). HarBraceJ.

Electrochemical Data, Vol. A, Pt. 1. Louis Meites & Petr Zuman. LC 74-14958. 742p. 1974. 65.00 o.p. (ISBN 0-471-59200-5). Krieger.

Electrochemical, Electrical & Magnetic Storage of Energy. Ed. by W. V. Hassenzahl. LC 81-6476. (Benchmark Papers on Energy: Vol. 8). 368p. 1982. 54.95 o.p. (ISBN 0-87933-376-6). Van Nos Reinhold.

Electrochemical Kinetics Theoretical Aspects. Klaus J. Vetter. 1967. 76.50 o.p. (ISBN 0-12-720250-1). Acad Pr.

Electrochemical Processes in Fuel Cells. M. W. Breiter. LC 69-17789. (Illus.). 1969. 34.00 o.p. (ISBN 0-387-04418-3). Springer-Verlag.

Electrochemical Systems. reference ed. John Newman. (International Series in the Physical Chemical Engineering Sciences). (Illus.). 448p. 1972. text ed. 54.00 o.p. (ISBN 0-13-248922-8). P-H.

Electrochemical Techniques for Inorganic Chemists. J. B. Headridge. 1969. 27.00 o.p. (ISBN 0-12-335650-4). Acad Pr.

Electrochemical Techniques in Corrosion Testing & Research. J. S. Scully. 1983. pap. 22.00 o.p. (ISBN 0-08-030540-7). Pergamon.

Electrochemical Test Methods for Stress Corrosion Cracking: Selected Papers from the Conference on Electrochemical Test Methods for Stress Corrosion Cracking, Firminy, France, Sept. 1980. Ed. by R. N. Parkins. (Illus.). 160p. 1981. pap. 18.75 o.p. (ISBN 0-08-026140-X). Pergamon.

Electrochemistry. Ed. by H. R. Thirsk. 1977. pap. 28.00 o.p. (ISBN 0-08-021676-5). Pergamon.

Electrochemistry: A Reformulation of the Basic Principles. H. G. Hertz. (Lecture Notes in Chemistry Ser.: Vol. 17). (Illus.). 254p. 1980. pap. 29.00 o.p. (ISBN 0-387-10008-3). Springer-Verlag.

Electrochemistry for Technologists. G. R. Palin. 1969. 60.00 o.p. (ISBN 0-08-013434-3); pap. 60.00 o.p. (ISBN 0-08-013433-5). Pergamon.

Electrodeposition of Chromium from Chromic Acid Solutions. George Dubpernell. LC 77-549. 1977. 25.00 o.p. (ISBN 0-08-021925-X). Pergamon.

Electrodiagnosis in Diseases of Nerve & Muscle: Principles & Practice. Jun Kimura. LC 82-17973. (Illus.). 672p. 1983. 70.00 o.p. (ISBN 0-8036-5341-7). Davis Co.

Electrodynamics of Magneto Electric Media. T. H. O'Dell. (Selected Topics in Solid State Physics Ser.: Vol. 11). 1970. 37.00 o.p. (ISBN 0-444-10013-X, North-Holland). Elsevier.

Electroforming. Peter Spiro. 335p. 1971. 70.00x o.p. (Pub. by Portcullio Pr). State Mutual Bk.

Electroless & Other Nonelectrolytic Plating Techniques: Recent Developments. Ed. by J. I. Duffy. LC 80-19494. (Chemical Tech. Rev. 171). (Illus.). 366p. 1981. 45.00 o.p. (ISBN 0-8155-0818-2). Noyes.

Electrolytes. Ed. by B. Pesce. 1962. 40.00 o.p. (ISBN 0-08-009597-6); pap. 24.00 o.p. (ISBN 0-08-013778-4). Pergamon.

Electromagnetic Ambients & Manmade Noise. John R. Herman. Ed. by Donald R. White. LC 79-84817. (Illus.). 265p. 1979. text ed. 42.00 o.p. (ISBN 0-932263-13-5). White Consult.

Electromagnetic Concepts & Applications. J. Skitok & Roger G. Marshall. 1981. pap. text ed. 53.33 o.p. (ISBN 0-13-248963-5). P-H.

Electromagnetic Distance Measurement: Aspects of Modern Land Surveying. C. D. Burnside. 117p. 1982. pap. text ed. 24.50x o.p. (ISBN 0-258-11624-2, Pub. by Granada England). Gower Pub Co.

Electromagnetic Fields & Waves. 3rd ed. Paul Lorrain et al. LC 86-31803. (Physics Ser.). (Illus.). 700p. 1987. 38.95 o.p. (ISBN 0-7167-1823-5); W H Freeman.
Electromagnetic Interactions & Field Theory: Proceedings of the International Universitaetswochen Fuer Kernphysik, 14, der Karlfranzens Universitaet, Schladming. International Universitaetswochen Fuer Kernph Staff. Ed. by P. Urban. (Acta Physica Austriaca: No. 14). (Illus.). v, 681p. 1975. 87.40 o.p. (ISBN 0-387-81333-0). Springer-Verlag.
Electromagnetic Interactions of Hadrons. Ed. by A. Donnachie & G. Shaw. LC 77-17811. (Nuclear Physics Monographs). (Illus.). 1978. Vol. 1, 458 Pgs. 75.00x o.p. (ISBN 0-306-31052-X, Plenum Pr); Vol. 2, 590 Pgs. 95.00x o.p. (ISBN 0-306-31106-2, Plenum Pr). Plenum Pub.
Electromagnetic Machines. R. Langlois-Berthelot. (Illus.). 550p. 1955. (ISBN 0-8022-0918-1). Philos Lib.
Electromagnetic Scattering. Ed. by Piergiorgio L. Uslenghi. 1978. 82.50 o.p. (ISBN 0-12-709650-7). Acad Pr.
Electromagnetics. 2nd ed. John D. Kraus. (Electrical & Electronic Engineering Ser.). (Illus.). 848p. 1973. text ed. 38.95 o.p. (ISBN 0-07-035396-4). McGraw.
Electromagnetism. V. Rossiter. 176p. 1979. 48.95 o.p. (ISBN 0-471-25992-6, Pub. by Wiley Heyden). Wiley.
Electromagnetism & Its Applications. B. Bolton. 1980. 33.95 o.p. (ISBN 0-442-30243-6). Van Nos Reinhold.
Electromagnetism & Life. Robert O. Becker & Andrew A. Marino. LC 81-9286. 211p. 1982. 66.50 o.p. (ISBN 0-87395-560-9); pap. 19.95 o.p. (ISBN 0-87395-561-7). State U NY Pr.
Electromagnetism & Quantum Theory. D. M. Grimes. (Electrical Science Ser.). 1969. 25.00 o.p. (ISBN 0-12-303150-8). Acad Pr.
Electron & Photon Interactions at High Energies. Ed. by H. Rollnik & W. E. Pfeil. 1974. 110.75 o.p. (ISBN 0-444-10626-X). Elsevier.
Electron & Photon Interactions with Atoms. Ed. by H. Kleinpoppen & M. R. MacDowell. LC 75-37555. (Illus.). 682p. 1976. 95.00x o.p. (ISBN 0-306-30846-0, Plenum Pr). Plenum Pub.
Electron & Positron Spectroscopies in Material Science & Engineering. Ed. by Otto Buck et al. (Materials Science Ser.). 1979. 70.50 o.p. (ISBN 0-12-139150-7). Acad Pr.
Electron-Atom & Electron-Molecule Collisions. Ed. by Juergen Hinze. LC 82-18927. (Physics of Atoms & Molecules Ser.). 362p. 1983. 62.50x o.p. (ISBN 0-306-41188-1, Plenum Pr). Plenum Pub.
Electron Beam Technology. Siegfried Schiller et al. LC 82-4774. 508p. 1983. 64.95 o.p. (ISBN 0-471-06056-9, Pub. by Wiley-Interscience). Wiley.
Electron Dynamics of Diode Regions. Charles K. Birdsall & William B. Bridges. (Electrical Science Ser). 1966. 69.00 o.p. (ISBN 0-12-099850-5). Acad Pr.
Electron Energy Bands in Solids. Joseph Callaway. (Solid State Reprint Ser.). 1964. 22.50 o.p. (ISBN 0-12-608450-5). Acad Pr.
Electron Gamemaster. Kay Ewbank et al. (Illus.). 162p. (Orig.). 1984. pap. 11.95 o.p. (ISBN 0-246-12514-4, Pub. by Granada England). Sheridan.
Electron Impact Phenomena. rev. ed. F. H. Field & J. L. Franklin. (Pure & Applied Physics Ser.: Vol. 1). 1957. 84.50 o.p. (ISBN 0-12-255450-7). Acad Pr.
Electron Microscopic Atlas of Lymph Node Cytology & Pathology. Y. Mori & K. Lennert. Tr. by K. Kuechemann. LC 73-79750. (Illus.). 1969. 153.40 o.p. (ISBN 0-387-04662-3). Springer-Verlag.
Electron Microscopy in Human Medicine: The Skin, Vol. 11a. Jan V. Johannessen. 412p. 1985. text ed. 80.00 o.p. (ISBN 0-07-032510-3). McGraw.
Electron Microscopy in Human Medicine: Vol. I, Instrumentation & Techniques. Jan V. Johannessen. (Electron Microscopy in Human Medicine). (Illus.). 1978. text ed. 60.00 o.p. (ISBN 0-07-032501-4). McGraw.
Electron Microscopy in Human Medicine, Vol. 10: Endocrine Organs. Jan V. Johannessen. 240p. 1982. text ed. 54.00 o.p. (ISBN 0-07-032509-X). McGraw.
Electron Microscopy in Human Medicine, Vol. 11: The Skin - Special Applications. Ed. by Jan V. Johannessen. (Electron Microscopy in Human Medicine). 250p. 1983. text ed. 65.00 o.p. (ISBN 0-07-032524-3). McGraw.
Electron Microscopy in Human Medicine: Vol. 2, Cellular Pathology. Jan V. Johannessen. (Illus.). 1978. text ed. 51.00 o.p. (ISBN 0-07-032502-2). McGraw.
Electron Microscopy in Human Medicine: Vol. 3, Infectious Agents. Jan V. Johannessen. (Electron Microscopy in Human Medicine Ser.). 325p. 1981. text ed. 88.50 o.p. (ISBN 0-07-032503-0). McGraw.
Electron Microscopy in Human Medicine: Vol. 4, Soft Tissues, Bones & Joints. Jan V. Johannessen. 325p. 1981. text ed. 78.00 o.p. (ISBN 0-07-032504-9). McGraw.
Electron Microscopy in Human Medicine: Vol. 5, Cardiovascular System, Lymphoreticular & Hematopoietic System. Jan V. Johannessen. 501p. 1982. text ed. 88.50 o.p. (ISBN 0-07-032505-7). McGraw.
Electron Microscopy in Human Medicine: Vol. 6, Nervous System, Sensory Organs, & Respiratory Tract. Jan V. Johannessen. (Electron Microscopy in Human Medicine Ser.). (Illus.). 368p. 1980. text ed. 78.00 o.p. (ISBN 0-07-032506-5). McGraw.
Electron Microscopy in Human Medicine, Vol. 7: Digestive System. Jan V. Johannessen. (Electron Microscopy in Human Medicine Ser.). 264p. 1980. text ed. 69.00 o.p. (ISBN 0-07-032507-3). McGraw.
Electron Microscopy in Human Medicine: Vol. 8, the Liver, Gallbladder & Biliary Ducts. Jan V. Johannessen. (Illus.). 1979. text ed. 65.00 o.p. (ISBN 0-07-032499-9). McGraw.
Electron Microscopy in Human Medicine, Vol. 9: Urogenital System & Breast. Jan V. Johannessen. (Illus.). 396p. 1980. text ed. 79.00 o.p. (ISBN 0-07-032508-1). McGraw.
Electron Microscopy in Material Science. Centre for Scientific Culture Ettore Majorana, International School of Electron Microscopy Staff. Ed. by U. Valdre. 1972. 127.00 o.p. (ISBN 0-12-780584-2). Acad Pr.
Electron Microscopy in Mineralogy. Ed. by H. R. Wenk et al. (Illus.). 590p. 1976. 59.00 o.p. (ISBN 0-387-07371-X). Springer-Verlag.
Electron Microscopy of Enzymes: Principles & Methods, Vol. 1. M. Arif Hayat. 1973. 26.95 o.p. (ISBN 0-442-25676-0). Van Nos Reinhold.
Electron Microscopy of Enzymes: Principles & Methods, Vol. 2. M. Arif Hayat. 200p. 1974. 24.95 o.p. (ISBN 0-442-25679-5). Van Nos Reinhold.
Electron Microscopy of Enzymes: Principles & Methods, Vol. 3. M. Arif Hayat. 190p. 1974. 24.95 o.p. (ISBN 0-442-25683-3). Van Nos Reinhold.
Electron Microscopy of Enzymes: Principles & Methods, Vol. 4. M. Arif Hayat. 1975. 29.95 o.p. (ISBN 0-442-25689-2). Van Nos Reinhold.
Electron Microscopy of Enzymes Principles & Methods, Vol. 5. M. Arif Hayat. 1977. 29.95 o.p. (ISBN 0-442-25690-6). Van Nos Reinhold.
Electron-Molecule Collisions & Photoionization Processes. Ed. by Vincent McKoy & H. Suzuki. (Illus.). 244p. 1984. lib. bdg. 24.95x o.p. (ISBN 0-89573-134-7). VCH Pubs.
Electron Optics, 2 pts. 2nd ed. P. Grivet. Incl. Pt. 1. Optics. 1972. pap. 100.00 o.p. (ISBN 0-08-016226-6); Pt. 2. Instruments. 1972. pap. text ed. 41.00 (ISBN 0-08-016228-2). 1972. Set. text ed. 79.00 o.p. (ISBN 0-08-016086-7). Pergamon.
Electron-Photon Shower Distribution Function: Tables for Lead, Copper & Air Absorbers. H. Messel & D. F. Crawford. LC 69-16049. 1970. 233.00 o.p. (ISBN 0-08-013374-6). Pergamon.
Electron Probe Microanalysis. 2nd ed. L. S. Birks. LC 79-9773. 204p. 1979. Repr. of 1971 ed. lib. bdg. 21.50 o.p. (ISBN 0-88275-952-3). Krieger.
Electron Scattering from Complex Nuclei Pts. A & B. Herbert Uberall. (Pure & Applied Physics Ser: Vol. 25). 1971. Pt. A. 79.50 o.p. (ISBN 0-12-705701-3); Pt. B. 77.00 o.p. (ISBN 0-12-705702-1). Acad Pr.
Electron Spectroscopy of Crystals. V. V. Nemoshkalenko & V. G. Aleshin. LC 78-12954. (Physics of Solids & Liquids Ser.). (Illus.). 374p. 1978. 69.50x o.p. (ISBN 0-306-40109-6, Plenum Pr). Plenum Pub.
Electron States & Optical Transitions in Solids. F. Bassani & Pastori Parravicini. 312p. 1975. 80.00 o.p. (ISBN 0-08-016846-9). Pergamon.
Electronic Absorption Spectra & Geometry of Organic Molecules. H. Suzuki. 1967. 104.00 o.p. (ISBN 0-12-678150-8). Acad Pr.
Electronic & Microprocessor - Controlled Security Projects. Vaughn Martin & Dean Davis. (Illus.). 240p. (Orig.). 1985. 21.95 o.p. (ISBN 0-8306-0957-1, 1957); pap. 14.60 o.p. (ISBN 0-8306-1957-7, 1957P). TAB Bks.
Electronic & Newer Ceramics. Ed. by J. J. Sves et al. 252p. 1983. 17.95 o.p. (ISBN 0-8436-0604-5). Van Nos Reinhold.
Electronic Aspects of Biochemistry: Proceedings. Ed. by Bernard Pullman. 1964. 89.50 o.p. (ISBN 0-12-566950-X). Acad Pr.
Electronic Business Machines. Leveson. 270p. 1960. (ISBN 0-8022-0964-5). Philos Lib.
Electronic Calculator: Student Guide. Charlotte Butsch. 1971. pap. text ed. 3.95 o.p. (ISBN 0-89420-055-0, 126877); cassette recordings 65.50 o.p. (ISBN 0-89420-143-3, 156780). Natl Book.
Electronic Calculators: A Mastery Approach Year. Juanita E. Carter & Darroch F. Young. 1981. pap. 16.95 o.p. (ISBN 0-395-29621-8). HM.
Electronic Circuit Analysis & Design. William H. Hayt & Gerold W. Nevdeck. LC 75-31032. (Illus.). 384p. 1976. text ed. 36.95 o.p. (ISBN 0-395-21919-1). HM.
Electronic Circuits & System Solutions. R. A. King. 103p. 1976. pap. 9.95 o.p. (ISBN 0-470-01399-0). Halsted Pr.
Electronic Circuits for Technicians. 2nd ed. Lloyd Temes. (Illus.). 1977. text ed. 44.95 o.p. (ISBN 0-07-063492-0). McGraw.
Electronic Circuits Manual. John Markus. 1971. text ed. 79.50 o.p. (ISBN 0-07-040444-5). McGraw.
Electronic Circuits Notebook: Proven Designs for Systems Applications. Electronics Magazine Editors & Samuel Weber. 344p. 1981. text ed. 44.50 o.p. (ISBN 0-07-019244-8). McGraw.
Electronic Communication Systems. 2nd ed. George Kennedy. (Illus.). 1977. text ed. 35.95 o.p. (ISBN 0-07-034052-8). McGraw.
Electronic Components, Instruments & Troubleshooting. Daniel L. Metzger. 1981. text ed. 37.33 o.p. (ISBN 0-13-250266-6). P-H.
Electronic Confessional: A Sex Book of the Eighties. Howard R. Lewis & Martha E. Lewis. Ed. by Jean Arbeiter. 320p. 1986. 16.95 o.p. (ISBN 0-87131-478-9). M Evans.
Electronic Connection Techniques & Equipment, 1968-69. Ed. by Geoffrey W. Dummer & J. M. Robertson. 1969. 195.00 o.p. (ISBN 0-08-013243-X). Pergamon.
Electronic Design & Construction of Alternate Energy Projects. R. Andrew Motes. (Illus.). 294p. (Orig.). 1985. 18.95 o.p. (ISBN 0-8306-0672-6, 1672); pap. 12.95 o.p. (ISBN 0-8306-1672-1, 1672P). TAB Bks.
Electronic Design Automation (EDA 84) (IEE Conference Publication: No. 232). 207p. 1984. pap. 75.00 o.s.i. (ISBN 0-85296-289-4). Inst Elect Eng.
Electronic Devices & Circuit Theory. 3rd ed. Robert L. Boylestad & Louis Nashelsky. (Illus.). 768p. 1982. text ed. 39.33 o.p. (ISBN 0-13-250324-7). P-H.
Electronic Devices & Circuits, Vols. 1-3. G. J. Pridham. LC 67-26692. 1972. Vol. 3. 1972. 95.00 o.p. (ISBN 0-08-016626-1); Vol. 1. 1968. 90.00 o.p. (ISBN 0-08-012549-2); Vol. 2. 1969. text ed. 27.00 o.p. (ISBN 0-08-013461-0); Vol. 3. pap. 95.00 o.p. (ISBN 0-08-016755-1); Vol. 1. pap. 9.25 o.p. (ISBN 0-08-012548-4); Vol. 2. pap. text ed. 11.25 o.p. (ISBN 0-08-013460-2). Pergamon.
Electronic Digital Computers: Their Uses in Science & Engineering. Franz L. Alt. (Applied Mathematics & Mechanics Ser: Vol. 4). 1958. 71.50 o.p. (ISBN 0-12-053650-1). Acad Pr.
Electronic Displays. I. Refioglu. 467p. 1983. 54.50X o.p. (ISBN 0-471-88175-9, Pub. by Wiley-Interscience). Wiley.
Electronic Drafting & Design. 4th ed. Nicholas M. Raskhodoff. (Illus.). 576p. 1982. text ed. 40.33 o.p. (ISBN 0-13-250621-1). P-H.
Electronic Drafting Techniques & Exercises. George Shiers. (Illus.). 1963. pap. text ed. (ISBN 0-13-250605-X). P-H.
Electronic Engineering Applications of Two Port Systems. H. B. Gatland. 1976. 85.00 o.p. (ISBN 0-08-018069-8); pap. 85.00 o.p. (ISBN 0-08-019866-X). Pergamon.
Electronic Equipment Wiring & Assembling: Part One. Ed. by D. Adams et al. (Engineering Craftsmen: No. G5). 1968. spiral bdg. 38.50x o.p. Trans-Atl Phila.
Electronic Equipment Wiring & Assembling: Part Two. Ed. by N. F. Clark et al. (Engineering Craftsmen: No. G25). (Illus.). 1969. spiral bdg. 47.50x o.p. (ISBN 0-89563-004-4). Trans-Atl Phila.
Electronic Filter Design Handbook. Arthur B. Williams. 1981. text ed. 61.95 o.p. (ISBN 0-07-070430-9). McGraw.
Electronic Flash. Jim Cornfield. (Petersen's Photographic Library Ser.: Vol. 3). (Illus.). 160p. (Orig.). 1980. pap. text ed. 8.95 o.p. (ISBN 0-8227-4041-9). Petersen Pub.
Electronic Fundamentals for Technicians. Robert L. Shrader. LC 77-37105. 1972. text ed. 31.00 o.p. (ISBN 0-07-057142-2, G). McGraw.
Electronic Funds Transfer System for Business Payments. Credit Research Foundation. 17p. 1973. 40.00 o.p. (ISBN 0-939050-22-6). Credit Res NYS.
Electronic Industries Information Sources. Ed. by Gretchen R. Randle. LC 67-31262. (Management Information Guide Ser.: No. 13). 1968. 65.00x o.p. (ISBN 0-8103-0813-4). Gale.
Electronic Information Publishing: Old Issues in a New Industry. Kurt D. Steele. 630p. 1984. pap. 15.00 o.p. (ISBN 0-317-27379-5, #G4-3753). PLI.
Electronic Inspection & Test, 2 vols. Ed. by D. Adams et al. (Engineering Craftsmen: No. G26). (Illus.). 1969. Set. s 69.95x o.p. (ISBN 0-85083-035-4). Trans-Atl Phila.
Electronic Library: Automation in Academic Libraries. Hugh F. Cline & Loraine T. Sinnott. LC 81-47871. 208p. 1983. 25.00X o.p. (ISBN 0-669-05113-6). Lexington Bks.
Electronic Logic Circuits. J. R. Gibson. (Illus.). 114p. 1981. text ed. write for info. o.p. (ISBN 0-205-07603-3, 207603). Wm C Brown.
Electronic Logic Systems. A. E. Almaini. (Illus.). 448p. 1986. pap. text ed. 46.00 o.p. (ISBN 0-13-251752-3). P-H.
Electronic Mail: A Revolution in Business Communications. Stephen Connell & Ian A. Galbraith. (Illus.). 152p. 1983. 18.95 o.p. (ISBN 0-442-21691-2). Van Nos Reinhold.
Electronic Maintenance, Vol. 1. Ed. by S. D. Coates et al. (Engineering Craftsmen: No. J4). (Illus.). 1969. spiral bdg. 45.00x o.p. Trans-Atl Phila.
Electronic Maintenance, Vol. 2. Ed. by I. Davidson et al. (Engineering Craftsmen: No. J24). (Illus.). 1970. spiral bdg. 43.50x o.p. (ISBN 0-89563-005-2). Trans-Atl Phila.
Electronic Materials & Devices. David H. Navon. 1975. text ed. 33.95 o.p. (ISBN 0-395-18917-9). HM.
Electronic Measurements & Instrumentation. Bernard M. Oliver & John M. Cage. (Illus.). 720p. 1971. text ed. 66.50 o.p. (ISBN 0-07-047650-0). McGraw.
Electronic Measurements Simplified. Clayton Hallmark. LC 73-879585. (Illus.). 240p. 1974. 7.95 o.p.; pap. 4.95 o.p. TAB Bks.
Electronic-Message Transfer & its Implications. Alfred M. Lee. LC 82-47683. 224p. 1983. 28.00x o.p. (ISBN 0-669-05555-7). Lexington Bks.
Electronic Money Machine: Profits from Your Home Computer. Haven Group Editors. 240p. 1984. pap. 5.95 o.p. (ISBN 0-380-86751-6, 86751). Avon.
Electronic Music Circuits. Barry Klein. LC 81-84278. 16.95 o.p. (ISBN 0-672-21833-X). Sams.
Electronic Music Synthesis. Hubert S. Howe, Jr. (Illus.). 272p. 1975. text ed. 18.95x o.p. (ISBN 0-393-09257-7). Norton.
Electronic Music Synthesizers. Delton T. Horn. (Illus.). 168p. 1980. 11.95 o.p. (ISBN 0-8306-9722-5); pap. 6.95 o.p. (ISBN 0-8306-1167-3, 1167). TAB Bks.
Electronic News Financial Fact Book & Directory, 1985. 24th ed. Fairchild Book Research Division Staff. 520p. 1985. pap. 125.00 o.p. (ISBN 0-87005-502-X). Fairchild.
Electronic News Financial Fact Book & Directory. 26th ed. Fairchild Book Research Department Staff. 500p. 1987. 125.00 o.p. (ISBN 0-87005-566-6). Fairchild.
Electronic News Financial Fact Book & Directory. 23rd ed. Fairchild Book Research Division Staff. 500p. 1984. pap. 125.00 o.p. (ISBN 0-87005-469-4). Fairchild.
Electronic News Financial Fact Book & Directory. 25th ed. Fairchild Book Research Division Staff. 500p. 1986. pap. 125.00 o.p. (ISBN 0-87005-536-4). Fairchild.
Electronic Office. Nancy B. Finn. (Illus.). 160p. 1983. pap. 16.95 o.p. (ISBN 0-13-251819-8). P-H.
Electronic Office: A Guide for Managers. John J. Stallard et al. LC 82-72866. 180p. 1982. 19.95 o.p. (ISBN 0-87094-256-5). Dow Jones-Irwin.
Electronic Prospecting. Charles Garrett et al. Ed. by Bettye Nelson. LC 76-11380. (Guidebook Ser.). (Illus.). 96p. (Orig.). 1980. pap. 4.95 o.p. (ISBN 0-915920-38-7). Ram Pub.
Electronic Publishing. Ed. by J. Kirst. (Communication Ser.). 224p. 1986. 31.00 o.p. (ISBN 0-7099-1575-6, Pub. by Croom Helm UK). Routledge Chapman & Hall.
Electronic Publishing Review: The International Journal of the Transfer of Published Information via Videotex & Online Media. Ed. by Harry Collier et al. 1984. per year 66.00 o.p. (ISBN 0-317-00229-5). Learned Info.
Electronic Refrigeration. H. J. Goldsmid. 230p. 1986. text ed. 70.00 o.p. (ISBN 0-85086-119-5, 1002, Pub. by Pion England). Routledge Chapman & Hall.
Electronic Reliability Electronics. Geoffrey W. Dummer. Ed. by N. B. Griffin. 1966. 60.00 o.p. (ISBN 0-08-011448-2); pap. 60.00 o.p. (ISBN 0-08-011447-4). Pergamon.
Electronic Shop Fabrication: A Basic Course. Robert S. Villanucci & Alexander W. Avtgis. (Illus.). 272p. 1982. text ed. 31.00 o.p. (ISBN 0-13-251959-3). P-H.
Electronic Spectra & Electronic Structure of Polyatomic Molecules see Molecular Spectra & Molecular Structure.

Titles

Electronic Structure & Properties of Hydrogen in Metals. Ed. by P. Jena & C. B. Satterthwaite. (NATO Conference Series VI, Materials Science: Vol. 6). 714p. 1983. 110.00x o.p. (ISBN 0-306-41130-X, Plenum Press). Plenum Pub.

Electronic Structure of Metals. N. B. Brandt & S. M. Chudinov. 336p. 1973. 6.45 o.p. (ISBN 0-8285-0778-3, Pub. by Mir Pubs USSR). Imported Pubns.

Electronic Structure of Molecules: Theory & Application to Inorganic Molecules, Vol. 3. G. Doggett. 1972. 70.00 o.p. (ISBN 0-08-016588-5). Pergamon.

Electronic Test Equipment: Operation & Applications. Ed. by A. M. Rudkin. 316p. 1981. text ed. 49.00x o.p. (ISBN 0-246-11478-9, Pub. by Granada England). Gower Pub Co.

Electronic Testing & Troubleshooting. George C. Loveday. LC 81-12948. 293p. 1982. (ISBN 0-471-08718-1). Wiley.

Electronic Transitions & the High Pressure Chemistry & Physics of Solids. H. G. Drickamer. (Studies in Chemical Physics). 1973. 35.00x o.p. (ISBN 0-412-11650-2, NO.6090, Pub. by Chapman & Hall). Routledge Chapman & Hall.

Electronic Transitions in Organometalloids. Brian G. Ramsey. (Organometallic Chemistry Ser). 1969. 77.00 o.p. (ISBN 0-12-576950-4). Acad Pr.

Electronic Transmission Technology: Lines, Waves & Antennas. William Sinnema. (Illus.). 1979. text ed. 41.00 o.p. (ISBN 0-13-252221-7). P-H.

Electronic Warfare & the U. S. S. R. Rubicon Consulting Staff. 1985. 395.00 o.p. (ISBN 0-938124-06-4). Rubicon.

Electronic Warfare: Element of Strategy & Multiplier of Combat Power. Don E. Gordon. (Pergamon Policy Studies on Security Affairs). (Illus.). 200p. 1982. 24.00 o.p. (ISBN 0-08-027189-8). Pergamon.

Electronic Warfare: 1985. Rubicon Consulting Staff. 1985. 395.00 o.p. (ISBN 0-938124-09-9). Rubicon.

Electronic Workshop Manual & Guide. Carl G. Grolle. 240p. 1977. text ed. 16.95 o.p. (ISBN 0-13-252502-X, Parker). P-H.

Electronically Hearing Computer Speech Recognition. John P. Cater. LC 84-50051. 13.95 o.p. (ISBN 0-672-22173-X). Sams.

Electronically Speaking: Computer Speech Generation. John C. Cater. 232p. 1982. pap. 14.95 o.p. (ISBN 0-672-21947-6, 21947). Sams.

Electronics. A. W. Keen. (Illus.). 256p. 1956. (ISBN 0-8022-0835-5). Philos Lib.

Electronics & Instrumentation for the Clinical Laboratory. Arthur A. Eggert. LC 83-10524. 432p. 1983. 28.50x o.p. (ISBN 0-471-86275-4, Pub. by Wiley Med). Wiley.

Electronics Applications. (ISBN 0-07-027998-5). McGraw.

Electronics Drafting Workbook. 3rd ed. E. Kirschner & K. M. Stone. (Illus.). 1978. text ed. 30.95 o.p. (ISBN 0-07-034890-1). McGraw.

Electronics for Technicians. P. W. Crane. 1971. pap. text ed. 9.00 o.p. (ISBN 0-08-016101-4). Pergamon.

Electronics: From Theory into Practice, 2 vols. 2nd ed. Jack Fisher & Bruce Gatland. 538p. 1976. Combined Ed. 135.00 o.p. (ISBN 0-08-019857-0); Vol. 1. pap. 65.00 o.p. (ISBN 0-08-019855-4); Vol. 2. pap. 70.00 o.p. (ISBN 0-08-019856-2). Pergamon.

Electronics in Everyday Life. William C. Vergara. (Popular Science Ser.). 235p. 1984. pap. 4.95 o.p. (ISBN 0-486-24576-4). Dover.

Electronics Instruments & Measurement. Paul B. Zbar & R. Orne. (Illus.). 1965. text ed. 29.95 o.p. (ISBN 0-07-072754-6). McGraw.

Electronics of Microwave Tubes. Werner J. Kleen. Tr. by P. A. Lindsay et al. 1958. 69.50 o.p. (ISBN 0-12-412550-6). Acad Pr.

Electronics Style Manual. John Markus. 1978. text ed. 5.95 o.p. (ISBN 0-07-040432-1). McGraw.

Electronics the Easy Way. (Easy Way Ser.). 225p. 1985. pap. 8.95 o.p. (ISBN 0-8120-2709-4). Barron.

Electrons & Chemical Bonding. Harry B. Gray. (Orig.). 1964. pap. 21.95 o.p. (ISBN 0-8053-3401-7). Benjamin-Cummings.

Electrons in Fluids: The Natural of Metal-Ammonia Solutions. Ed. by J. Jortner & N. R. Kestner. LC 73-8484. (Illus.). 493p. 1973. 72.00 o.p. (ISBN 0-387-06310-2). Springer-Verlag.

Electrons in Solids: An Introductory Survey. Richard H. Bube. LC 80-1689. 229p. 1980. 27.50 o.p. (ISBN 0-12-138650-3). Acad Pr.

Electrophoresis in the Separation of Biological Macromolecules. O. Gaal et al. LC 77-28502. 422p. 1980. 135.00 o.p. (ISBN 0-471-99602-5). Wiley.

Electrostatic Experiments: Encyclopedic Description of 417 Classical Experiments from the Golden Age of Electrostatics. G. W. Francis. Orig. Title: Electrical Experiments. (Illus.). 360p. Date not set. 25.00 o.p. (ISBN 0-917406-03-6); pap. 18.00 o.p. (ISBN 0-917406-04-4). Electret Sci.

Electrostatic Precipitation of Fly Ash. Air Pollution Control Association. (APCA Reprint Ser.: Vol. 8). 72p. 1977. 6.00 o.p. (ISBN 0-318-12253-7, RS-8); members 4.50 o.p. (ISBN 0-318-12254-5). Air & Waste.

Electrostatic Precipitator Manual. Jack R. McDonald & Alan H. Dean. LC 82-3449. (Pollution Tech. Rev.: No. 91). (Illus.). 484p. 1982. 48.00 o.p. (ISBN 0-8155-0895-6). Noyes.

Electrosurgery in Dentistry. 2nd ed. Maurice J. Oringer. LC 70-186952. (Illus.). 1150p. 1975. text ed. (ISBN 0-7216-7001-6). Saunders.

Electroweak Interactions-Theory & Phenomenology: Proceedings of the Lectures Held at Trieste, Italy, Summer 1982. S. Love et al. (International School for Advanced Studies Lecture Ser.: No. 1). 360p. 1989. 35.00 o.p. (ISBN 9971-950-51-0); pap. 21.00 o.p. (ISBN 9971-950-52-9). World Scientific Pub.

Elegant & Easy: Decorative Ideas for Food Presentations. Jean F. Nicolas. (Illus.). 140p. 1983. 24.95 o.p. (ISBN 0-8436-2266-0); pap. 18.95 o.p. (ISBN 0-8436-2267-9). Van Nos Reinhold.

Elegant Art: Fashion & Fantasy in the Eighteenth Century. Edward Maeder et al. (Illus.). 256p. 1983. 45.00x o.p. (ISBN 0-317-66608-8). Abrams.

Elegant Glassware of the Depression Era. Gene Florence. 1982. 17.95 o.p. (ISBN 0-89145-220-6). Collector Bks.

Elegant Hors d'Oeuvre. Margon Edney & Ede Grimm. Ed. by Elizabeth Rand & Diane Polster. LC 77-86167. (Illus.). 1977. plastic comb 5.95 o.p. (ISBN 0-914488-13-9). Rand-Tofua.

Elegant Japanese House: Traditional Sukiya Architecture. Teiji Itoh. (Illus.). 220p. 80.00 o.p. (ISBN 0-317-54980-4). Apollo.

Elegy Andinforno. Nedward Gross, Jr. 1955. (ISBN 0-8022-0636-0). Philos Lib.

Elegy for Stanley Gorski. Emanuel Fried. LC 86-50412. (Drama Ser.). 114p. (Orig.). 1986. pap. 3.95 o.p. (ISBN 0-938838-18-0). Textile Bridge.

Elektrochemie: Vol. 1 Grundlagen & Anwendungen, Vol 1. 2nd rev. ed. Guilio Milazzo. (Chemische Reihe Ser.: No. 26). 548p. (Ger.). 1980. 70.95x o.p. (ISBN 0-8176-1129-0). Birkhauser.

Elektrolyte und Spurenelemente der Intensivmedizin: Colloquium November 11, 1972 in Klinikum Steglitz der Freien Universitaet Berlin. Ed. by Ulrich Henneberg & Hans-Wolfgang Reinhardt. 1974. 22.50 o.p. (ISBN 3-11-004552-4). De Gruyter.

Elementals. Michael McDowell. 1981. pap. 2.95 o.p. (ISBN 0-380-78360-6, 78360-6). Avon.

Elementary Algebra. Michael E. Bennett et al. LC 80-21563. 400p. 1981. text ed. write for info. o.p. (ISBN 0-87150-303-4, 2391, Prindle). PWS-Kent Pub.

Elementary Algebra. 3rd ed. Vivian S. Groza. LC 80-53936. (Illus.). 660p. 1981. pap. text ed. 28.95x o.p. (ISBN 0-03-057719-5). HR&W.

Elementary Algebra. L. Murphy Johnson & Arnold R. Steffensen. 1985. text ed. write for info. o.p. (ISBN 0-673-15940-X). Scott F.

Elementary Algebra. 2nd ed. Charles P. McKeague. 1981. 27.00 o.p. (ISBN 0-12-484755-2). study guide 8.75 o.p. (ISBN 0-12-484764-1). Acad Pr.

Elementary Algebra: A Guided Inquiry. Sherman Stein & Calvin Crabill. LC 78-17913. 96p. (Orig.). 1972. text ed. 23.50 o.p. (ISBN 0-395-12669-X). HM.

Elementary Algebra: A Straightforward Approach. 2nd ed. Martin M. Zuckerman. 400p. 1982. 35.33 o.p. (ISBN 0-205-07624-6, 567624X); tchr's. ed. avail. o.p. (ISBN 0-205-07625-4, 5676258); study guide avail. o.p. (ISBN 0-205-07626-2, 5676266). Allyn.

Elementary Algebra by Example. William Brett & Michael Sentlowitz. LC 76-11979. (Illus.). 1977. pap. 28.50 o.p. (ISBN 0-395-24425-0). HM.

Elementary Algebra for College Students. Mary P. Dolciani & Robert H. Sorgenfrey. LC 78-146720. 1972. text ed. 15.70 o.p. (ISBN 0-395-12069-1). HM.

Elementary Algebra for College Students. 6th ed. Irving Drooyan & William Wooton. LC 83-3556. 433p. 1984. text ed. (ISBN 0-471-87387-X). Wiley.

Elementary Amiga BASIC. 29.95 o.p. (ISBN 0-87455-057-2). Compute Pubns.

Elementary Analysis, Vol. 2. K. S. Snell & J. B. Morgan. 1966. text ed. 24.00 o.p. (ISBN 0-08-011777-5); pap. 10.75 o.p. (ISBN 0-08-011776-7). Pergamon.

Elementary & Secondary Education Indicators in Brief, 1987. (Education Department Publication IS 87 Ser.: No. 106). (Illus.). 77p. (Orig.). 1987. pap. 3.00 o.p. (ISBN 0-318-22896-3, S/N 065-000-00290-6). USGPO.

Elementary Applied Partial Differential Equations. Richard Haberman. (Illus.). 560p. 1983. text ed. (ISBN 0-13-252833-9). P-H.

Elementary Business Statistics: The Modern Approach. 4th ed. John E. Freund & Frank J. Williams. (Illus.). 576p. 1982. pap. text ed. (ISBN 0-13-253120-8). P-H.

Elementary Calculus for Business, Economics & Social Sciences. Chaney Anderson & R. C. Pierce, Jr. 1975. text ed. 23.50 o.p. (ISBN 0-395-18960-8). HM.

Elementary Calculus: Student Supplement. H. Jerome Kiesler. 1976. pap. text ed. write for info. o.p. (ISBN 0-87150-230-5, PWS 1756, Prindle). PWS-Kent Pub.

Elementary Chemical Thermodynamics. Bruce H. Mahan. (Orig.). 1963. pap. text ed. 18.95 o.p. (ISBN 0-8053-6801-9). Benjamin-Cummings.

Elementary College Mathematics. Sol Weiss. 1977. text ed. write for info. o.p. (ISBN 0-87150-217-8, PWS 1771, Prindle). PWS-Kent Pub.

Elementary Composition Practice, Book 2. Linda L. Blanton. LC 78-5736. 160p. 1979. pap. text ed. 11.50 o.p. (ISBN 0-88377-128-4). Newbury Hse.

Elementary Composition Practice Book 1. Linda L. Blanton. 100p. 1978. pap. text ed. 11.50 o.p. (ISBN 0-88377-112-8). Newbury Hse.

Elementary Differential Equations. 6th ed. E. D. Rainville & P. E. Bedient. 1981. write for info. o.p. (ISBN 0-02-397770-1). Macmillan.

Elementary Differential Equations. R. L. Schwarzenberger. 1969. pap. 6.95x o.p. (ISBN 0-412-09580-7, NO.6247, Pub. by Chapman & Hall). Routledge Chapman & Hall.

Elementary Forms of the New Religious Life. Roy Wallis. LC 83-11092. (International Library of Sociology). 171p. 1984. 26.95x o.p. (ISBN 0-7100-9890-1). Routledge Chapman & Hall.

Elementary Functions. Carl B. Allendoerfer et al. 1977. text ed. 29.95 o.p. (ISBN 0-07-001371-3). McGraw.

Elementary Functions. Adil Yaqub. 368p. 1975. text ed. 21.95 o.p. (ISBN 0-395-17093-1). HM.

Elementary General Relativity. C. Clarke. 131p. 1980. pap. 29.95x o.p. (ISBN 0-470-26930-8). Halsted Pr.

Elementary Guide to Reliability. 2nd ed. Geoffrey W. Dummer & R. C. Winton. LC 73-16199. 66p. 1973. pap. text ed. 8.50 o.p. (ISBN 0-08-017821-9). Pergamon.

Elementary Harmony. 3rd ed. Robert W. Ottman. 416p. 1983. pap. text ed. 37.00 o.p. (ISBN 0-13-257436-5). P-H.

Elementary Human Anatomy Laboratory Textbook. 2nd ed. John P. Harley. 1977. pap. text ed. 11.95 o.p. (ISBN 0-8403-0906-6). Kendall-Hunt.

Elementary Illustrations of the Differential & Integral Calculus. Augustus De Morgan. 152p. 1943. 16.95 o.p. (ISBN 0-87548-158-2). Open Court.

Elementary Keyboard Harmony. Maurice Lieberman. (Illus.). 1964. 8.95x o.p. (ISBN 0-393-09628-9, NortonC). Norton.

Elementary Knowledge: A Story of the Creation of the Hebrew Alaphabet. Peter Haden. (Illus.). 68p. 1981. 25.00x o.p. (ISBN 0-87663-357-2). Universe.

Elementary Language Arts: Strategies for Teaching & Learning. Ohio Department of Education Staff. 52p. 1982. 4.00 o.p. (ISBN 0-8141-1312-5). NCTE.

Elementary Linear Algebra. 4th ed. Howard Anton. LC 83-27382. 464p. 1984. (ISBN 0-471-09890-6). Wiley.

Elementary Linear Algebra. 3rd ed. Stanley I. Grossman. 446p. 1987. text ed. (ISBN 0-534-07422-7). Wadsworth Pub.

Elementary Linear Algebra. J. A. Thorpe & P. G. Kumpel. LC 83-14442. 433p. 1984. text ed. 41.25x o.p. (ISBN 0-03-061249-7). SCP.

Elementary Linear Algebra with Applications. Marc Konvisser. 350p. 1981. write for info. o.p. (ISBN 0-87150-295-X, 2331, Prindle). PWS-Kent Pub.

Elementary Mathematical Methods. 3rd ed. Diane Thiessen et al. 1003p. 1988. text ed. write for info. o.p. (ISBN 0-02-390320-1). Macmillan.

Elementary Mathematics. 2nd ed. Robert E. Willcutt & Donald D. Paige. 1978. text ed. write for info. o.p. (ISBN 0-87150-242-9, PWS 1961, Prindle). PWS-Kent Pub.

Elementary Mathematics. V. Zaitsev et al. 590p. 1978. 10.00 o.p. (ISBN 0-8285-0719-8, Pub. by Mir Pubs USSR). Imported Pubns.

Elementary Mathematics: A Fundamentals & Techniques Approach. Samuel R. Filippone & Michael Z. Williams. LC 75-19539. (Illus.). 448p. 1976. text ed. 25.95 o.p. (ISBN 0-395-20028-8). HM.

Elementary Mathematics: Teaching Suggestions & Strategies. Sol Weiss. LC 77-28616. (Illus.). 1978. pap. text ed. write for info. o.p. (ISBN 0-87150-251-8, PWS 2062, Prindle). PWS-Kent Pub.

Elementary Matrix Algebra. 3rd ed. Franz E. Hohn. 1973. text ed. write for info. o.p. (ISBN 0-02-355950-0). Macmillan.

Elementary Matrix Algebra with Applications. 2nd ed. Richard J. Painter & Richard C. Yantis. 1977. text ed. write for info. o.p. (ISBN 0-87150-227-5, PWS 1801, Prindle). PWS-Kent Pub.

Elementary Mechanics of Solids. P. P. Benham. (Illus.). 1966. text ed. 70.00 o.p. (ISBN 0-08-011216-1). Pergamon.

Elementary Numerical Techniques for Ordinary Differential Equations. John L. Van Iwaarden. 207p. 1980. pap. 7.95 o.p. (ISBN 0-933694-14-8). COMPress.

Elementary Particle Physics (Multiparticle Aspects) Proceedings of the International University Courses on Nuclear Physics, 11th, Schladming, Austria, 1972. International University Courses on Nuclear Physics Staff. Ed. by P. Urban. LC 72-87907. (Acta Physica Austriaca: Suppl. 9). (Illus.). ix, 909p. 1972. 116.90 o.p. (ISBN 0-387-81103-6). Springer-Verlag.

Elementary Particle Theories: Proceedings. International University Courses on Nuclear Physics, 5th, Schladming, Austria, 1966. Ed. by P. Urban. (Acta Physica Austriaca Ser.: Suppl. 3). (Illus.). 1966. 56.70 o.p. (ISBN 0-387-80755-1). Springer-Verlag.

Elementary Particles: Science, Technology & Society. Ed. by Luke C. Yuan & Chien-Shiung Wu. 1971. 81.00 o.p. (ISBN 0-12-774850-4). Acad Pr.

Elementary Physical Education: Toward Inclusion. Don Morris. (Brighton Series in Health & Physical Education). (Illus.). 372p. 1980. pap. text ed. 21.00 o.p.; pap. 25.00 o.p. Pub Horizons.

Elementary Physical Science. Huey. 1957. 3.00 o.p. (ISBN 0-15-225381-5, HJ). HarBraceJ.

Elementary Plane Surveying. 4th ed. Raymond E. Davis & J. W. Kelly. (Illus.). 1967. text ed. 49.95 o.p. (ISBN 0-07-015771-5). McGraw.

Elementary Political Analysis. 2nd ed. Herbert Jacob & Robert Weissberg. (Illus.). 320p. 1975. text ed. 29.95 o.p. (ISBN 0-07-032136-1). McGraw.

Elementary Principal's Handbook. 2nd ed. Hughes. 1985. 39.95 o.p. (ISBN 0-205-08107-X, 238107). Allyn.

Elementary Principal's Handbook: New Approaches to Administrative Action. Reynold Bean & Harris Clemes. 1978. text ed. 26.95 o.p. (ISBN 0-13-259473-0, Parker). P-H.

Elementary Principles of Philosophy. Georges Politzer. LC 76-21231. 180p. 1976. pap. 2.95 o.p. (ISBN 0-7178-0469-0). Intl Pubs Co.

Elementary Processes at High Energy, Pts. A-B, Pts. A-b. Ed. by A. Zichichi. 1972. 85.00 ea. o.p. (ISBN 0-12-780586-9) (ISBN 0-12-780587-7). Acad Pr.

Elementary Quantum Mechanics. Nevill Mott & M. Berry. LC 76-189453. (Wykeham Science Ser.: No. 22). 130p. 1972. 9.95x o.p. (ISBN 0-8448-1124-6, Pub. by Crane Russak & Co). Taylor & Francis.

Elementary Reader in English. rev. ed. Robert J. Dixson. (Illus., Orig.). (gr. 9-12). 1971. pap. text ed. 3.25 o.p. (ISBN 0-88345-044-5, 17977); cassettes 40.00 o.p. (ISBN 0-685-19790-5). Prentice ESL.

Elementary Reading Instruction. Edward Fry. 1977. text ed. 31.95 o.p. (ISBN 0-07-022585-0). McGraw.

Elementary School Guidance & Counseling: A Composite View. Ed. by William H. Van Hoose et al. (Illus.). 300p. 1973. text ed. 16.75 o.p. (ISBN 0-395-12673-8, 3-57497). HM.

Elementary School Health Education: Ecological Perspectives. 2nd ed. Donald B. Stone et al. 480p. 1980. pap. text ed. write for info. o.p. (ISBN 0-697-07385-8). Wm C Brown.

Elementary School Health Instruction. Marion B. Pollock & Kathleen Middleton. (Illus.). 544p. 1984. text ed. 31.95 o.p. (ISBN 0-8016-3957-3). Mosby.

Elementary School in the United States. Ed. by Harold G. Shane & John I. Goodlad. (National Society for the Study of Education Yearbooks Ser: No. 72, Pt. 2). 1973. lib. bdg. 9.50x o.s.i. (ISBN 0-226-60113-7). U of Chicago Pr.

Elementary School Kids' Book of Lists. Kids' Stuff People Staff. LC 81-80910. 154p. (gr. 1-8). 1981. pap. text ed. 4.95 o.p. (ISBN 0-86530-047-X, IP 47X). Incentive Pubns.

Elementary School Physical Education: An Educational Experience. Grace E. Figley et al. 1977. pap. text ed. 17.95 o.p. (ISBN 0-8403-1761-1). Kendall-Hunt.

Elementary Spanish: A First Year College Textbook. Jose M. Goicoecha. 121p. 1969. pap. text ed. 6.95x o.p. (ISBN 0-8290-1093-9). Irvington.

Elementary Spoken Swedish. Martin Soderback. 84p. 1947. pap. 3.75x o.p. (ISBN 0-8006-1078-4, 1-1078, Fortress). Augsburg Fortress.

Elementary Statistical Analysis. Samuel S. Wilks. 1948. 26.50x o.p. (ISBN 0-691-07957-9). Princeton U Pr.

Elementary Statistical Methods in Psychology & Education. 2nd ed. Paul J. Blommers & Robert A. Forsyth. LC 76-11983. (Illus.). 608p. 1977. text ed. 21.95 o.p. (ISBN 0-395-24340-8). HM.

Elementary Statistical Physics. Charles Kittel. LC 58-12495. (Illus.). 228p. 1958. 37.95x o.p. (ISBN 0-471-49005-9). Wiley.

Elementary Statistics. 2nd ed. Robert Johnson. LC 75-43078. 1976. write for info. o.p. (ISBN 0-87872-102-9, Duxbury Pr). PWS-Kent Pub.

Elementary Statistics. 3rd ed. Mario F. Triola. (Illus.). 625p. (For additional information on STATDISK adoption contact publisher). 1986. text ed. 33.95 o.p. (ISBN 0-8053-9327-7); instr's. guide 6.95 o.p. (ISBN 0-8053-9332-3); student solutions manual by Mason 6.95 o.p. (ISBN 0-8053-9328-5); statdisk lab. manual 6.95 o.p. (ISBN 0-8053-9329-3); IBM STATDISK pkg. avail. o.p. (ISBN 0-8053-9334-X); Apple statdisk pkg. avail. o.p. (ISBN 0-8053-9344-7). Benjamin-Cummings.

Elementary Statistics: A Workbook. K. Hope. 1967. 18.00 o.p. (ISBN 0-08-012132-2); pap. 35.00 o.p. (ISBN 0-08-012131-4). Pergamon.

Elementary Statistics for Business. Siskin Johnson. LC 78-13691. (Illus.). 1979. text ed. write for info. o.p. (ISBN 0-87872-188-6, Duxbury Pr); write for info. study guide o.p. (ISBN 0-686-65910-4). PWS-Kent Pub.

Elementary Structural Analysis. Robert G. Boggs. 1984. text ed. 38.95 o.p. (ISBN 0-03-063933-6). HR&W.

Elementary Studies for Piano. J. B. Duvernoy. Ed. by Hans T. Seifert. (Carl Fischer Music Library: No. 506). (Illus.). 1908. pap. 4.00 o.p. (ISBN 0-8258-0129-X). Fischer Inc NY.

Elementary Survey Sampling. William Mendenhall et al. 1971. (ISBN 0-685-26508-0). PWS-Kent Pub.

Elementary Symbolic Logic. William Gustason & Dolph E. Ulrich. LC 81-70028. 280p. 1982. Repr. of 1973 ed. text ed. 18.95x o.p. (ISBN 0-917974-78-6). Waveland Pr.

Elementary Teachers Guide to Free Curriculum Materials. 44th ed. 1987. 22.75 o.p. (ISBN 0-87708-181-6). Ed Prog.

Elementary Teachers Guide to Free Curriculum Materials. 45th ed. 1988. 23.00 o.p. (ISBN 0-87708-193-X). Ed Prog.

Elementary Teachers' Music Almanack: Timely Lesson Plans for Every Day of the School Year. Marvin S. Adler & Jesse C. McCarroll. (Illus.). 1978. text ed. 15.50x o.p. (ISBN 0-13-260836-7, Parker). P-H.

Elementary Technical Mathematics. 3rd ed. Ewen & Nelson. 546p. (ISBN 0-534-02861-6). Watts.

Elementary Technical Mathematics. 3rd ed. Frank L. Juszli & Charles A. Rodgers. (Illus.). 1980. text ed. (ISBN 0-13-260869-3). P-H.

Elementary: The Cartoonist Did It. Robert Mankoff. 128p. 1980. pap. 4.95 o.p. (ISBN 0-380-75317-0, 75317-0). Avon.

Elementary Theory of Elastic Plates. L. G. Jaeger. 1964. text ed. 17.75 o.p. (ISBN 0-08-010342-1); pap. 7.75 o.p. (ISBN 0-08-010341-3). Pergamon.

Elementary Theory of Structures. 2nd ed. Yuan-Yu Hsieh. (Illus.). 448p. 1982. pap. text ed. 48.00 o.p. (ISBN 0-13-261545-2). P-H.

Elementary Topology: A Combinatorial & Algebraic Approach. D. W. Blackett. 1982. 26.00 o.p. (ISBN 0-12-103060-1). Acad Pr.

Elementary Vectors. 3rd ed. E. E. Wolstenholme. 1971. text ed. 9.90 o.p. (ISBN 0-08-016569-9); pap. text ed. 2.75 o.p. (ISBN 0-08-016570-2). Pergamon.

Elements in a Theory of Industrial Relations. Charles McCarthy. 144p. 1984. 32.50x o.p. (ISBN 0-7165-2363-9, BBA 05254, Pub. by Irish Academic Pr Ireland). Biblio Dist.

Elements of a Two-Process Theory of Learning. J. A. Gray. 1975. 59.50 o.p. (ISBN 0-12-296850-6). Acad Pr.

Elements of Analytical Dynamics. Rudolf Kurth. 200p. 1976. text ed. 30.00 o.p. (ISBN 0-08-019848-1). Pergamon.

Elements of Banking. 3rd ed. F. E. Perry. 400p. 1981. pap. 11.95x o.p. (ISBN 0-416-32080-5, NO.3538). Routledge Chapman & Hall.

Elements of BASIC. National Computing Centre, Ltd. Staff. (Computers & the Professional Ser.). 100p. 1979. pap. 25.00x o.s.i. (ISBN 0-85012-118-3). Intl Pubns Serv.

Elements of BASIC FORTRAN IV Programming. 2nd ed. Wilson T. Price. 1975. pap. text ed. 20.95 o.p. (ISBN 0-03-089502-2). HR&W.

Elements of BASIC Plus Programming. Wilson T. Price. 1982. pap. text ed. 23.95 o.p. (ISBN 0-03-060148-7). HR&W.

Elements of Biochemistry. Larry G. Scheve. 500p. 1984. 46.00 o.s.i. (ISBN 0-205-07909-1, 687909); net o.p. 31.50 o.s.i.; instr's. manual avail. o.s.i. Allyn.

Elements of Biological Science. 2nd ed. William T. Keeton. (Illus.). 1973. text ed. 20.95x o.p. (ISBN 0-393-09346-8). Norton.

Elements of Biological Science. William T. Keeton. 1968. 8.50x o.p. (ISBN 0-393-09830-3, NortonC). Norton.

Elements of Biology. 4th ed. Robert M. Brenner. 1977. study guide 18.95 o.p. (ISBN 0-07-069138-X). McGraw.

Elements of Biology. 4th ed. Paul B. Weisz & Richard N. Keogh. 1977. text ed. 37.95 o.p. (ISBN 0-07-069137-1). McGraw.

Elements of Business. Robert A. Lynn & James P. O'Grady. LC 77-75881. (Illus.). 1978. text ed. 31.95 o.p. (ISBN 0-395-25107-9). HM.

Elements of Business & Statistics: Learning by Objectives. Harry E. McAllister. LC 74-23909. 566p. 1975. 34.00 o.p. (ISBN 0-471-58120-8). Krieger.

Elements of Business Statistics. Byrkit. PWS-Kent Pub.

Elements of Calculus: With Contemporary Applications. Marcus M. McWaters & James H. Reed. 1976. text ed. 17.95 o.p. (ISBN 0-15-522063-2, HC). HarBraceJ.

Elements of Chromatography. T. I. Williams. (Illus.). 96p. 1955. (ISBN 0-8022-1888-1). Philos Lib.

Elements of Civil Procedure, Cases & Materials: 1982 Suplement. 3rd ed. Maurice Rosenberg et al. (University Casebook Ser.). 157p. 1982. pap. text ed. 5.50 o.p. (ISBN 0-88277-082-9). Foundation Pr.

Elements of Classical Physics. M. C. Martin & C. A. Hewett. LC 73-3450. 1975. 42.00 o.p. (ISBN 0-08-017098-6). Pergamon.

Elements of Complex Analysis. B. Choudhary. LC 83-12820. 262p. 1983. 23.95x o.p. (ISBN 0-470-27492-1). Halsted Pr.

Elements of Computer Process Control with Advanced Control Applications. Pradeep B. Deshpande & Raymond H. Ash. LC 80-82117. 424p. 1981. text ed. 49.95x o.p. (ISBN 0-87664-449-3). Instru Soc.

Elements of Critical Theory. Wayne Shumaker. LC 74-9398. (Perspectives in Criticism I Ser.). 131p. 1975. Repr. of 1952 ed. lib. bdg. 22.50x o.p. (ISBN 0-8371-7663-8, SHCT). Greenwood.

Elements of Cryptanalysis. William F. Friedman. LC 76-19947. (Cryptographic Ser.). 1976. lib. bdg. 26.80 o.p. (ISBN 0-89412-002-6); pap. 18.80 o.p. (ISBN 0-89412-100-6). Aegean Park Pr.

Elements of Cytology. 2nd ed. Norman S. Cohn. (Illus.). 1969. text ed. 14.50 o.p. (ISBN 0-15-522076-4, HC). HarBraceJ.

Elements of Data Processing. Marxer. LC 75-153725. 215p. 1974. pap. 16.00 o.p. (ISBN 0-8273-0410-2); tchr's. manual o.s.i. 3.60 o.p. (ISBN 0-8273-0411-0). Delmar.

Elements of Data Processing Mathematics. 2nd ed. Wilson T. Price & M. Miller. LC 71-140239. 1971. text ed. 29.95 o.p. (ISBN 0-03-084745-1, HoltC). HR&W.

Elements of Early Reading Instruction. R. Baird Shuman. 96p. 1979. pap. 7.95 o.p. (ISBN 0-8106-1623-8). NEA.

Elements of Elasticity. D. S. Dugdale. 1968. 40.00 o.p. (ISBN 0-08-012634-0); pap. 40.00 o.p. (ISBN 0-08-012633-2). Pergamon.

Elements of Electronics. 4th ed. Henry V. Hickey & William M. Villines, Jr. LC 79-13830. (Illus.). 1980. text ed. 41.95 o.p. (ISBN 0-07-028695-7). McGraw.

Elements of Engineering Electromagnetics. N. Narayana Rao. (Illus.). 1977. pap. text ed. 52.00 o.p. (ISBN 0-13-264150-X). P-H.

Elements of English Architecture. Hugh Braun. (Illus.). 212p. 1980. Repr. 22.95 o.p. (ISBN 0-7153-5775-1). David & Charles.

Elements of Ethology: A Textbook of Agricultural & Veterinary Students. D. G. Wood-Gush. LC 82-243446. (Illus.). 225p. 1983. 38.00 o.p. (ISBN 0-412-23160-3, NO. 6793, Pub. by Chapman & Hall); pap. 16.95 o.p. (ISBN 0-412-23170-0, NO. 6792). Routledge Chapman & Hall.

Elements of Experimental Stress Analysis: SI Edition. A. W. Hendry. LC 76-54580. 1977. text ed. 20.00 o.p. (ISBN 0-08-021301-4); pap. text ed. 8.50 o.p. (ISBN 0-08-021300-6). Pergamon.

Elements of Explosives Production. James Glackin. 60p. 1976. pap. 5.00 o.p. (ISBN 0-87364-083-7). Paladin Pr.

Elements of Export Marketing & Management. Alan E. Branch. 1984. pap. 19.95 o.p. (ISBN 0-412-23150-6, Pub. by Chapman & Hall England, NO. 6838). Routledge Chapman & Hall.

Elements of Export Practice. Alan E. Branch. 400p. 1977. pap. 16.95 o.p. (ISBN 0-412-15610-5, NO.6042, Pub. by Chapman & Hall England). Routledge Chapman & Hall.

Elements of Film. 2nd ed. Lee R. Bobker. (Illus.). 400p. (Orig.). 1974. pap. text ed. 10.95 o.p. (ISBN 0-15-522095-0, HC). HarBraceJ.

Elements of Finance for Managers. B. K. Watts. (Illus.). 256p. 1976. pap. 16.95x o.p. (ISBN 0-7121-0551-4, Pub. by Macdonald & Evans England). Trans-Atl Phila.

Elements of Financial Records see Accounting Ten-Twelve.

Elements of Food Engineering. John C. Harper. (Illus.). 1976. pap. 21.95 o.p. (ISBN 0-87055-299-6). AVI.

Elements of Food Technology. Desrosier. 1977. pap. 32.95 o.s.i. (ISBN 0-87055-284-8). Van Nos Reinhold.

Elements of Genetics. Irwin H. Herskowitz. 1979. write for info. o.p. (ISBN 0-02-353950-X). Macmillan.

Elements of Hereditary Solid Mechanics. Yu Rabotnov. 387p. 1980. 9.95 o.p. (ISBN 0-8285-1537-9, Pub. by Mir Pubs USSR). Imported Pubns.

Elements of Human & Social Geography (Some Anthropological Perspectives) Eric Sunderland. LC 73-10060. 120p. 1973. 19.75 o.p. (ISBN 0-08-017689-5); pap. 9.25 o.p. (ISBN 0-08-017690-9). Pergamon.

Elements of Human Genetics. 2nd ed. L. L. Cavalli-Sforza. LC 76-58969. 1977. text ed. 26.95 o.p. (ISBN 0-8053-1872-0); pap. text ed. 19.95 o.p. (ISBN 0-8053-1874-7). Benjamin-Cummings.

Elements of Income Tax. 2nd rev. ed. B. B. Lal. 1980. text ed. 35.00x o.p. (ISBN 0-7069-0701-9, Pub. by Vikas India). Advent NY.

Elements of Intelligence. Ed. by Roy Godson. (Intelligence Requirements for the 1980's Ser.: Vol. I). 124p. (Orig.). 1979. pap. 4.95 o.p. (ISBN 0-87855-826-8). Transaction Pubs.

Elements of Intelligence, Vol. I. rev. ed. Ed. by Roy Godson. (Intelligence Requirements for the 1980's: Vol. VI). 150p. 1983. pap. 6.50 o.p. (ISBN 0-87855-954-X). Transaction Pubs.

Elements of International Strategy: A Primer for the Nuclear Age. Louis J. Halle. (American Values Projected Abroad Ser.: Vol. 10). 134p. (Orig.). 1984. lib. bdg. 14.75 o.p. (ISBN 0-8191-3700-6, Co-pub. by White Miller Center); pap. text ed. 8.75 o.p. (ISBN 0-8191-3701-4, Co-pub. by White Miller Center). U Pr of Amer.

Elements of Lettering. 2nd ed. John H. Benson & A. G. Carey. 1962. text ed. 30.95 o.p. (ISBN 0-07-004775-8). McGraw.

Elements of Loadbearing Brickwork. D. Lenczner. 125p. 1972. 35.00 o.p. (ISBN 0-08-016814-0). Pergamon.

Elements of Logic. 3rd ed. Stephen F. Barker. (Illus.). 1979. text ed. 27.95 o.p. (ISBN 0-07-003720-5). McGraw.

Elements of Marine Ecology. E. V. Tait. (Illus.). 1974. 17.60 o.p. (ISBN 0-387-91113-8). Springer-Verlag.

Elements of Mathematical Logic. 2nd ed. J. Lukasiewicz. (International Series in Pure & Applied Mathematics: Vol. 31). 1964. 35.00 o.p. (ISBN 0-08-010393-6); pap. 35.00 o.p. (ISBN 0-08-013695-8). Pergamon.

Elements of Mathematical Logic & Set Theory. J. Slupecki & L. Borkowski. 1967. text ed. 35.00 o.p. (ISBN 0-08-011096-7). Pergamon.

Elements of Medical Genetics. 7th ed. Alan E. Emery. (Illus.). 1988. pap. text ed. 18.50 o.p. (ISBN 0-443-02724-2). Churchill.

Elements of Modern Management. Eugene J. Benge. LC 76-25179. 232p. 1979. pap. 5.95 o.p. AMACOM.

Elements of Moral Science, 2 vols. James Beattie. Ed. by Rene Wellek. LC 75-11195. (British Philosophers & Theologians of the 17th & 18th Centuries: Vol. 2). 1976. Repr. of 1793 ed. Set. lib. bdg. 101.00 o.p. (ISBN 0-8240-1751-X); lib. bdg. write for info. o.p. Garland Pub.

Elements of Music: A Programmed Approach. 2nd ed. Michelle G. Worthing. 304p. 1983. write for info. wire coil o.p. (ISBN 0-697-03564-6). Wm C Brown.

Elements of Neutron Interaction Theory. Anthony Foderaro. LC 79-103896. 1971. text ed. 40.00x o.p. (ISBN 0-262-06033-7). MIT Pr.

Elements of Organic Photochemistry. Ed. by D. O. Cowan & R. L. Drisko. LC 75-28173. (Illus.). 586p. 1976. 49.50x o.p. (ISBN 0-306-30821-5, Plenum Pr). Plenum Pub.

Elements of Petroleum Reservoirs. 250p. 1969. 26.00x o.s.i. (ISBN 0-317-32915-4). Soc Petrol Engineers.

Elements of Philosophy: An Introduction. Samuel E. Stumpf. 1979. text ed. 27.95 o.p. (ISBN 0-07-062216-7). McGraw.

Elements of Photogrammetry. Paul R. Wolf. (Illus.). 1974. text ed. 35.00 o.p. (ISBN 0-07-071337-5, C). McGraw.

Elements of Physical Geology. James H. Zumberge & Clemens A. Nelson. LC 75-26843. 412p. 1976. (ISBN 0-471-98674-7). Wiley.

Elements of Physical Oceanography. H. J. McLellan. 1965. 40.00 o.p. (ISBN 0-08-011320-6). Pergamon.

Elements of Political Economy. 3rd, rev. ed. James Mill. LC 65-24376. Repr. of 1844 ed. 35.00x o.p. (ISBN 0-678-00008-5). Kelley.

Elements of Position Classification in Local Government. Esther C. Lawton & Harold Suskin. 1976. 6.00 o.p. (ISBN 0-317-00536-7). Intl Personnel Mgmt.

Elements of Practical Coal Mining. LC 72-86921. 1973. 16.50x o.p. (ISBN 0-89520-018-X). SMM&E Inc.

Elements of Probability & Mathematical Statistics. Frederick H. Steen. 512p. 1982. text ed. write for info. o.p. (ISBN 0-87872-299-8, 6075, Duxbury Pr). PWS-Kent Pub.

Elements of Probability Theory. L. Z. Rumshiskii. 1965. 45.00 o.p. (ISBN 0-08-010534-3); pap. text ed. 12.75 o.p. (ISBN 0-08-013609-5). Pergamon.

Elements of Quantity Surveying. 7th ed. Arthur Willis & Christopher Willis. 254p. 1978. pap. 18.00x o.p. (ISBN 0-246-11471-1, Pub by Granada England). Sheridan.

Elements of Quantity Surveying. 7th ed. Arthur J. Willis & Christopher J. Willis. 254p. 1978. pap. text ed. 22.75x o.p. (ISBN 0-258-97098-7, Pub. by Granada England). Gower Pub Co.

Elements of Radio Servicing. 3rd ed. William Marcus & Alex Levy. (gr. 9-12). 1967. text ed. 45.95 o.p. (ISBN 0-07-040290-6). McGraw.

Elements of Ship Design. R. Munro-Smith. 145p. 1976. pap. 13.50x o.p. (ISBN 0-900976-39-X, Pub. by Inst Marine Eng). Intl Spec Bk.

Elements of Social Organization. Raymond Firth. (ISBN 0-8022-0506-2). Philos Lib.

Elements of Soil Mechanics for Civil & Mining Engineers. 4th ed. G. N. Smith. 424p. 1978. pap. text ed. 17.50x o.p. (ISBN 0-258-97106-1, Pub. by Granada England). Gower Pub Co.

Elements of Soil Mechanics for Civil & Mining Engineers. 5th ed. G. N. Smith. 493p. 1982. pap. text ed. 21.75x o.p. (ISBN 0-246-11765-6, Pub. by Granada England). Gower Pub Co.

Elements of Speech Communication: Achieving Competency. David M. Jabusch & Stephen Littlejohn. LC 80-82760. (Illus.). 464p. 1980. text ed. 22.95 o.p. (ISBN 0-395-29730-3). HM.

Elements of Steelmaking Practice. J. D. Sharp. 1966. 65.00 o.p. (ISBN 0-08-011437-7); pap. 65.00 o.p. (ISBN 0-08-011436-9). Pergamon.

Elements of Structural Geology. 2nd ed. E. S. Hills. 1972. pap. 25.00x o.p. (ISBN 0-412-20750-8, NO.6300, Pub. by Chapman & Hall). Routledge Chapman & Hall.

Elements of System-Dynamics Simulation. T. J. Ferrari. 93p. 1978. pap. 11.00 o.p. (ISBN 90-220-0668-9, PDC143, Pudoc). UNIPUB.

Elements of Systems Analysis. 3rd ed. Marvin Gore & John Stubbe. 568p. 1983. text ed. write for info. o.p. (ISBN 0-697-08169-9). instrs.' resource manual avail. o.p. (ISBN 0-697-08178-8); alternate casebook avail. o.p. (ISBN 0-697-00092-3); solutions manual to alternate casebook avail. o.p. (ISBN 0-697-00267-5). Wm C Brown.

Elements of the Mechanical Behavior of Solids. Suh. 614p. 1975. 21.95 o.p. (ISBN 0-89116-520-7). Hemisphere Pub.

Elements of the Philosophy of the Human Mind. Dugald Stewart. 1986. Repr. of 1792 ed. lib. bdg. 30.00x o.p. (ISBN 0-935005-65-X). Ibis Pub VA.

Elements of the Science of Nutrition. Graham Lusk. (Nutrition Foundations Reprint Ser.). 844p. 1982. 45.00 o.p. (ISBN 0-12-460460-9). Acad Pr.

Elements of Thermodynamics & Heat Transfer. 2nd ed. Edward F. Obert & Robert L. Young. LC 79-23780. 558p. 1980. Repr. of 1962 ed. lib. bdg. 39.50 o.p. (ISBN 0-89874-005-3). Krieger.

Elements of Truth. Joseph H. Hinshaw. LC 67-13370. 160p. 1967. (ISBN 0-8022-0726-X). Philos Lib.

Elements of Wave Propagation in Random Media. Barry J. Uscinski. (Illus.). 1977. text ed. 48.95 o.p. (ISBN 0-07-066650-4). McGraw.

Elena. Thomas H. Cook. 435p. 1986. 18.45 o.p. (ISBN 0-395-35632-6). HM.

Elena: A Love Story of the Russian Revolution. Judith Egan. LC 80-39613. 320p. 1981. 11.95 o.p. (ISBN 0-89919-028-6). Ticknor & Fields.

Elena's Secrets of Mexican Cooking. Elena Zelayeta. 1968. pap. 6.50 o.p. (ISBN 0-385-00197-5, Dolp). Doubleday.

Elephant. Byron Barton. LC 74-154301. (Illus.). (ps-3). 1979. 4.95 o.p. (ISBN 0-395-28764-2, Clarion). HM.

Elephant & His Secret: Based on a Fable by Gabriela Mistral. Tr. by Doris Dana. LC 73-75432. (Illus.). 32p. (ps-3). 1974. 5.95 o.p. (ISBN 0-689-30430-7, Atheneum). Macmillan.

Elephant Bangs Train. William Kotzwinkle. 1981. pap. 2.95 o.p. (ISBN 0-380-01161-1, 56549-8, Bard). Avon.

Elephant Eats the Profits. Jacquelyn Reinach & Ruth L. Perle. LC 77-7254. (Sweet Pickles Ser.). (Illus.). (gr. k-2). 1977. 2.95 o.p. (ISBN 0-03-021426-2). H Holt & Co.

Elephant Herds & Rhino Horns. Don Torgersen. LC 81-10158. (Animal Safari Nature Library). (Illus.). (gr. 4 up). 1982. PLB 11.93 o.p. (ISBN 0-516-00652-5); pap. 3.95 o.p. (ISBN 0-516-40652-3). Childrens.

Elephant Is Soft & Mushy. Sam Gross. (Illus.). 128p. 1982. pap. 4.95 o.p. (ISBN 0-380-57679-1, 57679-1). Avon.

Elephant Man. Bernard Pomerance. LC 79-7792. 1979. pap. 4.25 o.p. (ISBN 0-394-17539-5, E744, Ever). Grove.

Elephants Can Remember. Agatha Christie. 1976. pap. 1.25 o.p. (ISBN 0-440-12329-1). Dell.

Elephants Never Jump. Violet Easton. (Illus.). 32p. (ps-2). 1986. 11.95 o.p. (ISBN 0-316-20401-3, Joy St Bks). Little.

Elevations of Love-to Women (Real & Imagined) Frank Winburne. 1977. 4.00 o.p. (ISBN 0-682-48783-X). Exposition-Phoenix.

Elevators & Escalators in Architectural Design: A Bibliography. Mary E. Huls. (Architecture Ser.: A 1511). 5p. 1985. 2.00 o.p. (ISBN 0-89028-661-2). Vance Biblios.

Eleven Essays in the European Novel. Richard P. Blackmur. LC 64-19367. (Orig.). 1964. pap. 2.95 o.p. (ISBN 0-15-628210-0, Harv). HarBraceJ.

Eleven Harrowhouse. Gerald A. Browne. LC 70-183382. 1972. 15.95 o.p. (ISBN 0-87795-024-5, Arbor Hse). Morrow.

Eleven Hundred Open Salts. Allan B. Smith et al. (Illus.). 1981. pap. 15.00 o.p. (ISBN 0-940554-07-0). Country Hse.

Eleven Hundred Words You Need to Know. Murray Bromberg & Melvin Gordon. LC 70-12919. 1971. pap. 5.95 o.p. (ISBN 0-8120-0405-1). Barron.

Eleven Million Mile High Dancer. Carol Hill. 496p. 1985. 16.95 o.p. (ISBN 0-03-070699-8). H Holt & Co.

Eleven Skagit Poets. Ed. by Samuel Green. 1987. 16.00 o.p. (ISBN 0-918116-43-0); pap. 8.00 o.p. (ISBN 0-918116-44-9). Brooding Heron Pr.

Eleven Times Seventeen Graphs. (Easy-to-Make Photocopier Bks.). (Orig.). 1983. pap. 14.95 o.p. (ISBN 0-87280-029-6, Asher-Gallant). Caddylak Systs.

Eleventh Commandment & Other Short Stories. Mary Silberman. 1978. pap. 4.00 o.p. (ISBN 0-682-49163-2). Exposition-Phoenix.

Eleventh Lacus Forum. Linguistic Association of Canada & the U. S. Staff. Ed. by Robert A. Hall. 1984. pap. text ed. 12.95 o.s.i. (ISBN 0-917496-25-6). Hornbeam Pr.

Eleventh National Passive Solar Conference Proceedings. 572p. 1986. 100.00 o.s.i. (ISBN 0-89553-202-6). Am Solar Energy.

Elfie Jingle: Santa's Right Hand Man. Warren W. Parker. (Illus.). 64p. 1980. 5.00 o.p. (ISBN 0-682-49628-6). Exposition-Phoenix.

Elgar-Atkins Friendship. E. Wulstan Atkins. (Illus.). 510p. 1984. 45.00 o.p. (ISBN 0-7153-8583-6). David & Charles.

Elias Practical Grammar. Elias. 2.95 o.p. (ISBN 0-686-18360-6). Kazi Pubns.

Elias Ries, Inventor. Estelle H. Ries. 1952. (ISBN 0-8022-1343-X). Philos Lib.

Elidor. Alan Garner. 160p. 1981. pap. 1.95 o.s.i. (ISBN 0-345-29042-9, Del Rey). Ballantine.

Eliel Saarinen: Finnish-American Architect & Educator. 2nd rev. ed. Albert Christ-Janer. LC 79-832. 1980. Repr. of 1948 ed. lib. bdg. 32.50x o.s.i. (ISBN 0-226-10464-8). U of Chicago Pr.

Eliel Saarinen: Finnish-American Architect & Educator. rev. ed. Albert Christ-Janer. LC 79-832. (Illus.). 190p. 1985. pap. 17.95 o.s.i. (ISBN 0-226-10465-6). U of Chicago Pr.

Eligibility for Trade Union Office. 86p. 1972. 4.55 o.p. (ISBN 92-2-100176-8). Intl Labour Office.

Eligible Connection. Elsie Lee. 1980. pap. 1.95 o.p. (ISBN 0-440-12821-8). Dell.

Elijah: Prophet of God. Leon J. Wood. 1968. 2.95 o.p. (ISBN 0-87227-020-3). Reg Baptist.

Elijah: Prophet of Power. Phillip Keller. 160p. 1980. 8.95 o.p. (ISBN 0-8499-0266-5). Word Bks.

Elijah the Slave. Isaac Bashevis Singer. (Illus.). 32p. (ps-3). 1981. pap. 1.95 o.p. (ISBN 0-590-31469-6). Scholastic Inc.

Eliot, Auden, Lowell: Aspects of the Baudelairean Inheritance. L. Mackinnon. 224p. 1982. pap. 38.50x o.p. (ISBN 0-391-02955-X). Humanities.

Eliseo Vivas: A Bibliography. Hugh M. Curtler. LC 80-9013. (American Literature Catolog Ser.). 150p. 1982. lib. bdg. 26.00 o.p. (ISBN 0-8240-9300-3). Garland Pub.

Elite Unit Insignia of the Vietnam War: An Illustrated Reference Guide for Collectors. Leroy Thompson. (Illus.). 60p. 1987. 14.95 o.p. (ISBN 0-85368-815-X, Pub. by Arms & Armour). Sterling.

Elites Against Democracy: Leadership Ideals in Bourgeois Political Thought in Germany, 1890-1933. Walter Struve. 484p. 1973. 58.50x o.p. (ISBN 0-691-07555-7); pap. 12.50 o.p. (ISBN 0-691-10020-9). Princeton U Pr.

Elitism. G. Lowell Field & John Higley. 1980. 18.50x o.p. (ISBN 0-7100-0487-7). Routledge Chapman & Hall.

Elizabeth Barrett Browning. Dorothy Hewlett. LC 72-4251. xiv, 388p. 1972. Repr. of 1952 ed. lib. bdg. 27.50x o.p. (ISBN 0-374-93883-0, Octagon). Hippocrene Bks.

Elizabeth Barrett Browning's Letters to Mrs. David Ogilvy. Elizabeth Barrett Browning. Ed. by Peter N. Heydon & Philip Kelley. LC 72-92081. 1973. 7.95 o.p. (ISBN 0-8129-0287-4). Times Bks.

Elizabeth Bayley Seton. Annabelle M. Melville. 1976. pap. 2.25 o.s.i. (ISBN 0-515-09682-2). Jove Pubns.

Elizabeth Cady Stanton. Martha Kendall. LC 86-7569. (Illus.). 72p. (Orig.). 1987. pap. 5.00 o.p. (ISBN 0-932334-29-6). Heart of the Lakes.

Elizabeth Cady Stanton - Susan B. Anthony Reader. Date not set. (ISBN 0-8052-3759-3). Random.

Elizabeth, Captive Princess. Margaret E. Irwin. (Illus.). 1948. 7.50 o.p. (ISBN 0-15-128361-3). HarBraceJ.

Elizabeth Catches a Fish. Jane R. Thomas. LC 76-28318. (Illus.). (gr. 1-4). 1979. 6.95 o.p. (ISBN 0-395-28827-4, Clarion). HM.

Elizabeth Gail & Double Trouble. Hilda Stahl. (No. 11). 1982. pap. 2.95 o.p. (ISBN 0-8423-0715-X). Tyndale.

Elizabeth Gail & the Frightened Runaways. Hilda Stahl. (No. 8). 1981. pap. 2.95 o.p. (ISBN 0-8423-0728-1). Tyndale.

Elizabeth Gail & the Holiday Mystery. Hilda Stahl. (No. 12). 1982. pap. 2.95 o.p. (ISBN 0-8423-0713-3). Tyndale.

Elizabeth Gail & the Missing Love Letters. Hilda Stahl. (No. 13). 1982. pap. 2.95 o.p. (ISBN 0-8423-0709-5). Tyndale.

Elizabeth Gail & the Music Camp Romance. Hilda Stahl. (Windrider Ser.: No. 14). 128p. (gr. 3-7). 1983. pap. 2.95 o.p. (ISBN 0-8423-0708-7). Tyndale.

Elizabeth Gail & the Mystery at the Johnson Farm. Hilda Stahl. (Windrider Ser.: No. 1). (gr. 5-9). 1979. pap. text ed. 2.95 o.p. (ISBN 0-8423-0720-6). Tyndale.

Elizabeth Gail & the Secret Box. Hilda Stahl. (Windrider Ser.: No. 2). (gr. 3-9). 1979. pap. 2.95 o.p. (ISBN 0-8423-0721-4). Tyndale.

Elizabeth Gail & the Strange Birthday Party. Hilda Stahl. (Windrider Ser.: No. 6). (gr. 4-6). 1980. 2.95 o.p. (ISBN 0-8423-0724-9). Tyndale.

Elizabeth Gail & the Time for Love. Hilda Stahl. (Windrider Ser.: No. 18). 120p. (gr. 3 up). 1983. pap. 2.95 o.p. (ISBN 0-8423-0732-X). Tyndale.

Elizabeth Gail & Trouble from the Past. Hilda Stahl. (No. 9). 1981. pap. 2.95 o.p. (ISBN 0-8423-0717-6). Tyndale.

Elizabeth Gail Gift Set. 1983. Set, 6 vol. No. 1. 16.95 o.p. (ISBN 0-8423-0748-6); Set, 6 vol. No. 2. 16.95 o.p. (ISBN 0-8423-0749-4); Set, 6 vol. No. 3. 16.95 o.p. (ISBN 0-8423-0747-8). Tyndale.

Elizabeth Gaskell. Angus Easson. 1979. 25.00x o.p. (ISBN 0-7100-0099-5). Routledge Chapman & Hall.

Elizabeth Gaskell. Coral Lansbury. (English Authors Ser.: No. 371). 1984. lib. bdg. 18.95 o.p. (ISBN 0-8057-6857-2, Twayne). G K Hall.

Elizabeth Gaskell: An Annotated Bibliography, 1929-1975. Jeffrey E. Welch. LC 75-42874. (Reference Library of the Humanities Ser.: Vol. 50). 1977. lib. bdg. 26.00 o.p. (ISBN 0-8240-9950-8). Garland Pub.

Elizabeth Gaskell: Four Short Stories. Ed. by Anna Walters. 128p. (Orig.). 1983. pap. 5.95 o.p. (ISBN 0-86358-001-7, Pandora Pr). Routledge Chapman & Hall.

Elizabeth Grotesque. Neil Rhodes. 208p. 1980. 30.00x o.p. (ISBN 0-7100-0599-7). Routledge Chapman & Hall.

Elizabeth Joy. Caroline Philps. 144p. 9.95 o.p. (ISBN 0-85648-907-7). Lion USA.

Elizabeth Macarthur & Her World. Hazel King. 230p. 1982. 21.95x o.p. (ISBN 0-424-00080-6, Pub. by Sydney U Pr Australia). Intl Spec Bk.

Elizabeth Our Queen. Richard Dimbleby. LC 78-12304. (Illus.). 1979. Repr. of 1953 ed. lib. bdg. 35.00x o.p. (ISBN 0-313-21096-9, DIEQ). Greenwood.

Elizabeth Taylor: The Last Star. Kitty Kelley. 1982. pap. 3.95 o.p. (ISBN 0-440-12410-7). Dell.

Elizabeth Vige Le Brun. Colin Baillie. (Illus.). 1988. write for info. o.p. Braziller.

Elizabethan Dumb Show. Dieter Mehl. (Library Reprints Ser.). 224p. 1982. 44.00 o.p. (ISBN 0-416-33980-8, NO. 3705). Routledge Chapman & Hall.

Elizabethan England. Peter Lane. (Visual Sources Ser.). (Illus.). 96p. (gr. 7-12). 1981. 17.95 o.p. (ISBN 0-7134-3566-6, Pub. by Batsford England). David & Charles.

Elizabethan Lyrics from the Original Texts. 3rd ed. Ed. by Norman Ault. Repr. of 1949 ed. 69.00x o.p. (ISBN 0-686-02251-3). Somerset Pub.

Elizabethan Madrigal: A Comparative Study. Joseph Kerman. 318p. Repr. of 1962 ed. lib. bdg. 49.00 o.p. (Pub. by Am Repr Serv). Reprint Servs.

Elizabethan Popular Theatre: Plays in Performance. Michael Hattaway. (Theatre Production Ser.). (Illus.). 234p. 1985. pap. 12.95x o.p. (ISBN 0-7102-0530-9). Routledge Chapman & Hall.

Elizabethan Puritan Movement. Patrick Collinson. (Library Reprints Ser.). 528p. 1982. 60.00x o.p. (ISBN 0-416-34000-8, NO. 3701). Routledge Chapman & Hall.

Elizabethan Shakespeare. John D. Wilson. 1982. lib. bdg. 42.50 o.p. (ISBN 0-686-81913-6). Bern Porter.

Elizabethans: Costume Cut-out Book. Sue Shields. (Illus.). 24p. (gr. 5-8). 1988. pap. 9.95 o.p. (ISBN 0-434-96316-X, Pub. by W Heinemann Ltd). David & Charles.

Eliza's Daddy. Ianthe Thomas. LC 75-41343. (Let Me Read Ser.). (Illus.). (gr. 1-5). 1976. 4.95 o.p. (ISBN 0-15-225400-5, HJ); pap. 1.65 o.p. (ISBN 0-15-225401-3, VoyB). HarBraceJ.

Elk Hunt. Alan E. Nourse. (Illus.). 352p. 1986. 19.95 o.p. (ISBN 0-02-590700-X). Macmillan.

Elkaz Kazan's Dilema. Johnny W. St. Ama. Ed. by Renais Hill. LC 88-70623. 182p. (Orig.). 1988. pap. 8.95 o.p. (ISBN 1-55666-022-7). Authors Unltd.

Elkhorn Tavern. Douglas C. Jones. LC 79-27818. 304p. 1980. 12.95 o.p. (ISBN 0-03-050926-2). H Holt & Co.

Elkhorn Tavern. Douglas C. Jones. LC 79-27818. 320p. 1984. pap. 5.95 o.s.i. (ISBN 0-03-000097-1, Owl Bks). H Holt & Co.

Ella: The Life & Times of Ella Fitzgerald. Sid Colin. (Illus.). 160p. 1987. 19.95 o.p. (ISBN 0-241-11754-2, Pub. by Hamish Hamilton England). David & Charles.

Elle Knitting Book. Elle Magazine Staff. (Illus.). 128p. 1984. 19.95 o.p. (ISBN 0-684-18219-X, ScribT). Scribner.

Ellen & Edy: A Biography of Ellen Terry & Her Daughter, Edith Craig, 1847-1947. Joy Melville. (Illus.). 298p. 1988. text ed. 32.50 o.p. (ISBN 0-86358-252-4, Pandora Pr); pap. text ed. 10.95 o.p. (ISBN 0-86358-078-5, Pandora Pr). Routledge Chapman & Hall.

Ellen Bray: A Novel of Superb Romance. Jane Julian. LC 85-31975. 256p. 1986. 16.95 o.p. (ISBN 0-688-06471-X). Morrow.

Ellen C. Sabin: Proponent of Higher Education for Women. Estelle Pau On Lau. 1978. pap. text ed. 10.00 o.p. (ISBN 0-8191-0469-8). U Pr of Amer.

Ellen G. White: Prophet of Destiny. Rene Noorbergen. LC 70-190456. 363p. 1970. text ed. 6.95 o.p. (ISBN 0-87983-014-X); pap. 2.50 o.p. (ISBN 0-87983-077-8); spanish version 1.95 o.p. (ISBN 0-87983-076-X). MMI Pr.

Ellen Glasgow: Centennial Essays. Ed. by M. Thomas Inge. LC 75-15976. 232p. 1976. 17.95x o.p. (ISBN 0-8139-0620-2). U Pr of Va.

Ellen Terry: Player in Her Time. Nina Auerbach. (Illus.). 448p. 1987. 22.00 o.p. (ISBN 0-393-02398-2). Norton.

Ellen Wilkinson, Eighteen Ninety-One to Nineteen Forty-Seven. Betty D. Vernon. 254p. 1982. pap. 14.00 o.p. (ISBN 0-7099-2603-0, Pub. by Croom Helm Ltd). Routledge Chapman & Hall.

Ellen's Lion: Twelve Stories. Crockett Johnson. LC 59-5791. (Illus.). 64p. (gr. 2 up). 1984. pap. 4.95 o.s.i. (ISBN 0-87923-509-8). Godine.

Ellery Queen's Champions of Mystery. Ed. by Ellery Queen. (Large Print Bks). 547p. 1987. lib. bdg. 18.95 o.s.i. (ISBN 0-8161-4108-8, Large Print Bks). G K Hall.

Ellery Queen's Memorable Characters. Davis Publications Staff & Ellery Queen. 1984. 12.95 o.p. (ISBN 0-385-19645-8, Dial). Doubleday.

Ellery Queen's Prime Crimes. Ellery Queen. LC 59-13341. 288p. 1984. 12.95 o.p. (ISBN 0-385-27954-X, Dial). Doubleday.

Ellery Queen's Prime Crimes Two. Davis Publications Staff & Ellery Queen. LC 59-13341. 288p. 1985. 12.95 o.p. (ISBN 0-385-19644-X, Dial). Doubleday.

Ellicott City, Maryland: Mill Town, U. S. A. Celia M. Holland. 273p. 1970. casebound 14.95 o.p. (ISBN 0-686-86318-6). MD Hist Pr.

Ellie: A Child's Fight Against Leukemia. Jonathan B. Tucker. LC 81-7181. (Illus.). 368p. 1982. 15.95 o.p. (ISBN 0-03-057662-8). H Holt & Co.

Elliott O'Donnell's Casebook of Ghosts. Ed. by Harry Ludlam. LC 73-84645. (Illus.). 1969. 8.95 o.s.i. (ISBN 0-8008-2385-0). Taplinger.

Elliptic Functions: A Primer. Eric H. Neville. Ed. by W. J. Langford. 211p. 1971. text ed. 27.00 o.p. (ISBN 0-08-016369-6). Pergamon.

Elliptischen Funktionen und Ihre Anwendungen, 2 Vols. Robert Fricke. LC 5-33590. 1971. Repr. of 1922 ed. Set. 95.00 o.p. (ISBN 0-384-16860-4). Johnson Repr.

Ellis Island. Fred M. Stewart. (General Ser.). 1983. lib. bdg. 18.95 o.p. (ISBN 0-8161-3538-X, Large Print Bks). G K Hall.

Ellis Island & Me. Thomas Terjeson. 72p. 1987. 7.75 o.p. (ISBN 0-8062-3080-0). Carlton.

Ellwood Tables for Real Estate Appraising & Financing. 650p. 20.00 o.p. (ISBN 0-318-15179-0, 21-1011). Natl Assoc Realtors.

Elly the Elephant. Norma Simon. Ed. by Kathleen Tucker. LC 81-23990. (Illus.). 40p. (ps-1). 1982. Repr. of 1962 ed. PLB 10.25 o.p. (ISBN 0-8075-1970-7). A Whitman.

Elmer, the Bucket-Mouthed Pelican. Betty Lou Burkart. (ps-1). 1977. 4.00 o.p. (ISBN 0-682-48824-0). Exposition-Phoenix.

Elmer the Elephant. Georgeanne Irvine. (Zoo Babies Ser.). (Illus.). 16p. (Orig.). (gr. k-6). 1983. pap. 1.25 o.p. (ISBN 0-8249-8056-5). Ideals.

Elmer's Diet. Claudia Jett. (gr. k-1). 1985. 4.95 o.p. (ISBN 0-533-06340-X). Vantage.

Elmo Doolan & the Search for the Golden Mouse. Shirley R. Murphy. 128p. (gr. 3-7). 1982. pap. 1.95 o.p. (ISBN 0-380-57109-9, 57109-9, Camelot). Avon.

Elmore Leonard's Dutch Treat. Elmore Leonard. 1985. 17.95 o.p. (ISBN 0-87795-768-1). Morrow.

Elodea. Tom Pier. 24p. 1986. pap. 5.00 o.p. (ISBN 0-911287-07-8). Blue Begonia.

Eloges see Oeuvre Poetique.

Eloquent April: New Poems & Prose. Melville Cane. LC 79-142105. 1971. 9.95 o.p. (ISBN 0-15-128528-4). HarBraceJ.

Elsevier's Banking Dictionary. 2nd ed. J. Ricci. 286p. (Eng., Fr., Ital., Span., Dutch. & Ger.). 1980. 102.75 o.p. (ISBN 0-444-41834-2). Elsevier.

Elsewhere Perhaps. Amos Oz. Tr. by Nicholas De Lange. (Helen & Kurt Wolff Bk.). 1973. 7.95 o.p. (ISBN 0-15-183746-5). HarBraceJ.

Elsie Lee's Book of Simple Gourmet Cookery. Elsie Lee. 1971. 6.95 o.p. (ISBN 0-87795-011-3, Arbor Hse). Morrow.

Elsie Lee's Party Cookbook. Elsie Lee. LC 73-93419. 1974. 7.95 o.p. (ISBN 0-87795-084-9, Arbor Hse). Morrow.

Elson's Music Dictionary. Louis C. Elson. LC 70-173097. 320p. 1972. Repr. of 1905 ed. 43.00x o.s.i. (ISBN 0-8103-3268-X). Gale.

Elucidation of Organic Electrode Processes. P. Zuman. (Current Chemical Concepts Ser.). 1969. 54.50 o.p. (ISBN 0-12-782750-1). Acad Pr.

Elusive Treasure. Brian Fagan. LC 77-8478. (Encore Edition). (Illus.). 1977. 7.95 o.p. (ISBN 0-684-16212-1, ScribT). Scribner.

Elves' Secret. Mary L. Thomas. (Illus.). 4p. (gr. 1-3). 1985. 4.95 o.p. (ISBN 0-533-06361-2). Vantage.

Elvis. Albert Goldman. LC 81-8130. (Illus.). 598p. 1981. text ed. 14.95 o.p. (ISBN 0-07-023657-7). McGraw.

Elvis. Albert Goldman. 736p. 1982. pap. 4.95 o.p. (ISBN 0-380-60350-0). Avon.

Elvis. Dave Marsh. LC 81-84901. (Illus.). 246p. 1982. 34.50 o.p. (ISBN 0-8129-0947-X). Times Bks.

Elvis. Dave Marsh. 1986. 14.98 o.p. (ISBN 0-517-60520-1). Crown.

Elvis Aaron Presley. C. L. Burns. (Illus.). 112p. 1984. pap. 5.00 o.p. (ISBN 0-682-40185-4). Exposition-Phoenix.

Elvis after Life: Unusual Psychic Experiences Surrounding the Death of a Superstar. Raymond A. Moody, Jr. LC 87-61477. 158p. 1987. 12.95 o.p. (ISBN 0-934601-40-2). Peachtree Pubs.

Elvis: His Life & Times in Poetry & Lines. Joan B. West. 1979. 4.00 o.p. (ISBN 0-682-49305-8). Exposition-Phoenix.

Elvis Image. Janice Cabaj. (Illus.). 224p. 1982. 10.00 o.p. (ISBN 0-682-49837-8). Exposition-Phoenix.

Elvis Presley: King of Kings. Ilona Panta. 1979. 10.00 o.p. (ISBN 0-682-49266-3). Exposition-Phoenix.

Elvis Presley's Graceland. Stanley Booth. LC 85-72540. 1986. 20.00 o.p. (ISBN 0-317-42627-3). Aperture.

Elwood's Stories of the Old Ringgold Cavalry, 1847-1865. John W. Elwood. (Illus.). 326p. 1985. Repr. of 1914 ed. perfect bdg. 17.95 o.p. (ISBN 0-933227-36-1). Closson Pr.

Emancipation & Equal Rights: Politics & Constitutionalism in the Civil War Era. Herman Belz. (Essays in American History). 1978. 10.95x o.p. (ISBN 0-393-05692-9); pap. 5.95x o.p. (ISBN 0-393-09016-7). Norton.

Emancipist: A Saga of the Early Days of Australia. Veronica G. Sweeney. 1056p. 1986. 19.45 o.p. (ISBN 0-671-60209-8). S&S.

Emanuel Swedenborg's Journal of Dreams. Emanuel Swedenborg. LC 86-70341. 1986. pap. 8.95 o.p. (ISBN 0-87785-133-6). Swedenborg.

Embankment Stabilization & Soil Mechanics. (Transportation Research Report Ser.). 74p. 1980. 6.00 o.p. (ISBN 0-309-03059-5). Transport Res Bd.

Embargoes, Surplus Disposal, & United States Agriculture. (Agricultural Economic Report Ser.: No. 564). (Illus.). 450p. 1987. pap. 22.00 o.p. (ISBN 0-318-22447-X, S/N 001-019-00500-9). USGPO.

Embarrassment of Riches. James H. Kunstler. LC 84-17671. 288p. 1985. 15.95 o.p. (ISBN 0-385-19696-2, Dial). Doubleday.

Embattled Confederacy: Eighteen Sixty-One to Eighteen Sixty-Five. National Historical Society Staff. LC 81-43240. (Image of War Ser.: Vol. III). (Illus.). 464p. 1982. pap. 19.95 o.p. (ISBN 0-385-15468-2). Doubleday.

Embattled Shadows: A History of Canadian Cinema, 1895-1939. Peter Morris. (Illus.). 1978. 19.95x o.p. (ISBN 0-7735-0322-6, McGill Canada); pap. 8.95 o.p. (ISBN 0-7735-0323-4, McGill Canada). U of Toronto Pr.

Embers of Desire. Patricia Pellicane. 400p. 1983. pap. 3.75 o.s.i. (ISBN 0-8439-2052-1, Pub. by Leisure Bks CT). Dorchester Pub Co.

Embezzler. Louis Auchincloss. 1966. 5.95 o.p. (ISBN 0-395-07362-6). HM.

Embezzler. Louis Auchincloss. 1980. pap. 3.95 o.p. (ISBN 0-395-29845-8). HM.

Emblem For an Era: Selected Images of American Victorian Womanhood. R. W. Lewis. (Illus., Orig.). 1982. pap. 3.00 o.s.i. (ISBN 0-89467-023-9). Yale Art Gallery.

Embrace of the Butcher. Anthony Burton. LC 83-23190. 224p. 1986. pap. 3.50 o.p. (ISBN 0-931773-64-4). Critics Choice Paper.

Embrace Tiger, Return to Mountain: The Essence of T'ai Chi. Al C. Huang. LC 73-80134. (Illus.). 185p. 1973. 10.00 o.p. (ISBN 0-911226-12-5); pap. 6.50 o.p. (ISBN 0-911226-13-3). Real People.

Embroiderer's Portfolio of Flower Designs. Eszter Haraszty. (Illus.). 1982. spiral bound 29.95 o.p. (ISBN 0-87140-643-8, A Liveright Bk). Norton.

Embroidery. Conran Octopus. 1986. pap. 9.95 o.p. (ISBN 0-345-33608-9, Pub. by Ballantine Trade). Ballantine.

Embroidery: A Complete Course in Embroidery Design & Technique. Pauline Brown. LC 86-40121. 1987. 19.95 o.s.i. (ISBN 0-394-75011-X, Pub. by Villard Bks). Random.

Embroidery & Nature. Jan Messent. (Illus.). 168p. 1980. pap. 18.25 o.s.i. (ISBN 0-8231-4258-2). Branford.

Embroidery of Mexico & Guatemala. Frances S. Goodman. (Encore Edition). 1976. 5.95 o.p. (ISBN 0-684-15946-5, ScribT). Scribner.

Embroidery of Ourha. M. Shakhbazyana & O. Ivanova. 150p. 1985. 9.95 o.p. (ISBN 0-8285-3173-0, Pub. by Sovetakan Grogh Yerevan). Imported Pubns.

Embroidery of Roses. Ondori Publishing Company Staff. (Illus.). 143p. 1980. pap. 7.25 o.p. (ISBN 0-87040-488-1). Japan Pubns USA.

Embryogenesis: Development & Some Anomalies of the Upper Respiratory Tract Including the Septo-Maxillary Syndrome & Its Treatment. C. J. Griffin & Philomena McGrath. 1978. 26.00x o.p. (ISBN 0-424-00049-0, Pub. by Sydney U Pr). Intl Spec Bk.

Embryology & Phylogeny in Annelids & Arthropods. D. L. Anderson. LC 73-1019. 492p. 1973. 54.00 o.p. (ISBN 0-08-017069-2). Pergamon.

Embryology of the Common Marmoset (Callithrix Jacchus) I. R. Phillips. Ed. by A. Brodal et al. (Advances in Anatomy, Embryology & Cell Biology Ser.: Vol. 52/5). 1976. soft cover 15.40 o.p. (ISBN 0-387-07955-6). Springer-Verlag.

Embryology of the Human Thyroid Gland Including the Ultimobranchial & Other Related Organs. S. Sugiyama. (Advances in Anatomy, Embryology & Cell Biology: Vol. 44, Pt. 2). (Illus.). 1971. pap. 42.50 o.p. (ISBN 0-387-05425-1). Springer-Verlag.

EMC Technology: 1982 Anthology. White Don, Consultants Staff. (Illus.). 200p. 1984. text ed. 42.00 o.p. (ISBN 0-932263-24-0). White Consult.

Emerald. Mario Soldati. Tr. by William Weaver. LC 76-54764. (Helen & Kurt Wolff Bks.). 1977. 8.95 o.p. (ISBN 0-15-128530-6). HarBraceJ.

Emerald Fire. Julia Grice. 1978. pap. 3.50 o.p. (ISBN 0-380-38596-1, 82347-0). Avon.

Emerald Station. Daoma Winston. 1976. pap. 3.50 o.p. (ISBN 0-380-00738-X, 63933-5). Avon.

Emergence of a Multiracial Society: The Sociology of Multiracism with Reference to Guyana. Iris D. Sukdeo. 224p. 1982. 9.50 o.p. (ISBN 0-682-49686-3, University). Exposition-Phoenix.

Emergence of Civilisation, the Cyclades & the Aegaen in the Third Millennium. Colin Renfrew. (Illus.). 1972. 99.00x o.p. (ISBN 0-416-16480-3, NO.2404). Routledge Chapman & Hall.

Emergence of Japan As a World Power, Eighteen Hundred Ninety-Five to Nineteen Hundred Twenty-Five. Morinosuke Kajima. LC 68-11079. 1967. 6.60 o.p. (ISBN 0-8048-0166-5). C E Tuttle.

Emergence of Lincoln: Douglas, Buchanan, & Party Chaos, 1857-1859 see Ordeal of the Union.

Emergence of Lincoln: Prologue to Civil War, 1859-1861 see Ordeal of the Union.

Emergence of Man. L. Lieberman. 1970. pap. text ed. 9.95x o.p. (ISBN 0-8290-1407-1). Irvington.

Emergence of Modern Lithuania. Alfred E. Senn. LC 74-14028. 272p. 1975. Repr. of 1959 ed. lib. bdg. 29.75x o.p. (ISBN 0-8371-7780-4, SEML). Greenwood.

Emergence of Order in Developing Systems: Proceedings of the Society for the Study of Developmental Biology, 27th Symposium. Society for the Study of Developmental Biology Staff. Ed. by Michael Locke. 1969. 61.50 o.p.; pap. 53.00 o.p. (ISBN 0-12-612966-5). Acad Pr.

Emergence of Society: A Prehistory of the Establishment. John Pfeiffer. LC 76-27308. (Illus.). 528p. 1977. text ed. 32.95 o.p. (ISBN 0-07-049758-3); text ed. 15.00 o.p. (ISBN 0-07-049759-1). McGraw.

Emergence of Sociological Theory. Jonathan E. Turner & Leonard Beeghley. 587p. 1981. 36.00x o.p. (ISBN 0-256-02416-2). Dorsey.

Emergence of the Eastern World. G. L. Seidler. 1968. 30.00 o.p. (ISBN 0-08-012637-5). Pergamon.

Emergence of the Great Powers. John B. Wolf. Ed. by William L. Langer. LC 83-10707. (Rise of Modern Europe Ser.). (Illus.). xv, 336p. 1983. Repr. of 1951 ed. lib. bdg. 48.50 o.p. (ISBN 0-313-24088-4, WOEM). Greenwood.

Emergence of the Jewish Problem, 1878-1939. James W. Parkes. 1971. Repr. of 1946 ed. lib. bdg. 22.50x o.p. (ISBN 0-8371-2794-7, PJPR). Greenwood.

Emergencies in Dental Practice: Prevention & Treatment. 3rd ed. Frank M. McCarthy. (Illus.). 767p. 1979. write for info. o.p. (ISBN 0-7216-5877-6). Saunders.

Emergencies in Obstetrics & Gynecology. Arnold W. Cohen. (Clinics in Emergency Medicine Ser.: Vol. 1). (Illus.). 224p. 1981. text ed. 30.00 o.p. (ISBN 0-443-08130-1). Churchill.

Emergency Care & Transportation of the Sick & Injured. 3rd ed. 448p. 1981. 12.00 o.p. (ISBN 0-317-36767-6, 4900009). Amer Acad Ortho Surg.

Emergency Care: Assessment & Intervention. 3rd ed. Carmen G. Warner. LC 81-18985. (Illus.). 693p. 1982. text ed. 34.95 o.p. (ISBN 0-8016-5352-5). Mosby.

Emergency Childbirth Handbook. B. Anderson & P. Shapiro. 1982. pap. 12.95 o.p. (ISBN 0-442-20979-7). Van Nos Reinhold.

Emergency Health Help: A Modern Grandma's Natural Guide to Health. Ada White. 1976. 4.50 o.p. (ISBN 0-682-48467-9). Exposition-Phoenix.

Emergency Medical Services Communications Design Manual. Systech Corporation Staff. 1980. 50.00 o.s.i. (ISBN 0-686-37969-1). Info Gatekeepers.

Emergency Medical Services Instructor Training Program: A National Standard Curriculum, Student Study Guide DOT HS 900 081. 79p. (Orig.). 1986. pap. 3.00 o.p. (ISBN 0-318-20103-8, S/N 050-003-00426-0). USGPO.

Emergency Medical Services Systems: A Guide to Information Sources. Ed. by Carlos Fernandez-Caballero & Marianne Fernandez-Caballero. (Health Affairs Information Guide Series, Gale Information Guide Library: Vol. 9). 200p. 1981. 68.00x o.p. (ISBN 0-8103-1503-3). Gale.

Emergency Medicine: A Comprehensive Study Guide. American College of Emergency Physicians Staff. Ed. by Ronald L. Krome & Robert J. Rothstein. (Illus.). 1053p. 1985. text ed. 110.00 o.p. (ISBN 0-07-001439-6). McGraw.

Emergency Medicine: Concepts & Clinical Practice, 2 vols. Peter Rosen et al. LC 82-18812. (Illus.). 1714p. 1983. text ed. 130.00 o.p. (ISBN 0-8016-3057-6). Mosby.

Emergency Nursing: A Guide to Comprehensive Care. Ed. by Janet G. Parker. LC 84-11971. 624p. 1984. 27.95 o.p. (ISBN 0-471-09907-4, Pub. by Wiley Med). Wiley.

Emergency Nursing: Principles & Practice. 2nd ed. Sheehy. 1985. 39.95 o.p. (ISBN 0-8016-0455-9). Mosby.

Emergency Pediatrics. 2nd ed. Barkin & Rosen. 1986. 42.00 o.p. (ISBN 0-8016-0479-6). Mosby.

Emergency Planning & Community Right-to-Know Act Handbook. 2nd ed. J. Gordon Arbuckle et al. (Emergency Planning & Community Right-to-Know Act Handbook Ser.). 340p. 1987. pap. 59.00 o.s.i. (ISBN 0-86587-730-0). Gov Insts.

Emergency Preparedness: Proceedings, American Nuclear Society Executive Conference. 304p. 37.00 o.p. (ISBN 0-89448-307-2, 650010). Am Nuclear Soc.

Emergency Removal of Patients & First Aid Fire Fighting in Hospitals. 3rd ed. Robert McGrath. (Illus.). 56p. 1974. pap. 6.25 o.p. (ISBN 0-87912-101-7, 129.59). Natl Safety Coun.

Emergency Room. Bob Wolfe & Diane Wolfe. LC 82-19878. (Carolrhoda Photo Bks.). (Illus.). 40p. (gr. k-4). 1983. PLB 9.95 o.p. (ISBN 0-87614-206-4). Carolrhoda Bks.

Emergency Room: An ABC Tour. Julie Steedman. LC 74-18335. (Illus.). (gr. k-3). 1975. pap. 3.95 o.p. (ISBN 0-914440-05-5). EPM Pubns.

Emergency Room: Confessions of an E. R. Doctor. Edith Alston & David Cutler. LC 84-10772. 368p. 1984. 19.95 o.p. (ISBN 0-15-128755-4). HarBraceJ.

Emergency Surgery. 10th ed. Dudley. 1032p. 1977. 93.50 o.p. (ISBN 0-7236-0448-7, Pub. by John Wright UK). Butterworth.

Emerging Adolescent: Characteristics & Educational Implications. Ed. by Donald R. Steer et al. Eichhorn & Epstein. 56p. 1980. 3.75 o.p. (ISBN 0-318-15782-9, NMSA-003). Natl Middle Schl.

Emerging Areas of Litigation Affecting Banks & Other Financial Institutions. Pennsylvania Bar Institute Staff. 269p. 1983. 25.00 o.p. (ISBN 0-318-02154-4, 232). PA Bar Inst.

Emerging Business: Managing for Growth. Seymour Jones & M. Bruce Cohen. LC 82-17650. 425p. 1983. 44.50x o.p. (ISBN 0-471-09800-0). Wiley.

Emerging Concepts in Management. 2nd ed. Max S. Wortmen, Jr. & Fred Luthans. (Illus.). 480p. 1975. write for info. o.p. (ISBN 0-02-430040-3); pap. write for info. o.p. Macmillan.

Emerging Death Mystique: The Challenge & the Promise. Harry G. Armstrong. 1978. 10.50 o.p. (ISBN 0-682-48936-0, Banner). Exposition-Phoenix.

Emerging Diseases of Animals. (Agricultural Planning Studies: No. 61). (Orig.). 1968. pap. 17.00 o.p. (ISBN 0-685-09378-6, F122, FAO). UNIPUB.

Emerging Energy Technologies: 1978. Ed. by W. B. Bradley et al. 1978. 20.00 o.p. (ISBN 0-685-66797-9, G00141). ASME.

Emerging Entertainment: The Drama of the American People to 1828. Walter J. Meserve. LC 77-74444. 352p. 1977. 25.00x o.p. (ISBN 0-253-37007-8). Ind U Pr.

Emerging Form in Architecture. F. Wilson. 1983. 27.95 o.p. (ISBN 0-8436-0150-7). Van Nos Reinhold.

Emerging Goddess: The Creative Process in Art, Science, & other Fields. Albert Rothenberg. LC 78-26486. (Illus.). 440p. 1982. pap. text ed. 12.50x o.s.i. (ISBN 0-226-72949-4). U of Chicago Pr.

Emerging Language Three. John T. Hatten et al. 72p. 1981. pap. 7.95 o.p. (ISBN 0-88450-003-9, 2028-B). Communication Skill.

Emerging Local Area Network Business. Business Communications Staff. (Illus.). 180p. 1986. pap. 1750.00 o.p. (ISBN 0-89336-438-X, G-074R). BCC.

Emerging Marine Economy of the Pacific. Ed. by Chennat Gopalakrishnan. (Illus.). 256p. 1984. text ed. 49.95 o.p. (ISBN 0-250-40637-3). Butterworth.

Emerging Nationalism in Portuguese Africa: A Bibliography of Documentary Ephemera Through 1965. Compiled by Ronald H. Chilcote. LC 71-155299. (Bibliographical Ser.: No. 39). 114p. 1969. 9.95x o.p. (ISBN 0-8179-2391-8); pap. 5.95x o.p. (ISBN 0-8179-2392-6). Hoover Inst Pr.

Emerging Nationalism in Portuguese Africa: Documents. Compiled by Ronald H. Chilcote. LC 71-155299. (Publications Ser.: No. 97). (Illus.). 646p. 1972. 25.00x o.p. (ISBN 0-8179-1971-6). Hoover Inst Pr.

Emerging Order: God in the Age of Scarcity. Jeremy Rifkin & Ted Howard. (Epiphany Bks.). 1983. pap. 2.95 o.s.i. (ISBN 0-345-30464-0). Ballantine.

Emerging Skills: Implications for Voc Ed. Harold Halfin & Orville Nelson. 39p. cancelled o.s.i. (ISBN 0-318-22088-1, IN234). Natl Ctr Res Voc Ed.

Emerging Social Issues: A Sociological Perspective. James A. Inciardi & Harvey A. Siegal. LC 73-19437. 204p. 1975. pap. text ed. 7.95 o.p. (ISBN 0-275-85090-0, HoltC). HR&W.

Emerging Technologies in Aerospace Structures, Design, Structural Dynamics & Materials. Ed. by J. R. Vinson. 326p. 1980. 40.00 o.p. (ISBN 0-686-69849-5, H00157). ASME.

Emerging Worker: Equality & Conflict in the Mass Consumption Society. William A. Westley & Margaret W. Westley. 160p. 1971. 8.50 o.p. (ISBN 0-7735-0075-8, McGill Canada). U of Toronto Pr.

Emerson in Concord. Edward W. Emerson. LC 79-78149. (Library of Lives & Letters). (Illus.). 272p. 1970. Repr. of 1889 ed. 40.00x o.p. (ISBN 0-8103-3601-4). Gale.

Emerson's Transcendental Vocabulary: A Concordance. Mary A. Ihirg. LC 81-47965. 280p. 1982. lib. bdg. 48.00 o.p. (ISBN 0-8240-9264-3). Garland Pub.

EMI Control in Aerospace Systems. Bernhard E. Keiser. Ed. by Donald R. White. LC 79-54649. (Illus.). 282p. 1979. text ed. 37.00 o.p. (ISBN 0-932263-15-1). White Consult.

EMI Control in Boats & Ships. Russell V. Carstensen. Ed. by Donald R. White. LC 80-51209. (Illus.). 280p. 1981. text ed. 37.00 o.p. (ISBN 0-932263-20-8). White Consult.

EMI Control in Medical Electronics. Michael F. Gard. Ed. by Donald R. White. LC 78-66192. (Illus.). 175p. 1979. text ed. 32.00 o.p. (ISBN 0-932263-19-4). White Consult.

EMI Control Methodology & Procedures. 3rd ed. Donald R. White. Ed. by Edward R. Price. LC 76-39643. 1982. text ed. 248.00 o.p. (ISBN 0-932263-10-0). White Consult.

EMI Control Methods & Techniques. 3rd ed. Donald R. White. LC 72-138444. (Electromagnetic Interference & Compatibility Ser.: Vol. 3). (Illus.). 668p. 1981. text ed. 111.00 o.p. (ISBN 0-932263-02-X). White Consult.

EMI Prediction & Analysis Techniques. Donald R. White & William G. Duff. LC 72-138444. (Electromagnetic Interference & Compatibility Ser.: Vol. 5). (Illus.). 573p. 1972. text ed. 94.00 o.p. (ISBN 0-932263-04-6). White Consult.

EMI Specifications, Standards & Regulations. 2nd ed. Donald R. White. LC 72-138444. (Electromagnetic Interference & Compatibility Ser.: Vol. 6). (Illus.). 1014p. 1981. text ed. 69.00 o.p. (ISBN 0-932263-05-4). White Consult.

EMI Test Methods & Procedures. 2nd ed. Donald R. White. LC 72-138444. (Electromagnetic Interference & Compatibility Ser.: Vol. 2). (Illus.). 520p. 1980. text ed. 88.00 o.p. (ISBN 0-932263-01-1). White Consult.

Emigrants: Early Travellers to the Antipodes. Hector Bolitho & John Mulgan. (Essay Index Reprint Ser.). 223p. 1982. Repr. of 1939 ed. lib. bdg. 15.00 o.p. (ISBN 0-686-79687-X). Irvington.

Emil Brunner. J. Edward Humphrey. Ed. by Bob E. Patterson. LC 75-36186. (Maker's of the Modern Theological Mind Ser.). 1976. 8.95 o.p. (ISBN 0-87680-453-9). Word Bks.

Emily Bronte, a Psychological Portrait. N. Crandall. Repr. of 1957 ed. 28.00 o.p. (ISBN 0-527-20400-5). Kraus Repr.

Emily Dickinson. Paul J. Ferlazzo. (United States Authors Ser.). 168p. 1984. lib. bdg. 13.50 o.s.i. (ISBN 0-8057-7180-8, Twayne); pap. 7.95 o.s.i. (ISBN 0-8057-7425-4). G K Hall.

Emily Dickinson: A Bibliography, 1850-1966. Sheila T. Clendenning. LC 67-65585. (Serif Ser.: No. 3). 175p. 1969. 10.00x o.p. (ISBN 0-87338-016-9). Kent St U Pr.

Emily Dickinson & Metaphysical Tradition. Anand R. Thota. 196p. 1982. text ed. 18.50x o.p. (ISBN 0-391-02460-4). Humanities.

Emily Dickinson & the Image of Home. Jean M. Mudge. LC 74-78979. (New England Writers Ser.). (Illus.). 316p. 1975. 22.50x o.p. (ISBN 0-87023-164-2). U of Mass Pr.

Emily Dickinson: The Mind of the Poet. Albert J. Gelpi. 1971. pap. 2.95 o.p. (ISBN 0-393-00555-0, Norton Lib.). Norton.

Emily Dickinson's Imagery. Rebecca Patterson. Ed. by Margaret H. Freeman. LC 79-4024. (New England Writers Ser.). 256p. 1980. lib. bdg. 20.00x o.p. (ISBN 0-87023-272-X). U of Mass Pr.

Emily Dickinson's Reading, 1836-1886. Jack L. Capps. LC 66-14439. 1966. 17.50x o.s.i. (ISBN 0-674-25050-8). Harvard U Pr.

Emin Pasha, His Life & Work, 2 Vols. Eduard Schnitzer. Ed. by George Schweitzer. LC 70-82071. (Illus.). Repr. of 1898 ed. Set. 31.00x o.p. (ISBN 0-8371-5090-6, SCE&, Pub. by Negro U Pr). Greenwood.

Eminent Domain, Taking for the Public Good: A Review of Legal Articles, 1980-1985. Dale E. Casper. (Public Administration Ser.: P 1822). 9p. 1985. 2.00 o.p. (ISBN 0-89028-672-8). Vance Biblios.

Eminent Edwardians. Piers Brendon. 1980. 10.95 o.p. (ISBN 0-395-29195-X). HM.

Eminent Victorian Soldiers: Seekers of Glory. Byron Farwell. (Illus.). 1985. 17.45 o.p. (ISBN 0-393-01884-9). Norton.

Emission, Absorption & Transfer of Radiation in Heated Atmospheres. B. H. Armstrong & R. W. Nicholls. 319p. 1972. 80.00 o.p. (ISBN 0-08-016774-8). Pergamon.

Emission Electronics. L. N. Dobretsov & M. V. Gomoyunova. 433p. 74.95x o.p. (ISBN 0-470-21680-8). Halsted Pr.

Emission Factors & Inventories. Air Pollution Control Association Specialty Conference, Anaheim, CA, 1978. 213p. 1979. 12.50 o.p. (ISBN 0-318-12255-3, SP-28); members 10.00 o.p. (ISBN 0-318-12256-1). Air & Waste.

Emission Spectroscopy. Ed. by Ramon M. Barnes. LC 75-30672. 1976. 87.50 o.p. (ISBN 0-12-786137-8). Acad Pr.

Emma in Winter. Penelope Farmer. LC 66-10071. (Illus.). (gr. 5-7). 1966. 5.75 o.p. (ISBN 0-15-225700-4, HJ). HarBraceJ.

Emma Lazarus: Poet of Liberty. Irving Gerber. (American Destiny Ser.: Jewish Americans). (Illus.). (gr. 4-12). 1979. of 10 9.95 set o.p. (ISBN 0-87594-183-4). Book Lab.

Emmanuelle One. Emmanuelle Arsan. Tr. by Lowell Bair from Fr. LC 78-139255. 1980. pap. 3.95 o.p. (ISBN 0-394-17657-X, B439, BC). Grove.

Emmanuelle Two. Emmanuelle Arsan. Tr. by Anselm Hollo from Fr. LC 74-24995. 1981. 4.50 o.s.i. (ISBN 0-394-17891-2, B453, BC). Grove.

Emma's Dilemma. Catherine Sefton. (Illus.). 96p. (gr. 4-6). 1983. 8.95 o.p. (ISBN 0-571-11841-0). Faber & Faber.

Emmeline. Judith Rossner. 1980. 12.95 o.p. (ISBN 0-671-22938-9). S&S.

Emmet Gowin - Petra: In the Hashemite Kingdom of Jordan. Emmet Gowin. 36p. (Orig.). 1986. pap. 20.00 o.p. (ISBN 0-938608-50-9). Pace Pubns.

Emmie. Jeanette Seymour. 1980. pap. write for info. o.p. PB.

Emmy Keeps a Promise. Madye L. Chastain. LC 56-9200. (gr. 4-6). 1956. 4.50 o.p. (ISBN 0-15-225739-X, HJ). HarBraceJ.

Emmy Keeps a Promise. Madye L. Chastain. LC 56-9200. (Illus.). (gr. 4-6). 1966. pap. 0.75 o.p. (ISBN 0-15-628776-5, AVB21, VoyB). HarBraceJ.

Emotion & Reproduction, Pt. A. Ed. by L. Carenza & L. Zichella. (Serono Symposia Ser.). 1979. 124.00 o.p. (ISBN 0-12-159401-7). Acad Pr.

Emotion & Reproduction: Proceedings of the International Congress of Psychosomatic Obstetrics & Gynecology, 5th, Vol. 20B, Pt. B. International Congress of Psychosomatic Obstetrics & Gynecology Staff. Ed. by L. Carenza & L. Zinchella. LC 78-54528. 1980. 124.00 o.p. (ISBN 0-12-159402-5). Acad Pr.

Emotional Care of the Facially Burned & Disfigured Patients. Norman R. Bernstein. pap. 16.50 o.p. Phoenix Soc.

Emotional Disorders: An Outline Guide to Diagnosis & Pharmacological Treatment. 3rd ed. A. DiMascio & H. Goldberg. 1980. 28.95 o.p. (ISBN 0-87489-255-4). Med Economics.

Emotional Problems of Development in Children. Martin Herbert. 1974. 44.00 o.p. (ISBN 0-12-341450-4). Acad Pr.

Emotional Structures in Organisations: A Study of the Process of Change. Per-Olof Berg. 287p. (Orig.). 1979. pap. text ed. 23.50 o.p. (ISBN 0-86238-022-7, Pub. by Chartwell-Bratt England). Gower Pub Co.

Emotional Ties. Laura Matthews. 240p. 1984. pap. 2.95 o.p. (ISBN 0-380-87361-3, 87361-3). Avon.

Emotionally Disturbed Child in the Classroom. 2nd ed. Hewett & Taylor. 416p. 1980. text ed. 33.33 o.s.i. (ISBN 0-205-06725-5, 2467259). Allyn.

Emotions As Resources: A Biblical & Pastoral Perspective. Bert Ghezzi & Mark Kinzer. 110p. 1983. pap. 6.95 o.p. (ISBN 0-89283-158-8). Servant.

Emotions: Outline of a Theory. Jean-Paull Sartre. (ISBN 0-8022-1482-7). Philos Lib.

Empathy & Birth Order: Some Experimental Explorations. Ezra Stotland et al. LC 71-149400. viii, 198p. 1971. 16.95x o.p. (ISBN 0-8032-0797-2). U of Nebr Pr.

Empathy & Confrontation in Pastoral Care. Ralph L. Underwood. LC 85-47722. (Theology & Pastoral Care Ser.). 128p. 1986. pap. 7.95 o.p. (ISBN 0-8006-1737-1, 1-1737, Fortress). Augsburg Fortress.

Emperor: Downfall of an Autocrat. Ryszard Kapuscinski. Tr. by William R. Brand & Katarzyna Mroczkowska-Brand. LC 82-47670. (Helen & Kurt Wolff Bk.). 180p. 1983. 12.95 o.p. (ISBN 0-15-128771-6). HarBraceJ.

Emperor Frederick Second. David G. Einstein. (ISBN 0-8022-0441-4). Philos Lib.

Emperor of Midnight. Edouard Roditi. LC 74-17017. 150p. (Orig.). 1974. pap. 5.00 o.p. (ISBN 0-87685-185-5). Black Sparrow.

Emperor's Games. Damion Hunter. 1984. pap. 3.95 o.s.i. (ISBN 0-345-29827-6). Ballantine.

Emperor's New Clothes. Hans Christian Andersen. LC 83-19610. (Illus.). 48p. (gr. k-3). 1973. PLB 7.95 o.p. (ISBN 0-395-18415-0). HM.

Emperor's New Clothes. Hans Christian Andersen. (Children's Classics Ser.). 32p. (gr. k-3). 1988. 5.95 o.p. (ISBN 0-8249-8260-6). Ideals.

Emperor's Pearl: A Judge Dee Mystery. Robert Van Gulik. 160p. 1981. pap. 2.95 rack size o.s.i. (ISBN 0-684-17318-2, ScribT). Scribner.

Empire & Commonwealth. Chester Martin. LC 74-9227. 385p. 1975. Repr. of 1929 ed. lib. bdg. 35.00x o.p. (ISBN 0-8371-7626-3, MAEC). Greenwood.

Empire in Brazil: A New World Experiment with Monarchy. C. H. Haring. 1968. pap. 3.95 o.p. (ISBN 0-393-00386-8, Norton Lib). Norton.

Empire of the Senseless. Kathy Acker. 1988. 17.95 o.p. (ISBN 0-8021-1079-7). Grove.

Empire of the Sun. J. G. Ballard. 320p. 1984. 16.45 o.p. (ISBN 0-671-53051-8). S&S.

Empire Or Independence, 1760-1776: A British-American Dialogue. Ian R. Christie & Benjamin W. Labaree. (Illus.). 1977. 12.50x o.p. (ISBN 0-393-05556-6, N854, Norton Lib); pap. 5.95 o.p. (ISBN 0-393-00854-1). Norton.

Empire Without End. Lidia S. Mazzolani. Tr. by Joan McConnell & Mario Pel. LC 76-20672. (Helen & Kurt Wolff Bk.). 1976. Repr. of 1972 ed. 10.95 o.p. (ISBN 0-15-128780-5). HarBraceJ.

Empirical Analysis of the Circular Dichroism of Chiral Olefins. John Hudec. 1977. pap. 35.00 o.p. (ISBN 0-08-021584-X). Pergamon.

Empirical Distributions & Processes: Selected Papers from a Meeting at Oberwolfach, Mar. 28-Apr. 3, 1976. Ed. by P. Ganssler & P. Revesz. (Lecture Notes in Mathematics Ser.: Vol. 566). 1977. soft cover 13.00 o.p. (ISBN 0-387-08061-9). Springer-Verlag.

Empirical Investigation of Farmers' Behavior under Uncertainty: Income, Price, & Yield Variability for Late 19th Century American Agriculture. Robert A. McGuire. Ed. by Stuart Bruchey. LC 84-48311. (American Economic History Ser.). 331p. 1985. lib. bdg. 45.00 o.p. (ISBN 0-8240-6659-6). Garland Pub.

Empirical Study of Education in Twenty-One Countries. Gilbert F. Peaker. 230p. (Orig.). 1975. pap. text ed. 17.00x o.p. Coronet Bks.

Empleo del Agua Oxigeuda de la Leche en Condiciones Dificiles. (Agricultural Planning Studies: No. 82). pap. 5.75 o.p. (F1287, FAO). UNIPUB.

Employee & Union Member Guide to Labor Law. National Labor Law Center. 1982. 150.00 o.p. Natl Lawyers Guild.

Employee Benefits. Pennsylvania Bar Institute Staff. LC 89-60079. 322p. 1989. 55.00 o.p. (ISBN 0-318-19038-9, 301). PA Bar Inst.

Employee Benefits Legislation 1984. Practising Law Institute Staff & Max J. Schwartz. LC 83-62932. (Tax Law & Estate Planning Ser.). 208p. 1984. 45.00 o.p. (J4-3554). PLI.

Employee Benefits under ERISA. (Tax Law & Estate Planning Course Handbook Ser.: Vol. 190). 168p. 1983. 45.00 o.p. (ISBN 0-317-11537-9, J4-3531). PLI.

Employee Communication: A Bibliography. Sarojini Balachandran. 1976. pap. 3.60 o.p. (ISBN 0-931874-04-1). Assn Busn Comm.

Employee Consultation & Information in Multinational Corporations. Ed. by Jacques Vandamme. LC 85-21264. 288p. 1986. 34.50 o.p. (ISBN 0-7099-2624-3, Pub. by Croom Helm Ltd). Routledge Chapman & Hall.

Employee: Contemporary Viewpoints. Ed. by Marie S. Ensign & Laurie N. Adler. LC 85-6243. (Human Resource Management Ser.). 247p. 1985. 39.00 o.p. (ISBN 0-87436-449-3). ABC-Clio.

Employee Counseling in Industry & Government: A Guide to Information Sources. Ed. by Theodore P. Peck. LC 79-16028. (Management Information Guide Ser.: No. 37). 138p. 1979. 68.00x o.p. (ISBN 0-8103-0837-1). Gale.

Employee Discipline & Arbitration. Morris Stone. 80p. 2.50 o.p. (ISBN 0-318-12379-7); members 1.50 o.p. (ISBN 0-318-12380-0). Am Arbitration.

Employee Dismissal Law & Practice. Henry H. Perritt, Jr. LC 84-3492. (Trial Practice Library: No. 1676). 465p. (Annual supplements avail.). 1984. text ed. 75.00x o.p. (ISBN 0-471-89025-1); Supplememt, 1986. pap. 33.00 o.p. (ISBN 0-471-84970-7). Wiley.

Employee Drug Abuse: A Manager's Guide for Action. Carl D. Chambers & Richard D. Heckman. LC 73-183372. 240p. 1983. 23.95 o.p. (ISBN 0-8436-0718-1). Van Nos Reinhold.

Employee Handbook & Personnel Policies Manual. 2nd. ed. Richard J. Simmons. 570p. 55.00 o.p. Castle Pubns.

Employee Motivation: Principles & Practices. Philip C. Grant. LC 84-90036. (Illus.). 159p. 1984. 14.95 o.p. (ISBN 0-533-06122-9). Vantage.

Employee Participation at the Level of the Enterprise: Labour Relations at the European Level & in Different Countries. Ed. by Roger Blanpain. (Bulletin of Comparative Labour Relations Ser.: No. 4). 1973. 12.00 o.p. (ISBN 90-31-20020-4). Kluwer Academic.

Employee Relations & Regulation in the 80's. Ed. by Herbert R. Northrup & Richard L. Rowan. LC 81-84823. (Labor Relations & Public Policy Ser.: No. 22). 464p. 1982. pap. 20.00 o.p. (ISBN 0-89546-035-1). Indus Res Unit-Wharton.

Employee Relations in the Academic Setting see Issues in the Public Employee Relations Library: Series 2.

Employee Relations Policy in Local Government see Issues in the Public Employee Relations Library: Series 4.

Employee Rights & the Employment Relationship. Howard M. Vollmer. LC 76-845. 175p. 1976. Repr. of 1960 ed. lib. bdg. 22.50x o.p. (ISBN 0-8371-8743-5, VOER). Greenwood.

Employee Stock Ownership Plans: A Decision Maker's Guide. David A. Peckman. 55p. 1983. (stapled cover) 10.00 o.p. (ISBN 0-86643-031-8). Employee Benefit.

Employee Stock Ownership Plans: A Selected Bibliography, 1974-1984. Joseph C. Santora. (Public Administration Ser.: Bibliography P 1649). 1985. pap. 2.25 o.p. (ISBN 0-89028-339-7). Vance Biblios.

Employee Welfare Benefit Plans. (Tax Law & Estate Planning Ser.). 486p. 1987. 45.00 o.p. (J4-3607). PLI.

Employees' Benefits in Florida. Florida Bar Staff. LC 79-51283. 597p. 1980. looseleaf 15.00 o.p. (ISBN 0-910373-23-X, 222). FL Bar Legal Ed.

Employer-Sponsored Career Development Programs. Anita S. Lancaster & Richard R. Berne. 64p. cancelled o.s.i. (ISBN 0-318-22089-X, IN231). Natl Ctr Res Voc Ed.

Employer's Guide to Strike Planning & Prevention. Mark A. Hutcheson et al. 420p. 1985. text ed. 25.00 o.p. (ISBN 0-317-14132-5, B1-1296). PLI.

Employing the Handicapped: A Practical Compliance Manual. A. B. Zimmer. 384p. 1981. 21.95 o.p.; pap. 5.95 o.p. AMACOM.

Employment & Economic Reform - Towards a Strategy for the Sudan: Report of a Mission Financed by the United Nations Development Programme & Organized by the ILO-Jobs & Skills Programme for Africa, August-September 1986. International Labour Office Staff. v, 172p. (Orig.). 1987. pap. 15.75 o.p. (ISBN 92-2-106221-X). Intl Labour Office.

Employment & Equilibrium: A Theoretical Discussion. Arthur C. Pigou. LC 78-13981. 1979. Repr. of 1941 ed. lib. bdg. 24.00x o.p. (ISBN 0-313-20741-0, PIEE). Greenwood.

Employment & Income Distribution in the African Economy. James Fry. 192p. 1979. 32.00 o.p. (ISBN 0-85664-715-2, Pub. by Croom Helm Ltd). Routledge Chapman & Hall.

Employment & Output in Protected Manufacturing Industries. Beatrice N. Vaccara. LC 79-27932. (Illus.). x, 107p. 1980. Repr. of 1960 ed. lib. bdg. 35.00x o.p. (ISBN 0-313-22302-5, VAEO). Greenwood.

Employment-at-Will. Joseph L. Cook & Earleen H. Cook. (Public Administration Ser.: Bibliography P 1630). 1985. pap. 3.75 o.p. (ISBN 0-89028-300-1). Vance Biblios.

Employment at Will & Employer Responsibility. Daniel Mackey. LC 86-14054. (AMA Research Study). 1986. 19.95 o.p. (ISBN 0-8144-3510-6). AMACOM.

Employment, Capital & Economic Policy: Great Britain 1918-1939. Alan Booth & Melvyn Pack. 256p. 1985. 55.00x o.p. (ISBN 0-631-13804-8). Basil Blackwell.

Employment Discrimination & Civil Rights in the Federal Courts: ALI-ABA Course of Study Materials. American Law Institute-American Bar Association Committee on Continuing Professional Education. LC 87-105914. 673p. Date not set. price not set o.p. Am Law Inst.

Employment Discrimination Law: Cases & Materials, Teacher's Manual. Joel W. Friedman & George M. Strickler, Jr. (University Casebook Ser.). 171p. 1985. pap. (ISBN 0-88277-269-4). Foundation Pr.

Employment Discrimination Law: Cases & Materials, 1985 Supplement. Joel W. Friedman & George M. Strickler, Jr. (University Casebook Ser.). 175p. 1985. pap. 8.95 o.p. (ISBN 0-88277-270-8). Foundation Pr.

Employment Discrimination Law: Cases & Materials. Joel Wm. Friedman et al. LC 82-21016. (University Casebook Ser.). 865p. 1982. text ed. 26.00 o.p. (ISBN 0-88277-096-9). Foundation Pr.

Employment, Growth & Basic Needs: A One-World Problem. 1976. pap. 11.50 o.p. (ISBN 92-2-101510-6, ILO80, ILO). UNIPUB.

Employment in Michigan: A Guide to Employment Practices & Regulations. M. G. Sautter. 1984. pap. 45.00 o.p. (ISBN 0-86678-382-2). Butterworth MN.

Employment Interviewing. 5th ed. John M. Fraser. (Illus.). 224p. 1978. pap. 18.95x o.p. (ISBN 0-7121-0570-0, Pub. by Macdonald & Evans England). Trans-Atl Phila.

Employment Law: New Problems in the Workplace. Practising Law Institute Staff & Joseph Barbash. LC 81-83454. (Litigation & Administrative Practice Ser.: No. 187). 264p. 1981. 35.00 o.p. (H4-4861). PLI.

Employment Litigation & Its Alternatives. (Litigation & Administrative Practice Course Handbook Ser.: Vol. 243). 466p. 1984. 15.00 o.p. (ISBN 0-317-11462-X, H4-5044). PLI.

Employment Patterns & Income Growth. Joseph J. Stern & Jeffrey D. Lewis. (Working Paper: No. 419). 70p. 1980. 5.00 o.p. (ISBN 0-686-36049-4, WP-0419). World Bank.

Employment Practices for the Professional Firm. Schachter et al. 1984. pap. 59.95 o.p. (ISBN 0-88057-268-X). Exec Ent Pubns.

Employment Problems in the Defense Industry: Proceedings of the Institute of Industrial Relations Conference. Institute of Industrial Relations Staff. 1971. 2.00 o.p. (ISBN 0-89215-037-8). U Cal LA Indus Rel.

Emporia: A Centennial Retrospective, 1897-1987. Travis C. McDonald. (Illus.). 142p. (Orig.). 1987. pap. 15.00 o.p. (ISBN 1-55618-023-3). Brunswick Pub.

Empowered: Living Experience of Talking with God. Boyce A. Bowdon. LC 77-15744. 1978. pap. 3.95 o.p. (ISBN 0-8042-2318-1, John Knox). Westminster John Knox.

Empowering Vision: For Your Service Business. 2nd ed. Marianne Weidlein & Stephanie Roth. Orig. Title: Visions & Business: Support & Tools for the Entrepreneur. (Illus.). 295p. 1988. pap. text ed. 19.95 o.p. (ISBN 0-942097-00-9). Megabks CO.

Empowerment. Ed. by Chogyam Trungpa. LC 76-17439. 1978. pap. 3.95 o.p. (ISBN 0-87773-705-3). Shambhala Pubns.

Empty Barn. large type ed. Arthur C. De Angeli & Marguerite De Angeli. (Illus.). (gr. k-3). 1966. 3.50 o.s.i. (ISBN 0-664-32362-6, Westminster). Westminster John Knox.

Empty Boxes. Harriet P. Crank. 96p. 1986. 8.95 o.p. (ISBN 0-8062-2860-1). Carlton.

Empty Copper Sea. John D. MacDonald. (Travis McGee Mystery Ser.). 1985. pap. 3.50 o.p. (ISBN 0-449-12913-6, GM). Fawcett.

Empty Hand, Loaded Gun: The Ultimate System for Close Combat. Dan Westerlin. (Illus.). 120p. (Orig.). 1984. pap. 8.00 o.p. (ISBN 0-87364-291-0). Paladin Pr.

Empty Mirror: Experiences in a Japanese Zen Monastery. Janwillem Van De Wetering. 1974. 7.95 o.p. (ISBN 0-395-18282-4). HM.

Empty Mirror: Experiences in a Japanese Zen Monastery. Janwillem Van De Wetering. LC 73-12235. 160p. 1975. pap. 3.95 o.p. (ISBN 0-395-20443-7). HM.

Empty Nest: A Novel of Intrigue & Romance. Elizabeth Cadell. Ed. by Jennifer Williams. LC 86-60043. 224p. 1986. 14.95 o.p. (ISBN 0-688-06219-9). Morrow.

Empty Room. Vincent A. McCrossen. 1955. Philos Lib.

Empyreal Sea-Live 1400 Years. Hilton Hotema. 52p. 1964. pap. text ed. 8.95 o.s.i. (ISBN 0-88697-046-6). Life Science.

En Bonne Forme. 3rd ed. Simone R. Dietiker. 416p. 1983. pap. 15.50net o.p. (ISBN 0-669-05255-8). Heath.

En Busca de Espana. Frank P. Casa. (Orig., Span.). 1968. pap. text ed. 10.95 o.p. (ISBN 0-15-522581-2, HC). HarBraceJ.

En Contacto: A First Course in Spanish. Pablo Valencia & Franca Merlonghi. 1982. pap. 25.95 o.p. (ISBN 0-395-27846-5); 3.95 o.p. HM.

En Contacto: Gramatica en Accion. 2nd ed. Mary McVey-Gill et al. (Span.). 1984. pap. text ed. 21.95 o.p. (ISBN 0-03-063887-9); lab manual 13.95 o.p. (ISBN 0-03-063888-7). HR&W.

En Contacto: Lecturas Intermedias. 2nd ed. Mary McVey-Gill et al. (Span.). 1980. pap. text ed. 15.95 o.p. (ISBN 0-03-063886-0); exercise manual 11.95 o.p. HR&W.

En el Cielo De Espana. F. Merono. 244p. (Span.). 6.45 o.p. (ISBN 0-8285-1746-0, Pub. by Progress Pubs USSR). Imported Pubns.

En la Ardiente Oscuridad. Antonio Buero Vallejo. Ed. by Samuel A. Wofsy. 196p. (Span.). 1954. pap. text ed. 9.95x o.p. (ISBN 0-02-422370-0, ScribC). Scribner.

En la Lucha, Tomo I: Palabras y Hechos 1936-1939. D. Ibarruri. 368p. (Span.). 1976. 7.95 o.p. (ISBN 0-8285-1677-4, Pub. by Progress Pubs USSR). Imported Pubns.

En Mi Alma Soy Libre. Paul Twitchell. 249p. 1983. pap. 5.95 o.p. (ISBN 0-88155-023-X). Illum Way Pub.

En Mon Ame Je Suis Libre. Paul Twitchell. Tr. by Yves Martin. 255p. 1983. pap. 3.95 o.p. (ISBN 0-88155-019-1). Illum Way Pub.

Enardo & Rosael. Alejandro Tapia & Rivera. 1952. (ISBN 0-8022-1691-9). Philos Lib.
Encancaranublado. Ana L. Vega. 141p. (Span.). 1983. pap. 7.50 o.s.i. (ISBN 0-317-15036-7, 3010). Ediciones Norte.
Enchanted Barn. Grace L. Hill. 352p. 1988. lib. bdg. 16.95x o.s.i. (ISBN 0-8161-4341-2, Large Print Bks). G K Hall.
Enchanted Canopy: A Journey of Discovery to the Last Unexplored Frontier, the Rainforests of the World. Andrew Mitchell. (Illus.). 288p. 1986. 29.95 o.p. (ISBN 0-02-585420-8). Macmillan.
Enchanted Closet. Beta. (Illus.). (gr. k-2). 1967. PLB 7.21 PLB o.p. (ISBN 0-87460-117-7). Lion Bks.
Enchanted Country: Northern Writers in the South, 1865-1910. Anne E. Rowe. LC 78-17048. xxiv, 160p. 1978. 20.00x o.p. (ISBN 0-8071-0453-1). La State U Pr.
Enchanted Encore. Rosalynn Carroll. (Rapture Romance Ser.: No. 63). 192p. 1984. pap. 1.95 o.p. (Sig). NAL.
Enchanted Island. Walter Lowrie. 1953. (ISBN 0-8022-1002-3). Philos Lib.
Enchanted Loom. Robert Jastrow. 1983. pap. 6.75 o.p. (ISBN 0-671-47068-X, Touchstone Bks). S&S.
Enchanted Orchard. Dorothy S. Carter. LC 78-187856. (Illus.). 128p. (Orig.). (gr. 3-7). 1973. 5.95 o.p. (ISBN 0-15-225955-4, HJ). HarBraceJ.
Enchanted Quill. Autumn Stanley. 1978. pap. 1.00 o.p. (ISBN 0-931832-10-1). Fithian Pr.
Enchanted Sea & Other Tales. Enid Blyton. (Read for Fun Ser.). (Illus.). 64p. (gr. k-3). 1987. 6.95 o.p. (ISBN 0-09-167200-7, Pub. by Century Hutchinson). David & Charles.
Enchanted Toys: A Glow-in-the-Dark Book. (Learning Curves Bks.). (Illus.). 10p. (ps-1). 1987. pap. 3.95 o.p. (ISBN 0-553-18359-1). Bantam.
Enchanted Wanderer & Other Stories. N. S. Leskov. 352p. 1974. 5.45 o.p. (ISBN 0-8285-1007-5, 180641, Pub. by Progress Pubs USSR). Imported Pubns.
Enchanter. Vladimir Nabokov. 128p. 1986. 16.95 o.p. (ISBN 0-399-13211-2, Perigee). Putnam Pub Group.
Enchantment. Anne Hampson. (Silhouette Romances Ser.). 1984. lib. bdg. 8.95 o.p. (ISBN 0-8398-2809-8, Gregg). G K Hall.
Enchantress. Han Suyin. (Large Print Books General Ser.). 1985. lib. bdg. 18.95 o.p. (ISBN 0-8161-3905-9). G K Hall.
Enchantress from the Stars. Sylvia L. Engdahl. LC 74-98609. 1970. sparton bdg. 9.95 o.p. (ISBN 0-689-20508-2, Atheneum). Macmillan.
Enciclopedia Basica Danae en Color, 2 vols. 4th ed. 1300p. (Span.). 1977. Set. leatherette 80.00 o.p. (ISBN 84-7060-429-5, S-50481). French & Eur.
Enciclopedia Biografica De Ciencia y Tecnologia. 2nd ed. Isaac Asimov. 800p. (Span.). 1974. 47.95 o.p. (ISBN 84-292-7004-3, S-50544). French & Eur.
Enciclopedia de Citas Morales y Religiosas. 456p. (Span.). 1976. 18.95 o.p. (ISBN 84-7228-251-1, S-50575). French & Eur.
Enciclopedia de la Construccion. G. Arosio. 1004p. (Span.). 1970. 58.00 o.p. (ISBN 84-224-0560-1, S-50541). French & Eur.
Enciclopedia De La Ensenanza General Basica, 10 vols. 2nd ed. (Span.). 1978. Set. 340.00 o.p. (ISBN 0-686-57359-5, S-50469). French & Eur.
Enciclopedia de la Magia y de la Brujeria. Constantino de Maria. 660p. (Span.). 1971. 35.95 o.p. (ISBN 84-315-0672-5, S-14961). French & Eur.
Enciclopedia De las Tecnicas Pictoricas. Maria Bazzi. 342p. (Span.). 1965. 12.25 o.p. (ISBN 84-279-4511-6, S-50549). French & Eur.
Enciclopedia Del Mar y De la Navegacion Deportiva. Gianni Cazzaroli. 396p. (Span.). 1975. 37.50 o.p. (ISBN 84-279-4516-7, S-50490). French & Eur.
Enciclopedia Practica de Floricultura y Jardineria. 2nd ed. Tina Cecchini. 588p. (Span.). 1978. pap. 28.50 o.p. (ISBN 84-315-0972-4, S-14572). French & Eur.
Enclosing Behavior. Robert B. Bechtel. LC 77-2850. (Community Development Ser.: Vol. 31). 1982. 34.95 o.p. (ISBN 0-87933-069-4). Van Nos Reinhold.
Encore. Monique R. High. 1982. pap. 3.95 o.p. (ISBN 0-440-12363-1). Dell.
Encounter. Crawford Power. 1972. pap. 1.25 o.p. (ISBN 0-380-01157-3, Bard). Avon.
Encounter Between Two Worlds. Calvin Williams. 80p. 1982. 5.50 o.p. (ISBN 0-682-49858-0). Exposition-Phoenix.
Encounter: Group Sensitivity Training Experience. Carl Goldberg. LC 70-133292. 1971. 25.00x o.p. (ISBN 0-87668-035-X). Aronson.
Encounter: Readings for Thinking, Talking, Writing. 2nd ed. Joan G. Roloff. LC 73-7356. (Illus.). 416p. 1974. pap. text ed. write for info. o.p. (ISBN 0-02-477150-3). Macmillan.
Encounter with a New World: A Reading-Writing Text for Speakers of English As a Second Language. D. Fassler & N. Lay. 1979. pap. text ed. 9.95 o.p. (ISBN 0-13-274910-6). P-H.
Encounter with Disaster: A Medical Diary of Hiroshima, 1945. Averill A. Liebow. (Illus.). 224p. 1985. pap. 5.70 o.p. (ISBN 0-393-30282-2). Norton.
Encounter with the Text: Form & History in the Hebrew Bible. Ed. by Martin J. Buss et al. LC 78-31182. (Semeia Studies). 232p. (Orig.). 1979. pap. 5.95 o.p. (ISBN 0-8006-1508-5, 1-1508, Fortress). Augsburg Fortress.
Encountering Aborigines, a Case Study: Anthropology & the Australian Aboriginal. Kenelm O. Burridge. LC 72-1191. 272p. 1974. text ed. 31.00 o.p. (ISBN 0-08-017071-4); pap. text ed. 12.00 o.p. (ISBN 0-08-017646-1). Pergamon.
Encountering Marx: Bonds & Barriers Between Christians & Marxists. Jan M. Lochman. Tr. by Edwin H. Robertson from Ger. LC 76-55827. 144p. 1977. pap. 2.00 o.p. (ISBN 0-8006-1249-3, 1-1249, Fortress). Augsburg Fortress.
Encountering Society: Introductory Readings in Sociology. Janet K. Mancini & Franklyn A. Robbins. LC 80-8253. 219p. 1980. pap. text ed. 13.50 o.p. (ISBN 0-8191-1181-3). U Pr of Amer.
Encounters. Kathleen Wiegner. 1972. pap. 8.00 o.p. (ISBN 0-87924-019-9). Membrane Pr.
Encounters: A Basic Reader. Paul Pimsleur & Donald Berger. (Illus.). 224p. (Orig.). 1974. pap. text ed. 9.95 o.p. (ISBN 0-15-522585-5, HC). HarBraceJ.
Encounters: A Basic Reader. 2nd ed. Paul Pimsleur et al. 206p. 1980. pap. text ed. 11.25 o.p. (ISBN 0-15-522588-X, HC). HarBraceJ.
Encounters: A Memoir. Dorothy Norman. (Helen & Kurt Wolff Bk Ser.). (Illus.). 1987. 19.95 o.p. (ISBN 0-15-128792-9). HarBraceJ.
Encounters in Experimental Chemistry. William L. Jolly. (Illus.). 157p. 1972. 14.95 o.p. (ISBN 0-15-522591-X, HC, HC). HarBraceJ.
Encounters in Yoga & Zen. Trevor Leggett. 1982. pap. 9.95 o.p. (ISBN 0-7100-9241-5). Routledge Chapman & Hall.
Encounters: Themes in Literature. 2nd ed. Ed. by G. Robert Carlsen et al. Anthony Tovatt. (Themes & Writers Ser). (Illus.). 768p. (gr. 10). 1972. text ed. 24.32 o.p. (ISBN 0-07-009904-9). McGraw.
Encounters Training. 2nd ed. Carlsen. Date not set. (ISBN 0-07-009910-3). McGraw.
Encounters with Books: Teaching Fiction 11-16. David Jackson. (Teaching Secondary English Ser.). 198p. 1984. 21.00x o.p. (ISBN 0-416-33060-6, NO. 4061); pap. 10.95x o.p. (ISBN 0-416-33070-3, NO. 4062). Routledge Chapman & Hall.
Encounters with Stravinsky. Paul Horgan. (Illus.). 336p. 1972. 7.95 o.p. (ISBN 0-374-14828-7). FS&G.
Encounters with the Jewish People. Chaim Raphael. LC 79-14424. 1979. pap. text ed. 6.95x o.p. (ISBN 0-87441-282-X). Behrman.
Encounters with the Self. 2nd ed. Don E. Hamachek. LC 78-357. 1978. pap. 20.95 o.p. (ISBN 0-03-019851-8, HoltC). HR&W.
Encounters with Unjust Authority. William A. Gamson et al. 186p. 1982. pap. text ed. (ISBN 0-534-10536-X). Wadsworth Pub.
Encouraging Talk. Lewis Knowles. LC 83-17390. (Teaching Secondary English Ser.). 250p. 1984. 21.00 o.p. (ISBN 0-416-33200-5, 4059); pap. 10.95 o.p. (ISBN 0-416-33210-2, 4060). Routledge Chapman & Hall.
Encouraging Writing. Robert Protherough. (Teaching English Ser.). 224p. 1983. 25.00x o.p. (ISBN 0-416-34050-4, NO. 3862); pap. 9.95x o.p. (ISBN 0-416-34060-1, NO. 3863). Routledge Chapman & Hall.
Encyclopaedia Britannica, 32 vols. 1988. Set. 1069.00 o.p. (ISBN 0-85229-473-5). Ency Brit Ed.
Encyclopaedia of Garden Plants & Flowers. Reader's Digest Association, London. (Illus.). 1977. 22.50 o.p. (ISBN 0-393-08780-8). Norton.
Encyclopaedia of Gardening. J. C. Loudon. Ed. by John D. Hunt. LC 79-56972. (English Landscape Garden Ser.). 1311p. 1982. lib. bdg. 200.00 o.p. (ISBN 0-8240-0176-1). Garland Pub.
Encyclopaedia of Indian Culture, Vol. 3. R. N. Saletore. 425p. 1983. text ed. 50.00x o.p. (ISBN 0-391-02332-2). Humanities.
Encyclopaedia of Religions. Maurice A. Canney. LC 75-123370. 412p. 1970. Repr. of 1921 ed. 53.00 o.p. (ISBN 0-8103-3856-4). Gale.
Encyclopaedic Dictionary of Science & War. Charles M. Beadnell. LC 74-164093. 314p. 1971. Repr. of 1943 ed. 43.00x o.p. (ISBN 0-8103-3753-3). Gale.
Encyclopedia Americana, 30 vols. Rev. ed. Ed. by David Holland. LC 85-24877. (Illus.). 1987. text ed. write for info. o.p. (ISBN 0-7172-0119-8). Grolier Inc.
Encyclopedia Buying Guide: A Consumer Guide to General Encyclopedia in Print. 3rd. ed. Kenneth F. Kister. 580p. pap. 19.95 o.p. (ISBN 0-8352-1409-5). Bowker.
Encyclopedia de l'Esoterisme. Jacques d' Ares. 217p. (Fr.). 1975. pap. 19.95 o.p. (ISBN 0-686-56900-8, M-6010). French & Eur.
Encyclopedia for Boys & Girls. Johnson. (ISBN 0-8022-0807-X). Philos Lib.
Encyclopedia for the TRS-80, Vol. 1. Bill Vick et al. Ed. by Nan McCarthy & Chris Crocker. (Illus.). 269p. (Orig.). 1981. 19.95 o.p. (ISBN 0-88006-025-5, EN8101); pap. text ed. 10.95 o.p. (ISBN 0-88006-026-3, EN8081). Wayne Green Ent.
Encyclopedia for the TRS-80, Vol. 2. Wayne Green. Ed. by Nan McCarthy et al. (Encyclopedia for the TRS-80 Ser.). (Illus.). 283p. 1981. text ed. 19.95 o.p. (ISBN 0-88006-029-8, EN8102); pap. text ed. 10.95 o.p. (ISBN 0-88006-030-1, EN8082). Wayne Green Ent.
Encyclopedia for the TRS-80, Vol. 3. Allan J. Domuret et al. Ed. by Katherine Putnam & Kate Comiskey. (Illus.). 265p. 1981. text ed. 19.95 o.p. (ISBN 0-88006-031-X, EN8103); pap. text ed. 10.95 o.p. (ISBN 0-88006-032-8, EN8083). Wayne Green Ent.
Encyclopedia for the TRS-80, Vol. 4. Ed. by Katherine Putnam & Kate Comiskey. (Illus.). 253p. (Orig.). 1981. 19.95 o.p. (ISBN 0-88006-033-6, EN8104); pap. 10.95 o.p. (ISBN 0-88006-034-4, EN8084). Wayne Green Ent.
Encyclopedia for the TRS-80, Vol. 5. John W. Blattner et al. Ed. by Katherine Putnam & Kate Comiskey. 239p. (Orig.). 1982. 19.95 o.p. (ISBN 0-88006-035-2, EN8105); pap. 10.95 o.p. (ISBN 0-88006-036-0, EN8085). Wayne Green Ent.
Encyclopedia for the TRS-80, Vol. 6. Fred Blechman et al. Ed. by Katherine Putnam & Kate Comiskey. (Illus.). 303p. 1982. 19.95 o.p. (ISBN 0-88006-040-9, EN8106); pap. 10.95 o.p. (ISBN 0-88006-041-7, EN8086). Wayne Green Ent.
Encyclopedia for the TRS-80, Vol. 7. Chuck Baird et al. Ed. by Katherine Putnam & Kate Comiskey. (Illus.). 265p. 1982. 19.95 o.p. (ISBN 0-88006-042-5, EN8107); pap. 10.95 o.p. (ISBN 0-88006-043-3, EN8087). Wayne Green Ent.
Encyclopedia for the TRS-80, Vol. 8. Ed. by Katherine Putnam & Kate Comiskey. 219p. (Orig.). 1982. 19.95 o.p. (ISBN 0-88006-044-1, EN8108); pap. 10.95 o.p. (ISBN 0-88006-045-X, EN8088). Wayne Green Ent.
Encyclopedia for the TRS-80, Vol. 9. Ed. by Katherine Putnam & Kate Comiskey. (Illus.). 253p. (Orig.). 1982. 19.95 o.p. (ISBN 0-88006-046-8, EN8109); pap. 10.95 o.p. (ISBN 0-88006-047-6, EN8089). Wayne Green Ent.
Encyclopedia for the TRS-80, Vol. 10. Ed. by Katherine Putnam & Kate Comiskey. (Illus.). 177p. (Orig.). 1982. 19.95 o.p. (ISBN 0-88006-048-4, EN8110); pap. 10.95 o.p. (ISBN 0-88006-049-2, EN8090). Wayne Green Ent.
Encyclopedia for the TRS-80, No. 10. Wayne Green Books Editors. (Illus.). 250p. (Orig.). 1981-82. 19.50 o.p. (ISBN 0-88006-056-5, EN8100); pap. 10.50 o.p. (ISBN 0-88006-057-3, EN8080). Wayne green Ent.
Encyclopedia for Today's Christian Woman. Compiled by Cecil B. Murphey. (Encyclopedias Ser.). 512p. 1984. 16.95 o.p. (ISBN 0-8007-1393-1). Revell.
Encyclopedia of Aberrations. Edward Podolsky. (ISBN 0-8022-1991-8). Philos Lib.
Encyclopedia of American Cars, 1930-1942. James Moloney. Ed. by George H. Dammann. LC 77-89427. (Automotive Ser.). (Illus.). 384p. 1977. 29.95 o.p. (ISBN 0-912612-12-6). Crestline.
Encyclopedia of American History. 3rd ed. Dushkin Publishing Group Staff. LC 73-88982. (Illus.). 344p. 1981. 15.95 o.p.; pap. text ed. 10.95 o.p. Dushkin Pub.
Encyclopedia of American Religions. 2nd ed. Ed. by J. Gordon Melton. 899p. 1986. 165.00x o.p. (ISBN 0-8103-2133-5). Gale.
Encyclopedia of American Religions: Supplement. 2nd ed. Ed. by J. Gordon Melton. 300p. 1987. 80.00x o.p. (ISBN 0-8103-2131-9). Gale.
Encyclopedia of Antiques. Harold Lewis Bond. LC 74-31297. (Illus.). 468p. 1975. Repr. of 1945 ed. 60.00x o.p. (ISBN 0-8103-4206-5). Gale.
Encyclopedia of Architectural Technology. Reference International Publishers Staff. (Illus.). 1979. text ed. 38.00 o.p. (ISBN 0-07-051740-1). McGraw.
Encyclopedia of Architecture. J. Wilt. Ed. by W. Papworth. (Illus.). 1392p. 1982. 14.98 o.s.i. (ISBN 0-517-37985-6, Bonanza). Outlet Bk Co.
Encyclopedia of Arts. Dagobert D. Runes. 1088p. 1965. (ISBN 0-8022-1434-7). Philos Lib.
Encyclopedia of Associations: Index. 22nd ed. Ed. by Susan Boyles-Martin & Karin Koek. 600p. 1987. 35.00x o.p. (ISBN 0-8103-2692-2). Gale.
Encyclopedia of Associations: International Organizations 1988, Vol. 4. Ed. by Karin E. Koek. (Encyclopedia of Associations Ser.). 1000p. cancelled o.s.i. (ISBN 0-8103-2694-9). Gale.
Encyclopedia of Associations Nineteen Eighty-Eight, Updating Service. 22nd ed. 1987. pap. text ed. 195.00x o.p. (ISBN 0-8103-2695-7). Gale.
Encyclopedia of Associations, Vol. 1: National Organizations of the U. S. 22nd ed. Ed. by Susan B. Martin & Karin Koek. (Encyclopedia of Associations Ser.). 2500p. 1987. 230.00x o.p. (ISBN 0-8103-2690-6). Gale.
Encyclopedia of Associations, Vol. 2: Geographic & Executive Index. 22nd ed. Ed. by Susan B. Martin & Karin Koek. (Encyclopedia of Associations Ser.). 800p. 1987. 210.00x o.p. (ISBN 0-8103-2691-4). Gale.
Encyclopedia of Associations, Vol. 3: New Associations & Projects. 22nd ed. Ed. by Susan Boyles-Martin & Karin Koek. 1987. pap. text ed. 220.00x o.p. (ISBN 0-8103-2693-0). Gale.
Encyclopedia of Australian Art. Alan McCulloch. (Illus.). 1327p. 125.00 o.p. (ISBN 0-317-54940-5). Apollo.
Encyclopedia of Aviation. Reference International. LC 77-72699. (Encore Edition). (Illus.). 1977. 5.95 o.p. (ISBN 0-684-16921-5, ScribT). Scribner.
Encyclopedia of Black Folklore & Humor. rev. ed. Henry D. Spalding. LC 73-16760. 1979. 16.95 o.p. (ISBN 0-8246-0129-7). Jonathan David.
Encyclopedia of British Pottery & Porcelian Marks. Geoffrey A. Godden. 765p. 1984. 35.00 o.p. (ISBN 0-257-65782-7, Pub. By Hutchinson Pub UK). Seven Hills Bk Dists.
Encyclopedia of Building & Construction Terms. Hugh Brooks. LC 82-21565. 416p. 1983. text ed. 39.95 o.p. (ISBN 0-13-275511-4). P-H.
Encyclopedia of Business Information Sources. 6th ed. Ed. by James Woy. 878p. 1986. 210.00x o.p. (ISBN 0-8103-0364-7). Gale.
Encyclopedia of Business Information Sources: Supplement. 6th ed. Ed. by James Woy. 160p. 1987. 80.00x o.p. (ISBN 0-8103-2115-7). Gale.
Encyclopedia of Child Guidance. Ralph B. Winn. (ISBN 0-8022-1903-9). Philos Lib.
Encyclopedia of Christian Marriage. 414p. 1983. 16.95 o.p. (ISBN 0-8007-1376-1). Revell.
Encyclopedia of Christian Parenting. 540p. 1982. 16.95 o.p. (ISBN 0-8007-1276-5). Revell.
Encyclopedia of Clinical Assessment. Ed. by Robert H. Woody. LC 80-10463. (Social & Behavioral Science Ser.). 1980. text ed. 75.00x o.p. (ISBN 0-87589-446-1). Jossey-Bass.
Encyclopedia of Computers & Electronics. (Encyclopedia Ser.). (Illus.). 144p. (gr. 4 up). 1983. 14.95 o.s.i. (ISBN 0-02-689200-6, Checkerboard Pr). Macmillan.
Encyclopedia of Criminology. V. C. Branham & S. B. Kutash. (ISBN 0-8022-0167-9). Philos Lib.
Encyclopedia of Cultivated Orchids. Alex D. Hawkes. (Illus.). 602p. 1965. 80.00 o.p. (ISBN 0-571-06502-3). Faber & Faber.
Encyclopedia of Duncan Glass. Gail Krause. 1976. 17.50 o.p. (ISBN 0-682-48527-6). Exposition-Phoenix.
Encyclopedia of Embroidery Stitches, Including Crewel. Marion Nichols. (Illus.). 12.00 o.p. (ISBN 0-8446-5232-6). Peter Smith.
Encyclopedia of Engineering Materials, Pt. A: Polymer Science & Tech, Vol. 3: Properties & Processing Operations. Cheremisinoff. 1989. write for info. o.p. (ISBN 0-8247-8004-3). Dekker.
Encyclopedia of Engineering Materials, 2 pts. Cheremisnoff. 816p. 1988. Set; Pt. A, Polymer Science & Technology; Pt. B, Polymer-Plastics Prop. 185.00 o.p. (ISBN 0-8247-7988-6). Dekker.
Encyclopedia of Engineering Materials, Vol. 1, Pt. A. Cheremisnoff. 1988. Pt. A, Polymer Science & Technology; Vol. 1, Synthesis & Properties. 185.00 o.p. (ISBN 0-8247-7858-8). Dekker.
Encyclopedia of Environmental Science. 2nd ed. McGraw-Hill Editors. 1980. text ed. 72.50 o.p. (ISBN 0-07-045264-4). McGraw.
Encyclopedia of Fishing Lures. Loring D. Wilson. LC 78-67468. (Illus.). 1980. 19.95 o.s.i. (ISBN 0-498-02337-0). A S Barnes.
Encyclopedia of Food Science, Vol. 3. Martin S. Peterson & Arnold H. Johnson. (Technologic Food Encyclopedia Ser.). (Illus.). 1978. 99.95 o.s.i. (ISBN 0-87055-227-9). AVI.
Encyclopedia of French Period Furniture Designs. Jose C. Rubira. LC 83-18220. (Illus.). 416p. (Orig.). 1983. pap. 16.95 o.p. (ISBN 0-8069-7750-7). Sterling.
Encyclopedia of Gardening. rev. ed. Ed. by Norman Taylor. (Illus.). 1974. 27.95 o.p. (ISBN 0-395-08237-4). HM.
Encyclopedia of Homonyms 'Sound-Alikes' Dora Newhouse. LC 76-27486. 1977. 16.95 o.s.i. (ISBN 0-918050-01-4). Newhouse Pr.

Titles

Encyclopedia of Indian Philosophies: Volume 1, Bibliography. Revised ed. Ed. by Karl H. Potter. LC 77-85558. 1023p. 1984. 60.00 o.p. (ISBN 0-691-07281-7). Princeton U Pr.

Encyclopedia of Information Systems & Services, International Volume. 7th ed. Ed. by Amy Lucas. 482p. 1986. 185.00x o.p. (ISBN 0-8103-2493-8). Gale.

Encyclopedia of Information Systems & Services, 1988, Vol. 1. 8th ed. Ed. by Amy Lucas & Annette Novallo. 1000p. 1987. 230.00x o.p. (ISBN 0-8103-2530-6). Gale.

Encyclopedia of Information Systems & Services, United States Volume. 7th ed. Ed. by Amy Lucas. 944p. 1986. 210.00x o.p. (ISBN 0-8103-2494-6). Gale.

Encyclopedia of Information Systems & Services: United States, International & Index Volume, 3 vols. Ed. by Amy Lucas. 2217p. 1986. 370.00x o.p. (ISBN 0-8103-2492-X). Gale.

Encyclopedia of Information Systems & Services, 1988: International Volume, Vol. 2. 8th ed. Ed. by Amy Lucas & Annette Novallo. 500p. 1987. 195.00x o.p. (ISBN 0-8103-2531-4). Gale.

Encyclopedia of Information Systems & Services, 1988: United States, International & Index, 3 vols. 8th ed. Ed. by Amy Lucas & Annette Novallo. Set. 400.00x o.p. (ISBN 0-8103-2532-2). Gale.

Encyclopedia of Iron & Steel Industry. A. K. Osborne. 1956. (ISBN 0-8022-1251-4). Philos Lib.

Encyclopedia of Islam, 4 vols. Ed. by B. Lewis et al. Incl. Vol. 1. A-B: Fasc. 1-22. Ed. by H. A. Gibb et al. 1960. text ed. 185.75x (ISBN 90-040-0530-7); Vol. 2. C-G: Fasc. 23-40. Ed. by B. Lewis et al. 1965. 185.75x o.p. (ISBN 90-040-0531-5); Vol. 3. H-Iram: Fasc. 41-60. 1969. text ed. 226.25x (ISBN 90-040-3275-4); Vols. 4 & 5. I-Ram &K-Ha: Fasc. 61-78. 1978. text ed. 275.50. Humanities.

Encyclopedia of Linguistics, Information & Control. A. R. Meetham. 1969. 185.00 o.p. (ISBN 0-08-012337-6). Pergamon.

Encyclopedia of Literature. Joseph T. Shipley. (ISBN 0-8022-1558-0). Philos Lib.

Encyclopedia of Live Foods. Charles O. Masters. (Illus.). 336p. 1975. 19.95 o.p. (ISBN 0-87666-093-6, PS-730). TFH Pubns.

Encyclopedia of Management. 3rd, rev. ed. Ed. by Carl Heyel. 1416p. 1982. 62.95 o.p. (ISBN 0-442-25165-3). Van Nos Reinhold.

Encyclopedia of Medicinal Herbs. Joseph M. Kadans. LC 79-158469. 256p. 1985. pap. 2.50 o.p. (ISBN 0-668-02487-9). Arco.

Encyclopedia of Modern Education. H. Rivlin. (ISBN 0-8022-1353-7). Philos Lib.

Encyclopedia of Morals. Vergilius Ferm. 1956. Philos Lib.

Encyclopedia of Mystery & Detection. Ed. by Chris Steinbrunner & Otto Penzler. LC 84-9131. (Illus.). 448p. 1984. pap. 13.95 o.p. (ISBN 0-15-628787-0, Harv). HarBraceJ.

Encyclopedia of New York City. Ed. by Kenneth T. Jackson. 1988. 50.00 o.p. (ISBN 0-317-68064-1). Yale U Pr.

Encyclopedia of Occultism & Parapsychology: Vols. 1 & 2. Leslie A. Shepard. 1980. pap. 19.90 boxed set o.p. (ISBN 0-380-50112-0, 50112); Vol. 1. pap. 9.95 o.p. (ISBN 0-380-48835-3, 48835); Vol. 2. pap. 9.95 o.p. (ISBN 0-380-48975-9, 48975). Avon.

Encyclopedia of Philosophy. Hegel. 1959. (ISBN 0-8022-0702-2). Philos Lib.

Encyclopedia of Philosophy. G. H. R. Parkinson et al. 880p. 1988. lib. bdg. 75.00x o.p. (ISBN 0-7099-4024-6, Pub. by Croom Helm UK). Routledge Chapman & Hall.

Encyclopedia of Physical Education, Fitness, & Sports: Training, Environment, Nutrition & Fitness. American Alliance for Health, Physical Education, Recreation & Dance Staff. 614p. 1980. 39.90 o.p. (ISBN 0-317-31995-7, 240-26754). AAHPERD.

Encyclopedia of Power Foods for Health & Longer Life. Carlson Wade. 1982. pap. 4.95 o.p. (ISBN 0-13-276121-1, Reward). P-H.

Encyclopedia of Professional Management. Lester R. Bittel. (Illus.). 1979. text ed. 52.50 o.p. (ISBN 0-07-005478-9). McGraw.

Encyclopedia of Psychology. P. L. Harriman. 912p. (ISBN 0-8022-0682-4). Philos Lib.

Encyclopedia of Radio & Television. J. H. Reyner. (Illus.). 736p. 1958. (ISBN 0-8022-1331-6). Philos Lib.

Encyclopedia of Real Estate Appraising Forms & Model Reports. Samuel T. Barash. LC 83-3029. 398p. 1983. text ed. 39.95 o.p. (ISBN 0-13-276212-9). P-H.

Encyclopedia of School Safety. 1973. spiral bdg. 16.30 o.p. (ISBN 0-87912-103-3, 429-07). Natl Safety Coun.

Encyclopedia of Sewing. Adele P. Margolis. LC 85-4342. (Illus.). 544p. 1987. 30.00 o.p.; pap. 30.00 o.p. (ISBN 0-385-14989-1). Doubleday.

Encyclopedia of Spanish Period Furniture Designs. Jose C. Rubira. LC 84-8862. (Illus.). 352p. (Orig.). 1985. pap. 16.95 o.p. (ISBN 0-8069-7902-X). Sterling.

Encyclopedia of Superstitions. Edwin Radford. (ISBN 0-8022-1301-4). Philos Lib.

Encyclopedia of Textiles. 3rd ed. Ed. by American Fabrics Magazine Staff. (Illus.). 656p. 1980. text ed. 49.95 o.p. (ISBN 0-13-276576-4, Busn). P-H.

Encyclopedia of the American Theatre. Edwin Bronner. LC 75-2439. (Illus.). 1980. 30.00 o.s.i. (ISBN 0-498-01219-0). A S Barnes.

Encyclopedia of the Modern Royal Airforce. 2nd ed. Terry Gander. (Illus.). 264p. 1987. 29.95 o.p. (ISBN 0-85059-859-1, Pub. by PSL P Stephens). Sterling.

Encyclopedia of the Papacy. Hans Kuhner. 249p. 1958. (ISBN 0-8022-0900-9). Philos Lib.

Encyclopedia of Track & Field. (ISBN 0-671-61915-2). Arco.

Encyclopedia of Track & Field. P-H.

Encyclopedia of Vocational Guidance, 2 vols. (ISBN 0-8022-0824-X). Philos Lib.

Encyclopedia of Wood. U. S. Department of Forestry Staff. LC 77-7728. (Illus.). 384p. 1980. pap. 13.95 o.p. (ISBN 0-8069-8890-8). Sterling.

Encyclopedia of Working with Glass. Milton K. Berlye. 1983. 29.95 o.p. (ISBN 0-89696-193-1, Everest House Book). Dodd.

Encyclopedia of World Architecture. Henri Stierlin. 416p. 1983. pap. 21.95 o.p. (ISBN 0-442-27957-4). Van Nos Reinhold.

Encyclopedia Science Supplement, 1984. Grolier, Inc. Staff. Ed. by Herbert Kondo. LC 64-7603. (Illus.). 1982. write for info. o.p. (ISBN 0-7172-1514-8). Grolier Inc.

Encyclopedic Dictionary of Mathematics for Engineers. Ed. by I. N. Sneddon. LC 73-6800. 1976. 240.00 o.p. (ISBN 0-08-021149-6). Pergamon.

Encyclopedic Dictionary of Physical Geography. Ed. by Andrew Goudie. 576p. 1985. 60.00x o.p. (ISBN 0-631-13292-9). Basil Blackwell.

Encyclopedie De l'Esoterisme1risme, 2: Religions Non Chretiennes. Jacques D'ares. Jacques d' Ares. 244p. (Fr.). 1975. pap. 19.95 o.p. (ISBN 0-686-56899-0, M-6009). French & Eur.

Encyclopedie Des Baissons. 512p. (Fr.). 1970. 27.50 o.p. (ISBN 0-686-57137-1, M-6192). French & Eur.

Encyclopedie Des Cuisines Regionales et Etrangeres. 512p. (Fr.). 1971. 27.50 o.p. (ISBN 0-686-57139-8, M-6194). French & Eur.

Encyclopedie Des Sports. 320p. 1976. 57.50 o.p. (ISBN 0-686-57148-7, M-6205). French & Eur.

Encyclopedie du Cinema: A-H, Vol. 1. R. Boussinot. (Fr.). 85.00 o.p. (ISBN 0-686-92236-0, F-79450). French & Eur.

Encyclopedie du Cinema: I-Z, Vol. II. R. Boussinot. (Fr.). 85.00 o.p. (ISBN 0-686-92242-5, F-79451). French & Eur.

Encyclopedie Francaise Permanente, 22 vols. (Fr.). Set. 1750.00 o.p. (ISBN 0-686-57273-4, F-12790). French & Eur.

Encyclopedie Internationale Des Sciences et Des Techniques, 11 vols. (Fr.). Set. 850.00 o.p. (ISBN 0-686-57161-4, M-6220). French & Eur.

Encyclopedie Medicale Quillet. (Fr.). 82.50 o.p. (ISBN 0-686-57163-0, M-6222). French & Eur.

Encylopedie Illustree Du Monde Vegetal. 600p. (Fr.). 14.95 o.p. (ISBN 0-686-57160-6, M-6219). French & Eur.

End. Skip Morrow. LC 82-83314. 96p. 1983. pap. 4.95 o.p. (ISBN 0-03-063401-6). H Holt & Co.

End. Carole S. Smith. 1978. pap. 1.75 o.p. (ISBN 0-380-01978-7, 38919). Avon.

End & a Beginning: The South Coast & Los Angeles, 1850-1887. Joseph S. O'Flaherty. LC 72-75481. 1972. 7.50 o.p. (ISBN 0-682-47476-2, Lochinvar). Exposition-Phoenix.

End of a Dark Road. Crystal Thrasher. LC 82-3958. 228p. (gr. 3-7). 1982. 12.95 o.s.i. (ISBN 0-689-50250-8, M K McElderry). Macmillan.

End of a Golden Age: Higher Education in a Steady State. Ed. by Edward Gross & John S. Western. (Scholars' Library). (Illus.). 144p. 1982. pap. text ed. 37.50x o.p. (ISBN 0-7022-1625-9). U of Queensland Pr.

End of Affluence: A Blueprint for Your Future. Paul R. Ehrlich & Anne H. Ehrlich. 320p. 1980. pap. 2.50 o.s.i. (ISBN 0-345-29049-6). Ballantine.

End of All Songs. Michael Moorcock. 1978. pap. 1.75 o.p. (ISBN 0-380-01964-7, 38471). Avon.

End of an Era. National Historical Society Staff. Ed. by William C. Davis & Bell I. Wiley. LC 82-45884. (Image of War 1861-1865 Ser.: Vol. VI). (Illus.). 496p. 1984. 19.95 o.p. (ISBN 0-385-18282-1). Doubleday.

End of Arcadia: Gordon Browning & Tennessee Politics. William R. Majors. 1982. 14.95x o.p. (ISBN 0-87870-098-6). Memphis St Univ.

End of Days, Nineteen Seventy-One to Two Thousand One: An Eschatological Study. Charles D. Willis. (Illus.). 1972. 7.50 o.p. (ISBN 0-682-47385-5). Exposition-Phoenix.

End of Ideology Theory: Illusions & Reality. L. N. Moskvichov. 191p. 1974. 3.95 o.p. (ISBN 0-8285-0225-0, Pub. by Progress Pubs USSR). Imported Pubns.

End of Isolation: British Foreign Policy, 1900-1907. George W. Monger. LC 75-36357. 343p. 1976. Repr. of 1963 ed. lib. bdg. 22.50x o.p. (ISBN 0-8371-8628-5, MOEI). Greenwood.

End of My Life. Vance Boufjaily. 1984. pap. 6.95 o.p. (ISBN 0-87795-603-0, Arbor Hse). Morrow.

End of Religion: Autobiographical Explorations. Dom A. Graham. LC 77-139461. 292p. 1973. pap. 2.85 o.p. (ISBN 0-15-628790-0, Harv). HarBraceJ.

End of Senility. Arthur S. Freese. LC 77-90662. 1978. 8.95 o.p. (ISBN 0-87795-173-X, Arbor Hse). Morrow.

End of Senility see Prime of Your Life: The Book That Makes Old Age Obsolete.

End of Summer. Bernice Grohskopf. 208p. (YA) (gr. 7 up). 1982. pap. 2.25 o.p. (ISBN 0-380-79293-1, Flare). Avon.

End of the Ages Has Come: An Early Interpretation of the Passion & Resurrection of Jesus. Dale C. Allison, Jr. LC 85-47732. 208p. 1985. 3.95 o.p. (ISBN 0-8006-0753-8, 1-753, Fortress). Augsburg Fortress.

End of the American Era. Andrew Hacker. LC 71-108823. 1971. pap. text ed. 3.95x o.s.i. (ISBN 0-689-70272-8, 178, Atheneum). Macmillan.

End of the Line? The Development of Christian Theology in the Last Two Centuries. John H. Kent. LC 82-7263. 144p. 1982. pap. 6.95 o.p. (ISBN 0-8006-1652-9, 1-1652, Fortress). Augsburg Fortress.

End of the Religious Life. Robert S. Faricy. 96p. 1983. pap. 6.95 o.p. (ISBN 0-86683-690-X). HarpR.

End of the River. B. L. Van Vors. 432p. 1983. pap. 3.95 o.p. (ISBN 0-380-83428-6, 83428-6). Avon.

End of the Taboos: An Ethics of Encounter. Gerard M. Fourez. LC 72-91522. (Illus.). 160p. (Orig.). 1973. pap. 3.75 o.p. (ISBN 0-8006-0148-3, Fortress). Augsburg Fortress.

End of the Trail. Leta May Smith. 1976. 10.00 o.p. (ISBN 0-682-48399-0, Lochinvar). Exposition-Phoenix.

End of the World, A.D. 2133. Lucio B. Silvestre. LC 83-90813. 233p. 1985. 12.95 o.p. (ISBN 0-533-05822-8). Vantage.

End of the World News. Anthony Burgess. 388p. 1983. text ed. 15.95 o.p. (ISBN 0-07-008965-5). McGraw.

End of Time: A Meditation on the Philosophy of History. Josef Pieper. 157p. 1982. Repr. of 1954 ed. lib. bdg. 18.00 o.p. (ISBN 0-374-96447-5, Octagon). Hippocrene Bks.

End the Arms Race - Fund Human Needs: Proceedings of Vancouver Centennial Peaces & Disarmament Symposium, 1986. Ed. by Thomas L Perry & James G. Foulks. 336p. 1987. pap. 9.95 o.p. (ISBN 0-295-96492-8). U of Wash Pr.

End Time-God's Glory. John W. Hartsaw. 112p. 1982. 6.50 o.p. (ISBN 0-682-49848-3). Exposition-Phoenix.

End Time Prophecy. Bob Yandian. 15p. 1983. wkbk. 3.95 o.s.i. (ISBN 0-914307-15-0, Dist. by Harrison Hse). R Tilton Ministries.

End to Silence: Uncensored Opinion in the Soviet Union from Roy Medvedev's Underground Magazine Political Diary. Roy A. Medvedev. Ed. by Stephen F. Cohen. 1982. 19.95 o.p. (ISBN 0-393-01491-6). Norton.

End-Use Markets for Thirteen Nonferrous Metals. 56p. (Orig.). 1986. pap. 3.00 o.p. (ISBN 0-318-21285-4, S/N 003-009-00479-9). USGPO.

Endangered Species. Sandra Hochman. 1979. pap. 2.25 o.p. (ISBN 0-380-42366-9, 42366). Avon.

Endearment. LaVyrle Spencer. 320p. (Orig.). 1984. pap. 3.95 o.p. (ISBN 0-440-02446-3, Emerald). Dell.

Enderby's Dark Lady: Or, No End to Enderby. Anthony Burgess. 160p. 1984. text ed. 14.95 o.p. (ISBN 0-07-008969-8). McGraw.

Endgame. Harvey Ardman. (Orig.). 1975. pap. 1.75 o.p. (ISBN 0-380-00352-X, 24299). Avon.

Endgame. Samuel Beckett. Tr. by Samuel Beckett from Fr. 1958. pap. 3.95 o.p. (ISBN 0-394-17208-6, E96, Ever). Grove.

Ending Hunger: Its Possible, It's Happening. pap. 5.50 o.p. (ISBN 0-686-95390-8). Am Fr Serv Comm.

Ending Up. Kingsley Amis. LC 74-10678. 1974. 6.95 o.p. (ISBN 0-15-128796-1). HarBraceJ.

Endless Adventure. Coman. 1978. pap. 3.95 o.p. (ISBN 0-89272-041-7). Down East.

Endless Chain of Nature: Experiment at Hubbard Brook. Patricia P. Sturges. LC 76-15962. (Illus.). 1976. 7.95 o.s.i. (ISBN 0-664-32597-1, Westminster). Westminster John Knox.

Endless Love. Scott Spencer. 400p. 1980. pap. 3.50 o.p. (ISBN 0-380-50823-0). Avon.

Endless Rapture: Rape, Romance, & the Female Imagination. Helen Hazen. 192p. 1983. 12.95 o.s.i. (ISBN 0-684-17917-2, ScribT). Scribner.

Endless Universe. Marion Zimmer Bradley. 1984. pap. 2.95 o.s.i. (ISBN 0-441-20668-9). Ace Bks.

Endless War: Fifty Years of Struggle in Vietnam. James P. Harrison. (Illus.). 384p. 1983. pap. text ed. 8.95 o.p. (ISBN 0-07-026836-3). McGraw.

Endless Waves. Geraldine C. Little. 50p. 1985. 4.95 o.p. (ISBN 0-934536-24-4). Merging Media.

Endocrine Disorders. Ed. by Helen Hamilton & Minnie B. Rose. LC 84-5509. (Nurse's Clinical Library). (Illus.). 192p. 1984. text ed. 19.95 o.p. (ISBN 0-916730-71-9). Springhouse Pub.

Endocrine Disorders & Tumors in Children: Pathology of Sexual Development, Vol. 16. Ed. by P. P. Rickham. (Progress in Pediatric Surgery). (Illus.). 206p. 1983. text ed. 27.50 o.p. (ISBN 0-8067-1516-2). Urban & S.

Endocrine Function of the Human Adrenal Cortex. Ed. by V. H. James et al. (Serono Symposium Ser.). 1979. 93.00 o.p. (ISBN 0-12-380160-5). Acad Pr.

Endocrine Function of the Human Ovary. Ed. by V. H. T. James et al. 1976. 98.00 o.p. (ISBN 0-12-380150-8). Acad Pr.

Endocrine Function of the Human Testis: Proceedings. Symposium at University of Florence, Italy Staff. Ed. by V. H. James et al. 1973. 82.50 o.p. (ISBN 0-12-380101-X). Acad Pr.

Endocrine Hypothalamus. Ed. by S. L. Jeffcoate & J. S. Hutchinson. 1979. 93.00 o.p. (ISBN 0-12-382150-9). Acad Pr.

Endocrine Lung in Health & Disease. Kenneth L. Becker & Adi Gazdar. (Illus.). 639p. 1984. write for info. o.p. (ISBN 0-7216-1007-2). Saunders.

Endocrine Treatment of Breast Cancer: A New Approach. Ed. by B. Henningsen et al. (Recent Results in Cancer Research: Vol. 71). (Illus.). 260p. 1981. 49.00 o.p. (ISBN 0-387-09781-3). Springer-Verlag.

Endocrines & Osmoregulation: A Comparative Account of the Regulation of Water & Salt in Vertebrates. Peter J. Bentley. LC 72-131549. (Zoophysiology & Ecology Ser.: Vol. 1). (Illus.). 1971. 36.00 o.p. (ISBN 0-387-05273-9). Springer-Verlag.

Endocrinology. P. Marsden & A. McCullagh. (Management of Common Diseases in Family Practice Ser.). (Illus.). 200p. 1985. 19.50 o.p. (ISBN 0-88416-527-2). Year Bk Med.

Endocrinology: A Logical Approach for Clinicians. William Jubiz. (Illus.). 1979. text ed. 30.00 o.p. (ISBN 0-07-033065-4). McGraw.

Endocrinology: A Logical Approach for Clinicians. William Jubiz. 1980. pap. text ed. 18.95 o.p. (ISBN 0-07-033066-2). McGraw.

Endocrinology & Metabolism. Philip Felig et al. 1981. text ed. 95.00 o.p. (ISBN 0-07-020387-3). McGraw.

Endocrinology, Neuroendocrinology, Neuropeptides-Part II: Proceedings of the 28th International Congress of Physiological Sciences, Budapest, 1980. Ed. by E. Stark et al. LC 80-42046. (Advances in Physiological Sciences Ser.: Vol. 14). (Illus.). 350p. 1981. 57.00 o.p. (ISBN 0-08-026871-4). Pergamon.

Endocrinology, Neuroendocrinology, Neuropeptides-Part 1: Proceedings of the 28th International Congress of Physiological Sciences, Budapest, 1980. Ed. by E. Stark et al. LC 80-42047. (Advances in Physiological Sciences: Vol. 13). (Illus.). 350p. 1981. 57.00 o.p. (ISBN 0-08-026827-7). Pergamon.

Endodontic Therapy. 3rd ed. Franklin S. Weine. LC 81-14194. (Illus.). 692p. 1982. text ed. 55.95 o.p. (ISBN 0-8016-5380-0). Mosby.

Endodontics. 2nd ed. Nicholls. 365p. 1977. 38.50 o.p. (ISBN 0-7236-0427-4, Pub. by John Wright UK). Butterworth.

Endogenous & Exogenous Opiate Agonists & Antagonists: Proceedings of the International Narcotic Club Conference, 11-15 June 1979, North Falmouth, Massachusetts, U. S. A. Ed. by E. Leong Way. (Book Supplement to Pergamon Journal Life Sciences). (Illus.). 600p. 1980. 155.00 o.p. (ISBN 0-08-025488-8). Pergamon.

Endometriosis: A Woman's Guide to a Common but Often Undetected Disease that Can Cause Infertility & Other Major Medical Problems. Julia Older. 240p. 1984. 15.95 o.s.i. (ISBN 0-684-18057-X, ScribT). Scribner.

Endoscopic Sphincterotomy of the Papilla of Vater. Ed. by L. Demling & M. Classen. LC 77-99149. 108p. 1978. pap. 27.50 o.p. (ISBN 0-88416-242-7). Year Bk Med.

Endoscopy in Primates & Other Experimental Animals. Ed. by R. M. Harrison. (Journal of Medical Primatology: Vol. 5, No. 2). (Illus.). 1976. 20.00 o.p. (ISBN 3-8055-2428-5). S Karger.

Ends & Means of Reducing Income Poverty. Robert J. Lampman. 1971. 19.50 o.p. (ISBN 0-12-435250-2). Acad Pr.
Ends & Odds: Dramatic Pieces. Samuel Beckett. 1976. pap. 3.95 o.p. (ISBN 0-394-17918-8, E680, Ever). Grove.
Endurance. Alfred Lansing. (YA) (gr. 7 up). 1976. pap. 1.75 o.p. (ISBN 0-380-00670-7, 29363). Avon.
Endurance Racing. Sylvia Wilkinson. LC 80-27450. (World of Racing Ser.). (Illus.). 48p. (gr. 4 up). 1981. PLB 11.93 o.p. (ISBN 0-516-04712-4); pap. 3.95 o.p. (ISBN 0-516-44712-2). Childrens.
Endure No Longer. Martha Albrand. 1973. pap. 1.25 o.p. (ISBN 0-380-01166-2, 17467). Avon.
Enduring Art of Japan. Langdon Warner. (Illus.). (YA) (gr. 9 up). 1971. pap. 7.95 o.p. (ISBN 0-394-17392-9, E579, Ever). Grove.
Enduring Hemingway: An Anthology of a Lifetime in Literature. Ernest Hemingway. Ed. by Charles Scribner. LC 73-15476. 857p. 1974. Encore Ed. 7.95 o.p. (ISBN 0-684-17310-7, ScribT). Scribner.
Enduring Hills. 2nd ed. Janice H. Giles. 1971. 7.95 o.p. (ISBN 0-395-12042-X). HM.
Enduring Hills. Janice H. Giles. 1984. lib. bdg. 17.50 o.p. (ISBN 0-8161-3648-3, Large Print Bks). G K Hall.
Enduring Passion. Irma Walker. (Orig.). 1987. pap. 3.95 o.p. (ISBN 0-440-12515-4). Dell.
Enduring Satisfaction. William P. McEwen. (ISBN 0-8022-1017-1). Philos Lib.
Enduring Values in a Changing Society. Mary J. McCormick. LC 75-18288. 1975. 10.00 o.p. (ISBN 0-87304-128-3). Family Serv.
Eneide de Virgile, Prince des Poetes Latines. Publius Vergilius Maro. Repr. of 1560 ed. 63.00 o.p. (ISBN 0-685-02159-9). Johnson Repr.
Enemies. Brian J. Royal. 1978. pap. 1.75 o.p. (ISBN 0-8439-0644-8, Pub. by Leisure Bks CT). Dorchester Pub Co.
Enemies: A Love Story. Isaac Bashevis Singer. 1981. pap. 2.95 o.p. (ISBN 0-449-24065-7, Crest). Fawcett.
Enemies of Poetry. W. B. Stanford. 181p. 1985. pap. 9.95x o.p. (ISBN 0-7102-0586-4). Routledge Chapman & Hall.
Enemies of Poetry. W. Bedell Stanford. 1980. 26.95x o.p. (ISBN 0-7100-0460-5). Routledge Chapman & Hall.
Enemies of Society. Paul Johnson. LC 76-54230. 1977. 9.95 o.p. (ISBN 0-689-10798-6, Atheneum). Macmillan.
Enemies of the System. Brian Aldiss. 112p. 1981. pap. 1.95 o.p. (ISBN 0-380-53793-1, 53793-1). Avon.
Enemy at Green Knowe. Lucy M. Boston. LC 78-71151. (Illus.). (gr. 4-7). 1979. pap. 4.95 o.p. (ISBN 0-15-628792-7, VoyB). HarBraceJ.
Enemy at Green Knowe see Adventures at Green Knowe.
Enemy Countries, Axis-Controlled Europe, 9 vols. (Axis A: Nos. 1-192). 1945. 710.00 o.p. (ISBN 3-601-00016-4). Kraus Intl.
Enemy in Sight. Bill Bragg. (Orig.). 1980. pap. 1.75 o.p. (ISBN 0-505-51530-X, Pub. by Tower Bks). Dorchester Pub Co.
Enemy in Sight. Bill Bragg. (Gunsmoke Western Ser.). 176p. 1988. text ed. 12.95 o.p. (ISBN 0-85997-859-1, Pub. by Firecrest Pub Ltd). Prescott Pr NH.
Enemy Is Listening. Aileen Clayton. (Ballantine Espionage Intelligence Library: No. 22). 416p. 1982. pap. 3.95 o.s.i. (ISBN 0-345-30250-8). Ballantine.
Enemy Seas. Gordon D. Shirreffs. (gr. 6-8). 1965. 3.50 o.s.i. (ISBN 0-664-32359-6, Westminster). Westminster John Knox.
Enemy Within. Steven Charles. (Private School Ser.: No. 5). (YA) (gr. 7 up). 1987. pap. 2.50 o.p. (ISBN 0-671-60330-2). Archway.
Enemy Within-Without. Alexander Duddington. 1985. 10.00x o.p. (ISBN 0-317-62052-5, Guild of Pastoral Psych). State Mutual Bk.
Enemy Within-Without Psychotherapy & Morals Psychotherapy-What It Is. William P. Kraemer. 1985. 10.00x o.p. (ISBN 0-317-62053-3, Guild of Pastoral Psych). State Mutual Bk.
Energetic Diabetic: A Personal Fitness Guide. Nell Armstrong & Diane Wakat. (Illus.). 304p. 1985. pap. 14.95 o.p. (ISBN 0-89303-437-1). P-H.
Energetics of Mitochondria. rev. ed. J. B. Chappell. Ed. by J. J. Head. LC 77-70873. (Carolina Biology Readers Ser.: No. 19). (Illus.). 32p. (gr. 10 up). 1979. pap. 2.30 o.p. (ISBN 0-89278-219-6, 45-9619). Carolina Biological.
Energi. Paul Williams. 1974. pap. 3.50 o.p. (ISBN 0-446-32445-0). Warner Bks.
Energie: Economie et Prospective. A. Gardel. LC 79-40986. (Illus.). 1979. 105.00 o.p. (ISBN 0-08-024782-2). Pergamon.
Energie et Societe. M. de Perrot. 1982. pap. 51.00 o.p. (ISBN 0-08-027078-6). Pergamon.
Energie Humaine see Human Energy.
Energie Nucleaire et Societe. M. de Perrot. 1982. pap. 26.00 o.p. (ISBN 0-08-027077-8). Pergamon.
Energie: Von der Tretmuhle zum Kernreaktor. Werner F. Striedieck. LC 65-12034. (Orig., Ger.). 1965. pap. text ed. 4.95x o.p. (ISBN 0-89197-141-6). Irvington.
Energies of Universe. Eugene Fritz. 1960. (ISBN 0-8022-0550-X). Philos Lib.
Energistic Materials Symposium: Proceedings, Chicago IL, 7-9 May 1968. (Science of Advanced Materials & Process Engineering Ser., Vol. 13). 470p. 20.00 o.p. (ISBN 0-938994-13-1). SAMPE.
Energizing Your Investments. Venita VanCaspel. 1981. 1.50 o.p. (ISBN 0-8359-1678-2, Reston). P-H.
Energy. Gerald M. Crawley. (Illus.). 320p. 1975. text ed. write for info. o.p. (ISBN 0-02-325580-3, 32558). Macmillan.
Energy: A Bibliography of Social Science & Related Literature. Denton E. Morrison. LC 74-4800. (Reference Library of Social Science: No. 9). 185p. 1975. lib. bdg. 28.00 o.p. (ISBN 0-8240-1096-5). Garland Pub.
Energy: A National Issue. Francis X. Murray. LC 76-52878. (Illus.). 1976. pap. text ed. 3.95 o.p. (ISBN 0-89206-001-8). CSI Studies.
Energy: A Strategy for International Action. John C. Campbell et al. (Triangle Papers: No. 6). 1974. pap. 6.00 o.p. Trilateral Comm.
Energy: An Issue of the Eighties. Ed. by Donna R. Plesser et al. (Information Plus Ser.). 120p. 1987. pap. 16.95 o.p. (ISBN 0-936474-65-3). Info Plus TX.
Energy: An Issue of the Eighty's. rev. ed. Ed. by Mark A. Siegel & Nancy R. Jacobs. (Instructional Aides Ser.). 106p. 1983. pap. text ed. 13.95 o.p. (ISBN 0-936474-28-9). Info Plus TX.
Energy & Combustion Science: Selected Papers from Progress in Energy & Combustion Science. Ed. by N. A. Chigier. LC 79-40860. (Illus.). 1979. 63.00 o.p. (ISBN 0-08-024781-4); pap. 21.00 o.p. (ISBN 0-08-024780-6). Pergamon.
Energy & Economic Myths. Nicholas Georgescu-Roegen. LC 76-10265. 1977. text ed. 34.00 o.p. (ISBN 0-08-021027-9); pap. text ed. 13.25 o.p. (ISBN 0-08-021056-2). Pergamon.
Energy & Education: Teaching Alternatives. Ed. by Fredrick E. Posthuma. 144p. 1978. pap. 10.95 o.p. (ISBN 0-8106-1492-8). NEA.
Energy & Environment. Allan R. Evans. 265p. 1980. pap. text ed. 8.95x o.p. (ISBN 0-933694-15-6). COMPress.
Energy & Finite Element Methods in Structural Mechanics. Irving H. Shames & Clive L. Dym. 732p. 1985. text ed. 46.95 o.p. (ISBN 0-07-056392-6). McGraw.
Energy & Housing: Symposium - Open University, Milton Keynes, Building Science, Suppl. Ed. by B. W. Jones. 160p. 1975. pap. 40.00 o.p. (ISBN 0-08-018968-7). Pergamon.
Energy & Resource Recovery from Waste. Stephen C. Schwarz & Calvin R. Brunner. LC 83-13110. (Energy Tech. Rev. No. 86; Pollution Tech. Rev. No. 102). 272p. 1984. 32.00 o.p. (ISBN 0-8155-0959-6). Noyes.
Energy & Sea Power - Challenge for the Decade. Ed. by Don Walsh & Marjorie Cappellari. (Illus.). 206p. 1981. 50.00 o.p. (ISBN 0-08-028035-8). Pergamon.
Energy & Social Change. James O'Toole. Ed. by Center for Futures Research. LC 76-44015. 1975. pap. 6.95 o.p. (ISBN 0-262-65011-8). MIT Pr.
Energy & Social Policy. Ed. by Jonathan Bradshaw & Toby Harris. 208p. (Orig.). 1983. pap. 13.95x o.p. (ISBN 0-7100-9503-1). Routledge Chapman & Hall.
Energy & the Chemical Sciences. S. D. Christian & J. J. Zuckerman. 1978. 45.00 o.p. (ISBN 0-08-022094-0). Pergamon.
Energy & the Earth Machine. Donald E. Carr. 288p. 1976. 12.95 o.p. (ISBN 0-393-06407-7). Norton.
Energy & the Environment. John M. Fowler. (Illus.). 480p. 1975. text ed. 26.95 o.p. (ISBN 0-07-021720-3). McGraw.
Energy & the Mitochondrion. David E. Green & Harold Baum. 1970. 14.25 o.p. (ISBN 0-12-297950-8). Acad Pr.
Energy Aspects of the Forest Industries: Proceedings of a Seminar Organized by the Timber Committee of the United Nations Economic Commission for Europe, Udine, Italy 13-17 Nov. 1978. United Nations Economic Commission for Europe, Geneva, Switzerland. LC 79-42869. (Illus.). 428p. 1979. 95.00 o.p. (ISBN 0-08-025661-9). Pergamon.
Energy Auditing for Commercial Buildings: A Selected Bibliography. Anthony G. White. (Architecture Ser.: A 1432). 7p. 1985. 2.00 o.p. (ISBN 0-89028-482-2). Vance Biblios.
Energy Audits Manual. Dale, Jack, & Associates, Staff. (Illus.). 332p. 1984. pap. 49.50 o.s.i. (ISBN 0-86587-031-4). Gov Insts.
Energy Balances of Developing Countries Nineteen Seventy-One tp Nineteen Eighty-Two. OECD Staff. 346p. (Orig.). 1984. pap. 30.00x o.p. (ISBN 92-64-02543-X). OECD.
Energy Balloon. Stewart Udall et al. LC 74-14903. 288p. 1974. text ed. 7.95 o.p. (ISBN 0-07-065732-7). McGraw.
Energy Bibliography & Index, Vol. 1. Texas A & M University Library Staff. LC 77-93150. 1384p. 1978. 375.00x o.p. (ISBN 0-87201-965-9). Gulf Pub.
Energy Choices in a Democratic Society. Nuclear & Alternative Energy Systems Committee, Consumption, Location & Occupational Patterns Resource Group Synthesis Panel. LC 80-81335. (Study of Nuclear & Alternative Energy Systems Ser.). xvii, 136p. 1980. pap. text ed. 7.95x o.p. (ISBN 0-309-03045-5). Natl Acad Pr.
Energy Conservation. (Ad Hoc Committee Reports). 14p. 1986. 2.00 o.p. (ISBN 0-318-17728-5). NARUC.
Energy Conservation. McGraw.
Energy Conservation Idea Handbook. 171p. (Orig.). 1980. pap. 12.00 o.p. (ISBN 0-89492-047-2). Acad Educ Dev.
Energy Conservation in Biological Membranes: April 6-8, 1978, Mosbach, Germany. Ed. by G. Schaefer & M. Klingenberg. (Colloquium Mosbach Ser.: Vol. 29). (Illus.). 1978. 48.00 o.p. (ISBN 0-387-09079-7). Springer-Verlag.
Energy Conservation in Building Heating & Air Conditioning Systems. Ed. by R. Gopal et al. 112p. 1978. 18.00 o.p. (ISBN 0-685-66798-7, H00116). ASME.
Energy Conservation in Buildings & Industrial Plants. Milton Meckler. (Illus.). 1980. text ed. 31.50 o.p. (ISBN 0-07-041195-6). McGraw.
Energy Conservation in Heating, Cooling & Ventilating Buildings: Proceedings of Heat & Mass Transfer in Buildings Summer Seminar, Dubrovnik, Yugoslavia, Aug. 29-Sept. 3, 1977, 2 vols. Heat & Mass Transfer in Buildings Summer Seminar Staff. Ed. by C. J. Hoogendoorn & N. Afgan. LC 78-1108. (Thermal & Fluids Engineering Ser.). 901p. 1978. Set. text ed. 195.00 o.p. (ISBN 0-89116-161-9). Hemisphere Pub.
Energy Conservation in Hot Climates. Dieter Holm. (Illus.). 160p. 1983. pap. 32.50 o.p. (ISBN 0-89397-159-6). Nichols Pub.
Energy Conservation in Industry, 3 Vols. Ed. by A. S. Strub & H. Ehringer. 1089p. 1984. 259.50 o.p. (ISBN 0-89116-447-2). Hemisphere Pub.
Energy Conservation Measures: Proceedings of the International Symposium, Kuwait, 6-8 February 1983. Ed. by J. D. Parker. LC 83-25137. 332p. 1984. 85.00 o.p. (ISBN 0-08-031141-5). Pergamon.
Energy Conservation: Proceedings of the Energy Research & Development Administration Conference Held at the University of Miami, Dec. 1975. Ed. by T. Nejat Veziroglu. 1977. pap. 170.00 o.p. (ISBN 0-08-022134-3). Pergamon.
Energy Conservation Standards: For Building Design, Construction & Operation. Fred S. Dubin & Chalmers G. Long, Jr. 432p. 1983. pap. text ed. 25.95 o.p. (ISBN 0-07-017884-4). McGraw.
Energy Conservation Through Building Design. Donald A. Watson. 1979. text ed. 29.95 o.p. (ISBN 0-07-068460-X). McGraw.
Energy Conservation Through Fluid Film Lubrication Technology: Frontiers in Research & Design. Ed. by S. Rohde. 224p. 1979. 30.00 o.p. (ISBN 0-317-33494-8, G00160); members 15.00 o.p. (ISBN 0-317-33495-6). ASME.
Energy Conservation Through Waste Utilization: Proceedings of 1978 National Waste Processing Conference. 500p. 1978. 90.00 o.p. (ISBN 0-685-92280-4, I00119). ASME.
Energy Conversion Engineering: Intersociety Energy Conversion Engineering Conference, 15th; Proceedings, 3 vols. 2669p. pap. 145.00 o.p. AIAA.
Energy Conversion Engineering: Proceedings, Fourteenth Intersociety Energy Conversion Engineering Conference, 2 vols. 2200p. softcover 121.00 o.p. (ISBN 0-8412-0513-2, 700039). Am Nuclear Soc.
Energy Conversion Engineering: Proceedings, Intersociety Energy Conversion Engineering Conference & American Nuclear Society Conference, Las Vegas, September 21-25, 1970, 2 Vols. 1300p. softcover 46.00 o.p. (ISBN 0-317-33008-X, 700003). Am Nuclear Soc.
Energy Conversion Engineering: Proceedings of the Intersociety Conference, 13th, San Diego, August 20-25, 3 vols. 3000p. soft 127.00 o.p. (ISBN 0-317-33020-9, 700029). Am Nuclear Soc.
Energy Cost & Consumption Report, 1980-1981 & 1981-1982. Higher Education Energy Task Force Staff. 180p. 15.00 o.p.; members 10.00 o.p. Assn Phys Plant Admin.
Energy Decision Making: The Interaction of Law & Policy. Joseph P. Tomain & Shelia S. Hollis. LC 81-47747. 224p. 1983. 26.50x o.p. (ISBN 0-669-04800-3). Lexington Bks.
Energy Deskbook. Samuel Glasstone. 464p. 1983. 37.95 o.p. (ISBN 0-442-22928-3). Van Nos Reinhold.
Energy Devices & Processes: Proceedings of a Workshop on the Second Law of Thermodynamics, Held at the George Washington University, Wash. D. C., 14-16 Aug. 1979. Ed. by A. B. Cambel. 300p. 1980. pap. 73.00 o.p. (ISBN 0-08-026704-1). Pergamon.
Energy Dictionary. V. Daniel Hunt. 1983. 32.95 o.p. (ISBN 0-442-27395-9); pap. 19.95 o.p. (ISBN 0-442-23787-1). Van Nos Reinhold.
Energy Directory 1983. Ed. by Joanne Terminello. LC 74-79869. 392p. 250.00 o.p. (ISBN 0-89947-014-9, EIC Intell). Bowker.
Energy, Ecology, Economy: A Framework for Environmental Policy. Gerald Garvey. (Illus.). 235p. 1972. pap. 4.95x o.p. (ISBN 0-393-09408-1). Norton.
Energy, Economic Growth, & the Environment. Ed. by Sam H. Schurr. 232p. 1973. pap. 9.95 o.p. (ISBN 0-317-60176-8). Resources Future.
Energy Economics & Management in Industry: Proceedings of the European Congress Held Algarve, Portugal, 2-5 April 1984. Ed. by D. A. Reay. 80p. 1985. pap. 22.00 o.p. (ISBN 0-08-032548-3). Pergamon.
Energy Education: Goals & Practices. Rodney F. Allen. LC 79-93115. (Fastback Ser.: No. 139). (Orig.). 1980. pap. 0.90 o.p. (ISBN 0-87367-139-2). Phi Delta Kappa.
Energy Education Programs: Perspectives for Community, Junior, & Technical Colleges. Mary Ann Settlemire. 1981. pap. 4.00 o.p. (ISBN 0-87117-104-X). Am Assn Comm Jr Coll.
Energy Efficiency & Conservation in the Asia-Pacific Region: Proceedings of the Fouth Workshop, Honolulu, Hawaii, June 2-5, 1981. Ed. by G. Y. Pauker. 200p. 1983. pap. 28.00 o.p. (ISBN 0-08-030532-6). Pergamon.
Energy-Efficient Church. Total Environmental Action, Inc. Staff. Ed. by Douglas Hoffman. LC 79-10432. (Illus.). 1979. pap. 4.95 o.p. (ISBN 0-8298-0362-9). Pilgrim NY.
Energy Efficient Electrical Steels: Proceedings TMS-AIME Fall Meeting, Pittsburgh, PA, 1980. Ed. by A. R. Marder & E. T. Stephenson. (Illus.). 219p. 26.00 o.p. (ISBN 0-89520-374-X); members 16.00 o.p. (ISBN 0-317-36238-0); student members 10.00 o.p. (ISBN 0-317-36239-9). ASM.
Energy-Efficient Site Design. Ed. by Gary O. Robinette. 176p. 1983. 29.95 o.p. (ISBN 0-442-22338-2). Van Nos Reinhold.
Energy, Electricity & Nuclear Power Estimates for the Period up to 2000: September, 1982. (Reference Data Ser.: No. 1). (Illus.). 57p. 1983. pap. 5.50 o.p. (ISBN 92-0-159182-9, IRDS1/2, IAEA). UNIPUB.
Energy Engineering. John W. Mitchell. LC 82-19977. 236p. 1983. 44.95 o.p. (ISBN 0-471-08772-6, Pub. by Wiley-Interscience). Wiley.
Energy Engineering & Management for Building Systems. William J. Coad. 320p. 1981. 41.95 o.p. (ISBN 0-442-25467-9). Van Nos Reinhold.
Energy Engineering Fundamentals: With Residential & Commercial Applications. Charles B. Schuder. 176p. 1982. 27.95 o.p. (ISBN 0-442-28109-9). Van Nos Reinhold.
Energy Evaluation of Energy Systems. Arthur P. Fraas. (Energy, Combustion & Environment Ser.). (Illus.). 704p. 1982. text ed. 54.95 o.p. (ISBN 0-07-021758-0). McGraw.
Energy Factbook. Richard C. Dorf. Ed. by Thomas J. Dembofsky. (Illus.). 256p. 1981. pap. text ed. 7.95 o.p. (ISBN 0-07-017629-9). McGraw.
Energy Factbook. Richard C. Dorf. 1981. text ed. 28.95 o.p. (ISBN 0-07-017623-X). McGraw.
Energy Finance, 1984. 88.00 o.p. (ISBN 0-8002-3164-3). Intl Pubns Serv.
Energy Flow Through the United States Economy: A Wall Chart. Center for Advanced Computation Staff. 1976. 15.00 o.p. (ISBN 0-252-00637-2). U of Ill Pr.
Energy for Development: Third World Options. Denis Hayes. LC 77-91821. (Worldwatch Papers). 1977. pap. 4.00 o.p. (ISBN 0-916468-14-3). Worldwatch Inst.
Energy, Forces & Resources. LC 83-26619. (Science Universe Ser.). (Illus.). 64p. (gr. 5 up). 1984. 9.95 o.p. (ISBN 0-668-06178-2, 6178-2). Arco.
Energy from Biological Processes. Office of Technology Assessment, Congress of the United States Staff. 200p. 1981. lib. bdg. 28.50x o.p. (ISBN 0-86531-171-4). Westview.
Energy from Heaven & Earth. Edward Teller. LC 79-4049. (Illus.). 322p. 1979. text ed. 21.95x o.p. (ISBN 0-7167-1063-3); pap. text ed. 13.95x o.p. (ISBN 0-7167-1064-1). W H Freeman.

Titles

Energy from the Sea: Marine Resource Readings. new ed. Ed. by Bernard L. Gordon. (Illus.). 1977. pap. 12.50 o.p. (ISBN 0-910258-07-4). Book & Tackle.

Energy from the Sun. (Wonders of Learning Kits Ser.). (gr. 3-6). 1980. incl. cass. & tchr's. guide 28.95 o.p. (ISBN 0-686-74409-8, 04973). Natl Geog.

Energy Guide: A Directory of Information Resources. Virginia Bemis. LC 77-10470. (Reference Library of Social Science: Vol. 43). 1977. lib. bdg. 33.00 o.p. (ISBN 0-8240-9870-6). Garland Pub.

Energy: Historical Development of the Concept. Ed. by R. Bruce Lindsay. LC 75-30719. (Benchmark Papers on Energy Ser.: Vol 1). 369p. 1975. 74.00 o.p. (ISBN 0-12-786963-8). Acad Pr.

Energy II: A Bibliography of 1975-1976 Social Science & Related Literature. Denton E. Morrison. (Reference Library of Social Science: Vol. 42). (Lc 76-052702). 1977. lib. bdg. 33.00 o.p. (ISBN 0-8240-9871-4). Garland Pub.

Energy in an Age of Limited Availability & Delimited Applicability. Philip Sporn. 1976. pap. 15.75 o.p. (ISBN 0-08-020857-6). Pergamon.

Energy in Mining: Proceedings of the First International Symposium on Energy in Mining, San Francisco California, 1982. Miller Freeman Publications, Inc. Staff. 250p. 1982. 3 ring binder 177.00 o.p. (ISBN 0-87930-145-7). Miller Freeman.

Energy in Packaging & Waste. A. V. Bridgwater & K. Lidgren. 1983. 64.50 o.p. (ISBN 0-442-30570-2). Van Nos Reinhold.

Energy in Perspective. 2nd ed. Jerry B. Marion & Marvin L. Roush. 1982. pap. 10.00 o.p. (ISBN 0-12-472276-8). Acad Pr.

Energy in the American Economy, 1850-1975: An Economic Study of Its History & Prospects. Sam Schurr & Bruce C. Netschert. LC 76-58896. (Resources for the Future, Inc.). 1977. Repr. of 1960 ed. lib. bdg. 49.00x o.p. (ISBN 0-8371-9471-7, SCEN). Greenwood.

Energy in the World of the Future. Hal Hellman. LC 72-90980. (World of the Future Ser.). (Illus.). 240p. (gr. 7 up). 1973. 6.95 o.p. (ISBN 0-87131-123-2). M Evans.

Energy in Transition: A Report on Energy Policy & Future Options. Mans Lonnroth & Peter Steen. LC 78-68827. 1980. 17.95x o.p. (ISBN 0-520-03881-9). U of Cal Pr.

Energy Information Locator: A Select Guide to Information Centers, Systems, Data Bases; Abstracing Services, Directories, Newsletters, Binder Services, & Journals. Ed. by Claire Mencke & Craig Horton. LC 74-79869. 1977. 35.00 o.p. (ISBN 0-89947-009-2, EIC Intell). Bowker.

Energy Investment Game: How to Play It & Win with Oil & Gas. W. A. Armfield, Jr. LC 80-19221. (Illus.). 222p. 1980. 24.95 o.p. (ISBN 0-87624-128-3, Inst Busn Plan); pap. 6.95 o.p. (ISBN 0-87624-127-5). P-H.

Energy Isn't Easy. Norman F. Smith. (Illus.). (gr. 6 up). 1984. 12.95 o.p. (ISBN 0-698-20584-7, Coward). Putnam Pub Group.

Energy Law in a Nutshell. Joseph P. Tomain. LC 81-11636. (Nutshell Ser.). 338p. 1981. pap. text ed. 9.95 o.p. (ISBN 0-314-60134-1). West Pub.

Energy-Linked Functions of Mitochondria. Ed. by Britton Chance. 1963. 54.00 o.p. (ISBN 0-12-167862-8). Acad Pr.

Energy Management & Conservation. Dale R. Patrick & Stephen W. Fardo. (Illus.). 304p. 1982. text ed. 39.00 o.p. (ISBN 0-13-277657-X). P-H.

Energy Management Principles: Applications, Benefits, Savings. Craig B. Smith. (Illus.). 400p. 1981. text ed. 75.00 o.p. (ISBN 0-08-028036-6); pap. text ed. 41.00 o.p. (ISBN 0-08-028811-1). Pergamon.

Energy Merchant. Rufus Jarman. (Social Studies Student Ser.). 1977. PLB 10.00 o.p. (ISBN 0-8239-0366-4). Rosen Group.

Energy Metabolism & the Regulation of Metabolic Processes in Mitochondria. Ed. by Myron A. Mehlman & Richard W. Hanson. 1972. 54.50 o.p. (ISBN 0-12-487850-4). Acad Pr.

Energy Metabolism: Proceedings, No. 11. Symposium on Energy Metabolism, Troon Scotland, 3d, 1964. Ed. by K. L. Blaxter. 1965. 72.00 o.p. (ISBN 0-12-105550-7). Acad Pr.

Energy Methods in Applied Mechanics. Henry L. Langhaar. LC 62-10925. 350p. 1962. 46.50x o.p. (ISBN 0-471-51711-9, Pub. by Wiley-Interscience). Wiley.

Energy Methods in Finite Element Analysis. Ed. by R. Glowinski et al. LC 78-13642. (Numerical Methods in Engineering Ser.). 361p. 1979. 102.00 o.p. (ISBN 0-471-99723-4, Pub. by Wiley-Interscience). Wiley.

Energy Modelling Studies & Conservation: Proceedings of a Seminar of the United Nations Economic Commission for Europe, Washington, D. C. 24-28 March 1980. UNECE Staff. (Illus.). 600p. 1982. 140.00 o.p. (ISBN 0-08-027416-1). Pergamon.

Energy-Money, Materials & Engineering: Proceedings of the Symposium Organised by the Institution of Chemical Engineers (in Conjunction with the American Institute of Chemical Engineers & Deutsche Vereinigung fur Chemie-und Verfahrenstechnik), London, U. K., October 12-15, 1982. Institution of Chemical Engineers Staff. (Institution of Chemical Engineers Symposium Ser.: No. 78). 475p. 1983. 75.00 o.s.i. (ISBN 0-08-028774-3). Pergamon.

Energy New Frontiers: Proceedings of the 22nd Intersociety Energy Conversion Engineering Conference (IECEC) 1987. 200.00 o.p. (ISBN 0-317-62913-1, P198). Soc Auto Engineers.

Energy Non-Crisis. 2nd, rev., enl. ed. Lindsey William & Clifford Wilson. 240p. pap. 3.95 o.p. (ISBN 0-89051-068-7). Master Bks.

Energy Options. Ed. by M. Barak & D. T. Swift-Hook. (IEE Conference Publication: No. 233). 421p. 1984. pap. 118.00 o.s.i. (ISBN 0-85296-290-8, IC233). Inst Elect Eng.

Energy Options & Policy Issues in Developing Countries. Darrel G. Fallen-Bailey & Trevor A. Byer. (Working Paper: No.350). vi, 107p. 1979. 5.00 o.p. (ISBN 0-686-36157-1, WP-0350). World Bank.

Energy Options: Real Economics & the Solar-Hydrogen System. John O. Bockris. LC 80-16311. 441p. 1980. 49.95x o.p. (ISBN 0-470-26915-4). Halsted Pr.

Energy Parks: Proceedings, American Nuclear Society Executive Conference, Arlington VA, 24-27 April 1977. 220p. 18.00 o.p. (ISBN 0-89448-303-X, 650004). Am Nuclear Soc.

Energy, Planning & Urban Form. Susan Owens. 118p. 1986. pap. 16.50 o.p. (ISBN 0-85086-118-7, 9918, Pub. by Pion England). Routledge Chapman & Hall.

Energy Planning for Buildings. Michael Sizemore et al. (Illus.). 1979. 14.00 o.p. (ISBN 0-913962-08-2); members 26.75 o.p. Am Inst Arch.

Energy-Policy Analysis & Congressional Action. Raymond C. Scheppach & Everett M. Ehrlich. LC 80-8993. (Illus.). 272p. 1982. 31.50x o.p. (ISBN 0-669-04490-3). Lexington Bks.

Energy Policy & Demand Management Policy. Mohan Munasinghe & Gunther Schramm. 464p. 1983. 37.95 o.p. (ISBN 0-442-25838-0). Van Nos Reinhold.

Energy Policy & Forecasting: Economic, Financial, & Technological Dimensions. Glenn R. DeSouza. LC 79-9671. (Arthur D. Little Bk.). 240p. 1981. 29.50x o.p. (ISBN 0-669-03614-5). Lexington Bks.

Energy Policy of the Soviet Union. Werner Gumpel. pap. 2.00 o.p. (ISBN 0-8179-4232-7). Hoover Inst Pr.

Energy Policy: The Global Challenge. Peter N. Nemetz. 1979. pap. text ed. 20.50x o.p. (ISBN 0-920380-30-1, Pub. by Inst Res Pub Canada). Gower Pub Co.

Energy R & D Decision Making for Canada. Karen Hartley. 108p. 1979. pap. text ed. 3.00x o.p. (ISBN 0-920380-40-9, Pub. by Inst Res Pub Canada). Gower Pub Co.

Energy, Regional Science & Public Policy. Ed. by M. Chatterji & P. Van Rompuy. 1976. pap. 20.00 o.p. (ISBN 0-387-07692-1). Springer-Verlag.

Energy Research & Development Activity 1974-1976. Smithsonian Science Information Exchange Inc. 1978. 100.00 o.p. (ISBN 0-08-023248-5). Pergamon.

Energy Research, Development & Demonstration in the IEA Countries, 1983. OECD Staff. 180p. (Orig.). 1984. pap. 22.00X o.p. (ISBN 92-64-12627-9). OECD.

Energy Research Programs Directory. Ed. by Jaques Cattell Press Staff. 444p. 1980. 75.00 o.p. (ISBN 0-8352-1242-4). Bowker.

Energy: Resource, Slave, Pollutant; a Physical Science Text. Robert S. Rouse & Robert O. Smith. 1975. write for info. o.p. (ISBN 0-02-404000-2). Macmillan.

Energy Resources. Andrew L. Simon. LC 74-28320. 176p. 1975. 36.00 o.p. (ISBN 0-08-018750-1); pap. 17.50 o.p. (ISBN 0-08-018751-X). Pergamon.

Energy Resources & Conservation Related to Built Environment: Proceedings of the International Conference, Dec. 7-12, 1980, Miami Beach, Florida, 2 vols. Ed. by Oktay Ural. (Pergamon Policy Studies on International Development). 1290p. 1981. Set. 270.00 o.p. (ISBN 0-08-027170-7). Pergamon.

Energy Risk Management. Ed. by G. T. Goodman & W. D. Rowe. LC 79-42931. 1980. 98.00 o.p. (ISBN 0-12-289680-7). Acad Pr.

Energy Saver Homes: Design Energy Consumption Versus Measured Energy Consumption of the 10 NAHB Energy Saver Homes. National Association of Home Builders Staff. 135p. 1983. pap. 10.00 o.p. (ISBN 0-86718-190-7). Nat Assn H Build.

Energy Saving Ideas for Mobile Equipment Designers. Society of Automotive Engineers Staff. LC 80-52982. 64p. 1980. Six papers. 18.00 o.p. (ISBN 0-89883-240-3, SP469). Soc Auto Engineers.

Energy Saving Lighting Systems. Prafulla C. Sorcar. 368p. 1982. 36.95 o.s.i. (ISBN 0-442-26430-5). Van Nos Reinhold.

Energy-Saving Projects. Sunset Magazine & Books Editors. LC 80-53485. (Illus.). 96p. (Orig.). 1981. pap. 4.95 o.p. (ISBN 0-376-01230-7, Sunset Bks.). Sunset-Lane.

Energy Storage & Redistribution in Molecules. Juergen Hinze. 610p. 1983. 115.00x o.p. (ISBN 0-306-41272-1, Plenum Pr). Plenum Pub.

Energy Storage, Compression, & Switching, Vol. 1. Ed. by W. H. Bostick et al. LC 75-42405. 538p. 1976. 85.00x o.p. (ISBN 0-306-30892-4, Plenum Pr). Plenum Pub.

Energy Storage, Compression, & Switching, Vol. 2. Ed. by V. Nardi et al. 1036p. 1982. 145.00x o.p. (ISBN 0-306-41014-1, Plenum Pr). Plenum Pub.

Energy Storage: Four Major Alternatives - Heat Storage, Cool Storage, Compressed Air Energy Storage & Underground Pumped Hydro Storage. Kenneth Pollack & Michael J. Gergen. Ed. by Perrin Stryker. LC 83-80664. 275p. (Orig.). pap. 29.50 o.p. (ISBN 0-918780-23-3). INFORM.

Energy Systems: An Analysis for Engineers & Policy Makers. James Bailey. (Energy Power & Environment: Vol. 2). 1978. 39.75 o.p. (ISBN 0-8247-6713-6). Dekker.

Energy Systems in the United States. Amr et al. (Energy, Power & Environment Ser.: Vol. 12). 512p. 1981. 89.75 o.p. (ISBN 0-8247-1275-7). Dekker.

Energy Technology Conference Proceedings. (Illus.). 211p. 1980. 30.00 o.p. (ISBN 0-915567-57-1, 52145). Natl Corrosion Eng.

Energy Technology Handbook. Douglas M. Considine. 1977. text ed. 92.50 o.p. (ISBN 0-07-012430-2). McGraw.

Energy Technology, No. 15: Repowering America. Ed. by Government Institutes, Inc. Staff. 964p. 1988. 87.00 o.s.i. (ISBN 0-86587-428-X). Gov Insts.

Energy Terminology: A Multi-Lingual Glossary. Ed. by World Energy Conference Staff. 275p. 1983. 120.00 o.p. (ISBN 0-08-029314-X, B110); pap. 44.00 o.p. (ISBN 0-08-029315-8). Pergamon.

Energy, the Biomass Options. Henry R. Bungay. LC 80-19645. (Alternate Energy Ser.). 347p. 1981. 48.95x o.p. (ISBN 0-471-04386-9). Wiley.

Energy: The Countdown: A Report to the Club of Rome. Thierry De Montbrial. LC 78-41103. (Illus.). 1979. 64.00 o.p. (ISBN 0-08-024225-1); pap. 18.75 o.p. (ISBN 0-08-024224-3). Pergamon.

Energy: The Imperative of a Trilateral Approach. John C. Campbell et al. (Triangle Papers: No. 5). 1974. pap. 6.00 o.p. Trilateral Comm.

Energy: The Power to Work. Joan Solomon. (Science in a Social Context Ser.). 1986. pap. text ed. 6.95x o.p. (ISBN 0-631-91010-7); tchr's guide 9.95 o.p. Basil Blackwell.

Energy: The Solar Hydrogen Alternative. J. O. Bockris. LC 75-19125. 365p. 1976. 47.95x o.p. (ISBN 0-470-08429-4). Halsted Pr.

Energy Use Management. J. C. Denton. 1983. pap. 45.00 o.p. (ISBN 0-08-030533-4). Pergamon.

Energy Use Management: Proceedings of the International Conference, 4 vols. Ed. by Rocco Fazzolare & C. B. Smith. LC 77-86455. 1978. Set. 705.00 o.p. (ISBN 0-08-021723-0). Pergamon.

Energy, Vol. 4 (incl. 1985-1987 Supplements) Ed. by Eleanor C. Goldstein. (Social Issues Resources Ser.). 1987. 30.00 o.p. (ISBN 0-89777-121-4). Soc Issues.

Energy War: Reports from the Front. Harvey Wasserman. LC 79-89989. 276p. 1979. 12.95 o.p. (ISBN 0-88208-105-5); pap. 5.95 o.p. (ISBN 0-88208-106-3). Chicago Review.

Enfant de la Haute Mer. Jules Supervielle. 170p. 1931. 4.95 o.p. (ISBN 0-686-55092-7). Schoenhof.

Enfant de la Haute Mer. Jules Supervielle. (Illus.). 152p. 1973. 8.95 o.p. (ISBN 0-686-55094-3). Schoenhof.

Enfants Humilies Journal (1939-1940) Georges Bernanos. pap. 9.95 o.p. (ISBN 0-685-23911-X). French & Eur.

Enforcement of Money Judgments. Louis A. Kass. 1964. pap. 3.50x o.p. (ISBN 0-87526-031-4). Gould.

Eng in America Book Pk, No. 10. (Our Nations Heritage Ser.). Date not set. (ISBN 0-07-375415-3). McGraw.

Engeldk-Svensk Pocket Dictionary (Prisma Modern) & Grammar. Gomer. 1985. pap. 14.00x o.p. (ISBN 91-518-1148-0, S208). Vanous.

Engels, Armies & Revolution: The Revolutionary Tactics of Classical Marxism. Martin Berger. LC 77-24300. 239p. 1977. 25.00 o.p. (ISBN 0-208-01650-3, Archon). Shoe String.

Engelsk-Svensk Ordbok (Prisma Modern) 3rd. ed. Bror Danielsson. 396p. (Orig.). 1986. text ed. 20.00x o.p. (ISBN 91-518-1296-7, S-205); Svensk-engelsk, 4th Ed. 1984. pap. text ed. 16.75x o.p. (SW-204). Vanous.

Engelsman's General Construction Cost Guide. Engelsman. 1985. pap. 39.95 o.p. (ISBN 0-442-26704-5). Van Nos Reinhold.

Engelsman's General Construction Cost Guide, 1984. Coert Engelsman. 1983. pap. 29.50 o.p. (ISBN 0-442-26678-2). Van Nos Reinhold.

Engelsman's Maintenance Manual for Condominiums: Cooperatives & Rental Apartment Complexes. Coert Englesman. 200p. 1983. pap. 43.95 o.p. (ISBN 0-442-22251-3). Van Nos Reinhold.

Engine & Tractor Power. Carroll E. Goering. 1986. text ed. 34.00 o.p. (ISBN 0-534-05814-0, 77F6068, PWS-Kent Ser Tech). PWS-Kent Pub.

Engine Emissions: Pollutant Formation & Measurement. Ed. by G. S. Springer & D. J. Patterson. LC 71-188716. 372p. 1973. 65.00x o.p. (ISBN 0-306-30585-2, Plenum Pr). Plenum Pub.

Engine Swapping. Ed. by Hot Rod Magazine Editors. (Hot Rod Shop Ser.). (Illus.). 176p. 1981. pap. 8.95 o.p. (ISBN 0-8227-6014-2). Petersen Pub.

Engineering. Alexander P. Gest. LC 63-10287. (Our Debt to Greece & Rome Ser). Repr. of 1930 ed. 17.50x o.p. (ISBN 0-8154-0078-0). Cooper Sq.

Engineering: A Decision Making Process. George E. Morris. LC 76-13090. (Illus.). 1977. pap. 13.50 o.p. (ISBN 0-395-24546-X). HM.

Engineering Acoustics & Noise Control. Conrad J. Hemond, Jr. (Illus.). 208p. 1983. text ed. 64.00 o.p. (ISBN 0-13-278911-6). P-H.

Engineering: An Introduction to a Creative Profession Instructor's Manual. 5th ed. George C. Beakley et al. 68p. 1986. write for info. o.p. (ISBN 0-02-307100-1). Macmillan.

Engineering & Scientific Microcomputers & Workstations. 221p. 1983. 985.00x o.p. (ISBN 0-88694-542-9). Intl Res Dev.

Engineering & Technical Handbook. reference ed. Donald G. McNeese & Albert L. Hoag. 1956. text ed. 39.33 o.p. (ISBN 0-13-277434-8). P-H.

Engineering & Technology Catalog, 1984. Ed. by Elsevier Science Publishing Company Staff. Date not set. write for info. o.p. Elsevier.

Engineering & Technology Degrees Fall 1986. R. A. Ellis. 230p. (Orig.). 1987. Set. pap. 230.00 o.p. (ISBN 0-87615-037-7). AAES.

Engineering & Technology Degrees, Fall 1986, 2 vols. R. A. Ellis & Engineering Manpower Commission Staff. 1987. Pt. I (By School), 50 pgs. 89.00 o.p. (ISBN 0-87615-047-4); Pt. II (By Minorities), 205 pgs. 115.00 o.p. AAES.

Engineering & Technology Degrees 1985: By Curriculum, Pt. III. Engineering Manpower Commission & R. A. Ellis. 86p. (Orig.). 1986. pap. 60.00 o.p. (ISBN 0-87615-065-2). AAES.

Engineering & Technology Degrees, 1986: By Curriculum, Pt. III. Engineering Manpower Commission & R. A. Ellis. 75p. (Orig.). 1987. pap. 89.00 o.p. (ISBN 0-87615-067-9). AAES.

Engineering & Technology Degrees, 1985: Complete Set. Engineering Manpower Commission & R. A. Ellis. (Orig.). 1986. Set. pap. 200.00 o.p. (ISBN 0-87615-036-9). AAES.

Engineering & Technology Degrees 1985: Pt. II by Minorities. Engineering Manpower Commission & R. A. Ellis. 145p. (Orig.). 1986. pap. 100.00 o.p. (ISBN 0-87615-056-3). AAES.

Engineering & Technology Degrees 1985: Pt. I by School. Engineering Manpower Commission & R. A. Ellis. 50p. (Orig.). 1986. pap. 75.00 o.p. (ISBN 0-87615-046-6). AAES.

Engineering & Technology Enrollments Fall 1985: Pt. I, Engineering Enrollments. Engineering Manpower Commission. Ed. by R. A. Ellis. 410p. 1984. pap. 100.00 o.p. (ISBN 0-87615-086-5). AAES.

Engineering & Technology Enrollments, Fall 1985: Pt. II-Technology Enrollments. Engineering Manpower Commission. Ed. by R. A. Ellis. 300p. 1985. pap. 100.00 o.p. (ISBN 0-87615-096-2). AAES.

Engineering & Technology Enrollments, Fall 1985. Engineering Manpower Commission & R. A. Ellis. (Orig.). 1985. pap. 195.00 o.p. (ISBN 0-87615-076-8). AAES.

Engineering Application Software. Ed. by Jim Fitzgerald. 400p. 1987. 125.00 o.p. DATA Busn Pub.

Engineering Applications of Fracture Analysis: Proceedings of the First National Conference on Fracture Held in Johannesburg, South Africa, 1979. Ed. by G. G. Garrett & D. L. Marriott. LC 80-41074. (International Ser. on the Strength & Fractures of Materials & Structures). (Illus.). 440p. 1980. 93.00 o.p. (ISBN 0-08-025437-3). Pergamon.

Engineering Applications of Holography: Proceeding of the SPIE Seminar, Los Angeles, 1972. Society of Photo-Optical Instrumentation Engineers Staff. 400p. 28.00 o.p. (ISBN 0-89252-097-3). SPIE.

Engineering Applications of Lasers & Holography. Winston E. Kock. LC 75-17507. (Optical Physics & Engineering Ser.). (Illus.). 400p. 1975. 65.00x o.p. (ISBN 0-306-30849-5, Plenum Pr). Plenum Pub.

Engineering Calculations in Radiative Heat Transfer. W. A. Gray & R. Muller. LC 73-17321. 176p. 1974. 45.00 o.p. (ISBN 0-08-017786-7); pap. 45.00 o.p. (ISBN 0-08-017787-5). Pergamon.

Engineering Challenges in the 1980's, Vol. 1. Frwd. by L. Maunder. (Proceedings of the Engineering Section of the British Association for the Advancement of Science Ser.). (Illus.). 192p. 1982. text ed. 97.50 o.p. (ISBN 0-89116-348-4, Pub. by Cambridge Info & Res Serv England). Hemisphere Pub.

Engineering Drawing for Advanced Students. P. M. Dunne. 1967. pap. text ed. 4.20 o.p. (ISBN 0-08-012135-7). Pergamon.

Engineering Drawing for Technicians, Vol. 1. O. Ostrowsky. (Illus.). 94p. 1979. pap. 21.00x o.p. (ISBN 0-7131-3408-9). Trans-Atl Phila.

Engineering Drawing for Technicians, Vol. 2. O. Ostrowsky. 96p. 1981. pap. 22.00x o.p. (ISBN 0-7131-3429-1). Trans-Atl Phila.

Engineering Drawing form the Beginning, Vol. 2. M. F. Cousins. 1970. 17.75 o.p. (ISBN 0-08-006853-7); text ed. 29.00 o.p. (ISBN 0-08-006854-5). Pergamon.

Engineering Drawing from the Beginning. M. F. Cousins. 1964. Vol. 1. 1964. 30.00 o.p. (ISBN 0-08-010839-3); pap. 12.00 o.p. (ISBN 0-08-010840-7). Pergamon.

Engineering Economics. James L. Riggs. (McGraw-Hill Ser. in Industrial Engineering & Management Science). (Illus.). 1977. text ed. 32.95 o.p. (ISBN 0-07-052860-8, C). McGraw.

Engineering Economics. Ollie Smidt. 7.00 o.p. (ISBN 0-317-06289-1). Intertec IL.

Engineering Economics for Professional Engineers' Examinations. 2nd ed. Max Kurtz. (Illus.). 288p. 1975. text ed. 39.95 o.p. (ISBN 0-07-035675-0). McGraw.

Engineering Economics: Problems & Solutions. Sam R. Davidson. LC 83-11792. 224p. (Orig.). 1983. pap. text ed. 12.00 o.p. (ISBN 0-668-05862-5, 5862). Arco.

Engineering Economy. 6th ed. Walter J. Fabrycky & Gerald J. Thuesen. (Illus.). 624p. 1984. text ed. 50.00 o.p. (ISBN 0-13-277723-1). P-H.

Engineering Electromagnetic Fields & Waves. Carl T. Johnk. LC 74-13567. 655p. 1975. (ISBN 0-471-44289-5). Wiley.

Engineering Electromagnetics. D. T. Thomas. 416p. 1973. 115.00 o.p. (ISBN 0-08-016778-0). Pergamon.

Engineering Equipment for Foundries: Proceedings. Seminar on Engineering Equipment for Foundries & Advanced Methods of Producing Such Equipment, Geneva, 1977. Ed. by United Nations Economic Commission for Europe, Geneva. (Illus.). 1979. 125.00 o.p. (ISBN 0-08-022421-0). Pergamon.

Engineering Evaluation of Nuclear Power Reactor Decommissioning Alternatives (AIF-NESP-009) Atomic Industries Forum, Inc., Nuclear Energy Services Division Staff. (National Environmental Studies Project: NESP Reports). 480p. 1976. 40.00 o.p. (ISBN 0-318-13569-8); NESP sponsors 20.00 o.p. (ISBN 0-318-13570-1). US Coun Energy Awareness.

Engineering Field Theory. A. J. Baden-Fuller. 272p. 1973. 65.00 o.p. (ISBN 0-08-017033-1); pap. 65.00 o.p. (ISBN 0-08-017034-X). Pergamon.

Engineering Field Theory: Text & Examples, 2 vols. A. J. Baden-Fuller. 1982. pap. 150.00 o.p. (ISBN 0-08-029320-4). Pergamon.

Engineering Fluid Mechanics. John J. Bertin. (Illus.). 576p. 1984. text ed. (ISBN 0-13-278812-8). P-H.

Engineering Fluid Mechanics. John A. Roberson & Clayton T. Crowe. 1975. text ed. 20.95 o.p. (ISBN 0-395-18607-2). HM.

Engineering Fluid Mechanics. 2nd ed. John A. Roberson & Clayton T. Crowe. LC 79-87855. (Illus.). 1980. text ed. 40.95 o.p. (ISBN 0-395-28357-4). HM.

Engineering for Architecture. Architectural Record Magazine Editors. Ed. by Robert E. Fischer. (Architectural Record Book Ser.). (Illus.). 224p. 1980. text ed. 37.50 o.p. (ISBN 0-07-002353-0). McGraw.

Engineering Formulas. 4th ed. Kurt Gieck. 260p. 1983. text ed. 18.95 o.p. (ISBN 0-07-023219-9). McGraw.

Engineering Fundamentals for Professional Engineers Exams. 2nd ed. Lloyd M. Polentz. LC 78-21927. (Illus.). 1981. text ed. 36.50 o.p. (ISBN 0-07-050380-X); pap. text ed. 17.95 o.p. (ISBN 0-07-050381-8). McGraw.

Engineering Fundamentals Quick Reference Cards. 2nd ed. Michael R. Lindeburg. (Engineering Review Manual Ser.). 40p. 1986. pap. text ed. 9.25 o.p. (ISBN 0-932276-63-6). Prof Pubns CA.

Engineering Geology Case Histories, Nos. 6-10 In One Volume. Ed. by George A. Kiersch et al. LC 74-77141. (Illus.). 1974. 12.50 o.p. (ISBN 0-8137-4202-1). Geol Soc.

Engineering Inspection, Measurement & Testing. H. C. Town & R. Colebourne. (Illus.). 196p. 1956. Philos Lib.

Engineering Know-How in Engine Design, Pt. 24. (Milwaukee Section Lecture Ser.). 52p. 1976. pap. 12.00 o.p. (ISBN 0-89883-185-7, SP411). Soc Auto Engineers.

Engineering Learning Through Creativity: Recycling Instructional Resources. Luretha F. Lucky & Nancy O. Miller. 1979. pap. text ed. 13.00 o.p. (ISBN 0-8191-0779-4). U Pr of Amer.

Engineering Management. David I. Cleland & Dundar F. Kocaoglu. (Industrial Engineering & Management Science Ser.). (Illus.). 528p. 1981. text ed. 47.95 o.p. (ISBN 0-07-011316-5). McGraw.

Engineering Management of Water Quality. P. H. McGauhey. LC 67-28085. 1968. text ed. 45.00 o.p. (ISBN 0-07-044975-9). McGraw.

Engineering Materials & Their Applications. 2nd ed. Richard A. Flinn & Paul K. Trojan. (Illus.). 753p. 1981. text ed. 37.95 o.p. (ISBN 0-395-29645-5). HM.

Engineering Materials & Their Applications. Richard A. Flinn & Paul K. Trojan. 1975. text ed. 24.60 o.p. (ISBN 0-395-18916-0). HM.

Engineering Mathematics. Blakey & Hutton. 600p. 1960. (ISBN 0-8022-0140-7). Philos Lib.

Engineering Mechanics, SI Version: Dynamics, Vol. 2. James L. Meriam. LC 77-24716. 1980. (ISBN 0-471-05559-X). Wiley.

Engineering Medicine Man: The New Pioneer. Margaret Harmon. LC 75-25690. (Illus.). (gr. 5-9). 1975. 6.95 o.s.i. (ISBN 0-664-32581-5, Westminster). Westminster John Knox.

Engineering: Modeling & Computation. Walter J. Gajda, Jr. & William E. Biles. LC 77-74378. (Illus.). 1982. text ed. 31.50 o.p. (ISBN 0-395-25585-6). HM.

Engineering Models for Agricultural Production. Donnell R. Hunt. 1985. 43.95 o.s.i. (ISBN 0-87055-494-8). AVI.

Engineering of Microprocessor Systems: Guidelines on System Development. ERA Staff. LC 79-40952. 1979. 34.00 o.p. (ISBN 0-08-025435-7); pap. 9.75 o.p. (ISBN 0-08-025434-9). Pergamon.

Engineering of Unconventional Protein Production. 127p. 1969. pap. 24.00 o.p. (ISBN 0-8169-0271-2, S-93). Am Inst Chem Eng.

Engineering Plasticity. G. R. Calladine. 1969. text ed. 27.00 o.p. (ISBN 0-08-013970-1); pap. text ed. 13.25 o.p. (ISBN 0-08-013969-8). Pergamon.

Engineering Plasticity: Theory of Metal Forming Processes. Ed. by H. Lippmann. (CISM International Centre for Mechanical Sciences Ser.: Vol. 139). (Illus.). 1979. pap. 57.90 o.p. (ISBN 0-387-81429-9). Springer-Verlag.

Engineering Principles for Electrical Technicians. K. M. Smith & P. Holroyd. 1969. text ed. 16.75 o.p. (ISBN 0-08-012986-2); pap. text ed. 7.75 o.p. (ISBN 0-08-012985-4). Pergamon.

Engineering Principles in Physiology, 2 vols. Ed. by J. H. U. Brown & Donald Gann. Vol. 1, 1973. 71.50 o.p. (ISBN 0-12-136201-9); Vol. 2, 1973. 84.50 o.p. (ISBN 0-12-136202-7). Acad Pr.

Engineering Properties of Soils & Their Measurements. 2nd ed. Joseph E. Bowles. (Illus.). 1978. text ed. 37.95 o.p. (ISBN 0-07-006752-X). McGraw.

Engineering Research Centers. 1031p. 300.00x o.p. (ISBN 0-582-90018-2, Longman Group). Gale.

Engineering, Science, & Computer Jobs 1985. 6th ed. Ed. by Christopher Billy. (Peterson's Annual Guides-Careers Ser.). 686p. (Orig.). 1984. pap. 14.95 o.p. (ISBN 0-87866-248-0). Petersons Guides.

Engineering, Science, & Computer Jobs 1987. 8th ed. (Peterson's Annual Guides to Jobs Ser.). 823p. (Orig.). 1986. pap. 17.95 o.p. (ISBN 0-87866-467-X). Petersons Guides.

Engineering, Science, & Computer Jobs 1988. 9th ed. (Peterson's Annual Guides to Jobs Ser.). 745p. (Orig.). 1987. lib. bdg. 24.95 o.p. (ISBN 0-87866-655-9); pap. 19.95 o.p. (ISBN 0-87866-576-5). Petersons Guides.

Engineering, Science & Computer Jobs 1983. 4th Ed. ed. Sandra Grundfest. LC 82-644127. (Peterson's Annual Guides Ser.). 787p. 1982. pap. 12.95 o.p. (ISBN 0-87866-204-9). Peterson's Guides.

Engineering, Science, & Computer Jobs 1984. 5th ed. Ed. by Sandra Grundfest. LC 82-644127. (Peterson's Annual Guide Ser.). 702p. 1983. 13.95 o.p. (ISBN 0-87866-253-7). Petersons Guides.

Engineering Science for Technicians, Vol. 1. 2nd ed. I. McDonagh et al. (Illus.). 256p. 1982. pap. text ed. 19.95x o.p. (ISBN 0-686-83107-1). Trans-Atl Phila.

Engineering Science for Technicians, Vol. 2. McDonagh et al. (Illus.). 1978. pap. 19.95x o.p. (ISBN 0-7131-3398-8). Trans-Atl Phila.

Engineering Tenders, Sales & Contracts: Standard Forms & Procedures. Andrew Pike. 462p. 1983. 70.00 o.p. (ISBN 0-419-12530-2, NO. 6764, E & FN Spon). Routledge Chapman & Hall.

Engineers & Industrial Growth: Higher Technical Education & the Engineering Profession During the 19th & Early 20th Centuries: France, Germany, Sweden & England. Goran Ahlstrom. (Illus.). 118p. 1982. 24.00 o.p. (ISBN 0-7099-0506-8, Pub. by Croom Helm Ltd). Routledge Chapman & Hall.

Engineers at Work: A Casebook. Carl H. Vesper. 1975. pap. 17.50 o.p. (ISBN 0-395-18407-X). HM.

Engineers Can Write Better. 20p. 1971. pap. 4.00 o.p. (ISBN 0-8169-0160-0, X-18). Am Inst Chem Eng.

Engineers' Metric Manual & Buyers' Guide. D. S. Lock. 1974. 355.00 o.p. (ISBN 0-08-018220-8). Pergamon.

Engineers' Salaries: Special Industry Report, 1987. R. A. Ellis & Engineering Manpower Commission Staff. 1988. pap. 230.00 o.p. (ISBN 0-87615-128-4). AAES.

Engineers' Salaries: Special Industry Report 1985. Engineering Manpower & Engineering Manpower Commission Staff. 220p. (Orig.). 1986. pap. 225.00 o.p. (ISBN 0-87615-126-8). AAES.

Engines for Homebuilt Aircraft & Ultralights. Joe Christy. (Illus.). 112p. 1984. pap. 8.70 o.p. (ISBN 0-8306-2347-7, 2347P). TAB Bks.

Engines of Creation. Eric Drexler. LC 85-25362. 312p. 1986. 17.95 o.s.i. (ISBN 0-385-19972-4, Anchor Pr). Doubleday.

Engines That Passed. C. Hamilton Ellis. LC 72-364512. (Illus.). 133p. 1968. lib. bdg. 17.95x o.p. (ISBN 0-678-06005-3). Kelley.

England. Stuart Rossiter. (Blue Guides). (Illus.). 24.95 o.p. (ISBN 0-393-01537-8); pap. 14.95 o.p. (ISBN 0-393-00090-7). Norton.

England & the Salt Trade in the Later Middle Ages. A. R. Bridbury. LC 73-9261. (Illus.). 198p. 1973. Repr. of 1955 ed. lib. bdg. 22.50x o.p. (ISBN 0-8371-7001-X, BRES). Greenwood.

England As It Is: Political, Social & Industrial in the Middle of the Nineteenth Century, 2 vols. William Johnston. (Development of Industrial Society Ser.). 750p. 1971. Repr. of 1851 ed. 65.00 set o.p. (ISBN 0-7165-1774-4, BBA 03546, Pub. by Irish Academic Pr). Biblio Dist.

England in Eighteen Fifteen & Eighteen Forty-Five. A. Alison. (Development of Industrial Society Ser.). 98p. 1971. Repr. of 1845 ed. 17.50x o.p. (ISBN 0-7165-1699-3, BBA 05044, Pub. by Irish Academic Pr Ireland). Biblio Dist.

England in Eighteen Thirty- Five, 3 vols. Frederick Von Raumer. 960p. 1971. Repr. of 1836 ed. 80.00x set o.p. (ISBN 0-7165-1780-9, BBA 03067, Pub. by Irish Academic Pr). Biblio Dist.

England in the Seventeenth Century. new ed. Maurice Ashley. 275p. 1980. 9.95x o.p. (ISBN 0-06-490228-5, 06319); pap. 9.95o. p. o.p. (ISBN 0-686-70948-9, 06320). B&N Imports.

England on Thirty-Five Dollars a Day. Darwin Porter. 540p. 1985. pap. 10.95 o.p. (ISBN 0-671-55416-6). S&S.

England since the Industrial Revolution, 1815-1848. J. Hampden Jackson. LC 75-7239. (Illus.). 298p. 1975. Repr. of 1949 ed. lib. bdg. 35.00x o.p. (ISBN 0-8371-8102-X, JAES). Greenwood.

England under George I: The Beginnings of the Hanoverian Dynasty. Michael Wolfgang. LC 81-6495. (Studies in Modern History). viii, 406p. 1981. Repr. of 1936 ed. lib. bdg. 35.00x o.p. (ISBN 0-313-23040-4, MIEG). Greenwood.

England under the Yorkists & Tudors 1471 - 1603. P. J. Helm. (Illus.). 1968. 12.50x o.p. (ISBN 0-7135-0541-9); pap. text ed. 15.00x o.p. (ISBN 0-7135-0542-7). Humanities.

England's Holy War: A Study of English Liberal Idealism During the Great War. Irene C. Willis. LC 70-147489. (Library of War & Peace; the Character & Causes of War). 1972. lib. bdg. 46.00 o.p. (ISBN 0-8240-0282-2). Garland Pub.

English Abbey: Its Life & Work in the Middle Ages. Frederick H. Crossley. LC 82-25127. (Illus.). xiv, 114p. 1983. Repr. of 1935 ed. lib. bdg. 48.50x o.p. (ISBN 0-313-23849-9, CRFE). Greenwood.

English & American Literature: A Guide to Reference Materials. R. C. Schweik & Dietner Riesner. pap. cancelled o.s.i. (ISBN 3-503-01236-2). Adlers Foreign Bks.

English & Colonial Bars in the Nineteenth Century. Daniel Duman. (Illus.). 228p. 1983. 30.00 o.p. (ISBN 0-85664-468-4, Pub. by Croom Helm Ltd). Routledge Chapman & Hall.

English & Continental Systems of Adminstrative Law. Z. M. Medjati & J. E. Trice. 1978. 42.00 o.p. (ISBN 0-444-85108-9); pap. 58.00 o.p. (ISBN 0-444-85198-4). Elsevier.

English & Dutch Ceramics. Lunsingh Scheurleer & Robert J. Charleston. LC 78-55079. (Masterpieces of Western & Near Eastern Ceramics: Vol. 7). (Illus.). 1979. 250.00 o.p. (ISBN 0-87011-348-8). Kodansha.

English & Japanese in Contrast. Taylor. 1979. 7.25 o.p. (ISBN 0-88345-356-8, 18477). Prentice ESL.

English-Arabic Conversational Dictionary. Richard Jaschke. 392p. 1987. pap. 7.95 o.p. (ISBN 0-8044-6311-5, 0093). Hippocrene Bks.

English Artist' Paper. John Krill. (Illus.). 160p. 39.50 o.s.i. (ISBN 0-89835-272-X). Abaris Bks.

English As a Second Language, Vol. I. Clara V. Velazquez. 240p. 1982. pap. text ed. 14.50 o.p. (ISBN 0-8403-2859-1). Kendall-Hunt.

English As a Second Language: An Interdisciplinary Approach, Vol. 3. Clara V. Velazquez. 288p. 1982. pap. text ed. 17.00 o.p. (ISBN 0-8403-2659-9). Kendall-Hunt.

English As an International Language. Ed. by British Council Staff. (English Lanuage Teaching Documents Ser.: Vol. 102). 72p. 1983. pap. 5.75 o.p. (ISBN 0-08-029480-4). Alemany Pr.

English As We Speak It in Ireland. Patrick W. Joyce. LC 68-26579. 1971. Repr. of 1910 ed. 55.00x o.p. (ISBN 0-8103-3356-2). Gale.

English Associations of Working Men. Joseph M. Baernreither. Tr. by A. Taylor. LC 66-28040. 492p. 1966. Repr. of 1889 ed. 46.00x o.p. (ISBN 0-8103-3078-4). Gale.

English at Your Fingertips. Rosella Nelson et al. 1975. pap. 6.95 o.p. (ISBN 0-87789-129-X); tchrs' manual 3.95 o.p. (ISBN 0-87789-141-9). ELS Educ Servs.

English Book-Illustration of To-Day: Appreciations of the Work of Living English Illustrators with Lists of Their Books. Rose E. Sketchley. LC 78-179655. (Illus.). xxx, 210p. 1974. Repr. of 1903 ed. 48.00x o.p. (ISBN 0-8103-4052-6). Gale.

English (British) for Spanish Travellers. Berlitz Editors. (Travellers Ser. for Non-English Speakers). 1971. pap. 4.95 o.p. (ISBN 0-02-966600-7, Berlitz). Macmillan.

English Brown Stoneware, Sixteen Seventy to Nineteen Hundred. Adrian Oswald & R. J. Hildyard. (Illus.). 296p. 1983. 64.95 o.p. (ISBN 0-571-11905-0). Faber & Faber.

English-Bulgarian Concise Technical Dictionary. A. Desov. (Eng. & Bulgarian.). 17.50 o.s.i. (ISBN 0-686-91776-6). E J Brill USA.

English Cameo Glass. Ray Grover & Lee Grover. (Illus.). 482p. 50.00 o.s.i. (ISBN 0-317-55001-2). Apollo.

English Ceramics from Northern California Collections. Michael Conforti et al. LC 80-65652. (Illus.). 56p. 1980. pap. 3.95 o.p. (ISBN 0-88401-035-X). Fine Arts Mus.

English Channel. Nigel Calder. 400p. 1986. 24.95 o.p. (ISBN 0-317-46589-9). Penguin USA.

English Chartist Circular & Temperance Record for England & Wales, 2 vols. in 1, Nos. 1-153. LC 68-20983. Repr. of 1844 ed. 95.00x o.p. (ISBN 0-678-08006-2). Kelley.

English Chinese Dictionary of Demography. Tian Xueyuan et al. 446p. 1985. pap. 7.95 o.p. (ISBN 0-8351-1616-6). China Bks.

English-Chinese Dictionary of Highway Engineering. rev. ed. 1141p. 1986. text ed. 99.50 o.p. (ISBN 0-317-64976-0, Pub. by A A Balkema). Gower Pub Co.

English-Chinese Dictionary of Metals & Their Heat Treatment. Science Press Staff. LC 81-1279. iii, 266p. 1981. pap. 27.50x o.p. (ISBN 0-8311-1081-3). Indus Pr.

English Christmas. 14.95 o.p. (ISBN 0-317-62759-7). H Holt & Co.

English Civic Pageantry, 1558-1642. David M. Bergeron. LC 70-163908. 338p. 1972. lib. bdg. 19.95x o.p. (ISBN 0-87249-238-9). U of SC Pr.

English Civil War: Conservatism & Revolution, 1603-1649. Robert Ashton. 464p. 1981. pap. 24.95 o.p. (ISBN 0-393-01207-7); pap. text ed. 7.95x o.p. (ISBN 0-393-95202-9). Norton.

English Collection, 1979. Arlene H. Eakle et al. 168p. 1979. pap. 10.00 o.p. (ISBN 0-940764-26-1). U of Utah Pr.

English Conversation Pictures of the 18th & Early 19th Centuries. G. C. Williamson. (Illus.). 120p. sewn bdg. 25.00 o.p. (ISBN 0-317-54952-9). Apollo.

English Cookery Book to 1850. Arnold Oxford. 20.00 o.p. (ISBN 0-87556-662-6). Saifer.

English Costume in the Age of Elizabeth. 2nd ed. I. Brooke. (English Costume Ser.). (Illus.). 1977. Repr. of 1950 ed. text ed. 9.95x o.p. (ISBN 0-7136-0156-6). Humanities.

English Costume of the Later Middle Ages. I. Brooke. (English Costume Ser.). (Illus.). 1977. text ed. 9.95x o.p. (ISBN 0-7136-0155-8). Humanities.

English Costume of the Seventeenth Century. 2nd ed. I. Brooke. (English Costume Ser.). (Illus.). 1977. Repr. of 1950 ed. text ed. 9.95x o.p. (ISBN 0-7136-0157-4). Humanities.

English Country Cooking. Caroline Conran. (Illus.). 1985. 16.45 o.p. (ISBN 0-394-54638-5, Pub. by Villard Bks). Random.

English Country House: An Art & Way of Life. Olive Cook & A. F. Kersting. (Illus.). 240p. 1984. pap. 10.95f o.s.i. (ISBN 0-500-27309-X). Thames-Hudson.

English Country Pubs. Derry Brabbs. 1986. 19.95 o.s.i. (ISBN 0-316-10498-1). Little.

English-Czech Dictionary, 3 vol. set. Karel Hais & Bretislav Hodek. 2880p. 1986. 120.00x o.p. (ISBN 0-87052-339-2). Hippocrene Bks.

English Diaries: A Review of English Diaries from the Sixteenth to the Twentieth Century with an Introduction on Diary Writing. Arthur Ponsonby. LC 75-152247. 458p. 1971. Repr. of 1923 ed. 44.00x o.p. (ISBN 0-8103-3711-8). Gale.

English Dolls' Houses of the Eighteenth & Nineteenth Centuries. rev. ed. Vivien Greene. (Illus.). 1980. encore ed. 11.95 o.p. (ISBN 0-684-17185-6, ScribT). Scribner.

English Drama to Sixteen Sixty (Excluding Shakespeare): A Guide to Information Sources. Ed. by F. Elaine Penninger. LC 73-16988. (American Literature, English Literature, & World Literatures in English Information Guide Ser.: Vol. 5). vi, 392p. 1976. 68.00x o.p. (ISBN 0-8103-1223-9). Gale.

English Eccentrics & Eccentricities. John Timbs. LC 69-18076. 596p. 1969. Repr. of 1875 ed. 43.00x o.p. (ISBN 0-8103-3556-5). Gale.

English Emblem Books. Rosemary Freeman. 1966. lib. bdg. 20.00x o.p. (ISBN 0-374-92888-6, Octagon). Hippocrene Bks.

English English. 2nd ed. Ed. by Norman W. Schur. LC 77-20390. 332p. 1980. 46.00x o.p. (ISBN 0-8103-1096-1). Gale.

English Epigrams. Ed. by William D. Adams. LC 74-77039. 442p. 1974. Repr. of 1878 ed. 37.00x o.p. (ISBN 0-8103-3700-2). Gale.

English Fairy & Other Folktales. Ed. by Edwin S. Hartland. LC 68-21772. 312p. 1968. Repr. of 1890 ed. 40.00x o.p. (ISBN 0-8103-3465-8). Gale.

English Farm Wagon: Origins & Structure. J. Geraint Jenkins. (Illus.). 264p. 1981. 24.95 o.p. (ISBN 0-7153-8119-9). David & Charles.

English Field Systems. Howard L. Gray. 568p. 1980. Repr. of 1915 ed. lib. bdg. 39.50x o.p. (ISBN 0-678-08069-0). Kelley.

English Florilegium. Date not set. (ISBN 0-89659-790-3). Abbeville Pr.

English Folk-Rhymes: A Collection of Traditional Verses Relating to Places & Persons, Customs, Superstitions, Etc. G. F. Northall. LC 67-23918. 584p. 1967. Repr. of 1892 ed. 46.00x o.p. (ISBN 0-8103-3455-0). Gale.

English for Business. Baty. 1966. pap. text ed. (ISBN 0-534-00657-4). PWs-Kent Pub.

English for Engineers. Clive Brasnett. 1969. pap. 6.95x o.p. (ISBN 0-423-84130-0, NO.2140). Routledge Chapman & Hall.

English for Medical Students. Clive Brasnett. 1976. pap. 6.95x o.p. (ISBN 0-423-49760-X, NO. 2771). Routledge Chapman & Hall.

English for Specific Purposes: Science & Technology. 15.00 o.p. (ISBN 0-8384-0599-1). Heinle & Heinle.

English for the Business World. Michael Dean. 192p. 1985. pap. 9.95x o.p. (ISBN 0-631-90070-5); cassette 14.95x o.p. (ISBN 0-631-90190-6). Basil Blackwell.

English-French Dictionary. 1984. pap. 1.95 o.p. (ISBN 0-89531-081-3). Sharon Pubns.

English Furniture. (Illus.). 1988. 34.95 o.p. (ISBN 0-7134-5842-9, Pub. by Batsford England). David & Charles.

English Furniture from Charles II to George II. R. W. Symonds. (Illus.). 269p. 1981. 89.50 o.p. (ISBN 0-902028-95-2). Antique Collect.

English Furniture, 1800-1851. Edward T. Joy. (Illus.). 320p. 1988. 65.00 o.p. (ISBN 0-7063-6676-X, Pub. by Ward Lock). David & Charles.

English-German Chemical Terminology: An Introduction to Chemistry in English & German. 5th ed. Hans Fromherz & Alexander King. LC 68-26705. 588p. (Eng. & Ger.). 1968. 46.30x o.p. (ISBN 3-527-25093-X). VCH Pubs.

English Gold Coins: Ancient to Modern Times. Emery M. Norweb. LC 68-9275. (Illus.). 96p. 1968. pap. 10.00x o.p. (ISBN 0-910386-44-7, Pub. by Cleveland Mus Art). Ind U Pr.

English Gothic Literature. Ed. by Derek Brewer & A. Norman Jeffares. LC 83-3016. (History of Literature Ser.). (Illus.). 328p. 1987. 28.50 o.s.i. (ISBN 0-8052-3861-1). Schocken.

English Grammar. Gordon Lish. (gr. 9-12). 1972. Vol. 1. pap. text ed. 9.00 o.s.i. (ISBN 0-8449-2700-7); Vol. 2. pap. text ed. 9.00 o.p.; tchrs'. manual 1.00 o.p.; test 1.00 o.p. Carroll CA.

English Grammar: A Linguistic Study of Its Classes & Structures. F. S. Scott. 1970. pap. text ed. 10.00x o.p. (ISBN 0-435-10790-9). Heinemann Ed.

English Grammar for the Vietnamese. Danh R. Duong. 400p. 1977. o.p. (ISBN 0-8044-0137-3); pap. 7.95x o.p. (ISBN 0-8044-6127-9). Ungar.

English Guide for Court Reporters. Lillian I. Morson. 11.95 o.p. (ISBN 0-533-00947-2). Vantage.

English Gypsies & Their Language. Charles G. Leland. LC 68-22035. 276p. 1969. Repr. of 1874 ed. 46.00x o.p. (ISBN 0-8103-3883-1). Gale.

English Handbook of Grammar, Style, & Composition. Rev. ed. Research & Education Association Staff. LC 83-62275. (Illus.). 224p. 1984. pap. text ed. 12.95 o.p. (ISBN 0-87891-552-4). Res & Educ.

English Handwriting see Society's Work.

English Historic Carpentry. Cecil A. Hewett. (Illus.). 352p. 1981. 40.00x o.p. (ISBN 0-8476-3809-X). Rowman.

English Historical Facts: 1603-1688. Chris Cook & John Wroughton. 231p. 1980. 32.50x o.p. (ISBN 0-8476-6295-0). Rowman.

English Humanism: Wyatt to Cowley. Ed. by Joanna Martindale. LC 84-17667. 292p. 1984. 31.00 o.p. (Pub. by Croom Helm Ltd); pap. 17.50 o.p. (ISBN 0-7099-2067-9). Routledge Chapman & Hall.

English-Hungarian Pocket Dictionary. 14th ed. L. Orszagh. 1987. pap. 8.50x o.p. (H272). Vanous.

English-Icelandic Dictionary. S. O. Bogason. (Eng. & Icelandic.). 75.00 o.p. (ISBN 0-685-29251-7). E J Brill USA.

English Idioms see Metaphor.

English Idioms & Americanisms for Foreign Students, Professionals & Physicians. J. E. Schmidt. 544p. 1972. 32.25 o.p. (ISBN 0-398-02400-6). C C Thomas.

English Imperative. Eirlys Davies. 288p. 1986. 43.00 o.p. (ISBN 0-7099-4513-2, Pub. by Croom Helm Ltd). Routledge Chapman & Hall.

English in America. (Our Nations Heritage Ser.). Date not set. (ISBN 0-07-375394-7). McGraw.

English Influence on the French Vocabulary see Metaphor.

English Influence on the French Vocabulary see Preliminary Announcement.

English-Irish Dictionary. T. De Bhardraithe. (Eng. & Irish.). 1959. 12.50x o.s.i. (ISBN 0-686-00860-X). Colton Bk.

English IV: Franco, Slav & Flank Defence. John L. Watson. (Contemporary Chess Openings Ser.). (Illus.). 112p. 1981. 22.95 o.p. (ISBN 0-7134-2688-8, Pub. by Batsford England). David & Charles.

English Journals, 1651-1652. L. Huygens et al. Ed. by A. G. Bachrach & H. Collmer. Tr. by A. G. Bachrach & H. Collmer. (Illus.). 1982. 40.00 o.p. (ISBN 90-04-06858-9). E J Brill USA.

English Journey: Or, The Road to Milton Keynes. Beryl Bainbridge. 158p. 1984. 12.95 o.s.i. (ISBN 0-8076-1101-8). Braziller.

English Language. Alex English & Gary Delsohn. 1986. pap. 7.95 o.p. (ISBN 0-8092-4827-1). Contemp Bks.

English Language: An Introduction. Nelson Francis. (gr. 12). 1965. 4.95x o.p. (ISBN 0-393-09629-7, NortonC); pap. text ed. 6.95x o.p. (ISBN 0-393-09925-3). Norton.

English Language & Orientation Programs in the United States. Institute of International Education, New York Staff. 174p. 1984. 8.95 o.s.i. (ISBN 0-318-16641-0). Tchrs Eng Spkrs.

English Language Arts in the Secondary School. Ed. by Angela M. Broening. LC 56-10731. (Illus.). 1956. 24.00x o.p. (ISBN 0-89197-142-4). Irvington.

English Language Skills Assessment in a Reading Context (Elsa Test AN) Donna Ilyin et al. 1980. 10.50 ea. o.p. (ISBN 0-88377-145-4); test material 6.95 o.p. (ISBN 0-686-86504-9). Newbury Hse.

English Language Sources for Reference Questions Related to Soviet Science (with an Emphasis on Chemistry) Gary Wiggins. (Occasional Papers: No. 102). 29p. 1972. pap. 2.00 o.p. (ISBN 0-317-58882-6). U of Ill Lib Info Sci.

English Law in India. A. C. Banerjee. 324p. 1984. text ed. 22.50x o.p. (ISBN 0-391-03008-6). Humanities.

English Lit Relit. Richard Armour. 1969. text ed. 5.95 o.p. (ISBN 0-07-002224-0); pap. 2.95 o.p. (ISBN 0-07-002282-8). McGraw.

English Literature, an Illustrated Record, 4 vols in 2. Richard Garnett & Edmund W. Gosse. Repr. of 1935 ed. 33.00 o.p. (ISBN 0-686-02073-1). Somerset Pub.

English Literature from Dryden to Burns. Alan D. McKillop. Repr. of 1948 ed. 69.00 o.p. (ISBN 0-403-04048-5). Somerset Pub.

English Literature, Sixteen Sixty to Eighteen Hundred: A Bibliography of Modern Studies, Vols. 5 & 6. Curtis A. Zimansky. LC 51-6868. 1972. Vol. 5, 1961-65. 45.50x o.p. (ISBN 0-691-06184-X); Vol. 6, 1966-70. 47.50x o.p. (ISBN 0-691-06185-8). Princeton U Pr.

English Lyrics Before Fifteen Hundred. Ed. by Theodore Silverstein. (York Medieval Texts). 1971. 14.95 o.s.i. (ISBN 0-8101-0353-2). Northwestern U Pr.

English Magical & Scientific Poems to 1700: An Annotated Bibliography. Robert M. Schuler. LC 78-68270. 120p. 1979. lib. bdg. 24.00 o.p. (ISBN 0-8240-9767-X). Garland Pub.

English Masters. Horace Shipp. (Illus.). 128p. 1956. (ISBN 0-8022-1562-9). Philos Lib.

English Medieval Theatre Fourteen Hundred to Fifteen Hundred. William Tydeman. (Theatre Production Studies). (Illus.). 218p. 1986. text ed. 42.50 o.p. (ISBN 0-7100-9850-2). Routledge Chapman & Hall.

English Mummers' Play. Alex Helm. (Folklore Society Mistletoe Ser.). (Illus.). 124p. 1981. 45.00x o.p. (ISBN 0-8476-7014-7). Rowman.

English Mystics of the Fourteenth Century. Thomas W. Coleman. LC 74-109723. 1971. Repr. of 1938 ed. lib. bdg. 35.00x o.p. (ISBN 0-8371-4213-X, COEM). Greenwood.

English-Norwegian Dictionary: Norweigian Dictionary. Ed. by Byerke & Sorass. 562p. 1963. 35.00x o.p. (N434). Vanous.

English Novel, from the Earliest Days to the Death of Joseph Conrad. Ford Madox Ford. Repr. of 1929 ed. 39.00x o.p. (ISBN 0-403-03879-0). Somerset Pub.

English Novel in Transition, Eighteen Eighty Five to Nineteen Forty. William C. Frierson. LC 65-29043. Repr. of 1942 ed. 25.00x o.p. (ISBN 0-8154-0074-8). Cooper Sq.

English-Pali Dictionary. Compiled by A. P. Mahathera. 588p. 1955. 33.50 o.p. (ISBN 0-7100-0202-5, Pali Text). Routledge Chapman & Hall.

English Peasant Farming: The Agrarian History of Lincolnshire from Tudor to Recent Times. Joan Thirsk. (Methuen Library Reprint Ser.). (Illus.). 368p. 1981. 55.00x o.p. (ISBN 0-416-30530-X, NO. 3584). Routledge Chapman & Hall.

English Perfect: Tense-Choice & Pragmatic Inferences. R. W. McCoard. (North-Holland Linguistic Ser: Vol. 38). 1978. 66.00 o.p. (ISBN 0-444-85154-2, North-Holland). Elsevier.

English Pistols. Howard L. Blackmore. (Illus.). 64p. 1985. 17.95 o.p. (ISBN 0-85368-712-9, Pub. by Arms & Armour). Sterling.

English Poems: The Elizabethan Age & the Puritan Period (1550-1660, Vol. 2. Ed. by Walter C. Bronson. LC 7-29843. (Granger Poetry Library). 1979. Repr. of 1909 ed. 36.50x o.p. (ISBN 0-89609-154-6). Roth Pub Inc.

English Poems: Vol. 3-Restoration & Eighteenth Century. Ed. by Walter C. Bronson. LC 7-29843. (Granger Poetry Library). 552p. 1982. Repr. of 1908 ed. 36.50x o.p. (ISBN 0-89609-227-5). Roth Pub Inc.

English Poetry, Nineteen Hundred to Nineteen Fifty: An Assessment. C. H. Sisson. LC 81-13024. 1982. pap. 8.95 o.p. (ISBN 0-416-32100-3, NO. 3567). Routledge Chapman & Hall.

English Poetry of the Nineteenth Century. Oscar J. Campbell. LC 75-154103. 1971. Repr. of 1929 ed. lib. bdg. 37.50x o.p. (ISBN 0-8371-6074-X, CAEP). Greenwood.

English Poetry of the Seventeenth Century. rev. ed. Ed. by Roberta F. Brinkley. 1936. pap. 8.95x o.p. (ISBN 0-393-09446-4, NortonC). Norton.

English Porcelain. Rev. ed. John Cushion. (Letts Collector's Guides). (Illus.). 72p. 1982. 9.95 o.p. (ISBN 0-85097-349-X, Pub by C Letts Bks UK). Seven Hills Bk Dists.

English Press in the Eighteenth Century. Jeremy Black. (Illus.). 352p. 1986. 43.00 o.p. (ISBN 0-7099-3924-8, Pub. by Croom Helm UK). Routledge Chapman & Hall.

English Prints for the Collector. Stephen Calloway. LC 80-19370. (Illus.). 240p. 1981. 85.00 o.p. (ISBN 0-87951-120-6). Overlook Pr.

English Pronunciation from the Fifteenth to the Eighteenth Century: A Handbook to the Study of Historical Grammar. Constance Bullock-Davies. LC 75-109726. Repr. of 1934 ed. lib. bdg. 35.00x o.p. (ISBN 0-8371-4216-4, DAEP). Greenwood.

English Proverbs & Proverbial Phrases. William C. Hazlitt. LC 67-23914. 606p. 1969. Repr. of 1907 ed. 42.00x o.p. (ISBN 0-8103-3199-3). Gale.

English Public Schools. James McConnell. (Illus.). 1985. 19.45 o.p. (ISBN 0-393-02244-7). Norton.

English Quakers & the First Industrial Revolution: A Study of the Quaker Community in Four Industrial Counties; York, Warwick, & Gloucester, 1750-1830. David H. Pratt. LC 84-46009. (British Economic History Ser.). 236p. 1985. lib. bdg. 28.00 o.p. (ISBN 0-8240-6689-8). Garland Pub.

English Religious Drama of the Middle Ages. Hardin Craig. LC 78-6893. 1978. Repr. of 1968 ed. lib. bdg. 37.50x o.p. (ISBN 0-313-20496-9, CRER). Greenwood.

English Religious Life in the Eighth Century. Thomas Allison. LC 75-106708. 1970. Repr. of 1929 ed. lib. bdg. 35.00x o.p. (ISBN 0-8371-3438-2, ALRL). Greenwood.

English Renaissance, Fifteen Ten to Sixteen Eighty-Eight. 2nd rev. ed. Vivian D. Pinto. Repr. of 1951 ed. 59.00x o.p. (ISBN 0-403-08601-9). Somerset Pub.

English Renaissance Poetry: A Collection of Shorter Poems from Skelton to Jonson. Ed. by John Williams. 400p. 1974. pap. 8.95 o.p. (ISBN 0-393-00726-X, N726, Norton Lib). Norton.

English Reserve - Italian Fire. Lillian V. Smith. 32p. 1987. 6.75 o.p. (ISBN 0-8062-2958-6). Carlton.

English Rivers & Canals. Paul Atterbury. (Illus.). 1984. 15.45 o.p. (ISBN 0-393-01829-6). Norton.

English Romanesque Lead Sculpture. George Zarnecki. (Illus.). 64p. 1957. (ISBN 0-8022-1952-7). Philos Lib.

English Romantic Poetry, Eighteen Hundred to Eighteen Thirty-Five: A Guide to Information Sources. Ed. by Donald Reiman. LC 74-11527. (American Literature, English Literature, & World Literatures in English Information Guide Ser.: Vol. 27). 320p. 1979. 68.00x o.p. (ISBN 0-8103-1231-X). Gale.

English Room. Derry Moore & Michael Pick. LC 84-15699. (Illus.). 144p. 1985. 19.95 o.p. (ISBN 0-517-55596-4). Crown.

English-Russian Dictionary of Environmental Control. Ed. by E. L. Milovanov & E. A. Veistman. 338p. (Eng. & Rus.). 1981. 44.00 o.p. (ISBN 0-08-023576-X). Pergamon.

English-Russian Physics Dictionary. Ed. by D. M. Tolstoi. LC 78-40718. (Eng. & Rus.). 1979. 120.00 o.p. (ISBN 0-08-023057-1). Pergamon.

English-Russian Polytechnical Dictionary. A. E. Chernukhin. 647p. 1976. 20.50 o.p. (ISBN 0-8285-0595-0, Pub. by Rus Lang Pubs USSR). Imported Pubns.

English Schools in the Middle Ages. Nicholas Orme. (Illus.). 367p. 1973. 55.00x o.p. (ISBN 0-416-16080-8, NO. 2357). Routledge Chapman & Hall.

English Serbian Croation Dictionary. 7th ed. M. Drvodelic. 880p. 1983. text ed. 27.50x o.p. (ISBN 0-89918-670-X, Y670). Vanous.

English Silver Spoons. rev. ed. Michael Snodin. (Letts Collectors' Guides Ser.). (Illus.). 80p. 1982. 9.95 o.p. (ISBN 0-85097-379-1, Pub. by C Letts Bks UK). Seven Hills Bk Dists.

English Sixth Form College: An Educational Concept. R. Wearing-King. 1969. pap. text ed. 5.50 o.p. (ISBN 0-08-013214-6). Pergamon.

English Skills Handbook: Reading & Writing. Harvey S. Wiener & Charles Bazerman. LC 76-14015. (Illus.). 1977. pap. 19.96 o.p. (ISBN 0-395-20595-6). HM.

English Song: Dowland to Purcell. Ian Spink. (Illus.). 320p. 1986. pap. 12.95 o.s.i. (ISBN 0-8008-2396-6). Taplinger.

English Structure in Focus. Polly Davis. 1977. pap. text ed. 13.25 o.p. (ISBN 0-88377-077-6); tchr's. manual 4.00 o.p. (ISBN 0-88377-095-4); answer key 4.00 o.p. (ISBN 0-88377-100-4). Newbury Hse.

English Structure Planning: A Commentary on Procedure & Practice in the Seventies. Ed. by D. T. Cross & M. R. Bristow. 1983. 32.00 o.p. (ISBN 0-85086-094-6, NO. 5053, Pub. by Pion). Routledge Chapman & Hall.

English Summer. Cornelia S. Parker. 1934. 3.50 o.p. (ISBN 0-87140-800-7). Liveright.

English Surnames, 2 Vols. 4th ed. Mark A. Lower. LC 68-22037. 590p. 1968. Repr. of 1875 ed. Set. 37.00x o.p. (ISBN 0-8103-3129-2). Gale.

English Synonyms. George Crabb. 1966. Repr. of 1916 ed. 27.50 o.p. (ISBN 0-7100-1234-9). Routledge Chapman & Hall.

English Syntax. alternate ed. Paul Roberts. (Orig.). 1964. pap. text ed. 7.95 o.p. (ISBN 0-15-522665-7, HC, HC). HarBraceJ.

English Table in History & Literature. Charles Cooper. LC 68-21760. 244p. 1968. Repr. of 1929 ed. 35.00x o.p. (ISBN 0-8103-3520-4). Gale.

English-Tagalog-Visayan Pocket Dictionary. Enriquez & Bautista. (Eng. & Tagalog.). 4.00x o.s.i. (ISBN 0-686-05265-X). Colton Bk.

English Teaching: Programs & Policies. Anthony Adams & Esmor Jones. (English, Language & Education Ser.). 192p. 1985. pap. 14.00 o.p. (ISBN 0-335-15074-8, Open Univ Pr). Taylor & Francis.

English Teaching Since 1965: How Much Growth? David Allen. (Orig.). 1980. pap. text ed. 15.00x o.p. (ISBN 0-435-10051-3). Heinemann Ed.

English the Easy Way. (Easy Way Ser.). 1982. 8.95 o.p. (ISBN 0-8120-2517-2). Barron.

English Tragedy Before Shakespeare. Wolfgang Clemen. 1980. 49.95x o.p. (ISBN 0-416-74380-3, NO.2976). Routledge Chapman & Hall.

English Traveller & the Movement of Ideas, 1660-1732. Ray W. Frantz. 1967. lib. bdg. 18.00x o.p. (ISBN 0-374-92870-3, Octagon). Hippocrene Bks.

English Traveller in America, 1785-1835. Jane L. Mesick. 1970. Repr. of 1922 ed. lib. bdg. 35.00x o.p. (ISBN 0-8371-4280-6, MEEN). Greenwood.

English Travellers Abroad, 1604-1667. John W. Stoye. LC 68-23130. (Maps). 1967. Repr. of 1952 ed. lib. bdg. 26.00x o.p. (ISBN 0-374-97638-4, Octagon). Hippocrene Bks.

English Urban Environment: Recent Writings, 1980-1983. Dale E. Casper. (Public Administration Ser.: Bibliography P 1643). 1985. pap. 2.00 o.p. (ISBN 0-89028-333-8). Vance Biblios.

English Usage. Ely Marquez & J. Donald Bowen. (Advanced Language Study). 192p. 1983. pap. text ed. 11.00 o.p. (ISBN 0-88377-285-X). Newbury Hse.

English Usage: A Guide to First Principles. Walter Nash. (Language, Education & Society Ser.). 161p. 1986. lib. bdg. 24.95 o.p. (ISBN 0-7102-0024-2). Routledge Chapman & Hall.

English Village Green. Brian Bailey. (Illus.). 208p. 18.95 o.s.i. (ISBN 0-317-54977-4). Apollo.

English Villagers of the Thirteenth Century. George C. Homans. 496p. 1975. pap. 7.95 o.p. (ISBN 0-393-00765-0, Norton Lib). Norton.

English Vowel Sounds see Society's Work.

English Weapons & Warfare: 1449-1660. A. V. Norman & Don Pottinger. (Illus.). 250p. 1985. 14.95 o.p. (ISBN 0-88029-044-7, Pub. by Dorset Pr). Hippocrene Bks.

English, Welsh & Scottish Country Inns & Castle Hotels. 2nd ed. Karen Brown. LC 79-54714. (Country Inns Travel Guide Ser.). (Illus., Orig.). 1979. pap. 9.95 o.p. (ISBN 0-930328-02-7). Travel Pr.

English, Welsh & Scottish Country Inns. rev., 2nd ed. Karen Brown & June Brown. (Karen Brown's European Country Inns Ser.). (Illus.). 286p. 1985. pap. 9.95 o.p. (ISBN 0-930328-10-8). Travel Pr.

English, Welsh, Scottish Country Inns. rev., 3rd ed. Karen Brown & June Brown. LC 85-51931. (Karen Brown's: European Country Inn Ser.). (Illus.). 290p. (Orig.). 1986. pap. 10.95 o.p. (ISBN 0-930328-17-5). Travel Pr.

English Whippet. E. G. Walsh & Mary Lowe. (Illus.). 1984. 27.00 o.p. (ISBN 0-85115-193-0, Pub. by Boydell & Brewer). Longwood Pub Group.

English Workshop: First Course. Fay Greiffenberg. 252p. 1978. pap. text ed. 4.50 o.p. (ISBN 0-15-522706-8, HC). HarBraceJ.

English Year. Roy Strong & Julia T. Oman. LC 82-804. (Illus.). 224p. 1982. 24.50 o.p. (ISBN 0-89919-122-3). Ticknor & Fields.

English 2200: A Programed Course in Grammar & Usage. 2nd ed. Joseph C. Blumenthal. 383p. 1976. pap. text ed. 9.74 o.p. (ISBN 0-15-522700-9, HC). HarBraceJ.

English 2600: A Programed Course in Grammar & Usage. 4th ed. Joseph C. Blumenthal. 1973. pap. text ed. 10.52 o.p. (ISBN 0-15-522690-8, HC). HarBraceJ.

English 3200: A Programed Course in Grammar & Usage. 2nd ed. Joseph C. Blumenthal. (Prog. Bk.). 1972. pap. text ed. 12.08 o.p. (ISBN 0-15-522675-4, HC, HC). HarBraceJ.

Englishing of French Words see Preliminary Announcement.

Englishman's Daughter. Peter Evans. 1984. pap. 3.50 o.s.i. (ISBN 0-345-31451-4). Ballantine.

Englishman's Greek Concordance of the New Testament: Numerically Coded to Strong's Exhaustive Concordance. rev. ed. (Gr.). 1980. Repr. 39.95 o.p. Baker Bk.

Englishness: National Identity in Arts, Politics & Society 1880-1920. Ed. by Philip Dodd & Robert Colls. 384p. 1987. text ed. 47.50x o.p. (Pub. by Croom Helm UK); pap. text ed. 16.95x o.p. (ISBN 0-317-64356-8, Pub. by Croom Helm UK). Routledge Chapman & Hall.

Englishwoman's Review of Social & Industrial Questions: An Index. Ed. by Janet H. Murray & Anna K. Clark. 1985. lib. bdg. 40.00 o.p. (ISBN 0-8240-3765-0). Garland Pub.

Engrammes of the Universe: Extra-Cerebral Memory, Reincarnation & Demonic Possession. J. M. Sanchez-Perez. 1980. 8.50 o.p. (ISBN 0-682-49474-7). Exposition-Phoenix.

Engraved Designs of William Blake. Lawrence Binyon. LC 67-25542. (Graphic Art Ser.). 1967. Repr. of 1926 ed. lib. bdg. 65.00 o.p. (ISBN 0-306-70956-2). Da Capo.

Enhanced Oil Recovery. F. J. Fayers. (Developments in Petroleum Science Ser.: Vol. 13). 596p. 1981. 110.75 o.p. (ISBN 0-444-42033-9). Elsevier.

Enhanced Recovery & Rotating Equipment: A Workbook for Petroleum Engineers. 86p. 1980. 25.00 o.p. (ISBN 0-317-33502-2, I00135); members 12.50 o.p. (ISBN 0-317-33503-0). ASME.

Enhancing Human Performance: Issues, Theories, & Techniques. Ed. by Daniel Druckman & Johns A. Swets. 312p. 1988. 32.50 o.p. (ISBN 0-309-03792-1); pap. text ed. 22.50 o.p. (ISBN 0-309-03787-5). Natl Acad Pr.

Enhancing Productivity: Proceedings of the Pacific Cascade Instrumentation '84 Symposium. Instrument Society of America Staff. 216p. 1984. pap. 39.50 o.p. (ISBN 0-87664-836-7). Instru Soc.

Enhancing Your Apple II & IIe, Vol. 2. Don Lancaster. 17.95 o.p. (ISBN 0-672-22425-9). Sams.

Enhancing Your Apple Two, Vol. I. 2nd ed. Don Lancaster. LC 83-51704. 15.95 o.p. (ISBN 0-672-21822-4). Sams.

Enigma of the Eighties: Environment, Economic, Energy. Thomas A. Dougherty. (Science of Advanced Materials Process Engineering Ser.). (Illus.). 1979. 55.00 o.p. (ISBN 0-686-15770-2). SAMPE.

Enigma of the Hereafter. Paul Siweck. 1953. (ISBN 0-8022-1581-5). Philos Lib.

Enigmas del Micromundo. V. Chernogorova. 317p. (Span.). 1977. pap. 3.45 o.p. (ISBN 0-8285-1694-4, Pub. by Mir Pubs USSR). Imported Pubns.

Enjoy Golf & Win: Mental Golf--Its Impact on Scoring & Enjoyment. R. Craig Smith. LC 81-50344. 60p. (Orig.). 1981. pap. 6.95 o.s.i. (ISBN 0-686-31629-0). Wordsmith Pubns.

Enjoying a Profitable Business. 2nd ed. A. C. Hazel & A. S. Reid. 251p. 1976. text ed. 18.50x o.p. (ISBN 0-220-66287-8, Pub. by Busn Bks England). Gower Pub Co.

Enjoying Birds Around New York City. Robert S. Arbib, Jr. 1966. pap. 2.45 o.p. (ISBN 0-395-07347-2). HM.

Enjoying the Arts: Theatre. Mary McGann. (Illus.). (YA) (gr. 7-12). 1977. PLB 10.97 o.p. (ISBN 0-8239-0388-5). Rosen Group.

Enjoying the Psalms, 2 vols. William MacDonald. 1977. pap. 7.00 ea. o.p. Vol. 1 (ISBN 0-937396-34-6). Vol. 2 (ISBN 0-937396-35-4). Walterick Pubs.

Enjoying the Signery. Bill MacRobbie. 1977. 4.00 o.p. (ISBN 0-682-48965-4). Exposition-Phoenix.

Enjoyment of Mathematics: Selections from Mathematics for the Amateur. Hans Rademacher & Otto Toeplitz. 24.00x o.p. (ISBN 0-691-07958-7); pap. 9.95x o.p. (ISBN 0-691-02351-4). Princeton U Pr.

Enjoyment of the Arts. Max Schoen. (ISBN 0-8022-1504-1). Philos Lib.

Enku: Sculptor of a Hundred Thousand Buddhas. Kazuaki Tanahashi. LC 81-50969. (Illus.). 122p. (Orig.). 1982. pap. 13.95 o.s.i. (ISBN 0-394-74882-4). Shambhala Pubns.

Enlarged Type Reprint of the Nineteen Seventy-Six Medical Devices Act P. L. 94-295. pap. cancelled o.s.i. (ISBN 0-914176-08-0); pap. cancelled o.s.i.; pap. cancelled o.s.i.; pap. cancelled o.s.i. Wash Busn Info.

Enlarging the Change: The Princeton Seminars in Literary Criticism, 1949-1951. Robert Fitzgerald. 261p. 1985. text ed. 19.95x o.p. (ISBN 0-930350-62-6). NE U Pr.

Enlightened England. rev. ed. Ed. by Wylie Sypher. (Illus.). 1962. 14.95x o.p. (ISBN 0-393-09425-1, NortonC). Norton.

Enlightenment. rev. ed. Peter Gay. 1985. pap. 15.95 o.p. (ISBN 0-671-21915-4, Touchstone Bks). S&S.

Enlightenment & English Literature: Prose & Poetry of the Eighteenth Century with Selected Modern Critical Essays. John L. Mahoney. 1980. text ed. 26.00 o.p. (ISBN 0-669-02321-3). Heath.

Enlightenment & Romanticism in Eighteenth-Century Prussia. Henri Brunschwig. Tr. by Frank Jellinek from Fr. LC 73-87299. 1977. pap. text ed. 11.00x o.s.i. (ISBN 0-226-07769-1). U of Chicago Pr.

Enlightenment & Scottish Literature: Progress & Poetry, Vol. I. John MacQueen. 1982. 15.00x o.p. (ISBN 0-7073-0290-0, Pub. by Scot Acad Pr). Longwood Pub Group.

Ennemonde et Autres Caracteres: Roman. Jean Giono. 13.50 o.p. (ISBN 0-685-34167-4). Schoenhof.

Eno Collection of New York City Views. New York Public Library Staff. Ed. by Frank Weitenkampf. LC 79-162522. (Illus.). 90p. 1971. Repr. of 1925 ed. 43.00x o.p. (ISBN 0-8103-3744-4). Gale.

Enormous Room. e. e. Cummings. LC 77-114387. 1970. 5.95 o.p. (ISBN 0-87140-956-9); pap. 3.25 o.p. (ISBN 0-87140-001-4, L-001). Liveright.

Enormous Room. E. E. Cummings. LC 34-2154. 332p. 1934. 5.95 o.s.i. (ISBN 0-394-60427-X). Modern Lib.

Enough Is Enough: A Biblical Call for Moderation in a Consumer Oriented Societed. John V. Taylor. LC 77-72456. 1977. pap. 5.95 o.p. (ISBN 0-8066-1584-2, 10-2083, Augsburg). Augsburg Fortress.

Enough Is Enough: Exploding the Myth of Having It All. Carol Orsborn. 1986. 15.95 o.p. (ISBN 0-399-13175-2). Putnam Pub Group.

Enquiry, 2 vols, No. 3. 1970. Repr. of 1945 ed. Set. lib. bdg. 11.75x o.p. (ISBN 0-8371-9166-1, EN00). Greenwood.

Enquiry Concerning the Principles of Natural Knowledge. Alfred N. Whitehead. (Western Philosophy & Religion Ser.). 207p. 1982. pap. 5.95 o.p. (ISBN 0-486-24343-5). Dover.

Enquiry Concerning the Principles of Natural Knowledge. Alfred North Whitehead. 1983. 12.75 o.p. (ISBN 0-8446-6013-2). Peter Smith.

Enquiry into the Ideas of Space & Time. Edmund Law. Ed. by Rene Wellek. LC 75-11230. (British Philosophers & Theologians of the 17th & 18th Century: Vol. 31). 1976. Repr. of 1734 ed. lib. bdg. 51.00 o.p. (ISBN 0-8240-1783-8). Garland Pub.

Enriched Uranium Poems-Bern Porter Interview. Robert G. Head & Phil Nurenberg. (White Paper Ser.: No. 5). 50p. (Orig.). 1983. pap. 3.00 o.p. (ISBN 0-912824-31-X). Vagabond Pr.

Enriching Your Reading Program. Marjorie R. Heyman. 1972. pap. 4.95 o.p. (ISBN 0-8224-2710-9). D S Lake Pubs.

Ensemble: Culture et Societe. 2nd ed. Raymond F. Comeau et al. LC 76-49630. 1982. pap. text ed. 15.95 o.p. (ISBN 0-03-060087-1, HoltC). HR&W.

Ensemble: Grammaire. 2nd ed. Raymond F. Comeau et al. LC 76-49636. 1982. text ed. 17.95 o.p. (ISBN 0-03-060082-0, HoltC); lab manual 11.95 o.p. (ISBN 0-03-060083-9). tapes avail. o.p. (ISBN 0-03-060084-7). HR&W.

Ensemble: Literature. 2nd ed. Raymond F. Comeau et al. LC 76-48930. 1982. pap. text ed. 15.95 o.p. (ISBN 0-03-060086-3, HoltC). HR&W.

Ensign Flandry. Poul Anderson. 1979. lib. bdg. 11.95 o.p. (ISBN 0-8398-2526-9, Gregg). G K Hall.

Ensor's Complete Graphic Work. Aug. Taevernier. (Illus.). 379p. 1973. 200.00 o.s.i. (ISBN 0-915346-81-8). A Wofsy Fine Arts.

Ensuring Data Base Integrity. William E. Perry. LC 82-25922. 378p. 1983. 50.00x o.p. (ISBN 0-471-86526-5). Wiley.

Ensuring Intensive Care. Ed. by Jean Robinson & Barbara McVan. LC 81-6995. (Nursing Photobook Ser.). (Illus.). 160p. 1981. 17.95 o.p. (ISBN 0-916730-37-9). Springhouse Pub.

Ensuring Program Quality. National Computing Centre, Ltd. Staff. Ed. by Bill Murphy et al. 64p. (Orig.). 1980. pap. 22.50x o.s.i. (ISBN 0-85012-235-X). Intl Pubns Serv.

ENT & Oral Surgery of the Dog & Cat: Veterinary Practitioner Handbook. J. G. Lane. 296p. 1982. text ed. 29.00 o.p. (ISBN 0-7236-0659-5). Butterworth.

Entailment: The Logic of Relevance & Necessity, Vol. 1. Alan R. Anderson & Nuel D. Belnap, Jr. LC 72-14016. 567p. 1975. 52.50x o.p. (ISBN 0-691-07192-6). Princeton U Pr.

Entangling Alliances: Christianity & Foreign Policy. James B. Jordan. cancelled o.s.i. (ISBN 0-930462-21-1). Am Bur Eco Res.

Entendamonos: Manual de Conversacion. 2nd ed. Carlos Garcia-Prada & William E. Wilson. (Span). 1959. pap. 9.50 o.p. (ISBN 0-395-04481-2). HM.

Enter. Jean-Daniel Dodin. Ed. by Keith Jarett. Tr. by Mary-Denise Dodin from Fr. LC 84-51380. 142p. 1984. pap. text ed. 5.95 o.s.i. (ISBN 0-9612174-2-1). Synthetix.

Enter a Free Man. Tom Stoppard. LC 72-81791. 96p. 1972. pap. 2.95 o.s.i. (ISBN 0-394-17779-7, E586, Ever). Grove.

Enter Dr. Nikola! Guy Boothby. (Dr. Nikola Ser: No. 1). 256p. 1975. pap. 5.95 o.p. (ISBN 0-87877-032-1, X-32). Newcastle Pub.

Enter the Saint. Leslie Charteris. (Saint Ser.). 256p. 1980. pap. 1.95 o.p. (ISBN 0-441-20727-8). Ace Bks.

Entering Higher Education in the United States: A Guide for Students from Other Countries. rev. ed. LC 73-99051. 50p. 1985. pap. 25.00 per package of 40 copies o.p. (221615). College Bd.

Entering Medicine: the Dynamics of Transition: A Seven Year Study of Medical Education in Israel. J. T. Shuval. LC 78-40930. 247p. 1980. 59.00 o.p. (ISBN 0-08-024272-3). Pergamon.

Entering Space: An Astronaut's Odyssey. Joseph P. Allen & Russell Martin. LC 84-2561. (Illus.). 224p. 1984. 24.95 o.p. (ISBN 0-941434-53-2). Stewart Tabori & Chang.

Entering the Remodeling Field: A Manual for Small-Volume Builders. Henri De Marne. 96p. 1977. pap. 8.00 o.p. (ISBN 0-86718-050-1). Nat Assn H Build.

Enterprise & Society. Vinayshil Gautam. 1979. text ed. 8.50x o.p. (ISBN 0-391-01861-2). Humanities.

Enterprise Organization: Cases, Statutes & Analysis on Licensing, Employment, Agency, Partnerships, Associations, & Corporations. 3rd ed. Alfred F. Conard et al. LC 82-10902. (University Casebook Ser.). 1243p. 1982. text ed. 27.50 o.p. (ISBN 0-88277-058-6); Editor's Notes. write for info. o.p. (ISBN 0-88277-108-6). Foundation Pr.

Enterprise Organization: Corporation & Partnership Statutes, Rules & Forms to Accompany 3rd. ed. Alfred F. Conrad et al. (University Casebook Ser.). 339p. 1982. pap. text ed. 5.50 o.p. (ISBN 0-88277-088-8). Foundation Pr.

Enterprise Versus Bureaucracy: The Development of Structural Air-Raid Precautions During the 2nd World War. Lord Baker of Windrush. LC 77-30397. 1978. 20.00 o.p. (ISBN 0-08-022149-1). Pergamon.

Enterprise Zones: A Bibliographic Update. Anthony G. White. (Public Administration Ser.: P 1729). 9p. 1985. 2.00 o.p. (ISBN 0-89028-499-7). Vance Biblios.

Enterprising Women: Their Contribution to the American Economy, 1776-1976. Caroline Bird. 256p. 1976. 12.95 o.p. (ISBN 0-393-08724-7). Norton.

Entertainers & the Entertained: Essays on Theater, Film & Television. John Houseman. 352p. 1986. 18.45 o.s.i. (ISBN 0-671-62233-1). S&S.

Entertaining Fast & Fresh. Susan Mitchell. (Illus.). 128p. (Orig.). 1985. pap. 7.95 o.p. (ISBN 0-8249-3037-1). Ideals.

Entertaining for All Seasons. Sunset Magazine & Books Editors. LC 83-82499. (Illus.). 168p. 1984. 14.95 o.p. (ISBN 0-376-02141-1, Sunset Bks). Sunset-Lane.

Entertaining in Jerusalem. Weisgal. 1985. 19.95 o.p. (ISBN 0-940646-22-6). Rossel Bks.

Entertaining with Style. Prue Leith & Polly Tyrer. LC 85-61142. (Cookbook Library). (Illus.). 224p. 1985. 19.95 o.p. (ISBN 0-688-04078-0). Morrow.

Entertainment of the Stage see Mr. Law's Unlawfulness of the Stage Entertainment Examin'd.

Enthusiast. Peter Hill. 1979. 7.95 o.p. (ISBN 0-395-27543-1). HM.

Enthusiast: A Life of Thornton Wilder. Gilbert A. Harrison. LC 83-5076. (Illus.). 416p. 1983. 19.45 o.p. (ISBN 0-89919-197-5). Ticknor & Fields.

Entity Process: The Accumulation of a Physical Property as a Function of Mortality & Magnitude of Rank. Frank Reynolds East. 1977. 10.00 o.p. (ISBN 0-682-48630-2, University). Exposition-Phoenix.

Entity-Relationship Approach to Information Modeling & Analysis: Proceedings of the Second International Conference on Entity-Relationship Approach, Washington, D. C., Oct. 12-14, 1981. Ed. by P. P. Chen. 602p. 1984. 84.25 o.p. (ISBN 0-444-86747-3, I-492-83, North Holland). Elsevier.

Entomological Information Storage & Retrieval. Ross H. Arnett, Jr. 210p. 1970. 4.95 o.p. (ISBN 0-916846-00-8). Flora & Fauna.

Entrance to Porlock. Frederick Buechner. LC 79-97132. 1970. 5.95 o.p. (ISBN 0-689-10052-3, Atheneum). Macmillan.

Entrapped. Edward Baskett. LC 75-41812. 160p. 1976. 6.50 o.p. (ISBN 0-88208-064-4). Chicago Review.

Entratiens avec le Professeur Y. Louis-Ferdinand D. Celine. 1976. pap. 12.95 o.p. (ISBN 0-686-50140-3). Schoenhof.

Entre la Vie et la Mort: Roman. Nathalie Sarraute. pap. 14.95 o.p. (ISBN 0-685-23939-X). Schoenhof.

Entre Picasso et Radiquet. Jean Cocteau. 194p. 1967. 9.95 o.p. (ISBN 0-686-54526-5). French & Eur.

Entrepreneur. I. G. Broat. LC 77-24921. 1978. 9.95 o.p. (ISBN 0-689-10818-4, Atheneum). Macmillan.

Entrepreneur & Gentleman: The Case History of a Japanese Business. Akira Sueno. Tr. by Neal Donner. LC 76-51611. (Illus.). 1977. 16.50 o.p. (ISBN 0-8048-1199-7). C E Tuttle.

Entrepreneurial Megabucks: The One-Hundred Greatest Entrepreneurs of the Last Twenty-Five Years. A. David Silver. LC 85-12089. (Small Business Management Ser.). 467p. 1985. 19.95 o.p. (ISBN 0-471-82184-5). Wiley.

Entrepreneurial Middle Class. Richard Scase & Robert Goffee. 1982. 33.00 o.p. (ISBN 0-7099-0450-9, Pub. by Croom Helm Ltd). Routledge Chapman & Hall.

Entrepreneurial Mothers. Phyllis Gillis. LC 82-42685. 384p. 1983-84. 16.95 o.p. (ISBN 0-89256-248-X); pap. 9.95 o.p. (ISBN 0-89256-256-0). Rawson Assocs.

Entrepreneurial Skills: Cases in Small Business Management. Philip W. Mahin. 1981. pap. 18.95x o.p. (ISBN 0-256-02562-2). Irwin.

Entrepreneurs in Corporations. Paul M. Connolly. (Studies in Productivity: No. 47). 79p. 1986. pap. 39.00 o.s.i. (ISBN 0-08-029519-3, PBI). Pergamon.

Entrepreneurs of Entrepreneurship. Wesley W. Watkins. 12p. cancelled o.s.i. (ISBN 0-318-22091-1, OC84). Natl Ctr Res Voc Ed.

Entrepreneurship. Ed. by D. Bos et al. (Zeitschrift fur Nationalokonomie Supplementum: 4). (Illus.). 220p. 1985. pap. 38.70 o.p. (ISBN 0-387-81830-8). Springer-Verlag.

Entrepreneurship. Joshua Ronen. LC 82-47950. 336p. 1982. 40.00x o.p. (ISBN 0-669-05715-0). Lexington Bks.

Entrepreneurship & Small Business Management. Kenneth R. Van Voorhis. 1980. text ed. 40.00 o.s.i. (ISBN 0-205-06682-8, 086682-2). Allyn.

Entrepreneurship & Venture Management: Text & Readings. Clifford M. Baumback & Joseph R. Mancuso. (Illus.). 368p. 1975. pap. text ed. (ISBN 0-13-283119-8). P-H.

Entrepreneurship in India's Small-Scale Industries: An Exploration of Social Contexts. Richard P. Taub & Doris L. Taub. LC 86-63597. 300p. 1989. 31.00 o.p. (ISBN 0-913215-19-8). Riverdale Co.

Entretiens avec Georges Charbonnier. Michel Butor. pap. 8.95 o.p. (ISBN 0-685-37246-4). French & Eur.

Entretiens avec les Mots. Paula Kane & Patricia Short. (Fr.). 1984. pap. text ed. 21.00 o.p. (ISBN 0-88377-380-5). Newbury Hse.

Entropy, Absolute Temperature & Coldness in Thermodynamics Boundary Conditions in Porous Material: Proceedings of CISM, Department of Mechanics of Solids, 1971. CISM (International Center for Mechanical Sciences), Department of Mechanics of Solids Staff. Ed. by I. Muller. (CISM Pubnlications: No. 76). (Illus.). 53p. 1973. pap. text ed. 8.20 o.p. (ISBN 0-387-81126-5). Springer-Verlag.

Entropy Effect. Vonda N. McIntyre. (Star Trek Ser.). 224p. 1984. lib. bdg. 10.95 o.p. (ISBN 0-8398-2831-4, Gregg). G K Hall.

Entropy Exhibition: Michael Moorcock & the British "New Wave" in Science Fiction. Colin Greenland. 244p. 1983. 26.95x o.p. (ISBN 0-7100-9310-1). Routledge Chapman & Hall.

Entry. Hans Holzer. 1981. pap. 2.50 o.s.i. (ISBN 0-505-51661-6, T51661, Pub. by Tower Bks). Dorchester Pub Co.

Entry Strategies for Foreign Markets: From Domestic to International Business. Franklin R. Root. LC 77-25345. 1977. 10.00 o.p. (ISBN 0-8144-2216-0). AMACOM.

Entry: The Hiring, Start-up & Supervision of Administrators. Barry C. Jentz. (Illus.). 256p. 1982. text ed. 21.15x o.p. (ISBN 0-07-032528-6). McGraw.

Entscheidungstheorie. K. Egle. (Interdisciplinary Systems Research Ser.: No. 5). 246p. (Ger.). 1975. pap. 27.95x o.p. (ISBN 0-8176-0776-5). Birkhauser.

Enumeration & Design. D. M. Jackson & S. A. Vanstone. 1984. 47.00 o.p. (ISBN 0-12-379120-0). Acad Pr.

Env-Sens Crack Prob in Nuc. Ed. by J. C. Scully. (Illus.). 190p. 1986. pap. 50.00 o.p. (ISBN 0-08-033418-0, PBL). Pergamon.

Environment & Behavior. C. J. Holahan. LC 77-25400. (Plenum Social Ecology Ser.). (Illus.). 206p. 1977. 32.50x o.p. (ISBN 0-306-31086-4, Plenum Pr). Plenum Pub.

Environment & Bilateral Aid. 1980. 4.50 o.p. (ISBN 0-905347-16-1). C I D E.

Environment & Energy: Environmental Aspects of Energy Production & Use with Particular Reference to New Technologies. United Nations Economic Commission for Europe, Geneva, Switzerland. LC 79-40550. 1979. 34.00 o.p. (ISBN 0-08-024468-8). Pergamon.

Environment & Man. 3rd ed. Richard H. Wagner. (Illus.). 606p. 1978. text ed. 22.95x o.p. (ISBN 0-393-09066-3). Norton.

Environment & Man. 2nd ed. Richard H. Wagner. (Illus.). 528p. 1974. 9.95x o.p. (ISBN 0-393-09317-4). Norton.

Environment & Man in Kansas: A Geographical Analysis. Huber Self. LC 77-5867. (Illus.). xvi, 288p. 1978. 19.95x o.p. (ISBN 0-7006-0162-7). U Pr of KS.

Environment & Man: The Built Environment, Vol. 8. Ed. by John Lenihan & William Fletcher. 1979. 39.50 o.p. (ISBN 0-12-443508-4). Acad Pr.

Environment & the Law. Irving J. Sloan. LC 79-156377. 120p. 1971. (ISBN 0-379-11077-6). Oceana.

Environment & Trade: The Relation of International Trade & Environmental Policy. Ed. by Seymour J. Rubin & Thomas R. Graham. LC 81-65012. (Illus.). 222p. 1982. text ed. 35.50x o.s.i. (ISBN 0-86598-032-2, Pub. by Allanheld). Rowman.

Environment & Utopia: A Synthesis. R. H. Moos & R. Brownstein. LC 77-23273. (Social Ecology Ser.). 294p. 1977. pap. 14.95x o.p. (ISBN 0-306-20024-4, Plenum Pr). Plenum Pub.

Environment & Utopia: A Synthesis. Rudolf Moos & Robert Brownstein. LC 77-23275. (Plenum Social Ecology Ser.). 294p. 1977. 39.50x o.p. (ISBN 0-306-30985-8, Plenum Pr). Plenum Pub.

Environment at Work. E. C. Poulton. (Illus.). 176p. 1979. 25.50x o.p. (ISBN 0-398-03848-1). C C Thomas.

Environment: Chinese & American Perspectives. Ed. by Laurence J. Ma & Allen G. Noble. 397p. 1981. 34.00x o.p. (ISBN 0-416-60301-7, NO. 3491). Routledge Chapman & Hall.

Environment in Engineering Education. (Studies in Engineering Education: No. 9). 120p. 1980. pap. 9.25 o.p. (ISBN 92-3-101793-4, U1028, UNESCO). UNIPUB.

Environment: International Aspects. K. Ananichev. 207p. 1976. pap. 2.45 o.p. (ISBN 0-8285-0430-X, Pub. by Progress Pubs USSR). Imported Pubns.

Environment of Early Man in the British Isles. John G. Evans. LC 74-29803. 256p. 1975. 40.00x o.p. (ISBN 0-520-02973-9). U of Cal Pr.

Environment of International Business: Concepts, Structures, & Strategies. Endel-Jakob Kolde. LC 81-17122. 483p. 1981. instr's. manual 27.95x o.p. (ISBN 0-534-01038-5). PWS-Kent Pub.

Environment of Medicine: Report of the Council on Long Range Planning & Development. LC 85-178765. 1985. 10.00 o.p. (ISBN 0-89970-249-X, OP-223-5). AMA.

Environment Regional Science & Interregional Modeling. Ed. by M. Chatterji & P. Van Rompuy. 1976. pap. 14.00 o.p. (ISBN 0-387-07693-X). Springer-Verlag.

Environment-Sensitive Fracture of Engineering Materials. Ed. by Z. A. Foroulis. LC 79-84173. 662p. 1979. 50.00 o.p. (ISBN 0-89520-353-7). Minerals Metals.

Environment-Sensitive Fracture of Engineering Materials: Proceedings of the TMS-AIME Fall Meeting, Chicago, IL, 1977. (Illus.). 672p. 50.00 o.p.; members 32.00 o.p. (ISBN 0-317-34868-X); student members 16.00 o.p. (ISBN 0-317-34869-8). ASM.

Environment: The Human Impact, Selections from the Science Teacher. Compiled by Rosemary E. Amidei. 1973. pap. 1.00 o.p. (ISBN 0-87355-001-3). Natl Sci Tchrs.

Environment 1988-89. 7th, rev. ed. Ed. by John Allen. LC 79-644216. (Annual Editions Ser.). (Illus.). 256p. 1988. pap. text ed. 9.95 o.p. (ISBN 0-87967-724-4). Dushkin Pub.

Environmental Administration in Thailand. Roy C. Stubbs. LC 81-9781. (East-West Environment & Policy Institute Research Report: No. 5). vi, 89p. (Orig.). 1981. pap. text ed. 3.00 o.p. (ISBN 0-86638-027-2). EW Ctr HI.

Environmental Analysis: For Land-Use & Site Planning. William M. Marsh. (Illus.). 1977. text ed. 44.50 o.p. (ISBN 0-07-040490-9). McGraw.

Environmental Analysis for Management. James P. Baughman et al. 1974. 33.95x o.p. (ISBN 0-256-01561-9). Irwin.

Environmental & Birth Defects. James G. Wilson. (Environmental Science: An Interdisciplinary Monograph). 1973. 83.00 o.p. (ISBN 0-12-757750-5). Acad Pr.

Environmental & Community Health see Individualized Health Incentive Program Modules For Physically Disabled Students.

Environmental & Land Use Law Section: 1984 Mid-Year Meeting & Seminars. 314p. 1984. 30.00 o.p. (ISBN 0-88129-135-8). Wash Bar CLE.

Environmental Archaeology. Myra Shackley. (Illus.). 256p. 1981. text ed. 40.00x o.p. (ISBN 0-04-913020-X); pap. text ed. 29.95x o.p. (ISBN 0-04-913021-8). Unwin Hyman.

Environmental Audits. 3rd ed. Lawrence B. Cahill. (Illus.). 240p. 1984. pap. 49.00 o.p. (ISBN 0-86587-066-7). Gov Insts.

Environmental Audits. 4th ed. Ed. by Lawrence B. Cahill et al. 397p. 1985. pap. 54.00 o.p. (ISBN 0-86587-129-9). Gov Insts.

Environmental Biology for Engineers: A Guide to Environmental Assessment. G. Camougis. 1980. text ed. 28.50 o.p. (ISBN 0-07-009677-5). McGraw.

Environmental Carcinogenesis; Occurrence Risk Evaluation & Mechanisms: Proceedings. International Conference on Environmental Carcinogensis, Amsterdam, May 1979. Ed. by P. Emmelot & E. Kriek. 402p. 1979. 107.50 o.p. (ISBN 0-444-80158-8, North Holland). Elsevier.

Environmental Compliance in a Changing Legal Environment. Practising Law Institute Staff & Joel H. Sachs. LC 82-82815. (Criminal Law & Urban Problems Course Handbook: Litigation & Administrative Practice Ser.: No. 129). 576p. 1983. 45.00 o.p. (C44163). PLI.

Environmental Concern: Personal Attitudes & Behavior Toward Environmental Problems. Ed. by Arvin W. Murch. 378p. 1974. text ed. 29.50x o.p. (ISBN 0-8422-5169-3); pap. text ed. 11.00x o.p. (ISBN 0-8422-0410-5). Irvington.

Environmental Considerations for Biomass Energy Development: Hawaii Case Study. Gerald G. Marten & Daryl Babor. LC 81-22046. (East-West Environment & Policy Institute Research Report: No. 9). vi, 58p. (Orig.). 1981. pap. text ed. 3.00 o.p. (ISBN 0-86638-031-0). EW Ctr HI.

Environmental Contamination by Radioactive Materials. (Proceedings Ser.). (Illus.). 736p. (Orig., Eng. , Fr. & Span.). 1969. pap. 53.75 o.p. (ISBN 92-0-020169-5, ISP226, IAEA). UNIPUB.

Environmental Controls! A Handbook for Realtors. 90p. 3.00 o.p. (ISBN 0-318-15180-4, 111-217). Natl Assoc Realtors.

Environmental Degradation of Materials in Nuclear Power Systems: Water Reactors, Monterey, CA September 2-12, 1985. 655p. Date not set. 85.00 o.p. (ISBN 0-89448-124-X, 700108). Am Nuclear Soc.

Environmental Design. Richard P. Dober. LC 75-11961. 288p. 1975. Repr. of 1969 ed. 24.50 o.p. (ISBN 0-88275-331-2). Krieger.

Environmental Economics. Thomas H. Tietenberg. 1984. text ed. (ISBN 0-673-15558-7). Scott F.

Environmental Economics: A Guide to Information Sources. Ed. by Barry C. Field & Cleve E. Willis. (Man & the Environment Information Guide Ser.: Vol. 8). 264p. 1979. 68.00x o.p. (ISBN 0-8103-1433-9). Gale.

Environmental Education: A Guide to Information Sources. Ed. by William B. Stapp & Mary D. Liston. LC 73-17542. (Man & the Environment Information Guide Ser.: Vol. 1). 238p. 1980. 68.00x o.p. (ISBN 0-8103-1337-5). Gale.

Environmental Education-Key Issues of the Future: Proceedings of the Conference Held at the College of Technology, Farnborough, England. Ed. by Hughes-Evans. LC 77-827. 1977. pap. 15.75 o.p. (ISBN 0-08-021490-8). Pergamon.

Environmental Education-Principles & Practice. Ed. by S. McB Carson. (Illus.). 1978. pap. 27.50x o.p. (ISBN 0-7131-0133-4). Trans-Atl Phila.

Environmental Effects of Atmospheric Heat-Moisture Releases: Cooling Towers, Cooling Ponds & Area Sources, No. H00110. K. E. Torrance. Ed. by R. G. Watts. 1978. pap. 18.00 o.p. (ISBN 0-685-99207-1). ASME.

Environmental Effects of Cooling Towers: AIF-NESP-026. Environmental Systems Corporation Staff. (National Environmental Studies Project: NESP Reports). 1983. 50.00 o.p. (ISBN 0-318-02234-6). US Coun Energy Awareness.

Environmental Effects on Composite Materials, Vol. 1. Ed. by George S. Springer. LC 81-50309. 203p. 1981. pap. 35.00 o.p. (ISBN 0-87762-300-7). Technomic.

Environmental Engineering. P. Aarne Vesilind. LC 81-70872. 1982. 37.95 o.p. (ISBN 0-250-40422-2). Butterworth.

Environmental Factor: An Approach for Managers. D. J. Davison. LC 77-20123. 183p. 1978. 42.95x o.p. (ISBN 0-470-99351-0). Halsted Pr.

Environmental Factors in Respiratory Disease. Ed. by Douglas H. Lee. (Environmental Science Ser.). 1972. 47.00 o.p. (ISBN 0-12-440655-6). Acad Pr.

Environmental Factors in the Heating of Buildings. L. E. Anapol'skaya. 248p. 1975. text ed. 49.00x o.p. (ISBN 0-7065-1511-0, Pub. by Keter Pub Jerusalem). Coronet Bks.

Environmental Factors in Urban Planning. E. Grandjean & A. Gilgen. 206p. 1976. text ed. 42.50x o.p. (ISBN 0-8290-0943-4). Irvington.

Environmental Factors in Urban Planning. E. Grandjean et al. 220p. 1976. 33.00x o.s.i. (ISBN 0-85066-084-X). Taylor & Francis.

Environmental Geology. Donald R. Coates. LC 80-21272. 731p. 1981. text ed. (ISBN 0-471-06379-7). Wiley.

Environmental Geomorphology & Landscape Conservation, 2. V. Ed. by Donald R. Coates. LC 72-77882. (Benchmark Papers in Geology Ser.). (Illus.). 1974. 66.00 o.p. (ISBN 0-12-786242-0). Acad Pr.

Environmental Geomorphology & Landscape Conservation: Non-Urban, Vol. 3. Ed. by D. R. Coates. LC 72-77882. (Benchmark Papers in Geology: Vol. 8). 483p. 1982. 61.95 o.p. (ISBN 0-87933-023-6). Van Nos Reinhold.

Environmental Geomorphology & Landscape Conservation: Prior to 1900, Vol. 1. Ed. by D. R. Coates. LC 72-77882. (Benchmark Papers in Geology: Vol.1). 485p. 1982. 61.95 o.p. (ISBN 0-87933-005-8). Van Nos Reinhold.

Environmental Glossary. 3rd ed. Ed. by G. William Frick. LC 84-81930. 336p. 1984. 38.00 o.p. (ISBN 0-86587-073-X). Gov Insts.

Environmental Guidelines Survey. 1983. 7.50 o.p. (ISBN 0-905347-40-4). C I D E.

Environmental Hazards-Air Pollution: A Bibliography. E. Willard Miller. (Public Administration Ser.: Bibliography P-1611). 54p. 1985. pap. 8.25 o.p. (ISBN 0-89028-261-7). Vance Biblios.

Environmental Hazards-Industrial & Toxic Wastes: A Bibliography. E. Willard Miller & Ruby M. Miller. (Public Administration Ser.: Bibliography P-1615). 99p. 1985. pap. 15.00 o.p. (ISBN 0-89028-265-X). Vance Biblios.

Environmental Hazards-Liquid Wastes: A Bibliography. E. Willard Miller & Ruby M. Miller. (Public Administration Ser.: Bibliography P-1614). 41p. 1985. pap. 6.00 o.p. (ISBN 0-89028-264-1). Vance Biblios.

Environmental Hazards-Radioactive Materials & Wastes: A Bibliography. E. Willard Miller & Ruby M. Miller. (Public Administration Ser.: Bibliography P-1616). 67p. 1985. pap. 9.75 o.p. (ISBN 0-89028-266-8). Vance Biblios.

Environmental Hazards-Solid Wastes: A Bibliography. E. Willard Miller & Ruby M. Miller. (Public Administration Ser: Bibliography P-1613). 43p. 1985. pap. 6.75 o.p. (ISBN 0-89028-263-3). Vance Biblios.

Environmental Hazards-Water Pollution: A Bibliography. E. Willard Miller & Ruby M. Miller. (Public Administration Ser.: Bibliography P-1612). 49p. 1985. pap. 7.50 o.p. (ISBN 0-89028-262-5). Vance Biblios.

Environmental Impact Assessment: A Practical Guide. Colin F. Porter. LC 84-3555. (Australian Environment Ser.: No. 9). (Illus.). 269p. 1985. text ed. 35.00x o.p. (ISBN 0-7022-1699-2). U of Queensland Pr.

Environmental Impact Assessment: Proceedings of a Seminar of the United Nations Economic Commission for Europe, Villach, Austria. United Nations Economic Commission for Europe. (ECE Seminars & Symposia). (Illus.). 368p. 1981. 74.00 o.p. (ISBN 0-08-024445-9). Pergamon.

Environmental Impact of Energy Strategies within the EEC. Environmental Resources, Ltd. Staff. 1980. pap. 42.00 flexi-cover o.p. (ISBN 0-08-025681-3). Pergamon.

Environmental Impacts of Artificial Ice Nucleating Agents. Donald A. Klein. LC 78-7985. 256p. 1982. 46.95 o.p. (ISBN 0-87933-334-0). Van Nos Reinhold.

Environmental Implications of Expanded Coal Utilization. Ed. by M. J. Chadwick & N. Lindman. LC 81-23560. (Illus.). 304p. 1982. 67.00 o.p. (ISBN 0-08-028734-4). Pergamon.

Environmental Information Sources. 230p. 1986. pap. text ed. 54.00 o.s.i. (ISBN 0-86587-140-X). Gov Insts.

Environmental Instrumentation. L. J. Fritschen & L. W. Gay. (Springer Advanced Texts in Life Sciences Ser.). (Illus.). 1979. 35.80 o.p. (ISBN 0-387-90411-5). Springer-Verlag.

Environmental Issues. Lawrence G. Hines & Christopher Hill. 1973. pap. 5.95x o.p. (ISBN 0-393-09331-X). Norton.

Environmental Issues in Chemical Perspective. Thomas G. Spiro & William M. Stigliani. LC 79-23756. 374p. 1980. 24.50x o.p. (ISBN 0-87395-427-0). State U NY Pr.

Environmental Issues-Scope Report 10. Ed. by Martin W. Holdgate & Gilbert F. White. LC 77-2667. 224p. 1977. 54.95 o.p. (ISBN 0-471-99503-7, Pub. by Wiley-Interscience). Wiley.

Environmental Law: A Guide to Information Sources. Mortimer Schwartz. LC 73-17541. (Man & the Environment Information Guide Ser.: Vol. 6). 208p. 1977. 68.00x o.p. (ISBN 0-8103-1339-1). Gale.

Environmental Law: An In-Depth Review. United Nations Environment Programme Staff. LC 82-121356. (UNEP Reports: No. 2). viii, 274p. Date not set. price not set. o.p. UN.

Environmental Law for Non-Lawyers. David B. Firestone & Frank C. Reed. LC 82-70697. (Illus.). 282p. 1983. 34.95 o.p. (ISBN 0-250-40529-6). Butterworth.

Environmental Law: Groundwater Protection & Industrial Contamination. Pennsylvania Bar Institute Staff. 220p. 1984. 30.00 o.p. (ISBN 0-318-02188-9, 246). PA Bar Inst.

Environmental Law Handbook. 8th ed. J. Gorden Arbuckle & G. William Frick. LC 76-41637. 586p. 1985. text ed. 49.50 o.p. (ISBN 0-86587-122-1). Gov Insts.

Environmental Law Handbook. 9th ed. J. Gordon Arbuckle et al. 600p. 1987. text ed. 57.95 o.s.i. (ISBN 0-86587-706-8). Gov Insts.

Environmental Law in a Nutshell. Roger W. Findley & Daniel A. Farber. LC 83-6764. (Nutshell Ser.). 343p. 1983. pap. text ed. 9.95 o.p. (ISBN 0-314-73633-6). West Pub.

Environmental Laws & Real Estate Handbook. Steven A. Tasher et al. 246p. 1987. pap. 69.00 o.s.i. (ISBN 0-86587-729-7). Gov Insts.

Environmental Leadership. Stuart Langton. LC 80-7445. 160p. 1984. 20.00x o.p. (ISBN 0-669-03698-6). Lexington Bks.

Environmental Management Handbook for the Hydrocarbon Processing Industries. Ed. by James D. Wall. LC 80-16294. 224p. (Orig.). 1980. pap. 25.00x o.p. (ISBN 0-87201-265-4). Gulf Pub.

Environmental Management in the Colorado River Basin. A. Berry Crawford & Dean F. Peterson. LC 74-121364. 313p. 1974. pap. 8.00 o.p. (ISBN 0-87421-068-2). Utah St U Pr.

Environmental Management in the South China Sea: Legal & Institutional Developments. Douglas M. Johnston. LC 82-11507. (East-West Environment & Policy Institute Research Report: No. 10). vi, 114p. (Orig.). 1982. pap. text ed. 4.00 o.p. (ISBN 0-86638-032-9). EW Ctr HI.

Environmental Management: Planning for Traffic. J. Antoniou. 1972. text ed. 41.50 o.p. (ISBN 0-07-094222-6). McGraw.

Environmental Mediation & Conflict Management: A Selection of Papers Presented at the 5th Annual Conference of the NAEP, Washington Dc, April 21-23 1980. Ed. by R. Rajagopal. 120p. 1981. pap. 12.00 o.p. (ISBN 0-08-026261-9). Pergamon.

Environmental Memory. Date not set. Random.

Environmental Modeling: Analysis & Management. Ed. by Pantell Daetz. LC 73-22191. (Benchmark Papers in Electric Engineering & Computer Science: Vol. 6). 407p. 1982. 59.95 o.p. (ISBN 0-87933-082-1); pap. 39.95 o.p. (ISBN 0-87933-138-0). Van Nos Reinhold.

Environmental Modification Convention of 1977: A Technical, Legal & Policy Appraisal. Ed. by Arthur Westing. 100p. 1984. pap. 21.00x o.p. Taylor & Francis.

Environmental Physics in Construction: Its Application in Architectural Design. Erich Schild et al. 211p. 1982. text ed. 65.00 o.p. (ISBN 0-246-11224-7, Pub. by Granada England). Gower Pub Co.

Environmental Physiology & Psychology in Arid Conditions: Proceeding of the Lucknow Symposium. (Arid Zone Research Ser.: No. 22). 400p. (Eng. & Fr.). 1964. 9.50 o.p. (ISBN 92-3-000566-5, U220, UNESCO). UNIPUB.

Environmental Physiology & Psychology in Arid Conditions: Review of Research. (Arid Zone Research Ser.: No. 22). 345p. 1963. 12.50 o.p. (ISBN 92-3-100531-6, U221, UNESCO); pap. write for info o.p. (ISBN 92-3-100532-4). UNIPUB.

Environmental Physiology of Desert Organisms. Neil F. Hadley. LC 75-14408. 283p. 1975. 58.50 o.p. (ISBN 0-12-786620-5). Acad Pr.

Environmental Physiology of Marine Animals. W. B. Vernberg & F. J. Vernberg. LC 70-183485. (Illus.). 346p. 1972. 30.00 o.p. (ISBN 0-387-05721-8). Springer-Verlag.

Environmental Physiology of Plants. A. H. Fitter & R. K. Hay. (Experimental Botany Ser.). 1981. 64.50 o.p. (ISBN 0-12-257760-4); pap. 27.00 o.p. (ISBN 0-12-257762-0). Acad Pr.

Environmental Physiology: Proceedings of the 28th International Congress of Physiological Sciences, Budapest, 1980 (Including the Satellite Symposium on Sports Physiology) Ed. by F. Obal & G. Benedek. LC 80-42102. (Advances in Physiological Sciences: Vol. 18). (Illus.). 375p. 1981. 57.00 o.p. (ISBN 0-08-027339-4). Pergamon.

Environmental Planning: Perception & Behavior. Thomas Saarinen. LC 75-19533. (Illus.). 288p. 1976. pap. 16.95 o.p. (ISBN 0-395-20618-9). HM.

Environmental Policy in Australia. Alan Gilpin. (Australian Environment Ser.: No. 8). (Illus.). 380p. 1981. text ed. 38.50x o.p. (ISBN 0-7022-1366-7); pap. text ed. 22.50x o.p. (ISBN 0-7022-1367-5). U of Queensland Pr.

Environmental Policy Law: Cases, Readings & Text. Thomas J. Schoenbaum. LC 82-7280. (University Casebook Ser.). 1065p. 1982. text ed. 26.00 o.p. (ISBN 0-88277-057-8). Foundation Pr.

Environmental Pollution. 2nd ed. Laurent Hodges. LC 76-27643. 1977. text ed. 38.95 o.p. (ISBN 0-03-089878-1, HoltC). HR&W.

Environmental Pollution in Montana. Ed. by Robert Bigart. LC 71-169032. 261p. 1972. 8.50 o.p. (ISBN 0-87842-037-1); pap. 4.95 o.p. (ISBN 0-87842-025-8). Mountain Pr.

Environmental Problems & Their International Implications. Ed. by Halis Odabasi & S. Erol Ulug. LC 73-87538. (Illus.). 1973. 19.50x o.p. (ISBN 0-87081-052-9). Univ Pr Colo.

Environmental Protection Hustle. Bernard J. Frieden. (Joint Center for Urban Studies). (Illus.). 1979. 25.00x o.p. (ISBN 0-262-06068-X); pap. 7.95x o.p. (ISBN 0-262-56022-4). MIT Pr.

Environmental Psychology: People & Their Physical Settings. 2nd ed. H. M. Proshansky et al. LC 76-2336. 1976. text ed. 24.95 o.p. (ISBN 0-03-089679-7, HoltC). HR&W.

Environmental Psychology: Selected Readings. Caroline T. Toepfer et al. LC 72-86362. 290p. 1972. 28.00x o.p. (ISBN 0-8422-5001-8); pap. text ed. 8.95x o.p. (ISBN 0-8422-0234-X). Irvington.

Environmental Quality. (Illus.). 745p. (Orig.). 1984. pap. 16.00 o.p. (ISBN 0-318-19969-6, S/N 041-011-00078-5). USGPO.

Environmental Quality: Global Aspects of Chemistry, Toxicology & Technology As Applied to the Environment, 5 vols. Ed. by F. Coulston & F. Korte. Vol. 1, 1972. 32.95 o.p. (ISBN 0-12-227001-0); Vol. 2, 1973. 40.00 o.p. (ISBN 0-12-227002-9); Vol. 3, 1974. 35.00 o.p. (ISBN 0-12-227003-7); Vol.4, 1975. 32.95 o.p. (ISBN 0-12-227004-5); Vol. 5, 1976. 32.95 o.p. (ISBN 0-12-227005-3). Acad Pr.

Environmental Radioactivity. 2nd ed. Merril Eisenbud. (Environmental Science: An Interdisciplinary Monograph). 1973. 89.00 o.p. (ISBN 0-12-235150-9). Acad Pr.

Environmental Regulation: Looking Ahead. (Technical & Economic Reports: Radiation Protection & Environmental Considerations). 365p. 1979. 30.00 o.p. (ISBN 0-318-13571-X); members 15.00 o.p. (ISBN 0-318-13572-8). US Coun Energy Awareness.

Environmental Research & Protection: Inorganic Analysis. Ed. by W Fresenius & I. Luderwald. 310p. 1984. pap. 17.50 o.p. (ISBN 0-387-13469-7). Springer Verlag.

Environmental Sanitation & Integrated Health Delivery Programs. Charles S. Pineo et al. 82p. 1979. 5.00x o.p. (ISBN 0-87553-126-1, 068). Am Pub Health.

Environmental Science. 3rd ed. Jonathan Turk & Amos Turk. 1984. text ed. 40.75 o.s.i. (ISBN 0-03-058467-1, CBS C); instr's manual 12.00 o.s.i. (ISBN 0-03-058468-X). SCP.

Environmental Science Handbook for Architects & Builders. Steven V. Szokolay. LC 79-25004. 532p. 1980. 102.95x o.p. (ISBN 0-470-26904-9). Halsted Pr.

Environmental Science Methods. Ed. by R. Haynes. (Illus.). 400p. 1982. 45.00x o.p. (ISBN 0-412-23280-4, NO. 6604, Pub. by Chapman & Hall England); pap. 19.95x o.p. (ISBN 0-412-23290-1, NO. 6603). Routledge Chapman & Hall.

Environmental Science: The Way the World Works. Bernard J. Nebel. (Illus.). 1981. text ed. (ISBN 0-13-283002-7). P-H.

Environmental Statutes. (Environmental Statutes Ser.). 1008p. 1987. text ed. 44.00 o.s.i. (ISBN 0-86587-152-3); pap. text ed. 29.50 o.s.i. (ISBN 0-86587-151-5). Gov Insts.

Environmental Statutes. Ed. by TFP Sullivan Staff. 731p. 1985. 38.95 o.p. (ISBN 0-86587-123-X). Gov Insts.

Environmental Statutes, 1986. 752p. 1986. text ed. 39.95 o.p. (ISBN 0-86587-133-7); pap. text ed. 27.95 o.p. (ISBN 0-86587-132-9). Gov Insts.

Environmental Statutes, 1988. 1072p. 1988. 48.50 o.p. (ISBN 0-86587-738-6); pap. 32.50 o.p. (ISBN 0-86587-737-8). Gov Insts.

Environmental Stress: Individual Human Adaptations. Ed. by Lawrence J. Folinsbee et al. 1978. 44.00 o.p. (ISBN 0-12-261350-3). Acad Pr.

Environmental Systems. G. H. Dury. LC 80-29151. (Orig.). 1981. 19.95x o.p. (ISBN 0-435-08001-6); instr's. manual 6.00x o.p. (ISBN 0-435-08002-4). Heinemann Ed.

Environmental Toxicology: A Guide to Information Sources. Robert L Rudd. LC 73-17540. (Man & the Environmrnt Information Guide Ser.: Vol. 7). 280p. 1977. 68.00x o.p. (ISBN 0-8103-1342-1). Gale.

Environmental Values, Eighteen Sixty to Nineteen Seventy-Two: A Guide to Information Sources. Ed. by Loren C. Owings. LC 73-17539. (Man & the Environment Information Guide Ser.: Vol. 4). 336p. 1976. 68.00x o.p. (ISBN 0-8103-1343-X). Gale.

Environmentalism see Psychology of School Learning.

Environmmental Aspects of Non-Conventional Energy Resources: Proceedings, American Nuclear Society Topical Meeting, Denver, September 26-28, 1978. 500p. softcover 47.00 o.p. (ISBN 0-317-33032-2, 700027). Am Nuclear Soc.

Environs of Leningrad. P. Kann. 133p. 1981. 7.95 o.p. (ISBN 0-8285-2704-0, Pub. by Progress Pubs USSR). Imported Pubns.

Envy: A Theory of Social Behaviour. Helmut Schoeck. Tr. by Michael Glenny & Betty Ross. LC 69-14842. (Helen & Kurt Wolff Bks.). Orig. Title: Neid. 408p. 1972. pap. 3.95 o.p. (ISBN 0-15-628798-6, HB241, Harv). HarBraceJ.

Envy & Other Works. Yuri Olesha. Tr. by Andrew R. MacAndrew. 320p. 1981. pap. 7.95 o.p. (ISBN 0-393-00042-7). Norton.

Enzo Cucchi. Diane Waldman. Ed. by Rizzoli International Staff. (Illus.). 192p. (Orig.). 1986. pap. text ed. 29.95 o.p. (ISBN 0-8478-0756-8). Rizzoli Intl.

Enzymatic Methods of Analysis. G. G. Guilbault. 1970. 65.00 o.p. (ISBN 0-08-006989-4). Pergamon.

Enzyme Activities & Aging. Roy E. Beauchene et al. LC 74-5496. 208p. 1974. text ed. 34.50x o.p. (ISBN 0-8422-7217-8). Irvington.

Enzyme Activities of Human Tissue. (Enzymologia Biologica et Clinica: Vol. 11, Nos. 1-2). 1970. pap. 35.50 o.p. (ISBN 3-8055-0824-7). S Karger.

Enzyme Engineering, Vol. 2. Ed. by E. Kendall Pye & Lemuel B. Wingard. LC 74-13768. 470p. 1974. 75.00x o.p. (ISBN 0-306-35282-6, Plenum Pr). Plenum Pub.

Enzyme Engineering, Vol. 3. Ed. by E. Kendall Pye & H. H. Weetall. LC 74-13768. 594p. 1977. 85.00x o.p. (ISBN 0-306-35283-4, Plenum Pr). Plenum Pub.

Enzyme Engineering, Vol. 4. Ed. by G. B. Broun et al. LC 74-13768. 512p. 1978. 75.00x o.p. (ISBN 0-306-40021-9, Plenum Pr). Plenum Pub.

Enzyme Engineering, Vol. 5. Ed. by Howard H. Weetall & Garfield P. Royer. LC 74-13768. 504p. 1979. 75.00 o.p. (ISBN 0-306-40471-0, Plenum Pr). Plenum Pub.

Enzyme Engineering, Vol. 6. Ed. by Ichiro Chibata & Saburo Fukui. LC 74-13768. 560p. 1982. 85.00x o.p. (ISBN 0-306-41121-0, Plenum Pr). Plenum Pub.

Enzyme Engineering: Future Directions. Ed. by Lemual B. Wingard et al. LC 80-12061. 536p. 1980. 85.00x o.p. (ISBN 0-306-40442-7, Plenum Pr). Plenum Pub.

Enzyme Histochemistry: A Laboratory Manual. Z. Lojda et al. (Illus.). 1979. pap. 47.00 o.p. (ISBN 0-387-09269-2). Springer-Verlag.

Enzyme Immunoassay. Eiji Ishikawa et al. LC 81-80938. (Illus.). 280p. 1981. 39.00 o.p. (ISBN 0-89640-055-7). Igaku-Shoin.

Enzyme Kinetics: The Steady-State Approach. 2nd ed. Paul C. Engel. LC 81-16864. (Outline Studies in Biology). 96p. 1982. pap. 8.50x o.p. (ISBN 0-412-23970-1, NO. 6628, Pub. by Chapman & Hall England). Routledge Chapman & Hall.

Enzyme Nomenclature 1978. Ed. by International Union of Biochemistry, Nomenclature Committee. 20.00 o.p. (ISBN 0-12-227160-2); pap. 8.95 o.p. (ISBN 0-12-227161-0). Acad Pr.

Enzyme Structure & Function. Blackburn. (Enzymology Ser.: Vol. 3). 1976. 99.75 o.p. (ISBN 0-8247-6326-2). Dekker.

Enzyme Technology. R. M. Lafferty. (Illus.). 350p. 1983. pap. 68.00 o.p. (ISBN 0-387-12479-9). Springer-Verlag.

Enzyme Technology: Preparation, Purification, Stabilization, Immobilization-Recent Advances. Ed. by S. Torrey. LC 83-13157. (Biotechnology Review No. 2; Chemical Technology Review No. 222). 308p. 1984. 42.00 o.p. (ISBN 0-8155-0956-1). Noyes.

Enzymes. H. Freidmann. 1982. 76.95 o.p. (ISBN 0-87933-067-7). Van Nos Reinhold.

Enzymes & Immobilized Cells in Biotechnology. Allen I. Laskin. 1985. 41.95 o.p. (ISBN 0-8053-6360-2). Benjamin-Cummings.

Enzymes & Isoenzymes: Structure, Properties & Function. Ed. by D. Shugar. 1970. 47.00 o.p. (ISBN 0-12-640860-2). Acad Pr.

Enzymes of Glutamine Metabolism. Ed. by Stanley Prusiner & Earl R. Stadtman. 1973. 65.50 o.p. (ISBN 0-12-566450-8). Acad Pr.

Enzymes of the Arterial Wall. John E. Kirk. 1969. 84.50 o.p. (ISBN 0-12-409650-6). Acad Pr.

Enzymology in the Practice of Laboratory Medicine. Ed. by Philip Blume & Esther Freier. 1974. 60.50 o.p. (ISBN 0-12-107950-3). Acad Pr.

Enzymology of the Cell Surface. A. Rothstein. Bd. with Tension at the Cell Surface. E. N. Harvey. (Protoplasmatologia: Vol. 2e, Pts. 4-5). (Illus.). iv, 116p. 1954. 24.80 o.p. (ISBN 0-387-80345-9). Springer-Verlag.

Eothen. A. W. Kinglake. (Century Classic Ser.). 226p. 1988. pap. 11.95 o.p. (ISBN 0-317-61166-6, Pub. by Century Hutchinson). David & Charles.

EPA Manual of Chemical Methods for Pesticides & Devices. Compiled by EPA Staff & State Labs Staff. (Illus.). 1363p. (Incl. 3 supplements & binder). 1983. in U.S. 68.50 o.p. (ISBN 0-935584-23-4); outside U.S. 71.50 o.p. (ISBN 0-318-17091-4). Assoc Official.

Epee Fencing. I. Vass. (Illus.). 1976. 12.50x o.p. (ISBN 963-13-3703-0, H-377). Vanous.

Epee Fencing. I. Vass. 392p. 18.00 o.s.i. (ISBN 9-6313-3703-0). Newbury Bks.

Ephemerides of Phialo. Stephen Gosson. LC 73-170404. (English Stage Ser.: Vol. 3). 1974. lib. bdg. 61.00 o.p. (ISBN 0-8240-0586-4). Garland Pub.

Ephesians & Colossians see Word Studies in the Greek New Testament, for the English Reader.

Ephesians, II Colossians, Thessalonians: Pastoral Epistles. J. Paul Sampley et al. LC 77-78652. (Proclamation Commentaries: the New Testament Witness for Preaching). 128p. 1978. pap. 4.95 o.p. (ISBN 0-8006-0589-6, 1-589, Fortress). Augsburg Fortress.

Ephraim of Israel: The Unknown Apostle. Paul Constant. 128p. 1956. (ISBN 0-8022-0289-6). Philos Lib.

Epic. Paul Merchant. (Critical Idiom Ser., Vol. 17). 1972. pap. 5.00 o.p. (ISBN 0-416-19700-0, NO. 2316). Routledge Chapman & Hall.

Epic Strain in the English Novel. rev. ed. Eustace M. Tillyard. LC 75-17891. (Illus.). 207p. 1975. Repr. of 1967 ed. lib. bdg. 22.50x o.p. (ISBN 0-8371-8195-X, TIES). Greenwood.

Epicoene see also Silent Woman.

Epicrisis Systematis Mycologici, Seu Synopsis Hymenomycetum. Elias M. Fries. 1965. Repr. of 1838 ed. 44.00 o.p. (ISBN 0-384-16950-3). Johnson Repr.

Epics of Espionage. Bernard Newman. 1951. (ISBN 0-8022-1204-2). Philos Lib.

Epidemic! The Story of the Disease Detectives. Jules Archer. LC 76-46790. 1977. 5.95 o.p. (ISBN 0-15-225980-5, HJ). HarBraceJ.

Epidemics in Colonial America. John Duffy. LC 53-9904. x, 274p. 1971. pap. text ed. 9.95 o.p. (ISBN 0-8071-0205-9). La State U Pr.

Epidemiological Evaluation of Drugs. Ed. by F. Colombo et al. LC 77-24938. (Illus.). 334p. 1977. 27.50 o.p. (ISBN 0-88416-217-6). Year Bk Med.

Epidemiologie, Diagnose, Klinik und Therapie Systemischer Pilzerkrankungen: Ancotil Roche 5-Fluorocytosin. Ed. by H. Schoenfeld. (Chemotherapy: Vol. 22, Suppl.). (Illus.). 100p. 1976. 30.00 o.p. (ISBN 3-8055-2289-4). S Karger.

Epidemiology & Control of Gastrointestinal Parasites of Cattle in Australia. Ed. by N. Anderson & P. J. Waller. (Illus.). xii, 90p. (Orig.). 1983. pap. text ed. 8.50x o.p. (ISBN 0-643-03517-6, Pub. by CSIRO). Intl Spec Bk.

Epidemiology & Detection of Lead Toxicity. Ed. by H. L. Hardy et al. LC 74-26934. (Lead Toxicity Ser.: Vol. 3). 147p. 1976. text ed. 29.50x o.p. (ISBN 0-8422-7261-5). Irvington.

Epidemiology & Public Health: PreTest Self-Assessment & Review. 3rd ed. PreTest Service, Inc. Staff et al. (Clinical Science Ser.). 272p. 1985. text ed. 13.95 o.p. (ISBN 0-07-051003-2). McGraw.

Epidemiology: Man & Disease. John P. Fox et al. (Illus.). 1970. text ed. write for info. o.s.i. (ISBN 0-02-339170-7). Macmillan.

Epidemiology of Cerebrovascular Disease. J. F. Kurtzke. LC 77-76725. (Illus.). 1969. 52.00 o.p. (ISBN 0-387-04591-0). Springer-Verlag.

Epidemiology of Neurologic & Sense Organ Disorders. Leonard T. Kurland et al. LC 72-90644. (Vital & Health Statistics Monographs, American Public Health Association). (Illus.). 801p. 1973. 29.50x o.s.i. (ISBN 0-674-25875-4). Harvard U Pr.

Epidemiology: Principles & Methods. Brian Macmahon & Thomas F. Pugh. 376p. 1970. text ed. 25.00 o.p. Little.

Epidermis: Proceedings. Ed. by William Montagna & Walter C. Lobitz, Jr. 1964. 89.50 o.p. (ISBN 0-12-505250-2). Acad Pr.

Epigrammatists: A Selection from the Epigrammatic Literature of Ancient, Mediaeval & Modern Times. Henry P. Dodd. LC 69-16801. 735p. 1969. Repr. of 1876 ed. 51.00x o.p. (ISBN 0-8103-3524-7). Gale.

Epilegomena to the Study of Greek Religion, & Themis: A Study of the Social Origins of Greek Religion. Jane Harrison. 1962. 10.00 o.p. (ISBN 0-8216-0075-3, Pub. by Univ Bks). Carol Pub Group.

Epilepsies. 3rd ed. John M. Sutherland & Mervyn Eadie. (Illus.). 176p. 1980. pap. text ed. 12.50 o.p. (ISBN 0-443-02184-8). Churchill.

Epilepsy. Letitia Fairfield. 160p. 1957. (ISBN 0-8022-0470-8). Philos Lib.

Epilepsy: A Clinical, Electroencephalographic, & Statistical Study 466 Patients. T. Tsuboi & W. Christian. (Neurology Ser.: Vol. 17). (Illus.). 1976. 36.00 o.p. (ISBN 0-387-07735-9). Springer-Verlag.

Epilepsy: A Personal Approach. Nancy C. Schumacher. LC 85-1965. 200p. 1985. 18.95 o.p. (ISBN 0-87073-469-5); pap. 11.25 o.p. (ISBN 0-87073-494-6). Schenkman Bks Inc.

Epilepsy & Motor System. Ed. by E. J. Speckmann & C. E. Elger. (Illus.). 359p. pap. text ed. 29.50 o.p. (ISBN 0-8067-1821-8). Urban & S.

Titles

Epilepsy Fact Book. Harry Sands & Frances C. Minters. (Illus.). 1979. pap. 4.95 o.s.i. (ISBN 0-684-16823-5, ScribT). Scribner.

Epilepsy in Young People: Symposium Held at the Holiday Inn, Portsmouth, June 1986. Ed. by Euan Ross et al. 169p. 1987. 45.00 o.p. (ISBN 0-471-91469-X, Dist. by A R Liss). Wiley.

Epileptics in Prison. Ed. by John Gunn. 1978. 46.50 o.p. (ISBN 0-12-306550-X). Acad Pr.

Epileptology: Proceedings. International Symposium on Epilepsy, 7th, West Berlin. Ed. by D. Janz. LC 76-9258. (Illus.). 460p. 1976. 37.00 o.p. (ISBN 0-88416-087-4). Year Bk Med.

Epiphany. Merrill R. Abbey & O. C. Edwards. LC 74-76935. (Proclamation 1: Aids for Interpreting the Lessons of the Church Year, Series A). 64p. (Orig.). 1974. pap. 2.95 o.p. (ISBN 0-8006-4062-4, 1-4062, Fortress). Augsburg Fortress.

Epiphany. Paul J. Achtemeier & Elizabeth R. Achtemeier. LC 73-79349. (Proclamation 1: Aids for Interpreting the Lessons of the Church Year, Series C). 64p. 1973. pap. 2.95 o.p. (ISBN 0-8006-4052-7, 1-4052, Fortress). Augsburg Fortress.

Epiphany. C. Fitzsimons Allison & Werner H. Kelber. LC 74-24900. (Proclamation 1: Aids for Interpreting the Lessons of the Church Year Ser.). 64p. 1974. pap. 2.95 o.p. (ISBN 0-8006-4072-1, 1-4072, Fortress). Augsburg Fortress.

Epiphany. Joseph A. Burgess & Albert C. Winn. Ed. by Elizabeth Achtemeier et al. LC 79-7377. (Proclamation 2: Aids for Interpreting the Lessons of the Church Year, Series A). 64p. (Orig.). 1980. pap. 3.75 o.p. (ISBN 0-8006-4092-6, 1-4092, Fortress). Augsburg Fortress.

Epiphany. David Buttrick. LC 84-18756. (Proclamation 3 C Ser.). 64p. 1985. pap. 3.75 o.p. (ISBN 0-8006-4126-4, Fortress). Augsburg Fortress.

Epiphany. Charles Carlston. Ed. by Elizabeth Achtemeier. LC 84-6012. (Proclamation 3: Aids for Interpreting the Lessons of the Church Year Series B). 64p. 1984. pap. 3.75 o.p. (ISBN 0-8006-4102-7, Fortress). Augsburg Fortress.

Epiphany. Marianne H. Micks. LC 84-18756. (Proclamation 3A Ser.). 64p. 1986. pap. 3.75 o.p. (ISBN 0-8006-4118-3, Fortress). Augsburg Fortress.

Epiphany. Richard I. Pervo & William J. Carl, III. Ed. by Elizabeth Achtemeier et al. LC 79-7377. (Proclamation 2: Aids for Interpreting the Lessons of the Church Year, Series C). 64p. 1979. pap. 3.75 o.p. (ISBN 0-8006-4085-3, 1-4085, Fortress). Augsburg Fortress.

Epiphany. Ernest W. Saunders & Fred B. Craddock. Ed. by Elizabeth Achtemeier et al. LC 79-7377. (Proclamation 2: Aids for Interpreting the Lessons of the Church Year, Series B). 64p. 1981. pap. 3.75 o.p. (ISBN 0-8006-4069-1, 1-4069, Fortress). Augsburg Fortress.

Episcopal Church Calendar. 56p. 1979. pap. 6.25 o.p. (ISBN 0-8192-3047-2). Morehouse Pub.

Episode: Report on the Accident Inside My Skull. Eric Hodgins. LC 81-3560. xi, 272p. 1981. pap. 6.95 o.p. (ISBN 0-689-70612-X, 271, Atheneum). Macmillan.

Episodes of Life. (Classics of the Victorian Imagination Ser.). 176p. 1986. pap. 7.95 o.p. (ISBN 0-394-62300-2, Ever). Grove.

Epistle of Comfort. Robert Southwell. Ed. by Margaret Waugh. LC 66-22384. 1966. 3.95 o.p. (ISBN 0-8294-0072-9). Loyola.

Epistle to Dr. Benjamin Franklin. G. Arthur Mihram. 1975. 4.00 o.p. (ISBN 0-682-48365-6, University). Exposition-Phoenix.

Epistles of John. F. F. Bruce. LC 78-22069. 1978. pap. 5.95 o.p. (ISBN 0-8028-1783-1). Eerdmans.

Epistles of Paul & Rudolf Steiner's Philosophy of Freedom. Frederick Hiebel. 1979. pap. 4.95 o.p. (ISBN 0-916786-41-2). St George Bk Serv.

Epistulae. Saint Hieronymus. (Corpus Scriptorum Ecclesiasticorum Latinorum Ser: Vols. 54-56). 1910-18. 121.00 o.p. (ISBN 0-384-23021-0). Johnson Repr.

Epistulae Imperatorum Pontificum Aliorum Inde Ab Anno. 367 Usque Ad Annum 553 Datae Avellana Quae Dicitur Collectio, 2 Pts. 1895-1898. 50.00 ea. o.p. (ISBN 0-384-14515-9). Johnson Repr.

Epitaph for Planet Earth: How to Survive the Approaching End of the Human Species. Milo D. Appleman. LC 81-70329. 240p. 1982. 14.95 o.p. (ISBN 0-8119-0447-4). Fell.

Epitaph of a Small Winner. Machado De Assis. 1978. pap. 2.25 o.p. (ISBN 0-380-01712-1, 59659-8, Bard). Avon.

Epoxy Resin Technology: Developments Since 1979. Ed. by J. I. DiStasio. LC 81-18926. (Chemical Technology Review Ser.: No. 204). (Illus.). 366p. (Orig.). 1982. 48.00 o.p. (ISBN 0-8155-0888-3). Noyes.

Epoxy Resins: Chemistry & Technology. Ed. by C. May & Y. Tanaka. 816p. 1973. 199.00 o.p. (ISBN 0-8247-1446-6). Dekker.

Epson, Epson, Read All about It! Julie Knott & Dave Prochnow. LC 84-28237. 1985. write for info. o.p. (ISBN 0-201-11640-5). Addison-Wesley.

Epstein-Barr Virus. Ed. by M. A. Epstein & B. G. Achong. (Illus.). 1979. 77.00 o.p. (ISBN 0-387-09272-2). Springer-Verlag.

Epstein-Barr Virus Diet. rev., 2nd ed. Ira Hunter. 19p. 1987. pap. 12.00x o.p. (ISBN 0-931918-03-0). Busn Psych.

Equal Access Act: Implications for Secondary School Policies. Christian Legal Society. 47p. (Orig.). 1984. pap. text ed. 2.00 o.p. (ISBN 0-944561-05-5). Chr Legal.

Equal Credit Opportunity Act: 1982 & 1986 Supplement. National Consumer Law Center Staff. LC 82-81233. 106p. 1982. pap. 48.00 o.p. (ISBN 0-943116-00-7). Nat Consumer Law.

Equal Employment Compliance Manual. Virgil Day. LC 77-14116. 1977. 260.00 o.p. (ISBN 0-317-20374-6). Callaghan.

Equal Employment Opportunities Commission. Ed. by Arthur M. Schlesinger, Jr. (Let's Visit Places & Peoples of the World Ser.). (Illus.). (gr. 5 up). 1989. 14.95 o.p. Chelsea Hse.

Equal Justice under Law: The Supreme Court in American Life. (Illus.). 159p. 1982. 8.50 o.p. (ISBN 0-318-23084-4, S/N 066-002-00001-2). USGPO.

Equal Opportunity Handbook for Hotels, Restaurants & Institutions. Arch Stokes. LC 79-859. 283p. 1983. 22.95 o.p. (ISBN 0-8436-2148-6). Van Nos Reinhold.

Equal Opportunity in Education. Ed. by Harold Silver. 1979. pap. 14.95x o.p. (ISBN 0-416-78540-9, NO.2512). Routledge Chapman & Hall.

Equal Opportunity in the Workplace: A Checklist, 1980-1983. Dale E. Casper. (Public Administration Series: Bibliography: No. P 1633). 16p. 1985. pap. 2.25 o.p. (ISBN 0-89028-303-6). Vance Biblios.

Equal Pay for Women. Barrie O. Pettman. LC 77-7335. (Illus.). 1977. text ed. 33.95x o.p. (ISBN 0-07-049735-4). McGraw.

Equal Time: Maintaining a Balance in Today's Intimate Relationships. Genevieve G. Marcus & Robert L. Smith. LC 81-68911. 224p. 1982. 14.95 o.p. (ISBN 0-8119-0443-1); pap. 8.95 o.p. (ISBN 0-8119-0446-6). Fell.

Equalities & Inequalities in Education: Proceedings of the Eugenics Society Annual Symposium, 11th, London, 1973. Eugenics Society Annual Symposium Staff. Ed. by Peter R. Cox et al. 1976. 45.50 o.p. (ISBN 0-12-194240-6). Acad Pr.

Equalities & Inequalities in Family Life. Ed. by R. Chester & J. Peel. 1978. 52.00 o.p. (ISBN 0-12-171650-3). Acad Pr.

Equality, 2 vols, No. 10. 1970. Repr. of 1940 ed. Set. lib. bdg. 54.00x o.p. (ISBN 0-8371-9167-X, EQ00). Greenwood.

Equality & Beyond: Housing Segregation & the Goals of the Great Society. George Grier & Eunice Grier. 116p. pap. 1.45 o.p. (ISBN 0-686-95014-3). ADL.

Equality, Development & Peace: Report. United Nations Decade for Women World Conference Staff. 238p. 1980. pap. 18.00 o.p. (E.80.IV.3). UN.

Equality, Justice & Rectification: An Exploration in Normative Sociology. D. L. Phillips. 1979. 51.50 o.p. (ISBN 0-12-554350-6). Acad Pr.

Equations over Finite Fields: An Elementary Approach. W. M. Schmidt. (Lecture Notes in Mathematics: Vol. 536). 1976. soft cover 17.00 o.p. (ISBN 0-387-07855-X). Springer-Verlag.

Equibbrium States & the Ergodic Theory of Anosov Diffeomorphisms. (Lecture Notes in Mathematics Ser.: Vol. 470). 108p. 1975. pap. 13.00 o.p. (ISBN 0-387-07187-3). Springer-Verlag.

Equilibrium Configurations of Degenerate Gaseous Masses. Gurgen S. Saakyan. Tr. by C. F. Hall from Rus. LC 74-13583. 294p. 1974. 76.95x o.p. (ISBN 0-470-74805-2). Halsted Pr.

Equilibrium Credit Rationing. William R. Keeton. LC 78-75066. (Outstanding Dissertations in Economics). 1980. lib. bdg. 36.00 o.p. (ISBN 0-8240-4142-9). Garland Pub.

Equilibrium of Wit: Essays for Odette de Mourgues. Ed. by Peter Bayley & Dorothy G. Coleman. LC 81-71433. (French Forum Monographs: No. 36). 286p. (Orig.). 1982. pap. 24.95x o.p. (ISBN 0-917058-35-6). French Forum.

Equilibrium Properties of Aqueous Solutions of Single Strong Electrolytes. E. A. Guggenheim & R. H. Stokes. LC 79-20329. 1969. 40.00 o.p. (ISBN 0-08-013445-9). Pergamon.

Equilibrium Properties of Fluid Mixtures, Vol. 1: A Bibliography of Data on Fluids of Cryogenic Interest. M. J. Hiza et al. LC 75-19000. 166p. 1975. 95.00x o.p. (ISBN 0-306-66001-6, IFI Plenum). Plenum Pub.

Equine Infectious Diseases III: Proceedings of the International Conference, 3rd. International Conference on Equine Infectious Diseases Staff. Ed. by J. T. Bryans & H. Gerber. 1973. 69.00 o.p. (ISBN 3-8055-1392-5). S Karger.

Equine Medicine & Surgery, Vols. I & II. Ed. by H. E. Amstutz et al. LC 81-70196. (Illus.). 1456p. 1982. 105.00 o.p. (ISBN 0-939674-04-1). Am Vet Pubns.

Equine Veterinary Manual. Tony Pavord & Rod Fisher. LC 86-27487. (Illus.). 208p. 1987. 19.95 o.s.i. (ISBN 0-87605-863-2). Howell Bk.

Equinox: A Gathering of T'ang Poets. Tr. by David Gordon from Chinese. LC 73-181682. xx, 88p. 1975. 9.95x o.p. (ISBN 0-8214-0162-9); pap. 3.50 o.s.i. (ISBN 0-8214-0173-4, 82-81636). Ohio U Pr.

Equipment Leasing. (Reports Ser.: No. 503). 212p. 1982. 1285.00x o.p. (ISBN 0-88694-503-8). Intl Res Dev.

Equipment Leasing. 2nd ed. Rev. by Peter K. Nevitt & Frank J Fabozzi. LC 85-70190. 1985. 50.00 o.p. (ISBN 0-87094-569-6). Dow Jones-Irwin.

Equipment Leasing 1985: Basics - Recent Developments - Advanced Issues & Case Studies, Vol 404. 508p. 1985. 15.00 o.p. (A4-4246). PLI.

Equipment Lists: Items Approved, Certified, or Accepted Under Marine Inspection & Navigation Laws. (Commandant Instruction Ser.: No. M 16714.3B). 234p. 1985. pap. 8.00 o.p. (ISBN 0-318-21947-6, S/N 050-012-00232-1). USGPO.

Equipment Planning Guide for Vocational & Technical Training & Education Programmes: Electronics, No. 10. (Equipment Planning Guides Ser.). v, 276p. (Orig.). 1981. pap. 28.00 o.p. (ISBN 92-2-102588-8). Intl Labour Office.

Equipping Adults Through Bible Study. Neal McBride. 32p. 1977. pap. 1.50 o.s.i. (ISBN 0-8307-0505-8, 9970118). Regal.

Equitable Distribution Law & Practice. Gerald D. McLellan. LC 85-6603. (Trial Practice Library). 352p. 1985. 85.00 o.p. (ISBN 0-471-88165-1). Wiley.

Equitable Distribution of Pensions. Pennsylvania Bar Institute Staff. 220p. 1985. 50.00 o.p. (ISBN 0-318-19043-5, 314). PA Bar Inst.

Equitable Distribution: Preparation, Trial & Appeal. 169p. 1984. 30.00 o.p. (ISBN 0-318-03915-X, 262). PA Bar Inst.

Equitation. Henry Wynmalen. (Illus.). 15.95 o.p. (ISBN 0-85131-138-5, BL2472, Pub. by J A Allen U K). S R Smith Sporting Bks.

Equity in Vocational Education: A Futures Agenda. Compiled by Lucille Campbell-Thrane. 80p. 1982. 5.50 o.p. (ISBN 0-318-22095-4, RD213). Natl Ctr Res Voc Ed.

Equivariant Pontrjagin Classes & Applications to Orbit Spaces. D. B. Zagier. LC 72-90185. (Lecture Notes in Mathematics: Vol. 290). 130p. 1972. pap. 9.00 o.p. (ISBN 0-387-06013-8). Springer-Verlag.

Equus. Peter Shaffer. 1977. pap. 1.95 o.p. (ISBN 0-380-00357-0, 51797-3, Bard). Avon.

Equus & Shrivings. Peter Shaffer. LC 74-77857. 1974. 7.95 o.p. (ISBN 0-689-10630-0, Atheneum). Macmillan.

Equus: The Creation of a Horse. Robert Vavra. LC 77-78061. (Illus.). 1977. 39.95 o.p. (ISBN 0-688-03239-7). Morrow.

Era of Good Feelings. George Dangerfield. LC 51-14815. 1963. pap. 5.50 o.p. (ISBN 0-15-629000-6, Harv). HarBraceJ.

Era of Reconstruction: 1863-1877. Forrest G. Wood. LC 74-13488. (American History Ser.). 1975. pap. 8.50x o.s.i. (ISBN 0-88295-771-6). Harlan Davidson.

Erdoel Lexicon. 5th ed. Karlheinz Kramer. (Eng. & Ger., Lexicon of Petroleum). 1972. 48.00 o.p. (ISBN 3-7785-0233-6, M-7366, Pub. by Heuthig). French & Eur.

Ere de Soupcon: Essais sur le roman. Nathalie Sarraute. 1964. pap. 6.50 o.p. (ISBN 0-685-11165-2). Schoenhof.

Ergebnisse der Inneren Medizin und Kinderheilkunde, Vol. 34. 180p. (New series). 1974. 73.20 o.p. (ISBN 0-387-06519-9). Springer Verlag.

Ergodesign' Eighty-Four: Proceedings of the International Symposium on Ergonomics & Design in the Electronic Office, Montreaux, Jan. 1984. Ed. by E. Grandjean. (Behaviour & Information Technology Special Issue Ser.: Vol. 3, No. 4). 208p. 1984. 31.00x o.p. Taylor & Francis.

Ergodic & Information Theory. Ed. by Robert M. Gray & Lee D. Davisson. (Benchmark Papers in Electrical Engineering & Computer Science: Vol. 19). 1977. 76.50 o.p. (ISBN 0-12-786590-X). Acad Pr.

Ergodic Theories. Ed. by P. Caldirola. (Italian Physical Society: Course 14). 1962. 82.50 o.p. (ISBN 0-12-368814-0). Acad Pr.

Ergodic Theory, Entropy. M. Smorodinsky. LC 75-171482. (Lecture Notes in Mathematics: Vol. 214). 1971. pap. 8.20 o.p. (ISBN 0-387-05556-8). Springer-Verlag.

Ergodic Theory: Introductory Lectures. P. Walters. LC 75-9853. (Lecture Notes in Mathematics Ser.: Vol. 458). 200p. 1975. pap. 11.40 o.p. (ISBN 0-387-07163-6). Springer-Verlag.

Ergodic Theory on Compact Spaces. M. Denker et al. (Lecture Notes in Mathematics: Vol. 527). 1976. soft cover 19.00 o.p. (ISBN 0-387-07797-9). Springer-Verlag.

Ergodic Theory: Proceedings of the Symposium, New Orleans, 1961. Ergodic Theory Symposium Staff. Ed. by Fred B. Wright. 1963. 60.50 o.p. (ISBN 0-12-765450-X). Acad Pr.

Ergogenic Aids & Muscular Performance. Ed. by Morgan. 1972. 72.50 o.p. (ISBN 0-12-506850-6). Acad Pr.

Ergonomic Design of the Electronic Office: A Special Issue of Behavior & Information Technology, Vol. 3, No. 4. Ed. by E. Grandjean. 208p. 1984. pap. 25.00x o.p. (ISBN 0-85066-987-1). Taylor & Francis.

Ergonomics in Advanced Manufacturing Technology. G. I. Johnson & J. R. Wilson. (Illus.). 64p. 1988. text ed. 45.00 o.p. (ISBN 0-408-02422-4). Butterworth.

Ergonomics: Man In His Working Environment. K. F. Murrell. 1980. 23.00x o.p. (ISBN 0-412-07800-7, NO. 2181, Pub. by Chapman & Hall); pap. 19.95x o.p. (ISBN 0-412-21990-5, NO. 6207). Routledge Chapman & Hall.

Ergonomics Problems in Process Operations: Proceedings of the Symposium, Birmingham, U. K., July 11-13, 1984. Ed. by Institution of Chemical Engineers Staff. (Institution of Chemical Engineers Symposium Ser.: Vol. 90). 235p. 1984. 31.00 o.s.i. (ISBN 0-08-030282-3). Pergamon.

Eric Berne, Master Gamesman: A Transactional Biography. Elizabeth W. Jorgensen & Henry I. Jorgensen. LC 83-49369. 312p. 1984. 22.50 o.p. (ISBN 0-394-53846-3, GP 897). Grove.

Eric Delderfield's Book of True Animal Stories. Eric R. Delderfield. LC 76-126288. (Illus.). (gr. 4-6). 4.95 o.s.i. (ISBN 0-8008-2510-1). Taplinger.

Eric Dickerson: Record-Breaking Rusher. Rich Roberts. LC 85-13234. (Sports Stars Ser.). (Illus.). 48p. (gr. 2-5). 1985. PLB 11.27 o.p. (ISBN 0-516-04349-8); pap. 2.95 o.p. (ISBN 0-516-44349-6). Childrens.

Eric Fischl Scenes Before the Eye: The Evolution of Year of the Drowned Dog & Floating Islands. Lucinda Barnes & Constance W. Glenn. Ed. by Jane K. Bledsoe. (Illus.). 96p. 1986. pap. 25.00 o.p. (ISBN 0-936270-25-X). CA St U LB Art.

Eric Flame. Frank R. Wallace. LC 76-139225. 1970. 30.00 o.p. (ISBN 0-911752-04-8). I & O Pub.

Eric Gill: Man of Flesh & Spirit. Malcolm Yorke. LC 81-71073. (Illus.). 304p. 1985. pap. 14.95 o.p. (ISBN 0-87663-883-3). Universe.

Eric Hoffer. James Baker. (United States Authors Ser.). 1982. lib. bdg. 14.50 o.p. (ISBN 0-8057-7359-2, Twayne). G K Hall.

Eric John Stark: Outlaw of Mars. Leigh Brackett. 208p. 1982. pap. 2.25 o.s.i. (ISBN 0-345-30515-9, Del Rey). Ballantine.

ERIC Update: Educational Technology in Adult, Career & Vocational Education. 53p. 1982. 3.80 o.p. (ISBN 0-318-23567-6, BB 56). Natl Ctr Res Voc Ed.

Eric Williams: The Man & the Leader. Ed. by Ken I. Boodhoo. 162p. (Orig.). 1986. lib. bdg. 26.00 o.p. (ISBN 0-8191-5103-3); pap. text ed. 12.25 o.p. (ISBN 0-8191-5104-1). U Pr of Amer.

Erica the Ecologist. Beverly S. Brown. LC 81-71554. (Illus.). 20p. (Orig.). (gr. 3-5). cancelled o.s.i. (ISBN 0-943864-13-5). Davenport.

Erich Fromm: The Courage to Be Human. Rainer Funk. 320p. 1982. 19.50 o.p. (ISBN 0-8264-0061-2). Continuum.

Erich's Sunrise see Destiny at Dawn.

Eridahn. Robert F. Young. 160p. (Orig.). 1983. pap. 1.95 o.s.i. (ISBN 0-345-30854-9, Del Rey). Ballantine.

Erie Canal. Samuel H. Adams. (Landmark Ser.: No. 34). (Illus.). (gr. 4-6). 1963. lib. bdg. 8.99 o.s.i. (ISBN 0-394-90334-X). Random.

Erik Erikson: The Growth of His Work. Robert Coles. (Series in Science). 462p. 1987. pap. 12.95 o.p. (ISBN 0-317-66484-0). Da Capo.

Erinnerungen und Erorterungen Von Karl Kautsky: Quellen und Untersuchungen Zur Geschichte Er Deutschen und Osterreichischen Arbeiterbewegung, No. 3. Benedikt Kautsky. 1960. 66.00x o.p. (ISBN 0-686-21241-X). Mouton.

ERISA & Bankruptcy. Harold S. Nowikoff & A. Richard Susko. LC 82-63148. (Commercial Law & Practice Course Handbook Ser.: No. 296). 1983. 45.00 o.p. (A44057). PLI.

ERISA Litigation. Practising Law Institute Staff & Max J. Schwartz. LC 82-61186. (Litigation & Administrative Practice Ser.: No. 207). 1982. 45.00 o.p. (H44883). PLI.

Erisa Plan Administrators Desk Book with Checklists & Guidelines for Successful Communications. 2nd ed. Thomas I. McCord & Raymond Doreian. LC 78-69719. 1978. 49.50 o.p. (ISBN 0-87624-133-X, Inst Busn Plan). P-H.

ERISA: Selected Legislative History, 1974-1985. 1986. 35.00 o.p. (ISBN 0-87179-530-2, 0530). BNA.

ERISA: The Law & the Code 1987 Edition. 05/1987 ed. Ed. by Anthony A. Harris & Kathleen D. Gill. LC 86-600411. 660p. 1987. pap. 40.00 o.p. (ISBN 0-87179-549-3). BNA.

ERISA: The Multiemployer Pension Plan Amendments Act 1980. Bert N. Obrentz & Arthur F. Woodard. LC 84-192042. (Tax Law Estate Planning Ser.). (Illus.). 112p. 1984. 45.00 o.p. (J43550). PLI.

Erle Stanley Gardner: A Checklist. E. H. Mundell. LC 70-97619. (Serif Ser.: No. 6). 91p. 1969. 10.00x o.p. (ISBN 0-87338-034-7). Kent St U Pr.

Ernest Hemingway: A Life Story. Carlos Baker. 1982. pap. 5.95 o.p. (ISBN 0-380-50039-6, 69822-6, Discus). Avon.

Ernest Hemingway: A Study in Narrative Technique. P. G. Rama Rao. 1980. text ed. 20.00x o.p. Coronet Bks.

Ernest Hemingway: A Study of His Rhetoric. Nageswar E. Rao. 134p. 1983. text ed. 12.50x o.p. (ISBN 0-391-02892-8). Humanities.

Ernest Hemingway: Five Decades of Criticism. Ed. by Linda W. Wagner. 325p. 1974. 15.95 o.p. (ISBN 0-87013-182-6). Mich St U Pr.

Ernest Hemingway: The Papers of a Writer. Bernard Oldsey. LC 80-9031. 1981. lib. bdg. 24.00 o.p. (ISBN 0-8240-9303-8). Garland Pub.

Ernest Jones: A Biography. Vincent Brome. (Illus.). 1983. 19.50 o.p. (ISBN 0-393-01594-7). Norton.

Ernest Pontifex see also Way of All Flesh.

Ernest Rutherford: Atom Pioneer. John Rowland. 160p. 1957. (ISBN 0-8022-1401-0). Philos Lib.

Ernst Damitz: 1805-1883. Esther Sparks. LC 76-56874. (Illus.). 56p. (Orig.). 1976. pap. 3.75 o.p. (ISBN 0-86559-021-4). Art Inst Chi.

Ernst Troeltsch: Writings on Theology & Religion. Ed. by Robert Morgan & Michael Pye. LC 77-79596. 1977. 17.50 o.s.i. (ISBN 0-8042-0554-X, John Knox). Westminster John Knox.

Eros the Bittersweet: An Essay. Anne Carson. LC 85-43371. 201p. 1986. text ed. 25.00x o.s.i. (ISBN 0-691-06681-7); pap. 12.95 o.s.i. (ISBN 0-691-01449-3). Princeton U Pr.

Erosion & Sediment Yield. Ed. by Jonathan Laronne & M. Paul Mosley. LC 81-6456. (Benchmark Papers in Geology: Vol. 63). 400p. 1982. 51.95 o.p. (ISBN 0-87933-409-6). Van Nos Reinhold.

Erosion Control on Highway Construction. (National Cooperative Highway Research Program Synthesis of Highway Practice). 52p. 1973. 4.00 o.p. (ISBN 0-309-02131-6). Transport Res Bd.

Erotic Fantasies. Phyllis Kronhausen & Eberhard Kronhausen. 1969. pap. 4.95 o.p. (ISBN 0-394-17401-1, B276, BC). Grove.

Erotic Fantasies: A Study of the Sexual Imagination. Phyllis Kronhausen & Eberhard Kronhausen. LC 87-215. 448p. 1987. pap. 10.95 o.p. (ISBN 0-8021-3006-2, Ever). Grove.

Erotic Interludes: Tales Told by Women. Lonnie G. Barbach. LC 86-6232. 288p. 1986. 15.95 o.s.i. (ISBN 0-385-23319-1). Doubleday.

Erotic Spirituality: The Integrative Tradition from Leone Ebreo to John Donne. T. Anthony Perry. 208p. 1980. 15.75 o.p. (ISBN 0-8173-0024-4). U of Ala Pr.

Erotic Theatre. John Elsom. LC 73-15277. (Illus.). 288p. 1974. 10.00 o.s.i. (ISBN 0-8008-2465-2). Taplinger.

Erotic World of Faery. Maureen Duffy. 1980. pap. 3.50 o.p. (ISBN 0-380-48108-1, 48108-1, Discus). Avon.

Erotica Japonica: Masterworks of Shunga Painting. Richard Lane. LC 85-81674. (Illus.). 160p. 1986. 50.00 o.p. (ISBN 0-87040-665-5). Japan Pubns USA.

Eroticism in Western Art. Edward Lucie-Smith. LC 84-51304. (World of Art Ser.). (Illus.). 288p. 1985. pap. 9.95 o.p. (ISBN 0-500-20121-8). Thames Hudson.

Errant Sleuth. Cyril Joyce. (Lythway Ser.). 200p. 1988. lib. bdg. 18.50x o.s.i. (ISBN 0-7451-0684-6, Pub. by Chivers Pr UK). G K Hall.

Errol Flynn: The Untold Story. Charles Higham. 1981. pap. 4.95 o.p. (ISBN 0-440-12307-0). Dell.

Error-Control Coding & Applications. Djimitri Wiggert. LC 78-23237. (Illus.). 203p. 1978. 25.00x o.p. (ISBN 0-89006-066-5). Artech Hse.

Error-Detecting Codes, Self-Checking Circuits & Applications. J. F. Wakerly. (Computer Design & Architecture Ser.). 232p. 1978. 19.50 o.p. (ISBN 0-444-00256-1, North-Holland); pap. 24.50 o.p. (ISBN 0-444-00259-6). Elsevier.

Errors of Observation & Their Treatment: SI Edition. 4th ed. J. Topping. 1972. pap. 8.50x o.p. (ISBN 0-412-21040-1, NO. 6291, Pub. by Chapman & Hall). Routledge Chapman & Hall.

Erte's Fashion Designs: Harper's Bazaar, 1918-1932. Erte. (Illus.). 1982. 18.00 o.p. (ISBN 0-8446-5884-7). Peter Smith.

Erte's Theatrical Costumes in Full Color. Erte. 16.50 o.p. (ISBN 0-8446-5757-3). Peter Smith.

Erythropoiesis: Regulatory Mechanisms & Developmental Aspects, Proceedings of the Tel Aviv University Conference, Petah Tikva, July 1970. Tel Aviv University Conference on Erythropoiesis Staff. Ed. by Yehuda Matoth. 1972. 56.50 o.p. (ISBN 0-12-480250-8). Acad Pr.

Es Lebe Mein Volkswagen. John Muir. Tr. by Ruth Shamai & Herbert Jeschke. (Illus.). 308p. 1978. pap. 10.00 o.p. (ISBN 3-980018-90-3). John Muir.

Esa communidad Lleamasha Iglesia see Community Called Church.

Escape. John McEwen. LC 83-91436. 157p. 1985. 11.95 o.p. (ISBN 0-533-06043-5). Vantage.

Escape! Sigurd Senje. Tr. by Evelyn Ramsden. LC 64-12509. (gr. 7 up). 1966. pap. 1.25 o.p. (ISBN 0-15-629041-3, VoyB). HarBraceJ.

Escape, No. 3. Metabooks, Inc. Staff. (Orig.). 1986. pap. 2.25 o.p. Bantam.

Escape from Auschwitz. Erich Kulka. (Illus.). 192p. (Orig.). 1986. 27.95 o.p. (ISBN 0-89789-088-4); pap. 12.95 o.p. (ISBN 0-89789-089-2). Bergin & Garvey.

Escape from Auschwitz. Rudolf Vrba & Alan Bestic. 364p. 1988. pap. 7.95 o.s.i. (ISBN 0-8021-3139-5). Grove.

Escape from Auschwitz: I Cannot Forgive. Rudolf Vrba & Alan Bestic. LC 64-16164. 352p. 1986. pap. 3.95 o.p. (ISBN 0-394-62133-6, BC). Grove.

Escape from Castle Quarras. Douglas Niles. LC 85-90159. (Super Endless Quest (Adventure Gamebook) Ser.). 189p. (Orig.). 1985. pap. 2.50 o.p. (ISBN 0-88038-252-X). TSR Inc.

Escape from Gulag Taria. Joseph Rosenberger. (Death Merchant Ser.: No. 67). (Orig.). 1986. pap. 2.75 o.p. (ISBN 0-440-12375-5). Dell.

Escape from Hell. Abas Korchari. 160p. 1987. 10.95 o.p. (ISBN 0-8062-3069-X). Carlton.

Escape from Loneliness. Paul Tournier. LC 61-14599. 192p. 1976. pap. 6.95 o.s.i. (ISBN 0-664-24592-7, Westminster). Westminster John Knox.

Escape from Sobibor. Richard Rashke. 389p. 1982. 15.45 o.p. (ISBN 0-395-31831-9). HM.

Escape from the Storm. Barbara Andrews. (Candlelight Supreme Ser.: No. 160). (Orig.). 1987. pap. 2.75 o.p. (ISBN 0-440-12424-7). Dell.

Escape into You. Marvin Bell. LC 79-162967. 1971. pap. 5.95 o.p. (ISBN 0-689-10472-3, Atheneum). Macmillan.

Escape Me Never. Sylvia Grieg. 1986. pap. 3.95 o.p. (ISBN 0-380-89737-7). Avon.

Escape of the Guilty: A Trial Judge Speaks out Against Crime. Ralph A. Fine. LC 86-8946. 320p. 1986. 17.95 o.p. (ISBN 0-396-08590-3). Dodd.

Escape of the Leopard. John Moffitt. LC 73-11415. 1974. 9.95 o.p. (ISBN 0-15-129050-4). HarBraceJ.

Escape on Skis. Amelia Walden. LC 74-23568. (gr. 6 up). 1975. 7.50 o.s.i. (ISBN 0-664-32560-2, Westminster). Westminster John Knox.

Escape the River. Roy Brown. LC 76-179440. 160p. (gr. 6 up). 1979. 5.95 o.p. (ISBN 0-395-28893-2, Clarion). HM.

Escape to Freedom. Joseph Mayer, Jr. 1979. 8.00 o.p. (ISBN 0-682-49378-3). Exposition-Phoenix.

Escape to Sea. pap. 3.75 o.p. (FN11, FNB). UNIPUB.

Escape to the Sea. Jack Kelly. 1977. 4.50 o.p. (ISBN 0-682-48791-0). Exposition-Phoenix.

Escape to Third Earth: A Thundercats Adventure. Cathy E. Dubowski. LC 85-1990. (Illus.). 32p. (gr. 5-8). 1985. 4.95 o.s.i. (ISBN 0-394-87467-6, BYR). Random.

Escape to Witch Mountain. Alexander Key. LC 68-11206. 192p. (gr. 5 up). 1984. pap. 2.50 o.p. (ISBN 0-671-54557-4). Archway.

Escape Velocity. Christopher Stasheff. 256p. 1986. pap. 2.95 o.s.i. (ISBN 0-441-21601-3, Pub. by Charter Bks). Ace Bks.

Eschatology & Ethics: Essays on the Theology & Ethics of the Kingdom of God. Carl E. Braaten. LC 74-77674. 192p. (Orig.). 1974. pap. 6.50 o.p. (ISBN 0-8066-1422-6, 10-2085, Augsburg). Augsburg Fortress.

Eschatology Handbook: The Bible Speaks to Us about Endtimes. Val J. Sauer, Jr. (Illus.). 180p. (Orig.). 1981. pap. 7.95 o.s.i. (ISBN 0-8042-0066-1, John Knox). Westminster John Knox.

Eschatology in Luke. E. Earle Ellis. Ed. by John Reumann. LC 72-75649. (Facet Bks.). 29p. 1972. pap. 0.50 o.p. (ISBN 0-8006-3070-X, 1-3070, Fortress). Augsburg Fortress.

Escort & Lynx, 1981 to 1982. Chilton Automotives Editorial Staff. (Illus.). 1981. pap. 13.50 o.p. (ISBN 0-8019-7055-5). Chilton.

Escort MK 1, 2, & 3: The Development & Competition History. Jeremy Walton. (Illus.). 375p. 1985. 19.95 o.p. (ISBN 0-85429-348-5, Pub. by G T Foulis Ltd). Haynes Pubns.

Escrima Self Defence: Stick, Empty Hand, Knife. rev. ed. Mark Romain. (Illus.). 112p. 1984. pap. text ed. 12.00 o.p. (ISBN 0-87364-382-8). Paladin Pr.

Escrito al Margen. Jose M. Oviedo. 383p. (Span.). 1982. pap. 12.50 o.s.i. (ISBN 0-317-46768-9, 3023). Ediciones Norte.

Escucha a los Animales. William L. Coleman. 144p. 1981. 3.25 o.p. (ISBN 0-88113-063-X). Edit Betania.

Esenin: A Biography in Memoirs, Letters, & Documents. Ed. by J. Davies. 286p. 1982. 30.00 o.p. Ardis Pubs.

Eskimo Legends. 2nd ed. Lela K. Oman. (Alaskana Book Ser.: No. 21). 1975. 8.00 o.p. Alaska Pacific.

Eskimo Legends & Other Stories of Alaska. Orma F. Long. (Illus.). 5.50 o.p. (ISBN 0-682-49089-X). Exposition-Phoenix.

Eskimo of Northwestern Alaska: A Biological Perspective. Ed. by P. L. Jamison & S. L. Zegura. LC 77-18941. (US-IBP Synthesis Ser.: Vol. 8). 319p. 1982. 54.95 o.p. (ISBN 0-87933-319-7). Van nos Reinhold.

Eskimo Prehistory. Hans-Georg Bandi. (Illus.). 226p. 1969. write for info. o.p. U of Alaska Pr.

Eskimos: Growing up in a Changing Culture. Carolyn Meyer. LC 77-8560. (Illus.). 224p. (gr. 7 up). 1977. 8.95 o.p. (ISBN 0-689-50078-5, Atheneum). Macmillan.

Esophageal Manometry: Methods & Clinical Practice. Weihrauch. LC 81-11430. (Illus.). 144p. 1981. text ed. 25.00 o.p. (ISBN 0-8067-2151-0). Urban & S.

ESOPS: An Analytical Report. new ed. Hewitt Associates Staff. 60p. 1975. pap. 10.00 o.s.i. (ISBN 0-911192-30-1). Profit Sharing.

ESOPs, TRASOPs, PAYSOPS & Other Employee Stock Ownership Plans. (Tax Law & Estate Planning Course Handbook Series 1982-83). 1982. pap. 45.00 o.p. (ISBN 0-685-90315-X, J4-3514). PLI.

Esoteric Substance of Voltarian Thought. Denise B. Quebedeau, pseud. LC 73-88706. 634p. 1974. (ISBN 0-8022-2135-1). Philos Lib.

ESP (English for Specific Purposes) The Present Position. Pauline C. Robinson. LC 79-41105. (Pergamon Institute of English). 1980. pap. text ed. 9.50 o.p. (ISBN 0-08-024585-4). Pergamon.

E.S.P. Ionage. William S. Doxey. 1979. pap. 1.95 o.p. (ISBN 0-505-51363-3, Pub. by Tower Bks). Dorchester Pub Co.

ESP McGee. Edward Packard. (Illus.). 96p. (gr. 2-6). 1983. pap. 2.25 o.p. (ISBN 0-380-84053-7, 84053, Camelot). Avon.

ESP McGee & the Dolphin's Message. Jesse Rodgers. 96p. (gr. 2-6). 1984. pap. 2.25 o.p. (ISBN 0-380-86132-1, Camelot). Avon.

ESP McGee & the Ghost Ship. Ian McMahan. 96p. (gr. 2-6). 1984. pap. 2.25 o.p. (ISBN 0-380-86116-X, Camelot). Avon.

ESP McGee & the Haunted Mansion. Jim Lawrence. 96p. (gr. 2-6). 1983. pap. 2.25 o.p. (ISBN 0-380-84061-8, Camelot). Avon.

ESP McGee & The Mysterious Magician. Kathryn Ernst. 96p. (gr. 2-6). 1983. pap. 2.25 o.p. (ISBN 0-380-84079-0, 84079-9, Camelot). Avon.

ESP McGee to the Rescue. George Shea. 96p. (gr. 2-6). 1984. pap. 2.25 o.p. (ISBN 0-380-86124-0, Camelot). Avon.

ESP Teacher: Role, Development & Prospects. (English Language Teaching Documents Ser.: Vol. 112). 142p. 1983. pap. text ed. 8.25 o.s.i. (ISBN 0-08-030302-1). Pergamon.

ESP: The Search Beyond the Senses. Daniel Cohen. LC 73-5238. (Illus.). (gr. 7 up). 1973. 6.50 o.p. (ISBN 0-15-226250-4, HJ). HarBraceJ.

ESP: The Search Beyond the Senses. Daniel Cohen. LC 77-3615. (Illus.). (gr. 7 up). 1977. pap. 1.75 o.p. (ISBN 0-15-629045-6, VoyB). HarBraceJ.

Espaliers & Vines for the Home Gardener. Harold O. Perkins. (Illus.). 1979. Repr. of 1964 ed. 9.95 o.p. (ISBN 0-8138-1030-2). Iowa St U Pr.

Espana en el siglo XX. Ed. by Antonio Regalado et al. 500p. (Orig.). 1974. pap. text ed. 12.95 o.p. (ISBN 0-15-522873-0, HC). HarBraceJ.

Espanol: A Descubrirlo, Learning Spanish the Modern Way. 3rd ed. Conrad J. Schmitt et al. 1971. text ed. 21.08 o.p. (ISBN 0-07-055375-0, W). McGraw.

Espanol Como Lengua Extranjera, Ensenanza de Idiomas y Traduccion tres calas Bibliograficas: Spanish as a Foreign Language. Ed. by Jose Polo. (Span.). pap. 15.00 o.s.i. (ISBN 0-686-46747-7). E J Brill USA.

Espanol en Espanol: La Lengua del Mundo Hispano. Nicholas Shumway & David Forbes. (Span.). 1984. text ed. 26.95 o.p. (ISBN 0-03-063144-0). HR&W.

Espanol Esencial: Un Repaso. Richard Woehr et al. (Span.). 1974. pap. text ed. 21.95 o.p. (ISBN 0-03-010316-9). HR&W.

Espanol Practico para los Negoclos. Nicholas F. Sallese & Julia Ortiz-Griffin. 496p. 1988. write for info. o.p. Macmillan.

Especially for Him: A Beginner's Cookbook for Men. 2nd ed. Hal Burbach. LC 82-50937. (Illus.). 224p. 1982. pap. 6.95x o.p. (ISBN 0-942320-07-7). Am Cooking.

Esperanto-English. M. C. Butler. 10.00 o.s.i. (ISBN 0-685-85558-9). E J Brill USA.

Espoir. Andre Malraux. 1972. 3.95 o.p. (ISBN 0-686-56323-9). Schoenhof.

Esquire's Wine & Liquor Handbook. Esquire Editors & David Laskin. 352p. 1984. pap. 8.95 o.p. (ISBN 0-380-88674-X). Avon.

Essais sur le Roman. Michel Butor. 1969. pap. 8.95 o.p. (ISBN 0-686-50135-7). French & Eur.

Essais sur les Essais. Michel Butor. pap. 4.95 o.p. (ISBN 0-685-37247-2). Schoenhof.

Essais sur les Modernes. Michel Butor. (Coll. Idees). pap. 3.95 o.p. (ISBN 0-685-37248-0). Schoenhof.

Essay. Michael F. Shugrue. 1980. pap. text ed. write for info. o.p. (ISBN 0-02-410380-2). Macmillan.

Essay Collections in International Relations: A Classified Bibliography. Moorhead Wright et al. (Reference Library of Social Science: Vol. 45). (LC 76-052692). 1977. lib. bdg. 29.00 o.p. (ISBN 0-8240-9868-4). Garland Pub.

Essay Concerning Human Understanding. John Locke. 1983. Repr. of 1976 ed. 8.95x o.p. (ISBN 0-460-00984-2, Evman); pap. 6.50x o.p. (ISBN 0-460-11332-1). Biblio Dist.

Essay of Genius. Alexander Gerard. 514p. Repr. of 1774 ed. cancelled o.s.i. (ISBN 3-7705-0043-1). Adlers Foreign Bks.

Essay on Christian Philosophy. Jacques Maritain. 1955. Philos Lib.

Essay on Criticism. Graham Hough. 1967. pap. 2.95x o.p. (ISBN 0-393-00415-5, Norton Lib). Norton.

Essay on Epic Poetry: in Five Epistles to the Rev. Mr. Mason. With Notes... see Ode, Inscribed to John Howard.

Essay on Man by Alexander Pope. Alexander Pope. Ed. by Maynard Mack. (Library Reprints Ser.). 288p. 1982. 49.95 o.p. (ISBN 0-416-34010-5, NO. 3703). Routledge Chapman & Hall.

Essay on Man, Crousaz see Popeiana.

Essay on Man, Crousaz Two see Popeiana.

Essay on Man, Warburton, Etc see Popeiana.

Essay on Mankind. Gerhard Hirschfeld. 1957. (ISBN 0-8022-0728-6). Philos Lib.

Essay on Painting: in Two Epistles to Mr. Romney...Third Edition Corrected & Enlarged see Ode, Inscribed to John Howard.

Essay on Rights. Hillel Steiner. 288p. 1985. 29.95 o.p. (ISBN 0-631-13165-5). Basil Blackwell.

Essay on the Military Architecture of the Middle Ages. Eugene Viollet-le-Duc. LC 74-12651. (Illus.). 1977. Repr. of 1860 ed. lib. bdg. 35.00 o.p. (ISBN 0-8371-7747-2, VIMA). Greenwood.

Essay on the Origin of Evil. William King. Bd. with Dissertations Concerning the Fundamental Principle & Immediate Criterion of Virtue. LC 75-11228. (British Philosophers & Theologians of the 17th & 18th Centuries Ser.). 391p. 1978. lib. bdg. 51.00 o.p. (ISBN 0-8240-1782-X). Garland Pub.

Essay on the Origin of Thought. Jurij Moskvitin. LC 72-85540. 297p. 1974. 15.00x o.p. (ISBN 0-8214-0156-4, 82-81086). Ohio U Pr.

Essay on the Principle of Population. Thomas R. Malthus. 320p. 1982. pap. text ed. 7.95x o.p. (ISBN 0-460-01692-X, Evman). Biblio Dist.

Essay on Transcendentalism. Charles M. Ellis. LC 70-91761. Repr. of 1954 ed. lib. bdg. 35.00x o.p. (ISBN 0-8371-3092-1, ELTR). Greenwood.

Essay on Truth. James Beattie. 1986. lib. bdg. 30.00x o.p. (ISBN 0-935005-36-6); pap. text ed. 16.50x o.p. (ISBN 0-935005-37-4). Ibis Pub VA.

Essay: Structure & Purpose. Richard L. Cherry et al. 1975. pap. 16.50 o.p. (ISBN 0-395-18610-2). HM.

Essay upon Harmony As It Relates Chiefly to Situation & Building with Elements: The Art of Laying Out of Pleasure Grounds. Robert Morris & John Trusler. Ed. by John D. Hunt. LC 79-56993. (English Landscape Garden Ser.). 121p. 1982. lib. bdg. 26.00 o.p. (ISBN 0-8240-0162-1). Garland Pub.

Essaying Montaigne: A Study of the Renaissance Institution of Writing & Reading. John O'Neill. (International Library of Phenomenology & Moral Sciences). 240p. 1982. 30.00x o.p. (ISBN 0-7100-0937-2). Routledge Chapman & Hall.

Essays & Studies-1972, Vol. 25. 125p. 1972. text ed. 12.50x o.p. (ISBN 0-391-00231-7). Humanities.

Essays & Studies-1973, Vol. 26. 112p. 1973. text ed. 12.50x o.p. (ISBN 0-391-00279-1). Humanities.

Essays & Studies-1978, Vol. 31. 130p. 1978. text ed. 18.00x o.p. (ISBN 0-391-00838-2). Humanities.

Essays & Studies, 1979, Vol. 32. (New Series of Essays & Studies). 1979. text ed. 18.00x o.p. (ISBN 0-391-01035-2). Humanities.

Essays & Studies-1981, Vol. 34. 147p. 1981. text ed. 21.25x o.p. (ISBN 0-391-02292-X). Humanities.

Essays & Studies, 1982. Ed. by S. Bushrui. 123p. 1982. text ed. 18.50x o.p. (ISBN 0-391-02622-4). Humanities.

Essays & Studies, 1983, Vol. 36. Beatrice White. (Essays & Studies). 100p. 1983. text ed. 22.50x o.p. (ISBN 0-391-02834-0). Humanities.

Essays: First & Second Series. Ralph Waldo Emerson. (Riverside Library). 16.95 o.p. (ISBN 0-395-08125-4). HM.

Essays for Exposition. Ed. by Carl Benson & Robert O'Neal. 358p. (Orig.). 1977. pap. text ed. 8.75 o.p. (ISBN 0-15-522890-0, HC). HarBraceJ.

Essays in Aesthetics. Jean-Paul Sartre. LC 63-11486. 104p. 1963. (ISBN 0-8022-1485-1). Philos Lib.

Essays in American History Dedicated to Frederick Jackson Turner. Turner. 12.75 o.p. (ISBN 0-8446-1451-3). Peter Smith.

Essays in Applied Price Theory. Reuben A. Kessel. Ed. by R. H. Coase & Merton Miller. LC 80-12974. (Midway Reprint Ser.). xii, 370p. 1982. pap. text ed. 17.50x o.s.i. (ISBN 0-226-43201-7). U of Chicago Pr.

Essays in Biography. John Maynard Keynes. 1963. pap. 3.25 o.p. (ISBN 0-393-00189-X, Norton Lib). Norton.

Essays in Design. J. Christopher Jones. 335p. 1984. pap. 27.95x o.p. (ISBN 0-471-90297-7, Pub. by Wiley-Interscience). Wiley.

Essays in Econometric History. Robert W. Fogel. LC 64-25069. (Illus.). 311p. 1970. pap. 9.95x o.p. (ISBN 0-8018-1148-1). Johns Hopkins.

Essays in Economic History, 3 vols. Ed. by Eleanora M. Carus-Wilson. Incl. Vol. 1. 1969. pap. 10.95 o.p. (ISBN 0-312-26005-9); Vol. 2. 1969. 14.95 o.p. (ISBN 0-312-26040-7); Vol. 3. 1969. (ISBN 0-687-01188-4); pap. 10.95 o.p. (ISBN 0-312-26110-1). 1969. pap. St Martin.

Essays in English History: World History in Six Dimensions. Paul Harrison Silfen. LC 74-80691. 1975. 4.00 o.p. (ISBN 0-682-48047-9, University). Exposition-Phoenix.

Essays in French & German History: World History in Six Dimensions. Paul Harrison Silfen. 1976. 6.50 o.p. (ISBN 0-682-48375-3, University). Exposition-Phoenix.

Essays in Gandhian Economics. Ed. by Romesh Diwan & Mark Lutz. xxv, 243p. 1985. text ed. 27.50x o.p. (ISBN 0-86590-789-7, Pub. by Gandhi Peace Found (New Delhi)). Apt Bks.

Essays in General Relativity. Ed. by Frank J. Tipler. LC 80-517. 1980. 49.50 o.p. (ISBN 0-12-691380-3). Acad Pr.

Essays in Gratitude. D. Elton Trueblood. LC 82-71215. 1982. 8.95 o.p. (ISBN 0-8054-6938-9). Broadman.

Essays in Greek & Roman History: World History in Six Dimensions. Paul Harrison Silfen. 1975. 4.50 o.p. (ISBN 0-682-48279-X, University). Exposition-Phoenix.

Essays in Honor of J. Dwight Pentecost. Ed. by Stanley D. Toussaint & Charles Dyer. 1986. text ed. 15.95 o.p. (ISBN 0-8024-2381-7). Moody.

Essays in Honour of Yigael Yadin. Ed. by Geza Vermes & Jacob Neusner. (Publications of the Oxford Centre for Postgraduate Hebrew Studies: Vol. 6). (Illus.). 618p. 1983. text ed. 45.00x o.s.i. (ISBN 0-86598-102-7, Pub. by Allanheld). Rowman.

Essays in Islamic Art & Architecture (In Honor of Katharina Otto-Dorn) Ed. by Abbas Daneshvari. LC 81-71740. (Islamic Art & Architecture Ser.: Vol. 1). (Illus.). x, 135p. (Orig., Fr.). 1981. 35.00x o.p. (ISBN 0-89003-111-8); pap. text ed. 25.00x o.p. (ISBN 0-89003-110-X). Mazda Pubs.

Essays in Jurisprudence in Honor of Roscoe Pound. American Society for Legal History Staff. Ed. by Ralph A. Newman. LC 73-10750. (Illus.). 670p. 1973. Repr. of 1962 ed. lib. bdg. 34.00x o.p. (ISBN 0-8371-7023-0, EJRP). Greenwood.

Essays in Law & Society. Ed. by Geoff Mungham & Zenon Bankowski. 216p. (Orig.). 1980. pap. 18.00x o.p. (ISBN 0-7100-0489-3). Routledge Chapman & Hall.

Essays in Metaphysics. Heidegger. LC 60-13645. 80p. 1960. (ISBN 0-8022-0703-0). Philos Lib.

Essays in Monetary Policy in Honor of Elmer Wood. Ed. by Pinkney C. Walker. LC 65-21793. 143p. 1965. 14.00 o.p. (ISBN 0-8262-0039-7). U of Mo Pr.

Essays in Normative Economics. Abram Bergson. LC 66-13177. (Illus.). 1966. 20.00x o.s.i. (ISBN 0-674-26500-9, Belknap Pr). Harvard U Pr.

Essays in Physics. Ed. by G. K. Conn & G. N. Fowler. Vol. 1. 1970. pap. 21.50 o.p. (ISBN 0-12-184801-9); Vol. 2. 1970. pap. 21.50 o.p. (ISBN 0-12-184802-7); Vol. 3. 1971. pap. 34.00 o.p. (ISBN 0-12-184803-5); Vol. 4. 1972. pap. 34.00 o.p. (ISBN 0-12-184804-3); Vol. 5, 1974. pap. 45.00 o.p. (ISBN 0-12-184805-1); Vol. 6, 1976. pap. 45.00 o.p. (ISBN 0-12-184806-X). Acad Pr.

Essays in Plant Taxonomy. Ed. by H. E. Street. 1978. 82.50 o.p. (ISBN 0-12-673360-0). Acad Pr.

Essays in Politics. Scott Buchanan. 1953. (ISBN 0-8022-0192-X). Philos Lib.

Essays in Presidential Rhetoric. Theodore O. Windt & Beth Ingold. 344p. 1983. pap. text ed. 14.95 o.p. (ISBN 0-8403-3242-4, 40324202). Kendall-Hunt.

Essays in Provocation. Glenn E. Hoover. 1951. (ISBN 0-8022-0741-3). Philos Lib.

Essays in Regional Economics. John F. Kain & John R. Meyer. LC 73-160024. (Illus.). 412p. 1971. 29.50x o.p. (ISBN 0-674-26562-9). Harvard U Pr.

Essays in Relating Theory to Practice in Education. 3rd ed. H. R. Weinstock. 1975. pap. text ed. 9.95x o.p. (ISBN 0-8422-0510-1). Irvington.

Essays in Russian History: World History in Six Dimensions. Paul Harrison Silfen. LC 74-80692. 1975. 4.00 o.p. (ISBN 0-682-48048-7, University). Exposition-Phoenix.

Essays in Science. Albert Einstein. 128p. (ISBN 0-8022-0437-6). Philos Lib.

Essays in Skepticism. Bertrand Russell. LC 62-18547. 1963. (ISBN 0-8022-1418-5). Philos Lib.

Essays in Supply Side Economics. Ed. by David G. Rayboy. 173p. 1982. 10.95 o.p. (ISBN 0-317-07524-1); pap. 5.95 o.p. (ISBN 0-317-07525-X). Heritage Found.

Essays in the History of Economics. George J. Stigler. LC 65-14426. (Phoenix Ser.). viii, 392p. 1966. lib. bdg. 25.00 o.s.i. (ISBN 0-226-77426-0, 206, Phoen); pap. 11.95 o.s.i. (ISBN 0-226-77427-9). U of Chicago Pr.

Essays in the History of Mechanics. C. A. Truesdell. LC 68-17860. (Illus.). 1969. 59.00 o.p. (ISBN 0-387-04367-5). Springer-Verlag.

Essays in the Humanities. Ed. by J. S. Gallegly et al. (Rice University Studies: Vol. 57, No. 1). 85p. 1971. pap. 10.00x o.p. (ISBN 0-89263-207-0). Rice Univ.

Essays in the Sociology of Perception. Ed. by Mary Douglas. 288p. (Orig.). 1982. pap. 17.95x o.p. (ISBN 0-7100-0881-3). Routledge Chapman & Hall.

Essays in Theoretical Physics: In Honor of Dirk ter Haar. Ed. by W. E. Parry. (Illus.). 352p. 1984. 63.00 o.p. (ISBN 0-08-026523-5). Pergamon.

Essays in Toxicology, Vols. 1-7. Ed. by F. R. Blood. Incl. Vol. 1. 1969. 22.50 o.p. (ISBN 0-12-107601-6); pap. 24.00 (ISBN 0-12-107651-2); Vol. 2. 1970. 50.00 (ISBN 0-12-107602-4); pap. 24.00 (ISBN 0-12-107652-0); Vol. 3. Wayland J. Hayes, Jr. 1972. 35.00 (ISBN 0-12-107603-2); pap. 24.00 (ISBN 0-12-107653-9); Vol. 4. 1973. 50.00 (ISBN 0-12-107604-0); pap. write for info.; Vol. 5. 1974. 49.00 (ISBN 0-12-107605-9); Vol. 6. 1975. 50.00 (ISBN 0-12-107606-7); lib. bdg. 72.00 o.p. (ISBN 0-12-107674-1); Vol. 7. 1976. 60.00 (ISBN 0-12-107607-5); lib. bdg. 75.00 o.p. (ISBN 0-12-107676-8). pap. Acad Pr.

Essays in Traditional Jewish Thought. Samuel Belkin. 1951. (ISBN 0-8022-0092-3). Philos Lib.

Essays in Twentieth Century American Diplomatic History Dedicated to Professor Daniel M. Smith. Ed. by Clifford L. Egan & Alexander W. Knott. LC 81-40030. (Illus.). 238p. (Orig.). 1982. PLB 29.75 o.p. (ISBN 0-8191-2125-8); pap. text ed. 13.50 o.p. (ISBN 0-8191-2126-6). U Pr of Amer.

Essays in World History from Antiquity to the Present. Paul Harrison Silfen. 1976. 17.50 o.p. (ISBN 0-682-48482-2, University). Exposition-Phoenix.

Essays, Moral & Political, 2 vols. Robert Southey. (Development of Industrial Society Ser.). 878p. 1971. Repr. of 1832 ed. 80.00x set o.p. (ISBN 0-7165-1589-X, BBA 03069, Pub. by Irish Academic Pr). Biblio Dist.

Essays of a String Teacher: Come Let Us Rosin Together. Clifford A. Cook. LC 73-77584. 1973. 7.50 o.p. (ISBN 0-682-47690-0). Exposition-Phoenix.

Essays of Philanthropos on Peace & War. William Ladd. LC 76-147434. (Library of War & Peace; Proposals for Peace: a History). 1972. lib. bdg. 46.00 o.p. (ISBN 0-8240-0221-0). Garland Pub.

Essays of William Graham Sumner, 2 Vols. William G. Sumner. Ed. by Albert G. Keller & Maurice R. Davie. xix, 499p. 1969. Repr. of 1934 ed. Set. 62.50 o.p. (ISBN 0-208-00628-1, Archon). Shoe String.

Essays on Analytical Chemistry: In Memory of Professor Anders Ringbom. Ed. by Erkki Wanninen. LC 77-4103. 1977. 150.00 o.p. (ISBN 0-08-021596-3). Pergamon.

Essays on Biblical Interpretation. Paul Ricoeur. Ed. by Lewis S. Mudge. LC 80-8052. 192p. (Orig.). 1980. pap. 4.95 o.p. (ISBN 0-8006-1407-0, 1-1407, Fortress). Augsburg Fortress.

Essays on Biblical Theology. Hartmut Gese. Tr. by Keith R. Crim. LC 81-65658. 256p. (Orig.). 1981. pap. 14.50 o.p. (ISBN 0-8066-1894-9, 10-2087, Augsburg). Augsburg Fortress.

Essays on Comparative Literature & Linguistics. Ed. by G. S. Amur et al. viii, 174p. 1984. text ed. 18.95x o.p. (ISBN 0-86590-228-3, Pub. by Sterling Pubs India). Apt Bks.

Essays on Econometrics & Planning. C. R. Rao. 1965. 65.00 o.p. (ISBN 0-08-011025-8). Pergamon.

Essays on Form & Interpretation. Noam Chomsky. (Studies in Linguistic Analysis: Vol. 2). 1977. 38.25 o.p. (ISBN 0-7204-8615-7, North-Holland). Elsevier.

Essays on Future Trends in Anaesthesia. A. Boba. LC 72-76388. (Anaesthesiology & Resuscitation Ser.: Vol. 61). (Illus.). 103p. 1972. pap. 12.20 o.p. (ISBN 0-387-05798-6). Springer-Verlag.

Essays on German Influence upon English Education & Science, 1850-1919. George Haines, 4th. (Connecticut College Monograph: No. 9). x, 188p. 1969. 22.50 o.p. (ISBN 0-208-00762-8, Archon). Shoe String.

Essays on Goldsmith by Scott, Macaulay & Thackeray, & Selections from His Writings. Oliver Goldsmith. Repr. of 1946 ed. 25.00x o.p. (ISBN 0-403-04056-6). Somerset Pub.

Essays on Haitian Literature. Leon F. Hoffmann. LC 82-50882. 269p. 1984. 17.00 o.p. (ISBN 0-89410-344-X); pap. 8.00 o.p. (ISBN 0-89410-345-8). Three Continents.

Essays on Hispanic Literature - Ensayos de Literatura Hispana: A Bilingual Anthology. Marguerite C. Suarez-Murias. LC 81-43911. 220p. (Orig., Eng. & Span.). 1982. lib. bdg. 30.50 o.p. (ISBN 0-8191-2600-4); pap. text ed. 13.25 o.p. (ISBN 0-8191-2601-2). U Pr of Amer.

Essays on Honesty, Morality, & Competition. Willard B. Arnold. 136p. 1985. 10.00 o.p. (ISBN 0-682-40235-4). Exposition-Phoenix.

Essays on Islamic Philosophy & Science. Ed. by George F. Hourani. LC 74-13493. 261p. 1974. 49.50x o.p. (ISBN 0-87395-224-3). State U Ny Pr.

Essays on Jung & the Study of Religion. Ed. by Luther H. Martin & James Goss. LC 85-17865. 214p. (Orig.). 1986. lib. bdg. 31.00 o.p. (ISBN 0-8191-4923-3); pap. text ed. 13.50 o.p. (ISBN 0-8191-4924-1). U Pr of Amer.

Essays on la Mujer. Ed. by Rosaura Sanchez & Rosa M. Cruz. (Anthology Ser.: No. 1). 200p. (Orig.). 1977. pap. 9.95 o.p. (ISBN 0-89551-020-0). Ucla Chicano Stud.

Essays on Literature & Politics 1932-1972. Philip Rahv. Ed. by Arabel J. Porter & Andrew J. Dvosin. 1978. 15.00 o.p. (ISBN 0-395-27270-X). HM.

Essays on Manuscripts & Rare Books. Cora E. Lutz. LC 75-2323. (Illus.). 177p. (Orig.). 1975. 19.50 o.p. (ISBN 0-208-01513-2, Archon). Shoe String.

Essays on Music. Romain Rolland. 371p. Repr. of 1948 ed. lib. bdg. 49.00 o.p. (Pub. by Am Repr Serv). Reprint Servs.

Essays on Music in the Western World. Oliver Strunk. (Illus.). 200p. 1974. 8.95 o.p. (ISBN 0-393-02178-5). Norton.

Essays on Nature & Grace. Joseph Sittler. LC 76-171505. 1972. 2.00x o.p. (ISBN 0-8006-0070-3, Fortress). Augsburg Fortress.

Essays on New Testament Themes. Ernst Kasemann. LC 81-70554. 200p. 1982. pap. 6.95 o.p. (ISBN 0-8006-1629-4, 1-1629, Fortress). Augsburg Fortress.

Essays on Oceanography: A Tribute to John Swallow. Ed. by J. Crease et al. (Illus.). 578p. 1984. 180.00 o.p. (ISBN 0-08-032339-1). Pergamon.

Essays on Old Testament Hermeneutics. rev. ed. Ed. by Claus Westermann. 1969. 9.95 o.p. (ISBN 0-8042-0108-0, John Knox). Westminster John Knox.

Essays on Old Testament Hermeneutics. Ed. by Claus Westermann & James L. Mays. LC 63-10637. 1979. pap. 8.95 o.p. (ISBN 0-8042-0107-2, John Knox). Westminster John Knox.

Essays on Other Minds. Ed. by Thomas O. Buford. LC 73-122911. 434p. 1970. 34.95 o.p. (ISBN 0-252-00123-0). U of Ill Pr.

Essays on Petroleum. Mana S. Al-Otaiba. 176p. 1982. 21.50 o.p. (ISBN 0-7099-1921-2, Pub. by Croom Helm Ltd). Routledge Chapman & Hall.

Essays on Philosophy & the Classics. John Stuart Mill. Ed. by John M. Robson. LC 63-25876. (Collected Works of John Stuart Mill Ser.). 1978. 45.00x o.p. (ISBN 0-8020-2283-9). U of Toronto Pr.

Essays on Political Economy. Matthew Carey. LC 66-21660. 1968. Repr. of 1822 ed. 49.50x o.s.i. (ISBN 0-678-00285-1). Kelley.

Essays on Power & Change in Jamaica. Ed. by Carl Stone & Aggrey Brown. 207p. (Orig.). 1977. pap. 8.95 o.p. (ISBN 0-87855-683-4). Transaction Pubs.

Essays on Reason, Will, Creativity, & Time: Studies in the Philosophy of Friedrich Nietzsche. Bernard D. Ouden. LC 82-45042. 124p. (Orig.). 1982. PLB 23.75 o. p. o.p. (ISBN 0-8191-2449-4); pap. text ed. 10.00 o.p. (ISBN 0-8191-2450-8). U Pr of Amer.

Essays on Rhythm, Music, Movement. Henrietta Rosenstrauch. LC 73-77959. 1973. spiral bdg. 5.95 o.p. (ISBN 0-913650-01-3). CPP Belwin.

Essays on Shakespeare & Elizabethan Drama: In Honor of Hardin Craig. Ed. by Richard Hosley. LC 62-12438. (Illus.). 391p. 1962. 39.00x o.p. (ISBN 0-8262-0014-1). U of Mo Pr.

Essays on the Active Powers of Man. Thomas Reid. Ed. by Rene Wellek. LC 75-11251. (British Philosophers & Theologians of the 17th & 18th Centuries: Vol. 50). 1977. Repr. of 1788 ed. lib. bdg. 51.00 o.p. (ISBN 0-8240-1802-8). Garland Pub.

Essays on the American West. Ed. by Harold M. Hollingsworth & Sandra L. Myres. LC 77-98406. (Walter Prescott Webb Memorial Lectures Ser.: No. 3). 114p. 1969. 10.95x o.p. (ISBN 0-292-70017-2). Tex A&M Univ Pr.

Essays on the Closing of the American Mind. Ed. by Robert L. Stone. 224p. 1989. pap. 11.95 o.p. (ISBN 1-55652-052-2). Chicago Review.

Essays on the Gita. Sri Aurobindo. 588p. 1983. 15.00 o.p. (ISBN 0-89071-231-X). Aurobindo Assn.

Essays on the History & Meaning of Checks & Balances. E. P. Panagopoulos. 314p. (Orig.). 1986. lib. bdg. 32.25 o.p. (ISBN 0-8191-4996-9); pap. text ed. 15.50 o.p. (ISBN 0-8191-4997-7). U Pr of Amer.

Essays on the Law & Economics of Local Governments. Ed. by Daniel Rubinfeld. (Papers on Public Economics: Vol. 3). 253p. (Orig.). 1980. pap. text ed. 12.00x o.p. (ISBN 0-87766-262-2, 27200). Urban Inst.

Essays on the Lord's Supper. Oscar Cullmann & Franz J. Leenhardt. LC 58-8979. 1958. pap. 4.95 o.p. (ISBN 0-8042-3748-4, John Knox). Westminster John Knox.

Essays on the Love Commandment. Luise Schottroff et al. Ed. & tr. by Reginald H. Fuller. LC 78-54550. 112p. 1978. 7.95 o.p. (ISBN 0-8006-0528-4, 1-528, Fortress). Augsburg Fortress.

Essays on the Monteverdi Mass & Vespers of 1610. Jeffrey Kurtzman. LC 78-66039. (Rice University Studies: Vol. 64, No.4). (Illus.). 182p. 1979. pap. 10.00x o.p. (ISBN 0-89263-238-0). Rice Univ.

Essays on the New Deal. Ed. by Harold M. Hollingsworth & William F. Holmes. LC 73-80898. (Walter Prescott Webb Memorial Lectures Ser.: No. 2). 116p. 1969. 10.95x o.p. (ISBN 0-292-78410-4). Tex A&M Univ Pr.

Essays on the Principles of Morality & Natural Religion. Henry Home & Lord Kames. LC 75-11228. (Philosophy of David Hume Ser.). 410p. 1976. lib. bdg. 51.00 o.p. (ISBN 0-8240-1781-1). Garland Pub.

Essays on the Reconstruction of Medieval History. Ed. by Vaclav Mudroch & G. S. Couse. 200p. 1974. 15.00x o.p. (ISBN 0-7735-0069-3, McGill Canada). U of Toronto Pr.

Essays on the Sermon on the Mount. Hans D. Betz. LC 84-47910. 192p. 1984. 3.95 o.p. (ISBN 0-8006-0726-0, 1-726, Fortress). Augsburg Fortress.

Essays on the Sources for Chinese History. Ed. by Donald D. Leslie et al. LC 74-10508. xii, 380p. 1975. 24.95x o.p. (ISBN 0-87249-329-6). U of SC Pr.

Essays on the Theory & Practice of Criminal Justice. Robert M. Rich. 319p. 1977. pap. text ed. 15.25 o.p. (ISBN 0-8191-0235-0). U Pr of Amer.

Essays, Plays & Sundry Verses. Abraham Cowley. 499p. Repr. of 1906 ed. 69.00x o.p. (ISBN 0-403-04057-4). Somerset Pub.

Essays Today Seven. William T. Moynihan. 224p. 1972. pap. text ed. 5.95 o.p. (ISBN 0-15-522946-X, HC). HarBraceJ.

Essence & Application: A View from Chiron. Zane B. Stein. (Illus.). 211p. (Orig.). 1986. pap. 11.00 o.p. CAO TIMES.

Essence Heritage. Martin A. Larson. LC 79-83606. 1980. Philos Lib.

Essence of Biometry. John Stanley. 162p. 1963. 6.50 o.p. (ISBN 0-7735-0013-8, McGill Canada). U of Toronto Pr.

Essence of Bruckner. Robert Simpson. 1978. 7.95 o.s.i. (ISBN 0-8008-2467-9, Crescendo). Taplinger.

Essence of Faith. Albert Schweitzer. LC 66-23987. (ISBN 0-8022-1519-X). Philos Lib.

Essence of Fiction: A Practical Handbook for Successful Writing. Malcolm L. McConnel. 221p. 1986. 14.45 o.p. (ISBN 0-393-02306-0). Norton.

Essence of Living. Zinka Saric. 1985. 7.95 o.p. (ISBN 0-533-06397-3). Vantage.

Essence of Music & Other Papers. Ferruccio Busoni. 200p. 1957. (ISBN 0-8022-0202-0). Philos Lib.

Essence of Opera. Ed. by Ulrich Weisstein. 1969. pap. 5.95 o.p. (ISBN 0-393-00498-8, Norton Lib). Norton.

Essence of the Bible. Paul Claudel. 128p. 1958. (ISBN 0-8022-0258-6). Philos Lib.

Essence of the Supply-Side Economics for the Benefit of Politicians & Businessmen. Gregorius Salisbury. (Research Center for Economic Psychology Library). (Illus.). 121p. 1983. 117.75 o.p. (ISBN 0-86654-060-1). Inst Econ Finan.

Essence of Yoga. Georg Feuerstein. LC 75-42897. 1976. pap. 3.95 o.p. (ISBN 0-394-17902-1, E671, Ever). Grove.

Essenes: The Elect of Israel & the Priests of Artemis. Allen H. Jones. (Illus.). 146p. (Orig.). 1985. lib. bdg. 24.75 o.p. (ISBN 0-8191-4744-3); pap. text ed. 10.00 o.p. (ISBN 0-8191-4745-1). U Pr of Amer.

Essential Algebra & Trigonometry. Doris S. Stockton. LC 77-76337. (Illus.). 1978. text ed. 40.36 o.p. (ISBN 0-395-25413-2); instr's. manual 1.56 o.p. (ISBN 0-395-25414-0). HM.

Essential Anaethesia. Ellis & Campbell. 1986. 21.00 o.p. (ISBN 0-8016-1514-3). Mosby.

Essential Anatomy. 3rd, rev. ed. J. P. Lumley et al. (Illus.). 1981. pap. text ed. 22.00 o.p. (ISBN 0-443-02003-5). Churchill.

Essential Aspects of Career Planning & Development. 2nd ed. J. C. Atherton & Anthony Mumphrey. LC 75-39156. 376p. (gr. 10-12). 1977. text ed. 14.95x o.p. (ISBN 0-8134-1786-4, 1786). Inter Print Pubs.

Essential Biology. Lee Chin-Chiu. LC 73-13537. 1973. pap. text ed. 6.00x o.p. (ISBN 0-8422-0353-2). Irvington.

Essential Catholicism. Tr. by Thomas Bokenkotter. LC 84-13631. 432p. 1985. 19.95 o.s.i. (ISBN 0-385-18357-7). Doubleday.

Essential Clinical Microbiology: An Introductory Text. E. M. Cooke & G. L. Gibson. 276p. 1983. pap. 16.95 o.p. (ISBN 0-471-90017-6, Dist. by A R Liss). Wiley.

Essential Clinical Virology. R. G. Sommerville. (Illus.). 190p. 1983. pap. text ed. 14.75 o.p. (ISBN 0-632-01085-1, B4748-7). Mosby.

Essential College Algebra. Doris S. Stockton. LC 78-69526. (Illus.). 1979. text ed. 36.36 o.p. (ISBN 0-395-26544-4); instr's. manual 1.96 o.p. (ISBN 0-395-26538-X). HM.

Essential Commodore 128 User's Guide. Jerry Willis. LC 85-81855. 208p. pap. 12.95 o.p. (ISBN 0-89586-239-5). Price Stern.

Essential Concepts in Immunology. Irving Weissman et al. LC 78-57262. 1978. 21.95 o.p. (ISBN 0-8053-4406-3). Benjamin-Cummings.

Essential CPA Law Review. 6th ed. George C. Thompson & Gerald P. Brady. LC 83-11994. 512p. 1984. text ed. 24.25 o.p. (ISBN 0-534-02797-0). PWS-Kent Pub.

Essential Cubism. Douglas Cooper & Gary Tinterow. LC 83-22348. (Illus.). 448p. 1984. 45.00 o.p. (ISBN 0-8076-1092-5). Braziller.

Essential Engineering Dynamics. J. C. Maltbaek. 359p. 1975. pap. text ed. 17.25x o.p. (ISBN 0-258-97070-7, Pub. by Granada England). Gower Pub Co.

Essential Exercises for the Childbearing Year: A Guide to Health & Comfort Before & After Your Baby Is Born. Elizabeth Noble. 1976. 12.95 o.p. (ISBN 0-395-24836-1); pap. 6.95 o.p. (ISBN 0-395-24835-3). HM.

Essential Guide to Timex-Sinclair Home Computers: The Only Book You'll Ever Need to Become an Expert at the Timex-Sinclair 1000 & 2000. Peter Morse et al. 1983. pap. 8.50 o.p. (ISBN 0-671-47069-8, Touchstone Bks). S&S.

Essential Idioms in English. rev. & enl. ed. Robert J. Dixson. (Illus., Orig.). (gr. 9 up). 1971. pap. text ed. 3.75 o.p. (ISBN 0-88345-048-8, 18013). Prentice ESL.

Essential Interactionism: On the Intelligibility of Prejudice. Barry Glassner. (International Library of Sociology). (Illus.). 1980. 22.95x o.p. (ISBN 0-7100-0381-1). Routledge Chapman & Hall.

Essential Japanese Grammar. Everett F. Bleiler. LC 63-17899. 1963. lib. bdg. 9.50x o.p. (ISBN 0-88307-578-4). Gannon.

Essential Landscape: The New Mexico Photographic Survey. Ed. by Steve A. Yates. LC 84-23754. (Illus.). 156p. 1985. 45.00 o.p. (ISBN 0-8263-0784-1). U of NM Pr.

Essential Left: Four Classic Texts on the Principles of Socialism. Karl Marx et al. (Unwin Books). 1960. pap. 9.95 o.p. (ISBN 0-04-335013-5). Unwin Hyman.

Essential Management of Obstetric Emergencies. T. F. Baskett. 1985. 35.00 o.p. (ISBN 0-471-90333-7, Dist. by A R Liss). Wiley.

Essential Math, Science, & Computer Terms for College Freshmen. William F. Shanahan. LC 79-3323. (Illus.). 1981. pap. 5.95 o.p. (ISBN 0-671-18435-0). Monarch Pr.

Essential Mathematics for College Physics with Calculus: A Self Study Guide. Michael Ram. 418p. (Orig.). 1984. pap. text ed. (ISBN 0-471-80876-8). Wiley.

Essential Mathematics with Applications. Vernon C. Barker & Richard N. Aufmann. LC 82-82928. 288p. 1982. pap. 14.95 o.p. (ISBN 0-395-33195-1). HM.

Essential Methods in Business Statistics. Edward N. Dubois. (Illus.). 1979. text ed. 37.95 o.p. (ISBN 0-07-017889-5). McGraw.

Essential of Structured COBOL Programming. Jan L. Mize & William W. Cotterman. LC 78-6609. 364p. 1978. pap. 19.95 o.p. (ISBN 0-534-00580-2). Krieger.

Essential Oils Analysis by Capillary Gas Chromatography & Carbon-13 NMR Spectroscopy. V. Formacek & K. H. Kubeczka. 373p. 1983. 159.95x o.p. (ISBN 0-471-26218-8, Pub. by Wiley Heyden). Wiley.

Essential OS-2. Judd Robbins. 367p. (Orig.). 1987. pap. 22.95 o.p. (ISBN 0-89588-478-X). Sybex.

Essential Paediatric Radiology. Steiner. (Illus.). 270p. 1983. 62.00 o.p. (ISBN 0-632-00957-8, B4841-6). Mosby.

Essential PC-DOS. Myril C. Shaw & Susan S. Shaw. LC 84-51218. 300p. 1985. pap. 16.95 o.p. (ISBN 0-89588-176-4). SYBEX.

Essential Primary Care. Street & Burch. 1986. 17.50 o.p. (ISBN 0-8016-4915-3). Mosby.

Essential Santa Fe. Rinaja Soleil. LC 87-18026. (Illus.). 148p. (Orig.). 1987. pap. 8.95 o.p. (ISBN 0-86534-116-8). Sunstone Pr.

Essential Self: An Introduction to Literature. Paul Berry. (Illus.). 480p. 1975. text ed. 24.95 o.p. (ISBN 0-07-005048-1). McGraw.

Essential Shakespeare: Nine Major Plays & the Sonnets. Ed. by Russel A. Fraser. (Illus.). 544p. 1972. pap. text ed. write for info. o.p. (ISBN 0-02-339550-8). Macmillan.

Essential Surgical Practice. A. Cuschieri et al. (Illus.). 1105p. 1982. 77.00 o.p. (ISBN 0-7236-0622-6). Butterworth.

Essential Theatre. 3rd ed. Oscar G. Brockett. 402p. 1984. pap. text ed. 20.95 o.p. (ISBN 0-03-063553-5, HoltC). HR&W.

Essential Trigonometry. Doris S. Stockton. LC 78-69543. (Illus.). 1979. text ed. 27.95 o.p. (ISBN 0-395-26539-8). HM.

Essential Wisdom of George Santayana. Thomas N. Munson. LC 83-12738. viii, 224p. 1983. Repr. of 1962 ed. lib. bdg. 35.00x o.p. (ISBN 0-313-24126-0, MUEW). Greenwood.

Essentials Guides to Wills, Estates, Trusts, & Death Taxes. Ed. by Alex J. Soled. 290p. pap. 12.95 o.p. (ISBN 0-318-23709-1). Am Assn Retire.

Essentials in Economics: Quick Access to the Important Facts & Concepts. Research & Education Association Staff. (Illus.). 96p. 1987. pap. text ed. 4.95 o.p. Res & Educ.

Essentials in Electronic Communications: Quick Access to the Important Facts & Concepts. Research & Education Association Staff. (Illus.). 96p. 1987. pap. text ed. 4.95 o.p. Res & Educ.

Essentials in Statistics: Quick Access to the Important Facts & Concepts. Research & Education Association Staff. (Illus.). 96p. 1987. pap. text ed. 4.95 o.p. (ISBN 0-87891-592-3). Res & Educ.

Essentials in Vector Analysis: Quick Access to the Important Facts & Concepts. Research & Education Association Staff. (Illus.). 96p. 1987. pap. text ed. 4.95 o.p. (ISBN 0-87891-595-8). Res & Educ.

Essentials of Accounting Theory. Wilford J. Eiteman. LC 61-8425. 1961. 4.50x o.s.i. (ISBN 0-912164-03-4). Masterco Pr.

Essentials of Advertising. Louis C. Kaufman. 538p. 1980. text ed. 24.00 o.p. (ISBN 0-15-524100-1, HC). HarBraceJ.

Essentials of Auto Mechanics. Charles Pearce. (Auto Mechanics Motivational Program). 1973. pap. text ed. 7.95 o.p. (ISBN 0-89036-816-3); tchrs' guide 1.50 o.p. (ISBN 0-89036-821-X); vocabulary 2.95 o.p. (ISBN 0-89036-818-X); unit tests 3.50 o.p. (ISBN 0-89036-817-1); study guide pap. 7.50 o.p. (ISBN 0-89036-820-1); guide bk. 2.95 o.p. (ISBN 0-89036-815-5). Hawkes Pub Inc.

Essentials of Bank Consumer Leasing. Ronald S. Loshin & Randall R. McCathren. LC 83-71932. 350p. 1985. 195.00 o.p. (ISBN 0-933355-00-9). Bank Lease Pubns.

Essentials of Basic Youth Ministry. Spencer Nordyke & Cyndy Nordyke. 49p. (Orig.). 1984. wkbk. 4.95 o.s.i. (ISBN 0-914307-21-5). R Tilton Ministries.

Essentials of Behavior. Clark L. Hull. LC 73-8150. 145p. 1974. Repr. of 1951 ed. lib. bdg. 22.50x o.p. (ISBN 0-8371-6956-9, HUEB). Greenwood.

Essentials of Biology: A Basic Text of Current Biological Thought. C. Leland Rodgers. LC 74-8166. (gr. 10-12). 1974. pap. 7.95 o.p. (ISBN 0-8120-0236-9). Barron.

Essentials of Business Math. Walter Gleason. 496p. 1982. pap. text ed. write for info. o.p. (ISBN 0-87150-350-6, 2752, Prindle). PWS-Kent Pub.

Essentials of Business Mathematics. 3rd ed. W. Alton Parish & William L. Kindsfather. 1983. pap. text ed. 27.95 o.p. (ISBN 0-03-062566-1). HR&W.

Essentials of Business Statistics. Wayne W. Daniel. LC 83-80247. 544p. 1984. text ed. 40.36 o.p. (ISBN 0-395-34274-0). HM.

Essentials of Cell & Molecular Biology. E. D. DeRobertis & E. M. DeRobertis, Jr. 1981. text ed. 36.95x o.s.i. (ISBN 0-03-057713-6, CBS C); study guide 10.95 o.s.i. (ISBN 0-03-059736-6); instr's manual 9.95 o.s.i. (ISBN 0-03-059734-X). SCP.

Essentials of Clinical Dental Assisting. 3rd ed. Joseph E. Chasteen. (Illus.). 432p. 1984. 33.50 o.p. (ISBN 0-8016-1127-X). Mosby.

Essentials of Clothing Construction. 2nd ed. Naomi Reich et al. (Illus.). 1978. pap. text ed. 21.33 o.p. (ISBN 0-13-284398-6). P-H.

Essentials of Communication Electronics. 3rd ed. Morris Slurzberg & William Osterheld. (Illus.). 784p. 1972. text ed. 45.95 o.p. (ISBN 0-07-058309-9). McGraw.

Essentials of Consumer Vehicle Leasing. Ronald S. Loshin & Randall R. McCathren. LC 85-71348. 350p. 1985. 195.00 o.p. (ISBN 0-317-19285-X). Bank Lease Pubns.

Essentials of Corporation Law. Leona Beane. 304p. 1984. pap. text ed. 17.95 o.p. (ISBN 0-8403-3264-5). Kendall Hunt.

Essentials of Data Processing. Nancy Floyd. 288p. 1986. pap. 22.95 o.p. (ISBN 0-8016-1660-3). Irwin.

Essentials of Dental Surgery & Pathology. 4th ed. R. A. Cawson. (Dental Ser.). (Illus.). 1984. pap. text ed. 33.00 o.p. (ISBN 0-443-02653-X). Churchill.

Essentials of Discipleship. Francis M. Cosgrove. LC 79-93015. 192p. 1980. pap. 5.95 o.p. (ISBN 0-89109-442-3). NavPress.

Essentials of Drafting. J. Bethune. 416p. 1977. text ed. 37.33 o.p. (ISBN 0-13-284430-3). P-H.

Essentials of Drivers Education. Charles Pearce. (Drivers Education Motivational Program). 1973. pap. 5.95 o.p. (ISBN 0-89036-811-2); study guide 5.95 o.p. (ISBN 0-89036-812-0); vocabulary 2.95 o.p. (ISBN 0-89036-813-9); sample tests 2.95 o.p. (ISBN 0-89036-814-7); guide bk. 2.95 o.p. Hawkes Pub Inc.

Essentials of Economic Theory. John B. Clark. LC 68-8972. (Illus.). xvi, 566p. 1968. Repr. of 1907 ed. 49.50x o.s.i. (ISBN 0-678-00425-0). Kelley.

Essentials of Economics. James D. Gwartney et al. 1981. 17.00i o.p. (ISBN 0-12-311030-0). Acad Pr.

Essentials of Economics: Instructor's Manual & Test Bank. 2nd ed. J. R. Clark. 1985. text ed. 10.00 o.s.i. (ISBN 0-12-311036-X, HC). HarBraceJ.

Essentials of Electronic Communications II: Quick Access to the Important Facts & Concepts. Research & Education Association Staff. (Illus.). 96p. 1987. pap. text ed. 4.95 o.p. (ISBN 0-317-60119-9). Res & Educ.

Essentials of Engineering Economics. Erick Kasner. (Illus.). 1979. text ed. 43.45 o.p. (ISBN 0-07-033323-8). McGraw.

Essentials of Farm Financial Management. S. S. Johl. 164p. 1970. 5.00 o.p. (ISBN 0-88065-140-7, Pub. by Messers Today & Tomorrow Printers & Publishers). Scholarly Pubns.

Essentials of FORTRAN. G. Gleason. LC 72-90224. 1973. pap. text ed. 14.95 o.p. (ISBN 0-03-091400-0, HoltC). HR&W.

Essentials of Gastrointestinal Radiology. Bronwyn Jones & John M. Braver. 1982. pap. (ISBN 0-7216-5207-7). Saunders.

Essentials of General Speech Communication. 4th ed. A. Craig Baird et al. (Speech Ser.). (Illus.). 288p. 1973. text ed. 38.95 o.p. (ISBN 0-07-003252-1). McGraw.

Essentials of Grammar. D. Parisi & F. Antinucci. (Language, Thought & Culture Ser.). 1976. 19.95 o.p. (ISBN 0-12-544650-0). Acad Pr.

Essentials of Human Anatomy & Physiology. Elaine Marieb. 1986. pap. 24.95 o.p. (ISBN 0-8053-6730-6); coloring wkbk. 14.95 o.p. (ISBN 0-8053-6731-4); instr's. guide 9.95 o.p. (ISBN 0-8053-6732-2). Benjamin-Cummings.

Essentials of Investments. C. Ronald Sprecher. LC 77-74380. (Illus.). 1978. text ed. 43.56 o.p. (ISBN 0-395-25454-X); instr's. manual 1.16 o.p. (ISBN 0-395-25455-8). HM.

Essentials of Lasers. L. Allen. 1969. text ed. 31.00 o.p. (ISBN 0-08-013320-7); pap. text ed. 11.25 o.p. (ISBN 0-08-013319-3). Pergamon.

Essentials of Logic: Being Ten Lectures on Judgment & Inference. Bernard Bosanquet. LC 4-3994. 1968. Repr. of 1895 ed. 18.00 o.p. (ISBN 0-527-10006-4). Kraus Repr.

Essentials of Macroeconomic Analysis. Bilas & Alessio. Irwin.

Essentials of Management. 2nd ed. W. Jack Duncan. LC 77-81236. 1978. text ed. 29.95x o.p. (ISBN 0-03-039826-6). Dryden Pr.

Essentials of Management. 3rd ed. Harold D. Koontz et al. (Management Ser.). 1982. text ed. 19.95x o.p. (ISBN 0-07-035419-7). McGraw.

Essentials of Management. 3rd, reference ed. Joseph L. Massie. (Essentials of Management Ser.). (Illus.). 1979. text ed. 25.67 o.p. (ISBN 0-13-286351-0); pap. text ed. 19.00 o.p. (ISBN 0-13-286344-8). P-H.

Essentials of Management Science. Meredith & Turban. 1982. pap. 23.95 o.p. (ISBN 0-256-02703-X). Irwin.

Essentials of Managerial Finance. 7th ed. J. Fred Weston & Eugene F. Brigham. 816p. 1985. text ed. 35.95x o.s.i. (ISBN 0-03-000227-3); study guide 12.95x o.s.i. (ISBN 0-03-000229-X). Dryden Pr.

Essentials of Marketing. Evans & Barry Berman. 1984. text ed. write for info. o.p. (ISBN 0-02-334590-X). Macmillan.

Essentials of Marketing Research Text, Readings, & Cases. Robert F. Hartley et al. 560p. 1983. text ed. write for info. o.p. (ISBN 0-02-351230-X). Macmillan.

Essentials of Materials Science. A. G Guy. 1976. text ed. 42.00 o.p. (ISBN 0-07-025351-X). McGraw.

Essentials of Maternity Nursing. Irene M. Bobak & Margaret D. Jensen. (Illus.). 1138p. 1984. cloth 37.95 o.p. (ISBN 0-8016-2486-X). Mosby.

Essentials of Mechanics: A Unified First Course. Donald F. Young et al. (Illus.). 582p. 1974. text ed. 15.50x o.p. (ISBN 0-8138-1110-4). Iowa St U Pr.

Essentials of Medical Mycology. E. G. V. Evans & J. C. Gentles. LC 84-23143. (Illus.). 195p. 1985. pap. text ed. 36.00 o.p. (ISBN 0-443-02505-3). Churchill.

Essentials of Medicine & Surgery for Dental Students. 4th ed. A. C. Kennedy & L. Blumgart. LC 81-68802. (Dental Ser.). (Illus.). 1982. pap. text ed. 27.00 o.p. (ISBN 0-443-02534-7). Churchill.

Essentials of Meteorology. D. H. McIntosh et al. (Wykeham Science Ser.: No. 3). 262p. 1973. pap. 11.75x o.p. (ISBN 0-8448-1354-0, Pub. by Crane Russak & Co). Taylor & Francis.

Essentials of Modern Physics Applied to the Study of the Infrared. A. Hadni. 1967. 69.00 o.p. (ISBN 0-08-011902-6). Pergamon.

Essentials of Nuclear Chemistry. H. J. Arnikar. LC 81-6818. 335p. 1982. 21.95 o.p. (ISBN 0-470-27176-0). Halsted Pr.

Essentials of Obstetrics & Gynaecology. 3rd ed. James Willocks. LC 85-19450. 277p. (Orig.). 1986. pap. 20.00 o.p. (ISBN 0-443-03367-6). Churchill.

Essentials of Organizational Behavior. Stephen P. Robbins. (Illus.). 256p. 1984. pap. text ed. (ISBN 0-13-286542-4). P-H.

Essentials of Paleobotany. 2nd ed. A. C. Shukla & S. P. Misra. (Illus.). 1982. text ed. 22.50x o.p. (ISBN 0-7069-1450-3, Pub. by Vikas India). Advent NY.

Essentials of Parasitology. 3rd ed. Marvin C. Meyer & O. Wilford Olsen. 288p. 1980. write for info. wire coil o.p. (ISBN 0-697-04684-2). Wm C Brown.

Essentials of Parenting in the First Years of Life. Barbara Gross & Bernard Shuman. LC 79-23739. 61p. (Orig.). 1980. pap. text ed. 7.95 o.p. (ISBN 0-87868-184-1, 1841). Child Welfare.

Essentials of Periodontology & Periodontics. 3rd. ed. I. MacPhee & G. Cowley. (Illus.). 338p. 1981. text ed. 47.75 o.p. (ISBN 0-632-00533-5, B 3103-3). Mosby.

Essentials of Philosophy. Nicholas Horvath. LC 73-18149. 1974. pap. text ed. 6.95 o.p. (ISBN 0-8120-0498-1). Barron.

Essentials of Physical Geography. 2nd ed. Robert E. Gabler & Robert J. Sager. 1982. text ed. 36.95 o.p. (ISBN 0-03-058551-1, CBS C). SCP.

Essentials of Physics. Marcel Wellner. 592p. 1986. pap. text ed. 38.95 o.p. (ISBN 0-8403-4114-8). Kendall Hunt.

Essentials of Plastic & Reconstructive Surgery with Notes on Clinical, Nursing & General Management. Brian Morgan & Margaret Wright. 250p. 1986. pap. 13.95 o.p. (ISBN 0-571-13275-8). Faber & Faber.
Essentials of Psychology. 3rd ed. Dennis Coon. (Illus.). 702p. 1985. pap. text ed. 31.50 o.p. (ISBN 0-314-85226-3). West Pub.
Essentials of Psychology. John P. Houston et al. 550p. 1981. 17.75i o.p. (ISBN 0-12-356858-7). test bank II (1500 items) o.p.; instrs' manual 10.00i o.p. (ISBN 0-12-356842-0). Acad Pr.
Essentials of Psychology. Spencer A. Rathus. 544p. 1986. text ed. 21.95 o.p. (ISBN 0-03-069871-5, HoltC). HR&W.
Essentials of Pulmonary Medicine. M. Williams. LC 81-50836. (Illus.). 190p. 1982. pap. write for info. o.p. (ISBN 0-7216-9394-6). Saunders.
Essentials of Real Estate Investment. 3rd ed. David Sirota. LC 83-19127. (Illus.). 298p. (Orig.). Date not set. pap. text ed. 31.95 o.p. (ISBN 0-88462-667-9, 1559-01, Real Estate Ed). Longman Finan.
Essentials of Solid State Electronics. Rodney B. Faber. LC 84-29113. 355p. 1985. 33.95 o.p. (ISBN 0-471-86575-3). Wiley.
Essentials of Stage Lighting. 2nd ed. Hunton D. Sellman & Merrill J. Lessley. (Illus.). 208p. 1982. text ed. (ISBN 0-13-289249-9). P-H.
Essentials of Statistics. R. Mason. 1976. pap. text ed. (ISBN 0-13-289561-7). P-H.
Essentials of Statistics in Marketing. C. S. Greensted & A. K. Jardine. 1978. pap. 24.95 o.p. (ISBN 0-434-90887-8, Pub. by W Heinemann Ltd). David & Charles.
Essentials of Syntactic Design. Leopold P. Begne. 232p. 1984. pap. text ed. 16.95x o.p. (ISBN 0-89917-412-4). Tichenor Pub.
Essentials of Technical Mathematics. 2nd ed. Richard S. Paul & M. Leonard Shaevel. (Illus.). 704p. 1982. text ed. (ISBN 0-13-288050-4). P-H.
Essentials of Technical Mathematics with Calculus. Richard S. Paul & M. Leonard Shaevel. LC 77-17582. (P-H Series in Technical Mathematics). (Illus.). 1978. Reference ed. text ed. (ISBN 0-13-289199-9). P-H.
Essentials of Textiles. 3rd ed. Marjory L. Joseph. 1984. 29.95 o.p. (ISBN 0-03-064243-4); pap. text ed. 25.95 o.p. (ISBN 0-03-062738-9). HR&W.
Essentials of Treasury Management. Peter Muller. 260p. 1981. 120.00 o.p. (ISBN 0-8002-3418-9). Intl Pubns Serv.
Essex Design Guide for Residential Areas: A Bibliography. Lindsay M. Smales & Brian Goodey. (Architecture Ser.: A 1426). 26p. 1985. 3.75 o.p. (ISBN 0-89028-476-8). Vance Biblios.
EST. Adelaide Bry. 1976. pap. 3.50 o.p. (ISBN 0-380-00697-9). Avon.
Establishing a Geriatric Service. Ed. by Davis Coakley. (Illus.). 236p. 1982. text ed. 35.00x o.p. (ISBN 0-7099-0700-1). Sheridan.
Establishing Quality Control & Normal Ranges in the Clinical Laboratory. Robert G. Hoffmann. LC 70-138367. 1971. 7.50 o.p. (ISBN 0-682-47167-4, University). Exposition-Phoenix.
Establishment of Spanish Rule in America. Bernard Moses. LC 65-21909. Repr. of 1898 ed. 22.50x o.p. (ISBN 0-8154-0156-6). Cooper Sq.
Establishment of the United Arab Emirates. Abdulah O. Taryam. 256p. 1986. 43.00 o.p. (ISBN 0-7099-4330-X, Pub. by Croom Helm UK). Routledge Chapman & Hall.
Estancia Life: Agricultural, Economic, & Cultural Aspects of Argentine Farming. Walter Larden. LC 73-78359. (Illus.). 320p. 1973. Repr. of 1911 ed. 18.00 o.p. (ISBN 0-87917-031-X). Ethridge.
Estate & Gift Tax after ERTA. Michael J. Weinberger. 431p. 1982. text ed. 40.00 o.p. (ISBN 0-686-97905-2, D3-0152). PLI.
Estate Planner's Guide to Business Agreements & Estate Documents. Frank B. Weisz. LC 81-66934. 223p. 1981. comb bdg. 12.95 o.p. (ISBN 0-87863-065-1). FS&G.
Estate Planner's Kit. Jack A. Kirby. LC 78-61307. (Estate Planning & Administration Ser.). 1978. 39.50 o.p. (ISBN 0-87624-140-2, Inst Busn Plan). P-H.
Estate Planning. Edward Milam & D. L. Crumbley. 1980. pap. 6.95 o.p. (ISBN 0-8144-7531-0). AMACOM.
Estate Planning: A Guide for Advisors & Their Clients. D. Larry Crumbley & Edward E. Milam. 200p. 1985. 25.00 o.p. (ISBN 0-87094-686-2). Dow Jones-Irwin.
Estate Planning & Will Drafting. 465p. 1983. 16.00 o.p. (ISBN 0-318-02399-7). ICLE Georgia.
Estate Planning: Complete Guide & Workbook. rev. ed. Alice F. Brod. 1984. 125.00 o.p. (ISBN 0-916592-49-9). Panel Pubs.
Estate Planning Desk Book. 5th ed. William H. Behrenfeld. LC 81-1980. 346p. 1981. 49.50 o.p. (ISBN 0-87624-139-9, Inst Busn Plan). P-H.
Estate Planning Desk Book. 4th ed. William H. Behrenfeld. LC 77-78606. 1977. 29.95 o.p. (ISBN 0-87624-138-0, Inst Busn Plan). P-H.
Estate Planning for Family Lawyers. Massachusetts Continuing Legal Education-New England Law Institute, Inc. Staff. LC 83-63414. 182p. write for info. o.p. Mass CLE.
Estate Planning for Owners of Closely-Held Corporations. Francis Brogan. 276p. 1982. 89.50 o.p. (ISBN 0-87624-136-4, Inst Busn Plan). P-H.
Estate Planning for Property Management & Health Care Financing for the Elderly. Pennsylvania Bar Institute Staff. 232p. 1985. 50.00 o.p. (ISBN 0-318-19042-7, 310). PA Bar Inst.
Estate Planning for the Aging or Incapacitated Client, 1986. LC 86-232545. (Tax Law & Estate Planning Ser.: No. 172). 351p. 1986. 45.00 o.p. (ISBN 0-317-58232-1). PLI.
Estate Planning for the General Practitioner. California Continuing Education of the Bar Staff. 889p. 1979. 70.00 o.p. (ISBN 0-88124-064-8, ES-33320). Cal Cont Ed Bar.
Estate Planning: Pennsylvania Legal Practice Course Materials. Pennsylvania Bar Institute Staff. 74p. 1984. 15.00 o.p. (ISBN 0-318-02170-6, PLP-85). PA Bar Inst.
Estate Planning Plus 1985 Supplement. 2nd ed. Jerome A. Manning. 480p. 1982. text ed. 60.00 o.p. (ISBN 0-317-18467-9, DI-0153). PLI.
Estate Planning: Proceedings of the UCLA CEB Estate Planning Institute, Los Angeles, April, 1982. UCLA-CEB Estate Planning Institute Staff. LC 80-69720. 320p. 1983. 65.00 o.p. (ISBN 0-88124-112-1). Cal Cont Ed Bar.
Estate Planning: 1980. California Continuing Education of the Bar Staff. LC 80-69720. 260p. 1980. 50.00 o.p. (ISBN 0-88124-073-7). Cal cont Ed Bar.
Estate Planning: 1983. Edward C. Halbach, Jr. et al. 485p. 1984. text ed. 65.00 o.p. (ISBN 0-88124-123-7). Cal Cont Ed Bar.
Estate Planning: 1986 Supplement. 5th ed. A. James Casner. 1986. write for info. o.p. (ISBN 0-316-13231-4). Little.
Esteban, Vol. 2. (This Is Animation Ser.: No. 2). (Illus.). 125p. 1984. 7.95 o.p. (ISBN 0-318-02669-4). Bks Nippan.
Estero, Florida 1882. E. E. Damkohler. LC 67-19575. 1974. pap. 1.00 o.p. (ISBN 0-87208-014-5). Island Pr Pubs.
Estes Famlies of Old Clay County, Missouri: Their Ancestors & Their Descendants. Annabelle C. McAllister. ix, 335p. 1972. 25.00 o.p. (ISBN 0-88490-133-5). VA State Lib.
Estey Reed Organs on Parade: A Pictorial Review of the Many Parlour, Boudoir, Philharmonic, & Other Types of Reed Organs Made Over a 100-Year Period by the Famous Estey Organ Company, Together with a Brief Corporate History. Robert B. Whiting. LC 81-7545. (Illus.). 156p. 1981. pap. 15.00 o.p. (ISBN 0-911572-21-X, A-295). Vestal.
Esther. Beatrice Hollenbeck. (Illus.). 29p. (gr. k-4). 1979. pap. text ed. 8.75 o.p. CEF Press.
Esther Scroll: Its Genesis, Growth, & Meaning. David J. Clines. (JSOT Supplement Ser.: No. 30). 260p. pap. text ed. 14.95x o.s.i. (Pub. by JSOT Pr England). Eisenbrauns.
Esther Waters. George Moore. (Black & Gold Library). 1942. 7.95 o.p. (ISBN 0-87140-872-4). Liveright.
Esthetic Animal: Man, the Art-Created Art Creator. Robert Joyce. LC 75-10619. (Illus.). 1975. 9.00 o.p. (ISBN 0-682-48300-1, University). Exposition-Phoenix.
Estimated Production of Pulp, Paper, & Paperboard in Certain Countries in 1976. (Forestry Papers: No. 28). 48p. 1977. pap. 7.50 o.p. (ISBN 0-686-92798-2, F1269, FAO). UNIPUB.
Estimated World Requirements of Narcotic Drugs in 1983: Supplement, No.6. International Narcotics Control Board Staff. 6p. (Eng., Fr. & Span.). 1983. pap. text ed. 1.00 o.p. (UN83/11/2S). UN.
Estimated World Requirements of Narcotic Drugs in 1983: Supplement, No. 7. International Narcotics Control Board Staff. 12p. (Eng., Span. & Fr.). 1983. pap. text ed. 1.00 o.p. (UN83/11/2S7). UN.
Estimates of the Population of the United States, By Age, Sex, & Race 1980-1985. (Current Population Reports Ser. P-25 Population Estimates & Projections: No. 985). 60p. 1986. pap. 3.00 o.p. (S/N 003-001-91482-4). USGPO.
Estimates of the Population of the United States, by Age, Sex, & Race: 1980 to 1986. (Current Population Reports P-25, Population Estimates & Projections: No. 1000). (Illus.). 63p. 1987. pap. 3.25 o.p. (ISBN 0-318-22625-1, S/N 803-004-00008-1). USGPO.
Estimating & Cost Control in Electrical Construction Design. William C. Miller. (Illus.). 1978. 32.95 o.p. (ISBN 0-442-12203-9). Van Nos Reinhold.
Estimating & Cost Control in Plumbing Design. William C. Miller & Leonard Gallina. 176p. 1980. 25.95 o.p. (ISBN 0-442-23347-7). Van Nos Reinhold.
Estimating Building Construction. 2nd ed. William J. Hornung. (Illus.). 320p. 1986. text ed. 40.00 o.p. (ISBN 0-13-289919-1). P-H.
Estimating for Keyboard Input to Photocomposition. 30.00 o.p. (ISBN 0-318-02596-5). Print Indus Am.
Estimating Manufacturing Costs: A Practical Guide for Managers & Estimators. Lawrence M. Matthews. (Illus.). 288p. 1983. text ed. 33.95 o.p. (ISBN 0-07-040951-X). McGraw.
Estimating Needs for Mental Health Care: A Contribution of Epidemiology. Ed. by H. Haefner. (Illus.). 1979. pap. 21.30 o.p. (ISBN 0-387-09425-3). Springer-Verlag.
Estimating Peak Runoff Rates from Ungaged Small Rural Watersheds. (National Cooperative Highway Research Program Report). 53p. 1972. 4.60 o.p. (ISBN 0-309-02021-2). Transport Res Bd.
Estimating Population & Income of Small Areas. National Research Council. 1981. pap. text ed. 14.25 o.p. (ISBN 0-309-03096-X). Natl Acad Pr.
Estimating Residential Construction. Alonzo Wass. (Illus.). 1980. text ed. 39.33 o.p. (ISBN 0-13-289942-6). P-H.
Estimation see Distributed Parameter Systems Theory.
Estimation of Recent Trends in Fertility & Mortality in the Republic of Korea. 1980. 4.25 o.p. (ISBN 0-309-02890-6). Natl Acad Pr.
Estimation of Seismic Risk in Canada: A Review. pap. 5.00 o.p. (SSC37, SSC). UNIPUB.
Estimator's Piping Man-Hour Manual. 3rd ed. John S. Page & Jim G. Nation. LC 75-28602. (Estimator's Man-Hour Library). 220p. 1976. 48.00x o.p. (ISBN 0-87201-700-1). Gulf Pub.
Estonian-English Dictionary. Paul F. Saagpakk. LC 81-43606. (Yale Linguistic Ser.). 1216p. (Estonian & Eng.). 1982. 170.00t o.p. (ISBN 0-300-02849-0). Yale U Pr.
Estonian General Reader. 2nd rev ed. Felix Oinas. LC 73-64410. (Uralic & Altaic Ser: Vol. 34). (Orig.). 1972. 15.00x o.p. (ISBN 0-87750-007-X); pap. text ed. 7.00 o.p. Res Ctr Lang Semiotic.
Estrogen Replacement Therapy. Don Gambrell, Jr. 1987. pap. 8.65 o.p. (ISBN 0-917634-23-3). Creative Infomatics.
Estrogen Therapy: Proceedings of the Workshop Conference, Geneva, October 1977. Estrogen Therapy Workshop Staff. Ed. by Ch Lauritzen & P. A. Van Keep. (Frontiers of Hormone Research: Vol. 5). (Illus.). 1978. 54.50 o.p. (ISBN 3-8055-2879-5). S Karger.
Estuarine & Wetland Processes with Emphasis on Modeling. Ed. by Peter Hamilton & Keith B. Macdonald. LC 80-14721. (Marine Science Ser.: Vol. 11). 666p. 1980. 105.00x o.p. (ISBN 0-306-40452-4, Plenum Pr). Plenum Pub.
Estuarine Oceanography. Council on Education in the Geological Sciences Staff & F. F. Wright. (Illus.). 80p. 1974. text ed. 20.95 o.p. (ISBN 0-07-012336-5). McGraw.
Estudio de la Biblia. John Tickle. Tr. by Olimpia Diaz, Sr. from Eng. 96p. 1980. pap. 1.95 o.p. (ISBN 0-89243-131-8). Liguori Pubns.
Estudio de la Biblia, Libro II. John Tickle. Tr. by Olimpia Diaz. 96p. (Span.). 1983. 3.95 o.p. (ISBN 0-89243-184-9). Liguori Pubns.
Esturarine Comparisons: Symposium. Ed. by Victor S. Kennedy. 1982. 47.50 o.p. (ISBN 0-12-404070-5). Acad Pr.
Et Al: A Collection of Short Stories. Gary Peterson. 64p. 1982. 5.00 o.p. (ISBN 0-682-49833-5). Exposition-Phoenix.
Et la Chine? Roland Barthes. 16p. 1976. 9.95 o.p. (ISBN 0-686-53935-4). French & Eur.
Etat De Siege. Albert Camus. (Coll. Soleil). 1949. 13.50 o.p. (ISBN 0-685-11172-5). Schoenhof.
Etching Compositions & Processes. Ed. by M. J. Collie. LC 82-7894. (Chemical Technology Review Ser.: No. 210). (Illus.). 308p. 1983. 42.00 o.p. (ISBN 0-8155-0913-8). Noyes.
ETCs, New Methods for U. S. Exporting. Leo G. Welt. LC 83-22487. (AMA Management Briefing). 1984. 10.00 o.p. (ISBN 0-8144-2300-0). AMACOM.
Ete: Essai. Albert Camus. 1954. pap. 6.50 o.p. (ISBN 0-685-11173-3). Schoenhof.
Eternal Drama. Richard Rosenheim. 1952. (ISBN 0-8022-1374-X). Philos Lib.
Eternal Duality. Arturo Alberni. (ISBN 0-8022-0016-8). Philos Lib.
Eternal Egypt. Clement Robichon & Alesandre Varille. (Illus.). 1956. (ISBN 0-8022-1359-6). Philos Lib.
Eternal Grit: Up-to-Heaven Insights & Down-to-Earth Wisdom. McKay Allphin. LC 78-70363. 138p. 1978. 7.95 o.p. (ISBN 0-88290-102-8). Horizon Utah.
Eternal Judgment. Derek Prince. (Foundation Ser.: Bk. VII). 1965-66. pap. 2.95 o.p. (ISBN 0-934920-06-0, B-16). Derek Prince.
Eternal Life: Why We Believe. L. Harold DeWolf. LC 79-21670. 112p. 1980. pap. 6.95 o.s.i. (ISBN 0-664-24288-X, Westminster). Westminster John Knox.
Eternal Slum: Housing & Social Policy in Victorian London. Anthony S. Wohl. (Studies in Urban History Ser.). (Illus.). 1977. lib. bdg. 29.95x o.p. (ISBN 0-7735-0311-0, McGill Canada). U of Toronto Pr.
Eternal Sonship: A Refutation According to Adam Clarke. David Campbell. (Illus.). 95p. (Orig.). 1977. pap. 1.95 o.p. (ISBN 0-912315-44-X). Word Aflame.
Eternal Thoughts from Christ the Teacher, 2 Vols. Richard J. Cushing. 1962. 3.50 ea. o.p. Vol. 1 (ISBN 0-8198-0606-4). Vol. 2 (ISBN 0-8198-0607-2). Dghtrs St Paul.
Eternal Triangle (You, Your Neighbour & God) Gary Price Todd. 1977. 6.50 o.p. (ISBN 0-682-48858-5). Exposition-Phoenix.
Ethan Frome. Edith Wharton. 192p. pap. 1.95 o.s.i. (ISBN 0-684-17487-1, ScribT). Scribner.
Ethan Frome. Edith Wharton. 48p. (Orig.). 1989. pap. 9.95 o.p. (ISBN 1-55651-225-2); audiocassette tape incl. o.p. Cram Cassettes.
Ethel Wright Mohamed. Ethel W. Mohamed. Ed. by Christine Wilson. (Illus.). pap. 9.95 o.p. (ISBN 0-938896-41-5). Mississippi Archives.
Etheldreda. Moyra Caldecott. 224p. 1987. pap. 8.95 o.p. (ISBN 1-85063-070-4, Pub. by Routledge UK). Routledge Chapman & Hall.
Ether Lipids: Chemistry & Biology. Ed. by Fred L. Snyder. 1972. 86.00 o.p. (ISBN 0-12-654150-7). Acad Pr.
Ethernet Sourcebook. 3rd ed. R. Shotwell. 550p. 1985. 120.25 o.p. (ISBN 0-444-00978-7, North-Holland). Elsevier.
Ethic of Democratic Capitalism: A Moral Reassessment. Robert Benne. LC 80-2385. 288p. 1981. pap. 11.95 o.p. (ISBN 0-8006-1445-3, 1-1445, Fortress). Augsburg Fortress.
Ethical Arguments for Analysis. 2nd ed. Robert J. Baum. LC 76-1952. 1976. pap. text ed. 19.95 o.p. (ISBN 0-03-089646-0, HoltC). HR&W.
Ethical Arguments for Analysis: Brief Edition. 2nd ed. Robert J. Baum. LC 78-10770. 1979. pap. text ed. 15.95 o.p. (ISBN 0-03-045011-X, HoltC). HR&W.
Ethical Decisions for Social Work Practice. 2nd ed. Frank M. Loewenberg & Ralph Dolgoff. LC 85-63090. 165p. 1985. pap. text ed. 9.95 o.p. (ISBN 0-87581-311-9). Peacock Pubs.
Ethical Dilemmas & the Education of Policymakers. Joel L. Fleishman & Bruce L. Payne. LC 80-10230. (Teaching of Ethics Ser.). 76p. 1980. pap. 4.00 o.p. (ISBN 0-916558-05-3). Hastings Ctr.
Ethical Dilemmas of Development in Asia. Ed. by Godfrey Gunatilleke & Nellan Tiruchelvan. LC 81-47964. 288p. 1983. 25.00x o.p. (ISBN 0-669-05147-0). Lexington Bks.
Ethical Inquiry. Kathleen Hynes. Ed. by Constance McKenna & Karen Johnson. 16p. pap. cancelled o.s.i. (ISBN 0-915365-07-3). Cath Free Choice.
Ethical Issues in Government. Ed. by Norman E. Bowie. 251p. 1981. 29.95 o.p. (ISBN 0-87722-165-0). Temple U Pr.
Ethical Issues in Human Genetics: Genetic Counseling & the Use of Genetic Knowledge. Ed. by Bruce Hilton et al. LC 72-93443. 468p. 1973. 45.00x o.p. (ISBN 0-306-30715-4, Plenum Pr). Plenum Pub.
Ethical Issues in Modern Medicine. 2nd ed. John Arras & Robert Hunt. LC 82-61239. 574p. 1983. pap. 23.95 o.p. (ISBN 0-87484-574-2). Mayfield Pub.
Ethical Man. Alane Mark. (Academy First Mystery Ser.). 200p. 1987. pap. 4.95 o.p. (ISBN 0-89733-223-7). Academy Chi Pubs.
Ethical Standards Casebook. Rev. ed. Ed. by Robert Callis et al. 116p. 1982. pap. text ed. 9.75 o.p. (ISBN 0-911547-37-1, 72125W34). Am Assn Coun Dev.
Ethics. Aristotle. Tr. by John Warrington. 1975. Repr. of 1963 ed. 14.95x o.p. (ISBN 0-460-00547-2, Evman). Biblio Dist.
Ethics, Vol. 3, (incl. 1987 Supplement) Ed. by Eleanor C. Goldstein. (Social Issues Resources Ser.). 1988. 15.00 o.p. (ISBN 0-89777-090-0). Soc Issues.
Ethics & Action. Peter Winch. (Studies in Ethics & the Philosophy of Religion). 240p. 1972. 20.00x o.p. (ISBN 0-7100-7438-7). Routledge Chapman & Hall.
Ethics & Bigness: Proceedings. Conference on Science-Philosophy & Religion in Their Religion to the Democratic Way of Life, 17th New York. 1962. 45.00 o.p. (ISBN 0-527-00664-5). Kraus Repr.
Ethics & Existentialism of Kierkegaard: Outlines for a Philosophy of Life. James J. Valone. 310p. (Orig.). 1983. lib. bdg. 30.00 o.p. (ISBN 0-8191-3443-0); pap. text ed. 15.25 o.p. (ISBN 0-8191-3444-9). U Pr of Amer.

Ethics & Infinity. Emmanuel Levinas. Tr. by Richard Cohen from Fr. LC 85-1542. 140p. 1985. pap. text ed. 9.50x o.p. (ISBN 0-8207-0178-5). Duquesne.

Ethics, Emotion & the Unity of Self. Oliver Letwin. 144p. 1987. lib. bdg. 42.50x o.p. (ISBN 0-7099-4110-2, Pub. by Croom Helm UK). Routledge Chapman & Hall.

Ethics for Science Policy: Proceedings. Ed. by T. Segerstedt. LC 79-40299. (Illus.). 1979. 51.00 o.p. (ISBN 0-08-024464-5); pap. 21.00 o.p. (ISBN 0-08-024463-7). Pergamon.

Ethics from a Theocentric Perspective: Theology & Ethics, Vol. 1. James M. Gustafson. LC 81-11603. 284p. 1981. 27.50x o.s.i. (ISBN 0-226-31110-4). U of Chicago Pr.

Ethics in a World of Power: The Political Ideas of Friedrich Meinecke. Richard W. Sterling. 1958. 38.00x o.p. (ISBN 0-691-07507-7). Princeton U Pr.

Ethics in Government. Peter A. French. 176p. 1983. pap. text ed. (ISBN 0-13-290908-1). P-H.

Ethics in Medicine: Historical Perspectives & Contemporary Concerns. Ed. by Stanley J. Reiser et al. 1977. text ed. 70.00x o.p. (ISBN 0-262-18081-2); pap. 29.95x o.p. (ISBN 0-262-68029-7). MIT Pr.

Ethics in Nigerian Culture. Elechi Amadi. 128p. (Orig.). 1982. pap. text ed. 12.50x o.p. (ISBN 0-435-89030-1). Heinemann Ed.

Ethics in the Education of Business Managers. Charles W. Powers & David Vogel. LC 80-10147. (Teaching of Ethics Ser.). 81p. 1980. pap. 5.00 o.p. (ISBN 0-916558-10-X). Hastings Ctr.

Ethics in the New Testament: Change & Development. Jack T. Sanders. LC 74-26342. 160p. 1975. 4.50 o.p. (ISBN 0-8006-0404-0, 1-404, Fortress). Augsburg Fortress.

Ethics of Ambiguity. Simone De Beauvoir. 1949. (ISBN 0-8022-0369-8). Philos Lib.

Ethics of Corporate Conduct. Ed. by Clarence C. Walton. LC 77-24172. (American Assembly Guides). (Illus.). 1977. 10.95 o.p. (ISBN 0-13-290544-2); pap. 4.95 o.p. (ISBN 0-13-290536-1). Am Assembly.

Ethics of Decision: An Introduction to Christian Ethics. George W. Forell. LC 55-7767. 176p. 1955. pap. 4.50 o.p. (ISBN 0-8006-1770-3, 1-1770, Fortress). Augsburg Fortress.

Ethics of Decision Making. Malcolm W. Eckel. LC 68-16116. (gr. 11 up). pap. 3.50 o.p. (ISBN 0-8192-1029-3). Morehouse Pub.

Ethics of Economics. Ed. by Ivan Hill. LC 76-5728. 352p. 1980. pap. 17.95 o.p. (ISBN 0-275-91493-3, B1493). Praeger.

Ethics of Enjoyment: The Christian's Pursuit of Happiness. Kenneth Cauthen. LC 75-13466. 128p. 1975. pap. 1.99 o.p. (ISBN 0-8042-0815-8, John Knox). Westminster John Knox.

Ethics of G. E. Moore & David Hume: The Treatise as a Response to Moore's Refutation of Ethical Naturalism. Richard J. Soghoian. LC 79-88306. 1979. pap. text ed. 10.00 o.p. (ISBN 0-8191-0774-3). U Pr of Amer.

Ethics of Health Care. Institute of Medicine Staff. Ed. by Laurence Tancredi. LC 74-28130. xi, 313p. 1974. pap. 9.75 o.p. (ISBN 0-309-02249-5). Natl Acad Pr.

Ethics of International Economics: An Innovative Approach to World Affairs. Sidney H. Scheuer. 192p. 1980. 8.50 o.p. (ISBN 0-682-49653-7). Exposition-Phoenix.

Ethics of the Talmud. 2nd ed. Aryeh Kaplan. 336p. 1981. pap. 2.95 o.p. (ISBN 0-940118-31-9). Maznaim.

Ethics, Politics, & Education. Isaac B. Berkson. LC 68-64524. 1968. 7.50 o.p. (ISBN 0-87114-020-9). U of Oreg Bks.

Ethics, Professionalism, & Maintaining Competence. Compiled by American Society of Civil Engineers Staff. 357p. 1977. pap. 19.00x o.p. (ISBN 0-87262-076-X). Am Soc Civil Eng.

Ethiopia: A Country Study. 3rd ed. Ed. by Irving Kaplan & Harold D. Nelson. LC 81-7928. (Area Handbook Ser.: No. 550-28). 396p. 1980. 12.00 o.p. (ISBN 0-318-21948-4, 008-020-00870-2). USGPO.

Ethiopia: Politics, Economics & Society. Peter Schwab. Ed. by Bogdan Szajkowski. LC 84-62184. (Marxist Regimes Ser.). (Illus.). 134p. 1985. lib. bdg. 25.00x o.p. (ISBN 0-931477-00-X); pap. text ed. 10.95x o.p. (ISBN 0-931477-01-8). Lynne Rienner.

Ethiopia: Population, Resources, Economy. G. Galperin. 286p. 1981. 7.00 o.p. (ISBN 0-8285-2106-9, Pub. by Progress Pubs USSR). Imported Pubns.

Ethiopia, the Study of a Polity, 1540-1935. David Mathew. LC 73-19309. (Illus.). 254p. 1974. Repr. of 1947 ed. lib. bdg. 22.50x o.p. (ISBN 0-8371-7324-8, MAET). Greenwood.

Ethiopian Romance. Heliodorus Of Emesa. Tr. by Moses Hadas. LC 76-28171. 1976. Repr. of 1957 ed. lib. bdg. 24.75x o.p. (ISBN 0-8371-9085-1, HEER). Greenwood.

Ethnic Costume from Guizhou: Clothing Designs & Decorations from Minority Ethnic Groups in Southwest China. Huang Shoubao. Tr. by Liu Bingwen from Chinese. (Illus.). 102p. (Orig.). 1987. pap. 19.95 o.p. (ISBN 0-8351-1738-3). China Bks.

Ethnic Factor in the Urban Polity. Richard A. Gabriel. LC 73-10260. 1973. 29.50x o.p. (ISBN 0-8422-5125-1); pap. text ed. 9.50x o.p. (ISBN 0-8422-0344-3). Irvington.

Ethnic Families in America. 2nd ed. Ed. by C. Mindel & R. W. Habenstein. 432p. 1981. pap. 23.00 o.p. (ISBN 0-444-99090-9). Elsevier.

Ethnic Groups, Vol. 3 (incl. 1985-1987 Supplements) Ed. by Eleanor C. Goldstein. (Social Issues Ser.). 1986. 15.00 o.p. (ISBN 0-89777-080-3). Soc Issues.

Ethnic Identity in Society. Arnold Dashefsky. 1976. pap. 16.50 o.p. (ISBN 0-395-30587-X). HM.

Ethnic Identity: The Case of the French Americans. James H. Parker. LC 82-23718. (Illus.). 80p. (Orig.). 1983. lib. bdg. 22.00 o.p. (ISBN 0-8191-2981-X); pap. text ed. 8.25 o.p. (ISBN 0-8191-2982-8). U Pr of Amer.

Ethnic Myth: Race, Ethnicity & Class in America. Stephen Steinberg. LC 80-69377. 1981. 14.95 o.s.i. (ISBN 0-689-11151-7, Atheneum). Macmillan.

Ethnic Myth: Race, Ethnicity, & Class in America. Stephen Steinberg. LC 81-70491. 282p. 1982. pap. 10.95x o.p. (ISBN 0-8070-4149-1, BP 635). Beacon Pr.

Ethnic Pluralism & Public Policy: Achieving Equality in the United States & Britain. Ed. by Nathan Glazer et al. LC 83-16283. 320p. 1984. 30.00x o.p. (ISBN 0-669-07345-8). Lexington Bks.

Ethnic Problems of Tropical Africa: Can They Be Solved? R. Magilova. 302p. 1978. 5.45 o.p. (ISBN 0-8285-3336-9, Pub. by Progress Pubs USSR). Imported Pubns.

Ethnic Separatism & World Politics. Ed. by Frederick L. Shiels. (Illus.). 322p. (Orig.). 1984. lib. bdg. 30.50 o.p. (ISBN 0-8191-3729-4); pap. text ed. 14.25 o.p. (ISBN 0-8191-3730-8). U Pr of Amer.

Ethnic Vegetarian Kitchen. Shanta N. Sacharoff. LC 84-5279. (Illus.). 192p. pap. 7.95 o.p. (ISBN 0-89286-238-6, One Hund One Prods). Ortho.

Ethnicity & Medical Care. Alan Harwood. LC 80-19339. (Commonwealth Fund Ser.). (Illus.). 544p. 1981. text ed. 34.50x o.s.i. (ISBN 0-674-26865-2). Harvard U Pr.

Ethnicity & the Media: An Analysis of Media Reporting in the United Kingdom, Ireland & Canada. (Illus.). 376p. 1978. pap. 25.50 o.p. (ISBN 92-3-101454-4, U808, UNESCO). UNIPUB.

Ethnicity, Birthplace, & Achievement: The Changing Hawaiian Mosaic. Paul Wright & Robert W. Gardner. LC 83-1619. (Papers of the East-West Population Institute: No. 82). v, 41p. (Orig.). 1983. pap. text ed. 1.50 o.p. (ISBN 0-86638-009-4). EW Ctr HI.

Ethnicity in an International Context. Ed. by Abdul A. Said & Luiz R. Simmons. LC 74-20193. 200p. 1975. 12.95x o.s.i. (ISBN 0-87855-110-7). Transaction Pubs.

Ethnography & Acculturation of the Chichimeca-Jonaz of Northeast Mexico. Harold E. Driver & Wilhelmine Driver. LC 63-62521. (General Publications Ser: Vol. 26). 1963. pap. text ed. 9.95x o.p. (ISBN 0-87750-116-5). Res Ctr Lang Semiotic.

Ethnolinguistics So Far. D. L. Olmstead. 1950. pap. 5.00 o.p. (ISBN 0-384-43285-9). Johnson Repr.

Ethnological Album of Weapons, Tools, Ornaments & Articles of Dress Etc. of the Natives of the Pacific Island, 2 vols. James Edge-Partington & Charles Heape. 200.00x o.p. (ISBN 0-87556-084-9). Saifer.

Ethnology in Folklore. George L. Gomme. LC 79-75802. 207p. 1969. Repr. of 1892 ed. 30.00x o.p. (ISBN 0-8103-3832-7). Gale.

Ethnomethodology: How People Make Sense. reference ed. Warren Handel. 176p. (Orig.). 1982. pap. text ed. (ISBN 0-13-291708-4). P-H.

Ethology & Nonverbal Communication in Mental Health: An Interdisciplinary Biopsychosocial Exploration. Samuel A. Corson & E. O'Leary Corson. LC 79-41689. (International Ser. in Biopsychosocial Sciences). (Illus.). 290p. 1980. 77.00 o.p. (ISBN 0-08-023728-2). Pergamon.

Ethos & Identity. A. L. Epstein. 1978. pap. 9.95 o.p. (ISBN 0-422-76370-5, NO. 3706, Pub. by Tavistock England). Routledge Chapman & Hall.

Ethos of the Bible. Birger Gerhardsson. Tr. by Stephen Westerholm from Swedish. LC 81-43077. 160p. 1981. pap. 8.95 o.p. (ISBN 0-8006-1612-X, 1-1612, Fortress). Augsburg Fortress.

Ethrane: Proceedings. Symposium on Modern Anesthetic Agents, 1st, Hamburg, Nov. 9-10, 1973. (Anaesthesiology & Resusatation Ser.: Vol. 84). (Illus.). 400p. 1974. pap. 37.80 o.p. (ISBN 0-387-06877-5). Springer-Verlag.

Ethylenethiourea. Ed. by P. C. Kearney. 14p. 1977. pap. 35.00 o.p. (ISBN 0-08-022026-6). Pergamon.

Etomidate: An Intravenous Hypnotic Agent. First Report on Clinical & Experimental Experience. Ed. by A. Doenicke. (Anesthesiology & Resuscitation Ser.: Vol. 106). (Illus.). 1977. pap. 25.50 o.p. (ISBN 0-387-08485-1). Springer-Verlag.

Etoposide (VP-Sixteen) Current Status & New Developments (Symposium) Brian F. Issell et al. 1984. 41.50 o.p. (ISBN 0-12-375350-3). Acad Pr.

Etranger au Bord de La Riviere. Paul Twitchell. 1979. pap. 5.95 o.p. (ISBN 0-914766-42-2). Illum Way Pub.

Etruscans. Alain Hus. LC 75-11425. (Illus.). 192p. 1975. Repr. of 1961 ed. lib. bdg. 22.50x o.p. (ISBN 0-8371-8189-5, HUTE). Greenwood.

Ettore Sottsass, Jr. Architect. Florita Z. Louis de Malave. (Architecture Ser.: A 1444). 13p. 1985. 2.00 o.p. (ISBN 0-89028-514-4). Vance Biblios.

Etude Simplifiee de Classiques. Gisele Shumake. (gr. 8-10). 1983. pap. 3.75x o.p. (ISBN 0-88334-167-0). Ind Sch Pr.

Etudes Africaines-African Studies: Catalogues et Inventaires. (Maison Des Sciences De L'homme, Service D'echange D'information Scientifiques, Publications Series: No. 3). 1970. pap. 14.00x o.p. (ISBN 90-2796-305-3). Mouton.

Etudes & Caprices for Violin. J. Dont. (Carl Fischer Music Library: No. 306). (Illus.). 1903. pap. 6.50 o.p. (ISBN 0-8258-0040-4). Fischer Inc NY.

Etudes de Femmes. Honore De Balzac. 142p. 1971. 9.95 o.p. (ISBN 0-686-53867-6). French & Eur.

Etudes Generales see Sociologie Du Developpement Latino-Americain: Tendances Actuelles De la Recherche et Bibliographie.

Etudes Sectorielles see Sociologie Du Developpement Latino-Americain: Tendances Actuelles De la Recherche et Bibliographie.

Eucalypts for Wood Production. Ed. by W. Edward Hillis & Alan G. Brown. 1984. 65.50 o.p. (ISBN 0-12-348760-9). Acad Pr.

Eucharist. Chiara Lubich. LC 77-82230. 93p. 1977. pap. 2.95 o.p. (ISBN 0-911782-30-3). New City.

Eucharist: God's Gift of Love. Sr. Marlene Brokamp & Sr. Marilyn Brokamp. (Illus.). 28p. (Orig.). 1976. pap. 1.95 o.p. (ISBN 0-912228-25-3). St Anthony Mess Pr.

Eucharistic Vessels of the Middle Ages see Exhibition Catalogues from the Fogg Art Museum.

Eucharistic Words of Jesus. Joachim Jeremias. Tr. by Norman Perrin from Ger. LC 77-78633. 280p. 1977. pap. 12.95 o.p. (ISBN 0-8006-1319-8, 1-1319, Fortress). Augsburg Fortress.

Eugene Debs: American Socialist. Ann T. White. LC 74-9350. (Illus.). 144p. (gr. 7 up). 1974. 6.95 o.p. (ISBN 0-88208-045-8). Chicago Review.

Eugene Labiche & Georges Feydeau. Leonard C. Pronko. LC 81-84703. (Modern Dramatists Ser.). 192p. (Orig.). 1982. pap. 9.95 o.s.i. (ISBN 0-394-17965-X, E795, Ever). Grove.

Eugene O'Neill. Normand Berlin. LC 82-47992. (Illus.). 184p. (Orig.). 1982. pap. 9.95 o.p. (ISBN 0-394-62418-1, E819, Ever). Grove.

Eugene O'Neill & the American Critic: A Bibliographical Checklist. 2nd ed. Jordan Y. Miller. LC 72-122403. xi, 553p. 1973. 42.50 o.p. (ISBN 0-208-00939-6, Archon). Shoe String.

Eugene the Brave. Ellen Conford. (Illus.). 32p. (gr. 1-3). 1978. 11.45 o.p. (ISBN 0-316-15292-7). Little.

Eugenics: Then & Now. Ed. by Carl J. Bajema. LC 75-43761. (Benchmark Papers in Genetics Ser: Vol. 5). 400p. 1976. 71.00 o.p. (ISBN 0-12-786110-6). Acad Pr.

Eugenie Grandet. Honore De Balzac. Tr. by Ellen Marriage. 1973. Repr. of 1907 ed. 9.95x o.p. (ISBN 0-460-00169-8, Evman). Biblio Dist.

Eukaryotic Genetics Systems: Proceedings of the ICN-UCLA Symposia on Molecular & Cellular Biology. ICN-UCLA Symposia Staff. Ed. by Gary Wilcox et al. 1977. 52.50 o.p. (ISBN 0-12-751550-X). Acad Pr.

Eunuch of Time & Other Stories. Sunita Jain. (Vikas Library of Modern Indian Writing: No. 24). 100p. 1982. text ed. 15.00x o.p. (ISBN 0-7069-1881-9, Pub. by Vikas India). Advent NY.

Euphausiacea Bibliography: A World Literature Survey. M. A. McWhinnie et al. 1981. 190.00 o.p. (ISBN 0-08-024649-4). Pergamon.

Eur New World Book, No. 10. (Our Nations Heritage Ser.). Date not set. (ISBN 0-07-375414-5). McGraw.

Eurail Guide: How to Travel Europe & All the World by Train, 1983. Rev., 1983 ed. Kathryn M. Saltzman & Marvin L. Saltzman. Ed. by Barbara F. Saltzman. LC 72-83072. 816p. pap. 10.95 o.p. (ISBN 0-912442-13-1). Eurail Guide.

Eurail Guide: How to Travel Europe & All the World by Train, 1984. 14th, rev. ed. Kathryn S. Turpin & Marvin L. Saltzman. Ed. by Barbara F. Saltzman. LC 72-83072. (Illus.). 816p. 1984. pap. 10.95 o.p. (ISBN 0-912442-14-X). Eurail Guide.

Eurail Guide: How to Travel Europe & All the World by Train 1985. 15th ed. Kathryn S. Turpin & Marvin L. Saltzman. Ed. by Barbara F. Saltzman. LC 72-83072. 816p. 1985. pap. 10.95 o.p. (ISBN 0-912442-15-8). Eurail Guide.

Eurail Guide: How to Travel Europe & All the World by Train 1987. 17th rev. ed. Kathryn S. Turpin & Marvin L. Saltzman. LC 72-83072. (Illus.). 816p. 1987. pap. 12.95 o.p. (ISBN 0-912442-17-4). Eurail Guide.

Eurail Guide: How to Travel Europe & All the World by Train, 1988. 18th ed. Kathryn S. Turpin & Marvin L. Saltzman. (Illus.). 816p. 1988. pap. 12.95 o.p. (ISBN 0-912442-18-2). Eurail Guide.

Eureka! Math Fun from Many Angles. David B. Lewis. LC 82-18997. 170p. (Orig.). 1983. pap. 6.95 o.p. (ISBN 0-399-50710-8, Perigee). Putnam Pub Group.

Eurekas. Albert Goldbarth. LC 80-28023. 24p. 1981. pap. 3.95 o.p. (ISBN 0-918518-21-0). Ion Books.

Euro-Arab Dialogue: The Relations Between the Two Cultures. Ed. by Derek Hopwood. LC 85-6688. 336p. 1985. 34.50 o.p. (ISBN 0-7099-1946-8, Pub. by Croom Helm Ltd). Routledge Chapman & Hall.

Euro Tunnel Nineteen Eighty-Three. 184p. 1983. pap. text ed. 72.95x o.p. (ISBN 0-317-19286-8, Pub. by Access Conferences England). Gower Pub Co.

Eurochem 'Eighty-Three-Chemical Engineering Today: The Challenge of Change. Ed. by Institution of Chemical Engineers Staff. LC 83-8121. (Institution of Chemical Engineers Symposium Ser.: No. 79). 616p. 1983. 95.00 o.s.i. (ISBN 0-08-030261-0, 1903, 1902, 1302, 1502). Pergamon.

Eurocommunism & the State. Santiago Carrillo. Tr. by Nan Green & A. M. Elliott. LC 78-51455. 180p. 1978. 8.95 o.s.i. (ISBN 0-88208-093-8); pap. 4.95 o.s.i. (ISBN 0-88208-094-6). Chicago Review.

Europa. Romain Gary. (Coll. Soleil). 18.50 o.p. (ISBN 0-685-85705-0). Schoenhof.

Europa Biographical Dictionary of British Women. Ed. by Anne Crawford. 424p. 1984. 55.00x o.s.i. (ISBN 0-8103-1789-3, Pub. by Europa England). Gale.

Europa y los Comunistas. Ed. by V. Zagladin. 319p. (Span.). 1977. 4.45 o.p. (ISBN 0-8285-1423-2, Pub. by Progress Pubs USSR). Imported Pubns.

Europa Year Book 1987, 2 vols. 28th ed. LC 59-2942. 3000p. 1988. 265.00x o.p. (ISBN 0-946653-32-1, Pub. by Europa England). Gale.

Europa Year Book 1988, 2 vols. 29th ed. 3000p. 1988. Set. 350.00x o.s.i. (Europa England). Gale.

Europa Yearbook 1985: A World Survey, Vols. 1 & 2. 1985. Set. pap. 210.00 o.p. (ISBN 0-905118-79-0, EUR49, Europa). Vol. 1, 1368p. Vol. 2, 2952p. UNIPUB.

Europa Yearbook, 1986, 2 vols. 235.00 o.p. (ISBN 0-946653-14-3). Intl Pubns Serv.

Europe. Bruce Jacobsen. 1984. pap. 5.95 o.p. (ISBN 0-914457-00-4). Mustang Pub.

Europe. Jules Romains. 86p. 1916. 3.95 o.p. (ISBN 0-686-55305-5). Schoenhof.

Europe ABC Europ Production: 1987. 4099p. 1987. 136.00 o.p. (ISBN 0-318-23573-0). Manufacturers.

Europe after De Gaulle. Hubert M. Gladwyn. Ed. by Brian Crozier. LC 70-86972. (World Realities Ser). (Orig.). 1969. 4.95 o.s.i. (ISBN 0-8008-2520-9). Taplinger.

Europe after Eighteen Fifteen. 5th ed. Rene Albrecht-Carrie. (Quality Paperback: No. 43). (Orig.). 1972. pap. 4.95 o.s.i. (ISBN 0-8226-0043-9, Helix Bks). Rowman.

Europe Against Poverty. Jane Dennett & Edward James. 256p. 1982. text ed. 26.75x o.p. (ISBN 0-7199-1074-9, Pub. by Bedford England). Gower Pub Co.

Europe & the American Civil War. Donaldson Jordan & Edwin J. Pratt. LC 74-75998. 1969. Repr. of 1931 ed. lib. bdg. 20.50x o.p. (ISBN 0-374-94370-2, Octagon). Hippocrene Bks.

Europe & the British Health Service. Lord Wade. 94p. 1974. pap. text ed. 2.50x o.p. (ISBN 0-7199-0890-6, Pub. by Bedford England). Gower Pub Co.

Europe & the Decline of Spain. R. A. Stradling. (Early Modern Europe Today Ser.). (Illus.). 224p. 1981. text ed. 14.95x o.p. (ISBN 0-04-940061-4). Unwin Hyman.
Europe & the Evolution of the International Monetary System. Ed. by A. K. Swoboda. 1973. 25.00 o.s.i. (ISBN 9-0286-0173-2). E J Brill USA.
Europe & the Middle Ages: A Short History. Edward M. Peters. (Illus.). 352p. 1983. pap. text ed. (ISBN 0-13-291914-1). P-H.
Europe & the World. new, rev. ed. Ed. by Trevor Cairns. LC 73-22523. (Cambridge Introduction to History Ser.). (Illus.). 104p. (gr. 5 up). 1975. PLB 10.95 o.p. (ISBN 0-8225-0805-2). Lerner Pubns.
Europe at School: A Study in Primary & Secondary Schools in France, West Germany, Italy, Portugal & Spain. Norman Newcombe. 1977. pap. 11.95x o.p. (ISBN 0-416-82890-6, NO. 2348). Routledge Chapman & Hall.
Europe Between Revolutions, 1815-1848. Jacques Droz. LC 80-66909. (History of Europe Ser.; Cornell Paperbacks Ser.). 288p. 1980. pap. 7.95x o.p. (ISBN 0-8014-9206-8). Cornell U Pr.
Europe by Rail. E. Foher. 580p. 1984. pap. 12.95 o.p. (ISBN 3-92327-825-X, Pub. by M Muller West Germany). Bradt Ent.
Europe by Rail. Eberhard Fuhrer. (Michael Mueller Publications). 1985. 12.95 o.p. (ISBN 3-923278-25-X). Riverdale Co.
Europe Confronts the Dollar: The Creation of the SDR, 1963-69. Dorothy M. Sobol. LC 80-8473. (Modern American History Ser.). 446p. 1981. lib. bdg. 61.00 o.p. (ISBN 0-8240-4868-7). Garland Pub.
Europe: Discovery Trips. 3rd ed. Sunset Magazine & Books Editors. LC 80-80855. (Illus.). 144p. 1980. pap. 7.95 o.p. (ISBN 0-376-06173-1, Sunset Bks). Sunset-Lane.
Europe et L'Amerique Comparees, 2 vols. Drouin De Bercy. (Illus.). 884p. 1968. Repr. of 1818 ed. Set. 45.00 o.p. (ISBN 0-8398-0369-9). Parnassus Imprints.
Europe for Business Travelers, 1985. Steve Birnbaum. (Stephen Birnbaum Travel Guides Ser.). 1984. pap. 7.70 o.p. (ISBN 0-395-36530-9). HM.
Europe for Business Travelers: 1987. Steve Birnbaum. (Illus.). 560p. 1986. pap. 8.70 o.s.i. (ISBN 0-395-42580-8). HM.
Europe in a Changing World. Ed. by E. Talmor. 84p. 1985. pap. 23.00 o.p. (ISBN 0-08-033405-9, Pub. by PPL). Pergamon.
Europe in New World. (Our Nations Heritage Ser.). Date not set. (ISBN 0-07-375393-9). McGraw.
Europe in the Caribbean. Harold P. Mitchell. LC 73-75777. (Illus.). xi, 211p. 1973. Repr. of 1963 ed. lib. bdg. 20.00x o.p. (ISBN 0-8154-0479-4). Cooper Sq.
Europe in the Twentieth Century. Robert O. Paxton. (Illus.). 651p. 1975. text ed. 27.00 o.p. (ISBN 0-15-524718-2, HC). HarBraceJ.
Europe in the Twentieth Century. Roland N. Stromberg. 1980. pap. text ed. (ISBN 0-13-291906-0). P-H.
Europe in Twenty-Two Days. Rick Steves. (Illus.). 112p. (Orig.). 1985. pap. 4.95 o.p. (ISBN 0-912528-43-5). John Muir.
Europe in Twenty-Two Days. rev. ed. Rick Steves. (Twenty-Two Days Ser.). (Illus.). 144p. 1987. pap. 6.95 o.p. (ISBN 0-912528-62-1). John Muir.
Europe, Italy & the Rebuilding of the Holy Roman Empire. Gaston De La Lavoissier. (Illus.). 131p. 1984. 97.85x o.p. Inst Econ Pol.
Europe: It's Choice: Soviet Invasion with the Death of the Empires. Auguste V. Robertson. (Illus.). 157p. 1988. 157.85 o.p. (ISBN 0-86722-174-7). Inst Econ Pol.
Europe-Major Cities: Winter Vacation Guide, 1989. (Illus.). cancelled o.s.i. Wrld Travel.
Europe, Nineteen Eight-Two. Steve Birnbaum. (Get 'em & Go Travel Guide Ser.). 1232p. 1981. pap. 12.95 o.p. (ISBN 0-395-31534-4). HM.
Europe, Nineteen Eighty. Steve Birnbaum. (Get 'em & Go Travel Guides). 1979. 17.50 o.p. (ISBN 0-395-27770-1); pap. 11.95 o.p. (ISBN 0-686-65212-6). HM.
Europe, Nineteen Eighty-One. Steve Birnbaum. (Get 'em & Go Travel Guides). 1980. 17.50 o.p. (ISBN 0-395-29754-0); pap. 11.95 o.p. (ISBN 0-395-29755-9). HM.
Europe of the Dictators, 1919-1945. Elizabeth Wiskemann. LC 80-66913. (Paperback Ser.). 287p. 1980. pap. 7.95x o.p. (ISBN 0-8014-9210-6). Cornell U Pr.
Europe on Twenty-Five Dollars a Day, 1985-86. Arthur Frommer. (Dollar-a-Day Guides Ser.). 744p. 1985. pap. 10.95 o.p. (ISBN 0-671-52473-9). Prentice Hall Pr.
Europe since Seventeen Fifteen: A Modern History. Eugen Weber. (Illus.). 790p. 1972. pap. text ed. 12.95x o.p. (ISBN 0-393-09404-9). Norton.
Europe since Waterloo. 3rd ed. Robert Ergang & Donald G. Rohr. 1967. text ed. 21.00 o.p. (ISBN 0-669-05205-1). Heath.
Europe Through the Back Door. Rick Steves. (Illus.). 364p. (Orig.). 1984. pap. 9.95 o.p. (ISBN 0-912528-37-0). John Muir.
Europe Through the Back Door. 7th, rev. ed. Rick Steves. (Back Door Ser.: No. 1). (Illus.). 400p. 1987. pap. 11.95 o.p. (ISBN 0-912528-60-5). John Muir.
Europe Versus America: Foreign Policy in the 1980's. Baard B. Knudsen. (Atlanta Papers Ser.: No. 56). 62p. 1985. pap. 7.00x o.p. (ISBN 0-8476-7366-9). Rowman.
Europe: Where the Fun Is. rev. ed. Rollin Riggs & Bruce Jacobsen. LC 84-62614. 176p. 1985. pap. 7.95 o.p. (ISBN 0-914457-07-1). Mustang Pub.
Europe Without Defense? Forty-Eight Hours That Could Change the Face of the World. Robert Close. LC 79-4693. (Pergamon Policy Studies). (Illus.). 1979. 70.00 o.p. (ISBN 0-08-023108-X). Pergamon.
Europe 101: History, Art & Culture for the Traveler. Rick Steves. (Illus.). 372p. (Orig.). 1985. pap. 9.95 o.p. (ISBN 0-912528-42-7). John Muir.
Europe, 1984. Steve Birnbaum. 1983. pap. 13.45 o.p. (ISBN 0-395-34626-6). HM.
Europe, 1985. Steve Birnbaum. (Stephen Birnbaum Travel Guides Ser.). 1984. pap. 13.45 o.p. (ISBN 0-395-36523-6). HM.
Europe: 1987. Steve Birnbaum. LC 85-45132. (Illus.). 1232p. 1986. pap. 13.45 o.s.i. (ISBN 0-395-42340-6). HM.
European Administrative Elite. John A. Armstrong. 400p. 1973. 50.50x o.p. (ISBN 0-691-07551-4); pap. 21.50x o.p. (ISBN 0-691-10016-0). Princeton U Pr.
European Allies, 1 vol. (Series D: Nos. 1-40). 1940. 83.00 o.p. (ISBN 3-601-00019-9). Kraus Intl.
European & American Art from the Princeton Alumni Collection: Publication of the Art Museum, Princeton University. Ed. by H. B. Landman. LC 74-188505. (Illus.). 188p. 1972. 31.50x o.p. (ISBN 0-691-03882-1). Princeton U Pr.
European Architectural Iron: A Selected Bibliography. Anthony G. White. (Architecture Ser.: A 1408). 8p. 1985. 2.00 o.p. (ISBN 0-89028-438-5). Vance Biblios.
European Architecture in the Twentieth Century, 1924-33. Whittick. (Illus.). 280p. 1955. (ISBN 0-8022-1872-5). Philos Lib.
European Bookdealers: A Directory of Dealers in Secondhand & Antiquarian Books on the Continent of Europe, 1982-1984. 5th ed. 276p. 1982. 21.00 o.p. (ISBN 0-900661-24-0, Pub. by Sheppard Press, Ltd.). Seven Hills Bk Dists.
European Challenge: From Atlantic Alliance to Pan-European Entente for Peace & Jobs. Andre G. Frank. LC 84-6588. 104p. 1984. pap. 5.95 o.p. (ISBN 0-88208-173-X). Chicago Review.
European Common Market: Problems & Prospects. Alva W. Stewart. (Public Administration Ser.: P 1665). 12p. 1985. 2.00 o.p. (ISBN 0-89028-375-3). Vance Biblios.
European Community: A Guide for Business & Government. Brian Morris et al. LC 81-47856. (Illus.). 320p. 1982. 32.50x o.p. (ISBN 0-253-32100-X). Ind U Pr.
European Community & Its Mediterranean Enlargement. Loukas Tsoukalis. 320p. 1981. text ed. 16.95x o.p. (ISBN 0-04-382030-1); pap. text ed. 16.95x o.p. (ISBN 0-04-382031-X). Unwin Hyman.
European Computer Survey Nineteen Sixty-Eight to Nineteen Sixty-Nine, 2 vols. 5th ed. Computer Consultants Ltd. 1968. 145.00 o.p. (ISBN 0-08-013372-X). Pergamon.
European Computer Survey Nineteen Sixty-Nine to Seventy. 6th ed. Computer Consultants Ltd. LC 74-102635. 1969. 145.00 o.p. (ISBN 0-08-016026-3). Pergamon.
European Computer Users Handbook, 1969-70. Computer Consultants Ltd. LC 63-25287. 1971. 65.00 o.p. (ISBN 0-08-016027-1); Pergamon.
European Conference of Ministers of Transport: (ECMT) 28th Annual Report-1981, Vol. 1. OECD Staff. (Activity of the Conference Ser.). 206p. 1982. pap. 18.00x o.p. OECD.
European Conquest & African Resistance, Pts. 1-2 see Tarikh.
European Council: Decision-Making in European Politics. Simon Bulmer & Wolfgang Wessels. 256p. 1986. text ed. 39.50x o.p. (ISBN 0-333-36841-X, Pub. by Macmillan London). Sheridan.
European Desserts. Lise Nikora. (Illus.). 80p. (Orig.). 1984. pap. 4.95 o.p. (ISBN 0-8249-3029-0). Ideals.
European Detours: A Travel Guide to Unusual Sights. Nino Lo Bello. LC 80-19901. (Illus.). 164p. 1981. 8.95 o.p. (ISBN 0-8437-3375-6). Hammond Inc.
European Diplomatic History 1815-1914: Documents & Interpretations. Herman N. Weill. LC 74-171719. 1972. 15.00 o.p. (ISBN 0-682-47375-8, University); pap. 5.00 o.p. (ISBN 0-682-47327-8). Exposition-Phoenix.
European Drama of the Early Middle Ages. Richard Axton. LC 74-24680. 1975. 22.95x o.p. (ISBN 0-8229-3301-2). U of Pittsburgh Pr.
European Economic History. 3rd ed. Shepard B. Clough. Orig. Title: Economic Development of Western Civilization. (Illus.). 640p. 1975. text ed. 48.95 o.p. (ISBN 0-07-011393-9). McGraw.
European Economy in the Nineteen Eighties: Proceedings. Ed. by Hans-Gert Braun et al. 257p. 1983. text ed. 44.95x o.p. (ISBN 0-566-00478-X). Gower Pub Co.
European Experience Since Eighteen Fifteen. Peter N. Stearns. (Illus.). 476p. 1972. pap. text ed. 9.95 o.p. (ISBN 0-15-524765-4, HC). HarBraceJ.
European Family: Patriarchy to Partnership from the Middle Ages to the Present. Michael Mitterauer & Reinhard Sieder. Tr. by Karla Oosterveen & Manfred Horzinger. LC 81-21954. 240p. 1982. lib. bdg. 25.00x o.s.i. (ISBN 0-226-53240-2). U of Chicago Pr.
European Firearms. J. F. Hayward. (Illus.). 58p. 1954. (ISBN 0-8022-0696-4). Philos Lib.
European Hand Firearms. Jackson & Whitelaw. 1978. 25.00 o.p. (ISBN 0-87556-154-3). Saifer.
European Hand Firearms of the 16th, 17th & 18th Century, with a Treatise on Scottish Hand Firearms by C. Whitlaw. H. Jackson. (Illus.). 125p. 1923. 25.00 o.p. (ISBN 0-317-03751-X). Saifer.
European Handbook of Advertising Agencies, 1984. 60.00 o.p. (ISBN 0-8002-3336-0). Intl Pubns Serv.
European History Seventeen Eighty-Nine to Nineteen Fourteen. C. A. Leeds. 448p. 1979. pap. 17.95x o.p. (ISBN 0-7121-0575-1, Pub. by Macdonald & Evans England). Trans-Atl Phila.
European Illustration: The Twelfth Annual. Ed. by Edward Booth-Clibborn. (Illus.). 228p. 1986. 45.00 o.p. (ISBN 0-8109-0877-8). Abrams.
European Illustration, 1983. Ed. by Edward Booth-Clibborn. 1983. 45.00 o.p. (ISBN 0-8109-0868-9). Abrams.
European Illustration: 1983. Ed. by Edward B. Clibborn. 1985. 45.00 o.p. (ISBN 0-8109-0868-9). Abrams.
European Immigration & Ethnicity in the United States & Canada: A Historical Bibliography. Ed. by David L. Brye. LC 82-24306. (Clio Bibliography Ser.: No. 7). 458p. 1983. 68.00 o.p. (ISBN 0-87436-258-X). ABC-Clio.
European Independence & the Approaching Third World Conflagration. Aurelian Banville. (Illus.). 171p. 1980. deluxe ed. 69.95x o.p. (ISBN 0-930008-67-7). Inst Econ Pol.
European Integration & the Common Fisheries Policy. Michael Leigh. (Illus.). 244p. 1984. 35.00 o.p. (ISBN 0-7099-1646-9, Pub. by Croom Helm Ltd). Routledge Chapman & Hall.
European Integration: Select International Bibliography of Theses & Disserations 1957-1977. Ed. by J. P. Siemers. 240p. 1979. 47.50x o.p. (ISBN 90-286-0166-X, Pub. by Sitjthoff Noordhoff). Kluwer Academic.
European Intellectual Revolution & the World of Man. G. B. Hall. (Illus.). 168p. 1986. 147.45 o.p. (ISBN 0-86722-135-6). Inst Econ Pol.
European Interests in ASEAN. Stuart Harris. Ed. by Brian Bridges. (Chatham House Papers on Foreign Policy). 96p. (Orig.). 1984. pap. 10.95x o.p. (ISBN 0-7100-9558-9). Routledge Chapman & Hall.
European Iron Age. Date not set. (ISBN 0-8052-3941-3). Random.
European Labor Relations: Text & Cases. M. Thomas Kennedy. LC 78-14155. 448p. 1980. 39.00x o.p. (ISBN 0-669-02663-8). Lexington Bks.
European Local Area Network Markets. International Resource Development, Inc. Staff. 180p. 1983. 1650.00x o.p. (ISBN 0-88694-583-6). Intl Res Dev.
European Marketing & Data Statistics 1987-88. 23rd ed. 350p. 1987. 180.00x o.p. (ISBN 0-86338-189-8, Pub. by Euromonitor Pubns). Gale.
European Markets. 1983. 150.00x o.p. (ISBN 0-934940-17-7). Gale.
European Monetary System: An Outsider's View. Benjamin J. Cohen. LC 81-4167. (Essays in International Finance Ser.: No. 142). 1981. pap. text ed. 4.50x o.p. (ISBN 0-88165-049-8). Princeton U Int Finan Econ.
European Monetary Unification. Giovanni Magnifico. LC 73-303. 227p. 1973. 45.95x o.p. (ISBN 0-470-56525-X). Halsted Pr.
European Neutrals & the Soviet Union. Swedish Institute of International Affairs. Ed. by Bo Huldt & Atis Lejins. 134p. (Orig.). 1986. pap. text ed. 24.00x o.p. (ISBN 91-7182-624-6). Coronet Bks.
European North Calotte. Ed. by W. Tietze. 96p. 1975. pap. 23.00 o.p. (ISBN 0-08-019668-3). Pergamon.
European Paint Manufacturers: Manufacturers of Paints, Varnishes, Enamels, Lacquers, Printing Inks, Solvents & Paint Removers in 16 Countries, 3rd Ed, 1977-1979. 1978. pap. 45.00 o.s.i. (ISBN 90-6156-514-6). E J Brill USA.
European Paintings in the Metropolitan Museum of Art, by Artists Born in or Before 1865: A Summary Catalogue. Katharine Baetjer. Ed. by Ellen Shultz. LC 80-17747. 878p. 1981. 75.00 o.p. (ISBN 0-87099-250-3). Metro Mus Art.
European Photography, 1983-84. Ed. by Edward Booth-Clibborn. (Illus.). 190p. 1984. 45.00 o.p. (ISBN 0-8109-0870-0). Abrams.
European Photography: 1983-84. Ed. by Edward B. Clibborn. 1985. 45.00 o.p. (ISBN 0-8109-0870-0). Abrams.
European Piano Atlas. H. K. Herzog. 102p. (Orig.). 1984. pap. 24.73 o.p. (ISBN 3-923639-61-9). Bold Strummer Ltd.
European Porcelain of the 18th Century. Peter W. Meister & Hort Reber. (Illus.). 320p. sewn bdg. 50.00 o.p. (ISBN 0-317-55026-8). Apollo.
European Powers & the German Question, 1848-1871. W. E. Mosse. LC 74-76002. 1969. Repr. of 1958 ed. lib. bdg. 34.50x o.p. (ISBN 0-374-95928-5, Octagon). Hippocrene Bks.
European Prehistory. Sarunas Milisauskas. (Studies in Archaeology Ser.). 1979. 29.50 o.p. (ISBN 0-12-497950-5). Acad Pr.
European Progress in Spatial Analysis. Ed. by R. J. Bennett. 305p. 1982. 28.00x o.p. (ISBN 0-85086-091-1, NO. 8005, Pub. by Pion Ltd England). Routledge Chapman & Hall.
European Regional Communities: A New Era on the Old Continent. Melvin G. Shimm. LC 62-20226. (Library of Law & Contemporary Problems Ser.). 253p. (Orig.). 1962. 10.00 o.p. (ISBN 0-379-11502-6); pap. 3.00 o.p. Oceana.
European Renaissance Since 1945. Maurice Crouzet. (History of European Civilization Library). (Illus.). 1970. pap. text ed. 6.95 o.p. (ISBN 0-15-524780-8, HC). HarBraceJ.
European Social Policy, Today & Tomorrow. Michael Shanks. 1977. 35.00 o.p. (ISBN 0-08-021444-4); pap. 10.25 o.p. (ISBN 0-08-021443-6). Pergamon.
European Sources of Scientific & Technical Information. 7th ed. Ed. by A. P. Harvey. 400p. 1986. 190.00x o.p. (ISBN 0-582-90153-7, Pub. by Longman). Gale.
European Theater of Operations see Combat World War II.
European Trade Fairs: A Guide for Exporters. L. R. Thomas. 81p. 1981. pap. 5.00 o.p. (S/N 003-009-00341-5). USGPO.
European Trade Goods from the Utz Site & the Search for Fort Orleans, Vol. 39. Robert T. Bray. (Missouri Archaeologist Ser.). (Illus.). 87p. (Orig.). 1978. pap. 4.00 o.p. (ISBN 0-943414-56-3). MO Arch Soc.
European-United States Trade Relations. Ed. by Robert E. Baldwin & Andre Sapir. 1987. U of Chicago Pr.
European Universities, Nineteen Seventy-Five to Eighty-Five: Proceedings of the 5th General Assembly of the Standing Conference of Rectors & Vice-Chancellors of the European Universities, Bologna, 1974. Ed. by Alain Nicollier. LC 75-4331. 1975. pap. 44.00 o.p. (ISBN 0-08-019710-8); French Ed. pap. 60.00 o.p. (ISBN 0-08-019711-6). Pergamon.
European Witness. Stephen Spender. LC 74-138186. 246p. 1971. Repr. of 1946 ed. lib. bdg. 35.00x o.p. (ISBN 0-8371-5643-2, SPEW). Greenwood.
European Yearbook, Vols. 1-31. Ed. by B. Landheer & A. H. Robertson. prices on application o.p. E J Brill USA.
European Yearbook, Vol. 24. Ed. by A. H. Robertson. 1976. 95.00 o.p. (ISBN 90-247-2043-5). E J Brill USA.
Europeans. Luigi Brazini. 304p. 1983. 15.50 o.p. (ISBN 0-671-24578-3). S&S.
Europeans. Richard Mayne. LC 70-39632. 206p. 1972. 16.95 o.p. (ISBN 0-912050-22-5, Library Pr). Open Court.
Europe's Free Trade Area Experiment. H. Corbet & D. Robertson. 1970. pap. text ed. 11.30 o.p. (ISBN 0-08-016233-9). Pergamon.
Europe's Future Food & Agriculture. Ed. by A. M. McFarquhar. (Asepelt Ser.: Vol. 3). 1971. 47.50 o.p. (ISBN 0-444-10052-0, North-Holland). Elsevier.
Europe's Nuclear Power Experiment: History of the OECD Dragon Project. E. N. Shaw. (Illus.). 300p. 1982. 37.00 o.p. (ISBN 0-08-029324-7). Pergamon.
Europe's Political Puzzle: A Study of the Fouchet Negotiations & the 1963 Veto. Alessandro Silj. (Occasional Papers in International Affairs: No. 17). 186p. 1984. pap. text ed. 11.25 o.p. (ISBN 0-8191-4048-1). U Pr of Amer.

Europe's Wonderful Little Hotels & Inns. 5th ed. Hilary Rubinstein. LC 82-19864. (Illus.). 624p. 1983. pap. 14.95 o.p. (ISBN 0-312-92193-4). Congdon & Weed.
Europe's Wonderful Little Hotels & Inns: 1985. Ed. by Hilary Rubinstein. LC 84-21515. 688p. 1985. pap. 16.95 o.p. (ISBN 0-312-92195-0). Congdon & Weed.
Europium. S. Sinha. LC 67-28186. (Anorganische & Allgemeine Chemie: Vol. 8). (Illus.). 1968. 29.00 o.p. (ISBN 0-387-03723-3). Springer-Verlag.
Europump Terminology -- Glossary of Pump Applications in English, German, French, Italian, & Spanish. (Illus.). 1979. 195.00x o.p. Coronet Bks.
Europump Terminology-Pump Applications. 500p. (Eng., Ger., Ital., Fr. & Span.). 1979. text ed. 107.00 o.p. (ISBN 0-85461-089-8). Gower Pub Co.
Eurythmics: Sweet Dreams-The Definitive Biography. Johnny Waller & Steve Rapport. (Illus.). 128p. 1985. pap. 9.95 o.p. (ISBN 0-88188-383-2, Robus Bks). H Leonard Pub Corp.
Eusebius of Caesarea & the Arian Crisis. Colm Luibheid. 136p. 1981. 22.50x o.p. (ISBN 0-7165-2277-2, BBA 03636, Pub. by Irish Academic Pr Ireland). Biblio Dist.
Euthanasia. Ed. by A. Carmi. LC 84-3099. (Medicolegal Library: Vol. 2). 160p. 1984. pap. 32.10 o.p. (ISBN 0-387-13251-1). Springer Verlag.
Eutrophication & Water Supply: Proceedings of the Specialised Conference of the IWSA held in Vienna, Austria, Oct. 7-9, 1981. Ed. by C Gomella & J. P. Mounier. (Illus.). 284p. 1983. pap. 73.00 o.p. (ISBN 0-08-030419-2). Pergamon.
Eva Peron. Nicholas Fraser & Marysa Navarro. (Illus.). 1981. 17.95 o.p. (ISBN 0-393-01457-6). Norton.
Evacuation Planning in Emergency Management. Ronald W. Perry et al. LC 81-47542. (Batelle Human Affairs Research Centers Ser.). (Illus.). 224p. 1981. 30.00x o.p. (ISBN 0-669-04650-7). Lexington Bks.
Evaluate & Grow. Harold J. Westing. 1984. pap. 5.95 o.p. (ISBN 0-88207-624-8). Victor Bks.
Evaluating & Improving Written Expression: A Practical Guide for Teachers. 2nd ed. Hall. 1987. 29.95 o.p. (ISBN 0-205-10548-3, Pub. by Longwood Div). Allyn.
Evaluating Bridge Structural Adequacy, Bituminous Pavement Maintenance, Roadside Management, Economic Impact of Highway Deicing, Hazardous Materials Transportion. (Transportation Research Report Ser.). 655p. 1977. 4.80 o.p. (ISBN 0-309-02676-8). Transport Res Bd.
Evaluating College Writing Programs. Lester Faigley & Stephen P. Witte. 136p. 1984. 10.95 o.p. (ISBN 0-317-37085-5). NCTE.
Evaluating Employer Satisfaction: Measurement of Satisfaction with Training & Job Performance of Former Vocational Education Students. Stephen J. Franchak & Larry L. Smiley. 79p. 1981. 5.50 o.p. (ISBN 0-318-15463-3, RD210). Natl Ctr Res Voc Ed.
Evaluating Knowledge: Engineering Tools. Paul Harmon & Ric Mayer. (Illus.). 75p. 1988. pap. text ed. 12.00 o.p. (ISBN 0-929280-14-8). Amer Artificial.
Evaluating Mental-Health Programs: The Progress Evaluation Scales. David Ihilevich & Goldine G. Gleser. LC 81-48627. (Illus.). 272p. 1982. 27.50x o.p. (ISBN 0-669-05464-X). Lexington Bks.
Evaluating Options in Statewide Transportation Planning-Programming: Issues, Techniques & Their Relationships. (National Cooperative Highway Research Program Report). 91p. 1977. 5.60 o.p. (ISBN 0-317-36080-9). Transport Res Bd.
Evaluating Primary Care: Some Experiments in Quality Measurement in an Academic Unit of Primary Medical Care. Ewen M. Clark & J. A. Forbes. (Illus.). 235p. 1979. 21.25 o.p. (ISBN 0-85664-856-6, Pub. by Croom Helm Ltd). Routledge Chapman & Hall.
Evaluating Research Plans in the Behavioral Sciences: A Guide. Joel R. Davitz & Lois L. Davitz. LC 77-20296. 1977. pap. 4.95x o.p. (ISBN 0-8077-2544-7). Tchrs Coll.
Evaluating Social Programs: Theory, Practice, & Politics. Ed. by Peter H. Rossi & Walter Williams. LC 75-183473. (Quantitative Studies in Social Relations). 320p. 1972. 19.95 o.p. (ISBN 0-12-785739-7). Acad Pr.
Evaluating Social Studies Programs: Focus on Law-Related Education. G. Dale Greenwald & Douglas P. Superka. 250p. (Orig.). 1982. pap. 9.95 o.p. (ISBN 0-89994-277-6). Soc Sci Ed.
Evaluating Statistical Validity of Research Reports: A Guide for Managers, Planners, & Researchers. Amanda Golbeck. (Forest Service General Technical Report PSW-87). (Illus.). 24p. 1986. pap. 1.50 o.p. (ISBN 0-318-21334-6, S/N 001-001-00623-8). USGPO.
Evaluating Student Satisfaction: Measurement of Training & Job Satisfaction of Former Vocational Education. Eliseo R. Ponce & Stephen J. Franchak. 123p. 1981. 8.25 o.p. (ISBN 0-318-15464-1, RD211). Natl Ctr Res Voc Ed.
Evaluating Tax Shelter Offerings 1984. (Tax Law & Estate Planning, Course Handbook Ser. 1983-1984). 1030p. 1984. 45.00 o.p. (ISBN 0-686-80237-3, J4-3541). PLI.
Evaluating Tax Shelters & Other Tax Oriented Investments in State. LC 86-165897. cancelled o.s.i. Natl Busn Inst.
Evaluating the Costs-Benefits of Data Bases. William E. Perry. LC 82-60700. (Data Base Monograph: No. 11). 125p. (Orig.). 1982. pap. 15.00x o.s.i. (ISBN 0-89435-060-9). QED Info Sci.
Evaluating the Curriculum in the 80's. Malcolm Skilbeck. (Studies in Teaching & Learning). 192p. (Orig.). 1984. pap. text ed. 19.95 o.s.i. (ISBN 0-340-35216-7). Princeton Bk Co.
Evaluating the FBC Option. Richard T. Sheahan. (Illus.). 253p. 1983. pap. 68.00 o.p. (ISBN 0-86587-117-5). Gov Insts.
Evaluating the FBC Option: 1984. Ed. by Richard T. Sheahan. (Illus.). 286p. 3-ring binder 69.00 o.p. (ISBN 0-86587-068-3). Gov Insts.
Evaluating the FBC Option, 1985. Ed. by Richard Sheahan. (Illus.). 279p. 1985. 65.00 o.p. (ISBN 0-86587-040-3). Gov Insts.
Evaluating the Impact of Nutrition & Health Programs. Ed. by Robert E. Klein et al. LC 79-11321. 476p. 1979. 69.50x o.p. (ISBN 0-306-40164-9, Plenum Pr). Plenum Pub.
Evaluating the New Bed. Ed. by Gerald Collier. 120p. 1978. pap. 16.00 o.p. (ISBN 0-900868-64-3, Open Univ Pr). Taylor & Francis.
Evaluating Transnational Programs in Government & Business. Ed. by Kenneth W. McHale et al. 1980. 65.00 o.p. (ISBN 0-08-025101-3). Pergamon.
Evaluating Transportation Proposals. (Transportation Research Report Ser.). 64p. 1979. 3.60 o.p. (ISBN 0-309-02986-4). Transport Res Bd.
Evaluating Victim Services. Ed. by Susan E. Salasin. LC 80-25440. (Sage Research Progress Series in Evaluation: Vol. 7). 168p. 1981. 20.00 o.p. (ISBN 0-8039-1525-X); pap. 9.95 o.p. (ISBN 0-8039-1526-8). Sage.
Evaluating Voc Ed Programs: A Handbook for Corrections Educators. Ida Halasz & Karen Behm. 98p. 1982. 7.95 o.p. (ISBN 0-318-22099-7, RD227). Natl Ctr Res Voc Ed.
Evaluating with Validity. Ernest R. House. LC 80-14695. (Illus.). 295p. 1980. 28.00 o.s.i. (ISBN 0-8039-1438-5); pap. 14.00 o.s.i. (ISBN 0-8039-1439-3). Sage.
Evaluation & Action in the Social Environment. Ed. by Richards H. Price & Peter E. Polister. LC 80-10960. 1980. 24.95 o.p. (ISBN 0-12-564650-X). Acad Pr.
Evaluation & Analysis of Flexible Pavement Component & Properties. (Transportation Research Report Ser.). 51p. 1980. 4.20 o.p. (ISBN 0-309-03068-4). Transport Res Bd.
Evaluation, Diagnosis, & Treatment of Occlusal Problems. Peter E. Dawson. LC 74-12409. (Illus.). 423p. 1974. cloth 73.50 o.p. (ISBN 0-8016-1216-0). Mosby.
Evaluation for Leisure Service Managers. Herberta M. Lundegren & Patricia Farrell. 296p. 1985. text ed. 24.95 o.p. (ISBN 0-03-059428-6). SCP.
Evaluation Handbook: Guidelines & Practices for Follow-Up Studies of Former Vocational Students, Vol. 1. Stephen J. Franchak & Janet E. Spirer. 230p. 1978. 13.00 o.p. (ISBN 0-318-15466-8, RD 171). Natl Ctr Res Voc Ed.
Evaluation in Education, Vol. 3. Ed. by B. H. Choppin & T. N. Postlethwaite. (Reviews in Educational Evaluation Ser.). 250p. 1980. 68.00 o.p. (ISBN 0-08-026066-7). Pergamon.
Evaluation in Education, Vol. 4, No. 3. Ed. by B. H. Choppin. LC 77-81507. (Illus.). 93p. 1981. pap. 25.00 o.p. (ISBN 0-08-027134-0). Pergamon.
Evaluation in Education, Vol. 6. Ed. by B. H. Choppin & T. N. Postlethwaite. (An International Review Ser.). (Illus.). 386p. 1984. 79.00 o.p. (ISBN 0-08-031493-7). Pergamon.
Evaluation in Education, Vol. 7. Ed. by H. J. Walberg. (International Review Ser.). (Illus.). 374p. 1985. 99.00 o.p. (ISBN 0-08-032320-0). Pergamon.
Evaluation in Education, Vol. 8. Ed. by H. J. Walberg & T. N. Postlethwaite. (International Review Ser.). (Illus.). 288p. 1985. 99.00 o.p. (ISBN 0-08-032732-X, Pub by PPL). Pergamon.
Evaluation in Education: An Experiment in Rural Primary Schools in Malaysia, Vol. 4, No. 2. Choppin. (Illus.). 121p. 1980. pap. 22.00 o.p. (ISBN 0-08-027138-3). Pergamon.
Evaluation in Education: Four Complete. Ed. by B. H. Choppin & T. N. Postlethwaite. (Illus.). 370p. 1981. 76.00 o.p. (ISBN 0-08-028404-3). Pergamon.
Evaluation in Education: Vol. 1, International Progress. Ed. by B. Choppin & N. Postlethwaite. 1979. 95.00 o.p. (ISBN 0-08-023352-X). Pergamon.
Evaluation in Physical Education. 2nd ed. Margaret J. Safrit. (Illus.). 1981. text ed. (ISBN 0-13-292250-9). P-H.
Evaluation in Student Affairs. George Kuh. 1980. 9.00 o.p. (ISBN 1-55620-015-3, 72601C). Am Assn Coun Dev.
Evaluation Indoctrination. Paul R. Lees-Haley. (Illus.). 257p. 1983. 395.00 o.p. (ISBN 0-938124-02-1). Rubicon.
Evaluation Interview. rev. 2nd ed. Richard A. Fear. (Illus.). 1978. 27.50 o.p. (ISBN 0-07-020201-X, P&RB). McGraw.
Evaluation of AASHO Interim Guides for Design of Pavement Structures. (National Cooperative Highway Research Project Report). 111p. 1972. 5.60 o.p. (ISBN 0-309-02009-3). Transport Res Bd.
Evaluation of Adolescent Self-Esteem Through the Coopersmith Self-Esteem Inventory & Graphometric Analysis of Handwriting. Patricia Wellingham-Jones. (Illus.). 40p. (Orig.). 1984. pap. 9.00 o.p. (ISBN 0-318-23126-3). Wellingham Jones.
Evaluation of an Environs Exposure Rate Monitoring System for Post-Accident Assessment: AIF-NESP 023. Science Applications, Inc. Staff. (National Environmental Studies Project: NESP Reports). 1981. 50.00 o.p. (ISBN 0-318-02231-1). US Coun Energy Awareness.
Evaluation of an Undergraduate Course Involving Student Placement in Institutional Settings. R. S. Ruskin. 1972. pap. text ed. 4.75x o.p. (ISBN 0-8422-0259-5). Irvington.
Evaluation of Archival Institutions: Services, Principles, & Guide to Self-Study. Task Force on Institutional Evaluation Staff. 48p. 1982. pap. text ed. 5.00 o.p. (ISBN 0-931828-55-4). Soc Am Archivists.
Evaluation of College of the Air Course, "The American Economy," on the Basis of a National Survey of High School Social Studies Teachers. Ann F. Brunswick. (Report Ser: No. 100). 1964. 1.50x o.p. (ISBN 0-932132-01-4). NORC.
Evaluation of Complex Systems. Ed. by Ronald J. Wooldridge. LC 80-84297. (Program Evaluation Ser.: No. 10). 1981. pap. text ed. 12.95x o.p. (ISBN 0-686-78534-7). Jossey-Bass.
Evaluation of Construction Control Procedures: Aggregate Gradation Variations & Effects. (National Cooperative Highway Research Program Reports). 58p. 1969. 2.80 o.p. (ISBN 0-317-36081-7, 1744). Transport Res Bd.
Evaluation of Database Management Systems. Judy King. 416p. 1981. 29.95 o.p. (ISBN 0-442-23994-7). Van Nos Reinhold.
Evaluation of Drug Activities: Pharmacometrics, 2 Vols. Ed. by D. R. Laurence & A. L. Bacharach. 1965. Vol. 1. 75.00 o.p. (ISBN 0-12-438301-7); Vol. 2. 75.00 o.p. (ISBN 0-12-438302-5). Acad Pr.
Evaluation of Employee Benefits: Theory, Practice & Implication for Tort Practice. James Lambrinos. 38p. 1986. 9.00 o.p. (ISBN 0-89154-321-X). Intl Found Employ.
Evaluation of Interstitial Nerve Cells in the Central Nervous System: A Correlative Study Using Acetylcholinesterase & Golgi Techniques. G. D. Das & G. W. Kreutzberg. LC 64-20582. (Advances in Anatomy, Embryology & Cell Biology: Vol. 41, Pt. 1). (Illus.). 1969. pap. 17.70 o.p. (ISBN 0-387-04091-9). Springer-Verlag.
Evaluation of Liver Function: A Multifaceted Approach to Clinical Diagnosis. Ed. by Laurence Demers & Leslie Shaw. LC 78-13314. (Illus.). 222p. 1978. text ed. 22.50 o.p. (ISBN 0-8067-0400-4). Urban & S.
Evaluation of Novel Protein Products. Ed. by A. E. Bender et al. LC 70-99794. 1970. 130.00 o.p. (ISBN 0-08-006635-6). Pergamon.
Evaluation of On-Line Searching in MEDLARS (AIM-TWX) by Biomedical Practitioners. F. Wilfrid Lancaster. (Occasional Papers: No. 101). 19p. 1972. pap. 2.00 o.p. (ISBN 0-317-58879-6). U of Ill Lib Info Sci.
Evaluation of Population Estimation Procedures for Counties: 1980. Gilbert R. Felton. (Current Population Reports Series P-25, Population Estimates & Projections, No. 964). (Illus.). 71p. (Orig.). 1986. pap. 3.50 o.p. (ISBN 0-318-21544-6, S/N 003-001-91481-6). USGPO.
Evaluation of Quality of Care in Psychiatry: Proceedings of a Symposium Held at the Queen St. Mental Health Centre, Toronto, Canada, June 22, 1979. A. G. Awad et al. LC 80-94280. 140p. 1981. 32.00 o.p. (ISBN 0-08-025364-4). Pergamon.
Evaluation of Sites & Services Projects: The Evidence from El Salvador. Michael Bamberger & Edgardo Gonzalez-Polio. (Working Paper: No. 549). 233p. (Eng. & Span.). 1982. pap. 10.00 o.p. (ISBN 0-8213-0116-0). World Bank.
Evaluation of Sites & Sevices Projects: The Experience from Lusaka, Zambia. Michael Bamberger & Bishwapriya Sanyal. (Working Paper: No. 548). 201p. 1982. pap. 10.00 o.p. (ISBN 0-8213-0115-2). World Bank.
Evaluation of Statistical Planning & Acquisitions for Small Businesses. Charles E. Couthen, Jr. 168p. 1987. 14.95 o.s.i. (ISBN 0-89227-056-X). Commonwealth Pr.
Evaluation of the Soviet Population Census, 1970. Ed. by V. V. Pokshishevsky. 100p. 1975. pap. 23.00 o.p. (ISBN 0-08-019672-1). Pergamon.
Evaluation of the Utility & Cost of Computerized Library Catalogues. J. L. Dolby. 1969. 27.50x o.p. (ISBN 0-262-04023-9). MIT Pr.
Evaluation of Thermophysical Property Measurement Methods & Standard Reference Materials. Ed. by CODATA Staff. (CODATA Bulletin). (Illus.). 62p. 1986. pap. 15.00 o.p. (ISBN 0-08-032526-2, Pub. by PPL). Pergamon.
Evaluation of Toxicological Data for the Protection of Public Health: Proceedings of an International Colloquium, Luxemburg, 1976. Ed. by W. J. Hunter & G. P. Smeets. 1977. pap. 89.00 o.p. (ISBN 0-08-021998-5). Pergamon.
Evaluation of Transportation Operational Improvement. (Transportation Research Report). 51p. 1977. 2.80 o.p. (ISBN 0-309-02655-5). Transport Res Bd.
Evaluation of Trawl Performance by Statistical Inference of the Catch. G. A. Motte & Y. Iitaka. (Marine Technical Report: No. 36). 1975. pap. 2.00 o.p. (ISBN 0-938412-08-6). Sea Grant Pubns.
Evaluation of Wing Design. (Illus.). 151p. 25.00 o.p. (ISBN 0-317-32140-4, SP802). AIAA.
Evaluations en Gerontologie, Vol. 1 & 2. Liliane Israel et al. xxviii, 668p. (Ital.). 1984. Set. 249.50 o.p. (ISBN 3-8055-3829-4). S Karger.
Evaluations en Gerontologie: Manuel de references des moyens d'Investigation et de Mesure des Fonctions Mentales, Vol. 1. Liliane Israel et al. (Limited Volume Ser.). xvi, 440p. (Ital.). 1984. bound 165.50 o.p. (ISBN 3-8055-3827-8). S Karger.
Evaluations en Gerontologie: Receuil des Instruments Analyses, Vol. 2. Liliane Israel et al. (Limited Volume Ser.). xii, 228p. (Ital.). 1984. bound 84.00 o.p. (ISBN 3-8055-3828-6). S Karger.
Evaluations of Drug Interactions. Ed. by Arthur F. Shinn et al. 1200p. (Updated 6 times per year). 1985. text ed. 52.95 loose-leaf o.p. (ISBN 0-317-58436-7). Mosby.
Evaluations of Drug Interactions EDI. Shinn. 1985. 54.95 o.p. (ISBN 0-8016-4046-6). Mosby.
Evaluations of Drug Interactions EDI-Student Version. Shinn. 1985. 41.95 o.p. (ISBN 0-8016-4044-X). Mosby.
Evaluations of Social Service Programs: An Annotated & Unannotated Bibliography. Donna L. Bramble & Dwight F. Davis. 1978. 5.50 o.p. (ISBN 0-686-22967-3). Univ OK Gov Res.
Evaluator's Handbook. Lynn L. Morris & Carol T. Fitz-Gibbon. LC 78-58658. (Program Evaluation Kit: Vol. 1). 160p. 1978. pap. 9.95 o.p. (ISBN 0-8039-1071-1). Sage.
Evangelical Challenge. Morris A. Inch. LC 77-12310. 166p. 1978. pap. 4.95 o.s.i. (ISBN 0-664-24177-8, Westminster). Westminster John KNox.
Evangelical Theology. A. A. Hodge. 1976. pap. 7.95 o.p. (ISBN 0-85151-236-4). Banner of Truth.
Evangelical Theology, Eighteen Thirty-Three to Eighteen Fifty-Six: A Response to Tractarianism. Ed. by Peter Toon & Peter Martin. LC 79-16701. (New Foundations Theological Library Ser.). 254p. 5.95 o.s.i. (ISBN 0-8042-3703-4, John Knox). Westminster John Knox.
Evangelical Witness: The Message Medium, Mission, & Method of Evangelism. Ralph W. Quere. LC 75-2839. 160p. 1975. pap. 3.75 o.p. (ISBN 0-8066-1485-4, 10-2100, Augsburg). Augsburg Fortress.
Evangelicals & Culture. Doreen Rosman. 262p. 1984. 29.00 o.p. (ISBN 0-7099-2253-1, Pub. by Croom Helm Ltd). Routledge Chapman & Hall.
Evangelicals & Jews in an Age of Pluralism. Ed. by Marc H. Tanenbaum & Marvin R. Wilson. 272p. 1984. pap. 9.95 o.p. (ISBN 0-8010-8871-2). Baker Bk.
Evangelicals at an Impasse: Biblical Authority in Practice. Robert K. Johnston. pap. 7.95 o.s.i. (ISBN 0-8042-2038-7, John Knox). Westminster John Knox.
Evangelicals on the Canterbury Trail: Why Evangelicals Are Attracted to the Liturgical Church. Robert E. Webber. 160p. 1985. 13.95 o.p. (ISBN 0-8499-0402-1, 04021). Word Bks.
Evangeline. Henry Wadsworth Longfellow. 1971. pap. 0.60 o.p. (ISBN 0-380-01169-7, Bard). Avon.

Evangelism As a Lifestyle. Jim Petersen. LC 80-83874. 144p. 1980. pap. 5.95 o.p. (ISBN 0-89109-475-X). NavPress.

Evangelism for Our Generation. Jim Petersen. 216p. 1985. pap. 5.95 o.p. (ISBN 0-89109-476-8). NavPress.

Evangelism in Perspective. Robert E. Coleman. LC 75-31306. 3.95 o.p. (ISBN 0-87509-080-X); pap. 2.00 o.p. (ISBN 0-87509-081-8). Chr Pubns.

Evangelism: The Ministry of the Church. Ed. by Richard Hughes & Joseph A. Serig. 1981. pap. 12.00 o.p. (ISBN 0-8309-0304-6). Herald Hse.

Evangelization: Mission & Ministry for Catholic Educators. 25p. 1979. 3.60 o.p. Natl Cath Educ.

Evangelizing Adults. Glen C. Smith. 404p. (Orig.). 1985. pap. 12.95 o.p. (ISBN 0-8423-0793-1). Tyndale.

Evangelizing Youth. Glenn C. Smith. 352p. (Orig.). 1985. pap. 12.95 o.p. (ISBN 0-8423-0791-5). Tyndale.

Evan's Histological Appearances of Tumours, 2 vols. 3rd ed. David J. Ashley. (Illus.). 900p. 1978. text ed. 161.50 o.p. (ISBN 0-443-01762-X). Churchill.

Evasive Peace. John Davis. LC 79-142227. 1970. pap. 6.00 o.p. (ISBN 0-911026-01-0). New World Press NY.

Eve of the Wedding. Lionel Black. 160p. 1981. pap. 2.25 o.p. (ISBN 0-380-55996-X, 55996). Avon.

Eve: The History of an Idea. J. A. Phillips. LC 83-48424. (Illus.). 192p. 1984. 12.45 o.p. (ISBN 0-06-066552-1). HarpR.

Eveline II. Intro. by Patrick Henden. LC 81-48545. 208p. (Orig.). 1982. pap. 3.50 o.p. (ISBN 0-394-17972-2, B-473, BC). Grove.

Even Cowgirls Get the Blues. Tom Robbins. 1976. pap. 4.95 o.p. (ISBN 0-395-24510-9). HM.

Even If I'm Bad: Sermons for Children. Orin D. Thompson. (Orig.). 1966. pap. 2.95 o.p. (ISBN 0-8066-0616-9, 10-2108, Augsburg). Augsburg Fortress.

Even-Tempered Angler. Louis D. Rubin, Jr. (Illus.). 96p. 1987. 12.95 o.p. (ISBN 0-8329-0445-7). Lyons & Burford.

Evening at Symphony. Janet Baker-Carr. 1977. 10.95 o.p. (ISBN 0-395-25697-6). HM.

Evening Colonnade. Cyril Connolly. LC 74-11475. 469p. 1975. 15.00 o.p. (ISBN 0-15-129387-2). HarBraceJ.

Evening Edged in Gold. Arno Schmidt. LC 79-3373. (Helen & Kurt Wolff Bk.). 224p. 1980. 74.95 o.p. (ISBN 0-15-129376-7). HarBraceJ.

Evening Meal. Tom Watson & Jenny Watson. LC 82-19909. (What the World Eats Ser.). (Illus.). 64p. (gr. 5 up). 1983. PLB 11.93 o.p. (ISBN 0-516-01858-2). Childrens.

Evening Performance. George Garrett. LC 85-1504. 528p. 1985. 18.95 o.p. (ISBN 0-385-19094-8). Doubleday.

Evening Stars: The Making of the Network News Anchor. Barbara Matusow. LC 83-321. (Illus.). 320p. 1983. 14.45 o.p. (ISBN 0-395-33968-5). HM.

Evenings Faces. Diana Cobbold. LC 81-71688. 1982. 13.95 o.p. (ISBN 0-87795-404-6, Arbor Hse). Morrow.

Evenings with the Orchestra. Hector Berlioz. Ed. & tr. by Jacques Barzun. LC 72-95224. 1973. pap. 5.95 o.s.i. (ISBN 0-226-04375-4, P499, Phoen). U of Chicago Pr.

Evenings with the Orchestra. Hector Berlioz. 376p. Repr. of 1959 ed. lib. bdg. 49.00 o.p. (Pub. by Am Repr Serv). Reprint Servs.

Events Which Have Occured since I Met Senator Richard B. Russell. Mary C. Brugmann. 1987. text ed. write for info. o.p. (ISBN 0-682-40325-3). Exposition-Phoenix.

Ever-Present Past. Edith Hamilton. 1967. 5.00 o.p. (ISBN 0-393-04264-2, Norton Lib); pap. 2.95x o.p. (ISBN 0-393-00425-2). Norton.

Everest: A Mountaineering History. Walt Unsworth. 592p. 1981. 30.00 o.p. (ISBN 0-395-31332-5). HM.

Everest House Complete Book of Gardening. Jack Kramer. LC 79-51198. (Illus.). 384p. 1982. 29.95 o.p. (ISBN 0-89696-041-2, Everest House Book). Dodd.

Everest: The Testing Place. John B. West. 256p. 1985. text ed. 18.95 o.p. (ISBN 0-07-069502-4). McGraw.

Everest: The Unclimbed Ridge. Chris Bonington & Charles Clarke. (Illus.). 1984. 24.45 o.p. (ISBN 0-393-01875-X). Norton.

Everest: The West Ridge. Thomas F. Hornbein. LC 80-16088. (Illus.). 248p. 1980. Repr. of 1965 ed. 17.50 o.s.i. (ISBN 0-916890-90-2). Mountaineers.

Everett Anderson's Friend. Lucille Clifton. LC 75-32251. (Illus.). 32p. (gr. k-3). 1976. reinforced bdg. 6.95 o.p. (ISBN 0-03-015161-9). H Holt & Co.

Everett Anderson's Nine Month Long. Lucille Clifton. LC 78-4202. (Illus.). (gr. 1-4). 1978. 6.95 o.p. (ISBN 0-03-043536-6). H Holt & Co.

Everett Anderson's Year. Lucille Clifton. LC 73-2244. (Illus.). 32p. (ps-3). 1974. reinforced bdg. 6.95 o.p. (ISBN 0-03-012736-X). H Holt & Co.

Everett Anderson's 1-2-3. Lucille Clifton. LC 76-25866. (Illus.). (gr. k-3). 1977. reinforced bdg. 6.95 o.p. (ISBN 0-03-017441-4). H Holt & Co.

Evergreen: A Guide to Basic Writing. Susan E. Fawcett & Alvin Sandberg. LC 79-89001. 1980. pap. 14.95 o.p. (ISBN 0-395-28694-8). HM.

Evergreen: A Guide to Writing. 2nd ed. Susan E. Fawcett & Alvin Sandberg. 400p. 1984. pap. 22.36 o.p. (ISBN 0-395-34107-8). HM.

Evergreen Form Studies: Design Characteristics of Conifers. Ed. by Gary O. Robinette. 336p. 1983. 31.95 o.p. (ISBN 0-442-22337-4). Van Nos Reinhold.

Evergreen Poems. Harry Pines. 80p. 1982. 5.00 o.p. (ISBN 0-682-49872-6). Exposition-Phoenix.

Evergreen Review, No. 98. Ed. by Barney Rosset & Fred Jordan. 158p. 1984. pap. 5.95 o.p. (ISBN 0-394-62001-1, E880, Ever). Grove.

Evergreen Review Reader, Vol. 2, 1962-1967. Ed. by Barney Rosset. (Illus.). 360p. 1981. pap. 12.50 o.p. (ISBN 0-394-17490-9, E741, Ever). Grove.

Evergreen Review Reader: Vol. 1. 1957-1961. Ed. by Barney Rosset. LC 79-52055. (Illus.). 400p. 1979. pap. 8.95 o.p. (ISBN 0-394-17095-4, E733, Ever). Grove.

Everlasting Cat. Mildred Kirk. LC 77-76561. (Illus.). 208p. 1977. 16.95 o.s.i. (ISBN 0-87951-063-3). Overlook Pr.

Every Brilliant Eye. Loren D. Estleman. 264p. 1986. 15.45 o.p. (ISBN 0-395-39428-7). HM.

Every Cliche in the Book. Peggy Rosenthal & George Dardess. Ed. by Maria D. Guarnaschelli. LC 86-23623. (Illus.). 144p. 1987. 14.95 o.p. (ISBN 0-688-06113-3). Morrow.

Every Day Is Father's Day. Bill Lee. 50p. 1984. pap. 4.95 o.p. (ISBN 0-531-09825-7). Watts.

Every Day Is Sunday. Ralph Schoenstein. 158p. 1986. 14.95 o.p. (ISBN 0-316-77428-6). Little.

Every Day with Andrew Murray. rev. ed. Andrew Murray. 208p. 1986. pap. 3.95 o.p. (ISBN 0-89283-302-5, Pub. by Vine Books). Servant.

Every Day with Jesus. George Duncan. 288p. 1984. pap. 6.95 o.p. (ISBN 0-89066-059-X). World Wide Pubs.

Every Day's a Matinee: Memoirs Scribbled on a Dressing Room Door. Max Wilk. (Illus.). 288p. 1975. 8.50 o.p. (ISBN 0-393-07491-9). Norton.

Every Employee a Manager. M. Scott Myers. Ed. by William R. Newton. (Illus.). 1980. text ed. 24.50 o.p. (ISBN 0-07-044269-X). McGraw.

Every Excuse in the Book. Cindy Kuris & Marc Kuris. 128p. 1988. pap. 2.95 o.p. (ISBN 1-55547-243-5). Critics Choice Paper.

Every Four Years: The American Presidency. rev. ed. LC 84-50290. (Illus.). 228p. 1984. 21.95 o.p. (ISBN 0-89599-015-6, Dist. by Norton). Smithsonian Bks.

Every Four Years: The American Presidency. Ed. by Robert C. Post. LC 80-80118. (Illus.). 228p. 1980. 21.95 o.p. (ISBN 0-89599-005-9, Dist. by Norton). Smithsonian Bks.

Every Good Boy Deserves Favor & Professional Foul. Tom Stoppard. LC 77-92786. 1978. 8.95 o.s.i. (ISBN 0-394-50157-8, GP703). Grove.

Every Goy's Guide to Common Jewish Expressions. Arthur Naiman. (Illus.). 185p. 1981. pap. 4.95 o.p. (ISBN 0-395-31560-3). HM.

Every Great Chess Player Was Once a Beginner. Brian Byfield & Alan Orpin. (Illus.). (gr. 2 up). 1974. 24.95 o.s.i. (ISBN 0-8184-0203-2). Carol Pub Group.

Every Man in His Humour see Jacobean Drama: An Anthology.

Every Man's Book of Saints. C. P. Clarke. 346p. 1969. (ISBN 0-8022-2280-3). Philos Lib.

Every Man's Book of Superstitions. Christine Chaudler. 192p. 1971. (ISBN 0-8022-2030-4). Philos Lib.

Every Man's Challenge. Daughters of St. Paul. 1988. 6.50 o.p. (ISBN 0-317-67491-9, ST0050); pap. 5.25 o.p. (ISBN 0-8198-2314-7). Dghtrs St Paul.

Every Night at Five: Susan Stamberg's "All Things Considered" Book. National Public Radio Staff & Susan Stamberg. (Illus.). 1982. pap. 9.95 o.p. (ISBN 0-394-70652-8). Pantheon.

Every Pastor's Worship Planning Book. Gary R. Shiplett. Ed. by Sheila Meyer. 155p. (Orig.). 1983. pap. text ed. 7.95 o.p. (ISBN 0-916260-24-0). Meriwether Pub.

Every Woman Has a Ministry. Regina Lambert. LC 79-84321. (Illus.). 1979. pap. 2.95 o.p. (ISBN 0-89221-062-1). New Leaf.

Every Woman in Her Humor: A Critical Edition. Archie M. Tyson. Ed. by Stephen Orgel. LC 79-54327. 300p. 1980. lib. bdg. 40.00 o.p. (ISBN 0-8240-4479-7). Garland Pub.

Every Woman's Pharmacy: A Guide to Safe Drug Use. William F. Rayburn & Fredrick P. Zuspan. LC 83-919. 1983. pap. text ed. 12.95 o.p. (ISBN 0-8016-4030-X). Mosby.

Everybody Can Know. Edith Schaeffer. 1978. 8.95 o.p. (ISBN 0-8423-0786-9). Tyndale.

Everybody Counts! A Workshop Manual to Increase Awareness of Handicapped People. Michael J. Ward et al. LC 79-63014. 80p. 1979. pap. 14.95 o.p. (ISBN 0-86586-027-0); pap. 12.71 o.p. Coun Exc Child.

Everybody's Business Scoreboard: Corporate America's Winner's, Loosers & Also-Rans. Ed. by Milton Moskowitz & Michael Katz. LC 82-48420. 160p. (Orig.). 1983. pap. 5.72i o.p. (ISBN 0-06-250626-9, CN4053). HarpR.

Everybody's Guide to Emotional Well-Being: Helping Yourself Get Help. J. Ingram Walker. 220p. (Orig.). 1982. 13.95 o.p. (ISBN 0-936602-35-X); pap. 9.95 o.p. (ISBN 0-936602-34-1). Kampmann.

Everybody's Guide to Great Wines under Five Dollars. 2nd ed. James Nelson. 1983. pap. text ed. 6.95 o.p. (ISBN 0-07-046222-4). McGraw.

Everybody's Guide to Small Claims Court, California Edition. 5th ed. Ralph Warner. LC 81-80355. (Illus.). 256p. 1985. pap. 9.95 o.p. (ISBN 0-917316-63-0). Nolo Pr.

Everybody's Guide to Small Claims Court, California Edition. Ralph Warner. 1986. pap. 10.95 o.p. (ISBN 0-87337-007-4). Nolo Pr.

Everybody's Guide to Small Claims Court. Ralph Warner. LC 80-455. (Illus.). 256p. 1980. 11.95 o.s.i. (ISBN 0-201-08303-5); pap. 8.95 o.s.i. (ISBN 0-201-08304-3). Addison-Wesley.

Everyday Art of India. Robert F. Bussabarger & Betty D. Robins. LC 68-20951. (Illus., Orig.). 1968. pap. 7.95 o.p. (ISBN 0-486-21988-7). Dover.

Everyday Chinese-English Dictionary. Beijing Language Institute Staff. 881p. 1989. 8.95 o.s.i. (ISBN 0-87052-291-4). Hippocrene Bks.

Everyday Death: The Case of Bernadette Powell. Ann Janes. 1985. 15.95 o.p. (ISBN 0-03-062976-4). H Holt & Co.

Everyday Details. Cecil C. Handisyde. (Illus.). 110p. 1976. 15.95 o.p. (ISBN 0-85139-213-X, Pub. by Architectural Pr). Nichols Pub.

Everyday Dialogues in English. Robert J. Dixson. (Illus., Orig.). (gr. 11 up). 1971. pap. text ed. 3.25 o.p. (ISBN 0-88345-051-8, 17979); cassettes 100.00 o.p. (ISBN 0-685-19793-X); tapes o.p. 70.00 o.p. (ISBN 0-685-19794-8). Prentice ESL.

Everyday Expressions in Japanese. Hideichi Ono. 1963. pap. 4.95 o.p. (ISBN 0-89346-025-7, Pub. by Hokuseido Pr). Heian Intl.

Everyday God. James Taylor. 116p. (Orig.). 1983. pap. 5.95 o.p. (ISBN 0-8358-0470-4). Upper Room.

Everyday Greek: Greek Words in English, Including Scientific Terms. Horace Addison Hoffman. (Midway Reprint). 1976. pap. text ed. 8.00x o.s.i. (ISBN 0-226-34787-7). U of Chicago Pr.

Everyday Insects. Gertrude E. Allen. (Illus.). (gr. k-3). 1973. reinforced bdg. 5.95 o.p. (ISBN 0-395-17891-6). HM.

Everyday Meteorology. A. Austin Miller & M. Parry. (Illus.). 288p. 1959. (ISBN 0-8022-1116-X). Philos Lib.

Everyday Prayers. Madeleine L'Engle. (Illus.). (ps-3). 1974. 1.35 o.p. (ISBN 0-8192-1154-0). Morehouse Pub.

Everyday Prayers for Everyday People. Bernadette M. Snyder. LC 83-63165. 132p. 1984. pap. 4.95 o.p. (ISBN 0-87973-604-6, 604). Our Sunday Visitor.

Everyday Problems. William Wegman. Ed. by Laurance Wieder. LC 84-71459. (Illus.). 84p. (Orig.). 1984. pap. 12.95 o.p. (ISBN 0-918305-04-7). Brightwaters.

Everyday Television: Nationwide. Charlotte Brunsdon & David Morley. (Television Monograph: No. 10). 94p. 1978. pap. 6.95 o.p. (ISBN 0-85170-080-2, Pub. by British Film Inst England). U of Ill Pr.

Everyday Turtles, Toads, & Their Kin. Gertrude E. Allen. (Illus.). (gr. k-3). 1970. reinforced bdg. 5.95 o.p. (ISBN 0-395-15601-7). HM.

Everyday Wildflowers. Gertrude E. Allen. (Illus.). (gr. k-3). 1965. lib. bdg. 5.95 o.p. (ISBN 0-395-17890-8). HM.

Everydays Chinese: Selected Prose Readings. Zhong Qin. 252p. (Orig.). 1985. pap. 11.95 o.p. (ISBN 0-8351-1396-5). China Bks.

Everyman. Ed. by A. C. Cawley. (Old & Middle English Texts). 47p. 1978. Repr. of 1961 ed. pap. 14.95x o.p. (ISBN 0-06-491012-1, 06391). B&N Imports.

Everyman Project: A World Report on the Resources from Humane Society. Robert Jungk. 1977. 10.95 o.p. (ISBN 0-87140-614-4). Liveright.

Everyman's Data Base Primer Featuring dBASE III Plus. R. A. Byers. 1986. pap. text ed. 19.95 o.p. (ISBN 0-07-912708-8). McGraw.

Everyman's Database Primer Featuring dBASE III. R. A. Byers. 1985. pap. text ed. 19.95 o.p. (ISBN 0-07-912631-6). McGraw.

Everyman's Database Primer: Featuring dBASE III. Robert A. Byers. 300p. 1984. pap. 19.95 o.p. (ISBN 0-912677-31-7). Tate Pub.

Everyman's Dictionary of Music. Eric Blom. 687p. Repr. of 1954 ed. lib. bdg. 79.00 o.p. (Pub. by Am Repr Serv). Reprint Servs.

Everyman's Dictionary of Non-Classical Mythology. rev. ed. Egerton Sykes. (Everyman's Reference Library). (Illus.). 298p. 1977. Repr. of 1968 ed. 13.50x o.p. (ISBN 0-460-03010-8, Pub. by J. M. Dent England). Biblio Dist.

Everyone Needs a Mountain: Or Skylife at Eidolon. Marguerite W. Zapoleon. LC 85-90021. (Illus.). 130p. 1985. 10.00 o.p. (ISBN 0-9614542-0-2). McClain.

Everyone's Guide to Preparing a Bill of Lading. William J. Haugh. 1979. pap. text ed. 6.50 o.p. (ISBN 0-87408-018-5). Intl Thom Trans Pr.

Everyone's Trash Problem: Nuclear Wastes. Margaret O. Hyde. LC 78-23859. 1979. text ed. 9.95 o.p. (ISBN 0-07-031551-5). McGraw.

Everyone's 1979 Tax. Lasser. 1978. pap. 2.95 o.p. (ISBN 0-15-629094-4, Harv). HarBraceJ.

Everything about Exchange Values for Foods. Pamela A. Cinnamon & Marilyn A. Swanson. LC 81-53064. 60p. 1981. 3.50 o.p. (ISBN 0-89301-083-9). U of Idaho Pr.

Everything & More. Jacqueline Briskin. (General Ser.). 1984. lib. bdg. 16.95 o.p. (ISBN 0-8161-3747-1, Large Print Bks). G K Hall.

Everything Book on Condominiums. Donnie Rudd. 64p. 1982. 5.00 o.p. (ISBN 0-682-49844-0). Exposition-Phoenix.

Everything but the Kitchen Sink: A Plan Ahead Cookbook. K. Eliason et al. LC 85-81839. (Illus.). 142p. 1986. pap. 7.95 o.p. (ISBN 0-89586-370-7). Price Stern.

Everything Happened to Susan. Barry Malzberg. 1978. pap. 1.50 o.p. (ISBN 0-505-51221-1, Pub. by Tower Bks). Dorchester Pub Co.

Everything in the Garden. Edward A. Albee. LC 68-16862. 1968. 5.95 o.p. (ISBN 0-689-10002-7, Atheneum). Macmillan.

Everything Is Just Great: A Story of Faith, Adventure, & Success. Robert B. Pamplin, Jr. LC 85-8788. 128p. 1985. 8.95 o.p. (ISBN 0-88070-118-8). Multnomah.

Everything Is Negotiable! Gavin Kennedy. 260p. 1983. text ed. 31.75x o.p. (ISBN 0-09-149770-1, Pub. by Busn Bks England). Gower Pub Co.

Everything That Rises Must Converge see Wise Blood.

Everything to Live For. Susan White-Bowden. 1985. 15.45 o.s.i. (ISBN 0-671-55732-7, Poseidon). PB.

Everything to Lose: A Diary 1945 to 1962. Frances Partridge. 19.95 o.p. (ISBN 0-316-69285-9). Little.

Everything You Always Wanted to Know about Elementary Statistics: But Were Afraid to Ask. J. Schutte. (Methods of Social Science Ser.). 1977. pap. text ed. (ISBN 0-13-293506-6). P-H.

Everything You Always Wanted to Know about Exchange Values for Foods. Pamela A. Cinnamon & Marilyn A. Swanson. 1976. 2.75 o.p. (ISBN 0-89301-034-0). U of Idaho Pr.

Everything You Ever Need to Know to Enhance the Sexual Response by Hypnosis but Didn't Know Whom to Ask. D. J. Mozzochi. 1986. 6.95 o.p. (ISBN 0-533-06738-3). Vantage.

Everything You Never Wanted to Know about Yourself or, the Cancer Syndrome. Terrence Gouedy. (Illus.). 64p. 1981. 12.50 o.p. (ISBN 0-682-49640-5). Exposition-Phoenix.

Everything You Want to Know about Cosmetics or What Your Friendly Clerk Didn't Tell You. Toni Stabile. LC 84-1514. 304p. 1984. 16.95 o.p. (ISBN 0-396-08358-7). Dodd.

Everything You Want to Know About TM Including How to Do It. White, John, Warren, Nineteen Thirty-Nine. 1976. pap. 1.95 o.s.i. (ISBN 0-671-80430-8). PB.

Everything You Wanted to Know about American Watches & Didn't Know Who to Ask: 1983 Price Guide. George Townsend. 1974. 8.00 o.p. (ISBN 0-913902-38-1). Heart Am Pr.

Everywoman's Money Book. Betty J. Wylie & Lynne MacFarlane. 208p. 1987. pap. 14.95 o.p. (ISBN 1-55013-021-8, Pub. by Key Porter Canada). U of Toronto Pr.

Eve's Little Friends. I. Sauer. LC 80-15297. 1981. text ed. 8.95 o.p. (ISBN 0-07-054830-7). McGraw.

Eve's New Rib: Twenty Faces of Sex, Marriage, & Family. Robert T. Francoeur. LC 78-182328. 256p. 1972. 6.50 o.p. (ISBN 0-15-129384-8). HarBraceJ.

Evidence & Methods, a Supplement see Time on the Cross: The Economics of Negro Slavery.

Evidence, Cases & Materials: Teachers' Manual. 5th ed. John Kaplan & Jon R. Waltz. (University Casebook Ser.). 279p. 1984. pap. text ed. (ISBN 0-88277-214-7). Foundation Pr.

Evidence, Cases Materials, Problems. 3rd ed. Edward W. Cleary & John W. Strong. LC 81-10426. (American Casebook Ser.). 1143p. 1981. text ed. 34.95 o.p. (ISBN 0-314-59847-2). West Pub.

Evidence, Cases on. 5th ed. Kaplan & Waltz. 1984. Foundation Pr.

Evidence Code-Federal. Gould Editorial Staff. 300p. (Supplemented annually). looseleaf 10.00 o.p. Gould.

Evidence for Gravitational Theories. C. Moller. (Italian Physical Society: Course 20). 1963. 71.50 o.p. (ISBN 0-12-368820-5). Acad Pr.

Evidence for Our Faith. 3rd ed. Joseph H. Cavanaugh. 1959. 12.95 o.p. (ISBN 0-268-00092-1). U. of Notre Dame Pr.

Evidence in Florida. 2nd ed. Florida Bar Staff. LC 77-71502. 226p. 1979. looseleaf, ringbinder 35.00 o.p. (ISBN 0-910373-12-4, 268). FL Bar Legal Ed.

Evidence Law of New York Quizzer 1981. Gould Editorial Staff. 1981. cancelled 7.50x o.p. (ISBN 0-87526-220-1). Gould.

Evidence Never Lies: The Casebook of a Modern Sherlock Holmes. Alfred A. Lewis & Herbert L. MacDonell. 288p. 1984. 16.95 o.s.i. (ISBN 0-03-071856-2). H Holt & Co.

Evidence of Satan in the Modern World. Leon Christiani. 1975. pap. 1.50 o.p. (ISBN 0-380-00413-5, 25122). Avon.

Evidence of Things Not Seen. James Baldwin. 144p. 1985. 11.95 o.p. (ISBN 0-03-005529-6). H Holt & Co.

Evidence Problems. 2nd ed. Kenneth S. Broun & Robert Meisenholder. LC 80-28083. (American Casebook Ser.). 304p. 1981. pap. text ed. 11.95 o.p. (ISBN 0-8299-2125-7); tchr's manual avail. o.p. (ISBN 0-314-60971-7). West Pub.

Evidence, Rules, & Statute Supplement, 1984. Jack B. Weinstein et al. (University Casebook Ser.). 377p. 1983. pap. text ed. 8.75 o.p. (ISBN 0-88277-154-X). Foundation Pr.

Evidence Technician Program Manual. James H. Jones & Joseph L. Peterson. (Orig.). 1976. pap. 2.95x o.p. (ISBN 0-89444-002-0). John Jay Pr.

Evidence That Wasn't There. C. S. Adler. 192p. (gr. 5-9). 1982. 10.00 o.s.i. (ISBN 0-89919-117-7, Clarion). HM.

Evidence Trial Manual for Texas Lawyers. Murl A. Larkin. 650p. 1984. 85.00 o.p. (ISBN 0-409-25012-0). Butterworth TX.

Evil & Danger of Stage Plays. Arthur Bedford. LC 72-170479. (English Stage Ser.: Vol. 43). lib. bdg. 61.00 o.p. (ISBN 0-8240-0626-7). Garland Pub.

Evil & the Christian God. Michael L. Peterson. LC 82-70465. 176p. (Orig.). 1982. pap. 7.95 o.p. (ISBN 0-8010-7070-8). Baker Bk.

Evil Hour. Jill McGown. 224p. 1988. pap. 2.95 o.p. (ISBN 1-55547-253-2). Critics Choice Paper.

Evil in the Morning of the World: Phenomenological Approaches to a Balinese Community. John S. Lansing. LC 74-620023. (Michigan Papers on South & Southeast Asia No. 6). (Illus.). x, 104p. (Orig.). 1974. pap. 6.50 o.p. (ISBN 0-89148-006-4). Ctr S&SE Asian.

Evil Is the Night. Joselyn Chadwick. 1974. pap. 0.95 o.p. (ISBN 0-380-00012-1, 19224). Avon.

Evil of Dark Harbor. Clarissa Ross. 1978. pap. 1.25 o.p. (ISBN 0-380-00478-X, 25486). Avon.

Evil Stalks the Night. Kathryn M. Griffith. 368p. 1984. pap. 3.50 o.p. (ISBN 0-8439-2063-7). Dorchester Pub Co.

Evil Star. Logan Robinson. 1986. 14.45 o.p. (ISBN 0-393-02293-5). Norton.

Evil That Men Do: The Story of the Nazis. Arnold P. Rubin. LC 77-2272. 224p. (YA) (gr. 7 up). 1977. lib. bdg. 10.79 o.s.i. (ISBN 0-671-32852-2). Messner.

Evil Water. Ian Watson. 200p. 1988. 19.95 o.p. (ISBN 0-575-03953-1, Pub. by Gollancz England). David & Charles.

Evinrude Service-Repair Handbook: 40-140 Hp, 1965-1981. Ed. by Eric Jorgensen. (Illus.). pap. 9.00 o.p. (ISBN 0-89287-218-7, B647). Clymer Pub.

Evinrude Service-Repair: 1.5 to 35 Hp, 1965-1983. (Illus.). pap. 9.00 o.p. Clymer Pub.

Evita: The Legend of Eva Peron, 1919-1952. Andrew Lloyd Webber & Tim Rice. 1979. pap. 5.95 o.p. (ISBN 0-380-46433-0, 46433-0). Avon.

Evoked Brain Potentials in Psychiatry. Charles Shagass. LC 76-157928. 286p. 1972. 39.50x o.p. (ISBN 0-306-30533-X, Plenum Pr). Plenum Pub.

Evoked Electrical Activity in the Auditory Nervous System. Ed. by Ralph F. Naunton. 1978. 63.50 o.p. (ISBN 0-12-514960-3). Acad Pr.

Evoked Potentials in Clinical Testing. Ed. by A. M. Halliday. LC 81-68936. (Clinical Neurology & Neurosurgery Monographs Vol. 3). (Illus.). 575p. 1983. text ed. 74.00 o.p. (ISBN 0-443-01791-3). Churchill.

Evolution. Theodore H. Eaton. 1969. 10.95x o.p. (ISBN 0-393-09921-0, NortonC). Norton.

Evolution. 3rd ed. Jay M. Savage. LC 76-26696. 1977. pap. text ed. 17.95 o.p. (ISBN 0-03-089536-7, HoltC). HR&W.

Evolution & Human Nature. Richard B. Morris. 208p. 1984. pap. 3.75 o.p. (ISBN 0-380-69120-5, 69120-5, Discus). Avon.

Evolution & Macroscopic Structure of Valley & Ridge Thrust Belt: Tennessee & Virginia. D. Roeder & O. E. Gilbert. (University of Tennessee Studies in Geology). (Illus.). 25p. 1978. pap. 8.50 o.p. (ISBN 0-910249-00-8). U of Tenn Geo.

Evolution & Modification of Behavior. Konrad Lorenz. LC 65-24436. 1967. pap. 8.00x o.p. (P534). U of Chicago Pr.

Evolution & the Human Population. Joan Solomon. (Science in a Social Context Ser.). 1986. pap. text ed. 6.95x o.p. (ISBN 0-631-91990-2); tchr's guide 9.95 o.p. Basil Blackwell.

Evolution & the Word of God. P. J. Bart-Williams. LC 83-91501. 87p. 1985. 8.95 o.p. (ISBN 0-533-06080-X). Vantage.

Evolution As Entropy: Toward a Unified Theory of Biology. Daniel R. Brooks & E. O. Wiley. LC 85-8544. (Science & its Conceptual Foundations Ser.). (Illus.). 1986. 25.00x o.s.i. (ISBN 0-226-07581-8). U of Chicago Pr.

Evolution as Revelation. Jacob Kohn. LC 62-15032. 192p. 1963. (ISBN 0-8022-0878-9). Philos Lib.

Evolution by Gene Duplication. S. Ohno. LC 78-112882. (Illus.). 1970. 32.00 o.p. (ISBN 0-387-05225-9). Springer-Verlag.

Evolution by Natural Selection. Charles Darwin & Alfred R. Wallace. LC 58-14868. 1971. Repr. of 1958 ed. 32.00 o.p. (ISBN 0-384-10875-X, B132). Johnson Repr.

Evolution by Sexual Select Theory. 1984. 51.95 o.p. (ISBN 0-442-21181-3). Van Nos Reinhold.

Evolution from Space: A Theory of Cosmic Creationism. Fred Hoyle & Chandra Wickramasinghe. 176p. 1984. pap. 5.75 o.p. (ISBN 0-671-49263-2, Touchstone). S&S.

Evolution Goes on Every Day. Dorothy H. Patent. LC 76-50525. (Illus.). 160p. (gr. 5 up). 1977. 10.95 o.p. (ISBN 0-8234-0297-5). Holiday.

Evolution in Textile Design from the Highlands of Guatemala. Margot B. Schevill. LC 86-2858. (Illus.). 84p. 1986. pap. 12.95 o.p. (ISBN 0-295-96448-0, Pub. by Lowie Mus Anthro). U of Wash Pr.

Evolution of a Contested Domestic Relations Case. 188p. 1984. 35.00 o.p. (ISBN 0-318-03924-9, 272). PA Bar Inst.

Evolution of a Valley: The Androscoggin Story. Page H. Jones. LC 74-81953. (Illus.). 192p. 1975. 7.95 o.p. (ISBN 0-914016-16-4). Phoenix Pub.

Evolution of American Electoral Systems. Paul Kleppner & Walter D. Burnham. LC 80-24632. (Contributions in American History Ser.: No. 95). (Illus.). xiii, 279p. 1982. pap. text ed. 9.95 o.p. (ISBN 0-313-23608-9, KEVPB). Greenwood.

Evolution of American Urban Society. 2nd ed. Howard P. Chudacoff. (Illus.). 256p. 1981. pap. text ed. (ISBN 0-13-293605-4). P-H.

Evolution of Anatomy see Short History of Anatomy & Physiology: From the Greeks to Harvey.

Evolution of Belief. Roger Webber. 89p. 1984. 8.95 o.p. (ISBN 0-533-05475-3). Vantage.

Evolution of Bioenergetic Processes. E. Broda. LC 75-6847. 220p. 1979. 61.00 o.p. (ISBN 0-08-024397-5); pap. 24.00 o.p. (ISBN 0-08-022651-5). Pergamon.

Evolution of Corporate Financial Reporting. T. Lee & R. Parker. 1982. 42.50 o.p. (ISBN 0-442-30710-1). Van Nos Reinhold.

Evolution of Cost Accounting. S. Paul Garner. LC 76-41238. (Accounting History Classics Ser.: Vol. 1). (Illus.). 432p. 1976. pap. 11.95 o.p. (ISBN 0-8173-8900-8). U of Ala Pr.

Evolution of Culture. Leslie A. White. 1959. pap. text ed. 4.95 o.p. (ISBN 0-07-069682-9). McGraw.

Evolution of Desert Biota. Ed. by David W. Goodall. (Illus.). 250p. 1976. 20.00x o.p. (ISBN 0-292-72015-7). U of Tex Pr.

Evolution of Economic Thought. 2nd ed. Jacob Oser. 1970. text ed. 15.95 o.p. (ISBN 0-15-525001-9, HC). HarBraceJ.

Evolution of Economic Thought. 3rd ed. Jacob Oser & William C. Blanchfield. 512p. 1975. text ed. 25.00 o.p. (ISBN 0-15-525002-7, HC). HarBraceJ.

Evolution of Electronic Music. David Ernst. LC 76-41624. (Illus.). 1977. pap. text ed. 15.95 o.s.i. (ISBN 0-02-870880-6). Schirmer Bks.

Evolution of Genetics. Arnold W. Ravin. (Illus., Orig.). 1965. 39.00 o.p. (ISBN 0-12-583450-0); pap. 16.00 o.p. (ISBN 0-12-583456-X). Acad Pr.

Evolution of Group Analysis. Ed. by Malcolm Pines. (International Library of Group Psychotherapy & Group Process). 280p. 1983. 35.00x o.p. (ISBN 0-7100-9290-3). Routledge Chapman & Hall.

Evolution of Industrial Systems: The Forking Paths. Timothy W. Leggatt. LC 84-29365. 256p. 1985. 29.95 o.p. (ISBN 0-7099-1603-5, Pub. by Croom Helm Ltd); pap. 14.95 o.p. (ISBN 0-7099-1670-1). Routledge Chapman & Hall.

Evolution of Insect Migration & Diapause. Ed. by H. Dingle. (Proceedings in Life Sciences). 1978. 29.00 o.p. (ISBN 0-387-90294-5). Springer-Verlag.

Evolution of Law. Alan Watson. LC 84-21835. 176p. 1985. text ed. 19.50x o.p. (ISBN 0-8018-2504-0). Johns Hopkins.

Evolution of Library Outreach 1960-75 & Its Effect on Reader Services. Kathleen Weibel. (Occasional Papers: No. 156). 28p. 1982. pap. 3.00 o.p. (ISBN 0-317-59003-0). U of Ill Lib Info Sci.

Evolution of Mammals. L. B. Halstead. (Illus.). 1981. 12.95 o.p. (ISBN 0-8467-0561-3, Pub. by Two Continents). Hippocrene Bks.

Evolution of Man: Two Hundred & Six Million Years on Earth. Mark-Age Staff. LC 71-147256. 160p. 1971. 13.00 o.p. (ISBN 0-912322-02-0). Mark-Age.

Evolution of Medieval Thought. 2nd ed. David Knowles. Ed. by D. E. Luscombe. Tr. by C. N. Brooke. 368p. 1988. pap. text ed. 19.95 o.p. (ISBN 0-582-49426-5). Longman.

Evolution of Modern Italy. Arthur J. Whyte. (Illus.). 1965. pap. 5.95x o.p. (ISBN 0-393-00298-5, Norton Lib). Norton.

Evolution of OPEC. Albert L. Danielsen. LC 81-85395. 305p. 1982. 19.95 o.p. (ISBN 0-15-129394-5). HarBraceJ.

Evolution of Pancreatic Islets. T. Adesanya Grillo et al. 1977. 95.00 o.p. (ISBN 0-08-021257-3). Pergamon.

Evolution of Particle Physics. Ed. by M. Conversi. 1970. 98.00 o.p. (ISBN 0-12-186150-3). Acad Pr.

Evolution of Play Behavior. Ed. by Dietland Muller-Schwarze. LC 77-2385. (Benchmark Papers in Animal Behavior: Vol. 10). 1982. 59.95 o.p. (ISBN 0-87933-272-7). Van Nos Reinhold.

Evolution of Protein Structure & Function: A Symposium in Honor of Prof. Emil L. Smith. Ed. by David S. Sigman & Mary Brazier. LC 80-18140. (UCLA Forum in Medical Science Ser.: Vol. 21). 1980. 32.50 o.p. (ISBN 0-12-643150-7). Acad Pr.

Evolution of Psychosomatic Concepts: Anorexia Nervosa: a Paradigm. Ed. by M. Ralph Kaufman et al. LC 64-16017. 379p. 1964. text ed. 42.50x o.s.i. (ISBN 0-8236-1780-7). Intl Univs Pr.

Evolution of Russia. Otto Hoetzsch. (History of European Civilization Library). (Illus., Orig.). 1966. pap. text ed. 10.95 o.p. (ISBN 0-15-525100-7, HC). HarBraceJ.

Evolution of Sedimentary Rocks. Robert M. Garrels & Fred T. Mackenzie. (Illus.). 1971. text ed. 14.95x o.p. (ISBN 0-393-09959-8, NortonC). Norton.

Evolution of Sex Determining Mechanisms. James Bull. 1983. 24.95 o.p. (ISBN 0-8053-0400-2). Benjamin-Cummings.

Evolution of Society: Selections from Herbert Spencer's "Principles of Sociology" Herbert Spencer. Ed. by Robert L. Carniero. LC 67-20581. (Midway Reprint Ser). 300p. 1974. pap. text ed. 10.50x o.s.i. (ISBN 0-226-76895-3). U of Chicago Pr.

Evolution of Soviet Security Strategy: 1965-1975. Avigdor Haselkorn. LC 77-85316. (Strategy Paper Ser.: No. 31). 139p. 1978. 9.95x o.p. (ISBN 0-8448-1273-0, Pub. by Crane Russak & Co); pap. 4.95x o.p. (ISBN 0-8448-1272-2). Taylor & Francis.

Evolution of the Biosphere. M. M. Kamshilov. Tr. by Minna Brodskaya. 1976. 6.45 o.p. (ISBN 0-8285-5167-7, Pub. by Mir Pubs USSR). Imported Pubns.

Evolution of the Black Nurse Midwife. Barbara M. Butler. 64p. 1983. 5.50 o.p. (ISBN 0-682-49966-8). Exposition-Phoenix.

Evolution of the Brain & Intelligence. Harry J. Jerison. 1973. 60.00 o.p. (ISBN 0-12-385250-1). Acad Pr.

Evolution of the Crystalline Rocks. Ed. by D. K. Bailey & R. MacDonald. 1977. 59.00 o.p. (ISBN 0-12-073450-8). Acad Pr.

Evolution of the Human Mind. Norman L. Munn. LC 75-146722. (Illus., Orig.). 1971. pap. 8.95 o.p. (ISBN 0-395-11149-8, 3-39665). HM.

Evolution of the Plio-Pleistocene African Suidae. J. M. Harris & T. D. White. LC 78-73167. (Transactions Ser.: Vol. 69, Pt. 2). (Illus.). 1979. pap. 15.00 o.p. (ISBN 0-87169-692-4). Am Philos.

Evolution of the United Nations. G. R. Bunting & M. J. Lee. 1964. pap. 35.00 o.p. (ISBN 0-08-010922-5). Pergamon.

Evolution of Theology in the Greek Philosophers, 2 Vols in 1. Edward Caird. LC 4-16272. (Gifford Lectures 1900-1902). 1968. Repr. of 1904 ed. 46.00 o.p. (ISBN 0-527-14130-5). Kraus Repr.

Evolution of Trotsky's Theory of Revolution. Curtis Stokes. LC 81-40930. 206p. (Orig.). 1982. lib. bdg. 30.75 o.p. (ISBN 0-8191-2235-1); pap. text ed. 12.50 o.p. (ISBN 0-8191-2236-X). U Pr of Amer.

Evolution of Wage Structure. Lloyd G. Reynolds et al. LC 56-5945. Repr. of 1956 ed. 21.00 o.p. (ISBN 0-08-022308-7). Pergamon.

Evolution or Extinction: The Choice Before Us-A Systems Approach to the Study of the Future. R. K. Curtis. 420p. 1982. 73.00 o.p. (ISBN 0-08-027933-3); pap. 34.00 o.p. (ISBN 0-08-027932-5). Pergamon.

Evolution: The History of an Idea. Peter J. Bowler. LC 83-5909. (Illus.). 413p. 1984. 40.00x o.p. (ISBN 0-520-04880-6); pap. 12.95 o.p. (ISBN 0-520-04890-3). U of Cal Pr.

Evolutionary Biology, Vol. 11. Ed. by Max K. Hecht et al. LC 67-11961. (Illus.). 682p. 1978. 69.50x o.p. (ISBN 0-306-40091-X, Plenum Pr). Plenum Pub.

Evolutionary Biology of the Primates. William C. Osman. 1973. 40.50 o.p. (ISBN 0-12-528750-X). Acad Pr.

Evolutionary Geology & the New Catastrophism. George M. Price. (Illus.). 352p. 1984. Repr. of 1926 ed. photocopy 16.95x o.p. (ISBN 0-915554-13-5). Sourcebook.

Evolutionary Principles of the Mammalian Middle Ear. G. Fleischer. (Advances in Anatomy, Embriology & Cell Biology: Vol. 55, Pt. 5). (Illus.). 1979. pap. 29.00 o.p. (ISBN 0-387-09140-8). Springer-Verlag.

Evolutionary Relationships, Osteology & Zoogeography of Leptodactyloid Frogs. John D. Lynch. (Miscellaneous Publications Ser.: No. 53). 238p. 1971. pap. 12.25 o.p. (ISBN 0-686-80374-4). U of KS Mus Nat Hist.

Evolutionary Significance of the Exine. Ed. by I. K. Ferguson & J. Muller. (Linnean Society Symposia Ser.: No. 1). 1976. 143.00 o.p. (ISBN 0-12-253650-9). Acad Pr.

Evolutionary Visions of the Future. Ed. by B. H. Banathy. (Illus.). 96p. 1985. pap. 18.25 o.p. (ISBN 0-08-032563-7, Pub. by PPL). Pergamon.

Evolving Earth. 2nd ed. F. J. Sawkins et al. 1978. write for info. o.p. (ISBN 0-02-406510-2, 40651). Macmillan.

Evolving Genes & Proteins: A Symposium. Ed. by Vernon Bryson & Henry J. Vogel. 1965. 92.00 o.p. (ISBN 0-12-138250-8). Acad Pr.

Evolving School Law Issues: Update '87 Trial Notebook. 600p. 1987. 200.00 o.p. (ISBN 0-88364-121-6). Natl Sch Boards.

Evolving Strategies & Tactics in Membrane Research. D. F. Wallach & R. J. Winzler. LC 73-21715. (Illus.). 450p. 1974. 49.00 o.p. (ISBN 0-387-06576-8). Springer-Verlag.

Evolving Universe. Rufus Phillips. 1952. (ISBN 0-8022-1966-7). Philos Lib.

Ex-Magician & Other Stories. Murilo Rubiao. Tr. by Thomas Colchie. 128p. 1984. pap. 2.95 o.p. (ISBN 0-380-69146-9, Bard). Avon.

Exact Categories & Categories of Sheaves. M. Barr et al. (Lecture Notes in Mathematics: Vol. 236). vii, 239p. 1972. pap. 9.00 o.p. (ISBN 0-387-05678-5). Springer-Verlag.

Exact Methods in Linguistic Research. O. S. Akhmanova et al. Tr. by David G. Haynes & Dolores V. Mohr. LC 63-19957. 1963. 44.00x o.p. (ISBN 0-520-00542-2). U of Cal Pr.

Exalt His Name: A Christmas Program. Muriel Browne. 1984. pap. 0.95 o.p. (ISBN 0-8024-3551-3). Moody.

Exaltation One Step at a Time. Ron Zeidner & Janie Zeidner. 107p. (YA) (gr. 11 up). 1981. 5.95 o.p. (ISBN 0-942241-15-0, 8313). Pubs Bk Sales.

Examination Haematology. A. H. Goldstone. (Illus.). 206p. 1978. pap. write for info. o.p. Saunders.

Examination into the Principles of Currency Involved in the Bank Charter Act of 1844. John E. Cairnes. LC 65-2094. 1966. Repr. of 1854 ed. 17.50x o.s.i. (ISBN 0-678-00106-5). Kelley.

Examination of Plato's Doctrines, 2 vols. I. M. Crombie. Incl. Vol. 1. Plato on Man & Society. 1962. text ed. 36.00x o.p. (ISBN 0-7100-3608-6); Vol. 2. Plato on Knowledge & Reality. 1963. text ed. 41.00x. (International Library of Philosophy & Scientific Method). Set. text ed. 40.50x o.p. (ISBN 0-391-01053-0). Humanities.

Examination of Water for Pollution Control: Handbook for Management & Analysts. M. J. Suess. (Illus.). 1500p. 1982. 475.00 o.p. (ISBN 0-08-025255-9). Pergamon.

Examination of Water for Pollution Control, Vol. 1: Sampling, Data Analysis & Laboratory Equipment: A Reference Handbook. Ed. by M. J. Suess. (Illus.). 360p. 1985. 165.00 o.p. (ISBN 0-08-032499-1, Pub. by PPL). Pergamon.

Titles

Examination of Water for Pollution Control, Vol. 2: Physical Chemical & Radiological Examination: A Reference Handbook. Ed. by M. J. Suess. (Illus.). 554p. 1985. 165.00 o.p. (ISBN 0-08-032500-9, Pub. by PPL). Pergamon.

Examination of Water for Pollution Control, Vol. 3: Biological, Bacteriological & Virological Examination: A Reference Handbook. Ed. by M. J. Suess. (Illus.). 530p. 1985. 160.00 o.p. (ISBN 0-08-032501-7, Pub. by PPL). Pergamon.

Examine Your Doctor: A Patient's Guide to Avoiding Medical Mishaps. Siegfried J. Kra. LC 82-5579. 256p. 1982. 12.95 o.p. (ISBN 0-89919-104-5). Ticknor & Fields.

Examining Financial Statements. 244p. 1984. 25.00 o.p. (ISBN 0-88129-126-9). Wash Bar CLE.

Examining Our Faith. YMCA of the U. S. A. Staff. 32p. 1980. pap. 4.95x o.s.i. (ISBN 0-88035-030-X, Pub. by YMCA USA). Human Kinetics.

Example of Melville. Warner Berthoff. 1972. pap. 2.25 o.p. (ISBN 0-393-00595-X, Norton Lib). Norton.

Example of Richard Wright. McCall. 1969. 7.95 o.p. (ISBN 0-15-129449-6). HarBraceJ.

Examples of Music Before Fourteen Hundred. 2nd ed. Harold Gleason & Warren Becker. 1987. pap. text ed. (ISBN 0-89917-035-8). Alfred Pub.

Examples of the CESMM. Martin Barnes. 106p. 1977. 6.50 o.p. Am Soc Civil Eng.

Examples of the Design of Buildings to CP 110 & Allied Codes. rev. ed. Charles E. Reynolds & James C. Steedman. (Viewpoint Publications Ser.). (Illus.). 1978. pap. 45.00x o.p. (ISBN 0-7210-1091-1, Pub. by C & CA London). Scholium Intl.

Excalibur! Kane & Jakes. 1980. pap. 3.50 o.p. (ISBN 0-440-12213-9). Dell.

Excavation & Grading Code Administration, Inspection & Enforcement. C. Michael Scullin. (Illus.). 448p. 1983. text ed. 58.00 o.p. (ISBN 0-13-293894-4). P-H.

Excavation of Fort Renville: An Archaeological Report. David W. Nystuen & Carla G. Lindeman. LC 77-91212. (MN Historic Archaeology Ser.). (Illus.). 58p. 1969. pap. 2.00 o.p. (ISBN 0-87351-050-X). Minn Hist.

Excavations at Kastelli, Chania, Greece, 1976. Hara Georgiou & Y. Tzedakis. (Occasional Paper: 2). (Illus.). 13p. 1978. 3.00x o.p. (ISBN 0-317-06620-X). UCLA Arch.

Excavations in Southeastern Guatemala: 1976-1978. Ed. by Lawrence H. Feldman & Garry R. Walters. (Miscellaneous Publications in Anthropology Ser.: No. 9, Reports 1 & 2). (Illus.). 1980. pap. 5.60x o.p. (ISBN 0-913134-80-5). Mus Anthro Mo.

Excellence in Leadership. Frank Goble. LC 72-79880. (Illus.). 1978. pap. 6.95 o.p. (ISBN 0-916054-84-5). Green Hill.

Excellence in Our Schools. 64p. 1982. 6.00 o.p. (ISBN 0-8106-1421-9). NEA.

Excellence of Exposition: Practical Procedure in Expository Preaching. Douglas M. White. 1977. pap. 4.95 o.p. (ISBN 0-87213-939-5). Loizeaux.

Excellence: Your Guide to Action Now. incl. 3 updates 24.95 o.p. (ISBN 0-87545-029-6, 411-13362). Natl Sch Pr.

Excelling: High School Superstars & How to Become One. Van R. Hutchinson. (Excelling Ser.). 173p. 1985. 10.97 o.p. (ISBN 0-8239-0636-1). Rosen Group.

Excelling in Sports: How to Train. Cordner Nelson. (Excelling Ser.). 118p. (gr. 7-12). 1985. 10.97 o.p. (ISBN 0-8239-0631-0). Rosen Group.

Excelling: Raising Your Grades with High Tech. Robert Shockley & Glen W. Cutlip. (Excelling Ser.). 114p. (gr. 7-12). 1985. 10.97 o.p. (ISBN 0-8239-0646-9). Rosen Group.

Excelling: The Nutritional Way to Good Health. Cecilia Maguire. (Excelling Ser.). 109p. (gr. 7-12). 1985. 10.97 o.p. (ISBN 0-8239-0635-3). Rosen Group.

Except for Me & Thee. Jessamyn West. 1974. pap. 1.25 o.p. (ISBN 0-380-01171-9, 18671). Avon.

Except for Me & Thee. Jessamyn West. LC 69-17171. 1969. 8.50 o.s.i. (ISBN 0-15-129454-2). HarBraceJ.

Exceptional Children & Youth. 2nd ed. Ed. by Edward L. Meyen. 511p. 1982. text ed. 27.95 o.p. (ISBN 0-89108-109-7). Love Pub Co.

Exceptional Children: Biological & Psychological Perspectives. James R. Frazier & Dianne M. Frazier. LC 74-12092. 339p. 1974. text ed. 29.50x o.p. (ISBN 0-8422-5198-7). Irvington.

Exceptional Children: Educational Resources & Perspectives. Samuel A. Kirk & Francis E. Lord. 464p. 1974. pap. 12.95 o.p. (ISBN 0-395-18027-9). HM.

Exceptional Children: Introduction to Special Education. 3rd ed. Daniel P. Hallahan & James M. Kauffman. (Illus.). 512p. 1986. text ed. (ISBN 0-13-294026-4). P-H.

Exceptional Free Library-Resource Materials. Carol Smallwood. LC 83-22166. 241p. 1984. lib. bdg. 18.50 o.p. (ISBN 0-87287-406-0). Libs Unl.

Exceptional Man. Michael Blankfort. LC 80-66008. 1980. 10.95 o.p. (ISBN 0-689-11072-3, Atheneum). Macmillan.

Exceptionality: Selected Readings. G. Nardi et al. 1972. pap. text ed. 4.75x o.p. (ISBN 0-8422-0207-2). Irvington.

Excerpts from Three Classical Chinese Novels. Yang Xianyi & Gladys Yang. (Panda Bks.). 295p. (Orig.). 1981. pap. 5.95 o.p. (ISBN 0-8351-0945-3). China Bks.

Excess of Love. Cathy C. Spellman. 526p. 1985. 16.95 o.p. (ISBN 0-385-29398-4). Delacorte.

Exchange. R. L. Brent. (Liquidator Ser.). 1978. pap. 1.75 o.p. (ISBN 0-441-22210-2). Ace Bks.

Exchange & Power in Social Life. Peter M. Blau. LC 64-23827. 352p. 1964. write for info. o.p. (ISBN 0-02-310820-7). Macmillan.

Exchange in Oceania. Per Hage & Frank Harary. (International Library of Anthropology). 280p. 1988. lib. bdg. 69.00 o.p. (ISBN 0-415-00413-6, Pub. by Routledge UK). Routledge Chapman & Hall.

Exchange Lists & Diet Patterns. Karen K. Arbogast. 352p. 1980. 21.95 o.p. (ISBN 0-442-25655-8). Van Nos Reinhold.

Exchange Rate Adjustment under Generalized Currency Floating: Comparative Analysis among Developing Countries. Romeo M. Bautista. (Working Paper: No. 436). 99p. 1980. 5.00 o.p. (ISBN 0-686-36172-5, WP-0436). World Bank.

Exchange Rate Enviroment. Simon Brooks & Keith Cuthertson. 320p. 1986. 60.00 o.p. (ISBN 0-7099-1762-7, Pub. by Croom Helm UK). Routledge Chapman & Hall.

Exchange-Rate Policy, Monetary Policy, & Real Exchange-Rate Variability. Pieter Korteweg. LC 80-39553. (Essays in International Finance Ser.: No. 140). 1980. pap. text ed. 4.50x o.p. (ISBN 0-88165-047-1). Princeton U Int Finan Econ.

Exchange Teacher. Agnes Sibley. LC 61-5293. 230p. 1961. pap. 2.50 o.p. (ISBN 0-87004-156-8). Caxton.

Exciplex. Ed. by M. Gordon & W. R. Ware. 372p. 1975. 72.50 o.p. (ISBN 0-12-290650-0). Acad Pr.

Exciting Electric Machine Inventions. Laithwaite. 1974. pap. 4.20 o.p. (ISBN 0-08-017249-0). Pergamon.

Excitons at High Density. Ed. by H. Haken & S. Nikitine. (Tracts in Modern Physics Ser.: Vol. 73). (Illus.). vi, 303p. 1975. 50.50 o.p. (ISBN 0-387-06943-7). Springer-Verlag.

Excitotoxins. Ed. by Kjell Fuxe et al. (Wenner-Gren International Symposium Ser.: Vol. 39). 376p. 1904. 65.00x o.p. (ISBN 0-306-41653-0, Plenum Pr). Plenum Pub.

Exclusionary & Inclusionary Zoning: A Bibliography. Mary E. Huls. (Public Administration Series: Bibliography P 1763). 1985. pap. 2.00 o.p. (ISBN 0-89028-563-2). Vance Biblios.

Exclusively Yours: Fashion Knits from the World's Top Designers. Frances Kennett. (Illus.). 128p. 1987. 19.95 o.p. (ISBN 0-13-293812-X). P-H.

Excursion Through the United States & Canada During the Years 1822-1823. William N. Blane. LC 68-58049. (Illus.). 1969. Repr. of 1824 ed. 35.00x o.p. (ISBN 0-8371-4978-9, BLA&, Pub. by Negro U Pr). Greenwood.

Excursions in Historical Geology: A Modular Approach. George D. Brown & George T. Ladd. 1973. pap. 13.95 o.p. (ISBN 0-395-16830-9). HM.

Excursions in Historical Geology: A Modular Approach, Units 1-12. George D. Brown & George T. Ladd. 1977. pap. 11.95 o.p. (ISBN 0-395-24243-6); Instr's. manual 5.75 o.p. (ISBN 0-686-97245-7); Student's manual avail. o.p. HM.

Exe Estuary: Wildlife in Camera. Thomas Davis. 1988. text ed. 50.00x o.p. (ISBN 0-86023-195-X, Pub. by Barracuda UK). State Mutual Bk.

Execution by Hunger: The Hidden Holocaust. Miron Dolot. LC 84-16568. 1985. 16.45 o.p. (ISBN 0-393-01886-5). Norton.

Execution of Charles Horman: An American Sacrifice. Thomas Hauser. LC 78-53864. 1978. 8.95 o.p. (ISBN 0-15-129456-9). HarBraceJ.

Executioner's Song. Norman Mailer. 1984. pap. 4.95 o.p. (ISBN 0-446-36353-7). Warner Bks.

Executive & Ownership Report. American Trucking Association Satistical Analysis Department. (Financial & Operating Statistics Ser.). 80p. 1988. pap. text ed. 175.00 o.p. (ISBN 0-88711-001-0). Am Trucking Assns.

Executive Baby: Creating a Truly Superior Child. Elizabeth Grey & Michael Grey. (Illus.). 128p. (Orig.). 1984. pap. 8.95 o.p. (ISBN 0-920792-36-7). Eden Pr.

Executive Body: A Complete Guide to Fitness & Stress Management for the Working Woman. Nancy Burstein. 1984. 16.45 o.p. (ISBN 0-671-49437-6). S&S.

Executive Compensation Strategy. Panel Publishers, Inc. Staff. 1985. 125.00 o.s.i. (ISBN 0-916592-55-3). Panel Pubs.

Executive Compensation 1983. Practicing Law Institute Staff & Yale D. Tauber. LC 83-62935. (Tax Law & Estate Planning Ser.: No. 192). (Illus.). 496p. 1983. 35.00 o.p. PLI.

Executive Computing: The IBM Personal Computer. John Zussman & David E. Cortesi. 1986. pap. text ed. 19.95 o.p. (ISBN 0-03-068914-7). HR&W.

Executive Control & Data Processing. Lowell H. Hattery. 1959. 10.00 o.p. (ISBN 0-910136-03-3). Anderson Kramer.

Executive Deskbook. Auren Uris. 330p. 1979. pap. 14.95 o.p. (ISBN 0-442-26107-1). Van Nos Reinhold.

Executive Dissent: How to Say No & Win. Auren Uris. LC 78-9802. 1978. 12.95 o.p. (ISBN 0-8144-5473-9). AMACOM.

Executive Guide to Copyright Protection for Information Products: Building a Copyright Policy for Your Company. 1987. pap. write for info. o.p. (ISBN 0-942774-21-3). Info Indus.

Executive Guide to Employment Practices. Thom K. Cope. LC 84-62043. 176p. (Orig.). 1984. pap. 19.95 o.p. (ISBN 0-939644-14-2). Media Prods & Mktg.

Executive Look. Mortimer Levitt. LC 80-66011. (Illus.). 320p. 1981. 16.95 o.p. (ISBN 0-689-11078-2, Atheneum). Macmillan.

Executive Memory Guide. Hermine Hilton. 160p. 1987. 14.70 o.p. (ISBN 0-671-60739-1). S&S.

Executive Sourcebook. Bert Darga. (Illus.). 288p. 1985. 17.45 o.p. (ISBN 0-671-47772-2). S&S.

Executive Suite. Date not set. pap. (ISBN 0-385-29470-0). Delacorte.

Executive Suite. Cameron Hawley. 352p. 1986. pap. 5.95 o.p. (ISBN 0-385-29470-0, Delta). Dell.

Executive Taxation & Employee Benefits. 484p. 1983. 25.00 o.p. (ISBN 0-88129-007-6). Wash Bar CLE.

Executive's & Professional's Guide to Pension & Retirement Benefits. Mayer Siegel & Carol I. Buckmann. 285p. 1982. 40.00 o.p. (ISBN 0-15-100019-0, H39964, Pub. by Law & Business). HarBraceJ.

Executive's Guide to Finding a Superior Job. William A. Cohen. 224p. 1983. 17.95 o.p. (ISBN 0-8144-5766-5). AMACOM.

Executives Guide to Meetings, Conferences & Audiovisual Presentations. J. R. Jeffries & J. D. Bates. 256p. 1983. text ed. 22.95 o.p. (ISBN 0-07-004060-5). McGraw.

Exegesis at Qumran: Four Q Florilegium in Its Jewish Context. George J. Brooke. (JSOT Supplement Ser.: No. 29). 370p. pap. text ed. 15.95x o.s.i. (Pub. by JSOT Pr England). Eisenbrauns.

Exempt Organizations: Tax Strategies & Legal Problems. William T. Hutton & Stephen Schwarz. LC 82-61802. (Tax Law & Estate Planning Ser.). 172p. 1984. 45.00 o.p. PLI.

Exercise in Diagnosis & Treatment of Coronary Heart Disease. Ed. by J. J. Kellermann. (Cardiology: Vol. 62, No. 3 (1977)). (Illus.). 1977. 20.00 o.p. (ISBN 3-8055-2805-1). S Karger.

Exercise Myth. Henry A. Solomon. LC 83-22672. 160p. 1984. 12.95 o.p. (ISBN 0-15-129458-5). HarBraceJ.

Exercise Myth. Henry A. Solomon. 144p. 1986. pap. 2.95 o.p. (ISBN 0-553-25731-5). Bantam.

Exercise Program. Richard Blonsky & Mary J. Givens. 38p. 1985. ring binder 24.95 o.p. (ISBN 0-317-69657-2, 000003). Demos Pubns Inc.

Exercise Testing of Cardiac Patients. M. Kaltenbach. 126p. 1976. pap. 13.95 o.p. (ISBN 0-683-04504-0). Krieger.

Exercise to a New Figure. (Purse Books). 1962. pap. 0.49 o.p. (ISBN 0-440-62404-5). Dell.

Exercises & Solutions Manual for Foundations in Biophysics. A. L. Stanford. 1977. 7.50 o.p. (ISBN 0-12-663352-5). Acad Pr.

Exercises for Change of Position. Gaylord Yost. 2.50 o.p. (ISBN 0-913650-53-6). CPP Belwin.

Exercises in Calculus. Mary H. Hutchinngs & William R. Cogswell. 146p. (gr. 9-12). 1981. pap. text ed. 6.25 o.p. (ISBN 0-88334-148-4). Ind Sch Pr.

Exercises in Diagnosing ECG Tracings. 3rd ed. Conover. 1984. pap. 18.95 o.p. (ISBN 0-8016-1238-1). Mosby.

Exercises in Diagnostic Radiology, Vol. 3: Bone. 2nd ed. Lucy F. Squire et al. (Illus.). 85p. 1981. pap. text ed. write for info. o.p. (ISBN 0-7216-8541-2). Saunders.

Exercises in Macroeconomics: Development of Concepts. William E. Mitchell et al. (Illus.). 432p. 1973. text ed. 26.95 o.p. (ISBN 0-07-042511-6). McGraw.

Exercises in Mathematics. Jean Bass. Tr. by Scripta Technica. 1966. 84.00 o.p. (ISBN 0-12-080750-5). Acad Pr.

Exercises in Organic Spectroscopy. 2nd ed. Ed. by Robert H. Shapiro & Charles H. Depuy. LC 76-44911. 1977. pap. text ed. 19.95 o.p. (ISBN 0-03-089712-2, HoltC). HR&W.

Exercises in Russian Syntax: The Compound & Complex Sentence. V. S. Belevitskaia-Khalizaieja. 343p. 1977. 2.40 o.p. (ISBN 0-8285-0547-0, Pub. by Progress Pubs USSR). Imported Pubns.

Exercises to Accompany American Heritage Dictionary. American Heritage Dictionary Editors. 1977. 1.40 o.p. (ISBN 0-395-26171-6). HM.

Exerstyle. Quarto Marketing, Ltd. Staff. 1985. 23.45 o.p. (ISBN 0-671-60142-3, Fireside); pap. 11.95 o.p. (ISBN 0-671-55204-X). S&S.

Exeter Book Riddles. Kevin Crossley-Holland. 1988. pap. 12.50 o.p. (ISBN 0-85991-260-4, Pub. by Boydell & Brewer). Longwood Pub Group.

Exhaustive Concordance of the Book of Mormon, Doctrine & Covenants & Pearl of Great Peace. R. Gary Shapiro. Orig. Title: Triple Concordance. 1977. 17.95 o.p. (ISBN 0-89036-085-5). Hawkes Pub Inc.

Exhibition Catalogue Manual in Use in the Library of the Metropolitan Museum of Art. Ed. by Lucy C. Ho. (Illus.). 40p. 1974. 2.50 o.p. (ISBN 0-87099-099-3). Metro Mus Art.

Exhibition Catalogues from the Fogg Art Museum, 10 vols. facsimile ed. Incl. Tiepolo: A Bicentenary Exhibition, 1770-1970. George Knox. 1978. lib. bdg. 67.00 (ISBN 0-8240-1954-7); Degas Monotypes: Essay, Catalogue & Checklist. Eugenia P. Janis. 1978. lib. bdg. 74.00 (ISBN 0-8240-1955-5); Ingres' Sculptural Sytle: A Group of Unknown Drawings. Phyllis Hattis. Repr. of 1973 ed. lib. bdg. 28.00 (ISBN 0-8240-1956-3); Three American Painters: Kenneth Noland, Jules Olitski, Frank Stella. Michael Fried. Repr. of 1965 ed. lib. bdg. 18.00 (ISBN 0-8240-1957-1); Gods & Heroes: Baroque Images of Antiquity. Eunice Williams. Repr. of 1968 ed. lib. bdg. 48.00 (ISBN 0-8240-1958-X); Frederick M. Watkins Collection. Repr. of 1973 ed. lib. bdg. 46.00 (ISBN 0-8240-1959-8); Eucharistic Vessels of the Middle Ages. Heidi R. Kaufmann et al. Repr. of 1975 ed. lib. bdg. 28.00 (ISBN 0-8240-1960-1); Works of Art from the Collection of Paul J. Sachs. Agnes Mongan. 1978. Repr. of 1966 ed. lib. bdg. 46.00 (ISBN 0-8240-1961-X); Harvard Honors Lafayette. Agnes Mongan et al. Repr. of 1976 ed. lib. bdg. 28.00 (ISBN 0-8240-1962-8); Benjamin Franklin: A Perspective. Louise T. Ambler. Repr. of 1975 ed. lib. bdg. 25.00 (ISBN 0-8240-1963-6). (Illus.). 1977. Garland Pub.

Exhibition of the Royal Academy of Arts, 4 vols. Royal Academy of Arts Staff. (History & Literature of Art Ser.). 1975. Repr. of 1901 ed. Set. lib. bdg. 295.00 o.s.i. (ISBN 0-306-70644-X). Da Capo.

Exil see Oeuvre Poetique.

Exile in Great Britain: Refugees from Hitler's Germany. G. Hirschfeld. 304p. 1984. text ed. 38.50x o.p. (ISBN 0-391-03121-X). Humanities.

Exile of Celine. Tom Clark. LC 86-10234. 224p. 1987. 16.45 o.p. (ISBN 0-394-55312-8). Random.

Exile: The Unquiet Oblivion of Richard M. Nixon. Robert S. Anson. 352p. 1984. 17.45 o.p. (ISBN 0-671-44021-7). S&S.

Exiled in Paradise: German Refugee Artists & Intellectuals from the 1930's to Present. Anthony Heilbut. LC 84-45071. 515p. 1984. pap. 13.95 o.p. (ISBN 0-8070-5411-9, BP677). Beacon Pr.

Exiles, Vol. 1. William S. Long. (Australians Ser.: Vol. I). 1984. lib. bdg. 12.95 o.p. (ISBN 0-8398-2824-1, Gregg). G K Hall.

Exiles: A Facsimile of Notes, Manuscripts & Galley Proofs. James Joyce. Ed. by Michael Groden. LC 77-18397. (James Joyce Archive Ser.). 1978. lib. bdg. 125.00 o.p. (ISBN 0-8240-2810-4). Garland Pub.

Existence: A New Dimension in Psychiatry & Psychology. Ed. by Rollo May et al. 1967. pap. 13.95 o.p. (ISBN 0-671-20314-2, Touchstone Bks). S&S.

Existence & Presence: The Dialectics of Divinity. Laurence L. Cassidy. LC 80-5881. 246p. 1981. lib. bdg. 25.50 o.p. (ISBN 0-8191-1486-3); pap. text ed. 12.50 o.p. (ISBN 0-8191-1487-1). U Pr of Amer.

Existential Christian, No. 1. James Park. (Existential Freedom Ser. No. 1). 1970. pap. 1.00x o.p. (ISBN 0-89231-001-4). Existential Bks.

Existential Christian, No. 2. James Park. (Existential Freedom Ser.: No. 2). 1971. pap. 5.00x o.p. (ISBN 0-89231-002-2). Existential Bks.

Existential Freedom, No. 3. James Park. 1973. pap. 5.00x o.p. (ISBN 0-89231-003-0). Existential Bks.

Existential Man: The Challenge of Psychotherapy. R. E. Johnson. 1971. 32.00 o.p. (ISBN 0-08-016325-4). Pergamon.

Existential Metaphysics. Alvin Thalheimer. LC 60-15963. 640p. 1960. (ISBN 0-8022-1707-9). Philos Lib.

Existential Phenomenology. rev. ed. W. A. Luijpen. LC 69-13437. (Philosophical Ser.: No. 12). 1969. pap. text ed. 17.50x o.p. (ISBN 0-391-00705-X). Duquesne.
Existential Psychoanalysis. Jean-Paul Sartre. 1953. (ISBN 0-8022-1483-5). Philos Lib.
Existential Sentences in English. Gary L. Milsark. Ed. by Jorge Hankamer. LC 78-66570. (Outstanding Dissertations in Linguistics Ser.). 1979. text ed. 36.00 o.p. (ISBN 0-8240-9678-9). Garland Pub.
Existentialism. Jean-Paul Sartre. 96p. 1947. (ISBN 0-8022-1484-3). Philos Lib.
Existentialism & Casework. Kirk A. Bradford. 1969. 5.50 o.p. (ISBN 0-682-46935-1, University). Exposition-Phoenix.
Existentialism & Education. George F. Kneller. 1958. (ISBN 0-8022-0871-1). Philos Lib.
Existentialism & Indian Thought. K. Guru Dutt. (ISBN 0-8022-0432-5). Philos Lib.
Existentialism & Thomism. Joseph C. Mihalich. 96p. 1960. (ISBN 0-8022-1113-5). Philos Lib.
Existentialism in American Literature. Ruby Chatterji. 176p. 1983. text ed. 12.50x o.p. (ISBN 0-391-02890-1). Humanities.
Existentialism, Religion & Death. Walter Kaufmann. 14.25 o.p. (ISBN 0-8446-6133-3). Peter Smith.
Existentialisme et la Sagesse Des Nations. Simone de Beauvoir. 14.95 o.p. (ISBN 0-686-54089-1). French & Eur.
Existentialist Essays. Don Wainwright. LC 65-11638. 72p. 1965. (ISBN 0-8022-1790-7). Philos Lib.
Existentialist Ethics. Hazel E. Barnes. LC 78-55038. (Midway Reprint Ser.). 1985. pap. 6.95x o.s.i. (ISBN 0-226-03728-2, P779, Phoen). U of Chicago Pr.
Existentialist Prolegomena: To a Future Metaphysics. Frederick Sontag. LC 68-11315. 1969. lib. bdg. 15.00x o.s.i. (ISBN 0-226-76819-8). U of Chicago Pr.
Exit Laughing. Irvin S. Cobb. LC 73-19798. 576p. 1974. Repr. of 1941 ed. 53.00x o.p. (ISBN 0-8103-3687-1). Gale.
Exit the King. Eugene Ionesco. Tr. by Donald Watson from Fr. (Illus., Orig.). 1967. pap. 2.95 o.p. (ISBN 0-394-17267-1, E456, Ever). Grove.
Exit to Eden. Anne Rampling. 1985. 17.95 o.p. (ISBN 0-87795-609-X, Arbor Hse). Morrow.
Exitalian Somaliliand. E. Sylvia Pankhurst. 1952. (ISBN 0-8022-1261-1). Philos Lib.
Exits off a Toll Road. Steven Lewis. LC 75-6211. 53p. 1975. pap. 5.00 o.p. (ISBN 0-915316-11-0); pap. 15.00 limited signed ed. o.p. (ISBN 0-685-56251-4). Pentagram.
Exodus. Ed. by Peter J. Lucas. 1977. 40.00x o.p. (ISBN 0-416-17170-2, NO. 2304). Routledge Chapman & Hall.
Exodus: A Hermeneutics of Freedom. J. Severino Croatto. LC 80-26148. 112p. (Orig.). 1981. pap. 4.95 o.p. (ISBN 0-88344-111-X). Orbis Bks.
Exodus & Beyond. Lyndon W. Cook & Donald W. Cannon. (Essays in Mormon History Ser.). 264p. 1980. pap. 7.95 o.p. (ISBN 0-89036-151-7). Hawkes Pub Inc.
Exodus from Hell. Jack Buchanan. (M.I.A. Hunter Ser.: No. 5). pap. 2.75 o.s.i. (ISBN 0-515-08544-8). Jove Pubns.
Exodusters: Black Migration to Kansas After Reconstruction. Nell I. Painter. (Illus.). 1979. pap. 4.95x o.p. (ISBN 0-393-00951-3). Norton.
Exogenous & Endogenous Influences on Metabolic & Neural Control, Vol. 1: Invited Lectures: Proceedings of the Third Congress of the European Society for Comparative Physiology & Biochemistry, August 31-September 3, 1981, Noorwijkerhout Netherlands. Ed. by A. D. Addink & N. Spronk. (Illus.). 432p. 1982. 110.00 o.p. (ISBN 0-08-027986-4). Pergamon.
Exogenous & Endogenous Influences on Metabolic & Neural Control, Vol. 2: Abstracts: Proceedings ot the Third Congress of the European Society for Comparative Physiology & Biochemistry, August 31-September 3, 1981, Noorwijkerhout, Netherlands. Ed. by A. D. Addink & N. Spronk. (Illus.). 260p. 1982. 73.00 o.p. (ISBN 0-08-028845-6). Pergamon.
Exorcism & the Healing of the Sick. Reginald M. Wooley. (Church Historical Society London N. S. Ser.: No. 8). Repr. of 1932 ed. 20.00 o.p. (ISBN 0-8115-3132-5). Kraus Repr.
Exorcism As a Christian Ministry. Elijah White. LC 74-80387. 128p. 1975. pap. 2.95 o.p. (ISBN 0-8192-1183-4). Morehouse Pub.
Exorcist. William P. Blatty. 416p. 1972. pap. 3.95 o.s.i. (ISBN 0-553-24769-7). Bantam.
Exotic Floral Patterns in Color. E. A. Seguy. (Illus.). 11.50 o.p. (ISBN 0-8446-5082-X). Peter Smith.
Exotic Japanese Stories. Ryunosuke Akutagawa. (Illus.). 480p. 1972. 6.95 o.p. (ISBN 0-87140-994-1); pap. 4.95 o.p. (ISBN 0-87140-264-5). Liveright.
Exotic Pasta: Seventy New Recipes for Very Different Pasta Dishes. Rosella De Angioy. LC 85-11606. (Illus.). 96p. 1985. 12.95 o.p. (ISBN 0-571-12543-3). Faber & Faber.
Exotic Species in Mariculture. Ed. by Roger Mann. (Illus.). 1979. text ed. 32.50x o.p. (ISBN 0-262-13155-2). MIT Pr.
Exotic Weapons. rev. ed. 1987. write for info. o.p. (ISBN 0-915179-58-X). Loompanics.
Exotic Weapons: An Access Book, 1982 Edition. Where & How to Buy Strange Weapons. Michael Hoy. (Illus.). 1982. pap. 9.95 o.p. (ISBN 0-686-23955-5). Loompanics.
Expanded Interest Tables. 3rd ed. Michael R. Lindeburg. (Engineering Review Manual Ser.). 112p. 1983. pap. 12.95 o.p. (ISBN 0-932276-35-0). Prof Pubns CA.
Expanding & Maintaining Your Apple Personal Computer. James Morrison. 1630p. 1984. pap. write for info. o.p. (ISBN 0-201-05157-5). Addison-Wesley.
Expanding Circle: Ethics & Sociobiology. Peter Singer. 190p. 1981. 10.95 o.p. (ISBN 0-374-15112-1). FS&G.
Expanding Earth. Pascual Jordan. Ed. by Arthur Beer. 224p. 1971. 37.00 o.p. (ISBN 0-08-015827-7). Pergamon.
Expanding Family: Childbearing. Carole L. Blair & Elizabeth M. Salerno. LC 75-30278. 1976. pap. text ed. 12.95 o.p. (ISBN 0-316-09915-5). Little.
Expanding Horizons in African Studies: Program of African Studies, Northwestern University, Proceedings of the Twentieth Anniversary Conference, 1968. Ed. by Gwendolen M. Carter & Ann Paden. 1969. 19.95x o.s.i. (ISBN 0-8101-0265-X). Northwestern U Pr.
Expanding Plastic Bag Market. Business Communications Staff. 1988. pap. 1950.00 o.p. (ISBN 0-89336-618-8, P-082). BCC.
Expanding Uses of Petroleum. Institute of Petroleum Staff. 1982. 48.95 o.p. (ISBN 0-471-26176-9). Wiley.
Expansion & Reform Eighteen Eighty Nine to Nineteen Twenty-Six. John S. Bassett. LC 72-137901. (American History & Culture in the Nineteenth Century Ser). 1971. Repr. of 1935 ed. 29.50x o.p. (ISBN 0-8046-1469-5, Pub. by Kennikat). Assoc Faculty Pr.
Expansion of Christianity. D. R. De Lacey. (Discovering the Bible Ser.). (YA) (gr. 8-10). pap. 9.95 o.p. (ISBN 0-7175-1163-4). Dufour.
Expansion of England. John R. Seeley. Ed. by John Gross. LC 73-152225. (Classics of British Historical Literature Ser). 1973. pap. text ed. 3.25 o.s.i. (ISBN 0-226-74429-9, P429, Phoen). U of Chicago Pr.
Expansion of God. Leslie G. Howard. LC 81-4521. 464p. (Orig.). 1981. pap. 3.74 o.p. (ISBN 0-88344-121-7). Orbis Bks.
Expansion of the Federal Union Eighteen Hundred One to Eighteen Forty-Eight. Wayne A. Frederick & Thomas T. Lyons. (Illus.). 296p. (Orig.). (gr. 10-12). 1978. pap. text ed. 6.75 o.p. (ISBN 0-88334-116-6). Ind Sch Pr.
Expansion of Thought. John D. Pickett. LC 74-76034. 1975. 25.00 o.p. (ISBN 0-682-47978-0, University). Exposition-Phoenix.
Expect a Miracle. Dale E. Galloway. 1982. pap. 4.95 o.p. (ISBN 0-8423-0822-9). Tyndale.
Expectant Creativity: The Action of Hope in Christian Ethics. Vincent J. Genovesi. LC 81-43807. 172p. (Orig.). 1982. lib. bdg. 29.25 o.p. (ISBN 0-8191-2407-9); pap. text ed. 12.25 o.p. (ISBN 0-8191-2408-7). U Pr of Amer.
Expectant Fathers. Sam Bittman & Sue R. Zalk. (Orig.). 1983. pap. 7.95 o.s.i. (ISBN 0-345-31763-7). Ballantine.
Expectations & Stability in Oligopoly Models. J. Okuguchi. (Lecture Notes in Economics & Mathematical Systems Ser.: Vol. 138). 1977. 11.00 o.p. (ISBN 0-387-08056-2). Springer-Verlag.
Expectations Approach: Improving Managerial Communication & Performance. John L. Machin. 352p. 1981. text ed. 39.95 o.p. (ISBN 0-07-084539-5). McGraw.
Expectations, Forecasting & Control: A Provisional Textbook of Macroeconomics: Vol. II, Prices, Market & Turning Points. William Frazer. LC 80-1361. 439p. 1980. lib. bdg. 37.50 o.p.; pap. text ed. 20.25 o.p. (ISBN 0-8191-1291-7). U Pr of Amer.
Expectations, Forecasting & Control: A Provisional Textbook of Macroeconomics, Vol. I: Monetary Matters, Keynesian & Other Models. William Frazer. LC 80-1361. 493p. 1980. pap. 37.75 o.p. (ISBN 0-8191-1144-9); pap. text ed. 20.75 o.p. (ISBN 0-8191-1145-7). U Pr of Amer.
Expedition. Wayne D. Barlowe. 1988. pap. 14.95 o.p. Workman Pub.
Expedition for the Survey of the Rivers Euphrates - Tigris, Carried Out by Order of the British Government in the Years 1835-1837, 2 vols. Francis R. Chesney. Incl. Geographical & Historical Notices of the Regions Situated Between the Rivers Nile & Indus; Vol. 1. lib. bdg. 35.00 (ISBN 0-8371-1479-9, CHEX); Vol. 2. lib. bdg. 35.00 (ISBN 0-8371-1483-7, CHEY). LC 68-55182. 1970. Repr. of 1850 ed. Set. lib. bdg. 63.50x o.p. (ISBN 0-8371-3796-9, CHET). Greenwood.
Expedition to Earth. Arthur C. Clarke. LC 78-95868. 181p. 1970. 6.95 o.s.i. (ISBN 0-15-129461-5). HarBraceJ.
Expeditions of John Charles Fremont Supplement: Proceedings of the Court Martial. John C. Fremont. Ed. by Mary L. Spence & Donald Jackson. LC 73-100374. 480p. 1973. 32.50 o.p. (ISBN 0-252-00403-5). U of Ill Pr.
Expeditions to Prussia & the Holy Land Made by Henry Earl of Derby. Richard Kyngeston. Ed. by L. T. Smith. 1965. Repr. of 1894 ed. 27.00 o.p. (ISBN 0-384-30775-2). Johnson Repr.
Expense Analysis: Condominiums, Cooperatives, & Planned Unit Developments. Ed. by Kenneth Anderson. 1978. pap. 10.00 o.p. (ISBN 0-912104-33-3). Inst Real Estate.
Expense Analysis: Condominiums, Cooperatives, & Planned Unit Developments. Ed. by Kenneth Anderson. 1979. lib. bdg. 10.00 o.p. (ISBN 0-912104-41-4). Inst Real Estate.
Expense Analysis: Condominiums, Cooperatives & Planned Unit Developments, 1984. Ed. by Kenneth Anderson & Stacey Ruiz. 152p. (Orig.). 1984. pap. 44.95 o.p. (ISBN 0-912104-79-1). Inst Real Estate.
Expense Analysis: Condominiums, Cooperatives, & Planned Unit Developments. Ed. by Kenneth R. Anderson & Stacey L. Ruiz. 136p. 1982. pap. 19.50 o.p. (ISBN 0-912104-63-5). Inst Real Estate.
Expense Analysis: Condominiums, Cooperatives, & Planned Unit Developments, 1983 Edition. Ed. by Kenneth R. Anderson & Stacey L. Ruiz. 152p. (Orig.). 1983. pap. 55.00 o.p. (ISBN 0-912104-74-0, 85803). Inst Real Estate.
Expense Analysis: Condominiums, Cooperatives, & Planned Unit Developments, 1981. Institute of Real Estate Management Staff. Ed. by Kenneth R. Anderson. 125p. 1981. pap. text ed. 15.00 o.p. (ISBN 0-912104-57-0). Inst Real Estate.
Expensive Analysis: Condominiums, Cooperatives & PUD's. 124p. 1981. softcover cancelled 30.00 o.p. (ISBN 0-317-34478-1). Inst Real Estate.
Expensive Habits. Maureen Howard. 422p. 1986. 17.45 o.s.i. (ISBN 0-671-50625-0). Summit Bks.
Experience & Faith. William Horden. LC 82-72653. 160p. 1983. pap. 10.95 o.p. (ISBN 0-8066-1960-0, 10-2133, Augsburg). Augsburg Fortress.
Experience & Identity: Birmingham & the West Midlands 1760-1800. John Money. 1977. lib. bdg. 18.00x o.p. (ISBN 0-7735-0290-4, McGill Canada). U of Toronto Pr.
Experience of Breastfeeding. Sheila Kitzinger. 255p. (Orig.). 1980. pap. 4.95 o.p. (ISBN 0-14-005591-6). Penguin.
Experience of Childbirth. 4th, rev ed. Sheila Kitzinger. (Illus.). 1968. pap. 3.95 o.p. (ISBN 0-14-020900-X, Pelican). Penguin.
Experience of Death. Paul L. Landsberg. 116p. 1953. (ISBN 0-8022-0915-7). Philos Lib.
Experience of Lent with the Risen Christ. Catherine Nerney. 1.95 o.p. (ISBN 0-8091-9308-6). Paulist Pr.
Experiences. Florence H. Morgan & Fred Morgan. (Illus.). 1975. pap. text ed. 8.75 o.p. (ISBN 0-15-525813-3, HC). HarBraceJ.
Experiences in Biochemical Perception. Ed. by L. Nicholas Ornston & Steve Sligar. LC 82-1614. 1982. 58.00 o.p. (ISBN 0-12-528420-9). Acad Pr.
Experiences in Communication. Wayne A. Shrope. 288p. (Orig.). 1974. pap. text ed. 9.95 o.p. (ISBN 0-15-525850-8, HC). HarBraceJ.
Experiences in Interpersonal Relationships. Vera G. Channels. 335p. 1975. pap. text ed. 4.95x o.p. (ISBN 0-8134-1703-1, 1703); teacher's manual 0.50 o.p. (ISBN 0-8134-1708-2, 1708). Inter Print Pubs.
Experiences in Language: Tools & Techniques for Language Arts. 4th ed. Walter T. Petty et al. 500p. 1984. pap. text ed. 35.00 o.p. (ISBN 0-205-08192-4, 238192). Allyn.
Experiences in Life Science: A Laboratory Guide. 2nd ed. Eugene H. Kaplan. (Illus.). 256p. 1976. pap. text ed. (ISBN 0-02-361770-5). Macmillan.
Experiences in Mathematical Ideas, 2 vols. National Council of Teachers of Mathematics Staff. LC 71-135151. (Illus.). (gr. 5-8). 1970. Vol. 1, 236p. incl. teaching pkgs. 15.75 ea. o.p. (ISBN 0-87353-051-9). Vol. 2, 154p (ISBN 0-87353-052-7). Vol. 2 (ISBN 0-87353-053-5). NCTM.
Experiences in Music for Young Children. M. C. Pugmire. LC 76-4304. 1977. pap. text ed. 13.95 o.p. (ISBN 0-8273-0567-2); 4.20 o.s.i. instr's. guide (ISBN 0-8273-0568-0); 5.95 o.s.i. cassette (ISBN 0-8273-0566-4). Delmar.
Experiences of a Physical Researcher. Raymond Bayless. 1972. 7.95 o.p. (ISBN 0-8216-0076-1, Pub. by Univ Bks). Carol Pub Group.
Experiences of God. Jurgen Moltmann. Tr. by Margaret Kohl from Ger. LC 80-8046. 96p. 1980. pap. 2.25 o.p. (ISBN 0-8006-1406-2, 1-1406, Fortress). Augsburg Fortress.
Experiences with God & His Messengers: The Key to God's Kingdom. Hendrik Th. Lilipaly. 1980. 6.00 o.p. (ISBN 0-682-49506-9). Exposition-Phoenix.
Experiences with the Monitoring & Evaluation of Training & Visit Extension in India. Gershon Feder & Roger Slade. (Working Paper Ser.: No. 595). 46p. 1983. 3.50 o.p. (ISBN 0-8213-0192-6, WP 0595). World Bank.
Experiences with Three Tillage Systems on a Marine Loam Soil I: 1972-1975. Westmaas Research Group on New Tillage Systems Staff. (Agricultural Research Reports: No. 899). 104p. 1980. pap. 18.50 o.p. (ISBN 90-220-0741-3, PDC219, PUDOC). UNIPUB.
Experiencia Historica De Desarollo No Capitalista. V. Solodovnikov & V. Bogoslovski. 254p. (Span.). 1975. 5.95 o.p. (ISBN 0-8285-1424-0, Pub. by Progress Pubs USSR). Imported Pubns.
Experiencing Accounting: A Study Guide for Personal Computing. Goodman & Mason. (Pt. 1). 1985. 24.67 o.s.i. (ISBN 0-205-08221-1, 058221). Allyn.
Experiencing Comprehensive Education: A Study of Bishop McGregor School. Robert G. Burgess. 288p. 1983. 24.00 o.p. (ISBN 0-416-35150-6, NO. 4037); pap. 11.95 o.p. (ISBN 0-416-35160-3, NO. 4038). Routledge Chapman & Hall.
Experiencing Shakespeare I. Center for Learning Staff. 188p. 1983. wire coil bdg. 34.95 o.p. (ISBN 0-697-01885-7). Wm C Brown.
Experiencing the Environment. Ed. by Seymour Wapner et al. LC 75-37839. (Illus.). 252p. 1976. 39.50x o.p. (ISBN 0-306-30873-8, Plenum Pr). Plenum Pub.
Experiential Definition of Psychology. Alan Richardson. 244p. 1985. 37.50x o.p. (ISBN 0-7022-1814-6). U of Queensland Pr.
Experiential Education Policy Guidelines. Experiential Education Advisory Panel Staff. Ed. by Richard J. Miguel. 54p. 1979. 4.50 o.p. (ISBN 0-318-15471-4, RD 160). Natl Ctr Res Voc Ed.
Experiential Learning: Rationale, Characteristics, & Assessment. Morris, Keeton T., & Associates Staff. LC 75-44884. (Higher Education Ser). (Illus.). 296p. 1976. 25.95 o.p. (ISBN 0-87589-277-9). Jossey-Bass.
Experiment Hope. Jurgen Moltmann. Tr. & intro. by M. Douglas Meeks. LC 74-26339. 208p. 1975. 8.95 o.p. (ISBN 0-8006-0407-5, Fortress). Augsburg Fortress.
Experiment in Autobiography: Discoveries & Conclusions in a Very Ordinary Brain (since 1866) H. G. Wells. 736p. 1984. 29.95 o.p. (ISBN 0-316-93031-8). Little.
Experiment in Depth: A Study of the Work of Jung, Eliot & Toynbee. P. W. Martin. 1976. pap. 9.95 o.p. (ISBN 0-7100-8393-9). Routledge Chapman & Hall.
Experiment in Independence: New Jersey in the Critical Period 1781-1789. Richard P. McCormick. 1950. 30.00x o.p. (ISBN 0-8135-0120-2). Rutgers U Pr.
Experiment in Wartime Intercultural Relations: Philippine Students in Japan, 1943-1945. Grant K. Goodman. 34p. 1962. pap. 2.00 o.p. (ISBN 0-87727-046-5, DP 46). Cornell SE Asia.
Experimental Analysis of Insect Behavior. Ed. by L. B. Browne. (Illus.). 370p. 1974. 20.90 o.p. (ISBN 0-387-06557-1). Springer-Verlag.
Experimental & Analytical Modeling of LWR Safety Experiments, HTD-Vol.7. Ed. by L. E. Hochreiter & G. L. Sozzi. 144p. 1980. 20.00 o.p. (ISBN 0-317-33508-1, G00167); members 10.00 o.p. (ISBN 0-317-33509-X). ASME.
Experimental & Clinical Interventions in Aging. Walker & Cooper. 472p. 1983. 75.00 o.p. (ISBN 0-8247-7012-9). Dekker.
Experimental Approach to Organization Development. 2nd ed. Donald F. Harvey & Donald R. Brown. (Illus.). 592p. 1982. pap. text ed. (ISBN 0-13-295360-9). P-H.
Experimental Approaches to Psychopathology. Ed. by Mitchell Kietzman et al. 1975. 65.50 o.p. (ISBN 0-12-406750-6). Acad Pr.

Experimental Cell Fusion. Eric Sidebottom & Nils Ringertz. Ed. by J. J. Head. LC 81-67982. (Carolina Biology Readers Ser.: No. 102). (Illus.). 32p. (gr. 10 up). 1984. pap. 2.30 o.p. (ISBN 0-89278-302-8, 45-9702). Carolina Biological.

Experimental Chemistry. 5th ed. Michell J. Sienko & Robert A. Plane. 1976. text ed. 21.95 o.p. (ISBN 0-07-057331-X). McGraw.

Experimental Control of Mitosis, 1: Radiation Effects on Mitosis. Janie Lesher. 1972. 28.50x o.p. (ISBN 0-8422-7040-X). Irvington.

Experimental Control of Mitosis, 2. J. J. McCormick et al. 1973. 28.50x o.p. (ISBN 0-8422-7027-2). Irvington.

Experimental Dimension of Psychology. Alan Richardson. LC 83-23335. 244p. 1987. pap. text ed. 14.50 o.p. (ISBN 0-7022-1937-1). U of Queensland Pr.

Experimental Electronics for Students. K. J. Close & J. Yarwood. 280p. 1979. 16.95x o.p. (ISBN 0-412-14760-2, NO. 6060, Pub. by Chapman & Hall England). Routledge Chapman & Hall.

Experimental Embroyognesis in Vascular Plants. V. Raghavan. (Experimental Botany Ser.). 1977. 103.50 o.p. (ISBN 0-12-575450-7). Acad Pr.

Experimental Food Chemistry. Nell I. Mondy. (Illus.). 1980. pap. 17.95 o.p. (ISBN 0-87055-343-7). AVI.

Experimental Foods Laboratory Manual. 2nd ed. Margaret McWilliams. (Illus.). 1981. spiral bdg. 15.95x o.p. (ISBN 0-8087-3416-4). Plycon Pr.

Experimental Hematology Today, 1985. Ed. by S. J. Baum et al. (Illus.). xv, 143p. 1986. pap. 39.00 o.p. (ISBN 0-387-96273-5). Springer-Verlag.

Experimental Hypnosis. Ed. by Leslie M. Le Cron. 1965. pap. 2.95 o.p. (ISBN 0-8065-0156-1, 206, Pub. by Citadel Pr). Carol Pub Group.

Experimental Mechanics: Proceedings, International Congress on Experimental Mechanics - 1st, Vols. 1 & 2. Ed. by B. E. Rossi. 1963. 105.00 o.p. (ISBN 0-08-013346-0). Pergamon.

Experimental Methods for Social Policy Research. George W. Fairweather & Louis G. Tornatzky. LC 76-25590. 1977. 110.00 o.p. (ISBN 0-08-021237-9); pap. 110.00 o.p. (ISBN 0-08-021236-0). Pergamon.

Experimental Methods in Heavy Ion Physics. Ed. by K. Bethge. LC 78-12583. (Lecture Notes in Physics: Vol. 83). 1978. pap. 20.00 o.p. (ISBN 0-387-08931-4). Springer-Verlag.

Experimental Microbiology. Ronald M. Atlas & Alfred E. Brown. 400p. 1984. pap. write for info. o.p. (ISBN 0-02-304530-2). Macmillan.

Experimental Music: Cage & Beyond. Michael Nyman. LC 74-4848. (Illus.). 1975. Repr. of 1974 ed. 16.95 o.s.i. (ISBN 0-02-871200-5). Schirmer Bks.

Experimental Music: Composition with an Electronic Computer. Lejaren A. Hiller & Leonard M. Isaacson. LC 79-21368. 1979. Repr. of 1959 ed. lib. bdg. 24.75x o.p. (ISBN 0-313-22158-8, HIEM). Greenwood.

Experimental Myopathies & Muscular Dystrophy. (Neurology Ser.: Vol. 16). 115p. 1975. 29.00 o.p. (ISBN 0-387-07376-0). Springer-Verlag.

Experimental Neutron Resonance Spectroscopy. Ed. by J. A. Harvey. 1970. 99.00 o.p. (ISBN 0-12-329850-4). Acad Pr.

Experimental Neutron Thermalization. P. A. Egelstaff & M. J. Poole. LC 79-86201. 1969. 87.00 o.p. (ISBN 0-08-006533-3). Pergamon.

Experimental Organic Chemistry. H. Dupont Durst & George W. Gokel. (Illus.). 1980. text ed. 34.95 o.p. (ISBN 0-07-018393-7). McGraw.

Experimental Physiology. Dennis A. Baeyens. 96p. (Orig.). 1981. lab manual 8.95x o.p. (ISBN 0-89459-131-2). Hunter Textbks.

Experimental Population Genetics. Ed. by Roger Milkman. (Benchmark Papers in Genetics: Vol. 13). 416p. 1983. 51.95 o.p. (ISBN 0-87933-100-3). Van Nos Reinhold.

Experimental Procedures in Elementary Qualitative Analysis. Esmarch S. Gilreath. 1968. text ed. 22.95 o.p. (ISBN 0-07-023213-X). McGraw.

Experimental Psychology. B. A. Farrell. 1955. (ISBN 0-8022-0476-7). Philos Lib.

Experimental Psychology. Barry H. Kantowitz & Henry L. Roediger, III. 1980. text ed. 26.50 o.p. (ISBN 0-395-30814-3). HM.

Experimental Psychology: A Manual of Laboratory Practice, 2 vols in 4 pts. Edward B. Titchener. LC 9-30853. Repr. of 1901 ed. Set. 125.00 o.p. (ISBN 0-384-60658-9). Johnson Repr.

Experimental Psychology: Research Tactics & Their Applications. D. Chris Anderson & John G. Borkowski. 1978. text ed. write for info. o.p. (ISBN 0-673-07866-3). Scott F.

Experimental Psychology: Tactics of Behavioral Research. John G. Borkowski & D. Chris Anderson. 1977. pap. write for info. o.p. (ISBN 0-673-15085-2). Scott F.

Experimental Psychology: Understanding Psychological Research. 2nd ed. Barry Kantowitz & Henry Roediger, III. (Illus.). 539p. 1984. text ed. 35.50 o.p. (ISBN 0-314-78017-3); tchr's. manual avail. o.p. (ISBN 0-314-78018-1); student guide 13.95 o.p. (ISBN 0-314-79060-8). West Pub.

Experimental Psychopathology: Recent Research & Theory. Ed. by H. D. Kimmel. 1971. 53.00 o.p. (ISBN 0-12-407250-X). Acad Pr.

Experimental Social Psychology. rev. ed. Gardner Murphy et al. 1970. Repr. of 1937 ed. lib. bdg. 42.50x o.p. (ISBN 0-8371-3341-6, MUES). Greenwood.

Experimental Social Psychology: Commentary & Readings. Chester A. Insko & John Schopler. 1972. text ed. 20.00 o.p. (ISBN 0-12-372650-6). Acad Pr.

Experimental Studies of Amphibian Development. E. Hadorn. Tr. by D. C. Turner. LC 74-2549. (Illus.). 160p. 1974. 12.00 o.p. (ISBN 0-387-06644-6). Springer-Verlag.

Experimental Studies of Freudian Theories. Hans J. Eysenck & Glenn D. Wilson. 1973. 39.95x o.p. (ISBN 0-416-78010-5, NO. 2196). Routledge Chapman & Hall.

Experimental Studies on Guinea Pig's Eczema: Their Significance in Human Eczema. N. Hunziker. LC 68-57875. (Illus.). 1969. 46.70 o.p. (ISBN 0-387-04564-3). Springer-Verlag.

Experimental Study of Food. 2nd ed. Ada M. Campbell & Marjorie Penfield. LC 78-69535. (Illus.). 1979. text ed. 36.95 o.p. (ISBN 0-395-26666-1). HM.

Experimental Study of Foods. Ruth M. Griswold. LC 62-5195. 1962. text ed. 14.95 o.p. (ISBN 0-395-04548-7, 3-20375). HM.

Experimental Study of Pituitary Tumors: Genesis. Cytology & Hormone Content. Kwa Hong Giok. (Illus.). 1961. pap. 20.70 o.p. (ISBN 0-387-02714-9). Springer-Verlag.

Experimental Techniques in Quantitative Chemical Analysis. Vinay Kumar. LC 80-69043. 183p. (Orig.). 1981. pap. text ed. 13.00 o.p. (ISBN 0-8191-1509-6). U Pr of Amer.

Experimental Theater. James Roose-Evans. 1971. pap. 1.65 o.p. (ISBN 0-380-01172-7, 11981, Bard). Avon.

Experimental Thymectomy, Possibilities & Limitations. Max W. Hess. LC 68-31624. (Experimental Medicine, Pathology & Clinic Ser.: Vol. 25). (Illus.). 1968. 33.70 o.p. (ISBN 0-387-04107-9). Springer-Verlag.

Experimental World Literacy Programme: A Critical Assessment. 195p. 1976. pap. 5.00 o.p. (ISBN 92-3-101314-9, U232, UNESCO). UNIPUB.

Experimentation: An Introduction to Measurement Theory & Experiment Design. David C. Baird. 1962. pap. text ed. (ISBN 0-13-295345-5). P-H.

Experimentation & Measurement. W. J. Youden. (National Bureau of Standards Special Publication Ser.: No. 672). 126p. 1984. pap. 3.75 o.p. (ISBN 0-318-11716-9, S/N 003-003-02575-5). USGPO.

Experimentation on Interpersonal Behavior: The Social Psychological Approach. T. Rywick. LC 72-86199. 1972. pap. text ed. 4.50x o.p. (ISBN 0-8422-0210-2). Irvington.

Experimenter's Guide to Solid State Electronics Projects. Alfred W. Barber. (Illus.). 1980. text ed. 17.95 o.p. (ISBN 0-13-295451-6, Parker). P-H.

Experimenting with Truth: The Fusion of Religion with Technology Needed for Humanity's Survival. Rustrum Roy. (Hibbert Lectures: 1979). (Illus.). 228p. 1981. 39.00 o.p. (ISBN 0-08-025820-4); pap. 13.75 o.p. (ISBN 0-08-025819-0). Pergamon.

Experiments & Demonstrations in Exercise Physiology. Wayne E. Sinning. LC 74-4591. (Illus.). 162p. 1975. pap. text ed. 18.95 o.p. (ISBN 0-7216-8313-4). HR&W.

Experiments & Research with Humans: Values in Conflicts. National Academy of Science, Academy Forum. LC 75-13985. (Illus.). 224p. 1975. pap. 8.50x o.p. (ISBN 0-309-02347-5). Natl Acad Pr.

Experiments in Animal Behaviour. Marguerite D. Hainsworth. (Illus., Orig.). (gr. 8-12). 1968. pap. 11.64 o.p. (ISBN 0-395-02682-2). HM.

Experiments in Digital Principles. 2nd ed. Donald P. Leach. (Illus.). 176p. 1981. text ed. 34.95 o.p. (ISBN 0-07-036916-X). McGraw.

Experiments in Form: A Foundation Course in Three-Dimensional Design. Peter Pearce & Susan Pearce. 160p. 1980. pap. 9.95 o.p. (ISBN 0-442-26497-6). Van Nos Reinhold.

Experiments in General, Organic & Biological Chemistry. 5th ed. J. R. Holum. 182p. 1979. lab manual o.p. (ISBN 0-471-04751-1). Wiley.

Experiments in Interviewing Techniques: Field Experiments in Health Reporting, 1971-1977. Charles F. Cannell et al. 446p. (Orig.). 1979. pap. 18.00x o.p. (ISBN 0-87944-247-6). Inst Soc Res.

Experiments in Microprocessors & Digital Systems. Douglas V. Hall & Marybelle B. Hall. (Illus.). 176p. 1981. text ed. 14.75 o.p. (ISBN 0-07-025576-8). McGraw.

Experiments in Physical Chemistry. 2nd ed. J. R. Wilson et al. 1968. 100.00 o.p. (ISBN 0-08-012541-7). Pergamon.

Experiments in Physical Chemistry. 2nd rev. ed. Ed. by J. R. Wilson et al. R. M. W. Rickett. LC 68-18536. 1978. pap. 18.00 o.p. (ISBN 0-08-023798-3). Pergamon.

Experiments in Physics. 3rd ed. Alan Cromer. 240p. 1984. pap. text ed. 12.95 o.p. (ISBN 0-8403-3388-9). Kendall-Hunt.

Experiments in Primary Education: Aspects of Project Follow-Through. Eleanor E. Maccoby & Miriam Zellner. 1970. pap. text ed. 7.95 o.p. (ISBN 0-15-526010-3, HC). HarBraceJ.

Experiments in Solid State Electronics. J. I. Matthews. 1972. text ed. 27.95 o.p. (ISBN 0-07-040961-7). McGraw.

Experiments with Bible Study. Hans-Ruedi Weber. LC 82-13398. 330p. 1983. pap. 12.95 o.s.i. (ISBN 0-664-24461-0, Westminster). Westminster John Knox.

Experiments with Everyday Objects: Science Activities for Children, Parents & Teachers. Kevin Goldstein-Jackson et al. LC 77-13232. (Illus.). 1978. 15.95 o.p. (ISBN 0-13-295287-4, Spec); pap. 3.95 o.p. (ISBN 0-13-295279-3, Spec). P-H.

Expert dBASE III PLUS. Date not set. (ISBN 0-89588-404-6). Sybex.

Expert Medical Witness: A Bibliography. Frederick Frankena. (Public Administration Ser.: P 1829). 16p. 1985. 2.25 o.p. (ISBN 0-89028-679-5). Vance Biblios.

Expert Witness: A General, Mostly Legal Bibliography. Frederick Frankena. 1985. pap. 3.00 o.p. (ISBN 0-89028-674-4). Vance Biblios.

Expert Witness Handbook-A Guide for Engineers. D. G. Sunar. (Engineering Career Advancedment Ser.). 80p. (Orig.). 1985. pap. text ed. 7.95 o.p. (ISBN 0-932276-51-2). Prof Pubns CA.

Expiremental Psychology. I. Pavlov. 1957. (ISBN 0-8022-1290-5). Philos Lib.

Expl New World Book, No. 10. (Our Nations Heritage Ser.). Date not set. (ISBN 0-07-375413-7). McGraw.

Explanation-Based Learning. Ed. by Gerald DeJong. 225p. 1988. pap. text ed. 20.00x o.p. (ISBN 0-929280-05-9). Amer Artificial.

Explanation of Culture Change: Models in Prehistory. Ed. by Colin Renfrew. LC 73-10034. 1974. 65.00x o.p. (ISBN 0-8229-1111-6). U of Pittsburgh Pr.

Explanation of Economic Recovery Tax Act of 1981. 128p. 1981. member 5.00 o.p. (ISBN 0-686-48354-5); non-member 7.00 o.p. (ISBN 0-686-48355-3). Am Consul Eng.

Explanation of Tax Equity & Fiscal Responsibility Act of 1982. 152p. 1982. member 7.00 o.p. (ISBN 0-686-48360-X); non-member 10.00 o.p. (ISBN 0-686-48361-8). Am Consul Eng.

Explanation of the Tax Reform Act of 1986. 672p. 1986. 30.00 o.p. (55); members 10.00 o.p. Am Consul Eng.

Explanation, Prediction & Planning: The Lowry Model. M. J. Webber. 250p. 1983. 25.00 o.p. (ISBN 0-85086-099-7, NO. 5056). Routledge Chapman & Hall.

Exploding Frog. McFarland. Date not set. (ISBN 0-316-55576-2). Little.

Exploding the Myth: Caregiving in America, A Study, January 1987. 61p. (Orig.). 1987. pap. 2.50 o.p. (ISBN 0-318-23456-4, S/N 052-070-06342-4). USGPO.

Exploitation, Conservation, Preservation: A Geographic Perspective on Natural Resource Use. Susan L. Cutter et al. LC 84-18298. (Illus.). 468p. 1985. 25.00x o.s.i. (ISBN 0-86598-129-9, Rowman & Allanheld). Rowman.

Exploitation of Illness in Capitalist Society. Howard Waitakin & Barbara Waterman. 1974. pap. text ed. (ISBN 0-02-424540-2). Macmillan.

Exploitation of Marine Communities. Ed. by R. M. May. (Dahlem Workshop Reports Ser.: Vol. 32). (Illus.). 370p. 1985. 24.00 o.p. (ISBN 0-387-15028-5). Springer-Verlag.

Exploits of Moominpappa. Tove Jansson. 1978. pap. 1.50 o.p. (ISBN 0-380-01910-8, 41665, Camelot). Avon.

Exploracion Intercultural: Una Guia para el Estudiante. Virginia V. Zanger. 1984. pap. text ed. 9.00 o.p. (ISBN 0-88377-430-5). Newbury Hse.

Exploration in Humans & Animals. J. Archer & L. Birke. 1983. 41.95 o.p. (ISBN 0-442-30527-3). Van Nos Reinhold.

Exploration of the Universe. 4th ed. George Abell. 1982. text ed. 36.95 o.p. (CBS C); instr's manual 21.50 o.s.i. (ISBN 0-03-058503-1). SCP.

Exploration of the Universe. 4th ed. George O. Abell. 1982. 39.95 o.p. (HoltC). HR&W.

Exploration of Time. R. N. Bowen. (Illus.). 138p. 1958. (ISBN 0-8022-0162-8). Philos Lib.

Exploration of Western America, Eighteen Hundred to Eighteen Fifty. Edmund W. Gilbert. LC 65-26291. (Illus.). 1966. Repr. of 1933 ed. 23.50x o.p. (ISBN 0-8154-0079-9). Cooper Sq.

Explorations in Aerospace Law: Selected Essays by John Cobb Cooper, 1946-1966. Ed. by Ivan A. Vlasic. 500p. 1968. 15.00x o.p. (ISBN 0-7735-0032-4, McGill Canada). U of Toronto Pr.

Explorations in Child Psychiatry. Ed. by E. James Anthony. LC 75-2308. 520p. 1975. 49.50x o.p. (ISBN 0-306-30819-3, Plenum Pr). Plenum Pub.

Explorations in Economics. James F. Willis & Martin L. Primack. LC 76-13973. (Illus.). 1977. text ed. 23.25 o.p. (ISBN 0-395-24524-9). HM.

Explorations in Ethnohistory: Indians of Central Mexico in the Sixteenth Century. Ed. by H. R. Harvey & Hanns J. Prem. LC 83-16853. (Illus.). 321p. 1984. 35.00x o.p. (ISBN 0-8263-0712-4). U of NM Pr.

Explorations in Ethnomusicology: Essays in Honor of David Mcallister. Ed. by Charlotte Erisbie. LC 86-21291. (Detroit Monographs in Musicology Ser.: No. 9). 1987. 35.00 o.p. (ISBN 0-89990-030-5). Harmonie Pk Pr.

Explorations in Hittite Asia Minor, Nineteen Twenty-Nine. Hans H. Von der Osten. LC 28-3839. (Oriental Institute Pubns. Ser). (Illus.). 1930. pap. text ed. 12.00x o.s.i. (ISBN 0-226-62324-6, OIC8). U of Chicago Pr.

Explorations in Personal Health. Michael S. Haro et al. LC 76-10900. (Illus.). 1977. text ed. 24.50 o.p. (ISBN 0-395-24478-1). HM.

Explorations in Sociolinguistics. 3rd ed. Ed. by Stanley Lieberson. LC 67-65323. (General Publications Ser: Vol. 44). (Orig.). 1971. pap. text ed. 15.00 o.p. (ISBN 0-87750-132-7). Res Ctr Lang Semiotic.

Explorations in Space & Time: A Series of Computer-Generated Astronomy Films, Filmnotes. M. L. Meeks. 1974. pap. 3.00 o.p. (ISBN 0-395-18866-0). HM.

Explorations in the Development of Writing: Theory, Research, & Practice. Ed. by Barry M. Kroll & Gordon Wells. LC 82-23774. 293p. 1983. 71.95x o.p. (ISBN 0-471-90136-9, Wiley-Interscience). Wiley.

Explorations in the Nonclassical Ion Area. Herbert C. Brown. 1976. pap. 12.75 o.p. (ISBN 0-08-020488-0). Pergamon.

Explorations in Time-Limited Counseling & Therapy. Charles J. Gelso & Deborah H. Johnson. (Guidance & Counseling Ser.). 300p. 1983. text ed. 25.95x o.p. (ISBN 0-8077-2726-1). Tchrs Coll.

Explorations in Urban Land Economics. Ed. by John J. Sullivan. LC 79-119693. 122p. 1970. pap. 2.50 o.s.i. (ISBN 0-686-01014-0). Lincoln Inst Land.

Explorations in Zoology. Larry G. Sellers et al. 203p. (Orig.). 1980. pap. 12.95 lab manual o.p. (ISBN 0-89459-122-3). Hunter Textbks.

Explorations into Teaching & Learning: School Based Teacher Education. Ed. by James R. Gress & James E. Kerber. 1976. pap. text ed. 5.00 o.p. (ISBN 0-89039-182-3). Ann Arbor Pubs.

Exploratory Drilling. B. Vozdvizhensky. 510p. 1982. 11.95 o.p. (ISBN 0-8285-2312-6, Pub. by Mir Pubs USSR). Imported Pubns.

Exploratory Electricity. Ed. by Joseph Arnold & Kenneth Schank. (gr. 9-12). 1960. text ed. 5.28 o.p. (ISBN 0-87345-276-3). Glencoe.

Exploratory Study on Responsibility, Liability & Accountability for Risks in Construction. Building Research Advisory Board Staff. 1978. pap. 8.25x o.p. (ISBN 0-309-02791-8). Natl Acad Pr.

Explore Australia: Touring for Leisure & Pleasure. 3rd. ed. Currey O'Neil. (Illus.). 400p. 1984. 29.95 o.p. (ISBN 0-85550-498-6). Salem Hse Pubs.

Explore Australia: Touring for Leisure & Pleasure. 5th ed. Currey O'Neil. (Illus.). 400p. 1987. 29.95 o.p. (ISBN 0-85550-494-3). Salem Hse Pubs.

Explore the Bible Yourself: Firsthand Joy. Richard V. Yohn. LC 81-83318. 72p. 1981. 3.95 o.p. (ISBN 0-89109-076-2). NavPress.

Explore the Word! Henry Morris, 3rd. LC 78-55611. 1978. pap. 7.95 o.p. (ISBN 0-89051-047-4). Master Bks.

Explore Your Psychic World. Ambrose A. Worrall & Olga N. Worrall. LC 79-85062. 1970. pap. 6.68i o.p. (ISBN 0-06-069686-9); pap. 3.95 o.p. (ISBN 0-686-96729-1, RD 156). HarpR.

Explorers of the Black Box: The Search for the Cellular Basis of Memory. Susan Allport. 1986. 17.45 o.p. (ISBN 0-393-02322-2). Norton.

Exploring a Career in Home Economics. James Hahn & Lynn Hahn. (Careers in Depth Ser.). 140p. (gr. 7-12). 1981. lib. bdg. 9.97 o.p. (ISBN 0-8239-0530-6). Rosen Group.

Exploring America's Valleys: From Shenandoah to the Rio Grande. Ed. by Donald J. Crump. (Special Publications Series 19: No. 1). 200p. 1984. 7.95 o.p. (ISBN 0-87044-476-X); PLB 9.50 o.p. (ISBN 0-87044-481-6). Natl Geog.

Exploring Biology with Microcomputers. Ed. by Christopher Smith. (Orig.). 1985. pap. text ed. 28.50x o.p. (ISBN 0-86184-129-8). Trans Atl Phila.

Exploring Black America. Marcella Thum. LC 74-19428. (gr. 7 up). 1975. 10.95 o.p. (ISBN 0-689-30462-5, Atheneum). Macmillan.

Exploring Books with Children. Iris M. Tiedt. LC 78-69530. (Illus.). 1979. text ed. 29.95 o.p. (ISBN 0-395-25498-1). HM.

Exploring Careers As a Carpenter. Marilyn Jones. (Careers Ser.). 139p. (gr. 7-12). 1985. 9.97 o.p. (ISBN 0-8239-0624-8). Rosen Group.

Exploring Careers As a Chiropractor. rev. ed. G. Howard Poteet & Michael A. Petti. (Careers in Depth Ser.). (YA) (gr. 7-12). 1984. PLB 9.97 o.p. (ISBN 0-8239-0383-4). Rosen Group.

Exploring Careers in Advertising. Jules Singer & Larry Deckinger. (Careers in Depth Ser.). 169p. (gr. 7-12). 1985. lib. bdg. 9.97 o.p. (ISBN 0-8239-0625-6). Rosen Group.

Exploring Careers in Cable-TV. David Berlyn. (Careers in Depth Ser.). (Illus.). 128p. 1985. lib. bdg. 10.97 o.p. (ISBN 0-8239-0666-3). Rosen Group.

Exploring Careers in Child Care. McKnight Staff. LC 74-82448. (gr. 8-12). 1974. text ed. 16.64 o.p. (ISBN 0-87345-573-8); teacher's guide 32.00 o.p. (ISBN 0-87345-576-2); activity manual 6.64 o.p. (ISBN 0-87345-574-6). Glencoe.

Exploring Careers in Child Care Services. rev. ed. Jean Ispa. (Careers in Depth Ser.). 126p. (gr. 7-12). 1986. lib. bdg. 9.97 o.p. (ISBN 0-8239-0556-X). Rosen Group.

Exploring Careers in Communications & Telecommunications. John Zacharis. 161p. (gr. 7-12). 1985. 9.97 o.p. (ISBN 0-8239-0644-2). Rosen Group.

Exploring Careers in Community & Public Health. Lois S. Sigel. (Careers in Depth Ser.). 135p. (gr. 7-12). 1984. lib. bdg. 10.95 o.p. (ISBN 0-8239-0621-3). Rosen Group.

Exploring Careers in Engineering. Deborah D. Stine. (Illus.). 153p. (gr. 7-12). 1986. lib. bdg. 9.97 o.p. (ISBN 0-8239-0660-4). Rosen Group.

Exploring Careers in Hospital & Health Services Administration. W. Richard Kirk. 1983. 9.97 o.p. (ISBN 0-8239-0552-7); lib. bdg. 7.97 o.p. Rosen Group.

Exploring Careers in Hospitality & Food Service. McKnight Staff. LC 75-18678. (gr. 8-12). 1975. text ed. 19.68 o.p. (ISBN 0-87345-605-X); teacher's guide 34.64 o.p. (ISBN 0-87345-606-8). Glencoe.

Exploring Careers in Industry. Miller et al. LC 74-14422. (gr. 7-9). 1975. text ed. 18.64 o.p. (ISBN 0-87345-108-2). Glencoe.

Exploring Careers in Library Science. Lynne Anderson. Ed. by R. Rosen. (Careers Ser.). 135p. (YA) (gr. 7-12). 1987. PLB 10.95 o.p. (ISBN 0-317-59345-5). Rosen Group.

Exploring Careers in Nursing. Jackie Heron. 1987. 10.95 o.p. (ISBN 0-8239-0689-2). Rosen Group.

Exploring Careers in Research & Development in Industry. Mary P. Lee. (Careers in Depth Ser.). (Illus.). 140p. (gr. 7-12). 1983. lib. bdg. 9.97 o.p. (ISBN 0-8239-0601-9). Rosen Group.

Exploring Careers in Tool & Die Making. Carl Fields. 136p. (gr. 7-12). 1985. 9.97 o.p. (ISBN 0-8239-0633-7). Rosen Group.

Exploring Careers in Word Processing. rev. ed. Phyllis Peck & Gilbert Konkel. Ed. by R. Rosen. (Exploring Careers Ser.). 113p. (YA) (gr. 7-12). 1985. PLB 9.97 o.p. (ISBN 0-317-59350-1). Rosen Group.

Exploring Careers Through Part-Time & Summer Employment. 2nd rev. ed. Charlotte Lobb. 144p. (gr. 7-12). 1982. PLB 9.97 o.p. (ISBN 0-8239-0371-0). Rosen Group.

Exploring Careers Through Volunteerism. Rev. ed. Charlotte Lobb. LC 75-28325. (gr. 7-12). 1979. 9.97 o.p. (ISBN 0-8239-0334-6). Rosen Group.

Exploring Clinical Methods for Social Research. David N. Berg & Kennwyn K. Smith. 1985. 30.00 o.p. (ISBN 0-8039-2432-1). Sage.

Exploring Construction Occupations. Charles S. Winn et al. (Careers in Focus Ser.). 1975. text ed. 13.76 o.p. (ISBN 0-07-071021-X). McGraw.

Exploring Contemporary Male-Female Roles: A Facilitator's Guide. Ed. by Clarke G. Carney & Sarah L. McMahon. LC 76-58237. 276p. 1977. pap. 7.95 o.p. (ISBN 0-88390-135-8). Univ Assocs.

Exploring Data Analysis: The Computer Revolution in Statistics. W. J. Dixon & W. L. Nicholson. LC 73-85786. 1974. 37.50x o.p. (ISBN 0-520-02470-2). U of Cal Pr.

Exploring Electricity & Electronics With Projects. John Edwards. (Illus.). 208p. (Orig.). 1983. 15.95 o.p. (ISBN 0-8306-0497-9, 1497); pap. 9.95 o.p. (ISBN 0-8306-1497-4). TAB Bks.

Exploring English with Microcomputers. Ed. by Daniel Chandler. (Orig.). 1983. pap. text ed. 14.95x o.p. (ISBN 0-86184-102-6). Trans Atl Phila.

Exploring Fabrics. McKnight Staff. LC 76-53072. (gr. 7-12). 1977. text ed. 18.36 o.p. (ISBN 0-87345-613-0); tchr's ed. 42.67 o.p. (ISBN 0-87345-615-7). Glencoe.

Exploring Geography with Microcomputers. Ed. by Deryn Watson. (Orig.). 1984. pap. text ed. 23.50x o.p. (ISBN 0-86184-119-0). Trans Atl Phila.

Exploring Hawaii, 2 bks. William Webb & Mary Webb. Incl. Bk. I. Ohau; Bk. II. Maui. (Illus.). 1978. pap. 2.95 ea. o.p. Island Heritage.

Exploring Health Occupations. Charles S. Winn et al. (Careers in Focus Ser.). 1976. text ed. 20.96 o.p. (ISBN 0-07-071027-9). McGraw.

Exploring History with Microcomputers. Ed. by John Wilkes. (Orig.). 1985. pap. text ed. 26.00x o.p. (ISBN 0-86184-137-9). Trans Atl Phila.

Exploring in Physics: A New Outlook on Problems in Physics. Reginald J. Stephenson. (Midway Reprint Ser). 1974. pap. text ed. 4.25x o.s.i. (ISBN 0-226-77276-4). U of Chicago Pr.

Exploring Junior High School Guidance. Indiana Public School Study Council Staff. LC 65-17603. 68p. 1965. pap. text ed. 1.50x o.p. (ISBN 0-8134-6202-9, 6202). Inter Print Pubs.

Exploring Korea. Ruth C. Burkholder & Carrie L. Goddard. (Illus.). 17p. (Orig.). 1984. pap. 3.95 o.p. (ISBN 0-377-00142-2). Friendship Pr.

Exploring Language. 4th ed. Gary Goshgarian. 1986. pap. text ed. write for info. o.p. (ISBN 0-673-39211-2); tchr's. manual avail. o.p. Scott F.

Exploring Language Arts in the Elementary Classroom. John W. Stewig. 1983. text ed. 31.95 o.p. (ISBN 0-03-057462-5). HR&W.

Exploring Living Environments. McKnight Staff. LC 77-82245. (gr. 7-12). 1977. text ed. 17.28 o.p. (ISBN 0-87345-619-X); tchr's ed. 38.60 o.p. (ISBN 0-87345-620-3). Glencoe.

Exploring Marketing Occupations. Charles S. Winn et al. (Careers in Focus Ser). (Illus.). 160p. (gr. 6-9). 1976. text ed. 14.88 o.p. (ISBN 0-07-071039-2). McGraw.

Exploring Mathematics with Microcomputers. Ed. by Nigel Bufton. (Orig.). 1986. pap. text ed. 26.00x o.p. (ISBN 0-86184-162-X). Trans Atl Phila.

Exploring Medical Language: A Student-Directed Approach. Lafleur & Starr. 1984. pap. 24.95 o.p. (ISBN 0-8016-2812-1). Mosby.

Exploring Military Service for Women. Mary M. Slappey. (Miltary Opportunity Ser.). (Illus.). 168p. (YA) (gr. 9-12). 1986. PLB 14.95 o.p. (ISBN 0-8239-0693-0). Rosen Group.

Exploring Nature with Your Child. Dorothy Shuttlesworth. (Illus.). 240p. (gr. k-12). 1983. pap. 9.95 o.p. (ISBN 0-86683-747-7, AY8383). HarpR.

Exploring New World. (Our Nations Heritage Ser.). Date not set. (ISBN 0-07-375392-0). McGraw.

Exploring Occupations in Agribusiness & Natural Resources. Charles S. Winn et al. (Careers in Focus Ser.). 1975. text ed. 14.88 o.p. (ISBN 0-07-071043-0). McGraw.

Exploring Occupations in Communication & Graphic Arts. Charles S. Winn et al. (Careers in Focus Ser.). 1976. text ed. 14.88 o.p. (ISBN 0-07-071031-7). McGraw.

Exploring Occupations in Electricity & Electronics. Charles S. Winn & L. Heath. (Careers in Focus Ser.). 1975. text ed. 14.88 o.p. (ISBN 0-07-071025-2). McGraw.

Exploring Occupations in Engineering & Manufacturing. Charles S. Winn et al. (Careers in Focus Ser.). 1976. text ed. 15.12 o.p. (ISBN 0-07-071035-X). McGraw.

Exploring Occupations in Food Service & Home Economics. Charles S. Winn & M. C. Baker. (Careers in Focus Ser.). 1975. text ed. 14.88 o.p. (ISBN 0-07-071041-4). McGraw.

Exploring Occupations in Personal Services, Hospitality & Recreation. Charles S. Winn & B. J. Vorndran. (Careers in Focus Ser.). 1975. text ed. 14.88 o.p. (ISBN 0-07-071033-3). McGraw.

Exploring Occupations in Public & Social Services. Charles S. Winn et al. (Careers in Focus Ser.). 1975. text ed. 14.88 o.p. (ISBN 0-07-071029-5). McGraw.

Exploring Occupations in Science, Fine Arts & Humanities. Charles S. Winn & L. M. Davis. (Careers in Focus Ser.). 1975. text ed. 14.88 o.p. (ISBN 0-07-071045-7). McGraw.

Exploring Offbeat Jobs. Marilyn Jones. Ed. by Ruth Rosen. (Careers Ser.). (Illus.). 144p. (gr. 7 up). 1987. lib. bdg. 9.97 o.p. (ISBN 0-8239-0690-6). Rosen Group.

Exploring Our Environment: Animals Student Materials One. Sally DeRoo. (Exploring Our Environment Ser.). (Illus.). 22p. (gr. 3-6). 1979. wkbk. 1.00 o.p. (ISBN 0-87879-828-5). Ann Arbor Pubs.

Exploring Photography. Robert Walker. 1983. 14.64 o.p. (ISBN 0-87006-430-4). Goodheart.

Exploring Primary Science & Technology with Microconputers. Ed. by Jan Stewart. (Orig.). 1985. pap. text ed. 21.50x o.p. (ISBN 0-86184-136-0). Trans Atl Phila.

Exploring Religious Meaning. 2nd ed. Robert C. Monk et al. (Illus.). 1980. pap. text ed. (ISBN 0-13-297515-7). P-H.

Exploring Science in the Elementary School. Donald P. Kauchak & Paul Eggen. 1980. pap. 26.95 o.p. (ISBN 0-395-30643-4). HM.

Exploring Social Psychology. 2nd ed. Robert A. Baron & Donn Byrne. 384p. pap. text ed. 28.00 o.p. (ISBN 0-205-07606-8, 797606); instr's. manual avail. o.p. (ISBN 0-205-07607-6). Allyn.

Exploring Solar Energy: Principles & Projects. Allan Kaufman. LC 86-60262. (Illus.). (YA) (gr. 7-12). 1986. pap. 7.95x o.p. (ISBN 0-911168-60-5). Prakken.

Exploring Space & Atoms. LC 83-26623. (Science Universe Ser.). (Illus.). 64p. (gr. 5 up). 1984. 9.95 o.p. (ISBN 0-668-06175-8, 6175-8). Arco.

Exploring Speech Communication: An Introduction. Mary Forrest & Margot Olson. 424p. 1981. pap. text ed. 25.00 o.p. (ISBN 0-8299-0381-X). West Pub.

Exploring Technology. E. Allen Bame & Paul Cummings. LC 79-53783. (Technology Series). (Illus.). 288p. 1980. text ed. 14.95 o.p. (ISBN 0-87192-112-X, 000-3); tchr's. guide 13.25 o.p. (ISBN 0-87192-114-6); activity manual 10.95 o.p. (ISBN 0-87192-113-8). Davis Mass.

Exploring the Basics: Readings in Psychology. D. Sanzotta et al. LC 73-6751. 1973. pap. text ed. 4.75x o.p. (ISBN 0-8422-0310-9). Irvington.

Exploring the Galaxies. Simon Mitton. LC 76-42913. (Encore Edition). (Illus.). 1978. pap. 1.95 o.p. (ISBN 0-684-16912-6, ScribT). Scribner.

Exploring the Great Basin. Gloria G. Cline. LC 83-22871. xviii, 254p. 1984. Repr. of 1963 ed. lib. bdg. 38.50x o.p. (ISBN 0-313-24241-0, CLEX). Greenwood.

Exploring the Heart: Discoveries in Heart Disease & High Blood Pressure. Julius H. Comroe, Jr. LC 83-2145. (Illus.). 352p. 1984. 18.45 o.p. (ISBN 0-393-01708-7). Norton.

Exploring the Little Rivers of New Jersey. 3rd rev. ed. Margaret Cawley & James Cawley. 1971. pap. 8.95 o.p. (ISBN 0-8135-0685-9). Rutgers U Pr.

Exploring the NEC PC 8201A. Marvin C. Mallon. LC 84-17516. 128p. 1985. pap. text ed. 14.95 o.p. (ISBN 0-03-000358-X, HoltC). HR&W.

Exploring the New Management. 3rd ed. Robert M. Fulmer & Theodore T. Herbert. 320p. 1983. text ed. write for info. o.p. (ISBN 0-02-340080-3). Macmillan.

Exploring the New Testament. Rachel Henderlite. (Orig.). (gr. 6 up). 1946. pap. 5.95 o.p. (ISBN 0-8042-0240-0, John Knox). Westminster John Knox.

Exploring the Ocean Depths. Edward H. Shenton. (Illus.). 1968. 6.95 o.p. (ISBN 0-393-06363-1). Norton.

Exploring the Old Testament. Rachel Henderlite. (Orig.). (gr. 6 up). 1945. pap. 5.95 o.p. (ISBN 0-8042-0120-X, John Knox). Westminster John Knox.

Exploring the Parenthood Choice: An Activities Guide for Educators. National Alliance for Optional Parenthood Staff. 78p. 1981. spiral bd. 8.95 o.p. (ISBN 0-941816-10-9). Network Pubns.

Exploring the PICK Operating System. Jonathan Sisk & Steven Van Arsdale. 29.95 o.p. (ISBN 0-8104-6286-9). Sams.

Exploring the Road Less Traveled. Walden Howard & Alice Howard. 1985. pap. 5.95 o.s.i. (ISBN 0-671-54292-3). S&S.

Exploring the Santa Barbara Back Country. Illus. by Dennis Gagnon. pap. text ed. 5.95 o.p. (ISBN 0-317-65369-5). Western Tanager.

Exploring the Violent Earth. Jonathan Rutland. LC 79-55265. (gr. 3-5). 1979. 2.95 o.p. (ISBN 0-531-09177-5, Warwick Press); PLB 7.90 o.p. (ISBN 0-531-09167-8). Watts.

Exploring the Visual Arts. Burton Wasserman. Ed. by George F. Horn & Sarita R. Rainey. LC 76-19938. (Books in Art Education). (Illus.). (YA) (gr. 10 up). 1976. 17.95 o.p. (ISBN 0-87192-085-9). Davis Mass.

Exploring the World of Plastics. Gerald L. Steele. LC 75-42964. (gr. 8-12). 1977. text ed. 19.96 o.p. (ISBN 0-87345-411-1). Glencoe.

Exploring Theatre & Education. Ed. by Ken Robinson. 1980. text ed. 12.50x o.p. (ISBN 0-435-18780-5); pap. text ed. 15.00x o.p. (ISBN 0-435-18781-3). Heinemann Ed.

Exploring Transportation Occupations. Charles S. Winn & Lawrence A. Walsh. (Careers in Focus Ser.). 1976. text ed. 14.88 o.p. (ISBN 0-07-071023-6). McGraw.

Exploring Tropical Isles & Seas: An Introduction for the Traveler & Amateur Naturalist. Frederic Martini. (Illus.). 384p. 1984. 27.95 o.p. (ISBN 0-13-295949-6); pap. 15.95 o.p. (ISBN 0-13-295931-3). P-H.

Exploring University Mathematics, 3 Vols. N. J. Hardiman. 1969. Vol. 2. 1968. 35.00 o.p. (ISBN 0-08-012567-0); Vol. 3. 1969. 35.00 o.p. (ISBN 0-08-012903-X); Vol. 1. 1967. 23.00 o.p. (ISBN 0-08-011990-5); Vol. 3 1969. pap. 35.00 o.p. (ISBN 0-08-012902-1); Vol. 1. pap. 9.25 o.p. (ISBN 0-08-011991-3); Vol. 2 1968. pap. text ed. 7.75 o.p. (ISBN 0-08-012566-2). Pergamon.

Explosion: The Day Texas City Died. Walter Brough & Michael Sutton. 1980. pap. 2.75 o.p. (ISBN 0-380-75838-5, 75838-5). Avon.

Explosions: Course, Prevention, Protection. W. Bartknecht. Tr. by H. Burg & T. Almond. (Illus.). 251p. 1981. 76.50 o.p. (ISBN 0-387-10216-7). Springer-Verlag.

Explosive Nucleosynthesis: Proceedings of the Conference on Explosive Nucleosynthesis Held in Austin, Texas, on April 2-3, 1973. Ed. by David N. Schramm & W. David Arnett. 313p. 1973. 17.95x o.p. (ISBN 0-292-72006-8); pap. 9.95x o.p. (ISBN 0-292-72007-6). U of Tex Pr.

Explosive Welding, Forming, Plugging, & Compaction. Ed. by I. Berman & J. W. Schroeder. (PVP: No. 44). 119p. 1980. 20.00 o.p. (ISBN 0-686-69850-9, H00171). ASME.

Export Finance. A. Dunn & M. Knight. 154p. 1983. pap. 120.00 o.p. (ISBN 0-8002-3400-6). Intl Pubns Serv.

Export of Capital. C. K. Hobson. LC 82-48309. (World Economy Ser.). 261p. 1983. lib. bdg. 33.00 o.p. (ISBN 0-8240-5364-8). Garland Pub.

Export Promotion Policies. Barend A. de Vries. (Working Paper: No. 313). v, 75p. 1979. 6.95 o.p. (ISBN 0-8213-9196-8, WP-0313). World Bank.

Export Trading Company Act of 1982. Pennsylvania Bar Institute Staff. 134p. 1983. 25.00 o.p. (ISBN 0-318-02161-7, 234). PA Bar Inst.

Exporter's Guide to Federal Resources for Small Business Exporters. Compiled by Stanley B. Parrish et al. 125p. (Orig.). 1988. pap. 3.50 o.p. (S/N 045-000-00248-9). USGPO.

Exporting: A Practical Manual for Developing Export Markets & Coping with Foreign Customs. 2nd ed. Ernest Y. Maitland. 150p. 1982. 12.50 o.p. (ISBN 0-88908-098-4). ISC Pr.

Exporting Behavior of Manufacturing Firms. Somkid Jatusripitak. Ed. by Richard Farmer. LC 85-22755. (Research for Business Decisions Ser.: No. 87). 130p. 1985. 39.95 o.p. (ISBN 0-8357-1723-2). UMI Res Pr.

Exporting for Small & Medium Sized Firms. Daniel Enet. 150p. 1977. text ed. 22.00x o.p. (ISBN 0-220-66329-7, Pub. by Busn Bks England). Gower Pub Co.

Exporting from the U. S. A. How to Develop Export Markets & Cope with Foreign Customs. A. B. Manning. 114p. (Orig.). 1981. pap. 12.95 o.p. (ISBN 0-88908-908-6, 9502, Pub. by Intl Self-Counsel Pr). TAB Bks.

Exporting: Practical Guide for Entrepreneurs & Managers. rev. ed. Allan J. Siposs. (Business & Management Bks.). (Illus., Orig.). Date not set. pap. 30.00 o.p. (ISBN 0-935402-26-8). IBMI Irvine.

Exposition Commemorative du 150e Anniversaire de la Mort de Balzac. Honore De Balzac. (Illus.). 144p. 17.50 o.p. (ISBN 0-686-53870-6). French & Eur.

Exposition: Critical Writing & Thinking. Robert J. Gula. 210p. 1984. pap. 5.95 o.p. (ISBN 0-88334-177-8). Ind Sch Pr.

Exposition of the Gospels, 2 vol. Philip Doddridge. 1986. Set. 37.50 o.p. (ISBN 0-8254-2456-9). Vol. I, 472pgs. Vol. II, 492pgs. Kregel.

Expository Dictionary of New Testament Words. W. E. Vine. 1396p. 14.95 o.p. (ISBN 0-8007-0089-9); thumb index ed. 16.95 o.p. (ISBN 0-8007-0090-2). Revell.

Expository Dictionary of New Testament Words. W. E. Vine. 1392p. (Orig.). 1981. pap. 12.95 o.p. (ISBN 0-310-33781-X, 6795P). Zondervan.

Expository Preaching. Robert Shannon & J. Michael Shannon. 128p. (Orig.). 1982. pap. 5.95 o.p. (ISBN 0-87239-605-3, 3020). Standard Pub.

Expression of Results in Quantum Chemistry. Ed. by D. H. Whiffen. 1978. pap. 35.00 o.p. (ISBN 0-08-022367-2). Pergamon.

Expression of the Emotions in Man & Animal. Charles Darwin. 416p. 1955. (ISBN 0-8022-0341-8). Philos Lib.

Expressionism. R. S. Furness. (Critical Idiom Ser.). 100p. 1973. pap. 5.50 o.p. (ISBN 0-416-75670-0, 2207). Routledge Chapman & Hall.

Expressionism in Art. new ed. Sheldon Cheney. LC 79-131276. (Illus.). 1970. 10.95x o.p. (ISBN 0-87140-530-X); pap. 5.95 o.p. (ISBN 0-87140-233-5, 1970). Liveright.

Expressions of Love & Nature. George W. Nelson, Jr. 80p. 6.00 o.p. (ISBN 0-682-40140-4). Exposition-Phoenix.

Exquisite Thing. Joyce MacIver. 1977. pap. 1.75 o.p. (ISBN 0-380-00923-4, 31856). Avon.

Extant Medieval Musical Instruments: A Provisional Catalogue by Types. Frederick Crane. LC 72-185993. (Illus.). 120p. 1972. text ed. 10.00x o.p. (ISBN 0-87745-022-6). U of Iowa Pr.

Extend: Youth Reaching Youth. Kenneth Fletcher et al. LC 74-77684. 112p. (Orig.). 1974. pap. 6.50 o.p. (ISBN 0-8066-1435-8, 10-2150, Augsburg). Augsburg Fortress.

Extended Wear Contact Lenses: For Aphakia & Myopia. Jack Hartstein. LC 85-18954. (Illus.). 288p. 1982. text ed. 46.00 cloth o.p. (ISBN 0-8016-2109-7). Mosby.

Extending Canadian Health Insurance: Options for Pharmacare & Denticare. R. G. Evans & M. F. Williamson. (Ontario Economic Council Research Studies). 1978. pap. 14.00x o.p. (ISBN 0-8020-3353-9). U of Toronto Pr.

Extending the Benefits of Vocational Education to Indian Populations: Integrated Planning Package. Carol J. Minugh & Miller R. Tiger. 175p. 1980. 15.00 o.p. (ISBN 0-318-15473-0, RD183). Natl Ctr Res Voc Ed.

Extending the Educational Ladder: The Quality & the Postdoctoral Study. William Zumeta. LC 83-49457. 288p. 1984. 25.00x o.p. (ISBN 0-669-07819-0). Lexington Bks.

Extending Workplace Democracy - An Overview of Participatory Decisionmaking Plans for Unionists. Compiled by Andrew Nickelhoff. 87p. 1981. comb. binding 5.00 o.p. (ISBN 0-87736-343-9). U of Mich Inst Labor.

Extension Education & Rural Development, Vol. 1: International Experience in Communication & Innovation. Ed. by Bruce R. Crouch & Shankarish Chamala. LC 79-41221. 371p. 1981. 91.95x o.p. (ISBN 0-471-27829-7, Pub. by Wiley-Interscience). Wiley.

Extensions of Linear-Quadratic Control, Optimization & Matrix Theory. D. H. Jacobson. 1977. 46.50 o.p. (ISBN 0-12-378750-5). Acad Pr.

External Bonding of a Nonbonded Fiber Lay. (Bibliographic Ser.: No. S27). 56p. 1967. 8.00 o.p. (ISBN 0-317-34381-5). Inst Paper Chem.

External Construction by Animals. Ed. by Nicholas E. Collias & Elsie C. Collias. LC 75-34185. (Benchmark Papers in Animal Behavior: Vol. 4). 1976. 63.00 o.p. (ISBN 0-12-786250-1). Acad Pr.

External Degree. Cyril O. Houle. LC 73-3775. (Higher Education Ser). 1973. 24.95x o.p. (ISBN 0-87589-175-6). Jossey-Bass.

Extinct & Vanishing Animals: A Biology of Extinction & Survival. V. Ziswiler. Tr. by F. Bunnell & P. Bunnell. (Heidelberg Science Library: Vol. 2). 1967. pap. 6.50 o.p. (ISBN 0-387-90003-9). Springer-Verlag.

Extinct & Vanishing Birds of the World. 2nd ed. James C. Greenway, Jr. (Illus.). 15.25 o.p. (ISBN 0-8446-2164-1). Peter Smith.

Extra Cash for Kids. Larry Belliston & Kurt Hanks. LC 82-6892. 192p. (Orig.). (gr. 4 up). 1982. pap. 6.95 o.p. (ISBN 0-89879-082-4). Writers Digest.

Extra Lesson: Exercises in Movement, Drawing & Painting for Helping Children in Difficulties with Writing, Reading & Arithmetic. Audrey E. McAllen. (Illus.). 1987. pap. 17.50 o.p. (ISBN 0-904625-00-1, Pub. by Steiner Schools Fellowship England). St George Bk Serv.

Extra-Special Crockery Pot Recipes. rev. ed. Lou S. Pappas. LC 75-9644. (Illus.). 192p. 1982. pap. 6.95 o.p. (ISBN 0-911954-69-4). Bristol Pub Ent CA.

Extracellular Matrix Influences on Gene Expression. Ed. by Harold C. Slavkin & Richard C. Grevlich. 1975. 87.50 o.p. (ISBN 0-12-648360-4). Acad Pr.

Extraction of Useful Chemical Derivatives from Coal. Philip D. Swann et al. LC 74-26746. (Energy Ser.: Vol. 2). 188p. 1976. text ed. 38.00x o.p. (ISBN 0-8422-7263-1). Irvington.

Extraction with Supercritical Gases. Ed. by G. M. Schneider et al. (Illus.). 189p. 1980. lib. bdg. 48.80x o.p. (ISBN 3-527-25854-X). VCH Pubs.

Extractive Metallurgy. Dennis. 370p. 1966. (ISBN 0-8022-0380-9). Philos Lib.

Extractive Metallurgy: Developments since 1980. Ed. by M. J. Collie. LC 83-21996. (Chemical Technology Review Ser.: No. 227). (Illus.). 323p. 1984. 45.00 o.p. (ISBN 0-8155-0978-2). Noyes.

Extractive Metallurgy Laboratory Exercises. Ed. by H. Alan Fine. 165p. 32.00 o.p. (ISBN 0-89520-392-8); members 20.00 o.p. (ISBN 0-317-36215-1); student members 12.00 o.p. (ISBN 0-317-36216-X). ASM.

Extractive Metallurgy of Cooper: Proceedings of the AIME Annual Meeting, Las Vegas, NV, 1976. (Illus.). 1055p. 45.00 o.p. (ISBN 0-89520-103-8); members 32.00 o.p. (ISBN 0-317-34870-1); student members 16.00 o.p. (ISBN 0-317-34871-X). ASM.

Extractive Metallurgy of Refactory Metals: Proceedings of the AIME Annual Meeting, Chicago, 1981. (Illus.). 475p. 36.00 o.p. (ISBN 0-89520-371-5); members 24.00 o.p. (ISBN 0-317-36209-7); students 15.00 o.p. (ISBN 0-317-36210-0). ASM.

Extracts from a Journal Written on the Coast of Chile, Peru, & Mexico in the Years Eighteen Twenty, Eighteen Twenty-One, Eighteen Twenty-Two, 2 vols. 3rd ed. Basil Hall. 752p. 1968. Repr. of 1824 ed. Set. 40.00 o.p. (ISBN 0-8398-0755-4). Parnassus Imprints.

Extracts from the Records of Colchester with Some Transcripts from the Recording of Michaell Taintor of "Brainford", Conn. Michaell Taintor. Intro. by Charles M. Taintor. 172p. 1986. pap. 12.50 o.p. (ISBN 1-55613-023-6). Heritage Bk.

Extracurricular Homemaker. Jean T. Carver. 1979. 4.00 o.p. (ISBN 0-682-49256-6). Exposition-Phoenix.

Extrahepatic Biliary Atresia. Daum. (Gastroenterology Ser.). 336p. 1983. 59.75 o.p. (ISBN 0-8247-7017-X). Dekker.

Extraordinaire: Little Tidbits. Alexis Pub. Staff. (Illus.). 64p. 1984. pap. 5.00 o.p. (ISBN 0-682-40156-0). Exposition-Phoenix.

Extraordinary Black Book. 2nd ed. John Wade. (Development of Industrial Society Ser.). 608p. 1971. Repr. of 1834 ed. 55.00x o.p. (ISBN 0-7165-1588-1, BBA 03540, Pub. by Irish Academic Pr). Biblio Dist.

Extraordinary Boston. Steve Dunwell. Ed. by James Patrick. (Illus.). 128p. 1986. 30.00 o.p. (ISBN 0-89909-098-2). Yankee Bks.

Extraordinary Care. Dennis L. Breo. LC 86-18777. (Illus.). 300p. 17.95 o.p. (ISBN 0-914091-95-6). Chicago Review.

Extraordinary Lives. Robert A. Caro et al. Intro. by William Zinsser. 252p. 1986. 16.45 o.p. (ISBN 0-8281-1206-1, Am Heritage). HM.

Extraordinary Synod 1985. Intro. by Bernard Law. 2.50 o.s.i. (ISBN 0-8198-2315-5). Dghtrs St Paul.

Extraordinary Writs in Florida. Florida Bar Staff. LC 77-83093. 104p. 1979. pap. 10.00 o.p. (ISBN 0-910373-22-1, 247). FL Bar Legal Ed.

Extraretinal Photoreception in Circadian Rhythms & Related Phenoma: Proceedings of a Symposium, Vancouver. Ed. by Michael Menaker. 1976. pap. 26.00 o.p. (ISBN 0-08-020965-3). Pergamon.

Extrasensory Perception. CIBA Foundation. Ed. by G. E. Woltenholme & Elaine C. Emiller. 1966. pap. 2.75 o.p. (ISBN 0-8065-0155-3, 212, Pub. by Citadel Pr). Carol Pub Group.

Extraterrestrial Picture Activity Book. (Illus.). 48p. (Orig.). (gr. 1-4). 1982. pap. 1.90 o.s.i. (ISBN 0-671-45574-5, Little Simon). S&S.

Extraterritorial Discovery in International Litigation. (Litigation & Administrative Practice Course Handbook Ser.: Vol. 248). 578p. 1984. 15.00 o.p. (ISBN 0-317-11465-4, H4-4932). PLI.

Extraterritoriality in China: The Case Against Abolition. H. G. Woodhead et al. LC 78-74343. 189p. (The Growth & Decline of Rural Industrial Enterprise in North China. Extent & Effects of Industrialization in China the Modern Chinese Economy). 1980. lib. bdg. 26.00 o.p. (ISBN 0-8240-4280-8). Garland Pub.

Extravagant Gestures. Carole B. Sager. 1985. 16.95 o.p. (ISBN 0-87795-765-7, Arbor Hse). Morrow.

Extraversion & Introversion: An Interactional Perspective. Larry W. Morris. Ed. by C. D. Spielberger & I. G. Sarason. LC 79-16168. (Clinical & Community Psychology Ser.). 217p. 1979. 24.95x o.p. (ISBN 0-470-26805-0). Halsted Pr.

Extreme Environments: Mechanisms of Microbial Adaptation. Ed. by Milton R. Heinrich. 1976. 65.00 o.p. (ISBN 0-12-337850-8). Acad Pr.

Extreme Games & Their Solutions. J. Rosenmuller. LC 77-6655. (Lecture Notes in Economics & Mathematical Systems Ser: Vol. 145). 1977. pap. 13.00 o.p. (ISBN 0-387-08244-1). Springer-Verlag.

Extreme Weather History & Climate Atlas from Alabama. E. A. Carter & V. G. Seaquist. 350p. (Orig.). 1984. 15.95 o.p. (ISBN 0-317-04384-6); pap. 10.95 o.p. Strode.

Extremism in the United States: A Teaching Resource Focusing on Neo-Nazism. 140p. 1983. 7.95 o.p. (ISBN 0-8106-1420-0). NEA.

Extremos de America see American Extremes.

Exurbs: Urban Residential Developments in the Countryside. Dinker I. Patel. LC 79-48040. 151p. 1980. text ed. 24.25 o.p. (ISBN 0-8191-1001-9); pap. text ed. 10.25 o.p. (ISBN 0-8191-1002-7). U Pr of Amer.

Eye: A Light Receiver. Wilburn L. Sooter. LC 81-68313. 1981. pap. 3.95 o.p. (ISBN 0-89051-076-8); tchr's guide 2.95x o.p. Master Bks.

Eye & Ocular Adnexae. Robert H. Sagerman & David H. Abramson. (Illus.). 242p. 1982. pap. 135.00 o.p. (ISBN 0-08-027467-6, H230). Pergamon.

Eye Fooled You. Roy Doty. (Illus.). 48p. (gr. 3-7). 1983. pap. 2.95 o.s.i. (ISBN 0-02-042980-0, Collier). Macmillan.

Eye Listens. Paul Claudel. (ISBN 0-8022-0259-4). Philos Lib.

Eye Movements, Vision & Behavior: A Hierarchical Visual Information Processing Model. Kenneth R. Gaarder. LC 74-14710. 156p. 1975. 16.00 o.p. (ISBN 0-470-28895-7, Pub. by Wiley). Krieger.

Eye of Cat. Roger Zelazny. 1982. 13.50 o.s.i. (ISBN 0-671-25519-3, Timescapape). PB.

Eye of the Artist. Jack Clifton. LC 81-896. 1973. pap. 14.95 o.p. (ISBN 0-89134-034-3). North Light Bks.

Eye of the Beholder. Philip Glazebrook. LC 70-134809. 256p. 1976. 7.95 o.p. (ISBN 0-689-10737-4, Atheneum). Macmillan.

Eye of The Queen. Phillip Mann. 225p. 1983. 13.50 o.p. (ISBN 0-87795-462-3, Arbor Hse). Morrow.

Eye of the Storm. Joseph P. Bishop. 128p. (Orig.). 1983. pap. 3.95 o.p. (ISBN 0-87123-263-4, 210263). Bethany Hse.

Eye of the Tiger. Wilbur Smith. 1977. pap. 1.95 o.p. (ISBN 0-440-12406-9). Dell.

Eye on Cavett. Dick Cavett & Christopher Porterfield. (Illus.). 256p. 1983. 15.95 o.p. (ISBN 0-87795-463-1, Arbor Hse). Morrow.

Eye on the World. K. S. Tan. (Writing in Asia Ser.). 1975. pap. text ed. 5.00 o.p. (ISBN 0-686-60351-6). Heinemann Ed.

Eye Signs & Symptoms in Brain Tumors. 3rd ed. Alfred Huber. LC 76-28437. (Illus.). 440p. 1976. 47.50 o.p. (ISBN 0-8016-2302-2). Mosby.

Eye Surgery (Stallard) 6th ed. M. J. Roper-Hall. (Illus.). 916p. 1980. 101.00 o.p. (ISBN 0-7236-0515-7, Pub. by John Wright UK). Butterworth.

Eyes. Felice Picano. LC 75-13409. 1976. 8.95 o.p. (ISBN 0-87795-123-3, Arbor Hse). Morrow.

Eyes & Seeing. Joan E. Rahn. LC 80-23988. (Illus.). 128p. (gr. 5-9). 1981. 10.95 o.s.i. (ISBN 0-689-30828-0, Atheneum Childrens Bks). Macmillan.

Eyes Have It. Maxine Williams. LC 62-15648. 146p. 1962. pap. 1.75 o.p. (ISBN 0-88243-495-0, 02-0495). Gospel Pub.

Eyes of Eternity: A Spiritual Autobiography. Vesna Krmpotic. LC 78-23591. 1979. 10.95 o.s.i. (ISBN 0-15-129627-8). HarBraceJ.

Eyes of Jehovah: Life of James A. Harding. Lloyd C. Sears. 8.50 o.p. (ISBN 0-89225-089-5). Gospel Advocate.

Eyes of Texas CookBook. The Staff & Viewers of The Eyes of Texas. (Illus.). 224p. 1987. pap. 11.95 o.p. (ISBN 0-940672-43-X). Shearer Pub.

Eyes on the Universe: A History of the Telescope. Isaac Asimov. LC 75-15830. 288p. 1975. 8.95 o.s.i. (ISBN 0-395-19427-X). HM.

Eyewitness. John Minahan. 176p. (Orig.). 1981. pap. 2.25 o.p. (ISBN 0-380-77388-0, 77388). Avon.

Ezekiel, Second Isaiah. James L. Mays. Ed. by Foster R. McCurley. LC 77-15239. (Proclamation Commentaries, The Old Testament Witnesses for Preaching). 96p. (Orig.). 1978. pap. 4.95 o.p. (ISBN 0-8006-0592-6, 1-592, Fortress). Augsburg Fortress.

Ezra Pound. James F. Knapp. (United States Author Ser.). 1979. 16.95 o.s.i. (ISBN 0-8057-7286-3, Twayne). G K Hall.

Ezra Pound. Ed. by Grace Schulman. 160p. (Orig.). 1974. pap. text ed. 2.25 o.p. (ISBN 0-07-055634-2). McGraw.

Ezra Pound & the Pisan Cantos. Anthony Woodward. 1980. 21.95x o.p. (ISBN 0-7100-0372-2). Routledge Chapman & Hall.

Ezra Pound Perspectives: Essays in Honor of His Eightieth Birthday. Ed. by Noel Stock. LC 75-40995. 1977. Repr. of 1965 ed. lib. bdg. 22.50x o.p. (ISBN 0-8371-8712-5, STEP). Greenwood.

Ezra Pound: The Last Rower. C. David Heymann. (Seaver-Grove Bk.). 1980. pap. 6.95 o.p. (Ever). Grove.

Ezra Pound: The Last Rower. A Political Profile. C. David Heymann. LC 80-52073. 320p. 1980. pap. 6.95 o.p. Seaver Bks.

Ezra Pound's Cathay. Yipp Wai-Lim. LC 68-56325. 1969. 30.50x o.p. (ISBN 0-691-06161-0). Princeton U Pr.

F

F. A. N. Y. The Story of the Women's Transport Service 1907-1984. Hugh Popham. (Illus.). 276p. 1985. 34.95 o.p. (ISBN 0-436-36310-0, Pub. by Secker & Warburg UK). David & Charles.

F. B. Meyer Bible Commentary. F. B. Meyer. 645p. 1979. cloth 16.95 o.p. (ISBN 0-8423-4250-8). Tyndale.

F-Centers in Alkali Halides. Jordon J. Markham. (Solid State Physics Ser.: Suppl. 8). 1966. 92.00 o.p. (ISBN 0-12-607768-1). Acad Pr.

F D R: The Other Side of the Coin. Hamilton Fish. 255p. 1976. pap. 8.00 o.p. (Inst Hist Rev). Noontide.

F. L. Y. E. R. S. Fun Loving Youth en Route to Success. Lawrence Graham & Lawrence Hamdan. 1985. pap. 4.95 o.p. (ISBN 0-671-60369-8, Fireside). S&S.

F-Plus Diet. Audrey Eyton. 288p. 1985. 13.95 o.p. (ISBN 0-517-55738-X). Crown.

F. R. Leavis. William Walsh. LC 80-7971. 192p. 1980. 20.00x o.p. (ISBN 0-253-19426-1). Ind U Pr.

F. Scott Fitzgerald. rev. ed. Kenneth E. Eble. (United States Authors Ser.: No. 36). 192p. 1984. pap. 7.95 o.s.i. (ISBN 0-8057-7423-8, Twayne). G K Hall.

F T C Superstar. Mary Anderson. LC 75-30565. (Illus.). 176p. (gr. 4-6). 1976. 7.95 o.p. (ISBN 0-689-30497-8, Atheneum). Macmillan.

F-111 Aardvark in Detail & Scale. Bert Kinzey. LC 82-6829. (Detail & Scale Ser.: Vol. 4). (Illus.). 72p. (Orig.). 1982. pap. 8.95 o.p. (ISBN 0-8168-5014-3, 25014, TAB-Aero). TAB Bks.

F-4 Phantom II. Robert C. Stern. (Warbirds Illustrated Ser.: No.27). (Illus.). 1984. pap. 9.95 o.p. (ISBN 0-85368-670-X, Arms & Armour Pr). Sterling.

F 4-U Corsair at War. Richard Abrams. (Illus.). 160p. 1981. pap. 10.95 o.s.i. (ScribT); pap. 3.50 Encore ed. o.s.i. (ISBN 0-684-17013-2). Scribner.

Faber Book of Animal Stories. Ed. by Johnny Morris. 207p. (gr. 5 up). 1978. pap. 7.95 o.p. (ISBN 0-571-11221-8). Faber & Faber.

Faberge & His Contemporaries: The India Early Minshall Collection of The Cleveland Museum of Art. Henry Hawley. LC 67-28951. (Illus.). 148p. 1967. 10.00x o.p. (ISBN 0-910386-10-2, Pub. by Cleveland Mus Art). Ind U Pr.

Fabian Essays in Socialism. Ed. by George Bernard Shaw. 1967. 11.50 o.p. (ISBN 0-8446-1403-3). Peter Smith.

Fabiola; or, the Church of the Catacombs, 1854. Nicholas P. Wiseman. Ed. by Robert L. Wolff. LC 75-454. (Victorian Fiction Ser). 1976. lib. bdg. 73.00 o.p. (ISBN 0-8240-1533-9). Garland Pub.

Fabled Lands. Time-Life Books Editors. (Enchanted World Ser.). (Illus.). 144p. (YA) (gr. 7 up). 1986. 19.93 o.p.; lib. bdg. 23.93 o.p. Time-Life.

Fables. Mikhail E. Saltykov. Tr. by Vera Volkhovsky from Rus. LC 74-14115. 257p. 1976. Repr. of 1941 ed. lib. bdg. 35.00x o.p. (ISBN 0-8371-7790-1, SAFA). Greenwood.

Fables & Fabulists, Ancient & Modern. Thomas Newbigging. LC 70-78212. 164p. 1971. Repr. of 1895 ed. 34.00x o.p. (ISBN 0-8103-3770-3). Gale.

Fables & Parables. N. Y. Wales. 1952. (ISBN 0-8022-1794-X). Philos Lib.

Fables, Tales, Stories. Leo Tolstoy. 122p. 1973. pap. text ed. 1.95 o.p. (ISBN 0-8285-0616-7, Pub. by Progress Pubs USSR). Imported Pubns.

Fabric Forming Systems. Peter Schwartz et al. LC 82-7967. (Textile Ser.). (Illus.). 175p. 1983. 24.00 o.p. (ISBN 0-8155-0908-1). Noyes.

Fabric Frames from Stretch Bars. Susan A. Grosskopf. (Illus.). 40p. 1983. pap. 5.00 o.p. (ISBN 0-943574-19-6). That Patchwork.

Fabric Games. Lynn Mayne. 1978. 12.95 o.p. (ISBN 0-395-27084-7); pap. 6.95 o.p. (ISBN 0-395-27209-2). HM.

Fabric of Chinese Society. Morton H. Fried. LC 76-75993. 1969. Repr. of 1953 ed. lib. bdg. 20.00x o.p. (ISBN 0-374-92926-2, Octagon). Hippocrene Bks.

Fabric of Ducile Strain. Ed. by M. R. Stauffer. (Illus.). 399p. 1983. 56.95 o.p. (ISBN 0-87933-442-8). Van Nos Reinhold.

Fabric of the ERA: Congressional Intent. Marjorie Childs. (Illus.). 144p. 1982. 10.00 o.p. (ISBN 0-682-49864-5). Exposition-Phoenix.

Fabric Painting in Tole, Vol. 1. Kay Burdette. (Illus., Orig.). 1982. pap. 7.95 o.p. (ISBN 0-941284-16-6). Deco Design Studio.

Fabrication of Refractory Metals. Walter D. Wilkinson. LC 70-115054. 429p. 1970. 34.00 o.p. (ISBN 0-685-58269-8, 450013). Am Nuclear Soc.

Fabrication of Thorium Fuel Elements. Weissert & Schileo. LC 68-25126. 1968. 13.00 o.p. (ISBN 0-89448-007-3, 300001). Am Nuclear Soc.

Fabrics for Historic Buildings. 2nd ed. Jane C. Nylander. (Illus.). 160p. pap. 12.95 o.p. (NT 3174). Preservation Pr.

FABTECH International Conference Proceedings. Society of Manufacturing Engineers Staff. Ed. by Fabricating Manufacturers Association Staff. LC 81-52608. (Illus.). 529p. 1981. pap. 35.00 o.p. (ISBN 0-87263-072-2). SME.

Fabulation & Metafiction. Robert Scholes. LC 78-10776. 231p. 1979. 22.95 o.p. (ISBN 0-252-00704-2); pap. 5.95 o.p. (ISBN 0-252-00761-1). U of Ill Pr.

Fabulous Cars of the 1920s & 1930s. Richard L. Knudson. LC 81-343. (Superwheels & Thrill Sports Bks.). (Illus.). (gr. 4 up). 1981. PLB 9.95 o.p. (ISBN 0-8225-0504-5, AACR1). Lerner Pubns.

Fabulous Chicago. rev. ed. Emmett Dedmon. LC 81-66024. (Illus.). 480p. 1983. 19.95 o.p. (ISBN 0-689-11197-5, Atheneum); pap. 9.95 o.p. (ISBN 0-689-70639-1, 288). Macmillan.

Fabulous Clipjoint. Frederic Brown. 1979. lib. bdg. 10.50 o.p. (ISBN 0-8398-2541-2, Gregg). G K Hall.

Fabulous Creature. Zilpha K. Snyder. LC 80-18977. 252p. (gr. 5-9). 1981. 10.95 o.s.i. (ISBN 0-689-30829-9, Atheneum Childrens Bks). Macmillan.

Fabulous Englishman. Robert McCrum. 274p. 1985. 14.45 o.p. (ISBN 0-395-37776-5). HM.

Fabulous Fiber Cookbook. Jeanne Jones. LC 77-742. (Illus.). 1977. 8.95 o.p. (ISBN 0-89286-110-X, One Hund One Prods); pap. 6.95 o.p. (ISBN 0-89286-155-X). Ortho.

Fabulous Fruit Desserts. Terence Janericco. Ed. by Neysa Hebbard & Sharon Smith. LC 85-51873. 296p. 1986. 16.95 o.p. (ISBN 0-89909-092-3). Yankee Bks.

Fabulous Gunman. Wayne D. Overholser. 1981. pap. 1.95 o.p. (ISBN 0-440-13191-X). Dell.

Fabulous Illustrated Story of Psychoactive Plants. Michael Starks. (Illus.). 1982. 16.95 o.p. (ISBN 0-317-03303-4). Loompanics.

Fabulous Lunts: A Biography of Alfred Lunt & Lynn Fontanne. Jared Brown. LC 85-43249. 512p. 1986. 24.95 o.p. (ISBN 0-689-11648-9, Atheneum). Macmillan.

Fabulous Makeovers for Ultimate Beauty. Linda McCrerey. Incl. Blonde. 96p (ISBN 0-02-081380-5); Brunette. 96p (ISBN 0-02-081390-2); Redhead. 96p (ISBN 0-02-081400-3). (Illus.). 1986. pap. 3.95 ea. o.p. (Collier). Macmillan.

Fabulous Riverboat. Philip Jose Farmer. (Science Fiction Ser.). 1980. lib. bdg. 13.50 o.p. (ISBN 0-8398-2619-2, Gregg). G K Hall.

Facades: A Bibliography. Mary Vance. (Architecture Ser.: A 1406). 14p. 1985. 2.25 o.p. (ISBN 0-89028-436-9). Vance Biblios.

Face. Pierre Boulle. 24p. 1953. 9.95 o.p. (ISBN 0-686-54100-6). French & Eur.

Face at the Window. Wolfgang Ecke. LC 79-15628. (Illus.). 128p. (gr. 5-9). 1983. pap. 4.95 o.s.i. (ISBN 0-13-299081-4, Pub. by Treehouse Bks). P-H.

Face Behind the Mask: A Novel. John Minahan. 1986. 13.45 o.p. (ISBN 0-393-02252-8). Norton.

Face Lifting by Exercise. 9th ed. Senta M. Runge. LC 56-6321. (Illus.). 1977. Repr. of 1961 ed. 18.00 o.p. (ISBN 0-9601042-1-6). Allegro Pub.

Face of China As Seen by Photographers or Travelers: 1860-1912. Nigel Cameron. LC 78-53932. (Illus.). 160p. 1978. 25.00 o.p. (ISBN 0-89381-029-0); pap. 14.95 o.p. (ISBN 0-89381-031-2). Aperture.

Face of Death. Lesley Grant-Adamson. 304p. 1986. 13.95 o.s.i. (ISBN 0-684-18588-1). Scribner.

Face of Love. Anne N. Reisser. (Candlelight Ecstacy Ser.: No. 20). (Orig.). 1986. pap. 1.50 o.p. (ISBN 0-440-12496-4). Dell.

Face of Man: Expressions of Universal Emotions in a New Guinea Village. Paul Ekman. LC 79-12934. 154p. 1980. lib. bdg. 30.00 o.p. (ISBN 0-8240-7130-1). Garland Pub.

Face of the City. Garry Fleming. 1960. (ISBN 0-8022-0512-7). Philos Lib.

Face of the Heavenly Mother. Josef Mindszenty. 1951. (ISBN 0-8022-1123-2). Philos Lib.

Face the Music, Bk. I. Margaret Dee. 1955. 1.75 o.p. (ISBN 0-913650-36-6). CPP Belwin.

Face the Music, Bk. II. Margaret Dee. 1955. 1.75 o.p. (ISBN 0-913650-37-4). CPP Belwin.

Face the Wind: The Art & Science of Motorcycle Riding. Frank Joseph. (Illus.). 208p. 1984. 13.50 o.p. (ISBN 0-682-40162-5, Exposition-Banner). Exposition-Phoenix.

Face to Face. Jackie M. Smith. LC 73-5352. 144p. (Orig.). 1973. pap. 3.75 o.p. (ISBN 0-8042-9017-2, John Knox). Westminster John Knox.

Face to Face: Fascism & Revolution in India. Lasse Berg & Lisa Berg. Tr. by Norman Kurtin from Swedish. LC 73-172283. (Illus.). 240p. 1972. 7.95 o.p. (ISBN 0-87867-014-9). Ramparts.

Face to Face with Asia. Pierre Mendes France. Tr. by Susan Danon. 1974. 8.95 o.p. (ISBN 0-87140-567-9). Liveright.

Face Value: The Politics of Beauty. Robin T. Lakoff & Raquel L. Scherr. 344p. 1986. pap. 6.95 o.p. (ISBN 0-86358-059-9). Routledge Chapman & Hall.

Faceless Enemy: A True Story of Injustice. Pir Nasir. 216p. 1985. 12.50 o.p. (ISBN 0-682-49975-7, Universidad de Oriente). Exposition-Phoenix.

Faces & Spirits. Stanley Noyes. LC 74-84844. 1974. pap. 2.25 o.p. (ISBN 0-913270-38-5). Sunstone Pr.

Faces in the Water. Phyllis R. Naylor. LC 80-24057. 180p. (gr. 6 up). 1981. PLB 9.95 o.p. (ISBN 0-689-30823-X, AThenum). Macmillan.

Faces of Change: Five Rural Societies in Transition: Bolivia, Kenya, Afghanistan, Taiwan, China Coast. Intro. by Norman N. Miller & Manon L. Spitzer. LC 78-60524. (Illus.). 424p. 1978. pap. text ed. 15.95 o.p. (ISBN 0-88333-005-9). U Field Staff Intl.

Faces of Communication: A New Approach to Interpersonal Development. Jesse C. Sawyer. (Illus.). 1980. 8.00 o.p. (ISBN 0-682-49482-8). Exposition-Phoenix.

Faces of God. James D. Hamilton. 100p. 1984. pap. 3.95 o.p. (ISBN 0-8341-0940-9). Beacon Hill.

Faces of John Lennon. Dezo Hoffmann. 160p. 1986. text ed. 24.95 o.p. (ISBN 0-07-029306-6, McGraw Hill). McGraw.

Faces of Nationalism. Boyd C. Shafer. LC 74-6068. 560p. 1974. pap. 5.45 o.p. (ISBN 0-15-629800-7, Harv). HarBraceJ.

Faces of New England. Ulrike Welsch. Ed. by Sharon Smith. LC 83-50088. (Illus.). 144p. 1983. 15.95 o.p. (ISBN 0-89909-015-X); pap. 12.95 o.p. (ISBN 0-89909-017-6). Yankee Bks.

Faces of Persian Youth: A Sociological Study. A. R. Arasteh. 1970. 30.00 o.p. E J Brill USA.

Faces of the Future: The Lessons of Science Fiction. Brian Ash. LC 74-21697. 224p. 1975. 8.95 o.s.i. (ISBN 0-8008-2583-7). Taplinger.

Facets of Hellenic Life. John Scarborough. LC 75-29704. (Illus.). 320p. 1976. text ed. 23.50 o.p. (ISBN 0-395-20368-6). HM.

Facets of Physics. Ed. by D. Allan Bromley & V. W. Hughes. 1970. 56.00 o.p. (ISBN 0-12-135350-8). Acad Pr.

Fachwoerterbuch des Versicherungswesen. S. Heinze. (Ger. & Eng., Dictionary of Insurance Terms, English-German). 1961. 12.00 o.p. (ISBN 3-87097-017-0, M-7393, Pub. by Brandstetter). French & Eur.

Fachworterbuch Verpackung. Johanes Hoffmann. (Ger., Eng., Fr., Ital., Span. & Rus., Dictionary of packaging). 1975. 89.50 o.p. (ISBN 3-7785-0497-5, M-7406, Pub. by Verlag Fuer Fachliteratur). French & Eur.

Facies Anatomy & Diagenesis of a Bahamian Ooid Shoal. P. M. Harris. (Sedimenta VII). (Illus.). 163p. 1979. 7.00 o.p. (ISBN 0-932981-06-2). Univ Miami CSL.

Facilitating Communication Change: An Interpersonal Approach to Therapy & Counseling. Ed. by Lawrence Bloom et al. 286p. 1986. 36.50 o.p. (ISBN 0-87189-358-4). Aspen Pub.

Facilitating Student's Career Development. Ed. by Vince Harren et al. LC 80-84301. (Student Services Ser.: No. 14). 1981. pap. text ed. 11.95x o.p. (ISBN 0-87589-862-9). Jossey-Bass.

Facilities & Plant Engineering Handbook. Bernard T. Lewis & J. P. Marron. 1974. text ed. 79.50 o.p. (ISBN 0-07-037560-7). McGraw.

Facilities for Conferences, Retreats & Outdoor Education. 66p. 1985. 8.95 o.p. (ISBN 0-87603-080-0). Am Camping.

Facilities in Ports for the Reception of Oil Residues: Results of an Enquiry Made in 1972, Supplement 1976. 27p. 1976. 7.00 o.p. (ISBN 0-686-70798-2, IMCO22, IMO). UNIPUB.

Facilities Management: A Manual for Plant Administration, 6 Pts. Ed. by Rex O. Dillow. 864p. 1984. 70.00 o.s.i. (ISBN 0-913359-02-5). Assn Phys Plant Admin.

Facility Design & Operational Effects. (Transportation Research Report Ser.). 54p. 1980. 5.40 o.p. (ISBN 0-309-03071-4). Transport Res Bd.

Facility Programming. Ed. by Wolfgang F. Preiser. LC 77-17881. (Community Development Ser.: Vol. 39). (Illus.). 1982. 51.95 o.p. (ISBN 0-87933-310-3). Van Nos Reinhold.

Facing Change: Strategies for Problem Solving in the Congregation. Joseph S. Zaccaria. LC 84-18552. 112p. (Orig.). 1984. pap. 5.95 o.p. (ISBN 0-8066-2097-8, 10-2156, Augsburg). Augsburg Fortress.

Facing Life: A Scientist's View of How Things Work. John F. Shultz. 1984. 7.95 o.p. (ISBN 0-533-05747-7). Vantage.

Facing Reality: Philosophical Adventures by a Brain Scientist. John C. Eccles. LC 76-121064. (Heidelberg Science Library: Vol. 13). (Illus.). 1970. pap. 15.00 o.p. (ISBN 0-387-90014-4). Springer-Verlag.

Facing the Challenges of the Future: The 1984 Presidents Academy Award Addresses. 1984. 6.00 o.p. (ISBN 0-317-40585-3). Am Assn Comm Jr Coll.

Facing the Issues, No. 2. William J. Krutza & Philip P. Dicicco. (Contemporary Discussion Ser.). pap. 3.50 o.p. (ISBN 0-8010-5326-9). Baker Bk.

Facing the Music. Harold C. Schonberg. 1981. 17.95 o.s.i. (ISBN 0-671-25406-5). Summit Bks.

Facing the Music: An Inside View of the Real Concert World. Henri Temianka. LC 72-92653. (Illus.). 272p. (Orig.). 1980. pap. 8.95 o.p. (ISBN 0-88284-109-2, 5076). Alfred Pub.

Facing Up. Judith Mattison. LC 79-7385. (Illus.). 96p. (Orig.). 1979. pap. 2.95 o.p. (ISBN 0-8006-1368-6, 1-1368, Fortress). Augsburg Fortress.

Facing up to Nuclear Power. Ed. by John Francis & Paul Abrecht. LC 76-42471. (Illus.). 1976. pap. 3.95 o.s.i. (ISBN 0-664-24129-8, Westminster). Westminster John Knox.

Facing Your Feelings: How to Get Your Emotions to Work for You. Bert Ghezzi. (Living as a Christian Ser.). 112p. 1983. pap. 3.95 o.p. (ISBN 0-89283-133-2). Servant.

Fact & Fancy in International Economic Relations: An Essay on International Monetary Reform. Thomas Balogh. LC 73-7993. 132p. 1973. 31.00 o.p. (ISBN 0-08-017740-9). Pergamon.

Fact & Fantasy in Freudian Theory. 2nd ed. Paul Kline. (Methuen's Manuals of Modern Psychology Ser.). 548p. 1981. 49.95x o.p. (ISBN 0-416-72640-2, NO. 3518). Routledge Chapman & Hall.

Fact & Fiction: The New Journalism & the Nonfiction Novel. John Hollowell. LC 76-20826. xiv, 190p. 1977. 20.00x o.p. (ISBN 0-8078-1281-1). U of NC Pr.

Fact & Theory. W. M. O'Neil. 1969. 20.00x o.p. (ISBN 0-424-05800-6, Pub by Sydney U Pr). Intl Spec Bk.

Fact Book of the American Public Library. Herbert Goldhor. (Occasional Papers: No. 150). 80p. 1981. pap. 3.00 o.p. (ISBN 0-317-58997-0). U of Ill Lib Info Sci.

Fact Book of United States Agriculture, 1986. rev. ed. (Agriculture Dept. Miscellaneous Publication: No. 1063). 139p. 1985. pap. 2.75 o.p. (ISBN 0-318-20106-2, S/N 001-000-04455-9). USGPO.

Fact Book of United States Agriculture, 1987. rev. ed. (Agriculture-Dept. Miscellaneous Publication Ser.: No. 1063). 177p. pap. 4.25 o.p. (ISBN 0-318-23553-6, S/N 001-000-04496-6). USGPO.

Fact-Book on Fermented Foods & Beverages. Beatrice T. Hunter. LC 73-76229. (Pivot Original Health Book). 128p. 1973. pap. 1.25 o.p. (ISBN 0-87983-055-7). Keats.

Fact-Finding Conference. Warren H. Schmidt & Richard Beckhand. 1956. 2.00 o.p. (ISBN 0-88379-014-9). A A A C E.

Fact-Finding in the Public Sector: A Case Study see Issues in the Public Employee Relations Library: Series 3.

Fact in Fiction: The Use of Literature in the Systematic Study of Society. Joan Rockwell. 211p. 1974. 19.95x o.p. (ISBN 0-7100-7877-3). Routledge Chapman & Hall.

Fact of Crystal. Abbie H. Evans. LC 61-7254. 1961. 9.95 o.p. (ISBN 0-15-129879-3). HarBraceJ.

Fact of Literature: Three Essays on Public Material. Frederic Will. 215p. (Orig.). 1973. pap. text ed. 20.00x o.p. (ISBN 9-0620-3377-6). Humanities.

Faction & Parliament: Essays on Early Stuart History. Ed. by Kevin Sharpe. (Orig.). 1985. pap. 13.95 o.p. (ISBN 0-416-39880-4, 9596). Routledge Chapman & Hall.

Factors Affecting Administration in United States Academic Libraries During the Period 1971-1975. Anne M. Allison. (Occasional Papers: No. 138). 31p. 1979. pap. 2.00 o.p. (ISBN 0-317-58980-6). U of Ill Lib Info Sci.

Factors Affecting Dispersal Distances of Small Organisms. D. O. Wolfenbarger. LC 73-92856. 1975. 15.00 o.p. (ISBN 0-682-47905-5, University). Exposition-Phoenix.

Factors Affecting the Use of Lumber. Truss Fabricators in the United States Staff. 80p. 1979. 12.00 o.p. (ISBN 0-935018-20-4); members 9.00 o.p. (ISBN 0-317-17412-6). Forest Prod.

Factors & Trends in Trip Length. (National Cooperative Highway Research Program Report). 70p. 1968. 3.20 o.p. (ISBN 0-317-36082-5, 1582). Transport Res Bd.

Factors in a Theory of Poetic Translating. R. de Beaugrande. (Approaches to Translation Studies: No. 5). 1978. pap. text ed. 17.50x o.p. (ISBN 90-232-1570-2). Humanities.

Factors In Formation & Regression of the Atherosclerotic Plaque. Ed. by Gustav R. Born et al. LC 82-12286. (NATO ASI Series A, Life Sciences: Vol. 51). 274p. 1982. 55.00x o.p. (ISBN 0-306-41035-4, Plenum Pr). Plenum Pub.

Factors Influencing Adrenergic Mechanisms in the Heart: Proceedings of a Satellite Symposium of the 28th International Congress of Physiological Sciences, Visegrad, Hungary, 1980. Ed. by M. Szentivanyi & A. Juhasz-Nagy. LC 80-42203. (Advances in Physiological Sciences Ser.: Vol. 27). (Illus.). 265p. 1981. 50.00 o.p. (ISBN 0-08-027348-3). Pergamon.

Factors Influencing Modal Trip Assignment. (National Cooperative Highway Research Program Report). 78p. 1968. 3.20 o.p. (ISBN 0-317-36083-3, 1711). Transport Res Bd.

Factors Influencing Myocardial Contractility. Ed. by Ralph D. Tanz et al. 1967. 99.00 o.p. (ISBN 0-12-683450-4). Acad Pr.

Factors Influencing Willingness to Pay for Use of Marine Recreational Facilities: Sand Beach. 52p. 1976. free o.p. (P503). Sea Grant Pubns.

Factors of Growth & Investment Policies: An International Approach. United Nations Economic Commission for Europe. 1978. pap. 34.00 o.p. (ISBN 0-08-021992-6). Pergamon.

Factors, Trends & Guidelines Related to Trip Length. (National Cooperative Highway Research Project Report). 59p. 1970. 3.20 o.p. (ISBN 0-309-01876-5). Transport Res Bd.

Factory Cast Prestressed Concrete: The Fire Fighter. Prestressed Concrete Institute Staff. 12p. Date not set. pap. 2.00 o.p. (ISBN 0-318-19817-7, MK-1-80). P-PCI.

Factory Electrification. Bartho & Pike. (Illus.). 400p. 1956. (ISBN 0-8022-0076-1). Philos Lib.

Factory Made: How Things Are Manufactured. Leonard Gottlieb. (Illus.). 144p. (gr. 5 up). 1978. 7.95 o.p. (ISBN 0-395-26450-2). HM.

Factory Store Guide to All New England. 5th ed. A. Miser & A. Pennypincher. LC 76-51130. 288p. (Orig.). 1981. pap. 5.95 o.p. (ISBN 0-87106-956-3). Globe Pequot.

Factory Workers in Tangku. Sung-Ho Lin. Ed. by Ramon H. Myers. LC 80-8823. (China During the Interregnum 1911-1949, The Economy & Society Ser.). 128p. 1982. lib. bdg. 22.00 o.p. (ISBN 0-8240-4678-1). Garland Pub.

Facts about Life All People Should Know. Grier L. Paden. 1983. 13.95 o.p. (ISBN 0-533-05789-2). Vantage.

Facts about Norway. 20th ed. Aftenposten. Ed. by Royal Ministry of Foreign Affairs Staff. 104p. 1987. 11.00x o.p. (ISBN 8-2516-1060-5, N451). Vanous.

Facts About Shakespeare. William A. Neilson & Ashley H. Thorndike. Repr. of 1931 ed. 49.00x o.p. (ISBN 0-403-03058-7). Somerset Pub.

Facts about Syphilis & Gonorrhea, 2 bks. (gr. 10-12). 1972. pap. text ed. 6.00 each o.s.i. (ISBN 0-8449-1228-X). Carroll CA.

Facts about the Fifty States. rev. ed. Sue R. Brandt. (First Bks.). (Illus.). (gr. 4 up). 1979. PLB 10.40 o.p. (ISBN 0-531-02899-2). Watts.

Facts & Faith: Reason, Science & Faith, Vol. 1. J. D. Thomas. 1966. 13.95 o.p. (ISBN 0-89112-011-4). Abilene Christ U.

Facts & Fantasies about Drugs. Shirley Schwarzrock & C. Gilbert Wrenn. (Coping with Ser.). (Illus.). (gr. 6-9). 1970. pap. text ed. 3.00 o.p. (ISBN 0-913476-12-9). Am Guidance.

Facts & Fantasies about Smoking. Shirley Schwarzrock & C. Gilbert Wrenn. (Coping with Ser.). (Illus.). 40p. (gr. 7-12). 1971. pap. text ed. 3.00 o.p. (ISBN 0-913476-14-5). Am Guidance.

Facts & Figures on Government Finance. 21st ed. 329p. (Orig., Biennial). 1981. pap. text ed. 15.00 o.p. (ISBN 0-318-16988-6). Tax Found.

Facts in the Case of E. A. Poe. Andrew Sinclair. LC 80-141477. 192p. 1980. 9.95 o.p. (ISBN 0-03-022091-2). H Holt & Co.

Facts of Awareness see Science of Education.

Facts of Everyday Life. Tony Osman. LC 84-28761. (Illus.). 160p. (Orig.). 1985. pap. 14.95 o.p. (ISBN 0-571-13513-7). Faber & Faber.

Facts of Flight. Jerry Grey. LC 72-12793. (Franklin Institute Bk). (Illus.). (gr. 7 up). 1973. 4.95 o.s.i. (ISBN 0-664-32526-2, Westminster); pap. 2.95 o.s.i. (ISBN 0-664-34004-0, Westminster). Westminster John Knox.

Facts of Life. R. D. Laing. 1984. pap. 3.95 o.p. (ISBN 0-394-71474-1). Pantheon.

Facts on Backs. Leonard Ring. Ed. by Doug Clarke. LC 81-83953. (Illus.). 1981. text ed. 22.00 o.p. (ISBN 0-88061-004-2). Inst Pub ILCI.

Titles

Facts on File Dictionary of Biology. Ed. by Elizabeth Tootill. 288p. 1981. 16.95 o.p. (ISBN 0-87196-510-0); pap. 5.95 o.p. (ISBN 0-87196-637-9). Facts on File.

Facts on File Directory of Major Public Corporations. 1648p. 1987. 110.00 o.p. (ISBN 0-8160-1529-5). Facts on File.

Faculty Directory of Higher Education, 12 vols. Ed. by CMG Information Services, Inc. Staff. cancelled o.s.i. (ISBN 0-8103-2750-3). Gale.

Faculty Directory of Higher Education, Vol. 10: Science & Mathematics. Ed. by CMG Imformation Services, Inc. Staff. 1056p. cancelled o.s.i. (ISBN 0-8103-2760-0). Gale.

Faculty Directory of Higher Education, Vol. 11: Social Sciences. Ed. by CMG Information Services, Inc. Staff. 748p. cancelled o.s.i. (ISBN 0-8103-2761-9). Gale.

Faculty Directory of Higher Education, Vol. 2: Communications. Ed. by CMG Information Services, Inc. Staff. 240p. cancelled o.s.i. (ISBN 0-8103-2752-X). Gale.

Faculty Directory of Higher Education, Vol. 3: Computer Science & Data Processing. Ed. by CMG Information Services, Inc. Staff. 320p. cancelled o.s.i. (ISBN 0-8103-2753-8). Gale.

Faculty Directory of Higher Education, Vol. 4: Education. Ed. by CMG Information Services, Inc. Staff. 752p. cancelled o.s.i. (ISBN 0-8103-2754-6). Gale.

Faculty Directory of Higher Education, Vol. 5: Engineering. Ed. by CMG Information Services, Inc. Staff. 400p. cancelled o.s.i. (ISBN 0-8103-2755-4). Gale.

Faculty Directory of Higher Education, Vol. 6: Fine & Applied Arts. Ed. by CMG Information Services, Inc. Staff. 688p. cancelled o.s.i. (ISBN 0-8103-2756-2). Gale.

Faculty Directory of Higher Education, Vol. 7: Hummanities. Ed. by CMG Information Services, Inc. Staff. 264p. cancelled o.s.i. (ISBN 0-8103-2757-0). Gale.

Faculty Directory of Higher Education, Vol. 8: Language & Literature. Ed. by CMG Information Services, Inc. Staff. 648p. cancelled o.s.i. (ISBN 0-8103-2758-9). Gale.

Faculty Directory of Higher Education, Vol. 9: Medicine & Nursing. Ed. by CMG Information Services, Inc. Staff. 848p. cancelled o.s.i. (ISBN 0-8103-2759-7). Gale.

Faculty Member's Guide to the U. S. Immigration Law. Eugene H. Smith & Marvin J. Baron. LC 87-120847. (Illus.). 53p. NAFSA Washington.

Facundo: Civilizacion y Barbarie. Sarmiento. (Span). 4.50x o.s.i. (ISBN 0-686-00864-2). Colton Bk.

Fad Diets Can Be Deadly: The Safe Sure, Way to Weight Loss & Good Nutrition. Frank Netter. LC 74-21446. 1975. 8.00 o.p. (ISBN 0-682-48144-0, Banner). Exposition-Phoenix.

Faded Mezzuzoth. Gershon Kranzler. saddle-stitched 5.00 o.p. (ISBN 0-87559-134-5). Shalom.

Fading American Newspaper. C. E. Lindstrom. 11.25 o.p. (ISBN 0-8446-1282-0). Peter Smith.

Fading, My Parmacheene Belle. Joanna Scott. 1987. 17.45 o.s.i. (ISBN 0-89919-451-6). Ticknor & Fields.

Fading of the Maoist Vision. Rhoads Murphey. 1980. 14.95 o.p. (ISBN 0-416-60201-0, NO. 2870). Routledge Chapman & Hall.

Faeriemound of Dragonkind. Jean Blashfield & James M. Ward. LC 86-91680. (Catacombs Gamebooks). (Illus.). 160p. 1987. 7.95 o.p. (ISBN 0-88038-449-2). TSR Inc.

Fahrenheit Four Fifty-One. Ray Bradbury. (Orig.). 1979. pap. 2.95 o.p. (ISBN 0-345-34200-3). Ballantine.

Fahrenheit Four Fifty-One. Ray Bradbury. 1967. 16.45 o.s.i. (ISBN 0-671-23977-5). S&S.

Failing Forward. Ted Roberts. 1985. pap. 4.95 o.p. (ISBN 0-89081-432-5). Harvest Hse.

Failure & Success in America: A Literary Debate. Martha Banta. LC 78-51156. text ed. 52.50x o.p. (ISBN 0-691-06366-4); pap. 24.50x o.p. (ISBN 0-691-10070-5). Princeton U Pr.

Failure Forecasting. Credit Research Foundation. 17p. 1977. 40.00 o.p. (ISBN 0-939050-25-0). Credit Res NYS.

Failure Modes in Composites II: Proceedings of the TMS-AIME Spring Meeting, Pittsburgh, 1976. TMS Staff & AIME Staff. Ed. by James N. Fleck & Richard L. Mehan. (Illus.). 302p. pap. 24.00 o.p. (ISBN 0-89520-122-4); pap. 15.00 members o.p. (ISBN 0-317-34872-8); pap. 9.00 student members o.p. (ISBN 0-317-34873-6). ASM.

Failure of Individualism: A Documented Essay. Richard S. Devane. LC 75-28664. (Illus.). 1976. Repr. lib. bdg. 35.00x o.p. (ISBN 0-8371-8484-3, DEFI). Greenwood.

Failure of the American Baptist Culture. Ed. by James B. Jordan. LC 82-82376. (Christianity & Civilization Ser.: No. 1). xiv, 304p. (Orig.). 1982. pap. 9.95 o.p. (ISBN 0-939404-04-4). Geneva Ministr.

Failure of the Environmental Movement. Barry Commoner. Date not set. price not set o.p. Pantheon.

Failure Prevention & Reliability, 1981. Ed. by F. T. Loo. 1981. 40.00 o.p. (ISBN 0-686-34485-5, 100142). ASME.

Failure: The Back Door to Success. Erwin Lutzer. LC 75-16177. 1977. pap. 3.50 o.p. (ISBN 0-8024-2516-X). Moody.

Faint Heart Never Kissed a Pig. Ann Drysdale. 170p. 1984. 15.00 o.p. (ISBN 0-7100-0972-0). Routledge Chapman & Hall.

Fair & Wilder. Anne Wilder. 64p. 1981. 5.00 o.p. (ISBN 0-682-49725-8). Exposition-Phoenix.

Fair Annie of Old Mule Hollow. Beverly C. Crook. (gr. 6 up). 1978. text ed. 7.95 o.p. (ISBN 0-07-014487-7). McGraw.

Fair Credit Reporting Act: 1982 & 1986 Supplement. National Consumer Law Center Staff. LC 82-6506. 169p. 1982. pap. 48.00 o.p. (ISBN 0-943116-03-1). Nat Consumer Law.

Fair Em: An Introduction & Critical Edition. Standish Henning. LC 79-3099. (Renaissance Drama Ser.). 150p. 1980. lib. bdg. 24.00 o.p. (ISBN 0-8240-4483-5). Garland Pub.

Fair Fights & Foul: A Dissenting Lawyer's Autobiography. Thurman Arnold. LC 65-14716. (Illus.). 1965. 5.95 o.p. (ISBN 0-15-129940-4). HarBraceJ.

Fair Game. Daisy Vivian. (Large Print Bks.) Nightingales Ser.). 300p. 1987. pap. 12.95 o.p. (ISBN 0-8161-4216-5). G K Hall.

Fair Game: A Hunter's Cookbook. Jane Hibler. Ed. by Betsy Lawrence. LC 83-71039. (Great American Cooking Schools Ser.). (Illus.). 84p. (Orig.). 1983. pap. 5.95 o.p. (ISBN 0-941034-15-1). I Chalmers.

Fair Haven: A Work in Defence of the Miraculous Element in Our Lord's Ministry Upon Earth. Samuel Butler. Ed. by Robert L. Wolff. LC 75-1503. (Victorian Fiction Ser.). 1977. Repr. of 1873 ed. lib. bdg. 73.00 o.p. (ISBN 0-8240-1578-9). Garland Pub.

Fair Housing & Families: Discrimination Against Children. Jim Buchanan. (Public Administration Ser.: P 1732). 11p. 1985. 2.00 o.p. (ISBN 0-89028-502-0). Vance Biblios.

Fair Land, Fair Land. A. B. Guthrie, Jr. 256p. 1982. 14.45 o.p. (ISBN 0-395-32511-0). HM.

Fair Penitent. Nicholas Rowe. Ed. by Malcolm Goldstein. LC 69-10354. (Regents Restoration Drama Ser.). xxii, 83p. 1969. 9.50x o.p. (ISBN 0-8032-0367-5); pap. 2.95x o.p. (ISBN 0-8032-5367-2, BB 270, Bison). U of Nebr Pr.

Fair Play for Frogs: The Waldie-Frobish Papers. Jerome Waldie & Nestle J. Frobish. LC 76-27418. 1977. 7.95 o.p. (ISBN 0-15-129961-7). HarBraceJ.

Fair Use & Free Inquiry: Copyright Law & the New Media. Ed. by John S. Lawrence & Bernard Timberg. (Communication & Information Science Ser.). 1980. 47.50x o.p. (ISBN 0-89391-028-7). Ablex Pub.

Fair Wages Resolutions. Brian Bercusson. (Studies in Labour & Social Law: Vol. 2). 566p. 1978. lib. bdg. 35.00x o.p. (ISBN 0-7201-0709-1). Mansell.

Fair Warning. George E. Simpson & Neal R. Burger. 1981. pap. 3.50 o.p. (ISBN 0-440-12478-6). Dell.

Fair-Weather Friends. Jack Gantos. LC 76-62500. (Illus.). (gr. k-3). 1977. reinforced bdg. 6.95 o.p. (ISBN 0-395-25156-7). HM.

Fair Wind of Love. Rosalind Laker. (Nightingale Ser.). 262p. 1988. pap. 12.95 o.p. (ISBN 0-8161-4409-5, Large Print Bks). G K Hall.

Fairchild's Financial Manual of Retail Stores. 60th ed. Fairchild Book Research Dept. 200p. (Orig.). 1987. pap. 60.00 o.p. (ISBN 0-87005-568-2). Fairchild.

Fairchild's Financial Manual of Retail Stores, 1984. 57th ed. Fairchild Book Research Division Staff. 255p. 1984. pap. 60.00 o.p. (ISBN 0-87005-471-6). Fairchild.

Fairchild's Financial Manual of Retail Stores. 58th ed. Fairchild Book Research Division Staff. 230p. 1985. pap. 60.00 o.p. (ISBN 0-87005-504-6). Fairchild.

Fairchild's Financial Manual of Retail Stores. 59th ed. Fairchild Book Research Division Staff. 200p. 1986. pap. 60.00 o.p. (ISBN 0-87005-538-0). Fairchild.

Fairchild's Textile & Apparel Financial Directory. 12th ed. Fairchild Book Research Division Staff. 160p. 1985. pap. 50.00 o.p. (ISBN 0-87005-503-8). Fairchild.

Fairchild's Textile & Apparel Financial Directory. 13th ed. Fairchild Book Research Division Staff. 150p. 1986. pap. 50.00 o.p. (ISBN 0-87005-537-2). Fairchild.

Fairchild's Textile & Apparel Financial Directory 1987. 14th ed. Fairchild Book Research Dept. 150p. (Orig.). 1987. pap. 50.00 o.p. (ISBN 0-87005-567-4). Fairchild.

Fairchild's Textile & Apparel Financial Directory, 1984. 11th ed. Fairchild Book Research Division Staff. 190p. 1984. pap. 50.00 o.p. (ISBN 0-87005-470-8). Fairchild.

Faire Maide of the Exchange. Karl E. Synder. LC 79-54329. (Renaissance Drama Ser.). 225p. 1980. lib. bdg. 31.00 o.p. (ISBN 0-8240-4477-0). Garland Pub.

Fairfield County: An Insider's Guide. Parke Cummings & Nora Lapin. LC 75-8337. 288p. 1975. pap. 3.95 o.p. (ISBN 0-88208-055-5). Chicago Review.

Fairfield Porter: Art in Its Own Terms-Selected Criticism 1935-1975. Rackstraw Downes. LC 78-57598. 1979. 15.00 o.s.i. (ISBN 0-8008-2586-1); pap. 7.95 o.s.i. (ISBN 0-8008-2587-X). Taplinger.

Fairies in Tradition & Literature. Katherine M. Briggs. 1977. pap. 8.95 o.p. (ISBN 0-7100-8687-3). Routledge Chapman & Hall.

Fairly Dangerous Thing. Reginald Hill. 12.95 o.s.i. (ISBN 0-88150-014-3, Foul Play). Countryman.

Fairly Good Time. Mavis Gallant. (Hall Fiction Ser.). 320p. 1986. pap. 6.95 o.p. (ISBN 0-8398-2896-9). G K Hall.

Fairly Lucky You Live Hawaii! Richard L. Rapson. LC 80-5530. 166p. 1980. lib. bdg. 20.75 o.p. (ISBN 0-8191-1167-8); pap. text ed. 8.25 o.p. (ISBN 0-8191-1168-6). U Pr of Amer.

Fairness & Justice: Law in the Service of Equality. Charles M. Haar & Daniel W. Fessler. LC 86-29775. 1987. pap. 9.95 o.s.i. (ISBN 0-671-63311-2, Touchstone Bks). S&S.

Fairshare: The Monthly Newsletter of Divorce, Alimony, & Division of Marital Property. 90.00 o.p. (ISBN 0-15-100020-4, N39810, Pub. by Law & Business). HarBraceJ.

Fairweather Friends. Stephen Roos. LC 86-17246. 128p. (YA) (gr. 9-12). 1987. 12.95 o.p. (Atheneum Childrens Bk.). Macmillan.

Fairy Mythology. Keightley. LC 74-16410. 578p. 1975. Repr. of 1870 ed. 54.00x o.p. (ISBN 0-8103-3466-6). Gale.

Fairy Smoke: Children's Poems. Marjorie K. Lawrence. (ps-3). 1974. 5.00 o.p. (ISBN 0-682-47898-9). Exposition-Phoenix.

Fairy Tale Land: Art Doll Illustration. Takako Takashi. (Illus.). 112p. 1988. 24.95 o.p. (ISBN 4-7661-0481-1, Pub. by Graphic Sha Japan). Bks Nippan.

Fairy Tale of New York. J. P. Donleavy. 384p. 1974. pap. 1.75 o.p. (ISBN 0-440-33233-8, LE). Dell.

Fairy Tale Super Fun Book. (Illus.). (ps-1). pap. 1.98 o.s.i. (ISBN 0-517-48235-5). Outlet Bk Co.

Fairy Tales & Children. Date not set. (ISBN 0-8052-3897-2). Random.

Fairy Tales & the Art of Subversion: The Classical Genre of Children & the Process of Civilization. Jack Zipes. 214p. 1985. 22.50 o.p. (ISBN 0-939544-13-X, 9689); pap. 9.95 o.p. (ISBN 0-939544-14-8, 9663). Routledge Chapman & Hall.

Fairy Tales & the Female Imagination. Jennifer Waelti-Walters. 225p. 1982. 18.95 o.p. (ISBN 0-920792-07-3). Eden Pr.

Fairy Tales by T. Jones. T. Jones. Date not set. (ISBN 0-8052-3807-7). Random.

Fairy Tales Near & Far. Felix Salten. (ISBN 0-8022-1472-X). Philos Lib.

Fairytale Book of Ballet. Rosanna Hansen. (Illus.). 80p. (gr. 1-7). 7.95 o.p. (ISBN 0-448-11499-2, G&D). Putnam Pub Group.

Fairytales. Cynthia Freeman. LC 76-50340. 1977. 8.95 o.p. (ISBN 0-87795-163-2, Arbor Hse). Morrow.

Faith: A Psalm of Active Trust & Quiet Confidence. Rev. G. K. Gould. 1976. 4.00 o.p. (ISBN 0-682-48515-2). Exposition-Phoenix.

Faith Active in Love. George W. Forell. LC 54-10896. 1954. kivar 8.95 o.p. (ISBN 0-8066-0186-8, 10-2165, Augsburg). Augsburg Fortress.

Faith & Belief. Wilfred C. Smith. LC 78-63601. 1979. 35.50x o.p. (ISBN 0-691-07232-9). Princeton U Pr.

Faith & Ferment: An Interdisciplinary Study of Christian Beliefs & Practices. Ed. by Robert S. Bilheimer. LC 83-70512. 352p. (Orig.). 1983. pap. 15.95 o.p. (ISBN 0-8066-2018-8, 10-2168, Augsburg). Augsburg Fortress.

Faith & Fragmentation: Christianity for a New Age. J. Philip Wogaman. LC 85-47712. 208p. 1985. pap. 10.95 o.p. (ISBN 0-8006-1864-5, 1-1864, Fortress). Augsburg Fortress.

Faith & Freedom: The Christian Faith According to the Lutheran Confessions. Charles S. Anderson. LC 76-27087. 1977. pap. 6.95 o.p. (ISBN 0-8066-1558-3, 10-2170, Fortress). Augsburg Fortress.

Faith & Fried Potatoes. Grayce Confer. 184p. 1982. pap. 4.95 o.p. (ISBN 0-8341-0732-5). Beacon Hill.

Faith & Learning: Christian Faith & Higher Education in Twentieth Century America. Alexander Miller. LC 77-23142. 1977. Repr. of 1960 ed. lib. bdg. 22.50x o.p. (ISBN 0-8371-9458-X, MIFL). Greenwood.

Faith & Love. R. Alexander & A. Steinbach. 128p. 1958. (ISBN 0-8022-1639-0). Philos Lib.

Faith & Moral Authority. Ben F. Kimpel. 1953. (ISBN 0-8022-0856-8). Philos Lib.

Faith & Piety in Early Judaism: Texts & Documents. George W. Nickelsburg & Michael E. Stone. LC 82-71830. 272p. 1983. 8.95 o.p. (ISBN 0-8006-0679-5, Fortress). Augsburg Fortress.

Faith & Process: The Significance of Process Thought for Christian Faith. Paul R. Sponheim. LC 78-66955. 1979. 12.50 o.p. (ISBN 0-8066-1680-6, 10-2179, Augsburg). Augsburg Fortress.

Faith & Reality. Wolfhart Pannenberg. LC 77-682. 148p. 1977. softcover 6.50 o.s.i. (ISBN 0-664-24755-5, Westminster). Westminster John Knox.

Faith & Science in an Unjust World, Vol. 1: Plenary Presentations. Ed. by Roger L. Shinn. LC 80-81141. 408p. 1980. pap. 12.95 o.p. (ISBN 0-8006-1390-2, 1-1390, Fortress). Augsburg Fortress.

Faith & Science in an Unjust World, Vol. 2: Reports & Recommendations. Ed. by Paul Abrecht. LC 80-81141. 224p. 1980. pap. 6.95 o.p. (ISBN 0-8006-1391-0, 1-1391, Fortress). Augsburg Fortress.

Faith & the Mystery of God. Maurice Wiles. LC 82-2451. 160p. 1982. pap. 6.95 o.p. (ISBN 0-8006-1651-0, 1-1651, Fortress). Augsburg Fortress.

Faith & the Prospect of Economic Collapse. Robert Lee. 170p. pap. 3.99 o.p. (ISBN 0-8042-0814-X, John Knox). Westminster John Knox.

Faith at Work. Dorothy Martin. (Peggy Ser.: No. 9). (gr. 7). 1985. pap. 3.50 o.p. (ISBN 0-8024-8309-7). Moody.

Faith Beyond Humanism. David R. Williams. LC 62-20877. (ISBN 0-8022-1885-7). Philos Lib.

Faith: Conversations with Contemporary Theologians. Ed. by Teofilo Cabestrero. Tr. by Donald D. Walsh from Span. LC 80-1431. Orig. Title: Coversationes sobre la fe. 192p. (Orig.). 1980. pap. 3.98 o.p. (ISBN 0-88344-126-8). Orbis Bks.

Faith Development in the Adult Life Cycle. 1983. 10.95 o.p. (ISBN 0-8215-9904-6). Sadlier.

Faith Enacted As History: Essays in Biblical Theology. Will Herberg. Ed. by Bernhard W. Anderson. LC 76-26899. 1976. 12.00 o.s.i. (ISBN 0-664-21335-9, Westminster). Westminster John Knox.

Faith, Feminism & the Christ. Patricia Wilson-Kastner. LC 83-5688. 160p. 1983. pap. 8.95 o.p. (ISBN 0-8006-1746-0, Fortress). Augsburg Fortress.

Faith for All Generations. Robert Flood. LC 86-70628. Orig. Title: Up with America. 96p. 1986. pap. 5.95 o.p. (ISBN 0-89636-214-0). Accent Bks.

Faith for Moderns. 2nd rev. ed. Robert Gordis. LC 76-136424. 1971. pap. 8.95x o.s.i. (ISBN 0-8197-0001-0, 10001). Bloch.

Faith, Hope & Love. Irose A. Roberts. LC 83-91504. 1985. 11.95 o.p. (ISBN 0-533-06087-7). Vantage.

Faith, Hope & Luck: A Sociological Study of Children Growing up with a Life-Threatening Illness. Charles Waddell. LC 82-24871. 104p. (Orig.). 1983. lib. bdg. 24.00 o.p. (ISBN 0-8191-3011-7); pap. text ed. 9.50 o.p. (ISBN 0-8191-3012-5). U Pr of Amer.

Faith in the Center Ring: An Elephantine Question. Joan P. Berry. LC 77-15227. (Illus., Orig.). 1978. pap. 3.50 o.p. (ISBN 0-8006-1323-6, Fortress). Augsburg Fortress.

Faith Is the Password: Meditations on Romans. W. A. Poovey. LC 79-50090. 1979. pap. 3.50 o.p. (ISBN 0-8066-1707-1, 10-2185, Augsburg). Augsburg Fortress.

Faith Is the Victory. Buell H. Kazee. 1983. pap. 4.95 o.p. (ISBN 0-8423-0844-X). Tyndale.

Faith It or Fake It? Fritz Ridenour. LC 73-120783. 176p. 1978. pap. 3.95 o.s.i. (ISBN 0-8307-0441-8, S114186). Regal.

Faith, Keyes, & Clark's Industrial Chemicals. 4th ed. Frederick A. Lowenheim & Marguerite K. Moran. LC 75-17951. 904p. 1975. 125.00 o.p. (ISBN 0-471-54964-9, Pub. by Wiley-Interscience). Wiley.

Faith of Christians. Denis Baly & Royal W. Rhodes. LC 84-47914. 256p. 1984. pap. 1.95 o.p. (ISBN 0-8006-1790-8, Fortress). Augsburg Fortress.

Faith of Our Fathers. Lawrence H. Waddy. 1975. pap. 3.95x o.p. (ISBN 0-8192-4063-X). Morehouse Pub.

Faith of Our Fathers. Spiro Zavos. LC 82-2060. 155p. 1983. text ed. 14.50 o.p. (ISBN 0-7022-1751-4); pap. 8.95 o.p. (ISBN 0-7022-1761-1). U of Queensland Pr.

Faith of Shi'a Islam. Muhammed R. Al-Muzaffar. 89p. (Orig.). 1986. pap. text ed. 8.95 o.p. (ISBN 0-7103-0157-X). Routledge Chapman & Hall.

Faith of the Christian Church. rev. ed. Gustaf Aulen. Tr. by Eric H. Wahlstrom from Swedish. LC 61-5302. 416p. 1973. pap. 8.95 o.p. (ISBN 0-8006-1655-3, 1-1655, Fortress). Augsburg Fortress.

Faith of the Fathers. Lawrence Waddy. 3.95 o.p. (ISBN 0-317-12186-3). Morehouse Pub.

Faith Once Given: The Apostle's Creed Interpreted for Today. George M. Ricker. 1978. pap. 4.95 o.s.i. (ISBN 0-664-24189-1, Westminster). Westminster John Knox.

Faith: Reflections on Experience, Theology & Fiction. Kent D. Smith. 114p. (Orig.). 1984. lib. bdg. 23.25 o.p. (ISBN 0-8191-3634-4); pap. text ed. 9.75 o.p. (ISBN 0-8191-3635-2). U Pr of Amer.

Faith, Science, & the Future. Ed. by Paul Abrecht. LC 79-7035. 240p. 1979. pap. 3.95 o.p. (ISBN 0-8006-1365-1, 1-1365, Fortress). Augsburg Fortress.

Faith Speaks. T. L. Osborn. 1982. pap. 2.95 o.p. (ISBN 0-89274-226-7, HH-226). Harrison Hse.

Faith That Makes a Difference. John W. Bachman. LC 83-70508. 128p. (Orig.). 1983. pap. 6.95 o.p. (ISBN 0-8066-2014-5, 10-2193, Augsburg). Augsburg Fortress.

Faith the Great Adventure. Helmut Thielicke. LC 84-48716. 160p. 1985. pap. 1.25 o.p. (ISBN 0-8006-1833-5, 1-1833, Fortress). Augsburg Fortress.

Faith to Change the World. Lester Sumrall. 173p. (Orig.). 1983. pap. 4.95 o.p. (ISBN 0-89274-306-9, HH-306). Harrison Hse.

Faith under Fire. Wellesley Muir. Ed. by Raymond H. Woolsey. 128p. (Orig.). (YA) (gr. 10-12). 1988. pap. 7.95 o.p. (ISBN 0-8280-0495-1). Review & Herald.

Faith under Fire: Biblical Interpretations of Suffering. Danile J. Simundson. LC 79-54119. 158p. 1980. pap. 7.95 o.p. (ISBN 0-8066-1756-X, 10-2195, Augsburg). Augsburg Fortress.

Faith We Hold: The Living Witness of Luther & the Augsburg Confession. James A. Nestingen. LC 83-70516. 96p. (Orig.). 1983. pap. 5.95 o.p. (ISBN 0-8066-2022-6, 10-2200, Augsburg). Augsburg Fortress.

Faithful Are the Wounds. May Sarton. 288p. 1972. 9.95 o.p. (ISBN 0-393-08439-6). Norton.

Fakers: Exploding the Myths of the Supernatural. Danny Korem & Paul Meier. LC 80-23180. (Illus.). 1981. 5.95 o.p. (ISBN 0-8010-5431-1); pap. 5.95 o.p. (ISBN 0-8010-5435-4). Baker Bk.

Falcon. Nigel Slater. LC 78-73086. 1979. 9.95 o.p. (ISBN 0-689-10928-8, Atheneum). Macmillan.

Falcon & the Snowman. Robert Lindsey. 1979. 12.95 o.p. (ISBN 0-671-24560-0). S&S.

Falconer's the Drug, the Nurse, the Patient. 7th ed. Eleanor Sheridan et al. (Illus.). 1008p. 1982. write for info. o.p. (ISBN 0-7216-8232-4). Saunders.

Falkners of Mississippi: A Memoir. Murry C. Falkner. LC 67-24417. (Illus.). xxvi, 206p. 1967. 25.00x o.p. (ISBN 0-8071-0446-9). La State U Pr.

Fall from Grace. Larry Collins. 1985. 17.45 o.p. (ISBN 0-671-43609-0). S&S.

Fall of a Doll's House: Three Generations of American Women & the Houses They Lived In. Jane Davison. 256p. 1982. pap. 3.50 o.p. (ISBN 0-380-57398-9, 57398-9, Discus). Avon.

Fall of a Doll's House: Three Generations of American Women & the Houses They Lived In. Jane Davison. LC 79-19053. 252p. 1980. 10.95 o.p. (ISBN 0-03-041676-0). H Holt & Co.

Fall of Camelot. Time-Life Books Editors. (Enchanted World Ser.). (Illus.). 144p. (YA) (gr. 7 up). 1986. 19.93 o.p.; lib. bdg. 23.93 o.p. (ISBN 0-8094-5258-8). Time-Life.

Fall of Christianity. Gerrit J. Heering. LC 77-147670. (Library of War & Peace; Relig. & Ethical Positions on War). 1973. lib. bdg. 46.00 o.p. (ISBN 0-8240-0428-0). Garland Pub.

Fall of Hitler; or, Where Is Thy Peace. Samuel Solomon. 99p. 1985. 8.95 o.p. (ISBN 0-533-06162-8). Vantage.

Fall of Kelvin Walker. Alisdair Gray. LC 87-182. 160p. 1987. pap. 7.95 o.s.i. (ISBN 0-8021-3004-6). Grove.

Fall of Rome: Can It Be Explained? 2nd ed. Ed. by Mortimer Chambers. LC 75-135290. (gr. 11 up). 1971. pap. text ed. 13.95 o.p. (ISBN 0-03-084478-9, HoltC). HR&W.

Fall of Saigon: Scenes from the Sudden End of a Long War. David Butler. (Illus.). 493p. 1985. 17.45 o.p. (ISBN 0-671-46675-5). S&S.

Fall of the American University. Adam Ulam. 217p. 1973. 9.95 o.p. (ISBN 0-912050-20-9, Library Pr). Open Court.

Fall of the Hermit Kingdom. Woonsang Choi. LC 66-11939. 192p. 1967. 10.00 o.p. (ISBN 0-379-00277-9). Oceana.

Fall of the Peacock Throne: The Story of Iran. William H. Forbis. (McGraw-Hill Paperbacks Ser.). (Illus.). 320p. 1981. pap. text ed. 6.95 o.p. (ISBN 0-07-021486-7). McGraw.

Fall of Valor. Charles Jackson. 310p. 1986. pap. 5.95 o.p. (ISBN 0-87795-834-3). Morrow.

Fall of Worlds. Francine Mezo. 320p. 1980. pap. 2.50 o.p. (ISBN 0-380-75564-5, 75564). Avon.

Fall of Yugoslavia. Ilija Jukic. Tr. by Dorian Cooke. LC 73-16431. 1974. 8.50 o.s.i. (ISBN 0-15-130100-X). HarBraceJ.

Fall Out of Heaven: An Autobiographical Journey. Alan Cheuse. (Illus.). 328p. 1987. 17.95 o.p. (ISBN 0-87905-273-2, Peregrine Smith). Gibbs Smith Pub.

Fallen Crown: Three French Mary Stuart Plays of the Seventeenth Century. Michael G. Paulson. LC 79-6812. 207p. 1980. text ed. 22.00 o.p. (ISBN 0-8191-0959-2); pap. text ed. 12.50 o.p. (ISBN 0-8191-0960-6). U Pr of Amer.

Fallible Forms & Symbols: Discourses on Method in a Theology of Culture. Bernard E. Meland. LC 76-7868. 240p. 1976. 11.95 o.p. (ISBN 0-8006-0453-9, Fortress). Augsburg Fortress.

Falling. Susan F. Schaeffer. 240p. 1982. pap. 3.50 o.p. (ISBN 0-380-59006-9, 59006-9, Bard). Avon.

Falling Angel. William Hjortsberg. LC 78-53866. 1978. 8.95 o.p. (ISBN 0-15-130118-2). HarBraceJ.

Falling Apart. Nicholas Salaman. 192p. 1986. 14.95 o.p. (ISBN 0-531-15021-6). Watts.

Falling Apart or Coming Together: How You Can Experience the Faithfulness of God. Lois W. Johnson. LC 83-72112. 128p. (Orig.). 1984. pap. 6.95 o.p. (ISBN 0-8066-2056-0, 10-2208, Augsburg). Augsburg Fortress.

Falling Arches: The Case Against Federal Intervention in the Practice of Medicine. Ben B. White. 1977. 6.00 o.p. (ISBN 0-682-48871-2). Exposition-Phoenix.

Falling in Love Again: Marlene Dietrich. Donald Spoto. 19.95 o.p. (ISBN 0-316-80724-9). Little.

Falling Star: A True Story of Romance in the Wilds of Africa. Betty Leslie-Melville. 252p. 1985. 16.95 o.p. (ISBN 0-02-583980-2). Macmillan.

Falling Stars. Farris K. Hendrix. 1985. 6.95 o.p. (ISBN 0-533-06557-7). Vantage.

Falling Towards England: Unreliable Memoirs II. Clive James. 1986. 15.45 o.p. (ISBN 0-393-02360-5). Norton.

Fallout Shelter Architecture: A Bibliography. Edward H. Teague. (Architecture Ser.: Bibliography A 1326). 1985. pap. 2.00 o.p. (ISBN 0-89028-276-5). Vance Biblios.

False Inspector Dew. Peter Lovesey. 1983. pap. 2.95 o.s.i. (ISBN 0-394-71338-9). Pantheon.

False Match. Henry Bean. 1982. 13.50 o.s.i. (ISBN 0-671-44251-1, Poseidon). PB.

False Messiah. Leonard Wolf. 1982. 13.45 o.p. (ISBN 0-395-32528-5). HM.

False Messiahs: Prophets of the Millennium. Jack Gratus. LC 75-29890. 284p. 1976. 10.95 o.s.i. (ISBN 0-8008-2588-8). Taplinger.

False Promises: The Shaping of American Working-Class Consciousness. Stanley Aronowitz. LC 73-5679. 480p. 1974. 12.50 o.p. (ISBN 0-07-002315-8); pap. text ed. 5.95 o.p. (ISBN 0-07-002316-6). McGraw.

False Science: Underestimating the Soviet Threat. Steven Rosefielde. LC 81-1050. 300p. 1982. text ed. 14.95 o.p. (ISBN 0-87855-868-3). Transaction Pubs.

Falta una Pagina Que Trate de Eso. Rodriguez De Llano. 61p. (Span.). 1978. 7.50 o.p. (ISBN 0-317-11653-3). Dawsons.

Fame & the Founding Fathers. Douglass Adair. Ed. & intro. by H. Trevor Colbourn. LC 73-17356. 315p. 1974. 14.95x o.p. (ISBN 0-393-05499-3). Norton.

Fame, Fraud & Fortune: Seventy-four Years in Wall Street. Jacques Coe. (Illus.). 264p. 1983. 9.95 o.p. (ISBN 0-682-49917-X). Exposition-Phoenix.

Fame Game. Rona Jaffe. 1980. pap. 2.50 o.p. (ISBN 0-440-13043-3). Dell.

Fame II. Brad Benedict. LC 84-80884. (Illus.). 112p. (Orig.). 1984. pap. 12.95 o.p. (ISBN 0-394-62303-7, E960, Ever). Grove.

Familiar Allusions: A Hand-Book of Miscellaneous Information. William A. Wheeler. LC 66-24371. 586p. 1966. Repr. of 1882 ed. 51.00x o.p. (ISBN 0-8103-0166-0). Gale.

Familiar Faces, Hidden Lives: The Story of Homosexual Men in America Today. Howard Brown. LC 76-24910. 1976. 8.95 o.p. (ISBN 0-15-130149-2). HarBraceJ.

Familiar Garden Birds of America: An Illustrated Guide to the Birds in Your Own Backyard. Henry H. Collins & Ned R. Boyajian. (Nonfiction Ser.). 1985. pap. 9.95 o.p. (ISBN 0-8398-2852-7). G K Hall.

Familiar Ground. Elizabeth Cox. LC 84-45055. 205p. 1984. 14.95 o.p. (ISBN 0-689-11474-5, Atheneum). Macmillan.

Familiar Problems in Mechanical Drawing. Thomas E. French & C. L. Svensen. 1973. text ed. 11.60 o.p. (ISBN 0-07-022312-2). McGraw.

Familiar Quotations. John Bartlett. 1958. (ISBN 0-8022-0077-X). Philos Lib.

Familias Conviven Mejor con Amor. Howard Hendricks. 48p. 1979. 1.65 o.p. (ISBN 0-88113-095-8). Edit Betania.

Families. Ed. by Ruth E. Fideler. (Illus.). (gr. k-1). 1979. PLB 39.50 o.p. (ISBN 0-88296-001-6); tchr's. guide incl. o.p. (ISBN 0-88296-316-3). Gateway Pr MI.

Families Across the Life Cycle. Kathleen A. Knafl & Helen K. Grace. 1978. pap. text ed. 8.95 o.p. (ISBN 0-316-49897-1). Little.

Families Against the City: Middle Class Homes of Industrial Chicago, 1872-1890. Richard Sennett. LC 73-115190. (Joint Center for Urban Studies Publications Ser). (Illus.). 1970. 17.50x o.p. (ISBN 0-674-29225-1). Harvard U Pr.

Families & Communities As Educators. Hope Leichter. LC 79-63. 1979. text ed. 11.95 o.p. (ISBN 0-8077-2560-9); pap. text ed. 14.95x o.p. (ISBN 0-8077-2559-5). Tchrs Coll.

Families & How to Survive Them. Robin Skynner & John Cleese. (Illus.). 302p. 1984. 19.95 o.p. (ISBN 0-413-52640-2, 9239). Heinemann Ed.

Families Around the World. rev. ed. Marion H. Smith & Carol S. Prescott. LC 76-17687. (Fideler Social Studies). (Illus.). 96p. (gr. 1-2). 1979. text ed. 6.20 ea. 1-4 copies o.p. (ISBN 0-88296-007-5); text ed. 4.96 ea. 5 or more copies o.p.; tchrs' ed 4.96 o.p. (ISBN 0-88296-322-8). Gateway Pr MI.

Families at Risk. Ed. by Nicola Madge. (SSRC-DHSS Studies in Deprivation & Disadvantage: No. 8). viii, 228p. 1983. text ed. 33.00x o.p. (ISBN 0-435-82568-2). Gower Pub Co.

Families in an Urban Mold: Policy Implications of an Australian-U.S. Comparison. Ludwig L. Geismar & Shirley Geismar. (Pergamon Policy Studies). 1979. 60.00 o.p. (ISBN 0-08-023379-1). Pergamon.

Families in Britain. British Family Research Committee. 350p. 1983. pap. 25.00x o.p. (ISBN 0-7100-9236-9). Routledge Chapman & Hall.

Families of Children with Special Needs: Early Intervention Techniques for the Practitioner. Alan A. Mori. LC 83-258. 274p. 1983. 34.50 o.p. (ISBN 0-89443-934-0). Aspen Pub.

Families, Politics, & Public Policy: A Feminist Dialogue on Women & the State. Irene Diamond. LC 82-20357. 432p. 1983. 17.95 o.p. (ISBN 0-582-28268-3). Longman.

Families Without Villains: American Families in an Era of Change. Laura Lein. LC 83-48190. 128p. 1984. 27.00x o.p. (ISBN 0-669-07046-7). Lexington Bks.

Family. Ed. by Alice S. Rossi et al. 1978. 10.95 o.p. (ISBN 0-393-01167-4); pap. 6.95x o.p. (ISBN 0-393-09064-7). Norton.

Family. Ed Sanders. 1972. pap. 1.95 o.p. (ISBN 0-380-00771-1, 24802). Avon.

Family. Adrian Wilson. Ed. by Patrick McNeill. (Society Now Ser.). 160p. 1985. pap. 6.50 o.p. (ISBN 0-422-79860-6, 9676, Pub. by Tavistock England). Routledge Chapman & Hall.

Family: A Novel in the Form of a Memoir. Herbert Gold. LC 81-66964. 1981. 11.95 o.p. (ISBN 0-87795-332-5, Arbor Hse). Morrow.

Family: A Sociological Interpretation. 3rd ed. Bert N. Adams. LC 81-80805. 530p. 1981. text ed. 28.50 o.p. (ISBN 0-395-30555-1). HM.

Family Adventures. Bruce Clanton. LC 80-51060. (ps-6). 1980. pap. 6.95 o.p. (ISBN 0-89390-018-4). Resource Pubns.

Family Album. Danielle Steel. 1985. 18.95 o.s.i. (ISBN 0-8161-3859-1, Large Print Bks). G K Hall.

Family Album: A Personal Selection from Four Generations of Churchills. Mary Soames. 1982. 22.45 o.p. (ISBN 0-395-32525-0). HM.

Family & Friends. Anita Brookner. LC 85-6373. 1985. 13.45 o.s.i. (ISBN 0-394-54616-4). Pantheon.

Family & Friends. Anita Brookner. (General Ser.). 272p. 1986. lib. bdg. 15.95 o.p. (ISBN 0-8161-4061-8, Large Print Bks). G K Hall.

Family & Human Development. Ed. by John Touliatos. LC 72-6350. 197p. 1972. 24.50x o.p. (ISBN 0-8422-5050-6); pap. text ed. 9.75x o.p. (ISBN 0-8422-0245-5). Irvington.

Family & Individual Development. Ed. by John A. Meacham. 134p. 1986. 33.75x o.p. (ISBN 3-8055-4037-X). Transaction Pubs.

Family & Mental Health Problems in a Deaf Population. 2nd ed. John D. Rainer et al. (Illus.). 320p. 1969. 40.00 o.p. (ISBN 0-398-01539-2). C C Thomas.

Family & Pastoral Care: Theology & Pastoral Care. Herbert Anderson. pap. 5.95 o.p. (ISBN 0-317-02963-0, Fortress). Augsburg Fortress.

Family & School. Daphne Johnson & Elizabeth Ransom. 147p. 1983. 24.50 o.p. (ISBN 0-7099-2236-1, Pub. by Croom Helm Ltd). Routledge Chapman & Hall.

Family & Social Change: A Study of Family & Kinship in a South Wales Town. Colin Rosser & C. C. Harris. (International Library of Sociology). 256p. 1983. pap. 11.95x o.p. (ISBN 0-7100-9434-5). Routledge Chapman & Hall.

Family & Social Change in an African City: A Study of Rehousing in Lagos. Peter Marris. (African Studies Ser.: No. 8). (Illus.). 1962. 22.95 o.s.i. (ISBN 0-8101-0156-4). Northwestern U Pr.

Family & the School: A Joint Systems Approach to Problems with Children. Emilia Dowling & Elsie Osborne. 208p. 1985. 24.95x o.p. (ISBN 0-7102-0613-5); pap. 14.95x o.p. (ISBN 0-7102-0166-4). Routledge Chapman & Hall.

Family Approach to Eating Disorders: Assessment & Treatment of Anorexia Nervosa & Bulimia. Ed. by W. Vandereycken & J. Vanderlinden. 288p. Date not set. 45.00 o.s.i. (ISBN 0-08-035147-6, PBI). Pergamon.

Family Bible Encyclopedia, 2 vols. Alvera Mickelsen & Berkley Mickelsen. Incl. Volume I (A-K (ISBN 0-89191-100-6); Volume II (L-Z (ISBN 0-89191-127-8). LC 78-55384. (Illus.). 1978. 9.95 ea. o.p.; Set. 12.95 o.p. (ISBN 0-89191-201-0). Cook.

Family Book of Camping Lists. Charles Farmer & Kathleen Farmer. LC 80-39689. (Illus.). 180p. (Orig.). 1981. pap. 9.95 o.p. (ISBN 0-8117-2136-1). Stackpole.

Family Book of Praise. Mary J. Tully. (Illus.). 128p. (Orig.). 1980. 8.95 o.p. (ISBN 0-8215-6543-5); pap. 5.94 o.p. (ISBN 0-8215-6542-7). Sadlier.

Family Business. Vincent Patrick. 1985. 16.45 o.s.i. (ISBN 0-671-46513-9, Poseidon). PB.

Family: Center of Love & Life. Pope John Paul II. 1988. 3.00 o.p. (ISBN 0-317-67498-6, EP0484); pap. 2.00 o.p. (ISBN 0-317-67499-4). Dghtrs St Paul.

Family-Centered Maternity-Newborn Care: A Basic Text. Celeste R. Phillips. LC 80-11522. (Illus.). 382p. 1980. pap. text ed. 19.95 o.p. (ISBN 0-8016-3920-4). Mosby.

Family Choice in Schooling: Issues & Dilemmas. Ed. by Michael E. Manley-Casimir. LC 81-47024. 224p. 1981. 25.00x o.p. (ISBN 0-669-04546-2). Lexington Bks.

Family Christmas Tree Book. Tomie DePaola. LC 80-12081. (Illus.). 32p. (gr. k-3). 1984. pap. 5.95 o.p. (ISBN 0-8234-0535-4). Holiday.

Family Circle Christmas Treasury, 1987. Family Circle Editors. Ed. by Ceri Hadda. 280p. 1987. 19.95 o.p. (ISBN 0-933585-04-7). Family Circle Bks.

Family Circle Cookbook, 1986. Family Circle Editors. Ed. by JoAnn Billowitz. (Illus.). 1986. 19.95 o.p. Family Circle Bks.

Family Circle Cookbook, 1987. The Family Circle Staff. Ed. by JoAnn Brett-Billowitz. 320p. 1986. 19.95 o.p. (ISBN 0-933585-03-9). Family Circle Bks.

Family Conspiracy. Joan Phipson. LC 64-11494. (Illus.). (gr. 4-6). 1964. 5.95 o.p. (ISBN 0-15-227110-4, HJ). HarBraceJ.

Family Conspiracy. Joan Phipson. LC 64-11494. (Illus.). (gr. 4-6). 1966. pap. 4.95 o.p. (ISBN 0-15-630150-4, VoyB). HarBraceJ.

Family Decision Making: An Ecosystem Approach. Beatrice Paolucci et al. LC 76-39953. 190p. 1977. pap. text ed. write for info. o.p. (ISBN 0-02-391370-3). Macmillan.

Family Encyclopedia of Art. Bernard L. Myers & Trewin Copplestone. LC 79-833. (Illus.). 320p. 1979. 19.95 o.s.i. (ISBN 0-03-049046-4). H Holt & Co.

Family Enrichment: A Manual for Promoting Family Togetherness. Esther Christian. Ed. by Don L. Sorenson. LC 82-70356. 160p. 1982. pap. text ed. 5.95x o.p. (ISBN 0-932796-12-5). Ed Media Corp.

Family Fare: Christian Activities for Every Season of the Year. Darlene McRoberts. LC 81-65642. (Illus.). 80p. (Orig.). 1981. pap. 6.95 o.p. (ISBN 0-8066-1878-7, 10-2247, Augsburg). Augsburg Fortress.

Family Financial Planner. rev. ed. Ed. by Financial Publishing Co. Staff. 160p. 1987. pap. 18.00 o.p. (ISBN 0-87600-508-3). Finan Pub.

Family Financial Planning: A Handbook for Family Stewardship. Ruth A. Schweyer. (Orig.). 1984. pap. 0.95 o.p. (ISBN 0-8066-2100-1, 23-1605, Augsburg). Augsburg Fortress.

Family Financial Planning Book. Richard Birch. (Illus.). 224p. 1987. pap. 16.95 o.p. (ISBN 1-55013-020-X, Pub. by Key Porter Canada). U of Toronto Pr.

Family First Aid & Medical Guide. James Bevan. 192p. 1984. pap. 7.95 o.p. (ISBN 0-671-50891-1). S&S.

Family Fortunes. John Neufeld. LC 87-19616. 320p. 1988. 18.95 o.p. (ISBN 0-689-11816-3, Atheneum). Macmillan.

Family Forum. Jay Kesler. 1984. 12.95 o.p. (ISBN 0-88207-820-8). Victor Bks.

Family Fun Cartoons. 2nd ed. William Armstrong. (Armstrong Cartoon Ser.). (Illus.). 48p. (Orig.). (ps up). 1971. pap. 1.00 o.p. (ISBN 0-913452-03-3). Jesuit Bks.

Family Fun with Rocks. Julia Craw & Bernada French. pap. 1.00 o.p. (ISBN 0-910652-16-3). Gembooks.

Family Guide to Estate Planning, Funeral Arrangements, & Settling an Estate after Death. Theodore E. Hughes & David Klein. 240p. 1983. 16.95 o.s.i. (ISBN 0-684-17920-2, ScribT). Scribner.

Family Handyman Home Improvement Book. Family Handyman Magazine Editors. (Encore Edition). (Illus.). 1979. pap. 4.95 encore ed. o.p. (ISBN 0-684-16897-9, ScribT). Scribner.

Family Happiness. Laurie Colwin. 1983. pap. 3.50 o.p. (ISBN 0-449-20275-5, Crest). Fawcett.

Family History & Local History: A Regional History of England. David Hey. (Illus.). 276p. 1987. text ed. 35.95 o.p. Longman.

Family Homestead Reflections. Emil Gunsch. 1985. 6.95 o.p. (ISBN 0-533-06707-3). Vantage.

Family Hope for the World. Pontifical Council for the Family Staff. 71p. pap. 3.50 o.p. (ISBN 0-317-46615-1). New City.

Family in History: Interdisciplinary Essays. Theodore K. Rabb & Robert I. Rotberg. 240p. 1976. Repr. of 1973 ed. lib. bdg. 17.00x o.p. (ISBN 0-374-96705-9, Octagon). Hippocrene Bks.

Family in Latin America. Ed. by Man S. Das & Clinton J. Jesser. 1980. text ed. 40.00x o.p. (ISBN 0-7069-0800-7, Pub. by Vikas India). Advent NY.

Family in Question: Changing Households & Familiar Ideologies. D. Gittins. LC 85-24853. 208p. 1986. text ed. 28.50x o.p. (ISBN 0-391-03360-3); pap. text ed. 9.95x o.p. Humanities.

Family in the Modern World. Ed. by Ailsa Burns & Gill Bottomley. (Studies in Society Ser.: No. 18). 220p. 1983. text ed. 28.50x o.p. (ISBN 0-86861-190-5); pap. text ed. 14.95 o.p. (ISBN 0-86861-198-0). Unwin Hyman.

Family in Today's Money World. 2nd ed. Frances L. Feldman. LC 75-279660. 409p. 1976. 13.95 o.p. (ISBN 0-87304-130-5); pap. 10.00 o.p. (ISBN 0-87304-131-3). Family Serv.

Family in Transition: Rethinking Marriage, Sexuality, Child Rearing, & Family Organizations. 5th ed. Arlene S. Skolnick & Jerome H. Skolnick. 1986. pap. text ed. (ISBN 0-673-39601-0). Scott F.

Family Investment Guide. John Dorfman. LC 81-66020. 1981. 14.95 o.p. (ISBN 0-689-11208-4, Atheneum). Macmillan.

Family Law. 489p. 1983. 7.00 o.p. (ISBN 0-318-02391-1). ICLE Georgia.

Family Law, Cases & Materials on: 1983 Supplement. Judith Areen. (University Casebook Ser.). 393p. 1982. pap. text ed. 8.95 o.p. (ISBN 0-88277-107-8). Foundation Pr.

Family Law Handbook. Ed. by S. Joel Kolko. 290p. 1985. pap. text ed. 25.00 o.p. (ISBN 0-87179-474-8, 0474). BNA.

Family Law Section: Mid-Year Meeting & Seminars. 1984. 30.00 o.p. (ISBN 0-88129-139-0). Wash Bar CLE.

Family Lawyer's Symposium. Pennsylvania Bar Institute Staff. 196p. 1985. 55.00 o.p. (ISBN 0-318-19045-1, 303). PA Bar Inst.

Family Legal Companion. Thomas Hauser. LC 84-26117. 240p. 1985. text ed. 15.95 o.p. (ISBN 0-07-027216-6). McGraw.

Family Lie. Georges Simenon. Tr. by Caroline Hillier. LC 78-53898. (Helen & Kurt Wolff Bks.). 1978. 7.95 o.p. (ISBN 0-15-156247-4). HarBraceJ.

Family Life. Russell Banks. (Orig.). 1985. pap. 3.45 o.p. (ISBN 0-380-00258-2, 22855). Avon.

Family Life & Morality: Studies in Black & White. William Gibson. LC 79-57076. 116p. 1980. pap. text ed. 10.00 o.p. (ISBN 0-8191-0969-X). U Pr of Amer.

Family Life & Sex Education: Curriculum & Instruction. Esther D. Schulz & Sally R. Williams. (Orig.). 1969. pap. text ed. 10.95 o.p. (ISBN 0-15-527090-7, HC). HarBraceJ.

Family Life: Book One. Helen R. Prevo. 1967. pap. 3.00 o.p. (ISBN 0-88323-010-0, 110); wkbk. 2.75x o.p. (ISBN 0-88323-011-9, 111). Pendergrass Pub.

Family Life: Book Two. Helen R. Prevo. 1969. pap. 3.00x o.p. (ISBN 0-88323-012-7, 112); wkbk. 2.75x o.p. (ISBN 0-88323-013-5, 113). Pendergrass Pub.

Family Life Cycle: A Framework for Family Therapy. Ed. by Elizabeth A. Carter & Monica McGoldrick. 1980. text ed. 29.50 o.p. (ISBN 0-89876-028-3). Gardner Pr.

Family Life Education: Focus on Student Involvement. K. B. Green. 3.00 o.p. (ISBN 0-317-52234-5, A261-08420). Home Econ Educ.

Family Life in the Seventeenth Century: The Verneys of Claydon. Miriam Slater. LC 83-11181. 224p. 1984. 21.95x o.p. (ISBN 0-7100-9477-9). Routledge Chapman & Hall.

Family Life in the U. S. A. Gladys Alesi & Dora Pantell. (gr. 9-12). 1987. pap. text ed. 4.50 o.p. (ISBN 0-13-301904-7, 17391). Prentice ESL.

Family Life Yours: Breaking the Patterns of Drug Abuse. Guillermo Bernal & James L. Sorensen. 192p. 1987. 15.95 o.p. (ISBN 0-06-250820-2). HarpR.

Family Madness: A Novel. Thomas Keneally. 288p. 1986. 17.45 o.s.i. (ISBN 0-671-61175-5). S&S.

Family Man. Joseph Monninger. LC 81-12870. 1982. 10.95 o.p. (ISBN 0-689-11235-1, Atheneum). Macmillan.

Family Man. Robin Moore & Milt Machlin. 608p. 1988. pap. 4.50 o.s.i. (ISBN 1-55785-045-3). Bart Books.

Family Mashber. Der Nister. Tr. by Leonard Wolf. 1987. 22.45 o.s.i. (ISBN 0-671-52768-1). Summit Bks.

Family Medical Guide: The Illustrated Medical & Health Advisor. Consumer Guide Editors. LC 83-13105. (Illus.). 576p. 1983. 12.95 o.p. (ISBN 0-688-02210-3). Morrow.

Family Medicine: A Guidebook for Practitioners of the Art. David B. Shires & Brian K. Hennen. (Illus.). 1980. text ed. 25.00 o.p. (ISBN 0-07-056920-7). McGraw.

Family Medicine: Principles & Practice. 2nd ed. Ed. by Robert B. Taylor et al. 2020p. 1983. 85.00 o.p. Soc Tchrs Fam Med.

Family Microcomputer-Microprocessor User's Manual: M 6805 HMOS-M 146805 CMOS. 2nd ed. Margaret Dickie. (Illus.). 272p. 1983. pap. 18.95 o.p. (ISBN 0-13-541375-3). P-H.

Family Moskat. Isaac Bashevis Singer. 608p. 1980. pap. 2.95 o.p. (ISBN 0-449-24066-5, Crest). Fawcett.

Family Occasions: A Cookbook. Ed. by Cooking Committee of Concord Alternative Residence, Inc. LC 83-51249. (Illus.). 216p. 1984. pap. 5.95 o.p. (ISBN 0-89909-029-X). Yankee Bks.

Family of Children. (Illus.). 192p. 1977. 14.95 o.p. (ISBN 0-448-14412-3, G&D); pap. 11.95 o.p. (ISBN 0-399-50965-8, G&D). Putnam Pub Group.

Family of God: A Sympolic Study of Christian Life in America. William L. Warner. LC 75-11494. (Illus.). 451p. 1975. Repr. of 1961 ed. lib. bdg. 25.25 o.p. (ISBN 0-8371-8206-9, WAFG). Greenwood.

Family of Man. Edward Steichen. (Illus.). 1955. popular ed. 12.50 o.p. (ISBN 0-671-24380-2). S&S.

Family of Pascual Duarte. Camilo J. Cela. 144p. 1976. pap. 1.45 o.p. (ISBN 0-380-01175-1, 60749-2, Bard). Avon.

Family of Strangers. Marian M. Poe. (Orig.). 1981. pap. 2.50 o.p. (ISBN 0-505-51648-9, Pub. by Tower Bks). Dorchester Pub Co.

Family Out-of-Pocket Expenditures for Health Care: United States, 1980. Jonathan H. Sunshine & Marvin Dicker. LC 87-7721. (DHHS Publication PHS Ser.). 313p. 1987. pap. 15.00 o.p. (ISBN 0-318-23745-8, 017-022-01010-1). USGPO.

Family Passions. Shelley Katz. 432p. (Orig.). 1983. pap. 3.95 o.p. (ISBN 0-440-12482-4). Dell.

Family Pilgrim's Progress. John Bunyan. Retold by Jean Watson. LC 83-50310. (Illus.). 128p. (gr. 3-5). 1983. 9.95 o.p. (ISBN 0-8423-0863-6). Tyndale.

Family Planning for Developing Countries. Eto I. Falola. (Illus.). 160p. 1982. 8.50 o.p. (ISBN 0-682-49759-2). Exposition-Phoenix.

Family Planning: Fundamentals for Health Professionals. Ann Cowper & Cyril Young. (Illus.). 160p. 1981. 25.00 o.p. (ISBN 0-85664-907-4, Pub. by Croom Helm Ltd); pap. 11.50 o.p. (ISBN 0-85664-908-2). Routledge Chapman & Hall.

Family Planning Programs: An Evaluation of Experience. Roberto Cuca. (Working Paper: No. 345). xii, 134p. 1979. 8.00 o.p. (ISBN 0-686-36195-4, WP-0345). World Bank.

Family Pocket Promise Book. Larry Christenson. LC 83-72175. 128p. (Orig.). 1983. pap. 2.95 o.p. (ISBN 0-87123-303-7, 200303). Bethany Hse.

Family, Politics & Social Theory. D. H. Morgan. 218p. 1985. 35.00 o.p. (ISBN 0-7100-9943-6). Routledge Chapman & Hall.

Family, Power, & Politics in Egypt: Sayed Bey Marei-His Clan, Clients & Cohorts. Robert Springborg. LC 81-43527. 288p. 1982. 36.95x o.p. (ISBN 0-8122-7835-6). U of Pa Pr.

Family Prayers. Frank Colquhoun. 80p. 1984. pap. 1.35 o.p. (ISBN 0-88028-040-9). Forward Movement.

Family Prayers. Ron Klug & Lyn Klug. LC 79-50081. 1979. pap. 4.95 o.p. (ISBN 0-8066-1708-X, 10-2258, Augsburg). Augsburg Fortress.

Family Problems & What to Do About Them. Wallace Denton. LC 71-139690. 1971. pap. 4.50 o.s.i. (ISBN 0-664-24908-6, Westminster). Westminster John Knox.

Family Psychology: Theory, Therapy, & Training. Luciano L'Abate. LC 82-20255. 328p. (Orig.). 1983. lib. bdg. 34.25 o.p. (ISBN 0-8191-2883-X); pap. text ed. 16.25 o.p. (ISBN 0-8191-2884-8). U Pr of Amer.

Family Reunion. T. S. Eliot. 1947. 4.95 o.p. (ISBN 0-15-130155-7). HarBraceJ.

Family Reunion. Joyce Harrington. 320p. 1983. pap. 2.95 o.p. (ISBN 0-380-63099-0, 63099-0). Avon.

Family Rituals. Compiled by Charla Honea. LC 81-52861. (Illus., Orig.). 1981. pap. 3.95x o.p. (ISBN 0-8358-0433-X). Upper Room.

Family Rooms, Dens & Studios. Sunset Magazine & Books Editors. LC 79-88159. (Illus.). 96p. 1979. pap. 5.95 o.p. (ISBN 0-376-01132-7, Sunset Bks). Sunset-Lane.

Family Roots of Adolescent Delinquency. Joseph F. Perez. 1978. 23.95 o.p. Van Nos Reinhold.

Family Secret. Joe Cumming & Doug Cumming. LC 82-83143. (Illus.). 76p. 1982. 8.95 o.p. (ISBN 0-931948-40-1). Peachtree Pubs.

Family Secrets: What You Need to Know to Build a Strong Christian Family. Gladys Hunt. 98p. 1985. pap. 3.95 o.p. (ISBN 0-89283-233-9, Pub. by Vine Books). Servant.

Family Security Through Estate Planning. 2nd ed. Arnold D. Kahn. LC 82-4673. 224p. 1983. text ed. 22.50 o.p. (ISBN 0-07-033216-9). McGraw.

Family, Society, & the Individual. 4th ed. William M. Kephart. LC 76-13094. (Illus.). 1977. text ed. 18.15 o.p. (ISBN 0-395-24247-9). HM.

Family, Society, & the Individual. 5th ed. William M. Kephart. LC 80-81847. (Illus.). 624p. 1980. text ed. 27.50 o.p. (ISBN 0-395-29760-5). HM.

Family Structure & Effective Health Behavior: The Energized Family. Lois Pratt. LC 75-29817. (Illus.). 256p. 1976. pap. 17.95 o.p. (ISBN 0-395-18702-8). HM.

Family Symphony. Virginia Clawson. LC 84-17524. 1984. 7.95 o.p. (ISBN 0-8054-5661-9). Broadman.

Family Systems in America. 3rd ed. Ira L. Reiss. LC 80-10168. 544p. 1980. text ed. 28.95 o.p. (ISBN 0-03-047246-6, HoltC). HR&W.

Family Themes & Hawthorne's Fiction: The Tenacious Web. Gloria C. Erlich. 190p. 1984. text ed. 30.00 o.p. (ISBN 0-8135-1028-7). Rutgers U Pr.

Family Therapy. M. Rolf Olsen. 244p. 1987. 29.95 o.p. (ISBN 0-422-79100-8, 1198, Pub. by Tavistock England). Routledge Chapman & Hall.

Family Through Literature. Nicholas Tavuchis & William J. Goode. LC 74-8935. (Sociology Ser.). 448p. 1974. text ed. 19.95 o.p. (ISBN 0-07-062919-6). McGraw.

Family Ties: Alex Gets the Business. Joe Claro. 112p. (Orig.). (YA) (gr. 7 up). 1986. pap. 2.95 o.p. (ISBN 0-380-75235-2). Avon.

Family Ties, Corporate Bonds: How We Act Out Family Roles in the Office. Paula R. Bernstein. 192p. 1987. pap. 7.95 o.p. (ISBN 0-8050-0114-X). H Holt & Co.

Family Ties That Bind: A Self-Help Guide to Change Through Family of Origin Therapy. Richard W. Richardson. 144p. 1984. pap. 7.95 o.p. (ISBN 0-88908-601-X, 9527). ISC Pr.

Family Trade. James Carroll. 1982. 14.95 o.p. (ISBN 0-316-13013-3). Little.

Family Trap. Hila Colman. 1982. cancelled o.s.i. Macmillan.

Family Work in Action: A Handbook for Social Workers. Ed. by Oded Manor & David Bell. 179p. 1984. 32.00 o.p. (ISBN 0-422-78750-7, 9016, Pub. by Tavistock England). Routledge Chapman & Hall.

Family's Construction of Reality. David Reiss. LC 81-2703. (Illus.). 448p. 1981. text ed. 29.50x o.p. (ISBN 0-674-29415-7). Harvard U Pr.

Famine en Afrique: Rapports de Conference d'un Groupe de Travail sur la Famine en Afrique a Kinshasha au Zaire en janvier 1980. Ed. by J. P. Carter. 46p. 1982. pap. 14.25 o.p. (ISBN 0-08-028885-5, H120). Pergamon.

Famished Land. Elizabeth Byrd. 1978. pap. 1.95 o.p. (ISBN 0-380-39313-1, 39313). Avon.

Famous All over Town. Danny Santiago. 288p. 1983. 14.50 o.p. (ISBN 0-671-43249-4). S&S.

Famous Criminal Trials. Andrew David. LC 79-17543. (On Trial Ser.). (Illus.). (gr. 5 up). 1979. PLB 8.95 o.p. (ISBN 0-8225-1427-3). Lerner Pubns.

Famous Curses. Daniel Cohen. LC 79-52039. (High Interest, Low Vocabulary Ser.). (Illus.). (gr. 4-9). 1979. 8.95 o.p. (ISBN 0-396-07712-9). Dodd.

Famous Duels & Assassinations. Lewis Melville & Reginald Hargreaves. LC 72-178619. (Illus.). 320p. 1974. Repr. of 1929 ed. 40.00x o.p. (ISBN 0-8103-3973-0). Gale.

Famous Faces: Price Guide & Catalog for Magazine Collectors. Frank R. Zawacki. LC 84-52051. (Illus.). 292p. 1985. 12.95 o.p. (ISBN 0-87069-433-2). Wallace-Homestead.

Famous Monkey Last Words. Paul White. (Jungle Doctor Picture Fable Ser.). 21p. (gr. k-5). 1986. pap. 26.50 o.p. (ISBN 0-85364-370-9, Pub. by Paternoster UK). Attic Pr.

Famous New Englanders Cookbook. Ed. by Sandra J. Taylor. LC 84-50426. (Illus.). 160p. 1984. 11.95 o.p. (ISBN 0-89909-037-0); pap. 8.95 o.p. (ISBN 0-89909-039-7). Yankee Bks.

Famous People: Grades Five to Thirteen. rev. ed. Lois S. Roets. 60p. 1985. tchrs.' ed. 8.00 o.p. (ISBN 0-911943-05-6). Leadership Pubs.

Famous Phrases from History. Charles F. Hemphill, Jr. LC 82-7217. 173p. 1982. pap. 16.95x o.p. (ISBN 0-89950-052-8). McFarland & Co.

Famous Sayings & Their Authors: A Collection of Historical Sayings in English, French, German, Greek, Italian, & Latin. Edward Latham. LC 68-26582. 278p. 1970. Repr. of 1904 ed. 40.00x o.p. (ISBN 0-8103-3141-1). Gale.

Famous Secret Societies. John H. Lepper. LC 73-143638. 360p. 1971. Repr. of 1932 ed. 43.00 o.p. (ISBN 0-8103-3648-0). Gale.

Famous Sergeants & Corporals in American History. Ed. by Walter Haan. (Illus.). 128p. (Orig.). 1988. pap. 9.95 o.p. (ISBN 0-913337-10-2). Southfarm Pr.

Fan Man. William Kotzwinkle. 1979. pap. 2.95 o.p. (ISBN 0-380-00790-8, 43125-4). Avon.

Fancy Footwork. Cory Kenyon. (Candlelight Ecstasy Ser.: No. 507). (Orig.). 1987. pap. 2.25 o.p. (ISBN 0-440-12445-X). Dell.

Fanfarlo: Bilingual Edition. Charles Baudelaire. Tr. by Greg Boyd. LC 85-47684. 128p. (Orig., Eng. & Fr.). 1986. pap. 6.95 o.p. (ISBN 0-88739-003-X, Pub. by Donald S Ellis, San Francisco). Creative Arts Bk.

Fanny Burney: An Annotated Bibliography. Joseph A. Grav. LC 80-9022. (British Literature Catalogue Ser.). 190p. 1981. lib. bdg. 36.00 o.p. (ISBN 0-8240-9325-9). Garland Pub.

Fanny Burney & Her Friends: Select Passages from Her Diary & Other Writings. Frances B. Arblay. LC 75-76135. 346p. 1969. Repr. of 1890 ed. 35.00x o.p. (ISBN 0-8103-3896-3). Gale.

Fanny Crosby's Story. S. Trevena Jackson. (Christian Biography Ser.). 198p. 1981. pap. 3.95 o.p. (ISBN 0-8010-5127-4). Baker Bk.

Fanny G. Lou Graham. (Orig.). 1980. pap. text ed. 2.25 o.p. (ISBN 0-505-51569-5, Pub. by Tower Bks). Dorchester Pub Co.

Fanny the Soccer Star. Martha T. Amos. (Illus.). 1979. 5.50 o.p. (ISBN 0-682-49455-0). Exposition-Phoenix.

Fans. Nancy Armstrong. 174p. 1985. 24.95 o.s.i. (ISBN 0-285-62591-8, Pub. by Souvenir Pr Ltd UK). Seven Hills Bk Dists.

Fans. W. C. Osborne. 1977. 60.00 o.p. (ISBN 0-08-021725-7); pap. 60.00 o.p. (ISBN 0-08-021726-5). Pergamon.

Fans: Design & Operation of Centrifugal, Axial Flow & Cross Flow Fans. B. Eck. LC 72-137613. 612p. 1974. 115.00 o.p. (ISBN 0-08-015872-2); Pergamon.

Fanshen. David Hare. 86p. 1976. pap. 6.95 o.p. (ISBN 0-571-11019-3). Faber & Faber.

Fantasists on Fantasy. Robert H. Boyer & Kenneth J. Zahorski. 304p. (Orig.). 1984. pap. 3.95 o.p. (ISBN 0-380-86553-X, 86553, Discus). Avon.

Fantastic Bicycle Book. Steven Lindblom. (gr. 1-12). 1979. 8.95 o.p. (ISBN 0-395-28481-3); pap. 3.95 o.p. (ISBN 0-395-28482-1). HM.

Fantastic in Literature. Eric S. Rabkin. LC 75-30201. 1976. 26.50 o.p. (ISBN 0-691-06301-X); pap. 10.50 o.p. (ISBN 0-691-01340-3). Princeton U Pr.

Fantastic Invasion: Notes on Contemporary Africa. Patrick Marnham. LC 79-2763. 1980. 10.95 o.p. (ISBN 0-15-130301-0). HarBraceJ.

Fantasticks. Harvey Schmidt & Tom Jones. (YA) (gr. 7 up). 1976. pap. 2.95 o.p. (ISBN 0-380-00915-3, 60047-1, Bard). Avon.

Fantasy Football. Adam Lerner. (Illus.). 72p. (gr. 4 up). 1984. PLB 8.95 o.p. (ISBN 0-8225-1501-6). Lerner Pubns.

Fantasy Football Digest, 1988. Cliff Charpentier. 1988. pap. 9.95 o.p. (ISBN 0-8225-0075-2). Lerner Pubns.

Fantasy Games. Peter Dally. 1976. pap. 1.75 o.p. (ISBN 0-380-00658-8, 29769). Avon.

Fantasy Hall of Fame. Ed. by Robert Silverberg & Martin H. Greenberg. 1983. 16.95 o.p. (ISBN 0-87795-521-2, Arbor Hse). Morrow.

Fantasy in Literature. John Aquino. 64p. 1977. pap. 6.95 o.p. (ISBN 0-8106-1817-6). NEA.

Fantasy in Verse. Grace Emmert Northrop. 1977. 4.00 o.p. (ISBN 0-682-48718-X). Exposition-Phoenix.

Fantasy Literature: An Approach to Reality. T. E. Apter. LC 82-47794. 176p. 1982. 20.00x o.p. (ISBN 0-253-32101-8). Ind U Pr.

Fantasy of Reason: The Life & Thought of William Godwin. Don Locke. (Illus.). 1980. 30.00x o.p. (ISBN 0-7100-0387-0). Routledge Chapman & Hall.

Fantasy Summer. Susan B. Pfeffer. (Perfect Image Ser.). 192p. (gr. 7 up). 1984. 10.95 o.p. (ISBN 0-399-21086-5, Putnam). Putnam Pub Group.

Fantazius Mallare: A Mysterious Oath. Ben Hecht. LC 78-6637. (Illus.). 1978. pap. 3.95 o.p. (ISBN 0-15-630160-1, Harv). HarBraceJ.

FAO Agricultural Commodity Projections to 1990. (FAO Economic & Social Development Paper Ser.: No. 62). (Illus.). 212p. (Orig.). 1986. pap. text ed. 16.25 o.p. (ISBN 92-5-102366-2, F2962, FAO). UNIPUB.

FAO Seed Review: 1979-80. (AGP-SIDP Ser.). 225p. (Eng. & Fr.). 1981. pap. 13.50 o.p. (ISBN 92-5-101149-4, F2276, FAO). UNIPUB.

FAO Trade Yearbook, 1984, Vol. 38. 370p. 1986. text ed. 34.50 o.p. (ISBN 92-5-002266-2, F2820, FAO). UNIPUB.

FAO-WHO Evaluation of Dieldrin Residues in Food. 99p. 1973. pap. 7.50 o.p. (ISBN 0-686-70617-X, F1978, FAO). UNIPUB.

FAO-WHO Food Additives Data System. 231p. (Orig.). pap. 12.00 o.p. (ISBN 92-5-101471-X, F2566, FAO). UNIPUB.

Far Away & Long Ago. W. H. Hudson. 318p. 1985. pap. 5.95x o.p. (ISBN 0-460-11956-7, Pub. by Evman England). Biblio Dist.

Far Beyond the Stars. Bhagwan Shree Rajneesh. Ed. by Ma Prem Maneesha. LC 82-229145. (Initiation Talks Ser.). (Illus.). 306p. (Orig.). 1980. 8.95 o.p. (ISBN 0-88050-059-X). Chidvilas Inc.

Far Cry. Michael Stewart. 1986. 13.95 o.p. (ISBN 0-317-53105-0, Large Print Bks). G K Hall.

Far East. 5th ed. Chester A. Bain. Ed. by June W. Bain. (Quality Paperback: No. 44). (Orig.). 1972. pap. 3.95 o.p. (ISBN 0-8226-0044-7). Littlefield.

Far East: A Concise History. F. C. Jones. 1966. 17.75 o.p. (ISBN 0-08-011642-6); pap. 7.75 o.p. (ISBN 0-08-011641-8). Pergamon.

Far East & Australasia, Nineteen Eighty-Eight. 19th ed. 1000p. 1987. 170.00x o.p. (ISBN 0-946653-36-4, Pub. by Europa England). Gale.

Far East & Australasia 1984-85. 16th ed. LC 74-417170. (Illus.). 945p. 1985. 145.00 o.p. (ISBN 0-946653-00-3, EUR54, EUR). UNIPUB.

Far East & Australasia 1987. 18th ed. 989p. 1986. 155.00x o.p. (ISBN 0-317-58276-3, Pub. by Europa England). Gale.

Far East & Australasia 1987. 18th ed. Taylor & Francis Inc Europa Staff. 98p. 1987. 155.00x o.p. (ISBN 0-946653-23-2, Pub. by Europe England). Intl Pubns Serv.

Far East One. (Everything Bks.). 128p. 1983. pap. 2.98 o.p. (ISBN 0-913428-76-0). Landfall Pr.

Far Eastern Lacquer. George Kuwayama. (Illus.). 128p. (Orig.). 1982. pap. 15.95 o.p. (ISBN 0-87587-108-9). LA Co Art Mus.

Far Eastern Languages Catalog, 22 vols. Library of Congress Staff. 1972. Set. lib. bdg. 2265.00 o.p. (ISBN 0-8161-0980-X, Hall Library). G K Hall.

Far Eastern Vendors Strategies ıʊr U. S. Microcomputer Markets. International Resource Development, Inc. Staff. 202p. 1983. 1850.00x o.p. (ISBN 0-88694-582-8). Intl Res Dev.

Far from Denmark. Peter Martins & Robert Cornfield. 1982. 24.95 o.p. (ISBN 0-316-54855-3). Little.

Far from the Sea. Evan Hunter. LC 82-71564. 320p. 1983. 12.95 o.p. (ISBN 0-689-11338-2). Macmillan.

Far Frontier. William O. Steele. LC 59-12905. (Illus.). (gr. 3-7). 1959. 5.50 o.p. (ISBN 0-15-227171-6, HJ). HarBraceJ.

Far-Infrared Techniques. M. F. Kimmitt. 1970. 15.95x o.p. (ISBN 0-85086-009-1, NO. 2911, Pub. by Pion England); pap. 9.50x o.p. (ISBN 0-85086-015-6, 2905). Routledge Chapman & Hall.

Far Out Isn't Far Enough. Tomi Ungerer. LC 83-49425. (Illus.). 176p. 1984. pap. 12.95 o.p. (ISBN 0-394-62189-1, E938, Ever). Grove.

Far Side of Paradise: A Biography of F. Scott Fitzgerald. rev. & enl. ed. Arthur Mizener. (Illus.). pap. 4.95 o.p. (ISBN 0-395-08395-8, 46, SenEd). HM.

Far Side of Victory. Joanne Greenberg. 233p. 1983. 14.95 o.p. (ISBN 0-03-063252-8). H Holt & Co.

Far Southwest, Eighteen Forty-Six to Nineteen Twelve: A Territorial History. Howard R. Lamar. (Illus.). 1970. pap. 6.95x o.p. (ISBN 0-393-00522-4, Norton Lib). Norton.

Far Tortuga. Peter Matthiessen. LC 87-40154. (Vintage Contemporaries Ser.). 416p. 1984. pap. 10.95 o.p. (ISBN 0-394-75667-3, Vin). Random.

FAR 121 & 63. Federal Aviation Administration Staff. 1987. pap. 9.95 o.p. (ISBN 0-940732-48-3, Pub. by ASA). Aviation.

FAR, 1988. Aviation Supplies & Academics Staff. 1988. pap. 5.95 o.p. (ISBN 0-940732-54-8, Pub. by ASA). Aviation.

Faraday As a Natural Philosopher. Joseph Agassi. LC 73-151130. 1972. lib. bdg. 23.00x o.s.i. (ISBN 0-226-01046-5). U of Chicago Pr.

Faraway Island. Barbara Corcoran. LC 76-25152. (gr. 5-9). 1977. PLB 6.95 o.p. (ISBN 0-689-30550-8, Atheneum). Macmillan.

Faraway Loves. Jan Gelman. (Follow Your Heart Romance Ser.: No. 5). 128p. (Orig.). (gr. 5 up). 1984. pap. 1.95 o.p. (ISBN 0-671-47579-7). Archway.

Farberware: World of Wok Cookery. Gail Piazza. LC 82-71462. (Illus.). 144p. 1982. 10.95 o.p. (ISBN 0-916752-57-7). Longman Trade.

Farce. Albert Bermel. 1983. pap. 9.50 o.p. (ISBN 0-671-25149-X, Touchstone Bks). S&S.

Farce: Amorous Intrigue & Deception 1. Ed. by Walter H. Rubsamen. (Ballad Opera Ser.). 1975. lib. bdg. 61.00 o.p. (ISBN 0-8240-0911-8). Garland Pub.

Farce: Amorous Intrigue & Deception 2. Ed. by Walter H. Rubsamen. (Ballad Opera Ser.). 1975. lib. bdg. 61.00 o.p. (ISBN 0-8240-0912-6). Garland Pub.

Farce, Broad or Satirical. Ed. by Walter H. Rubsamen. (Ballad Opera Ser.). 1974. lib. bdg. 61.00 o.p. (ISBN 0-8240-0910-X). Garland Pub.

Farce: From Aristophanes to Woody Allen. Albert Bermel. 1982. 19.95 o.p. (ISBN 0-671-25148-1). S&S.

Farce: Magical Transformation & Necromancy. Ed. by Walter H. Rubsamen. (Ballad Opera Ser.). 1974. lib. bdg. 61.00 o.p. (ISBN 0-8240-0909-6). Garland Pub.

Farewell, Babylon. Naim Kattan. Tr. by Sheila Fischman from Fr. LC 79-25580. 192p. 1980. 9.95 o.s.i. (ISBN 0-8008-2598-5). Taplinger.

Farewell in June: Four Russian Plays. A. Vampilov et al. Tr. by Kevin Windle & Amanda Metcalf. LC 82-11161. (Contemporary Russian Writing Ser.). 273p. 1983. 14.50 o.p. (ISBN 0-7022-1862-6). U of Queensland Pr.

Farewell Ministry of Christ: John 13-17. Ernest T. Wilson. LC 81-316. 96p. (Orig.). 1981. pap. 2.50 o.p. (ISBN 0-87213-965-4). Loizeaux.

Farewell the Ivory Tower: Universities in Transition. J. A. Corry. LC 70-124985. 130p. 1970. 8.25 o.p. (ISBN 0-7735-0076-6, Pub. by McGill Canada). U of Toronto Pr.

Farewell the Trumpets: The Decline of an Empire. James Morris. LC 79-24253. (Illus.). 576p. 1978. 14.95 o.p. (ISBN 0-15-130404-1). HarBraceJ.

Farewell to Arms. Ernest Hemingway. 336p. 1983. 14.95 o.s.i. (ISBN 0-684-10236-6, ScribT). Scribner.

Farewell to European History: or, the Conquest of Nihilism. Alfred Weber. Ed. by R. F. Hull. LC 76-52396. 1977. Repr. of 1948 ed. lib. bdg. 35.00x o.p. (ISBN 0-8371-9447-4, WEFA). Greenwood.

Farewell to Fear. Nelson L. Price. (Orig.). 1983. pap. 5.95 o.p. (ISBN 0-8054-5533-7). Broadman.

Farewell to France. Noel Barber. 832p. 1984. pap. 4.75 o.p. (ISBN 0-380-68064-5, 68064-5). Avon.

Farewell to Manzanar. Jeanne W. Houston & James D. Houston. (San Francisco Book Co. Bk.). 1973. 8.95 o.p. (ISBN 0-395-17215-2). HM.

Farewell to Russia. Richard Hugo. (Orig.). 1989. pap. 4.50 o.p. (ISBN 1-55817-165-7). Pinnacle Bks.

Farm. Louis Bromfield. 1980. pap. 2.50 o.p. (ISBN 0-380-41715-4, 41715). Avon.

Farm. Dorothy Lowell. 96p. 1986. 6.95 o.p. (ISBN 0-8062-2797-4). Carlton.

Farm see My Toys, My First Book, Baby Animals, the Farm.

Farm Accounting & Business Analysis Workbook. Sydney James. (Illus.). 1975. pap. 7.50x workbook o.p. (ISBN 0-8138-0610-0). Iowa St U Pr.

Farm Animal Health & Disease Control. 2nd ed. John K. Winkler. LC 81-18656. (Illus.). 230p. 1982. text ed. 21.00 o.p. (ISBN 0-8121-0843-4). Lea & Febiger.

Farm Animal Management & Poultry Production. 2nd ed. N. S. Sastry & C. K. Thomas. (Illus.). xv, 539p. 1982. text ed. 40.00x o.p. (ISBN 0-7069-1730-8, Pub by Vikas India). Advent NY.

Farm Animals. (Chubby Panoramas Ser.). (Illus.). 1983. 2.85 o.s.i. (ISBN 0-671-47665-3, Little Simon). S&S.

Farm Animals. Dorothy Rose. (Chubby Banana Split Board Bks.). (ps). 1984. 2.95 o.s.i. (ISBN 0-671-50957-8, Little Simon). S&S.

Farm Builder's Handbook. 3rd ed. R. J. Lytle. 1981. text ed. 29.95 o.p. (ISBN 0-07-039276-5). McGraw.

Farm Cook & Rule Book: The Golden Anniversary Edition. Nell B. Nichols. LC 76-932. 320p. 1976. 12.95 o.p. (ISBN 0-15-130406-8). HarBraceJ.

Farm Cook & Rule Book: The Golden Anniversary Edition. Nell B. Nichols. LC 76-932. 1976. pap. 6.95 o.p. (ISBN 0-15-130407-6, Harv). HarBraceJ.

Farm Electrification. Robert H. Brown. (Agricultural Engineering Ser). 1956. text ed. 40.95 o.p. (ISBN 0-07-008462-9). McGraw.

Farm Estate & Business Planning. 9th ed. Neil E. Harl. LC 84-70455. 394p. 1984. pap. 14.95 o.p. (ISBN 0-930264-52-5). Century Comm.

Farm Friends. (Animals & Their Babies Ser.). (Illus.). 32p. (ps-3). 1987. pap. 5.95 o.s.i. (ISBN 0-671-63489-5, Little Simon). S&S.

Farm Giants. Ross R. Olney. LC 82-1798. (Illus.). 48p. (ps-3). 1982. 12.95 o.s.i. (ISBN 0-689-30937-6, Atheneum Childrens Bks). Macmillan.

Farm Holiday Guide to England. 40th ed. (Illus.). 512p. (Orig.). 1987. pap. 12.95 o.p. (ISBN 0-935161-97-X). Hunter Pub NY.

Farm Implements & Machinery: Multilingual Illustrated Dictionary. 4th ed. H. Steinmetz. 512p. 1982. pap. text ed. 24.95x o.p. (Pub. by H Steinmetz). Agribookstore.

Farm Income Tax Manual. 8th ed. John C. O'Byrne & Charles Davenport. 1987. pap. text ed. 65.00x o.p. (ISBN 0-87473-258-1). Michie Co.

Farm Journal's Best Ever Pies. Farm Journal Editors & Patricia A. Ward. LC 81-43122. (Illus.). 228p. 1981. 17.95 o.p. (ISBN 0-385-17729-1). Doubleday.

Farm Journal's Choice Chocolate Recipes. Farm Journal Editors. 1982. pap. 2.50 o.s.i. (ISBN 0-345-30184-6). Ballantine.

Farm Machinery. 9th ed. Claude Culpin. (Illus.). 416p. 1977. 36.95x o.p. (ISBN 0-8464-0403-6); 19.95 o.p. Beekman Pubs.

Farm Machinery. 10th ed. Claude Culpin. (Illus.). 464p. 1981. pap. text ed. 24.50x o.p. (ISBN 0-246-11539-4, Pub. by Granada England). Gower Pub Co.

Farm Management Glossary. (Agricultural Services Bulletins: No. 63). 221p. (Eng., Fr. & Span.). 1985. pap. 17.00 o.p. (ISBN 92-5-002195-X, F2778, FAO). UNIPUB.

Farm Management: Principles, Planning, Budgets. John Herbst. 1986. pap. text ed. 16.80x o.p. (ISBN 0-87563-276-9). Stipes.

Farm Mechanization for Profit. Bill Butterworth & John Nix. 269p. 1983. pap. text ed. 24.95 o.p. (ISBN 0-246-11562-9, Granada England). Gower Pub Co.

Farm on the River of Emeralds. Moritz Thomsen. 1978. 10.95 o.p. (ISBN 0-395-26311-5). HM.

Farm Plan. Elizabeth H. Bente. 114p. 1981. 6.00 o.p. (ISBN 0-682-49671-5). Exposition-Phoenix.

Farm Policies & Politics in the Truman Years. Allen J. Matusow. LC 67-12101. 1970. pap. text ed. 3.25x o.p. (ISBN 0-689-70250-7, 163, Atheneum). Macmillan.

Farm Policy in Australia. R. K. Hefford. (Illus.). 432p. 1985. text ed. 39.50 o.p. (ISBN 0-7022-1698-4). U of Queensland Pr.

Farm Policy Perspectives: Setting the Stage for 1985 Agricultural Legislation. 262p. 1984. 6.50 o.p. (ISBN 0-318-23080-1, 052-070-05924-9). USGPO.

Farm Population of the United States: 1986. (Current Population Reports Series P-27, Farm Population: No. 60). 38p. (Orig.). 1987. pap. 2.25 o.p. (S/N 803-005-20001-9). USGPO.

Farm Town: A Memoir of the Nineteen Thirties. J. W. McManigal & Grant Heilman. LC 73-86031. (Illus.). 100p. 1974. (ISBN 0-8289-0205-4); pap. 9.95 o.p. (ISBN 0-8289-0204-6). Greene.

Farm Vegetarian Cookbook. rev. ed. Ed. by Louise Hagler. LC 78-110794. (Illus.). 1979. 6.95 o.p. (ISBN 0-913990-18-3). Book Pub Co.

Farm Women: Work, Farm & Family in the United States. Rachel A. Rosenfeld. LC 85-13945. (Institute for Research in Social Science Ser.). xiii, 354p. 1987. 26.00x o.p.; pap. 9.95x o.p. (ISBN 0-8078-4193-5). U of NC Pr.

Farm Workshop & Maintenance. Ed. by Farmers Weekly. (Illus.). 192p. 1972. text ed. 15.95x o.p. (ISBN 0-8464-0404-4). Beekman Pubs.

Farmer in the Dell. Illus. by Diane Zuromskis. (Illus.). (gr. 1-3). 1978. 10.95 o.p. (ISBN 0-316-98889-8). Little.

Farmer's & Housekeeper's Cyclopaedia of 1888. Ed. by Stephen Lewandowski. LC 77-23827. 644p. 25.00 o.p. (ISBN 0-912278-90-0, C1977); pap. 12.95 o.p. (ISBN 0-912278-91-9). Crossing Pr.

Farmer's Cookbook: A Collection of Favorite Recipes, Economical Meal Planning Methods & Other Tips & Pointers from America's Farm Kitchens. Mitzi Ayala. (Illus.). 240p. 1981. 15.00 o.p. (ISBN 0-936602-16-3). Kampmann.

Farmhouse. Illus. by Carolyn Bracken & Nina Barbaresi. (Busy Bubble Bks.). (Illus.). (ps). 1984. pap. 2.85 o.s.i. (ISBN 0-671-47670-X, Little Simon). S&S.

Farming the Lord's Land: Christian Perspectives on American Agriculture. Charles P. Lutz. LC 80-80285. 208p. (Orig.). 1980. pap. 9.95 o.p. (ISBN 0-8066-1785-3, 10-2264, Augsburg). Augsburg Fortress.

Farmington Plan Survey: A Summary of the Seperate Studies of 1957-1961. Robert Vosper. (Occasional Papers: No. 77). 46p. 1965. pap. 1.00 o.p. (ISBN 0-317-58859-1). U of Ill Lib Info Sci.

Farms & Farmers. Linda Inman. (Illus.). 64p. (gr. 4-8). 1985. wkbk. 6.95 o.p. (ISBN 0-86653-320-6). Good Apple.

Farms & Farmers in an Urban Age. Edward C. Higbee. LC 73-15578. (Twentieth Cent. Fund Ser.). 183p. 1973. Repr. of 1963 ed. 12.00 o.p. (ISBN 0-527-40450-0). Kraus Repr.

Farms, Farmers & Society. G. E. Fussell. 1976. 15.00x o.p. (ISBN 0-87291-077-6). Coronado Pr.

Faroe: The Emergence of a Nation. John F. West. LC 77-151438. 1973. 10.00 o.p. (ISBN 0-8397-2063-7). Eriksson.

Farther Defence of Dramatick Poetry see Defence of Dramatick Poetry.

Farthing's Fortunes. Richard Wright. LC 76-11860. 1976. 10.00 o.p. (ISBN 0-689-10756-0, Atheneum). Macmillan.

FASB, Current Text As of June 1, 1987: General Standards. 1988. 23.50 o.p. (ISBN 0-256-06249-8). Irwin.

FASB, Current Text As of June 1, 1987: Industry Standards. 1988. 18.50 o.p. (ISBN 0-256-06248-X). Irwin.

FASB, Original Pronouncements: Issued Through July 1973 to June 1, 1987. 1988. 23.50 o.p. (ISBN 0-256-06247-1). Irwin.

FASB, Original Prouncements: Issued Through June 1973. 1988. 17.50 o.p. (ISBN 0-256-06245-5). Irwin.

FASB, Statement of Financial Accounting Concepts 1-6. 1988. 10.95 o.p. (ISBN 0-256-06250-1). Irwin.

Fascinating Facts: Weird Bits of Information on Practically Everything. David Lewis. (Illus.). 1977. 10.00 o.p. (ISBN 0-517-53051-1); pap. 6.95 o.p. (ISBN 0-517-53052-X). Crown.

Fascinating Tales of the Pacific, 6 bks. Glen Wright. Ed. by Carol Murphy. (Illus.). (gr. 3-6). 1981. Set. PLB 40.00 o.p. (ISBN 0-89868-110-3, Read Res); Set. pap. 28.00 o.p. (ISBN 0-89868-117-0, Read Res). ARO Pub.

Fascinations. David N. Cooperman. 96p. 1984. pap. 4.50 o.p. (ISBN 0-682-40150-1). Exposition-Phoenix.

Fascism: An Informal Introduction to Its Theory & Practice. Renzo De Felice. LC 76-13006. 128p. 1977. 5.95x o.p. 1976 (ISBN 0-87855-190-5); pap. 8.95x o.s.i. 1977 (ISBN 0-87855-619-2). Transaction Pubs.

Fascism & the Industrial Leadership in Italy, 1919-1940: A Study in the Expansion of Private Power Under Fascism. Roland Sarti. LC 79-138636. 1971. 38.50x o.p. (ISBN 0-520-01855-9). U of Cal Pr.

Fascism in Europe. Ed. by S. J. Woolf. 416p. 1981. 29.95x o.p. (ISBN 0-416-30230-0, NO. 3553); pap. 12.95x o.p. (ISBN 0-416-30240-8, NO. 3542). Routledge Chapman & Hall.

Fascist Challenge & the Policy of Appeasement. Ed. by Lothar Kettenacker & Wolfgang J. Mommsen. 416p. 1983. text ed. 39.95x o.p. (ISBN 0-04-940068-1). Unwin Hyman.

Fashion Accessories: Men's & Women's. Fairchild Market Research Division Staff. (Fairchild Fact Files Ser.). (Illus.). 55p. 1985. pap. 17.50 o.p. (ISBN 0-87005-521-6). Fairchild.

Fashion & Color. Kojiro Kumagai. (Illus.). 144p. 1986. pap. 20.00 o.p. (ISBN 0-8161-8812-2, Pub. by Graphic-Sha Pub Co Ltd Japan). G K Hall.

Fashion & Fetishism: A Social History of the Corset, Tight-Lacing & Other Forms of Body-Sculpture in the West. David Kunzle. LC 80-14872. (Illus.). 384p. 1982. 36.50 o.s.i. (ISBN 0-8476-6276-4). Rowman.

Fashion Art for the Fashion Industry. Rita Gersten. (Illus.). 128p. 1989. pap. 25.00 o.p. (ISBN 0-87005-676-X). Fairchild.

Fashion Drawing in Vogue. William Packer. LC 83-2035. (Illus.). 240p. 1983. 29.95 o.p. (ISBN 0-698-11242-3, Coward). Putnam Pub Group.

Fashion: From Concept to Consumer. Virginia S. Frings. (Illus.). 320p. 1982. text ed. (ISBN 0-13-306605-3). P-H.

Fashion Illustration in New York. Pater Sato. (Illus.). 127p. 1986. pap. 20.00 o.p. (ISBN 0-8161-8807-6, Pub. by Graphic-Sha Pub Co Ltd Japan). G K Hall.

Fashion Innovation & Marketing. Kathryn M. Greenwood & Mary F. Murphy. (Illus.). 1978. write for info. o.p. (ISBN 0-02-346950-1). Macmillan.

Fashion Knitting. Conran Octopus. 1986. pap. 9.95 o.p. (ISBN 0-345-33609-7, Pub. by Ballantine Trade). Ballantine.

Fashion: The Inside Story. Barbaralee Diamonstein. LC 85-42865. (Illus.). 200p. 1985. pap. 29.95 o.p. (ISBN 0-8478-0610-3). Rizzoli Intl.

Fashion Your Figure: The Ten-Minutes-A-Day Program for Fitness. Toni Beck & Patsy Swank. LC 72-80418. Orig. Title: Your Moves to Make. 1970. 4.95 o.p. (ISBN 0-395-07399-5). HM.

Fashionable First Courses. Arabella Boxer. LC 86-16542. 80p. 1987. pap. 9.95 o.p. (ISBN 0-385-23812-6). Doubleday.

Fashions of the Heart. Yvonne Lehman. (Chime Ser.). (YA) 1981. pap. 2.50 o.p. (ISBN 0-89191-372-6, 53728). Cook.

Fassbinder. Ronald Hayman. LC 84-5456. 192p. 1984. 17.45 o.p. (ISBN 0-671-52373-2); pap. 9.95 o.p. (ISBN 0-671-52380-5). S&S.

Fassbinder. Tr. by Ruth McCormick from Ger. (Illus.). 256p. 1981. 16.95 o.p. (ISBN 0-934378-17-7); pap. 7.95 o.p. (ISBN 0-934378-18-5). Tanam Pr.

Fast Access Wordperfect 5.0. Rhyder McClure. 1988. pap. 15.95 o.p. (ISBN 0-13-197153-0). Brady Bks.

Fast & Fresh Cooking Basics. Susan Mitchell. (Illus.). 128p. (Orig.). 1984. pap. 7.95 o.p. (ISBN 0-8249-3036-3). Ideals.

Fast & Loose: A Novelette by David Olivieri. Edith Wharton. LC 76-58438. 1977. ltd. boxed 50.00x o.p. (ISBN 0-8139-0599-0). U Pr of Va.

Fast Carriers: The Forging of an Air Navy. Clark G. Reynolds. LC 77-10914. 522p. 1978. Repr. of 1968 ed. 29.50 o.p. (ISBN 0-88275-608-7). Krieger.

Fast Food Gets an "A" in School Lunch. Len Fredrick. LC 76-54649. 1983. 22.95 o.p. (ISBN 0-8436-2073-0). Van Nos Reinhold.

Fast Foods Facts. Marion J. Franz. 60p. 1985. pap. 3.50 o.p. (ISBN 0-937721-02-6). DCI Publishing.

Fast-Growth Management: How to Improve Profits with Entrepreneurial Stategies. Mack Hanan. (Illus.). 1980. 14.95 o.p. (ISBN 0-8144-5559-X). AMACOM.

Fast Lane Diet: The Fourteen-Day Weight Loss Program for Everyone on the Fast Track to Success. Dottie Dekko. 224p. 1985. text ed. 14.95 o.p. (ISBN 0-07-016298-0). McGraw.

Fast Life. Cynthia Wilkerson. 1979. pap. 2.25 o.p. (ISBN 0-505-51350-1, Pub. by Tower Bks). Dorchester Pub Co.

Fast-n-Easy Phrase Book. Carolyn M. Heard. (Illus.). 320p. 1984. 6.95 o.p. (ISBN 0-671-46673-9). Prentice Hall Pr.

Fast Pulsed & Burst Reactors: A Comprehensive Account of the Physics of Both Single Burst & Repetitively Pulsed Reactors. E. P. Shabalin. (Illus.). 1979. 105.00 o.p. (ISBN 0-08-022708-2). Pergamon.

Fast Reactor Fuel Element Technology: Proceedings, American Nuclear Society Conference, New Orleans, April 13-15, 1971. 940p. 43.00 o.p. (ISBN 0-317-33009-8, 700004). Am Nuclear Soc.

Fast Reactor Physics. Ed. by M. M. Williams. N. J. McCormick. (Illus.). 136p. 1985. pap. 51.00 o.p. (ISBN 0-08-033236-6, Pub. by PPL). Pergamon.

Fast Sam, Cool Clyde, & Stuff. W. Myers. (YA) (gr. 7 up). 1978. pap. 1.50 o.p. (ISBN 0-380-01943-4, 52761-8, Flare). Avon.

Fast Sooner Hound. Arna Bontemps & Jack Conroy. (Illus.). 32p. (gr. 4-8). 1978. PLB 10.95 o.p. (ISBN 0-395-18657-9). HM.

Fast Times at Ridgemont High: A True Story. Cameron Crowe. 1981. 14.95 o.p. (ISBN 0-671-25290-9); pap. 5.95 o.p. (ISBN 0-671-25291-7). S&S.

Fast Track: Texans & Other Strivers. Nicholas Lemann. 1981. 12.95 o.p. (ISBN 0-393-01436-3). Norton.

Fast Track: The Super Achievers & How They Make It to Early Success. Mary A. Kellogg. 1978. text ed. 9.95 o.p. (ISBN 0-07-033507-9). McGraw.

Fastest, Cheapest, Best Way to Clean Everything. Consumer Guide Editors. 288p. 1982. pap. 8.70 o.p. (ISBN 0-671-25468-5, Fireside). S&S.

Fasting for Regeneration: The Short Cut. Julia Seton. 70p. pap. 8.95 o.s.i. (ISBN 0-88697-024-5). Life Science.

Fasting in the New Testament. Joseph F. Wimmer. LC 81-83183. 160p. (Orig.). 1982. pap. 8.95 o.p. (ISBN 0-8091-2420-3). Paulist Pr.

Fasting Rediscovered: A Guide to Health & Wholeness for Your Body-Spirit. Thomas Ryan. LC 80-81581. 160p. (Orig.). 1981. pap. 6.95 o.p. (ISBN 0-8091-2323-1). Paulist Pr.

Fat & Sodium Control Cookbook: A Handy & Authoritative Guide for Those on Sodium Restricted or Fat-Controlled Diets-Including Suggestions for Controlling Carbohydrate, Cholesterol & Saturated Fats. 4th rev ed. Alma Payne & Dorothy Callahan. 1975. 16.95 o.p. (ISBN 0-316-69542-4). Little.

Fat Cats, Cousin Scraggs & the Monster Mice. Barbara S. Hazen. LC 84-20457. (Illus.). 48p. (gr. 3-7). 1985. 11.95 o.s.i. (ISBN 0-689-31092-7, Atheneum Childrens Bks). Macmillan.

Fat Consumption & Coronary Disease. T. Cleave. 1958. (ISBN 0-8022-0261-6). Philos Lib.

Fat Destroyer Foods: The Magic Metabolizer Diet. Sidney Petrie & Robert B. Stone. 1975. 10.95 o.p. (ISBN 0-13-308098-6, Reward); pap. 4.95 o.p. (ISBN 0-13-308080-3). P-H.

Fat-Free Recipes. Nevada Lampen. 1977. pap. 4.95 o.p. (ISBN 0-571-11026-6). Faber & Faber.

Fat Gopal. Jacquelin Singh. LC 82-21258. (Illus.). 48p. (ps-3). 1984. 12.95 o.p. (ISBN 0-15-227372-7, HJ). HarBraceJ.

Fat Is in Your Head. Charlie W. Shedd. 1977. pap. 1.95 o.p. (ISBN 0-380-01761-X, 48876). Avon.

Fat Mutton & Liberty of Conscience. Carl Bridenbaugh. LC 74-6573. (Illus.). 1976. pap. text ed. 3.95x o.p. (ISBN 0-689-70535-2, 224, Atheneum). Macmillan.

Fat of the Land: What's Behind Your Shrinking Food Dollar, & What You Can Do about It. Fred Powledge. 1984. 15.45 o.p. (ISBN 0-671-42435-1). S&S.

Fat Tuesday. R. Wright Campbell. LC 82-19264. 384p. 1983. 15.45 o.p. (ISBN 0-89919-158-4). Ticknor & Fields.

Fata Morgana. Andre Breton. Tr. by Clark Mills. (Illus.). 36p. (Fr.). pap. cancelled o.s.i. (ISBN 0-941194-01-9). Black Swan Pr.

Fatal Affair. Velda Johnston. 244p. 1987. 16.95 o.s.i. (ISBN 0-8161-4288-2). G K Hall.

Fatal Beauty. John Godey. LC 84-3068. 312p. 1984. 14.95 o.p. (ISBN 0-689-11481-8, Atheneum). Macmillan.

Fatal Choice: The Teenage Suicide Crisis. John Q. Baucom. 1986. text ed. 10.95 o.p. (ISBN 0-8024-2533-X). Moody.

Fatal Environment: The Myth of the Frontier in the Age of Industrialization 1800-1890. Richard Slotkin. LC 83-45084. 688p. 1985. 37.50 o.p. (ISBN 0-689-11410-9, Atheneum). Macmillan.

Fatal Flower. Lynn Benedict. 1973. pap. 0.75 o.p. (ISBN 0-380-01177-8, 15909). Avon.

Fatal Flowers: On Sin, Sex & Suicide in the Deep South. Rosemary Daniell. 288p. 1981. pap. 3.50 o.p. (ISBN 0-380-54254-4, 65946, Discus). Avon.

Fatal Friendship: A Novel; by a Lady, 1771, 2 vols. in 1. Ed. by Michael F. Shugrue. (Flowering of the Novel, 1740-1775 Ser: Vol. 95). 1975. lib. bdg. 61.00 o.p. (ISBN 0-8240-1194-5). Garland Pub.

Fatal Run. Ernest Clark. 240p. 1985. pap. 3.50 o.p. (ISBN 0-440-11783-6). Dell.

Fate & Effects of Petroleum Hydrocarbons in Marine Organisms & Ecosystems. Ed. by Douglas A. Wolfe. LC 77-76464. 1977. 120.00 o.p. (ISBN 0-08-021613-7). Pergamon.

Fate Is the Hunter. 2nd ed. Ernest K. Gann. 1984. pap. 9.95 o.s.i. (ISBN 0-671-50400-2). S&S.

Fate Keeps on Happening: Adventures of Lorelei Lee & Other Writings. Anita Loos. Ed. by Ray P. Corsini. (Illus.). 336p. 1984. 16.95 o.p. (ISBN 0-396-08398-6). Dodd.

Fate of Drugs in the Organism: A Bibliographic Survey, Vol. 1. Compiled by Societe Francaise des Sciences et Techniques Pharmaceutiques Working Group Staff & J. L. Hirtz. 600p. 1974. 125.00 o.p. (ISBN 0-8247-6133-2). Dekker.

Fate of Drugs in the Organism: A Bibliographic Survey, Vol. 4. Jean L. Hirtz. 640p. 1977. 125.00 o.p. (ISBN 0-8247-6587-7). Dekker.

Fate of French-E in English: The Plural of Nouns Ending in-th, Vol. 7. C. T. Onions et al. Ed. by Steele Commager. Incl. Basic; Problems of Spelling Reform; Pure English of the Soil; Inflected English; Critique of Pure English; Retrospect. (Society of Pure English Ser.). 1979. lib. bdg. 50.00 o.p. (ISBN 0-8240-3671-9). Garland Pub.

Fate of the Badger. Richard Meyer. (Illus.). 128p. 1987. 35.95 o.p. (ISBN 0-7134-5189-0, Pub. by Batsford England); pap. 19.95 o.p. (ISBN 0-7134-5504-7, Pub. by Batsford England). David & Charles.

Fate Stepped In. D. L. Stasio. 256p. 1981. 10.50 o.p. (ISBN 0-682-49726-6). Exposition-Phoenix.

Fate Worse Than Death: A Novel of Suspense. Sheila Radley. 224p. 1986. 13.95 o.p. (ISBN 0-684-18582-2). Scribner.

Father & Child: Developmental & Clinical Perspectives. Stanley Cath et al. 1982. text ed. 33.00 o.p. (ISBN 0-316-13196-2). Little.

Father & Children. Date not set. (ISBN 0-8052-3835-2). Random.

Father Christmas Letters. J. R. R. Tolkien. (Illus.). 48p. 1976. 8.95 o.p. (ISBN 0-395-24981-3). HM.

Father Christmas Letters. rev. ed. J. R. R. Tolkien. Ed. by Baille Tolkien. 1979. pap. 4.95 o.p. (ISBN 0-395-28262-4). HM.

Father Clement, 1823. Grace Kennedy. Ed. by Robert L. Wolff. Bd. with Father Oswald 1842. LC 75-445. (Victorian Fiction Ser). 1976. lib. bdg. 73.00 o.p. (ISBN 0-8240-1525-8). Garland Pub.

Father-Daughter Rape. Elizabeth Ward. LC 84-73205. 252p. 1985. 17.50 o.p. (ISBN 0-394-54632-6, GP-971). Grove.

Father Divine. Robert Weisbrot. LC 84-45084. (Illus.). 241p. 1984. pap. 10.95x o.p. (ISBN 0-8070-0901-6, BP684). Beacon Pr.

Father Figure. Ed. by Lorna McKee & Margaret O'Brien. LC 81-22298. 300p. 1982. 27.00x o.p. (ISBN 0-422-77720-X, NO. 3627, Pub. by Tavistock); pap. 12.95x o.p. (ISBN 0-422-77730-7, NO. 3628). Routledge Chapman & Hall.

Father Goose. Gene Fowler. 1974. pap. 1.95 o.p. (ISBN 0-380-01179-4, 15966). Avon.

Father in Primitive Psychology. Bronislaw Malinowski. 1966. pap. 2.95 o.p. (ISBN 0-393-00332-9, Norton Lib). Norton.

Father Knickerbocker Rebels: New York City During the Revolution. Thomas J. Wertenbaker. LC 68-57282. (Illus.). Repr. of 1948 ed. 24.50x o.p. (ISBN 0-8154-0286-4). Cooper Sq.

Father of Texas Geology: Robert T. Hill. Nancy Alexander. LC 76-2621. (No. 4). (Illus.). 332p. 1976. 16.95 o.p. (ISBN 0-87074-152-7); pap. 15.95 o.p. (ISBN 0-87074-002-4). SMU Press.

Father of the Wesleys. Franklin Wilder. LC 72-146917. 1971. 6.00 o.p. (ISBN 0-682-47238-7). Exposition-Phoenix.

Father Oswald 1842 see Father Clement, 1823.

Father Pig. Burt Hirschfeld. LC 76-184883. 1972. 6.95 o.p. (ISBN 0-87795-028-8, A4321, Arbor Hse). Morrow.

Father Time & the Day Boxes. George E. Lyon. LC 85-4132. (Illus.). 32p. (ps-2). 1985. 12.95 o.s.i. (ISBN 0-02-761370-4). Bradbury Pr.

Father Was a Tenor. Anna M. Hamlin. 1978. 5.00 o.p. (ISBN 0-682-48956-5). Exposition-Phoenix.

Fatherbond. Don Osgood. 1989. pap. 6.95 o.p. Tyndale.

Fatherhood: A Personal Journal with Quotes. Running Press Staff. (Illus.). 96p. (Orig.). 1987. pap. 5.95 o.p. (ISBN 0-89471-548-8); lib. bdg. 15.90 o.p. (ISBN 0-89471-549-6). Running Pr.

Fatherhood of God & the Victorian Family: The Social Gospel in America. Janet F. Fishburn. LC 81-43090. 220p. 1982. 4.95 o.p. (ISBN 0-8006-0671-X, Fortress). Augsburg Fortress.

Fathers. Herbert Gold. 1983. 16.95 o.p. (ISBN 0-87795-549-2, Arbor Hse); pap. 8.95 o.p. (ISBN 0-87795-550-6). Morrow.

Fathers & Daughters in Roman Society & the Elite Family. Judith P. Hallett. LC 83-43074. 352p. 1984. 44.50 o.p. (ISBN 0-691-03570-9); pap. 13.95x o.p. (ISBN 0-691-10160-4). Princeton U Pr.

Fathers & Family Work in Two Cultures: Antecedents & Concomitants of Fathers' Participation in Child Care & Household Work in Germany, Israel, Sweden, United States & Wales. Karin Sandqvist. (Stockholm Institute of Education, Studies in Education & Psychology: No. 23). 236p. (Orig.). 1987. pap. 28.50x o.p. (ISBN 91-22-01162-5, Pub. by Almqvist & Wiksell). Coronet Bks.

Fathers & Sons. Lewis Yablonsky. 1982. 13.95 o.p. (ISBN 0-671-25461-8). S&S.

Fathers & Sons. Lewis Yablonsky. 224p. 1984. pap. 8.95 o.p. (ISBN 0-671-25462-6, Fireside). S&S.

Father's Days. Katherine Brady. pap. 2.95 o.p. (ISBN 0-440-12475-1). Dell.

Fathers of the Church on Prayer & the Spiritual Life , Quotations from the. pap. 5.95 o.p. (ISBN 0-317-60789-8). Eastern Orthodox.

Fathers Playing Catch with Sons. Donald Hall. 1986. pap. 3.95 o.p. (ISBN 0-440-32438-6, LE). Dell.

Fathers: There at the Birth. Tim Spacek. LC 85-11684. 1985. 12.95 o.p. (ISBN 0-914091-80-8); pap. 6.95 o.p. (ISBN 0-914091-79-4). Chicago Review.

Father's Words. Richard Stern. 1986. 14.95 o.p. (ISBN 0-87795-791-6). Morrow.

Fatigue Crack Growth: Proceedings of a Conference on Fatigue Crack Growth, Cambridge, U. K. 09-20-1984. Ed. by R. A. Smith. (Illus.). 250p. 1986. 49.00 o.p. (ISBN 0-08-032547-5, Pub. by PPL). Pergamon.

Fatigue, Creep, & Pressure Vessels for Elevated Temperature Service. Ed. by C. W. Lawton & R. R. Seeley. (MCP Ser.: Vol. 17). 206p. 1981. 40.00 o.p. (ISBN 0-686-34500-2, H00210). ASME.

Fatigue Design Handbook. (Advances in Engineering Series). 132p. 1968. 40.00 o.p. (ISBN 0-89883-004-4, AE-4). Soc Auto Engineers.

Fatigue Design of Machine Components. L. Sors. 224p. 1971. 45.00 o.p. (ISBN 0-08-016138-3); xerox copyflo o.p. Pergamon.

Fatigue: Environment & Temperature Effects. Ed. by John J. Burke & Volker Weiss. (Sagamore Army Materials Research Conference Proceedings Ser.: Vol. 27). 410p. 1983. 75.00x o.p. (ISBN 0-306-41101-6, Plenum Pr). Plenum Pub.

Fatigue of Metals. R. Cazaud. (Illus.). 348p. 1953. (ISBN 0-8022-0227-6). Philos Lib.

Fatima Secret. Emmett Culligan. 1975. pap. 1.50 o.p. (ISBN 0-89555-052-0). TAN Bks Pubs.

Fatness to Fitness. Zona H. Cornelison. 1985. pap. 5.95 o.p. (ISBN 0-89274-364-6). Harrison Hse.

Fatras. Jacques Prevert. 16.95 o.p. (ISBN 0-685-37049-6). Schoenhof.

Faulkner: Fifty Years after "The Marble Faun" Ed. by George H. Wolfe. LC 75-40380. 192p. 1976. 12.95 o.p. (ISBN 0-8173-7609-7). U of Ala Pr.

Faulkner: Jimmy, That Is. Sandra B. Taylor. LC 84-50099. (Illus.). 200p. 1984. 14.95 o.p. (ISBN 0-87397-262-7). Strode.

Faulkner: Myth & Motion. Richard P. Adams. 1968. 29.00 o.p. (ISBN 0-691-06141-6). Princeton U Pr.

Faulkner: The House Divided. Eric J. Sundquist. LC 82-8923. 200p. 1983. pap. 22.50x o.p. (ISBN 0-8018-2898-8). Johns Hopkins.

Faulkner's Art & Characters. Walter K. Everett. LC 68-31478. (Orig.). (gr. 9 up). 1969. pap. text ed. 5.95 o.p. (ISBN 0-8120-0392-6). Barron.

Faulkner's As I Lay Dying. Andre Bleikasten. Tr. by Roger Little. LC 72-79904. (Midland Bks.: No. 159). (Illus.). 192p. 1973. 8.50x o.p. (ISBN 0-253-32150-6); pap. 3.95x o.p. (ISBN 0-253-20159-4). Ind U Pr.

Faulkner's Early Literary Reputation in America. O. B. Emerson. Ed. by A. Walton Litz. LC 83-18321. (Studies in Modern Literature: No. 30). 430p. 1984. 49.95 o.p. (ISBN 0-8357-1467-5). UMI Res Pr.

Faulkner's "Negro" Art & the Southern Context. Thadious M. Davis. LC 82-7327. 266p. 1982. o. p. 25.00x o.p. (ISBN 0-8071-0147-7); pap. 12.95x o.p. (ISBN 0-8071-1064-7). La State U Pr.

Faunal Affinities, Systematics & Bionomics of the Orthoptera of the California Channel Islands. D. C. Rentz & David B. Weissman. (UC Publications in Entomology: Vol. 94). 1982. 29.95x o.p. (ISBN 0-520-09640-1). U of Cal Pr.

Faune Ichthyologique Du London Clay: Text & Atlas. Edgar Casier. (Illus.). xiv, 496p. 1966. 100.00x o.p. (ISBN 0-565-00654-1, Pub. by Brit Mus Nat Hist England). Sabbot-Natural Hist Bks.

Faust. Goethe. 1958. (ISBN 0-8022-0601-8). Philos Lib.

Faust I & II. Johann Wolfgang von Goethe. 48p. (Orig.). 1989. pap. 9.95 o.p. (ISBN 1-55651-277-5); audiocassette tape incl. o.p. (ISBN 1-55651-278-3). Cram Cassettes.

Faust Legend in Music. James W. Kelly. LC 74-75893. (Detroit Reprints in Music). 1976. 10.00 o.p. (ISBN 0-911772-81-2). Harmonie Pk Pr.

Faust: Sources, Works, Criticism. Ed. by Paul A. Bates. (Harbrace Sourcebook Ser.). 240p. (Orig.). 1969. pap. text ed. 8.95 o.p. (ISBN 0-15-527102-4, HC). HarBraceJ.

Fausto. 4th ed. Goethe. (Biblioteca Basica De Cultura Ser.). (Span.). pap. 5.00 o.p. (ISBN 0-8477-0722-9); pap. 3.75 o.p. (ISBN 0-8477-0723-7). U of PR Pr.

Fauvism Reexamined. Ellen C. Oppler. LC 75-23805. (Outstanding Dissertations in the Fine Arts - 20th Century). (Illus.). 1976. lib. bdg. 55.00 o.p. (ISBN 0-8240-1999-7). Garland Pub.

Faux-Monnayeurs: Rompin. Andre Gide. 1956. 11.50 o.p. (ISBN 0-685-11181-4). Schoenhof.

Favorite Andrew Lang Fairy Tale Books in Many Colors: Red, Green, Yellow & Blue Fairy Tale Books, 4 vols. Andrew Lang. (Illus.). 500p. (gr. 2 up). 1979. pap. 23.80 boxed set o.p. (ISBN 0-486-23407-X). Dover.

Favorite Brand Name Recipes, Appetizers, Dips & Snacks. Consumer Guide Editors. 144p. (Orig.). 1982. pap. 2.50 o.s.i. (ISBN 0-449-24568-3, Crest). Fawcett.

Favorite Brand Name Recipes: Desserts. Consumer Guide Editors. 1944. pap. 2.50 o.p. (ISBN 0-449-20211-9, Crest). Fawcett.

Favorite Brands Name Recipes, Soups & Sandwiches. Consumer Guide Editors. 144p. (Orig.). 1982. pap. 2.50 o.s.i. (ISBN 0-449-24571-3, Crest). Fawcett.

Favorite Children's Parties. Linda DeGraw & Barbara J. Wallin. 96p. (Orig.). 1985. pap. 6.95 o.s.i. (ISBN 0-934318-49-2). Falcon Pr MT.

Favorite Christmas Stories. Ed. by Frances Cavanah. (gr. 3 up). 1948. 5.95 o.p. (ISBN 0-448-02376-8, G&D). Putnam Pub Group.

Favorite Christmas Stories. Laura M. Hawkes. 64p. 1973. pap. 2.50 o.p. (ISBN 0-89036-015-4). Hawkes Pub Inc.

Favorite Daytrips in New England. 2nd ed. Michael Schuman. LC 83-50697. (Magazine Guidebook Ser.). (Illus.). 192p. 1984. pap. 8.95 o.p. (ISBN 0-89909-024-9). Yankee Bks.

Favorite Fairy Tales Told in India. Virginia Haviland. LC 71-117019. (Illus.). 96p. (gr. k-3). 1973. 7.95g o.p. (ISBN 0-316-35055-9). Little.

Favorite Fairy Tales Told in Norway. Virginia Haviland. (Illus.). (gr. 2-6). 1961. 7.95 o.p. (ISBN 0-316-35053-2). Little.

Favorite Nursery Rhymes. Ed. by Diane Namm. LC 85-19628. (Illus.). (gr. 1-4). 1986. pap. 14.95 o.s.i. (ISBN 0-671-60264-0, Little Simon). S&S.

Favorite Recipes. 2nd ed. Sunset Editors. LC 69-14226. (Illus.). 112p. 1969. pap. 5.95 o.p. (ISBN 0-376-02176-4, Sunset Bks.). Sunset-Lane.

Favorite Recipes from Hudson & Halls. Peter Hudson & David Halls. (Illus.). 248p. 1986. 29.95 o.p. (ISBN 0-317-52637-5, Pub. by Whitcoulls NZ). Intl Spec Bk.

Favorite Recipes from Pepperidge Farm. (Illus.). 160p. 1980. 8.95 o.p. (ISBN 0-916752-34-8). Dorison Hse.

Favorite Recipes Giftpack. 1982. 11.90 o.p. (ISBN 0-376-02155-1). Sunset-Lane.

Favorite Restaurant Recipes. (Illus.). 256p. 1982. 25.00 o.p. (ISBN 0-89535-100-5). Knapp Pr.

Favorite Seafood Recipes. Sally M. Morris. (Illus.). 216p. (Orig.). 1983. pap. 6.95 o.p. (ISBN 0-911954-78-3). Bristol Pub Ent CA.

Favorite Stories from Old Korea. Irene-Anne Monteiro. (Illus.). vi, 58p. 1984. pap. text ed. 2.50x o.p. (ISBN 9971-64-042-2, 00325). Heinemann Ed.

Favorite Stories from Sri Lanka. Indi Rani. (Favorite Stories Ser.). (Illus.). vi, 46p. 1983. pap. text ed. 2.50x o.p. (ISBN 9971-64-039-2). Heinemann Ed.

Favorite Stories from the Maoris. Irene-Anne Monteiro. (Illus.). viii, 60p. (Orig.). pap. text ed. 2.50x o.p. (ISBN 9971-64-043-0). Heinemann Ed.

Favorite Tales by Thornton Burgess. Thornton W. Burgess. (Platt & Munk Pandabacks Ser.). (Illus.). 24p. (ps-3). 1979. pap. 1.25 o.p. (ISBN 0-448-49613-5, G&D). Putnam Pub Group.

Favorite Tales of Hans Andersen. Hans Christian Andersen. Tr. by M. R. James from Danish. (Illus.). 168p. (gr. 4-8). 1986. pap. 6.95 o.p. (ISBN 0-571-13927-2). Faber & Faber.

Favorite Vermont Ski Inns & Lodging Guide. Rudyard Colter & Janet Colter. (McGraw-Hill Paperbacks). 1977. pap. text ed. 5.95 o.p. (ISBN 0-07-012085-4). McGraw.

Favour of Your Company: Invitations to London Social Events, 1750 to 1850. Victoria Moger. (Illus.). 48p. pap. 13.95 o.p. (ISBN 0-913720-09-7, Sandstone). Beil.

Favourite Chinese Stories. Retold by Leon Comber. 1967. pap. text ed. 2.50x o.p. (ISBN 0-686-60353-2). Heinemann Ed.

Favourite Stories from Asia. bilingual ed. Leon Comber. (Favourite Stories Ser.). (Orig.). 1981. pap. text ed. 2.50x o.p. (ISBN 9-97164-007-4). Heinemann Ed.

Favourite Stories from Bali. Retold by Suarti Levine & David Stuart-Fox. (Favourite Stories Ser.). 1978. pap. text ed. 2.50x o.p. (ISBN 0-686-60354-0). Heinemann Ed.

Favourite Stories from Borneo. Retold by Leon Comber. (Favourite Stories Ser.). 1975. pap. text ed. 2.50x o.p. (ISBN 0-686-60355-9). Heinemann Ed.

Favourite Stories from Burma. Retold by Marguerite Siek. (Favourite Stories Ser.). 1975. pap. text ed. 2.50x o.p. (ISBN 0-686-60356-7). Heinemann Ed.

Favourite Stories from Central Asia. Irene-Anne Monteiro. (Favourite Stories Ser.). (Illus.). viii, 60p. 1984. pap. text ed. 2.50x o.p. (ISBN 9971-64-044-9). Heinemann Ed.

Favourite Stories from Hong Kong. Retold by Leon Comber. (Favourite Stories Ser.). 1978. pap. text ed. 2.50x o.p. (ISBN 0-686-60358-3). Heinemann Ed.

Favourite Stories from India. Retold by Marguerite Siek. (Favourite Stories Ser.). 1975. pap. text ed. 2.50x o.p. (ISBN 0-686-60359-1). Heinemann Ed.

Favourite Stories from Indonesia. Retold by Marguerite Siek. (Favourite Stories Ser.). 1972. pap. text ed. 2.50x o.p. (ISBN 0-686-60360-5). Heinemann Ed.

Favourite Stories from Japan. Retold by Ilse Pordes. (Favourite Stories Ser.). 1975. pap. text ed. 2.50x o.p. (ISBN 0-686-60424-5). Heinemann Ed.

Favourite Stories from Malaysia. Retold by Leon Comber. (Favourite Stories Ser.). 1972. pap. text ed. 2.50x o.p. (ISBN 0-686-60425-3). Heinemann Ed.

Favourite Stories from Persia. Cynthia Helms. (Favourite Stories Ser.). (Illus.). ix, 61p. (Orig.). 1982. pap. text ed. 2.50x o.p. (ISBN 9971-64-041-4). Heinemann Ed.

Favourite Stories from Singapore. Retold by Irene-Anne Monteiro. (Favourite Stories Ser.). 1977. pap. text ed. 2.50x o.p. (ISBN 0-686-60427-X). Heinemann Ed.

Favourite Stories from Taiwan. Leon Comber & Charles Shuttleworth. (Illus., Orig.). 1975. pap. text ed. 2.50x o.p. (ISBN 0-686-97707-6). Heinemann Ed.

Favourite Stories from Thailand. Retold by Jenny Watson. (Favourite Stories Ser.). 1976. pap. text ed. 2.50x o.p. (ISBN 0-686-60428-8). Heinemann Ed.

Favourite Stories from the Philippines. Retold by Leon Comber. (Favourite Stories Ser.). 1978. pap. text ed. 2.50x o.p. (ISBN 0-686-60426-1). Heinemann Ed.

Fawn Zeller's Porcelain Dollmaking Techniques. Sybill McFadden. (Illus.). 105p. 1984. pap. 10.95 o.p. (ISBN 0-87588-217-X, 2908). Hobby Hse.

FBI & the CIA: Secret Agents & American Democracy. James Munves. LC 75-10136. (Illus.). 186p. (gr. 7 up). 1975. 7.50 o.p. (ISBN 0-15-227423-5, HJ). HarBraceJ.

FCC Rule Book. Ed. by Rick Palm. 1984. 3.00 o.p. (ISBN 0-87259-002-X). Am Radio.

FDR. Ted Morgan. 905p. 1985. 22.45 o.p. (ISBN 0-671-45495-1). S&S.

FDR: The Other Side of the Coin. Hamilton Fish. (Illus.). 256p. 1976. 11.00 o.p. (ISBN 0-686-76164-2); pap. 8.00 o.p. Inst Hist Rev.

Fear. James C. Moloney. 1957. (ISBN 0-8022-1136-4). Philos Lib.

Fear & Trembling. Gholam-Hossein Sa'edi. Tr. by Minoo Southgate from Farsi. xxxi, 121p. 1984. 18.00 o.p. (ISBN 0-89410-287-7); pap. 10.00 o.p. (ISBN 0-89410-288-5). Three Continents.

Fear Brokers. Thomas J. McIntyre & John C. Obert. LC 79-4255. 1979. 11.95 o.p. (ISBN 0-8298-0357-2). Pilgrim NY.

Fear, Faith, & the Future: Affirming Christian Hope in the Face of Doomsday Prophecies. Ted Peters. LC 79-54120. 128p. 1980. pap. 5.95 o.p. (ISBN 0-8066-1755-1, 10-2272, Augsburg). Augsburg Fortress.

Fear in Animals & Man. W. Sluckin. 330p. 1979. 26.95 o.p. (ISBN 0-442-30164-2). Van Nos Reinhold.

Fear in Battle. John Dollard & Donald Horton. LC 77-2970. 1977. Repr. of 1944 ed. lib. bdg. 24.75x o.p. (ISBN 0-8371-9579-9, DOFB). Greenwood.

Fear: Learning to Cope. Albert G. Forgione et al. 1978. 17.95 o.p. (ISBN 0-442-26388-0). Van Nos Reinhold.

Fear of Cooking: The Absolute Foolproof Cookbook for Beginners (& Everyone Else) Bob Scher. LC 83-22535. (Illus.). 367p. 1984. pap. 9.70 o.p. (ISBN 0-395-32216-2). HM.

Fear of Filing: A Beginner's Guide to Tax Preparation & Record Keeping for Artists, Performers, Writers & Freelance Professionals. Volunteer Lawyers for the Arts. Ed. by Theodore W. Striggles. 128p. 1983. 12.95 o.p. (ISBN 0-396-08210-6). Dodd.

Fear of Flying. Erica Jong. LC 73-3697. 320p. 1973. 12.95 o.s.i. (ISBN 0-03-010731-8). H Holt & Co.

Fear of Women. Wolfgang Lederer. LC 68-16305. (Illus.). 1970. pap. 4.95 o.p. (ISBN 0-15-630419-8, HB184, Harv). HarBraceJ.

Fearful Joy. Papers from the Thomas Gray Bicentenary Conference at Carleton University. Ed. by James Downey & Ben Jones. (Illus.). 324p. 1974. 11.50x o.p. (ISBN 0-7735-0132-0, McGill Canada). U of Toronto Pr.

Fearless Flying: The Complete Program for Relaxed Air Travel. Albert G. Forgione & Frederic M. Bauer. 1980. 11.95 o.p. (ISBN 0-395-29123-2); pap. 6.95 o.p. (ISBN 0-395-30059-2). HM.

Fearless Love. Stephanie Andrews. (Dawn of Love Ser.: No. 4). (YA) (gr. 7 up). pap. 2.25 o.p. (ISBN 0-671-55158-2). Archway.

Fearless Spectator: A Selective Collection of the Columns of the Late Charles McCabe. Charles McCabe. LC 78-133452. 290p. (Orig.). 1984. pap. 8.95 o.p. (ISBN 0-87701-313-6). Chronicle Bks.

Fears & Phobias. Margaret O. Hyde. (gr. 9-12). 1977. text ed. 11.95 o.p. (ISBN 0-07-031648-1). McGraw.

Fearsome Inn. Isaac Bashevis Singer. LC 67-23693. (Illus.). 48p. (Orig.). (gr. 3-6). 1984. pap. 4.95 o.s.i. (ISBN 0-689-70769-X, Aladdin). Macmillan.

Feasibility of a Global Observation & Analysis Experiment. National Academy of Sciences. 1966. pap. 5.00x o.p. (ISBN 0-309-01290-2). Natl Acad Pr.

Feasibility of Fertility Planning: Micro Perspectives. Ed. by T. Scarlett Epstein & Darrell Jackson. 1977. 48.00 o.p. (ISBN 0-08-021452-5); pap. 18.25 o.p. (ISBN 0-08-021837-7). Pergamon.

Feast for Lent. Delia Smith. LC 84-51652. 96p. pap. 3.95 o.p. (ISBN 0-89622-220-9). Twenty-Third.

Feast Is Finished. Denise Robins. (Lythway Ser.). 1987. lib. bdg. 17.50 o.p. (ISBN 0-7451-0584-X, Pub. by Chivers Pr UK). G K Hall.

Feast Made for Laughter. Craig Claiborne. (Illus.). 432p. 1983. pap. 7.95 o.s.i. (ISBN 0-03-064007-5, Owl Bks.). H Holt & Co.

Feast of All Saints. Anne Rice. 640p. 1981. pap. 2.95 o.p. (ISBN 0-449-24378-8, Crest). Fawcett.

Feast of Ashes. Sally Rosenbluth. LC 80-13195. 1980. 12.95 o.p. (ISBN 0-689-11071-5, Atheneum). Macmillan.

Feast of Blood. Charles M. Collins. 1975. pap. 1.25 o.p. (ISBN 0-380-00474-7, 25460). Avon.

Feast of Scotland. Janet Warren. LC 79-84819. (Illus.). 1979. 17.45 o.p. (ISBN 0-316-92348-6). Little.

Feast of Snakes. Harry Crews. LC 76-8206. 1976. 7.95 o.p. (ISBN 0-689-10729-3, Atheneum). Macmillan.

Feast of Vegetables. John Tovey. (Illus.). 156p. 1986. 29.95 o.p. (ISBN 0-7126-0780-3, Pub. by Century Hutchinson). David & Charles.

Feast on a Diabetic Diet. rev. ed. Euell Gibbons & Joe Gibbons. 336p. 1982. pap. 2.95 o.p. (ISBN 0-449-23853-9, Crest). Fawcett.

Feast Without Fuss. Pamela Harlech. LC 77-3559. 1977. 12.95 o.p. (ISBN 0-689-10787-0, Atheneum). Macmillan.

Feasting Free on Wild Edibles. Bradford Angier. LC 72-6088. (Illus.). 320p. 1972. pap. 11.95 o.p. (ISBN 0-8117-2006-3). Stackpole.

Feasts for a Farthing. Molly Finn. Ed. by Dennis Dinan. LC 85-50086. (Illus.). 272p. (Orig.). 1985. pap. 10.95 o.p. (ISBN 0-89909-066-4). Yankee Bks.

Feather Star. Patricia Wrightson. LC 63-7901. (Illus.). (gr. 7 up). 1963. 4.95 o.p. (ISBN 0-15-227501-0, HJ). HarBraceJ.

Feathers from Sand Dune Cave: A Basketmaker Cave Near Navajo Mountain, Utah. Lydon L. Hargrave. (Technical Ser.). 52p. 1970. pap. 2.00 o.p. (TS-9). Mus Northern Ariz.

Feathers on the Wind. 2nd ed. Walter Nelms. LC 82-61096. (Illus.). 96p. 1982. 5.95 o.p. (ISBN 0-938232-13-4). Winston-Derek.

Features of Person & Society in Swat-Collected Essays on Pathans: Selected Essays of Frederik Barth, Vol. II. Fredrik Barth. (International Library of Anthropology Ser.). 208p. 1981. 33.00x o.p. (ISBN 0-7100-0620-9). Routledge Chapman & Hall.

Featuring the Saint. Leslie Charteris. 1980. pap. 1.95 o.s.i. (ISBN 0-441-23155-1). Ace Bks.

Febrile Child: Clinical Management of Fever & Other Types of Pyrexia. Martin I. Lorin. LC 82-85550. 262p. 1982. 38.00 o.p. (ISBN 0-471-08329-1, JW). Krieger.

Federal Administrative Procedure Sourcebook: Statutes & Related Materials. Administrative Conference of the U. S. Staff. 984p. (Orig.). 1985. pap. 21.00 o.p. (ISBN 0-318-18756-6, S/N 052-003-00989-7). USGPO.

Federal Aviation Regulations: Air Taxi Operators & Commerical Operators of Small Aircraft, Pt. 135. Federal Aviation Administration Staff. Ed. by Aviation Book Company. 1979. pap. 5.95 o.p. (ISBN 0-911720-56-1). Aviation.

Federal Aviation Regulations for Aircraft Mechanics: An Extract. rev. ed. FAA Staff. 600p. 1987. pap. 15.95 o.p. (ISBN 0-89100-292-8, EA-FAR-1M). IAP.

Federal Aviation Regulations for Pilots, (FAR) Aero Staff. Ed. by Ernest J. Gentle. LC 60-10472. 112p. 1984. pap. 5.25 o.p. (ISBN 0-8168-5740-7, 25740P, TAB-Aero). TAB Bks.

Federal Aviation Regulations for Pilots. 12th, rev. ed. Federal Aviation Administration Staff. Ed. by Walter P. Winner. LC 83-25663. 216p. 1987. pap. 5.95 o.p. (ISBN 0-916413-07-1). Aviation.

Federal Aviation Regulations for 1987. TAB-Aero Staff. 128p. 1987. pap. 5.95 o.p. (ISBN 0-8306-8742-4, 25742, TAB-Aero). TAB Bks.

Federal Benefits for Veterans & Dependents. 91p. 1987. pap. 2.25 o.p. (ISBN 0-318-22430-5, S/N 051-000-00185-1). USGPO.

Federal Budget & the Nonprofit Sector. Lester M. Salamon & Alan J. Abramson. (Nonprofit Sector Ser.). 116p. (Orig.). 1982. pap. text ed. 13.75 o.p. (ISBN 0-87766-318-1). Urban Inst.

Federal Bureau of Investigation. Max Lowenthal. LC 70-139139. 1971. Repr. of 1950 ed. lib. bdg. 22.50x o.p. (ISBN 0-8371-5755-2, LOFB). Greenwood.

Federal Civil Trial Practice & Procedure. 314p. 1983. 15.007 o.p. (ISBN 0-318-02485-3). ICLE Georgia.

Federal Client. 58p. 1983. incl. client list 20.00 o.p. (34); members 10.00 o.p.; avail. separately 7.00 o.p. Am Consul Eng.

Federal Communications Commission Reports: Second Series, Vol. 97. 1388p. 1986. 37.00 o.p. (ISBN 0-318-22378-3, S/N 004-000-00453-1). USGPO.

Federal Communications Commission Reports: Second Series, Vol. 98. 1437p. 1986. 38.00 o.p. (ISBN 0-318-22379-1, S/N 004-000-00454-0). USGPO.

Federal Contract Compliance Manual. 470p. 1983. 19.00 o.p. (30840-3). P-H.

Federal Copyright Records, Seventeen Ninety to Eighteen Hundred. Ed. by James Gilreath & Elizabeth Carter. LC 86-600334. (Illus.). 181p. 1987. 13.00 o.p. (ISBN 0-8444-0540-X, S/N 030-000-00184-2). USGPO.

Federal Court Awards of Attorney's Fees. Richard E. Larson. 544p. 1981. 40.00 o.p. (ISBN 0-15-100021-2, H400087, Pub. by Law & Business). HarBraceJ.

Federal Courts: Cases, Comments & Questions. Martin H. Redish. LC 82-24763. (American Casebook Ser.). 884p. 1983. text ed. 29.95 o.p. (ISBN 0-314-71146-5). West Pub.

Federal Courts, Cases, Comments & Questions: 1986 Supplement. Martin H. Redish. (American Casebook Ser.). 210p. 1985. pap. text ed. 8.95 o.p. (ISBN 0-314-96535-1). West Pub.

Federal Courts, Jurisdiction & Practice. Theodore Schussler. 152p. (Orig.). 1982. pap. 7.50x o.p. (ISBN 0-87526-036-5). Gould.

Federal Departmentalization: A Critique of Theories of Organization. S. C. Wallace. LC 79-152615. 251p. 1972. Repr. of 1941 ed. lib. bdg. 22.50x o.p. (ISBN 0-8371-6050-2, WAFE). Greenwood.

Federal Efforts for Developing New Evaluative Methods. Ed. by Nick Smith. LC 81-80074. (Program Evaluation Ser.: No. 12). 1981. pap. text ed. 9.95x o.p. (ISBN 0-87589-859-9). Jossey-Bass.

Federal Employment Relations Manual. 1987. (ISBN 0-87179-909-X). BNA.

Federal Estate & Gift Taxation in a Nutshell. 3rd ed. John K. McNulty. LC 82-24726. (Nutshell Ser.). 509p. 1983. pap. text ed. 11.95 o.p. (ISBN 0-314-71766-8). West Pub.

Federal Ethics Handbook. Michie Company Editorial Staff. 372p. 1981. looseleaf 75.00 o.p. (ISBN 0-87215-356-8); Suppl. 1984. 37.50 o.p. (ISBN 0-87215-730-X). Michie Co.

Federal Evaluation Policy: Analyzing the Effects of Public Programs. Joseph S. Wholey et al. 134p. 1970. pap. 6.50 o.p. (ISBN 0-87766-003-4). Urban Inst.

Federal Executive: The President & the Bureaucracy. Thomas A. Timberg. LC 77-17490. (Orig.). 1978. pap. text ed. 7.95x o.p. (ISBN 0-89197-641-8). Irvington.

Federal Fast Finder. 10th ed. Washington Researchers Publishing Staff. (Briefcase Ser.: Bk. 1). 1988. pap. 25.00 o.p. (ISBN 0-934940-63-0). Wash Res Pub.

Federal Fast Finder. IX ed. Washington Researchers Staff. (Briefcase Ser.: Vol. 1). 66p. 1986. pap. 25.00 o.p. (ISBN 0-934940-51-7). Wash Res Pub.

Federal Fertility in the Stream of Commerce. Elihu D. Ryden. LC 72-86198. 56p. 1972. pap. text ed. 3.50x o.p. (ISBN 0-8422-0220-X). Irvington.

Federal Finance & Economic Development in India. R. N. Tripathy. 288p. 1984. text ed. 30.00x o.p. (ISBN 0-86590-171-6, Pub. by Sterling Pubs India). Apt Bks.

Federal Food, Drug, & Cosmetic Act as Amended & Related Laws. Gerard P. Walsh. LC 81-601313. 195p. 1986. 4.75 o.p. (ISBN 0-318-23078-X, 017-012-00324-9). USGPO.

Federal Government Information Technology: Electronic Record Systems & Individual Privacy. LC 86-600524. (OTA-CIT Ser.: No. 296). 162p. (Orig.). 1986. pap. 7.50 o.p. (ISBN 0-318-21287-0, S/N 052-003-01038-1). USGPO.

Federal Government Information Technology: Electronic Surveillance & Civil Liberties. Illus. by John H. Gibbons. LC 85-600609. (OTA-CIT-293). 80p. (Orig.). 1985. pap. text ed. 3.00 o.p. (ISBN 0-318-18757-4, S/N 052-003-01015-1). USGPO.

Federal Government Information Technology: Management, Security, & Congressional Oversight. LC 86-600507. (Illus.). 198p. 1986. pap. 7.50 o.p. (ISBN 0-318-22380-5, S/N 052-003-01026-7). USGPO.

Federal Health Programs: Improving the Health-Care System? Ed. by Stuart Altman & Harvey M. Sapolsky. LC 79-48059. (University Health Policy Consortium Ser.). 272p. 1981. pap. text ed. 14.00x o.p. (ISBN 0-669-06371-1). Lexington Bks.

Federal Historic Preservation Case Law: A Special Report. Charlotte R. Bell. 88p. (Orig.). 1985. pap. 3.25 o.p. (ISBN 0-318-18758-2, S/N 052-003-01000-3). USGPO.

Federal Hospital Phone Book: 1983-84. Ed. by Stanley Alperin. pap. 24.99 o.p. (ISBN 0-916524-19-1). US Direct Serv.

Federal Hotel-Motel Discount Directory. 112p. 1987. pap. 5.50 o.p. (ISBN 0-318-22624-3, S/N 022-003-01140-4). USGPO.

Federal Income Tax Project. American Law Institute Staff. LC 84-155263. AM Law Inst.

Federal Income Taxation: A Law Student Guide to the Leading Cases & Concepts. 3rd ed. Marvin A. Chirelstein. LC 82-4990. (University Textbook Ser.). 348p. 1982. pap. text ed. 15.50 o.p. (ISBN 0-88277-059-4). Foundation Pr.

Federal Income Taxation Cases & Materials. Alan Gunn. LC 81-1502. (American Casebook Ser.). 785p. 1981. text ed. 24.95 o.p. (ISBN 0-314-58805-1); pap. text ed. incl. 1983 suppl. avail. o.p.; tchr's. manual avail. o.p. (ISBN 0-314-63144-5). West Pub.

Federal Income Taxation, Cases & Materials: 1985 Legislative Supplement, Vol. II. 2nd ed. Stanley S. Surrey et al. (University Casebook Ser.). 101p. 1985. pap. text ed. 5.95 o.p. (ISBN 0-88277-261-9). Foundation Pr.

Federal Income Taxation, Cases & Other Materials, 1985 Supplement. Alan Gunn. (American Casebook Ser.). 77p. 1984. pap. text ed. 3.95 o.p. West Pub.

Federal Income Taxation of Estates & Beneficiaries: 1984 Supplement. M. Carr Ferguson et al. LC 70-79882. 195p. 1984. pap. 25.00 o.p. (ISBN 0-316-27908-0). Little.

Federal Income Taxation of Individuals in a Nutshell. 3rd ed. John K. McNulty. LC 83-6509. (Nutshell Ser.). 487p. 1983. pap. text ed. 11.95 o.p. (ISBN 0-314-74082-1). West Pub.

Federal Income Taxation, Principles & Policies: 1983 Supplement. Erwin N. Griswold & Michael J. Graetz. (University Casebook Ser.). 363p. 1983. pap. text ed. 3.63 o.p. (ISBN 0-88277-156-6). Foundation Pr.

Federal Income Taxation: 1983 Supplement. Lawrence M. Stone. 1983. pap. text ed. write for info. o.p. Little.

Federal Intervention in the Mortgage Markets: An Analysis. Douglas Hearth. Ed. by Richard N. Farmer. LC 83-17880. (Research for Business Decisions Ser.: No. 64). 110p. 1983. 37.95 o.p. (ISBN 0-8357-1484-5). UMI Res Pr.

Federal Judiciary Almanac 1986. W. Stuart Dornette & Robert R. Cross. (Federal Law Practice Ser.). 1109p. 1986. 85.00 o.p. (ISBN 0-471-83901-9); Supplement 1. pap. 30.00 o.p. (ISBN 0-471-85666-5). Wiley.

Federal Legislation for Libraries. Ed. by Winifred Ladley. (Allerton Park Institute Ser.: No. 13). 104p. 1967. 4.00x o.p. (ISBN 0-87845-008-4). U of Ill Lib Info Sci.

Federal Organization & Administrative Management. Herbert Emmerich. LC 75-135704. 314p. 1971. 18.00 o.p. (ISBN 0-8173-4813-1). U of Ala Pr.

Federal Philadelphia, 1785-1825: The Athens of the Western World. Beatrice B. Garvan. (Illus.). 96p. (Orig.). 1987. pap. 12.95 o.p. (ISBN 0-87633-069-3). Phila Mus Art.

Federal Public Land & Resources Law. George C. Coggins & Charles F. Wilkinson. LC 80-28034. (University Casebook Ser.). 849p. 1981. text ed. 24.50 o.p. (ISBN 0-88277-022-5); Supplement, 215p. write for info. o.p. (ISBN 0-88277-144-2). Foundation Pr.

Federal Records of World War II, 2 vols. LC 72-307. 1982. Repr. of 1950 ed. Set. 130.00x o.p. (ISBN 0-8103-0998-X); Vol. 1, Civilian Agencies; 1073 Pp. Vol. 2, Military Agencies; 1061 Pp. Gale.

Federal Regulation of Consumer-Creditor Relations. Kenneth R. Redden & James McClellan. 666p. 1982. 45.00x o.p. (ISBN 0-87215-441-6). Michie Co.

Federal Regulation of Employment Service, 11 binders. LC 76-22821. Lawyers Co-Op.

Federal Regulation of Family Law. Kenneth R. Redden. (Federal Law Library). 457p. 1982. 40.00x o.p. (ISBN 0-87215-557-9). Michie Co.

Federal Regulatory Directory: 1983-1984. Congressional Quarterly, Inc. Staff. LC 79-644368. 893p. 1983. 35.95 o.p. (ISBN 0-87187-250-1). Congr Quarterly.

Federal Regulatory Process: Agency Practices & Procedures. Gary J. Edles & Jerome Nelson. 698p. 1981. 65.00 o.p. (ISBN 0-15-100022-0, H39891, Pub. by Law & Business). HarBraceJ.

Federal Reorganization: What Have We Learned? Ed. by Peter Szanton. LC 80-29280. (Chatham House Series on Change in American Politics). 184p. 1981. pap. text ed. 14.95x o.p. (ISBN 0-934540-11-X). Chatham Hse Pubs.

Federal Reserve & Our Manipulated Dollar. Martin A. Larson. 288p. Date not set. pap. 6.50 o.p. (ISBN 0-317-53254-5). Noontide.

Federal Rules of Civil Appellate & Supreme Court. Law School ed. West Publishing Co. Editorial Staff. (Criminal Procedure 1985 Ser.). 852p. 1985. pap. text ed. 9.95 o.p. (ISBN 0-314-93952-0). West Pub.

Federal Rules of Civil-Appellate-Criminal Procedure: Law School Edition, 1982. West Publishing Company Staff. 383p. 1982. pap. text ed. 7.95 o.p. (ISBN 0-314-68826-9). West Pub.

Federal Rules of Civil Procedure. 450p. 1985. looseleaf 12.95 o.p. Gould.

Federal Rules of Civil Procedure-1984. Kevin M. Clermont. 456p. 1984. pap. text ed. 10.50 o.p. (ISBN 0-88277-183-3). Foundation Pr.

Federal Rules of Civil Procedure, 1986. 450p. 1986. pap. 11.00 o.p. (ISBN 0-88277-330-5). Foundation Pr.

Federal Rules of Criminal Procedure: 1986 Law School Edition. West Publishing Co. Editorial Staff. 459p. 1986. pap. text ed. 5.95 o.p. (ISBN 0-314-24862-5). West Pub.

Federal Rules of Evidence. 300p. 1985. looseleaf 10.00 o.p. (ISBN 0-87526-301-1). Gould.

Federal Rules Service Third: 1958-1959, 22 vols. Ed. by Pike & Fischer. 895.00 o.p. (ISBN 0-317-44847-1). Callaghan.

Federal Special Court Litigation. University of Virginia School of Law Staff & Kenneth R. Redden. LC 82-81710. xxi, 520p. 1982. 40.00 o.p. (ISBN 0-87215-421-1). Michie Co.

Federal Tax Policy. rev. ed. Joseph A. Pechman. (Brookings Institute Studies of Government Finance). 1971. pap. text ed. 5.95x o.p. (ISBN 0-393-09987-3). Norton.

Federal Tax Research: Guide to Materials & Techniques. Gail L. Richmond. LC 81-68691. (University Textbook Ser.). 503p. 1981. pap. text ed. 2.75 o.p. (ISBN 0-88277-055-1). Foundation Pr.

Federal Tax Treatment of Income from Oil & Gas. Stephen L. McDonald. LC 79-29702. (Brookings Institution, National Committee on Government Finance, Studies of Government Finance). (Illus.). xv, 163p. 1980. Repr. of 1963 ed. lib. bdg. 35.00x o.p. (ISBN 0-313-22289-4, MCFT). Greenwood.

Federal Taxation of Estates, Gifts, & Trusts. Joint Comittee on Continuing Legal Education et al. Date not set. price not set o.p. Am Law Inst.

Federal Taxation of Estates, Trusts & Gifts: Principles & Planning. Joseph M. Dodge. LC 81-11602. (American Casebook Ser.). 771p. 1981. 29.95 o.p. (ISBN 0-314-59848-0); supplement avail. o.p. (ISBN 0-314-69793-4). West Pub.

Federal Taxation, 1988. James W. Pratt et al. 1988. 46.95 o.p. (ISBN 0-256-06458-X). Irwin.

Federal Taxation, 1989. James Pratt et al. 1988. 51.50 o.p. (ISBN 0-256-06716-3); study guide 15.50 o.p. (ISBN 0-256-06717-1); practice set 13.50 o.p. (ISBN 0-256-06719-8); practice set 2 13.50 o.p. (ISBN 0-256-06718-X). Irwin.

Federal Taxes & Management Decisions, 1987-88. Ray M. Sommerfeld. 1987. 33.95x o.p. (ISBN 0-256-03612-8). Irwin.

Federal Trade Commission: A Study in Administrative Law & Prcedure. Gerard C. Henderson. LC 68-16354. 1968. Repr. of 1924 ed. 12.00x o.p. (ISBN 0-87586-006-0). Agathon.

Federalism & Resource Development: The Australian Case. Ed. by Peter Drysdale & Hirofumi Shibata. 264p. 1985. text ed. 25.95x o.p. (ISBN 0-86861-734-2). Unwin Hyman.

Federalism in Central & Eastern Europe. Rudolf Schlesinger. 1970. Repr. of 1945 ed. lib. bdg. 35.00x o.p. (ISBN 0-8371-3402-1, SCFE). Greenwood.

Federalism Today: Approaches, Issues & Trends. Sharada Rath. ix, 208p. 1985. text ed. 25.00x o.p. (ISBN 0-86590-505-3, Pub. by Sterling Pubs India). Apt Bks.

Federalist Delaware: 1775-1815. John A. Munroe. 286p. 1980. Repr. of 1954 ed. 20.50 o.p. (ISBN 0-374-96024-0, Octagon). Hippocrene Bks.

Federalist System: Seventeen Eighty-Nine to Eighteen Hundred & One. John S. Bassett. LC 68-19308. 1968. Repr. of 1906 ed. 22.50x o.p. (ISBN 0-8154-0017-9). Cooper Sq.

Federalists: A Study in Administrative History. Leonard D. White. LC 77-18058. 1978. Repr. of 1948 ed. lib. bdg. 37.75 o.p. (ISBN 0-313-20101-3, WHFE). Greenwood.

Federico Garcia Lorca. Reed Anderson. (Modern Dramatists Ser.). 192p. 1984. 19.50 o.s.i. (ISBN 0-394-54137-5, GP952). Grove.

Federico Garcia Lorca. Reed Anderson. (Modern Dramatists Ser.). 192p. 1984. pap. 7.95 o.p. (ISBN 0-394-62264-2, Ever). Grove.

Fee-For-Services Medicine: The Overlooked Alternative. American Medical Association Staff. 24p. (Orig.). 1987. pap. 8.00 o.p. (ISBN 0-89970-305-4, OP-155). AMA.

Feed Information & Animal Production. 320p. 1983. text ed. 41.30 o.p. (ISBN 0-85198-522-X). CAB Intl.

Feed My Sheep: Questions & Answers for the Christian & the Potential Christian. Marjorie H. Robbins. 1979. 4.50 o.p. (ISBN 0-682-49281-7). Exposition-Phoenix.

Feed My Sheep: Sermons on Contemporary Issues in Pastoral Care. Ed. by Gregory J. Johanson. 6.95 o.p. Paulist Pr.

Feed Your Kids Bright. Francine Prince & Harold Prince. 336p. 1987. 17.45 o.s.i. (ISBN 0-671-60522-4). S&S.

Feed Your Kids Right: Dr. Smith's Program for Your Child's Total Health. Lendon Smith. 1979. text ed. 10.95 o.p. (ISBN 0-07-058496-6). McGraw.

Feed Yourself Right. Lendon Smith. LC 83-959. 464p. 1983. text ed. 14.95 o.p. (ISBN 0-07-058499-0). McGraw.

Feedback Circuits & Op-Amps. D. Horrocks. 1983. 22.95 o.p. (ISBN 0-442-30554-0). Van Nos Reinhold.

Feedback from Tomorrow. John Dakin. (Research in Planning & Design Ser.). 492p. 1980. 35.00x o.p. (ISBN 0-85086-071-7, NO. 3020, Pub. by Pion England). Routledge Chapman & Hall.

Feedback Loop. Roy Alcock. 1984. 7.95 o.p. (ISBN 0-533-05880-5). Vantage.

Feeding a Crowd. Girl Scouts of the U. S. A. Staff. 50p. (gr. 4-12). 1973. pap. 1.00 package of six o.p. (ISBN 0-88441-125-7, 19-977). Girl Scouts USA.

Feeding & Digestion. Gwynne Vevers. LC 83-18757. (Your Body Ser.: No. 3). (Illus.). 24p. (gr. 1-4). 1984. 8.25 o.p. (ISBN 0-688-02830-6); PLB 7.63 o.p. (ISBN 0-688-02831-4). Lothrop.

Feeding & Nutrition of Nonhuman Primates. Ed. by Robert S. Harris. 1970. 72.50 o.p. (ISBN 0-12-327360-9). Acad Pr.

Feeding & Survival Strategies of Estuarine Organisms. Ed. by N. V. Jones & W. J. Wolff. LC 81-12005. (Marine Science Ser.: Vol. 15). 316p. 1981. 59.50x o.p. (ISBN 0-306-40813-9, Plenum Pr). Plenum Pub.

Feeding Strategy for the High Yielding Dairy Cow. W. H. Broster & Henry Swan. 432p. 1979. text ed. 45.00x o.p. (ISBN 0-258-97126-6, Pub. by Granada England). Gower Pub Co.

Feeding the Horse. (Illus.). 127p. 1974. lib. bdg. 10.75 o.p. (ISBN 0-936032-04-9). Blood-Horse.

Feeding the World of the Future. Hal Hellman. LC 70-179085. (World of the Future Ser.). (Illus.). 224p. (gr. 7 up). 1972. 6.95 o.p. (ISBN 0-87131-107-0). M Evans.

Feeling Child. Arthur Janov. 1975. pap. 5.95 o.p. (ISBN 0-671-22022-5, Touchstone Bks). S&S.

Feeling Fit in Your Forty's: How to Get the Most from the Best Years of Your Life. Richard Benyo & Rhonda Provost. LC 86-47679. 288p. 1987. 14.95 o.p. (ISBN 0-689-11581-4, Atheneum). Macmillan.

Feeling Great. Jeanne Segal. 176p. 1983. pap. 7.95 o.p. (ISBN 0-87877-069-0). Newcastle Pub.

Feeling of Jazz. George T. Simon. (Illus.). 1961. 5.00 o.p. S&S.

Feelings from Within. Bobbi. 1980. 5.00 o.p. (ISBN 0-682-49659-6). Exposition-Phoenix.

Feet of a Snake. Barry Chubin. 1984. 14.95 o.p. (ISBN 0-87795-571-9, Arbor Hse). Morrow.

Feis Tighe Chonuin Chinn-Shleibhe. Ed. by Nicholas O'Kearney. 215p. Repr. of 1855 ed. 19.00 o.p. (ISBN 0-384-43005-8). Johnson Repr.

Feldenkrais Method: Teaching by Handling, A Technique for Individuals. Yochanan Rywerant. LC 83-47734. (Ginger Bk.). 256p. 1983. 16.45 o.p. (ISBN 0-06-250750-8). HarpR.

Feldspar Minerals, Vol. 2: Chemical & Textural Properties. J. V. Smith. LC 73-15294. (Illus.). 690p. 1974. 87.00 o.p. (ISBN 0-387-06516-4). Springer-Verlag.

Felice: God's Little Lamb in Making Friends. Jill Wolf. (Illus.). 22p. (ps-3). 1985. 2.95 o.p. (ISBN 0-89954-333-2). Antioch Pub Co.

Felicien Rops: The Complete Graphic Work, 2 vols. Maurice Exsteens. (Illus.). 464p. 1986. Repr. of 1928 ed. 195.00 set o.p. (ISBN 0-915346-91-5). Vol. 1, 480p; Vol. 2, 464p. A Wofsy Fine Arts.

Feline Medicine. Ed. by Paul W. Pratt. LC 82-82939. (Illus.). 687p. 1983. 49.50 o.p. (ISBN 0-939674-00-9). Am Vet Pubns.

Felipe Angeles & the Mexican Revolution. Matthew T. Slattery. LC 82-91102. (Illus.). 214p. (Orig.). 1982. 12.95 o.p. (ISBN 0-932970-35-4); pap. 8.95 o.p. (ISBN 0-932970-34-6). Greenbriar Bks.

Felipe the Bullfighter. Robert Vavra. LC 68-10006. (Illus.). (gr. 4-6). 1968. 4.95 o.p. (ISBN 0-15-227510-X, HJ). HarBraceJ.

Felisa Rincon: Woman of the Americas. Irving Gerber. (American Destiny Ser.: Puerto Ricans). (Illus.). (gr. 4-12). 1979. of ten 12.95 set o.p. (ISBN 0-87594-179-6, 4612). Book-Lab.

Felix Culpa. Joseph S. Abela. 1977. 6.50 o.p. (ISBN 0-682-48745-7). Exposition-Phoenix.

Felix H. Man. C. M. Kauffman. (Orig.). pap. 2.95 o.p. (ISBN 0-317-02544-9, Pub. by Victoria & Albert Mus UK). Faber & Faber.

Felix Holt, the Radical. George Eliot. 1967. 14.95x o.p. (ISBN 0-460-00353-4, DEL 04130, Evman); pap. text ed. 4.95x o.p. (ISBN 0-460-11353-4, Evman). Biblio Dist.

Felix Mendelssohn: His Life, His Family, His Music. Herbert Kupferberg. LC 72-1172. (Encore Edition). 1972. 2.95 o.p. (ISBN 0-684-15414-5, ScribT). Scribner.

Fell Terrier. D. Brian Plummer. (Illus.). 244p. 1983. 22.00 o.p. (ISBN 0-85115-181-7, Pub. by Boydell & Brewer). Longwood Pub Group.

Fellini's Faces. Ed. by Christian Strich. 1982. pap. 12.95 o.s.i. (ISBN 0-03-061479-1, Owl Bks). H Holt & Co.

Fellow Travellers. T. C. Worsley. 247p. (Orig.). 1984. 18.00 o.p. (ISBN 0-907040-51-9, Pub. by GMP England); pap. 7.50 o.p. (ISBN 0-907040-45-4). Alyson Pubns.

Fellow-Travellers: Intellectual Friends of Communism. rev. & updated ed. David Caute. Date not set. 35.00 o.p.; pap. 17.95 o.p. Yale U Pr.

Fellowship. Mary C. Romine & Aden F. Romine. 384p. (Orig.). 1984. pap. 3.75 o.s.i. (ISBN 0-8439-2142-0, Pub. by Leisure Bks CT). Dorchester Pub Co.

Fell's Guide to College Money: For the Asking in Florida. Charles T. Mangrum, II et al. 224p. (Orig.). (YA) (gr. 9-12). 1987. pap. 13.95 o.p. (ISBN 0-8119-0706-6). Fell.

Fell's Guide to Commercial Art. Roy P. Nelson & Byron Ferris. LC 66-14801. 118p. (gr. 10 up). 1966. 19.95 o.p. (ISBN 0-8119-0041-X). Fell.

Felony Arrests: Their Prosecution & Disposition in New York City's Courts. (Vera Studies in Criminal Justice (Professional Studies)). (Illus.). 192p. (Orig.). 1981. 17.50x o.p. (ISBN 0-582-28195-4); pap. text ed. 9.95x o.p. (ISBN 0-582-28187-3). Longman.

Felsic Plutonic Rocks & Associated Mineralization of the Kingdom of Saudi Arabia. Ed. by A. R. Drysdall et al. 292p. 1986. pap. 51.00 o.p. (ISBN 0-08-032634-X, Pub. by PPL). Pergamon.

Feltmaking: Techniques & Projects. Inge Evers. LC 87-80486. (Illus.). 87p. (Orig.). 1987. pap. 6.95 o.s.i. (ISBN 0-937274-34-8, Dist. by Sterling Publishing Co.). Lark Bks.

Female Complaints: Lydia Pinkham & the Business of Women's Medicine. Sarah Stage. (Illus.). 304p. 1981. pap. 4.95 o.p. (ISBN 0-393-00033-8). Norton.

Female Complaints: Lydia Pinkham & the Business of Women's Medicine. Sarah Stage. (Illus.). 1979. 14.95 o.p. (ISBN 0-393-01178-X). Norton.

Female Criminals in India. Shubhra Ghosh. 1986. 22.50 o.p. (Pub. by Uppal Pub Hse New Deli). South Asia Bks.

Female Desires: How They Are Sought, Bought, & Packaged. Rosalind Coward. LC 84-73207. 256p. 1985. pap. 5.95 o.p. (ISBN 0-394-62367-3, E977, Ever). Grove.

Female Eunuch. Germaine Greer. 1971. text ed. 9.95 o.p. (ISBN 0-07-024372-7). McGraw.

Female Fix. Muriel Nellis. 1980. 8.95 o.p. (ISBN 0-395-27786-8). HM.

Female Gothic. Ed. by Juliann Fleenor. 250p. (Orig.). pap. 12.95 o.p. (ISBN 0-920792-06-5). Eden Pr.

Female Hand: Palmistry for Today's Woman. Lori Reid. (Illus.). 208p. (Orig.). 1987. pap. 8.99 o.p. (ISBN 0-85030-516-0, Pub. by Aquarian Pr England). Sterling.

Female Homosexuality: A Psychodynamic Study of Lesbianism. Frank S. Caprio. 1967. pap. 2.25 o.p. (ISBN 0-8065-0151-0, 258, Pub. by Citadel Pr). Carol Pub Group.

Female Imagination. Patricia M. Spacks. 1976. pap. 3.50 o.p. (ISBN 0-380-00599-9, 62901, Discus). Avon.

Female Labor Force in the United States: Demographic & Economic Factors Governing its Growth & Changing Composition. Valerie K. Oppenheimer. (Population Monograph Ser.: No. 5). xii, 197p. 1976. pap. text ed. 6.95 o.p. (ISBN 0-8371-9408-3, OPL). Greenwood.

Female Offender. Caesar Lombrosso. (Illus.). 320p. 1958. (ISBN 0-8022-0993-9). Philos Lib.

Female Parts: One Woman Plays. Dario Fo & Franca R. Rame. 48p. (Orig.). 1981. pap. 3.95 o.p. (ISBN 0-86104-220-4). Routledge Chapman & Hall.

Female Quixote. Charlotte Lennox. (Mother of the Novel Reprint Ser.). 400p. 1986. pap. 7.95 o.p. (ISBN 0-86358-080-7, Pandora Pr). Routledge Chapman & Hall.

Female Scholars: A Tradition of Learned Women Before 1800. Ed. by Jeanie R. Brink. (Illus.). 1980. 17.95 o.p. (ISBN 0-920792-02-2). Eden Pr.

Female Sexuality Following Spinal Cord Injury. 1978. (ISBN 0-915708-07-8). Cheever Pub.

Female Sterilization. Herbert P. Brown & Stephan N. Schanzer. 126p. 1982. text ed. 19.50 o.p. (ISBN 0-88416-356-3). Year Bk Med.

Female Sterilization: Prognosis for Qualified Outpatient Procedures. Ed. by Gordon W. Duncan et al. (Illus.). 1972. 43.00 o.p. (ISBN 0-12-224050-2). Acad Pr.

Female Strategies. Evelyn Shaw & Joan Darling. 1986. pap. 6.95 o.p. (ISBN 0-671-42354-1, Touchstone Bks). S&S.

Female-to-Male Transsexualism: Historical, Clinical, Theoretical Issues. Leslie M. Lothstein. 352p. 1983. 26.95 o.p. (ISBN 0-7100-9476-0). Routledge Chapman & Hall.

Female Transport. Steve Gooch. 1984. pap. 6.95 o.p. (ISBN 0-902818-62-7, NO. 4140). Routledge Chapman & Hall.

Feminine Consciousness in the Modern British Novel. Sydney J. Kaplan. LC 75-2179. 182p. 1975. 17.95 o.p. (ISBN 0-252-00463-9). U of Ill Pr.

Feminine Dimension of the Divine. Joan C. Engelsman. LC 79-13884. 204p. 1979. pap. 9.95 o.s.i. (ISBN 0-664-24268-5, Westminster). Westminster John Knox.

Feminine Mind & Body. J. Dudley Chapman. LC 66-20216. 1967. (ISBN 0-8022-0232-2). Philos Lib.

Feminine Mind Is Magnificent & Exacting: An Aesthetic Realism Lesson of Two College Girls. Eli Siegel. 17p. 1965. pap. 2.00x o.p. (ISBN 0-911492-06-2). Aesthetic Realism.

Feminine Mystique. Betty Friedan. 1963. 10.00 o.p. (ISBN 0-393-08436-1). Norton.

Feminine Mystique. 2nd ed. Betty Friedan. 430p. 1974. 10.00 o.p. (ISBN 0-393-08685-2). Norton.

Femininity. Susan Brownmiller. 288p. 1984. 16.50 o.p. (ISBN 0-671-24692-5, Linden Pr). S&S.

Feminism & Socialism in China. Elisabeth J. Croll. 1978. 27.50 o.p. (ISBN 0-7100-8816-7). Routledge Chapman & Hall.

Feminism for Girls: An Adventure Story. Ed. by Angela McRobbie & Trisha McCabe. (Illus.). 256p. (Orig.). 1981. pap. 11.50 o.p. (ISBN 0-7100-0961-5). Routledge Chapman & Hall.

Feminism in Canada: From Pressure to Politics. Ed. by Angela Miles & Geraldine Finn. 315p. 1982. 29.95 o.p. (ISBN 0-919619-02-9, Dist by U of Toronto Pr); pap. 14.95 o.p. (ISBN 0-919619-00-2, Dist. by U of Toronto Pr). Black Rose Bks.

Feminism on Trial: The Ginny Foat Case & Its Meaning for the Future of the Women's Movement. Ellen Hawkes. 430p. 1986. 18.95 o.p. (ISBN 0-688-04850-1). Morrow.

Feminist Challenge. Date not set. (ISBN 0-8052-0806-2). Random.

Feminist Dictionary. Cheris Kramarae & Paula A. Treichler. 587p. 1986. text ed. 28.95 o.p. (ISBN 0-86358-060-2); pap. text ed. 12.95 o.p. (ISBN 0-86358-015-7). Routledge Chapman & Hall.

Feminist Theatre. Helene Keyssar. LC 85-70226. 192p. 1985. 22.50 o.s.i. (ISBN 0-394-54631-8, GP-970). Grove.

Feminist Theatre. Helene Keyssar. LC 85-70226. 192p. 1985. pap. 7.95 o.p. (ISBN 0-394-62059-3, E-989, Ever). Grove.

Feminization of American Culture. Ann Douglas. 1978. pap. 3.95 o.p. (ISBN 0-380-01968-X, 60434-5, Discus). Avon.

Femmes d'Amis. Georges Courteline. 1972. 8.95 o.p. (ISBN 0-686-54629-6). French & Eur.

Fen Country: Twenty-Six Stories. Edmund Crispin. (Crime Ser.). 160p. 1981. pap. 3.95 o.p. (ISBN 0-14-005946-6). Penguin.

Fence. Daniel Harris. 288p. 1982. 12.00 o.p. (ISBN 0-682-49893-9). Exposition-Phoenix.

Fencin' Tool Bible. Bill Marquis. 1977. 10.95 o.p. (ISBN 0-89015-209-8). Eakin Pr.

Fencing. Jo Shaff. LC 81-66031. (Illus.). 1982. 9.95 o.p. (ISBN 0-689-11182-7, Atheneum). Macmillan.

Fender Stratocaster. Andre Duchossior. (Illus.). 48p. (Fr.). 1985. pap. 6.95 o.p. (ISBN 0-88188-388-3). H Leonard Pub Corp.

Feng-Shui: The Science of Sacred Landscape. Ernest J. Eitel. (Illus.). 96p. 1985. pap. 5.95 o.p. (ISBN 0-907791-09-3). Synerg AZ.

Fengate. Francis Pryor. (Shire Archaeology Ser.: No. 20). (Illus.). 1982. pap. 5.95 o.p. (ISBN 0-85263-577-X, Pub. by Shire Pubns England). Seven Hills Bk Dists.

Fennoscandian Tundra Ecosystems, Pt. 2: Animals & Systems Analysis. Ed. by F. E. Wielgolaski et al. (Ecological Studies: Vol. 17). (Illus.). 370p. 1976. 77.00 o.p. (ISBN 0-387-07551-8). Springer-Verlag.

Fenris Option. R. D. Jones. (Orig.). 1981. pap. 2.50 o.p. (ISBN 0-505-51640-3, Pub. by Tower Bks). Dorchester Pub Co.

Fenwomen: A Portrait of Women in an English Village. Mary Chamberlain. (History Workshop Ser.). (Illus.). 192p. 1983. pap. 9.95 o.p. (ISBN 0-7100-9567-8). Routledge Chapman & Hall.

Fer-de-Dance. Rex Stout. 1987. pap. 2.95 o.p. (ISBN 0-553-24918-5). Bantam.

Feral. Berton Roueche. 128p. 1983. pap. 2.50 o.p. (ISBN 0-380-65508-X, 65508). Avon.

Feral Classroom: High School Students' Construction of Reality. James MacPherson. (Routledge Education Bks.). 224p. 1983. 17.50x o.p. (ISBN 0-7100-9514-7). Routledge Chapman & Hall.

Fergus Lamont. Robin Jenkins. LC 79-63120. 293p. 1980. pap. 3.95 o.s.i. (ISBN 0-8008-2623-X, Pivot). Taplinger.

Ferguson's Castle: A Dream Remembered. Robert B. King. 1978. 10.00 o.p. (ISBN 0-682-49154-3). Exposition-Phoenix.

Fermentation Advances. Ed. by D. Perlman. 1969. 79.50 o.p. (ISBN 0-12-550850-6). Acad Pr.

Fernhurst, Q. E. D., & Other Early Writings. Gertrude Stein. LC 71-148664. 1983. pap. 6.95 o.p. Liveright.

Fernpickers. Bill Foster. 1977. 4.00 o.p. (ISBN 0-682-48744-9). Exposition-Phoenix.

Ferrari Legend: Sports Cars & Prototypes. Antoine Prunet. (Illus.). 1983. 49.50 o.p. (ISBN 0-393-01799-0). Norton.

Ferrari: The Man, the Machines. Ed. by Stan Grayson. (Marque History Bks.). (Illus.). 348p. 1982. 29.95 o.s.i. (ISBN 0-915038-05-6). Auto Quarterly.

Ferrari 308, 328, Mondial Autohistory. Geoff Willoughby. (Autohistory Ser.). (Illus.). 136p. Repr. of 1982 ed. 17.95 o.p. (ISBN 0-85045-832-3, Pub. by Osprey England). Motorbooks Intl.

Ferraris for the Road. Henry Rasmussen. (Survivor's Ser.). (Illus.). 1980. 12.98 o.p. (ISBN 0-87938-117-5). Motorbooks Intl.

Ferraro: My Story. Geraldine A. Ferraro & Linda B. Francke. (Illus.). 590p. 1986. lib. bdg. 19.95 o.p. (ISBN 0-8161-4098-7, Large Print BKs). G K Hall.

Ferret. George Markstein. 336p. (Orig.). 1983. pap. 3.50 o.s.i. (ISBN 0-345-30043-2). Ballantine.

Ferrets & Ferreting. Iain Brodie. (Illus.). 80p. (Orig.). 1987. pap. 8.95 o.p. (ISBN 0-7137-1831-5, Pub. by Blanford Pr England). Sterling.

Ferro & Antiferroelectric Substances. T. Mitsui et al. Ed. by K. H. Hellwege & A. M. Hellwege. LC 62-53136. (Landolt-Bornstein Ser.: Group 3, Vol. 9). (Illus.). vii, 496p. 1974. 212.10 o.p. (ISBN 0-387-06580-6). Springer-Verlag.

Ferroelectrics & Antiferroelectrics. Werner Kanzig. (Solid State Reprints Ser.). 1964. 30.00 o.p. (ISBN 0-12-608462-9). Acad Pr.

Ferrolysis: A Soil-Forming Process in Hydromorphic Conditions. (Agricultural Research Reports: 887). 1979. pap. 16.00 o.p. (ISBN 90-220-0699-9, PDC114, PUDOC). UNIPUB.

Ferromagnetodynamics: The Dynamics of Magnetic Bubbles Domains & Domain Walls. T. H. O'Dell. LC 80-25331. 230p. 1981. 69.95x o.p. (ISBN 0-470-27084-5). Halsted Pr.

Ferrous Production Metallurgy. A. T. Peters. LC 81-11710. 299p. 1982. 59.95x o.p. (ISBN 0-471-08597-9, Pub. by Wiley-Interscience). Wiley.

Ferry Tale: Crossing the Delaware on the Cape May-Lewes Ferry. William J. Miller, Jr. Ed. by Kathy K. Demarest. (Illus.). 120p. (Orig.). 1984. pap. 5.95 o.p. (ISBN 0-911293-03-5); 9.95 o.p. (ISBN 0-911293-04-3). Delapeake Pub Co.

Ferryboat Across the Kirenga. V. Shugaev et al. 1980. 8.95 o.p. (ISBN 0-8285-1854-8, Pub. by Progress Pubs USSR). Imported Pubns.

Ferryboat Islands: A Practical Guide to Washington State's San Juan Islands. Gordon Keith. (Illus.). 240p. (Orig.). 1988. pap. 9.95 o.p. Dolphin Bay.

Fertility: A Comprehensive Guide to Natural Family Planning. Elizabeth Clubb & Jane Knight. (Take Control Ser.). 192p. (Orig.). 1988. pap. 9.95 o.p. (ISBN 0-7153-8956-4, Pub. by David & Charles Pub England). Sterling.

Fertility & Family Planning in a Canadian Metropolis. T. R. Balakrishnan et al. (Illus.). 208p. 1975. 14.50x o.p. (ISBN 0-7735-0204-1, McGill Canada). U of Toronto Pr.

Fertility Control & the Medical Profession. Jean Aitken-Swan. 238p. 1977. 30.00 o.p. (ISBN 0-85664-463-3, Pub. by Croom Helm Ltd). Routledge Chapman & Hall.

Fertility Control Methods. Ed. by Gordon W. Duncan et al. 1973. 46.00 o.p. (ISBN 0-12-224060-X). Acad Pr.

Fertility in Massachusetts from the Revolution to the Civil War. Maris A. Vinovskis. LC 81-12686. (Studies in Social Discontinuity). 1981. 19.95 o.p. (ISBN 0-12-722040-2). Acad Pr.

Fertility of American Women: June Nineteen Eighty-Five. (Current Population Reports Series; P-20 Population Characteristics: No. 406). 69p. 1986. pap. 3.50 o.p. (S/N 003-001-90805-1). USGPO.

Fertilizer Industry. (UNIDO Guides to Information Sources: No. 21). pap. 4.00 o.p. (ISBN 0-686-93257-9, EID/164). UN.

Fertilizer Technology & Resources in the United States. Ed. by Kenneth D. Jacob. (Agronomy Ser.: Vol. 3). 1953. 66.00 o.p. (ISBN 0-12-379750-0). Acad Pr.

Fervent Years: The Group Theatre & the Thirties. Harold Clurman. (Quality Paperbacks Ser.). (Illus.). 352p. 1983. pap. 10.95 o.p. (ISBN 0-306-80186-8). Da Capo.

Fervent Years: The Story of the Group Theatre & the Thirties. Harold Clurman. LC 74-17485. (Illus.). 329p. 1975. pap. 4.95 o.p. (ISBN 0-15-630511-9, Harv). HarBraceJ.

Fest: The Transformation of Everday. Gerhard M. Martin. Tr. by M. Douglas Meeks. LC 76-7865. 96p. 1976. pap. 2.95 o.p. (ISBN 0-8006-1233-7, Fortress). Augsburg Fortress.

Festival. Humphreys Academy Patrons Staff. (Illus.). 320p. 1983. pap. 11.95 o.p. (ISBN 0-9610058-0-7). Wimmer Bks.

Festival! An Experiment in Living. Gladis DePree. 208p. 1985. 14.95 o.p. (ISBN 0-310-44110-2, 9488). Zondervan.

Festival of Art. Gerard Pottebaum. LC 79-135224. (Illus.). (ps-2). 1971. 5.50 o.p. (ISBN 0-8066-1107-3, 10-2287, Augsburg). Augsburg Fortress.

Festival of Christmas. Mary Hinderlie & Edna Hong. 48p. 1954. pap. 2.25 o.p. (ISBN 0-8066-0156-6, 10-2290, Augsburg). Augsburg Fortress.

Festival of Dressage. Jane Kidd. LC 86-10575. (Illus.). 144p. 1986. lib. bdg. 19.95 o.s.i. (ISBN 0-87605-859-4). Howell Bk.

Festival of Hope. Pontifical Council for the Laity Staff. 179p. pap. 6.00 o.p. (ISBN 0-317-46617-8). New City.

Festival Summer. Kathleen Gooding. 176p. (gr. 7 up). 1984. 15.95 o.p. (ISBN 0-571-13352-5). Faber & Faber.

Festivals & Costumes in the World. Ed. by H. Haga. 158p. (Orig.). 1985. pap. 24.95 o.p. (ISBN 4-766-10270-3, Pub. by Graphic Sha Japan). Bks Nippan.

Festivals in Classical China: New Year & Other Annual Observations During the Han Dynasty 206 B. C. - A. D. 220. Derk Bodde. (Illus.). xv, 439p. 1975. pap. 42.50x o.p. (ISBN 962-201-001-6, Pub. by Chinese U HK). Coronet Bks.

Festive Famularo Kitchen: An International Cookbook with a Continental Flavor. Joe Famularo & Louise Imperiale. LC 76-30498. 1977. 15.00 o.p. (ISBN 0-689-10750-1, Atheneum). Macmillan.

Fetal & Maternal Medicine. Ed. by E. J. Quilligan & Norman Kretchmer. LC 79-4345. 696p. 1980. 60.00 o.p. (ISBN 0-471-50737-7, JW). Krieger.

Fetal Ultrasonography: The Secret Prenatal Life. Ed. by Franco Borrutto et al. 144p. 1982. 32.00x o.p. (ISBN 0-471-10162-1, Dist. by A R Liss). Wiley.

Fete Fatale. Robert Barnard. (Nightingales Ser.). 296p. 1987. pap. 12.95x o.p. (ISBN 0-8161-4217-3, Large Print Bks.). G K Hall.

Fetes et Rites De la Confusion. Fernando Arrabal. 172p. 1974. 9.95 o.p. (ISBN 0-686-54454-4). French & Eur.

Feud. Giles A. Lutz. 208p. 1983. pap. 2.25 o.s.i. (ISBN 0-345-30255-9). Ballantine.

Feud at Mendoza. Marshall Grover. 1977. pap. 1.25 o.s.i. (ISBN 0-505-51187-8, Pub. by Tower Bks). Dorchester Pub Co.

Feudalism. John Critchley. 1977. text ed. 22.50x o.p. (ISBN 0-04-909009-7); pap. text ed. 9.95x o.p. (ISBN 0-04-909010-0). Unwin Hyman.

Feudalism to Capitalism: Peasant & Landlord in English Agrarian Development. John Martin. (Studies in Historical Sociology). 212p. 1982. text ed. 38.50x o.p. (ISBN 0-391-02766-2). Humanities.

Fever, Squalor & Vice: Sanitation & Social Policy in Victorian Sydney. A. J. Mayne. LC 82-2054. (Scholars' Library). (Illus.). 263p. 1982. text ed. 34.50x o.p. (ISBN 0-7022-1950-9). U of Queensland Pr.

Fevre Dream. George R. Martin. 384p. 1982. 14.50 o.s.i. (ISBN 0-671-45577-X, Poseidon); pap. 3.95 o.s.i. (ISBN 0-671-43185-4). PB.

Few Good Men. Tom Suddick. (Vietnam Ser.). 144p. 1978. pap. 2.95 o.p. (ISBN 0-380-01866-7, 87270-6). Avon.

Few Minutes with Andy Rooney. Andrew A. Rooney. LC 81-66015. 1981. 12.95 o.s.i. (ISBN 0-689-11194-0, Atheneum). Macmillan.

Few Particle Problems in the Nuclear Interaction. Proceedings of the International Conference, Los Angeles, 1972 et al. Ed. by Steven A. Moszkowski & Roy P. Haddock. 1973. 105.25 o.p. (ISBN 0-444-10439-9, North-Holland). Elsevier.

Few Practical Suggestions see Preliminary Announcement.

Feynman Path Integrals: Proceedings, International Colloquium, Marseilles May 1978. Ed. by W. Beiglbeeck et al. (Lecture Notes in Physics: Vol. 106). 1979. pap. 26.00 o.p. (ISBN 0-387-09532-2). Springer-Verlag.

FHA & FHA-GPM Mortgage Payment Tables, No. 721. Financial Publishing Company Staff. 208p. 1985. 7.50 o.s.i. (ISBN 0-87600-721-3). Finan Pub.

Fiat Money Inflation in France. Andrew D. White. 1945. 2.95 o.p. (ISBN 0-87004-172-X). Caxton.

Fiat Service-Repair Handbook: 131 Series, 1975-1977. Ed. by Eric Jorgensen. (Illus.). pap. 11.95 o.p. (ISBN 0-89287-197-0, A158). Clymer Pub.

Fiat: 128 & X1-9, 1971-1982--Service, Repair Handbook. Ed. by Eric Jorgensen. (Illus.). pap. 11.95 o.p. (ISBN 0-89287-282-9, A157). Clymer Pub.

Fiber Bundle Techniques in Gauge Theory: Lectures in Mathematical Physics at the University of Texas at Austin. W. Drechsler & M. E Mayer. Ed. by A. Boehm & J. D. Dollard. LC 77-25936. (Lecture Notes in Physics: Vol. 67). 1981. pap. text ed. 18.00 o.p. (ISBN 0-387-08350-2). Springer-Verlag.

Fiber Glass. Gerald L. Steele. (Illus.). (gr. 11-12). 1962. text ed. 14.64 o.p. (ISBN 0-87345-174-0). Glencoe.

Fiber Optic Markets. International Resource Development, Inc. Staff. 184p. 1983. 985.00x o.p. (ISBN 0-88694-557-7). Intl Res Dev.

Fiber Optics & Market Trends in Japan. Information Gatekeepers, Inc. Staff. 1982. 200.00 o.s.i. (ISBN 0-686-39229-9). Info Gatekeepers.

Fiber Optics & Satellites in Local Broadband & Computer Networks. 1980. 225.00 o.p. (ISBN 0-686-33027-7). Info Gatekeepers.

Fiber Optics Comes of Age: Proceedings of the SPIE Seminar, San Mateo, 1972, Vol. 013. Society of Photo-Optical Instrumentation Engineers Staff. (SPIE Seminar Proceedings). 134p. 1972. 14.00 o.p. (ISBN 0-89252-042-6). SPIE.

Fiber Optics Communications. Ed. by Henry F. Taylor. LC 83-72776. (Illus.). 320p. 1983. 55.00 o.p. (ISBN 0-89006-127-0). Artech Hse.

Fiber Optics for Communication & Sensors. Pradeep Wahi & K. C. Gupta. 1987. text ed. price not set o.p. (ISBN 0-89006-180-7). Artech Hse.

Fiber Optics in the Nuclear Environment. 25.00 o.p. (ISBN 0-686-32960-0). Info Gatekeepers.

Fiber Optics Operating Systems. 25.00 o.p. (ISBN 0-686-32963-5). Info Gatekeepers.

Fiberarts Design Book Two. Ed. by Fiberarts Magazine Staff. LC 80-67315. (Illus.). 176p. (Orig.). 1980. 24.95 o.p. (ISBN 0-937274-00-3); pap. 15.95 o.p. (ISBN 0-937274-01-1). Lark Bks.

Fiberglass-Reinforced Plastic Pressure Vessels. (Boiler & Pressure Vessel Code Ser.: Sec. X). 1977. 40.00 o.p. (ISBN 0-685-76830-9, R00100); pap. 60.00 loose-leaf o.p. (ISBN 0-685-76831-7, W00100). ASME.

Fiberoptics & Laser Handbook. Edward L. Safford, Jr. (Illus.). 364p. (Orig.). 1984. 21.95 o.p. (ISBN 0-8306-0671-8); pap. 16.95 o.s.i. (ISBN 0-8306-1671-3, 1671). TAB Bks.

Fibers in Friction Materials Symposium. 1987. 48.00 o.p. (ISBN 0-89883-461-9, P201). Soc Auto Engineers.

Fibre Bundles & Differential Geometry. J. L. Koszul. (Tata Institute of Fundamental Research, Lectures: Vol. 20). iv, 127p. 1987. pap. 12.60 o.p. (ISBN 0-387-12876-X). Springer-Verlag.

Fibre Concrete Roofing: A State of the Art Report. (Illus.). 146p. (Orig.). 1986. pap. 17.95x o.p. (ISBN 3-908001-05-6, Pub. by Intermed Tech England). Intermediate Tech.

Fibre Optics: Theory & Practice. W. B. Allan. LC 72-95066. (Optical Physics & Engineering Ser.). 248p. 1973. 49.50x o.p. (ISBN 0-306-30735-9, Plenum Pr). Plenum Pub.

Fibrinolysis: Current Fundamental & Clinical Concepts. P. J. Gaffney. Ed. by S. Balkuv-Ulutin. 1978. 73.00 o.p. (ISBN 0-12-273050-X). Acad Pr.

Ficcion De Luis Romero. Luis Gonzalez-del-Valle & Antolin Gonzalez-del-Valle. LC 76-22177. (Literary Criticism Ser.: No. 101). 1976. pap. 5.00 o.p. (ISBN 0-89295-000-5). Society Sp & Sp-Am.

Ficciones. Jorge L. Borges. Ed. & intro. by Anthony Kerrigan. 1962. pap. 6.95 o.p. (ISBN 0-394-17244-2, E368, Ever). Grove.

Ficciones: Four Stories & a Play, Vol. 7. M. De Unamuno. Tr. by Anthony Kerrigan from Span. Ed. by Martin Nozick. LC 67-22341. (Bollingen Ser.: Selected Works of Miguel De Unamuno, No. LXXXU17). 340p. 1975. 32.00 o.p. (ISBN 0-691-09930-8). Princeton U Pr.

Fichier Augustinien, 4 vols. Institut des Etudes Augustiniennes, Paris Staff. (Augustine Bibliography). 1978. Set. 355.00 o.p. (ISBN 0-8161-0947-8, Hall Library). G K Hall.

Fichier Augustinien, First Supplement. Institut des Etudes Augustiniennes, Paris Staff. 1981. lib. bdg. 125.00 o.p. (ISBN 0-8161-0365-8, Hall Library). G K Hall.

Fiction from Prison: Gathering up the Past. Dietrich Bonhoeffer. Tr. by Clifford Green from Ger. LC 80-2378. 228p. 1981. 15.95 o.p. (ISBN 0-8006-0663-9, 1-663, Fortress). Augsburg Fortress.

Fiction! Interviews with Northern California Novelists. Dan Tooker & Roger Hofheins. LC 76-28744. (Illus.). 1976. pap. 3.95 o.p. (ISBN 0-15-130651-6, Harv). HarBraceJ.

Fiction! Interviwes with Northern California Novelist. Ed. by Dan Tooker & Roger Hofheins. 200p. 1976. 8.95 o.p. (ISBN 0-15-130650-8). HarBraceJ.

Fiction One Hundred. 4th ed. James H. Pickering. 1120p. 1985. pap. text ed. write for info o.p. (ISBN 0-02-395540-6). Macmillan.

Fiction Writer's Help Book. Maxine Rock. LC 82-13502. 197p. 1982. 12.95 o.p. (ISBN 0-89879-090-5). Writers Digest.

Fiction Writer's Market, 1984-1985. 3rd ed. Ed. by Jean Fredette. 624p. 1984. 17.95 o.p. (ISBN 0-89879-134-0). Writers Digest.

Fiction Writer's Market, 1985. 5th ed. 624p. (Orig.). 1985. 17.95 o.p. (ISBN 0-89879-174-X). Writers Digest.

Fiction Writer's Market 1986. 6th ed. Ed. by Jean M. Fredette. 648p. 1986. 18.95 o.p. (ISBN 0-89879-216-9). Writers Digest.

Fiction Writer's Market 1987. 7th ed. Laurie Henry. 648p. 1987. 18.95 o.p. (ISBN 0-89879-267-3). Writers Digest.
Fiction Writer's Market '88. 8th ed. Ed. by Laurie Henry. 624p. 1988. 19.95 o.p. (ISBN 0-89879-310-6). Writers Digest.
Fictions. Joseph F. Trimmer & C. Wade Jennings. 1264p. 1985. pap. text ed. 18.00 net o.p. (ISBN 0-15-527325-6, HC). HarBraceJ.
Fictions from the Self: Poems. Michael Burkard. 1987. 15.45 o.p. (ISBN 0-393-02507-1). Norton.
Fiddleheads & Mustard Blossoms. Derevitzky. (Illus.). 1979. pap. 4.95 o.p. (ISBN 0-89272-074-3). Down East.
Fiddlin' Around. Peggy J. Schoenhofer. 1977. 4.50 o.p. (ISBN 0-682-48724-4). Exposition-Phoenix.
Fidelity of Protein Synthesis & Transfer RNA During Aging. Fay Dingley et al. LC 74-5496. 174p. 1975. text ed. 34.50x o.p. (ISBN 0-8422-7220-8). Irvington.
Fidelity's Flight. Sandra DuBay. 448p. (Orig.). 1982. pap. (ISBN 0-505-51825-2, Pub. by Tower Bks). Dorchester Pub Co.
Fidelity's Flight. Sandra DuBay. 464p. 1983. pap. 3.75 o.p. (ISBN 0-8439-2031-9, Pub. by Leisure Bks CT). Dorchester Pub Co.
Fiduciary Income Taxes. Pennsylvania Bar Institute Staff. 32p. 1983. incl. audiocassette 20.00 o.p. (ISBN 0-318-02186-2, 224). PA Bar Inst.
Fiduciary Law. 472p. 1983. 16.00 o.p. (ISBN 0-318-02404-7). ICLE Georgia.
Field Archaeology in Britain. John Coles. 267p. 1972. pap. 14.95x o.p. (ISBN 0-416-76540-8, NO. 2621). Routledge Chapman & Hall.
Field Assessments of Innovative Evaluation Methods. Ed. by Nick L. Smith. LC 81-48487. (Program Evaluation Ser.: No. 13). 1982. pap. text ed. 12.95x o.p. (ISBN 0-87589-915-3). Jossey-Bass.
Field Auditor's Manual & Guide. Stephen R. Novak. LC 79-88806. 776p. 1980. 79.50 o.p. (ISBN 0-87624-149-6, Inst Busn Plan). P-H.
Field Book of Mountaineering & Rock Climbing. Tom Lyman & Bill Riviere. LC 78-50762. (Illus.). 1978. pap. 1.95 o.p. (ISBN 0-684-15584-2, ScribT); pap. 1.95 encore ed. o.p. (ISBN 0-684-16910-X). Scribner.
Field-Coupled Surface Waves: A Comparative Study of Surface-Coupled EHD & MHD Systems. James R. Melcher. 1963. 22.50x o.p. (ISBN 0-262-13015-7). MIT Pr.
Field Crop Diseases Handbook. Robert F. Nyvall. (Illus.). 1979. 47.95 o.s.i. (ISBN 0-87055-336-4). AVI.
Field Days: Journal of an Itinerant Biologist. Roger B. Swain. LC 83-11507. 224p. 1983. 13.95 o.p. (ISBN 0-684-17989-X, ScribT). Scribner.
Field Equations for Thermoelastic Bodies with Uniform Symmetry - Acceleration Waves in Thermoelastic Bodies. CISM (International Center for Mechanical Sciences), Department of Mechanics of Solids Staff. Ed. by C. C. Wang. (CISM Pubnslications: No. 112). 41p. 1973. pap. 6.70 o.p. (ISBN 0-387-81180-X). Springer-Verlag.
Field Geology. 6th ed. Frederick H. Lahee. 1961. text ed. 61.95 o.p. (ISBN 0-07-035808-7). McGraw.
Field Guide to Astronomy Without a Telescope. W. A. Dexter. (Earth Science Curriculum Project Pamphlet Ser.). (gr. 11-12). 1971. pap. 5.76 o.p. (ISBN 0-395-02623-7). HM.
Field Guide to Australian Birds: The Passerines, Vol. 2. Peter Slater. LC 70-131130. (Illus.). 1972. 29.50 o.p. Harrowood Bks.
Field Guide to Australian Birds, Vol. 1: The Non-Passerines. Peter Slater. LC 70-131130. (Illus.). 1971. 29.50 o.p. Harrowood Bks.
Field Guide to Beaches. J. H. Hoyt. (Earth Science Curriculum Project Pamphlet Ser.). 1971. pap. 5.76 o.p. (ISBN 0-395-02621-0, 2-14607). HM.
Field Guide to Birds of Prey of Australia. Frank T. Morris. 124p. 29.95 o.p. (ISBN 0-686-62178-6). Eastview.
Field Guide to Florida Media. rev. ed. Del Marth & Martha Marth. Date not set. 15.95 o.s.i. (ISBN 0-318-21791-0). Trend Bk Div.
Field Guide to Fossils. J. R. Beerbower. (Earth Science Curriculum Project Pamphlet Ser). 1971. pap. 5.76 o.p. (ISBN 0-395-02618-0). HM.
Field Guide to Inland Fishes of Western Australia. G. R. Allen. (Illus.). 92p. 1982. pap. 15.00x o.p. (ISBN 0-7244-8409-4, Pub. by U of West Austral Pr). Intl Spec Bk.
Field Guide to Layered Rocks. T. Freeman. (Earth Science Curriculum Project Pamphlet Ser). 1971. pap. 5.76 o.p. (ISBN 0-395-02617-2). HM.
Field Guide to Mountain Flowers of New England. (Illus.). 188p. pap. cancelled o.s.i. (ISBN 0-317-33367-4); pap. 3.95 members o.s.i. (ISBN 0-317-33368-2). AMC Books.
Field Guide to Plutonic & Metamorphic Rocks. W. D. Romey. (Earth Science Curriculum Project Pamphlet Ser). 1971. pap. 5.76 o.p. (ISBN 0-395-02619-9). HM.
Field Guide to Rock Weathering. R. E. Boyer. (Earth Science Curriculum Project Pamphlet Ser). 1971. pap. 5.76 o.p. (ISBN 0-395-02615-6, 2-14601). HM.
Field Guide to Soils. H. Foth & H. S. Jacobs. (Earth Science Curriculum Project Pamphlet Ser). 1971. pap. 5.76 o.p. (ISBN 0-395-02616-4). HM.
Field Guide to Some Carbonate Rock Environments: Florida Keys & Western Bahamas, 1977. H. Gray Multer. LC 76-50173. (Illus.). 1977. pap. text ed. 19.95 o.p. (ISBN 0-8403-1646-1). Kendall-Hunt.
Field Guide to the Birds. 2nd ed. Roger T. Peterson. (Illus.). 1947. 9.95 o.p. (ISBN 0-395-08082-7). HM.
Field Guide to the Birds. Roger T. Peterson. (Illus., Orig.). 1978. pap. 5.95 o.p. (ISBN 0-395-08083-5). HM.
Field Guide to the Butterflies of the Pacific Northwest. James R. Christensen. LC 80-52967. (Illus.). 200p. (Orig.). 1981. pap. 16.95 o.p. (ISBN 0-89301-074-X). U of Idaho Pr.
Field Guide to the Geology of San Salvador. 3rd ed. R. W. Adams et al. Ed. by D. T. Gerace. 172p. 1983. pap. text ed. 12.50 o.p. (ISBN 0-935909-08-7). CCFL Bahamian.
Field Guide to the Insects of Britain & Northern Europe. Michael Chinery. 1974. 9.95 o.p. (ISBN 0-395-18229-8). HM.
Field Guide to the Larger Mammals of Africa. Jean Dorst. (Peterson Field Guide Ser). (Illus.). 1973. 8.50 o.p. (ISBN 0-395-10839-X). HM.
Field Guide to the Vascular Plants of Grand Teton National Park & Teton County, Wyoming. Richard J. Shaw. LC 75-26537. (Illus.). 300p. 1976. 8.00 o.p. (ISBN 0-87421-081-X). Utah St U Pr.
Field Guide to the Vegetation of San Salvador Island, Bahamas. Robert R. Smith. 135p. 1982. pap. text ed. 7.50 o.p. (ISBN 0-935909-03-6). CCFL Bahamian.
Field Guide to Trail Building Maintenance. 2nd ed. (Illus.). 250p. pap. cancelled o.s.i. (ISBN 0-317-33369-0) (ISBN 0-317-33370-4). AMC Books.
Field Hockey: The Coach & the Player. 2nd ed. Mildred J. Barnes & Richard G. Kentwell. 1978. text ed. 30.00 o.s.i. (ISBN 0-205-06512-0, 626512). Allyn.
Field Ionization & Field Desorption Mass Spectroscopy. H. D. Beckey. 1978. 85.00 o.p. (ISBN 0-08-020612-3). Pergamon.
Field-Marshal's Memoirs: From the Diary, Correspondence, & Reminiscences of Alfred Count Von Waldersee. Alfred H. Waldersee. (Illus.). 1978. Repr. of 1924 ed. lib. bdg. 27.50x o.p. (ISBN 0-8371-5326-3, WAFM). Greenwood.
Field Matter Interactions in Thermoelastic Solids. K. Hutter & A. A. Van De Ven. (Lecture Notes in Physics: Vol. 88). 1979. pap. 15.00 o.p. (ISBN 0-387-09105-X). Springer-Verlag.
Field of Blood. Gerald Seymour. LC 85-4821. 1985. 14.45 o.p. (ISBN 0-393-02214-5). Norton.
Field of Diamonds. Compiled by Joe Johnson. LC 73-87067. 12.95 o.p. (ISBN 0-8054-5133-1). Broadman.
Field of Linguistics. G. I. Trager. pap. 5.00 o.p. (ISBN 0-384-61330-6). Johnson Repr.
Field of Social Work. 7th ed. Arthur E. Fink. LC 77-89733. 1978. 23.95 o.p. (ISBN 0-03-022196-X, HoltC). HR&W.
Field-Proven Programs for Better Public Relations. 1980. 5.95 o.p. (ISBN 0-910170-14-2). Assn Sch Busn.
Field Sales Management: Text & Cases. H. Robert Dodge. 1973. 19.95x o.p. (ISBN 0-256-01453-1). Irwin.
Field Study in Behavior & Ecology: A Field Study in Behavior & Ecology. Dennis C. Turner. LC 74-24396. (Illus.). 160p. 1975. 20.00x o.p. (ISBN 0-8018-1680-7). Johns Hopkins.
Field Theoretical Methods in Particle Physics. Ed. by Werner Ruhl. LC 80-11773. (NATO ASI Series B, Physics: Vol. 55). 608p. 1980. 97.50x o.p. (ISBN 0-306-40444-3, Plenum Pr). Plenum Pub.
Field Theory in Elementary Particles. Ed. by Arnold Perlmutter. (Studies in the Natural Sciences: Vol. 19). 480p. 1983. 82.50x o.p. (ISBN 0-306-41345-0, Plenum Pr). Plenum Pub.
Field Theory in Social Science. Kurt Lewin. (Midway Reprint Ser.). 1976. pap. text ed. 15.00x o.s.i. (ISBN 0-226-47650-2). U of Chicago Pr.
Field Trip Guide: AAG San Antonio 1982. Ed. by Peter J. Hugill & Robin W. Doughty. (Illus.). 165p. (Orig.). 1982. pap. 4.00 o.p. (ISBN 0-89291-165-4). Assn Am Geographers.
Field Trip Guide, 1984. Association of American Geographers. 1984. 4.00 o.p. (ISBN 0-89291-180-8). Assn Am Geographers.
Field Trips: A Guide for Planning & Conducting Educational Experiences. Wayne J. Krepel & Charles R. Duvall. 56p. 1981. 6.95 o.p. (ISBN 0-8106-1683-1). NEA.
Field Trips: An Adventure in Learning. Rev. ed. Ed. by Rhoda Redleaf. (Illus.). 75p. 1984. pap. text ed. 10.50x o.p. (ISBN 0-934140-14-6). Toys N Things.
Fieldbook. LC 84-72053. (Illus.). 640p. (YA) (gr. 8 up). 1984. pap. 7.95 o.p. (ISBN 0-8395-3200-8, 3200). BSA.
Fielder's Choice: An Anthology of Baseball Fiction. Ed. by Jerome Holtzman. LC 79-24261. 395p. 1980. pap. 4.95 o.p. (ISBN 0-15-630652-2, Harv). HarBraceJ.
Fielder's Choice: An Anthology of Baseball Fiction. Jerry Holtzman. 1979. 12.95 o.p. (ISBN 0-15-130681-8). HarBraceJ.
Fielding's Bermuda & the Bahamas. Rachel J. Christmas & Walter Christmas. (Illus.). 224p. (Orig.). 1984. pap. 7.95 o.p. (ISBN 0-688-02433-5, Pub. by Fielding). Morrow.
Fielding's Bermuda & the Bahamas, 1985. Rachel J. Christmas & Walter Christmas. (Illus.). 256p. 1984. 7.95 o.p. (ISBN 0-688-03965-0). Fielding Travel Bks.
Fielding's Bermuda & the Bahamas, 1986. rev. ed. Rachel J. Christmas & Walter Christmas. (Illus.). 256p. (Orig.). 1985. pap. 7.95 o.p. (ISBN 0-688-04463-8). Fielding Travel Bks.
Fielding's Bermuda & the Bahamas, 1987. Rachel J. Christmas & Walter Christmas. (Illus.). 272p. 1986. pap. 7.95 o.p. (ISBN 0-688-04464-6). Fielding Travel Bks.
Fielding's Bermuda & the Bahamas, 1988. rev. ed. Rachel J. Christmas & Walter Christmas. (Illus.). 277p. 1987. pap. 7.95 o.p. (ISBN 0-688-07131-7). Fielding Travel Bks.
Fielding's Caribbean 1984. 6th, rev. ed. Margaret Zellers. LC 79-64115. (Illus.). 768p. (Orig.). 1984. pap. 12.95 FPT o.p. (ISBN 0-688-02445-9, Pub. by Fielding). Morrow.
Fielding's Caribbean, 1985. Margaret Zellers. (Illus.). 784p. 1984. 12.95 o.p. (ISBN 0-688-03961-8). Fielding Travel Bks.
Fielding's Caribbean, 1986. rev. ed. Margaret Zellers. (Illus.). 784p. (Orig.). 1985. pap. 12.95 o.p. (ISBN 0-688-05117-0). Fielding Travel Bks.
Fielding's Caribbean, 1987. Margaret Zellers. (Illus.). 816p. 1987. pap. 12.95 o.p. (ISBN 0-688-06415-9). Fielding Travel Bks.
Fielding's Caribbean, 1988. rev. ed. Margaret Zellers. (Illus.). 816p. 1987. pap. 12.95 o.p. (ISBN 0-688-07134-1). Fielding Travel Bks.
Fielding's Discover Europe: Off the Beaten Path, 1986. rev. ed. Margaret Zellers. Orig. Title: Fielding's Sightseeing Guide to Europe. 496p. (Orig.). 1985. pap. 12.95 o.p. (ISBN 0-688-02316-9). Fielding Travel Bks.
Fielding's Discover Europe off the Beaten Path 1987. Margaret Zellers. (Illus.). 516p. 1986. pap. 12.95 o.p. (ISBN 0-688-06500-7). Fielding Travel Bks.
Fielding's Economy Caribbean 1984. Margaret Zellers. (Illus.). 256p. (Orig.). 1984. pap. 8.95 o.p. (ISBN 0-688-02512-9, Pub. by Fielding). Morrow.
Fielding's Economy Caribbean, 1985. Margaret Zellers. (Illus.). 272p. 1984. 8.95 o.p. (ISBN 0-688-03964-2). Fielding Travel Bks.
Fielding's Economy Caribbean, 1986. rev. ed. Margaret Zellers. (Illus.). 272p. (Orig.). 1985. pap. 8.95 o.p. (ISBN 0-688-05263-0). Fielding Travel Bks.
Fielding's Economy Caribbean, 1987. Margaret Zellers. (Illus.). 272p. 1987. pap. 8.95 o.p. (ISBN 0-688-06416-7). Fielding Travel Bks.
Fielding's Economy Europe 1984. 18th, rev. ed. Joseph Raff. (Illus.). 896p. (Orig.). 1984. pap. 8.95 FPT o.p. (ISBN 0-688-02438-6, Pub. by Fielding). Morrow.
Fielding's Economy Europe, 1985. Joseph Raff & Judith Raff. (Illus.). 576p. 1984. pap. 9.95 o.p. (ISBN 0-688-03953-7). Fielding Travel Bks.
Fielding's Economy Europe, 1986. rev. ed. Joseph Raff & Judith Raff. Orig. Title: Fielding's Low-Cost Europe. (Illus.). 576p. (Orig.). 1985. pap. 9.95 o.p. (ISBN 0-688-04677-0). Fielding Travel Bks.
Fielding's Economy Europe, 1987. Joseph Raff & Judith Raff. (Illus.). 592p. 1986. pap. 9.95 o.p. (ISBN 0-688-04678-9). Fielding Travel Bks.
Fielding's Economy Europe 1988. rev. ed. Joseph Raff & Judith Raff. 592p. pap. 9.95 o.p. (ISBN 0-688-04679-7). Fielding Travel Bks.
Fielding's Europe 1984. 37th, rev. ed. Joseph Raff. 884p. (Orig.). 1984. pap. 12.95 FPT o.p. (ISBN 0-688-02266-9, Pub. by Fielding). Morrow.
Fielding's Europe, 1985. Joseph Raff. 880p. 1984. 12.95 o.p. (ISBN 0-688-03951-0). Fielding Travel Bks.
Fielding's Europe, 1986. rev. ed. Joseph Raff. 848p. (Orig.). 1985. pap. 12.95 o.p. (ISBN 0-688-04667-3). Fielding Travel Bks.
Fielding's Europe, 1987: Hotel Charts. Joseph Raff. 848p. 1986. pap. 12.95 o.p. (ISBN 0-688-04668-1). Fielding Travel Bks.
Fielding's Europe, 1988. rev. ed. Joseph Raff. 848p. 1987. pap. 12.95 o.p. (ISBN 0-688-04669-X). Fielding Travel Bks.
Fielding's Folly. Frances P. Keyes. 1976. pap. 1.50 o.p. (ISBN 0-380-00241-8, 22533). Avon.
Fielding's Low-Cost Europe see Fielding's Economy Europe, 1986.
Fielding's Mexico 1984. Lynn V. Foster & Lawrence Foster. (Illus.). 688p. (Orig.). 1984. pap. 12.95 FPT o.p. (ISBN 0-688-02439-4). Morrow.
Fielding's Mexico, 1985. Lynn V. Foster & Lawrence Foster. (Illus.). 704p. 1984. 12.95 o.p. (ISBN 0-688-03959-6). Fielding Travel Bks.
Fielding's Mexico, 1986. rev. ed. Lynn V. Foster & Lawrence Foster. (Illus.). 704p. (Orig.). 1985. pap. 12.95 o.p. (ISBN 0-688-04758-0). Fielding Travel Bks.
Fielding's Mexico, 1987: Maps, Hotels & Photos. Lynn V. Foster & Lawrence Foster. (Illus.). 720p. 1986. pap. 12.95 o.p. (ISBN 0-688-06594-5). Fielding Travel Bks.
Fielding's People's Republic of China, 1987. 3rd, rev. ed. Ruth L. Malloy & Priscilla L. Hsu. Orig. Title: Morrow Travel Guide to the People's Republic of China. (Illus.). 400p. 1986. pap. 13.95 o.p. (ISBN 0-688-05879-5). Fielding Travel Bks.
Fielding's Selective Shopping Guide to Europe 1984. 28th, rev. ed. Joseph Raff & Judith Raff. 304p. (Orig.). 1984. pap. 5.95 o.p. (ISBN 0-688-02437-8, Pub. by Fielding). Morrow.
Fielding's Selective Shopping Guide to Europe, 1985. Joseph Raff & Judith Raff. 320p. 1984. pap. 5.95 o.p. (ISBN 0-688-03956-1). Fielding Travel Bks.
Fielding's Selective Shopping Guide to Europe, 1986. rev. ed. Joseph Raff & Judith Raff. 320p. (Orig.). 1985. pap. 5.95 o.p. (ISBN 0-688-04672-X). Fielding Travel Bks.
Fielding's Selective Shopping Guide to Europe, 1987. Joseph Raff & Judith Raff. 352p. 1986. pap. 6.95 o.p. (ISBN 0-688-04673-8). Fielding Travel Bks.
Fielding's Sightseeing Guide to Europe see Fielding's Discover Europe: Off the Beaten Path, 1986.
Fielding's Tom Jones. A. J. Hassall. (Sydney Studies in Literature: No. 8). 1979. 21.00x o.p. (ISBN 0-424-00054-7, Pub. by Sydney U Pr). Intl Spec Bk.
Fielding's Worldwide Cruises. 3rd, rev. ed. Antoinette DeLand. (Illus.). 400p. 1986. pap. 12.95 o.p. (ISBN 0-688-06391-8). Fielding Travel Bks.
Fielding's Worldwide Guide to Cruises. rev. ed. Antoinette DeLand. LC 82-62320. (Illus.). 416p. 1982. pap. 12.95 o.p. (ISBN 0-688-01648-0). Morrow.
Fields. William Kurelek. (Illus.). 28p. (ps up). 1976. pap. 5.95 o.p. (ISBN 0-88776-070-8). Tundra Bks.
Fields, Factories & Workshops or Industry Combined with Agriculture & Brain Work with Manual Work. Petr A. Kropotkin. LC 68-28589. (Illus.). 1968. Repr. of 1901 ed. lib. bdg. 35.00x o.p. (ISBN 0-8371-0135-2, KRBM). Greenwood.
Fields of Change among the Iteso of Kenya. Ivan Karp. (International Library of Anthropology). 1978. 22.95x o.p. (ISBN 0-7100-8863-9). Routledge Chapman & Hall.
Fields of Gold. Compiled by Priscilla Shepard. LC 75-1641. 164p. 1975. boxed 16.95 o.p. (ISBN 0-8378-1862-1). Gibson.
Fields, Particles & Currents. A. H. Voelkel. LC 77-23001. (Lecture Notes in Physics: Vol. 66). 1977. pap. text ed. 22.00 o.p. (ISBN 0-387-08347-2). Springer-Verlag.
Fieldwork. Maria Danielle. 224p. 1981. pap. 2.25 o.p. (ISBN 0-380-78162-X, 78162-X). Avon.
Fiend. Margaret Millar. 1974. pap. 1.25 o.p. (ISBN 0-380-01180-8, 17962). Avon.
Fierce Eden. Jennifer Blake. (General Ser.). 602p. 1986. lib. bdg. 19.95 o.p. (ISBN 0-8161-4039-1, Large Print Bks). G K Hall.
Fiery Furnace. Lawrence Williams. 1960. 3.95 o.p. S&S.
Fiesta. Sesyle Joslin & John Alcorn. LC 67-18872. (Illus., Span.). (gr. k-3). 1967. 7.50 o.p. (ISBN 0-15-243575-1, HJ). HarBraceJ.
Fifteen Contemporary New Zealand Poets. Ed. by Alistair Paterson. LC 82-47994. 224p. 1982. 19.50 o.s.i. (ISBN 0-394-52881-6, GP858). Grove.
Fifteen Contemporary New Zealand Poets. Ed. by Alistair Paterson. LC 82-47994. 224p. 1982. pap. 9.95 o.s.i. (ISBN 0-394-17999-4, E816, Ever). Grove.
Fifteen-Minute Meals: Fresh, Fantastic & Nutritious Recipes. Emalee Chapman. LC 81-9567. (Illus.). 168p. (Orig.). 1981. pap. 7.95 o.p. (ISBN 0-89286-192-4, One Hund One Prods). Ortho.

Fifteen Poems from a Classical Tamil Anthology. Tr. by A. K. Ramanujan. (Translated from Tamil). 8.00 o.p. (ISBN 0-89253-774-4). Ind-US Inc.

Fifteen Three-Part Inventions for Piano. J. S. Bach. Ed. by Carl Czerny. (Carl Fischer Music Library: No. 255). (Illus.). 63p. 1912. pap. 4.95 o.p. (ISBN 0-8258-0099-4). Fischer Inc NY.

Fifteenth Annual Institue on Securities Regulation. 565p. 1984. 15.00 o.p. (B2-1294). PLI.

Fifteenth Century: The Prospect of Europe. Margaret Aston. (History of European Civilization Library). (Illus., Orig.). 1968. pap. text ed. 6.95 o.p. (ISBN 0-15-527355-8, HC). HarBraceJ.

Fifth Annual Microcomputers in Education Conference. Donna Craighead. LC 85-3749. (Computers in Education Ser.). 339p. 1985. 35.00 o.p. (ISBN 0-88175-097-2, Computer Sci Pr). W H Freeman.

Fifth Army at War. George Forty. (Illus.). 144p. 1980. encore ed 6.95 o.p. (ISBN 0-684-17539-8, ScribT). Scribner.

Fifth Avenue: A Very Special History. Kate Simon. LC 79-11996. (Illus.). 1979. 12.95 o.p. (ISBN 0-15-130702-4); pap. 4.95 o.p. (ISBN 0-15-630712-X). HarBraceJ.

Fifth Breeders' Cup: Annual Supplement to Blood-Horse. Blood-Horse Staff. (Illus.). 110p. 1988. pap. 6.00 o.p. (ISBN 0-939049-22-8). Blood-Horse.

Fifth Direction. Theodore Enslin. (Orig.). 1980. 35.00 o.p. (ISBN 0-915316-81-1); pap. 10.00 o.p. (ISBN 0-915316-80-3). Pentagram.

Fifth European Electro-Optics Conference: Proceedings of the SPIE Seminar, Utrecht, 1980. (SPIE Seminar Proceedings: Vol. 236). 512p. 40.00 o.p. (ISBN 0-89252-265-8); members 34.00 o.p. (ISBN 0-317-34640-7). SPIE.

Fifth Horseman of the Apocalypse. Jesse M. Hendley. LC 85-19795. 236p. (Orig.). 1985. pap. 10.95 o.p. (ISBN 0-8254-2849-1). Kregel.

Fifth Infantry Division in the ETO. (Divisional Ser.: No. 18). (Illus.). 254p. 1981. Repr. of 1945 ed. 27.50 o.p. (ISBN 0-89839-042-7). Battery Pr.

Fifth LACUS Forum: Proceedings. Linguistic Association of Canada & the U. S. Staff. Ed. by Wolfgang Woelck & Paul L. Garvin. 1978. pap. text ed. 12.95 o.s.i. (ISBN 0-917496-12-4). Hornbeam Pr.

Fifth National Ground Water Quality Symposium. 1980. 31.25 o.p. (ISBN 0-318-23008-9). Natl Water Well.

Fifth National Symposium & Exposition on Aquifer Restoration: Proceedings. 1985. 43.75 o.p. (ISBN 0-318-23016-X). Natl Water Well.

Fifth Old House Catalogue. Compiled by Lawrence Grow. LC 86-23659. (Illus.). 256p. (Orig.). 1986. 20.00 o.p. (ISBN 1-55562-001-9); pap. 12.95 o.p. (ISBN 1-55562-000-0). Main Street.

Fifth Pillar: The Story of a Pilgrimage to Mecca & Medina. Saida M. Khalifa. 1977. 7.50 o.p. (ISBN 0-682-48772-4). Exposition-Phoenix.

Fifth Quarter. E. Gabrilovich. 288p. 1984. pap. 3.95 o.p. (ISBN 0-8285-2622-2, Pub. by Progress Pubs USSR). Imported Pubns.

Fifth Republic. Ferdinand A. Hermens. 1960. pap. 3.95x o.p. (ISBN 0-268-00098-0). U of Notre Dame Pr.

Fifth Sally. Daniel Keyes. 1980. 10.95 o.p. (ISBN 0-395-29449-5). HM.

Fifth Season. Michael Sheridan. LC 78-7507. 52p. 1978. 8.50 o.p. (ISBN 0-8214-0405-9); pap. 4.95 o.p. (ISBN 0-8214-0407-5). Ohio U Pr.

Fifth Social Service: A Critical Analysis of the Seebohn Proposal. Ed. by Peter Townsend. 160p. 1970. (ISBN 0-7163-4011-9); (ISBN 0-7163-4010-0). Transaction Pubs.

Fifth Sun: Aztec Gods, Aztec World. Burr C. Brundage. (Texas Pan American Ser.). (Illus.). 283p. 1979. pap. 17.95 o.p. (ISBN 0-292-72427-6). U of Tex Pr.

Fifties: From Notebooks & Diaries of the Period. Edmund Wilson. Ed. & intro. by Leon Edel. 1987. pap. 12.95 o.p. (ISBN 0-374-52066-6). FS&G.

Fifties in Vogue. Nicholas Drake. LC 86-27769. 1987. 24.95 o.p. (ISBN 0-8050-0324-X). H Holt & Co.

Fifties: Photographs of America. Magnum Photos, Inc. Staff. LC 84-18948. (Illus.). 1985. 24.50 o.s.i. (ISBN 0-394-54064-6); pap. 14.95 o.s.i. (ISBN 0-394-72720-7). Pantheon.

Fifties Style: Then & Now. Richard Horn. LC 87-43244. (Illus.). 176p. 1988. 14.98 o.p. (ISBN 0-89471-624-7, Pub. by Courage Bks.). Running Pr.

Fifty Best American Short Stories 1915-1965. Ed. by Martha Foley & David Burnett. 1965. 15.00 o.p. (ISBN 0-395-07687-0). HM.

Fifty Best of Baltimore & Ohio Railroad, Bk. 1. Howard N. Barr. (Illus.). 1977. 12.00 o.p. (ISBN 0-934118-16-7). Barnard Roberts.

Fifty Best of Baltimore & Ohio Railroad, Bk. 5. Bob Lorenz. (Illus.). 1979. 12.00 o.p. (ISBN 0-934118-04-3). Barnard Roberts.

Fifty Biking Holidays. Illus. by Joan Jackson. pap. text ed. 4.95 o.p. (ISBN 0-913548-45-6). Western Tanager.

Fifty Birds of Town & City. (Illus.). 54p. 1978. pap. 7.50 o.p. (ISBN 0-318-21951-4, S/N 024-010-00382-1). USGPO.

Fifty Counted Thread Embroidery Stitches. Coats, J. & P. Ltd. Staff. LC 78-50729. (Illus.). 1978. pap. 2.25 o.s.i. (ISBN 0-684-15643-1, SL797, ScribT). Scribner.

Fifty Craft Ideas with Patterns. Loretta Reese. LC 80-53363. (Illus.). 64p. (Orig.). pap. 4.95 o.p. (ISBN 0-87239-427-1, 2144). Standard Pub.

Fifty Daily Telegraph Brain-Twisters. D. S. Barnard. 128p. (Orig.). 1986. pap. 3.95 o.p. (ISBN 0-7137-1612-6, Pub. by Javelin England). Sterling.

Fifty-Eight Home Shelving & Storage Projects. Percy W. Blandford. (Illus.). 288p. (Orig.). 1985. text ed. 25.95 o.p. (ISBN 0-8306-0844-3, 1844); pap. 14.60 o.p. (ISBN 0-8306-1844-9). TAB Bks.

Fifty-Eight Lonely Men: Southern Federal Judges & School Desegregation. Jack W. Peltason. LC 61-12350. 1961. 4.95 o.p. (ISBN 0-15-130707-5). HarBraceJ.

Fifty Faces of Football: The American Game & What has Made it Great. Harold Rosenthal. LC 81-66009. (Illus.). 320p. 1981. 12.95 o.p. (ISBN 0-689-11218-1, Atheneum). Macmillan.

Fifty Favorite Bible Stories. Ed. by Ernest H. Hayes. 1963. pap. text ed. 4.55 o.s.i. (ISBN 0-08-006196-6, Religious Educ Pr). Pergamon.

Fifty Feet in Paradise: The Booming of Florida. David Nolan. LC 84-529. (Illus.). 352p. 1984. 15.95 o.p. (ISBN 0-15-130748-2). HarbraceJ.

Fifty-Fifth Avenuers. Melvene De Lord. 1979. 7.00 o.p. (ISBN 0-682-49364-3). Exposition-Phoenix.

Fifty-Five: A Decade of Experience. National Research Council. 262p. 1984. pap. text ed. 14.00x o.p. (ISBN 0-309-03664-X). Natl Acad Pr.

Fifty-Five Advanced Computer Programs in BASIC. W. Scott Watson. (Illus.). 252p. 16.95 o.p. (ISBN 0-8306-0012-4); pap. 9.95 o.p. (ISBN 0-8306-1295-5, 1295). TAB Bks.

Fifty-Five Hundred Questions & Answers on the Holy Bible. 192p. 1974. pap. 4.95 o.p. (ISBN 0-310-24361-0, 9666P). Zondervan.

Fifty-Five Miles per Hour. Philip J. Pines. (Illus.). 240p. 1982. 10.50 o.p. (ISBN 0-682-49793-2). Exposition-Phoenix.

Fifty-Five Years of Recorded Country Western Music. Jerry Osborne. 1976. pap. 9.95 o.p. (ISBN 0-89019-060-7). Norwalk Pr.

Fifty-Four SuperCalc Models: Finance, Statistics, Mathematics. Robert H. Flast. 288p. (Orig.). 1983. pap. text ed. 15.95 o.p. (ISBN 0-07-881118-X). Osborne-McGraw.

Fifty-Four VisiCalc Models. 1983. pap. text ed. 15.95 o.p. (ISBN 0-07-881100-7). McGraw.

Fifty Front Pages of the Rarest & Most Valuable Books on Wall Street & the Stock Market. Ed. by Howard K. May. (Illus.). 91p. 1980. plastic spiral binding 27.50 o.p. (ISBN 0-89266-240-9). Am Classical Coll.

Fifty Hikes in Connecticut: A Guide to Short Walks & Day Hikes Around the Nutmeg State. Gerry Hardy & Sue Hardy. LC 77-94006. (Fifty Hikes Ser.). (Illus.). 152p. 1982. pap. 8.95 o.p. (ISBN 0-942440-05-6). Backcountry Pubns.

Fifty Hikes in Eastern Pennsylvania: Day Hikes & Backpacks from the Susquehanna to the Poconos. Carolyn Hoffman. LC 82-4004. (Fifty Hikes Ser.). (Illus.). 224p. (Orig.). 1982. pap. 9.95 o.p. (ISBN 0-942440-02-1). Backcountry Pubns.

Fifty Hikes in the Adirondacks: Short Walks, Day Trips & Backpacks Throughout the Park. Barbara McMartin. LC 79-92569. (Fifty Hikes Ser.). (Illus.). 252p. 1982. pap. 9.95 o.p. (ISBN 0-942440-00-5). Backcountry Pubns.

Fifty Hikes in Vermont: Walks, Day Hikes & Backpacking Trips in the Green Mountain State. 2nd ed. Ruth Sadlier & Paul Sadlier. LC 79-92572. (Fifty Hikes Ser.). (Illus.). 184p. 1983. pap. 7.95 o.p. (ISBN 0-942440-08-0). Backcountry Pubns.

Fifty Hours. Eugene Richards & Dorothea Lynch. LC 83-49420. 48p. 1984. pap. 12.95 o.p. (ISBN 0-394-62023-2, E932, Ever). Grove.

Fifty Key Words: Comparative Religion. Eric J. Sharpe. LC 70-161840. (Fifty Key Words Ser). (Orig.). 1971. pap. 2.45 o.p. (ISBN 0-8042-3897-9, John Knox). Westminster John Knox.

Fifty Key Words: The Bible. Julian Charley. LC 76-143419. (Fifty Key Words Ser). (Orig.). 1971. pap. 2.45 o.p. (ISBN 0-8042-3890-1, John Knox). Westminster John Knox.

Fifty Key Words: Theology. Frederick G. Healey. (Fifty Key Words Ser.). (Orig.). 1967. pap. 2.45 o.p. (ISBN 0-8042-3895-2, John Knox). Westminster John Knox.

Fifty-Minute Supervisor. 1988. 6.95 o.p. (114). Am Bartenders.

Fifty Pascal Programs. Bruce H. Hunter. LC 84-50351. 338p. 1984. pap. 18.95 o.p. (ISBN 0-89588-110-1). SYBEX.

Fifty Selected Piano Studies. J. B. Cramer. Ed. by Hans Von Bulow. (Carl Fischer Music Library: No. 52). 53p. 1908. pap. 1.00 o.p. (ISBN 0-8258-0133-8). Fischer Inc NY.

Fifty Simple Ready-To-Run VIC-20 Programs. Barbara Fulgham. (Illus.). 176p. (Orig.). 1984. 12.95 o.p. (ISBN 0-8306-0754-4); pap. 6.70 o.p. (ISBN 0-8306-1754-X, 1754). TAB Bks.

Fifty Strategies for Experiential Learning: Book One. Ed. by Louis Thayer. LC 75-27735. Orig. Title: Affective Education: Strategies for Experiential Learning. 230p. 1976. pap. 7.95 o.p. (ISBN 0-88390-108-0). Univ Assocs.

Fifty Strategies for Experiential Learning: Book Two. Ed. by Louis Thayer. LC 80-54160. 336p. 1981. pap. 15.95 o.p. (ISBN 0-88390-164-1). Univ Assocs.

Fifty Texas Artists: A Critical Selection of Painters & Sculptors Working in Texas. Annette Carlozzi. LC 86-14704. (Illus.). 128p. (Orig.). 1986. 35.00 o.p. (ISBN 0-87701-399-3); pap. 18.95 o.p. (ISBN 0-87701-372-1). Chronicle Bks.

Fifty Thousand Words Divided & Spelled. Harry Sharp. LC 81-85507. 434p. 1978. pap. 2.95 o.p. (ISBN 0-317-65282-6). New Century.

Fifty-Three Space-Saving Built-In Furniture Projects. Percy W. Blandford. (Illus.). 400p. (Orig.). 1983. 21.95 o.p. (ISBN 0-8306-0504-5, 1504); pap. 16.95 o.p. (ISBN 0-8306-1504-0). TAB Bks.

Fifty Villas of Our Time. R. Aloi. (Illus.). 1970. 40.00 o.p. E J Brill USA.

Fifty Years a Medium. Estelle Roberts. (Illus.). 224p. 1972. pap. 0.95 o.p. (ISBN 0-380-01182-4, 07286). Avon.

Fifty Years in the Law Business. Advocatus Diaboli. (ISBN 0-8022-0391-4). Philos Lib.

Fifty Years Later: The New Deal Evaluated. Ed. by Harvard Sitkoff. 272p. 1985. 29.95 o.p. (ISBN 0-87722-371-8). Temple U Pr.

Fifty Years of Citrus: The Florida Citrus Exchange, 1909-1959. James T. Hopkins. LC 60-10227. (Illus.). 1960. 6.00 o.p. (ISBN 0-8130-0114-5). U Presses Fla.

Fifty Years of Collecting: An Anniversary Selection. Painting by Modern Masters. Thomas M. Messer. (Fifty Years of Collecting: An Anniversary Selection: Vol. I). (Illus.). 151p. (Orig.). 1987. pap. 20.00 o.p. (ISBN 0-89207-064-1). S R Guggenheim.

Fifty Years of Eternal Vigilance. Carolyn Thorman. 192p. 1988. 14.95 o.p. (ISBN 0-934601-62-3). Peachtree Pubs.

Fifty Years of Medicine. Lord Horder. 72p. 1954. (ISBN 0-8022-0743-X). Philos Lib.

Fifty Years of Outdoor Resident Education. William M. Hammerman. 129p. 1980. pap. 15.00 o.p. (ISBN 0-87603-047-9). Am Camping.

Fifty Years of Political & Economic Planning: Looking Forward 1931-1981. Ed. by John Pinder. xii, 228p. 1981. text ed. 24.50x o.p. (ISBN 0-435-83690-0). Gower Pub Co.

Fifty Years of the History of the Republic in South Africa, 1795-1845, 2 vols. Johan C. Voight. LC 76-77214. (Illus.). 1970. Repr. of 1899 ed. Set. lib. bdg. 32.00x o.p. (ISBN 0-8371-9955-7, VOR&, Pub. by Negro U Pr); Vol. 1. lib. bdg. 15.00 o.p. (ISBN 0-8371-1306-7, VOS&, Pub. by Negro U Pr); Vol. 2. lib. bdg. 15.00 o.p. (ISBN 0-8371-1307-5, VOT&, Pub. by Negro U Pr). Greenwood.

Fifty Years of Vaudeville. Ernest Short. LC 78-16385. (Illus.). 1978. Repr. of 1946 ed. lib. bdg. 27.75 o.p. (ISBN 0-313-20576-0, SHFY). Greenwood.

Fifty Years of World Revolution, An International Symposium. 2nd ed. Ernest Mandel et al. Tr. by Gerald Pual. LC 68-58443. 1970. Repr. of 1968 ed. 27.00 o.p. (ISBN 0-87348-016-3). Path Pr NY.

Fifty Years of Yoknapatawpha: Faulkner & Yoknapatawpha, 1979. Ed. by Doreen Fowler & Ann J. Abadie. LC 80-12255. (Faulkner & Yoknapatawpha Ser.). 1980. 15.95x o.p. (ISBN 0-87805-121-X); pap. 7.95 o.p. (ISBN 0-87805-122-8). U Pr of Miss.

Fifty Years with Father. David Unwin. 150p. 1982. 18.00 o.p. (ISBN 0-913720-39-9). Beil.

Fifty Years with Music. Sigmund Spaeth. LC 77-13488. 1977. Repr. of 1959 ed. lib. bdg. 35.00x o.p. (ISBN 0-8371-9862-3, SPFY). Greenwood.

Fight Against Slavery. Terence Brady & Evan Jones. (Illus.). 1977. 7.95 o.p. (ISBN 0-393-05659-7). Norton.

Fight Against Time. Steven Clark. LC 78-20353. (Illus.). 1979. 8.95 o.p. (ISBN 0-689-10953-9, Atheneum). Macmillan.

Fight City Hall. Anthony Constantino. (Illus.). 44p. 1981. 5.00 o.p. (ISBN 0-682-49785-1). Exposition-Phoenix.

Fight City Hall & Win. Dolores M. Reed. 1986. 6.75 o.p. (ISBN 0-8062-2777-X). Carlton.

Fight for Shelton Bar. Ed. by Peter Cheeseman. 1981. pap. 6.95 o.p. (ISBN 0-413-38040-8, NO. 6469). Heinemann Ed.

Fight for the Panama Route. Dwight C. Miner. 1966. lib. bdg. 31.50x o.p. (ISBN 0-374-95776-2, Octagon). Hippocrene Bks.

Fight for Union. Margaret L. Coit. (Illus.). (gr. 7 up). 1961. 7.95 o.p. (ISBN 0-395-06715-4). HM.

Fight in the Mountains. Christian Bernhardsen. Tr. by Franey Sinding. LC 68-28800. (gr. 7 up). 1968. 4.50 o.p. (ISBN 0-15-227523-1, HJ). HarBraceJ.

Fight or Die. Todhunter Ballard. Orig. Title: Westward the Monitors Roar. 1977. pap. 1.50 o.s.i. (ISBN 0-505-51184-3, Pub. by Tower Bks). Dorchester Pub Co.

Fight That Ticket in British Columbia. 6th ed. Steve Harrison. 94p. 1984. 5.95 o.p. (ISBN 0-88908-166-2). ISC Pr.

Fight That Ticket in Oregon. Michael T. Bailey. 87p. 1977. 1.95 o.p. (ISBN 0-88908-800-4). ISC Pr.

Fighter Pilot: Aerial Combat Aces from Nineteen-Fourteen to the Present Day. Rev. ed. Stanley Ulanoff. (Illus.). 336p. 1986. 24.95 o.p. (ISBN 0-13-314816-5). P-H.

Fighter Pilots. Robert Jackson. 1977. pap. 1.50 o.p. (ISBN 0-505-51192-4, Pub. by Tower Bks). Dorchester Pub Co.

Fighter Pilots of World War II. Robert Jackson. (Inflation Fighters Ser.). 176p. 1982. pap. 1.50 o.p. (ISBN 0-8439-1138-7, Pub. by Leisure Bks CT). Dorchester Pub Co.

Fighting Arts. Michael Croucher & Howard Reid. (Illus.). 1983. 19.45 o.s.i. (ISBN 0-671-47158-9); pap. 12.95 o.s.i. (ISBN 0-671-47273-9). S&S.

Fighting Back. William Tavoulereas & Ben Stein. LC 85-22284. 253p. 1986. 15.45 o.p. (ISBN 0-671-46966-5). S&S.

Fighting Chance. Mignon G. Eberhart. LC 85-25596. 256p. 1986. 14.95 o.p. (ISBN 0-394-55082-X). Random.

Fighting Chance: The Moral Use of Nuclear Weapons. Joseph P. Martino. 276p. (Orig.). 1987. pap. 15.95 o.p. (ISBN 0-89870-181-3). Ignatius Pr.

Fighting Computer Crime. Donn B. Parker. (Illus.). 352p. 1983. 19.95 o.s.i. (ISBN 0-684-17796-X, ScribT). Scribner.

Fighting for Our Lives. Kit Mouat. (Illus.). 160p. (Orig.). 1981. pap. 4.95 o.p. (ISBN 0-946097-14-3, Pub. by GMP England). Alyson Pubns.

Fighting for Peace: The War Resistance Movement. William J. Chamberlain. (Library of War & Peace; Non-Resis. & Non-Vio.). 1972. lib. bdg. 46.00 o.p. (ISBN 0-8240-0373-X). Garland Pub.

Fighting for Time. National Historical Society Staff. Ed. by William C. Davis & Bell I. Wiley. LC 82-45363. (Image of War (1861-1865) Ser.: Vol. 4). (Illus.). 464p. 1983. 19.95 o.p. (ISBN 0-385-18280-5). Doubleday.

Fighting Forces of Rhodesia, No. 4. 55p. 1988. pap. 6.00 o.p. (ISBN 0-929757-11-4). WW Milit Exch.

Fighting Gear of World War One: Equipment & Weapons of the American Doughboy. C. B. Colby. (Illus.). (gr. 4-7). 1961. PLB 6.99 o.p. (ISBN 0-698-30077-7, Coward). Putnam Pub Group.

Fighting Gear of World War Two: Equipment & Weapons of the American G. I. C. B. Colby. (Illus.). (gr. 4-7). 1961. PLB 6.99 o.p. (ISBN 0-698-30078-5, Coward). Putnam Pub Group.

Fighting Gundam. (Roman Album Ser.: No. 42). (Illus.). 1984. 8.95 o.p. (ISBN 0-318-02647-3). Bks Nippan.

Fighting Sail. A. B. Whipple & Time-Life Books Editors. (Seafarers Ser.). (Illus.). 1978. 13.95 o.p. (ISBN 0-8094-2654-4). Time-Life.

Fighting Sexual Harassment: An Advocacy Handbook. rev. ed. Alliance Against Sexual Coersion Staff. 96p. (Orig.). 1981. pap. 3.95 o.p. (ISBN 0-932870-14-7). Alyson Pubns.

Fighting Ships of the Rising Sun: The Drama of the Imperial Japanese Navy, 1895-1945. Stephen Howarth. LC 83-45076. (Illus.). 448p. 1983. 19.95 o.p. (ISBN 0-689-11402-8, Atheneum). Macmillan.

Fighting to Win: Business Political Power. Edward A. Grefe. 280p. 1981. 35.00 o.p. (ISBN 0-15-100023-9, H39956, Pub. by Law & Business). HarBraceJ.

Fighting with Gandhi: Step-by-Step Strategy for Resolving Everyday Conflicts. Mark Juergensmeyer. LC 83-48419. 160p. 1984. 12.45i o.p. (ISBN 0-06-250438-X). HarpR.

Fighting Words: Imperial Censorship & the Russian Press, 1804-1906. Charles A. Ruud. 352p. 1982. 35.00x o.p. (ISBN 0-8020-5565-6). U of Toronto Pr.

Figs & Fury. 2nd ed. Phyllis Tickle. 82p. 1976. 4.25 o.p. (ISBN 0-918518-04-0, St Luke TN). Peachtree Pubs.

Figurative Language of the Tragedies of Shakespeare's Chief Sixteen-Century Contemporaries: An Index. Louis C. Stagg. LC 82-49173. (Reference Library of the Humanities). 750p. 1984. lib. bdg. 104.00 o.p. (ISBN 0-8240-9176-0). Garland Pub.

Figure Drawing: The Structure, Anatomy, & Expressive Design of Human Form. Nathan Goldstein. (Illus.). 330p. 1981. pap. text ed. 29.67 o.p. (ISBN 0-13-314435-6). P-H.

Figure-Eight. Reese Williams. (Illus.). 128p. 1981. 12.95 o.p. (ISBN 0-934378-19-3); pap. 5.95 o.p. (ISBN 0-934378-20-7). Tanam Pr.

Figure in Hiding. Franklin W. Dixon. (Hardy Boys Ser: Vol. 16). (gr. 5-9). 1937. 4.50 o.p. (ISBN 0-448-08916-5, G&D); PLB 3.29 o.p. (ISBN 0-448-18916-X, G&D). Putnam Pub Group.

Figure Painting. Hans Schwarz. LC 79-84662. (Start to Paint Ser.). (Illus.). 1979. pap. 3.95 o.s.i. (ISBN 0-8008-2717-1, Pentalic). Taplinger.

Figures. Jean C. Knaff. LC 88-15163. (Illus.). 36p. (ps up). write for info. o.s.i. (ISBN 0-88708-076-6). Picture Bk Studio.

Figures of Dead Men. Leonard Baskin. LC 68-19668. (Illus.). 80p. 1968. signed woodcut ltd ed 150.00x o.p. U of Mass Pr.

Figures of Desire: A Theory & Analysis of Surrealist Film. Linda Williams. LC 80-27490. (Illus.). 228p. 1981. 22.95 o.p. (ISBN 0-252-00878-2). U of Ill Pr.

File. Penn Kimball. LC 83-12574. 368p. 1983. 14.95 o.p. (ISBN 0-15-130952-3). HarBraceJ.

File. Penn Kimball. 1985. pap. 3.95 o.p. (ISBN 0-380-69999-0, Bard). Avon.

File & Database Management Programs for the IBM-PC. Myron Hecht. LC 85-5340. (IBM-PC Ser.). 304p. 1985. pap. 17.95 o.p. (ISBN 0-471-80975-6). Wiley.

File Management Techniques. Billy G. Claybrook. 247p. 1983. text ed. 45.00 o.s.i. Assn Inform & Image Mgmt.

File on Stanley Patton Buchta. Irvin Faust. 256p. 1973. pap. 1.50 o.p. (ISBN 0-380-01183-2, 14647, Bard). Avon.

File Structures Using Ada. Nancy E. Miller & Charles G. Petersen. (Illus.). 600p. text ed. cancelled o.s.i. (ISBN 0-8053-0440-1); instr's. guide avail. o.s.i. (ISBN 0-8053-0442-8); software avail. o.s.i. (ISBN 0-8053-0441-X). Benjamin-Cummings.

File Techniques for Data Base Organization in COBOL. Leroy F. Johnson & Rodney H. Cooper. (P-H Software Ser.). (Illus.). 384p. 1981. text ed. 34.00 o.p. (ISBN 0-13-314039-3). P-H.

Filibusterismo see Subversive.

Filing Systems & Database for the BBC Micro. A. P. Stephenson & D. J. Stephenson. (Illus.). 219p. (Orig.). 1984. pap. 15.95 o.p. (ISBN 0-246-12423-7, Pub. by Granada England). Sheridan.

Filipino Lippi's Strozzi Chapel in Santa Maria Novella. J. Russell Sale. Ed. by Sydney J. Freedberg. LC 78-74376. (Outstanding Dissertations in the Fine Arts Ser.). (Illus.). 1979. lib. bdg. 57.00 o.p. (ISBN 0-8240-3963-7). Garland Pub.

Filipinos on Oahu, Hawaii. Benjamin V. Carino. LC 81-5382. (Papers of the East-West Population Institute: No. 72). vii, 46p. (Orig.). 1981. pap. text ed. 1.50 o.p. (ISBN 0-86638-019-1). EW Ctr HI.

Filipo Brunelleschi: The Cupola of Santa Maria Del Fiore. Howard Saalman. (Studies in Architecture). (Illus.). 391p. 1980. 140.00 o.p. (ISBN 0-8390-0268-8). Abner Schram Ltd.

Filipo Lippi Studies: Naturalism Style Andiconography in Early Renaissance Art. Jeffrey Ruda. LC 79-57498. (Outstanding Dissertations in the Fine Arts Ser.: No. 5). 235p. 1981. lib. bdg. 40.00 o.p. (ISBN 0-8240-3940-8). Garland Pub.

Fill My Cup, Lord: Meditations on Word Pictures in the New Testament. Mildred Tengbom & Luverne Tengbom. LC 78-66944. 1979. pap. 5.95 o.p. (ISBN 0-8066-1681-4, 10-2308, Augsburg). Augsburg Fortress.

Fille Mal Gardee. Ivor F. Guest. 71p. Repr. of 1960 ed. lib. bdg. 39.00 o.p. (Pub. by Am Repr Serv). Reprint Servs.

Filling Up Your Think Tank. Bill Stearns. 144p. (gr. 9-12). 1986. 4.50 o.p. (ISBN 0-89693-264-8). Victor Bks.

Film & Education. Godfrey Elliott. (ISBN 0-8022-0447-3). Philos Lib.

Film & Video. (Fact Bks). 96p. (gr. 4-7). pap. 3.50 o.p. (ISBN 0-528-87176-5, Checkerboard Pr). Macmillan.

Film Appreciation. Allan Casebier. (Illus., Orig.). 1976. pap. text ed. 8.75 o.p. (ISBN 0-15-527370-1, HC). HarBraceJ.

Film As a Subversive Art. Amos Vogel. 1976. pap. 10.95 o.s.i. (ISBN 0-394-73207-3). Random.

Film Career of Alain Robbe-Grillet. William F. Van Wert. 1977. lib. bdg. 25.00 o.p. (ISBN 0-8161-7992-1, Hall Reference). G K Hall.

Film Catalog: A List of Film Holdings in the Museum of Modern Art. (Library Catalogs & Supplements Ser.). (Illus.). 462p. 1985. lib. bdg. 60.00 o.s.i. (ISBN 0-8161-0443-3). G K Hall.

Film Flam: Essays on Hollywood. Larry McMurtry. 1987. 16.45 o.s.i. (ISBN 0-671-64308-8). S&S.

Film Idea. Stanley J. Solomon. (Illus.). 403p. 1972. pap. text ed. 9.95 o.p. (ISBN 0-15-527375-2, HC). HarBraceJ.

Film in the Language Arts Classes. John Aquino. 56p. 1976. 6.95 o.p. (ISBN 0-8106-1811-7). NEA.

Film Index of Work Measurement & Methods Engineering Subjects. Ed. by Benjamin S. Fried. 1980. 11.00 o.p. (ISBN 0-89806-027-3); members 7.00 o.p. Inst Indus Eng.

Film on the Left: American Documentary Film from 1931 to 1942. W. Alexander. LC 80-8534. (Illus.). 364p. 1981. 36.00 o.p. (ISBN 0-691-04678-6, LPE); pap. 12.50x L.P.E. o.p. (ISBN 0-691-10111-6). Princeton U Pr.

Film Preparation & Etching Using Vacuum or Plasma Technology: Proceedings of the SIRA International Seminar, Brighton, U. K., 22-24 March 1983. Ed. by B. Williams. 100p. 1984. pap. 30.00 o.p. (ISBN 0-08-031150-4). Pergamon.

Film Scriptwriting. Dwight V. Swain. 384p. 1976. 24.95 o.p. (ISBN 0-240-50968-4); pap. 22.95 o.p. (ISBN 0-240-51198-0). Focal Pr.

Film Semiotics, Metz, & Leone's Trilogy. Lane Roth. Ed. by Garth S. Jowett. LC 81-48352. (Dissertations on Film Ser.). 231p. 1983. lib. bdg. 36.00 o.p. (ISBN 0-8240-5110-6). Garland Pub.

Film Study Collections: A Guide to Their Development & Use. Nancy Allen. LC 78-20935. 1979. 25.00 o.p. (ISBN 0-8044-2001-7). Ungar.

Film Technique & Film Acting. V. I. Pudovkin. Ed. & tr. by Ivor Montagu. 1970. pap. 6.95 o.p. (ISBN 0-394-17457-7, E683, Ever). Grove.

Film: The Medium & the Maker. James Scott. LC 74-26611. 1975. text ed. 9.95 o.p. (ISBN 0-03-079445-5, HoltC). HR&W.

Film Yearbook 1983. Al Clark. (Illus.). 192p. (Orig.). 1983. pap. 12.95 o.p. (ISBN 0-394-62465-3, E853, Ever). Grove.

Film Yearbook, 1985. Al Clark. LC 83-644931. (Illus.). 192p. 1984. pap. 12.95 o.p. (ISBN 0-394-62321-5, Ever). Grove.

Filmed Books & Plays: 1928-1974. rev. ed. A. G. Enser. 1975. 70.50 o.p. (ISBN 0-12-785201-8). Acad Pr.

Filmgoer's Companion. Leslie L. Halliwell. 1978. pap. 7.95 o.p. (ISBN 0-380-00430-5, 50419-7). Avon.

Filmmakers in Conversation. Ed. by Anthony Loeb. (Illus.). 123p. (Orig.). 1983. pap. 5.95 o.p. (ISBN 0-932026-08-7). Chicago Review.

Films & Filmstrips for Language Arts: An Annotated Bibliography. Jill P. May. LC 81-11084. 103p. 1981. pap. 6.95 o.p. (ISBN 0-8141-1726-0). NCTE.

Films Ex Libris: Literature in 16mm & Video. Salvatore J. Parlato. LC 80-10181. (Illus.). 283p. 1980. lib. bdg. 19.95x o.p. (ISBN 0-89950-006-4). McFarland & Co.

Films in the Mathematics Classroom. Barbara J. Bestgen & Robert E. Reys. LC 82-3442. 90p. 1982. pap. 6.00 o.p. (ISBN 0-87353-195-7). NCTM.

Films of Clark Gable. Gabe Essoe. (Illus.). 1970. 12.00 o.p. (ISBN 0-8065-0011-5, Pub. by Citadel Pr); pap. 7.95 o.p. (ISBN 0-8065-0273-8). Carol Pub Group.

Films of Jeannette MacDonald & Nelson Eddy. Philip Castanza. (Illus.). (gr. 7 up). 1978. 14.95 o.p. (ISBN 0-8065-0600-8, Pub. by Citadel Pr). Carol Pub Group.

Films of Paul Newman. Lawrence J. Quirk. (Illus.). 1971. 9.95 o.p. (ISBN 0-8065-0233-9, Pub. by Citadel Pr); pap. 6.95 o.p. (ISBN 0-8065-0385-8). Carol Pub Group.

Films of Shirley Maclaine. Christopher Denis. (Illus.). 1980. 14.95 o.p. (Pub. by Citadel Pr). Carol Pub Group.

Films Stars Don't Die in Liverpool. Peter Turner. (Illus.). 144p. 1987. 15.95 o.s.i. (ISBN 0-8021-0042-2). Grove.

Filostrato of Giovanni Boccaccio. Giovanni Boccaccio. Tr. by Nathaniel E. Griffin & Arthur B. Myrick. LC 72-120232. 1973. Repr. lib. bdg. 40.00x o.p. (ISBN 0-374-90730-7, Octagon). Hippocrene Bks.

Fils De Personne. Henri De Montherlant. Bd. with Incompris. 1944. 13.25 o.p. (ISBN 0-685-35872-0). Schoenhof.

Fils de Personne: Avec: Un Incompris. Henry de Montherlant. 222p. (Soleil). 1944. 9.95 o.p. (ISBN 0-686-55518-X). Schoenhof.

Filters & Filtration. R. H. Warring. (Illus.). 1969. 35.00x o.p. Coronet Bks.

Filters & Filtration. R. H. Warring. 250p. 1969. 125.00x o.p. (ISBN 0-85461-025-1, Pub by Trade & Tech England). Gower Pub Co.

Filtration, Pt. 2. Clyde Orr. (Chemical Processing & Engineering; an International Ser.: Vol. 10). 424p. 1979. 89.75 o.p. (ISBN 0-8247-6763-2). Dekker.

Final Act Adopted at the Ninth Session of the Contracting Parties & Protocol Amending Part 1 & Articles 29 & 30 of the General Agreement on the Organization for Trade Cooperation. 1955. pap. 5.00 o.s.i. (G128, GATT). UNIPUB.

Final Command. Warren C. Norwood. 252p. 1986. pap. 2.95 o.p. (ISBN 0-553-25554-1, Spectra). Bantam.

Final Curtain. Ngaio Marsh. 1983. pap. 3.50 o.p. (ISBN 0-515-07074-2, Medallion). Jove Pubns.

Final Cut: Dreams & Disasters in the Making of Heaven's Gate. Steven Bach. LC 85-4983. (Illus.). 420p. 1985. 19.95 o.p. (ISBN 0-688-04382-8). Morrow.

Final Days. Bob Woodward & Bernstein. 1977. pap. 4.95 o.p. (ISBN 0-380-00844-0, 69708-8). Avon.

Final Dress. John Houseman. LC 83-423. 512p. 1983. 19.25 o.p. (ISBN 0-671-42031-3). S&S.

Final Dress. John Houseman. 592p. 1984. pap. 9.95 o.p. (ISBN 0-671-42032-1, Touchstone Bks). S&S.

Final Entries 1945: The Diaries of Joseph Goebbels. Ed. by Hugh Trevor-Roper. 1979. pap. 2.75 o.p. (ISBN 0-380-42408-8, 42408-8). Avon.

Final Epidemic: Physicians & Scientists on Nuclear War. Ed. by Bulletin of the Atomic Scientists Staff. 252p. 1982. pap. 4.95 o.s.i. (ISBN 0-226-03874-2). U of Chicago Pr.

Final Frontier. Diane Carey. 416p. (Orig.). pap. 4.50 o.p. (ISBN 0-671-64752-0). Archway.

Final Harbor. Harry Homewood. 1980. text ed. 11.95 o.p. (ISBN 0-07-029694-4). McGraw.

Final Harbor. David Martin. LC 84-559. 336p. 1984. pap. 15.95 o.p. (ISBN 0-03-069504-X, Owl Bks). H Holt & Co.

Final Judgment: My Life as a Soviet Defense Attorney. Dina Kaminskaya. Tr. by Michael Glenny from Rus. 416p. 1983. 18.25 o.p. (ISBN 0-671-24739-5). S&S.

Final Moments. Emma Page. LC 86-24090. (Crime Club Ser.). 192p. 1987. 12.95 o.s.i. (ISBN 0-385-23802-9). Doubleday.

Final Offer Arbitration - Concepts, Developments, & Techniques. Peter Feville. (Public Employee Relations Library: No. 50). 1975. pap. 14.00 non-members o.p. (ISBN 0-685-56577-7); pap. 12.00 members o.p. Intl Personnel Mgmt.

Final Reflection. John M. Ford. (Gregg Fiction Star Trek Ser.). 1985. lib. bdg. 11.95 o.p. (ISBN 0-8398-2885-3, Gregg). G K Hall.

Final Report: NCHRP Project 20-3D, FY'70, Freeway Traffic Management. 60p. 1979. 4.00 o.p. (ISBN 0-309-02919-8). Transport Res Bd.

Final Report on the WPA Program, 1935-1943. U. S. Federal Works Agency Staff. LC 75-35362. (U. S. Government Documents Program Ser.). 145p. 1976. Repr. of 1947 ed. lib. bdg. 35.00x o.p. (ISBN 0-8371-8600-5, USWP). Greenwood.

Final Treatment: The File on Dr. X. Matthew Lifflander. 1979. 11.95 o.p. (ISBN 0-393-08833-2). Norton.

Final Turning Point. Paul Van Maanen & Marj Van Maanen. 1984. 20.95 o.p. (ISBN 0-533-06046-X). Vantage.

Final Witness. Roger E. Swaybill. 256p. 1983. pap. 2.75 o.p. (ISBN 0-380-81422-6, 81422-6). Avon.

Final Yamato. (Big Little Bks.: No. 138). (Illus.). 350p. 1984. 6.95 o.p. (ISBN 0-318-02736-4). Bks Nippan.

Final Years: NYO&W. John Krause & Ed Crist. (Carstens Hobby Bks). (Illus.). 1977. pap. 9.95 o.p. (ISBN 0-911868-32-1). Carstens Pubns.

Finalists. Russell Braddon. LC 77-3869. 1977. 7.95 o.p. (ISBN 0-689-10801-X, Atheneum). Macmillan.

Finality of Faith, & Christianity Among the World Religions. Nels F. Ferre. LC 78-11979. 1979. Repr. of 1963 ed. lib. bdg. 35.00x o.p. (ISBN 0-313-21182-5, FEFF). Greenwood.

Finally the Pawn. Jada Thacker. 304p. 1986. pap. 3.50 o.p. (ISBN 0-380-89918-3). Avon.

Finally...I'm a Doctor. Neil Shulman. LC 76-14605. 1976. pap. text ed. 11.95 o.p. (ISBN 0-684-14601-0, Pub. by Scribner). Hemisphere Pub.

Finance. Herbert B. Mayo. 512p. 1982. text ed. 31.95x o.p. (ISBN 0-03-059572-X); instr's. manual 19.95 o.p. (ISBN 0-03-059573-8); study guide 12.95x o.p. (ISBN 0-03-060121-5). Dryden Pr.

Finance & Economic Growth in Developing Countries. K. L. Gupta. LC 84-14307. 242p. 1984. 31.00 o.p. (ISBN 0-7099-3803-9, Pub. by Croom Helm Ltd). Routledge Chapman & Hall.

Finance Capital: A Study of the Latest Phase of Capitalist Development. Rudolf Hilferding. Tr. by Tom Bottomore from Ger. 500p. 1981. 50.00x o.p. (ISBN 0-7100-0618-7). Routledge Chapman & Hall.

Finance for Mine Management. R. M. Wanless. (Illus.). 200p. 1983. 35.00 o.p. (ISBN 0-412-24060-2, NO. 6761, Pub. by Chapman & Hall). Routledge CHapman & Hall.

Finance for the Purchasing Executive. L. E. Rockley. 191p. 1978. text ed. 29.50x o.p. (ISBN 0-220-66362-9, Pub. by Busn Bks England). Gower Pub Co.

Finance in China. Srinvas Wagel. LC 78-74334. (Modern Chinese Economy Ser.). 447p. 1980. lib. bdg. 67.00 o.p. (ISBN 0-8240-4268-9). Garland Pub.

Finance of British Industry, Nineteen Eighteen to Nineteen Twenty-Six. W. A. Thomas. 351p. 1978. 55.00x o.p. (ISBN 0-416-67420-8, NO. 2543); pap. 14.95 o.p. (ISBN 0-416-34300-7, NO. 3709). Routledge Chapman & Hall.

Finance of Cities in West Germany. R. J. Bennett. (Illus.). 62p. 1983. pap. 22.00 o.p. (ISBN 0-08-031462-7). Pergamon.

Finance of International Trade. 4th ed. D. P. Whiting. 278p. 1981. pap. 29.50x o.p. (ISBN 0-7121-0637-5). Trans-Atl Phila.

Financial Accounting. 7th ed. James J. Benjamin et al. LC 83-70548. 651p. 1988. 36.95x o.p. (ISBN 0-87393-075-4); study guide 11.95x o.p. (ISBN 0-87393-076-2); Vol. I. working papers 9.95x o.p. (ISBN 0-87393-079-7); Vol. II. working papers 9.95x o.p. (ISBN 0-87393-080-0). Dame Pubns.

Financial Accounting. R. Brockington. (Higher Business Education Ser.). (Illus.). 240p. 1983. text ed. 32.50x o.p. (ISBN 0-7121-0644-8); pap. 27.50x o.p. (ISBN 0-7121-0639-1). Trans-Atl Phila.

Financial Accounting. 4th ed. Sidney Davidson et al. 896p. 1985. text ed. 35.95 o.s.i. (ISBN 0-03-071318-8). Dryden Pr.

Financial Accounting. Roger H. Hermanson et al. 1981. text ed. 19.50x o.p. (ISBN 0-256-02556-8); avail. study guide o.p.; avail. working papers o.p.; practice set 5.50 o.p. (ISBN 0-256-02573-8). Irwin.

Financial Accounting. 3rd ed. Roger H. Hermanson et al. 1987. 37.95 o.p. (ISBN 0-317-61191-7); study guide 12.95 o.p. (ISBN 0-317-61192-5); working papers 12.95 o.p. (ISBN 0-317-61193-3); practice set 10.95 o.p. (ISBN 0-317-61194-1). Irwin.

Financial Accounting. Eugene J. Laughlin. LC 83-19781. 824p. 1984. text ed. (ISBN 0-471-88720-X). Wiley.

Financial Accounting. Belverd E. Needles, Jr. 1983. text ed. 30.95 o.p. (ISBN 0-395-32470-X). HM.

Financial Accounting: A Basic Approach. Albert Slavin et al. 756p. 1980. text ed. 33.95x o.p. (ISBN 0-03-048906-7); instr's. manual 10.00 o.p. (ISBN 0-03-052241-2); study guide 13.95x o.p. (ISBN 0-03-052246-3); working papers 13.95x o.p. (ISBN 0-03-052261-7); x practice set 12.95 o.p. (ISBN 0-03-052256-0); test bank 10.00 o.p. (ISBN 0-03-052251-X). Dryden Pr.

Financial Accounting: An Introduction. 3rd ed. Harold Bierman, Jr. & Allan R. Drebin. LC 77-75531. (Illus.). 1978. text ed. 31.95x o.s.i. (ISBN 0-7216-1704-2); study guide 12.95x o.s.i. (ISBN 0-7216-1717-4). Dryden Pr.

Financial Accounting: An Introduction. 3rd ed. Paul H. Walgenbach et al. 665p. 1977. text ed. 21.95 o.p. (ISBN 0-15-527381-7, HC). HarBraceJ.

Financial Accounting & Reporting. Paul R. Berney et al. 1980. text ed. 34.95x o.p. (ISBN 0-256-02418-9). Irwin.

Financial Accounting & Reporting: A Contemporary Emphasis. reference ed. John Dearden & John Shank. (Illus.). 544p. 1975. text ed. 44.00 o.p. (ISBN 0-13-314757-6). P-H.

Financial Accounting: Concepts & Principles. David F. Fetyko. 746p. 1980. text ed. 21.95x o.p. (ISBN 0-534-00753-8, Kent Pub); guide 6.95xstudy o.p. (ISBN 0-534-00851-8); papers 6.95xworking o.p. (ISBN 0-534-00846-1). PWS-Kent Pub.

Financial Accounting Standards Board Current Text 1982-1984: International. Financial Accounting Standards Board. 1800p. 1983. text ed. 300.00 looseleaf ed. o.p. (ISBN 0-07-020902-2). McGraw.

Financial Accounting: The Main Ideas. 2nd ed. Arthur L. Thomas. 768p. 1975. (ISBN 0-534-00390-7). PWS-Kent Pub.

Financial Accounting Theory Two: Issues & Controversies. Thomas F. Keller & Stephen A. Zeff. 1969. pap. text ed. 16.95 o.p. (ISBN 0-07-033496-X). McGraw.

Financial Advisory: Hundreds of Ways to Save & Invest Your Money. Milton Pierce. (Illus.). 256p. (Orig.). 1985. pap. 9.95 o.p. (ISBN 0-399-50983-6, Perigee). Putnam Pub Group.

Financial Aid for Graduate & Professional Education 1987. 3rd ed. Patricia McWade. 13p. (Orig.). 1987. pap. 1.25 o.p. (ISBN 0-87866-534-X). Petersons Guides.

Financial Aid for Graduate & Professional Education 1988. 4th ed. Patricia McWade. 13p. (Orig.). 1988. pap. 1.50 o.p. (ISBN 0-87866-701-6). Petersons Guides.

Financial Analysis for Decision Making. Curtis J. Blecke & Daniel L. Gotthilf. 272p. 1980. text ed. 39.95 o.p. (ISBN 0-13-315234-0). P-H.

Financial Analysis of Investor-Owned Electric Utilities. (DOE-EIA-0499 Ser.). (Illus.). 116p. 1986. pap. 5.50 o.p. (S/N 061-003-00508-0). USGPO.

Financial Analysis Using Calculators: Time Value of Money. Elbert B. Greynolds & J. S. Aronfsky. 1980. pap. text ed. 24.95 o.p. (ISBN 0-07-024690-4). McGraw.

Financial Analyst's Handbook. Ed. by Summer N. Levine. Incl. Vol. 1. Portfolio Management. 1492p. 65.00 (ISBN 0-87094-082-1); Vol. 2. Analysis by Industry. 1032p. (ISBN 0-87094-083-X). LC 74-81386. 1975. Dow Jones-Irwin.

Financial & Accounting Handbook for the Service Industries. Jerome Solomon. 482p. 1983. 38.95 o.p. (ISBN 0-8436-0854-4). Van Nos Reinhold.

Financial & Corporate Public Relations: The Integrated Approach. E. Kopel. 1983. text ed. 24.95 o.p. (ISBN 0-07-084586-7). McGraw.

Financial & Operating Results of Department & Specialty Stores 1983 Results. 1987. pap. 69.00 o.p. (ISBN 0-87102-120-X, 26-4134). Natl Ret Merch.

Financial Control in Health Care. David W. Young. LC 83-71735. 250p. 1984. 35.00 o.p. (ISBN 0-87094-445-2). Dow Jones-Irwin.

Financial Freedom on Five Dollars a Day. 3rd ed. 170p. 1986. 7.95 o.p. (ISBN 0-88908-613-3). ISC Pr.

Financial Futures. 200p. 1984. 120.00 o.p. (ISBN 0-8002-3166-X). Intl Pubns Serv.

Financial Futures & Investment Strategy. Arthur L. Rebell et al. LC 83-73719. 380p. 1984. 40.00 o.p. (ISBN 0-87094-491-6). Dow Jones-Irwin.

Financial Handbook. 5th ed. Ed. by Edward I. Altman. LC 81-10473. 1344p. 1981. 69.95x o.p. (ISBN 0-471-07727-5, Pub. by Ronald Pr). Wiley.

Financial Health of the Electric Utility Industry. (Ad Hoc Committee Reports Ser.). 71p. 1982. 8.00 o.p. (ISBN 0-318-16979-7). NARUC.

Financial Information Services: Online Teledelivery. International Resource Development, Inc. Staff. 162p. 1983. 1285.00x o.p. (ISBN 0-88694-559-3). Intl Res Dev.

Financial Ingredient in Foodservice Management. National Institute for Food Service Industry Staff et al. 224p. 1981. pap. text ed. write for info. o.p. (ISBN 0-697-00473-2); instrs.' manual avail. o.p. (ISBN 0-697-05229-X); student manual avail. o.p. (ISBN 0-697-05228-1). Wm C Brown.

Financial Institutions. Peter S. Rose & Donald R. Fraser. 1980. 18.95x o.p. (ISBN 0-256-02205-4). Irwin.

Financial Institutions. 2nd ed. Peter S. Rose & Donald R. Fraser. 1985. 36.95 o.p. (ISBN 0-256-02882-6). Irwin.

Financial Institutions & Markets. 2nd ed. Murray E. Polakoff & Thomas A. Durkin. LC 80-82758. (Illus.). 673p. 1981. text ed. 47.56 o.p. (ISBN 0-395-29191-7). HM.

Financial Institutions & Markets. Murray E. Polakoff et al. 1970. text ed. 23.50 o.p. (ISBN 0-395-05062-6). HM.

Financial Institutions & Markets in a Changing World. 3rd ed. Donald R. Fraser & Peter S. Rose. 1987. pap. 21.95 o.p. (ISBN 0-317-61186-0). Irwin.

Financial Institutions & Markets in a Changing World. Ed. by Donald R. Fraser & Peter S. Rose. 1980. pap. 12.95x o.p. (ISBN 0-256-02201-1). Irwin.

Financial Institutions, Markets, & Money. 2nd ed. David S. Kidwell & Richard L. Peterson. 704p. 1984. text ed. 33.95x o.p. (ISBN 0-03-063821-6); instr's. manual 19.95 o.p. (ISBN 0-03-063822-4). Dryden Pr.

Financial Intermediaries: An Introduction. Benton E. Gup. LC 75-31005. (Illus.). 416p. 1976. text ed. 17.50 o.p. (ISBN 0-395-19828-3). HM.

Financial Intermediaries: An Introduction. 2nd ed. Benton E. Gup. LC 79-87858. 1980. text ed. 31.50 o.p. (ISBN 0-395-28138-5). HM.

Financial Invasion of the U. S. A. A Threat to American Society? Earl H. Fry. (Illus.). 1979. text ed. 18.50 o.p. (ISBN 0-07-022591-5). McGraw.

Financial Keys to Small Business Profitability. Edward N. Rausch. 176p. 1982. 15.95 o.p. (ISBN 0-8144-5615-4). AMACOM.

Financial Management. 5th ed. Robert W. Johnson & Ronald W. Melicher. 725p. 1982. text ed. 40.00 o.p. (ISBN 0-205-07708-0); study guide avail. o.p. (ISBN 0-205-07822-2); instr's. manual avail. o.p. (ISBN 0-205-07709-9); test manual avail. o.p. (ISBN 0-205-07812-5). Allyn.

Financial Management. Ed. by M. Olsen. 50p. 1984. pap. 23.00 o.p. (ISBN 0-08-031290-X). Pergamon.

Financial Management & Policy. 7th ed. James C. Van Horne. (Illus.). 768p. 1986. text ed. 49.00 o.p. (ISBN 0-13-316761-5). P-H.

Financial Management Classics. Carroll D. Aby & Donald E. Vaughn, Jr. LC 79-10710. (Illus.). 1979. pap. text ed. (ISBN 0-673-16168-4). Scott F.

Financial Management in Agriculture. 3rd ed. Ed. by John A. Hopkin et al. Peter J. Barry & C. B. Baker. (Illus.). 530p. 1983. 30.60 o.p. (ISBN 0-8134-2291-4); text ed. 22.95x o.p. Inter Print Pubs.

Financial Management of Commercial Banks. John M. Mason. LC 78-24809. 442p. 1982. 40.00 o.p. (ISBN 0-471-87745-X); tchr's. guide o.p. (ISBN 0-471-89511-3). Wiley.

Financial Management of Financial Institutions. George Hempel & Jess B. Yawitz. (Illus.). 1977. write for info. o.p. (ISBN 0-13-315978-7); pap. text ed. 12.95 o.p. (ISBN 0-13-315960-4). P-H.

Financial Management of the Hospital Food Service Department. Faisal A. Kaud. LC 83-12238. (Illus.). 88p. 1983. pap. 30.00 o.p. (ISBN 0-87258-411-9, 046205). AHPI.

Financial Management of Your Law Practice. 96p. 1984. 20.00 o.p. (ISBN 0-88129-130-7). Wash Bar CLE.

Financial Management Strategies for Arts Organizations. Frederick J. Turk & Robert P. Gallo. LC 84-12352. (Illus.). 200p. 1984. casebound 17.95 o.s.i. (ISBN 0-915400-40-5). Am Council Arts.

Financial Management: Theory & Practice. 4th ed. Eugene F. Brigham. 1152p. 1985. text ed. 41.95x o.s.i. (ISBN 0-03-071693-4); study guide 13.95x o.s.i. (ISBN 0-03-071696-9). Dryden Pr.

Financial Management: Theory & Strategies. Edwin H. Neave & John C. Wiginton. (Illus.). 416p. 1981. text ed. 41.67 o.p. (ISBN 0-13-316109-9). P-H.

Financial Markets & Institutions. Robert D. Auerbach. 640p. 1983. text ed. write for info. o.p. (ISBN 0-02-304610-4). Macmillan.

Financial Officer's Manual & Guide. Thomas Vickman. LC 82-15793. 384p. 1983. text ed. 49.95 o.p. (ISBN 0-87624-151-8, Inst Busn Plan). P-H.

Financial Planner's Guide to Using a Personal Computer. Colin K. Mick & Jerry Ball. LC 83-73713. 300p. 1984. 22.50 o.p. (ISBN 0-87094-469-X). Dow Jones-Irwin.

Financial Planning: A Home Study Course. Dianne M. Rankin. (Home Study Ser.). 43p. 1984. wkbk. & audio tape 24.00 o.p. (ISBN 0-939926-24-5); audio tape o.p. (ISBN 0-939926-23-7). Fruition Pubns.

Financial Planning for the Utterly Confused. Joel J. Lerner. 224p. 1986. pap. text ed. 8.95 o.p. (ISBN 0-07-037224-1). McGraw.

Financial Planning under the New Rules. Wyatt. 1987. 36.95 o.p. (ISBN 0-88462-575-3, 56506-12, Reald Estate Ed). Longman Finan.

Financial Reform in the 1980s. Thomas F. Cargill & Gillian G. Garcia. (Publication Ser.: No. 313). xx, 214p. 1985. o.p. 19.95 o.p.; pap. 10.95 o.p. (ISBN 0-8179-8132-2). Hoover Inst Pr.

Financial Reporting & Bookkeeping in Girl Scouting. (Illus.). 112p. 1982. pap. 12.00 o.p. (ISBN 0-88441-446-9, 26-174). Girl Scouts USA.

Financial Reporting in India. Claire Marston. (International Accounting Ser.). 176p. 1986. 34.50 o.p. (ISBN 0-7099-4611-2, Pub. by Croom Helm Ltd). Routledge Chapman & Hall.

Financial Self-Assessment: A Workbook for Colleges. Nathan Dickmeyer & K. Scott Hughes. 73p. 1980. pap. text ed. 20.00, 1 copy o.p. (ISBN 0-915164-11-6); pap. text ed. 17.50 each, 2-4 copies o.p.; pap. text ed. 12.50 each, 5 or more copies o.p. NACUBO.

Financial Services: Changing Institutions & Government Policy. Ed. by George Benston. LC 83-13995. 290p. 1983. 14.95 o.p. (ISBN 0-13-316513-2); pap. 7.95 o.p. (ISBN 0-13-316505-1). Am Assembly.

Financial Side of Industrial Research Management. Lynn W. Ellis. LC 83-19658. 250p. 1984. 44.95x o.p. (ISBN 0-471-89056-1, Pub. by Wiley-Interscience). Wiley.

Financial Sourcebook. Alexander Hamilton Institute,Inc. 1984. Binder 110.00 o.p. (ISBN 0-88057-116-0). Exec Ent Pubns.

Financial Statement Analysis. George Foster. (Illus.). 1978. text ed. 38.33 o.p. (ISBN 0-13-316273-7). P-H.

Financial Statement Analysis. Charles H. Gibson & Patricia A. Boyer. LC 78-17716. 456p. 1979. text ed. 20.95x o.p. (ISBN 0-8436-0755-6); instr's manual 3.95 o.p. (ISBN 0-686-79900-3); test bank 2.25 o.p. (ISBN 0-686-79901-1). PWS-Kent Pub.

Financial Times Mining Yearbook, 1988. 1988. 105.00 o.p. (ISBN 0-912289-89-9); Standing Order. 94.50 o.p. St James Pr.

Financial Times Oil & Gas Yearbook, 1988. 1988. 105.00 o.p. (ISBN 0-912289-93-7); Standing Order. 94.50 o.p. St James Pr.

Financial Times World Hotel Directory. 1987. 105.00 o.p. (ISBN 0-912289-90-2); Standing Order. 94.50 o.p. St James Pr.

Financial Times World Hotel Directory. 750p. 1989. 125.00 o.p. (ISBN 1-55862-006-0); Standing Order. 112.50 o.p. St James Pr.

Financial Times World Insurance Yearbook, 1987. 1987. 105.00 o.p. (ISBN 0-912289-88-0); Standing Order. 94.50 o.p. St James Pr.

Financial Times World Insurance Yearbook, 1989. 550p. 1989. 125.00 o.p. (ISBN 1-55862-002-8); Standing Order. 112.50 o.p. St James Pr.

Financial Tools for Marketing Administration. L. G. Rayburn. 1982. 10.95 o.p. (ISBN 0-8144-7567-1). AMACOM.

Financially Free: Add 30,000 Dollars a Year to Your Income Through Part Time Real Estate Investing. Marc S. Garrison. 1986. 17.45 o.s.i. (ISBN 0-671-61731-1). S&S.

Financier: The Biography of Andre Meyer. Cary Reich. LC 83-8291. (Illus.). 460p. 1983. 15.95 o.p. (ISBN 0-688-01551-4). Morrow.

Financing & Charges for Wastewater Systems ('73) Water Pollution Control Federation Staff. (Illus.). 68p. pap. 8.00 o.p. (ISBN 0-943244-25-0). Water Pollution.

Financing & Investing in Hi-Tech. Ed. by Fred B. Renwick. LC 82-48008. (Salomon Brothers Center for the Study of Financial Institutions). cancelled o.s.i. (ISBN 0-669-05832-7). Lexington Bks.

Financing Black Economic Development. Timothy Bates & William Bradford. (Institute for Research on Poverty Policy Analysis Ser.). 1979. 24.50 o.p. (ISBN 0-12-081650-4); pap. 12.50 o.p. (ISBN 0-12-081652-0). Acad Pr.

Financing Business Transactions. 676p. 1984. 45.00 o.p. (ISBN 0-88129-133-1). Wash Bar CLE.

Financing Capital Formation for Local Governments. Ann R. McWatters. LC 79-10333. (Research Report: No. 79-3). 1979. pap. 3.00x o.p. (ISBN 0-87772-266-8). UCB IGS.

Financing Income-Producing Real Estate. Ed. by James A. Britton, Jr. & Lewis O. Kerwood. (Illus.). 1977. text ed. 34.95 o.p. (ISBN 0-07-007926-9, T&D). McGraw.

Financing Modern Government. William H. Anderson. LC 72-9040. 1973. text ed. 19.50 o.p. (ISBN 0-395-14349-7, 3-01000). HM.

Financing of Public Enterprises in Developing Countries. Ed. by Praxy Fernandes. 148p. 1981. pap. 20.00x o.p. (ISBN 92-9038-020-9, Pub. by Intl Ctr Pub Yugoslavia). Kumarian Pr.

Financing of State Plans. Jagannath Mirsha & R. K. Sinha. 334p. 1984. text ed. 45.00x o.p. (ISBN 0-317-07709-0, Pub. by Sterling Pubs India). Apt Bks.

Financing of Technological Change. Lorne Switzer. Ed. by Fred Bateman. LC 85-16419. (Research in Business Economics & Public Policy Ser.: No. 10). 86p. 1985. 39.95 o.p. (ISBN 0-8357-1689-9). UMI Res Pr.

Financing of Terror. James Adams. 352p. 1986. 18.45 o.s.i. (ISBN 0-671-49700-6). S&S.

Financing Politics, Money, Elections & Political Reform. 3rd ed. Herbert E. Alexander. LC 83-21079. 232p. 1984. pap. 10.95 o.p. (ISBN 0-87187-280-3). Congr Quarterly.

Financing Public Tennis Courts. Rev. ed. U. S. Tennis Association, Education & Research Center Staff. 88p. 1979. 2.50 o.p. (ISBN 0-938822-21-7). USTA-CERT.

Financing Real Estate: Analysis & Application. Alan R. Winger & Margaret R. Thomas. 363p. 1982. text ed. 19.00 o.p. (ISBN 0-15-575842-X, HC). HarBraceJ.

Financing Rental Construction After Tax Reform: A Builder's Guide. National Association of Home Builders Staff. 80p. 1986. pap. 12.50 o.p. (ISBN 0-86718-288-1). Nat Assn H Build.

Financing Residential Real Estate. 5th ed. Joseph E. Schram, Jr. et al. (Illus.). 343p. 1987. pap. 29.95 o.p. (ISBN 0-915799-32-4). Natl Real Estate Inst.

Financing the International Petroleum Industry. Norman A. White. LC 79-51576. 1979. 40.00 o.p. (ISBN 0-8144-5572-7). AMACOM.

Financing Urban Development in Mexico City: A Case Study of Property Tax, Land Use, Housing, & Urban Planning. Oliver Oldman et al. Ed. by Lawrence M. Herrmann & Laurence D. Lee. LC 67-20878. (Harvard Law School International Tax Program Ser). 1967. 27.00x o.s.i. (ISBN 0-674-30150-1). Harvard U Pr.

Finch's Fortune. Mazo De La Roche. 1976. pap. 1.50 o.s.i. (ISBN 0-449-23053-8, Crest). Fawcett.

Find a Safe Place. Alex Lazzarino & E. Kent Hayes. 1984. text ed. 15.95 o.p. (ISBN 0-07-036782-5). McGraw.

Find a Word. Ed. by Norman Goldfind. (Leisure Fun Ser.: No. 19). 128p. (Orig.). 1988. pap. 2.50 o.s.i. (ISBN 1-55785-044-5). Bart Books.

Find Debbie! Roy Brown. LC 75-25511. 160p. (gr. 6 up). 1979. 7.95 o.s.i. (ISBN 0-395-28894-0, Clarion). HM.

Find the Cat. Elaine Livermore. (Illus.). 48p. (gr. k up). 1979. pap. 1.95 o.p. (ISBN 0-395-28595-X). HM.

Find the Kirillian. Seth McEvoy. (Be an Interplanetary Spy Ser.: No. 1). 128p. 1985. pap. 1.95 o.p. (ISBN 0-553-23506-0). Bantam.

Find Waldo. Martin Handford. (ps up). 1988. 9.95 o.p. Little.

Find Your Self in the Bible: A Guide to Relational Bible Study for Small Groups. Karl A. Olsson. LC 73-88605. 128p. (Orig.). 1974. pap. 6.50 o.p. (ISBN 0-8066-1408-0, 10-2318, Augsburg). Augsburg Fortress.

Find Yourself, Give Yourself. Dick Wulf. LC 83-61819. 162p. 1983. pap. 5.95 o.p. (ISBN 0-89109-496-2). NavPress.

Finders Keepers. Lucienne S. Bloch. 225p. 1982. 11.95 o.p. (ISBN 0-395-32040-2). HM.

Finder's Keepers. Arthur Collins & Michael Collins. LC 85-63396. 185p. 1986. 17.95 o.s.i. (ISBN 0-933341-34-2). Quinlan Pr.

Finding a Position: Strategies for Library School Graduates. Robert F. Delzell. (Occasional Papers: No. 153). 27p. 1982. pap. 3.00 o.p. (ISBN 0-317-58999-7). U of Ill Lib Info Sci.

Finding & Helping the Able Child. Ed. by Trevor Kerry. (Illus.). 240p. 1983. 25.25 o.p. (ISBN 0-7099-1514-4, Pub. by Croom Helm Ltd). Routledge Chapman & Hall.

Finding Birds Around the World. Peter Alden & John Gooders. (Illus.). 704p. 1981. 17.95 o.p. (ISBN 0-395-29114-3). HM.

Finding Company Intelligence: A Case Study. LC 84-42965. (Business Research Ser.: Vol. 6). 1984. pap. 85.00 o.p. (ISBN 0-934940-28-2). Wash Res Pub.

Finding Facts: Interviewing, Observing, Using Reference Sources. William L. Rivers. 1975. pap. text ed. (ISBN 0-13-316364-4). P-H.

Finding Fossil Man. Robin Place. (Illus.). 128p. 1957. (ISBN 0-8022-1984-5). Philos Lib.

Finding Hope Again: A Pastor's Guide to Counseling Depressed Persons. Roy W. Fairchild. LC 79-2988. 160p. 1980. 9.45 o.p. (ISBN 0-06-062325-X). HarpR.

Finding Hoseyn. Colin MacKinnon. 320p. 1986. 15.95 o.p. (ISBN 0-87795-741-X, Arbor Hse). Morrow.

Finding Is the First Act: Trove Folktales & Jesus' Treasure Parable. John D. Crossan. Ed. by William E. Beardslee et al. LC 79-9898. (Semeia Studies). 160p. (Orig.). 1980. pap. 4.95 o.p. (ISBN 0-8006-1509-3, Fortress). Augsburg Fortress.

Finding Love: Practical Advice for Men & Women. Sally J. Raphael & M. J. Abadie. 1984. pap. 7.95 o.p. (ISBN 0-87795-588-3, Arbor Hse); (12-copy prepack) o. p. 95.40 o.p. (ISBN 0-87795-618-9). Morrow.

Finding Money. Rev. ed. James G. Hellmuth. LC 83-15337. 248p. 1985. 50.00 o.p. (ISBN 0-932648-47-9). Boardroom.

Finding Our Father. Diogenes Allen. LC 73-16917. 128p. 1974. 6.00 o.p. (ISBN 0-8042-0557-4, John Knox). Westminster John Knox.

Finding Out about Life in Britain in the Second World War. Madeline Jones. (Finding Out About Ser.). (Illus.). 72p. (gr. 7-12). 1983. 18.95 o.p. (ISBN 0-7134-3665-4, Pub. by Batsford England). David & Charles.

Finding Out: Conducting & Evaluating Social Research. June A. True. 433p. 1983. pap. text ed. (ISBN 0-534-01168-3). Wadsworth Pub.

Finding the Clown In Yourself. Jack Krall & Jan Kalberer. LC 86-62620. 98p. 1987. pap. 8.95 o.s.i. (ISBN 0-89390-090-7). Resource Pubns.

Finding the Missing Link. Robert Broom. LC 75-11916. 104p. 1975. Repr. of 1951 ed. lib. bdg. 35.00x o.p. (ISBN 0-8371-8141-0, BRFM). Greenwood.

Finding the Old Testament in the New. Henry M. Shires. LC 73-19600. 224p. 1974. 7.50 o.s.i. (ISBN 0-664-20993-9, Westminster). Westminster John Knox.

Finding the Treasure Within You. Jim Lewis. LC 81-70339. 128p. 1982. pap. 4.75 o.p. (ISBN 0-87516-469-2). DeVorss.

Finding True North. W. M. Ransom. LC 73-92744. 51p. 1973. pap. 5.00 o.p. (ISBN 0-914742-02-7). Copper Canyon.

Finding Your Job, 6 units. Finney Company. Incl. Unit IC. 1980. (ISBN 0-912486-45-7); Unit 2B. 1974 (ISBN 0-912486-11-2); Unit 3B. 1975 (ISBN 0-912486-12-0); Unit 4B. 1977 (ISBN 0-912486-31-7); Unit 5B. 1978 (ISBN 0-912486-40-6); Unit 6B. 1979 (ISBN 0-912486-42-2). LC 66-40358. (Illus.). (gr. 7 up). Set. 207.00 o.p. (ISBN 0-912486-09-0); 34.50 ea o.p. Finney Co.

Finding Your Roots. Jeane E. Westin. LC 76-62675. 1985. pap. 3.95 o.s.i. (ISBN 0-345-32554-0). Ballantine.

Findings: A Book of Poems. Richard Howard. LC 71-145629. 1971. pap. 3.95 o.s.i. (ISBN 0-689-10391-3, Atheneum). Macmillan.

Titles

Findings of Research in Miscue Analysis: Classroom Implications. Ed. by P. David Allen & Dorothy J. Watson. LC 76-45092. 1976. 11.25 o.p. (ISBN 0-8141-1733-3). NCTE.

Fine. Samuel Shem. 1986. pap. 3.95 o.p. (ISBN 0-440-12510-3). Dell.

Fine & Pleasant Misery. Patrick F. McManus. 1982. pap. 6.25 o.s.i. (ISBN 0-03-059172-4). H Holt & Co.

Fine Art of Food. David W. Steadman. (Illus.). 1974. 1.00 o.p. (ISBN 0-915478-43-9). Galleries Coll.

Fine Book Binding in the Twentieth Century. Roy H. Lewis. LC 84-9375. (Illus.). 148p. 1985. 29.95 o.p. (ISBN 0-668-06084-0, 6084). Arco.

Fine Companion. Shakerly Marmion. Ed. by Richard Sonnershein & Stephen Orgel. LC 78-66827. (Renaissance Drama Ser.). 1979. lib. bdg. 40.00 o.p. (ISBN 0-8240-9731-9). Garland Pub.

Fine Crochet Lace. Nihon Vogue Staff. LC 81-85009. (Illus.). 90p. 1982. pap. 11.95 o.p. (ISBN 0-87040-503-9). Japan Pubns USA.

Fine Fresh Food-Fast. Michele Urvater. Ed. by Richard Atcheson. LC 81-68836. (Great American Cooking Schools Ser.). (Illus.). 84p. 1981. pap. 5.95 o.p. (ISBN 0-941034-02-X). I Chalmers.

Fine Gossoon: Saga of a Proud Irishman. Ellen M. Hayes. 160p. 1981. 8.00 o.p. (ISBN 0-682-49782-7). Exposition-Phoenix.

Fine-Line Lithography. R. Newman. (Materials Processing Theory & Practice Ser.: Vol. 1). 1980. 131.75 o.p. (ISBN 0-444-85351-0, North-Holland). Elsevier.

Fine Lines: The Best of Ms. Fiction. Ed. by Ruth Sullivan. 256p. 1981. 12.95 o.s.i. (ISBN 0-684-17143-0, ScribT); pap. 5.95 o.s.i. (ISBN 0-684-17650-5). Scribner.

Fine Mechanisms & Precision Instruments, Principles of Design. W. Trylinski. 1971. 130.00 o.p. (ISBN 0-08-006361-6). Pergamon.

Fine Needle Aspiration Biopsy of the Rat Liver - Cytological, Cytochemical & Biochemical Methods: Proceedings of a Workshop on Technique & Application of Fine Needle Aspiration Biology in Experimental Toxicology, Zurich, 1979. Ed. by G. Zbinden. (Illus.). 70p. 1980. 46.00 o.p. (ISBN 0-08-025508-6). Pergamon.

Fine Particulate Pollution. United Nations Economic Commission for Europe. 1979. 35.00 o.p. (ISBN 0-08-023399-6). Pergamon.

Fine Red Rain: An Inspector Porfiry Rostnikov Mystery. Stuart M. Kaminsky. 1987. 14.95 o.p. (ISBN 0-684-18666-7). Scribner.

Fine Structure History of Science: Lessons for Methodology. G. Buchdahl. 1981. pap. 16.25 o.p. (ISBN 0-08-028930-4). Pergamon.

Fine Things. Date not set. (ISBN 0-385-29527-8). Delacorte.

Fine Things. Danielle Steel. 408p. 1987. pap. 18.95 o.p. (ISBN 0-385-29527-8). Delacorte.

Fine Woodworking Techniques One. Fine Woodworking Magazine. (Illus.). 1978. 9.95 o.p. (ISBN 0-918804-02-7, ScribT). Scribner.

Fine Writing see Persian Words in English.

Finer Points of Riding. rev. ed. A. K. Frederiksen. (Illus.). pap. 5.95 o.p. (ISBN 0-85131-323-X, BL2403, Pub. by J A Allen U K). S R Smith Sporting Bks.

Finest Kind: The Fisherman of Gloucester. Kim Bartlett. (Illus.). 1977. 8.95 o.p. (ISBN 0-393-08797-2). Norton.

Finger Acupressure. Pedro Chan. 1976. pap. 3.95 o.p. (ISBN 0-8431-0344-2). Borden.

Fingerboard Foundation for the Classical GNR. Darrel Irving. (Illus.). 96p. (Orig.). 1978. pap. 14.95 o.s.i. (ISBN 0-317-66183-3, Pub. by Calliope Music). Bold Strummer Ltd.

Fingermath, Bk. 1. Peter K. Gurau & E. A. Lieberthal. 1979. text ed. 5.72 pupil's ed. o.p. (ISBN 0-07-025221-1). McGraw.

Fingerprints & Other Stories. Seth Gilkerson. 1979. 8.00 o.p. (ISBN 0-682-49430-5). Exposition-Phoenix.

Fingerprints: History, Law & Romance. George W. Wilton. LC 70-164057. 340p. 1971. Repr. of 1938 ed. 43.00x o.p. (ISBN 0-8103-3755-X). Gale.

Fingertip Reference for Dental Materials. Sandra P. Hall & Felice L. Hirsch. LC 79-54689. (Dental Assisting Ser.). 161p. 1981. pap. text ed. 14.95 o.p. (ISBN 0-8273-1863-4). Delmar.

Finishing Technology. rev. ed. George A. Soderberg. (gr. 10-12). 1969. text ed. 21.28 o.p. (ISBN 0-87345-016-7). Glencoe.

Finishing Touches. Thomas Tessier. LC 85-18683. 256p. 1986. 14.95 o.p. (ISBN 0-689-11746-9, Atheneum). Macmillan.

Finist the Falcon Prince. Tr. by Lydia Regehr. LC 72-186860. (Illus.). 40p. (gr. 2-5). 1973. PLB 4.95g o.p. (ISBN 0-87614-032-0). Carolrhoda Bks.

Finite Element & Allied Methods for Reactor Physics & Shielding Calculations: Proceedings of a Seminar Held at the Inperial College of Science & Technology, London, U. K., 18-20th September 1985. Ed. by A. J. Goddard. 200p. 1986. pap. 100.00 o.p. (ISBN 0-08-034128-4, PBL). Pergamon.

Finite Element Approximation of the Navier-Stokes Equations. rev. ed. V. Girault & P. A. Raviart. (Lecture Notes in Mathematics Ser.: Vol. 749). 202p. 1979. pap. 17.00 o.p. (ISBN 0-387-09557-8). Springer-Verlag.

Finite Element Computational Fluid Mechanics. A. J. Baker. 544p. 1983. text ed. 48.95 o.p. (ISBN 0-07-003465-6). McGraw.

Finite Element Method for Elliptic Problems. P. G. Ciarlet. (Studies in Mathematics & Its Applications: Vol. 4). 530p. 1978. 110.75 o.p. (ISBN 0-444-85028-7, North-Holland); pap. 44.75 o.p. (ISBN 0-444-86016-9). Elsevier.

Finite Element Method: Fundamentals & Applications. Ed. by Douglas H. Norrie & Gerard DeVries. 1973. 71.00 o.p. (ISBN 0-12-521650-5). Acad Pr.

Finite Element Methods for Convection Dominated Flows, Bk. No. G00151. Ed. by T. J. Hughes. LC 90-75379. (Applied Mechanics Division Ser.: Vol. 34). 240p. 1979. 30.00 o.p. (ISBN 0-686-62956-6). ASME.

Finite Element Methods in Radiation Physics: Proceedings of the International Seminar, Imperial College of Science Technology, UK. Williams. Ed. by A. J. Goddard. 160p. 1981. pap. 45.00 o.p. (ISBN 0-08-028694-1). Pergamon.

Finite Elements in Geomechanics. G. Gudehus. (Wiley Series in Numerical Methods in Engineering). 573p. 1977. 135.00 o.p. (ISBN 0-471-99446-4). Wiley.

Finite Geometries. P. Dembowski. (Ergebnisse Er Mathematik und Ihrer Grenzgebiete: Vol. 44). 1968. 43.70 o.p. (ISBN 0-387-04100-1). Springer-Verlag.

Finite Markov Processes & Applications. Marius Iosifescu. LC 79-42726. 295p. 1980. 63.95x o.p. (ISBN 0-471-27677-4). Wiley.

Finite Mathematics. Martin Eisen & Carole Eisen. 1979. text ed. write for info. o.p. (ISBN 0-02-472450-5). Macmillan.

Finite Mathematics. 3rd ed. Margaret L. Lial & Charles D. Miller. 1985. text ed. write for info. o.p. (ISBN 0-673-18023-9). Scott F.

Finite Mathematics: An Elementary Approach. 2nd ed. Lawrence Gilligan & Robert B. Nenno. 1979. text ed. write for info. o.p. (ISBN 0-673-16235-4). Scott F.

Finite Mathematics & Its Applications. 2nd ed. Larry J. Goldstein & David Schneider. (Illus.). 528p. 1984. pap. text ed. (ISBN 0-13-317313-5). P-H.

Finite Mathematics & Its Applications. Robert E. Rector & Earl J. Zwick. LC 78-69547. (Illus.). 1979. text ed. 29.95 o.p. (ISBN 0-395-27206-8). HM.

Finite Mathematics: For Business & Social Science. William J. Adams. LC 73-84448. 368p. 1974. 22.50 o.p. (ISBN 0-536-00986-4). Krieger.

Finite Mathematics for Business, Economics, & Social Science. James Radlow. LC 78-13783. (Illus.). 1979. write for info. o.p. (ISBN 0-87872-182-7, Duxbury Pr). PWS-Kent Pub.

Finite Mathematics for the Managerial, Social, & Life Sciences. Lane F. Hardy. (Illus.). 559p. 1984. text ed. 39.75 o.p. (ISBN 0-314-77900-0). West Pub.

Finite Mathematics with Applications. John J. Costello et al. 524p. 1981. text ed. 20.75 o.p. (ISBN 0-15-527400-7, HC). HarBraceJ.

Finite Mathematics with BASIC: A Liberal Arts Approach. Rev. ed. Irving A. Dodes. LC 78-31505. (Illus.). 372p. 1981. lib. bdg. 23.00 o.p. (ISBN 0-88275-862-4). Krieger.

Finite Resources & the Human Future: Population-Food-Energy. Ed. by Ian G. Barbour et al. LC 76-3864. 144p. 1976. pap. 4.75 o.p. (ISBN 0-8066-1526-5, 10-2325, Augsburg). Augsburg Fortress.

Finite Simple Groups: Proceedings. London Mathematical Society Instructional Conference Staff. Ed. by M. B. Powell & G. Higman. 1971. 60.50 o.p. (ISBN 0-12-563850-7). Acad Pr.

Finite State Markovian Decision Processes. Cyrus Derman. (Mathematics in Science & Engineering Ser.: Vol. 67). 1970. 54.50 o.p. (ISBN 0-12-209250-3). Acad Pr.

Finite Strip Method in Structural Analysis. Y. K. Cheung. Ed. by B. G. Neal. 130p. 1976. text ed. 47.00 o.p. (ISBN 0-08-018308-5). Pergamon.

Finlandia: Pictures of Finland. K. Siikala. (Illus.). 1981. 65.00 o.p. (ISBN 951-26-2039-1). E J Brill USA.

Finn the Wolfhound. A. J. Dawson. LC 63-7894. (gr. 7-9). 1966. pap. 0.75 o.p. (ISBN 0-15-630998-X, VoyB). HarBraceJ.

Finnegans Wake Gazetteer. Louis O. Mink. LC 77-74443. 600p. 1978. 27.50x o.p. (ISBN 0-253-32210-3). Ind U Pr.

Finnish Conversational Exercises: Elementary Level. V. Kallioinen. 1974. pap. 11.50 o.p. (ISBN 9-5171-7028-9). E J Brill USA.

Finnish-English, English-Finnish Dictionary. 2nd, rev. ed. A. Wuolle. (Eng. & Finnish.). text ed. 30.00 o.p. (ISBN 951-99126-1-4). E J Brill USA.

Finnish-English General Dictionary. R. Hurme et al. 1446p. 1984. 135.00x o.p. (ISBN 951-0-12157-6, F575). Vanous.

Finnish Folk Poetry: Epic. Matti Kuusi et al. (Illus.). 1977. lib. bdg. 35.00x o.p. (ISBN 0-7735-0289-0, McGill Canada). U of Toronto Pr.

Finnish for Foreigners, Pt. 3. Aalitio Reader. 1975. pap. 18.50x o.p. (ISBN 9-5110-1919-8, F-566). Vanous.

Finnish for Foreigners, Pt. 1: Lessons 1-25. M. J. Aaltio. (Illus.). 236p. 1985. pap. text ed. 22.00x o.p. (F561); 2 Cassettes 52.50x o.p. (F552). Vanous.

Finnish for Foreigners: Pt 2, Lessons 26 to 40. 8th rev. ed. M-H Aaltio. (Illus.). 192p. 1976. pap. text ed. 20.00x o.p. (ISBN 95-110-1483-8, F 562). Vanous.

Finnish General Dictionary: English-Finnish. 2nd ed. R. Hurme & M. Pesonen. 1984. 135.00x o.p. (ISBN 9-5100-8553-7, F-565). Vanous.

Finnish Literary Reader. Paavo Ravila. LC 65-63019. (Uralic & Altaic Ser.: Vol. 44). (Orig.). 1965. pap. text ed. 7.95x o.p. (ISBN 0-87750-012-6). Res Ctr Lang Semiotic.

Finnish-Soviet Armistice Negotiations of 1944. Thede Palm. 160p. (Orig.). 1971. pap. text ed. 16.50x o.p. Coronet Bks.

Finnish Structural Sketch. Robert T. Harms. LC 64-64593. (Uralic & Altaic Ser: Vol. 42). (Orig.). 1964. pap. text ed. 3.00x o.p. (ISBN 0-87750-011-8). Res Ctr Lang Semiotic.

Finno-Ugric, Siberian Mythology. Uno Holmberg. (Mythology of All Races Ser: Vol. Iv). (Illus.). Repr. of 1932 ed. 30.00x o.p. (ISBN 0-8154-0116-7). Cooper Sq.

Fins & the Fifties. Mike Key & Tony Thacker. (Illus.). 128p. 1988. 19.95 o.p. (ISBN 0-85045-810-2, Pub. by Osprey England). Motorbooks Intl.

Fior, Son of the King. Jenny Robertson. LC 76-27080. (gr. 4 up). 1976. pap. 2.25 o.p. (ISBN 0-8066-1559-1, 10-2330, Augsburg). Augsburg Fortress.

Fiorello LaGuardia. Ida Meltzer. (American Destiny Ser.: Italian Americans). (Illus.). (gr. 4-12). 1979. of 10 12.95 set o.p. (ISBN 0-87594-188-5). Book Lab.

Fir-Flower Tablets. Tr. by Florence Ayscough & Amy Lowell. LC 73-862. (China Studies: From Confucius to Mao Ser.). (Illus.). xcv, 227p. 1973. Repr. of 1921 ed. 23.50 o.s.i. (ISBN 0-88355-058-X). Hyperion Conn.

Fire. John W. Lyons. LC 85-2185. (Scientific American Library). (Illus.). 170p. 1987. 32.95 o.p. (ISBN 0-7167-5010-4, Dist. by W H Freeman). Sci Am Bks.

Fire & Arson Photography. Eastman Kodak Company. 1977. pap. 2.50 o.p. (ISBN 0-87985-187-2, M-67). Eastman Kodak.

Fire & Forest Meteorology Conference, 6th: Proceedings. Ed. by Robert E. Martin et al. 304p. (Orig.). 1980. pap. 10.00 o.p. (ISBN 0-939970-20-1). Soc Am Foresters.

Fire & Spirit. Bernie Claus. 64p. 1986. 6.75 o.p. (ISBN 0-8062-2564-5). Carlton.

Fire & Sword in the Sudan. Rudolf C. Slatin. Tr. by Francis R. Wingate. LC 79-82470. 1969. Repr. of 1896 ed. lib. bdg. 33.00x o.p. (ISBN 0-8371-1639-2, SLF&, Pub. by Negro U Pr). Greenwood.

Fire & the Glory: Lafayette & America's Fight for Freedom. Virginia O. Beahrs. LC 76-5848. 190p. 1976. 8.95 o.s.i. (ISBN 0-664-32592-0, Westminster). Westminster John Knox.

Fire & the Gold. Phyllis A. Whitney. 1985. pap. 2.25 o.p. (ISBN 0-449-70059-3, Juniper). Fawcett.

Fire & Water - A Night at the Bar. Dorothy Faircloth. 56p. 1983. 5.50 o.p. (ISBN 0-682-49989-7). Exposition-Phoenix.

Fire Apparatus Practices. 6th ed. IFSTA Committee. Ed. by Gene P. Carlson & Charles Orton. LC 80-82822. 217p. 1980. pap. text ed. 11.00 o.p. (ISBN 0-87939-040-9). Fire Protect Pubns.

Fire Code Inspections & Fire Prevention: What Methods Lead to Success? John R. Hall et al. (Illus.). 122p. (Orig.). 1979. pap. text ed. 7.50 o.p. (ISBN 0-87766-127-8). Urban Inst.

Fire Dawn. Virginia Coffman. LC 76-39720. 1977. 8.95 o.p. (ISBN 0-87795-159-4, Arbor Hse). Morrow.

Fire Demon. Gary Gygax & Flint Dille. (Sagard the Barbarian Gamebooks: No. 4). (YA) (gr. 7 up). pap. 2.25 o.p. (ISBN 0-671-55490-5). Archway.

Fire Department Cartoons. 48p. (ps up). 1.00 o.p. (ISBN 0-913452-07-6). Jesuit Bks.

Fire Department Hydraulics. Eugene F. Mahoney. 1978. 32.67 o.p. (ISBN 0-205-06563-5, 826563). Allyn.

Fire from Within. Carlos Castaneda. 320p. 1984. 17.45 o.p. (ISBN 0-671-49205-5). S&S.

Fire Gospel. Da Free John. 224p. (Orig.). 1982. pap. 14.95 o.s.i. (ISBN 0-913922-73-0). Dawn Horse Pr.

Fire Hazard Analysis from Plastic Insulation in Exterior Walls of Buildings. Donald W. Belles. 1982. 5.35 o.p. (ISBN 0-686-37665-X, TR 82-1). Society Fire Protect.

Fire Hose Practices. International Fire Services Training Association Committee. Ed. by Everett Hudiburg & Charles E. Thomas. (Illus.). 275p. 1974. pap. text ed. 8.00 o.p. (ISBN 0-87939-003-4). Fire Protect Pubns.

Fire in Heaven: A Novel. Malcolm Bosse. 608p. 1986. 18.45 o.p. (ISBN 0-671-47080-9). S&S.

Fire in His Bones. Benson Idahosa. (Orig.). 1986. pap. 4.95 o.p. (ISBN 0-89274-429-4). Harrison Hse.

Fire in the Birdbath & Other Disturbances. William Allen. LC 85-10556. 155p. 1986. 13.45 o.p. (ISBN 0-393-02249-8). Norton.

Fire in the Blood. Mary K. Simmons. 1977. pap. 1.95 o.s.i. (ISBN 0-671-80913-X). PB.

Fire in the Brand: An Introduction to the Creative Work & Theology of John Wesley. Howard A. Slaatte. 1963. 4.00 o.p. (ISBN 0-682-41125-6). Exposition-Phoenix.

Fire in the Embers. Burt Hirschfeld. 1976. pap. 2.75 o.p. (ISBN 0-380-00312-0, 76885). Avon.

Fire in the Morning. Elizabeth Spencer. 288p. 1987. pap. 4.95 o.p. (ISBN 0-380-70105-7). Avon.

Fire Inside. J. L. Williams. 1984. 6.50 o.p. (ISBN 0-89536-654-1, 0634). CSS of Ohio.

Fire Island. Burt Hirschfeld. 512p. 1977. pap. 3.50 o.p. (ISBN 0-380-00232-9, 88104-7). Avon.

Fire of Life: The Smithsonian Book of the Sun. LC 80-28422. (Illus.). 262p. 1981. 24.95 o.p. (ISBN 0-89599-006-7, Dist. by Norton). Smithsonian Bks.

Fire of Sinai. Aaron Soloveitchik. (Annual Fryer Memorial Lecture Ser.). 0.75 o.p. (ISBN 0-914131-20-6, 132). Torah Umesorah.

Fire of Your Life: A Solitude Shared. Maggie Ross. LC 82-61420. 128p. 1983. pap. 6.95 o.p. (ISBN 0-8091-2513-7). Paulist Pr.

Fire on the Earth. Ralph Martin. 1975. pap. 3.50 o.p. (ISBN 0-89283-021-2). Servant.

Fire on the Mountain. Edward Abbey. 192p. 1982. pap. 2.75 o.p. (ISBN 0-380-59519-2, 59519-2, Flare). Avon.

Fire over the Holy Land. Gordon Lindsay. 1.25 o.p. (ISBN 0-89985-185-1). Christ Nations.

Fire Prevention & Inspection. 4th ed. International Fire Service Training Association Staff. Ed. by Everett Hudiburg & Charles Thomas. (Illus.). 182p. 1974. pap. text ed. 8.00 o.p. (ISBN 0-87939-010-7). Fire Protect Pubns.

Fire Problem & Its Solution. Charles V. Walsh. 384p. 1987. 26.95 o.p. (ISBN 0-8062-2927-6). Carlton.

Fire Resistance Manual. 63p. 1984. 3.00 o.p. (GA-600-84). Gypsum Assn.

Fire Service First Aid Practices, IFSTA Committee. 5th ed. Ed. by John Peige et al. LC 77-75409. 269p. 1977. pap. text ed. 11.00 o.p. (ISBN 0-87939-009-3). Fire Protect Pubns.

Fire Song. Roberta Gellis. (General Ser.). 1984. lib. bdg. 18.95 o.p. (ISBN 0-8161-3749-8, Large Print Bks). G K Hall.

Fire! The Library Is Burning! Cytron. Date not set. 10.95 o.p. (ISBN 0-940646-57-9). Rossel Bks.

Fireball. Paul Davies. 1989. 19.95 o.p. (ISBN 0-434-17701-6). Bentley.

Firebird. Tyres. 1987. pap. 3.50 o.p. (ISBN 0-553-26716-7, Spectra). Bantam.

Firebird: A Study of D. H. Lawrence. Dallas Kenmare. 1952. (ISBN 0-8022-0843-6). Philos Lib.

Firebolt. Patrick Clay. (Sargeant Hawk Ser.: No. 5). 240p. (Orig.). 1982. pap. 2.25 o.p. (ISBN 0-8439-1169-7, Pub. by Leisure Bks CT). Dorchester Pub Co.

Firebrand for Justice: A Biography of Louis Dembitz Brandeis. Iris Noble. LC 69-10867. (gr. 7 up). 1969. 4.50 o.s.i. (ISBN 0-664-32431-2, Westminster). Westminster John Knox.

Firebug! Evelyn W. Minshull. LC 74-1366. (gr. 6-9). 1974. 5.50 o.s.i. (ISBN 0-664-32548-3, Westminster). Westminster John Knox.

Fired. Khamal S. Opoku. 132p. 1980. pap. 5.00 o.p. (ISBN 0-682-49636-7). Exposition-Phoenix.

Firefighting & Fires. Currier & Ives Portfolios. (Chronicles of America Ser.). (Illus.). 32p. pap. 4.95 o.p. (ISBN 0-8437-2978-3). Hammond Inc.

Fireflies. Max Bolliger. Tr. by Rosenna Hoover. LC 77-98615. (Illus.). (ps-2). 1970. 4.95 o.p. (ISBN 0-689-20498-1, Atheneum). Macmillan.

Fireflies in the Dark. Tr. by Abdullah Al-Udhari. 1974. saddlestitched in wrappers 1.25 o.p. (ISBN 0-685-78971-3, Pub. by Menard Pr). Small Pr Dist.

Firefleod & Other Stories. Vonda N. McIntyre. 288p. 1979. 10.95 o.p. (ISBN 0-395-28422-8). HM.

Firefly Named Torchy. Bernard Waber. LC 74-122906. (Illus.). (gr. k-3). 1970. reinforced bdg. 9.95 o.p. (ISBN 0-395-18656-0). HM.

Firehouse Mystery. Mary Adrian. (Illus.). (gr. 4-6). 1950. 4.25 o.p. (ISBN 0-395-06536-4). HM.

Firelands Art Review 1977. Joel Rudinger. (Anthology of the Arts Ser.: No. 2). 1977. pap. 3.00x o.p. (ISBN 0-918342-04-X). Cambric.

Firelands Art Review 1978. Ed. by Joel Rudinger. (Cambric Press Anthology of the Arts AA-3). (Illus.). 1978. pap. 3.00x o.p. (ISBN 0-918342-05-8). Cambric.

Firelands Review 1979. Ed. by Joel Rudinger. (Cambric Press Anthology of the Arts: Aa-4). (Illus.). 1979. pap. 3.00x o.p. (ISBN 0-918342-09-0). Cambric.

Fireplaces: How to Build. rev ed. Sunset Editors. LC 79-90337. (Illus.). 96p. 1980. pap. 4.95 o.p. (ISBN 0-376-01155-6, Sunset Bks). Sunset-Lane.

Fireplaces: The Owner-Builder's Guide. Ken Kern & Steve Magers. 1978. pap. 7.95 o.s.i. (ISBN 0-684-15885-X, ScribT). Scribner.

Fires & Human Behaviour. David Canter. LC 79-41489. 338p. 1980. 64.95 o.p. (ISBN 0-471-27709-6, Pub. by Wiley-Interscience). Wiley.

Fires at Midnight. Marie Flasschoen. (Velvet Glove Ser.: No. 12). 176p. 1984. pap. 2.25 o.p. (ISBN 0-380-89482-3). Avon.

Fires in the in-Basket: The ABC's of the State Department. John P. Leacacos. LC 75-36097. 1977. Repr. of 1968 ed. lib. bdg. 35.00x o.p. (ISBN 0-8371-8623-4, LEFI). Greenwood.

Fires of Hell. Harvey R. Saunders. LC 72-164911. 1972. (ISBN 0-8022-2060-6). Philos Lib.

Fires of Spring. James A. Michener. 1984. pap. 4.95 o.p. (ISBN 0-449-20649-1, Crest). Fawcett.

Firesetter in Residential Treatment: Psychological Test Results. 1985. pap. 4.50 o.s.i. (ISBN 0-317-27067-2). Child Welfare.

Fireship. C. Northcote Parkinson. 192p. 1975. 6.95 o.p. (ISBN 0-395-20428-3). HM.

Fireside Reader. Ed. by Reader's Digest Editors. LC 77-76319. (Illus.). 640p. 1978. 17.97 o.p. (ISBN 0-89577-099-7). RD Assn.

Fireweed. Jill P. Walsh. (YA) (gr. 7 up). 1978. pap. 1.50 o.p. (ISBN 0-380-01185-9, 49536-8, Flare). Avon.

Fireworks. Rosemary Edelman. LC 78-72923. 1979. 9.95 o.p. (ISBN 0-87795-213-2, Arbor Hse). Morrow.

Fireworks Source Book: Your Mail Order Guide to Supplies & Services for the Fiber Arts. Bobbi A. McRae. (Illus.). 232p. 1988. pap. 12.95 o.p. (ISBN 0-932620-79-5). Betterway Pubns.

First Advisory Committee Meeting on the Human & Social Development Programme: A Report, Mexico City, Mexico. 1979. UNIPUB.

First Afghan War. Florentia Sale. Ed. by Patrick Macrory. LC 75-373. (Military Memoirs Ser). (Illus.). xix, 186p. 1969. 19.50 o.p. (ISBN 0-208-00830-6, Archon). Shoe String.

First Aid Book. 223p. 1980. pap. 7.00 o.p. (ISBN 0-318-11720-7, S/N 029-017-00003-4). USGPO.

First Aid Book. Alton L. Thygerson. (Illus.). 288p. 1982. pap. text ed. 20.33 o.p. (ISBN 0-13-318006-9). P-H.

First Aid for Backpackers & Campers. Lowell J. Thomas & Joy L. Sanderson. LC 77-212197. (Illus.). 1979. 8.95 o.p. (ISBN 0-03-021106-9); pap. 3.95 o.p. (ISBN 0-03-021111-5). H Holt & Co.

First Aid for Boaters & Divers. Sea Grant. 128p. 1980. pap. 6.95 o.p. (ISBN 0-8329-1425-8). New Century.

First Aid for Health Emergencies. 3rd ed. Brent Q. Hafen. 604p. pap. text ed. 26.50 o.p. (ISBN 0-314-78012-2). West Pub.

First Aid for House Plants. Shirley Ross. LC 75-37763. 175p. 1976. (ISBN 0-07-053869-7); pap. text ed. 6.95 o.p. (ISBN 0-07-053868-9). McGraw.

First Aid for Hypochondriacs. James Gorman. LC 82-60060. (Illus.). 160p. 1982. 4.95 o.s.i. (ISBN 0-89480-173-2, 489). Workman Pub.

First Aid Manual for Chemical Accidents: For Use with Nonpharmaceutical Chemicals. Ed. by M. J. Lefevre. Tr. by Solvay American Corporation & Ernest I. Becker. LC 80-17518. 218p. 1982. pap. 24.95 o.s.i. (ISBN 0-87933-336-7). Van Nos Reinhold.

First Amendment in the Federal Courts: Freedom of Speech & the Press. Alva W. Stewart. (Public Administration Ser.: P 1780). 11p. 1985. 2.00 o.p. (ISBN 0-89028-580-2). Vance Biblios.

First American Peace Movement. Incl. War Inconsistent with the Religion of Jesus Christ. David L. Dodge; Lawfulness of War for Christians Examined. James Mott; Solemn Review of the Custom of War. Noah Worcester. LC 73-147428. (Library of War & Peace; Proposals for Peace: a History). 1973. lib. bdg. 46.00 o.p. (ISBN 0-8240-0220-2). Garland Pub.

First among Equals. Jeffrey Archer. 1984. 16.45 o.p. (ISBN 0-671-50406-1, Linden Pr). S&S.

First among Equals. Jeffrey Archer. (General Ser.). 1984. lib. bdg. 17.95 o.p. (ISBN 0-8161-3758-7, Large Print Bks); pap. 10.95 o.s.i. (ISBN 0-8161-3778-1). G K Hall.

First & Last Gravelsburg Spelling Bee. Marian Bartch et al. 48p. 1986. 5.95 o.p. Carlton.

First & Second Kings, a Commentary. rev. ed. 2nd ed. John Gray. LC 73-134271. (Old Testament Library). (Illus.). 826p. 1978. 27.50 o.s.i. (ISBN 0-664-20898-3, Westminster). Westminster John Knox.

First & Second Samuel, A Commentary. Hans W. Hertzberg. LC 65-10074. (Old Testament Library). 416p. 1965. 22.95 o.s.i. (ISBN 0-664-20541-0, Westminster). Westminster John Knox.

First Annual Educational Conference on Prepaid Legal Services: October Nineteen Eighty-One. 1981. 95.00 o.p. (ISBN 0-317-40262-5, 3-007); 16 tapes avail. o.p. Am Prepaid.

First Annual Family Law Institute. 152p. 1983. 7.00 o.p. (ISBN 0-318-02388-1). ICLE Georgia.

First Assessment of Reading, 1970-71: Assessment, Released Exercise Set. National Assessment of Educational Progress Staff. 331p. 1979. Repr. of 1973 ed. 10.35 o.p. (ISBN 0-318-13993-6, Natl Assessment Ed Progress). Ed Comm States.

First Astrowitches. Marian T. Place. (gr. 3-7). 1985. pap. 2.50 o.p. (ISBN 0-380-70056-5, Camelot). Avon.

First Australians. Ronald Berndt & Catherine Berndt. (Illus.). 144p. 1954. (ISBN 0-8022-0114-8). Philos Lib.

First Baron Herbert of Cherbury. Herbert Edward. Ed. by Rene Wellek. (British Philosophers & Theologians of the 17th & 18th Centuries Ser.). 1979. 51.00 o.p. (ISBN 0-8240-1779-X). Garland Pub.

First Blood: The Story of Fort Sumter. W. A. Swanberg. (Illus.). 384p. 1984. pap. 12.95 o.p. (ISBN 0-684-18200-9, ScribT). Scribner.

First Boer War. Joseph Lehmann. (Echoes of War Ser.). 1987. pap. 10.95 o.p. (ISBN 0-907675-53-0, Pub. by Buchan & Enright England). Seven Hills Bk Dists.

First Book of Animal Life: First Nature Book. Cork Wheeler. (gr. 2-5). 1982. 10.95 o.p. (ISBN 0-86020-632-7, Usbore-Hayes). EDC.

First Book of Josef: An Introduction to Computer Programming. Ivan Tomek. (Illus.). 320p. 1983. pap. 23.95 o.p. (ISBN 0-13-318287-8). P-H.

First Book of the Cabinet of the President of the U. S. James Eichner. LC 69-11536. (First Bks). (gr. 4-6). PLB 6.45 o.p. (ISBN 0-531-00491-0). Watts.

First Book of the Civil War. rev. ed. Dorothy Levenson. LC 77-7153. (First Bks.). (Illus.). (gr. 4-7). 1977. lib. bdg. 10.40 s&l o.p. (ISBN 0-531-01291-3). Watts.

First Born. John Katzenbach. LC 83-45078. 320p. 1984. 14.95 o.s.i. (ISBN 0-689-11404-4, Atheneum). Macmillan.

First Canadian-American Conference on Hydrogeology: Proceedings. 1985. 43.75 o.p. (ISBN 0-318-23042-9). Natl Water Well.

First Casualty: From the Crimea to Vietnam: The War Correspondent As Hero, Propagandist, & Myth Maker. Phillip Knightley. LC 75-11684. (Illus.). 465p. 1975. 12.95 o.p. (ISBN 0-15-131264-8). HarBraceJ.

First Catch Your Tiger. Oliver Graham-Jones. LC 72-8320. 1973. 7.95 o.s.i. (ISBN 0-8008-2739-2). Taplinger.

First Certification of Changes to Schedules to the General Agreement on Tariffs & Trade. 154p. (Orig., Eng. & Fr.). 1969. pap. 8.50 o.p. (ISBN 0-685-20807-9, G43, GATT). UNIPUB.

First Child, Second Child: Your Birth Order Profile. Wilson & Edington. 1981. text ed. 12.95 o.p. (ISBN 0-07-070756-1). McGraw.

First Christians: Their Beginnings, Writings, & Beliefs. Eduard Lohse. LC 82-7454. 128p. (Orig.). 1983. pap. 1.95 o.p. (ISBN 0-8006-1646-4, 1-1646, Fortress). Augsburg Fortress.

First Christmas: The True & Unfamiliar Story in Words & Pictures. Paul L. Maier. LC 76-163162. (Illus.). 1971. 10.45i o.p. (ISBN 0-06-065396-5). HarpR.

First Circuits Course for Engineering Technology. Charles Belove. 1982. text ed. 32.95 o.p. (ISBN 0-03-057851-5). HR&W.

First Collected Insights of the Prophet O. C. O. C. Smith, Jr. 1978. 4.00 o.p. (ISBN 0-682-48784-8). Exposition-Phoenix.

First Corinthians. (Erdmans Commentaries Ser.). pap. 3.95 o.p. (ISBN 0-8010-3394-2). Baker Bk.

First Corinthians: A Translation with Notes. Paul R. Caudill. LC 82-71220. 1983. 5.95 o.p. (ISBN 0-8054-1391-X). Broadman.

First Course in College Mathematics. 4th ed. Margaret Willerding. 1980. text ed. 28.00 o.p. (ISBN 0-87150-285-2, Prindle); pap. text ed. PWS-Kent Pub.

First Course in Differential Equations with Applications. 2nd ed. Dennis G. Zill. 540p. 1982. text ed. write for info. o.p. (ISBN 0-87150-319-0, 33L-2514, Prindle). PWS-Kent Pub.

First Course in Geometry: A Modern Textbook for the High School. Myrtle Edwards. 1965. text ed. 7.50 o.p. (ISBN 0-682-43014-5, University). Exposition-Phoenix.

First Course in Linear Algebra. Raymond A. Beauregard & John B. Fraleigh. LC 72-5648. 1973. text ed. 27.95 o.p. (ISBN 0-395-14017-X). HM.

First Course in Linear Algebra. P. B. Bhattacharya et al. 190p. 1983. pap. 23.95x o.p. (ISBN 0-470-27442-5). Halsted Pr.

First Course in Linear Regression. 2nd ed. MarySue Younger. 1985. text ed. write for info. o.p. (ISBN 0-87150-865-6, 36G5030, Duxbury Pr). PWS-Kent Pub.

First Course in Probability. 2nd ed. Sheldon Ross. 400p. 1984. text ed. write for info. o.p. (ISBN 0-02-403910-1). Macmillan.

First Course in Programming with Pascal. Bert Mendelson. 385p. 1982. scp 20.75 o.p. (ISBN 0-205-07823-0, 207823). Wm C Brown.

First Course in Quantum Mechanics. rev. ed. H. Clark. 1982. pap. 14.95 o.p. (ISBN 0-442-30173-1). Van Nos Reinhold.

First Course in Written & Spoken German: A Review & Exercise Book. 2nd ed. Edwin Zeydel. 1948. text ed. 9.95x o.p. (ISBN 0-8290-2365-8); pap. text ed. 4.95x o.p. (ISBN 0-89197-560-8). Irvington.

First Course on Electrical Drives. S. K. Pillai. LC 82-224149. 208p. 1982. 17.95 o.p. (ISBN 0-470-27531-6). Halsted Pr.

First Crossing: A Personal Log. Malcolm McConnell & Carol McConnell. LC 83-42681. 1983. 18.45 o.p. (ISBN 0-393-03282-5). Norton.

First Days at School: A Co-operative Reader for Child & Adult. Marion J. Kaminkow. 58p. 1985. pap. 5.00 o.p. (ISBN 0-317-43216-8). Magna Carta Bk.

First Days of Life. Russell Freedman. LC 74-7573. (Illus.). 64p. (gr. 3-6). 1974. 5.50 o.p. (ISBN 0-8234-0249-5). Holiday.

First Easter: The True & Unfamiliar Story in Words & Pictures. Paul L. Maier. LC 72-81346. (Illus.). 1973. 10.95i o.p. (ISBN 0-06-065397-3). HarpR.

First Editions of John Buchan: A Collector's Bibliography. Robert G. Blanchard. LC 81-10902. x, 246p. 1981. 35.00 o.p. (ISBN 0-208-01905-7, Archon). Shoe String.

First Elizabeth. Carolly Erickson. 464p. 1983. 19.25 o.s.i. (ISBN 0-671-41746-0). Summit Bks.

First Emancipation: The Abolition of Slavery in the North. Arthur Zilversmit. LC 67-15954. 1971. pap. text ed. 2.75 o.s.i. (ISBN 0-226-98332-3, P398, Phoen). U of Chicago Pr.

First Emperor of China: The Greatest Archeological Find of Our Time. Arthur Cotterell. LC 81-4347. (Illus.). 208p. 1981. 25.00 o.p. (ISBN 0-03-059889-3). H Holt & Co.

First Encounter. John Dos Passos. (ISBN 0-8022-0411-2). Philos Lib.

First Epistle of St. Peter. 2nd ed. Edward G. Selwyn. (Thornapple Commentaries Ser.). 517p. 1981. pap. 14.95 o.p. (ISBN 0-8010-8199-8). Baker Bk.

First Epistle to the Corinthians. Eugen Walter. Ed. by John L. McKenzie. LC 81-605. (New Testament for Spiritual Reading Ser.). 200p. 1981. 10.00 o.p.; pap. 4.95 o.s.i. Crossroad NY.

First Experiments in Psychology. John M. Gardiner & Zofia Kaminska. (Essential Psychology Ser.). 1975. pap. 4.50x o.p. (ISBN 0-416-81690-8, NO. 2732). Routledge Chapman & Hall.

First Family: George Washington & His Intimate Relations. Miriam A. Bourne. (Illus.). 160p. 1982. 14.95 o.p. (ISBN 0-393-01531-9). Norton.

First Family Paper Doll & Cut Out Book. Jim Fitzgerald & John Boswell. (Orig.). 1981. pap. 4.95 o.p. (ISBN 0-440-52632-9, Dell Trade Pbks). Dell.

First FGGE Results from Satellites. Ed. by T. Tanczer. (Advances in Space Research: Vol. 1, No. 4). (Illus.). 331p. 1981. pap. 48.00 o.p. (ISBN 0-08-027160-X). Pergamon.

First Fifty Years: The Cleveland Museum of Art 1916-1966. Carl Wittke. LC 66-21227. (Illus.). 176p. 1966. 10.00x o.p. (ISBN 0-910386-09-9, Pub. by Cleveland Mus Art). Ind U Pr.

First Firefly: New Poems & Prose. Melville Cane. LC 73-16006. 1974. 5.95 o.p. (ISBN 0-15-131280-X). HarBraceJ.

First Five Years: Dr. Hugh Jolly Answers Questions from Parents. Hugh Jolly. (Winston Family Handbooks Ser.). 96p. (Orig.). 1985. pap. 9.95 o.p. (ISBN 0-86683-848-1, AY8493). HarpR.

First Four Books of Poems: Including a Mask for Janus, the Dancing Bear, Green with Beasts, the Drunk in the Furnace. W. S. Merwin. LC 75-4079. 288p. 1975. 12.50 o.p. (ISBN 0-689-10668-8, Atheneum); pap. 10.95 o.s.i. (ISBN 0-689-10694-7). Macmillan.

First Franciscans & the Gospel. Duane V. Lapsanski. 1976. 6.95 o.p. (ISBN 0-8199-0568-2). Franciscan Herald.

First French Republic, Seventeen Ninety-Two to Eighteen Four. M. J. Sydenham. 1974. 40.00x o.p. (ISBN 0-520-02577-6). U of Cal Pr.

First Generation: The School & Society in Early Australia. John F. Cleverley. LC 72-166084. 168p. 1971. 21.00x o.p. (ISBN 0-424-06230-5, Pub. by Sydney U Pr); pap. 16.00x o.p. (ISBN 0-424-06250-X, Pub. by Sydney U Pr). Intl Spec Bk.

First Harvest: An Institute for Policy Studies Reader, 1963-1983. Ed. by John S. Friedman. LC 83-48306. 368p. 1983. 22.50 o.s.i. (ISBN 0-394-53501-4, GP-879). Grove.

First Harvest: An Institute for Policy Studies Reader, 1963-1983. Ed. by John S. Friedman. LC 83-48306. 368p. 1983. pap. 8.95 o.p. (ISBN 0-394-62491-2, E870, Ever). Grove.

First Industrial Nation: An Economic History of Britain, 1700-1914. 2nd ed. Peter Mathias. 480p. 1983. 30.00 o.p. (ISBN 0-416-33290-0, NO. 3831); pap. 12.95 o.p. (ISBN 0-416-33300-1, NO. 3830). Routledge Chapman & Hall.

First International Congress on Clinical Pharmacy Education: Proceedings July 13-16, Minneapolis, Minnesota, 1976. LC 76-75010. 1976. 6.00 o.p. (ISBN 0-937526-04-5). AACP Alexandria.

First Iron-Clad Naval Engagement in the World: The Merrimac & the Monitor. Elsberry V. White. (Illus.). 1906. wrappers 15.00x o.p. (ISBN 0-686-17397-X). R S Barnes.

First Joint Robots Conference: Proceedings of the International Conference on Industrial Robot Technology, 3rd, University of Nottingham, Eng., March 1976. International Conference on Industrial Robot Technology Staff & International Symposium on Industrial Robots, 6th, Univ. Nottingham, Eng., Mar. 1976. Ed. by T. E. Brock. 530p. 1977. softbound 75.00x o.p. (ISBN 0-685-89046-5). Scholium Intl.

First Labour Party Nineteen Six to Nineteen Fourteen. Ed. by K. D. Brown. LC 85-4190. 297p. 1985. 31.00 o.p. (ISBN 0-7099-3209-X, Pub. by Croom Helm Ltd). Routledge Chapman & Hall.

First LACUS Forum: Proceedings. Linguistic Association of Canada & the U. S. Staff. Ed. by Adam Makkai & Valerie Makkai. 1974. pap. text ed. 12.95 o.s.i. (ISBN 0-917496-04-3). Hornbeam Pr.

First Ladies. 3rd ed. Margaret B. Klapthor. LC 81-50261. 91p. 1981. 8.00 o.p. (ISBN 0-318-11783-5, S/N 066-000-00009-5). USGPO.

First Ladies of the Restoration. Frances H. Mulliken. 1985. pap. 6.50 o.p. (ISBN 0-8309-0419-0). Herald Hse.

First Lady from Plains. Rosalynn Carter. LC 84-548. (Illus.). 357p. 1984. 17.45 o.s.i. (ISBN 0-395-35294-0). HM.

First Lessons in Beekeeping. Dadant & Sons Inc., Staff. (Illus.). 128p. 1982. pap. 4.95 o.s.i. (ISBN 0-684-17423-5, ScribT). Scribner.

First Lessons in Beekeeping. rev. ed. Dadant & Sons, Inc., Staff & C. P. Dadant. (Illus.). 128p. 1980. 7.95 o.s.i. (ISBN 0-684-16747-6, ScribT). Scribner.

First Lessons in Black & White Photography. Michael Simon & Dennis Moore. 239p. 1978. pap. text ed. 21.95x o.p. (ISBN 0-03-021011-9). H Holt & Co.

First Letters. Peter K. Shreck. (Macmillan Learning Window Bks.). (Illus.). 48p. (ps-k). 1982. 7.95 o.s.i. (ISBN 0-02-782590-6). Macmillan.

First Light. Ann G. O'Barr. LC 83-70211. (Orig.). 1984. pap. 5.95 o.p. (ISBN 0-8054-7305-X). Broadman.

First Light: A Novel of a Daughter's Reluctant Understanding of Her Mother's Life. Emily Ellison. LC 84-27237. 256p. 1985. 14.95 o.p. (ISBN 0-688-04949-4). Morrow.

First Light: Sojourns with People of the Outer Hebrides, the Sierra Madre, the Himalayas & Other Remote Places. Ethan Hubbard. LC 85-29894. (Illus.). 200p. 1986. 29.95 o.p. (ISBN 0-930031-04-0). Chelsea Green Pub.

First Lincoln Campaign. Reinhard H. Luthin. 1964. 11.25 o.p. (ISBN 0-8446-1292-8). Peter Smith.

First-Line Management: Approaching Supervision Effectively. 3rd. ed. Lawrence L. Steinmetz & H. Ralph Todd, Jr. 1983. pap. 18.95 o.p. (ISBN 0-256-02883-4). Irwin.

First-Line Management: The Foreman's Role in Manufacturing, Vol. 4. Ed. by Ivan R. Vernon. LC 70-144105. (Manufacturing Management Ser). (Illus.). 1972. text ed. 12.50 o.p. (ISBN 0-87263-028-5). SME.

First Love. Ronald F. Bridges. 1987. 6.95 o.p. (ISBN 0-89109-143-2). NavPress.

First Love & Other Shorts. Samuel Beckett. Tr. by Samuel Beckett from Fr. (Incl. From An Abandoned Work; Enough; Imagination Dead Imagine; Breath; & Not I). 1974. pap. 7.95 o.p. (ISBN 0-394-17850-5, E623, Ever). Grove.

First Love, True Love. Anne Emery. LC 56-5376. 192p. (gr. 7-10). 1956. 8.95 o.s.i. (ISBN 0-664-32140-2, Westminster). Westminster John Knox.

First Mayday: The Haymarket Speeches 1895-1910. Voltairine De Cleyre. (Illus.). 53p. (Orig.). 1982. pap. 2.50 o.p. (ISBN 0-904564-35-5). Left Bank.

First Mishna & the Controversies of the Tannaim. David Hoffmann. Tr. by Paul Forchheimer from German. Incl. Highest Court in the City of Sanctuary. LC 77-98683. 1977. 17.50 o.p. (ISBN 0-87203-072-5). Hermon.

First Morning: New Poems. Peter R. Viereck. LC 70-178791. 120p. 1972. Repr. lib. bdg. 22.50x o.p. (ISBN 0-8371-6284-X, VIFM). Greenwood.

First New Deal. Raymond Moley. LC 66-22282. (Illus.). 1966. 12.50 o.p. (ISBN 0-15-131290-7). HarBraceJ.

First Nine Months of Life. Geraldine L. Flanagan. 1962. 11.95 o.s.i. (ISBN 0-671-26105-3). S&S.

First of All. McCullough. 1981. pap. 5.95 o.s.i. (ISBN 0-03-050941-6). H Holt & Co.

First of All Persons: A New Look at Men-Women Relationships. Elizabeth S. Genne & William H. Genne. (Orig.). 1973. pap. 1.95 o.p. (ISBN 0-377-03041-4). Friendship Pr.

First of Midnight. Marjorie Darke. LC 77-13435. 192p. (gr. 6 up). 1979. 6.95 o.p. (ISBN 0-395-28854-1, Clarion). HM.

First on Everest: The Mystery of Mallory & Irvine. Tom Holzel & Audrey Salkeld. 1986. 19.95 o.p. (ISBN 0-8050-0303-7). H Holt & Co.

First on Mars, No. 18. Rex Gordon. (Science Fiction Rediscovery Ser.). 1976. pap. 2.45 o.p. (ISBN 0-380-00572-7, 28084-1). Avon.

First on the Land: The North Carolina Indians. Ruth Y Wetmore. LC 74-84151. (Illus.). 196p. 1977. 10.95 o.p. (ISBN 0-910244-80-4). Blair.

First Orchid for Pat. Anne Emery. (gr. 5-9). 1957. 5.50 o.s.i. (ISBN 0-664-32174-7, Westminster). Westminster John Knox.

First-Order Categorical Logic: Model-Theoretical Methods in the Theory of Topoi & Related Categories. M. Makkai & G. Reyes. LC 77-13221. (Lecture Notes in Mathematics: Vol. 611). 1977. pap. text ed. 22.00 o.p. (ISBN 0-387-08439-8). Springer-Verlag.

First-Order Logic. R. M. Smullyan. LC 68-13495. (Ergebnisse der Mathematik und Ihrer Grenzgebiete: Vol. 43). 1968. Repr. 23.00 o.p. (ISBN 0-387-04099-4). Springer-Verlag.

First Overland Mail. Robert Pinkerton. (Landmark Ser.: No. 40). (Illus.). (gr. 4-6). 1963. lib. bdg. 8.99 o.s.i. (ISBN 0-394-90340-4). Random.

First Palenque Round Table, 1973, Part 2. Ed. by Merle Greene Robertson. LC 74-83484. (Palenque Round Table Ser.: Vol. II). (Illus.). 143p. (Orig.). 1974. pap. text ed. 15.00x o.p. (ISBN 0-292-76465-0, Stevenson Sch). U of Tex Pr.

First Paperback Poets Anthology. Roger McDonald. 1974. 19.95x o.p. (ISBN 0-7022-0916-3); pap. 7.95x o.p. (ISBN 0-7022-0917-1). U of Queensland Pr.

First Penthouse Dwellers of America. Ruth Underhill. LC 75-23849. (Illus.). 1976. lib. bdg. 15.00x o.p. (ISBN 0-88307-525-3); pap. 4.95 o.p. (ISBN 0-88307-526-1). Gannon.

First Person. Lehman Strauss. LC 67-20931. 1967. 7.95 o.s.i. (ISBN 0-87213-815-1). Loizeaux.

First Person Rural. Hodding Carter. LC 77-10014. 1977. Repr. lib. bdg. 35.00x o.p. (ISBN 0-8371-9727-9, CAFI). Greenwood.

First Person Rural: Essays of a Sometime Farmer. Noel Perrin. LC 77-94109. (Illus.). 144p. 1978. 8.95 o.s.i. (ISBN 0-87923-232-3). Godine.

First Person Singular: A Review of the Life & Work of Mr. Sherlock Holmes, the Worlds First Consulting Detective. Roger Butters. 1984. 10.00 o.p. (ISBN 0-533-05646-2). Vantage.

First Peter, 2 vols. John Brown. 1980. 39.95 o.p. (ISBN 0-85151-204-6); Vol. 1, 577 Pp. (ISBN 0-85151-205-4); Vol. 2, 640 Pp. (ISBN 0-85151-206-2). Banner of Truth.

First Peter see Word Studies in the Greek New Testament, for the English Reader.

First Peter: An Expositional Commentary. D. Edmond Hiebert. 1984. pap. 35.95x o.p. (ISBN 0-8024-0275-5). Moody.

First Philosophers. 2nd ed. George Thomson. (Studies in Ancient Society). (Illus.). 1961-1977. pap. text ed. 7.95 o.p. (ISBN 0-85315-406-6). Humanities.

First Pictorial History of the American Oil & Gas Industry, 1859-1983. Ruth S. Knowles. LC 82-22485. (Illus.). x, 171p. 1983. 15.95 o.p. (ISBN 0-8214-0693-0). Ohio U Pr.

First Place: Skills & Activities for Early Learning. 07/1982 ed. Dorothy Michener & Beverly Muschlitz. LC 82-82050. (Illus.). 96p. (ps-2). pap. text ed. 6.95 o.p. (ISBN 0-86530-057-7, IP 57-7). Incentive Pubns.

First Poems of Childhood. Illus. by Tasha Tudor. LC 67-4523. (Illus.). 24p. (ps-3). 1978. 5.95 o.p. (ISBN 0-448-40505-9, G&D); PLB 3.79 o.p. (ISBN 0-448-13021-1, G&D). Putnam Pub Group.

First Pony. Toni Webber. (Illus.). 96p. 1988. 14.95 o.p. (ISBN 0-7063-6434-1, Pub. by Ward Lock). David & Charles.

First Prayers. Illus. by Anna M. Magagna. LC 82-60742. (Illus.). 64p. (ps-2). 1983. 8.95 o.s.i. (ISBN 0-02-762120-0). Macmillan.

First Pregnancy: An Integrating Principle in Female Psychology. Jellemieke C. Hees-Stauthamer. Ed. by Peter E. Nathan. LC 85-5791. (Research in Clinical Psychology Ser.: No. 13). 190p. 1985. 34.95 o.p. (ISBN 0-8357-1657-0). UMI Res Pr.

First Prize Quilts. Demetra Makris. 1984. 22.45 o.p. (ISBN 0-671-46938-X). S&S.

First Prize Quilts. Dimetra Markis. (Illus.). 1985. pap. 12.95 o.p. (ISBN 0-671-60278-0, Fireside). S&S.

First Psychodramatic Family. J. L. Moreno. pap. 10.00 o.p. Beacon Hse.

First Questions about Transport. Keith Faulkner. (Illus.). 61p. (gr. 2 up). 1986. 11.95 o.p. (ISBN 0-340-32904-1, Pub. by Hodder & Stoughton UK). David & Charles.

First R: Elementary Reading Today. 2nd ed. Wilma H. Miller. LC 76-23175. 1977. pap. text ed. 18.95 o.p. (ISBN 0-03-089877-3, HoltC). HR&W.

First Report of the Commission on Merchant Marine & Defense: Findings & Conclusions, 1987. (Illus., Orig.). 1987. pap. 4.25 o.p. (ISBN 0-318-23748-2, S/N 040-000-00517-0). USGPO.

First Ride. Janice Kaplan. 128p. (YA) (gr. 7 up). 1982. pap. 1.95 o.p. (ISBN 0-380-78055-0, 78055-0, Flare). Avon.

First Rotarian: The Life & Times of Percy Paul Harris, Founder of Rotary. James P. Walsh. Ed. by Harry Treadwell. (Illus.). 351p. 1979. 40.00 o.s.i. E J Brill USA.

First Russian Radical: Alexander Radischev, 1749-1802. David M. Lang. LC 77-5516. (Illus.). 1977. Repr. of 1959 ed. lib. bdg. 35.00x o.p. (ISBN 0-8371-9637-X, LAFRR). Greenwood.

First Season: Advent, Christmas, Epiphany. Wayne Saffen. LC 73-79325. (Illus.). 96p. (Orig.). 1973. pap. 0.50 o.p. (ISBN 0-8006-0166-1, Fortress). Augsburg Fortress.

First, Second & Third Symphonies in Full Orchestral Score. Ludwig van Beethoven. 368p. 1976. pap. 9.95 o.p. (ISBN 0-486-23377-4). Dover.

First Sentences. Peter K. Shreck. (Macmillan Learning Window Bks.). (Illus.). 48p. (ps-k). 1982. 7.95 o.s.i. (ISBN 0-02-782570-1). Macmillan.

First Serve. Mary Towne. LC 76-100. (Illus.). (gr. 5-9). 1976. 6.95 o.p. (ISBN 0-689-30532-X, Atheneum). Macmillan.

First Seven Thousand Years: A Study in Bible Chronology. Charles G. Ozanne. LC 73-114063. (Illus.). 1970. 5.00 o.p. (ISBN 0-682-47084-8, Testament). Exposition-Phoenix.

First Snow. Y. Bryl. 288p. 1982. 9.45 o.p. (ISBN 0-8285-2489-0, Pub. by Progress Pubs USSR). Imported Pubns.

First Special Service Force: A War History of the North Americans 1942-1944. Robert D. Burhans. (Elite Unit Ser.: No. 1). (Illus.). 376p. 1981. Repr. of 1947 ed. 22.00 o.p. (ISBN 0-89839-050-8). Battery Pr.

First Stargazers: An Introduction to the Origins of Astronomy. James Cornell. 1981. 15.95 o.s.i. (ISBN 0-684-16799-9, ScribT). Scribner.

First Steps. John Cusick. 48p. 1984. pap. 2.00 o.p. (ISBN 0-914070-26-6). ACTA Pubns.

First Steps in BASIC. Ray Curnow & Susan Curran. (Clear & Simple Home Computer Ser.: Vol. II). (Illus.). 192p. 1984. pap. 9.50 o.p. (ISBN 0-671-49443-0, Fireside). S&S.

First Steps in Counted Crosstitch. Leslie Linsley. LC 86-16719. (Illus.). 144p. 1987. 19.95 o.p. (ISBN 0-385-19882-5); pap. 12.95 o.p. (ISBN 0-385-24100-3). Doubleday.

First Steps in Quilting. Leslie Linsley. (Illus.). 144p. 1986. 15.95 o.p. (ISBN 0-385-19880-9). Doubleday.

First Steps in Reading & Writing. rev. ed. Jack Wigfield. 192p. 1988. pap. text ed. 7.95 o.p. (ISBN 0-06-632570-6). Newbury Hse.

First Steps in Ritual: Safe, Effective Techniques for Experiencing the Inner Worlds. Dolores Ashcroft-Nowicki. LC 86-18829. 96p. 1986. lib. bdg. 19.95x o.p. (ISBN 0-8095-7010-6). Borgo Pr.

First Steps in Stenciling. Leslie Linsley. LC 86-2108. (Illus.). 144p. 1986. 19.95 o.p. (ISBN 0-385-19879-5); pap. 12.95 o.p. (ISBN 0-385-23801-0). Doubleday.

First Story. Peter K. Shreck. (Macmillan Learning Window Bks.). (Illus.). 48p. (ps-k). 1982. 7.95 o.s.i. (ISBN 0-02-782580-9). Macmillan.

First Strike. Douglas Terman. 1979. 10.95 o.p. (ISBN 0-684-16383-7, ScribT). Scribner.

First Supplement of the Catalogue of the Book Library of the British Film Institute. British Film Inst. Staff. 1983. lib. bdg. 240.00 o.p. (ISBN 0-8161-0388-7, Hall Library). G K Hall.

First Supplement to the Subject Catalogue of the Royal Commonwealth Society. D. H. Simpson. 1977. lib. bdg. 250.00 o.p. (ISBN 0-8161-0075-6, Hall Library). G K Hall.

First the Egg. Louise Moeri. 96p. (gr. 7-10). 1984. pap. text ed. 1.75 o.p. (ISBN 0-671-47525-8). Archway.

First Theory Book. Angela Diller. 1921. pap. 10.95 o.s.i. (ISBN 0-02-870720-6). Schirmer Bks.

First Things First - Meeting the Basic Needs of the People of Nigeria: Report to the Government of Nigeria by a JASPA Basic Needs Mission - Jobs & Skills Programme for Africa. International Labour Office Staff & Jobs & Skills Programme for Africa Staff. x, 256p. (Orig.). 1981. pap. 16.10 o.p. (ISBN 92-2-102682-5). Intl Labour Office.

First Three Internationals: Their History & Lessons. George Novack et al. LC 74-79908. 192p. 1974. 23.00 o.p. (ISBN 0-87348-367-7). Path Pr NY.

First Three Years of Life: A Guide to Physical, Emotional, & Intellectual Growth of Your Baby. Burton L. White. 304p. 1984. pap. 3.95 o.p. (ISBN 0-380-68296-6). Avon.

First-Time Cookbook. Evelyn Rose & Judi Rose. LC 83-61273. 207p. 1984. 9.95 o.p. (ISBN 0-88186-125-1). Parkwest Pubns.

First-Time Investor. Bob Madigan & Lawrence Kasoff. (Illus.). 320p. 1986. text ed. 17.95 o.p. (ISBN 0-13-942384-2). P-h.

First Time Manager. L. Belker. 1983. pap. 9.95 o.p. (ISBN 0-8144-7588-4). AMACOM.

First Time Manager. 2nd ed. Loren B. Belker. LC 78-12993. 1979. 14.95 o.p. (ISBN 0-8144-5492-5). AMACOM.

First to Twenty-First Annual Reports. Massachusetts Anti-Slavery Society. LC 74-91265. 1833-1853. Repr. 70.00x o.p. (ISBN 0-8371-2485-9, MBA&, Pub. by Negro U Pr). Greenwood.

First Voyages. Ed. by Damon Knight et al. 384p. 1981. pap. 2.95 o.p. (ISBN 0-380-77586-7, 77586). Avon.

First Words. Peter K. Shreck. (Macmillan Learning Window Bks.). (Illus.). 48p. (ps-k). 1982. 7.95 o.s.i. (ISBN 0-02-782560-4). Macmillan.

First World Disarmament: And Why It Failed. Lord Noel-Baker. 1979. 10.50 o.p. (ISBN 0-08-023365-1). Pergamon.

First World War. John Ray. (History Broadsheets Ser.). 1976. pap. text ed. 11.50x o.p. (ISBN 0-435-31748-2). Heinemann Ed.

First-Year French: Debuts Culturels. Jeannette Bragger & Robert P. Shupp. LC 77-433. 1977. pap. text ed. 11.75 o.p. (ISBN 0-03-015016-7, HoltC). HR&W.

First Year of Forever. B. D. Van Vechten. LC 82-45171. 224p. 1982. 12.95 o.p. (ISBN 0-689-11317-X, Atheneum). Macmillan.

First Year of Greek. rev. ed. James T. Allen. 1931. text ed. write for info. o.p. (ISBN 0-02-301750-3). Macmillan.

First Year of Life. G. Curtis Jenkins & R. Newton. (Library of General Practice). (Illus.). 260p. 1981. pap. text ed. 21.50 o.p. (ISBN 0-443-01717-4). Churchill.

First Years Together. Ruth Sanford. 140p. (Orig.). 1983. pap. 5.95 o.p. (ISBN 0-89283-134-0). Servant.

First Your Penny. Donna Hill. LC 84-20459. 228p. (gr. 5 up). 1985. 12.95 o.s.i. (ISBN 0-689-31093-5, Atheneum Childrens Bks). Macmillan.

Fiscal Federalism. Wallace E. Oates. (Harbrace Business & Economics Ser.). (Illus.). 256p. 1972. text ed. 11.95 o.p. (ISBN 0-15-527452-X, HC). HarBraceJ.

Fiscal Federalism & Grants-in-Aid. Ed. by Peter Mieszkowski & William Oakland. (Papers on Public Economics Ser.: Vol.1). 166p. (Orig.). 1979. pap. text ed. 12.00x o.p. (ISBN 0-87766-254-1, 26300). Urban Inst.

Fiscal System of Hong Kong. H. C. Y Ho. 182p. 1979. 38.00 o.p. (ISBN 0-85664-686-5, Pub. by Croom Held Ltd). Routledge Chapman & Hall.

Fiscal Tiers: The Economics of Multi-Level Government. David King. 320p. 1984. text ed. 39.95x o.p. (ISBN 0-04-336081-5); pap. text ed. 16.95x o.p. (ISBN 0-04-336084-X). Unwin Hyman.

Fish. Monroe Engel. LC 81-7975. 1981. 12.95 o.p. (ISBN 0-689-11219-X, Atheneum). Macmillan.

Fish. (Insight Ser.). (Illus.). 40p. (gr. 4up). 1983. PLB 12.40 o.p. (ISBN 0-531-03474-7). Watts.

Fish & Flips. Jacquelyn Reinach. Ed. by Ruth L. Perle. LC 77-14577. (gr. k-2). 1978. 2.95 o.p. (ISBN 0-03-042016-4). H Holt & Co.

Fish & Shellfish Hygiene. WHO Staff. 62p. 1975. pap. 6.00 o.p. (ISBN 0-685-54032-4, F170, FAO). UNIPUB.

Fish & Shellfish Pathology. Anthony E. Ellis. 1985. 87.50 o.p. (ISBN 0-12-237490-8). Acad Pr.

Fish Catching Methods of the World. rev. & enlarged edition ed. A. Von Brandt. (Illus.). 1972. 35.00 o.s.i. (ISBN 0-685-12016-3). E J Brill USA.

Fish for My People. Robert L. Howell. (Orig.). 1968. pap. 4.95 o.p. (ISBN 0-8192-1097-8). Morehouse Pub.

Fish from Japan. Elizabeth K. Cooper et al. LC 69-11595. (Illus.). (gr. 3-6). 1969. 5.50 o.p. (ISBN 0-15-228056-1, HJ); 5.50 o.p. (ISBN 0-15-228057-X). HarBraceJ.

Fish Handling & Preservation at Sea: A Fisherman's Guide to Various Methods of Handling & Preserving Fish on Board Fishing Vessels. D. Amos. (Marine Bulletin Ser.: No. 45). 1981. 2.00 o.p. (ISBN 0-938412-23-X, P889). Sea Grant Pubns.

Fish in a Stream in a Cave. Ralph Maloney. 160p. 1972. 5.95 o.p. (ISBN 0-393-08455-8). Norton.

Fish in Nutrition. Ed. by E. Heen & R. Kreuzer. 1962. 7.50 o.p. (ISBN 0-685-36359-7, FN76, FAO). UNIPUB.

Fish in Research. Ed. by O. W. Neuhaus & J. E. Halver. LC 74-107020. 1969. 59.00 o.p. (ISBN 0-12-515850-5). Acad Pr.

Fish of the Atlantic. Ed Ricciuti. (Illus.). 95p. pap. 3.50 o.s.i. (ISBN 0-88839-155-2). Hancock House.

Fish Pathology. H. H. Reichenbach-Klinke. (Illus.). 512p. (Orig.). 1973. pap. text ed. 29.95 o.p. (ISBN 0-87666-074-X, PS-204). TFH Pubns.

Fish Physiology, Vol. 10: Gills. Ed. by W. S. Hoar & D. J. Randall. 1984. 59.00 o.p. (ISBN 0-12-350460-0). Acad Pr.

Fish Population Dynamics. John A. Gulland. LC 75-45094. 372p. 1977. 97.95 o.p. (ISBN 0-471-01575-X). Wiley.

Fish Saving. C. L. Cutting. (Illus.). 374p. 1956. (ISBN 0-8022-0331-0). Philos Lib.

Fish-Shape Paumanok. Robert C. Murphy. LC 63-22603. (Memoirs Ser.: Vol. 58). (Illus.). 1964. 10.00 o.p. (ISBN 0-87169-058-6). Am Philos.

Fisher Guide to Italy. Wilma Pezzini. 1983. pap. 11.95 o.p. (ISBN 0-8116-0004-1). Garrard.

Fisheries & Aquatic Sciences in Canada: An Overview. (Fisheries Research Board of Canada Reports). 53p. 1979. pap. 5.50 o.p. (ISBN 0-660-01195-6, SSC134, SSC). UNIPUB.

Fisheries Biology: A Study in Population Dynamics. D. H. Cushing. (Illus.). 1968. write for info o.p. (ISBN 0-299-04740-7). U of Wis Pr.

Fisheries Ecology. Tony J. Pitcher & Paul J. Hart. (Illus.). 1982. 36.95 o.p. (ISBN 0-87055-405-0). AVI.

Fisheries of the United States, 1986. (Current Fishery Statistics: No. 8385). (Illus.). 133p. 1987. pap. 6.50 o.p. (ISBN 0-318-22898-X, S/N 003-020-00155-6). USGPO.

Fisherman & His Wife. Retold by I. M. Richardson. (Fairy Tales Ser.). (Illus.). (gr. k-4). 1987. PLB 9.79 o.p.; pap. 1.95 o.p. Troll Assocs.

Fisherman & His Wife see Magic Fish.

Fisherman & His Wife with Benjy & Bubbles. Ruth L. Perle. LC 78-55629. (Read with Me Ser.). (Illus.). 32p. (gr. k-3). 1979. 2.95 o.p. (ISBN 0-03-044971-5). H Holt & Co.

Fisherman & the Bird. Sonia Levitin. (Illus.). 48p. (gr. k-3). 1982. 10.95 o.s.i. (ISBN 0-395-31860-2). HM.

Fisherman Knits: The Classics. Janet Mysse. 206p. 1984. 29.50 o.s.i. (ISBN 0-934318-43-3). Falcon Pr MT.

Fisherman's Diary. McClane. 1978. 10.00 o.p. (ISBN 0-15-131300-8). HarBraceJ.

Fisherman's Guide: A Systems Approach to Creativity & Organization. Robert Campbell. 1985. 9.95 o.s.i. (ISBN 0-394-72334-1). Shambhala Pubns.

Fishermen's Digest. 11th ed. Mark Thiffault. LC 75-148727. (Illus.). 256p. (Orig.). 1984. pap. 12.95 o.p. (ISBN 0-910676-70-4). DBI.

Fishers of Men. William Barclay. LC 66-22246. 120p. 1979. pap. 4.95 o.s.i. (ISBN 0-664-24224-3, Westminster). Westminster John Knox.
Fishery. (Sector Policy Paper). 1982. pap. 5.00 o.p. (ISBN 0-8213-0138-1). World Bank.
Fishery Management & Extended Maritime Jurisdiction: The Philippine Tuna Fishery Situation. Virginia L. Aprieto. LC 81-3262. (East-West Environment & Policy Institute Research Report: No. 4). vi, 78p. (Orig.). 1981. pap. text ed. 3.00 o.p. (ISBN 0-86638-026-4). EW Ctr HI.
Fishes: An Introduction to Ichthyology. Peter B. Moyle & Joseph J. Cech. (Illus.). 720p. 1982. text ed. (ISBN 0-13-319723-9). P-H.
Fishes of the English Chalk, Part 1-7, Vols. 56-56, 61-65, Nos. 263, 266, 291, 300, 308, 313, 320. A. Smith Woodward. Repr. of 1912 ed. Set. 64.00 o.p. (ISBN 0-384-69212-5). Johnson Repr.
Fishes of the Old Red Sandstone, Pt. 2, Nos. 2-4. R. H. Traquair. Repr. of 1914 ed. Set. 20.00 o.p. (ISBN 0-384-61370-5). Johnson Repr.
Fishing Basics. John Randolph. (Illus.). (gr. 3-7). 1981. 9.95 o.s.i. (ISBN 0-13-319707-7). P-H.
Fishing: Dry Flies for Trout on Rivers & Streams. Art Lee. LC 81-66449. 1982. 19.95 o.p. (ISBN 0-689-10959-8, Atheneum). Macmillan.
Fishing for the Beginner. John Fabian. LC 74-77842. 150p. 1974. 6.95 o.p. (ISBN 0-689-10614-9, Atheneum). Macmillan.
Fishing Hotspots 1987-Midwest Region. 212p. (Orig.). 1987. pap. 7.95 o.p. (ISBN 0-528-84586-1). Rand McNally.
Fishing in Troubled Waters: Research on the Chinese Fishing Industry in West Malaysia. (Asian Folklore & Social Life Monographs: Vol. 100). 1977. 22.00x o.p. (ISBN 0-89986-319-1). Oriental Bk Store.
Fishing the Flats. Mark Sosin & Lefty Kreh. LC 82-20158. (Illus.). 160p. 1983. 16.95 o.p. (ISBN 0-8329-0278-0); pap. 12.95 o.p. (ISBN 0-8329-0280-2). Lyons & Burford.
Fishing with Artificial Lures. David Sternberg. 160p. 1985. 16.95 o.p. (ISBN 0-13-319740-9). P-H.
Fishing with Dad. James Flora. LC 67-18865. (Illus.). (gr. 1-4). 1967. 4.50 o.p. (ISBN 0-15-228100-2, HJ). HarBraceJ.
Fishing with Live Bait. Dick Sternberg. (Hunting & Fishing Library). 1985. 16.95 o.p. (ISBN 0-13-319716-6). P-H.
Fishing with the Experts. Ed. by Charles Wade. 1977. 9.95 o.p. (ISBN 0-285-62189-0, Pub. by Souvenir Pr). Intl Spec BK.
Fishless Days, Angling Nights. Sparse G. Hackle. LC 83-3551. (Illus.). 224p. 1983. pap. 12.95 o.p. (ISBN 0-8329-0327-2). Lyons & Burford.
Fisica: Curso Introductorio. A. V. Piorishkin. 596p. (Span.). 1974. 8.95 o.p. (ISBN 0-8285-1454-2, Pub. by Mir Pubs USSR). Imported Pubns.
Fist of the North Star. Buronson & Tetsuo Hara. Ed. by Seiji Horibuchi. Tr. by Satoru Fujii & Fred Burke. (Illus.). 48p. (Orig.). 1989. pap. 2.95 o.p. (ISBN 0-929279-26-3). Viz Commns Inc.
Fist of the North Star, Vol. 2. Buronson & Tetsuo Hara. Ed. by Seiji Horibuchi. Tr. by Satoru Fujii & Fred Burke. (Illus.). 48p. (Orig.). 1989. pap. 2.95 o.p. Viz Commns Inc.
Fist of the North Star, Vol. 3. Buronson & Tetsuo Hara. Ed. by Seiji Horibuchi. Tr. by Satoru Fujii & Fred Burke. (Illus.). 48p. (Orig.). 1989. pap. 2.95 o.p. Viz Commns Inc.
Fist of the North Star, Vol. 4. Buronson & Tetsuo Hara. Ed. by Seiji Horibuchi. Tr. by Satoru Fujii & Fred Burke. (Illus.). 48p. (Orig.). 1989. pap. 2.95 o.p. Viz Commns Inc.
Fist of the North Star, Vol. 5. Buronson Hara & Tetsuo Hara. Ed. by Seiji Horibuchi. Tr. by Satoru Fujii & Fred Burke. (Illus.). 48p. (Orig.). 1989. pap. 2.95 o.p. (ISBN 0-929279-37-9). Viz Commns Inc.
Fist of the North Star, Vol. 6. Buronson Hara & Tetsuo Hara. Ed. by Seiji Horibuchi. Tr. by Satoru Fujii & Fred Burke. (Illus.). 48p. (Orig.). 1989. pap. 2.95 o.p. (ISBN 0-929279-38-7). Viz Commns Inc.
Fist of the North Star, Vol. 7. Buronson Hara & Tetsuo Hara. Ed. by Seiji Horibuchi. Tr. by Satoru Fujii & Fred Burke. (Illus.). 48p. (Orig.). 1989. pap. 2.95 o.p. (ISBN 0-929279-39-5). Viz Commns Inc.
Fist of the North Star, Vol. 8. Buronson Hara & Tetsuo Hara. Ed. by Seiji Horibuchi. Tr. by Satoru Fujii & Fred Burke. (Illus.). 48p. (Orig.). 1989. pap. 2.95 o.p. (ISBN 0-929279-40-9). Viz Commns Inc.
Fit & Proper Persons: Ideal & Reality in Nineteenth-Century Urban Government. E. P. Hennock. (Studies in Urban History: No. 2). (Illus.). 416p. 1973. 22.00x o.p. (ISBN 0-7735-0154-1, McGill Canada). U of Toronto Pr.
Fit for the Future: The Guide for Women Who Want to Live Well. Jeanette Winterspoon. 126p. 1986. pap. 8.95 o.p. (ISBN 0-86358-072-6, 80726). Routledge Chapman & Hall.
Fit to Fly: A Medical Handbook for Pilots. BALPA Medical Study Group Staff. 80p. 1980. pap. text ed. 5.50x o.p. (ISBN 0-246-11401-0, Pub. by Granada England). Gower Pub Co.
Fitness & Figure Control: The Creation of You. 2nd ed. Linda Garrison et al. LC 81-81277. (Illus.). 113p. 1981. pap. 7.95 o.p. (ISBN 0-87484-549-1). Mayfield Pub.
Fitness for College & Life. Charles A. Bucher & William E. Prentice. 1985. pap. 14.95 o.p. (ISBN 0-8016-0884-8). Mosby.
Fitness for Every Body. Linda Garrison & Ann K. Read. LC 79-91831. (Illus.). 138p. 1980. pap. 8.95 o.p. (ISBN 0-87484-444-4). Mayfield Pub.
Fitness in America--the Perrier Study: A National Research Report of Behavior, Knowledge, & Opinions Concerning the Taking up of Sports & Exercise. Harris, Louis, & Associates Staff. LC 82-49184. (Reference Library of Social Science Ser.). 60p. 1983. lib. bdg. 20.00 o.p. (ISBN 0-8240-9143-4). Garland Pub.
Fitness in the Elementary Schools. 1986. 9.95 o.p. (ISBN 0-88314-331-3). AAHPERD.
Fitness Program with Spine Motion. 11th ed. Paul C. Bragg & Patricia Bragg. pap. 3.95 o.p. (ISBN 0-87790-020-5). Health Sci.
Fitting the Task to the Man: An Ergonomic Approach. 3rd ed. Etienne Grandjean. LC 79-3855. (Illus.). 379p. (Orig.). 1982. 42.00x o.p. (ISBN 0-8002-2225-3); pap. 25.00x o.p. (ISBN 0-85066-192-7). Taylor & Francis.
Fitzgeralds & the Kennedys. Doris K. Goodwin. (Illus.). 1008p. 1987. 22.45 o.s.i. (ISBN 0-671-23108-1). S&S.
Fitzwilliam Virginal Book, 2 vols. William Byrd et al. Ed. by J. A. Maitland & W. B. Squire. (Illus.). 974p. 1949. Repr. of 1899 ed. 25.00x o.p. (ISBN 0-8450-0102-7). Broude.
Five Against the Odds. C. H. Frick. LC 55-8676. (gr. 7 up). 1955. 6.50 o.p. (ISBN 0-15-228245-9, HJ). HarBraceJ.
Five Ages of the Cinema. Charles H. Tarbox. (Illus.). 90p. 1980. 20.00 o.p. (ISBN 0-682-49618-9, Banner). Exposition-Phoenix.
Five Articles: Serve the People. Mao Tse-Tung. 1968. pap. 1.95 o.p. (ISBN 0-8351-0970-4). China Bks.
Five Biblical Portraits. Elie Wiesel. LC 81-40458. 168p. 1981. 9.95 o.p. (ISBN 0-268-00957-0). U of Notre Dame Pr.
Five Books of Moses. Oswald T. Allis. 1977. pap. 7.95 o.p. (ISBN 0-8010-0108-0). Baker Bk.
Five California Architects. Esther McCoy. 1982. pap. 10.00 o.s.i. (ISBN 0-275-71720-8). H Holt & Co.
Five Cent, Five Cent (Liberia) Edna W. Chandler. LC 67-17414. (Illus.). (gr. 1-3). 1967. PLB 9.50 o.p. (ISBN 0-8075-2463-8). A Whitman.
Five Centuries of Map Printing. David Woodward. LC 74-11635. 1977. pap. 7.95 o.s.i. (ISBN 0-226-90726-0, P723, Phoen). U of Chicago Pr.
Five Clocks. Martin Joos. LC 62-62715. 108p. 1967. pap. 3.95 o.p. (ISBN 0-15-631380-4, Harv). HarBraceJ.
Five Days to a High School Diploma. Jack Rudman. (Admission Test Ser.: ATS-81). 300p. (Cloth bdg. avail. on request). 1988. pap. 13.95 o.p. Natl Learning.
Five Decades: Poems, Nineteen Twenty-Five to Nineteen-Seventy. Pablo Neruda. Ed. & tr. by Ben Belitt. (Bilingual ed.). 1974. pap. 8.95 o.s.i. (ISBN 0-394-17869-6, E636, Ever). Grove.
Five Eyes. Abdeslam Boulaich et al. Ed. by Paul Bowles. 125p. 1979. 14.00 o.p. (ISBN 0-87685-409-9); pap. 5.00 o. p. o.p. (ISBN 0-87685-408-0). Black Sparrow.
Five Feet to the Line. Nita K. Beck. 1977. 4.00 o.p. (ISBN 0-682-48716-3). Exposition-Phoenix.
Five Fifty-Nine to Damascus. Roland S. Jefferson. LC 85-61374. 288p. 1985. 16.00 o.p. Exposition-Phoenix.
Five Flights of the Starfire. Edwin Mumford. 1974. pap. 3.00 o.p. (ISBN 0-682-47882-2). Exposition-Phoenix.
Five Fur Traders of the Northwest. Ed. by Charles M. Gates. LC 65-63528. 296p. 1965. Repr. of 1933 ed. 7.25 o.p. (ISBN 0-87351-024-0). Minn Hist.
Five Go Adventuring Again. Enid Blyton. 1986. 15.95 o.s.i. (ISBN 0-317-53106-9, Large Print Bks). G K Hall.
Five Hundred & Four Absolutely Essential Words. rev. ed. Murray Bromberg et al. LC 74-5052. 1975. pap. 5.50 o.p. (ISBN 0-8120-0525-2). Barron.
Five Hundred Club. The Philadelphia Daily News Staff. (Illus.). 144p. (Orig.). 1988. pap. 2.95 o.s.i. (ISBN 1-55785-024-0). Bart Books.
Five Hundred Contractors Receiving the Largest Dollar Volume of Prime Contract Awards for RDT & E, Fiscal Year 1985. (Illus.). 41p. (Orig.). 1986. pap. 2.25 o.p. (ISBN 0-318-20108-9, S/N 008-000-00452-8). USGPO.
Five Hundred Delinquent Women. S. Glueck & Eleanor Glueck. Repr. of 1934 ed. 39.00 o.p. (ISBN 0-527-34080-4). Kraus Repr.
Five Hundred Fifty-Five IC Project Book. Robert J. Traister. (Illus.). 224p. (Orig.). 1985. 18.95 o.p. (ISBN 0-8306-0996-2, 1996); pap. 11.60 o.p. (ISBN 0-8306-1996-8). TAB Bks.
Five Hundred Five Jokes You Can Tell. Winston K. Pendleton. LC 77-17199. 1978. pap. 5.95 o.p. (ISBN 0-8272-1008-6). CBP.
Five Hundred Four Absolutely Essential Words. 2nd ed. Murray Bromberg et al. 139p. 1984. pap. 6.95 o.p. (ISBN 0-8120-2338-2). Barron.
Five Hundred Games. Compiled by Peter L. Cave. (Illus.). 160p. 1983. PLB 4.59 o.p. (ISBN 0-448-13619-8, G&D); pap. 2.95 o.p. (ISBN 0-448-02159-5, G&D). Putnam Pub Group.
Five Hundred Thirty-Four Ways to Raise Money. J. Thomas Hay. 256p. 1983. 15.50 o.p. (ISBN 0-671-47167-8); pap. 6.75 o.p. (ISBN 0-671-47286-0). S&S.
Five Hundred Years of Travel Books about Scotland, 1296-1796. Arthur Mitchell. 1982. pap. 25.00 o.p. (ISBN 0-686-37955-1). Saifer.
Five Language Dictionary of Surface Coatings, Platings, Product Finishing, Plastics & Rubber. R. W. Santholzer. 1969. 145.00 o.p. (ISBN 0-08-012336-8). Pergamon.
Five Lessons: The Modern Fundamentals of Golf. Ben Hogan. 127p. 1985. 16.45 o.p. (ISBN 0-671-61291-3). S&S.
Five-Line Frolics: Two Hundred Ten Original Limericks. Martin B. Smith. 80p. 1982. 5.50 o.p. (ISBN 0-682-49862-9). Exposition-Phoenix.
Five Little Monkeys. Juliet Kepes. (Illus.). 32p. (gr. k-3). 1952. PLB 6.95 o.p. (ISBN 0-395-19112-2). HM.
Five Little Monkeys. Juliet Kepes. (gr. k-3). 1978. pap. 2.25 o.p. (ISBN 0-395-26688-2). HM.
Five Little Peppers & How They Grew. Margaret Sidney. (Illus.). (gr. 4-6). PLB 5.95 o.p. (ISBN 0-448-05808-1, G&D); deluxe ed. 11.95 o.p. (ISBN 0-448-06008-6); pap. 5.95 o.p. (ISBN 0-448-11008-3); lib. bdg. 2.95 o.p. (ISBN 0-448-16303-9). Putnam Pub Group.
Five Manuscript Newspapers from Early Nevada. Stephen A. Kinsey et al. (Nevada Monographs: No. 1). (Illus.). 24p. (Orig.). 1981. pap. text ed. 6.50 o.p. (ISBN 0-936332-07-7). Falcon Hill Pr.
Five Men under One Umbrella: And Other Ready-to-Read Riddles. Joseph Low. LC 74-20615. (Ready-to-Read Ser.). (Illus.). 64p. (gr. 1-3). 1975. 6.95 o.s.i. (ISBN 0-02-761460-3). Macmillan.
Five Million Dollar Prince. Michael Butterworth. LC 85-46077. (Crime Club Ser.). 192p. 1986. 12.95 o.p. (ISBN 0-385-23542-9). Doubleday.
Five-Minute Lessons in Successful Selling: Increase Your Sales Skills Without Going Back to School. Rodney Young. 208p. 1985. 16.95 o.p. (ISBN 0-13-321670-5); pap. 7.95 o.p. (ISBN 0-13-321662-4). P H.
Five Minute Phobia Cure. Roger Callahan. 1985. 19.95 o.p. (ISBN 0-913864-89-7). Enterprise Del.
Five Models of Foster Family Group Homes. Elizabeth A. Lawder et al. LC 74-75756. 97p. (Orig.). 1974. pap. 6.60 o.p. (ISBN 0-87868-122-1, 1221). Child Welfare.
Five More. Ner Littner. LC 80-80866. (Orig.). 1980. pap. text ed. 3.95 o.p. (ISBN 0-87868-189-2, CW-33). Child Welfare.
Five O'Clock Comes Early: A Ballplayer's Battle with Alcoholism. Bob Welch & George Vecsey. LC 81-16772. (Illus.). 256p. 1982. 12.95 o.p. (ISBN 0-688-00810-0). Morrow.
Five O'Clock Comes Early: A Young Man's Battle with Alcoholism. Bob Welch & George Vecsey. LC 85-24455. 224p. 1986. pap. 6.95 o.p. (ISBN 0-688-06273-3, Quill). Morrow.
Five on a Treasure Island. Enid Blyton. 1985. 11.95 o.p. (ISBN 0-317-53107-7, Large Print Bks). G K Hall.
Five Patients. Michael Crichton. 224p. 1981. pap. 2.75 o.p. (ISBN 0-380-57364-4, 62919-4). Avon.
Five Place Tables of Elliptical Functions. Max Schuler & H. Gebelein. Tr. by L. S. Larsen. (Illus., Eng. & Ger.). 1955. 23.10 o.p. (ISBN 0-387-01952-9). Springer-Verlag.
Five Plays about King John. May Mattsson. 1977. pap. text ed. 19.75x o.p. (ISBN 91-554-067-0X). Humanities.
Five Plays by Ronald Ribman. Ronald Ribman. 1978. pap. 2.95 o.p. (ISBN 0-380-40006-5, 65342, Bard). Avon.
Five Poems, Fourteen Seventy-Eighteen Seventy: An Elementary Essay on the Background of English Literature. Eustace M. Tillyard. Repr. of 1948 ed. 29.00x o.p. (ISBN 0-403-07216-6). Somerset Pub.
Five Ports to Danger. Vivian Connolly. (Orig.). 1980. pap. 1.75 o.p. (ISBN 0-505-51518-0, Pub. by Tower Bks). Dorchester Pub Co.
Five Red Herrings. Dorothy L. Sayers. 1976. pap. 2.75 o.p. (ISBN 0-380-01187-5, 62109-6). Avon.
Five Secrets of Living. Warren Wiersbe. 1978. pap. 2.95 o.p. (ISBN 0-8423-0870-9). Tyndale.
Five Sparrows: A Japanese Folktale. Patricia M. Newton. LC 82-3881. (Illus.). 32p. (ps-3). 1982. 11.95 o.s.i. (ISBN 0-689-30936-8, Atheneum Childrens Bks). Macmillan.
Five-Star Basketball Drills. Ed. by Howard Garfinkel. (Illus.). 272p. 1987. pap. 12.95 o.p. (ISBN 0-940279-09-6). Masters Pr MI.
Five Steps Toward a Better Marriage. David A. Thompson. 96p. (Orig.). 1980. pap. 5.95 o.p. (ISBN 0-87123-164-6, 210164). Bethany Hse.
Five Stories of Ferrara. Giorgio Bassani. LC 76-153681. (Helen & Kurt Wolff Bk). 216p. 1971. 5.95 o.p. (ISBN 0-15-131400-4). HarBraceJ.
Five Straight Errors on Ladies Day. Walter H. Nagle. LC 65-17946. 140p. 1965. 4.95 o.p. (ISBN 0-87004-109-6). Caxton.
Five Ten (k) Register, 1986. LC 86-81817. 779p. pap. cancelled o.s.i. (ISBN 0-914176-31-5). Wash Busn Info.
Five: The Evolution of the Russian School of Music. Mikhael Zetlin. Ed. & tr. by George Panin. LC 73-1439. (Illus.). 344p. 1975. Repr. of 1959 ed. lib. bdg. 38.50 o.p. (ISBN 0-8371-6797-3, ZETF). Greenwood.
Five Thousand & One Hard to Find Publishers & Their Addresses. 2nd ed. 80p. 1987. lib bdg 40.00 o.p. (ISBN 0-317-61514-9). A Armstrong.
Five Thousand One Hard to Find Publishers & Their Addresses. 2nd ed. 80p. 1984. lib. bdg. 25.00 o.p. (ISBN 0-946291-06-3). A Armstrong.
Five Thousand One Nights at the Movies: A Guide from A to Z. Pauline Kael. 1982. 25.00 o.p. (ISBN 0-03-042606-5). H Holt & Co.
Five Thousand Personalities of the World. 1st ed. Ed. by J. M. Evans. 600p. 1986. 75.00 o.s.i. (ISBN 0-934544-30-1). Am Biog Inst.
Five Year Cumulative Index to Journal of APCA. 96p. 1978. 15.00 o.p. (ISBN 0-318-12257-X, JIV); members 10.00 o.p. (ISBN 0-318-12258-8). Air & Waste.
Five-Year Plan for Meeting the Automatic Data Processing & Telecommunication Needs of the Federal Government, Vol. 1. (Illus.). 316p. 1987. pap. 15.00 o.p. (ISBN 0-318-23824-1, 041-001-00325-8). USGPO.
Five-Year Plan for Meeting the Automatic Data Processing & Telecommunications Needs of the Federal Government, Vol. 2. 1987. pap. 29.00 o.p. (ISBN 0-318-23515-3, S/N 041-001-00324-0). USGPO.
Fives Wild. Walter Winward. LC 75-41850. 256p. 1976. 8.95 o.p. (ISBN 0-689-10711-0, Atheneum). Macmillan.
Fivescourt: A Novel in Reverse. Hilya Harsch. 1979. 6.50 o.p. (ISBN 0-682-49382-1). Exposition-Phoenix.
Fix. Dorian Fliegel. 1978. 8.95 o.p. (ISBN 0-395-25700-X). HM.
Fix It. Robert Brightman. 1981. write for info. o.p. (ISBN 0-916752-18-6). Longman Trade.
Fix Your Chevrolet. rev. ed. Bill Toboldt. LC 62-12426. (Illus.). 384p. 1981. 8.00 o.p. (ISBN 0-87006-329-4). Goodheart.
Fixed Bridge Prosthesis. 2nd ed. O. Roberts. 300p. 1980. 35.00 o.p. (ISBN 0-7236-0545-9, Pub. by John Wright UK). Butterworth.
Fixed by Camel. Jacquelyn Reinach. LC 76-43091. (Sweet Pickles Ser.). (Illus.). (gr. k-2). 1977. 2.95 o.p. (ISBN 0-03-018096-1). H Holt & Co.
Fixed Communications System Service Demand Assessment: 18 to 30 GHz. Exec. Summary. 20.00 o.p. (ISBN 0-686-33011-0); Final Report. 100.00 o.p. (ISBN 0-686-33012-9); Appendix. 100.00 o.p. (ISBN 0-686-33013-7). Info Gatekeepers.
Fixed-Film Biological Processes for Wastewater Treatment. Ed. by Yeun C. Wu & Ed D. Smith. LC 83-13126. (Pollution Technology Review No. 104). (Illus.). 493p. 1984. 48.00 o.p. (ISBN 0-8155-0963-4). Noyes.
Fixed Interval Work Sampling. Ed. by Chester L. Brisley. (Reprinted from the Journal of Industrial Engineering). 1969. pap. text ed. 13.00 o.p. (ISBN 0-89806-025-7, 115). Inst Indus Eng.
Fixed Point Theory & Its Applications. Ed. by S. Swaminathan. 1976. 40.50 o.p. (ISBN 0-12-678650-X). Acad Pr.
Fixed Restorative Techniques. Henry V. Murray & Troy B. Sluder. (Dental Laboratory Technical Manuals Ser). viii, 308p. 1972. pap. text ed. 18.00x o.p. (ISBN 0-8078-7904-5). U of NC Pr.
Fixing Fences. Bruce Wannamaker. LC 84-7037. (Illus.). 32p. (gr. 2-3). 1984. lib. bdg. 4.95 o.p. (ISBN 0-89693-226-5). Dandelion Hse.
Fizzles. Samuel Beckett. 1976. pap. 1.95 o.p. (ISBN 0-394-17917-X, E681, Ever). Grove.
Flag at the Pole. Paxton Davis. LC 76-81. (Illus.). 128p. (gr. 8-12). 1976. 5.95 o.p. (ISBN 0-689-30522-2, Atheneum). Macmillan.

Flags. Brenda Thompson & Rosemary Giesen. LC 76-22431. (Lerner First Fact Bks.). (Illus.). (gr. k-3). 1977. PLB 4.95 o.p. (ISBN 0-8225-1355-2). Lerner Pubns.

Flags of American History. David D. Crouthers. LC 77-26205. (Hammond Profile Ser.). (gr. 6 up). 1973. 9.95 o.p. (ISBN 0-8437-3080-3). Hammond Inc.

Flagstad Manuscript (by) Louis Biancolli. Kirsten Flagstad. 293p. Repr. of 1952 ed. lib. bdg. 39.00 o.p. (Pub. by Am Repr Serv). Reprint Servs.

Flagstad: Singer of the Century. Howard Vogt. (Illus.). 352p. 1988. 39.95 o.s.i. (ISBN 0-436-55800-9, Pub. by Secker & Warburg UK). David & Charles.

Flair in the Kitchen. 1980. pap. 4.95 o.p. (ISBN 0-930756-58-4, 532003K). Aglow Pubns.

Flambard's Confession. Marilyn Durham. LC 82-2978. 784p. 1982. 17.95 o.p. (ISBN 0-15-131453-5). HarBraceJ.

Flame. R. V. Cassill. LC 80-66505. 1980. 11.95 o.p. (ISBN 0-87795-280-9, Arbor Hse). Morrow.

Flame into Being: The Life & Work of D. H. Lawrence. Anthony Burgess. 278p. 1985. 15.00 o.p. (ISBN 0-87795-766-5, Arbor Hse). Morrow.

Flame of Recognition. new ed. Ed. by Nancy Newhall. LC 65-2407. (Illus.). 104p. 1971. pap. 15.00 o.s.i. (ISBN 0-912334-02-9). Aperture.

Flame-Retardant Polymeric Materials, Vol. 1. Ed. by Menachem Lewin et al. LC 75-26781. 458p. 1975. 75.00x o.p. (ISBN 0-306-30840-1, Plenum Pr). Plenum Pub.

Flame-Retardant Polymeric Materials, Vol. 2. Ed. by Menachem Lewin et al. LC 75-26781. (Illus.). 345p. 1978. 69.50x o.p. (ISBN 0-306-32212-9, Plenum Pr). Plenum Pub.

Flame Trees of Thika. Elspeth Huxley. LC 87-73807. (Illus.). 288p. 1987. 22.50 o.s.i. (ISBN 1-55584-144-9). Weidenfeld.

Flameout. Basil Jackson. 1976. 7.95 o.p. (ISBN 0-393-08740-9). Norton.

Flames of Desire. Vanessa Royall. 1978. pap. 2.25 o.p. (ISBN 0-440-14637-2). Dell.

Flames: Their Structure, Radiation & Temperature. 4th ed. A. G. Gaydon & H. G. Wolfhard. 1979. 63.00 o.p. (ISBN 0-412-15390-4, NO. 6119, Pub. by Chapman & Hall). Routledge Chapman & Hall.

Flaming Arrows. William O. Steele. LC 57-6791. (Illus.). (gr. 4-6). 1957. 5.95 o.p. (ISBN 0-15-228424-9, HJ). HarBraceJ.

Flaming Arrows. William O. Steele. LC 57-6791. (Illus.). (gr. 4-8). 1972. pap. 1.15 o.p. (ISBN 0-15-631550-5, VoyB). HarBraceJ.

Flaming Center: A Theology of the Christian Mission. Carl E. Braaten. LC 76-62605. 176p. 1977. 4.25 o.p. (ISBN 0-8006-0490-3, 1-490, Fortress). Augsburg Fortress.

Flaming Prophet: The Story of Samuel Zwemer. J. Christy Wilson. LC 76-130778. (Bold Believers Ser). (Orig.). 1970. pap. 0.95 o.p. (ISBN 0-377-84201-X). Friendship Pr.

Flaming Tree. Phyllis A. Whitney. LC 85-1601. 288p. 1986. 15.95 o.p. (ISBN 0-385-23095-8). Doubleday.

Flaming Tree. Phyllis A. Whitney. (Large Print Bks (General Ser.)). 367p. 1986. lib. bdg. 18.95 o.p. (ISBN 0-8161-4126-6). G K Hall.

Flanagan's Run. Tom McNab. 448p. 1983. pap. 3.95 o.p. (ISBN 0-380-63149-0, 63149-0). Avon.

Flaneur des Deux Rives. Guillaume Apollinaire. pap. 7.95 o.p. (ISBN 0-685-37170-0). Schoenhof.

Flannery O'Connor's South. Robert Coles. LC 79-23057. (Walter Lynwood Fleming Lectures in Southern History). xii, 228p. 1980. 25.00 o.p. (ISBN 0-8071-0655-0). La State U Pr.

Flannery Row. Karen Ackerman. (Illus.). 32p. (ps-2). 1986. lib. bdg. 12.95 o.s.i. (ISBN 0-316-00647-5, Joy St Bks). Little.

Flappers & Philosophers. F. Scott Fitzgerald. 1959. 5.95 o.p. (ISBN 0-684-10153-X, ScribT); pap. 2.95 o.p. (ISBN 0-684-12958-2, SL371, ScribT). Scribner.

Flare Bestseller. Bruce Hart & Carole Hart. 1982. pap. 10.90 Boxed Set o.s.i. (ISBN 0-380-81331-9, 81331). Avon.

Flare Stars. G. A. Gurzadyan. LC 79-41746. (International Series on Natural Philosophy). (Illus.). 344p. 1980. 100.00 o.p. (ISBN 0-08-023035-0). Pergamon.

Flare Young Love, 5 vols. 1984. Boxed Set. pap. 11.25 o.p. (ISBN 0-380-88435-6, Flare). Avon.

Flash & Filigree. Terry Southern. LC 58-12116. (Library of Contemporary Americana). 204p. 1984. pap. 6.95 o.p. (ISBN 0-87795-648-0, Arbor Hse). Morrow.

Flash Photolysis & Pulse Radiolysis: Contributions to the Chemistry of Biology & Medicine. R. V. Bensasson & T. G. Truscott. (Illus.). 272p. 1983. 65.00 o.p. (ISBN 0-08-024949-3). Pergamon.

Flashlight & Other Poems. Judith Thurman. LC 75-29442. (Illus.). 48p. (gr. 2-6). 1976. 6.95 o.p. (ISBN 0-689-30515-X, Atheneum Childrens Bk). Macmillan.

Flashmaps Instant Guide to Chicago. rev. ed. Toy Lasker. (Illus.). 80p. 1977. pap. 3.95 o.p. (ISBN 0-03-064054-7). Flashmaps Pubns.

Flashmaps Instant Guide to Dallas-Fort Worth. Toy Lasker. (Flashmaps Instant Guide Ser.). (Illus.). 72p. (Orig.). 1982. pap. 3.95 o.p. (ISBN 0-942226-00-3). Flashmaps Pubns.

Flashmaps Instant Guide to New York. 1988. pap. 4.95 o.p. (ISBN 0-942226-25-9). McKay.

Flashmaps Instant Guide to New York. rev. ed. Toy Lasker. LC 79-77622. (Flashmaps Instant Guide Ser.). (Illus.). 80p. 1986. pap. 4.95 o.p. (ISBN 0-942226-01-1). Flashmaps Pubns.

Flashmaps Instant Guide to Washington, D. C. rev. ed. Toy Lasker. LC 75-6206. (Flashmaps Instant Guide Ser.). (Illus.). 80p. 1986. pap. 4.95 o.p. (ISBN 0-942226-02-X). Flashmaps Pubns.

Flask of Fields. Ed. by Richard J. Anobile. 1973. pap. 4.45 o.p. (ISBN 0-380-01189-1, 17533). Avon.

Flat on My Face. Julia First. (gr. 4-6). 1984. pap. 1.25 o.p. (ISBN 0-380-00204-3, 52324-8, Camelot). Avon.

Flauta de Dios. Paul Twitchell. Tr. by Mario Proano et al from Span. 216p. (Orig.). 1980. pap. 3.95 o.p. (ISBN 0-914766-49-X, 0926). Illum Way Pub.

Flavio. Gordon Parks. (Illus.). 1978. 8.95 o.p. (ISBN 0-393-08806-5). Norton.

Flavonoids: Advances in Research, 1975-1981. J. B. Harborne & T. J. Mabry. (Illus.). 650p. 1982. 79.95x o.p. (ISBN 0-412-22480-1, NO. 6698, Pub. by Chapman & Hall). Routledge Chapman & Hall.

Flavor Bears Scratch 'n' Sniff: Fantastic Flavor Factory. (gr. 2-3). pap. 2.95 o.p. (ISBN 0-89954-368-5). Antioch Pub Co.

Flavor Bears Scratch 'n' Sniff: Voyage to Huggle Land. (gr. 2-3). pap. 2.95 o.p. (ISBN 0-89954-380-4). Antioch Pub Co.

Flavor Bears: The Wild Flavor Chase. (gr. 2-3). 2.95 o.p. (ISBN 0-89954-381-2). Antioch Pub Co.

Flavors of Hungary. Charlotte S. Biro. LC 73-81085. (Illus.). 192p. (Orig.). 1973. pap. 6.95 o.p. (ISBN 0-912238-37-2, One Hund One Prods). Ortho.

Flavors of India. Shanta N. Sacharoff. LC 79-182418. (Illus.). 192p. (Orig.). 1972. pap. 7.95 o.p. (ISBN 0-912238-16-X, One Hund One Prods). Ortho.

Flavors of Japan. Delphine Hirasuna & Diane J. Hirasuna. LC 81-11039. (Illus.). 192p. (Orig.). 1981. pap. 6.95 o.p. (ISBN 0-89286-190-8, One Hund One Prods). Ortho.

Flavors of Mexico: Authentic Recipes from South of the Border. Angeles De La Rosa & C. Gandia Fernandez. LC 78-11397. (Illus.). 1978. pap. 5.95 o.p. (ISBN 0-89286-142-8, One Hund One Prods). Ortho.

Flaw in Japanese Management. Haruo Takagi. Ed. by Richard Farmer. LC 85-20832. (Research for Business Decisions Ser.: No. 83). 119p. 1985. 39.95 o.p. (ISBN 0-8357-1718-6). UMI Res Pr.

Flaws in the Social Fabric: Homosexuals & Society in Sydney. Denise Thompson. 220p. 1985. text ed. 34.95x o.p. (ISBN 0-86861-676-1); pap. text ed. 14.95x o.p. (ISBN 0-86861-684-2). Unwin Hyman.

Flaxman & Europe: The Outline Illustrations & Their Influence. Sarah Symmons. LC 83-48691. (Theses from the Courtauld Institute of Art Ser.). (Illus.). 420p. 1984. lib. bdg. 50.00 o.p. (ISBN 0-8240-5987-5). Garland Pub.

Flayderman's Guide to Antique American Firearms...& Their Values. 3rd ed. Ed. by Norm Flayerman. LC 75-36418. (Illus.). 624p. 1983. pap. 19.95 o.p. (ISBN 0-910676-58-5). DBI.

Flea Market America: The Bargain Hunter's Guide. Cree McCree. LC 83-60096. (Illus.). 180p. 1983. pap. 6.35 o.p. (ISBN 0-912528-31-1). John Muir.

Flea Market Price Guide. 4th ed. Robert W. Miller. (Illus.). 272p. pap. 7.95 o.p. (ISBN 0-87069-381-6). Wallace-Homestead.

Flea Story. Robert Tallon. LC 77-3168. (Illus.). (ps-3). 1977. reinforced bdg. 6.95 o.p. (ISBN 0-03-021531-5). H Holt & Co.

Flea Trainer. Illus. by Mary B. Schwark. (Zig Ziglar Ser.). (Illus.). 48p. 1988. pap. 2.50 o.p. (ISBN 0-8423-8846-X). Tyndale.

Fleas, Flukes, & Cuckoos. Miriam Rothschild & Theresa Clay. 1952. (ISBN 0-8022-1384-7). Philos Lib.

Fleas, Ticks & Cockroaches: Disease Transmitters. Walter Weber. (Illus.). 1987. pap. 12.00 o.p. Thomson Pubns.

Flee the Captor. Herbert Ford. (Orion Ser). 1979. pap. 4.95 o.p. (ISBN 0-8127-0219-0). Review & Herald.

Fleecing of America. William Proxmire. 1980. 10.95 o.p. (ISBN 0-395-29133-X). HM.

Fleet Admiral: The Story of William F. Halsey. Lawrence A. Keating. (Illus.). (gr. 7 up). 1965. 3.95 o.s.i. (ISBN 0-664-32343-X, Westminster). Westminster John Knox.

Fleet: Its River, Prison, & Marriages. John Ashton. LC 68-21753. 410p. 1969. Repr. of 1888 ed. 43.00x o.p. (ISBN 0-8103-3414-3). Gale.

Fleet Owners Maintenance Shop Design Book. Fleet Owner Magazine Staff. 256p. 1981. text ed. 32.50 o.p. (ISBN 0-07-021260-0). McGraw.

Fleet Papers: Being Letters from Richard Oastler with Occasional Communications from Friends, 4 vols. 1841-44. Repr. Set. lib. bdg. 91.00x o.p. (ISBN 0-8371-9168-8, FP00); Vol. 1. lib. bdg. 28.00 o.p. (ISBN 0-313-21634-7, FP01); Vol. 2. lib. bdg. 28.00 o.p. (ISBN 0-313-21635-5, FP02); Vol. 3. lib. bdg. 28.00 o.p. (ISBN 0-313-21636-3, FP03); Vol. 4. lib. bdg. 28.00 o.p. (ISBN 0-313-21637-1, FP04). Greenwood.

Fleeting Shadows & Faint Echoes of Las Huertas. Bill F. Gurule. 128p. 1987. 9.95 o.p. (ISBN 0-8062-2938-1). Carlton.

Flesh & Blood. C. K. Williams. 132p. 1987. 14.95 o.p. (ISBN 0-374-15636-0); pap. 8.95 o.p. (ISBN 0-374-52090-9). FS&G.

Flesh of My Flesh. Una Kroll. 112p. 1975. pap. 6.50 o.p. (ISBN 0-232-51336-8). Attic Pr.

Fletcher Corporation Forms Annotated: 1958-1988, 17 vols. 12th ed. LC 79-9226. 525.00 o.p. (ISBN 0-317-11811-0). Callaghan.

Fletcher Cyclopedia of Corporations: 1959, 33 vols. LC 31-11602. 1175.00 o.p. Callaghan.

Fleur de Lis. Dorothy E. Taylor. 288p. 1984. pap. 2.95 o.p. (ISBN 0-380-87619-1, 87619-1). Avon.

Fleurs Animees see Court of Flora.

Fleurs Bleues. Raymond Queneau. (Folio 1000). 1978. pap. 3.95 o.p. (ISBN 0-686-54673-3). Schoenhof.

Flexease. rev. ed. Taylor Hay. (Illus.). 118p. Date not set. pap. 12.95 o.p. Haymaker Bk Co.

Flexible Benefits: A How-to-Guide. Richard E. Johnson. LC 86-80999. 163p. (Orig.). 1986. pap. 25.00 o.p. (ISBN 0-89154-301-5). Intl Found Employ.

Flexible Compensation Plans, 1984. (Tax Law & Estate Planning Course Handbook Ser.: Vol. 204). 307p. 1984. 45.00 o.p. (ISBN 0-317-11448-4, J4-3545). PLI.

Flexible Pavement Design & Management: Materials Characterization. (National Cooperative Highway Research Program Report). 118p. 1973. 5.60 o.p. (ISBN 0-309-02128-6). Transport Res Bd.

Flexible Pavement Design & Management: Systems Approach & Implementation. (National Cooperative Highway Research Program Report). 53p. 1975. 4.00 o.p. (ISBN 0-309-02339-4). Transport Res Bd.

Flexible Pavement Design & Management: Systems Formulation. (National Cooperative Highway Research Program Report). 64p. 1973. 4.40 o.p. (ISBN 0-309-02127-8). Transport Res Bd.

Flexible Weapons. John Sanchez. (Illus.). 80p. 1981. pap. 8.00 o.p. (ISBN 0-87364-219-8). Paladin Pr.

Flexible Work Schedule: An Innovation in the Quality of Work Life. Simcha Ronen. (Illus.). 352p. 1981. text ed. 33.95 o.p. (ISBN 0-07-053607-4). McGraw.

Flick & I. Ralph J. Batschelet. 176p. 1981. 9.00 o.p. (ISBN 0-682-49717-7). Exposition-Phoenix.

Flicks. Tomie De Paola. LC 79-87514. (Illus.). (ps-3). 1979. 11.95 o.s.i. (ISBN 0-15-228487-7, HJ). HarBraceJ.

Flight & Barr Worcester: Seventeen Eighty-Three to Eighteen Forty. Henry Sandon. (Illus.). 245p. 1978. 39.50 o.p. (ISBN 0-902028-75-8). Antique Collect.

Flight Attendant. Alice Musbach & Barbara Davis. (Illus.). 288p. 1980. 12.95 o.p. (ISBN 0-517-54068-1); pap. 9.95 o.s.i. (ISBN 0-517-54069-X). Crown.

Flight Engineer Question Book. (FAA-T-8080-8A Ser.). (Illus.). 219p. 1986. pap. 8.00 o.p. (ISBN 0-318-19961-0, S/N 050-007-00722-1). USGPO.

Flight Engineer Question Book. (FAA-T-8080-8B Ser.). (Illus.). 243p. 1988. pap. 11.00 o.p. (S/N 050-007-00789-2). USGPO.

Flight Engineer Turboset-Basic Written Test Guide. Federal Aviation Administration Staff. 144p. 1977. pap. text ed. 4.00 o.p. (ISBN 0-939158-18-3). Flightshops.

Flight Facts for Private Pilots. 2nd ed. Rev. by Don Downie. Morgan R. Rodney. 1983. pap. 10.95 o.p. (ISBN 0-8168-5804-7, 25804, TAB-Aero). TAB Bks.

Flight Facts for Private Pilots. 2nd rev. & enl. ed. Rev. by Don Downie & Morgan R. Rodney. 216p. 1984. pap. 10.95 o.p. (25804, TAB-Aero). TAB Bks.

Flight from Paris. Noah Webster. LC 86-24092. (Crime Club Ser.). 192p. 1987. 12.95 o.s.i. (ISBN 0-385-23560-7). Doubleday.

Flight from Sorrow: The Life & Death of Tamara Wall. Felicity Barringer. LC 83-45063. 288p. 1984. 15.95 o.p. (ISBN 0-689-11389-7, Atheneum). Macmillan.

Flight Guide Airport & Frequency Manual, Vol. 2: Eastern & Central States. Airguide Publications Staff. Ed. by Monte Navarre. 1984. small binder 28.00 o.p. (ISBN 0-911721-15-0, Pub. by Airguide). Aviation.

Flight in America, Nineteen Hundred to Nineteen Eighty-Three: From the Wrights to the Astronauts. Roger E. Bilstein. LC 83-24822. (Illus.). 386p. 1984. 39.50x o.p. (ISBN 0-8018-2973-9). Johns Hopkins.

Flight Instructor Airplane Written Test Guide. rev. ed. Federal Aviation Administration Staff. 138p. 1979. pap. text ed. 7.00 o.p. (ISBN 0-939158-15-9). Flightshops.

Flight Instructor Instrument-Airplane Written Test Guide. rev. ed. Federal Aviation Administration Staff. 86p. 1980. pap. text ed. 4.00 o.p. (ISBN 0-939158-13-2). Flightshops.

Flight Instructor Murders. George Redder. 1977. 8.00 o.p. (ISBN 0-682-48941-7). Exposition-Phoenix.

Flight Instructor Practical Test Guide. rev. ed. Federal Aviation Administration Staff. 17p. 1978. pap. text ed. 1.75 o.p. (ISBN 0-939158-12-4). Flightshops.

Flight Instructor Practical Test Guide (AC 61-58A) Federal Aviation Administration Staff. 17p. 1979. pap. 1.75 o.p. (ISBN 0-86677-011-9, Pub. by Cooper Aviation). Aviation.

Flight Instructor Question Book. (FAA-T-8080-3A Ser.). (Illus.). 72p. 1986. pap. 3.25 o.p. (ISBN 0-318-19960-2, S/N 050-007-00719-1). USGPO.

Flight Instructor Test Book. Aviation Supplies & Academics. 1986. pap. text ed. 11.95 o.p. (Pub. by ASA). Aviation.

Flight of Birds. Crawford H. Greenewalt. LC 75-7170. (Transactions Ser.: Vol. 65, Pt. 4). (Illus.). 1975. pap. 10.00 o.p. (ISBN 0-87169-654-1). Am Philos.

Flight of Butterflies. (Illus.). 60p. 1982. 9.95 o.p. (ISBN 0-87099-206-6). Metro Mus Art.

Flight of Cranes. Christine Bruckner. Tr. by Ruth Hein from Ger. LC 81-22176. Orig. Title: Nirgendwo ist Poenichen. 384p. 1982. 14.95 o.p. (ISBN 0-88064-001-4). Fromm Intl Pub.

Flight of Peter Fromm. Martin Gardner. LC 73-1932. 286p. 1973. 9.95x o.p.; pap. 6.95 o.p. (ISBN 0-913232-77-7). W Kaufmann.

Flight of Splendor. Joellyn Carroll. (Candlelight Ecstasy Ser.: No. 159). (Orig.). 1983. pap. 1.95 o.p. (ISBN 0-440-12858-7). Dell.

Flight of the Dragonfly. Robert L. Forward. 1984. 17.45 o.s.i. (ISBN 0-671-49939-4, Timescape); pap. 7.70 o.s.i. (ISBN 0-671-49944-0, Timescape). PB.

Flight of the Falcon. Daphne Du Maurier. 288p. 1985. pap. 3.50 o.p. (ISBN 0-380-69868-4). Avon.

Flight of the Falcon. Robert Lindsey. 1983. 15.50 o.p. (ISBN 0-671-45159-6). S&S.

Flight of the Fox. Shirley R. Murphy. LC 78-5436. (Illus.). (gr. 4-6). 1978. 8.95 o.p. (ISBN 0-689-30662-8, Atheneum). Macmillan.

Flight of the Mew Gull. Alex Henshaw. 306p. 1987. 17.95 o.p. (ISBN 0-88186-127-8). Parkwest Pubns.

Flight of the Pterosaurs. Keith Moseley. 1986. 13.95 o.s.i. (ISBN 0-671-62232-3). S&S.

Flight of the Sparrow. Julia Cunningham. 128p. (YA) (gr. 7 up). 1982. pap. 1.95 o.p. (ISBN 0-380-57653-8, 57653-8, Camelot). Avon.

Flight of the Starfire. Edwin Mumford. 1972. 4.00 o.p. (ISBN 0-682-47432-0). Exposition-Phoenix.

Flight of the Vin Fiz. E. P. Stein. 1985. 15.95 o.p. (ISBN 0-87795-672-3, Arbor Hse). Morrow.

Flight of the Wild Gander. Joseph Campbell. Penguin USA.

Flight School Handbook. Randall Brink. (Illus.). 210p. 1982. pap. 8.95 o.p. (ISBN 0-8306-2329-9, 2329). TAB Bks.

Flight Theory for Pilots. 2nd ed. Charles E. Dole. (Illus.). 283p. 1988. pap. 12.95 o.p. Aviation.

Flight to America: The Social Background of 300,000 Danish Emigrants. Kristian Hvidt. 1975. 41.00 o.p. (ISBN 0-12-785348-0). Acad Pr.

Flight to Canada. Ishmael Reed. 1977. pap. 2.75 o.p. (ISBN 0-380-01798-9, 52019, Bard). Avon.

Flight to Lucifer: A Gnostic Fantasy. Harold Bloom. 236p. 1979. 9.95 o.p. (ISBN 0-374-15644-1). FS&G.

Flights of Victory: Songs in Celebration of the Nicaraguan Revolution. Ernesto Cardenal. Ed. & tr. by Marc Zimmerman. LC 84-5278. 123p. (Orig., Span. & Eng.). pap. 9.95 o.p. (ISBN 0-88344-131-4). Orbis Bks.

Flights: Readings in Magic, Mysticism, Fantasy & Myth. David A. Leeming. 388p. (Orig.). 1974. pap. text ed. 9.50 o.p. (ISBN 0-15-527556-9, HC). HarBraceJ.

Fling. Pamela Beck & Patti Massman. LC 84-4043. 288p. Date not set. 13.95 o.p. (ISBN 0-317-65060-2). M Evans.

Flintlock & Tomahawk: New England in King Philip's War. Douglas E. Leach. 1966. pap. 4.95 o.p. (ISBN 0-393-00340-X, Norton Lib). Norton.

Flintlock: Its Origin & Development. Torsten Lenk. 55.00 o.p. (ISBN 0-87556-149-7). Saifer.

Flintstone's Fun & Activity Book. (Elephant Bks). 1.25 o.p. (ISBN 0-448-12291-X, G&D). Putnam Pub Group.

Flipside Fiction Library, 7 vols. (gr. 8 up). 1988. Set. lib. bdg. 90.65 o.p. (ISBN 0-8239-0832-1). Rosen Group.

Flirting with Destiny. Samuel H. Jameson. 1979. 9.00 o.p. (ISBN 0-682-49386-4). Exposition-Phoenix.

Floater. Joseph Koenig. 288p. 1987. pap. 3.50 o.p. (ISBN 0-445-40598-8). Mysterious Pr.

Floater. Calvin Trillin. LC 80-17337. 216p. 1980. 9.95 o.p. (ISBN 0-89919-017-0). Ticknor & Fields.

Floaters. Tish O. Ezekiel. LC 83-45498. 256p. 1984. 14.95 o.p. (ISBN 0-689-11446-X, Atheneum). Macmillan.

Floater's Guide to Montana. Hank Fisher. LC 79-52411. (Illus.). 160p. (Orig.). 1979. pap. 6.95 o.p. (ISBN 0-934318-89-1). Falcon Pr MT.

Floating. Hugo Leckey. (Illus.). 1982. 18.95 o.p. (ISBN 0-393-03272-8). Norton.

Floating Admiral. The Detection Club. 320p. 1984. pap. 2.95 o.s.i. (ISBN 0-441-24098-4, Pub. by Charter Bks). Ace Bks.

Floating Island: A Tale of Washington. Garrett Epps. 1985. 14.45 o.p. (ISBN 0-395-37702-1). HM.

Floating Rate Notes. Georges Ugeux. 170p. 1981. 120.00 o.p. (ISBN 0-8002-3426-X). Intl Pubns Serv.

Flock of Words: An Anthology of Poetry for Children & Others. Ed. by David Mackay. LC 77-91070. 1970. 8.50 o.p. (ISBN 0-15-228599-7, HJ). HarBraceJ.

Flogging of Phineas McIntosh: A Tale of Colonial Folly & Injustice, Bechuanaland 1933. Michael Crowder. Date not set. 27.50 o.p. Yale U Pr.

Flohy-Mikenas System, English Opening. Paul Janicki & Jerzy Konikowsky. 83p. (Orig.). 1987. pap. 5.00 o.s.i. (ISBN 0-931462-63-0). Chess Ent Inc.

Flood. Champ Clark. (Planet Earth Ser.). (Illus.). 176p. (YA) (gr. 7 up). 1982. 18.60 o.p. (ISBN 0-8094-4310-4); lib. bdg. 22.60 o.p. Time-Life.

Flood & Noah's Ark. Andre Parrott. 1956. (ISBN 0-8022-1271-9). Philos Lib.

Flood Damage Prevention: Monographs. Mary Vance. (Public Administration Ser.: Bibliography P 1639). 1985. pap. 3.00 o.p. (ISBN 0-89028-329-X). Vance Biblios.

Flood of November Fourth, 1985. McClain Printing Company Staff. 112p. 1985. 9.95 o.p. (ISBN 0-87012-477-3). McClain.

Flood of Thirty-Seven. Mable M. Bartlett. 1979. 4.50 o.p. (ISBN 0-682-49317-1). Exposition-Phoenix.

Floors & Floorcoverings: A Bibliography. Edward H. Teague. (Architecture Ser.: A 1448). 9p. 1985. 2.00 o.p. (ISBN 0-89028-538-1). Vance Biblios.

Flora & Vegetation of Britain: Origins & Change. J. L. Harley & D. H. Lewis. 1985. pap. 10.00 o.p. (ISBN 0-12-325570-8). Acad Pr.

Flora of the South Indian Hill Stations Ootacamund Coonoor, Kotagiri, 2 vols. P. F. Fyson. (Illus.). 1339p. 1977. Set. 100.00 o.p. (ISBN 0-88065-089-3, Pub. by Messers Today & Tomorrow Printers & Publishers). Scholarly Pubns.

Floral Art Book of Reference. Helen Cox. LC 70-91462. 1970. text ed. 17.75 o.p. (ISBN 0-08-007100-7). Pergamon.

Floral Embroidery. Ondori Publishing Company Staff. (Ondori Handicrafts Ser). (Illus.). 64p. 1976. pap. 5.50 o.p. (ISBN 0-87040-365-6). Japan Pubns USA.

Floral Evolution in Relation to Pollination Ecology. E. E. Leppik. (International Bioscience Monographs: No. 3). (Illus.). 215p. 1977. 15.00 o.s.i. (ISBN 0-88065-151-2, Pub. by Messers Today & Tomorrow Printers & Publishers). Scholarly Pubns.

Floral Patterns for Stencilling. Susan M. Britton & Jackie N. Looney. LC 85-27718. (Illus.). 168p. (Orig.). 1986. 19.95 o.p. (ISBN 0-8069-4728-4); pap. 12.95 o.p. (ISBN 0-8069-4730-6). Sterling.

Floramel & Esteban. Emilie Buchwald. LC 81-7135. (Illus.). 72p. 1982. 9.95 o.p. (ISBN 0-15-228678-0, HJ). HarBraceJ.

Florence. Alta Macadam. (Blue Guides Ser.). (Illus.). 1982. 24.95 o.p. (ISBN 0-393-01538-6); pap. 14.95 o.p. (ISBN 0-393-00091-5). Norton.

Florence: A Traveler's Anthology. Ed. by Toby Cole. LC 81-80430. 312p. 1981. 12.95 o.p. (ISBN 0-88208-126-8). Chicago Review.

Florence & Tuscany: Phaidon Cultural Guides. 1986. text ed. 14.95 o.p. (ISBN 0-13-322512-7). P-H.

Florence Fabricant's Pleasures of the Table: Innovative Menus for Entertaining, Easily Prepared Recipes, & the Wines to Serve Them with. Intro. by Sam Aaron. (Illus.). 176p. 1986. 24.95 o.p. (ISBN 0-8109-1488-3). Abrams.

Florence Farr, Bernard Shaw & W. B. Yeats. Ed. by Clifford Bax. 104p. 1971. Repr. of 1941 ed. 15.00x o.p. (ISBN 0-7165-1394-3, BBA 02046, Pub. by Cuala Press Ireland). Biblio Dist.

Florence in Transition, 2 vols. Marvin B. Becker. Incl. Vol. 1. The Decline of the Commune. 263p. 1967 (ISBN 0-8018-0062-5); Vol. 2. Studies in the Rise of the Territorial State. 275p. 1968 (ISBN 0-8018-0063-3). LC 66-28027. 20.00x ea. o.p. Johns Hopkins.

Florence Nightingale. Cecil Woodham-Smith. LC 83-45126. (Illus.). 384p. 1983. pap. 11.95 o.s.i. (ISBN 0-689-70652-9, 296, Atheneum). Macmillan.

Florence Travel Guide. Berlitz Editors. (Travel Guides for English Speakers Ser.). 1978. pap. 6.95 o.p. (ISBN 0-02-969210-5, Berlitz). Macmillan.

Florentine Painting & Its Social Background. Frederick Antal. LC 48-10125. Repr. cancelled o.s.i. (ISBN 0-403-07218-2). Somerset Pub.

Flores en la Tarde. Ernesto F. Flores. Tr. by Juan Hernandez. Ed. by Richard L. Fricker. 1985. pap. 3.00 o.p. (ISBN 0-317-60608-5). Latitudes Pr.

Florestan: The Life & Work of Robert Schumann. Robert H. Schauffler. 574p. Repr. of 1945 ed. lib. bdg. 69.00 o.p. (Pub. by Am Repr Serv). Reprint Servs.

Florida. Carole Chester. (Rand McNally Pocket Guide). (Illus.). 126p. 1985. pap. 5.95 o.p. (ISBN 0-528-84873-9). Rand McNally.

Florida. Dana Facaros & Michael Pauls. 120p. (Orig.). 1985. pap. 5.95 o.p. (ISBN 0-87052-138-1). Hippocrene Bks.

Florida Almanac, 1983-84 Edition. 5th ed. Ed. by Del Marth & Martha J. Marth. LC 71-618243. 444p. 1983. pap. 9.95 o.p. (ISBN 0-88289-322-X). Pelican.

Florida Almanac, 1986-1987. Del Marth. 1985. pap. 10.95 o.p. (ISBN 0-88289-484-6). Pelican.

Florida Almanac, 1986-1987. Ed. by Del Marth & Martha Marth. 444p. (Orig.). (gr. 7-12). pap. 10.95 o.p. Pelican.

Florida & Federal Securities Regulation. 2nd ed. Florida Bar Staff. LC 79-51286. 323p. 1981. casebound 30.00 o.p. (ISBN 0-910373-24-8, 280). FL Bar Legal Ed.

Florida & the American Motion Picture Industry, 1898-1980. Richard A. Nelson. Ed. by Garth S. Jowett. LC 81-48350. (Dissertations on Film Ser.). 798p. 1983. lib. bdg. 176.00 o.p. (ISBN 0-8240-5108-4). Garland Pub.

Florida & the Southeast 1985. Sylvia T. McNair. Ed. by Robert C. Fisher. (Fisher Annotated Travel Guides Ser.). 304p. 1984. pap. 12.95 o.p. (ISBN 0-8116-0062-9). NAL.

Florida Anthropology. Charles H. Fairbanks. pap. 7.00 o.p. (ISBN 0-685-02245-5). Johnson Repr.

Florida Aquatic Habitat & Fishery Resources. Ed. by William Seaman, Jr. (Illus.). 543p. (Orig.). 1985. pap. text ed. 15.00 o.p. (ISBN 0-9616676-0-5). Am Fish Fl.

Florida Archaeology. Jerald T. Milanich & Charles H. Fairbanks. LC 80-524. (New World Archaeological Record Ser.). 1980. 25.00 o.p. (ISBN 0-12-495960-1). Acad Pr.

Florida Burn. Stephen Grave. (Miami Vice Ser.: No. 1). 1985. pap. 2.95 o.p. (ISBN 0-380-89930-2). Avon.

Florida Enchantments. Anthony Weston Dimock & Julian A. Dimock. LC 74-13789. (Illus.). 334p. 1975. Repr. of 1908 ed. 43.00x o.p. (ISBN 0-8103-4061-5). Gale.

Florida Famous Restaurants. Joyce LaFray. 9.95 o.s.i. (ISBN 0-942084-06-3). Trend Bk Div.

Florida, Images of the Landscape. James Valentine. (Illus.). 160p. 1988. 35.00 o.p. Westcliffe Pubs Inc.

Florida Insight Guide. (Illus.). 15.95 o.s.i. Trend Bk Div.

Florida Keys: A History & Guide. Joy Williams. LC 85-2341. 1987. pap. 9.95 o.s.i. (ISBN 0-394-72958-7). Random.

Florida Landscape Plants: Native & Exotic. rev. ed. John V. Watkins & Thomas J. Sheehan. LC 75-22365. (Illus.). 1975. 12.95 o.p. (ISBN 0-8130-0529-9). U Presses Fla.

Florida Manufacturers Register, 1988. 688p. 1988. 85.00 o.p. (ISBN 0-318-22804-1, Pub. by Manufacturers' News Inc). Manufacturers.

Florida Media List. Florida Clipping Service. 10.00 o.p. (ISBN 0-317-17493-2). Trend Bk Div.

Florida One-Day Trip Book: Fifty-Two Off-Beat Excursions in & Around Orlando. Edward Hayes. (Illus.). 160p. 1981. pap. 4.95 o.p. (ISBN 0-914440-50-0). EPM Pubns.

Florida Real Estate Principles, Practices & Law. 10th ed. George Gaines & David Coleman. LC 86-10057. 208p. 1986. pap. text ed. 22.50 o.p. (ISBN 0-88462-427-7, 1610-01, Real Estate Ed). Longman Finan.

Florida Real Estate Principles, Practices & Law. 8th ed. George Gaines, Jr. & David S. Coleman. (Illus.). 480p. 1984. pap. text ed. 22.95 o.p. (ISBN 0-88462-474-9, 1610-01, Real Estate Ed). Longman Finan.

Florida Real Estate Principles, Practices & Law. 11th ed. George Gaines, Jr. & David S. Coleman. (G & C Learning Ser.). (Illus.). 472p. 1987. pap. 23.95 o.p. (ISBN 0-88462-670-9, Real Estate Ed); pap. text ed. 15.95 o.p. (Real Estate Ed). Longman Finan.

Florida Real Property Practice II. 2nd ed. Florida Bar Staff. LC 73-156745. 849p. 1975. casebound 50.00 o.p. (ISBN 0-910373-04-3, 256). FL Bar Legal ED.

Florida Restaurant Guide: Broward - Palm Beach Edition. Robert Tolf. 4.95 o.p. (ISBN 0-317-17501-7). Trend Bk Div.

Florida: Restitution. suppl. 6.00 o.p. Am Law Inst.

Florida Retirees' Handbook: Answers to Your Legal & Financial Questions. Elwood Phillips. LC 84-1693. (Florida Living Ser.). 176p. (Orig.). 1984. pap. 5.95 o.p. (ISBN 0-910923-13-2). Pineapple Pr.

Florida Statistical Abstract, 1973. Ed. by Ralph B. Thompson. 631p. (LC A67-7393). 1973. 12.50x o.p. (ISBN 0-8130-0394-6); pap. 8.50 o.p. (ISBN 0-8130-0511-6). U Presses Fla.

Florida Statistical Abstract, 1974. Ed. by Ralph B. Thompson. (LC A67-7393). 1974. 12.50x o.p. (ISBN 0-8130-0489-6); pap. 8.50 o.p. (ISBN 0-8130-0510-8). U Presses Fla.

Florida Statistical Abstract, 1986. 19.95 o.s.i. (ISBN 0-318-22291-4). Trend Bk Div.

Florida: Torts, Vols. 1-2. suppl. 6.00 o.p. Am Law Inst.

Florida Trails: As Seen from Jacksonville to Key West & from November to April Inclusive. Winthrop Packard. LC 83-139152. (Illus.). 300p. 1983. pap. 9.95 o.s.i. (ISBN 0-910923-02-7). Pineapple Pr.

Florida: Trusts. 8.50 o.p. (ISBN 0-686-90683-7). Am Law Inst.

Florida Underwater Gourmet. Joyce LaFray. 9.95 o.s.i. Trend Bk Div.

Florida: Winter Vacation Guide, 1989. (Illus.). cancelled o.s.i. Wrld Travel.

Florida Zoning & Land Use Planning. Florida Bar Staff. LC 80-68722. 398p. 1980. looseleaf o.p. 45.00 o.p. (ISBN 0-910373-33-7, 229). FL Bar Legal Ed.

Florida's Heritage. Kathleen Montpelier. LC 81-18338. (Illus.). 152p. 1982. text ed. 15.00 o.p. (ISBN 0-87905-115-9). Gibbs Smith Pub.

Flotation, 2 vols. Ed. by M. C. Fuerstenau. LC 76-19745. 1976. 39.00x o.p. (ISBN 0-89520-032-5). SMM&E Inc.

Flote Gottes. Paul Twitchell. Tr. by Eckankar Studiengruppe Munchen. 228p. (Orig., Ger.). 1980. pap. 6.95 o.p. (ISBN 0-88155-001-9, 0526). Illum Way Pub.

Flounder. Gunter Grass. 1980. pap. 3.95 o.p. (ISBN 0-449-24180-7, Crest). Fawcett.

Flow & Fracture at Elevated Temperatures. Ed. by Rishi Raj. 1985. 121.00 o.p. (ISBN 0-87170-201-0). ASM.

Flow in Primary Non-Rotating Passages in Turbomachines. Ed. by H. J. Herring & W. G. Steltz. 224p. 1979. 30.00 o.p. (ISBN 0-317-33518-9, G00165); members 15.00 o.p. (ISBN 0-317-33519-7). ASME.

Flow Induced Heat Exchanger Tube Vibration-1980, HTD-Vol.9. Ed. by J. Chewoweth. 72p. 1980. 16.00 o.p. (ISBN 0-317-33520-0, G00182); 8.00 o.p. (ISBN 0-317-33521-9). ASME.

Flow-Induced Vibration Design Guidelines. Ed. by P. Y. Chen. (PVP Ser.: Vol. 52). 143p. 1981. 30.00 o.p. (ISBN 0-686-34512-6, H00188). ASME.

Flow-Induced Vibration of Circular Cylindrical Structures 1982. Ed. by S. S. Chen & M. P. Paidoussis. (PVP Ser.: Vol. 63). 223p. 1982. 44.00 o.p. (H00220). ASME.

Flow-Induced Vibration of Power Plant Components. Ed. by M. K. Au-Yang. (PVP: No. 41). 176p. 1980. 24.00 o.p. (ISBN 0-686-69851-7, H00168). ASME.

Flow Injection Analysis, Vol. 62. Jaromir Ruzicka & Elo H. Hansen. LC 75-4460. (Chemical Analysis: A Series of Monographs on Analytical Chemistry & Its Applications). 207p. 1981. 65.00 o.p. (ISBN 0-471-08192-2, Pub. by Wiley-Interscience). Wiley.

Flow, Mixing & Heat Transfer in Furnaces, Vol. 2. Ed. by Khalil. 1978. 60.00 o.p. (ISBN 0-08-022695-7). Pergamon.

Flow of Art. Henry McBride. LC 75-13774. 1975. 12.50 o.p. (ISBN 0-689-10692-0, Atheneum). Macmillan.

Flow of News in the Gulf. (New Communication Order Ser.: No. 3). 69p. 1982. pap. 9.00 o.p. (ISBN 0-686-95490-4, UPB121, UPB). UNIPUB.

Flow Visualization. T. Asanuma. 1979. text ed. 69.50 o.p. (ISBN 0-07-002378-6). McGraw.

Flow Visualization. Wolfgang Merzkirch. 1974. 80.00 o.p. (ISBN 0-12-491350-4). Acad Pr.

Flow Visualization Two. Ed. by Wolfgang Merzkirch. LC 81-6406. (Illus.). 803p. 1982. text ed. 149.95 o.p. (ISBN 0-89116-232-1). Hemisphere Pub.

Flowcharting & BASIC. Perry Edwards & Bruce Broadwell. 214p. (Orig.). 1974. pap. text ed. 11.00 o.p. (ISBN 0-15-527661-1, HC). HarBraceJ.

Flowcharting & FORTRAN IV. Perry Edwards. (Illus.). 132p. 1973. text ed. 14.15 o.p. (ISBN 0-07-019042-9, G). McGraw.

Flowcharting for Bank Auditors: A Basic Guide. 56p. 1980. 30.00 o.p. (ISBN 0-317-33777-7, 209). Bank Admin Inst.

Flower & Bird Painting. 1987. 14.95 o.p. (FLBIPA). China Bks.

Flower & the Nettle: Diaries & Letters of Anne Morrow Lindbergh 1936-1939. Anne M. Lindbergh. LC 75-25708. (Helen & Kurt Wolff Bk.). (Illus.). 605p. 1976. 12.95 o.s.i. (ISBN 0-15-131501-9). HarBraceJ.

Flower Arranger's Bible. Derek Bridges. (Illus.). 144p. 1986. 34.95 o.p. (ISBN 0-7126-0789-7, Pub. by Century Hutchinson). David & Charles.

Flower Decoration in the House. G. Jekyll. 1982. 29.50 o.s.i. Apollo.

Flower Decoration in the House. Gertrude Jekyll. (Illus.). 171p. 1982. 29.50 o.p. (ISBN 0-907462-31-6). Antique Collect.

Flower Essences & Vibrational Healing. 2nd ed. Gurudas. 314p. 1985. pap. 12.95 o.p. (ISBN 0-914732-09-9). Bro Life Inc.

Flower Lore. Hilderic Friend. (Illus.). 704p. 1981. pap. 10.95 o.p. (ISBN 0-914918-32-X). Whitford Pr.

Flower of Asia see Triumph of Failure.

Flower of Contemplation. Adah F. Shifrin. (Illus.). 66p. 1974. pap. 1.25 o.p. (ISBN 0-913078-20-4). Sheriar Pr.

Flower of Gold. Kenn Smith. 304p. (Orig.). 1982. pap. 3.25 o.p. (ISBN 0-505-51836-8, Pub. by Tower Bks). Dorchester Pub Co.

Flower of Love. Rachel North. (Orig.). 1980. pap. 2.50 o.p. (ISBN 0-505-51525-3, Pub. by Tower Bks). Dorchester Pub Co.

Flower of Silence. Joanne Marshall. 1975. pap. 0.95 o.p. (ISBN 0-380-00304-X, 19455). Avon.

Flower Ornament Scripture, Vol. 1. Tr. by Thomas Cleary from Chinese. LC 83-2370. 703p. 1986. 49.45 o.p. (ISBN 0-87773-299-X). Shambhala Pubns.

Flower Painting. Jenny Rodwell. (Illus.). 192p. 1985. 19.95 o.p. (ISBN 0-89134-158-7). North Light Bks.

Flower Painting. Clare Sydney. LC 85-43478. (Illus.). 80p. 1986. pap. 19.95 o.p. (ISBN 0-8478-0695-2). Rizzoli Intl.

Flower Painting for Beginners. Kenneth Jameson. LC 79-84663. (Start to Paint Ser.). (Illus.). 1979. pap. 3.95 o.s.i. (ISBN 0-8008-2808-9, Pentalic). Taplinger.

Flower Show. Dennis Stock. LC 86-42741. (Illus.). 112p. 1986. slipcased 50.00 o.p. (ISBN 0-8478-0730-4). Rizzoli Intl.

Flower That's Free: A Novel. Sarah Harrison. 1985. 17.45 o.p. (ISBN 0-671-55205-8). S&S.

Flower Veils the Sun. Zizo Attia. (Illus.). 68p. 1979. 7.50 o.p. (ISBN 0-682-49418-6). Exposition-Phoenix.

Flowering. Agnes S. Turnbull. 1972. 9.95 o.p. (ISBN 0-395-13947-3). HM.

Flowering Dust. Lloyd F. Merrell. LC 61-17968. 68p. 1962. (ISBN 0-8022-1103-8). Philos Lib.

Flowering of New England, 1815-1865. Van Wyck Brooks. 1981. pap. 7.95 o.s.i. (ISBN 0-395-30522-5). HM.

Flowering of the Bamboo: A Bizarre International Mystery. William Triplett. LC 85-51266. 300p. 1985. 14.95 o.p. (ISBN 0-933149-01-8). Woodbine House.

Flowering Plant Index of Illustration & Information. Garden Center of Greater Cleveland Staff. 1979. lib. bdg. 210.00 o.p. (ISBN 0-8161-0301-1, Hall Library). G K Hall.

Flowering Plants from Cuban Gardens. Women's Club of Havana Staff. (Illus.). 1958. 22.95 o.p. (ISBN 0-87599-131-9). S G Phillips.

Flowering Plants of the World. V. H. Heywood. 1985. 39.95 o.p. (ISBN 0-13-322405-8). P-H.

Flowers & Plants in Embroidery. Valerie Campbell-Harding. (Illus.). 144p. 1988. 29.95 o.p. (ISBN 0-7134-1313-1, Pub. by Batsford England). David & Charles.

Flowers by Giorgio Morandi. Jean M. Folon. LC 85-60992. (Illus.). 84p. 1985. 30.00 o.p. (ISBN 0-8478-0639-1). Rizzoli Intl.

Flowers for the Executioner. Bernardo Teixeira. 272p. (Orig.). 1982. pap. 2.75 o.p. (ISBN 0-380-79376-8, 79376). Avon.

Flowers for the Living. Catharine Brandt. LC 77-72449. 1977. pap. 3.95 o.p. (ISBN 0-8066-1585-0, 10-2345, Augsburg). Augsburg Fortress.

Flowers from a Painter's Garden: The Watercolors of Paul Gell. Commentaries by Paul Gell. Tr. by Ronald King. (Illus.). 144p. 1983. 29.95 o.p. (ISBN 0-8109-1479-4). Abrams.

Flowers in Hell: An Investigation into Women & Crime. Barney Bardsley. 470p. 1988. text ed. write for info. o.p. (ISBN 0-86358-065-3, Pub. by Pandora Pr); pap. write for info. o.p. (ISBN 0-86358-197-8, Pub. by Pandora Pr). Routledge Chapman & Hall.

Flowers of Anger. Lynn Hall. (YA) (gr. 7 up). 1978. pap. 1.95 o.p. (ISBN 0-380-01882-9, 59212-6, Flare). Avon.

Flowers of the Amazon. Margaret Mee. (Illus.). 108p. 1983. limited ed. 675.00 o.s.i. (ISBN 0-87951-185-0). Overlook Pr.

Flowers of the Desert. C. A. Haddad. (Orig.). 1982. pap. 3.50 o.p. (ISBN 0-440-12718-1). Dell.

Flowers of the Forest. Ruth D. MacDougall. LC 80-22415. 1981. 11.95 o.p. (ISBN 0-689-11124-X, Atheneum). Macmillan.

Flows in Internal Combustion Engines. Ed. by T. Uzkan. 1982. 24.00 o.p. (H00245). ASME.

Floyd Clymer's Historical Motor Scrapbook: Ford Model T Edition. Floyd Clymer. Ed. by Clymer Publications. (Historical Motor Scrapbook Ser.). (Illus.). 1954. pap. 7.00 o.p. (ISBN 0-89287-259-4, H512). Clymer Pub.

Fluctuation of Glaciers, 3 vols. Incl. Vol. 1. 1959-1965. Peter Kasser. 1967. pap. o.p. (ISBN 92-3-100643-6, U251). UNIPUB; Vol. 2. 1965-1970. Peter Kasser. 357p. 1974. pap. 22.75 o.p. (ISBN 92-3-101045-X, U252). UNIPUB; Vol. 3. 1970-1975. Fritz Muller. 269p. 1977. pap. 44.75 (ISBN 92-3-101462-5, U848). UNIPUB. (Co-published with the International Commission on Snow & Ice of IAHS, UNESCO). UNIPUB.

Fluctuation Phenomena in Solids. Ed. by R. E. Burgess. (Pure & Applied Physics Ser.: Vol. 19). 1964. 94.50 o.p. (ISBN 0-12-143650-0). Acad Pr.

Fluctuations & Non-Linear Wave Interactions in Plasmas. A. G. Sitenko. Tr. by O. D. Kocherga. LC 80-41990. (International Series in Natural Philosophy: Vol. 107). (Illus.). 290p. 1982. 83.00 o.p. (ISBN 0-08-025051-3, C135). Pergamon.

Fluid-Bed Heat Transfer: Gas-Fluidized Bed Behavior & Its Influence on Bed Thermal Properties. J. S. Botterill. 1975. 55.00 o.p. (ISBN 0-12-118750-0). Acad Pr.

Fluid Conductors & Connectors. 156p. 1982. pap. 22.00 o.p. (ISBN 0-89883-406-6, HS150). Soc Auto Engineers.

Fluid Dynamics of Jet Amplifiers: Proceedings of CISM, Department of Hydro Gasdynamics, Technical Univ. of Turin, 1970. CISM (International Center for Mechanical Sciences), Department of Hydro & Gasdynamics Staff. Ed. by A. Romiti. (CISM Publications: No. 66). (Illus.). 1973. pap. 12.60 o.p. (ISBN 0-387-81152-4). Springer-Verlag.

Fluid Flow & Heat Transfer. Aksel L. Lydersen. LC 78-18467. 357p. 1979. 115.00 o.p. (ISBN 0-471-99697-1); pap. 34.95x o.p. (ISBN 0-471-99696-3, Pub. by Wiley-Interscience). Wiley.

Fluid Logic Controls & Industrial Automation. Daniel Bouteille. LC 73-520. 194p. 1973. 24.00 o.p. (ISBN 0-471-09172-3, Pub. by Wiley). Krieger.

Fluid Mechanics & Its Applications. James Murdock. LC 75-31024. (Illus.). 384p. 1976. text ed. 30.50 o.p. (ISBN 0-395-20626-X). HM.

Fluid Mechanics for Civil Engineers. N. B. Webber. 354p. 1971. pap. 13.95x o.p. (ISBN 0-412-10600-0, NO. 6585, Pub. by Chapman & Hall England). Routledge Chapman & Hall.

Fluid Mechanics for Engineering Technology. 2nd ed. Irving Granet. (Illus.). 416p. 1981. text ed. (ISBN 0-13-322610-7). P-H.

Fluid Mixing. Institution of Chemical Engineers. 1982. 46.50 o.s.i. (ISBN 0-08-028762-X). Pergamon.

Fluid Mixing: Proceedings of the Symposium Held at Bradford University, U. K., 3-5 April 1984, No. 2. Ed. by Institution of Chemical Engineers Staff. (Institution of Chemical Engineers Symposium Ser.: Vol. 89). 207p. 1984. 55.00 o.s.i. (ISBN 0-08-031416-3). Pergamon.

Fluid Mixing Technology. James Y. Oldshue. (Chemical Engineering Ser.). 400p. 1983. text ed. 52.50x o.p. (ISBN 0-07-047685-3). McGraw.

Fluid Power with Applications. Anthony Esposito. (Illus.). 1980. text ed. 36.67 o.p. (ISBN 0-13-322701-4). P-H.

Fluid-Structure Interaction Phenomena in Pressure Vessel & Piping Systems, Series PVP-PB-026. Ed. by M. K. Au-Yang & S. J. Brown, Jr. 1977. pap. text ed. 16.00 o.p. (ISBN 0-685-86866-4, G00130). ASME.

Fluid Thermodynamic Properties for Light Petroleum Systems. Kenneth E. Starling. LC 70-184683. 270p. 1973. 45.00x o.s.i. (ISBN 0-87201-293-X). Gulf Pub.

Fluid Transmission Line Dynamics. Ed. by M. E. Franke & T. M. Drzewiecki. 122p. 1981. 24.00 o.p. (ISBN 0-686-34490-1, H00200). ASME.

Fluidic Applications. CISM (International Center for Mechanical Sciences) Staff. Ed. by G. Belforte. (CISM International Centre for Mechanical Sciences, Courses & Lectures: No. 60). (Illus.). 156p. 1974. pap. 16.90 o.p. (ISBN 0-387-81220-2). Springer-Verlag.

Fluidic Components & Equipment, 1968-69. Ed. by Geoffrey W. Dummer & J. M. Robertson. 1969. 210.00 o.p. (ISBN 0-08-013446-7). Pergamon.

Fluidized Bed Combustion & Applied Technology. Ed. by Robert G. Schwieger. (Illus.). 636p. 1984. text ed. 102.50 o.p. (ISBN 0-89116-383-2). Hemisphere Pub.

Fluidized Bed Combustion: Technical, Financial & Regulatory Issues. Richard T. Sheahan. (Illus.). 281p. 1983. 3-ring binder 48.00 o.p. (ISBN 0-86587-105-1). Gov Insts.

Fluids & Applied Mathematics. S. G. Rimon. 1983. pap. 54.00 o.p. (ISBN 0-08-030531-8). Pergamon.

Fluids for Power Systems. R. H. Warring. (Illus.). 1970. 52.50x o.p. Coronet Bks.

Fluorescence: Theory, Instrumentation, & Practice. Ed. by G. G. Guilbault. 1967. 95.00 o.p. (ISBN 0-8247-1260-9). Dekker.

Fluorescent Luminaries. 1980. 5.00 o.p. (ISBN 0-318-18022-7, LE 1-1974). Natl Elec Mfrs.

Fluorine Chemistry, 5 vols. Ed. by J. H. Simons. 1950-64. Vol. 1, 1950. 93.50 o.p. (ISBN 0-12-643901-X); Vol. 2, 1954. 93.50 o.p. (ISBN 0-12-643902-8); Vol. 3, 1963. 77.00 o.p. (ISBN 0-12-643903-6); Vol. 4, 1965. 104.00 o.p. (ISBN 0-12-643904-4); Vol. 5, 1964. 88.00 o.p. (ISBN 0-12-643905-2). Acad Pr.

Fluoropolymers. Leo A. Wall. LC 74-165023. (High Polymers Ser.: Vol. 25). 562p. 1972. 46.50 o.p. (ISBN 0-471-39350-9, JW). Krieger.

Flute. Philip Bate. (Illus.). 1969. 10.00x o.p. (ISBN 0-393-02071-1). Norton.

Flute. rev. ed. Philip Bate. (Instruments of the Orchestra Ser.). 1979. 17.95x o.p. (ISBN 0-393-01292-1). Norton.

Flute Book: A Complete Guide for Students & Performers. Nancy Toff. (Illus.). 1985. 35.00 o.p. (ISBN 0-684-18241-6, ScribT). Scribner.

Flute De Dieu. Paul Twitchell. 1975. pap. 5.95 o.p. (ISBN 0-914766-93-7). Illum Way Pub.

Flute Manual: A Comprehensive Text & Resource Book for Both the Teacher & the Student. Thomas E. Rainey, Jr. LC 85-11133. (Illus.). 238p. (Orig.). 1985. lib. bdg. 27.25 o.p. (ISBN 0-8191-4776-1); pap. text ed. 12.50 o.p. (ISBN 0-8191-4777-X). U Pr of Amer.

Flutie! The Story of Boston College Quaterback Doug Flutie, Winner of the 1984 Heisman Trophy. Ian Thomsen. LC 84-63145. (Illus.). 152p. (Orig.). 1985. pap. 6.95 o.p. (ISBN 0-87106-881-8). Globe Pequot.

Flutterby. Stephen Cosgrove. (Illus.). 672p. (Fr. & Span.). pns o.p. (S-12416). French & Eur.

Fly & Survive: Safety in General Aviation. Ed. by Leslie Hurst & Ronald Hurst. (Illus.). 208p. 1985. 29.50x o.p. (ISBN 0-00-383029-2, Pub. by Collins England). Sheridan.

Fly Away Home. Marge Piercy. 448p. 1984. 17.45 o.s.i. (ISBN 0-671-49419-8). Summit Bks.

Fly Away with E. T. Ed. by Kate Klimo. (Tubbies Ser.). (Illus.). 10p. 1983. pap. 2.95 o.s.i. (ISBN 0-671-46437-X, Little). S&S.

Fly Fishing. Viscount Grey. 224p. (Orig.). 1986. pap. 16.95 o.p. (ISBN 0-941130-16-9). Lyons & Burford.

Fly-Fishing Heresies. Leonard M. Wright, Jr. (Illus.). 240p. pap. 5.95 o.p. (ISBN 0-88317-083-3). Stoeger Pub Co.

Fly Fishing in Salt Water. rev. ed. Lefty Kreh. (Illus.). 250p. 1986. 19.95 o.p. (ISBN 0-8329-0426-0). Lyons & Burford.

Fly Fishing Strategy. Doug Swisher & Carl Richards. LC 84-63022. (Illus.). 192p. 1985. pap. 17.95 o.p. (ISBN 0-8329-0379-5). Lyons & Burford.

Fly Fishingest Gentlemen. Keith C. Russell. (Illus.). 288p. 1986. 17.95 o.p. (ISBN 0-8329-0403-1, Pub. by Winchester Pr); slipcased, ltd. ed. o.p. 30.00 o.p. (ISBN 0-8329-0430-9, Pub. by Winchester Pr). New Century.

Fly Free. Joan Phipson. LC 79-14661. 160p. (gr. 7 up). 1979. 7.95 o.p. (ISBN 0-689-50149-8, Atheneum). Macmillan.

Fly into Danger. Joan Phipson. LC 76-28717. 160p. (gr. 7 up). 1977. 6.95 o.p. (ISBN 0-689-50080-7, Atheneum). Macmillan.

Fly on the Wall. Tony Hillerman. Ed. by J. Barzun & W. H. Taylor. LC 81-47384. (Crime Fiction 1950-1975 Ser.). 212p. 1983. lib. bdg. 18.00 o.p. (ISBN 0-8240-4993-4). Garland Pub.

Fly Tying Problems. John Veniard. (ISBN 0-8329-0248-9). Lyons & Burford.

Fly Tying Techniques. Jacqueline Wakeford. LC 80-1274. (Illus.). 160p. 1985. pap. 17.95 o.p. (ISBN 0-8329-0415-5). Lyons & Burford.

Flying Bomber. Peter G. Cooksley. (Encore Edition). (Illus.). 1979. 3.95 o.p. (ISBN 0-684-17542-8, ScribT). Scribner.

Flying Corpse Headquarters 1914-18. Maurice Baring. (Echoes of War Ser.). 1987. pap. 11.95 o.p. (ISBN 0-907675-44-1, Pub. by Buchan & Enright England). Seven Hills Bk Dists.

Flying Hawaii: A Pilot's Guide to the Islands. Peter N. Forman. (Illus.). 160p. (Orig.). 1983. pap. 10.25 o.p. (ISBN 0-8306-2361-2, 2361). TAB Bks.

Flying High: Inside Big-Time Drug Smuggling. Wayne Greenhaw. 256p. 1984. 15.95 o.p. (ISBN 0-396-08360-9). Dodd.

Flying Machine: A Stagecoach Journey in 1774. John J. Loeper. LC 75-13772. (Illus.). 80p. (gr. 3-5). 1976. 4.95 o.p. (ISBN 0-689-30491-9, Atheneum). Macmillan.

Flying Saucers: A Modern Myth of Things Seen in the Sky. C. G. Jung. pap. 6.95 o.p. (ISBN 0-691-01822-7). Princeton U Pr.

Flying the Bahamas: The Weekend Pilot's Guide. Frank K. Smith. (Illus.). 240p. (Orig.). 1983. pap. 11.15 o.p. (ISBN 0-8306-2351-5, 2351P). TAB Bks.

Flying VFR in Marginal Weather. Paul Garrison. pap. 11.60 o.p. (ISBN 0-8306-2282-9, 2282). TAB Bks.

Flying with Loran C. Bill Givens. (Illus.). 208p. (Orig.). 1985. pap. 15.60 o.p. (ISBN 0-8306-2370-1, 2370P). TAB Bks.

FlyRide Europe 1986. rev. ed. Ed. by Consumer Report Book Editors. Ed Perkins. 304p. 1986. pap. 12.00 o.p. (ISBN 0-89043-036-5). Consumer Reports.

FM & Repeaters for the Radio Amateur. American Radio Relay League Staff. LC 72-96087. pap. 5.00 o.p. (ISBN 0-87259-454-8). Am Radio.

Foal Creek. Peter Z. Cohen. LC 72-75266. (Illus.). (gr. 5-9). 1972. 5.95 o.p. (ISBN 0-689-30048-4, Atheneum). Macmillan.

Foams. J. J. Bikerman. LC 72-94700. (Applied Physics & Engineering: Vol. 10). (Illus.). 320p. 1973. 47.50 o.p. (ISBN 0-387-06108-8). Springer-Verlag.

Focal Aspects of the Industrial Revolution: 1826-42, Five Pamphlets. (Development of Industrial Society Ser.). 198p. 1971. Repr. of 1842 ed. 27.50x o.p. (ISBN 0-7165-1562-8, BBA 03063, Pub. by Irish Academic Pr England). Biblio Dist.

Focke-Wulf 190 D. J. Richard Smith et al. Ed. by Thomas H. Hitchcock. LC 85-63199. (Monogram Close-Up 10 Ser.: No. 10). (Illus.). 32p. 1986. 6.95 o.s.i. (ISBN 0-914144-10-3). Monogram Aviation.

Focus. Arthur Miller. LC 84-71472. (Library of Contemporary Americana). 224p. 1984. pap. 6.95 o.p. (ISBN 0-87795-649-9, Arbor Hse). Morrow.

Focus: A College English Handbook. Kim Flachmann. LC 80-82699. (Illus.). 448p. 1981. pap. 22.36 o.p. (ISBN 0-395-29728-1). HM.

Focus, Coherence & Emphasis. Paul Werth. 304p. 1984. 29.95 o.p. (ISBN 0-7099-2790-8, Pub. by Croom Helm Ltd). Routledge Chapman & Hall.

Focus for Evangelism: The Evangelical Implications of Ministry. Dennis Orsen. 48p. (Orig.). 1985. pap. 3.95 o.p. (ISBN 0-8066-2199-0, 23-1601, Augsburg). Augsburg Fortress.

Focus on Dance: Dance for the Handicapped, Vol. 9. 104p. 5.95 o.p. AAHPERD.

Focus on Forster's "A Passage to India" Indian Essays in Criticism. Ed. by V. A. Shahane. 158p. 1981. 40.00x o.p. (ISBN 0-86125-074-5, Pub. by Orient Longman Ltd India). Apt Bks.

Focus on Infusion: Proceedings of the American Instructor's of the Deaf, 50th Biennial Meeting, Rochester, NY, June 1981, Vol. I. American Instructors of the Deaf Staff. Ed. by Frances Solano et al. (Illus.). 1982. pap. (ISBN 0-942896-00-9). Con Am Inst Deaf.

Focus on Southeastern Ground Water Issues, 1987: Proceedings. LC 86-31163. 1986. 43.75 o.p. (ISBN 0-318-23041-0). Natl Water Well.

Focus on Southwestern Ground Water Issues, 1987: Proceedings. LC 86-31162. 1987. 43.75 o.p. (ISBN 0-318-23040-2). Natl Water Well.

Focus on Symphony Macros. Alan Simpson. 239p. (Orig.). 1986. pap. 19.95 o.p. (ISBN 0-89588-351-1). Sybex.

Focus on the Teacher-Communicative Approaches to Teacher Training. (English Language Teaching Documents Ser.: Vol. 110). 88p. 1983. pap. text ed. 5.75 o.s.i. (ISBN 0-08-030300-5). Pergamon.

Fodor's Alaska 1984. (Illus.). 224p. 1983. pap. 8.95 traveltex o.p. (ISBN 0-679-00972-8). McKay.

Fodor's Alaska 1985. 1985. pap. 8.95 traveltex o.p. (ISBN 0-679-01075-0). McKay.

Fodor's Alaska 1986. 1986. pap. 8.95 o.p. (ISBN 0-679-01196-X). McKay.

Fodor's Alaska 1988. 1988. pap. 8.95 o.p. (ISBN 0-679-01462-4). McKay.

Fodor's American Cities on a Budget 1986. 1985. pap. 12.95 o.p. (ISBN 0-679-01195-1). McKay.

Fodor's Amsterdam 1985. 1985. pap. 5.95 o.p. (ISBN 0-679-01177-3). McKay.

Fodor's Amsterdam, 1988. 1988. pap. 6.95 o.p. (ISBN 0-679-01464-0, Fodor). McKay.

Fodor's Arizona 1988. 1987. pap. 7.95 o.p. (ISBN 0-679-01465-9). McKay.

Fodor's Australia & New Zealand, 1987. 1986. pap. 15.95 o.p. (ISBN 0-679-01314-8, Fodor). McKay.

Fodor's Australia, New Zealand & the Pacific 1985. 1984. pap. 14.95 traveltex o.p. (ISBN 0-679-01076-9). McKay.

Fodor's Australia, New Zealand & the South Pacific, 1984. (Illus.). 576p. 1983. pap. 13.95 traveltex o.p. (ISBN 0-679-00973-6). McKay.

Fodor's Australia, New Zealand & the South Pacific 1986. 1985. pap. 14.95 o.p. (ISBN 0-679-01198-6). McKay.

Fodor's Australia, New Zealand & the South Pacific 1988. 1987. pap. 15.95 o.p. (ISBN 0-679-01466-7, Fodor). McKay.

Fodor's Austria 1984. (Illus.). 400p. 1983. pap. 11.95 traveltex o.p. (ISBN 0-679-00974-4). McKay.

Fodor's Austria 1985. 1984. pap. 12.95 traveltex o.p. (ISBN 0-679-01077-7). McKay.

Fodor's Austria 1986. 1985. pap. 13.95 o.p. (ISBN 0-679-01199-4). McKay.

Fodor's Austria, 1987. 1986. pap. 13.95 o.p. (ISBN 0-679-01315-6, Fodor). McKay.

Fodor's Austria 1988. 1987. pap. 13.95 o.p. (ISBN 0-679-01467-5, Fodor). McKay.

Fodor's Bahamas 1986. 1985. pap. 6.95 o.p. (ISBN 0-679-01200-1). McKay.

Fodor's Bahamas, 1987. 1986. pap. 7.95 o.p. (ISBN 0-679-01442-X, Fodor). McKay.

Fodor's Bahamas 1988. 1987. pap. 8.95 o.p. (ISBN 0-679-01468-3, Fodor). McKay.

Fodor's Beijing, Guangzhou, & Shanghai, 1984. (Illus.). 176p. 1983. pap. 6.95 o.p. (ISBN 0-679-01054-8). McKay.

Fodor's Beijing, Guangzhou & Shanghai 1985. 1985. pap. 6.95 o.p. (ISBN 0-679-01078-5). McKay.

Fodor's Beijing, Guangzhou, & Shanghai 1986. 1986. pap. 7.95 o.p. (ISBN 0-679-01201-X). McKay.

Fodor's Beijing, Guangzhou & Shanghai 1988. 1988. pap. 7.95 o.p. (ISBN 0-679-01470-5, Fodor). McKay.

Fodor's Belgium & Luxembourg, 1981. 1981. pap. 12.95 o.p. (ISBN 0-679-00671-0). McKay.

Fodor's Belgium & Luxembourg 1984. (Illus.). 336p. 1983. pap. 12.95 traveltex o.p. (ISBN 0-679-00975-2). Mckay.

Fodor's Belgium & Luxembourg 1985. 1984. pap. 12.95 traveltex o.p. (ISBN 0-679-01079-3). McKay.

Fodor's Belgium & Luxembourg 1986. 1985. pap. 13.95 o.p. (ISBN 0-679-01202-8). McKay.

Fodor's Belgium & Luxembourg 1988. 1987. pap. 13.95 o.p. (ISBN 0-679-01471-3, Fodor). McKay.

Fodor's Bermuda 1984. (Illus.). 192p. 1983. pap. 7.95 traveltex o.p. (ISBN 0-679-00976-0). McKay.

Fodor's Bermuda 1985. 1984. pap. 8.95 traveltex o.p. (ISBN 0-679-01080-7). McKay.

Fodor's Bermuda 1986. 1985. pap. 8.95 o.p. (ISBN 0-679-01203-6). McKay.

Fodor's Bermuda, 1987. 1986. pap. 8.95 o.p. (ISBN 0-679-01448-9, Fodor). McKay.

Fodor's Bermuda 1988. 1987. pap. 8.95 o.p. (ISBN 0-679-01472-1, Fodor). McKay.

Fodor's Boston 1986. 1986. pap. 7.95 o.p. (ISBN 0-679-01204-4). McKay.

Fodor's Boston, 1987. 1986. pap. 7.95 o.p. (ISBN 0-679-01321-0, Fodor). McKay.

Fodor's Boston, 1988. 1987. pap. 7.95 o.p. (ISBN 0-679-01473-X, Fodor). McKay.

Fodor's Brazil 1984. (Illus.). 160p. 1983. pap. 6.95 traveltex o.p. (ISBN 0-679-00977-9). McKay.

Fodor's Brazil 1985. 1984. pap. 6.95 traveltex o.p. (ISBN 0-679-01082-3). McKay.

Fodor's Brazil 1986. 1985. pap. 6.95 o.p. (ISBN 0-679-01205-2). McKay.

Fodor's Brazil, 1988. 1987. pap. 8.95 o.p. (ISBN 0-679-01474-8, Fodor). McKay.

Fodor's Budget Britain 1984. (Illus.). 224p. 1983. pap. 7.95 o.p. (ISBN 0-679-00979-5). McKay.

Fodor's Budget Britain 1985. 1984. pap. 7.95 o.p. (ISBN 0-679-01083-1). McKay.

Fodor's Budget Canada 1984. 1983. pap. 8.95 o.p. (ISBN 0-679-00980-9). McKay.

Fodor's Budget Canada 1985. 1984. pap. 8.95 o.p. (ISBN 0-679-01084-X). McKay.

Fodor's Budget Caribbean, 1983. 1982. pap. 8.95 o.p. (ISBN 0-679-00877-2, Fodor). McKay.

Fodor's Budget Caribbean 1984. (Illus.). 320p. 1983. pap. 8.95 o.p. (ISBN 0-679-00981-7). McKay.

Fodor's Budget Caribbean 1985. 1984. pap. 8.95 o.p. (ISBN 0-679-01085-8). McKay.

Fodor's Budget Europe 1984. (Illus.). 688p. 1983. pap. 11.95 traveltex o.p. (ISBN 0-679-00982-5). McKay.

Fodor's Budget Europe 1985. 1984. pap. 11.95 traveltex o.p. (ISBN 0-679-01086-6). McKay.

Fodor's Budget Europe 1986. 1985. pap. 11.95 o.p. (ISBN 0-679-01209-5). McKay.

Fodor's Budget Europe, 1987. 1986. pap. 12.95 o.p. (ISBN 0-679-01326-1, Fodor). McKay.

Fodor's Budget Europe 1988. 1987. pap. 12.95 o.p. (ISBN 0-679-01478-0, Fodor). McKay.

Fodor's Budget France 1984. 1983. pap. 6.95 o.p. (ISBN 0-679-00983-3). McKay.

Fodor's Budget France '85. 1985. pap. 6.95 o.p. (ISBN 0-679-01087-4). McKay.

Fodor's Budget Germany 1984. 1983. pap. 7.95 o.p. (ISBN 0-679-00984-1). McKay.

Fodor's Budget Germany '85. 1985. pap. 7.95 o.p. (ISBN 0-679-01088-2). McKay.

Fodor's Budget Hawaii 1984. (Illus.). 128p. 1983. pap. 4.95 o.p. (ISBN 0-679-00985-X). McKay.

Fodor's Budget Hawaii 1985. 1984. pap. 5.95 o.p. (ISBN 0-679-01089-0). McKay.

Fodor's Budget Italy 1984. (Illus.). 176p. 1983. pap. 6.95 o.p. (ISBN 0-679-00986-8). McKay.

Fodor's Budget Italy 1985. 1984. pap. 6.95 o.p. (ISBN 0-679-01090-4). McKay.

Fodor's Budget Japan, 1981. 1980. pap. 4.95 o.p. (ISBN 0-679-00655-9). McKay.

Fodor's Budget Japan 1984. (Illus.). 192p. 1983. pap. 6.95 o.p. (ISBN 0-679-00987-6). McKay.

Fodor's Budget Japan '85. 1985. pap. 6.95 o.p. (ISBN 0-679-01091-2). McKay.

Fodor's Budget London 1984. 1983. pap. 6.95 o.p. (ISBN 0-679-01057-2). McKay.

Fodor's Budget London 1985. 1985. pap. 7.95 o.p. (ISBN 0-679-01092-0). McKay.

Fodor's Budget Mexico, 1981. 1981. pap. 5.95 o.p. (ISBN 0-679-00660-5). McKay.

Fodor's Budget Mexico 1984. (Illus.). 256p. 1983. pap. 7.95 o.p. (ISBN 0-679-00988-4). McKay.

Fodor's Budget Mexico 1985. 1984. pap. 7.95 o.p. (ISBN 0-679-01093-9). McKay.

Fodor's Budget Scandinavia 1984. 1983. pap. 7.95 o.p. (ISBN 0-679-00989-2). McKay.

Fodor's Budget Scandinavia 1985. 1984. pap. 7.95 o.p. (ISBN 0-679-01095-5). McKay.

Fodor's Budget Spain, 1981. 1981. pap. 4.95 traveltex o.p. (ISBN 0-679-00653-2). McKay.

Fodor's Budget Spain 1984. (Illus.). 224p. 1983. pap. 6.95 o.p. (ISBN 0-679-00990-6). McKay.

Fodor's Budget Spain 1985. 1985. pap. 6.95 o.p. (ISBN 0-679-01096-3). McKay.

Fodor's Budget Travel Britain 1986. 1985. pap. 5.95 o.p. (ISBN 0-679-01206-0). McKay.

Fodor's Budget Travel Canada 1986. 1986. pap. 6.95 o.p. (ISBN 0-679-01207-9). McKay.

Fodor's Budget Travel Caribbean 1986. 1985. pap. 6.95 o.p. (ISBN 0-679-01208-7). McKay.

Fodor's Budget Travel France 1986. 1986. pap. 5.95 o.p. (ISBN 0-679-01210-9). McKay.

Fodor's Budget Travel Germany 1986. 1985. pap. 5.95 o.p. (ISBN 0-679-01211-7). McKay.

Fodor's Budget Travel Hawaii 1986. 1985. pap. 5.50 o.p. (ISBN 0-679-01212-5). McKay.

Fodor's Budget Travel in America, 1984. (Illus.). 720p. 1983. pap. 11.95 traveltex o.p. (ISBN 0-679-00991-4). McKay.

Fodor's Budget Travel in America 1985. 1984. pap. 11.95 traveltex o.p. (ISBN 0-679-01097-1). McKay.

Fodor's Budget Travel Italy 1986. 1985. pap. 5.95 o.p. (ISBN 0-679-01213-3). McKay.

Fodor's Budget Travel Japan 1986. 1986. pap. 6.95 o.p. (ISBN 0-679-01214-1). McKay.

Fodor's Budget Travel London 1986. 1985. pap. 5.95 o.p. (ISBN 0-679-01215-X). McKay.

Fodor's Budget Travel Mexico 1986. 1985. pap. 5.95 o.p. (ISBN 0-679-01216-8). McKay.

Fodor's Budget Travel Spain 1986. 1986. pap. 5.95 o.p. (ISBN 0-679-01219-2). McKay.

Fodor's California 1984. (Illus.). 576p. 1983. pap. 11.95 traveltex o.p. (ISBN 0-679-00992-2). McKay.

Fodor's California 1985. 1984. pap. 11.95 traveltex o.p. (ISBN 0-679-01098-X). McKay.

Fodor's California 1986. 1985. pap. 11.95 o.p. (ISBN 0-679-01220-6). McKay.

Fodor's California, 1988. 1987. pap. 12.95 o.p. (ISBN 0-679-01487-X, Fodor). McKay.

Fodor's Canada, 1984. Bernadine Kreis. 1983. pap. 11.95 o.p. (ISBN 0-679-00993-0, Fodor). McKay.

Fodor's Canada 1985. 1984. pap. 12.95 traveltex o.p. (ISBN 0-679-01099-8). McKay.

Fodor's Canada 1986. 1985. pap. 12.95 o.p. (ISBN 0-679-01221-4). McKay.

Fodor's Canada, 1987. 1986. pap. 13.95 o.p. (ISBN 0-679-01336-9, Fodor). McKay.

Fodor's Canada 1988. 1987. pap. 13.95 o.p. (ISBN 0-679-01488-8, Fodor). McKay.

Fodor's Canada's Maritime Provinces 1986. 1986. pap. 6.95 o.p. (ISBN 0-679-01222-2). McKay.

Fodor's Canada's Maritime Provinces 1988. 1987. pap. 7.95 o.p. (ISBN 0-679-01489-6, Fodor). McKay.

Fodor's Cancun, Cozumel, Merida & the Yucatan 1988. 1987. pap. 8.95 o.p. (ISBN 0-679-01490-X, Fodor). McKay.

Fodor's Cape Cod & the Islands of Martha's Vineyard & Nantucket. 1983. pap. 7.95 Traveltex o.p. (ISBN 0-679-00840-3). McKay.

Fodor's Cape Cod, 1984. (Fodor's Modern Guides Ser.). (Orig.). 1983. pap. 8.95 traveltex o.p. (ISBN 0-679-00994-9). McKay.

Fodor's Cape Cod, 1985. 1985. pap. 8.95 traveltex o.p. (ISBN 0-679-01101-3). McKay.

Fodor's Cape Cod 1986. 1986. pap. 8.95 o.p. (ISBN 0-679-01223-0). McKay.

Fodor's Cape Cod, 1988. (Travel Guides). 1988. pap. 8.95 o.p. (ISBN 0-679-01491-8, Fodor). McKay.

Fodor's Caribbean & Bahamas 1985. 1984. pap. 12.95 traveltex o.p. (ISBN 0-679-01102-1). McKay.

Fodor's Caribbean & the Bahamas. 1982. pap. 11.95 o.p. (ISBN 0-679-00904-3, Fodor). McKay.

Fodor's Caribbean & the Bahamas 1984. (Illus.). 544p. 1983. pap. 12.95 traveltex o.p. (ISBN 0-679-00995-7). McKay.

Fodor's Caribbean 1986. 1985. pap. 12.95 o.p. (ISBN 0-679-01224-9). McKay.

Fodor's Caribbean, 1987. 1986. pap. 12.95 o.p. (ISBN 0-679-01445-4, Fodor). McKay.

Fodor's Caribbean 1988. 1987. pap. 13.95 o.p. (ISBN 0-679-01492-6, Fodor). McKay.

Fodor's Chesapeake, 1988. (Travel Guides). 1988. pap. 7.95 o.p. (ISBN 0-679-01494-2, Fodor). McKay.

Fodor's Chicago & the Great Lakes Recreation Areas. 1983. pap. 7.95 traveltex o.p. (ISBN 0-679-00838-1). McKay.

Fodor's Chicago, 1984. (Illus.). 160p. 1983. pap. 8.95 traveltex o.p. (ISBN 0-679-00996-5). McKay.

Fodor's Chicago 1985. 1985. pap. 7.95 traveltex o.p. (ISBN 0-679-01104-8). McKay.

Fodor's Chicago 1986. 1986. pap. 6.95 o.p. (ISBN 0-679-01226-5). McKay.

Fodor's Chicago 1988. 1988. pap. 6.95 o.p. (ISBN 0-679-01495-0, Fodor). McKay.

Fodor's Colorado, 1981. 1980. pap. 6.95 o.p. (ISBN 0-679-00602-8). McKay.

Fodor's Colorado 1984. (Illus.). 144p. 1983. pap. 7.95 traveltex o.p. (ISBN 0-679-00997-3). Mckay.

Fodor's Colorado 1985. 1984. pap. 7.95 traveltex o.p. (ISBN 0-679-01106-4). McKay.

Fodor's Colorado 1986. 1985. pap. 7.95 o.p. (ISBN 0-679-01228-1). McKay.

Fodor's Colorado, 1987. 1986. pap. 8.95 o.p. (ISBN 0-679-01343-1, Fodor). McKay.

Fodor's Colorado 1988. 1987. pap. 8.95 o.p. (ISBN 0-679-01496-9, Fodor). McKay.

Fodor's Dallas - Fort Worth, 1988. (Travel Guides). 1988. pap. 6.95 o.p. (ISBN 0-679-01497-7, Fodor). McKay.

Fodor's Dallas-Fort Worth, 1985. 1985. pap. 4.95 o.p. (ISBN 0-679-01107-2). McKay.

Fodor's Dallas-Fort Worth 1986. 1986. pap. 5.95 o.p. (ISBN 0-679-01229-X). McKay.

Fodor's Eastern Europe, 1984. 1983. pap. 14.95 traveltex o.p. (ISBN 0-679-00999-X). McKay.

Fodor's Eastern Europe 1985. 1984. pap. 15.95 traveltex o.p. (ISBN 0-679-01108-0). McKay.

Fodor's Eastern Europe 1986. 1985. pap. 15.95 o.p. (ISBN 0-679-01230-3). McKay.

Fodor's Eastern Europe, 1988. 1987. pap. 16.95 o.p. (ISBN 0-679-01498-5, Fodor). McKay.

Fodor's Egypt 1984. (Illus.). 272p. 1983. pap. 11.95 traveltex o.p. (ISBN 0-679-01000-9). McKay.

Fodor's Egypt 1985. 1984. pap. 12.95 traveltex o.p. (ISBN 0-679-01109-9). McKay.

Fodor's Egypt 1986. 1985. pap. 12.95 o.p. (ISBN 0-679-01231-1). McKay.

Fodor's Egypt, 1987. 1986. pap. 12.95 o.p. (ISBN 0-679-01346-6, Fodor). McKay.

Fodor's Egypt 1988. 1987. pap. 12.95 o.p. (ISBN 0-679-01499-3, Fodor). McKay.

Fodor's Europe, 1983. 1982. pap. 12.95 o.p. (ISBN 0-679-00910-8, Fodor). McKay.

Fodor's Europe 1984. (Illus.). 864p. 1983. pap. 15.95 o.p. (ISBN 0-679-01002-5); pap. 12.95 traveltex o.p. (ISBN 0-679-01001-7). McKay.

Fodor's Europe 1985. 1984. pap. 13.95 traveltex o.p. (ISBN 0-679-01110-2). McKay.

Fodor's Europe 1986. 1985. pap. 13.95 o.p. (ISBN 0-679-01232-X). McKay.

Fodor's Europe 1988. 1987. pap. 14.95 o.p. (ISBN 0-679-01500-0, Fodor). McKay.

Fodor's Far West, 1981. 1980. pap. 8.95 o.p. (ISBN 0-679-00604-4). McKay.

Fodor's Far West, 1984. 1984. pap. 10.95 o.p. (ISBN 0-679-01003-3, Fodor). McKay.

Fodor's Far West 1985. 1985. pap. 11.95 traveltex o.p. (ISBN 0-679-01111-0). McKay.

Fodor's Far West 1986. 1986. pap. 12.95 o.p. (ISBN 0-679-01233-8). McKay.

Fodor's Far West 1988. 1988. pap. 13.95 o.p. (ISBN 0-679-01501-9, Fodor). McKay.

Fodor's Far West,1982. 1981. pap. 9.95 Traveltex o.p. (ISBN 0-679-00785-7). McKay.

Fodor's Florida, 1984. (Illus.). 332p. 1983. pap. 8.95 traveltex o.p. (ISBN 0-679-00971-X). McKay.

Fodor's Florida, 1985. 1984. pap. 9.95 traveltex o.p. (ISBN 0-679-01112-9). McKay.

Fodor's Florida 1986. 1985. pap. 9.95 o.p. (ISBN 0-679-01234-6). McKay.

Fodor's Florida 1988. 1987. pap. 10.95 o.p. (ISBN 0-679-01502-7, Fodor). McKay.

Fodor's France 1983. (Illus.). 592p. 1983. pap. 12.95 traveltex o.p. (ISBN 0-679-00914-0). McKay.

Fodor's France, 1984. (Illus.). 576p. 1983. pap. 12.95 traveltex o.p. (ISBN 0-679-01004-1). McKay.

Fodor's France 1985. 1984. pap. 13.95 traveltex o.p. (ISBN 0-679-01113-7). McKay.

Fodor's France 1986. 1986. pap. 13.95 o.p. (ISBN 0-679-01235-4). McKay.

Fodor's France, 1987. 1986. pap. 13.95 o.p. (ISBN 0-679-01350-4, Fodor). McKay.

Fodor's France 1988. 1987. pap. 13.95 o.p. (ISBN 0-679-01503-5, Fodor). McKay.

Fodor's Fun in Acapulco. 1985. pap. 5.50 o.p. (ISBN 0-679-01167-6). McKay.

Fodor's Fun in Acapulco, 1987. 1986. pap. 5.95 o.p. (ISBN 0-679-01351-2, Fodor). McKay.

Fodor's Fun in Acapulco 1988. 1987. pap. 6.95 o.p. (ISBN 0-679-01504-3, Fodor). McKay.

Fodor's Fun in Disney World & the Orlando Area 1988. 1987. pap. 6.95 o.p. (ISBN 0-679-01512-4, Fodor). McKay.

Fodor's Fun in Las Vegas 1988: Including Reno & Lake Tahoe. 1987. pap. 6.95 o.p. (ISBN 0-679-01508-6, Fodor). McKay.

Fodor's Fun in London. 1985. pap. 5.50 o.p. (ISBN 0-679-01173-0). McKay.

Fodor's Fun in London, 1987. 1986. pap. 5.95 o.p. (ISBN 0-679-01353-9, Fodor). McKay.

Fodor's Fun in London 1988. 1987. pap. 6.95 o.p. (ISBN 0-679-01509-4, Fodor). McKay.

Fodor's Fun in Maui. 1986. pap. 6.95 o.p. (ISBN 0-679-01354-7, Fodor). McKay.

Fodor's Fun in Montreal. 1985. pap. 5.50 o.p. (ISBN 0-679-01168-4). McKay.

Fodor's Fun in Montreal 1988. 1987. pap. 6.95 o.p. (ISBN 0-679-01510-8, Fodor). McKay.

Fodor's Fun in New Orleans. 1986. pap. 5.95 o.p. (ISBN 0-679-01356-3, Fodor). McKay.

Fodor's Fun in New York City 1988. 1987. pap. 6.95 o.p. (ISBN 0-679-01511-6, Fodor). McKay.

Fodor's Fun in Paris 1988. 1987. pap. 6.95 o.p. (ISBN 0-679-01513-2, Fodor). McKay.

Fodor's Fun in Puerto Rico. 1985. pap. 5.50 o.p. (ISBN 0-679-01179-X). McKay.

Fodor's Fun in Rio. 1986. pap. 6.95 o.p. (ISBN 0-679-01358-X, Fodor). McKay.

Fodor's Fun in St. Martin-St. Maarten 1988. 1987. pap. 6.95 o.p. (ISBN 0-679-01514-0, Fodor). McKay.

Fodor's Fun in San Francisco, 1988. 1987. pap. 6.95 o.p. (ISBN 0-679-01515-9, Fodor). McKay.

Fodor's Fun in the Bahamas, 1987. 1986. pap. 5.95 o.p. (ISBN 0-679-01352-0, Fodor). McKay.

Fodor's Fun in the Bahamas 1988. 1987. pap. 5.95 o.p. (ISBN 0-679-01505-1, Fodor). McKay.

Fodor's Fun in Waikiki. 1985. pap. 5.50 o.p. (ISBN 0-679-01169-2). McKay.

Fodor's Fun in Waikiki, 1987. 1986. pap. 5.95 o.p. (ISBN 0-679-01362-8, Fodor). McKay.

Fodor's Germany, 1983. (Illus.). 544p. 1983. pap. 12.95 traveltex o.p. (ISBN 0-679-00916-7). Mckay.

Fodor's Germany, 1984. (Illus.). 544p. 1983. pap. 12.95 traveltex o.p. (ISBN 0-679-01005-X). McKay.

Fodor's Germany 1985. 1985. pap. 13.95 traveltex o.p. (ISBN 0-679-01114-5). McKay.

Fodor's Germany 1986. 1986. pap. 13.95 o.p. (ISBN 0-679-01236-2). McKay.

Fodor's Germany, 1987. 1986. pap. 13.95 o.s.i. (ISBN 0-679-01363-6, Fodor). McKay.

Fodor's Germany 1988. 1987. pap. 13.95 o.p. (ISBN 0-679-01517-5, Fodor). McKay.

Fodor's Grand Canyon. (Illus.). 224p. pap. 8.95 traveltex o.p. (ISBN 0-679-00917-5). McKay.

Fodor's Great Britain 1983. (Illus.). 528p. 1983. pap. 15.95 o.p. (ISBN 0-679-00918-3); pap. 12.95 traveltex o.p. (ISBN 0-679-00919-1). McKay.

Fodor's Great Britain, 1984. (Illus.). 528p. 1983. pap. 15.95 o.p. (ISBN 0-679-01007-6); pap. 12.95 traveltex o.p. (ISBN 0-679-01006-8). McKay.

Fodor's Great Britain 1985. 1984. pap. 13.95 traveltex o.p. (ISBN 0-679-01116-1). McKay.

Fodor's Great Britain 1986. 1985. pap. 13.95 o.p. (ISBN 0-679-01237-0). McKay.

Fodor's Great Britain, 1987. 1986. pap. 13.95 o.p. (ISBN 0-679-01364-4, Fodor). McKay.

Fodor's Great Britain 1988. 1987. pap. 13.95 o.p. (ISBN 0-679-01518-3, Fodor). McKay.

Fodor's Great Travel Values: Caribbean. (Great Travel Values Ser.). 1988. pap. 7.95 o.p. (ISBN 0-679-01477-2, Fodor). McKay.

Fodor's Great Travel Values, 1988: American Cities. (Great Travel Values Ser.). 1987. pap. 13.95 o.p. (ISBN 0-679-01463-2, Fodor). McKay.

Fodor's Great Travel Values, 1988: Hawaii. 1987. pap. 5.95 o.p. (ISBN 0-679-01481-0, Fodor). McKay.

Fodor's Greater Miami & the Gold Coast 1986. 1985. pap. 5.95 o.p. (ISBN 0-679-01238-9). McKay.

Fodor's Greater Miami & the Gold Coast 1988. 1987. pap. 5.95 o.p. (ISBN 0-679-01519-1, Fodor). McKay.

Fodor's Greater Miami, 1987. 1986. pap. 5.95 o.p. (ISBN 0-679-01365-2, Fodor). McKay.

Fodor's Greece Travel, 1984. 1983. pap. 11.95 o.p. (ISBN 0-679-01008-4, Fodor). McKay.

Fodor's Greece 1983. (Illus.). 384p. 1983. pap. 11.95 traveltex o.p. (ISBN 0-679-00921-3). Mckay.

Fodor's Greece, 1984. (Illus.). 332p. 1983. traveltex 11.95 o.p. McKay.

Fodor's Greece 1985. 1984. pap. 12.95 traveltex o.p. (ISBN 0-679-01117-X). McKay.

Fodor's Greece 1986. 1985. pap. 13.95 o.p. (ISBN 0-679-01239-7). McKay.

Fodor's Greece, 1987. 1986. pap. 13.95 o.p. (ISBN 0-679-01366-0, Fodor). McKay.

Fodor's Greece 1988. 1987. pap. 13.95 o.p. (ISBN 0-679-01520-5, Fodor). McKay.

Fodor's Hawaii Travel, 1984. 1983. pap. 10.95 o.p. (ISBN 0-679-01009-2, Fodor). McKay.

Fodor's Hawaii, 1983. 1983. pap. 13.95 o.p. (ISBN 0-679-00922-1); pap. 10.95 traveltex o.p. (ISBN 0-679-00923-X). McKay.

Fodor's Hawaii, 1984. (Illus.). 352p. 1983. pap. 13.95 o.p. (ISBN 0-679-01010-6). McKay.

Fodor's Hawaii 1985. 1984. pap. 11.95 traveltex o.p. (ISBN 0-679-01118-8). McKay.

Fodor's Hawaii 1986. 1985. pap. 11.95 o.p. (ISBN 0-679-01240-0). McKay.

Fodor's Hawaii, 1987. 1986. pap. 11.95 o.p. (ISBN 0-679-01447-0, Fodor). McKay.

Fodor's Hawaii 1988. 1987. pap. 11.95 o.p. (ISBN 0-679-01521-3, Fodor). McKay.

Fodor's Holland 1982. 1983. pap. 11.95 Traveltex o.p. (ISBN 0-679-00797-0). McKay.

Fodor's Holland 1983. 336p. 1983. pap. 12.95 o.p. (ISBN 0-679-00924-8). McKay.

Fodor's Holland, 1984. 1983. pap. 12.95 traveltex o.p. (ISBN 0-679-01050-5). McKay.

Fodor's Holland 1985. 1985. pap. 13.95 traveltex o.p. (ISBN 0-679-01119-6). McKay.

Fodor's Holland 1986. 1986. pap. 13.95 o.p. (ISBN 0-679-01241-9). McKay.

Fodor's Holland 1988. 1987. pap. 13.95 o.p. (ISBN 0-679-01522-1, Fodor). McKay.

Fodor's Hong Kong & Macau 1986. 1985. pap. 10.95 o.p. (ISBN 0-679-01242-7, Fodor). McKay.

Fodor's Hong Kong & Macau 1988. 1987. pap. 10.95 o.p. (ISBN 0-679-01523-X, Fodor). McKay.

Fodor's Houston & Galveston, 1985. 1985. pap. 5.95 o.p. (ISBN 0-679-01121-8). McKaY.

Fodor's Houston & Galveston 1986. 1986. pap. 5.95 o.p. (ISBN 0-679-01243-5). McKay.

Fodor's Houston & Galveston, 1988. (Travel Guides). 1988. pap. 6.95 o.p. (ISBN 0-679-01524-8, Fodor). McKay.

Fodor's India & Nepal, 1982. 1981. pap. 15.95 o.p. (ISBN 0-679-00798-9). McKay.

Fodor's India, Nepal & Sri Lanka, 1984. (Illus.). 640p. 1983. pap. 16.95 traveltex o.p. (ISBN 0-679-01013-0). Mckay.

Fodor's India, Nepal, & Sri Lanka 1985. 1984. pap. 16.95 traveltex o.p. (ISBN 0-679-01122-6). McKay.

Fodor's India, Nepal & Sri Lanka 1986. 1985. pap. 16.95 o.p. (ISBN 0-679-01244-3). McKay.

Fodor's Interstate - 95. 1986. pap. 6.95 o.s.i. (ISBN 0-679-01373-3, Fodor). McKay.

Fodor's Ireland 1983. (Illus.). 320p. 1983. pap. 11.95 traveltex o.p. (ISBN 0-679-00927-2). McKay.

Fodor's Ireland, 1984. (Illus.). 320p. 1983. pap. 11.95 traveltex o.p. (ISBN 0-679-01014-9). McKay.

Fodor's Ireland 1985. 1984. pap. 12.95 traveltex o.p. (ISBN 0-679-01123-4). McKay.

Fodor's Ireland 1986. 1986. pap. 12.95 o.p. (ISBN 0-679-01245-1). McKay.

Fodor's Ireland, 1987. 1986. pap. 12.95 o.p. (ISBN 0-679-01374-1, Fodor). McKay.

Fodor's Ireland 1988. 1987. pap. 13.95 o.p. (ISBN 0-679-01526-4, Fodor). McKay.

Fodor's Israel 1983. (Illus.). 368p. 1983. pap. 11.95 traveltex o.p. (ISBN 0-679-00929-9). McKay.

Fodor's Israel, 1984. (Illus.). 368p. 1983. pap. 12.95 traveltex o.p. (ISBN 0-679-01015-7). McKay.

Fodor's Israel 1985. 1984. pap. 13.95 traveltex o.p. (ISBN 0-679-01124-2). McKay.

Fodor's Israel 1986. 1985. pap. 13.95 o.p. (ISBN 0-679-01246-X). McKay.

Fodor's Israel 1988. 1987. pap. 13.95 o.p. (ISBN 0-679-01527-2, Fodor). McKay.

Fodor's Italy, 1982. 1981. pap. 13.95 o.p. (ISBN 0-679-00803-9); pap. 10.95 o.p. (ISBN 0-679-00804-7). McKay.

Fodor's Italy 1983. (Illus.). 528p. 1983. pap. 12.95 traveltex o.p. (ISBN 0-679-00931-0). McKay.

Titles

Fodor's Italy, 1984. (Illus.). 528p. 1983. pap. 12.95 traveltex o.p. (ISBN 0-679-01016-5). McKay.
Fodor's Italy 1985. 1984. pap. 13.95 traveltex o.p. (ISBN 0-679-01125-0). McKay.
Fodor's Italy 1986. 1985. pap. 13.95 o.p. (ISBN 0-679-01247-8). McKay.
Fodor's Italy, 1987. 1986. pap. 13.95 o.p. (ISBN 0-679-01376-8, Fodor). McKay.
Fodor's Italy 1988. 1987. pap. 13.95 o.p. (ISBN 0-679-01528-0, Fodor). McKay.
Fodor's Japan & Korea, 1982. 1981. pap. 14.95 o.p. (ISBN 0-679-00805-5); pap. 11.95 o.p. (ISBN 0-679-00806-3). McKay.
Fodor's Japan 1983. (Illus.). 480p. 1983. pap. 15.95 o.p. (ISBN 0-679-00932-9); pap. 12.95 traveltex o.p. (ISBN 0-679-00933-7). McKay.
Fodor's Japan, 1984. (Illus.). 544p. 1983. pap. 14.95 traveltex o.p. (ISBN 0-679-01017-3). McKay.
Fodor's Japan, 1985. 1985. pap. 14.95 traveltex o.p. (ISBN 0-679-01126-9). McKay.
Fodor's Japan 1986. 1986. pap. 14.95 o.p. (ISBN 0-679-01248-6). McKay.
Fodor's Japan 1988. 1987. pap. 15.95 o.p. (ISBN 0-679-01529-9, Fodor). McKay.
Fodor's Korea 1985. 1984. pap. 9.95 traveltex o.p. (ISBN 0-679-01128-5). McKay.
Fodor's Korea 1986. 1986. pap. 9.95 traveltex o.p. (ISBN 0-679-01250-8). McKay.
Fodor's Korea 1988. 1988. pap. 11.95 o.p. (ISBN 0-679-01531-0, Fodor). McKay.
Fodor's Lisbon 1985. 1985. pap. 5.95 o.p. (ISBN 0-679-01129-3). McKay.
Fodor's Lisbon 1986. 1986. pap. 5.95 o.p. (ISBN 0-679-01251-6). McKay.
Fodor's Lisbon, 1988. (Travel Guides). 1988. pap. 6.95 o.p. (ISBN 0-679-01532-9, Fodor). McKay.
Fodor's London, 1982. 1982. pap. 7.95 Traveltex o.p. (ISBN 0-679-00808-X). McKay.
Fodor's London 1983. 256p. 1983. pap. 7.95 o.p. (ISBN 0-679-00935-3). McKay.
Fodor's London, 1984. (Illus.). 256p. 1983. pap. 7.95 traveltex o.p. (ISBN 0-679-01020-3). McKay.
Fodor's London 1985. 1984. pap. 8.95 o.p. (ISBN 0-679-01130-7). McKay.
Fodor's London 1986. 1985. pap. 8.95 o.p. (ISBN 0-679-01252-4). McKay.
Fodor's London, 1987. 1986. pap. 8.95 o.p. (ISBN 0-679-01382-2, Fodor). McKay.
Fodor's London 1988. 1987. pap. 8.95 o.p. (ISBN 0-679-01533-7, Fodor). McKay.
Fodor's Los Angeles & Nearby Attractions 1988. 1987. pap. 8.95 o.p. (ISBN 0-679-01534-5, Fodor). McKay.
Fodor's Los Angeles, 1984. (Illus.). 528p. 1983. pap. 9.95 traveltex o.p. (ISBN 0-679-01018-1). McKay.
Fodor's Los Angeles 1985. 1984. pap. 8.95 traveltex o.p. (ISBN 0-679-01131-5). McKay.
Fodor's Los Angeles 1986. 1985. pap. 8.95 o.p. (ISBN 0-679-01253-2). McKay.
Fodor's Madrid, 1984. 1983. pap. 4.95 o.p. (ISBN 0-679-01063-7). McKay.
Fodor's Madrid, 1985. 1985. pap. 5.95 o.p. (ISBN 0-679-01132-3). McKay.
Fodor's Madrid 1986. 1986. pap. 5.95 o.p. (ISBN 0-679-01254-0). McKay.
Fodor's Madrid, 1988. (Travel Guides). 1988. pap. 6.95 o.p. (ISBN 0-679-01535-3, Fodor). McKay.
Fodor's Mexico City & Acapulco. (Illus.). 144p. 1983. pap. 4.95 o.p. (ISBN 0-679-01053-X). McKay.
Fodor's Mexico City & Acapulco 1985. 1984. pap. 5.95 o.p. (ISBN 0-679-01134-X). McKay.
Fodor's Mexico City & Acapulco 1986. 1985. pap. 5.95 o.p. (ISBN 0-679-01256-7). McKay.
Fodor's Mexico City & Acapulco 1988. 1987. pap. 6.95 o.p. (ISBN 0-679-01539-6, Fodor). McKay.
Fodor's Mexico, 1983: Traveltext. 1982. pap. 11.95 o.p. (ISBN 0-679-00938-8, Fodor). McKay.
Fodor's Mexico, 1984. (Illus.). 640p. 1983. pap. 15.95 o.p. (ISBN 0-679-01021-1); pap. 12.95 traveltex o.p. (ISBN 0-679-01022-X). Mckay.
Fodor's Mexico 1985. 1984. pap. 13.95 traveltex o.p. (ISBN 0-679-01133-1). McKay.
Fodor's Mexico 1986. 1985. pap. 13.95 o.p. (ISBN 0-679-01255-9). McKay.
Fodor's Mexico, 1987. 1986. pap. 13.95 o.p. (ISBN 0-679-01385-7, Fodor). McKay.
Fodor's Mexico 1988. 1987. pap. 13.95 o.p. (ISBN 0-679-01538-8, Fodor). McKay.
Fodor's Munich, 1985. 1985. pap. 5.95 o.p. (ISBN 0-679-01136-6). McKay.
Fodor's Munich 1986. 1986. pap. 6.95 o.p. (ISBN 0-679-01258-3). McKay.
Fodor's Munich 1988. 1988. pap. 6.95 o.p. (ISBN 0-679-01540-X, Fodor). McKay.
Fodor's New England, 1982. 1981. pap. 8.95 Traveltex o.p. (ISBN 0-679-00811-X). McKay.
Fodor's New England, 1984. (Illus.). 512p. 1983. pap. 10.95 traveltex o.p. (ISBN 0-679-01023-8). McKay.
Fodor's New England 1985. 1984. pap. 10.95 traveltex o.p. (ISBN 0-679-01137-4). McKay.
Fodor's New England 1986. 1985. pap. 10.95 o.p. (ISBN 0-679-01259-1). McKay.
Fodor's New England, 1987. 1986. pap. 11.95 o.p. (ISBN 0-679-01450-0, Fodor). McKay.
Fodor's New England 1988. 1987. pap. 12.95 o.p. (ISBN 0-679-01541-8, Fodor). McKay.
Fodor's New Mexico, 1988. (Travel Guides). 1988. pap. 7.95 o.p. (ISBN 0-679-01542-6, Fodor). McKay.
Fodor's New Orleans 1986. 1985. pap. 7.95 o.p. (ISBN 0-679-01261-3). McKay.
Fodor's New Orleans 1988. 1987. pap. 7.95 o.p. (ISBN 0-679-01543-4, Fodor). McKay.
Fodor's New York City & Nearby Attractions, 1984. (Illus.). 506p. 1983. pap. 9.95 travletex o.p. (ISBN 0-679-01024-6). McKay.
Fodor's New York City 1983. 480p. 1983. pap. 8.95 o.p. (ISBN 0-679-00940-X). McKay.
Fodor's New York City 1985. 1984. pap. 8.95 traveltex o.p. (ISBN 0-679-01139-0). McKay.
Fodor's New York City 1986. 1985. pap. 8.95 o.p. (ISBN 0-679-01262-1). McKay.
Fodor's New York City 1988. 1987. pap. 8.95 o.p. (ISBN 0-679-01544-2, Fodor). McKay.
Fodor's New York State, 1988. (Travel Guides). 1988. pap. 9.95 o.p. (ISBN 0-679-01545-0, Fodor). McKay.
Fodor's New Zealand 1986. 1986. pap. 7.95 o.p. (ISBN 0-679-01305-9). McKay.
Fodor's New Zealand, 1988. (Travel Guides). 1988. pap. 7.95 o.p. (ISBN 0-679-01546-9, Fodor). McKay.
Fodor's North Africa, 1983. 1982. pap. 14.95 o.p. (ISBN 0-679-00941-8, Fodor). McKay.
Fodor's North Africa, 1983. 1986. pap. 16.95 o.p. (ISBN 0-679-01392-X, Fodor). McKay.
Fodor's North Africa, 1984. (Illus.). 416p. 1983. pap. 15.95 traveltex o.p. (ISBN 0-679-01025-4). McKay.
Fodor's North Africa 1985. 1984. pap. 15.95 traveltex o.p. (ISBN 0-679-01140-4). McKay.
Fodor's North Africa 1986. 1985. pap. 15.95 o.p. (ISBN 0-679-01263-X). McKay.
Fodor's North Africa 1988. 1987. pap. 16.95 o.p. (ISBN 0-679-01547-7, Fodor). McKay.
Fodor's Pacific North Coast 1986. 1986. pap. 9.95 o.p. (ISBN 0-679-01264-8). McKay.
Fodor's Pacific North Coast, 1988. (Travel Guides). 1988. pap. 9.95 o.p. (ISBN 0-679-01548-5, Fodor). McKay.
Fodor's Paris 1983. 288p. 1983. pap. 7.95 o.p. (ISBN 0-679-00942-6). McKay.
Fodor's Paris, 1984. (Illus.). 288p. 1983. pap. 7.95 traveltex o.p. (ISBN 0-679-01027-0). McKay.
Fodor's Paris 1985. 1985. pap. 8.95 traveltex o.p. (ISBN 0-679-01142-0). McKay.
Fodor's Paris 1986. 1985. pap. 8.95 o.p. (ISBN 0-679-01265-6). McKay.
Fodor's Paris, 1987. 1986. pap. 8.95 o.s.i. (ISBN 0-679-01394-6, Fodor). McKay.
Fodor's Paris 1988. 1987. pap. 8.95 o.p. (ISBN 0-679-01549-3, Fodor). McKay.
Fodor's Pennsylvania. rev. ed. (Illus.). 176p. 1983. pap. 7.95 traveltex o.p. (ISBN 0-679-00943-4). McKay.
Fodor's People's Republic of China, 1983. (Illus.). 560p. 1983. pap. 14.95 traveltex o.p. (ISBN 0-679-00944-2). McKay.
Fodor's People's Republic of China, 1984. (Illus.). 624p. 1983. pap. 14.95 traveltex o.p. (ISBN 0-679-01028-9). McKay.
Fodor's People's Republic of China 1985. 1984. pap. 15.95 traveltex o.p. (ISBN 0-679-01105-6). McKay.
Fodor's People's Republic of China 1986. 1985. pap. 15.95 o.p. (ISBN 0-679-01227-3). McKay.
Fodor's People's Republic of China 1988. 1988. pap. 16.95 o.p. (ISBN 0-679-01550-7, Fodor). McKay.
Fodor's Philadelphia, 1988. (Travel Guides). 1988. pap. 7.95 o.p. (ISBN 0-679-01551-5, Fodor). McKay.
Fodor's Portugal 1983. (Illus.). 320p. 1983. pap. 11.95 traveltex o.p. (ISBN 0-679-00945-0). McKay.
Fodor's Portugal, 1984. (Illus.). 320p. 1983. pap. 11.95 traveltex o.p. (ISBN 0-679-01030-0). McKay.
Fodor's Portugal 1985. 1984. pap. 12.95 traveltex o.p. (ISBN 0-679-01144-7). McKay.
Fodor's Portugal 1986. 1985. pap. 12.95 o.p. (ISBN 0-679-01267-2, Fodor). McKay.
Fodor's Portugal 1988. 1987. pap. 13.95 o.p. (ISBN 0-679-01552-3, Fodor). McKay.
Fodor's Rome 1983. 220p. 1983. pap. 7.95 o.p. (ISBN 0-679-00946-9). McKay.
Fodor's Rome, 1984. (Illus.). 220p. 1983. pap. 7.95 traveltex o.p. (ISBN 0-679-01031-9). Mckay.
Fodor's Rome 1985. 1985. pap. 8.95 traveltex o.p. (ISBN 0-679-01145-5). McKay.
Fodor's Rome 1986. 1985. pap. 8.95 o.p. (ISBN 0-679-01268-0). McKay.
Fodor's Rome, 1987. 1986. pap. 8.95 o.p. (ISBN 0-679-01398-9, Fodor). McKay.
Fodor's Rome 1988. 1987. pap. 8.95 o.p. (ISBN 0-679-01554-X, Fodor). McKay.
Fodor's San Diego, 1984. 1983. pap. 8.95 traveltex o.p. (ISBN 0-679-01032-7). McKay.
Fodor's San Diego, 1985. 1985. pap. 7.95 traveltex o.p. (ISBN 0-679-01146-3). McKay.
Fodor's San Diego 1986. 1986. pap. 7.95 o.p. (ISBN 0-679-01269-9). McKay.
Fodor's San Diego, 1988. (Travel Guides). 1988. pap. 7.95 o.p. (ISBN 0-679-01556-6, Fodor). McKay.
Fodor's San Francisco, 1984. (Illus.). 416p. 1983. pap. 9.95 traveltex o.p. (ISBN 0-679-01033-5). McKay.
Fodor's San Francisco 1986. 1986. pap. 7.95 o.p. (ISBN 0-679-01270-2, Fodor). McKay.
Fodor's San Francisco, 1988. (Travel Guides). 1988. pap. 7.95 o.p. (ISBN 0-679-01557-4, Fodor). McKay.
Fodor's Scandinavia 1983. (Illus.). 512p. 1983. pap. 12.95 o.p. (ISBN 0-679-00950-7). McKay.
Fodor's Scandinavia 1984. (Illus.). 512p. 1983. pap. 13.95 traveltex o.p. (ISBN 0-679-01034-3). McKay.
Fodor's Scandinavia 1985. 1984. pap. 14.95 traveltex o.p. (ISBN 0-679-01149-8). McKay.
Fodor's Scandinavia 1986. 1986. pap. 14.95 o.p. (ISBN 0-679-01271-0). McKay.
Fodor's Scandinavia 1988. 1987. pap. 15.95 o.p. (ISBN 0-679-01558-2, Fodor). McKay.
Fodor's Scotland, 1984. 1983. pap. 9.95 traveltex o.p. (ISBN 0-679-01035-1). McKay.
Fodor's Scotland, 1985. 1985. pap. 10.95 traveltex o.p. (ISBN 0-679-01150-1). McKay.
Fodor's Scotland 1986. 1985. pap. 10.95 o.p. (ISBN 0-679-01272-9). McKay.
Fodor's Scotland, 1987. 1986. pap. 12.95 o.p. (ISBN 0-679-01402-0, Fodor). McKay.
Fodor's Scotland 1988. 1987. pap. 12.95 o.p. (ISBN 0-679-01559-0, Fodor). McKay.
Fodor's Singapore 1988. 1987. pap. 7.95 o.p. (ISBN 0-679-01560-4, Fodor). McKay.
Fodor's South America 1983. (Illus.). 676p. 1983. pap. 15.95 o.p. (ISBN 0-679-00952-3); pap. 12.95 traveltex o.p. (ISBN 0-679-00953-1). McKay.
Fodor's South America, 1984. (Illus.). 576p. 1983. pap. 13.95 traveltex o.p. (ISBN 0-679-01037-8). McKay.
Fodor's South America 1985. 1984. pap. 14.95 traveltex o.p. (ISBN 0-679-01152-8). McKay.
Fodor's South America 1986. 1985. pap. 14.95 o.p. (ISBN 0-679-01274-5). McKay.
Fodor's South America, 1987. 1986. pap. 14.95 o.p. (ISBN 0-679-01406-3, Fodor). McKay.
Fodor's South America 1988. 1987. pap. 14.95 o.p. (ISBN 0-679-01562-0, Fodor). McKay.
Fodor's South Pacific 1986. 1986. pap. 7.95 o.p. (ISBN 0-679-01307-5). McKay.
Fodor's South Pacific, 1988. (Travel Guides). 1988. pap. 8.95 o.p. (ISBN 0-679-01563-9, Fodor). McKay.
Fodor's South, 1984. (Illus.). 496p. 1983. pap. 11.95 traveltex o.p. (ISBN 0-679-01036-X). McKay.
Fodor's South 1985. 1984. pap. 12.95 traveltex o.p. (ISBN 0-679-01151-X). McKay.
Fodor's South 1986. 1985. pap. 12.95 o.p. (ISBN 0-679-01273-7). McKay.
Fodor's South 1988. 1987. pap. 12.95 o.p. (ISBN 0-679-01561-2, Fodor). McKay.
Fodor's Southeast Asia 1983. (Illus.). 512p. 1983. pap. 12.95 traveltex o.p. (ISBN 0-679-00955-8). McKay.
Fodor's Southeast Asia, 1984. 1983. pap. 13.95 o.p. (ISBN 0-679-01049-1, Fodor). McKay.
Fodor's Southeast Asia, 1984. 1986. pap. 15.95 o.p. (ISBN 0-679-01408-X, Fodor). McKay.
Fodor's Southeast Asia 1985. 1984. pap. 14.95 traveltex o.p. (ISBN 0-679-01153-6). McKay.
Fodor's Southeast Asia 1986. 1985. pap. 14.95 o.p. (ISBN 0-679-01275-3). McKay.
Fodor's Southeast Asia 1988. 1987. pap. 15.95 o.p. (ISBN 0-679-01564-7, Fodor). McKay.
Fodor's Soviet Union 1983. (Illus.). 464p. 1983. pap. 14.95 traveltex o.p. (ISBN 0-679-00956-6). McKay.
Fodor's Soviet Union, 1984. (Illus.). 462p. 1983. pap. 14.95 traveltex o.p. (ISBN 0-679-01039-4). McKay.
Fodor's Soviet Union 1985. 1984. pap. 15.95 traveltex o.p. (ISBN 0-679-01154-4). McKay.
Fodor's Soviet Union 1986. 1986. pap. 15.95 o.p. (ISBN 0-679-01276-1). McKay.
Fodor's Soviet Union 1988. 1987. pap. 16.95 o.p. (ISBN 0-679-01565-5, Fodor). McKay.
Fodor's Spain 1983. (Illus.). 448p. 1983. pap. 11.95 traveltex o.p. (ISBN 0-679-00958-2). McKay.
Fodor's Spain, 1984. 1983. pap. 12.95 o.p. (ISBN 0-679-01040-8, Fodor). McKay.
Fodor's Spain 1985. 1984. pap. 13.95 traveltex o.p. (ISBN 0-679-01155-2). McKay.
Fodor's Spain 1988. 1987. pap. 13.95 o.p. (ISBN 0-679-01566-3, Fodor). McKay.
Fodor's Stockholm, Copenhagen, Oslo, Helsinki & Reykjavik, 1984. 1983. pap. 5.95 o.p. (ISBN 0-679-01064-5). McKay.
Fodor's Stockholm, Copenhagen, Oslo, Helsinki & Reykjavik 1985. 1985. pap. 5.95 o.p. (ISBN 0-679-01156-0). McKay.
Fodor's Stockholm, Copenhagen, Oslo, Helsinki & Reykjavik 1988. 1988. pap. 7.95 o.p. (ISBN 0-679-01567-1, Fodor). McKay.
Fodor's Sweden 1986. 1986. pap. 6.95 o.p. (ISBN 0-679-01309-1). McKay.
Fodor's Sweden 1988. 1988. pap. 6.95 o.p. (ISBN 0-679-01568-X, Fodor). McKay.
Fodor's Switzerland 1983. (Illus.). 352p. 1983. pap. 11.95 traveltex o.p. (ISBN 0-679-00959-0). McKay.
Fodor's Switzerland, 1984. (Illus.). 336p. 1983. pap. 11.95 traveltex o.p. (ISBN 0-679-01041-6). McKay.
Fodor's Switzerland 1985. 1984. pap. 12.95 traveltex o.p. (ISBN 0-679-01157-9). McKay.
Fodor's Switzerland, 1987. 1986. pap. 13.95 o.p. (ISBN 0-679-01413-6, Fodor). McKay.
Fodor's Switzerland 1988. 1987. pap. 13.95 o.p. (ISBN 0-679-01569-8, Fodor). McKay.
Fodor's Sydney, 1988. (Travel Guides). 1988. pap. 7.95 o.p. (ISBN 0-679-01570-1, Fodor). McKay.
Fodor's Texas 1985. 1985. pap. 9.95 traveltex o.p. (ISBN 0-679-01158-7). McKay.
Fodor's Texas 1986. 1986. pap. 8.95 o.p. (ISBN 0-679-01281-8). McKay.
Fodor's Texas 1988. 1988. pap. 8.95 o.p. (ISBN 0-679-01571-X, Fodor). McKay.
Fodor's Tokyo & Vicinity, 1984. (Illus.). 144p. 1983. pap. 5.95 o.p. (ISBN 0-679-01052-1). McKay.
Fodor's Tokyo & Vicinity 1985. 1985. pap. 5.95 o.p. (ISBN 0-679-01159-5). McKay.
Fodor's Tokyo 1986. 1986. pap. 6.95 o.p. (ISBN 0-679-01282-6). McKay.
Fodor's Tokyo, 1988. (Travel Guides). 1988. pap. 6.95 o.p. (ISBN 0-679-01572-8, Fodor). McKay.
Fodor's Toronto 1986. 1985. pap. 7.95 o.p. (ISBN 0-679-01283-4, Fodor). McKay.
Fodor's Toronto 1988. 1987. pap. 7.95 o.p. (ISBN 0-679-01573-6, Fodor). McKay.
Fodor's Turkey 1983. (Illus.). 400p. 1983. pap. 12.95 o.p. (ISBN 0-679-00961-2). McKay.
Fodor's Turkey, 1984. (Illus.). 500p. 1983. pap. 13.95 traveltex o.p. (ISBN 0-679-01043-2). McKay.
Fodor's Turkey 1985. 1984. pap. 13.95 traveltex o.p. (ISBN 0-679-01161-7). McKay.
Fodor's Turkey 1986. 1985. pap. 14.95 o.p. (ISBN 0-679-01284-2). McKay.
Fodor's Turkey, 1987. 1986. pap. 16.95 o.p. (ISBN 0-679-01424-1, Fodor). McKay.
Fodor's Turkey 1988. 1987. pap. 16.95 o.p. (ISBN 0-679-01574-4, Fodor). McKay.
Fodor's U. S. A. Traveltext. 1982. pap. 12.95 o.p. (ISBN 0-679-00963-9, Fodor). McKay.
Fodor's U. S. A., 1984. (Illus.). 928p. 1983. pap. 13.95 traveltex o.p. (ISBN 0-679-01044-0). McKay.
Fodor's U. S. A., 1985. 1984. pap. 14.95 traveltex o.p. (ISBN 0-679-01162-5). McKay.
Fodor's U. S. A. 1986. 1985. pap. 14.95 o.p. (ISBN 0-679-01285-0). McKay.
Fodor's U. S. A. 1988. 1987. pap. 15.95 o.p. (ISBN 0-679-01575-2, Fodor). McKay.
Fodor's Vienna 1985. 1985. pap. 5.95 o.p. (ISBN 0-679-01163-3). McKay.
Fodor's Vienna 1986. 1986. pap. 5.95 o.p. (ISBN 0-679-01286-9). McKay.
Fodor's Vienna 1988. 1987. pap. 6.95 o.p. (ISBN 0-679-01576-0, Fodor). McKay.
Fodor's Virgin Islands 1988. 1987. pap. 8.95 o.p. (ISBN 0-679-01577-9, Fodor). McKay.
Fodor's Virginia, 1988. (Travel Guides). 1988. pap. 7.95 o.p. (ISBN 0-679-01578-7, Fodor). McKay.
Fodor's Washington, D. C., 1984. (Illus.). 272p. 1983. pap. 8.95 traveltex o.p. (ISBN 0-679-01046-7). McKay.
Fodor's Washington, D. C. 1985. 1985. pap. 8.95 traveltex o.p. (ISBN 0-679-01164-1). McKay.
Fodor's Washington, D. C. 1986. 1986. pap. 7.95 o.p. (ISBN 0-679-01287-7). McKay.
Fodor's Washington, D. C. 1988. 1988. pap. 7.95 o.p. (ISBN 0-679-01579-5, Fodor). McKay.
Fodor's Washington, D.C. 1983. 224p. 1983. pap. 7.95 o.p. (ISBN 0-679-00964-7). McKay.
Fodor's Yugoslavia 1984. (Illus.). 320p. 1983. pap. 13.95 traveltex o.p. (ISBN 0-679-01047-5). McKay.
Fodor's Yugoslavia 1985. 1984. pap. 13.95 traveltex o.p. (ISBN 0-679-01166-8). McKay.
Fodor's Yugoslavia 1986. 1985. pap. 13.95 o.p. (ISBN 0-679-01288-5). McKay.
Fodor's Yugoslavia 1988. 1987. pap. 14.95 o.p. (ISBN 0-679-01580-9, Fodor). McKay.
Fog. Mildred Lee. LC 72-81259. 256p. (gr. 6 up). 1979. 9.95 o.s.i. (ISBN 0-395-28911-4, Clarion). HM.
Fog Comes on Little Pig Feet. Rosemary Well. 1973. pap. 1.50 o.p. (ISBN 0-380-01192-1, 53249). Avon.
Foil Around & Stay Fit: Exercise Secrets of a Fencer. Camille Lownds & Tony August. LC 76-54896. (Illus.). 1977. 12.95 o.p. (ISBN 0-15-132227-9). HarBraceJ.

Foil Around & Stay Fit: Exercise Secrets of a Fencer. Camille Lownds & Tony August. LC 76-54896. (Illus.). 1977. pap. 5.95 o.p. (ISBN 0-15-132228-7, Harv). HarBraceJ.
Foiling the System Breakers: Computer Security & Access Control. J. Lobel. 288p. 1986. text ed. 37.50 o.p. (ISBN 0-07-038357-X). McGraw.
Fokker Fighters of World War One. Alex Imrie. (Vintage Warbirds Ser.: No. 6). (Illus.). 68p. (Orig.). 1987. pap. 9.95 o.p. (ISBN 0-85368-782-X, Pub. by Arms & Armour). Sterling.
Fokker, the Man & the Aircraft. Henri Hengener. Ed. by B. Robertson. LC 61-10595. (Harleyford Ser). (Illus.). 1961. 24.95 o.p. (ISBN 0-8168-6370-9, 26370, TAB-Aero). TAB Bks.
Folate Antagonisms As Therapeutics Agents: Vol. 2: Pharmacology, Experimental & Clinical Therapeutics. F. M. Sirotnak et al. LC 83-15774. 1984. 70.50 o.p. (ISBN 0-12-646902-4). Acad Pr.
Folate Antagonists As Therapeutics Agents: Biochemistry, Molecular Actions, & Synthetic Design, Vol. 1. Ed. by F. M. Sirotnak et al. LC 83-15774. 1984. 82.50 o.p. (ISBN 0-12-646901-6). Acad Pr.
Folding & Fracturing of Rocks. John G. Ramsay. (International Ser. in Earth & Planetary Sciences). (Illus.). 1967. text ed. 73.95 o.p. (ISBN 0-07-051170-5). McGraw.
Folio Annual, 1979: Supplement to the Handbook of Magazine Publishing. 1979. 20.00 o.p. (ISBN 0-918110-04-1). Hanson Pub Grp.
Folio for Violin & Piano. A. Corelli. Ed. by Ferd David & Leopold Auer. (Carl Fischer Music Library: No. 877). 1922. pap. 6.00 o.p. (ISBN 0-8258-0093-5). Fischer Inc NY.
Folio Verse: Attacks, Defences, & Imitations see Popeiana.
Folk Architecture of Louisiana: A Selected Bibliography. Coralie G. Davis. (Architecture Ser.: A 1464). 9p. 1985. 2.00 o.p. (ISBN 0-89028-554-3). Vance Biblios.
Folk Costume of Eastern Europe. Lilla M. Fox. LC 76-51358. (Illus.). 1977. 7.95 o.p. (ISBN 0-8238-0213-2). Plays.
Folk Dances of the Greeks. Theodore Petrides & Elfleida Petrides. 1961. 6.00 o.p. (ISBN 0-682-40070-X, Banner). Exposition-Phoenix.
Folk Dancing. Mary B. Jensen & Clayne R. Jensen. LC 73-4771. (Illus.). 148p. 1973. pap. 4.95 o.p. (ISBN 0-8425-0458-3). Brigham.
Folk Directory: 1987. The English Folk Dance & Song Society Staff. 96p. 1987. pap. 9.95 o.p. (ISBN 0-85418-147-4). Princeton Bk Co.
Folk Festivals & the Foreign Community. Dorothy G. Spicer. LC 70-167201. 162p. 1976. Repr. of 1923 ed. 40.00x o.p. (ISBN 0-8103-4301-0). Gale.
Folk Literature of the Chamacoco Indians, Vol. 63. Johannes Wilbert. LC 87-2659. 744p. pap. 41.95 o.p. (ISBN 0-317-65406-3). UCLA Lat Am Ctr.
Folk-Lore of China, & Its Affinities with That of the Aryan & Semitic Races. Nicholas B. Dennys. LC 79-89262. (Illus.). iv, 184p. 1972. Repr. of 1876 ed. 43.00x o.p. (ISBN 0-8103-3932-3). Gale.
Folk-Lore of Plants. Thomas F. Thiselton-Dyer. LC 68-22054. 336p. 1968. Repr. of 1889 ed. 40.00x o.p. (ISBN 0-8103-3554-9). Gale.
Folk-Lore, Old Customs & Superstitions in Shakespeare Land. J. Harvey Bloom. LC 73-2830. viii, 180p. 1973. Repr. of 1930 ed. 31.00x o.p. (ISBN 0-8103-3269-8). Gale.
Folk Medicine. D. C. Jarvis. 1982. pap. 5.95 o.s.i. (ISBN 0-449-90066-5, Columbine). Fawcett.
Folk Music of Hungary. Zoltan Kodaly. 195p. Repr. of 1972 ed. lib. bdg. 39.00 o.p. (Pub. by Am Repr Serv). Reprint Servs.
Folk Music with an Overdrive. Flatt & Scruggs. pap. 2.50 o.p. (ISBN 0-686-09066-7, Pub. by Peer-Southern). CPP Belwin.
Folk of the Air. Peter S. Beagle. 1986. 16.45 o.p. (ISBN 0-345-33782-4, Del Rey). Ballantine.
Folk Tales from Korea. Ed. & tr. by Zong In-Sob. LC 53-12953. 1979. pap. 6.95 o.p. (ISBN 0-394-17096-2, E738, Ever). Grove.
Folk Tales from the Russian. Vera De Blumenthal. LC 78-74512. (Children's Literature Reprint Ser.). (Illus.). (gr. 4-5). 1979. Repr. of 1903 ed. 16.75x o.p. (ISBN 0-8486-0216-1). Roth Pub Inc.
Folklore As A Historical Science. George L. Gomme. LC 67-23898. (Illus.). 392p. 1968. Repr. of 1908 ed. 37.00x o.p. (ISBN 0-8103-3432-1). Gale.
Folklore, Myths & Legends of Britain. (Automobile Association of England Ser.). 1979. 22.95 o.p. (ISBN 0-393-01231-X). Norton.
Folklore of Fairy-Tale. Macleod Yearsley. LC 68-31517. 256p. 1968. Repr. of 1924 ed. 40.00x o.p. (ISBN 0-8103-3457-7). Gale.
Folklore of Rajasthan. Ed. by Jawarharlal Handoo. 1985. 6.00x o.p. (ISBN 0-8364-1395-4, Pub. by Ctrl Inst). South Asia Bks.
Folklore of the Jews. Angelo S. Rappoport. LC 71-167125. 288p. Repr. of 1937 ed. 40.00x o.p. (ISBN 0-8103-3864-5). Gale.
Folks from Dixie. facsimile ed. Paul L. Dunbar. LC 78-78572. (Illus.). 263p. lib. bdg. 12.50 o.p. (ISBN 0-8290-2367-4); pap. text ed. 6.95x o.p. (ISBN 0-89197-761-9). Irvington.
Folksong & Music Hall. Edward Lee. (Routledge Popular Music Ser.). (Illus.). 148p. 1982. 13.95x o.p. (ISBN 0-7100-0902-X). Routledge Chapman & Hall.
Folksongs of the Upper Thames. Alfred Williams. LC 68-31150. (Illus.). 312p. 1968. Repr. of 1923 ed. 40.00x o.p. (ISBN 0-8103-3421-6). Gale.
Folktales of Chile. Ed. by Yolando Pino-Saavedra. Tr. by Rockwell Gray. LC 67-25585. (Folktales of the World Ser). 1968. lib. bdg. 14.00x o.s.i. (ISBN 0-226-66873-8). U of Chicago Pr.
Folktales of France. Genevieve Massignon. LC 68-14008. (Folktales of the World Ser). 1968. 14.00x o.s.i. (ISBN 0-226-50965-6). U of Chicago Pr.
Folktales of Hungary. Ed. by Linda Degh. Tr. by Judit Halasz. LC 64-19846. (Folktales of the World Ser). 1969. lib. bdg. 14.00x o.s.i. (ISBN 0-226-14023-7); pap. text ed. 6.95x o.s.i. (ISBN 0-226-14024-5, FW6). U of Chicago Pr.
Folkways & Mores. Date not set. (ISBN 0-8052-0631-0). Random.
Follow Me: A Pocket Guide to Daily Scriptual Prayer. David Rosage. 256p. 1987. 7.95 o.p. (ISBN 0-89283-362-9). Servant.
Follow the Fox. Elaine Livermore. (Illus.). 48p. (gr. k-3). 1981. 7.95 o.s.i. (ISBN 0-395-31672-3). HM.
Follow the Leaders. Richard Blackman. (Illus.). 1978. 9.95 o.p. (ISBN 0-671-22471-9). S&S.
Follow the Line. Demi. LC 81-4072. (Illus.). 48p. 1981. 4.95 o.p. (ISBN 0-03-059112-0). H Holt & Co.
Follow the North Star. Harriette DeJarnette. 384p. (Orig.). 1982. pap. 3.25 o.p. (ISBN 0-8439-1073-9, Pub. by Leisure Bks CT). Dorchester Pub Co.
Follow the Saint. Leslie Charteris. (Saint Ser.). (Illus.). 288p. 1982. pap. 2.50 o.s.i. (ISBN 0-441-24211-1). Ace Bks.
Follow the Shadows. Jocelyn Carew. 1979. pap. 2.75 o.p. (ISBN 0-380-44776-2, 44776). Avon.
Follow the Sharks. William G. Tapply. (Brady Coyne Mystery Ser.). 224p. 1985. 13.95 o.p. (ISBN 0-684-18446-X, ScribT). Scribner.
Follow the Water. Varley Lang. LC 61-16637. (Illus.). 222p. 1961. 2.98 o.p. (ISBN 0-910244-24-3). Blair.
Followers of the Cross. Harry N. Huxhold. LC 85-22823. 80p. (Orig.). 1985. pap. 4.95 o.p. (ISBN 0-8066-2184-2, 10-2346, Augsburg). Augsburg Fortress.
Following Christ: Prayers from Imitation of Christ. Ronald Klug. LC 80-25260. (Illus.). 63p. 1981. pap. 3.95 o.p. (ISBN 0-570-03826-X, 12-2791). Concordia.
Following Jesus: A Woman's Workshop on Luke. Evelyn Bence. (Woman's Workshop Ser.). 112p. 1986. pap. 4.50 o.p. (ISBN 0-310-44781-X, 11314P). Zondervan.
Following Jesus: Discipleship in the Gospel of Mark. E. A. Best. (Journal for the Study of the New Testament, Supplement Ser.: No. 4). 283p. pap. text ed. 14.95x o.s.i. (Pub. by JSOT Pr England). Eisenbrauns.
Following the Frontier: American Transportation in the Nineteenth Century. Leonard F. James. LC 68-13811. (Curriculum Related Bks.). (Illus.). (gr. 5-8). 1968. 4.95 o.p. (ISBN 0-15-228827-9, HJ). HarBraceJ.
Following the Way: The Setting of John's Gospel. Bruce E. Schein. LC 79-54121. 224p. 1980. 15.95 o.p. (ISBN 0-8066-1758-6, 10-2348, Augsburg). Augsburg Fortress.
Following Through: Herbert Warren Wind on Golf. Herbert W. Wind. 384p. 1985. 19.50 o.p. (ISBN 0-89919-398-6). Ticknor & Fields.
Folyl & Antifolyl Polyglutamates. Ed. by I. David Goldman et al. LC 82-24628. (Advances in Experimental Medicine & Biology Ser.: Vol. 163). 436p. 1983. 69.50x o.p. (ISBN 0-306-41262-4, Plenum Pr). Plenum Pub.
Fonemas Tacana Vy Modelos de Acentuacion. Donald Van Wynen & Mabel Van Wynen. (Notas Linguisticas de Bolivia Ser.: No. 6). 32p. 1962. pap. 0.75 o.s.i. (ISBN 0-88312-763-6). Summer Inst Ling.
Fonotacticas del Cayuvava. Harold Key. (Notas Linguisticas De Bolivia Ser.: No. 4). 72p. 1962. pap. 0.75 o.s.i. (ISBN 0-88312-764-4). Summer Inst Ling.
Fons Sapientiae: Garden Fountains in Illustrated Books, Sixteen-Eighteenth Centuries. Elisabeth B. MacDougall & Naomi Miller. LC 77-76011. (Illus.). 1977. pap. 5.00x o.p. (ISBN 0-88402-073-8). Dumbarton Oaks.
Fontana Economic History of Europe: The Middle Ages. Ed. by Carlo M. Cipolla. LC 75-26027. (Fontana Ser.: Vol. 1). (Illus.). 389p. 1976. text ed. 26.50x o.p. (ISBN 0-06-492176-X, 06467). B&N Imports.
Fontana Economic History of Europe: The Twentieth Century. Ed. by Carlo M. Cipolla. LC 75-26207. (Fontana Ser.: Vol. 5, Pt. 1). (Illus.). 402p. 1977. Repr. of 1976 ed. text ed. 26.50x o.p. (ISBN 0-06-492181-6, 06472). B&N Imports.
Food. Root Waverley. 608p. 1986. pap. 15.95 o.p. (ISBN 0-671-62795-3, Fireside). S&S.
Food, Vol. 4 (Incl. 1987 Supplement) Ed. by E. Goldstein. 1988. 15.00 o.p. (ISBN 0-89777-128-1). Soc Issues.
Food Additive Control in Canada. (Food Additive Control Ser.: No. 1). pap. 5.75 o.p. (F178, FAO). UNIPUB.
Food Additive Control in the United Kingdom. (Food Additive Control Ser.: No. 2). pap. 5.75 o.p. (F182, FAO). UNIPUB.
Food Aid & Education. (World Food Programme Studies: No. 6). (Orig.). 1965. pap. 5.75 o.p. (ISBN 0-685-09382-4, F185, FAO). UNIPUB.
Food Allergy. Frederic Speer. LC 76-45950. (Illus.). 176p. 1978. 17.50 o.p. (ISBN 0-88416-184-6). Year Bk Med.
Food Analysis Theory & Practice. rev. ed. Pomeranz. 1978. 32.95 o.p. (ISBN 0-87055-238-4). Van Nos Reinhold.
Food & Cooking of Russia. Lesley Chamberlain. (Handbooks Ser.). 336p. 1986. pap. 7.95 o.s.i. (ISBN 0-14-046471-9). Penguin.
Food & Drink of Mexico. George C. Booth. 12.75 o.p. (ISBN 0-8446-5481-7). Peter Smith.
Food & Heat Producing Solar Greenhouse. rev. ed. Bill Yanda & Rick Fisher. LC 79-91276. (Illus.). 208p. (Orig.). 1980. pap. 6.00 o.p. (ISBN 0-912528-20-6). John Muir.
Food & Menu Dictionary. C. Dahl. LC 77-123002. 160p. 1983. 12.50 o.p. (ISBN 0-8436-0556-1). Van Nos Reinhold.
Food As a Crutch. Shirley Schwarzrock & C. Gilbert Wrenn. (Coping with Ser.). (Illus.). (gr. 7-12). 1971. pap. text ed. 3.00 o.p. (ISBN 0-913476-18-8). Am Guidance.
Food Aversion Learning. Ed. by N. W. Milgram et al. LC 77-21965. (Illus.). 280p. 1977. 35.00x o.p. (ISBN 0-306-31040-6, Plenum Pr). Plenum Pub.
Food Buying Guide for Child Nutrition Programs. (Illus.). 150p. 1984. pap. 4.50 o.p. (ISBN 0-318-22381-3, S/N 001-000-04382-0). USGPO.
Food Colloids. H. D. Graham. (Illus.). 1977. 62.95 o.p. (ISBN 0-87055-201-5). AVI.
Food Coloring Red, No. 20. Date not set. (ISBN 0-07-521032-0). McGraw.
Food Composition: Tables for Use in the Middle East. P. L. Pellet & Sossy Shadarevian. 1970. pap. 11.95x o.p. (ISBN 0-8156-6032-4, Am U Beirut). Syracuse U Pr.
Food Consumption, Prices, & Expenditures, 1985. (Agriculture Department Statistical Bulletin Ser.: No. 749). 124p. 1987. pap. 5.50 o.p. (ISBN 0-318-22382-1, S/N 001-019-00499-1). USGPO.
Food Costs-Farm Prices: A Compilation or Information Relating to Agriculture. U. S. Congress, House Committee on Agriculture. (Illus.). x, 128p. 1973. Repr. of 1970 ed. 35.00x o.p. (ISBN 0-8103-3278-7). Gale.
Food Deprivation. (Landmark Ser.). 1979. 29.00x o.p. (ISBN 0-8422-4127-2). Irvington.
Food Drying: Proceedings of a Workshop Held at Edmonton, Alberta, 6-9 July 1981. Gordon Yaciuk. 104p. 1982. pap. 8.00 o.p. (ISBN 0-88936-333-1, IDRC195, IDRC). UNIPUB.
Food Editors' Favorites Cookbook. Ed. by Jane Baker & Barbara G. Ostmann. LC 83-6199. 160p. 1983. pap. 8.95 o.p. (ISBN 0-8437-3396-9). Hammond Inc.
Food Editors' Hometown Favorites Cookbook: American Regional & Local Specialties. Ed. by Jane Baker & Barbara G. Ostmann. LC 83-6199. 160p. (Orig.). 1984. pap. 8.95 o.p. (ISBN 0-8437-3398-5). Hammond Inc.
Food, Energy & Future of Society. David Pimentel. 1980. pap. 3.50x o.p. (ISBN 0-87081-089-8). Univ Pr Colo.
Food Equipment Facts: A Handbook for the Food Service Industry. Carl Scriven & James Stevens. LC 81-24977. 6429p. 1982. text ed. 19.95 o.p. (ISBN 0-471-86819-1). Wiley.
Food First: Beyond the Myth of Scarcity. Francis M. Lappe & Joseph Collins. 1977. 11.95 o.p. (ISBN 0-395-25347-0). HM.
Food First Curriculum Sampler. Laurie Rubin. (Illus.). pap. text ed. 1.00 o.p. (ISBN 0-317-02667-4). Inst Food & Develop.
Food for Beginners. Susan George & Nigel Paige. (Illus.). 175p. pap. 4.95 o.s.i. Inst Food & Develop.
Food for Champions: How to Eat to Win. Ned Bayrd & Chris Quilter. LC 81-20285. (Illus.). 224p. 1982. 11.95 o.p. (ISBN 0-395-31820-3). HM.
Food for Fifty. 7th ed. Grace Shugart et al. LC 84-13109. 676p. 1985. text ed. 52.00 o.p. (ISBN 0-02-411060-4). Macmillan.
Food for Knapsackers & Other Trail Travellers. Hasse Bunnelle. LC 74-162395. (Totebooks Ser.). 144p. 1971. pap. 4.95 o.s.i o.s.i. (ISBN 0-87156-049-6). Sierra.
Food for Life: The Cancer Prevention Cookbook. Richard Bohannon et al. 352p. 1986. 17.95 o.p. (ISBN 0-8092-5029-2). Contemp Bks.
Food for Sport. Nathan J. Smith. LC 76-4092. (Berkeley Series in Nutrition). (Illus.). 1976. pap. 6.95 o.p. (ISBN 0-915950-03-0). Bull Pub.
Food for Thought. Capon. 1978. 7.95 o.p. (ISBN 0-15-127267-0). HarBraceJ.
Food for Thought. 2nd ed. Theodore P. Labuza & A. Elizabeth Sloan. (Illus.). 1977. pap. 13.95 o.s.i. (ISBN 0-87055-244-9). AVI.
Food for Thought from God's Kettle. V. Gladys Shutt. 1982. 8.95 o.p. (ISBN 0-533-05178-9). Vantage.
Food for Tomorrow. C. Dean Freudenberger. LC 83-72119. 176p. 1984. pap. 11.95 o.p. (ISBN 0-8066-2063-3, 10-2333, Augsburg). Augsburg Fortress.
Food from Farm to Table: Yearbook of Agriculture, 1982. LC 82-60049. (Illus.). 413p. 1982. 12.00 o.p. (ISBN 0-318-21952-2, 001-000-04298-0). USGPO.
Food from Windmills. Peter Fraenkel. (Illus.). 75p. (Orig.). 1975. pap. 4.50x o.p. (ISBN 0-903031-25-6, Pub. by Intermed Tech England). Intermediate Tech.
Food Import Dependence in Somalia: Magnitude, Causes, & Policy Options. Y. Hossein Farzin. (Discussion Paper Ser.: No. 23). 42p. 1988. 5.00 o.p. (ISBN 0-8213-1024-0, DP0023). World Bank.
Food in Perspective: Third International Conference of Ethnological Food Research. Alexander Fenton & Trefor Owen. (Illus.). 425p. 1981. text ed. 50.00x o.p. (ISBN 0-85976-044-8). Humanities.
Food in the Social Order: Studies of Food & Festivities in Three American Communities. Ed. by Mary Douglas. 312p. 1987. pap. (ISBN 0-88738-691-1). Transaction Pubs.
Food Industry Benefit Plans 1984. Ed. by Catherine C. Hayne. 41p. (Orig.). 1984. pap. 9.00 o.p. (ISBN 0-89154-268-X). Intl Found Employ.
Food Industry: Economics & Policies. Ed. by J. Burns et al. 307p. 1983. text ed. 42.00 o.p.; pap. 25.20 o.p. CAB Intl.
Food Industry Institute Proceedings April 18-21, 1982. Ed. by Becky A. Wright. 99p. (Orig.). 1982. pap. 10.00 o.p. (ISBN 0-89154-197-7). Intl Found Employ.
Food Intolerance: Are the Foods You Eat Making You Sick. John Honter et al. Ed. by Jacqueline Sharkey. LC 86-81046. 127p. (Orig.). pap. 6.95 o.p. (ISBN 0-89586-447-9, Body Press). Price Stern.
Food Is More Than Cooking: A Basic Guide for Young Cooks. Jean Anderson. LC 67-17732. (Illus.). (gr. 7 up). 1968. 7.95 o.s.i. (ISBN 0-664-32397-9, Westminster). Westminster John Knox.
Food Is Your Best Medicine. Henry G. Bieler. 256p. 1988. pap. 3.50 o.p. (ISBN 0-345-00624-0). Ballantine.
Food Law Handbook. Harold W. Schultz. (Illus.). 1981. 48.95 o.s.i. (ISBN 0-87055-372-0). AVI.
Food Lobbyists: Behind the Scenes of Food & Agri-Politics. Harold D. Guither. LC 79-6734. 352p. 1980. 32.00x o.p. (ISBN 0-669-03539-4). Lexington Bks.
Food Lover's Guide to Paris. Patricia Wells. LC 83-40537. (Illus.). 320p. (Orig.). 1984. pap. 9.95 o.p. (ISBN 0-89480-658-0, 658). Workman Pub.
Food Makes the Difference: A Parent's Guide to Raising a Healthy Child. Patricia Kane. 1985. 16.45 o.p. (ISBN 0-671-54323-7). S&S.
Food, Man, & Society. Ed. by D. N. Walcher et al. LC 76-28698. 304p. 1976. 45.00x o.p. (ISBN 0-306-30974-2, Plenum Pr). Plenum Pub.
Food Marketing Review, 1986. Anthony E. Gallo et al. (Agriculture Economic Report 565). (Illus.). 87p. 1987. pap. 4.25 o.p. (ISBN 0-318-22623-5, S/N 001-019-00503-3). USGPO.
Food, People & Nutrition. Eleanor F. Eckstein. (Illus.). 1980. pap. 25.95 o.p. (ISBN 0-87055-355-0). AVI.
Food, Pharmaceutical & Bioengineering - 1976-77. 256p. 1978. pap. 27.00 o.p. (ISBN 0-8169-0101-5, S-172). Am Inst Chem Eng.
Food Policies. John R. Tarrant. LC 79-40740. (Wiley Series on Studies in Environmental Management & Resources Development). 338p. 1980. 88.95 o.p. (ISBN 0-471-27656-1, Pub. by Wiley-Interscience). Wiley.
Food: Politics, Economics, Nutrition & Research. Ed. by Philip H. Abelson. 1976. 30.00 o.p. (ISBN 0-12-041652-2); pap. 22.00 o.p. (ISBN 0-12-041653-0). Acad Pr.
Food Power. George Schwartz. 1979. text ed. 10.95 o.p. (ISBN 0-07-055673-3). McGraw.

Food Preparation for Hotels, Restaurants, & Cafeterias. 2nd ed. R. G. Haines. (Illus.). 1973. 17.76 o.p. (ISBN 0-8269-4422-1). Am Technical.

Food Processing Waste Management. John H. Green & Amihud Kramer. (Illus.). 1979. 60.95 o.s.i. (ISBN 0-87055-331-3). AVI.

Food Processor Cookbook: Sunbeam. LC 79-65556. (Illus.). 1979. 9.95 o.p. (ISBN 0-916752-35-6). Longman Trade.

Food Processor Cookery: Step-by-Step Guide to Success. Margaret D. Murphy. LC 78-72950. 1978. 9.95 o.p. (ISBN 0-916752-30-5). Longman Trade.

Food Products Formulary, Vol. 1: Meats, Poultry, Fish & Shellfish. 2nd ed. Lucy Long et al. (Illus.). 1982. 78.95 o.p. (ISBN 0-87055-392-5). AVI.

Food Repair Handbook: Culinary First-Aid Manual. Michelle Berriedale-Johnson. (Illus.). 136p. (Orig.). 1986. pap. 17.50x o.p. (ISBN 0-356-10405-2, Pub. by MacD & Co). Trans-Atl Phila.

Food Sanitation. 2nd ed. Rufus K. Guthrie. (Illus.). 1980. 24.95 o.p. (ISBN 0-87055-361-5). AVI.

Food Sanitation: Study Course. Anna K. Jernigan. LC 73-146936. (Illus.). 78p. 1971. pap. text ed. 9.95x o.p. (ISBN 0-8138-0815-4). Iowa St U Pr.

Food Science. 2nd ed. Gordon G. Birch et al. 1977. text ed. 25.00 o.p. (ISBN 0-08-021347-2); pap. text ed. 13.75 o.p. (ISBN 0-08-021346-4). Pergamon.

Food Security in Asia & the Pacific Rim: Perspectives & Policy Issues. Ed. by Anthony H. Chisholm & Rodney Tyers. LC 81-48396. (Illus.). 384p. 1982. 32.50x o.p. (ISBN 0-669-05356-2). Lexington Bks.

Food Security Issues in the Arab Near East: A Report of the United Nations Economic Commission for Western Asia. A. A. El-Sherbini. LC 79-40254. (Illus.). 1979. 59.00 o.p. (ISBN 0-08-023447-X). Pergamon.

Food Service & Restaurant Marketing. Robert Reid. 320p. 1983. 27.95 o.s.i. (ISBN 0-8436-2263-6). Van nos Reinhold.

Food Service for Fitness. Jeanne E. Polak. 84p. (Orig.). 1981. spiral 7.95 o.p. (ISBN 0-8087-3418-0, Feffer & Simons). Burgess MN Intl.

Food Service Productivity & Profit Ideabook. William L. Kahrl. LC 75-8918. (Illus.). 192p. 1983. 21.95 o.p. (ISBN 0-8436-0594-4). Van Nos Reinhold.

Food Service Supervisor-School Lunch Manager. Linda Bernbach. LC 79-15860. 1980. pap. 8.00 o.p. (ISBN 0-668-04819-0, 4819-0). Arco.

Food Sleuth Handbook. Sandra K. Friday & Heidi S. Hurwitz. LC 81-68133. (Illus.). 288p. 1982. 15.95 o.p. (ISBN 0-689-11246-7, Atheneum). Macmillan.

Food Stamps, & Income Maintenance. Maurice MacDonald. (Poverty Policy Analysis Ser.). 1977. 19.50 o.p. (ISBN 0-12-464050-8); pap. 10.00 o.p. (ISBN 0-12-464052-4). Acad Pr.

Food Theory & Applications. Ed. by Pauline C. Paul et al. LC 79-172953. 1972. write for info. o.p. (ISBN 0-02-393210-4). Macmillan.

Food Web. S. L. Pimm. LC 82-1306. (Population & Community Biology Ser.). 1982. 39.95x o.p. (ISBN 0-412-23100-X, NO. 6438, Pub. by Chapman & Hall); pap. 18.95 o.p. (ISBN 0-412-23110-7, NO. 6575). Routledge Chapman & Hall.

Food with the Famous. Jane Grigson. LC 79-55605. 1980. 15.95 o.p. (ISBN 0-689-11040-5, Atheneum). Macmillan.

Foodborne & Waterborne Diseases: Their Epidemiological Characteristics. I. Jackson Tartakow & John H. Vorperian. (Illus.). 1981. 38.95 o.s.i. (ISBN 0-87055-368-2). AVI.

Foodborne Disease & Food Safety. LC 81-20681. 1981. 19.50 o.p. (ISBN 0-89970-106-X, OP-150). AMA.

Foods. Gloria Truitt. Ed. by Patricia Mahany. (Nature Riddle Coloring Bks.). (Illus.). 16p. (Orig.). (ps-4). 1982. pap. 0.95 o.p. (ISBN 0-87239-599-5, 2386). Standard Pub.

Foods for One or Two - or More. Amy G. Ireson & Shirley F. Lipscomb. LC 77-75158. (Illus.). 1978. text ed. 29.50 o.p. (ISBN 0-395-25820-0). HM.

Foods from the Founding Fathers: Recipes from Five Colonial Seaports. Helen N. Burke. (Illus.). 1978. 10.00 o.p. (ISBN 0-682-48585-3, Banner). Exposition-Phoenix.

Foods of the Frontier. Gertrude Harris. LC 72-77565. (Illus.). 192p. 1972. pap. 4.95 o.s.i. (ISBN 0-912238-25-9, One Hund One Prods). Ortho.

Foods Oils & Their Uses. 2nd ed. Theodore J. Weiss. (Illus.). 1983. 37.95 o.p. (ISBN 0-87055-420-4). AVI.

Foodservice Facilities Planning. 2nd ed. Edward A. Kazarian. (Illus.). 1983. 29.95 o.p. (ISBN 0-87055-436-0). AVI.

Foodservice Systems Administration. Mary J. Hitchcock. (Illus.). 1980. text ed. write for info. o.p. (ISBN 0-02-354650-6). Macmillan.

Fool of God: Jacopone Da Todi. George T. Peck. LC 79-16713. (Illus.). 288p. 1980. 22.50 o.p. (ISBN 0-8173-0022-8). U of Ala Pr.

Foolish Dinosaur Fiasco. Scott Corbett. (Illus.). (gr. 1-3). 1978. 10.45 o.p. (ISBN 0-316-15657-4, Pub. by Atlantic Monthly Pr). Little.

Foolish Tortoise. Richard Buckley. LC 85-12099. (Illus.). 24p. (ps up). 1985. pap. 4.95 o.p. (ISBN 0-88708-002-2). Picture Bk Studio.

Fools & Heroes: The Changing Role of Communist Intellectuals in Czechoslovakia. Peter Hruby. 1980. 51.00 o.p. (ISBN 0-08-024276-6); pap. 31.00 o.p. (ISBN 0-08-026790-4). Pergamon.

Fool's Crow. Thomas E. Mails. 1980. pap. 3.50 o.p. (ISBN 0-380-52175-X, 52175-X, Discus). Avon.

Fool's Gold. Ted Wood. 192p. 1986. 13.95 o.s.i. (ISBN 0-684-18568-7). Scribner.

Fools in Town Are on Our Side. Ross Thomas. 384p. 1976. pap. 1.75 o.p. (ISBN 0-380-00687-1, 59964-3). Avon.

Fools in Town Are on Our Side. Ross Thomas. 384p. 1987. pap. 3.95 o.p. (ISBN 0-445-40560-0). Mysterious Pr.

Fool's Mercy. Henry Allen. 312p. 1982. 12.95 o.p. (ISBN 0-395-32039-9). HM.

Foot in Diabetes: Proceedings of the First National Conference on the Diabetic Foot, Malvern, 1986. Ed. by H. Connor et al. LC 86-32514. 1987. 25.55 o.p. (ISBN 0-471-91190-9, Dist. by A R Liss). Wiley.

Foot Reflexology. Ina Bryant. LC 81-11016. 1981. pap. 4.95 o.p. (ISBN 0-89019-076-3). Norwalk Pr.

Foot Talk: A Complete Guide to the Good Health & Care of the Feet. Barry H. Block. (Illus.). 1984. 13.95 o.p. (ISBN 0-87795-522-0, Arbor Hse). Morrow.

Foot Throws Karate, Judo & Self-Defense. Hayward Nishioka. LC 72-93269. (Japanese Arts Ser.). (Illus.). 204p. 1972. pap. text ed. 9.95x o.p. (ISBN 0-89750-025-3, Dist. by Wehman). Ohara Pubns.

Foot Troubles. T. T. Stamm. (Illus.). 128p. 1957. (ISBN 0-8022-1629-3). Philos Lib.

Football. Cass R. Sandak. (Easy-Read Sports Bks). (Illus.). 48p. (gr. 1-3). 1982. PLB 10.40 o.p. (ISBN 0-531-04376-2). Watts.

Football see Heinemann Guided Readers.

Football-Access. pap. 4.95 o.p. (ISBN 0-671-60377-9). S&S.

Football-Access. Ed. by Richard S. Wurman. (Sports Ser.). (Illus.). 72p. 1982. pap. 4.95 o.p. (ISBN 0-915461-03-X). Access Pr.

Football by the Numbers 1986. George Ignatin & Allen Barra. 192p. 1986. pap. 9.95 o.p. (ISBN 0-13-938937-7). P-H.

Football Coaching. Compiled by American Football Coaches Association Staff. 224p. 1981. 19.95 o.s.i. (ISBN 0-684-17149-X, ScribT). Scribner.

Football Fantasy 1988. Charpen. pap. 9.95 o.p. (ISBN 0-8225-9955-4). Lerner Pubns.

Football for Young Champions. 2nd ed. Robert J. Antonacci & Jene Barr. LC 75-10825. (Illus.). 160p. (gr. 4-6). 1976. text ed. 10.95 o.p. (ISBN 0-07-002154-6). McGraw.

Football Greats. R. Broeg & Weeb Ewbank. LC 77-7592. (Illus.). 1977. pap. 4.95 o.p. (ISBN 0-8272-1007-8). CBP.

Football: Records, Stars, Feats & Facts. Louis Phillips & Arnie Markoe. LC 79-87526. (Illus.). (gr. 4-7). 1979. 2.95 o.p. (ISBN 0-15-228947-X, HJ). HarBraceJ.

Football Rules in Pictures. rev. ed. Don Schiffer & Lud Duroska. (Illus.). 80p. 1983. pap. 6.95 o.p. (ISBN 0-399-50840-6, G&D). Putnam Pub Group.

Football Strength & Conditioning Program for all Seasons. Rich Tuten & Clancy Moore. (Illus.). 134p. (Orig.). 1983. pap. text ed. 8.95x o.p. (ISBN 0-89459-206-8). Hunter Textbks.

Football's New Master Defense Guide. Bob Troppmann. LC 83-2401. 204p. 1983. pap. text ed. 17.95 plastic comb binding o.p. (ISBN 0-13-324244-7, Parker). P-H.

Footlight Summer. John W. Chambers. LC 83-2628. 204p. (gr. 5-9). 1983. 10.95 o.s.i. (ISBN 0-689-30980-5, Atheneum Childrens Bks). Macmillan.

Footnote to History. Si-lan C. Leyda. LC 82-83630. (Illus.). 317p. 49.95 o.p. (ISBN 0-87127-134-6, Pub. by Dance Horiz). Princeton Bk Co.

Footprints: Chilling Drama of Two Bigfoot. Gordon Jones. 1977. 7.00 o.p. (ISBN 0-682-48829-1). Exposition-Phoenix.

Footprints in the Refrigerator. Selma Boyd & Pauline Boyd. LC 82-7112. (Easy-Read Story Bks). (Illus.). (gr. k-3). 1982. 3.95 o.p. (ISBN 0-531-03554-9); PLB 10.40 o.p. (ISBN 0-531-04450-5). Watts.

Footprints: Poems. Denise Levertov. LC 72-80972. 64p. 1972. pap. 4.95 o.p. (ISBN 0-8112-0455-3, NDP344). New Directions.

Footprints under the Window. Franklin W. Dixon. (Hardy Boys Ser: Vol. 12). (gr. 5-9). 1933. 3.29 o.p. (ISBN 0-448-18912-7, G&D). Putnam Pub Group.

Footprints: Walking Through the Passages of Life. Howard Hendricks & Jeanne Hendricks. LC 80-25868. (Illus.). 96p. 1981. pap. 5.95 o.p. (ISBN 0-930014-55-3). Multnomah.

Footsore One: Walks & Hikes Around Puget Sound. 2nd ed. Harvey Manning. (Footsore Ser.). (Illus.). 240p. 1982. pap. 9.95 o.p. (ISBN 0-89886-065-2). Mountaineers.

Footsore Two: Walks & Hikes Around Puget Sound. 2nd ed. Harvey Manning. LC 77-23727. (Footsore Ser.). (Illus.). 224p. (Orig.). 1978. pap. 9.95 o.p. (ISBN 0-916890-54-6). Mountaineers.

Footsteps in the Sea: A Biography of Archbishop Athenagoras Cavadas. George Poulos. (Illus.). 186p. 1979. 7.95 o.p. (ISBN 0-916586-36-7); pap. 10.95 o.p. (ISBN 0-916586-35-9). Holy Cross Orthodox.

Footsteps of St. Peter. John R. MacDuff. 648p. lib. bdg. 24.95 o.p. (ISBN 0-8254-5166-3). Kregel.

Footwear (Men's, Women's, Boys' & Girls') Fact File 1985. 9th ed. Fairchild Market Research Division Staff. (Fairchild Fact Files Ser.). (Illus.). 50p. 1985. pap. 17.50 o.p. (ISBN 0-87005-524-0). Fairchild.

Footwear, Nineteen Eighty-Six: Men's, Women's, Boys' & Girls' 10th ed. Fairchild Market Research Division Staff. (Failrchild Fact Files Ser.). (Illus.). 50p. 1986. pap. 20.00 o.p. (ISBN 0-87005-556-9). Fairchild.

Footwork. Ian McMahan. 416p. 1986. 18.95 o.p. (ISBN 0-531-15023-2). Watts.

Foozles & Frauds. Harold Russell. LC 76-58739. 1977. text ed. 15.00 o.p. (ISBN 0-89413-044-7). Inst Inter Aud.

For a Child: Great Poems Old & New. Ed. by Wilma McFarland. (Illus.). (gr. k-3). 1947. 4.50 o.s.i. (ISBN 0-664-32001-5, Westminster). Westminster John Knox.

For a New Novel: Essays on Fiction. Alain Robbe-Grillet. Tr. by Richard Howard from Fr. 1966. pap. 2.25 o.s.i. (ISBN 0-394-17107-1, B112, BC). Grove.

For a Restructuring of International Economic Relations. I. I. Dioumoulen et al. 182p. 1983. pap. 2.95 o.p. (ISBN 0-8285-2592-7, Pub. by Progress Pubs USSR). Imported Pubns.

For Adults Only. George W. Gunn. (Illus., Orig.). (gr. 12). 1967. pap. 1.25 o.p. (ISBN 0-8042-9349-X, John Knox). Westminster John Knox.

For All It May, or May Not Mean! Lynda K. Thomas. (Illus.). 1984. 6.95 o.p. (ISBN 0-533-05867-8). Vantage.

For All Seasons. Charles H. Numrich. 43p. 1981. pap. text ed. 6.25 o.p. (ISBN 0-89536-490-5, 0600). CSS of Ohio.

For Always Only. Ellen P. Davidson. 136p. 1973. 5.95 o.p. (ISBN 0-393-08374-8). Norton.

For Art's Sake. Jack Cross. (Classroom Close-Ups Ser.). (Illus.). 1977. text ed. 16.50x o.p. (ISBN 0-04-371051-4); pap. text ed. 6.95x o.p. (ISBN 0-04-371052-2). Unwin Hyman.

For Better or Worse. Linda R. Wisdom. (Candlelight Ecstasy Ser.: No. 249). 192p. (Orig.). 1984. pap. 1.95 o.s.i. (ISBN 0-440-12558-8). Dell.

For Every Body: Exercise, Nutrition & Health for Young Christians. Steve Swanson. LC 80-67804. 128p. (Orig.). 1981. pap. 3.50 o.p. (ISBN 0-8066-1866-3, 10-2349, Augsburg). Augsburg Fortress.

For Fear of Little Men. James A. FitzGerald. LC 76-52151. 1977. 10.00 o.p. (ISBN 0-682-48753-8). Exposition-Phoenix.

For Friends at Home: A Scottish Emigrant's Letters from Canada, California, & the Cariboo, 1844-1864. Ed. by Richard A. Preston. (Illus.). 352p. 1975. 12.95 o.p. (ISBN 0-7735-0147-9, McGill Canada). U of Toronto Pr.

For Gourmets with Ulcers. Toni M. Bruyere & Sidney J. Robey. LC 78-152655. 1971. 6.95 o.p. (ISBN 0-393-08645-3). Norton.

For Heaven's Sake. Peter Kreeft. LC 86-8773. 192p. 1986. 12.95 o.p. (ISBN 0-8407-5494-9). Nelson.

For Honor's Lady. Rosanne Kohake. 544p. 1984. pap. 3.95 o.p. (ISBN 0-380-85480-5, 85480). Avon.

For Humans & Angels. E. Winifred Singleton. 1977. 5.00 o.p. (ISBN 0-682-48846-1). Exposition-Phoenix.

For I Am! The Reaching. Aroen. (For I Am Ser.). 1980. 8.50 o.p. (ISBN 0-682-49512-3). Exposition-Phoenix.

For I Will Consider My Cat Jeoffry. Christopher Smart. LC 83-15660. (Illus.). 32p. (ps up). 1984. 10.95 o.s.i. (ISBN 0-689-31026-9, Atheneum Childrens Bks). Macmillan.

For Immediate Realease. 61p. 1979. member 6.00 o.p. (ISBN 0-686-48369-3); non-member 12.00 o.p. (ISBN 0-686-48370-7). Am Consul Eng.

For Keeps? Carol Stanley. 1988. pap. 2.95 o.p. (ISBN 0-380-75442-8). Avon.

For Love Alone. Christina Stead. LC 78-23847. 491p. 1979. pap. 5.95 o.p. (ISBN 0-15-632535-7, Harv). HarBraceJ.

For Love of a Wild Thing. Ernest Dudley. LC 74-80816. 224p. 1974. 10.00 o.p. (ISBN 0-8397-2325-3). Eriksson.

For Love of Her. Emily Dickinson. (Illus.). 1974. pap. 4.95 o.p. (ISBN 0-517-51488-5, C N Potter Bks). Crown.

For Love of Imabelle. Chester Himes. 192p. 1973. Repr. of 1965 ed. 7.95x o.p. (ISBN 0-911860-33-9). Chatham Bkseller.

For Love or Money: How to Succeed in Spite of Yourself. Fred Labowitz. 286p. 1982. 12.95 o.p. (ISBN 0-936602-46-5). Kampmann.

For Love's Sake. Leroy Brownlow. 1975. gift ed. 6.95 o.p. (ISBN 0-915720-15-9). Brownlow Pub Co.

For Mary, with Love. Thomas Savage. 288p. 1983. 15.45i o.p. (ISBN 0-316-77158-9). Little.

For Mature Adults Only. Norman C. Habel. LC 68-58159. (Orig.). 1969. pap. 1.95 o.p. (ISBN 0-8006-1971-4, Fortress). Augsburg Fortress.

For Max Jacob. Andrei Codrescu. LC 74-24555. 32p. (Orig.). 1975. pap. 5.00 o.p. (ISBN 0-686-10820-5). Tree Bks.

For Melba. Keorapetse Kgositsile. 1970. pap. 1.50 o.p. (ISBN 0-88378-007-0). Third World.

For My Country. Jules-Paul Tardivel. Tr. by Sheila Fischman. LC 75-6862. (Social History of Canada Ser.). Orig. Title: Pour la Patrie. 1975. pap. 8.95 o.p. (ISBN 0-8020-6267-9). U of Toronto Pr.

For Parents Only: Are Your Children Flowers or Weeds? Doris B. Tonks. 1984. 7.95 o.p. (ISBN 0-533-05771-X). Vantage.

For Pete's Sake. Bradford Street. (Fiction Movie Tie-in). 1974. pap. 1.25 o.p. (ISBN 0-380-00051-2, 19760). Avon.

For Queen & Country: Victorian England. Margaret Drabble. LC 78-9782. (Illus.). (gr. 6 up). 1979. 8.95 o.p. (ISBN 0-395-28960-2, Clarion). HM.

For Sale by Owner. Russell Oddy. (ISBN 0-88908-595-1). ISC Pr.

For Sale: Minnesota: Organized Promotion of Scandinavian Immigration, 1866-1873. Lars Ljungmark. 304p. 1971. pap. 7.50 o.p. (ISBN 0-318-16615-1, SP11). Swedish-Am.

For Self-Examination. Soren Kierkegaard. Tr. by Edna Hong & Howard Hong. (Orig.). 1940. pap. 4.50 o.p. (ISBN 0-8066-0075-6, 10-2350, Augsburg). Augsburg Fortress.

For Spirits & Kings: African Art from the Paul & Ruth Tishman Collection. Ed. by Susan Vogel. LC 81-4368. (Illus.). 256p. 1981. 35.00 o.p. (ISBN 0-87099-267-8); pap. 19.95 o.p. (ISBN 0-87099-268-6). Metro Mus Art.

For Sylvia: An Honest Account. Valentine Ackland. 1986. 13.45 o.p. (ISBN 0-393-02297-8). Norton.

For Tatiana: When Love Triumphed over the Kremlin. Edward Lozansky. LC 85-30568. (Illus.). 320p. 1986. pap. 17.95 o.p. (ISBN 0-03-005064-2). H Holt & Co.

For the Birds. Skip Morrow. LC 81-21284. (Illus.). 96p. (Orig.). 1982. pap. 3.95 o.p. Seaver Bks.

For the Birds. Skip Morrow. 1982. pap. 3.95 o.s.i. (ISBN 0-394-17646-4, Ever). Grove.

For the Birds & Other Stories. Edward Thomas. LC 84-90173. 71p. 1985. 7.95 o.p. (ISBN 0-533-06241-1). Vantage.

For the Defense. F. L. Bailey & John Greenya. LC 75-741. 384p. 1975. 10.95 o.p. (ISBN 0-689-10667-X, Atheneum). Macmillan.

For the Duration... The United States Goes to War, Pearl Harbor-1942. Lee Kennett. (Illus.). 256p. 1985. 15.95 o.s.i. (ISBN 0-684-18239-4, ScribT). Scribner.

For the Inward Journey: The Writings of Howard Thurman. Howard Thurman. Intro. by Vincent Harding & Anne S. Thurman. LC 83-26366. 352p. 1984. 17.95 o.p. (ISBN 0-15-132656-8). HarBraceJ.

For the Loneliest of Reasons. David Kalugin. (Illus.). 1979. soft cover 4.95 o.p. (ISBN 0-933586-03-5). Book Promo Pr.

For the Love of God. Janet Dailey. (Nightingale Paperbacks Ser.). 1984. pap. 9.95 o.p. (ISBN 0-8161-3697-1, Large Print Bks). G K Hall.

For the Love of My Daughter. Mary E. Ton. LC 77-87253. 1978. pap. 2.95 o.p. (ISBN 0-89191-104-9). Cook.

For the Love of St. Maarten. Will S. Johnson. 160p. 1987. 9.95 o.p. (ISBN 0-8062-2824-5). Carlton.

For the New Year. Eric Pankey. LC 84-45241. 1984. 12.95 o.p. (ISBN 0-689-11507-5, Atheneum); pap. 7.95 o.p. (ISBN 0-689-11506-7, Atheneum). Macmillan.

For the Record: Selected Statements, 1977 to 1980. Henry A. Kissinger. 288p. 1981. 15.45 o.p. (ISBN 0-316-49663-4). Little.

For the Shape of Your Life. Felicia Scherer. (Illus.). 1976. pap. text ed. 2.95 o.p. (ISBN 0-918734-14-2). Reymont.

For the Time Being. Sydney J. Harris. 1972. 8.95 o.p. (ISBN 0-395-14001-3). HM.

For the Tutor. 123p. 1970. pap. 3.00 o.p. (ISBN 0-912041-02-1). Natl Comm Res Youth.

For the Welfare of Children. Children's Defense Fund Staff. 40p. (Orig.). 1978. pap. 2.50 o.p. (ISBN 0-938008-17-X). Children's Defense.

For the Woman over Fifty. Adele Nudel. 1979. pap. 2.95 o.p. (ISBN 0-380-44685-5, 44685-5). Avon.

For the Woman over Fifty: A Practical Guide for a Full & Vital Life. Adele Nudel. LC 77-91047. 1978. 12.50 o.p. (ISBN 0-8008-2967-0). Taplinger.

For These or Such Like Reasons: John Holt's Attack on Benjamin Franklin. Intro. by Charles Wetherell. 1979. pap. 3.50x o.p. (ISBN 0-912296-42-9, Dist. by U Pr of Va). Am Antiquarian.

For Those Who Would Be President: Sixteen Management Skills for the Top Job. Neil R. Sweeney. 192p. 1986. pap. 12.95 o.p. (ISBN 0-673-15958-2). Scott F.

For Weber: Essays in the Sociology of Fate. Bryan S. Turner. 360p. 1981. 30.00x o.p. (ISBN 0-7100-0780-9). Routledge Chapman & Hall.

For Whom the Bell Tolls. Ernest Hemingway. 48p. (Orig.). 1989. pap. 9.95 o.p. (ISBN 1-55651-279-1); audiocassette tape incl. o.p. (ISBN 1-55651-280-5). Cram Cassettes.

For Whom the Duck Tolls. Keith C. Russell et al. (Illus.). 288p. 1987. pap. 17.95 o.p. (ISBN 0-317-66834-X, Pub. by Winchester Pr). New Century.

For Whom the Ducks Toll: A Select Gathering of Memorable Waterfowling Tales. Keith C. Russell. LC 84-7446. (Illus.). 288p. 1984. slipcased, ltd. ed. o.s.i. 30.00 o.p. (ISBN 0-8329-0314-0, Pub. by Winchester Pr); 17.95 o.p. (ISBN 0-8329-0357-4, Pub. by Winchester Pr). New Century.

For Whom You Search. J. Lee White. 208p. 1982. 9.00 o.p. (ISBN 0-682-49889-0). Exposition-Phoenix.

For Women Only. Evelyn Petersen & J. Allan Petersen. pap. 7.95, 1974 o.p. (ISBN 0-8423-0896-2); pap. 4.95 1982 o.p. (ISBN 0-8423-0897-0). Tyndale.

For Women: Opportunities Unlimited. 4.00 o.p. (ISBN 0-686-31048-9, 29707). Rough Notes.

For Your Eyes Only. Ian Fleming. (James Bond Ser.). 192p. 1981. pap. 3.50 o.s.i. (ISBN 0-425-08167-2). Jove Pubns.

Foraging Vacation: Edibles from Maine's Sea & Shore. Raquel Boehmer. (Illus.). 150p. (Orig.). 1982. pap. 7.95 o.p. (ISBN 0-89272-139-1, PIC488). Down East.

Foraminifera, Vol. 1. Ed. by R. H. Hedley & C. G. Adams. 1974. 84.00 o.p. (ISBN 0-12-336401-9). Acad Pr.

Foraminifera, Vol. 2. Ed. by R. H. Hedley & C. G. Adams. 1977. 72.00 o.p. (ISBN 0-12-336402-7). Acad Pr.

Forbidden Dreams. Jolene Prewit-Parker. (Velvet Glove Ser.: No. 10). 176p. (Orig.). 1984. pap. 2.25 o.p. (ISBN 0-380-89466-1). Avon.

Forbidden Game: A Social History of Drugs. Brian Inglis. LC 75-12382. 1975. 8.95 o.s.i. (ISBN 0-684-14428-X, ScribT). Scribner.

Forbidden Lands. Gordon Cooper. (Illus.). 176p. 1955. (ISBN 0-8022-0298-5). Philos Lib.

Forbidden Love. Karen Robards. 384p. 1983. pap. 3.50 o.s.i. (ISBN 0-8439-2024-6, Pub. by Leisure Bks CT). Dorchester Pub Co.

Forbidden Passion. Marilyn Cunningham. (Candlelight Ecstasy Ser.: No. 515). (Orig.). 1987. pap. 2.25 o.p. (ISBN 0-440-12660-6). Dell.

Forbidden Planet. W. J. Stuart. 157p. Date not set. pap. 3.95 o.p. (ISBN 0-374-52082-8). FS&G.

Forbidden Tower. Marion Zimmer Bradley. 1979. lib. bdg. 14.00 o.p. (ISBN 0-8398-2405-X, Gregg). G K Hall.

Forbidden Voyage. Earle L. Reynolds. LC 74-27390. (Illus.). 281p. 1975. Repr. of 1961 ed. lib. bdg. 27.50x o.p. (ISBN 0-8371-7906-8, REFV). Greenwood.

Force Concept in Chemistry. B. M. Deb. 480p. 1981. 43.95 o.p. (ISBN 0-442-26106-3). Van Nos Reinhold.

Force of Order & Methods... An American View into the Dutch Directed Society. M. C. Blanken. (Studies in Social Life: Vol. 19). 1976. pap. 32.50 o.p. (ISBN 9-0247-1849-X). E J Brill USA.

Force of Tradition: A Case Study of Women Priests in Sweden. Brita Stendahl. LC 84-48713. (Illus.). 208p. 1985. pap. 19.95 o.p. (ISBN 0-8006-1808-4, 1-1808, Fortress). Augsburg Fortress.

Force Play. Anthony Stuart. LC 78-73870. 1979. 8.95 o.p. (ISBN 0-87795-224-8, Arbor Hse). Morrow.

Forced Labor: Maternity Care in the United States. Nancy S. Shaw. 1975. 24.00 o.p. (ISBN 0-08-017835-9); pap. 13.00 o.p. (ISBN 0-08-017834-0). Pergamon.

Forces of Freedom in Spain 1974-1979. Samuel D. Eaton. LC 80-8383. (Illus.). 192p. 1981. pap. 11.95x o.p. (ISBN 0-8179-7452-0, P-245). Hoover Inst Pr.

Forces of Love. Clayton W. Fountain. LC 86-70142. 420p. pap. 15.95 o.p. (ISBN 0-931494-90-7). Brunswick Pub.

Forcing, Arithmetic, Division Rings. J. Hirschfeld & W. H. Wheeler. (Lecture Notes in Mathematics Ser.: Vol. 454). vii, 266p. 1975. pap. 17.00 o.p. (ISBN 0-387-07157-1). Springer-Verlag.

Ford Agency: A Pictorial History. Henry Dominguez. LC 81-1440. (Illus.). 1981. pap. 14.95 o.p. (ISBN 0-87938-095-0). Motorbooks Intl.

Ford Anglia Owners Workshop Manual: '59 Thru '68. J. H. Haynes & S. F. Page. (Owners Workshop Manuals Ser.: No. 001). 1979. 15.95 o.p. (ISBN 0-900550-01-5). Haynes Pubns.

Ford Bronco, Nineteen Sixty-Six to Nineteen Eighty-One. Chilton Automotives Editorial Staff. (Illus.). 1981. pap. 13.50 o.s.i. (ISBN 0-8019-7140-3). Chilton.

Ford Car Tune-Up Maintenance: 1969-1981. Ed. by Eric Jorgensen. pap. 8.95 o.p. (ISBN 0-89287-135-0, A-170). Clymer Pub.

Ford Falcon, Comet, Fairlane. (A160). Clymer Pub.

Ford Fiesta 1978-1980 Shop Manual. Ed. by Eric Jorgensen & Eric Jorgensen. (Illus.). pap. text ed. 12.95 o.p. (ISBN 0-89287-299-3, A173). Clymer Pub.

Ford Madox Brown & the Pre-Raphaelite History-Picture. Lucy F. Rabin. LC 77-94725. (Outstanding Dissertations in the Fine Arts Ser.). 364p. 1978. lib. bdg. 37.00 o.p. (ISBN 0-8240-3246-2). Garland Pub.

Ford Model A Album. Ed. by Floyd Clymer. (Illus.). pap. 5.00 o.p. (ISBN 0-89287-261-6, H521). Clymer Pub.

Ford Model A Service Manual & Handbook of Repair & Maintenance. Victor W. Page. Ed. by Clymer Publications. 1961. pap. 9.00 o.p. (ISBN 0-89287-265-9, H525). Clymer Pub.

Ford Model T Manual: 1922. Ed. by Ford Motor Company. (Illus.). 1949. pap. 4.00 o.p. (ISBN 0-89287-255-1, H505). Clymer Pub.

Ford Models' Crash Course in Looking Great. Eileen Ford & Joan Heilman. 1985. 18.45 o.p. (ISBN 0-671-49961-0). S&S.

Ford Mustang. (A291). Clymer Pub.

Ford, Not a Lincoln. Richard Reeves. LC 75-22195. 212p. 1975. 8.95 o.p. (ISBN 0-15-132302-X). HarBraceJ.

Ford Owner's Handbook: Models T & a Nineteen Hundred & Eight to Nineteen Twenty-Eight. Victor W. Page. Ed. by Clymer Publications. (Illus.). 1958. pap. 9.00 o.p. (ISBN 0-89287-258-6, H509). Clymer Pub.

Ford Pick-Ups 1965-84: RTUG. Chilton Automotives Editorial Staff. LC 83-45303. 312p. 1984. pap. 13.50 o.p. (ISBN 0-8019-7461-5). Chilton.

Ford Pickup Repair. Ed. by Spence Murray. LC 78-65688. (Pickups & Vans Ser.). (Illus.). 1979. pap. text ed. 4.95 o.p. (ISBN 0-8227-5042-2). Petersen Pub.

Ford Spotter's Guide: 1920-1980. Ted Burness. LC 81-9495. (Illus.). 9.95 o.p. (ISBN 0-87938-150-7). Motorbooks Intl.

Ford Tune-up & Maintenance: Vans & Pickups, 1969-1978. Mike Bishop. Ed. by Eric Jorgensen. (Illus.). 1978. pap. 7.00 o.p. (ISBN 0-89287-231-4, A242). Clymer Pub.

Ford White House: The Diary of a Speechwriter. John J. Casserly. LC 77-82185. (Illus.). 1977. 17.50 o.p. (ISBN 0-87081-106-1). Univ Pr Colo.

Ford Y-Block. J. C. Eickman. LC 84-19041. (Illus.). 120p. 1984. pap. 12.95 o.p. (ISBN 0-87938-185-X). Motorbooks Intl.

Fore! The Best of Wodehouse on Golf. P. G. Wodehouse. Ed. by D. R. Bensen. LC 83-5097. 256p. 1983. 13.45 o.p. (ISBN 0-89919-212-2). Ticknor & Fields.

Forecast for Love. Renee Shann. (Lythway Ser.). 264p. 1988. lib. bdg. 19.50x o.s.i. (ISBN 0-7451-0720-6, Pub. by Chivers Pr UK). G K Hall.

Forecasting. S. Makridakis. Ed. by S. C. Wheelwright. (TIMS Studies in the Management Sciences: Vol. 12). 373p. 1980. pap. 50.50 o.p. (ISBN 0-444-85294-8, North Holland). Elsevier.

Forecasting Accounts Receivable for a Manufacturing Corporation. 20p. 1980. pap. 40.00 o.p. (ISBN 0-939050-28-5). Credit Res NYS.

Forecasting & Time Series Analysis. Douglas C. Montgomery & Lynwood A. Johnson. 1976. text ed. 33.95 o.p. (ISBN 0-07-042857-3). McGraw.

Forecasting Economic Time Series. Ed. by C. W. Granger. (Economic Theory & Math. Economics Ser.). 1977. 35.00 o.p. (ISBN 0-12-295150-6). Acad Pr.

Forecasting in Business & Economics. C. W. Granger. LC 79-91742. (Economic Theory, Econometrics & Mathematical Econometrics Ser.). 1979. 29.95 o.p. (ISBN 0-12-295180-8). Acad Pr.

Forecasting Local Government Spending. Claudia D. Scott. 142p. 1972. 8.50 o.p. (ISBN 0-87766-023-9). Urban Inst.

Forecasting Passenger & Freight Travel. (Transportation Research Report Ser.). 86p. 1977. 3.80 o.p. (ISBN 0-309-02664-4). Transport Res Bd.

Forecasting Process Leader's Guide. Levenbach. 1984. pap. (ISBN 0-534-03009-2). Van Nos Reinhold.

Forecasting Your Future: How to Prepare Your Own Astrological Time-Scan. Rupert J. Sewell. 96p. (Orig.). 1987. pap. 5.99 o.p. (ISBN 0-85030-572-1, Pub. by Aquarian Pr England). Sterling.

Forefathers. Nancy Cato. 1984. pap. 3.95 o.p. (ISBN 0-451-12798-6, Sig). NAL.

Forehanding & Backhanding-If You're Lucky. Gary Paulsen. LC 77-27046. (Sports on the Light Side Ser.). (Illus.). (gr. 4-6). 1978. PLB 14.25 o.p. (ISBN 0-8172-1158-6). Raintree Pubs.

Forehead, Breath & Smile: An Anthology of Devotional Readings from the Spiritual Teaching of Master Da Free John. Da Free John. 1982. 20.95 o.p. (ISBN 0-913922-70-6). Dawn Horse Pr.

Foreign & American Folk Sayings, Realities & Philosophies. Henry P. Keuls. (Illus.). 1986. 7.95 o.p. (ISBN 0-533-06714-6). Vantage.

Foreign Business Practices: Materials on Practical Aspects of Exporting, International Licensing & Investing. 96p. 1985. pap. 3.50 o.p. (ISBN 0-318-18763-9, S/N 003-009-00460-8). USGPO.

Foreign Business Practices: Materials on Practical Aspects of Exporting, International Licensing & Investing. U. S. Department of Commerce Staff. 1981. 50.00 o.s.i. (ISBN 0-686-37967-5). Info Gatekeepers.

Foreign Commerce & the Antitrust Laws: 1985 Supplement. Wilbur L. Fugate. 1985. pap. 42.50 o.p. (ISBN 0-316-29539-6). Little.

Foreign Commerce & the Antitrust Laws: 1986 Supplement. 3rd ed. Wilbur L. Fugate. LC 81-83240. 228p. 1986. write for info. o.p. (ISBN 0-316-29541-8). Little.

Foreign Consular Offices in the United States, 1987. rev. ed. (State Department Publication Ser.). 92p. 1987. pap. 4.50 o.p. (ISBN 0-318-23749-0, 044-000-02171-4). USGPO.

Foreign Correspondent Looks at Taiwan. J. J. Nerbonne. (Illus.). 1973. 12.50 o.p. E J Brill USA.

Foreign Corrupt Practices Act: Anatomy of a Statute. George C. Greanias. LC 81-48265. (Illus.). 208p. 1982. 26.00x o.p. (ISBN 0-669-05254-X). Lexington Bks.

Foreign Debt & Economic Performance: Special Topics. Ed. by Jeffrey D. Sachs. 1988. U of Chicago Pr.

Foreign Debt & Latin American Economic Development. Ed. by Antonio Jorge et al. 200p. 1983. 50.00 o.p. (ISBN 0-08-029411-1). Pergamon.

Foreign Devils. Irvin Faust. LC 72-97685. 1973. 7.95 o.p. (ISBN 0-87795-056-3, Arbor Hse). Morrow.

Foreign Devils on the Silk Road: The Search for the Lost Cities & Treasures of Chinese Central Asia. Peter Hopkirk. (Illus.). 264p. 1981. 30.00x o.p. (ISBN 0-87023-234-7). U of Mass Pr.

Foreign Direct Investments in the United States: 1985 Transactions. (Illus.). 102p. 1986. pap. 5.00 o.p. (ISBN 0-318-22622-7, S/N 003-009-00488-8). USGPO.

Foreign Engineers in the United States: Immigration or Importation? Institute of Electrical Electronic Engineers Staff et al. LC 85-154979. 1984. write for info. o.p. Inst Electrical.

Foreign Exchange & the Corporate Treasurer. John Heywood. LC 79-50620. 1979. 16.95 o.p. (ISBN 0-8144-5556-5). AMACOM.

Foreign Exchange Control in the Arab World & Repatriation of Capital & Profits: Ninety Seventy-Eight. (Arab World & Iran Business Guides Ser.). 1978. pap. 10.00 o.p. (ISBN 0-931000-04-1). Suburban Pub CT.

Foreign Exchange Dealer's Handbook. 2nd ed. Raymond G. Coninx. 150p. 1985. 35.00 o.p. (ISBN 0-87094-886-5). Dow Jones-Irwin.

Foreign Exchange Management. R. McRae & D. Walker. 1980. text ed. 32.00 o.p. (ISBN 0-13-325357-0). P-H.

Foreign Exchange Risk Management. Alan C. Shapiro. LC 78-10628. 1978. pap. 7.50 o.p. (ISBN 0-8144-2229-2). AMACOM.

Foreign Exchange Yearbook, 1980. Ed. by Trevor Underwood. 264p. 1980. pap. 79.95x o.p. (ISBN 0-470-26982-0). Halsted Pr.

Foreign Films. CineBooks Staff. LC 89-60765. (Home Library Ser.). 288p. (Orig.). 1989. pap. 9.95 o.p. (ISBN 0-933997-22-1). CineBooks.

Foreign Finance in Continental Europe & the U. S. A., 1815-1870: Quantities, Origins, Function & Distribution. D. C. Platt. 224p. 1984. text ed. 37.95x o.p. (ISBN 0-04-330336-6). Unwin Hyman.

Foreign Flavors. LC 85-70349. 235p. 1985. 8.95 o.p. (ISBN 0-87509-360-4). Chr Pubns.

Foreign Investment in South Africa & Namibia: A Directory of U. S., Canadian & British Corporations Operating in South Africa & Namibia. Anne Newman & Cathy Bowers. Ed. by Carolyn Mathiasen. 279p. 1984. pap. 35.00 o.p. (ISBN 0-931035-00-7). IRRC Inc DC.

Foreign Investment in U. S. Real Estate. Ronald S. Barak. 561p. 1981. 55.00 o.p. (ISBN 0-15-100024-7, H39905, Pub. by Law & Business). HarBraceJ.

Foreign Investment Regulations & Labour Employment Conditions in the Arab World. Arab World & Iran Business Guides. 1978. pap. 12.50 o.p. (ISBN 0-931000-03-3). Suburban Pub CT.

Foreign Jobs: The Most Popular Countries. Curtis W. Casewit. 160p. 1984. pap. 8.95 o.p. (ISBN 0-671-49295-0). Monarch Pr.

Foreign Loans: Material Published 1980-1984. Mary Vance. (Public Administration Ser.: P 1698). 32p. 1985. 4.50 o.p. (ISBN 0-89028-448-2). Vance Biblios.

Foreign Market Entry Strategies. Franklin R. Root. 304p. 1982. 24.95 o.p. (ISBN 0-8144-5734-7). AMACOM.

Foreign Mud: The Opium Imbroglio at Canton in the 1830's & the Anglo-Chinese War. Maurice Collis. (Library Ser). (Illus.). 1968. pap. 4.25x o.p. (ISBN 0-393-00462-7, Norton Lib). Norton.

Foreign Ownership of U. S. Farmland. David N. Laband. LC 83-48639. 144p. 1984. 27.00x o.p. (ISBN 0-669-07305-9). Lexington Bks.

Foreign Patent Litigation. (Patents, Copyrights, Trademarks & Literary Property Course Handbook Ser.: Vol. 171). 327p. 1983. 15.00 o.p. (ISBN 0-317-11430-1, G4-3734). PLI.

Foreign Pension Plans 1985: The New Section Rules under IRC Section 404A. 319p. 1985. 15.00 o.p. (J4-3572). PLI.

Foreign Policy Analysis. Feliks Gross. 1954. (ISBN 0-8022-0634-4). Philos Lib.

Foreign Policy & the Democratic Dilemmas. 3rd ed. John Spanier & Eric M. Uslaner. 1982. pap. text ed. 16.95 o.p. (ISBN 0-03-060141-X). HR&W.

Foreign Policy for a New Age. Robert G. Wesson. LC 76-13999. (Illus.). 1977. text ed. 27.95 o.p. (ISBN 0-395-24652-0). HM.

Foreign Policy in World Politics. 6th ed. Roy C. Macridis. (Illus.). 416p. 1985. pap. text ed. (ISBN 0-13-326497-1). P-H.

Foreign Policy Is Your Business. Theodore R. Weber. LC 74-37769. (Christian Ethics for Modern Man Ser.). (Illus.). 128p. (Orig.). 1972. pap. 1.95 o.p. (ISBN 0-8042-9091-1, John Knox). Westminster John Knox.

Foreign Policy Making. 4th ed. John Spanier. 336p. 1985. pap. text ed. 16.95 o.p. (ISBN 0-03-070839-7, HoltC). HR&W.

Foreign Policy Making in the Middle East: Domestic Influences on Policy in Egypt, Iraq, Israel, & Syria. R. D. McLaurin et al. LC 76-24360. (Special Studies). 330p. 1977. text ed. 34.95 o.p. (ISBN 0-275-23870-9); pap. 17.95 o.p. (ISBN 0-275-91681-2, B1681). Praeger.

Foreign Policy, 1985 Annual. Ed. by Bruno Leone et al. (Opposing Viewpoints SOURCES Ser.). 100p. 1985. pap. text ed. 9.95 o.p. (ISBN 0-89908-510-5). Greenhaven.

Foreign Policy, 1986 Annual. Ed. by Bruno Leone et al. (Opposing Viewpoints SOURCES Ser.). 100p. 1986. pap. text ed. 9.95 o.p. (ISBN 0-89908-521-0). Greenhaven.

Foreign Statistical Documents: A Bibliography of General, International Trade & Agricultural Statistics, Including Holdings of the Stanford University Libraries. Ed. by Joyce Ball. (Bibliographical Ser.: No. 28). 1967. pap. 7.95x o.p. (ISBN 0-8179-2282-2). Hoover Inst Pr.

Foreign Unfair Competition: Practice & Procedure. Eugene T. Rossides. (Corporation Practice Ser.: No. 28). 1982. 92.00 o.p. (ISBN 0-317-55281-3). BNA.

Foreigner. David Plante. LC 84-45039. 256p. 1984. 12.95 o.p. (ISBN 0-689-11491-5, Atheneum). Macmillan.

Foreigner. Nahid Rachlin. 1978. 8.95 o.p. (ISBN 0-393-08819-7). Norton.

Forensic Geology: Earth Sciences & Criminal Investigation. R. C. Murray & John C. Tedrow. 1975. 33.06x o.p. (ISBN 0-8135-0794-4). Rutgers U Pr.

Forensic Handbook see Crime Scene & Evidence Collection Handbook.

Forensic Medicine, 3 vols. Ed. by Cesare G. Tedeschi et al. LC 74-4593. (Illus.). 1680p. 1977. Vol. 1. write for info. o.p. (ISBN 0-7216-8772-5); Vol. 2. write for info. o.p. (ISBN 0-7216-8773-3); Vol. 3. write for info. o.p. (ISBN 0-7216-8774-1); Set. write for info. o.p. (ISBN 0-7216-8771-7). Saunders.

Forensic Medicine for Lawyers. J. K. Mason. xv, 453p. 1978. 25.00x o.p. (ISBN 0-7236-0455-X, Pub by J Wright & Sons England). Rothman.

Forensic Science. Ed. by Geoffrey Davies. LC 75-9986. (ACS Symposium Ser.: No. 13). 1975. 23.95 o.p. (ISBN 0-8412-0280-X). Am Chemical.

Forensic Toxicology. Ballantyne. 168p. 1974. 18.50 o.p. (ISBN 0-7236-0356-1, Pub. by John Wright UK). Butterworth.

Forerunners of Drake. Gordon Connell-Smith. LC 75-7237. (Royal Empire Society Imperial Studies Ser). (Illus.). 264p. 1975. Repr. of 1954 ed. lib. bdg. 35.00x o.p. (ISBN 0-8371-8100-3, COFOD). Greenwood.

Forerunners of Jesus. Leroy Waterman. 168p. 1960. (ISBN.0-8022-1814-8). Philos Lib.

Forerunners of the Reformation: The Shape of Late Medieval Thought. Heiko A. Oberman. Tr. by Paul L. Nyhus. LC 81-66518. 352p. 1981. pap. 12.95 o.p. (ISBN 0-8006-1617-0, 1-1617, Fortress). Augsburg Fortress.

Forest. Roger Caras. 1980. pap. 4.95 o.p. (ISBN 0-395-29611-0). HM.

Forest & Shade Trees of Iowa. Peter J. Vander Linden & Donald R. Farrar. (Illus.). 133p. (gr. 9-12). 1984. 25.00 o.p. (ISBN 0-8138-0731-X). Iowa St U Pr.

Forest City: An Illustrated History of London, Canada. Frederick Armstrong. Ed. by Jerry Mosher. LC 86-23434. (Illus.). 336p. 1986. 29.95 o.p. (ISBN 0-89781-180-1). Windsor Pubns Inc.

Forest Environments in Tropical Life Zones: A Pilot Study. L. R. Holdridge et al. LC 75-129847. 1971. 265.00 o.p. (ISBN 0-08-016340-8). Pergamon.

Forest Firefighting. Daniel R. Simone. 32p. 6.95 o.p. (ISBN 0-8062-3039-8). Carlton.

Forest Folklore, Mythology & Romance. Alexander Porteous. LC 68-26597. 322p. 1968. Repr. of 1928 ed. 34.00x o.p. (ISBN 0-8103-3456-9). Gale.

Forest Genetics & Tree Improvement in the People's Republic of China. Stanley L. Krugman et al. LC 82-62310. 84p. (Orig.). 1983. pap. 3.00 o.p. (ISBN 0-939970-18-X, SAF 83-02). Soc Am Foresters.

Forest Island Dynamics in Man-Dominated Landscapes. Ed. by R. L. Burgess & S. M. Sharpe. (Ecological Studies: Vol. 41). (Illus.). 310p. 1981. 37.00 o.p. (ISBN 0-387-90584-7). Springer Verlag.

Forest People. Colin M. Turnbull. LC 61-12850. (Illus.). 1968. pap. 9.95 o.s.i. (ISBN 0-671-20153-0, Touchstone Bks). S&S.

Forest Pest Management in the People's Republic of China. Max W. McFadden et al. LC 82-50539. 86p. (Orig.). 1982. pap. 5.00 o.p. (ISBN 0-939970-14-7, SAF 82-03). Soc Am Foresters.

Forest Resource Economics. G. Robinson Gregory. 548p. 1972. (ISBN 0-471-06833-0, 40503). Wiley.

Forest Rose: A Tale of the Frontier. Facs. of 1885 Ed. Emerson Bennett. LC 72-96394. li, 118p. 1973. 4.95 o.p. (ISBN 0-8214-0128-9). Ohio U Pr.

Forest Service & the Civilian Conservation Corps: 1933-42. Alison T. Otis et al. (Forest Service 395 Ser.). (Illus.). 225p. 1986. pap. 11.00 o.p. (ISBN 0-318-21545-4, S/N 001-001-00625-4). USGPO.

Forest Soils: Properties & Processes. K. A. Armson. 1977. 30.00c o.p. (ISBN 0-8020-2265-0). U of Toronto Pr.

Forest Trees of the Pacific Slope. George B. Sudworth. (Illus.). 16.75 o.p. (ISBN 0-8446-3031-4). Peter Smith.

Foresters' Future: Leaders or Followers. (SAF Convention Proceedings Ser.). (Illus.). 1986. 20.00 o.p. Soc Am Foresters.

Forestlands: Public & Private. Robert T. Deacon & M. Bruce Johnson. LC 84-22699. (Illus.). 332p. 1985. 34.95 o.s.i. (ISBN 0-88410-391-9); pap. 12.95 o.s.i. (ISBN 0-88410-392-7). PRIPP.

Forestry Education in America Today & Tomorrow. Samuel Trask et al. LC 63-21251. (Illus.). 402p. 1963. 5.00 o.p. (ISBN 0-939970-12-0). Soc Am Foresters.

Forests of Ireland: History, Distribution & Silviculture. Niall O'Carroll. (Turoe Press Ser.). (Illus.). 128p. 1984. pap. 17.95 o.p. (ISBN 0-905223-49-7, Dist. by Kampmann). M Boyars Pubs.

Forests of Norbio. Guiseppe Dessi. LC 74-30087. 1975. 7.95 o.p. (ISBN 0-15-132505-7). HarBraceJ.

Forever & Always. Mildred Lawrence. LC 61-10111. 1961. 5.95 o.p. (ISBN 0-15-228961-5, HJ). HarBraceJ.

Forever Building: The Life & Ministry of Paul E. Martin. Walter N. Vernon. LC 73-88016. (Illus.). 160p. 1973. 12.95x o.p. (ISBN 0-87074-142-X). SMU Press.

Forever Families. Annette Bradshaw & Gwyn Franson. 48p. (Orig.). pap. write for info. o.p. (ISBN 0-88290-180-X, 2804). Horizon Utah.

Forever Feminine: Women's Magazines & the Cult of Femininity. Marjorie Ferguson. xi, 243p. 1983. text ed. 28.50x o.p. (ISBN 0-435-82301-9). Gower Pub Co.

Forever Free. Joy Adamson. LC 63-8081. (Helen & Kurt Wolff Bks.). (Illus.). (gr. 10 up). 1963. 9.50 o.p. (ISBN 0-15-132550-2). HarBraceJ.

Forever Island: A Novel. Patrick D. Smith. (Illus.). 192p. 1973. 5.95 o.p. (ISBN 0-393-08528-7). Norton.

Forever Sad the Hearts. Patricia L. Walsh. (Vietnam Ser.). 400p. 1982. pap. 2.95 o.p. (ISBN 0-380-78378-9, 88518-2). Avon.

Forever Yours. Arlene Cook. (Rhapsody Romance Ser.). 1984. pap. 2.95 o.p. (ISBN 0-89081-438-4). Harvest Hse.

Forevermore: Nuclear Waste in America. Donald L. Barlett & James B. Steele. LC 84-22761. (Illus.). 352p. 1985. 17.45 o.p. (ISBN 0-393-01920-9). Norton.

Forge & the Forest. Betty Underwood. LC 74-29448. (Illus.). 240p. (gr. 6 up). 1975. 6.95 o.p. (ISBN 0-395-20492-5). HM.

Forge of Fury. Jack Hoffenberg. 1967. pap. 1.75 o.p. (ISBN 0-380-00453-4, 26914). Avon.

Forgery, Perjury, & an Enormous Fortune: 2303 Claimants to the Ella Wendell Estate (1931) Mervin Rosenman. LC 84-238075. write for info. o.p. Persea Bks.

Forget All the Rules about Graphic Design: Including the Ones in This Book. Bob Gill. (Illus.). 168p. 1985. pap. 17.95 o.p. (ISBN 0-8230-1864-4). Watson-Guptill.

Forget Me Knots. Owen Brookes. 1986. 15.95 o.p. (ISBN 0-03-002702-0). H Holt & Co.

Forget the Dust: Let's Paint. Nancy Michael. (Illus.). 40p. 1986. pap. 6.95 o.s.i. (ISBN 0-317-47686-6). Deco Design Studio.

Forgetful Bears. Lawrence Weinberg. (Illus.). 32p. (ps-2). 1982. 8.95 o.p. (ISBN 0-89919-068-5, Clarion). HM.

Forging & Welding. rev. ed. Robert E. Smith. (Illus.). (gr. 7 up). 1956. text ed. 17.28 o.p. (ISBN 0-87345-120-1). Glencoe.

Forgive & Be Free: Healing the Wounds of Past & Present. Richard P. Walters. 144p. 1983. pap. 7.95 o.p. (ISBN 0-310-42611-1, 12339P). Zondervan.

Forgive, Forget & Be Free. rev. ed. Jeanette Lockerbie. 160p. 1984. pap. 5.95 o.p. (ISBN 0-89840-068-6). Heres Life.

Forgive Me No Longer: The Liberation of Martha. Esther Fibush & Martha Morgan. LC 75-27965. 442p. 1977. 15.95 o.p. (ISBN 0-87304-148-8). Family Serv.

Forgiveness & Confession: Keys to Renewal. Alvin N. Rogness. LC 75-121960. 1970. pap. 1.75 o.p. (ISBN 0-8066-1012-3, 10-2355, Augsburg). Augsburg Fortress.

Forgiveness Is a Work As Well As a Grace. Edna Hong. LC 84-6470. 128p. (Orig.). 1984. pap. 6.95 o.p. (ISBN 0-8066-2081-1, 10-2356, Augsburg). Augsburg Fortress.

Forgotten Art of Building & Using a Brick Bake Oven. Richard M. Bacon. LC 77-74809. (Forgotten Arts Ser.). (Illus.). 64p. (Orig.). 1977. pap. 4.95 o.p. (ISBN 0-911658-76-9). Yankee Bks.

Forgotten Arts, Bk. 3. Richard M. Bacon. LC 75-10770. (Forgotten Arts Ser.). (Illus.). 64p. 1976. pap. 4.95 o.p. (ISBN 0-911658-71-8). Yankee Bks.

Forgotten Arts: Making Old-Fashioned Pickles, Relishes, Chutneys, Sauces & Catsups, Mincemeats, Beverages & Syrups. Ed. by Cherry Pyron & Clarissa M. Silitch. LC 78-54880. (Forgotten Arts Ser.). (Illus.). 64p. (Orig.). 1978. pap. 5.95 o.p. (ISBN 0-911658-84-X). Yankee Bks.

Forgotten Bear. Consuelo Joerns. LC 78-1546. (Illus.). (gr. k-3). 1978. 6.95 o.s.i. (ISBN 0-02-747990-0, Four Winds). Macmillan.

Forgotten Beasts of Eld. Patricia A. McKillip. (YA) (gr. 7 up). 1976. pap. 2.50 o.p. (ISBN 0-380-00480-1, 62505-9). Avon.

Forgotten Books of the American Nursery. Rosalie V. Halsey. LC 68-31084. 256p. 1969. Repr. of 1911 ed. 30.00x o.p. (ISBN 0-8103-3483-6). Gale.

Forgotten Door. Alexander Key. LC 65-10170. 124p. (gr. 7 up). 1965. 9.95 o.s.i. (ISBN 0-664-32342-1, Westminster). Westminster John Knox.

Forgotten Dreams: Rituals in American Popular Art. Thomas St. John. 1985. 11.95 o.p. (ISBN 0-533-06686-7). Vantage.

Forgotten Empire-Vijayanagar: A Contribution to the History of India. Robert T. Sewell. (Illus.). 450p. 1972. Repr. of 1900 ed. 37.50x o.p. (ISBN 0-7165-2137-7, BBA 03055, Pub. by Irish Academic Pr). Biblio Dist.

Forgotten Females: Women of African & Indian Descent in Colonial Chile, 1535-1800. Della M. Flusche & Eugene H. Korth. LC 82-24269. 112p. 1983. 16.50 o.p. (ISBN 0-87917-085-9). Ethridge.

Forgotten Kingdom. C. Leonard Woolley. (Illus.). 1968. pap. 1.95x o.p. (ISBN 0-393-00450-3, Norton Lib). Norton.

Forgotten Language. Erich Fromm. 1956. pap. 4.95 o.p. (ISBN 0-394-17483-6, E47, Ever). Grove.

Forgotten Language. Erich Fromm. 1951. pap. 4.95 o.p. (ISBN 0-03-018436-3). H Holt & Co.

Forgotten Legions: Sheep in the Rio Grande Plain of Texas. Val W. Lehmann. LC 76-102787. 1969. 10.00 o.p. (ISBN 0-87404-022-1). Tex Western.

Forgotten Man's Almanac: Rations of Common Sense from William Graham Sumner. William G. Sumner. Ed. by A. G. Keller. LC 70-141268. 1971. Repr. of 1943 ed. lib. bdg. 35.00x o.p. (ISBN 0-8371-5828-1, SUFM). Greenwood.

Forgotten Men: The Civilian Conservation Corps. Robert A. Ermentrout. 112p. 1982. 6.50 o.p. (ISBN 0-682-49805-X). Exposition-Phoenix.

Forgotten Musicians. Paul Nettl. 1951. (ISBN 0-8022-1194-1). Philos Lib.

Forgotten Ones: A Sociological Study of Anglo & Chicano Retardates. Anne-Marie Henshel. 285p. 1972. 17.50x o.p. (ISBN 0-292-72403-9). U of Tex Pr.

Forgotten People: A History of the South Platte Trail. Nell Propst. LC 79-26567. (Illus.). 1979. 24.95 o.p. (ISBN 0-87108-555-0). Pruett.

Forgotten People: The Woodland Erie. Harry F. Lupold. 1975. 6.75 o.p. (ISBN 0-682-48390-7, University); pap. 4.50 o.p. (ISBN 0-682-48391-5). Exposition-Phoenix.

Forgotten Railways: South-East England. H. P. White. (Forgotten Railway Series). (Illus.). 192p. 1988. 29.95 o.p. (ISBN 0-317-60142-3). David & Charles.

Forgotten Railways: South Wales. J. H. Page. (Illus.). 228p. 1989. 24.95 o.p. (ISBN 0-946537-44-5). David & Charles.

Forgotten Railways: West Midlands. Rex Christiansen. (Forgotten Railways of Great Britain Ser.). (Illus.). 192p. 1985. 29.95 o.p. (ISBN 0-946537-01-1). David & Charles.

Forgotten Religions see Ancient Religions.

Forgotten Republics. Clarence A. Manning. 1952. (ISBN 0-8022-1047-3). Philos Lib.

Forgotten Sector: The Training of Ancillary Staff in Hospitals. D. N. Smith. 1969. 50.00 o.p. (ISBN 0-08-013379-7); pap. 50.00 o.p. (ISBN 0-08-013378-9); Pergamon.

Forgotten Texas. Griffin Smith, Jr. & Reagan Bradshaw. Ed. by Barbara Rodriquez. (Illus.). 160p. 1983. 45.00 o.p. (ISBN 0-932012-58-2). Texas Month Pr.

Forgotten Victim: A History of the Civilian. Richard S. Hartigan. 173p. 1985. pap. text ed. 16.95 o.p. (ISBN 0-317-18526-8). Precedent Pub.

Forgotten War: America in Korea 1950-1953. Clay Blair. 896p. 1988. 29.95 o.p. (ISBN 0-317-63103-9). Times Bks.

Forgotten Writings of Mark Twain. Henry Suskis. LC 62-20869. 1963. (ISBN 0-8022-0431-7). Philos Lib.

Fork in the Road. Marguerite M. Rowe. 416p. 1987. 16.95 o.p. (ISBN 0-8062-2926-8). Carlton.

Fork-Tailed Devil: The P-38. Martin Caidin. (Illus.). 1983. pap. 3.50 o.s.i. (ISBN 0-345-31292-9). Ballantine.

Form & Fable in American Fiction. x1961 ed. Daniel Hoffman. 384p. 1973. pap. 2.95 o.p. (ISBN 0-393-00673-5, Norton Lib). Norton.

Form & Function: Japanese Brushes. Illus. by Masao Usui. LC 78-71255. (Form & Function Ser.: Vol. 1). (Illus.). 80p. 1979. pap. 10.95 o.p. (ISBN 0-87011-370-4). Kodansha.

Form & Function: Japanese Knives. Illus. by Masao Usui. LC 78-71255. (Form & Function Ser.: Vol. 2). (Illus.). 80p. 1979. pap. 10.95 o.p. (ISBN 0-87011-371-2). Kodansha.

Form & Function: Japanese Spoons & Ladles. Illus. by Masao Usui. LC 78-71255. (Form & Function Ser.: Vol. 3). (Illus.). 80p. 1979. pap. 10.95 o.p. (ISBN 0-87011-372-0). Kodansha.

Form & Meaning of the Fall Narrative. Norman C. Nabel. 153p. 1965. Concordia Schl Grad Studies.

Form & Purpose: Is The Emperor Naked. Moshe Safdie. (Illus.). 144p. 1982. 19.95 o.p. (ISBN 0-395-31663-4); pap. 9.95 o.p. (ISBN 0-395-31664-2). HM.

Form & Style: Theses, Reports, Term Papers. 5th ed. William G. Campbell & Stephen V. Ballou. LC 77-75137. (Illus.). 1978. pap. 8.95 o.p. (ISBN 0-395-25442-6). HM.

Form & Style: Theses, Reports, Term Papers. 6th ed. William G. Campbell et al. LC 81-82571. 1981. pap. 11.95 o.p. (ISBN 0-395-31689-8). HM.

Form & Technique of Psychotherapy. I. H. Paul. LC 78-3181. 1979. 23.00x o.s.i. (ISBN 0-226-64999-7). U of Chicago Pr.

Form & Thought in Prose. 4th ed. Ed. by Wilfred Stone & Robert Hoopes. 1977. text ed. write for info. o.p. (ISBN 0-673-15726-1). Scott F.

Form of Housing. Sam Davis. (Illus.). 1977. 28.95x o.p. (ISBN 0-442-22007-3). Van Nos Reinhold.

Form of Time. Elliott Jaques. LC 81-17510. 252p. 1982. 32.00x o.p. (ISBN 0-8448-1394-X, Pub. by Crane Russak & Co). Taylor & Francis.

Form, Style, Tradition: Reflections on Japanese Art & Society. Shuichi Kato. Tr. by John Bester from Japanese. LC 81-84908. (Illus.). 216p. 1982. pap. 5.95 o.p. (ISBN 0-87011-510-3). Kodansha.

Formability: Analysis, Modeling & Experimentation: Proceedings of the TMS-AIME Fall Meeting, Chicago, IL, 1977. TMS Staff & AIME Staff. Ed. by S. S. Hecker et al. (Illus.). 284p. 20.00 o.p. (ISBN 0-89520-144-5); members 14.00 o.p. (ISBN 0-317-34874-4); student members 9.00 o.p. (ISBN 0-317-34875-2). ASM.

Formable HSLA & Dual-Phase Steels: Proceedings of the TMS-AIME Fall Meeting, Chicago, IL, 1977. TMS Staff & AIME Staff. Ed. by A. T. Davenport. (Illus.). 248p. 28.00 o.p. (ISBN 0-89520-351-0); members 17.00 o.p. (ISBN 0-317-34876-0); student members 9.00 o.p. (ISBN 0-317-34877-9). ASM.

Formal Aspects Cognitive Processes: Proceedings. Interdisciplinary Conference, Ann Arbor, March 1973. Ed. by T. Storer & D. Winter. LC 74-32111. (Lecture Notes in Computer Science: Vol. 22). v, 214p. 1975. pap. 15.00 o.p. (ISBN 0-387-07016-8). Springer-Verlag.

Formaldehyde: Toxicology-Epidemiology-Mechanisms. Ed. by John J. Clary et al. (Illus.). 304p. 1983. 58.00 o.p. (ISBN 0-8247-7025-0). Dekker.

Formalization of Natural Languages. P. Kummel. LC 77-6812. (Communication & Cybernetics Ser: Vol. 15). 1979. 48.00 o.p. (ISBN 0-387-08271-9). Springer-Verlag.

Forman Hanna, Pictorial Photographer of the Southwest. Mark Sawyer. LC 85-52009. (Illus.). 144p. (Orig.). 1986. pap. 14.95 o.s.i. (ISBN 0-87358-396-5). Northland.

Formation & Fate of Cell Organelles. International Society for Cell Biology Staff. Ed. by Katherine B. Warren. (Proceedings: Vol. 6). 1968. 74.50 o.p. (ISBN 0-12-611906-6). Acad Pr.

Formation & Perception of the Modern Arab World: Studies by Marwan R. Buheiry. Marwan R. Buheiry. Ed. by Lawrence I. Conrad et al. 600p. 1989. 24.95 o.p. (ISBN 0-87850-064-2). Darwin Pr.

Formation & Powers of National Banking Associations - A Legal Primer. 255p. 1983. 5.50 o.p. (ISBN 0-318-23085-2, S/N 052-070-05853-6). USGPO.

Formation & Role of Excited States in Radiolysis: Special Issue of International Journal for Radiation Physics & Chemistry, Vol. 8, Nos. 1 & 2. Ajit Singh. 1976. pap. 51.00 o.p. (ISBN 0-08-019986-0). Pergamon.

Formation & Trapping of Free Radicals. Ed. by Arnold M. Bass & H. P. Broida. (Illus.). 1960. 85.50 o.p. (ISBN 0-12-080350-X). Acad Pr.

Formation & Use of Compound Epithets in English Poetry see Persian Words in English.

Formation of Christian Understanding: An Essay in Theological Hermeneutics. Charles M. Wood. LC 81-5103. 126p. 1981. pap. 7.95 o.s.i. (ISBN 0-664-24373-8, Westminster). Westminster John Knox.

Formation of Faith. Bernard Cooke. LC 65-27619. (Pastoral Ser). 1965. pap. 2.00 o.p. (ISBN 0-8294-0014-1). Loyola.

Formation of Modern Lebanon. Meir Zamir. LC 85-358. 309p. 1985. 43.00 o.p. (ISBN 0-7099-3002-X, Pub. by Croom Helm Ltd). Routledge Chapman & Hall.

Formation of the American Catholic Minority, 1820-1860. Thomas T. McAvoy. Ed. by Richard C. Wolf. LC 67-22985. (Facet Bks). 1967. pap. 0.50 o.p. (ISBN 0-8006-3042-4, 1-3042, Fortress). Augsburg Fortress.

Formation of the Christian Bible. Hans Von Campenhausen. Tr. by J. A. Baker from Ger. LC 73-171495. 360p. 1977. pap. 2.95 o.p. (ISBN 0-8006-1263-9, 1-1263, Fortress). Augsburg Fortress.

Formation of the Economic Thought of Karl Marx. Ernest Mandel. Tr. by Brian Pearce from Fr. LC 71-142990. 224p. 1971. 7.95 o.p. (ISBN 0-85345-151-6); pap. 4.50 o.p. (ISBN 0-85345-187-7). Monthly Rev.

Formation of the Gospel According to Mark. Etienne Trocme. Tr. by Pamela Gaughan. LC 75-15510. 1975. 12.95 o.s.i. (ISBN 0-664-20803-7, Westminster). Westminster John Knox.

Formation of the Lutheran Church in America. Johannes Knudsen. LC 77-15235. 132p. 1978. 3.00 o.p. (ISBN 0-8006-0517-9, 1-517, Fortress). Augsburg Fortress.

Formation of the New Testament. H. F. Sparks. 172p. 1953. (ISBN 0-8022-1615-3). Philos Lib.

Formation of the Polish State: The Period of Ducal Rule, 963-1194. Tadeusz Manteuffel. Tr. by Andrew Gorski. LC 81-115830. 171p. 1982. 22.50x o.p. (ISBN 0-8143-1682-4). Wayne St U Pr.

Formation of the Resurrection Narratives. Reginald H. Fuller. LC 79-8885. 240p. 1980. pap. 3.95 o.p. (ISBN 0-8006-1378-3, 1-1378, Fortress). Augsburg Fortress.

Formation of the Soviet Union: Communism & Nationalism 1917-1923. rev. ed. Richard Pipes. LC 64-21284. (Illus.). 1968. pap. text ed. 5.95x o.p. (ISBN 0-689-70158-6, 124, Atheneum). Macmillan.

Formations of Nations & People. Ed. by Formations Editorial Collective Staff. (Routledge Formations Ser.). (Illus.). 240p. (Orig.). 1983. pap. 14.95 o.p. (ISBN 0-7102-0044-7). Routledge Chapman & Hall.

Formative Years of the Jewish Labor Movement in the United States: (1890-1900) Abraham M. Rogoff. LC 78-21163. 1979. Repr. of 1945 ed. lib. bdg. 35.00x o.p. (ISBN 0-313-20881-6, ROFJ). Greenwood.

Former Marine Tells It Like It Was, & Is. Alfred Schiani. 104p. 1987. 7.95 o.p. (ISBN 0-8062-3081-9). Carlton.

Forming the American Minds: Early School Books & Their Compilers (1783-1837) Michael V. Belok. 1973. 12.50 o.p. E J Brill USA.

Formosa: Licensed Revolution & the Home Rule Movement, 1895-1945. George H. Kerr. LC 73-91458. (Illus.). 283p. 1974. 16.00x o.p. (ISBN 0-8248-0323-X). UH Pr.

Forms - Froms. Dennis Barone. 72p. (Orig.). 1988. pap. 7.00 o.p. (ISBN 0-937013-22-6). Potes Poets.

Forms & Techniques of Altruistic & Spiritual Growth: A Symposium. P. A. Sorokin. Repr. of 1954 ed. 28.00 o.p. (ISBN 0-527-84810-7). Kraus Repr.

Forms in English Literature. Philip J. McFarland et al. LC 75-144318. (Literature Ser.). (Illus.). 816p. (gr. 12). 1972. text ed. 18.32 o.p. (ISBN 0-395-11202-8, 2-26560). HM.

Forms Manual to Accompany Cases & Materials on Oil & Gas Law. Eugene O. Kuntz et al. (American Casebook Ser.). 200p. 1986. pap. 6.95 o.p. (ISBN 0-314-33934-5). West Pub.

Forms of Drama. Ed. by Robert W. Corrigan & Glenn M. Loney. LC 74-150136. 906p. (Orig.). 1972. pap. 17.50 o.p. (ISBN 0-395-04327-1). HM.

Forms of Poetry: A Pocket Dictionary of Verse. rev. ed. Ed. by Louis Untermeyer. LC 26-12381. 1948. 7.95 o.p. (ISBN 0-15-132639-8). HarBraceJ.

Forms of Roman Legislation. David Daube. LC 78-12308. 111p. 1979. Repr. of 1956 ed. lib. bdg. 24.75x o.p. (ISBN 0-313-21146-9, DAFR). Greenwood.

Forms of the Essay: The American Experience. Deanne K. Milan & Naomi C. Rattner. 344p. 1979. pap. text ed. 12.00 o.p. (ISBN 0-15-527970-X, HC). HarBraceJ.

Forms upon the Frontier: Folklife & Folk Arts in the United States. Ed. by Austin Fife et al. (Illus.). 189p. (Orig.). 1969. pap. 6.50 o.p. (ISBN 0-87421-036-4). Utah St U Pr.

Formula Book. Norman Stark. 1977. pap. 1.75 o.p. (ISBN 0-380-00840-8, 31047). Avon.

Formula Budgeting: An Approach to Facilities Funding. David L. McClintock. 50p. 5.00 o.p. (ISBN 0-913359-05-X); 3.50, members o.p. Assn Phys Plant Admin.

Formula for Action: A Report to the President on Defense Acquisition. 45p. (Orig.). 1986. pap. 4.25 o.p. (ISBN 0-318-20109-7, S/N 040-000-00495-5). USGPO.

Formulary 1987: Veterinary Hospital Pharmacy, Washington State University. Compiled by Christine S. Schultz. 156p. 1986. pap. 17.95 spiral bound o.p. (ISBN 0-87422-031-9). Wash St U Pr.

Formulas & Theorems for the Special Functions of Mathematical Physics. 3rd ed. W. Magnus et al. (Grundlehren der Mathematischen Wissenschaften: Vol. 52). 1966. 46.00 o.p. (ISBN 0-387-03518-4). Springer-Verlag.

Formulas for Stress & Strain. 5th ed. Raymond J. Roark & Warren C. Young. (Illus.). 512p. 1976. text ed. 62.50 o.p. (ISBN 0-07-053031-9). McGraw.

Forrest Mims's Computer Projects. Forrest M. Mims, III. 200p. (Orig.). 1985. pap. text ed. 14.95 o.p. (ISBN 0-07-881193-7). Osborne-McGraw.

Fort Ancient. R. Morgan. (Illus.). 40p. 1970. pap. 1.00 o.s.i. (ISBN 0-318-00858-0). Ohio Hist Soc.

Fort Bliss, An Illustrated History. Leon C. Metz. Ed. by Frank Mangan. LC 81-82224. (Illus.). 180p. 1981. 34.95 o.p. (ISBN 0-930208-10-2). Mangan Bks.

Fort Bridger: Island in the Wilderness. Fred R. Gowans & Eugene E. Campbell. LC 75-5827. (Illus.). 150p. 1975. 4.95 o.p. (ISBN 0-8425-0419-2); pap. 4.95 o.p. (ISBN 0-8425-0420-6). Brigham.

Fort Holmes. Brian L. Dunnigan. Ed. by David A. Armour. LC 85-129297. (Reports in Mackinac History & Archaeology: No. 10). (Illus.). 40p. (Orig.). 1984. pap. 5.00 o.p. (ISBN 0-911872-51-5). Mackinac Island.

Fort Knox-Fortress in Maine. John E. Cayford. LC 83-71723. (Illus.). 104p. (Orig.). 1983. 17.50 o.p. (ISBN 0-941216-10-1); pap. 10.00 o.p. (ISBN 0-941216-14-4). Cay Bel.

Fort Osage. Rhoda Wooldridge. LC 82-11712. (Illus.). (gr. 4-6). 1983. pap. 8.00 o.p. (ISBN 0-8309-0351-8). Ind Pr MO.

Fort Pendleton's Finest: Love Among the Ruins. Kenneth W. Cheeseman. 1979. 5.00 o.p. (ISBN 0-682-49376-7). Exposition-Phoenix.

Fort Robinson, Outpost on the Plains. Roger T. Grange. (Nebraska History Magazine Reprints: Vol. 39, No. 3). 241p. 1958. 3.00 o.p. (ISBN 0-318-17581-9). Nebraska Hist.

Fort Rock Basin: Prehistory & Environment. Stephen Bedwell. LC 74-169230. 1973. 10.00 o.p. (ISBN 0-87114-058-6). U of Oreg Bks.

Fort Supply: Brigham Young's Green River Experiment. Fred R. Gowans & Eugene E. Campbell. 1976. pap. 2.95 o.p. (ISBN 0-8425-0248-3). Brigham.

Fort Wayne Story: A Pictorial History. John Ankenbruck. 232p. 1980. 22.95 o.s.i. (ISBN 0-89781-015-5). Windsor Pubns Inc.

Forth into Light. Gordon Merrick. 1976. pap. 4.95 o.p. (ISBN 0-380-01195-6, 89417-3). Avon.

Forth Road Bridge. 273p. 1967. 10.00x o.p. (ISBN 0-901948-19-5). Am Soc Civil Eng.

Fortie's & Fiftie's Collectibles. William Ketchum. LC 85-80121. 96p. pap. 7.95 o.p. (ISBN 0-89586-248-4). Price Stern.

Fortieth Anniversary Issue. National Deans, Administrators & Counselors. 1977. pap. 3.00 o.p. (ISBN 0-686-23289-5). Natl Assn Women.

FORTRAN Coloring Book. Roger Kaufman. LC 78-998. 1978. pap. 8.95 o.p. (ISBN 0-262-61026-4). MIT Pr.

FORTRAN Cookbook. Thomas P. Dence. (Illus.). 336p. pap. 12.50 o.p. (ISBN 0-8306-1187-8, 1187). TAB Bks.

FORTRAN IV Programming. M. G. Chopra & Ram Kumar. 248p. 1986. 30.00x o.p. (ISBN 0-7069-3008-8, Pub. by Vikas India); pap. 15.00x o.p. (ISBN 0-7069-1535-6). Advent NY.

FORTRAN IV Programming. 2nd ed. Wilfred P. Rule. 1973. pap. text ed. write for info. o.p. (ISBN 0-685-19590-2, PWS 549, Prindle). PWS-Kent Pub.

FORTRAN IV Programming: Based on the IBM System 1130. Robert V. Jamison. LC 70-96241. (Illus.). 1970. text ed. 31.25 o.p. (ISBN 0-07-032270-8). McGraw.

FORTRAN IV with WATFOR & WATFIV. reference ed. P. Cress et al. 1970. pap. text ed. (ISBN 0-13-329433-1). P-H.

FORTRAN Programming: A Spiral Approach. Charles B. Kreitzberg & Ben Shneiderman. 1975. 16.95 o.p. (ISBN 0-15-528012-0). HarbraceJ.

FORTRAN Programming: A Supplement for Calculus Course (Universitext) W. R. Fuller. LC 77-12129. (Illus.). 1977. pap. text ed. 12.00 o.p. (ISBN 0-387-90283-X). Springer-Verlag.

FORTRAN Programs for Scientists & Engineers. Alan R. Miller. LC 82-80263. (Scientists & Engineers Ser.: No. 3). (Illus.). 280p. 1982. pap. 19.95 o.p. (ISBN 0-89588-082-2, F440). SYBEX.

FORTRAN with Style: Programming Proverbs. Henry F. Ledgard & Louis J. Chmura. (Computer Programming Ser.). (gr. 12 up). 1978. pap. text ed. 10.95x o.p. (ISBN 0-8104-5682-6). Sams.

FORTRAN 77: Elements of Programming Style. William M. Fuori et al. 358p. 1987. pap. 22.95. o.p. (ISBN 0-8104-6397-0). Sams.

FORTRAN 77 for Engineers & Scientists. Barnard & Skillicorn. 550p. 1987. pap. text ed. 30.76 net o.p. (ISBN 0-205-11098-3). Wm C Brown.

Fortress for Well-Being: Baha'i Teachings on Marriage. (Comprehensive Deepening Program Ser.: Gift Ed.). 1974. 12.95 o.p. (ISBN 0-87743-093-4, 364-010); pap. 5.00 o.p. (ISBN 0-87743-153-1, 364-011). Baha'i.

Forts & Supplies: The Role of the Army in the Economy of the Southwest, 1846-1861. Robert W. Frazer. LC 83-17051. (Illus.). 263p. 1983. 22.50 o.p. (ISBN 0-8263-0630-6). U of NM Pr.

Fort's Law. Joe L. Hensley. LC 87-13484. (Crime Club Ser.). 192p. 1987. 12.95 o.p. (ISBN 0-385-23830-4). Doubleday.

Fortunate Grandchild. Read. (Illus.). 1983. 11.45 o.p. (ISBN 0-395-34419-0). HM.

Fortunate Strangers. Cornelius Beukenkamp. 1971. pap. 5.95 o.p. (ISBN 0-87877-000-3, S-0). Newcastle Pub.

Fortune. Michael McDowell. (Blackwater Ser.: Pt. V). 176p. 1983. pap. 2.95 o.p. (ISBN 0-380-82784-0, 82784-0). Avon.

Fortune & Men's Eyes. John Herbert. LC 67-31624. (Photos). 1968. pap. 4.95 o.p. (ISBN 0-394-17357-0, E457, Ever). Grove.

Fortune at Your Feet: How You Can Make Money with Real Estate in Good Times & Bad. A. D. Kessler. LC 80-84231. 1981. 10.95 o.p. (ISBN 0-15-132668-1). HarBraceJ.

Fortune-Building Secrets of the Rich. Duane G. Newcomb. LC 82-18837. 215p. 1982. pap. 5.95 o.p. (ISBN 0-13-329102-2, Reward). P-H.

Fortune-Building Secrets of the Rich. Duane G. Newcomb. LC 82-18837. 215p. 1983. 14.95 o.p. (Parker). P-H.

Fortune du Tasse en France. Chandler B. Beall. 1942. pap. 2.00 o.p. (ISBN 0-87114-001-2). U of Oreg Bks.

Fortune Hunter. Cory Kenyon. (Candlelight Ecstasy Ser.: No. 422). 1986. pap. 2.25 o.p. (ISBN 0-440-12665-7). Dell.

Fortune Wheel. Valerie Bradstreet. 160p. 1981. pap. 2.25 o.p. (ISBN 0-380-78303-7, 78303-7). Avon.

Fortunes & Failures: White-Collar Mobility in 19th-Century San Francisco. Peter R. Decker. LC 77-12557. (Studies in Urban History). 1978. 27.00x o.s.i. (ISBN 0-674-31118-3). Harvard U Pr.

Fortunes & Misfortunes of Moll Flanders see also Moll Flanders.

Fortunes & Misfortunes of the Famous Moll Flanders see also Moll FLANDERS.

Fortunes of Nigel. Walter Scott. Ed. by Frederick M. Link. LC 65-18715. xlii, 488p. 1965. pap. 9.95x o.p. (ISBN 0-8032-5176-9, BB 321, Bison). U of Nebr Pr.

Fortunes of War. David Fraser. 1985. 15.45 o.p. (ISBN 0-393-01973-X). Norton.

Forty Acres & No Mule. Janice H. Giles. 1967. 7.95 o.p. (ISBN 0-395-07736-2). HM.

Forty Computer Games. Ed. by Emily A. Gibbs & Jim Perry. (Illus.). 148p. 1980. pap. text ed. 7.95 o.p. (ISBN 0-88006-023-9, BK7381). Wayne Green Ent.

Forty Computer Games from Kilobaud Microcomputing. Ed. by Emily A. Gibbs & Jim Perry. 148p. 1980. 7.95 o.p. (ISBN 0-88006-023-9, BK1381). Wayne Green Ent.

Forty Educational Games for the BBC Micro. Apps. (Illus.). 204p. (Orig.). 1984. pap. 11.95 o.p. (ISBN 0-246-12317-6, Pub. by Granada England). Sheridan.

Forty-Eighth Annual Report of the National Labor Relations Board for the Fiscal Year Ended September 30, 1983. annual ed. (Illus.). 235p. 1986. pap. 11.00 o.p. (ISBN 0-318-21546-2, S/N 031-000-00253-2). USGPO.

Forty Elementary Exercises for Violin. Franz Wohlfahrt. Ed. by Hans Sitt. (Carl Fischer Music Library: L553). (Illus.). 1915. pap. 3.50 o.p. (ISBN 0-8258-0073-0). Fischer Inc NY.

Forty-Five Mercy Street. Anne Sexton. Ed. by Linda G. Sexton. 1976. 8.95 o.p. (ISBN 0-395-24295-9); pap. 3.95 o.p. (ISBN 0-395-24294-0). HM.

Forty-Five Years of Cancer Incidence in Connecticut: 1935-79. Ed. by Jean F. Heston et al. 763p. 1986. 37.00 o.p. (ISBN 0-318-20372-3, S/N 017-042-00187-1). USGPO.

Forty-Four Terrific Woodworking Plans & Projects. Raymond D. Brown. 21.95 o.p. (ISBN 0-8306-0762-5, 1762); pap. 11.95 o.p. TAB Bks.

Forty-Fourth Electric Furnace Conference Proceedings. Collective Work Staff. LC 46-22879. 408p. 1987. 60.00 o.p. (ISBN 0-932897-17-7). Iron & Steel.

Forty Innovative Programs in Early Childhood Education. Compiled by Berlie J. Fallon. LC 72-95010. 1973. pap. 6.75 o.p. (ISBN 0-8224-3075-4). D S Lake Pubs.

Forty-Nine Year Old Rookie. Simon Marder. 144p. 1986. 11.95 o.p. (ISBN 0-8062-2942-X). Carlton.

Forty-One Hiking Trails, Northwest California. Don Lowe & Roberta Lowe. (Illus.). 96p. (Orig.). 1981. pap. 7.95 o.s.i. (ISBN 0-911518-62-2). Touchstone Oregon.

Forty-One Sonnet-Poems Eighty-Two. Anthony Cronin. 47p. 1981. pap. 4.95 o.p. (ISBN 0-906897-28-9). Dufour.

Forty-Second Omelet Guaranteed! Howard Helmer & Joan O'Sullivan. LC 81-70072. 1982. 12.95 o.p. (ISBN 0-689-11288-2, Atheneum). Macmillan.

Forty-Thousand Selected Words Organized by Letter, Sound & Syllable. Joan Frazer et al. 1987. text ed. 21.95 o.p. (ISBN 0-88450-799-8, 3083-B); pap. text ed. 16.95 o.p. (ISBN 0-88450-798-X, 2506-B). Communication Skill.

Forty to Sixty-How We Waste the Middle Aged. Michael Fogarty. 250p. 1975. pap. text ed. 9.75x o.p. (ISBN 0-7199-0904-X, Pub. by Bedford England). Gower Pub Co.

Forty to Sixty Year Old Male: A Guide for Men & the Women in Their Lives to See Them Through the Crises of the Male Middle Years. Michael E. McGill. 204p. 1982. pap. 7.95 o.p. (ISBN 0-671-25134-1, Fireside). S&S.

Forty-Two British Watercolours. John Murdoch. (Illus.). 88p. (Orig.). 1984. pap. 6.95 o.p. (ISBN 0-901486-99-X, Pub. by Victoria & Albert Mus UK). Faber & Faber.

Forty-Two Years in the White House. Irwin H. Hoover. LC 74-7938. (Illus.). 332p. 1974. Repr. of 1934 ed. lib. bdg. 22.75x o.p. (ISBN 0-8371-7602-6, HOFY). Greenwood.

Forty Ways to Fortify Your Faith. James R. Bjorge. LC 83-72115. 128p. (Orig.). 1984. pap. 5.95 o.p. (ISBN 0-8066-2059-5, 10-2358, Augsburg). Augsburg Fortress.

Forty Ways to Say Thank You, Lord. James R. Bjorge. LC 80-67802. 96p. (Orig.). 1981. pap. 5.95 o.p. (ISBN 0-8066-1864-7, 102361, Augsburg). Augsburg Fortress.

Forty Years a Guinea Pig. E. Frederic Morrow. LC 80-16657. 236p. 1980. 10.95 o.p. (ISBN 0-8298-0399-8). Pilgrim NY.

Forty Years of Spy. Leslie Ward. LC 70-81512. 374p. 1969. Repr. of 1915 ed. 46.00x o.p. (ISBN 0-8103-3575-1). Gale.

Forty Years with the Silent Billion. Frank C. Laubach. 501p. 1970. 6.50 o.p. (ISBN 0-317-35463-9). New Readers.

Forum on the Public Library Inquiry. Ed. by Lester Asheim. LC 76-106680. 1970. Repr. of 1950 ed. lib. bdg. 35.00x o.p. (ISBN 0-8371-3351-3, ASPL). Greenwood.

Forum: Religious Faith Speaks to American Issues. Ed. by William A. Norgren. (Orig.). 1975. pap. 2.95 o.p. (ISBN 0-377-00044-2). Friendship Pr.

Forward Surgeon. Luther H. Wolff. LC 84-90249. 211p. 1985. 13.95 o.p. (ISBN 0-533-06288-8). Vantage.

Fossil Algae: Recent Results & Developments. Ed. by E. Flugel. LC 76-46461. (Illus.). 1977. 54.00 o.p. (ISBN 0-387-07974-2). Springer-Verlag.

Fossil Factory. Niles Eldridge. Date not set. price not set o.p. Addison-Wesley.

Fossil Malacostracous Crustacea. T. Bell. pap. 6.00 o.p. (ISBN 0-384-03838-7). Johnson Repr.

Fossil Rodents from the Neogene Siwalik Deposits, Pakistan. Louis L. Jacobs. (Bulletin Ser.). 116p. 1978. pap. 6.50 o.p. (BS-52). Mus Northern Ariz.

Fossil Snake. L. M. Boston. LC 75-26997. 64p. (gr. 3-7). 1976. 5.95 o.p. (ISBN 0-689-50037-8, Atheneum). Macmillan.

Fossil Vertebrates of Africa, 3 vols. Ed. by L. S. Leakey et al. Vol. 1, 1969. 55.50 o.p. (ISBN 0-12-440401-4); Vol. 2, 1971. 63.50 o.p. (ISBN 0-12-440402-2). Acad Pr.

Fossil Vertebrates of Africa, Vol. 4. Ed. by L. Leakey & R. Savage. 1976. 81.00 o.p. (ISBN 0-12-440404-9). Acad Pr.

Fossils & the Life of the Past. E. Thenius. Tr. by B. M. Crook from Ger. LC 76-183484. (Heidelberg Science Library: Vol. 14). (Illus.). 194p. 1973. pap. 8.60 o.p. (ISBN 0-387-90039-X). Springer-Verlag.

Fossils of Iowa: Field Guide to Paleozoic Deposits. Robert C. Wolf. (Illus.). 198p. 1983. pap. 9.95 o.p. (ISBN 0-8138-1334-4). Iowa St U Pr.

Foster & Laurie. Al Silverman. 1974. 14.45 o.p. (ISBN 0-316-79116-4). Little.

Foster Care in the 1980s. Deborah McDaniel. 174p. 1981. pap. 16.75 o.p. (ISBN 0-08-028096-X). Pergamon.

Foster Care of Children: Nurture & Treatment. Draza Kline & Helen-Mary F. Overstreet. LC 78-186386. (Studies of the Child Welfare League of America). 316p. 1972. 37.50x o.p. (ISBN 0-231-03601-9); pap. 17.00x o.p. (ISBN 0-231-08337-8). Columbia U Pr.

Foster Child. Marion D. Bauer. LC 76-54291. 168p. (gr. 6 up). 1979. 7.95 o.p. (ISBN 0-395-28889-4, Clarion). HM.

Foster-Child Health Care. Florence Kavaler & Margaret R. Swire. LC 81-47184. 224p. 1983. 26.00x o.p. (ISBN 0-669-04561-6). Lexington Bks.

Fostering the Capital-Goods Sector in LDCs: A Survey of Evidence & Requirements. Howard Pack. (Working Paper: No. 376). v, 59p. 1980. 5.00 o.p. (ISBN 0-686-36183-0, WP-0376). World Bank.

Foucault Reader. Michel Foucault. Ed. by Paul Rabinow. LC 83-19510. 1984. 9.95 o.p. (ISBN 0-394-52904-9); pap. 10.95 o.p. (ISBN 0-394-71340-0). Pantheon.

Foujita. Jean Selz. 96p. 1981. 14.95 o.p. (ISBN 0-517-54429-6). Crown.

Foul Shot. Doug Hornig. 272p. 1984. 13.95 o.s.i. (ISBN 0-684-18187-8, ScribT). Scribner.

Fouling in Heat Exchange Equipment. Ed. by J. M. Chenoweth & M. Impagliazzo. 105p. 1981. 20.00 o.p. (ISBN 0-686-34494-4, G00206). ASME.

Fouling of Heat Transfer Equipment. Ed. by Euan F. Somerscales & James G. Knudsen. LC 80-28694. (Illus.). 743p. 1981. text ed. 98.50 o.p. (ISBN 0-89116-199-6). Hemisphere Pub.

Foundation & Structure of Sartrean Ethics. Thomas C. Anderson. LC 79-11762. x, 186p. 1979. 22.50x o.p. (ISBN 0-7006-0191-0). U Pr of KS.

Foundation Book of Astrology. Theodor Laurence. 10.00 o.p. (ISBN 0-8216-0204-7, Pub. by Univ Bks). Carol Pub Group.

Foundation: Building Sentence Skills. Thomas Neuberger. 1982. pap. 17.95 o.p. (ISBN 0-395-31805-X). HM.

Foundation Engineering. Ed. by G. A. Leonards. (Civil Engineering Ser.). 1962. text ed. 76.50 o.p. (ISBN 0-07-037198-9). McGraw.

Foundation Engineering for Difficult Subsoil Conditions. 2nd ed. Leonardo Zeevaert. 688p. 1982. 49.95 o.p. (ISBN 0-442-20169-9). Van Nos Reinhold.

Foundation Engineering Handbook. Ed. by Hans F. Winterkorn & F. Y. Fang. 736p. 1975. 67.95 o.s.i. (ISBN 0-442-29564-2). Van Nos Reinhold.

Foundation for Expressive Drawing. 2nd ed. E. J. Tomasch & Oscar Larmer. 206p. 1983. pap. text ed. write for info o.p. (ISBN 0-8087-2076-7). Burgess MN Intl.

Foundation for Faith. Derek Prince. (Foundation Ser.: Bk. I). 1965-66. pap. 2.95 o.p. (ISBN 0-934920-00-1, B-10). Derek Prince.

Foundation Grants Index. 17th ed. The Foundation Center Staff. Ed. by Ruth Kovacs. LC 72-76018. (Annual Publication). 1056p. (Orig.). 1988. pap. text ed. 55.00 o.p. (ISBN 0-87954-241-1). Foundation Ctr.

Foundation Grants to Individuals. Foundation Center Staff. Ed. by Loren Renz. 1986. pap. text ed. 18.00 o.p. (ISBN 0-317-43186-2). Foundation Ctr.

Foundation in Physics, Vol. 1. S Malhotra et al. 303p. 1986. pap. text ed. 10.95x o.p. (ISBN 0-7069-2456-8, Pub. by Vikas India). Advent NY.

Foundation of Euclidean & Non-Euclidean Geometries According to F. Klein. L. Redei. (International Series in Pure & Applied Mathematics: Vol. 97). 1968. 52.00 o.p. (ISBN 0-08-011965-4). Pergamon.

Foundation of Home Economics Research: A Human Ecology Approach. Norma Compton & Olive Hall. LC 72-81810. 401p. (Orig.). 1972. pap. 13.95x o.p. (ISBN 0-8087-0338-2, Feffer & Simons). Burgess MN Intl.

Foundation of Management. Peter Anthony. 220p. 1986. pap. text ed. 17.95 o.p. (ISBN 0-422-78930-5, 98685, Pub. by Tavistock England). Routledge Chapman & Hall.

Foundation of Moral Goodness, 2 vols. in 1. John Blaguy. Ed. by Rene Wellek. LC 75-11194. (British Philosophers & Theologians of the 17th & 18th Centuries Ser.: Vol. I). 1976. Repr. of 1729 ed. lib. bdg. 51.00 o.p. (ISBN 0-8240-1750-1). Garland Pub.

Foundation Studies in Fugue. Hugo Norden. 1977. pap. 6.95 o.s.i. (ISBN 0-8008-2978-6, Crescendo). Taplinger.

Foundation Trilogy. Isaac Asimov. 1976. pap. 6.95 o.p. (ISBN 0-380-00101-2, 54403-2). Avon.

Foundations & Concrete Works. E. Dobson. (Illus.). 130p. 1986. pap. 20.00 o.p. (ISBN 0-87556-699-5). Saifer.

Foundations & Piling: A Revision of A-71. Mary Vance. (Architecture Ser.: A 1499). 32p. 1985. 4.50 o.p. (ISBN 0-89028-649-3). Vance Biblios.

Foundations for Christian Growth. 2nd ed. Ronald D. Tucker & Richard A. Hufton. (Illus.). 322p. cancelled o.s.i. (ISBN 0-933643-16-0). Grace Ch St Louis.

Foundations for Curriculum Development & Evaluation in Art Education. Ed. by George W. Hardiman & Theodore Zernich. 484p. 1981. pap. text ed. 14.80x o.p. (ISBN 0-87563-202-5). Stipes.

Foundations for Dams. 480p. 1974. pap. 28.00x o.p. (ISBN 0-87262-100-6). Am Soc Civil Eng.

Foundations for Policy in Guidance & Counseling. Edward Herr & Nancy Pinson. 221p. 1982. pap. 9.25 o.p. (ISBN 0-911547-41-X, 72008W34). Am Assn Coun Dev.

Foundations for Sociology. Diane R. Shapiro. 1980. pap. 19.50 o.p. (ISBN 0-395-30742-2). HM.

Foundations in the Dust: The Story of Mesopotamian Exploration. rev. & enl. ed. Seton Lloyd. (Illus.). 216p. 1980. 19.95 o.p. (ISBN 0-500-05038-4). Thames Hudson.

Foundations of Analysis: Landau Revisited. C. J. Mozzochi. LC 75-46243. 1976. text ed. 7.50 o.p. (ISBN 0-682-48511-X, University). Exposition-Phoenix.

Foundations of Behavioral Research: Educational, Psychological, & Sociological Inquiry. 2nd ed. Frederick N. Kerlinger. LC 72-91751. 1973. text ed. 38.95 o.p. (ISBN 0-03-085462-8, HoltC). HR&W.

Foundations of Brazilian Economic Growth. Donald E. Syvrud. LC 74-11812. (Publications Ser.: No. 141). 295p. 1974. 15.00x o.p. (ISBN 0-8179-6411-8). Hoover Inst Pr.

Foundations of Capitalism. O. C. Cox. 1959. Philos Lib.

Foundations of Chemistry. Jesse S. Binford, Jr. (Illus.). 334p. 1985. pap. text ed. 23.95 o.p. (ISBN 0-931541-03-4). Bk Pubs.

Foundations of Chemistry: A Laboratory Manual. Clark E. Bricker. 1966. pap. text ed. 10.95 o.p. (ISBN 0-15-528275-1, HC). HarBraceJ.

Foundations of Child Psychiatry. Ed. by E. Miller. 1968. 175.00 o.p. (ISBN 0-08-011826-7). Pergamon.

Foundations of Citizenship, 2 Bks. 1971 ed. Bernard Shawn. Bk. 1. fabrikoid 8.95 o.p. (ISBN 0-88323-015-1, 115); Bk. 2. fabrikoid 8.95 o.p. (ISBN 0-88323-016-X, 116); combo fabrikoid o.p. 12.95 o.p. (ISBN 0-88323-017-8, 117); tchr's guide 1.25 o.p. (ISBN 0-88323-018-6, 118). Pendergrass Pub.

Foundations of Citizenship: Adult Education Editon. pap. 2.95x o.p. (ISBN 0-88323-019-4, 119). Pendergrass Pub.

Foundations of Classical & Quantum Statistical Mechanics. R. Jancel. 1969. 81.00 o.p. (ISBN 0-08-012823-8). Pergamon.

Foundations of Cognitive Process in Remedial & Special Education. Lester Mann & David A. Sabatino. 304p. 1985. 35.00 o.p. (ISBN 0-87189-115-8). Aspen Pub.

Foundations of Computer Science. M. Carberry et al. LC 78-27891. (Computer Software Engineering Ser.). 317p. 1979. text ed. 29.95 o.p. (ISBN 0-914894-18-8, Computer Sci Pr). W H Freeman.

Foundations of Conditioning. Ed. by Harold B. Falls et al. 1970. text ed. 8.00i o.p. (ISBN 0-12-248055-4). Acad Pr.

Foundations of Developmental Psychology. Richard La Barba. LC 80-615. 1981. 29.70i o.p. (ISBN 0-12-432350-2). Acad Pr.

Foundations of Distance Education. Desmond Keegan. LC 85-21274. 256p. 1986. 34.50 o.p. (ISBN 0-7099-1547-0, Pub. by Croom Helm Ltd). Routledge Chapman & Hall.

Foundations of Drama. C. J. Gianakaris. 1975. pap. 10.75 o.p. (ISBN 0-395-18611-0). HM.

Foundations of Economic Analysis. Paul A. Samuelson. LC 65-11953. 1965. pap. text ed. 4.95x o.p. (ISBN 0-689-70177-2, 80, Atheneum). Macmillan.

Foundations of Economic Development: Intelligence vs. Capital. Pablo E. Victoria. (Illus.). 128p. 1983. 7.50 o.p. (ISBN 0-682-49932-3, University). Exposition-Phoenix.

Foundations of Electrical Engineering. K. Simonyi. 1964. 215.00 o.p. (ISBN 0-08-010204-2); pap. 215.00 o.p. (ISBN 0-08-019001-4). Pergamon.

Foundations of Emergency First Aid Services: Skill Class Workbook. 3rd ed. John Pappa et al. 96p. 1985. pap. text ed. 8.50 o.p. (ISBN 0-317-54558-2). Kendall-Hunt.

Foundations of English Administrative Law: Certiorari & Mandamus in the Seventeenth Century. Edith G. Henderson. LC 63-11421. (Ames Foundation Publications Ser). 1963. 16.00x o.s.i. (ISBN 0-674-31351-8). Harvard U Pr.

Foundations of Ethology. Konrad Lorenz. 1983. pap. 9.50 o.p. (ISBN 0-671-44573-1, Touchstone Bks). S&S.

Foundations of Experimental Psychology. Ed. by James W. Kalat. LC 72-86187. 493p. 1972. 48.50x o.p. (ISBN 0-8422-5027-1). Irvington.

Foundations of Financial Management. 4th ed. Stanley B. Block & Geoffrey A. Hirt. 1987. 40.95 o.p. (ISBN 0-256-03622-5); study guide 13.95 o.p. (ISBN 0-256-03623-3). Irwin.

Foundations of Financial Management: First Canadian Edition. Stanley Black et al. 1987. 42.95 o.p. (ISBN 0-256-05632-3). Irwin.

Foundations of Fluid Mechanics. Shao Yuan. 1967. pap. text ed. 48.00 o.p. (ISBN 0-13-329813-2). P-H.

Foundations of Genetics: A Science for Society. Anna C. Pai. (Illus.). 320p. 1974. text ed. 18.95 o.p. (ISBN 0-07-048093-1, C); text ed. 31.95 o.p. (ISBN 0-07-048092-3). McGraw.

Foundations of Infinitesimal Calculus. H. Jerome Keisler. 1976. pap. text ed. write for info. o.p. (ISBN 0-87150-215-1, PWS1753, Prindle). PWS-Kent Pub.

Foundations of Language Development a Multidisciplinary Approach, 2 vols. E. H. Lenneberg. Ed. by Elizabeth Lenneberg. 1975. Vol. 1. 39.95 o.p. (ISBN 0-12-443701-X); Vol. 2. 39.95 o.p. (ISBN 0-12-443702-8); Set. 60.00 o.p. Acad Pr.

Foundations of Leninism. Joseph Stalin. 127p. (Orig.). 1939. pap. 1.95 o.p. (ISBN 0-7178-0070-9). Intl Pubs Co.

Foundations of Life-Long Education, Vol. 1. Ed. by Ravindra H. Dave. 1976. text ed. 55.00 o.p. (ISBN 0-08-021192-5); pap. text ed. 23.00 o.p. (ISBN 0-08-021191-7). Pergamon.

Foundations of Marxist Aesthetics. A. Zis. 298p. 1977. 6.95 o.p. (ISBN 0-8285-0193-9, Pub. by Progress Pubs USSR). Imported Pubns.

Foundations of Mathematical Biology, 3 vols. Ed. by Robert Rosen. Incl. Vol. 1. Subcellular Systems. 1972. 57.50 (ISBN 0-12-597201-6); Vol. 2. Cellular Systems. 1972. 65.00 (ISBN 0-12-597202-4); Vol. 3. 1973. 74.50 (ISBN 0-12-597203-2). Set. 198.50 o.p. Acad Pr.

Foundations of Metaphysics in Science. Errol E. Harris. LC 83-3502. 510p. 1983. pap. text ed. 22.00 o.p. (ISBN 0-8191-3169-5). U Pr of Amer.

Foundations of Modern Art. A. Ozenfant. Tr. by John Rodker. (Illus.). 16.00 o.p. (ISBN 0-8446-0834-3). Peter Smith.

Foundations of Modern Historical Thought: From Machiavelli to Vico. Paul Avis. 192p. 1986. 34.50 o.p. (ISBN 0-7099-0581-5, Pub. by Croom Helm Ltd). Routledge Chapman & Hall.

Foundations of Modern Potential Theory. N. S. Landkof. Tr. by A. P. Doohovskoy from Rus. LC 77-186131. (Grundlehren der Mathematischen Wissenschaften: Vol. 180). 440p. 1973. 58.00 o.p. (ISBN 0-387-05394-8). Springer-Verlag.

Foundations of Modern Sociology. 4th ed. Metta Spencer & Alex Inkeles. (Illus.). 608p. 1985. text ed. (ISBN 0-13-329996-1). P-H.

Foundations of Multivariate Analysis: A Unified Approach by Means of Projection onto Linear Subspaces. Kei Takeuchi et al. 500p. 1982. 35.95x o.p. (ISBN 0-470-27311-9). Halsted Pr.

Foundations of Nigeria's Financial Infrastructure. Ed. by J. K. Onoh. 320p. 1980. 29.95 o.p. (ISBN 0-7099-0448-7, Pub. by Croom Helm Ltd). Routledge Chapman & Hall.

Foundations of Non-Stationary Dynamic Programming with Discrete Time Parameter. Karl Hinderer. (Lecture Notes in Operations Research & Mathematical Systems: Vol. 33). 1970. pap. 10.90 o.p. (ISBN 0-387-04956-8). Springer-Verlag.

Foundations of Ontology. Otto Samuel. 1952. (ISBN 0-8022-1478-9). Philos Lib.

Foundations of Optimization. M. S. Bazaraa & C. M. Shetty. (Lecture Notes in Economics & Mathematical Systems Ser.: Vol. 122). 1979. pap. 13.00 o.p. (ISBN 0-387-07680-8). Springer-Verlag.

Foundations of Parasitology. 3rd ed. Gerald D. Schmidt & Larry S. Roberts. LC 81-1342. (Illus.). 260p. 1985. text ed. 41.95 casebound o.p. (ISBN 0-8016-4385-6). Mosby.

Foundations of Paul Samuelson's Revealed Preference Theory: A Study by the Method of Rational Reconstruction. Stanley Wong. 1978. 34.95x o.p. (ISBN 0-7100-8643-1). Routledge Chapman & Hall.

Foundations of Personnel. 2nd ed. John M. Ivancevich & William F. Glueck. 1983. 30.50x o.p. (ISBN 0-256-02694-7); study guide 10.95 o.p. (ISBN 0-256-02901-6). Irwin.

Foundations of Personnel-Human Resource Management. 3rd ed. Ivancevich & Glueck. 1986. 38.95 o.p. (ISBN 0-256-03425-7); study guide 12.95 o.p. (ISBN 0-256-03426-5). Irwin.

Foundations of Physical Education. Richard Rivenes et al. LC 77-75155. (Illus.). 1978. text ed. 25.95 o.p. (ISBN 0-395-25389-6). HM.

Foundations of Physics. M. Bunge. (Springer Tracts in Natural Philosophy: Vol. 10). (Illus.). 1967. 37.00 o.p. (ISBN 0-387-03983-X). Springer-Verlag.

Foundations of Practical Harmony & Counterpoint. 2nd ed. Reginald O. Morris. LC 79-10541. (Illus.). xii, 148p. 1980. Repr. of 1931 ed. lib. bdg. 35.00x o.p. (ISBN 0-313-21465-4, MOPH). Greenwood.

Foundations of Psychobiology. Daniel N. Robinson & William R. Utall. 384p. 1983. text ed. write for info. o.p. (ISBN 0-02-402460-0). Macmillan.

Foundations of Psychology. Gary S. Belkin & Ruth H. Skydell. LC 78-69566. (Illus.). 1980. pap. 38.76 o.p. (ISBN 0-395-25363-2). HM.

Foundations of Psychopathology. rev. ed. John Nemiah. LC 73-81222. 352p. 1973. 30.00x o.p. (ISBN 0-87668-100-3). Aronson.

Foundations of Quantum Dynamics. S. M. Blinder. 1974. 58.50 o.p. (ISBN 0-12-106050-0). Acad Pr.

Foundations of Quantum Mechanics & Ordered Linear Spaces. Ed. by A. Hartkaemper & H. Neumann. LC 74-2859. (Lecture Notes in Physics: Vol. 29). vi, 355p. 1974. pap. 18.00 o.p. (ISBN 0-387-06725-6). Springer-Verlag.

Foundations of Quantum Theory. Sol Wieder. 1973. 32.00 o.p. (ISBN 0-12-749050-7). Acad Pr.

Foundations of Radio. M. G. Scroggie. (Illus.). 320p. 1957. (ISBN 0-8022-1525-4). Philos Lib.

Foundations of Retailing. J. Barry Mason & Morris L. Mayer. 1981. text ed. 18.50x o.p. (ISBN 0-256-02546-0). Irwin.

Foundations of Social Research. N. Lin. 1976. text ed. 38.95 o.p. (ISBN 0-07-037867-3). McGraw.

Foundations of Sociology. David C. King & Marvin R. Koller. LC 74-23219. 1975. text ed. 15.95 o.p. (ISBN 0-03-007756-7, HoltC). HR&W.

Foundations of Space-Time Theories. Ed. by John S. Earman et al. LC 77-83503. (Studies in the Philosopy of Science: Vol. 8). (Illus.). 1977. 29.50 o.p. (ISBN 0-8166-0807-5). U of Minn Pr.

Foundations of Special Relativity: Kinematic Axioms for Minkowski Space-Time. J. W. Schutz. (Lecture Notes in Mathematics: Vol. 361). (Illus.). 314p. 1973. pap. 17.00 o.p. (ISBN 0-387-06591-1). Springer-Verlag.

Foundations of Statistical Mechanics: A Deductive Treatment. O. Penrose. LC 70-89513. (International Series in Natural Philosophy: Vol. 22). (Illus.). 1970. 70.00 o.p. (ISBN 0-08-013314-2). Pergamon.

Foundations of Structural Geology. R. G. Park. (Illus.). 135p. 1982. 38.00 o.p. (ISBN 0-412-00181-0, NO. 5025, Chapman & Hall); pap. 17.95 o.p. (ISBN 0-412-00191-8, NO. 5026, Chapman & Hall). Routledge Chapman & Hall.

Foundations of the Australian Monetary System, 1788-1851. S. Butlin. 1969. 27.00x o.p. (ISBN 0-424-05830-8, Pub by Sydney U Pr). Intl Spec Bk.

Foundations of the Mathematical Theory of Structures. CISM (International Center for Mechanical Sciences) Staff. Ed. by E. De Arantes Oliveira. (CISM Pubs. Ser: No. 121). (Illus.). 223p. 1976. pap. 26.00 o.p. (ISBN 0-387-81312-8). Springer-Verlag.

Foundations of the Origin of Species. Charles Darwin. Ed. by Francis Darwin. LC 10-1422. 1909. 21.00 o.p. (ISBN 0-527-21610-0). Kraus Repr.

Foundations of the South African Cheap Labour System. Norman Levy. (International Library of Sociology). 300p. 1982. 32.50x o.p. (ISBN 0-7100-0909-7). Routledge Chapman & Hall.

Foundations of the Theory of Signs. Charles W. Morris. LC 70-132776. (Foundations of the Unity of Science Ser: Vol. 1, No. 2). 1938. pap. 3.50x o.p. (ISBN 0-226-57577-2, P401, Phoen). U of Chicago Pr.

Foundations of Tudor Policy. William G. Zeeveld. LC 81-6868. (Illus.). vii, 291p. 1981. Repr. of 1948 ed. lib. bdg. 35.00 o.p. (ISBN 0-313-22890-6, ZEFT). Greenwood.

Foundations of Vocational Education: Social & Philosophical Concepts. reference ed. J. Thompson. (Illus.). 1972. pap. text ed. (ISBN 0-13-330068-4). P-H.

Foundations Today: Facts & Figures on Private Foundations. 5th ed. Ed. by Loren Renz. 38p. 1988. pap. 7.50 o.p. (ISBN 0-87954-280-2). Foundation Ctr.

Founders of Electrochemistry. Samuel Ruben. 107p. 1975. pap. 8.95 o.p. (ISBN 0-87548-370-4). Open Court.

Founding Family: The Pickneys of South Carolina. Francis L. Williams. LC 77-92548. (Illus.). 576p. 1978. 19.95 o.p. (ISBN 0-15-131503-5). HarBraceJ.

Founding Fathers of Israel. Gershon Winer. LC 79-136422. 1971. price not set o.p. (ISBN 0-8197-0264-1). Bloch.

Founding of New Societies. Louis Hartz. LC 64-11535. 1964. 6.50 o.p. (ISBN 0-15-132775-0). HarBraceJ.

Founding Principles of American Government: Two Hundred Years of Democracy on Trial. rev. ed. George J. Graham, Jr. & Scarlett G. Graham. LC 83-21085. 400p. 1984. pap. text ed. 14.95x o.p. (ISBN 0-934540-25-X). Chatham Hse Pubs.

Founding the Life Divine: An Introduction to the Integral Yoga of Sri Aurobindo. Morwenna Donnelly. LC 74-2430. 250p. 1976. pap. 7.95 o.s.i. (ISBN 0-913922-13-7). Dawn Horse Pr.

Founding Theory of American Sociology 1881-1915. Roscoe C. Hinkle. (International Library of Sociology). 1980. 36.95x o.p. (ISBN 0-7100-0401-X). Routledge Chapman & Hall.

Foundry Equipment Planning Guides for Vocational & Technical Training, Vol. 7. (Technical Training & Education Programme). pap. 22.80 o.p. (ISBN 92-2-105778-X, ILO241, ILO). UNIPUB.

Foundryman's Handbook. 8th ed. Foundry Services, Ltd. Staff. 1975. text ed. 18.25 o.p. (ISBN 0-08-018020-5). Pergamon.

Fountain of Justice: A Study of the Natural Law. John C. Wu. 287p. 1980. 5.95 o.p. (ISBN 0-89955-183-1, Pub. by Mei Ya China). Intl Spec Bk.

Fountain of Life. Solomon I. Gabriol. Tr. by Harry E. Wedeck. LC 61-18056. (ISBN 0-8022-0556-9). Philos Lib.

Fountain Press Price Guide to Collectible Cameras. (Illus.). 191p. (Orig.). 1987. pap. 15.95 o.p. (ISBN 0-86343-014-7, Pub. by Fountain Pr UK). Seven Hills Bk Dists.

Fountain Square. (Everything Bks.). 128p. 1983. pap. 2.98 o.p. (ISBN 0-913428-78-7). Landfall Pr.

Fountaine of Ancient Fiction see Golden Booke of the Leaden Gods.

Fountains of Paradise. Arthur C. Clarke. LC 78-14072. 1979. 10.00 o.s.i. (ISBN 0-15-132773-4). HarBraceJ.

Four Ages of Music. Walter Wiora. Tr. by M. Herter Norton. (Illus.). 1967. pap. 4.95 o.p. (ISBN 0-393-00427-9, Norton Lib). Norton.

Four & Twenty Blackbirds. Francis Brabazon. (Illus.). 52p. (gr. 1-5). 1975. pap. 2.25 o.p. (ISBN 0-913078-22-0). Sheriar Pr.

Four Centuries of European Jewelry. Ernle Bradford. (Illus.). 224p. 1953. (ISBN 0-8022-0166-0). Philos Lib.

Four Centuries of Shakespearian Criticism. Ed. by Frank Kermode. 1974. pap. 2.45 o.p. (ISBN 0-380-00058-X, 20131-3, Discus). Avon.

Four Centuries of Southern Indians. Ed. by Charles M. Hudson. LC 73-85028. 184p. 1975. 14.00x o.p. (ISBN 0-8203-0332-1). U of Ga Pr.

Four Clever Brothers: A Story by the Brothers Grimm. Jacob Grimm & Wilhelm K. Grimm. LC 67-6007. (Illus.). 32p. (gr. k-3). 1967. 6.95 o.p. (ISBN 0-15-229100-8, HJ). HarBraceJ.

Four Concepts: An English Workbook. Ann C. Lewis & Thomas E. Bambrey. LC 80-16256. 340p. 1980. Repr. of 1977 ed. 13.50 o.p. (ISBN 0-89874-186-6). Krieger.

Four Creeks. Robert McArthur. (Illus.). 1980. lib. bdg. 25.00 o.p. (ISBN 0-916908-36-4); pap. 3.50 o.p. (ISBN 0-916908-12-7). Place Herons.

Four-D Funhouse. Clayton Emery & Earl Wajenberg. LC 85-51044. (Amazing Stories Ser.). 219p. (Orig.). 1985. pap. 2.95 o.p. (ISBN 0-88038-255-4). TSR Inc.

Four Days. Gloria Goldreich. LC 79-3352. 384p. 1980. 10.95 o.p. (ISBN 0-15-132802-1). HarBraceJ.

Four Days: A Novel of Burma 1945. William Crook. LC 79-55600. 1980. 9.95 o.p. (ISBN 0-689-11033-2, Atheneum). Macmillan.

Four Days of Mayaguez. Roy Rowan. (Illus.). 224p. 1975. 7.95 o.p. (ISBN 0-393-05564-7). Norton.

Four Days: The Historical Record of the Death of President Kennedy. UPI Staff & American Heritage Magazine Staff. 1983. pap. 9.50 o.p. (ISBN 0-671-50046-5). S&S.

Four-Dimensional Geometry: Introduction. Adrien L. Hess. LC 77-4310. (Illus.). 32p. 1977. pap. 3.00 o.s.i. (ISBN 0-87353-117-5). NCTM.

Four Dubliners: Wilde, Yeats, Joyce & Beckett. Richard Ellman. LC 85-600321. 118p. 1986. 7.00 o.p. (ISBN 0-8444-0522-1, S/N 030-000-00178-8). USGPO.

Four-Fold Health. Harriette Curtiss & F. Homer. 1936. 4.95 o.p. (ISBN 0-87516-304-1). DeVorss.

Four-Foot Forks. Illus. by Mary B. Schwark. (Zig Ziglar Ser.). (Illus.). 48p. 1988. pap. 2.50 o.p. (ISBN 0-8423-8847-8). Tyndale.

Four French Plays. Tr. by W. S. Merwin from Fr. LC 84-70390. 288p. 1985. pap. 10.95 o.s.i. (ISBN 0-689-11501-6, Atheneum). Macmillan.

Four French Renaissance Plays. Ed. by Arthur P. Stabler. (Illus.). 368p. 1978. pap. 8.00 o.p. (ISBN 0-87422-014-9). Wash St U Pr.

Four Fundamental Concepts of Psycho-Analysis. Jacques Lacan. 1978. 19.95x o.p. (ISBN 0-393-01170-4). Norton.

Four Good Things. James McMichael. (New Poetry Ser.). 96p. 1980. 8.95 o.p. (ISBN 0-395-29913-6); pap. 4.95 o.p. (ISBN 0-395-29914-4). HM.

Four Gospels. 5.00 o.p. (ISBN 0-317-46838-3); 3.50 o.p. (ISBN 0-317-46839-1). Dghtrs St Paul.

Four Gospels & the Revelation. Tr. by Richmond Lattimore from Gr. 320p. 1979. 14.95 o.p. (ISBN 0-374-15801-0). FS&G.

Four Gospels As One. David H. Yarn. 281p. 1982. 8.95 o.p. (ISBN 0-87747-948-8). Deseret Bk.

Four Hazardous Journeys of Reverend Jonathan Blanchard. Raymond P. Fischer. 352p. Date not set. 14.95 o.p. (ISBN 0-8423-0914-4). Tyndale.

Four in a Wild Place. John Stallard. LC 79-152674. 1971. 6.95 o.p. (ISBN 0-393-08649-6). Norton.

Four-Language Technical Dictionary of Chromatography: English, German, French, Russian. H. Angele. LC 76-103000. (Eng., Ger., Fr. & Rus.). 1970. 65.00 o.p. (ISBN 0-08-015865-X). Pergamon.

Four-Language Technical Dictionary of Heating, Ventilation & Sanitary Engineering: English, German, French, Russian. W. Lindeke. LC 79-81248. 1970. 39.00 o.p. (ISBN 0-08-006426-4). Pergamon.

Four-Leaf Clover. Will & Nicolas. LC 59-8956. (Illus.). 32p. (gr. k-3). 1959. 5.95 o.p. (ISBN 0-15-229140-7, HJ). HarBraceJ.

Four Lectures on Marxism. Paul M. Sweezy. LC 81-81694. 96p. 1981. 12.00 o.p. (ISBN 0-85345-583-X). Monthly Rev.

Four Legged Helpers see Animales Que Ayudan.

Four Little Troubles, 4 bks. James Marshall. Incl. Eugene. 32p; Someone Is Talking About Hortense. 32p; Sing Out Irene. 32p; Snake - His Story. 32p. (Illus., Orig.). (ps-2). 1975. boxed 3.95 o.p. (ISBN 0-395-19880-1). HM.

Four Loves. C. S. Lewis. LC 60-10920. 1960. 9.95 o.s.i. (ISBN 0-15-132915-X). HarBraceJ.

Four Marines & Other Portraits. Photos by Jack Shear. (Illus.). 96p. 1985. 40.00 o.p. (ISBN 0-942642-19-8). Twelvetrees Pr.

Four-Minute Sell. Janet G. Elsea. 1984. 12.70 o.p. (ISBN 0-671-49194-6). S&S.

Four, Oh! A Change of Values. Reginald N. Fickett. LC 84-91274. 123p. 1985. 10.00 o.p. (ISBN 0-533-06356-6). Vantage.

Four Persistent Issues: Essays on California's Land Ownership Concentration, Water Deficits, Sub-State Regionalism, & Congressional Leadership. Paul W. Gates et al. LC 78-17964. 1978. pap. 5.75x o.p. (ISBN 0-87772-257-9). UCB IGS.

Four Plays. Gunter Grass. Tr. by Ralph Manheim & A. Leslie Willson. Incl. Flood; Mister, Mister; Only Ten Minutes to Buffalo; The Wicked Cooks. LC 67-11968. 289p. 1968. pap. 3.25 o.p. (ISBN 0-15-633150-0, HB138, Harv). HarBraceJ.

Four Plays by Bernard Shaw. George Bernard Shaw. Incl. Candida. 1953; Caesar & Cleopatra; Pygmalion; Heartbreak House. 1962. 3.95 o.s.i. (ISBN 0-394-60019-3, M19). Modern Lib.

Four Prentices of London. Mary A. Gasior. LC 79-54340. (Renaissance Drama Ser.). 200p. 1980. lib. bdg. 26.00 o.p. (ISBN 0-8240-4458-4). Garland Pub.

Four Quartets. T. S. Eliot. LC 43-7996. 1943. 5.95 o.p. (ISBN 0-15-133053-0). HarBraceJ.

Four Quartets. T. S. Eliot. 1988. pap. 5.95 o.p. HarBraceJ.

Four Reformers: Luther, Melanchthon, Zwingli, Calvin. Kurt Aland. Tr. by James L. Schaaf. LC 79-50091. 176p. 1979. pap. 5.95 o.p. (ISBN 0-8066-1709-8, 10-2364, Augsburg). Augsburg Fortress.

Four Screenplays of Ingmar Bergman. Ingmar Bergman. 1969. pap. 9.50 o.s.i. (ISBN 0-671-20353-3, Touchstone Bks). S&S.

Four Seasons Cookbook. Tom G. Margittai & Paul Kovi. 596p. 1986. pap. 12.95 o.s.i. (ISBN 0-671-62796-1, Fireside). S&S.

Four Seasons of the Year. Tang Lufeng & Chen Huilian. (Illus.). 19p. (gr. 1-3). 1984. pap. 2.95 o.p. (ISBN 0-8351-1413-9). China Bks.

Four Seasons: Splendid Recipes from the World-Famous Restaurant. Tom G. Margittai & Paul Kovi. 1980. 35.00 o.p. (ISBN 0-671-25022-1). S&S.

Four Sergeants. Zeno. LC 76-25232. 1977. 8.95 o.p. (ISBN 0-689-10765-X, Atheneum). Macmillan.

Four Sonatas; Andante, Theme & Variations; & Adagio for Piano. Alexander Reinagle. (Music Reprint Ser.). 100p. 1987. Repr. of 1786 ed. lib. bdg. 24.50 o.p. (ISBN 0-306-76254-4). Da Capo.

Four-Star Kitchen: Classic Recipes from New York's Great Restaurants. Arthur Hettich & Ann Seranne. LC 86-1418. (Illus.). 352p. 1986. 22.00 o.s.i. (ISBN 0-8129-1227-6). Times Bks.

Four Stories. Gabriel Josipovici. 1977. pap. 3.00 o.p. (ISBN 0-685-84023-9, Pub. by Menard Pr). Small Pr Dist.

Four Stories. Constance G. Taylor. 1984. 6.95 o.p. (ISBN 0-533-06223-3). Vantage.

Four Thousand Years of Mexican Architecture. Ed. by Society of Mexican Architects. (Illus.). 1956. 60.00 o.s.i. (ISBN 0-685-39858-7). E J Brill USA.

Four Verse Plays. Maxwell Anderson. Incl. High Tor; Winterset; Elizabeth the Queen; Mary of Scotland. LC 59-1731. 560p. (Orig.). 1959. pap. 9.95 o.p. (ISBN 0-15-633329-5, Harv). HarBraceJ.

Four Views of China. Ed. by Robert A. Kapp. (Rice University Studies: Vol. 59, No. 4). 96p. 1974. pap. 10.00 o.p. (ISBN 0-89263-218-6). Rice Univ.

Four Villages-Architecture in Nepal: Studies of Village Life. Katherine D. Blair. LC 81-71007. (Illus.). 72p. 1985. pap. 10.00 o.p. (05594-9, Pub. by Craft & Folk Art Museum). U of Chicago Pr.

Four Ways of Politics: State & Nation in Italy, Somalia, Israel, Iran. E. A. Bayne. LC 65-14723. 316p. 1965. 7.50 o.p. (ISBN 0-910116-60-1). U Field Staff Intl.

Four Weeks with God & Your Neighbor. Jay E. Adams. pap. 2.50 o.p. (ISBN 0-8010-0140-4). Baker Bk.

Four Words see Metaphor.

Four Years after High School: A Capsule Description of 1980 Senior. Calvin C. Jones et al. (Education Department Publication CS: No. 210). 61p. 1986. pap. 3.25 o.p. (ISBN 0-318-21681-7, S/N 065-000-00257-4). USGPO.

Fourier Transform & Its Applications. 2nd ed. R. N. Bracewell. (Electrical Engineering Ser.). (Illus.). 1978. text ed. 50.95 o.p. (ISBN 0-07-007013-X). McGraw.

Fourier Transform Nuclear Magnetic Resonance Techniques: A Practical Approach. K. Mullen & P. S. Pregosin. 1977. 40.50 o.p. (ISBN 0-12-510450-2). Acad Pr.

Fourier Transform Spectroscopy: Proceedings of the International Conference, Durham, U. K., 19-22 September, 1983. Ed. by J. R. Birch. 290p. 1984. pap. 70.00 o.p. (ISBN 0-08-030265-3). Pergamon.

Fourier Transforms & Their Physical Applications. D. C. Champeney. (Techniques of Physics Ser.: No. 1). 1973. 73.00 o.p. (ISBN 0-12-167450-9). Acad Pr.

Fourteen Day Conspiracy. Jean Gilliland. LC 80-51212. 224p. 1980. pap. 6.95 o.s.i. (ISBN 0-934616-09-4). Valkyrie Pub Hse.

Fourteen Days to a Healthy Heart. Frederick T. Zugibe. (Illus.). 224p. 1986. 17.95 o.p. (ISBN 0-02-633610-3). Macmillan.

Fourteen Days to a Healthy Heart. Frederick T. Zugibe. 288p. 1987. pap. 4.50 o.p. (ISBN 0-380-70282-7). Avon.

Fourteen Days to Midnight. Jerry Jenkins. (Bradford Family Adventures Ser.). (Illus.). 112p. (gr. 3-6). 1985. 2.95 o.p. (ISBN 0-87239-943-5, 2993). Standard Pub.

Fourteen Women's Programs: Making Your House a Home. Wilma Shaffer. 96p. (Orig.). 1984. pap. 3.95 o.p. (ISBN 0-87239-743-2, 2974). Standard Pub.

Fourteenth Annual Institute on Employment Law. 612p. 1985. 15.00 o.p. (H4-4973). PLI.

Fourteenth International Cancer Congress, Budapest, August 1986: Abstracts of Lectures, Symposia & Free Communications. xlviii, 1350p. 1986. pap. 66.00 o.p. (ISBN 3-8055-4434-0). S Karger.

Fourteenth International Symposium on Industrial Robots, 14th: Proceedings. 1984. lib. bdg. 114.00 o.p. (ISBN 0-903608-75-8, Pub. by IFS Pubns UK). Air Sci Co.

Fourth & Fifth Symphonies in Full Orchestral Score. Ludwig van Beethoven. 260p. 1976. pap. 7.95 o.p. (ISBN 0-486-23378-2). Dover.

Fourth & Long Gone. Pepper Rodgers. 296p. 1984. 12.95 o.p. (ISBN 0-931948-61-4). Peachtree Pubs.

Fourth Angel. John Rechy. 160p. 1983. pap. 6.95 o.p. (ISBN 0-394-62469-6). Seaver Bks.

Fourth Annual Microcomputers in Education Conference: Literacy Plus. Ed. by Ruth Camuse. LC 84-17597. (Computers in Education Ser.). 463p. 1984. text ed. 35.00 o.p. (ISBN 0-88175-077-8, Computer Sci Pr). W H Freeman.

Fourth Book of Good Boats. Roger C. Taylor. LC 83-48724. (Illus.). 256p. 1984. 8.95 o.p. (ISBN 0-87742-171-4, F380). Intl Marine.

Fourth Breeders' Cup, 1988. pap. 6.00 o.p. (ISBN 0-939049-16-3). Blood Horse.

Fourth Certification of Changes to Schedules to the General Agreement on Tariffs & Trade. 517p. 1980. pap. 25.00 o.p. (ISBN 0-686-63036-X, G139, GATT). UNIPUB.

Fourth Deadly Sin. Lawrence Sanders. 1986. 18.95 o.p. (ISBN 0-8161-3989-X, Large Print Bks). G K Hall.

Fourth Dimension: Toward a Geometry of Higher Reality. Rudy Rucker. LC 84-6529. (Illus.). 228p. 1984. 17.45 o.p. (ISBN 0-395-34420-4). HM.

Fourth Evangelist & His Gospel: An Examination of Contemporary Scholarship. Robert Kysar. LC 75-22711. 320p. (Orig.). 1975. pap. 11.95 o.p. (ISBN 0-8066-1504-4, 10-2365, Augsburg). Augsburg Fortress.

Fourth Flight of the Starfire. Edwin Mumford. 1972. 4.00 o.p. (ISBN 0-682-47574-2). Exposition-Phoenix.

Fourth Generation. Hugo. (Infotech Computer State of the Art Reports). 501p. 1971. 310.00x o.p. (ISBN 0-08-028550-3). Pergamon.

Fourth Generation: A Call for New Understanding for the Growing Numbers over Age 75. John M. Mason. LC 78-52195. 1978. pap. 3.95 o.p. (ISBN 0-8066-1664-4, 10-2375). Augsburg Fortress.

Fourth Generation Preacher's Kid. Colleen Reese. LC 81-2943. 1982. pap. 7.50 o.p. (ISBN 0-8309-0314-3). Herald Hse.

Fourth King. Glen Petrie. LC 86-47660. 384p. 1986. 17.95 o.p. (ISBN 0-689-11765-5, Atheneum). Macmillan.

Fourth LACUS Forum: Proceedings. Linguistic Association of Canada & the U. S. Staff. Ed. by Michel Paradis. 1977. pap. text ed. 12.95 o.s.i. (ISBN 0-917496-09-4). Hornbeam Pr.

Fourth Man. Andrew Boyle. 464p. 1980. pap. 3.50 o.s.i. Bantam.

Fourth National Symposium on Aquifer Restoration: Proceedings. 1984. 43.75 o.p. (ISBN 0-318-23103-4). Natl Water Well.

Fourth Old House Catalogue. Lawrence Grow. LC 84-15488. (Illus.). 224p. (Orig.). 1984. pap. 11.95 o.p. (ISBN 0-915590-52-2). Main Street.

Fourth Report on the Excavation of the Roman Fort at Richborough, Kent. Joscelyn P. Bushe-Fox. (Reports of the Research Committee of the Society of Antiquaries of London Ser.: no. 16). pap. cancelled o.s.i. (ISBN 0-317-28015-5, 2025574). Bks Demand UMI.

Fourth Session of the Sixth National People's Congress. Zhao Ziyang et al. 197p. (Orig.). 1986. pap. 4.95 o.p. (ISBN 0-8351-1854-1). China Bks.

Fowl & Game Bird Cookery. James A. Beard. LC 78-71061. (Illus.). 1982. pap. 5.95 o.p. (ISBN 0-15-633340-6, Harv). HarBraceJ.

Fox & Heggie. Sandra E. Guzzo. Ed. by Kathleen Tucker. LC 83-16672. (Illus.). 32p. (gr. k-3). 1983. PLB 10.25 o.p. (ISBN 0-8075-2546-4). A Whitman.

Fox & the Buffalo. Brian Swann. Ed. by Green Tiger Press Staff. (Illus.). 12p. (Orig.). 1985. pap. 2.50 o.p. (ISBN 0-88138-003-2, Pub. by Envelope Bks). Green Tiger Pr.

Fox & the Hound. Heather Simon. (Illus.). (gr. 3-6). 1981. pap. 2.25 o.p. (ISBN 0-671-47236-4). Archway.

Fox Dancer. Robert J. Steelman. 1976. pap. 0.95 o.p. (ISBN 0-8439-0370-8, Pub. by Leisure Bks CT). Dorchester Pub Co.

Fox in the Ball Park. Harold Longman. LC 79-24063. 128p. (gr. 7-9). 1980. text ed. 9.95 o.p. (ISBN 0-07-038681-1). McGraw.

Fox Talbot, Photographer. Robert Lassam. (Illus.). 94p. 1981. 22.50x o.p. (ISBN 0-900193-74-3, Pub. by Compton Pr England); pap. 9.95 o.p. (ISBN 0-900193-77-8). Kent St U Pr.

Fox Two! America's First Ace in Vietnam. Randy Cunningham et al. (Illus.). 160p. 1984. pap. 8.95 o.p. (ISBN 0-912173-01-7). Champlin Museum.

Fox Woman & Other Stories. Abraham Merritt. 1977. pap. 1.50 o.p. (ISBN 0-380-01709-1, 33845). Avon.

Foxcatcher. William H. Hallahan. LC 85-21753. 320p. 1986. 16.95 o.p. (ISBN 0-688-04686-X). Morrow.

Foxe's Book of Martyrs. John Foxe. 400p. pap. 3.95 o.p. (ISBN 0-8007-8013-2, Spire Bks). Revell.

Foxes of Harrow. Date not set. pap. (ISBN 0-385-29512-X). Delacorte.

Foxes of Harrow. Frank Yerby. 544p. 1986. pap. 6.95 o.p. (ISBN 0-385-29512-X, Delta). Dell.

Foxfire, Vols. 7-9. Eliot Wigginton. 1986. Boxed set. 34.85 o.s.i. (ISBN 0-385-23721-9, Anchor Pr). Doubleday.

Foxfire Books, 3 vols, Bks. 1-3. Eliott Wigginton. (Illus.). 1312p. 1975. Set. pap. 27.85 o.s.i. (ISBN 0-385-11253-X, Anch). Doubleday.

Foxfire Light. Janet Dailey. (Nightingale Ser.). 1983. pap. 9.95 o.p. (ISBN 0-8161-3494-4, Large Print Bks). G K Hall.

Foxglove Tales. Alison Uttley. Selected by Lucy Meredith. (Illus.). 192p. (gr. 4 up). 1984. 11.95 o.p. (ISBN 0-571-13354-1). Faber & Faber.

Fox's Lair. Ian McMahan. (Microkid Mystery Ser.: No. 2). 96p. 1985. pap. 2.50 o.p. (ISBN 0-380-69833-1, Camelot). Avon.

Fra Girolamo Savonarola, Florentine Art & Renaissance Historiography. Ronald Steinberg. LC 76-8304. (Illus.). 151p. 1977. 14.00x o.p. (ISBN 0-8214-0202-1). Ohio U Pr.

Fracas Factor. Mack Reynolds. 1978. 1.50 o.s.i. (ISBN 0-8439-0602-2, Pub. by Leisure Bks CT). Dorchester Pub Co.

Fractional Calculus & Its Applications: Proceedings of the International Conference, June 1974. International Conference, New Haven Staff. Ed. by B. Ross. (Lecture Notes in Mathematics: Vol. 457). 380p. 1975. pap. 21.00 o.p. (ISBN 0-387-07161-X). Springer-Verlag.

Fractional Prentage Methods for Ionisation of Open Shells of D & F Electrons see Photoelectron Spectrometry.

Fracture & Failure: Analyses, Mechanisms & Applications. P. P. Tung et al. 1981. 47.00 o.p. (ISBN 0-87170-113-8). ASM.

Fracture & Fatigue Control in Structures: Applications of Fracture Mechanics. Stanley T. Rolfe & John M. Barson. (Illus.). 1977. pap. text ed. (ISBN 0-13-329953-8). P-H.

Fracture & Fatigue-Elasto-Plasticity, Thin Sheet & Micro-Mechanisms: Proceedings of the Third European Colloquium on Fracture, London, 8-10 September 1980. J. C. Radon. LC 80-40915. (Illus.). 450p. 1980. 91.00 o.p. (ISBN 0-08-026161-2). Pergamon.

Fracture & Society, Vol. 4: Fracture & Society see Industrial Systems Engineering & Management in Developing Countries: Proceedings of the International Conference, 3-6 November 1980, Asian Institute of Technology, Bangkok, Thailand.

Fracture Management: A Practical Approach. J. Ted Hartman. LC 77-24292. (Illus.). 338p. 1978. text ed. 21.50 o.p. (ISBN 0-8121-0601-6). Lea & Febiger.

Fracture Mechanics. Ed. by Nicholas Perrone et al. LC 78-16063. (Illus.). 722p. 1978. 30.00x o.p. (ISBN 0-8139-0802-7). U Pr of Va.

Fracture Mechanics, Current Status, Future Prospects: Proceedings of a Conference Held at Cambridge University, March 16, 1979. Ed. by R. A. Smith. (Illus.). 128p. 1979. 65.00 o.p. (ISBN 0-08-024766-0). Pergamon.

Fracture Mechanics in China: A Selection of Chinese Papers & Abstracts. H. Li Huazong. 158p. 1983. pap. 68.00 o.p. (ISBN 0-08-028726-3, A115, A145). Pergamon.

Fracture Problems & Solutions in the Energy Industry: Proceedings of the 5th Canadian Fracture Conference (CFC5), Winnipeg, Canada, September 3-4, 1981. Ed. by L. A. Simpson. (Illus.). 260p. 1982. 73.00 o.p. (ISBN 0-08-028671-2, A145, B110). Pergamon.

Fractures, Dislocations & Sprains. Alan E. Nourse. LC 78-6855. (First Bks). (Illus.). (gr. 4 up). 1978. PLB 10.40 s&l o.p. (ISBN 0-531-01494-0). Watts.

Fractures of the Mandible. 2nd ed. Killey. 74p. 1974. pap. 9.95 o.p. (ISBN 0-7236-0395-2, Pub. by John Wright UK). Butterworth.

Fraggle Rock. Stevenson. 1984. pap. 3.95 o.p. (ISBN 0-03-071472-9). H Holt & Co.

Fragile Alliance: An Orientation to the Psychiatric Treatment of the Adolescent. 3rd ed. John E. Meeks. LC 74-32258. 416p. 1980. lib. bdg. 23.50 o.p. (ISBN 0-88275-982-5). Krieger.

Fragile Beauty. John Nichols. (Illus.). 160p. 1987. 15.00 o.p. (ISBN 0-87905-282-1). Gibbs Smith Pub.

Fragile Deception. Jane Atkin. (Candlelight Supreme Ser.). (Orig.). 1986. pap. 2.75 o.p. (ISBN 0-440-12695-9). Dell.

Fragile Presence: Transcendence in Modern Literature. John Killinger. LC 72-91520. 176p. 1973. pap. 0.50x o.p. (ISBN 0-8006-0165-3, Fortress). Augsburg Fortress.

Fragments. Lou Graham. 288p. (Orig.). 1981. pap. 2.50 o.p. (ISBN 0-505-51708-6, Pub. by Tower Bks). Dorchester Pub Co.

Fragments: A Selection from the Notebooks of Paolo Soleri. Paolo Soleri. LC 79-3587. (Illus.). 224p. 1981. 12.45 o.p. (ISBN 0-06-250810-5). HarpR.

Fragments of a Faith Forgotten. 2nd ed. G. R. Mead. 633p. 1906. pap. 39.95 o.s.i. (ISBN 0-88697-011-3). Life Science.

Fragments of Ancient Japanese Ornamental Findings. (Illus.). 1983. pap. 12.50 o.p. (ISBN 0-686-47343-4). Saifer.

Fragments of the Mexican Revolution: Personal Accounts from the Border. Ed. by Oscar J. Martinez. LC 83-12370. (Illus.). 329p. 1983. 24.95x o.p. (ISBN 0-8263-0694-2); pap. 12.50x o.p. (ISBN 0-8263-0709-4). U of NM Pr.

Fragrance: The Story of Perfume from Cleopatra to Chanel. Edwin T. Morris. (Illus.). 256p. 1985. 24.95 o.p. (ISBN 0-684-18195-9, ScribT). Scribner.

Fragrant Garden: A Book About Sweet Scented Flowers & Leaves. Louise B. Wilder. 14.25 o.p. (ISBN 0-8446-5099-4). Peter Smith.

Frailties. Nancy Geyer. LC 85-18050. 1986. 17.95 o.p. (ISBN 0-316-30892-7). Little.

Frame Analysis: An Essay on the Organization of Experience. Erving Goffman. LC 74-4644. 1974. 27.00x o.s.i. (ISBN 0-674-31656-8). Harvard U Pr.

Frames of Meaning: The Social Construction of Extraordinary Science. H. M. Collins & T. J. Pinch. 256p. 1982. 29.95 o.p. (ISBN 0-7100-9011-0). Routledge Chapman & Hall.

Framework: A Developer's Handbook. Forefront Corporation Staff. 1985. pap. text ed. 24.95 o.p. (ISBN 0-07-912624-3). McGraw.

Framework: A Programmer's Reference. Forefront Corporation Staff. Ed. by Ashton-Tate. 300p. 1984. pap. 24.95 o.p. (ISBN 0-912677-21-X). Tate Pub.

Framework: A Programmer's Reference. Forefront Corporation Staff. 1985. pap. text ed. 24.95 o.p. (ISBN 0-07-912621-9). McGraw.

Framework: An Introduction. B. Harrison. 1985. pap. text ed. 15.95 o.p. (ISBN 0-07-912620-0). McGraw.

Framework: An Introduction. Bill Harrison. (Framework Bks.). 300p. 1984. pap. 15.95 o.p. (ISBN 0-912677-20-1). Tate Pub.

Framework: An Introduction to Programming. Forefront Corporation Staff. 1985. pap. text ed. 24.95 o.p. (ISBN 0-07-912623-5). McGraw.

Framework for Evaluating an Internal Audit Function. Alan S. Glazer & Henry J. Jaenicke. (Illus.). 1980. pap. text ed. 16.00 o.p. (ISBN 0-89413-082-X). Inst Inter Aud.

Framework for II Writers. Frederick Williams. 1985. pap. 15.95 o.p. (ISBN 0-912677-54-6). Tate Pub.

Framework for Political Analysis. David Easton. LC 78-71147. 1979. pap. text ed. 4.50x o.s.i. (ISBN 0-226-18015-8, P834, Phoen). U of Chicago Pr.

Framework II: An Introduction. B. Harrison. 1986. pap. text ed. 15.95 o.p. (ISBN 0-07-912710-X). McGraw.

Framework of Criminal Justice. Michael King. 159p. 1981. 30.00 o.p. (ISBN 0-7099-0430-4, Pub. by Croom Helm Ltd); pap. 11.00 o.p. (ISBN 0-7099-1500-4). Routledge Chapman & Hall.

Framework: On-the-Job Applications. Expert Systems Staff. Ed. by Ashton-Tate Staff. (Framework Books). 300p. 1984. pap. 19.95 incl. disk o.p. (ISBN 0-912677-22-8). Tate-Pub.

Framework: On-the-Job Applications. Expert Systems Staff & ProQuest Staff. 1985. pap. text ed. 19.95 o.p. (ISBN 0-07-912622-7). McGraw.

Framing Feminism: Art & the Women's Movement, 1970-1985. Intro. by Rozsika Parker & Griselda Pollack. 49.95 o.p. (ISBN 0-317-65246-X, Pandora Pr); pap. 15.95 o.p. (ISBN 0-317-65247-8, Pandora Pr). Routledge Chapman & Hall.

Framing the Sign: Criticism & its Institutions. Jonathan Culler. 224p. Date not set. text ed. 49.95 o.p. (ISBN 0-631-15895-2); pap. 14.95 o.p. (ISBN 0-631-15896-0). Basil Blackwell.

Framley Parsonage. Anthony Trollope. 1978. pap. 3.95x o.p. (ISBN 0-460-01181-2, Evman). Biblio Dist.

Francais a Vivre, Learning French the Modern Way, Level 2. 3rd ed. Mary S. Metz & Jo Helstrom. (Illus.). (gr. 10-12). 1972. text ed. 21.00 o.p. (ISBN 0-07-041710-5). McGraw.

Francais: Continuons. Josee P. Okin & Conrad J. Schmitt. (gr. 8-10). 1970. text ed. 21.52 o.p. (ISBN 0-07-047515-6, W). McGraw.

Francaise et la France. Jean Giraudoux. pap. 9.95 o.p. (ISBN 0-685-33913-0). French & Eur.

France. rev. ed. Virginia Creed. LC 77-83911. (World Culture Ser.). (Illus.). 168p. (gr. 6 up). 1978. text ed. 11.20 ea. 1-4 copies o.s.i. (ISBN 0-88296-188-8); text ed. 8.96 ea. 5 or more copies o.s.i.; tchrs'. guide 8.94 o.s.i. (ISBN 0-686-85956-1). Gateway Pr MI.

France. (Self-Guided Ser.). (Illus.). 1989. pap. 12.95 o.p. (ISBN 0-88729-202-X). Langenscheidt.

France. (AA Road Map Ser.). (Illus.). Date not set. (ISBN 0-86145-015-9, Pub. by Auto Assn England). Salem Hse Pubs.

France. F. George Kay. LC 79-89185. (Rand McNally Pocket Guide). (Illus., Orig.). 1980. pap. 5.95 o.p. (ISBN 0-528-84875-5). Rand McNally.

France. Time-Life Books Editors. (Library of Nations). (Illus.). 160p. 1984. 23.93 o.p. (ISBN 0-8094-5304-5). Time-Life.

France: A Cultural Review Grammar. Rebecca M. Valette & Jean P. Valette. (Illus., Orig.). 1973. text ed. 13.95 o.p. (ISBN 0-15-528760-5, HC). HarBraceJ.

France-a Hugo Phrase Book. (Hugo's Language Courses Ser.: No. 560). 96p. 1970. pap. 3.25 o.p. (ISBN 0-8226-0560-0). Littlefield.

France a la Carte. Richard Binns. (Illus.). 144p. 1982. 7.95 o.p. (ISBN 0-89919-106-1). Ticknor & Fields.

France: A Phaidon Cultural Guide. Phaidon Press Limited Staff. (Illus.). 864p. 1985. 16.95 o.p. (ISBN 0-13-330580-5). P-H.

France, a Short History. Albert L. Guerard. 1946. 8.50x o.p. (ISBN 0-393-05229-X, NortonC). Norton.

France Actuelle. rev. ed. Camille Bauer. (Illus.). 1971. text ed. 11.95 o.p. (ISBN 0-395-04150-3, 3-03207). HM.

France: An Applied Geography. J. W. House. (Illus.). 1978. 55.00x o.p. (ISBN 0-416-15080-2, NO. 2243). Routledge Chapman & Hall.

France & Soviet Union. rev. ed. Virginia Creed & W. A. Douglas Jackson. LC 77-83892. (World Cultures Ser.). (Illus.). 298p. (gr. 6 up). 1978. text ed. 12.43 ea. 1-4 copies o.p. (ISBN 0-88296-154-3); text ed. 9.94 ea. 5 or more copies o.p.; tchrs'. guide 8.96 o.p. (ISBN 0-88296-369-4). Gateway Pr MI.

France & the United States: Their Diplomatic Relations, 1789-1914. Henry Blumenthal. 1972. pap. 2.95 o.p. (ISBN 0-393-00625-5, Norton Lib). Norton.

France, Europe & the Two World Wars. Rene Albrecht-Carrie. LC 74-6775. 346p. 1975. Repr. of 1961 ed. lib. bdg. 22.50x o.p. (ISBN 0-8371-7568-2, ALFR). Greenwood.

France, Historic Houses, Castles & Gardens, Open to the Public. Compiled by France, Ministry of Culture Staff. (Illus.). 450p. (Orig.). 1986. pap. 14.95 o.p. (ISBN 2-85822-070-0, Pub. by Ministere de la Culture Paris). Seven Hills Bk Dists.

France in Africa see Tarikh.

France Motorway Atlas. 8th ed. Michelin Guides & Maps Division. pap. 3.95 o.p. (ISBN 2-06-700400-X). Michelin.

France Nineteen Eighty-Seven. Steve Birnbaum. (Illus.). 784p. 1986. pap. 12.70 o.s.i. (ISBN 0-395-42339-2). HM.

France Observed: In the Seventeenth Century by British Travellers. John Lough. (Illus.). 352p. 1985. 79.95x o.p. (ISBN 0-85362-218-3, Oriel). Routledge Chapman & Hall.

France of Louis XIV. W. K. Ritchie. Ed. by Marjorie Reeves. (Then & There Ser.). (Illus.). 96p. (Orig.). (gr. 7-12). 1977. pap. text ed. 4.75 o.p. (ISBN 0-582-20540-9). Longman.

France on the Eve of Revolution: British Travellers' Observations 1763-1788. John Lough. 338p. 1987. text ed. (ISBN 0-534-10678-1); pap. text ed. (ISBN 0-534-10681-1). Wadsworth Pub.

France Reviews: Its Revolutionary Origins. Paul Farmer. 1963. lib. bdg. 16.50x o.p. (ISBN 0-374-92698-0, Octagon). Hippocrene Bks.

France: Ses Grandes Heures Litteraires. Andre Maman et al. (Level 4 or 5). (gr. 9-12). 1968. text ed. 43.95 o.p. (ISBN 0-07-039851-8). McGraw.

France since Nineteen Eighteen. Herbert Tint. 1970. 24.00 o.p. (ISBN 0-7134-3455-4, Pub. by Batsford England); pap. 12.50 o.p. (ISBN 0-7134-3448-1). David & Charles.

France: The Tragic Years. Sisley Huddleston. 297p. Date not set. pap. 5.00 o.p. (ISBN 0-317-53244-8). Noontide.

France Today: Introductory Studies. 5th ed. Ed. by J. E. Flower. 259p. 1983. pap. 10.95x o.p. (ISBN 0-416-35010-0, NO. 4036). Routledge Chapman & Hall.

France, 1985. Steve Birnbaum. (Stephen Birnbaum Travel Guides). 1984. pap. 11.70 o.p. (ISBN 0-395-36524-4). HM.

Frances Farmer: Shadowland. William Arnold. 1984. pap. 3.95 o.s.i. (ISBN 0-425-05761-5). Berkley Pub.

Francexport, 1987-1988. 8th ed. 1236p. 115.00 o.p. (ISBN 0-318-21497-0). Addor.

Franchise. Peter Gent. 576p. 1984. pap. 3.95 o.s.i. (ISBN 0-345-28299-X). Ballantine.

Franchise Affair. Josephine Tey. 1984. pap. 3.95 o.s.i. (ISBN 0-671-50812-1, RE). WSP.

Franchise Opportunities Handbook 1986. 20th ed. Compiled by Andrew Kostecka. 294p. 1986. pap. 15.00 o.p. (S/N 003-008-00201-3). USGPO.

Franchise Option: Expanding Your Business Through Franchises. Henward M. DeBands & William Ginalski. (Illus.). 236p. 1986. write for info. o.p. Intl Franchise Assn.

Franchise Restaurants: A Statistical Appendix to Foodservice Trends. National Restaurant Association Staff. 74p. 1986. pap. 30.00 o.p. (ISBN 0-317-57911-8, CS207). Natl Restaurant Assn.

Franchiser. Stanley Elkin. LC 79-92109. 360p. 1980. pap. 10.95 o.s.i. (ISBN 0-87923-323-0, Nonpareil Bks). Godine.

Franchising in New York. Practising Law Institute Staff & David J. Kaufman. LC 84-137672. (New York Law Course Handbook Ser.: No. 58). write for info. o.p. PLI.

Franchising in New York 1985: Compliance & Strategies for National & Local Franchisors: A Course Handbook. David J. Kaufmann. 460p. 1985. pap. 45.00 o.p. (F4-3709). PLI.

Franchising in the Economy 1985-1987. 16th annual ed. Andrew Kostecka. (Illus.). 101p. 1987. pap. 4.75 o.p. (ISBN 0-318-22620-0, S/N 003-008-00202-1). USGPO.

Franchising in the U. S. Pros & Cons. Michael M. Coltman. 148p. 1982. pap. text ed. 5.95 o.p. (ISBN 0-88908-909-4, 9504). ISC Pr.

Franchising Nineteen Eighty-Seven: Business Strategies & Legal Compliance. David J. Kaufmann. 920p. 1987. 45.00 o.s.i. (ISBN 0-317-66109-4). Intl Franchise Assn.

Francie's Paper Puppy. Achim Broger. LC 83-24987. (Illus.). 28p. (gr. 1 up). 1984. 12.95 o.p. (ISBN 0-907234-56-9). Picture Bk Studio.

Francis Asbury's America: An Album of Early American Methodism. Ed. by Terry O. Bilhartz. LC 83-18275. 128p. 1984. 9.95 o.p. (ISBN 0-310-44790-9); pap. 4.95 o.p. (ISBN 0-310-44791-7, 18275P). Zondervan.

Francis Bacon, Philosopher of Industrial Science. Benjamin Farrington. 1979. Repr. of 1949 ed. lib. bdg. 18.00x o.p. (ISBN 0-374-92706-5, Octagon). Hippocrene Bks.

Francis Bacon: The Early & Middle Years, 1928-1958. Hugh M. Davies. LC 77-94731. (Outstanding Dissertations in the Fine Arts Ser.). 325p. 1978. lib. bdg. 37.00 o.p. (ISBN 0-8240-3224-1). Garland Pub.

Francis Bitter: Selected Papers & Commentaries. Ed. by Thomas Erber & Clarence M. Fowler. 1969. 40.00x o.p. (ISBN 0-262-05006-4). MIT Pr.

Francis: Brother of the Universe. Roy Gasnick. (Illus.). 1.00 o.p. (NCR602). Paulist Pr.

Francis Ford Coppola: A Guide to References & Resources. Joel S. Zuker. 1984. lib. bdg. 43.95 o.s.i. (ISBN 0-8161-8446-1, Hall Reference). G K Hall.

Francis Galton: The Life & Work of a Victorian Genius. D. W. Forrest. LC 74-5819. (Illus.). 280p. 1974. 14.95 o.s.i. (ISBN 0-8008-2682-5). Taplinger.

Francis J. Weber: The Monsignor of the Archives. Doyce B. Nunis, Jr. 35p. 1983. 18.00 o.p. (ISBN 0-317-11642-8). Dawsons.

Francis Joseph & the Italians: 1849-1859. William A. Jenks. LC 78-5727. 1978. 17.95x o.p. (ISBN 0-8139-0758-6). U Pr of Va.

Francis Marion. Cynthia Klingel & Dan Zadra. (We the People Ser.). (Illus.). 32p. PLB 10.45 o.p. Creative Ed.

Francis of Assisi: A Prophet for Our Time. N. Van Doornik. 1978. 8.95 o.p. (ISBN 0-8199-0695-6). Franciscan Herald.

Francis Poulenc. Henri Hell. 118p. Repr. of 1959 ed. lib. bdg. 39.00 o.p. (Pub. by Am Repr Serv). Reprint Servs.

Francis Schaeffer: The Man & His Message. Louis G. Parkhurst, Jr. 288p. 1985. pap. 8.95 o.p. (ISBN 0-8423-0923-3); 12.95 o.p. (ISBN 0-8423-0932-2). Tyndale.

Francis William Edmonds: Mammon & Art. Maybelle Mann. LC 76-23638. (Outstanding Dissertations in the Fine Arts - American). (Illus.). 1977. Repr. of 1972 ed. lib. bdg. 50.00 o.p. (ISBN 0-8240-2708-6). Garland Pub.

Franciscan Cartoons. Wm. Armstrong. (Armstrong Cartoon Ser.). (Illus., Orig.). 1974. pap. 1.00 o.p. (ISBN 0-913452-24-6). Jesuit Bks.

Franciscans & Italian Immigration in America. Leonard Bacigalupo. LC 76-50676. 1977. 4.50 o.p. (ISBN 0-682-48741-4, University). Exposition-Phoenix.

Francisco de Quevedo: La Vida del Buscon Llamado Don Pablos. Francisco De Quevedo & Barry Ife. 1977. 42.00 o.p. (ISBN 0-08-021855-5). Pergamon.

Francisco: Hermano del Universo. Roy Gasnick. (Span.). 1.00 o.p. (NCR458). Paulist Pr.

Francisco Ribalta & His Followers: A Catalogue Raisonne. David M. Kowal. Ed. by S. J. Freedberg. (Outstanding Dissertations in Fine Arts Ser.). (Illus.). 660p. 1985. Repr. of 1981 ed. 75.00 o.p. (ISBN 0-8240-6860-2). Garland Pub.

Francisco Romero on Problems of Philosophy. Marjorie S. Harris. 128p. 1960. (ISBN 0-8022-0685-9). Philos Lib.

Franck. Laurence Davies. (Master Musicians Ser.). (Illus.). 160p. 1975. 17.95x o.p. (ISBN 0-460-03134-1, Pub. by J. M. Dent England). Biblio Dist.

Franco & the Spanish Civil War. L. E. Snellgrove. (Modern Times Ser.). (Illus.). 134p. (Orig.). (gr. 9-12). 1980. pap. text ed. 4.95 o.p. (ISBN 0-582-20422-4). Longman.

Francois Boucher's Early Development As a Draughtsman: 1720-1734. Beverly Schreiber-Jacoby. Ed. by S. J. Freedberg. (Outstanding Dissertations in Fine Arts Ser.). (Illus.). 450p. 1985. Repr. of 1983 ed. 60.00 o.p. (ISBN 0-8240-6875-0). Garland Pub.

Francois Hers: A Tale. Francois Hers & Jean-Francois Chevrier. LC 83-72970. (Illus.). 176p. 1984. 35.00f o.s.i. (ISBN 0-500-54091-8). Thames Hudson.

Francois Maurian. Elsie Pell. (ISBN 0-8022-1960-8). Philos Lib.

Francois Rabelais. Donald M. Frame. LC 76-62519. 1977. 12.95 o.p. (ISBN 0-15-133465-X). HarBraceJ.

Francois X. Aubry. Donald Chaput. (Illus.). 1975. 30.00 o.p. (ISBN 0-87062-110-6). A H Clark.

Franju: Movie Edition. Raymond Durgnat. LC 68-31139. 144p. 1967. pap. 5.95 o.p. (ISBN 0-520-00367-5). U of Cal Pr.

Frank & Christine Zane's Super Bodies in 12 Weeks. Frank Zane & Christine Zane. 1982. 14.95 o.s.i. (ISBN 0-671-42077-1). S&S.

Frank & Ernest. Bob Thaves. 64p. 1983. pap. 3.95 o.p. (ISBN 0-03-063552-7). H Holt & Co.

Frank & Maisie: A Memoir with Parents. Wilfred Sheed. 1985. 17.45 o.p. (ISBN 0-671-44990-7). S&S.

Frank & Maisie: A Memoir with Parents. Wilfrid Sheed. 304p. 1986. pap. 7.95 o.s.i. (ISBN 0-671-62813-5, Touchstone Bks). S&S.

Frank Barr, Bush Pilot in Alaska & the Yukon. Ed. by Dermot Cole. LC 86-3633. (Illus.). pap. 7.95 o.p. (ISBN 0-88240-314-1). Alaska Northwest.

Frank Bridge: Radical & Conservative. Anthony Payne. 96p. 1984. text ed. 15.00x o.p. (ISBN 0-87663-423-4). Universe.

Frank C. Laubach: Teacher of Millions. David Mason. 329p. 1968. 3.50 o.p. (ISBN 0-317-35464-7). New Readers.

Frank Lloyd Wright in Print 1959-1970 see American Association of Architectural Bibliographers' Papers.

Frank Norris: A Literary Legend. S. N. Verma. 241p. 1987. text ed. 27.50x o.p. (ISBN 0-7069-3336-2, Pub. by Vikas Pub Hse India). Advent NY.

Frank O'Hara: A Comprehensive Bibliography. Alexander Smith, Jr. LC 77-83403. (Garland Reference Library of the Humanities: No. 107). 1979. lib. bdg. 48.00 o.p. (ISBN 0-8240-9833-1). Garland Pub.

Frank Sinatra: A Celebration. Derek Jewell. 19.95 o.p. (ISBN 0-316-46304-3). Little.

Frank Sinatra: Ol' Blue Eyes. Associated Press Staff & Norm Goldstein. 1982. pap. 8.95 o.p. (ISBN 0-03-061921-1, Owl Bks). H Holt & Co.

Frank Two Hundred Seven Poems. Raphael Rudnik. LC 81-16914. viii, 61p. 1982. 14.95x o.p. (ISBN 0-8214-0634-5); pap. 7.95 o.p. (ISBN 0-8214-0635-3). Ohio U Pr.

Frank Waters: A Bibliography. Terence A. Tanner. 45.00x o.p. Ohio U Pr.

Frankenstein. Ed. by Richard J. Anobile. (Film Classics Library). (Illus.). 256p. 1974. pap. 5.50 o.p. (ISBN 0-380-01196-4, 19117, Flare). Avon.

Frankenstein. Mary Wollstonecraft Shelley. 1982. pap. 2.95x o.p. (ISBN 0-460-01616-4, Evman). Biblio Dist.

Frankenstein see New Method Supplementary Readers: Bestseller Pack.

Frankenstein: The True Story. Christopher Isherwood & Don Bachardy. 1973. pap. 1.25 o.p. (ISBN 0-380-01197-2, 17970). Avon.

Frankenstein's Aunt. Alan R. Pettersson. 132p. (gr. 3-7). 1982. pap. 2.50 o.p. (ISBN 0-380-60020-X, Camelot). Avon.

Frankie Say: The Rise of Frankie Goes to Hollywood. Danny Jackson. 1985. pap. 6.95 o.p. (ISBN 0-671-60093-1, Pub. by Fireside). S&S.

Frankish Institutions under Charlemagne. Francois L. Ganshof. 1970. pap. 3.95 o.p. (ISBN 0-393-00500-3, Norton Lib). Norton.

Franklin County, Ohio, History. Franklin Co., Chapter OGS Staff & W. I. Martin. 1.50 o.s.i. (ISBN 0-935057-47-1). OH Genealogical.

Franklin Scare. Jerome Charyn. LC 77-79529. 1977. 8.95 o.p. (ISBN 0-87795-167-5, Arbor Hse). Morrow.

Franklin Stein. Ellen Raskin. LC 75-175560. (Illus.). (ps-3). 1972. 5.95 o.p. (ISBN 0-689-30035-2, Atheneum). Macmillan.

Frantz Fanon: A Critical Study. 2nd ed. Irene L. Gendzier. 312p. (Orig.). 1983. pap. 8.95 o.p. (ISBN 0-394-62453-X, E846, Ever). Grove.

Frantz Fanon's Uneven Ribs with Poems More & More. Taban L. Liyong. (African Writers Ser.). 1971. pap. text ed. 6.50 o.p. (ISBN 0-435-90090-0). Heinemann Ed.

Franz Boas Reader: Shaping of American Anthropology, 1883-1911. Franz Boas. Ed. by George W. Stocking. LC 81-21851. xiv, 354p. 1982. pap. text ed. 12.00x o.s.i. (ISBN 0-226-77490-2). U of Chicago Pr.

Franz Kafka of Prague. Date not set. (ISBN 0-8052-0748-1). Random.

Franz Schubert & the Essence of Melody. Hans Gal. 1977. 8.95 o.s.i. (ISBN 0-8008-2992-1, Crescendo). Taplinger.

Fraser of North Cape: The Life of Admiral of the Fleet Lord Fraser, 1888-1981. Richard Humble. LC 83-8723. (Illus.). 386p. 1983. 29.95 o.p. (ISBN 0-7100-9555-4). Routledge Chapman & Hall.

Fratricides. Nikos Kazantzakis. 1985. pap. 7.95 o.s.i. (ISBN 0-671-27221-7, Touchstone Bks). S&S.

Fraudulent Financial Reporting: A Corporate Perspective. Kenneth A. Merchant. LC 87-80813. 83p. (Orig.). 1987. pap. 10.00 o.p. (ISBN 0-317-61825-3). Finan Exec.

Frayn: Plays One. Michael Frayn. (World Dramatists Ser.). 400p. pap. 6.95 o.p. (ISBN 0-317-39293-X, 9809). Routledge Chapman & Hall.

Freak. Michael Collins. 216p. 1983. 10.95 o.p. (ISBN 0-396-08104-5). Dodd.

Freaks, Myths & Images of the Secret Self. Leslie A. Fiedler. (Illus.). 1978. 14.95 o.p. (ISBN 0-671-22505-7). S&S.

Freaks: Myths & Images of the Secret Self. Leslie A. Fiedler. 368p. 1984. pap. 9.95 o.p. (ISBN 0-671-24847-2, Touchstone Bks). S&S.

Freaks of Fanaticism & Other Strange Events. Sabine Baring-Gould. LC 68-21754. 284p. 1968. Repr. of 1891 ed. 40.00x o.p. (ISBN 0-8103-3503-4). Gale.

Freaky Facts. Louis Phillips. (Funnybones Ser.). (Illus.). 64p. 1981. pap. 1.50 o.s.i. (ISBN 0-671-42247-2). Wanderer Bks.

Freddie Freightliner Goes to Hawaii. David L. George. Ed. by Carol Murphy. (Illus.). (gr. k-6). 1983. 6.50 o.p. (ISBN 0-89868-136-7); pap. 3.95 o.p. (ISBN 0-89868-137-5). ARO PUB.

Freddie Freightliner Goes to Hollywood. David L. George. Ed. by Carol Murphy. (Illus.). (gr. k-6). 1982. 6.50 o.p.; pap. 3.95 o.p. (ISBN 0-686-91784-7). ARO Pub.

Freddie Freightliner Goes to Kennedy Space Center. David L. George. Ed. by Carol Murphy. (Illus.). (gr. k-6). 1982. 5.95 o.p.; pap. 6.50 o.p. (ISBN 0-89868-133-2). ARO PUB.

Freddie Freightliner Helps the Fire Department. David L. George. Ed. by Carol Murphy. (Illus.). (gr. k-6). 1983. 6.50 o.p.; pap. 3.95 o.p. (ISBN 0-89868-135-9). ARO PUB.

Freddie Freightliner Learns to Talk. David L. George. Ed. by Carol Murphy. (Illus.). (gr. k-6). 1981. 6.50 o.p. (ISBN 0-89868-126-X); pap. 3.95 o.p. (ISBN 0-89868-127-8). ARO PUB.

Freddie Freightliner Series. David L. George. Ed. by Carol Murphy. (Illus.). (gr. k-6). 35.00 set o.p. (ISBN 0-89868-124-3); pap. 23.00 set o.p. (ISBN 0-89868-125-1). ARO PUB.

Freddie Freightliner to the Rescue. David L. George. Ed. by Carol Murphy. (Illus.). (gr. k-6). 1982. 6.50 o.p.; pap. 3.95 o.p. (ISBN 0-89868-131-6). ARO PUB.

Freddus Elephantus et Horatius Porcus Saltans Cincinnatis. Edvardus C. Echols. 129p. (Orig., Lat.). (gr. 10-11). 1980. pap. text ed. 4.95x o.p. (ISBN 0-88334-139-5). Ind Sch Pr.

Freddy's Book. John Neufeld. (gr. 2-7). 1976. pap. 1.75 o.p. (ISBN 0-380-00203-5, 53298-0, Camelot). Avon.

Frederic Harrison. Harry R. Sullivan. (English Authors Ser.). 1983. lib. bdg. 21.95 o.s.i. (ISBN 0-8057-6827-0, Twayne). G K Hall.

Frederic Joliot-Curie. Maurice Goldsmith. 1976. text ed. 17.50x o.p. (ISBN 0-85315-342-6). Humanities.

Frederic Remington: An Essay & Catalog to Accompany a Retrospective Exhibition. Peter H. Hassrick. LC 72-96833. (Illus.). 48p. 1973. pap. 3.00 o.p. (ISBN 0-88360-021-8, Dist by Univ. of Texas Pr). Amon Carter.

Frederic Remington & the West: With the Eye of the Mind. Ben M. Vorpahl. LC 77-25953. (Illus.). 312p. 1978. 17.95 o.p. (ISBN 0-292-78703-0). U of Tex Pr.

Frederic Remington, the Camera & the Old West. Estelle Jussim. LC 82-71186. (Anne Burnett Tandy Lectures in American Civilization: No. 3). (Illus.). 112p. 1983. 19.95 o.p. (ISBN 0-88360-044-7); pap. 10.95 o.p. (ISBN 0-88360-047-1). Amon Carter.

Frederic William Maitland & the History of English Law. James R. Cameron. LC 77-677. (Illus.). xvi, 214p. 1977. Repr. of 1961 ed. lib. bdg. 22.50x o.p. (ISBN 0-8371-9499-7, CAFWM). Greenwood.

Frederica Fare. Compiled by Parent's Association of Frederica Academy Staff. 8.95 o.p. (ISBN 0-918544-86-6). Wimmer Bks.

Frederick Denison Maurice: Rebellious Conformist, 1805-1872. Olive J. Brose. LC 74-141380. xxiii, 308p. 1971. 16.00x o.p. (ISBN 0-8214-0092-4). Ohio U Pr.

Frederick Douglass. Benjamin Quarles. LC 68-16416. (Studies in American Negro Life). (Illus.). 1968. pap. text ed. 4.95x o.p. (ISBN 0-689-70162-4, NL4, Atheneum). Macmillan.

Frederick Douglass, Great Abolitionist. Ida S. Meltzer. Ed. by Nestina Thomas. (American Destiny Ser.: Black Americans). (Illus.). 32p. (Orig.). (gr. 4-12). 1972. pap. text ed. 12.95 set of ten o.p. (ISBN 0-87594-174-5). Book-Lab.

Frederick II of Hohenstaufen. Georgina Masson. 1973. lib. bdg. 24.00x o.p. (ISBN 0-374-95297-3, Octagon). Hippocrene Bks.

Frederick Law Olmstead, Sr. Founder of Landscape Architecture. Julius G. Fabos et al. Date not set. price not set o.p. U of Mass Pr.

Frederick Law Olmsted & the American Environmental Tradition. Albert Fein. LC 72-75831. (Planning & Cities Ser.). (Illus.). 160p. 1972. 10.00 o.p. (ISBN 0-8076-0650-2); pap. 7.95 o.p. (ISBN 0-8076-0649-9). Braziller.

Frederick M. Watkins Collection see Exhibition Catalogues from the Fogg Art Museum.

Frederick the Great: The Magnificent Enigma. Robert B. Asprey. (Illus.). 656p. 1986. 29.45 o.p. (ISBN 0-89919-352-8). Ticknor & Fields.

Frederick Wiseman: A Guide to References & Resources. Liz Ellsworth. 1979. lib. bdg. 32.50 o.p. (ISBN 0-8161-8066-0, Hall Reference). G K Hall.

Fred's First Day. Cathy Warren. LC 83-25153. (Illus.). 32p. (gr. k up). 1984. 12.00 o.p. (ISBN 0-688-03813-1); PLB 11.04 o.p. (ISBN 0-688-03814-X). Lothrop.

Fred's Pyramid. Stewart Moskowitz. Ed. by Kate Klimo. (Moskowitz Bks.). (Illus.). 32p. 1983. pap. 4.80 o.s.i. (ISBN 0-671-44563-4, Little Simon). S&S.

Fred's Pyramid. Stewart Moskowitz. LC 82-7910. (Illus.). 32p. (gr. k-3). 1982. lib. bdg. 7.97 o.s.i. (ISBN 0-671-45889-2). Messner.

Free & Ennobled: Source Readings in the Development of Victorian Feminism. Ed. by Carol Bauer & Lawrence Ritt. (Illus.). 1979. 59.00 o.p. (ISBN 0-08-022272-2); pap. 26.00 o.p. (ISBN 0-08-022271-4). Pergamon.

Free & Equal Cookbook. Carole Kruppa. LC 85-2626. (Illus.). 128p. (Orig.). 1985. pap. 5.95 o.p. (ISBN 0-9609516-5-2, Dist. by Publishers Group). Surrey Bks.

Free Black Heads of Households in the New York State Federal Census, 1790 to 1830. Ed. by Alice Eichholz & James M. Rose. (Genealogy & Local History Ser.: Vol. 14). 336p. 68.00x o.p. (ISBN 0-8103-1468-1). Gale.

Free City of Krakow. William H. Keith, Jr. (Twilight: 2000 Ser.). (Illus.). 49p. (Orig.). 1985. pap. 7.00 o.s.i. (ISBN 0-943580-51-X). Game Designers.

Free Discussion of the Doctrine of Materialism and Philosophical Necessity, 1778. Richard Price. Ed. by Rene Wellek. LC 75-11247. (British Philosophers & Theologians of the 17th & 18th Centuries Ser.). 1978. lib. bdg. 51.00 o.p. (ISBN 0-8240-1798-6). Garland Pub.

Free Enquirer, 10 vols. Incl. Series 1, Vol. 1. lib. bdg. 28.00 (ISBN 0-313-21624-X, FE11); Series 1, Vol. 2. lib. bdg. 28.00 (ISBN 0-313-21625-8, FE12); Series 1, Vol. 3. lib. bdg. 28.00 (ISBN 0-313-21626-6, FE13); Series 2, Vol. 1. lib. bdg. 28.00 (ISBN 0-313-21627-4, FE21); Series 2, Vol. 2. lib. bdg. 28.00 (ISBN 0-313-21628-2, FE22); Series 2, Vol. 3. lib. bdg. 28.00 (ISBN 0-313-21629-0, FE23); Series 2, Vol. 4. lib. bdg. 28.00 (ISBN 0-313-21630-4, FE24); Series 2, Vol. 5. lib. bdg. 28.00 (ISBN 0-313-21631-2, FE25); Series 3, Vol. 1. lib. bdg. 28.00 (ISBN 0-313-21632-0, FE31); Series 3, Vol. 2. lib. bdg. 28.00 (ISBN 0-313-21633-9, FE32). 1969. Repr. of 1835 ed. Set. lib. bdg. 250.00x o.p. (ISBN 0-8371-9172-6, FE00). Greenwood.

Free Enterprise, Fair Employment. Elliott Jaques. LC 82-8038. 200p. cancelled o.s.i. (ISBN 0-8448-1417-2, Pub. by cRane Russak & Co). Taylor & Francis.

Free Fall in Crimson. John D. MacDonald. 288p. 1985. pap. 3.50 o.p. (ISBN 0-449-12894-6, GM). Fawcett.

Free Fire Zone. Rob Riggan. LC 83-42649. 416p. 1984. 15.45 o.p. (ISBN 0-393-01800-8). Norton.

Free Flight. Douglas C. Terman. 1980. 11.95 o.p. (ISBN 0-684-16723-9). Scribner.

Free Grass. Ernest Haycox. 333p. 1986. lib. bdg. 14.95x o.p. (ISBN 0-8161-3882-6, Large Print Bks). G K Hall.

Free Lance. George Shipway. LC 75-2379. 304p. 1975. 7.95 o.p. (ISBN 0-15-133476-5). HarBraceJ.

Free Like a Dream. Robert C. Sluzis. 1977. 4.50 o.p. (ISBN 0-682-48893-3). Exposition-Phoenix.

Free Magazines for Libraries. Adeline M. Smith. LC 80-15557. 280p. 1980. lib. bdg. 17.95x o.p. (ISBN 0-89950-021-8). McFarland & Co.

Free Man of Color: The Autobiography of Willis Augustus Hodges. Ed. by Willard B. Gatewood. LC 82-2032. (Illus.). 168p. 1982. text ed. 17.95x o.p. (ISBN 0-87049-353-1). U of Tenn Pr.

Free Men All: The Personal Liberty Laws of the North, 1780-1861. Thomas D. Morris. LC 73-8126. 265p. 1974. 27.50x o.p. (ISBN 0-8018-1505-3). Johns Hopkins.

Free Negro Labor & Property Holding in Virginia, 1830-1860. Luther P. Jackson. LC 69-15524. (Studies in American Negro Life Ser). 1969. pap. 3.45 o.s.i. (ISBN 0-689-70107-1, NL15, Atheneum). Macmillan.

Free Not to Love. Anne Emery. LC 74-20764. (gr. 7 up). 1975. 5.75 o.s.i. (ISBN 0-664-32563-7, Westminster). Westminster John Knox.

Free Order: National Goal & World Goal. Hamilton Hadley. 523p. 1973. Repr. of 1963 ed. lib. bdg. 35.00 o.p. (ISBN 0-8371-6582-2, HAFO). Greenwood.

Free Radical Telomerization. Charles Starks. 1974. 72.50 o.p. (ISBN 0-12-663650-8). Acad Pr.

Free Speech in the Church. Karl Rahner. LC 79-8717. Orig. Title: Freie Wort in der Kirche. 112p. 1981. Repr. of 1959 ed. lib. bdg. 35.00x o.p. (ISBN 0-313-20849-2, RAFS). Greenwood.

Free Stuff for Kids. 9th, rev. ed. Free Stuff Editors. LC 81-2416. (Illus.). 120p. pap. 3.50 o.p. (ISBN 0-671-60569-0). Meadowbrook.

Free the North Wind. Frank Driskill. 1980. 11.95 o.p. (ISBN 0-89015-237-3). Eakin Pr.

Free Things for Teachers. Susan Osborn. LC 81-17844. (Free Things! A Bargain Hunter's Bonanza Ser.). 128p. 1982. pap. 4.95 o.p. (ISBN 0-399-50606-3, Perigee). Putnam Pub Group.

Free to Be... You & Me. Marlo Thomas et al. LC 73-14784. (Illus.). 144p. 1974. text ed. 12.95 o.p. (ISBN 0-07-064223-0); pap. text ed. 9.95 o.p. (ISBN 0-07-064224-9). McGraw.

Free to Choose: A Personal Statement. Milton Friedman & Rose Friedman. 352p. 1985. pap. 7.95 o.p. (ISBN 0-380-69879-X). Avon.

Free Trade & Protection in Germany, 1868-79. Ivo N. Lambi. 267p. (Orig.). 1963. pap. text ed. 46.50x o.p. (ISBN 3-515-00304-5, Pub. by Franz Steiner). Coronet Bks.

Free Trade in Ideas: A Constitutional Imperative. (ACLU Public Policy Reports). 1984. pap. 2.50 o.p. (ISBN 0-86566-035-2). Ctr Natl Security.

Free Verse: An Essay on Prosody. Charles O. Hartman. LC 80-10782. 216p. 1986. text ed. 25.00 o.s.i. (ISBN 0-691-10185-X); pap. 12.50 o.s.i. Princeton U Pr.

Free Will: A Defence Against Neuro-Physiological Determinism. John Thorp. (International Library of Philosophy). 208p. 1980. 20.00x o.p. (ISBN 0-7100-0565-2). Routledge Chapman & Hall.

Free World & Free Trade. Harry S. Truman. LC 63-21185. 36p. 1963. boxed 8.95x o.p. (ISBN 0-87074-117-9). SMU Press.

Free Yourself from Pain. David E. Bresler & Richard Trubo. 1979. 15.95 o.p. (ISBN 0-671-24071-4). S&S.

Free Yourself from Pain. David E. Bresler & Richard Trubo. 1986. pap. 10.95 o.s.i. (ISBN 0-671-62334-6, Fireside). S&S.

Freedom: An Anarchist Monthly, 2 vols, No. 4. 1970. Repr. of 1934 ed. Set. lib. bdg. 39.00x o.p. (ISBN 0-8371-9173-4, FD00). Greenwood.

Freedom & Authority: A Study of English Thought in the Early Seventeenth Century. Gerald R. Cragg. LC 75-4946. 1975. 15.00 o.s.i. (ISBN 0-664-20738-3, Westminster). Westminster John Knox.

Freedom & Authority in Our Time: Proceeding. Conference on Science-Philosophy & Religion in Their Relation to the Democratic Way of Live, 12th, New York. 1953. 56.00 o.p. (ISBN 0-527-00659-9). Kraus Repr.

Freedom & Determinism. Ed. by Keith Lehrer. 204p. 1976. pap. text ed. 19.95x o.p. (ISBN 0-391-00537-5). Humanities.

Freedom & Growth in Marriage. 2nd ed. James L. McCary. LC 79-17199. 498p. 1980. write for info. o.p. (ISBN 0-02-379040-7); write for info. tchrs' manual o.p. (ISBN 0-02-379050-4). Macmillan.

Freedom & History. Hywel D. Lewis. 1962. text ed. 17.50x o.p. (ISBN 0-04-323007-5). Humanities.

Freedom & Plenty: Ours to Save. Wilfrid S. Bronson. LC 52-13252. (gr. 1-5). 1953. 5.25 o.p. (ISBN 0-15-229498-8, HJ). HarBraceJ.

Freedom & Resentment & Other Essays. P. F. Strawson. 220p. 1976. pap. 12.95 o.p. (ISBN 0-416-63430-3, NO. 2534). Routledge Chapman & Hall.

Freedom & Stability in the World Economy. D. Evans & R. Body. 128p. 1976. 15.00 o.p. (ISBN 0-85664-119-7, Pub. by Croom Helm Ltd). Routledge Chapman & Hall.

Freedom Condemned. Jean-Paul Sartre. LC 60-13659. 160p. 1960. (ISBN 0-8022-1491-6). Philos Lib.

Freedom, Equality & the Market: Arguments on Social Policy. Barry Hindess. 170p. 1987. text ed. 39.95 o.p. (ISBN 0-422-79470-8, 1149, Pub. by Tavistock England); pap. text ed. 12.95 o.p. (ISBN 0-422-79480-5, 1176). Routledge Chapman & Hall.

Freedom Fighter's Manual. Central Intelligence Agency Staff. (Illus.). 16p. (Orig., Eng. & Span.). 1984. pap. 2.00 o.p. (ISBN 0-394-62035-6, Ever). Grove.

Freedom For the Gods. Henry Johnsen. 40p. 1986. 6.50 o.p. (ISBN 0-8062-2837-7). Carlton.

Freedom Force. Tom De Haven. (U. S. A. Ser.). 1987. (Flare). Avon.

Freedom from Bad Habits. Charles Cerling. LC 84-62384. 141p. (Orig.). 1984. pap. 5.95 o.p. (ISBN 0-89840-079-1). Heres Life.

Freedom Inside the Organization: Bringing Civil Liberties to the Workplace. David W. Ewing. 1978. pap. text ed. 4.95 o.p. (ISBN 0-07-019847-0). McGraw.

Freedom Is an Inside Job. Vera Channels & Mary Vestermark. LC 77-15745. 1978. 5.95 o.p. (ISBN 0-8042-2060-3, John Knox). Westminster John Knox.

Freedom: Its History, Nature & Varieties. Robert E. Dewey & James A. Gould. 1970. pap. text ed. write for info. o.p. (ISBN 0-02-329500-7, 32950). Macmillan.

Freedom Now. Francine Klagsbrun. LC 72-2757. (Illus.). 240p. (gr. 5 up). 1972. 6.95 o.p. (ISBN 0-395-14326-8). HM.

Freedom of Forgiveness. David Augsburger. 128p. 1973. pap. 3.95 o.p. (ISBN 0-8024-2875-4). Moody.

Freedom of Obedience. Martha Thatcher. (Christian Character Library). 179p. 1986. hdbk. 8.95 o.p. (ISBN 0-89109-541-1). NavPress.

Freedom of the News Media. Olga G. Hoyt & Edwin P. Hoyt. LC 72-93809. 192p. (gr. 6 up). 1979. 6.95 o.p. (ISBN 0-395-28910-6, Clarion). HM.

Freedom of the Press & Fair Trial: Final Report with Recommendations. Association of the Bar of the City of New York Staff & H. R. Medina. LC 67-15897. 99p. 1967. 21.50x o.p. (ISBN 0-231-03054-1). Columbia U Pr.

Freedom or Death. Nikos Kazantzakis. 320p. 1983. pap. 8.50 o.s.i. (ISBN 0-671-49260-8, Touchstone). S&S.

Freedom Plays the Flute: A Selection from the Folk Poetry of Modern Greece. Carrie C. Dulakis. 144p. 1982. 7.50 o.p. (ISBN 0-682-49867-X). Exposition-Phoenix.

Freedom Road: 1944-1945. Richard Collier. LC 83-45066. (Illus.). 336p. (Orig.). 1984. 17.95 o.p. (ISBN 0-689-11392-7, Atheneum). Macmillan.

Freedom to Live. Ernest Holmes. Ed. by Willis H. Kinnear. 96p. 1969. pap. 4.50 o.p. (ISBN 0-911336-35-4). Sci of Mind.

Titles

Freedom under Planning. Barbara Wooton. LC 78-9994. 1979. Repr. of 1945 ed. lib. bdg. 35.00 o.p. (ISBN 0-313-21099-3, WOFU). Greenwood.
Freedom Versus Organization: 1814-1914. Bertrand Russell. 1962. pap. 5.95 o.p. (ISBN 0-393-00136-9, Norton Lib). Norton.
Freedom with Justice: Catholic Social Thought & Liberal Institutions. Michael Novak. LC 84-47731. 272p. 1984. 17.45 o.p. (ISBN 0-06-066317-0). HarpR.
Freedom Within: The Prison Notes of Stefan Cardinal Wyszynski. Stefan Wyszynski. Tr. by Barbara Krzywick-Herburt & Walter Ziemba. LC 83-12878. (Illus.). 384p. 1984. 16.95 o.p. (ISBN 0-15-133466-8). HarBraceJ.
Freedom's First Generation: Black Hampton, Virginia, 1861-1890. Robert F. Engs. LC 79-5046. (Illus.). 1980. 13.95x o.p. (ISBN 0-8122-7768-6). U of Pa Pr.
Freedom's Holy Light: Like the Country She Symbolizes, She Stands Tall & Proud, Upholding... Richard H. Schneider. (Illus.). 128p. 1985. 14.95 o.p. (ISBN 0-8407-5497-3). Nelson.
Freedom's Thunder. Michael Foster. 1976. pap. 1.95 o.p. (ISBN 0-380-00660-X, 29058). Avon.
Freelance Jobs for Writers. Ed. by Kirk Polking. LC 80-16070. 280p. 1984. pap. 8.95 o.p. (ISBN 0-89879-142-1). Writers Digest.
Freelance Pallbearers. Ishmael Reed. 1977. pap. 1.75 o.p. (ISBN 0-380-00987-0, 32649-3, Bard). Avon.
Freelance Pallbearers. Ishmael Reed. 155p. 1975. Repr. of 1967 ed. 7.50x o.p. (ISBN 0-911860-46-0). Chatham Bkseller.
Freelance Photographer's Handbook. Frederik D. Bodin. (Illus.). 160p. 1981. pap. text ed. 14.95 o.p. (ISBN 0-240-51761-X). Focal Pr.
Freelon Starbird. Richard F. Snow. LC 75-43901. (Illus.). 240p. (gr. 7 up). 1976. 7.95 o.p. (ISBN 0-395-24275-4). HM.
Freely Chosen Reality. Ralph A. Powell. LC 82-21943. 194p. (Orig.). 1983. lib. bdg. 28.50 o.p. (ISBN 0-8191-2924-0); pap. text ed. 12.50 o.p. (ISBN 0-8191-2925-9). U Pr of Amer.
Freemasonry Through Six Centuries, 2 vols. Henry W. Coil. 600p. 1976. Repr. of 1966 ed. text ed. 27.50 slipcase o.p. (ISBN 0-88053-034-0, M 083). Macoy Pub.
Freemason's Pocket Reference Book. Fred L. Pick & Norman Knight. 304p. 1956. (ISBN 0-8022-1971-3). Philos Lib.
Freer Gallery of Art, Washington D. C. John A. Pope et al. LC 80-82645. (Oriental Ceramics Ser.: Vol. 9). (Illus.). 180p. 1981. 65.00 o.p. (ISBN 0-87011-448-4). Kodansha.
Freer Gallery of Art, Washington DC see Oriental Ceramics: The World's Great Collections.
Freestyle Windsurfing with Gary Eversole. Roger Jones. LC 82-48931. (Illus., Orig.). 1983. pap. 10.95 o.p. (ISBN 0-06-250725-7, CN4061). HarpR.
Freethinkers Handbook. Joan Stein. 208p. 1982. 7.95 o.p. (ISBN 0-917802-07-1). Theoscience Found.
Freeway Entry, Flow & Control: Ten Reports. (Transportation Research Report Ser.). 69p. 1975. 5.60 o.p. (ISBN 0-309-02384-X). Transport Res Bd.
Freeways. Vina Delmar. LC 70-153685. 256p. 1971. 5.95 o.p. (ISBN 0-15-133485-4). HarBraceJ.
Freeways, Automatic Vehicle Identification & Effects of Geometrics. (Transportation Research Report Ser.). 85p. 1976. 3.80 o.p. (ISBN 0-309-02570-2). Transport Res Bd.
Freezer to Oven to Table. Ceil Dyer. LC 75-31075. 224p. 1976. 9.95 o.p. (ISBN 0-87795-128-4, Arbor Hse); pap. 3.95 o.p. (ISBN 0-87795-134-9). Morrow.
Frege & Godel: Two Fundamental Texts in Mathematical Logic. abr. ed. Jean Van Heijenoort. LC 71-116736. 1970. 11.00x o.p. (ISBN 0-674-31844-7); pap. 7.95x o.p. (ISBN 0-674-31845-5). Harvard U Pr.
Frege Philosophy of Language. Michael Dummett. LC 80-29692. 752p. 1981. text ed. 42.00x o.s.i. (ISBN 0-674-31930-3). Harvard U Pr.
Frei Otto: A Bibliography & Building List. Edward H. Teague. (Architecture Ser.: A 1452). 6p. 1985. 2.00 o.p. (ISBN 0-89028-542-X). Vance Biblios.
Freie Wort in der Kirche see Free Speech in the Church.
Freight Transportation Characteristics. (Transportation Research Report Ser.). 50p. 1976. 2.80 o.p. (ISBN 0-309-02560-5). Transport Res Bd.
Fremde Am Fluss. Paul Twitchell. 1979. pap. 5.95 o.p. Illum Way Pub.
Fremont Cannon: High Up & Far Back. Ernest A. Lewis. LC 80-69260. (Frontier Military Ser.: No. XI). (Illus.). 168p. 1981. 32.50 o.p. (ISBN 0-87062-138-6). A H Clark.
French. W. Maureen Miller. 640p. (Orig.). 1983. pap. 3.95 o.p. (ISBN 0-440-02737-3, Emerald). Dell.
French Academies of the Sixteenth Century. Frances A. Yates. (Warburg Institute Studies: Vol. 15). Repr. of 1948 ed. 44.00 o.p. (ISBN 0-8115-1391-2). Kraus Repr.
French Affair. Marion Chesney. (Nightingales Ser.). 298p. 1987. pap. 11.95x o.p. (ISBN 0-8161-4185-1, Large Print Bks.). G K Hall.
French Art & Music since Fifteen Hundred. Anthony Blunt & Edward Lockspeiser. 1974. pap. 5.95x o.p. (ISBN 0-416-81650-9, NO. 2095). Routledge Chapman & Hall.
French Atlantic Affair. Ernest Lehman. LC 77-5199. 1977. 10.95 o.p. (ISBN 0-689-10803-6, Atheneum). Macmillan.
French Baroque Music. James R. Anthony. (Illus.). 468p. 1981. pap. 8.95 o.p. (ISBN 0-393-00967-X). Norton.
French Baroque Music. James R. Anthony. (Illus.). 1973. 20.00x o.p. (ISBN 0-393-02173-4). Norton.
French Baroque Music: From Beaujoyeulx to Rameau. James R. Anthony. 1978. 22.50x o.p. (ISBN 0-393-02198-X). Norton.
French-Canadian Idea of Confederation, Eighteen Sixty-Four to Nineteen Hundred. A. I. Silver. 280p. 1981. o. p. 32.50x o.p. (ISBN 0-8020-5557-5); pap. 12.95c o.p. (ISBN 0-8020-6441-8). U of Toronto Pr.
French Cat. Sine. 160p. 1982. pap. 2.40 o.p. (ISBN 0-671-45693-8, Fireside). S&S.
French Cinema of the Occupation & Resistance: The Birth of a Critical Esthetic. Andre Bazin. Tr. by Stanley Hochman. 174p. 1984. pap. 8.95 o.p. (ISBN 0-8044-6024-8). Ungar.
French Clocks the World Over: Part 1-From Their Beginnings to the Louis XV-Louis XVI Transition Period. English ed. Tardy. Tr. by Alexander Ballantyne. (Illus.). 356p. 1981. 85.00 o.s.i. (ISBN 0-911403-03-5, 2390179, Pub. by Tardy FR). Seven Hills Bk Dists.
French Clocks the World Over: Part 2-From Louis XVI Style to Louis XVIII-Charles X Period. English ed. Tardy. Tr. by Alexander Ballantyne. (Illus.). 392p. 1981. 85.00 o.s.i. (ISBN 0-911403-24-8, 2930189, Pub. by Tardy FR). Seven Hills Bk Dists.
French Clocks, the World Over: Part 3. English ed. Tardy. Tr. by Alexander Ballantyne. (Illus.). 524p. 1982. 105.00 o.s.i. (ISBN 2-901622-00-3, 2390199, Pub. by Tardy FR). Seven Hills Bk Dists.
French Collection, 1980. 433p. 1980. pap. 20.00 o.p. (ISBN 0-940764-28-8). U of Utah Pr.
French Colonial Lobby, 1889-1938. Stuart M. Persell. (Publication Ser.: No. 283). 184p. 1983. 24.95x o.p. (ISBN 0-8179-7831-3). Hoover Inst Pr.
French Company Handbook 1988. 192p. 1988. 56.00 o.p. (ISBN 2-905437-03-0). Addor.
French Cooking for the People Who Can't. Julia Hayes. LC 78-53800. (Illus.). 1979. 11.95 o.p. (ISBN 0-689-10914-8, Atheneum). Macmillan.
French Cooking Simplified with a Food Processor. Ruth Howse. LC 77-13150. (Illus.). 1977. pap. 5.95 o.s.i. (ISBN 0-89286-129-0, One Hund One Prods). Ortho.
French Country Favorites. Bon Appetit Magazine Editors. (Cooking with Bon Appetit Ser.). 1987. 12.95 o.p. (ISBN 0-89535-181-1). Knapp Pr.
French Country Inns & Chateau Hotels. 3rd rev. ed. Karen Brown. (Karen Brown's Country Inns Travel Guide Ser.). (Illus.). 288p. (Orig.). 1985. pap. 9.95 o.p. (ISBN 0-930328-09-4). Travel Pr.
French Country Inns & Chateau Hotels. 2nd ed. Karen A. Brown. LC 77-32024. (Illus., Orig.). 1982. pap. 9.95 o.p. (ISBN 0-930328-03-5). Travel Pr.
French Country Inns & Chateau Hotels see French Country Inns & Chateaux.
French Country Inns & Chateaux. rev. 4th ed. Karen Brown. LC 85-51930. (Karen Brown's: European Country Inns Ser.). Orig. Title: French Country Inns & Chateau Hotels. (Illus.). 288p. 1986. pap. 10.95 o.p. (ISBN 0-930328-15-9). Travel Pr.
French Country Welcome. (Nineteen Eighty-Seven Travel Guides Ser.). 1987. pap. 11.95 o.p. (ISBN 2-904394-23-0). Faber & Faber.
French Diplomacy in the Caribbean & the American Revolution. R. John Singh. 1977. 10.00 o.p. (ISBN 0-682-48891-7, University). Exposition-Phoenix.
French Economic Planning. John S. Harlow. 104p. 1966. 9.00x o.p. (ISBN 0-87745-010-2); pap. 4.95x o.p. (ISBN 0-87745-011-0). U of Iowa Pr.
French-English Chemical Terminology: An Introduction to Chemistry in French & English. Hans Fromherz & Alexander King. 561p. (Fr. & Eng.). 1968. 46.30x o.p. (ISBN 3-527-25095-6). VCH Pubs.
French-English Science & Technology Dictionary. 4th ed. Louis DeVries & Stanley Hochman. (Fr. & Eng.). 1976. text ed. 46.10 o.p. (ISBN 0-07-016629-3). McGraw.
French Ensor Chadwick: Selected Letters & Papers. Doris D. Maguire. LC 81-40169. 656p. (Orig.). 1982. lib. bdg. 41.50 o.p. (ISBN 0-8191-1923-7); pap. text ed. 28.25 o.p. (ISBN 0-8191-1924-5). U Pr of Amer.
French False Friends. C. W. E. Kirk-Greene. 272p. 1981. 14.95 o.p. (ISBN 0-7100-0741-8). Routledge Chapman & Hall.
French Farm & Village Holiday Guide. Duo Publishing Staff. 1986. pap. 12.95 o.p. (ISBN 0-906318-14-9). Bradt Ent.
French Farm & Village Holiday Guide. (Illus.). 384p. (Orig.). 1987. pap. 12.95 o.p. (ISBN 0-935161-96-1). Hunter Pub NY.
French Farm & Village Holiday Guide 1988. (Illus.). 384p. (Orig.). 1988. pap. 12.95 o.p. (ISBN 1-55650-015-7). Hunter Pub NY.
French Faust: Henri De Saint Simon. Mathurian Dondo. 260p. 1956. (ISBN 0-8022-0410-4). Philos Lib.
French Five Hundred. William G. Sibley. 120p. 1968. pap. 2.50 o.s.i. (ISBN 0-318-00861-0). Ohio Hist Soc.
French for English Idioms & Figurative Phrases. J. O. Kettridge. (Fr. & Eng.). 1966. Repr. of 1940 ed. 16.00 o.p. (ISBN 0-7100-1669-7). Routledge Chapman & Hall.
French for Oral Written Review. 3rd ed. Charles Carlut & Walter Meiden. 1983. text ed. 19.95 o.p. (ISBN 0-03-062318-9); practice manual 11.95 o.p. (ISBN 0-03-062319-7); tapes 180.00 o.p. (ISBN 0-03-062321-9). HR&W.
French for Spanish Travellers. Berlitz Editors. 1977. pap. 4.95 o.p. (ISBN 0-02-966610-4, Berlitz). Macmillan.
French Foreign Legion Mines & Booby Traps. French Foreign Legion Staff. (Illus.). 120p. (Orig.). 1985. pap. 12.00 o.p. (ISBN 0-87364-344-5). Paladin Pr.
French Foreign Legion: Nineteen-Forty to the Present. Yves L. Cadiou & Tibor Szecske. (Uniforms Illustrated Ser.: No. 15). (Illus.). 72p. (Orig.). 1986. pap. 9.95 o.p. (ISBN 0-85368-806-0, Pub. by Arms & Armour). Sterling.
French Foreign Legion: The Inside Story of the World Famous Fighting Force. John R. Young. LC 84-50777. (Illus.). 212p. 1984. 35.00 o.p. (ISBN 0-500-01342-X). Thames Hudson.
French Founders of North America & Their Heritage. Sabra Holbrook. LC 75-13574. 272p. (YA) 1976. 7.95 o.p. (ISBN 0-689-30490-0, Atheneum). Macmillan.
French History & Society: The Wars of Religion to the Fifth Republic. Roger S. Mettam & Douglas Johnson. LC 75-2861. 168p. 1974. pap. 6.95x o.p. (ISBN 0-416-81620-7, NO. 2317). Routledge Chapman & Hall.
French Horn. 2nd ed. R. Morley-Pegge. (Illus.). 222p. 1973. 13.95x o.p. (ISBN 0-393-02171-8). Norton.
French Horn. R. Morley-Pegge. (Illus.). 194p. 1960. (ISBN 0-8022-1151-8). Philos Lib.
French Huguenots. Janet G. Gray. LC 81-67172. 200p. (Orig.). 1981. pap. 8.95 o.p. (ISBN 0-8010-3758-1). Baker Bk.
French Idioms & Figurative Phrases: With Many Quotations. J. O. Kettridge. 1970. Repr. of 1949 ed. 18.00 o.p. (ISBN 0-7100-1668-9). Routledge Chapman & Hall.
French in Review. 2nd ed. Rene Daudon. 433p. 1962. text ed. 17.00 o.p. (ISBN 0-15-528850-4, HC, HC). HarBraceJ.
French: Language & Life Styles. Diane Butturff & Mary E. Coffman. (Illus.). 512p. 1975. text ed. 30.95 o.p. (ISBN 0-07-009455-1, C). McGraw.
French Leave. Richard Binns. (Illus.). 224p. 1982. 6.95 o.p. (ISBN 0-89919-101-0). Ticknor & Fields.
French Leave. 3rd ed. Richard Binns. (Illus.). 336p. 1983. pap. 9.70 o.p. (ISBN 0-89919-196-7). Ticknor & Fields.
French Lieutenant's Woman: A Screenplay. Harold Pinter. 1981. 14.95 o.p. (ISBN 0-316-70851-8). Little.
French Literary Imagination & Dostoevsky & Other Essays. Henri Peyre. LC 74-28294. (Studies in the Humanities: No. 10). 192p. 1975. 13.50 o.p. (ISBN 0-8173-7324-1). U of Ala Pr.
French Literature in Early American Translation: A Bibliographical Survey of Books & Pamphlets Printed in the United States from 1668 Through 1820. Compiled by Forrest Bowe & Mary F. Daniels. (Reference Library of the Humanities: Vol. 77). (Illus., LC 76-052680). 1977. lib. bdg. 76.00 o.p. (ISBN 0-8240-9893-5). Garland Pub.
French Lyric Poetry: An Anthology. Frank S. Giese & Warren F. Wilder. 117p. 1965. pap. text ed. write for info. o.p. (ISBN 0-02-342500-8). Macmillan.
French Mathematical Seminars. rev. ed. Ed. by Nancy D. Anderson. LC 78-10797. 200p. 1989. 34.00 o.p. (ISBN 0-8218-3116-X, FRENCHSEM). Am Math.
French Menu Cookbook: A Revised & Updated Edition of a Culinary Classic. Richard Olney. LC 85-71046. 320p. 1987. 12.95 o.p. Godine.
French Novel from Gide to Camus. Germaine Bree & Margaret Guiton. LC 62-21467. 241p. 1962. pap. 2.25 o.p. (ISBN 0-15-633480-1, Harv). HarBraceJ.
French Occupation of the Champlain Valley: From 1609-1759 with Added Index. Guy O. Coolidge. LC 79-13458. 1979. Repr. of 1938 ed. 19.50 o.p. (ISBN 0-916346-34-X). Harbor Hill Bks.
French Official Publications. Gloria Westfall. LC 80-40418. (Guides to Official Publications: Vol. 6). (Illus.). 223p. 1980. 55.00 o.p. (ISBN 0-08-021838-5). Pergamon.
French Opinion on War & Diplomacy During the Second Empire. Lynn M. Case. LC 70-120242. 1972. Repr. of 1954 ed. lib. bdg. 26.00x o.p. (ISBN 0-374-91302-1, Octagon). Hippocrene Bks.
French Pensions. Tony Lynes. 163p. 1967. pap. text ed. 5.00x o.p. (ISBN 0-686-70846-6, Pub. by Bedford England). Gower Pub Co.
French Piano Music: An Anthology, Forty-Four Pieces by Twenty-Eight Composers. Ed. by Isidor Philipp. 13.25 o.p. (ISBN 0-8446-5602-X). Peter Smith.
French Policy Towards the Chinese in Madagascar. Leon M. Slawecki. (Foreign Area Studies Ser.: No. 13). (Illus.). 265p. 1971. 28.00 o.p. (ISBN 0-208-01251-6). Shoe String.
French Politics & Political Institutions. 2nd ed. Roy Pierce. LC 83-5948. (Illus.). 382p. 1983. pap. text ed. 15.25 o.p. (ISBN 0-8191-3087-7). U Pr of Amer.
French Politics & Public Policy. Ed. by Philip G. Cerny & Martin A. Schain. 1981. pap. 10.95x o.p. (ISBN 0-416-30850-3, NO. 2381). Routledge Chapman & Hall.
French Pre-Revolution, 1787-1788. Jean Egret. Tr. by Wesley D. Camp from Fr. LC 77-78776. (Illus.). 1978. Repr. of 1972 ed. lib. bdg. 27.00x o.s.i. (ISBN 0-226-19142-7). U of Chicago Pr.
French Prose: An Intermediate Reader. A. M. Galpin & Edward E. Milligan. 1965. text ed. write for info. o.p. (ISBN 0-02-340250-4). Macmillan.
French Prose Writers of the Fourteenth & Fifteenth Centuries. J. M. Ferrier. 1966. pap. text ed. 11.75 o.p. (ISBN 0-08-011301-X). Pergamon.
French Provincial Cooking. Elizabeth David. (Handbook Ser.). 1964. pap. 9.95 o.p. (ISBN 0-14-046099-3). Penguin.
French Renaissance Fountains. Naomi Miller. LC 76-23645. (Outstanding Dissertations in the Fine Arts - 16th Century). (Illus.). 1977. Repr. of 1966 ed. lib. bdg. 76.00 o.p. (ISBN 0-8240-2713-2). Garland Pub.
French Revolution. Graham Bearman. (History Broadsheets Ser.). (Illus.). 1977. pap. text ed. 11.50x o.p. (ISBN 0-435-31749-0). Heinemann Ed.
French Revolution. Gerald P. Dartford. (gr. 9-12). 1972. pap. text ed. 4.95x o.p. (ISBN 0-88334-046-1). Ind Sch Pr.
French Revolution. Gaetano Salvemini. 1962. pap. 2.25x o.p. (ISBN 0-393-00179-2, Norton Lib). Norton.
French Revolution: Conflicting Interpretations. 3rd ed. Frank A. Kafker. Ed. by James M. Laux. LC 82-9878. 298p. 1983. pap. 15.00 o.p. (ISBN 0-89874-517-9). Krieger.
French Revolution in San Domingo. T. Lothrop Stoddard. 410p. 1986. pap. 6.50 o.p. (ISBN 0-317-53268-5). Noontide.
French Revolution: Introductory Documents. Ed. by D. Wright. 1974. pap. 9.95x o.p. (ISBN 0-7022-0923-6). U of Queensland Pr.
French Revolution of 1870-1871. Roger L. Williams. (Revolutions in the Modern World Ser.). 1969. pap. 5.95x o.p. (ISBN 0-393-09837-0, NortonC). Norton.
French Sculptors of the Seventeenth & Eighteenth Centuries: The Region of Louis XIV. Francois Souchal. LC 78-320398. (Reign of Louis XIV Catalogue Raisonne Ser.: Vol. 1, A-F). (Illus.). 400p. 1977. 135.00 o.p. (ISBN 0-85181-062-4). Faber & Faber.
French Socialist & Communist Party under the Fifth Republic, 1958-1981: From Opposition to Power. Wayne Northcutt. 172p. 1985. text ed. 29.95x o.p. (ISBN 0-8290-1057-2); pap. text ed. 14.95x o.p. (ISBN 0-8290-1538-8). Irvington.
French Songs, Poems & Proverbs. Ed. by Arthur B. Forster & Lucille Lenoir. 1934. pap. text ed. 2.75x o.p. (ISBN 0-89197-502-0). Irvington.
French Speaking Switzerland Travel Guide. Berlitz Editors. (Berlitz Travel Guides). (Illus.). 1982. pap. 4.95 o.p. (ISBN 0-02-969740-9, Berlitz). Macmillan.
French Stage in the Eighteenth Century, 2 vols. Frederick W. Hawkins. LC 68-57608. (Illus.). 1970. Repr. of 1888 ed. Set. lib. bdg. (ISBN 0-8371-2746-7, HASE); Vol. 1. lib. bdg. (ISBN 0-8371-2747-5, HASF); Vol. 2. lib. bdg. (ISBN 0-8371-2748-3, HASG). Greenwood.

French Struggle for the West Indies, 1665-1713. Nellis M. Crouse. 1966. lib. bdg. 20.50x o.p. (ISBN 0-374-91938-0, Octagon). Hippocrene Bks.

French Syntax: The Transformational Cycle. Richard S. Kayne. LC 75-4681. (Current Studies in Linguistics: No. 6). 464p. 1975. text ed. 37.50x o.p. (ISBN 0-262-11055-5). MIT Pr.

French Theatre 1918-1939. Bettina L. Knapp. Ed. by Bruce King & Adele King. LC 85-47543. (Modern Dramatists Ser.). 180p. 1986. 27.50 o.p. (ISBN 0-394-54719-5). Grove.

French Theatre 1918-1939. Bettina L. Knapp. Ed. by Bruce King & Adele King. LC 85-47543. (Modern Dramatists Ser.). 1986. pap. 11.95 o.p. (ISBN 0-394-62068-2, Ever). Grove.

French Thought since Sixteen Hundred. Ed. by D. C. Potts & D. G. Charlton. LC 75-2862. 96p. 1974. pap. 5.95x o.p. (ISBN 0-416-81630-4, NO. 2390). Routledge Chapman & Hall.

French Workers' Movement: Economic Crisis & Political Change. Mark Kesselman. LC 84-9238. 400p. 1984. text ed. 39.95x o.p. (ISBN 0-04-331095-8). Unwin Hyman.

Frenchman's Creek. Daphne Du Maurier. 1977. pap. 0.95 o.p. (ISBN 0-380-00979-X, 32565). Avon.

Frequency Engineering in Mobile Radio Bands. W. M. Pannell. 356p. 1979. 50.00 o.p. (ISBN 0-906782-00-7). Taylor & Francis.

Frequency Modulation Receivers. J. D. Jones. (Illus.). 118p. 1957. (ISBN 0-8022-0815-0). Philos Lib.

Frequency Response Testing in Nuclear Reactors. T. W. Kerlin. (Nuclear Science & Technology Ser.). 1974. 68.50 o.p. (ISBN 0-12-404850-1). Acad Pr.

Frescoes in Siena's Palazzo Pubblico, Twelve Eighty-Nine to Fifteen Thirty-Nine: Studies in Imagery & Relations to Other Communal Palaces in Tuscany. Edna C. Southard. LC 78-74381. (Fine Arts Dissertations, Fourth Ser.). (Illus.). 1979. lib. bdg. 80.00 o.p. (ISBN 0-8240-3967-X). Garland Pub.

Frescoes of the Skull: The Later Prose & Drama of Samuel Beckett. James Knowlson & John Pilling. LC 79-6153. 320p. (Orig.). 1980. pap. 9.50 o.p. (ISBN 0-394-17610-3, E735, Ever). Grove.

Fresh, Fast, & Fabulous. Ed. by Carole N. McCrone & Marga Rose-Hancock. 190p. 1982. pap. 8.95 o.s.i. (ISBN 0-89716-122-X). Peanut Butter.

Fresh Garden Vegetables. Libby Hillman. Ed. by Robin Beckhardt. LC 81-68833. (Great American Cooking Schools Ser.). (Illus.). 84p. 1981. pap. 5.95 o.p. (ISBN 0-941034-04-6). I Chalmers.

Fresh Paint: The Houston School. Susie Kalil & Barbara Rose. Ed. by Scott Lubeck. (Illus.). 224p. 1985. 29.95 o.p. (ISBN 0-87719-000-3); pap. 19.95 o.p. (ISBN 0-87719-001-1). Texas Month Pr.

Fresh Water Friends & Foes. Will Barker. Date not set. 3.95 o.p. (ISBN 0-317-63433-X). Acropolis.

Fresh Ways with Fish & Shellfish. Time-Life Books Editors. (Health Home Cooking Ser.). 144p. (YA) (gr. 7 up). 1986. 19.93 o.p.; lib. bdg. 22.60 o.p. (ISBN 0-8094-5817-9). Time-Life.

Freshwater: A Comedy. Virginia Woolf. LC 76-1902. 128p. 1976. 6.95 o.p. (ISBN 0-15-133487-0). HarBraceJ.

Freshwater: A Comedy. Virginia Woolf. Ed. by Lucio P. Ruotolo. LC 85-912. (Illus.). 96p. 1985. 9.95 o.p. (ISBN 0-15-133488-9). HarBraceJ.

Freshwater & Terrestrial Radioecology: A Selected Bibliography. Ed. by A. W. Klement & V. Schultz. LC 80-22169. 587p. 1982. 53.95 o.p. (ISBN 0-87933-389-8). Van Nos Reinhold.

Freshwater Angler's Clinic. Hal Scharp. 1979. 9.95 o.p. (ISBN 0-671-24631-3). S&S.

Freshwater Biological Monitoring: Proceedings of a Specialized Conference, Cardiff, U. K., Sept. 12-14, 1984. Ed. by D. Pascoe & R. W. Edwards. LC 82-645900. (Advances in Water Pollution Control Ser.). 168p. 1984. 45.00 o.p. (ISBN 0-08-032313-8). Pergamon.

Freshwater Fish Farming: How to Begin. (Better Farming Ser.: No. 27). 43p. 1979. pap. 5.00 o.p. (ISBN 92-5-100606-7, F1834, FAO). UNIPUB.

Freshwater Pollution, Canadian Style. Peter A. Larkin. (Environmental Damage & Control in Canada Ser.: Vol. 3). (Illus.). 168p. 1974. 5.00 o.p. (ISBN 0-7735-0197-5, McGill Canada); pap. 4.95 o.p. (ISBN 0-7735-0208-4, McGill Canada). U of Toronto Pr.

Freshwater Studies. John Gee. Ed. by Morton Jenkins. LC 85-15668. (Practical Ecology Ser.). (Illus.). 96p. 1986. pap. text ed. 10.95x o.p. (ISBN 0-04-574024-0). Unwin Hyman.

Freshwater Vegetation Management. Edward O. Gangstad. 380p. 35.00 o.p. (ISBN 0-317-54020-3). Thomson Pubns.

Fretting Corrosion. R. B. Waterhouse. 1973. 65.00 o.p. (ISBN 0-08-016902-3). Pergamon.

Freud & Future Religious Experience. Anthony J. De Luca. (Quality Paperback Ser: No. 330). 263p. 1977. pap. 4.95 o.p. (ISBN 0-8226-0330-6). Littlefield.

Freud & His Time. Fritz Wittels. 1931. 6.95 o.p. (ISBN 0-87140-807-4). Liveright.

Freud & Society. Yiannis Gabriel. (International Library of Group Psychotherapy & Group Process). 330p. 1983. 29.95x o.p. (ISBN 0-7100-9410-8). Routledge Chapman & Hall.

Freud & the Mind. Ilham Dilman. 224p. 1986. pap. 14.95x o.p. (ISBN 0-631-15005-6). Basil Blackwell.

Freud: Character & Consciousness. Israel Rosenfeld. 5.95 o.p. (ISBN 0-8216-0080-X, Pub. by Univ Bks). Carol Pub Group.

Freud, Jung & Occultism. Nandor Fodor. 1971. 7.95 o.p. (ISBN 0-8216-0081-8, Pub. by Univ Bks). Carol Pub Group.

Freud Rediscovered. Lucy Freeman. LC 79-52251. 1980. 11.95 o.p. (ISBN 0-87795-227-2, Arbor Hse). Morrow.

Freude Am Lesen: A German Reader. Ed. by Robert M. Browning. (Orig., Ger.). 1964. pap. text ed. 7.95x o.p. (ISBN 0-89197-180-7). Irvington.

Friar Bacon & Friar Bungay. Robert Greene. Ed. by J. A. Lavin. (New Mermaid Ser.). 1976. pap. 2.95x o.p. (ISBN 0-393-90013-4). Norton.

Fric-Frac: The Great Riviers Train Robbery. Albert Spaggiari. 1979. 8.95 o.p. (ISBN 0-395-27764-7). HM.

Friction Materials: Recent Advances. L. B. Newman. LC 77-15219. (Chemical Technology Review Ser.: No. 100). (Illus.). 358p. 1978. 36.00 o.p. (ISBN 0-8155-0688-0). Noyes.

Friction, Wear, Lubrication, Vols. 1 & 2. I. V. Kragelsky & V. V. Alisin. 1986. Vol. 1, 348 p. 12.95 o.p. (ISBN 0-8285-3223-0, Pub. by Mir Pubs USSR); Vol. 2, 280 p. 12.95 o.p. (ISBN 0-8285-3258-3, Pub. by Mir Pubs USSR). Imported Pubns.

Friday. Robert A. Heinlein. LC 81-13221. 384p. 1982. 14.95 o.s.i. (ISBN 0-03-061516-X); deluxe ed. 50.00 ltd. ed. o.p. (ISBN 0-03-061553-4). H Holt & Co.

Friday's Daughter. Mary R. Myers. 1984. pap. 3.50 o.s.i. (ISBN 0-345-30448-9). Ballantine.

Friedman on Leases, 3 vols. 2nd ed. Milton R. Friedman. 1773p. 1983. text ed. 185.00 o.p. (ISBN 0-686-43894-9, N6-1350). PLI.

Friedman on Leases, Vol. 3. Milton R. Friedman. 1978. 40.00 o.p. (ISBN 0-685-31251-8, N1-1312). PLI.

Friedman on Leases: 1987 Supplement. Milton R. Friedman. 334p. (Orig.). 1987. pap. text ed. 50.00 o.p. (ISBN 0-317-18592-6, NS-1539). PLI.

Friedrich Froebel & English Education. Evelyn Lawrence. (Illus.). 248p. 1953. (ISBN 0-8022-0937-8). Philos Lib.

Friedrich Schiller. John D. Simons. (World Authors Ser.). 1981. 18.95 o.p. (ISBN 0-8057-6445-3, Twayne). G K Hall.

Friedrich Schleiermacher. Stephen Sykes. LC 75-158145. (Makers of Contemporary Theology Ser). (Orig.). 1971. pap. 3.45 o.p. (ISBN 0-8042-0556-6, John Knox). Westminster John Knox.

Friend in Deed. Robert Jagoda. 1977. 7.95 o.p. (ISBN 0-393-08789-1). Norton.

Friend in the Police. John Givins. LC 79-1822. 1980. 10.95 o.p. (ISBN 0-15-133538-9). HarBraceJ.

Friend Indeed. D. J. Arneson. LC 80-23062. (gr. 4 up). 1981. PLB 8.90 o.p. (ISBN 0-531-04257-X). Watts.

Friend Is Someone Who Likes You. Joan W. Anglund. LC 58-8624. (Illus.). (gr. k-3). 1958. 6.95 o.p. (ISBN 0-15-229677-8, HJ). HarBraceJ.

Friend: The Story of George Fox & the Quakers. Jane H. Yolen. LC 74-171865. 192p. (gr. 6 up). 1979. 6.95 o.p. (ISBN 0-395-28932-7, Clarion). HM.

Friendly Beasts. Laura N. Baker. (Illus.). 28p. (gr. k-3). 1957. Repr. 4.95 o.p. (ISBN 0-395-27662-4). HM.

Friends. Terry Berger. LC 80-25940. (Illus.). 64p. (gr. 3 up). 1981. 9.29 o.p. (ISBN 0-671-42165-4, 158). Messner.

Friends. Ed. by San Diego Zoological Society Staff. (San Diego Zoo Series of Picture Bks.). (Illus.). 12p. (ps-2). bds. 2.95 o.p. (ISBN 0-89346-237-3). Heian Intl.

Friends: A Handbook about Getting Along Together. Sandra Ziegler. LC 80-17529. (Living the Good Life Ser.). (Illus.). 112p. (Orig.). (gr. 1-6). 1980. pap. 5.95 o.p. (ISBN 0-89565-174-2). Childs World.

Friends along the Way. Julia Markus. 264p. 1985. 15.45 o.p. (ISBN 0-395-35357-2). HM.

Friends & Lovers. Helen MacInnes. LC 47-4756. 1971. 6.95 o.s.i. (ISBN 0-15-133550-8). HarBraceJ.

Friends from the Forest. Joy Adamson. LC 81-47295. (Helen & Kurt Wolff Bk.). 96p. 1981. 9.95 o.p. (ISBN 0-15-133645-8). HarBraceJ.

Friends of the Road. Virginia Sorensen. LC 77-17293. 192p. (gr. 5-9). 1978. 6.95 o.p. (ISBN 0-689-50093-9, Atheneum). Macmillan.

Friends with God. Catherine Marshall. (Illus.). (gr. 2-4). 1980. pap. 1.95 o.p. (ISBN 0-380-01199-9, 52803-7). Avon.

Friendship: A Study in Theological Ethics. Gilbert C. Meilaender. LC 81-50459. 118p. 1981. text ed. 10.95 o.p. (ISBN 0-268-00956-2). U of Notre Dame Pr.

Friendship & Other Poems. Marguerite De Angeli. LC 79-6857. (Illus.). 48p. 1981. 6.95a o.p. (ISBN 0-385-15854-8). Doubleday.

Friendship in the Lord. Paul Hinnebusch. LC 73-90411. 144p. 1974. pap. 2.75 o.p. (ISBN 0-87793-065-1). Ave Maria.

Friendship of Christ. Robert H. Benson. (Thomas More Books to Live Ser.). 156p. 1984. 10.95 o.p. (ISBN 0-88347-171-X). Thomas More.

Frigates. Time-Life Books Editors & Henry Gruppe. (Seafarers Ser.). (Illus.). 1980. 13.95 o.p. (ISBN 0-8094-2715-X). Time-Life.

Frightened Forest. Ann Turnbull. LC 74-19358. 128p. (gr. 3-6). 1979. 7.95 o.p. (ISBN 0-395-28884-3, Clarion). HM.

Frightening Angels: A Study of U. S. Multinationals in Developing Nations. rev. ed. Anant R. Negandhi & Benjamin S. Prasad. LC 74-30491. (Illus.). 268p. 1975. 20.00x o.p. (ISBN 0-87338-169-6). Kent St U Pr.

Frigidity: Its Cure with Hypnosis. Gilbert S. MacVaugh. LC 78-26958. 1979. 47.00 o.p. (ISBN 0-08-021748-6). Pergamon.

Fringe Benefits for Librarians: A Selected Bibliography. Lorna Peterson. (Public Administration Ser.: P 1725). 5p. 1985. 2.00 o.p. (ISBN 0-89028-495-4). Vance Biblios.

Fringes of Power: Ten Downing Street Diaries, 1939-1955. John Colville. LC 85-10468. (Illus.). 775p. 1985. 24.50 o.p. (ISBN 0-393-02223-4). Norton.

Frisbee. Stancil E. Johnson. LC 75-9881. (Illus.). 244p. (Orig.). 1975. pap. 4.95 o.p. (ISBN 0-911104-53-4, 069). Workman Pub.

Frisbee Fun. Margaret Poynter. (gr. 3-6). 1978. pap. 1.25 o.p. (ISBN 0-671-29885-2); pap. 7.29 o.p. Archway.

Frisky in the Morning. Philip F. Nelson. 1980. 5.50 o.s.i. (ISBN 0-682-49571-9). Exposition-Phoenix.

Fritz Lang. Ed. by Stephen Jenkins. (British Film Institute Bks.). (Illus.). 173p. 1981. 14.95 o.p. (ISBN 0-85170-108-6); pap. 9.95 o.p. (ISBN 0-85170-109-4). U of Ill Pr.

Fritz Schumacher: A Bibliography. Edward H. Teague. (Architecture Ser.: A 1469). 5p. 1985. 2.00 o.p. (ISBN 0-89028-599-3). Vance Biblios.

Frivolities of Courtiers & Footprints of Philosophers. John Of Salisbury. Tr. by Joseph B. Pike. LC 77-159199. x, 436p. 1971. Repr. of 1938 ed. lib. bdg. 29.00x o.p. (ISBN 0-374-94213-7, Octagon). Hippocrene Bks.

Frobisch's Angel: A Novel. Doris Rochlin. 336p. 1987. 16.95 o.s.i. (ISBN 0-8008-3058-X). Taplinger.

Frog & the Scorpion. A. E. Maxwell. 224p. 1987. pap. 3.50 o.p. (ISBN 0-553-26876-7). Bantam.

Frog Band & the Onion Seller. Jim Smith. (Frog Band Ser.). (Illus.). 32p. (gr. 1-3). 1977. 8.95 o.p. (ISBN 0-316-80005-8); pap. 3.95 o.p. (ISBN 0-316-80006-6). Little.

Frog Pond. Joyce MacIver. 1977. pap. 1.95 o.p. (ISBN 0-380-00957-9, 32334). Avon.

Frog Princess. I Bilibin. (Illus.). 12p. 1979. pap. 2.45 o.p. (ISBN 0-8285-1147-0, Pub. by Goznak Pubs USSR). Imported Pubns.

Frog Queen. K. Kubilinskas. (Illus.). 82p. 1974. 3.45 o.p. (ISBN 0-8285-1148-9, Pub. by Progress Pubs USSR). Imported Pubns.

Frog Who Drank the Waters of the World. Patricia M. Newton. LC 83-2594. (Illus.). 32p. (ps-3). 1983. 9.95 o.s.i. (ISBN 0-689-30993-7, Atheneum Childrens Bks). Macmillan.

Frogmorton. Susan Colling. (Illus.). (gr. 3-7). 1966. lib. bdg. 4.99 o.p. (ISBN 0-394-91175-X). Knopf.

From a Bare Hull. Ferenc Mate. 1975. 24.95 o.p. (ISBN 0-920256-00-7). Norton.

From a Broken Web: Separation, Sexism, & Self. Catherine Keller. LC 86-47508. 224p. 1986. 21.95 o.p. (ISBN 0-8070-6732-6). Beacon Pr.

From a Doctor's Heart. Eugene F. Snyder. 1951. (ISBN 0-8022-1607-2). Philos Lib.

From a Gun to a Flower: Messages Through the Mediumship of Zaher P. Kury. Zaher P. Kury. (Illus.). 192p. 1984. 10.00 o.p. (ISBN 0-682-40160-9). Exposition-Phoenix.

From a High Place. Edward Mathis. (Dan Roman Mystery Ser.). 256p. 1985. 13.95 o.s.i. (ISBN 0-684-18492-3, ScribT). Scribner.

From a Mighty Fortress: Prints, Drawings, & Books in the Age of Luther, 1483-1546. Christiane Andersson & Charles Talbot. (Illus.). 412p. (Orig.). 1983. pap. 15.00 o.p. (ISBN 0-89558-091-8). Detroit Inst Arts.

From a Ruined Garden. Date not set. (ISBN 0-8052-3867-0). Random.

From a Woman's Heart. Judith Mattison. LC 77-84804. 1969. 3.50 o.p. (ISBN 0-8066-0917-6, 10-2465, Augsburg). Augsburg Fortress.

From Abacus to Zeus: A Handbook of Art History. James Pierce. 1977. pap. text ed. (ISBN 0-13-331686-6). P-H.

From Absolutism to Revolution: 1648-1848. 2nd ed. Ed. by Herbert H. Rowen. (Ideas & Institutions in Western Civilization, Vol. 4). 1968. pap. text ed. write for info. o.p. (ISBN 0-02-404110-6). Macmillan.

From Adam's Rib to Women's Lib & Other Ventures. Elinor G. Black. 1974. 4.00 o.p. (ISBN 0-682-48123-8). Exposition-Phoenix.

From Adolescent to Adult. Percival M. Symonds & Arthur R. Jensen. LC 75-31472. 413p. 1976. Repr. of 1961 ed. lib. bdg. 24.75x o.p. (ISBN 0-8371-8531-9, SYAA). Greenwood.

From Ape Man to Homer. H. E. Mellersh. LC 73-8567. (Illus.). 222p. 1974. Repr. of 1962 ed. lib. bdg. 35.00x o.p. (ISBN 0-8371-6962-3, MEAM). Greenwood.

From Apology to Protest: The Black American Novel. Noel Schraufnagel. LC 72-95180. 1973. lib. bdg. 25.00 o.p. (ISBN 0-912112-02-6). Everett-Edwards.

From Approximately Coast to Coast...It's the Bob & Ray Show. Bob Elliott & Ray Goulding. LC 83-45069. (Illus.). 1983. 13.95 o.s.i. (ISBN 0-689-11395-1, Atheneum). Macmillan.

From Approximately Coast to Coast...It's the Bob & Ray Show. Bob Elliott & Ray Goulding. (General Ser.). 1984. lib. bdg. 14.95 o.p. (ISBN 0-8161-3644-0, Large Print Bks). G K Hall.

From Atoms to Quarks. James S. Trefil. (Illus.). 288p. 1980. 12.95 o.s.i. (ISBN 0-684-16484-1, ScribT). Scribner.

From Author to Reader: A Social Study of Books. Peter Mann. 160p. 1982. 17.95x o.p. (ISBN 0-7100-9089-7). Routledge Chapman & Hall.

From Babylon to Bethlehem: The People of God from the Exile to the Messiah. H. L. Ellison. LC 78-71044. (Orig.). 1979. pap. 4.95 o.p. (ISBN 0-8042-0034-3, John Knox). Westminster John Knox.

From BASIC to C. Harley M. Templeton. 1986. pap. 16.95 o.p. (ISBN 0-87455-026-2). Compute Pubns.

From Beethoven to Shostakovich. Max Graf. 474p. 1947. (ISBN 0-8022-0613-1). Philos Lib.

From Behavioral Science to Behavior Modification. Harry I. Kalish. (Illus.). 448p. 1981. text ed. 31.50 o.p. (ISBN 0-07-033245-2). McGraw.

From Birth to One Year. Marilyn Segal. Ed. by Betty Bardige. (Nova University Play & Learn Program). (Illus.). 67p. (gr. 9-12). pap. text ed. 5.95x o.p. (ISBN 0-935266-00-3). Jalmar Pr.

From Bondage to Freedom. James Sprunt et al. (Orig.). 1968. pap. 4.95 o.p. (ISBN 0-8042-9020-2, John Knox); tchrs' guide pap. 3.00 o.p. (ISBN 0-686-76880-9). Westminster John Knox.

From Brown to Bradley: School Desegregation 1954-1974. 15.00 o.p. Anderson Pub Co.

From Brown to Bunter: The Life & Death of the School Story. P. W. Musgrave. (Illus.). 275p. 1986. 24.95 o.p. (ISBN 0-7102-0529-5). Routledge Chapman & Hall.

From Bush to City: A Look at the New Africa. Marc Bernheim & Evelyne Bernheim. LC 66-10069. (gr. 7 up). 1966. 6.50 o.p. (ISBN 0-15-230258-1, HJ). HarBraceJ.

From Bust to Bra: A Survey of Women's Corsetry. Rosemary Hawthorne & Mary Want. (Illus.). 160p. 1987. (ISBN 0-7104-3032-9, Pub. by Costello UK). Seven Hills Bk Dists.

From Camel to Truck: The Bedouin in the Modern World. Dawn Chatty. 1985. 14.50 o.p. (ISBN 0-317-28892-X). Vantage.

From Camelot to Kent State: The Sixties Experience in the Words of Those Who Lived It. Joan Morrison & Robert K. Morrison. (Illus.). 320p. 1987. pap. 12.95 o.p. (ISBN 0-317-63092-X). Times Bks.

From Carriage to Spaceship. S. Mikhalkov. (Illus.). 16p. 1975. pap. 1.99 o.p. (ISBN 0-8285-1150-0, Pub. by Progress Pubs USSR). Imported Pubns.

From Chicago. Russell Bowman. Ed. by Pace Gallery Publications Staff. (Illus.). 15p. (Orig.). 1982. fold out brochure 6.00 o.p. (ISBN 0-938608-20-7). Pace Pubns.

From Chips to Systems: An Introduction to Microprocessors. Rodnay Zaks. LC 81-51126. (Illus.). 552p. 1981. pap. 20.95 o.p. (ISBN 0-89588-063-6, C201A). SYBEX.

From Chusan to Sea Princess. Malcolm R. Gordon. (Illus.). 184p. 1985. 24.95 o.p. (ISBN 0-86861-736-9). Unwin Hyman.

From Columbus to Aquarius: An Interpretive History, 2 vols. G. E. Frakes & W. Royce Adams. LC 74-2800. 1976. Vol. 1. pap. text ed. 17.95 o.p. (ISBN 0-03-014191-5, HoltC); Vol. 2. pap. text ed. 16.95 o.s.i. (ISBN 0-03-014196-6). HR&W.

From Comiskey to the Domes: An Architectural History of the Ball Parks. Jeffrey M. Lambert. (Architecture Ser.: A 1431). 11p. 1985. 2.00 o.p. (ISBN 0-89028-481-4). Vance Biblios.

From Concept to Context: Approaches to Asian & Islamic Calligraphy. Shen Fu. (Illus.). 165p. 1986. pap. 21.00 o.p. (ISBN 0-318-21325-7, S/N 047-000-00403-9). USGPO.

From Concertation to Consensus: Proceedings of the UNESCO General Conference, 20th Session, 1978. UNESCO General Conference Staff. Ed. by Amadou-Mahtar M'Bow. (UNESCO & the Solidarity of Nations Ser.: No. 2). 200p. 1979. pap. 7.00 o.p. (ISBN 0-686-93877-1, UNESCO). UNIPUB.

From Conflict to Cooperation: A Manager's Guide to Mediation. Beverly A. Potter. 160p. (Orig.). 1987. pap. 9.95 o.p. (ISBN 0-914171-05-4). Ronin Pub.

From Conquest to Collapse: European Empires from Eighteen Fifteen to Nineteen Sixty. V. G. Kiernan. LC 82-47883. 285p. 1982. 16.45 o.p. (ISBN 0-394-50959-5). Pantheon.

From Continent to Continent: In Search of a New Life. Linford Schultz. (ISBN 0-682-49574-3). Exposition-Phoenix.

From Copernicus to Einstein. Hans Reichenbach. (ISBN 0-8022-1318-9). Philos Lib.

From Copying to Creating. Helen H. Gordon. 237p. 1981. pap. text ed. 14.95 o.p. (ISBN 0-03-053551-4, HoltC). HR&W.

From Cotswolds to High Sierras. George E. Franklin. LC 66-20373. (Illus.). 167p. 1966. 4.00 o.p. (ISBN 0-87004-046-4). Caxton.

From Court to Capital: A Tentative Interpretation of the Origins of the Japanese Urban Tradition. Paul Wheatley & Thomas See. LC 76-25637. (Illus.). 1978. lib. bdg. 17.50x o.s.i. (ISBN 0-226-89430-4). U of Chicago Pr.

From Cultural Rebellion to Counterrevolution: The Politics of Maurice Barres. C. Stewart Doty. LC 75-15337. 294p. 1976. 16.00x o.p. (ISBN 0-8214-0191-2). Ohio U Pr.

From Cyclotrons to Cytochromes: Essays in Molecular Biology & Chemistry. Ed. by Nathan O. Kaplan & Arthur Robinson. LC 82-1785. 1982. 84.00 o.p. (ISBN 0-12-397580-8). Acad Pr.

From Darkness into Light: Women's Emancipation in Iran. Badr ol-Moluk Bamdad. Ed. & tr. by F. R. Bagley. LC 76-50308. 1977. 8.00 o.p. (ISBN 0-682-48705-8, University). Exposition-Phoenix.

From Darkness to Light-Poems & Parables: The Collected Works of Krishnamurti, Vol. I. J. Krishnamurti. LC 79-2985. 144p. 1980. 15.00i o.p. (ISBN 0-06-064832-5). HarpR.

From Death Row to Freedom. David Wainapel. LC 84-71905. 181p. 1984. pap. 8.95 o.s.i. (ISBN 0-8197-0496-2). Bloch.

From Death to Birth. Edmund A. Steimle. LC 73-79327. 144p. 1973. pap. 1.00 o.p. (ISBN 0-8006-1037-7, Fortress). Augsburg Fortress.

From Death Unto Life. F. A. Walton. 1977. 5.00 o.p. (ISBN 0-682-48750-3). Exposition-Phoenix.

From Descartes to Hume: Continental Metaphysics & the Development of Modern Philosophy. Louis E. Loeb. 382p. 1981. 39.95x o.p. (ISBN 0-8014-1289-7). Cornell U Pr.

From Despotism to Revolution, 1763-1789. Leo Gershoy. LC 83-10734. (Rise of Modern Europe Ser.). (Illus.). xvi, 355p. 1983. Repr. of 1944 ed. lib. bdg. 48.50x o.p. (ISBN 0-313-24080-9, GEDE). Greenwood.

From Distant Shores. Bruce Nicolaysen. (Novel of New York Ser.: Vol. 1). 480p. 1980. pap. 2.50 o.p. (ISBN 0-380-75424-X, 75424-X). Avon.

From DNA to Protein: The Transfer of Genetic Information. Maria Szekely. LC 79-11894. 284p. 1982. pap. 24.95x o.p. (ISBN 0-470-27155-8). Halsted Pr.

From DNA to Protein: The Transfer of Genetic Information. Maria Szekely. LC 79-11894. 284p. 1980. 59.95x o.p. (ISBN 0-470-26687-2). Halsted Pr.

From Dreams to Reality: Adventures in Careers. Girl Scouts of the U. S. A. Staff. (From Dreams to Reality Ser.). 64p. (gr. 7-12). 1978. pap. 2.75 o.p. (ISBN 0-88441-319-5, 20-810). Girl Scouts USA.

From Dreams to Reality: Leaders' Guide. 16p. 1978. pap. 1.80 o.p. (ISBN 0-88441-321-7, 20-812). Girl Scouts USA.

From Drinking to Alcoholism: A Sociological Commentary. David Robinson. LC 75-26597. 211p. 1976. 59.95x o.p. (ISBN 0-471-01357-9); pap. text ed. 11.95 o.p. (ISBN 0-471-01358-7). Wiley.

From Earth to Heaven. Isaac Asimov. 256p. 1983. pap. 1.75 o.p. (ISBN 0-380-42184-4, 42184-4, Discus). Avon.

From Edinburgh to the Antarctic. Burn Murdoch. (Antarctic Classics Ser.). (Illus.). 384p. 1987. Repr. of 1894 ed. 40.00 o.s.i. (ISBN 0-9506104-6-1). Archival Facsimiles.

From Evolution to Creation: A Scientist Changes. Gary E. Parker. LC 77-78020. 1978. pap. 1.00 o.p. (ISBN 0-89051-035-0). Master Bks.

From Existence to Life. D. C. Anjaria. 1984. 5.95 o.p. (ISBN 0-533-05657-8). Vantage.

From Experience to Expression: A College Rhetoric. 2nd ed. Joseph J. Comprone. LC 80-82348. (Illus.). 528p. 1980. pap. 27.56 o.p. (ISBN 0-395-29310-3). HM.

From Failing Hands: The Story of Presidential Succession. John D. Feerick. LC 65-14917. xvi, 368p. 1965. 35.00 o.p. (ISBN 0-8232-0635-1). Fordham.

From Fear to Friendship: Australia's Policies Towards the People's Republic of China 1966-1982. Edmund S. Fung & Colin Mackerras. LC 84-11956. 351p. 1985. text ed. 37.50x o.p. (ISBN 0-7022-1738-7). U of Queensland Pr.

From Fiction to Metafiction: Essays in Honor of Carmen Martin Gaite. Ed. by Mirella Servodidio & Marcia L. Welles. LC 82-61181. 200p. (Orig.). 1983. 25.00 o.p. (ISBN 0-89295-023-4). Society Sp & Sp-Am.

From Florence to Brest, Fourteen Thirty-Nine to Fifteen Ninety-Six. 2nd ed. Oscar Halecki. LC 68-26103. 456p. 1968. 39.50 o.p. (ISBN 0-208-00702-4, Archon). Shoe String.

From Flowchart to Program. Richard G. Todd. LC 85-8093. (Illus.). 192p. (Orig.). 1985. 19.95 o.p. (ISBN 0-8306-0862-1, 1862); pap. 12.60 o.p. (ISBN 0-8306-1862-7, 1862P). Tab Bks.

From Football to Finance: The Story of Brady Keys Jr. Eric B. Roberts. LC 70-151026. (Illus.). 112p. (gr. 7 up). 1971. 4.75 o.p. (ISBN 0-15-230265-4, HJ). HarBraceJ.

From Freedom to Freedom: A Student's Guide. Morris Johnson et al. 1977. 4.50 o.p. (ISBN 0-394-32078-6). Random.

From Gene to Protein: Information Transfer in Normal & Abnormal Cells. Ed. by Thomas R. Russell et al. (Miami Winter Symposia Ser.: Vol. 16). 1979. 60.50 o.p. (ISBN 0-12-604450-3). Acad Pr.

From Greek to Graffiti: English Words That Survive & Thrive. Robert C. Goodspeed. (Illus.). 308p. (Orig.). 1981. 15.00 o.p. (ISBN 0-682-49696-0, University); pap. 10.00 o.p. (ISBN 0-682-49706-1, University). Exposition-Phoenix.

From Hegel to Nietzsche. Karl Lowith. LC 83-48512. (Philosophy of Hegel Ser.). 477p. 1984. lib. bdg. 55.00 o.p. (ISBN 0-8240-5635-3). Garland Pub.

From Hegel to Terrorism & Other Essays on the Dynamic Nature of Philosophy. James Feibleman. 144p. 1985. text ed. 17.50 o.p. (ISBN 0-391-03057-4). Humanities.

From Helgoland to Hollywood. Lawrence S. Telford. 160p. 1981. 8.00 o.p. (ISBN 0-682-49738-X). Exposition-Phoenix.

From Hell to Heaven. Leonard S. Smithfield, Jr. 1976. 6.50 o.p. (ISBN 0-682-48586-1). Exposition-Phoenix.

From Here to Eternity. James Jones. 1978. pap. 2.50 o.p. (ISBN 0-380-00338-4, 41830). Avon.

From Holland with Love: Delicious Dutch Recipes. Jan Morgan. (Illus.). 1980. 12.50x o.s.i. (ISBN 0-911268-48-0). E J Brill USA.

From Horses to Horsepower: Life in Kansas, 1900-1925. Everett Dick. LC 84-80212. (Illus.). 210p. 1986. 29.95 o.s.i. (ISBN 0-87726-026-5). Kansas St Hist.

From Human Sentience to Drama: Principles of Critical Analysis, Tragic & Comedic. Richard Pollard & Hazel B. Pollard. LC 73-85447. ix, 310p. 1974. 14.00x o.p. (ISBN 0-8214-0135-1). Ohio U Pr.

From Ice Set Free. Bruce Clements. LC 70-184703. 224p. (gr. 7 up). 1972. 5.50 o.p. (ISBN 0-374-32468-9). FS&G.

From India to the Planet Mars. Theodore Floumey. 10.00 o.p. (ISBN 0-8216-0083-4, Pub. by Univ Bks). Carol Pub Group.

From Italy to Muscovy: The Life & Works of Maxim the Greek. Jack V. Haney. 194p. bds. cancelled o.s.i. (ISBN 3-7705-0925-0). Adlers Foreign Bks.

From J.A.P. to Jewish Mother. 36p. 1988. 1.95 o.p. (ISBN 0-317-66694-0). Spevack.

From Jordan to Pentecost, Bk. III. Derek Prince. (Foundation Ser.). pap. 2.95 o.p. (ISBN 0-934920-02-8, B-12). Derek Prince.

From Justinian to Charlemagne. European Art, 565-787: An Annotated Bibliography. Ness Lawrence. 1985. lib. bdg. 61.00 o.s.i. (ISBN 0-8161-8328-7). G K Hall.

From Last to First (Neil Bonnett Auto Racing) Ned Webb. LC 79-66524. (Illus.). 250p. 9.95 o.p. (ISBN 0-87397-153-1). Strode.

From Lupita's Hill. Bettie Forsman. LC 72-86936. 272p. (gr. 4-6). 1973. 6.50 o.p. (ISBN 0-689-30085-9, Atheneum). Macmillan.

From Luther to Fifteen Eighty: A Pictorial Account. Ingetraut Ludolphy. (Illus.). 1977. 16.95 o.p. (ISBN 0-570-03264-4, 15-2710). Concordia.

From Mama's Honey Jar. Catharine P. Smith. Ed. by James Kuse & D. Ralph Luedtke. 1978. pap. 3.95 o.p. (ISBN 0-89542-607-2). Ideals.

From Management Theory to Business Sense: The Myths & Realities of People at Work. David A. Whitsett & Lyle Yorks. 352p. 1984. 23.95 o.p. (ISBN 0-8144-5765-7); pap. 17.95 o.p. (ISBN 0-8144-7610-4). AMACOM.

From Manager to Innovator: Using Information to Become an Ideal Entrepenuer. William H. Fonvielle. 80p. 1987. 16.95 o.s.i. Admin Mgmt.

From Many Lands. Alberta Eiseman. LC 72-115068. (Illus.). (gr. 5-9). 1970. PLB 6.95 o.p. (ISBN 0-689-20598-8, Atheneum). Macmillan.

From Memory to Written Record in England, 1066-1307. M. T. Clanchy. (Illus.). 1979. text ed. 27.00x o.p. (ISBN 0-674-32510-9). Harvard U Pr.

From Mesmer to Christian Science: A Short History of Mental Healing. Frank Podmore. 10.00 o.p. (ISBN 0-8216-0034-6, Pub. by Univ Bks). Carol Pub Group.

From Metternich to Hitler: Aspects of British & Foreign History, 1814-1939. Ed. by W. N. Medlicott. LC 83-10688. (Historical Association Essays Ser.). viii, 267p. 1983. Repr. of 1963 ed. lib. bdg. 38.50x o.p. (ISBN 0-313-24085-X, MEME). Greenwood.

From Molecules to Man. Ed. by Morris Pollard. (Perspectives in Virology: Vol. 7). 1971. 61.50 o.p. (ISBN 0-12-560540-4). Acad Pr.

From Moses to Elisha: Israel to the End of the Ninth Century B. C. Leonard E. Elliott-Binns. LC 78-10639. (Illus.). 1979. Repr. of 1929 ed. lib. bdg. 35.00 o.p. (ISBN 0-313-21015-2, EBFM). Greenwood.

From Muleback to Super Jet with the Gospel. Marshall Keeble. 2.50 o.p. (ISBN 0-89225-091-7). Gospel Advocate.

From Murk to Masterpiece. Geraldine Henze. 1985. pap. 9.95x o.p. (ISBN 0-256-03159-2). Irwin.

From Music Boxes to Street Organs. Romke De Waard. LC 67-27808. (Illus.). 1967. 12.95 o.p. (ISBN 0-911572-04-X, A-43). Vestal.

From My Texan Log Cabin. Lisa Kahn. 72p. 1985. 5.95 o.p. (ISBN 0-89015-453-8). Eakin Pr.

From Myth to Icon: Reflections of Greek Ethical Doctrine in Literature & Art. Helen North. LC 79-7619. (Cornell Studies in Classical Philology: Vol. XL). (Illus.). 288p. 1979. 29.95x o.p. (ISBN 0-8014-1135-1). Cornell U Pr.

From Nicaea to Chalcedon: A Guide to the Literature & Its Background. Frances M. Young. LC 83-1760. 416p. 1983. 22.95 o.p. (ISBN 0-8006-0711-2, 1-711, Fortress). Augsburg Fortress.

From Now to Eternity: Sermons from Revelation. Nathan M. Meyer. pap. 6.00 o.s.i. (ISBN 0-88469-035-0). BMH Bks.

From Obote to Obote. Akena Adoko. (Illus.). xx, 336p. 1983. text ed. 40.00x o.p. (ISBN 0-7069-2262-X, Pub. by Vikas India). Advent NY.

From One Language to Another: Functional Equivalence in Bible Translation. Jan de Waard & Eugene A. Nida. LC 86-16328. 224p. 1986. 15.95 o.p. (ISBN 0-8407-7555-5). Nelson.

From One Life to Another. Shirley Kaufman. LC 78-23502. (Pitt Poetry Ser.). 1979. pap. 6.95 o.p. (ISBN 0-8229-5300-5). U of Pittsburgh Pr.

From One to Two Years. Don Adcock & Marilyn Segal. LC 80-13835. (Play & Learn Ser.). (Illus.). 104p. 1980. pap. 4.95 o.s.i. (ISBN 0-916392-51-1). Oak Tree Pubns.

From One to Two Years. rev. ed. Marilyn Segal & Don Adcock. Ed. by Ruth Spiegel. (Nova University Play & Learn Ser.). (Illus.). 98p. (gr. 9-12). 1977. pap. text ed. 6.95x o.p. (ISBN 0-935266-01-1). Jalmar Pr.

From Orphans to Champions: The Story of Dematha's Morgan Wootten. Morgan Wootten & Bill Gilbert. LC 79-63847. (Illus.). 1979. 8.95 o.p. (ISBN 0-689-11011-1, Atheneum). Macmillan.

From Outrage to Action: The Story of the National Audubon Society. Ed. by Patrice Benneward. (Illus., Orig.). 1982. pap. write for info. o.p. (ISBN 0-930698-15-0). Natl Audubon.

From Paragraph to Theme. Herman Hudson & Maurice L. Imhoof. Orig. Title: Understanding & Expressing Convictions Through Paragraph & Essay. (Illus.). 160p. 1972. pap. text ed. write for info. o.p. (ISBN 0-02-357800-9). Macmillan.

From Parlor to Prison: Five American Suffragists Talk About Their Lives. Ed. by Sherna Gluck. 1976. pap. 3.95 o.p. (ISBN 0-394-71642-6, Vin). Random.

From Parry to Britten: British Music in Letters 1900-1945. Ed. by Lewis Foreman. (Illus.). 248p. 1988. 39.95 o.p. (ISBN 0-931340-03-9). Am Inst Psych.

From Pearl Harbor to Okinawa. Bruce Bliven, Jr. (Landmark Ser.: No. 94). (Illus.). (gr. 5-9). 1963. lib. bdg. 8.99 o.s.i. (ISBN 0-394-90394-3, BYR). Random.

From Performance. Robert Stearns. (Illus.). 1980. pap. 2.00 o.s.i. (ISBN 0-917562-14-3). Contemp Arts.

From Perry to Pearl Harbor: The Struggle for Supremacy in the Pacific. Edwin A. Falk. LC 73-21285. (Illus.). 362p. 1974. Repr. of 1943 ed. lib. bdg. 22.50x o.p. (ISBN 0-8371-6161-4, FAPP). Greenwood.

From Pigeons to People: A Look at Behavior Shaping. Elizabeth Hall. (Illus.). 144p. (gr. 5 up). 1975. 6.95 o.p. (ISBN 0-395-21894-2). HM.

From Primer to Pleasure in Reading. Mary K. Thwaite. LC 72-82182. (Illus.). 340p. 1972. 14.95 o.p. (ISBN 0-87675-275-X). Horn Bk.

From Prison to the Major Leagues: The Picture Story of Ron Leflore. Ron Knapp. LC 80-19233. (Illus.). 64p. (gr. 4-6). 1980. lib. bdg. 9.29 o.s.i. (ISBN 0-671-34059-X). Messner.

From Project to Production. A. Brichta & P. E. Sharp. LC 79-97830. 1970. 33.00 o.p. (ISBN 0-08-006638-0); pap. 17.50 o.p. (ISBN 0-08-006639-9). Pergamon.

From Puppets to Eternity. Sparky Chance. 1976. 4.00 o.p. (ISBN 0-682-48573-X). Exposition-Phoenix.

From Reconstruction to Revolution: The Blacks' Struggle for Equality. Joseph A. Alvarez. LC 71-154747. (Illus.). 1971. 6.50 o.p. (ISBN 0-689-10485-5, Atheneum). Macmillan.

From Religion to Philosophy. A Study of the Origins of Western Speculation. F. M. Cornford. 275p. 1979. text ed. (ISBN 0-391-01238-X); pap. text ed. 12.50x o.p. (ISBN 0-391-01239-8). Humanities.

From Research to Practice. Ed. by H. L. Pick et al. LC 78-16932. (Illus.). 402p. 1978. 50.00x o.p. (ISBN 0-306-31132-1, Plenum Pr). Plenum Pub.

From Right to Left: An Autobiography. Frederick V. Field. LC 82-23407. 336p. 1983. 16.95 o.p. (ISBN 0-88208-162-4); pap. 8.95 o.p. (ISBN 0-88208-161-6). Chicago Review.

From Sambo to Superspade: The Black Experience in Motion Pictures. Daniel Leab. LC 75-11948. 1975. 15.00 o.p. (ISBN 0-395-19402-4). HM.

From Sambo to Superspade: The Black Experience in Motion Pictures. Daniel Leab. LC 75-11948. 1976. pap. 6.95 o.p. (ISBN 0-395-24895-7). HM.

From Scarface to Scarlett: American Films in the 1930s. Roger Dooley. LC 80-8745. (Illus.). 704p. 1981. 25.00 o.p. (ISBN 0-15-133789-6). HarBraceJ.

From Scarface to Scarlett: American Films in the 1930s. Roger Dooley. LC 80-8745. 704p. 1984. pap. 14.95 o.p. (ISBN 0-15-633998-6, Harv). HarBraceJ.

From Sea & Stream: An International Fish Cookbook. rev. ed. Lou S. Pappas. LC 86-18171. (Illus.). 144p. (Orig.). 1986. pap. 7.95 o.p. (ISBN 0-89286-266-1, One Hund One Prods). Ortho.

From Shtetl to Suburbia: The Family in Jewish Literary Imagination. Sol Gittleman. LC 78-53646. 1978. 12.95x o.p. (ISBN 0-8070-6364-9). Beacon Pr.

From Sight to Insight: Steps in the Writing Process. 2nd ed. Jeff Rackham. LC 83-12876. 1984. pap. text ed. 17.95 o.p. (ISBN 0-03-062444-4). HR&W.

From Sin to Wholeness. Brian W. Grant. LC 81-16122. 174p. 1982. pap. 8.95 o.s.i. (ISBN 0-664-24399-1, Westminster). Westminster John Knox.

From Society to Nature: A Study of Doris Lessing's "Children of Violence" Ingrid Holmquist. (Gothenburg Studies in English: No. 46). 1980. pap. 22.50x o.p. (ISBN 91-7346-083-4). Humanities.

From Spacelab to Space Station: Fifth DGLR-AAS Symposium, Oct. 3-5, 1984, Hamburg, Gemany. Ed. by H. Stoewer & P. M. Bainum. (Advances in the Astronautical Sciences Ser.: Vol. 56). 270p. 1984. 40.00 o.p. (ISBN 0-87703-209-2). Univelt Inc.

From Start to Finish. Selma F. Stonberg. (Illus., Orig.). 1972. pap. 12.50 o.p. (ISBN 0-395-05438-9). HM.

From Talbot to Stieglitz: Masterpieces of Early Photography from the New York Public Library. Julia Van Haaften. LC 81-52310. (Illus.). 128p. 1982. 29.95 o.s.i. (ISBN 0-500-54077-2). Thames Hudson.

From Tenancy to Home Ownership: A Comparative Study of Tenure Conversions & Their Effects. Lennart J. Lundqvist. 288p. 1986. 37.75 o.p. (ISBN 0-7099-1676-0, Pub. by Croom Helm Ltd). Routledge Chapman & Hall.

From Text to Sermon: Responsible Use of the New Testament in Preaching. Ernest Best. LC 77-79584. 1978. 8.95 o.p. (ISBN 0-8042-0245-1, John Knox). Westminster John Knox.

From the Abyss of Its Inhabitants by One of Them. C. F. Masterman. LC 79-56963. (English Working Class Ser.). 1980. lib. bdg. 15.00 o.p. (ISBN 0-8240-0115-X). Garland Pub.

From the Boundary Waters. Gordon Osing. (Illus.). 72p. 1981. 8.95 o.p. (ISBN 0-87870-207-5). Memphis St Univ.

From the Country of Eight Islands: An Anthology of Japanese Poetry, Japanese. Ed. by Hiroaki Sato & Burton Watson. LC 80-1077. 480p. 1981. 25.00x o.p. (ISBN 0-295-95798-0). U of Wash Pr.

From the Diaries of Felix Frankfurter. Ed. by Joseph P. Lash. 366p. 1975. 12.50 o.p. (ISBN 0-393-07488-9). Norton.

From the Diary of a Snail. Gunter Grass. Tr. by Ralph Manheim from Ger. LC 75-29309. 310p. 1976. pap. 3.95 o.s.i. (ISBN 0-15-633950-1, Harv). HarBraceJ.

From the Earliest Times to the End of the Middle Kingdom see Scepter of Egypt: A Background for the Study of Egyptian Antiquities in the Metropolitan Museum of Art.

From the Exile to Christ: Historical Introduction to Palestinian Judaism. Werner Foerster. Ed. by Gordon E. Harris. LC 64-18151. 264p. 1964. pap. 3.95 o.p. (ISBN 0-8006-0978-6, 1-978, Fortress). Augsburg Fortress.

From the Fifteenth District. Mavis Gallant. (Hall Fiction Paperbacks). 256p. 1986. pap. 5.95 o.p. (ISBN 0-8398-2897-7). G K Hall.

From the Frontline: Speeches of Sir Seretse Khama. Ed. by Gwendolen M. Carter & E. Philip Morgan. (Special Project Ser.: No. 27). 252p. 1980. 26.95x o.p. Hoover Inst Pr.

From the Ghetto: The Fiction of Abraham Cahan. Jules Chametzky. Date not set. price not set o.p. U of Mass Pr.

From the Heart. June C. Cash. 192p. 1987. 12.95 o.p. (ISBN 0-13-530767-8). P-H.

From the Hinterland of Ecuador to the Shores of Galapagos. Margaret Nesheim. (Illus.). 154p. 1981. 10.00 o.p. (ISBN 0-682-49673-1). Exposition-Phoenix.

From the Jungles of Belfast: A Footnote to History, 1904-1972. Denis Ireland. 176p. (Orig.). 1973. pap. 4.50 o.p. (ISBN 0-85640-034-3, Pub. by Blackstaff Pr). Longwood Pub Group.

From the Life of a Researcher. W. W. Coblentz. (ISBN 0-8022-0271-3). Philos Lib.

From The Magic Mountain: Mann's Later Masterpieces. Henry Hatfield. LC 78-74213. (Illus.). 256p. 1979. 27.50x o.p. (ISBN 0-8014-1204-8). Cornell U Pr.

From the Mixed-up Files of Mrs. Basil E. Frankweiler. E. L. Konigsburg. (Illus.). (gr. 3-7). 1972. pap. 3.95 o.s.i. (ISBN 0-689-70308-2, Aladdin). Macmillan.

From the Nolichucky to Memphis: Reminiscences of a Tennessee Doctor. Samuel F. Strain. LC 79-129552. (Twentieth Century Reminiscence Ser.: No. 2). (Illus.). 1979. 13.95 o.p. (ISBN 0-87870-064-1). Memphis St Univ.

From the Picture Press. Ed. by John Szarkowski. LC 72-82886. (Illus.). 96p. 1973. pap. 5.95 o.p. (ISBN 0-87070-334-X). Museum Mod Art.

From the Realm of Morpheus: A Mesmerizing Tour of the Human Imagination. Steven Millhauser. LC 86-5395. 384p. 1986. 17.95 o.p. (ISBN 0-688-06501-5). Morrow.

From the Rising of the Sun: Christians & Society in Contemporary Japan. James M. Phillips. LC 80-24609. 320p. (Orig.). 1981. pap. 14.95 o.p. (ISBN 0-88344-145-4). Orbis Bks.

From the Shadow of Insight. Joseph Wanefsky. LC 73-82166. 160p. 1973. 7.95 o.p. (ISBN 0-8022-2128-9). Philos Lib.

From the Shadow of the Insight. Joseph Wanefsty. LC 73-82166. 1974. 7.95 o.p. (ISBN 0-317-65279-6). Philos Lib.

From the Shamrock Shore. Ian Kavanaugh. 1982. pap. 3.50 o.p. (ISBN 0-440-02798-5, Emerald). Dell.

From the Silent Earth: A Report of the Greek Bronze Age. Joseph W. Alsop. LC 81-4122. (Illus.). xviii, 296p. 1981. Repr. of 1964 ed. lib. bdg. 39.00x o.p. (ISBN 0-313-23014-5, ALFS). Greenwood.

From the Slave Cabin of Yani. Virgil S. Powell. LC 77-74872. 1977. 10.00 o.p. (ISBN 0-682-48781-3, Banner). Exposition-Phoenix.

From the Smithsonian: More Science Activities. Illus. by Simms Taback. (gr. 2-7). 1988. pap. 9.95 o.p. Galison.

From the Tigris to the Tiber: An Introduction to Ancient History. 3rd ed. Tom B. Jones. 1983. pap. text ed. (ISBN 0-534-10609-9). Wadsworth Pub.

From the Underside: Evangelism from a Third World Vantage Point. James A. Armstrong. LC 81-9509. 112p. (Orig.). 1981. pap. 4.95 o.p. (ISBN 0-88344-146-2). Orbis Bks.

From the Vedas to the Manu-Samhita: A Cultural Study. V. B. Mishra. 160p. 1982. text ed. 19.95x o.p. (ISBN 0-391-02705-0). Humanities.

From the Walls In. Charles Wing. LC 78-26354. (Illus.). 1979. pap. 14.95 o.p. (ISBN 0-316-94740-7, Pub. by Atlantic Monthly Pr). Little.

From the World of the Cabbalah. Ben Z. Bokser. 1954. (ISBN 0-8022-0147-4). Philos Lib.

From These Beginnings. Date not set. (ISBN 0-8052-3908-1). Random.

From This Day. Nora Roberts. (Nightingale Large Print Ser.). 1985. pap. text ed. 9.95 o.p. (ISBN 0-8161-3743-9, Large Print Bks). G K Hall.

From This Good Ground. Edna Hong. LC 74-77685. (Illus.). 128p. (Orig.). 1974. pap. 3.50 o.p. (ISBN 0-8066-1436-6, 10-2470, Augsburg). Augsburg Fortress.

From Thought to Theme. 7th ed. William F. Smith & Raymond D. Liedlich. 439p. 1983. pap. text ed. 13.95 o.p. (ISBN 0-15-529217-X, HC). HarBraceJ.

From Thought to Theme: A Rhetoric & Reader for College English. 4th ed. William F. Smith & Raymond D. Liedlich. 1974. pap. text ed. 8.95 o.p. (ISBN 0-15-529211-0, HC). HarBraceJ.

From Thought to Theme: A Rhetoric & Reader for College English. 6th ed. William F. Smith & Raymond D. Liedlich. 467p. 1980. pap. text ed. 11.95 o.p. (ISBN 0-15-529215-3, HC). HarBraceJ.

From Tires to Teeth see Getting along Series of Skills.

From Tourist to Hostage: A Traveler's Tale of Terrorism. Leo C. Byron. Ed. by James T. Ziegenfuss, Jr. 234p. 1988. 21.95 o.p. (ISBN 0-9621456-0-2). BoneKemper Typesetting.

From Tradition to Political Reality: A Study of the Ideas Set Forth in Support of the Commonwealth Government in England, 1649-1653. Margaret A. Judson. LC 79-209788. (Studies in British History & Culture: Vol. Vii). x, 121p. 1980. 17.50 o.p. (ISBN 0-208-01836-0, Archon). Shoe String.

From Trash to Treasure: How to Make Money at the Swaps. Godfrey Harris & Barbara DeKovner-Mayer. 7.95 o.p. (ISBN 0-935047-00-X). Americas Group.

From Trunk to Tail: Elephants Legendary & Real. Suzanne Jurmain. LC 78-52848. (Illus.). (gr. 4-6). 1978. 6.95 o.p. (ISBN 0-15-230268-9, HJ). HarBraceJ.

From Two to Three Years Old-Play & Learning. Marilyn Segal & Don Adcock. Ed. by Susan Talpins. (Nova University Play & Learn Program). (Illus.). 81p. (Orig.). 1979. pap. text ed. 6.95x o.p. (ISBN 0-935266-02-X). Jalmar Pr.

From Under the Earth: America's Metals, Fuels, & Minerals. Howard E. Smith, Jr. LC 67-18546. (Curriculum Related Bks.). (Illus.). (gr. 5 up). 1967. 5.25 o.p. (ISBN 0-15-230270-0, HJ). HarBraceJ.

From Uniformity to Unity, 1662-1962. Ed. by Geoffrey F. Nuttall & O. Chadwick. LC 63-2539. 1962. 20.00x o.p. (ISBN 0-8401-1746-9). A R Allenson.

From Voluntarism to Conscription: Congress & Selective Service, 1940-1945. John O'Sullivan. Ed. by Frank Freidel. LC 80-8476. (Modern American History Ser.). 375p. 1982. lib. bdg. 55.00 o.p. (ISBN 0-8240-4865-2). Garland Pub.

From Whence Came You? Morton Deutsch. 1958. (ISBN 0-8022-0383-3). Philos Lib.

From Where I Stand. Susan Price. LC 83-20827. 128p. (gr. 6 up). 1984. 11.95 o.p. (ISBN 0-571-13247-2). Faber & Faber.

From Word to Story. Wallace Graves & William G. Leary. 1971. pap. text ed. 8.95 o.p. (ISBN 0-15-529225-0, HC). HarBraceJ.

From Writers to Writing. Lee Kirby & John Scarry. 1978. pap. text ed. write for info. o.p. (ISBN 0-673-15693-1). Scott F.

Frommer's Amsterdam & Holland. rev. ed. Burnham. (Frommer's City Guide Ser.). 1986. pap. 5.95 o.p. (ISBN 0-671-62352-4). P-H.

Frommer's Australia on Thirty-Five Dollars A Day. John Godwin. (Dollars-a-Day Guides). 1986. pap. 10.95 o.p. (ISBN 0-671-55604-5). P-H.

Frommer's Dollarwise Guide to Austria & Hungary. Rev. & expanded ed. Darwin Porter. (Frommer's Dollarwise Guides Ser.). 610p. 1986. pap. 11.95 o.p. (ISBN 0-671-62057-6). P-H.

Frommer's Dollarwise Guide to California & Las Vegas. Rev. & updated ed. Mary Rakauskas. 312p. 1987. pap. 13.95 o.p. (ISBN 0-671-62532-2). P-H.

Frommer's Dollarwise Guide to Cruises: Including Alaska, Canada, the Carribean, Hawaii, Mexico, Panama & the U. S. Rev. & updated ed. Marylyn Springer & Don A. Schultz. (Formmer's Dollarwise Guides). 408p. 1986. pap. 13.95 o.p. (ISBN 0-671-62343-5). P-H.

Frommer's Dollarwise Guide to England & Scotland. rev. ed. Darwin Porter. (Frommer's Dollarwise Guides). 744p. 1986. pap. 13.95 o.p. (ISBN 0-671-62060-6). P-H.

Frommer's Dollarwise Guide to France. Rev., expanded & updated ed. Darwin Porter. (Frommer's Dollarwise Guides). 660p. 1986. pap. 13.95 o.p. (ISBN 0-671-62059-2). P-H.

Frommer's Dollarwise Guide to Italy. rev., expanded & updated ed. Darwin Porter. (Frommer's Dollarwise Guides). 576p. 1986. pap. 13.95 o.p. (ISBN 0-671-62058-4). P-H.

Frommer's Dollarwise Guide to Japan & Hong Kong. Beth Reiber. (Frommer Travel Guides Ser.). (Illus.). 384p. 1986. pap. 12.95 o.p. (ISBN 0-671-55776-9). S&S.

Frommer's Dollarwise Guide to Skiing in Europe: The Top Resorts in Austria, France, Italy & Switzerland. Catherine Foreht & Peter Foreht. (Frommer's Dollarwise Guides). 276p. 1986. pap. 12.95 o.p. (ISBN 0-671-62417-2). P-H.

Frommer's Dollarwise Guide to the Northwest. Marilyn Springer & Don A. Schultz. (Frommer's Dollarwise Guides). (Illus.). 420p. 1987. pap. 11.95 o.p. (ISBN 0-671-62344-3). P-H.

Frommer's Dollarwise Guide to the Southwest. Roy Bongertz. (Frommer's Dollarwise Guides). 528p. 1987. pap. 11.95 o.p. (ISBN 0-671-62345-1). P-H.

Frommer's Europe on Five Dollars a Day. Arthur Frommer. (Frommer Ser.). 1988. write for info. o.p. Prentice Hall Pr.

Frommer's Europe on Twenty-Five Dollars a Day. Rev. ed. Arthur Frommer. (Frommers Dollar-A-Day Guides). 768p. 1987. pap. 12.95 o.p. (ISBN 0-671-62347-8). P-H.

Frommer's Europe on Twenty-Five Dollars a Day. rev. ed. Arthur Frommer. (Frommer's Dollar-a-Day Guides). (Illus.). 1987. pap. 13.95 o.p. (ISBN 0-13-291833-1). Prentice Hall Pr.

Frommer's Guide to Athens. rev. ed. Keown. (Frommer's City Guide Ser.). 1986. pap. 5.95 o.p. (ISBN 0-671-62353-2). P-H.

Frommer's Guide to Atlantic City & Cape May. rev. ed. Gloria S. McDarrah. (Frommer's City Guide Ser.). 1986. pap. 5.95 o.p. (ISBN 0-671-62349-4). P-H.

Frommer's Guide to Cancun, Cozumel, & the Yucatan. Tom Brosnahan. (Frommers City Guides). 224p. 1986. pap. 5.95 o.p. (ISBN 0-671-62432-6). P-H.

Frommer's Guide to London. rev. ed. Darwin Porter. (Frommer's City Guides Ser.). 1986. pap. 5.95 o.p. (ISBN 0-671-62338-9). P-H.

Frommer's Guide to Mexico City & Acapulco. rev. ed. Tom Brosnahan. (Fommer's City Guide). 1987. pap. 5.95 o.p. (ISBN 0-671-62460-1). P-H.

Frommer's Guide to Montreal & Quebec City. rev. ed. Brosnahan. (Frommer's City Guide). 1986. pap. 5.95 o.p. (ISBN 0-671-62356-7). P-H.

Frommer's Guide to New York. rev. ed. Sylvan Levey. (Frommer's City Guide Ser.). 1987. pap. 5.95 o.p. (ISBN 0-671-62336-2). P-H.

Frommer's Guide to San Francisco. rev. ed. Mary Rakauskas. (Frommer's City Guide Ser.). 1987. pap. 5.95 o.p. (ISBN 0-671-62543-8). P-H.

Frommer's Guide to Washington D. C. rev. ed. Rena Bulkin. (Frommer's City Guide Ser.). 1987. pap. 5.95 o.p. (ISBN 0-671-62363-X). P-H.

Frommer's Hawaii on Forty-Five Dollars a Day. rev. ed. Faye Hammel & Sylvan Levey. (Frommer's Dollar-A-Day Guides). 396p. 1986. pap. 10.95 o.p. (ISBN 0-671-62341-9). P-H.

Frommer's Mexico on Twenty Dollars a Day: Including a Special Section on Guatemala. rev. ed. Tom Brosnahan. (Frommer's Dollar-A-Day Guides). 504p. 1986. pap. 12.95 o.p. (ISBN 0-671-62351-6). P-H.

Frommer's Scandinavia on Forty Dollars a Day. rev. ed. Darwin Porter. (Frommer's Dollar-A-Day Guides). 480p. 1987. pap. 12.95 o.p. (ISBN 0-671-62456-3). P-H.

Frontera: The United States Border with Mexico. Alan Weisman. (Illus.). 224p. 1986. 29.95 o.s.i. (ISBN 0-15-147315-3). HarBraceJ.

Frontier Crossroads II: The People of Newport, Vermont. Emily M. Nelson. LC 77-8624. (Illus.). 1978. 15.00x o.p. (ISBN 0-914016-49-0). Phoenix Pub.

Frontier Literature: Images of the American West. Ed. by Dan Jaffe & John Knoepfle. (Patterns in Literary Art Ser.). (gr. 9-12). 1979. text ed. 15.20 o.p. (ISBN 0-07-032187-6). McGraw.

Frontier Politics: Alaska's James Wickersham. Evangeline Atwood. LC 79-71140. (Illus.). 1979. 14.95 o.p. (ISBN 0-8323-0317-8). Binford-Metropolitan.

Frontier Technology in Mineral Processing. Ed. by John F. Spisak & Gerald V. Jergensen, II. LC 84-52515. (Illus.). 175p. 1985. pap. 45.00x o.p. (ISBN 0-89520-433-9, 433-9). SMM&E Inc.

Frontier Town. Peter Seymour. LC 82-80754. (Illus.). (gr. 1-4). 1982. 7.75 o.p. (ISBN 0-03-062077-5). H Holt & Co.

Frontieres Du Gothique: Librairie De Medicis 1945. Pierre Francastel. (Reeditions: No. 9). 1971. 21.60x o.p. (ISBN 90-2796-772-5). Mouton.

Frontiers in Catecholamine Research: Proceedings, International Catecholamine Symposium, 3rd, Strasbourg, France, May, 1973. Ed. by Earl Usdin & Solomon Snyder. 1974. 300.00 o.p. (ISBN 0-08-017922-3). Pergamon.

Frontiers in Chemistry: Proceedings. International Congress of Pure & Applied Chemistry 28th, Vancouver, BC, Canada, 16-22 August 1981. Ed. by Laidler. (IUPAC Symposium Ser.). (Illus.). 350p. 1982. 95.00 o.p. (ISBN 0-08-026220-1). Pergamon.

Frontiers in Physicochemical Biology. Ed. by Bernard Pullman. 1979. 72.50 o.p. (ISBN 0-12-566960-7). Acad Pr.

Frontiers in Physiological Psychology. Ed. by Roger W. Russell. 1967. 19.95 o.p. (ISBN 0-12-604250-0). Acad Pr.

Frontiers in the Teaching of Physiology: Computer Literacy & Simulation. 64p. 1981. 7.50 o.s.i. (ISBN 0-318-12931-0). Am Physiological.

Frontiers in Visual Science: Proceedings of the University of Houston College of Optometry Dedication Symposium, Houston Texas, March, 1977. Ed. by J. Cool & E. L. Smith. LC 78-24191. (Springer Series in Optical Sciences: Vol. 8). (Illus.). 1978. 54.00 o.p. (ISBN 0-387-09185-8). Springer-Verlag.

Frontiers of Alcoholism. Ed. by Morris E. Chafetz et al. LC 79-91171. 1970. 30.00x o.p. (ISBN 0-87668-026-0). Aronson.

Frontiers of Applied Geometry: Proceedings of a Symposium, Las Cruces, New Mexico, 1980. Ed. by Robin J. McLeod & Eugene L. Wachspress. 128p. 1981. pap. 29.00 o.p. (ISBN 0-08-026487-5). Pergamon.

Frontiers of Criminology. Ed. by H. J. Klare & D. Haxby. 1967. 40.00 o.p. (ISBN 0-08-011579-9). Pergamon.

Frontiers of Healing: New Dimensions in Parapsychology. Ed. by Nicholas M. Regush. 1977. pap. 2.75 o.p. (ISBN 0-380-00707-X, 76554-7). Avon.

Frontiers of Human Knowledge: Lectures Held at the Quincentenary Celebrations of Uppsala University 1977. Ed. by Torgny Segerstedt. (Illus.). 1978. pap. text ed. 32.50 o.p. (ISBN 91-554-0791-9). Humanities.

Frontiers of Pattern Recognition: Proceedings of the International Conference on Frontiers of Pattern Recognition, Jan. 1971. Ed. by S. Watanabe. 1972. 72.00 o.p. (ISBN 0-12-737140-0). Acad Pr.

Frontiers of Planned Unit Development. Robert W. Burchell. 300p. 1973. text ed. 15.00x o.p. (ISBN 0-87855-095-X). Transaction Pubs.

Frontiers of Psychology. G. K. Yacorznski. LC 62-20876. 240p. 1963. (ISBN 0-8022-1947-0). Philos Lib.

Frontiers of Quantitative Economics. Ed. by M. D. Intriligator. LC 70-134645. (Contributions to Economic Analysis Ser.: Vol. 71). 471p. 1975. pap. 40.50 o.p. (ISBN 0-7204-0373-1, North-Holland). Elsevier.

Frontiers of Science & Philosophy. Ed. by Robert G. Colodny. LC 61-9401. (Philosophy of Science Ser.). 1962. 26.95x o.p. (ISBN 0-8229-3100-1). U of Pittsburgh Pr.

Frontline Theology. Ed. by Dean G. Peerman. 1967. 4.50 o.p. (ISBN 0-8042-0570-1, John Knox). Westminster John Knox.

Frost, Drought & Heat Resistance. J. Levitt. (Protoplasmatologia: Vol. 8, Pt. 6). (Illus.). 1958. pap. 30.70 o.p. (ISBN 0-387-80490-0). Springer-Verlag.

Frost in the Sun. Claire Lorrimer. 534p. 1988. 22.95 o.p. (ISBN 0-7126-9490-0, Pub. by Century Hutchinson). David & Charles.

Frost, Moisture & Erosion: Nine Reports. (Transportation Research Report Ser.). 105p. 1975. 4.60 o.p. (ISBN 0-309-02380-7). Transport Res Bd.

Froth Floatation. 1962. 18.00x o.p. (ISBN 0-89520-029-5). SMM&E Inc.

Frozen Assets. Barrie Keeffe. 1981. pap. 4.95 o.p. (ISBN 0-413-45730-3, NO. 2072). Heinemann Ed.

Frozen Image: Scandinavian Photography. Martin Friedman et al. LC 82-72450. (Illus.). 208p. 1982. 35.00 o.p. (ISBN 0-89659-311-8); pap. 24.95 o.p. (ISBN 0-89659-312-6). Abbeville Pr.

Frozen Lady. Susan Arnout. LC 81-71662. 581p. 1983. 15.95 o.p. (ISBN 0-87795-368-6, Arbor Hse). Morrow.

Frozen Snakes & Dinosaur Bones: Exploring a Natural History Museum. Margery Facklam. LC 75-41394. (Illus.). 128p. (gr. 3-7). 1976. 6.95 o.p. (ISBN 0-15-230275-1, HJ). HarBraceJ.

Titles

Frozen Stakes: The Future of Antarctic Minerals. 1980. 3.80 o.p. (ISBN 0-905347-45-5). C I D E.

Frozen Waves. Robert E. Vardeman. (Jade Demon Ser.: No. 2). 208p. 1985. pap. 2.95 o.p. (ISBN 0-380-89799-7). Avon.

Frugal Fish Cookbook: 300 Delicious Recipes for All Seasons. Robert Ackart. 320p. 1983. 17.45i o.p. (ISBN 0-316-00646-7). Little.

Frugal Shopper: Save Money on Everything with Coupons, Refunds, Rebates & Free Offers. Marion Joyce. 128p. 1986. pap. 6.95 o.p. (ISBN 0-399-51278-0, Perigee). Putnam Pub Group.

Frugal Woodworker. Rick Liftig. (Illus.). 240p. 1986. 22.95 o.p. (ISBN 0-8306-0202-X, NO. 2702); pap. 12.60 o.p. (ISBN 0-8306-2702-2). TAB Bks.

Fruit & Vegetable Exports from the Mediterranean Area to the EEC. Rkobert D. Hunt. (Working Paper: No. 321). 90p. 1979. 5.00 o.p. (ISBN 0-686-36208-X, WP-0321). World Bank.

Fruit Book. Cynthia Overbeck. LC 74-12744. (Early Nature Picture Bks.). (Illus.). 32p. (gr. k-3). 1975. PLB 6.95 o.p. (ISBN 0-8225-0295-X). Lerner Pubns.

Fruit Cookbook. Suzanne Topper. 1980. pap. 3.45 o.p. (ISBN 0-380-01202-2, 14803-X). Avon.

Fruit of the Spirit. H. Ray Dunning. 38p. 1982. pap. 1.95 o.p. (ISBN 0-8341-0806-2). Beacon Hill.

Fruit Preservation. Ed. by Duru Jagtiani. 128p. 1980. pap. 3.95x o.p. (ISBN 0-7069-1039-7, Pub. by Vikas India). Advent NY.

Fruits & Vegetables. Erica Jong. LC 74-138876. 1971. 5.95 o.p. (ISBN 0-03-085998-0); pap. 3.95 o.p. (ISBN 0-03-085999-9). H Holt & Co.

Fruits d'Or. Nathalie Sarraute. 1963. pap. 8.50 o.p. (ISBN 0-685-23938-1). Schoenhof.

Fruits for the Home Garden. U. P. Hedrick. (Illus.). 14.50 o.p. (ISBN 0-8446-4753-5). Peter Smith.

Fruits of Enlightenment. Leo Tolstoy. Tr. by Michael Frayn from Rus. 99p. 1979. pap. 6.95 o.p. (ISBN 0-413-45830-X, NO. 3013). Heinemann Ed.

Fry Cooking. Ser-Vol-Tel Institute Staff. (Foodservice Career Education Ser.). 1983. pap. 8.95 o.p. (ISBN 0-8436-2028-5). Van Nos Reinhold.

FS Consumers & Con. Date not set. (ISBN 0-07-641213-X). McGraw.

FS-CS Infant Care, No. 1. Date not set. (ISBN 0-07-102221-X). McGraw.

FS-CS Set European G. Webster. Date not set. (ISBN 0-07-102908-7). McGraw.

FS-CS Set Natr Disas. Date not set. (ISBN 0-07-102786-6). McGraw.

FS Dimensioning, Pt. 2. Date not set. (ISBN 0-07-691795-9). McGraw.

FS Dividing Work. Date not set. (ISBN 0-07-641215-6). McGraw.

FS Earth Science SRS. Webster. Date not set. (ISBN 0-07-101747-X). McGraw.

FS Enjoying Ourselves. Date not set. (ISBN 0-07-641218-0). McGraw.

FS Making Decisions. Date not set. (ISBN 0-07-641216-4). McGraw.

FS Making Rules &, Makiru. Date not set. (ISBN 0-07-641219-9). McGraw.

FS Meeting Our Needs. Date not set. (ISBN 0-07-641212-1). McGraw.

FS Producers & Pro. Date not set. (ISBN 0-07-641214-8). McGraw.

FS Protecting Ourselves. Date not set. (ISBN 0-07-641217-2). McGraw.

FS Slavery in a Divi. Date not set. (ISBN 0-07-405363-9). McGraw.

FS with CS Advanc, Set 2. Date not set. (ISBN 0-07-102246-5). McGraw.

F.T.C. & Company. Mary Anderson. LC 78-12097. (Illus.). (gr. 4-6). 1979. 8.95 o.p. (ISBN 0-689-30673-3, Atheneum). Macmillan.

F.T.L. Further Than Life. Michael L. Williams. 336p. 1987. pap. 3.50 o.p. (ISBN 0-380-89632-X). Avon.

Fuck Journal. Bob Flanagan. 94p. 1988. 4.95 o.p. (ISBN 0-937815-11-X). Hanuman Bks.

Fuel Alcohol: Energy & Environment in a Hungry World. 1981. 5.50 o.p. (ISBN 0-905347-29-3). C I D E.

Fuel-Coolant Interactions. Ed. by M. L. Corradini & A. A. Bishop. (HTD Ser.: Vol. 19). 113p. 1981. 24.00 o.p. (ISBN 0-686-34493-6, H00204). ASME.

Fuel Element Experience in Nuclear Power Reactors. Massoud Simnad. LC 78-131892. 620p. 1971. 43.00 o.p. (ISBN 0-677-03260-9, 455016). Am Nuclear Soc.

Fuel Ethanol & Agriculture: An Economic Assessment. Earle E. Gavett. (Agriculture Economic Ser: No. 562). 70p. 1986. pap. 3.25 o.p. (ISBN 0-318-21963-8, S/N 001-019-00482-7). USGPO.

Fuel, Furnaces & Refractories. 2nd ed. J. D. Gilchrist. 1977. 100.00 o.p. (ISBN 0-08-020430-9); pap. 100.00 o.p. (ISBN 0-08-020429-5). Pergamon.

Fuel Gases from Coal. Frank J. Schora et al. 203p. 1976. text ed. 34.50x o.p. (ISBN 0-8422-7266-6). Irvington.

Fuelling the Fire: U. S. Policy & the Western Sahara Conflict. Leo Kamil. 108p. 1988. 150.00x o.p. (Pub. by Spokesman UK); pap. 50.00x o.p. (Pub. by Spokesman UK). State Mutual Bk.

Fuels & Fuel Technology. 2nd ed. W. Francis & M. C. Peters. (Illus.). 608p. 1980. 170.00 o.p. (ISBN 0-08-025249-4); pap. text ed. 46.00 o.p. (ISBN 0-08-025250-8). Pergamon.

Fuels from Biomass. Ed. by P. B. Weisz & J. F. Marshall. 136p. 1980. 495.00 o.p. (ISBN 0-8247-6964-3). Dekker.

Fuel's Gold. Steve Jackson. LC 86-90227. (Car Wars(R) Gamebook: No. 2). 192p. (Orig.). 1986. pap. 2.95 o.p. (ISBN 0-88038-298-8). TSR Inc.

Fuelwood: The Energy Crisis That Won't Go Away. LC 86-139823. 1984. 6.00 o.p. (ISBN 0-905347-55-2). C I D E.

Fugitive - A Magazine of Verse: April 1922 to December 1925, 4 vols. in 1. Intro. by Donald Davidson. authorized ed. 18.00 o.p. (ISBN 0-8446-1192-1). Peter Smith.

Fugitive Emissions & Controls. Howard E. Hesketh & Frank L. Cross, Jr. LC 82-72348. (Environment & Energy Handbook Ser.). (Illus.). 145p. 1983. 29.95 o.p. (ISBN 0-250-40448-6). Butterworth.

Fugitive Facts. 2nd ed. Ed. by Robert Thorne. LC 69-19882. 496p. 1969. Repr. of 1889 ed. 43.00x o.p. (ISBN 0-8103-3750-9). Gale.

Fugitive Trail. Zane Grey. 1984. pap. 2.95 o.s.i. (ISBN 0-671-50658-7). PB.

Fulfilling the Circle: A Study of John Donne's Thought. Terry G. Sherwood. 231p. 1984. 27.50x o.p. (ISBN 0-8020-5621-0). U of Toronto Pr.

Fulfillment of Book of Mormon Prophecies. Ross Warner. 1975. pap. 4.95 o.p. (ISBN 0-89036-081-2). Hawkes Pub Inc.

Fulke Greville. Charles R. Larson. (English Authors Ser.). 1980. lib. bdg. 15.95 o.p. (ISBN 0-8057-6794-0, Twayne). G K Hall.

Full Blessing of Pentecost. Andrew Murray. 128p. 1987. pap. 3.95 o.p. (ISBN 0-310-55102-1, 19010P). Zondervan.

Full Circle. Erich M. Remarque. LC 74-1190. 1974. 6.95 o.p. (ISBN 0-15-134100-1). HarBraceJ.

Full Circle. Erich M. Remarque. LC 74-1190. 116p. 1974. pap. 2.95 o.p. (ISBN 0-15-634020-8, HB282, Harv). HarBraceJ.

Full Circle. Danielle Steel. (General Ser.). 1984. lib. bdg. 17.95 o.s.i. (ISBN 0-8161-3759-5, Large Print Bks). G K Hall.

Full Color Collection of Modern Art in Its Most Representative Offerings. Ed. by Victor De St. Martin. (Illus.). 131p. 1988. 137.45 o.p. (ISBN 0-86650-244-0). Gloucester Art.

Full Color Most Beloved Paintings of Flowers in the Art History of Mankind. Anthony De Vecellius. (Illus.). 118p. 1988. 127.55 o.p. (ISBN 0-86650-253-X). Gloucester Art.

Full-Contact Karate. Jean Y. Theriault & Joseph Jennings. (Illus.). 192p. (Orig.). 1983. pap. 9.95 o.p. (ISBN 0-8092-5597-9). Contemp Bks.

Full Dentures. A. Mack. (Dental Practitioner Handbook Ser.: No. 13). (Illus.). 106p. 1971. pap. text ed. 10.50 o.p. (ISBN 0-7236-0475-4, Pub. by John Wright UK). Butterworth.

Full Disclosure. William Safire. 1978. pap. 2.50 o.s.i. (ISBN 0-345-27195-5). Ballantine.

Full House: The Story of the Anderson Quintuplets. Karen Anderson & Jo Robinson. (Illus.). 282p. 1986. 16.95 o.p. (ISBN 0-316-03953-5). Little.

Full Potential: Your Career & Life Planning Workbook. R. J. Radin. 240p. 1983. pap. text ed. 7.95 o.p. (ISBN 0-07-051091-1). McGraw.

Full Term. J. I. M. Stewart. 1979. 12.95 o.p. (ISBN 0-393-01282-4). Norton.

Fully Human: A Program in Human Sexuality for Use with Persons Who Are Developmentally Disabled. rev. ed. Nancy Howes. 1985. 3 ribg bdg. 35.00 o.p. (ISBN 0-940050-04-8). Sun Rose.

Fulton's Footprints in Fiji. Eric B. Hare. 1985. pap. 6.50 o.p. (ISBN 0-8163-0583-8). Pacific Pr Pub Assn.

Fumbling for Words. David P. Brunet. LC 83-21378. (Orig.). 1984. pap. 2.25 o.p. (ISBN 0-9603840-6-5). Andrew Mtn Pr.

Fumigacion En Tante Que Traitment Insecticide. (Agricultural Planning Studies: No. 79). pap. 25.00 o.p. (F1291, FAO). UNIPUB.

Fun & Pleasure of Experimental Botany. Frank O. Payne. (Illus.). 201p. 1986. 117.75 o.p. (ISBN 0-86650-215-7). Gloucester Art.

Fun City. Burt Hirschfeld. (Orig.). 1985. pap. 2.95 o.p. (ISBN 0-440-02771-3, Emerald). Dell.

Fun City: Gertrude's Follies Comes to Town. Tom Hachtman. 1985. 6.95 o.p. (ISBN 0-87795-699-5, Arbor Hse). Morrow.

Fun Fact Fill-Ins. Louis Phillips & Karen Markoe. (Magic Answer Bks.). (Illus.). 64p. (gr. 3-7). 1984. pap. 2.95 o.s.i. (ISBN 0-671-44919-2). Wanderer Bks.

Fun for the Not So Young. Hedges. 1958. (ISBN 0-8022-0700-6). Philos Lib.

Fun House Terrors. Hilary Milton. Ed. by Betty Schwartz. (Plot It Yourself Horror Stories Ser.: No. 6). (Illus.). 128p. (Orig.). (gr. 3-7). 1984. pap. 2.95 o.s.i. (ISBN 0-671-52406-2). Wanderer Bks.

Fun in Fern Hollow. (Fern Hollow Board Bks.). (Illus.). (ps). 1985. bds. 1.49 o.s.i. (ISBN 0-318-12070-4). Outlet Bk Co.

Fun-In-Learning about Passover. Alfred J. Kolatch. LC 74-175489. (Illus.). (gr. 2-8). 1972. pap. 3.95 o.p. (ISBN 0-8246-0133-5). Jonathan David.

Fun Way into Electronics. Dick Smith. 72p. (Orig.). 1986. pap. 9.95 ea. o.p. Vol. 1, 72pps (ISBN 0-672-22548-4). Vol. 2, 128pps (ISBN 0-672-22549-2). Vol. 3, 96pps (ISBN 0-672-22550-6). Sams.

Fun with Bargello. Mira Silverstein. LC 76-162776. (Encore Editions). (Illus.). 1972. 2.95 o.p. (ISBN 0-684-15001-8, ScribT). Scribner.

Fun with Chinese Characters, Vol. 1. Tan Huay Peng. (Illus.). 192p. 1982. pap. 8.95 o.p. (ISBN 9971-4-6072-6). Hippocrene Bks.

Fun with Chinese Horoscopes. Repr. of 1987 ed. 6.95 o.p. (FUWICI). China Bks.

Fun with Growing Things. Joan Eckstein & Joyce Gleit. (Illus.). 1982. pap. 3.45 o.p. (ISBN 0-380-00344-9, 23861, Flare). Avon.

Fun with Making Things: An Activity Book for Kids. Joan Eckstein. 36p. (gr. 3-7). 1979. pap. 1.50 o.p. (ISBN 0-380-43315-X, 43315-X, Camelot). Avon.

Fun with Maths & Physics. Y. A. Perelman. 355p. 1984. 9.95 o.s.i. (ISBN 0-8285-2894-2, Pub. by Mir Pubs USSR). Imported Pubns.

Fun with Pens. Christopher Jarman. (Illus.). 1979. pap. 2.95 o.s.i. (ISBN 0-8008-3094-6, Pentalic). Taplinger.

Fun with the Alphabet. Zokeisha. (Puppet Story Board Bks.). (Illus.). 12p. (ps-2). 1981. 2.95 o.s.i. (ISBN 0-671-42646-X, Little Simon). S&S.

Fun with the Funnies: Fifty Motivating Activities for Language Arts, Writing, & Social Studies, Grades 4-6. John Guenther. 1983. pap. 7.95 o.p. (ISBN 0-673-15637-0). Scott F.

Function & Analysis of Capital Market Rates. reference ed. James C. Van Horne. LC 73-99453. 1970. pap. text ed. 20.00 o.p. (ISBN 0-13-331934-2). P-H.

Function & Form in the Sloth. M. Goffart. 1971. 60.00 o.p. (ISBN 0-08-016090-5). Pergamon.

Function of Naturally Occuring Polyamines. Uriel Bachrach. 1973. 58.50 o.p. (ISBN 0-12-070650-4). Acad Pr.

Function of Quinones in Energy Conserving Systems. Ed. by Bernard L. Trumpower. 1982. 88.50 o.p. (ISBN 0-12-701280-X). Acad Pr.

Functional Administration in Physical & Health Education. Marion L. Johnson. LC 76-13089. (Illus.). 1977. text ed. 23.50 o.p. (ISBN 0-395-20635-9). HM.

Functional Analysis & Its Applications. Ed. by H. G. Garnir et al. (Lecture Notes in Mathematics: Vol. 399). xvii, 565p. 1974. pap. 28.00 o.p. (ISBN 0-387-06869-4). Springer-Verlag.

Functional Analysis in Modern Applied Mathematics. Ed. by Ruth Curtain & A. J. Pritchard. 1977. 61.50 o.p. (ISBN 0-12-196250-4). Acad Pr.

Functional Analysis: Proceedings. Ed. by Carroll O. Wilde. 1970. 47.00 o.p. (ISBN 0-12-751750-2). Acad Pr.

Functional Anatomy of Marine Mammals, Vol. 1. Ed. by R. J. Harrison. 1973. 78.50 o.p. (ISBN 0-12-328001-X). Acad Pr.

Functional Anatomy of the Spermatazoan. Ed. by B. Afzelius. 1975. 120.00 o.p. (ISBN 0-08-018006-X). Pergamon.

Functional & Structural Nature of Biomembranes: I. Hartmut Glossman et al. LC 73-1290. (Illus.). 184p. 1972. text ed. 24.00x o.p. (ISBN 0-8422-7044-2). Irvington.

Functional & Structural Nature of Biomembranes: II. Ralph A. Reisfeld et al. LC 73-1290. (Illus.). 214p. 1973. text ed. 24.00x o.p. (ISBN 0-8290-2369-0). Irvington.

Functional Competencies for Adapting to the World of Work. Nina Selz et al. 58p. 1980. 4.50 o.p. (ISBN 0-318-22106-3, SN30). Natl Ctr Res Voc Ed.

Functional Differential Equations & Bifurcations: Proceedings. Ed. by A. F. Ize. (Lecture Notes in Mathematics: Vol. 799). 409p. 1980. pap. 28.00 o.p. (ISBN 0-387-09986-7). Springer-Verlag.

Functional English for Writers. 2nd ed. Kevin G. Burne et al. 1978. pap. write for info. o.p. (ISBN 0-673-15105-0). Scott F.

Functional Integration: Theory & Applications. Ed. by Jean-Pierre Antoine & Enrique Tirapegui. LC 80-21935. 366p. 1980. 65.00x o.p. (ISBN 0-306-40573-3, Plenum Pr). Plenum Pub.

Functional Language Intervention, 2 vols. Ed. by Thomas M. Longhurst. LC 74-6246. 1974. Vol. 1. text ed. 12.00x o.p. (ISBN 0-8422-5174-X); Vol. 2. text ed. 14.00x o.p. (ISBN 0-8422-5192-8); Vol. 1. pap. text ed. 16.95x o.p. (ISBN 0-8422-0405-9); Vol. 2. pap. text ed. 16.95x o.p. (ISBN 0-8422-0450-4). Irvington.

Functional Lessons in Singing. 2nd ed. Ivan Trusler & Walter Ehret. LC 73-180598. (Illus.). 240p. 1972. Reference ed. pap. text ed. 27.67 o.p. (ISBN 0-13-331801-X). P-H.

Functional Medical Laboratory Technology: Hematology & Urinalysis. Stanley L. Lamberg & Robert Rothstein. (Illus.). 1978. pap. 15.95 o.p. (ISBN 0-87055-268-6). AVI.

Functional Model for Fourth Generation Languages. Gary E. Fisher. LC 86-600545. (NBS Special Publication Computer Science & Technology Ser.: No. 500-133). (Illus., Orig.). 1985. pap. 2.25 o.p. (S/N 003-003-02731-6). USGPO.

Functional Morphology & Classification of Teleostean Fishes. William A. Gosline. LC 77-151454. (Illus.). 216p. 1971. pap. text ed. 10.00x o.p. (ISBN 0-87022-300-3). UH Pr.

Functional Organization of Descending Supraspinal Fibre Systems to the Spinal Cord: Anatomical Observations & Physiological Correlations. R. Nyberg-Hansen. (Advances in Anatomy, Embryology & Cell Biology: Vol. 39, Pt. 2). (Illus.). 1966. pap. 11.30 o.p. (ISBN 0-387-03494-3). Springer-Verlag.

Functional Piano. Carmen P. Rummo. 1972. 5.00 o.p. (ISBN 0-913650-41-2). CPP Belwin.

Functional Plant Planning, Layout & Materials Handling. Merle C. Nutt. LC 70-114266. (Illus.). 1970. text ed. 18.95 o.p. (ISBN 0-682-47092-9, University). Exposition-Phoenix.

Functional Writing. A. D. Van Nostrand et al. LC 77-74098. (Illus.). 1978. pap. 13.50 o.p. (ISBN 0-395-25294-6). HM.

Functioning of the Yugoslav Economy. Ed. by Radmila Stojanovic. LC 82-770. 220p. 1982. 40.00 o.p. (ISBN 0-87332-207-X). M E Sharpe.

Functions of a Complex Variable, Operational Calculus, & Stability Theory. M. L. Krasnov et al. 373p. 1985. 7.95 o.p. (ISBN 0-8285-2947-7, Pub. by Mir Pubs USSR). Imported Pubns.

Functions of Algebra & Trigonometry. Kenneth P. Bogart. LC 76-11984. (Illus.). 1977. text ed. 17.75 o.p. (ISBN 0-395-20468-2). HM.

Functions of Biological Membranes. M. Davies. (Outline Studies in Biology). 1973. pap. 7.50 o.p. (ISBN 0-412-11350-3, NO. 6080, Pub. by Chapman & Hall). Routledge Chapman & Hall.

Functions of Several Variables. B. D. Craven. 144p. 1981. 23.00x o.p. (ISBN 0-412-23330-4, NO. 6607, Pub by Chapman & Hall England); pap. 13.95x o.p. (ISBN 0-412-23340-1, NO. 6606). Routledge Chapman & Hall.

Fund Accounting: Theory & Practice. 2nd ed. Edward S. Lynn & Robert J. Freeman. (Illus.). 896p. 1983. text ed. (ISBN 0-13-332411-7). P-H.

Fund Advisors Institute, July 1980, Williamsburg, Va. Proceedings. Ed. by Elizabeth Hieb. 80p. (Orig.). 1980. pap. 8.00 o.p. (ISBN 0-89154-137-3). Intl Found Employ.

Fund Raising. Systems & Procedures Exchange Center Staff. (SPEC Kit & Flyer Ser.: No. 94). 103p. 1983. 20.00 o.p. (ISBN 0-318-03462-X). Assn Res Lib.

Fund Raising for Libraries: A Selective Bibliography. Lorna Peterson. (Public Administration Ser.: P 1726). 7p. 1985. 2.00 o.p. (ISBN 0-89028-496-2). Vance Biblios.

Fund-Raising, Grants, & Foundations: A Comprehensive Bibliography. Charlotte-Georgi & Terry Fate. LC 84-21821. 204p. 1985. lib. bdg. 27.50 o.p. (ISBN 0-87287-441-9). Libs Unl.

Fund Raising Letter Collection. William E. Sheppard. 150p. 1978. 35.00 o.p. Fund Raising.

Fundamental Computer Programming Using FORTRAN 77. Jarrell C. Grout. (Software Ser.). (Illus.). 432p. 1983. pap. text ed. (ISBN 0-13-335141-6). P-H.

Fundamental Concepts of Algebra. Claude Chevalley. (Pure and Applied Mathematics Ser.: Vol. 7). 1957. 59.00 o.p. (ISBN 0-12-172050-0). Acad Pr.

Fundamental Concepts of Estate Planning 1984. (Tax Law & Estate Planning Course Handbook Ser.: Vol. 149). 467p. 1984. 45.00 o.p. (ISBN 0-317-11435-2, D4-5169). PLI.

Fundamental Concepts of Mathematics. 2nd ed. R. L. Goodstein. 1979. 69.00 o.p. (ISBN 0-08-021665-X); pap. 25.00 o.p. (ISBN 0-08-021666-8). Pergamon.

Fundamental Constants & Quantum Electrodynamics. B. N. Taylor et al. (Reviews of Modern Physics Monographs). 1969. 46.50 o.p. (ISBN 0-12-684050-4). Acad Pr.

Fundamental Duties: A Volume of Essays by Present & Former Members of the Law Faculty of the University of Exeter to Commemorate the Silver Jubilee of the University. Ed. by D. Lasok et al. LC 80-40933. 269p. 1980. 43.00 o.p. (ISBN 0-08-024048-8); pap. 16.75 o.p. (ISBN 0-08-024049-6). Pergamon.

Fundamental Fulfillment. James Park. (Existential Freedom Ser.: No. 7). 1975. pap. 5.00x o.p. (ISBN 0-89231-007-3). Existential Bks.

Fundamental Harmony. Hugo Norden. LC 73-123576. 7.50 o.s.i. (ISBN 0-8008-3103-9, Crescendo). Taplinger.

Fundamental Harmony Workbook. Edward J. Madden. pap. 2.50 o.s.i. (ISBN 0-8008-3101-2, Crescendo). Taplinger.

Fundamental Interactions: Cargese 1981. Ed. by J. L. Basdevant & R. Gastmans. LC 82-10164. (NATO ASI Series B, Physics: Vol. 85). 714p. 1982. 105.00x o.p. (ISBN 0-306-41116-4, Plenum Pr). Plenum Pub.

Fundamental Issues in Present-day China. Xiaoping Deng. 202p. 1987. 9.95 o.p.; pap. 5.95 o.p. China Bks.

Fundamental Laws of Mechanics. I. E. Irodov. 1980. pap. 6.45 o.p. (ISBN 0-8285-1803-3, Pub. by Mir Pubs USSR). Imported Pubns.

Fundamental Laws of the State of Israel. Ed. by Joseph Badi. LC 61-8605. 451p. 1961. text ed. 56.00x o.p. (ISBN 0-8290-0174-3). Irvington.

Fundamental Legal Documents of Communist China. Ed. by Albert P. Blaustein. xxix, 603p. 1962. 20.00x o.p. (ISBN 0-8377-0300-X). Rothman.

Fundamental Motor Patterns. 3rd ed. Ralph L. Wickstrom. LC 82-21659. (Illus.). 250p. 1983. text ed. 17.50 o.p. (ISBN 0-8121-0879-5). Lea & Febiger.

Fundamental of Play Directing. 4th ed. Alexander Dean & Lawrence Carra. LC 79-26236. 417p. 1980. text ed. 25.95 o.p. (ISBN 0-03-021551-X, HoltC). HR&W.

Fundamental Physics of Radiology. 3rd ed. W. Meredith & J. Massey. 718p. 1977. 50.00 o.p. (ISBN 0-7236-0778-8, Pub. by John Wright UK). Butterworth.

Fundamental Principles of Heat Transfer. S. Whitaker. 1977. text ed. 38.50 o.p. (ISBN 0-08-017866-9). Pergamon.

Fundamental Processes in Energetic Atomic Collisions. Ed. by H. O. Lutz et al. (NATO ASI Series B, Physics: Vol. 103). 678p. 1983. 120.00x o.p. (ISBN 0-306-41465-1, Plenum Pr). Plenum Pub.

Fundamental Relationships & Their Logical Formulations. Fred S. Johnston. LC 73-91714. 231p. 1974. (ISBN 0-8022-2134-3). Philos Lib.

Fundamental Research in Homogeneous Catalysis, Vol. 1. Ed. by M. Tsutsui & R. Ugo. LC 77-13024. 252p. 1977. 55.00x o.p. (ISBN 0-306-34441-6, Plenum Pr). Plenum Pub.

Fundamental Research in Homogeneous Catalysis, Vol. 2. Ed. by Y. Ishii & M. Tsutsui. LC 77-13024. 306p. 1978. 59.50x o.p. (ISBN 0-306-40033-2, Plenum Pr). Plenum Pub.

Fundamental Research in Homogeneous Catalysis, Vol. 3. Ed. by M. Tsutsui. LC 77-13024. 1072p. 1979. 145.00x o.p. (ISBN 0-306-40199-1, Plenum Pr). Plenum Pub.

Fundamental Research in Organometallic Chemistry. Ed. by Minoru Tsutsui & Yoshio Ishii. 1008p. 1982. 72.95 o.p. (ISBN 0-442-27216-2). Van Nos Reinhold.

Fundamental Research on Estuaries. 96p. 1983. 6.95x o.p. (ISBN 0-309-03378-0). Natl Acad Pr.

Fundamental Statistics for Psychology. 2nd ed. Robert B. McCall. 1975. text ed. 18.95 o.p. (ISBN 0-15-529413-X, HC). HarBraceJ.

Fundamental Statistics for Psychology. 3rd ed. Robert B. McCall. 420p. 1980. text ed. 20.75 o.p. (ISBN 0-15-529417-2, HC). HarBraceJ.

Fundamental Techniques in Virology. Ed. by K. Habel & N. P. Salzman. 1969. 97.00 o.p. (ISBN 0-12-312650-9). Acad Pr.

Fundamental Techniques of Plastic Surgery. 7th ed. Ian A. McGregor. (Illus.). 324p. 1980. pap. text ed. 36.00 o.p. (ISBN 0-443-01828-6). Churchill.

Fundamental Things Apply: Reflecting on Christian Basics. Clyde F. Crews. LC 83-71005. 104p. (Orig.). 1983. pap. 3.95 o.p. (ISBN 0-87793-272-7). Ave Maria.

Fundamentalism. James Barr. LC 77-14512. 396p. 1978. pap. 9.50 o.s.i. (ISBN 0-664-24191-3, Westminster). Westminster John Knox.

Fundamentals Learning Through Making Music. Jay Zorn & James Hanshumaker. Ed. by Sandy Feldstein. LC 79-25768. 1980. pap. 13.50 o.p. (ISBN 0-88284-105-X). Alfred Pub.

Fundamentals of Abnormal Psychology. Frederick G. Mears & Robert J. Gatchel. 1979. text ed. 40.36 o.p. (ISBN 0-395-30674-4). HM.

Fundamentals of Accounting. 5th ed. Sidney Davidson & James Schinder. LC 74-80399. 1975. text ed. 31.95x o.s.i. (ISBN 0-03-082803-1); instr's. manual 20.00 o.s.i. (ISBN 0-03-089652-5). Dryden Pr.

Fundamentals of Aerospace Instrumentation & Fundamentals of Test Measurement: Tutorial Proceedings of the International Instrumentation Symposium, 28th, 1982, Vol. 13 & Vol. 8. International Instrumentation Symposium Staff. LC 68-59468. 112p. 1982. pap. text ed. 25.00x o.p. (ISBN 0-87664-692-5). Instru Soc.

Fundamentals of Aerospace Instrumentation & Fundamentals of Test Measurement: Tutorial Proceedings of the 29th International Instrumentation Symposium, Vol. 14 & Vol. 9. International Instrumentation Symposium Staff. LC 68-59468. 112p. 1983. pap. text ed. 25.00x o.p. (ISBN 0-87664-757-3). Instru Soc.

Fundamentals of Aerospace Instrumentation, Vol. 11 & Fundamentals of Test Measurement, Vol. 6: Tutorial Proceedings of the International Instrumentation Symposium, 25th, Anaheim, California, 1979. International Instrumentation Symposium Staff. LC 68-59468. 97p. 1979. pap. text ed. 15.00x o.p. (ISBN 0-87664-435-3). Instru Soc.

Fundamentals of Aerospace Instrumentation, Vol. 12 & Fundamentals of Test Measurement, Vol. 7: Tutorial Proceedings of the International Instrumentation Symposium, 26th, Seattle, Washington, 1980. International Instrumentation Symposium Staff. LC 68-59468. 128p. 1980. pap. text ed. 18.00x o.p. (ISBN 0-87664-474-4). Instru Soc.

Fundamentals of Aerospace Instrumentation, Vol. 15 & Fundamentals of Test Measurement, Vol. 10: Tutorial Proceedings of the International Instrumentation Symposium, 30th. International Instrumentation Symposium Staff. LC 68-59468. 32p. 1984. pap. text ed. 12.00x o.p. (ISBN 0-87664-807-3). Instru Soc.

Fundamentals of Algebra: An Integrated Text-Workbook. Robert Donaghey & JoAnna Ruddel. (Illus.). 559p. 1978. pap. text ed. 22.00 o.p. (ISBN 0-15-529420-2, HC). HarBraceJ.

Fundamentals of Analytical Chemistry. 4th ed. Douglas A. Skoog & Donald M. West. 1982. text ed. 55.75x o.p. (ISBN 0-03-058459-0, CBS C); solns. manual 14.00 o.p. (ISBN 0-03-058461-2). SCP.

Fundamentals of Analytical Flame Spectroscopy. Cornelis T. Alkemade & Roland Herrmann. LC 79-4376. 442p. 1979. 112.00 o.p. (ISBN 0-470-26710-0). Halsted Pr.

Fundamentals of Angiography. Marianne R. Tortorici. LC 81-18803. (Illus.). 304p. 1982. text ed. 31.95 o.p. (ISBN 0-8016-5014-3). Mosby.

Fundamentals of Applied Physics. C. Thomas Olivo & Thomas P. Olivo. LC 77-79381. 1978. text ed. 29.95 o.p. (ISBN 0-8273-1300-4); instr's. guide 8.50 o.p. (ISBN 0-8273-1301-2). Delmar.

Fundamentals of Aseptic Technique 1987. (User's Guide for Computer Software Ser.). 24p. 1987. 299.00 o.p. (ISBN 0-939583-31-3). Assn Oper Rm Nurses.

Fundamentals of Astrodynamics. R. R. Bate et al. (Illus.). 16.00 o.p. (ISBN 0-8446-0025-3). Peter Smith.

Fundamentals of Biochemical Pharmacology. Ed. by Z. M. Bacq et al. LC 75-135101. 1973. text ed. 62.00 o.p. (ISBN 0-08-016453-6); pap. 150.00 o.p. (ISBN 0-08-017775-1). Pergamon.

Fundamentals of Bonding: A Manual on Fidelity & Surety. David Porter. cancelled o.s.i. (ISBN 0-686-31029-2, 26570). Rough Notes.

Fundamentals of Botany. K. S. Bilgrami et al. 706p. 1986. text ed. 45.00x o.p. (ISBN 0-7069-2893-8, Pub. by Vikas India). Advent NY.

Fundamentals of Business Mathematics. 3rd ed. Walter E. Williams & James H. Reed. 736p. 1984. text ed. write for info o.p. (ISBN 0-697-08069-2). Wm C Brown.

Fundamentals of Chemical Reaction Engineering. Charles D. Holland & Raymond G. Anthony. (International Series in the Physical & Chemical Engineering Sciences). (Illus.). 1979. text ed. 59.00 o.p. (ISBN 0-13-335596-9). P-H.

Fundamentals of Chemistry. 2nd ed. James E. Brady & John R. Holum. LC 83-21796. 960p. 1984. (ISBN 0-471-87548-1). Wiley.

Fundamentals of Chemistry. Edward Kostiner & Jesse R. Rea. 480p. 1979. text ed. 18.50 o.p. (ISBN 0-15-529430-X, HC). HarBraceJ.

Fundamentals of Chemistry. Fred H. Redmore. (Illus.). 1979. Reference ed. text ed. 39.33 o.p. (ISBN 0-13-335158-0). P-H.

Fundamentals of Chemistry. Michael Wartell & Jack Cummins. 450p. 1980. pub net 22.50 o.p. (ISBN 0-87150-736-6, W6 4271). Brooks-Cole.

Fundamentals of Chemistry: A Modern Introduction. 3rd ed. Frank Brescia et al. 1975. 7.50 o.p. (ISBN 0-12-132332-3); tchr's. manual 1976 1.00 o.p. (ISBN 0-12-132373-0). Acad Pr.

Fundamentals of Chemistry in the Laboratory. Francis M. Pottenger et al. 1976. pap. write for info. o.p. (ISBN 0-673-07877-9). Scott F.

Fundamentals of Child Counseling. Donald B. Keat. 300p. 1974. text ed. 23.95 o.p. (ISBN 0-395-17827-4). HM.

Fundamentals of Child Development. 2nd ed. Harry Munsinger. LC 74-23601. (Illus.). 1975. text ed. 19.95 o.p. (ISBN 0-03-091881-2, HoltC). HR&W.

Fundamentals of Circuits, Electronics, & Signal Analysis. Kendall L. Su. LC 77-74147. (Illus.). 1978. text ed. 44.50 o.p. (ISBN 0-395-25038-2). HM.

Fundamentals of Civil Litigation Preparation: Research, Pleadings, & Paper Discovery. Massachusetts Continuing Legal Education, Inc. Staff. LC 84-61755. 1985. 25.00 o.p. Mass CLE.

Fundamentals of Civil Motion Practice. Massachusetts Continuing Legal Education, Inc. Staff. LC 84-61765. (Illus.). 120p. 1985. 25.00 o.p. Mass CLE.

Fundamentals of Clinical Nutrition. Rebecca Shoden & Sue Griffin. (Illus.). 1980. text ed. 11.95 o.p. (ISBN 0-07-056991-6). McGraw.

Fundamentals of Clinical Trials. 2nd ed. L. Friedman et al. 320p. 1985. 31.00 o.p. (ISBN 0-88416-499-3). Year Bk Med.

Fundamentals of College Algebra & Trigonometry. Robert Ellis & Denny Gulick. 448p. 1984. text ed. 25.00 net o.p. (ISBN 0-15-529350-8, HC). HarBraceJ.

Fundamentals of Communication. John R. Bittner. (Illus.). 560p. 1985. pap. text ed. (ISBN 0-13-335217-X). P-H.

Fundamentals of Compressible Flow. S. M. Yahya. LC 81-13390. 358p. 1982. 26.95x o.p. (ISBN 0-470-27282-1). Halsted Pr.

Fundamentals of Computer Education. Janice L. Flake et al. 396p. 1985. pap. text ed. write for info., Incl. disk o.p. (ISBN 0-534-04764-5). Wadsworth Pub.

Fundamentals of Computer Logic. David Hutchison. LC 80-42028. (Ellis Horwood Series in Computers & their Applications). 214p. 1981. 79.95x o.p. (ISBN 0-470-27117-5). Halsted Pr.

Fundamentals of Concept Formation in Empirical Science. Carl G. Hempel. (Foundations of the Unity of Science Ser: Vol. 2, No. 7). 1952. pap. text ed. 2.25x o.s.i. (ISBN 0-226-57597-7, P416, Phoen). U of Chicago Pr.

Fundamentals of Construction Estimating & Cost Accounting. Keith Collier. (Illus.). 400p. 1974. pap. text ed. 39.33 o.p. (ISBN 0-13-335604-3). P-H.

Fundamentals of Corporate Organization. Massachusetts Continuing Legal Education, Inc. Staff. LC 84-61751. (Illus.). 336p. 1985. 35.00 o.p. Mass CLE.

Fundamentals of Counseling. 2nd ed. Bruce E. Shertzer & Shelley C. Stone. 544p. 1974. text ed. 17.75 o.p. (ISBN 0-395-17580-1). HM.

Fundamentals of Crane Design. J. Kogan. 560p. 1975. text ed. 110.00x o.p. (ISBN 0-7065-1450-5, Pub. by Keter Pub Jerusalem). Coronet Bks.

Fundamentals of Dairy Chemistry. 2nd ed. Ed. by Byron H. Webb et al. 1974. 69.95 o.p. (ISBN 0-87055-143-4). AVI.

Fundamentals of Dental Hygiene Instrumentation. Jill S. Nield & Ginger H. O'Connor. (Illus.). 368p. 1983. pap. (ISBN 0-7216-6778-3). Saunders.

Fundamentals of Dental Radiography. 2nd ed. Lincoln R. Manson-Hing. LC 84-12594. (Illus.). 236p. 1985. text ed. 24.75 o.p. (ISBN 0-8121-0960-0). Lea & Febiger.

Fundamentals of Digital Filtering with Applications in Geophysical Prospecting for Oil. A. Mesko. LC 83-5835. 512p. 1984. 74.95x o.p. (ISBN 0-470-27444-1). Halsted Pr.

Fundamentals of Digital Systems Design. V. Thomas Rhyne. LC 72-6903. (Illus.). 560p. 1973. text ed. 55.00 o.p. (ISBN 0-13-336156-X). P-H.

Fundamentals of Dimensional Metrology. Busch & Wilkie Brothers Foundation Staff. LC 64-12593. 428p. 1966. 21.95 o.p. (ISBN 0-8273-0193-6). Delmar.

Fundamentals of Dual-Phase Steels: Proceedings of the AIME Meeting, Chicago, IL, 1981. Ed. by Richard A. Kot & Bruce L. Bramfitt. (Illus.). 502p. 48.00 o.p. (ISBN 0-89520-383-9); members 32.00 o.p. (ISBN 0-317-36240-2); student members 18.00 o.p. (ISBN 0-317-36241-0). ASM.

Fundamentals of Electricity & Automotive Electrical Systems. Thomas Weathers & Claud Hunter. (Illus.). 256p. 1981. pap. text ed. 29.00 o.p. (ISBN 0-13-337030-5). P-H.

Fundamentals of Electricity for Agriculture. Gustafson. 1980. 25.95 o.p. (ISBN 0-87055-481-6). Van Nos Reinhold.

Fundamentals of Electro-Optical Remote Sensing. Irving W. Ginsberg. 1988. price not set o.p. Orbit Bk Co.

Fundamentals of Electrochemical Analysis. Z. Galus. Tr. by G. F. Reynolds from Pol. LC 76-5838. (Series in Analytical Chemistry). 520p. 1976. 121.95 o.p. (ISBN 0-470-15080-7). Halsted Pr.

Fundamentals of Employee Benefit Programs. 2nd ed. Employee Benefit Research Institute Staff. LC 85-6764. 235p. 1985. 28.00 o.p. (ISBN 0-86643-042-3); pap. 15.00 o.p. (ISBN 0-86643-041-5). Employee Benefit.

Fundamentals of Energy Engineering. Fairmount Press, Inc. Staff & Albert Thumann. (Illus.). 400p. 1984. text ed. 43.00 o.p. (ISBN 0-13-338327-X). P-H.

Fundamentals of Engineering Drawing. Cecil H. Jensen & Jay Helsel. 1979. text ed. 35.95 o.p. (ISBN 0-07-032517-0). McGraw.

Fundamentals of English Grammar. Mildred R. Jenkins. (Illus.). 208p. 1983. 10.50 o.p. (ISBN 0-682-49904-8). Exposition-Phoenix.

Fundamentals of Entomology. John N. Belkin. 220p. 1976. pap. 12.95x o.p. (ISBN 0-916846-10-5). Flora & Fauna.

Fundamentals of Entomology. 2nd ed. Richard J. Elzinga. (Illus.). 464p. 1981. pap. text ed. (ISBN 0-13-338194-3). P-H.

Fundamentals of Entomology & Plant Pathology. 2nd ed. Louis L. Pyenson. (Illus.). 1980. 27.95 o.p. (ISBN 0-87055-334-8). AVI.

Fundamentals of Estate Planning. rev. ed. Jack Keir & Carl P. Lundy. Rev. by Bernhart R. Snyder. LC 79-92663. 1982. 11.95 o.p. (ISBN 0-87863-037-6, Farnsworth Pub Co). Longman Finan.

Fundamentals of Financial Management. 3rd ed. Eugene F. Brigham. 832p. 1983. 35.95x o.p. (ISBN 0-03-062619-6); instr's. manual 20.00 o.p. (ISBN 0-03-062621-8). Dryden Pr.

Fundamentals of Flight. Richard S. Shevell. (Illus.). 464p. 1983. text ed. 57.00 o.p. (ISBN 0-13-339093-4). P-H.

Fundamentals of Fluid Power. William D. Wolansky et al. LC 76-13963. (Illus.). 1977. text ed. 36.50 o.p. (ISBN 0-395-18956-X). HM.

Fundamentals of Food Freezing. Norman W. Desrosier & Donald K. Tressler. (Illus.). 1977. pap. 29.95 o.s.i. (ISBN 0-87055-290-2). AVI.

Fundamentals of Food Process Engineering. Romeo T. Toledo. (Illus.). 1980. pap. 27.95 o.p. (ISBN 0-87055-338-0). AVI.

Fundamentals of Food Processing Operations: Ingredients, Methods & Packaging. John L. Heid & Maynard A. Joslyn. (Illus.). 1967. pap. 45.95 o.p. (ISBN 0-87055-014-4). AVI.

Fundamentals of Formation Evaluation. Donald P. Helander. (Illus.). 344p. 1983. 48.00 o.p. (P-7049). Oil & Gas.

Fundamentals of Gas Dynamics. Robert P. Benedict. LC 83-1273. 272p. 1983. text ed. (ISBN 0-471-09193-6); solutions manual o.p. (ISBN 0-471-87340-3). Wiley.

Fundamentals of Gas-Surface Interactions: Proceedings. Ed. by Howard Saltsburg et al. 1967. 79.50 o.p. (ISBN 0-12-616950-0). Acad Pr.

Fundamentals of Genetics. 2nd ed. A. S. Islam. 520p. 1982. text ed. 30.00x o.p. (ISBN 0-7069-1798-7, Pub. by Vikas India). Advent NY.

Fundamentals of Good Writing. Cleanth Brooks & Robert Penn Warren. LC 50-7936. 1950. 14.50 o.s.i. (ISBN 0-15-134157-5). HarBraceJ.

Fundamentals of Guidance. 3rd ed. Bruce E. Shertzer & Shelley C. Stone. LC 75-31026. (Illus.). 576p. 1976. text ed. 20.30 o.p. (ISBN 0-395-20621-9). HM.

Fundamentals of Guidance. 4th ed. Bruce E. Shertzer & Shelley C. Stone. LC 80-81917. (Illus.). 576p. 1980. text ed. 36.36 o.p. (ISBN 0-395-29712-5). HM.

Fundamentals of Harmony. Siegmund Levarie. LC 84-67829. xiii, 151p. 1984. Repr. of 1954 ed. lib. bdg. 35.00x o.p. (ISBN 0-313-24526-6, LEFU). Greenwood.

Fundamentals of Heat Transfer. Lindon Thomas. (Illus.). 1980. text ed. 59.00 o.p. (ISBN 0-13-339903-6). P-H.

Fundamentals of Holography. Yu. N. Denisyuk. 136p. 1985. pap. 3.95 o.s.i. (ISBN 0-8285-2876-4, Pub. by Mir Pubs USSR). Imported Pubns.

Fundamentals of Human Lymphoid Cell Culture. Glick. 176p. 1980. 45.00 o.p. (ISBN 0-8247-6988-0). Dekker.

Fundamentals of Human Sexuality. 3rd ed. Herant Katchadourian & Donald T. Lunde. LC 80-10603. 534p. 1980. pap. text ed. 27.95 o.p. (ISBN 0-03-042941-2, HoltC). HR&W.

Fundamentals of Hydraulic Engineering Systems. Ned H. Hwang. (P-H Ser. in Environmental Sciences). (Illus.). 352p. 1981. text ed. (ISBN 0-13-340000-X). P-H.

Fundamentals of Idaho Real Estate. David L. Rockwell et al. (Illus.). 458p. (Orig.). 1985. pap. 29.95 o.p. (ISBN 0-915799-15-4). Natl Real Estate Inst.

Fundamentals of Income Tax Return Preparation with Related Planning Considerations. Massachusetts Continuing Legal Education-New England Law Institute, Inc. Staff. LC 84-62953. 298p. write for info. o.p. Mass CLE.

Fundamentals of Infection Control: An In-Service Orientation Program. Charles P. Craig. 280p. 1983. pap. 27.95 o.p. (ISBN 0-87489-187-6). Med Economics.

Fundamentals of Inferential Statistics for Business Analysis. 2nd ed. Howard B. Baltz. 416p. 1985. pap. text ed. 22.95 o.p. (ISBN 0-8403-2217-8). Kendall-Hunt.

Fundamentals of Instructing - Basic Ground Instructor Test Book. cancelled o.s.i. (ISBN 0-940732-34-3, ASA-FOI-BGI-B). Av Suppl & Acad.

Fundamentals of Instructing & Ground Instructor, Basic-Advanced, Question Book. (FAA-T-8080-4A Ser.). (Illus.). 104p. 1986. pap. 4.25 o.p. (ISBN 0-318-19955-6, S/N 050-007-00720-5). USGPO.

Fundamentals of Instructing Flight & Ground Instructors Written Test Guide. Federal Aviation Administration Staff. 36p. 1979. pap. text ed. 2.25 o.p. (ISBN 0-939158-17-5). Flightshops.

Fundamentals of Instructing, Flight Instructor, Ground Instructor, Basic & Advanced, Question Book. (FAA-T-8080-3B Ser.). (Illus.). 162p. 1988. pap. 8.50 o.p. (S/N 050-007-00790-6). USGPO.

Fundamentals of Integrated GC-Ms, Pt. I: Gas Chromatograpghy. B. J. Gudzinowicz et al. (Chromatographic Science Ser.: Vol. 7). 1976. 99.75 o.p. (ISBN 0-8247-6365-3). Dekker.

Fundamentals of Internal Medicine. Donald Kaye & Louis F. Rose. LC 82-3600. (Illus.). 1344p. 1982. pap. 39.95 o.p. (ISBN 0-8016-2622-6). Mosby.

Fundamentals of International Taxation. 2nd ed. Jon E. Bischel & Robert Feinschreiber. LC 77-78052. 1985. text ed. 35.00 o.p. (ISBN 0-685-85339-X, J1-1416). PLI.

Fundamentals of Investing: Student Guide. Iris F. Hartley. (FLMI Insurance Education Program Ser.). 1984. 7.00 o.p. (ISBN 0-915322-67-6). LOMA.

Fundamentals of Investments. 3rd ed. Richard A. Stevenson. Ed. by Edward H. Jennings. (Illus.). 662p. 1984. text ed. 39.75 o.p. (ISBN 0-314-77825-X); instr's. manual avail. o.p. (ISBN 0-314-77826-8). West Pub.

Fundamentals of Legal Drafting (1965) Reed Dickerson. 1965. 18.00 o.p. (ISBN 0-316-18394-6). Little.

Fundamentals of Linear Algebra. Katsumi Nomizu. LC 77-7468. 1979. text ed. 19.95 o.p. (ISBN 0-8284-0276-0). Chelsea Pub.

Fundamentals of Linear Algebra & Analytical Geometry. Y. S. Bugrov & S. M. Nikolsky. Tr. by Leonid Levant. 189p. 1982. pap. 3.45 o.p. (ISBN 0-8285-2445-9, Pub. by Mir Pubs USSR). Imported Pubns.

Fundamentals of Linguistic Analysis. Ronald W. Langacker. 375p. 1972. text ed. 15.95 o.p. (ISBN 0-15-529455-5, HC). HarBraceJ.

Fundamentals of Logic. 3rd ed. James D. Carney & Richard K. Scheer. (Illus.). 1980. text ed. write for info. o.p. (ISBN 0-02-319480-4). Macmillan.

Fundamentals of Management: Functions, Behavior, Models. 4th ed. James Donnelly et al. 1981. 18.50x o.p. (ISBN 0-256-02073-6). Irwin.

Fundamentals of Management Science. 3rd ed. Turban & Meredith. 1985. 42.95x o.p. (ISBN 0-256-03078-2); study guide 12.95x o.p. (ISBN 0-256-03079-0). Irwin.

Fundamentals of Management Science. rev. ed. Efraim Turban & Jack Meredith. 1981. 22.50x o.p. (ISBN 0-686-77310-1). Irwin.

Fundamentals of Management: Selected Readings. 4th ed. Ed. by James H. Donnelly, Jr. et al. 1981. pap. 11.95 o.p. (ISBN 0-256-02426-X). Irwin.

Fundamentals of Mathematical Analysis, 2 vols. G. M. Fikhtengol'ts. 1965. Vol. 2. 33.00 o.p. (ISBN 0-08-010060-0); Vol. 1. text ed. 27.00 o.p. (ISBN 0-08-010059-7); Vol. 2. pap. 23.00 o.p. (ISBN 0-08-013474-2); Vol. 1. pap. text ed. 18.75 o.p. (ISBN 0-08-013473-4). Pergamon.

Fundamentals of Mathematics. rev. ed. 154p. 1981. Text. training materials 3400.00x o.p. (ISBN 0-87683-050-5); 60.00x o.p. (ISBN 0-87683-051-3). GP Pub.

Fundamentals of Mathematics: Outline & Review Problems for Electronic Circuit Fundamentals. Walter J. Weir & Gregory Weir. (Illus.). 192p. 1987. pap. text ed. 13.00 o.p. (ISBN 0-13-341090-0). P-H.

Fundamentals of Men's Fashion Design: A Guide to Tailored Clothes. rev. ed. Masaaki Kawashima. LC 73-91066. (Illus.). 224p. 1976. 18.50x o.p. (ISBN 0-87005-105-9). Fairchild.

Fundamentals of Metal Machining & Machine Tools. Boothroyd. 350p. 1975. 42.50 o.p. (ISBN 0-89116-473-1). Hemisphere Pub.

Fundamentals of Metallurgical Processes. L. Coudurier & I. Wilkomirsky. 1978. text ed. 62.00 o.p. (ISBN 0-08-019612-8); pap. text ed. 18.75 o.p. (ISBN 0-08-019654-3). Pergamon.

Fundamentals of Microalloying Forging Steels. Ed. by G. Krauss & S. Banerji. LC 87-5664. 1987. 62.00 o.p. (ISBN 0-87339-062-8). Minerals Metals.

Fundamentals of Microelectronics. I. P. Stepanenko. 455p. 1982. 10.95 o.p. (ISBN 0-8285-2512-9, Pub. by Mir Pubs USSR). Imported Pubns.

Fundamentals of Microprocessors. Henry O. Daley. 1983. text ed. 30.95 o.p. (ISBN 0-03-059934-2). HR&W.

Fundamentals of Modern Business. Swindle. 1977. (ISBN 0-534-00506-3); (ISBN 0-534-00509-8). PWS-Kent Pub.

Fundamentals of Montana Real Estate. David L. Rockwell et al. (Illus.). 462p. (Orig.). 1985. pap. 29.95 o.p. (ISBN 0-915799-19-7). Natl Real Estate Inst.

Fundamentals of Municipal Bonds. Public Securities Association Staff. LC 80-83540. (Illus.). 208p. 1982. text ed. 17.00 o.s.i. (ISBN 0-9605198-0-7). Pub Securities.

Fundamentals of Municipal Borrowing. 320p. 1984. 30.00 o.p. (ISBN 0-318-03914-1, 261). PA Bar Inst.

Fundamentals of Music. 3rd ed. Raymond Elliott. LC 76-139599. (Illus.). 1987. pap. text ed. (ISBN 0-13-341305-5). P-H.

Fundamentals of Music. Richard Wink. LC 76-20867. (Illus.). 1977. pap. 23.95 o.p. (ISBN 0-395-20598-0). HM.

Fundamentals of Music Theory. Sterling P. Cossaboom. LC 72-87760. 1973. pap. 2.50 o.s.i. (ISBN 0-8008-3102-0, Crescendo). Taplinger.

Fundamentals of Network Analysis & Synthesis. Behrouz Peikari. LC 82-4708. 512p. 1982. Repr. of 1974 ed. PLB 35.50 o.p. (ISBN 0-89874-538-1). Krieger.

Fundamentals of Numerical Computation: International Conference. Ed. by G. Alefeld & R. D. Crigorieff. (Computing Supplementum: No. 2). (Illus.). 250p. 1980. pap. 57.90 o.p. (ISBN 0-387-81566-X). Springer-Verlag.

Fundamentals of Nursing: Concepts, Process & Practice. Potter & Perry. 1985. 44.95 o.p. (ISBN 0-8016-3828-3). Mosby.

Fundamentals of Nutrition. Martha D. Dunn. (Illus.). 580p. 1983. 26.95 o.p. (ISBN 0-8436-2284-9). Van Nos Reinhold.

Fundamentals of Occlusion & Temporomandibular Disorders. Jeffrey P. Okeson. (Illus.). 512p. 1985. 49.95 o.p. (ISBN 0-8016-3707-4). Mosby.

Fundamentals of Orofacial Myology. Marvin L. Hanson & Richard H. Barrett. (Illus.). 440p. 1989. text ed. 54.75x o.p. (ISBN 0-398-05518-1). C C Thomas.

Fundamentals of Paleontology: Mammals. Ed. by Y. A. Orlov. 592p. 1968. text ed. 117.50x o.p. (ISBN 0-7065-0494-1, Pub. by Keter Pub Jerusalem). Coronet Bks.

Fundamentals of Paleontology: Porifera, Archaeocyatha, Coelentera, Vermes. Ed. by Y. A. Orlov. 912p. 1971. text ed. 180.00x o.p. (ISBN 0-317-46492-2, Pub. by Keter Pub Jerusalem). Coronet Bks.

Fundamentals of Physical Science. 6th ed. Konrad B. Krauskopf & Arthur Beiser. LC 76-152006. (Illus.). 1971. text ed. 34.95 o.p. (ISBN 0-07-035440-5, +007). McGraw.

Fundamentals of Physics. 5th ed. Henry Semat & Philip Baumel. LC 73-19985. 593p. 1974. text ed. 23.95 o.p. (ISBN 0-03-084747-8, HoltC). HR&W.

Fundamentals of Physics, 2 vols. B. M. Yavorsky & A. A. Pinsky. 1030p. 1974. Set. 11.50 o.p. (ISBN 0-8285-0781-3, Pub. by Mir Pubs USSR). Imported Pubns.

Fundamentals of Plant Genetics & Breeding. James R. Welsh. LC 80-14638. 304p. 1981. 38.95 o.p. (ISBN 0-471-02862-2). Wiley.

Fundamentals of Political Economy. M. N. Ryndina et al. 1980. 7.95 o.p. (ISBN 0-8285-1776-2, Pub. by Progress Pubs USSR). Imported Pubns.

Fundamentals of Political Science. A. M. Yakovlev. 559p. 1979. 5.45 o.p. (ISBN 0-8285-0227-7, Pub. by Progress Pubs USSR). Imported Pubns.

Fundamentals of Portland Cement Concrete - A Quantitative Approach: Fresh Concrete, Vol. 1. Ed. by Sandor Popovics. LC 81-2796. 477p. 1982. 65.50x o.p. (ISBN 0-471-86217-7, Pub. by Wiley-Interscience). Wiley.

Fundamentals of Press Tool Design. W. F. Walker. (Illus.). 150p. 1956. (ISBN 0-8022-1797-4). Philos Lib.

Fundamentals of Programming Languages. 2nd ed. E. Horowitz. (Illus.). xv, 446p. 1983. 29.50 o.p. (ISBN 0-387-12944-8). Springer-Verlag.

Fundamentals of Programming Languages. Ellis Horowitz. 1983. 26.95 o.p. (ISBN 0-914894-37-4, Computer Sci Pr). W H Freeman.

Fundamentals of Property & Casualty Insurance: Your Passkey to the Licensing Exam. 2nd ed. LC 86-11850. 1987. 27.95 o.p. (ISBN 0-88462-680-6, 5311-07, Reus Real Estate). Longman Finan.

Fundamentals of Psychiatry. Robert Waldinger. LC 86-3327. 496p. 1986. text ed. 24.95x o.p. (ISBN 0-88048-208-7, 48-208-7). Am Psychiatric.

Fundamentals of Psychoanalysis. Franz Alexander. 1963. pap. 4.95x o.p. (ISBN 0-393-00206-3, N206, Norton Lib). Norton.

Fundamentals of Quantum Mechanics. V. Fock. 375p. 1978. 8.45 o.p. (ISBN 0-8285-5197-9, Pub. by Mir Pubs USSR). Imported Pubns.

Fundamentals of Radiobiology. 2nd ed. Z. M. Bacq & P. Alexander. 1961. 150.00 o.p. (ISBN 0-08-009406-6). Pergamon.

Fundamentals of Radiography, Module 26-5. (Nondestructive Examination Techniques I Ser.). (Illus.). 84p. 1979. spiral bdg. 9.00x o.p. (ISBN 0-87683-094-7). GP Pub.

Fundamentals of Russian. rev. ed. Horace G. Lunt. 1968. 11.00x o.p. (ISBN 0-393-09695-5, NortonC); test & tape set 90.00 o.p. (ISBN 0-393-99113-X). Norton.

Fundamentals of Scientific Communism. V. Afansyev. 214p. 1981. 3.95 o.p. (ISBN 0-8285-2234-0, Pub. by Progress Pubs USSR). Imported Pubns.

Fundamentals of Semiconductor Devices. Edward S. Yang. (Illus.). 1978. text ed. 49.95 o.p. (ISBN 0-07-072236-6). McGraw.

Fundamentals of Sensation & Perception. Michael W. Levine & Jeremy M. Shefner. (Illus.). 528p. 1981. text ed. 23.00 o.p. (ISBN 0-394-34772-2, RanC). Random.

Fundamentals of Special Radiographic Procedures. Albert M. Snopek. (Illus.). 352p. 1975. text ed. 39.95 o.p. (ISBN 0-07-059515-1). McGraw.

Fundamentals of Speech Communication: The Credibility of Ideas. 4th ed. Bert Bradley. 432p. 1984. pap. text ed. write for info o.p. (ISBN 0-697-04247-2). Wm C Brown.

Fundamentals of Sports Biomechanics. Charles Simonian. (Illus.). 224p. 1981. text ed. 26.67 o.p. (ISBN 0-13-344499-6). P-H.

Fundamentals of Sports Training. L. Mateveyev. 310p. 1981. 8.00 o.p. (ISBN 0-8285-2120-4, Pub. by Progress Pubs USSR). Imported Pubns.

Fundamentals of Statistics in the Biological, Medical, & Health Sciences. Richard P. Runyon. 393p. 1985. text ed. 27.00 o.p. (ISBN 0-87150-839-7, Duxbury Pr). PWS-Kent Pub.

Fundamentals of Structured COBOL Programming. 4th ed. Carl Feingold. 880p. 1983. pap. text ed. write for info. o.p. (ISBN 0-697-08173-7). Wm C Brown.

Fundamentals of Survey Measurement & Analysis. M. A. Cooper. (Aspects of Modern Land Surveying Ser.). 107p. 1974. text ed. 17.00x o.p. (ISBN 0-258-96871-0, Pub. by Granada England). Gower Pub Co.

Fundamentals of the Design of Fluid Film Bearings. Ed. by S. M. Rohde et al. (Bk. no. H00145). 1979. 24.00 o.p. (ISBN 0-685-95760-8). ASME.

Fundamentals of the Legislation of the U. S. S. R. & the Union Republics. 387p. 1974. 5.45 o.p. (ISBN 0-8285-0334-6, Pub. by Progress Pubs USSR). Imported Pubns.

Fundamentals of the Theory of Electricity. I. E. Tamm. 684p. 1979. 20.00 o.p. (ISBN 0-8285-1964-1, Pub. by Mir Pubs USSR). Imported Pubns.

Fundamentals of Theoretical Chemistry. R. Daudel. 1968. 60.00 o.p. (ISBN 0-08-012300-7). Pergamon.

Fundamentals of Transonic Flow. H. Moulden Trevor. LC 84-7381. 332p. 1984. 54.50x o.p. (ISBN 0-471-04661-2, Pub. by Wiley Interscience). Wiley.

Fundamentals of Ultrasonic Testing, Module 32-1. (Nondestructive Examination Techniques II Ser.). 84p. 1979. spiral bdg. 9.00x o.p. (ISBN 0-87683-098-X). GP Pub.

Fundamentals of Utah Real Estate. David L. Rockwell et al. (Illus.). 495p. (Orig.). 1985. pap. 29.95 o.p. (ISBN 0-915799-20-0). Natl Real Estate Inst.

Fundamentals of Voice & Diction. 7th ed. Lyle V. Mayer. 304p. 1985. pap. text ed. write for info. o.p. (ISBN 0-697-04257-X). Wm C Brown.

Fundamentals of Voluntary Health Care. George B. De Huszar. LC 61-9382. 1962. 6.00 o.p. (ISBN 0-87004-070-7). Caxton.

Fundamentals of Washington Real Estate. 4th, rev. ed. David L. Rockwell et al. (Illus.). 530p. 1987. pap. 29.95 o.p. (ISBN 0-915799-24-3). Natl Real Estate Inst.

Fundamentals of Waves, Optics & Modern Physics. 2nd ed. Hugh D. Young. 1975. text ed. 42.95 o.p. (ISBN 0-07-072521-7). McGraw.

Fundamentals of Well-Log Interpretation. 3rd ed. M. R. Wyllie. 1963. 49.50 o.p. (ISBN 0-12-767253-2). Acad Pr.

Fundamentals of World Peace. A. Hamer Hall. 1954. (ISBN 0-8022-0658-1). Philos Lib.

Fundamentos de la Electronica. I. P. Zherebstov. 543p. (Span.). 1976. 7.95 o.p. (ISBN 0-8285-1685-5, Pub. by Mir Pubs USSR). Imported Pubns.

Fundamentos de la Estetica Marxista. A. Zis. 287p. (Span.). 1976. 5.95 o.p. (ISBN 0-8285-1336-8, Pub. by Progress Pubs USSR). Imported Pubns.

Fundamentos de la Teoria de los Numeros. I. Vinogradov. 107p. (Span.). 1977. 6.45 o.p. (ISBN 0-8285-1686-3, Pub. by Mir Pubs USSR). Imported Pubns.

Fundamentos del Comunismos Cientifico. V. Afanasiev. 294p. (Span.). 1977. 7.45 o.p. (ISBN 0-8285-1658-8, Pub. by Progress Pubs USSR). Imported Pubns.

Fundamentos Matematicos de la Cibernetica. Y. M. Korshunov. 326p. (Span.). 1979. 7.45 o.p. (ISBN 0-8285-1453-4, Pub. by Mir Pubs USSR). Imported Pubns.

Funded Welfare Benefit Plans. 466p. 1985. 45.00 o.p. (J4-3579). PLI.

Funding Education: Problems, Patterns, Solutions. David Listokin. 107p. 1972. pap. (ISBN 0-87855-551-X). Transaction Pubs.

Funds for Decentralized Energy Systems RD&D: An Annotated Bibliography. Frederick Frankena. (Public Administration Ser.: P 1694). 7p. 1985. 2.00 o.p. (ISBN 0-89028-424-5). Vance Biblios.

Funds Statement. Arthur D. Little. LC 84-81458. (Allen Seed III Ser.). 220p. 1984. 12.00 o.p. (ISBN 0-910586-55-1). Finan Exec.

Funds Transfer Bank Contact Directory, 1984. 1986. 27.00 o.p. (ISBN 0-318-03381-X, 654). Bank Admin Inst.

Funeral Games. Mary Renault. 1981. 14.00 o.p. (ISBN 0-394-52068-8). Pantheon.

Funeral Makers. Cathie Pelletier. 365p. 1986. 16.95 o.p. (ISBN 0-02-595480-6). Macmillan.

Funeral Rites. Jean Genet. Tr. by Bernard Frechtman from Fr. 1969. pap. 5.95 o.p. (ISBN 0-394-17163-2, B239, BC). Grove.

Funerals: Consumers' Last Rights. Ed. by Consumer Reports. 1978. 14.95 o.p. (ISBN 0-393-08816-2). Norton.

Fungal Infection in the Compromised Patient. Ed. by D. W. Warnock & M. D. Richardson. LC 81-21952. 260p. 1982. 45.00 o.p. (ISBN 0-471-10204-0, Dist. by A R Liss). Wiley.

Fungal Lipid Biochemistry. John D. Weete. LC 74-8457. (Monographs in Lipid Research). (Illus.). 406p. 1974. 69.50x o.p. (ISBN 0-306-35801-8, Plenum Pr). Plenum Pub.

Fungal Pathogenicity & the Plant's Response: Proceedings of the Long Ashton Research Station Symposium, University of Bristol, September 1971. Long Ashton Research Station Symposium Staff. Ed. by R. J. Byrde & C. V Cutting. 1973. 134.50 o.p. (ISBN 0-12-148850-0). Acad Pr.

Fungi of the Faeros, 2 pts. F. H. Moeller. Incl. Pt. 1. Basidiomycetes. 1945; Pt. 2. Myxomycetes, Archimycetes, Phycomycetes, Asomycetes, & Fungi Imperfecti (with Appendix to Pt. 1) 1958. (Illus.). 15.00x set o.p. (ISBN 0-934454-42-6). Lubrecht & Cramer.

Fungicides: An Advanced Treatise, Vols. 1-2. Ed. by Dewayne C. Torgeson. 1967. Vol. 1. 99.00 o.p. (ISBN 0-12-695601-4); Vol. 2, 1969. 99.00 o.p. (ISBN 0-12-695602-2). Acad Pr.

Funk & Wagnalls Standard Dictionary. 1986. pap. 3.50 o.p. (ISBN 0-451-12540-1). NAL.

Funk & Wagnall's Standard Dictionary. 1040p. 1987. pap. 3.95 o.p. (ISBN 0-451-14277-2, Sig). NAL.

Funny Business: A Senile Executive's Guide to Power & Success. E. Alfred Osborne. LC 78-20828. (Illus.). 1979. 10.95 o.p. (ISBN 0-8144-5511-5). AMACOM.

Funny Car Racing for Beginners. I. G. Edmonds. LC 81-6936. (Illus.). 224p. (gr. 4-9). 1982. 10.95 o.p. (ISBN 0-03-059047-7). H Holt & Co.

Funnyman & the Penny Dodo. Stephen Mooser. LC 84-2185. (Easy Read Story Book Ser.). (Illus.). 32p. (gr. k-3). 1984. lib. bdg. 10.40 o.p. Watts.

Funtastic Tales for Young People. Howard S. Jamieson. (Illus.). (gr. 5 up). 1981. 6.50 o.p. (ISBN 0-682-49769-X). Exposition-Phoenix.

FUP. Jim Dodge. 1984. 7.75 o.p. (ISBN 0-671-50910-1). S&S.

Fur-Trade & Early Western Exploration. Clarence A. Vandiveer. LC 73-145876. (Illus.). 1971. Repr. of 1929 ed. lib. bdg. 23.50x o.p. (ISBN 0-8154-0381-X). Cooper Sq.

Furies & the Flame. Ingrid Rimland. 224p. 1984. 15.00 o.p. (ISBN 0-87879-418-2, Arena Press). Acad Therapy.

Furniture & Bedding. 6th ed. Fairchild Market Research Division Staff. (Fairchild Facts Files). (Illus.). 50p. 1986. pap. 20.00 o.p. (ISBN 0-87005-549-6). Fairchild.

Furniture Doctor. George Grotz. LC 62-7640. 1962. 14.95 o.p. (ISBN 0-385-01444-9). Doubleday.

Furniture Making, Repairing & Finishing: Monographs. Mary Vance. (Architecture Ser.: A 1404). 18p. 1985. 3.00 o.p. (ISBN 0-89028-434-2). Vance Biblios.

Furo: The Japanese Bath. Peter Grilli. LC 85-40063. (Illus.). 176p. 1985. 45.00 o.s.i. (ISBN 0-87011-601-0). Kodansha.

Further Adventures of Manko-Delights & Frights see Manko of Mankoland.

Further Adventures of Solar Pons. Basil Copper. 256p. 1987. pap. 5.95 o.p. (ISBN 0-89733-273-3). Academy Chi Pubs.

Further Adventures of the Little Mouse Trapped in a Book. Monique Felix. Date not set. 5.95 o.p. (ISBN 0-310-57030-1, 16103). Zondervan.

Further Documents & Correspondence of John Constable R. A. Ed. by R. B. Beckett. (Correspondence & Discourses of John Constable, R. A. Ser.). (Illus.). 371p. 1972. 27.00 o.p. (ISBN 0-900716-17-7, Pub. by Boydell & Brewer). Longwood Pub Group.

Further Education Today. rev. ed. Leonard Cantor & I. F. Roberts. 256p. 1983. pap. text ed. 14.95x o.p. (ISBN 0-7100-9501-5). Routledge Chapman & Hall.

Further Favourite Stories from Asia. bilingual ed. Leon Comber. (Favourite Stories Ser.). (gr. 5). 1981. pap. text ed. 2.50x o.p. (ISBN 0-686-73756-3). Heinemann Ed.

Further Letters of John Butler Yeats. John B. Yeats. Ed. by Lennox Robinson. 100p. 1971. Repr. of 1920 ed. 15.00x o.p. (ISBN 0-7165-1355-2, BBA 02086, Pub. by Cuala Press Ireland). Biblio Dist.

Further Phonics Fun. Compiled by Constance McAllister. (Illus., Orig.). (gr. 2-6). 1979. pap. 2.95 o.p. (ISBN 0-87534-175-6). Highlights.

Further Record. P. D. Ouspensky. 352p. 1987. pap. 13.95 o.p. (ISBN 1-85063-056-9, 30569, Ark Paperbks). Routledge Chapman & Hall.

Fury of Passions. Virgil S. Powell. (Illus.). 176p. 1984. 10.00 o.p. (ISBN 0-682-40117-X). Exposition-Phoenix.

Fusarium: A Laboratory Guide to the Indentification of the Major Species. C. Booth. (Illus.). 58p. 1977. pap. text ed. 10.00x o.p. (ISBN 0-317-60205-5). Lubrecht & Cramer.

Fusion of Psychiatry & Social Science. Harry S. Sullivan. Ed. by Helen S. Perry. 1971. pap. 5.95x o.p. (ISBN 0-393-00603-4, Norton Lib). Norton.

Fusion Reactor Materials: Proceedings, American Nuclear Society Winter Meeting. 308p. 1976. 23.00 o.p. (ISBN 0-317-33050-0, 120017). Am Nuclear Soc.

Fusion Technology Nineteen Seventy-Eight: Proceedings, 2 vols. Commission of the European Communities, Luxembourg. LC 79-40553. (Commission of the European Communities: Eur 6215). (Illus.). 1979. Set. pap. 280.00 o.p. (ISBN 0-08-023439-9). Pergamon.

Fusion Technology: Proceedings of the 11th Symposium, Oxford, England, Sept. 15-19, 1980, 2 vols. Commission of the European Communities, Luxembourg. (Illus.). 1000p. 1981. Set. pap. 200.00 o.p. (ISBN 0-08-025697-X). Pergamon.

Fusion Technology: Proceedings of the 12th Symposium (SOFT), Julich Laboratory, Federal Republic of Germany, 13-17 September 1982, 2 Vols. Ed. by Commission of the European Communities, Luxembourg. (International School of Fusion Reactor Technology (CEC) Ser.). 1564p. 1983. Set. pap. 395.00 o.p. (ISBN 0-08-029977-6). Pergamon.

Fussball Perfekt see Soccer: Techniques & Tactics.

Futile: The Magazine for Adult Dating. Sara Parriot. LC 83-40036. (Illus.). 88p. 1983. pap. 5.95 o.p. (ISBN 0-89480-576-2, 576). Workman Pub.

Future. Ed. by John Souter. 96p. Date not set. pap. 4.95 o.p. (ISBN 0-8423-0979-9). Tyndale.

Future Broker Home Study Course. 6th ed. Lyn M. Sennholz & Robert F. Sennholz. 298p. 1987. wkbk. 125.00 o.p. (ISBN 0-915513-08-0). Ctr Futures Ed.

Future Cities: Spatial Analysis of Energy Issues. John R. Beaumont & Paul Keys. (Geography & Public Policy Research Studies). 198p. 1982. 59.95x o.p. (ISBN 0-471-10451-5, Pub. by Res Stud Pr). Wiley.

Future Coal Supply for the World Energy Balance. Ed. by M. Grenon. (International Institute for Applied Systems Analysis. Proceedings). 1979. 175.00 o.p. (ISBN 0-08-023437-2). Pergamon.

Future Energy Consumption of the Third World-with Special Reference to Nuclear Power: An Individual & Comprehensive Evaluation of 156 Countries. M. Fritz. 393p. 1981. 67.00 o.p. (ISBN 0-08-026168-X). Pergamon.

Future File. Paul Dickson. 1979. pap. 1.95 o.p. (ISBN 0-380-42242-5, 42242). Avon.

Future for Insecticides: Needs & Prospects. Ed. by Robert L. Metcalf, Jr. & John J. McKelvey. LC 75-33225. 540p. 1976. 31.50 o.p. Krieger.

Future for Ocean Technology. C. A. Niblett et al. (Future for Science & Technology Ser.). 175p. 1986. 29.95 o.p. (ISBN 0-86187-522-2, Pub. by Croom Helm UK). Routledge Chapman & Hall.

Future for the City Centre. Ed. by Ross L. Davies & Anthony G. Champion. (Special Publications of the Institute of British Geographers Ser.: No. 14). 1983. 41.00 o.p. (ISBN 0-12-206240-X). Acad Pr.

Future for the Historical Jesus: The Place of Jesus in Preaching & Theology. Leander E. Keck. LC 81-43081. 280p. 1981. pap. 10.95 o.p. (ISBN 0-8006-1613-8, 1-1613, Fortress). Augsburg Fortress.

Future Information Processing Technology. Ed. by Peg Kay & Patricia Powell. (National Bureau of Standards Special Pub. 500-103. Computer Science & Technology Ser.). 251p. 1983. pap. 6.50 o.p. (ISBN 0-318-11721-5, S/N 003-003-02504-6). USGPO.

Future Is Now: The Significance of Precognition. 6.00 o.p. (ISBN 0-8216-0082-6, Pub. by Univ Bks). Carol Pub Group.

Future of Being Human. Paul Olson. LC 74-31004. 192p. Date not set. 6.95 o.p. (ISBN 0-317-65061-0). M Evans.

Future of Biology: Proceedings of the Rockefeller University & State Univesity of New York Conference on the Future of Biology, Nov. 26-27, 1965. Rockefeller University Staff et al. Ed. by Detlev W. Bronk. LC 67-63223. 1966. pap. 19.50x o.p. (ISBN 0-87395-268-5). State U NY Pr.

Future of Boston's Capital Plant. George Peterson et al. LC 80-54775. (America's Urban Capital Stock Ser.: Vol. 6). (Illus.). 69p. (Orig.). 1981. pap. text ed. 6.00 o.p. (ISBN 0-87766-291-6). Urban Inst.

Future of Broadcasting. Ed. by Richard Hoggart & Janet Morgan. 166p. 1984. 29.50 o.p. (ISBN 0-8419-5090-3). Holmes & Meier.

Future of Business - Annual Review 1980-81: Practical Issues. Center for Strategic & International Studies, Georgetown University Staff. Ed. by G. Sterling Slappey. LC 79-24081. (Pergamon Policy Studies). 110p. 1980. 35.00 o.p. (ISBN 0-08-025585-X); pap. 35.00 o.p. (ISBN 0-08-025584-1). Pergamon.

Future of Church-Related Higher Education. Edgar M. Carlson. LC 77-84081. 1977. pap. 6.50 o.p. (ISBN 0-8066-1606-7, 10-2475, Augsburg). Augsburg Fortress.

Future of Cincinnati's Capital Plant. N. Humphrey et al. (America's Urban Capital Stock Ser.: Vol. 3). 66p. (Orig.). 1980. pap. 6.00x o.p. (ISBN 0-87766-264-9, 27400). Urban Inst.

Future of Cleveland's Capital Plant. N. Humphrey et al. (America's Urban Capital Stock Ser.: Vol. 2). 77p. (Orig.). 1979. pap. text ed. 6.00x o.p. (ISBN 0-87766-258-4, 26900). Urban Inst.

Future of Council Housing. Ed. by John English. (Illus.). 208p. 1982. 26.50 o.p. (ISBN 0-7099-0900-4, Pub. by Croom Helm Ltd). Routledge Chapman & Hall.

Future of Creation: Collected Essays. Jurgen Moltmann. Tr. by Margaret Kohl from Ger. LC 79-7388. 208p. 1979. 10.95 o.p. (ISBN 0-8006-0627-2, 1-627, Fortress). Augsburg Fortress.

Future of Federalism. Nelson A. Rockefeller. LC 62-17224. 1963. pap. 1.95 o.p. (ISBN 0-689-70165-9, 46, Atheneum). Macmillan.

Future of Federalism. Nelson A. Rockefeller. LC 62-17224. (Godkin Lectures Ser: 1962). 1962. 9.95x o.p. (ISBN 0-674-33800-6). Harvard U Pr.

Future of Franchising: Looking Twenty-Five Years Ahead to the Year 2010. 27p. 1986. 10.00 o.p. (ISBN 0-317-66118-3). Intl Franchise Assn.

Future of Gas & Oil from the Sea. Gerard J. Mangone. 240p. 1983. 39.95 o.p. (ISBN 0-442-26164-0). Van Nos Reinhold.

Future of International Education. (UNITAR Lecture Ser.). pap. 1.00 o.p. (ISBN 92-1-157001-8, E.75.XV.LS.4). UN.

Future of Labor Arbitration in America. American Arbitration Association Staff & Benjamin Aaron. LC 76-18440. 304p. 1976. pap. 5.00 o.p. (ISBN 0-943001-15-3). Am Arbitration.

Future of Music. E. J. Dent. 1965. pap. text ed. 5.75 o.p. (ISBN 0-08-011354-0). Pergamon.

Future of Muslim Civilisation. Ziauddin Sardar. 224p. 1979. 25.00 o.p. (ISBN 0-85664-800-0, Pub. by Croom Helm Ltd). Routledge Chapman & Hall.

Future of New York City's Capital Plant. David A. Grossman. (America's Urban Capital Stock Ser.: Vol. 1). 112p. (Orig.). 1979. pap. text ed. 6.00x o.p. (ISBN 0-87766-249-5, 25700). Urban Inst.

Future of Nonfuel Minerals in the U. S. & World Economy: Input-Output Projections, 1980 to 2030. Wassily Leontief et al. LC 82-48956. (Illus.). 512p. 1983. 45.00x o.p. (ISBN 0-669-06377-0). Lexington Bks.

Future of Oakland's Capital Plant. George Peterson et al. LC 80-54776. (America's Urban Capital Stock Ser.: Vol. 5). 80p. (Orig.). 1981. pap. text ed. 6.00x o.p. (ISBN 0-87766-290-8). Urban Inst.

Future of Oil: World Oil Resources & Use. 2nd ed. Peter R. Odell & Kenneth E. Rosing. 224p. 1983. pap. 25.00 o.p. (ISBN 0-89397-146-4). Nichols Pub.

Future of Religion. James O. Unwin. 1973. 4.50 o.p. (ISBN 0-682-47605-6). Exposition-Phoenix.

Future of Science. Bertrand Russell. 96p. (ISBN 0-8022-1419-3). Philos Lib.

Future of Social Studies: A Report & Summary of Project SPAN. Project SPAN Staff. (Project SPAN Reports Ser.). 96p. (Orig.). 1982. pap. 9.95 o.p. (ISBN 0-89994-273-3). Soc Sci Ed.

Future of Socialist Economic Integration. rev. ed. Kalman Pecsi. Ed. by Paul Marer. Tr. by George Hajdu & Keith Crane. LC 81-2524. 190p. 1981. 35.00 o.p. (ISBN 0-87332-186-3). M E Sharpe.

Future of the Automobile in an Oil-Short World. Lester R. Brown et al. LC 79-67316. (Worldwatch Papers). 1979. pap. 4.00 o.p. (ISBN 0-916468-31-3). Worldwatch Inst.

Future of the Automobile in an Oil-Short World. (Worldwatch Institute Papers: No. 32). 64p. 1979. pap. 2.95 o.p. (WW32, WW). UNIPUB.

Future of the Great Planet Earth: What Does Biblical Prophecy Mean for You? Richard S. Hanson. LC 72-78554. 128p. 1972. pap. 4.50 o.p. (ISBN 0-8066-1222-3, 10-2485, Augsburg). Augsburg Fortress.

Future of the Word Processor. Derek Painter. Ed. by P. J. Hills. (Communication Ser.). 144p. 1987. 24.00 o.p. (ISBN 0-7099-2058-X, Pub. by Croom Helm UK). Routledge Chapman & Hall.

Future Position of the English-Speaking Peoples in World Prophecy & Events. Julian B. Shealy. 1975. 10.00 o.p. (ISBN 0-682-48107-6). Exposition-Phoenix.

Future Present: The Phenomenon of Christian Worship. Marianne H. Micks. LC 75-103844. 1970. pap. 6.95 o.p. (ISBN 0-8164-2109-9). HarpR.

Future Quest. Ed. by Roger Elwood. (Orig.). 1973. pap. 0.95 o.p. (ISBN 0-380-01204-9, 16808). Avon.

Future Role of the New York State Library in Statewide Audiovisual Activities: A Survey with Recommendations. Harold Goldstein. (Occasional Papers: No. 70). 29p. 1964. pap. 1.00 o.p. (ISBN 0-317-58851-6). U of Ill Lib Info Sci.

Future Shape of Preaching. Thor Hall. LC 77-157537. (Orig.). 1971. pap. 1.00x o.p. (ISBN 0-8006-0019-3, Fortress). Augsburg Fortress.

Future Story. Fiona French. LC 83-22317. (Illus.). 32p. (gr. 1-9). 1983. 11.95 o.p. (ISBN 0-911745-35-1). P Bedrick Bks.

Future Studies in the K-Twelve Curriculum. John D. Haas. LC 79-28708. 100p. (Orig.). 1980. pap. 11.95 o.p. (ISBN 0-89994-245-8). Soc Sci Ed.

Future That Will Work: Competitiveness & Compassion. David Owen. 192p. 1985. pap. 12.95 o.p. (ISBN 0-275-91811-4, B1811). Praeger.

Future Trends in Chemotheraphy: Proceedings of the International Symposium, Tirrenia, May 6-7, 1974, 4 vols. Ed. by A. Bertelli. 0.00 o.p. Vol. 4, 1980-1982. 85.00 o.p. (ISBN 2-88079-001-8); Vol 5, 1982-1984. 95.00 o.p. (ISBN 2-88079-004-2); Vol. 6, 1984-1986. 115.00 o.p. E J Brill USA.

Future Trends in Fiber Optics Markets & Technology: Yearly Update. 225.00 o.p. (ISBN 0-686-33026-9). Info Gatekeepers.

Future Trends in Geomathematics. Ed. by R. G. Craig & M. L. Labovitz. 1982. 28.00x o.p. (ISBN 0-85086-080-6, NO. 8002, Pub by Pion England). Routledge Chapman & Hall.

Future While It Happened. Samuel Lubell. 162p. 1973. pap. 2.95x o.p. (ISBN 0-393-09321-2). Norton.

Future World, Vol. 3. Ruth Norman. 525p. (Orig.). 1988. pap. 15.95 o.p. (ISBN 0-932642-85-3). Unarius Pubns.

Futuredays: A Nineteenth-Century Vision of the Year 2000. Isaac Asimov. LC 86-80186. (Illus.). 96p. 1986. pap. 12.95 o.p. (ISBN 0-8050-0120-4). H Holt & Co.

Futures. Freda Bright. 1983. 14.50 o.s.i. (ISBN 0-671-44114-0, Pub by Poseidon). S&S.

Futures for a Declining City: Simulations for the Cleveland Area. Katherine Bradbury et al. LC 81-10857. (Studies in Urban Economics). 1981. 25.95 o.p. (ISBN 0-12-123580-7). Acad Pr.

Futures for Natural Non-Chemical Pest Control. Business Communications Staff. 1988. 1950.00 o.p. (ISBN 0-89336-562-9, C-082). BCC.

Futures for the Welfare State. Ed. by Norman Furniss. LC 85-45959. 288p. 1986. 29.50x o.p. (ISBN 0-253-32440-8). Ind U Pr.

Futures: The Anti-Inflation Investment. Mike Geczi. 1980. pap. 2.95 o.p. (ISBN 0-380-75713-3, 75713-3, Discus). Avon.

Futurework. Diane Butler. 1984. 16.95 o.p. (ISBN 0-03-061984-X); pap. 8.95 o.p. (ISBN 0-03-064098-9). H Holt & Co.

Futurism. Rosa T. Clough. LC 60-15952. (Illus.). 298p. (ISBN 0-8022-0267-5). Philos Lib.

Futurological Congress. Stanislaw Lem. 1976. pap. 2.75 o.p. (ISBN 0-380-00584-0, 58289-9, Bard). Avon.

Fuzzy Information, Knowledge Representation & Decision Analysis: Proceedings of the IFAC-IFIP-IFORS Symposium, Marseille, France, July 1983. E. Sanchez. Ed. by M. M. Gupta. 500p. 1984. 170.00 o.p. (ISBN 0-08-030583-0). Pergamon.

Fuzzy Set & Possibility Theory: Recent Developments. Ed. by Ronald R. Yager. (Illus.). 672p. 1982. 160.00 o.p. (ISBN 0-08-026294-5, D110). Pergamon.

Fuzzy Sets & Their Applications to Cognitive & Decision Processes. Ed. by Zadeh & King-Sun Fu. 1975. 65.50 o.p. (ISBN 0-12-775260-9). Acad Pr.

FYI... Resources on Local Government, 1983-1986. Ed. by Mary A. Schellinger. 274p. 1987. pap. 16.50 o.s.i. (ISBN 0-87326-944-6). Intl City Mgt.

G

G. I. The American Soldier in World War II. Lee Kennett. (Illus.). 288p. 1987. 20.95 o.s.i. (ISBN 0-684-18491-5). Scribner.

G. K. Chesterton & Hilaire Belloc: The Battle Against Modernity. Jay P. Corrin. LC 81-4756. xvi, 262p. 1981. text ed. 24.95x o.p. (ISBN 0-8214-0604-3). Ohio U Pr.

G. K. Chesterton: Radical Populist. Margaret Canovan. LC 77-73045. 1977. 10.95 o.p. (ISBN 0-15-135700-5). HarBraceJ.

G-L CBASIC. (ISBN 0-07-931024-9). McGraw.

G. P. S. A Case Study in Generality & Problem Solving. George W. Ernst & Allen Newell. (ACM Monograph Ser). 1969. 69.00 o.p. (ISBN 0-12-241050-5). Acad Pr.

G Spot: & Other Recent Discoveries about Human Sexuality. Alice K. Ladas & Beverly Whipple. 1982. 11.95 o.p. (ISBN 0-03-061831-2). H Holt & Co.

G. Washington Bear. Rachel N. Pittman. (Illus.). 23p. (Orig.). (ps-5). 1984. pap. 4.95 o.p. (ISBN 0-9615382-0-1). Lubrecht & Cramer.

GAAP: A Transaction Approach. Patrick R. Delaney & James R. Adler. 500p. 1984. text ed. 24.95 o.p. (ISBN 0-471-86144-8). Wiley.

GAAP 1987: Interpretation & Application. Patrick R. Delaney et al. 1986. pap. 24.95 o.p. (ISBN 0-471-84931-6). Wiley.

GABA in Nervous System Function. Ed. by E. Roberts et al. 1975. 40.75 o.p. (ISBN 0-7204-7567-8, North Holland). Elsevier.

GABA-Neurotransmitters. Ed. by P. Krogsgaard-Larsen et al. (Alfred Benson Symposium Ser.: No. 12). 1979. 95.00 o.p. (ISBN 0-12-426730-0). Acad Pr.

Gabby Hartnett Story: From a Mill Town to Cooperstown. James M. Murphy. (Illus.). 104p. 1983. 8.00 o.s.i. (ISBN 0-682-49991-9). Exposition-Phoenix.

Gabby's Grand Opening. Pete Kersten & Rick Lersten. (Kersten Brothers' Critter Tales Picture Bks.). 32p. (ps-3). 1986. 7.95 o.p. (ISBN 0-316-49005-9). Little.

Gabo: Constructions, Structure, Paintings, Drawings & Engravings. Naum Gabo. LC 58-1904. 193p. 1957. Repr. 49.00 o.p. (ISBN 0-403-04073-6). Somerset Pub.

Gabor Peterdi: Paintings. Burt Chernow. LC 82-50989. (Illus.). 120p. 1983. 29.95 o.s.i. (ISBN 0-8008-3121-7). Taplinger.

Gabriel Marcel. Sam Keen. LC 67-11288. (Makers of Contemporary Theology Ser). 1967. pap. 3.45 o.p. (ISBN 0-8042-0584-1, John Knox). Westminster John Knox.

Gabriel Marcel & His Critics: An International Bibliography (1935-1976) Francois H. Lapointe & Clarie C. Lapointe. LC 76-24736. (Reference Library of the Humanities Ser.: Vol. 57). 1977. lib. bdg. 39.00 o.p. (ISBN 0-8240-9941-9). Garland Pub.

Gabriel Renville, Young Sioux Warrior: The Adventures of an Indian Boy in Early Minnesota. Donald D. Parker. LC 73-86547. 1973. 7.00 o.p. (ISBN 0-682-47719-2, Lochinvar). Exposition-Phoenix.

Gabriel Tellez: El Condenado por Desconfiado. Ed. by D. Rogers. LC 73-7964. 172p. 1974. 24.00 o.s.i. (ISBN 0-08-017247-4); pap. 14.00 o.s.i. (ISBN 0-08-017248-2). Pergamon.

Gabrielle & Selena. Peter Desbarats. LC 68-11498. (Illus.). (gr. k-3). 1968. 5.50 o.p. (ISBN 0-15-230514-9, HJ). HarBraceJ.

Gabrielle & Selena. Peter Desbarats. LC 73-14661. (Illus.). 32p. (gr. k-3). 1974. pap. 0.95 o.p. (ISBN 0-15-634080-1, AVB87, VoyB). HarBraceJ.

Gabriel's Girl. Norma Johnston. LC 83-2631. 192p. (gr. 5-9). 1983. 12.95 o.s.i. (ISBN 0-689-30989-9, Atheneum Childrens Bks). Macmillan.

Gadabouts & Stick-at-Home: Wild Animals & Their Habitats. Lorus J. Milne & Margery Milne. LC 79-20743. (Illus.). (gr. 4 up). 1980. 8.95 o.s.i. (ISBN 0-684-16473-6, Pub. by Scribner). Macmillan.

Gadgets. Martin Schwartz. (Illus.). 144p. 1986. pap. 14.95 o.p. Pharos Bks NY.

Gaelic Vision in Scottish Culture. Malcolm Chapman. 1979. 21.50x o.p. (ISBN 0-7735-0506-7, McGill Canada). U of Toronto Pr.

GAG: A Practical Compiler Generator. U. Kastens et al. (Lecture Notes in Computer Science Ser.: Vol. 141). 156p. 1982. pap. 12.00 o.p. (ISBN 0-387-11591-9). Springer-Verlag.

Gage Blocks, Mechanical Comparators, & Electronic Comparators. (Metrology Ser.: Module 27-3). (Illus.). 68p. 1979. spiral bdg. 6.00x o.p. (ISBN 0-87683-082-3). GP Pub.

Gahan Wilson's America. Gahan Wilson. 1985. 14.70 o.p. (ISBN 0-671-55512-X). S&S.

Gahan Wilson's America. Gahan Wilson. (Illus.). 128p. 1986. pap. 7.95 o.p. (ISBN 0-671-62789-9, Fireside). S&S.

Gaietes de l'Escadron. Georges Courteline & Francis Pruner. 192p. 1962. 8.95 o.p. (ISBN 0-686-54630-X). French & Eur.

Gaiety of Grace. Edna Hong. LC 77-176484. 124p. 1979. pap. 4.50 o.p. (ISBN 0-8066-1775-6, 10-2541, Augsburg). Augsburg Fortress.

Gaijin. Marc Olden. 1986. 17.95 o.p. (ISBN 0-87795-788-6). Morrow.

Gaining Consistent Profits in Stock Market Charts. C. M. Flumiani. (Illus.). 151p. 1988. 77.75 o.p. (ISBN 0-86654-272-8). Inst Econ Finan.

Gaining Ground: The Renewal of America's Small Farms. J. Tevere MacFadyen. 1984. 16.95 o.s.i. (ISBN 0-03-069563-5). H Holt & Co.

Gaining Momentum for Board Action. Arty Trost & Judy Rauner. 104p. pap. 10.50x o.s.i. (NO. 3400). Am Council Arts.

Gains & Losses: Errors in Trace Analysis. Ed. by R. A. Chalmers. 90p. 1983. pap. 30.00 o.p. (ISBN 0-08-030239-4). Pergamon.

Gainsharing. 34.95 o.p. (ISBN 0-89806-040-0, NO. 134). Inst Indus Eng.

Gainsharing & Productivity: A Guide to Planning, Implementation & Development. Robert J. Doyle. 288p. 1983. 24.95 o.p. (ISBN 0-8144-5764-9). AMACOM.

Gaints' Bread. Agatha Christie. LC 72-97688. 1982. pap. 5.95 o.p. (ISBN 0-87795-387-2, Arbor Hse). Morrow.

Gala. William Lewis. 1989. pap. 3.95 o.p. (ISBN 0-7701-0912-8). PaperJacks US.

Galactic Empires, Vol. I. Ed. by Brian Aldiss. (YA) (gr. 7 up). 1979. pap. 2.25 o.p. (ISBN 0-380-42341-3, 42341). Avon.

Galactic Empires, Vol. II. Ed. by Brian Aldiss. (YA) (gr. 7 up). 1979. pap. 2.25 o.p. (ISBN 0-380-42879-2, 42879). Avon.

Galactic Nebulae & Interstellar Matter. Jean Dufay. (Illus.). 400p. (ISBN 0-8022-0421-X). Philos Lib.

Galactic Structure. Ed. by Adriaan Blaauw & Maarten Schmidt. LC 64-23428. (Stars & Stellar Systems Ser.: Vol. 5). (Illus.). 1965. lib. bdg. 50.00x o.s.i. (ISBN 0-226-45957-8). U of Chicago Pr.

Galapagos. Kurt Vonnegut, Jr. LC 85-4581. (Illus.). 295p. 1985. 16.95 o.p. (ISBN 0-385-29416-6, Sey Lawr); signed ltd. 75.00 o.p. (ISBN 0-385-29420-4). Delacorte.

Galatians see Word Studies in the Greek New Testament, for the English Reader.

Galatians-Ephesians, Vol. VIII. Beacon Bible Expositions Staff. 228p. 1981. text ed. 6.95 o.p. (ISBN 0-8010-0820-4). Baker Bk.

Galatians-Philemon, Vol. IX. Beacon Bible Commentary Staff. 15.95 o.p. (ISBN 0-8010-0696-1). Baker Bk.

Galaxien. Timothy Ferris. Tr. by Anita Ehlers from Eng. 184p. (Ger.). 1981. 94.00 o.p. (ISBN 0-8176-1250-5). Birkhauser.

Galaxies. Timothy Ferris. LC 80-13139. (Illus.). 200p. 1980. o.s.i 75.00 o.s.i. (ISBN 0-87156-273-1). Sierra.

Galaxies. rev. ed. Harlow Shapley. LC 61-7393. (Illus.). 1967. pap. text ed. 2.45x o.s.i. (ISBN 0-689-70179-9, 100, Atheneum). Macmillan.

Galaxies & the Universe, Vol. IX. Ed. by Allan Sandage & Mary Sandage. LC 74-7559. (Stars & Stellar Systems Midway Reprint Ser.). (Illus.). 818p. 1983. pap. text ed. 40.00x o.s.i.; pap. text ed. 40.00x o.p. (ISBN 0-226-45970-5). U of Chicago Pr.

Galaxies: Structure & Evolution. R. J. Taylor. (Wykeham Science Ser.: No. 49). 204p. pap. (ISBN 0-85109-670-0). Taylor & Francis.

Galaxy of Funny Gags, Puns, Quips & Putdowns. Leopold Fechtner. 1982. pap. 5.95 o.p. (ISBN 0-13-345959-4, Reward). P-H.

Galaxy of Games & Activities for the Kindergarten. Joyce Lewallen. (Illus.). 1978. text ed. 14.95x o.p. (ISBN 0-13-346106-8, Parker). P-H.

Galbraith Viewpoint in Perspective: Critical Commentary on "The Age of Uncertainty" Television Series. Ed. by Gerald L. Musgrave. LC 77-92085. (Hoover Special Project Ser). 1978. pap. 4.95x o.p. (ISBN 0-8179-4212-2). Hoover Inst Pr.

Gale Directory of Publications Update, 1988. 120th ed. Ed. by Kay Gill & Donald P. Boyden. pap. text ed. cancelled o.s.i. (ISBN 0-8103-2546-2). Gale.

Gale Directory of Publications Update 1989. Ed. by Kay Gill & Donald P. Boyden. cancelled o.s.i. (ISBN 0-8103-2891-7). Gale.

Gale Directory of Publications, 1987. 1453p. 1987. 135.00x o.p. (ISBN 0-8103-1498-3). Gale.

Gale Directory of Publications, 1988. 120th ed. Ed. by Kay Gill & Donald P. Boyden. 1500p. 1987. 145.00x o.p. (ISBN 0-8103-2544-6). Gale.

Galerkin Finite Element Methods for Parabolic Problems. V. Thomee. (Lecture Notes in Mathematics Ser.: Vol. 1054). vii, 237p. 1984. pap. 17.00 o.p. (ISBN 0-387-12911-1). Springer-Verlag.

Galicia: A Historical Survey & Bibliographic Guide. Paul R. Magocsi. (Illus.). 319p. 1983. 24.95x o.p. (ISBN 0-8020-2482-3). U of Toronto Pr.

Galileo at Work: His Scientific Biography. Stillman Drake. LC 78-5239. xxiv, 536p. 1981. pap. 9.95 o.s.i. (ISBN 0-226-16227-3). U of Chicago Pr.

Galileo Galilei, His Life & Work. Raymond J. Seeger. (Men of Physics Ser.). 1966. 75.00 o.p. (ISBN 0-08-012025-3); pap. 7.75 o.p. (ISBN 0-08-012024-5). Pergamon.

Galileo Galilei: "Two New Sciences" Tr. by Stillman Drake from Lat. 366p. 1974. info. 30.00xfor o.p. (ISBN 0-299-06400-X). U of Wis Pr.

Galileo's Early Notebooks. William A. Wallace. LC 77-89766. 1977. text ed. 24.95x o.p. (ISBN 0-268-00998-8). U of Notre Dame Pr.

Galina: A Russian Story. Galina Vishnevskaya. Tr. by Guy Daniels from Rus. LC 84-10943. 416p. 1984. 19.95 o.p. (ISBN 0-15-134250-4). HarBraceJ.

Gallant Passion. Helene M. Lehr. 320p. (Orig.). 1984. pap. 2.95 o.p. (ISBN 0-380-86074-0, 86074). Avon.

Gallery. John H. Burns. 1985. 6.95 o.p. (ISBN 0-87795-709-6, Arbor Hse). Morrow.

Gallery of Ghosts: An Anthology of Reported Experience. Ed. by Andrew MacKenzie. LC 73-2019. 160p. 1973. 7.95 o.s.i. (ISBN 0-8008-3122-5). Taplinger.

Gallery of New Testament Rogues: From Herod to Satan. John R. Bodo. LC 78-13984. 152p. 1979. pap. 6.95 o.s.i. (ISBN 0-664-24227-8, Westminster). Westminster John Knox.

Gallery of Sinister Perspectives: Ten Crimes & a Scandal. Albert Borowitz. LC 81-19352. 175p. 1982. 0.00 o.p. (ISBN 0-87338-264-1); pap. 6.75 o.p. (ISBN 0-87338-271-4). Kent St U Pr.

Gallery of Turned Objects. Albert LeCoff. LC 81-10187. 98p. 1981. 7.95 o.p. (ISBN 0-8425-1978-5). Brigham.

Galley Guide to Fine Food. Richard Bock. 1977. pap. 5.95 o.p. (ISBN 0-89328-009-7). Lorenz Corp.

Gallium Arsenide Microwave Bulk & Transit-Time Devices. Ed. by Lester F. Eastman. LC 72-77827. (Modern Frontiers in Applied Science Ser.). (Illus.). 253p. 1972. pap. 15.00x o.p. (ISBN 0-89006-014-2). Artech Hse.

Galloping Gertrude. John J. Loeper. LC 79-21974. (Illus.). (gr. 4-6). 1980. 6.95 o.p. (ISBN 0-689-30749-7, Atheneum). Macmillan.

Gallup Study: Images of Community Colleges. Compiled by Gallup Organization, Inc. Staff. 40p. (Orig.). 1981. pap. 10.00 o.p. (ISBN 0-87117-121-X, 1019). Am Assn Comm Jr Coll.

Gallup Survey of Britain, 1985. Ed. by Gordon Heald & Robert J. Wybrow. 320p. 1986. 34.50 o.p. (ISBN 0-7099-3846-2, Pub. by Croom Helm Ltd). Routledge Chapman & Hall.

Gambler in Love. Patricia Matthews. 1985. lib. bdg. 17.95 o.p. (ISBN 0-8161-3849-4). G K Hall.

Gambler, the Gunfighter & Other Poems & Ballads. Vincent M. O'Connell. 1979. 5.00 o.p. (ISBN 0-682-49425-9). Exposition-Phoenix.

Gambler's Bedside Book. Ed. by John K. Hutchens. LC 74-20212. 1977. 12.95 o.s.i. (ISBN 0-8008-3123-3). Taplinger.

Gambling: A Guide to Information Sources. Jack I. Gardner. LC 79-23797. (Sports, Games, & Pastimes Information Guide Ser.: Vol. 8). 304p. 1980. 68.00x o.p. (ISBN 0-8103-1229-8). Gale.

Gambling: Crime or Recreation. Donna R. Plesser et al. (Information Aids Ser.). 88p. 1986. pap. 15.95 o.p. (ISBN 0-936474-56-4). Info Plus TX.

Gambling-Crime or Recreation? Ed. by Mark A. Siegel et al. (Information Aids Ser.). 1986. pap. 14.95 o.p. (ISBN 0-936474-38-6). Info Plus TX.

Gambling in Australia. Ed. by Geoffery Caldwell et al. 240p. 1985. 24.95 o.p. (ISBN 0-949614-17-3, Pub. by Croom Helm Ltd). Routledge Chapman & Hall.

Gambling Professional's Textbook: Winning Statistics for Las Vegas. Stuart D. Waymire. 165p. (Orig.). 1988. pap. 19.95 o.p. Thundblt Pr NV.

Gambling World. Rouge Et Noir Staff. LC 68-22047. 384p. 1968. Repr. of 1898 ed. 43.00x o.p. (ISBN 0-8103-3551-4). Gale.

Game Bird Carving. 3rd ed. Bruce Burk. (Illus.). 400p. 1987. 37.95 o.p. (Pub. by Winchester Pr). New Century.

Game Buyer's Guide. Compiled by Frank Mentzer & James M. Ward. LC 85-51045. 300p. (Orig.). 1985. pap. 5.95 o.p. (ISBN 0-88038-144-2). TSR Inc.

Game Cookbook. Geraldine Steindler. (Illus.). 240p. pap. 8.95 o.p. (ISBN 0-88317-000-0). Stoeger Pub Co.

Game Fish of the Rocky Mountains: A Guide to Identification. Michel Pijoan. LC 84-62424. (Illus.). 64p. (Orig.). 1985. 6.95 o.p. (ISBN 0-87358-372-8). Northland.

Game of Chess. Richard Scott. 1955. (ISBN 0-8022-1524-6). Philos Lib.

Game of Hearts. Marlaine Kayle. (Candlelight Regency Ser.: No. 705). 1982. pap. 1.95 o.p. (ISBN 0-440-12912-5). Dell.

Game of Soldiers. Stuart Jackman. LC 81-14950. 1982. 11.95 o.p. (ISBN 0-689-11237-8, Atheneum). Macmillan.

Game of the Pink Pagoda. Roger Moss. 1987. pap. 8.95 o.p. (ISBN 0-345-34179-1). Ballantine.

Game Plan for Disaster. Clark R. Mollenhoff. 384p. 1976. 9.95 o.p. (ISBN 0-393-05543-4). Norton.

Game Playing with Digital Computer. Thomas William. Repr. lib. bdg. cancelled o.s.i. Reprint Servs.

Game Theory & Experimental Games: The Study of Strategic Interaction. A. Colman. (International Series in Experimental Social Psychology: Vol. 4). 300p. 1982. 51.00 o.p. (ISBN 0-08-026070-5); pap. text ed. 22.00 o.p. (ISBN 0-08-026069-1). Pergamon.

Game Theory & Its Application. L. C. Thomas. LC 83-26673. (Mathematics & Its Applications Ser.: 1-176). 279p. 1984. 65.95x o.p. (ISBN 0-470-27507-3). Halsted Pr.

Games. Vera Cowie. 384p. 1987. pap. 3.95 o.p. (ISBN 0-380-70326-2). Avon.

Games. Carolyn Pitcher. LC 84-51222. (Make-It-Yourself Ser.). (Illus.). 32p. 1984. lib. bdg. 11.90 o.p. (ISBN 0-531-04813-6). Watts.

Games & Activities to Reinforce Reading Skills. Florence Shankman. 1972. pap. 3.75x o.p. (ISBN 0-8422-0260-9). Irvington.

Games & Gadgets for the Church School. Donna Skinner. 1983. pap. 5.95 o.p. (ISBN 0-570-03914-2, 12-2853). Concordia.

Games & Graphics for the TI 99-4A. Thomas Thompson, Jr. 128p. pap. 8.95 o.p. (6407). Sams.

Games & Ideas for Teaching Spanish. Burlington Willes. LC 66-28929. 1967. pap. 2.95 o.p. (ISBN 0-8224-3235-8). D S Lake Pubs.

Games & Puzzles. Barbara Angell. 1978. pap. 4.50 o.p. (ISBN 0-914946-08-0). Cleveland St Univ Poetry Ctr.

Games & Simulations in Science Education. H. I. Ellington et al. 180p. 1981. 27.50x o.p. (ISBN 0-89397-093-X). Nichols Pub.

Games at Twilight. Anita Desai. 144p. 1983. pap. 5.95 o.s.i. (ISBN 0-14-005348-4). Penguin.

Games Authors Play. P. Hutchinson. LC 83-12177. 131p. 1983. 22.00 o.p. (ISBN 0-416-73060-4, NO. 6523); pap. 10.00 o.p. (ISBN 0-416-73070-1, NO. 6524). Routledge Chapman & Hall.

Games Cells Play. Max D. Lechtman et al. LC 78-57373. 1979. text ed. 16.95 o.p. (ISBN 0-8053-6094-8). Benjamin-Cummings.

Games for One Player. Pick. (Illus.). 144p. 1954. (ISBN 0-8022-1974-8). Philos Lib.

Games for the Not So Young. Sid G. Hedges. 128p. 1957. (ISBN 0-8022-0701-4). Philos Lib.

Games for Young People. Alfred Froh & Margaret King. 1943. pap. 2.95 o.p. (ISBN 0-8066-0080-2, 10-2515, Augsburg). Augsburg Fortress.

Games from an Edwardian Childhood. Rosaleen Cooper & Ann Palmer. (Illus.). 96p. 1983. 12.95 o.p. (ISBN 0-7153-8317-5). David & Charles.

Games: Games Activities Measures Exercises in Speech. Glynis H. Strause & Marcus L. Ambrester. (Illus.). 90p. (Orig.). 1986. pap. 7.95x o.p. (ISBN 0-88133-202-X). Sheffield Wisc.

Games! Games! Games! Jeane Chipman & George Chipman. LC 83-18993. 1983. 7.95 o.p. (ISBN 0-87747-983-6, Pub. by Shadow Mountain). Deseret Bk.

Games, Graphics & Sound. Ray Curnow & Susan Curnou. (Clear & Simple Home Computer Ser.: Vol. III). (Illus.). 128p. 1984. pap. 9.50 o.p. (ISBN 0-671-49444-9, Fireside). S&S.

Games in Education & Development. Loyda M. Shears & Eli M. Bower. (Illus.). 392p. 1974. 30.75 o.p. (ISBN 0-398-02608-4). C C Thomas.

Games Killers Play. Alfred Hitchcock. 1980. pap. 2.95 o.p. (ISBN 0-440-12790-4). Dell.

Games Magazine Book of Crossword Puzzles. Ed. by Will Shortz. (Games Magazine Bks.: No. 2). 96p. (Orig.). 1985. pap. 5.95 o.p. (ISBN 0-89480-840-0, 840). Workman Pub.

Games, Sport & Power. Gregory P. Stone. 230p. 1972. (ISBN 0-87855-003-8); pap. 9.95x o.p. (ISBN 0-87855-503-X). Transaction Pubs.

Games, Sports & Exercises for the Physically Handicapped. 3rd. ed. Ronald C. Adams et al. LC 81-7288. (Illus.). 430p. 1982. pap. 28.50 o.p. (ISBN 0-8121-0785-3). Lea & Febiger.

Game's the Same. John Smythe. 104p. 1957. (ISBN 0-8022-1604-8). Philos Lib.

Games They Played. Richard B. Lyttle. LC 82-1749. (Illus.). 160p. (gr. 5 up). 1982. 11.95 o.s.i. (ISBN 0-689-30928-7, Atheneum Childrens Bks). Macmillan.

Games We All Play & Shouldn't. 1974. 5.95 o.p. (ISBN 0-88088-208-5). Peter Pauper.

Gamesman Bridge: Play Better with Kantar. Edwin B. Kantar & Jackson Stanley. (Illus.). 1972. 5.95 o.p. (ISBN 0-87140-543-1). Liveright.

Gamines: How to Adopt from Latin America. Jean Nelson-Erichsen & Heino R. Erichsen. LC 79-26965. (Illus.). 1981. 15.95 o.p. (ISBN 0-87518-197-X). Dillon.

Gamma & X-Ray Spectrometry Techniques & Applications. K. Debertin & W. B. Mann. 1983. pap. 28.00 o.p. (ISBN 0-08-029159-7). Pergamon.

Gamma-Ray Angular Correlations. R. D. Gill. 1975. 67.50 o.p. (ISBN 0-12-283850-5). Acad Pr.

Gammage Cup. Carol Kendall. LC 59-8953. (Illus.). (gr. 4-6). 1959. 6.95 o.s.i. (ISBN 0-15-230572-6, HJ). HarBraceJ.

Gandhi. Olivia Coolidge. (Illus.). (gr. 7 up). 1971. 7.95 o.p. (ISBN 0-395-12573-1). HM.

Gandhi. Hugh Owen. (Leaders of Asia Ser.). 1984. pap. 4.95 o.p. (ISBN 0-318-12095-X). U of Queensland Pr.

Gandhi: A Memoir. William Shirer. 1981. pap. 7.75 o.p. (ISBN 0-671-25080-9, Touchstone). S&S.

Gandhi & the Struggle for India's Independence. F. W. Rawding. LC 81-14241. (Cambridge Topic Bks.). (Illus.). 52p. (gr. 5-10). 1982. PLB 8.95 o.p. (ISBN 0-8225-1225-4). Lerner Pubns.

Gandhi: Screenplay for the Film by Richard Attenborough. John Briley. LC 83-80383. 192p. 1983. 6.95 o.p. (ISBN 0-394-62471-8, E856, Ever). Grove.

Gandhi: Soldier of Nonviolence. Calvin Kytle. LC 82-10633. (Illus.). 208p. 1983. 13.95 o.p. (ISBN 0-932020-18-6); pap. 8.95 o.s.i. (ISBN 0-932020-19-4). Seven Locks Pr.

Gandhi's Children. Trevor Fishlock. (Illus.). 208p. 1983. text ed. 16.50x o.p. (ISBN 0-87663-436-6, 83-4904); pap. 8.95 o.s.i. (ISBN 0-87663-593-1). Universe.

Gandhi's Religious Thought. Margaret Chatterjee. LC 83-5841. 224p. 1984. text ed. 19.95x o.p. (ISBN 0-268-01009-9, 85-10091). U of Notre Dame Pr.

Ganglion-Blocking & Ganglion-Stimulating Agents. Ed. by D. A. Kharkevich. 1967. 90.00 o.p. (ISBN 0-08-011929-8). Pergamon.

Gang's Weigh. Miriam Gang & Arthur Gang. 88p. (Orig.). 1986. pap. 9.95 o.s.i. (ISBN 0-941850-24-2). Liturgical Pubns.

Ganjifa, Playing Cards India. Rudolph Von Leyden. (Illus.). 144p. (Orig.). pap. 9.95 o.p. (ISBN 0-905209-17-6, Pub. by Victoria & Albert Mus UK). Faber & Faber.

Ganoid Fishes of British Carboniferous Formations, Pt. 1., Nos. 2-7. R. H. Traquair. Repr. of 1914 ed. Set. 41.00 o.p. (ISBN 0-384-61380-2). Johnson Repr.

Garbage Delight. Dennis Lee. (Illus.). 64p. (gr. k-3). 1978. 6.95 o.p. (ISBN 0-395-27201-7). HM.

Garbage World. Charles Platt. 1977. pap. 1.25 o.s.i. (ISBN 0-505-51164-9, Pub. by Tower Bks). Dorchester Pub Co.

Garcons. Henry De Montherlant. 19.25 o.p. (ISBN 0-685-36980-3). Schoenhof.

Garcons. Henry de Montherlant. 384p. 1969. 11.95 o.p. (ISBN 0-686-55520-1). Schoenhof.

Garcons: Texte Integral. Henry de Montherlant. (Illus.). 552p. 1973. 195.00 o.p. (ISBN 0-686-55519-8). Schoenhof.

Garden As Fine Art. F. R. Cowell. 1978. 20.00 o.p. (ISBN 0-395-27065-0). HM.

Garden, Ashes. Danilo Kis. LC 75-15769. 170p. 1975. 7.95 o.p. (ISBN 0-15-134287-3). HarBraceJ.

Garden, Ashes. Danilo Kis. Tr. by William J. Hannaher. LC 78-7508. 1978. pap. 2.95 o.p. (ISBN 0-15-634548-X, Harv). HarBraceJ.

Garden Books, Old & New. Mary Evans. LC 71-162512. 88p. 1971. Repr. of 1926 ed. 35.00x o.p. (ISBN 0-8103-3743-6). Gale.

Garden Construction Know-How. 1977. pap. 5.95 o.p. (ISBN 0-917102-69-X). Ortho.

Garden Fresh Cooking: Hundreds of Wonderful Ways to Cook, Serve, & Store Your Favorite Vegetables & Fruits. Rodale Food Center Staff & Judith Hurley. Ed. by Anne Halpin & Charlie Gerras. 224p. 1987. 19.95 o.p. (ISBN 0-87857-694-0); pap. 14.95 o.p. (ISBN 0-87857-695-9). Rodale Pr Inc.

Garden Is Doing Fine. Carol Farley. LC 75-9516. 192p. (gr. 5-7). 1975. 7.95 o.p. (ISBN 0-689-30475-7, Atheneum). Macmillan.

Garden of Eden. Ernest Hemingway. 1987. 11.95 o.p. (ISBN 0-8161-4153-3, Large Print Bks). G K Hall.

Garden of the Brave in War: Recollections of Iran. Terence O'Donnell. 1980. 10.95 o.p. (ISBN 0-89919-016-2). Ticknor & Fields.

Garden of the Sphinx: One Hundred Fifty Challenging & Instructive Puzzles. Pierre Berloquin. (Illus.). 224p. 1985. 11.95 o.s.i. (ISBN 0-684-18342-0). Scribner.

Garden Planning & Design. P-H.

Garden Pools. Leonard C. Betts. (Illus.). 1952. pap. 2.95 o.p. (M-513). TFH Pubns.

Garden Pools, Fountains & Waterfalls. 2nd ed. Sunset Editors. LC 73-89588. (Illus.). 80p. 1974. pap. 5.95 o.p. (ISBN 0-376-01224-2, Sunset Bks.). Sunset-Lane.

Garden Projects. P-H.

Garden Rooms: Greenhouses, Sunrooms & Solariums. Ogden Tanner. 1986. 24.95 o.p. (ISBN 0-671-60274-8, Linden Pr). S&S.

Garden Song. The Vanessa-Ann Collection Staff. Ed. by Margaret Marti. (Illus.). 96p. 1983. pap. text ed. 8.95 o.p. (ISBN 0-913921-29-7). Vanessa-Ann Collec.

Garden Spice & Wild Pot-Herbs: An American Herbal. Walter C. Muenscher & Myron A. Rice. LC 78-56899. (Comstock Ser.). (Illus.). 218p. 1978. pap. 12.95 o.p. (ISBN 0-8014-9174-6). Cornell U Pr.

Gardener's Answer Book. Sunset Magazine & Books Editors. LC 82-83214. (Illus.). 160p. 1983. pap. 7.95 o.p. (ISBN 0-376-03186-7, Sunset Bks). Sunset-Lane.

Gardener's Art Through the Ages, 2 vols. 7th ed. Horst De La Croix & Richard G. Tansey. 922p. 1980. Set. text ed. 26.50 o.p. (ISBN 0-15-503758-7, HC); Vol. I - Ancient, Medieval, & Non-European Art. pap. text ed. 17.50 o.p. (ISBN 0-15-503759-5); Vol. II - Renaissance & Modern Art. pap. text ed. 17.50 o.p. (ISBN 0-15-503760-9). HarBraceJ.

Gardener's Catalog, No. 2. rev. ed. Gardener's Catalog Editors. (Illus.). 320p. 1983. pap. 12.95 o.p. (ISBN 0-688-01238-8, Quill NY). Morrow.

Gardener's Grandchildren. Barbara Willard. LC 78-23637. (gr. 6-12). 1979. text ed. 7.95 o.p. (ISBN 0-07-070291-8). McGraw.

Gardener's Guide to Propagating Food Plants. Franklin H. Fitz. (Illus.). 160p. 1983. 11.95 o.s.i. (ISBN 0-684-17655-6, ScribT). Scribner.

Gardeners Labyrinth. Dydymus Mountaine, pseud. Ed. by John D. Hunt. LC 79-57008. (English Landscape Garden Ser.). 281p. 1982. lib. bdg. 46.00 o.p. (ISBN 0-8240-0150-8). Garland Pub.

Gardening Ants, the Attines. Neal A. Weber. LC 76-184169. (Memoirs Ser.: Vol. 92). (Illus.). 1972. 10.00 o.p. (ISBN 0-87169-092-6). Am Philos.

Gardening as Therapy: A Resource Manual for Development of Horticultural Therapy Programs for the Spring Season. Margaret E. Coxon et al. (Illus.). 32p. (Orig.). 1978. pap. 4.25 o.p. (ISBN 0-89955-377-X, Pub. by U BC Pr Canada). Intl Spec Bk.

Gardening as Therapy: A Resource Manual of Horticultural Therapy Programs for the Summer Season. Margaret E. Coxon. (Illus.). 32p. 1979. pap. 4.25 o.p. (ISBN 0-89955-378-8, Pub. by U BC Pr Canada). Intl Spec Bk.

Gardening Book: Indoors & Outdoors. Anne B. Walsh. LC 75-28272. (Illus.). 112p. (gr. 4-7). 1976. 6.95 o.p. (ISBN 0-689-50042-4, Atheneum). Macmillan.

Gardening for Health & Nutrition: An Introduction to the Method of Bio-Dynamic Gardening Inaugurated by Rudolf Steiner. John Philbrick & Helen Philbrick. (Illus.). 93p. 1971. pap. 4.50 o.p. (ISBN 0-8334-1715-0, Pub. by Steinerbooks NY). Anthroposophic.

Gardening for People: Who Think They Don't Know How. Doug Moon. LC 74-84449. (Illus.). 265p. (Orig.). 1975. pap. 4.50 o.p. (ISBN 0-912528-10-9). John Muir.

Gardening in Containers. 3rd ed. Sunset Editors. LC 76-46651. (Illus.). 80p. 1977. pap. 3.95 o.p. (ISBN 0-376-03205-7, Sunset Bks.). Sunset-Lane.

Gardening in the City: Backyards, Balconies, Terraces & Penthouses. Carla Wallach. LC 76-3429. (Illus.). 192p. 1976. 8.95 o.p. (ISBN 0-15-134288-1). HarBraceJ.

Gardening on the Eastern Seashore. R. Marilyn Schmidt. (Illus.). 235p. (Orig.). 1983. pap. 10.95 o.p. (ISBN 0-937996-02-5). Barnegat.

Gardening with Color. Ed. by Ortho Books Editorial Staff. LC 77-89690. (Illus.). 1978. pap. 5.95 o.p. (ISBN 0-917102-58-4). Ortho.

Gardening with Perennials. Joseph Hudak. Orig. Title: Gardening with Perennials Month by Month. (Illus.). xvi, 398p. 1985. Repr. of 1976 ed. 24.95 o.p. (ISBN 0-88192-018-5). Timber.

Gardening with Perennials Month by Month see Gardening with Perennials.

Gardening with Wildflowers. Frances Tenenbaum. 208p. (Orig.). 1986. pap. 8.95 o.p. (ISBN 0-345-32606-7). Ballantine.

Gardening Without Poisons. 2nd ed. Beatrice T. Hunter. 1973. 6.95 o.p. (ISBN 0-395-13522-2). HM.

Gardens & Scenic Spots of Beijing. Ed. by Beijing Administration of Gardens & Parks Staff. (Illus.). 45p. (Orig.). 1986. pap. text ed. 14.95 o.p. (ISBN 0-8351-1793-6). China Bks.

Gardens in Time. John Oldham & Ray Oldham. (Illus.). 288p. 1980. pap. 35.00 o.p. (ISBN 0-318-14683-5, Landscape Architecture); pap. 24.50 Holiday price o.p. (ISBN 0-318-14684-3). Am Landscape Arch.

Gardens: Monographs Published 1970-1984. Mary Vance. (Architecture Ser.: A 1428). 46p. 1985. 6.75 o.p. (ISBN 0-89028-478-4). Vance Biblios.

Gardens of Stone. Nicholas Proffitt. 437p. 1984. pap. 3.95 o.p. (ISBN 0-88184-076-9). Carroll & Graf.

Gardens of the Heart. Hulda C. Miller. 102p. 1984. 4.95 o.p. (ISBN 0-86544-025-5). Salv Army Suppl South.

Gardner's Art Through the Ages. 3rd ed. Horst De la Croix & Richard G. Tansey. 1948. 6.50 o.p. (ISBN 0-15-503750-1). HarbraceJ.

Garelli Moped Owner Service-Repair: 1976-1978. Ed Scott. (Illus.). pap. 6.00 o.p. (ISBN 0-89287-200-4, M435). Clymer Pub.

Garelli Mopeds '72 to '78. Mervyn Bleach. 13.50 o.p. (189). Haynes Pubns.

Gargoyle Conspiracy. Marvin H. Albert. 288p. 1982. pap. 1.95 o.p. (ISBN 0-440-15239-9). Dell.

Garibaldi's Defence of the Roman Republic, 1848-9. George M. Trevelyan. LC 76-156214. (Illus.). 1971. Repr. of 1912 ed. lib. bdg. 35.00x o.p. (ISBN 0-8371-6165-7, TRGD). Greenwood.

Garimus File. Gary Stanley. LC 82-72301. (Illus., Orig.). 1983. pap. 6.95 o.p. (ISBN 0-86605-107-4). Heres Life.

Garish Days. Lynn Caraganis. LC 87-8293. 224p. 1988. 15.95 o.s.i. (ISBN 1-55584-037-X). Weidenfeld.

Garland for Gandhi. Helen P. Jacob. LC 68-21993. (Illus.). (gr. 2-5). 1968. 5.95 o.p. (ISBN 0-395-27651-9, Pub. by Parnassus). HM.

Garlinghouse Portfolio of Custom Home Plan. Ed. by Garlinghouse Publication Inc., Staff. (Illus.). 432p. (Orig.). 1987. pap. 27.50 o.p. (ISBN 0-938708-17-1). L F Garlinghouse Co.

Garner's Gizmos & Gadgets. Phillip Garner. (Illus.). 80p. 1987. pap. 6.95 o.p. (ISBN 0-399-51343-4, Perigee). Putnam Pub Group.

Garnishes, Relishes & Sauces for Foodservice Menu Planning. Eulalia C. Blair. LC 77-3292. (Foodservice Menu Planning Ser.). 320p. 1983. 18.95 o.p. (ISBN 0-8436-2173-7). Van Nos Reinhold.

Garrett Collection, the Johns Hopkins University: Auction of Ancient Roman, Latin American, Far Eastern, Islamic, Indian, Canadian, Australian & African Coins, Pt. I. 1984. 15.00 o.p. (ISBN 0-318-19614-X). Numismatic Fine Arts.

Garrett Wade Woodworking Tools Catalogue 1988. (Illus.). 196p. (Orig.). 1987. pap. 4.00 o.p. (ISBN 0-8069-6622-X). Sterling.

Garrett Wade Woodworking Tools Catalogue, 1989. (Illus.). 196p. (Orig.). 1988. pap. 4.00 o.p. (ISBN 0-8069-6906-7). Sterling.

Garrison's & Morton's a Medical Bibliography: An Annotated Check-List of Texts Illustrating the History of Medicine. 4TH ed. Ed. by Leslie T. Morton. 1022p. 1983. 52.00x o.p. (ISBN 0-686-46682-9, 05810-6, Pub by Gower Pub Co England). Lexington Bks.

Garvin of the OBSERVER. David Ayerst. LC 84-23767. 314p. 1985. 43.00 o.p. (ISBN 0-7099-0560-2, Pub. by Croom Helm Ltd). Routledge Chapman & Hall.

Gary Carter; The Kid. Ray Buck. LC 83-21084. (Sports Stars Ser.). (Illus.). 48p. (gr. 2-8). 1984. lib. bdg. 10.33 o.p. (ISBN 0-516-04337-4); pap. 2.95 o.p. (ISBN 0-516-44337-2). Childrens.

Gary Coleman Show: The Lost Dog Adventure. (Saturday Morning Bks.). (Illus.). 24p. (gr. 3-6). 1983. pap. 1.95 o.p. (ISBN 0-89954-224-7). Antioch Pub Co.

Gary Coleman Show: The Mansion Mystery. (Saturday Morning Bks.). (Illus.). 12p. (gr. 2-6). 1983. pap. 2.95 o.p. (ISBN 0-89954-225-5). Antioch Pub Co.

Gary Coleman Show: What If Elephants Had Pink Stripes? Illus. by Joan Corbitt. (Saturday Morning Bks.). (Illus.). 22p. (ps-2). 1983. 2.50 o.p. (ISBN 0-89954-223-9). Antioch Pub Co.

Gary Cooper: Legends. Richard Schickel. 14.95 o.p. (ISBN 0-316-77307-7). Little.

Gary Yanker's Sportwalking. Gary Yanker. (Illus.). 160p. (Orig.). 1987. pap. 9.95 o.p. (ISBN 0-8092-4966-9). Contemp Bks.

Garza County History. Garza County Historical Society Staff. 1980. 25.00 o.p. (ISBN 0-89015-266-7). Eakin Pr.

Gas Chemistry in Nuclear Reactors & Large Industrial Plants. Ed. by Edwin A. Dyer. 296p. 1980. pap. 73.95x o.p. (ISBN 0-471-25663-3, Pub. by Wiley Heyden). Wiley.

Gas Chromatography. Ed. by Donald R. Coates. 1960. 87.50 o.p. (ISBN 0-12-177350-7). Acad Pr.

Gas Discharges & Their Applications. (PPL Conference Publications Ser.: No. 20). (Illus.). 536p. (Orig.). 1982. pap. 98.00 o.s.i. (ISBN 0-906048-86-9, PC020). Inst Elect Eng.

Gas, Food, & Lodging. John Baeder. LC 81-5427. (Illus.). 132p. 1982. 29.95 o.p. (ISBN 0-89659-308-8). Abbeville Pr.

Gas Industry & the Environment: Proceedings of the United Nations Economic Commission for Europe, Commission on Gas, Minsk, U. S. S. R., 1977. United Nations Economic Commission for Europe, Commission on Gas. 1978. 90.00 o.p. (ISBN 0-08-022412-1). Pergamon.

Gas Lasers. C. S. Willet. 1974. 155.00 o.p. (ISBN 0-08-017803-0). Pergamon.

Gas Lighting. David Gledhill. (Shire Album Ser.: No. 65). (Illus.). 32p. (Orig.). pap. 2.95 o.p. (ISBN 0-85263-539-7, Pub. by Shire Pubns England). Seven Hills Bk Dists.

Gas Phase Chromatography of Steroids. K. B. Eik-Nes & E. C. Horning. LC 68-18620. (Monographs on Endocrinology: Vol. 2). (Illus.). 1968. 35.00 o.p. (ISBN 0-387-04277-6). Springer-Verlag.

Gas-Phase Electron Diffraction. A. Haaland et al. (Topics in Current Chemistry Ser.: Vol. 53). (Illus.). iv, 119p. 1975. 29.00 o.p. (ISBN 0-387-07051-6). Springer-Verlag.

Gas-Phase Oxidation of Hydrocarbons. V. Y. Shtern. Ed. by B. P. Mullins. 1964. 175.00 o.p. (ISBN 0-08-010202-6). Pergamon.

Gas Situation in the EEC Region Around the Year 1990. United Nations Economic Commission for Europe. (European Committee for Economic Perspectives ser.: Vol. 18). 1979. 105.00 o.p. (ISBN 0-08-024465-3). Pergamon.

Gas Solubilities. W. Gerrard. 1980. 125.00 o.p. (ISBN 0-08-025248-6). Pergamon.

Gas! The Battle for Ypres, 1915. J. McWilliams & R. J. Steel. 224p. 18.95 o.s.i. (ISBN 0-920277-01-2). Janes Info Group.

Gas Tracer Study of Roof-Vent Effluent Diffusion at Millstone Nuclear Power Station AIF-NESP-007B. Stanford Research Institute Staff. (National Environmental Studies Project: NESP Reports). 295p. 1975. 20.00 o.p. (ISBN 0-318-13573-6); to NESP sponsors 10.00 o.p. (ISBN 0-318-13574-4). US Coun Energy Awareness.

Gas Turbine Combustion. Arthur H. Lefebvre. (Energy, Combustion, & Environment Ser.). (Illus.). 416p. 1983. text ed. 46.95 o.p. (ISBN 0-07-037029-X). McGraw.

Gas Turbine Heat Transfer: 1978. Ed. by V. L. Erickson & H. L. Julien. 1978. 18.00 o.p. (ISBN 0-685-66801-0, H00125). ASME.

Gas Turbine System Technician, Electrical 3 & 2. Robert W. Gosner & James M. Pluth. (Illus.). 624p. (Orig.). 1985. pap. 17.00 o.p. (ISBN 0-318-19954-8, S/N 008-047-00380-3). USGPO.

Gas Turbines & Jet Propulsion. G. Geoffrey Smith. (Illus.). 350p. 1955. (ISBN 0-8022-1594-7). Philos Lib.

Gaschromatographie der Pflanzenschutzmittel: Tabellarische Literaturreferate Berlin-Dahlem, 5 vols. new ed. Federal Institute for Biology in Agriculture & Forestry Staff & Institute for Plant Protection Agent Research Staff. (Ger.). Vol. I, 1970. 20.00 o.p. (ISBN 0-913106-09-7); Vol. II, 1972. 15.00 o.p. (ISBN 0-913106-10-0); Vol. III. 15.00 o.p. (ISBN 0-913106-11-9); Vol. IV. 15.00 o.p. (ISBN 0-913106-12-7); Vol. V, 1975. 15.00 o.p. (ISBN 0-913106-13-5). PolyScience.

Gaseous Dielectrics II: Proceedings of the Second International Symposium on Gaseous Dielectrics, Knoxville, Tenn., U. S. A., March 9-13, 1980. Ed. by Loucas G. Christophorou. 506p. 1980. 125.00 o.p. (ISBN 0-08-025978-2). Pergamon.

Gaseous Electronics. Ed. by J. W. McGowan & P. K. John. 132p. 1975. pap. 26.50 o.p. (ISBN 0-444-10777-0, North-Holland). Elsevier.

Gaseous Electronics & Gas Lasers. B. E. Cherrington. 1979. text ed. 69.00 o.p. (ISBN 0-08-020622-0). Pergamon.

Gases & Airs. Elementary Science Study Staff. 1975. tchr's. guide 21.00 o.p. (ISBN 0-07-018519-0). McGraw.

Gasifiers: Fuel for Siege Economies. 1983. 5.50 o.p. (ISBN 0-905347-42-0). C I D E.

Gasoline Alley. Dick Moores. (Illus.). 1976. pap. 3.95 o.p. (ISBN 0-380-00761-4, 30486). Avon.

Gasp IV Simulation Language. A. Alan Pritsker. LC 74-3281. 451p. 1974. 41.50x o.p. (ISBN 0-471-70045-2, Pub. by Wiley-Interscience). Wiley.

Gassendi's View of Knowledge: A Study of the Epistemological Basis of His Logic. Howard T. Egan. LC 83-23345. 190p. (Orig.). 1984. lib. bdg. 28.50 o.p. (ISBN 0-8191-3737-5); pap. text ed. 14.25 o.p. (ISBN 0-8191-3738-3). U Pr of Amer.

Gastric Brooding Frog. Ed. by Michael J. Tyler. (Illus.). 163p. 1983. 33.00 o.p. (ISBN 0-7099-2425-9, Pub. by Croom Helm Ltd). Routledge Chapman & Hall.

Gastric Motility: A Selectively Annotated Bibliography. Ed. by Robert M. Stern & Christopher M. Davis. LC 82-12173. 191p. 1982. 29.95 o.p. (ISBN 0-87933-430-4). Van Nos Reinhold.

Gastric Secretion: Proceedings of the Symposium, Frankfurt Am Main, 1971. Gastric Secretion Symposium Staff. Ed. by George Sachs. 1972. 71.50 o.p. (ISBN 0-12-613750-1). Acad Pr.

Gastrin & the Vagus. Ed. by J. F. Rehfeld & E. Amdrup. 1979. 79.50 o.p. (ISBN 0-12-584750-5). Acad Pr.

Gastro-Intestinal Ultrastructure: An Atlas of Scanning & Transmission Electron Micrographs. Carl J. Pfeiffer et al. 1974. 95.50 o.p. (ISBN 0-12-553750-6). Acad Pr.

Gastroenterology: A Problem-Oriented Approach. C. R. Kannan. 1985. pap. text ed. 33.25 o.p. (ISBN 0-87488-760-7). Med Exam.

Gastrointestinal & Hepatic Complications in Pregnancy. Vinod K. Rustgi & James N. Cooper. LC 85-91281. 292p. 1986. 39.95 o.p. (ISBN 0-471-80913-6). Wiley.

Gastrointestinal Defence Mechanisms: Proceedings of a Satellite Symposium of the 28th International Congress of Physiological Sciences, Budapest, 1980. Ed. by Gy. Mozsik et al. LC 80-41883. (Advances in Physiological Sciences: Vol. 29). (Illus.). 590p. 1981. 100.00 o.p. (ISBN 0-08-027350-5). Pergamon.

Gastrointestinal Diseases: Focus on Clinical Diagnosis. 2nd ed. Khursheed N. Jeejeebhoy. 1984. text ed. 51.25 o.p. (ISBN 0-87488-395-4). Med Exam.

Gastrointestinal Disorders. Ed. by Helen Hamilton & Minnie B. Rose. (Nurse's Clinical Library). (Illus.). 192p. 1985. text ed. 19.95 o.p. (ISBN 0-916730-75-1). Springhouse Pub.

Gastrointestinal Hormones: A Symposium. Ed. by James C. Thompson. LC 75-3573. (Illus.). 680p. 1975. 27.50x o.p. (ISBN 0-292-72704-6). U of Tex Pr.

Gastrointestinal Problems, Vol. 4. Julie M. Strange. (RN Nursing Assessment Ser.). 180p. 1984. pap. 15.95 o.p. (ISBN 0-87489-285-6). Med Economics.

Gastrointestinal Tract Cancer. Ed. by Martin Lipkin & Robert A. Good. LC 78-1964. (Sloan-Kettering Institute Cancer Ser.). (Illus.). 620p. 1978. 89.50x o.p. (ISBN 0-306-31098-8, Plenum Pr). Plenum Pub.

Gastronomic Bibliography. K. Bitting. 718p. 1939. 60.00 o.p. (ISBN 0-87556-723-1). Saifer.

Gate Behind the Wall. Samuel Heilman. 192p. 1985. 15.45 o.s.i. (ISBN 0-671-52489-5). Summit Bks.

GATE: Containing Results from the GARP Atlantic Tropical Experiment (GATE) Including the Proceedings of the GATE Symposium on Oceanography & Surface Layer Meteorology, Kiel May 1978. G. Siedler et al. 1980. 180.00 o.p. (ISBN 0-08-023983-8). Pergamon.

Gate of Heaven. Ralph McInerny. 1976. pap. 1.75 o.p. (ISBN 0-380-00568-9, 28217). Avon.

Gate: The True Story of the Design & Construction of the Golden Gate Bridge. John Van der Zee. (Illus.). 384p. 1987. 19.45 o.p. (ISBN 0-671-60205-5). S&S.

Gated River. Lucy Ferriss. 416p. 1986. 16.95 o.p. (ISBN 0-531-15007-0). Watts.

Gatekeeper. William Page. LC 81-9040. 48p. (Orig.). 1983. pap. 3.95 o.p. (ISBN 0-918518-07-5). Ion Books.

Gatekeeping: The Denial, Dismissal & Distortion of Women. Ed. by D. Spender & L. Spender. 101p. 1984. pap. 19.25 o.p. (ISBN 0-08-031307-8). Pergamon.

Gates. Muriel Rukeyser. LC 76-20738. 1976. text ed. 7.95 o.p. (ISBN 0-07-054268-6); pap. text ed. 4.95 o.p. (ISBN 0-07-054269-4). McGraw.

Gates' Jigs, Fixtures, Tools & Gauges. 6th ed. Ed. by G. H. Ryder. (Illus.). 1973. 35.00x o.p. Trans-Atl Phila.

Gates of Creation. Philip Jose Farmer. 224p. 1981. pap. 2.75 o.s.i. (ISBN 0-441-27390-4). Ace Bks.

Gates of Death. Terry Phillips. LC 86-91529. (Advanced Dungeons & Dragons Adventure Gamebks.: No. 13). 192p. 1987. pap. 2.95 o.p. (ISBN 0-88038-433-6). TSR Inc.

Gates of Freedom: A Passover Haggadah. Chaim Stern. LC 81-84191. (Illus.). 130p. 1986. pap. 6.95 o.p. (ISBN 0-940646-21-8). Rossel Bks.

Gates of Sagittarius. Roland Cutler. 304p. 1981. pap. 2.75 o.p. (ISBN 0-380-56085-2, 56085). Avon.

Gates of the Forest. Elie Wiesel. (YA) (gr. 7 up). 1976. pap. 1.95 o.p. (ISBN 0-380-01206-5, 51821, Bard). Avon.

Gateway to Oblivion: The Great Lakes Vortex. Hugh F. Cochrane. 1981. pap. 2.50 o.p. (ISBN 0-380-54817-8, 54817). Avon.

Gateway to Survival Is Storage. Walter D. Batchelor. 128p. 1974. pap. 3.95 o.p. (ISBN 0-89036-127-4). Hawkes Pub Inc.

Gateways to Science, Level 1. 3rd ed. Neal J. Holmes et al. 1982. text ed. 11.32 o.p. (ISBN 0-07-029801-7). McGraw.

Gathas of Zarathustra: A Reconstruction of the Text. M. C. Monna. 1978. pap. text ed. 35.00x o.p. (ISBN 90-6203-582-5). Humanities.

Gather Back the Dream. William V. Sieller. LC 73-89135. 80p. 1973. 4.00 o.p. (ISBN 0-8233-0198-2). Golden Quill.

Gather 'Round. Ed. by Paul F. Page. 1976. 8.95 o.p. (ISBN 0-89390-000-1). Resource Pubns.

Gather 'Round Too! Ed. by Paul F. Page. 1977. 8.95 o.p. (ISBN 0-89390-003-6). Resource Pubns.

Gathered into One. William R. Davies. 1975. pap. 3.50 o.p. (ISBN 0-8192-1191-5). Morehouse Pub.

Gatherer. Owen Brookes. 1982. 13.95 o.p. (ISBN 0-03-059531-2). H Holt & Co.

Gathering God's People: Signs of a Successful Parish. 265p. 1982. 9.55 o.p. (ISBN 0-318-00782-7). Natl Cath Educ.

Gathering of Gunmen. Howard R. Simpson. LC 86-29283. (Crime Club Ser.). 192p. 1987. 12.95 o.p. (ISBN 0-385-24216-6). Doubleday.

Gathering of Hope. Helen Hayes. LC 83-1728. 112p. 1983. 9.95 o.p. (ISBN 0-8006-0705-8, Fortress). Augsburg Fortress.

Gathering of Horsemen. James L. Burke. (Orig.). 1982. pap. PB.

Gathering of Strangers: Understanding the Life of Your Church. Robert C. Worley. LC 76-21091. 112p. 1976. pap. 5.95 o.s.i. (ISBN 0-664-24124-7, Westminster). Westminster John Knox.

Gathering of Wolves. Michael Hammonds. 1976. pap. 1.25 o.p. (ISBN 0-685-72564-2, LB393, Pub. by Leisure Bks CT). Dorchester Pub Co.

Gathering Time. Deirdra B. Baldwin. (Ser. One). 1975. pap. 7.00 o.p. (ISBN 0-931846-00-5). Wash Writers Pub.

Gating & Rising: State of the Art. 1982. 30.00 o.p. (ISBN 0-686-44987-8). Steel Founders.

Gatt Actividades (1986) 107p. 1987. pap. text ed. 7.95 o.p. (ISBN 92-870-3027-8, G201/G200) (ISBN 92-870-2027-2). UNIPUB.

GATT Activities in 1969-70. annual Incl. GATT Activities in 1970-71. 59p. (Orig., Eng., Fr. & Span.). 1972. pap. 5.00 (G100, GATT). UNIPUB; GATT Activities in 1972. 51p. (Orig., Eng., Fr. & Span.). 1973. pap. 5.00 (G36, GATT). UNIPUB; GATT Activities in 1973. 66p. (Orig., Eng., Fr. & Span.). 1974. pap. 5.50 (G37, GATT). UNIPUB; GATT Activities in 1974. (Eng., Fr. & Span.). 1975. pap. 7.50 (G38, GATT). UNIPUB; GATT Activities in 1975. 70p. (Eng., Fr. & Span.). 1976. pap. 7.50 (G39, GATT). UNIPUB; GATT Activities in 1976. (Eng., Fr. & Span.). 1977. pap. 7.50 (G40, GATT). UNIPUB; GATT Activities 1977. (Eng., Fr. & Span.). 1977. pap. 7.50 (G117, GATT). UNIPUB; GATT Activities in 1978 & Results of the Tokyo Round Multilateral Trade Negotiations. (Eng., Fr. & Span.). 1979. pap. 7.50 (G125, GATT). UNIPUB; GATT Activities in 1979 & Conclusion of the Tokyo Round Multilateral Trade Negotations. 87p. 1980. pap. 7.50 (G140, GATT). UNIPUB; GATT Activities in 1980. 65p. 1981. pap. 8.00 o.p. (ISBN 92-870-1001-3, G146, GATT). UNIPUB; GATT Activities in 1981. 61p. 1982. pap. 7.50 (ISBN 92-870-1004-8, G151, GATT). UNIPUB; GATT Activities in 1982. 87p. 1983. pap. text ed. 7.50 (ISBN 92-870-1008-0, G162, GATT). UNIPUB; GATT Activities in 1983. 69p. 1985. pap. 7.50 (ISBN 92-870-1011-0, G162, GATT). UNIPUB; 1984. 75p. 1986. pap. 7.50 (G169). UNIPUB. (Orig., Eng., Fr. & Span.). 1971. pap. 1.50 o.p. (ISBN 0-685-11715-4, G98, GATT). UNIPUB.

GATT Activities in 1970-71 see GATT Activities in 1969-70.

GATT Activities in 1972 see GATT Activities in 1969-70.

GATT Activities in 1973 see GATT Activities in 1969-70.

GATT Activities in 1974 see GATT Activities in 1969-70.

GATT Activities in 1975 see GATT Activities in 1969-70.

GATT Activities in 1976 see GATT Activities in 1969-70.

GATT Activities in 1978 & Results of the Tokyo Round Multilateral Trade Negotiations see GATT Activities in 1969-70.

GATT Activities in 1979 & Conclusion of the Tokyo Round Multilateral Trade Negotations see GATT Activities in 1969-70.

GATT Activities in 1980 see GATT Activities in 1969-70.

GATT Activities in 1981 see GATT Activities in 1969-70.

GATT Activities in 1982 see GATT Activities in 1969-70.

GATT Activities in 1983 see GATT Activities in 1969-70.

GATT Activities 1977 see GATT Activities in 1969-70.

GATT Negotiations & United States Trade Policy. (CBO Study Ser.). (Illus.). 155p. (Orig.). 1987. pap. 6.50 o.p. (ISBN 0-318-23752-0, S/N 052-070-06336-0). USGPO.

GATT Status of Legal Instruments: Supplement, No. 9. 86p. 1981. pap. 5.00 o.p. (ISBN 0-686-79001-4, G147, GATT). UNIPUB.

Gaudy Night. Dorothy L. Sayers. 1976. pap. 3.50 o.p. (ISBN 0-380-01207-3, 65037). Avon.

Gauge Theories, Massive Neutrinos & Proton Decay. Ed. by Behram Kursunoglu & Arnold Perlmutter. LC 81-11923. (Studies in the Natural Sciences: Vol. 18). 402p. 1981. 72.50x o.p. (ISBN 0-306-40821-X, Plenum Pr). Plenum Pub.

Gauguin's Religious Themes. Ziva Amishai-Maisels. Ed. by S. J. Freedberg. (Outstanding Dissertations in Fine Arts Ser.). (Illus.). 670p. 1985. Repr. of 1970 ed. 75.00 o.p. (ISBN 0-8240-6863-7). Garland Pub.

Gauquelin Book of American Charts. Michel Gauquelin & Francoise Gauquelin. 384p. (Orig.). 1982. pap. 15.95 o.p. (ISBN 0-917086-33-3). A C S Pubns Inc.

Gaussian Measures in Banauch Spaces. H. H. Kuo. (Lecture Notes in Mathematics Ser.: Vol. 463). vi, 224p. 1975. pap. 16.00 o.p. (ISBN 0-387-07173-3). Springer-Verlag.

Gay Bunch. Oleta Gay. 1979. 5.50 o.p. (ISBN 0-682-49232-9). Exposition-Phoenix.

Gay Novel: The Male Homosexual Image in America. James Levin. 350p. 1983. 39.50x o.p. (ISBN 0-8290-1065-3). Irvington.

Gay Novel: The Male Homosexual Image in America. James Levin. 350p. 1984. pap. 14.95 o.p. (ISBN 0-8290-1559-0). Irvington.

Gay Place. William Brammer. 1978. 11.95 o.p. (ISBN 0-932012-05-1). Texas Month Pr.

Gay Trivia Quiz Book. James Aaron. 224p. (Orig.). 1985. pap. 5.95 o.p. (ISBN 0-87795-638-3, Arbor Hse). Morrow.

Gay: What Teenagers Should Know about Homosexuality & the AIDS Crisis. Morton Hunt. LC 87-23626. 256p. (YA) (gr. 8-12). 1987. pap. 6.95 o.p. (R& S Bks.). FS&G.

Gay: What You Should Know About Homosexuality. Morton Hunt. LC 77-76806. 210p. (gr. 5 up). 1977. 7.95 o.p. (ISBN 0-374-38754-0). FS&G.

Gayan. 4th ed. Hazrat Inayat Khan. 172p. 1978. pap. 3.95 o.p. (ISBN 0-900217-10-3, Pub. by Sufi Pub Co England). Hunter Hse.

Gayan, Vadan, Nirtan. Hazrat I. Khan. LC 80-52801. (The Collected Works of Hazrat Inayat Khan Ser.). 304p. 1980. 7.50 o.p. (ISBN 0-930872-21-5, 1006H); pap. 5.95 o. p o.p. (ISBN 0-930872-16-9, 1006P). Omega Pr NY.

Gayelord Hauser's New Treasury of Secrets. rev. ed. Gayelord Hauser. LC 74-22102. 424p. 1974. 8.95 o.p. (ISBN 0-374-22150-2). FS&G.

Gayety of Grace. Edna Hong. LC 77-176484. 128p. 1972. 3.95 o.p. (ISBN 0-8066-1213-4, 10-2540, Augsburg). Augsburg Fortress.

Gaylord's Badge. Richard Meade. 1976. pap. 1.25 o.p. (ISBN 0-505-50974-1, BT50974, Pub. by Tower Bks). Dorchester Pub Co.

Gaynor Women. Virginia Coffman. LC 77-90664. 1978. 8.95 o.p. (ISBN 0-87795-180-2, Arbor Hse). Morrow.

GBL's, How to Prepare & Process United States Government Bills of Lading. (Illus.). 51p. 1987. pap. 2.50 o.p. (ISBN 0-318-22619-7, S/N 022-000-00200-7). USGPO.

G.E. Nine Hundred Ninety-Nine (T.V.) (Big Little Bks.: No. 40). (Illus.). 350p. 1984. 6.95 o.p. (ISBN 0-318-02692-9). Bks Nippan.

G.E. Nine Hundred Ninety-Nine (T.V., Vol. 2. (Big Little Bks.: No. 53). (Illus.). 350p. 1984. 6.95 o.p. (ISBN 0-318-02698-8). Bks Nippan.

G.E. Nine Hundred Ninety-Nine (T.V., Vol. 3. (Big Little Bks.: No. 60). (Illus.). 350p. 1984. 6.95 o.p. (ISBN 0-318-02702-X). Bks Nippan.

G.E. Nine Hundred Ninety-Nine (T.V., Vol. 4. (Big Little Bks.: No. 89). (Illus.). 350p. 1984. 6.95 o.p. (ISBN 0-318-02719-4). Bks Nippan.

Gear Design & Performance. 1984. 26.00 o.p. (ISBN 0-89883-805-3, SP584). Soc Auto Engineers.

Gear Processing & Manufacturing. 2nd ed. Society of Manufacturing Engineers Staff. 260p. 1984. 33.00 o.p. (ISBN 0-87263-167-2). SME.

GED - Mathematics Test 5. 1976. pap. 7.65 o.p. (ISBN 0-8092-8112-0). Contemp Bks.

GED: How to Prepare for the High School Equivalency Examination. 1978. pap. 8.95 o.s.i. (ISBN 0-8092-5136-1). Contemp Bks.

GED Mathematics Test Preparation Guide: High School Equivalency Examination. Deborah Moran et al. (Cliffs Test Preparation Ser.). 182p. (gr. 10 up). 1983. pap. 3.95 o.p. (ISBN 0-8220-2016-5). Cliffs.

GED Reading Skills Test Preparation Guide: High School Equivalency Examination. William A. Covino & Margaret Coda-Messerle. (Cliffs Test Preparation Ser.). 105p. (Orig.). (gr. 10 up). 1981. pap. 2.95 o.p. (ISBN 0-8220-2014-9). Cliffs.

GED-Reading Skills Test 4. 1976. pap. 6.00 o.p. (ISBN 0-8092-8113-9). Contemp Bks.

GED Science Test Preparation Guide: High School Equivalency Examination. Harold D. Nathan. (Cliffs Test Preparation Ser.). 164p. (Orig.). (gr. 10 up). 1980. pap. 3.95 o.p. (ISBN 0-8220-2010-6). Cliffs.

GED Social Studies Test Preparation Guide: High School Equivalency Examination. Stephen Fisher. (Cliff Test Preparation Ser.). 218p. (Orig.). (gr. 10 up). 1980. pap. 3.95 o.p. (ISBN 0-8220-2012-2). Cliffs.

GED Writing Skills Test Preparation Guide: High School Equivalency Examination. Loraine J. Weber & Willam A. Covino. (Cliffs Test Preparation Ser.). 151p. (Orig.). (gr. 10 up). 1981. pap. 3.95 o.p. (ISBN 0-8220-2015-7). Cliffs.

Gedichte Aus Den Jahren 1908-1945. Franz Werfel. 1946. 15.00 o.p. (ISBN 0-685-57210-2). M S Rosenberg.

Gedichte Von Osterreich. (Ger.). 3.25 o.p. (ISBN 0-911862-41-2). Hungarian Rev.

Geek. Craig Nova. 224p. 1984. pap. 3.95 o.s.i. (ISBN 0-440-33092-0, LE). Dell.

Gegenseitige Beeinflussung und Temperatur-Wirkung bei tropischen und subtropischen Pflanzen: Bericht ueber neue experimentelle Untersuchungen an Nutzpflanzen und Arten der spontanen Vegetation. Ruediger Knapp. (Illus.). 1967. pap. 12.50x o.p. (ISBN 3-7682-0576-2). Lubrecht & Cramer.

Gehydrology of the Dakota Sandstone Aquifer. 1984. 31.25 o.p. (ISBN 0-318-23046-1). Natl Water Well.

Gel Chromatography: Theory, Methodology & Application. T. Kremmer & L. Boross. LC 77-24994. 299p. 1979. 104.00 o.p. (ISBN 0-471-99548-7, Pub. by Wiley-Interscience). Wiley.

Geldwertstabilitat und Wirtschaftswachstum. Ed. by Hans Seidel. 240p. 1984. write for info. o.s.i. (ISBN 3-525-13169-0). Intl Monetary.

Geller Effect. Uri Geller & Guy L. Playfair. LC 86-33551. 1987. 17.95 o.s.i. (ISBN 0-8050-0465-3). H Holt & Co.

Gem in the Wire. Vittorio Conti. Tr. by Barbara E. Lewis from Ital. 101p. 1984. 8.95 o.p. (ISBN 0-533-05810-4). Vantage.

Gem Stones of the United States. Dorothy Schlegel. (Shorey Prospecting Ser.). 52p. 1975. pap. 2.50 o.p. (ISBN 0-8466-8007-6, G-7). Shorey.

Gemini. Domini Taylor. LC 84-20389. 240p. 1985. 13.95 o.p. (ISBN 0-689-11535-0, Atheneum). Macmillan.

Gemma. Noel Streatfeild. (Orig.). (gr. 3-6). 1986. pap. 3.25 o.s.i. (ISBN 0-440-42859-9, YB). Dell.

Gems & Jewelry. Arem. 1987. pap. 4.95 o.p. (ISBN 0-553-25140-6). Bantam.

Gems of Truth. Myrtle S. Jessup. 64p. 1981. 5.00 o.p. (ISBN 0-682-49688-X). Exposition-Phoenix.

Gems of Wisdom. Bawa R. Muhaiyaddeen. 125p. 1982. 4.95 o.s.i. (ISBN 0-914390-21-X). Fellowship Pr PA.

Gen Ind Ed Training. Groneman. Date not set. (ISBN 0-07-024976-8). McGraw.

Gendai Chato Taikan: A General View of Contemporary Tea Ceremony & Ceramic Ware, 6 vols. Ed. by Shufunotomo Editorial Staff & Tetsuzo Tanikawa. (Illus., Japanese.). 1979. Set. 200.00 o.p. (ISBN 4-07-909839-1, Pub. by Shufunotomo Co Ltd Japan). Vol. 1, 152p. Vol. 2, 164p. Vol. 3, 186p. Vol. 4, 186p. Vol. 5, 186p. Vol. 6, 200p. C E Tuttle.

Gendarme Est Sans Pitie: Avec: La Peur des Coupes, Theodore Cherche des Allumettes, La Couche. Georges Courteline. 1974. 8.95 o.p. (ISBN 0-686-54631-8). French & Eur.

Gender. Ivan Illich. 1985. pap. 6.95 o.p. (ISBN 0-394-71587-X). Pantheon.

Gender Advertisements. Erving Goffman. LC 78-23351. (Illus.). 1979. 16.00x o.s.i. (ISBN 0-674-34191-0). Harvard U Pr.

Gender & Sex in Society. Lucile Duberman et al. LC 73-10658. 274p. 1975. pap. text ed. 13.95 o.p. (ISBN 0-275-85070-6, HoltC). HR&W.

Gender Chameleons: Androgeny in Rock 'n Roll. Steven Simels. 1985. 12.95 o.p. (ISBN 0-87795-694-4, Arbor Hse). Morrow.

Gender, Class & Education. Ed. by Len Barton & Stephen Walker. 210p. 1983. 30.00x o.p. (ISBN 0-905273-42-7, Falmer Pr); pap. 16.00x o.p. (ISBN 0-905273-41-9). Taylor & Francis.

Gender, Politics & Fiction: Twentieth Century Australian Women's Novels. Ed. by Carole Ferrier. LC 84-22051. 262p. 1985. text ed. 32.50 o.p. (ISBN 0-7022-1796-4). U of Queensland Pr.

Gender, Sex & the Law. Ed. by Susan Edwards. LC 84-29309. 222p. 1985. 29.00 o.p. (ISBN 0-7099-0938-1, Pub. by Croom Helm Ltd). Routledge Chapman & Hall.

Gendered Subjects: The Dynamics of Feminist Teaching. Ed. by Margo Culley & Catherine Portuges. 128p. 1985. 24.95x o.p. (ISBN 0-7102-0608-9); pap. 12.95 o.p. (ISBN 0-7100-9907-X). Routledge Chapman & Hall.

Gene Activity in Early Development. Eric H. Davidson. 1977. 36.50 o.p. (ISBN 0-12-205160-2). Acad Pr.

Gene Age: Genetic Engineering & the Industrial Revolution. Edward J. Sylvester & Lynn C. Klotz. (Illus.). 224p. 1983. 15.95 o.p. (ISBN 0-684-17950-4, ScribT). Scribner.

Gene Cloning in Organisms Other Than E. Coli. Ed. by P. H. Hofschneider & W. Goebel. (Current Topics in Microbiology & Immunology Ser.: Vol. 96). (Illus.). 260p. 1981. 46.00 o.p. (ISBN 0-387-11117-4). Springer-Verlag.

Gene-Enzyme Systems in Drosophila. W. J. Dickinson & D. T. Sullivan. LC 74-17430. (Results & Problems in Cell Differentiation: Vol. 6). (Illus.). xii, 163p. 1975. 37.00 o.p. (ISBN 0-387-06977-1). Springer-Verlag.

Gene Function: Proceedings of the 12th FEBS Meeting, Dresden, 1978. Ed. by S. Rosenthal et al. (Federation of European Biochemical Society Ser.: Vol. 51). (Illus.). 1979. 93.00 o.p. (ISBN 0-08-023175-6). Pergamon.

Gene Hovis's Uptown, Down Home Cookbook. Gene Hovis & Sylvia Rosenthal. 1987. 17.95 o.p. (ISBN 0-316-37443-1). Little.

Gene McCarthy's Minnesota. Eugene J. McCarthy. (Illus.). 144p. 1982. 12.95 o.p. (ISBN 0-86683-682-9); pap. 6.95 o.p. (ISBN 0-86683-681-0). HarpR.

Gene Mapping in Laboratory Animals. R. Robinson. Incl. Pt. A. 160p. 32.50x (ISBN 0-306-37551-6); Pt. B. 486p. 49.50x o.p. (ISBN 0-306-37552-4). 1972 (Plenum Pr). Plenum Pub.

Gene Therapy: Fact & Fiction. Ed. by Theodore Friedmann. LC 83-24063. 131p. (Orig.). 1983. pap. 4.95x o.p. (ISBN 0-87969-215-4). Cold Spring Harbor.

Genealogical Evidence: A Guide to the Standard of Proof Relating to Pedigrees, Ancestry, Heirship & Family History. Noel C. Stevenson. LC 79-53622. (Orig.). 1979. lib. bdg. 26.80 o.p. (ISBN 0-89412-101-4); pap. 18.80 o.p. (ISBN 0-89412-036-0). Aegean Park Pr.

Genealogical Index of the Newberry Library, Chicago, 4 vols. Newberry Library, Chicago Staff. 1970. Set. lib. bdg. 345.00 o.p. (ISBN 0-8161-0498-0, Hall Library). G K Hall.

Genealogical Research, Vol. 1: Methods & Sources. rev. ed. Rubincam. 579p. Date not set. 17.50 o.p. Genealog Pub.

Genealogists Guide to Charleston County, South Carolina. Richard N. Cote. (Illus.). 52p. 1981. pap. 10.00 o.p. (ISBN 0-89308-245-7). Southern Hist Pr.

Genealogy of the Bostwick Family in America. Henry A. Bostwick. 1172p. 1987. pap. 60.00 o.p. (ISBN 0-317-59258-0). Heritage Bk.

Geneen. Robert J. Schoenberg. LC 84-5957. (Illus.). 1985. 19.45 o.p. (ISBN 0-393-01858-X). Norton.

Genera of Amaryllidaceae. Hamilton P. Traub. (Illus.). 85p. 10.00 o.p. (ISBN 0-930653-03-3). Am Plant Life.

General & Historical Geology. Y. M. Vasiliev. 382p. 1981. 15.00 o.p. (ISBN 0-8285-2070-4, Pub. by Mir Pubs USSR). Imported Pubns.

General & Introductory View of Professor Kant's Principles. Friedrich A. Nitsch. Ed. by Rene Wellek. LC 75-11240. (British Philosophers & Theologians of the 17th & 18th Centuries: Vol. 40). 1977. Repr. of 1796 ed. lib. bdg. 51.00 o.p. (ISBN 0-8240-1792-7). Garland Pub.

General & Restricted Problems of Three Bodies: Proceedings of the CISM, Department for General Mechanics, 1973. CISM (International Center for Mechanical Sciences), Department for General Mechanics Staff. Ed. by V. Szebehely. (CISM International Centre for Mechanical Sciences Ser.: No. 170). (Illus.). 53p. 1974. pap. 6.20 o.p. (ISBN 0-387-81264-4). Springer-Verlag.

General Animal Ecology. T. N. Krishnan. 1976. 11.00x o.p. (ISBN 0-8364-0405-X); pap. 8.00x o.p. (ISBN 0-8364-0406-8). South Asia Bks.

General Bibliographical Dictionary, 4 vols. Friedrich A. Ebert. LC 68-19956. 1076p. 1968. Repr. of 1837 ed. 210.00x o.p. (ISBN 0-8103-3304-X). Gale.

General Biology Laboratory Manual. 4th ed. William H. Mason & Norton L. Marshall. 192p. 1988. pap. 13.95 manual o.p. (ISBN 0-8403-3353-6). Kendall-Hunt.

General Biology Laboratory Manual Biology I. Dorothy C. Dunning. 109p. 1985. pap. text ed. 10.95 o.s.i. (ISBN 0-89917-460-4, Pub. by College Town Pr). Tichenor Pub.

General Botany. B. Dwain Vance. 92p. (Orig.). 1981. pap. 7.95 lab manual o.p. (ISBN 0-89459-218-1). Hunter Textbks.

General Catalogue of Printed Books to 1900 Grenoble Public Reference Library, 12 Vols. Ed. by Grenoble Public Reference Library Staff. 1981. lib. bdg. 2075.00 o.p. (ISBN 3-598-10160-0). K G Saur.

General Catalogue of Thirty Three Thousand Three Hundred Forty-Two Stars for the Epoch 1950, 5 vols. Carnegie Institution of Washington, Department of Meridian Astronomy Staff. Ed. by Benjamin Boss et al. 1937. Set. 150.00 o.p. (ISBN 0-384-07706-4). Johnson Repr.

General Catechetical Directory: Proceedings of the Sacred Congregation of the Clergy on the Official English Translation of the Latin Document, April 11, 1971. Sacred Congregation of the Clergy Staff. pap. 3.75 o.s.i. (ISBN 1-55586-173-3); pap. 3.00 Latin text o.p. (ISBN 0-686-18987-6). US Catholic.

General Censuses & Vital Statistics in the Americas: An Annotated Bibliography of the Historical Censuses & Current Vital Statistics of the 21 American Republics. United States Library of Congress, Census Library Project Staff. LC 73-81474. 151p. 1974. Repr. of 1943 ed. 13.50x o.p. (ISBN 0-87917-036-0). Ethridge.

General Chemistry. Ralph S. Becker & Wayne Wentworth. LC 72-5642. 1973. text ed. 19.50 o.p. (ISBN 0-395-16002-2, 3-03295). HM.

General Chemistry. 2nd ed. Ralph S. Becker & Wayne E. Wentworth. LC 79-87864. 1980. text ed. 33.95 o.p. (ISBN 0-395-25316-0). HM.

General Chemistry. Darrell D. Ebbing. 928p. 1984. text ed. 55.16 o.p. (ISBN 0-395-31489-5). HM.

General Chemistry, 2 vols. N. L. Glinka. 768p. 1981. 16.50 set o.p. (ISBN 0-8285-2119-0, Pub. by Mir Pubs USSR). Imported Pubns.

General Chemistry. 4th ed. Ralph H. Petrucci. 798p. 1985. text ed. write for info. o.p. (ISBN 0-02-394790-X); study guide avail. o.p. (ISBN 0-02-394830-2). Macmillan.

General Chemistry Examination Questions. K. J. Johnson & L. M. Epstein. 367p. (Orig.). 1978. text ed. 6.95x o.p. (ISBN 0-8087-1057-5, Feffer & Simons). Burgess MN Intl.

General Chemistry Laboratory Manual. 3rd ed. Seymour Dondes & Steven W. Lurie. (Illus.). 1981. 14.95x o.p. (ISBN 0-89529-154-1). Avery Pub.

General Chemistry Laboratory Operation. 3rd ed. Lawrence E. Conroy et al. 1977. pap. write for info. o.p. (ISBN 0-02-324330-9, 32433). Macmillan.

General Chemistry: Principles & Structure. 3rd ed. James E. Brady & Gerard E. Humiston. LC 84-16162. 826p. 1983. 39.45 o.p. (ISBN 0-471-07806-9); text ed. 37.95 SI version o.p. (ISBN 0-471-86739-X); pap. text ed. SI version o.p. (ISBN 0-471-86660-1). Wiley.

General Chemistry Problem Solving II. Steven S. Zumdahl. LC 80-54375. 323p. 1984. pap. text ed. 11.00 o.p. (ISBN 0-669-08215-5). Heath.

General Chemistry with Qualitative Analysis. 2nd ed. Kenneth W. Whitten & Kenneth D. Gailey. 1984. text ed. 49.25 o.s.i. (ISBN 0-03-063827-5, CBS C); instr's. manual 21.50 o.s.i. (ISBN 0-03-069574-0); study guide 17.50 o.s.i. (ISBN 0-03-063569-1); lecture outline 18.75 o.s.i. (ISBN 0-03-063577-2); solution manual 15.00 o.s.i. (ISBN 0-03-063573-X); problems bk. 17.50 o.s.i. (ISBN 0-03-063576-4). SCP.

General Climatology. 3rd ed. Howard J. Critchfield. (Illus.). 416p. 1974. ref. ed. 26.95 o.p. (ISBN 0-13-350264-3). P-H.

General Council of the First International, 5 vols. K. Marx et al. 2704p. 1974. 18.00 o.p. (ISBN 0-8285-0458-X, Pub. by Progress Pubs USSR). Imported Pubns.

General Crisis of Capitalism. V. Trepelkov. 168p. 1984. pap. 1.45 o.p. (Pub. by Progress Pubns USSR). Imported Pubns.

General Crook & the Apache Wars. 2nd ed. Charles Lummis. LC 65-17580. (Illus.). 168p. 1985. 14.95 o.p.; pap. 11.95 o.p. (ISBN 0-87358-392-2). Northland.

General Crook & the Apache Wars. Charles Lummis. (Illus.). 168p. 1986. pap. 11.95 o.p. (ISBN 0-87358-387-6). Northland.

General Dermatology. Franklin S. Glickman. LC 77-78229. (Illus.). 368p. 1979. 34.00 o.p. (ISBN 0-88416-195-1). Year Bk Med.

General Drafting. 4th ed. Verne C. Fryklund & Frank R. Kepler. LC 78-81375. (Illus.). (gr. 9-10). 1969. text ed. 14.63 o.p. (ISBN 0-87345-095-7). Glencoe.

General Dynamical Processes: A Mathematical Introduction. Thomas G. Windeknect. (Mathematics in Science & Engineering Ser). 1971. 54.50 o.p. (ISBN 0-12-759550-3). Acad Pr.

General Dynamics F-16. 2nd ed. William G. Holder & William D. Siuru, Jr. LC 82-70929. (Aero Ser.: No. 26). (Illus.). 104p. 1983. pap. 9.95 o.p. (ISBN 0-8168-0597-0, 20597, TAB-Aero). TAB Bks.

General Ecology. 2nd ed. S. J. McNaughton & Larry L. Wolf. LC 78-23200. 702p. 1979. text ed. 34.95 o.p. (ISBN 0-03-019801-1, HoltC). HR&W.

General Economic Theory of Francois Perroux. Ducarmel Bocage. 216p. (Orig.). 1985. lib. bdg. 23.25 o.p. (ISBN 0-8191-4381-2); pap. text ed. 12.25 o.p. (ISBN 0-8191-4382-0). U Pr of Amer.

General Education. Thomas R. McConnell. (National Society for the Study of Education Yearbooks Ser: No. 51, Pt. 1). 1952. lib. bdg. 6.50x o.s.i. (ISBN 0-226-60017-3); pap. text ed. 4.50x o.s.i. (ISBN 0-226-60018-1). U of Chicago Pr.

General Education in a Free Society. Harvard Committee. LC 45-4180. 1945. 16.00x o.s.i. (ISBN 0-674-34251-8). Harvard U Pr.

General Education in Two-Year Colleges. Ed. by B. Lamar Johnson. LC 81-48568. (Community College Ser.: No. 40). 1982. pap. text ed. 12.95x o.p. (ISBN 0-87589-886-6). Jossey-Bass.

General Electronic Circuits. 2nd ed. J. J. DeFrance. LC 75-25718. 1976. text ed. 28.95 o.p. (ISBN 0-03-015481-2, HoltC). HR&W.

General English Tests Elementary One Pack. B. J. Carroll. (Illus.). 8p. 1982. pap. 100.00 o.p. (ISBN 0-08-029432-4). Alemany Pr.

General English Tests Instruction Booklet. B. J. Carroll. (Illus.). 14p. 1983. pap. 2.00 o.p. (ISBN 0-08-028659-3). Alemany Pr.

General Environmental Guidelines for Evaluating & Reporting the Effects of Nuclear Power Plant Site Preparation, Plant & Transmission Facilities Construction (AIF-NESP-003) Hittman Associates, Inc. (National Environmental Studies Project: NESP Reports). 150p. 1974. 6.50 o.p. (ISBN 0-318-13575-2). US Coun Energy Awareness.

General Equilibrium, Growth & Trade: Essays in Honor of Lionel McKenzie. Ed. by Jerry Green & Jose A. Scheinkman. LC 79-50216. (Economic Theory, Econometrics & Mathematical Economics Ser.). 1979. 43.00 o.p. (ISBN 0-12-298750-0). Acad Pr.

General Field Test Plan for Evaluation of Roof-Vent Effluent Diffusion from Reactor & Turbine Buildings (AIF-NESP-007A) Stanford Research Institute Staff. (National Environmental Studies Project: NESP Reports). 110p. 1975. 20.00 o.p. (ISBN 0-318-13576-0); to NESP sponsors 10.00 o.p. (ISBN 0-318-13577-9). US Coun Energy Awareness.

General Geology Eleven Laboratory Manual. Fred B. Keller et al. 9.95 o.p. (ISBN 0-88725-008-4). Hunter Textbks.

General George H. Thomas, the Indomitable Warrior. Wilbur Thomas. 1964. 25.00 o.p. (ISBN 0-682-42066-2, Lochinvar). Exposition-Phoenix.

General Guide on Protection Against Ionising Radiations see Manual of Industrial Radiation Protection.

General Guide to Paris Street Atlas. Raymond Denaes. 1980. pap. 10.95 o.p. (ISBN 0-933982-04-6, Pub by Editions L'indispensable). Bradt Ent.

General Handbook for the Dental Office. Joan O. McCarn. 40p. 1987. 5.75 o.p. (ISBN 0-8062-2849-0). Carlton.

General History of Music, From the Earliest Ages to the Present Period (1789, 2 Vols. Charles Burney. Repr. of 1957 ed. lib. bdg. 108.00 o.p. (Pub. by Am Repr Serv). Reprint Servs.

General History of the Robberies & Murders of the Most Notorious Pyrates. Charles Johnson. LC 71-170563. (Foundations of the Novel Ser.: Vol. 44). 1972. lib. bdg. 61.00 o.p. (ISBN 0-8240-0556-2). Garland Pub.

General Ind Ed Sg. 2nd ed. Groneman. Date not set. (ISBN 0-07-024968-7). McGraw.

General Industry: OSHA Safety & Health Standards Digest. rev. ed. (OSHA Ser.: No. 2201). 83p. 1983. pap. 2.75 o.p. (ISBN 0-318-11725-8, S/N 029-016-00072-1). USGPO.

General Information Concerning Patents: A Brief Introduction to Patent Matters. (Illus.). 45p. 1986. pap. 2.00 o.p. (ISBN 0-318-22385-6, S/N 003-004-00626-9). USGPO.

General Intensive Care. Goodland. 112p. 1978. pap. 10.50 o.p. (ISBN 0-7236-0503-3, Pub. by John Wright UK). Butterworth.

General Interest & Education Videolog. LC 78-74187. 318p. 1981. pap. 39.50 o.p. (ISBN 0-88432-071-5, Video-Forum). J Norton Pubs.

General James "Pete" Longstreet. Wilbur D. Thomas. 1979. 21.00 o.p. (ISBN 0-87012-330-0). McClain.

General Leathercraft. 4th ed. Raymond Cherry. (gr. 9 up). 1955. pap. text ed. 3.30 o.p. (ISBN 0-87345-151-1). Glencoe.

General License Study Guide. Timothy M. Daniel. Ed. by Si Dunn. 82p. 1982. pap. 6.95 o.p. (ISBN 0-88006-017-4, SG7358). Wayne Green Ent.

General Management. Norman A. Berg. 1984. 19.95 o.p. (ISBN 0-256-02910-5). Irwin.

General Management Agreement. rev. ed. 1979. 9.95 o.p. (ISBN 0-686-46422-2, 980). Inst Real Estate.

General Mathematical Ability: Preparation & Review for the Mathematics Part of the High School Equivalency Diploma Test. E. Guercio et al. LC 74-19738. (GED Preparation Ser.). 160p. (Orig.). 1975. lib. bdg. 7.00 o.p. (ISBN 0-668-03841-1); pap. 6.00 o.p. (ISBN 0-668-03689-3). Arco.

General Mechanic: A Capstan Guide: Fast-Track Method Ser. rev. ed. Dale Crane. (Illus.). 128p. pap. text ed. cancelled o.s.i. (27-3). Av Suppl & Acad.

General Medical Aspects of Scoliosis. Ed. by P. A. Zorab. 1977. 76.00 o.p. (ISBN 0-12-781850-2). Acad Pr.

General Microbiology. Robert F. Boyd. (Illus.). 960p. 1984. 38.95 o.p. (ISBN 0-8016-0900-3). Mosby.

General Microbiology Laboratory Manual. 2nd Ed. ed. Geraldine Luginbuhl. 1981. lab manual 7.95 o.p. (ISBN 0-89459-219-X). Hunter Textbks.

General Microbiology: Study Guide. Wright. 1984. pap. 10.95 o.p. (ISBN 0-8016-5691-5). Mosby.

General Mirobiology: Laboratory Manual. Wright. 1984. pap. 16.95 o.p. (ISBN 0-8016-5664-8). Mosby.

General Motors F Units the Locos: That Revolutionized Railroading. Daniel Mulhearn & John Taibi. 1983. pap. 9.95 o.p. (ISBN 0-915276-39-9). Quadrant Pr.

General Motors X Cars Tune-up & Repair. 156p. (Orig.). 1981. pap. 6.95 o.p. (ISBN 0-8227-5058-9). Petersen Pub.

General Orders of George Washington: Commander-in-Chief of the Army of Revolution Issued at Newburgh on the Hudson, 1782-1783. new ed. United States Army, Continental Army Staff. Ed. by Edward C. Boynton. LC 73-16354. (Illus.). 160p. 1974. Repr. of 1883 ed. 11.50 o.p. (ISBN 0-916346-04-8). Harbor Hill Bks.

General Organizational & Administrative Concepts for University Police. Swen C. Nielsen. 96p. 1971. 17.00 o.p. (ISBN 0-398-02164-3). C C Thomas.

General Parasitology. Thomas C. Cheng. 1973. text ed. 49.95i o.p. (ISBN 0-12-170750-4). Acad Pr.

General Plastics: Projects & Procedures. rev. ed. Raymond Cherry. (Illus.). (gr. 10-12). 1967. text ed. 16.64 o.p. (ISBN 0-87345-162-7). Glencoe.

General Practice for Students of Medicine. R. Harvard Davis. (Monographs for Students of Medicine Ser.). 1975. 28.00 o.p. (ISBN 0-12-328850-9). Acad Pr.

General Practice in Australia. Ed. by N. Anderson et al. 170p. 1986. pap. 25.00 o.p. (ISBN 0-424-00122-5, Pub. by Sydney U Pr). Intl Spec Bk.

General Practice Insurance Law, Cases, Materials & Problems, 1985. Kenneth H. York & John W. Whelan. (American Casebook Ser.). 119p. 1985. pap. text ed. 7.50 o.p. (ISBN 0-314-92941-X). West Pub.

General Practice Medicine. 2nd ed. Ed. by J. H. Barber. (Illus.). 389p. 1984. pap. text ed. 56.00 o.p. (ISBN 0-443-02693-9). Churchill.

General Practice Revisited: A Second Study of Patients & Their Doctors. Ann Cartwright & Robert Anderson. 1981. 28.95x o.p. (ISBN 0-422-77360-3, NO. 3440, Pub. by Tavistock). Routledge Chapman & Hall.

General Principles of English Law. 6th ed. P. W. Redmond & I. N. Stevens. 400p. 1988. pap. 32.50x o.p. (ISBN 0-7121-0747-9, Pub. by Pitman Pub Ltd London). Trans-Atl Phila.

General Principles of Food Hygiene: 1969. pap. 5.75 o.p. (ISBN 92-5-100234-7, F658, FAO). UNIPUB.

General Principles of Geology. J. F. Kirkaldy. (Illus.). 327p. 1955. (ISBN 0-8022-0866-5). Philos Lib.

General Problem of the Motion of Coupled Rigid Bodies About a Fixed Point. E. Leimanis. (Springer Tracts in Natural Philosophy: Vol. 7). (Illus.). 1965. 36.00 o.p. (ISBN 0-387-03408-0). Springer-Verlag.

General Selections from the Works of Sigmund Freud. Sigmund Freud. Ed. by John Rickman. 1967. 6.95 o.p. (ISBN 0-87140-927-5). Liveright.

General Shop Woodworking. rev. ed. Verne C. Fryklund & Armand J. LaBerge. (gr. 9-10). 1972. text ed. 15.28 o.p. (ISBN 0-87345-031-0). Glencoe.

General Statutes of North Carolina, Rules Volume. Michie Company Editorial Staff. 761p. 1984. 35.00 o.p. (ISBN 0-87215-877-2). Michie Co.

General Studies: First Handbook for Technical Students. I. J. Finch. 1965. text ed. 16.25 o.p. (ISBN 0-08-011106-8); pap. text ed. 7.00 o.p. (ISBN 0-08-011105-X). Pergamon.

General Surgery in Gynaecological Practice. Simmons & Luck. (Illus.). 176p. 1971. 9.50 o.p. (ISBN 0-632-05340-2, B-4628-6). Mosby.

General Survey of Events, Sources, Persons & Movements in Continental Legal History. (Continental Legal History Ser.: Vol. 1). (Illus.). liii, 754p. 1968. Repr. of 1912 ed. 37.50x o.p. (ISBN 0-8377-2201-2). Rothman.

General Systems & Organization: Methodological Aspects. Ed. by Arlyn J. Melcher. LC 74-11584. 120p. 1975. 9.50x o.p. (ISBN 0-87338-165-3, Pub. by Comp. Adm. Research Inst.). Kent St U Pr.

General Systems Approach: Contributions Toward an Holistic Conception of Social Work. Ed. by Gordon Hearn. Date not set. 3.00 o.s.i. (68-300-41). Coun Soc WK Ed.

General Systems Theory: Mathematical Foundations. M. D. Mesarovic & Y. Takahara. 1975. 69.50 o.p. (ISBN 0-12-491540-X). Acad Pr.

General Theory of Furnaces. M. A. Glinkov & G. M. Glinkov. 1980. 8.45 o.p. (ISBN 0-8285-1799-1, Pub. by Mir Pubs USSR). Imported Pubns.

General Theory of Law. L. S. Jawitsch. 293p. 1981. cloth 6.90 o.p. (ISBN 0-8285-1969-2, 230142, Pub. by Progress Pubs USSR). Imported Pubns.

General Theory of Magic. Marcel Mauss. 160p. 1975. pap. 4.95 o.p. (ISBN 0-393-00779-0, Norton Lib). Norton.

General Theory of Noiseless Channels: Proceedings of the CISM, Department of Automation & Information, 1970. CISM (International Center for Mechanical Sciences), Department of Automation & Information Staff. Ed. by G. Katona. (CISM International Center for Mechanical Sciences Ser.: No. 31). 69p. 1975. pap. 12.40 o.p. (ISBN 0-387-81167-2). Springer-Verlag.

General Theory of Relativity. C. W. Kilmister. LC 73-7639. 376p. 1973. text ed. 35.00 o.p. (ISBN 0-08-017639-9); pap. 11.75 o.p. (ISBN 0-08-017645-3). Pergamon.

General Thoracic Surgery. 2nd ed. Ed. by Thomas W. Shields. LC 82-17942. (Illus.). 1072p. 1983. text ed. 118.00 o.p. (ISBN 0-8121-0782-9). Lea & Febiger.

General Topology. A Csasar. Ed. by P. M. Cohn. 1978. 94.00x o.p. (ISBN 0-85274-275-4, Pub. by A Hilger UK). Taylor & Francis.

General Welding & Cutting. Ed. by J. Bell et al. (Engineering Craftsmen: No. F10). (Illus.). 1976. spiral bdg. 49.95x o.p. (ISBN 0-85083-330-2). Trans-Atl Phila.

General Zoology Laboratory Guide: Complete Version. 8th ed. J. E. Wodsedalek & Charles F. Lytle. 304p. 1981. wire coil o.p. (ISBN 0-697-04599-4). Wm C Brown.

General Zoology Laboratory Manual. Stephen A. Miller. 272p. 1985. write for info. wire coil o.p. (ISBN 0-697-00318-3). Wm C Brown.

Generalic. Grgo Gamulin. (Illus.). 136p. 1987. 22.50 o.p. (ISBN 0-87052-396-1). Hippocrene Bks.

Generalization in Ethics: An Essay in the Logic of Ethics, with the Rudiments of a System of Moral Philosophy. Marcus G. Singer. LC 61-10824. 1971. pap. text ed. 3.45x o.p. (ISBN 0-689-70278-7, 183, Atheneum). Macmillan.

Generalized Analytic Functions. I. N. Vekua. 1962. 30.00 o.p. (ISBN 0-08-009693-X). Pergamon.

Generalizing from Laboratory to Life. Ed. by Irwin Silverman. LC 80-84295. (Methodology of Social & Behavioral Science Ser.: No. 8). 1981. pap. text ed. 13.95x o.p. (ISBN 0-87589-852-1). Jossey-Bass.

Generalizing from the Experimental Housing Allowance Program: An Assessment of Site Characteristics. Jeanne E. Goedert. write for info. o.p. Urban Inst.

Generals in Politics: Pakistan 1958-1982. Mohammed A. Khan. 226p. 1983. text ed. 18.95x o.p. (ISBN 0-7069-2215-8, Pub. by Vikas India). Advent NY.

Generals Wear Cork Hats: An Amazing Adventure That Made World History. Ben L. Burman. LC 63-18337. (Illus.). 1963. 5.00 o.s.i. (ISBN 0-8008-3150-0). Taplinger.

Generation Gap: Implications for Labor-Management Relations: Proceedings of the Annual Research Conference, 13th, UCLA, 1970. Annual Research Conference Staff. 2.00 o.p. (ISBN 0-89215-031-9). U Cal LA Indus Rel.

Generation in Motion: Popular Music & Culture in the 1960's. David Pichaske. LC 78-63033. (Illus.). 1979. 17.50 o.p. (ISBN 0-02-871860-7); pap. 6.95 o.p. (ISBN 0-02-871850-X). Schirmer Bks.

Generation of Electricity by Wind Power. Rev. ed. E. W. Golding. 1976. 29.95x o.p. (ISBN 0-419-11070-4, NO. 6127, Pub. by E & FN Spon). Routledge Chapman & Hall.

Generation of Electricity by Wind Power. E. W. Golding. (Illus.). 330p. 1956. (ISBN 0-8022-0603-4). Philos Lib.

Generation of Motion Pictures. William A. Short. Ed. by Bruce S. Kupelnick. LC 76-52129. (Classics of Film Literature Ser.). 1978. lib. bdg. 31.00 o.p. (ISBN 0-8240-2894-5). Garland Pub.

Generation of Victors. Burt Hirschfeld. LC 73-82180. 1973. 7.95 o.p. (ISBN 0-87795-061-X, Arbor Hse). Morrow.

Generations. John Egerton. 212p. 1986. pap. 8.95 o.s.i. (ISBN 0-671-62833-X, Touchstone). S&S.

Generations: An Introduction to Drama. M. S. Barranger & Daniel B. Dodson. (Illus.). 1971. pap. text ed. 7.95 o.p. (ISBN 0-15-529534-9, HC). HarBraceJ.

Generative Phonology: Description & Theory. Michael Kenstowicz & Charles Kisseberth. LC 79-319. 1979. 50.00 o.p. (ISBN 0-12-405160-X). Acad Pr.

Generic Assessment of Barge Transportation of Spent Nuclear Fuel (AIF-NESP-014) Science Applications, Inc. Staff. (National Environmental Studies Project: NESP Reports). 267p. 1978. 60.00 o.p. (ISBN 0-318-13578-7); to NESP sponsors 20.00 o.p. (ISBN 0-318-13579-5). US Coun Energy Awareness.

Generic Methodology for Assessment of Radiation Doses from Groundwater Migration of Radionuclides in LWR Wastes in Shallow Land Burial Trenches (AIF-NESP-013) rev. ed. Dames & Moore. (National Environmental Studies Project-AIF-Inforum: NESP Reports). 207p. 1979. 60.00 o.p. (ISBN 0-318-13580-9); to NESP sponsors 20.00 o.p. (ISBN 0-318-13581-7). US Coun Energy Awareness.

Generic Substitution & Prescription Drug Prices: Economic Effects of State Drug Product Selection Laws. Alison Masson & Robert L. Steiner. 350p. 1986. pap. 10.00 o.p. (S/N 018-000-00314-7). USGPO.

Generous Man. Reynolds Price. LC 66-16357. 1966. 4.95 o.p. (ISBN 0-689-00024-3, Atheneum). Macmillan.

Genes. 2nd ed. Benjamin Lewin. LC 84-15350. 716p. 1985. (ISBN 0-471-80789-3); pap. (ISBN 0-471-82068-7). Wiley.

Genes & Populations. Paul Geisert. (EMI Programmed Biology Ser.). (gr. 9 up). 1967. pap. text ed. 4.50 o.s.i. (ISBN 0-88462-019-0, 3304-19, Ed Methods). Longman Finan.

Genes & Proteins. Ed. by Robert P. Wagner. LC 75-8851. (Benchmark Papers in Genetics Ser: Vol. 2). 395p. 1975. 77.00 o.p. (ISBN 0-12-787710-X). Acad Pr.

Genes of Ambition. F. L. Neely. LC 86-91114. (Illus.). 416p. 1986. text ed. 20.00 o.p. (ISBN 0-682-40292-3). Exposition-Phoenix.

Genesis, Vol. I. James M. Boice. 352p. 1982. Chapter 1-11. 20.95 o.p. (ISBN 0-310-21540-4, 10486). Zondervan.

Genesis. Date not set. (ISBN 0-8052-3778-X). Random.

Genesis Accounts of Creation. Claus Westermann. Ed. by Norman E. Wagner. LC 64-11858. (Facet Ser.). 1964. pap. 1.35 o.p. (ISBN 0-8006-3007-6, 1-3007, Fortress). Augsburg Fortress.

Genesis: An Expositional Commentary, Vol. 2. James M. Boice. 352p. 1985. 20.95 o.p. (ISBN 0-310-21560-9, 10487). Zondervan.

Genesis: An Expositional Commentary, Vol. 3, Genesis Thirty-Seven thru Fifty Twenty-Six. James M. Boice. 368p. 1987. text ed. 20.95 o.p. (ISBN 0-310-21590-0, 10488). Zondervan.

Genesis Debate: Persistent Questions about Creation & the Flood. Ed. by Ronald Youngblood. LC 86-17998. 240p. 1986. pap. 12.95 o.p. (ISBN 0-8407-7517-2). Nelson.

Genesis-Deuteronomy, Vol. I. Beacon Bible Commentary Staff. 15.95 o.p. (ISBN 0-8010-0688-0). Baker Bk.

Genesis, Exodus, Leviticus, Numbers. Foster R. McCurley. LC 78-14670. (Proclamation Commentaries: the Old Testament Witness for Preaching). 128p. 1979. pap. 4.95 o.p. (ISBN 0-8006-0593-4, 1-593, Fortress). Augsburg Fortress.

Genesis of New Weapons: Decision Making for Military R&D. Ed. by Franklin A. Long & Judith Reppy. LC 80-12243. 1980. 55.00 o.p. (ISBN 0-08-025973-1). Pergamon.

Genesis of Religion. Margaret Murray. 88p. 1963. (ISBN 0-8022-1179-8). Philos Lib.

Genesis of Russophobia in Great Britain. John H. Gleason. LC 70-159189. ix, 314p. 1971. Repr. of 1950 ed. lib. bdg. 21.50x o.p. (ISBN 0-374-93156-9, Octagon). Hippocrene Bks.

Genesis of the Soviet Federative State: 1917-1925. M. Iroshnikov. 317p. 1982. 8.45 o.p. (ISBN 0-8285-2477-7, Pub. by Progress Pubs USSR). Imported Pubns.

Genesis Principle for Parents. Pat H. Owen. 224p. 1985. pap. 6.95 o.p. (ISBN 0-8423-0996-9). Tyndale.

Genesis Rejuvenated. rev. ed. Carlo Suares. Tr. by Edouard Roditi. 1973. saddlestitched in wrappers 2.00 o.p. (ISBN 0-685-78973-X, Pub. by Menard Pr). Small Pr Dist.

Genetic Analysis of the Cell Surface. Ed. by P. Goodfellow. (Receptors & Recognition Series B: Vol. 16). 300p. 1984. text ed. 59.95 o.p. (ISBN 0-412-25070-5, NO. 9009, Pub by Chapman & Hall England). Routledge Chapman & Hall.

Genetic Analysis of the X Chromosome: Studies of Duchenne Muscular Dystrophy & Related Disorders. Ed. by Henry F. Epstein & Stewart Wolf. LC 82-15037. (Advances in Experimental Medicine & Biology: Vol. 154). 222p. 1982. 49.50x o.p. (ISBN 0-306-41129-6, Plenum Pr). Plenum Pub.

Genetic & Reproductive Engineering. Darrel S. English et al. LC 73-22048. 1974. 29.75x o.p. (ISBN 0-8422-5157-X); pap. text ed. 9.50x o.p. (ISBN 0-8422-0383-4). Irvington.

Genetic Approaches to Microbial Pathogenicity. Ed. by W. Goebel. (Current Topics in Microbiology & Immunology Ser.: Vol. 118). (Illus.). 310p. 1985. 89.00 o.p. (ISBN 0-387-15597-X). Springer-Verlag.

Genetic Basis of Development. Alistair D. Stewart & David M. Hunt. LC 81-11591. (Tertiary Level Biology Ser.). 200p. 1981. 31.95x o.p. (ISBN 0-470-27234-1); pap. 29.95 o.p. Halsted Pr.

Genetic Basis of Morphological Variation: An Evaluation & Application of the Twin Study Method. Richard H. Osborne & Frances V. De George. LC 59-15743. (Commonwealth Fund Publications Ser). 1959. 16.00x o.s.i. (ISBN 0-674-34600-9). Harvard U Pr.

Genetic Control of Immune Responsiveness: Relationship to Disease Susceptibility. Ed. by Hugh O. McDevitt & Maurice Landy. (Perspectives in Immunology Ser). 1973. 76.50 o.p. (ISBN 0-12-483250-4). Acad Pr.

Genetic Control of Insect Pests. G. Davidson. 1974. 46.00 o.p. (ISBN 0-12-205750-3). Acad Pr.

Genetic Control of Natural Resistance to Infection & Malignancy. Ed. by Emil Skamene. (Perspectives in Immunology Ser.). 1980. 59.00 o.p. (ISBN 0-12-647680-2). Acad Pr.

Genetic Counseling. Arno G. Motulsky et al. 256p. 1974. text ed. 21.50x o.p. (ISBN 0-8422-7150-3). Irvington.

Genetic Counseling in Relation to Mental Retardation. J. M. Berg. 1971. pap. 9.00 o.p. (ISBN 0-08-016315-7). Pergamon.

Genetic Damage in Man Caused by Environmental Agents. Ed. by Kare Berg. LC 79-414. 1979. 56.50 o.p. (ISBN 0-12-089550-1). Acad Pr.

Genetic Engineering-Biotechnology Sourcebook. Newsletter Publications Center Staff. Ed. by Robert Pergolizzi. 333p. 1982. text ed. 105.00 o.p. (ISBN 0-07-049321-9). McGraw.

Genetic Engineering for Nitrogen Fixation. Ed. by Alexander Hollaender. LC 77-8998. (Basic Life Sciences Ser.: Vol. 9). 550p. 1977. 85.00x o.p. (ISBN 0-306-36509-X, Plenum Pr). Plenum Pub.

Genetic Engineering of Symbiotic Nitrogen Fixation & Conservation of Fixed Nitrogen. Ed. by J. M. Lyons et al. LC 81-4683. (Basic Life Sciences Ser.: Vol. 17). 712p. 1981. 95.00x o.p. (ISBN 0-306-40730-2, Plenum Pr). Plenum Pub.

Genetic Epistemology. Jean Piaget. Tr. by Eleanor Duckworth. 1971. pap. 5.95 o.p. (ISBN 0-393-00596-8, Norton Lib.). Norton.

Genetic Exchange: A Celebration & a New Generation. Ed. by Uldis N. Streips et al. (Genetic & Cellular Technology Ser.: Vol. 1). (Illus.). 392p. 1982. 69.50 o.p. (ISBN 0-8247-1418-0). Dekker.

Genetic Manipulation As It Affects the Cancer Problem. Ed. by J. Schultz & W. J. Whelan. 1977. 43.50 o.p. (ISBN 0-12-632755-6). Acad Pr.

Genetic Markers of Human Immunoglobulins. R. Grubb. LC 72-121989. (Molecular Biology, Biochemistry & Biophysics Ser.: Vol. 9). (Illus.). 1970. 31.00 o.p. (ISBN 0-387-05211-9). Springer-Verlag.

Genetic Mechanisms of Sexual Development. Ed. by H. Lawrence Vallet & Ian H. Porter. LC 78-25762. (Birth Defects Institute Symposium Ser.: No. 7). 1979. 53.50 o.p. (ISBN 0-12-710550-6). Acad Pr.

Genetic Mosaics & Cell Differentiation. W. J. Gehring. (Results & Problems in Cell Differentiation: Vol. 9). (Illus.). 1978. 51.00 o.p. (ISBN 0-387-08882-2). Springer-Verlag.

Genetic Organization, Vol. 1. Ed. by E. W. Caspari & A. W. Ravin. 1969. 109.00 o.p. (ISBN 0-12-163301-2). Acad Pr.

Genetic Polymorphisms & Diseases in Man. Ed. by Bracha Ramot. 1974. 66.00 o.p. (ISBN 0-12-577140-1). Acad Pr.

Genetic Recombination & Rearrangement. Ed. by John H. Wilson. 1985. text ed. 35.95 o.p. (ISBN 0-8053-9790-6). Benjamin-Cummings.

Genetic Technology: A Guide to Key R & D Projects. rev. ed. Technical Insights, Inc. Staff. LC 84-52608. 280p. 1985. 337.00 o.p. (ISBN 0-914993-10-0). Tech Insights.

Genetic Variation among Influenza Viruses. Ed. by Debi S. Nayak. LC 81-14845. (ICN-UCLA Symposia on Molecular & Cellular Biology Ser.: Vol. 21). 1981. 75.00 o.p. (ISBN 0-12-515080-6). Acad Pr.

Genetical Structures of Populations. K. Mather. 1973. 16.95x o.p. (ISBN 0-412-12140-9, NO. 6191, Pub. by Chapman & Hall). Routledge Chapman & Hall.

Genetics. 2nd ed. John B. Jenkins. LC 78-69608. (Illus.). 1979. text ed. 27.50 o.p. (ISBN 0-395-26502-9). HM.

Genetics. George P. Redei. 1982. text ed. write for info. o.p. (ISBN 0-02-398850-9). Macmillan.

Genetics. William D. Stansfield. (Schaum Outline Ser.). 1969. pap. 9.95 o.p. (ISBN 0-07-060842-3). McGraw.

Genetics. 3rd ed. Monroe W. Strickberger, Jr. 256p. 1985. text ed. write for info. o.p. (ISBN 0-02-418130-7); write for info. study guide o.p. Macmillan.

Genetics: A Basic Guide. I. J. Pedder & E. G. Wynne. 183p. 1974. pap. text ed. 5.95x o.p. (ISBN 0-393-09267-4). Norton.

Genetics: A Human Concern. H. Eldon Sutton & Robert P. Wagner. 432p. 1985. text ed. write for info. o.p. (ISBN 0-02-418320-2). Macmillan.

Genetics: A Molecular Approach. Laura Mays. 1981. text ed. write for info. o.p. (ISBN 0-02-378320-6). Macmillan.

Genetics: A Survey of the Principles of Heredity. 5th ed. A. M. Winchester. LC 76-14001. (Illus.). 1977. text ed. 38.50 o.p. (ISBN 0-395-24557-5). HM.

Genetics & Breast Cancer. Henry T. Lynch. 256p. 1981. 32.95 o.p. (ISBN 0-442-24919-5). Van Nos Reinhold.

Genetics & Heterogeneity of Common Gastrointestinal Disorders. Ed. by Jerome I. Rotter et al. 1980. 65.50 o.p. (ISBN 0-12-598760-9). Acad Pr.

Genetics & Morphogenesis in the Basidiomycetes. Ed. by Marvin N. Schwalb & Philip G. Miles. 1978. 36.00 o.p. (ISBN 0-12-632050-0). Acad Pr.

Genetics & Social Structure: Mathematical Structuralism in Population Genetics & Social Theory. Ed. by Paul A. Ballanoff. LC 73-20412. (Benchmark Papers in Genetics Ser.: Vol. 1). 504p. 1982. 59.95 o.p. (ISBN 0-87933-067-8). Van Nos Reinhold.

Genetics & the Quality of Life. Ed. by C. Birch & P. Albrecht. 1976. 60.00 o.p. (ISBN 0-08-018210-0); pap. 60.00 o.p. (ISBN 0-08-019861-9). Pergamon.

Genetics, Environment & Behavior: Implications for Educational Policy. Ed. by Lee Ehrmann & Gilbert S. Omenn. 1972. 44.00 o.p. (ISBN 0-12-233450-7). Acad Pr.

Genetics for Aquarists. Johannes H. Schroder. (Illus.). 1976. pap. 9.95 o.p. (ISBN 0-87666-461-3, PS-656). TFH Pubns.

Genetics: Human Aspects. Arthur P. Mange & Elaine J. Mange. 1980. text ed. 35.95 o.s.i. (ISBN 0-03-056751-3, CBS C); instr's manual 6.95 o.s.i. (ISBN 0-03-056752-1). SCP.

Genetics in Aquaculture. Ed. by N. P. Wilkins & E. M. Gosling. (Developments in Aquaculture & Fisheries Science Ser.: Vol. 12). 436p. 1983. 118.50 o.p. (ISBN 0-444-42209-9). Elsevier.

Genetics, Law, & Social Policy. Philip Reilly. 1977. 18.50x o.s.i. (ISBN 0-674-34657-2). Harvard U Pr.

Genetics of Aging. Ed. by E. L. Schneider. LC 78-28. (Illus.). 440p. 1978. 65.00x o.p. (ISBN 0-306-31100-3, Plenum Pr). Plenum Pub.

Genetics of Diabetes Mellitus. Ed. by W. Creutzfeldt et al. 1976. pap. 20.80 o.p. (ISBN 0-387-07651-4). Springer-Verlag.

Genetics of Host-Parasite Interaction. P. R. Day. 238p. 1974. 25.95 o.p. (ISBN 0-317-63560-3). W H Freeman.

Genetics of Human Histocompatibility Antigens & Their Relation to Disease. E. Thorsby et al. (Illus.). 220p. 1973. text ed. 29.50x o.p. (ISBN 0-8422-7062-0). Irvington.

Genetics of Industrial Management: Proceedings of the Symposium, 2nd. Genetics of Industrial Mangement Symposium Staff. Ed. by K. D. Macdonald. 1976. 129.00 o.p. (ISBN 0-12-464350-7). Acad Pr.

Genetics of Livestock Improvement. 3rd, reference ed. John F. Lasley. LC 77-22807. (Illus.). 1978. text ed. 44.67 o.p. (ISBN 0-13-351106-5). P-H.

Genetics of Man. 2nd ed. Paul A. Moody. (Illus.). 525p. 1975. text ed. 11.95x o.p. (ISBN 0-393-09228-3). Norton.

Genetics of Man. Paul A. Moody. (Illus.). 1967. 9.95x o.p. (ISBN 0-393-09577-0, NortonC). Norton.

Genetics of Sex Differentiation. Ursula Mittwoch. 1973. 55.00 o.p. (ISBN 0-12-501040-0). Acad Pr.

Genetics of the Immune Response. Ed. by Erna Moller & Goran Moller. LC 82-24695. 324p. 1983. 59.50x o.p. (ISBN 0-306-41252-7, Plenum Pr). Plenum Pub.

Genetics, Paleontology & Evolution. Ed. by Glenn L. Jepsen et al. LC 49-9873. (Illus.). 1963. pap. 1.95 o.p. (ISBN 0-689-70110-1, 35, Atheneum). Macmillan.

Genetics, Revised Edition. Charlotte Avers. 657p. 1980. text ed. (ISBN 0-87150-759-5, Pub. by Willard Grant Pr). PWS-Kent Pub.

Genetics, Structure & Function of Blood Cells: Proceedings of the 28th International Congress of Physiological Sciences, Budapest, 1980. S. R. Hollan et al. LC 80-41876. (Advances in Physiological Sciences: Vol. 6). (Illus.). 310p. 1981. 57.00 o.p. (ISBN 0-08-026818-8). Pergamon.

Geneva Bible: A Facsimile of the Fifteen-Sixty Edition. Intro. by Lloyd E. Berry. 1274p. 1969. 95.00x o.p. (ISBN 0-299-05251-6). U of Wis Pr.

Geneva Protocol to the General Agreement on Tariffs & Trade, 1979: Schedule of Concessions, Tokyo Round, 1979, 4 Vols. Incl. Vol. 1. Canada, Czechoslovakia, New Zealand, Norway, South Africa (G127 1). UNIPUB; Vol. 2. United States, Finland, Sweden (G127 2). UNIPUB; Vol. 3. Austria, Japan, Spain, Yugoslavia, Switzerland (G127 3). UNIPUB; Vol. 4. Iceland, Argentina, Jamaica, Romania, Hungary, European Communities (G127 4). UNIPUB. 3670p. Set. pap. 120.00 o.p. (ISBN 0-686-93158-0, G127, GATT); pap. 32.50 ea. o.p. UNIPUB.

Genevieve & Alexander. Marjorie Franco. LC 81-69147. (Illus.). 256p. 1982. 12.95 o.p. (ISBN 0-689-11259-9, Atheneum). Macmillan.

Genic Psychology: Method & Theory. Archie B. Carran. 183p. 1972. 29.50x o.p. (ISBN 0-8422-5011-5); pap. text ed. 9.95x o.p. (ISBN 0-8422-0189-0). Irvington.

Genie du Lieu, II. Michel Butor. 17.50 o.p. (ISBN 0-685-37250-2). French & Eur.

Genito-Urinary Problems in Childhood. P. P. Rickham et al. (Progress in Pediatric Surgery Ser.: Vol. 17). (Illus.). 213p. 1983. 27.50 o.p. (ISBN 0-8067-1517-0). Urban & S.

Genitourinary Cancer Surgery. Ed. by E. David Crawford & Thomas A. Borden. LC 81-23624. (Illus.). 575p. 1982. text ed. 98.50 o.p. (ISBN 0-8121-0812-4). Lea & Febiger.

Genitourinary Problems, Vol. 6. Nancy Reilly & Joan Doyle. (RN Assessment Ser.). 180p. 1984. pap. 15.95 o.p. (ISBN 0-87489-286-4). Med Economics.

Genius & Creative Intelligence. Nathaniel Hirsch. 1969. (ISBN 0-8022-2271-4). Philos Lib.

Genius Nobody Knew. Zig Ziglar. (Zig Ziglar Ser.: No. 4). 48p. (Orig.). (ps-7). 1987. pap. 2.50 o.p. (ISBN 0-8423-1001-0). Tyndale.

Genius of American Politics, Nineteen Fifty-eight. Daniel J. Boorstin. (Walgreen Foundation Lectures). 1953. lib. bdg. 10.50x o.s.i. (ISBN 0-226-06490-5, Phoen). U of Chicago Pr.

Genius of Charles James. Elizabeth A. Coleman. (Illus.). 176p. 1982. 25.50 o.p. (ISBN 0-03-062588-2). H Holt & Co.

Genius of George Washington. Edmund S. Morgan. 1981. 12.95 o.p. (ISBN 0-393-01440-1). Norton.

Genius of Paul: A Study in History. Samuel Sandmel. LC 79-7392. 256p. 1979. pap. 5.95 o.p. (ISBN 0-8006-1370-8, 1-1370, Fortress). Augsburg Fortress.

Genius of Shaw. Michael Holroyd. LC 78-31306. (Illus.). 256p. 1979. 18.95 o.p. (ISBN 0-03-043541-2). H Holt & Co.

Genius of the Few: The Story of Those who Founded the Garden of Eden. Christian O'Brien. 320p. 1985. pap. 12.95 o.p. (ISBN 0-85500-214-X). Newcastle Pub.

Genji Days. Edward G. Seidensticker. LC 76-44157. 256p. 1984. pap. 5.25 o.p. (ISBN 0-87011-640-1). Kodansha.

GENMIX: A General Computer Program for Two-Dimensional Parabolic Flow. Ed. by Dudley B. Spalding. LC 77-7978. 1978. 95.00 o.p. (ISBN 0-08-021708-7). Pergamon.

Genocide. A. Galkin et al. 244p. 1985. pap. 3.95 o.p. (ISBN 0-8285-3096-3, Pub. by Progress Pubs USSR). Imported Pubns.

Genocide: State Power & Mass Murder. 2nd ed. Ed. by Irving L. Horowitz. 96p. 1977. pap. 5.95 o.p. (ISBN 0-87855-620-6). Transaction Pubs.

Genome & Chromatin - Organization, Evolution, Function: Symposium, Kaiserslautern, October 13-15, 1978. Ed. by W. Nagl & F. Ehrendorfer. (Plant Systematics & Evolution: Supplement 2). (Illus.). 1979. 87.40 o.p. (ISBN 0-387-81539-2). Springer-Verlag.
Genome Organization & Expression In Plants. Ed. by C. J. Leaver. LC 79-28255. (NATO ASI Series A, Life Sciences: Vol. 29). 618p. 1980. 95.00x o.p. (ISBN 0-306-40340-4, Plenum Pr). Plenum Pub.
Genre for the Gospels: The Biographical Character of Matthew. Philip L. Shuler. LC 81-71384. 144p. 1982. 3.50 o.p. (ISBN 0-8006-0677-9, Fortress). Augsburg Fortress.
Genre Painting in the Hungarian National Gallery. Magdolna B. Supka. (Illus.). 1975. 14.00 o.s.i. (ISBN 0-912728-88-4). Newbury Bks.
Genre Painting of Eastman Johnson: The Sources & Development of His Styles & Themes. Patricia Hills. LC 76-23627. (Outstanding Dissertations in the Fine Arts-American Ser.). (Illus.). 270p. 1977. Repr. of 1973 ed. lib. bdg. 58.00 o.p. (ISBN 0-8240-2697-7). Garland Pub.
Gens De la Parole: Essai Sur la Condition et le Role Des Griots Dans la Societe Malinke. Sory Camara. (Fr.). 1976. pap. text ed. 16.80x o.p. (ISBN 90-2797-954-5). Mouton.
Gentile Reactions to Jewish Ideals. J. S. Raisin. 1953. (ISBN 0-8022-1306-5). Philos Lib.
Gentilz: Artist of the Old Southwest. Dorothy S. Kendall & Carmen Perry. (Elma Dill Russell Spencer Foundation Ser.: No. 6). (Illus.). 141p. 1974. pap. 22.50 o.p. (ISBN 0-292-72705-4). U of Tex Pr.
Gentle Americans, Eighteen Sixty-Four to Nineteen Sixty: Biography of a Breed. Helen H. Howe. LC 78-24027. (Illus.). 1979. Repr. of 1965 ed. lib. bdg. 37.50x o.p. (ISBN 0-313-20826-3, HOGA). Greenwood.
Gentle Architecture. Malcolm Wells. (Illus.). 192p. 1981. text ed. 32.95 o.p. (ISBN 0-07-069245-9). McGraw.
Gentle Art of Faking Furniture. H. Cescinsky. (Illus.). 16.50 o.p. (ISBN 0-8446-1830-6). Peter Smith.
Gentle Barbarian: The Life & Work of Turgenev. V. S. Pritchett. (Illus.). 1978. pap. 3.95 o.p. (ISBN 0-394-72526-3, Vin). Random.
Gentle Breeze of Jesus. Mel Tari & Noni Tari. LC 78-64960. 1978. pap. 2.95 o.p. (ISBN 0-89221-056-7, 056-7). New Leaf.
Gentle Desperado. Max Brand. (Large Print Bks (General Ser.)). 338p. 1986. lib. bdg. 15.95x o.p. (ISBN 0-8161-4049-9). G K Hall.
Gentle Feuding. Johanna Lindsey. (General Ser.). 1984. lib. bdg. 14.95 o.p. (ISBN 0-8161-3750-1, Large Print Bks). G K Hall.
Gentle Pirate. Jayne Castle. (Candelight Ecstasy Ser.: No. 2). 1986. pap. 1.50 o.p. (ISBN 0-440-12981-8). Dell.
Gentle Tasaday: A Stone Age in the Philippine Rain Forest. John Nance. 1988. pap. 12.95 o.p. Godine.
Gentle Tasaday: A Stone Age People in the Philippine Rain Forest. John Nance. Ed. by J. Ferrone. LC 76-40221. 1977. pap. 8.95 o.p. (ISBN 0-15-634712-1, Harv). HarBraceJ.
Gentle Tigress. C. O. Lamp. 320p. 1984. pap. 3.25 o.p. (ISBN 0-8439-2139-0, Pub. by Leisure Bks CT). Dorchester Pub Co.
Gentle Tyrant. Larry A. Long. 1982. 4.50 o.p. (ISBN 0-682-49797-5). Exposition-Phoenix.
Gentlefolk in the Making: Studies in the History of English Courtesy Literature & Related Topics from 1531 to 1774. J. E. Mason. LC 74-120648. 1970. Repr. lib. bdg. 26.00x o.p. (ISBN 0-374-95296-5, Octagon). Hippocrene Bks.
Gentleman from Maryland: The Conscience of a Gay Conservative. Robert Bauman. 320p. 1986. 17.95 o.p. (ISBN 0-87795-686-3). Morrow.
Gentleman of Renaissance France. William L. Wiley. LC 75-152622. (Illus.). 1971. Repr. of 1954 ed. lib. bdg. 35.00 o.p. (ISBN 0-8371-6169-X, WIGR). Greenwood.
Gentleman Savage: The Life of Mansfield Parkyns, 1823-1894. Duncan Cumming. 176p. 1988. 39.95 o.p. (ISBN 0-7126-1734-5, Pub. by Century Hutchinson). David & Charles.
Gentleman Traitor. Alan Williams. LC 75-15791. 312p. 1975. 8.95 o.p. (ISBN 0-15-135015-9). HarBraceJ.
Gentleman's Agreement. Laura Z. Hobson. 1983. 16.95 o.p. (ISBN 0-87795-551-4, Arbor Hse); pap. 8.95 o.p. (ISBN 0-87795-552-2). Morrow.
Gentleman's Country House & Its Plan 1835-1914. Jill Franklin. (Illus.). 272p. 1981. 42.50 o.p. (ISBN 0-7100-0622-5). Routledge Chapman & Hall.
Gentleman's Magazine Biographical & Obituary Notices, 1781-1819: An Index. Benjamin Nangle. LC 80-907. (Garland Reference Library of the Humanities). 450p. 1980. 67.00 o.p. (ISBN 0-8240-9510-3). Garland Pub.
Gentlemen & Tradesmen: The Values of Economic Catastrophe. Charles Hampden-Turner. 281p. 1984. 19.95x o.p. (ISBN 0-7100-9579-1). Routledge Chapman & Hall.
Gentlemen of Adventure. Ernest K. Gann. 512p. 1983. 15.95 o.p. (ISBN 0-87795-465-8, Arbor Hse). Morrow.
Gentlemen of Sixteen July. Maurice & Ken Follett. LC 80-52012. 1980. 9.95 o.p. (ISBN 0-87795-298-1, Arbor Hse). Morrow.
Gentlemen Prefer Blondes. Anita Loos. (Illus.). 1963. 5.95 o.p. (ISBN 0-87140-888-0). Liveright.
Gently Through the Woods. (Scene of the Crime Ser.: No. 46). 1982. pap. 2.25 o.p. (ISBN 0-440-13055-7). Dell.
Gently Touch the Milkweed. Lynn Hall. (YA) (gr. 7 up). 1977. pap. 1.50 o.p. (ISBN 0-380-00982-X, 49353-5). Avon.
Gently with the Innocents. Alan Hunter. (Scene of the Crime Mystery Ser.: No. 28). 1981. pap. 2.25 o.p. (ISBN 0-440-12834-X). Dell.
Gentrification of Inner Melbourne: A Political Geography of Inner City Housing. William S. Logan. LC 84-17382. (Scholars' Library). (Illus.). 328p. 1985. text ed. 37.50x o.p. (ISBN 0-7022-1729-8). U of Queensland Pr.
Genus Fields of Algebraic Number Fields. M. Ishida. (Lecture Notes in Mathematics: Vol. 555). 1977. soft cover 13.00 o.p. (ISBN 0-387-08000-7). Springer-Verlag.
Genus Frullania Subgenus Frullania in Latin America. R. E. Stotler. 1970. 24.00x o.p. (ISBN 3-7682-0679-3). Lubrecht & Cramer.
Genus Fusarium: A Pictorial Atlas. Wolfgang Gerlach & Helgard Nirenberg. (Mitteilungen aus der Biologischen Bundesanstalt fuer Land- und Fortswirtschaft Berlin Dahlem: No. 209). (Illus.). 406p. 1982. pap. text ed. 42.00x o.p. (ISBN 3-489-20900-1). Parey Sci Pubs.
Genus Lentinus: A World Monograph. D. N. Pegler. (Orig.). 1983. text ed. 29.50x o.s.i. (ISBN 0-916422-68-2, Pub. by HMSO London). Mad River.
Genus Porella in Latin America. L. F. Swails, Jr. (Illus.). 1970. 24.00x o.p. (ISBN 3-7682-0674-2). Lubrecht & Cramer.
Geobotany I. Ed. by Robert C. Romans. LC 76-51249. 308p. 1977. 55.00x o.p. (ISBN 0-306-31007-4, Plenum Pr). Plenum Pub.
Geobotany II. Ed. by Robert C. Romans. LC 81-13992. 272p. 1981. 55.00x o.p. (ISBN 0-306-40832-5, Plenum Pr). Plenum Pub.
Geochemistry & the Origin of Life. Ed. by K. A. Kvenvolden. LC 74-24685. (Benchmark Papers in Geology Ser: Vol. 14). 500p. 1975. 77.00 o.p. (ISBN 0-12-786895-X). Acad Pr.
Geochemistry of Bismuth. Ed. by E. D. Angino & D. T. Long. LC 78-24291. (Benchmark Papers in Geology: Vol. 49). 432p. 1982. 62.95 o.p. (ISBN 0-87933-234-4). Van Nos Reinhold.
Geochemistry of Boron. C. T. Walker. LC 75-4645. (Benchmark Papers in Geology: Vol. 23). 457p. 1975. 80.50 o.p. (ISBN 0-12-787719-3). Acad Pr.
Geochemistry of Germanium. Ed. by Jon N. Weber. LC 73-12621. (Benchmark Papers in Geology Ser). 480p. 1982. 67.95 o.p. (ISBN 0-87933-058-9). Van Nos Reinhold.
Geochemistry of Organic Molecules. Ed. by Keith A. Kvenvolden. LC 79-18201. (Benchmark Papers in Geology Ser.: Vol. 52). 357p. 1982. 51.95 o.p. (ISBN 0-87933-353-7). Van Nos Reinhold.
Geochemistry of Organic Substances. S. M. Manskaya & T. V. Drozdova. 1968. 65.00 o.p. (ISBN 0-08-012404-6). Pergamon.
Geochemistry of the Lithosphere. A. A. Beus. 1976. 10.00 o.p. (ISBN 0-8285-1817-3, Pub. by Mir Pubs USSR). Imported Pubns.
Geochronology of North America. National Research Council. 1965. pap. 7.00x o.p. (ISBN 0-309-01276-7). Natl Acad Pr.
Geodetic Surveying. A. V. Maslov et al. Tr. by V. V. Kuznetsov. 652p. 1985. 13.95 o.p. (ISBN 0-8285-2789-X, Pub. by Mir Pubs USSR). Imported Pubns.
Geoffrey Bawa. Brian B. Taylor. 1985. 30.00 o.p. (ISBN 0-89381-235-8). Aperture.
Geographers Biobibliographical Studies, Vol. 1. Ed. by T. W. Freeman et al. Marguerita Oughton & Philippe Pinchemel. (Illus.). 138p. 1977. pap. 34.00x o.p. (ISBN 0-7201-0637-0). Mansell.
Geographers: Biobibliographical Studies, Vol. 3. Ed. by T. W. Freeman et al. (Illus.). 184p. 1979. pap. 34.00x o.p. (ISBN 0-7201-0927-2). Mansell.
Geographic Living-Cost Differentials. Richard J. Cebula. LC 82-48096. 208p. 1983. 37.00X o.p. (ISBN 0-669-05968-4). Lexington Bks.
Geographic Perspectives on Global Problems: An Introduction to Geography. Ronald R. Boyce. LC 81-11639. 362p. 1982. text ed. (ISBN 0-471-09336-X); tchr's. manual o.p. (ISBN 0-471-86928-7); study guide o.p. (ISBN 0-471-09337-8). Wiley.
Geographical & Historical Notices of the Regions Situated Between the Rivers Nile & Indus see Expedition for the Survey of the Rivers Euphrates - Tigris, Carried Out by Order of the British Government in the Years 1835-1837.
Geographical Atlas of World Weeds. Leroy Holm et al. LC 78-24280. 394p. 1979. 53.50 o.p. (ISBN 0-471-04393-1, Pub. by Wiley-Interscience). Wiley.
Geographical Economics. Patrick O'Sullivan. LC 80-39881. 199p. 1981. 37.95x o.p. (ISBN 0-470-27122-1). Halsted Pr.
Geographical Introduction to History. Lucien Febvre & Lionel Bataillon. Tr. by E. G. Mountford & J. H. Paxton. LC 72-11735. Orig. Title: Earth & Human Evolution. (Illus.). 388p. 1975. Repr. of 1925 ed. lib. bdg. 22.50x o.p. (ISBN 0-8371-6710-8, FEGI). Greenwood.
Geographical Mobility: Mar. Nineteen Eighty-Five. (Current Population Reports Series P-20, Population Characteristics: No. 420). 71p. (Orig.). 1987. pap. 3.50 o.p. (S/N 803-005-00013-3). USGPO.
Geographical Mobility: March 1983 to March 1984. Annual ed. (Current Population Reports Series P-20, Population Characteristics: No. 407). (Illus.). 156p. 1986. pap. 8.00 o.p. (003-001-90806-9). USGPO.
Geography & Capital. K. A. Boesler. 1975. pap. text ed. 44.00 o.p. (ISBN 0-08-019712-4). Pergamon.
Geography & History for the Young Child: The Montessori Approach. Tim Seldin. (Illus.). 208p. (Orig.). 1982. pap. text ed. 10.95 o.p. (ISBN 0-8425-1990-4). Brigham.
Geography & Soil Properties. A. F. Pitty. 1979. 15.95 o.p. (ISBN 0-416-75380-9, NO. 2374); pap. 17.95x o.p. (ISBN 0-416-71540-0, NO. 2375). Routledge Chapman & Hall.
Geography & the Urban Environment: Progress in Research & Applications, 3 vols. Ed. by D. T. Herbert & R. J. Johnston. LC 77-13555. 1979. Vol. 1. 69.95 o.p. (ISBN 0-471-99575-4, Pub. by Wiley-Interscience); Vol. 2, 308p. 81.95x o.p. (ISBN 0-471-99725-0); Vol. 3, 428p. 79.95 o.p. (ISBN 0-471-27632-4). Wiley.
Geography & the Urban Environment: Progress in Research & Applications, Vol. 4. D. T. Herbert & R. J. Johnston. LC 77-13555. (Geography & the Urban Environment Ser.). 354p. 1982. 77.00 o.p. (ISBN 0-471-28051-8, Pub. by Wiley-Interscience). Wiley.
Geography & the Urban Environment: Progress In Research & Development, Vol. 5. D. T. Herbert & R. J. Johnston. LC 78-647093. 386p. 1983. 104.00 o.p. (ISBN 0-471-10225-3). Wiley.
Geography & the Urban Environment: Progress in Research & Applications, Vol. 6. J. F. Hughes & R. J. Johnston. (Geography & the Urban Environment: Progress in Research & Applications Ser.: No. 2-428). 380p. 1984. 100.00 o.p. (ISBN 0-471-90417-1). Wiley.
Geography Encyclopedia. LC 84-60401. (Encyclopedia Brown Ser.). (Illus.). 144p. (gr. 4 up). 14.95 o.s.i. (ISBN 0-02-689199-9, Checkerboard Pr). Macmillan.
Geography of Agriculture. P. A. R. Newbury. (Illus.). 336p. 1980. pap. text ed. 26.50x o.p. (ISBN 0-7121-0733-9). Trans-Atl Phila.
Geography of Australian Corporate Power. Michael Taylor. 230p. 1984. 24.95 o.p. (ISBN 0-949614-06-8, Pub. by Croom Helm Ltd). Routledge Chapman & Hall.
Geography of Colorado. Joy Clapp & Paul C. Stevens. 96p. pap. 4.00x o.p. (ISBN 0-933472-34-X). Johnson Bks.
Geography of Economic Activity. 3rd, rev. ed. Richard S. Thoman & Peter Corbin. LC 74-5756. (Illus.). 528p. 1974. text ed. 39.00 o.p. (ISBN 0-07-064207-9). McGraw.
Geography of Economic Systems. ref. ed. Brian J. Berry & Edgar C. Conkling. 544p. 1976. pap. text ed. (ISBN 0-13-351296-7). P-H.
Geography of English Politics: The 1983 British Election. R. J. Johnston. LC 84-27512. (Geography & Environment Ser.). 358p. 1985. 43.00 o.p. (ISBN 0-7099-1441-5, Pub. by Croom Helm Ltd). Routledge Chapman & Hall.
Geography of Housing. Larry S. Bourne. LC 80-19908. (Scripta Series in Geography). 288p. 1981. 52.95x o.p. (ISBN 0-470-27058-6); pap. 28.95x o.p. (ISBN 0-470-27059-4). Halsted Pr.
Geography of Living Things. M. S. Anderson. 1952. (ISBN 0-8022-0033-8). Philos Lib.
Geography of Marketing: Concepts & Methodology. H. M. Saxena. (Illus.). 151p. 1984. text ed. 20.00x o.p. (ISBN 0-86590-547-9, Pub. by Sterling Pubs India). Apt Bks.
Geography of Post-War France: A Social & Economic Approach. Hugh D. Clout. 180p. 1972. text ed. 20.00 o.p. (ISBN 0-08-016765-9); pap. text ed. 10.00 o.p. (ISBN 0-08-016766-7). Pergamon.
Geography of the Soviet Union. V. V. Pokshishevsky. 279p. 1974. 6.45 o.p. (ISBN 0-8285-0518-7, Pub. by Progress Pubs USSR). Imported Pubns.
Geography: Regions & Concepts. 4th ed. Harm J. De Blij & Peter O. Muller. LC 80-13010. 587p. 1984. text ed. (ISBN 0-471-88596-7). Wiley.
Geography 1988-89. 3rd, rev. ed. Ed. by Gerald R. Pitzl. (Annual Editions Ser.). (Illus.). 256p. 1988. pap. text ed. 9.95x o.p. (ISBN 0-87967-719-8). Dushkin Pub.
Geological Evolution of Australia & New Zealand. D. S. W. Brown et al. 1968. 34.00 o.p. (ISBN 0-08-012278-7); pap. 20.00 o.p. (ISBN 0-08-012277-9). Pergamon.
Geological-Geophysical Atlas of the Indian Ocean. Ed. by G. B. Udintsev. 1976. 175.00 o.p. (ISBN 0-08-020939-4). Pergamon.
Geological Map of Ethiopia & Somalia. G. Merla et al. 1980. 89.00 o.p. (ISBN 0-08-024028-3). Pergamon.
Geology & Ourselves. F. H. Edmunds. 1956. (ISBN 0-8022-0433-3). Philos Lib.
Geology & Virginia. Richard V. Dietrich. LC 76-110752. (Illus.). xiv, 213p. 1971. 17.95x o.p. (ISBN 0-8139-0289-4). U Pr of Va.
Geology, Earthquake Hazards & Land Use in the Helena Area, Montana: A Review. Robert G. Schmidt. (Geological Survey Professional Paper: No. 1316). (Illus.). 68p. 1986. pap. 7.50 o.p. (ISBN 0-318-21682-5, S/N 024-001-03547-2). USGPO.
Geology for Development, Mineral Resources & Exploration Potential of Africs (GSA '82) Proceedings of the General Conference on African Geology, 6th, Nairobi, Africa, December 1982. Ed. by C. A. Kogbe. 190p. 1984. pap. 36.00 o.p. (ISBN 0-08-031424-4). Pergamon.
Geology of Continental Margins. Ed. by C. A. Burk & C. L. Drake. LC 74-16250. (Illus.). xiii, 1009p. 1977. 69.30 o.p. (ISBN 0-387-06866-X). Springer-Verlag.
Geology of Great Exuma Island: Field Guide for Second Symposium on the Geology of the Bahamas. Steven Mitchell. 45p. 1984. pap. text ed. 4.00 o.p. (ISBN 0-935909-13-3). CCFL Bahamian.
Geology of Libya, 3 vols. Ed. by M. J. Salem & M. T. Busrewil. 1981. 82.00 ea. o.p. Vol. 1 (ISBN 0-12-615501-1). Vol. 2 (ISBN 0-12-615502-X). Vol. 3 (ISBN 0-12-615503-8). Acad Pr.
Geology of Scotland. 2nd ed. Ed. by C. Y. Craig. 472p. 1983. 61.95x o.p. (ISBN 0-470-27260-0). Halsted Pr.
Geology of the Great Lakes. Jack L. Hough. LC 58-6995. (Illus.). 322p. 1958. 24.95 o.p. (ISBN 0-252-72441-0). U of Ill Pr.
Geology of Washington. U. S. Geological Survey Staff. (Reprint Ser.: No. 12). 1978. Repr. 0.50 o.p. (ISBN 0-686-36916-5). WA Div Geol.
Geology of Wisconsin & Upper Michigan: Including Parts of Adjacent States. Rachel K. Paull & Richard A. Paull. LC 76-27036. (Illus.). 1977. pap. text ed. 13.95 o.p. (ISBN 0-8403-1596-1). Kendall-Hunt.
Geology: The Paradox of Earth & Man. Keith Young. 416p. 1975. text ed. 27.95 o.p. (ISBN 0-395-05561-X). HM.
Geology: The Science of a Changing Earth. 7th ed. Ira S. Allison & Donald F. Palmer. (Illus.). 1980. text ed. 28.95 o.p. (ISBN 0-07-001123-0); pap. text ed. 29.95x o.p. (ISBN 0-07-001121-4). McGraw.
Geomagnetic Pulsations: Proceedings of the Orr European Geophysical Symposium, Budapest, August 1980. Orr European Geophysical Symposium Staff. Ed. by D. Orr. 100p. 1983. pap. 30.00 o.p. (ISBN 0-08-026508-1). Pergamon.
Geomathematical & Petrophysical Studies in Sedimentology, an International Symposium: Proceedings of Papers Presented at Sessions Sponsored by the International Association for Mathematical Geology at the Tenth International Congress on Sedimentology in Jerusalem, July 1979. Dan Gill & Daniel F. Merriam. (Computers & Geology Ser.: Vol. 3). (Illus.). 285p. 1979. 63.00 o.p. (ISBN 0-08-023832-7). Pergamon.
Geomechanics Applications in Underground Hardrock Mining. Ed. by William G. Pariseau. LC 84-72183. (Illus.). 256p. 1984. 35.00 o.p. (ISBN 0-89520-432-0, 432-0). SMM&E Inc.
Geometric Algebra. E. Artin. (Pure & Applied Mathematics Ser.). 224p. 1957. 37.95x o.p. (ISBN 0-470-03432-7, Pub. by Wiley-Interscience). Wiley.
Geometric & Engineering Drawing. 2nd ed. K. Morling. (Illus.). 1974. pap. 27.50x o.p. (ISBN 0-7131-3319-8). Trans-Atl Phila.
Geometric Applications of Homotopy Theory I: Proceedings, Evanston, March 21-26, 1977. Ed. by M. B. Barratt & M. E. Mahowald. LC 78-16038. (Lecture Notes in Mathematics: Vol. 657). 1978. pap. 25.00 o.p. (ISBN 0-387-08858-X). Springer-Verlag.

Geometric Applications of Homotopy Theory II: Proceedings, Evanston, March 21-26, 1977. Ed. by M. B. Barratt & M. E. Mahowald. LC 78-16038. (Lecture Notes in Mathematics: Vol. 658). 1978. pap. 25.00 o.p. (ISBN 0-387-08859-8). Springer-Verlag.

Geometric Exercises in Paper Folding. rev. ed. T. S. Row. Ed. by W. W. Berman & D. E. Smith. (Illus.). 13.25 o.p. (ISBN 0-8446-2840-9). Peter Smith.

Geometric Functional Analysis & Its Applications. R. B. Holmes. LC 75-6803. (Graduate Texts in Mathematics Ser.: Vol. 24). vii, 485p. 1975. 28.00 o.p. (ISBN 0-387-90136-1). Springer-Verlag.

Geometric Highway & Culvert Design: Six Reports. (Transportation Research Report Ser.). 64p. 1974. 2.60 o.p. (ISBN 0-309-02363-7). Transport Res Bd.

Geometric Invariant Theory. D. Mumford. (Ergebnisse der Mathematik und Ihrer Grenzgebiete: Vol. 34). (Illus.). 1965. 22.50 o.p. (ISBN 0-387-03284-3). Springer-Verlag.

Geometric Playthings. Jean Pedersen & Kent Pedersen. (Illus.). 32p. 1973. pap. 3.95 o.p. (ISBN 0-8431-1716-8, 35-3). Troubador Pr.

Geometric Selections for Elementary & Middle School Teachers. Douglas B. Aichele & Melfried Olson. 96p. 1981. 11.95 o.p. (ISBN 0-8106-1720-X). NEA.

Geometric Theory of Diffraction. Robert C. Hansen. LC 81-6198. 406p. 1981. 44.95x o.p. (ISBN 0-471-09842-6, Pub. by Wiley-Interscience); pap. 29.50x o.p. (ISBN 0-471-09841-8, Pub. by Wiley-Interscience). Wiley.

Geometric Theory of Semilinear Parabolic Equations. D. Henry. (Lecture Notes in Mathematics Ser.: Vol. 840). 348p. 1981. pap. 24.00 o.p. (ISBN 0-387-10557-3). Springer-Verlag.

Geometric Topology. James C. Cantrell. LC 78-31631. 1979. 80.50 o.p. (ISBN 0-12-158860-2). Acad Pr.

Geometric Topology in Dimensions 2 & 3. E. E. Moise. LC 76-49892. (Graduate Texts in Mathematics Ser.: Vol. 47). 1977. 34.00 o.p. (ISBN 0-387-90220-1). Springer-Verlag.

Geometrical Lectures. Isaac Barrow. Ed. by J. M. Child. 218p. 1916. 14.95 o.p. (ISBN 0-912050-54-3). Open Court.

Geometrical Optics. C. L. Martin. 1956. (ISBN 0-8022-1067-8). Philos Lib.

Geometrical Solutions Derived from Mechanics. Archimedes. Tr. by J. L. Heiberg. 30p. pap. 2.95 o.p. (ISBN 0-87548-167-1). Open Court.

Geometrical Study of the Elementary Catastrophes. T. Poston & A. E. Woodcock. LC 73-22575. (Lectures Notes in Mathematics: Vol. 373). (Illus.). v, 257p. 1977. pap. 18.00 o.p. (ISBN 0-387-06681-0). Springer-Verlag.

Geometrics, Water Treatment, Utility Practices, Safety Appurtenances & Outdoor Adverfisement. (Transportation Research Report Ser.). 95p. 1977. 4.00 o.p. (ISBN 0-309-02656-3). Transport Res Bd.

Geometry: A Guided Inquiry. Don Chakerian et al. LC 71-179132. 1972. text ed. 21.50 o.p. (ISBN 0-395-13148-0, 3-53528). HM.

Geometry & Topology. Ed. by M. Do Carmo. (Lecture Notes in Mathematics: Vol. 597). 1977. 35.00 o.p. (ISBN 0-387-08345-6). Springer-Verlag.

Geometry for Teachers. C. Patrick Collier. LC 75-25017. (Illus.). 352p. 1976. text ed. 21.95 o.p. (ISBN 0-395-20661-8). HM.

Geometry for the Practical Worker. 2nd ed. J. E. Thompson. 256p. 1982. pap. 9.95 o.p. (ISBN 0-442-28272-9). Van Nos Reinhold.

Geometry for Today. Mervin L. Keedy et al. (Illus.). 608p. text ed. (ISBN 0-87150-500-2, Prindle); tchr's ed. 12.98 o.p. (ISBN 0-686-64030-6). PWS-Kent Pub.

Geometry in Architecture. William Blackwell. LC 83-10281. 185p. 1984. 37.50x o.p. (ISBN 0-471-09683-0, Pub. by Wiley-Interscience). Wiley.

Geometry in the Mathematics Curriculum: 36th Yearbook. National Council of Teachers of Mathematics Staff. LC 73-16458. (Illus.). 480p. 1973. 24.00 o.p. (ISBN 0-87353-016-0). NCTM.

Geometry of Banach Spaces - Selected Topics. J. Diestel. LC 75-25771. (Lecture Notes in Mathematics: Vol. 485). xi, 282p. 1975. pap. 14.00 o.p. (ISBN 0-387-07402-3). Springer-Verlag.

Geometry of Iterated Loop Spaces. J. P. May. LC 72-85090. (Lecture Notes in Mathematics: Vol. 271). ix, 175p. 1972. pap. 7.00 o.p. (ISBN 0-387-05904-0). Springer-Verlag.

Geometry of Manifolds. Richard L. Bishop & R. J. Crittenden. (Pure and Applied Mathematics Ser.: Vol. 15). 1964. text ed. 19.50 o.p. (ISBN 0-12-102450-4). Acad Pr.

Geometry of Metric & Linear Spaces: Proceedings. Ed. by L. M. Kelly. (Lecture Notes in Mathematics: Vol. 490). x, 244p. 1975. pap. 17.00 o.p. (ISBN 0-387-07417-1). Springer-Verlag.

Geometry of the Stars. James P. Calk. 1975. 5.00 o.p. (ISBN 0-682-47189-5, Banner). Exposition-Phoenix.

Geometry Problems My Students Have Written. Ruth C. Kespohl. LC 79-13880. (Illus.). 87p. 1979. pap. 6.00 o.p. (ISBN 0-87353-142-6). NCTM.

Geometry's Oldest Challenges. Antonio Pedagno. 60p. 1987. 6.50 o.p. (ISBN 0-8062-2779-6). Carlton.

Geomorphology & Soils. Ed. by K. Richards et al. (Illus.). 500p. 1985. text ed. 60.00x o.p. (ISBN 0-04-551093-8). Unwin Hyman.

Geomorphology & Time. John Thornes & Denys Brunsden. 1977. 15.95x o.p. (ISBN 0-416-80080-7, NO. 6289). Routledge Chapman & Hall.

Geomorphology: Geomorphic Processor & Surficial Geology. Robert Ruhe. 1975. text ed. 27.95 o.p. (ISBN 0-395-18553-X). HM.

GeoRef Thesaurus & Guide to Indexing. 4th ed. Ed. by Crystal S. Palmer. LC 85-73613. 522p. 1986. pap. text ed. 65.00 o.p. (ISBN 0-913312-78-9). Am Geol.

GeoRef Thesaurus & Guide to Indexing. 3rd ed. Ed. by Sharon J. Riley. 468p. 1981. 45.00 o.p. (ISBN 0-913312-53-3). Am Geol.

Georg Buchner. Julian Hilton. LC 81-84702. (Modern Dramatists Ser.). 168p. (Orig.). 1982. pap. 8.95 o.p. (ISBN 0-394-17967-6, E796, Ever). Grove.

Georg Buchner: The Complete Collected Works. Georg Buchner. Ed. by Henry J. Schmidt. 1977. pap. 2.95 o.p. (ISBN 0-380-01815-2, 35725-9, Bard). Avon.

George A. Meyers Papers: An Inventory to the Microfilm Edition. Thomas J. Rieder. 32p. 1974. 2.50 o.p. (ISBN 0-318-03220-1). Ohio Hist Soc.

George Abbot, Archbishop of Canterbury, 1562-1633: A Bibliography. Richard A. Christophers. LC 65-27845. 1966. 7.50x o.p. (Biblio. Soc., U of Va.). U Pr of Va.

George Ade: Warmhearted Satirist. Fred C. Kelly. LC 76-52441. (Illus.). 1977. Repr. of 1947 ed. lib. bdg. 24.75x o.p. (ISBN 0-8371-9443-1, KEGA). Greenwood.

George Auriol. Armond Fields. LC 85-2511. (Illus.). 192p. (Orig.). 1985. pap. 19.95 o.p. (ISBN 0-87905-200-7). Gibbs Smith Pub.

George Bellows: Painter of America. Charles H. Morgan. LC 78-27285. (Illus.). 1979. Repr. of 1965 ed. 45.00 o.p. (ISBN 0-527-65050-1). Kraus Repr.

George Bernard Shaw. Arthur Ganz. LC 83-48304. (Modern Dramatists Ser.). (Illus.). 180p. 1984. 17.50 o.s.i. (ISBN 0-394-53502-2, GP-880). Grove.

George Bernard Shaw. Arthur Ganz. LC 83-48304. (Modern Dramatists Ser.). (Illus.). 180p. 1984. pap. 9.95 o.p. (ISBN 0-394-62492-0, E871, Ever). Grove.

George Bernard Shaw: His Life & Personality. Hesketh Pearson. LC 63-4164. 1963. pap. 1.95 o.p. (ISBN 0-689-70149-7, 36, Atheneum). Macmillan.

George C. Marshall Nineteen Forty-Seven to Nineteen Forty-Nine. Robert H. Ferrell. LC 72-197304. (American Secretaries of State & Their Diplomacy, New Ser.: Vol. 15). 1966. 23.50x o.p. (ISBN 0-8154-0070-5). Cooper Sq.

George Cadbury. Walter Stranz. (Lifelines Ser.: No. 22). (Illus.). 64p. (Orig.). 1983. pap. 3.50 o.p. (ISBN 0-85263-236-3, Pub. by Shire Pubns England). Seven Hills Bk Dists.

George E. P. Box: The Selected Works, 2 vols. George E. Box. Ed. by George C. Tiao. 1984. Vol. I, 650 pp. write for info. o.p. (ISBN 0-534-03307-5); Vol. II, 700 pp. write for info. o.p. (ISBN 0-534-03308-3). Brooks-Cole.

George Eliot & Flaubert: Pioneers of the Modern Novel. Barbara Smalley. LC 73-85446. ix, 240p. 1974. 13.50x o.p. (ISBN 0-8214-0136-X). Ohio U Pr.

George Eliot Calender: Diary 1986. Hill Starr. 1985. pap. 12.95 o.p. (ISBN 0-15-634718-0). HarBraceJ.

George Eliot-George Henry Lewes Library: An Annotated Bibliography of Their Books at Dr. William's Library. William Baker. LC 76-24744. (Reference Library of the Humanities Ser.: Vol. 67). 1977. lib. bdg. 55.00 o.p. (ISBN 0-8240-9931-1). Garland Pub.

George Eliot: Her Beliefs & Her Art. Neil Roberts. LC 75-956. 1975. 24.95x o.p. (ISBN 0-8229-1121-3). U of Pittsburgh Pr.

George F. Hoar & the Half-Breed Republicans. Richard E. Welch, Jr. LC 70-133214. 1971. 27.00x o.s.i. (ISBN 0-674-34876-1). Harvard U Pr.

George Foster Story. rev. ed. Malka Drucker & George Foster. LC 80-11437. (Illus.). 128p. (gr. 5 up). 1980. 8.95 o.p. (ISBN 0-8234-0413-7). Holiday.

George Fox's Book of Miracles. George Fox. Ed. by Henry J. Cadbury. LC 73-735. 161p. 1973. Repr. of 1948 ed. lib. bdg. 16.50x o.p. (ISBN 0-374-92825-8, Octagon). Hippocrene Bks.

George Frederic Handel. Paul H. Lang. (Illus.). 1977. 22.95 o.p. (ISBN 0-393-02131-9, Norton Lib); pap. 15.95 o.p. (ISBN 0-393-00815-0). Norton.

George Gascoigne's A Hundredth Sundrie Flowres. George Gascoigne. Repr. of 1942 ed. 23.50 o.p. (ISBN 0-403-04077-9). Somerset Pub.

George Gershwin: His Journey to Greatness. David Ewen. LC 77-6821. (Illus.). 1977. Repr. of 1970 ed. lib. bdg. 25.00x o.p. (ISBN 0-8371-9663-9, EWGG). Greenwood.

George Grosz: His Life & Work. Uwe M. Schneede et al. Tr. by Susanne Flatauer. LC 78-64969. (Illus.). 184p. 1980. 12.50x o.s.i. (ISBN 0-87663-333-5); pap. 10.00 o.p. (ISBN 0-87663-990-2). Universe.

George Herbert Mead on Social Psychology. George H. Mead. Ed. by Anselm Strauss. LC 64-23419. (Heritage of Sociology Ser.). 1964. lib. bdg. 22.50x o.s.i. (ISBN 0-226-51664-4). U of Chicago Pr.

George Jones: The Saga of an American Singer. Bob Allen. LC 84-1541. (Illus.). 312p. 1984. 15.95 o.p. (ISBN 0-385-27906-X). Doubleday.

George MacDonald. Richard H. Reis. LC 71-125820. (Twayne's English Authors Ser.). 1972. lib. bdg. 17.95 o.p. (ISBN 0-8057-1356-5). Irvington.

George Meredith: An Annotated Bibliography 1925-1975. John C. Olmsted. LC 77-83354. (Reference Library of the Humanities Ser.: No. 99). 1978. lib. bdg. 28.00 o.p. (ISBN 0-8240-9841-2). Garland Pub.

George Meriton. Sir Henry Spelman. Anon. Charles Fearne. Ed. by David S. Berkowitz & Samuel E. Thorne. (English Legal History Ser.: Vol. 137). 370p. 1979. lib. bdg. 61.00 o.p. (ISBN 0-8240-3174-1). Garland Pub.

George Morrison. Dragos Kostich. LC 75-45210. (Story of an American Indian Ser.). (Illus.). 68p. (gr. 5 up). 1976. PLB 7.95 o.p. (ISBN 0-87518-110-4). Dillon.

George Orwell: A Life. Bernard Crick. (Illus.). 1981. 17.95 o.p. (ISBN 0-316-16112-8, Pub. by Atlantic Monthly Pr). Little.

George Orwell & 1984: The Man & the Book. LC 84-600333. 160p. (Orig.). 1985. pap. 3.50 o.p. (ISBN 0-318-18764-7, S/N 030-000-00171-1). USGPO.

George Orwell: The Ethical Imagination. Sant S. Bal. 144p. 1981. text ed. 15.00x o.p. (ISBN 0-391-02202-4). Humanities.

George Sand: A Biographical Portrait. Ruth Jordan. LC 76-5190. (Illus.). 1976. 12.50 o.s.i. (ISBN 0-8008-3199-3). Taplinger.

George Sand: A Biography. Curtis Cate. (YA) (gr. 7 up). 1976. pap. 3.50 o.p. (ISBN 0-380-00700-2, 56242-1, Discus). Avon.

George Silverman's Explanation. Charles Dickens. Ed. by Harry Stone. (Illus.). 80p. 1985. 85.00 o.p. (ISBN 0-937048-36-4). CSUN.

George Stubbs: Seventeen Twenty-Four to Eighteen Six. Ed. by Tate Gallery, London Staff. (Illus.). 240p. 1985. pap. 45.00 o.p. (ISBN 0-88162-038-6). Salem Hse Pubs.

George Third & William Pitt, 1783-1806. Donald G. Barnes. 1965. lib. bdg. 37.50x o.p. (ISBN 0-374-90399-9, Octagon). Hippocrene Bks.

George Washington & Religion. Paul F. Boller, Jr. LC 63-9755. 248p. 1963. 12.95 o.p. (ISBN 0-87074-021-0). SMU Press.

George Washington Arrington: Civil War Spy, Texas Ranger, Sheriff & Rancher. Jerry Sinise. 1980. 7.95 o.p. (ISBN 0-89015-216-0). Eakin Pr.

George Washington Himself. John C. Fitzpatrick. LC 75-18398. (Illus.). 544p. 1975. Repr. of 1933 ed. lib. bdg. 25.75x o.p. (ISBN 0-8371-8338-3, FIGW). Greenwood.

George Washington Noble. James C. Neace. 80p. 1986. 6.95 o.p. (ISBN 0-8062-2891-1). Carlton.

George Washington: The Image & the Man. W. E. Woodward. LC 70-184103. 1972. 7.95 o.p. (ISBN 0-87140-806-6); pap. 3.95 o.p. (ISBN 0-87140-269-6). Liveright.

George Washington Williams: The Massachusetts Years. John H. Franklin. 1983. pap. 3.50 o.p. (ISBN 0-912296-58-5, Dist. by U Pr of Va). Am Antiquarian.

Georges Sorel & the Sociology of Virtue. Arthur L. Greil. LC 80-69046. 262p. (Orig.). 1982. lib. bdg. 26.75 o. p. o.p. (ISBN 0-8191-1988-1); pap. text ed. 13.50 o.p. (ISBN 0-8191-1989-X). U Pr of Amer.

Georgetown University Round Table on Language & Linguistics: Applied Linguistics & the Preparation of Second Language Teachers-Toward a Rationale. Ed. by James E. Alatis et al. LC 58-31607. (Georgetown Univ. Round Table Ser.). 416p. (GURT 1983). 1984. pap. 13.95 o.s.i. (ISBN 0-87840-118-0). Georgetown U Pr.

Georgette Klinger's Skincare. Georgette Klinger & Barbara Rowes. 1981. pap. 3.50 o.p. (ISBN 0-380-55863-7, 65094-0, Flare). Avon.

Georgia. Photos by James Valentine. LC 77-76964. (Belding Imprint Ser.). (Illus.). 192p. (Text by Charles Wharton). 1977. 32.50 o.s.i. (ISBN 0-912856-35-1). Gr Arts Ctr Pub.

Georgia: Agency. 2nd ed. 1983. 18.00 o.p. (ISBN 0-686-90434-6). Am Law Inst.

Georgia Almanac. Ed. by James Crutchfield. LC 86-25981. 1986. 14.95 o.p. (ISBN 0-934395-33-0); pap. 9.95 o.p. (ISBN 0-934395-34-9). Rutledge Hill Pr.

Georgia Basic Practice Handbook. 1478p. 1984. looseleaf 55.00 o.p. (ISBN 0-318-02378-4). ICLE Georgia.

Georgia Citizens & Soldiers of the American Revolution. Robert S. Davis, Jr. 350p. 1979. 30.00 o.p. (ISBN 0-89308-169-8); pap. 27.00 o.p. (ISBN 0-89308-411-5). Southern Hist Pr.

Georgia: Contracts. 1983. 9.50 o.p. (ISBN 0-686-90441-9). Am Law Inst.

Georgia Corporate Practice. 406p. 1981. 6.00 o.p. (ISBN 0-318-02383-0). ICLE Georgia.

Georgia Creditor's Rights, 3 vols. 600p. 1986. 180.00 o.p. D & S Pub.

Georgia Federal Rules of Court, Vol. 1. 1987. 50.00 o.p. (ISBN 0-409-26577-2). D & S Pub.

Georgia-Georgia Tech Joke Book. S. C. Lee. 104p. pap. 2.95 o.p. (ISBN 0-87397-083-7). Strode.

Georgia Landlord-Tenant Law. 350p. 1986. write for info. o.p. D & S Pub.

Georgia Life & Accident & Sickness Insurance. Ed. by Merritt Company Staff. 230p. 1984. write for info. o.p. (ISBN 0-930868-44-7). Merritt Co.

Georgia Manufacturing Directory, 1989. 400p. 1988. pap. 69.00 o.p. (ISBN 0-318-02859-X). Manufacturers.

Georgia O'Keeffe: A Portrait by Alfred Stieglitz. (Illus.). 1978. museum edition 45.00 o.p. (ISBN 0-87099-182-5). Metro Mus Art.

Georgia Psychic: Ellen Evans. Ruth B. Wilvert. 1979. 6.00 o.p. (ISBN 0-682-49475-5). Exposition-Phoenix.

Georgia Scenes, Characters, Incidents, &c., in the First Half Century of the Republic. Augustus Longstreet. 260p. 1988. pap. 9.95 o.p. (ISBN 1-55709-113-7). Applewood.

Georgia Sketch Book. Ouida Canaday. LC 81-84168. (Illus.). 1981. 1.98 o.p. (ISBN 0-931948-29-0). Peachtree Pubs.

Georgia: Torts, Vols. 1-4. 1983. 15.50 o.p. (ISBN 0-686-90694-2). Am Law Inst.

Georgia Voices: A Documentary History to 1872. Spencer B. King, Jr. LC 66-27890. 370p. 1966. pap. 8.50x o.p. (ISBN 0-8203-0352-6). U of Ga Pr.

Georgian: A Reading Grammar. Howard I. Aronson. (Illus.). 526p. 1982. 27.95 o.p. (ISBN 0-89357-100-8). Slavica.

Georgian at Princeton. Ed. by Robert M. Myers. LC 75-33772. 365p. 1976. 12.95 o.p. (ISBN 0-15-135105-8). HarBraceJ.

Georgian Buildings of Bath from Seventeen Hundred to Eighteen Thirty. rev. ed. Walter Ison. (Illus.). 1979. 35.00 o.p. (ISBN 0-906230-21-7, Pub. by Kingsmead Pr England). Eastview.

Georgian Delights: The Pursuit of Happiness. J. H. Plumb. (Illus.). 160p. 1980. 12.95 o.p. (ISBN 0-316-71128-4). Little.

Georgian Dublin: Architectural Restoration. Kevin C. Kearns. (Illus.). 224p. 1983. 34.95 o.p. (ISBN 0-7153-8440-6). David & Charles.

Georgian Society Records, 5 vols. Georgia Society. 1987. Set. 300.00 o.p. (ISBN 0-7165-0320-4, Pub. by Irish Academic Pr Ireland). Biblio Dist.

Georgian Triumph: Seventeen Hundred to Eighteen Thirty. Michael Reed. (Making of Britain Ser.). (Illus.). 224p. 1983. 24.95x o.p. (ISBN 0-7100-9414-0). Routledge Chapman & Hall.

Georgie the Giraffe. Georgeanne Irvine. (Zoo Babies Ser.). (Illus.). 16p. (Orig.). (gr. k-6). 1983. pap. 1.25 o.p. (ISBN 0-8249-8053-0). Ideals.

Georgie's Christmas Carol. Robert Bright. LC 74-4832. (Illus.). 48p. (ps-k). 1975. 9.95 o.s.i. (ISBN 0-385-02344-8). Doubleday.

Georgina & the Dragon. Lee Kingman. LC 70-184249. (Illus.). 112p. (gr. 2-5). 1973. 6.95 o.p. (ISBN 0-395-13730-6). HM.

Geostatistics. Pierre F. Mousset-Jones. 180p. 1980. text ed. 33.50 o.p. (ISBN 0-07-043568-5). McGraw.

Geotechnical Engineering Handbook. M. Carter. (Illus.). 244p. 1982. 35.00 o.p. (ISBN 0-412-00341-4, NO. 5041, Chapman & Hall). Routledge Chapman & Hall.

Geotechnical Practice for Stability in Open Pit Mining. LC 72-86923. 1971. 5.00x o.p. (ISBN 0-89520-013-9). SMM&E Inc.

Geotechnology: An Introductory Text for Students & Engineers. Albert F. Roberts. LC 76-45440. 1977. 76.00 o.p. (ISBN 0-08-019602-0); pap. 30.00 o.p. (ISBN 0-08-021594-7). Pergamon.

Geotectonic Development of California, Vol. 1. Ed. by W. G. Ernst. (Illus.). 720p. 1981. text ed. (ISBN 0-13-353938-5). P-H.

Geothermal Energy: A Hot Prospect. Augusta Goldin. LC 80-8800. (Illus.). (gr. 7 up). 1981. 11.95 o.p. (ISBN 0-15-230662-5, HJ). HarBraceJ.

Gerald's Party: A Novel. Robert Coover. 320p. 1986. 17.45 o.s.i. (ISBN 0-671-60655-7, Linden Pr). S&S.

Gerard de Nerval, Eighteen Hundred Eight to Eighteen Fifty-Five. S. A. Rhodes. (ISBN 0-8022-1332-4). Philos Lib.

Gerard Manley Hopkins. Jerome Bump. (English Authors Ser.). 1982. lib. bdg. 15.95 o.p. (ISBN 0-8057-6819-X, Twayne). G K Hall.

Gerard Manley Hopkins. Kenyon Critics. LC 77-28228. 1978. Repr. of 1945 ed. lib. bdg. 24.75x o.p. (ISBN 0-313-20255-9, HOKC). Greenwood.

Gerard Manley Hopkins. Paddy Kitchen. LC 78-56337. (Illus.). 1979. 11.95 o.p. (ISBN 0-689-10930-X, Atheneum). Macmillan.

Gerard Manley Hopkins. G. F. Lahey. LC 77-120638. 1970. Repr. of 1930 ed. lib. bdg. 18.50x o.p. (ISBN 0-374-94709-0, Octagon). Hippocrene Bks.

Gerard Manley Hopkins Meets Walt Whitman in Heaven & Other Poems. Philip Dacey. (Illus.). 100p. 1982. 22.50 o.p. (ISBN 0-915778-43-2); signed ed. o.p. 75.00 o.p. (ISBN 0-915778-44-0); pap. 8.50 o.p. (ISBN 0-915778-45-9). Penmaen Pr.

Gerber Baby Encyclopedia. Craig Norback & Co. Staff. (Orig.). 1983. pap. (ISBN 0-440-53292-2). Dell.

Gerhard von Rad. James Crenshaw. (Makers of the Modern Theological Mind Ser.). 1978. 8.95 o.p. (ISBN 0-8499-0112-X). Word Bks.

Gerhardt's Children. Jerrold Mundis. LC 76-7359. 1976. 9.95 o.p. (ISBN 0-689-10732-3, Atheneum). Macmillan.

Geri. Geri Jewell & Stewart Weiner. 224p. 1984. pap. 3.50 o.s.i. (ISBN 0-345-30639-2). Ballantine.

Geriatric Medicine Annual, 1986. Richard J. Ham. 288p. 1986. casebound 35.95 o.p. (ISBN 0-87489-390-9). Med Economics.

Geriatric Nutrition. Daphne A. Roe. (Illus.). 304p. 1983. pap. text ed. (ISBN 0-13-354035-9). P-H.

Geriatric Orthopaedics. Ed. by M. Devas. 1977. 55.50 o.p. (ISBN 0-12-213750-7). Acad Pr.

Geriatric Prescriber. Coni et al. 1986. 14.25 o.p. (ISBN 0-8016-1312-4). Mosby.

Geriatric Psychology. Richard A. Hussian. 256p. 1981. 23.95 o.p. (ISBN 0-442-21916-4). Van Nos Reinhold.

Germ-Free Animal in Research. Marie E. Coates. LC 68-24698. (Illus.). 1968. 90.00 o.p. (ISBN 0-12-177150-4). Acad Pr.

German: A Comprehensive Course. rev. ed. John W. Kurtz & Heinz Politzer. 1966. 9.95x o.p. (ISBN 0-393-09688-2). Norton.

German Africa: A Select Annotated Bibliography. Jon Bridgman & David E. Clarke. LC 64-7917. (Bibliographical Ser.: No. 19). 120p. 1965. pap. 6.95x o.p. (ISBN 0-8179-2192-3). Hoover Inst Pr.

German Air Aces of World War One. Alex Imrie. (Vintage Warbirds Ser.: No. 8). (Illus.). 64p. (Orig.). 1988. pap. 9.95 o.p. (ISBN 0-85368-792-7, Pub. by Arms & Armour). Sterling.

German-American History & Life: A Guide to Information Sources. Ed. by Michael Keresztesi & Gary Cocozzoli. LC 79-24065. (Ethnic Studies Information Guide Ser.: Vol. 4). 392p. 1980. 68.00x o.p. (ISBN 0-8103-1459-2). Gale.

German & Austrian Ceramics. Gunter Reinheckel. Ed. by Robert J. Charleston. LC 78-55079. (Masterpieces of Western & Near Eastern Ceramics Ser: Vol. 8). (Illus.). 1978. 250.00 o.p. (ISBN 0-87011-349-6). Kodansha.

German & Netherlandish Sculpture, 1280-1800: The Harvard Collections. Charles L. Kuhn. LC 65-19824. (Illus.). 1965. 17.50x o.s.i. (ISBN 0-674-35000-6). Harvard U Pr.

German Books in Print: Author-Title-Catchword Catalogue 1985-86, 4 Vols. 15th ed. Verlag Vereinigung Staff. 8719p. 1985. lib. bdg. 200.00 o.p. (ISBN 3-7657-1294-9). K G Saur.

German Books in Print: ISBN Index to Spring Supplement 1985-86. 15th ed. Verlag Vereinigung Staff. 120p. 1986. lib. bdg. 20.00 o.p. (ISBN 3-7657-1298-1, Pub. by Buchhandler-Vereinigung GmbH). K G Saur.

German Books in Print: ISBN Index 1985-86. 15th ed. Verlag Vereinigung Staff. 800p. 1985. lib. bdg. 90.00 o.p. K G Saur.

German Books in Print: Spring Supplement, 1985-86. 15th ed. Verlag Vereinigung Staff. 700p. 1983. lib. bdg. 45.00 o.p. (ISBN 3-7657-1297-3, Pub. by Buchhandler-Vereinigung GmbH). K G Saur.

German Books in Print: Subject Guide to German Books in Print 1985-86, 4 Vols. 8th ed. Verlag Vereinigung Staff. 6500p. 1985. lib. bdg. 150.00 o.p. (ISBN 3-7657-1296-5, Pub. by Buchhandler-Vereinigung GmbH). K G Saur.

German Books in Print 1988-1989 - Verzeichnis Lieferbarer Bucher 1988-1989: Author-Title-Catchword, 5 vols. 18th ed. 9300p. 1988. 325.00 o.p. (ISBN 3-7657-1476-3). K G Saur.

German Center Party, 1870-1933: A Study in Political Catholicism. Ellen L. Evans. LC 80-27668. 448p. 1981. 35.00x o.p. (ISBN 0-8093-0997-1). S Ill U Pr.

German Colonists in Houston. Dorothy E. Justman. (Illus.). 384p. 1974. 15.95 o.p. (ISBN 0-89015-075-3). Eakin Pr.

German Conversational Practice. Gerald E. Logan. 1974. pap. text ed. 7.25 students bk o.p. (ISBN 0-88377-012-1); tchr's bk 6.00 o.p. (ISBN 0-88377-015-6). Newbury Hse.

German Design 1870-1918. John Heskett. (Illus.). 160p. 1986. 22.50 o.s.i. (ISBN 0-8008-3208-6). Taplinger.

German-English, English-German Medical Dictionary. rev. & enl. 8th ed. D. W. Unseld. (Ger. & Eng.). 27.50 o.p. (ISBN 3-8047-0661-4). E J Brill USA.

German-English, English-German Patent Terminological Dictionary. E. B. Klaften & F. C. Allison. (Ger. & Eng.). 75.00 o.s.i. (ISBN 0-685-12020-1). E J Brill USA.

German-English, English-German Welding Engineering Dictionary. A. W. Kleiber. (Ger. & Eng.). 35.00 o.s.i. (ISBN 0-685-00398-1). E J Brill USA.

German-English Science Dictionary. 4th ed. Louis DeVries & Leon Jacolev. (Ger. & Eng.). 1978. text ed. 37.95 o.p. (ISBN 0-07-016602-1). McGraw.

German Engravings, Etchings & Woodcuts: 1400-1700, Vols. 1-28. Ed. by F. W. Hollstein. (Illus.). write for info o.p. E J Brill USA.

German Expressionist Drama: Ernst Toller & Georg Kaiser. Renate Benson. (Modern Dramatists Ser.). 192p. 1984. 19.50 o.p. (ISBN 0-394-54135-9, GP-936). Grove.

German Expressionist Drama: Ernst Toller & Georg Kaiser. Renate Benson. (Modern Dramatists Ser.). 192p. 1984. pap. 7.95 o.p. (ISBN 0-394-62268-5, Ever). Grove.

German Folk Art. Ernst Schlee. LC 79-92578. (Illus.). 326p. 1980. 85.00 o.s.i. (ISBN 0-87011-356-9). Kodansha.

German Grammar. Elke Gschossman. (Schaum Outline Ser.). 256p. 1975. pap. text ed. 4.95 o.p. (ISBN 0-07-025090-1). McGraw.

German Grammar Workbook. Robert O. Roseler & Joseph R. Reichard. (Orig.). 1956. pap. text ed. 4.95x o.p. (ISBN 0-89197-533-0). Irvington.

German Humanism. Eckhard Bernstein. (World Authors Ser.). 1983. lib. bdg. 21.95 o.s.i. (ISBN 0-8057-6537-9, Twayne). G K Hall.

German in Review. 4th ed. Robert O. Roseler. (gr. 9-12). 1967. text ed. 13.95 o.p. (ISBN 0-03-061735-9, HoltC). HR&W.

German in Review. Kimberly Sparks & Van H. Vail. 317p. 1967. text ed. 16.00 o.p. (ISBN 0-15-529590-X, HC, HC). HarBraceJ.

German Influence on the English Vocabulary see Persian Words in English.

German Made Simple. Eugene Jackson & Adolph Geiger. LC 65-10615. (Made Simple Ser.). pap. 4.95 o.p. (ISBN 0-385-00129-0). Doubleday.

German Masters of the Nineteenth Century: Paintings & Drawings from the Federal Republic of Germany. Gert Schiff & Stephen Waetzoldt. (Illus.). 280p. 1981. 45.00 o.p. (ISBN 0-8109-0979-0). Abrams.

German Masters of the Nineteenth Century: Paintings & Drawings from the Federal Republic of Germany. Stephan Waetzoldt et al. Ed. by Emily Walter. (Illus.). 280p. 1981. 8.95 o.p. (ISBN 0-87099-263-5); pap. 5.95 o.p. (ISBN 0-87099-264-3). Metro Mus Art.

German Mind of the Nineteenth Century: A Literary & Historical Anthology. Ed. by Hermann Glaser. 416p. 1981. 17.50 o.p. (ISBN 0-8264-0041-8); pap. 8.95x o.p. (ISBN 0-8264-0044-2). Continuum.

German Opposition to Hitler: An Appraisal. Hans Rothfels. Tr. by Lawrence Wilson. LC 75-40929. 166p. 1976. Repr. of 1962 ed. lib. bdg. 48.50x o.p. (ISBN 0-8371-8696-X, ROGO). Greenwood.

German People: A Social Portrait to 1914. Robert H. Lowie. 1972. lib. bdg. 16.50x o.p. (ISBN 0-374-95137-3, Octagon). Hippocrene Bks.

German Pioneers in Texas. Don H. Biggers. (Illus.). 230p. Repr. of 1925 ed. 11.95 o.p. (ISBN 0-89015-385-X). Eakin Pr.

German Poetry Nineteen Ten to Nineteen Seventy-Five. Ed. by Michael Hamburger. (Persea Ser.). 533p. (Orig.). 10.95 o.s.i. (ISBN 0-89255-050-3). Persea Bks.

German Polity. 3rd ed. David P. Conradt. (Illus.). 304p. 1985. pap. text ed. 14.95 o.p. (ISBN 0-582-28497-X). Longman.

German Revolutions. Friedrich Engels. LC 67-15314. 256p. 1967. pap. text ed. 2.95x o.s.i. (ISBN 0-226-20869-9, P256, Phoen). U of Chicago Pr.

German-Romance Contact: Name-Giving in Walser Settlements. Peter N. Richardson. LC 74-79043. (Amsterdamer Publikationen Zur Sprache und Literatur: No. 15). 372p. (Orig.). 1974. pap. text ed. 35.00x o.p. (ISBN 90-6203-221-4). Humanities.

German-Russian Dictionary. Rahmanoba. 556p. (Ger. & Rus.). 1957. 4.95 o.p. (ISBN 0-686-92465-7, M-9105). French & Eur.

German Secret Weapons of World War II. (Illus.). 64p. 1985. pap. 6.00 o.p. (ISBN 0-87364-345-3). Paladin Pr.

German Social Democratic Party, 1875-1933. W. L. Guttsman. (Illus.). 1981. text ed. 39.95x o.p. (ISBN 0-04-943024-6). Unwin Hyman.

German Song. Elisabeth Schumann. LC 79-4136. (Illus.). 1980. Repr. of 1948 ed. lib. bdg. 24.75x o.p. (ISBN 0-313-20999-5, SCGE). Greenwood.

German Sturm und Drang. Roy Pascal. 1953. (ISBN 0-8022-1281-6). Philos Lib.

German Toys, Nineteen Twenty-Four to Nineteen Twenty-Six: Der Universal-Spielwaren-Katalog. (Illus.). 1986. 9.98 o.p. (ISBN 0-87588-251-X, 2956). Hobby Hse.

German Trade Fairs: A Handbook for American Exhibitors & Exporters. 94p. 1986. pap. 4.50 o.p. (S/N 003-009-00477-2). USGPO.

German University: A Heroic Ideal in Conflict with the Modern World. Daniel Fallon. LC 80-66184. 120p. 1980. 8.95 o.p. (ISBN 0-87081-165-7). Univ Pr Colo.

German Wars Nineteen Fourteen to Nineteen Forty-Five. Donald J. Goodspeed. LC 77-4967. 1977. 17.50 o.p. (ISBN 0-395-25713-1). HM.

German Women Writers of the Twentieth Century. Ed. by Elizabeth R. Herrmann & Edna H. Spitz. LC 78-40139. 1978. text ed. 33.00 o.p. (ISBN 0-08-021827-X); pap. text ed. 18.75 o.p. (ISBN 0-08-021828-8). Pergamon.

German Yearbook on Business History, 1983. Ed. by W. Engels & H. Pohl. Tr. by E. Martin from Ger. 160p. 1984. 27.30 o.p. (ISBN 0-387-13061-6). Springer Verlag.

Germanic People. Francis Owen. 1960. pap. 9.95x o.p. (ISBN 0-8084-0145-9). New Coll U Pr.

Germans: The Biography of an Obsession. George Bailey. 1978. pap. 4.95 o.p. (ISBN 0-380-00140-3, Discus). Avon.

Germany. rev. 1985 ed. Carole Chester. LC 79-89186. (Pocket Guide Ser.). (Illus., Orig.). 1980. pap. 5.95 o.p. (ISBN 0-528-84876-3). Rand McNally.

Germany. rev. ed. Gerhart H. Seger. LC 77-83909. (World Cultures Ser.). (Illus.). 188p. (gr. 6 up). 1978. text ed. 11.20 ea. 1-4 copies o.s.i. (ISBN 0-88296-180-2); text ed. 8.96 ea. 5 or more copies o.s.i.; tchrs'. guide o.s.i. 8.94 o.s.i. (ISBN 0-686-85958-8). Gateway Pr MI.

Germany. Time-Life Books Editors. (Library of Nations). (Illus.). 160p. (YA) (gr. 7 up). 1984. lib. bdg. 23.93 o.p. Time-Life.

Germany: A Phaidon Cultural Guide. Phaidon Press Limited Staff. (Illus.). 832p. 1985. 16.95 o.p. (ISBN 0-13-354143-6). P-H.

Germany & the American Revolution: A Sociohistorical Investigation of Late Eighteenth-Century Political Thinking. Horst Dippel. Tr. by Bernhard A. Uhlendorf. LC 77-367. (Institute of Early American History & Culture Ser.). (Illus.). xxiv, 448p. 1977. 32.50x o.p. (ISBN 0-8078-1301-X). U of NC Pr.

Germany & the Great Powers, 1866-1914: A Study in Public Opinion & Foreign Policy. E. Malcolm Carroll. 852p. 1975. Repr. of 1938 ed. lib. bdg. 54.50x o.p. (ISBN 0-374-91299-8, Octagon). Hippocrene Bks.

Germany & World Politics in the Twentieth Century. Ludwig Dehio. 1967. pap. 1.55x o.p. (ISBN 0-393-00391-4, NortonC). Norton.

Germany, Austria & Switzerland in Twenty-Two Days. Rick Steves. (Twenty-Two Days Ser.). (Illus.). 136p. (YA) (gr. 7-12). 1987. pap. 6.95 o.p. (ISBN 0-912528-66-4). John Muir.

Germany: Economic & Labour Conditions under Fascism. Jurgen Kuczynski. LC 68-30824. (Illus.). 1968. Repr. of 1945 ed. lib. bdg. 35.00x o.p. (ISBN 0-8371-0519-6, KUGE). Greenwood.

Germany from the Reformation to the Present Day. Minna R. Falk. LC 57-1470. (ISBN 0-8022-0471-6). Philos Lib.

Germany in Western Civilization. William H. Maehl. LC 77-1394. 832p. 1979. 27.50 o.p. (ISBN 0-8173-5707-6). U of Ala Pr.

Germany: Seventeen Eighty-Nine to Nineteen Nineteen. Agatha Ramm. (Library Reprints Ser.). 516p. 1982. 57.00x o.p. (ISBN 0-416-33990-5, NO. 3702). Routledge Chapman & Hall.

Germany Today: A Personal Report. Walter Laqueur. 240p. 1984. 16.95 o.p. (ISBN 0-316-51453-5). Little.

Germany Tried Democracy: A Political History of the Reich, 1918-1933. S. William Halperin. 1965. pap. 6.95 o.p. (ISBN 0-393-00280-2, Norton Lib). Norton.

Germany's Aims in the First World War. Fritz Fischer. 1968. pap. 8.95x o.p. (ISBN 0-393-09798-6, NortonC). Norton.

Germany's Colonial Demands. Oxford University, British Commonwealth Group Staff. Ed. by A. L. Bullock. LC 75-8482. (Illus.). 274p. 1975. Repr. of 1939 ed. lib. bdg. 35.00x o.p. (ISBN 0-8371-8154-2, BUGC). Greenwood.

Germfree Life & Gnotobiology. Thomas D. Luckey. 1963. 84.50 o.p. (ISBN 0-12-458750-X). Acad Pr.

Germfree Research: Biological Effects of Gnotobiotic Environments. Ed. by James B. Heneghan. 1973. 70.50 o.p. (ISBN 0-12-340650-1). Acad Pr.

Geronimo. Matthew G. Grant. LC 73-12203. (We the People Ser.). 1974. PLB 6.95 o.p. (ISBN 0-87191-267-8). Creative Ed.

Gerontologic Human Resources: The Role of the Paraprofessional. Joan Settin. LC 81-6315. 192p. 1982. 24.95x o.p. (ISBN 0-89885-042-8). Human Sci Pr.

Gerontological Pharmacology: A Resource for Health Practitioners. Joan E. Oppeneer & Thora M. Vervoren. LC 82-14423. (Illus.). 257p. 1983. pap. 21.95 o.p. (ISBN 0-8016-3739-2). Mosby.

Gerontology. Rooke. 1978. 17.75 o.p. (ISBN 0-8191-0232-6). U Pr of Amer.

Gerontology: Social & Behavioural Perspectives. Ed. by D. B. Bromley. LC 84-17490. 254p. 1984. 27.00 o.p. (ISBN 0-7099-3283-9, Pub. by Croom Helm Ltd). Routledge Chapman & Hall.

Gerrit & His Dog & the Royal Law. (Children's Summit Bks.). 1978. pap. 1.95 o.p. (ISBN 0-8010-0139-0). Baker Bk.

Gerry Frank's "Where to Find It, Buy It, Eat It in New York" rev., 4th ed. Gerald W. Frank. 1985. pap. 10.95 o.p. (ISBN 0-9612578-3-0); pap. 5.95 pocket ed. o.p. (ISBN 0-9612578-2-2). G's Frankly Speaking.

Gershon Kranzler's Ten Stories. Gershon Kranzler. 24.50 o.p. (ISBN 0-87559-126-4). Shalom.

Gershwins. Robert E. Kimball & Alfred E. Simon. LC 73-80749. (Illus.). 1973. 25.00 o.p. (ISBN 0-689-10569-X, Atheneum). Macmillan.

Gertrude Jekyll on Gardening. Gertrude Jekyll. Ed. by Penelope Hobhouse. LC 83-48521. (Illus.). 336p. 1984. 20.00 o.s.i. (ISBN 0-87923-496-2). Godine.

Gertrude Stein: A Composite Portrait. Ed. by Linda Simon. (Orig.). 1974. pap. 1.65 o.p. (ISBN 0-380-00169-1, 20115). Avon.

Gertrude Stein: An Annotated Critical Bibliography. Maureen Liston. LC 78-21971. (Serif Ser.: No. 35). 220p. 1979. 15.00x o.p. (ISBN 0-87338-221-8). Kent St U Pr.

Gertrude Stein on Picasso. Gertrude Stein. Ed. by Edward Burns. LC 78-131273. (Illus.). 1970. 19.75 o.p. (ISBN 0-87140-513-X). Liveright.

Gertrude Stein's America. Gilbert A. Harrison. LC 65-21871. 103p. 1974. 15.95 o.p. (ISBN 0-87140-589-X); pap. 4.95 o.p. (ISBN 0-87140-288-2). Liveright.

Gertrude Stephens' Crossword Dictionary. Gertrude Stephens. 48p. 1987. 6.95 o.p. (ISBN 0-8062-2951-9). Carlton.

Gesammelte Mathematische und Physikalische Werke, 3 vols in 6 pts. Hermann Grassmann. (Ger). Repr. of 1911 ed. Set. 195.00 o.p. (ISBN 0-384-09730-8). Johnson Repr.

Gesammelte Werke, 7 vols. Salomon Maimon. Set. cancelled o.s.i. (ISBN 3-487-00882-3). Adlers Foreign Bks.

Gesammelte Werke: Nineteen Twenty-Four to Nineteen Thirty-Five. Otto von Bismarck. (Ger.). 869.00 o.p. (ISBN 0-686-47439-2). Kraus Repr.

Geschichte der Classischen Philologie in Deutschland Von Den Anfangen Bis Zur Gegenwart. Konrad Bursian. 1965. Repr. of 1883 ed. 65.00 o.p. (ISBN 0-384-06603-8). Johnson Repr.

Geschichte der Geologie und Paleontologie. K. A. Von Zittel. 1889. 50.00 o.p. (ISBN 0-384-71020-4). Johnson Repr.

Geschichte der Germanischen Philologie Vorzugsweise in Deutschland. Rudolf H. Von Raumer. (Akademie der Wissenschaften, Muenich. Historische Kommission Ser: Geschichte der Wissenschaften in Deutschland. Neuere Zeit. 9. Bd.). xii, 743p. Repr. of 1870 ed. 30.00 o.p. (ISBN 0-384-49680-6). Johnson Repr.

Geschichte der Physik Von Den Altesten Zeitem Bis Zum Ausgange Des Achtzehnten Jahrhunderts. Ernst Gerland. Repr. of 1913 ed. 50.00 o.p. (ISBN 0-384-18180-5). Johnson Repr.

Geschichte der Zoologie Bis Auf Johann Mueller und Charles Darwin. Julius V. Carus. Repr. of 1872 ed. 50.00 o.p. (ISBN 0-384-07825-7). Johnson Repr.

Titles

Geschichtschreiber der Husitischen Bewegung in Bohmen, Vols. 2, 6, 7. Ed. by Karl A. Hofler. (Ger). pap. 65.00 ea. vol. 2, 6 o.p.; pap. 23.00 vol. 7 o.p. (ISBN 0-384-23810-6). Johnson Repr.

Gesellschaft Fur Informatik 6, Jahrestagung 29, September-1. Oktober 1976. Ed. by E. J. Neuhold. (Informatik-Fachberichte: Band 5). 1976. soft cover 23.10 o.p. (ISBN 0-387-07912-2). Springer-Verlag.

Gesellschaftliche Verhaltnisse der Ngadha. Paul Arndt. Repr. of 1954 ed. 46.00 o.p. (ISBN 0-384-02114-X). Johnson Repr.

Gesetzgebende Kommission Katharinas Second. Georg Sacke. Repr. of 1940 ed. 14.00 o.p. (ISBN 0-384-52895-3). Johnson Repr.

Geshikhte Fun der Yidisher Arbeterbavegung, Vol. 2. Ed. by Elias Tcherikower. LC 45-13072. (Illus., Yiddish.). 1945. 20.00 o.p. (ISBN 0-914512-18-8). Yivo Inst.

Geshikhte fun der yidisher shprakh see History of the Yiddish Language.

Gespaltene Himmel see Heavens Are Cleft Asunder.

Gespraechsbuch I mit Uebungen, "Unterwegs" see Deutsch X 3.

Gespraechsbuch II "Meine Meinung" see Deutsch X 3.

Gestalt Psychology. new ed. Wolfgang Kohler. LC 72-114375. 1970. pap. 5.95 o.p. (ISBN 0-87140-218-1). Liveright.

Gestapo: Instrument of Tyranny. Edward Crankshaw. LC 79-21687. Repr. of 1956 ed. 16.95 o.p. (ISBN 0-89201-086-X). Zenger Pub.

Geste De Monglane. Ed. by David M. Dougherty & E. B. Barnes. LC 66-9253. 1966. 10.00 o.p. (ISBN 0-87114-012-8). U of Oreg Bks.

Gestodene: The Development of a New Gestodene - Containing Low Dose Oral Contraceptive. Ed. by M. Elstein. (Illus.). 350p. 1987. 45.00 o.p. (ISBN 0-940813-05-X). Parthenon NJ.

Gestures. Francis Poole. pap. 3.00 o.p. (ISBN 0-938078-10-0). Anhinga Pr.

Get Acquainted Book, Bk. I. Margaret Dee. 1953. 1.75 o.p. (ISBN 0-913650-32-3). CPP Belwin.

Get off My Ship: Ensign Berg vs. the U. S. Navy. E. Lawrence Gibson. 1978. pap. 4.95 o.p. (ISBN 0-380-40071-5, 40071-5). Avon.

Get Out of Your Own Way. Bhagwan Shree Rajneesh. Ed. by Ma Yoga Pratima. LC 83-181935. (Initation Talks Ser.). (Illus.). 374p. (Orig.). 1977. 8.95 o.p. (ISBN 0-88050-066-2). Chidvilas Inc.

Get Personal with Your TI 99. William A. Manning & Lon Ingalsbe. (Illus.). 198p. 1983. pap. 2.95 o.p. (ISBN 0-88056-098-3). Weber Systems.

Get Rich on Other People's Money: Real Estate Investment Secrets. William H. Pivar. LC 81-2019. 208p. 1981. 11.95 o.p. (ISBN 0-668-05144-2); pap. 6.95 o.p. (ISBN 0-668-05152-3). Arco.

Get Rich on the Obvious: How to Turn Your Everyday Observations into Stock Market Profits. Thomas J. Taylor. LC 81-47899. 180p. 1982. 12.95 o.p. (ISBN 0-15-135250-X). HarBraceJ.

Get Set for Math Success. Imogene Forte. (Get Set Ser.). (Illus.). 64p. (ps-1). 1985. guide 4.95 o.p. (ISBN 0-86530-105-0). Incentive Pubns.

Get Set... Go! James R. Sherman. LC 83-62907. 67p. 1983. pap. 2.95 o.p. (ISBN 0-935538-05-4). Pathway Bks.

Get the Message Out: Communication Techniques for Congregations. Russell Tokheim. 40p. (Orig.). 1983. pap. 3.95 o.p. (ISBN 0-8066-2028-5, 10-2544, Augsburg). Augsburg Fortress.

Get These Men Out of the Hot Sun. Herbert Mitgang. LC 71-188941. 204p. 1972. 6.00 o.p. (ISBN 0-87795-035-0, A4378, Arbor Hse). Morrow.

Get up & Go. Daisy Hepburn. LC 84-3362. (Life with Spice Bible Study Ser.). 64p. 1984. 2.95 o.s.i. (ISBN 0-8307-0946-0, 6101833). Regal.

Get up & Grow. Daisy Hepburn. LC 84-3361. (Life with Spice Bible Study Ser.). 64p. 1984. 2.95 o.s.i. (ISBN 0-8307-0942-8, 6101800). Regal.

Get Well Hotel. Burstein. 113p. 1980. text ed. 4.95 o.p. (ISBN 0-07-009244-3). McGraw.

Get Your Head Out of the Fridge: How to Stop Being a Foodaholic. Jerry L. Walke & Angela Y. Whitt. 224p. 1987. pap. 7.95 o.p. (ISBN 0-399-51370-1, Perigee). Putnam Pub Group.

Getaway Guide I: Short Vacations in the Pacific Northwest. 2nd, rev. & enl. ed. Jake Rankin & Marni Rankin. LC 82-18784. 223p. 1983. pap. 9.95 o.p. (ISBN 0-914718-76-2). Globe Pequot.

Getaway Guide III: Short Vacations in Northern California. Marni Rankin & Jake Rankin. LC 81-11228. (Illus.). 253p. (Orig.). 1981. pap. 8.95 o.p. (ISBN 0-914718-63-0). Pacific Search.

Getaway Guide IV: Short Vacations in Southern California. Jake Rankin & Marni Rankin. LC 82-19060. (Illus.). 248p. (Orig.). 1983. pap. 9.95 o.p. (ISBN 0-914718-77-0). Pacific Search.

Getriebe-Worterbuch. Herbert Bucksch. (Ger. & Eng., Dictionary of Transmissions). 1976. 132.00 o.p. (ISBN 0-686-56477-4, M-7423, Pub. by Bauverlag). French & Eur.

Getting a Better Job. David Gootnick. (Illus.). 1978. pap. text ed. 6.95 o.p. (ISBN 0-07-023745-X). McGraw.

Getting a Grip on Time Management. Les Christie. 64p. 1984. pap. 5.95 o.p. (ISBN 0-88207-192-0). Victor Bks.

Getting Along in English. Adrian S. Palmer & Margot C. Kimball. (English As a Second Language Bks.). pap. text ed. 6.50 o.p. (ISBN 0-582-79723-3). Longman.

Getting along Series of Skills, 5 vols. Thomas Mooney. Incl. Vol. I. After School Is Out. 1963 (ISBN 0-88323-021-6, 121); Vol. II. Al Looks for a Job. 1964 (ISBN 0-88323-022-4, 122); Vol. III. Job at Last. 1964 (ISBN 0-88323-023-2, 123); Vol. IV. Money in the Pocket. 1965 (ISBN 0-88323-024-0, 124); Vol. V. From Tires to Teeth. 1965 (ISBN 0-88323-025-9, 125). wkbk. 2.75x ea. o.p. Pendergrass Pub.

Getting along with Difficult People. Friedrich Schmitt. Tr. by Erich R. Schultz from Ger. LC 79-114244. (Orig.). 1970. pap. 1.00 o.p. (ISBN 0-8006-0010-X, Fortress). Augsburg Fortress.

Getting & Keeping Members. (Leadership Pamphlet Ser.: No. 12). 1956. 1.40 o.p. (ISBN 0-88379-024-6). A A A C E.

Getting Away with Murder? Anne Morice. (Nightingale Paperbacks). 1985. pap. 10.95 o.p. (ISBN 0-317-19809-2, Large Print Bks). G K Hall.

Getting Born. Russell Freedman. LC 78-6673. (Illus.). 40p. (gr. 1-4). 1978. 9.95 o.p. (ISBN 0-8234-0336-X). Holiday.

Getting Control of Your Inner Self. Rick Vohn. 176p. 1982. pap. 2.95 o.p. (ISBN 0-8423-0999-3). Tyndale.

Getting Even. Paul Kropp. (Illus.). 1986. pap. 2.50 o.p. (ISBN 0-671-62419-9). Archway.

Getting Free: A Handbook for Women in Abusive Relationships. Ginny Nicarthy. LC 82-80723. (New Leaf Ser.). 304p. 1982. pap. 8.95 o.p. (ISBN 0-931188-13-X). Seal Pr Feminist.

Getting Free: Women & Psychotherapy. Ann P. Hinton et al. (Fred Jordan Bk.). 1982. pap. 8.95 o.p. (ISBN 0-394-17982-X, Ever). Grove.

Getting from Twenty to Thirty: Surviving Your First Decade in the Real World. Mike Edelhart. LC 82-21007. 240p. 1983. 10.95 o.p. (ISBN 0-87131-381-2); pap. 6.95 o.p. (ISBN 0-87131-382-0). M Evans.

Getting Great Graphics. Cary N. Prague. (Illus.). 192p. (Orig.). 1985. 25.95 o.p. (ISBN 0-8306-0876-1, 1876); pap. 17.95 o.p. (ISBN 0-8306-1876-7, 1876P). TAB Bks.

Getting High on Creativity. Marilyn Jones. (Exploring Careers Ser.). 140p. 1982. lib. bdg. 8.97 o.p. (ISBN 0-8239-0548-9). Rosen Group.

Getting in Shape: A Primer for Nutrition, Fitness & Weight Loss. 2nd ed. Cindy Pemberton. LC 83-72832. (Illus.). 125p. (Orig.). 1983. pap. 5.95 o.p. (ISBN 0-916870-68-5). Creative Arts Bk.

Getting in Shape: An Optimum Approach to Fitness & Weight Control. Frank I. Katch et al. 1979. 7.95 o.p. (ISBN 0-395-27782-5). HM.

Getting in Shape for Skin & Scuba Diving. Curtis Mitchell. LC 81-11227. (Illus.). 176p. 1981. pap. 6.95 o.p. (ISBN 0-8329-0114-8). New Century.

Getting into Life. Hala Beloff. 165p. 1987. 39.95 o.p. (ISBN 0-416-40850-8, 1064). Routledge Chapman & Hall.

Getting into the Formula of Concord. Eugene F. Klug. 1977. pap. 3.75 o.p. (ISBN 0-570-03742-5, 12-2646). Concordia.

Getting into the Story of Concord. David Scaer. 1978. pap. 3.95 o.p. (ISBN 0-570-03768-9, 12-2703). Concordia.

Getting into the Theology of Concord. Robert Preus. 1978. pap. 3.95 o.p. (ISBN 0-570-03767-0, 12-2702). Concordia.

Getting into VSAM: An Introduction & Technical Reference. Michael P. Bouros. LC 84-19610. 435p. 1985. text ed. 37.95x o.p. (ISBN 0-471-81237-4). Wiley.

Getting into Your Wok with Annette Annechild. Annette Annechild. 1980. pap. 9.95 o.s.i. (ISBN 0-671-79137-0). PB.

Getting Involved with Jesus. Charles B. Hodge, Jr. LC 78-140289. (Twentieth Century Sermons Ser.). 1970. 11.95 o.p. (ISBN 0-89112-304-0). Abilene Christ U.

Getting It Right. Joyce Vogelman. 208p. 1981. pap. 2.25 o.p. (ISBN 0-380-77685-5, 77685). Avon.

Getting It Together: Black Businessmen in America. John Seder & Berkeley G. Burrell. LC 70-142096. 1971. 6.95 o.p. (ISBN 0-15-135275-5). HarBraceJ.

Getting More from Your Bible. Hall. 1984. 6.95 o.p. (ISBN 0-88207-300-1). Victor Bks.

Getting More from Your Food Processor. Kostick. (Illus.). 144p. 1984. 10.95 o.p. (ISBN 0-916752-63-1). Dorison Hse.

Getting More Out of Church. Wayne Kiser. 168p. 1986. pap. 6.95 o.p. (ISBN 0-89693-530-2). Victor Bks.

Getting Motivated: The Secret Behind Individual Motivations by the Man Who Was Not Afraid to Ask "Why?" Ernest Dichter. LC 78-21168. (Illus.). 1979. 50.00 o.p. (ISBN 0-08-023687-1). Pergamon.

Getting Nations Together: A Case Study of the European Community. William A. Nesbitt. (Illus.). 74p. (Orig.). 1979. pap. text ed. 3.00x o.p. (ISBN 0-936876-04-2). LRIS.

Getting Older & Staying Young. D. D. Stonecypher, Jr. 352p. 1974. 8.95 o.p. (ISBN 0-393-01102-X). Norton.

Getting Organized: Time & Paperwork. Stephanie Winston. 1980. pap. 7.95 o.s.i. (ISBN 0-446-38212-4). Warner Bks.

Getting Publicity. David M. Rees. 96p. 1984. 14.95 o.p. (ISBN 0-7153-8525-9). David & Charles.

Getting Ready for Living Together. Richard Langsdale. LC 74-76918. (Illus.). 96p. (Orig.). 1974. pap. 1.95 o.p. (ISBN 0-8006-1302-3, 1-1302, Fortress). Augsburg Fortress.

Getting Ready for Marriage see Loving.

Getting Ready for My First Day of School. William L. Coleman. 123p. (Orig.). (gr. k). 1983. pap. 4.95 o.p. (ISBN 0-87123-274-X, 210274). Bethany Hse.

Getting Ready for Phonics. Compiled by Constance McAllister. (Illus., Orig.). (ps-1). 1978. pap. 2.95 o.p. (ISBN 0-87534-170-5). Highlights.

Getting Ready for Your Baby. Helen R. Kime & Shari H. Wynkoop. 1978. pap. text ed. 3.50x o.p. (ISBN 0-88323-143-3, 233). Pendergrass Pub.

Getting Ready to Bargain see Issues in the Public Employee Relations Library: Series 2.

Getting Rid of Richard. Joyce Elbert. LC 77-183381. 1972. 6.95 o.p. (ISBN 0-87795-026-1, A4314, Arbor Hse). Morrow.

Getting Sales: A Practical Guide to Getting More Sales for Your Business. Richard D. Smith & Ginger Dick. 112p. 1983. 14.95 o.p. (ISBN 0-88908-089-5, 9519). ISC Pr.

Getting Schools Involved with Parents. Roger L. Kroth & Geraldine T. Scholl. 69p. 1978. pap. text ed. 4.50 o.p. (ISBN 0-86586-036-X). Coun Exc Child.

Getting Serious, Stories. Gordon Weaver. LC 80-17737. x, 118p. 1980. 14.95x o.p. (ISBN 0-8071-0777-8); pap. 9.95 o.p. (ISBN 0-8071-0778-6). La State U Pr.

Getting, Spending, Borrowing, Lending: What You Must Know about Government Regulation of Consumer Transactions, 2 vols. Pennsylvania Bar Institute Staff. 319p. 1984. 25.00 o.p. (ISBN 0-318-02200-1, 256). PA Bar Inst.

Getting Started in Tennis. Arthur Ashe. Ed. by Louie Robinson. LC 77-5199. (Illus.). 1979. 6.95 o.p. (ISBN 0-689-10826-5, Atheneum); pap. 3.95 o.p. (ISBN 0-689-70582-4, 245). Macmillan.

Getting Started with PC's & Compatibles. rev., & exp. ed. David Arnold & PC World Editors. 1988. pap. 18.95 o.p. Brady Bks.

Getting Strong, Looking Strong: A Guide to Successful Bodybuilding. Boyer Coe & Bob Summer. LC 78-20352. (Illus.). 1979. 7.95 o.p. (ISBN 0-689-10954-7, Atheneum). Macmillan.

Getting the Business: The Rewards & Hazards of Self-Employment. Albert J. Pollard. 64p. 1980. 6.50x o.p. (ISBN 0-682-49661-8, Banner). Exposition-Phoenix.

Getting the Most from Your Bank. Catherine Stribling. 320p. 1984. pap. 2.95 o.s.i. (ISBN 0-345-30651-1). Ballantine.

Getting the Most from Your Micro. Ernest E. Mau. 288p. pap. 14.95 o.p. (6264). Sams.

Getting the Most from Your Personal Computer. Ernest E. Mau. 256p. 1983. pap. 14.95 o.p. (ISBN 0-317-00358-5). Sams.

Getting the Most from Your Pocket Computer. Stephen F. Nowak & Gary J. Muswick. (Illus.). 336p. (Orig.). 1984. 14.95 o.p. (ISBN 0-8306-0723-4, 1723); pap. 9.70 o.p. (ISBN 0-8306-1723-X). TAB Bks.

Getting There from Here. Walt W. Rostow. 1978. text ed. 14.95 o.p. (ISBN 0-07-053898-0). McGraw.

Getting There: Frontier Travel Without Power. Suzanne Hilton. LC 79-23196. (Junior Literary Guild Selection Ser.). (Illus.). 192p. (gr. 5-9). 1980. 10.95 o.s.i. (ISBN 0-664-32657-9, Westminster). Westminster John Knox.

Getting Thin: All about Fat-How You Get it, How You Lose It, How You Keep It Off for Good. Gabe Mirkin & Laure Foreman. (Illus.). 320p. 1983. 18.95 o.p. (ISBN 0-316-57437-6). Little.

Getting Things Done. Edwin C. Bliss. 144p. 1983. pap. 6.95 o.s.i. (ISBN 0-684-17982-2, ScribT). Scribner.

Getting Things Done: The ABC's of Time Management. Edwin C. Bliss. LC 76-1363. (Illus.). 128p. 1976. 9.95 o.s.i. (ISBN 0-684-14644-4, ScribT); pap. 6.95 o.s.i. Scribner.

Getting Things from God. Charles A. Blanchard. (Classic Elective Ser.: No. 1). 168p. 1985. pap. 6.95 o.p. (ISBN 0-89693-520-5); pap. 0.95 o.p. Victor Bks.

Getting Through the Going Through Stage. Robert A. Schuller. LC 86-8770. 192p. 1986. 14.95 o.p. (ISBN 0-8407-5445-0). Nelson.

Getting to Know Pictures. Barbara Whelpton. (Illus.). 144p. 1960. (ISBN 0-8022-1856-3). Philos Lib.

Getting to Know the General: The Story of an Involvement. Graham Greene. LC 84-14013. 192p. 1984. 14.70 o.p. (ISBN 0-671-54160-9). S&S.

Getting to Know the Holy Spirit. David Mains. (Chapel Talks Ser.). 64p. 0.95 o.p. (ISBN 0-89191-262-2, 52621). Cook.

Getting to Know Your Bible. Hans-Georg Lubkoll & Eugen Wiesnet. Tr. by David L. Scheidt from Ger. LC 75-34527. (Illus.). 64p. 1976. pap. 1.95 o.p. (ISBN 0-8006-1217-5, 1-1217, Fortress). Augsburg Fortress.

Getting Together. Toby Stein. LC 79-55597. 1980. 10.95 o.p. (ISBN 0-689-11027-8, Atheneum). Macmillan.

Getting Tough on Gateway Drugs: A Guide for the Family. LC 84-14595. 1984. pap. 6.50 o.p. Am Psychiatric.

Getting Up: Subway Graffiti in New York. Craig Castleman. (Illus.). 164p. 1982. 18.00x o.p. (ISBN 0-262-03089-6). MIT Pr.

Getting Your Act Together. Bob Donahue & Marilyn Donahue. (Windrider Ser.: No. 4). 108p. (gr. 7-9). 1983. pap. 3.95 o.p. (ISBN 0-8423-1005-3). Tyndale.

Getting Yours. Letty C. Pogrebin. (YA) (gr. 7 up). 1976. pap. 1.75 o.p. (ISBN 0-380-00600-6, 27789). Avon.

Gettysburg: Eighteen Sixty-Three & Today. Charles R. Nitchkey. (Illus.). 1979. 8.50 o.p. (ISBN 0-682-49495-X, Banner). Exposition-Phoenix.

Ghana & the Ivory Coast: The Impact of Colonialism in an African Setting. David Guyer. 1971. 5.00 o.p. (ISBN 0-682-47203-4, University). Exposition-Phoenix.

Ghana: History & Traditional Customs of a Proud People. Joseph A. Mensah. 1980. 12.50 o.p. (ISBN 0-682-49471-2, University). Exposition-Phoenix.

Ghent Altarpiece & the Art of Jan Van Eyck. Lotte B. Philip. LC 73-113007. (Illus.). 380p. 1981. 52.50x o.p. (ISBN 0-691-03870-8); pap. 16.50 o.p. (ISBN 0-691-00316-5). Princeton U Pr.

Ghettos & Barrios. Ed. by Robert McCabe & Sally Anthony. 254p. 1969. pap. text ed. 9.50x o.p. (ISBN 0-8290-1408-X). Irvington.

Ghita of Alizarr. 2nd ed. Frank Thorne. (Ghita of Alizarr Ser.). (Illus.). 124p. 1985. pap. 10.95 o.p. (ISBN 0-87416-011-1). Catalan Communs.

Ghita Two: The Thousand Wizards of Urd. Frank Thorne. (Ghita of Alizarr Ser.). (Illus.). 128p. (Orig.). 1985. pap. 10.95 o.p. (ISBN 0-87416-010-3). Catalan Communs.

Ghost. J. N. Williamson. 288p. 1984. pap. 2.95 o.s.i. (ISBN 0-8439-2074-2, Pub. by Leisure Bks CT). Dorchester Pub Co.

Ghost & Bertie Boggin. Catherine Sefton. 94p. (gr. 2-6). 1982. 8.95 o.p. (ISBN 0-571-11524-1). Faber & Faber.

Ghost at Skeleton Rock. rev. ed. Franklin W. Dixon. (Hardy Boys Ser: Vol. 37). (gr. 5-9). 1958. 4.50 o.p. (ISBN 0-448-08937-8, G&D). Putnam Pub Group.

Ghost Dance Religion: Shakers of Puget Sound - Extracts. facsimile ed. James Mooney. (Shorey Indian Ser.). 21p. pap. 3.50 o.s.i. (ISBN 0-8466-0003-X, S3). Shorey.

Ghost Dance Religion: Smohalla. facs. ed. (Shorey Historical Soc). 40p. pap. 3.95 o.s.i. (ISBN 0-8466-0002-1, S2). Shorey.

Ghost Doll. Bruce McMillan. LC 83-8386. (Illus.). 32p. (ps-2). 1983. 8.70 o.s.i. (ISBN 0-395-33073-4). HM.

Ghost Fox. James Houston. (YA) (gr. 7 up). 1978. pap. 4.50 o.p. (ISBN 0-380-01816-0, 69161-2). Avon.

Ghost Fox. James Houston. LC 76-24907. 1977. 8.95 o.p. (ISBN 0-15-135300-X, HJ). HarBraceJ.

Ghost Garden. Hila Feil. LC 75-29277. (Illus.). 256p. (gr. 4-6). 1976. 7.95 o.p. (ISBN 0-689-30501-X, Atheneum). Macmillan.

Ghost in the Lagoon. Natalie S. Carlson. LC 83-25114. (Illus.). 40p. (gr. 2-4). 1984. 9.75 o.p. (ISBN 0-688-03794-1); lib. bdg. 9.12 o.p. (ISBN 0-688-03795-X). Lothrop.

Ghost in the Mirror. Marcia Kruchten. 96p. (gr. 5-8). 1985. 2.25 o.s.i. (ISBN 0-87406-040-0). Willowisp Pr.

Ghost in the Music. John Nichols. LC 79-657. 240p. 1979. 9.95 o.p. (ISBN 0-03-042576-X). H Holt & Co.
Ghost in the Park. Beatrice S. Smith. LC 75-39149. (Mini-Mysteries Ser.). (Illus.). 32p. (gr. 1-4). 1976. PLB 5.95 o.p. (ISBN 0-87614-056-8). Carolrhoda Bks.
Ghost Knights of Camelot. David A. Kraft. (Wizards, Warriors & You Ser.: Bk. 4). 112p. (Orig.). (gr. 4 up). 1984. pap. 2.25 o.p. (ISBN 0-380-89276-6, Flare). Avon.
Ghost Lane. Jane L. Curry. LC 78-73399. 144p. (gr. 5-9). 1979. 9.95 o.p. (ISBN 0-689-50129-3, Atheneum). Macmillan.
Ghost-Maker. Kathleen Kilgore. 176p. 1986. pap. 2.50 o.p. (ISBN 0-380-70057-3, Flare). Avon.
Ghost of a Chance. Linda Crawford. 1985. 15.95 o.p. (ISBN 0-87795-677-4, Arbor Hse). Morrow.
Ghost of Amador. Illus. by John R. Andrews. pap. text ed. 3.95 o.p. (ISBN 0-913548-54-5). Western Tanager.
Ghost of Five Owl Farm. Wilson Gage. (gr. 4-8). 1969. pap. 1.75 o.s.i. (ISBN 0-671-56085-9); pap. 2.50 o.p. (ISBN 0-671-63323-6). Archway.
Ghost of Follonsbee's Folly. Florence Hightower. (Illus.). (gr. 4-6). 1958. 5.95 o.p. (ISBN 0-395-06814-2). HM.
Ghost of Lucrece. Thomas Middleton. Repr. of 1937 ed. 29.00x o.p. (ISBN 0-403-07246-8). Somerset Pub.
Ghost of Thomas Kempe. Penelope Lively. 1986. 11.95 o.p. (ISBN 0-317-53108-5, Large Print Bks). G K Hall.
Ghost Paddle: A Northwest Coast Indian Tale. James Houston. LC 72-72364. (Illus.). 64p. (gr. 2-6). 1972. 5.50 o.p. (ISBN 0-15-230760-5, HJ). HarBraceJ.
Ghost Plane of Blackwater. William F. Hallstead. LC 74-17071. 156p. (gr. 7 up). 1975. pap. 1.75 o.p. (ISBN 0-15-634730-X, AVB95, VoyB). HarBraceJ.
Ghost Plane of Blackwater. William F. Hallstead. LC 73-17248. 156p. (gr. 7up). 1974. 5.95 o.p. (ISBN 0-15-230770-2, HJ). HarBraceJ.
Ghost Plane Over Hartley Field. Larry Sutton. LC 80-69286. (Carolrhoda Mini-Mysteries). (Illus.). 32p. (gr. 1-4). 1981. PLB 5.95 o.p. (ISBN 0-87614-135-1). Carolrhoda Bks.
Ghost Stories from the American South. Compiled by W. K. McNeil. LC 84-45638. (Illus.). 176p. 1985. 19.95 o.p. (ISBN 0-935304-83-5); pap. 7.95 o.p. (ISBN 0-935304-84-3). August Hse.
Ghost Toasties. Michael J. Pellowski. (Illus.). 24p. (ps-2). 1986. 1.95 o.s.i. (ISBN 0-87406-137-7). Willowisp Pr.
Ghost Tower. Jean Blashfield. LC 84-91359. (Super Endless Quest (Adventure Gamebook) Ser.). 189p. (Orig.). 1985. pap. 2.50 o.p. (ISBN 0-88038-215-5). TSR Inc.
Ghost Town for Sale. Mary P. Warren. 176p. (gr. 4-6). 1973. 5.50 o.s.i. (ISBN 0-664-32521-1, Westminster). Westminster John Knox.
Ghost Town Gold. William C. MacDonald. 1974. pap. 0.95 o.p. (ISBN 0-380-00130-6, 20560). Avon.
Ghost Towns of British Columbia (1975) Bruce Ramsay. (Illus.). pap. 7.50 o.s.i. (ISBN 0-685-86893-1). E J Brill USA.
Ghost Towns of California. Donald C. Miller. LC 78-7788. (Western Ghost Town Ser.: Bk. 5). (Illus.). 1978. 14.95 o.p. (ISBN 0-87108-517-8). Pruett.
Ghost Towns of Idaho. Donald C. Miller. LC 76-42297. (Western Ghost Town Ser.). 1976. price not set o.p. (ISBN 0-87108-205-5). Pruett.
Ghost Towns of Nevada. Donald C. Miller. LC 79-20228. (Western Ghost Town Ser.: Bk. 6). 1979. 14.95 o.p. (ISBN 0-87108-541-0). Pruett.
Ghost Towns of the Pacific. 1987. 9.98 o.p. (ISBN 0-8317-3900-2, Gallery Bks). Smith Pubs.
Ghost Towns of the Southwest: Arizona, New Mexico & Utah. Donald C. Miller. LC 80-22898. (Western Ghost Town Ser.). 1980. 14.95 o.p. (ISBN 0-87108-565-8). Pruett.
Ghost Vision. Jeanie Kortum & Dugald Stermer. LC 82-19410. (Sierra Club Books for Young Readers). (Illus.). 144p. (gr. 5-9). o.s.i 10.95 o.s.i.; PLB 10.99 o.s.i. Sierra.
Ghost Walker. R. D. Lawrence. LC 82-12111. 256p. 1983. 15.95 o.s.i. (ISBN 0-03-061594-1). H Holt & Co.
Ghost with the Halloween Hiccups. Stephen Mooser. (Easy-Read Storybooks). (Illus.). (gr. k-3). 1977. Repr. lib. bdg. 9.40 s&l o.p. (ISBN 0-531-01316-2). Watts.
Ghostboat. George E. Simpson & Neal R. Burger. 1985. pap. 1.95 o.p. (ISBN 0-440-15421-9). Dell.
Ghostbusters Training Manual. Christopher Brown. 24p. (gr. 3-7). 1985. pap. 1.95 o.p. (ISBN 0-89954-358-8). Antioch Pub Co.
Ghostly Terrors. Daniel Cohen. (gr. 4 up). 1983. pap. 1.95 o.p. (ISBN 0-671-45856-6). Archway.
Ghosts. Bernard Brett. LC 82-13373. (Chiller Ser.). (Illus.). 128p. (gr. 8-12). 1983. lib. bdg. 9.29 o.s.i. (ISBN 0-671-46746-8). Messner.
Ghosts. Barbara Hayes. LC 86-17755. (Enchanted World of...Ser.). (Illus.). (ps-3). Date not set. PLB 8.95 o.p. (ISBN 0-86592-319-1). Rourke Corp.
Ghosts. Henrik Ibsen. 1965. pap. 0.95 o.p. (ISBN 0-380-01213-8, 22152, Bard). Avon.
Ghosts. Henrik Ibsen. (Student Editions Ser.). 144p. (Orig.). 1985. pap. text ed. 3.95 o.p. (ISBN 0-413-54460-5, 9051). Heinemann Ed.
Ghosts of Africa. William Stevenson. 1981. pap. 2.95 o.s.i. (ISBN 0-345-29793-8). Ballantine.
Ghosts of Africa. William Stevenson. LC 80-7943. 576p. 1980. 12.95 o.p. (ISBN 0-15-135338-7). HarBraceJ.
Ghosts of Old Mobile. May R. Beck. (Illus.). 184p. 1946. o.p. (ISBN 0-940882-02-7). HB Pubns.
Ghosts of the Carolinas. Nancy Roberts & Bruce Roberts. pap. 5.95 o.p. (ISBN 0-87461-953-X). Bright Mtn Bks.
Ghosts: Vintage Aircraft of World War II. Photos by Philip Makanna. LC 87-50469. 120p. 1987. 36.00 o.s.i. (ISBN 0-934738-29-7). Thomasson-Grant.
Giacometti: A Biography. James Lord. (Illus.). 376p. 1986. pap. 14.95 o.p. (ISBN 0-374-52006-2). FS&G.
Giacomo Zanella: Poet, Essayist, & Critic of the "Risorgimento" Philip J. Spartano. 24.00 o.p. (ISBN 0-916379-02-7). Scripta.
GIANT Handbook of Electronic Circuits. Ed. by Raymond A. Collins. (Illus.). 882p. 1980. 24.95 o.p. (ISBN 0-8306-9673-3, 1300); pap. 24.60 o.p. (ISBN 0-8306-9662-8, 1300). TAB Bks.
Giant Horse of Oz. Ruth P. Thompson. 1985. pap. 5.95 o.p. (ISBN 0-345-32359-9, Del Rey). Ballantine.
Giant in Texas o.p. Stanley Scott & Levi Davis. 1976. 6.95 o.p. (ISBN 0-89015-080-X). Eakin Pr.
Giant Journey. Steven Kroll. LC 80-20512. (Illus.). 32p. (ps-3). 1981. reinforced bdg. 7.95 o.p. (ISBN 0-8234-0381-5). Holiday.
Giant Killers. Michael Pertschuk. LC 86-5419. 1986. 17.45 o.p. (ISBN 0-393-02354-0). Norton.
Giant Molecular Clouds in the Galaxy. P. M. Solomon & M. G. Edmunds. (Illus.). 348p. 1980. 77.00 o.p. (ISBN 0-08-023068-7). Pergamon.
Giant on Horseback. Lewis B. Patten. 224p. 1985. pap. 2.50 o.s.i. Ace Bks.
Giant Poems. Ed. by Daisy Wallace. LC 77-21038. (Illus.). 32p. (gr. 1-4). 1978. reinforced bdg. 5.95 o.p. (ISBN 0-8234-0326-2). Holiday.
Giant Steps. Barry N. Kaufman. 352p. 1980. pap. 2.50 o.p. (ISBN 0-449-24290-0, Crest). Fawcett.
Giant Steps. Ed. by Warren W. Wiersbe. 496p. 1981. 15.95 o.p. (ISBN 0-8010-9648-0). Baker Bk.
Giants. Jack Ansell. LC 75-11149. 1975. 9.95 o.p. (ISBN 0-87795-110-X, Arbor Hse). Morrow.
Giants. (Illus.). 48p. (gr. 1-7). 1980. 5.95 o.p. (ISBN 0-448-47486-7, G&D); PLB 5.29 o.p. (ISBN 0-448-13623-6, G&D). Putnam Pub Group.
Giants. J. M. LeClezio. LC 75-13628. 1975. 10.00 o.p. (ISBN 0-689-10661-0, Atheneum). Macmillan.
Giants: An Unforgettable Season. Photos by National Football League Staff. (Illus.). 160p. 1987. 24.95 o.p. (ISBN 0-02-589020-4). Macmillan.
Giants & Ogres. Barbara Hayes. LC 86-17688. (Enchanted World of...Ser.). (Illus.). (ps-3). Date not set. PLB 8.95 o.p. (ISBN 0-86592-316-7). Rourke Corp.
Giants & Ogres. Time-Life Books Editors. (Enchated World Ser.). (Illus.). 144p. (YA) (gr. 7 up). 1985. 19.93 o.p.; lib. bdg. 23.93 o.p. Time-Life.
Giants Bread. Mary Westmacott. LC 72-97688. 1973. 6.95 o.p. (ISBN 0-87795-058-X, Arbor Hse). Morrow.
Giant's Bread. Mary Westmacott, pseud. 320p. 1982. pap. 2.50 o.p. (ISBN 0-440-12871-4). Dell.
Giants' Bread. Mary Westmacott, pseud. LC 72-97688. 1982. 5.95 o.p. (Arbor Hse). Morrow.
Giants' Farm. Jane H. Yolen. LC 76-58317. (Illus.). 48p. (ps-3). 1979. 6.95 o.p. (ISBN 0-395-28834-7, Clarion). HM.
Giants for Justice: Bethune, Randolph & King. Beth P. Wilson. LC 77-88971. (gr. 5 up). 1978. 6.95 o.p. (ISBN 0-15-230781-8, HJ). HarBraceJ.
Giants Go Camping. Jane H. Yolen. LC 78-17928. (Illus.). (gr. 1-3). 1979. 6.95 o.p. (ISBN 0-395-28955-6, Clarion). HM.
Giants: Russia & America. Richard J. Barnet. 1978. 10.95 o.p. (ISBN 0-671-22741-6, Touchstone Bks); pap. 7.95 o.p. (ISBN 0-671-24403-5). S&S.
GIB. L. Dean Carper. 111p. (gr. 5 up). 1985. pap. 6.00 o.p. (ISBN 0-8309-0413-1). Herald Hse.
Gibbon & His Roman Empire. David P. Jordan. LC 78-141515. 260p. 1971. 24.95 o.p. (ISBN 0-252-00152-4). U of Ill Pr.
Gibboniana, 17 vols. Incl. Vol. 1 (ISBN 0-8240-1338-7); Vol. 2 (ISBN 0-8240-1339-5); Vol. 3 (ISBN 0-8240-1340-9); Vol. 4 (ISBN 0-8240-1341-7); Vol. 5 (ISBN 0-8240-1342-5); Vol. 6 (ISBN 0-8240-1343-3); Vol. 7 (ISBN 0-8240-1344-1); Vol. 8 (ISBN 0-8240-1345-X); Vol. 9 (ISBN 0-8240-1346-8); Vols. 10 & 11. Set (ISBN 0-8240-1347-6); Vol. 12 (ISBN 0-8240-1348-4); Vol. 13 (ISBN 0-8240-1349-2); Vol. 14 (ISBN 0-8240-1350-6); Vol. 15 (ISBN 0-8240-1351-4); Vol. 16 (ISBN 0-8240-1352-2); Vol. 17 (ISBN 0-8240-1353-0). (Life & Times of Seven Major British Writers Ser). 1975. lib. bdg. 60.00 ea. o.p. Garland Pub.
Gibbons of Siberut. Tony Whitten. 224p. 1982. 45.00x o.p. (ISBN 0-460-04476-1, Pub. by Dent Australia). State Mutual Bk.
Gideon's Spring: A Man & His Kibbutz. Zerubavel Gilead & Dorothea Krook. 1985. 19.45 o.p. (ISBN 0-89919-308-0). Ticknor & Fields.
Gift. Peter Dickinson. 192p. (gr. 7-12). 1974. 12.45 o.p. (ISBN 0-316-18427-6, Pub. by Atlantic Monthly Pr.). Little.
Gift from a Sheep. Alberta Eiseman & Nicole Eiseman. LC 79-10629. (Illus.). (gr. 2-5). 1979. 9.95 o.p. (ISBN 0-689-30707-1, Atheneum). Macmillan.
Gift in Secret. Caroline Light. LC 87-9163. (Starlight Romance Ser.). 384p. 1987. 16.95 o.s.i. (ISBN 0-385-23992-0, GC Large Print). Doubleday.
Gift of a Virgin: Women, Marriage & Ritual in a Bengali Society. Lina M. Fruzzetti. (Illus.). 170p. 1982. 27.00 o.p. (ISBN 0-8135-0939-4). Rutgers U Pr.
Gift of Dreams: A Christian View. Kathryn Lindskoog. LC 78-19504. 1979. 8.95i o.p. (ISBN 0-06-065248-9). HarpR.
Gift of Freedom: A Study of the Economic & Social Status of Wage Earners in the United States. United States Bureau of Labor Statistics Staff. LC 78-10339. (Illus.). 1979. Repr. of 1949 ed. lib. bdg. (ISBN 0-313-20687-2, USGF). Greenwood.
Gift of God. Gary Moore. Ed. by Mary H. Wallace. 96p. (Orig.). 1981. pap. 3.50 o.p. (ISBN 0-912315-37-7). Word Aflame.
Gift of Healing. A. Worrall & O. Worrall. LC 65-26006. 1976. pap. 6.95i o.p. (ISBN 0-06-069687-7, RD 154). HarpR.
Gift of Hope: How We Survive Our Tragedies. Robert L. Veninga. 14.95 o.p. (ISBN 0-316-89904-6). Little.
Gift of Hope: How We Survive Our Tragedies. Robert L. Veninga. (Large Print Bks.). 404p. 1986. lib. bdg. 16.95 o.p. (ISBN 0-8161-4101-0, Large Print Bks). G K Hall.
Gift of Laughter. Estelle W. Thomas. (gr. 7 up). 1967. 4.50 o.s.i. (ISBN 0-664-32395-2, Westminster). Westminster John Knox.
Gift of Life. Nancy Martzlufft. LC 85-62552. 132p. (Orig.). 1985. pap. 4.95 o.p. (ISBN 0-934134-42-1). Sheed & Ward MO.
Gift of Life. Sally L. Palmer. LC 80-14696. 152p. 1980. pap. 7.95 o.s.i. (ISBN 0-664-24319-3, Westminster). Westminster John Knox.
Gift of Love, 5 vols. Joan W. Anglund. (Illus.). 32p. 1980. Set. pap. 8.95 o.p. (ISBN 0-15-634741-5, VoyB). HarBraceJ.
Gift of Love: Marriage As a Spiritual Journey. Ann T. Linthorst. 9.95 o.p. (ISBN 0-8091-0299-4). Paulist Pr.
Gift of Love: Remembering the Old Anew. Patrick Mooney. (Greeting Book Line Ser.). 48p. (Orig.). 1983. pap. 1.50 o.p. (ISBN 0-89622-168-7). Twenty-Third.
Gift of Mirrorvax. Malcolm MacCloud. LC 81-1399. 204p. (gr. 6 up). 1981. PLB 9.95 o.p. (ISBN 0-689-30849-3, Atheneum). Macmillan.
Gift of Music. Ed. by Louise Bachelder. 1975. 5.95 o.p. (ISBN 0-88088-218-2). Peter Pauper.
Gift of Music. Jane S. Smith & Betty Carlson. LC 83-70798. 255p. 1983. pap. 7.95 o.p. (ISBN 0-89107-293-4, Crossway Bks). Good News.
Gift of Poverty. Otis Evelyn Neblett. 1979. 5.00 o.p. (ISBN 0-682-49488-7). Exposition-Phoenix.
Gift of Simplicity. June H. McEwen. LC 84-6327. 1984. pap. 3.95 o.p. (ISBN 0-8054-5914-6). Broadman.
Gift of the Deer. Helen Hoover. 1981. pap. 4.95 o.p. (ISBN 0-395-30534-9). HM.
Gift of the Greeks: Art & Civilization of Ancient Greece. Huntington Art Gallery Staff. 1982. 10.00 o.s.i. (ISBN 0-317-40554-3). Trillium Pr.
Gift of the Magi & Other Stories. O. Henry. LC 87-60922. (Illus.). 240p. 1987. 12.95 o.p. (ISBN 0-89577-266-3). RD Assn.
Gift of the Spiderwoman: Southwestern Textiles. Joe B. Wheat. (University of Pennsylvania Museum Ser.). (Illus.). 48p. 1986. pap. 14.95 o.p. (ISBN 0-8122-0950-8). U of Pa Pr.
Gift Pilze Kompass: Die Giftigen Pilze und Ihre Geniessbaren Doppelgaenger Sicher Bestimmen. E. Garnweidner. (Illus.). 79p. (Ger.). 1984. pap. 7.50x o.p. (ISBN 3-7742-2214-2). Lubrecht & Cramer.
Gift Wrap, Please. Elizabeth W. Watson. (Orig.). 1966. pap. 1.95 o.p. (ISBN 0-8054-9710-2). Broadman.
Gifted Children: A Guide for Teachers & Parents. Virginia Ehrlich. 224p. 1982. 14.95 o.p. (ISBN 0-13-356121-6); 6.95 o.p. (ISBN 0-13-356113-5). P-H.
Gifted Education: A Comprehensive Roadmap. Patricia Alexander & Joseph Muia. LC 81-12707. 323p. 1982. text ed. 34.00 o.p. (ISBN 0-89443-383-0). Aspen Pub.
Giftpflanzenkompass: Giftige Pflanzen und Ihre Fruechte Sicher Bestimmen. M. Pahlow. (Illus.). 76p. (Ger.). 1984. pap. 7.50x o.p. (ISBN 3-7742-4217-8). Lubrecht & Cramer.
Gifts & Crafts from the Garden. Maggie Oster. Date not set. price not set o.p. Rodale Pr Inc.
Gifts for Alcestis. Illus. by Eleanor C. Anderson. (Illus.). 93p. 1985. 9.95 o.p. (ISBN 0-533-05798-1). Vantage.
Gifts from a Country Kitchen. Marion N. Ham. Ed. by Jeanne Voltz. (Illus.). 168p. 1984. 19.95 o.p. (ISBN 0-668-06258-4, 6258-4). Arco.
Gifts from above. Doris M. Walsh. 1977. 5.00 o.p. (ISBN 0-682-48981-6). Exposition-Phoenix.
Gifts from Eykis. Wayne Dyer. 1983. 12.50 o.p. (ISBN 0-671-46066-8). S&S.
Gifts from Korea. Larry Wilkinson & Dorcas Wilkinson. 1983. pap. 7.00 o.p. (ISBN 0-8309-0376-3). Herald Hse.
Gifts from the Kitchen. Bon Appetit Magazine Editors. LC 86-27191. (Cooking with Bon Appetit Ser.). 1987. 12.95 o.p. (ISBN 0-89535-179-X). Knapp Pr.
Gifts in Good Taste. Helen Hecht & Linda L. Mushlin. LC 79-51354. 1979. 10.95 o.p. (ISBN 0-689-10997-0, Athenem). Macmillan.
Gifts of Deceit: Sun Myung Moon, Tongsun Park & the Korean Scandal. Robert Boettcher & Gordon L. Freedman. LC 79-20192. 408p. 1980. 14.95 o.p. (ISBN 0-03-044576-0). H Holt & Co.
Gifts of Healing. H. L. Cayce. 1976. pap. 1.95 o.p. (ISBN 0-87604-070-9). ARE Pr.
Gifts of Power: The Writings of Rebecca Jackson, Black Visionary, Shaker Eldress. Ed. by Jean M. Humez. LC 81-4684. (Illus.). 376p. 1981. 22.50x o.p. (ISBN 0-87023-299-1). U of Mass Pr.
Gifts of Silence. Daniel B. Wessler & M. Jenelyn Wessler. LC 75-32942. (Illus., Orig.). 1977. pap. 3.95 o.p. (ISBN 0-8042-1613-4, John Knox). Westminster John Knox.
Gifts of the Earth: Fifty-Five Authentic Indian American Recipes from Fifteen Tribes. Juli S. Trapp. LC 82-7672. (Illus.). 40p. (Orig.). 1982. pap. 6.95 o.p. (ISBN 0-87108-632-8). Pruett.
Gifts of the Magi. J. L. Schrader. 1988. write for info. o.p. Metro Mus Art.
Gifts of the Spirit. Frank B. Stanger. 1974. pap. 1.25 o.p. (ISBN 0-87509-084-2). Chr Pubns.
Gifts of the Spirit. Lela Mawdsky Traver. 1972. 4.00 o.p. (ISBN 0-682-47423-1). Exposition-Phoenix.
Gifts of the Spirit & the Body of Christ: Perspectives on the Charismatic Movement. Ed. by J. Elmo Agrimson. LC 73-88608. 112p. (Orig.). 1974. pap. 2.95 o.p. (ISBN 0-8066-1411-0, 10-2550, Augsburg). Augsburg Fortress.
Giftwish. Graham D. Martin. 224p. (gr. 4-6). 1981. 8.95 o.p. (ISBN 0-395-30348-6). HM.
Gil Vicente: Farces & Festival Plays. Thomas R. Hart. LC 73-115231. 1972. 8.00 o.p. (ISBN 0-87114-055-1). U of Oreg Bks.
Gilagae. Hazel L. Cowle. 462p. 1986. 15.95 o.p. (ISBN 0-8062-2716-8). Carlton.
Gilbert & George: The Complete Pictures, 1971-1985. Carter Ratcliff. 1987. 45.00 o.p. (ISBN 0-8478-0774-6); pap. 29.95 o.p. (ISBN 0-8478-0779-7). Rizzoli Intl.
Gilbert Ryle: An Introduction to His Philosophy. William Lyons. (Harvester Studies in Philosophy: No. 21). 1980. text ed. 30.00x o.p. (ISBN 0-391-01800-0). Humanities.
Gildaen: The Heroic Adventures of a Most Unusual Rabbit. Emilie Buchwald. LC 72-91231. (Illus.). 192p. (gr. 3-7). 1973. 5.50 o.p. (ISBN 0-15-230800-8, HJ). HarBraceJ.
Gilded Needles. Michael McDowell. 352p. 1980. pap. 2.50 o.p. (ISBN 0-380-76398-2, 76398). Avon.
Gilera 50: Mopeds '72 Thru '78. Mansur Darlington. (Illus.). pap. 13.50 o.p. (ISBN 0-85696-257-0, 257). Haynes Pubns.
Gilgal Theophany. Yoseph. 1985. 6.95 o.p. (ISBN 0-533-06448-1). Vantage.
Gilgamesh the King. Robert Silverberg. LC 84-12434. 290p. 1984. 16.95 o.p. (ISBN 0-87795-599-9, Arbor Hse). Morrow.
Gilles & Jeanne. Michel Tournier. Tr. by Alan Sheridan from Fr. LC 87-393. 128p. 1989. 15.95 o.p. (ISBN 0-8021-0021-X). Grove.

Titles

Titles

Gilliane. Roberta Gellis. (Roselynde Chronicles Ser.). 1984. lib. bdg. 13.95 o.p. (ISBN 0-8398-2863-2, Gregg). G K Hall.
Gillie & the Flattering Fox. Lisl Weil. LC 77-21248. (Illus.). (ps-2). 1978. 7.95 o.p. (ISBN 0-689-30637-7, Atheneum). Macmillan.
Gillig's Guide to Turning Unprofitable Real Estate into Moneymakers. Harry Gillig. 1979. 24.95 o.p. (ISBN 0-87624-166-6, Inst Busn Plan). P-H.
Gilt-Edged Market. Jeremy J. Wormell. (Illus.). 1985. text ed. 39.95x o.p. (ISBN 0-04-332103-8). Unwin Hyman.
Gimme a Break! Warner Wolf & William Taaffe. 200p. 1984. pap. 3.50 o.p. (ISBN 0-380-69138-8). Avon.
Gimme a Break! Warner Wolf on Sports. Warner Wolf. 1983. text ed. 14.95 o.p. (ISBN 0-07-071537-8). McGraw.
Gimme Shelter: Three Plays. Barrie Keeffe. LC 79-52013. 1979. pap. 3.95 o.p. (ISBN 0-394-17419-4, E731, Ever). Grove.
Gina Farina & the Prince of Mintz. Nancy Patz. LC 85-16382. (Illus.). 32p. (ps-3). 1986. 13.95 o.p. (ISBN 0-15-230815-6, HJ). Harbracej.
Ginger & Pickles. Beatrix Potter. LC 85-13641. (Illus.). (ps-2). 1909. 4.95 o.p. (ISBN 0-7232-0609-0). Warne.
Ginger Man. J. P. Donleavy. (Penguin Fiction Ser.). 352p. 1986. pap. 4.95 o.p. (ISBN 0-14-002705-X). Penguin.
Gingerbread Boy. Illus. by Kathy Wilburn. (Pudgy Pals Ser.). (Illus.). 16p. (ps). 1984. 3.95 o.p. (ISBN 0-448-10217-X, G&D). Putnam Pub Group.
Ginger's Star. John C. Elkins. 80p. 1986. 6.95 o.p. (ISBN 0-8062-2770-2). Carlton.
Gingham Dog. Lanford Wilson. LC 76-88015. 110p. 1969. 5.25 o.p. (ISBN 0-8090-4950-3). Hill & Wang.
Gingivitis. 2nd ed. Cross. 52p. 1977. pap. 12.50 o.p. (ISBN 0-7236-0452-5, Pub. by John Wright UK). Butterworth.
Ginseng Maiden. 1980. 1.95 o.p. (ISBN 0-8351-0842-2). China Bks.
Giono: Master of Fictional Modes. Norma L. Goodrich. LC 72-4041. 344p. 1973. 34.00 o.p. (ISBN 0-691-06239-0). Princeton U Pr.
Giorgio De Chirico's Graphic Work. Alfonso Ciranna. (Illus.). 214p. 1969. ltd. ed. 400.00 o.p. (ISBN 0-915346-94-X). A Wofsy Fine Arts.
Giorgio Ghisi: The Engravings. Suzanne Boorsch et al. (Illus.). 208p. 1985. 50.00 o.p. (ISBN 0-87099-396-8); pap. 25.00 o.p. (ISBN 0-87099-397-6). Metro Mus Art.
Giorgio Vasari, Architect: A Selected Bibliography of Books & Articles. Carole Cable. (Architecture Ser.: A 1387). 7p. 1985. 2.00 o.p. (ISBN 0-89028-397-4). Vance Biblios.
Giovanni Antonio Bazzi - "Il Sodoma" Andree Hayum. LC 75-23794. (Outstanding Dissertations in the Fine Arts - 16th Century). (Illus.). 1976. lib. bdg. 50.00 o.p. (ISBN 0-8240-1989-X). Garland Pub.
Giovanni Battista Sammartini's "Sonate a tre Stromenti:" Six Notturnos for String Trio, Op. 7. Bathia Churgin. LC 80-12339. (Early Musical Masterworks Ser.). 81p. 1981. 25.00x o.p. (ISBN 0-8078-1446-6). U of NC Pr.
Giraffe Hooves & Antelope Horns. Don Torgersen. LC 81-15508. (Animal Safari Nature Library). (Illus.). (gr. 4 up). 1982. PLB 11.93 o.p. (ISBN 0-516-00655-X); pap. 3.95 o.p. (ISBN 0-516-40655-8). Childrens.
Giraffe Went to School. (gr. k-3). 1971. 0.79 o.p. (ISBN 0-8431-4104-2). Wonder.
Giraldi Cinthio on Romances. Cinthio Giraldi. Tr. by Henry L. Snuggs. LC 68-12971. 216p. 1968. 20.00x o.p. (ISBN 0-8131-1158-7). U Pr of Ky.
Giri. Marc Olden. LC 82-72061. 1982. 13.95 o.p. (ISBN 0-87795-422-4, Arbor Hse). Morrow.
Girl Beneath the Lion. Andre P. De Mandiargues. Tr. by Richard Howard from Fr. (Orig.). 1980. pap. 4.95 o.s.i. (ISBN 0-7145-0251-0). Riverrun NY.
Girl Can Dream. Betty Cavanna. (Illus.). (gr. 5-9). 1948. 5.75 o.s.i. (ISBN 0-664-32043-0, Westminster). Westminster John Knox.
Girl from the Emeraline Island. Robert S. Blum. 288p. 1984. pap. 2.95 o.s.i. (ISBN 0-345-30847-6, Del Rey). Ballantine.
Girl Green As Elderflower. Randolph Stow. LC 84-8905. 158p. 1984. pap. 5.95 o.s.i. (ISBN 0-8008-3269-8). Taplinger.
Girl Grows Up. 4th ed. Ruth Fedder. (Illus.). (gr. 9 up). 1967. text ed. 5.95 o.p. (ISBN 0-07-020294-X). McGraw.
Girl in the Hairy Paw. Ed. by Ronald Gottesman & Harry Geduld. 1976. pap. 6.45 o.p. (ISBN 0-380-00610-3, 28688-2). Avon.
Girl in the Photograph. Lygia F. Telles. 256p. 1982. pap. 3.95 o.p. (ISBN 0-380-80176-0, 80176-0, Bard). Avon.
Girl in the Plain Brown Wrapper. John D. MacDonald. (Travis McGee Ser.). 1985. pap. 3.50 o.p. (ISBN 0-449-12915-2, GM). Fawcett.
Girl in the White Coat on the Delta Eagle. Gary Youree. 1979. 9.95 o.p. (ISBN 0-393-01278-6). Norton.
Girl in the White Ship. Peter Townsend. LC 82-3110. 224p. 1983. 15.95 o.p. (ISBN 0-03-057787-X). H Holt & Co.
Girl in Winter. Philip Larkin. 1985. 13.95 o.p. (ISBN 0-317-53110-7, Large Print Bks). G K Hall.
Girl on the Motorcycle. Andre P. De Mandiargues. Tr. by Richard Howard from Fr. (Orig.). 1981. pap. 10.95 o.p. (ISBN 0-7145-0253-7). Riverrun NY.
Girl on the Outside. Mildred P. Walter. LC 82-267. 150p. (gr. 6 up). 1982. 11.75 o.p. (ISBN 0-688-01438-0). Lothrop.
Girl Scout Council Self-Evaluation. rev. ed. 64p. 1982. pap. 6.50 o.p. (ISBN 0-88441-449-3, 26-175). Girl Scouts USA.
Girl Scout on the Move. 1980. pap. 6.50 pkg. of 5 o.p. (ISBN 0-686-88529-5, 26-632-005). Girl Scouts USA.
Girl Who Cried Flowers: And Other Tales. Jane Yolen. LC 80-26140. (Illus.). 64p. (YA) (gr. 10 up). 1981. pap. 7.95 o.s.i. (ISBN 0-8052-0666-3). Schocken.
Girl Who Got All the Breaks. Carol E. Rinzler. 176p. 1981. pap. 2.25 o.p. (ISBN 0-380-56077-1, 56077). Avon.
Girl Who Heard Dragons. Anne McCaffrey. 176p. 1988. 13.95 o.p. Tor Bks.
Girl Who Lived on the Ferris Wheel. Louise Moeri. 112p. (YA) (gr. 7 up). 1980. pap. 1.95 o.p. (ISBN 0-380-52506-2, 65045-2, Flare). Avon.
Girl Who Would Rather Climb Trees. Miriam Schlein. LC 75-11591. (Illus.). 32p. (gr. k-2). 1975. 4.95 o.p. (ISBN 0-15-230978-0, HJ). HarBraceJ.
Girl with a Squint. Georges Simenon. 1978. 7.95 o.p. (ISBN 0-15-135692-0). HarBraceJ.
Girl with the Golden Lion. Desmond Meiring. 1985. 10.00 o.p. (ISBN 0-533-05652-7). Vantage.
Girl Without a Name. Gunnel Beckman. Tr. by Anne Parker from Swedish. LC 75-124840. (Illus.). (gr. 4-6). 1970. 5.50 o.p. (ISBN 0-15-230980-2, HJ). HarBraceJ.
Girlfriends. Dallas Miller. 1977. pap. 1.75 o.p. (ISBN 0-380-00890-4, 31591). Avon.
Girls & Sex. rev. ed. Wardell B. Pomeroy. LC 81-65500. 192p. (YA) (gr. 7 up). 1981. 10.95 o.p. (ISBN 0-385-28330-X). Delacorte.
Girls' Christian Names: Their History, Meaning & Association. Helena Swan. LC 68-17935. 536p. 1968. Repr. of 1900 ed. 37.00x o.p. (ISBN 0-8103-3135-7). Gale.
Girls Growing up in Late Victorian & Edwardian England. Carol Dyhouse. (Studies in Social History). 224p. 1981. 22.95x o.p. (ISBN 0-7100-0821-X). Routledge Chapman & Hall.
Girls' Guide to Menstruation. Ellen Voelckers. LC 74-20590. (MS Ser.). (Illus.). 128p. (YA) (gr. 7-12). 1975. lib. bdg. 9.97 o.p. (ISBN 0-8239-0313-3). Rosen Group.
Girls in the Velvet Frame. Adele Geras. LC 79-12352. (gr. 4-7). 1979. 8.95 o.p. (ISBN 0-689-30729-2, Atheneum). Macmillan.
Girls in White. Vida Butterworth. LC 78-10862. 1979. pap. 6.50 o.p. (ISBN 0-8309-0230-9). Herald Hse.
Girls of Huntington House. Blossom Elfman. 1973. 11.95 o.p. (ISBN 0-395-13951-1). HM.
Girodet-Trioson: An Iconographical Study. George Levitine. LC 77-94702. (Outstanding Dissertations in the Fine Arts Ser.). 1978. lib. bdg. 63.00 o.p. (ISBN 0-8240-3235-7). Garland Pub.
Giselle. Geoffrey Ashton. (Stories of the Ballets Ser.). (Illus.). 48p. 1985. 8.95 o.p. (ISBN 0-8120-5673-6). Barron.
Gissing. Colin Partridge. (Critical Heritage Ser.). 582p. 1985. pap. 15.00 o.p. (ISBN 0-7102-0598-8). Routledge Chapman & Hall.
Gist of Music. George A. Wedge. 1936. 3.00 o.p. (ISBN 0-02-872780-0). Schirmer Bks.
Gitaway Box. Hilary Milton. (gr. 4-9). 1980. pap. 3.25 o.p. (ISBN 0-89191-243-6). Cook.
Gitter's Twenty-Four Hour New York. Michael Gitter. 1987. pap. 5.95 o.s.i. (ISBN 0-671-65710-0, Fireside). S&S.
Giulio Parigi's Stage Designs: Florence & the Early Baroque Spectacle. Arthur Blumenthal. Ed. by S. J. Freedberg. (Outstanding Dissertations in Fine Arts Ser.). (Illus.). 500p. 1985. Repr. of 1984 ed. 60.00 o.p. (ISBN 0-8240-6874-2). Garland Pub.
Giuseppe Castiglione: A Jesuit Painter at the Court of the Chinese Emperors. Michel Beurdeley. LC 77-157257. (Illus.). 1972. 25.00 o.p. (ISBN 0-8048-0987-9). C E Tuttle.
Giuseppe Porta. David McTavish. LC 79-57500. (Outstanding Dissertations in the Fine Arts Ser.: No. 5). 600p. 1985. lib. bdg. 88.00 o.p. (ISBN 0-8240-3938-6). Garland Pub.
Give & Take. Tricia Springstubb. 228p. (gr. 6). 1981. 14.95 o.p. (ISBN 0-316-80785-0). Little.
Give Me a Child Until He's Two: Then You Take Him till He's Four! Marilyn McGinnis. LC 80-54005. 176p. 1981. pap. 5.95 o.s.i. (ISBN 0-8307-0785-9, 5414801). Regal.
Give Me Your Good Ear. Maureen Brady. LC 78-66097. 140p. 1979. pap. 4.50 o.p. (ISBN 0-933216-00-9). Spinsters Aunt Lute.
Give Peace a Chance: A Catalog of the Exhibition at the Peace Museum, Chicago. Peace Museum Staff. Ed. by Marianne Philbin. LC 83-15117. (Illus.). 136p. 1983. pap. 8.95 o.p. (ISBN 0-914091-35-2). Chicago Review.
Give Sorrow Words: Maryse Holder's Letters from Mexico. Maryse Holder. LC 78-74551. 1979. 10.00 o.p. (ISBN 0-394-50621-9, GP826). Grove.
Give Up? William Cole. (Illus.). 48p. 1981. pap. 1.95 o.p. (ISBN 0-380-56069-0, 56069-0, Camelot). Avon.
Give Us Each Day: The Diary of Alice Dunbar-Nelson. Alice Dunbar-Nelson. Ed. by Gloria T. Hull. (Illus.). 480p. 1986. pap. 8.70 o.p. (ISBN 0-393-30311-X). Norton.
Give Us Each Day: The Diary of Alice Dunbar-Nelson. Ed. by Gloria T. Hull. (Illus.). 1985. 19.45 o.p. (ISBN 0-393-01893-8). Norton.
Give Us This Day. Ernest Holmes. pap. 0.75 o.p. (ISBN 0-87516-144-8). DeVorss.
Give Us This Day - A Cautionary Tale. James L. O'Bryant. 40p. 1986. 7.00 o.p. (ISBN 0-8062-2802-4). Carlton.
Give Your Child a Head Start in Reading. Fitzhugh Dodson. 192p. 1981. pap. 7.95 o.s.i. (ISBN 0-671-43641-4, Fireside). S&S.
Give Your Child a Superior Mind. Siegfried Engelmann & Therese Engelmann. 1966. 10.95 o.p. (ISBN 0-671-28670-6). S&S.
Givers & Takers. Megan Hughes & Frank Ohrbach. 1979. pap. 1.95 o.p. (ISBN 0-8439-0623-5, Pub. by Leisure Bks CT). Dorchester Pub Co.
Giving A Children's Party: Planning, Ideas, Food & Games For One to Ten Year Olds. June Cable-Alexander et al. (Illus.). 80p. 1984. bds. 12.95 laminated o.p. (ISBN 0-7207-1482-6). Salem Hse Pubs.
Giving & Receiving. Mary Jean McFayden et al. (Themepaks Ser.). (gr. 1-6). 1977. 4.95 o.p. (ISBN 0-8042-1457-3, John Knox). Westminster John Knox.
Giving & Taking: Across the Foundation Desk. John M. Russell. LC 77-4865. 1977. pap. text ed. 4.95 o.p. (ISBN 0-8077-2526-9). Tchrs Coll.
Giving Away Success: How Women Get Stuck & What to Do About It. S. Schenkel. 1984. text ed. 15.95 o.p. (ISBN 0-07-055261-4); pap. text ed. 7.95 o.p. (ISBN 0-07-055260-6). McGraw.
Giving Cardiac Care. Ed. by Richard West & Barbara McVan. LC 80-27519. (Nursing Photobook). (Illus.). 160p. 1981. text ed. 17.95 o.p. (ISBN 0-916730-28-X). Springhouse Pub.
Giving Cardiovascular Drugs Safely. 2nd ed. Ed. by Patti Urosevich & Barbara McVan. (Illus.). 188p. 1985. 14.95 o.p. (ISBN 0-916730-70-0). Springhouse Pub.
Giving Emergency Care Competently. 2nd ed. Ed. by Susan Williams & Barbara McVan. LC 78-52929. (New Nursing Skillbook Ser.: Vol. 1). (Illus.). 192p. 1983. text ed. 14.95 o.p. (ISBN 0-916730-59-X). Springhouse Pub.
Giving Good Food. Deborah Navas. LC 84-50425. (Illus.). 144p. (Orig.). 1984. pap. 7.95 o.p. (ISBN 0-89909-036-2). Yankee Bks.
Giving Time a Chance: The Secret of a Lasting Marriage. Ronna Romney & Beppie Harrison. LC 83-16382. 288p. 1983. 13.95 o.p. (ISBN 0-87131-416-9). M Evans.
Giving up for Good. Howard Williams. (Illus.). 128p. (Orig.). 1987. pap. 5.95 o.p. (ISBN 0-7137-1733-5, Pub. by Javelin). Sterling.
Giving up the Gun: Japan's Reversion to the Sword, 1543-1879. Noel Perrin. LC 80-50744. (Illus.). 122p. 1980. pap. 6.95 o.p. (ISBN 0-87773-184-5). Shambhala Pubns.
Giving Youth a Better Chance: Options for Education, Work, & Service. Carnegie Council on Policy Studies in Higher Education Staff. LC 79-90851. (Higher Education Ser. & the Carnegie Council Ser.). 1980. 25.95x o.p. (ISBN 0-87589-441-0). Jossey-Bass.
Glacial Isostasy. J. Andrews. 1982. 59.95 o.p. (ISBN 0-87933-051-1). Van Nos Reinhold.
Glacier Bay Concerto. Richard Dauenhauer. (Alaskana Book Ser.: No. 38). (Illus.). 120p. (Orig.). 1980. 12.95 o.p. (ISBN 0-935094-02-4); pap. 4.95 o.p. (ISBN 0-935094-04-0). Alaska Pacific.
Glad Reunion. John Claypool. 144p. 1985. 8.95 o.p. (ISBN 0-8499-0469-2, 0469-2). Word Bks.
Glad to Be Me: Building Self-Esteem in Yourself & Others. Ed. by Dov P. Elkins. 1985. pap. 10.00 o.p. (ISBN 0-13-357319-2). Growth Assoc.
Gladstone, Disraeli & Later Victorian Politics, 2E. Paul Adelman. 1970. pap. text ed. 7.25 o.p. (ISBN 0-582-35332-7). Longman.
Gladstone: Volume I, Eighteen Hundred Nine to Eighteen Sixty-Five. Richard Shannon. 600p. 1986. pap. 16.95 o.p. (ISBN 0-416-36870-0, 9763). Routledge Chapman & Hall.
Glamour's Success Book. Barbara Coffey. 1983. pap. 9.50 o.p. (ISBN 0-671-46263-6, Fireside). S&S.
Glanville: Scepticism. Sascha Talmor. 112p. 1981. 26.00 o.p. (ISBN 0-08-027407-2). Pergamon.
Glas des 20. Jahrhunderts: Jugendstil--Art Deco. Gustav E. Pazaurek & Walter Spiegl. (Illus.). 263p. (Ger.). 1985. 80.00 o.p. (ISBN 3-7814-0219-3, Pub. by Klinkhardt & Biermann WG). Seven Hills Bk Dists.
GLAS: General Ledger Accounting System for SuperCalc. Sheldon W. Philips & Brian L. King. LC 83-10413. (Key-By-Key Ser.). (Illus.). 240p. 1983. pap. (ISBN 0-534-02851-9); PWS-Kent Pub.
GLAS: General Ledger Accounting System for VisiCalc. (Key-By-Key Ser.). (Illus.). 240p. 1983. pap. write for info. o.p. (ISBN 0-534-02881-0); write for info. o.p. PWS-Kent Pub.
GLAS: Payroll for SuperCalc. Sheldon W. Philips & Brian L. King. (Key-By-Key Ser.). (Illus.). 170p. 1983. write for info. o.p. (ISBN 0-534-02857-8); write for info. o.p. PWS-Kent Pub.
GLAS: Payroll for VisiCalc. Sheldon W. Philips & Brian L. King. (Key-By-Key Ser.). (Illus.). 150p. 1983. pap. write for info. o.p. (ISBN 0-534-02882-9); write for info. templates on disk o.p. PWS-Kent Pub.
Glasgow: The Making of a City. Andrew Gibb. (Illus.). 197p. 1983. 25.25 o.p. (ISBN 0-7099-0161-5, Pub. by Croom Helm Ltd); pap. 11.95 o.p. (ISBN 0-7099-1169-6). Routledge Chapman & Hall.
Glass Bead Game; Magister Ludi. Hermann Hesse. LC 63-12171. 1969. 9.95 o.p. (ISBN 0-03-081851-6). H Holt & Co.
Glass Cage. Georges Simenon. LC 72-91840. (Helen & Kurt Wolff Bk.). 1973. 5.50 o.p. (ISBN 0-15-135800-1). HarBraceJ.
Glass Children & Other Essays. Daisaku Ikeda. Tr. by Burton Watson. LC 78-65720. Orig. Title: Japanese. 172p. 1983. pap. 4.95 o.p. (ISBN 0-87011-608-8). Kodansha.
Glass Dove. Sally Carrighar. 1978. pap. 1.75 o.p. (ISBN 0-380-01829-2, 36194). Avon.
Glass Flowers. Kredel. 1946. 2.75 o.p. (ISBN 0-15-135813-3). HarBraceJ.
Glass Highway. Loren D. Estleman. (Amos Walker Mystery Ser.). 179p. 1983. 13.45 o.p. (ISBN 0-395-34636-3). HM.
Glass House. John Hix. (Illus.). 208p. 1974. pap. 13.95 o.p. (ISBN 0-262-58044-6). MIT Pr.
Glass House Tapes. Citizens Research & Investigation Committee Staff & Louis Tackwood. Ed. by Donald Freed. 1973. pap. 1.75 o.p. (ISBN 0-380-01215-4, 14555). Avon.
Glass in the Collections of the Metropolitan Museum of Art. Compiled by Jane Hayward & Amy Horbar. (Illus.). 20p. (Orig.). 1982. pap. 3.25 o.p. (ISBN 0-87099-306-2). Metro Mus Art.
Glass Menagerie & a Streetcar Named Desire. Tennessee Williams. 48p. (Orig.). 1989. pap. 9.95 o.p. (ISBN 1-55651-333-X); audiocassette tape incl. o.p. (ISBN 1-55651-334-8). Cram Cassettes.
Glass Microelectrodes. M. Lavallee et al. LC 68-9252. 446p. 1969. 39.00 o.p. (ISBN 0-471-51885-9, Pub. by Wiley). Krieger.
Glass of Blessings. Barbara Pym. (Large Print Bks (General Ser.)). 427p. 1986. lib. bdg. 17.95 o.p. (ISBN 0-8161-3841-9). G K Hall.
Glass of Lalique: A Collector's Guide. Christopher V. Percy. (Illus.). 192p. 1983. 35.00 o.p. (ISBN 0-684-15603-2, ScribT). Scribner.
Glass Paperweights. rev. ed. Patricia McCawley. (Letts Collectors' Guides). (Illus.). 71p. 1982. 9.95 o.p. (ISBN 0-85097-374-0, Pub. by C Letts Bks UK). Seven Hills Bk Dists.
Glass Reinforced Plastics. P. Morgan. (Illus.). 1957. (ISBN 0-8022-1144-5). Philos Lib.
Glass-Steagall Act: Banks & the Securities Business. Martin E. Lowy & Cantwell F. Muckenfuss. LC 84-61950. (Corporate Law & Practice Course Handbook Ser. No. 463). 15.00 o.p. PLI.
Glass-Steagall Act 1985: Banks & the Securities Business. 304p. 1985. 15.00 o.p. (B4-6729). PLI.
Glasshouse Tomatoes. New Zealand Ministry of Agriculture & Fisheries Staff. 86p. 1978. pap. 3.50 o.p. (ISBN 0-477-01037-7, Pub. by New Zealand Gov Pub). Ag Access Pub.
Glauber Rocha & the Cinema Novo in Brazil: A Study of His Films & Critical Writing. Burnes S. Hollyman. Ed. by Garth S. Jowett. LC 81-48354. (Dissertations on Film Ser.). 220p. 1983. lib. bdg. 31.00 o.p. (ISBN 0-8240-5103-3). Garland Pub.
Glaucoma Update: Proceedings. International Glaucoma Symposium, Nara, Japan, May 7-11, 1978. Ed. by G. K. Krieglstein & W. Leydecker. LC 79-10747. (Illus.). 1979. pap. 33.00 o.p. (ISBN 0-387-09350-8). Springer-Verlag.

GLC Good Practice Details. Greater London Council Department of Architecture & Civic Design Staff. (Illus.). 148p. 1980. 26.50 o.p. (ISBN 0-85139-241-5); pap. 17.50 o.p. (ISBN 0-85139-242-3). Nichols Pub.

GLC Preferred Dwelling Plans. 2nd ed. Greater London Council, Department of Architecture & Civic Design Staff. (Illus.). 83p. 1981. 18.50 o.p. (ISBN 0-85139-252-0). Nichols Pub.

Gleanings along Life's Way. Lillie V. Brown. LC 85-90132. 74p. 1985. 6.95 o.p. (ISBN 0-533-06639-5). Vantage.

Gleanings among the Sheaves. C. H. Spurgeon. 98p. pap. 1.95 o.p. (ISBN 0-8010-8110-6). Chr Pubns.

Gleanings for the Curious from the Harvest Fields of Literature: A Melange of Excerpta. Charles C. Bombaugh. LC 68-23465. 868p. 1970. Repr. of 1875 ed. 54.00x o.p. (ISBN 0-8103-3086-5). Gale.

Gleanings from the New Testament. Archibald M. Hunter. LC 75-33652. 1976. pap. 4.95 o.s.i. (ISBN 0-664-24794-6, Westminster). Westminster John Knox.

Gleanings in Old Garden Literature. William C. Hazlitt. LC 68-21773. 272p. 1968. Repr. of 1887 ed. 35.00x o.p. (ISBN 0-8103-3509-3). Gale.

Glengarry Glenn Ross. David Mamet. 1984. 17.50 o.p. (ISBN 0-394-53857-9). Grove.

Glenn's Complete Bicycle Manual: Selection, Maintenance, Repair. Clarence W. Coles & Harold T. Glenn. (Illus.). 352p. 1973. 9.95 o.p. (ISBN 0-517-50092-2); pap. 11.95 o.p. (ISBN 0-517-50093-0). Crown.

Glenrannoch. Rona Randall. 224p. 1981. pap. 2.50 o.p. (ISBN 0-380-78311-8, 78311). Avon.

Glickman's Clinical Periodontology: Prevention, Diagnosis & Treatment of Periodonal Disease in the Practice of General Dentistry. 5th ed. Fermin A. Carranza. LC 77-16991. (Illus.). 1979. text ed. write for info. o.p. (ISBN 0-7216-2440-5). Saunders.

Glimpse of Nothingness: Experiences in an American Zen Commune. Janwillem Van de Wetering. LC 74-31078. 192p. 1975. 8.95 o.p. (ISBN 0-395-20442-9). HM.

Glimpses of China from a Galloping Horse (a Woman's Journal). Norma L. Djerassi. LC 74-19098. 1975. 11.75 o.p. (ISBN 0-08-018215-1). Pergamon.

Glimpses of Colonial Society & Life at Princeton College, 1766-1773, by One of the Class of 1763. William Paterson. Ed. by W. Jay Mills. LC 72-179711. (Illus.). 184p. (Six songs). 1972. Repr. of 1903 ed. 40.00x o.p. (ISBN 0-8103-3810-6). Gale.

Glimpses of Glory: Scripture Poems. Nan Dobson Saye. (Illus.). 64p. 1980. 5.00 o.p. (ISBN 0-682-49584-0). Exposition-Phoenix.

Glimpses of the Moon. Edmund Crispin. 1979. pap. 2.95 o.p. (ISBN 0-380-45062-3, 69021-7). Avon.

Glitz. Elmore Leonard. 407p. 1985. lib. bdg. 15.95 o.p. (ISBN 0-8161-3834-6, Large Print Bks); pap. 9.95 o.p. (ISBN 0-8161-3835-4, Large Print Bks). G K Hall.

Global Analysis: A Data Scheme & Deck for Univariate & Bivariate Analysis. Philip M. Burgess & James E. Harf. (CISE Learning Package Ser.: No. 7). (Illus.). 70p. (Orig.). 1975. pap. text ed. 3.50x o.p. (ISBN 0-936876-23-9). LRIS.

Global & Large Scale System Models: Proceedings. Ed. by B. Lazarevic & B. Lazarevic. (Lecture Notes in Control & Information Sciences: Vol. 19). 1979. pap. 17.00 o.p. (ISBN 0-387-09637-X). Springer-Verlag.

Global Approch to Geology: The Background of a Mineral Exploration Strategy Based on Significant Form in the Patterning of the Earth's Crust. B. B. Brock. 388p. 1972. text ed. 76.50 o.p. (ISBN 0-317-64997-3, Pub. by A A Balkema). Gower Pub Co.

Global Carbon Cycle. Ed. by B. Bolin et al. LC 78-16261. (SCOPE Ser. (Scientific Committee on Problems of the Environment): Report 13). 491p. 1979. pap. 85.00 o.p. (ISBN 0-471-99710-2, Pub. by Wiley-Interscience). Wiley.

Global Chemical Cycles & Their Alterations by Man, PCSR 2. Ed. by Werner Stumm. (Physical & Chemical Sci. Rsch. Rept. Ser.: No. 2). (Illus.). 347p. 1977. 40.00x o.p. (ISBN 0-89573-084-7). VCH Pubs.

Global Communication & Understanding. National Association for Women Deans, Administrators, & Counselors. 1978. pap. 6.00 o.p. (ISBN 0-686-12124-4). Natl Assn Women.

Global Connection: Local Action for World Justice. Dennis E. Shoemaker. (Orig.). 1977. pap. 3.95 o.p. (ISBN 0-377-00069-8). Friendship Pr.

Global Demands on Language & the Mission of the Language Academies. Pref. by John Lihani. 219p. (Orig.). 1988. pap. 12.90 o.p. KY Foreign Language Conference.

Global Differentiable Dynamics, Proceedings. Ed. by O. Hajek et al. (Lecture Notes in Mathematics.: Vol. 235). (Illus.). x, 140p. 1972. pap. 9.00 o.p. (ISBN 0-387-05674-2). Springer-Verlag.

Global Edge: How Your Company Can Win in the International Marketplace. Sondra Snowdon. 396p. 1986. 19.45 o.p. (ISBN 0-671-60122-9). S&S.

Global Environmental Monitoring. Branislav Gosovic. (United Nations & Its Agencies Ser.). 256p. 1988. lib. bdg. 62.50 o.p. (ISBN 0-415-00458-6). Routledge Chapman & Hall.

Global Implications of Space Activities, AAS9. LC 82-16289. (Illus.). 151p. 1982. 20.00 o.p. (ISBN 0-915928-68-X). AIAA.

Global Insecurity: A World Plan for Energy & Econonic Upheaval. Ed. by Daniel H. Yergin & Martin Hillenbrand. 420p. 1982. 15.95 o.p. (ISBN 0-395-30517-9). HM.

Global Issues: Activities & Resources for the High School Teacher. Kenneth A. Switzer & Paul Mulloy. LC 79-22885. (Illus.). 168p. 1979. pap. 8.95 o.p. (ISBN 0-89994-240-7). Soc Sci Ed.

Global Issues in the Intermediate Classroom, Grades 5-8. Jacquelyn Johnson & John Benegar. (Illus.). 152p. (Orig.). 1981. 9.95 o.p. (ISBN 0-89994-265-2). Soc Sci Ed.

Global Issues 1988-89. 4th, rev. ed. Ed. by Robert Jackson. LC 85-658006. (Annual Editions Ser.). (Illus.). 256p. 1988. pap. text ed. 9.95 o.p. (ISBN 0-87967-733-3). Dushkin Pub.

Global Living Here & Now. James A. Scherer. 1974. pap. 2.25 o.p. (ISBN 0-377-00003-5). Friendship Pr.

Global Models & the International Economic Order. Sam Cole. LC 77-30175. 1978. 17.50 o.p. (ISBN 0-08-022991-3); pap. 7.25 o.p. (ISBN 0-08-022025-8). Pergamon.

Global Perspectives of an International Tax Lawyer. Mitchell B. Carroll. 1978. 8.00 o.p. (ISBN 0-682-49133-0). Exposition-Phoenix.

Global Policy: Challenge of the Eighties. Ed. by Morton A. Kaplan. LC 83-61051. 281p. 1983. pap. 12.95 o.s.i/ o.s.i. (ISBN 0-88702-000-3, Pub. by Wash Inst Pr). Paragon Hse.

Global Politics. James L. Ray. LC 78-69552. (Illus.). 1979. text ed. 19.50 o.p. (ISBN 0-395-26542-8). HM.

Global Politics. 2nd ed. James L. Ray. LC 82-81582. 416p. 1983. pap. 20.95 o.p. (ISBN 0-395-32781-4). HM.

Global Possible: Resources Development & the New Century. Ed. by Robert Repetto et al. LC 85-8209. 538p. (Orig.). 1985. pap. text ed. 13.95 o.p. (ISBN 0-300-03534-9). Yale U Pr.

Global Predicament: Ecological Perspectives on World Order. Ed. by David W. Orr & Marvin S. Soroos. LC 78-10207. xvi, 398p. 1979. 27.50x o.p. (ISBN 0-8078-1346-X); pap. 10.95x o.p. (ISBN 0-8078-1349-4). U of NC Pr.

Global Review of Human Settlements & Statistical Annex, 2 vols. Compiled by United Nations Statistical Office Staff. 1976. 250.00 o.p. (ISBN 0-08-021045-7). Pergamon.

Global Risk Assessments: Issues, Concepts & Applications, Bk. 14. Ed. by Jerry Rogers. (Illus.). 250p. 1987. pap. 32.50 o.p. (ISBN 0-317-61734-6). Global Risk.

Global Stability. Gerald R. Ford. 25p. 1982. limited signed ed. 50.00 o.s.i. (ISBN 0-935716-14-9). Lord John.

Global Studies: Africa. 2nd ed. Jo Sullivan. LC 86-73041. (Illus.). 256p. 1987. pap. text ed. 9.95 o.p. (ISBN 0-87967-690-6). Dushkin Pub.

Global Studies: Africa, 1984. Jane Martin. (Illus.). 256p. pap. 8.95 o.p. (ISBN 0-87967-493-8). Dushkin Pub.

Global Studies: China. 2nd ed. William Joseph. LC 84-72320. (Illus.). 224p. 1987. pap. text ed. 9.95 o.p. (ISBN 0-87967-691-4). Dushkin Pub.

Global Studies: China, 1984. Suzanne Ogden. (Illus.). 176p. 1984. pap. 8.95 o.p. (ISBN 0-87967-494-6). Dushkin Pub.

Global Studies: Latin America. 2nd ed. Paul Goodwin. LC 85-72086. 256p. 1986. pap. 8.95 o.p. (ISBN 0-87967-619-1). Dushkin Pub.

Global Systems Dynamics. Ed. by E. O. Attinger. 353p. 1970. 46.00 o.p. (ISBN 0-471-03640-4). Halsted Pr.

Global Textile Industry. B. Toyne et al. (World Industry Studies: No. 2). 248p. 1984. text ed. 59.95 o.p. (ISBN 0-04-338110-3). Unwin Hyman.

Global Theory of Dynamical Systems: Proceedings. Ed. by Z. Nitecki & C. Robinson. (Lecture Notes in Mathematics Ser.: Vol. 819). 499p. 1980. pap. 34.00 o.p. (ISBN 0-387-10236-1). Springer-Verlag.

Global Trends in Migration: Theory & Research in International Population Movements. Ed. by Mary M. Kritz et al. LC 80-68399. 532p. 1981. 14.95 o.p. (ISBN 0-913256-54-4); pap. text ed. 9.95 o.p. (ISBN 0-934733-08-2). Ctr Migration.

Global Universal Encyclopedia, 21 vols. rev. ed. LC 85-27032. (Illus.). 1987. text ed. write for info. o.p. (ISBN 0-7172-2022-2). Grolier Inc.

Globalism: America's Demise. William Bowen, Jr. LC 84-80408. 222p. (Orig.). 1984. 8.95 o.p.; pap. 6.95 o.p. (ISBN 0-910311-24-2). Huntington Hse Inc.

Globe Illustrated Shakespeare. William Shakespeare. (Illus.). 1983. 29.95 o.p. (ISBN 0-517-40776-0). Crown.

Globe Restored: A Study of the Elizabethan Theatre. rev. ed. C. Walter Hodges. (Illus.). 256p. 1973. pap. 2.95 o.p. (ISBN 0-393-00691-3, Norton Lib). Norton.

Globe Restored: A Study of the Elizabethan Theatre. Cyril W. Hodges. Repr. of 1953 ed. 39.00 o.p. (ISBN 0-403-07241-7). Somerset Pub.

Gloire des Rois see Oeuvre Poetique.

Gloomy Louie. Phyllis Green. Ed. by Ann Fay. LC 79-28533. (Illus.). (gr. 3-6). 1980. PLB 7.50 o.p. (ISBN 0-8075-2962-1). A Whitman.

Gloria Chipmunk, Star! Joan L. Nixon. LC 79-23431. (Illus.). 48p. (gr. 1-4). 1980. 6.95 o.p. (ISBN 0-395-29103-8, Clarion). HM.

Glorious Failure: Black Congressman Robert Brown Elliott & the Reconstruction in South Carolina. Peggy Lamson. (Illus.). 336p. 1974. pap. 3.95x o.p. (ISBN 0-393-00733-2, Norton Lib). Norton.

Glorious Hour of Lieutenant Monroe. James Hanser. LC 75-13573. (Illus.). 208p. (gr. 4-6). 1976. 7.95 o.p. (ISBN 0-689-30495-1, Atheneum). Macmillan.

Glorious Life & Actions of St. Whigg see Perfidious P.

Glorious Morning. Julia Ellis. LC 82-72068. 1982. 14.95 o.p. (ISBN 0-87795-431-3, Arbor Hse). Morrow.

Glorious Noodle: A Culinary Tour Around the World. Linda Merinoff. 416p. 1986. 16.45 o.s.i. (ISBN 0-671-52355-4, Poseidon). PB.

Glorious Presence. Joy Fuller. LC 81-65753. 168p. (Orig.). 1981. pap. 2.95 o.p. (ISBN 0-87516-449-8). DeVorss.

Glorious Revolution in America: Documents on the Colonial Crisis of 1689. Ed. by Michael G. Hall et al. 1972. pap. text ed. 4.95x o.p. (ISBN 0-393-09398-0). Norton.

Glorious Technicolor: The Movies' Magic Rainbow. Fred E. Basten. LC 78-67469. (Illus.). 1980. 30.00 o.s.i. (ISBN 0-498-02317-6). A S Barnes.

Glorious Third. Cynthia P. Seton. 208p. 1980. pap. 3.95 o.p. (ISBN 0-393-00987-4). Norton.

Glorious Third. Cynthia P. Seton. 1979. 8.95 o.p. (ISBN 0-393-08845-6). Norton.

Glory. Vladimir Nabokov. (McGraw-Hill Paperback Ser.). 228p. 1980. pap. text ed. 4.95 o.p. (ISBN 0-07-045727-1). McGraw.

Glory. Vladimir Nabokov. 1971. pap. text ed. 6.95 o.p. (ISBN 0-07-045733-6). McGraw.

Glory & Shame of England, 2 vols. C. Edwards Lester. (Development of Industrial Society Ser.). 620p. 1971. Repr. of 1866 ed. 42.50x set o.p. (ISBN 0-7165-1789-2, BBA 03549, Pub. by Irish Academic Pr). Biblio Dist.

Glory Beyond All Comparison. Betty S. Cloyd. LC 81-52216. 1981. pap. 4.50x o.p. (ISBN 0-8358-0423-2). Upper Room.

Glory Days: Alex Wyllie & the Canterbury Ranfurly Shield Team 1982-85. Kevin McMenamin. 238p. 1986. 29.95 o.p. (ISBN 0-7233-0795-4, Pub. by Whitcoulls NZ). Intl Spec Bk.

Glory Days with the Dodgers: And Other Days with Others. John Roseboro & Bill Libby. LC 77-23697. 1978. 9.95 o.p. (ISBN 0-689-10864-8, Atheneum). Macmillan.

Glory for Fanchon: Five Years in Fascinating Mexico. Camille Mirepoix Stegmuller. (Illus.). 160p. 1980. 7.50 o.p. (ISBN 0-682-49587-5). Exposition-Phoenix.

Glory Game. Janet Dailey. 1985. 16.45 o.s.i. (ISBN 0-671-55544-8). S&S.

Glory in the Flower. Norma Johnston. LC 73-84830. 208p. (gr. 5-9). 1974. 6.95 o.p. (ISBN 0-689-30140-5, Atheneum). Macmillan.

Glory in the Flower. John H. Wilson, Jr. 1979. 10.00 o.p. (ISBN 0-682-49316-3, Banner). Exposition-Phoenix.

Glory of God's Will. Elisabeth Elliot. 1982. pap. 1.50 o.p. (ISBN 0-89107-271-3). Good News.

Glory of Israel: The Theology & Provenience of the Isaiah Targum. Bruce D. Chilton. (JSOT Supplement Ser.: No. 23). ix, 178p. pap. text ed. 18.50 o.s.i. (Pub. by JSOT Pr England). Eisenbrauns.

Glory of the Journey. Isobel I. Young. LC 85-71207. (Illus.). 80p. (Orig.). 1985. pap. 7.95 o.p. (ISBN 0-89227-109-4). Commonwealth Pr.

Glory Road: Josh White. Julia Siegel. LC 82-47939. 219p. (YA) (gr. 7 up). 1982. 10.95 o.p. (ISBN 0-15-231056-8, HJ). HarBraceJ.

Glory to God: A Candlelight Service for Christmas. Steven Bomely. 1983. pap. 2.25 o.p. (ISBN 0-89536-625-8, 0733). CSS of Ohio.

Glory Within You: Modern Man & the Spirit. Duncan E. Littlefair. LC 72-8972. 224p. 1973. 5.95 o.s.i. (ISBN 0-664-20960-2, Westminster). Westminster John Knox.

Glossar III, Einsprachig Deutsch see Deutsch X 3.

Glossary for International Communications, Vol. III. Media Institute Staff & Leonard R. Sussman. LC 83-62432. (Communications in a Changing World Ser.). 112p. 1983. pap. 10.00 o.p. (ISBN 0-937790-18-4). Media Inst.

Glossary I, German-English see Deutsch X 3.

Glossary II, German-English see Deutsch X 3.

Glossary of Chinese Archaeology. Zhang Xinglian. Ed. by Zhao Shuhan. 199p. (Orig., Chinese & Eng.). 1983. 4.95 o.p. (ISBN 0-8351-1210-1); pap. 3.95 o.p. (ISBN 0-8351-1082-6). China Bks.

Glossary of Environmental Terms (Terrestrial) U. S. Army, Natick Labs. Staff. LC 73-2851. 158p. 1973. Repr. of 1968 ed. 40.00x o.p. (ISBN 0-8103-3277-9). Gale.

Glossary of Geology. 2nd ed. Ed. by Robert L. Bates & Julia A. Jackson. LC 79-57360. 749p. 1980. 60.00 o.p. (ISBN 0-913312-15-0). Am Geol.

Glossary of Harpsichord Terms: English-Deutch, Deutch-English. S. Costa. 116p. 1988. pap. 29.35 o.p. (ISBN 3-920-11277-6). Bold Strummer Ltd.

Glossary of Liturgical & Ecclesiastical Terms. Frederick G. Lee. LC 76-174069. (Tower Bks.). (Illus.). xl, 492p. 1972. Repr. of 1877 ed. 44.00x o.p. (ISBN 0-8103-3949-8). Gale.

Glossary of Marine Technology Terms. Institute of Marine Engineers Staff. 178p. 1980. pap. 17.50x o.p. (ISBN 0-434-90840-1). Sheridan.

Glossary of Mining Geology. G. Amstutz. 196p. (Eng., Span., Fr. & Ger.). 1971. 36.50 o.p. (ISBN 3-432-01667-0, M-7428, Pub. by F. Enke). French & Eur.

Glossary of Neurotraumatology. Ed. by E. S. Gurdjian et al. LC 78-15626. (Acta Neurochirurgica: Supplementum 25). 63p. (Eng., Ger., Fr. & Span.). 1979. pap. 11.70 o.p. (ISBN 0-387-81481-7). Springer-Verlag.

Glossary of Senate Terms: A Guide for TV. 19p. (Orig.). 1986. pap. 1.00 o.p. (S/N 052-070-06124-3). USGPO.

Glossary of Terms & Phrases. Henry P. Smith. LC 79-175746. x, 534p. 1972. Repr. of 1889 ed. 51.00x o.p. (ISBN 0-8103-3816-5). Gale.

Glossary of Terms Used in Pasture & Range Survey Research, Ecology, Management. 153p. 1976. pap. 13.25 o.p. (ISBN 0-685-68955-7, F925, FAO). UNIPUB.

Gloucester Clipper Fishing Schooners. Erik A. Ronnberg, Jr. Ed. by Ernest J. Gentle. (Moonraker Publications Ser.). (Illus.). 96p. 1985. pap. 10.95 o.p. (ISBN 0-8168-0013-8, 20013, TAB-Aero). TAB Bks.

Gloves: Their Annals & Associations. S. William Beck. LC 75-75801. 284p. 1969. Repr. of 1883 ed. 27.00 o.p. (ISBN 0-8103-3825-4). Gale.

Glow. Brooks Stanwood. 1979. text ed. 9.95 o.p. (ISBN 0-07-060879-2). McGraw.

Glow in the Dark. Rick Bundschuh. LC 86-31350. (Illus.). 148p. (Orig.). 1985. pap. 4.95 o.s.i. (ISBN 0-8307-1091-4, S182323). Regal.

Glowing in the Dark. Arline Strong. LC 75-8874. (Illus.). 64p. (ps-4). 1975. 4.95 o.p. (ISBN 0-689-30485-4, Atheneum). Macmillan.

Glutamine: Metabolism, Enzymology & Regulation. Ed. by Jaime Mora & Rafael Palacios. 1980. 29.95 o.p. (ISBN 0-12-506040-8). Acad Pr.

Glutathione: A Symposium. Ed. by Sidney P. Colowick et al. 1954. 77.00 o.p. (ISBN 0-12-181876-4). Acad Pr.

Glycoconjugates: Glyconproteins, Glycolipides & Proteoglycans. Ed. by Martin Horowitz. LC 77-4086. 392p. 1982. 65.00 ea. o.p. Vol. III: Pt. A: 392 pgs (ISBN 0-12-356103-5). Vol. IV: Pt. B: 82-45134: 384 pgs (ISBN 0-12-356104-3). Acad Pr.

Glycoconjugates: Mammalian Glycoproteins & Glycolipids, Vol. 1. Ed. by Martin Horowitz & Ward Pigman. LC 76-27445. 1977. 85.00 o.p. (ISBN 0-12-356101-9). Acad Pr.

Glycogen & Its Related Enzymes of Metabolism in the Central Nervous System. M. Z. Ibrahim. (Advances in Anatomy, Embryology & Cell Biology: Vol. 52, Pt. 1). (Illus.). 90p. 1975. pap. 33.10 o.p. (ISBN 0-387-07454-6). Springer-Verlag.

Glycolysis & Respiration of Tumors. Alan C. Aisenberg. 1960. 57.50 o.p. (ISBN 0-12-046250-8). Acad Pr.

GM A-Body, 1982-85. Chilton Automotives Editorial Staff. LC 84-45469. 224p. (Orig.). 1985. pap. 13.95 o.p. (ISBN 0-8019-7586-7). Chilton.

GM X-Bodies. (Popular Mechanics-Motor Car Care Guide Ser.). (Illus.). 176p. pap. 6.95 o.p. (ISBN 0-87851-929-7). Hearst Bks.

Gnomes. Barbara Hayes. LC 86-17687. (Enchanted World of...Ser.). (Illus.). (ps-3). Date not set. PLB 8.95 o.p. (ISBN 0-86592-317-5). Rourke Corp.

Gnomes--One Hundred, Dragons--Zero. Jean Blashfield & James M. Ward. LC 86-91726. (Catacombs Gamebooks: No. 2). 160p. (Orig.). (gr. 4 up). 1987. pap. 7.95 o.p. (ISBN 0-88038-503-0). TSR Inc.

Gnostic Paul. Elaine H. Pagels. LC 74-26350. 192p. 1975. 10.95 o.p. (ISBN 0-8006-0403-2, Fortress). Augsburg Fortress.

GNP: An Overview of Source Data & Estimating Methods. Carol S. Carson. (Methodology Papers: United States National Income & Product Accounts: No. BEA-MP-4). 34p. 1987. pap. 2.00 o.p. (ISBN 0-318-23826-8, 003-010-00179-8). USGPO.

Go Ask Alice. LC 74-159446. 159p. (gr. 3 up). 1971. 11.95 o.s.i. (ISBN 0-13-357111-4). P-H.

Go Away, Warts! Norma Simon. Ed. by Kathleen Tucker. LC 79-28534. (Albert Whitman Concept Bks.: Level 2). (Illus.). (gr. 3-6). 1980. PLB 10.25 o.p. (ISBN 0-8075-2970-2). A. Whitman.

Go Fly a Sailplane. Linda Morrow & Ray Morrow. LC 80-65995. (Illus.). 128p. 1981. 10.95 o.p. (ISBN 0-689-11080-4, Atheneum). Macmillan.

Go for Broke. Arnold Palmer & Barry Furlong. LC 72-90399. 1973. 7.95 o.p. (ISBN 0-671-21478-0). S&S.

Go for It! Gayle Olinekova. 144p. 1982. pap. 9.50 o.p. (ISBN 0-671-45692-X, Fireside). S&S.

Go for It: How to Win at Love, Work & Play. Irene C. Kassorla. 320p. 1985. pap. 3.95 o.p. (ISBN 0-440-12752-1). Dell.

Go Make Disciples. Rolf A. Syrdal. LC 77-84077. 1979. pap. 4.50 o.p. (ISBN 0-8066-1603-2, 10-2555, Augsburg). Augsburg Fortress.

Go Out in Joy. Nina Herrmann. LC 76-44972. 1977. 7.95 o.p. (ISBN 0-8042-2073-5, John Knox). Westminster John Knox.

Go, Phillips, Go! Amelia Walden. LC 73-15959. 208p. (gr. 6 up). 1974. 6.50 o.s.i. (ISBN 0-664-32541-6, Westminster). Westminster John Knox.

Go Slow Now: Faulkner & the Race Question. Charles D. Peavy. LC 72-185291. 1971. 6.50 o.p. (ISBN 0-87114-056-X). U of Oreg Bks.

Go Tell It. Sherwood Wirt. 63p. 1979. pap. 1.95 o.p. (ISBN 0-8341-0580-2). Beacon Hill.

Go to the Widowmaker. James Jones. 1979. pap. 2.75 o.p. (ISBN 0-440-12942-7). Dell.

Go To Your Room! Bil Keane. 128p. 1982. pap. 1.95 o.p. (ISBN 0-449-14469-0, GM). Fawcett.

Go up the Road. Evelyn S. Lampman. LC 79-190556. (Illus.). (gr. 5-9). 1972. 5.50 o.p. (ISBN 0-689-30307-6, Athenum). Macmillan.

Go with Haste into the Mountains. Cornelia M. Flaherty. 230p. (Orig.). 1984. 9.95 o.s.i. (ISBN 0-934318-42-5); pap. write for info. o.s.i. Falcon Pr MT.

Go with the Gospel. David W. Preus. LC 76-27075. 1977. pap. 3.95 o.p. (ISBN 0-8066-1560-5, 10-2557, Augsburg). Augsburg Fortress.

Go with the Poem. Lilian Moore. (gr. 4 up). 1979. text ed. 10.95 o.p. (ISBN 0-07-042880-8). McGraw.

Goa. (Illus.). 120p. 1983. text ed. 50.00x o.p. (ISBN 0-7069-2385-5, Pub. by Vikas India). Advent NY.

Goal of Economic Growth. rev. ed. Ed. by Edmund S. Phelps. LC 69-13019. (Problems of the Modern Economy Ser). 1969. pap. 4.95x o.p. (ISBN 0-393-09838-9, NortonC). Norton.

Goalguide: A Minicourse in Writing Goals & Behavioral Objectives for Special Education. Herbert R. Padzensky & Jane Gibson. 1975. instructors manual, (free with participant's manual & wkbk.) 1.50 o.p. (ISBN 0-8224-3487-3). D S Lake Pubs.

Goals, Aims, Objectives: Duquesne University: a Case Study. Sigmund Nosow & Frederick R. Clark. LC 76-41370. (Orig.). 1976. pap. text ed. 6.00x o.p. (ISBN 0-391-00669-X). Humanities.

Goals for Americans. President's Commission on National Goals. LC 60-53566. 3.50 o.p. (ISBN 0-936904-08-9); pap. 1.00 o.p. (ISBN 0-936904-09-7). Am Assembly.

Goals in Male Reproductive Research: Proceedings of Conference on Future Goals in Reproductive Medicine & Surgery, 20 September, 1979, Bethesda, Md. Ed. by Saul Boyarsky & Kenneth Polakoski. 144p. 1981. 42.00 o.p. (ISBN 0-08-025910-3). Pergamon.

Goannas & Goblins: Whimsey & Satire for Older Children. Ian D. Simmonds. LC 84-91291. (Illus.). 40p. 1985. 5.95 o.p. (ISBN 0-533-06387-6). Vantage.

Goat Production & Research in the Tropics. Ed. by J. W. Copland. (Proceedings Ser.: No. 7). 118p. (Orig.). 1985. pap. text ed. 18.00 o.p. (ISBN 0-949511-10-2). Agribookstore.

Goats. Wilfrid S. Bronson. LC 59-6029. (Illus.). (gr. 1-5). 1959. 5.50 o.p. (ISBN 0-15-231109-2, HJ). HarBraceJ.

Goats of Agadez. Victor Englebert. LC 72-76363. (Illus.). 48p. (gr. k-4). 1973. 5.50 o.p. (ISBN 0-15-231118-1, HJ). HarBraceJ.

Gobbledygook. Steven Kroll. (Snuggle & Read Story Bks.). 32p. (ps-3). 1985. pap. 2.50 o.p. (ISBN 0-380-89769-5, Camelot). Avon.

Gobierno De Puerto Rico. 2nd rev. ed. Carmen R. De Santiago. pap. 14.00 o.p. (ISBN 0-8477-2226-0). U of PR Pr.

Goblin Aeroplane: And Other Tales. Enid Blyton. (Read for Fun Ser.). (Illus.). 64p. (gr. k-3). 1987. 6.95 o.p. (ISBN 0-09-167190-6, Pub. by Century Hutchinson). David & Charles.

Goblins of Labyrinth. Brian Froud & Terry Jones. (Illus.). 144p. 1986. 25.00 o.p. (ISBN 0-03-008499-7, Owl Bks); pap. 16.95 o.p. (ISBN 0-03-007318-9). H Holt & Co.

God. Robert Hicks & Richard Bewes. (Understanding Bible Truth Ser.). (Orig.). 1981. pap. 0.95 o.p. (ISBN 0-89840-024-4). Heres Life.

God. Heinrich Ott. LC 73-5350. 128p. 1974. pap. 5.95 o.p. (ISBN 0-8042-0590-6, John Knox). Westminster John Knox.

God & Abortion. Vivian De Danois. (Science of Man Library Bk). 1979. 97.75 o.p. (ISBN 0-89266-160-7). Am Classical Coll Pr.

God & Country. Charles Schoenfeld. 128p. 1955. (ISBN 0-8022-1508-4). Philos Lib.

God & Human Suffering: An Excercise in the Theology of the Cross. Douglas J. Hall. LC 86-7964. 224p. 1986. text ed. 16.95 o.p. (ISBN 0-8066-2223-7, 10-2640, Augsburg). Augsburg Fortress.

God & Man in Modern Spirituality. Finbarr Connolly. 276p. Date not set. pap. 9.95 o.p. (ISBN 0-87061-108-9). Chr Classics.

God & Marriage. Geoffrey W. Bromiley. 96p. (Orig.). 1980. pap. 4.95 o.p. (ISBN 0-8028-1851-X). Eerdmans.

God & Production in a Guatemalan Town. Sheldon Annis. (Illus.). 213p. 1987. pap. 27.50x o.p. (ISBN 0-292-72736-4). U of Tex Pr.

God & Space Time. Alfred P. Stiernotte. 1954. (ISBN 0-8022-1647-1). Philos Lib.

God & the Grotesque. Carl Skrade. LC 74-10972. 1974. 7.50 o.s.i. (ISBN 0-664-20710-3, Westminster). Westminster John Knox.

God & the Interior Life. John Sullivan. 1962. 3.50 o.p. (ISBN 0-8198-0047-3); pap. 2.50 o.p. (ISBN 0-8198-0048-1). Dghtrs St Paul.

God & the New Haven Railway. George D. O'Brien. LC 86-47554. 144p. 1986. 14.95 o.p. (ISBN 0-8070-1010-3). Beacon Pr.

God & the New Physics. Paul Davies. 320p. 1983. 17.45 o.s.i. (ISBN 0-671-47688-2). S&S.

God & the Universe. Helger C. Langmack. 1953. (ISBN 0-8022-0920-3). Philos Lib.

God & Vitamins. Marjorie Holmes. 368p. 1982. pap. 3.95 o.p. (ISBN 0-380-56994-9, 68536-1). Avon.

God & You Unlimited. Nola Stevens. (Illus.). 144p. 1980. 7.00 o.p. (ISBN 0-682-49642-1). Exposition-Phoenix.

God at Work. James Parkes. (ISBN 0-8022-1265-4). Philos Lib.

God Believes in Me, Director Guide. William V. Coleman & Patricia R. McLemore. (Illus.). 24p. (Orig.). (gr. 2-6). 1975. pap. 1.25 o.p. (ISBN 0-87793-082-1); simplified family ed. gr. 2-3 0.95 o.p. (ISBN 0-87793-080-5). Ave Maria.

God Between. Charles E. Bradford. Ed. by Richard W. Coffen. 96p. 1984. pap. 5.95 o.p. (ISBN 0-8280-0243-6). Review & Herald.

God Bless Grandparents. Catharine Brandt. LC 78-52189. (Illus.). 1978. pap. 5.50 o.p. (ISBN 0-8066-1658-X, 10-2559, Augsburg). Augsburg Fortress.

God Calls. Mary L. Boney. (Orig.). (gr. 7-9). 1964. pap. 3.45 o.p. (ISBN 0-8042-9230-2, John Knox). Westminster John Knox.

God Calls Us Together. Victor Frohne & Mrs. Victor Frohne. 1976. pap. 1.15 o.p. (ISBN 0-8042-1243-0, John Knox); tchrs' ed 2.35 o.p. (ISBN 0-8042-1244-9); resource kit 6.95 o.p. (ISBN 0-685-73037-9). Westminster John Knox.

God Cares for Me. Diane Stortz. (Wipe-Clean Bks.). (Illus.). 12p. (ps). 1985. pap. 1.39 o.p. (ISBN 0-87239-951-6, 3511). Standard Pub.

God Chaser. Pat E. Taylor. (Illus.). 300p. (Orig.). 1986. write for info. o.p. (ISBN 0-941720-32-2); pap. 7.95 o.p. (ISBN 0-941720-31-4). Slough Pr TX.

God, Country & Family Stuff. Clara M. Wolfe. LC 84-91296. 85p. 1985. 7.95 o.p. (ISBN 0-533-06382-5). Vantage.

God Created Me Too! Dot Cachiaras. (Happy Day Bks.). (Illus.). 32p. (gr. k-2). 1987. 1.59 o.p. (ISBN 0-87403-274-1, 3774). Standard Pub.

God First: What It Means to Love God Above All Things. Ken Wilson. (Living As a Christian Ser.). 85p. 1980. pap. 3.50 o.p. (ISBN 0-89283-089-1). Servant.

God Game. Andrew Greeley. 320p. 1987. write for info. o.p. (Dist. by St Martin's Pr & Warner Pub Servs). Tor Bks.

God, Goods & the Common Good: Eleven Perspectives on Economic Justice in Dialog with the Roman Catholic Bishops' Pastoral Letter. Ed. by Charles P. Lutz. LC 87-70240. 176p. (Orig.). 1987. pap. 9.95 o.p. (ISBN 0-8066-2286-5, 10-2563, Augsburg). Augsburg Fortress.

God Has a Story Too: Biblical Sermons in Context. James A. Sanders. LC 77-15244. 160p. 1979. pap. 3.95 o.p. (ISBN 0-8006-1353-8, 1-1353, Fortress). Augsburg Fortress.

God Helps David. Marjorie Palmer. (My Bible Story Reader Ser.: Vol. I). (Illus.). (gr. 2 up). 1983. pap. 1.95 o.p. (ISBN 0-8024-0191-0). Moody.

God Holds Your Tomorrows. Roger C. Palms. LC 76-3855. 104p. (Orig.). 1976. pap. 3.50 o.p. (ISBN 0-8066-1527-3, 10-2565, Augsburg). Augsburg Fortress.

God-Illuminated Cook: The Practice of the Presence of God. Brother Lawrence. (East Ridge Press Ser.). (Illus.). 142p. 1980. pap. 4.50 o.p. (ISBN 0-89345-217-3). Garber Comm.

God in the High Country. Otis D. Richardson. 1980. 10.00 o.p. (ISBN 0-682-49644-8). Exposition-Phoenix.

God in the Mountain. Colin Thubron. 1978. 9.95 o.p. (ISBN 0-393-08785-9). Norton.

God in the Present Tense. D. Shelby Corlett. 156p. 1974. 1.95 o.p. (ISBN 0-8341-0248-X). Beacon Hill.

God: Incidences or Divine Providence. Mary Light. 1975. pap. 1.00 o.p. (ISBN 0-910924-69-4). Macalester.

God Is. John Bisagno. 1981. 5.50 o.p. (ISBN 0-88207-345-1). Victor Bks.

God Is a Lousy Strategist. John P. Kemp. LC 84-90212. 85p. 1985. 7.95 o.p. (ISBN 0-533-06267-5). Vantage.

God Is Alive & Well. 2nd rev. ed. Oneal Carman. 1976. 4.75 o.p. (ISBN 0-682-48521-7). Exposition-Phoenix.

God Is at Work. Henrietta T. Wilkinson. (Illus., Orig.). (gr. 5-7). 1965. pap. 3.95 o.p. (ISBN 0-8042-9410-0, John Knox). Westminster John Knox.

God Is Blue & Other Stories. Gerry Pratt. LC 78-818. 150p. 1978. 8.50 o.p. (ISBN 0-917304-38-1); pap. 7.50 o.p. (ISBN 0-917304-56-X). Timber.

God Is Everywhere: Fifteen Stories to Help Children Know God. Compiled by Theresa Hayes. (Illus.). 80p. (gr. 3-5). 1986. 7.95 o.p. (ISBN 0-87403-097-8, 3617). Standard Pub.

God Is Great, God Is Good: Devotions for Families. Rolf Aaseng. LC 75-176470. (Orig.). 1972. 4.95 o.p. (ISBN 0-8066-1200-2, 10-2567, Augsburg). AugsburG Fortress.

God Is in Control. Mathilde W. Duke. 1979. 4.00 o.p. (ISBN 0-682-49261-2). Exposition-Phoenix.

God Is in the Night. Connie Abrams. (Happy Day Bks.). (Illus.). 24p. (ps-2). 1984. 1.59 o.p. (ISBN 0-87239-733-5, 3703). Standard Pub.

God Is My Feurer. Martin Niemoeller. (ISBN 0-8022-1218-2). Philos Lib.

God Is My Fuehrer. Gordon C. Bennett. (Orig.). 1970. pap. 1.50 o.p. (ISBN 0-377-80611-0). Friendship Pr.

God Is Not a Gentleman & I Am That One. Da Free John. LC 83-73178. 1983. 12.95 o.s.i. (ISBN 0-913922-85-4). Dawn Horse Pr.

God Is the Answer. Dana Gattin. 1984. pap. 6.95 o.p. (ISBN 0-317-03625-4). Unity School.

God Kind of Marriage. Karrel Hughes. 61p. (Orig.). 1984. pap. 2.95 o.p. (ISBN 0-89274-328-X). Harrison Hse.

God Knows. Joseph Heller. LC 84-47747. 353p. 1984. 19.45 o.p. (ISBN 0-394-52919-7). Knopf.

God Listens & Knows. Edith Eckblad. LC 80-67808. 32p. 1980. pap. 3.50 o.p. (ISBN 0-8066-1871-X, 10-2578, Augsburg). Augsburg Fortress.

God Loves All People. Grace M. Overholser & Madeline H. Beck. (Illus.). 96p. (gr. 1-3). 1975. pap. 3.95 o.p. (ISBN 0-8042-9428-3, John Knox); tchrs' ed 3.95 o.p. (ISBN 0-8042-9429-1); resource kit 10.00 o.p. (ISBN 0-8042-9430-5). Westminster John Knox.

God Loves His People see Bible Pop-O-Rama Books.

God Loves You. Catherine Marshall. (gr. 2-4). 1973. pap. 0.95 o.p. (ISBN 0-380-01221-9, 14712). Avon.

God Made Alaska for the Indians. Ishmael Reed. LC 81-48415. 200p. 1982. lib. bdg. 31.00 o.p. (ISBN 0-8240-9384-4). Garland Pub.

God Made Animals. (Baby's First Cloth Bks.). 6p. (ps). 1.98 o.p. (ISBN 0-8307-0814-6, 5608003). Regal.

God Made Everything. Debra Stuckey. (God's Creatures Ser.). (Illus.). (ps-1). 4.95 o.p. (ISBN 0-570-04109-0, 56-1484). Concordia.

God Made Families. Debra K. Stuckey. (God's Creatures Ser.). (Illus.). 24p. (ps-1). 1986. 4.95 o.p. (ISBN 0-570-04118-X). Concordia.

God Made Farm Animals. Sue T. Hayes. (Happy Day Bks.). (Illus.). 24p. (ps-2). 1984. 1.59 o.p. (ISBN 0-87239-735-1, 3705). Standard Pub.

God Made It All! Mary T. Blanton. LC 83-7345. (Illus.). 32p. (ps-k). 1983. PLB 4.95 o.p. (ISBN 0-89693-209-5). Dandelion Hse.

God Made Known. Mervyn A. Warren. Ed. by Gerald Wheeler. LC 83-17677. (Illus.). 94p. (Orig.). 1983. pap. 5.95 o.p. (ISBN 0-8280-0230-4). Review & Herald.

God Made Me. (Baby's First Cloth Bks.). 6p. (ps). 1981. 1.98 o.p. (ISBN 0-8307-0816-2, 5608021). Regal.

God Made Me. Debra Stuckey. (God's Creatures Ser.). (Illus.). (ps-1). 1985. 4.95 o.p. (ISBN 0-570-04108-2, 56-1483). Concordia.

God Made Me: I'm Glad. Dorothy L. Dysard. (CPA Vacation Venture Ser). (gr. k-1). 1975. pap. 1.00 student bk. o.s.i. (ISBN 0-664-24970-1, Westminster); pap. 2.35 leader's guide o.s.i. (ISBN 0-664-24971-X, Westminster); kindergarten resource packet 6.95, o.s.i. (ISBN 0-664-29795-1). Westminster John Knox.

God Made Prayer. Debra K. Stuckey. (God Made...Ser.). (Illus.). 24p. (ps-1). 1985. 1.58 o.p. (ISBN 0-570-04117-1, 56-1528). Concordia.

God Made the Sea, the Sand & Me. Elizabeth E. Watson. (Illus.). (gr. k-3). 1979. 5.95 o.p. (ISBN 0-8054-4254-5, 4242-54). Broadman.

God Made Us a Good World. Gertrude A. Priester. (Through-The-Week Ser). 1970. pap. 1.75 pupil's bk o.s.i. (ISBN 0-664-24873-X, Westminster); tchrs' ed. 3.45 o.s.i. (ISBN 0-664-24872-1, Westminster). Westminster John Knox.

God Makers. Frank Herbert. 1983. pap. 2.95 o.s.i. (ISBN 0-425-06388-7, Medallion). Berkley Pub.

God Makes Old Age Young. Erling Ruud. Tr. by J. Melvin Moe from Norwegian. LC 75-22720. 176p. 1976. pap. 6.50 o.p. (ISBN 0-8066-1506-0, 10-2585, Augsburg). Augsburg Fortress.

God Meets Man: A Theology of the Sabbath & the Second Advent. Sakae Kubo. LC 78-6616. (Anvil Ser.). 1978. pap. 8.95 o.p. (ISBN 0-8127-0171-2). Review & Herald.

God Never Said We'd Be Leading at the Half. Dean Spencer & Dean Nelson. 116p. (Orig.). 1980. pap. 2.95 o.p. (ISBN 0-8341-0766-X). Beacon Hill.

God of Forgiveness & Healing in the Theology of Karl Rahner. J. Norman King. LC 81-40932. 100p. (Orig.). 1982. lib. bdg. 25.25 o.p. (ISBN 0-8191-2237-8); pap. text ed. 8.75 o.p. (ISBN 0-8191-2238-6). U Pr of Amer.

God of Glory. Ronald F. Hogan. 1984. pap. 5.95 o.p. (ISBN 0-87213-333-8). Loizeaux.

God of Mirrors. Robert Reilly. Ed. by Peter Davison. LC 85-20145. 403p. 1986. 17.95 o.p. (ISBN 0-87113-029-7). Atlantic Monthly.

God of Untold Tales. Michael E. Moynahan. LC 79-64823. 1979. pap. 4.95 o.p. (ISBN 0-89390-009-5). Resource Pubns.

God on Our Minds. Patrick Henry & Thomas F. Stransky. LC 81-70593. 176p. 1982. pap. 6.95 o.p. (ISBN 0-8006-1600-6, 1-1600, Fortress). Augsburg Fortress.

God, Power, & Evil: A Process Theodicy. David R. Griffin. LC 76-21631. 1976. 17.50 o.s.i. (ISBN 0-664-20753-7, Westminster). Westminster John Knox.

God Related. Sarah Faye. 1985. 7.95 o.p. (ISBN 0-533-06726-X). Vantage.

God Save the Mark. Donald E. Westlake. 208p. 1987. pap. 3.95 o.p. (ISBN 0-445-40612-7). Mysterious Pr.

God Sends the Rain. Lane D. Endicott. 96p. 1987. 7.95 o.p. (ISBN 0-8062-2955-1). Carlton.

God, Sex & You. M. O. Vincent. 192p. 1985. pap. 4.95 o.p. (ISBN 0-916441-25-3). Barbour & Co.

God Speaks to Me. Pauline P. Meek. (Illus.). 96p. (Orig.). (gr. 3-4). 1972. pap. 2.95 o.p. (ISBN 0-8042-9494-1, John Knox); tchrs' ed. 2.95 o.p. (ISBN 0-8042-9495-X). Westminster John Knox.

God Stalk. P. C. Hodgell. LC 82-1672. 228p. 1982. 13.95 o.s.i. (ISBN 0-689-30844-2, Atheneum Childrens Bks). Macmillan.

God-Talk: An Examination of the Language & Logic of Theology. John Macquarrie. 1979. pap. 7.95 o.p. (ISBN 0-8164-2205-2). HarpR.

God-the Cornerstone of Our Life. John C. Krol. 1978. 5.50 o.p. (ISBN 0-8198-0531-9); pap. 3.95 o.p. (ISBN 0-8198-0532-7). Dghtrs St Paul.

God the Father: Theology & Patriarchy in the Teaching of Jesus, No. 4. Robert Hamerton-Kelly. Ed. by Walter Brueggemann & John R. Donahue. LC 78-54551. (Overtures to Biblical Theology Ser.). 144p. 1979. pap. 8.95 o.p. (ISBN 0-8006-1528-X, 1-1528, Fortress). Augsburg Fortress.

God: The Question & the Quest. Paul R. Sponheim. LC 85-47737. 224p. 1986. 3.95 o.p. (ISBN 0-8006-0756-2, Fortress). Augsburg Fortress.

God the Son. Donald Senior. LC 81-69109. (Illus.). 95p. 1982. pap. 5.95 o.s.i. (ISBN 0-89505-065-X). Tabor Pub.

God the Stranger: Reflections about Resurrection. Edmund A. Steimle. LC 78-14674. 80p. 1979. pap. 4.95 o.p. (ISBN 0-8006-1354-6, 1-1354, Fortress). Augsburg Fortress.

God vs We the People. John A. Sinclair. 1977. 7.50 o.p. (ISBN 0-682-48746-5). Exposition-Phoenix.

God Wants You Rich: And Other Enticing Doctrines. Florence Bulle. 223p. (Orig.). 1983. pap. 5.95 o.p. (ISBN 0-87123-264-2, 210264). Bethany Hse.

God Wants You to Be Well. Laurence H. Blackburn. 160p. 1974. pap. 3.75 o.p. (ISBN 0-8192-1189-3). Morehouse Pub.

God Was Here but He Left Early. Irwin Shaw. LC 72-87047. 1973. 7.95 o.p. (ISBN 0-87795-055-5, Arbor Hse). Morrow.

God Was Here but He Left Early. Irwin Shaw. LC 72-87047. (Priam Ser.). 1980. pap. 6.95 o.p. (ISBN 0-87795-239-6, Arbor Hse). Morrow.

God Was There but He Left Early. Irwin Shaw. 1983. pap. 6.95 o.p. (Arbor Hse). Morrow.

God: What People Have Said about Him. Ed. by Lothar Kahn. 320p. 1980. 9.95 o.p. (ISBN 0-8246-0251-X). Jonathan David.

God Who Cares: A Christian Looks at Judaism. Frederick Holmgren. LC 78-52445. (Orig.). 1979. pap. 4.95 o.p. (ISBN 0-8042-0588-4, John Knox). Westminster John Knox.

God Who Is Rich in Mercy. Ed. by P. T. O'Brien & D. G. Peterson. 1987. 21.95 o.p. (ISBN 0-8010-6711-1). Baker Bk.

God Who Responds. H. D. McDonald. 200p. (Orig.). 1986. pap. 5.95 o.p. (ISBN 0-87123-840-3, 210840). Bethany Hse.

God with Us: A Theology of Transpersonal Life. Joseph Haroutunian. LC 65-19279. 318p. 1980. pap. 7.95 o.s.i. (ISBN 0-664-24291-X, Westminster). Westminster John Knox.

God Would Have Done It If He'd Had the Money. George Fisher. (Illus.). 1983. pap. 9.95 o.p. (ISBN 0-914546-49-X). Rose Pub.

God Writes Straight with Crooked Lines. Ernest A. Fitzgerald. LC 80-65997. 144p. 1981. 7.95 o.p. (ISBN 0-689-11073-1, Atheneum). Macmillan.

Goddaughter. Adrian Reid. 1980. pap. 2.25 o.p. (ISBN 0-380-47571-5, 47571). Avon.

Godden's Guide to Mason's China & the Ironstone Wares. Geoffrey A. Godden. (Illus.). 316p. 1980. 69.50 o.s.i. (ISBN 0-902028-86-3). Antique Collect.

Goddess: The Secret Lives of Marilyn Monroe. Anthony Summers. (Large Print Bks (Special Ser.)). 723p. 1986. lib. bdg. 20.95x o.p. (ISBN 0-8161-4116-9); pap. 12.95x o.p. (ISBN 0-8161-4154-1). G K Hall.

Goddesses in Ancient India. P. K. Agrawala. 180p. 1983. text ed. 50.00x o.p. (ISBN 0-391-02960-6). Humanities.

Goddesses in Everywoman: A New Psychology of Women. Jean S. Bolen. LC 83-48990. 334p. 1984. 15.45 o.p. (ISBN 0-06-250082-1). HarpR.

Godfather. Mario Puzo. 1985. lib. bdg. 19.95 o.p. (ISBN 0-8161-3875-3, Large Print Bks). G K Hall.

Godforgotten. Gladys Schmitt. LC 77-182333. 312p. 1972. 6.95 o.p. (ISBN 0-15-136065-0). HarBraceJ.

Godly Exhortation by Occasion of the Late Judgement of God at Parris Garden see Treatise of Daunces.

Godly Kings & Early Ethics. Tertius Chandler. 1976. 12.50 o.p. (ISBN 0-682-48452-0, University). Exposition-Phoenix.

Godly Man. Gene Warr. 1978. pap. 3.95 o.p. (ISBN 2-01064-105-1, 40121). Word Bks.

Godly Woman. Irma Warr. 1978. pap. 5.95 o.p. (ISBN 2-01064-201-5, 40123). Word Bks.

Godparents, Why? Marilyn J. Bomgren. 1981. 2.50 o.p. (ISBN 0-89536-473-5, 0717). CSS of Ohio.

Godric. Frederick Buechner. LC 80-66014. 1980. 10.95 o.p. (ISBN 0-689-11086-3, Atheneum). Macmillan.

God's Abundant Supply. D. E. Thompson. (Illus., Orig.). 1984. pap. 4.95 o.p. (ISBN 0-912315-75-X). Word Aflame.

Gods & Heroes: Baroque Images of Antiquity see Exhibition Catalogues from the Fogg Art Museum.

Gods & Mortals in Classic Mythology: Dictionary. Michael Grant & John Hazel. 320p. 1985. 19.95 o.s.i. (ISBN 0-88029-036-6, Pub. by Dorset Pr). Hippocrene Bks.

Gods & Rituals: Readings in Religious Beliefs & Practices. Ed. by John Middleton. LC 75-44032. (Texas Press Sourcebooks in Anthropology Ser.: No. 6). 480p. 1976. pap. 13.95 o.p. (ISBN 0-292-72708-9). U of Tex Pr.

God's Angels Need No Wings. Claus Westermann. Tr. by David L. Scheidt. LC 78-14676. 128p. 1979. 2.95 o.p. (ISBN 0-8006-0535-7, 1-535, Fortress). Augsburg Fortress.

God's Banker: Account of the Life & Death of Roberto Calvi. Rupert Cornwell. (Illus.). 260p. 1984. 15.95 o.p. (ISBN 0-396-08295-5). Dodd.

God's Best Secrets. Andrew Murray. 1986. pap. 9.95 o.p. (ISBN 0-310-29711-7, 10391P). Zondervan.

God's Board: A Manual for Holy Communion. 1939. 3.25 o.p. (ISBN 0-8192-1093-5). Morehouse Pub.

God's Boot Camp. Norvel Hayes. 30p. (Orig.). 1979. pap. 1.50 o.p. (ISBN 0-89274-277-1). Harrison Hse.

God's Bullies: Power Politics & Religious Tyranny. Perry D. Young. 1982. 13.50 o.p. (ISBN 0-03-059706-4). H Holt & Co.

God's Call to Public Responsibility. Ed. by George W. Forell & William H. Lazareth. LC 77-78651. (Justice Bks). 64p. 1978. pap. 1.95 o.p. (ISBN 0-8006-1551-4, 1-1551, Fortress). Augsburg Fortress.

Gods Can Die. Edwin Thumboo. (Writing in Asia Ser.). 1977. pap. text ed. 3.50x o.p. (ISBN 0-686-60436-9, 00223). Heinemann Ed.

God's Care Is Everywhere. Bruce Wannamaker. LC 82-7244. (Illus.). 32p. (ps-k). 1982. PLB 4.95 o.p. (ISBN 0-89693-202-8). Dandelion Hse.

God's Cathedral. Virginia Neuhausel. 1958. (ISBN 0-8022-1198-4). Philos Lib.

God's Children Praying. L. M. Borchardt. (Learning Awareness Ser.). 16p. (gr. 1-2). pap. 0.78 o.p. (ISBN 0-570-04352-2, 61HH2016). Concordia.

God's Co-Workers: Your Importance to God. Clyde W. Rathwick. 1985. 10.00 o.p. (ISBN 0-682-40223-0). Exposition-Phoenix.

God's Covenant: The One Story of the Bible. Dolores M. Malone. (Illus.). 160p. (Orig.). (gr. 3-4). 1973. pap. 3.95 o.p. (ISBN 0-8042-9466-6, John Knox). Westminster John Knox.

God's Daughter in Nassau. Stephen G. Burrows. 186p. 1980. 8.50 o.p. (ISBN 0-682-49497-6). Exposition-Phoenix.

God's Everlasting Arms of Love. Ruth M. Thorndike. 1977. 6.50 o.p. (ISBN 0-682-48736-8). Exposition-Phoenix.

God's Family in God's World. Grace M. Overholser. (Illus., Orig.). (gr. 1-3). 1965. pap. 1.95 o.p. (ISBN 0-8042-9433-X, John Knox). Westminster John Knox.

God's Fool. Lawrence D. Moon. 12.95 o.p. (ISBN 0-531-09946-6). Watts.

God's Gift of Tongues: The Nature, Purpose, & Duration of Tongues As Taught in the Bible. George W. Zeller. LC 78-100. (Orig.). 1978. pap. 2.50 o.p. (ISBN 0-87213-985-9). Loizeaux.

God's Gold Mines. C. Roy Angell. LC 62-9194. 1962. 7.95 o.p. (ISBN 0-8054-5113-7). Broadman.

God's Guidance at Dawn. Mary Light. pap. 1.00 o.p. (ISBN 0-910924-68-6). Macalester.

Gods in the Making: And Other Writings. W. H. Church. (Illus.). 216p. (Orig.). 1983. pap. text ed. 6.95 o.p. (ISBN 0-87604-148-9). ARE Pr.

God's Joy in My Heart. R. Y. Nelson & Karen Hess. LC 80-65544. 256p. (Orig.). 1980. pap. 9.95 o.p. (ISBN 0-8066-1789-6, 10-2677, Augsburg). Augsburg Fortress.

God's Little House. Sandol Stoddard. (Orig.). 1984. pap. 1.95 o.p. (ISBN 0-8091-6553-8). Paulist Pr.

Gods, Men, & Ghosts. Lord Dunsany. (Illus.). 13.50 o.p. (ISBN 0-8446-0081-4). Peter Smith.

Gods, Men & Ghosts: The Best Supernatural Fiction of Lord Dunsany. Lord Dunsany. Ed. by E. F. Bleiler. LC 75-164735. (Illus.). 1971. pap. 4.95 o.p. (ISBN 0-486-22808-8). Dover.

God's Message to Me. Lyn Bigelow. (Illus.). 8p. (gr. k-4). pap. text ed. cancelled o.s.i. CEF Press.

God's Moving Spirit. T. Ralph Morton. 108p. (Orig.). 1973. pap. 2.50 o.p. (ISBN 0-8192-1167-2). Morehouse Pub.

God's Numbers in Creation, Vol. 1. Ed. by Don Kistler. 1986. pap. 4.95 o.p. (ISBN 0-940532-03-4). AOG.

Gods of Aquarius: UFO's & the Transformation of Man. Brad Steiger. LC 76-20616. (Illus.). 1976. 8.95 o.p. (ISBN 0-15-136415-X). HarBraceJ.

Gods of Bell. Robert Gately. 1979. 7.00 o.p. (ISBN 0-682-49298-1). Exposition-Phoenix.

Gods of Foxcroft. D. Levy. 1970. 6.95 o.p. (ISBN 0-87795-003-2, Arbor Hse). Morrow.

Gods of Goodness: The Sophisticated Idolatry of the Main Line Churches. Bruce L. Blackie. LC 74-19096. 1975. 5.95 o.s.i. (ISBN 0-664-20719-7, Westminster). Westminster John Knox.

Gods of Greece. Arianna Stassinopoulos & Roloff Beny. (Illus.). 216p. 1983. 40.00 o.p. (ISBN 0-8109-0958-8). Abrams.

Gods of the Greataway. Michael Coney. (Song of the Earth Ser.: Vol. II). 1984. 15.45 o.p. (ISBN 0-395-35337-8). HM.

God's Other Son: The Life & Times of the Reverend Billy Sol Hargus. Don Imus. 1981. 12.95 o.s.i. (ISBN 0-671-22537-5); pap. 5.95 o.s.i. (ISBN 0-671-43167-6). S&S.

God's Own Junkyard. Peter Blake. LC 63-22178. (Illus.). 1979. pap. 12.95 o.p. (ISBN 0-03-047431-0). H Holt & Co.

God's Parable. Frederick H. Borsch. LC 75-22443. 1976. softcover 3.50 o.s.i. (ISBN 0-664-24786-5, Westminster). Westminster John Knox.

God's People in Christ: New Testament Perspectives on the Church & Judaism, No. 7. Daniel J. Harrington. Ed. by Walter Brueggemann & John R. Donahue. LC 79-7380. (Overtures to Biblical Theology Ser.). 144p. 1980. pap. 8.95 o.p. (ISBN 0-8006-1531-X, 1-1531, Fortress). Augsburg Fortress.

God's People Our Story: Bible Stories from the New Testament. DeVere Ramsay. LC 83-51404. 128p. (gr. 3-7). 1984. 6.50 o.p. (ISBN 0-8358-0480-1). Upper Room.

God's Pilgrims. Phillip Mauro. 192p. 1969. pap. 3.00 o.p. (ISBN 0-87509-090-7). Chr Pubns.

God's Plan for Christian Service. Ronald D. Tucker & Richard A. Hufton. (Illus.). 418p. cancelled o.s.i. (ISBN 0-933643-17-9). Grace Ch St Louis.

God's Plan for Financial Success. Leroy Brownlow. 1979. pap. 2.95 o.p. (ISBN 0-915720-49-3). Brownlow Pub Co.

God's Plan for Marriage. Stanley C. Brown. LC 77-6674. 1977. 4.95 o.s.i. (ISBN 0-664-24758-X, Westminster). Westminster John Knox.

God's Plan for the Human Race. Paul L. Giroux. 1980. 5.00 o.p. (ISBN 0-682-49270-1). Exposition-Phoenix.

God's Plot: The Paradoxes of Puritan Piety, Being the Autobiography & Journal of Thomas Shepard. Ed. by Michael McGiffert. LC 71-181364. (Commonwealth Ser.: Vol. 1). (Illus.). 264p. 1972. 20.00x o.p. (ISBN 0-87023-100-6). U of Mass Pr.

God's Power Through the Laying On of Hands. Norvel Hayes. 45p. 1982. pap. 2.50 o.p. (ISBN 0-89274-280-1). Harrison Hse.

God's Promise for Today. Benjamin DeJong. 1974. Repr. 3.25 o.p. (ISBN 0-89081-212-8). Harvest Hse.

God's Promises to Preachers. Aaron Isaiah Jones. LC 81-67128. 1982. 5.50 o.p. (ISBN 0-8054-2240-4). Broadman.

God's Purpose for Man: The Spirit & the Flesh. Mollie Colbert-Thornton. 141p. 1984. 8.95 o.p. (ISBN 0-533-05913-5). Vantage.

God's Rainbow. Margaret H. Johnson. 72p. 1982. 5.00 o.p. (ISBN 0-682-49907-2). Exposition-Phoenix.

God's Revolution: The Witness of Eberhard Arnold. Eberhard Arnold. Ed. by Hutterian Society of Brothers Staff & John H. Yoder. pap. 8.95 o.p. (ISBN 0-8091-2609-5). Paulist Pr.

God's Secret for Getting Things Done. Bruce Cook. 117p. 1983. pap. 5.50 o.p. (ISBN 0-89693-173-0). Victor Bks.

God's Smuggler. Brother Andrew et al. (Illus.). 224p. 1968. pap. 2.95 o.p. (ISBN 0-8007-8016-7, Spire Bks); pap. 0.79 o.p. (ISBN 0-8007-8501-0, Spire Comics). Revell.

God's Song in My Heart: Daily Devotions. Ruth Y. Nelson. LC 56-11912. 432p. 1957. 8.95 o.p. (ISBN 0-8006-0254-4, 1-254, Fortress). Augsburg Fortress.

God's Stewards. Helge Brattgard. LC 63-16594. (Orig.). 1963. pap. 3.95 o.p. (ISBN 0-8066-0317-8, 10-2710, Augsburg). Augsburg Fortress.

God's Story & Modern Literature: Reading Fiction in Community. Carl Ficken. LC 84-48705. 176p. 1985. pap. 1.50 o.p. (ISBN 0-8006-1823-8, 1-1823, Fortress). Augsburg Fortress.

Gods, the Little Guys & the Police. Humberto Costantini. Tr. by Toby Talbott. 240p. 1985. pap. 3.95 o.p. (ISBN 0-380-69839-0, Bard). Avon.

Gods Themselves. Isaac Asimov. 288p. 1982. pap. 2.50 o.p. (ISBN 0-449-23756-7, Crest). Fawcett.

Gods Who Walk the Rainbow. Swami Sivananda Radha. LC 81-9410. (Illus.). 240p. (Orig.). 1981. pap. 8.95 o.p. (ISBN 0-931454-07-7). Timeless Bks.

God's Will Is Prosperity. Gloria Copeland. pap. 2.95 o.p. (ISBN 0-89274-090-6, HH-090). Harrison Hse.

God's Wonderful World: Twenty Six Lessons for Primary Church. Carolyn Lehman. (Children's Church Ser.). (Illus.). 144p. 1985. wkbk 8.95 o.p. (ISBN 0-87239-839-0, 3316). Standard Pub.

God's Word A. D. LeRoy Lawson. LC 83-348. 112p. (Orig.). 1984. pap. 2.95 o.p. (ISBN 0-87239-668-1, 41022). Standard Pub.

God's Word & Me, Vol. I. Beatrice Hollenbeck. (Illus.). 37p. (gr. k-4). 1979. pap. text ed. 12.65 o.p. CEF Press.

God's Word & Me, Vol. II. Beatrice Hollenbeck. (Illus.). 70p. (gr. k-4). 1979. pap. text ed. 12.65 o.p. CEF Press.

God's Word B. C. John W. Wade. LC 83-349. (Orig.). 1983. pap. 2.95 o.p. (ISBN 0-87239-667-3, 41020). Standard Pub.

God's Word in a Child's World: Messages & Guidelines for Sharing the Gospel with Children. Eldon Weisheit. LC 86-3442. 128p. (Orig.). 1986. pap. 7.95 o.p. (ISBN 0-8066-2214-8, 10-2745, Augsburg). Augsburg Fortress.

God's Work of Art: Images of the Church in Ephesians. Lamar Williamson, Jr. (Orig.). 1971. pap. 1.25 o.p. (ISBN 0-8042-9064-4, John Knox). Westminster John Knox.

God's Work of Liberation: A Journey Through the Old Testament with the Liberation Heroes of Israel. Robert Bennett. (Illus., Orig.). 1976. pap. text ed. 5.95 o.p. (ISBN 0-8192-4067-2); tchr's guide 2.25x o.p. (ISBN 0-8192-4068-0). Morehouse Pub.

God's Works Through Elvis. Marvin R. Long. 1979. 4.00 o.p. (ISBN 0-682-49294-9). Exposition-Phoenix.

God's Young Church. William Baraclay. LC 70-110082. 120p. 1970. pap. 2.65 o.s.i. Westminster John Knox.

God's Young Church. William Barclay. 1970. pap. 2.65 o.s.i. (ISBN 0-664-24884-5, Westminster). Westminster John Knox.

Godwin Sideboard. John Malcolm. (Tim Simpson Mystery Ser.). 176p. 1985. 13.95 o.s.i. (ISBN 0-684-18398-6, ScribT). Scribner.

Godwin's Practical Encyclopedia of Cabalistic Magick. 2nd, rev. & expanded ed. David Godwin. Ed. by Carl L. Weschcke. (Sourcebook Ser.). 500p. 1987. pap. 15.00 o.p. (ISBN 0-87542-292-6, L-292). Llewellyn Pubns.

Gody Emigratsii (Years of Emigration) Mark Vishniak. LC 71-82306. (Foreign Language Ser.: No. 6). (Rus). 1970. 12.00x o.p. (ISBN 0-8179-4061-8). Hoover Inst Pr.

Goethe As a Critic of Literature. Ed. by Karl J. Fink & Max L. Baeumer. 236p. (Orig.). 1985. lib. bdg. 27.50 o.p. (ISBN 0-8191-4280-8); pap. text ed. 13.25 o.p. (ISBN 0-8191-4281-6). U Pr of Amer.

Goethe Centenary Papers. Ed. by Martin Schutze. (Illus.). 174p. 1933. 7.95 o.p. (ISBN 0-87548-256-2). Open Court.

Goffredo Petrassi. John S. Weissmann. 79p. Repr. of 1957 ed. lib. bdg. 39.00 o.p. (Pub. by Am Repr Serv). Reprint Servs.

Goggle-Eyed Pirates. Lee Falk. 1974. pap. 0.95 o.p. (ISBN 0-380-01223-5, 18184). Avon.

Goggles. Ezra J. Keats. LC 70-78081. (Illus.). (gr. k-2). 1969. 12.95 o.s.i. (ISBN 0-02-749590-6). Macmillan.

Goggles. Ezra J. Keats. LC 70-78081. 32p. (ps-3). 1971. pap. 4.95 o.s.i. (ISBN 0-02-044100-2, Collier). Macmillan.

Gogol's Forgotten Book: Selected Passages & Its Contemporary Readers. Ruth Sobel. LC 80-8292. 1981. lib. bdg. 23.50 o.p. (ISBN 0-8191-1630-0); pap. text ed. 13.50 o.p. (ISBN 0-8191-1631-9). U Pr of Amer.

Goin' Railroading. Sam Speas & Margeret Coel. LC 85-19099. (Illus.). 312p. 1985. 34.95 o.p. (ISBN 0-87108-692-1). Pruett.

Goin' Up Gandy. Don Teter. 1977. pap. 6.00 o.p. (ISBN 0-87012-284-3). McClain.

Going Alone: Woman's Guide to Travel Know How. Carol Chester. (Illus.). 176p. 1987. pap. 8.95 o.s.i. (ISBN 0-87052-431-3). Hippocrene Bks.

Going Bust: Inside the British Bankruptcy Business. Stephen Aris. 194p. 1985. 20.95 o.p. (ISBN 0-233-97693-0, Pub. by A Deutsch England). David & Charles.

Going Co-op. Coughlan & Franke Staff. 248p. 1983. 9.00 o.p. (ISBN 0-318-17890-7, H09B, Pub. by Beacon Pr). NASCO.

Going CO-OP: The Complete Guide to Buying & Owning Your Own Apartment. William Coughlan & Monte Franke. LC 82-72501. 224p. 1983. pap. 9.95 o.p. (ISBN 0-8070-0869-9, BP 650). Beacon Pr.

Going Crazy. Otto Freidrich. 1977. pap. 1.95 o.p. (ISBN 0-380-00888-2). Avon.

Going for Broke: Gambling with Taxpayers' Money. John Redwood. 160p. 1984. 45.00x o.p. (ISBN 0-631-13525-1). Basil Blackwell.

Going for It! How to Succeed As an Entrepreneur. Victor Kiam. LC 85-61762. 264p. 1986. 16.95 o.p. (ISBN 0-688-06060-9). Morrow.

Going for the Gold. Tim Wendel. LC 80-81802. (Illus.). 144p. 1980. 10.00 o.p. (ISBN 0-88208-116-0). Chicago Review.

Going, Going, Gone: A Mystery Introducing Helen Greene. Eliza G. Collins. 224p. 1986. 13.95 o.s.i. (ISBN 0-684-18616-0). Scribner.

Going Home. Peter Simpson & Ruth Levitt. (Illus.). 400p. 1981. pap. text ed. 19.50 o.p. (ISBN 0-443-01839-1). Churchill.

Going Metric: Guidelines for the Mathematics Teacher, Grades K-8. Walter W. Leffin. LC 75-31956. 48p. 1975. pap. 3.75 o.s.i. (ISBN 0-87353-055-1). NCTM.

Going Metric in Catering. J. H. Croft. 1969. pap. 5.50 o.p. (ISBN 0-08-006512-0). Pergamon.

Going My Way? Stan Applebaum & Victoria Cox. LC 76-8492. (Let Me Read Ser.). (Illus.). (gr. 1-5). 1976. 4.95 o.p. (ISBN 0-15-231125-4, HJ). HarBraceJ.

Going My Way? Stan Applebaum & Victoria Cox. LC 76-8492. (Let Me Read Ser.). (Illus.). (gr. k-3). 1976. pap. 1.65 o.p. (ISBN 0-15-231126-2, VoyB). HarBraceJ.

Going Native in Hawaii: A Poor Man's Guide to Paradise. Timothy E. Head. LC 65-14212. (Illus., Orig.). pap. 3.25 o.p. (ISBN 0-8048-0209-2). C E Tuttle.

Going Nowhere. Alvin Greenberg. 1973. pap. 1.65 o.p. (ISBN 0-380-01224-3, 15081, Bard). Avon.

Going on Like This. John R. Gardiner. LC 82-73016. 224p. 1983. 12.95 o.p. (ISBN 0-689-11347-1, Atheneum). Macmillan.

Going on Sixteen. Betty Cavanna. LC 46-2683. (Illus.). 220p. (gr. 7-10). 1946. 8.95 o.s.i. (ISBN 0-664-32011-2, Westminster). Westminster John Knox.

Going Places: A Traveller's Journal. The Metropolitan Museum of Art Staff. (Illus.). 160p. 1986. 7.95 o.s.i. (ISBN 0-684-18739-6). Scribner.

Going Potty. Kay Matthews. (Illus.). 23p. (ps-k). 1985. 4.95 o.p. (ISBN 0-533-06368-X). Vantage.

Going Shopping. Sarah Garland. (Illus.). 32p. (ps-k). 1985. 6.95 o.p. (ISBN 0-316-30433-6, Joy St Bks). Little.

Going Steady. Anne Emery. 190p. (gr. 5-9). 1950. 8.95 o.s.i. (ISBN 0-664-32066-X, Westminster). Westminster John Knox.

Going to China? 1979. pap. 9.95 incl. cassette o.p. (ISBN 0-8351-0825-2). China Bks.

Going to School. Suzanne Green. LC 86-32819. (Perlorians Ser.). (Illus.). 32p. (ps-k). 1987. pap. 6.95 o.p. (ISBN 0-385-23509-7). Doubleday.

Going to the Opera. Lionel Salter. (Illus.). 160p. 1956. (ISBN 0-8022-1473-8). Philos Lib.

Going to the Zoo with Roger Caras. Roger Caras. LC 72-88167. (Illus.). 128p. (gr. 3-7). 1973. 5.95 o.p. (ISBN 0-15-231130-0, HJ). HarBraceJ.

Going Too Far. Tony Hendra. (Illus.). 504p. 1987. pap. 19.95 o.p. (ISBN 0-385-23223-3, Dolp). Doubleday.

Going Up! Pompey Season, 1986-1987. Mike Neasom & Murray Sanders. (Illus.). 128p. 1987. pap. 9.95 o.p. (Pub. by Milestone Pubns UK). Seven Hills Bk Dists.

Going Vegetarian: A Guide for Teenagers. Sada Fretz. LC 82-14230. (Illus.). 280p. (gr. 7up). 1983. 11.75 o.p. (ISBN 0-688-01713-4). Morrow.

Going...Teach. Ed. by C. Bonivento. 1988. 19.95 o.p. (ISBN 0-317-67489-7, RA0114). Dghtrs St Paul.

Goju Ryu. Morio Higaonna. Japan Pubns USA.

Gold & Black Gold: Basic Value Investing for the New Economic Era. Leslie Snyder. LC 74-84433. 1974. 7.50 o.p. (ISBN 0-682-48094-0, Banner). Exposition-Phoenix.

Gold & Jewels. Brenda Thompson & Rosemary Giesen. LC 76-22437. (Lerner First Fact Bks.). (Illus.). (gr. k-3). 1977. PLB 4.95 o.p. (ISBN 0-8225-1356-0). Lerner Pubns.

Gold & Prices. George F. Warren & Frank A. Pearson. LC 82-48216. (Gold, Money, Inflation & Deflation Ser.). 481p. 1983. lib. bdg. 61.00 o.p. (ISBN 0-8240-5261-7). Garland Pub.

Gold & Silver Leaching, Recovery & Economics. Ed. by W. J. Schlitt & W. C. Larson. LC 81-68558. (Illus.). 148p. 1981. text ed. 20.00x o.p. (ISBN 0-89520-289-1). SMM&E Inc.

Gold & the Glory. Chet Cunningham. 1977. pap. 1.75 o.p. (ISBN 0-8439-0450-X, Pub. by Leisure Bks CT). Dorchester Pub Co.

Gold Availability, World: A Mineral Availability Appraisal. (Mines Bureau Information Circular Ser.: No. 9070). (Illus.). 95p. 1986. pap. 4.50 o.p. (S/N 024-004-02164-1). USGPO.

Gold Coin. Reidar Brodtkorb. Tr. by L. W. Kingsland. LC 66-11198. (Illus.). (gr. 5 up). 1966. 4.95 o.p. (ISBN 0-15-231155-6, HJ). HarBraceJ.

Gold Country. Shirley Kaufman. LC 73-5542. (Pitt Poetry Ser.). 1973. 15.95x o.p. (ISBN 0-8229-3269-5); pap. 6.95 o.p. (ISBN 0-8229-5238-6). U of Pittsburgh Pr.

Gold Deadline. Herbert Resnicow. 192p. 1985. pap. 2.95 o.p. (ISBN 0-380-69923-0). Avon.

Gold Disc of Coosa. Virginia P. Brown. LC 75-24616. 7.95 o.p. (ISBN 0-87397-085-3). Strode.

Gold Flower & the Bear. 1979. 1.95 o.p. (ISBN 0-8351-0672-1). China Bks.

Gold Frame. Herbert Resnicow. 248p. 1986. pap. 2.95 o.p. (ISBN 0-380-70048-4). Avon.

Gold in History & Modern Times & Labour in History & in Modern Times. Walter J. Stein. 1986. pap. 6.95 o.p. (ISBN 0-916786-88-9). St George Bk Serv.

Gold in the Black Hills. Steve Mensing. (Orig.). 1981. pap. 1.75 o.p. (ISBN 0-505-51644-6, Pub. by Tower Bks). Dorchester Pub Co.

Gold in the Woodpile: An Informal History of Banking in Oregon. O. K. Burrell. LC 68-63377. (Illus.). 1967. 8.50 o.p. (ISBN 0-87114-015-2). U of Oreg Bks.

Gold-Lined Box. Marjory Hall. LC 68-17150. 198p. (gr. 5-9). 1968. 4.25 o.s.i. (ISBN 0-664-32420-7, Westminster). Westminster John Knox.

Gold Mine of Money-Making Ideas. Marguerite Brunner. 1977. 7.95 o.p. (ISBN 0-89328-015-1); pap. 4.95 o.p. (ISBN 0-89328-017-8). Lorenz Corp.

Gold Mining in the American West. John A. Burton. 104p. 1986. 8.95 o.p. (ISBN 0-8062-2924-1). Carlton.

Gold Mining 87: Proceedings of the First International Conference on Gold Mining. Pref. by C. O. Brawner. LC 87-62247. (Illus.). 600p. 1987. 70.00x o.p. (ISBN 0-87335-072-3, 072-3). SMM&E Inc.

Gold of the Gods. Glen Wright. Ed. by Carol Murphy. (Illus.). (gr. 3-6). 1981. PLB 6.95 o.p. (ISBN 0-89868-113-8, Read Res); pap. text ed. 4.95 o.p. (ISBN 0-89868-120-0, Read Res). ARO Pub.

Gold, Prices & Wages Under the Greenback Standard. Wesley C. Mitchell. pap. 35.00 o.p. (ISBN 0-384-39220-2). Johnson Repr.

Gold Seekers. J. Mark Bond. 432p. 1984. pap. 3.75 o.s.i. (ISBN 0-8439-2183-8, Pub. by Leisure Bks CT). Dorchester Pub Co.

Gold, Silver, Uranium & Coal - Geology, Mining, Extraction, & Environment. Ed. by Maurice C. Fuerstenau & R. B. Palmer. LC 82-73914. (Illus.). 526p. 1983. pap. text ed. 40.00x o.p. (ISBN 0-89520-406-1, 406-1). SMM&E Inc.

Gold Solutions. Herbert Resnicow. 192p. 1984. pap. 2.75 o.p. (ISBN 0-380-69278-3, 69287-3). Avon.

Gold Standard in Theory & History. Ed. by Barry Eichengreen. 320p. 1985. pap. 11.95 o.p. (ISBN 0-416-39110-9, 9614). Routledge Chapman & Hall.

Gold Strike. Peter McCurtin. (Sundance Ser.: No. 35). 1980. pap. 1.75 o.p. (ISBN 0-8439-0819-X, Pub. by Leisure Bks CT). Dorchester Pub Co.

Gold Trails of Big Bear Valley. George J. Williams, III. (Western Americana History Ser.). (Illus., Orig.). 1985. pap. 3.95 o.p. Tree by River.

Gold Wagon. Chet Cunningham. 1980. pap. 1.50 o.p. (ISBN 0-505-51460-5, Pub. by Tower Bks). Dorchester Pub Co.

Gold Was the Mortar: The Economics of Cathedral Building. Henry Kraus. (Illus.). 1979. 37.95x o.p. (ISBN 0-7100-8728-4). Routledge Chapman & Hall.

Golda. William Gibson. LC 77-15889. 1978. 8.95 o.p. (ISBN 0-689-10876-1, Atheneum). Macmillan.

Goldberg Street: Short Plays & Monologues. David Mamet. LC 84-7310. 156p. 1985. 15.00 o.p. (ISBN 0-394-54610-5, GP-964). Grove.

Golden Age. Constantine FitzGibbon. 189p. 1975. 7.95 o.p. (ISBN 0-393-08683-6). Norton.

Golden Age. Kenneth Grahame. (Illus.). 1975. pap. 4.95 o.p. (ISBN 0-380-00289-2, 23986). Avon.

Golden Age: Dutch Painters of the Seventeenth Century. Bob Haak. Tr. by Elizabeth Willems-Treeman from Dutch. (Illus.). 536p. 1984. 75.00 o.p. (ISBN 0-8109-0956-1); 65.00 o.p. Abrams.

Golden Age of American Anthropology. Ed. by Margaret Mead & Ruth L. Bunzel. LC 60-11668. (Golden Age Ser). 12.50 o.p. (ISBN 0-8076-0122-5). Braziller.

Golden Age of British Photography, 1839-1900, from the Collection of the Victoria & Albert Museum. Mark Haworth-Booth et al. (Illus.). 192p. 1987. pap. 29.95 o.p. (ISBN 0-89381-277-3). Aperture.

Golden Age of Italian Music. Grace O'Brien. (ISBN 0-8022-1236-0). Philos Lib.

Golden Age of Naples: Art & Civilization under the Bourbons 1734-1805. (Illus.). 472p. 1981. Set. pap. 30.00 o.p. (ISBN 0-89558-086-1). Detroit Inst Arts.

Golden Age of Opera. Robert Tuggle. LC 83-7895. (Illus.). 256p. 1983. 35.00 o.s.i. (ISBN 0-03-057778-0, Owl Bks.). H Holt & Co.

Golden Age of Russian Literature. Ivar Spector. LC 43-4556. (Illus.). 1952. 6.00 o.p. (ISBN 0-87004-163-0). Caxton.

Golden Age of Style. Julian Robinson. 1976. 12.95 o.p. (ISBN 0-15-136085-5). HarBraceJ.

Golden Age of the Poster. Ed. by Hayward Cirker & Blanche Cirker. (Illus.). 15.25 o.p. (ISBN 0-8446-0059-8). Peter Smith.

Golden Apple. (Sharazad Stories Ser.). (Illus., Arabic.). (gr. 4-6). pap. 3.50x o.p. (ISBN 0-86685-251-4). Intl Bk Ctr.

Golden Apples. Eudora Welty. LC 49-10054. 244p. 1949. 12.95 o.s.i. (ISBN 0-15-136089-8). HarBraceJ.

Golden Apples of the Sun. Ed. by Chris Wallace-Crabbe. 288p. 1980. 15.50x o.p. (ISBN 0-522-84192-9, Pub. by Melbourne U Pr Australia). Intl Spec Bk.

Golden Asse. rev. ed. Lucius Apuleius. Tr. by Adlington. (Black & Gold Lib). 1973. 6.95 o.p. (ISBN 0-87140-989-5). Liveright.

Golden Bats & Pink Pigeons: A Journey to the Flora & Fauna of a Unique Island. Gerald Durrell. 1984. pap. 6.75 o.p. (ISBN 0-671-50757-5, Touchstone Bks). S&S.

Golden Blue of the Sunset. Jessie B. Schleisman. LC 86-914230. 128p. 1987. text ed. 7.50 o.p. (ISBN 0-682-40327-X). Exposition-Phoenix.

Golden Book of Management. L. Urwick & W. Wolf. LC 82-71319. 448p. 1984. text ed. 50.00 o.p. (ISBN 0-8144-5561-1). AMACOM.

Golden Book of Original Contemporary Poems for Adults & Children. Martha K. Johnson-McHenry. 1985. 6.95 o.p. (ISBN 0-533-06546-1). Vantage.

Golden Book of Theology. Billy J. Tolson. 1978. 5.50 o.p. (ISBN 0-682-49233-7). Exposition-Phoenix.

Golden Booke of the Leaden Gods, Repr. Of 1577 Ed. Stephen Batman. Bd. with Third Part of the Countess of Pembroke's Yvychurch. Abraham Fraunce. Repr. of 1592 ed; Fountaine of Ancient Fiction. Richard Lynche. Repr. of 1599 ed. LC 75-27856. (Renaissance & the Gods Ser.: Vol. 13). (Illus.). 1976. lib. bdg. 88.00 o.p. (ISBN 0-8240-2062-6). Garland Pub.

Golden Boy. William Gibson & Clifford Odets. LC 74-77624. 1965. 3.95 o.p. (ISBN 0-689-10217-8, Atheneum). Macmillan.

Golden Century of Italian Opera: From Rossini to Puccini. William Weaver. (Illus.). 256p. 1980. 35.00 o.p. (ISBN 0-500-01240-7). Thames Hudson.

Golden Century of Venetian Painting. Terisio Pignatti. Ed. by Kenneth Donahue. Tr. by Murtha Baca from Ital. (Illus.). 1979. 14.95x o.p. (ISBN 0-87587-088-0). LA Co Art Mus.

Golden Chain. Ed. by Carole G. Silver. (Illus.). vii, 149p. 1982. 11.00x o.s.i. (ISBN 0-931332-04-4); pap. 6.00x o.s.i. (ISBN 0-931332-03-6). Wedgestone Pr.

Golden Chersonese. Bird. (Century Classic). 1988. pap. 13.95 o.p. (ISBN 0-317-61288-3, Pub. by Century Hutchinson). David & Charles.

Golden Chersonese. Isabella Bird. (Travel Classics Ser.). 384p. 1985. lib. bdg. 23.95 o.p. (ISBN 0-317-19639-1, Pub. by Century Pubs UK). Hippocrene Bks.

Golden Circle. David Collins & Evelyn Witter. LC 82-51215. (Illus.). 94p. (gr. 4-8). 1983. lib. bdg. 5.95 o.p. (ISBN 0-938232-47-9, Dist. by Baker & Taylor). Winston-Derek.

Golden Circle. Lee Falk. (Phantom Ser., No. 5). 1973. pap. 0.75 o.p. (ISBN 0-380-01225-1, 14894). Avon.

Golden Clan: The Murrays, the McDonnells, & the Irish American Aristocracy. John Corry. 1977. 8.95 o.p. (ISBN 0-395-25146-X). HM.

Golden Conch. Wang Qizhong. (Illus.). 38p. (gr. 3-5). 1986. pap. 2.95 o.p. (ISBN 0-8351-1489-9). China Bks.

Golden Country. Shusaku Endo. Tr. by Francis Mathy. LC 70-123898. 1970. 5.25 o.p. (ISBN 0-8048-0213-0). C E Tuttle.

Golden Cup. Date not set. (ISBN 0-385-29508-1). Delacorte.

Golden Cup. Belva Plain. 384p. 1986. 17.95 o.p. (ISBN 0-385-29508-1). Delacorte.

Golden Dawn: An Account of the Teachings, Rites & Ceremonies of the Order of the Golden Dawn. 4th ed. Israel Regardie. LC 83-80167. (Illus.). 1200p. 1984. 35.00 o.p. (ISBN 0-87542-664-6). Llewellyn Pubns.

Golden Dawn: Twilight of the Magicians. R. A. Gilbert. LC 86-15993. 144p. 1986. lib. bdg. 19.95x o.p. (ISBN 0-8095-7003-3). Borgo Pr.

Golden Days. Carolyn See. 224p. 1987. pap. price not set o.p. HR&W.

Golden Days in Egypt: A Beginner's History of Rights & Duties. Roy Cochrane. (Illus.). 1979. 7.50 o.p. (ISBN 0-682-49287-6). Exposition-Phoenix.

Golden Door. Arthur De Ponceau. 272p. 1986. 14.95 o.p. (ISBN 0-8062-2868-7). Carlton.

Golden Door: The United States from 1865 to 1918. Isaac Asimov. LC 77-21385. (Illus.). 288p. (gr. 7 up). 1977. 10.95 o.s.i. (ISBN 0-395-25798-0). HM.

Golden Dozen. Jessyca R. Gaver. 1976. pap. 1.25 o.p. (ISBN 0-685-69151-9, LB348ZK, Pub. by Leisure Bks CT). Dorchester Pub Co.

Golden Dragon: By Clipper Ship Around the Horn. John J. Loeper. LC 78-5085. (Illus.). 80p. (gr. 3-7). 1978. 6.95 o.p. (ISBN 0-689-30658-X, Atheneum). Macmillan.

Golden Eagle Years. Mike Tomkies. (Illus.). 208p. (Orig.). 1982. 29.95 o.p. (ISBN 0-434-78801-5, Pub. by W Heinemann Ltd). David & Charles.

Golden Egg. James Pollak. Ed. by Bruce S. Kupelnick. LC 76-52124. (Classics of Film Literature Ser.). 1978. lib. bdg. 24.00 o.p. (ISBN 0-8240-2890-2). Garland Pub.

Golden Egg: The Personal Income Tax, Where It Came from, How It Grew. Gerald Carson. 1977. 10.00 o.p. (ISBN 0-395-25177-X). HM.

Golden Flutes & Great Escapes - Apple. Delton T. Horn. (No. 2). 10.95 o.p. (ISBN 0-88056-050-9). Weber Systems.

Golden Flutes & Great Escapes - Commodore 64. Delton T. Horn. 10.95 o.p. (ISBN 0-88056-051-7, Dist. by Weber Systems). Weber Systems.

Golden Gate. Vikram Seth. LC 85-8395. 320p. 1986. 17.45 o.s.i. (ISBN 0-394-54974-0). Random.

Golden Gate Counties Street Atlas 1986. Thomas Bros. Maps Staff. (Illus.). 326p. pap. 29.95 o.p. Thomas Bros Maps.

Golden Gate: Marin, San Francisco, San Mateo & Santa Clara Counties Street Guide & Directory, 1987. Thomas Bros. Maps Staff. (Illus.). 388p. 1987. pap. 29.95 o.p. (ISBN 0-88130-205-8). Thomas Bros Maps.

Golden Gate Street Atlas & Directory, 1987. rev. ed. Thomas Bros. Maps Staff. (Illus.). Date not set. pap. 29.95 o.p. (ISBN 0-88130-153-1). Thomas Bros Maps.

Golden Gate Street Guide & Directory 1988. Thomas Bros. Maps Staff. (Illus.). 390p. 1988. pap. 29.95 o.p. (ISBN 0-88130-286-4). Thomas Bros Maps.

Golden Gates. Jean Conrad. 224p. 1987. pap. 5.95 o.p. (ISBN 0-310-47811-1, 15658P). Zondervan.

Golden Girls: True Stories of Olympic Women Stars. Carli Laklan. LC 79-24052. (Illus.). (gr. 7-10). 1980. text ed. 9.95 o.p. (ISBN 0-07-036074-X). McGraw.

Golden Guitar & Other Poems. John G. Caserta. 72p. 1985. 7.50 o.p. (ISBN 0-682-40212-5). Exposition-Phoenix.

Golden Hive. Harry Behn. LC 66-12587. (Illus.). (gr. 3 up). 1966. 4.50 o.p. (ISBN 0-15-231200-5, HJ). HarBraceJ.

Golden Ingots. Jane M. Brams. (Illus.). 1980. 5.00 o.p. (ISBN 0-682-49562-X). Exposition-Phoenix.

Golden Journey. Agnes S. Turnbull. 1974. pap. 1.25 o.p. (ISBN 0-380-00154-3, 20792). Avon.

Golden Journey. Agnes S. Turnbull. 1984. lib. bdg. 14.95 o.p. (ISBN 0-8161-3612-2, Large Print Bks). G K Hall.

Golden Kingdom. Steve Dewitt. LC 83-81903. (Illus.). 299p. 1984. pap. text ed. 4.95 o.p. (ISBN 0-88155-026-4). Illum Way Pub.

Golden Lamb. Irene Gough. LC 68-20643. (Foreign Lands Bks.). (Illus.). (gr. 3-6). 1968. PLB 3.95g o.p. (ISBN 0-8225-0360-3). Lerner Pubns.

Golden Lasso. Fern Michaels. (Nightingale Large Print Ser.). 1985. pap. text ed. 9.95 o.p. (ISBN 0-8161-3742-0, Large Print Bks). G K Hall.

Golden Lemon: A Collection of Special Recipes. Doris Tobias & Mary Merris. LC 77-88908. viii, 210p. 1981. pap. 6.95 o.p. (ISBN 0-689-70609-X, 268, Atheneum). Macmillan.

Golden Lion. Pamela Haines. 500p. 1986. 19.95 o.s.i. (ISBN 0-684-18731-0). Scribner.

Golden Lotus: A Translation of the Chinese Novel, Chin P'ing Mei, 4 vols. Tr. by Clement Egerton from Chinese. 1572p. 1972. Set. 80.00 o.p. (ISBN 0-7100-7349-6); 22.00 ea. o.p. Routledge Chapman & Hall.

Golden Lucky Bag. U. S. Naval Academy, Class of 1934 Staff. Ed. by Arthur R. Gralla. (Illus.). 336p. 1984. write for info. o.p. JostGls.

Golden Millet Dream & Other Stories Ser. Liu Lanyun. Tr. by Yu Fanqin & Wang Mingjie. (Chinese-English Readers). (Illus.). 296p. (Orig.). 1982. pap. 6.95 o.p. (ISBN 0-8351-1102-4). China Bks.

Golden Mountain, No. 13. Paul Radin. (Asian Folklore & Social Life Monograph). 1971. 14.00x o.p. (ISBN 0-89986-016-8). Oriental Bk Store.

Golden Notebook. Doris Lessing. 1984. 24.45 o.p. (ISBN 0-671-28770-2). S&S.

Golden Nuggets see Word Studies in the Greek New Testament, for the English Reader.

Golden Number. M. Borrisavlietvitch. (Illus.). 96p. 1958. (ISBN 0-8022-0157-1). Philos Lib.

Golden Opportunity. Edith Begner. 288p. 1980. pap. 2.50 o.p. (ISBN 0-380-75085-6, 75085). Avon.

Golden Page. Alma M. Myer. LC 77-71602. 1977. 10.00 o.p. (ISBN 0-682-48742-2, Lochinvar). Exposition-Phoenix.

Golden Porcupine. Muriel R. Bolton. 1977. pap. 1.95 o.p. (ISBN 0-380-01657-5, 33258). Avon.

Golden Precepts: A Guide to Enlightened Living. rev. 3rd ed. G. De Purucker. Ed. by Helen Todd & W. Emmett Small. 170p. 1971. 3.50 o.p. (ISBN 0-686-86619-3); pap. 2.50 o.p. (ISBN 0-913004-02-2, 913004-02). Point Loma Pub.

Golden Reckoning. Jean Nash. 320p. 1987. pap. 3.95 o.p. (ISBN 0-380-89873-X). Avon.

Golden Shames. Gershon Kranzler. saddle-stitched 5.00 o.p. (ISBN 0-87559-128-0). Shalom.

Golden Sovereigns. Jocelyn Carew. 408p. 1976. pap. 1.95 o.p. (ISBN 0-380-00845-9, 47381-X). Avon.

Golden Spike. Ted Morrisby. (Illus.). 240p. 1986. 14.95 o.s.i. (ISBN 0-8008-3335-X). Taplinger.

Golden State Warriors. Frank MacDonald. (NBA Today Ser.). (Illus.). 48p. (gr. 4 up). 1983. PLB 10.45 o.p. (ISBN 0-87191-977-X). Creative Ed.

Golden Thread. Jean Nash. (Orig.). 1980. pap. 2.25 o.p. (ISBN 0-505-51483-4, Pub. by Tower Bks). Dorchester Pub Co.

Golden Throng: A Book about Bees. Edwin W. Teale. (Illus.). 160p. 1982. Repr. 16.50x o.p. (ISBN 0-87663-407-2). Universe.

Golden Torc. Julian May. (Saga of Pliocene Exile Ser.: Vol. II). 448p. 1982. 13.95 o.p. (ISBN 0-395-31261-2). HM.

Golden Unicorn. Phyllis A. Whitney. LC 75-41676. 336p. 1976. 7.95 o.p. (ISBN 0-385-12088-5). Doubleday.

Golden Urchin. Madeleine Brent. LC 86-8959. 336p. 1987. 16.95 o.s.i. (ISBN 0-385-23015-X). Doubleday.

Golden Vanity. John Langstaff & David Gentleman. LC 76-167835. (Illus.). (gr. k-3). 1972. 4.95 o.p. (ISBN 0-15-231500-4, HJ). HarBraceJ.

Golden Venture. Jane Flory. LC 75-43899. (Illus.). 224p. (gr. 5-9). 1976. 7.95 o.p. (ISBN 0-395-24377-7). HM.

Golden Warrior. Hope Muntz. 1949. 8.95 o.s.i. (ISBN 0-684-13585-X, ScribT). Scribner.

Goldenberg Who Couldn't Dance. Everett Greenbaum. LC 79-3353. 160p. 1980. 8.95 o.p. (ISBN 0-15-136174-6). HarBraceJ.

Goldengrove. Jill P. Walsh. 1985. pap. 0.95 o.p. (ISBN 0-380-01227-8, 50435-9). Avon.

Goldenrod. Mary Towne. LC 77-1578. (gr. 4-6). 1977. 6.95 o.p. (ISBN 0-689-30597-4, Atheneum). Macmillan.

Goldfinger. Ian Fleming. (James Bond Ser.). 272p. (Orig.). 1980. pap. 3.50 o.s.i. (ISBN 0-425-08165-6). Jove Pubns.

Goldilocks. Ed McBain. LC 77-80173. 1978. 8.95 o.p. (ISBN 0-87795-177-2, Arbor Hse). Morrow.

Goldilocks & the Three Bears. (Favorite Tale Pop-Up Bks.). (Illus.). 1.98 o.p. (ISBN 0-517-46233-8). Outlet Bk Co.

Goldseekers. William S. Long. (Gregg Fiction, The Australians Ser.: Vol. VII). 356p. 1985. lib. bdg. 12.95 o.p. (ISBN 0-8398-2884-5, Gregg). G K Hall.

Goldsmith: The Critical Heritage. G. S. Rousseau. 412p. 1985. pap. 15.00 o.p. (ISBN 0-7102-0511-2). Routledge Chapman & Hall.

Goldsmiths: An Main und Neckar Daten - Werke -Zeichen. Wolfgang Scheffler. 128p. (Ger.). 18.50 o.p. (ISBN 3-921811-01-5, Pub. by Kunst & Antiquitaten West Germany). Seven Hills Bk Dists.

Goldsmith's & Silversmith's Handbook. 2nd rev. ed. S. Abbey. (Illus.). 1968. 17.50 o.p. (ISBN 0-685-12021-X). E J Brill USA.

Goldsmiths: Des Ostallgaus Daten - Werke - Zeichen. Wolfgang Scheffler. 127p. (Ger.). 18.50 o.p. (ISBN 3-921811-12-0, Pub. by Kunst & Antiquitaten West Germany). Seven Hills Bk Dists.

Goldstein Trial Technique: Nineteen Sixty-Nine to Nineteen Eighty-Four, 3 vols. 2nd ed. Irving Goldstein & Fred Lane. LC 84-23915. Set. 200.00 o.p. (ISBN 0-317-12038-7); Suppl., 1986. 60.00 o.p.; Suppl., 1983. 69.00 o.p. Callaghan.

Goldsworthy Lowes Dickinson. E. M. Forster. LC 73-5944. (Illus.). 277p. 1973. pap. 3.95 o.s.i. (ISBN 0-15-636150-7, Harv). HarBraceJ.

Golem Legend: Origins & Implications. Byron L. Sherwin. LC 84-21948. (Illus.). 60p. (Orig.). 1985. lib. bdg. 18.75 o.p. (ISBN 0-8191-4402-9); pap. text ed. 7.25 o.p. (ISBN 0-8191-4403-7). U Pr of Amer.

Golem Remembered 1909-1980: Variations of a Jewish Legend. Arnold L. Goldsmith. LC 81-74580. (Illus.). 181p. 1981. 22.50x o.p. (ISBN 0-8143-1683-2). Wayne St U Pr.

Golem: The Story of a Legend. Ed. by Elie Wiesel. Tr. by Anne Borchardt. LC 83-9304. (Illus.). 105p. 1983. 12.50 o.s.i. (ISBN 0-671-45483-8); Special ed., signed, limited. 50.00 o.s.i. (ISBN 0-671-49624-7). Summit Bks.

Golf. Gary Wiren. (Sport Ser.). (Illus.). (gr. 10 up). 1971. text ed. 4.95 ref. ed. o.p. (ISBN 0-13-358028-8); pap. text ed. 13.67 ref. ed. o.p. (ISBN 0-13-358010-5). P-H.

Golf: A Guide to Information Sources. Ed. by Joseph S. Murdoch & Janet Seagle. LC 79-23270. (Sports, Games & Pastimes Information Guide Ser.: Vol. 7). 1979. 65.00x o.p. (ISBN 0-8103-1457-6). Gale.

Golf Book. Michael Bartlett. LC 80-67625. (Illus.). 1980. 22.95 o.p. (ISBN 0-87795-297-3, Arbor Hse) (ISBN 0-686-64654-1). Morrow.

Golf Courses of Colorado: A Guide to Public & Resort Courses. Don Gallup & Jim Gallup. LC 84-70834. (Illus.). 328p. 1984. pap. 8.95 o.p. (ISBN 0-9613458-0-2). Colo Leisure.

Golf Digest Almanac, 1984. Ed. by Golf Digest. (Annual Ser.). 771p. 1984. 14.95 o.p. (ISBN 0-914178-66-0). Golf Digest.

Golf Digest Almanac, 1985. Golf Digest Editors. LC 84-645998. 893p. 1985. pap. 12.95 o.p. (ISBN 0-914178-74-1). Golf Digest.

Golf Digest Almanac, 1986. 3rd ed. Golf Digest Editors. LC 84-81382. 640p. 1986. pap. 14.95 o.p. (ISBN 0-914178-87-3). Golf Digest.

Golf for the Young. Eddie Merrins & Michael McTeigue. LC 83-45081. (Illus.). 112p. (YA) (gr. 10 up). 1983. pap. 9.95 o.s.i. (ISBN 0-689-70659-6, Atheneum). Macmillan.

Golf Is a Four-Letter Word: The Intimate Confessions of a Hooked Slicer. Richard Armour. (Illus.). 1962. pap. text ed. 3.95 o.p. (ISBN 0-07-002259-3). McGraw.

Golf My Way. Jack Nicklaus & Ken Bowden. (Illus.). 1974. 15.50 o.p. (ISBN 0-671-21702-X). S&S.

Golf Records, Facts & Champions. Donald Steel. (Illus.). 248p. 1988. 19.95 o.p. (ISBN 0-85112-847-5, Pub. by Guinness Superlatives England). Sterling.

Golf Secret. Henry A. Murray. (Illus.). 1954. 12.95 o.p. (ISBN 0-87523-093-8). Emerson.

Golf Shot. Michael W. Biddulph. LC 79-19060. (Illus.). 116p. 1980. 10.95 o.p. (ISBN 0-393-01312-X). Norton.

Golf Swing of the Future. Mindy Blake. (Illus.). 124p. 1973. 10.95 o.p. (ISBN 0-393-08376-4). Norton.

Golf: The Technique Barrier. Mindy Blake. (Illus.). 1979. 10.95 o.p. (ISBN 0-393-08825-1). Norton.

Golf Widow's Revenge. Patricia J. Smith. (Illus.). 160p. 1987. 13.95 o.p. (ISBN 0-8092-4802-6). Contemp Bks.

Golfer's Stroke Saving Handbook. Craig Shankland et al. LC 77-20905. (Illus.). 1978. 19.95 o.p. (ISBN 0-316-78260-2). Little.

Golfing Mind. Vivien Saunders. (Illus.). 192p. 1988. 19.95 o.s.i. (ISBN 0-689-12032-X, Atheneum). Macmillan.

Golf's Golden Grind: The History of the Tour. Al Barkow. 1974. 8.95 o.p. (ISBN 0-15-190885-0). HarBraceJ.

Golf's Supershots. George Peper. LC 81-66018. 1982. 17.95 o.p. (ISBN 0-689-11135-5, Atheneum). Macmillan.

Golf's Supershots: How the Pros Played Them - How You Can Play Them. George Peper. LC 81-66018. (Illus.). 160p. 1984. pap. 12.95 o.p. (ISBN 0-689-70671-5, 313, Atheneum). Macmillan.

Golgotha. Eugene D. Evans. 160p. 1982. 8.00 o.p. (ISBN 0-682-49856-4, Banner). Exposition-Phoenix.

Golgotha & the Church of the Holy Sepulchre. Andre Parrott. 1957. (ISBN 0-8022-1269-7). Philos Lib.

Golgotha Falls. Frank De Felitta. 1984. 15.45 o.p. (ISBN 0-671-50775-3). S&S.

Goliad Massacre: A Tragedy of Texas Revolution. Jakie L. Pruett & Everett B. Cole. (Illus.). 160p. 1985. 10.95 o.p. (ISBN 0-89015-476-7). Eakin Pr.

Goliaths of the World. John A. Bonar. Ed. by James Beasley. 89p. 1981. pap. 7.00 o.p. (ISBN 0-936204-22-2). Jelm Mtn.

Gollancz-Sunday Times SF Competition Stories. 192p. 1988. 19.95 o.p. (ISBN 0-575-04074-2, Pub. by Gollancz England). David & Charles.

Gombo Comes to Philadelphia. Edward L. Tinker. 32p. 1957. pap. 3.00x o.p. (ISBN 0-912296-26-7, Dist. by U Pr of Va). Am Antiquarian.

Gonadal Steroids & Brain Function: IUPS-Satellite Symposium 1980. Ed. by W. Wuttke & R. Horowski. (Experimental Brain Research Ser.: Supplementum 3). (Illus.). 325p. 1981. pap. 41.90 o.p. (ISBN 0-387-10606-5). Springer-Verlag.

Gonadotrophins: Current Research, 3 vols, Vol. 2. G. E. Seidel et al. 1974. text ed. 21.50x o.p. (ISBN 0-8422-7205-4). Irvington.

Gonadotrophins: Current Research, 3 vols, Vol. 3. Ed. by K. J. Ranadive et al. 1974. text ed. 21.50x o.p. (ISBN 0-685-55782-0). Irvington.

Gonadotropins & Gonadal Function. N. R. Moudgal. 1974. 65.00 o.p. (ISBN 0-12-508850-7). Acad Pr.

Gonds of Andhra Pradesh: Tradition & Change in an Indian Tribe. Christoph Von Furer Haimendorf. (Illus.). 569p. 1981. 40.00x o.p. (ISBN 0-7069-0718-3, Pub. by Vikas India). Advent NY.

Gondwana Stratigraphy: IUGS Symposium, Buenos Aires, 1967. (Earth Sciences Ser.: No. 2). (Illus.). 173p. (Orig., Eng. & Span.). 1969. pap. 15.75 o.p. (ISBN 92-3-000770-6, U267, UNESCO). UNIPUB.

Gone Man. Brad Solomon. 1980. pap. 2.25 o.p. (ISBN 0-380-49577-5, 49577-5). Avon.

Gone the Dreams & Dancing. Douglas C. Jones. 320p. 1984. 15.95 o.p. (ISBN 0-03-060043-X). H Holt & Co.

Gone Tomorrow: Zen Inspired Poetry. Ken Noyle. LC 66-20573. (Orig.). 1966. pap. 3.50 o.p. (ISBN 0-8048-0217-3). C E Tuttle.

Gone with the Wish. Eileen Goudge. (Swept Away Ser.: No. 1). 176p. 1986. pap. 2.50 o.p. (ISBN 0-380-75128-3, Flare). Avon.

Gonorrhoea: Epidemiology & Pathogenesis. Ed. by F. A. Skinner et al. 1978. 69.00 o.p. (ISBN 0-12-648055-9). Acad Pr.

Gonzalo De Tapia, 1561-1594: Founder of the First Permanent Jesuit Mission in North America. William E. Shiels. LC 74-12835. (U. S. Catholic Historical Society Monograph: No. XIV). 1978. Repr. of 1934 ed. lib. bdg. 35.00x o.p. (ISBN 0-8371-7758-8, SHGT). Greenwood.

Good. Date not set. pap. 7.95 o.p. (ISBN 0-413-50250-3). Heinemann Ed.

Good Advice. William Safire & Leonard Safir. LC 81-84897. 382p. 1982. 16.45 o.s.i. (ISBN 0-8129-1013-3). Times Bks.

Good Age Cookbook: Recipes from the Institute for Creative Aging. Jan Harlow et al. 1979. 10.95 o.p. (ISBN 0-395-27781-7). HM.

Good Apple & Career Education. Cindi Gahris. (Illus.). 144p. (gr. 3-7). 1983. wkbk. 9.95 o.p. (ISBN 0-86653-110-6, GA 463). Good Apple.

Good Apple & Creative Writing Fun. Howard Knopf & Kate A. Dunaway. (gr. 3-7). 1981. 9.95 o.p. (ISBN 0-86653-054-1, GA 255). Good Apple.

Good Apple & Grammar Fun. John Artman. (Illus.). 144p. (gr. 3-7). 1983. wkbk. 9.95 o.p. (ISBN 0-86653-128-9, GA 466). Good Apple.

Good As Gold. Joseph Heller. 1979. 12.95 o.p. (ISBN 0-671-22923-0). S&S.

Good Beer Guide, 1986 see Best Pubs of Great Britain, 1987-1988.

Good Beginning for Babies: Guidelines for Group Care. Anne Willis & Henry Ricciuti. LC 74-25867. (Illus.). 213p. 1975. pap. text ed. 7.00 o.p. (ISBN 0-912674-43-1, NAEYC #212). Natl Assn Child Ed.

Good Bibliographic Practice. James Negus. 60p. Softbound. 2.00 o.p. (ISBN 0-318-12927-2). Am Philatelic Society.

Good Books: A Book Lover's Companion. Steven Gilbar. LC 82-5554. 464p. 1982. 19.50 o.p. (ISBN 0-89919-127-4); pap. 9.70 o.p. (ISBN 0-89919-132-0). Ticknor & Fields.

Good Breakfast Book: A Bringing-Back-Breakfast Cookbook. Nikki Goldbeck & David Goldbeck. LC 74-21211. (Illus.). 224p. (Orig.). 1976. pap. 5.95 o.p. (ISBN 0-399-50705-1, Perigee). Putnam Pub Group.

Good Cat Book. Mordecai Siegal. 352p. 1982. pap. 8.50 o.p. (ISBN 0-671-45623-7, Fireside). S&S.

Good Cents. Amazing Life Games Staff. (Illus.). 1974. pap. 3.95 o.p. (ISBN 0-395-19501-2, Sandpiper). HM.

Good Cents: Every Kid's Guide to Making Money. Amazing Life Games Staff. LC 74-9378. (Illus.). 128p. (gr. 4-6). 1974. 7.95 o.p. (ISBN 0-395-19500-4). HM.

Good Cheer: The Romance of Food & Feasting. Frederick W. Hackwood. LC 68-9571. 424p. 1968. Repr. of 1911 ed. 34.00x o.p. (ISBN 0-8103-3508-5). Gale.

Good Citizens Alphabet. Bertrand Russell. (Illus.). 32p. 1958. (ISBN 0-8022-1420-7). Philos Lib.

Good Dog, Bad Dog. Matthew Margolis & Mordecai Siegal. LC 72-78139. 1973. 8.95 o.p. (ISBN 0-03-001421-2). H Holt & Co.

Good Earth & Country Cooking. 2nd ed. Betty Groff & Jose Wilson. LC 73-23128. (Illus.). 256p. 1974. pap. 14.95 o.p. (ISBN 0-8117-2066-7). Stackpole.

Good Enough to Dream. Roger Kahn. LC 85-1596. 360p. 1985. 16.95 o.p. (ISBN 0-385-18912-5). Doubleday.

Good Fish Dinner. Barbara Walker. LC 78-11152. (Illus.). 40p. (ps-3). 1979. 5.95 o.s.i. (ISBN 0-8193-0983-4); PLB 5.95 o.s.i. (ISBN 0-8193-0984-2). Parents.

Good Food for a Sober Life: A Diet & Nutrition Book for Recovering Alcoholics- & Those Who Love Them. Jack Mumey & Anne S. Hatcher. 192p. 1987. 16.95 o.p. (ISBN 0-8092-4804-2). Contemp Bks.

Good Food from a Japanese Temple. Soei Yoneda. Tr. by Kim Schuefftan from Japanese. LC 82-80734. (Illus.). 208p. 1982. 18.95 o.p. (ISBN 0-87011-527-8). Kodansha.

Good-for-Nothings. Jacob Grimm & Wilhelm K. Grimm. 1957. 3.25 o.p. (ISBN 0-15-232183-7, HJ). HarBraceJ.

Good Goodies. Stanley Dworkin & Florence Dworkin. 1980. pap. 2.50 o.p. (ISBN 0-449-23964-0, Crest). Fawcett.

Good Greenwood. Eric Rhodin. LC 72-150382. (gr. 7 up). 1971. 4.75 o.s.i. (ISBN 0-664-32495-9, Westminster). Westminster John Knox.

Good Guys, Bad Guys. Martin Lubin. 312p. 1981. text ed. 12.95 o.p. (ISBN 0-07-038913-6). McGraw.

Good Guys Finish First: Success Strategies from the Book of Proverbs for Business Men & Women. Clinton W. McLemore. LC 83-14708. 142p. 1983. pap. 7.95 o.s.i. (ISBN 0-664-26004-7, Westminster). Westminster John Knox.

Good Health Kit. Richard Smith & Ron Van Der Meer. 1987. 24.95 o.p. (ISBN 0-8050-0389-4). H Holt & Co.

Good Heart Diet Cookbook. Ellen Stern & Jonathan Michaels. LC 81-8938. 256p. 1982. 12.95 o.p. (ISBN 0-89919-053-7). Ticknor & Fields.

Good Hope Poems. Mark Harris. 85p. (Orig.). 1985. pap. 6.95x o.p. (ISBN 0-932269-22-2). Wyndham Hall.

Good Housekeeping Encyclopedia of House Plants. Robert Herwig. LC 84-47793. (Illus.). 288p. 1984. 19.95 o.p. (ISBN 0-688-03321-0, Hearst Bk). Morrow.

Good Housekeeping Family Health & Medical Guide. Good Housekeeping Magazine Editors. LC 78-51129. (Illus.). 960p. 1979. 25.45 o.p. (ISBN 0-87851-023-0). Hearst Bks.

Good Housekeeping International Cookbook. Good Housekeeping Staff. pap. 1.75 o.p. (ISBN 0-380-01211-1, 30783). Avon.

Good Housekeeping Woman's Medical Guide. David Rorvik. 1976. pap. 1.95 o.p. (ISBN 0-380-00566-2, 28886). Avon.

Good Husband. Pamela H. Johnson. 1979. 8.95 o.s.i. (ISBN 0-684-16157-5, ScribT). Scribner.

Good Journey. Simon J. Ortiz. LC 84-8458. (Sun Tracks Ser.: No. 12). 165p. 1984. pap. 8.95 o.p. (ISBN 0-8165-0883-6). U of Ariz Pr.

Good King Richard? An Account of Richard III & His Reputation. Jeremy Potter. 1983. text ed. 32.50x o.s.i. (ISBN 0-09-464630-9, Pub. by Constable Pubs UK). Trans-Atl Phila.

Good Life Good Death: A Doctor's Case for Euthanasia & Suicide. Christiaan Barnard. LC 80-18839. 120p. 1980. 7.95 o.s.i. (ISBN 0-13-360370-9). P-H.

Good Man Is Hard to Find. Flannery O'Connor. LC 55-7423. 1955. 7.95 o.p. (ISBN 0-15-136503-2). HarBraceJ.

Good Man's Not Hard to Find. Kiki Olson. 1985. pap. 5.95 o.p. (ISBN 0-671-54676-7, Pub. by Fireside). S&S.

Good Manufacturing Practices for Pharmaceuticals. Willig. (Drugs & the Pharmaceutical Sciences Ser.). 312p. 1982. 55.00 o.p. (ISBN 0-8247-1664-7). Dekker.

Good Mixer Cookbook. Diana Campbell. LC 81-69077. (Illus.). 160p. 1982. 9.95 o.p. (ISBN 0-916752-49-6). Longman Trade.

Good Morning, 3 vols. 1969. Repr. of 1921 ed. Set. lib. bdg. 39.00x o.p. (ISBN 0-8371-9175-0, GM00). Greenwood.

Good Morning, I'm Joan Lunden. Joan Lunden & Ardy Freidberg. 1986. 17.95 o.p. (ISBN 0-399-13126-4). Putnam Pub Group.

Good Morning Judy! Jeanine Steuck. LC 78-52173. 1978. pap. 4.95 o.p. (ISBN 0-8066-1673-3, 10-2801, Augsburg). Augsburg Fortress.

Good Morning, Lord: Devotions for College Students. Louis O. Caldwell. (Good Morning Lord Ser.). 1971. 4.95 o.p. (ISBN 0-8010-2324-6). Baker Bk.

Good Morning, Lord: Devotions for Young Mothers. Mary F. Loeks. (Good Morning, Lord Ser.). 1977. 4.95 o.p. (ISBN 0-8010-5566-0). Baker Bk.

Good Morning, Lord: Meditations for Modern Marrieds. Louis O. Caldwell. (Good Morning Lord Ser.). 1974. 3.95 o.p. (ISBN 0-8010-2351-3). Baker Bk.

Good Morning, Lord: More Devotions for Teens. Paul Martin. (Good Morning Lord Ser.). (gr. 7-12). 1973. 4.95 o.p. (ISBN 0-8010-5915-1). Baker Bk.

Good Morning, Merry Sunshine. Bob Greene. 1985. lib. bdg. 17.95 o.p. (ISBN 0-8161-3803-6, Large Print Bks). G K Hall.

Good Morning, Merry Sunshine: A Father's Journal of His Child's First Year. Bob Greene. LC 83-45510. 320p. 1984. 14.95 o.p. (ISBN 0-689-11434-6, Atheneum). Macmillan.

Good Morning, Revolution: Uncollected Writings of Social Protest. Langston Hughes. Ed. by Faith Berry. LC 73-81747. 160p. 1973. 8.50 o.s.i. (ISBN 0-88208-023-7); pap. 5.95 o.s.i. (ISBN 0-88208-024-5). Chicago Review.

Good Morning to You, Valentine. Ed. by Lee B. Hopkins. LC 75-11650. (Illus.). 32p. (gr. 1-5). 1976. 11.95 o.p. (ISBN 0-15-232134-9, HJ). HarBraceJ.

Good Morrow. Gunilla Norris. (Illus.). (gr. 3-7). 1969. PLB 5.25 o.p. (ISBN 0-689-20670-4, Atheneum). Macmillan.

Good-Natured Man: The Evolution of a Moral Ideal, 1660-1800. John K. Sheriff. LC 81-14758. 144p. 1982. text ed. 13.50 o.p. (ISBN 0-8173-0097-X). U of Ala Pr.

Good Neighbors U. S. A. Cookbook. Ed. by Clarissa M. Silitch. LC 84-51677. (Illus.). 320p. 1985. 15.95 o.p. (ISBN 0-89909-060-5). Yankee Bks.

Good News! Beth Neuberger. (Happy Day Bks.). (Illus.). 24p. (ps-2). 1984. 1.59 o.p. (ISBN 0-87239-736-X, 3706). Standard Pub.

Good News about Jesus As Told by Mark. Thomas Smith. Ed. by Alphonsus Pluth. LC 77-89324. (Illus.). 101p. 1977. pap. 3.95 o.p. (ISBN 0-88489-095-3); tchrs' ed 1.00 o.p. (ISBN 0-88489-116-X). St Mary's.

Titles

Good News About Jesus As Told by Mark. Thomas J. Smith. LC 77-89324. 1978. pap. 3.95 o.p. (ISBN 0-8042-0248-6, John Knox). Westminster John Knox.
Good News Anyone. Jean L. Smith. (Orig.). 1970. pap. 1.95 o.p. (ISBN 0-377-00451-0). Friendship Pr.
Good News, Bad News. Michael Savage. 1986. pap. 4.95 o.p. (ISBN 0-89480-294-1). Workman Pub.
Good News from John: Visual Messages for Children. Harold J. Uhl. LC 79-50094. (ps-4). 1979. pap. 6.95 o.p. (ISBN 0-8066-1712-8, 10-2811, Augsburg). Augsburg Fortress.
Good News Is the Bad News Is Wrong. Ben J. Wattenberg. LC 84-10574. 431p. 1984. 17.45 o.p. (ISBN 0-671-47545-2). S&S.
Good News Is the Bad News Is Wrong. rev. & updated ed. Ben J. Wattenberg. 1985. pap. 8.95 o.p. (ISBN 0-671-60641-7, Touchstone Bks.). S&S.
Good News: Mark. W. E. McCumber. 184p. 1981. pap. 4.95 o.p. (ISBN 0-8341-0699-X). Beacon Hill.
Good News to the Poor: Wealth & Poverty in Luke-Acts. Walter E. Pilgrim. LC 81-65653. 208p. (Orig.). 1981. pap. 10.95 o.p. (ISBN 0-8066-1889-2, 10-2807, Augsburg). Augsburg Fortress.
Good Night, Little Wrinkle. Photos by Anita Shevett. LC 86-62245. (Wrinkles Board Bks.). (Illus.). 12p. (ps-1). 1987. pap. 2.95 o.s.i. (ISBN 0-394-88680-1, BYR). Random.
Good Night, Lord. Paul Martin. 64p. 1974. 1.95 o.p. (ISBN 0-8341-0241-2). Beacon Hill.
Good Night, Orange Monster. Betty J. Lifton. LC 72-75275. (gr. 1-3). 1972. 5.95 o.s.i. (ISBN 0-689-30055-7, Atheneum). Macmillan.
Good Night's Sleep: A Step-by-Step Program for Overcoming Insomnia & Other Sleep Problems. Jerrold S. Maxman. (Illus.). 1981. 14.95 o.p. (ISBN 0-393-01437-1). Norton.
Good Old Ernie. Bartch-Mallett. (Bartch & Mallett's Ernie Ser.: Bk. 1). 7.95 o.p. (ISBN 0-8062-0932-1). Carlton.
Good People of Gomorrah. Ed. by Gordon Osing. LC 78-31841. (Illus.). 1979. pap. 6.95x o.p. (ISBN 0-918518-13-X, St Luke TN). Peachtree Pubs.
Good Samaritan. LC 76-47914. (Sunshine Bks.). (Illus.). 1977. pap. 1.50 o.p. (ISBN 0-8006-1578-6, 1-1578, Fortress). Augsburg Fortress.
Good School. Date not set. pap. (ISBN 0-385-29365-8). Delacorte.
Good School. Richard Yates. 192p. 1984. pap. 8.95 o.p. (ISBN 0-385-29365-8, Delta). Dell.
Good Sex: A Healthy Man's Guide to Sexual Fulfillment. Gary F. Kelly. LC 78-22257. 1979. 8.95 o.p. (ISBN 0-15-136685-3). HarBraceJ.
Good Son. Craig Nova. 448p. 1983. pap. 4.50 o.s.i. (ISBN 0-440-33091-2, LE). Dell.
Good Sport, Bad Sport. Jerry Jenkins. (Bradford Family Adventures Ser.). (Illus.). 112p. (gr. 3-6). 1985. 2.95 o.p. (ISBN 0-87239-944-3, 2994). Standard Pub.
Good Stones. Anne M. Epstein. (Illus.). 274p. (gr. 5-9). 1977. 6.95 o.p. (ISBN 0-395-25154-0). HM.
Good Stories for Great Holidays. Francis J. Olcott. (Illus.). (gr. 4-6). 1914. 6.95 o.p. (ISBN 0-395-06967-X). HM.
Good Taste Begins with You. Alton E. Frazier. Ed. by Arthur F. Ide. LC 79-9441. (Illus., Orig.). 1980. pap. 39.00 set o.s.i. (ISBN 0-86663-250-6). Ide Hse.
Good Things for Babies. Sandy Jones. LC 75-34209. 1975. 8.95 o.s.i. (ISBN 0-395-20728-2); pap. 4.95 o.p. (ISBN 0-395-21501-3). HM.
Good Things for Babies. 2nd rev. ed. Sandy Jones. (Illus.). 1980. 12.95 o.p. (ISBN 0-395-29197-6); pap. 6.95 o.p. (ISBN 0-395-29198-4). HM.
Good Time Charlie's Back in Town. Alfred Silver. 1978. pap. 1.75 o.p. (ISBN 0-380-39065-5, 39065). Avon.
Good Times, Bad Times. Harold Evans. LC 83-48833. 1984. 17.95 o.p. (ISBN 0-689-11465-6, Atheneum). Macmillan.
Good Times, Bad Times. James Kirkwood. 1981. pap. 2.95 o.p. (ISBN 0-449-23975-6, Crest). Fawcett.
Good Times Game Book: Good Things for Youth Leaders. Compiled by Douglas Kamstra. 1981. pap. 5.95 o.p. (ISBN 0-8010-7705-2). Baker Bk.
Good to Eat: Riddles of Food & Culture. Marvin Harris. 288p. 1986. 17.45 o.p. (ISBN 0-671-50366-9). S&S.
Good Tour Guide. Date not set. Salem Hse Pubs.
Good Vibrations: The Complete Guide to Vibrators. Joani Blank. LC 80-26761. 52p. 1982. pap. 4.50 o.p. (ISBN 0-940208-05-9). Down There Pr.
Good Writing: An Informal Manual of Style. Alan Vrooman. LC 66-18229. 1967. pap. text ed. 3.95x o.p. (ISBN 0-689-70567-0, Atheneum). Macmillan.
Goodbye, Blues: A Guide to Breaking the Tranquilizer Habit the Natural Way. Bernard Green & Ted Schwarz. LC 80-21551. 224p. 1982. text ed. 10.95 o.p. (ISBN 0-07-024337-9); pap. text ed. 5.95 o.p. (ISBN 0-07-024338-7). McGraw.
Goodbye, California. Alistair MacLean. 1983. pap. 2.95 o.p. (ISBN 0-449-20302-6, Crest). Fawcett.
Goodbye, Columbus. Philip Roth. 1959. 9.95 o.p. (ISBN 0-395-08138-6). HM.
Goodbye, Funny Dumpy-Lumpy. Bernard Waber. LC 76-14349. (gr. 1-4). 1977. reinforced bdg. 6.95 o.p. (ISBN 0-395-24735-7). HM.
Goodbye, Goliath. Elliott Chaze. 192p. 1983. 11.95 o.s.i. (ISBN 0-684-17844-3, ScribT). Scribner.
Goodbye, Grandpa. Ron Koch. LC 74-14183. 96p. (gr. 2 up). 1975. pap. 5.95 o.p. (ISBN 0-8066-1465-X, 10-2816, Augsburg). Augsburg Fortress.
Goodbye, Secret Place. Kathy G. Roe. LC 81-20108. 176p. (gr. 5-9). 1982. 7.95 o.p. (ISBN 0-395-31864-5). HM.
Goodbye to Arthritis. Patricia Byrivers. 1986. 13.50 o.p. (ISBN 0-8166-0317-0, Large Print Books). G K Hall.
Goodbye to Bedlam: Understanding Mental Illness & Retardation. John Langone. 160p. (gr. 7-12). 1974. 14.95 o.p. (ISBN 0-316-51421-7). Little.
Goodbye to Goodtime Charlie: American Governorship Transformed. 2nd ed. Larry Sabato. LC 82-22033. 243p. 1983. pap. 12.95 o.p. (ISBN 0-87187-249-8). Congr Quarterly.
Goodbye to Some. Gordon Forbes. (War Library). 272p. 1982. pap. 2.50 o.s.i. (ISBN 0-345-30641-4). Ballantine.
Goodbye to the Low Profile: The Art of Creative Confrontation. Herbert Schmertz & William Novak. (Illus.). 242p. 1986. 16.95 o.p. (ISBN 0-316-77366-2). Little.
Goodbye, Yesterday. Joan W. Anglund. LC 74-77621. (Illus.). 1974. 3.95 o.p. (ISBN 0-689-10610-6, Atheneum). Macmillan.
Goode's World Atlas. 16th ed. Ed. by Edward B. Espenshade, Jr. Joel Morrison. LC 73-21108. 384p. 1978. text ed. 19.95 o.p. (ISBN 0-528-83125-9); pap. text ed. 15.95 o.p. (ISBN 0-528-63007-5). Rand McNally.
Goodly Heritage, the Episcopal Church in Florida, 1821-1892. Joseph D. Cushman, Jr. LC 65-28693. (Illus.). 1965. 7.50 o.p. (ISBN 0-8130-0054-8). U Presses Fla.
Goodnight, Good Day. Zokeisha. (Puffies Ser.). (Illus.). 8p. (ps). 1982. pap. 3.40 o.s.i. (ISBN 0-671-45079-4, Little Simon). S&S.
Goodnight, Little Rabbit. Marie Wabbes. (Illus.). (ps). 1987. pap. 4.95 o.s.i. (ISBN 0-87113-127-7, Joy St Bks). Little.
Goodwill Ambassador. Thomas J. Bennett. 1980. pap. 3.50 o.p. (ISBN 0-682-49496-8). Exposition-Phoenix.
Goody Hall. Natalie Babbitt. LC 73-149221. (Illus.). 176p. (gr. 4 up). 1971. 10.95 o.p. (ISBN 0-374-32745-9, Sunburst); pap. 3.95 o.p. FS&G.
Gooficon: A Repair Manual for English. Marina K. Burt & Carol Kiparsky. 1972. pap. 8.25 o.p. (ISBN 0-912066-07-5). Newbury Hse.
Goofy. LC 79-11365. (Walt Disney Best Comics Ser.). (Illus.). 184p. (YA) (gr. 7 up). 1979. 15.95 o.p. (ISBN 0-89659-033-X). Abbeville Pr.
Goori Goori Bird. Grahame L. Walsh. (Illus.). 56p. (gr. 3 up). 1986. 15.95 o.p. (ISBN 0-7022-1777-8). U of Queensland Pr.
Goose & the Golden Coins. Lorinda B. Cauley. LC 80-24591. (Illus.). 48p. (ps-3). 1981. pap. 5.95 o.p. (ISBN 0-15-232207-8, VoyB). HarBraceJ.
Goose & the Golden Coins. Ed. by Lorinda B. Cauley. LC 80-24591. (Illus.). 48p. (ps-3). 1981. 11.95 o.p. (ISBN 0-15-232206-X, HJ). HarBraceJ.
Goose Dinner. Eve Bunting. LC 80-39747. (Let Me Read Ser.). (Illus.). 32p. (ps-3). 1981. 7.95 o.p. (ISBN 0-15-232224-8, HJ). HarBraceJ.
Goose Dinner. Eve Bunting. LC 80-39747. (Let Me Read Ser.). (Illus.). 32p. (ps-3). 1981. pap. 2.95 o.p. (ISBN 0-15-232225-6, VoyB). HarBraceJ.
Goose Goofs Off. Jacquelyn Reinach. LC 76-44313. (Sweet Pickles Ser.). (Illus.). (gr. k-2). 1977. 2.95 o.p. (ISBN 0-03-018086-4). H Holt & Co.
Gooseberries to Oranges. Barbara Cohen. (Illus.). (gr. 1-3). 1982. 11.75 o.p. (ISBN 0-688-00690-6); PLB 11.88 o.p. (ISBN 0-688-00691-4). Lothrop.
Gopher Reader I. Ed. by A. Hermina Poatgieter & James T. Dunn. LC 58-62565. 308p. 1958. pap. 7.50 o.p. (ISBN 0-87351-138-7). Minn Hist.
Gordon Craig's Paris Diary 1932 - 1933. Gordon Craig. Ed. by Colin Franklin. (Illus.). 154p. 1986. 185.00x o.p. (ISBN 0-8139-1121-4, Bird & Bull Pr). U Pr of Va.
Gordon Solie: Master of the Ring. Gordon Solie & Dee Forbes. LC 84-62145. (Illus.). 128p. 1984. pap. 7.95 o.p. (ISBN 0-88427-056-4). North River.
Gordon's Print Price Annual, 1988. Date not set. 300.00 o.p. (ISBN 0-317-57511-2). Editions Pub.
Gore Vidal: A Primary & Secondary Bibliography. Robert J. Stanton. 1978. lib. bdg. 31.50 o.p. (ISBN 0-8161-8109-8, Hall Reference). G K Hall.
Gorey Cats Paper Dolls. Ed. by Malcolm Whyte. (Illus.). 40p. (Orig.). 1982. pap. 3.95 o.p. (ISBN 0-89844-086-6). Troubador Pr.
Gorga, the Space Monster. Edward Packard. (Choose Your Own Adventure Ser.: No. 5). 64p. (gr. 1-8). 1982. pap. 2.25 o.s.i. (ISBN 0-553-15507-5). Bantam.
Gorgle V. (Big Little Bks.: No. 129). (Illus.). 350p. 1984. 6.95 o.p. (ISBN 0-318-02733-X). Bks Nippan.
Gorgon, 49 vols. 1969. Repr. of 1819 ed. Set. lib. bdg. 18.25x o.p. (ISBN 0-8371-9176-9, GG00). Greenwood.
Gorilla Did It. Barbara S. Hazen. LC 73-84828. (Illus.). (ps-1). 1978. pap. 3.95 o.p. (Aladdin). Macmillan.
Gorilla Wants to Be the Baby. Barbara S. Hazen. LC 78-5972. (Illus.). (ps-1). 1978. 6.95 o.p. (ISBN 0-689-30654-7, Atheneum). Macmillan.
Gorlin Clinic. Barbara Harrison. 1975. pap. 1.75 o.p. (ISBN 0-380-00446-1, 27052). Avon.
Gospel. Jack Ansell. LC 72-82169. 1973. 7.95 o.p. (ISBN 0-87795-038-5, Arbor Hse). Morrow.
Gospel. Date not set. (ISBN 0-8052-3875-1). Random.
Gospel According to Andy Capp. D. P. McGeachy, 3rd. LC 73-5347. (Illus.). 132p. (Orig.). 1973. pap. 2.95 o.p. (ISBN 0-8042-1955-9, John Knox). Westminster John Knox.
Gospel According to Barabbas. Salvatore Grillo. Tr. by Nino Cavoto from Ital. LC 82-72703. Orig. Title: Vangelo Secondo Barabba. 294p. (Orig.). 1982. pap. 4.95 o.p. (ISBN 0-89944-041-X, P 041-X). Don Bosco Multimedia.
Gospel According to Genesis. Charles C. Cochrane. 96p. (Orig.). 1984. pap. 4.95 o.p. (ISBN 0-8028-1971-0). Eerdmans.
Gospel According to Matthew. James Morison. 706p. lib. bdg. 24.95 o.p. (ISBN 0-8254-5190-6). Kregel.
Gospel According to St. Matthew. A. H. McNeile. (Thornapple Commentaries Ser.). 484p. 1980. pap. 8.95 o.p. (ISBN 0-8010-6099-0). Baker Bk.
Gospel & the Ambiguity of the Church. Ed. by Vilmos Vajta. LC 73-88358. 256p. 1974. 0.50x o.p. (ISBN 0-8006-0278-1, Fortress). Augsburg Fortress.
Gospel & the Church. Alfred Loisy. Tr. by Christopher Home from Ger. LC 75-13050. (Lives of Jesus Ser.). 352p. 1976. pap. 3.00 o.p. (ISBN 0-8006-1274-4, 1-1274, Fortress). Augsburg Fortress.
Gospel & the Poor. Wolfgang Stegemann. Tr. by Dietlinde Elliott from Ger. LC 83-48915. 80p. 1984. pap. 0.95 o.p. (ISBN 0-8006-1783-5, 1-1783, Fortress). Augsburg Fortress.
Gospel As History. Ed. by Vilmos Vajta. LC 74-26348. 256p. 1975. text ed. 2.00x o.p. (ISBN 0-8006-0410-5, Fortress). Augsburg Fortress.
Gospel in Leviticus. Joseph Seiss. LC 80-8078. 400p. 1981. 12.95 o.p. (ISBN 0-8254-3743-1). Kregel.
Gospel in Madison Avenue. Peter Rudowski. 1983. 3.85 o.p. (ISBN 0-89536-644-4, 0741). CSS of Ohio.
Gospel in the Last Days. J. M. Little. LC 84-90258. 143p. 1985. 10.95 o.p. (ISBN 0-533-06299-3). Vantage.
Gospel Message & Hellenistic Culture. Tr. by John A. Baker. (History of Early Christian Doctrine Before the Council of Nicaea: Vol. 2). 17.50 o.p. (ISBN 0-664-20961-0, Westminster). Westminster John Knox.
Gospel of John & Judaism. C. K. Barrett. Tr. by D. M. Smith. LC 75-15435. 112p. 1975. 3.95 o.p. (ISBN 0-8006-0431-8, 1-431, Fortress). Augsburg Fortress.
Gospel of Luke. Bo Reicke. LC 64-12263. (Orig.). 1964. pap. 1.95 o.p. (ISBN 0-8042-3400-0, John Knox). Westminster John Knox.
Gospel of Mark: A Translation for Children. Tr. by Wayne W. Martin. LC 84-50838. 112p. (Orig.). (gr. 3-7). 1984. pap. 5.00 o.p. (ISBN 0-8358-0493-3). Upper Room.
Gospel of Matthew. William R. Cannon. LC 82-50948. 128p. (Orig.). 1983. pap. 4.95 o.p. (ISBN 0-8358-0450-X). Upper Room.
Gospel Power: Toward the Revitalization of Preaching. John Burke. LC 77-14517. 1978. pap. 4.95 o.p. (ISBN 0-8189-0359-7). Alba.
Gospel Singer. Nathaniel A. Dikens. 1987. 11.95 o.p. (ISBN 0-533-07387-1). Vantage.
Gospel Unified. Tamer Fakhry. 1984. 15.00 o.p. (ISBN 0-533-05126-6). Vantage.
Gospels: A First Commentary. F. G. Herod. LC 77-79590. (Bible Speaks to Us Today Ser.). 1977. pap. 2.95 o.p. (ISBN 0-8042-0255-9, John Knox). Westminster John Knox.
Gospels & Contemporary Biographies in the Greco-Roman World. Clyde W. Votaw. LC 79-135748. (Facet Bks.). 72p. 1970. pap. 0.50 o.p. (ISBN 0-8006-3061-0, 1-3061, Fortress). Augsburg Fortress.
Goss China Arms, Decorations & Their Values. Nicholas Pine. (Illus.). 120p. 1985. 17.95 o.p. (ISBN 0-903852-24-1, Pub. by Milestone Pubns UK). Seven Hills Bk Dists.
Goss China: 1986 Price Guide. Nicholas Pine. (Illus.). 120p. 1985. 17.95 o.p. (ISBN 0-903852-74-8, Pub. by Milestone Pubns UK). Seven Hills Bk Dists.
Gossamer Fly. Meira Chand. LC 79-27033. 192p. 1980. 8.95 o.p. (ISBN 0-89919-002-2). Ticknor & Fields.
Gossamer Odyssey: The Triumph of Human-Powered Flight. Morton Grosser. (Illus.). 288p. 1981. 14.95 o.p. (ISBN 0-395-30531-4). HM.
Gossip from the Forest. Thomas Keneally. LC 75-34484. 220p. 1976. 8.95 o.p. (ISBN 0-15-136705-1). HarBraceJ.
Gossip from Thrush Green. Miss Read. 1982. 13.00 o.p. (ISBN 0-395-32215-4). HM.
Gossip in the First Decade of Victoria's Reign. John Ashton. LC 67-23942. 332p. 1968. Repr. of 1903 ed. 30.00x o.p. (ISBN 0-8103-3249-3). Gale.
Gossip Trivia Quiz Book. Bruce Solomon & Michael Uslan. 1985. 6.95 o.p. (ISBN 0-87795-701-0, Arbor Hse). Morrow.
Gothic Ai & Av. Richard J. D'Alquen. LC 72-94440. (Janua Linguarum, Series Practica: No. 151). 182p. 1974. pap. text ed. 36.80x o.p. (ISBN 0-686-22578-3). Mouton.
Gothic Cathedral in France & England: Style, Form, & Sources. Carole Cable. (Architecture Ser.: A 1383). 7p. 1985. 2.00 o.p. (ISBN 0-89028-393-1). Vance Biblios.
Gothic Cathedral: Origins of Gothic Architecture & the Medieval Concept of Order. Otto Von Simson. LC 72-11946. (Bollingen Ser.: No. 48). (Illus.). 300p. 1973. 31.00 o.p. (ISBN 0-691-09741-0); pap. 9.50 o.p. (ISBN 0-691-01789-1). Princeton U Pr.
Gothic Pursuit. John Malcolm. (Tim Simpson Mystery Ser.). 208p. 1987. 14.95 o.p. (ISBN 0-684-18833-3, Scribner). Scribner.
Gothic Revival in Architecture, Art & Literature. Mary Vance. (Architecture Ser.: A 1498). 13p. 1985. 2.00 o.p. (ISBN 0-89028-648-5). Vance Biblios.
Gothic Stained Glass: 1200-1300. Louis Grodecki & Catherine Brisac. Tr. by Barbara D. Boehm from Fr. LC 85-71277. (Illus.). 288p. 1985. 75.00x o.p. (ISBN 0-8014-1809-7). Cornell U Pr.
Gotta Dance! Beth Joiner. LC 84-91373. 1985. 7.95 o.p. (ISBN 0-533-06411-2). Vantage.
Gotta Run, My Government Is Collapsing. Garry Trudeau. 128p. 1982. pap. 2.25 o.p. (ISBN 0-449-24524-1, Crest). Fawcett.
Gottfried's Tristan. 35.00x o.p. (ISBN 0-317-58094-9). Camden Hse.
Gourman Report: A Rating of Graduate & Professional Programs in American & International Universities. 3rd, rev. ed. Jack Gourman. LC 85-62132. 197p. 1985. pap. 9.95 o.p. (ISBN 0-918192-09-9). Natl Ed Stand.
Gourmet Cookbook for Those Interested in Weight Control. Caroline Weiss et al. (Illus.). 1986. pap. 2.99 o.p. (ISBN 0-686-65552-4). Budlong.
Gourmet Cooking Confidential. Ralph Varketta. LC 74-21449. (Illus.). 1975. 6.75 o.p. (ISBN 0-682-48154-8). Exposition-Phoenix.
Gourmet Guide to Water Cookery. Jay Heyman. 128p. 1983. pap. 4.95 o.p. (ISBN 0-380-81935-X, 81935-X). Avon.
Gourmet Italian Cooking for Large Appetites & Small Budgets: With Special Sections on Outdoor & Teenage Cooking. Frank Lanza. 1979. 7.50 o.p. (ISBN 0-682-49234-5, Banner). Exposition-Phoenix.
Gourmet Preserves: Sweet or Savory, Spread, Sauce or Condiment, a Complete Guide to Delicious & Unique Preserving. Judith Choate. LC 86-18951. (Illus.). 192p. 1987. 15.95 o.p. (ISBN 0-317-56474-9). Weidenfeld.
Gourmet Woodburner. Freddie Peirce. LC 84-27394. (Illus.). 188p. 1986. pap. 14.95 o.p. (ISBN 0-87842-175-0). Mountain Pr.
Gout I: Recent Studies. Jack L. Katz et al. 200p. 1974. text ed. 21.50x o.p. (ISBN 0-8422-7191-0). Irvington.
Gout II: Recent Studies. R. W. E. Watts et al. 1974. 21.50x o.p. (ISBN 0-8422-7208-9). Irvington.
Governance of Colleges & Universities: Modernizing Structure & Processes. 2nd. ed. John J. Corson. 1975. text ed. 21.95 o.p. (ISBN 0-07-013205-4). McGraw.
Governess: Or Little Female Academy. Sarah Fielding. pap. 8.95 o.p. (ISBN 0-317-65251-6, Pandora Pr). Routledge Chapman & Hall.
Governing America. Joseph A. Califano, Jr. 1982. pap. 8.50 o.p. (ISBN 0-671-25429-4, Touchstone Bks). S&S.

Governing America: An Introduction. Robert Sherrill et al. (Illus.). 654p. 1978. text ed. 28.00 net o.p. (ISBN 0-15-529629-9, HC). HarBraceJ.

Governing New York City. Wallace S. Sayre & Herbert Kaufman. 1965. pap. 11.95x o.p. (ISBN 0-393-09657-2, NortonC). Norton.

Governing Urban America. 5th ed. Charles R. Adrian & Charles Press. 1977. text ed. 35.95 o.p. (ISBN 0-07-000446-3). McGraw.

Government Accounting & Supplements 1 & 2. (Orig.). 1987. Set. text ed. 27.00 o.p. (ISBN 0-11-560008-6, HM265, Pub. by Her Maj Station Ofc); Supplement No. 1. text ed. 3.42 o.p. (ISBN 0-11-560010-8, HM266); Supplement No. 2. text ed. 6.45 o.p. (ISBN 0-11-560011-6, HM267). UNIPUB.

Government & Administration of Mississippi. Robert B. Highsaw & Charles N. Fortenberry. Ed. by W. Brooke Graves. LC 80-11136. (American Commonwealths Ser.: Vol. 22). (Illus.). xiv, 414p. 1980. Repr. of 1954 ed. lib. bdg. 35.00x o.p. (ISBN 0-313-22369-6, HIGA). Greenwood.

Government & Economic Choice: An Introduction to Public Finance. Thomas F. Pogue & Larry G. Sgontz. LC 77-75157. (Illus.). 1978. text ed. 36.50 o.p. (ISBN 0-395-25112-5). HM.

Government & Economy in British West Africa. David E. Carney. (Orig.). 1961. pap. 9.95x o.p. (ISBN 0-8084-0147-5). New Coll U Pr.

Government & Industry Relationships: The Lubbock Memorial Lectures, 1975. Ed. by David G. Lethbridge. 200p. 1976. 38.00 o.p. (ISBN 0-08-019733-7); pap. text ed. 23.00 o.p. (ISBN 0-08-019732-9). Pergamon.

Government & Labor in Early America. Richard B. Morris. LC 81-9525. 579p. 1981. pap. 10.95x o.p. (ISBN 0-930350-24-3). NE U Pr.

Government & Politics of California. 4th ed. Henry Turner & J. Vieg. 1971. text ed. 10.95 o.p. (ISBN 0-07-065580-4); pap. text ed. (ISBN 0-07-065581-2). McGraw.

Government & Politics of France. 2nd ed. Vincent Wright. 350p. 1987. text ed. 37.50 o.p. (ISBN 0-8419-0871-0); pap. text ed. 16.95 o.p. (ISBN 0-8419-0872-9). Holmes & Meier.

Government & Rebellions in Southeast Asia. Ed. by Chandran Jeshurun. (Issues in Southeast Asian Security Ser.). 306p. 1986. text ed. 42.50x o.p. (ISBN 9971-988-10-0, Pub. by Inst Southeast Asian Stud). Gower Pub Co.

Government & Technical Progress: Cross-Industry Analysis. Ed. by Richard R. Nelson. (Technical Policy & Economic Growth Ser.). (Illus.). 512p. 1982. 125.00 o.p. (ISBN 0-08-028837-5, L110). Pergamon.

Government & the Governed. Douglas Wass. LC 83-26877. (BBC Reith Lecture Ser.: 1983). 120p. 1984. 19.95x o.p. (ISBN 0-7102-0312-8). Routledge Chapman & Hall.

Government at the Grass-Roots. 3rd ed. George S. Blair. LC 80-84554. (Illus.). 1981. 15.95 o.p. (ISBN 0-913530-25-5); pap. 10.95x o.p. (ISBN 0-913530-24-7). Palisades Pub.

Government by Contract. John Hanrahan. 1983. 16.50 o.p. (ISBN 0-393-01717-6). Norton.

Government by the People. rev. ed. Katie Baer. 72p. 1982. 5.50 o.p. (ISBN 0-88336-489-1). New Readers.

Government by the People, 3 pts. 11th ed. James M. Burns et al. Incl. National, State, Local. 800p. text ed. 24.95 o.p. (ISBN 0-13-361253-8); wkbk. 8.50 o.p. (ISBN 0-13-361295-3); Basic. 480p. text ed. 22.95 o.p. (ISBN 0-13-361238-4); National. 640p. text ed. 23.95 o.p. (ISBN 0-13-361246-5); study guide 7.95 o.p. (ISBN 0-13-361287-2). (Illus.). 1981. study guide 7.95 o.p. (ISBN 0-13-361279-1). P-H.

Government by the People: Basic. 12th ed. James M. Burns et al. (Illus.). 480p. 1984. text ed. (ISBN 0-13-361360-7). P-H.

Government by the People: Basic. 12th, alternate ed. James M. Burns et al. (Illus.). 512p. 1985. text ed. (ISBN 0-13-361502-2). P-H.

Government by the People: National. 12th ed. James M. Burns et al. (Illus.). 592p. 1984. text ed. (ISBN 0-13-361378-X). P-H.

Government by the People: National, State & Local. 12th ed. James M. Burns et al. (Illus.). 752p. 1984. text ed. (ISBN 0-13-361386-0). P-H.

Government by the People: National, State, Local. 12th, alternate ed. James M. Burns et al. (Illus.). 800p. 1985. text ed. (ISBN 0-13-361544-8). P-H.

Government by the People: National, State, & Local. 12th ed. Raymond L. Lee & Dorothy A. Palmer. 288p. 1985. pap. text ed. (ISBN 0-13-361411-5). P-H.

Government Contracting & Subcontracting. Frank M. Rapoport et al. 117p. 1985. manual 40.00 o.p. (50628). PES Inc WI.

Government Controlled Enterprises: International Strategic & Policy Decisions. R. Mazzolini. LC 78-10961. 400p. 1979. 77.00 o.p. (ISBN 0-471-99727-7, Pub. by Wiley-Interscience). Wiley.

Government Finance Statistics Yearbook. International Monetary Fund Staff. 1987. 20.00 o.s.i. (ISBN 1-55775-004-1). Intl Monetary.

Government Grants: A Guide for Voluntary Organizations. 46p. (Orig.). 1983. pap. text ed. 8.75x o.p. (ISBN 0-7199-1106-0, Pub. by Bedford England). Gower Pub Co.

Government Grants: A Guide for Voluntary Organisations. Maggie Jones. 56p. 1985. pap. text ed. 7.90x o.p. (ISBN 0-7199-1159-1, Pub. by Bedford England). Gower Pub Co.

Government in America: People, Politics & Policies. 3rd ed. Robert L. Lineberry. 1986. text ed. write for info. o.p. (ISBN 0-673-39458-1); pap. text ed. write for info. o.p. (ISBN 0-673-39459-X). Scott F.

Government in Britain. G. T. Popham. 1969. text ed. 70.00 o.p. (ISBN 0-08-013418-1); pap. text ed. 70.00 o.p. (ISBN 0-08-013417-3). Pergamon.

Government in France: An Introduction to the Executive Power. M. Anderson. 1970. 31.00 o.p. (ISBN 0-08-015562-6); pap. 15.25 o.p. (ISBN 0-08-015561-8). Pergamon.

Government in Pre-Colonial Africa see Tarikh.

Government in Spain: The Executive at Work. Kenneth M. Medhurst. 1973. pap. 22.00 o.p. (ISBN 0-08-016940-6). Pergamon.

Government in Sweden: The Executive at Work. N. C. Elder. 1970. 35.00 o.p. (ISBN 0-08-015534-0); pap. text ed. 14.25 o.p. (ISBN 0-08-015533-2). Pergamon.

Government Intervention in Agriculture: Measurement, Evaluation, & Implications for Trade Negotiations. Nicole Ballenger. (Foreign Agriculture Economic Report: No. 229). 56p. 1987. pap. 2.75 o.p. (ISBN 0-318-22751-7, S/N 001-019-00520-3). USGPO.

Government of China, 1644-1911. Pao C. Hsieh. 1966. lib. bdg. 24.00x o.p. (ISBN 0-374-93991-8, Octagon). Hippocrene Bks.

Government of Elizabethan England. Ed. by Alan G. Smith. LC 68-23117. (Foundations of Modern History Ser). 1968. pap. 2.95x o.p. (ISBN 0-393-09816-8, NortonC). Norton.

Government of France. 2nd ed. Gwendolen M. Carter. (Illus., Orig.). 1972. pap. text ed. 10.95 o.p. (ISBN 0-15-529636-1, HC). HarBraceJ.

Government of Germany. 2nd ed. John H. Herz. (Illus.). 208p. (Orig.). 1972. pap. text ed. 8.95 o.p. (ISBN 0-15-529641-8, HC). HarBraceJ.

Government of Socialist China. John Yin. 574p. (Orig.). 1984. lib. bdg. 42.75 o.p. (ISBN 0-8191-3976-9); pap. text ed. 25.50 o.p. (ISBN 0-8191-3977-7). U Pr of Amer.

Government of the Fifth Republic. J. A. Laponce. LC 76-2005. (Illus.). 415p. 1976. Repr. of 1961 ed. lib. bdg. 35.00x o.p. (ISBN 0-8371-8763-X, LAGF). Greenwood.

Government of the Soviet Union. 3rd ed. Gwendolen M. Carter. (Illus., Orig.). 1972. pap. text ed. 8.95 o.p. (ISBN 0-15-529644-2, HC). HarBraceJ.

Government of the United Kingdom. 3rd ed. Gwendolen M. Carter. (Illus., Orig.). 1972. pap. text ed. 10.95 o.p. (ISBN 0-15-529647-7, HC). HarBraceJ.

Government Policy & Development of Financial Markets: The Case of Korea. Arvind Virmani. (Working Paper Ser.: No. 747). 114p. 1985. 5.00 o.p. (ISBN 0-8213-0587-5, WP 0747). World Bank.

Government Publications, Vol. 1. Vladimir M. Palic. 1977. 57.00 o.p. (ISBN 0-08-021457-6). Pergamon.

Government Reference Books Eighty to Eighty-One: A Biennial Guide to U. S. Government Publications-7th Biennial Volume. Walter L. Newsome. 430p. 1982. 42.50 o.p. (ISBN 0-87287-291-2). Libs Unl.

Government Reference Books Seventy-Eight to Seventy-Nine: A Biennial Guide to U. S. Government Publications, 6th Biennial Volume. Compiled by Walter L. Newsome. LC 76-146307. 536p. 1980. lib. bdg. 35.00 o.p. (ISBN 0-87287-242-4). Libs Unl.

Government Reference Books, 1982-1983: A Biennial Guide to U. S. Government Publications. LeRoy C. Schwarzkopf. 394p. 1984. lib. bdg. 47.50x o.p. (ISBN 0-87287-467-2). Libs Unl.

Government Regulation & Business. Allyn D. Strickland. 1981. text ed. 38.36 o.p. (ISBN 0-395-30751-1). HM.

Government Regulation of Business Including Antitrust Information Sources. Ed. by Beatrice S. McDermott & Freada A. Coleman. LC 67-25294. (Management Information Guide Ser.: No. 11). 236p. 1967. 68.00x o.p. (ISBN 0-8103-0810-X). Gale.

Government Regulation of Private Schools: A Bibliography. Jim Buchanan. (Public Administration Ser.: P 1711). 19p. 1985. 3.00 o.p. (ISBN 0-89028-461-X). Vance Biblios.

Government Regulation: Scope, Growth, Process. W. T. Stanbury. 267p. 1980. pap. text ed. 10.95x o.p. (ISBN 0-920380-48-4, Pub. by Inst Res Pub Canada). Gower Pub Co.

Government Research Directory. 4th ed. Ed. by Kay Gill & Susan E. Tufts. 977p. 1986. 350.00x o.p. (ISBN 0-8103-0473-2). Gale.

Government Research Directory: Supplement. 4th ed. Ed. by Kay Gill & Susan E. Tufts. 250p. 1987. pap. 210.00x o.p. (ISBN 0-8103-2514-4). Gale.

Government Spending & the Nonprofit Sector in Cook County - Chicago. Kristen A. Gronbjerg et al. (Nonprofit Sector Ser.). 79p. (Orig.). 1985. pap. text ed. 12.95x o.p. (ISBN 0-87766-348-3). Urban Inst.

Government Spending & the Nonprofit Sector in San Francisco. Paul Harder et al. (Nonprofit Sector Ser.). 75p. (Orig.). 1984. pap. text ed. 12.95 o.p. (ISBN 0-87766-365-3). Urban Inst.

Government Spending & the Nonprofit Sector in Two Michigan Communities: Flint - Genesee County & Tuscola County. James C. Musselwhite, Jr. & Lauren K. Saunders. Ed. by Lester Salamon. (Nonprofit Sector Ser.). 123p. (Orig.). 1984. pap. text ed. 12.95x o.p. (ISBN 0-87766-377-7). Urban Inst.

Governmental Finances in 1983-1984. (GF 84-5. Government Finances). (Illus.). 107p. 1985. pap. 4.00 o.p. (ISBN 0-318-18767-1, S/N 003-024-06364-6). USGPO.

Governmental Regulation of Industrial Relations: A Comparative Study of United States & British Experience. Hywell Evans. 128p. 1961. pap. 2.50 o.p. (ISBN 0-87546-016-X). ILR Pr.

Governments & Leaders: An Approach to Comparative Politics. Edward Feit. LC 77-77977. (Illus.). 1978. text ed. 33.50 o.p. (ISBN 0-395-25367-5). HM.

Governor Alfred E. Smith: The Politician As Reformer. Paula Eldot. Ed. by Frank Freidel. LC 80-8469. (Modern American History Ser.). 420p. 1981. lib. bdg. 61.00 o.p. (ISBN 0-8240-4855-5). Garland Pub.

Governor O. Max Gardner: A Power in North Carolina & New Deal Washington. Joseph L. Morrison. LC 74-132253. (Illus.). xvi, 323p. 1971. 19.95 o.p. (ISBN 0-8078-1153-X). U of NC Pr.

Governors of Arkansas: Essays in Political Biography. Ed. by Timothy P. Donovan & Willard B. Gatewood, Jr. LC 81-50374. 320p. 1981. text ed. 20.00x o.s.i. (ISBN 0-938626-00-0). U of Ark Pr.

Governors of Virginia, Eighteen Sixty to Nineteen Seventy-Eight. Ed. by Edward Younger & James T. Moore. LC 81-16359. (Illus.). 428p. 1982. 20.00x o.p. (ISBN 0-8139-0920-1). U Pr of Va.

Gower Handbook of Management. Ed. by Dennis Lock & Nigel Farrow. 1153p. 1983. text ed. 64.95x o.p. (ISBN 0-566-02333-4). Gower Pub Co.

Goya. Jose Gudiol. (Masters of Art Ser.). (Illus.). 128p. 1985. 19.95 o.p. (ISBN 0-8109-0992-8). Abrams.

Goya Then & Now: Paintings, Portraits, & Frescoes. Oto Bihalji-Merin. Tr. by John E. Woods. LC 81-47299. (Helen & Kurt Wolff Bk.). (Illus.). 312p. 1981. 100.00 o.p. (ISBN 0-15-136712-4). HarBraceJ.

GPSS FORTRAN. B. Schmidt. LC 80-40968. (Computing Ser.). 523p. 1980. 73.95 o.p. (ISBN 0-471-27881-5). Wiley.

Grace All the Way Home. Mark Trotter. LC 81-52860. 1982. pap. 4.95 o.p. (ISBN 0-8358-0434-8). Upper Room.

Grace & Faith in the Old Testament. Ronald M. Hals. LC 79-54128. 96p. 1980. pap. 5.50 o.p. (ISBN 0-8066-1759-4, 10-2883, Augsburg). Augsburg Fortress.

Grace & Mercy in Her Wild Hair. Ramprasad Sen. Tr. by Leonard Nathan & Clinton Seely. LC 82-904. 100p. (Orig.). 1982. pap. write for info. o.p. (ISBN 0-87773-761-4). Shambhala Pubns.

Grace & Torah. J. M. Myers. LC 74-26343. 96p. 1975. pap. 3.95 o.p. (ISBN 0-8006-1099-7, 1-1099, Fortress). Augsburg Fortress.

Grace at Point Zero. Loren E. Halvorson. (Orig.). 1972. pap. 1.75 o.p. (ISBN 0-377-02111-3). Friendship Pr.

Grace in Experience & Theology. Harold H. Ditmanson. LC 77-72447. 1977. pap. 8.50 o.p. (ISBN 0-8066-1587-7, Augsburg, 10-2880). Augsburg Fortress.

Grace Notes & Other Fragments. Joseph A. Sittler. Ed. by Robert M. Herhold & Linda M. Delloff. LC 80-8055. 128p. (Orig.). 1981. pap. 5.95 o.p. (ISBN 0-8006-1404-6, 1-1404, Fortress). Augsburg Fortress.

Grace of Law. Ernest F. Kevan. pap. 9.95 o.p. (ISBN 0-8010-5373-0). Baker Bk.

Grace to You. Mark Mensendiek. 20p. (Orig.). pap. cancelled o.s.i. (ISBN 0-933643-22-5). Grace Ch St Louis.

Graceful Courage: A Venture in Christian Humanism. Roger Hazelton. LC 84-48706. 128p. 1985. pap. 1.00 o.p. (ISBN 0-8006-1850-5, 1-1850, Fortress). Augsburg Fortress.

Gracie Square. Bruce Nicolaysen. (Novel of New York Ser.: Vol. V). 624p. (Orig.). 1984. pap. 4.50 o.p. (ISBN 0-380-86058-9, 86058). Avon.

Gracious Living: How to Enjoy Being a Woman. Adele Williams. LC 76-29227. 1976. 8.95 o.p. (ISBN 0-87795-149-7, Arbor Hse). Morrow.

Graded Exercises in English. rev. ed. Robert J. Dixson. (Orig.). (gr. 8-10). 1971. pap. text ed. 3.75 o.p. (ISBN 0-88345-058-5, 18009); answer key 1.50 o.p. (ISBN 0-685-19797-2). Prentice ESL.

Graded Readers for Students of English As a Second Language. Incl. Jack London's The Call of the Wild. Ed. by Winifred E. Jones. (3000 word level). pap. 3.25 o.p. (ISBN 0-87789-075-7); Selected Stories by American Authors. Ed. by Kenneth Croft & Edith F. Croft. (2000 word level). pap. 2.95 o.p. (ISBN 0-87789-074-9); Stephen Crane's The Red Badge of Courage. Ed. by Winifred E. Jones. (3000 word level). pap. 3.25 o.p. (ISBN 0-87789-079-X); Stories by Edgar Allan Poe. Ed. by David P. Harris. (4000 word level). pap. 3.50 o.p. (ISBN 0-87789-080-3); Stories by Edith Wharton. Ed. by Kenneth Croft & Edith F. Croft. (3000 word level). pap. 3.25 o.p. (ISBN 0-87789-078-1); Stories by Jack London. Ed. by Kenneth Croft & Edith F. Croft. (3000 word level). pap. 3.25 o.p. (ISBN 0-87789-076-5); Stories by O. Henry. Ed. by Mildred H. Larson. (3000 word level). pap. 3.25 o.p. (ISBN 0-87789-077-3); Stories by Washington Irving. Ed. by Kenneth Croft & Edith F. Croft. (2000 word level). pap. 2.95 o.p. (ISBN 0-87789-073-0); Stories of the American West. Ed. by Sara Withers. (4000 word level). pap. 3.50 o.p. (ISBN 0-87789-082-X); Two Short Novels by Henry James. Ed. by Corbin S. Carnell. (4000 word level). pap. 3.50 o.p. (ISBN 0-87789-081-1); Castaway's. Frank Stockton. Ed. by Geo McCallum. (1500 word level). pap. 2.95 o.p. (ISBN 0-89285-150-3); Huckleberry Finn. Mark Twain. Ed. by Corbin S. Carnell. pap. 3.50 o.p. (ISBN 0-89285-151-1). 1973. pap. ELS Educ Servs.

Grades, What's So Important about Them, Anyway? Shirley Schwarzrock & C. Gilbert Wrenn. (Coping with Ser.). (Illus.). 33p. (gr. 7-12). pap. text ed. 3.00 o.p. (ISBN 0-913476-34-X). Am Guidance.

Gradual Vegetarian: For Everyone Finally Ready to Make the Change. Lisa Tracy. LC 84-28629. 300p. 1985. 17.95 o.p. (ISBN 0-87131-452-5). M Evans.

Gradualia, Bks.1 & 2. William Byrd et al. Ed. by P. C. Buck. (Tudor Church Music: Vol. 7). 1963. Repr. of 1927 ed. 85.00x o.p. Broude.

Graduate & Professional Programs: An Overview 1985. 19th ed. Ed. by Diane Conley. (Annual Guides-Graduate Study Ser.). 885p. (Orig.). 1984. pap. 15.95 o.p. (ISBN 0-87866-234-0). Petersons Guides.

Graduate & Professional Programs: An Overview 1984. 18th ed. Charles Granade. LC 77-641915. (Graduate Study). 799p. 1983. pap. 14.95 o.p. (ISBN 0-87866-217-0). Petersons Guides.

Graduate & Professional Programs: An Overview 1987, Bk. 1. 21st ed. LC 86-642931. (Peterson's Annual Guides to Graduate Study Ser). 1065p. (Orig.). 1986. pap. 17.95 o.p. (ISBN 0-87866-471-8). Petersons Guides.

Graduate Guides Set, 1989, 6 vols. Date not set. Set. 241.00 o.p. (ISBN 0-87866-756-3); Set. pap. 155.50 o.p. Petersons Guides.

Graduate Management Admission Test. 3rd ed. Arco Editorial Board. LC 79-1214. (Arco Professional Career Examination Ser.). (Illus.). 408p. (Orig.). 1980. pap. 6.95 o.p. (ISBN 0-668-04914-6, 4914); lib. bdg. 10.00 o. p. o.p. (ISBN 0-668-04917-0). Arco.

Graduate Management Admission Test (GMAT) Gino Crocetti & David Ellis. LC 83-8794. 352p. 1983. pap. 6.95 o.p. (ISBN 0-668-05679-7, 5679). Arco.

Graduate Programs in Engineering & Applied Sciences, 1985. 19th ed. Ed. by Diane Conley & Charles Granade. (Annual Guides to Graduate Study Ser.). 885p. (Orig.). 1984. pap. 21.95 o.p. (ISBN 0-87866-238-3). Petersons Guides.

Graduate Programs in Engineering & Applied Sciences, 1986. 20th ed. Ed. by Amy J. Goldstein & Charles Granade. (Peterson's Annual Guides to Graduate Study Ser.). 986p. (Orig.). 1985. pap. 24.95 o.p. (ISBN 0-87866-346-0). Petersons Guides.

Graduate Programs in Engineering & Applied Sciences 1987, Bk. 5. 21st ed. LC 86-642942. (Peterson's Annual Guides to Graduate Study Ser.). 1090p. (Orig.). 1986. pap. 26.95 o.p. (ISBN 0-87866-425-4). Petersons Guides.

Graduate Programs in the Biological, Agricultural, & Health Sciences, 1985. 19th ed. Ed. by Diane Conley & Barbara C. Ready. (Annual Guides-Graduate Study Ser.). 2038p. (Orig.). 1984. pap. 25.95 o.p. (ISBN 0-87866-236-7). Petersons Guides.

Graduate Programs in the Humanities & Social Sciences, 1985. 19th ed. Ed. by Diane Conley & Amy J. Goldstein. (Annual Guides to Graduate Study Ser.). 1576p. (Orig.). 1984. pap. 22.95 o.p. (ISBN 0-87866-235-9). Petersons Guides.

Graduate Programs in the Humanities & Social Sciences 1987, Bk. 2. 21st ed. LC 86-642933. (Peterson's Annual Guides to Graduate Study Ser.). 2095p. (Orig.). 1986. pap. 27.95 o.p. (ISBN 0-87866-472-6). Petersons Guides.

Graduate Programs in the Physical Sciences & Mathematics, 1985. 19th ed. Ed. by Diane Conley & Charles Granade. (Annual Guides to Graduate Study Ser.). 640p. (Orig.). 1984. pap. 19.95 o.p. (ISBN 0-87866-237-5). Petersons Guides.

Graduate Programs in the Physical Sciences & Mathematics 1987, Bk. 4. 21st ed. LC 86-642939. (Peterson's Annual Guides to Graduate Study Ser). 700p. (Orig.). 1986. pap. 24.95 o.p. (ISBN 0-87866-474-2). Petersons Guides.

Graduate Research in Arid & Semi-Arid Lands at Texas Tech University: 1928-1972. Compiled by Grace Eaton Lee. 186p. 1974. 1.70 o.s.i. (ISBN 0-318-14555-3, 74-2). Intl Ctr Arid & Semi-Arid.

Graduate Student Finances, 1963: A Survey of Thirty-Seven Fields of Study. Seymour Warkov et al. (Report Ser: No. 103). 1963. 2.50x o.p. (ISBN 0-932132-04-9). NORC.

Graduate Studies 1985-86: Guide to Postgraduate Studies in The U. K. 1985. 180.00 o.p. (ISBN 0-86021-703-5). Intl Pubns Serv.

Graduate Study in Education: 50th Yearbook, Pt. 1. National Society for the Study of Education Staff. Ed. by Ralph W. Tyler. LC 51-6258. 1951. pap. text ed. 4.50x o.s.i. (ISBN 0-226-60014-9). U of Chicago Pr.

Graduate Study in Psychology & Associated Fields, 1986 Edition with 1987 Addendum. Ed. by American Psychological Association Staff. 658p. 1987. pap. 18.50 o.p. (ISBN 0-912704-81-0, 4270011). Am Psychol.

Graduated Robot & Other Stories. J. Hunter Holly et al. Ed. by Roger Elwood. LC 73-21477. (Illus.). 48p. (gr. 4-8). 1974. PLB 3.95g o.p. (ISBN 0-8225-0956-3). Lerner Pubns.

Graduation Issue in Trade Policy Towards LDCs. Isaiah Frank. (Working Paper Ser.: No. 334). 30p. 1979. 3.50 o.p. (ISBN 0-317-58558-4, WP 0334). World Bank.

Gradus ad Parnassum. Ed. by Caspar Koch. 1950. 3.95 o.p. (ISBN 0-913650-50-1). CPP Belwin.

Gradus ad Parnassum: Twenty-Nine Selected Studies for Piano. Muzio Clementi. (Carl Fischer Music Library: No. 388). 76p. 1983. pap. 7.50 o.p. (ISBN 0-8258-0119-2, L 388). Fischer Inc NY.

Grady Barr. Jack Donahue & Michel T. Halbouty. LC 81-66961. 352p. 1981. 12.95 o.p. (ISBN 0-87795-329-5, Arbor Hse). Morrow.

Grafting on Polyamides see Polymerization Reactions.

Graham Greene. John Spurling. (Contemporary Writers Ser.). 96p. 1983. pap. 5.95x o.p. (ISBN 0-416-31850-9, NO.3554). Routledge Chapman & Hall.

Graham Greene: A Bibliography & Guide to Research. R. A. Wobbe. LC 78-68307. 478p. 1979. lib. bdg. 61.00 o.p. (ISBN 0-8240-9760-2). Garland Pub.

Graham Sutherland: A Biography. Roger Berthoud. (Illus.). 352p. 1982. 26.95 o.p. (ISBN 0-571-11882-8). Faber & Faber.

Grail. Philip Michaels. 336p. 1982. pap. 3.50 o.p. (ISBN 0-380-79921-9, 79921-9). Avon.

Grain of Salt. Grigory Vinokur. LC 80-17406. 184p. 1981. 9.95 o.p. (ISBN 0-8119-0330-3). Fell.

Grain Refinement in Castings & Welds. Ed. by S. A. David. LC 83-61027. (Proceedings). 293p. 1983. 10.00 o.p. (ISBN 0-89520-457-6). Minerals Metals.

Grain Trade, How It Works. James Schonberg. 1956. text ed. 15.00 o.p. (ISBN 0-682-40084-X, University). Exposition-Phoenix.

Grain Trade in the Old Northwest. John G. Clark. LC 80-18227. (Illus.). xi, 324p. 1980. Repr. of 1966 ed. lib. bdg. 35.00x o.p. (ISBN 0-313-22419-6, CLGT). Greenwood.

Gram-Negative Bacterial Infections & Mode of Endotoxin Actions - Pathophysiologic, Immunologic, & Clinical Aspects. Ed. by B. Urbaschek & R. Urbaschek. LC 74-34099. (Illus.). 550p. 1975. 45.00 o.p. (ISBN 0-387-81292-X). Springer-Verlag.

Grammaire a l'Oeuvre. 3rd ed. John Barson. LC 80-27639. 249p. 1981. pap. text ed. 18.95x o.p. (ISBN 0-03-050891-6, HoltC). HR&W.

Grammar. Frank Palmer. 1972. pap. 2.50 o.p. (ISBN 0-14-021333-3, Pelican). Penguin.

Grammar & Style Guide see World Book Desk Reference Set.

Grammar & the Teaching of English. Ed. by Joel Siegel et al. 87p. 1970. pap. text ed. 7.95x o.p. (ISBN 0-8290-1676-7). Irvington.

Grammar in Plain English. rev. ed. Harriet Diamond & Phyllis Dutwin. LC 75-2487. (gr. 9-12). 1977. pap. text ed. 8.95 o.p. (ISBN 0-8120-0545-7). Barron.

Grammar of Biloxi. Paula F. Einaudi. LC 75-25114. (American Indian Linguistics Ser.). 1976. lib. bdg. 51.00 o.p. (ISBN 0-8240-1965-2). Garland Pub.

Grammar of Conducting. rev. ed. Max Rudolf. 1969. 10.95 o.s.i. (ISBN 0-02-872210-8). Schirmer Bks.

Grammar of Headlines in the Times: 1870-1970. A. M. Simon-Vandenbergen. (Royal Flemish Academy of Science, Literature, Proceedings 1981 Ser.). 364p. (Orig.). 1981. pap. 60.00x o.p. (ISBN 90-6569-300-9, Pub by Brepols Belgium). Benjamins North Am.

Grammar of Modern English. W. H. Mittins. 1967. pap. 11.95x o.p. (ISBN 0-416-69810-7, NO. 2325). Routledge Chapman & Hall.

Grammar of Pawnee. Douglas R. Parks. LC 75-25121. (American Indian Linguistics Ser.). 1976. lib. bdg. 51.00 o.p. (ISBN 0-8240-1971-7). Garland Pub.

Grammar of Tuscarora. Marianne M. Williams. LC 75-25124. (American Indian Linguistics Ser.). 1976. lib. bdg. 51.00 o.p. (ISBN 0-8240-1974-1). Garland Pub.

Grammar of Vai. William E. Welmers. (UC Publications in Linguistics: Vol. 84). 1977. pap. 18.50x o.p. (ISBN 0-520-09555-3). U of Cal Pr.

Gramma's Stories & Rhymes for Little Christians. Margaret A. Lang. (Illus.). 104p. (ps-5). 1982. 9.95 o.p. Lang Pubns.

Grammatical Basis of Linguistic Performance: Language Use & Acquisition. Robert C. Berwick & Amy S. Weinberg. (Current Studies in Linguistics). 288p. 1983. text ed. 35.00x o.p. (ISBN 0-262-02192-7). MIT Pr.

Grammatical Basis of Linguistic Performance: Language Use & Acquisition. Robert C. Berwick & Amy S. Weinberg. 344p. 1986. pap. text ed. 9.95x o.p. (ISBN 0-262-52110-5). MIT Pr.

Grammatical Man: Information, Entropy, Language, & Life. Jeremy Campbell. 320p. 1982. 16.50 o.p. (ISBN 0-671-44061-6). S&S.

Grammatical Miscellany of Fourteen Twenty-Seven to Fourteen Sixty-Five: From Bristol & Wiltshire. Nicholas Orme. 26p. 1982. pap. 4.00 o.p. (ISBN 0-8232-0008-6). Fordham.

Gramsci: An Alternative Communism? Luciano Pellicani. Tr. by Mimi Watts from Ital. LC 80-8329. (Publication Ser.: No. 243). 136p. (Orig.). 1981. pap. 8.95x o.p. (ISBN 0-8179-7432-6). Hoover Inst Pr.

Gramsci & Italy's Passive Revolution. Ed. by John A. Davis. LC 79-53440. (Illus.). 278p. 1979. text ed. 28.50x o.p. (ISBN 0-06-491609-X). B&N Imports.

Grand Ambassadors of Achievement Internation. Ed. by J. M. Evans. 250p. 1988. write for info. o.p. (ISBN 0-934544-51-4). Am Biog Inst.

Grand Canaria & Eastern Canary Islands. Mary Tisdall & Archie Tisdall. 220p. (Orig.). 1984. pap. 10.95 o.p. (ISBN 0-903909-27-8, Pub. by Roger Lascelles England). Bradt Ent.

Grand Canyon: Early Impressions. Ed. by Paul Schullery. LC 80-66185. 130p. 1981. 15.00 o.p. (ISBN 0-87081-086-3); pap. 7.95 o.p. (ISBN 0-87081-087-1). Univ Pr Colo.

Grand Canyon: The Story Behind the Scenery. rev. ed. Merrill D. Beal. LC 75-14775. (Illus.). 64p. 1978. 8.95 o.p. (ISBN 0-916122-31-X); pap. 4.50 o.p. (ISBN 0-916122-06-9). KC Pubns.

Grand Celebration. The Vanessa-Ann Collection Staff. Ed. by Margaret Marti. (Illus.). 96p. 1983. pap. text ed. 8.95 o.p. (ISBN 0-913921-28-9). Vanessa-Ann Collec.

Grand Central...the World's Greatest Railway Terminal. William D. Middleton. LC 77-24507. (Illus.). 216p. 1977. 22.95 o.p. (ISBN 0-87095-071-1). Gldn West Bks.

Grand Homes of Texas. Texas Homes Editors. Ed. by Ann Richardson. (Illus.). 200p. 1982. 45.00 o.p. (ISBN 0-932012-36-1). Texas Month Pr.

Grand Huckster: Houston's Judge Roy Hofheintz, Genius of the Astrodome. Edgar Ray. (Illus.). 1980. 19.95 o.p. (ISBN 0-87870-069-2); deluxe ed. 29.95 o.p. (ISBN 0-87870-195-8). Memphis St Univ.

Grand Jubilee. Suzette H. Elgin. 240p. 1983. pap. 2.50 o.s.i. (ISBN 0-425-06045-4). Berkley Pub.

Grand Jury. Elizabeth Rose. 1974. pap. 1.50 o.p. (ISBN 0-380-01230-8, 18002). Avon.

Grand National. John Welcome. 1977. 8.95 o.p. (ISBN 0-671-22452-2). S&S.

Grand National Racer. Margaret Ogan & George Ogan. LC 75-54662. (Hiway Bks.: A High Interest-Low Reading Level Book). 114p. (gr. 7 up). 1977. 7.50 o.s.i. (ISBN 0-664-32608-0, Westminster). Westminster John Knox.

Grand Old Ladies: North Carolina Architecture During the Victorian Era. Ed. by Marguerite Schumann. LC 84-48035. (Illus.). 128p. 1984. 19.95 o.p. (ISBN 0-88742-013-3). Globe Pequot.

Grand Opening. Richard W. Bimler. 1983. 3.75 o.p. (ISBN 0-89536-589-8, 0731). CSS of Ohio.

Grand Passion. Mary Mackey. 1986. 17.45 o.p. (ISBN 0-671-54077-7). S&S.

Grand Prix of Canada. Gerald Donaldson. 128p. 1984. pap. 14.95 o.p. (ISBN 0-380-87080-0, 87080-0). Avon.

Grand Recueil: Methodes, Vol. 2. Francis Ponge. 308p. 1961. 21.95 o.p. (ISBN 0-686-54888-4). Schoenhof.

Grand Recueil: Pieces, Vol. 3. Francis Ponge. 220p. 1961. 18.95 o.p. (ISBN 0-686-54889-2). Schoenhof.

Grand Street Reader. Ed. by Ben Sonnenberg. 448p. 1986. 18.45 o.s.i. (ISBN 0-671-60623-9); pap. 10.95 o.s.i. (ISBN 0-671-62969-7). Summit Bks.

Grand Tour & Other Poems. Mary F. Lindsley. 1952. (ISBN 0-8022-0980-7). Philos Lib.

Grand Troupeau. Jean Giono. 1972. 3.95 o.p. (ISBN 0-686-53966-4). Schoenhof.

Grandes Ecoles, Pourquoi Faire? Honore De Balzac. 1973. pap. text ed. 9.95 o.p. (ISBN 0-686-53877-3). French & Eur.

Grandes Epreuves De l'Esprit see Major Ordeals of the Mind & the Countless Minor Ones.

Grandeur of God. C. Samuel Storms. 80p. 1985. pap. 6.95 o.p. (ISBN 0-8010-8254-4). Baker Bk.

Grandfather Stories, Vol. I. Vada Carlson & Gary Witherspoon. 123p. Date not set. price not set o.s.i. (ISBN 0-89019-006-2). Navajo Curr.

Grandfathers: God's Gift to Children. Mary B. Christian. 1982. pap. 1.00 o.p. (ISBN 0-570-04069-8, 56-1372). Concordia.

Grandfather's Stories. Donna Roland. (Illus., Orig.). (gr. 1-3). 1982. pap. 4.50 o.s.i. (ISBN 0-941996-00-X). Open My World.

Grandison Mather. Henry Harland, pseud. Ed. by Ian Fletcher & John Stokes. LC 76-24391. (Decadent Consciousness Ser.). 1977. lib. bdg. 46.00 o.p. (ISBN 0-8240-2768-X). Garland Pub.

Grandissimo Pavarotti. Mayer Martin. LC 86-2042. (Illus.). 224p. 1986. 40.00 o.p. (ISBN 0-385-23138-5). Doubleday.

Grandma Haley. Aleda Renken. (Haley Adventures Bks.). (gr. 3-9). 1981. pap. 1.75 o.p. (ISBN 0-570-07234-4, 39-1069). Concordia.

Grandma Moses American Songbook. (Illus.). 256p. (Paintings by Grandma Moses). 1985. 24.95 o.p. (ISBN 0-8109-0990-1). Abrams.

Grandma's Country Cooking. Ideals Staff. (Illus.). 64p. (Orig.). 1984. pap. 3.95 o.p. (ISBN 0-8249-3033-9). Ideals.

Grandma's Large Type Knitting Book. Joan R. Heilman. 80p. 1986. pap. 10.95 o.s.i. (ISBN 0-87523-205-1). Emerson.

Grandma's Letters to God. Ruth Y. Nelson. LC 83-72109. 112p. 1984. pap. 5.50 o.p. (ISBN 0-8066-2053-6, 10-2886, Augsburg). Augsburg Fortress.

Grandma's Secret Letter. Maggie S. Davis. LC 80-23331. (Illus.). 32p. (ps-3). 1982. 12.95 o.p. (ISBN 0-8234-0382-3). Holiday.

Grandmasters of Chess. Harold C. Schonberg. (Illus.). 1981. 18.95 o.p. (ISBN 0-393-01403-7). Norton.

Grandmother. Georges Simenon. Tr. by Jean Stewart. LC 80-14918. (Helen & Kurt Wolff Bk.). 192p. 1980. Repr. of 1959 ed. 8.95 o.p. (ISBN 0-15-136738-8). HarBraceJ.

Grandmother Goes up the Mountain. Margaret Kitchen. (Illus.). 156p. (gr. 4-8). 1986. 10.95 o.p. (ISBN 0-233-97749-X). Andre Deutsch.

Grandmother Oma. Ilse Kleberger. LC 67-10459. (Illus.). (gr. 2-5). 1967. PLB 5.95 o.p. (ISBN 0-689-20201-6, Atheneum). Macmillan.

Grandmother Remembers Family Recipes. Judith Levy & Judy Pelikan. (Illus.). 96p. 1984. 14.95 o.p. (ISBN 0-941434-46-X). Stewart Tabori & Chang.

Grandmothers. Glenway Wescott. LC 50-6732. 1962. pap. 1.45 o.p. (ISBN 0-689-70205-1, 11, Atheneum). Macmillan.

Grandmothers. Glenway Wescott. 1986. write for info. o.p. (ISBN 0-87795-799-1). Morrow.

Grandmothers Book. 1984. 6.98 o.p. (ISBN 0-517-46121-8). Crown.

Grandmothers' Club. Alan Cheuse. 326p. 1986. 18.95 o.p. (ISBN 0-87905-253-8, Peregrine Smith). Gibbs Smith Pub.

Grandmothers: God's Gift to Children. Mary B. Christian. 1982. pap. 1.00 o.p. (ISBN 0-570-04068-X, 56-1371). Concordia.

Grandmother's Pictures. Sam Cornish. (Illus.). 1978. pap. 0.95 o.p. (ISBN 0-380-01912-4, 37416, Camelot). Avon.

Grandparent's Book. Milton Kamen. 1981. pap. 12.95 o.p. (ISBN 0-89586-151-8). Price Stern.

Grandparents' Handbook: A Practical Guide to Enjoying the New Generation. Hugh Jolly. (Winston Family Handbooks Ser.). 96p. (Orig.). 1984. pap. 9.95 o.p. (ISBN 0-86683-847-3, AY8492). HarpR.

Grandpa's Farm. James Flora. LC 65-19989. (Illus.). (gr. 1-4). 1965. 6.95 o.p. (ISBN 0-15-232340-6, HJ). HarBraceJ.

Grands Chemins. Jean Giono. (Coll. Soleil). 1964. 14.95 o.p. (ISBN 0-685-11222-5). Schoenhof.

Grange Master's America: In Defense of Freedom. Winton Weydemeyer. 272p. 1981. 12.50 o.p. (ISBN 0-682-49677-4). Exposition-Phoenix.

Granger's Index to Poetry. 7th ed. Ed. by William J. Smith. 1982. 155.00 o.p. (ISBN 0-231-05002-X). Columbia U Pr.

Granny see Broken Star-the Warburgs of Altona: Their Life in Germany & Their Death in the Holocaust.

Granny Bouncer's Rescue. (Tales from Fern Hollow Ser.). (Illus.). 22p. (ps-1). 1985. 1.98 o.p. (ISBN 0-517-45798-9). Outlet Bk Co.

Granny Glee & Sockabye Land. Lavina Rahmlow. (Illus.). 64p. (gr. k-2). 1984. 5.50 o.p. (ISBN 0-682-40167-6). Exposition-Phoenix.

Granny Glee & Whoppity Sock. Lavina Rahmlow. (Illus.). (gr. 2-4). 1979. 5.00 o.p. (ISBN 0-682-49457-7). Exposition-Phoenix.

Granny Iliko, Illarion, & I. N. Dumbadze. 173p. 1985. 7.95 o.p. (ISBN 0-8285-3032-7, Pub. by Raduga Pubs USSR). Imported Pubns.

Granny, the Baby & the Big Gray Thing. Peggy Parish. LC 78-185148. (Ready-to-Read Ser.). (Illus.). 40p. (gr. 1-3). 1974. pap. 1.25 o.s.i. (ISBN 0-02-044790-6, Collier). Macmillan.

Grant: A Biography. William S. McFeely. (Illus.). 1981. 25.00 o.p. (ISBN 0-393-01372-3). Norton.

Grant Seekers Guide National Network of Grantmakers. rev. ed. Jill R. Shellow. 550p. (Orig.). 1985. 24.95x o.p. (ISBN 0-918825-05-9, Dist. by Consortium Book Sales); pap. 16.95 o.p. (ISBN 0-918825-10-5). Moyer Bell Limited.

Grantley Manor: A Tale, 1847. Georgiana Fullerton. Ed. by Robert L. Wolff. LC 75-451. (Victorian Fiction Ser.). 1975. lib. bdg. 73.00 o.p. (ISBN 0-8240-1531-2). Garland Pub.

Grants for Arts & Cultural Programs. (COMSEARCH: Broad Topics Ser.). 1987. pap. 35.00 o.p. (ISBN 0-87954-201-2). Foundation Ctr.

Grants for Business & Employment. (COMSEARCH: Broad Topics Ser.). 1987. pap. 35.00 o.p. (ISBN 0-87954-202-0). Foundation Ctr.

Grants for Business & Employment. (COMSEARCH: Broad Topics Ser.). 1989. pap. 45.00 o.p. (ISBN 0-87954-306-X). Foundation Ctr.

Grants for Children & Youth. (COMSEARCH: Broad Topics Ser.). 1987. pap. 35.00 o.p. (ISBN 0-87954-203-9). Foundation Ctr.

Grants for Children & Youth. (COMSEARCH: Broad Topics Ser.). 1989. pap. 45.00 o.p. (ISBN 0-87954-307-8). Foundation Ctr.

Grants for Community & Urban Development. (COMSEARCH: Broad Topics Ser.). 1987. pap. 35.00 o.p. (ISBN 0-87954-216-0). Foundation Ctr.

Grants for Community & Urban Development. (COMSEARCH: Broad Topics Ser.). 1989. pap. 45.00 o.p. (ISBN 0-87954-318-3). Foundation Ctr.

Grants for Crime & Law Enforcement. (COMSEARCH: Broad Topics Ser.). 1987. pap. 35.00 o.p. (ISBN 0-87954-220-9). Foundation Ctr.

Grants for Crime & Law Enforcement. (COMSEARCH: Broad Topics Ser.). 1989. pap. 45.00 o.p. (ISBN 0-87954-322-1). Foundation Ctr.

Grants for Elementary & Secondary Education. (COMSEARCH: Broad Topic Ser.). 1987. pap. 35.00 o.p. (ISBN 0-87954-217-9). Foundation Ctr.

Grants for Elementary & Secondary Education. (COMSEARCH: Broad Topics Ser.). 1989. pap. 45.00 o.p. (ISBN 0-87954-319-1). Foundation Ctr.

Grants for Environmental Law, Protection & Education. (COMSEARCH: Broad Topics Ser.). 1987. pap. 35.00 o.p. (ISBN 0-87954-221-7). Foundation Ctr.

Grants for Environmental Law, Protection & Education. (COMSEARCH: Broad Topics Ser.). 1989. pap. 45.00 o.p. (ISBN 0-87954-323-X). Foundation Ctr.

Grants for Family Services. LC 87-29495. (COMSEARCH: Broad Topics Ser.). 1987. pap. 35.00 o.p. (ISBN 0-87954-222-5). Foundation Ctr.

Grants for Family Services. (COMSEARCH: Broad Topics Ser.). 1989. pap. 45.00 o.p. (ISBN 0-87954-324-8). Foundation Ctr.

Grants for Film, Media & Communications. (COMSEARCH: Broad Topics Ser.). 1989. pap. 45.00 o.p. (ISBN 0-87954-321-3). Foundation Ctr.

Grants for Graduate Students 1986-88. 395p. (Orig.). 1986. pap. 29.95 o.s.i. (ISBN 0-87866-483-1). Petersons Guides.

Grants for Higher Education. (COMSEARCH: Broad Topics Ser.). 1987. pap. 35.00 o.p. (ISBN 0-87954-204-7). Foundation Ctr.

Grants for Hospital & Medical Care Programs. (COMSEARCH: Broad Topics Ser.). 1989. pap. 45.00 o.p. (ISBN 0-87954-329-9). Foundation Ctr.

Grants for Hospitals & Medical Care Programs. (COMSEARCH: Broad Topics Ser.). 1987. pap. 35.00 o.p. (ISBN 0-87954-205-5). Foundation Ctr.

Grants for International & Foreign Programs. (COMSEARCH: Broad Topics Ser.). 1987. pap. 35.00 o.p. (ISBN 0-87954-210-1). Foundation Ctr.

Grants for International & Foreign Programs. (COMSEARCH: Broad Topics Ser.). 1989. pap. 45.00 o.p. (ISBN 0-87954-312-4). Foundation Ctr.

Grants for Libraries & Information Services. (COMSEARCH: Broad Topics Ser.). 1989. pap. 45.00 o.p. (ISBN 0-87954-327-2). Foundation Ctr.

Grants for Matching & Challenge Support. (COMSEARCH: Broad Topics Ser.). 1989. pap. 45.00 o.p. (ISBN 0-87954-320-5). Foundation Ctr.

Grants for Medical & Professional Health Education. (COMSEARCH: Broad Topics Ser.). 1987. pap. 35.00 o.p. (ISBN 0-87954-223-3). Foundation Ctr.

Grants for Medical & Professional Health Education. (COMSEARCH: Broad Topics Ser.). 1989. pap. 45.00 o.p. (ISBN 0-87954-325-6). Foundation Ctr.

Grants for Minorities. (COMSEARCH: Broad Topics Ser.). 1989. pap. 45.00 o.p. (ISBN 0-87954-313-2). Foundation Ctr.

Grants for Minorities: COMSEARCH: Broad Topics Ser. 1987. pap. 35.00 o.p. (ISBN 0-87954-211-X). Foundation Ctr.

Grants for Museums. (COMSEARCH: Broad Topics Ser.). 1987. pap. 35.00 o.p. (ISBN 0-87954-206-3). Foundation Ctr.

Grants for Museums. (COMSEARCH: Broad Topics Ser.). 1989. pap. 45.00 o.p. (ISBN 0-87954-308-6). Foundation Ctr.

Grants for Physically & Mentally Disabled. (COMSEARCH: Broad Topics Ser.). 1987. pap. 35.00 o.p. (ISBN 0-87954-224-1). Foundation Ctr.

Grants for Physically & Mentally Disabled. (COMSEARCH: Broad Topics Ser.). 1989. pap. 45.00 o.p. (ISBN 0-87954-326-4). Foundation Ctr.

Grants for Public & Political Science. (COMSEARCH: Broad Topics Ser.). 1987. pap. 35.00 o.p. (ISBN 0-87954-214-4). Foundation Ctr.

Grants for Public Health. (COMSEARCH: Broad Topics Ser.). 1987. pap. 35.00 o.p. (ISBN 0-87954-213-6). Foundation Ctr.

Grants for Public Health. (COMSEARCH: Broad Topics Ser.). 1989. pap. 45.00 o.p. (ISBN 0-87954-315-9). Foundation Ctr.

Grants for Public Policy & Political Science. (COMSEARCH: Broad Topics Ser.). 1989. pap. 45.00 o.p. (ISBN 0-87954-316-7). Foundation Ctr.

Grants for Recreation. (COMSEARCH: Broad Topics Ser.). 1989. pap. 45.00 o.p. (ISBN 0-87954-317-5). Foundation Ctr.

Grants for Religion & Religious Education. (COMSEARCH: Broad Topics Ser.). 1987. pap. 35.00 o.p. (ISBN 0-87954-212-8). Foundation Ctr.

Grants for Religion & Religious Education. (COMSEARCH: Broad Topics Ser.). 1989. pap. 45.00 o.p. (ISBN 0-87954-314-0). Foundation Ctr.

Grants for Science & Technology Programs. (COMSEARCH: Broad Topics Ser.). 1989. pap. 45.00 o.p. (ISBN 0-87954-309-4). Foundation Ctr.

Grants for Science Programs. (COMSEARCH: Broad Topics Ser.). 1987. pap. 35.00 o.p. (ISBN 0-87954-207-1). Foundation Ctr.

Grants for Social Science Programs. (COMSEARCH: Broad Topics Ser.). 1987. pap. 35.00 o.p. (ISBN 0-87954-208-X). Foundation Ctr.

Grants for Social Science Programs. (COMSEARCH: Broad Topics Ser.). 1989. pap. 45.00 o.p. (ISBN 0-87954-310-8). Foundation Ctr.

Grants for the Child. Public Management Institute Staff. LC 80-80575. 930p. 1980. directory 200.00 o.p. (ISBN 0-916664-27-9). Public Management.

Grants for Women & Girls. (COMSEARCH: Broad Topics Ser.). 1987. pap. 35.00 o.p. (ISBN 0-87954-209-8). Foundation Ctr.

Grants for Women & Girls. (COMSEARCH: Broad Topics Ser.). 1989. pap. 45.00 o.p. (ISBN 0-87954-311-6). Foundation Ctr.

Grants Game: How to Get Free Money. Lawrence Lee. 224p. 1981. 12.95 o.p. (ISBN 0-936602-18-X); pap. 8.95 o.p. (ISBN 0-936602-03-1). Kampmann.

Grants of Matching & Challenge Support. (COMSEARCH: Broad Topics Ser.). 1987. pap. 35.00 o.p. (ISBN 0-87954-219-5). Foundation Ctr.

Grants Survival Library. 2nd ed. Donald Levitan. (Public Administration Ser.: P 1836). 27p. 1985. 3.75 o.p. (ISBN 0-89028-686-8). Vance Biblios.

Grantspro. Public Management Institute Staff. 65p. 1984. manual, incl. diskette 200.00x o.s.i. (ISBN 0-916664-39-2). Public Management.

Grapes: A Vintage View of Hockey. Don Cherry & Stan Fischler. 1983. pap. 3.50 o.p. (ISBN 0-380-65177-7, 65177). Avon.

Grapes & Grapevines of California. Bosqui & Co. Staff. LC 81-4775. (Illus.). 64p. 1981. 29.95 o.p. (ISBN 0-15-136786-8). HarBraceJ.

Grapes of Wrath: A Collection of Critical Essays. Ed. by Robert C. Davis. 157p. 1982. 15.95 o.p. (ISBN 0-13-363358-6); pap. 4.95 o.p. (ISBN 0-13-363341-1). P-H.

Graph-Grammars & Their Application to Computer Science. Ed. by H. Ehrig et al. (Lecture Notes in Computer Science: Vol. 153). 452p. 1983. pap. 22.50 o.p. (ISBN 0-387-12310-5). Springer-Verlag.

Graph Theory & Applications. H. N. Temperley. LC 81-6933. (Mathematics & Its Applications Ser.). 130p. 1981. 52.95x o.p. (ISBN 0-470-27296-1); pap. 15.95 o.p. (ISBN 0-470-20120-7). Halsted Pr.

Graph Theory & Applications: Proceedings of Conference on Graph Theory, Western Michigan University, Kalamazoo, 1972. Conference on Graph Theory Staff. Ed. by Y. Alavi et al. LC 72-95978. (Lecture Notes in Mathematics: Vol. 303). 329p. 1973. pap. 16.00 o.p. (ISBN 0-387-06096-0). Springer-Verlag.

Graphic Arts. McKnight Staff & Wilbur R. Miller. LC 78-53390. (Basic Industrial Arts Ser.). (Illus.). 1978. 7.28 o.p. (ISBN 0-87345-795-1); softbound 5.28 o.p. (ISBN 0-87345-787-0). Glencoe.

Graphic Arts Photography: Black & White. John Cogoli et al. LC 80-84800. (Illus.). 412p. 1981. 35.00 o.p. (ISBN 0-88362-036-7, 1503). Graphic Arts Tech Found.

Graphic Communication & Design in Contemporary Cartography, Vol. 2. D. R. Taylor. 314p. 1982. 92.95 o.p. (ISBN 0-471-10316-0). Wiley.

Graphic Communications for the Performing Arts. Ed. by David J. Skal. LC 81-51181. (Illus.). 160p. (Orig.). 1981. pap. 14.95 o.p. (ISBN 0-930452-11-9). Theatre Comm.

Graphic Design: A Problem Solving Approach to Visual Communication. Elizabeth Resnick. (Illus.). 160p. 1984. 15.95 o.p. (ISBN 0-13-363267-9); pap. 9.95 o.p. (ISBN 0-13-363259-8). P-H.

Graphic Design in Japan, Vol. 1. Japan Graphic Designers Association Staff. LC 82-645590. (Illus.). 200p. 1982. 59.50 o.p. (ISBN 0-87011-516-2). Kodansha.

Graphic Design in Japan, Vol. 5. Japan Graphic Designers Association Staff. LC 82-645590. (Illus.). 226p. 1985. 80.00 o.p. (ISBN 0-87011-730-0). Kodansha.

Graphic Engineering Geometry. John R. Bedford. LC 78-67438. 160p. (Orig.). 1979. pap. 12.00x o.p. (ISBN 0-87201-325-1). Gulf Pub.

Graphic Excellence. Studio Magazine Staff. LC 87-61203. (Illus.). 256p. 1987. 49.95 o.p. (ISBN 0-86636-050-6). PBC Intl Inc.

Graphic Guide to Industrialized Building Elements. Raymond Sluzas & Anne Ryan. LC 77-13121. (Illus.). 176p. 1983. 23.95 o.p. (ISBN 0-8436-0163-9); pap. 18.95 o.p. (ISBN 0-8436-0164-7). Van Nos Reinhold.

Graphic Illustration: Tools & Techniques for Beginning Illustrators. Marta Thoma. (Illus.). 175p. 1982. 29.95 o.p. (ISBN 0-13-363374-8); pap. 14.95 o.p. (ISBN 0-13-363366-7). P-H.

Graphic Imaging Device Comparison Charts: 1987 Edition. Harold Durbin. 1987. pap. 25.00 o.p. (ISBN 0-936786-13-2). Durbin Assoc.

Graphic Reproduction. William P. Spence & David G. Vequist. 1981. 32.50 o.p. (ISBN 0-684-16764-6, ScribT). Scribner.

Graphic Symbols for Arc Welding Apparatus. 1983. 7.50 o.p. (ISBN 0-318-18034-0, EW 4-1982). Natl Elec Mfrs.

Graphic Thinking for Architects & Designers. Paul Laseau. 224p. 1980. 22.50 o.p. (ISBN 0-442-26247-7); pap. 18.95 o.p. (ISBN 0-442-25698-1). Van Nos Reinhold.

Graphic Works: 209 Lithographs, Etchings Engravings. Odillon Redon. (Illus.). 17.25 o.p. (ISBN 0-8446-0872-6). Peter Smith.

Graphicacy & Geography Teaching. David Boardman. (Illus.). 184p. 1983. pap. 19.50 o.p. (ISBN 0-7099-0644-7, Pub. by Croom Helm Ltd). Routledge Chapman & Hall.

Graphical Engineering Aid for VLSI Systems. Paul J. Drongowski. Ed. by Harold Stone. LC 85-1041. (Computer Science Series: Computer Architecture & Design: No. 4). 226p. 1985. 44.95 o.p. (ISBN 0-8357-1656-2). UMI Res Pr.

Graphical Methods for Data Analysis. John M. Chambers et al. 416p. 1983. pap. text ed. write for info o.p. (ISBN 0-87150-413-8, 5020, Duxbury Pr). PWS-Kent Pub.

Graphics & Sound for Your Personal Computer. Mike McMahan. LC 85-719. (Illus.). 192p. 1985. pap. 19.95 o.p. (ISBN 0-915381-66-4); optional diskette 10.00 o.p. WordWare Pub.

Graphics & Sounds on the Commodore 64 Knight. LC 83-51183. 128p. 1984. pap. 8.95 o.p. (ISBN 0-672-22278-7). Sams.

Graphics for the Macintosh: An Idea Book. John P. Grillo & J. Douglas Robertson. 1985. 17.95 o.p. (ISBN 0-03-000477-2). HR&W.

Graphics Generator: Business & Technical Graphics for the IBM Personal Computer. Larry J. Goldstein. (Illus.). 155p. 1982. 95.00 o.p. (ISBN 0-89303-266-2); diskettes 95.00 o.p. (ISBN 0-89303-495-9). Brady Bks.

Graphics in Engineering Design. 3rd ed. Alexander Levens & William Chalk. LC 79-17291. 304p. 1980. 45.50x o.p. (ISBN 0-471-01478-8). Wiley.

Graphics with the IBM PC. Kenniston W. Lord, Jr. (Illus.). 288p. 1985. pap. 19.95 o.p. (ISBN 0-673-15971-X). Scott F.

Graphis Annual Reports 86-87. Ed. by B. Martin Pedersen. (Illus.). 240p. 1988. 65.00 o.p. (ISBN 0-8230-2101-7). Watson-Guptill.

Graphis Annual: 1986-1987. Ed. by Walter Herdeg. (Illus.). 256p. 1986. 59.50 o.p. (ISBN 0-8230-2130-0). Watson-Guptill.

Graphis Posters Eighty-Six: The International Annual of Poster Art. Ed. by Walter Herdeg. (Illus.). 204p. 1986. 59.50 o.p. (ISBN 0-8230-2131-9). Watson-Guptill.

Graphite Furnace Technology & Atomic Absorption Spectroscopy: Commemorating the 25th Anniversary of the Publication of the First Paper by B. V. L'vov. Ed. by W. Slavin. 400p. 1984. pap. 61.00 o.p. (ISBN 0-08-031405-8). Pergamon.

Graphiti (Four Quadrants) Steve Goldberg. (gr. 5-9). 1976. pap. 3.50 o.p. (ISBN 0-918932-64-5). Activity Resources.

Graphiti (One Quadrant) Steve Goldberg. (gr. 2-4). 1976. pap. 3.50 o.p. Activity Resources.

Graphologists Alphabet. Eric Singer. 1952. (ISBN 0-8022-1578-5). Philos Lib.

Graphology Student's Workbook. 2nd ed. Ruth Gardner. (Illus.). 85p. 1975. 4.95 o.p. (ISBN 0-87542-250-0). Llewellyn Pubns.

Graphs & Applications: Proceedings of the First Colorado Symposium on Graph Theory. Ed. by Frank Harary & John S. Maybee. LC 84-20819. 347p. 1985. 47.50 o.p. (ISBN 0-471-88772-2). Wiley.

Graphs & Charts. (Basic Academic Ser.: Module 5). (Illus.). 110p. 1982. spiral bdg. 19.50x o.p. (ISBN 0-87683-229-X); instr's. manual o.p. 15.00 o.p. (ISBN 0-87683-240-0). GP Pub.

Graphs & Questionnaires. C. F. Picard. (Mathematical Studies Ser.: Vol. 32). 1980. pap. 63.25 o.p. (ISBN 0-444-85239-5, North-Holland). Elsevier.

Graphs As Mathematical Models. Gary Chartrand. 1977. text ed. write for info. o.p. (ISBN 0-87150-236-4, PWS 1901, Prindle). PWS-Kent Pub.

Grasping Imagination: The American Writings of Henry James. Peter Buitenhuis. LC 79-149323. 1970. 25.00x o.p. (ISBN 0-8020-5244-4); pap. 6.50 o.p. (ISBN 0-8020-6225-3). U of Toronto Pr.

Grass Beyond the Mountains. Richmond P. Hobson, Jr. LC 85-25303. 256p. (Orig.). 1986. pap. 9.95 o.p. (ISBN 0-934878-69-2). Dembner Bks.

Grass Is Green Again. May Andrews. 1979. pap. 5.00 o.p. (ISBN 0-682-49525-5). Exposition-Phoenix.

Grass Is Greener. Amy Paul. (Illus.). 96p. (Orig.). 1981. pap. 1.95 o.p. (ISBN 0-380-78576-5, 78576-5, Flare). Avon.

Grass Productivity. Andre Voisin. (Illus.). 350p. 1959. (ISBN 0-8022-1781-8). Philos Lib.

Grass Roof. new ed. Younghill Kang. Bd. with Yalu Flows. Mirok Li. 352p. 1975. pap. 3.95 o.p. (ISBN 0-393-00766-9, Norton Lib). Norton.

Grass Skiing: A Complete Beginner's Book. Lavada Weir. LC 80-24927. (Illus.). 128p. (gr. 4 up). 1981. lib. bdg. 9.79 o.s.i. (ISBN 0-671-33012-8). Messner.

Grass Tower. Shirley R. Murphy. LC 75-23151. (Illus.). (gr. 7 up). 1976. 7.95 o.p. (ISBN 0-689-30512-5, Atheneum). Macmillan.

Grasses of Southern Queensland. 2nd ed. J. C. Tothill & J. B. Hacker. LC 82-8512. (Illus.). 475p. 1983. text ed. 32.50x o.p. (ISBN 0-7022-1881-2). U of Queensland Pr.

Grasshopper Book. Wilfrid S. Bronson. LC 43-51236. (Illus.). (gr. 3-7). 1943. 4.95 o.p. (ISBN 0-15-232362-7, HJ). HarBraceJ.

Grasshopper Trap. Patrick F. McManus. (General Ser.). 339p. 1986. lib. bdg. 16.95 o.p. (ISBN 0-8161-4043-X, Large Print Bks); pap. 9.95 o.p. (ISBN 0-8161-4070-7, Large Print Bks.). G K Hall.

Grasslands. Clyde M. Brundy. 496p. 1980. pap. 2.50 o.p. (ISBN 0-380-75499-1, 75499-1). Avon.

Grassroots Conservation of Biological Diversity in the U. S. Background Paper, No. 1. LC 85-600633. (OTA-BP-F-38 Ser.). (Illus.). 75p. (Orig.). 1986. pap. 3.50 o.p. (ISBN 0-318-19952-1, S/N 052-003-01019-4). USGPO.

Grassroots: The Writer's Handbook. 2d ed. Susan E. Fawcett & Alvin Sandberg. 288p. 1982. pap. 23.16 o.p. (ISBN 0-395-32572-2). HM.

Grassroots: The Writer's Workbook, Form A. Susan E. Fawcett & Alvin Sandberg. LC 75-37475. 30p. 1976. pap. 14.95 o.p. (ISBN 0-395-24063-8). HM.

Grave for a Russian. Charles C. Vance. 1985. pap. 3.25 o.p. (ISBN 0-380-89631-1). Avon.

Grave Must Be Deep. Theodore Roscoe. (Facsimile Fiction Ser.: Vol. 1). 1988. 17.95x o.p. (ISBN 1-55742-041-6); pap. 8.95x o.p. (ISBN 1-55742-040-8). Starmont Hse.

Graven Stones of Lower Accomack County, VA. Jean M. Mihalyka & Faye D. Wilson. xlvii, 302p. (Orig.). 1986. pap. 16.50 o.p. (ISBN 0-917890-98-1). Heritage Bk.

Graves of Academe. Richard Mitchell. 1981. 14.95 o.p. (ISBN 0-316-57508-9). Little.

Gravestones of Early New England: And the Men Who Made Them. Harriette M. Forbes. (Thanatology Service Ser.). 200p. 1987. Repr. of 1927 ed. 22.95 o.p. (ISBN 0-930194-03-9). Ctr Thanatology.

Graveyard. Marek Hlasko. Tr. by Norbert Guterman from Pol. LC 74-27463. 126p. 1975. Repr. of 1959 ed. lib. bdg. 35.00x o.p. (ISBN 0-8371-7897-5, HLGR). Greenwood.

Gravitation & Elementary Particle Physics. Ed. by A. A. Logunov. Tr. by Valerii Ilyushchenko. 294p. 1984. pap. 8.95 o.p. (Pub. by Mir Pubs USSR). Imported Pubns.

Gravitation & Relativity. M. G. Bowler. 1976. 45.00 o.p. (ISBN 0-08-020567-4); pap. 45.00 o.p. (ISBN 0-08-020408-2). Pergamon.

Gravitation, Quanta & the Universe: Proceedings of the Einstein Centenary Symposium Held at Ahmedabad, India 29 January to 3 February, 1979. Ed. by A. R. Prasanna et al. LC 80-17051. 326p. 1980. 62.95x o.p. (ISBN 0-470-27007-1). Halsted Pr.

Gravitational Physiology: Proceedings of the 28th International Congress of Physiological Sciences, Budapest, 1980. LC 80-42103. (Advances in Physiological Sciences: Vol. 19). (Illus.). 350p. 1981. 57.00 o.p. (ISBN 0-08-027340-8). Pergamon.

Gravity & Levity. Alan McGlashen. 1976. 6.95 o.p. (ISBN 0-395-24762-4). HM.

Gravity & Magnetics for Geologists & Seismologists. L. L. Nettleton. (SEG Monographs: No. 1). 121p. 1971. pap. 7.50 o.p. (ISBN 0-931830-10-9). Soc Expl Geophys.

Gravity: Black Holes & the Universe. I. Nicolson. 264p. 1981. 33.95x o.p. (ISBN 0-470-27111-6). Halsted Pr.

Gravity Flow & Transportation of Solids in Suspension. Alexely Stepanoff. LC 72-91156. (Materials Handling & Packaging Ser). 191p. 1969. text ed. 14.50 o.p. (ISBN 0-471-82202-7, Pub. by Wiley). Krieger.

Gravity Park. Dana A. Eastwood. 1978. 4.00 o.p. (ISBN 0-682-49110-1). Exposition-Phoenix.

Gravure de Mode Feminine en France. Raymond Gaudriault. (Illus.). 223p. 1985. 55.00 o.p. (ISBN 2-85917-030-8, Pub. by Editions de L'Amateur Fr). Seven Hills Bk Dists.

Gray Herbarium Index, 10 Vols. Harvard University, Gray Herbarium Staff. 1970. Set. lib. bdg. 860.00 o.p. (ISBN 0-8161-0754-8, Hall Library). G K Hall.

Gray Prince. Jack Vance. 1975. pap. 1.25 o.p. (ISBN 0-380-00555-7, 26799). Avon.

GRE Literature in English. Research & Education Association Staff. (Illus.). 384p. 1987. pap. text ed. 15.95 o.p. (ISBN 0-87891-634-2). Res & Educ.

Greasy Thumb Automechanics Manual for Women. Barb Wyatt. (Illus.). 225p. 1976. pap. 8.00 o.p. (ISBN 0-918040-00-0). Spinsters Aunt Lute.

Great Abnormals. Theophilus B. Hyslop. LC 79-162514. xxviii, 318p. 1971. Repr. of 1925 ed. 43.00x o.p. (ISBN 0-8103-3797-5). Gale.

Great Alone. Janet Dailey. 768p. 1986. 18.45 o.s.i. (ISBN 0-671-61276-X, Poseidon). S&S.

Great American Baseball Lineup Quiz Book. Richard L. Chilton. LC 83-45528. 288p. 1984. pap. 9.95 o.p. (ISBN 0-689-70673-1, Atheneum). Macmillan.

Great American Candy Bar Book. Ray Broekel. 1982. pap. 9.70 o.p. (ISBN 0-395-32502-1). HM.

Great American Chefs Institute. Ed. by Sandy Lesberg. (American Recipe Collection). (Illus.). 192p. pap. 9.95 (North) o.p. (ISBN 0-936320-25-7). pap. 9.95 (West) o.p. (ISBN 0-936320-28-1). Fell.

Great American Families. Gore Vidal et al. (Illus.). 1977. 15.95 o.p. (ISBN 0-393-08752-2). Norton.

Great American Inventors. C. R. Gibbs. 120p. (YA) (gr. 6-12). 1988. PLB 11.95 o.p. (ISBN 0-87460-389-7). Lion Bks.

Titles

Great American Novel. Philip Roth. 400p. 1973. pap. 7.95 o.p. (ISBN 0-374-51584-0). FS&G.

Great American Quilts, 1987. (Illus.). 128p. 1987. 19.95 o.p. (ISBN 0-8487-0696-X). Oxmoor Hse.

Great American Sculptures. William J. Clark. LC 75-28869. (Art Experience in Late 19th Century America Ser.: Vol. 5). (Illus.). 1976. Repr. of 1878 ed. lib. bdg. 53.00 o.p. (ISBN 0-8240-2229-7). Garland Pub.

Great American Soccer Book. Harvey Frommer. LC 79-2037. (Illus.). 1980. 9.95 o.p. (ISBN 0-689-10993-8, Atheneum). Macmillan.

Great American Stomach Book. Maureen Mylander. LC 82-3238. 288p. 1982. 15.95 o.p. (ISBN 0-89919-092-8); pap. 8.95 o.p. (ISBN 0-89919-108-8). Ticknor & Fields.

Great American Success Story. George Gallup, Jr. & Alec M. Gallup. 1985. 14.95 o.p. (ISBN 0-87094-601-3). Dow Jones-Irwin.

Great & Glorious Romance: The Story of Carl Sandburg & Lilian Steichen. Helga Sandburg. LC 77-84394. 352p. 1978. 12.95 o.s.i. (ISBN 0-15-136894-5). HarBraceJ.

Great Awakening: Documents on the Revival of Religion, 1740-1745. Ed. by Richard L. Bushman. (Documentary Problems in Early American History Ser.). 192p. 1971. pap. text ed. 4.25x o.p. (ISBN 0-393-09401-4). Norton.

Great Awakening: Documents on the Revival of Religion, 1740-1745. Ed. by Richard L. Bushman. LC 84-10383. (Institute of Early American History & Culture Ser.). xiv, 174p. 1970. 17.50x o.p. (ISBN 0-8078-1181-5). U of NC Pr.

Great Barzhoon. Cecil Roche. (Illus.). 44p. (gr. 2 up). 1985. 4.95 o.p. (ISBN 0-533-06186-5). Vantage.

Great Baseball Stories Today & Yesterday. Bill Gutman. LC 78-480. (Messner Sports Bks.). (Illus.). 192p. (YA) (gr. 7 up). 1978. lib. bdg. 8.79 o.s.i. (ISBN 0-671-32881-6). Messner.

Great Bazaar. Leslie Lindsay & John Aron. (Orig.). 1982. pap. 9.95 o.s.i. (ISBN 0-440-53077-6, Delta). Dell.

Great Bear Scare. John Barrett. (Bear Bks). (Illus.). 32p. (gr. k-4). 1981. PLB 11.93 o.p. (ISBN 0-516-09191-3). Childrens.

Great Beyond. Maurice Maeterlinck. (ISBN 0-8022-1036-8). Philos Lib.

Great Beyond: A Pastoral Approach to Death. J. Moulton Thomas. 1980. 6.75 o.p. (ISBN 0-682-49556-5). Exposition-Phoenix.

Great Big Joke & Riddle Book. Ed. by Oscar Weigle. LC 79-129734. (Illus.). 224p. (gr. 1-5). 1981. 6.99 o.p. (ISBN 0-448-02584-1, G&D); PLB 6.99 o.p. (ISBN 0-448-03167-1, G&D). Putnam Pub Group.

Great Black Magic Stories. Ed. by Michel Parry. LC 77-76574. 1977. 8.95 o.s.i. (ISBN 0-8008-3618-9). Taplinger.

Great Book of Currier & Ives' America. Walton Rawls. (Illus.). 488p. sewn bdg. 49.95 o.s.i. (ISBN 0-317-54926-X). Apollo.

Great Book of Inside Knowledge. Ed. by Marion Buhagiar. LC 86-31050. 416p. 1986. 50.00 o.p. (ISBN 0-932648-74-6). Boardroom.

Great Books of Hashish, Vol. I, Bk. I. Laurence Cherniak. LC 79-17557. (Illus.). 176p. 1979. pap. 14.95 o.p. (ISBN 0-915904-41-1). And-Or Pr.

Great Bridge. rev. ed. David W. McCullough. (Illus.). 640p. 1976. pap. 5.95 o.p. (ISBN 0-380-00753-3, 49718). Avon.

Great Bridge Scandal. Alan Truscott. 1969. 6.95 o.p. (ISBN 0-682-46964-5). Exposition-Phoenix.

Great Britain & Ireland. (AA Road Map Ser.). (Illus.). Date not set. (ISBN 0-86145-108-2, Pub. by Auto Assn England). Salem Hse Pubs.

Great Britain & Ireland: A Phaidon Cultural Guide. Phaidon Press Limited Staff. (Illus.). 644p. 1985. 16.95 o.p. (ISBN 0-13-363755-7). P-H.

Great Britain & Ireland Nineteen Eighty-Two. Steve Birnbaum. (Get 'em & Go Travel Guide Ser.). 704p. 1981. pap. 10.95 o.p. (ISBN 0-395-31535-2). HM.

Great Britain & Ireland Nineteen Eighty-Seven. Steve Birnbaum. (Illus.). 800p. 1986. pap. 12.70 o.s.i. (ISBN 0-395-42338-4). HM.

Great Britain & Ireland 1983. Steve Birnbaum. (Get 'em & Go Travel Guide Ser.). 1982. pap. 11.45 o.p. (ISBN 0-395-32871-3). HM.

Great Britain & Ireland 1984. Steve Birnbaum. (Get'em & Go Travel Guide Ser.). 1983. pap. 11.45 o.p. (ISBN 0-395-34630-4). HM.

Great Britain & the American Colonies, 1606-1763. Ed. by Jack P. Greene. LC 78-95257. (Documentary History of the United States Ser). xlvii, 312p. 1970. 19.95x o.p. (ISBN 0-87249-167-6). U of SC Pr.

Great Britain Great Empire. W. Ross Johnston. (Scholars' Library). (Illus.). 207p. 1982. text ed. 37.50x o.p. (ISBN 0-7022-1576-7). U of Queensland Pr.

Great Britain in Twenty-Two Days. Rick Steves. 104p. (Orig.). 1986. pap. 4.95 o.p. (ISBN 0-912528-52-4). John Muir.

Great Britain, 1985. Steve Birnbaum. (Stephen Birnbaum Travel Guides Ser.). 1984. pap. 11.70 o.p. (ISBN 0-395-36522-8). HM.

Great Britain's Woodyard: British America & the Timber Trade 1763-1867. Arthur R. Lower. (Illus.). 292p. 1973. 16.95 o.p. (ISBN 0-7735-0096-0, McGill Canada). U of Toronto Pr.

Great British Picture Show. George Perry. 19.95 o.p. (ISBN 0-316-70000-2). Little.

Great Buildings of Boston. George M. Cushing, Jr. 1983. 15.50 o.p. (ISBN 0-8446-5951-7). Peter Smith.

Great Campaigns--Reform & War in America Nineteen Hundred to Nineteen Twenty-Eight. Otis L. Graham, Jr. & Leon Litwack. LC 79-24302. 400p. 1980. pap. 12.50 o.p. (ISBN 0-89874-022-3). Krieger.

Great Camps of the Adirondacks. Harvey Kaiser. LC 79-90360. (Illus.). 1982. 45.00 o.s.i. (ISBN 0-87923-308-7). Godine.

Great Canadian Character Anthology. Ed. by Bill Brownstein et al. (Illus.). 128p. (Orig.). 1985. pap. 12.95 o.s.i. (ISBN 0-920792-54-5). Eden Pr.

Great Cases in Psychotherapy. Ed. by Dan Wedding & Raymond J. Corsini. LC 78-61878. 314p. 1979. pap. text ed. 15.95 o.p. (ISBN 0-87581-234-1). Peacock Pubs.

Great Chain of Life. Joseph W. Krutch. (Illus.). 1978. pap. 3.95 o.p. (ISBN 0-395-25943-6). HM.

Great Chefs of Chicago. Tele-Record Productions Staff. (Great Chefs Ser.). 112p. 1985. pap. 9.95 o.p. (ISBN 0-380-89696-6). Avon.

Great Chefs of New Orleans II. Tele-Record Productions Staff. 112p. 1984. pap. 9.95 o.p. (ISBN 0-380-87973-5, 87973-5). Avon.

Great Chefs of San Francisco. Tele-Record Productions Staff. 96p. 1984. pap. 9.95 o.p. (ISBN 0-380-87072-X, 87072). Avon.

Great Chicago Bar & Saloon Guide. rev. ed. Dennis B. McCarthy. 176p. pap. 3.95 o.p. (ISBN 0-914091-68-9). Chicago Review.

Great Christ Debate: A Quest for the Theological Reconciliation of Judaism, Christianity, & Islam. Etomar Ben Roffman. 1978. 8.50 o.p. (ISBN 0-682-49123-3). Exposition-Phoenix.

Great Churches-Today's Essentials. Don R. Pegram. 1982. pap. 1.25 o.p. (ISBN 0-89265-083-4). Randall Hse.

Great Circle. Conrad Aiken. 1985. 6.95 o.p. (ISBN 0-87795-706-1, Arbor Hse). Morrow.

Great Code: The Bible & Literature. Northrop Frye. LC 81-47303. 320p. 1982. 14.95 o.p. (ISBN 0-15-136902-X). HarBraceJ.

Great Columbia Plain: A Historical Geography, 1805-1910. Donald W. Meinig. LC 68-11044. (Emil & Kathleen Sick Lecture-Book Series in Western History & Biography). (Illus.). 598p. (Orig.). 1983. pap. 14.95 o.p. (ISBN 0-295-96044-2). U of Wash Pr.

Great Comedians. Larry Wilde. 384p. 1973. pap. 3.95 o.p. (ISBN 0-8065-0388-2, Pub. by Citadel Pr). Carol Pub Group.

Great Communicator. Jim Borgman. (Illus.). 160p. 1985. pap. 8.95 o.p. (ISBN 0-9609632-1-9). Chicago Review.

Great Compassion Dharma Transmission Verses of the 42 Hands & Eyes. Tripitaka Master Hua. Tr. by Buddhist Text Translation Society. (Illus.). 100p. (Orig.). 1983. pap. 16.00 o.p. (ISBN 0-88139-002-X). Buddhist Text.

Great Concert Music: Philip Hale's Boston Symphont Programme Notes. Philip Hale. Ed. by John N. Burk. LC 75-109742. xix, 400p. 1971. Repr. of 1939 ed. lib. bdg. 35.00x o.p. (ISBN 0-8371-4232-6, HACM). Greenwood.

Great Contemporaries. Winston S. Churchill. LC 73-77128. (Illus.). 1976. pap. 4.95 o.s.i. (ISBN 0-226-10631-4, P692, Phoen). U of Chicago Pr.

Great Cooking. 29.95 o.p. (ISBN 0-317-62763-5). H Holt & Co.

Great Crash, Nineteen Twenty-Nine. 50th Anniv. ed. John Kenneth Galbraith. 1979. 11.95 o.p. (ISBN 0-395-28420-1); pap. 3.45 o.p. (ISBN 0-395-08359-1). HM.

Great Crash of Nineteen Twenty-Nine. John Kenneth Galbraith. 1980. pap. 2.75 o.p. (ISBN 0-380-50799-4, 63842-8, Discus). Avon.

Great Decisions, 1983. Foreign Policy Association Staff. LC 58-59828. (Illus.). 96p. 1983. pap. 8.00 o.p. (ISBN 0-87124-080-7). Foreign Policy.

Great Decisions, 1984. 96p. 1984. 8.00 o.p. (ISBN 0-317-04558-X). Foreign Policy.

Great Decisions, 1985. Foreign Policy Association Staff. LC 58-59828. (Illus.). 96p. (Orig.). 1985. 15.00 o.p. (ISBN 0-87124-095-5); pap. 8.00 o.p. (ISBN 0-87124-085-8). Foreign Policy.

Great Decisions 1986. Foreign Policy Association Staff. LC 58-59828. (Illus.). 96p. (Orig.). 1986. pap. 8.00 o.p. (ISBN 0-87124-101-3). Foreign Policy.

Great Decisions 1987. LC 58-59828. 96p. 1987. pap. 8.00 o.p. (ISBN 0-87124-110-2). Foreign Policy.

Great Decisions 86 Activity Book. Heidi Hurch et al. (Illus.). 50p. (gr. 11-12). 1986. pap. 7.95 o.p. (ISBN 0-943804-62-0). U of Denver Teach.

Great Deluge: A Yeats Bibliography. John E. Stoll. LC 78-161084. 1971. 7.50x o.p. (ISBN 0-87875-010-X). Whitston Pub.

Great Diamond Robbery. Leon A. Harris. LC 85-7965. (Illus.). 32p. (gr. 3). 1985. 10.95 o.s.i. (ISBN 0-689-31188-5, Atheneum Childrens Bks). Macmillan.

Great Discoveries & the First Colonial Empires. Charles E. Nowell. (Development of Western Civilization Ser). (Illus.). 150p. 1954. pap. 5.95x o.p. (ISBN 0-8014-9848-1). Cornell U Pr.

Great Dissenters. Norman Thomas. 1970. pap. 3.95x o.p. (ISBN 0-393-00529-1, Norton Lib). Norton.

Great Dr. Burney: His Life, His Travels, His Works, His Family & His Friends, 2 vols. Percy A. Scholes. LC 74-104254. (Illus.). 1971. Repr. of 1948 ed. lib. bdg. 35.50x o.p. (ISBN 0-8371-4017-X, SCDB); Vol. 1. lib. bdg. 19.50 o.p. (ISBN 0-8371-6242-4, SCDC). Greenwood.

Great Dramas of the Bible. William E. Cameron. LC 81-71560. 305p. 1982. 6.95 o.p. (ISBN 0-87159-047-6). Unity School.

Great Draughtsmen from Pisanello to Picasso. Jakob Rosenberg. LC 59-7661. (Illus.). 1959. 21.00x o.s.i. (ISBN 0-674-36200-4). Harvard U Pr.

Great Dying: A Cosmic Catastrophe Demolishes the Dinosaurs & Rocks the Theory of Evolution. Kenneth J. Hsu. LC 86-9979. 356p. 1986. 17.95 o.p. (ISBN 0-15-136904-6). HarBraceJ.

Great Educators: Readings for Leaders in Education. Hugh C. Black et al. LC 72-88717. 799p. 1972. 29.95x o.s.i. (ISBN 0-911012-48-6). Nelson-Hall.

Great English Story Poems: Collections. Ed. by Harriet K. Ross. 160p. (YA) (gr. 5-12). 1989. PLB 10.95 o.p. (ISBN 0-87460-390-0); pap. 8.95 o.p. (ISBN 0-87460-364-1). Lion Bks.

Great Escape. Paul Brickhill. (Illus.). 1950. 12.95 o.p. (ISBN 0-393-08445-0). Norton.

Great Escape from Your Dead End Job. John J. Komar. 1981. pap. 2.25 o.s.i. (ISBN 0-345-29343-6). Ballantine.

Great Expectations. Kathy Acker. LC 83-48312. 128p. 1983. 14.95 o.p. (ISBN 0-394-53497-2, GP-873). Grove.

Great Expectations. Leigh Adams & Lynda Madara. 1980. pap. 7.95 o.p. (ISBN 0-395-29460-6). HM.

Great Expectations. 2nd ed. Charles Dickens. LC 72-177918. (Rinehart Editions). 1972. pap. text ed. 12.95 o.p. (ISBN 0-03-077900-6, HoltC). HR&W.

Great Expectations. Charles Dickens. LC 84-62236. (Illus.). 432p. 1985. 12.95 o.p. (ISBN 0-89577-205-1). RD Assn.

Great Expectations: The Psychology of Money. Henry C. Lindgren. LC 80-14177. 262p. 1980. 13.95 o.p. (ISBN 0-913232-82-3). W Kaufmann.

Great Expectorations: Advertising & the Tobacco Industry. Simon Chapman. (Comedia Ser.). (Illus.). 144p. (Orig.). 1987. pap. 7.50 o.p. (ISBN 0-906890-86-1). M Boyars Pubs.

Great Explorers. rev. ed. Joyce Grosseck. LC 80-69168. (American History & Culture Ser.). (Illus.). (gr. 4 up). 1981. text ed. 9.95 ea. 1-4 copies o.s.i. (ISBN 0-88296-031-8); text ed. 7.96 5 or more copies o.s.i. (ISBN 0-88296-031-8). Gateway Pr MI.

Great Fake Book. Vance Bourjaily. LC 86-10998. 320p. 1987. 17.95 o.s.i. (ISBN 1-55584-003-5). Weidenfeld.

Great Fear of 1789. G. Lefebvre. 1982. 35.00 o.p. (ISBN 0-691-05356-1); pap. 8.95 o.p. (ISBN 0-691-00793-4). Princeton U Pr.

Great Flower Painters: Four Centuries of Floral Art. Peter Mitchell. LC 72-95231. (Illus.). 276p. 1973. 85.00 o.p. (ISBN 0-87951-008-0). Overlook Pr.

Great Formosan Imposter. Frederic J. Foley. 126p. 1980. 7.50 o.p. (ISBN 0-89955-148-3, Pub. by Mei Ya China). Intl Spec Bk.

Great Free Enterprise Gambit. James A. Baar. 1980. 8.95 o.p. (ISBN 0-395-29115-1). HM.

Great Game. Mairi Huntington. LC 83-82072. (Illus.). 173p. (Orig.). 1985. pap. text ed. 4.95 o.p. (ISBN 0-88155-027-2, 0199). Illum Way Pub.

Great Game for a Girl. Tristram P. Coffin. 124p. 1980. 7.00 o.p. (ISBN 0-682-49566-2). Exposition-Phoenix.

Great Gatsby. F. Scott Fitzgerald. (Portico Ser.). pap. 1.25 o.p. (ISBN 0-671-08077-6). Monarch Pr.

Great Geographical Atlas. Rand McNally & Company Staff. 464p. 1982. 75.00 o.p. (ISBN 0-528-83079-1). Rand McNally.

Great Ghost Show. (Real Ghostbuster Storybooks). (gr. 1-5). 1987. pap. 2.25 o.s.i. (ISBN 0-671-64569-2). Wanderer Bks.

Great Ghost Stories. Ed. by Betty Schwartz. LC 85-8271. (Illus.). 192p. (gr. 5 up). 1985. lib. bdg. 9.97 o.s.i. (ISBN 0-671-60622-0). Messner.

Great Gillis Hopkins. Katherine Paterson. 1983. pap. 2.25 o.p. (ISBN 0-380-65219-6, Flare). Avon.

Great Gilly Hopkins. Katherine Paterson. 156p. (gr. 5 up). 1979. pap. 2.50 o.p. (ISBN 0-380-45963-9, Camelot). Avon.

Great God Mogadon & Other Plays. Barry Oakley. 119p. 1980. pap. 17.50x o.p. (ISBN 0-7022-1436-1); pap. 7.95x o.p. (ISBN 0-7022-1437-X). U of Queensland Pr.

Great Golden Gate Bridge Trivia Book: A Half-Century Compendium of Astounding Facts, Superlative Statistics & Fanciful Lore. E. J. Knapp. LC 86-28408. (Illus.). 144p. (Orig.). 1987. pap. 4.95 o.p. (ISBN 0-87701-433-7). Chronicle Bks.

Great Good Fortune: How Harvard Makes Its Money. Carl Vigeland. 1986. 18.45 o.p. (ISBN 0-395-36231-8). HM.

Great Gradepoint Mystery. Barbara Bartholomew. (Microkid Mystery Ser.: No. 1). 96p. (ps-5). 1985. pap. 2.50 o.p. (ISBN 0-380-69834-X, Camelot). Avon.

Great-Grandfather, the Baby, & Me. Howard Knotts. LC 78-2940. (Illus.). (ps-3). 1978. 6.95 o.p. (ISBN 0-689-30656-3, Atheneum). Macmillan.

Great Grandpapa Billie. May R. Beck. (Illus.). 281p. 1958. o.p. (ISBN 0-940882-08-6). HB Pubns.

Great Hamster Hunt. Lenore Blegvad & Erik Blegvad. LC 69-13780. (Illus.). (gr. k-3). 1969. 5.95 o.p. (ISBN 0-15-232500-X, HJ). HarBraceJ.

Great Harry. Carolly Erickson. LC 79-21868. 1980. 14.95 o.s.i. (ISBN 0-671-40017-7). Summit Bks.

Great Hinckley Fire. Clark C. Peterson. (Illus.). 1980. 7.50 o.p. (ISBN 0-682-49569-7). Exposition-Phoenix.

Great Hollywood Movies. Ted Sennett. 1983. 49.50 o.p. (ISBN 0-8109-0980-4). Abrams.

Great Horse Race. Fred Grove. LC 76-50907. (Double D Western Ser.). 1977. 5.95 o.p. (ISBN 0-385-12101-6). Doubleday.

Great Ideas in Communications. A. Brown. 1968. 45.00 o.p. (ISBN 0-08-007073-6). Pergamon.

Great Ideas in Engineering. E. Larson. 1968. 45.00 o.p. (ISBN 0-08-007078-7). Pergamon.

Great Ideas in Information Theory, Language & Cibernetics. Jagjit Singh. 15.25 o.p. (ISBN 0-8446-2946-4). Peter Smith.

Great Ideas in Music. P. Young. 1967. 55.00 o.p. (ISBN 0-08-007072-8); pap. (Reproduction on Demand) o.p. Pergamon.

Great Ideas of Science. Isaac Asimov. LC 70-82476. (Illus.). 144p. (gr. 7 up). 1969. 6.95 o.p. (ISBN 0-395-06580-1). HM.

Great Inertia: Scientific Stagnation in Traditional China. Wen-yuan Qian. LC 84-14217. 156p. 1985. 27.50 o.p. (ISBN 0-7099-2104-7, Pub. by Croom Helm Ltd). Routledge Chapman & Hall.

Great Inns of America. William E. Gilbert. LC 86-14690. 176p. (Orig.). 1986. pap. 12.95 o.p. (ISBN 0-931790-72-7). Brick Hse Pub.

Great International Disaster Book. 3rd ed. James Cornell. (Illus.). 464p. 1982. encore ed. 5.95 o.p. (ISBN 0-684-17345-X, ScribT). Scribner.

Great International Disaster Book. James Cornell. LC 76-20752. (Encore Editions). (Illus.). 432p. 1976. 5.95 o.p. (ISBN 0-684-16894-4, ScribT). Scribner.

Great Jehoshaphat & Gully Dirt! Jewell E. Smith. LC 75-33778. 226p. 1975. 3.98 o.p. (ISBN 0-910244-86-3). Blair.

Great Jewish Chess Champions. Harold U & Meir Z. Ribalow. (Illus.). 120p. 1987. 8.95 o.p. (ISBN 0-87052-305-8). Hippocrene Bks.

Great Jewish Plays. Ed. by Joseph C. Landis. 1980. pap. 4.45 o.p. (ISBN 0-380-00123-3, 51573-3, Bard). Avon.

Great Jews I Have Known. Max Raisin. 1952. Philos Lib.

Great Jurists of the World: From Gaius to Von Ihering. Ed. by John Macdonnell & Edwards Manson. (Continental Legal History Ser.: Vol. 2). xxxii, 608p. 1968. Repr. of 1914 ed. 37.50x o.p. (ISBN 0-8377-2425-2). Rothman.

Great Lakes State of America. Neal R. Peirce & John Keefe. (Illus.). 1980. 16.95 o.p. (ISBN 0-393-05619-8). Norton.

Great Lion of God. Taylor Caldwell. 704p. 1982. pap. 3.95 o.p. (ISBN 0-449-24096-7, Crest). Fawcett.

Great Literature & the Good Life. Sterling W. Sill. Ed. by Iris Syndergaard. LC 85-80542. 112p. 7.95 o.p. (ISBN 0-88290-305-5). Horizon Utah.

Great Love. Alexandra Kollontai. Tr. by Cathy Porter. 160p. 1982. pap. 4.95 o.p. (ISBN 0-393-30028-5). Norton.

Great Lover: Herbert Beerbohm Tree. Madelene Bingham. LC 78-65197. (Illus.). 1979. 11.95 o.p. (ISBN 0-689-10963-6, Atheneum). Macmillan.

Great Lover's Manifesto. Dave Grant. LC 85-60124. 160p. (Orig.). 1986. 9.95 o.p. (ISBN 0-89081-481-3). Harvest Hse.

Great Luxury Liners, Nineteen Twenty-Seven to Nineteen Fifty-Four: A Photographic Record. William H. Miller, Jr. (Illus.). 18.00 o.p. (ISBN 0-8446-5906-1). Peter Smith.

Great McGoniggle Rides Shotgun. Corbett. Date not set. (ISBN 0-316-15729-5). Little.

Great McGoniggle's Gray Ghost. Scott Corbett. (Illus.). (gr. 1-3). 1975. 10.45i o.p. (ISBN 0-316-15725-2, Pub. by Atlantic Monthly Pr). Little.

Great Mail Order Bazaar. Irvin Molotsky. LC 85-16489. (Illus.). 302p. 1986. pap. 14.95 o.p. (ISBN 0-87795-641-3, Arbor Hse). Morrow.

Great Maria. Cecelia Holland. 1987. pap. 8.95 o.p. (ISBN 0-345-34110-4). Ballantine.

Great Masters. Giorgio Vasari. Ed. by Michael Sonino. Tr. by Gaston Du C. De Vere. (Illus.). 384p. 1986. 75.00 o.p. (ISBN 0-88363-686-7). H L Levin.

Great Masters of the Violin. Boris Schwarz. 496p. 1983. 24.00 o.s.i. (ISBN 0-671-22598-7). S&S.

Great Me. James Gasper. 48p. 1986. 6.50 o.p. (ISBN 0-317-60859-2). Carlton.

Great Medical Bibliographers: A Study in Humanism. John F. Fulton. LC 76-30508. (Historical Library, Yale University School of Medicine: No. 26). (Illus.). 1977. Repr. of 1951 ed. lib. bdg. 35.00x o.p. (ISBN 0-8371-9436-9, FUGM). Greenwood.

Great Microwave Dessert Cookbook. Thelma Pressman. (Illus.). 176p. 1987. pap. 8.95 o.p. (ISBN 0-8092-4740-2). Contemp Bks.

Great Misconceptions: People with Disabilities. Archdiocese of San Francisco. 48p. 1982. saddle stitched 6.95 o.p. (ISBN 0-8403-2674-2). Kendall-Hunt.

Great Moments in Mathematics Before 1650. Howard Eves. LC 80-81046. (Dolciani Mathematical Exposition Ser.: No. 5). 1981. cloth 25.50 o.p. (ISBN 0-88385-305-1). Math Assn.

Great Moments in Sports Car Racing. David J. Abodaher. LC 80-26026. (Illus.). 96p. (gr. 4-6). 1981. PLB 9.29 o.p. (ISBN 0-671-33090-X). Messner.

Great Moments in the Indy 500. Edward F. Dolan, Jr. (Triumph Bks.). (Illus.). (gr. 6 up). 1982. PLB 11.90 o.p. (ISBN 0-531-04407-6). Watts.

Great Movie Directors. Ted Sennett. (Illus.). 320p. 1986. 35.00 o.p. (ISBN 0-8109-0718-6). Abrams.

Great Muppet Caper. (Illus.). 59p. 1981. 7.95 o.s.i. (ISBN 0-89524-144-7, 2505). Cherry Lane.

Great Myths & Legends. Ed. by World Book, Inc. Staff. LC 65-25105. (Childcraft-The How & Why Library). 310p. (gr. 3-7). 1984. PLB write for info. o.p. (ISBN 0-7166-0684-4). World Bk.

Great National Park Vacations. 1987. pap. 10.95 o.p. (ISBN 0-317-56581-8). Rand McNally.

Great New British Cooking. Jane Garmey. LC 85-14287. 220p. 1985. 16.45 o.p. (ISBN 0-671-53258-8). S&S.

Great New England Churches: Sixty-Five Houses of Worship That Changed Our Lives. Robert Mutrux. LC 81-80425. (Illus.). 288p. (Orig.). 1981. pap. 14.95 o.p. (ISBN 0-87106-950-4). Globe Pequot.

Great October Socialist Revolution. 496p. 1977. 8.95 o.p. (ISBN 0-8285-0468-7, Pub. by Progress Pubs USSR). Imported Pubns.

Great Operas of Mozart. Nathan Broder. 1962. 9.95 o.p. (ISBN 0-02-870440-1). Schirmer Bks.

Great Operas of Mozart. Ed. by Nathan Broder. 1964. 4.95 o.p. (ISBN 0-393-00256-X, N256, Norton Lib). Norton.

Great Orm of Loch Ness. F. W. Holiday. LC 68-15754. (Illus.). 1969. 6.95 o.p. (ISBN 0-393-06345-3). Norton.

Great Paintings from the Ringling Museum of Art: Fortieth Anniversary Celebration. Anthony F. Janson. LC 85-81062. (Illus.). 120p. 1986. pap. 14.95 o.p. (ISBN 0-916758-21-4). Ringling Mus Art.

Great Peasant Dishes of the World. Howard Hillman. 174p. 1983. 14.45 o.p. (ISBN 0-395-32210-3); pap. 8.70 o.p. (ISBN 0-395-34073-X). HM.

Great Pianists. rev. ed. Harold C. Schoenberg. 1987. 20.45 o.p. (ISBN 0-671-64200-6). S&S.

Great Po Sein: A Chronicle of the Burmese Theater. Kenneth Sein & J. A. Withey. LC 75-46553. 170p. 1976. Repr. of 1966 ed. lib. bdg. 35.00x o.p. (ISBN 0-8371-8737-0, SEGP). Greenwood.

Great Port: A Passage Through New York. James Morris. LC 70-84872. (Helen & Kurt Wolff Bk). (Illus.). 1969. 5.95 o.p. (ISBN 0-15-136945-3). HarBraceJ.

Great Power Competition for Overseas Bases. Robert E. Harkavy. (Pergamon Policy Studies On Security Affairs Ser.). 360p. 1982. 95.00 o.p. (ISBN 0-08-025089-0, T130). Pergamon.

Great Power Triangle & Asian Security. Ed. by Raju G. Thomas. LC 82-49053. 208p. 1983. 25.00x o.p. (ISBN 0-669-06405-X). Lexington Bks.

Great Powers & the End of the Ottoman Empire. Ed. by Marian Kent. (Illus.). 240p. 1984. text ed. 37.95x o.p. (ISBN 0-04-956013-1). Unwin Hyman.

Great Pretender. James Atlas. LC 85-48127. 320p. 1986. 14.95 o.p. (ISBN 0-689-11800-7, Atheneum). Macmillan.

Great Profundo & Other Stories. Bernard M. Laverty. 1988. 15.95 o.p. (ISBN 0-8021-1048-7). Grove.

Great Public Gardens of the Eastern United States: A Guide to Their Beauty & Botany. Doris M. Stone. (Illus.). 248p. 1982. pap. 12.95 o.p. (ISBN 0-394-70664-1). Pantheon.

Great Quillow. James Thurber. LC 75-6613. (Illus.). 54p. (gr. 2-3). 1975. pap. 1.95 o.p. (ISBN 0-15-636490-5, VoyB). HarBraceJ.

Great Rabbit Rip-Off. E. W. Hildick. LC 76-46296. (McGurk Mystery Ser.). 112p. (gr. 3-6). 1977. 9.95 o.p. (ISBN 0-02-743820-1). Macmillan.

Great Racehorses in Art. John Fairley. (Illus.). 224p. 75.00 o.p. (ISBN 0-317-54954-5). Apollo.

Great Rail Non-Journeys of Australia. Colin Taylor. LC 85-24514. (Illus.). 233p. 1987. text ed. 29.50x o.p. (ISBN 0-7022-1949-5). U of Queensland Pr.

Great Railway Stations of Britain. Gordon Biddle. (Illus.). 240p. 1987. 39.95 o.p. (ISBN 0-7153-8263-2). David & Charles.

Great Rat Island Adventure. Charlene J. Talbot. LC 77-1055. (Illus.). (gr. 4-6). 1977. 7.95 o.p. (ISBN 0-689-30596-6, Atheneum). Macmillan.

Great Rebel: Che Guevara in Bolivia. Luis J. Gonzales & Gustavo A. Sanchez Salazar. 1969. pap. 1.45 o.p. (ISBN 0-394-17156-X, B227, BC). Grove.

Great Reform Act of 1832. E. J. Evans. (Lancaster Pamphlet Ser.). 60p. 1983. pap. 3.95 o.p. (ISBN 0-416-34450-X, NO. 3849). Routledge Chapman & Hall.

Great Religious Thinkers, 6 bks. E. L. Allen. (ISBN 0-8022-0022-2). Philos Lib.

Great Religious Thinkers: Creation & Grace - A Guide to the Thought of Emil Brunner. E. L. Allen. Philos Lib.

Great Religious Thinkers: Freedom in God. L. E. Allen. 1951. Philos Lib.

Great Religious Thinkers: The Self & Its Hazards - A Guide to the Thought of Karl Jaspers. E. L. Allen. 1951. Philos Lib.

Great Religious Thinkers: The Sovereignty of God & the Word of God - A Guide to the Thought of Karl Barth. E. L. Allen. 1951. Philos Lib.

Great Republic: A History of the American People. Bernard Bailyn et al. 1977. 39.95 o.p. (ISBN 0-316-07672-4). Little.

Great Resorts of America. Reid, Robert, Associates Staff. 160p. 1983. 19.95 o.s.i. (ISBN 0-03-063391-5). H Holt & Co.

Great Ringtail Garbage Caper. Timothy Foote. (Illus.). 80p. (gr. 3-6). 1980. 6.70 o.p. (ISBN 0-395-28759-6). HM.

Great River: Art & Society of the Connecticut Valley. (Illus.). 528p. 1985. pap. 35.00 o.p. (ISBN 0-918333-03-2). Wadsworth Atheneum.

Great Rivers of the World. Ed. by Alexander Frater. LC 83-83383. (Illus.). 224p. 1984. 24.95 o.p. (ISBN 0-316-29222-2). Little.

Great Russian Short Stories. Ed. by Stephen Graham. 1021p. 1975. pap. 6.95 o.p. (ISBN 0-87140-105-3). Liveright.

Great Sacrifice. Fred Pruitt. 31p. 1982. pap. 0.25 o.p. (ISBN 0-686-36262-4); pap. 1.00 5 copies o.p. (ISBN 0-686-37284-0). Faith Pub Hse.

Great Santini. Pat Conroy. 1977. pap. 3.95 o.p. (ISBN 0-380-00991-9, 65961-1). Avon.

Great Sermons. Ed. & illus. by Frank L. Bouquet. 100p. (Orig.). lib. bdg. 80.00 o.s.i. (ISBN 0-937041-47-5); text ed. 60.00 o.s.i.; pap. text ed. 25.00 o.s.i. (ISBN 0-937041-35-1). Systems Co.

Great Short Stories of the World. Ed. by Reader's Digest Editors. LC 72-81158. 800p. 1972. 17.97 o.p. (ISBN 0-89577-008-3). RD Assn.

Great Shorter Works of Pascal. Blaise Pascal. Ed. by John C. Blankenagel & Emile Cailliet. LC 73-21179. 231p. 1974. Repr. of 1948 ed. lib. bdg. 22.50x o.p. (ISBN 0-8371-6072-3, PASW). Greenwood.

Great Siege. Bradford. 1962. 6.50 o.p. (ISBN 0-15-136950-X). HarBraceJ.

Great Singers. Henry Pleasants. (Illus.). 390p. 1985. pap. 11.95 o.p. (ISBN 0-671-42160-3, Fireside). S&S.

Great Smoky Mountains Picture Book. Jim Doane. Ed. by George Castaldo. (Color Pictorial of Great Smoky Mountains Ser.: No. 1). (Illus.). 72p. (Orig.). (ps-12). 1981. 10.95 o.p. (ISBN 0-936672-13-7); pap. 7.50 o.p. (ISBN 0-936672-14-5). Aerial Photo.

Great Stone Face & Other Tales of the White Mountains. Nathaniel Hawthorne. (Illus.). (gr. 7 up). 6.95 o.p. (ISBN 0-395-07787-7). HM.

Great Stories about Animals. Compiled by Harriet Ross. LC 67-17991. (Illus.). 160p. (gr. 3-9). 1982. PLB 9.95 o.p. (ISBN 0-87460-198-3); pap. 3.95 o.p. (ISBN 0-87460-199-1). Lion Bks.

Great Stories of Mystery & Suspense, 2 vols. Ed. by Reader's Digest Editors. LC 73-76284. (Open-ended Ser.). (Illus.). 1294p. 1981. Set. 19.95 o.p. (ISBN 0-89577-083-0). RD Assn.

Great Stories of Mystery & Suspense, 2 vols. Ed. by Reader's Digest Editors. LC 73-76284. (Open-Ended Ser.). (Illus.). 1290p. 1977. Set. 19.95 o.p. (ISBN 0-89577-136-5). RD Assn.

Great Sunflower. Clifford Stone. 1977. pap. 1.50 o.p. (ISBN 0-380-01809-8, 35659). Avon.

Great Sweaters to Knit. Fabbri Magazine Editors Staff. (Illus.). 80p. 1983. pap. 9.95 o.p. (ISBN 0-684-17973-3, ScribT). Scribner.

Great Systems of Yoga. Ernest Wood. 1954. (ISBN 0-8022-1922-5). Philos Lib.

Great Tales of the Sea. Reader's Digest Editors. LC 77-81738. (Illus.). 640p. 1978. 16.98 o.p. (ISBN 0-89577-016-4). RD Assn.

Great Television Plays. Ed. by William I. Kaufman. (Orig.). 1969. pap. 2.75 o.p. (ISBN 0-440-33207-9, LE). Dell.

Great Tortoise Stories. Olatunde Ojomo. (Illus.). (gr. 1-3). 1985. 4.95 o.p. (ISBN 0-533-05455-9). Vantage.

Great Town & Country Bicycle Balloon Chase. Barbara Douglass. LC 83-14877. (Illus.). 32p. (gr. k-3). 1984. 11.75 o.p. (ISBN 0-688-02231-6); PLB 11.88 o.p. (ISBN 0-688-02232-4). Lothrop.

Great Tradition in English Literature. Rubenstein. pap. 1.95 o.p. (ISBN 0-8065-0309-2, Pub. by Citadel Pr). Carol Pub Group.

Great Truths to Live by see Word Studies in the Greek New Testament, for the English Reader.

Great Urge Downward. Gordon Merrick. 432p. (Orig.). 1984. pap. 4.95 o.p. (ISBN 0-380-88971-4). Avon.

Great Victorian Collection. Brian Moore. LC 75-5553. 213p. 1975. 7.95 o.p. (ISBN 0-374-16656-0). FS&G.

Great Visions of Philosophy. William P. Montague. (Paul Carus Lecture Ser.). 501p. 1950. 29.95 o.p. (ISBN 0-87548-098-5). Open Court.

Great Walking Adventure. Hamish Brown. (Great Adventure Ser.). (Illus.). 256p. 1986. 13.95 o.p. (ISBN 0-946609-12-8, Pub. by Oxford Ill Pr). Haynes Pubns.

Great Western Coaches from the Eighteen Nineties. Michael Harris. (Illus.). 160p. 1985. 42.95 o.p. (ISBN 0-7153-8050-8). David & Charles.

Great Western Locomotive Design: A Critical Appreciation. John C. Gibson. (Illus.). 160p. 1984. 24.95 o.p. (ISBN 0-7153-8606-9). David & Charles.

Great Western Railway: A New History. Frank Booker. (Illus.). 206p. 1986. pap. 12.95 o.p. (ISBN 0-946537-21-6). David & Charles.

Great Western Railway: One Hundred Fifty Glorious Years. David S. Thomas & P. B. Whitehouse. (Illus.). 208p. 1985. pap. 20.95 o.p. (ISBN 0-7153-8763-4). David & Charles.

Great Western Railway: One Hundred Fifty Glorious Years. Patrick Whitehouse & David S. Thomas. (Illus.). 208p. 1984. 39.95 o.p. (ISBN 0-7153-8530-5). David & Charles.

Great Whale Rescue: An American Folk Epic. Tom Tiede & Jack Findleton. (Illus.). 156p. 1986. pap. 14.95 o.p. (ISBN 0-345-33912-6). Pharos Bks NY.

Great Wheadle Tragedy. Alexander Theroux. LC 74-30911. (Illus.). 40p. (gr. 5 up). 1975. 4.95 o.s.i. (ISBN 0-87923-136-X). Godine.

Great Wheel: The World, Monetary System; a Reinterpretation. Sidney E. Rolfe & James L. Burtle. LC 73-79929. (McGraw-Hill Paperbacks). 304p. 1975. pap. text ed. 4.95 o.p. (ISBN 0-07-053562-0). McGraw.

Great White Shark. Eve Bunting. LC 82-3415. (Jem (High Interest-Low Vocabulary) Ser.). 64p. (gr. 4 up). 1983. lib. bdg. 9.29 o.s.i. (ISBN 0-671-44004-7); lib. bdg. 4.95 o.s.i. (ISBN 0-671-49472-4). Messner.

Great Wines of Bordeaux. James Seely. 1986. 29.95 o.p. (ISBN 0-316-77973-3). Little.

Great Wines of France: Margaux. Bernard Ginestet. 19.95 o.p. (ISBN 0-03-006014-1). H Holt & Co.

Great Wines of France: Saint-Julien. Bernard Ginestet. 19.95 o.p. (ISBN 0-03-006017-6). H Holt & Co.

Great Works of Edgar Allan Poe: Tales. Edgar Allan Poe. 1984. 12.98 o.p. (ISBN 0-517-45372-X). Crown.

Great Works of Sir Arthur Doyle: The Illustrated Sherlock Holmes Treasury. Arthur Conan Doyle. (Illus.). 1987. 12.98 o.p. (ISBN 0-517-64282-4). Crown.

Great Writing in Marketing. 2nd ed. Howard A. Thompson. 682p. 1981. pap. text ed. write for info. o.p. (ISBN 0-02-420630-X). Macmillan.

Great Yachts & Their Designers. Jonathan Eastland. LC 87-45388. (Illus.). 256p. 1987. 45.00 o.p. (ISBN 0-8478-0828-9). Rizzoli Intl.

Great Year of Zarathustra, 1881-1981. Ed. by David Goicoechea. LC 83-14732. 384p. 1984. lib. bdg. 31.50 o.p. (ISBN 0-8191-3497-X); pap. text ed. 16.50 o.p. (ISBN 0-8191-3498-8). U Pr of Amer.

Greater Ethiopia: The Evolution of a Multiethnic Society. Donald N. Levine. 1974. lib. bdg. 16.00x o.s.i. (ISBN 0-226-47558-1). U of Chicago Pr.

Greater Good: Potentials for an Intelligent Economy. Robert B. Zevin. 1983. 15.45 o.p. (ISBN 0-395-32530-7). HM.

Greater Look at Greater Buffalo. Jim Bisco. LC 86-26717. (Illus.). 480p. 1986. 34.95 o.p. (ISBN 0-89781-198-4). Windsor Pubns Inc.

Greater Medieval Historians: A Reader. Ed. by Indrikis Sterns. LC 82-15919. 472p. (Orig.). 1983. lib. bdg. 40.25 o.p. (ISBN 0-8191-2752-3); pap. text ed. 18.50 o.p. (ISBN 0-8191-2753-1). U Pr of Amer.

Greater Phoenix Street Maps Book. 96p. 1986. pap. 3.50 o.p. (ISBN 0-914846-18-3). Golden West Pub.

Greater Than Our Hearts: Prayers & Reflections. Ulrich Schaffer. LC 81-47434. 128p. 1981. 1.00 o.p. (ISBN 0-06-067088-6). HarpR.

Greatest American Woman, Lucretia Mott. Lloyd C. Hare. LC 76-109327. (Illus.). 307p. 1970. Repr. of 1937 ed. lib. bdg. 22.50x o.p. (ISBN 0-8371-3593-1, HLM&). Greenwood.

Greatest Breakthrough since Lunchtime. Colin Douglas. LC 78-27167. 1979. 8.95 o.s.i. (ISBN 0-8008-3649-9). Taplinger.

Greatest Cattle Drive. Paul I. Wellman. (North Star Bks.). (Illus.). (gr. 5-9). 1964. 2.95 o.p. (ISBN 0-395-07259-X). HM.

Greatest Crime. Sloan Wilson. (Adventure & Suspense Ser.). 11.50 o.p. (ISBN 0-87795-296-5, Arbor Hse). Morrow.

Greatest Crusade: Roosevelt, Churchill, & the Naval Wars. Richard Hough. LC 85-15442. (Illus.). 288p. 1986. 17.95 o.p. (ISBN 0-688-04309-7). Morrow.

Greatest Game Ever Played. Jerry Izenberg. 1987. 15.95 o.p. (ISBN 0-8050-0513-7). H Holt & Co.

Greatest Hits of the World Almanac. Ed. by World Almanac Editors. Date not set. pap. 6.95 o.s.i. (ISBN 0-345-33722-0). Ballantine.

Greatest Indian Stories. Zane Grey. 1978. pap. 1.50 o.s.i. (ISBN 0-505-51303-X, Pub. by Tower Bks). Dorchester Pub Co.

Greatest Men's Party on Earth: Inside the Bohemian Grove. John Van der Zee. LC 73-20143. 1974. 5.95 o.p. (ISBN 0-15-136905-4). HarBraceJ.

Greatest Revue Sketches. Ed. by Donald Oliver. 480p. (Orig.). 1982. pap. 4.95 o.p. (ISBN 0-380-79194-3, 79194-3, Bard). Avon.

Greatest Shoe on Earth. Jeff MacNelly. 128p. 1985. pap. 7.95 o.p. (ISBN 0-03-005613-6). H Holt & Co.

Greatest Thing in the World. (Gifts of Gold Ser.). 5.95 o.p. (ISBN 0-88088-628-5). Peter Pauper.

Greatness of Flaubert. Maurice Nadeau. Tr. by Barbara Bray. 309p. 1973. pap. 4.95 o.p. (ISBN 0-87548-325-9, Library Pr). Open Court.

Greco-Roman Wrestling. M. Briggs Hunt. LC 72-95485. pap. 5.95 o.p. (ISBN 0-87095-047-9, Athletic). Gldn West Bks.

Greece. rev. 1986 ed. John Harrison & Shirley Harrison. LC 80-50995. (Rand McNally Pocket Guide Ser.). (Illus.). 1980. pap. 5.95 o.p. (ISBN 0-528-84841-0). Rand McNally.

Greece. Stuart Rossiter. (Blue Guides Ser.). (Illus.). Date not set. 29.95 o.p. (ISBN 0-393-01539-4); pap. 14.95 o.p. (ISBN 0-393-00092-3). Norton.

Greece: A Phaidon Cultural Guide. Phaidon Press Limited Staff. (Illus.). 600p. 1985. 16.95 o.p. (ISBN 0-13-365131-2). P-H.

Greece on Twenty-Five Dollars a Day. 1984. pap. 9.95 o.p. (ISBN 0-671-47598-3). Prentice Hall Pr.

Greece on Twenty-Five Dollars a Day: Including Istanbul & Turkey's Aegean Coast. John Levy & Kyle McCarthy. 552p. 1986. pap. 10.95 o.p. (ISBN 0-671-55605-3). S&S.

Greed & Glory on Wall Street: The Fall of House of Lehman. Ken Auletta. (Large Print Bks.). 428p. 1987. lib. bdg. 21.95 o.p. (ISBN 0-8161-4189-4, Large Print Bks); pap. 11.95 o.p. (ISBN 0-8161-4255-6, Large Print Bks). G K Hall.

Greedy Mariani: And Other Folktales of the Antilles. Ed. by Dorothy S. Carter. LC 73-85318. (Illus.). (gr. 3-7). 1974. 5.50 o.p. (ISBN 0-689-30425-0, Athenum). Macmillan.

Greedy Python. Richard Buckley. LC 85-12054. (Illus.). 24p. (ps up). 1985. pap. 4.95 o.p. (ISBN 0-88708-001-4). Picture Bk Studio.

Greedy Shopkeeper. Irene Mirkovic. LC 80-13034. (Illus.). 32p. (gr. k-3). 1980. 7.95 o.p. (ISBN 0-15-232551-4, HJ). HarBraceJ.

Greedy Shopkeeper. Irene Mirkovic. LC 80-13034. (Illus.). 32p. (gr. k-3). 1980. pap. 2.95 o.p. (ISBN 0-15-232552-2, VoyB). HarBraceJ.

Greek Adventure: Byron & Other Characters of the Greek War of Independence. David Howarth. LC 75-13678. 1976. 10.00 o.p. (ISBN 0-689-10653-X, Atheneum). Macmillan.

Greek & Roman Coins & the Study of History. Joseph G. Milne. LC 75-109793. 1971. Repr. of 1939 ed. lib. bdg. 35.00x o.p. (ISBN 0-8371-4283-0, MIGR). Greenwood.

Greek & Roman Gold & Silver Plate. D. E. Strong. (Library Reprints Ser.). (Illus.). 256p. 1977. 69.95x o.p. (ISBN 0-416-72510-4, 2824). Routledge Chapman & Hall.

Greek & Roman Portraits in the J. Paul Getty Museum 1. Ed. by Jiri Frel. (Occasional Papers on Antiquities: No. 2). (Illus.). 160p. 1987. pap. write for info. o.p. (ISBN 0-89236-071-2). J P Getty Trust.

Greek & Roman Slavery: A Source Book. Thomas Wiedemann. LC 80-25432. 304p. 1981. text ed. 32.50x o.p. (ISBN 0-8018-2515-6); pap. text ed. 9.95x o.p. (ISBN 0-8018-2514-8). Johns Hopkins.

Greek Art. Arthur Fairbanks. LC 63-10265. (Our Debt to Greece & Rome Ser.). (Illus.). Repr. of 1930 ed. 17.50x o.p. (ISBN 0-8154-0062-4). Cooper Sq.

Greek Art & the Idea of Freedom. Denys Haynes. LC 80-53168. (Illus.). 108p. 1985. pap. 8.95 o.s.i. (ISBN 0-500-27356-1). Thames Hudson.

Greek Art of the Aegean Islands. Dietrich Von Bothmer & Joan R. Mertens. (Illus.). 238p. 1979. pap. 1.95 o.p. (ISBN 0-87099-216-3). Metro Mus Art.

Greek Athletes & Athletics. Harold A. Harris. LC 78-10139. (Illus.). 1979. Repr. of 1966 ed. lib. bdg. 37.50x o.p. (ISBN 0-313-20754-2, HAGR). Greenwood.

Greek Biology & Greek Medicine. Henry O. Taylor. LC 63-10282. (Our Debt to Greece & Rome Ser). Repr. of 1930 ed. 18.50x o.p. (ISBN 0-8154-0235-X). Cooper Sq.

Greek City-States. Kathleen Freeman. (Illus.). 1963. pap. 4.95 o.p. (ISBN 0-393-00193-8, Norton Lib). Norton.

Greek Coins. Harold N. Fowler. 94p. 3.50 o.p. (ISBN 0-86516-017-1). Bolchazy-Carducci.

Greek Communist Party, 1940-1944. John C. Loulis. (Illus.). 256p. 1982. 27.50 o.p. (ISBN 0-7099-1612-4, Pub. by Croom Helm Ltd). Routledge Chapman & Hall.

Greek Cooking for Everyone. Theoni Pappas & Elvira Monroe. LC 85-51196. (Illus.). 167p. (Orig.). 1986. pap. 7.95 o.p. (ISBN 0-933174-29-2). Wide World-Tetra.

Greek Cooking for the Gods. Eva Zane. LC 59-15454. (Illus., Orig.). 1970. pap. 6.95 o.p. (ISBN 0-912238-02-X, One Hund One Prods). Ortho.

Greek-English, English-Greek Dictionary, 2 vols. C. Patsis. (Gr. & Eng.). Set. 50.00 o.s.i. (ISBN 0-685-79111-4). E J Brill USA.

Greek Experiment: Imperialism & Social Conflict, 800-400 B. C. Robert J. Littman. Ed. by Geoffrey Barraclough. (History of European Civilization Library). (Illus.). 180p. (Orig.). 1974. pap. text ed. 8.00 o.p. (ISBN 0-15-529684-1, HC). HarBraceJ.

Greek Islands. Derek A. C. Davies. LC 73-158639. (This Beautiful World Ser.: Vol. 27). (Illus.). 130p. (Orig.). 1971. pap. 4.95 o.p. (ISBN 0-87011-154-X). Kodansha.

Greek Islands Travel Guide. Berlitz Editors. (Travel Guides Ser.). 1979. pap. 4.95 o.p. (ISBN 0-317-12277-0, Berlitz). Macmillan.

Greek Ivory-Carving in the Orientalizing & Archaic Periods. Jane Burr Carter. Ed. by S. J. Freedberg. (Outstanding Dissertations in Fine Arts Ser.). (Illus.). 380p. 1985. Repr. of 1984 ed. 50.00 o.p. (ISBN 0-8240-6851-3). Garland Pub.

Greek Lyric Poetry. Tr. by Willis Barnstone from Gr. LC 67-25140. (Illus.). 320p. 1972. 11.00x o.p. (ISBN 0-8052-3447-0); pap. 10.95 o.p. (ISBN 0-8052-0339-7). Schocken.

Greek Patristic Theolgy, Vol. 1: Eleven Studies in Eastern Orthodox Doctrine Spirituality. Constance N. Tsirpanlis. 170p. 1979. pap. 9.95 o.p. (ISBN 0-686-36327-2). EO Pr.

Greek Personality in Archaic Sculpture. George H. Karo. 1970. Repr. of 1948 ed. lib. bdg. 24.25x o.p. (ISBN 0-8371-3115-4, KAGP). Greenwood.

Greek Philosophers. W. K. Gurthrie. (ISBN 0-8022-0649-2). Philos Lib.

Greek Piety. Martin P. Nilsson. 1969. pap. 2.95 o.p. (ISBN 0-393-00265-9, Norton Lib.). Norton.

Greek Political Theory: The Image of Man in Thucydides & Plato. David Grene. 90p. 1965. pap. text ed. 1.95x o.s.i. (ISBN 0-226-30787-5, P201, Phoen). U of Chicago Pr.

Greek Revival. Firth Haring. 350p. 1987. pap. 3.95 o.p. (ISBN 1-55547-137-4). Critics Choice Paper.

Greek Revival Architecture in America. Talbot Hamlin. (Illus.). 16.50 o.p. (ISBN 0-8446-2196-X). Peter Smith.

Greek Sculptural Groups: Archaic & Classical. Holly L. Schanz. LC 78-74971. (Outstanding Dissertations in the Fine Arts Ser.). 190p. 1980. lib. bdg. 26.00 o.p. (ISBN 0-8240-3973-4). Garland Pub.

Greek Spirit in Renaissance Art. Lucie Simpson. 1953. (ISBN 0-8022-1576-9). Philos Lib.

Greek Stones Speak: The Story of Archaeology in Greek Lands. Paul MacKendrick. 1979. pap. 7.95 o.p. (ISBN 0-393-00932-7). Norton.

Greek Text of Jeremiah: A Revised Hypothesis. Sven Soderlund. (JSOT Supplement Ser.: No. 47). 304p. pap. text ed. 15.95 o.s.i. (Pub. by JSOT Pr England). Eisenbrauns.

Greek Tragedy & the Emotions. W. B. Stanford. 192p. 1986. pap. text ed. 14.95 o.p. (ISBN 0-7102-0882-0). Routledge Chapman & Hall.

Greek Vegetarian Cookery. Jack Santa Maria. LC 85-2416. (Illus.). 160p. 1985. 8.95 o.p. (ISBN 0-87773-332-5, 74197-8). Shambhala Pubns.

Greek Way. Edith Hamilton. 1981. pap. 2.25 o.p. (ISBN 0-380-00816-5, 53140-2, Discus). Avon.

Greek Way. Edith Hamilton. 1948. 19.95 o.p. (ISBN 0-393-04162-X). Norton.

Greek Word Roots: A Practical List with Greek & English Derivatives. Thomas Rogers. 32p. (Gr. & Eng.). 1981. pap. 2.50 o.p. (ISBN 0-8010-7707-9). Baker Bk.

Greeks. Janet Van Duyn. (Library of the Early Civilizations). (Illus.). 192p. (gr. 10 up). 1972. text ed. 10.95 o.p. (ISBN 0-07-067038-2, 67038). McGraw.

Greeks in Bactria & India. 2nd ed. W. Tarn. 1951. 39.00x o.p. Coronet Bks.

Green Andrew Green. Isabelle Holland. LC 84-2402. (Illus.). 80p. (gr. 4 up). 1984. 9.95 o.s.i. (ISBN 0-664-32714-1, Westminster). Westminster John Knox.

Green Bay Packers. James R. Rothaus. (NFL Today Ser.). (gr. 4 up). 1986. 10.45 o.p. (ISBN 0-88682-033-2). Creative Ed.

Green Blades Rising: The Anglo-Saxons. Kevin C. Crossley-Holland. LC 75-4576. (Illus.). 144p. (gr. 6 up). 1979. 8.95 o.s.i. (ISBN 0-395-28902-5, Clarion). HM.

Green Bond. Adrian Bell. 124p. 1976. 10.00x o.p. (ISBN 0-8476-1421-2). Rowman.

Green Christmas. Theodora Kroeber. (Illus.). 40p. (gr. k-3). 1967. Repr. 6.95 o.p. (ISBN 0-395-27659-4). HM.

Green Circle Blues. Scott Haring. LC 86-1769. (Car Wars Adventure Gamebook Ser.: No. 5). 192p. (Orig.). 1987. pap. 2.95 o.p. (ISBN 0-88038-445-X). TSR Inc.

Green Corn & Violets: Amerindian Recipes for Camp & Kitchen. Compiled by Judi Johnson. Frances King. 53p. 1976. pap. 1.75x o.p. (ISBN 0-89792-080-5). Ill St Museum.

Green Darkness. Anya Seton. 1973. 8.95 o.p. (ISBN 0-395-13937-6). HM.

Green Figs & Tender Grapes. Rachel C. Burhard. LC 85-51572. 81p. (Orig.). 1985. pap. 10.95x o.p. (ISBN 0-932269-60-5). Wyndham Hall.

Green Fun. Maryanne Gjersvik. LC 74-75042. 1975. pap. 6.95 o.p. (ISBN 0-85699-104-X). Chatham Pr.

Green Ginger Jar. Clara I. Judson. (Illus.). 224p. (gr. 4-6). 1949. 6.95 o.p. (ISBN 0-395-06847-9). HM.

Green Gold for America. Roderic M. Olzendam & Gordon Keith. LC 81-67805. (Illus.). 12.50 o.p. (ISBN 0-8323-0396-8); pap. 8.95 o.p. (ISBN 0-8323-0397-6). Binford-Metropolitan.

Green Gold Harvest: A History of Logging & Its Products. Whatcom Museum of History & Art Staff. LC 72-10060. (Whatcom Museum Ser.). (Illus.). 78p. 1969. pap. 5.00 o.p. (ISBN 0-295-95577-5). U of Wash Pr.

Green Grow the Dollars. Emma Lathen. 1982. 12.95 o.p. (ISBN 0-671-44130-2). S&S.

Green Harvest. Pamela Oldfield. 379p. 1988. 19.95 o.p. (ISBN 0-7126-0077-9, Pub. by Century Hutchinson). David & Charles.

Green House. Mario V. Llosa. 1984. pap. 2.25 o.p. (ISBN 0-380-01233-2, 60533-3, Bard). Avon.

Green House Gardener. P-H.

Green Ice. Gerald A. Browne. pap. 2.95 o.p. (ISBN 0-440-13224-X). Dell.

Green Immigrants. Claire S. Haughton. 1978. 12.95 o.p. (ISBN 0-15-137034-6). HarBraceJ.

Green Immigrants: The Plants That Transformed America. Claire S. Haughton. LC 79-24258. (Illus.). 450p. 1980. pap. 5.95 o.p. (ISBN 0-15-636492-1, Harv). HarBraceJ.

Green Inheritance: The World Wildlife Fund Book of Plants. Anthony Huxley. LC 84-12466. 192p. 1985. 19.95 o.p. (ISBN 0-385-19603-2, Anchor). Doubleday.

Green Is for Galanx. Josephine R. Stone. LC 79-23290. 1980. 8.95 o.p. (ISBN 0-689-30737-3, Atheneum). Macmillan.

Green Knight. Vera Chapman. (YA) 1978. pap. 1.50 o.p. (ISBN 0-380-01704-0, 33795-9). Avon.

Green Lady. Leigh Ellis. 208p. 1981. pap. 2.25 o.p. (ISBN 0-380-77701-0, 77701). Avon.

Green Machine & Frog Crusade. Date not set. (ISBN 0-385-29529-4). Delacorte.

Green Machine & the Frog Crusade. Stephen Tchudi. LC 86-24120. 216p. (gr. 5 up). 1987. 14.95 o.p. (ISBN 0-385-29529-4). Delacorte.

Green Man. Kingsley Amis. LC 76-95862. 1970. 5.95 o.p. (ISBN 0-15-137040-0). HarBraceJ.

Green Mare. Marcel Ayme. Tr. by Norman Denny. LC 55-8038. 1963. pap. 1.45 o.p. (ISBN 0-689-70006-7, 42, Atheneum). Macmillan.

Green Monday. Michael Thomas. 1980. 12.95 o.s.i. (ISBN 0-671-61002-3, Wyndam Bks). S&S.

Green Odyssey. Philip Jose Farmer. (Science Fiction Ser.). 1978. lib. bdg. 9.00 o.p. (ISBN 0-8398-2414-9, Gregg). G K Hall.

Green Pastures. Marc Connelly. (Illus.). 123p. 1963. 10.95 o.p. (ISBN 0-910278-14-8). Boulevard.

Green Ripper. John D. MacDonald. 228p. 1985. pap. 3.50 o.p. (ISBN 0-449-13042-8, GM). Fawcett.

Green Rose. Warren A. Silver. 304p. 1987. pap. 3.95 o.p. (ISBN 1-55547-201-X). Critics Choice Paper.

Green Stick. Malcolm Muggeridge. LC 81-17689. (Chronicles of Wasted Time Ser.: Vol. 1). 288p. 1982. pap. 7.25 o.p. (ISBN 0-688-00952-2, Quill NY). Morrow.

Green Stone. Nanette Simon. 1985. 7.95 o.p. (ISBN 0-533-06073-7). Vantage.

Green Tourist Guide: Greece. (Fr.). 1985. pap. 9.95 o.p. (ISBN 2-06-005190-8). Michelin.

Green Tourist Guide: Londres. 1985. pap. 9.95 o.p. (ISBN 2-06-005421-4). Michelin.

Green Train. Herbert Lieberman. 1986. 18.95 o.p. (ISBN 0-399-13127-2). Putnam Pub Group.

Green Train. Herbert Lieberman. 464p. 1987. pap. 3.95 o.p. (ISBN 0-380-70344-0). Avon.

Green Water for a Granite Valley. William V. Sieller. LC 78-115214. 1970. 4.00 o.p. (ISBN 0-8233-0144-3). Golden Quill.

Greenberg's American Flyer Numerical Parts List. Ernst W. Wullenweber, Jr. 24p. 1985. pap. 9.95 o.p. (ISBN 0-89778-025-6, 6550). Greenberg Pub Co.

Greenberg's American Flyer Numerical Pocket Guide. Jack Fazenbaker. 64p. (Orig.). text ed. 5.95 o.p. (ISBN 0-89778-099-X, 10-7065). Greenberg Pub Co.

Greenberg's American Flyer S Gauge Pocket Guide. rev. ed. Jack Fazenbaker. 64p. 1987. pap. 5.95 o.p. (ISBN 0-89778-082-5, 10-7025). Greenberg Pub Co.

Greenberg's Enjoying Lionel- Fundimensions Trains. Philip K. Smith & Stan Shantar. Ed. by Linda Greenberg. LC 82-80708. 48p. 1982. pap. 7.95 o.p. (ISBN 0-686-91985-8). Greenberg Pub.

Greenberg's Guide to American Flyer S Gauge. 3rd ed. Jack Fazenbaker. (Pocket Guide Ser.: No. 3). 31p. 1986. pap. text ed. 4.95 o.p. (ISBN 0-89778-043-4, 6750). Greenberg Pub Co.

Greenberg's Guide to LGB. John Ottley. Ed. by Linda Greenberg. (Illus.). 100p. (Orig.). 1986. 25.00 o.p. (ISBN 0-89778-002-7, 6580). Greenberg Pub Co.

Greenberg's Guide to Lionel Layout Plans. Cliff Lang. (Illus.). 32p. (Orig.). 1986. pap. 4.50 o.p. (ISBN 0-89778-050-7, 6660). Greenberg Pub Co.

Greenberg's Guide to Marx Trains. Ed. by Marsha Davis. 32p. (Orig.). 1986. pap. 5.95 o.p. (ISBN 0-89778-052-3). Greenberg Pub Co.

Greenberg's Price Guide to American Flyers S Gauge Trains 1945-1966. 2nd ed. Jim Patterson. Ed. by Linda Greenberg. (Illus.). 192p. 1984. 35.00 o.p. (ISBN 0-89778-004-3, 6411). Greenberg Pub Co.

Greenberg's Price Guide to Lionel Fundimensions Trains 1970-1985. Bruce Greenberg & Roland LaVoie. (Illus.). 192p. (Orig.). 1985. pap. 25.95 o.p. (ISBN 0-89778-022-1, 6535). Greenberg Pub Co.

Greenberg's Price Guide to Lionel Trains: Prewar & Postwar, 1901-86. rev. ed. Bruce C. Greenberg. 80p. pap. 6.95 o.p. (ISBN 0-89778-083-3, 10-6960). Greenberg Pub Co.

Greenberg's Repair & Operating Manual for Prewar Lionel Trains. John G. Hubbard. (Illus.). 96p. 1985. pap. 10.95 o.p. (ISBN 0-89778-041-8, 6585). Greenberg Pub Co.

Greene & Greene, 2 vols. Randell L. Makinson. (Illus.). 478p. 1984. Set. slip case 39.90 o.p. (ISBN 0-87905-167-1, Peregrine Smith). Gibbs Smith Pub.

Greene County Marriages, 1783 to 1868. Goldene F. Burgner. 396p. 1981. 30.00 o.p. (ISBN 0-89308-202-3). Southern Hist Pr.

Greene on Grains. Bert Greene. 1988. 22.95 o.p.; pap. 14.95 o.p. Workman Pub.

Greene's Biographical Encyclopedia of Composers. David M. Greene. LC 79-6863. (Illus.). 1392p. 1985. pap. 30.00 o.p. (ISBN 0-385-14278-1). Doubleday.

Greenham Women Everywhere: Dreams, Ideas & Actions from the Womens' Peace Movement. Alice Cook & Gwyn Kirk. 128p. 1983. pap. 6.50 o.p. (ISBN 0-89608-199-0). South End Pr.

Greenhouse Management. J. J. Hanan et al. LC 77-21211. (Advanced Series in Agricultural Sciences: Vol 5). 1978. 53.00 o.p. (ISBN 0-387-08478-9). Springer-Verlag.

Greenhousing for Purple Thumbs. Fenten. LC 76-26055. (Illus.). 192p. (Orig.). 1976. 4.95 o.s.i. (ISBN 0-89286-105-3, One Hund One Prods); pap. 4.95 o.s.i. (ISBN 0-89286-104-5). Ortho.

Greenlaw Index of the New England Historic Genealogical Society. New England Historical Genealogical Society Staff. 1979. lib. bdg. 205.00 o.p. (ISBN 0-8161-0312-7, Hall Library). G K Hall.

Greensleeves. Eloise J. McGraw. LC 68-25191. (gr. 7 up). 1968. 6.50 o.p. (ISBN 0-15-232564-6, HJ). HarBraceJ.

Greenstone. Yvonne Kalman. 544p. 1983. pap. 3.95 o.p. (ISBN 0-380-62414-1, 62414-1). Avon.

Greenville: Woven from the Past. Nancy V. Ashmore. Ed. by Jerry Mosher. LC 86-22483. (Illus.). 280p. 1986. 24.95 o.p. (ISBN 0-89781-193-3). Windsor Pubns Inc.

Greenwich Killing Time: A Thrilling Murder Mystery. Kinky Friedman. LC 86-2339. 1986. 13.95 o.p. (ISBN 0-688-06409-4, Pub. by Beech Tree Bks). Morrow.

Greenwich Observatory, 3 Vols. Eric G. Forbes et al. LC 75-15269. 1975. Boxed set. 60.00x o.p. (ISBN 0-684-14456-5). Scribner.

Greenwich Village, 1920-1930: A Comment on American Civilization in the Post-War Years. Caroline F. Ware. LC 76-51282. 1977. Repr. lib. bdg. 34.50x o.p. (ISBN 0-374-98230-9, Octagon). Hippocrene Bks.

Greetings from Christmas Past. Bevis Hillier. (Illus.). 96p. 1982. 6.95 o.p. (ISBN 0-87663-409-9). Universe.

Gregg Expert Speed Building. Charles E. Zoubek. (Diamond Jubilee Ser.). 1968. text ed. 36.25 o.p. (ISBN 0-07-073050-4). McGraw.

Gregg Shorthand, Functional Method. Louis A. Leslie & Charles E. Zoubek. (Diamond Jubilee Ser.). 1963. text ed. 18.76 o.p. (ISBN 0-07-037310-8). McGraw.

Gregg Shorthand Structured Learning Method. E. Skimin & P. McMurtrie. (Diamond Jubilee Ser.). 1971. text ed. 26.95 o.p. (ISBN 0-07-057895-8). McGraw.

Gregg Typing for Colleges: Complete Course. Ed. by Audrey S. Rubin. (Gregg College Typing Ser.: Series 4). 1979. text ed. 30.40 o.p. (ISBN 0-07-038251-4). McGraw.

Gregg Typing for Colleges: Intensive Course. Alan C. Lloyd et al. (Gregg College Typing Ser.: Series 4). 1979. pap. text ed. 23.70 o.p. (ISBN 0-07-038252-2). McGraw.

Gregorc Style Delineator, Developmental, Technical, & Administration Manual. Anthony F. Gregorc. 43p. (Orig.). 1986. pap. text ed. 15.95 o.p. (ISBN 0-934481-03-2). Gregorc Assocs.

Gregory Ain. Lamia Doumato. (Architecture Ser.: A 1434). 14p. 1985. 2.25 o.p. (ISBN 0-89028-484-9). Vance Biblios.

Gregory Griggs & Other Nursery Rhyme People. Arnold Lobel. LC 77-22209. (Illus.). 48p. (gr. k-3). 1978. 9.95 o.p. (ISBN 0-688-80128-5); PLB 12.88 o.p. (ISBN 0-688-84128-7). Greenwillow.

Gremlins. George Gipe. 278p. 1984. pap. 3.50 o.p. (ISBN 0-380-86561-0, 86561-0). Avon.

Grendel: Devil by the Deed. Matthew Wagner. (Illus.). 48p. (Orig.). 1986. pap. 6.95 o.p. (ISBN 0-938965-01-8). Comico Comic Co.

Gretchen, I Am. Carroll E. Jay. 1979. pap. 2.25 o.p. (ISBN 0-380-42820-2, 42820-2). Avon.

Gretchen's World. Alice Hoffer. LC 80-83354. (Illus.). 48p. (gr. k-3). 1981. 5.95 o.p. (ISBN 0-448-16560-0, G&D); PLB 11.85 o.p. (ISBN 0-448-13491-8, G&D). Putnam Pub Group.

Gretzky: From the Backyard Rink to the Stanley Rink. Wayne Gretzky & Jim Taylor. 1985. pap. 3.95 o.p. (ISBN 0-380-70103-0). Avon.

Grevisse's Correct French: A Practical Guide. Maurice Grevisse. Tr. by Christopher Kendris from Fr. (gr. 11-12). 1982. pap. text ed. 10.95 o.p. (ISBN 0-8120-2169-X). Barron.

Grey Beginning. Barbara Michaels. (General Ser.). 1985. lib. bdg. 15.95 o.p. (ISBN 0-8161-3787-0, Large Print Bks). G K Hall.

Grey Goose of Kilnevin. Patricia Lynch. (Illus.). 285p. (gr. 4-8). 1984. Repr. of 1939 ed. 12.95 o.p. (ISBN 0-900068-78-7). Irish Bks Media.

Grey King. Susan Cooper. (Illus.). (gr. 7 up). 1978. pap. 3.95 o.s.i. (ISBN 0-689-70448-8, Aladdin). Macmillan.

Grey Mane of Morning. Joy Chant. 1977. 12.50 o.p. (ISBN 0-04-823137-1). Unwin Hyman.

Grief Work. Juanita Ponce-Montoya. 1978. 5.50 o.p. (ISBN 0-682-49038-5). Exposition-Phoenix.
Grieg. John Horton. (Master Musicians: No. M169). (Illus.). 1975. pap. 7.95 o.p. (ISBN 0-8226-0711-5). Littlefield.
Grievance Arbitration in the Public Sector see Issues in the Public Employee Relations Library: Series 5.
Grievance Procedure in an American Enterprise. Yves Delamotte. (Fr.). 1966. 3.00 o.p. (ISBN 0-89215-051-3). U Cal LA Indus Rel.
Griffe de Tigre. Paul Twitchell. 192p. 1975. pap. 5.95 o.p. (ISBN 0-88155-000-0). Illum Way Pub.
Griffin, Williams, & Larson's Advanced Accounting. Canadian Edition. Peter D. Chant et al. 1983. 44.50 o.p. (ISBN 0-256-02395-6). Irwin.
Grim Phoenix: Reconstructing Thomas Pynchon. William M. Plater. LC 77-12833. 288p. 1978. 17.50x o.p. (ISBN 0-253-32670-2). Ind U Pr.
Grimani Breviary. Intro. by Mario Salmi. LC 74-78138. (Illus.). 276p. 1974. 195.00 o.s.i. (ISBN 0-87951-022-6). Overlook Pr.
Grimm's Fairy Tales. Jacob Grimm & Wilhelm K. Grimm. LC 68-10477. (Illus.). 128p. (gr. k-6). 1984. pap. 9.95 o.p. (ISBN 0-7100-9997-5); 13.95 o.p. (ISBN 0-7100-0912-7). Routledge Chapman & Hall.
Grin on the Moon. Leonard Peterson. (Orig.). 1966. pap. 0.75 o.p. (ISBN 0-377-80051-1). Friendship Pr.
Grinding, Vol. 1. Ed. by J. Allen et al. (Engineering Craftsmen: No. H5). 1968. spiral bdg. 38.50x o.p. Trans-Atl Phila.
Grinding, Vol. 2. Ed. by D. W. Barlow et al. (Engineering Craftsmen: No. H.31). 1972. spiral bdg. 49.95x o.p. (ISBN 0-85083-380-9). Trans-Atl Phila.
Grinding Machine Operations. Richard R. Kibbe. LC 84-11815. 294p. 1985. spiral 17.95 o.p. (ISBN 0-471-89021-9). Wiley.
Grinding Technology. S. F. Krar & J. W. Oswald. LC 72-7935. 1974. pap. text ed. 16.50 o.p. (ISBN 0-8273-0208-8). Delmar.
Gringo Yanqui. Hugh C. Stuntz. 192p. (Orig.). 1983. pap. 6.50 o.p. (ISBN 0-682-49933-1). Exposition-Phoenix.
Griselda. Antonio Vivaldi. Ed. by Howard M. Brown. LC 76-20997. (Italian Opera 1640-1770 Ser.: Vol. 35). 1978. lib. bdg. 35.00 o.p. (ISBN 0-8240-2634-9). Garland Pub.
Griselda's New Year. Marjorie W. Sharmat. LC 79-11375. (Ready-to-Read Ser.). (Illus.). 64p. (gr. 1-4). 1979. 6.95 o.s.i. (ISBN 0-02-782420-9). Macmillan.
Grishin. Hans Herlin. Tr. by J. Maxwell Brownjohn. LC 86-29072. 360p. 1987. 17.95 o.p. (ISBN 0-385-23696-4). Doubleday.
Grist from Adams' Mill. Jay E. Adams. LC 83-7388. 96p. 1983. pap. 2.50 o.p. (ISBN 0-87552-079-0). Presby & Reformed.
Grit & Clay. M. D. Picard. 358p. 1975. pap. 12.00 o.p. (ISBN 0-444-41305-7). Elsevier.
Grit, Grief & Gold. F. B. Whiting. (Shorey Historical Ser.). 296p. pap. 14.95 o.s.i. (ISBN 0-8466-0148-6, S148). Shorey.
Grizzard Advice Book Floor Dump. Lewis Grizzard. 1989. 222.40 o.p. (ISBN 0-929264-23-1). Longstreet Pr Inc.
Groceries. Herbert Scott. LC 76-4974. (Pitt Poetry Ser.). 1976. 15.95 o.p. (ISBN 0-8229-3332-2); pap. 6.95 o.p. (ISBN 0-8229-5270-X). U of Pittsburgh Pr.
Grocery Retailing in the Eighties. Progressive Grocer Magazine Staff. (Illus.). 1980. 14.95 o.p. (ISBN 0-911790-75-6). Prog Grocers Trade.
Grocery Store Botany. Joan E. Rahn. LC 74-75567. (Illus.). 64p. (gr. 4-6). 1974. 6.95 o.p. (ISBN 0-689-30435-8, Atheneum). Macmillan.
Grocery Store Zoology: Bones & Muscles. Joan E. Rahn. LC 76-26599. (Illus.). (gr. 5-9). 1977. 6.95 o.p. (ISBN 0-689-30560-5, Atheneum). Macmillan.
Grolier Academic Encyclopedia, 21 vols. rev. ed. LC 85-27032. (Illus.). 1987. text ed. write for info. o.p. (ISBN 0-7172-2017-6). Grolier Inc.
Grolle's Complete Guide to Electronic Troubleshooting. Carl G. Grolle. 224p. 1979. text ed. 17.95 o.p. (ISBN 0-13-365080-4, Parker). P-H.
Groomed for Murder. Vivian Rhodes. 1983. pap. 2.50 o.s.i. (ISBN 0-345-30732-1). Ballantine.
Groove Your Golf Swing My Way. Lee Trevino & Dick Aultman. LC 75-41853. 1976. 12.95 o.p. (ISBN 0-689-10723-4, Atheneum). Macmillan.
Groping Through the Maze: Foreign Experience Applied to the U. S. Problem of Coordinating Development Controls. Ed. by John H. Noble et al. LC 77-70427. (Illus.). 165p. 1977. 13.50 o.p. (ISBN 0-89164-041-X). Conservation Foun.
Grossman's Guide to Wines, Beers, & Spirits. 6th rev. ed. Harold J. Grossman. (Illus.). 1977. 32.50 o.s.i. (ISBN 0-684-15033-6, ScribT). Scribner.
Groteske und Hyperbolische Stil Des Mittelhochdeutschen Volksepos. Leo Wolf. (Ger). 18.00 o.p. (ISBN 0-384-69045-9); pap. 13.00 o.p. (ISBN 0-685-02157-2). Johnson Repr.
Grotesque. Philip Thomson. (Critical Idiom Ser.). 1979. pap. 5.50x o.p. (ISBN 0-416-08180-0, NO. 2544). Routledge Chapman & Hall.
Grotesque in Church Art. Thomas T. Wildridge. LC 68-30633. 240p. 1969. Repr. of 1899 ed. 35.00x o.p. (ISBN 0-8103-3077-6). Gale.
Grotowski. Raymond Temkine. 1972. pap. 1.65 o.p. (ISBN 0-380-01232-4, 12278, Bard). Avon.
Ground Control in Room & Pillar Mining. Ed. by Yoginder P. Chugh. LC 82-74112. (Illus.). 157p. 1983. 5.00 o.p. (ISBN 0-89520-407-X). SMM&E Inc.
Ground Engineering Equipment & Methods. F. Harris. 1983. text ed. 43.50 o.p. (ISBN 0-07-026747-2). McGraw.
Ground Engineering Equipment & Methods. Frank Harris. 281p. 1983. text ed. 29.95x o.p. (ISBN 0-246-11239-5, Pub. by Granada England). Gower Pub Co.
Ground Rent, Not Taxes: The Natural Source of Revenue for the Government. John C. Lincoln. 1972. pap. 0.75 o.s.i. (ISBN 0-686-17291-4). Lincoln Inst Land.
Ground Studies for Pilots. S. E. Taylor & H. A. Parmar. Incl. Vol. I. Radio Aids. 3rd ed. 200p. 1979. text ed. 26.50x o.p. (ISBN 0-246-11169-0); Vol. II. Plotting & Flight Planning. 130p. 1976. text ed. 19.95x o.p. (ISBN 0-246-11176-3); Vol. III. Navigation General. 232p. 1979. text ed. 26.50x o.p. (ISBN 0-246-11177-1). Gower Pub Co.
Ground Water Management. Compiled by American Society of Civil Engineers Staff. (Manual & Report on Engineering Practice Ser.: No. 40). 230p. 1972. pap. 24.00x o.p. (ISBN 0-87262-216-9). Am Soc Civil Eng.
Ground-Water Mining in the United States. Gordon Sloggett & Clifford Dickason. (Agricultural Economic Report: No. 555). (Illus.). 23p. 1986. pap. 1.25 o.p. (ISBN 0-318-21683-3, S/N 001-019-00484-3). USGPO.
Ground Water Quality Atlas. (Illus.). 72p. 20.00 o.p. (ISBN 0-318-15911-2). Natl Water Well.
Grounded in Love: Sacramental Theology in an Ecumenical Perspective. Frans J. Van Beeck. LC 81-40117. 162p. (Orig.). 1982. lib. bdg. 27.50 o.p. (ISBN 0-8191-2040-5); pap. text ed. 12.00 o.p. (ISBN 0-8191-2041-3). U Pr of Amer.
Groundhog's Day at the Doctor. Judy Delton. LC 80-20327. (Illus.). 48p. (ps-3). 1981. 5.95 o.s.i. (ISBN 0-8193-1041-7); PLB 5.95 o.s.i. (ISBN 0-8193-1042-5). Parents.
Groundwater: A Community Action Guide. Ed. by Susan Boyd et al. 22p. (Orig.). 1984. pap. text ed. 3.00 o.p. (ISBN 0-937345-01-6). Concern.
Groundwater Contamination from Hazardous Wastes. Eric F. Wood & Princeton Water Resources Group Staff. (Illus.). 192p. 1984. text ed. 42.67 o.p. (ISBN 0-13-366286-1). P-H.
Groundwater Management: Part of the Proceedings of the Specialized Conference of the IWSA Held in Berlin, FRG, 22-28 April 1985. Ed. by R. Urbistondo & L. R. Bays. (Illus.). 254p. 1985. pap. 73.00 o.p. (ISBN 0-08-033231-5, Pub. by PPL). Pergamon.
Groundwater: Strategies for State Action. Timothy Henderson et al. LC 84-10208. 375p. 1984. 24.95 o.p. (ISBN 0-911937-16-1). Environ Law Inst.
Group. Mary McCarthy. LC 63-15316. 378p. 1963. 8.50 o.p. (ISBN 0-15-137280-2). HarBraceJ.
Group Accounts. Robertson. 1980. pap. 16.95 o.p. (ISBN 0-85258-190-4). Van Nos Reinhold.
Group & Family Therapy: A Model for Psychotherapeutic Nursing Practice. Gwen M. Van Servellen. LC 83-1006. (Illus.). 315p. 1983. pap. text ed. 19.95 o.p. (ISBN 0-8016-5254-5). Mosby.
Group & the Unconscious. Didier Anzieu. Tr. by Benjamin Kiborne from Fr. (International Library of Group Psychotherapy & Group Process). 288p. 1984. 45.00X o.p. (ISBN 0-7100-0693-4). Routledge Chapman & Hall.
Group Counseling. 2nd ed. Merle M. Ohlsen. LC 76-51307. 1977. text ed. 29.95 o.p. (ISBN 0-03-089848-X, HoltC). HR&W.
Group Counseling: A Developmental Approach. 3rd ed. George M. Gazda. 1984. text ed. 35.00 o.p. (ISBN 0-205-08142-8, 248142). Allyn.
Group Counseling in the Schools. Clarence A. Mahler. LC 72-1723. (Orig.). 1972. text ed. 14.95 o.p. (ISBN 0-395-04818-4, 3-34210). HM.
Group Decision Making & Effectiveness: An Experimental Study. Andrew H. Van De Ven. LC 74-23134. 110p. 1975. 9.50x o.p. (ISBN 0-87338-163-7, Pub. by Comp. Adm. Research Inst.). Kent St U Pr.
Group Discussion: A Practical Guide to Participation & Leadership. Gerald M. Phillips et al. LC 78-56441. (Illus.). 1979. text ed. 30.76 o.p. (ISBN 0-395-25415-9). HM.
Group Discussion: Theory & Technique. 2nd ed. R. Victor Harnack et al. (Illus.). 1977. text ed. (ISBN 0-13-365247-5). P-H.
Group Dynamics for Student Activities. Russell D. Robinson. 1977. pap. 6.00 o.p. (ISBN 0-88210-082-3). Natl Assn Principals.
Group Homes in Perspective. 48p. (Eight papers reprinted from "Child Welfare"). 1964. pap. 3.95 o.p. (ISBN 0-87868-055-1, 0551). Child Welfare.
Group Insurance: Readings. Ed. by Roxana M. Matter. (FLMI Insurance Education Program Ser.). 1987. pap. text ed. 5.00 o.p. (ISBN 0-915322-94-3). LOMA.
Group Legal Service Plans: Organization, Operation & Management. The National Resource Center for Consumers of Legal Services Staff. 704p. 1981. 40.00 o.p. (ISBN 0-15-100025-5, H39972, Pub. by Law & Business). HarBraceJ.
Group Life. Marshall C. Greco. (ISBN 0-8022-0622-0). Philos Lib.
Group Life & Health Insurance, Vols. 1 & 2. Robert W. Batten & George M. Hider. LC 78-71257. (FLMI Insurance Education Program Ser.). 1979. Set. pap. text ed. 25.00 o.p. (ISBN 0-915322-31-5). LOMA.
Group Portrait with Lady. Heinrich Boll. Tr. by Leila Vennewitz from Ger. LC 72-8835. 320p. 1973. text ed. 8.95 o.p. (ISBN 0-07-006423-7). McGraw.
Group Practice Administration: Current & Future Roles. Edward K. Morita et al. (Illus.). 96p. (Orig.). 1977. 8.50 o.p. (ISBN 0-933948-50-6). Med Group Mgmt.
Group Procedures for Counselors in Educational & Community Settings. Richard J. Malnati & Edward L. Trembley. 1974. 24.50x o.p. (ISBN 0-8422-5161-8); pap. text ed. 8.95x o.p. (ISBN 0-8422-0385-0). Irvington.
Group Procedures: Purposes, Processes, & Outcomes. Richard C. Diedrich & H. Allan Dye. 1972. pap. 26.50 o.p. (ISBN 0-395-04364-6). HM.
Group Process As a Helping Technique. S. Thompson & J. H. Kahn. LC 79-124667. 1970. text ed. 22.00 o.p. (ISBN 0-08-016220-7); pap. text ed. 9.25 o.p. (ISBN 0-08-016219-3). Pergamon.
Group Processes in the Classroom. 4th ed. Richard A. Schmuck & Patricia A. Schmuck. 400p. 1982. pap. text ed. write for info o.p. (ISBN 0-697-06093-4). Wm C Brown.
Group Psychoanalysis. Wassell. 320p. 1959. Philos Lib.
Group Psychotherapies for Children: A Textbook. S. R. Slavson & Mortimer Schiffer. LC 74-23272. 1975. text ed. 52.50x o.s.i. (ISBN 0-8236-2250-9). Intl Univs Pr.
Group Psychotherapy for Students & Teachers: A Selective Bibliography, 1946-1979. Jerald Grobman. LC 81-43339. 125p. 1982. lib. bdg. 22.00 o.p. (ISBN 0-8240-9291-0). Garland Pub.
Group Representations in Mathematics & Physics: Battelle Seattle 1969 Rencontres. Ed. by V. Bargmann. LC 75-146233. (Lecture Notes in Physics: Vol. 6). 1970. pap. 18.80 o.p. (ISBN 0-387-05310-7). Springer-Verlag.
Group Symmetries in Nuclear Structure. J. C. Parikh. LC 77-17451. (Nuclear Physics Monographs Ser.). (Illus.). 288p. 1978. 49.50x o.p. (ISBN 0-306-31043-0, Plenum Pr). Plenum Pub.
Group Technology: An Integrated Planning & Implementation Concept for Small & Medium Batch Production. E. A. Arn. (Illus.). vi, 200p. 1975. pap. 31.90 o.p. (ISBN 0-387-07505-4). Springer-Verlag.
Group Technology at Work. Society of Manufacturing Engineers Staff. Ed. by Nancy Hyer. (Illus.). 254p. 1987. 35.00 o.p. (ISBN 0-87263-154-0). SME.
Group Theoretic Methods in Bifurcation Theory. D. H. Sattinger. (Lecture Notes in Mathematics: Vol. 762). 241p. 1979. pap. 16.00 o.p. (ISBN 0-387-09715-5). Springer-Verlag.
Group Theoretical Methods in Physics, Vol. 94. Ed. by W. Beiglboeck et al. (Lecture Notes in Physics Ser.). 1979. pap. 28.00 o.p. (ISBN 0-387-09238-2). Springer-Verlag.
Group Theory in Quantum Mechanics. V. Heine. 1963. 120.00 o.p. (ISBN 0-08-009242-X). Pergamon.
Groups in Harmony & Tension. Muzafer Sherif & Carolyn W. Sherif. 1966. lib. bdg. 21.50x o.p. (ISBN 0-374-97334-2, Octagon). Hippocrene Bks.
Groups in Social Work: An Ecological Approach. Pallassana R. Balgopal & Thomas V. Vassil. 300p. 1983. text ed. write for info. o.p. (ISBN 0-02-305530-8). Macmillan.
Groups of Automarphisms of Manifolds. D. Burghelea & R. Lashof. (Lecture Notes in Mathematics Ser.: Vol. 473). 156p. 1975. pap. 13.00 o.p. (ISBN 0-387-07182-2). Springer-Verlag.
Groups of Cohomological Dimension One. D. E. Cohen. LC 77-139950. (Lecture Notes in Mathematics: Vol. 245). 99p. 1972. pap. 9.00 o.p. (ISBN 0-387-05759-5). Springer-Verlag.
Groups: Theory & Experience. 2nd ed. Rodney W. Napier & Matti K. Gershenfeld. LC 80-82844. (Illus.). 448p. 1981. text ed. 27.95 o.p. (ISBN 0-395-29703-6). HM.
Groups: Theory & Experience. Rodney W. Napier & Matti K. Gershenfeld. LC 72-7925. 325p. 1973. text ed. 19.25 o.p. (ISBN 0-395-12658-4, 3-40200). HM.
Groups, Trees & Projective Modules. W. Dicks. (Lecture Notes in Mathematics: Vol. 790). 127p. 1980. pap. 13.00 o.p. (ISBN 0-387-09974-3). Springer-Verlag.
Groups: Understanding People Gathered Together. Tom Douglas. LC 83-406. 252p. 1983. 22.00 o.p. (ISBN 0-422-77660-2, NO.3856, Pub. by Tavistock); pap. 9.95 o.p. (ISBN 0-422-77670-X, NO. 3857). Routledge Chapman & Hall.
Groupwork Guide for Discussion Leaders to the Cure Is in the Cause. Wallace D. Labanna. 1972. 1.00x o.p. (ISBN 0-89039-003-7). Ann Arbor Pubs.
Grouse & Woodcock: An Upland Hunter's Book. Nick Sisley. LC 79-15388. (Illus.). 192p. 1980. 13.95 o.p. (ISBN 0-8117-0717-2). Stackpole.
Grouse of the North Shore. Gordon Gullion. (Illus.). 160p. 1984. 45.00 o.s.i. (ISBN 0-932558-19-4). Willow Creek Pr.
Groves of Academe. Mary McCarthy. 240p. 1981. pap. 2.95 o.p. (ISBN 0-380-52522-4, 52522-0). Avon.
Groves of Academe. Mary McCarthy. LC 52-7255. 320p. 1952. 9.50 o.s.i. (ISBN 0-15-137331-0). HarBraceJ.
Grow, Christian, Grow: Student. Knofel Staton. LC 77-82120. (New Life Ser.). (Illus.). 1978. pap. 2.25 o.p. (ISBN 0-87239-177-9, 39999). Standard Pub.
Grow It. Richard Langer. (YA) (gr. 7 up). 1978. pap. 4.95 o.p. (ISBN 0-380-01234-0, 33688-X). Avon.
Grow Strong with Words. William J. Crowley. LC 85-90993. (Illus.). 80p. (Orig.). (gr. 2). 1985. pap. 8.50 o.p. (ISBN 0-682-40269-9). Exposition-Phoenix.
Grow up Cupid. Date not set. (ISBN 0-385-29544-8). Delacorte.
Grow up, Cupid. June Oldham. LC 86-19662. 160p. (gr. 7 up). 1987. pap. 14.95 o.p. (ISBN 0-385-29544-8). Delacorte.
Grow Your Own Energy. Ed. by Michael Cross. (New Scientist Guides Ser.). (Illus.). 256p. 1984. 39.95x o.p. (ISBN 0-85520-731-0); pap. 15.95 o.p. (ISBN 0-85520-730-2). Basil Blackwell.
Growing. Evelyn Bence. 32p. (gr. 6-9). 1985. 4.95 o.p. (ISBN 0-8378-2043-X). Gibson.
Growing. Stewart Lee. 1978. 6.50 o.p. (ISBN 0-682-49225-6). Exposition-Phoenix.
Growing a Soul: The Story of A. Frank Smith. Norman W. Spellman. LC 78-20876. 1979. 17.95x o.p. (ISBN 0-87074-171-3). SMU Press.
Growing & Declining Urban Areas: A Fiscal Comparison. Thomas Muller. 121p. 1975. pap. 6.50 o.p. (ISBN 0-87766-154-5). Urban Inst.
Growing & Showing Geraniums. Alan Shellard. (Illus.). 68p. 1984. 12.95 o.s.i. (ISBN 0-7153-8575-5). David & Charles.
Growing Azaleas Commercially. Ed. by Anton M. Kofranek & Roy A. Larson. 1975. pap. 7.50x o.s.i. (ISBN 0-931876-12-5, 4058). ANR Pubns CA.
Growing Companies: Tax & Business Planning for the '80s (ALI-ABA Course of Study Materials) University of Missouri-Kansas City School of Law Staff et al. LC 83-169830. 1983. write for info. o.p. Am Law Inst.
Growing Herbs in Pots. John Brimer. 1976. 6.95 o.s.i. (ISBN 0-671-22252-X). S&S.
Growing Impact of Wideband Communication. (Reports Ser.: No. 172). 190p. 1981. 985.00x o.p. (ISBN 0-88694-172-5). Intl Res Dev.
Growing in Faith: Devotions for Parent-Child Interaction. Luther S. Cross. 32p. (Orig.). 1984. pap. 2.95 o.p. (ISBN 0-8066-2070-6, 23-1606, Augsburg). Augsburg Fortress.
Growing in Joy: God's Way to Increase Joy in All of Life. Ron Klug. LC 82-72637. 128p. 1983. pap. 6.95 o.p. (ISBN 0-8066-1943-0, 10-2902, Augsburg). Augsburg Fortress.
Growing in the Fruit of the Spirit. John Blattner. (Living As A Christian Ser.). 96p. 1984. pap. 3.95 o.p. (ISBN 0-89283-177-4). Servant.
Growing Knowing Jesus. Ian Cowie. LC 79-87736. 1979. pap. 2.95 o.p. (ISBN 0-8042-2336-X, John Knox). Westminster John Knox.
Growing Love: Meditations on Marriage & Commitment. Ulrich Schaffer. LC 76-62951. (Illus.). 1977. pap. 3.95i o.p. (ISBN 0-06-067079-7, RD-325). HarpR.

Growing of America: Seventeen Eighty-Nine to Eighteen Forty-Eight. Raymond Robinson. LC 78-67275. 1979. pap. text ed. 13.95x o.s.i. (ISBN 0-88273-112-2). Forum Pr IL.

Growing Old Alive. Han Yu. Tr. by Kenneth O. Hanson from Chinese. 1978. 10.00 o.p. (ISBN 0-914742-33-7); pap. 5.00 o.p. Copper Canyon.

Growing Old in America. Ed. by Beth B. Hess. LC 76-1778. 500p. 1976. text ed. 14.95 o.p. (ISBN 0-87855-140-9); pap. text ed. 6.95x o.p. (ISBN 0-87855-604-4). Transaction Pubs.

Growing Old in America. Elaine Landau. LC 84-27244. (Illus.). 160p. (gr. 7 up). 1985. lib. bdg. 9.79 o.p. (ISBN 0-671-42409-2). Messner.

Growing Old in America: Information Aids Ser. Donna R. Plesser et al. 104p. 1986. pap. 15.95 o.p. (ISBN 0-936474-59-9). Info Plus TX.

Growing Old Is a Family Affair. Dorothy B. Fritz. LC 78-37420. (Orig.). (YA) 1972. pap. 2.95 o.p. (ISBN 0-8042-2078-6, John Knox). Westminster John Knox.

Growing Old: The Social Problems of Aging. Elizabeth S. Johnson & John B. Williamson. LC 78-67459. 196p. 1980. pap. text ed. 16.95 o.p. (ISBN 0-03-040316-2, HoltC). HR&W.

Growing Pains. Paul R. Erickson. LC 85-52429. (Illus.). 74p. (gr. 4-8). 1985. 5.95 o.p. (ISBN 0-938232-61-4). Winston-Derek.

Growing Pains. Albert Frigone. Ed. by S. Michele McFadden. (Illus.). (gr. 4-10). 1977. pap. text ed. 37.50 30 copy pack 1.25 ea. o.p. (ISBN 0-89262-014-5). Career Pub.

Growing Pains. Audrey M. Raphael. (Illus.). 68p. 1985. 6.95 o.p. (ISBN 0-533-06210-1). Vantage.

Growing Pains. Cheryl Zach. (Smyth vs. Smyth Ser.: Bk. 6). 160p. (Orig.). 1989. pap. 2.95 o.p. (ISBN 1-55802-076-4). Lynx Bks.

Growing Season. Martha W. Hickman. LC 80-68983. 128p. (Orig.). 1980. pap. 4.50x o.p. (ISBN 0-8358-0411-9). Upper Room.

Growing Season. Jan C. Speas. 1979. pap. 2.25 o.p. (ISBN 0-380-44131-4, 44131). Avon.

Growing, Sharing, Serving. Jo Berry. LC 78-73461. 1979. pap. 3.95 o.p. (ISBN 0-89191-073-5). Cook.

Growing Strong Inside. Jane B. Moncure. LC 83-7443. (Illus.). 32p. (ps-k). 1983. PLB 4.95 o.p. (ISBN 0-89693-211-7). Dandelion Hse.

Growing Through Divorce: Working Guide. Jim Smoke & Lisa Guest. 96p. (Orig.). 1985. pap. 3.25 o.p. (ISBN 0-89081-477-5). Harvest Hse.

Growing through Rejection. Elizabeth Skoglund. 1983. pap. 3.95 o.p. (ISBN 0-8423-1239-0). Tyndale.

Growing Together. John Trent. 156p. 1985. pap. 6.95 o.p. (ISBN 0-89693-323-7). Victor Bks.

Growing Together: Prayers for Married People. Leslie Brandt & Edith Brandt. LC 75-2830. 96p. (Orig.). 1975. pap. 5.95 o.p. (ISBN 0-8066-1476-5, 10-2903, Augsburg). Augsburg Fortress.

Growing Tree. rev. ed. B. F. Wilson. LC 70-123535. 1971. 10.00x o.p. (ISBN 0-87023-067-0); pap. 6.50x o.p. (ISBN 0-87023-075-1). U of Mass Pr.

Growing up: A Bar Mitzvah Story. David Rosoff. (gr. 6-8). 1984. 13.00 o.p. (ISBN 0-87306-370-8). Feldheim.

Growing up Addicted: Why Our Children Abuse Alcohol & Drugs & What We Can Do about It. Tim Timmons & Stephen Arterburn. 320p. (Orig.). 1987. 15.45 o.p. (ISBN 0-345-33235-0, Pub. by Ballantine Epiphany). Ballantine.

Growing up Divorced: Children of the Eighties. Linda B. Francke. 1983. 15.50 o.p. (ISBN 0-671-25516-9, Linden Pr). S&S.

Growing up During the Norman Conquest. Frances Wilkins. LC 79-56440. (Growing Up Ser.). (gr. 7-9). 1980. text ed. 19.95 o.p. (ISBN 0-7134-3360-4, Pub. by Batsford England). David & Charles.

Growing up in a Hurry. Winifred Madison. (gr. 7 up). 1973. 6.95 o.p. (ISBN 0-316-54355-1). Little.

Growing up in America. Carol Foster et al. (Information Plus Ser.). 120p. 1987. pap. 16.95 o.p. (ISBN 0-936474-69-6). Info Plus TX.

Growing up in Christ. Eugene H. Peterson. pap. 5.50 o.p. (ISBN 0-8042-2026-3, John Knox). Westminster John Knox.

Growing up in France. Sabra Holbrook. LC 79-22101. (Illus.). (gr. 6-9). 1980. 8.95 o.p. (ISBN 0-689-30745-4, Atheneum). Macmillan.

Growing up in Hollywood. Robert Parrish. LC 75-29174. (Illus.). 1976. 10.00 o.p. (ISBN 0-15-137473-2). HarBraceJ.

Growing up in Hollywood. Robert Parrish. LC 77-4120. 1977. pap. 3.95 o.p. (ISBN 0-15-637315-7, Harv). HarBraceJ.

Growing up in Society. Tony Booth. (Essential Psychology Ser.). 1975. pap. 4.50x o.p. (ISBN 0-416-81900-1, NO. 2606). Routledge Chapman & Hall.

Growing up in the James Family: Henry James, Sr. As Son & Father. Katherine Weissbourd. Ed. by Peter E. Nathan. LC 84-29779. (Research in Clinical Psychology Ser.: No. 14). 134p. 1985. 34.95 o.p. (ISBN 0-8357-1652-X). UMI Res Pr.

Growing up in the Nineteen Sixties. Richard Tames. (Growing Up Ser.). (Illus.). 72p. (gr. 7-12). 1983. 17.95 o.s.i. (ISBN 0-7134-1342-5, Pub. by Batsford England). David & Charles.

Growing up in the Playground: The Social Development of Children. Andy Sluckin. (Social Worlds of Childhood Ser.). 160p. 1981. 22.50x o.p. (ISBN 0-7100-0788-4). Routledge Chapman & Hall.

Growing up on a Farm in Missouri. Mary T. Pilcher. 78p. 1985. 8.95 o.p. (ISBN 0-533-06322-1). Vantage.

Growing up on the Chocolate Diet: A Memoir with Recipes. Lora A. Brody. 320p. 1985. 16.45i o.p. (ISBN 0-316-10897-9). Little.

Growing up on the Chocolate Diet: A Memoir with Recipes. Lora A. Brody. 272p. 1986. pap. 8.95 o.p. (ISBN 0-8050-0119-0). H Holt & Co.

Growing up Puerto Rican. Ed. by Paulette Cooper. LC 79-184881. 256p. 1972. 6.95 o.p. (ISBN 0-87795-033-4, A4319, Arbor Hse). Morrow.

Growing up Smart & Happy: What Every Parent Should Know. Julius Segal & Zelda Segal. 272p. 1985. text ed. 14.95 o.p. (ISBN 0-07-056057-9). McGraw.

Growing up to Be Violent: A Longitudinal Study of the Development of Agression. M. M. Lefkowitz et al. 1977. 28.00 o.p. (ISBN 0-08-019515-6); pap. 14.50 o.p. (ISBN 0-08-019514-8). Pergamon.

Growing up under the Weimar Republic, 1918-1933. Wolfgang Von Leyden. LC 83-90284. (Illus.). 164p. 1984. 12.95 o.p. (ISBN 0-533-05777-9). Vantage.

Growing up with Roy & Dale. Roy Rogers & Karen A. Wojahn. LC 86-6524. (Illus.). 168p. 1986. text ed. 12.95 o.s.i. (ISBN 0-8307-1169-4, 5111629). Regal.

Growing up with the North American Indians. Pat Hodgeson. (Growing Up Ser.). (Illus.). 72p. (gr. 5 up). 1982. 17.95 o.p. (ISBN 0-7134-2732-9, Pub. by Batsford England). David & Charles.

Growing Ups & Downs. Henry Beard & Roy McKie. 1988. 10.95 o.p. (ISBN 0-317-66702-5). Workman Pub.

Growing When You Don't Feel Like It. Joyce M. Smith. (Good Life Bible Studies). 64p. (YA) (gr. 7-11). 1985. pap. 2.95 o.p. (ISBN 0-8423-1229-3). Tyndale.

Growing Wild Mushrooms. Bob Harris. (Illus.). pap. 7.95 o.p. (ISBN 0-914728-17-2). Wingbow Pr.

Growing Years: A Study Guide for the Televised Course. 2nd ed. Phillip Kaushall & Kiki Skagen-Munshi. (Illus.). 1979. pap. text ed. 11.95 o.p. (ISBN 0-07-033459-5). McGraw.

Growing Young. Ashley Montagu. (Illus.). 1983. text ed. 12.95 o.p. (ISBN 0-07-042841-7); pap. text ed. 6.95 o.p. (ISBN 0-07-042844-1). McGraw.

Growth & Development of the Full-Term & Premature Infant. J. H. P. Jonxis. (Jonxis Lectures Ser.: Vol. 1). 1978. 46.00 o.p. (ISBN 0-444-90050-0). Elsevier.

Growth & Development of the Preadolescent. Arthur W. Blair & William H. Burton. 1951. 39.00x o.p. (ISBN 0-89197-490-3). Irvington.

Growth & Properties. Ed. by H. C. Freyhardt. (Crystals-Growth, Properties & Applications Ser.: Vol. 2). (Illus.). 1980. 54.00 o.p. (ISBN 0-387-09697-3). Springer-Verlag.

Growth & Regulation of Animal Populations. Lawrence B. Slobodkin. (Illus.). 1980. pap. 7.95 o.p. (ISBN 0-486-63958-4). Dover.

Growth Centres in Spatial Planning. Malcolm Moseley. LC 74-9962. 1974. 50.00 o.p. (ISBN 0-08-018055-8). Pergamon.

Growth Counseling for Marriage Enrichment: Pre-Marriage & the Early Years. Howard J. Clinebell. Ed. by Howard W. Stone. LC 74-26335. (Creative Pastoral Care & Counseling Ser.). 96p. 1975. pap. 4.50 o.p. (ISBN 0-8006-0551-9, 1-551, Fortress). Augsburg Fortress.

Growth Counseling for Mid-Years Couples. Howard J. Clinebell. Ed. by Howard W. Stone. LC 76-7863. (Creative Pastoral Care & Counseling Ser.). 1977. pap. 0.50 o.p. (ISBN 0-8006-0558-6, 1-558, Fortress). Augsburg Fortress.

Growth Disorders in Infants, Children & Adolescents. Marvin L. Rallison. LC 85-6487. 476p. 1986. 37.50x o.p. (ISBN 0-471-08567-7). Wiley.

Growth, Distribution & Prices. Stephen A. Marglin. (Harvard Economic Studies: No. 155). (Illus.). 584p. 1984. text ed. 25.00x o.p. (ISBN 0-674-36415-5). Harvard U Pr.

Growth Factors. Ed. by K. W. Kastrup & J. Hoiriis-Nielson. LC 77-30607. (Federation of European Biochemical Societies Ser.: Vol. 48). 128p. 1978. 37.00 o.p. (ISBN 0-08-022629-9). Pergamon.

Growth Hormone Deficiency. M. B. Ranke & J. R. Bierch. 192p. 1983. pap. 20.00 o.p. (ISBN 0-317-65612-0). Urban & S.

Growth in Ministry. Ed. by Thomas E. Kadel. LC 79-8902. 176p. 1980. pap. 6.95 o.p. (ISBN 0-8006-1383-X, 1-1383, Fortress). Augsburg Fortress.

Growth in Open Economics. J. A. Hanson. (Lecture Notes in Economics & Mathematical Systems: Vol. 59). (Illus.). 135p. 1971. pap. 10.70 o.p. (ISBN 0-387-05671-8). Springer-Verlag.

Growth, Migration & the Balance of Payments in a Small Open Economy: Portugal. Manuel P. Barbosa. LC 79-53646. (Outstanding Dissertions in Economics Ser.). 330p. 1984. lib. bdg. 36.00 o.p. (ISBN 0-8240-4169-0). Garland Pub.

Growth, Nutrition & Metabolism of Cells in Culture. Ed. by George H. Rothblat & Vincent J. Christofalo. Vol. 1, 1972. 84.50 o.p. (ISBN 0-12-598301-8); Vol. 2, 1972. 78.50 o.p. (ISBN 0-12-598302-6); Vol. 3, 1977. 68.00 o.p. (ISBN 0-12-598303-4). Acad Pr.

Growth of Crystals from the Vapour. M. M. Faktor & I. Garrett. 1974. 35.00x o.p. (ISBN 0-412-11320-1, NO. 6106, Pub. by Chapman & Hall). Routledge Chapman & Hall.

Growth of East African Exports & Their Effect on Economic Development. Leslie Stein. 272p. 1979. 31.00 o.p. (ISBN 0-85664-948-1, Pub. by Croom Helm Ltd). Routledge Chapman & Hall.

Growth of Federal Power in American History. Ed. by Rhodri Jeffreys-Jones & Bruce Collins. 100p. 1983. 16.00x o.p. (ISBN 0-7073-0326-5, Pub. by Scot Acad Pr). Longwood Pub Group.

Growth of Human Behavior. 3rd ed. Norman L. Munn. 512p. 1974. text ed. 24.50 o.p. (ISBN 0-395-17017-6). HM.

Growth of Integrated Oil Companies. John G. McLean & Robert W. Haigh. Repr. of 1954 ed. 54.00 o.s.i. (ISBN 0-08-022306-0). Pergamon.

Growth of Japanese Churches in Brazil. John Mizuki. LC 78-5415. (Illus.). 212p. 1978. pap. 8.95 o.p. (ISBN 0-87808-323-5). William Carey Lib.

Growth of Judicial Power: Perspectives on "The Least Dangerous Branch" League of Women Voters Education Fund Staff. (Federalist Papers Reexamined: No. 5). 33p. 1977. pap. 1.00 o.p. (ISBN 0-89959-041-1, 332). LWV US.

Growth of Medical Thought. Lester S. King. (Midway Reprint Ser). 1974. pap. text ed. 14.00x o.s.i. (ISBN 0-226-43703-5). U of Chicago Pr.

Growth Opportunities in Wire, Cable & Fiber Optics: G-070. Business Communications Staff. 105p. 1983. 1250.00 o.p. (ISBN 0-89336-337-5). BCC.

Growth Points in Nuclear Physics, Vol. 1. P. E. Hodgson. (Illus.). 1980. 28.00 o.p. (ISBN 0-08-023080-6); pap. 12.75 o.p. (ISBN 0-08-023079-2). Pergamon.

Growth Points in Nuclear Physics, Vol. 2. P. E. Hodgson. (Illus.). 1980. 28.00 o.p. (ISBN 0-08-023082-2); pap. 12.75 o.p. (ISBN 0-08-023081-4). Pergamon.

Growth Points in Nuclear Physics, Vol. 3. P. E. Hodgson. (Illus.). 200p. 1981. 25.00 o.p. (ISBN 0-08-026485-9); pap. 13.75 o.p. (ISBN 0-08-026484-0). Pergamon.

Growth Pole Strategy & Regional Development Policy: Asian Experiences & Alternative Approaches. Ed. by Lo Fu-Chen & K. Salih. (Illus.). 1978. 55.00 o.p. (ISBN 0-08-021984-5). Pergamon.

Growth Policies & the International Order. Lincoln Gordon. (Council on Foreign Relations 1980's Project). (Illus.). 1979. text ed. 20.95 o.p. (ISBN 0-07-023812-X). McGraw.

Growth Policies & the International Order. Lincoln Gordon. 1979. pap. text ed. 9.95 o.p. (ISBN 0-07-023813-8). McGraw.

Growth to Selfhood: The Sufi Contribution to Islam. A. Reza Arasteh. (Orig.). 1980. pap. 7.95 o.p. (ISBN 0-7100-0355-2). Routledge Chapman & Hall.

Gruenfeld Defense, Russian Variations. Eric Schiller. 83p. (Orig.). 1985. pap. 5.50 o.p. (ISBN 0-931462-44-4). Chess Ent Inc.

Grumman F8F "Bearcat" B. R. Jackson & T. E. Doll. LC 73-123470. (Aero Ser.: Vol. 20). (Illus., Orig.). 1970. pap. 5.95 o.p. (ISBN 0-8168-0576-8, 20576, TAB-Aero). TAB Bks.

Grumpy Prophet & 22 other Bible Stories to Read & Tell. John C. Reid. 80p. (gr. 1-6). 1986. casebound 7.95 o.p. (ISBN 0-87239-917-6, 3370). Standard Pub.

GTW Class Kit L-K. 2nd ed. Date not set. (ISBN 0-07-029680-4). McGraw.

GTW Class Kit L-1. 2nd ed. Date not set. (ISBN 0-07-029681-2). McGraw.

GTW Class Kit L-2. 2nd ed. Date not set. (ISBN 0-07-029682-0). McGraw.

GTW Class Kit L-3. 2nd ed. Date not set. (ISBN 0-07-029683-9). McGraw.

GTW Class Kit L-4. 2nd ed. Date not set. (ISBN 0-07-029684-7). McGraw.

GTW Class Kit L-5. 2nd ed. Date not set. (ISBN 0-07-029685-5). McGraw.

GTW Class Kit L-6. 2nd ed. Date not set. (ISBN 0-07-029686-3). McGraw.

Gtwy L-K Demo Kit. 2nd ed. Date not set. (ISBN 0-07-029740-1). McGraw.

Gtwy L-1 Demo Kit. 2nd ed. Date not set. (ISBN 0-07-029741-X). McGraw.

Gtwy L-2 Demo Kit. 2nd ed. Date not set. (ISBN 0-07-029742-8). McGraw.

Gtwy L-2 Repl Kit. 2nd ed. Date not set. (ISBN 0-07-029752-5). McGraw.

Gtwy L-3 Demo Kit. 2nd ed. Date not set. (ISBN 0-07-029743-6). McGraw.

Gtwy L-3 Repl Kit. 2nd ed. Date not set. (ISBN 0-07-029753-3). McGraw.

Gtwy L-4 Demo Kit. 2nd ed. Date not set. (ISBN 0-07-029744-4). McGraw.

Gtwy L-4 Repl Kit. 2nd ed. Date not set. (ISBN 0-07-029754-1). McGraw.

Gtwy L-5 Demo Kit. 2nd ed. Date not set. (ISBN 0-07-029745-2). McGraw.

Gtwy L-5 Repl Kit. 2nd ed. Date not set. (ISBN 0-07-029755-X). McGraw.

Gtwy L-6 Demo Kit. 2nd ed. Date not set. (ISBN 0-07-029746-0). McGraw.

Gtwy L-6 Repl Kit. 2nd ed. Date not set. (ISBN 0-07-029756-8). McGraw.

Gtwy Level 2 TE. Date not set. (ISBN 0-07-029512-3). McGraw.

Guaman Poma: Writing & Resistance in Colonial Peru. Rolena Adorno. (Latin American Monographs: No. 68). (Illus.). 199p. 1986. text ed. 22.50x o.p. (ISBN 0-292-72452-7). U of Tex Pr.

Guangzhou Conference, 1980: Proceedings, Vols. 1 & 2. Science Press Staff. 1980. 99.95 o.p. (ISBN 0-442-20273-3). Van Nos Reinhold.

Guaranteed Income Funds: Labour Relations at the European Level. Ed. by Roger Blanpain. (Bulletin of Comparative Labour Relations Ser.: No. 3). 1972. 12.00 o.p. (ISBN 90-31-20019-0). Kluwer Academic.

Guard & Reserve in the Total Force: The First Decade, 1973-1983. Ed. by Bennie J. Wilson. 357p. 1985. 8.00 o.p. (ISBN 0-318-20111-9, S/N 008-020-01040-5). USGPO.

Guard! Society's Professional Prisoner. Robert J. Wicks. LC 79-28663. 150p. (Orig.). 1980. pap. 9.00x o.p. (ISBN 0-87201-343-X). Gulf Pub.

Guardian Angel. Linda R. Wisdom. (Candlelight Ecstasy Ser.: No. 196). (Orig.). 1983. pap. 1.95 o.s.i. (ISBN 0-440-13274-6). Dell.

Guardian of Boston: William Monroe Trotter. Stephen R. Fox. LC 78-108822. (Studies in American Negro Life). 1971. pap. text ed. 3.45x o.s.i. (ISBN 0-689-70256-6, Atheneum, NL26). Macmillan.

Guardians of the House. L. M. Boston. LC 74-18177. (Illus.). 64p. (gr. 3-7). 1975. 5.95 o.p. (ISBN 0-689-50016-5, Atheneum). Macmillan.

Guardrail Crash Test Evaluation: New Concepts & End Designs. (National Cooperative Highway Research Project Report). 89p. 1972. 4.80 o.p. (ISBN 0-309-02010-7). Transport Res Bd.

Guards Illustrated. 4th ed. National Safety Council. LC 80-83322. 94p. 1981. pap. 14.95 o.p. (ISBN 0-87912-032-0, 130.02). Natl Safety Coun.

Guarneri: Story of a Genius. Leonard Wibberley. LC 74-8142. 160p. (gr. 5 up). 1974. 5.95 o.p. (ISBN 0-374-32822-6). FS&G.

Guatemala in Rebellion: Unfinished History. Ed. by Jonathan L. Fried & Marvin E. Gettleman. (Latin America Ser.: No. 2). 368p. 1983. pap. 12.50 o.p. (ISBN 0-394-62455-6, E844, Ever). Grove.

Guatemalan Collection, 1981. 533p. 1981. pap. 20.00 o.p. (ISBN 0-940764-29-6). U of Utah Pr.

Gudrun. Alma J. Koenig. Tr. by Anthea Bell. LC 79-917. (gr. 7 up). 1979. 11.75 o.p. (ISBN 0-688-41899-6); PLB 11.88 o.p. (ISBN 0-688-51899-0). Lothrop.

Guerilla Street Theatre. Ed. by Henry Lesnick. 1973. pap. 2.45 o.p. (ISBN 0-380-01236-7, 15198, Discus). Avon.

Guerilla Warfare: From Nineteen Thirty-Nine to the Present Day. Robin Corbett. (Illus.). 224p. 1986. 32.50x o.p. (ISBN 0-85613-469-4, Pub. by MacD & Co). Trans-Atl Phila.

Guerilleres. Monique Witlig. 1976. pap. 2.95 o.p. (ISBN 0-380-00817-3, 54957, Bard). Avon.

Guernica. Fernando Arrabal. 192p. 1975. 9.95 o.p. (ISBN 0-686-54455-2). French & Eur.

Guernica: Studies - Postscripts. Schapiro. 20.00 o.p. (ISBN 0-8076-0983-8). Braziller.

Guerras de las Estrellas: Ilusiones y Peligros. U. S. S. R. Minutes of Defense Staff. 561p. 1985. pap. 1.75 o.p. (ISBN 0-317-47699-8, Pub. by Progress Pubs USSR). Imported Pubns.

Guerre Civile. Henri De Montherlant. 1965. 13.25 o.p. (ISBN 0-685-11226-8). Schoenhof.

Guerre Civile. Henry de Montherlant. 248p. (Soleil). 1965. 9.95 o.p. (ISBN 0-686-55521-X). Schoenhof.

Guerre et la Paix, 2 vols. Pierre-Joseph Proudhon. LC 70-147438. (Library of War & Peace; Proposals for Peace: a History). 1972. lib. bdg. 76.00 o.p. (ISBN 0-8240-0227-X). Garland Pub.

Guerrilla Warfare: Cause & Conflict (A 21st Century Success Story?) (National Security Essay Ser: No. 81-3). 93p. 1981. pap. 4.50 o.p. (ISBN 0-318-20112-7, S/N 008-020-00867-2). USGPO.

Guess a Rhyme: Poems to Complete! Riddles to Solve! Larry Weinburg. LC 81-15689. (Picturebacks Ser.). (Illus.). 32p. (gr. 1-4). 1982. pap. 1.95 o.s.i. (ISBN 0-394-85062-9). Random.

Guess What I Am, Vol. 2. (Vegetable Puppets Ser.). (Illus.). 10p. (ps). 1979. 2.50 o.p. (ISBN 0-89346-117-2, Pub. by Froebel-Kan Japan). Heian Intl.

Guest. James Marshall. LC 74-29445. (Illus.). 40p. (gr. k-3). 1975. reinforced bdg. 11.70 o.s.i. (ISBN 0-395-20277-9). HM.

Guest Book. (Illus.). 64p. 1986. 16.95 o.p. (ISBN 0-317-62027-4). H L Levin.

Guest Book. Metropolitan Museum of Art Staff. 80p. 1983. 19.95 o.s.i. (ISBN 0-684-17806-0, ScribT). Scribner.

Guest for the Night. S. Y. Agnon. Tr. by Misha Louvish from Hebrew. LC 68-13723. 492p. 1968. pap. 8.95 o.p. (ISBN 0-8052-0646-9). Schocken.

Guesthouses, Farmhouses & Inns in Britain. British Automobile Association Staff. (British Automobile Association Accommodation Guides Ser.). 368p. (Orig.). 1984. pap. 9.95 o.p. (ISBN 0-86145-186-4, Pub. by Automobile Assn Brit). Salem Hse Pubs.

Guests at the Villa. Alice Hesse. 1977. 5.00 o.p. (ISBN 0-682-48691-4, Banner). Exposition-Phoenix.

Guia de Studios Essential Arithmetic: Spanish Study Guide for Essential Arithmetic. Alberto Beron et al. 174p. Watts.

Guia-Diccionario del Quijote. Justo Caballero. (Span.). 12.50 o.p. (ISBN 0-686-56697-1, S-5649). French & Eur.

Guia Introductory al SAS, Edicion Revisada. SAS Institute, Inc. Staff. 94p. (Orig.). 1983. pap. 9.95 o.p. (ISBN 0-917382-42-0). SAS Inst.

Guia Para Leer el Antiguo Testamento: Segunda Parte, el Esenario Esta Puesto. Ed. by Life in Christ Staff. Tr. by Monica Villa Gomez. (Una Guia Para la Lectura De la Biblia). (Illus., Span.). 1977. pap. 1.25 o.p. (ISBN 0-914070-09-6). ACTA Pubns.

Guidance, an Examination. Harvard Educational Review Staff. 1962. pap. 8.00 o.p. (ISBN 0-384-21530-0). Johnson Repr.

Guidance: an Introduction. John J. Pietrofesa et al. 1980. text ed. 36.36 o.p. (ISBN 0-395-30699-X). HM.

Guidance & Control, PAAS8. Ed. by R. E. Roberson & J. S. Farrior. LC 62-13119. (Illus.). 670p. 1962. 59.50 o.p. (ISBN 0-317-36828-1). AIAA.

Guidance & Counseling in Colleges & Universities. S. K. Kochhar. 176p. 1984. pap. text ed. 13.95x o.p. (ISBN 0-86590-277-1, Pub. by Sterling Pub India). Apt Bks.

Guidance & Counseling in the Elementary School. R. Nelson. LC 79-185783. 1972. text ed. 17.95 o.p. (ISBN 0-03-084848-2, HoltC). HR&W.

Guidance & Counseling in the Schools: Perspective on the Past, Present & Future. Edwin L. Herr. 242p. 1979. 9.25 o.p. (ISBN 0-911547-44-4, 72124W34). Am Assn Coun Dev.

Guidance Function & Counseling Roles in an Adult Education Program. Adult Education Association Staff. 70p. 5.00 o.p. (ISBN 0-317-36199-6). A A A C E.

Guidance Function in Education. 2nd ed. Percival W. Hutson. LC 68-16462. (Illus.). 1968. 29.50x o.p. (ISBN 0-89197-195-5); pap. text ed. 12.95x o.p. (ISBN 0-89197-780-5). Irvington.

Guidance on Requirements Analysis for Office Automation Systems. Ed. by Lynne S. Rosenthal. (National Bureau of Standards Special Publication 500-147. Computer Science & Technology Ser.). (Illus.). 110p. 1987. pap. 5.00 o.p. (ISBN 0-318-22617-0, S/N 003-003-02791-0). USGPO.

Guidance on Software Package Selection. Ed. by Sheila Frankel. LC 86-600593. (National Bureau of Standards Special Publication 500-144. Computer Science & Technology Ser.). (Illus.). 120p. (Orig.). 1986. pap. 6.00 o.p. (003-003-02773-1). USGPO.

Guidance, Selection, & Training: Ideas & Applications. Peter Morea. 1972. 26.95x o.p. (ISBN 0-7100-7236-8). Routledge Chapman & Hall.

Guidance Services in the Modern School. 2nd ed. Merle M. Ohlsen. 450p. 1974. text ed. 11.95 o.p. (ISBN 0-15-570552-0, HC). HarBraceJ.

Guidargus de la Peinture de XIXe Siecle a Nos Jours. Gerald Schurr. (Illus.). 605p. (Fr.). 1983. 85.00 o.p. (ISBN 2-85917-028-6, 2390239, Pub. by Editions de l'Amateur FR). Seven Hills Bk Dists.

Guidargus de la Peinture du XIX Siecle a Nos Jours. G. Schurr. (Illus.). 687p. 1984. 90.00 o.p. (ISBN 2-85917-032-4, Pub. by Editions de l'Amatuer FR). Seven Hills Bk Dists.

Guidargus de L'Antiquite. Yves Gairaud. (Illus.). 461p. (Fr.). 1982. 42.00 o.s.i. (ISBN 2-85917-026-X, 2390109, Pub. by Editions de l'Amateur FR). Seven Hills Bk Dists.

Guidargus des Poupees de Collection. Francois Theimer. (Illus.). 254p. 1985. 50.00 o.p. (ISBN 2-85917-031-6, Pub. by Editions de l'Amateur FR). Seven Hills Bk Dists.

Guide Book of Mexican Coins Eighteen Twenty-Two to date. rev. ed. T. V. Buttrey & Clyde Hubbard. LC 76-49264. (Illus.). 256p. 1986. pap. 11.00 o.s.i. (ISBN 0-87341-089-0). Krause Pubns.

Guide Book of Mexican Coins, 1822 to Date. 2nd ed. T. V. Buttrey & Clyde Hubbard. 288p. 1988. pap. 12.95 o.p. (ISBN 0-87431-108-X). Krause Pubns.

Guide-Book to Mathematics. I. N. Bronshtein & K. A. Semendyayev. Tr. by J. Jaworowsky & M. N. Bleicher. LC 60-16788. (Illus.). 783p. 1972. 14.00 o.p. (ISBN 0-387-91106-5). Springer-Verlag.

Guide for Artists, Art Students, Travellers, Etc; see United States Art Directory & Year-Book.

Guide for Dating Early Published Music: A Manual of Bibliographical Practices. International Association of Music Libraries Staff. Ed. by Don W. Krummel. (Illus.). 1974. 26.00 o.p. (ISBN 0-913574-25-2, EAKRUM). Eur-Am Music.

Guide for Games. C. Joynson. 302p. 1957. (ISBN 0-8022-0819-3). Philos Lib.

Guide for Improving Locally Developed Career Education Measures. N. L. Mc Caslin & Jerry P. Walker. 52p. 1979. 3.80 o.p. (ISBN 0-318-15479-X, RD 167). Natl Ctr Res Voc Ed.

Guide for Selecting Microcomputer Data Management Software. Charles L. Sheppard. LC 85-600598. (NBS Special Publication Computer Science & Technology Ser.: No. 500-131). (Illus.). 66p. (Orig.). 1985. pap. 2.50 o.p. (S/N 003-003-02682-4). USGPO.

Guide for Teacher Recording in Day Care Agencies. rev. ed. 24p. 1965. 2.60 o.p. (ISBN 0-87868-028-4, 0284). Child Welfare.

Guide for the Hydroponic & Soilless Culture Grower. J. Benton Jones. (Illus.). 170p. 1983. pap. text ed. 19.95x o.p. (ISBN 0-917304-49-7). Timber.

Guide for the Misguided. Ezra Brudno. (ISBN 0-8022-0187-3). Philos Lib.

Guide for the Organization & Operation of a Religious Resource Center. John T. Corrigan. (Illus.). 1977. pap. 2.50 o.p. (ISBN 0-87507-004-3). Cath Lib Assn.

Guide for the Selection & Use of Microcomputers. 69p. (Orig.). 1987. pap. 4.00 o.p. (S/N 022-003-01141-2). USGPO.

Guide for Time Studies. Goldie Levenson. 55p. 1982. 12.95 o.p. (ISBN 0-88737-089-6, 21-1886). Natl League Nurse.

Guide of the Perplexed. abr. ed. Moses Maimonides. Ed. by Julius W. Guttman. Tr. by Chaim Rabin. 1978. pap. text ed. 6.95 o.s.i. (ISBN 0-85222-208-4, East & West Lib). Hebrew Pub.

Guide on Data Entity Naming Conventions. Judith J. Newton. (National Bureau of Standards Special Publication 500-149. Computer Science & Technology). (Illus.). 58p. (Orig.). 1987. pap. 3.00 o.p. (ISBN 0-318-23554-4, S/N 003-003-02818-5). USGPO.

Guide on Evaluation & Attenuation of Traffic Noise. 1974. pap. 3.00 o.p. (ISBN 0-686-20955-9, GTN-1). AASHTO.

Guide on Protection Against Ionising Radiations in Industrial Radiography & Fluoroscopy see Manual of Industrial Radiation Protection.

Guide on Protection Against Ionising Radiations in the Application of Luminous Compounds see Manual of Industrial Radiation Protection.

Guide on Selecting ADP Backup Processing Alternatives. Irene E. Isaac. LC 83-600618. (Computer Science & Technology. NBS Special Publication Ser.: No. 500-134). (Illus.). 40p. (Orig.). 1985. pap. 1.75 o.p. (ISBN 0-318-19571-2, S/N 003-003-02701-4). USGPO.

Guide on Workload Forecasting: National Bureau of Standards Special Publication 500-123. Helen Letmanyi. LC 85-600504. (Computer Science & Technology Ser.). (Illus.). 66p. (Orig.). 1985. pap. 3.00 o.p. (ISBN 0-318-21586-1, S/N 003-003-02634-4). USGPO.

Guide Rouge Swiss 1986-87. Alban Verlag. 308p. (Orig.). 1986. pap. 19.95 o.p. (ISBN 3-905037-00-9, Pub. by Alban Verlag Zurich). Bradt Ent.

Guide Specification for Glass Fiber Reinforced Concrete Panels. 14p. pap. 4.00 o.p. (ISBN 0-686-39961-7, SPC-120-82). P-PCI.

Guide to a Counselor-in-Training Program. Ed. by American Camping Association Publications Committee. 32p. 1974. pap. 2.00 o.p. (ISBN 0-87603-020-7). Am Camping.

Guide to a Course in Government Documents. Helen Q. Schroyer. (Occasional Papers: No. 135). 51p. 1978. pap. 2.00 o.p. (ISBN 0-317-58975-X). U of Ill Lib Info Sci.

Guide to a Regional Dissection & Study of the Human Body. 5th ed. Roger C. Crafts & Robert T. Binhammer. LC 85-16795. 148p. 1985. pap. 7.00 o.p. (ISBN 0-471-83857-8, Pub by Wiley Medical). Wiley.

Guide to a Year's Reading in Luther's Works. George Kraus. (Continued Applied Christianity Ser.). 1983. pap. 1.25 o.p. (ISBN 0-570-03902-9, 12-2984). Concordia.

Guide to Accounting Principles, Practices & Systems for Nursing Homes. Henry Posyniak. LC 77-80740. 1978. pap. 10.00 o.p. (ISBN 0-87125-040-3). Cath Health.

Guide to Adirondack Trails: Central Region. Bruce Wadsworth. Ed. by Neal S. Burdick. LC 86-3417. (ADK Forest Preserve Ser.: Vol. III). (Illus.). 224p. 1986. pap. 12.95 o.p. (ISBN 0-935272-30-5). ADK Mtn Club.

Guide to Adirondack Trails: Eastern Region. Betsy Tisdale. Ed. by Neal S. Burdick. LC 87-1241. (Forest Preserve Ser.: Vol. VI). 224p. 1987. pap. 12.95 o.p. (ISBN 0-935272-41-0). ADK Mtn Club.

Guide to Adirondack Trails: High Peaks Region. 11th ed. Ed. by Neal S. Burdick & Tony Goodwin. LC 85-4102. (Forest Preserve Ser.: Vol. I). (Illus.). 310p. 1985. pap. 12.95 o.p. (ISBN 0-935272-25-9). ADK Mtn Club.

Guide to Adirondack Trails: Northern Region. Peter V. O'Shea. Ed. by Neal S. Burdick. LC 85-30839. (ADK Forest Preserve Ser.: Vol. II). (Illus.). 164p. 1986. pap. 12.95 o.p. (ISBN 0-935272-29-1). ADK Mtn Club.

Guide to Adirondack Trails: The Northville-Placid Trail. Bruce Wadsworth. Ed. by Neal S. Burdick. LC 86-23126. (Forest Preserve Ser.: Vol. IV). (Illus.). 184p. 1987. pap. 12.95 o.p. (ISBN 0-935272-34-8). ADK Mtn Club.

Guide to Adirondack Trails: West-Central Region. 2nd ed. Art Haberl. Ed. by Neal S. Burdick. LC 87-27053. (Forest Preserve Ser.: Vol. V). (Illus.). 296p. 1987. pap. 12.95 o.p. (ISBN 0-935272-40-2). ADK Mtn Club.

Guide to Aegean & Mediterranean Turkey. Diane Darke. (Michael Haag Guides). (Illus.). 168p. (Orig.). 1986. pap. 14.95 o.p. (ISBN 0-87052-245-0). Hippocrene Bks.

Guide to Alcohol & Drug Dependence. Madden. 256p. 1979. pap. 20.00 o.p. (ISBN 0-7236-0504-1, Pub. by John Wright UK). Butterworth.

Guide to American Biography, 2 vols. in 1. Marion Dargan. LC 73-13455. 1973. Repr. of 1949 ed. lib. bdg. 24.75x o.p. (ISBN 0-8371-7134-2, DAAB). Greenwood.

Guide to American Catholic History. 2nd, rev. ed. John T. Ellis & Robert Trisco. LC 81-17585. 265p. 1982. lib. bdg. 31.00 o.p. (ISBN 0-87436-318-7). ABC-Clio.

Guide to American History Manuscript Collections in Libraries of the United States. Ray A. Billington. pap. 2.00 o.p. (ISBN 0-8446-1077-1). Peter Smith.

Guide to Ancient Sites in Britain. Janet Bord & Colin Bord. (Illus.). 183p. 1981. pap. 12.95 o.p. (ISBN 0-586-08309-X, Pub. by Granada England). Academy Chi Pubs.

Guide to Antibiotic Use in Dental Practice. Ed. by Michael Newman & Anthony Goodman. 200p. 1984. pap. 21.50 o.p. (ISBN 0-86715-149-8). Quint Pub Co.

Guide to Apartment House Management. Mary M. Holt. LC 70-159493. 1971. 6.00 o.p. (ISBN 0-682-47269-7, Banner). Exposition-Phoenix.

Guide to Art Museums: Midwest Edition. Michael Beatty & James Nulte. LC 84-81547. (Illus.). 200p. (Orig.). 1984. pap. 9.95 o.s.i. (ISBN 0-89708-128-5). And Bks.

Guide to Bank Taxation & 1987 Tax Preparation. 1987. 75.00 o.p. (ISBN 1-55520-054-0, 816). Bank Admin Inst.

Guide to Baseball Literature. Ed. by Anton Grobani. LC 74-17223. 380p. 1975. 48.00x o.p. (ISBN 0-8103-0962-9). Gale.

Guide to Basic Riding Instruction. Anne Lewis. (Illus.). pap. 2.95 o.p. (ISBN 0-85131-218-7, 6788, Pub. by J A Allen U K). S R Smith Sporting Bks.

Guide to Better Acol Bridge. Ron Klinger. 192p. 1988. pap. 15.95 o.p. (ISBN 0-575-04379-2, Pub. by Gollancz England). David & Charles.

Guide to Bird Finding East of the Mississippi. 2nd ed. Olin S. Pettingill, Jr. 1980. pap. 7.95 o.s.i. (ISBN 0-395-29132-1). HM.

Guide to British Parliamentary Papers. Frank Rodgers & Rose B. Phelps. (Occasional Papers: No. 82). 37p. 1967. pap. 1.00 o.p. (ISBN 0-317-58863-X). U of Ill Lib Info Sci.

Guide to Bronchial Asthma. H. Herxheimer. 1976. 45.50 o.p. (ISBN 0-12-343850-0). Acad Pr.

Guide to Buddhist Religion. Frank E. Reynolds et al. 440p. 1981. lib. bdg. 57.50 o.p. (ISBN 0-8161-7900-X, Hall Reference). G K Hall.

Guide to Buying, Selling & Starting a Travel Agency. rev. ed. Laurence Stevens. LC 75-30002. 100p. 1978. pap. 9.95 o.p. (ISBN 0-916032-00-0). Delmar.

Guide to Cairo: Including the Pyramids & Saqqara. 2nd, rev. ed. Michael Haag. (Michael Haag Travel Guides Ser.). (Illus.). 144p. 1987. pap. 9.95 o.s.i. (ISBN 0-87052-371-6, Pub. by Michael Haag UK). Hippocrene Bks.

Guide to California. Bob Thompson. (American Express Pocket Guides Ser.). (Illus.). 1983. 7.95 o.p. (ISBN 0-671-45374-2). S&S.

Guide to Camera Equipment. (Petersen's Photographic Library: Vol. 6). 160p. 1981. softcover 9.95 o.p. (ISBN 0-8227-4055-9). Petersen Pub.

Guide to Catalina Island. Chicki Mallan. (Illus.). 142p. (Orig.). 1984. 5.95 o.p. (ISBN 0-9603322-6-X). Moon Pubns CA.

Guide to Child Health: A Practical Guide. Vernon Coleman. 256p. (Orig.). 1985. pap. 9.95 o.p. (ISBN 0-7102-0269-5). Routledge Chapman & Hall.

Guide to Christian Colleges. 150p. 1984. 12.95 o.p. (ISBN 0-318-17496-0). Christ Coll Coal.

Guide to Classroom Observation. Robert Walker & Clem Adelman. (Illus.). 1975. pap. 12.95x o.p. (ISBN 0-416-81210-4, NO. 2570). Routledge Chapman & Hall.

Guide to Clinical Reasoning. Maurice Kraytman. 560p. 1981. text ed. 19.95 o.p. (ISBN 0-07-035451-0). McGraw.

Guide to Close Combat for Infantry Soldier. A. J. Advincular. LC 87-50246. 200p. (Orig.). pap. cancelled o.s.i. (ISBN 0-86568-094-9). Unique Pubns.

Guide to College Reading. Kathleen T. McWhorter. 1986. pap. text ed. write for info. o.p. (ISBN 0-673-39283-X). Scott F.

Guide to Colleges for Hearing Impaired & Deaf Students. Mary Ann Liscio. 1986. pap. 26.95 o.p. (ISBN 0-12-452241-6). Acad Pr.

Guide to Colleges for Learning Disabled Students. Ed. by Mary A. Liscio. 1984. 26.95 o.p. (ISBN 0-12-452240-8). Acad Pr.

Guide to Colleges for Learning Disabled Students. rev. ed. Ed. by Mary A. Liscio. 430p. 1986. pap. 26.95 o.p. (ISBN 0-12-452244-0). Acad Pr.

Guide to Colleges for Mobility Impaired Students. Mary Ann Liscio. 1986. pap. 26.95 o.p. (ISBN 0-12-452242-4). Acad Pr.

Guide to Colleges for Visually Impaired Students. Mary Ann Liscio. (Academic Press Professional-Technical Bk). 1986. pap. 26.95 o.p. (ISBN 0-12-452243-2). Acad Pr.

Guide to Colleges with Programs for the Learning Disabled. Date not set. Petersons Guides.

Guide to Common Insects & Diseases of Forest Trees in the Northeastern United States. (Illus.). 127p. 1979. pap. 6.00 o.p. (ISBN 0-318-21836-4, S/N 001-001-00501-1). USGPO.

Guide to Conditional Relations Part I: Being a Guide to Pages 1-12 of "Conditional Relations" Patthana. U. Narada. (Pali Text Society Ser.). 241p. 1979. 25.00x o.p. (ISBN 0-7100-0280-7). Routledge Chapman & Hall.

Guide to Congress: Congress & the Nation, 5 Vols. 3rd ed. 1983. (ISBN 0-87187-301-X). Congr Quarterly.

Guide to Contemporary French Literature from Valery to Sartre. Wallace Fowlie. 11.00 o.p. (ISBN 0-8446-2077-7). Peter Smith.

Guide to Contracting for the Sale of Goods. Robert Akroyd. 208p. (Orig.). 1984. pap. 17.95x o.p. (ISBN 0-7102-0005-6). Routledge Chapman & Hall.

Guide to Corporate Giving in the Arts, Vol. 3. Ed. by Robert Porter. 592p. 1983. 10.00 o.s.i. (ISBN 0-915400-39-1, 3800). Am Council Arts.

Guide to Corporate Giving in the Arts, Two. 2nd ed. Ed. by Robert A. Porter. 378p. 1981. 15.00 o.p. (ISBN 0-915400-23-5, NO. 340). Am Council Arts.

Guide to Criterion-Referenced Test Construction. Ed. by Ronald A. Berk. LC 84-47955. 1984. text ed. 37.50x o.p. (ISBN 0-8018-2417-6). Johns Hopkins.

Guide to Current Latin American Periodicals: Humanities & Social Sciences. Irene Zimmerman. 1961. 20.00 o.p. (ISBN 0-910824-00-2); pap. 15.00 o.p. (ISBN 0-910824-01-0). Kallman.

Guide to Curriculum Development in Social Studies. Connecticut Board of Education Staff. 122p. 1982. pap. 9.95 o.p. (ISBN 0-89994-276-8). Soc Sci Ed.

Guide to Daily Prayer. William Barclay. LC 62-11473. 1974. pap. 6.95 o.p. (ISBN 0-06-060401-8, RD75). HarpR.

Titles

Guide to Database Distribution: Legal Aspects & Model Contracts. Joseph Bremner & Peggy Miller. 1987. 160.00 o.p. (ISBN 0-317-60270-5). NFAIS.
Guide to Decoration in the Early American Manner. Nadine C. Wilson. LC 64-24587. (Illus.). 1965. 6.75 o.p. (ISBN 0-8048-0224-6). C E Tuttle.
Guide to Dental Radiography. 2nd ed. Rita A. Mason. (Illus.). 176p. 1982. pap. 22.00 o.p. (ISBN 0-7236-0623-4). Butterworth.
Guide to Departments of Anthropology 1986-87. 25th ed. (Anthropological Studies). 1986. 25.00 o.p. (ISBN 0-913167-14-2). Am Anthro Assn.
Guide to Dining on the Outer Banks of North Carolina: 1985-86 Edition. Linda Berger. (Guide to Dining Ser.). (Illus.). 42p. 1985. pap. 2.95 o.p. (ISBN 0-912367-08-3). Insiders Guide.
Guide to Doing Business in the ASEAN Region: Brunei, Indonesia, Malaysia, Philippines, Singapore, Thailand. 71p. 1986. pap. 1.75 o.p. (ISBN 0-318-20113-5, S/N 003-009-00450-1). USGPO.
Guide to Doing Business on the Arabian Peninsula. Quentin W. Fleming. 128p. 1981. 29.95 o.p. (ISBN 0-8144-5666-9); comb-bound 29.95 o.p. (ISBN 0-8144-7012-2). AMACOM.
Guide to Doing Business with the Department of State. rev. ed. (Department of State Publication Ser.: No. 9335). 49p. 1987. pap. 1.50 o.p. (ISBN 0-318-22900-5, S/N 044-000-02166-8). USGPO.
Guide to Doing Business with the Department of State. rev. ed. (State Department Publication Ser.: No. 9335). 1988. pap. 1.50 o.p. (S/N 044-000-02216-8). USGPO.
Guide to Early Chinese Communist Historical Materials: The Keio Collection. (Chinese Research Aid Ser.: No. 3). 1972. 4.00x o.p. (ISBN 0-912966-43-2). IEAS.
Guide to East Africa: Kenya, Tanzania & Seychells. rev. & 3rd ed. Nina Cassimati. (Travelaid Guide Ser.). 192p. 1986. pap. 11.95 o.s.i. (ISBN 0-87052-246-9). Hippocrene Bks.
Guide to Eastern Canada. Frederick Pratson. LC 81-86603. (Illus.). 480p. 1983. pap. 10.95 o.p. (ISBN 0-87106-967-9). Globe Pequot.
Guide to Eastern Canada. 2nd ed. Frederick Pratson. LC 86-2296. (Illus.). 496p. 1986. pap. 10.95 o.s.i. (ISBN 0-87106-890-7). Globe Pequot.
Guide to Effective Public Relations. 77p. 2.00 o.p. (ISBN 0-318-15182-0, 111-874). Natl Assoc Realtors.
Guide to Effective Scripture Study. Duane S. Crowther. LC 75-5321. (Scripture Guide Ser). 147p. 1975. pap. 4.95 o.p. (ISBN 0-88290-004-8). Horizon Utah.
Guide to Effective Study. Edwin A. Locke. LC 74-79409. 201p. 1975. pap. text ed. 15.95 o.p. (ISBN 0-8261-1580-2). Springer Pub.
Guide to Egypt. 3rd ed. Michael Haag. (Travelaid Guide Bks.). (Illus.). 352p. 1985. pap. 14.95 o.p. (ISBN 0-902743-14-7). Hippocrene Bks.
Guide to Electrical Installation & Repair. (McGraw-Hill Paperbacks Home Improvement Ser.). (Illus., Orig.). 1979. pap. text ed. 3.95 o.p. (ISBN 0-07-045964-9). McGraw.
Guide to Electronic Components. William Segallis. LC 75-2065. 256p. 1983. 41.95 o.p. (ISBN 0-8436-0208-2). Van Nos Reinhold.
Guide to Electronics in the Home: 1986. Ed. by Consumer Report Book Editors. Monte Florman. 336p. 1986. pap. 7.00 o.p. (ISBN 0-89043-045-4). Consumer Reports.
Guide to English Educational Terms. Date not set. (ISBN 0-8052-3922-7). Random.
Guide to Equine Facilities & Services: The List, 1987. Ed. by The Blood-Horse, Inc. Staff. (Illus.). 500p. 1987. pap. 26.50 o.p. (ISBN 0-939049-13-9). Blood-Horse.
Guide to Evaluation of Training. Ed. by Lloyd H. Stanley. (ICPE Training Ser.). 59p. 1984. pap. 10.00x o.p. (ISBN 92-9038-402-6, Pub. by Intl Ctr Pub Ent Yugoslavia). Kumarian Pr.
Guide to Federal Funding. Ed. by Susan B. Quarles. LC 86-10014. 480p. (Orig.). 1986. pap. text ed. 24.95x o.p. (ISBN 0-87154-699-X). Russell Sage.
Guide to Federal Labor Relations Authority Law & Practice. 2nd ed. Peter B. Broida. 900p. 1988. pap. 75.00 o.p. (ISBN 0-9615053-5-4). Dewey Pubns.
Guide to Federal Sector Equal Employment Law & Practice. Ernest C. Hadley. 400p. 1988. pap. 65.00 o.p. (ISBN 0-9615053-6-2). Dewey Pubns.
Guide to Festschriften. New York Public Library Staff & Library of Congress Staff. (Festschriften Collection of the New York Public Library). 1977. lib. bdg. 155.00 o.p. (ISBN 0-8161-0069-1, Hall Library). G K Hall.
Guide to Films about the Soviet Union. 2nd ed. 1987. 5.00 o.p. Comm Natl Security.
Guide to Films about the Soviet Union. National Security Committee & Harriman, W. Averell, Institute for Advanced Study of the Soviet Union Staff. Ed. by Kim Lamberty & Bernardine Joselyn. 75p. 1986. special punched 5.00 o.p. (ISBN 0-937115-01-0). Comm Natl Security.
Guide to Florence & Tuscany. Sheila Hale. (American Express Pocket Guides Ser.). (Illus.). 1983. 7.95 o.p. (ISBN 0-671-45368-8). S&S.
Guide to Florida Legal Research. Florida Bar Staff. LC 80-68019. 113p. 1980. pap. 25.00 o.p. (ISBN 0-910373-34-5, 279). FL Bar Legal Ed.
Guide to Florida Lighthouses. Elinor De Wire. LC 87-16835. (Illus.). 96p. 1987. 17.95 o.p. (ISBN 0-910923-44-2). Pineapple Pr.
Guide to Football Literature. Ed. by Anton Grobani. LC 75-1478. xvi, 336p. 1975. 40.00x o.p. (ISBN 0-8103-0964-5). Gale.
Guide to Fossil Man. 3rd rev. ed. Michael H. Day. LC 77-10517. 1978. Repr. of 1965 ed. lib. bdg. 24.00x o.s.i. (ISBN 0-226-13888-7). U of Chicago Pr.
Guide to Four-Year Colleges 1984. 14th ed. Ed. by Kim R. Kaye. (Peterson's Annual Guides-Undergraduate Study Ser.). 2028p. 1983. pap. 11.95 o.p. (ISBN 0-87866-215-4). Petersons Guides.
Guide to Four-Year Colleges 1987. 17th ed. (Peterson's Annual Guides to Undergraduate Study Ser.). 2289p. (Orig.). 1986. pap. 14.95 o.p. (ISBN 0-87866-527-7). Petersons Guides.
Guide to Four-Year Colleges 1988. 18th ed. (Peterson's Annual Guides to Undergraduate Study Ser.). 2381p. (Orig.). 1987. lib. bdg. 20.95 o.p. (ISBN 0-87866-647-8); pap. 15.95 o.p. (ISBN 0-87866-549-8). Petersons Guides.
Guide to Franchising. 3rd ed. M. Mendelsohn. LC 78-40961. 1982. text ed. 28.00 o.p. (ISBN 0-08-025845-X). Pergamon.
Guide to Free Computer Materials. 5th ed. 1987. 30.25 o.p. (ISBN 0-87708-177-8). Ed Prog.
Guide to Free Computer Materials. 6th ed. 1988. 30.25 o.p. (ISBN 0-87708-189-1). Ed Prog.
Guide to Furniture Refinishing & Antiquing. (McGraw-Hill Paperbacks Home Improvement Ser.). (Illus.). 112p. 1980. pap. text ed. 3.95 o.p. (ISBN 0-07-045973-8). McGraw.
Guide to Garden Shrubs & Trees. Ed. by Norman Taylor. 1965. 9.95 o.p. (ISBN 0-395-08238-2). HM.
Guide to General Toxicology. Ed. by F. Homburger & J. A. Hayes. (Karger Continuing Education Series: Vol. 5). (Illus.). x, 410p. 1983. 39.75 o.p. (ISBN 3-8055-3606-2). S Karger.
Guide to God's Minstrel: St. Francis of Assisi. Mary S. Podles & Vicki Porter. Ed. by Carol Strohecker. (Illus.). 24p. (Orig.). 1982. pap. 1.50 o.p. (ISBN 0-911886-23-0). Walters Art.
Guide to Golf Courses Britain, '88. Date not set. (ISBN 0-86145-774-9, Pub. by Auto Assn England). Salem Hse Pubs.
Guide to Graduate Business Schools. 5th. ed. Eugene Miller. 752p. 1986. pap. 12.95 o.p. (ISBN 0-8120-3650-6). Barron.
Guide to Graduate Business Schools. 4th ed. Ed. by Eugene Miller. 1984. pap. 12.95 o.p. (ISBN 0-8120-2770-1). Barron.
Guide to Graduate Education in Speech-Language Pathology & Audiology, 1985. 276p. 1985. 35.00 o.p. (ISBN 0-910329-20-6); manual avail. o.p. Am Speech Lang Hearing.
Guide to Great Resorts of the World. Steven B. Stern. (Illus.). 256p. 1985. 23.95 o.p. (ISBN 0-13-369711-8); pap. 14.95 o.p. (ISBN 0-13-369703-7). P-H.
Guide to Greece. Peter Sheldon. (American Express Pocket Guides Ser.). (Illus.). 1983. 7.95 o.p. (ISBN 0-671-45373-4). S&S.
Guide to Ham Radio. Larry Kahaner. 48p. 1978. pap. 4.95 o.p. (ISBN 0-88006-016-6, BK 7321). Wayne Green Ent.
Guide to Hand Lettering. 2nd ed. Mario G. Semere. (Illus.). 208p. 1977. pap. text ed. 16.95 o.p. (ISBN 0-8403-1780-8). Kendall-Hunt.
Guide to Hindu Religion. David J. Dell et al. 1981. lib. bdg. 47.00 o.p. (ISBN 0-8161-7903-4, Hall Reference). G K Hall.
Guide to Historical Method. Gilbert J. Garraghan. Ed. by Jean Delanglez. LC 73-13415. 482p. 1974. Repr. of 1946 ed. lib. bdg. 31.00x o.p. (ISBN 0-8371-7132-6, GAHM). Greenwood.
Guide to Hollywood & Beverly Hills: The Best Driving Tours, Walks, Restaurants, Homes, Shopping, Sights & Architecture. Charles Lockwood. LC 83-14341. 1984. pap. 7.95 o.p. (ISBN 0-517-55036-9). Crown.
Guide to Homebuilts. 9th ed. Peter M. Bowers. (Illus.). 224p. 1984. 17.95 o.p. (ISBN 0-8306-0364-6, 2364). TAB Bks.
Guide to Hospital Management of Injuries from Exposure to or Involving Ionizing Radiation. 41p. 1984. pap. 7.50 o.p. (ISBN 0-89970-251-1, OP-335). AMA.
Guide to Hungarian Studies, 2 vols. Elemer Bako. LC 79-152422. (Bibliographical Ser.: No. 52). 1218p. 1973. PLB 45.00x o.p. (ISBN 0-8179-2521-X). Hoover Inst Pr.
Guide to Hunting in Texas. John Wootters. LC 79-19642. (Illus.). 128p. (Orig.). 1979. pap. 9.95x o.p. (ISBN 0-88415-369-X, Lone Star Bks). Gulf Pub.
Guide to Income Tax Preparation: 1988 Edition. Warren H. Esanu et al. 640p. (Orig.). 1987. pap. 9.95 o.p. (ISBN 0-89043-096-9). Consumer Reports.
Guide to Independent Secondary Schools 1986-87. 7th ed. LC 80-645111. (Peterson's Annual Guides Ser). 1271p. (Orig.). 1986. pap. 15.95 o.p. (ISBN 0-87866-466-1). Petersons Guides.
Guide to Independent Secondary Schools 1987-88. 8th ed. LC 80-645111. (Annual Guides Ser.). 1290p. (Orig.). 1987. pap. 17.95 o.p. (ISBN 0-87866-491-2); lib. bdg. 22.95 o.p. (ISBN 0-87866-658-3). Petersons Guides.
Guide to Independent Secondary Schools 1984-85. 5th ed. Ed. by Rebecca A. Shepherd & Joan H. Hunter. (Peterson's Annual Guides Ser.). 1050p. 1984. pap. 13.95 o.p. (ISBN 0-87866-258-8). Petersons Guides.
Guide to Infectious Diseases of Mice & Rats. National Research Council. 370p. 1988. text ed. 40.00x o.p. (ISBN 0-309-03794-8). Natl Acad Pr.
Guide to International Congress Reports in Musicology, 1900-1975. John Tyrrell & Rosemary Wise. LC 77-83364. 350p. 1979. lib. bdg. 55.00 o.p. (ISBN 0-8240-9839-0). Garland Pub.
Guide to INTERPOL: The International Criminal Police Organization in the United States. 32p. 1987. pap. text ed. 8.00 o.p. (ISBN 0-87364-416-6). Paladin Pr.
Guide to Ireland. Date not set. (ISBN 0-905522-71-0). Salem Hse Pubs.
Guide to Jane Austen. Michael Hardwick. 228p. 1982. pap. 6.95 o.s.i. (ISBN 0-684-17652-1, ScribT). Scribner.
Guide to Landscape & Lawn Care. (McGraw-Hill Paperbacks Home Improvement Ser.). (Illus.). 112p. 1980. pap. text ed. 3.95 o.p. (ISBN 0-07-045972-X). McGraw.
Guide to Language & Study Skills, for College Students of English As a Second Language. McChesney et al. 1977. pap. text ed. (ISBN 0-13-370452-1). P-H.
Guide to Legal Research with 1966 Supplement. Erwin C. Surrency et al. LC 59-14272. 128p. (Orig.). 1959. pap. 6.00 o.p. (ISBN 0-379-00111-X). Oceana.
Guide to Legislative Leadership. Lucinda Simon. 52p. 1981. 5.00 o.s.i. (ISBN 1-55516-715-2). Natl Conf State Legis.
Guide to Life Insurance. Robert B. Brown. 1981. 15.00 o.p. (ISBN 0-686-31055-1, 29121). Rough Notes.
Guide to London Keep-Fit Clubs & Dance Centres. Debbie Thompson. 124p. pap. cancelled o.s.i. (ISBN 0-7045-0531-2, Pub. by Gower Pub England). Gower Pub Co.
Guide to Managing Information with Your Personal Computer. Beverly Hunter et al. (Illus.). 224p. 1985. 14.95 o.p. (ISBN 0-673-15945-0). Scott F.
Guide to Marine Photography. Peter R. Smyth. (Illus.). 144p. 1974. 12.50 o.p. (ISBN 0-393-03182-9). Norton.
Guide to Mars. Patrick Moore. (Illus.). 1978. 14.95 o.p. (ISBN 0-393-06432-8). Norton.
Guide to Maryland Negligence Cases. Charles O. Fisher & Richard C. Murray. 449p. 1982. 30.00x o.p. (ISBN 0-87215-472-6). Michie Co.
Guide to Materials about Public Aid to Religious Schools. Jim Buchanan. (Public Administration Ser.: Bibliography P 1621). 1985. pap. 3.75 o.p. (ISBN 0-89028-291-9). Vance Biblios.
Guide to Meeting Reading Competency Requirements: Effective Diagnosis & Correction of Difficulties. Donald C. Cushenbery. LC 81-9524. 264p. 1981. text ed. 17.50x o.p. (ISBN 0-13-370353-3, Parker). P-H.
Guide to Merit Systems Protection Board Law & Practice. 5th ed. Peter B. Broida. 1500p. 1988. pap. 85.00 o.p. (ISBN 0-9615053-4-6). Dewey Pubns.
Guide to Metrication. M. J. Jones. 1969. pap. text ed. 7.00 o.p. (ISBN 0-08-006539-2). Pergamon.
Guide to Microforms in Print 1986: Author-Title Incorporating International Microforms in Print. 1986. lib. bdg. 224.50x o.p. (ISBN 0-88736-068-8). Meckler Corp.
Guide to Microforms in Print, 1988. 1988. lib. bdg. 149.50x o.p. (ISBN 0-88736-280-X). Meckler Corp.
Guide to Military Installations. Dan Cragg. 416p. 1983. pap. 14.95 o.p. (ISBN 0-8117-2169-8). Stackpole.
Guide to Mobilizing Ethnic Minority Communities for Drug Abuse Prevention. (DHHS Publication ADM: No. 86-1465). 45p. 1986. pap. 1.50 o.p. (ISBN 0-318-21636-1, S/N 017-024-01301-3). USGPO.
Guide to Municipal Official Statements. Joseph C. Daley. 478p. 1980. 75.00 o.p. (ISBN 0-15-100026-3, H39824, Pub. by Law & Business). HarbraceJ.
Guide to Music for the Church Year. 4th ed. 1974. 4.95 o.p. (ISBN 0-8066-0930-3, 11-9195, Augsburg). Augsburg Fortress.
Guide to Myth & Religion in European Painting 1270-1700. Satia Bernen & Robert Bernen. LC 72-96070. 288p. 1973. 8.95 o.p. (ISBN 0-8076-0683-9); pap. 4.95 o.p. (ISBN 0-8076-0682-0). Braziller.
Guide to Napkin Folding. James A. Ginders. 1983. pap. 13.95 o.p. (ISBN 0-8436-2140-0). Van Nos Reinhold.
Guide to National Practices in Western Europe. Parkland Research Staff. 224p. 1983. 28.95 o.p. (ISBN 0-685-88894-0). Van Nos Reinhold.
Guide to Neurological & Neurosurgical Nursing. Ed. by Mariah Snyder. LC 82-17402. 613p. 1983. 29.95 o.p. (ISBN 0-471-09835-3, Pub. by Wiley Med). Wiley.
Guide to North American Waterfowl. Paul A. Johnsgard. LC 78-20612. (Midland Bks: No. 291). (Illus.). 272p. 1979. 15.95x o.p. (ISBN 0-253-12789-0); pap. 7.95 o.p. (ISBN 0-253-20291-4). Ind U Pr.
Guide to North Carolina Historical Highway Markers. Jerry Cashion. (Illus.). x, 262p. 1979. pap. 3.00 o.s.i. (ISBN 0-86526-079-6). NC Archives.
Guide to Nursing Management. 2nd ed. Ann Marriner. (Illus.). 288p. 1984. pap. text ed. 19.95 o.p. (ISBN 0-8016-3157-2). Mosby.
Guide to Opera & Dance on Videocassette. Robert Levine & Consumer Reports Books Editors. (Illus.). 256p. 1989. pap. 14.95 o.p. (ISBN 0-89043-261-9). Consumer Reports.
Guide to Operational Research. 3rd ed. Walter E. Duckworth et al. 1977. 12.95 o.p. (ISBN 0-412-13500-0, NO. 6092, Pub. by Chapman & Hall). Routledge Chapman & Hall.
Guide to Oral Interpretation: Solo & Group Performance. 2nd ed. Louise M. Scrivner & Danny R. Robinette. 270p. 1980. pap. text ed. (ISBN 0-02-408400-X). Macmillan.
Guide to Organizing a Health Care Fiscal Services Division with Job Descriptions for Key Functions. 2nd ed. Russell A. Caruana. 94p. 1981. pap. 8.50 o.p. (ISBN 0-930228-13-8). Healthcare Fin Man Assn.
Guide to Osterley Park House. John Hardy. (Illus.). 80p. 1985. 2.95 o.p. (ISBN 0-948107-14-6, Pub. by Victoria & Albert Mus UK). Faber & Faber.
Guide to Owl Watching in North America. Donald S. Heintzelman. LC 84-13067. (Illus.). 144p. (Orig.). 1984. pap. 8.95 o.p. (ISBN 0-8329-0361-2, Pub. by Winchester Pr). New Century.
Guide to Packaged Systems. R. V. Head. LC 73-148504. 116p. 1971. pap. 13.50 o.p. (ISBN 0-471-36600-5). Krieger.
Guide to Pattaya & Southern Thailand. Steve Van Beek. (Thailand Area Guides Ser.: Vol. 1). (Illus.). 150p. (Orig.). 1981. pap. 4.95 o.p. (ISBN 962-7035-05-X, Pub. by Hong Kong Pub Co Ltd). C E Tuttle.
Guide to PC & MS DOS. Alan Hoenig. (Microcomputer Bookshelf Ser.). 1985. pap. write for info. o.p. (ISBN 0-673-39103-5). Scott F.
Guide to Pennsylvania Politics. Edward F. Cooke & G. Edward Janosik. LC 79-14132. (Illus.). 1980. Repr. of 1957 ed. lib. bdg. 35.00x o.p. (ISBN 0-313-21994-X, COGP). Greenwood.
Guide to Personal Risk Taking. Richard E. Byrd. (AMACOM Executive Books). 1978. pap. 7.95 o.p. (ISBN 0-8144-7505-1). AMACOM.
Guide to Philosophy. Cyril E. Joad. LC 57-2470. lib. bdg. 16.50x o.p. (ISBN 0-88307-158-4). Gannon.
Guide to Photo Equipment You Can Make, Vol. 1. PhotoGraphic Magazine Editors & Parry C. Yob. LC 73-82539. (Photography How-to Ser.). (Illus.). 80p. (Orig.). 1973. pap. 3.95 o.p. (ISBN 0-8227-0020-4). Petersen Pub.
Guide to Planning Alcoholism Treatment Programs. Dixie P. McGough & Margaret H. Hindman. 100p. 1986. pap. 2.25 o.p. (ISBN 0-318-20114-3, S/N 017-024-01277-7). USGPO.
Guide to Planning for Manpower Development. Ed. by Stane Mozina. (ICPE Training Ser.). 67p. 1984. pap. 10.00x o.p. (ISBN 92-9038-403-4, Pub. by Intl Ctr Pub Ent Yugoslavia). Kumarian Pr.
Guide to Planning the Farm Estate: With Checklists & Forms. 2nd ed. Paul Douglass. (IBP Ser. in Estate Planning & Administration). 1979. text ed. 39.50 o.p. (ISBN 0-87624-172-0, Inst Busn Plan). P-H.
Guide to Planning the Farm Estate, with Checklists & Forms. Paul Douglass. LC 78-52430. (Estate Planning & Administration Ser.). 1978. 29.95 o.p. (ISBN 0-87624-171-2, Inst Busn Plan). P-H.
Guide to Plastics. C. A. Redfarn. (Illus.). 128p. 1958. (ISBN 0-8022-1316-2). Philos Lib.

Guide to Playing the Scrabble Brand Crossword Game: How to Improve Your Skills & Strategies. Gyles Brandreth. 192p. 1985. pap. 6.95 o.p. (ISBN 0-671-50652-8, Fireside). S&S.
Guide to Post-Cranial Bones of East African Animals: Mrs. Walker's Bone Book. Rikki Walker. (Illus.). 285p. text ed. 34.95 o.p. (ISBN 0-86542-321-0). Blackwell Sci.
Guide to Postal Exam. Corey. (Illus.). 144p. 1980. pap. text ed. 9.95 o.p. (ISBN 0-8359-2639-7, Reston). P-H.
Guide to Practical Pastoring. C. Sumner Wemp. LC 82-12562. 1982. 15.95 o.p. (ISBN 0-8407-5271-7). Nelson.
Guide to Practical Radio Chemistry, Vol. 1. A. N. Nesmeyanov. 312p. 1984. 9.00 o.p. (ISBN 0-8285-2887-X, Pub. by Mir Pubs USSR). Imported Pubns.
Guide to Practical Radio Chemistry, Vol. 2. A. N. Nesmeyanov. 446p. 1984. 9.00 o.p. (ISBN 0-8285-2888-8, Pub. by Mir Pubs USSR). Imported Pubns.
Guide to Pregnancy & Childbirth. William G. Birch. (Illus.). 1986. 2.99 o.p. (ISBN 0-317-39371-5). Budlong.
Guide to Prehistoric Ruins of the Southwest. Norman T. Oppelt. LC 81-5156. 200p. (Orig.). 1981. pap. 8.95 o.p. (ISBN 0-87108-587-9). Pruett.
Guide to Private Schools of the Northeast. Ruth Alden. 250p. (Orig.). 1988. pap. 11.95 o.p. (ISBN 0-937359-41-6). HDL Pubs.
Guide to Professional Benefit Plan Management & Administration. Lee F. Jost & C. Bruce Sutherland. 405p. (Orig.). 1980. pap. 35.00 o.p. (ISBN 0-89154-096-2). Intl Found Employ.
Guide to Professional Organizations for Teachers of Language & Literature. Joseph Gibaldi & Walter S. Achtert. vii, 62p. 1978. pap. 5.00x o.p. (ISBN 0-87352-125-0, W325). Modern Lang.
Guide to Professional Services in Speech-Language Pathology & Audiology 1983-84. 208p. 1983. pap. text ed. 28.00 o.p. (ISBN 0-910329-11-7). Am Speech Lang Hearing.
Guide to Programming in Applesoft. 3rd ed. Bruce Presley. 1987. softcover 22.50 o.p. (ISBN 0-931717-28-0); tchr's. guide & resource package 29.95 o.p. (ISBN 0-931717-30-2); pap. 19.95 o.p.; diskette 12.95 o.p. (ISBN 0-931717-31-0). Lawrenceville Pr.
Guide to Programming in Applesoft. 3rd ed. Bruce Presley. 1986. 25.95 o.p. (ISBN 0-931717-16-7). Lawrenceville Pr.
Guide to Prose Fiction in the Tatler & the Spectator. James E. Evans & John E. Wall. LC 76-24751. (Reference Library of the Humanities Ser.: Vol. 71). 1977. lib. bdg. 61.00 o.p. (ISBN 0-8240-9926-5). Garland Pub.
Guide to Radiographic Evaluation of Discontinuities in Aluminum Casting. General Dynamics Staff. 143p. 1973. 33.75 o.p. (ISBN 0-318-17204-6, 212). Am Soc Nondestructive.
Guide to Rapid Revision. 3rd ed. Daniel D. Pearlman et al. 128p. 1984. pap. text ed. write for info. wkbk. o.p. (ISBN 0-02-393250-3). Macmillan.
Guide to Recent Criminal Legislation. C. F. Shoolbred. LC 68-22498. 1968. text ed. 16.25 o.p. (ISBN 0-08-012895-5); pap. 7.00 o.p. (ISBN 0-08-012894-7). Pergamon.
Guide to Recommended Country Inns of New England. 8th, rev. & exp. ed. Elizabeth Squier. 384p. 1983. pap. 7.95 o.p. (ISBN 0-87106-976-8). Globe Pequot.
Guide to Recommended Country Inns of the Rocky Mountain Region (Colorado, Utah, Idaho, Montana, Nevada & Wyoming) Doris Kennedy. LC 87-8691. (Guide to the Recommended Country Inn Ser.). (Illus.). 300p. (Orig.). 1987. pap. 9.95 o.s.i. (ISBN 0-87106-816-8). Globe Pequot.
Guide to Recommended Country Inns of the West Coast, (California, Oregon, Washington) Julianne Belote. LC 86-14977. (Country Inn Ser.). (Illus.). 408p. (Orig.). 1986. pap. 10.95 o.s.i. (ISBN 0-87106-810-9). Globe Pequot.
Guide to Record Collecting. Jerry Osborne. LC 79-1022. 1979. pap. 5.95 o.p. (ISBN 0-89019-068-2). Norwalk Pr.
Guide to Reference Material: Science & Technology, Vol. 1. 4th ed. A. J. Walford. 650p. 1980. 60.00 o.p. (L611-8). ALA.
Guide to Research Writing. 3rd ed. Griffith T. Pugh. 1968. pap. 6.50 o.p. (ISBN 0-395-05079-0). HM.
Guide to Reviews of Books from & about Hispanic America 1981. Antonio Mates. 2285p. 1983. 110.00 o.p. (ISBN 0-87917-087-5). Ethridge.
Guide to Reviews of Books from & about Hispanic America, 1982. Antonio Matos. LC 66-96537. 1985. 110.00 o.p. (ISBN 0-87917-089-1). Ethridge.
Guide to Reviews of Books from & about Hispanic America, 1980. Ed. by Antonio Matos. LC 66-96537. 1780p. 1982. 90.00 o.p. (ISBN 0-87917-084-0). Ethridge.
Guide to Reviews of Books from & About Hispanic America, 1975: Guia a las Resenas de Libros de y Sobre Hispanoamerica, 1975. Antonio Matos. LC 66-96537. 1977. 55.00 o.p. (ISBN 0-87917-063-8). Ethridge.
Guide to Reviews of Books from & About Hispanic America, 1979: Guia a las Resenas de Libros de y Sobre Hispanoamerica, 1979. Antonio Matos. LC 66-96537. 1981. 90.00 o.p. (ISBN 0-87917-080-8). Ethridge.
Guide to Reviews of Books from & About Hispanic America, 1978: Guia a las Resenas de Libros de y sobre Hispanoamerica, 1978. Antonio Matos. LC 66-96537. 1980. 80.00 o.p. (ISBN 0-87917-073-5). Ethridge.
Guide to Reviews of Books from & About Hispanic America, 1974: Guia a las Resenas de Libros de y Sobre Hispanoamerica, 1974. Antonio Matos. LC 66-96537. (Eng. & Span.). 1977. 55.00 o.p. (ISBN 0-87917-060-3). Ethridge.
Guide to Reviews of Books From & About Hispanic America, 1977: Guia a las resenas de libros de y sobre Hispanoamerica, 1977. Antonio Matos. LC 66-96537. 1981. 10.00 o.p. (ISBN 0-87917-071-9). Ethridge.
Guide to Reviews of Books from & About Hispanic America, 1972: Guia a las Resenas De Libros De y Sobre Hispanoamerica, 1972. Ed. by Antonio Matos. LC 66-96537. 924p. (Eng. & Span.). 1976. 45.00 o.p. (ISBN 0-87917-044-1). Ethridge.
Guide to Reviews of Books from & About Hispanic America 1973: Guia a las Resenas De Libros De y Sobre Hispanoamerica 1973. Ed. by Antonio Matos. LC 66-96537. 980p. 1976. 45.00 o.p. (ISBN 0-87917-046-8). Ethridge.
Guide to Reviews of Books from & About Hispanic America, 1976: Guia a las Resenas de Libros de y sobre Hispanoamerica. Ed. by Antonio Matos. LC 66-96537. 1978. 65.00 o.p. (ISBN 0-87917-065-4). Ethridge.
Guide to Riding & Horse Care. Elaine Knox-Thompson & Suzanne Dickens. (Illus.). 144p. 1985. 16.95 o.s.i. (ISBN 0-87605-852-7). Howell Bk.
Guide to Russian Silver Hallmarks. Paul L. Paulson. (Illus.). pap. 25.00 o.s.i. (ISBN 0-317-55084-5). Apollo.
Guide to Safety & Health in Dock Work. x, 287p. 1976. 22.75 o.p. (ISBN 92-2-101081-3). Intl Labour Office.
Guide to Selected Microform Series & Their Indexes. Peter Olevnik. (Occasional Papers: No. 106). 63p. 1973. pap. 2.00 o.p. (ISBN 0-317-58890-7). U of Ill Lib Info Sci.
Guide to Services Selection in Low Rise Buildings. Jim Alder. (Illus.). 160p. 1983. 32.50 o.s.i. (ISBN 0-89397-153-7). Nichols Pub.
Guide to Seventeenth-Century American Poetry: A Reference Guide. William J. Scheick & Joella Doggett. 1978. lib. bdg. 21.00 o.p. (ISBN 0-8161-7983-2, Hall Reference). G K Hall.
Guide to Seventy-Five Tests for Special Education. 1983. pap. 22.95 o.p. (ISBN 0-8224-3583-7). D S Lake Pubs.
Guide to Shakespeare's Best Plays. Ed. by Valerie Levy. 960p. 1983. pap. 9.95 o.p. (ISBN 0-671-45871-X). Monarch Pr.
Guide to Shark Repellant & Golden Parachute Clauses. Ed. by Robert H. Winter et al. 1983. 75.00 o.p. (ISBN 0-15-100027-1, H42868, Pub. by Law & Business). HarBraceJ.
Guide to Small Business Management. A. Thomas Hollingsworth & Herbert H. Hand. 1979. 27.95x o.p. (ISBN 0-7216-4744-8). Dryden Pr.
Guide to Starting & Operating a Successful Travel Agency. Laurence Stevens. LC 83-61822. (Travel Management Library). 432p. 1984. 29.95 o.p. (ISBN 0-916032-21-3). Delmar.
Guide to State Legislative Materials. 3rd ed. Mary L. Fisher. LC 85-19261. (American Association of Law Libraries Publications Ser.: No. 15). ix, 327p. 1985. loose-leaf 32.50x o.p. (ISBN 0-8377-0123-6). Rothman.
Guide to Strategic Planning. Benton Gup. (McGraw-Hill Series in Finance). (Illus.). 1980. text ed. 25.95 o.p. (ISBN 0-07-025210-6). McGraw.
Guide to Structured COBOL with Efficiency Techniques & Special Algorithms. Pacifico A. Lim. (Data Processing Ser.). 272p. 1980. 27.95 o.p. (ISBN 0-442-24585-8). Van Nos Reinhold.
Guide to Structured COBOL with Efficiency Techniques & Special Algorithms. Pacifico A. Lim. 286p. 1982. pap. 15.95 o.p. (ISBN 0-442-24589-0). Van Nos Reinhold.
Guide to Studies in Spanish American Literature. Nina L. Weisinger. LC 78-18646. (Illus.). 120p. 1972. Repr. of 1940 ed. lib. bdg. 35.00x o.p. (ISBN 0-8371-6010-3, WESA). Greenwood.
Guide to Successful Consulting with Forms, Letters, & Checklists. Steven C. Stryker. (Illus.). 288p. 1984. 31.95 o.p. (ISBN 0-13-371104-8). P-H.
Guide to Successful Phonathons. rev. 1984 ed. Compiled by Nelson Cover. 95p. 1984. 16.50 o.p. (ISBN 0-89964-227-6). Coun Adv & Supp Ed.
Guide to Summer Camps & Summer Schools. 24th ed. Ed. by Porter Sargent Staff. (Handbook Ser.). (Illus.). 464p. 1985. 23.00 o.s.i. (ISBN 0-87558-113-7); pap. 18.00 o.s.i. (ISBN 0-87558-114-5). Porter Sargent.
Guide to the Addiction Severity Index: Background, Administration, & Field Testing Results. Thomas A. McLellan. (DHHS Publication ADM 86-1419). 57p. 1985. pap. 3.00 o.p. (ISBN 0-318-21585-3, S/N 017-024-01308-1). USGPO.
Guide to the Analysis of Alcohols by Gas Chromatography. 2nd ed. Seaton T. Preston, Jr. & Ronald Pankratz. 1976. 35.00 o.p. (ISBN 0-913106-06-2). PolyScience.
Guide to the Analysis of Fatty Acids & Their Esters by Gas Chromatography. Seaton T. Preston, Jr. 1971. spiral bdg 35.00 o.p. (ISBN 0-913106-08-9). PolyScience.
Guide to the Analysis of Hydro-Carbons by Gas Chromatography. 2nd ed. Seaton T. Preston, Jr. 1976. spiral bdg 45.00 o.p. (ISBN 0-913106-02-X). PolyScience.
Guide to the Analysis of Ketones & Aldehydes by Gas Chromatography. Seaton T. Preston, Jr. & Ronald E. Pankratz. 196p. (Orig.). 1986. pap. 35.00 o.p. (ISBN 0-913106-27-5). PolyScience.
Guide to the Analysis of Phenols by Gas Chromatography. Seaton T. Preston, Jr. & Ronald Pankratz. 1978. spiral bdg 25.00 o.p. (ISBN 0-913106-04-6). PolyScience.
Guide to the Antique Shops of Britain 1987. Ed. by R. Ferguson & C. Adams. 1000p. 1988. 25.00 o.p. (ISBN 1-85149-004-3). Antique Collect.
Guide to the Antique Shops of Britain 1988. Ed. by Rosemary Ferguson & Carol Adams. 1000p. 1987. 25.00 o.p. (ISBN 1-85149-045-0). Antique Collect.
Guide to the Antique Shops of Britain, 1982. Ed. by Rosemary Ferguson & Stella King. 1116p. 1981. 16.00 o.p. (ISBN 0-907462-03-0). Antique Collect.
Guide to the Antique Shops of Great Britain 1986. Ferguson & Adams. (Illus.). 1985. 16.00 o.p. (ISBN 0-907462-81-2). Antique Collect.
Guide to the Antique Shops of Great Britain 1985. Ed. by Rosemary Ferguson & Stella King. (Illus.). 1984. 16.00 o.p. (ISBN 0-907462-67-7). Antique Collect.
Guide to the Architecture of Metro Phoenix. American Institute of Architects Central Arizona Chapter Staff. (Illus.). 200p. 1986. pap. 12.00 o.p. (ISBN 0-87905-224-4). Gibbs Smith Pub.
Guide to the Archives, Vol. IV. Maria R. Astuni. 44p. 1981. 9.95 o.s.i. (ISBN 0-913256-56-0, 5.4). Ctr Migration.
Guide to the Archives, Vol. II. Olha Della Cava. 38p. 1977. 9.95 o.s.i. (ISBN 0-913256-31-5, 5.2). Ctr Migration.
Guide to the Archives of the Archdiocese of Boston. James O'Toole. LC 80-8989. 300p. 1981. lib. bdg. 61.00 o.p. (ISBN 0-8240-9359-3). Garland Pub.
Guide to the Atlantic Monthly Contributors' Club. George Monteiro & Philip Eppard. (Reference Bks.). 1983. lib. bdg. 40.50 o.s.i. (ISBN 0-8161-8492-5, Hall Reference). G K Hall.
Guide to the Best Buys in Package Tours. Ed. by Paige Palmer. LC 85-29724. 48p. 1986. pap. 3.95 o.p. (ISBN 0-87576-124-0). Pilot Bks.
Guide to the Cataloged Collections in the Manuscript Department of the William R. Perkins Library, Duke University. Ed. by Richard C. Davis & Linda A. Miller. LC 79-28688. 1005p. 1980. lib. bdg. 31.75 o.p. (ISBN 0-87436-299-7). ABC-Clio.
Guide to the Cruise Vacation. rev. ed. Steven B. Stern. LC 84-8411. 224p. 1984. 16.95 o.p. (ISBN 0-13-369331-7); pap. 8.95 o.p. (ISBN 0-13-369323-6). P-H.
Guide to the Defense Contracting Regulation for Small Business, Small Disadvantaged Business, Women-Owned Small Business. 2nd ed. 57p. 1985. pap. 2.25 o.p. (ISBN 0-318-21837-2, S/N 008-000-00411-1). USGPO.
Guide to the East Slavonic Languages: Guide to the Slavonic Languages, Part 3. 3rd rev. ed. Reginald G. De Bray. 254p. 1980. 25.95 o.p. (ISBN 0-89357-062-1). Slavica.
Guide to the Eastern Adirondacks: Lake George, Pharaoh Lake & Beyond. Barbara McMartin. LC 81-7955. (Illus.). 208p. 1981. pap. 8.95 o.p. (ISBN 0-935272-16-X). ADK Mtn Club.
Guide to the Falkland Islands & Their Natural History. Ian J. Strange. (Illus.). 160p. 1987. 29.95 o.p. (ISBN 0-87052-437-2). Hippocrene Bks.
Guide to the Federal Service Labor-Management Relations Statute. (Illus.). 76p. 1987. pap. 2.00 o.p. (ISBN 0-318-24018-1, 063-000-00032-9). USGPO.
Guide to the Federal Service Labor-Management Statute. rev. ed. (FLRA Doc. 1213). 54p. 1984. pap. 2.00 o.p. (ISBN 0-318-18769-8, S/N 063-000-00021-3). USGPO.
Guide to the Flags of the World. Mauro Talocci. Ed. by Whitney Smith. LC 82-3528. (Illus.). 271p. 1982. 17.50 o.p. (ISBN 0-688-01103-9). Morrow.
Guide to the General Conduct of Ethnographic Research. Roy F. Ellen. (Research Methods Social Anthropology Ser.: No. 1). 1984. 57.00 o.p. (ISBN 0-12-237180-1). Acad Pr.
Guide to the History of Psychology. John D. Lawry. (Quality Paperback Ser.: No. 361). 128p. 1981. pap. text ed. 6.95 o.p. (ISBN 0-8226-0361-6). Littlefield.
Guide to the Literature of the Sugar Industry. M. Schalit. 1970. 26.50 o.p. (ISBN 0-444-40839-8). Elsevier.
Guide to the Local Records in the South Carolina Archives. South Carolina Department of Archives & History Staff. 325p. 1988. text ed. 14.95x o.p. (ISBN 0-87249-607-4). U of SC Pr.
Guide to the Maintenance Repair & Alteration of Historic Buildings. Frederick A. Stahl. 1984. 26.95 o.p. (ISBN 0-442-28105-6). Van Nos Reinhold.
Guide to the Manuscript Collection of the Tamiment Library. Dorothy T. Swanson. LC 76-52595. (Reference Library of Social Science: Vol. 49). (Illus.). 1977. lib. bdg. 24.00 o.p. (ISBN 0-8240-9859-5). Garland Pub.
Guide to the Manuscript Collections of the Bancroft Library, Vols. 1 & 2. Ed. by George P. Hammond. Incl. Vol. I. Pacific & Western Manuscripts (Except California) Ed. by Dale L. Morgan & George P. Hammond. 1963. o.p. (ISBN 0-520-00882-0); Vol. II. Mexican & Central American Manuscripts. Ed. by George P. Hammond. 1973. 50.00x (ISBN 0-520-01991-1). U of Cal Pr.
Guide to the Manuscripts in the National Maritime Museum: The Personal Collections, Vol. 1. Ed. by R. J. Knight. 258p. 1977. lib. bdg. 37.00x o.p. (ISBN 0-7201-0714-8). Mansell.
Guide to the Mental Health Act, 1983. Robert Bluglass. LC 83-7635. 1983. pap. text ed. 21.75 o.p. (ISBN 0-443-03017-0). Churchill.
Guide to the National Electrical Code, 1984. rev., 3rd ed. Thomas L. Harman. (Illus.). 400p. 1984. pap. text ed. 37.33 o.p. (ISBN 0-13-370420-3). P-H.
Guide to the Official Publications of Other American Republics: Washington, 1945-48, 2 vols. U. S. Library of Congress Staff. Repr. of 1948 ed. Set. 90.00 o.p. (ISBN 0-384-63000-6). Johnson Repr.
Guide to the Pianist's Repertoire. Maurice Hinson. Ed. by Irwin Freundlich. LC 72-75983. 880p. 1973. 32.50x o.p. (ISBN 0-253-32700-8). Ind U Pr.
Guide to the Queen Charlotte Islands. 8th, rev. ed. Neil G. Carey. LC 81-12794. (Illus.). 1986. pap. 6.95 o.s.i. (ISBN 0-88240-252-8). Alaska Northwest.
Guide to the Radiotherapy & Oncology Department. T. Deeley. (Illus.). 116p. 1979. pap. 12.00 o.p. (ISBN 0-7236-0506-8, Pub. by John Wright UK). Butterworth.
Guide to the Recommended Country Inns of Arizona, New Mexico & Texas. Eleanor Morris. LC 87-8541. (Guide to the Recommended Country Inn Ser.). (Illus.). 312p. (Orig.). 1987. pap. 9.95 o.s.i. (ISBN 0-87106-836-2). Globe Pequot.
Guide to the Recommended Country Inns of New England. 9th, rev. ed. Elizbeth Squier. LC 73-83255. (Illus.). 444p. 1985. pap. 9.95 o.p. (ISBN 0-87106-867-2). Globe Pequot.
Guide to the Recommended Country Inns of New England, (Connecticut, Rhode Island, Massachusetts, Vermont, New Hampshire & Maine) 10th ed. Elizabeth Squier. LC 73-83253. (Voyager Book Ser.). (Illus.). 480p. 1987. pap. 10.95 o.s.i. (ISBN 0-87106-819-2). Globe Pequot.
Guide to the Recommended Country Inns of the Mid-Atlantic States & Chesapeake Region, (Delaware, Maryland, New Jersey, New York, Pennsylvania, Virginia, Washington, D. C. and West Virginia) 2nd ed. Brenda Chapin. LC 87-24. (Guide to the Recommended Country Inn Ser.). (Illus.). 300p. (Orig.). 1987. pap. 9.95 o.s.i. (ISBN 0-87106-818-4). Globe Pequot.
Guide to the Recommended Country Inns of the Midwest (Ohio, Indiana, Illinois, Missouri, Iowa, Minnesota, Wisconsin & Michigan) Bob Puhala. LC 86-31954. (Guide to the Recommended Country Inn Ser.). (Illus.). 324p. (Orig.). 1987. pap. 9.95 o.s.i. (ISBN 0-87106-814-1). Globe Pequot.

Guide to the Recommended Country Inns of the South (North Carolina, South Carolina, Georgia, Florida, Alabama, Mississippi, Louisiana, Arkansas, Kentucky & Tennessee) Sara Pitzer. LC 86-31896. (Country Inn Ser.). (Illus.). 312p. (Orig.). 1987. pap. 9.95 o.s.i. (ISBN 0-87106-812-5). Globe Pequot.

Guide to the Recommended Thrift Shops of New England: Financial Survival in the 1980s. Julie Hatfield et al. LC 81-86606. (Illus.). 518p. 1982. pap. 5.95 o.p. (ISBN 0-87106-969-5). Globe Pequot.

Guide to the Retention & Preservation of Records with Destruction Schedules. 6th ed. 1981. pap. 12.50 o.p. (ISBN 0-930228-15-4). Healthcare Fin Man Assn.

Guide to the Romanization of Standard Chinese. Yale University Library Staff. 1975. 9.50 o.p. (ISBN 0-88710-027-9). Yale Far Eastern Pubns.

Guide to the Small & Historic Lodgings of Florida. Herbert L. Hiller. LC 86-15132. (Illus.). 300p. 1986. pap. 12.95 o.p. (ISBN 0-910923-30-2). Pineapple Pr.

Guide to the Solar Corona. Donald E. Billings. 1966. 68.00 o.p. (ISBN 0-12-098550-0). Acad Pr.

Guide to the South of France. John Ardagh. (American Express Pocket Guides Ser.). (Illus.). 1983. 7.95 o.p. (ISBN 0-671-45367-X). S&S.

Guide to the South Slavonic Languages: Guide to the Slavonic Languages, Part 1. 3rd, rev. ed. Reginald G. De Bray. 399p. 1980. 26.95 o.p. (ISBN 0-89357-060-5). Slavica.

Guide to the Soviet Navy. 3rd ed. Norman Polmar. (Illus.). 768p. 1983. 36.95 o.p. (ISBN 0-87021-239-7). Naval Inst Pr.

Guide to the Stars. Hectar Macpherson. (Illus.). 160p. 1955. (ISBN 0-8022-1033-3). Philos Lib.

Guide to the Study of Animal Pysulations. James T. Janner. Date not set. write for info. o.p. U of Tenn Pr.

Guide to the Study of Electrode Kinetics. H. R. Thirsk & J. A. Harrison. 1972. 33.00 o.p. (ISBN 0-12-687750-5). Acad Pr.

Guide to the Successful Thesis & Dissertation, Vol. 19. Mauch & Birch. (Library & Informations Ser.). 256p. 1983. 25.00 o.p. (ISBN 0-8247-1800-3). Dekker.

Guide to the Use of Atlas: Standard 771-1984. 2nd ed. 302p. 1985. 31.00 o.p. (ISBN 0-471-82746-0, SHO9191). Wiley.

Guide to the Use of Books & Libraries. 4th ed. Jean K. Gates. (Illus.). 1979. text ed. 21.50 o.p. (ISBN 0-07-022986-4, C); pap. text ed. 18.95 o.p. (ISBN 0-07-022985-6). McGraw.

Guide to the Weimaraner. Gillian Burgoin. (Illus.). 198p. 1985. 22.50 o.p. (ISBN 0-85115-414-X, Pub. by Boydell & Brewer). Longwood Pub Group.

Guide to the West Slavonic Languages: Guide to the Slavonic Languages, Part 2. 3rd rev. ed. Reginald G. DeBray. 483p. 1980. 29.95 o.p. (ISBN 0-89357-061-3). Slavica.

Guide to the Works of John Dewey. Ed. by Jo Ann Boydston. LC 70-112383. (Arcturus Books Paperbacks). 413p. 1972. pap. 7.95x o.p. (ISBN 0-8093-0561-5). S Ill U Pr.

Guide to the World's Mountains. 2nd ed. Michael Kelsey. 679p. 1983. 19.95 o.p. Bradt Ent.

Guide to the Wrightsman Galleries at The Metropolitan Museum of Art. James Parker & Clare Le Corbeiller. LC 78-21154. 1979. pap. 3.95 o.p. (ISBN 0-87099-186-8). Metro Mus Art.

Guide to Thermoformed Plastic Packaging: Sales Builder-Cost Cutter. Stanley E. Farnham. LC 72-156481. 472p. 1983. 29.95 o.p. (ISBN 0-8436-1206-1). Van Nos Reinhold.

Guide to Thomas Aquinas. Josef Pieper et al. Tr. by Richard Winston & Clara Winston. 182p. 1982. Repr. of 1962 ed. lib. bdg. 20.50 o.p. (ISBN 0-374-96448-3, Octagon). Hippocrene Bks.

Guide to Track & Field Injuries. Arnd Kruger & Helmut Oberdieck. (Orig.). 1978. pap. 6.00 o.p. (ISBN 0-911520-85-6). Tafnews.

Guide to Training Needs Assessment. Ed. by Lloyd H. Stanley. (ICPE Training Ser.). 65p. 1984. pap. 10.00x o.p. (Pub. by Intl Ctr Pub Ent Yugoslavia). Kumarian Pr.

Guide to Travel Agency Accounting. M. J. Batham. LC 78-60276. 1979. 12.00 o.p. (ISBN 0-916032-05-1). Delmar.

Guide to Travel & Residence Expenses for the Multinational Executive, 1979. Travel & Living Costs Worldwide, Inc. Staff. 1978. pap. 60.00 o.p. (ISBN 0-685-66513-5). Suburban Pub CT.

Guide to Trivial Names, Trade Names & Synonyms for Substances Used in Analytical Chemistry. Ed. by H. M. Irving. 1978. pap. 35.00 o.p. (ISBN 0-08-022382-6). Pergamon.

Guide to Tuning Musical Instruments. John Meffen. (Illus.). 160p. 1983. 20.95 o.p. (ISBN 0-7153-8169-5). David & Charles.

Guide to Tutoring. Jeanette Driskell. LC 77-83053. 32p. 1977. 1.95 o.p. (ISBN 0-89301-050-2). U of Idaho Pr.

Guide to Twentieth-Century Literature in English. Ed. by Harry Blamires. 325p. 1983. 35.00 o.p. (ISBN 0-416-56180-2, NO. 4034); pap. 17.95 o.p. (ISBN 0-416-36450-0, NO. 4035). Routledge Chapman & Hall.

Guide to Two-Year Colleges 1984. 14th ed. Ed. by Kim R. Kaye. (Undergraduate Study Ser.). 376p. 1983. pap. 8.95 o.p. (ISBN 0-87866-216-2). Petersons Guides.

Guide to Two-Year Colleges 1987. 17th ed. (Peterson's Annual Guides to Undergraduate Study Ser.). 536p. (Orig.). 1986. pap. 10.95 o.p. (ISBN 0-87866-528-5). Petersons Guides.

Guide to Two-Year Colleges 1988. 18th ed. (Peterson's Annual Guides to Undergraduate Study Ser.). 620p. (Orig.). 1987. lib. bdg. 16.95 o.p. (ISBN 0-87866-648-6); pap. 11.95 o.p. (ISBN 0-87866-575-7). Petersons Guides.

Guide to Undergraduate Projective Geometry. A. F. Horadam. LC 71-110243. 1971. 80.00 o.p. (ISBN 0-08-017479-5). Pergamon.

Guide to Understanding Audit in Trusted Systems, 1987. 1987. pap. 1.50 o.p. (ISBN 0-318-23753-9, S/N 008-000-00484-6). USGPO.

Guide to U. S. Coins, 1987. Rev. ed. Charles F. French. (Illus.). 192p. 1986. pap. 4.95 o.p. (ISBN 0-671-62685-X, Fireside). S&S.

Guide to U. S. Government Scientific & Technical Resources. Rao Aluri & Judith Robinson. LC 83-14991. 259p. 1983. lib. bdg. 23.50 o.p. (ISBN 0-87287-377-3). Libs Unl.

Guide to Urban Wildlife Management. National Institute for Urban Wildlife Staff et al. 42p. 1984. 3.00 o.p. (ISBN 0-318-04276-2). Natl Inst Urban Wildlife.

Guide to Used Cars 1986. Ed. by Consumer Report Book Editors. Alex Markovich. 576p. 1986. pap. 8.00 o.p. (ISBN 0-89043-038-1). Consumer Reports.

Guide to Used Cars, 1987. Alex Markovich & Consumer Reports Books Editors. 624p. 1987. pap. 8.00 o.p. (ISBN 0-89043-081-0). Consumer Reports.

Guide to Vegetable Gardening & Food Preserving. (Home Improvement Ser.). (Illus.). 112p. 1980. pap. text ed. 3.95 o.p. (ISBN 0-07-045969-X). McGraw.

Guide to Warehouse Design, Conservation & Restoration. Coppa & Avery Consultants Staff. (Architecture Ser.: A 1370). 10p. 1985. 2.00 o.p. (ISBN 0-89028-360-5). Vance Biblios.

Guide to Welsh Literature, Vol. 2. Ed. by A. O. Jarman & G. R. Hughes. 1980. text ed. 40.00x o.p. (ISBN 0-7154-0457-1). Humanities.

Guide to West Africa. Michael Haag. (Travelaid Ser.). 256p. (Orig.). 1986. pap. 11.95 o.p. (ISBN 0-87052-244-2). Hippocrene Bks.

Guide to Western Wildlife. Buddy Mays. LC 77-22043. (Illus.). 224p. (Orig.). 1977. pap. 6.95 o.p. (ISBN 0-87701-103-6). Chronicle Bks.

Guide to Worker Productivity Experiments in the United States, 1971-1975. 186p. 1981. 17.50 o.p. Moffat Pub.

Guide to Writing & Using Printing Contracts. 24.95 o.p. (ISBN 0-318-02537-X). Print Indus Am.

Guide Yourself Through Old Age. Oren Arnold. LC 76-9712. 128p. 1976. pap. 3.50 o.p. (ISBN 0-8006-1239-6, Fortress). Augsburg Fortress.

Guidebook. Ed. by Donna Wetmore. LC 68-126162. 1982. 175.00 o.p. (ISBN 0-911790-20-9). Prog Grocers Trade.

Guidebook for Alcoholics. Drake Weston. 1964. 7.00 o.p. (ISBN 0-682-48821-6). Exposition-Phoenix.

Guidebook for International Trainers in Business & Industry: Co-Published with the American Society for Training & Development, Inc. Vincent A. Miller. 1979. 26.95 o.p. (ISBN 0-442-25392-3). Van Nos Reinhold.

Guidebook for North Carolina Registers of Deeds. rev. ed. Ed. by William A. Campbell. 109p. 1982. pap. 7.00 o.p. (ISBN 0-686-17568-9). Institute Government.

Guidebook for Speech Practice. Milton Dickens & James H. McBath. 1961. pap. text ed. 6.50 o.p. (ISBN 0-15-530031-8, HC). HarBraceJ.

Guidebook for Spiritual Friends. Barry A. Woodbridge. LC 84-51827. 96p. (Orig.). 1985. pap. 4.95 o.p. (ISBN 0-8358-0498-4). Upper Room.

Guidebook for Teaching United States History: Earliest Times to the Civil War, Pt. 1. Tedd Levy & Donna C. Krasnow. 1979. pap. text ed. 27.95 o.s.i. (ISBN 0-205-06503-1, 236503). Allyn.

Guidebook for Technology Assessment & Impact Analysis. A. R. Porter et al. LC 79-12699. (Systems Sciences & Engineering Ser.: Vol. 4). 544p. 1980. 42.50 o.p. (ISBN 0-444-00314-2, North Holland). Elsevier.

Guidebook of Franklin Mint Issues. 9th ed. Chester L. Kraus. LC 76-53857. 300p. 1982. for info. 13.95 o.s.i. (ISBN 0-87341-069-6). Krause Pubns.

Guidebook to Adventure. Jan Owen. LC 84-61640. (Illus.). 96p. 1984. pap. 17.95 o.p. (ISBN 0-13-368820-8). P-H.

Guidebook to Improved Financial Management for Small Cities & Other Governmental Units. Municipal Finance Officers Association Staff. LC 78-71709. (Illus.). 115p. 1978. 9.00 o.p. (ISBN 0-686-84362-2). Municipal.

Guidebook to Nutritional Factors in Foods. David A. Phillips. LC 79-10010. 1979. pap. 5.95 o.p. (ISBN 0-912800-71-2). Woodbridge Pr.

Guidebook to Revelations. Sylvester Hutchinson. 1977. 4.00 o.p. (ISBN 0-682-48708-2). Exposition-Phoenix.

Guidebook to the Central Llano Estacado: Friends of the Pleistocene South-Central Cell, 1983 Field Trip. Ed. by Vance T. Holliday. 165p. 1983. 7.00 o.s.i. (ISBN 0-318-17670-X, 83-2). Intl Ctr Arid & Semi-Arid.

Guided Course in English Composition. T. C. Jupp & John Milne. 1969. pap. text ed. 7.50x o.p. (ISBN 0-435-28480-0); tchr's ed. 5.50x o.p. (ISBN 0-435-28481-9). Heinemann Ed.

Guided Paragraph Writing. T. C. Jupp & John Milne. 1972. pap. text ed. 7.50x o.p. (ISBN 0-435-28491-6). Heinemann Ed.

Guided Weapons. Lee et al. (Brassey's Battlefield Weapons Systems & Technology: Vol. 8). 160p. 1983. text ed. 33.00 o.p. (ISBN 0-08-028336-5); pap. text ed. 14.25 o.p. (ISBN 0-08-028337-3). Pergamon.

Guideline for Design & Analysis of Nuclear Safety Related Earth Structures. 35p. 1983. pap. 16.00x o.p. (ISBN 0-87262-375-0, N-725). Am Soc Civil Eng.

Guidelines. Keating. 1983. text ed. write for info. o.p. (ISBN 0-02-362300-4). Macmillan.

Guidelines for Ad Hoc Collaboration Agreements Between Consulting Firms. American Consulting Engineers Council Staff. 54p. 1977. 15.00 o.p. (ISBN 0-686-48326-X). Am Consul Eng.

Guidelines for Childrens Sports. 1979. 4.15x o.p. (ISBN 0-88314-093-4). AAHPERD.

Guidelines for Computer Managers. National Computing Centre, Ltd. Staff. 265p. (Orig.). 1981. pap. 40.00x o.s.i. (ISBN 0-85012-248-1). Intl Pubns Serv.

Guidelines for Day Care Service. LC 74-181780. 32p. 1972. pap. 3.25 o.p. (ISBN 0-87868-091-8, 0918). Child Welfare.

Guidelines for Handling Library Orders for Serials & Periodicals. American Library Association, Resources & Technical Division, Bookdealer-Library Relations Committee. LC 74-11137. (Acquisitions Guidelines: No. 2). 16p. 1974. pap. text ed. 3.00x o.p. (ISBN 0-8389-3158-8). ALA.

Guidelines for Interpretive Building Design. 68p. 3.00 o.p. (ISBN 0-317-35025-0). Natl Audubon.

Guidelines for Living. Harold J. Sala. (Direction Bks.). 80p. (Orig.). 1982. pap. 2.95 o.p. (ISBN 0-8010-8219-6). Baker Bk.

Guidelines for Medial & Marginal Access Control on Major Roadways. (National Cooperative Highway Research Program Report). 147p. 1970. 6.20 o.p. (ISBN 0-309-01880-3). Transport Res Bd.

Guidelines for Perinatal Care. American Academy of Pediatrics, Committee on Fetus & Newborn. LC 83-71148. 288p. 1983. pap. text ed. 25.00 o.p. (ISBN 0-910761-04-3). AM Acad Pediat.

Guidelines for Pharm.D Programs. Conference of U.S. Schools of Pharmacy, Oct. 1975. 5.00 o.p. (ISBN 0-937526-05-3). AACP Alexandria.

Guidelines for Predicting Crop Water Requirements. Rev. ed. (Irrigation & Drainage Papers: No. 24). (Illus.). 156p. (Eng., Fr. & Span.). 1977. pap. 15.75 o.p. (ISBN 92-5-100279-7, F993, FAO). UNIPUB.

Guidelines for Preparation of the Uniform Franchise Offering Circular & Related Documents. Midwest Securities Commissioners Association. Date not set. 30.00 o.s.i. (ISBN 0-317-66122-1). Intl Franchise Assn.

Guidelines for Prescription Pricing Systems. D. C. Huffman. 34p. 1983. pap. 12.00 o.s.i. (ISBN 0-910769-13-3). Am Coll Apothecaries.

Guidelines for Research in Business Communication. Ed. by C. Glenn Pearce et al. 1977. pap. 6.00 o.p. (ISBN 0-931874-05-X). Assn Busn Comm.

Guidelines for Selected Personnel Practices in Catholic Schools II. 58p. 1977. 4.55 o.p. (ISBN 0-686-29246-4). Natl Cath Educ.

Guidelines for Selecting Bias-Free Textbooks & Storybooks. Council on Interracial Books for Children, Inc. Staff. LC 80-165903. 105p. 1980. pap. 7.95 o.s.i. (ISBN 0-930040-33-3). CIBC.

Guidelines for Selecting Bias-Free Textbooks & Storybooks. Council on Interracial Books for Children, Inc. Staff. (Orig.). 1980. pap. 7.95 o.p. Friendship Pr.

Guidelines for Sex-Fair Vocational Education Materials. Women on Words & Images Staff. 32p. 1978. 4.95 o.p. (ISBN 0-318-22109-8, SSN22). Natl Ctr Res Voc Ed.

Guidelines for the Establishment of Industrial Estates in Developing Countries. pap. 6.00 o.p. (ISBN 0-686-94493-3, UN78/2B13, UN). UNIPUB.

Guidelines for the Planning & Organization of School Library Media Centres. Rev. ed. Frances Laverne Carroll & Patricia F. Beilke. 52p. 1982. pap. 9.50 o.p. (ISBN 0-686-95502-1, UPB116, UNESCO). UNIPUB.

Guidelines for the Preparation of the Material Safety Data Sheet for Welding Consumables & Related Products. 1982. 7.00 o.p. (ISBN 0-318-18035-9, EW 5-1982). Natl Elec Mfrs.

Guidelines for Watershed Management. (Conservation Guides: No. 1). (Illus.). 306p. (Eng. & Fr., 3rd Printing 1983). 1977. pap. 22.00 o.p. (ISBN 92-5-100242-8, F741, FAO). UNIPUB.

Guidelines on Citizen Participation in Transportation Planning, 1978. 97p. pap. 7.00 o.p. (ISBN 0-686-32374-2, GCP-1). AASHTO.

Guidelines on Pregnancy & Work. 3.00 o.p. (ISBN 0-686-24123-1). Am Coll Obstetric.

Guidelines to Assess Computerized Time & Billing Systems for Use in CPA Firms. (Computer Services Guidelines Ser.). 55p. 1980. pap. 8.00 o.p. (ISBN 0-686-70234-4). Am Inst CPA.

Guidelines to Orthopedic Nursing. rev. ed. St. Mary's Memorial Hospital, Knoxville, Tennessee Staff. LC 74-18943. 1975. 8.50 o.p. (ISBN 0-87125-023-3). Cath Health.

Guidelines to Safe Drinking. Nicholas A. Pace & Wilbur Cross. 176p. 1984. text ed. 14.95 o.p. (ISBN 0-07-048052-4). McGraw.

Guides to the Evaluation of Permanent Impairment. 2nd ed. American Medical Association Staff. LC 74-151606. (Illus.). 245p. 1984. 27.50 o.p. (ISBN 0-89970-161-2). AMA.

Guiding Growth & Change: A Handbook for the Massachusetts Citizen. Sarah Peskin. (Illus.). 168p. 1978. pap. 3.50 o.p. (ISBN 0-910146-15-2). AMC Books.

Guiding Human Misfits. Alexandra Adler. 1952. (ISBN 0-8022-0006-0). Philos Lib.

Guiding the Mentally Retarded Person to Success: Basic Behavior Principles & Practice. rev. ed. John T. Neisworth & Robert M. Smith. LC 84-1724. (Illus.). 232p. 1984. pap. 19.00x o.p. (ISBN 0-936104-37-6, 0492). Pro Ed.

Guiding the Normal Child. Agatha Bowley. (ISBN 0-8022-0164-4). Philos Lib.

Guiding Your Child: A 60-Point Checklist for Parents. Elliott D. Landau & M. Winston Egan. LC 78-70361. 48p. 1978. pap. 3.95 o.p. (ISBN 0-88290-103-6). Horizon Utah.

Guiding Yourself into a Spiritual Reality: A Workbook. Peggy D. Burkan. LC 83-91310. 96p. (Orig.). 1985. pap. 7.95 o.p. (ISBN 0-935616-06-3). Reunion Pr.

Guidlines for Preparing Proposals. Roy Meador. 116p. 1985. 19.95 o.p. (ISBN 0-317-66012-8, Pub. by T Telford UK). Am Soc Civil Eng.

Guilford County, North Carolina, Will Abstracts, 1771-1841. Irene B. Webster. 216p. 1979. pap. 22.50 o.p. (ISBN 0-89308-352-6). Southern Hist Pr.

Guillaume Tell, 2 vols. Gioachino Rossini. Ed. by Phillip Gossett & Charles Rosen. LC 76-49192. (Early Romantic Opera Ser.: No. 17). 1979. lib. bdg. 180.00 o.p. (ISBN 0-8240-2916-X). Garland Pub.

Guilt & Grace. Paul Tournier. LC 62-7305. 1962. 11.95i o.p. (ISBN 0-06-068330-9). HarpR.

Guilt: Curse or Blessing. Arthur H. Becker. LC 77-72455. 1977. 9.50 o.p. (ISBN 0-8066-1599-0, 10-2913, Augsburg); pap. 5.50 o.p. (ISBN 0-8066-1588-5, 10-2912). Augsburg Fortress.

Guilt: The Grey Eminence behind Character, History & Culture. John Carroll. 288p. 1985. 36.00x o.p. (ISBN 0-7102-0357-8). Routledge Chapman & Hall.

Guilt: Theory & Therapy. Edward V. Stein. 1968. 6.00 o.s.i. (ISBN 0-664-20819-3, Westminster). Westminster John Knox.

Guilty & the Innocent. William Bixley. (Illus.). 176p. 1957. (ISBN 0-8022-0135-0). Philos Lib.

Guinea Pigs, All About Them. Alvin Silverstein & Virginia Silverstein. LC 74-148487. (Illus.). 96p. (gr. 3-7). 1972. 7.25 o.p. (ISBN 0-688-41664-0); PLB 10.88 o.p. (ISBN 0-688-51664-5). Lothrop.

Guinness Book of Names. rev. ed. Leslie A. Dunkling. (Illus.). 192p. (Orig.). 1986. pap. 9.95 o.p. (ISBN 0-85112-469-0, Pub. by Guinness Superlatives England). Sterling.

Guinness Book of World Records. 21st ed. Norris McWhirter. 1983. pap. 3.95 o.s.i. (ISBN 0-553-23111-1). Bantam.

Guinness Book of World Records 1984. Norris McWhirter. 704p. 1984. pap. text ed. 3.95 o.s.i. (ISBN 0-553-23990-2). Bantam.

Guinness Book of World Records 1986. Norris McWhirter. (Orig.). 1986. pap. 4.50 o.p. (ISBN 0-553-25454-5). Bantam.

Guinness Book of World Records 1987. Ed. by Alan Russell et al. LC 64-4984. (Illus.). 480p. 1986. 14.95 o.p. (ISBN 0-8069-4768-3); lib. bdg. 17.79 o.p. (ISBN 0-8069-4769-1). Sterling.

Guinness Book of World Records, 1988. Ed. by Alan Russel & David A. Boehm. LC 64-4984. (Illus.). 480p. 1987. 15.95 o.p. (ISBN 0-8069-6598-3); lib. bdg. 18.79 o.p. (ISBN 0-8069-6599-1). Sterling.

Guinness Sports Record Book 1987-1988. Ed. by David Boehm & Jim Benagh. LC 82-642136. (Illus.). 320p. 1987. 14.95 o.p. (ISBN 0-8069-6452-9); pap. 9.95 o.p. (ISBN 0-8069-6454-5). Sterling.

Guinness Sports Record Book 1988-89. Ed. by David A. Boehm. LC 82-642136. (Illus.). 256p. (YA) (gr. 10-12). 1988. 16.95 o.p. (ISBN 0-8069-6811-7); pap. 10.95 o.p. (ISBN 0-8069-6810-9). Sterling.

Guitar Bibliography: An International Listing of Literature on Classical Guitar from the Beginning to the Present. Werner Schwarz & Monica Haringer. (Illus.). xxxii, 257p. (Ger.). Date not set. Repr. of 1984 ed. lib. bdg. 45.00 o.p. K G Saur.

Guitar in Fourths Based upon a Uniform System of Tuning & Fingering. rev. ed. Bob Bianco. (Illus.). 64p. pap. 9.95 o.s.i. (ISBN 0-317-66184-1, Pub. by Calliope Music). Bold Strummer Ltd.

Guitar Player Book. rev. ed. Ed. by Jim Crockett. LC 79-2350. (Illus.). 416p. 1979. pap. 9.95 o.p. (ISBN 0-394-17169-1, E739, Ever). Grove.

Guitar-Plus. Ralph DeJay. (Illus.). 1979. pap. 4.00 o.p. (ISBN 0-682-49408-9). Exposition-Phoenix.

Guitar Repair: A Manual of Repair for Guitars & Fretted Instruments. Irving Sloane. LC 84-8543. (Illus.). 96p. (Orig.). 1985. pap. 9.95 o.p. (ISBN 0-8069-7934-8). Sterling.

Guitar Songbook. Frederick M. Noad. (Illus.). 1969. pap. 7.95 o.p. (ISBN 0-02-871730-9). Schirmer Bks.

Guitar Songbook with Instructions. Beverly McKeown. 1975. pap. 23.50 o.p. (ISBN 0-395-18648-X). HM.

Guitar: The History, the Music, the Players. Allan Kozinn et al. LC 83-62354. (Illus.). 1984. pap. 12.95 o.p. (ISBN 0-688-01973-0, Quill NY). Morrow.

Guitarrero Cave: Early Man in the Andes. Ed. by Thomas F. Lynch. LC 79-8868. (Studies in Archaeology). 1980. 29.95 o.p. (ISBN 0-12-460580-X). Acad Pr.

Guitars: The Tsumura Collection. Akira Tsumura. LC 87-81682. (Illus.). 1988. 50.00 o.s.i. (ISBN 0-87011-839-0). Kodansha.

Gulf of Maine: First Reader. Gary Lawless. 1977. pap. 4.95 o.p. (ISBN 0-942396-22-7). Blackberry ME.

Gulf Star Forty-Five. Kim Bartlett. 1979. 9.95 o.p. (ISBN 0-393-01265-4). Norton.

Gullah: Negro Life in the Carolina Sea Islands. Mason Crum. LC 68-28592. 1969. Repr. of 1940 ed. lib. bdg. 22.50 o.p. (ISBN 0-8371-0897-7, CRG&, Pub. by Negro U Pr). Greenwood.

Gulliver House. John Leggett. 1979. 10.95 o.p. (ISBN 0-395-27759-0). HM.

Gulliver's Travels. Date not set. (ISBN 0-8052-3904-9). Random.

Gulliver's Travels. Jonathan Swift. 352p. 1961. pap. 3.50 o.p. (ISBN 0-440-33308-3, LE). Dell.

Gulliver's Travels. Jonathan Swift. Ed. by Robert A. Greenberg. (Critical Edition). 1965. 5.50 o.p. (ISBN 0-393-05321-0, NortonC). Norton.

Gulliver's Travels. Jonathan Swift. LC 83-1033. (Illus.). 96p. (gr. 1up). 1983. 10.25 o.p. (ISBN 0-688-02044-5); lib. bdg. 10.88 o.p. (ISBN 0-688-02045-3). Morrow.

Gulliver's Travels. Jonathan Swift. 48p. (Orig.). 1988. pap. 9.95 o.s.i. (ISBN 1-55651-331-3); audiocassette tape incl. o.p. (ISBN 1-55651-332-1). Cram Cassettes.

Gulliver's Travels & Other Writings. Jonathan Swift. Ed. & intro. by Ricardo Quintana. LC 58-6364. 1958. 6.95 o.p. Modern Lib.

Gumdrop & the Secret Switches. Val Biro. LC 82-14786. (Gumdrop Ser.). (Illus.). 32p. (ps up). PLB 9.95 o.p. Creative Ed.

Gumdrop Finds a Friend. Val Biro. LC 82-17688. (Gumdrop Ser.). (Illus.). 32p. (ps up). PLB 9.95 o.p. Creative Ed.

Gumdrop Finds a Ghost. Val Biro. LC 82-17686. (Gumdrop Ser.). (Illus.). 32p. (ps up). PLB 9.95 o.p. Creative Ed.

Gumdrop Gets His Wings. Val Biro. LC 82-17717. (Gumdrop Ser.). (Illus.). 32p. (ps up). PLB 9.95 o.p. Creative Ed.

Gumdrop Has a Birthday. Val Biro. LC 82-14779. (Gumdrop Ser.). (Illus.). 32p. (ps up). PLB 9.95 o.p. Creative Ed.

Gums & Stabilisers for the Food Industry II: Application of Hydrocolliods; Proceedings of the International Conference, Clwyd, Wales, U. K., 11-15 July, 1983. Ed. by G. Phillips et al. LC 82-3863. (Illus.). 578p. 1984. 145.00 o.p. (ISBN 0-08-029819-2). Pergamon.

Gums & Stabilizers for the Food Industry: Interactions of Hydrocolloids. Ed. by G. O. Phillips & D. J. Wedlock. (Illus.). 420p. 1982. 170.00 o.p. (ISBN 0-08-026843-9). Pergamon.

Gun & Its Development. W. W. Greener. (Illus.). 848p. 1987. 35.00 o.p. (ISBN 0-85368-073-6, Pub. by Arms & Armour). Sterling.

Gun & the Glory of Granite Hendley. Ned Conquest. 1979. pap. 1.25 o.p. (ISBN 0-8439-0685-5, Pub. by Leisure Bks CT). Dorchester Pub Co.

Gun & the Olive Branch. Hirst. 1977. 12.95 o.p. (ISBN 0-15-138299-9). HarBraceJ.

Gun & the Olive Branch: The Roots of Violence in the Middle East. 2nd ed. David Hirst. LC 83-5554. 400p. 1984. 19.95 o.p. (ISBN 0-571-18079-5). Faber & Faber.

Gun Collector's Handbook of Values. 14th ed. Charles E. Chapel. (Illus.). 504p. 1983. 19.95 o.p. (ISBN 0-698-11240-7, Coward). Putnam Pub Group.

Gun Control: Restricting Rights or Protecting People? Carol D. Foster et al. (Information Plus Ser.). 104p. 1987. pap. 16.95 o.p. (ISBN 0-936474-67-X). Info Plus TX.

Gun Digest Book of Gun Care, Cleaning & Refinishing, Book 1: Handguns. J. B. Wood. LC 84-71764. (Illus.). 192p. (Orig.). 1984. pap. 9.95 o.p. (ISBN 0-910676-78-X). DBI.

Gun Digest Book of Gun Care, Cleaning & Refinishing, Book 2: Long Guns. J. B. Wood. LC 84-71764. (Illus.). 192p. (Orig.). 1984. pap. 9.95 o.p. (ISBN 0-910676-82-8). DBI.

Gun Digest Book of Modern Gun Values. 5th ed. Jack Lewis. LC 75-10067. (Illus.). 432p. (Orig.). 1985. pap. 14.95 o.p. (ISBN 0-910676-83-6). DBI.

Gun Digest Book of Modern Gun Values. 6th ed. Jack Lewis. (Illus.). 448p. (Orig.). 1987. pap. 15.95 o.p. (ISBN 0-87349-006-1). DBI.

Gun Digest Book of Scopes & Mounts: Scopes & Mounts. Bob Bell. LC 83-72345. (Illus.). 224p. (Orig.). 1983. pap. 11.95 o.p. (ISBN 0-910676-61-5). DBI.

Gun Digest Book of Sporting Dogs. Carl P. Wood. LC 84-62678. (Illus.). 256p. (Orig.). 1985. pap. 11.95 o.p. (ISBN 0-910676-72-0). DBI.

Gun Digest Book of Trap & Skeet Shooting. Art Blatt. LC 83-70143. (Illus.). 256p. (Orig.). 1984. pap. 12.95 o.p. (ISBN 0-910676-66-6). DBI.

Gun Digest Hunting Annual 1984. Robert S. Anderson. 224p. 1983. pap. 9.95 o.p. (ISBN 0-910676-68-2). DBI.

Gun Digest Hunting Annual 1985. 2nd ed. Ed. by Robert S. Anderson. (Illus.). 224p. (Orig.). 1984. pap. 10.95 o.p. (ISBN 0-910676-77-1). DBI.

Gun Digest Hunting Annual 1986. 3rd ed. Ed. by Robert S. Anderson. (Illus.). 256p. 1985. pap. 12.95 o.p. (ISBN 0-910676-90-9). DBI.

Gun Digest Hunting Annual, 1988. 5th ed. Ed. by Robert S. Anderson. (Illus.). 256p. (Orig.). 1987. pap. 13.95 o.p. (ISBN 0-87349-012-6). DBI.

Gun Digest, 1985. 39th ed. Ken Warner. (Illus.). 472p. 1984. pap. 14.95 o.p. (ISBN 0-910676-75-5). DBI.

Gun Digest 1986. 40th ed. Ed. by Ken Warner. LC 44-3588. (Illus.). 496p. 1985. pap. 15.95 o.p. (ISBN 0-910676-88-7). DBI.

Gun Digest, 1987. 41st ed. Ed. by Ken Warner. LC 44-3588. (Illus.). 480p. 1986. pap. 16.95 o.p. (ISBN 0-87349-001-0). DBI.

Gun Digest, 1988. 42nd ed. Ed. by Ken Warner. LC 44-32588. (Illus.). 480p. (Orig.). 1987. pap. 16.95 o.p. (ISBN 0-87349-010-X). DBI.

Gun Dogs: Their History, Breeding & Training. Date not set. (ISBN 0-948253-17-7). Howell Bk.

Gun Gamble. Christian Kassel. (Orig.). 1981. pap. 1.95 o.s.i. (ISBN 0-505-51701-9, Pub. by Tower Bks). Dorchester Pub Co.

Gun Lust. W. L. Fieldhouse. 208p. (Orig.). 1982. pap. 2.25 o.p. (ISBN 0-505-51778-7, Pub. by Tower Bks). Dorchester Pub Co.

Gun Patents 1864. George Daw. 1982. 25.00x o.p. (ISBN 0-87556-251-5). Saifer.

Gun Trader's Guide. 10th ed. Paul Wahl. Ed. by John Traister. 416p. 1982. pap. 11.95 o.p. (ISBN 0-88317-113-9). Stoeger Pub Co.

Gun Trader's Guide. 11th ed. Paul Wahl. (Illus.). 416p. (Orig.). 1984. pap. 12.95 o.p. (ISBN 0-88317-123-6). Stoeger Pub Co.

Gun Trader's Guide. 12th ed. Paul Wahl. 464p. 1986. pap. 13.95 o.p. (ISBN 0-88317-135-X). Stoeger Pub Co.

Gunbelt. John Benteen. (Sundance Ser.: No. 23). 1977. pap. 1.50 o.s.i. (ISBN 0-8439-0494-1, Pub. by Leisure Bks CT). Dorchester Pub Co.

Gunblaze. Lee Bishop. 1978. pap. 1.75 o.s.i. (ISBN 0-8439-0604-9, Pub. by Leisure Bks CT). Dorchester Pub Co.

Gunboat Diplomacy Eighteen Ninety-Five to Nineteen Hundred Five: Great Power Pressure in Venezuela. Miriam Hood. 208p. (Orig.). 1983. pap. text ed. 11.95 o.p. (ISBN 0-04-987002-5). Unwin Hyman.

Gundam, Vol. II. (Big Little Bks.: No. 92). (Illus.). 350p. 1984. 6.95 o.p. (ISBN 0-318-02720-8). Bks Nippan.

Gundam, Vol. III. (Big Little Bks.: No. 114). (Illus.). 350p. 1984. 6.95 o.p. (ISBN 0-318-02727-5). Bks Nippan.

Gundog Training. Keith Erlandson. (Popular Dog Ser.). (Illus.). 224p. 1988. 29.95 o.p. (ISBN 0-09-161340-X, Pub. by Century Hutchinson). David & Charles.

Gunfight at Powder River. Lawrence Cortesi. (Orig.). 1980. pap. text ed. 1.95 o.p. (ISBN 0-505-51585-7, Pub. by Tower Bks). Dorchester Pub Co.

Gunfighters. H. B. Broome. LC 86-19864. (Double D Western Ser.). 192p. 1986. 12.95 o.s.i. (ISBN 0-385-23516-X). Doubleday.

Gunfire at Timberline. C. E. Parker. 208p. 1982. pap. 2.25 o.s.i. (ISBN 0-8439-1078-X, Pub. by Leisure Bks CT). Dorchester Pub Co.

Gunn-Hilsum Effect. M. P. Shaw et al. LC 76-45995. 1979. 44.50 o.p. (ISBN 0-12-638350-2). Acad Pr.

Gunnar Birkerts: A Bibliography. Mary E. Huls. (Architecture Ser.: A 1493). 6p. 1985. 2.00 o.p. (ISBN 0-89028-623-X). Vance Biblios.

Gunnar Myrdal: A Bibliography, 1919-1981. Kerstin Assarsson-Rizzi & Harold Bohrn. (Reference Library of Social Science). 240p. 1983. lib. bdg. 33.00 o.p. (ISBN 0-8240-9256-2). Garland Pub.

Gunnysack Castle. Julian Silva. LC 83-11406. vi, 254p. 1983. 15.95 o.s.i. (ISBN 0-8214-0743-0); pap. 6.95 o.p. (ISBN 0-8214-0744-9). Ohio U Pr.

Guns & How They Work. Ivan Hogg. LC 78-53013. (Illus.). 1979. 16.95 o.p. (ISBN 0-89696-023-4, An Everest House Book). Dodd.

Guns Don't Die -- People Do: The Pros, the Cons, the Facts. Pete Shields. LC 81-67522. 1981. 12.95 o.p. (ISBN 0-87795-361-9, Arbor Hse); pap. 5.95 o.p. (ISBN 0-87795-347-3). Morrow.

Guns for Home Defense. Ed. by Garry James. LC 74-25603. (Petersen Books Sports & Hobbies Ser.). (Illus.). 1975. pap. 3.95 o.p. (ISBN 0-8227-0088-3). Petersen Pub.

Guns from the East. Dick Taylor. 224p. (Orig.). 1982. pap. 2.25 o.s.i. (ISBN 0-505-51824-4, Pub. by Tower Bks). Dorchester Pub Co.

Guns Illustrated 1984. 16th ed. Harold A. Murtz. (Illus.). 344p. 1983. pap. 11.95 o.p. (ISBN 0-910676-60-7). DBI.

Guns Illustrated 1985. 17th ed. Ed. by Harold A. Murtz. (Illus.). 328p. (Orig.). 1984. pap. 12.95 o.p. (ISBN 0-910676-76-3). DBI.

Guns Illustrated 1986. 18th ed. Ed. by Harold A. Murtz. LC 69-11342. (Illus.). 320p. 1985. pap. 13.95 o.p. (ISBN 0-910676-89-5). DBI.

Guns Illustrated, 1987. 19th ed. Ed. by Harold A. Murtz. LC 69-11342. (Illus.). 320p. 1986. pap. 14.95 o.p. (ISBN 0-87349-002-9). DBI.

Guns Illustrated, 1988. 20th ed. Ed. by Harold A. Murtz. LC 69-11342. (Illus.). 320p. (Orig.). 1987. pap. 14.95 o.p. (ISBN 0-87349-011-8). DBI.

Guns of Darkness. Ann Schlee. LC 73-84834. 240p. (gr. 5-9). 1974. 5.95 o.p. (ISBN 0-689-30145-6, Atheneum). Macmillan.

Guns of Sixty-Two. National Historical Society Staff. Ed. by William C. Davis. LC 81-43151. (Image of War, Eighteen Sixty-One - Eighteen Sixty-Five Ser.: Vol. 2). (Illus.). 464p. 1982. 19.95 o.p. (ISBN 0-385-15467-4). Doubleday.

Gunsmoke River. Owen Rountree. 176p. 1985. pap. 2.50 o.s.i. (ISBN 0-345-31456-5). Ballantine.

Gunstock Finishing & Care. A. Donald Newell. (Illus.). 512p. 1949. 22.95 o.p. (ISBN 0-8117-0780-6). Stackpole.

Gunter Grass. Ronald Hayman. (Contemporary Writers Ser.). 96p. 1985. pap. 5.95 o.p. (ISBN 0-416-35490-4, 9471). Routledge Chapman & Hall.

Gunter Grass Symposium. Ed. by A. Leslie Willson. (Department of German Language Ser.). 103p. 1972. 7.95x o.p. (ISBN 0-292-70121-7). U of Tex Pr.

Gunther Papers. Jack Gunther. (Illus.). 1975. pap. 4.45 o.p. (ISBN 0-380-01238-3, 24000-9, Flare). Avon.

Guptill Geneology. Mildred Jacobson. 188p. 1985. 12.50 o.s.i. Ye Galleon.

Gurdjieff: An Approach to His Ideas. Michael Waldberg. Tr. by Steve Cox. 160p. (Orig.). 1981. pap. 8.95 o.p. (ISBN 0-7100-0811-2). Routledge Chapman & Hall.

Guru. Manly P. Hall. 1959. (ISBN 0-8022-0660-3). Philos Lib.

Guru & the Policemen: A Novel. E. S. Modak. 150p. 1982. pap. text ed. 8.95x o.p. (ISBN 0-686-81224-7, Pub. by Vikas India). Advent NY.

Gurung-Nepali-English Glossary. Deu B. Gurung et al. 223p. (Nepali & Eng.). 1976. pap. 3.00x o.s.i. (ISBN 0-88312-854-3); microfiche (3) 6.00 o.s.i. (ISBN 0-88312-391-6). Summer Inst Ling.

Gurus, Godman & Good People. Khushwant Singh. (Illus.). 134p. 1975. text ed. 13.95x o.p. (ISBN 0-86125-087-7, Pub. by Orient Longman Ltd India). Apt Bks.

Gustav Stickley: Collected Works. (Illus.). 168p. 1985. pap. 17.50 o.p. (ISBN 0-87905-409-3). Gibbs Smith Pub.

Gustave Courbet: a Study of Style & Society. Linda Nochlin. LC 75-23803. (Outstanding Dissertations in the Fine Arts - 19th Century Ser.). (Illus.). 1976. lib. bdg. 50.00 o.p. (ISBN 0-8240-1998-9). Garland Pub.

Gustave Moreau: The Watercolors. Pierre-Louis Mathieu. LC 85-14732. (Illus.). 112p. 1985. 75.00 o.p. (ISBN 0-933920-31-8, Dist. by Rizzoli). Hudson Hills.

Gustavo Gutierrez. Robert M. Brown. LC 80-82185. (Makers of Contemporary Theology Ser.). 89p. 1981. pap. 3.95 o.p. (ISBN 0-8042-0651-1, John Knox). Westminster John Knox.

Gut Defences in Clinical Practice. Ed. by M. S. Losowsky & R. V. Heatley. LC 85-24263. 318p. 1986. text ed. 90.00 o.p. (ISBN 0-443-03212-2). Churchill.

Gut Hormones. 2nd ed. Ed. by S. R. Bloom. J. M. Polack. (Illus.). 605p. 1981. text ed. 78.00 o.p. (ISBN 0-443-02323-9). Churchill.

Guy & the Flowering Plum Tree. Robin Stemp. LC 80-67029. (Illus.). 32p. (ps-3). 1981. 8.95 o.p. (ISBN 0-689-50188-9, Atheneum). Macmillan.

Guy De Maupassant: Contes du surnaturel. Ed. by A. Kellett. LC 70-93731. 1969. 3.38 o.p. (ISBN 0-08-006792-1). Pergamon.

GWAI-83. Ed. by B. Neumann. (Informatik-Fachberichte: Band 76). 240p. (Eng. & Ger.). 1984. pap. 16.00 o.p. (ISBN 0-387-12871-9). Springer Verlag.

Gwen John Sculpture. John Malcolm. 208p. 1986. 13.95 o.p. (ISBN 0-684-18574-1). Scribner.

GWR Locomotive Allocations, 1922-67. J. W. Rowledge. 176p. 1986. 18.95 o.p. (ISBN 0-7153-8820-7). David & Charles.

GWR Stars Castle & Kings. O. S. Nock. LC 80-66419. (Illus.). 304p. 1980. 35.95 o.p. (ISBN 0-7153-7977-1). David & Charles.

GWR Two Cylinder 4-6-0s & 2-6-9s. Rodger Bradley. (Illus.). 96p. 1988. 22.95 o.p. (ISBN 0-7153-8894-0). David & Charles.

Gyascutus: Studies in Antebellum Southern Humorous & Sporting Writings. Ed. by James L. West. (Costerus New Ser.: No. 5-6). 1978. pap. text ed. 22.50x o.p. (ISBN 90-6203-522-1). Humanities.

Gymnastics. Ross R. Olney. (Illus.). 64p. (gr. 4-7). 1980. pap. 2.25 o.p. (ISBN 0-380-49213-X, Camelot). Avon.

Gymnastics Guide Nineteen Eighty-Five to Eighty Nine. 1985. 8.95 o.p. (ISBN 0-88314-311-9). AAHPERD.

Gynaecology Pocket Consultant. Wood. 1986. 16.50 o.p. (ISBN 0-8016-5640-0). Mosby.

Gynecologic Decision Making. Beth Israel Hospital Staff & Emanuel A. Friedman. 256p. 1983. text ed. 38.00 o.p. (ISBN 0-941158-08-X, D1681-6). Mosby.

Gynecologic Laser Surgery. Ed. by J. H. Bellina. LC 81-7323. 492p. 1981. 75.00x o.p. (ISBN 0-306-40741-8, Plenum Pr). Plenum Pub.

Gynecologic Oncology Case Studies. Samuel Lifshitz & Herbert Buchsbaum. 1978. spiral bdg. 32.00 o.p. (ISBN 0-87488-005-X). Med Exam.

Gynecology: A Concise Textbook. Ralph W. Hale & John A. Krieger. (Concise Textbook Ser.). 1983. pap. text ed. 23.75 o.p. (ISBN 0-87488-585-X). Med Exam.

Gynecology: A Textbook for Students. F. K. Beller et al. LC 73-77004. (Illus.). 385p. 1974. pap. 18.00 o.p. (ISBN 0-387-90087-X). Springer-Verlag.

Gynecology & Obstetrics: Abstracts from the 8th World Congress Held in Mexico, 1976. Ed. by Cast Elazo-Ayala & C. MacGregor. (International Congress Ser.: No. 396). 1976. pap. 48.50 o.p. (ISBN 0-444-15235-0, Excerpta Medica). Elsevier.

Gynecology & Obstetrics: The Health Care of Women. 2nd ed. Ed. by Seymour Romney et al. (Illus.). 1981. text ed. 65.00 o.p. (ISBN 0-07-053582-5). McGraw.

Gynecology of Childhood & Adolescence. 2nd ed. John W. Huffman et al. (Illus.). 588p. 1981. text ed. (ISBN 0-7216-4816-9). Saunders.

Gypsies. Josef Koudelka. LC 75-13611. (Illus.). 144p. 30.00 o.p. (ISBN 0-912334-74-6); pap. 19.95 o.p. (ISBN 0-912334-97-5). Aperture.

Gypsies. National Geographic Society Staff & Bart McDowell. LC 70-125339. (Special Publications Series 5). (Illus.). 1970. 7.95 o.p. (ISBN 0-87044-088-8). Natl Geog.

Gypsies. Jan Yoors. 256p. 1983. pap. 6.75 o.p. (ISBN 0-671-49335-3, Touchstone). S&S.

Gypsies & Government Policy in England. Barbara Adams et al. 1975. text ed. 27.50x o.p. (ISBN 0-435-85080-6). Gower Pub Co.

Gypsies & Other Bohemians: The Myth of the Artist in Nineteenth-Century France. Marilyn R. Brown. Ed. by Stephen Foster. LC 85-8427. (Studies in the Fine Arts: The Avant-Garde: No. 51). 230p. 1985. 44.95 o.p. (ISBN 0-8357-1704-6). UMI Res Pr.

Gypsies: The Secret People. Godfrey E. Webb. LC 73-1437. (Illus.). 189p. 1974. Repr. of 1960 ed. lib. bdg. 22.50x o.p. (ISBN 0-8371-6794-9, WEGY). Greenwood.

Gypsies, Tinkers, & Other Travellers. Ed. by Farnham Rehfisch. 1975. 60.00 o.p. (ISBN 0-12-585850-7). Acad Pr.

Gypsies: Waggon Time & After. Denis Harvey. (Illus.). 144p. 1980. 30.95 o.p. (ISBN 0-7134-1548-7, Pub. by Batsford England). David & Charles.

Gypsy: A Memoir. Gypsy Rose Lee. 1986. pap. 8.95 o.p. (ISBN 0-671-62286-2, Fireside). S&S.

Gypsy & Me: At Home & on the Road with Gypsy Rose Lee. Erik L. Preminger. (Illus.). 288p. 1984. 17.45i o.p. (ISBN 0-316-71776-2). Little.

Gypsy Bibliography. George F. Black. LC 74-149780. 248p. 1971. Repr. of 1914 ed. 34.00x o.p. (ISBN 0-8103-3708-8). Gale.

Gypsy Demons & Divinities: The Magic & Religion of the Gypsies. Elwood B. Trigg. 256p. 1974. 7.95 o.p. (ISBN 0-8065-0379-3, Pub. by Citadel Pr). Carol Pub Group.

Gypsy Fires in America. Irving H. Brown. LC 74-1035. 284p. Repr. of 1924 ed. 40.00x o.p. (ISBN 0-8103-3942-0). Gale.

Gypsy in Amber. Martin C. Smith. 192p. 1982. pap. 2.50 o.s.i. (ISBN 0-345-30614-7). Ballantine.

Gypsy in My Verse. Adam C. Zimmerman. 1976. 6.00 o.p. (ISBN 0-682-48460-1). Exposition-Phoenix.

Gypsy Laddie. Dorothy Rice. LC 75-156794. (gr. 1-4). 1972. 5.50 o.p. (ISBN 0-689-20694-1, Atheneum). Macmillan.

Gypsy Music. B. Sarosi. (Illus.). 1978. 17.50 o.p. (ISBN 963-13-3657-3). E J Brill USA.

Gypsy Sixpence. Edison Marshall. 1976. pap. 1.75 o.p. (ISBN 0-380-00706-1, 28837). Avon.

Gyrodynamics. CISM (International Center for Mechanical Sciences) Staff. Ed. by K. Magnus. (CISM Intl. Centre for Mechanical Science, Courses & Lectures Ser.: No. 53). (Illus.). x, 280p. 1974. pap. 15.40 o.p. (ISBN 0-387-81229-6). Springer-Verlag.

Gyrodynamics. Ed. by Hans Ziegler. (Illus., Eng. & Fr.). 1963. 46.70 o.p. (ISBN 0-387-03017-4). Springer-Verlag.

Gyroscope Applied. K. I. Richardson. (Illus.). 384p. 1955. (ISBN 0-8022-1338-3). Philos Lib.

H

H. D. The Life & Work of an American Poet. Janice S Robinson. (Illus.). 480p. 1982. 17.95 o.p. (ISBN 0-395-31855-6). HM.

H. Dickon Arkwright's Digest of a Journey Lately Undergone. William Cheney. viii, 20p. 1977. Repr. of 1960 ed. cloth 10.00 o.p. (ISBN 0-317-11647-9). Dawsons.

H. G. Wells. Norman MacKenzie & Jeanne MacKenzie. (Illus.). 1973. 12.50 o.p. (ISBN 0-671-21520-5). S&S.

H. G. Wells. Patrick Parrinder. (Critical Heritage Ser.). 351p. 1985. pap. 15.00 o.p. (ISBN 0-7102-0515-5). Routledge Chapman & Hall.

H. G. Wells: His Turbulent Life & Times. Lovat Dickson. LC 68-12534. 1969. pap. 3.45 o.p. (ISBN 0-689-70274-4, 180, Atheneum). Macmillan.

H. G. Wells in Love: Postscript to an Experiment in Autobiography. Ed. by G. P. Wells. (Illus.). 224p. 1984. 16.95 o.p. (ISBN 0-316-93034-2). Little.

H. L. Mencken. W. H. Williams. (United States Authors Ser.: No. 297). 1977. lib. bdg. 13.50 o.s.i. (ISBN 0-8057-7200-6, Twayne). G K Hall.

H. L. Mencken: A Bibliography. Bernard H. Porter. 1986. 42.50 o.p. (ISBN 0-317-55099-3). Bern Porter.

H. M. S. Hood vs. Bismarck: The Battleship Battle. Theodore Taylor. (World War II Ser.: Bk. 2). 144p. 1982. pap. 2.50 o.p. (ISBN 0-380-81174-X, 81174-X, Flare). Avon.

H. Richard Niebuhr. Lonnie Kliever. LC 77-92452. (Makers of the Modern Theological Mind Ser.). 1978. 8.95 o.p. (ISBN 0-8499-0078-6, 0078-6). Word Bks.

H. Rider Haggard: A Bibliography. D. E. Whatmore. 288p. 1986. 66.00 o.p. Mansell.

Ha-Hayim ha-Ketsarim see Short Life: A Novel.

Haakon. C. F. Griffin. 1979. pap. 2.50 o.p. (ISBN 0-380-43745-7, 43745-7). Avon.

Habib Bourguiba, Islam & the Creation of Tunisia. Norma Salem. LC 84-45235. 256p. 1984. 28.00 o.p. (ISBN 0-7099-3319-3, Pub. by Croom Helm Ltd). Routledge Chapman & Hall.

Habilitation of the Mentally Retarded Individual. Joe E. Walthall & Harold D. Love. (Illus.). 224p. 1974. 17.00 o.p. (ISBN 0-398-02908-3). C C Thomas.

Habitat: Areas of Communication, No. 3. Marta Ribalta. (Illus.). 264p. 1982. pap. 9.95 o.p. (ISBN 84-7031-447-5, Pub. by Editorial Blume Spain). Intl Spec Bk.

Habitat: Human Settlements in an Urban Age. Angus M. Gunn. 1978. 35.00 o.p. (ISBN 0-08-021487-8); pap. 20.00 o.p. (ISBN 0-08-021486-X). Pergamon.

Habitat: The Living Room, No. 1. Marta Ribalta. (Illus.). 86p. 1982. pap. 9.95 o.p. (ISBN 84-7031-229-4, Pub. by Editorial Blume Spain). Intl Spec Bk.

Habitat, Vol. 3 (incl. 1985-1987 Supplements) Ed. by Eleanor Goldstein. (Social Issues Resources Ser.). 1987. 45.00 o.p. (ISBN 0-89777-081-1). Soc Issues.

Habitations of Man in All Ages. Eugene E. Viollet-Le-Duc. Tr. by Benjamin Bucknall. LC 74-146922. 414p. 1971. Repr. of 1876 ed. 65.00x o.p. (ISBN 0-8103-3787-8). Gale.

Habitations of the Word: Essays. William H. Gass. 368p. 1985. 17.45 o.p. (ISBN 0-671-52726-6). S&S.

Habitations of the Word: Essays. William H. Gass. 288p. 1986. pap. 8.95 o.p. (ISBN 0-671-61769-9, Touchstone). S&S.

Habits, Not Diets: The Real Way to Weight Control. James M. Ferguson. LC 76-4098. 1976. pap. 9.95 o.p. (ISBN 0-915950-06-5). Bull Pub.

Habits of Health. Donald Norfolk. 1978. pap. 1.95 o.p. (ISBN 0-380-01935-3, 37846). Avon.

Habla Espanol? An Introductory Course. 2nd ed. Edward D. Allen et al. LC 80-23174. 502p. 1981. text ed. 26.95 o.p. (ISBN 0-03-057196-0, HoltC); instr's manual 19.95 o.p. (ISBN 0-03-057197-9); wkbk. 11.95 o.p. (ISBN 0-03-057198-7); lab manual 11.95 o.p. (ISBN 0-03-057199-5); tapes 350.00 o.p. (ISBN 0-03-057201-0). HR&W.

Habla Espanol: Essentials. 2nd ed. Edward D. Allen et al. (Span.). 1982. text ed. 25.95 o.p. (ISBN 0-03-058304-7); instr's. manual 19.95 o.p. (ISBN 0-03-058858-8); lab manual 11.95 o.p. (ISBN 0-03-058859-6); tapes avail. o.p. (ISBN 0-03-058861-8). HR&W.

Habsburg Twilight. Sarah Gainham. LC 78-73085. 1979. 11.95 o.p. (ISBN 0-689-10957-1, Atheneum). Macmillan.

Habsburg und Rom in Den Jahren 1708-1709. Hans Kramer. Repr. of 1936 ed. 14.00 o.p. (ISBN 0-384-30400-1). Johnson Repr.

Hacia Donde Va la Familia? Larry Christenson. 32p. 1978. 0.50 o.p. (ISBN 0-88113-110-5). Edit Betania.

Hackers: Heros of the Computer Revolution. Steven Levy. LC 84-6188. (Illus.). 480p. 1984. 17.95 o.p. (ISBN 0-385-19195-2, Anchor Pr). Doubleday.

Hackh's Chemical Dictionary. 4th ed. Julius Grant. 1969. text ed. 74.00 o.p. (ISBN 0-07-024064-7). McGraw.

Hacks & Dunces: Pope, Swift & Grub Street. Pat Rogers. 1980. pap. 11.95x o.p. (ISBN 0-416-74240-8, NO. 6418). Routledge Chapman & Hall.

Had You Been Born a Muslim. J. B. Irving. pap. 1.50 o.p. (ISBN 0-686-18471-8). Kazi Pubns.

Hadha ad-Din. Sayyid Qutb. 96p. (Orig., Arabic.). 1978. pap. 1.75x o.s.i. (ISBN 0-939830-18-3, Pub. by IIFSO Kuwait). New Era Pubns MI.

Hadronic Interactions of Electronics & Photons. Ed. by J. Cummings & H. Osborn. 95.00 o.p. (ISBN 0-12-198750-7). Acad Pr.

Hadrons & Their Interactions: Current - Field Algebra, Soft Pions, Supermultiplets, & Related Topics. Ed. by A. Zichichi. 1968. 104.00 o.p. (ISBN 0-12-780540-0). Acad Pr.

Haemostasis & Thrombosis. Neri G. G. Serneri & C. Prentice. LC 78-72545. (Proceedings of the Serono Symposia Ser.: No. 15). 1980. 138.00 o.p. (ISBN 0-12-516150-6). Acad Pr.

Hafetz Hayyim on the Siddur. Tr. by C. Wengrow. 12.95 o.p. (ISBN 0-87306-996-X). Feldheim.

Haffertee Finds a Place of His Own. (Haffertee Series of Four Gift Set). 61p. (gr. 3-7). 3.95 o.p. (ISBN 0-89191-149-9). Cook.

Haffertee Goes Exploring. (Haffertee Series of Four Gift Set). 61p. (gr. 3-7). 3.95 o.p. (ISBN 0-89191-150-2). Cook.

Haffertee Hamster Series. Incl. Haffertee Hamster Diamond (ISBN 0-89191-148-0); Haffertee's First Christmas (ISBN 0-89191-151-0). (Illus.). (ps-4). 1978. 3.95 ea. o.p. Cook.

Hagakure: The Book of the Samurai. Yamamoto Tsuneyomo. Tr. by William S. Wilson. 192p. 1981. pap. 2.95 o.p. (ISBN 0-380-54569-1, 54569-1, Discus). Avon.

Hagan & Bruner's Infectious Diseases of Domestic Animals. 7th rev. ed. James H. Gillespie & John F. Timoney. LC 80-15937. (Illus.). 912p. 1981. 49.50x o.p. (ISBN 0-8014-1333-8). Cornell U Pr.

Hah-Nee. Mary Buff & Conrad Buff. (gr. 4-6). 1965. reinforced bdg. 5.95 o.p. (ISBN 0-395-15081-7). HM.

Hahnemann Sequela. Harold King. 1984. 15.95 o.p. (ISBN 0-87795-564-6, Arbor Hse). Morrow.

Haidah Indians of Queen Charlotte Islands. James G. Swan. (Shorey Indian Ser.). (Illus.). 36p. (YA) (gr. 7 up). Repr. of 1874 ed. 7.95 o.s.i. (ISBN 0-8466-0034-X, S34). Shorey.

Haiku: The Mood of the Earth. Ann Atwood. LC 70-162737. (Illus.). (gr. 3 up). 1971. PLB 9.95 o.s.i. (ISBN 0-684-12494-7, Pub. by Scribner); pap. 4.95 o.s.i. (ISBN 0-684-16214-8, Pub. by Scribner). Macmillan.

Hail & Farewell. George Moore. Ed. by Richard Cave. (Illus.). 774p. 1980. text ed. 45.00x o.p. (ISBN 0-7705-1467-7). Humanities.

Hail, Hail, Camp Timberwood. Ellen Conford. (Illus.). (gr. 4-6). 1980. pap. 2.25 o.s.i. (ISBN 0-671-42685-0); pap. 2.25 o.p. (ISBN 0-671-47356-5). Archway.

Hail Mary. rev. ed. H. Leo Eddleman. 134p. 1983. pap. 4.00 o.p. (ISBN 0-682-40143-9). Exposition-Phoenix.

Hail Mary, Are You Heeding the Blessed Virgin? In Defense of Public Schools. H. Leo Eddleman. (Orig.). 1982. pap. 4.00 o.p. (ISBN 0-682-49899-8). Exposition-Phoenix.

Hair Magic. P-H.

Hair of the Dog. Ginny T. 1978. 6.50 o.p. (ISBN 0-682-49174-8). Exposition-Phoenix.

Hair Research: Status & Future Aspects. Ed. by C. E. Orfanos et al. (Illus.). 650p. 1981. 102.40 o.p. (ISBN 0-387-10798-3). Springer-Verlag.

Hairdressing in Theory & Practice. 6th, rev. ed. T. W. Masters. (Illus.). 1984. pap. 25.00 o.p. (ISBN 0-291-39624-0). E J Brill USA.

Hairy Cell Leukaemia. Ed. by J. C. Cawley et al. (Recent Results in Cancer Research Ser.: Vol. 72). (Illus.). 180p. 1980. 37.00 o.p. (ISBN 0-387-09920-4). Springer-Verlag.

Haiti: A Country Study. Thomas E. Weil. LC 73-600155. (DA Pam 550-164. Area Handbook Ser.). 204p. 1985. Repr. of 1973 ed. 9.00 o.p. (ISBN 0-318-20116-X, S/N 008-020-01065-1). USGPO.

Haiti: The Calvary of a Soldier. Demosthenes P. Calixte. LC 75-98715. Repr. of 1939 ed. 35.00x o.p. (ISBN 0-8371-2760-2, CAJ&, Pub. by Negro U Pr). Greenwood.

Haj. Leon Uris. 1985. lib. bdg. 19.95 o.p. (ISBN 0-8161-3788-9, Large Print Bks). G K Hall.

Hakluyt Voyages, Vol. 1. Richard Hakluyt. 1962. Repr. of 1907 ed. 14.95x o.p. (ISBN 0-460-00264-3, Evman). Biblio Dist.

Hakon of Rogen's Saga. Erik C. Haugaard. (Illus.). (gr. 7 up). 1963. 6.95 o.p. (ISBN 0-395-06803-7). HM.

Hakon of Rogen's Saga. Erik C. Haugaard. LC 63-10901. (Illus.). 132p. (gr. 6 up). 1973. pap. 0.95 o.p. (ISBN 0-395-16037-5, Sandpiper). HM.

Hal Borland's Book of Days. Hal Borland. 1985. pap. 9.70 o.p. (ISBN 0-393-30281-4). Norton.

Hal Borland's Twelve Moons of the Year. Hal Borland. (Nonfiction Ser.). 1985. pap. 9.95 o.p. (ISBN 0-8398-2867-5). G K Hall.

Hal Swiggett on North American Deer. Hal Swiggett. LC 79-65959. (Illus.). 1980. pap. 8.95 o.p. (ISBN 0-89149-047-7). Jolex.

Halas, Hef, the Beatles, & Me. Jack Mabley. 224p. 1987. 16.95 o.p. (ISBN 0-8092-4792-5). Contemp Bks.

Half Century of Polish Mathematics: Remembrances & Reflections. K. Kuratowski. (International Series in Pure & Applied Mathematics: Vol. 108). (Illus.). 212p. 1980. 42.00 o.p. (ISBN 0-08-023046-6). Pergamon.

Half Jew. Robert Beauvais. Tr. by Harold J. Salemson from Fr. LC 79-26039. 224p. 1980. 9.95 o.s.i. (ISBN 0-8008-3799-1). Taplinger.

Half Lines & Repetitions in Virgil. John Sparrow. Ed. by Steele Commager. LC 77-70823. (Latin Poetry Ser.). 1977. lib. bdg. 19.00 o.p. (ISBN 0-8240-2979-8). Garland Pub.

Half-Lives. Erica Jong. LC 72-11067. 1973. 6.95 o.p. (ISBN 0-03-007426-6); pap. 3.95 o.p. (ISBN 0-03-007411-8). H Holt & Co.

Half Magic. Edward Eager. LC 84-19816. (Illus.). 228p. (gr. 3-6). 1970. pap. 4.95 o.p. (ISBN 0-15-637990-2, VoyB). HarBraceJ.

Half-Mother. Emma Tennant. 176p. 1985. 14.45i o.p. (ISBN 0-316-83728-8). Little.

Half of Two Lives. A. Waley. 368p. 1983. text ed. 16.95 o.p. (ISBN 0-07-067807-3). McGraw.

Half-Past Tomorrow. Ruth C. Carlsen. (Illus.). 176p. (gr. 3-7). 1973. 3.95 o.p. (ISBN 0-395-16036-7). HM.

Halfway Houses. Robert Z. Apte. 125p. 1968. pap. text ed. 5.00x o.p. (ISBN 0-7135-1522-8, Pub. by Bedford England). Gower Pub Co.

Halfway Houses & Group Homes. Earleen H. Cook & Joseph L. Cook. (Public Administration Ser.: P 1713). 37p. 1985. 5.25 o.p. (ISBN 0-89028-463-6). Vance Biblios.

Hall of Light. William E. Southill. 1952. (ISBN 0-8022-1610-2). Philos Lib.

Hall of Mirrors. Robert Stone. 416p. 1981. pap. 5.95 o.s.i. (ISBN 0-395-30543-8). HM.

Hallelujah. Ella Thorp Ellis. LC 76-4810. (Illus.). 224p. (gr. 6-9). 1976. 7.95 o.p. (ISBN 0-689-30536-2, Atheneum). Macmillan.

Halley's Bible Handbook. Henry H. Halley. 1976. 10.95 o.p. (ISBN 0-310-25720-4, 9744); pap. 13.95 Large print o.p. (ISBN 0-310-25727-1, 12564L); large print kivar o.p. 19.95 o.p. (ISBN 0-310-41390-7, 9840). Zondervan.

Halley's Comet! Francis Reddy. LC 85-1396. (Illus.). 58p. (Orig.). 1985. pap. 5.95 o.p. (ISBN 0-913135-02-X). Kalmbach.

Halley's Comet. Donald Tattersfield. (Illus.). 166p. 1985. 24.95x o.p. (ISBN 0-631-14551-6). Basil Blackwell.

Halley's Comet: Memories of 1910. Roberta Etter & Stuart Schneider. LC 85-15666. 96p. 1985. 19.95 o.p. (ISBN 0-89659-588-9). Abbeville Pr.

Halliwell's Film & Video Guide. 6th ed. Leslie Halliwell. (Illus.). 1200p. 1988. 47.50 o.s.i. (ISBN 0-684-18928-3). Scribner.

Halliwell's Film & Video Guide. 5th ed. Leslie L. Halliwell. 1987. pap. 19.95 o.s.i. (ISBN 0-684-18826-0). Scribner.

Halliwell's Film Guide. 2nd ed. Leslie L. Halliwell. 1981. 36.00 o.p. (ISBN 0-684-16467-1, ScribT); encore ed. 19.95 o.p. (ISBN 0-684-17546-0). Scribner.

Halliwell's Film Guide. Leslie L. Halliwell. (Illus.). 1979. 24.95 o.p. (ISBN 0-684-16056-0, ScribT). Scribner.

Halliwell's Film Guide. 4th ed. Leslie L. Halliwell. 1000p. 1985. pap. 19.95 o.s.i. (ISBN 0-684-18468-0, ScribT). Scribner.

Halliwell's Film Guide: And Music. 5th ed. Leslie L. Halliwell. (Illus.). 1152p. 1986. 42.50 o.s.i. (ISBN 0-684-18634-9). Scribner.

Halliwell's Filmgoer's Companion. 8th ed. Leslie L. Halliwell. (Illus.). 1000p. 1985. 42.50 o.s.i. (ISBN 0-684-18183-5, ScribT). Scribner.

Halliwell's Harvest. Leslie L. Halliwell. 208p. 1986. pap. 12.95 o.p. (ISBN 0-684-18518-0, ScribT). Scribner.

Halliwell's Hundred: A Nostalgic Choice of Films from the Golden Age. Leslie L. Halliwell. LC 81-84272. 403p. 1982. 25.00 o.p. (ISBN 0-684-17447-2). Scribner.

Hallmarks on Pewter. 21.00 o.s.i. (ISBN 0-911403-05-1, Pub. by Tardy Fr.). Seven Hills Bk Dists.

Hallo Deutschland! Gerald E. Logan & David Braswell. LC 78-660. 1978. pap. text ed. 6.00 o.p. (ISBN 0-88377-101-2). Newbury Hse.

Halloween. Ben Greer. 176p. 1980. pap. 1.95 o.p. (ISBN 0-380-49619-4, 49619-4). Avon.

Hallucinogens: Cross-Cultural Perspectives. Marlene D. De Rios. LC 84-7244. (Illus.). 265p. 1984. 22.50x o.p. (ISBN 0-8263-0737-X). U of NM Pr.

Halo. Elizabeth Williams. LC 86-71932. 230p. (Orig.). 1987. pap. 9.95 o.p. (ISBN 1-55666-008-1). Authors Unltd.

Halogenated Benzenes: Mutual Solubility of Liquids. Horuath. (Solubility Data Ser.). 1985. 110.00 o.p. (ISBN 0-08-023926-9). Pergamon.

Halsman: Portraits. Philippe Halsman. Selected by Yvonne Halsman. (Illus.). 160p. 1985. 50.00 o.p. (ISBN 0-8109-1092-6). Abrams.

Ham House Kitchen. Caroline Davidson. (Illus.). 64p. (Orig.). 1985. pap. 6.95 o.p. (ISBN 0-905209-93-1, Pub. by Victoria & Albert Mus UK). Faber & Faber.

Ham Reporter. Robert J. Randisi. LC 87-19640. (Double D Western Ser.). 384p. 1987. 16.95 o.s.i. (ISBN 0-385-23991-2, GC Large Print). Doubleday.

Hambro Euromoney Directory: 1986. 15th ed. 1300p. 1986. pap. 120.00 o.p. (ISBN 0-8002-4069-3). Intl Pubns Serv.

Hamburger Heaven. James Trivers. (YA) 1979. pap. 1.75 o.p. (ISBN 0-380-48355-6, 48355-6). Avon.

Hamburger Hill. William Pelfrey. 208p. 1987. pap. 3.50 o.p. (ISBN 0-380-75403-7). Avon.

Hamburger Madness. Jack Ziegler. LC 78-53915. (Illus.). 1978. 7.95 o.p. (ISBN 0-15-138417-7). HarBraceJ.

Hamburger Madness. Jack Ziegler. LC 79-18424. 1980. pap. 5.95 o.p. (ISBN 0-15-638174-5, Harv). HarBraceJ.

Hamid & the Sultan's Son. Anne Rose. LC 75-11996. (Illus.). 48p. (gr. 2-5). 1975. 6.25 o.p. (ISBN 0-15-270101-X, HJ). HarBraceJ.

Hamilton. Robert N. Peck. (Illus.). 32p. (gr. 1-3). 1976. 13.45i o.p. (ISBN 0-316-69653-6). Little.

Hamilton Stark. Russell Banks. 1978. 9.95 o.p. (ISBN 0-395-26471-5). HM.

Hamiltonian Approach to Dynamic Economics. Ed. by David Cass & Karl Shell. (Economic Theory, Econometrics, & Mathematical Economics Ser.). 1976. 39.50 o.p. (ISBN 0-12-163650-X). Acad Pr.

Hamilton's Principles & Physical Systems. Ben R. Gossick. (Orig.). 1967. pap. 16.00 o.p. (ISBN 0-12-293346-X). Acad Pr.

Hamish's Groats End Walk: One Man & His Dog on a Hill Route Through Britain & Ireland. Hamish Brown. (Illus.). 1981. 29.95 o.p. (ISBN 0-575-03029-1, Pub. by Gollancz England). David & Charles.

Hamito-Semitica: Proceedings of the Colloquium of the Linguistics Association of Great Britian, Historical Section, Univsity of London, March 18-20, 1970. Colloquium of Linguistics Assocation of Great Britain, Historical Section, University of London Staff. Ed. by James Bynon & Theodora Bynon. LC 74-81134. (Janua Linguarum, Series Practice: No. 200). (Illus.). 518p. (Orig.). 1975. 88.00x o.p. (ISBN 0-686-22584-8); pap. 67.50x o.p. (ISBN 90-2793-092-9). Mouton.

Hamlet see also Tragedy of Hamlet.

Hamlet. William Shakespeare. Ed. by George B. Harrison. LC 62-21849. 1963. pap. 1.85 o.p. (ISBN 0-15-638410-8, Harv). HarBraceJ.

Hamlet. William Shakespeare. Ed. by G. A. Wilkes. (Challis Shakespeare Ser.). 204p. (Orig.). 1985. pap. text ed. 9.00x o.p. (ISBN 0-424-00094-6, Pub. by Sydney U Pr). Intl Spec Bk.

Hamlet by William Shakespeare. 48p. (Orig.). 1988. pap. 9.95 o.p. (ISBN 1-55651-377-1); cassette o.p. (ISBN 1-55651-378-X). Cram Cassettes.

Hamlet's Mousetrap. Arthur Wormhoudt. 1957. (ISBN 0-8022-1936-5). Philos Lib.

Hammer. Armand Hammer & Neil Lydon. (Illus.). 544p. 1988. pap. 9.95 o.p. (ISBN 0-399-51441-4, Perigee Bks). Putnam Pub Group.

Hammer: A Witness to History. Armand Hammer & Neil Lyndon. (Illus.). 512p. 1987. 22.95 o.p. (ISBN 0-399-13275-9, Putnam). Putnam Pub Group.

Hammer of Darkness. L. E. Modesitt, Jr. 336p. 1985. pap. 2.95 o.p. (ISBN 0-380-89798-9). Avon.

Hammer of the Gods: The Led Zeppelin Saga. Stephen Davis. LC 84-24776. (Illus.). 352p. 1985. 15.95 o.p. (ISBN 0-688-04507-3). Morrow.

Hammer on the Rock: A Darshan Diary. Bhagwan Shree Rajneesh. (Illus.). 464p. 1979. pap. 8.95 o.s.i. (ISBN 0-394-17090-3, E730, Ever). Grove.

Hammerlocke. Jack Barnao. 240p. 1986. 13.95 o.s.i. (ISBN 0-684-18683-7). Scribner.

Hammer's Slammers. David Drake. 288p. 1987. pap. 2.95 o.s.i. (ISBN 0-441-31602-6, Pub. by Ace Science Fiction). Ace Bks.

Hammock: How to Make Your Own & Lie in It. 2nd ed. Denison Andrews. LC 77-18433. (Illus.). 120p. 1978. pap. 2.95 o.p. (ISBN 0-89480-028-0, 178). Workman Pub.

Hammond Road Atlas & Vacation Guide 1987. rev ed. Ed. by Hammond Staff. LC 82-8117. (Illus.). 48p. 1987. pap. 2.50 o.p. Hammond Inc.

Hammond World Atlas. (New World Dictionaries Ser.). 288p. 1984. 19.95 o.p. (ISBN 0-671-53097-6). S&S.

Hamper & Trivet Catalog. Mark Drop & Steven Spiegel. (Illus.). 1986. pap. 5.95 o.p. (ISBN 0-671-61132-1, Fireside). S&S.

Hampton Court Palace. June Osborne. (Illus.). 160p. 1984. 24.95 o.p. (ISBN 0-7182-4402-8, Pub. by Kaye & Ward); pap. 20.95 o.p. (ISBN 0-7182-4401-X, Pub. by Kaye & Ward). David & Charles.

Hamptons: America's East End. Ken Robbins. (Illus.). 1984. pap. 9.75 o.p. (ISBN 0-912999-00-4, Pushcart Pr). Norton.

Hamsters, Gerbils, Guinea Pigs, Pet Mice & Pet Rats. James Hahn & Lynn Hahn. (Illus.). 72p. 1980. pap. 1.95 o.p. (ISBN 0-380-49239-3, 63784-7, Camelot). Avon.

Hancock's Half Hour. Ray Galton & Alan Simpson. (Entertainers Ser.). (Illus.). 136p. 1974. 8.50x o.p. (ISBN 0-7130-0087-2, Pub. by Woburn Pr England). Biblio Dist.

Hand. 4th ed. Birch & Brooks. (Rob & Smith's Operative Surgery Ser.). 1984. 99.95 o.p. (ISBN 0-8016-4408-9, C-4408-9). Mosby.

Hand. 2nd ed. Lee Milford. LC 82-3428. (Illus.). 368p. 1982. 60.00 o.p. (ISBN 0-8016-3450-4). Mosby.

Hand & Machine Knitting. Tessa Lorant. 1981. 4.95 o.p. (ISBN 0-684-16770-0, ScribT); 4.95 o.p. (ISBN 0-684-17716-1). Scribner.

Hand Block Printing & Resist Dying. P-H.

Hand-Book for Active Service. Egbert L. Viele. 1969. Repr. of 1861 ed. lib. bdg. 22.50 o.p. (ISBN 0-8371-0731-8, VIAS). Greenwood.

Hand-book of Games. Ed. by Henry G. Bohn. LC 73-84610. 632p. 1969. Repr. of 1850 ed. 43.00x o.p. (ISBN 0-8103-3570-0). Gale.

Hand Dynamics. Daim Batangtaris. (Illus.). 224p. 1983. pap. 12.95 o.p. (ISBN 0-87040-532-2). Japan Pubns USA.

Hand in Hand. Margery M. Johnson. (Illus., Orig.). (gr. 1-2). 1968. pap. 2.95 o.p. (ISBN 0-8042-9710-X). Westminster John Knox.

Hand in Psychological Diagnosis. Charlotte Wolff. 1952. (ISBN 0-8022-1919-5). Philos Lib.

Hand List of Illuminated Oriental Christian Manuscripts. Hugo Buchtal & Otto Kurz. (Warburg Institute Studies: Vol. 12). Repr. of 1942 ed. 20.00 o.p. (ISBN 0-8115-1389-0). Kraus Repr.

Hand Loom Weaving. Luther Hooper. LC 78-21372. (Illus.). 1979. pap. 9.95 o.s.i. (ISBN 0-8008-3805-X, Pentalic). Taplinger.

Hand Me Down the Dawn, No. 13. Mary H. Sayler. (Serenade-Saga Ser.). 1985. pap. 1.95 o.p. (ISBN 0-310-46652-0, 15524P). Zondervan.

Hand of Destiny: The Folk-Lore & Superstition of Everyday Life. C. J. Thompson. LC 70-125600. 306p. 1970. Repr. of 1932 ed. 46.00x o.p. (ISBN 0-8103-3419-4). Gale.

Hand of the Potter. Horace J. Prescod. 416p. 1987. 12.95 o.p. (ISBN 0-8062-2800-8). Carlton.

Hand-Picked Tours of Britain. Automobile Association of England. (Illus.). 1979. 22.95 o.p. (ISBN 0-393-01228-X). Norton.

Hand Splinting: Principles & Methods. Elaine Fess et al. LC 80-17398. (Illus.). 336p. 1980. text ed. 45.00 o.p. (ISBN 0-8016-1569-0). Mosby.

Hand That Holds Me. Michael Rogness. LC 84-14449. 112p. (Orig.). 1984. pap. 6.95 o.p. (ISBN 0-8066-2093-5, 10-2943, Augsburg). Augsburg Fortress.

Handbook & Guide for Selecting a Career & Preparing for the Future. rev. ed. Research & Education Association Staff. LC 84-60060. (Illus.). 576p. 1987-88. 15.95 o.p. (ISBN 0-87891-553-2). Res & Educ.

Handbook Assess Suppl Training. 1979. text ed. 5.95 o.p. (ISBN 0-07-013352-2). McGraw.

Handbook for Administrators & Teachers: Reading in the Kindergarten. Ed. by Lloyd O. Ollila. 107p. (Orig.). 1980. pap. text ed. 4.50 o.p. (ISBN 0-87207-728-4, 728). Intl Reading.

Handbook for A.R.E. Study Groups. rev. ed. 1971. pap. 3.95 o.p. (ISBN 0-87604-052-0). ARE Pr.

Handbook for Auditors. James A. Cashin. 1971. text ed. 89.50 o.p. (ISBN 0-07-010200-7). McGraw.

Handbook for Automatic Computation: Vol. 1. Pt. A. Description of ALGOL 60. H. Rutishauser. Ed. by F. L. Bauer et al. (Grundlehren der Mathematischen Wissenschaften: Vol. 135). (Illus.). 1967. 40.00 o.p. (ISBN 0-387-03826-4). Springer-Verlag.

Handbook for Benefit Plan Professionals, 1983. Becky A. Wright. 142p. (Orig.). 1983. pap. 10.00 o.p. (ISBN 0-89154-214-0). Intl Found Employ.

Handbook for Citizenship. Margaret Seely. (Illus.). 70p. 1981. pap. text ed. 5.95x o.p. (ISBN 0-88084-009-9). Alemany pr.

Handbook for Coaching Cross-Country & Running Events. George R. Colfer. 1977. text ed. 19.95 o.p. (ISBN 0-13-377051-6, Parker). P-H.

Handbook for College Admissions. Thomas C. Hayden. LC 80-66009. 1981. 12.95o.p. (ISBN 0-689-11095-2, Atheneum); pap. 7.95 o.p. (ISBN 0-689-11166-5). Macmillan.

Handbook for Community Manpower Surveys. J. Morton. 116p. 1972. pap. 2.00 o.p. (ISBN 0-911558-43-8). W E Upjohn.

Handbook for Conducting Workshop on the Counseling Needs of the Elderly. Compiled by Mary Ganikos et al. 47p. 1979. pap. text ed. 3.75 o.p. (ISBN 0-911547-45-2, 72137W34). Am Assn Coun Dev.

Handbook for Construction Accounting & Auditing. Henry G. Pansza. LC 83-9568. 285p. 1983. text ed. 39.95 o.p. (ISBN 0-13-372573-1). P-H.

Handbook for Corporate Directors. E. P. Mattar & M. Ball. 640p. 1985. text ed. 51.95 o.p. (ISBN 0-07-040936-6). McGraw.

Handbook for Dental Hygienists. 2nd ed. Collins et al. 320p. 1978. 19.00 o.p. (ISBN 0-7236-0497-5, Pub. by John Wright UK). Butterworth.

Handbook for Dental Surgical Assistants & Other Ancillary Workers. 2nd ed. S. Gelbier & Copley. 260p. 1977. 14.00 o.p. (ISBN 0-7236-0464-9, Pub. by John Wright UK). Butterworth.

Handbook for Development Officers at Independent Schools. 2nd ed. Ed. by Donald J. Whelan. 350p. 1982. 35.00 o.p. (ISBN 0-89964-194-6). Coun Adv & Supp Ed.

Handbook for Educating in the New Age. Walene James. (Illus.). 1977. pap. 4.95 o.p. (ISBN 0-87604-095-4). ARE Pr.

Handbook for Effective Supervision of Instruction. 3rd ed. Ross L. Neagley & N. Dean Evans. 1980. text ed. (ISBN 0-13-372672-X). P-H.

Handbook for Electronic Engineering Technicians. Milton Kaufman & Arthur H. Seidman. 1976. text ed. 35.00 o.p. (ISBN 0-07-033401-3). McGraw.

Handbook for Environmental Planning: The Social Consequences of Environmental Change. James McEvoy, III & Thomas Dietz. LC 76-57239. 354p. 1977. 32.00 o.p. (ISBN 0-471-58389-8, JW). Krieger.

Handbook for Episcopalians. William B. Williamson. LC 61-14387. 1961. pap. 4.95 o.p. (ISBN 0-8192-1080-3). Morehouse Pub.

Handbook for Family Analysis. Gordon Shipman. LC 82-47579. 400p. 1982. 30.00x o.p. (ISBN 0-669-05548-4); pap. 20.00x o.p. (ISBN 0-669-05549-2). Lexington Bks.

Handbook for Georgia Legislators. 9th ed. Vinson, Carl, Institute of Government Staff et al. LC 83-24573. 220p. (Orig.). 1984. 14.95 o.p. (ISBN 0-317-02454-X). U of GA Inst Govt.

Handbook for Latchkey Children & Their Parents: A Complete Guide for Latchkey Kids & Their Working Parents. Lynette Long & Thomas Long. 356p. 1983. 16.95 o.p. (ISBN 0-87795-506-9, Arbor Hse); pap. 7.95 o.p. (ISBN 0-87795-507-7). Morrow.

Handbook for Mangrove Area Management. Ed. by Lawrence S. Hamilton & Samuel C. Snedaker. xii, 123p. 1984. avail. o.s.i. (ISBN 0-86638-055-8). EW Ctr HI.

Handbook for Modern Language Teachers. Ed. by Alan W. Hornsey. 449p. 1982. 39.95x o.p. (ISBN 0-423-89690-3, NO. 2762); pap. 17.95 o.p. (ISBN 0-423-51050-9, NO. 3711). Routledge Chapman & Hall.

Handbook for No-Load Fund Investors. No-Load Fund Investor Staff. 1984. pap. text ed. 29.00 o.p. (ISBN 0-07-046854-0). McGraw.

Handbook for No-Load Fund Investors, 1987. S. Jacobs. 400p. 1987. pap. text ed. 24.95 o.p. (ISBN 0-07-032160-4). McGraw.

Handbook for Private Schools. 67th ed. Ed. by Porter Sargent Staff. (Handbook Ser.). (Illus.). 1986. 40.00 o.s.i. (ISBN 0-87558-115-3). Porter Sargent.

Handbook for Radiologic Technologists & Special Procedures Nurses in Radiology. N. W. Powell. (Illus.). 104p. 1974. 18.00 o.p. (ISBN 0-398-03066-9). C C Thomas.

Handbook for Recreation. rev. 1959 ed. U. S. Children's Bureau Staff. LC 74-174126. (Children's Bureau Publication Ser.: No. 231). (Illus.). x, 158p. 1975. Repr. of 1960 ed. 36.00x o.p. (ISBN 0-8103-4267-7). Gale.

Handbook for Single Adoptive Parents. Rev. 1982, 1985, & 1987 ed. Ed. by Hope Marindin. 70p. 8.00 o.p. (ISBN 0-318-13716-X). Comm Single Adopt.

Handbook for Skippers. Boy Scouts of America. (Illus.). (gr. 9-12). pap. cancelled o.s.i. (ISBN 0-8395-3233-4, 3233). BSA.

Handbook for Space Colonists. G. Harry Stine. (Illus.). 288p. 1985. pap. 11.95 o.p. (ISBN 0-03-070741-2, Owl Bks). H Holt & Co.

Handbook for Student Writers. John R. Willingham & Donald F. Warders. 348p. 1978. pap. text ed. 10.95 o.p. (ISBN 0-15-530810-6, HC). HarBraceJ.

Handbook for the Amateur Theatre. Peter Cotes. (Illus.). 430p. 1958. (ISBN 0-8022-0306-X). Philos Lib.

Handbook for the Design of Instruction in Pharmacy Education. Ed. by Thomas E. Cyrs, Jr. 200p. 6.50 o.p. (ISBN 0-937526-06-1). AACP Alexandria.

Handbook for the Design of Instruction in Pharmacy Education. Ed. by Thomas E. Cyrs, Jr. 200p. 1977. 6.50 o.p. (ISBN 0-686-83878-5). AACP Alexandria.

Handbook for the Disabled. Susanne Lunt. (Illus.). 288p. 1984. pap. 9.95 o.p. (ISBN 0-684-18030-8, ScribT). Scribner.

Handbook for the Lectionary. Horace T. Allen, Jr. LC 80-19735. 254p. 1980. softcover 8.95 o.s.i. (ISBN 0-664-24347-9, Westminster). Westminster John Knox.

Handbook for the Medical Secretary. 4th ed. Miriam Bredow. (Illus.). 1959. pap. text ed. 4.50 o.p. (ISBN 0-07-007413-5). McGraw.

Handbook for the Rolling Resistance of Pneumatic Tires. S. K. Clark & R. N. Dodge. (Illus.). 78p. 1979. 12.00 o.p. (ISBN 0-938654-26-8, TIRES). Indus Dev Inst Sci.

Handbook for the Study of Drama. rev. ed. Lynn Altenbernd & Leslie L. Lewis. (Orig.). 1966. pap. text ed. write for info. o.p. (ISBN 0-02-301940-9, 30194). Macmillan.

Handbook for the Study of Poetry. rev. ed. Lynn Altenbernd & Leslie L. Lewis. (Orig.). 1966. pap. text ed. write for info. o.p. (ISBN 0-02-301930-1, 30193). Macmillan.

Handbook for the Trial of Contract Lawsuits: Strategies & Techniques. Edward J. Imwinkelried. LC 81-7330. 379p. 1981. text ed. 37.50 o.p. (ISBN 0-13-382606-6, Busn). P-H.

Handbook for Trainers in Educational Management, with Special Reference to Countries in Asia & the Pacific. U Pareek & T. V. Rao. 273p. 1981. pap. 9.95 o.p. (ISBN 0-686-81858-X, UB106, UNESCO). UNIPUB.

Handbook for Translating from English into Russian. Galina Kruberg. 172p. 1982. pap. text ed. 14.95x o.p. (ISBN 0-8020-2473-4). U of Toronto Pr.

Handbook for Typists: Operation of the Selectric Typewriter, Technical Information, Format Illustrations & Procedures. Ellen Pate & Barbara Spengler. 162p. (Orig.). 1985. pap. text ed. 11.95 o.p. (ISBN 0-8403-2967-9, 40296702). Kendall-Hunt.

Handbook for Youth & Student Leadership. Elliott Masie & Michele Stein. (National Student Leadership Center). 200p. (Orig.). pap. 19.95 o.p. (ISBN 0-913393-18-5). Tools Trg.

Handbook of Abnormal Psychology. Richard Nice. 1959. (ISBN 0-8022-1216-6). Philos Lib.

Handbook of Accepted Roofing Knowledge. 88p. 6.00 o.p. (ISBN 0-317-33660-6); 4.25 o.p. (ISBN 0-317-33661-4). Assn Phys Plant Admin.

Handbook of Accounts Receivable Financing: A Dynamic Approach to Cash Flow & Profits. Bryan E. Milling. LC 78-1252. 1978. 19.95 o.p. (ISBN 0-87624-200-X, Inst Busn Plan). P-H.

Handbook of Adult Education 1970. Ed. by Robert Smith & J. Roby Kidd. 594p. 16.95 o.p. (ISBN 0-317-32115-3). A A A C E.

Handbook of Advanced Wastewater Treatment. 2nd ed. Russell L. Culp & George M. Wesner. 1978. 42.50 o.p. (ISBN 0-442-21784-6). Van Nos Reinhold.

Handbook of Air Pollution Analysis. Ed. by Roger Perry & Robert J. Young. 1977. 79.95x o.p. (ISBN 0-412-12660-5, NO. 6220, Pub. by Chapman & Hall). Routledge Chapman & Hall.

Handbook of American English Spelling. Lee C. Deighton. LC 78-6272. 1978. pap. 1.95 o.p. (ISBN 0-15-638672-0, Harv). HarBraceJ.

Handbook of Applied Behavior Analysis: Social & Instructional Processes. Ed. by A. Charles Catania & Thomas A. Brigham. 750p. 1978. text ed. 74.50x o.s.i. (ISBN 0-8290-0857-8). Irvington.

Handbook of Applied Hydraulics. 3rd ed. Calvin V. Davis & K. E. Sorensen. (Illus.). 1968. text ed. 98.00 o.p. (ISBN 0-07-015538-0). McGraw.

Handbook of Architectural Practice & Management. 4th ed. Ed. by John Powell. 1979. 34.00x o.p. (ISBN 0-900630-67-1, Pub. by RIBA). Intl Spec Bk.

Handbook of Atomic Elements. LC 78-92089. 1970. (ISBN 0-8022-2340-0). Philos Lib.

Handbook of Aviculture. Frank Woolham. (Illus.). 368p. 1987. 75.00 o.p. (ISBN 0-7137-1428-X, Pub. by Blandford Pr England). Sterling.

Handbook of Avoiding Probate (With Legal Forms) Barbara R. Stock. (Illus.). 228p. 1987. pap. 29.95 o.p. (ISBN 0-913455-10-5). Linch Pub.

Handbook of BASIC for the IBM PC. David I. Schneider. LC 83-15508. 512p. 1983. pap. 22.95 o.p. (ISBN 0-89303-506-8); bk. & diskette 44.95 o.p. (ISBN 0-89303-508-4); diskette 25.00 o.p. (ISBN 0-89303-507-6). Brady Bks.

Handbook of Basic Writing Skills. Cora L. Robey et al. 345p. 1978. pap. text ed. 10.95 o.p. (ISBN 0-15-529170-X, HC). HarBraceJ.

Handbook of Bibliographies on Law in the Developing Countries. Ralph Lanski. 621p. 60.00 o.p. (ISBN 0-317-07343-5). Transnatl Pubs.

Handbook of Biomedical Plastics. Henry Lee & Kris Neville. (Illus.). 575p. 1971. 65.00 o.p. (ISBN 0-686-48256-5, 1702). T-C Pubns CA.

Handbook of British Pottery & Porcelain Marks. Geoffrey A. Godden. (Illus.). 193p. 1983. pap. 11.50 o.p. (ISBN 0-214-20192-9, Pub. by Hutchinson Pub UK). Seven Hills Bk Dists.

Handbook of Budgeting. H. W. Sweeny & Robert Rachlin. LC 80-39887. (Systems & Controls for Financial Management Ser.). 778p. 1981. 59.95 o.p. (ISBN 0-471-05621-9, Pub. by Ronald Pr). Wiley.

Handbook of Business Finance & Capital Sources. 3rd ed. Dileep Rao. LC 84-45976. 650p. 1985. 95.00 o.p. (ISBN 0-8144-5811-4). AMACOM.

Handbook of Business Formulas & Controls. Spencer A. Tucker. (Illus.). 1979. text ed. 49.50 o.p. (ISBN 0-07-065421-2). McGraw.

Handbook of Cancer Diagnosis & Staging: A Clinical Atlas. Seth A. Borg & Susan Rosenthal. LC 83-14597. 271p. 1984. 35.00 o.p. (ISBN 0-471-87073-0). Wiley.

Handbook of Cancer Immunology, Vol. 1: Basic Cancer-Related Immunology. new ed. Harold Waters. (LC 76-052693). 1978. lib. bdg. 60.00x o.p. (ISBN 0-8240-9864-1, Garland STPM Pr). Garland Pub.

Handbook of Cancer Immunology, Vol. 2: Cellular Escape from Immune Destruction. new ed. Harold Waters. (LC 76-052693). 1978. lib. bdg. 52.50x o.p. (ISBN 0-8240-7001-1, Garland STPM Pr). Garland Pub.

Handbook of Cancer Immunology, Vol. 3: Immune Status in Cancer Treatment & Prognosis, Pt. A. new ed. Harold Waters. (LC 76-052693). 1978. lib. bdg. 77.50x o.p. (ISBN 0-8240-7002-X, Garland STPM Pr). Garland Pub.

Handbook of Cancer Immunology, Vol. 4: Immune Status in Cancer Treatment & Prognosis, Pt. B. new ed. Harold Waters. (LC 76-052693). 1978. lib. bdg. 60.00x o.p. (ISBN 0-8240-7003-8, Garland STPM Pr). Garland Pub.

Handbook of Cancer Immunology, Vol. 5: Immunotherapy. new ed. Harold Waters. (LC 76-052693). 1978. lib. bdg. 82.50x o.p. (ISBN 0-8240-7004-6, Garland STPM Pr). Garland Pub.

Handbook of Career Education Activities: For Use by Secondary Counselors & Classroom Teachers. Joyce D. Jensen & Stella G. Cooley. 114p. 1982. spiral bdg. 17.75x o.p. (ISBN 0-398-04768-5). C C Thomas.

Handbook of Career Planning for Special Needs Students. Thomas F. Harrington. LC 82-11419. 384p. 1982. 34.00 o.p. (ISBN 0-89443-661-9). Aspen Pub.

Handbook of Chemical Property Estimation Methods. W. J. Lyman & W. F. Reehl. 976p. 1982. text ed. 65.00 o.p. (ISBN 0-07-039175-0). McGraw.

Handbook of Child Psychopathology. Ed. by Michel Hersen & Thomas H. Ollendick. 538p. 1983. 60.00x o.p. (ISBN 0-306-40938-0, Plenum Pr). Plenum Pub.

Handbook of Christian Feasts & Customs. Francis X. Weiser. LC 58-10908. 1958. 9.50 o.p. (ISBN 0-15-138435-5). HarBraceJ.

Handbook of Circulation Management. Ed. by Barbara Love. 1980. 49.95 o.p. (ISBN 0-918110-02-5). Hanson Pub Grp.

Handbook of Clinical Drug Data. 5th, rev. ed. James E. Knoben et al. LC 82-22145. 669p. 1983. 29.50 o.p. (ISBN 0-914768-41-7). Drug Intell Pubns.

Handbook of Clinical Drug Research. Glenny & Nelmes. 1986. 27.00 o.p. (ISBN 0-8016-1829-0). Mosby.

Handbook of Clinical Nutrition: Clinician's Manual for the Diagnosis & Management of Nutritional Problems. Roland L. Weinsier & C. E. Butterworth, Jr. LC 80-20161. (Illus.). 231p. 1980. pap. text ed. 15.95 o.p. (ISBN 0-8016-5406-8). Mosby.

Handbook of Clinical Pharmacokinetics. Ed. by L. F. Prescott & M. Gibaldi. 1200p. text ed. 89.50 o.p. (ISBN 0-86792-004-1, Pub by Adis Pr Australia). Year Bk Med.

Handbook of COBOL Techniques. 3rd ed. Computer Partners, Inc. Staff. LC 87-25864. 106p. 1982. pap. 29.50x o.p. (ISBN 0-89435-229-6). QED Info Sci.

Handbook of COBOL Techniques & Programming Standards. Computer Partners, Inc. 154p. pap. 29.50 o.p. (ISBN 0-89435-227-X). Qed Info Sci.

Handbook of Communication. Wilbur Schramm et al. 1973. text ed. 55.00 o.p. (ISBN 0-395-30728-7). HM.

Handbook of Community Gardening. Boston Urban Gardeners. Ed. by Susan Naimark. (Illus.). 1982. 14.95 o.s.i. (ISBN 0-684-17466-9, ScribT); pap. 7.95 o.s.i. (ISBN 0-684-17843-5). Scribner.

Handbook of Components for Electronics. Charles A. Harper. 1977. text ed. 79.50 o.p. (ISBN 0-07-026682-4). McGraw.

Handbook of Computers & Data Processing. Research & Education Association Staff. LC 83-61837. (Illus.). 480p. 1983. 19.85 o.s.i. (ISBN 0-87891-546-X). Res & Educ.

Handbook of Connecticut Evidence: 1986 Supplement. Colin C. Tait & Joseph A. LaPlante. LC 76-7648. 244p. 1986. 35.00 o.p. Little.

Handbook of Construction Resources & Support Services. Professional Publications Staff. Ed. by Joseph A. MacDonald. LC 79-90746. (Orig.). 1980. pap. 49.50 o.p. (ISBN 0-932836-02-X). Prof Pubns NY.

Handbook of Contemporary English. Walter E. Meyers. 500p. 1974. text ed. 10.95 o.p. (ISBN 0-15-530848-3, HC). HarBraceJ.

Handbook of Controls & Instrumentation. John D. Lenk. (Illus.). 1980. pap. text ed. 39.00 o.p. (ISBN 0-13-377069-9). P-H.

Handbook of Corrosion Experiments. (Illus.). 83p. 25.00 o.p. (ISBN 0-915567-56-3, 52191). Natl Corrosion Eng.

Handbook of Cost Accounting Methods. Ed. by Jacob K. Lasser. LC 74-10672. (Illus.). vii, 1344p. 1971. Repr. of 1949 ed. lib. bdg. 59.25x o.p. (ISBN 0-8371-3546-X, LACA). Greenwood.

Handbook of Cotton Weaving, 2 Vols. E. Onikov. 501p. 1981. 15.00 set o.p. (ISBN 0-8285-2079-8, Pub. by Mir Pubs USSR). Imported Pubns.

Handbook of Creative Learning Exercises. Herbert Engel. LC 73-75394. (Building Blocks of Human Potential Ser.). 276p. 1973. 19.00x o.p. (ISBN 0-87201-162-3). Gulf Pub.

Handbook of Creativity. Judy Dorsett. (Illus.). 128p. 1985. pap. 7.95 o.p. (ISBN 0-87239-729-7, 3226). Standard Pub.

Handbook of Criminology. Daniel Glaser. 1974. text ed. 65.00 o.p. (ISBN 0-395-30603-5). HM.

Handbook of Cross-Cultural Human Development. Ruth H. Munroe et al. LC 79-12028. 900p. 1980. lib. bdg. 88.00 o.p. (ISBN 0-8240-7045-3). Garland Pub.

Handbook of Current English. 7th ed. Jim W. Corder & John J. Ruszkiewicz. 1985. text ed. write for info. o.p. (ISBN 0-673-15968-X). Scott F.

Handbook of Curriculum Evaluation. pap. 14.75 o.p. (UM33, UM). UNIPUB.

Handbook of Cyclical Indicators, 1984: A Supplement to the Business Conditions Digest. (Illus.). 195p. (Orig.). 1984. pap. 5.50 o.p. (ISBN 0-318-11728-2, S/N 003-010-00127-5). USGPO.

Handbook of Dam Engineering. Ed. by Alfred R. Golze. 1977. 69.95 o.p. (ISBN 0-442-22752-3). Van Nos Reinhold.

Handbook of Data Communication & Computer Networks. Dimitris N. Chorafas. (Illus.). 600p. 1985. text ed. 59.95 o.p. (ISBN 0-89433-244-9). Petrocelli.

Handbook of Data Processing Administration, Operations, & Procedures. new ed. S. R. Mixon. LC 75-38914. (Illus.). 396p. 1976. 29.95 o.p. (ISBN 0-8144-5400-3). AMACOM.

Handbook of Dental Local Anaesthesia. Hans Evers & Glenn Haegerstam. (Illus.). 208p. 1981. 29.50 o.p. (ISBN 0-907789-00-5). Year Bk Med.

Handbook of Depreciation Methods, Formulas & Tables. James M. Johnson. 704p. 1982. text ed. 49.95 o.p. (ISBN 0-13-377390-6, Busn). P-H.

Handbook of Designs & Devices. 2nd ed. C. P. Hornung. (Illus.). 14.25 o.p. (ISBN 0-8446-0706-1). Peter Smith.

Handbook of Diagnostic & Prescriptive Teaching. David Sabatino & Lester Mann. LC 82-4106. 353p. 1982. 35.00 o.p. (ISBN 0-89443-692-9). Aspen Pub.

Handbook of Digital IC Applications. David L. Heiserman. 1980. text ed. 42.00 o.p. (ISBN 0-13-372698-3). P-H.

Handbook of Dreams: Research, Theories & Applications. Ed. by Benjamin B. Wolman. 512p. 1983. pap. 16.95 o.p. (ISBN 0-442-29351-8). Van Nos Reinhold.

Handbook of Drug Therapy in Psychiatry. 2nd ed. Jerrold G. Bernstein. (Illus.). 352p. 1987. (ISBN 0-7236-7028-5). Butterworth.

Handbook of Ear, Nose & Throat Emergencies. Ed. by M. Haskell Newman et al. 1973. spiral bdg. 11.95 o.p. (ISBN 0-87488-639-2). Med Exam.

Handbook of Early American Sheet Music: 1768-1889. Harry Dichter & Elliot Shapiro. (Illus.). 17.25 o.p. (ISBN 0-8446-5570-8). Peter Smith.

Handbook of Economic Statistics, 1986, a Reference Aid. (CPAS 86-10002 Ser.). (Illus.). 242p. (Orig.). 1986. pap. 19.00 o.p. (ISBN 0-318-21547-0, S/N 041-015-00165-5). USGPO.

Handbook of Educational Technology: A Practical Guide for Teachers. Fred Percival & Henry Ellington. LC 82-24655. 150p. 1984. 26.50 o.p. (ISBN 0-89397-150-2). Nichols Pub.

Handbook of Electromedicine: Basic Principles, Applications, Equipment. 3rd, rev. ed. Siemens Staff. LC 85-12329. 300p. 1985. pap. 52.00 o.p. (ISBN 0-471-90407-4, Dist. by A R Liss). Wiley.

Handbook of Electronic Design & Analysis Procedures Using Programmable Calculators. Bruce K. Murdock. (Electrical-Computer Science & Engineering Ser.). 1979. 42.95 o.p. (ISBN 0-442-26137-3). Van Nos Reinhold.

Handbook of Electronics Calculations. Milton Kaufman & Arthur H. Seidman. (Illus.). 1979. text ed. 47.95 o.p. (ISBN 0-07-033392-0). McGraw.

Handbook of Electronics Packaging Design & Engineering. Bernard S. Matisoff. 400p. 1982. 45.95 o.s.i. (ISBN 0-442-20171-0). Van Nos Reinhold.

Handbook of Elliptic Integrals for Engineers & Scientists. 2nd ed. P. F. Byrd & M. D. Friedman. LC 72-146515. (Grundlehren der Mathematischen Wissenschaften: Vol. 67). (Illus.). 1971. 42.00 o.p. (ISBN 0-387-05318-2). Springer-Verlag.

Handbook of Emergency Care & Rescue. rev. ed. Lawrence W. Erven. 1976. text ed. write for info. o.p. (ISBN 0-02-472630-3). Macmillan.

Handbook of Endocrinology: Diagnosis & Management of Endocrine & Metabolic Disorders. 2nd ed. Richard S. Dillon. LC 79-10531. (Illus.). 760p. 1980. text ed. 52.00 o.p. (ISBN 0-8121-0642-3). Lea & Febiger.

Handbook of Energy Technology: Trends & Perspectives. V. Daniel Hunt. 992p. 1981. 68.95 o.p. (ISBN 0-442-22555-5). Van Nos Reinhold.

Handbook of Engine Swapping. Clymer Publications. (Illus.). 1960. pap. 4.00 o.p. (ISBN 0-89287-271-3, A263). Clymer Pub.

Handbook of English. Clarence Stratton. LC 74-19222. 360p. 1975. Repr. of 1940 ed. 51.00x o.p. (ISBN 0-8103-4112-3). Gale.

Handbook of Environmental Health & Safety: Principles & Practices. Herman Koren. 1980. 175.00 o.p. (ISBN 0-08-023900-5). Pergamon.

Handbook of Enzyme Inhibitors (1965-1977) Mahendra K. Jain. LC 82-2595. 447p. 1982. 130.00x o.p. (ISBN 0-471-86727-6). Wiley.

Handbook of Evaluation Research, Vol. 1. Ed. by Elmer L. Struening & Marcia Guttentag. LC 74-15764. 1975. 35.00 o.p. (ISBN 0-8039-0428-2). Sage.

Handbook of Family Law. 4th, Rev. ed. Stuart J. Faber. 484p. 1982. pap. text ed. 41.50 o.p. (ISBN 0-686-34400-6). Lega Bks.

Handbook of Family Planning. Ed. by Nancy Loudon & John Newton. (Illus.). 334p. 1985. pap. text ed. 34.00 o.p. (ISBN 0-443-02480-4). Churchill.

Handbook of Farm & Ranch Estate Planning. Jim G. Polson. 270p. 1982. text ed. 39.95 o.p. (ISBN 0-13-377952-1, Busn). P-H.

Handbook of Federal World War Agencies & Their Records, 1917-1921. U. S. National Archives Staff. LC 75-35366. (U. S. Government Documents Program Ser.: No.24). 666p. 1976. Repr. of 1943 ed. lib. bdg. 41.50x o.p. (ISBN 0-8371-8602-1, USHW). Greenwood.

Handbook of Fillers & Reinforcements for Plastics. Harry S. Katz & John V. Milewski. (Illus.). 1978. 49.50 o.p. (ISBN 0-442-25372-9). Van Nos Reinhold.

Handbook of Films, Sheets & Laminates. 85.00 o.p. (ISBN 0-686-48144-5, 0305). T-C Pubns CA.

Handbook of Financial Markets: Securities, Options and Futures. Frank J. Fabozzi & Frank G. Zarb. LC 80-70448. 825p. 1981. 50.00 o.p. (ISBN 0-87094-216-6). Dow Jones-Irwin.

Handbook of Fixed Income Securities. Ed. by Frank J. Fabozzi & Irving M. Pollack. LC 82-71874. 850p. 1983. 55.00 o.p. (ISBN 0-87094-306-5). Dow Jones-Irwin.

Handbook of Flame Spectroscopy. M. L. Parsons et al. LC 75-17865. 476p. 1975. 75.00x o.p. (ISBN 0-306-30856-8, Plenum Pr). Plenum Pub.

Handbook of Fluid Dynamics. Victor L. Streeter. 1961. text ed. 98.00 o.p. (ISBN 0-07-062178-0). McGraw.

Handbook of Fluids in Motion. Ed. by Nicholas P. Cheremisinoff & Ramesh Gupta. LC 82-70706. (Illus.). 1200p. 1983. 99.95 o.p. (ISBN 0-250-40458-3). Butterworth.

Handbook of Geriatric Drug Therapy for Health Care Professionals. Edward D. Sumner. LC 83-13592. (Illus.). 208p. 1983. pap. 14.00 o.p. (ISBN 0-8121-0904-X). Lea & Febiger.

Handbook of Geriatric Psychiatry. Ed. by Ewald W. Busse & Dan G. Blazer. 560p. 1979. 41.95 o.p. (ISBN 0-442-20896-0). Van Nos Reinhold.

Handbook of German East Africa. Great Britain, Admiralty Staff. LC 75-90114. (Illus.). 1969. Repr. of 1920 ed. 20.75 o.p. (ISBN 0-8371-2034-9, HGE&, Pub. by Negro U Pr). Greenwood.

Handbook of Gerontological Services. Monk. 1985. 41.95 o.p. (ISBN 0-442-27806-3). Van Nos Reinhold.

Handbook of Group Therapy. Martin Grotjahn & Frank M. Kline. 320p. 1982. 33.95 o.p. (ISBN 0-442-21939-3). Van Nos Reinhold.

Handbook of Hard Metals. Dawihl. 1957. (ISBN 0-8022-0363-9). Philos Lib.

Handbook of Heat Transfer. Warren M. Rohsenow & James P. Hartnett. 1504p. 1973. text ed. 89.50 o.p. (ISBN 0-07-053576-0). McGraw.

Handbook of Heavy Construction. 2nd ed. J. Havers & F. Stubbs. 1971. text ed. 99.00 o.p. (ISBN 0-07-027278-6). McGraw.

Handbook of HeI Photoelectron Spectra of Fundamental Organic Molecules. Katsumi Kimura et al. LC 81-6449. 268p. 1981. 54.95x o.p. (ISBN 0-470-27200-7). Halsted Pr.

Handbook of Histology. 5th ed. Karl A. Stiles. (Illus.). 1968. text ed. 25.00 o.p. (ISBN 0-07-061426-1). McGraw.

Handbook of Hose, Pipes, Couplings & Fittings. (Illus.). 500p. 1984. text ed. 128.00x o.p. (ISBN 0-85461-091-X). Gower Pub Co.

Handbook of Hypergeometric Integrals: Theory, Applications, Tables, Computer Programs. Harold Exton. LC 78-40120. (Mathematics & Its Applications Ser.). 316p. 1978. 84.95x o.p. (ISBN 0-470-26342-3). Halsted Pr.

Handbook of Hypnosis for Professionals. Roy Udolf. 384p. 1980. 32.95 o.p. (ISBN 0-442-28881-6). Van Nos Reinhold.

Handbook of Illinois Evidence: 1986 Supplement. Michael H. Graham. 1986. 28.00 o.p. (ISBN 0-316-32302-0). Little.

Handbook of Immunology for Students & House Staff. Ed. by Senih M. Fikrig. LC 82-6878. (Illus.). 203p. 1982. pap. 28.50x o.p. (ISBN 0-89573-111-8). VCH Pubs.

Handbook of Inductively-Coupled Plasma Spectrometry. Michael Thompson & J. N. Walsh. LC 83-7212. 230p. 1983. 85.00 o.p. (ISBN 0-412-00371-6, NO. 5039, Pub. by Chapman & Hall). Routledge Chapman & Hall.

Handbook of Industrial & Organizational Psychology. Marvin D. Dunnette. 1976. text ed. 64.75 o.p. (ISBN 0-395-30859-3). HM.

Handbook of Industrial Energy Conservation. S. Hu. 1982. 50.95 o.p. (ISBN 0-442-24426-6). Van Nos Reinhold.

Handbook of Industrial Fire Protection & Security. Ed. by Trade & Technical Press, Ltd. Staff. 150.00x o.p. (ISBN 0-85461-059-6). Trans-Atl Phila.

Handbook of Industrial Infrared Analysis. Robert G. White. LC 64-7506. 440p. 1964. 75.00x o.p. (ISBN 0-306-30174-1, Plenum Pr). Plenum Pub.

Handbook of Industrial Materials. Trade & Technical Press Editors. 600p. 1977. 120.00x o.p. (ISBN 0-85461-060-X, Pub by Trade & Tech England). Gower Pub Co.

Handbook of Industrial Materials: Ferrous & Non-Ferrous Metals, Non-Metallic Materials, Plastics & Adhesives. 1978. 150.00x o.p. Coronet Bks.

Handbook of Industrial Psychology. May Smith. (ISBN 0-8022-1599-8). Philos Lib.

Handbook of Industrial Residues. Jon C. Dyer & Nicholas A. Mignone. LC 82-19082. (Environment Engineering Ser.). (Illus.). 453p. 1983. 54.00 o.p. (ISBN 0-8155-0924-3, Noyes Pubns). Noyes.

Handbook of Industrial Waste Disposal. Richard A. Conway & Richard D. Ross. 576p. 1980. 39.50 o.p. (ISBN 0-442-27053-4). Van Nos Reinhold.

Handbook of Industrial Wastes Pretreatment. Jon C. Dyer. LC 79-25702. 280p. 1980. lib. bdg. 36.00 o.p. (ISBN 0-8240-7066-6). Garland Pub.

Handbook of Information, Computer & Communications Activities of Major International Organizations. OECD Staff. (Information Computer Communications Policy (ICCP) Ser.: No. 4). 233p. (Orig.). 1980. pap. 14.50x o.p. (ISBN 92-64-12035-1, 93-80-01-1). OECD.

Handbook of Instructional Resources & References for Teaching the Gifted. 2nd ed. Frances A. Karnes & Emily C. Collins. 196p. 1984. pap. 37.95 o.s.i. (ISBN 0-205-08151-7, 248151, Pub. by Longwood Div). Allyn.

Handbook of Instrumentation & Controls: A Practical Manual for the Mechanical Services. Howard Kallen. 1961. text ed. 79.50 o.p. (ISBN 0-07-033235-5). McGraw.

Handbook of Instruments & Instrumentation. Trade & Technical Press Editors. 650p. 1977. 129.50 o.p. (Pub by Trade & Tech England). Gower Pub Co.

Handbook of Insurance Terms & Concepts. Marshall W. Reavis. 208p. 1983. pap. 9.95 o.p. (ISBN 0-88462-630-X, 4101-10, Pub. by Longman Fin Serv Pub). Longman Finan.

Handbook of Interactive Video. Ed. by Steve Floyd & Beth Floyd. LC 82-12690. (Video Bookshelf Ser.). 168p. 1982. professional 37.95 o.p. (ISBN 0-86729-019-6). Knowledge Indus.

Handbook of Intercultural Training: Issues in Theory & Design, Vol. I. Ed. by Dan Landis. (Pergamon General Psychology Ser.: No. 116). (Illus.). 300p. 1983. 63.00 o.p. (ISBN 0-08-027533-8). Pergamon.

Handbook of Intermediate Metabolism of Aromatic Compounds. B. L. Goodwin. 1976. 60.00x o.p. (ISBN 0-412-12920-5, NO. 6130, Pub. by Chapman & Hall). Routledge Chapman & Hall.

Handbook of International Trade & Development Statistics, 1983-84 United Nations. 62.50 o.p. (ISBN 0-8002-3176-7). Intl Pubns Serv.

Handbook of Japanese Grammar. Harold G. Henderson. LC 43-15405. 1948. text ed. 8.95 o.p. (ISBN 0-395-04589-4, 3-23710). HM.

Handbook of Latin American & Caribbean National Archives. Ann K. Nauman. LC 83-15837. 1983. pap. 9.50 o.p. (ISBN 0-87917-088-3). Ethridge.

Handbook of Latin American Art, Bibliographic Compilation: General References & Art of the 19th & 20th Centuries, North America, 2 pts, Vol. I. Ed. by Joyce W. Bailey et al. LC 83-26656. 1984. Pt. 1: North America, 579pgs. lib. bdg. 75.00 o.p. (ISBN 0-87436-384-5); Pt. 2: South America, 616pgs. pap. 75.00 o.p. (ISBN 0-87436-385-3). ABC-Clio.

Handbook of Latin American Art, Vol. III: The Ancient Period. cancelled o.s.i. (ISBN 0-87436-390-X). ABC-Clio.

Handbook of Learned Societies & Institutions: America. LC 66-20613. viii, 606p. 1966. Repr. of 1908 ed. 44.00x o.p. (ISBN 0-8103-3079-2). Gale.

Handbook of Legendary & Mythological Art. Clara E. Clement. LC 68-26616. (Illus.). 587p. 1969. Repr. of 1881 ed. 45.00x o.p. (ISBN 0-8103-3175-6). Gale.

Handbook of Leprosy. 3rd ed. W. H. Jopling. 160p. 1984. pap. text ed. 27.50x o.p. (ISBN 0-433-17567-2, Pub. by W. Heinemann Med Bks). Sheridan Med Bks.

Handbook of Literary Terms. Jones E. Yelland. 1951. (ISBN 0-8022-1949-7). Philos Lib.

Handbook of Magazine Publishing. Ed. by Folio Magazine Editors. 1977. 59.95 o.p. (ISBN 0-918110-00-9). Hanson Pub Grp.

Handbook of Major Appliance Trouble-Shooting & Repair. David L. Heiserman. LC 76-10684. (Illus.). 1977. pap. text ed. 32.00 o.p. (ISBN 0-13-380295-7). P-H.

Handbook of Management Accounting. Ed. by David Fanning. 496p. (Orig.). 1983. text ed. 59.95x o.p. (ISBN 0-566-02236-2). Gower Pub Co.

Handbook of Management Games. 3rd ed. Chris Elgood. 352p. 1984. text ed. 46.50x o.p. (ISBN 0-566-02442-X). Gower Pub Co.

Handbook of Materials & Processes for Electronics. Charles A. Harper. 1970. text ed. 69.50 o.p. (ISBN 0-07-026673-5). McGraw.

Handbook of Maternity Care: A Guide for Nursing Practice. Margaret Jensen & Irene Bobak. LC 79-18163. (Illus.). 294p. 1980. pap. text ed. 19.95 o.p. (ISBN 0-8016-2490-8). Mosby.

Handbook of Mathematical Calculations for Science Students & Researchers. Karen Assaf & Said Assaf. (Illus.). 310p. 1974. text ed. 6.50x o.p. (ISBN 0-8138-1135-X). Iowa St U Pr.

Handbook of Mathematics. L. Kuipers & R. Timman. 1969. 205.00 o.p. (ISBN 0-08-011857-7); pap. text ed. 29.00 o.p. (ISBN 0-08-018996-2). Pergamon.

Handbook of Mechanical Power Drives. Trade & Technical Press Editors. 777p. 1977. 129.50 o.p. (Pub by Trade & Tech England). Gower Pub Co.

Handbook of Medical Emergencies in the Dental Office. 2nd ed. Stanley F. Malamed. LC 81-18687. (Illus.). 411p. 1982. pap. text ed. 32.95 o.p. (ISBN 0-8016-3075-4). Mosby.

Handbook of Medical Parasitology. V. Zaman. 200p. 1982. pap. text ed. 28.50 o.p. (ISBN 0-86792-000-9, Pub by Adis Pr Australia). Year Bk Med.

Handbook of Medical Sociology. 3rd ed. Howard E. Freeman et al. 1979. text ed. (ISBN 0-13-380253-1). P-H.

Handbook of Medical-Surgical Nursing. Elizabeth A. Mahoney & Jean P. Flynn. LC 83-12377. (Red Books: 1-627). 848p. 1983. pap. 19.95 o.p. (ISBN 0-471-86982-1). Wiley.

Handbook of Methodology for the Assessment of Air Pollution Effects on Vegetation. Air Pollution Control Association Specialty Conference, Minneapolis, 1978. 350p. 1979. 15.00 o.p. (ISBN 0-318-12259-6, SP-29); members 12.00 o.p. (ISBN 0-318-12260-X). Air & Waste.

Handbook of Methods of Approximate Fourier Transformation & Inversion of Laplace Transformaton. V. A. Krylov. 247p. 1977. 6.45 o.p. (ISBN 0-8285-0723-6, Pub. by Mir Pubs USSR). Imported Pubns.

Handbook of Microcomputer Interfacing. Steve Leibson. (Illus.). 272p. 1983. 21.95 o.p. (ISBN 0-8306-0501-0, 1501); pap. 16.60 o.p. (ISBN 0-8306-1501-6, 1501). TAB Bks.

Handbook of Microwave Ferrite Materials. Ed. by Wilhelm H. Von Aulock. (Illus.). 1965. 78.00 o.p. (ISBN 0-12-723350-4). Acad Pr.

Handbook of Middle American Indians: Ethnology, Vol. 7 & 8 (Pts. 1 & 2) Ed. by Robert Wauchope. write for info. o.p. U of Tex Pr.

Handbook of Modern Manufacturing Management. Harold B. Maynard. 1970. text ed. 95.00 o.p. (ISBN 0-07-041087-9). McGraw.

Handbook of Modern Marketing. Ed. by Victor P. Buell et al. LC 78-96238. (Illus.). 1504p. 1970. text ed. 83.95 o.p. (ISBN 0-07-008838-1). McGraw.

Handbook of Modern Personnel Administration. Joseph J. Famularo. (Illus.). 1280p. 1972. text ed. 73.50 o.p. (ISBN 0-07-019912-4). McGraw.

Handbook of Municipal Waste Management Systems: Planning & Practice. Barbara J. Stevens. (Environmental Engineering Ser.). 320p. 1980. 37.95 o.p. (ISBN 0-442-23362-0). Van Nos Reinhold.

Handbook of Museum Technology. Research & Education Association Staff. LC 82-80747. (Illus.). 416p. (Orig.). 1982. pap. text ed. 12.05 o.s.i. (ISBN 0-87891-540-0). Res & Educ.

Handbook of Natural Beauty. Virginia Castleton. LC 75-25828. 1975. 12.95 o.p. (ISBN 0-87857-100-0). Rodale Pr Inc.

Handbook of Natural Gas Engineering. D. L. Katz. 1959. text ed. 110.00 o.p. (ISBN 0-07-033384-X). McGraw.

Handbook of Natural Remedies for Common Ailments. Linda Clark. 1983. pap. 3.50 o.s.i. (ISBN 0-671-49204-7). PB.

Handbook of Neonatal Intensive Care. Merenstein & Gardner. 1984. pap. 27.95 o.p. (ISBN 0-8016-1739-1). Mosby.

Handbook of Noise & Vibration Control. 4th ed. Trade & Technical Press Editors. 850p. 1982. Repr. of 1979 ed. 129.50 o.p. (Pub by Trade & Tech England). Gower Pub Co.

Handbook of Non-Verbal Group Exercises. Kenneth T. Morris & Kenneth M. Cinnamon. LC 74-12328. 300p. 1975. pap. 7.95 o.p. (ISBN 0-398-03239-4). Univ Assocs.

Handbook of Nursing. Ed. by Jeanne Howe et al. LC 83-25942. 1776p. 1984. 39.95 o.p. (ISBN 0-471-89524-5). Wiley.

Handbook of Nutritional Contents of Foods. U. S. Department of Agriculture Staff. 14.75 o.p. (ISBN 0-8446-5252-0). Peter Smith.

Handbook of Ocean & Underwater Engineering. Ed. by John J. Myers. LC 67-27280. 1969. text ed. 94.00 o.p. (ISBN 0-07-044245-2). McGraw.

Handbook of Ocular Pharmacology. 3rd ed. Marvin B. Smith. LC 77-94882. (Illus.). 256p. 1984. spiral bd. 23.50 o.p. (ISBN 0-88416-451-9). Year Bk Med.

Handbook of Ocular Toxicity. Marvin B. Smith. LC 75-12027. 526p. 1976. 25.00 o.p. (ISBN 0-88416-114-5). Year Bk Med.

Handbook of Ohio School Law. 1987-88. Text only. 40.00 o.p. Anderson Pub Co.

Handbook of Operant Behavior. Ed. by Werner K. Honig & J. Staddor. LC 76-26034. (Century Psychology Ser.). 1977. text ed. 95.00 o.p. (ISBN 0-13-380535-2). P-H.

Handbook of Organic Waste Conversion. Ed. by Michael W. Bewick. (Van Nostrand Reinhold Environmental Engineering Ser.). 432p. 1980. 39.95 o.p. (ISBN 0-442-20679-8). Van Nos Reinhold.

Handbook of Organosilicon Compounds: Advances Since 1961, Vol. 2. Ed. by Vladimir Bazant et al. 628p. 1975. 135.00 o.p. (ISBN 0-8247-6267-3). Dekker.

Handbook of Oriental Collections in Finland: Manuscripts, Xylographs, Inscriptions & Russian Minority Literature. Harry Halen. (Scandinavian Institute of Asian Studies Monograph: No. 31). 1978. pap. 17.50 o.p. (ISBN 0-7007-0105-2). Humanities.

Handbook of Orthoptic Principles. 4th ed. G. T. Cashell & I. M. Durran. (Illus.). 1981. pap. text ed. 18.50 o.p. (ISBN 0-443-02200-3). Churchill.

Handbook of Ozone Technology & Applications, Vol. 1. Rip G. Rice & Ahaton Netzer. LC 81-70869. 386p. 1982. 64.95 o.p. (ISBN 0-250-40324-2). Butterworth.

Handbook of Ozone Technology & Applications, Vol. 2. Ed. by Rip G. Rice & Aharon Netzer. LC 81-70869. (Illus.). 325p. 1984. 64.95 o.p. (ISBN 0-250-40577-6). Butterworth.

Handbook of Paint Raw Materials. Ernest W. Flick. LC 81-18937. 340p. (Orig.). 1982. 45.00 o.p. (ISBN 0-8155-0881-6). Noyes.

Handbook of Pediatric Nursing. Laura L. Hayman & Eileen Sporing. LC 85-3183. (Red Book Ser.). 1985. pap. 22.50 o.p. (ISBN 0-471-88667-X). Wiley.

Handbook of Physical Calculations. 2nd ed. Jan J. Tuma. (Illus.). 512p. 1983. text ed. 44.50 o.p. (ISBN 0-07-065439-5). McGraw.

Handbook of Physical Medicine & Rehabilitation. 3rd ed. Frederic J. Kottke et al. LC 77-139429. (Illus.). 1982. (ISBN 0-7216-5571-8). Saunders.

Handbook of Physics. B. Yavorsky & A. Detlaf. 965p. 1975. 15.00 o.p. (ISBN 0-8285-0786-4, Pub. by Mir Pubs USSR). Imported Pubns.

Handbook of Physics for Radiologists & Radiographers. Derek Gifford. 632p. 1984. text ed. 32.00 o.p. (ISBN 0-471-90172-5, Dist. by A R Liss). Wiley.

Handbook of Politics from 1868-94. Edward McPherson. Incl. Vol. 1. 1868. 17.75 (ISBN 0-8371-2223-6, MDB&); Vol. 2. 1870. 17.75 (ISBN 0-8371-2224-4, MDC&); Vol. 3. 1872. 17.75 (ISBN 0-8371-2225-2, MDD&); Vol. 4. 1874. 17.75 (ISBN 0-8371-2226-0, MDE&); Vol. 5. 1876. 17.75 (ISBN 0-8371-2227-9, MDF&); Vol. 6. 1878. 17.75 (ISBN 0-8371-2228-7, MDG&); Vol. 7. 1880. 17.75 (ISBN 0-8371-2229-5, MDH&); Vol. 8. 1882. 17.75 (ISBN 0-8371-2230-9, MDI&); Vol. 9. 1884. 17.75 (ISBN 0-8371-2231-7, MDJ&); Vol. 10. 1886. 17.75 (ISBN 0-8371-2232-5, MDK&); Vol. 11. 1888. 17.75 (ISBN 0-8371-2233-3, MDL&); Vol. 12. 1890. 17.75 (ISBN 0-8371-2234-1, MDM&); Vol. 13. 1892. 17.75 (ISBN 0-8371-2235-X, MDN&); Vol. 14. 1894. 17.75 (ISBN 0-8371-2236-8, MDO&). LC 74-92751. 1868-1894. Repr. 220.00x o.p. (ISBN 0-8371-2484-0, MDA&, Pub. by Negro U Pr). Greenwood.

Handbook of Portuguese Nyasaland. Great Britain, Admiralty Staff. LC 79-90115. 1969. Repr. of 1920 ed. 22.50 o.p. (ISBN 0-8371-2033-0, HPN&, Pub. by Negro U Pr). Greenwood.

Handbook of Power Generation: Transformers & Generators. John E. Traister. (Illus.). 272p. 1983. text ed. 37.33 o.p. (ISBN 0-13-380816-5). P-H.

Handbook of Practical Solid State Troubleshooting. John D. Lenk. (Illus.). 1978. ref. ed. 32.00 o.p. (ISBN 0-13-380642-1); pap. 12.95 o.p. (ISBN 0-13-380725-8). P-H.

Handbook of Preschool Special Education: Programming, Curriculum, Training. Allen A. Mori & Jane E. Olive. LC 80-14199. 528p. 1980. 35.00 o.p. (ISBN 0-89443-276-1). Aspen Pub.

Handbook of Pressure-Sensitive Adhesive Technology. Ed. by Donastas Satas. 680p. 1982. 42.95 o.p. (ISBN 0-442-25724-4). Van Nos Reinhold.

Handbook of Private Schools. 68th ed. Ed. by Porter Sargent Staff. LC 15-12869. (Handbook Ser.). (Illus.). 1987. 45.00 o.s.i. (ISBN 0-87558-117-X). Porter Sargent.

Handbook of Private Television: A Complete Guide for Video Facilities & Networks Within Corporations, Nonprofit Institutions & Government Agencies. Nathan J. Sambul. (Illus.). 400p. 1982. text ed. 83.50 o.p. (ISBN 0-07-054516-2). McGraw.

Handbook of Probability & Statistics with Tables. 2nd ed. Richard S. Burington & Donald C. May, Jr. 1970. text ed. 42.00 o.p. (ISBN 0-07-009030-0). McGraw.

Handbook of Probate Law, 2 vols. 4th, rev. ed. Robert O. Angle. 659p. 1983. pap. text ed. 51.50 o.p. (ISBN 0-89074-089-5). Lega Bks.

Handbook of Process Stream Analysis. Kenneth J. Clevett. LC 73-14416. (Analytical Chemistry Ser.). (Illus.). 470p. 1974. 83.95x o.p. (ISBN 0-470-16048-9). Halsted Pr.

Handbook of Proton Ionization Heats. James J. Christensen et al. LC 76-16511. 269p. 1976. lib. bdg. 32.50 o.p. (ISBN 0-471-01991-7, Pub. by John Wiley). Krieger.

Handbook of Psychatric & Mental Health Nursing. Catherine G. Adams & Alberta Macione. (Red Books Ser.). (Illus.). 495p. (Orig.). 1983. pap. 18.50 o.p. (ISBN 0-471-86983-X). Wiley.

Handbook of Psychiatric Diagnostic Procedures, Volume 1. Ed. by R. C. Hall & T. P. Beresford. 343p. 1987. 45.00 o.s.i. (ISBN 0-08-034962-5, PBI). Pergamon.

Handbook of Psychiatric Diagnostic Procedures, Volume 2. Ed. by R. C. Hall & T. P. Beresford. 376p. 1986. 45.00 o.s.i. (ISBN 0-08-035167-0). Pergamon.

Handbook of Psychiatric Rating Scales. Research & Education Association Staff. LC 81-50760. (Illus.). 256p. 1981. pap. text ed. 13.30 o.p. (ISBN 0-87891-527-3). Res & Educ.

Handbook of Psychonomics, 2 Vols. Ed. by J. A. Michon et al. 1979. Set. 244.25 o.p. (ISBN 0-444-85201-8, North Holland); Vol. 1. 147.50 o.p. (ISBN 0-444-85109-7); Vol. 2. 147.50 o.p. (ISBN 0-444-85194-1). Elsevier.

Handbook of Pulp & Paper Technology. 2nd ed. Kenneth W. Britt. (Illus.). 1979. pap. 19.95 o.p. (ISBN 0-442-15645-6); pap. 22.95 o.p. (ISBN 0-442-26176-4). Van Nos Reinhold.

Handbook of R. H. Burnes' Cetacean Dissections. R. H. Burnes. (Illus.). 1952. 20.00x o.p. (ISBN 0-565-00162-0, Pub. by Brit Mus Nat Hist Engalnd). Sabbot-Natural Hist Bks.

Handbook of Railway Photography. R. E. Siviter. (Illus.). 128p. 1983. 30.95 o.p. (ISBN 0-7153-8265-9). David & Charles.

Handbook of Real Estate Mathematics. Leonard Kleeman. (Illus.). 1978. 24.95 o.p. (ISBN 0-13-380717-7, Busn). P-H.

Handbook of Regular Patterns: An Introduction to Symmetry in Two Dimensions. Peter S. Stevens. (Illus.). 384p. 1981. 47.50 o.p. (ISBN 0-262-19188-1). MIT Pr.

Handbook of Remote Control & Automation Techniques. 2nd ed. John E. Cunningham & Delton T. Horn. (Illus.). 350p. 1984. 21.95 o.p. (ISBN 0-8306-0777-3); pap. 18.60 o.p. (ISBN 0-8306-1777-9, 1777). TAB Bks.

Handbook of Reporting Methods. Maxwell McCombs et al. LC 75-31009. (Illus.). 1976. text ed. 18.95 o.p. (ISBN 0-395-18958-6). HM.

Handbook of Resource Room Teaching. Judith H. Cohen. LC 81-20599. 348p. 1982. text ed. 36.00 o.p. (ISBN 0-89443-653-8). Aspen Pub.

Handbook of Separation Techniques for Chemical Engineers. Philip A. Schweitzer. (Illus.). 1979. text ed. 72.00 o.p. (ISBN 0-07-055790-X). McGraw.

Handbook of Silicone Rubber Fabrication. Wilfred Lynch. 1978. 42.95 o.p. (ISBN 0-442-24962-4). Van Nos Reinhold.

Handbook of Simplified Radio, Phono & Tape Recorder Repairs: An Illustrated Troubleshooting Guide. James E. Keogh & Beu Suntag. LC 81-1258. (Illus.). 236p. 1981. text ed. 18.95 o.p. (ISBN 0-13-381673-7, Parker). P-H.

Handbook of Social & Cultural Anthropology. John J. Honigman. 1973. text ed. 67.00 o.p. (ISBN 0-395-30631-0). HM.

Handbook of Socialization Theory & Research. David A. Goslin. 1969. text ed. 55.00 o.p. (ISBN 0-395-30611-6). HM.

Handbook of Software Engineering. Ed. by Charles R. Vick. C. V. Ramamoorthy. 768p. 1984. 69.95 o.p. (ISBN 0-442-26251-5). Van Nos Reinhold.

Handbook of Special Education. Ed. by James M. Kauffman & Daniel P. Hallahan. (Illus.). 992p. 1981. text ed. (ISBN 0-13-381756-3). P-H.

Handbook of Special Vocational Needs Education. Gary Meers et al. LC 80-17759. 408p. 1980. 36.00 o.p. (ISBN 0-89443-288-5). Aspen Pub.

Handbook of Stage Lighting Graphics. William B. Warfel. LC 73-16421. (Illus.). 48p. 1974. pap. 7.95 o.s.i. (ISBN 0-910482-47-0). Drama Bk.

Handbook of Standard Structural Details for Buildings. Milo S. Ketchum. 1956. text ed. 46.00 o.p. (ISBN 0-13-381822-5). P-H.

Handbook of State Trading Organizations of Developing Countries. (ISBN 0-8002-3177-5). Intl Pubns Serv.

Handbook of Statistical Distributions. J. K. Patel et al. (Statistics: Textbooks & Monographs: Vol. 20). 1976. pap. 49.75 o.p. (ISBN 0-8247-7202-4). Dekker.

Handbook of Statistical Organization, Vol. 1. pap. 8.00 o.p. (ISBN 0-686-94557-3, UN79 17 17, UN). UNIPUB.

Handbook of Strategic Growth Through Mergers & Acquisitions. William K. Smith. 119p. 1985. text ed. 34.95 o.p. (ISBN 0-13-381815-2, Busn). P-H.

Handbook of Surgical Diathermy. 2nd ed. Mitchell & Lumb. 142p. 1978. 26.00 o.p. (ISBN 0-7236-0449-5, Pub. by John Wright UK). Butterworth.

Handbook of Survey Research. Ed. by Peter H. Rossi et al. (Quantitative Studies in Social Relations). 1983. 68.00 o.p. (ISBN 0-12-598226-7). Acad Pr.

Handbook of the Al Sa'ud Ruling Family of Saudi Arabia. Brian Lees. 55.00x o.s.i. Intl Bk Ctr.

Handbook of the Cleveland Museum of Art. Cleveland Museum of Art Staff. LC 76-54618. (Illus.). 456p. 1978. soft cover 20.00x o.p. (ISBN 0-910386-31-5, Pub. by Cleveland Mus Art). Ind U Pr.

Handbook of the Daily News Sweated Industries Exhibition. Ed. by Richard Mudie-Smith. LC 79-56964. (English Working Class Ser.). 1980. lib. bdg. 21.00 o.p. (ISBN 0-8240-0116-8). Garland Pub.

Handbook of the Indians of California. A. L. Kroeber. LC 76-19514. (Illus.). 1976. lib. bdg. 22.50x o.p. (ISBN 0-88307-585-7). Gannon.

Handbook of the Law under the Uniform Commercial Code. 2nd ed. James J. White & Robert S. Summers. LC 79-27189. (Hornbook Ser.). 1287p. 1980. text ed. 28.95 o.p. (ISBN 0-8299-2082-X). West Pub.

Handbook of the Nations. 7th ed. (Illus.). 352p. 1987. 80.00x o.p. (ISBN 0-8103-1593-9). Gale.

Handbook of the Papacy. William S. Kerr. 1951. (ISBN 0-8022-0845-2). Philos Lib.

Handbook of the Theatre. 2nd ed. Esme Crampton. (Illus.). 264p. (Orig.). 1973. pap. text ed. 13.50x o.p. (ISBN 0-435-18185-8). Heinemann Ed.

Handbook of Thermal Insulation Design Economics for Pipes & Equipment. William C. Turner & John F. Malloy. 1980. text ed. 81.50 o.p. (ISBN 0-07-065510-3). McGraw.

Handbook of Thermodynamic Tables & Charts. Kuzman Raznjevic. 400p. 1976. text ed. 69.50 o.p. (ISBN 0-07-051270-1). McGraw.

Handbook of Tools for Community Economic Change. Ed. by Ward Morehouse. (Illus.). 201p. 1983. looseleaf, spiralbound hardcover binder 25.00 o.p. (ISBN 0-942850-02-5). Intermediate Tech.

Handbook of Traps & Tricks. 2nd ed. Ed. by Ben R. Ezzell & Mary M. Ezzell. (Illus.). 104p. (Orig.). 1981. pap. 9.95 o.p. (ISBN 0-940918-01-3, STK 81-002). Dragon Tree.

Handbook of Unit Operations. D. A. Blackadder & R. M. Nedderman. 1971. 54.50 o.p. (ISBN 0-12-102950-6). Acad Pr.

Handbook of Utilization of Aquatic Plants: A Review of World Literature. E. C. Little. (Fisheries Technical Papers: No. 187). 181p. 1979. pap. 12.25 o.p. (ISBN 92-5-100825-6, F1863, FAO). UNIPUB.

Handbook of Vacuum Physics. A. H. Beck. 1965. Vol. 2, Pt. 1 1965. pap. 50.00 o.p. (ISBN 0-08-010888-1); Vol. 3, Pts. 1-3. 1965. pap. 50.00 o.p. (ISBN 0-08-011051-7). Pergamon.

Handbook of Valves, Piping & Pipelines. (Illus.). 530p. 1982. text ed. 146.25x o.p. (ISBN 0-85461-087-1). Gower Pub Co.

Handbook of Verbal Group Exercises. Kenneth T. Morris & Kenneth M. Cinnamon. LC 73-15524. 384p. 1974. pap. 7.95 o.p. (ISBN 0-398-03011-1). Univ Assocs.

Handbook of Vitamins, Minerals & Hormones. 2nd ed. Roman J. Kutsky. 1981. 36.95 o.p. (ISBN 0-442-24557-2). Van Nos Reinhold.

Handbook of Water Purification. Walter Lorch. (Illus.). 768p. 1981. text ed. 96.50 o.p. (ISBN 0-07-084555-7). McGraw.

Handbook of Weather Folk-Lore: Being a Collection of Proverbial Sayings in Various Languages Relating to the Weather. Charles Swainson. LC 73-5513. xii, 288p. 1974. Repr. of 1873 ed. 40.00x o.p. (ISBN 0-8103-3980-3). Gale.

Handbook of Wiring, Cabling, & Interconnecting for Electronics. Charles A. Harper. LC 72-4069. 1152p. 1972. text ed. 69.50 o.p. (ISBN 0-07-026674-3). McGraw.

Handbook of Woodworking Plans, Patterns & Projects. Abe Finkelstein & Bert Holtje. LC 79-26025. 256p. 1980. 12.95 o.p. (ISBN 0-13-382853-0, Parker). P-H.

Handbook of Work, Organization & Society. Robert Dubin. 1068p. 1976. text ed. 55.00 o.p. (ISBN 0-395-30591-8). HM.

Handbook of Writing & Revision. John M. Kierzek & Walker Gibson. 1967. pap. text ed. write for info. o.p. (ISBN 0-02-362990-8). Macmillan.

Handbook of 1985 Living Will Laws. Society for the Right to Die Staff. 128p. (Orig.). 1986. pap. 5.00x o.p. (ISBN 0-9613825-2-X). Soc Right to Die.

Handbook on Basic Trial Evidence. Joseph M. Pellicciotti. 262p. (Orig.). 1985. lib. bdg. 31.00 o.p. (ISBN 0-8191-4829-6); pap. text ed. 13.25 o.p. (ISBN 0-8191-4830-X). U Pr of Amer.

Handbook on Biotelemetry & Radio Tracking: International Conference: Biotelemetry & Radio Tracking in Biology & Medicine, Oxford, 20-22 March 1979. Ed. by C. Amlaner & D. Macdonald. LC 79-41234. (Illus.). 826p. 1980. 185.00 o.p. (ISBN 0-08-024928-0). Pergamon.

Handbook on Correctional Classification: Programming for Treatment & Reintegration. American Correctional Association Staff & Leonard J. Hippchen. LC 78-65636. (Criminal Justice Ser.). 172p. 1978. pap. text ed. 10.50 o.p. (ISBN 0-87084-005-3). Anderson Pub Co.

Handbook on Injectable Drugs. 4th ed. Lawrence A. Trissel. 625p. 1985. 45.00 o.p. (ISBN 0-930530-62-4); pap. 40.00 spiral bound o.p. (ISBN 0-930530-61-6). Am Soc Hosp Pharm.

Handbook on Material & Energy Balance Calculations in Metallurgical Processes. H. Alan Fine & Gordon H. Geiger. LC 79-93329. 572p. 1983. Repr. of 1979 ed. 45.00 o.p. (ISBN 0-89520-360-X). Minerals Metals.

Handbook on Material & Energy Balance Calculations in Metallurgical Processes. H. Alan Fine & Gordon H. Geiger. (Illus.). 572p. 45.00 o.p.; members 30.00 o.p. (ISBN 0-317-36220-8); student members 20.00 o.p. (ISBN 0-317-36221-6). ASM.

Handbook on Nonpayment of War Taxes. Peacemakers Staff. 64p. 1981. 3.00 o.p. (ISBN 0-318-15970-8). NISBCO.

Handbook on Patents, Trademarks & Copyrights. New York County Lawyers' Association Staff. LC 82-1135. 1982. pap. 25.00 o.p. (ISBN 0-87632-372-7). Clark Boardman.

Handbook on the Placement of Foreign Graduate Students: Graduate Handbook, Part 3. 184p. 1984. 7.00 o.s.i. (ISBN 0-317-34996-1). NAFSA Washington.

Handbook to Plants in Victoria, Vol. 2: Dicotyledons. J. H. Willis. 1972. 40.00x o.p. (ISBN 0-522-84037-X, Pub by Melbourne U Pr Australia). Intl Spec Bk.

Handbook to the Gospels: A Guide to the Gospel Writings & the Life & Times of Jesus. John Wijngaards. (Illus.). 300p. 1983. pap. 8.95 o.p. (ISBN 0-89283-118-9). Servant.

Handbook to the Works of Robert Browning. 6th rev. ed. Alexandra Orr. LC 4-13923. 1969. Repr. of 1902 ed. 35.00 o.p. (ISBN 0-527-68530-5). Kraus Repr.

Handbuch der Musikalischen Litteratur (the 1817 Edition & the Ten Supplements, 1818-27) Carl F. Whistling & Friedrich Hofmeister. Intro. by & intro. by Neil Ratliff. LC 74-23416. (Reference Library of the Humanities: No. 21). 1427p. 1975. lib. bdg. 182.00 o.p. (ISBN 0-8240-1064-7). Garland Pub.

Handbuch der Regionalen Geologie, Nos. 1-30. 1910-44. 400.00 o.p. (ISBN 0-384-21285-9). Johnson Repr.

Handcraft Centers of New England. Ed. by Sharon Smith. LC 80-85481. (Yankee Magazine Guidebook Ser.). (Illus.). 176p. (Orig.). 1981. pap. 7.95 o.p. (ISBN 0-911658-26-2). Yankee Bks.

Handcraft for Baby: Cotton Wares up to Two Years Old. Ondori Publishing Company Staff. (Illus.). 94p. (Orig.). 1984. pap. 8.95 o.p. (ISBN 0-87040-606-X). Japan Pubns USA.

Handel. Christopher Hogwood. LC 84-72765. (Illus.). 312p. 1985. 19.95 o.p. (ISBN 0-500-01355-1). Thames Hudson.

Handel. Richard A. Streatfeild. LC 77-28261. (New Library of Music). 1978. Repr. of 1909 ed. lib. bdg. 35.00x o.p. (ISBN 0-313-20248-6, STHA). Greenwood.

Handel. 2nd rev. ed. Herbert Weinstock. LC 78-11991. 1979. Repr. of 1959 ed. lib. bdg. 35.00x o.p. (ISBN 0-313-21109-4, WEHD). Greenwood.

Handel's Messiah. 2nd ed. Jens P. Larsen. Tr. by Major Bayliss et al from Danish. (Illus.). 336p. 1972. pap. 5.50 o.p. (ISBN 0-393-00657-3, Norton Lib). Norton.

Handel's Messiah: A Devotional Commentary. Joseph E. McCabe. LC 77-25860. 120p. 1978. pap. 5.95 o.s.i. (ISBN 0-664-24192-1, Westminster). Westminster John Knox.

Handful of Sand. Takuboku Ishikawa. Tr. by Shio Sakanishi from Japanese. LC 76-48221. (Modern Japanese Poets Ser.). (Illus.). 1977. Repr. of 1934 ed. lib. bdg. 24.75x o.p. (ISBN 0-8371-9318-4, ISHS). Greenwood.

Handful of Stars. Barbara Girion. 176p. (gr. 7 up). 1981. 11.95 o.s.i. (ISBN 0-684-17167-8, Pub. by Scribner). Macmillan.

Handgun Competition. George C. Nonte. LC 82-73789. (Illus.). 1978. 16.95 o.p. (ISBN 0-8329-2536-5, Pub. by Winchester Pr). New Century.

Handicap: A Study of Physically Handicapped Children & Their Families. Joan K. McMichael. LC 77-189858. (Contemporary Community Health Ser.). 1972. 18.95x o.p. (ISBN 0-8229-1106-X). U of Pittsburgh Pr.

Handicapism & Equal Opportunity: Teaching about the Disabled in Social Studies. James K. Shaver & Charles K. Curtis. 85p. 1981. pap. 7.50 o.p. (ISBN 0-939068-01-X). Coun Exc Child.

Handicapped & Their Rehabilitation. Harry A. Pattison. (Illus.). 976p. 1957. 118.00 o.p. (ISBN 0-398-04384-1). C C Thomas.

Handicapped Children: Early Detection, Intervention, & Education: Selected Case Studies from Argentina, Canada, Denmark, Jamaica, Jordan, Nigeria, Sri Lanka, Thailand & the United Kingdom. 142p. 1982. pap. 17.50 o.p. (ISBN 0-686-95507-2, UPB118, UNESCO). UNIPUB.

Handicapped Children in Residential Care: A Study of Policy Failure. Ann Shearer. 114p. 1980. pap. text ed. 12.25 o.p. (ISBN 0-7199-1035-8, Pub. by Bedford England). Gower Pub Co.

Handicapped Married Couples: A Welsh Study of Couples Handicapped from Birth by Mental, Physical or Personality Disorder. Ann Craft & Michael Craft. 1979. 25.00x o.p. (ISBN 0-7100-0411-7). Routledge Chapman & Hall.

Handicapped Person in the Community. Ed. by David M. Boswell. Janet M. Wingrove. 1974. pap. 17.95x o.p. (ISBN 0-422-74760-2, NO. 2605, Pub. by Tavistock England). Routledge Chapman & Hall.

Handicapped Students in the Social Studies Classroom: Teaching. Ed. by Terry Shaw. 64p. 1981. 8.95 o.p. (ISBN 0-8106-3180-6). NEA.

Handicapped Students Science: Teaching. Ed. by Marshall Corrick. 88p. 1981. 8.95 o.p. (ISBN 0-8106-3179-2). NEA.

Handicapped...How Does It Feel. Gregory S. LaMore. (Jalmar Creative Teaching Ser.). (Illus.). 70p. (gr. 1-5). 1981. pap. text ed. 7.95 o.p. (ISBN 0-935266-06-2). Jalmar Pr.

Handicapping Conditions & Services Directory. 248p. 1981. Repr. of 1980 ed. 58.00x o.p. (ISBN 0-8103-0995-5). Gale.

Handicapping Conditions in Children. Ed. by Bill Gillham. LC 85-22444. (Croom Helm Special Education Ser.). 128p. (Orig.). 1986. pap. 13.50 o.p. (ISBN 0-7099-0285-9, Pub. by Croom Helm Ltd). Routledge Chapman & Hall.

Handle with Care: A Question of Alzheimer's. Dorothy S. Brown. LC 84-61253. 120p. 1985. 16.95 o.p. (ISBN 0-87975-271-8); pap. 10.95 o.p. (ISBN 0-87975-272-6). Prometheus Bks.

Handling & Prevention of Fair Representation & Breach of Labor Contract Cases: Management & Union Viewpoints. Practising Law Institute Staff & Paul I. Weiner. LC 85-60067. (Litigation & Administrative Practice Ser.). PLI.

Handling Employee Grievances see Issues in the Public Employee Relations Library: Series 1.

Handling Employment Discrimination Cases, Vol. 1. Lee Modjeska. LC 78-70830. 1980. 79.50 o.p. (ISBN 0-686-29230-8); Suppl. 1987. 27.00 o.p.; Suppl. 1986. 22.50 o.p. Lawyers Co-Op.

Handling of Chemical Data. P. D. Lark et al. LC 66-17264. 1968. 100.00 o.p. (ISBN 0-08-011849-6). Pergamon.

Handling of Words & Other Studies in Literary Psychology. Vernon Lee. 8.00 o.p. (ISBN 0-8446-2442-X). Peter Smith.

Handling Problem Employees: How to Take Corrective Action, Trainer's Edition. Desk Top Seminars Staff. (Professional Development Program Ser.). 192p. 1983. 125.00 o.p. (ISBN 0-471-88936-9). Wiley.

Handling Small Pets: Step by Step. Giovonnia Ferguson. (Illus.). 1979. 4.00 o.p. (ISBN 0-682-49209-4). Exposition-Phoenix.

Handling Tax Disputes with the IRS 24th Annual Tax School. Pennsylvania Bar Institute Staff. 134p. 1985. 50.00 o.p. (ISBN 0-318-19048-6, 320). PA Bar Inst.

Handling, Transportation & Storage of Fruits & Vegetables: Vegetables & Melons, Vol. 1. 2nd ed. A. Lloyd Ryall & Werner J. Lipton. (Illus.). 1979. 62.95 o.p. (ISBN 0-87055-264-3). AVI.

Handlist of Italian Cookery Books. Lord Westbury. 262p. 1983. 35.00 o.p. (ISBN 0-87556-715-0). Saifer.

Handloader's Digest. 9th ed. Ed. by Ken Warner. LC 62-15069. (Illus.). 320p. 1981. pap. 10.95 o.p. (ISBN 0-910676-33-X). DBI.

Handloading for Hunters. Don Zutz. LC 77-21574. 1982. pap. 12.95 o.p. (ISBN 0-8329-3460-7, Pub. by Winchester Pr). New Century.

Handmade in America: Conversations with Fourteen Craftmasters. Barbaralee Diamonstein. LC 82-13941. (Illus.). 224p. 1983. 49.50 o.p. (ISBN 0-8109-1083-7). Abrams.

Handmade Silk Flowers. Bruce W. Miller & Mary C. Donnelly. (Illus.). 144p. 1986. 24.95 o.p. (ISBN 0-671-60731-6). S&S.

Hands All Around: Making Cooperative Quilts. Judy Robbins & Gretchen Thomas. (Illus.). 128p. 1986. pap. 14.95 o.p. (ISBN 0-13-372350-X). P-H.

Hands for Others. Sr. Louis Passero. 80p. 1988. pap. 0.75 o.s.i. (ISBN 0-317-67492-7, ST0070). Dghtrs St Paul.

Hands in Clay: An Introduction to Ceramics. Charlotte F. Speight. (Illus.). 348p. 1979. pap. 18.95 o.p. (ISBN 0-87484-645-5). Mayfield Pub.

Hands of a Stranger. Robert Daley. 418p. 1985. 16.45 o.p. (ISBN 0-671-49962-9). S&S.

Hands of a Stranger. Robert Daley. 615p. 1986. lib. bdg. 19.95 o.p. (ISBN 0-8161-4032-4, Large Print Bks); pap. 10.95 o.s.i. (ISBN 0-8161-4071-5, Large Print Bks). G K Hall.

Hands of Fate. Jean Chelin. LC 84-90014. 57p. 1985. 7.95 o.p. (ISBN 0-317-17448-7). Vantage.

Hands On: A Manipulative Curriculum for Teaching Multiple Handicapped Hearing Impaired Students. Patricia A. Potocki & Barbara L. Miller. 1980. 3-ring binder 45.00 o.p. (ISBN 0-88450-722-X, 3124-B). Communication Skill.

Hands-on BASIC for Kids Using the Commodore 64. J. G. Reh. (Illus.). 320p. (gr. 5 up). 1984. pap. 12.95 o.p. (ISBN 0-89303-511-4). Brady Bks.

Hands-on Paradox. Steven S. Cobb et al. Ed. by Marjorie M. Phifer & Linda Baughman. LC 87-70442. (Illus.). 304p. (Orig.). 1987. pap. 49.00 o.p. (ISBN 0-317-61509-2). Cobb Group.

Hands-On QuickBASIC. Larry J. Goldstein. (Illus.). 400p. 1989. pap. 19.95 o.p. Brady Bks.

Handwriting Analysis. David Ord. 60p. 1957. (ISBN 0-8022-1242-5). Philos Lib.

Handwriting Analyzer. Jerome S. Meyer. 1974. pap. 6.95 o.p. (ISBN 0-671-21757-7, Fireside). S&S.

Handwriting for Today. Tom Gourdie. 1978. pap. 3.95 o.s.i. (ISBN 0-8008-3812-2, Pentalic). Taplinger.

Handwriting Made Easy: A Simple Modern Approach. Tom Gourdie. LC 87-50225. (Illus.). 64p. 1981. pap. 3.95 o.s.i. (ISBN 0-8008-4597-8). Taplinger.

Handwriting Resource Book: Grades 1-7. British Columbia, Ministry of Education Staff. 91p. 1981. 8.50 o.p. (ISBN 0-8141-2038-5). NCTE.

Handwrought Jewelry. Lois Franke & William L. Udell. (gr. 7 up). 1962. text ed. 19.96 o.p. (ISBN 0-87345-175-9). Glencoe.

Handy Book of American Authors. Louis H. Peet. LC 75-156928. 328p. 1971. Repr. of 1907 ed. 48.00x o.p. (ISBN 0-8103-3360-0). Gale.

Handy Guide to Stowage. W. A. Flere. 1970. 11.50 o.s.i. (ISBN 0-85288-005-7). E J Brill USA.

Handy Hound. Bernard Wiseman. (Puntown Bks.). (Illus.). 48p. (gr. 1-3). 1987. pap. 11.95 o.p. (ISBN 0-316-94858-6). Little.

Handy Medical Guide for Seafarers: Fishermen, Trawlermen & Yachtsmen. R. W. Scott. (Illus.). 96p. 11.25 o.p. (ISBN 0-85238-007-0, FN52, FNB). UNIPUB.

Hang the Consequences. M. R. Meek. (Lennox Kemp Mystery Ser.). 160p. 1985. 12.95 o.s.i. (ISBN 0-684-18465-6, ScribT). Scribner.

Hang Tough, Paul Mather. Alfred Slote. (gr. 3-5). 1976. pap. 1.75 o.p. (ISBN 0-380-00225-6, 54999-9, Camelot). Avon.

Hangar Tales & War Stories: The Humor & Adventure of Flying. Jeff W. Griffin. (Illus.). 154p. (Orig.). 1984. pap. 9.95 o.p. (ISBN 0-8306-2355-8, 2355). TAB Bks.

Hanging at Tyburn. Gilbert B. Cross. LC 83-6331. 252p. (gr. 5-9). 1983. 11.95 o.s.i. (ISBN 0-689-31007-2, Atheneum). Macmillan.

Hanging Book. Bob Nilson. 1982. pap. 3.95 o.s.i. (ISBN 0-03-061783-9, Owl Bks). H Holt & Co.

Hanging by a Thread & Other Literary Essays see Writing on the Wall & Other Literary Essays.

Hanging in There: How to Resist Retirement from Life & Avoid Being Put Out to Pasture. Peter Schwed. 1977. 6.95 o.p. (ISBN 0-395-25694-1). HM.

Hanging On. Robert G. Beason. 1984. 15.95 o.p. (ISBN 0-15-138440-1). HarBraceJ.

Hanging on. Hila Colman. LC 76-53405. 1977. 8.95 o.p. (ISBN 0-689-10788-9, Atheneum). Macmillan.

Hanging Week. Jerome Gardner. 176p. 1988. lib. bdg. 19.95x o.s.i. (ISBN 0-7451-0781-8, Pub. by Chivers Pr UK). G K Hall.

Hangman's Dozen. Alfred Hitchcock. 1976. pap. 1.25 o.p. (ISBN 0-440-13428-5). Dell.

Hangman's Holiday. Dorothy L. Sayers. 1979. pap. 2.50 o.p. (ISBN 0-380-01240-5, 60048-X). Avon.

Hangman's Knot. Peter McCurtin. (Sundance Ser.). 176p. 1986. pap. 2.50 o.p. (ISBN 0-8439-2337-7, Pub. by Leisure Bks CT). Dorchester Pub Co.

Hank & Oogie. Nicki Weiss. (Snuggle & Read Story Bks.). (Illus.). 32p. (ps-3). 1985. pap. 2.50 o.p. (ISBN 0-380-69872-2, Camelot). Avon.

Hank Williams. Robert K. Krishef. LC 77-90157. (Country Music Bks.). (Illus.). (gr. 5 up). 1978. PLB 5.95 o.p. (ISBN 0-8225-1402-8). Lerner Pubns.

Hanna & Walter. Hanna Kohner et al. (Large Print Books). 1985. lib. bdg. 14.95 o.p. (ISBN 0-8161-3818-4). G K Hall.

Hannah Hereafter. Sutherland. 1978. 7.95 o.p. (ISBN 0-15-138448-7). HarBraceJ.

Hannah Herself. Ruth Franchere. (YA) (gr. 7-11). 1977. pap. 1.25 o.p. (ISBN 0-380-01647-8, 33050). Avon.

Hannah: Nightingale Ser. Betty Neels. 253p. 1987. pap. 10.95x o.p. (ISBN 0-8161-4269-6, Large Print Bks). G K Hall.

Hannibal & His Thirty-Seven Elephants. Marilyn Hirsh. LC 77-590. (Illus.). 32p. (gr. 1-3). 1977. reinforced bdg. 5.95 o.p. (ISBN 0-8234-0300-9). Holiday.

Hannibal, Man of Destiny. Mirza Taleb. LC 72-97060. 300p. 1974. 15.00 o.p. (ISBN 0-8283-1501-9). Branden Pub Co.

Hanoi. Mary McCarthy. LC 68-54313. 1968. pap. 1.45 o.p. (ISBN 0-15-138450-9). HarBraceJ.

Hans & Peter. Heidrun Petrides. LC 63-1031. (Illus.). (gr. k-3). 1963. 5.95 o.p. (ISBN 0-15-233275-8, HJ). HarBraceJ.

Hans Andersen's Fairy Tales. Hans Christian Andersen. Ed. by Naomi Lewis. (Puffin Classics). (Illus.). 176p. (gr. 4-6). 1981. pap. 2.95 o.p. (ISBN 0-14-030333-2, Puffin). Penguin.

Hans Baldung Grien: Eve, the Serpent & Death. Robert A. Koch. (Masterpieces in the National Gallery of Canada Ser.). 1974. pap. 3.25 o.p. (ISBN 0-88884-244-9, 56380-4, Pub. by Natl Gallery Canada). U of Chicago Pr.

Hans Christian Andersen: The Complete Fairy Tales & Stories. Erik C. Haugaard. LC 73-83883. (Anchor Folktale Library). 1128p. 1983. 10.95 o.p. (ISBN 0-385-18951-6, Anch). Doubleday.

Hans Hartung: Paintings, 1971-1975. Intro. by Henry Geldzahler. LC 75-31609. (Illus.). 1975. pap. 0.50 o.p. (ISBN 0-87099-145-0). Metro Mus Art.

Hans in Gluck see Hans in Luck.

Hans in Luck. Retold by & illus. by Paul Galdone. LC 79-16154. (Illus.). 48p. (ps-3). 1980. 5.95 o.s.i. (ISBN 0-8193-1011-5); PLB 5.95 o.s.i. (ISBN 0-8193-1012-3). Parents.

Hans in Luck. Jacob Grimm & Wilhelm K. Grimm. Ed. by Felix Hoffmann. LC 74-18184. Orig. Title: Hans in Gluck. (Illus.). 32p. (ps-2). 1975. 7.95 o.p. (ISBN 0-689-50020-3, Atheneum). Macmillan.

Hans Memlinc's Paintings for the Hospital of Saint John in Bruges. Vida J. Hull. LC 79-57503. (Outstanding Dissertations in the Fine Arts Ser.: No.5). 327p. 1982. lib. bdg. 46.00 o.p. (ISBN 0-8240-3936-X). Garland Pub.

Hans Nielsen Hauge: His Life & Message. Andreas Aarflot. LC 77-84101. 1979. pap. 9.95 o.p. (ISBN 0-8066-1627-X, 10-2965, Augsburg). Augsburg Fortress.

Hansel & Gretel. Jacob Grimm & Wilhelm K. Grimm. Tr. by Elizabeth D. Crawford from Ger. LC 79-989. (Illus.). 25p. (gr. k-3). 1980. 11.25 o.p. (ISBN 0-688-22198-X); PLB 11.88 o.p. (ISBN 0-688-32198-4). Morrow.

Hansel & Gretel. Jacob Grimm & Wilhelm K. Grimm. LC 83-61778. (Illus.). 22p. (gr. 1 up). 1983. pap. 5.95 o.p. (ISBN 0-907234-46-1). Picture Bk Studio.

Hansel & Gretel. Jacob Grimm & Wilhelm K. Grimm. 48p. (ps-3). 1986. 12.95 o.p. (ISBN 0-385-28387-3). Delacorte.

Hansel & Gretel. William Wiesner. LC 78-154302. (Illus.). (gr. k-3). 1979. 6.50 o.p. (ISBN 0-395-28829-0, Clarion). HM.

Hansel & Gretel, the Seven Ravens, & the Little Red Cap. Jacob Grimm & Wilhelm K. Grimm. (Illus.). 66p. (gr. 1 up). 1983. Repr. of 1979 ed. pap. 15.95 slipcased set o.p. (ISBN 0-907234-49-6). Picture Bk Studio.

Hanta Yo. Ruth B. Hill. LC 77-16922. 1979. 14.95 o.s.i. (ISBN 0-385-13554-8). Doubleday.

Hanukkah Latkes & Rothschild's Millions. David Schwartz. 1961. 14.95x o.p. New Coll U Pr.

Hapana Mbale. Tamara Braun. 240p. 1986. 15.00 o.p. (ISBN 0-8062-2823-7). Carlton.

Haphazard Amorist. Graham Jackson. 127p. 1981. text ed. 14.95 o.p. (ISBN 0-7022-1497-3); pap. 6.00 o.p. (ISBN 0-7022-1498-1). U of Queensland Pr.

Haplochromine Fishes of the East African Lakes. P. H. Greenwood. 839p. 1981. lib. bdg. 70.00 o.p. (ISBN 3-601-00483-6). Kraus Intl.

Happily Appley: A Leader's Guide to Food Fun with Young Children. Elizabeth Munz. (Illus.). 64p. 1975. spiral bdg. 1.00 o.p. (ISBN 0-88441-133-8, 19-995). Girl Scouts USA.

Happiness in Marriage see Works.

Happinism: A Goal for All Humanity. Howard O. Eaton. 1976. 4.00 o.p. (ISBN 0-682-48540-3). Exposition-Phoenix.

Happinism Revisited. 2nd rev. & enlarged ed. Howard O. Eaton. 1978. 4.50 o.p. (ISBN 0-682-49012-1). Exposition-Phoenix.

Happy Are the Meek. Andrew M. Greeley. 373p. 1986. lib. bdg. 16.95 o.p. (ISBN 0-8161-4029-4, Large Print Bks). G K Hall.

Happy Birthday. Myra C. Livingston & Erik Blegvad. LC 64-11492. (Illus.). (ps-3). 1964. 4.50 o.p. (ISBN 0-15-233370-3, HJ). HarBraceJ.

Happy Birthday, Moon. Frank Asch. (Illus.). 32p. (ps-3). 1982. 10.95 o.s.i. (ISBN 0-13-383687-8). P-H.

Happy Birthday, Moon. Frank Asch. (Illus.). 32p. (gr. k-3). 1985. pap. 4.95 o.s.i. (ISBN 0-13-383696-7). P-H.

Happy Birthday Oliver! Pierre Le-Tan. LC 77-79847. (Illus.). (ps-1). 1979. 3.95 o.p. (ISBN 0-394-83788-6, BYR); lib. bdg. 4.99 o.p. (ISBN 0-394-93788-0). Random.

Happy Birthday to You. R. G. Austin. (Which Way Secret Door Bks.). (Illus., Orig.). (gr. 1-3). 1983. pap. 1.95 o.p. (ISBN 0-671-47569-X). Archway.

Happy Birthday Unicorn. Jacquelyn Reinach et al. Ed. by Jacquelyn Reinach & Ruth L. Perle. LC 78-9585. (Sweet Pickles Ser.). (Illus.). (ps-2). 1979. 2.95 o.p. (ISBN 0-03-042066-0). H Holt & Co.

Happy Book of Christmas Stories. William J. Lederer. (Illus.). 1984. 7.45 o.p. (ISBN 0-393-01414-2). Norton.

Happy Day Ranch. Rena B. Carney. 1978. 6.95 o.p. (ISBN 0-682-48916-6). Exposition-Phoenix.

Happy Days. Samuel Beckett. 1961. 10.00 o.p. (ISBN 0-394-47507-0, GP647). Grove.

Happy Days. Samuel Beckett. (Orig.). 1961. pap. 4.95 o.p. (ISBN 0-394-17233-7, E318, Ever). Grove.

Happy Deathday. Hugh Fox. (Chapbook: No. 7). 28p. 1977. pap. 1.00 o.p. (ISBN 0-912824-16-6). Vagabond Pr.

Happy Ending: The Collected Lyrics of Louise I. Guiney. Louise I. Guiney. LC 78-11678. 1979. Repr. of 1927 ed. lib. bdg. 35.00x o.p. (ISBN 0-313-20702-X, GUHE). Greenwood.

Happy Endings. Margaret Logan. 1979. 7.95 o.p. (ISBN 0-395-27591-1). HM.

Happy English Child. Ursula Zilinsky. LC 87-21935. (Crime Club Ser.). 192p. 1988. pap. 12.95 o.p. (ISBN 0-385-24322-7). Doubleday.

Happy Gardener. Clarissa Start. Ed. by Gregory M. Franzwa. LC 85-3654. (Illus.). 142p. (Orig.). 1985. pap. 6.95 o.p. (ISBN 0-935284-37-0, 85-3654). Patrice Pr.

Happy Hannah. Yvonne Patterson. (Happy Day Bible Stories Bks.). (Illus.). 24p. (ps-2). 1984. 1.59 o.p. (ISBN 0-87239-764-5, 3724). Standard Pub.

Happy Jack's Go-Buggy: A WW 11 Fighter Pilot's Personal Document. Jack Ilfrey & Max Reynolds. 1979. 8.00 o.p. (ISBN 0-682-49236-1). Exposition-Phoenix.

Happy Lion. Louise Fatio. (Illus.). (gr. k-3). 1964. text ed. 12.95 o.p. (ISBN 0-07-020044-0). McGraw.

Happy Lioness. Louise Fatio. 113p. 1980. text ed. 9.95 o.p. (ISBN 0-07-020069-6). McGraw.

Happy Owls. Celestino Piatti. LC 64-11895. (Illus.). (ps-3). 1964. 7.95 o.p. (ISBN 0-689-20337-3, Atheneum). Macmillan.

Happy People: What Happiness Is, Who Has It & Why. Jonathan Freedman. LC 77-91477. 256p. 1978. 8.95 o.p. (ISBN 0-15-138476-2). HarBraceJ.

Happy Person. Harold Greenwald & Elizabeth Rich. 192p. 1985. pap. 3.95 o.p. (ISBN 0-380-69850-1). Avon.

Happy Prince & Other Stories. Oscar Wilde. (Illus.). (gr. 4-7). 1962. pap. 2.25 o.p. (ISBN 0-14-030164-X, Puffin). Penguin.

Happy Tales, Fables & Plays. Gordon C. Bennett. LC 75-13464. (Illus.). 120p. 1976. pap. 6.95 o.p. (ISBN 0-8042-1947-8, John Knox). Westminster John Knox.

Happy Times with Happy Seeds. Sally Cowell. (Happy Day Bks.). (Illus.). 24p. (ps-2). 1984. 1.59 o.p. (ISBN 0-87239-738-6, 3708). Standard Pub.

Happy to Be Here. Garrison Keillor. LC 81-66033. 1982. 11.95 o.p. (ISBN 0-689-11201-7, Atheneum). Macmillan.

Hapsburg Monarchy: 1867-1914. Arthur J. May. 1968. pap. 6.95 o.p. (ISBN 0-393-00460-0, Norton Lib). Norton.

Hara Kei in the Politics of Compromise 1905-1915. Tetsuo Najita. LC 67-27090. (East Asian Ser: No. 31). (Illus.). 1967. 24.50x o.s.i. (ISBN 0-674-37250-6). Harvard U Pr.

Hara: The Vital Centre of Man. Karlfried Von Duerckheim. Tr. by Sylvia-Monica Van Kospoth & Estelle R. Healey. (Unwin Paperbacks). 1977. pap. 11.95 o.p. (ISBN 0-04-290011-5). Unwin Hyman.

Harald Deilmann, Architect. Florita Z. Louis de Malave. (Architecture Ser.: Bibliography A-1304). 6p. 1985. pap. 2.00 o.p. (ISBN 0-89028-234-X). Vance Biblios.

Haraszthy at the Mint. Brian McGinty. (Famous California Trials: Vol. 10). (Illus.). 60p. 1975. 15.00 o.p. (ISBN 0-87093-092-3). Dawsons.

Harbor of Refuge. Stephen Jones. (Illus.). 1981. 24.95 o.p. (ISBN 0-393-01417-7). Norton.

Harbors, Anchorages & Marinas. R. H. Smith. LC 81-69410. (Southern California Edition Ser.: Vol. 1). 190p. (Orig.). 1983. 16.95 o.p. (ISBN 0-941786-01-3). C Bks.

Harbrace College Handbook. 7th ed. John C. Hodges & Mary E. Whitten. 532p. 1972. text ed. 8.95 o.p. (ISBN 0-15-531817-9, HC). HarBraceJ.

Harbrace College Handbook. 8th ed. John C. Hodges & Mary E. Whitten. 1977. 10.95 o.p. (ISBN 0-15-531824-1); correction chart 1.00 o.p. HarbraceJ.

Harbrace College Handbook: 1984. 9th ed. John C. Hodges & Mary E. Whitten. 586p. 1984. text ed. 11.25 o.p. (ISBN 0-15-531847-0, HC). HarBraceJ.

Harbrace College Reader. 4th ed. Mark Schorer et al. Ed. by Philip Durham & Everett L. Jones. 1972. text ed. 8.50 o.p. (ISBN 0-15-532411-X, HC). HarBraceJ.

Harbrace College Reader. 5th ed. Ed. by Mark Schorer et al. 598p. (Orig.). 1976. pap. text ed. 12.95 o.p. (ISBN 0-15-532412-8, HC). HarBraceJ.

Harbrace College Workbook, Form 7A. Sheila Y. Graham. 180p. 1972. pap. text ed. 6.95 o.p. (ISBN 0-15-531820-9, HC). HarBraceJ.

Harbrace College Workbook, Form 7B. Sheila Y. Graham & Mrs. John C. Hodges. 176p. 1973. pap. text ed. 6.95 o.p. (ISBN 0-15-531822-5, HC). HarBraceJ.

Harbrace College Workbook: Form 8A. Sheila Y. Graham. 1977. 8.95 o.p. (ISBN 0-15-531828-4). HarbraceJ.

Harbrace College Workbook: Form 8B. Sheila Y. Graham. 1978. pap. text ed. 8.95 o.p. (ISBN 0-15-531831-4, HC). HarBraceJ.

Harbrace College Workbook: Form 8C. Sheila Y. Graham. 1979. 8.95 o.p. (ISBN 0-15-531833-0). HarbraceJ.

Harbrace College Workbook, Form 9A. Sheila Y. Graham. 337p. 1982. pap. text ed. 8.75 o.p. (ISBN 0-15-531841-1, HC). HarBraceJ.

HarBrace College Workbook: Form 9C, Writing for the World of Work. Sheila Y. Graham. 339p. 1982. pap. text ed. 8.75 o.p. (ISBN 0-15-531845-4, HC). HarBraceJ.

Harbrace Guide to the Library & the Research Paper. 3rd ed. Donald A. Sears. 129p. (Orig.). 1973. pap. text ed. 8.95 o.p. (ISBN 0-15-535064-1, HC). HarBraceJ.

Harcourt Brace Intermediate Dictionary. LC 68-1860. (Illus.). (gr. 5-9). 1968. 7.50 o.p. (ISBN 0-15-233405-X, HJ). HarBraceJ.

Harcourt Brace Jovanovich Federal Tax Course, 1986. Ray M. Sommerfeld et al. 864p. 1985. pap. 25.50 o.p. (ISBN 0-15-535306-3, HC). HarBraceJ.

Hard Aground: The Story of the Argo Merchant Oil Spill. Ron Winslow. 1978. 10.95 o.p. (ISBN 0-393-05687-2). Norton.

Hard at Work, Andy Capp. Reginald Smythe. 128p. 1981. pap. 1.75 o.p. (ISBN 0-449-13725-2, GM). Fawcett.

Hard Choices: Four Critical Years in Managing America's Foreign Policy. Cyrus R. Vance. LC 83-592. 320p. 1983. 19.25 o.p. (ISBN 0-671-44339-9). S&S.

Hard-Core: A Study of the Unemployables in Contemporary American Society. James R. Smith. 100p. (Orig.). 1970. pap. text ed. 8.95x o.p. (ISBN 0-686-94119-5). Irvington.

Hard Country. Sharon Doubiago. 250p. (Orig.). 1982. pap. 9.95 o.p. (ISBN 0-931122-25-2). West End.

Hard Feelings. Don Bredes. LC 76-42213. 1977. 8.95 o.p. (ISBN 0-689-10745-5, Atheneum). Macmillan.

Hard Hitting Songs for Hard-Hit People. Alan Lomax. 368p. Repr. of 1967 ed. lib. bdg. 49.00 o.p. (Pub. by Am Repr Serv). Reprint Servs.

Hard Hours. Anthony Hecht. LC 67-25474. (Illus., Orig.). 1967. pap. 6.95 o.p. (ISBN 0-689-10115-5, Atheneum). Macmillan.

Hard of Hearing Children in Regular Schools. Mark Ross. (Illus.). 272p. 1982. text ed. (ISBN 0-13-383802-1). P-H.

Hard Right: The Rise of Jesse Helms. Ernest B. Furgurson. LC 86-2366. 1986. 18.45 o.p. (ISBN 0-393-02325-7). Norton.

Hard Times. Charles Dickens. 1974. Repr. of 1907 ed. 9.95x o.p. (ISBN 0-460-01292-4, Evman); pap. 3.95x o.p. (ISBN 0-460-11292-9, Evman). Biblio Dist.

Hard Times. Charles Dickens. 48p. (Orig.). 1989. pap. 9.95 o.p. (ISBN 1-55651-385-2); audiocassette tape incl. o.p. (ISBN 1-55651-386-0). Cram Cassettes.

Hard Times Catalog for Youth Ministry. Marilyn Benson & Dennis Benson. LC 82-81332. (Illus.). 288p. (Orig.). 1982. pap. 14.95 o.p. (ISBN 0-936664-06-1). Group Pub.

Hard Trade. Arthur Lyons. LC 83-150. 264p. 1983. pap. 3.95 o.p. (ISBN 0-03-063333-8). H Holt & Co.

Hardball Job Hunting Tactics. Dick Wright. LC 82-18357. (Work-In-America Institute Bk.). 192p. 1983. 16.95 o.p. (ISBN 0-87196-134-2); pap. 7.95 o.p. (ISBN 0-8160-1188-5). Facts on File.

Hardball Job Hunting Tactics. Dick Wright. 190p. 1983. 11.95 o.p. Work in Amer.

Hardball: The Education of a Baseball Commissioner. Bowie K. Kuhn. LC 86-5892. (Illus.). 352p. 1987. 19.45 o.s.i. (ISBN 0-8129-1278-0). Times Bks.

Hardcore Bodybuilder's Source Book. Robert Kennedy & Vivian Mason. LC 84-8821. 1984. 19.95 o.p. (ISBN 0-8069-4186-3); pap. 12.95 o.p. (ISBN 0-8069-7894-5). Sterling.

Hardcover. Wayne Warga. 256p. 1985. 15.95 o.p. (ISBN 0-87795-749-5, Arbor Hse). Morrow.

Hardenability Concepts with Applications to Steels: Proceedings of the TMS-AIME Fall Meeting, Chicago, IL, 1977. TMS Staff & AIME Staff. Ed. by D. V. Doane & J. S. Kirkaldy. (Illus.). 626p. 36.00 o.p. (ISBN 0-89520-141-0); members 22.00 o.p. (ISBN 0-317-34878-7); student members 12.00 o.p. (ISBN 0-317-34879-5). ASM.

Harder They Come. Michael Thelwell. 1980. pap. 7.95 o.p. (ISBN 0-394-17599-9, E749, Ever). Grove.

Hardinge of Penshurst: A Study in the Old Diplomacy. Briton C. Busch. (Conference on British Studies Biography: Vol. 1). (Illus.). 381p. 1980. 27.50 o.p. (ISBN 0-208-01830-1, Archon). Shoe String.

Hardness of Drinking Water & Public Health: Proceedings. Ed. by R. Amavis et al. 1976. pap. 140.00 o.p. (ISBN 0-08-020898-3). Pergamon.

Hardscrabble Letters. Richard E. Yates. LC 81-52943. 94p. 1981. 15.00 o.p. (ISBN 0-914546-39-2). Rose Pub.

Hardware & Software Concepts in VLSI. Guy Rabbat. Ed. by Guy Rabbat. (Van Nostrand Electrical-Computer Science & Engineering Ser.). (Illus.). 512p. 1983. 48.95 o.p. (ISBN 0-442-22538-5). Van Nos Reinhold.

Hardware-Software Design of Digital Systems. R. Bywater. 1981. text ed. 41.67 o.p. (ISBN 0-13-383950-8). P-H.

Hardy Classes on Riemann Surfaces. M. Heins. LC 75-84833. (Lecture Notes in Mathematics: Vol. 98). (Orig.). 1969. pap. 10.90 o.p. (ISBN 0-387-04617-8). Springer-Verlag.

Hardy Race of Men: America's Early Indians. Eileen T. Callan. LC 70-88111. (Curriculum Related Bks.). (Illus.). (gr. 7 up). 1970. 4.95 o.p. (ISBN 0-15-233411-4, HJ). HarBraceJ.

Hare Krishna Cookbook. Ed. by Krsna devi dasi & Sama devi dasi. LC 73-83769. (Illus.). 1973. pap. 4.50 o.p. (ISBN 0-685-48060-7). Bhaktivedanta.

Hare Krishna Hare Krishna: Five Distinguished Scholars in Religion Discuss the Krishna Movement in the West. Ed. by Steven Gelberg. LC 82-21055. (Press Eastern Philosophy & Literature Ser.). 224p. (Orig.). 1983. pap. 7.95 o.p. (ISBN 0-394-62454-8, E845, Ever). Grove.

Harem Games. Elliot Tokson. 304p. 1984. pap. 3.50 o.p. (ISBN 0-380-86579-3, 86579-3). Avon.

Harim & the Purdah: Studies of Oriental Women. Elizabeth Cooper. LC 68-23147. 312p. 1975. Repr. of 1915 ed. 43.00x o.p. (ISBN 0-8103-3167-5). Gale.

Hark! Hark! the Dogs Do Bark: And Other Rhymes About Dogs. Ed. by Lenore Blegvad. LC 75-9788. (Illus.). (ps-3). 1976. 5.95 o.p. (ISBN 0-689-50035-1, Atheneum). Macmillan.

Harlan Ellison Presents the Best of the New Wave. Ed. by Arthur B. Cover et al. (Illus.). 576p. 1986. 19.95 o.s.i. (ISBN 0-312-94028-9). Bluejay Bks.

Harlem: Negro Metropolis. Claude McKay. LC 40-32205. (Illus.). 1972. pap. 2.95 o.p. (ISBN 0-15-638946-0, HB224, Harv). HarBraceJ.

Harlequin in His Element: The English Pantomime, 1806-1836. David Mayer, 3rd. LC 79-88809. (Illus.). 1969. 29.50x o.s.i. (ISBN 0-674-37275-1). Harvard U Pr.

Harley-Davidson Motor Company. David Wright. LC 83-5332. (Illus.). 280p. 1983. 24.95 o.p. (ISBN 0-87938-103-5). Motorbooks Intl.

Harley Davidson Owners Workshop Manual: Super & Electraglide '74 Thru '77. (Owners Workshop Manuals Ser.: No. 330). 1979. 13.50 o.p. (ISBN 0-85696-330-5). Haynes Pubns.

Harley Davidson Owners Workshop Manual: Sportster '70 Thru '76. Jeff Clew. (Owners Workshop Manuals Ser.: No. 250). 1979. 13.50 o.p. (ISBN 0-85696-250-3). Haynes Pubns.

Harley Davidson: The Cult Lives On. Gerald Foster. (Illus.). 120p. (Orig.). 1986. pap. 4.98 o.p. (ISBN 0-85045-577-4). Motorbooks Intl.

Harlots, Rakes, & Bawds. Ed. by Walter H. Rubsamen. (Ballad Opera Ser.). 1974. lib. bdg. 61.00 o.p. (ISBN 0-8240-0902-9). Garland Pub.

Harmful Psychotherapy. Judi Striano. LC 87-61144. 128p. (Orig.). 1987. pap. text ed. 15.95 o.p. (ISBN 0-943659-01-9). Professional SBCA.

Harmonic Analysis. V. K. Dobrev et al. (Lecture Notes in Physics: Vol. 63). 1977. pap. 18.00 o.p. (ISBN 0-387-08150-X). Springer-Verlag.

Harmonic Analysis on Reductive P-adic Groups. Harish-Chandra. LC 79-138810. (Lecture Notes in Mathematics: Vol. 162). 1970. pap. 9.00 o.p. (ISBN 0-387-05189-9). Springer-Verlag.

Harmonic Analysis on Totally Disconnected Sets. J. Benedetto. LC 77-163741. (Lecture Notes in Mathematics: Vol. 202). 1971. pap. 14.00 o.p. (ISBN 0-387-05488-X). Springer-Verlag.

Harmonic & Minimal Maps: With Applications in Geometry & Physics. Gabor Toth. (Mathematics & Its Applications Ser.). 342p. 1984. 74.95 o.p. (ISBN 0-470-20127-4). Halsted Pr.

Harmonic Maps of Manifolds with Boundary. R. S. Hamilton. (Lecture Notes in Mathematics Ser.: Vol. 471). 168p. 1975. pap. 14.00 o.p. (ISBN 0-387-07185-7). Springer-Verlag.

Harmonic Materials of Modern Music: Resources of the Tempered Scale. Howard Hanson. LC 58-8138. (Eastman School of Music Ser.). (Illus.). 1960. 44.00x o.s.i. (ISBN 0-89197-207-2). Irvington.

Harmonic Practice. Roger Sessions. 465p. 1951. text ed. 22.95 o.p. (ISBN 0-15-531509-9, HC). HarBraceJ.

Harmonic Study Editions of Six Early Keyboard Classics. Richard McClanahan. 1977. pap. 4.95 o.s.i. (ISBN 0-8008-3808-4, Crescendo). Taplinger.

Harmonie Universelle: The Books on Instruments. Marin Mersenne. 596p. Repr. of 1957 ed. lib. bdg. 69.00 o.p. (Pub. by Am Repr Serv). Reprint Servs.

Harmonienlehre des Klaudios Ptolemaios. Ingemar During. Bd. with Porphyrios Kommentar zur Harmonienlehre des Ptolemaios. LC 78-66554. (Ancient Philosophy Ser.). 513p. 1982. lib. bdg. 62.00 o.p. (ISBN 0-8240-9600-2). Garland Pub.

Harmonization at the Piano. 4th ed. Arthur Frackenpohl. 275p. 1981. write for info. plastic comb binding o.p. (ISBN 0-697-03559-X); instrs' manual avail. o.p. (ISBN 0-697-03560-3). Wm C Brown.

Harmonization of Collaborative Analytical Studies: International Symposium on Harmonization of Collaborative Analytical Studies, Helsinki Finland, 20-21 September 1981. Ed. by H. Egan & T. S. West. (IUPAC Symposium Ser.). (Illus.). 260p. 1982. pap. 50.00 o.p. (ISBN 0-08-026228-7). Pergamon.

Harmony. 4th ed. Walter Piston. Ed. by Mark De Voto. (Illus.). 500p. 1978. text ed. 24.95x o.p. (ISBN 0-393-09034-5). Norton.

Harmony. 3rd ed. Walter Piston. (Illus.). 1962. 9.95x o.p. (ISBN 0-393-09737-4, NortonC). Norton.

Harmony & Voice Leading, Vol. I. Edward Aldwell & Carl Schachter. 302p. 1978. text ed. 18.00 net o.p. (ISBN 0-15-531515-3, HC). HarBraceJ.

Harmony & Voice Leading, Vol. 2. Edward Aldwell & Carl Schachter. 276p. 1979. text ed. 18.00 net o.p. (ISBN 0-15-531517-X, HC). HarBraceJ.

Harmony Illustrated Encyclopedia of Rock. 4th ed. Mike Clifford. (Illus.). 1984. 19.95 o.p. (ISBN 0-517-55261-2, Harmony); pap. 14.95 o.p. (ISBN 0-517-55262-0). Crown.

Harmony Illustrated Encyclopedia of Rock. 5th ed. Mike Clifford. (Illus.). 256p. 1986. 22.95 o.p. (ISBN 0-517-56264-2, Harmony); pap. 14.95 o.p. (ISBN 0-517-56265-0). Crown.

Harmony Illustrated Encyclopedia of Rock. 3rd ed. Salamander Books. (Illus.). 288p. 1982. 7.98 o.p. (ISBN 0-517-54661-2, Harmony); pap. 11.95 o.p. (ISBN 0-517-53985-3). Crown.

Harmony in Western Music. Richard F. Goldman. 1965. 11.95x o.p. (ISBN 0-393-09746-3, NortonC). Norton.

Harmony of Reason: A Study in Kant's Aesthetics. Francis X. Coleman. LC 74-4520. 1974. 19.95x o.p. (ISBN 0-8229-3282-2). U of Pittsburgh Pr.

Harness Horse & Strategic Win Betting. Dick Schneider. LC 76-44186. 1977. 10.00 o.p. (ISBN 0-682-48693-0, Banner). Exposition-Phoenix.

Harnessed Atom. (Nuclear Energy & Electricity Ser.). (Illus.). 143p. (Orig.). (YA) (gr. 6-8). 1986. pap. text ed. 7.00 o.p. (ISBN 0-318-21339-7, S/N 061-000-00678-8). USGPO.

Harnessed Atom: Nuclear Energy & Electricity, Teacher's Edition. 425p. 1986. pap. 18.00 o.p. (ISBN 0-318-21367-2, S/N 061-000-00677-0). USGPO.

Harnessing Peacocks. Mary Wesley. 288p. 1986. 16.95 o.p. (ISBN 0-684-18637-3). Scribner.

Harnessing the Sun: The Story of Solar Energy. David C. Knight. (Illus.). 128p. (gr. 5-9). 1976. PLB 11.88 o.p. (ISBN 0-688-32070-8). Morrow.

Harold Nicolson Diaries & Letters Nineteen Thirty to Nineteen Sixty-Four. Stanley Olson. LC 80-66005. 1980. 15.00 o.p. (ISBN 0-689-11097-9, Atheneum). Macmillan.

Harold Nicolson: Diaries & Letters 1930-1939. Harold G. Nicolson. Ed. by N. Nicolson. LC 66-23571. (Illus.). 1966. 10.00 o.p. (ISBN 0-689-10209-7, Atheneum). Macmillan.

Harold Pinter. Guido Almansi & Simon Henderson. LC 82-22902. (Contemporary Writers Ser.). 96p. 1983. pap. 5.95 o.p. (ISBN 0-416-31710-3, NO. 3560). Routledge Chapman & Hall.

Harold Pinter. Bernard F. Dukore. LC 81-84705. 160p. 1982. pap. 7.95 o.p. (ISBN 0-394-17964-1, E797, Ever). Grove.

Harold Pinter: An Annotated Bibliography. Stephen H. Gale. (Reference Publications). 1980. lib. bdg. 32.50 o.s.i. (ISBN 0-8161-8014-8, Hall Reference). G K Hall.

Harold Washington: A Political Biography. Florence H. Levinsohn. LC 83-15418. 308p. 1983. pap. 8.95 o.p. (ISBN 0-914091-41-7). Chicago Review.

Harp. Roslyn Rensch. (ISBN 0-8022-1329-4). Philos Lib.

Harper's Bible Dictionary. Rev. ed. Madeleine S. Miller & J. Lane. 1974. 21.95 o.p. (ISBN 0-06-065674-3); indexed 21.95i o.p. HarpR.

Harper's Topical Concordance. Ed. by Charles R. Joy. LC 62-11129. 640p. 1976. pap. 10.95 o.p. (ISBN 0-06-064229-7, RD 132). HarpR.

Harpoon: A Novel. C. W. Nicol. 512p. 1987. 22.95 o.p. (ISBN 0-399-13177-9, Putnam). Putnam Pub Group.

Harriet Beecher Stowe: A Reference Guide. Jean Ashton. 1978. lib. bdg. 24.00 o.p. (ISBN 0-8161-7833-X, Hall Reference). G K Hall.

Harriet Love's Guide to Vintage Chic. Harriet Love. (Illus.). 1982. 21.50 o.p. (ISBN 0-03-056238-4); pap. 12.50 o.p. (ISBN 0-03-056239-2, Owl Bks). H Holt & Co.

Harriet Martineau und Ihre Sittlich Religiose Weltschau. Gertrud Von Petzold. 1941. pap. 7.00 o.p. (ISBN 0-384-46100-X). Johnson Repr.

Harris Postage Stamp Catalog: 1987 Edition. rev. ed. David S. Macdonald. (Illus.). 342p. 1986. perfect bdg. 3.95 o.p. (ISBN 0-937458-43-0). Harris & Co.

Harrison Ford. Minty Clinch. (Illus.). 214p. 1988. 24.95 o.s.i. (ISBN 0-450-39940-0, Pub. by Hodder & Stoughton UK). David & Charles.

Harrison's Principles of Internal Medicine Patient Management Problems: PreTest Self-Assessment & Review, Vol. 2. PreTest Service, Inc. Staff. Ed. by A. J. Bollet. (Illus.). 260p. 1984. text ed. 39.95 o.p. (ISBN 0-07-051929-3). McGraw.

Harrison's Principles of Internal Medicine: Update One. 9th ed. Kurt J. Isselbacher et al. (Illus.). 304p. 1981. text ed. 35.00 o.p. (ISBN 0-07-032131-0). McGraw.

Harrison's Principles of Internal Medicine: Update Three. Kurt J. Isselbacher et al. (Illus.). 272p. 1982. text ed. 35.00 o.p. (ISBN 0-07-032133-7). McGraw.

Harrison's Principles of Internal Medicine: Update VI. Ed. by Robert G. Petersdorf et al. (Illus.). 400p. 1985. text ed. 35.00 o.p. (ISBN 0-07-049617-X). McGraw.

Harrison's Principles of Internal Medicine: Update 2. 9th ed. Kurt J. Isselbacher et al. (Illus.). 1982. text ed. 35.00 o.p. (ISBN 0-07-032132-9). McGraw.

Harrison's Principles of Internal Medicine: Update 4. 9th ed. Kurt J. Isselbacher & Raymond D. Adams. (Updates to Harrison's Principles of Internal Medicine Ser.). (Illus.). 320p. 1983. text ed. 35.00 o.p. (ISBN 0-07-032134-5). McGraw.

Harrods Book of Cakes & Desserts. Pat Alburey. LC 86-8020. (Illus.). 1986. 12.95 o.p. (ISBN 0-87795-819-X). Morrow.

Harrod's Librarians' Glossary & Handbook. Ray Prytherch. Ed. by L. M. Harrod. LC 83-17174. 880p. 1983. text ed. 69.95x o.p. (ISBN 0-566-03460-3). Gower Pub Co.

Harrow Sparrow. Jill Briscoe. LC 85-5097. (Illus.). 144p. (gr. 2-4). 1985. 8.95 o.p. (ISBN 0-8407-5428-0). Nelson.

Harrowing of Hell. William L. Hendricks. 1977. saddlewire 1.95 o.p. (ISBN 0-8054-9730-7). Broadman.

Harry Anderson: The Man Behind the Paintings. Raymond H. Woolsey & Ruth Anderson. LC 76-15700. (Illus.). 1976. 9.95 o.p. (ISBN 0-8280-0047-6). Review & Herald.

Harry Hoyle's Giant Jumping Bean. William Van Horn. LC 77-21112. (Illus.). (ps-2). 1978. 8.95 o.p. (ISBN 0-689-30636-9, Atheneum). Macmillan.

Harry the Hider. Carol Nicklaus. (Illus.). 32p. (gr. k-3). 1980. pap. 1.50 o.p. (ISBN 0-380-49189-3, 49189-3, Camelot). Avon.

Harsh & Dreadful Love: Dorothy Day & the Catholic Worker Movement. William D. Miller. 1973. 9.95 o.p. (ISBN 0-87140-558-X). Liveright.

Hart Crane: A Reference Guide. Joseph Schwartz. 1983. 43.50 o.s.i. (ISBN 0-8161-8493-3, Hall Reference). G K Hall.

Hartford: An Illustrated History of Connecticut's Capital. Glenn Weaver. LC 82-17606. (Illus.). 208p. 1982. 24.95 o.p. (ISBN 0-89781-052-X). Windsor Pubns Inc.

Hartford, Connecticut. (Panel Advisory Service Report Ser.). 62p. 1983. pap. 10.00 o.p. (ISBN 0-317-06732-X, HC2). Urban Land.

Harvard Century: The Making of a University to a Nation. Richard N. Smith. 1986. 22.45 o.p. (ISBN 0-671-46035-8). S&S.

Harvard College in the Seventeenth Century, 2 Vols. Samuel E. Morison. LC 36-6926. (Illus.). 1936. Set. 42.00x o.s.i. (ISBN 0-674-37450-9). Harvard U Pr.

Harvard Crimson Anthology. Ed. by Greg Lawless. 1980. 16.95 o.p. (ISBN 0-395-27607-1). HM.

Harvard Entrepreneurs Society's Guide to Making Money: Or the Tycoon's Handbook. Edward A. Gazvoda, Jr. & William M. Haney, III. 160p. 1983. pap. 6.70i o.p. (ISBN 0-316-30590-1); 6.95i o.p. Little.

Harvard Guide to Modern Psychiatry. Ed. by Armand M. Nicholi, Jr. (Illus.). 864p. 1978. 40.00x o.p. (ISBN 0-674-37566-1). Belknap Pr.

Harvard Honors Lafayette see Exhibition Catalogues from the Fogg Art Museum.

Harvard Library of Computer Graphics, Mapping Collection, 19 vols. Laboratory for Computer Graphics & Spatial Analysis, Harvard University Graduate School of Design Staff. (Illus.). 1981. Set. pap. 139.95 o.p. (ISBN 0-8122-1180-4). U of Pa Pr.

Harvard Project Manager-Total Project Manager: Controlling Your Resources. Lawrence S. Kasevich. 1986. 21.95 o.p. (ISBN 0-8306-0678-5, 2678); pap. 16.60 o.p. (ISBN 0-8306-2678-6). TAB Bks.

Harvest Gold. (Nostalgia Gift Set Ser.). (gr. 3-7). write for info. o.p. Cook.

Harvest of Fear. Charles M. Collins. 1975. pap. 1.25 o.p. (ISBN 0-380-00412-7, 25114). Avon.

Harvest of Honey. Ed. by Annette Gohlke. LC 83-63230. 66p. 1984. pap. 3.95 o.s.i. (ISBN 0-89821-058-5). Reiman Assocs.

Harvest of Stories: From a Half Century of Writing. Dorothy Canfield. LC 56-11298. 1956. 8.50 o.p. (ISBN 0-15-138987-X). HarBraceJ.

Harvest of the Sun: An Illustrated History of Riverside County. James T. Brown. LC 85-64117. 248p. 1985. 24.95 o.p. (ISBN 0-89781-145-3). Windsor Pubns Inc.

Harvest the Day. Margot Bickel & Hermann Steigert. Ed. by Gerhard E. Frost. (Illus.). 64p. (Orig.). pap. 7.95 o.p. (ISBN 0-86683-730-2). HarpR.

Harvesters & Harvesting, Eighteen Forty to Nineteen Hundred: A Study of the Rural Proletariat. David H. Morgan. Ed. by Frances Nuti. 224p. 1982. 28.00 o.p. (ISBN 0-7099-1735-X, Pub. by Croom Helm Ltd). Routledge Chapman & Hall.

Harvestime Pulpit Library: Let Them Know, Vol. 2. Ed. by Mary H. Wallace. (Illus.). 379p. (Orig.). 1984. pap. 8.95 o.p. (ISBN 0-912315-67-9). Word Aflame.

Harvesting of Krill. G. Eddie. (Southern Ocean Fisheries Survey Programmes: GLO-SO-77-2). 82p. (Eng. & Span., 2nd Printing 1978). 1977. pap. 7.50 o.p. (ISBN 92-5-100415-3, F1309, FAO). UNIPUB.

Harvesting the Sun: Photosynthesis in Plant Life. Ed. by Anthony San Pietro et al. 1967. 48.50 o.p. (ISBN 0-12-618956-0). Acad Pr.

Harvey Couch: An Entrepreneur Brings Electricity to Arkansas. Stephen Wilson. LC 86-22323. (Illus.). 128p. 1986. 13.95 o.p. (ISBN 0-87483-025-7); leather edition o.p. 20.00 o.p. (ISBN 0-87483-026-5). August Hse.

Harvey Cushing's Seventieth Birthday Party, April 8, 1939: Speeches, Letters, & Tributes. Cushing, Harvery Society Staff. (Illus.). 156p. 1939. photocopy ed. 15.50x o.p. (ISBN 0-398-04240-3). C C Thomas.

Has Rome Converted. Henri Fesquet. Tr. by Harold J. Salemson. 1968. 9.50 o.p. (ISBN 0-685-11959-9). Heineman.

Has Trade Protection Revitalized Domestic Industries? (CBO Study). 127p. (Orig.). 1986. pap. 5.50 o.p. (ISBN 0-318-22394-5, S/N 052-070-06206-1). USGPO.

Hashar. Elton Fax. 1980. 5.95 o.p. (ISBN 0-8285-1845-9, Pub. by Progress Pubs USSR). Imported Pubns.

Hasidic Anthology. Date not set. (ISBN 0-8052-4030-6). Random.

Hasidic Communication. Date not set. (ISBN 0-8052-0209-9). Random.

Hasidic Prayer. Date not set. pap. (ISBN 0-8052-0604-3). Random.

Hasidic Tales of the Holocaust. Yaffa Eliach. 336p. 1983. pap. 4.95 o.p. (ISBN 0-380-64725-7, Discus). Avon.

Hasidism. Martin Buber. (ISBN 0-8022-0191-1). Philos Lib.

Hastening Time, Vol. 4. Pat Spillman. 1988. pap. 3.50 o.p. (ISBN 0-317-66643-6). Herald Hse.

Hastings Conspiracy. Alfred Coppel. LC 80-10366. 352p. 1980. 12.95 o.s.i. (ISBN 0-03-056058-6). H Holt & Co.

Hasty Pudding & Barbary Pirates: A Life of Joel Barlow. Esther M. Douty. LC 74-22023. (Illus.). 144p. (gr. 3-6). 1975. 5.95 o.s.i. (ISBN 0-664-32559-9, Westminster). Westminster John Knox.

Hat. Faith Hubley & John Hubley. LC 74-1197. 48p. (gr. 2-5). 1974. 5.95 o.p. (ISBN 0-15-233611-7, HJ). HarBraceJ.

Hat Pin & Tie Pins. Alexandra M. Rhodes. Ed. by Noel Riley. (Antique Pocket Guides). (Illus.). 64p. 1982. pap. 5.95 o.p. (ISBN 0-7188-2540-3, Pub. by Lutterworth Pr UK). Seven Hills Bk Dists.

Hat-Shaking Dance & Other Ashanti Tales from Ghana. Harold Courlander & Albert K. Prempeh. LC 56-5872. (Illus.). (gr. 3-7). 1957. 5.75 o.p. (ISBN 0-15-233615-X, HJ). HarBraceJ.

Hatch! Karyn Henley. LC 79-91306. (Carolrhoda on My Own Bks.). (Illus.). (gr. k-4). 1980. PLB 8.95 o.p. (ISBN 0-87614-122-X). Carolrhoda Bks.

Hatha Yoga As Taught in Siddha Meditation Ashrams. rev. ed. LC 81-51182. (Illus.). 96p. 1981. pap. 8.00 o.s.i. (ISBN 0-914602-72-1). SYDA Found.

Hatha Yoga for Kids: A Guidebook for Parents & Children. Suresh T. Bhamre. (Illus.). (gr. k up). 1985. 8.00 o.p. (ISBN 0-682-40164-1). Exposition-Phoenix.

Hatteras Light: A Novel. Philip Gerard. 240p. 1986. 14.95 o.s.i. (ISBN 0-684-18730-2). Scribner.

Hatter's Phantoms. Georges Simenon. Tr. by Willard R. Trask. LC 76-18254. (Helen & Kurt Wolff Bk). 1976. 6.95 o.p. (ISBN 0-15-139270-6). HarBraceJ.

Hattie & the Fox. Mem Fox. LC 86-18849. (Illus.). 32p. (ps-2). 1987. 12.95 o.p. (ISBN 0-02-735470-9). Bradbury Pr.

Hauling Heavyweights: Moving Extra Large Loads by Road. Bob Tuck. (Illus.). 136p. (Orig.). 1988. pap. 12.95 o.p. (ISBN 0-85059-827-3, Pub. by PSL P Stephens England). Sterling.

Haunted & the Haunters: Tales of Ghosts & Other Apparitions. Ed. by Kathleen Lines. LC 75-20361. 288p. (gr. 7 up). 1975. 10.95 o.p. (ISBN 0-374-32900-1). FS&G.

Haunted Bookshop. Christopher Morley. 256p. 1983. pap. 4.95 o.p. (ISBN 0-380-62695-0, 62695-0). Avon.

Haunted Castle of Ravencurse. Lynn Beach. (Wizards, Warriors & You Ser.: Bk. 5). 112p. (gr. 4 up). 1985. pap. 2.25 o.p. (ISBN 0-380-89523-4). Avon.

Haunted Dolls. Seon Manley & Gogo Lewis. LC 79-7608. (Illus.). 336p. 1980. 10.95a o.p. (ISBN 0-385-15363-5, Pub by Zephyr-Bfyr); pap. 10.95 o.p. (ISBN 0-385-15654-5). Doubleday.

Haunted Heartland. Beth Scott & Michael Norman. LC 84-16308. 504p. (Orig.). 1985. 19.95 o.p. (ISBN 0-88361-092-2). Stanton & Lee.

Haunted Houses. Camille Flammarion. LC 76-159957. (Tower Bks.). 1971. Repr. of 1924 ed. 43.00x o.p. (ISBN 0-8103-3911-0). Gale.

Haunted Houses. L. B. Taylor, Jr. LC 82-20145. (Chiller Ser.). 128p. (gr. 8-12). 1983. lib. bdg. 8.79 o.s.i. (ISBN 0-671-46783-2). Messner.

Haunted Man & the Haunted House. Charles Dickens. 128p. 1985. pap. 4.95 o.p. (ISBN 0-86299-214-1). Academy Chi Pubs.

Haunted Night. Joan Phipson. LC 70-96320. (gr. 7 up). 1970. 5.50 o.p. (ISBN 0-15-233641-9, HJ). HarBraceJ.

Haunted Places. Betsy Hoffman. LC 81-16875. (Illus.). 96p. (gr. 4 up). 1982. lib. bdg. 8.97 o.p. (ISBN 0-671-34005-0). Messner.

Haunted Summer. Hope D. Jordan. (gr. 7-9). 1969. pap. 1.95 o.p. Archway.

Haunted Wisconsin. Beth Scott & Michael Norman. LC 80-22151. (Illus.). 256p. (Orig.). 1980. pap. 10.95 o.p. (ISBN 0-88361-082-5). Stanton & Lee.

Haunting at Lost Lake. Eleana Oliphant. 224p. (Orig.). pap. (ISBN 0-505-51721-3, Pub. by Tower Bks). Dorchester Pub Co.

Haunting of America: Ghost Stories from Our Past. Jean Anderson. LC 73-5864. (Illus.). 176p. (gr. 5 up). 1973. 6.95 o.p. (ISBN 0-395-17518-6). HM.

Haunting of Julie Unger. Valerie A. Lutters. LC 77-1575. (gr. 4-6). 1977. 7.95 o.p. (ISBN 0-689-30590-7, Atheneum). Macmillan.

Haunting of Suzanna Blackwell. Richard Setlowe. LC 83-10833. 355p. 1984. 14.95 o.p. (ISBN 0-03-057786-1). H Holt & Co.

Hausa Architecture in Northern Nigeria. James C. Moughtin. LC 85-20105. (Illus.). 180p. 1985. text ed. 24.95x o.p. (ISBN 0-936508-14-0). Barber Pr.

Hausa Language: A Descriptive Grammar, Vol. 4. M. A. Smirnova. (Languages of Asia & Africa Ser.). 100p. (Orig.). 1982. pap. 14.95x o.p. (ISBN 0-7100-9076-5). Routledge Chapman & Hall.

Hausa Reader: Cultural Materials with Helps for Use in Teaching Intermediate & Advanced Hausa. Charles H. Kraft. LC 70-161997. 1974. pap. 35.00x o.p. (ISBN 0-520-02067-7). U of Cal Pr.

Haute Surveillance. Jean Genet. 1965. pap. 12.25 o.p. (ISBN 0-685-11229-2). Schoenhof.

Havana X. Shelly Gross. LC 77-90665. 1978. 8.95 o.p. (ISBN 0-87795-182-9, Arbor Hse). Morrow.

Have a Good Day at the Office, Dear. Bill Lee. 80p. 1983. lib. bdg. 4.95 o.p. (ISBN 0-531-09803-6). Watts.

Have a Nice Day: Over 30 Pop-ups for "Adults" Simon Bond. (Illus.). 1986. 12.95 o.p. (ISBN 0-517-56319-3, C N Potter Bks). Crown.

Have a Very Merry Christmas! Skits for Elementary Schools & Families. Mabel J. Gabbott. LC 80-83034. 56p. (Orig.). 1981. pap. 4.95 o.p. (ISBN 0-88290-163-X, 2044). Horizon Utah.

Have a Word on Me. Willard Espy. 1981. 13.95 o.p. (ISBN 0-671-25255-0). S&S.

Have a Word on Me: A Celebration of Language. Willard Espy. 1984. pap. 6.70 o.p. (ISBN 0-671-50772-9, Touchstone Bks). S&S.

Have Healthy Teeth & Gums. Mervyn Pichel & Neal Curtis. (Illus.). 128p. (Orig.). 1986. pap. 5.95 o.p. (ISBN 0-7137-1431-X, Pub. by Javelin England). Sterling.

Have His Carcase. Dorothy L. Sayers. 1976. pap. 2.75 o.p. (ISBN 0-380-00939-0, 58305-4). Avon.

Have Jump Shot Will Travel. Charles Rosen. LC 74-18158. 204p. 1976. 6.95 o.p. (ISBN 0-87795-106-3, Arbor Hse). Morrow.

Have Mercy Upon Me see Confession: The Road to Forgiveness.

Have You Got the Energy? Proceedings. Junior Liaison Organization Annual Conference, London, 1974. 130p. 1975. pap. 35.00 o.p. (ISBN 0-08-019651-9). Pergamon.

Have You Heard This One? A Lifetime of Jokes Compiled with an Elastic Memory, Somewhat Depraved Sense of Humor, & a Pair of Scissors. Culver Sherrill. 1978. 4.00 o.p. (ISBN 0-682-49178-0). Exposition-Phoenix.
Haven of the Masses: A Study of the Pentecostal Movement in Chile. Christian L. D'Epinay. Tr. by Marjorie Sandle. (World Studies of Churches in Mission). 1969. pap. 4.95 o.p. (ISBN 0-377-82931-5, Pub. by Lutterworth England). Friendship Pr.
Havens of Refuge: The Sanctuary Movement & the Law. 1985. 1.00 o.p. Natl Lawyers Guild.
Haviland China, Vol. 2: A Pattern Identification Guide. Gertrude T. Jacobson. (Illus.). 208p. 12.95 o.p. (ISBN 0-87069-291-7). Wallace-Homestead.
Having a Baby Without a Man. Susan Robinson & F. H. Pizer. 166p. 1985. pap. 7.95 o.p. (ISBN 0-671-55146-9, Fireside). S&S.
Having a Picnic. Sarah Garland. (Illus.). 32p. (ps-k). 1985. 6.95 o.p. (ISBN 0-316-30434-4, Joy St Bks). Little.
Having Been There. Ed. by Alan Luks. 1979. 1.95 o.p. (ISBN 0-684-16170-2, ScribT); 1.95 o.p. (ISBN 0-684-17240-2). Scribner.
Having It All: A Practical Guide to Overcoming the Career Woman's Blues. Joyce Gabriel & Bettye Baldwin. LC 79-23283. 252p. 1979. 8.95 o.p. (ISBN 0-87131-302-2). M Evans.
Having It All: Love Success Sex-Money. Helen G. Brown. 1982. 15.50 o.p. (ISBN 0-671-45813-2, Linden Pr). S&S.
Having It Your Way: The Strategy of Settling Everyday Conflicts. Robert Bell. (Illus.). 1977. 8.95 o.p. (ISBN 0-393-01164-X). Norton.
Having Your Baby at Home. Kathy Fielding. 1980. softcover 3.95 o.p. (ISBN 0-912216-23-9). Angel Pr.
Havoc. Michael S. Huna. LC 82-90626. 40p. 1985. 5.95 o.p. (ISBN 0-533-05541-5). Vantage.
Havoc in Islandia. Mark Saxton. LC 81-20139. 256p. 1982. 12.95 o.p. (ISBN 0-395-31833-5). HM.
Hawaii. (Nick Carter Ser.). (Orig.). 1979. pap. 1.95 o.p. (ISBN 0-441-31845-2). Ace Bks.
Hawaii. Gordon Sager. LC 69-16369. (This Beautiful World Ser.: Vol. 8). (Illus.). 1969. pap. 5.25 o.p. (ISBN 0-87011-072-1). Kodansha.
Hawaii: A Woman's Guide. Shirley Van Campen. LC 79-83734. 1979. pap. 5.95 o.p. (ISBN 0-916032-07-8). Delmar.
Hawaii-Access. (Access Travel Guides Ser.). 1986. 9.95 o.p. (ISBN 0-671-60338-8). P-H.
Hawaii-Access. 2nd ed. Ed. by Richard S. Wurman. (Access Guidebook Ser.). (Illus.). 144p. 1985. pap. 9.95 o.p. (ISBN 0-915461-10-2). Access Pr.
Hawaii & Other Poems. Samuel Solomon. 1982. 6.95 o.p. (ISBN 0-533-05301-3). Vantage.
Hawaii Environmental Laws & Regulations, 2 vols. & supplements. rev ed. Hawaii, Office of Environmental Quality Control Staff & University of Hawaii, Environomental Center Staff. 1976. Set. 62.00x o.p. (ISBN 0-8248-0445-7). UH Pr.
Hawaii Nineteen Eighty-Seven. Steve Birnbaum. (Illus.). 456p. 1986. pap. 12.70 o.s.i. (ISBN 0-395-42337-6). HM.
Hawaii on Fifty Dollars a Day. rev. ed. Faye Hammel & SYlvan Levey. (Frommer's Dollar-A-Day Ser). (Illus.). 1987. pap. 12.95 o.p. (ISBN 0-13-384538-9). P-H.
Hawaii on Thirty-Five Dollars a Day, 1985-86. 382p. 1984. 9.95 o.p. (ISBN 0-671-52443-7). Prentice Hall Pr.
Hawaii Pono: A Social History. Lawrence H. Fuchs. LC 61-13347. (Illus.). 1961. 14.95 o.p. (ISBN 0-15-139539-X). HarBraceJ.
Hawaii: Travel Guide. 5th ed. Sunset Editors. LC 74-20023. (Illus.). 160p. 1975. pap. 5.95 o.p. (ISBN 0-376-06308-4, Sunset Bks.). Sunset-Lane.
Hawaii: Winter Vacation Guide, 1989. (Illus.). cancelled o.s.i. Wrld Travel.
Hawaii 1983. Steve Birnbaum. (Get 'em & Go Travel Guide Ser.). 1982. pap. 11.45 o.p. (ISBN 0-395-32872-1). HM.
Hawaii 1984. Steve Birnbaum. (Get'em & Go Travel Guide Ser.). 1983. pap. 11.45 o.p. (ISBN 0-395-34629-0). HM.
Hawaii, 1985. Steve Birnbaum. (Get 'em & Go Travel Guide Ser.). 1984. pap. 11.70 o.p. (ISBN 0-395-36521-X). HM.
Hawaiian Americans: An Account of the Mingling of Japanese, Chinese, Polynesian, & American Cultures. Edwin G. Burrows. LC 73-122394. 228p. 1970. Repr. of 1947 ed. 25.00 o.p. (ISBN 0-208-00949-3, Archon). Shoe String.
Hawaiian Flowers & Flowering Trees. Loraine E. Kuck & Richard C. Tongg. LC 58-7494. (Illus.). 1958. boxed 19.50 o.p. (ISBN 0-8048-0237-8). C E Tuttle.
Hawaiian Furniture & Hawaii's Cabinetmakers 1820-1940. Irving Jenkins. (U. S. Rights Except in Hawaii Ser.). (Illus.). 354p. 1985. 185.00 o.p. (ISBN 0-7103-0114-6, Kegan Paul). Routledge Chapman & Hall.
Hawaiian Herbs of Medicinal Value. D. M. Kaaiakamanu & J. K. Akina. Tr. by Akaiko Akana. LC 76-177367. 1972. pap. 4.75 o.p. (ISBN 0-8048-1019-2). C E Tuttle.
Hawaiian Prophet: Alexander Hume Ford. Valerie Noble. (Illus.). 1980. 15.00 o.p. (ISBN 0-682-49540-9, Banner). Exposition-Phoenix.
Hawaiian Tramways. Robert Ramsay. (Illus.). 36p. 1976. pap. 4.00 o.s.i. (ISBN 0-87095-062-2). Gldn West Bks.
Hawk High. Betty K. Levine. LC 79-22668. (Illus.). (gr. 4-6). 1980. 7.95 o.p. (ISBN 0-689-30748-9, Atheneum). Macmillan.
Hawk in Silver. Mary Gentle. LC 84-20145. 240p. (gr. 4 up). 1985. 10.25 o.p. (ISBN 0-688-04213-9). Lothrop.
Hawk of May. Gillian Bradshaw. 1980. 10.95 o.p. (ISBN 0-671-25093-0). S&S.
Hawk Over Hollyhedge Manor. Dorothy Dowdell. 1973. pap. 0.75 o.p. (ISBN 0-380-01242-1, 15040). Avon.
Hawk That Dare Not Hunt by Day. Scott O'Dell. 272p. (gr. 7 up). 1975. 7.95 o.p. (ISBN 0-395-21892-6). HM.
Hawker Hurricane in Action. Robert Jackson. (Illus.). 160p. 1988. 29.95 o.p. (ISBN 0-7137-1683-5, Pub. by Blandford Pr England). Sterling.
Hawk's Dream & Other Poems. Donald E. Axinn. LC 82-48002. (Poetry Ser.). 128p. 1982. pap. 5.95 o.p. (ISBN 0-394-62419-X, E812, Ever); 12.50 o.p. (ISBN 0-394-52828-X). Grove.
Hawks in Flight: A Guide to the Identification of Migrant Raptors. Pete Dunne & Clay Sutton. LC 87-18929. (Illus.). 288p. 1988. 17.95 o.s.i. (ISBN 0-395-42388-0). HM.
Hawkstone: A Tale of & for England in 1840, 1845. William Sewell. Ed. by Robert L. Wolff. LC 75-446. (Victorian Fiction Ser.). 1976. lib. bdg. 73.00 o.p. (ISBN 0-8240-1526-6). Garland Pub.
Hawthorn Conspiracy. Stephen Hesla. 246p. 1986. pap. 3.95 o.p. (ISBN 0-931773-65-2). Critics Choice Paper.
Hawthorne: A Critical Study. rev. ed. Hyatt H. Waggoner. LC 63-17215. 1963. 19.50x o.s.i. (ISBN 0-674-38250-1, Belknap Pr). Harvard U Pr.
Hawthorne at Auction 1894-1971. Ed. by C. E. Frazer Clark, Jr. LC 70-38939. (Bruccoli Clark Book, Authors at Auction Ser.). 442p. 1972. 44.00x o.p. (ISBN 0-8103-0919-X). Gale.
Hawthorne's Influence on Dickens & George Eliot. Edward Stokes. LC 84-3509. (Scholar's Library). 244p. 1985. pap. text ed. 37.50x o.p. (ISBN 0-7022-1689-5). U of Queensland Pr.
Hawthorne's Inviolable Circle: The Problem of Time. 2nd ed. Robert H. Fossum. LC 74-172791. 229p. 1973. lib. bdg. 25.00 o.p. (ISBN 0-912112-10-7). Everett-Edwards.
Haydn: Symphony No. One Hundred & Three in E-Flat Major (Drum Roll) Haydn. Ed. by Karl Geiringer. LC 73-20231. (Critical Scores Ser.). (Illus.). 116p. 1974. pap. 8.95x o.p. (ISBN 0-393-09349-2). Norton.
Hayek on Liberty. John Gray. 200p. 1984. 45.00x o.p. (ISBN 0-631-14813-2). Basil Blackwell.
Haynes General Motors J Car Owners Workshop Manual 1982 thru 1987. rev. ed. J. H. Haynes. LC 87-80836. (Illus.). 320p. 1988. pap. 15.95 o.p. (ISBN 0-317-65664-3). Haynes Pubns.
Haynes GM-A Cars Owners Workshop Manual 1982 thru 1987. rev. ed. J. H. Haynes. LC 87-80835. (Illus.). 320p. 1988. pap. 15.95 o.p. (ISBN 1-85010-390-9). Haynes Pubns.
Hayyim see Stories & Parables of the Hafetz Hayyim.
Hazard. Gerald A. Browne. LC 72-82171. 1973. 7.95 o.p. (ISBN 0-87795-040-7, Arbor Hse). Morrow.
Hazard Control Policy in Britain. John C. Chicken. LC 75-12900. 204p. 1975. 42.00 o.p. (ISBN 0-08-019739-6). Pergamon.
Hazardous Chemicals Information Annual, No. 1. Sax. 1986. pap. 75.95 o.s.i. (ISBN 0-442-28135-8). Van Nos Reinhold.
Hazardous Materials Handbook. James H. Meidl. (Fire Science Ser). 1972. pap. text ed. (ISBN 0-02-476370-5, 47637). Macmillan.
Hazardous Materials Transportation & Highway Maintenance: Planning, Budgeting, & Performing - 28 Reports. 74p. 1975. 3.40 o.p. (ISBN 0-309-02460-9). Transport Res Bd.
Hazardous Waste Handbook. 5th ed. Watson et al. 796p. 1984. 98.00 o.p. (ISBN 0-86587-121-3). Gov Insts.
Hazardous Waste Litigation 1985, Vol. 283. Practising Law Institute Staff. 633p. 1985. pap. 40.00 o.p. (ISBN 0-317-27606-9, H4-4969). PLI.
Hazardous Waste Processing Technology. Yen-Hsiung Kiang & Amir Metry. LC 81-69070. (Illus.). 549p. 1982. text ed. 49.95 o.p. (ISBN 0-250-40411-7). Butterworth.
Hazardous Waste Sites in the U. S. Ed. by A. Alan Pishdad. 175p. 1981. pap. 46.00 o.p. (ISBN 0-08-026274-0). Pergamon.
Hazards of Learning: An International Symposium on the Crisis of the University. George Urban. LC 76-3094. 316p. 1977. 12.95 o.p. (ISBN 0-87548-339-9). Open Court.
Hazards of Walking & other Memos from Your Bureaucrats. Ed. by Carol Trueblood & Donna Fenn. 1982. pap. 3.80 o.p. (ISBN 0-395-32592-7). HM.
Hazlitt Sampler: Selections from His Familiar, Literary & Critical Essays. William Hazlitt. Ed. by H. M. Sikes. 11.25 o.p. (ISBN 0-8446-0688-X). Peter Smith.
HB Chemistry & Physics. 67th ed. Robert C. Weast. 2424p. 1986. 69.95 o.p. (ISBN 0-8493-0467-9). CRC Pr.
HBJ Federal Tax Course 1985. Ray M. Sommerfeld et al. 726p. 1984. text ed. 27.95 o.p. (ISBN 0-15-535302-0, HC). HarBraceJ.
HBJ Federal Tax Course 1987. Ray M. Sommerfeld et al. 797p. 1986. text ed. 27.00 o.p. (ISBN 0-15-535309-8); Update for Tax 1987 1.25 o.p. (ISBN 0-317-56565-6). HarBraceJ.
HDE Manual of Fine Restaurant Service. Dennis Beznoska et al. LC 85-90980. (Illus.). 1985. 20.00 o.p. (ISBN 0-682-40243-5). Exposition-Phoenix.
He Hit Me First: When Brothers & Sisters Fight. Gessell Institute of Human Development Staff et al. LC 82-1565. 1982. 14.95 o.s.i. (ISBN 0-934878-18-8). Dembner Bks.
He Is Here. Riley R. Ballard. (Illus.). 80p. 1982. 5.50 o.p. (ISBN 0-682-49855-6). Exposition-Phoenix.
He Rode Alone. Steve Frazee. 160p. 1981. pap. 1.75 o.s.i. (ISBN 0-449-14103-9, Crest). Fawcett.
He-She. Herbert Gold. LC 79-5709. 1980. 9.95 o.p. (ISBN 0-87795-264-7, Arbor Hse). Morrow.
He Speaks Softly. Bob Benson. 160p. 1985. 10.99 o.p. (ISBN 0-8499-0449-8, 0449-8). Word Bks.
He Swings a Straight Stick. Paul Weinman. 20p. 1985. pap. 1.50 o.p. (ISBN 0-317-39900-4). Samisdat.
He Took Me to Heaven. Ruth B. Barker. 96p. 1984. 6.50 o.p. (ISBN 0-682-40195-1). Exposition-Phoenix.
He Was One of Us: The Life of Jesus of Nazareth. Rien Poortvliet. LC 85-29270. 128p. 1986. 14.95 o.s.i. (ISBN 0-385-13576-9). Doubleday.
He Who Cannot - A Teacher's Lament. F. C. Miller. 208p. 1982. 9.50 o.p. (ISBN 0-682-49866-1). Exposition-Phoenix.
He Who Rides a Tiger. Bhabani Bhattacharya. 245p. 1977. pap. 5.00 o.s.i. (ISBN 0-86578-072-2). Ind-US Inc.
Head Accountant-Audit Clerk. Jack Rudman. (Career Examination Ser.: C-2009). (Cloth bdg. avail. on request). pap. 16.00 o.p. Natl Learning.
Head & Neck Anatomy: With Clinical Correlations. Royce L. Montgomery. (Illus.). 352p. 1981. text ed. 32.00 o.p. (ISBN 0-07-042853-0). McGraw.
Head & Neck Cancer, Vol. 2. Ed. by Robert E. Wittes. LC 84-15351. (Cancer Investigation & Management Ser.). 350p. 1985. 75.00 o.p. (ISBN 0-471-10539-2, Dist. by A R Liss). Wiley.
Head & Neck Imaging: Excluding the Brain. Thomas R. Bergeron et al. (Illus.). 1983. 135.00 o.p. (ISBN 0-8016-0622-5). Mosby.
Head & Neck Injuries in Football: Mechanisms, Treatment & Prevention. Richard C. Schneider. LC 73-4197. 272p. 1973. 22.50 o.p. (ISBN 0-683-07573-X, WW). Krieger.
Head & Neck Surgery, 3 vols. H. H. Naumann. LC 79-3798. (Illus.). Vol. 1, 473 Pp. text ed. 105.00 o.p. (ISBN 0-7216-6663-9); Vol. 2, 475 Pp. 105.00 o.p. (ISBN 0-7216-6664-7); Vol. 3: Ear. 105.00 o.p. (ISBN 0-7216-6667-1). Saunders.
Head & Neck Surgery. Clarence T. Sasaki & Bruce W. Jafek. (Comprehensive Surgical Atlases in Otolaryngology & Head & Neck Surgery Ser.: Vol. 2). 1983. 99.00 o.p. (ISBN 0-8089-1596-7, 793792). Grune.
Head & Neck Surgery: Indications, Techniques & Pitfalls, Vol. 4. H. H. Naumann. (Illus.). 905p. 1984. The Neck. write for info. o.p. (ISBN 0-7216-6668-X). Saunders.
Head & Spine Imaging. Carlos F. Gonzelez et al. Ed. by Joseph C. Masdeu & C. Barrie Grossman. LC 84-15172. 952p. 1985. text ed. 150.00 o.p. (ISBN 0-471-89747-7). Wiley.
Head First: A Yellowthread Street Mystery. William Marshall. LC 85-27357. (Rinehart Suspense Novel Ser.). 192p. 1986. 14.95 o.p. (ISBN 0-8050-0061-5). H Holt & Co.
Head Injury. Louis Bakay et al. 1980. text ed. 37.50 o.p. (ISBN 0-316-07774-7). Little.
Head over Heels. Lurlene McDaniel. (Impressions Ser.). 112p. (Orig.). (gr. 6-8). 1987. pap. 2.25 o.s.i. (ISBN 0-87406-263-2). Willowisp Pr.
Head over Heels. Francine Pascal. (Sweet Valley High Ser.: No. 18). (Orig.). (gr. 5). 1985. pap. 2.75 o.p. (ISBN 0-553-26687-X). Bantam.
Head over Wheels. Lee Kingman. 224p. (gr. 5 up). 1978. 8.95 o.p. (ISBN 0-395-27202-5). HM.
Head Sharp: Step-by-Step Exercises to Develop Your Brain Power. Jack Maguire. 1985. 16.95 o.p. (ISBN 0-87795-740-1, Arbor Hse). Morrow.
Headbirths: Or the Germans Are Dying Out. Gunter Grass. Tr. by Ralph Manheim. 144p. 1982. 9.95 o.s.i. (ISBN 0-15-139600-0). HarBraceJ.
Headcase: An Anna Lee Mystery. Liza Cody. 196p. 1986. 13.95 o.s.i. (ISBN 0-684-18586-5). Scribner.
Headhunter. Michael Slade. LC 84-27173. 480p. 1985. 17.95 o.p. (ISBN 0-688-04710-6). Morrow.
Heading for the Holocaust: A History of War. John Rydjord. 272p. 1983. 12.00 o.p. (ISBN 0-682-49972-2). Exposition-Phoenix.
Heading Home. Paul Tsongas. 297p. 1985. lib. bdg. 14.95 o.p. (ISBN 0-8161-3954-7, Large Print Bks). G K Hall.
Heading Toward Omega: In Search of the Meaning of the Near-Death Experience. Kenneth Ring. LC 84-4650. (Illus.). 288p. 1984. 15.95 o.p. (ISBN 0-688-03910-3). Morrow.
Headlands. Bruce Beaver. LC 85-1132. 73p. 1987. 12.50 o.p. (ISBN 0-7022-1788-3). U of Queensland Pr.
Headless Ghost: True Tales of the Unexplained. William E. Warren. (Illus.). 160p. (gr. 5 up). 1986. 12.95 o.s.i. (ISBN 0-13-384280-0). P-H.
Headlights & Markers. Frank Donovan & Seth Henry. LC 68-8776. (Illus.). 1968. 17.95 o.p. (ISBN 0-87095-006-1). Gldn West Bks.
Headlines. Malcolm Hall. (Break-of-Day Bk.). (Illus.). 64p. (gr. 1-3). 1973. PLB 6.99 o.p. (ISBN 0-698-30482-9, Coward). Putnam Pub Group.
Headlines & Deadlines. April Koral. LC 80-28173. (Illus.). 64p. (gr. 4-7). 1981. lib. bdg. 9.29 o.s.i. (ISBN 0-671-42317-7). Messner.
Headman & I: Ambiguity & Ambivalence in the Fieldworking Experience. Jean-Paul Dumont. (Texas Pan American Ser.). (Illus.). 229p. 1978. text ed. 14.95x o.p. (ISBN 0-292-73007-1). U of Tex Pr.
Heads. Alex Kayser. LC 85-6007. (Illus.). 132p. 1985. pap. 19.95 o.p. (ISBN 0-89659-524-2). Abbeville Pr.
Heads: A Metafictional History of Western Civilization 1762-1975. Alan Goldfein. LC 73-9296. 1973. pap. 2.95 o.p. (ISBN 0-688-05177-4). Morrow.
Heads & Tails. Dorothy Rose. (Chubby Banana Split Board Bks.). (ps). 1984. 2.95 o.s.i. (ISBN 0-671-50958-6, Little Simon). S&S.
Heads Bowed Together. Ed. by Ann Simon. (Illus.). (gr. 9 up). 1966. pap. 1.95 o.p. (ISBN 0-377-36001-5). Friendship Pr.
Heads of Families, First Census of the United States, 1790: Connecticut. U. S. Bureau of the Census Staff. LC 64-62655. 1961-64. pap. 20.00 o.s.i. (ISBN 0-87152-019-2). Reprint.
Heads of Families, First Census of the United States, 1790: Maine. U. S. Bureau of the Census Staff. LC 64-60351. 1961-64. pap. 12.50 o.p. (ISBN 0-87152-351-5). Reprint.
Heads of Families, First Census of the United States, 1790: Rhode Island. U. S. Bureau of the Census Staff. LC 64-60349. 1961-64. Repr. of 1908 ed. 12.50 o.s.i. (ISBN 0-87152-016-8). Reprint.
Heads of Families, First Census of the United States, 1790: Vermont. U. S. Bureau of the Census Staff. LC 64-60350. 1961-64. pap. 12.50 o.p. (ISBN 0-87152-015-X). Reprint.
Headsparks. Robert Coles. (gr. 7 up). 1975. 5.95 o.p. (ISBN 0-316-15156-4, An Atlantic Little, Brown Book). Little.
Headstart Book of Knowing & Naming. Shari Lewis & Jacquelyn Reinach. (Young Pioneer Bks.). (ps). 1966. text ed. 4.95 o.p. (ISBN 0-07-078002-1). McGraw.
Heal the Sick. Reginald East. LC 77-80678. 160p. (Orig.). 1977. pap. 2.95 o.p. (ISBN 0-87123-232-4, 200232). Bethany Hse.
Heal Your Body. rev. ed. Louise L. Hay. 48p. 1984. pap. 3.00 o.p. (ISBN 0-937611-00-X). Hay House.
Healer. Peter Dickinson. LC 84-17454. 192p. (gr. 7 up). 1985. pap. 14.95 o.p. (ISBN 0-385-29372-0). Delacorte.
Healer. Date not set. (ISBN 0-385-29372-0). Delacorte.
Healer. Leonard Levitt. 240p. 1981. pap. 2.95 o.p. (ISBN 0-380-56531-5, 56531-5). Avon.
Healers. Henry Denker. 464p. 1984. pap. 4.50 o.p. (ISBN 0-380-67405-X, 67405). Avon.

Titles

Healer's Art. Eric J. Cassell. 240p. 1985. pap. 8.95 o.p. (ISBN 0-262-53062-7). MIT Pr.
Healing: A Forever-Settled Subject. Kenneth Hagin, Jr. 1981. pap. 0.50 mini bk. o.p. (ISBN 0-89276-707-3). Hagin Ministries.
Healing: A Spiritual Adventure. Mary E. Peterman. LC 74-80416. 104p. 1974. pap. 3.95 o.p. (ISBN 0-8006-1086-5, 1-1086, Fortress). Augsburg Fortress.
Healing Alcoholism. Claude M. Steiner. LC 79-2320. 208p. 1981. pap. 4.95 o.p. (ISBN 0-394-17923-4, B457, BC). Grove.
Healing & the Abundant Life. Malcolm Miner. LC 79-7614. 108p. 1979. pap. 3.95 o.p. (ISBN 0-8192-1258-X). Morehouse Pub.
Healing Choice. Ron L. Davis. 160p. 1986. 9.95 o.p. (ISBN 0-8499-0466-8, 0466-8). Word Bks.
Healing Christ. rev. ed. S. D. Gordon. 160p. (Orig.). 1985. pap. 3.95 o.p. (ISBN 0-89283-271-1, Pub. by Vine Books). Servant.
Healing Devotions. Anne S. White. LC 75-5218. 138p. 1975. pap. 3.95 o.p. (ISBN 0-8192-1192-3). Morehouse Pub.
Healing, Energy, Prayer & Relaxation. Israel Regardie. LC 82-83292. 80p. 1982. pap. 7.95 o.s.i. (ISBN 0-941404-02-1). Falcon Pr Az.
Healing for Everyone. 2nd, rev. ed. Evarts G. Loomis & Sig Paulson. LC 74-345. (Illus., Orig.). 1979. pap. 5.95 o.p. (ISBN 0-87516-377-7). DeVorss.
Healing from the War: Trauma & Transformation after Vietnam. Arthur Egendorf. LC 85-11801. 318p. 1985. 15.45 o.p. (ISBN 0-395-37701-3). HM.
Healing Gardens. Arden Rizer, Jr. Ed. by American Spiritualist Assembly Staff. 42p. (Orig.). 1987. pap. 9.00x o.p. (ISBN 0-939795-17-5). Amer Spirit.
Healing Love: The Inner Power of All Things. Ken L. Evensen. 9.95 o.p. (ISBN 0-533-04807-9). Vantage.
Healing Massage Techniques: A Study of Eastern & Western Methods. Frances Tappan. (Illus.). 1978. 18.95 o.p. (ISBN 0-8359-2821-7); pap. 14.95 o.p. (ISBN 0-8359-2819-5). Appleton & Lange.
Healing Miracles. Walter Rudolf Lange. 1977. 7.50 o.p. (ISBN 0-682-48668-X). Exposition-Phoenix.
Healing of America. Richard Cornuelle. LC 82-24015. 208p. 1983. 14.95 o.p. (ISBN 0-399-12785-2, Seaview). Putnam Pub Group.
Healing Power of Love. Joseph Murphy. pap. 1.00 o.p. (ISBN 0-87516-334-3). DeVorss.
Healing the Pain of Everyday Loss. Ira J. Tanner. 188p. 1980. pap. 4.95 o.p. (ISBN 0-03-057849-3). HarpR.
Healing the Wounds: A Physician Looks at His Work. David Hilfiker. 240p. 1985. 14.45 o.s.i. (ISBN 0-394-54283-5). Pantheon.
Healing Touch. Michael W. Fox. LC 82-22476. Orig. Title: Dr. Michael Fox's Massage Program for Cats & Dogs. 160p. 1983. pap. 6.95 o.p. (ISBN 0-937858-18-8). Newmarket.
Healing with Time & Love: A Guide for Visiting the Elderly. Patricia Murphy. (Andrus Gerontology Center Bk.). 56p. 1979. pap. 2.95x o.p. (ISBN 0-88474-092-7, 05742-8). Lexington Bks.
Healing Yourself. Joy Gardner. LC 86-19663. (Health Ser.). 66p. (Orig.). 1986. pap. 5.95 o.p. (ISBN 0-89594-213-5, C1982). Crossing Pr.
Health. brief ed. Benjamin A. Kogan. (Illus., Orig.). 1976. pap. text ed. 10.95 o.p. (ISBN 0-15-535586-4, HC). HarBraceJ.
Health. Benjamin A. Kogan. 1970. 11.95 o.p. (ISBN 0-15-535580-5). HarbraceJ.
Health. 4th ed. John LaPlace. (Illus.). 576p. 1984. pap. text ed. (ISBN 0-13-385435-3). P-H.
Health: A Concern for Every American. Donna R. Plesser & Mark A. Siegel. (Information Plus Ser.). 120p. 1987. pap. 16.95 o.p. (ISBN 0-936474-66-1). Info Plus TX.
Health: A Concern for Every American. rev. ed. Ed. by Mark A. Siegel & Nancy R. Jacobs. (Instructional Aides Ser.). 96p. 1983. pap. 13.95 o.p. (ISBN 0-936474-29-7). Info Plus TX.
Health Administration: Laws, Regulations, & Guidelines. National Health Publishing Staff. 1000p. 1980. 120.00 o.p. (ISBN 0-932500-00-5, 1106). Healthcare Fin Mgmt Assn.
Health & Fitness in Wisconsin. Ed. by Susan J. Montgomery et al. 200p. (Orig.). 1988. pap. Montgomery Media.
Health & Healing: Understanding Conventional & Alternative Medicine. Andrew Weil. 1984. 13.45 o.p. (ISBN 0-395-34430-1). HM.
Health & Human Nature. Paul Snyder. LC 78-14627. 256p. 1980. pap. 10.95 o.p. (ISBN 0-8019-6798-8). Chilton.
Health & Medical Economics: A Guide to Information Sources. Ed. by Ted J. Ackroyd. LC 73-17567. (Economics Information Guide Ser.: Vol. 7). 168p. 1977. 68.00x o.p. (ISBN 0-8103-1390-1). Gale.
Health & Population in Developing Countries: Selected Papers from the 5th Bellagio Populaion Conference, Rockefeller Foundation, Bellagio, 1979. Ed. by S. J. Segal & B. Winikoff. 100p. 1980. pap. 24.00 o.p. (ISBN 0-08-026101-9). Pergamon.
Health & Safety for Toxicity Testing. Douglas Walters & C. W. Jameson. 352p. 1984. text ed. 42.95 o.p. (ISBN 0-250-40546-6). Butterworth.
Health & Safety in Ceramics. Institute of Ceramics. 1980. pap. text ed. 5.50 o.p. (ISBN 0-08-026173-6). Pergamon.
Health & Social Work: Special Issue on Alcohol Problems. 248p. 1979. 6.00 o.p. (ISBN 0-317-35020-X). Natl Assn Soc Wkrs.
Health & Social Work: Special Issue on Long Term Care & Aging. 224p. 1979. 6.00 o.p. (ISBN 0-317-35021-8). Natl Assn Soc Wkrs.
Health & the Nature of Man. R. S. Rathbone & E. Rathbone. 1971. 19.95 o.p. (ISBN 0-07-051205-1, C); pap. text ed. 13.95 o.p. (ISBN 0-07-051206-X). McGraw.
Health & Wellness Confidential. Boardroom's Experts & Editors. LC 86-13678. 430p. 1986. 50.00 o.p. Boardroom.
Health Aspects of Wastewater Recharge: A State-of-the-Art Review. California State Water Resources Control Board Staff et al. LC 78-69808. (Illus.). 1978. Repr. 26.00 o.p. (ISBN 0-912394-18-8). Water Info.
Health Auxiliaries & the Health Team. Ed. by Muriel Skeet & Katherine Elliott. 222p. 1978. 30.00 o.p. (ISBN 0-85664-634-2, Pub. by Croom Helm Ltd). Routledge Chapman & Hall.
Health-Care. Ed. by Gordon Gebert. 40p. 1981. pap. 20.00 o.p. (ISBN 0-08-028091-9). Pergamon.
Health Care Administration: A Guide to Information Sources. Ed. by Dwight A. Morris & Lynne D. Morris. LC 78-53431. (Health Affairs Information Guide Ser.: Vol. 1). 280p. 1978. 68.00x o.p. (ISBN 0-8103-1378-2). Gale.
Health Care & Consciousness: Think of Yourself Now & Then. Julian Silverman. 1983. text ed. 22.00x o.s.i. (ISBN 0-8290-1335-0). Irvington.
Health Care & the Changing Economic Environment. Alan Sorkin. LC 84-47976. 176p. 1985. 25.00x o.p. (ISBN 0-669-09016-6). Lexington Bks.
Health Care & Traditional Medicine in China, 1800-1982. Sheila Hillier & John Jewell. 600p. 1983. 50.00 o.p. (ISBN 0-7100-9425-6). Routledge Chapman & Hall.
Health Care Construction: A Bibliography. Clarence E. Chrisholm & Clarence Toomer. (Architecture Ser.: Bibliography A 1323). 1985. pap. 2.00 o.p. (ISBN 0-89028-273-0). Vance Biblios.
Health Care Cost Containment Seminar November 7-10, 1982, Hollywood, Florida. Ed. by Becky A. Wright. 170p. (Orig.). 1983. pap. text ed. 17.50 o.p. (ISBN 0-89154-206-X). Intl Found Employ.
Health Care Cost Containment: Seminar Proceedings-Oct. 11-14, 1981, Palm Springs, CA. 78p. (Orig.). 1982. pap. text ed. 10.00 o.p. (ISBN 0-89154-169-1). Intl Found Employ.
Health Care Cost Containment, 1983. Ed. by Becky A. Wright. 90p. (Orig.). 1984. pap. text ed. 17.50 o.p. (ISBN 0-89154-219-1). Intl Found Employ.
Health Care Cost Explosion. Ed. by David Ehrlich. 264p. 1975. pap. 18.25 o.p. (ISBN 0-683-02789-1, Pub. by W & W). Krieger.
Health Care Cost Survey Results. Robert D. Cooper. 10p. 1981. 5.00 o.p. (ISBN 0-89154-166-7). Intl Found Employ.
Health Care Costs & Financing: A Guide to Information Sources. Ed. by Rita M. Keintz. LC 80-23862. (Health Affairs Information Guide Ser.: Vol. 6). 280p. 1981. 68.00x o.p. (ISBN 0-8103-1482-7). Gale.
Health Care Delivery in Anesthesia. Ed. by Harry Wollman et al. (Illus.). 1980. text ed. 16.00x o.p. (ISBN 0-89313-014-1). G F Stickley Co.
Health Care Financing in Developing Countries. Dieter K. Zschock. 82p. 1979. 5.00x o.p. (ISBN 0-87553-133-4, 065). Am Pub Health.
Health Care for Mothers & Infants in Rural & Isolated Areas: Proceedings. 2.75 o.p. (ISBN 0-686-24131-2). Am Coll Obstetric.
Health Care in a Context of Civil Rights. National Research Council, Institute of Medicine. 1981. pap. 11.50x o.p. (ISBN 0-309-03195-8). Natl Acad Pr.
Health Care in the European Community. Alan Maynard. LC 74-17701. (Contemporary Community Health Ser.). 1975. 27.95x o.p. (ISBN 0-8229-1119-1). U of Pittsburgh Pr.
Health Care: Its Psychosocial Dimensions. Jurrit Bergsma & David Thomasma. LC 81-9733. Orig. Title: Other Side of Medicine. (Illus.). 225p. 1981. text ed. 15.50x o.p. (ISBN 0-391-01630-X). Duquesne.
Health Care: Legal Responses to New Economic Forces. Practising Law Institute Staff & Robert M. McNaire. LC 86-103013. (Commercial Law & Practice Course Handbook Ser.: No. 371). 376p. 1985. 45.00 o.p. (A44138). PLI.
Health Care Management: A Text in Organization Theory & Behavior. Stephen M. Shortell & Arnold D. Kaluzny. LC 83-10194. (Health Service Ser.). 533p. 1983. 28.50 o.p. (ISBN 0-471-87567-8, Pub. by Wiley Med). Wiley.
Health Care Marketing Plans: From Strategy to Action. Steven G. Hillestad & Eric W. Berkowitz. LC 83-71842. 175p. 1984. 35.00 o.p. (ISBN 0-87094-462-2). Dow Jones-Irwin.
Health Care Priorities & Management. Gwyn Bevan et al. (Illus.). 294p. 1980. 30.00 o.p. (ISBN 0-7099-0093-7, Pub. by Croom Helm Ltd). Routledge Chapman & Hall.
Health Care Puzzle in New York State: A Citizen Guide. League of Women Voters of New York State Staff. Ed. by Katherine Stuligross. LC 84-52698. (Illus.). 35p. (Orig.). 1985. pap. 3.00 o.p. (ISBN 0-938588-06-0). LWV NYS.
Health Care Supervisor's Handbook. 2nd ed. Norman Metzger. LC 82-6764. 191p. 1982. 28.95 o.p. (ISBN 0-89443-696-1). Aspen Pub.
Health Care Survival Curve: Competition & Cooperation in the Marketplace. Irwin Miller. LC 83-73714. 250p. 1984. 35.00 o.p. (ISBN 0-87094-481-9). Dow Jones-Irwin.
Health Careers Guidebook, 1979. (United States Employment Service Career Guidebook Ser.). 231p. (Orig.). 1979. pap. 7.50 o.p. (S/N 029-000-00343-2). USGPO.
Health Consequences of Involuntary Smoking: A Report of the Surgeon General. (DHHS Publication CDC: No. 87-8398). 379p. 1987. pap. 11.00 o.p. (ISBN 0-317-62856-9, S-N 017-001-00458-8). USGPO.
Health Consequences of Using Smokeless Tobacco: A Report of the Advisory Committee to the Surgeon General. 221p. 1986. pap. 6.00 o.p. (ISBN 0-318-21292-7, S/N 017-042-00192-7). USGPO.
Health Detective's Handbook: A Guide to the Investigation of Environmental Health Hazards by Nonprofessionals. Ed. by Marvin S. Legator et al. LC 84-20105. 272p. 1985. text ed. 27.50x o.p. (ISBN 0-8018-2444-3); pap. text ed. 12.95x o.p. (ISBN 0-8018-2466-4). Johns Hopkins.
Health Devices Sourcebook, 1987. Robert Mosenkis & Dorothy Wood. 1294p. 1987. text ed. 140.00 o.p. (ISBN 0-941417-00-X). ECRI.
Health Devices Sourcebook, 1988. Intro. by Robert Mosenkis & Dorothy Wood. 1482p. 1988. text ed. 165.00 o.p. (ISBN 0-941417-02-6). ECRI.
Health, Doctors, & Social Workers. Zofia Butrym & John Horder. (Library of Social Work). 192p. (Orig.). 1983. pap. 10.95x o.p. (ISBN 0-7100-9403-5). Routledge Chapman & Hall.
Health Education by T.V. & Radio: Contibution to an International Conference Selected Bibliography. 476p. 1981. 18.00 o.p. (ISBN 3-598-20203-2). K G Saur.
Health Education Curriculum. J. Keogh Rash & R. Morgan Pigg, Jr. 299p. 1979. pap. text ed. write for info. o.p. (ISBN 0-02-398470-8). Macmillan.
Health Education: Foundations for the Future. Rubinson & Alles. 1983. 26.95 o.p. (ISBN 0-8016-4233-7). Mosby.
Health Effects of Nitrates, Nitrites, & N-Nitroso Compounds. National Research Council, Assembly of Life Sciences Staff. 544p. 1981. pap. text ed. 14.95x o.p. (ISBN 0-309-03230-X). Natl Acad Pr.
Health, Food & Population. Joan Solomon. (Science in a Social Context Ser.). 1986. pap. text ed. 6.95x o.p. (ISBN 0-631-91020-4). Basil Blackwell.
Health for Effective Living. 6th ed. Edward B. Johns et al. (Illus.). 512p. 1975. text ed. 31.95 o.p. (ISBN 0-07-032572-3). McGraw.
Health from the Hedgerow: Encyclopedia of Medicinal Plants. Dennis Furnell. (Illus.). 192p. 1985. 20.95 o.p. (ISBN 0-7134-4712-5, Pub. by Batsford England). David & Charles.
Health, Illness & Medicine: A Reader in Medical Sociology. Gary L. Albrecht & Paul C. Higgins. 1979. pap. 20.50 o.p. (ISBN 0-395-30557-8). HM.
Health in Elementary Schools. 6th ed. Harold J. Cornacchia et al. LC 82-24000. (Illus.). 479p. 1983. text ed. 26.95 o.p. (ISBN 0-8016-1076-1). Mosby.
Health in the City: Environmental & Behavioral Influences. Malcolm S. Weinstein. (Habitat Text Ser.). (Illus.). 1980. 35.00 o.p. (ISBN 0-08-023375-9). Pergamon.
Health in the Elementary School: Teaching for Relevance. Walter H. Greene et al. (Illus.). 1978. write for info. o.p. (ISBN 0-02-346590-5). Macmillan.
Health in the Round: Voluntary Action & Antenatal Services. Rosemary Allen & Andrew Purkis. 104p. (Orig.). 1983. pap. text ed. 12.25 o.p. (ISBN 0-7199-1077-3, Pub. by Bedford England). Gower Pub Co.
Health Information for International Travel: 1987. (DHHS Publication CDC: No. X7-8280). (Illus.). 171p. 1987. pap. 4.75 o.p. (S/N 017-023-00177-9). USGPO.
Health Information Systems Evaluation: Fish, Other Aquatic Life, & Wildlife - Report, 1968. U. S. Department of the Interior, Federal Water Pollution Control Administration, Committtee on Water Quality Criteria et al. Ed. by Leonard L. Hurst & Gerald A. Giebink. LC 74-75391. (Illus.). 352p. 1974. text ed. 22.50x o.p. (ISBN 0-87081-060-X). Univ Pr Colo.
Health Instruction: Theory & Application. 3rd ed. John T. Fodor & Gus T. Dalis. LC 80-24484. (Illus.). 150p. 1981. text ed. 9.75 o.p. (ISBN 0-8121-0776-4). Lea & Febiger.
Health Insurance & Canadian Public Policy: The Seven Decisions That Created the Canadian Health Insurance System. Malcolm Taylor. (Canadian Public Administration Ser.). 1978. 25.00x o.p. (ISBN 0-7735-0307-2, McGill Canada); pap. 11.95 o.p. (ISBN 0-7735-0308-0, McGill Canada). U of Toronto Pr.
Health Insurance Fundamentals: To Prepare for the Health Insurance License Examination. Prudential Insurance Company of America Staff. LC 76-17650. 170p. 1976. pap. text ed. 6.50 o.p. Krieger.
Health Maintenance Organizations. 185p. pap. 6.00 o.p. (ISBN 0-89970-127-2, OP-158). AMA.
Health Maintenance Through Physical Conditioning. Ed. by Robert C. Cantu. LC 80-15622. 180p. 1981. 13.00 o.p. (ISBN 0-88416-312-1). Year Bk Med.
Health: Man in a Changing Environment. 2nd ed. Benjamin A. Kogan. (Illus.). 1974. text ed. 13.95 o.p. (ISBN 0-15-535583-X, HC). HarBraceJ.
Health Management Briefing: Consumer Satisfaction with Health Care Services. American Hospital Association Staff. 72p. (Orig.). 1986. pap. 30.00 o.p. (ISBN 0-87258-440-2, 001502). Am Hospital.
Health Management Briefing: Hospital-Physician Joint Ventures. American Hospital Association Staff. 72p. (Orig.). 1986. pap. 30.00 o.p. (ISBN 0-87258-439-9, 001501). Am Hospital.
Health Management Briefing: Selective Contracting for Medicaid. American Hospital Association Staff. 72p. (Orig.). 1986. pap. 30.00 o.p. (ISBN 0-87258-441-0, 001503). Am Hospital.
Health, Medicine & the Faith Traditions: An Inquiry into Religion & Medicine. Martin E. Marty & Kenneth L. Vaux. LC 81-71383. 416p. 1982. pap. 17.95 o.p. (ISBN 0-8006-1636-7, 1-1636, Fortress). Augsburg Fortress.
Health Needs & Health Services in Rural Ghana. Conference on Blood Viscosity in Heart Disease, Thromboembolism & Cancer, Sydney Australia, May, 1978. Ed. by E. De Kadt et al. 140p. 1981. pap. 18.00 o.p. (ISBN 0-08-028136-2). Pergamon.
Health Occupations. John Latkiewicz et al. vii, 88p. (Orig.). 1984. pap. text ed. 7.50x o.p. (ISBN 0-435-08106-3). Heinemann Ed.
Health Occupations Education Curriculum. ERIC Clearinghouse on Adult, Career, & Vocational Education Staff. 56p. 1983. 4.95 o.p. (ISBN 0-318-22110-1, BB63). Natl Ctr Res Voc Ed.
Health of Americans. Ed. by Boisfeuillet Jones. LC 70-120793. 1970. 5.95 o.p. (ISBN 0-13-385070-6); pap. 2.45 o.s.i. (ISBN 0-13-385062-5). Am Assembly.
Health of America's Children: Maternal & Child Health Data Book. Dana Hughes et al. 242p. (Orig.). 1987. pap. 9.95 o.s.i. (ISBN 0-938008-57-9). Children's Defense.
Health of China. Ruth Sidel & Victor W. Sidel. LC 81-68353. 228p. 1983. pap. 11.95x o.p. (ISBN 0-8070-2161-X, BP651). Beacon Pr.
Health Physics Fundamentals. rev. ed. (Illus.). 178p. 1981. 3400.00x o.p. (ISBN 0-87683-325-3); 60.00x o.p. (ISBN 0-87683-326-1); lesson plans 2250.00x o.p. (ISBN 0-87683-327-X); transparencies 750.00x o.p. (ISBN 0-87683-328-8); question bank 1175.00x o.p. (ISBN 0-87683-329-6). GP Pub.
Health Planning & Community Participation: Case Studies in Southeast Asia. Susan B. Rifkin. LC 85-361. 184p. 1985. 22.50 o.p. (ISBN 0-7099-2276-0, Pub. by Croom Helm Ltd). Routledge Chapman & Hall.
Health Planning in the U. S, Vol. 1. National Research Council Institute of Medicine. 1981. pap. 9.75x o.p. (ISBN 0-309-03144-3). Natl Acad Pr.
Health Planning in the U. S, Vol. 2. National Research Council, Institute of Medicine. 1981. pap. 11.75x o.p. (ISBN 0-309-03145-1). Natl Acad Pr.

Health Policy & the Bureaucracy: Politics & Implementation. Frank J. Thompson. 252p. 1981. 40.00x o.p. (ISBN 0-262-20041-4). MIT Pr.

Health Problems in Australia & New Zealand. Ed. by N. D. McGlashan. 180p. 1980. pap. 24.00 o.p. (ISBN 0-08-026103-5). Pergamon.

Health Professions. Marcia V. Boyles et al. LC 77-11331. (Illus.). 465p. 1982. pap. (ISBN 0-7216-1904-5). Saunders.

Health Promotion in Nursing Practice. Nola Pender. (Illus.). 448p. 1982. pap. 23.95 o.p. (ISBN 0-8385-3668-9). Appleton & Lange.

Health, Race & Ethnicity. Ed. by Tom Rathwell & David Phillips. 288p. 1986. 31.00 o.p. (ISBN 0-7099-4221-4, Pub. by Croom Helm Ltd). Routledge Chapman & Hall.

Health Research: The Systems Approach. Ed. by Harriet Werley et al. LC 73-92207. (Illus.). 330p. 1976. text ed. 23.95 o.p. (ISBN 0-8261-1710-4). Springer Pub.

Health Risks. Elliot J. Howard & Susan A. Roth. 228p. (Orig.). 1986. 19.95 o.p. (ISBN 0-89586-442-8, Body Press); lib. bdg. 19.95 o.p. (ISBN 0-317-66062-4); pap. 8.95 o.p. (ISBN 0-89586-484-3). Price Stern.

Health, Safety & First Aid: A Guide for Training Child Care Workers. rev. ed. Audrey Robertson. 115p. (Orig.). 1984. pap. 14.95x o.p. (ISBN 0-934140-04-9). Toys N Things.

Health, Safety, & Nutrition for the Young Child. Lynn Marotz et al. LC 84-23845. 432p. 1985. pap. text ed. 23.95 o.p. (ISBN 0-8273-2052-3). Delmar.

Health Sciences & Services: A Guide to Information Sources. Ed. by Lois F. Lunin. LC 77-80614. (Management Information Guide Ser.: No. 36). 1979. 65.00x o.p. (ISBN 0-8103-0836-3). Gale.

Health Sciences Videolog. LC 78-74188. 1981. pap. 49.50 o.p. (ISBN 0-88432-069-3, Norton-Forum). J Norton Pubs.

Health Services. Elliott Jacques. (Brunel Institute of Organization & Social Studies). 1978. text ed. 40.00x o.p. (ISBN 0-435-82474-0). Heinemann Ed.

Health Services for Ethnic Minorities. Date not set. 2.50 o.s.i. Coun Soc Wk Ed.

Health Services Management: A Book of Cases. 2nd ed. Ed. by Anthony R. Kovner & Duncan Neuhauser. LC 85-24889. 288p. 1986. pap. text ed. 20.00x o.p. (ISBN 0-910701-11-3, 0836). Health Admin Pr.

Health Services Performance: Effectiveness & Efficiency. Ed. by Andrew F. Long & Stephen Harrison. LC 85-1310. 269p. 1985. 29.00 o.p. (ISBN 0-7099-1672-8, Pub. by Croom Helm Ltd). Routledge Chapman & Hall.

Health Services Research. Institute of Medicine Staff. 1979. pap. text ed. 6.95x o.p. (ISBN 0-309-02875-2). Natl Acad Pr.

Health Statistics on Older Pesons: United States, 1986. Richard J. Havlik et al. LC 87-600084. (DHHS publication PHS: No. 87-1409). 165p. 1987. pap. 8.50 o.p. (ISBN 0-317-62857-7, S-N 017-022-01002-0). USGPO.

Health Status & Use of Medical Services: Evidence on the Poor, the Black, & the Rural Elderly. Lynn Paringer et al. 111p. 1980. pap. 8.00 o.p. (ISBN 0-87766-241-X, 24800). Urban Inst.

Health Status of the Disadvantaged Chartbook, 1986. (Illus.). 138p. 1986. pap. 9.00 o.p. (ISBN 0-318-22614-6, S/N 017-022-00968-4). USGPO.

Health Teaching in Secondary Schools. 3rd ed. Carl Willgoose. 1982. text ed. 29.95 o.p. (ISBN 0-03-058493-0, CBS C). SCP.

Health, United States, Nineteen Eighty-Five. 180p. 1985. pap. 6.50 o.p. (ISBN 0-318-19948-3, S/N 017-022-00900-5). USGPO.

Health, United States, 1987. 12th ed. (DHHS Publication PHS Ser.: No. 88-1232). (Illus.). 215p. 1988. pap. 13.00 o.p. (S/N 017-022-01032-1). USGPO.

Health Visiting Practice. M. Saunders. 1968. 17.75 o.p. (ISBN 0-08-012899-8); pap. text ed. 5.75 o.p. (ISBN 0-08-012898-X). Pergamon.

Health, Vol. 3 (incl. 1984-1987 Supplements) Ed. by Eleanor Goldstein. (Social Issues Resources Ser.). 1987. 60.00 o.p. (ISBN 0-89777-077-3). Soc Issues.

Health 1988-89. 9th, rev. ed. Ed. by Rick Yarian. LC 81-64382. (Annual Editions Ser.). (Illus.). 256p. 1988. pap. text ed. 9.95x o.p. (ISBN 0-87967-718-X). Dushkin Pub.

Healthkin Food Train. Jane B. Moncure. LC 82-14710. (Healthkins Ser.). (gr. k-3). 1982. 10.35 o.p. (ISBN 0-516-06311-1). Childrens.

Healthkins Help. Jane B. Moncure. LC 82-14713. (Healthkins Ser.). (gr. k-3). 1982. 10.35 o.p. (ISBN 0-516-06313-8). Childrens.

Healthy Adolescent: A Parents Manual. Barry Lauton & Artur S. Freese. 224p. 1981. encore ed. 3.95 o.p. (ISBN 0-684-16819-7, ScribT). Scribner.

Healthy Children: Investing in the Future. LC 87-619858. (Illus., Orig.). 1988. pap. 13.00 o.p. (S/N 052-003-01081-0). USGPO.

Healthy Holidays: No-Cholesterol Vegetarian Recipes. Debra Wasserman & Charles Stahler. (Illus.). 80p. (Orig.). 1984. pap. 4.95 o.p. (ISBN 0-931411-00-9). Vegetarian Resc.

Healthy Living in an Unhealthy World. Edward Calabrese & Michael Dorsey. 224p. 1985. pap. 5.95 o.p. (ISBN 0-671-55452-2, Fireside). S&S.

Healthy Living in an Unhealthy World: What You Can Do Now to Reduce the Risks of Cancer & Other Environmentally Induced Diseases for Yourself & Your Family. Edward Calabrese & Michael Dorsey. 320p. 1984. 15.50 o.p. (ISBN 0-671-44759-9). S&S.

Healthy Mothers Coalition Directory of Educational Materials. 3rd ed. 188p. 1986. pap. 9.50 o.p. (ISBN 0-318-21628-0, S/N 017-001-00455-3). USGPO.

Healthy Mothers, Healthy Babies: A Compendium of Program Ideas for Serving Low-Income Women. (DHHS Publication PHS: No. 86-50209). 178p. 1986. pap. 9.00 o.p. (ISBN 0-318-21840-2, S/N 017-001-00456-1). USGPO.

Healthy People in Unhealthy Places: Stress & Fitness at Work. Kenneth R. Pelletier. (Merloyd Lawrence Bk.). 240p. 1984. 16.95 o.s.i. (ISBN 0-385-29275-9, Sey Lawr). Delacorte.

Healthy People in Unhealthy Places: Stress & Fitness at Work. Kenneth R. Pelletier. (Merloyd Lawrence Bk.). 268p. 1985. pap. 8.95 o.p. (ISBN 0-385-29393-3, Delta). Dell.

Healthy Snacks for Kids. Penny Warner. (Illus.). 216p. 1983. 7.95 o.p. (ISBN 0-911954-80-5). Bristol Pub Ent CA.

Healthy Way to Die. Michael Kenyon. 192p. 1987. pap. 2.95 o.p. (ISBN 0-380-70380-7). Avon.

Heap of Ashes. Ananta T. Pramoedya. (Asian & Pacific Writing Ser.). 1975. 22.50x o.p. (ISBN 0-7022-1060-9); pap. 10.95 o.p. (ISBN 0-7022-1071-4). U of Queensland Pr.

Hear Me Talkin' to Ya. Nat Shapiro & N. Hentoff. LC 66-28271. 14.00 o.p. (ISBN 0-8446-2928-6). Peter Smith.

Hear Me, White Man! William Dinsmore. 1985. 8.95 o.p. (ISBN 0-533-06621-2). Vantage.

Hear, Oh Israel. Samuel Rosenblatt. 1958. 7.50 o.s.i. (ISBN 0-87306-106-3). Feldheim.

Hear the Children Cry. Ruby J. Jensen. 288p. 1981. pap. 2.50 o.p. (ISBN 0-8439-0968-4, Pub. by Leisure Bks CT). Dorchester Pub Co.

Hear the Word of the Lord. Neely D. McCarter. (Illus., Orig.). (gr. 11-12). 1964. pap. 3.95 tchrs' guide o.p. (ISBN 0-8042-9210-8, John Knox). Westminster John Knox.

Hearing-Impaired Child in the Ordinary School. Alec Webster & John Ellwood. LC 84-23682. 182p. 1985. 26.00 o.p. (ISBN 0-7099-3629-X, Pub. by Croom Helm Ltd); pap. 15.50 o.p. (ISBN 0-7099-3630-3). Routledge Chapman & Hall.

Hearing Impairment among Aging Persons. Raymond H. Hull. LC 77-70100. (Cliffs Speech & Hearing Ser.). (Illus.). 1977. pap. text ed. 4.95 o.p. (ISBN 0-8220-1826-8). Cliffs.

Hearing Loss Help: How You Can Help Someone with Hearing Loss & How They Can Help Themselves. Alec Combs. LC 86-1135. (Illus.). 176p. (Orig.). 1986. pap. 12.95 o.p. (ISBN 0-935997-07-5). Alpenglow Pr.

Hearing, Speech & Communication Disorders. Compiled by Information Center for Hearing, Speech & Disorders of Human Communication of the Johns Hopkins Medical Institution Staff. Incl. Cumulated Citations: 1973. 772p. 1974. 85.00x (ISBN 0-306-67311-8); Cumulated Citations: 1974. 790p. 1975. 95.00x (ISBN 0-306-67312-6). LC 74-9879. 772p (IFI Plenum). Plenum Pub.

Hearse for Dark Harbor. Clarissa Ross. (Orig.). 1974. pap. 0.95 o.p. (ISBN 0-380-00117-9, 20461). Avon.

Heart. 3rd ed. Ed. by J. Willis Hurst & R. Bruce Logue. (Illus.). 1600p. 1974. text ed. 45.00 o.p. (ISBN 0-07-031471-3, HP). McGraw.

Heart. 5th ed. J. Willis Hurst et al. (Illus.). 352p. 1982. text ed. 85.00 o.p. (ISBN 0-07-031481-0). McGraw.

Heart, 2 vol. ed. 5th ed. J. Willis Hurst et al. 2120p. 1982. Set. text ed. 95.00 o.p. (ISBN 0-07-079033-7); Vol. 1. text ed. (ISBN 0-07-031483-7); Vol. 2. text ed. (ISBN 0-07-031484-5). McGraw.

Heart & the Scarab. Marguerite Kloepfer. 288p. 1981. pap. 2.50 o.p. (ISBN 0-380-77610-3, 77610). Avon.

Heart Attack (Mine... & Yours?) Kenneth E. Geary. 1979. 4.00 o.p. (ISBN 0-682-49348-1). Exposition-Phoenix.

Heart Disease. Braunwald. 1989. (ISBN 0-7216-2803-6). Saunders.

Heart Disease & Rehabilitation. 2nd ed. Ed. by Michael L. Pollock & Donald H. Schmidt. LC 85-12008. 752p. 1986. 47.50 o.p. (ISBN 0-471-09562-1). Wiley.

Heart Disease in the Elderly, Vol. 2. Ed. by Anthony Martin & A. John Camm. (Disease Management in the Elderly Ser.). 273p. 1984. 52.00 o.p. (ISBN 0-471-90126-1, Dist. by A R Liss). Wiley.

Heart Echoes in Verse. Mabel Glenn Haldeman. 1977. 8.50 o.p. (ISBN 0-682-48857-7). Exposition-Phoenix.

Heart Failure. Ed. by Alfred P. Fishman. (Illus.). 1978. text ed. 29.95 o.p. (ISBN 0-07-021118-3). McGraw.

Heart for God. Sinclair Ferguson. (Christian Character Library). 150p. 1985. hdbk. 8.95 o.p. (ISBN 0-89109-507-1). NavPress.

Heart Gifts from Helen Steiner Rice. Helen S. Rice. LC 68-28438. (Illus.). 96p. 1968. 8.95 o.p. (ISBN 0-8007-0133-X). Revell.

Heart in Hypertension: Symposium. Ed. by B. E. Strauer. (International Boehringer Mannheim Symposia Ser.). (Illus.). 484p. 1981. pap. 42.40 o.p. (ISBN 0-387-10496-8). Springer-Verlag.

Heart Is No Stranger. Luciano Comici. (Orig.). 1981. pap. 2.75 o.s.i. (ISBN 0-515-04801-1). Jove Pubns.

Heart: Its Function in Health & Disease. rev. ed. Arthur Selzer. (Perspectives in Medicine: No. 1). 1968. 27.50x o.p. (ISBN 0-520-01162-7). U of Cal Pr.

Heart Listens. Helen Van Slyke. 1986. pap. 4.50 o.s.i. (ISBN 0-446-31391-2). Warner Bks.

Heart Machine: A Personal Account of Open-Heart Surgery. James O. Ross. LC 73-6183. 144p. 1973. 5.50 o.s.i. (ISBN 0-8008-3821-1). Taplinger.

Heart of a Distant Forest: A Novel. Philip L. Williams. 224p. 1984. 12.45 o.p. (ISBN 0-393-01836-9). Norton.

Heart of a Dog. Mikhail Bulgakov. Tr. by Mirra Ginsburg from Rus. 1968. pap. 2.95 o.s.i. (ISBN 0-394-17442-9, B193, BC). Grove.

Heart of a Dog. Mikhail Bulgakov. Tr. by Mirra Ginsburg. 1987. 6.95 o.p. (ISBN 0-394-62380-0). Grove.

Heart of a Friend. 5.95 o.p. (ISBN 0-88088-289-1). Peter Pauper.

Heart of Darkness. rev. ed. Joseph Conrad. Ed. by Robert Kimbrough. LC 78-152308. (Norton Critical Edition Series). 1972. pap. 4.95x o.p. (ISBN 0-393-09773-0, NortonC). Norton.

Heart of Darkness & the Secret Sharer. Joseph Conrad. 48p. (Orig.). 1988. pap. 9.95 o.p. (ISBN 1-55651-381-X); audocassette tape incl. o.p. (ISBN 1-55651-382-8). Cram Cassettes.

Heart of Enterprise. Stafford Beer. LC 79-40532. 582p. 1980. 51.95 o.p. (ISBN 0-471-27599-9). Wiley.

Heart of Europe. Trilateral Comm.

Heart of Our Cities. Victor Gruen. 1972. pap. 4.45 o.p. (ISBN 0-671-21307-5, Touchstone Bks). S&S.

Heart of Qu'ran & Perfect Mizan. Shaykh F. Haeri. 140p. 1987. pap. 18.95 o.p. (ISBN 0-7103-0222-3, Kegan Paul). Routledge Chapman & Hall.

Heart of Rock & Roll. Steve Rabey. 96p. 1986. 8.95 o.p. (ISBN 0-8007-1483-0). Revell.

Heart of the Country. Greg Matthews. 1986. 17.45 o.p. (ISBN 0-393-02289-7). Norton.

Heart of the Dragon. Alasdair Clayre. (Illus.). 304p. 1985. 29.45 o.s.i. (ISBN 0-395-35336-X). HM.

Heart of the Empire: Discussions of Problems of Modern City Life in England with an Essay on Imperialism. C. F. Masterman. Ed. by B. Gilbert. (Society & the Victorians). 1973. Repr. text ed. 12.50x o.p. (ISBN 0-901759-82-1). Humanities.

Heart of the Flame. Araby Scott. 304p. 1982. pap. 3.50 o.p. (ISBN 0-380-79459-4, 79459-4). Avon.

Heart of the Garfish. Kathy Callaway. LC 81-70217. (Pitt Poetry Ser.). 60p. 1982. 15.95x o.p. (ISBN 0-8229-3458-2); pap. 6.95 o.p. (ISBN 0-8229-5338-2). U of Pittsburgh Pr.

Heart of the Gospel. 2nd rev. ed. George Townshend. 160p. (ISBN 0-85398-025-X); pap. 3.95 o.p. (ISBN 0-85398-020-9). G Ronald Pub.

Heart of the Healing. Bruce Davis & Genny W. Davis. 208p. 1985. pap. 6.95 o.p. (ISBN 0-553-34222-3). Bantam.

Heart of the Hunter. Linda P. Sandifer. 336p. 1987. pap. 3.95 o.p. (ISBN 0-380-75421-5). Avon.

Heart of the Lion. Jean Plaidy. 320p. 1982. pap. 2.95 o.s.i. (ISBN 0-449-24490-3, Crest). Fawcett.

Heart of the Matter. Pierre Teilhard De Chardin. Tr. by Rene Hague. LC 78-7093. (Helen & Kurt Wolff Bks). 276p. 1979. 8.95 o.p. (ISBN 0-15-139812-7). HarBraceJ.

Heart of The Rose. June Barraclough. 256p. 1988. pap. 3.50 o.p. (ISBN 1-55547-221-4). Critics Choice Paper.

Heart of the Storm. Jillian Hunter. (Avon Romance Ser.). 1985. pap. 3.50 o.p. (ISBN 0-380-89956-6). Avon.

Heart of War. John Masters. LC 80-12491. (Loss of Eden Ser.). 608p. 1980. text ed. 13.95 o.p. (ISBN 0-07-040782-7). McGraw.

Heart Perfusion, Energetics, & Ischemia. Ed. by Leopold Dintenfass et al. LC 83-876. (NATO ASI Series A, Life Sciences: Vol. 62). 718p. 1983. 110.00x o.p. (ISBN 0-306-41278-0, Plenum Pr). Plenum Pub.

Heart: Pretest Self-Assessment & Review. 2nd ed. J. Willis Hurst & Pretest Services, Inc. Staff. 240p. 1982. text ed. 32.00 o.p. (ISBN 0-07-050993-X). McGraw.

Heart: Pretest Self-Assessment & Review with CME Examination. 2nd ed. J. Willis Hurst & Pretest Services, Inc. 240p. 1982. text ed. 80.00 o.p. (ISBN 0-07-079097-3). McGraw.

Heart Smart: A Plan for Low-Cholesterol Living. Gail L. Becker. 224p. 1985. pap. 5.95 o.s.i. (ISBN 0-671-55521-9, Fireside). S&S.

Heart So Wild. Johanna Lindsey. 400p. 1987. 18.95 o.p. (ISBN 0-8161-4301-3, Large Print Bks). G K Hall.

Heart Songs. Laurel Winslow. 192p. 1984. pap. 2.50 o.p. (ISBN 0-380-85365-5, 85365). Avon.

Heart Speaks Many Ways. Madelaine A. Polland. 1983. pap. 3.95 o.p. (ISBN 0-440-13629-6). Dell.

Heart Strings, No. 3. Cassie Edwards. (Leisure First Romance Ser.). 192p. (gr. 6-12). 1982. pap. 1.95 o.p. (ISBN 0-8439-1153-0, Pub. by Leisure Bks CT). Dorchester Pub Co.

Heart to Heart: The Cleveland Clinic Guide to Understanding Heart Disease & Open-Heart Surgery. Norman V. Richards. LC 86-47694. (Illus.). 288p. 1987. 14.95 o.p. (ISBN 0-689-11854-6, Atheneum). Macmillan.

Heart to the Hawks. Don Moser. LC 74-18190. 224p. (gr. 7 up). 1975. 6.95 o.p. (ISBN 0-689-50024-6, Atheneum). Macmillan.

Heart Too Proud. Laura London. 1985. pap. 2.95 o.p. (ISBN 0-440-13498-6). Dell.

Heart: Update I. Ed. by J. Willis Hurst. 1979. text ed. 35.00 o.p. (ISBN 0-07-031490-X). McGraw.

Heart: Update II. J. Willis Hurst. (Illus.). 1979. text ed. 35.00 o.p. (ISBN 0-07-031491-8). McGraw.

Heart: Update IV. J. Willis Hurst. (Updates Ser.). (Illus.). 224p. 1981. text ed. 35.00 o.p. (ISBN 0-07-031493-4). McGraw.

Heart: Update V. J. Willis Hurst. (Illus.). 304p. 1981. text ed. 35.00 o.p. (ISBN 0-07-031495-0). McGraw.

Heartbeat of Evangelism. Robert E. Coleman. 32p. 1985. pap. 1.95 o.p. (ISBN 0-89109-400-8). NavPress.

Heartbreak Hotel: A Novel. Gabrielle Burton. 304p. 1986. 15.95 o.p. (ISBN 0-684-18594-6). Scribner.

Heartbreak House. George Bernard Shaw. Ed. by Stanley Weintraub & Anne Wright. LC 79-56710. (Bernard Shaw Early Texts: Play Manuscripts in Facsimile). 1981. lib. bdg. 67.00 o.p. (ISBN 0-8240-4585-8). Garland Pub.

Heartbreak Tennis. Amelia Walden. LC 76-30817. 168p. (gr. 7 up). 1977. 7.95 o.s.i. (ISBN 0-664-32607-2, Westminster). Westminster John Knox.

Heartbreak: The Losing Struggle of the Middle Years. Margaret R. Meyerer. 38p. 1985. 5.95 o.p. (ISBN 0-533-06554-2). Vantage.

Hearth & the Eagle. Anya Seton. 1973. 10.00 o.p. (ISBN 0-395-08172-6). HM.

Hearthsong: Rhyme & Reason. Margaret Paxson. 1980. 5.00 o.p. (ISBN 0-682-49476-3). Exposition-Phoenix.

Heartland. Mort Sahl. LC 75-46551. 160p. 1976. 7.95 o.p. (ISBN 0-15-139820-8). HarBraceJ.

Heartland & Hinterland: A Geography of Canada. Ed. by Larry D. McCann. 150p. 1984. text ed. (ISBN 0-13-385146-X). P-H.

Heartless. Stephen P. Cohen. LC 86-5199. 320p. 1986. 15.95 o.p. (ISBN 0-688-06089-7). Morrow.

Hearts & Dollars: How to Beat the High Cost of Falling In & Out of Love. Steven R. Lake. LC 83-7632. 250p. 1983. 12.95 o.p. (ISBN 0-914091-26-3); pap. 8.95 o.p. (ISBN 0-914091-25-5). Chicago Review.

Hearts & Minds: The Anatomy of Racism from Roosevelt to Reagan. Harry Ashmore. 1982. text ed. 15.95 o.p. (ISBN 0-07-002456-1). Mcgraw.

Heart's Citadel & Other Poems. Archibald Rutledge. 1953. 3.00 o.p. (ISBN 0-87517-031-5). Dietz.

Heart's Desire. Deborah Chester. 1983. pap. 2.50 o.p. (ISBN 0-380-84798-1, 84798). Avon.

Hearts in the Clouds. Ann J. Johnson. 1977. 7.50 o.p. (ISBN 0-682-48825-9). Exposition-Phoenix.

Heart's Possession. Veronica Gregory. 368p. (Orig.). 1987. pap. 3.95 o.p. (ISBN 0-380-75330-8). Avon.

Heart's Surrender. Dorothy Martin. (Peggy Ser.: No. 6). (gr. 7). 1985. pap. 3.50 o.p. (ISBN 0-8024-8306-2). Moody.

Heartsease. Date not set. (ISBN 0-385-29451-4). Delacorte.

Heartstorm. Carol B. Gerrond. 224p. 1987. pap. 5.95 o.p. (ISBN 0-310-47601-1, 15612P). Zondervan.

Heartthrobs. Douglas H. Ragin. 1984. 6.95 o.p. (ISBN 0-533-06052-4). Vantage.

Hearty Helpings. Ed. by Annette Gohlke. LC 83-63231. 64p. 1984. pap. 3.95 o.s.i. (ISBN 0-89821-059-3). Reiman Assocs.

Heat & Concentration Waves: Analysis & Applications. G. Alan Turner. 1972. 63.50 o.p. (ISBN 0-12-704050-1). Acad Pr.

Heat & Fluid Flow in Power System Components. Ed. by A. M. Rezk. (Heat & Mass Transfer: Vol. 3). (Illus.). 300p. 1980. 85.00 o.p. (ISBN 0-08-024235-9). Pergamon.

Heat & Its Workings see Concept of Heat & Its Workings.

Heat & Mass Transfer. A. V. Luikov. 623p. 1980. 21.00 o.p. (ISBN 0-8285-2084-4, Pub. by Mir Pubs USSR). Imported Pubns.

Heat & Mass Transfer During Cooling & Storage of Agricultural Products As Influenced by Natural Convection. 158p. 1980. pap. 32.50 o.p. (ISBN 90-220-0728-6, PDC208, Pudoc). UNIPUB.

Heat & Mass Transfers in Flows with Separated Regions. Ed. by Z. Zaric. LC 72-85858. 232p. 1975. pap. 60.00 o.p. (ISBN 0-08-017156-7). Pergamon.

Heat Death. Stephen Dobyns. LC 79-55592. 1980. 10.00 o.p. (ISBN 0-689-11034-0, Atheneum); pap. 5.95 o.p. (ISBN 0-689-11063-4). Macmillan.

Heat Exchangers: Design & Theory. N. H. Afgan & E. U. Schlunder. (Illus.). 928p. 1974. text ed. 92.50 o.p. (ISBN 0-07-000460-9). McGraw.

Heat Exchangers: Thermal-Hydraulic Fundamentals & Design. Ed. by S. Kakac et al. 1131p. 1985. Repr. 115.00 o.p. (ISBN 0-89116-225-9). Hemisphere Pub.

Heat Lighting. William R. Jordan, Sr. Ed. by Sherrian P. Wilson & Janie W. Oliver. 1984. 5.95 o.p. (ISBN 0-533-05922-4). Vantage.

Heat of the Day. Elizabeth Bowen. (Penguin Fiction Ser.). 336p. 1986. pap. 6.95 o.p. (ISBN 0-14-001844-1). Penguin.

Heat of Winter. Howard Hirt. LC 83-228. 320p. 1984. 16.95 o.p. (ISBN 0-15-139860-7). HarbraceJ.

Heat Pipes & Thermosyphons for Heat Recovery: Proceedings of the International Heat Pipe Conference, 4th, London, Sept. 7-10, 1981. International Heat Pipe Conference Staff & D. A. Reay. 64p. 1982. pap. 31.00 o.p. (ISBN 0-08-028693-3). Pergamon.

Heat Pumps. D. A. Reay & D. B. MacMichael. 1979. text ed. 85.00 o.p. (ISBN 0-08-022716-3); pap. 25.00 o.p. (ISBN 0-08-024748-2). Pergamon.

Heat Recovery Systems: A Directory of Equipment & Techniques. David A. Reay. LC 79-10877. (Energy Ser.). 590p. 1979. 75.00x o.p. (ISBN 0-419-11400-9, NO. 6231, Pub. by E & FN Spon England). Routledge Chapman & Hall.

Heat Transfer. 2nd ed. B. Gebhart. 1971. text ed. 45.95 o.p. (ISBN 0-07-023127-3). McGraw.

Heat Transfer. V. P. Isachenko et al. 493p. 1977. 13.00 o.p. (ISBN 0-8285-1761-4, Pub. by Mir Pubs USSR). Imported Pubns.

Heat Transfer & Fluid Flow in Nuclear Systems. Ed. by Henri Fenech. LC 81-8670. 300p. 1981. 150.00 o.p. (ISBN 0-08-027181-2). Pergamon.

Heat Transfer-Current Application of Air Conditioning. International Institute of Refrigeration. Ed. by A. Van Iherbeek. 1971. 150.00 o.p. (ISBN 0-08-016597-4). Pergamon.

Heat Transfer Equipment. (Principles of Steam Generation Ser.: Module 8). (Illus.). 90p. 1982. spiral bdg. 18.50 o.p. (ISBN 0-87683-258-3); instr's. manual o.p. 15.00x o.p. (ISBN 0-87683-279-6). GP Pub.

Heat Transfer in Cold Climates. Virgil J. Lunardini. 704p. 1981. 49.95 o.p. (ISBN 0-442-26250-7). Van Nos Reinhold.

Heat Transfer: In Counterflow, Parallel Flow & Cross Flow. 2nd ed. Helmuth Hausen. Tr. by M. S. Sayer from Ger. (Illus.). 544p. 1982. text ed. 72.50 o.p. (ISBN 0-07-027215-8). McGraw.

Heat Transfer in Nuclear Waste Disposal: HTD-Vol. 11. Ed. by F. Kulacki & R. W. Lyczkowski. 118p. 1980. 18.00 o.p. (ISBN 0-317-33534-0, G00184); members 9.00 o.p. (ISBN 0-317-33535-9). ASME.

Heat Transfer Nineteen Seventy-Four: Proceedings of the International Conference, 5th, Tokyo, 7 vols. International Heat Transfer Conference Staff. Ed. by T. Mizushina. LC 75-12763. (Illus.). 2300p. 1974. pap. text ed. 245.00 o.p. (ISBN 0-89116-001-9). Hemisphere Pub.

Heat Transfer: Proceedings of the U. K. National Conference, 1st, Leeds, U. K., July 3-5, 1984, No. 1. Ed. by Institution of Chemical Engineers Staff. (Institution of Chemical Engineers Symposium Ser.: Vol. 86). 1324p. 1984. 125.00 o.s.i. (ISBN 0-08-030281-5). Pergamon.

Heat Transfer Reviews, Nineteen Seventy to Nineteen Seventy-One. E. R. Eckert & T. F. Irvine, Jr. 1977. 46.00 o.p. (ISBN 0-08-021737-0). Pergamon.

Heat Transfer Textbook. John Lienhard. (Illus.). 480p. 1981. pap. text ed. (ISBN 0-13-385112-5). P-H.

Heat Treatment of Ferrous Alloys. Brooks. 262p. 1979. 52.50 o.p. (ISBN 0-89116-474-X). Hemisphere Pub.

Heat Treatment Seventy-Nine. 248p. 1980. text ed. 80.00x o.p. (ISBN 0-904357-25-2, Pub. by Inst Metals). Gower Pub Co.

Heat Wave. Sara Orwig. (Loveswept Ser.: No. 42). 192p. (Orig.). 1984. pap. text ed. 2.25 o.s.i. (ISBN 0-553-21655-4). Bantam.

Heath Introduction to Fiction. 2nd ed. John J. Clayton. 820p. 1983. pap. text ed. 11.50 o.p. (ISBN 0-669-06444-0). Heath.

Heath Introduction to Literature. 2nd ed. Ed. by Alice S. Landy. 1984. pap. text ed. 11.00 o.p. (ISBN 0-669-05378-3). Heath.

Heath Introduction to Poetry. 2nd ed. Joseph De Roche. 464p. 1983. pap. text ed. 9.00 o.p. (ISBN 0-669-06446-7). Heath.

Heath-Zenith Z100 User's Guide. Hugh Kenner. (Illus.). 208p. 1984. pap. 15.95 o.p. (ISBN 0-89303-516-5). Brady Bks.

Heather's Feathers. Leatie Weiss. (Illus.). 32p. (gr. k-3). 1978. pap. 2.25 o.p. (ISBN 0-380-40279-3, 65425-3, Camelot). Avon.

Heating & Cooling Load Calculations. P. G. Down. 1969. 65.00 o.p. (ISBN 0-08-013001-1). Pergamon.

Heating & Cooling Safety. V. Paul Lang. LC 76-24983. 1977. pap. 8.95 o.p. (ISBN 0-8273-1011-0); 2.20 o.s.i. instr's. guide (ISBN 0-8273-1012-9). Delmar.

Heating & Hot Water Services in Buildings. D. Kut. 1968. 110.00 o.p. (ISBN 0-08-012218-3). Pergamon.

Heating & Hot-Water Services: Selected Subjects with Worked Examples in SI Units. 4th ed. E. W. Shaw. 241p. pap. text ed. 25.00x o.p. (ISBN 0-246-11229-8, Pub. by Granada England). Gower Pub Co.

Heating Boilers. (Boilers & Pressure Vessel Code Ser.: Sec. 4). 1980. 65.00 o.p. (ISBN 0-686-70392-8, P00040); pap. 85.00 loose-leaf o.p. (ISBN 0-686-70393-6, V00040). ASME.

Heating in Toroidal Plasmas II: Proceedings of the 2nd Joint Grenoble-Varenna International Symposium, 2 vols. Ed. by E. Canobbio. (Committee of the European Communities Ser.). 1230p. 1982. pap. 220.00 o.p. (ISBN 0-08-029347-6, C135, B120). Pergamon.

Heating in Toroidal Plasmas III: Proceedings of the 3rd Joint Varenna-Grenoble International Symposium, Grenoble, France, 22-26 March 1982, 3 vols. Ed. by C. Gormezano & G. G. Leotta. 1224p. 1982. pap. 220.00 set o.p. (ISBN 0-08-029984-9). Pergamon.

Heating in Toroidal Plasmas: Proceedings, 2 vols. Commission of the European Communities, Joint Varenna-Grenoble International Symposium on Heating in Toroidal Plasmas, Grenoble, July 1978. 1979. pap. 200.00 o.p. (ISBN 0-08-023400-3). Pergamon.

Heating, Ventilating & Air Conditioning: Analysis & Design. 2nd ed. Faye C. McQuiston & Jerald D. Parker. LC 81-3004. 666p. 1982. (ISBN 0-471-08259-7). Wiley.

Heaven. V. C. Andrews. 1985. 16.45 o.s.i. (ISBN 0-671-60536-4, Poseidon). PB.

Heaven. V. C. Andrews. 588p. 1986. lib. bdg. 19.95 o.p. (ISBN 0-8161-4078-2, Large Print Bks); pap. 10.95 o.p. (ISBN 0-8161-4079-0, Large Print Bks.). G K Hall.

Heaven & Earth: Album Leaves from a Ming Encyclopedia. John Goodall. LC 79-64329. (Illus.). 192p. 1979. 39.50 o.s.i. (ISBN 0-87773-168-3). Shambhala Pubns.

Heaven Has a Floor. Evelyn Roberts. LC 79-9731. (Illus.). 32p. 1979. 10.95 o.p. (ISBN 0-385-27062-3, Dial). Doubleday.

Heaven: How to Get There. D. L. Moody. 112p. 1982. pap. text ed. 2.95 o.p. (ISBN 0-88368-115-3). Whitaker Hse.

Heaven in My Hand. Alice L. Humphreys. 5.95 o.p. (ISBN 0-8042-2352-1, John Knox). Westminster John Knox.

Heaven in the Eye. Clyde Rice. 368p. 1985. pap. 7.95 o.p. (ISBN 0-380-69919-2). Avon.

Heaven on the Halfshell: Edible Treasures from the Sea. Tom Chapman. (Illus.). 108p. 1988. 29.95 o.p. (ISBN 0-87701-502-3); pap. 16.95 o.p. (ISBN 0-87701-488-4). Chronicle Bks.

Heaven Sword. Jeanne Williams. 464p. 1985. pap. 3.95 o.p. (ISBN 0-380-89851-9). Avon.

Heaven: The Heart's Deepest Longing. Peter J. Kreeft. LC 80-7747. 160p. 1980. 10.00 o.p. (ISBN 0-06-064776-0). HarpR.

Heavenly Visions: The Art of Minnie Evans. Mitchell Kahan. (Illus.). 52p. (Orig.). 1986. 8.00 o.p. (ISBN 0-88259-951-8). NCMA.

Heaven's Answer for the Home. rev. ed. Lowell Lundstrom. 142p. 1985. pap. 3.95 o.p. (ISBN 0-938220-16-0). Whitaker Hse.

Heavens Are Cleft Asunder. rev. ed. Huschmand Sabet. Tr. by Oliver Coburn from Ger. Orig. Title: Gespaltene Himmel. (Eng.). 1975. (ISBN 0-85398-055-1, 332-014). G Ronald Pub.

Heaven's Command: An Imperial Progress. James Morris. LC 73-13965. (Helen & Kurt Wolff Bk.). (Illus.). 1973. 11.50 o.p. (ISBN 0-15-139900-X). HarBraceJ.

Heaven's My Destination. Thornton Wilder. 1984. pap. 1.65 o.p. (ISBN 0-380-00331-7, 49395, Bard). Avon.

Heavens Speak in Astrology Marvelous Things. Julian B. Shealy. 1974. 7.50 o.p. (ISBN 0-682-47827-X). Exposition-Phoenix.

Heavy Bread. Nancy J. Kauffman & Elizabeth J. Kauffman. LC 73-75087. (Pivot Family Reader Ser). 192p. (Orig.). 1973. pap. 1.25 o.p. (ISBN 0-87983-030-1). Keats.

Heavy Clay Technology. 2nd ed. F. H. Clews. 1969. 61.00 o.p. (ISBN 0-12-176350-1). Acad Pr.

Heavy Construction Cost File 1984: Unit Prices. Coert Engelsman. 260p. 1983. pap. 29.50 o.p. (ISBN 0-442-26680-4). Van Nos Reinhold.

Heavy Construction Cost File, 1985: Unit Prices. Coert Engelsman. 256p. 1985. pap. 41.95 o.p. (ISBN 0-442-26703-7). Van Nos Reinhold.

Heavy Construction: Equipment & Methods. Stuart Wood, Jr. (Illus.). 1977. text ed. 40.00 o.p. (ISBN 0-13-386086-8). P-H.

Heavy Current Electricity in the United Kingdom. Hinton. 1979. 23.00 o.p. (ISBN 0-08-023246-9); pap. 9.25 o.p. (ISBN 0-08-023247-7). Pergamon.

Heavy Current Fluidics. D. Bain. (CISM, International Centre for Mechanical Sciences Ser.: Vol. 45). (Illus.). 82p. 1975. pap. 10.00 o.p. (ISBN 0-387-81148-6). Springer-Verlag.

Heavy Element Properties: Proceedings of the Joint Session of the Baden Meetings, Sept. 1975. new ed. Ed. by W. Muller & H. Blank. LC 75-44241. (Illus.). 1976. 18.50 o.p. (ISBN 0-444-11048-8, North Holland). Elsevier.

Heavy Feather. A. L. Barker. LC 78-26479. 234p. 1979. Repr. of 1978 ed. 8.95 o.s.i. (ISBN 0-8076-0911-0). Braziller.

Heavy Metals in the Brain. F. M. Haug. (Advances in Anatomy, Embryology & Cell Biology: Vol. 47, Pt. 4). (Illus.). 70p. 1973. pap. 29.00 o.p. (ISBN 0-387-06213-0). Springer-Verlag.

Heavy Vehicle Fitting. R. Aylen et al. (Illus.). 251p. 1980. spiral 49.95x o.p. (ISBN 0-85083-510-0). Trans-Atl Phila.

Heavyhands: The Ultimate Exercise System. Leonard Schwartz. 1982. 15.45i o.p. (ISBN 0-316-77557-6). Little.

Hebb's Textbook of Psychology: Study Guide. 3rd ed. Charles C. Torrey. 1972. pap. text ed. 8.95 o.p. (ISBN 0-7216-8881-0). HR&W.

Hebdromdaires. Jacques Prevert & Andre Pozner. 192p. 1972. 12.50 o.p. (ISBN 0-686-54908-2). Schoenhof.

Hebrew Grammar. 60-13662 ed. Baruch Spinoza. 1963. (ISBN 0-8022-1618-8). Philos Lib.

Hebrew Impact on Western Civilization. Dagobert D. Runes. (ISBN 0-8022-1436-3). Philos Lib.

Hebrew Inscriptions & Stamps from Gibeon. James B. Pritchard. (University Museum Monographs: No. 17). (Illus.). 32p. 1959. 5.00x o.p. (ISBN 0-934718-10-5). Univ Mus of U PA.

Hebrew Marriage. David R. Mace. 288p. 1953. (ISBN 0-8022-1026-0). Philos Lib.

Hebrew Myths. Robert Graves & Raphael Patai. 1966. pap. text ed. 5.95 o.p. (ISBN 0-07-024125-2). McGraw.

Hebrew Pocket Dictionary. (Hebrew & Eng.). 12.50 o.s.i. (ISBN 0-88431-122-8). E J Brill USA.

Hebrew Union College-Jewish Institute of Religion at One Hundred Years. Karff. Date not set. 20.00 o.p. Ktav.

Hebrew Vocabularies. J. Barton Payne. (Hebrew.). pap. 4.95 o.p. (ISBN 0-8010-6949-1). Baker Bk.

Hebrews. David L. Eubanks & Robert C. Shannon. (Standard Bible Studies). 128p. 1986. pap. text ed. 5.95 o.p. (ISBN 0-87403-171-0, 40111). Standard Pub.

Hebrews see Word Studies in the Greek New Testament, for the English Reader.

Hebrews: A Good News Commentary. Donald A. Hagner. LC 82-48410. (Good News Commentary Ser.). 288p. 1983. pap. 9.95 o.p. (ISBN 0-06-063555-X, RD-425). HarpR.

Hebrews, James, I-II Peter, Vol. XI. Beacon Bible Expositions Staff. 8.95 o.p. (ISBN 0-8010-0677-5). Baker Bk.

Hebrews, James, 1 & 2 Peter, Jude, Revelation. Reginald H. Fuller et al. Ed. by Gerhard Krodel. LC 76-7864. (Proclamation Commentaries). 132p. 1977. pap. 4.95 o.p. (ISBN 0-8006-0584-5, 1-584, Fortress). Augsburg Fortress.

Hebrews-Revelation, Vol. X. Beacon Bible Commentary Staff. 15.95 o.p. (ISBN 0-8010-0698-8). Baker Bk.

Hector Berlioz: Rational Romantic. John Crabbe. LC 78-68765. 192p. 1980. 9.95 o.s.i. (ISBN 0-8008-0718-9, Crescendo). Taplinger.

Hector, the Accordion-Nosed Dog. John Stadler. LC 81-7713. (Illus.). 32p. (ps-2). 1984. 10.95 o.s.i. Bradbury Pr.

Hedda Gabler. Henrik Ibsen. Ed. by Henry Popkin. Tr. by Kai Jurgensen & Robert Schenkkan. (Orig.). 1975. pap. 0.95 o.p. (ISBN 0-380-00365-1, 24620, Bard). Avon.

Hedgehog & the Fox. Isaiah Berlin. 96p. 1986. pap. 4.95 o.s.i. (ISBN 0-671-60601-8, Touchstone). S&S.

Hedgehog Surprises. Betty Jo Stanovich. LC 83-26820. (Illus.). 48p. (gr. 1-3). 1984. 9.25 o.p. (ISBN 0-688-02690-7); lib. bdg. 8.59 o.p. (ISBN 0-688-02691-5). Lothrop.

Hedgehog's New House. Ding Yuzher. (Illus.). 18p. (gr. 3-5). pap. 1.95 o.p. (ISBN 0-8351-1182-2). China Bks.

Hee Haw. Ann McGovern. LC 75-86294. (Illus.). (gr. k-3). 1969. dolphin bdg. 6.95 o.p. (ISBN 0-395-06910-6). HM.

Hegel: A Re-Examination. John N. Findlay. (Muirhead Library of Philosophy Ser.). 1964. Repr. of 1958 ed. text ed. 19.95 o.p. (ISBN 0-391-00893-5). Humanities.

Hegel, Marx & Dialectic: A Debate. Richard Norman & Sean Sayers. (Philosophy Now Ser.: No. 10). 1980. text ed. 38.50x o.p. (ISBN 0-391-01779-9); pap. text ed. 12.00x o.p. (ISBN 0-391-01874-4). Humanities.

Hegel's Dialectical Method. William Young. LC 72-89398. 1972. pap. 4.95 o.p. (ISBN 0-87552-855-4). Presby & Reformed.

Hegel's Phenomenology: Dialogues on the Life of Mind. Jacob Loewenberg. LC 65-15621. 392p. 1965. 24.95 o.p. (ISBN 0-87548-022-5). Open Court.

Hegel's Phenomenology of Spirit. Werner Marx. LC 74-4635. 144p. 1975. pap. 4.50xi o.p. (ISBN 0-06-065463-5, RD88). HarpR.

Heidegger & Wittgenstein: The Poetics of Silence. Steven L. Bindeman. LC 80-6066. 159p. 1980. lib. bdg. 24.25 o.p. (ISBN 0-8191-1350-6); pap. text ed. 10.00 o.p. (ISBN 0-8191-1351-4). U Pr of Amer.

Heidi. Johanna Spyri. Ed. by Wendy Barish. (Illus.). 336p. 1982. 14.50 o.s.i. (ISBN 0-671-43790-9). Wanderer Bks.

Heidi. Johanna Spyri. (gr. k-3). 1978. 0.79 o.p. (ISBN 0-8431-4178-6). Wonder.

Heights of Desire. Molly Katz. (Candlelight Ecstasy Ser.: No. 402). (Orig.). 1986. pap. 2.25 o.p. (ISBN 0-440-13615-6). Dell.

Heights of Rimring. Duff Hart-Davis. LC 80-69379. 1981. 12.95 o.p. (ISBN 0-689-11148-7, Atheneum). Macmillan.

Heilige Caecilia in der Roemischen Kirche Des Altertums. Johann P. Kirsch. 1910. pap. 8.00 o.p. (ISBN 0-384-29610-6). Johnson Repr.

Heinemann Guided Readers. Ed. by John Milne. Incl. Beginner Level. Rich Man, Poor Man. T. C. Jupp. 1976. pap. text ed. 3.00x (ISBN 0-435-27022-2); Beginner Level. Death of a Soldier. Philip Prowse. 1976. pap. text ed. 3.00x (ISBN 0-435-27036-2); Beginner Level. Marco. Mike Esplen. 1976. pap. text ed. 3.00x (ISBN 0-435-27023-0); Dangerous Journey. Alwyn Cox. 1976. pap. text ed. 3.00x (ISBN 0-435-27021-4); Beginner Level. Money for a Motorbike. John Milne. 1976. pap. text ed. 3.00x (ISBN 0-435-27035-4); Beginner Level. Truth Machine. Norman Whitney. 1976. pap. text ed. 3.00x (ISBN 0-435-27037-0); Elementary Level. Road to Nowhere. John Milne. 1975. pap. text ed. 3.00x (ISBN 0-435-27013-3); Elementary Level. Black Cat. John Milne. 1975. pap. text ed. 3.00x (ISBN 0-435-27012-5); Elementary Level. Star for a Day. Philip Prowse. 1976. pap. text ed. 3.00x (ISBN 0-435-27034-6); Intermediate Level. Bristol Murder. Philip Prowse. pap. text ed. 3.00x (ISBN 0-435-27003-6); Intermediate Level. Smuggler. Piers Plowright. pap. text ed. 3.00x (ISBN 0-435-27005-2); Intermediate Level. Football. Duncan Forbes. pap. text ed. 3.00x (ISBN 0-435-27004-4); Intermediate Level. Woman Who Disappeared. Philip Prowse. 1975. pap. text ed. 3.00x (ISBN 0-435-27011-7); Intermediate Level. Raid. Glyn Frewer. 1976. pap. text ed. 3.00x (ISBN 0-435-27017-6); Upper Level. Money for Sale. Michael Hardcastle. 1975. pap. text ed. 3.00x (ISBN 0-435-27020-6); Upper Level. Story of Pop. John Byrne. 1975. pap. text ed. 3.00x (ISBN 0-435-27025-7); Upper Level. Olympic Games. Bruce Tulloh. 1976. pap. text ed. 3.00x (ISBN 0-435-27027-3). pap. text ed. 3.00x 1977 handbook o.p. (ISBN 0-435-27039-7). Heinemann Ed.

Heinemann New Family Medical Encyclopedia. Paul Paxton et al. (Illus.). 304p. 1984. 32.95 o.p. (ISBN 0-434-65410-8, Pub. by W Heinemann Ltd). David & Charles.

Heinkel 177 "Greif" Uwe Feist & R. S. Hirsch. LC 67-16732. (Aero Ser: Vol. 13). (Illus.). 1967. pap. 5.95 o.p. (ISBN 0-8168-0548-2, 20548, TAB-Aero). TAB Bks.

Heinrich Heine: A Biography. E. M. Butler. (Illus.). 296p. 1958. (ISBN 0-8022-0204-7). Philos Lib.

Heinrich Heine: A Biography. Eliza M. Butler. LC 70-106684. 1970. Repr. of 1956 ed. lib. bdg. 35.00x o.p. (ISBN 0-8371-3607-5, BUHH). Greenwood.

Heinrich Heine: A Selected Critical Bibliography of Secondary Literature, 1956-1980. Jeffrey L. Sammons. LC 81-43346. 200p. 1982. lib. bdg. 36.00 o.p. (ISBN 0-8240-9286-4). Garland Pub.

Heinrich Schutz: His Life & Work. Hans J. Moser. 740p. Repr. of 1959 ed. lib. bdg. 89.00 o.p. (Pub. by Am Repr Serv). Reprint Servs.

Heir Not Apparent. Suzanne Finstad. Ed. by Barbara Rodriquez. (Illus.). 288p. 1984. 17.95 o.p. (ISBN 0-932012-57-4). Texas Month Pr.

Heir of Sea & Fire. Patricia A. McKillip. LC 77-4650. 192p. (gr. 7 up). 1977. 13.95 o.s.i. (ISBN 0-689-30606-7, Atheneum Childrens Bks). Macmillan.

Heiress of Ardara. Margaret Porter. LC 87-21928. (Starlight Romance Ser.). 192p. 1988. pap. 12.95 o.p. (ISBN 0-385-24491-6). Doubleday.

Heirloom Quilts You Can Make. Maggie Malone. LC 83-24363. (Illus.). 288p. 1984. 19.95 o.p. (ISBN 0-8069-5508-2); pap. 10.95 o.p. (ISBN 0-8069-7838-4). Sterling.

Heirloom: Sermons, Lectures & Studies. Leo Jung. 1961. 7.50 o.s.i. (ISBN 0-87306-107-1). Feldheim.

Heirs of a Promise. new ed. Allen C. Deeter. 48p. 1972. pap. 1.95 o.s.i. (ISBN 0-87178-359-2). Brethren.

Heirs of Darkness. Zilpha K. Snyder. LC 78-53799. 1978. 8.95 o.p. (ISBN 0-689-10913-X, Atheneum). Macmillan.

Heirs of Love. Barbara F. Johnson. 1980. pap. 2.95 o.p. (ISBN 0-380-75739-7, 75739-7). Avon.

Heirs of the Kingdom. H. Kennedy Hudner. 288p. 1981. 12.95 o.p. (ISBN 0-03-049831-7). H Holt & Co.

Heirs with the Prince. Stephen Brown. LC 85-13810. 176p. 1985. 10.95 o.p. (ISBN 0-8407-5939-8). Nelson.

Held Captive by Indians: Selected Narratives, 1642-1836. Ed. by Richard VanDerBeets. LC 73-3448. (Illus.). 1973. 34.95x o.p. (ISBN 0-87049-145-8). U of Tenn Pr.

Helen. Maria Edgeworth. (Mothers of the Nove Reprint Ser.). 480p. 1986. pap. 8.95 o.p. (ISBN 0-86358-104-8, 81048, Pandora Pr). Routledge Chapman & Hall.

Helen & Teacher. Joseph P. Lash. 750p. 1986. pap. 6.95 o.s.i. (ISBN 0-385-28399-7, Delta). Dell.

Helen Corbitt Cooks for Company. Helen L. Corbitt. LC 74-599. 1975. 14.95 o.p. (ISBN 0-395-18491-6). HM.

Helen Gurley Brown's Outrageous Opinions. Helen Gurley Brown. 1982. pap. 2.95 o.p. (ISBN 0-380-63289-6, 63289-6). Avon.

Helen Hunt Jackson: A Lonely Voice of Conscience. Antoinette May. LC 87-6572. (Literary West Ser.). (Illus.). 160p. (Orig.). 1987. pap. 5.95 o.p. (ISBN 0-87701-376-4). Chronicle Bks.

Helen: The Story of Helen Keller. Geoffrey Hanks. 1977. pap. text ed. 1.85 o.s.i. (ISBN 0-08-021235-2). Pergamon.

Helicopter Aerodynamics. Rotor & Wing International Staff & R. W. Prouty. (Illus.). 174p. Date not set. pap. 19.95 o.p. Aviation.

Helicopters & Autogyros of the World. Paul Lambermont. (Illus.). 256p. 1959. (ISBN 0-8022-0905-X). Philos Lib.

Helirescue Manual: Personal Safety & SAR Operations Around Helicopters. Rick Lavalla. (Illus.). 73p. pap. 5.00 o.p. (ISBN 0-913724-27-0). Emerg Response Inst.

Helium & Neon. Clever. 1979. 110.00 o.p. (ISBN 0-08-022351-6). Pergamon.

Helium Four. Z. M. Galasiewicz. 1971. 37.00 o.p. (ISBN 0-08-015816-1). Pergamon.

Helix. Desmond Ryan & Joel Shurkin. 1979. 10.95 o.p. (ISBN 0-393-01250-6). Norton.

Hell above & Hell Below: A Real Life Story of an American Airman. Richard H. Lewis. As told to & as told to William R. Larson. LC 85-7067. (Illus.). 192p. 1985. 15.95 o.p. (ISBN 0-911293-05-1). Delapeake Pub Co.

Hell above Water. Harry McKeever. 288p. pap. 2.95 Cancelled o.p. (ISBN 0-8439-2396-2, Pub. by Leisure Bks CT). Dorchester Pub Co.

Hell-Holes & Hangings. Fred Harrison. 1968. 10.95 o.p. (ISBN 0-89015-047-8). Eakin Pr.

Hell No. Robert Emmett Love. 1976. 4.00 o.p. (ISBN 0-682-48549-7). Exposition-Phoenix.

Hellas: A Portrait of Greece. Nicholas Gage. LC 86-40120. 1986. 17.45 o.s.i. (ISBN 0-394-55694-1, Pub. by Villard Bks). Random.

Hellbent on Insanity. Ed. by Joey Green & Bruce Handy. 1982. pap. 9.95 o.s.i. (ISBN 0-03-059981-4, Owl Bks). H Holt & Co.

Hellenes. Basil C. Rodes. 1985. 9.95 o.p. (ISBN 0-8062-2419-3). Carlton.

Hellenic Perspectives: Essays in the History of Greece. Ed. by John T. Koumoulides. LC 80-5475. 398p. 1980. lib. bdg. 26.25 o.p. (ISBN 0-8191-1107-4); pap. text ed. 16.75 o.p. (ISBN 0-8191-1108-2). U Pr of Amer.

Hellenistic Age. J. B. Bury et al. 1970. pap. 2.95 o.p. (ISBN 0-393-00544-5, Norton Lib). Norton.

Heller Report: The National Plan for Science Abstracting & Indexing Services. Heller Associates Staff. 1963. 15.00 o.p. (ISBN 0-942308-01-8). NFAIS.

Helliconia Summer. Brian W. Aldiss. LC 83-45062. 384p. 1983. 16.95 o.p. (ISBN 0-689-11388-9, Atheneum). Macmillan.

Helliconia Winter. Brian W. Aldiss. LC 84-45607. 384p. 1985. 17.95 o.p. (ISBN 0-689-11541-5, Atheneum). Macmillan.

Hello Everybody, I'm Lindsey Nelson. Lindsey Nelson. LC 85-9070. (Illus.). 1985. 18.95 o.p. (ISBN 0-688-04186-8, Pub. by Beech Tree Bks). Morrow.

Hello Friend: Reflections for the New Student. Patti Simpson. LC 81-80176. 208p. (Orig.). 1981. pap. 4.95 o.p. (ISBN 0-914766-64-3, 0191). Illum Way Pub.

Hello, God! Prayers for Small Children. Lois W. Johnson. LC 75-4157. (Illus.). 32p. (ps-5). 1980. pap. 3.50 o.p. (ISBN 0-8066-1873-6, 10-2999, Augsburg). Augsburg Fortress.

Hello, Goodbye. David Lloyd. (First Words Ser.). (Illus.). 32p. (ps-2). 1983. 1.50 o.s.i. (ISBN 0-671-47103-1, Little Simon). S&S.

Hello Neighbor. H. E. Douglass. (Outreach Ser.). 16p. 1983. pap. 0.25 o.p. (ISBN 0-8163-0523-4). Pacific Pr Pub Assn.

Hello Star: The One Minute Word Star Word Processing Manual. Robert Banning. (Illus.). 1983. lab manual 24.95 o.p. (ISBN 0-934832-34-X). Word Power.

Hello to Bodega. Chester Aaron. LC 74-18176. (gr. 5 up). 1976. 6.95 o.p. (ISBN 0-689-50015-7, Atheneum). Macmillan.

Hell's Angels: The Motor Cycle Gangs. Hunter S. Thompson. 1967. 8.95 o.p. (ISBN 0-345-42819-6, RanC); pap. 2.95 o.p. (ISBN 0-345-30113-7). Random.

Helmut Pfeuffer: Trauma & Drama. Ed. by Gottfried Knapp. (Illus.). 156p. (Ger.). 1985. 42.00 o.p. (ISBN 3-7913-0715-0, Pub. by Prestel). TeNeues.

Heloise & Abelard, 2 Vols. in One. George Moore. (Black & Gold Lib). 1945. 7.95 o.p. (ISBN 0-87140-871-6). Liveright.

Heloise's Beauty Book: A Helpful Hints Approach to Looking & Feeling Your Best. Heloise. 308p. 1985. 18.95 o.p. (ISBN 0-87795-654-5, Arbor Hse). Morrow.

Heloise's Handy Book: Nineteen Eighty-Four Home & Away Calendar-Organizer. Heloise. 196p. 1983. pap. 7.50 o.p. (ISBN 0-87795-508-5, Arbor Hse). Morrow.

Heloise's Handy Book: Nineteen Eighty-Five Home & Away Calendar-Organizer. (Illus.). 1983. pap. 7.95 o.p. (ISBN 0-87795-591-3, Arbor Hse); (12-copy prepack) o. p. 95.40 o.p. (ISBN 0-87795-616-2). Morrow.

Help Book. J. L. Barkas. 1979. 19.95 o.s.i. (ISBN 0-684-15194-4, ScribT); pap. 3.50 o.s.i. (ISBN 0-684-17717-X). Scribner.

Help! For Elementary School Substitutes & Beginning Teachers. Mary L. Morrow. LC 73-22029. 1974. pap. 3.95 o.s.i. (ISBN 0-664-24984-1, Westminster). Westminster John Knox.

Help for Job Hunters. Joe Karmos et al. LC 80-69041. 188p. (Orig.). 1982. lib. bdg. 25.00 o.p. (ISBN 0-8191-2281-5); pap. text ed. 9.75 o.p. (ISBN 0-8191-2282-3). U Pr of Amer.

Help for the Evangelistic Preacher. James E. Carter. LC 83-70371. 1985. pap. 6.50 o.p. (ISBN 0-8054-6243-0). Broadman.

Help for the Hyperactive Child. Sydney Walker, 3rd. 1978. 8.95 o.p. (ISBN 0-395-25722-0). HM.

Help for the Reading Teacher: New Directions in Research. Ed. by William D. Page. 110p. 1975. 7.00 o.p. (ISBN 0-8141-2064-4) (ISBN 0-317-35272-5). NCTE.

Help for Troubled Americans see Timely & Profitable Help for Troubled Americans.

Help for Your Grief. Date not set. Random.

Help! From Heloise. Heloise. LC 80-70543. (Illus.). 500p. 1981. 14.95 o.p. (ISBN 0-87795-318-X, Arbor Hse). Morrow.

Help! From Heloise. Heloise. 544p. 1985. pap. 7.95 o.p. (ISBN 0-380-69853-6). Avon.

Help! I Just Found Out I'm a Pig! Don Klein. LC 83-40532. (Illus.). 96p. (Orig.). 1984. pap. 3.95 o.p. (ISBN 0-89480-671-8, 671). Workman Pub.

Help: I Run a Sunday School. Mary Duckert. LC 77-158124. 1971. pap. 2.65 o.s.i. (ISBN 0-664-24930-2, Westminster). Westminster John Knox.

Help I'm a Camp Counselor! Norman Wright. LC 85-28120. 240p. (Orig.). 1969. pap. 6.95 o.p. (5418700). Regal.

Help! I'm a Woman! Beverly Mattox. LC 77-21631. 1984. pap. 3.45 o.p. (ISBN 0-87227-053-X). Reg Baptist.

Help! In Solving Problems Creatively at Home & School. Bob Eberle. (Illus.). 80p. 1984. wkbk 5.50 o.p. (ISBN 0-317-43020-3). Good Apple.

Help Is on the Way: Overcoming Barriers to Spirit-Assisted Prayer. Robert G. Tuttle. LC 83-80412. 128p. (Orig.). 1983. pap. 4.95 o.p. (ISBN 0-8358-0461-5). Upper Room.

Help! I've Got Problems. Ed. by Marjorie Miller. (Standard Ideas Bks). 1978. pap. 1.95 ea. o.p. Standard Pub.

Help! Let Me Out! David L. Porter. LC 82-1110. (Illus.). 32p. (gr. k-3). 1982. 8.70 o.s.i. (ISBN 0-395-32438-6). HM.

Help Lord! a Guide to Public & Private Prayer. D. P. McGeachy. LC 77-79592. 1978. 5.95 o.p. (ISBN 0-8042-2358-0, John Knox). Westminster John Knox.

Help Me Adapt, Lord: Discovering New Blessings While Learning to Live with Less. Judith Mattison. LC 80-67797. 96p. (Orig.). 1981. pap. 4.50 o.p. (ISBN 0-8066-1859-0, 10-3007, Augsburg). Augsburg Fortress.

Help Me Understand. Amy R. Mumford. (Accent Expressions Ser.). 24p. (Orig.). (gr. 3-7). 1984. pap. 4.95 o.s.i. (ISBN 0-89636-142-X). Accent Bks.

Help Me Understand, Lord: Prayer Response to the Gospel of Mark. Neely D. McCarter. LC 77-14511. 1978. pap. 4.95 o.s.i. (ISBN 0-664-24180-8, Westminster). Westminster John Knox.

Help My Faith Grow, Lord! Glen Kuck. (Continued Applied Christianity Ser.). 1983. pap. 2.50 o.p. (ISBN 0-570-03894-4, 12-2976). Concordia.

Help Starts Here: The Maladjusted Child in the Ordinary School. I. Kolvin et al. LC 81-14184. (Illus.). 320p. 1981. 59.95x o.p. (ISBN 0-422-77380-8, NO. 3569, Pub by Tavistock England). Routledge Chapman & Hall.

Help Starts Here: The Maladjusted Child in the Ordinary School. Israel Kolvin et al. 436p. 1986. pap. text ed. 29.95 o.p. (ISBN 0-422-77390-5, 3568, Pub. by Tavistock England). Routledge Chapman & Hall.

Help Thy Neighbor: How Counseling Works & When It Doesn't. Linda Scheffler. LC 83-48300. 256p. 1983. 22.50 o.s.i. (ISBN 0-394-53504-9, GP-882). Grove.

Help Thy Neighbor: How Counseling Works & When It Doesn't. Linda Scheffler. LC 83-48300. 256p. 1983. pap. 7.95 o.s.i. (ISBN 0-394-62495-5, E875, Ever). Grove.

Help Your Child Succeed with a Computer: Choosing & Using the Right Computer for Your Child. Carol Klitzner & Herb Klitzner. 210p. 1984. 15.45 o.p. (ISBN 0-671-49418-X). S&S.

Helpful Hattie. Janet Quin-Harkin. LC 82-15723. (Let Me Read Ser.). (Illus.). 64p. (ps-3). 1983. 9.95 o.p. (ISBN 0-15-233756-3, HJ). HarBraceJ.

Helpful Hattie. Janet Quin-Harkin. LC 82-15723. (Let-Me-Read Ser.). (Illus.). 32p. (ps-3). 1983. pap. 4.95 o.p. (ISBN 0-15-233757-1, VoyB). HarBraceJ.

Helpful Hints for Your Pregnancy. Carol Barkin & Elizabeth James. Ed. by Kathi Paton. 128p. (Orig.). 1984. pap. 7.75 o.p. (ISBN 0-671-46779-4, Fireside). S&S.

Helping. Marian Bennett. (Wipe-Clean Bks.). (Illus.). 12p. (ps). 1985. pap. 1.39 o.p. (ISBN 0-87239-952-4, 3512). Standard Pub.

Helping a Child Understand Death. Linda J. Vogel. LC 74-26325. 96p. 1975. pap. 3.50 o.p. (ISBN 0-8006-1203-5, 1-1203, Fortress). Augsburg Fortress.

Helping Children Grow: The Adults Role. Bruce Grossman & Carol Keyes. 1978. pap. 12.95x o.p. (ISBN 0-89529-034-0). Avery Pub.

Helping Children Learn to Read. Lyndon W. Searfoss & John E. Readence. (Illus.). 480p. 1985. text ed. (ISBN 0-13-386947-4). P-H.

Helping Children Reach Their Potential: A Teachers' Resource Book. rev. ed. Gladys G. Jenkins. 1971. pap. write for info. o.p. (ISBN 0-673-08610-0). Scott F.

Helping Clumsy Children. Ed. by Neil Gordon & Ian McKinlay. (Illus.). 200p. 1980. pap. text ed. 18.50 o.p. (ISBN 0-443-01868-5). Churchill.

Helping Destitute Men. John Leech & John Wing. 1980. 25.00x o.p. (ISBN 0-422-76760-3, NO. 6366, Pub. by Tavistock England). Routledge Chapman & Hall.

Helping Geriatric Patients. Ed. by Jean Robinson & Barbara McVann. LC 82-11959. (Nursing Photobook Ser.). (Illus.). 160p. 17.95 o.p. (ISBN 0-916730-46-8). Springhouse Pub.

Helping Hospital Trustees Understand Physicians. Richard E. Thompson. LC 79-21428. 96p. (Orig.). 1979. pap. 15.00 o.p. (ISBN 0-87258-287-6, AHA-196115). AHPI.

Helping Interview. 2nd ed. Alfred D. Benjamin. 1974. pap. 8.50 o.p. (ISBN 0-395-18604-8). HM.

Helping Is. Jane Buerger & Jennie Davis. LC 84-7042. (Illus.). 32p. (ps-k). 1984. lib. bdg. 4.95 o.p. Dandelion Hse.

Helping Leaders Help Girls Grow. Girl Scouts of the U. S. A. 1972. boxed kit 4.00 o.p. (ISBN 0-88441-252-0, 19-978). Girl Scouts USA.

Helping: Origins & Development of the Major Psychotherapies. David R. Cole. 390p. 1983. pap. 19.95x o.p. (ISBN 0-409-82407-0, NO. 5071). Routledge Chapman & Hall.

Helping People Change: A Textbook of Methods. 2nd ed. Ed. by Frederick H. Kanfer & Arnold P. Goldstein. LC 79-17929. 560p. 1980. text ed. 46.00 o.p. (ISBN 0-08-025098-X); pap. text ed. 17.50 o.p. (ISBN 0-08-025097-1). Pergamon.

Helping Special Student Groups. Ed. by Lester N. Wildon. LC 80-84261. (College Learning Assistance Ser.: No. 7). 1982. pap. text ed. 13.95x o.p. (ISBN 0-87589-879-3). Jossey-Bass.

Helping the Fearful Child: A Guide to Everyday & Problem Anxieties. Jonathan Kellerman. 1981. 13.95 o.p. (ISBN 0-393-01392-8). Norton.

Helping the Teacher. Findley B. Edge. 1959. 15.95 o.p. (ISBN 0-88243-520-5, 02-0520). Gospel Pub.

Helping Young Children Cope with Crisis: A Guide for Training Child Care Workers. rev. ed. Ed. by Ardis Kysar & Elizabeth Overstad. 69p. (Orig.). 1985. pap. text ed. 9.50x o.p. (ISBN 0-934140-12-X). Toys N Things.

Helping Your Business Grow: One Hundred One Dynamic Ideas in Marketing. Brooks Fenno, Jr. 224p. 1982. 15.95 o.p. (ISBN 0-8144-5733-9). AMACOM.

Helping Your Child. Donald B. Keat, II & Louise Guerney. 204p. 1980. pap. text ed. 11.25 o.p. (ISBN 0-911547-46-0). Am Assn Coun Dev.

Helping Your Child Grow Slim. Warren P. Silberstein & Lawrence Galton. 160p. 1983. pap. 8.50 o.p. (ISBN 0-671-49433-3, Fireside). S&S.

Helping Your Child Know Right from Wrong. Patricia Galvin. LC 79-91138. (Redemptorist Pastoral Publications). (gr. 3-5). 1980. pap. 2.95 o.p. (ISBN 0-89243-117-2, 39900). Liguori Pubns.

Helping Your Child Learn Right from Wrong. Simon & Olds. 1976. 7.95 o.p. (ISBN 0-671-22220-1). S&S.

Helping Your Child Read. National Education Association Staff. 1983. pap. 1.95 o.p. (ISBN 0-380-82693-3, 82693). Avon.

Helping Your Diabetic Child: A Guide to Parents & to Their Children Who Have Diabetes. John M. Court. LC 78-18312. 1974. 8.95 o.s.i. (ISBN 0-8008-3823-8); pap. 4.95 o.s.i. (ISBN 0-8008-3824-6). Taplinger.

Helping Your Elderly Patients: A Guide for Nursing Assistants. Judith M. Conahan. LC 75-40507. (Illus.). 128p. 1976. pap. 5.95 o.p. (ISBN 0-913292-29-X). Tiresias Pr.

Helping Your Exceptional Baby: A Practical & Honest Approach to Raising a Mentally Handicapped Baby. Cliff Cunningham & Patricia Sloper. (Illus.). 1981. pap. 6.95 o.p. (ISBN 0-394-73867-5). Pantheon.

Helping Your Handicapped Child. George Paterson. LC 74-14185. 112p. (Orig.). 1975. pap. 5.95 o.p. (ISBN 0-8066-1467-6, 10-3005, Augsburg). Augsburg Fortress.

Helping Youth in Conflict. Francis I. Frellick. LC 65-11884. (Successful Pastoral Counseling Series). (Orig.). 1968. pap. 0.50 o.p. (ISBN 0-8006-5019-0, Fortress). Augsburg Fortress.

Helps & Hints at Bible Study. Louis M. Perschke. 176p. 1981. 8.50 o.p. (ISBN 0-682-49733-9, Testament). Exposition-Phoenix.

Helps for Identifying & Teaching the Problem Reader. Lydia P. Zink. LC 74-80695. 1975. 10.00 o.p. (ISBN 0-682-47989-6, University). Exposition-Phoenix.

Helsinki Travel Guide. (Berlitz Travel Guides). (Illus.). 1982. pap. 4.95 o.p. (ISBN 0-02-969230-X, Berlitz). Macmillan.

Helter Skelter: The True Story of the Manson Murders. Vincent Bugliosi & Curt Gentry. (Illus.). 502p. 1974. 15.00 o.p. (ISBN 0-393-08700-X). Norton.

Helvetius: A Study in Persecution. David W. Smith. LC 82-15841. (Illus.). viii, 250p. 1982. lib. bdg. 38.50x o.p. (ISBN 0-313-23744-1, SMHL). Greenwood.

Hematologic Problems in the Newborn. 3rd ed. Frank A. Oski & J. Lawrence Naiman. (Major Problems in Clinical Pediatrics: Vol. 4). (Illus.). 376p. 1982. write for info. o.p. (ISBN 0-7216-7022-9). Saunders.

Hematology. Ed. by William G. Figueroa. LC 81-10310. 430p. 1981. 40.00 o.p. (ISBN 0-471-09515-X). Krieger.

Hematology Case Studies. Ed. by John B. Harley et al. 1973. 17.00 o.p. Med Exam.

Hematology for Medical Technologists: PreTest Self-Assessment & Review. Ed. by Barbara L. Garrick. LC 78-51704. (Illus.). 208p. 1979. pap. 10.95 o.p. (ISBN 0-07-051573-5). McGraw-Pretest.

Titles

Hematology for Practitioners. Marshall A. Lichtman. 1978. text ed. 36.00 o.p. (ISBN 0-316-52480-8). Little.

Hematopoietic Agents. J. C. Dreyfus & B. Dreyfus. 1971. 100.00 o.p. (ISBN 0-08-016211-8). Pergamon.

Hemes & Hemoproteins. Ed. by Britton Chance et al. 1967. 88.00 o.p. (ISBN 0-12-167856-3). Acad Pr.

Hemingway: Direct & Oblique. Richard Peterson. LC 68-23810. (Studies in American Literature: No. 14). 1969. text ed. 20.80x o.p. (ISBN 90-2797-527-2). Mouton.

Hemingway in Michigan. Constance Cappel. (Great Lakes Bks.). (Illus.). 224p. Date not set. 29.95x o.s.i. (ISBN 0-8143-2059-7, Great Lakes Bks); pap. 14.95x o.s.i. (ISBN 0-8143-2060-0, Great Lakes Bks). Wayne St U Pr.

Hemingway Women. Bernice Kert. (Illus.). 1983. 19.50 o.p. (ISBN 0-393-01720-6). Norton.

Hemingway's Paris. Robert E. Gajdusek. LC 78-17214. (Illus.). 1978. encore ed. 5.95 o.p. (ISBN 0-684-16684-4, ScribT). Scribner.

Hemingway's Paris. Robert E. Gajdusek. (Illus.). 192p. 1982. pap. 12.95 o.p. (ISBN 0-684-17785-4, ScribT). Scribner.

Hemmings' Vintage Auto Almanac. 6th ed. David Brownell. LC 76-649715. 320p. 1984. pap. 9.95 o.s.i. (ISBN 0-917808-07-X). Hemmings.

Hemodialysis: Principles & Practice. Ed. by George L. Bailey. 1972. 81.50 o.p. (ISBN 0-12-072950-4). Acad Pr.

Hemodynamics & Aging. Bernard T. Engel et al. 166p. 1977. text ed. 29.50x o.p. (ISBN 0-8422-7252-6). Irvington.

Hemoglobin: Structure, Function, Evolution & Pathology. R. E. Dickerson & I. Geis. 1983. 36.95 o.p. (ISBN 0-8053-2411-9). Benjamin-Cummings.

Hemoglobinopathies in Children. Ed. by Elias Schwartz & Carl Pochedly. LC 78-55277. (Progress in Pediatric Hematology & Oncology Ser.). (Illus.). 400p. 1980. 39.00 o.p. (ISBN 0-88416-204-4). Year Bk Med.

Hemolytic Anemia in Disorders of Red Cell Metabolism. Ernest Beutler. LC 78-2391. (Topics in Hematology Ser.). (Illus.). 280p. 1978. 49.50x o.p. (ISBN 0-306-31112-7, Plenum Med Bk). Plenum Pub.

Hemoperfusion: Kidney & Liver Support & Detoxification, Proceedings of the Meeting, Haifa, August 25-26, 1979, Pt. 1. Meeting on Hemoperfusion, Kidney & Liver Supports & Detoxification Staff. Ed. by Samuel Sideman & T. M. Chang. LC 80-14154. 496p. 1980. text ed. 59.95 o.p. (ISBN 0-89116-152-X). Hemisphere Pub.

Hemophilia in Children. Ed. by Margaret W. Hilgartner. LC 76-3895. (Progress in Pediatric Hematology & Oncology Ser.). 222p. 1976. 22.50 o.p. (ISBN 0-88416-138-2). Year Bk Med.

Hemorheology & Thrombosis: Proceedings of the U. S. Japan Seminar, Kobe Japan. Ed. by A. Copley & S. Okamoto. 1976. 215.00 o.p. (ISBN 0-08-020872-X). Pergamon.

Hemorheology: Proceedings of the First International Conference. Ed. by A. Copley. 1968. 215.00 o.p. (ISBN 0-08-013171-9). Pergamon.

Hempstead Plan: Sensible Approach to Dieting & Nutrition. Grace DeJose. (Illus.). 1980. 7.50 o.p. (ISBN 0-682-49516-6). Exposition-Phoenix.

Hen Harrier. Donald Watson. (Illus.). 1977. 35.00 o.p. (ISBN 0-85661-015-1, Pub by T & A D Poyser). Buteo.

Henderson: The Rain King. Saul Bellow. 1976. pap. 2.50 o.p. (ISBN 0-380-00832-7, 58313-5). Avon.

Henderson the Rain King. Saul Bellow. 1976. pap. 4.95 o.p. (ISBN 0-14-004229-6). Penguin.

Hendrix: A Biography. Chris Welch. LC 73-83767. (Illus.). 1982. pap. 6.95 o.p. (ISBN 0-399-41004-X, 030901, Perigee). Putnam Pub Group.

Hennage: A Social System in Miniature. Clement Harris. Ed. by George Spindler & Louise Spindler. (Case Studies in Cultural Anthropology). 112p. 1982. pap. text ed. 6.95x o.p. (ISBN 0-8290-0314-2). Irvington.

Henri & the Crocodile. Louise Kantenwein. (Illus.). 64p. (gr. 1-4). 1981. 5.00 o.p. (ISBN 0-682-49732-0). Exposition-Phoenix.

Henri Christophe & Thomas Clarkson, a Correspondence. Henri Christophe. Ed. by Earl L. Griggs & Clifford H. Praton. LC 68-23281. (Illus.). 1968. Repr. of 1952 ed. lib. bdg. 22.50x o.p. (ISBN 0-8371-0091-7, CHCC). Greenwood.

Henri de Toulouse-Lautrec: W. H. B. Sands Correspondence. Herbert D. Schimmel & Phillip D. Cate. (Illus.). 224p. 1983. 35.00 o.p. (ISBN 0-396-08192-4). Dodd.

Henri Matisse: Master of Color. Volkmar Esser. (Illus.). 96p. (Orig.). 1987. pap. 7.95 o.p. (ISBN 0-317-56517-6). Parkwest Pubns.

Henri Rousseau. N. Brodskaya. 1983. pap. 7.95 o.p. (ISBN 0-8285-2637-0, Pub. by Aurora Pubs USSR). Imported Pubns.

Henrietta's War: News from the Home Front. Joyce Dennys. (Illus.). 160p. 1985. 15.95 o.p. (ISBN 0-233-97829-1, Pub. by A Deutsch England). David & Charles.

Henrik Ibsen. David Thomas. LC 83-49385. (Modern Dramatists Ser.). 224p. 1984. 19.50 o.s.i. (ISBN 0-394-53862-5, GP 904). Grove.

Henrik Ibsen. David Thomas. LC 83-49385. (Modern Dramatists Ser.). 224p. 1984. pap. 9.95 o.s.i. (ISBN 0-394-62157-3, E924, Ever). Grove.

Henry Austin & the Italian Villa Style in American Architecture: A Selected Bibliography. Bibliographic Research Library Staff. (Architecture Ser.: A 1400). 6p. 1985. 2.00 o.p. (ISBN 0-89028-430-X). Vance Biblios.

Henry Bacon's Lincoln Memorial. Lamia Doumato. (Architecture Ser.: Bibliography A 1324). 1985. pap. 2.00 o.p. (ISBN 0-89028-274-9). Vance Biblios.

Henry David Thoreau: Essays, Journals & Poems. Henry David Thoreau. Ed. by Dean S. Flower. 640p. (Orig.). 1975. pap. 2.50 o.p. (ISBN 0-449-22378-7, L2378, Crest). Fawcett.

Henry E. Sigerist: Autobiographical Writings. Ed. by Nora S. Beeson. 1967. 6.25 o.p. (ISBN 0-7735-0017-0, McGill Canada). U of Toronto Pr.

Henry Eighth see also King Henry Eighth.

Henry Eighth see also Life of King Henry Eighth.

Henry Eighth. William Shakespeare. Ed. by Louis B. Wright & Virginia A. LaMar. (Folger Lib. Ser). 320p. (gr. 11-12). 1968. pap. text ed. 2.95 o.p. (ISBN 0-671-82660-3). WSP.

Henry Explores the Jungle. Mark Taylor. LC 68-18461. (ps-2). 1968. PLB 7.95 o.p. (ISBN 0-689-20626-7, Atheneum). Macmillan.

Henry Fielding: A Reference Guide. L. J. Morrissey. 1980. lib. bdg. 36.50 o.p. (ISBN 0-8161-8139-X, Hall Reference). G K Hall.

Henry Fifth see also King Henry Fifth.

Henry Fifth see also Life of King Henry Fifth.

Henry Fonda. Norm Goldstein & The Associated Press. LC 82-48627. (Illus.). 124p. 1982. pap. 7.95 o.p. (ISBN 0-03-063353-2, Owl Bks). H Holt & Co.

Henry Fourth, Pt. 1 see also King Henry Fourth, Pt. 1.

Henry Fourth, Pt. 2 see also King Henry Fourth, Pt. 2.

Henry Freisher: "Talanta" Issue. Ed. by H. A. Mottola. (Illus.). 160p. 1985. pap. 31.00 o.p. (ISBN 0-08-032639-0, Pub. by PPL). Pergamon.

Henry George in the British Isles. Elwood P. Lawrence. LC 57-9034. 203p. 1957. 5.00 o.p. (ISBN 0-911312-25-0, Michigan State University Press). Schalkenbach.

Henry Hobson Richardson & His Works. Mariana G. Van Rensselaer. (Illus.). 16.50 o.p. (ISBN 0-8446-5843-X). Peter Smith.

Henry Howard, Earl of Surrey. William A. Sessions. (Twayne English Authors Ser.: No. 429). 192p. 1986. lib. bdg. 19.95x o.p. (ISBN 0-8057-6920-X, Twayne). G K Hall.

Henry in Shadowland. Laszlo Varvasovszky. (Illus.). 32p. 1989. 15.95 o.p. (ISBN 0-87923-785-6). Godine.

Henry IV, Pt. 1. William Shakespeare. 48p. (Orig.). 1988. pap. 9.95 o.p. (ISBN 1-55651-383-6); audiocassette tape incl. o.p. (ISBN 1-55651-384-4). Cram Cassettes.

Henry James: A Study in the Aesthetics of the Novel. Rama K. Asthana. 130p. 1980. Repr. of 1936 ed. text ed. 12.50x o.p. (ISBN 0-391-02180-X). Humanities.

Henry James & Germany. Evelyn A. Hovanec. (Costerus: New Ser.: No. XIX). 1979. pap. text ed. 17.50x o.p. (ISBN 90-6203-902-2). Humanities.

Henry James & Impressionism. James J. Kirschke. LC 80-52732. 357p. 1981. 22.50x o.p. (ISBN 0-87875-206-4). Whitston Pub.

Henry James in Northampton: Vision & Revision. Dean Flower. (Illus.). 28p. 1971. pap. 3.00 o.p. (ISBN 0-87391-027-3). Smith Coll.

Henry James: Stories of the Supernatural. Henry James. Ed. by Leon Edel. LC 78-125479. 1980. pap. 9.95 o.s.i. (ISBN 0-8008-3829-7). Taplinger.

Henry James: The Early Novels, The Late Novels, 2 vols. Ed. by James W. Gargano. 1987. Set. 60.00 o.s.i. (ISBN 0-8161-8882-3). G K Hall.

Henry James: The Master. Leon Edel. 1978. pap. 2.95 o.p. (ISBN 0-380-39685-8, 39685-3, Discus). Avon.

Henry James: The Untried Years. Leon Edel. 1978. pap. 2.95 o.p. (ISBN 0-380-39107-4, 39107-4, Discus). Avon.

Henry James's Ultimate Narrative: The Golden Bowl. R. B. Wilson. xii, 329p. 1982. text ed. 34.95x o.p. (ISBN 0-7022-1593-7). U of Queensland Pr.

Henry Kissinger: The Anguish of Power. John G. Stoessinger. LC 76-22585. 1977. pap. text ed. 4.95x o.p. (ISBN 0-393-09153-8). Norton.

Henry Lee McFee. Frwd. by Frederick Hard. (Illus.). 72p. 1950. 3.00 o.s.i. (ISBN 0-915478-00-5). Galleries Coll.

Henry Moore: An Illustrated Biography. William Packer. LC 85-80475. (Illus.). 200p. 1985. 22.50 o.p. (ISBN 0-394-55050-1). Grove.

Henry Ossawa Tanner: American Artist. Marcia M. Mathews. LC 69-19279. (Negro American Biographies & Autobiographies Ser). 1969. lib. bdg. 17.50x o.s.i. (ISBN 0-226-51005-0). U of Chicago Pr.

Henry Sixth, Pt. 1 see also King Henry Sixth, Pt. 1.

Henry Sixth, Pt. 2 see also King Henry Sixth, Pt. 2.

Henry Sixth, Pt. 3 see also King Henry Sixth, Pt. 3.

Henry Villard & the University of Oregon. George N. Belknap. 1976. pap. 2.00 o.p. (ISBN 0-87114-083-7). U of Oreg Bks.

Henry Wiggen's Books. Mark J. Harris. 1977. pap. 2.95 o.p. (ISBN 0-380-01688-5, Bard). Avon.

Henrys: A Family of Artists. Bruce Henry. (Illus.). 128p. 1986. 43.00 o.p. (ISBN 0-7099-3764-4, Pub. by Croom Helm Ltd). Routledge Chapman & Hall.

Henry's Fabulous Model A Ford. Leslie R. Henry. Ed. by Clymer Publications. pap. 6.00 o.p. (ISBN 0-89287-260-8, H520). Clymer Pub.

Henry's Fork. Charles E. Brooks. LC 86-3055. (Illus.). 220p. 1986. 27.95 o.p. (ISBN 0-8329-0425-2); pap. text ed. 40.00 o.p. (ISBN 0-8329-0449-X). Lyons & Burford.

Heparin: Structure, Cellular Functions, & Clinical Applications. Ed. by Norman M. McDuffie. LC 78-31254. 1979. 43.50 o.p. (ISBN 0-12-484850-8). Acad Pr.

Hepatic Tumors & Oral Contraceptives. (Landmark Ser.). 1979. 22.50x o.p. (ISBN 0-8422-4128-0). Irvington.

Hepatitis Viruses of Man. Arie Zuckerman & Colin Howard. LC 79-40894. (Experimental Virology Ser.). 1980. 69.00 o.p. (ISBN 0-12-782150-3). Acad Pr.

Heptarchia Mystica of John Dee. Robert Turner. 128p. 1986. pap. 13.95 o.p. (ISBN 0-85030-470-9, Pub. by Thorsons UK). Weiser.

Hepzibah. Peter Dickinson. LC 80-65425. (Illus.). 32p. (gr. 2-7). 1980. 8.95 o.s.i. (ISBN 0-87923-334-6). Godine.

Her Ladyship's Companion. Joanna W. Bourne. (Regency Romance Ser.). 224p. 1983. pap. 2.75 o.p. (ISBN 0-380-81596-6, 81596-6). Avon.

Her Name Was Sojourner Truth. Hertha Pauli. (YA) (gr. 7-11). 1976. pap. 1.50 o.p. (ISBN 0-380-00719-3, 29074). Avon.

Her Victory. Allan Sillitoe. 592p. pap. 6.95 o.p. (ISBN 0-586-05655-6, Pub. by Granada England). Academy Chi Pubs.

Her Work: Stories by Texas Women. Ed. by Lou H. Rodenberger. LC 82-60562. 347p. 1982. 16.95 o.p. (ISBN 0-940672-05-7); pap. 8.95 o.p. (ISBN 0-940672-04-9). Shearer Pub.

Heraclitean Fragments: A Companion Volume to the Heidegger-Fink Seminar on Heraclitus. John Sallis & Kenneth Maly. 208p. 1980. 18.50 o.p. (ISBN 0-8173-0027-9). U of Ala Pr.

Heraclitus Seminar, Nineteen Sixty-Six to Nineteen Sixty-Seven. Martin Heidegger & Eugen Fink. Tr. by Charles H. Seibert. 181p. 1979. 18.75 o.p. (ISBN 0-8173-6628-8). U of Ala Pr.

Herald. Michael Shaara. 224p. 1984. pap. 2.95 o.p. (ISBN 0-380-61382-4, 61382). Avon.

Herald to the Trades Advocate & Cooperative Journal, Nos. 1-36. 1970. Repr. lib. bdg. 32.00x o.p. (ISBN 0-8371-9380-X, HA00). Greenwood.

Heraldic Alphabet. J. P. Brooke-Little. (Illus.). 218p. 1987. pap. 7.95 o.p. (ISBN 0-317-58445-6). Parkwest Pubns.

Heraldik in Diensten der Shakespeare-Forschung. Alfred Von Mauntz. LC 68-57296. 344p. 1969. Repr. of 1903 ed. 40.00x o.p. (ISBN 0-8103-3886-6). Gale.

Heraldry & Floral Forms As Used in Decoration. Herbert Cole. LC 74-164180. (Tower Bks). (Illus.). 248p. 1971. Repr. of 1922 ed. 46.00x o.p. (ISBN 0-8103-3913-7). Gale.

Heraldry Index of the St. Louis Public Library. St. Louis Public Library Staff. 1980. lib. bdg. 495.00 o.p. (ISBN 0-8161-0311-9, Hall Library). G K Hall.

Herb Cookery. Alan Hooker. LC 77-174183. (Illus., Orig.). 1971. pap. 7.95 o.s.i. (ISBN 0-912238-10-0, One Hund One Prods). Ortho.

Herb Denenberg's Smart Shopper's Guide. Herb Dennenberg. LC 80-66978. 208p. 1980. pap. 6.95 o.p. (ISBN 0-8019-7003-2). Chilton.

Herb Gardening. Claire Loewenfeld. (Illus.). 256p. 1964. 9.95 o.p. (ISBN 0-571-06024-2); pap. 5.50 o.p. (ISBN 0-571-09475-9). Faber & Faber.

Herb Growing Book. Rosemary Verey. (Illus.). 48p. (gr. 5 up). 1981. 10.45i o.p. (ISBN 0-316-89974-7). Little.

Herb Handbook. Dawn MacLeod. pap. 3.00 o.p. (ISBN 0-87980-051-8). Wilshire.

Herb-Lore for Housewives. Constance Romanne-James. LC 71-180978. (Illus.). 280p. 1974. Repr. of 1938 ed. 40.00x o.p. (ISBN 0-8103-3976-5). Gale.

Herb Lubalin: A Retrospective. Date not set. price not set o.p. Am Showcase.

Herbaceous Plants. Steven Still. (Illus.). 203p. 1982. pap. text ed. 24.80 o.p. (ISBN 0-87563-212-2); pap. text ed. 18.80x o.p. (ISBN 0-87563-211-4). Stipes.

Herbert & Hortense. Betty Bates. Ed. by Kathleen Tucker. LC 84-2387. (Just for Fun Bks.). (Illus.). 32p. (gr. 1-4). 1984. PLB 10.25 o.p. (ISBN 0-8075-3222-3). A Whitman.

Herbert Hated Being Small. Karla Kuskin. (Illus.). 32p. (gr. k-3). 1979. 6.95 o.p. (ISBN 0-395-26462-6). HM.

Herbert Hoover: A Public Life. David Burner. LC 83-45517. (Illus.). 448p. 1984. pap. 12.95 o.s.i. (ISBN 0-689-70669-3, 311, Atheneum). Macmillan.

Herbert Hoover & the Great Depression. Harris G. Warren. 1967. pap. 5.95 o.p. (ISBN 0-393-00394-9, Norton Lib). Norton.

Herbert Hoover & the Republican Era: A Reconsideration. Ed. by Carl E. Krog & William R. Tanner. LC 84-17317. 280p. (Orig.). 1984. lib. bdg. 31.00 o.p. (ISBN 0-8191-4288-3); pap. text ed. 15.50 o.p. (ISBN 0-8191-4289-1). U Pr of Amer.

Herbert Read-Formlessness & Form: An Introduction to His Aesthetics. David Thistlewood. 176p. 1984. 16.95x o.p. (ISBN 0-7102-0147-8). Routledge Chapman & Hall.

Herbert Spencer on Social Evolution. Herbert Spencer. Ed. by J. D. Peel. LC 76-172616. (Heritage of Sociology Ser.). lii, 270p. 1975. pap. text ed. 2.95 o.s.i. (ISBN 0-226-76892-9, P454, Phoen). U of Chicago Pr.

Herbert Von Karajan: A Biographical Portrait. Roger Vaughan. (Illus.). 1986. 16.45 o.p. (ISBN 0-393-02224-2). Norton.

Herbicides & Plant Growth Regulation. W. W. Fletcher & R. C. Kirkwood. (Illus.). 384p. 1983. 55.00x o.p. (ISBN 0-412-00271-X, NO. 5028, Pub. by Chapman & Hall England). Routledge Chapman & Hall.

Herblock Special Report. Herbert Block. (Illus.). 1976. 7.95 o.p. (ISBN 0-393-08708-5); pap. 3.95 o.p. (ISBN 0-393-00838-X). Norton.

Herblock Through the Looking Glass. Herbert Block. (Illus.). 287p. 1984. 12.45 o.p. (ISBN 0-393-01929-2). Norton.

Herblock thru Looking Glass. 1985. pap. 6.70 o.p. (ISBN 0-393-30216-4). Norton.

Herbs: An Indexed Bibliography, 1971-1980. James Simon et al. LC 82-24493. (Scientific Literature on Selected Herbs, Aromatic, & Medicinal Plants of the Temperate Zone). 632p. 1984. 69.50 o.p. (ISBN 0-208-01990-1, Archon). Shoe String.

Herbs & Herb Gardening. Eleanour S. Rohde. LC 70-180975. (Illus.). 244p. 1976. Repr. of 1936 ed. 48.00x o.p. (ISBN 0-8103-4303-7). Gale.

Herbs & Medicinal Plants. Madge Hooper. (Illus.). 126p. (Orig.). 1986. pap. 6.95 o.p. (ISBN 0-668-06569-9). Arco.

Herbs for Prostate & Bladder Troubles. Sarah Beckett. LC 80-50751. (Everybody's Home Herbal Ser.). (Illus.). 63p. (Orig.). 1980. 1.95 o.s.i. (ISBN 0-394-73944-2). Shambhala Pubns.

Herbs for Rheumatism & Arthritis. Sarah Beckett. LC 80-50752. (Everybody's Home Herbal Ser.). (Illus.). 62p. (Orig.). 1980. pap. 1.95 o.p. (ISBN 0-394-73943-4). HarpR.

Herbs for Use & for Delight: An Anthology from the Herbarist. Herb Society of America Staff. (Illus.). 10.00 o.p. (ISBN 0-8446-5199-0). Peter Smith.

Herbs That Heal. William A. Thompson. LC 77-72361. (Encore Edition). (Illus.). 1977. pap. 1.95 o.p. (ISBN 0-684-16928-2, ScribT). Scribner.

Herbst Dictionaries of Commercial, Financial & Legal Terms, Vol. 3. Robert Herbst & Alan G. Readett. (Three-Language Ser.). 980p. 1982. text ed. 98.95x o.p. (ISBN 0-686-98023-9). Birkhauser.

Herbst Dictionaries of Commercial, Financial & Legal Terms: Deutsch-Englisch. Ed. by Robert Herbst & Alan G. Readett. (Two-Language Ser.: Vol. B). 906p. (Ger. & Eng.). 1976. text ed. 24.95x o.p. (ISBN 0-686-92258-1). Birkhauser.

Herbst Dictionaries of Commercial, Financial & Legal Terms: English-German. Robert Herbst & Alan G. Readett. (Two-Language Ser.: Vol. A). 688p. (Eng. & Ger.). 1975. text ed. 24.95 o.p. (ISBN 0-686-92254-9). Birkhauser.

Herbst Dictionaries of Commercial, Financial & Legal Terms Vol. I. Robert Herbst & Alan G. Readett. (Herbst Dictionaries; 3-Language Ser.). 1138p. (Eng., Ger. & Fr.). 1979. text ed. 98.95 o.p. (ISBN 3-85942-000-3). Birkhauser.

Herbst Dictionaries of Commercial, Financial & Legal Terms Vol. 2. Ed. by Robert Herbst & Alan G. Readett. (Herbst Dictioaries; 3-Language Ser.). 1106p. (Ger., Eng. & Fr.). 1979. text ed. 98.95 o.p. (ISBN 3-85942-006-2). Birkhauser.

Herbst Dictionary of Commercial, Financial & Legal Terms. Ed. by Robert Herbst & Alan G. Readett. (Three-Language Ser.: Vol. 3). 980p. (Fr., Eng. & Ger.). 1979. text ed. 98.95 o.p. (ISBN 3-85942-002-X). Birkhauser.

Here Am I; Send Aaron! Jill Bricose. 1984. pap. 2.95 o.p. (ISBN 0-89693-712-7). Victor Bks.

Here Be Dragons. Sharon K. Penman. LC 84-23480. (Illus.). 704p. 1985. 19.95 o.p. (ISBN 0-03-062773-7). H Holt & Co.

Here Come the Purim Players! Barbara Cohen. LC 83-14878. (Illus.). 32p. (gr. 1-4). 1984. 12.00 o.p. (ISBN 0-688-02106-9); PLB 11.88 o.p. (ISBN 0-688-02108-5). Lothrop.

Here Comes Adventure. Robert H. Pierson. Ed. by Gerald Wheeler. (Banner Ser.). (Illus.). 192p. (Orig.). 1984. pap. 6.95 o.p. (ISBN 0-8280-0244-4). Review & Herald.

Here Comes Alex Pumpernickel. Fernando Krahn. (Illus.). 32p. (ps up). 1981. 9.70i o.p. (ISBN 0-316-50311-8, Atlantic-Little, Brown). Little.

Here Comes Charlie Brown: Selected Cartoons from "Good Ol' Charlie Brown, Vol. 2. Charles M. Schulz. (Peanuts Ser.). (Illus.). 1983. pap. 1.95 o.p. (ISBN 0-449-20235-6, Crest). Fawcett.

Here Comes Jesus. Ed Stewart. LC 77-90584. 160p. 1977. pap. 3.95 o.s.i. (ISBN 0-8307-0553-8, S101157). Regal.

Here Comes Peter Cottontail. Steve Nelson & Jack Rollins. (Illus.). (gr. 3-8). pap. 2.95 incl. lyrics o.p. (ISBN 0-317-43568-X). FS&G.

Here Comes the Clones: A Guide to IBM-PC Compatible Computers & Software. Melody Newrock. (BYTE Book). (Illus.). 1984. pap. text ed. 18.95 o.p. (ISBN 0-07-046458-8). McGraw.

Here I Am, Em B! 96p. (gr. 3 up). 1981. pap. 6.95 o.p. (ISBN 0-8280-0028-X). Review & Herald.

Here I Am: Forty-Five & Still Going. Samuel V. White. 1984. 6.95 o.p. (ISBN 0-533-05955-0). Vantage.

Here I Am, Wasn't I! The Inevitable Disruption of Easy Times. Sheldon B. Kopp. 160p. (Orig.). 1986. pap. 3.95 o.p. (ISBN 0-553-25424-3). Bantam.

Here I Stand. Paul Robeson. LC 70-159847. 1971. pap. 6.95 o.p. (ISBN 0-8070-6407-6, BP410). Beacon Pr.

Here Is France. Claire H. Bishop. LC 69-20376. (Illus.). 240p. (gr. 7 up). 1969. 10.95 o.p. (ISBN 0-374-32970-2). FS&G.

Here is Haiti. Ruth Wilson. 1957. (ISBN 0-8022-1894-6). Philos Lib.

Here Lies Duffy Baker. C. Hampton Gilbert. 1978. 8.00 o.p. (ISBN 0-682-49047-4). Exposition-Phoenix.

Here Lies the Body. Scott Corbett. (Illus.). 128p. (gr. 4-6). 1974. 12.45 o.p. (ISBN 0-316-15717-1, Pub. by Atlantic Monthly Pr.). Little.

Here No Evil. Ruth Malone. 144p. (gr. 6-9). 1973. 4.75 o.s.i. (ISBN 0-664-32522-X, Westminster). Westminster John Knox.

Here or Nowhere. Renee Hermanson. LC 83-51401. 128p. (Orig.). 1984. pap. 5.50 o.p. (ISBN 0-8358-0478-X). Upper Room.

Here They Dug the Gold: Colorado's Gold Rush, 1859-1869. George F. Willison. (Illus.). 368p. pap. cancelled o.s.i. (ISBN 0-87380-158-X). Rio Grande.

Here to Get My Baby. Louise Shivers. 1985. 13.95 o.p. (ISBN 0-317-53112-3, Large Print Bks). G K Hall.

Here Today. Zoe Fairbairns. 256p. 1984. pap. 3.95 o.p. (ISBN 0-380-89497-1). Avon.

Here Today & Gone Tomorrow: The Story of World's Fairs & Expositions. Suzanne Hilton. LC 78-8636. (Junior Literary Guild Selection Ser.). (Illus.). 192p. 1978. 8.95 o.s.i. (ISBN 0-664-32633-1, Westminster). Westminster John Knox.

Heredity. Patricia Storace. LC 86-47861. (Barnard New Women Poets Ser.). 96p. 1987. 20.00 o.p. (ISBN 0-8070-6800-4); pap. 7.95 o.p. (ISBN 0-8070-6801-2, BP 741). Beacon Pr.

Heredity & Evolution in Human Populations. rev. ed. Leslie C. Dunn. LC 65-11617. 1965. pap. text ed. 1.95x o.p. (ISBN 0-689-70065-2, 71, Atheneum). Macmillan.

Heredity & Evolution in Human Populations. rev. ed. Leslie C. Dunn. LC 65-11617. (Books in Biology: No. 1). (Illus.). 1965. 9.95x o.s.i. (ISBN 0-674-38950-6). Harvard U Pr.

Heredity & Human Affairs. 3rd ed. James J. Nagle. LC 82-25906. (Illus.). 448p. 1983. pap. 20.95 o.p. (ISBN 0-8016-3626-4). Mosby.

Heredity & Society: Proceedings of the New York State Department of Health, Birth Defects Institute Symposium, 2nd, Oct. 1971. New York State Department of Health, Birth Defects Institute Symposium Staff. Ed. by Ian H. Porter et al. 1973. 52.50 o.p. (ISBN 0-12-562850-1). Acad Pr.

Heredity & Variation in Microorganisms: Proceedings, Vol. 11. Cold Spring Harbor Symposia on Quantitative Biology Staff. Repr. of 1946 ed. 27.00 o.p. (ISBN 0-384-22570-X). Johnson Repr.

Herein Lies the Treasure-Trove, Vol. 1. Triptaka Master Hua. Tr. by Buddhist Text Translation Society. (Illus.). 160p. (Orig.). 1983. pap. 6.50 o.p. (ISBN 0-88139-001-1). Buddhist Text.

Herencia. Joaquin Calvo-Sotelo. Ed. by Richard B. Klein. 112p. 1976. pap. text ed. 4.50x o.p. (ISBN 0-88334-075-5). Ind Sch Pr.

Heresies Right & Left: Some Political Assumptions Reexamined. Reo M. Christenson. LC 83-5848. 196p. 1983. pap. text ed. 10.25 o.p. (ISBN 0-8191-3086-9). U Pr of Amer.

Heresy, Crusade, & Inquisition in Southern France, 1100-1250. Walter L. Wakefield. 1974. 40.00x o.p. (ISBN 0-520-02380-3). U of Cal Pr.

Heretical Cosmology: The Catastrophic Dislocations of Galaxies, Stars & Planets. Louis Jacot. LC 86-91194. (Illus.). 192p. 1986. text ed. 9.50 o.p. (ISBN 0-682-40175-7). Exposition-Phoenix.

Hereticus Papers. Ed. by Robert M. Brown. LC 79-10409. (Collected Writings of St. Hereticus: Vol. 2). 156p. 1979. pap. 5.95 o.s.i. (ISBN 0-664-24265-0, Westminster). Westminster John Knox.

Heritage. Lewis Orde. LC 81-66968. 384p. 1981. 13.95 o.p. (ISBN 0-87795-337-6, Arbor Hse). Morrow.

Heritage of American Paintings. William J. Williams. (Illus.). 256p. 30.00 o.p. (ISBN 0-317-54884-0). Apollo.

Heritage of Bhikkhu. Walpola Rahula. 1974. pap. 3.95 o.s.i. (ISBN 0-394-17823-8, E622, Ever). Grove.

Heritage of Buddha. LuZanne Boozer. 1953. (ISBN 0-8022-0156-3). Philos Lib.

Heritage of Buddhist Poetry. W. Crown. 1986. 6.95 o.p. (ISBN 0-533-06003-6). Vantage.

Heritage of Canada. (Illus.). 1979. 24.95 o.p. (ISBN 0-393-01288-3, Pub. by Reader's Digest). Norton.

Heritage of Deceit. Elizabeth Sarant. 1981. 5.00 o.p. (ISBN 0-682-49611-1). Exposition-Phoenix.

Heritage of Hastur. Marion Zimmer Bradley. (Science Fiction Ser.). 1977. Repr. of 1975 ed. lib. bdg. 14.00 o.p. (ISBN 0-8398-2363-0, Gregg). G K Hall.

Heritage of Hellenism: The Greek World from 323 to 31 BC. John Ferguson. (History of European Civilization Library). (Illus., Orig.). 1973. pap. text ed. 6.95 o.p. (ISBN 0-15-535723-9, HC). HarBraceJ.

Heritage of Horror: The English Gothic Cinema, 1946-1972. David Pirie. 1974. pap. 2.95 o.p. (ISBN 0-380-00069-5, 20099, Equinox). Avon.

Heritage of Japanese Art. Masao Ishizawa & Ichimatsu Tanaka. LC 81-80995. (Illus.). 208p. 1986. pap. 35.00 o.p. (ISBN 0-87011-787-4). Kodansha.

Heritage of Japanese Art. Masao Ishizawa & Ichimatsu Tanaka. (Illus.). 208p. 1982. 60.00 o.s.i. (ISBN 0-87011-481-6). Kodansha.

Heritage of Musical Style. Donald H. Van Ess. LC 73-101138. (Illus.). text ed. 29.50x o.p. (ISBN 0-03-081241-0). Irvington.

Heritage of Shadows. Madeleine Brent. LC 83-45164. 312p. 1984. 15.95 o.p. (ISBN 0-385-19041-7). Doubleday.

Heritage of Western Civilization, 2 vols. 5th ed. Oliver A. Johnson & John L. Beatty. 464p. 1982. Vol. I. pap. text ed. (ISBN 0-13-387225-4); Vol. II. pap. text ed. (ISBN 0-13-387233-5). P-H.

Heritier de Biraque, 2 vols. facsimile ed. Honore De Balzac. 1961. 37.50 ea. o.p. French & Eur.

Herma. MacDonald Harris. LC 81-66005. 1981. 16.95 o.p. (ISBN 0-689-11179-7, Atheneum). Macmillan.

Herman Johannes Lam 1892-1977: The Life & Work of a Dutch Botanist. M. Jacobs. 271p. 1984. pap. 22.50x o.p. (ISBN 90-6203-545-0). Humanities.

Herman Melville. Mumford. 1963. pap. 2.45 o.p. (ISBN 0-15-640072-3, Harv). HarBraceJ.

Hermann Weyl Selecta. 592p. (Ger.). 1965. 56.95x o.p. (ISBN 0-8176-0414-6). Birkhauser.

Hermetica: The Ancient Greek & Latin Writings Which Contain Religious or Philosophic Teachings Ascribed to Hermes Trismegistus, 4 vols. Ed. & tr. by Walter Scott. LC 85-8198. 1985. Vol. 4; 576p. 17.95 o.s.i. (ISBN 0-87773-341-4); Vol 1; 630p. pap. 15.95 o.s.i. (ISBN 0-394-74225-7); Vol. 2; 482p. pap. 15.95 o.s.i. (ISBN 0-394-74227-3); Vol. 3; 632p. pap. 17.95 o.s.i. Shambhala Pubns.

Hermit. Eugene Ionesco. Tr. by Richard Seaver from Fr. LC 80-52072. 169p. 1980. pap. 4.95 o.p. (ISBN 0-394-17746-0). Seaver Bks.

Hermit Kingdom: Ladakh. H. P. Ahluwalia. (Illus.). 180p. 1981. text ed. 75.00x o.p. (ISBN 0-7069-1022-2, Pub. by Vikas India). Advent NY.

Hermitage Collection: Western European Paintings. (Illus.). 190p. 28.00 o.s.i. (ISBN 0-912729-23-6). Newbury Bks.

Hermitage Within: Spirituality of the Desert. Tr. by Alan Neame. 160p. 1982. pap. 6.95 o.p. (ISBN 0-8091-2428-9). Paulist Pr.

Hermitian & Kahlerian Geometry in Relativity. E. J. Flaherty. (Lecture Notes in Physics: Vol. 46). 1976. pap. 17.60 o.p. (ISBN 0-387-07540-2). Springer-Verlag.

Hermits & Anchorites of England. Rotha M. Clay. LC 68-21759. (Illus.). 292p. 1968. Repr. of 1914 ed. 40.00x o.p. (ISBN 0-8103-3424-0). Gale.

Hernan Cortes: Conquistador in Mexico. John Wilkes. LC 76-22436. (Cambridge Topic Bks.). (Illus.). (gr. 5-10). 1977. PLB 8.95 o.p. (ISBN 0-8225-1205-X). Lerner Pubns.

Hero Ain't Nothin' but a Sandwich. Alice Childress. 100p. (gr. 5-9). 1973. 8.95 o.p. (ISBN 0-698-20278-3, Coward). Putnam Pub Group.

Hero in History: Myth, Power, or Moral Ideal. Sidney Hook. pap. 1.00 o.p. Hoover Inst Pr.

Hero in Scandinavian Literature: From Peer Gynt to the Present. Ed. by John M. Weinstock & Robert T. Rovinsky. LC 74-26815. (Germanic Languages Symposia Ser.). (Illus.). 238p. 1975. 17.50x o.p. (ISBN 0-292-73001-2). U of Tex Pr.

Hero Is More Than Just a Sandwich. Sonya Friedman. 1986. 16.95 o.p. (ISBN 0-399-13204-X). Putnam Pub Group.

Hero Machine. (Big Little Bks.: No. 58). (Illus.). 350p. 1984. 6.95 o.p. (ISBN 0-318-02701-1). Bks Nippan.

Hero Mechas. (Big Little Bks.: No. 141). (Illus.). 350p. 1984. 6.95 o.p. (ISBN 0-318-02738-0). Bks Nippan.

Hero of My Life: Essays on Dickens. Bert G. Hornback. (Illus.). xii, 159p. 1981. text ed. 18.95x o.p. (ISBN 0-8214-0587-X). Ohio U Pr.

Hero of New York. T. Glen Coughlin. LC 85-8791. 1986. 14.45 o.p. (ISBN 0-393-02262-5). Norton.

Hero of Our Time. Mihail Lermontov. Tr. by Vladimir Nabokov & Dmitri Nabokov. (Anchor Literary Library). 1982. pap. 4.95 o.p. (ISBN 0-385-09344-6, Anch). Doubleday.

Hero of the Waverley Novels. Alexander Welsh. LC 68-9825. 1968. pap. text ed. 2.45x o.p. (ISBN 0-689-70203-5, 135, Atheneum). Macmillan.

Hero One: Advanced Programming & Interfacing. Mark J. Robillard. LC 83-50379. (Illus.). 240p. 1983. pap. 16.95 o.p. (ISBN 0-672-22165-9, 22165). Sams.

Hero Rises up. John Arden & Margaretta D'Arcy. 105p. 1969. pap. 6.95 o.p. (ISBN 0-416-13960-4, NO. 2982). Routledge Chapman & Hall.

Hero Robot. (Big Little Bks.: No. 7). (Illus.). 350p. 1984. 6.95 o.p. (ISBN 0-318-02685-6). Bks Nippan.

Hero Robot, Vol. 2. (Big Little Bks.: No. 85). (Illus.). 350p. 1984. 6.95 o.p. (ISBN 0-318-02717-8). Bks Nippan.

Hero Robot, Vol. 3. (Big Little Bks.: No. 106). (Illus.). 350p. 1984. 6.95 o.p. (ISBN 0-318-02725-9). Bks Nippan.

Hero Tales from American Life. Francis T. Miller. LC 71-174081. (Illus.). 484p. 1971. Repr. of 1909 ed. 43.00x o.p. (ISBN 0-8103-3800-9). Gale.

Herod Antipas: A Contemporary of Jesus Christ. new ed. Harold W. Hoehner. 456p. 1980. pap. 15.95 o.p. (ISBN 0-310-42251-5, 10842P). Zondervan.

Herodon Peri Politeias. Herodes Atticus. 124p. pap. 8.00 o.p. (ISBN 0-384-22585-3). Johnson Repr.

Herodotus. J. A. Evans. (World Authors Ser.). 1982. lib. bdg. 16.95 o.p. (ISBN 0-8057-6488-7, Twayne). G K Hall.

Heroes. (Big Little Bks.: No. 132). (Illus.). 350p. 1984. 6.95 o.p. (ISBN 0-318-02734-8). Bks Nippan.

Heroes. Charles Kingsley. (Dent's Illustrated Children's Classics Ser.). (Illus.). 219p. (gr. 4 up). 1975. Repr. of 1965 ed. 11.00x o.p. (ISBN 0-460-05058-3, BKA 01605, Pub. by J. M. Dent, England). Biblio Dist.

Heroes. David Shields. 343p. 1984. 16.45 o.p. (ISBN 0-671-52564-6). S&S.

Heroes of Israel. William G. Blaikie. 520p. lib. bdg. 19.95 o.p. (ISBN 0-8254-5030-6). Kregel.

Heroes of Soccer. Larry Adler. LC 80-10209. (Illus.). 96p. (gr. 4-6). 1980. lib. bdg. 8.29 o.s.i. (ISBN 0-671-33095-0). Messner.

Heroes, Villains, & Ghosts: Folklore of Old California. Hector Lee. LC 84-7707. (Illus.). 189p. (Orig.). 1984. pap. 8.95 o.s.i. (ISBN 0-88496-223-7). Capra Pr.

Heroes Who Fell from Grace. G. Lee Tippin & Charles Patterson. LC 85-16196. 320p. 1985. 16.95 o.p. (ISBN 0-938936-37-9). Daring Bks.

Heroic Age: A Novel. Stratis Haviaras. 352p. 1984. 15.45 o.p. (ISBN 0-671-49291-8). S&S.

Heroic Mexico. William W. Johnson. LC 83-22856. 480p. 1984. pap. 8.95 o.p. (ISBN 0-15-640080-4, Harv). HarBraceJ.

Heroin Addiction. Gerry V. Stimson & Edna Oppenheimer. 300p. 1982. 33.00 o.p. (ISBN 0-422-77890-7, NO. 3690, Pub. by Tavistock). Routledge Chapman & Hall.

Heroin Addiction: Theory, Research & Treatment, Vol. 1. Second Ed. ed. Jerome J. Platt. LC 83-19584. 462p. lib. bdg. 34.50 o.p. (ISBN 0-89874-694-9). Krieger.

Heroin & Behavior. Gerry V. Stimson. LC 73-174. 246p. 1973. 25.95x o.p. (ISBN 0-470-82530-8). Halsted Pr.

Heroine's Journey. Helene K. Joy. 160p. 1986. 9.50 o.p. (ISBN 0-8062-2782-6). Carlton.

Heroines of Dixie: Confederate Women Tell Their Story of the War. Ed. by Katherine M. Jones. LC 73-8160. (Illus.). 430p. 1973. Repr. of 1955 ed. lib. bdg. 25.50x o.p. (ISBN 0-8371-6949-6, JOHD). Greenwood.

Herold. Michel Butor. pap. 9.95 o.p. (ISBN 0-685-37251-0). French & Eur.

Heron. Giorgio Bassani. LC 70-95855. (Helen & Kurt Wolff Bk). 1970. 5.95 o.p. (ISBN 0-15-140095-4). HarBraceJ.

Herpes: How to Live with It, How to Treat It, How Not to Treat It see Herpes: Identification, Treatment & Prevention.

Herpes: Identification, Treatment & Prevention. rev. ed. Raymond P. Kennedy. Orig. Title: Herpes: How to Live with It, How to Treat It, How Not to Treat It. 137p. 1985. pap. 24.50 o.p. (ISBN 0-942028-17-1). R D Anderson.

Herpes in Focus. R. K. Landow. (Illus.). 288p. 17.95 o.p. (ISBN 0-8065-0837-X, Pub. by Citadel Pr). Carol Pub Group.

Herpes Perplex. 1984. pap. 0.25 o.p. (ISBN 0-89230-189-9). Do It Now.

Herpesviruses. Ed. by Albert S. Kaplan. 1974. 96.00 o.p. (ISBN 0-12-397050-4). Acad Pr.

Herr Raiffeisen among Chinese Farmers. China International Famine Relief Commission. LC 78-74320. (Modern Chinese Economy Ser.: Vol. 22). 140p. 1980. lib. bdg. 20.00 o.p. (ISBN 0-8240-4270-0). Garland Pub.

Herself. Hortense Calisher. LC 72-82174. 420p. 1972. 10.00 o.p. (ISBN 0-87795-042-3, Arbor Hse). Morrow.

Hersey's Executive Memory Program. Bill Hersey. 226p. 1987. text ed. 21.95 o.p. (ISBN 0-13-387168-1); pap. 9.95 o.p. (ISBN 0-13-387143-6). P-H.

Hershey's Cookies, Bars, & Brownies. Hershey's Kitchens Staff. (Illus.). 80p. 1983. pap. 4.95 o.p. (ISBN 0-8249-3023-1). Ideals.

Hershey's Kidsnacks. Hershey's Kitchens Staff. (Illus.). 64p. (Orig.). 1984. pap. 3.95 o.p. (ISBN 0-8249-3034-7). Ideals.

Hersheys Time-Less Desserts. Hershey's Kitchens Staff. (Illus.). 80p. (Orig.). 1985. pap. 4.95 o.p. (ISBN 0-8249-3046-0). Ideals.

Hertfordshire: A Shell Guide. R. M. Healey. (Illus.). 1986. pap. 11.95 o.p. (ISBN 0-571-13948-5). Faber & Faber.

Herzog's Bankruptcy Forms & Practice. 7th ed. Asa S. Herzog et al. LC 80-18209. 1984. 150.00 o.p. (ISBN 0-87632-011-6). Clark Boardman.

He's Coming! Hilton Sutton. 149p. (Orig.). 1983. pap. 2.95 o.p. (ISBN 0-89274-256-9). Harrison Hse.

Het Hoogste Wezen Bij De Manggaraiers. J. A. Verheijen. Repr. of 1951 ed. 46.00 o.p. (ISBN 0-384-64290-X). Johnson Repr.

Heteroatom Ring Systems & Polymers. H. R. Allcock. 1967. 81.00 o.p. (ISBN 0-12-050550-9). Acad Pr.

Heteroepitaxial Semiconductors for Electronic Devices. Ed. by G. W. Cullen & C. C. Wang. LC 77-21749. (Illus.). 1978. 98.00 o.p. (ISBN 0-387-90285-6). Springer-Verlag.

Heterogeneity of Polypeptide Hormones. Ed. by David Rabinowitz & Jesse Roth. 1975. 48.50 o.p. (ISBN 0-12-573801-3). Acad Pr.

Heterogeneous Catalysis: Proceedings of the Annual Symposia of the Industry-University Chemistry Program (IUCCP) of Tex A&M Univ Chemistry Department, No. 2. Ed. by B. L. Shapiro. LC 84-40141. (Illus.). 432p. 1984. 40.00x o.p. (ISBN 0-89096-201-4). Tex A&M Univ Pr.

Hew Against the Grain. Betty S. Cummings. LC 76-25593. 180p. (gr. 6-9). 1977. 6.95 o.s.i. (ISBN 0-689-30551-6, Atheneum). Macmillan.

Hexagone, C'Est la France. Jacques Poletti & Louise Lillard. (Fr.). 1984. pap. text ed. 16.95 o.p. (ISBN 0-03-062021-X). HR&W.

Hey Diddle Diddle. Ray Marshall & Korky Paul. Ed. by Kate Klimo. (Chubby Pop-Ups Ser.). (Illus.). 10p. 1983. 3.80 o.s.i. (ISBN 0-671-46239-3, Little Simon). S&S.

Hey, Didi Darling. S. A. Kennedy. LC 83-12774. 192p. (gr. 5up). 1983. 11.70 o.s.i. (ISBN 0-395-34555-3). HM.

Titles

Hey Girls, Let's Go Fishing. Frances C. Jenkins. 1978. 5.00 o.p. (ISBN 0-682-49045-8). Exposition-Phoenix.
Hey Hey Man. Sid Fleischman. (Illus.). (gr. 1-3). 1979. 12.95 o.p. (ISBN 0-316-26001-0, Joy St Bks). Little.
Hey-How for Halloween! Ed. by Lee B. Hopkins. LC 74-5601. (Illus.). 32p. (gr. 1-5). 1974. 4.95 o.p. (ISBN 0-15-233900-0, HJ). HarBraceJ.
Hey Joe! The Portrait of a Wisconsin Woodsman. Ken La Pointe. 1979. 7.50 o.p. (ISBN 0-682-49452-6). Exposition-Phoenix.
Hey Junior! Using IBM's Home Computer. David E. Arnold & David Cortesi. (IBM PCjr Home Computer Ser.). 250p. 1984. pap. 14.95 o.p. (ISBN 0-03-071772-8). HR&W.
Hey, Kid! Rita G. Gelman. (Illus.). 32p. (gr. k-3). 1978. pap. 1.25 o.p. (ISBN 0-380-40261-0, 56812-8, Camelot). Avon.
Hey, That's My Soul You're Stomping on. Barbara Corcoran. LC 77-13499. 144p. (gr. 5-9). 1978. pap. 7.95 o.s.i. (ISBN 0-689-30617-2, Atheneum). Macmillan.
Hey Traveler! Wanna Ride? V. Gladys Shutt. 1983. 10.95 o.p. (ISBN 0-533-05694-2). Vantage.
Hezekiah Speaks the Word of God in the Last Testament. Hezekiah. 1978. 4.00 o.p. (ISBN 0-682-49186-1). Exposition-Phoenix.
HFM Readings. Healthcare Financial Management Association Staff. 103p. 1983. pap. text ed. 8.95 o.s.i. (ISBN 0-930228-19-7). Healthcare Fin Mgmt Assn.
HHC User Guide. (ISBN 0-07-931087-7). McGraw.
Hi Butterfly. Taro Gomi. LC 84-1100. (Illus.). 40p. (ps-1). 1985. 10.25 o.p. (ISBN 0-688-04137-X, Morrow Junior Books); PLB 10.88 o.p. (ISBN 0-688-04138-8, Morrow Junior Books). Morrow.
Hi, Cat! Ezra J. Keats. (Illus.). 32p. (gr. k-3). 1988. pap. 4.95 o.s.i. (ISBN 0-02-044120-7, Aladdin Bks). Macmillan.
Hi, Daddy, Here I Am. Grete J. Hertz. LC 64-2541. (Foreign Lands Bks.). (Illus.). (gr. k-3). 1964. PLB 3.95g o.p. (ISBN 0-8225-0351-4). Lerner Pubns.
Hi Hai High: Zen & the Art of Backpacking. Fil Lewitt. (Illus.). 1979. 6.00 o.p. (ISBN 0-682-49524-7). Exposition-Phoenix.
Hi! Have a Nice Day. Norman C. Habel. LC 74-171498. (Open Book Ser.). (Illus.). 96p. (Orig.). 1972. pap. 1.00 o.p. (ISBN 0-8006-0109-2, Fortress). Augsburg Fortress.
Hi Ho the Rattlin' Bog: And Other Folk Songs for Group Singing. Ed. by John Langstaff. LC 75-76616. (Illus.). (gr. 6 up). 1969. 5.50 o.p. (ISBN 0-15-234400-4, HJ). HarBraceJ.
Hi Res-Double Hi Res Graphics for the Apple IIc & Apple II Family. William H. DeWitt. LC 85-26018. 192p. 1986. pap. 16.95 o.p. (ISBN 0-471-83183-2). Wiley.
Hi There! What Is Your Name? CARA Staff. 96p. 1987. pap. text ed. 9.95 o.p. (ISBN 0-682-40339-3). Exposition-Phoenix.
Hickcox's Monthly Catalog of U. S. Government Publications, 1885-1894 with Superintendent of Documents Classification Numbers Added. Ed. by Research Publications, Inc. Staff. write for info. o.p. (ISBN 0-8408-0018-5). Res Pubns CT.
Hickethier Color Atlas. Alfred Hickethier. 1974. 65.95 o.p. (ISBN 0-442-23409-0). Van Nos Reinhold.
Hidden Assets. C. Peterson. 1981. pap. 2.95 o.p. (ISBN 0-380-78535-8, 78535-8). Avon.
Hidden Childhood: A Jewish Girl's Sanctuary in a French Convent, 1942-1945. Frida Weinstein. LC 85-800. 160p. 1985. 13.95 o.p. (ISBN 0-8090-5444-2). Hill & Wang.
Hidden Corners of California. Camaro Editors. (Guide to Old California Ser.). (Illus.). 1979. pap. 5.95 o.s.i. (ISBN 0-913290-20-3). Camaro Pub.
Hidden Country Villages of California. Frances Coleberd. LC 77-21926. (Illus.). 180p. 1982. pap. 7.95 o.p. (ISBN 0-87701-252-0). Chronicle Bks.
Hidden Crisis in American Politics. Samuel Lubell. LC 69-17630. 1971. 5.95 o.p. (ISBN 0-393-05370-9); pap. text ed. 4.95x o.p. (ISBN 0-393-09886-9, NortonC). Norton.
Hidden Depths see Use & Abuse.
Hidden Factors in Technological Change. Ed. by Edward Semper & Philip Coggin. 1976. pap. text ed. 10.00 o.p. (ISBN 0-08-021007-4). Pergamon.
Hidden Fortunes: How to Profit from the New Opportunities of the 1980s. Albert J. Lowry. 352p. 1983. 17.45 o.s.i. (ISBN 0-671-42721-0). S&S.
Hidden France. Richard Binns. (Illus.). 160p. 1983. 8.95 o.p. (ISBN 0-89919-157-6). Ticknor & Fields.
Hidden Frontier: Ecology & Ethnicity in an Alpine Valley. John W. Cole & Eric R. Wolf. (Studies in Social Discontinuity Ser.). 1974. 24.95 o.p. (ISBN 0-12-785132-1). Acad Pr.
Hidden Harbor. Kathrene S. Pinkerton. LC 76-18900. (Illus.). (gr. 9 up). 1966. 3.95 o.p. (VoyB); pap. 0.75 o.p. (ISBN 0-15-640185-1). HarBraceJ.
Hidden Hawaii: The Adventurer's Guide. 3rd, rev. ed. Ray Riegert. Ed. by Sayre V. Young & Leslie Henriques. (Illus.). 396p. 1985. pap. 11.95 o.p. (ISBN 0-915233-01-0). Ulysses Pr.
Hidden Heart. Laura Kinsale. (Avon Romance Ser.). 352p. 1986. pap. 3.50 o.p. (ISBN 0-380-75008-2). Avon.
Hidden in Plain Sight. Kenneth R. Montgomery. 262p. 1986. 12.95 o.p. (ISBN 0-8062-2809-1). Carlton.
Hidden Life of Flowers. J. M. Guilcher. 96p. 1954. (ISBN 0-8022-0643-3). Philos Lib.
Hidden Manna Revealed by the Comforter. Gladys Cuss. 200p. 1981. 9.00 o.p. (ISBN 0-682-49768-1). Exposition-Phoenix.
Hidden Minorities: The Persistence of Ethnicity in American Life. Ed. by Joan H. Rollins. LC 81-40137. 268p. (Orig.). 1982. lib. bdg. 27.25r o.p. (ISBN 0-8191-2052-9); pap. text ed. 14.00 o.p. (ISBN 0-8191-2053-7). U Pr of Amer.
Hidden Profits in Stamping: A Creative Materials Management Guide. Jack Gilchrist. LC 77-2145. 128p. 1983. 28.95 o.p. (ISBN 0-8436-0818-8). Van Nos Reinhold.
Hidden San Francisco & Northern California: The Adventurer's Guide. Ray Riegert. (Illus.). 420p. 1984. pap. 9.95 o.p. (ISBN 0-915233-00-2). Ulysses Pr.
Hidden Script: Writing & the Unconscious. David Punter. 208p. 1985. 24.95x o.p. (ISBN 0-7100-9951-7). Routledge Chapman & Hall.
Hidden Staircase. Carolyn Keene. (Nancy Drew Ser.: Vol. 2). (gr. 4-7). 1930. 4.50 o.p. (ISBN 0-448-09502-5, G&D); PLB 3.29 o.p. (ISBN 0-448-19502-X, G&D). Putnam Pub Group.
Hidden Story of Scientology. Omar V. Garrison. 232p. 1974. 8.50 o.p. (ISBN 0-8065-0440-4, Pub. by Citadel Pr). Carol Pub Group.
Hidden Sun: Solar Eclipses & Astrophotography. James Lowenthal. (Illus.). 128p. 1984. pap. 5.95 o.p. (ISBN 0-380-86959-4, 86959). Avon.
Hidden Symptoms. Deirdre Madden. Ed. by Upton B. Brady. 142p. 1987. 14.95 o.p. (ISBN 0-87113-065-3). Atlantic Monthly.
Hidden Target. Helen MacInnes. LC 80-7953. 448p. 1980. 12.95 o.s.i. (ISBN 0-15-140198-5). HarBraceJ.
Hidden Treasure: Parables for Kids. Margaret Freeman. LC 81-16669. (Illus.). 96p. (Orig.). (gr. 4-9). 1982. pap. 3.95 o.p. (ISBN 0-87239-499-9, 2728). Standard Pub.
Hidden Valleys & Unknown Shores. Marie Keesing. LC 77-88963. (Illus.). (gr. 4-7). 1978. 6.95 o.p. (ISBN 0-15-232582-4, HJ). HarBraceJ.
Hidden Wholeness: The Visual World of Thomas Merton. John H. Griffin. 1979. pap. 7.95 o.p. (ISBN 0-395-28520-8). HM.
Hidden Window Mystery. rev. ed. Carolyn Keene. LC 75-1582. (Nancy Drew Ser.: Vol. 34). (Illus.). 196p. (gr. 4-7). 1975. 4.50 o.p. (ISBN 0-448-09534-3, G&D); PLB 3.29 o.p. (ISBN 0-448-19534-8, G&D). Putnam Pub Group.
Hidden World: Life under a Rock. Laurence Pringle. LC 76-47641. (Exploring an Ecosystem Ser.). (Illus.). 64p. (gr. 3-6). 1977. 9.95 o.s.i. (ISBN 0-02-775340-9, 77534). Macmillan.
Hide & Seek. Ellen Devlin. 1986. 17.95 o.p. (ISBN 0-399-13173-6). Putnam Pub Group.
Hide & Seek. Jack Ketchum. 208p. (Orig.). 1984. pap. 2.95 o.s.i. (ISBN 0-345-31237-6). Ballantine.
Hide & Seek. Jessamyn West. LC 72-88797. 1973. 7.50 o.s.i. (ISBN 0-15-140215-9). HarBraceJ.
Hide & Seek Birthday: A Lift-the-Flap Book. (Learning Curves Bks.). (Illus.). 24p. (ps-1). 1987. pap. 5.95 o.p. (ISBN 0-553-18353-2). Bantam.
Hide & Seek with Wilma Worm. Demi. LC 82-63207. (Follow-Me Bks.). (Illus.). 26p. (ps). 1983. 3.50 o.p. (ISBN 0-394-86020-9). Random.
Hiding. Norma Klein. (gr. 7-9). 1977. pap. 2.25 o.p. (ISBN 0-671-50809-1). Archway.
Hiding House. Judith Vigna. Ed. by Ann Fay. LC 79-17251. (Albert Whitman Concept Bks.: Level I). (Illus.). 32p. (gr. 1-3). 1979. PLB 11.25 o.p. (ISBN 0-8075-3275-4). A Whitman.
Hiding the Bell. Ruth N. Moore. (Illus.). (gr. 4-6). 1968. 5.25 o.s.i. (ISBN 0-664-32412-6, Westminster). Westminster John Knox.
Hidy Ochiai's Living Karate. Hidy Ochiai. 176p. (Orig.). 1986. pap. 9.95 o.p. (ISBN 0-8092-4841-7). Contemp Bks.
Hierarchical Structures in Guajajara. David Bendor-Samuel. (Publications in Linguistics & Related Fields: No. 37). 214p. 1972. pap. 2.25 o.p. (ISBN 0-88312-039-9); microfiche (3) 6.00 o.p. (ISBN 0-88312-439-4). Summer Inst Ling.
Hierarchy of Formulas in Set Theory. Azriel Levy. LC 52-42839. (Memoirs Ser.: No. 57). 76p. 1974. pap. 13.00 o.p. (ISBN 0-8218-1257-2, MEMO-57). Am Math.
Hierbas al Rescate (Herbs to the Rescue) LaDean Griffin. (Span.). Date not set. pap. 2.95 o.p. (ISBN 0-913923-50-8). Woodland UT.
Hieroglyphics of a New Speech: Cubism, Stieglitz, & the Early Poetry of William Carlos Williams. Bram Dijkstra. LC 69-18054. 1969. 26.50 o.p. (ISBN 0-691-06169-6). Princeton U Pr.
Hieronimus Bosch: The Temptation of Saint Anthony. Anne F. Francis. (Illus.). 1980. 15.00 o.p. (ISBN 0-682-48910-7, University). Exposition-Phoenix.
Hieronymous Bosch: His Picture-Writing Deciphered. D. Bax. Tr. by M. A Bax-Botha from Dutch. (Illus.). 1979. 65.00 o.s.i. (ISBN 0-8390-0231-9). Abner Schram Ltd.
Hieronymus Bosch: An Annotated Bibliography. Walter S. Gibson. 211p. 1983. lib. bdg. 37.50 o.p. (ISBN 0-8161-8347-3, Hall Reference). G K Hall.
Hieronymus Bosch: The Complete Works. Roger H. Marijnissen. (Illus.). 516p. 1987. 175.00 o.s.i. (ISBN 1-55660-032-1). A Wofsy Fine Arts.
Hieronymus Bosch: The Complete Works. Roger H. Marijnissen. (Illus.). 516p. 1987. 175.00 o.s.i. A Wofsy Fine Arts.
Hieronymus Cock: Printmaker & Publisher. Timothy A. Riggs. LC 76-23706. (Outstanding Dissertations in the Fine Arts Ser.). 1977. lib. bdg. 88.00 o.p. (ISBN 0-8240-2724-8). Garland Pub.
High above the Holy Land. Tim Dowley. Ed. by Earl O. Roe. LC 86-6422. (Illus.). 64p. 1986. 15.95 o.s.i. (ISBN 0-8307-1153-8, 5111590). Regal.
High Adventure: The First Seventy-Five Years of Civil Aviation. Joe Christy. LC 84-16453. (Illus.). 234p. (Orig.). 1984. pap. 16.60 o.p. (ISBN 0-8306-2387-6, 2387). TAB Bks.
High Altitude Cookbook. Beverly A. Nemiro & Donna M. Hamilton. LC 67-12738. 1969. 18.95 o.p. (ISBN 0-394-51308-8). Random.
High & Wild: A Mountaineer's World. Galen Rowell. LC 79-13000. (Illus.). 160p. 1979. 29.95 o.s.i. (ISBN 0-87156-263-4). Sierra.
High Blood Pressure. rev. ed. Nancy R. Hull et al. LC 83-9714. (Illus.). 40p. (Orig.). (gr. 8-10). 1983. pap. text ed. 3.00 o.p. (ISBN 0-939838-13-3). Pritchett & Hull.
High Church. Frederick W. Robinson. Ed. by Robert L. Wolff. LC 75-498. (Victorian Fiction Ser.). 1975. Repr. of 1860 ed. lib. bdg. 73.00 o.p. (ISBN 0-8240-1573-8). Garland Pub.
High Citadel. Joel Seligman. 1978. 10.95 o.p. (ISBN 0-395-26301-8). HM.
High Cost of Indifference: Leader's Guide. John Hambrick. (Study & Grow Electives). 64p. 1985. pap. 3.95 o.s.i. (ISBN 0-8307-1019-1, 6102038). Regal.
High-Cost Oil & Gas Resources. Jerome D. Davis. (Illus.). 266p. 1981. 40.00 o.p. (ISBN 0-85664-588-5, Pub. by Croom Held Ltd). Routledge Chapman & Hall.
High Crimes & Misdemeanors. Joanne Greenberg. LC 79-11111. 228p. 1980. 9.95 o.s.i. H Holt & Co.
High Crimes & Misdemeanors: The Untold & Dramatic Story of the Rodino Committee. Howard Fields. 1978. 10.95 o.p. (ISBN 0-393-05681-3). Norton.
High Crusade. Paul Z. Anderson. 176p. 1983. pap. 2.50 o.s.i. (ISBN 0-425-06277-5). Berkley Pub.
High Crystal. Martin Caidin. LC 73-91500. 1974. 6.95 o.p. (ISBN 0-87795-079-2, Arbor Hse). Morrow.
High-Density Digital Recording. Ed. by Ford Kalil. Al Buschman. LC 85-8926. (NASA Reference Publications: No. 1111). (Illus.). 320p. (Orig.). 1985. pap. 11.00 o.p. (ISBN 0-318-19572-0, S/N 033-000-00967-4). USGPO.
High Density Lipoproteins. Day. 728p. 1981. 115.00 o.p. (ISBN 0-8247-1220-X). Dekker.
High Density Lipoproteins & Atherosclerosis: Proceedings of the 3rd Argenteuil Symposium Held Under the Auspices of the Foundation Cardiologique Princesse Liliane in Waterloo, Belgium, Nov., 1977. Ed. by A. M. Gotto et al. (Argenteuil Symposia Ser.: Vol. 3). 1978. 42.75 o.p. (ISBN 0-444-80047-6, Biomedical Pr). Elsevier.
High Empire. Clyde M. Brundy. 432p. 1983. pap. 3.50 o.p. (ISBN 0-380-00040-7, 85290-X). Avon.
High Energy Astrophysics. L. Gratton. (Italian Physical Society: Course 35). 1967. 82.50 o.p. (ISBN 0-12-368835-3). Acad Pr.
High Energy Electrons in Radiation Therapy. Ed. by A. Zuppinger et al. (Illus.). 130p. 1980. pap. 29.10 o.p. (ISBN 0-387-10188-8). Springer-Verlag.
High Energy Physics, 5 vols. Ed. by E. H. Burhop. (Pure & Applied Physics Ser.: Vol. 25). Vol. 1, 1967. 87.50 o.p. (ISBN 0-12-144301-9); Vol. 2, 1967. 87.50 o.p. (ISBN 0-12-144302-7); Vol. 3, 1969. 87.50 o.p. (ISBN 0-12-144303-5); Vol. 4, 1969. 87.50 o.p. (ISBN 0-12-144304-3); Vol. 5, 1972. 87.50 o.p. (ISBN 0-12-144305-1). Acad Pr.
High Energy Physics & Nuclear Structure: Proceedings of the 5th International Conference, Uppsala, Sweden-1973. Ed. by G. Tibell. 1974. 84.25 o.p. (ISBN 0-444-10688-X, North-Holland). Elsevier.
High Explosives & Propellants. 2nd ed. S. Fordham. 1980. text ed. 35.00 o.p. (ISBN 0-08-023834-3); pap. 14.50 o.p. (ISBN 0-08-023833-5). Pergamon.
High Frontier. Keith Oliver. LC 86-50483. 224p. 1986. 15.00 o.p. (ISBN 0-682-40302-4). Exposition-Phoenix.
High Ideals? James Harris. LC 77-13737. 1978. 8.95 o.p. (ISBN 0-15-140221-3). HarBraceJ.
High Ideals? James Harris. LC 77-13737. 1978. pap. 3.95 o.p. (ISBN 0-15-640195-9, Harv). HarBraceJ.
High Impact Resumes & Letters. 2nd ed. Ronald L. Krannich & William J. Banis. (Illus.). 154p. 1987. pap. 9.95 o.p. (ISBN 0-942710-12-6). Impact VA.
High-Intensity Memory Power. Michael Kellett. LC 85-26283. (Illus.). 160p. (Orig.). 1986. pap. 4.95 o.p. (ISBN 0-8069-6310-7). Sterling.
High Intensity Workshop for Prepaid Plan Administrators: November Nineteen Seventy-Nine. 320p. 1979. 35.00 o.p. (ISBN 0-317-40264-1, 3-004). Am Prepaid.
High-Interest Books for Teens: A Guide to Book Reviews & Bibliographic Sources. Ed. by Adele Sarkissian. 300p. 1981. 85.00x o.p. (ISBN 0-8103-0599-2). Gale.
High Interest-Easy Reading: For Junior & Senior High School Students. 4th, rev. ed. ABA, Committee to Study Foreign Investment in U.S., Corporation, Banking & Business Law Section. Ed. by Hugh Agee. 96p. (gr. 7-12). 1984. pap. 5.25 o.p. (ISBN 0-8141-2095-4). NCTE.
High Interest Rates, Spreads & the Costs of Intermediation. James A. Hanson & Roberto Rocha. (Industry & Finance Paper Ser.: No. 18). 94p. 1986. 6.95 o.p. (ISBN 0-8213-0835-1, BK 0835). World Bank.
High Jinks Down under: It Happened One Night at Mulubat. Robbie Cass. 1978. 6.50 o.p. (ISBN 0-682-49137-3). Exposition-Phoenix.
High-Latitude Space Plasma Physics. Bengt Hultgvist & Tor A. Hagfors. LC 82-22518. 546p. 1983. 95.00x o.p. (ISBN 0-306-41241-1, Plenum Pr). Plenum Pub.
High-Level Languages for Microprocessor Projects. National Computing Centre, Ltd. Staff. Ed. by David Taylor & Lyndon Morgan. (Illus.). 279p. (Orig.). 1980. pap. 37.50x o.s.i. (ISBN 0-85012-233-3). Intl Pubns Serv.
High Lysine & Fiber Cancer Prevention Cookbook. Cory Ser Vass & Charlotte Turgeon. 128p. 12.95 o.p. (ISBN 0-8007-1436-9). Revell.
High Middle Ages. Trevor Rowley. (Making of Britian Ser.). 256p. 1986. text ed. 37.50 o.p. (ISBN 0-7100-9815-4, 98154, Pub. by Routledge UK). Routledge Chapman & Hall.
High Museum of Art. (Illus.). 80p. 29.95 o.p. (ISBN 0-939802-18-X); pap. 19.95 o.p. High Mus Art.
High Note, Low Note. Anne Emery. (gr. 5-9). 1954. 3.95 o.s.i. (ISBN 0-664-32107-0, Westminster). Westminster John Knox.
High on a Hilltop. Marjorie Kahl Lawrence. 1973. 3.00 o.p. (ISBN 0-682-47624-2). Exposition-Phoenix.
High on Gold. Lee Richmond. 1974. pap. 1.50 o.p. (ISBN 0-380-01249-9, 18267). Avon.
High on the Energy Bridge. Eric K. Goodman. LC 79-1930. 264p. 1980. 11.95 o.p. (ISBN 0-03-047166-4); pap. 6.95 o.s.i. (ISBN 0-03-056841-2). H Holt & Co.
High Pavement Blues. Bernard Ashley. (Julia Macrae BKs). (Illus.). 176p. (gr. 6 up). PLB 9.50 o.p. (ISBN 0-531-04607-9). Watts.
High-Paying Jobs in Six Months or Less. Anne Cardoza & Suzee J. Vlk. 160p. (Orig.). 1984. pap. 7.95 o.p. (ISBN 0-671-50414-2, Pub. by Monarch Pr). S&S.
High Performance. Lawrence Field. (Harold Robbins Ser.). 256p. (Orig.). pap. 3.95 o.p. (ISBN 0-671-64083-6). Archway.
High-Performance Graphics System Architecture: A Methodology for Design & Evaluation. Ingrid Carlbom. Ed. by Harold S. Stone. LC 84-2673. (Computer Science: Systems Programming Ser.: No. 21). 182p. 1984. 42.95 o.p. (ISBN 0-8357-1595-7). UMI Res Pr.
High Performance Liquid Chromatography. H. Engelhardt. Tr. by G. Gutnikov from Ger. LC 78-22002. (Chemical Laboratory Practice Ser.). (Illus.). 1979. 34.00 o.p. (ISBN 0-387-09005-3). Springer-Verlag.

High-Pitched Laugh of a Painted Lady. Lewis W. Green. LC 80-16382. 176p. 1980. 4.50 o.p. (ISBN 0-89587-017-7); pap. 2.98 o.p. (ISBN 0-89587-020-7). Blair.

High Plains Route. Richard C. Kistler. Ed. by James J. Reisdorff. (Illus.). 112p. 1986. pap. 20.00 o.p. (ISBN 0-9609568-7-5). South Platte.

High Pressure Effects on Cellular Processes. Arthur M. Zimmerman. (Cell Biology Ser.). 1970. 77.00 o.p. (ISBN 0-12-781250-4). Acad Pr.

High Pressure Liquid Chromatography in Clinical Chemistry. Ed. by P. F. Dixon et al. 1976. 64.50 o.p. (ISBN 0-12-218450-5). Acad Pr.

High Pressure Science & Technology: Proceedings of the International AIRAPT Conference, Le Creuset, France, July 30-Aug. 3, 1979. International AIRAPT Conference Staff. Ed. by B. Vodar & P. Marteau. (Illus.). 1200p. 1980. 355.00 o.p. (ISBN 0-08-024774-1). Pergamon.

High Profile. Melville Garton. LC 84-90065. 210p. 1984. 13.95 o.p. (ISBN 0-533-06146-6). Vantage.

High Resolution Displays & HDTV. International Resource Development, Inc. Staff. 178p. 1983. 1850.00x o.p. (ISBN 0-88694-553-4). Intl Res Dev.

High-Resolution Infrared & Submillimetre Spectroscopy: A Selection of Papers Presented at a Workshop Held in Bonn, 1977. Ed. by G. Schultz & T. S. Moss. 1978. pap. 28.00 o.p. (ISBN 0-08-021675-7). Pergamon.

High-Resolution Laser Spectroscopy. Ed. by K. Shimoda. (Topics in Applied Physics Ser.: Vol. 13). (Illus.). 1976. 60.00 o.p. (ISBN 0-387-07719-7). Springer-Verlag.

High Resolution NMR in Solids. M. Mehring. LC 76-10680. (NMR Ser.: Vol. 11). 1976. 30.70 o.p. (ISBN 0-387-07704-9). Springer-Verlag.

High Resolution NMR of Macromolecules. Frank A. Bovey. 1972. 99.50 o.p. (ISBN 0-12-119740-9). Acad Pr.

High Resolution Nuclear Magnetic Resonance Spectroscopy. J. W. Emsley et al. 1966. 290.00 o.p. (ISBN 0-08-011824-0). Pergamon.

High Risk Pregnancy & Child. Ed. by Z. Stembera et al. Tr. by M. Schierlova from Czech. (Illus.). 308p. 1976. 27.50 o.p. (ISBN 90-247-1924-0, Pub. by Nijhoff). Year Bk Med.

High Road. Ben Bova. 288p. 1981. 11.95 o.p. (ISBN 0-395-31288-4). HM.

High Road to Pyrrhonism. Richard H. Popkin. Ed. by R. A. Watson & J. E. Force. LC 78-10493. (Studies in Hume & Scottish Philosophy). 1980. 25.00x o.p. (ISBN 0-89690-002-9); pap. 10.00x o.p. (ISBN 0-89690-003-7). Austin Hill Pr.

High School & Beyond Student Financial Assistance: Student Loans. Cynthia L. Brown et al. (Education Publication CS: No. 87-341c). 54p. 1987. pap. 2.75 o.p. (ISBN 0-317-62861-5, S-N 065-000-00297-3). USGPO.

High School Diploma As a Terminal Degree: Contractor Report. Theodore C. Wagenhaar. (Education Dept. Publication CS Ser.: No. 86-202). 112p. 1986. pap. 5.00 o.p. (ISBN 0-318-21684-1, S/N 065-000-00267-1). USGPO.

High School English Instruction Today: The National Study of High School English Programs. James R. Squire & Roger K. Applebee. LC 68-22030. (Illus.). 1968. text ed. 22.50x o.p. (ISBN 0-89197-210-2); pap. text ed. 7.95x o.p. (ISBN 0-89197-211-0). Irvington.

High School Graduate Guide for Scoring High on Civil Service Tests. Solomon Wiener. 240p. (Orig.). (gr. 12). 1981. pap. 9.95 o.p. (ISBN 0-671-42776-8). Monarch Pr.

High School Rebel: Readings in Adolescent School Rebellion. G. Louis Heath. 75p. 1969. pap. text ed. 6.50x o.p. (ISBN 0-8290-1397-0). Irvington.

High School Stage Band. George Taylor. (Careers in Depth Ser.). (YA) (gr. 7-12). 1978. PLB 9.97 o.p. (ISBN 0-8239-0415-6). Rosen Group.

High School Typewriting. Kenneth Zimmer. LC 74-9198. 320p. text ed. cancelled o.s.i. (ISBN 0-02-479730-8); cancelled o.s.i. (ISBN 0-02-479780-4); text ed. cancelled o.s.i. (ISBN 0-02-479740-5); cancelled o.s.i. (ISBN 0-686-61289-2). Glencoe.

High School Vocational Graduates: Which Doors Are Open? Paul B. Campbell et al. 28p. 1982. 3.75 o.p. (ISBN 0-318-22125-X, RD226). Natl Ctr Res Voc Ed.

High Sierra. W. R. Burnett. 224p. 1986. pap. 3.50 o.p. (ISBN 1-55547-133-1). Critics Choice Paper.

High Sierra Hiking Guide to Pinecrest. Ben Schifrin. LC 75-38173. (High Sierra Hiking Guide Ser.). (Illus.). 128p. (Orig.). 1976. pap. 7.95 o.p. (ISBN 0-911824-48-0). Wilderness Pr.

High Speed Can Manufacture, 2 vols. Ed. by G. F. Allard et al. (Engineering Craftsmen Ser.: No. H301). (Illus.). 1972. Set. spiral bdg. 69.95x o.p. Trans-Atl Phila.

High Speed CMOS Logic Circuits Data Book. Texas Instruments Engineering Staff. LC 82-74480. 800p. 1984. pap. 11.95 o.p. (ISBN 0-89512-114-X, SCLD001A). Tex Instr Inc.

High-Speed Photography. 60p. 1981. pap. 6.75 o.p. (ISBN 0-87985-165-1, G44). Eastman Kodak.

High Speed Photography: Proceedings of the SPIE International Congress, 9th, Denver, 1970. 621p. 30.00 o.p. (ISBN 0-317-34650-4). SPIE.

High Speed Pulse & Digital Techniques. Arpad Barna. LC 79-26264. 185p. 1980. 31.95x o.p. (ISBN 0-471-06062-3, Pub. by Wiley-Interscience). Wiley.

High Speed Pulse Technique. J. A. Coekin. Ed. by P. Hammond. 263p. 1975. 55.00 o.p. (ISBN 0-08-018774-9); pap. text ed. 55.00 o.p. (ISBN 0-08-018773-0). Pergamon.

High Speed Small Craft. Peter Du Crane. (Illus.). 336p. 1958. (ISBN 0-8022-0212-8). Philos Lib.

High-Speed Wind Tunnel Testing. Alan Pope & Kenneth L. Goin. LC 78-15823. 486p. 1978. Repr. of 1965 ed. lib. bdg. 35.50 o.p. (ISBN 0-88275-727-X). Krieger.

High Spy. Robert Coulson. LC 87-50414. (Lazer Tag Ser.: No. 1). 128p. (Orig.). (gr. 4 up). 1987. pap. 2.95 o.p. (ISBN 0-88038-514-6). TSR Inc.

High Stakes. Eleanor Woods. (Candlelight Ecstasy Ser.: No. 270). 192p. (Orig.). 1984. pap. 1.95 o.p. (ISBN 0-440-13600-8). Dell.

High Stand. Hammond Innes. LC 86-3477. 336p. 1986. 17.95 o.p. (ISBN 0-689-11850-3, Atheneum). Macmillan.

High Street. Andre Ernotte & Elliott Tiber. 1977. pap. 1.50 o.p. (ISBN 0-380-00927-7, 31898). Avon.

High Strength Concrete. (PCI Journal Reprints Ser.). 20p. pap. 5.00 o.p. (ISBN 0-686-40032-1, JR100). P-PCI.

High-Strength Powder Metallurgy: Aluminum: Proceedings of the AIME Annual Meeting, Dallas, TX, 1982. Ed. by Michael J. Koczak & Gregory J. Hildeman. (Illus.). 425p. 50.00 o.p. (ISBN 0-89520-453-3); members 32.00 o.p. (ISBN 0-317-36302-6); student members 16.00 o.p. (ISBN 0-317-36303-4). ASM.

High-Tech Bits. Robert J. Martin. 1984. pap. 1.25 ea. o.p. (ISBN 0-8010-6170-9). Baker Bk.

High Tech Filtration. Business Communications Staff. 253p. 1984. 1750.00 o.p. (ISBN 0-89336-360-X, C-046). BCC.

High-Tech Fitness. J. Patrick Netter. LC 84-40317. (Illus.). 288p. (Orig.). 1984. pap. 12.95 o.p. (ISBN 0-89480-771-4, 771). Workman Pub.

High-Tech Growth Opportunities: A Special Report on Significant, New Developments Available for License. LC 86-50598. 185p. 1986. 615.00 o.p. (ISBN 0-914993-29-1). Tech Insights.

High Tech: How to Find & Profit from Today's New Super Stock. Albert Toney & Thomas Tilling. 387p. 1983. 16.50 o.s.i. (ISBN 0-671-46235-0). S&S.

High Tech Real Estate: Planning, Adapting & Operating Buildings in the Computer & Telecommunications Age. Ed. by Robert F. Cushman et al. 640p. 1985. 55.00 o.p. (ISBN 0-87094-611-0). Dow Jones-Irwin.

High Tech Training. Bill Dobbins. 1982. 19.25 o.p. (ISBN 0-671-43860-3); pap. 9.50 o.p. (ISBN 0-671-43861-1). S&S.

High Technology Careers. Texe W. Marrs. 225p. 1985. pap. 9.95 o.p. (ISBN 0-87094-589-0). Dow Jones-Irwin.

High Technology in the Work Place: Japan & the United States, A Seminar Report. 40p. 1984. 4.00 o.s.i. (ISBN 0-317-06766-4). Japan Soc.

High Technology Industries: Profiles & Outlooks, the Computer Industry. (High Technology Industries: Profiles & Outlooks Ser.). (Illus.). 70p. (Orig.). 1983. pap. 4.50 o.p. (ISBN 0-318-21692-2, S/N 003-009-00360-1). USGPO.

High Technology Industries: Profiles & Outlooks: The Robotics Industry. (High Technology Industries: Profiles & Outlooks Ser.). (Illus.). 64p. (Orig.). 1983. pap. 4.00 o.p. (ISBN 0-318-21583-7, S/N 003-009-00363-6). USGPO.

High Technology Industries: Profiles & Outlooks: The Semiconductor Industry. (High Technology Industries: Profiles & Outlooks Ser.). 32p. (Orig.). 1983. pap. 3.50 o.p. (ISBN 0-318-21584-5, S/N 003-009-00361-0). USGPO.

High Temperature Materials: Papers Presented at the Sixth Plansee Seminar. Plansee Seminar De Re Metallica - 6th - Reutte-1968. Ed. by F. Benesovsky. (Illus.). 1969. 82.60 o.p. (ISBN 0-387-80916-3). Springer-Verlag.

High-Temperature Protective Coating. Ed. by Subhash C. Singhal. LC 82-63096. 363p. 1982. 50.00 o.p. (ISBN 0-89520-455-X). Minerals Metals.

High Temperature Protective Coatings: Proceedings of the AIME Annual Meeting, Atlanta, 1983. Ed. by S. C. Singhal. (Illus.). 390p. 50.00 o.p. (ISBN 0-89520-455-X); members 32.00 o.p. (ISBN 0-317-36304-2); student members 16.00 o.p. (ISBN 0-317-36305-0). ASM.

High Temperature Structural Composites: Synthesis, Characterization & Properties. Ed. by M. J. Luton & R. S. Polizzotti. LC 87-43114. 300p. 1988. 90.00 o.p. (ISBN 0-87339-032-6). Minerals Metals.

High Temperature Technology-3: Proceedings of an International Symposium, Pacific Grove, Calif., 1967. International Union of Pure & Applied Chemistry. 764p. 1976. 185.00 o.p. (ISBN 0-08-020760-X). Pergamon.

High Temperature Vapors: Science & Technology. John W. Hastie. (Materials Science & Technology Ser.). 1975. 91.00 o.p. (ISBN 0-12-331950-1). Acad Pr.

High Touch Selling. John Savage. 1986. 14.95 o.p. (ISBN 0-88462-677-6). Little.

High Treason at Catfish Bend. Ben L. Burman. 144p. (gr. 3-5). 1981. pap. 1.95 o.p. (ISBN 0-380-53512-2, 53512-2, Camelot). Avon.

High Voltage Engineering. N. S. Naidu & V. Kamaraju. 384p. 1983. text ed. 4.10 o.p. (ISBN 0-07-451786-4). McGraw.

High Walls of Jerusalem: A History of the Balfour Declaration & the Birth of the British Mandate for Palestine. Ronald Sanders. LC 82-23265. (Illus.). 768p. 1983. 24.95 o.p. (ISBN 0-03-053971-4). H Holt & Co.

High Water at Catfish Bend. Ben L. Burman. 132p. (gr. 3-5). 1981. pap. 1.95 o.p. (ISBN 0-380-53470-3, 53470-3, Camelot). Avon.

High Water at Catfish Bend. Ben. L. Burman. 2.95 o.s.i. (ISBN 0-685-36539-5). Taplinger.

High Water at Catfish Bend see Three from Catfish Bend.

High, Wide & Lonesome: Growing up on the Colorado Frontier. Hal Borland. 1984. pap. 6.95 o.p. (ISBN 0-8398-2850-0). G K Hall.

Highbinders. Tom Lord. (Ash Tallman Ser.: No. 1). 176p. 1984. pap. 2.25 o.p. (ISBN 0-380-86249-2, 86249). Avon.

Highbinders. F. M. Parker. LC 86-29278. 336p. 1987. 16.95 o.s.i. (ISBN 0-385-23984-X, GC Large Print). Doubleday.

Higher Criticism of the Pentateuch. William H. Green. (Twin Brooks Ser.). 1978. pap. 4.95 o.p. (ISBN 0-8010-3723-9). Baker Bk.

Higher Education & Manpower Planning: A Comparative Study of Planned & Market Economies. O. Fulton & A. Gordon. 127p. 1982. 13.00 o.p. (ISBN 92-2-102973-5). Intl Labour Office.

Higher Education & the Older Volunteer: A Place for Everyone. Ed. by Holly Jellison. (Orig.). 1980. pap. 6.00 o.p. (ISBN 0-87117-098-1). Am Assn Comm Jr Coll.

Higher Education in America: Problems, Priorities & Prospects. Algo D. Henderson & Jean G. Henderson. LC 73-21071. (Higher Education Ser.). 1974. 23.95x o.p. (ISBN 0-87589-227-2). Jossey-Bass.

Higher Education in the People's Republic of China: Report of the Stanford University Delegation. Ed. by Thomas Fingar. (Special Report of the Northeast Asia-United States Forum on International Policy, Stanford University). 129p. 1980. pap. 6.50 o.p. (ISBN 0-935371-01-X). ISIS.

Higher Education in Twentieth-Century America. William C. DeVane. LC 65-13839. (Library of Congress Series in American Civilization). 1965. 16.00x o.s.i. (ISBN 0-674-39150-0). Harvard U Pr.

Higher Education Opportunities for Minorities & Women: Annotated Selections, 1985-86. William C. Young. 113p. 1986. pap. 5.50 o.p. (ISBN 0-318-20374-X, S/N 065-000-00252-3). USGPO.

Higher Geometry. N. V. Efimov. 1980. 11.00 o.p. (ISBN 0-8285-1903-X, Pub. by Mir Pubs USSR). Imported Pubns.

Higher Ground. Meredith S. Willis. 1981. 12.95 o.s.i. (ISBN 0-684-17225-9, ScribT). Scribner.

Higher Learning in Colorado: A Historical Study, 1860-1940. Michael McGiffert. LC 64-18746. 307p. 1964. 14.95 o.p. (ISBN 0-8040-0085-9, SB). Ohio U Pr.

Higher Set Theory: Proceeding, Oberwolfach Germany, April 13-23, 1977. Ed. by G. H. Mueller & D. S. Scott. (Lecture Notes in Mathematics Ser.: Vol. 669). 1978. pap. 29.00 o.p. (ISBN 0-387-08926-8). Springer-Verlag.

Higher Than the Arrow. Judy Van Der Veer. (gr. 4-6). 1975. pap. 1.50 o.p. (ISBN 0-380-00194-2, 44859-9, Camelot). Avon.

Highest Apple: Sappho & the Lesbian Poetic Tradition. Judy Grahn. LC 84-51941. 160p. (Orig.). 1985. pap. 6.95 o.p. (ISBN 0-933216-12-2). Spinsters Aunt Lute.

Highest Court in the City of Sanctuary see First Mishna & the Controversies of the Tannaim.

Highland Railway: The History of the Railways of the Scottish Highlands, Vol. 2. H. A. Vallance. (Illus.). 200p. 1985. 25.95 o.p. (ISBN 0-946537-23-2). David & Charles.

Highland Settler: A Portrait of the Scottish Gael in Nova Scotia. Charles W. Dunn. LC 53-7025. 1953. pap. 7.95 o.p. (ISBN 0-8020-6094-3). U of Toronto Pr.

Highland Velvet. Jude Deveraux. (General Ser.). 1985. lib. bdg. 16.95 o.p. (ISBN 0-8161-3794-3, Large Print Bks). G K Hall.

Highlanders of Arunachal Pradesh. Christoph Von Furer-Haimendorf. (Illus.). 224p. 1982. text ed. 27.50x o.p. (ISBN 0-7069-1367-1, Pub. by Vikas India). Advent NY.

Highlights from Drugs & American High School Students, 1975-1983. Lloyd Johnson. 141p. 1984. pap. 4.00 o.p. (ISBN 0-318-11788-6, S/N 017-024-01208-4). USGPO.

Highlights in Microbiology Nineteen Seventy-Nine to Eighty, Vol. 3. American Society for Microbiology, Education & Training Board Staff. (Highlights Ser.). 1981. 5.00 o.p. (ISBN 0-686-95718-0). Am Soc Microbio.

Highlights of Persian Art. Ed. by Richard Ettinghausen & Ehsan Yarshater. LC 79-4746. (Persian Art Ser.: Vol. 1). (Illus.). 390p. 1982. 65.00 o.s.i. (ISBN 0-8390-0282-3). Abner Schram Ltd.

Highlights of the Bible: New Testament. William L. Lane. LC 80-50543. 160p. 1980. pap. 3.95 o.s.i. (ISBN 0-8307-0676-3, S343118). Regal.

Highlights of the Off-Season. Peter J. Smith. 336p. 1986. 16.45 o.s.i. (ISBN 0-671-62503-9). S&S.

Highlights of the Untermyer Collection of English & Continental Decorative Arts. LC 77-12235. (Illus.). 1977. pap. 1.95 o.p. (ISBN 0-87099-169-8). Metro Mus Art.

Highlights of the Watergate Tapes. R. Kent Horsley. 1974. pap. 2.00 o.p. (ISBN 0-89036-038-3). Hawkes Pub Inc.

Highlights of Tibetan History. Wang Furen et al. Tr. by Xu Jian. (China Studies). (Illus.). 206p. (Orig.). 1984. pap. 6.95 o.p. (ISBN 0-8351-1170-9). China Bks.

Highly Flavoured Ladies. Patricia Angadi. 219p. 1988. 19.95 o.p. (ISBN 0-575-04001-7, Pub. by Gollancz England). David & Charles.

Highly Parallel Processing. George S. Almasi & Allan Gottlieb. 350p. text ed. 32.95x o.p. (ISBN 0-8053-0177-1). Benjamin-Cummings.

Highway & the City. Lewis Mumford. LC 63-10598. (Orig.). 1963. pap. 2.35 o.p. (ISBN 0-15-640216-5, HB62, Harv). HarBraceJ.

Highway Capacity & Level of Service. (Transportation Research Report Ser.). 60p. 1979. 3.40 o.p. (ISBN 0-309-02844-2). Transport Res Bd.

Highway Capacity, Measures of Effectiveness & Flow Theory. (Transportation Research Report Ser.). 83p. 1978. 5.00 o.p. (ISBN 0-317-36086-8). Transport Res Bd.

Highway Capacity, Traffic Flow, & Traffic Control Devices. Transportation Research Board Staff. (Transportation Research Report Ser.). 137p. 1977. 7.80 o.p. (ISBN 0-309-02673-3). Transport Res Bd.

Highway Collision Reconstruction. Ed. by E. A. Moffat & C. A. Moffat. 124p. 1980. pap. text ed. 18.00 o.p. (ISBN 0-317-02624-0, G00190). ASME.

Highway Engineering Handbook. Kenneth B. Woods. 1960. text ed. 92.00 o.p. (ISBN 0-07-071735-4). McGraw.

Highway Heavy Metal: The World's Trucks at Work. Arthur Ingram & Martin Phippard. (Illus.). 160p. 1986. 19.95 o.p. (ISBN 0-7137-1614-2, Pub. by Blandford Pr England). Sterling.

Highway Noise: A Design Guide for Highway Engineers. (National Cooperative Highway Research Project Report). 79p. 1971. 4.60 o.p. (ISBN 0-309-01895-1). Transport Res Bd.

Highway Number One: A Vietnamese Odyssey in Verse. James M. Cantwell. 64p. 1980. pap. 4.00 o.p. (ISBN 0-682-49595-6). Exposition-Phoenix.

Highway to the North. Frank Illingworth. (Illus.). 294p. 1955. (ISBN 0-8022-0774-X). Philos Lib.

Highways & Our Environment. J. Robinson. 1971. text ed. 59.50 o.p. (ISBN 0-07-053315-6). McGraw.

Hiking. Calvin Rutstrum. LC 83-26485. (Illus.). 136p. (Orig.). 1980. pap. 8.95 o.p. (ISBN 0-934802-20-3). ICS Bks.

Hiking from Inn to Inn: Wilderness Walking Tours with Comfortable Overnight Lodging from Maine to Virginia. David MacInnes & Kathleen MacInnes. LC 81-17336. (Illus.). 192p. 1982. pap. 7.95 o.p. (ISBN 0-914788-49-3). Globe Pequot.

Hiking Guide to Acadia National Park & Mount Desert Island. Robert Moran. (Islander Guide Ser.). (Illus.). 24p. 1988. 2.25 o.p. Acadia Pub Co.

Titles

Hiking Kauai: The Garden Isle. 3rd ed. Robert Smith. LC 83-60684. (Illus.). 120p. 1983. pap. 7.95 o.p. (ISBN 0-89997-031-1). Wilderness Pr.

Hiking Light. Marlyn Doan. (Illus.). 204p. 1982. pap. 8.95 o.p. (ISBN 0-89886-036-9). Mountaineers.

Hiking Maui: The Valley Isle. 3rd ed. Robert Smith. LC 83-51475. (Illus.). 144p. 1984. pap. 7.95 o.p. (ISBN 0-89997-037-0). Wilderness Pr.

Hiking Trails of Central Colorado. Bob Martin. LC 82-25067. (Illus.). 1983. pap. 9.95 o.p. (ISBN 0-87108-635-2). Pruett.

Hiking Trails of the Boulder Mountain Area. Vici Dehan. LC 79-87492. (Illus.). 1984. pap. 8.95 o.p. (ISBN 0-87108-678-6). Pruett.

Hiking Virginia's National Forests. Rev. ed. Karin Wuertz-Schaefer. LC 77-70414. (Illus.). 204p. 1977. pap. 7.95 o.p. (ISBN 0-914788-05-1). Globe Pequot.

Hilaire Belloc. A. N. Wilson. LC 83-45504. (Illus.). 320p. 1984. 17.95 o.p. (ISBN 0-689-11440-0, Atheneum). Macmillan.

Hilarion. Daniel Curley. (gr. 5-9). 1979. 6.95 o.p. (ISBN 0-395-28268-3). HM.

Hilary Knight's the Twelve Days of Christmas. Hilary Knight. LC 81-2599. (Illus.). 34p. (ps up). 1981. 9.95 o.s.i. (ISBN 0-02-750870-6). Macmillan.

Hilbert. Constance Reid. LC 76-97989. (Illus.). 1970. 29.50 o.p. (ISBN 0-387-04999-1). Springer-Verlag.

Hilda, the Hen Who Wouldn't Give up. Jill Tomlinson. LC 79-3764. (Illus.). 96p. (gr. 1-5). 1980. Repr. of 1967 ed. 5.95 o.p. (ISBN 0-15-234455-1, HJ). HarBraceJ.

Hill of Evil Counsel. Amos Oz. LC 77-92543. 216p. 1978. 7.95 o.p. (ISBN 0-15-140234-5). HarBraceJ.

Hill Smoke. L. P. Holmes. 1986. pap. 2.95 o.s.i. (ISBN 0-446-31360-2). Warner Bks.

Hillbilly. Eli Young. LC 84-91335. 80p. 1985. 6.95 o.p. (ISBN 0-533-06432-5). Vantage.

Hillbilly Women. Kathy Kahn. 1985. pap. 1.50 o.p. (ISBN 0-380-00171-3, 48371, Discus). Avon.

Hills of Faraway: A Guide to Fantasy. Diane Waggoner. LC 76-900. 1978. 16.95 o.p. (ISBN 0-689-10846-X, Atheneum). Macmillan.

Hillslope Analysis. Ian Statham & Brian Finlayson. LC 80-40564. (Sources & Methods in Geography Ser.). 176p. 1980. pap. text ed. 12.95 o.p. (ISBN 0-408-10622-0). Butterworth.

Hilltop Housewife Cookbook. Hazel B. Corliss. (Illus.). 258p. 1973. pap. 4.95x o.p. (ISBN 0-9600712-4-5). Sourcebook.

Hillyars & the Burtons. Henry Kingsley. (Australian Literary Reprints Ser.). 464p. 1973. 21.00x o.p. (ISBN 0-424-06490-1, Pub. by Sydney U Pr); pap. 7.50x o.p. (ISBN 0-424-06500-2). Intl Spec Bk.

Himalaya: Trekking from Sikkim to Pakistan. Ann Mitcalfe & Doug Wilson. (Illus.). 159p. 1988. pap. 39.95 o.p. (ISBN 0-340-40117-6, Pub. by Hodder & Stoughton UK). David & Charles.

Himalayan Gateway-History & Culture of Sikkim. G. Kotturan. 1983. text ed. 15.00x o.p. (ISBN 0-391-02941-X). Humanities.

Himalayan Pilgrimage: A Study of Tibetan Religion. David Snellgrove. LC 81-10540. (Illus.). 326p. (Orig.). 1981. pap. 14.95 o.p. (ISBN 0-87773-720-7, Prajna). Shambhala Pubns.

Himalayan Wonderland: Travels in Lahaul-Spiti. M. S. Gill. (Illus.). 1979. 15.95x o.p. (Pub. by Vikas India). Advent NY.

Himalayas. concise ed. Yoshikazu Skirakawa. (Illus.). 1977. 25.00 o.p. (ISBN 0-8109-1051-9). Abrams.

Himaraya Torekkingu see Trekking in the Himalayas.

Himmels Leiter. Willy Prins. 1977. text ed. 11.95 o.p. (ISBN 3-7672-0458-4). M S Rosenberg.

Hindi-English, English-Hindi Pocket Dictionary, 2 vols. 17.50 set o.p. E J Brill USA.

Hindi-English, English-Hindi Standard Illustrated Dictionary, 2 vols. Ed. by R. C. Pathak. (Illus.). Set. 50.00 o.p. Vol. 1, Hindi-Eng. Vol. 2. Eng.-Hindi, E J Brill USA.

Hindi on Trial. S. Dwivedi. 250p. 1980. text ed. 30.00x o.p. (ISBN 0-7069-1210-1, Pub by Vikas India). Advent NY.

Hindu Gods & Goddesses. Swami Harshananda. (Illus., Orig.). 1985. pap. 4.25 o.p. (ISBN 0-87481-522-3, Pub. by Ramakrishna Math Madras India). Vedanta Pr.

Hindu Metaphysics. Balbir Singh. 256p. 1986. text ed. 25.00x o.p. (ISBN 0-391-03408-1). Humanities.

Hindu Monastic Life: The Monks & Monasteries of Bhubaneswar. David M. Miller & Dorothy C. Wertz. (Illus.). 320p. 1976. 25.00x o.p. (ISBN 0-7735-0190-8, McGill Canada); pap. 9.95 o.p. (ISBN 0-7735-0247-5, McGill Canada). U of Toronto Pr.

Hindu Philosophy. Theos Bernard. 1953. Philos Lib.

Hindu Tradition. World Religions Development Center. (Illus.). 108p. 1978. pap. 6.95 o.p. (ISBN 0-89505-005-6); pap. 3.75 guide bk. o.p. (ISBN 0-89505-004-8). Tabor Pub.

Hindu View of Christ. Swami Akhikananda. (ISBN 0-8022-0012-5). Philos Lib.

Hindu Yogi Science of Breath. Yogi Ramacharaka. 88p. 1905. pap. text ed. 5.95 o.s.i. (ISBN 0-88697-047-4). Life Science.

Hinduism: An Introduction. Margaret Stutley. 192p. 1985. pap. 11.95 o.p. (ISBN 0-85030-348-6, Pub. by Thorsons UK). Weiser.

Hinduism & Buddhism. Ananda Coomaraswamy. 86p. 1960. (ISBN 0-8022-0292-6). Philos Lib.

Hinduism: Essence & Consequence. Arun Shourie. 1980. text ed. 40.00x o.p. (ISBN 0-7069-0834-1, Pub. by Vikas India). Advent NY.

Hindustan Gadar Party: A Short History. Sohan S. Josh. 1977. 9.00x o.p. (ISBN 0-8364-0089-5). South Asia Bks.

Hindustan under Free Lances: Seventeen Seventy to Eighteen Twenty. H. G. Keene. (Illus.). 276p. 1972. Repr. of 1907 ed. 27.50x o.p. (ISBN 0-7165-2128-8, BBA 03052, Pub. by Irish Academic Pr). Biblio Dist.

Hink Pink Book. Marilyn Burns. (Illus.). (gr. 1 up). 1981. 11.95 o.p. (ISBN 0-316-11744-7, Joy St Bks). Little.

Hinterland. Edmund Waterbridge. 448p. 1988. 19.95 o.p. (ISBN 0-933031-15-7). Coun Oak Bks.

Hints & Kinks. American Radio Relay League Staff. LC 33-14685. 4.00 o.s.i. (ISBN 0-87259-710-5). Am Radio.

Hints from Heloise. Heloise. LC 79-56019. 1980. 12.95 o.p. (ISBN 0-87795-260-4, Arbor Hse). Morrow.

Hints in Haiku. Norimoto Iino. LC 66-26967. 1967. (ISBN 0-8022-0770-7). Philos Lib.

Hints to Philanthropists. W. Davis. 176p. 1971. Repr. of 1821 ed. 22.50x o.p. (ISBN 0-7165-1564-4, Pub. by Irish Academic Pr Ireland). Biblio Dist.

Hints Toward a Select & Descriptive Bibliography of Education. G. Stanley Hall & John M. Mansfield. LC 72-10907. xx, 151p. 1973. Repr. of 1886 ed. 48.00x o.p. (ISBN 0-8103-3176-4). Gale.

Hip Disorders in Infants & Children. Ed. by Stanley M. Chung. LC 81-1549. (Illus.). 396p. 1981. text ed. 40.00 o.p. (ISBN 0-8121-0706-3). Lea & Febiger.

Hip Pocket Guide to Mexico, Belize, Guatemala & the French Antilles. Ed. by Philippe Gloaguen & Pierre Josse. (Collier World Traveler Ser.). (Illus.). 192p. 1985. pap. 6.95 o.p. (ISBN 0-02-097020-X, Collier). Macmillan.

Hip: Proceedings of the 10th Open Scientific Meeting of the Hip Society,1982. The Hip Society. LC 73-7515. (V10). (Illus.). 255p. 1982. 56.00 o.p. (ISBN 0-8016-0064-2). Mosby.

Hip: Proceedings of the 11th Open Scientific Meeting of the Hip Society, 1983. text ed. Ed. by The Hip Society. (Illus.). 368p. 1983. 57.00 o.p. (ISBN 0-8016-0074-X). Mosby.

Hip: Proceedings of the 12th Open Scientific Meeting of the Hip Society 1982. The Hip Society. 1984. 59.00 o.p. (ISBN 0-8016-0079-0). Mosby.

Hippies: A Study of Their Drug Habits & Sexual Customs in India. Tribhuwan Kapur. 200p. 1981. text ed. 20.00x o.p. (ISBN 0-7069-1368-X, Pub. by Vikas India). Advent NY.

Hippo Jogs for Health. J Reinach. Ed. by Ruth L. Perle. LC 77-16320. (Illus.). (gr. k-2). 1978. 2.95 o.p. (ISBN 0-03-042026-1). H Holt & Co.

Hippo Learns His Name. Rod Hunt. (Little Stories Ser.). (Illus.). 32p. (ps-k). 1987. 5.95 o.p. (ISBN 0-09-167220-1, Pub. by Century Hutchinson). David & Charles.

Hippo Leaves Home. Roger Hargreaves. LC 81-84546. (Illus.). 32p. (ps-1). 1982. 3.95 o.p. (ISBN 0-448-12317-7, G&D). Putnam Pub Group.

Hippocampus. Ed. by Robert L. Isaacson & Karl H. Pribram. Incl. Vol. 1, Structure & Developmemnt. 436p (ISBN 0-306-37535-4); Vol. 2, Neurophysiology & Behavior. 464p (ISBN 0-306-37536-2). LC 75-28121. (Illus.). 1975. 55.00 ea. o.p. (Plenum Pr). Plenum Pub.

Hippolytus. David Rudkin. (Orig.). 1980. pap. text ed. 9.50x o.p. (ISBN 0-435-23780-2). Heinemann Ed.

Hippopotame a Mange la Maitresse. Mike Thaler. (Illus.). 32p. (Fr.). (ps-3). 1982. pap. 1.95 o.p. (ISBN 0-380-81273-8, 81273-8, Camelot). Avon.

Hippo's Tips on Hips. David N. Bruskin. (Story Bus Subseries: City Bus). (Illus.). 10p. (ps-2). 1988. bds. 14.95 o.p. (ISBN 1-55929-011-0). Bound Fun Inc.

Hiram Powers & His Ideal Sculpture. Donald M. Reynolds. LC 76-23685. (Outstanding Dissertations in the Fine Arts - American Ser.). (Illus.). 1977. Repr. of 1975 ed. lib. bdg. 76.00 o.p. (ISBN 0-8240-2720-5). Garland Pub.

Hiroshige. Isaburo Oka. Tr. by Stanleigh H. Jones. LC 81-84836. (Great Japanese Art Ser.). (Illus.). 48p. 1982. 22.95 o.p. (ISBN 0-87011-509-X). Kodansha.

Hiroshige: A Shoal of Fishes. Ando Hiroshige. (Illus.). 54p. 1981. 14.95 o.p. (ISBN 0-87099-237-6, Co-pub. by Viking). Metro Mus Art.

Hiroshige's Woodblock Prints. Edward F. Strange. 1984. 16.75 o.p. (ISBN 0-8446-6097-3). Peter Smith.

Hiroshima Joe. Martin Booth. LC 85-30747. 442p. 1986. 17.95 o.p. (ISBN 0-87113-056-4). Atlantic Monthly.

Hiroshima, Mon Amour. Marguerite Duras. Tr. by Richard Seaver from Fr. (Illus., Text for the film). 1969. pap. 7.95 o.p. (ISBN 0-394-17227-2, E284, Ever). Grove.

His Battalion & Live until Dawn: Contemporary Russian Writing. Vasil Bykov. Tr. by Jennifer Woodhouse & Robert Woodhouse. 412p. 1982. 19.95 o.p. (ISBN 0-7022-1605-4). U of Queensland Pr.

His Butler's Story. Edward Limonov. Ed. by Fred Jordan. Tr. by Judson Rosengrant from Rus. 352p. 1987. 17.95 o.s.i. (ISBN 0-394-55607-0). Grove.

His Irish Connection. Andre J. Kehoe. (Illus.). 1980. 8.50 o.p. (ISBN 0-682-49575-1, Banner). Exposition-Phoenix.

His Lordship's Patronage: Offices of Profit in Colonial Maryland. Donnell M. Owings. 214p. 1953. 10.00 o.s.i. (ISBN 0-686-36830-4). Md Hist.

His Majesty's Agent. David Shahar. Tr. by Dalya Bilu. LC 80-7940. (Helen & Kurt Wolff Bks.). 416p. 1980. 14.95 o.p. (ISBN 0-15-140356-2). HarBraceJ.

His Majesty's Opposition, Seventeen Fourteen to Eighteen Thirty. Archibald S. Foord. LC 79-14245. 1979. Repr. of 1964 ed. lib. bdg. 42.50x o.p. (ISBN 0-313-21974-5, FOHM). Greenwood.

His Master's Voice. Stanislaw Lem. Tr. by Michael Kandel. LC 82-47668. (Helen & Kurt Wolff Bk.). 228p. 1983. 12.95 o.p. (ISBN 0-15-140360-0). HarBraceJ.

His Name Shall Be Joseph: Ancient Prophecies of the Latter-Day Seer. Joseph F. McConkie. 240p. 1980. 9.95 o.p. (ISBN 0-89036-152-5). Hawkes Pub Inc.

His Name Was Not Listed. B. Vassilyev. 293p. 1978. 7.95 o.p. (ISBN 0-8285-1067-9, Pub. by Progress Pubs USSR). Imported Pubns.

His Nameless Love. V. Tyayanov. 357p. 1974. 7.95 o.p. (ISBN 0-8285-1081-4, Pub. by Progress Pubs USSR). Imported Pubns.

His Only Son Our Lord. Kent S. Knutson. LC 66-13051. (Orig.). 1966. pap. 6.50 o.p. (ISBN 0-8066-9351-7, 10-3040, Augsburg). Augsburg Fortress.

His Own Man: Essays in Honour of Arthur Reginald Marsden Lower. Ed. by Welf H. Heick & Roger Graham. 1974. 7.50x o.p. (ISBN 0-7735-0212-2, McGill Canada). U of Toronto Pr.

His Promises. Nellie Britt. 50p. 1987. 8.95 o.p. (ISBN 0-682-40355-5). Exposition-Phoenix.

His Servants Speak: Statements by Latter-day Saint Leaders on Contemporary Topics. R. Clayton Brough. LC 75-17101. 298p. 1975. 10.95 o.p. (ISBN 0-88290-054-4). Horizon Utah.

His Stubborn Love. Joyce Landorf. pap. 3.95 o.p. (ISBN 0-310-27122-3, 9991P). Zondervan.

His Toy, His Dream, His Rest. John Berryman. 317p. 1968. 6.50 o.p. (ISBN 0-374-17028-2). FS&G.

Hispanic Furniture: An American Collection from the Southwest. Sali Katz. (Illus.). 1985. 27.95 o.p. (ISBN 0-8038-3064-5). Hastings.

Hispanic Studies in Honor of Alan D.Deyermond: A North American Tribute. Ed. by John S. Miletich. 1986. 28.00x o.p. (ISBN 0-317-65344-X). Hispanic Seminary.

Hispanico. J. M. Sanchez-Perez. LC 73-86548. 1974. 5.00 o.p. (ISBN 0-682-47818-0). Exposition-Phoenix.

Hispano-Classical Translations: Printed Between 1482 & 1699. Theodore S. Beardsley, Jr. Ed. by J. Koren. LC 72-107356. (Duquesne Philological Ser.: No. 12). 1970. text ed. 15.00x o.p. (ISBN 0-8207-0115-7). Humanities.

Hispanoamerica Moderna. Frederick S. Richard. (Illus.). 276p. (Span.). 1972. pap. text ed. 9.95 o.p. (ISBN 0-15-536110-4, HC). HarBraceJ.

Histamine: Mechanisms of Regulation of the Biogenic Amines Level in the Tissues with Special Reference to Histamine. Ed. by C. Maslinski. LC 72-95941. 370p. 1974. 64.50 o.p. (ISBN 0-12-787052-0). Acad Pr.

Histocompatibility Antigens. Ed. by B. Parham & J. S. Stominger. (Receptors & Recognition Series B.: Vol. 14). 350p. 1982. 62.00 o.p. (ISBN 0-412-22410-0, NO. 6713, Pub. by Chapman & Hall). Routledge Chapman & Hall.

Histoenzymology of the Endocrine Gland. L. Arvy. 1971. 135.00 o.p. (ISBN 0-08-015649-5). Pergamon.

Histoire D'Amour. Jean Giono. (Illus.). 60p. 1969. 25.00 o.p. (ISBN 0-686-53968-0). French & Eur.

Histoire de Canada, de Son Eglise et De Ses Missions. E. Ch. Brasseur De Bourbourg. (Canadiana Avant 1867: No. 4). 1968. 44.40x o.p. (ISBN 90-2796-333-9). Mouton.

Histoire De France. Henri Grimal & Lucien Moreau. (Illus.). (gr. 8-10). 1969. pap. text ed. 1.00 o.p. (ISBN 0-88345-062-3, 17758). Prentice ESL.

Histoire de France illustree. J. Beauregard. 1968. 19.75 o.p. (ISBN 0-08-013198-0); pap. 9.25 o.p. (ISBN 0-08-013197-2). Pergamon.

Histoire de la Revolution Francaise: Livres I a VIII, Vol. 1. Michelet. 1568p. 41.50 o.p. (ISBN 0-686-56541-X). Schoenhof.

Histoire de la Revolution Francaise: Livres IX a XXI-Tableau Chronologique, Vol. 2. Michelet. 1696p. 42.95 o.p. (ISBN 0-686-56542-8). Schoenhof.

Histoire de l'Empereur. facsimile ed. Honore De Balzac. (Illus.). 1970. 29.95 o.p. (ISBN 0-686-53878-1). French & Eur.

Histoire de l'Imprimerie. Paul Dupont. 1164p. (Fr.). Date not set. Repr. of 1854 ed. text ed. 99.36x o.p. (ISBN 0-576-72401-7, Pub. by Gregg Intl Pubs England). Gregg Intl.

Histoire de l'Imprimerie en France au XVe et au XVIe Siecle, 4 vols. Anatole Claudin. (Illus., Fr.). Set. 540.00 o.p. (ISBN 0-8115-0031-4). Kraus Repr.

Histoire De Piaf see Piaf.

Histoire du Capitalism see History of Capitalism, 1500-1980.

Histoire du Livre en France depuis les Temps les Plus Recules Jusqu'en, 1789. Edmond Werdet. 2048p. (Fr.). Date not set. Repr. of 1862 ed. text ed. 248.40x o.p. (ISBN 0-576-72404-1, Pub. by Gregg Intl Pubs England). Gregg Intl.

Histoire et Absolu: Essai Sur Kierkegaard. Colette. 19.95 o.p. (ISBN 0-686-54575-3). French & Eur.

Histoire et Commerce des Colonies Angloises Dans L'amerique Septentrionale, (Londres, 1755) Georges M. Butel-Dumont. (Canadiana Avant 1867: No. 5). 1966. 24.40x o.p. (ISBN 90-2796-325-8). Mouton.

Histoires. Jacques Prevert. 1965. 8.95 o.p. (ISBN 0-685-23898-9). Schoenhof.

Histological & Cytological Typing of Neoplastic Diseases of Haematopoietic & Lymphoid Tissues. G. Mathe & H. Rappaport. (World Health Organization: International Histological Classification of Tumours Ser.: No. 14). (Illus.). 45p. 1976. 52.00 o.p. (ISBN 92-4-176014-1, 70-1-014-20); incl. slides 139.00 o.p. (ISBN 0-89189-126-9, 70-1-014-00). Am Soc Clinical.

Histological Studies of the Human Thyroid Gland. S. Sugiyama. (Advances in Anatomy, Embryology & Cell Biology Ser.: Vol. 39, Pt. 3). (Illus.). 1967. pap. 18.90 o.p. (ISBN 0-387-03767-5). Springer-Verlag.

Histological Techniques. M. Gabe. Tr. by R. E. Blackith & A. Kovoor. (Illus.). 1976. 65.80 o.p. (ISBN 0-387-90162-0). Springer-Verlag.

Histological Techniques for Electron Microscopy. 2nd ed. Daniel C. Pease. 1965. 53.50 o.p. (ISBN 0-12-548456-9). Acad Pr.

Histological Typing of Bone Tumours. F. Schajowicz et al. (World Health Organization: International Histological Classification of Tumours Ser.: No. 6). (Illus.). 1972. incl. slides 125.00 o.p. (ISBN 0-89189-110-2, 70-1-006-00). Am Soc Clinical.

Histological Typing of Breast Tumours. 2nd. ed. R. W. Scarff & H. Torloni. (World Health Organization: International Histological Classification of Tumours Ser.: No. 2). (Illus.). 1977. 27.00 o.p. (ISBN 0-89189-111-0, 70-1-002-20); incl. slides 102.00 o.p.; slides 75.00 o.p. Am Soc Clinical.

Histological Typing of Endocrine Tumours. E. D. Williams & R. E. Siebenmann. (World Health Organization: No. 23). 33.50 o.p. (ISBN 0-686-95504-8, 70-1-023-20); 118.00 o.p. (ISBN 0-686-99516-3). Am Soc Clinical.

Histological Typing of Female Genital Tract Tumours. (World Health Organization: International Histological Classification of Tumours Ser.: No. 13). (Illus.). 1975. 52.00 o.p. (ISBN 92-4-176013-3, 70-1-013-20); incl. slides 139.00 o.p. (ISBN 0-89189-127-7, 70-1-013-00). Am Soc Clinical.

Histological Typing of Gastric & Oesophageal Tumors. K. Oota. (World Health Organization: International Histological Classification of Tumours Ser.: No. 18). (Illus.). 1977. text ed. 33.00 o.p. (ISBN 92-4-176018-4, 70-1-018-20). Am Soc Clinical.

Histological Typing of Intestinal Tumours. B. C. Morson. (International Histological Classification of Tumors Ser.: No. 15). (Illus.). 69p. 1976. text ed. 56.00 o.p. (ISBN 92-4-176015-X, 70-1-015-20, World Health Organization). Am Soc Clinical.

Histological Typing of Odontogenic Tumours, Jaw Cysts & Allied Lesions. J. J. Pindborg & I. R. Kramer. (World Health Organization: International Histological Classification of Tumours Ser.: No. 5). (Illus.). 1971. incl. slides 118.00 o.p. (ISBN 0-89189-115-3, 70-1-005-00). Am Soc Clinical.

Histological Typing of Ovarian Tumours. S. F. Serov & R. F. Scully. (World Health Organization: International Histological Classification of Tumours Ser.: No. 9). (Illus.). 1973. 38.50 o.p. (ISBN 0-89189-117-X, 70-1-009-20); incl. slides 118.00 o.p. (ISBN 0-89189-118-8, 70-1-009-00). Am Soc Clinical.

Histological Typing of Salivary Gland Tumours. (World Health Organization: International Histological Classification of Tumours Ser.: No. 7). (Illus.). 1972. incl. slides 51.00 o.p. (ISBN 0-89189-119-6, 70-1-007-00). Am Soc Clinical.

Histological Typing of Skin Tumours. R. E. Ten Seldam & E. B. Helwig. (World Health Organization: International Histological Classification of Tumours Ser.: No.12). (Illus.). 1977. 73.50 o.p. (ISBN 9-2417-6012-5, 70-1-012-20); incl. slides 166.50 o.p. (ISBN 0-89189-128-5, 70-1-012-00). Am Soc Clinical.

Histological Typing of Testis Tumours. F. K. Mostofi. (World Health Organization: International Histological Classification of Tumours Ser.: No. 16). (Illus.). 1976. pap. text ed. 62.50 o.p. (ISBN 92-4-176016-8, 70-1-016-20). Am Soc Clinical.

Histological Typing of Thyroid Tumours. C. Hedinger. (World Health Organization: International Histological Classification of Tumours Ser.: No. 11). (Illus.). 1974. 20.00 o.p. (ISBN 92-4-176011-7, 70-1-011-20); incl. slides 51.00 o.p. (ISBN 0-89189-120-X, 70-1-011-00). Am Soc Clinical.

Histological Typing of Tumors of the Central Nervous System, No. 21. K. J. Zulch. (WHO Ser.). 66p. 1980. 34.00 o.p. (ISBN 92-4-176021-4, 70-1-021-20); with bk. & slide 143.50 o.p. (ISBN 0-89189-131-5, 70-1-021-00). Am Soc Clinical.

Histological Typing of Tumors of the Liver, Biliary Tract & Pancreas. J. B. Gibson. (World Health Organization: International Histological Classification of Tumours Ser.: No. 20). (Illus.). 1978. text ed. 42.00 o.p. (ISBN 92-4-176020-6, 70-1-020-20). Am Soc Clinical.

Histological Typing of Tumours of the Eye & its Adnexa. L. E. Zimmerman & L. H. Sobin. (World Health Organization: International Histological Classification of Tumors: No. 24). (Illus.). 82p. 31.50 o.p. (ISBN 0-686-95509-9, 70-1-024-20); text ed. 111.50 incl. slides o.p. (70-1-024-00). Am Soc Clinical.

Histological Typing of Upper Respiratory Tract Tumors. K. Shanmugaratnam. (World Health Organization: International Histological Classification of Tumours Ser.: No. 19). (Illus.). 1978. text ed. 62.50 o.p. (ISBN 92-4-176019-2, 70-1-019-20). Am Soc Clinical.

Histology & Cytology: Functional Medical Laboratory Manual. Stanley L. Lamberg & Robert Rothstein. (Illus.). 1978. 15.95 o.p. (ISBN 0-87055-272-4). AVI.

Histology: Cell & Tissue Biology. 5th ed. Ed. by Leon Weiss & Lambert Lansing. (Illus.). 1220p. 1983. 61.75 o.p. (ISBN 0-444-00716-4, Biomedical Pr). Elsevier.

Histology of the Fowl. R. D. Hodges. 1974. 130.50 o.p. (ISBN 0-12-351350-2). Acad Pr.

Histology of the Human Eye. Michael J. Hogan et al. LC 78-135327. (Illus.). 1971. write for info. o.p. (ISBN 0-7216-4720-0). Saunders.

Histology Review. Fred J. Roisen & Linda Hsu. (Basic Science Review Bks.). 1975. 16.95 o.p. (ISBN 0-87488-219-2). Med Exam.

Histones & Other Nuclear Proteins. Harris Busch. 1965. 54.00 o.p. (ISBN 0-12-147656-1). Acad Pr.

Histopathology of Non-Hodgkin Lymphomas: Kiel Classification. K. Lennert. (Illus.). 130p. 1981. 48.00 o.p. (ISBN 0-387-10445-3). Springer-Verlag.

Historia de la Inquisicion. I. Grigulevich. 414p. (Span.). 1980. 8.95 o.p. (ISBN 0-8285-1813-0, Pub. by Progress Pubs USSR). Imported Pubns.

Historia de la Isla de Cuba. Carlos M. Sterling & Manuel M. Sterling. (Illus.). 392p. (Span.). (gr. 12 up). 1976. pap. 8.95 o.p. (ISBN 0-88345-251-0). Prentice ESL.

Historia del Descubrimiento y Exploracion De Latinoamerica. I. P. Maguidovich. 396p. (Span.). 1979. 7.45 o.p. (ISBN 0-8285-1440-2, Pub. by Progress Pubs USSR). Imported Pubns.

Historia Histrionica: An Historical Account of the English Stage. James Wright. Bd. with Roscius Anglicanus: An Historical Review of the Stage. John Downes. LC 70-170465. (English Stage Ser.: Vol. 38). 1974. lib. bdg. 61.00 o.p. (ISBN 0-8240-0621-6). Garland Pub.

Historia Naturalis of Pliny. Joyce Whalley. (Illus.). 48p. 1984. 17.95 o.p. (ISBN 0-905209-21-4, Pub. by Victoria & Albert Mus UK). Faber & Faber.

Historian & the Computer: A Practical Guide. Edward Shorter. (Illus.). 160p. 1975. pap. 2.95x o.p. (ISBN 0-393-00732-4). Norton.

Historian's Conscience: The Correspondence of Arnold J. Toynbee & Columba Cary-Elwes, Monk of Ampleforth. Ed. by Christian B. Peper. LC 85-47952. 750p. 1986. 29.95 o.p. (ISBN 0-8070-5000-8). Beacon Pr.

Historian's Introduction to Early American Music. Richard Crawford. (Illus.). 1980. pap. 4.00 o.p. (ISBN 0-912296-44-5, Dist. by U Pr of Va). Am Antiquarian.

Historians of Medieval India: Studies in Indo-Muslim Historical Writing. Peter Hardy. LC 81-23724. v, 146p. 1982. Repr. of 1966 ed. lib. bdg. 35.00x o.p. (ISBN 0-313-23452-3, HAHM). Greenwood.

Historiarum Adversum Paganos Libri, Bk. 1. Paulus Orosius. Ed. by C. Zangemeister. (Corpus Scriptorum Ecclesiasticorum Latinorum Ser: Vol. VII). Repr. of 1882 ed. 50.00 o.p. (ISBN 0-384-43720-6). Johnson Repr.

Historias Extranas de Brujeria. Roger Elwood. Tr. by George Lockward from Eng. 112p. (Span.). 1974. pap. 1.95 o.p. (ISBN 0-89922-028-2). Edit Caribe.

Historic Architecture in Mississippi. 3rd ed. Mary W. Crocker. LC 72-92483. (Illus.). 256p. 1982. 17.50 o.p. (ISBN 0-87805-022-1). U Pr of Miss.

Historic Architecture of the Caribbean. David Buisseret. (Orig.). 1980. pap. text ed. 17.50x o.p. (ISBN 0-435-98131-5). Heinemann Ed.

Historic Buildings: Monographs Published since 1970. Mary Vance. (Architecture Series: Bibliography A 1461). 169p. 1985. pap. 18.75 o.p. (ISBN 0-89028-551-9). Vance Biblios.

Historic Buildings of Massachusetts. Scribner's, Charles, & Sons Staff. LC 76-12600. 1976. 14.95 o.s.i. (ISBN 0-684-14567-7, ScribT). Scribner.

Historic Country Hotels of England: A Select Guide. Wendy Arnold. 1985. 19.95 o.p. (ISBN 0-03-004132-5); pap. 11.95 o.p. (ISBN 0-03-004133-3). H Holt & Co.

Historic Country House Hotels 1987: Great Britain & Ireland. rev. ed. Sigourney Welles & Jill Darbey. (Illus.). 179p. 1987. pap. 11.95 o.p. (ISBN 0-88742-103-2). Globe Pequot.

Historic Country Inns of California. Jim Crain. LC 77-727. 170p. 1980. pap. 6.95 o.p. (ISBN 0-87701-208-3). Chronicle Bks.

Historic Devices, Badges, & War-Cries. Fanny M. Palliser. LC 68-18030. (Illus.). 440p. 1971. Repr. of 1870 ed. 51.00x o.p. (ISBN 0-8103-3381-3). Gale.

Historic Dress of the Old West. Ernest L. Reedstrom. (Illus.). 128p. 1987. 24.95 o.p. (ISBN 0-7137-1529-4, Pub. by Blandford Pr England). Sterling.

Historic Hotels of London. Arnold. 19.95 o.p. (ISBN 0-03-007303-0). H Holt & Co.

Historic Hotels of London. Wendy Arnold. LC 85-27074. 96p. 1986. 11.95 o.s.i. (ISBN 0-03-007304-9). H Holt & Co.

Historic House Museums. Laurence V. Coleman. LC 71-175318. (Illus.). xii, 200p. 1973. Repr. of 1933 ed. 43.00x o.p. (ISBN 0-8103-3118-7). Gale.

Historic Houses, Castles & Gardens: Great Britain & Ireland, 1987. (Illus.). 235p. (Orig.). 1987. pap. 11.95 o.p. (ISBN 0-935161-80-5). Hunter Pub NY.

Historic Houses, Castles & Gardens in Great Britain & Ireland, 1988. (Illus.). 235p. (Orig.). 1988. pap. 12.95 o.p. (ISBN 1-55650-013-0). Hunter Pub NY.

Historic Houses, Castles & Gardens in France. (Illus.). 376p. (Orig.). 1987. pap. 15.95 o.p. (ISBN 0-317-59323-4). Hunter Pub NY.

Historic Huntsville: A City of New Beginnings. Elise H. Stephens & Sarah Shouse. LC 84-21599. (Illus.). 216p. 1984. 22.95 o.p. (ISBN 0-89781-096-1). Windsor Pubns Inc.

Historic Models of Early America, & How to Make Them. C. J. Maginley. LC 47-11432. (Illus.). (gr. 4-6). 1947. 5.95 o.p. (ISBN 0-15-234689-9, HJ). HarBraceJ.

Historic Models of Early America: & How to Make Them. C. J. Maginley. LC 47-11432. (Illus.). (gr. 4-6). 1966. pap. 0.60 o.p. (ISBN 0-15-640371-4, VoyB). HarBraceJ.

Historic Ninepins. John Timbs. LC 68-22057. 360p. 1969. Repr. of 1869 ed. 34.00x o.p. (ISBN 0-8103-3539-5). Gale.

Historic Organs in France. Ch. W. Lindow. Tr. by Homer D. Blanchard. LC 80-138201. (Little Organ Books Ser.: No. 1). (Illus.). 1980. pap. 21.00 o.p. (ISBN 0-930112-03-2). Organ Lit.

Historic Preservation. James M. Fitch. (Illus.). 448p. 1982. text ed. 44.50 o.p. (ISBN 0-07-021121-3). McGraw.

Historic Preservation. 339p. 1984. 35.00 o.p. (ISBN 0-318-03920-6, 268). PA Bar Inst.

Historic Preservation in Foreign Countries: France, England, Ireland, the Netherlands, & Denmark, Vol. 1. Anthony Dale. Ed. by Robert E. Stipe. (Illus.). 153p. (Orig.). 1984. members 12.00 o.p. (ISBN 0-911697-00-4); 14.00 o.p. US ICOMOS.

Historic Preservation Law & Tax Planning for Old & Historic Buildings. National Trust for Historic Preservation in the United States & American Law Institute-American Bar Association Committee for Continuing Professional Education. LC 87-107412. (ALI-ABA Course of Study Materials Ser.). Date not set. price not set o.p. Am Law Inst.

Historic Preservation: Monographs. Mary Vance. (Architecture Series: Bibliography A 1460). 105p. 1985. pap. 15.25 o.p. (ISBN 0-89028-550-0). Vance Biblios.

Historic Preservation Plans: An Annotated Bibliography. 48p. 1976. pap. 3.95 o.p. (ISBN 0-89133-038-0). Preservation Pr.

Historic Ship Models. Wolfram Z. Mondfelt. (Illus.). 352p. 1985. 24.95 o.p. (ISBN 0-8069-5732-8). Sterling.

Historic Spots in California. 2nd rev. ed. Mildred B. Hoover et al. (Illus.). 1966. 19.50 o.p. (ISBN 0-8047-0079-6). Stanford U Pr.

Historic Texas Hotels & Country Inns I. Sally Ross & Linda Johnson. 1982. 8.95 o.p. (ISBN 0-89015-322-1). Eakin Pr.

Historic White Plains. John Roesch. LC 75-45366. (Illus.). 1976. Repr. of 1939 ed. 11.95 o.p. (ISBN 0-916346-16-1). Harbor Hill Bks.

Historic Whitman. Joseph J. Rubin. LC 72-1067. 416p. 1973. 32.00x o.s.i. (ISBN 0-271-01117-3). Pa St U Pr.

Historica de la Sociedad Sovietica. V. Lelchuk. 429p. (Span.). 1977. 5.45 o.p. (ISBN 0-8285-1477-1, Pub. by Progress Pubs USSR). Imported Pubns.

Historical Account of the Belief in Witchcraft in Scotland. Charles K. Sharpe. LC 74-8196. 268p. 1974. Repr. of 1884 ed. 48.00x o.p. (ISBN 0-8103-3590-5). Gale.

Historical & Cultural Agencies & Museums in Illinois, 1985. Congress of Illinois Historical Societies & Museums. 1985. pap. 2.00 o.p. (ISBN 0-912226-16-1). Ill St Hist Soc.

Historical & Patriotic Subjects, Vol. II. Ed. by Walter H. Rubsamen. (Ballad Opera Ser.). 1974. lib. bdg. 61.00 o.p. (ISBN 0-8240-0901-0). Garland Pub.

Historical Archaeology. Ivor Noel-Hume. (Illus.). 384p. 1975. pap. 5.95 o.p. (ISBN 0-393-00783-9, N783, Norton Lib). Norton.

Historical Aspects of Organic Evolution. Philip G. Fothergill. 455p. 1953. (ISBN 0-8022-0522-4). Philos Lib.

Historical Atlas & Chronology of County Boundaries, 1788-1980, 5 vols. Smith Center for the History of Cartography Staff & John H. Long. 1984. Set. lib. bdg. 475.00 o.p. (ISBN 0-8161-0431-X, Hall Library); Vol. 1 - Delaware, Maryland, New Jersey, Pennsylvania. lib. bdg. 99.00 o.p. (ISBN 0-8161-0449-2); Vol. 2 - Illinois, Indiana, Ohio. lib. bdg. 99.00 o.p. (ISBN 0-8161-0450-6); Vol. 3 - Michigan & Wisconsin. lib. bdg. 99.00 o.p. (ISBN 0-8161-0451-4); Vol. 4 - Iowa & Missouri. lib. bdg. 99.00 o.p. (ISBN 0-8161-0452-2); Vol. 5 - Minnesota, North Dakota, South Dakota. lib. bdg. 99.00 o.p. G K Hall.

Historical Atlas of Alabama. Donald B. Dodd. LC 73-36. (Illus.). 173p. 1974. 12.50 o.p. (ISBN 0-8173-5226-0). U of Ala Pr.

Historical Atlas of Latin America: Political, Geographic, Economic, Cultural. rev. ed. A. Curtis Wilgus. LC 66-30784. Orig. Title: Latin America in Maps. (Illus.). 1967. Repr. of 1943 ed. 22.50x o.p. (ISBN 0-8154-0256-2). Cooper Sq.

Historical Background of the Dead Sea Scrolls. Cecil Roth. 96p. 1959. (ISBN 0-8022-1383-9). Philos Lib.

Historical Catalogue of Printed Editions of the English Bible: 1525-1961. A. S. Herbert. 589p. 1968. 40.00 o.s.i. (ISBN 0-686-87735-7). A Wofsy Fine Arts.

Historical Commentary on St. Paul's Epistle to the Galatians. William M. Ramsay. (William M. Ramsay Library Ser.). 1979. pap. 6.95 o.p. (ISBN 0-8010-7680-3). Baker Bk.

Historical Consciousness. Date not set. (ISBN 0-8052-3841-7). Random.

Historical Cost Indexes, 1986. 6th ed. Means, R. S., Company, Inc. Staff. Ed. by Dean Entwistle. 20p. 1985. pap. 16.95 o.p. (ISBN 0-87629-011-X). R S Means.

Historical Criticism & Theological Interpretation of Scripture: Towards a Hermeneutic of Consent. Peter Stuhlmacher. Tr. & intro. by Roy A. Harrisville. LC 76-62606. 96p. 1977. pap. 3.25 o.p. (ISBN 0-8006-1258-2, 1-1258, Fortress). Augsburg Fortress.

Historical Directory of Minnesota Homes for the Aged. Ethel McClure. LC 68-65927. 25p. 1968. pap. 1.00 o.p. (ISBN 0-87351-042-9). Minn Hist.

Historical Farms & Agricultural Museum: A Bibliography. Mary Vance. (Architecture Ser.: A 1381). 5p. 1985. 2.00 o.p. (ISBN 0-89028-391-5). Vance Biblios.

Historical Film Catalog, 1894-1915. 2nd ed. 1979. pap. 2.50 o.p. (ISBN 0-913986-00-3). Renovare Co.

Historical Geography of Canada: A Selected Bibliography. Thomas A. Rumney. (Public Administration Ser.: P 1760). 34p. 1985. 5.25 o.p. (ISBN 0-89028-560-8). Vance Biblios.

Historical Geography of England & Wales. Ed. by R. A. Dodgshon & R. A. Butlin. 1978. 63.50 o.p. (ISBN 0-12-219250-8); pap. 29.50 o.p. (ISBN 0-12-219252-4). Acad Pr.

Historical Guide to Utah Ghost Towns. Stephen L. Carr. 166p. 1972. (ISBN 0-914740-01-6); pap. 7.95 o.p. (ISBN 0-914740-02-4). Western Epics.

Historical Index to the Pickering Papers. Massachusetts Historical Society Staff. Repr. of 1896 ed. 40.00 o.p. (ISBN 0-384-35810-1). Johnson Repr.

Historical Interpretation. J. J. Bagley. Incl. Vol. 1. Sources of English Medieval History, 1066-1540. 285p. 1973. 10.00 o.p. (ISBN 0-312-38045-3); Vol. 2. Sources of English History, 1540 to Present Day. 296p. 1973. 10.00 o.p. (ISBN 0-312-38080-1). LC 72-85263. (Illus.). 1973. St Martin.

Historical Introduction to Modern Psychology. 3rd ed. Gardner Murphy & Joseph K. Kovach. 526p. 1972. text ed. 27.00 net o.p. (ISBN 0-15-536245-3, HC). HarBraceJ.

Historical Investigation & New Testament Faith. Ferdinand Hahn. Ed. by Edgar Krentz. Tr. by Robert Maddox from Ger. LC 82-48547. 112p. 1983. pap. 7.50 o.p. (ISBN 0-8006-1691-X, 1-1691, Fortress). Augsburg Fortress.

Historical Jurisprudence: An Introduction to the Systematic Study of the Development of Law. Guy C. Lee. xvi, 517p. 1981. Repr. of 1900 ed. lib. bdg. 37.50x o.p. (ISBN 0-8377-0810-9). Rothman.

Historical Lights, 2 vols. 3rd ed. Charles E. Little. LC 68-27175. 966p. 1968. Repr. of 1886 ed. Set. 44.00x o.p. (ISBN 0-8103-3186-1). Gale.

Historical Manuscript Depositories in Pennsylvania. Irwin Richman. LC 65-65225. 73p. 1965. 5.95 o.p. (ISBN 0-911124-08-X). Pa Hist & Mus.

Historical Maps & Charts of China. Set. 2.00 o.p. (ISBN 0-88710-029-5). Yale Far Eastern Pubns.

Historical Museum, Moscow: Jewellery. M. Postnikova-Loseva et al. 167p. 1985. 11.95 o.p. (ISBN 0-8285-3384-9, Pub. by Aurora Pubs USSR). Imported Pubns.

Historical Musicology: A Reference Manual for Research in Music. Lincoln B. Spiess. LC 78-60147. (Musicological Studies: No. 4). xiii, 294p. 1980. Repr. of 1963 ed. lib. bdg. 45.50x o.p. (ISBN 0-313-20548-5, SPHM). Greenwood.

Historical Note-Book. E. Cobham Brewer. LC 66-23191. 1010p. 1966. Repr. of 1891 ed. 74.00x o.p. (ISBN 0-8103-0152-0). Gale.

Historical Novel. George Lukacs. 1978. Repr. of 1962 ed. text ed. 15.00x o.p. (ISBN 0-85036-068-4). Humanities.

Historical Novel & Other Essays. Brander Matthews. LC 68-30586. 336p. 1969. Repr. of 1901 ed. 30.00x o.p. (ISBN 0-8103-3218-3). Gale.

Historical Perspective on Light Infantry. Scot R. McMicheal. (Illus.). 1987. pap. 11.00 o.p. (ISBN 0-318-23827-6, 008-020-01125-8). USGPO.

Historical Plant Geography. Philip Stott. (Illus.). 192p. 1981. text ed. 39.95x o.p. (ISBN 0-04-580010-3); pap. text ed. 19.95x o.p. (ISBN 0-04-580011-1). Unwin Hyman.

Historical Reviews & Recent Advances in Perinatal Medicine. George F. Smith & Dharmapuri Vidyasagar. (Illus.). 402p. 1985. 29.50 o.p. (ISBN 81-85017-20-4). Year Bk Med.

Historical Revolution: English Historical Writing & Thought 1580-1640. F. Smith Fussner. LC 75-40916. 1976. Repr. of 1962 ed. lib. bdg. 24.75x o.p. (ISBN 0-8371-8684-6, FUHR). Greenwood.

Historical Sets, Collected Editions, & Monuments of Music: A Guide to their Contents. Anna H. Heyer. 573p. Repr. of 1969 ed. lib. bdg. 69.00 o.p. (Pub. by Am Repr Serv). Reprint Servs.

Historical Sociology. Hatry E. Barnes. (ISBN 0-8022-0063-X). Philos Lib.

Historical Studies: Selected Articles. J. J. Eastwood & F. B. Smith. 1975. pap. 10.00x o.p. (ISBN 0-522-83588-0, Pub. by Melbourne U Pr Australia). Intl Spec Bk.

Historical Studies Today. Ed. by Felix Gilbert. LC 70-163367. 480p. 1972. pap. 10.95x o.p. (ISBN 0-393-09402-2). Norton.

Historical Study of Staten Island, New York During the American Revolution see History of Staten Island, New York, During the American Revolution.

Historical Study of the Mother Tongue. Henry C. Wyld. 1969. Repr. of 1906 ed. lib. bdg. 35.00 o.p. (ISBN 0-8371-1873-5, WYMT). Greenwood.

Historical Supernovae. Ed. by D. H. Clark & F. R. Stephenson. LC 76-44364. 1977. 42.00 o.p. (ISBN 0-08-020914-9); pap. 17.25 o.p. (ISBN 0-08-021639-0). Pergamon.

Historical Topics in Algebra. National Council of Teachers of Mathematics Staff. LC 79-171459. (Illus.). 74p. 1971. pap. 5.00 o.p. (ISBN 0-87353-058-6). NCTM.

Historical Transactions, 1893 to 1943. Society of Naval Architects & Marine Engineers Staff. LC 81-6610. (Illus.). vi, 544p. 1981. Repr. of 1945 ed. lib. bdg. 60.50x o.p. (ISBN 0-313-23139-7, SOHT). Greenwood.

Historical Understanding in the Thought of Wilhelm Dilthey. Theodore Plantinga. 1980. 22.50x o.p. (ISBN 0-8020-5475-7). U of Toronto Pr.

Historical View of Hindu Astronomy. John Bentley. 316p. Repr. of 1825 ed. text ed. 32.50x o.p. Coronet Bks.

Historical Writing in England: C. 550 to C. 1307. Antonia Gransden. LC 73-3732. 634p. 1974. 75.00x o.p. (ISBN 0-8014-0770-2). Cornell U Pr.

Histories of Polybius, 2 vols. Polybius. Tr. by Evelyn S. Shuckburgh. LC 72-6204. (Indiana University Greek & Latin Classics Ser.). 1974. Repr. of 1962 ed. Set. lib. bdg. 45.00x o.p. (ISBN 0-8371-6468-0, POHP); Vol. 1. lib. bdg. 25.00 o.p. (ISBN 0-8371-6479-6, POHQ); Vol. 2. lib. bdg. 25.00 o.p. (ISBN 0-8371-6480-X, POHR). Greenwood.

Historiettes, 2 vols. Tallemant Des Reaux. Vol. 1. 39.95 o.p. (ISBN 0-686-56577-0); Vol. 2. 42.95 o.p. (ISBN 0-686-56578-9). Schoenhof.

Historism: The Rise of a New Historical Outlook. Friedrich Meinecke. 524p. 1972. 32.00 o.p. (ISBN 0-7100-7045-4). Routledge CHapman & Hall.

History. Robert Lowell. 208p. 1973. 7.95 o.p. (ISBN 0-374-17044-4); pap. 3.95 o.p. (ISBN 0-374-51288-4). FS&G.

History: A Workbook of Skill Development. Conal Furay & Michael J. Salevouris. 1979. pap. 9.95 o.p. (ISBN 0-531-05620-1). Watts.

History & Development of Advertising. Frank S. Presbrey. LC 68-8071. (Illus.). 1969. Repr. of 1929 ed. lib. bdg. 52.75x o.p. (ISBN 0-8371-0622-2, PRHA). Greenwood.

History & Development of Small Arms: British Sporting Rifle, Vol. 3. George A. Hoyem. LC 80-67532. (Illus.). 236p. 1985. 39.50 o.p. (ISBN 0-9604982-7-3). Armory Pubns.

History & Human Nature: A Philosophical Review of European History & Culture, 1750-1850. Robert C. Solomon. LC 79-1846. (Illus.). 1979. 18.95 o.p. (ISBN 0-15-140547-6). HarBraceJ.

History & Implementation of Employee Assistance Programs: A Bibliography. Mary E. Huls. (Public Administration Ser.: P 1723). 9p. 1985. 2.00 o.p. (ISBN 0-89028-493-8). Vance Biblios.

History & Memory: A Statesman's Perceptions of the Twentieth Century. Charles W. Yost. (Illus.). 1980. 14.95 o.p. (ISBN 0-393-01408-8). Norton.

History & Nature of Sociological Theory. Daniel W. Rossides. (Illus., LC 77-074382). 1978. text ed. 28.50 o.p. (ISBN 0-395-25059-5). HM.

History & Origin of Language. A. S. Diamond. 296p. 1959. (ISBN 0-8022-0395-7). Philos Lib.

History & Philosophy of Technology. Ed. by George Bugliarello & Dean B. Doner. LC 78-26846. 392p. 1979. 27.50 o.p. (ISBN 0-252-00462-0). U of Ill Pr.

History & Philosophy of the Social Sciences. Peter T. Manicas. 352p. 1987. text ed. 29.95x o.p. (ISBN 0-631-15258-X). Basil Blackwell.

History & Power: The Social Relevance of History. Harold E. Davis. LC 83-12385. 170p. 1983. lib. bdg. 26.25 o.p. (ISBN 0-8191-3412-0); pap. text ed. 12.00 o.p. (ISBN 0-8191-3413-9). U Pr of Amer.

History & Practice of Falconry. Allan Oswald. (Illus.). 129p. 12.50 o.p. (ISBN 0-87556-661-8). Saifer.

History & Religion of Israel. William L. Wardle. LC 78-11741. (Clarendon Bible, Old Testament Ser.: Vol. I). (Illus.). 1979. Repr. of 1942 ed. lib. bdg. 35.00x o.p. (ISBN 0-313-21016-0, WAHR). Greenwood.

History & Romance of the Horse. Arthur Vernon. LC 70-185379. (Illus.). xviii, 544p. 1975. Repr. of 1939 ed. 46.00x o.p. (ISBN 0-8103-3982-X). Gale.

History & Theology in Second Isaiah: A Commentary on Isaiah 35, 40-66. James D. Smart. 1965. 6.50 o.s.i. (ISBN 0-664-20647-6, Westminster). Westminster John Knox.

History & Traditions of Tikopia. Raymond Firth. 311p. 1961. text ed. 10.00x o.p. (ISBN 0-8248-0585-2). UH Pr.

History & Truth. Adam Schaff. 230p. 1976. 70.00 o.p. (ISBN 0-08-020579-8). Pergamon.

History & Truth in Hegel's Phenomenology. Merold Westphal. 1979. text ed. 15.00x o.p. (ISBN 0-391-00557-X). Humanities.

History As a Tool in Critical Interpretation: A Symposium. Ed. by Thomas F. Rugh & Erin R. Silva. LC 78-24729. 1978. pap. 2.50 o.p. (ISBN 0-8425-1291-8). Brigham.

History for Pupils with Learning Difficulties. Michael Wilson. 176p. 1985. pap. text ed. 19.95 o.s.i. (ISBN 0-340-35949-8). Princeton Bk Co.

History Highlights: Bridgewater, Massachusetts, a Commemorative Journal. Ed. by Katherine M. Doherty. LC 76-2972. (Illus.). 1976. 12.00 o.p. (ISBN 0-88492-014-3). W S Sullwold.

History in the Teaching of Physics: Proceedings. International Working Seminar on the Role of the History of Physics in Physics Education Staff. Ed. by Stephen G. Brush & Allen L. King. LC 71-188602. 128p. 1972. 10.00x o.p. (ISBN 0-87451-065-1). U Pr of New Eng.

History of Accounting in America: An Historical Interpretation of the Cultural Significance of Accounting. Gary J. Previts & Barabara D. Merino. LC 79-616. 378p. 1979. 49.95 o.p. (ISBN 0-471-05172-1, Pub by Ronald Pr). Wiley.

History of Albania: From Its Origins to the Present Day. Stefanaq Pollo & Arben Puto. (Illus.). 1980. 50.00x o.p. (ISBN 0-7100-0365-X). Routledge Chapman & Hall.

History of American Colleges & Their Libraries in the Seventeenth & Eighteenth Centuries: A Bibliographical Essay. David S. Zubatsky. (Occasional Papers: No. 140). 66p. 1979. pap. 2.00 o.p. (ISBN 0-317-58985-7). U of Ill Lib Info Sci.

History of American Economic Life. 4th ed. Edward C. Kirkland. LC 69-13070. 1969. 39.50x o.s.i. (ISBN 0-89197-214-5); pap. text ed. 19.95x o.s.i. (ISBN 0-89197-215-3). Irvington.

History of Ancient Geography: Among the Greeks & Romans from the Earliest Ages till the Fall of the Roman Empire, 2 vols. E. H. Bunbury. (Illus.). 1979. Repr. of 1879 ed. Set. text ed. 185.00x o.p. (ISBN 90-7026-511-7). Humanities.

History of Anthropology: A Research Bibliography. Robert V. Kemper & John F. Phinney. LC 76-24766. (Reference Library of Social Science: Vol. 31). 1977. lib. bdg. 29.00 o.p. (ISBN 0-8240-9911-7). Garland Pub.

History of Antisubmarine Warfare. Norman Friedman. (Illus.). 528p. 1987. 44.95 o.p. (ISBN 0-87021-274-5). Naval Inst Pr.

History of Apologetics. Avery Dulles. LC 74-107039. (Theological Resources Ser). 1971. 9.95 o.p. (ISBN 0-664-20911-4, Westminster). Westminster John Knox.

History of Architecture: Selected List of Books Published in Great Britain from 1974-1984. Mary Vance. (Architecture Ser., Bibliography: A 1479). 80p. 1985. pap. 12.00 o.p. (ISBN 0-89028-609-4). Vance Biblios.

History of Art As a History of Ideas. Max Dvorak. (Illus.). 256p. (Ger.). 1984. 27.95x o.p. (ISBN 0-7100-9969-X). Routledge Chapman & Hall.

History of Art for Young People. 2nd, rev., & enl. ed. H. W. Janson & Samuel Cauman. Rev. by Anthony F. Janson. (Illus.). 440p. 22.50 o.p. (ISBN 0-8109-0700-3). Abrams.

History of Art: From Twenty-Five Thousand B.C. to the Present. Marshall B. Davison. LC 83-16110. (Random House Library of Knowledge). (Illus.). 112p. (gr. 5 up). 1984. lib. bdg. 9.99 o.s.i. (ISBN 0-394-95181-6, BYR); pap. 8.95 o.s.i. (ISBN 0-394-85181-1). Random.

History of Australian Vegetation. J. M. Smith. 216p. 1982. text ed. 18.50 o.p. (ISBN 0-07-072953-0). McGraw.

History of Babeuf's Conspiracy for Equality. Philippe Buonarroti. Tr. by Bronterre O'Brien. LC 64-7661. 1965. Repr. of 1836 ed. 49.50x o.s.i. (ISBN 0-678-00087-5). Kelley.

History of Baldwin County Georgia. Anna M. Cook. LC 78-13226. 1978. Repr. of 1925 ed. 25.00 o.s.i. (ISBN 0-87152-279-9). Reprint.

History of Banking Theory in Great Britain & the United States. Lloyd W. Mints. 1945. lib. bdg. 20.00x o.s.i. (ISBN 0-226-53047-7). U of Chicago Pr.

History of Booksellers, the Old & the New. Henry Curwen. LC 68-19656. (Illus.). 490p. 1968. Repr. of 1873 ed. 37.00x o.p. (ISBN 0-8103-3300-7). Gale.

History of Brazil. 2nd ed. E. Bradford Burns. 1980. 65.00 o.p. (ISBN 0-231-04748-7); pap. 18.50x o.p. (ISBN 0-231-04749-5). Columbia U Pr.

History of British Empirical Sociology. Raymond Kent. 228p. 1981. 41.50 o.p. (ISBN 0-566-00415-1). Gower Pub Co.

History of Building. Jack Bowyer. 275p. 1973. pap. text ed. 12.35x o.p. (ISBN 0-258-96854-0, Pub. by Granada England). Gower Pub Co.

History of Burma. Godfrey E. Harvey. 1967. lib. bdg. 35.00x o.p. (ISBN 0-88254-839-5, Octagon). Hippocrene Bks.

History of Canada: An Annotated Bibliography. Ed. by Dwight L. Smith. LC 82-24307. (Clio Bibliography Ser.: No. 10). 327p. 1983. lib. bdg. 64.00 o.p. (ISBN 0-87436-047-1). ABC-Clio.

History of Capitalism, 1500-1980. Michel Beaud. Tr. by Tom Dickman & Anny Lefebvre. LC 83-42522. Orig. Title: Histoire du Capitalism. 288p. 1983. 22.00 o.p. (ISBN 0-85345-626-7); pap. 10.00 o.p. (ISBN 0-85345-627-5). Monthly Rev.

History of Caricature. Bohun Lynch. LC 74-6414. (Illus.). 184p. 1975. Repr. of 1927 ed. 35.00x o.p. (ISBN 0-8103-4044-5). Gale.

History of Children's Reading & Literature. Alec Ellis. 1968. pap. 60.00 o.p. (ISBN 0-08-012586-7). Pergamon.

History of China's Internal Loan Issues: Shanghai, 1934. Eduard A. Kann. Bd. with China's Currency Reform, 1941. Lin Yu Shen. LC 78-74317. (Modern Chinese Economy Ser.: Vol. 26). 288p. 1980. lib. bdg. 40.00 o.p. (ISBN 0-8240-4274-3). Garland Pub.

History of Chinese Dance. Wang Kefen. (Illus.). 150p. (Orig.). 1985. pap. 9.95 o.p. (ISBN 0-8351-1186-5). China Bks.

History of Chinese Educational Institutions, Vol. I: To the End of the Five Dynasties (A. D. 960) H. S. Galt. 1951. 30.00 o.p. E J Brill USA.

History of Christian Doctrine. Ed. by Hubert Cunliffe-Jones & Benjamin Drewery. LC 79-21689. 616p. 1980. 14.95 o.p. (ISBN 0-8006-0626-4, 1-626, Fortress). Augsburg Fortress.

History of Christian Thought: From Apostolic Times to Saint Augustine. John R. Willis. LC 76-16237. 1976. 16.00 o.p. (ISBN 0-682-48583-7, University). Exposition-Phoenix.

History of Christianity, 2 vols. Ed. by Clyde L. Manschreck & Ray C. Petry. pap. text ed. 45.00 o.p. (ISBN 0-8010-7067-8). Baker Bk.

History of Citrus in the Riverside Area. Ester Klotz & H. Lawton. (Illus.). 55p. 1969. pap. 3.50 o.p. Riverside Mus.

History of Civilization: Prehistory to 1715, Vol. I. 6th ed. Crane Brinton et al. (Illus.). 608p. 1984. pap. text ed. (ISBN 0-13-389866-0). P-H.

History of Civilization: Vol. 1, Prehistory to 1715. 5th ed. Crane Brinton et al. 1976. pap. text ed. (ISBN 0-13-389007-4); study guide 5.95 o.p. P-H.

History of Civilization: 1648 to the Present, Vol. II. 6th ed. Crane Brinton & John B. Christopher. (Illus.). 608p. 1984. pap. text ed. (ISBN 0-13-389874-1). P-H.

History of Codes & Ciphers in the United States During World War I. Ed. by Wayne G. Barker. (Cryptographic Ser.). (Illus.). 1979. lib. bdg. 28.80 o.p. (ISBN 0-89412-103-0); pap. 20.80 o.p. (ISBN 0-89412-031-X). Aegean Park Pr.

History of Codes & Ciphers in the United States Prior to World War I. Ed. by Wayne G. Barker. (Cryptographic Ser.). 1978. lib. bdg. 24.80 o.p. (ISBN 0-89412-104-9); pap. 16.80 o.p. (ISBN 0-89412-026-3). Aegean Park Pr.

History of Communist Party of the U. S. S. R., Past & Present. Rudolf Schlesinger. 432p. 1977. text ed. 30.00x o.p. (ISBN 0-86125-099-0, Pub. by Orient Longman Ltd India). Apt Bks.

History of Comparative Anatomy: From Aristotle to the Eighteenth Century. F. J. Cole. LC 75-12173. (Illus.). 544p. 1975. pap. 8.50 o.p. (ISBN 0-486-60224-9). Dover.

History of Composing Machines see Mechanism of the Linotype.

History of Counseling Psychology. John M. Whiteley. 1980. 7.25 o.p. (ISBN 1-55620-019-6, 71008C). Am Assn Coun Dev.

History of Croatia. Stephen Gazi. LC 72-96110. (Illus.). 284p. 1973. (ISBN 0-8022-2108-4). Philos Lib.

History of Currency in the United States. rev. ed. Alonzo B. Hepburn. LC 67-27411. xxiv, 573p. 1967. Repr. of 1924 ed. 45.00x o.s.i. (ISBN 0-678-00311-4). Kelley.

History of Davis & Canaan Valley. Pearle G. Mott. 1972. 15.00 o.p. (ISBN 0-87012-117-0). McClain.

History of Dickens County: Ranches & Rolling Plains. Fred Arrington. 19.95 o.p. Eakin Pr.

History of Doll Houses. Flora G. Jacobs. LC 65-24648. 1965. pap. 14.95 o.s.i. (ISBN 0-684-14538-3, ScribT). Scribner.

History of Drag Racing. Ed. by Hot Rod Magazine Editors. (Illus.). 160p. (Orig.). 1981. pap. 8.95 o.p. (ISBN 0-8227-5066-X, Dist. by Kampmann). Petersen Pub.

History of Dress: Late Gothic Europe, 1400-1500, Vol 1. Margaret Scott. (The History of Dress Ser.). (Illus.). 256p. 1981. text ed. 65.00 o.p. (ISBN 0-391-02148-6). Humanities.

History of Dutchess County, New York: 1683-1882. James H. Smith. 808p. Date not set. Repr. of 1882 ed. deluxe ed. 60.00 o.s.i. (ISBN 0-932334-35-0). Heart of the Lakes.

History of Economic Analysis. William K. Hutchinson. LC 73-17578. (Economics Information Guide Ser.: Vol. 3). 256p. 1976. 68.00x o.p. (ISBN 0-8103-1295-6). Gale.

History of Economic Theory & Method. Robert B. Ekelund & R. H. Hebert. 1975. text ed. 35.95 o.p. (ISBN 0-07-019143-3, C). McGraw.

History of Education in Tolland, Connecticut. Suzanne Prose. (Connecticut Educational History Ser.). 1984. 1.50 o.p. (ISBN 0-317-12721-7). I N Thut World Educ Ctr.

History of England. Jasper Ridley. 331p. 1985. pap. 8.95 o.p. (ISBN 0-7102-0579-1). Routledge Chapman & Hall.

History of England. 3rd ed. David H. Willson & Stuart E. Prall. 702p. 1984. text ed. 32.95x o.p. (ISBN 0-03-062358-8). H Holt & Co.

History of England, Vol. 2. Thomas B. Macaulay. 1980. Repr. of 1906 ed. 14.95x o.p. (ISBN 0-460-00035-7, Evman). Biblio Dist.

History of England, Vol. 3. Thomas B. Macaulay. 1968. Repr. of 1906 ed. 14.95x o.p. (ISBN 0-460-00036-5, Evman). Biblio Dist.

History of England: From the Accession of James II, Vol. 1. Thomas B. Macaulay. 1980. Repr. of 1906 ed. 14.95x o.p. (ISBN 0-460-00034-9, Evman). Biblio Dist.

History of England from the Accession of Edward Sixth to the Death of Elizabeth, 1547-1603. Albert F. Pollard. LC 69-14037. 1969. Repr. of 1910 ed. lib. bdg. 20.00 o.p. (ISBN 0-8371-1026-2, POHE). Greenwood.

History of England from the Defeat of the Armada to the Death of Elizabeth, 2 vols. Edward P. Cheyney. Set. 26.00 o.p. (ISBN 0-8446-1112-3). Peter Smith.

History of England, Vol. I: The Making of England 55 B. C. to 1399. 4th ed. Lacey B. Smith. Ed. by C. W. Hollister. 320p. 1983. pap. text ed. 10.50 o.p. (ISBN 0-669-04377-X). Heath.

History of England, Vol. IV: Britain Yesterday & Today 1830 to Present. Walter L. Arnstein. 304p. 1983. pap. text ed. 11.00 o.p. (ISBN 0-669-04380-X). Heath.

History of English & Irish Glass to 1969. W. A. Thorpe. 100.00x o.p. (ISBN 0-87556-334-1). Saifer.

History of English Electoral Law in the Middle Ages. Ludwig Riess. LC 73-18151. 107p. 1973. Repr. of 1940 ed. lib. bdg. 16.50x o.p. (ISBN 0-374-96804-7, Octagon). Hippocrene Bks.

History of English Gardening, Chronological, Biographical, Literary & Critical. George W. Johnson. Ed. by John D. Hunt. LC 79-56974. (English Landscape Garden Ser.). 449p. 1982. lib. bdg. 67.00 o.p. (ISBN 0-8240-0175-3). Garland Pub.

History of English Lotteries. John Ashton. LC 67-23945. (Illus.). 374p. 1969. Repr. of 1893 ed. 40.00x o.p. (ISBN 0-8103-3250-7). Gale.

History of English Opera. Eric W. White. LC 83-1599. (Illus.). 472p. 1983. 59.95 o.p. (ISBN 0-571-10788-5). Faber & Faber.

History of English Romanticism in the Eighteenth Century. Henry A. Beers. 1968. pap. 5.50 o.p. (ISBN 0-486-21940-2). Dover.

History of Engraving & Etching: From the Fifteenth Century to the Year 1914. A. M. Hind. (Illus.). 15.25 o.p. (ISBN 0-8446-2256-7). Peter Smith.

History of Esthetics. rev. & en. ed. Katherine E. Gilbert & Helmut Kunn. 613p. 1956. Repr. of 1956 ed. lib. bdg. 85.00 o.p. (ISBN 0-8495-2103-3). Am Inst Psych.

History of Exeter, N.H. 2nd, rev. ed. Charles H. Bell. LC 79-1226. (Illus.). 1979. Repr. of 1888 ed. 42.50 o.p. (ISBN 0-917890-14-0). Heritage Bk.

History of Fashion. rev. ed. J. Anderson Black & Madge Garland. LC 80-82797. (Illus.). 304p. 1980. 15.95 o.p. (ISBN 0-688-05835-3). Morrow.

History of Film. John L. Fell. LC 78-16203. 1979. pap. text ed. 19.95 o.p. (ISBN 0-275-64670-X, HoltC). HR&W.

History of Foreign-Language Dictionaries. R. L. Collison. (Language Library). 214p. 1982. pap. 24.95x o.p. (ISBN 0-233-97310-9). Basil Blackwell.

History of French-Canadian Literature. 2nd ed. Gerard Tougas. Tr. by Alta L. Cook from Fr. LC 76-7977. 1976. Repr. of 1966 ed. lib. bdg. 24.75x o.p. (ISBN 0-8371-8858-X, TOHF). Greenwood.

History of Gambling in England. John Ashton. LC 68-21520. 296p. 1968. Repr. of 1899 ed. 30.00x o.p. (ISBN 0-8103-3501-8). Gale.

History of Gardening in England. Alicia A. Rockley. LC 68-21522. 424p. 1969. Repr. of 1896 ed. 40.00x o.p. (ISBN 0-8103-3845-9). Gale.

History Of Genesee County, New York 1890-1982. Ed. by Mary McCully. LC 85-5431. (Illus.). 432p. 1985. deluxe ed. 35.00 o.p. (ISBN 0-932334-51-2). Heart of the Lakes.

History of Georgetown County, South Carolina. George C. Rogers, Jr. LC 70-95260. xviii, 582p. 1970. 24.95x o.p. (ISBN 0-87249-143-9). U of SC Pr.
History of Glass. Ed. by Dan Klein & Ward Lloyd. (Illus.). 288p. 75.00 o.s.i. (ISBN 0-317-54997-9). Apollo.
History of Glass in Japan. Dorothy Blair. LC 72-94022. (Illus.). 480p. 1973. 85.00 o.p. Kodansha.
History of Glass in Japan. Dorothy Blair. (Illus.). 479p. 1973. 60.00x o.p. (Corning Museum of Glass). U Pr of Va.
History of Graphic Design & Communications: A Sourcebook. Clive Ashwin. (Pembridge History of Design Ser.). 279p. 1983. 29.50 o.p. (ISBN 0-86206-005-2, Pub. by Pembridge Pr UK). Shoe String.
History of Greek Religion. 2nd ed. Martin P. Nilsson. (Orig.). 1964. pap. 4.45 o.p. (ISBN 0-393-00287-X, Norton Lib). Norton.
History of GWR Goods Wagons. A. G. Atkins et al. (Illus.). 224p. 1986. 30.95 o.p. (ISBN 0-7153-8725-1). David & Charles.
History of Hamilton County, Tennessee. James W. Livingood. 512p. 1981. 17.50 o.p. (ISBN 0-87870-204-0). Memphis St Univ.
History of Henderson, Chester, McNairy, Decatur & Hardin Counties, Tennessee. Goodspeed Publishing Company Staff. 1978. Repr. of 1886 ed. 17.50 o.p. (ISBN 0-89308-097-7). Southern Hist Pr.
History of Hollywood. Edwin Palmer. Ed. by Bruce S. Kupelnick. LC 76-52118. (Classics of Film Literature Ser.). 1978. lib. bdg. 28.00 o.p. (ISBN 0-8240-2886-4). Garland Pub.
History of Holy Russia. Gustave Dore. Tr. by Daniel Weissbort from Fr. LC 65-161410. 209p. 1971. 14.95 o.p. (ISBN 0-912050-11-X, Library Pr). Open Court.
History of Housing in the U. S., 1930-1980. Joseph B. Mason. (Illus.). 192p. 1982. 25.00x o.p. (ISBN 0-87201-365-0). Gulf Pub.
History of Hungarian Literature. Frederick Riedl. Tr. by C. A. Ginever. LC 68-26602. 306p. 1968. Repr. of 1906 ed. 40.00x o.p. (ISBN 0-8103-3221-3). Gale.
History of Israel from Alexander the Great to Bar Kochba. Henk Jagersma. Tr. by J. H. Kok. LC 85-45497. 256p. 1986. pap. 12.95 o.p. (ISBN 0-8006-1890-4, 1-1890, Fortress). Augsburg Fortress.
History of Israel in Old Testament Times. 2nd, rev. & enl. ed. Siegfried Herrmann. Tr. by John Bowden from Ger. LC 81-43092. 456p. 1981. pap. 16.95 o.p. (ISBN 0-8006-1499-2, 1-1499, Fortress). Augsburg Fortress.
History of Israel in Old Testament Times. Siegfried Herrmann. Tr. by John Bowden from Ger. LC 74-24918. 384p. 1975. 15.50x o.p. (ISBN 0-8006-0405-9, 1-405, Fortress). Augsburg Fortress.
History of Israel in the Old Testament Period. Henk Jagersma. Tr. by John Bowden. LC 82-48548. 320p. 1983. pap. 13.95 o.p. (ISBN 0-8006-1692-8, Fortress). Augsburg Fortress.
History of Italian Fascism. Federico Chabod. Tr. by Muriel Grindrod from Ital. 192p. 1975. Repr. of 1963 ed. 25.00x o.p. (ISBN 0-86527-095-3). Fertig.
History of Italian Painting. rev. ed. Frank J. Mather. Repr. of 1951 ed. lib. bdg. 48.50x o.p. (ISBN 0-8371-2534-0, MAIP). Greenwood.
History of Italian Renaissance Art. 2nd ed. Frederick N. Hartt. (Illus.). 1979. text ed. 35.95 o.p. (ISBN 0-13-392043-7). P-H.
History of Italy Seventeen Hundred to Eighteen Sixty: The Social Constraints of Political Change. Stuart Woolf. 1979. 55.00x o.p. (ISBN 0-416-80880-8, NO. 2602). Routledge Chapman & Hall.
History of Italy, Seventeen Hundred to Eighteen Sixty: The Social Constraints of Political Change. Stuart Woolf. 520p. 1986. pap. text ed. 23.00 o.p. (ISBN 0-416-80890-5, 1031). Routledge Chapman & Hall.
History of King Philip's War. Benjamin Church. LC 72-78674. 1867. 19.00 o.p. (ISBN 0-403-01937-0). Somerset Pub.
History of Lagos, Nigeria: The Shaping of an African City. Takiu Folami. (Illus.). 256p. 1982. 8.50 o.p. (ISBN 0-682-49772-X, University). Exposition-Phoenix.
History of Latin Literature, 2 vols. George A. Simcox. LC 78-113307. Repr. of 1883 ed. lib. bdg. 175.00 set o.p. (ISBN 0-8046-1204-8). Irvington.
History of Lauderdale, Tipton, Haywood & Crockett Counties. Goodspeed Publishing Company Staff. 1978. Repr. of 1886 ed. 20.00 o.p. (ISBN 0-89308-099-3). Southern Hist Pr.
History of Literary Criticism in the Renaissance. Joel E. Spingarn. LC 76-27737. 1976. lib. bdg. 27.50x o.p. (ISBN 0-8371-9025-8, SPLC). Greenwood.
History of Local Government of the United Kingdom. John J. Clarke. LC 77-23552. 1978. Repr. of 1955 ed. lib. bdg. 23.50x o.p. (ISBN 0-8371-9701-5, CLLG). Greenwood.
History of London. Robert Gray. LC 78-22605. 1979. 9.95 o.s.i. (ISBN 0-8008-3884-X); pap. 7.95 o.s.i. (ISBN 0-8008-3885-8). Taplinger.
History of Lumbering in Maine, 1861-1960. David C. Smith. 1972. 15.00 o.s.i. (ISBN 0-89101-024-6). U Maine Pr.
History of Luminescence from the Earliest Times Until 1900. E. Newton Harvey. LC 57-8124. (Memoirs Ser.: Vol. 44). (Illus.). 1980. Repr. of 1957 ed. 20.00 o.p. (ISBN 0-87169-044-6). Am Philos.
History of Magic. Richard Cavendish. LC 76-56613. (Illus.). 1980. pap. 5.95 o.s.i. (ISBN 0-8008-3887-4). Taplinger.
History of Man-Powered Flight. David A. Reay. 1977. 85.00 o.p. (ISBN 0-08-021738-9). Pergamon.
History of Mary Prince: Written by Herself. Mary Prince. 128p. 1987. pap. 8.95 o.p. (ISBN 0-86358-117-X, Pandora Pr). Routledge Chapman & Hall.
History of Mathametics. Hofmann. 1957. (ISBN 0-8022-0734-0). Philos Lib.
History of Mathematical Notations, 2 vols. Florian Cajori. Incl. Vol. 1. Notations in Elementary Mathematics. 467p. 1951. pap. 10.95 (ISBN 0-87548-154-X); Vol. 2. Notations Mainly in Higher Mathematics. 384p. 1952. 24.95 (ISBN 0-87548-172-8). (Illus.). Open Court.
History of Mediaeval Jewish Philosophy. Isaac Husik. LC 58-8533. (Temple Bks.). 1969. pap. text ed. 5.95x o.p. (ISBN 0-689-70102-0, T5, Atheneum). Macmillan.
History of Medical Group Management Association Nineteen Twenty-six to Nineteen Seventy-six. Edward B. Stevens. 135p. 1976. 8.00 o.p. (ISBN 0-317-34831-0, 100004); members 4.00 o.p. (ISBN 0-317-34832-9). Med Group Mgmt.
History of Medical Psychology. Gregory Zilboorg. 1967. pap. 5.95x o.p. (ISBN 0-393-00383-3, Norton Lib). Norton.
History of Medical Psychology. Gregory Zilboorg & George W. Henry. (Illus.). 1941. 12.50x o.p. (ISBN 0-393-01011-2, NortonC). Norton.
History of Medicine. 4th ed. Fielding H. Garrison. LC 29-3665. (Illus.). 1960. Repr. of 1929 ed. write for info. o.p. (ISBN 0-7216-4030-3). Saunders.
History of Melody. Bence Szabolcsi. 312p. Repr. of 1965 ed. lib. bdg. 49.00 o.p. (Pub. by Am Repr Serv). Reprint Servs.
History of Men's Clothing Industry-Colonial Through Modern Times. 370p. 20.00 o.p. (ISBN 0-318-19674-3). Clothing Mfrs.
History of Messianic Speculation in Israel from the First Through the Seventeenth Centuries. Abba H. Silver. 11.75 o.p. (ISBN 0-8446-2937-5). Peter Smith.
History of Metals in Colonial America. James A. Mulholland. LC 80-15130. (Illus.). xiv, 208p. 1981. text ed. 18.75 o.p. (ISBN 0-8173-0052-X); pap. text ed. 8.95 o.p. (ISBN 0-8173-0053-8). U of Ala Pr.
History of Mexican Americans in Lubbock County, Texas. Andres A. Tijerina. (Graduate Studies: No. 18). 73p. 1979. pap. 5.00 o.s.i. (ISBN 0-89672-067-5). Tex Tech Univ Pr.
History of Mexican Literature. 3rd ed. Carlos G. Pena. Tr. by Gusta B. Nance & Florene J. Dunstan. LC 68-24078. (No. 2). 552p. 1968. 19.95x o.p. (ISBN 0-87074-063-6); pap. 12.95x o.p. (ISBN 0-87074-064-4, MB2). SMU Press.
History of MGMA, Nineteen Twenty-Six to Nineteen Seventy-Six. Edwards B. Stevens. 135p. 1976. 8.00 o.p. (ISBN 0-317-34833-7, 100004); members 4.00 o.p. (ISBN 0-317-34834-5). Med Group Mgmt.
History of Mineola. Lucille Jones. 1972. 9.95 o.p. (ISBN 0-89015-024-9). Eakin Pr.
History of Miss Clarinda Cathcart & Miss Fanny Renton, 1765, 2 vols. in 1. Jean Marishall. (Flowering of the Novel, 1740-1775 Ser: Vol. 71). 1975. lib. bdg. 61.00 o.p. (ISBN 0-8240-1170-8). Garland Pub.
History of Modern Art: Painting, Sculpture, & Architecture. rev. ed. H. H. Arnason. LC 68-26863. (Illus.). 1977. 45.00 o.p. (ISBN 0-8109-0181-1). Abrams.
History of Modern Bulgarian Literature. Clarence A. Manning & Roman Smal-Stocki. LC 73-21262. 198p. 1974. Repr. of 1960 ed. lib. bdg. 27.50x o.p. (ISBN 0-8371-6130-4, MAHM). Greenwood.
History of Modern Culture. Maurice Parmelee. 1960. (ISBN 0-8022-1267-0). Philos Lib.
History of Modern Economic Analysis. Roger Backhouse. 470p. 1985. 49.95x o.p. (ISBN 0-631-14314-9). Basil Blackwell.
History of Modern Ireland: With a Sketch of Earlier Times. Giovanni Costigan. 1970. pap. text ed. write for info. o.p. (ISBN 0-02-325350-9). Macmillan.
History of Modern Thailand. B. J. Terwiel. LC 83-4089. (Histories of Southeast Asia Ser.). (Illus.). 379p. 1984. text ed. 29.95 o.p. (ISBN 0-7022-1892-8); pap. 17.95x o.p. (ISBN 0-7022-1902-9). U of Queensland Pr.
History of Mughal Architecture Akbar (1556-1605) The Age of Personality Architecture Vol. II. R. Nath. (History of Mughal Architecture Ser.: Vol. 2). (Illus.). 352p. 1985. text ed. 120.00x o.p. (ISBN 0-391-02681-X). Humanities.
History of Music & Musical Style. Homer Ulrich & Paul A. Pisk. (Illus.). 696p. 1963. text ed. 21.50 o.p. (ISBN 0-15-537720-5, HC). HarBraceJ.
History of Musical Instruments. Curt Sachs. (Illus.). 1940. 19.50x o.p. (ISBN 0-393-02068-1, NortonC). Norton.
History of My Life, Vols. 1 & 2. Giacomo Casanova. Tr. by Willard R. Trask. LC 66-22274. (Helen & Kurt Wolff Bk.). (Illus.). 679p. 1966. slipcase 10.00 o.s.i. (ISBN 0-15-141080-1). HarBraceJ.
History of My Life, Vols. 3 & 4. Giacomo Casanova. Tr. by Willard R. Trask. LC 66-22274. (Helen & Kurt Wolff Bk.). (Illus.). 704p. 1967. 10.00 o.s.i. (ISBN 0-15-141081-X). HarBraceJ.
History of My Life, Vols. 5 & 6 Combined. Giacomo Casanova. Tr. by Willard R. Trask. LC 66-22274. (Helen & Kurt Wolff Bks.). (Illus.). 1968. 10.00 o.s.i. (ISBN 0-15-141082-8). HarBraceJ.
History of My Life, Vols. 7 & 8 Combined. Giacomo Casanova. Tr. by Willard R. Trask. LC 66-22274. (Helen & Kurt Wolff Bk.). (Illus.). 1969. 10.00 o.s.i. (ISBN 0-15-141083-6). HarBraceJ.
History of My Life, Vols. 9 & 10. Giacomo Casanova. LC 66-22274. (Helen & Kurt Wolff Bks.). (Illus.). 1970. 10.00 o.s.i. (ISBN 0-15-141084-4). HarBraceJ.
History of My Life, Vols. 11 & 12 Combined. Giacomo Casanova. LC 66-22274. (Helen & Kurt Wolff Bks.). 768p. 1971. 10.00 o.s.i. (ISBN 0-15-141085-2). HarBraceJ.
History of Navajo Clans. Regina H. Lynch. write for info. o.s.i. (ISBN 0-936008-27-X). Navajo Curr.
History of Negro Education in the South: From 1619 to the Present. Henry A. Bullock. LC 67-20873. 1967. 24.50x o.s.i. (ISBN 0-674-39950-1). Harvard U Pr.
History of Negro Servitude in Illinois & of the Slavery Agitation in That State, 1719-1864. Norman D. Harris. LC 77-76855. (Illus.). 1969. 35.00 o.p. (ISBN 0-8371-1163-3, HNS&, Pub. by Negro U Pr). Greenwood.
History of New Testament Times. Robert H. Pfeiffer. LC 77-138125. 561p. 1972. Repr. of 1949 ed. lib. bdg. 23.00x o.p. (ISBN 0-8371-3559-1, PFNT). Greenwood.
History of Ohio. 2nd ed. E. H. Roseboom & F. P. Weisenberger. (Illus.). 443p. 1977. 16.95 o.s.i. (ISBN 0-318-00829-7). Ohio Hist Soc.
History of Old Sheffield Plate. Frederick Bradbury. (Illus.). 539p. 1983. Repr. of 1912 ed. 125.00 o.p. (ISBN 0-901100-03-X, Pub by JW Northend England). Seven Hills Bk Dists.
History of Our Lord As Exemplified in Works of Art; with That of His Type; St. John the Baptist; & Other Persons of the Old & New Testament, 2 vols. Anna B. Jameson. LC 92-167006. (Illus.). 942p. 1976. Repr. of 1890 ed. Set. 70.00x o.p. (ISBN 0-8103-4304-5). Gale.
History of Palestine & Syria to the Macedonian Conquest. Albert T. Olmstead. LC 73-152599. 1972. Repr. of 1931 ed. lib. bdg. 35.00x o.p. (ISBN 0-8371-6034-0, OLHP). Greenwood.
History of Parliamentary Elections & Electioneering: From the Stuarts to Queen Victoria. Joseph Grego. LC 73-141755. (Illus.). 504p. 1974. Repr. of 1892 ed. 70.00x o.p. (ISBN 0-8103-4030-5). Gale.
History of Pennsylvania, from Its Discovery by Europeans to the Declaration of Independence in 1776. Thomas F. Gordon. LC 66-25100. 1967. Repr. of 1829 ed. 25.00 o.s.i. (ISBN 0-87152-036-2). Reprint.
History of Pepsi Cola MBC. Wythe M. Hull, Jr. LC 85-73444. 76p. 1986. 17.00 o.p. (ISBN 0-89227-113-2). Commonwealth Pr.
History of Peru. Clements R. Markham. LC 68-8069. (Illus.). 1969. Repr. of 1892 ed. lib. bdg. 26.00x o.p. (ISBN 0-8371-0159-X, MAHP). Greenwood.
History of Pharmacy & the Pharmaceutical Industry. Patrice Boussel et al. (Illus.). 284p. 1983. 79.95 o.p. Thieme Med Pubs.
History of Philosophical Ideas in America. William H. Werkmeister. LC 80-24507. xvi, 599p. 1981. Repr. of 1949 ed. lib. bdg. 52.50x o.p. (ISBN 0-313-22743-8, WEHI). Greenwood.
History of Philosophical Systems. Vergilius Ferm. 662p. (ISBN 0-8022-0491-0). Philos Lib.
History of Philosophy in Australia. S. A. Grave. LC 83-23321. (Scholar's Library). 252p. 1985. text ed. 37.50 o.p. (ISBN 0-7022-1697-6). U Of Queensland Pr.
History of Philosophy: Modern Philosophy: Descartes to Leibnitz, Vol. 4. Frederick J. Copleston. pap. 5.50 o.p. (ISBN 0-385-01633-6, Im). Doubleday.
History of Physiology: Proceedings of the 28th International Congress of Physiological Sciences, Budapest 1980. Ed. by E. Schultheisz. LC 80-42207. (Advances in Physiological Sciences Ser.: Vol. 21). (Illus.). 210p. 1981. 36.00 o.p. (ISBN 0-08-027342-4). Pergamon.
History of Playing Cards & a Bibliography of Cards & Gaming. Catherine P. Hargrave. (Illus.). 18.00 o.p. (ISBN 0-8446-2205-2). Peter Smith.
History of Playing Cards, with Anecdotes of Their Use in Conjuring, Fortune-Telling, & Card-Sharking. Ed. by Ed S. Taylor. LC 72-89739. 1973. pap. 7.95 o.p. (ISBN 0-8048-1026-5). C E Tuttle.
History of Plene Spelling. Weinberg. Date not set. 15.00 o.p. Ktav.
History of Polish Emigration & Polish Communities in North & South Americas in the 19th & 20th Century. Jagiellonian University Staff. 525p. 9.00 o.s.i. (ISBN 0-317-36709-9). Kosciuszko.
History of Political Philosophy. 2nd ed. Leo Strauss & Joseph Cropsey. LC 80-26907. xii, 850p. 1981. pap. text ed. 21.00x o.s.i. (ISBN 0-226-77690-5). U of Chicago Pr.
History of Political Theories, 3 vols. William A. Dunning. Repr. of 1902 ed. Vol. 1 Ancient & Medieval,1902. 120.00 ea. o.p. (ISBN 0-384-13340-1). Vol. 2 From Luther To Montesquieu, 1905. Vol. 3, From Rousseau To Spencer, 1920. Johnson Repr.
History of Psychology. Thomas H. Leahey. (Illus.). 1980. text ed. 34.00 o.p. (ISBN 0-13-391755-X). P-H.
History of Psychology & Psychiatry. A. A. Roback. LC 61-10613. 435p. 1961. 8.95 o.p. (ISBN 0-8022-1354-5). Philos Lib.
History of Public Libraries in Great Britain. Thomas Kelly. 1977. 33.00 o.p. (ISBN 0-85365-239-2). Nichols Pub.
History of Punch. M. H. Spielmann. LC 69-16069. 608p. 1969. Repr. of 1895 ed. 53.00x o.p. (ISBN 0-8103-3553-0). Gale.
History of Religious Sectarianism in Russia (1860s-1917) A. I. Klibanov. Ed. by Stephen P. Dunn. LC 81-12180. (Illus.). 380p. 1982. 65.00 o.s.i. (ISBN 0-08-026794-7). Pergamon.
History of Renaissance Architecture. Bruce Allsop. LC 59-2405. 228p. Repr. cancelled o.s.i. (ISBN 0-403-04103-1). Somerset Pub.
History of Ridgefield, Connecticut. George L. Rockwell. LC 79-21199. 1979. Repr. of 1927 ed. 29.50 o.p. (ISBN 0-916346-37-4). Harbor Hill Bks.
History of Rock 'n Roll. Ritchie Yorke. (Illus.). 176p. (Orig.). (YA) (gr. 9-12). 1977. pap. 5.95 o.p. (ISBN 0-413-37640-0, NO. 0038). Routledge Chapman & Hall.
History of Rockland County N. Y. Ed. by David Cole. (Illus.). 555p. Repr. 45.00 o.p. (ISBN 0-911183-24-8). Rockland County Hist.
History of Rome. Mommsen. 576p. (ISBN 0-8022-1139-9). Philos Lib.
History of Royal Blue Express Services. R. C. Anderson & G. G. Frankis. (Illus.). 218p. 1985. 25.95 o.p. (ISBN 0-7153-8654-9). David & Charles.
History of Russia. 2nd ed. John T. Lawrence. 1962. pap. 1.50 o.p. (MW1318, Ment). NAL.
History of San Bernardino & San Diego Counties. Wallace W. Elliot. (Illus.). 204p. 18.00 o.p. (ISBN 0-935661-02-6); 3 copies or more 14.00 ea. o.p. Riverside Mus Pr.
History of San Bernardino & San Diego Counties. W. W. Elliott. (Illus.). 204p. 1965. Repr. of 1883 ed. 20.00 o.p. (ISBN 0-935661-01-8). Riverside Mus Pr.
History of Science, One: Ancient Science Through the Golden Age of Greece. George Sarton. 1970. pap. 7.95 o.p. (ISBN 0-393-00525-9, Norton Lib). Norton.
History of Science, Two: Hellenistic Science & Culture in the Last Three Centuries B.C. George Sarton. 1970. pap. 5.95 o.p. (ISBN 0-393-00526-7, Norton Lib). Norton.
History of Scotland. 2nd ed. R. Mitchison. (Illus.). 468p. 1982. 29.95x o.p. (ISBN 0-416-33220-X, NO. 3630); pap. 14.95x o.p. (ISBN 0-416-33080-0, NO. 3631). Routledge Chapman & Hall.
History of Scottish Poetry. David Irving. Ed. by J. A. Carylye. 1971. Repr. of 1861 ed. 37.00 o.p. (ISBN 0-384-25960-X, F426). Johnson Repr.
History of Sexuality, Vol. 1: An Introduction. Michel Foucault. Tr. by Robert Hurley from Fr. LC 78-51804. 1978. 8.95 o.p. (ISBN 0-394-41775-5). Pantheon.
History of Song. Dennis W. Stevens. LC 82-11781. 491p. 1982. Repr. of 1960 ed. lib. bdg. 41.55x o.p. (ISBN 0-313-22933-3, STHS). Greenwood.
History of Soviet Russia. 2nd ed. M. K. Dziewanowski. (Illus.). 432p. 1985. pap. text ed. (ISBN 0-13-392143-3). P-H.

History of Staten Island, New York, During the American Revolution. Harlow McMillen. Orig. Title: Historical Study of Staten Island, New York During the American Revolution. (Illus.). 1976. pap. 3.00 o.p. (ISBN 0-686-20332-1). Staten Island.

History of Steamboating on the Upper Missouri River. William E. Lass. LC 62-14663. (Landmark Ed. Ser.). (Illus.). xvi, 215p. 1962. 19.95x o.p. (ISBN 0-8032-0100-1). U of Nebr Pr.

History of Surnames of the British Isles: A Concise Account of Their Origin, Evolution, Etymology & Legal Status. Cecil H. Ewen. LC 68-30597. 528p. 1968. Repr. of 1931 ed. 45.00x o.p. (ISBN 0-8103-3124-1). Gale.

History of Taste: An Account of the Revolutions of Art Criticism & Theory in Europe. Frank P. Chambers. LC 76-136057. (Illus.). 1971. Repr. of 1932 ed. lib. bdg. 41.50x o.p. (ISBN 0-8371-5207-0, CHHT). Greenwood.

History of Tattooing & Its Significance, with Some Account of Other Forms of Corporal Marking. Wilfrid D. Hambly. LC 73-174052. (Illus.). 346p. 1975. Repr. of 1925 ed. 56.00x o.p. (ISBN 0-8103-4024-0). Gale.

History of Taxation & Expenditure in the Western World. Carolyn Webber & Aaron Wildavsky. 653p. 1986. 24.45 o.p. (ISBN 0-671-54617-1). S&S.

History of Technology: Fourth Annual Volume, 1979. Ed. by A. Rupert Hall & Norman Smith. 192p. 1979. 35.00 o.p. (ISBN 0-7201-0916-7). Mansell.

History of Tennessee Illustrated, History of Thirty East Tenn. Counties. Goodspeed Publishing Company Staff. 526p. 1979. Repr. of 1887 ed. 35.00 o.p. (ISBN 0-89308-188-4). Southern Hist Pr.

History of the Alphabet. David Diringer & H. Freeman. 78p. 1978. casebound ed. 35.00x o.p. (ISBN 0-905418-12-3, Pub. by Gresham England); pap. 10.95 o.p. (ISBN 0-905418-13-1). State Mutual Bk.

History of the American Economy. 3rd ed. Ross M. Robertson. (Illus.). 1973. text ed. 18.95 o.p. (ISBN 0-15-536501-0, HC). HarBraceJ.

History of the American Economy. 4th ed. Ross M. Robertson & Gary M. Walton. 586p. 1979. text ed. 21.95 o.p. (ISBN 0-15-536504-5, HC). HarBraceJ.

History of the American Film. Christopher Durang. 1978. pap. 1.95 o.p. (ISBN 0-380-39271-2, Bard). Avon.

History of the American People. Farhat J. Ziadeh & I. Freiji. (Arabic.). 1947. 38.00 o.p. (ISBN 0-691-04584-4). Princeton U Pr.

History of the American Theatre, 1700-1950. Glenn Hughes. 560p. 1951. 9.00 o.p. (ISBN 0-573-69015-4). French.

History of the Ancient World, 2 Vols. Mikhail Rostovtsev. Tr. by J. D. Duff from Rus. LC 73-109834. 1971. Repr. of 1926 ed. lib. bdg. 55.75x o.p. (ISBN 0-8371-4325-X, ROAW). Greenwood.

History of the Arab State of Zanzibar. Norman R. Bennett. (Studies in African History). 1978. 19.95x o.p. (ISBN 0-416-55080-0, NO. 2814). Routledge Chapman & Hall.

History of the Bank of England & Its Financial Services to the State. Eugen Philippovich Von Philippsberg. Tr. by Christabel Meredith. LC 79-1588. 1980. 22.50 o.p. (ISBN 0-88355-893-9). Hyperion Conn.

History of the Baptists in Missouri. R. S. Duncan. 1981. Repr. of 1882 ed. 44.00 o.p. (ISBN 0-686-77695-X). Church History.

History of the Boers in South Africa. George M. Theal. LC 79-81378. (Illus.). 1970. Repr. of 1887 ed. 35.00x o.p. (ISBN 0-8371-1661-9, THB&, Pub. by Negro U Pr). Greenwood.

History of the British Secret Service. Richard Deacon. 512p. 6.95 o.p. (ISBN 0-586-05116-3). Academy Chi Pubs.

History of the Brooklyn Art Association with an Index of Exhibitions. Marlor. 1970. 50.00 o.p. (ISBN 0-686-43147-2). Apollo.

History of the Christmas Card. George Buday. LC 74-174012. (Tower Bks.). (Illus.). xxiii, 330p. 1972. Repr. of 1954 ed. 50.00x o.s.i. (ISBN 0-8103-3931-5). Gale.

History of the Church of Blackburnshire. John E. Wallis. (Church Historical Society London, New Ser.: No. 7). Repr. of 1932 ed. 40.00 o.p. (ISBN 0-8115-3131-7). Kraus Repr.

History of the Colonization of Africa by Alien Races. Harry H. Johnston. LC 66-26825. 1966. Repr. of 1913 ed. 26.50 o.p. (ISBN 0-8154-0122-1). Cooper Sq.

History of the Colored Race in America, Containing Also Their Ancient & Modern Life in Africa, the Origin & Development of Slavery, the Civil War. 2nd ed. William T. Alexander. LC 68-55867. (Illus.). 1970. Repr. of 1887 ed. lib. bdg. 28.00x o.p. (ISBN 0-8371-0283-9, ALC&, Pub. by Negro U Pr). Greenwood.

History of the Common Law of England. Matthew Hale. Ed. by Charles M. Gray. LC 70-155856. (Classics of British Historical Literature Ser.). 1973. pap. text ed. 2.45x o.s.i. (ISBN 0-226-31305-0, P428, Phoen). U of Chicago Pr.

History of the Communist Party of the United States. William Z. Foster. LC 68-30821. 1968. Repr. of 1952 ed. lib. bdg. 30.50x o.p. (ISBN 0-8371-0423-8, FOHC). Greenwood.

History of the Conquest of Mexico. abridged ed. William H. Prescott. Ed. by C. Harvey Gardiner. LC 66-20592. 1966. lib. bdg. 12.00x o.s.i. (ISBN 0-226-67999-3). U of Chicago Pr.

History of the Contemporary Jews from 1900 to the Present. Solomon Grayzel. LC 60-15542. (Temple Books). 1969. pap. text ed. 4.95x o.p. (ISBN 0-689-70080-6, T3, Atheneum). Macmillan.

History of the Creeds. 2nd ed. Francis J. Badcock. (Church Historical Society, London, Ser.: No. 35). Repr. of 1938 ed. 55.00 o.p. (ISBN 0-8115-3158-9). Kraus Repr.

History of the Croatian People, 2 vols. Francis R. Preveden. (Illus.). Vol. 1, 1962, 256pp. Vol. 2, 1956, 152pp. (ISBN 0-8022-2014-2). Philos Lib.

History of the Cure of Souls. John T. McNeill. LC 76-62926. (Orig.). 1977. pap. 10.53i o.p. (ISBN 0-06-065540-2, RD-212). HarpR.

History of the Defense Systems Management College: Center of Excellence in Acquistion Management Education & Research. David D. Acker. Ed. by Catherine M. Clark. LC 85-73923. (Illus.). 470p. 1986. 28.00 o.p. (ISBN 0-318-21293-5, S/N 008-020-01077-4). USGPO.

History of the Ecumenical Movement: 1517 to 1948. 2nd ed. Ed. by Ruth Rouse & Stephen C. Neill. 1967. 12.50 o.s.i. (ISBN 0-664-20751-0, Westminster). Westminster John Knox.

History of the English Language. George L. Brook. 1964. pap. 3.95 o.p. (ISBN 0-393-00248-9, Norton Lib). Norton.

History of the English Language. Oliver F. Emerson. LC 70-145520. 432p. 1971. Repr. of 1909 ed. 45.00x o.p. (ISBN 0-8103-3666-9). Gale.

History of the English People. Elie Halevy. 1987. Vol. I. pap. 13.95 o.p. (ISBN 0-7448-0067-6, Pub. by Routledge UK). Routledge Chapman & Hall.

History of the English People in the Nineteenth Century: The Liberal Awakening, Vol. 2. Elie Halevy. 324p. 1987. pap. 13.95 o.p. (ISBN 0-7448-0069-2, Ark Paperbacks). Routledge Chapman & Hall.

History of the English People in the Nineteenth Century, Vol. 3: The Triumph of Reform. Elie Halevy. 385p. 1988. pap. text ed. 14.95 o.p. (ISBN 0-7448-0070-6, Pub. by Ark Paperbks). Routledge Chapman & Hall.

History of the Expedition to Jerusalem, 1095-1127. Foucher Of Chartres. Ed. by Sr. Harold S. Fink. 1972. pap. text ed. 6.95x o.p. (ISBN 0-393-09423-5). Norton.

History of the First Dakota-District of the Evangelical-Lutheran Synod of Iowa & Other States. C. G. Eisenberg. Tr. by Anton H. Richter from Ger. LC 82-17645. 268p. (Orig.). 1983. lib. bdg. 30.75 o.p. (ISBN 0-8191-2798-1); pap. text ed. 14.50 o.p. (ISBN 0-8191-2799-X). U Pr of Amer.

History of the First New York Regiment 1775-1783. T. W. Egly, Jr. (Illus.). 388p. 1981. 19.95 o.p. (ISBN 0-914339-04-4). P E Randall Pub.

History of the Ford Rotunda 1934-1962-Dearborn's Pride of the Past. Thomas Burke. 1977. 4.50 o.p. (ISBN 0-682-48730-9). Exposition-Phoenix.

History of the Formation of the Constitution of the United States of America, 2 vols. George Bancroft. 1983. Repr. of 1882 ed. Set. lib. bdg. 85.00x o.p. (ISBN 0-8377-0338-7). Rothman.

History of the Forty-Third Infantry Division. Joseph Zimmer. (Divisional Ser.: No. 23). (Illus.). 96p. 1982. Repr. of 1946 ed. 22.50 o.p. (ISBN 0-89839-068-0). Battery Pr.

History of the Free Churches. Paul Sangster. (Illus.). 224p. 1984. 30.95 o.p. (Pub. by W Heinemann Ltd). David & Charles.

History of the French Language. Urban T. Holmes & Alexander H. Schutz. 1938. 12.00 o.p. (ISBN 0-8196-0218-3). Biblo.

History of the French Revolution. Jules Michelet. Ed. by Gordon Wright. Tr. by Charles Cocks. (Classical European Historians Ser.). 1967. lib. bdg. 25.00x o.s.i. (ISBN 0-226-52332-2). U of Chicago Pr.

History of the Great Trains. Christopher Cook. LC 77-73046. (Illus.). 1977. 14.95 o.p. (ISBN 0-15-140930-7). HarBraceJ.

History of the Great War, 4 vols. John Buchan. 1987. Set. 165.00 o.p. (ISBN 0-933852-77-0). Nautical & Aviation.

History of the Greek & Roman Theater. rev. ed. Margaret Bieber. (Illus.). 360p. 1980. 63.00 o.p. (ISBN 0-691-03521-0); pap. 18.95 o.p. (ISBN 0-691-00212-6). Princeton U Pr.

History of the Greek World: 323-146 B.C. 2nd rev. ed. Max Cary. (History of the Greek & Roman World Ser). (Illus.). 446p. 1972. pap. 16.95x o.p. (ISBN 0-416-70200-7, NO. 2125). Routledge Chapman & Hall.

History of the Highland Clearances: Vol. I, Agrarian Transformation & the Evictions 1746-1886. Eric Richards. (Illus.). 532p. 1982. pap. 18.00 o.p. (ISBN 0-7099-2249-3, Pub. by Croom Held Ltd). Routledge Chapman & Hall.

History of the Highland Clearances: Vol. 2: Emigration, Protest, Reasons. Eric Richards. LC 81-208122. 528p. 1985. 43.00 o.p. (ISBN 0-7099-2259-0, Pub. by Croom Helm Ltd). Routledge Chapman & Hall.

History of the Human Heart; or, the Adventures of a Young Gentleman, 1749. Ed. by Michael F. Shugrue. (Flowering of the Novel, 1740-1775 Ser: Vol. 26). 1975. lib. bdg. 61.00 o.p. (ISBN 0-8240-1125-2). Garland Pub.

History of the ICC from Panacea to Palliative. Ari Hoogenboom & Olive Hoogenboom. (Norton Essays in American History Ser.). 224p. 1976. text ed. 10.00x o.p. (ISBN 0-393-05565-5); pap. text ed. 3.95x o.p. (ISBN 0-393-09204-6). Norton.

History of the Iconoclastic Controversy. Edward J. Martin. (Church Historical Society London N. S. Ser.: No. 2). Repr. of 1930 ed. 55.00 o.p. (ISBN 0-8115-3126-0). Kraus Repr.

History of the Library Association 1877-1977. W. A. Munford. (Library Association Centenary Volume). 1976. 22.50 o.p. (ISBN 0-85365-488-3). Nichols Pub.

History of the Lumber Business at Davis, West Virginia. Ben Thompson. 1974. 3.00 o.p. (ISBN 0-87012-188-X). McClain.

History of the Microscope. Reginald S. Clay & T. H. Court. (Illus.). 60.00 o.p. (ISBN 0-87556-605-7). Saifer.

History of the Modern British Chemical Industry. D. W. Hardie & J. Davidson Pratt. 1966. 29.00 o.p. (ISBN 0-08-011687-6); pap. 14.25 o.p. (ISBN 0-08-011686-8). Pergamon.

History of the Modern Movement: Art, Architecture, Design. Kurt Rowland. LC 73-7117. (Illus.). 240p. 1973. pap. 22.50 o.p. (ISBN 0-442-27172-7). Hennessey.

History of the Modern Taste in Gardening with Journals of Visits to Country Seats. Horace Walpole. Ed. by John D. Hunt. LC 79-56986. (English Landscape Garden ser.). 158p. 1982. lib. bdg. 24.00 o.p. (ISBN 0-8240-0166-4). Garland Pub.

History of the Navy of the United States, 2 vols. in 1. James Fenimore Cooper. LC 79-104432. Repr. of 1839 ed. lib. bdg. 39.00 o.p. (ISBN 0-8398-0277-3). Irvington.

History of the New Testament in Plain Language. Clayton Harrop. 192p. 1984. 10.99 o.p. (ISBN 0-8499-0432-3, 0432-3). Word Bks.

History of the Niagara River. Archer B. Hulbert. LC 78-12656. (Illus.). 1978. Repr. of 1908 ed. 19.50 o.p. (ISBN 0-916346-29-3). Harbor Hill Bks.

History of the Nineteenth Century in Caricature. Arthur B. Maurice & Frederick T. Cooper. LC 73-125160. (Illus.). 1970. Repr. of 1904 ed. 27.50x o.p. (ISBN 0-8154-0342-9). Cooper Sq.

History of the Public School Kindergarten in North Carolina. Ed. by Rebecca Murray. 91p. 1974. pap. text ed. 7.95x o.p. (ISBN 0-8422-0414-8). Irvington.

History of the Rhode Island Combat Units in the Civil War, 1861-1865. Harold R. Barker. (Illus.). 338p. 1964. 12.95 o.p. (ISBN 0-917012-44-5). RI Pubns Soc.

History of the Ridiculous Extravagancies of Monsieur Oufle Occasion'd by His Reading Books Treating of Magick, the Black-Art Demoniacks... & Other Superstitious Practices. Abbe L. Bordelon. LC 76-170524. (Foundations of the Novel Ser.: Vol. 17). 1973. lib. bdg. 61.00 o.p. (ISBN 0-8240-0529-5). Garland Pub.

History of the Rise & Progress of the Arts of Design in the U. S. William Dunlap. Ed. by Rita Weiss. (Illus.). Repr. of 1834 ed. Vol. 1. 15.00 o.p. (ISBN 0-8446-0598-0); Vol. 2, Pt. 1. 15.00 o.p.; Vol. 2, Pt. 2. 15.00 o.p. Peter Smith.

History of the Roman Law During the Middle Ages, Vol. 1. Friedrich K. Savigny. Tr. by E. Cathcart. LC 78-72146. 1979. Repr. of 1829 ed. 38.50 o.p. (ISBN 0-88355-815-7). Hyperion Conn.

History of the Roman World: 753-146 BC. 4th ed. H. H. Scullard. xiv, 480p. 1980. 35.00x o.p. (ISBN 0-416-71480-3, NO. 2901); pap. 16.95x o.p. (ISBN 0-416-71490-0, NO. 2900). Routledge Chapman & Hall.

History of the Romanian Communist Party. Robert R. King. (Publication Ser.: No. 233). 206p. (Orig.). 1980. pap. 8.95x o.p. (ISBN 0-8179-7332-X). Hoover Inst Pr.

History of the Royal Army Veterinary Corps. 1919-1961. J. Clabby. (Illus.). 244p. 1963. 35.00x o.p. (ISBN 0-87556-053-9). Saifer.

History of the Shoshone-Paiutes of the Duck Valley Indian Reservation. Whitney McKinney. LC 82-23240. (Illus.). 176p. 1982. 15.95 o.p. (ISBN 0-935704-10-8). Howe Brothers.

History of the Sixteen Karmapas of Tibet. Karma Thinley. Ed. by David Stott. LC 80-179. (Illus.). 150p. 1980. pap. write for info. o.p. (ISBN 0-87773-716-9, Prajna). Shambhala Pubns.

History of the Society of Jesus. William V. Bangert. LC 78-188687. (Original Studies Composed in English Ser.: No. 3). (Illus.). 570p. 1972. 14.75 o.p. (ISBN 0-912422-05-X); pap. 9.00 o.p. (ISBN 0-912422-23-8). Inst Jesuit.

History of the Study of Landforms; or, the Development of Geomorphology, Vol. 2: The Life & Work of William Morris Davis. R. J. Chorley et al. 874p. 1973. 75.00x o.p. (ISBN 0-416-26890-0, NO. 2139). Routledge Chapman & Hall.

History of the Telescope. Henry C. King. (Illus.). 19.00 o.p. (ISBN 0-8446-5780-8). Peter Smith.

History of the Theories of Aether & Electricity. Whittaker. (ISBN 0-8022-1867-9). Philos Lib.

History of the Universe. Jennifer Bartlett. (Illus.). 256p. 1985. 15.95 o.p. (ISBN 0-918825-12-1, Dist. by Kampmann & Co.). Moyer Bell Limited.

History of the Western World, 3 vols. 2nd ed. Bruce Lyon & Herbert H. Rowen. 1980. pap. 16.50 ea. o.p.; pap. 16.50 Vol. I o.p. (ISBN 0-395-30662-0); pap. 14.95 o.p. (ISBN 0-395-30663-9); pap. 16.50 Vol. III o.p. (ISBN 0-395-30664-7). HM.

History of the Women's Peace Party. Marie L. Degen. LC 76-147442. (Library of War & Peace; Histories of the Organized Peace Movement). 1972. lib. bdg. 46.00 o.p. (ISBN 0-8240-0232-6). Garland Pub.

History of the World Cup. Brian Glanville. (Illus.). 288p. 1984. pap. 10.95 o.p. (ISBN 0-571-13245-6). Faber & Faber.

History of the Writings of Beatrix Potter. Beatrix Potter. Ed. by Leslie Linder. LC 78-145549. 1971. 30.00 o.p. (ISBN 0-7232-1334-8). Warne.

History of the Yiddish Language, 2 vols. Max Weinreich. Tr. by Shlomo Noble & Joshua A. Fishman. LC 76-8097. (Illus.). 1980. 60.00x o.s.i. (ISBN 0-226-88604-2). U of Chicago Pr.

History of the Yiddish Language. Max Weinreich. Tr. by Shlomo Noble & Joshua A. Fishman. LC 76-8097. Orig. Title: Geshikhte fun der yidisher shprakh. (Illus.). 833p. 1980. 45.00 o.p. (ISBN 0-914512-39-0). Yivo Inst.

History of the Zulu War & Its Origin. Frances E. Colenso. LC 70-132643. 1971. Repr. of 1880 ed. lib. bdg. 28.00x o.p. (ISBN 0-8371-3654-7, CZW&, Pub. by Negro U Pr). Greenwood.

History of Transylvania. Stefan Pascu. Tr. by D. Robert Ladd. LC 82-66690. (Illus.). 344p. 1982. 35.00X o.p. (ISBN 0-8143-1722-7). Wayne St U Pr.

History of Tucker County. Homer F. Fansler. 1977. Repr. of 1962 ed. 25.00 o.p. (ISBN 0-87012-056-5). McClain.

History of Twiggs County, Georgia. Mrs. Hugh L. Faulk & Billy W. Jones. (Illus.). 1970. Repr. of 1960 ed. 17.50 o.s.i. (ISBN 0-89308-009-8). Southern Hist Pr.

History of UNCTAD 1964-1984. 294p. 1986. 5.00 o.p. (ISBN 92-1-112189-2, E.85.II.D.6). UN.

History of Union Parish, Louisiana: A Genealogical Profile of Its Pioneer Men & Women, Slaves & Ex-Slaves, & Immigrants. Max H. Williams. LC 86-47619. 250p. cancelled o.s.i. (ISBN 0-88164-516-8); pap. cancelled o.s.i. (ISBN 0-88164-517-6). ABBE Pubs Assn.

History of Wages in the United States from Colonial Times to 1928 with Supplement, 1929-1933. United States Bureau of Labor Statistics Staff. LC 67-13749. 1966. Repr. of 1934 ed. 50.00x o.p. (ISBN 0-8103-3363-5). Gale.

History of Watauga County, North Carolina. John P. Arthur. (Illus.). 443p. 1976. Repr. of 1915 ed. 37.50 o.p. (ISBN 0-89308-001-2). Southern Hist Pr.

History of Western Music. rev. ed. Donald J. Grout. (Illus.). 1973. text ed. 18.95x o.p. (ISBN 0-393-09416-2). Norton.

History of Western Music. rev. ed. Donald J. Grout. (Illus.). 540p. 1973. 15.95x o.p. (ISBN 0-393-09358-1). Norton.

History of Western Music. 3rd, shorter ed. Donald J. Grout & Claude Palisca. (Illus.). 1981. 26.95x o.p. (ISBN 0-393-95142-1). Norton.

History of Western Ontology from Thales to Heidegger. Rodolfo Ahumada. LC 78-60794. 1978. pap. text ed. 13.50 o.p. (ISBN 0-8191-0507-4). U Pr of Amer.

History of Western Philosophy: Philosophy from St. Augustine to Ockham. Ralph M. McInerny. LC 63-20526. 1970. 12.00x o.p. (ISBN 0-268-00417-X). U of Notre Dame Pr.
History of Western Society. 2nd ed. John P. McKay & Bennett D. Hill. LC 82-81316. 1072p. 1982. text ed. 30.95 o.p. (ISBN 0-395-32804-7). HM.
History of Western Society, 2 vols. 2nd ed. John P. McKay & Bennett D. Hill. LC 82-81320. 592p. 1983. Vol. 1. pap. 21.95 o.p. (ISBN 0-395-32798-9); Vol. 2. pap. 21.95 o.p. (ISBN 0-395-32799-7). HM.
History of Western Society, 3 vols. 2nd ed. John P. McKay & Bennett D. Hill. LC 82-81321. 416p. 1984. Vol. A. pap. 19.50 o.p. (ISBN 0-395-32800-4); Vol. B. pap. 19.50 o.p. (ISBN 0-395-32801-2); Vol. C. pap. 19.50 o.p. (ISBN 0-395-32802-0); Set of Vol. B & C. pap. 27.50 o.p. (ISBN 0-395-34249-X); transparencies 82.36 o.p. (ISBN 0-395-36247-4). HM.
History of Western Society. John P. McKay et al. LC 78-69592. (Illus.). 1980. pap. 23.50 o.p. (ISBN 0-395-27276-9); pap. text ed. 17.50 ea. 2-vol. ed. o.p.; pap. text ed. 15.50 ea. 3-vol. ed. o.p. HM.
History of Wildlife in America. Hal Borland. Ed. by Russell Bourne & Alma D. MacConomy. LC 75-15494. (Illus.). 208p. 1975. 14.95 o.p. (ISBN 0-912186-20-8). Natl Wildlife.
History of Witchcraft & Demonology. Montague Summers. 1956. cloth 10.00 o.p. (ISBN 0-8216-0038-9, Pub. by Univ Bks). Carol Pub Group.
History of Witchcraft: Sorcerers, Heretics & Pagans. Jeffrey B. Russell. (Illus.). 1982. pap. 11.95 o.p. (ISBN 0-500-27242-5). Thames Hudson.
History of Writing. Albertine Gaur. LC 84-52468. (Illus.). 224p. 1985. 25.00 o.p. (ISBN 0-684-18422-2, ScribT). Scribner.
History of Yaballaha III. Ed. by James A. Montgomery. 1967. lib. bdg. 14.00x o.p. (ISBN 0-374-95814-9, Octagon). Hippocrene Bks.
History of Yoga. Vivian Worthington. 176p. 1982. pap. 8.95 o.p. (ISBN 0-7100-9258-X). Routledge Chapman & Hall.
History, People, & Relevancy. Ed. by W. Bennett Jordan. 75p. 1972. pap. text ed. 4.95x o.p. (ISBN 0-8422-0268-4). Irvington.
History Preserved. Date not set. (ISBN 0-8052-0544-6). Random.
History vs. Anti-History. N. Mikeshin. 197p. 1977. 4.45 o.p. (ISBN 0-8285-0477-6, Pub. by Progress Pubs USSR). Imported Pubns.
History's Carnival: A Dissident's Autobiography. Leonid Plyushch. LC 77-92544. 1979. 14.95 o.p. (ISBN 0-15-141614-1). HarBraceJ.
Hit Me Again: More after Dinner Stories from the Houses of Parliament. Jack Aspinwall. 1987. pap. 8.95 o.p. (ISBN 0-907675-31-X, Pub. by Buchan & Enright England). Seven Hills Bk Dists.
Hit Parade, Nineteen Twenty to Nineteen Seventy. Richard M. Greene. LC 85-90721. 57p. (Orig.). 1985. pap. 10.50 o.p. Greene Co.
Hitchcock. Francois Truffaut. 1969. pap. 11.50 o.s.i. (ISBN 0-671-20346-0, Touchstone Bks). S&S.
Hitchcock. rev. ed. Francois Truffaut & Helen G. Scott. 320p. 1984. 19.45 o.s.i. (ISBN 0-671-52601-4). S&S.
Hitchhikers. Thompson. (Triumph Bks.). (gr. 6 up). 1980. PLB 11.90 o.p. (ISBN 0-531-04115-8, B17). Watts.
Hitchhiker's Guide to Africa & Arabia. David H. Childress. LC 84-1714. (Illus.). 304p. 1984. pap. 8.95 o.s.i. (ISBN 0-914091-42-5). Chicago Review.
Hitchhiker's Guide to Europe: The 1986 Guidebook for People on a Hitchhiking Budget. Ken Welsh. LC 86-382. 412p. 1986. pap. 7.95 o.p. (ISBN 0-394-62154-9, Ever). Grove.
Hitler. Joachim Fest. Tr. by Richard Winston & Clara Winston. LC 73-18154. (Helen & Kurt Wolff Bk). (Illus.). 1974. 15.00 o.p. (ISBN 0-15-141650-8). HarBraceJ.
Hitler. Ed. by Herbert Walther. (Illus.). 256p. 1983. 12.98 o.p. (ISBN 0-8119-0518-7, Pub. by Bison Bks). Fell.
Hitler's Master Plan: The Secret Conquest Strategy. Douglas S. Sherwen. 1979. 5.00 o.p. (ISBN 0-682-49336-8). Exposition-Phoenix.
Hitler's Mistakes. Ronald Lewin. LC 85-13757. 224p. 1986. 14.95 o.p. (ISBN 0-688-05821-3). Morrow.
Hitler's Secret Book. Adolf Hitler. LC 83-81374. 224p. 1983. pap. 7.95 o.p. (ISBN 0-394-62003-8, E881, Ever). Grove.
Hitler's Son. Wolfen Browne. 1987. 11.95 o.p. (ISBN 0-533-06912-2). Vantage.
Hitler's War Aims: Ideology, the Nazi State, & the Course of Expansion. Norman Rich. (Illus., Orig.). 1973. Vol. 1. 12.95x o.p. (ISBN 0-393-05454-3). Norton.
Hitler's War Aims: The Establishment of the New Order. Norman Rich. (Illus.). 548p. 1974. Vol. 2. 14.95x o.p. (ISBN 0-393-05509-4). Norton.
Hive. Camilo J. Cela. LC 81-11540. (Neglected Books of the 20th Century Ser.). (Illus.). 257p. 1983. pap. 6.95 o.p. (ISBN 0-88001-004-5). Ecco Pr.
Hive & the Honey Bee. rev. ed. Ed. by Dadant & Sons Inc., Staff. LC 63-15838. (Illus.). 3740p. 1976. 19.95 o.s.i. (ISBN 0-684-14790-4, ScribT). Scribner.
Hivers: Alien Module 7. J. Andrew Keith, Jr. (Traveller Ser.). (Illus.). 49p. (Orig.). 1986. pap. 7.00 o.p. (ISBN 0-943580-11-0). Game Designers.
HLA in Endocrine & Metabolic Disorders. Ed. by Nadir R. Farid. LC 80-70600. 1981. 72.50 o.p. (ISBN 0-12-247780-4). Acad Pr.
HMO-Hueckel Molecular Orbitals. E. Heilbronner & P. A. Straub. 1966. looseleaf bdg 58.00 o.p. (ISBN 0-387-03566-4). Springer-Verlag.
Hoard of the Himalayas. Larry Healey. 160p. (gr. 7 up). 1981. PLB 7.95 o.p. (ISBN 0-396-07978-4). Putnam Pub Group.
Hob Goblin & the Skeleton. Alice Schertle. LC 80-19521. (Illus.). 32p. (ps-3). 1982. 10.25 o.p. (ISBN 0-688-00279-X); PLB 10.88 o.p. (ISBN 0-688-00282-X). Lothrop.
Hob Goblin & the Skeleton. Alice Schertle. (ps-3). 1982. 10.25 o.p.; PLB 10.88 o.p. Lothrop.
Hobbes & Modernity: Five Exercises in Political Philosophical Exegesis. Aryeh Botwinick. LC 83-6536. 78p. (Orig.). 1983. lib. bdg. 22.00 o.p. (ISBN 0-8191-3210-1); pap. text ed. 8.25 o.p. (ISBN 0-8191-3211-X). U Pr of Amer.
Hobbit. collector's ed. J. R. R. Tolkien. (Illus.). 336p. 1973. slip cased 24.45 o.s.i. (ISBN 0-395-17711-1). HM.
Hobbit's Travels. Green. LC 78-15318. 96p. pap. 4.95 o.p. (ISBN 0-89471-040-0); 12.90 o.p. (ISBN 0-89471-041-9). Running Pr.
Hobble-de-hoy: The Word Game for Geniuses. Elizabeth Seymour. 1986. pap. 5.70 o.p. (ISBN 0-393-30331-4). Norton.
Hobby Computers Are Here! Wayne Green et al. 96p. 1976. pap. 4.95 o.p. (ISBN 0-88006-020-4, BK 7322). Wayne Green Ent.
Hobby Handbook: Macross Model World. (Illus.). 1984. 4.95 o.s.i. (ISBN 0-318-02675-9). Bks Nippan.
Hobby Metalcraft. Charles F. Pracna. 1978. 5.00 o.p. (ISBN 0-682-49048-2). Exposition-Phoenix.
Hobereaute. Jacques Audiberti. 9.95 o.p. (ISBN 0-686-54488-9). French & Eur.
Hobo on the Way to Heaven. Art Linkletter & George Bishop. 212p. 6.95 o.p. (ISBN 0-89191-337-8, 53371). Cook.
Hoby & Stub. Mary C. Dunne. LC 80-18449. 168p. (gr. 5-9). 1981. PLB 9.95 o.p. (ISBN 0-689-30806-X, Atheneum). Macmillan.
Hockey Coaching. Amateur Hockey Association of the U. S. Staff. (Illus.). 248p. 1982. 29.95 o.s.i. (ISBN 0-684-17457-X, ScribT). Scribner.
Hockey I Love. Vladislav Tretyak & V. Snegirev. Tr. by Anatole Konstantin from Rus. LC 77-9486. (Illus.). 192p. 1977. 7.50 o.p. (ISBN 0-88208-080-6). Chicago Review.
Hockey Scouting Report, Nineteen Eighty-Six to Nineteen Eighty-Seven. Michael Berger et al. (Illus.). 450p. 1986. pap. 14.95 o.p. (ISBN 0-02-028020-3, Collier). Macmillan.
Hockey Trick. Scott Corbett. (Trick Ser.). (Illus.). 112p. (gr. 4-6). 1974. lib. bdg. 13.95 o.p. (ISBN 0-316-15716-3, Joy St Bks). Little.
Hockey's Hall of Fame. Tim Moriarty. 1974. pap. 1.50 o.p. (ISBN 0-380-00165-9, 43463). Avon.
Hockey's Top Scorers. Richard Rainbolt. LC 74-27471. (Sports Heroes Library). (Illus.). 72p. (gr. 4 up). 1975. PLB 7.95 o.p. (ISBN 0-8225-1056-1). Lerner Pubns.
Hodge Cycles, Motives, & Shimura Varieties. P. Deligne et al. (Lecture Notes in Mathematics: Vol. 900). 414p. 1982. pap. 24.00 o.p. (ISBN 0-387-11174-3). Springer-Verlag.
Hodgkin's Disease. Mortimer J. Lacher. LC 75-25644. 508p. 1976. 50.50 o.p. (ISBN 0-471-51149-8). Krieger.
Hoer Gut Zu: A Beginning German Audio-Lingual Reader. Gerard F. Schmidt. 1964. text ed. (ISBN 0-02-407700-3). Macmillan.
Hoffa's Man: The Rise & Fall to James R. Hoffa as Witnessed by His Strongest Arm. Joseph Franco & Richard Hammer. (Illus.). 356p. 1987. 17.95 o.p. (ISBN 0-13-517764-2). P-H.
Hoffer's America. James Koerner. LC 73-82782. 143p. 1973. 9.95 o.p. (ISBN 0-912050-45-4, Library Pr). Open Court.
Hoffman on Pairs Play. Martin Hoffman. (Illus.). 184p. 1982. 15.95 o.p. (ISBN 0-571-11750-3). Faber & Faber.
Hofmannsthal Issue of Journal of the International A. Schnizler Research Foundation. Ed. by R. Hirsch & E. Weber. 1976. 7.50x o.p. (ISBN 0-685-73309-2). M S Rosenberg.
Hofmekler's People. Ori Hofmekler. LC 82-83651. (Illus.). 128p. 1983. pap. 9.95 o.p. (ISBN 0-03-063371-0). H Holt & Co.
Hog Butcher. Ronald L. Fair. LC 66-19486. 1966. 6.95 o.p. (ISBN 0-15-141702-4). HarBraceJ.
Hog Wild: The Autobiography of Frank Broyles. Frank Broyles & James Bailey. (Illus.). 1979. 13.95 o.p. (ISBN 0-87870-065-X). Memphis St Univ.
Hogarth: His Art & His World. Jack Lindsay. LC 78-21289. (Illus.). 1979. 14.95 o.s.i. (ISBN 0-8008-3916-1). Taplinger.
Hoghead. Frederick C. Gamst. (Case Studies in Cultural Anthropology). 128p. 1980. pap. text ed. 9.95 o.p. (ISBN 0-03-052636-1, HoltC). HR&W.
Hoisting Conference: 1975. 10.50x o.p. (ISBN 0-89520-026-0). SMM&E Inc.
Hoists, Cranes, & Derricks. Herbert S. Zim & James R. Skelly. LC 74-79098. (How Things Work Ser.). (Illus.). (gr. 3-7). 1974. PLB 8.16 o.p. (ISBN 0-688-31395-7); pap. 1.25 o.p. (ISBN 0-688-26395-X). Morrow.
Holcroft Covenant. Robert Ludlum. (Special Editions Ser.). 672p. 1986. lib. bdg. 19.95 o.p. (ISBN 0-8161-4060-X, Large Print Bks); pap. 11.95 o.p. (ISBN 0-8161-4074-X, Large Print Bks.). G K Hall.
Hold Back the Sunset. Jo Gersbach. 1979. 7.00 o.p. (ISBN 0-682-49407-0). Exposition-Phoenix.
Hold Fast to Love. Jo A. Simon. 288p. 1982. pap. 3.95 o.p. (ISBN 0-380-80945-1, 80945-1). Avon.
Hold the Dream. Barbara Taylor Bradford. (Large Print Books (General Ser.)). 1074p. 1985. lib. bdg. 19.95 o.p. (ISBN 0-8161-3980-6, Large Print Bks); pap. 11.95 o.p. (ISBN 0-8161-3981-4, Large Print Bks). G K Hall.
Holding out for the Moon. Peter Baroschini. 1986. write for info. o.p. (ISBN 0-87795-773-8). Morrow.
Holding Wonder. Zenna Henderson. 304p. 1986. pap. 1.50 o.p. (ISBN 0-380-01251-0, 44081). Avon.
Hole in the Fabric: Science, Contemporary Literature, & Henry James. Strother B. Purdy. LC 76-6667. (Critical Essays in Modern Literature Ser.). 1977. 23.95x o.p. U of Pittsburgh Pr.
Hole in the Wall. Arthur Morrison. 179p. 1983. pap. 8.95 o.s.i. (ISBN 0-85115-205-8, Pub. by Boydell & Brewer). Academy Chi Pubs.
Hole in the Wall. Arthur Morrison. 179p. pap. 8.95 o.s.i. (Pub. by Boydell & Brewer). Academy Chi Pubs.
Holes. Justin Sutcliffe. 96p. 1980. pap. 3.95 o.p. (ISBN 0-380-75325-1, 75325). Avon.
Holiday Cook. Lillian Langseth-Christensen. LC 69-18917. (Illus.). (gr. 5-12). 1969. PLB 10.95 o.p. (ISBN 0-87460-087-1). Lion Bks.
Holiday Cooking for Kids. Janet Wilk. (Cookbooks for Kids Ser.). (Illus.). (gr. 1-4). 1982. PLB 10.60 o.p. (ISBN 0-516-09227-8). Childrens.
Holiday Cooking for Kids. Janet Wilk. (Illus.). 64p. 1982. pap. 3.95 o.p. Ideals.
Holiday Guide to Scotland. Date not set. (ISBN 0-86145-648-3, Pub. by Auto Assn England). Salem Hse Pubs.
Holiday Handicraft. Nina R. Jordan. LC 38-27801. (Illus.). 245p. (gr. 4-6). 1938. 6.95 o.p. (ISBN 0-15-234868-9, HJ). HarBraceJ.
Holiday Parties. Judith Streb. LC 85-8806. (Illus.). 96p. (gr. 4-6). 1985. PLB 10.90 o.p. (ISBN 0-531-10041-3). Watts.
Holiday Sea Sonnets. John Blight. LC 84-28076. 100p. 1985. 14.95 o.p. (ISBN 0-7022-1865-0). U of Queensland Pr.
Holiday Song Book. Ed. & illus. by Robert Quackenbush. LC 77-5895. (Illus.). (gr. 1 up). 1977. 13.50 o.p. (ISBN 0-688-41820-1); PLB 13.88 o.p. (ISBN 0-688-51820-6). Lothrop.
Holidays in Cross-stitch, 1987. Vanessa-Ann Collection Staff. (Illus.). 128p. 1987. 19.95 o.p. (ISBN 0-8487-0697-8). Oxmoor Hse.
Holidays in England, Wales & Ireland, 1988. (Illus.). 568p. (Orig.). 1988. pap. 14.95 o.p. (ISBN 1-55650-019-X). Hunter Pub NY.
Holiness. Donald Nicholl. 176p. (Orig.). 1981. pap. 8.95 o.p. (ISBN 0-8164-2336-9). HarpR.
Holiness & the Will of God: Perspectives on the Theology of Tertullian. Gerald L. Bray. LC 79-5211. (New Foundations Theological Library). 1980. 3.25 o.s.i. (ISBN 0-8042-3705-0, John Knox). Westminster John Knox.
Holiness: Every Christian's Calling. Roger Roberts. LC 85-11330. 1985. pap. 5.95 o.p. (ISBN 0-8054-1956-X). Broadman.
Holiness in the Church. John A. Hardon. 1976. 3.50 o.s.i. (ISBN 0-8198-0417-7); pap. 2.50 o.s.i. (ISBN 0-8198-0418-5). Dghtrs St Paul.
Holistic Assessment of the Healthy Aged. Miriam M. Schrock. LC 80-10198. 174p. 1980. pap. 17.95 o.p. (ISBN 0-471-05597-2, Pub. by Wiley Med). Wiley.
Holistic Education: A Wellness Manual. Ed. by David C. Stilson et al. (Illus.). 74p. (Orig.). 1985. pap. text ed. 7.95x o.p. (ISBN 0-88133-138-4). Sheffield Wisc.
Holistic Gardener. Margaret Elphinstone & Julia Langley. (Illus.). 336p. (Orig.). 1988. pap. 9.99 o.p. (ISBN 0-7225-1267-8, Pub. by Thorsons (England)). Sterling.
Holistic Health Handbook. Berkeley Holistic Health Center. LC 78-54344. (Illus.). 1978. pap. 12.95 o.p. (ISBN 0-915904-32-2). And-Or Pr.
Holistic Health Handbook: A Tool for Attaining Wholeness of Body, Mind & Spirit. Compiled by Berkeley Holistic Health Center Staff. (Illus.). 488p. 1984. pap. 12.95 o.p. (ISBN 0-8289-0542-8). Greene.
Holistic Medicine. Tracy Deliman & John Smolowe. 1982. text ed. 27.95 o.p. (ISBN 0-8359-2844-6, R2844-0); pap. 19.95 o.p. (ISBN 0-8359-2843-8, R2843-2). Appleton & Lange.
Holistic Running: Beyond the Threshold of Fitness. Joel Henning. LC 78-3191. 1978. 7.95 o.p. (ISBN 0-689-10924-5, Atheneum). Macmillan.
Holland. Phillip Bergson. (World Cinema Ser.: No. 3). (Illus.). 1988. 24.95 o.s.i. (ISBN 0-948911-50-6, Pub. by Flicks Books England). U of Ill Pr.
Holland. 3rd ed. John Tomes. (Blue Guides Ser.). (Illus.). 1982. 29.95 o.p. (ISBN 0-393-01540-8); pap. 15.95 o.p. (ISBN 0-393-00093-1). Norton.
Holland, Belgium & Luxembourg. (Rand McNally Pocket Guides Ser.). (Illus.). 5.95 o.p. (ISBN 0-528-84313-3, 84313-3). Rand McNally.
Holland-Inside Information: The Complete Guide to Holland. 2nd ed. C. Gelderman-Curtis. (Illus.). 1980. pap. 17.50 o.p. E J Brill USA.
Holland Phaidon Cultural Guide. (Phaidon Cultural Guides Ser.). (Illus.). 1987. 17.95 o.p. (ISBN 0-13-611401-6). P-H.
Holli & Pandi's Hospital Adventure. Peggy R. Williams. (Illus.). 80p. (ps-3). 1987. text ed. 10.00 o.p. (ISBN 0-682-40311-3). Exposition-Phoenix.
Hollins College: An Illustrated History. Frances J. Niederer. LC 72-97863. (Illus.). 217p. 1973. 12.50x o.p. (ISBN 0-8139-0472-2). U Pr of Va.
Hollow Crown: A Life of Richard II. Harold F. Hutchison. LC 79-40750. (Library Reprints Ser.). (Illus.). 296p. 1979. 45.00x o.p. (ISBN 0-416-72540-6, NO. 2822). Routledge Chapman & Hall.
Hollow Detente: Anglo-German Relations in the Balkans, 1911-1914. Richard Crampton. (Illus.). 250p. 1980. text ed. 18.75x o.p. (ISBN 0-391-02159-1). Humanities.
Hollow Earth. Raymond Bernard. (Illus.). 1969. 6.95 o.p. (ISBN 0-8216-0090-7, Pub. by Univ Bks). Carol Pub Group.
Hollow Lands. Michael Moorcock. 1977. pap. 1.50 o.p. (ISBN 0-380-01794-6, 35386-5). Avon.
Hollow Tree. Ed. by Thom Roberts & Albert B. Paine. (Illus.). (gr. 3-7). 1973. pap. 1.50 o.p. (ISBN 0-380-01252-9, 44867, Camelot). Avon.
Hollow Woman. Simon Ritchie. 256p. 1987. 14.95 o.p. (ISBN 0-684-18702-7). Scribner.
Holly Hobbie's Nursery Rhymes. (Illus.). 48p. (gr. 1-7). 1978. PLB 5.99 o.p. (ISBN 0-448-13029-7, G&D). Putnam Pub Group.
Holly's Farm Animals. Jill Krementz. LC 86-60110. (Tough Enough Bks.). (Illus.). 24p. (ps-1). 1986. 3.95 o.s.i. (ISBN 0-394-88237-7, BYR). Random.
Hollywood & the Great Fan Magazines. Ed. by Martin Levin. LC 70-122641. 1971. pap. 5.95 o.p. (ISBN 0-87795-006-7, Arbor Hse). Morrow.
Hollywood Destinies: European Directors in America 1922-1931. Graham Petrie. (Cinema & Society Ser.). (Illus.). 288p. 1985. 29.95 o.p. (ISBN 0-7102-0161-3). Routledge Chapman & Hall.
Hollywood Education: Tales of Movie Dreams & Easy Money. David Freeman. 256p. 1986. 17.95 o.p. (ISBN 0-399-13044-6). Putnam Pub Group.
Hollywood Exiles. John Baxter. LC 75-34734. (Illus.). 232p. 1976. 14.95 o.s.i. (ISBN 0-8008-3918-8). Taplinger.
Hollywood Film Acting. Theodore Noose. LC 78-69633. 1979. 8.95 o.p. (ISBN 0-498-02207-2). A S Barnes.
Hollywood Goes to War. Colin Shindler. (Cinema & Society Ser.). (Illus.). 1979. 25.00 o.p. (ISBN 0-7100-0290-4). Routledge Chapman & Hall.
Hollywood Heartbreak: The Tragic & Mysterious Deaths of Hollywood's Most Remarkable Legends. Laurie Jacobson. (Illus.). 224p. (Orig.). 1984. pap. 10.95 o.p. (ISBN 0-671-49998-X, Fireside). S&S.
Hollywood in the Twenties. David Robinson. LC 68-24002. (Hollywood Ser.). 1968. pap. 5.95 o.s.i. (ISBN 0-498-06926-5). A S Barnes.

Hollywood Is a Four Letter Town. James Bacon. 1977. pap. 1.95 o.p. (ISBN 0-380-01671-0, 33399). Avon.

Hollywood Jr. High. Bonnie Towne. 128p. (gr. 5-8). 1985. 2.25 o.s.i. (ISBN 0-87406-041-9). Willowisp Pr.

Hollywood on the Palisades: A Filmography of Silent Feaures Made in Fort Lee, New Jersey 1903-1927. Rita E. Altomara. 120p. 1983. lib. bdg. 42.00 o.p. (ISBN 0-8240-9225-2). Garland Pub.

Hollywood Professionals, Vol. 2: Wood, King & Milestone. Tony Thomas et al. LC 73-3764. (International Film Guide Ser.). 192p. 1974. pap. 4.95 o.s.i. (ISBN 0-498-01394-4). A S Barnes.

Hollywood Professionals, Vol. 4: Browning & Siegel. Stuart Rosenthal & Judith M. Kass. LC 74-14266. (Illus.). 192p. 1976. pap. 4.95 o.s.i. (ISBN 0-498-01665-X). A S Barnes.

Hollywood Screenwriter. Ed. by Richard Corliss. (Orig.). 1972. pap. 1.95 o.p. (ISBN 0-380-01244-8, 12450, Bard). Avon.

Hollywood: Stars & Starlets, Tycoons & Flesh-Peddlers, Moviemakers & Moneymakers, Frauds & Geniuses, Hopefuls & Has-beens, Great Lovers & Sex Symbols. Garson Kanin. LC 83-27547. 408p. 1984. pap. 8.95 o.p. (ISBN 0-87910-010-9). Limelight Edns.

Hollywood Stuntpeople. Karin Ireland. LC 80-18346. (Illus.). 128p. (gr. 4-6). 1980. lib. bdg. 9.29 o.s.i. (ISBN 0-671-34062-X). Messner.

Hollywood: The Years of Innocence. John Kobal. LC 85-5970. (Illus.). 192p. 1985. 29.95 o.p. (ISBN 0-89659-578-1). Abbeville Pr.

Hollywood Trivia. David P. Strauss & Fred L. Worth. 352p. (Orig.). 1984. pap. 2.75 o.s.i. (ISBN 0-446-95492-6); pap. 3.95 o.s.i. (ISBN 0-446-32593-7). Warner Bks.

Hollywood Unreel: Fantasies About Hollywood & the Movies. Ed. by Martin H. Greenberg & Charles Waugh. LC 81-16742. 304p. 1982. 14.95 o.s.i. (ISBN 0-8008-3197-7). Taplinger.

Hollywood Wives. Jackie Collins. LC 83-4772. 512p. 1983. 16.50 o.p. (ISBN 0-671-47406-5). S&S.

Hollywood's Children: An Inside Account of the Child Star Era. Diana S. Cary. 1979. 11.95 o.p. (ISBN 0-395-27095-2). HM.

Hollywood's Irish Rose. Nora Bernard. 1979. pap. 1.95 o.p. (ISBN 0-380-41061-3, 41061). Avon.

Hollywood's Mother Goose. Rosalie Gustafson. 1985. 6.95 o.p. (ISBN 0-533-06626-3). Vantage.

Holmes-Laski Letters, the Correspondence of Justice Oliver Wendell Holmes & Harold J. Laski 1916-1935, 2 Vols. Ed. by Mark D. Howe. LC 63-24385. 1963. pap. 2.65 ea. o.p. (Atheneum). Vol. 1 (ISBN 0-689-70097-0, 43A). Vol. 2 (ISBN 0-689-70098-9, 43B). Macmillan.

Holocaust. Seymour Rossel. 160p. (gr. 9 up). 1981. lib. bdg. 11.90 o.p. (ISBN 0-531-04351-7). Watts.

Holocaust: A History of the Jews of Europe During the Second World War. Martin Gilbert. LC 85-5523. 1987. pap. 12.95 o.p. (ISBN 0-8050-0348-7). H Holt & Co.

Holocaust: An Annotated Bibliography. Harry J. Cargas & John T. Corrigan. 1977. pap. text ed. 4.00 o.p. (ISBN 0-87507-005-1). Cath Lib Assn.

Holocaust Survivors: Psychological & Social Sequelae. Ed. by Wilfred Quaytman. LC 80-80071. (Special Issue of Journal of Contemporary Psychotherapy: Vol. 11, No. 1). 88p. 1981. pap. 9.95 o.p. (ISBN 0-89885-016-9). Human Sci Pr.

Holography in Medicine & Biology. Ed. by G. Von Bally. (Springer Ser. in Optical Sciences: Vol. 18). (Illus.). 269p. 1979. 48.00 o.p. (ISBN 0-387-09793-7). Springer-Verlag.

Holst. 2nd. rev. ed. Imogen Holst. (Great Composers Ser.). (Illus.). 96p. (gr. 7 up). 1981. 12.95 o.p. (ISBN 0-571-18032-9). Faber & Faber.

Holsters & Other Gun Leather: Gun Digest Bk. Roger Combs. LC 83-70139. (Illus.). 256p. (Orig.). 1983. pap. 11.95 o.p. (ISBN 0-910676-55-0). DBI.

Holt Algebra Two with Trigonometry. Eugene D. Nichols et al. 1978. text ed. 20.76 o.p. (ISBN 0-03-018911-X, Holte E). HR&W.

Holt Geometry. Eugene D. Nichols et al. 1978. text ed. 18.32 o.p. (ISBN 0-03-018921-7, Holte E). HR&W.

Holt Handbook. Laurie G. Kirszner & Stephen R. Mandell. 832p. 1986. pap. text ed. 13.95 o.p. (ISBN 0-03-062762-1, HoltC). HR&W.

Holt Intermediate Dictionary of American English. Holt Editorial Staff. (gr. 4-9). 1967. text ed. 17.60 s.p. 4.20 o.p. (ISBN 0-03-067320-8, Holte E). HR&W.

Holt Workbook. Nancy Martinez & Joseph Martinez. 416p. 1986. text ed. 11.95 o.p. (ISBN 0-03-002967-8, HoltC). HR&W.

Holy Communion: The Lord's Supper in Changing Times. John Reumann et al. LC 79-8901. pap. (ISBN 0-8006-1382-1, 1-1382, Fortress). Augsburg Fortress.

Holy Days: The World of a Hasidic Family. Lis Harris. LC 85-14784. 266p. 1985. 18.45 o.s.i. (ISBN 0-671-46296-2). Summit Bks.

Holy Disorders. Edmund Crispin. 240p. 1980. pap. 2.95 o.p. (ISBN 0-380-51508-3). Avon.

Holy Family of Father Moon. Joseph H. Fichter. LC 84-82549. 155p. (Orig.). 1985. pap. 7.95 o.p. (ISBN 0-934134-13-8, Leaven Pr). Sheed & Ward MO.

Holy Grail: From the Works of Rudolf Steiner. Rudolf Steiner. Ed. by Steven Roboz. 40p. 1979. pap. 2.95 o.p. (ISBN 0-88010-049-4, Pub. by Steiner Book Centre Canada). Anthroposophic.

Holy Holy Land. Compiled by Charles L. Wallis. LC 79-85046. 1969. 6.95i o.p. (ISBN 0-06-069015-1). HarpR.

Holy Island. 2nd ed. James W. Kennedy. 144p. 1984. pap. 1.70 o.p. (ISBN 0-88028-028-X). Forward Movement.

Holy Moments. Robert T. Young. 112p. (Orig.). 1985. pap. 5.95 o.p. (ISBN 0-8358-0513-1). Upper Room.

Holy Nativity. Harvey B. Hatcher. LC 57-10298. (Orig.). 1957. pap. 1.95 o.p. (ISBN 0-8054-9702-1). Broadman.

Holy Nature of Man. Miguel F. Godreau. 1956. (ISBN 0-8022-0600-X). Philos Lib.

Holy Pictures. Claire Boylan. 208p. 1983. 13.50 o.s.i. (ISBN 0-671-46750-6). Summit Bks.

Holy Pretence. George L. Mosse. LC 68-14552. 1968. 23.50x o.p. (ISBN 0-86527-099-6). Fertig.

Holy Qur'an. Tr. by S. V. Ali from Arabic. 550p. 1981. text ed. 9.00 o.p. (ISBN 0-940368-08-0); pap. 4.95 o.p. (ISBN 0-940368-07-2). Tahrike Tarsile Quran.

Holy Qur'an. Mahomodali H. Shakir. 320p. 1986. text ed. 29.95 o.p. (ISBN 0-7103-0162-6); pap. text ed. 20.00 o.p. (ISBN 0-7103-0161-8). Routledge Chapman & Hall.

Holy Russia. Fitzroy Maclean. LC 78-72963. 1979. 13.95 o.p. (ISBN 0-689-10948-2, Atheneum). Macmillan.

Holy Spirit. H. Leo Boles. 10.95 o.p. (ISBN 0-89225-102-6). Gospel Advocate.

Holy Spirit. Glenn Clark. pap. 0.50 o.p. (ISBN 0-910924-07-4). Macalester.

Holy Spirit. Billy Graham. 1978. 4.99 o.p. (ISBN 0-8499-4153-9). Word Bks.

Holy Spirit. Robert Hicks & Richard Bewes. (Understanding Bible Truth Ser.). (Orig.). 1981. pap. 0.95 o.p. (ISBN 0-89840-021-X). Heres Life.

Holy Spirit. Eduard Schweizer. LC 79-8892. 144p. 1980. 10.95 o.p. (ISBN 0-8006-0629-9, 1-629, Fortress). Augsburg Fortress.

Holy Spirit in Action. F. J. Sheed. 148p. 1981. pap. 4.95 o.p. (ISBN 0-89283-109-X). Servant.

Holy Spirit in the Life of the Church: From Biblical Times to the Present. Paul D. Opsahl. LC 77-84099. 1978. pap. 12.95 o.p. (ISBN 0-8066-1625-3, 10-3160, Augsburg). Augsburg Fortress.

Holy Spirit, Lord & Life-Giver: A Biblical Introduction to the Doctrine of the Holy Spirit. John Williams. LC 79-27891. 1980. 8.50 o.p.; pap. 5.95 o.p. (ISBN 0-87213-951-4); study guide 3.25 o.p. (ISBN 0-87213-952-2). Loizeaux.

Holy Spirit-Shy Member of the Trinity. Frederick D. Bruner & William E. Hordern. LC 83-72124. 112p. (Orig.). 1984. pap. 6.95 o.p. (ISBN 0-8066-2068-4, 10-3070, Augsburg). Augsburg Fortress.

Holy Spirit: The Key to Supernatural Living. Bill Bright. 200p. 1980. 8.95 o.p. (ISBN 0-918956-67-6); pap. 5.95 o.p. (ISBN 0-918956-66-8). Campus Crusade.

Holy Terror. Date not set. pap. (ISBN 0-385-29286-4). Delacorte.

Holy Terror: The Fundamentalist War on America's Freedoms in Religion, Politics, & Our Private Lives. Flo Conway & Jim Siegelman. 504p. 1984. pap. 10.95 o.p. (ISBN 0-385-29286-4, Delta). Dell.

Holy War. John Bunyan. (Summit Bks). 1977. pap. 5.95 o.p. (ISBN 0-8010-0714-3). Baker Bk.

Holy Week. Richard J. Clifford & Hays H. Rockwell. Ed. by Elizabeth Achtemeier. LC 79-7377. (Proclamation 2, Ser. C). 1980. pap. 3.75 o.p. (ISBN 0-8006-4088-8, 1-4088, Fortress). Augsburg Fortress.

Holy Week. Reginald H. Fuller. Ed. by Elizabeth Achtemeier. LC 84-6011. (Proclamation 3: Aids for Interpreting the Lessons of the Church Year Ser. B). 64p. 1984. pap. 3.75 o.p. (ISBN 0-8006-4104-3, Fortress). Augsburg Fortress.

Holy Week. Roy Harrisville. LC 84-18756. (Proclamation 3 C Ser.). 64p. 1985. pap. 3.75 o.p. (ISBN 0-8006-4128-0, Fortress). Augsburg Fortress.

Holy Week. Roy A. Harrisville & Charles D. Hackett. Ed. by Elizabeth Achtemeier et al. LC 79-7377. (Proclamation 2: Aids for Interpreting the Lessons of the Church Year, Ser. B). 64p. 1981. pap. 3.75 o.p. (ISBN 0-8006-4086-1, 1-4086, Fortress). Augsburg Fortress.

Holy Week. Richard L. Jeske & Browne Barr. Ed. by Elizabeth Achtemeier et al. LC 79-7377. (Proclamation 2: Aids for Interpreting the Lessons of the Church Year, Ser. A). 64p. (Orig.). 1980. pap. 3.75 o.p. (ISBN 0-8006-4094-2, 1-4094, Fortress). Augsburg Fortress.

Holy Week. William C. McFadden & Reginald H. Fuller. LC 74-24932. (Proclamation 1: Aids for Interpreting the Lessons of the Church Year, Ser. B). 64p. 1975. pap. 2.95 o.p. (ISBN 0-8006-4074-8, 1-4074, Fortress). Augsburg Fortress.

Holy Week. Krister Stendahl. LC 74-76926. (Proclamation 1: Aids for Interpreting the Lessons of the Church Year, Ser. A). 64p. (Orig.). 1974. pap. 2.95 o.p. (ISBN 0-8006-4064-0, 1-4064, Fortress). Augsburg Fortress.

Holy Week. Daniel B. Stevick & Ben Johnson. LC 73-79351. (Proclamation 1: Aids for Interpreting the Lessons of the Church Year, Ser. C). 64p. 1973. pap. 2.95 o.p. (ISBN 0-8006-4054-3, 1-4054, Fortress). Augsburg Fortress.

Holy Week. Samuel Terrien. LC 84-18756. (Proclamation 3A Ser.). 64p. 1986. pap. 3.75 o.p. (ISBN 0-8006-4120-5, Fortress). Augsburg Fortress.

Holy Week Preaching. Krister Stendahl. LC 84-48714. (Resources for Preaching Ser.). 64p. 1985. pap. 0.95 o.p. (ISBN 0-8006-1851-3, 1-1851, Fortress). Augsburg Fortress.

Holy Year Prayer Book. Peter Coughlan. 1976. 2.95 o.p. (ISBN 0-685-77517-8, 221608). Franciscan Herald.

Holzman's New Guide to the Accumulated Earnings Tax. Robert S. Holzman. LC 81-10654. 289p. 1981. text ed. 27.95 o.p. (ISBN 0-13-392621-4, Busn). P-H.

Homage to Barcelona: The City & Its Art 1888-1936. Intro. by Marilyn McCully. (Illus.). 328p. 1987. pap. 22.50 o.s.i. (ISBN 0-500-27415-0). Thames Hudson.

Homage to Mistress Bradstreet & Other Poems. John Berryman. LC 63-24596. 1968. pap. 3.50 o.p. (ISBN 0-374-50660-4). FS&G.

Homage to My Father, a Pioneer in Central America. Bertha Giani. 128p. 1986. 9.50 o.p. (ISBN 0-8062-3006-1). Carlton.

Homage to the Sun. Kyriacos C. Markides. 272p. (Orig.). 1987. pap. 10.95 o.p. (ISBN 1-85063-072-0, Pub. by Routledge UK). Routledge Chapman & Hall.

Homage to the Tragic Muse. Angelos Terzakis. Tr. by Athan Anagnostopoulos from Gr. 1978. 8.95 o.p. (ISBN 0-395-27088-X). HM.

Home. Jan Pienkowski. Ed. by Kate Klimo. (Pienkowski Concept Bks.). (Illus.). 32p. (ps-k). 1983. 4.80 o.s.i. (ISBN 0-671-46246-6, Little Simon). S&S.

Home see **Changing Room.**

Home Alternative to Hospitals & Nursing Homes. Mara Covell et al. 1985. pap. 9.95 o.p. (ISBN 0-03-003922-3, Owl Bks). H Holt & Co.

Home & Building Maintenance. J. C. Woodin & Louis Hayes. 18.64 o.p. (ISBN 0-87345-466-9). Glencoe.

Home & Community Influences on Young Children. Karen D. Vander Ven. LC 76-14092. 1977. pap. text ed. 14.95 o.p. (ISBN 0-8273-0569-9). Delmar.

Home & Hospital Psychiatric Treatment: An Interdisciplinary Experiment. Fred R. Fenton et al. LC 81-16354. (Contemporary Community Health Ser.). (Illus.). 240p. 1982. 21.95x o.p. (ISBN 0-8229-1142-6). U of Pittsburgh Pr.

Home & School Partnerships in Exceptional Education. Carol T. Michaelis. LC 80-23920. 348p. 1981. text ed. 35.00 o.p. (ISBN 0-89443-330-X). Aspen Pub.

Home at Last: A Young Cat's Tale. Patricia Lauber. (Illus.). 48p. (gr. 3-5). 1980. 6.95 o.p. (ISBN 0-698-20507-3, Coward). Putnam Pub Group.

Home-Based Training Resource Handbook. 3rd rev. ed. Ed. by Debra Fish. (Illus.). 392p. 1984. GBC binding 32.50x o.p. (ISBN 0-934140-13-8). Toys N Things.

Home Before Midnight: A Traditional Verse. Illus. by Bobby Lewis. LC 81-6072. (Illus.). 32p. (ps-1). 1984. 11.75 o.p. (ISBN 0-688-00530-6); PLB 11.88 o.p. (ISBN 0-688-00731-7). Lothrop.

Home Book of Quotations: Classical & Modern. 10th ed. Burton Stevenson. 2816p. 1984. 39.95 o.s.i. (ISBN 0-396-08340-4). Dodd.

Home Book of Verse. 10th ed. Burton E. Stevenson. 45.00 o.p. (ISBN 0-03-028035-4). H Holt & Co.

Home Builders Publicity Manual - A-Step-by-Step Guide for Successful Public Relations. National Association of Home Builders Staff & Deborah Johnson. 35p. 1984. pap. 9.00 o.p. (ISBN 0-86718-208-3). Nat Assn H Build.

Home Building after Tax Reform: A Builder's Guide. National Association of Home Builders Staff. 118p. 1986. pap. 12.50 o.p. (ISBN 0-86718-285-7). Nat Assn H Build.

Home Built Aircraft. David B. Thurston. (Illus.). 224p. 1982. text ed. 29.95 o.p. (ISBN 0-07-064552-3, P&RB). McGraw.

Home Care for the Stroke Patient. Margaret Johnstone. (Illus.). 132p. 1980. pap. text ed. 12.00 o.p. (ISBN 0-443-02118-X). Churchill.

Home Care Guide to Accreditation & Quality Assurance. 65p. pap. cancelled o.s.i. (ISBN 0-86688-177-8). Joint Comm Hlthcare.

Home Centered Care: Designing a Family Day Care Program. Ronda Garcia. Ed. by L. Thompson & M. McDonald. Reg Garcia. (Illus., Orig.). 1985. pap. text ed. 8.95 o.p. (ISBN 0-937711-00-4). Child Council SF.

Home Computer Basics: An Introduction for Young People. Jack Rothfeder. (Illus.). 48p. (gr. 3-7). 1983. 9.95 o.s.i. (ISBN 0-13-392845-4). P-H.

Home Computer Handbook. Ian Graham & Helen Varley. 224p. 1984. 12.70 o.p. (ISBN 0-671-47221-6). S&S.

Home Computers: A Manual of Possibilities. Richard Koff. 1979. 7.95 o.p. (ISBN 0-15-142163-3). HarBraceJ.

Home Computers: Two to the Tenth Power Questions & Answers, Vol. 2: Software. Richard Didday. LC 77-9285. 230p. 1977. pap. 11.95 o.p. (ISBN 0-918398-01-0). Dilithium Pr.

Home Computers: Two to the Tenth Question & Answers, Vol. 1: Hardware. Rich Didday. LC 77-9285. 265p. 1977. 11.95 o.p. (ISBN 0-918398-00-2). Dilithium Pr.

Home Cooking in a Hurry. Sarah Howell. 1985. 7.95 o.p. (ISBN 0-8054-7002-6). Broadman.

Home Cooking... On Your Own: Recipes for Students, Newlyweds, & Those Who Live Alone. Madeline Westover et al. LC 84-72518. 128p. 1984. pap. 6.95 o.p. (ISBN 0-87747-860-0, Pub. by Shadow Mountain). Deseret Bk.

Home Economics Education. Martha L. Blankenship & Barbara D. Moer Chen. LC 78-69595. (Illus.). 1979. text ed. 32.95 o.p. (ISBN 0-395-26700-5). HM.

Home Economics Education Curriculum. National Center for Research in Vocational Education Staff. 55p. 1984. 4.95 o.p. (ISBN 0-318-22126-8, BB72). Natl Ctr Res Voc Ed.

Home Education Resource Guide. Don Hubbs. (Illus.). 88p. 1985. pap. 10.00 o.p. (ISBN 0-9615578-1-8). Blue Bird Pub.

Home Electrical Wiring & Maintenance Made Easy. American Association of Vocational Instructional Materials Staff. (Illus.). 272p. 1986. 28.95 o.p. (ISBN 0-8306-0473-1, 2673); pap. 19.60 o.p. (ISBN 0-8306-2673-5). Tab Bks.

Home Fires. Charlotte Mayerson. 1985. 15.95 o.p. (ISBN 0-87795-674-X, Arbor Hse). Morrow.

Home Fires: Stories by Writers from Byelorussia. Ed. by E. Moroz. 326p. 1986. 9.95 o.p. (Pub. by Raduga Pubs USSR). Imported Pubns.

Home for a Stranger. Joan T. Weiss. LC 79-3766. (Illus.). 120p. (gr. 4-6). 1980. 7.95 o.p. (ISBN 0-15-235224-4, HJ). HarBraceJ.

Home for the Homeless: A Sociological Exegesis of 1 Peter, Its Solution & Strategy. John H. Elliot. LC 80-2394. 320p. 1981. 9.95 o.p. (ISBN 0-8006-0659-0, 1-659, Fortress). Augsburg Fortress.

Home Free. James C. Schaap. LC 85-70470. 160p. 1986. pap. 6.95 o.p. (ISBN 0-89107-363-9, Crossway Bks). Good News.

Home Free: The No-Nonsense Guide to House Care. Ann Guilfoyle. LC 83-42666. (Illus.). 1984. 12.45 o.p. (ISBN 0-393-01778-8). Norton.

Home from Exile: An Approach to Post-Existentialist Philosophizing. Denis Hickey. LC 82-20059. 504p. (Orig.). (gr. 2-5). 1983. lib. bdg. 39.25 o.p. (ISBN 0-8191-2848-1); pap. text ed. 19.75 o.p. (ISBN 0-8191-2849-X). U Pr of Amer.

Home Front: Notes from the Family War Zone. L. Armstrong. 240p. 1983. text ed. 14.95 o.p. (ISBN 0-07-002276-3). McGraw.

Home Gardener's Book of Ferns. John Mickel & Evelyn Fiore. LC 78-14418. (Illus.). 1979. 12.95 o.p. (ISBN 0-03-045736-X); pap. 7.95 o.p. (ISBN 0-03-045741-6). H Holt & Co.

Home Gardening Wisdom. Dick Raymond & Jan Raymond. LC 82-3050. (Illus.). 320p. (Orig.). 1982. pap. 9.95 o.s.i. (ISBN 0-88266-265-1, Garden Way Pub). Storey Comm Inc.

Home Ground. Lynn Freed. 1986. 16.45 o.s.i. (ISBN 0-671-61965-9). Summit Bks.

Home Gunsmithing Digest. 3rd ed. Tommy L. Bish. (Illus.). 256p. (Orig.). 1984. pap. 12.95 o.p. (ISBN 0-910676-71-2). DBI.

Home Gym: A Guide to Fitness Equipment. Michael Lafavore. (Illus.). 192p. (Orig.). 1984. pap. 8.95 o.p. (ISBN 0-380-87965-4, 87965-4). Avon.

Home Health Care: Current Practice. Stanhope et al. 1987. 29.95 o.p. (ISBN 0-8016-4914-5). Mosby.

Home Healthcare. Allen D. Spiegel. 711p. 1983. text ed. 52.00 o.p. (ISBN 0-932500-22-6). Natl Hlth Pub.

Home Help. Janet Marks. 112p. 1975. pap. text ed. 7.50x o.p. (Pub. by Bedford England). Gower Pub Co.

Home Help Service. Margaret Dexter & Wally Harbert. 232p. 1983. 25.00x o.p. (ISBN 0-422-78680-2, NO. 4055); pap. 12.95x o.p. (ISBN 0-422-78690-X, NO. 4056). Routledge Chapman & Hall.

Home How-to Sourcebook. Mike McClintock. LC 83-20219. 384p. 1984. 24.95 o.p. (ISBN 0-684-18015-4, ScribT); pap. 14.95 o.p. (ISBN 0-684-18045-6, ScribT). Scribner.

Home in the Wilds. Kathrene Pinkerton. LC 76-11117. (Illus.). (YA) (gr. 10 up). 1976. 9.95 o.s.i. (ISBN 0-8008-3922-6). Taplinger.

Home Inspection Workbook. Steve Hunter. LC 79-28692. (Illus., Orig.). 1980. pap. 5.95 o.p. (ISBN 0-8437-3345-4). Hammond Inc.

Home Insulation Bible. S. Blackwell Ducan. 16.95 o.p. (ISBN 0-8306-0040-X, 1348); pap. 9.95 o.p. (ISBN 0-8306-1348-X). TAB Bks.

Home Is the Hunter. Helen MacInnes. LC 64-22669. 1964. 5.95 o.s.i. (ISBN 0-15-142039-4). HarBraceJ.

Home Landscape: The Art of Home Landscaping. rev. & enl. ed. Garrett Eckbo. (Illus.). 1978. text ed. 33.50 o.p. (ISBN 0-07-018879-3). McGraw.

Home Life. Pat Hodgson. (History in Focus Ser.). (Illus.). 72p. (gr. 7-12). 1982. 17.95 o.p. (ISBN 0-7134-4085-6, Pub. by Batsford England). David & Charles.

Home Life in China. Isaac T. Headland. LC 79-177278. (Illus.). xii, 334p. 1971. Repr. of 1914 ed. 51.00x o.p. (ISBN 0-8103-3822-X). Gale.

Home Lighting. Sunset Magazine & Books Editors. LC 82-81371. (Illus.). 96p. (Orig.). 1982. pap. 5.95 o.p. (ISBN 0-376-01312-5, Sunset Bks). Sunset-Lane.

Home: Love It or Leave It. David J. Wayne & Nancy N. Rue. (Orig.). 1983. pap. 4.95 o.p. (ISBN 0-8010-9662-6). Baker Bk.

Home-Made Baby Toys. Sara K. Swan. 1977. pap. 4.95 o.p. (ISBN 0-395-25410-8). HM.

Home Maintenance: A Guide to Taking Better Care of Your House. William Weiss. (Illus.). 1978. 3.95 o.p. (ISBN 0-684-15594-X, ScribT); Encore ed. 3.95 o.p. (ISBN 0-684-16697-6). Scribner.

Home Makers. Ivy Strick. LC 78-20706. 1980. 8.95 o.s.i. (ISBN 0-8008-3923-4). Taplinger.

Home Management Context & Concepts. Ruth E. Deacon & Francille M. Firebaugh. 1975. text ed. 17.95 o.p. (ISBN 0-395-18915-2). HM.

Home of the Learned Man: A Symposium on the Immigrant Scholar in America. Franx Adler et al. Ed. by John Kosa. LC 68-22380. 1968. 14.95x o.p. (ISBN 0-8084-0160-2). New Coll U Pr.

Home on the Range. Karol Jackowski. LC 82-71758. 96p. (Orig.). 1982. spiral bd. 4.95 o.p. (ISBN 0-87793-255-7). Ave Maria.

Home Operated Business Opportunities for the Disabled. 1977. (ISBN 0-915708-04-3). Cheever Pub.

Home Owner's Journal: What I Did & When I Did It. Colleen M. Jenkins. 132p. (Orig.). pap. 7.95 o.p. (ISBN 0-911493-09-3). Blue Sky.

Home Place. Wright Morris. LC 48-1792. (Illus.). xii, 178p. 1968. pap. 7.95 o.p. (ISBN 0-8032-5139-4, BB 386, Bison). U of Nebr Pr.

Home Place: A Memory & a Celebration. Robert Drake. LC 80-24110. (Illus.). 192p. 1980. 14.95 o.p. (ISBN 0-87870-198-2). Memphis St Univ.

Home Plans Book. 3rd ed. Murray Armor. Orig. Title: Home Plans of the Eighties. 288p. 1988. 14.95 o.p. (Pub. by Prism Pr). Avery Pub.

Home Plans of the Eighties see Home Plans Book.

Home Plumbing Made Easy: An Illustrated Manual. James L. Kittle. (Illus.). 272p. (Orig.). 1987. 24.95 o.p. (ISBN 0-8306-0397-2); pap. 14.60 o.p. (ISBN 0-8306-2797-9). TAB Bks.

Home Refinancing: How You Can Cash in on Today's Low Rates. Don DeBat. (Illus.). 96p. (Orig.). 1986. pap. 5.95 o.p. (ISBN 0-8092-4891-3). Contemp Bks.

Home Remedies for Candida. Betsy Russell-Manning. (Illus.). 112p. 1987. pap. text ed. 11.95 o.p. (ISBN 0-930165-15-2). Greensward Pr.

Home Rule on the Range: Early Days of the Grazing Service. Marvin Klemme. 1983. 10.95 o.p. (ISBN 0-533-05692-6). Vantage.

Home Run: Baseball's Greatest Hits & Hitters. Associated Features Inc. Editors. Ed. by Zander Hollander. LC 83-19200. (Random House Sports Library). (Illus.). 144p. (gr. 5-9). 1984. pap. 2.50 o.p. (ISBN 0-394-86488-3, BYR). Random.

Home Satellite TV Installation & Troubleshooting Manual. Frank Baylin & Brent Gale. LC 85-71662. 340p. 1985. pap. 29.95 o.p. (ISBN 0-917893-02-6, Baylin Gale). Consol.

Home Satellite TV Installation & Troubleshooting Manual. Frank Baylin & Brent Gale. 320p. 1986. pap. 29.95 o.p. (ISBN 0-672-22496-8, 22496). Sams.

Home Sausage Making. Charles Reavis. LC 80-39703. (Illus.). 128p. 1980. pap. 7.95 o.p. (ISBN 0-88266-246-5, Garden Way Pub). Storey Comm Inc.

Home School & Leisure in the Soviet Union. Ed. by Jenny Brine et al. (Illus.). 304p. 1980. text ed. 28.50x o.p. (ISBN 0-04-335040-2). Unwin Hyman.

Home Security Handbook. Popular Mechanics Editors. 1984. 12.50 o.p. (ISBN 0-87851-213-6, Hearst Bk). Morrow.

Home Sense. Mike McClintock. 224p. (Orig.). 1986. pap. 10.95 o.p. (ISBN 0-684-18656-X); 19.95 o.p. (ISBN 0-394-18655-9). Scribner.

Home Stretch. Rogers & Thatcher. 160p. 1986. 9.95 o.p. (ISBN 0-8499-0344-0). Word Bks.

Home Study Course. Jack Rudman. (Career Examination Ser.: CS-1). 1988. pap. 14.00 o.p. (ISBN 0-317-62918-2). Natl Learning.

Home Style Chinese Cooking in Pictures. Sumi Hatano. (Illus.). 1980. 10.50 o.p. (ISBN 0-87040-471-7). Japan Pubns USA.

Home Style Italian Cookery. Pauline Barrese. 1981. pap. 2.95 o.p. (ISBN 0-440-13718-7). Dell.

Home Team: BA-II & You, P. Joseph Klock. Ed. by Helene Berlin. (Illus.). 64p. (Orig.). 1984. pap. text ed. 9.55 o.s.i. (ISBN 0-913652-55-5). Realtors Natl.

Home Textiles. Fairchild Market Research Division Staff. (Fairchild Fact Files). (Illus.). 50p. 1986. pap. 20.00 o.p. (ISBN 0-87005-553-4). Fairchild.

Home to My Island. David Hurd. (Illus.). 192p. 1981. 9.50 o.p. (ISBN 0-682-49727-4). Exposition-Phoenix.

Home to the Mountain. Brenda B. Canary. 224p. 1982. pap. 2.75 o.p. (ISBN 0-380-61127-9, 61127-9). Avon.

Home to the Wilderness. Sally Carrighar. (Illus.). 1973. 7.95 o.p. (ISBN 0-395-15461-8). HM.

Home Video Handbook. 3rd ed. Charles Bensinger. LC 82-62202. 392p. 1982. 13.95 o.p. (ISBN 0-672-22052-0). Sams.

Home: Where Life Makes Up Its Mind see Standing Out: Being Real in an Unreal World.

Home with Aunt Florry. Charlene J. Talbot. LC 74-75572. 208p. (gr. 5-8). 1974. 7.25 o.p. (ISBN 0-689-30440-4, Atheneum). Macmillan.

Homebuilts: A Handbook for the First-Time Builder. Frank J. O'Brien. (Illus.). 176p. (Orig.). 1985. pap. 14.60 o.p. (ISBN 0-8306-2375-2, 2375). TAB Bks.

Homecoming. Julia Alvarez. Ed. by Robert Pack. LC 83-49391. (Poetry Ser.). 96p. 1984. 12.50 o.s.i. (ISBN 0-394-53855-2, GP889); pap. 7.95 o.s.i. (ISBN 0-394-62052-6). Grove.

Homecoming. Earl Hamner, Jr. 1973. pap. 0.95 o.p. (ISBN 0-380-01254-5, 36004). Avon.

Homecoming. James Pattinson. 190p. 1986. pap. 2.95 o.p. (ISBN 1-55547-113-7). Critics Choice Paper.

Homefront: America During World War II. Mark J. Harris et al. (Illus.). 256p. 1985. pap. 8.95 o.p. (ISBN 0-399-51124-5, Perigee). Putnam Pub Group.

Homegrown Music. Marc Bristol. LC 82-17217. (Illus.). 144p. (Orig.). 1983. pap. 8.95 o.p. (ISBN 0-914842-91-9). Madrona Pubs.

Homeless Borstal Boys. Roger Hood. 103p. 1966. pap. text ed. 5.00 Brit. pds. o.p. (ISBN 0-686-70847-4, Pub. by Bedford England). Gower Pub Co.

Homeless in America: Health Care & Human Needs. Institute of Medicine. 165p. 1988. text ed. 29.95x o.p. (ISBN 0-309-03835-9); pap. text ed. 19.95x o.p. (ISBN 0-309-03832-4). Natl Acad Pr.

Homeless Mentally Ill: No Longer Out of Sight & Out of Mind. National Conference of State Legislatures Staff. (State Legislative Report: Vol. 10, No. 13). 16p. 1985. pap. 5.00 o.p. (ISBN 1-55516-155-3). Natl Conf State Legis.

Homemade Beer Book. Vrest Orton. LC 72-89742. (Illus.). 1973. pap. 4.95 o.p. (ISBN 0-8048-1086-9). C E Tuttle.

Homemade Cookies. Ideals Staff. (Illus.). 64p. (Orig.). 1984. pap. 3.95 o.p. (ISBN 0-8249-3031-2). Ideals.

Homemade Desserts. Ideals Staff. (Illus.). 64p. 1984. pap. 3.95 o.p. (ISBN 0-8249-3035-5). Ideals.

Homemade Dolls in Foreign Dress. Nina R. Jordan. LC 39-27666. (Illus.). (gr. 3-7). 1939. 5.50 o.p. (ISBN 0-15-235405-0, HJ). HarBraceJ.

Homemade Money: The Definitive Guide to Success in a Home Business. Barbara Brabec. LC 83-21483. (Illus.). 272p. (Orig.). 1984. pap. 12.95 o.p. (ISBN 0-932620-31-0). Betterway Pubns.

Homemade Money: The Definitive Guide to Success in a Homebased Business. 2nd ed. Barbara Brabec. LC 86-17634. (Illus.). 304p. 1986. pap. 14.95 o.p. (ISBN 0-932620-67-1). Betterway Pubns.

Homeopathic Medicine: A Doctor's Guide to Remedies for Common Ailments. Trevor Smith. 256p. 1983. pap. 8.95 o.p. (ISBN 0-7225-0735-6). Inner Tradit.

Homeopathic Treatment of Emotional Illness. Trevor Smith. 208p. (Orig.). 1984. pap. 8.95 o.p. (ISBN 0-7225-0812-3). Inner Tradit.

Homeopathy: Nature's Healing Law. M. L. Scott. 19p. 1870. pap. 3.95 o.s.i. (ISBN 0-88697-026-1). Life Science.

Homeostasis in Injury & Shock: Proceedings of a Satellite Symposium of the 28th International Congress of Physiological Sciences, Budapest, Hungary, 1980. Ed. by Z. Biro et al. LC 80-42104. (Advances in Physiological Sciences: Vol. 26). (Illus.). 360p. 1981. 57.00 o.p. (ISBN 0-08-027347-5). Pergamon.

Homeostasis: Origins of the Concept. Lee L. Langley. (Benchmark Papers in Human Physiology Ser.: Vol. 1). 362p. 1982. 54.95 o.p. (ISBN 0-87933-007-4). Van Nos Reinhold.

Homeowner Income Tax Provisions & Metropolitan Housing Markets: A Simulation Study. Michael W. Andreassi & C. Duncan MacRae. LC 81-51624. 78p. 1981. pap. 9.00 o.p. (ISBN 0-87766-297-5, URI 29900). Urban Inst.

Homeowner's Almanac. Thomas Ervin & Don Hart. LC 80-66065. (Illus.). 128p. (Orig.). 1980. pap. write for info. o.p. (ISBN 0-936682-00-0). Conquest Corp MI.

Homeowner's Encyclopedia of House Construction. Morris Krieger. (Illus.). 1978. text ed. 36.50 o.p. (ISBN 0-07-035497-9). McGraw.

Homeowner's Handbook: What You Need to Know about Buying, Maintaining, Improving, & Running Your Home Successfully. Michael McClintock. (Illus.). 1980. 3.95 o.p. (ISBN 0-684-16145-1, ScribT); encore ed. 3.95 o.p. (ISBN 0-684-17548-7). Scribner.

Homeownership Effects of Alternative Mortgage Instruments. James Follain & Raymond Struyk. 95p. 1977. pap. 6.00 o.p. (ISBN 0-87766-193-6, 18900). Urban Inst.

Homer. Andre Michalopoulos. (World Authors Ser.). 1966. lib. bdg. 16.95 o.s.i. (ISBN 0-8057-2432-X, Twayne). G K Hall.

Homer & the Heroic Tradition. Cedric H. Whitman. 1965. pap. 4.95 o.p. (ISBN 0-393-00313-2, Norton Lib). Norton.

Homeric Hymns. Daryl Hine. LC 72-82685. 1972. 7.95 o.p. (ISBN 0-689-10515-0, Atheneum). Macmillan.

Homes & Homebuilding 1984. 17th ed. National Association of Home Builders Staff. 212p. 1984. 15.00 o.p. (ISBN 0-86718-205-9). Nat Assn H Build.

Homes & Homebuilding 1986. 19th ed. National Association of Home Builders Staff. 239p. 1986. pap. 15.00 o.p. (ISBN 0-86718-262-8). Nat Assn H Build.

Homes & Homebuilding, 1988. 250p. 1988. 15.00 o.p. (ISBN 0-86718-316-0). Nat Assn H Build.

Homes for the Nineteen-Eighties: An Energy & Construction Design Aid. C. Keeler Chapman & John E. Traister. LC 82-5929. (Illus.). 256p. (Orig.). 1982. pap. 17.95 o.p. (ISBN 0-8306-1425-7, 1425). TAB Bks.

Homes of the Kings: The Grand Tour. Flavio Conti. LC 77-88245. (Illus.). 1978. 14.95 o.p. (ISBN 0-15-142165-X). HarBraceJ.

Homespun. Ed. by Anita Browne. LC 78-73481. (Granger Poetry Library). 1979. Repr. of 1936 ed. 32.50x o.p. (ISBN 0-89609-108-2). Roth Pub Inc.

Homespun Schools. Raymond Moore & Dorothy Moore. 1982. 9.95 o.p. (ISBN 0-8499-0326-2). Word Bks.

Homestead. Keith Wilson. (Illus.). 72p. 1969. 5.00 o.p. Kayak.

Homestead Grays. James Wylie. 1978. pap. 1.95 o.p. (ISBN 0-380-38604-6, 38604). Avon.

Homestead Your House: California Edition. 6th, rev. ed. Ralph Warner & Toni Ihara. LC 80-117976. (Illus.). 1986. pap. 8.95 o.p. Nolo Pr.

Homeward Winds the River. Barbara F. Johnson. 1979. pap. 3.50 o.p. (ISBN 0-380-42952-7, 82016-1). Avon.

Homewood Trilogy. John E. Wideman. 496p. 1984. pap. 8.95 o.p. (ISBN 0-380-89564-1). Avon.

Homework: How to Study & Remember. Herbert L. Collier. (Illus.). 144p. 1976. 7.95 o.p. (ISBN 0-89019-054-2). Norwalk Pr.

Homeworks: The Complete Guide to Displaying Your Possessions. Robin Guild. 1979. 29.95 o.p. (ISBN 0-442-24576-9). Van Nos Reinhold.

Homeworks: The Complete Guide to Displaying Your Possessions. Robin Guild. (Illus.). 264p. 1984. pap. 19.95 o.p. (ISBN 0-442-22775-2). Van Nos Reinhold.

Homicide Investigation Techniques: Personal Experience Accounts of Professionals & Experts. Southwestern Law Enforcement Institute Staff. (Illus.). 144p. 1961. 15.95x o.p. (ISBN 0-398-01814-6). C C Thomas.

Homilies of St. John Chrysostom on the Letters of St. Paul to Titus & Philemon. Blake Goodall. (Univ. of California Publications in Classical Studies: Vol. 20). 1979. pap. 19.95x o.p. (ISBN 0-520-09596-0). U of Cal Pr.

Homing in the Presence: Meditations for Daily Living. Gerhard E. Frost. 125p. 1978. pap. 5.95 o.p. (ISBN 0-86683-756-6). HarpR.

Hominid Evolution & Community Ecology. Robert Foley. LC 83-72771. (Studies in Archaeology). 1984. 64.00 o.p. (ISBN 0-12-261920-X). Acad Pr.

Homme d'etat russe, Nicolas Miliutine, d'apres sa correspondance inedite. A. Leroy-Beaulieu. (Russian Ser.: Vol. 14). Repr. of 1884 ed. 20.00 o.p. (ISBN 0-87569-010-6). Academic Intl.

Homme Revolte: Essai. Albert Camus. (Coll. Soleil). 1951. 16.50 o.p. (ISBN 0-685-11234-9); pap. 4.95 o.p. (ISBN 0-686-66425-6). Schoenhof.

Hommes De Bonne Volonte, 4 tomes. Jules Romains. 1956. Set. 150.00 o.p. (ISBN 0-685-11235-7). Schoenhof.

Homo Faber: A Study of Man's Mental Evolution. G. N. Tyrrell. LC 73-13026. 205p. 1973. Repr. of 1951 ed. lib. bdg. 35.00x o.p. (ISBN 0-8371-7110-5, TYHF). Greenwood.

Homo Sapiens in Decline: A Reappraisal of Natural Selection. Gerhard Kraus. 189p. 1973. text ed. 8.00x o.p. (ISBN 0-7121-5601-1). Humanities.

Homo Sovieticus. Alexander Zinoviev. 206p. 1986. 17.95 o.p. (ISBN 0-87113-080-7). Atlantic Monthly.

Homology in Group Theory. U. Stammbach. LC 73-19547. (Lecture Notes in Mathematics: Vol. 359). 183p. 1973. pap. 19.00 o.p. (ISBN 0-387-06569-5). Springer-Verlag.

Homology of Classical Groups Over Finite Fields & Their Associated Infinite Loop Spaces. Z. Fiedorowicz & S. Priddy. LC 78-12091. (Lecture Notes in Mathematics: Vol. 674). 1978. pap. 27.00 o.p. (ISBN 0-387-08932-2). Springer-Verlag.

Homopoietic Colonies. D. Metcalf. (Recent Results in Cancer Research: Vol. 61). 1977. 32.90 o.p. (ISBN 0-387-08232-8). Springer-Verlag.

Homosexual Behaviour: Therapy & Assessment. M. P. Feldman & M. J. Macculloch. 1971. 100.00 o.p. (ISBN 0-08-016244-4). Pergamon.

Homosexual Matrix. C. A. Tripp. LC 75-6987. 336p. 1975. text ed. 13.95 o.p. (ISBN 0-07-065201-5). McGraw.

Homosexual: Oppression & Liberation. Dennis Altman. 1984. pap. 1.95 o.p. (ISBN 0-380-01256-1, 27425, Discus). Avon.

Homosexualities & French Literature: Cultural Contexts, Critical Texts. Ed. by George Stambolian & Elaine Marks. LC 78-25659. 368p. 1979. 38.50x o.p. (ISBN 0-8014-1186-6). Cornell U Pr.

Homosexuality: A Biblical Perspective. Greg L. Bahnsen. LC 78-62911. 1978. pap. 4.95 o.p. (ISBN 0-8010-0744-5). Baker Bk.

Homosexuality & Counseling. Clinton R. Jones. LC 74-76922. 144p. (Orig.). 1974. pap. 1.50 o.p. (ISBN 0-8006-1301-5, 1-1301, Fortress). Augsburg Fortress.

Homosexuality & the Catholic Church. Ed. by Jeannine Gramick. 1983. pap. 8.95 o.p. (ISBN 0-88347-149-3). Thomas More.

Homosexuality in Greek Myth. Bernard Sergent. Tr. by Arthur Goldhammer from Fr. LC 85-73369. 344p. 1986. 24.95 o.p. (ISBN 0-8070-5700-2). Beacon Pr.

Homosexuality in Renaissance England. Alan Bray. 149p. (Orig.). 1982. 15.00 o.p. (ISBN 0-907040-16-0, Pub. by GMP England); pap. 7.50 o.p. (ISBN 0-907040-13-6). Alyson Pubns.

Homosexuality: The Psychology of the Creative Process. Paul Rosenfels. LC 78-146467. 1971. 5.95 o.p. (ISBN 0-87212-002-3). Libra.

Homosexualization of America. Dennis Altman. LC 82-73959. 256p. 1983. pap. 10.95 o.p. (ISBN 0-8070-4143-2, BP-654). Beacon Pr.

Homosexuals: As Seen by Themselves & Thirty Authorities. Aron M. Krich. 1962. pap. 2.25 o.p. (ISBN 0-8065-0123-5, Pub. by Citadel Pr). Carol Pub Group.

Homotopical Algebra. D. G. Quillen. (Lecture Notes in Mathematics: Vol. 43). (Orig.). 1967. pap. 13.10 o.p. (ISBN 0-387-03914-7). Springer-Verlag.

Homotopy Equivalence of Three-Manifolds with Boundaries. K. Johannson. (Lecture Notes in Mathematics: Vol. 761). 303p. 1979. pap. 23.00 o.p. (ISBN 0-387-09714-7). Springer-Verlag.

Homotopy Invariant Algebraic Structures on Topological Spaces. J. M. Boardman & R. M. Vogt. LC 73-13427. (Lecture Notes in Mathematics: Vol. 347). 1973. pap. 17.00 o.p. (ISBN 0-387-06479-6). Springer-Verlag.

Honcho. Jack Slade. (Sundance Ser.: No. 13). 1978. pap. 1.50 o.p. (ISBN 0-8439-0587-5, Pub. by Leisure Bks CT). Dorchester Pub Co.

Honda. LC 80-80769. (Popular Mechanic Motor Car Care Guides). (Illus.). 176p. 12.95 o.p. (ISBN 0-87851-935-1); pap. 6.95 o.p. (ISBN 0-87851-927-0). Hearst Bks.

Honda CB250 & 350 Twins '68 - '70. Stewart Wilkins. (Owners Workshop Manuals Ser.: No. 133). 1979. 13.50 o.p. (ISBN 0-85696-133-7). Haynes Pubns.

Honda CB350 & CB500 Fours '73 - '75. Mark Reynolds. (Owners Workshop Manuals Ser.: No. 132). 1979. 11.50 o.p. (ISBN 0-85696-132-9). Haynes Pubns.

Honda CD-CM 185, 200 & 250 Twins '77-'80. Martyn Meek. pap. 13.50 o.p. (798). Haynes Pubns.

Honda CD-CM 185, 200 & 250 Twins '78-'80. Martyn Meek. (Owners Workshop Manual Ser.). 13.50 o.p. (ISBN 0-85696-572-3, 572). Haynes Pubns.

Honda C50, C70 & C90 '72 - '81. Mervyn Bleach. (Illus.). pap. 13.50 o.p. (ISBN 0-85696-324-0, 324). Haynes Pubns.

Honda Express: 1977-1980 Service-Repair-Performance. Ed. by Eric Jorgensen. (Illus.). pap. text ed. 11.95 o.p. (ISBN 0-89287-194-6, M314). Clymer Pub.

Honda Hawk 400 Twins '78-'81. Curt Choate & J. H. Haynes. pap. 13.50 o.p. (ISBN 0-85696-701-7, 701). Haynes Pubns.

Honda Motor: The Men, the Management, the Machines. Tetsuo Sakiya. (Illus.). 260p. (Orig.). 1987. pap. 5.95 o.p. (ISBN 0-87011-826-9). Kodansha.

Honda Owner's Workshop Manual: XR75 Dirt Bikes '72 - '78. Mervyn Bleach. (Owners Workshop Manuals Ser.: No. 287). 1979. 13.50 o.p. (ISBN 0-85696-287-2). Haynes Pubns.

Honda Service-Repair Handbook: 250-350cc Scrambler Twins, All Years. Clymer Publications Staff. (Illus.). pap. text ed. 11.95 o.p. (ISBN 0-89287-010-9, M331). Clymer Pub.

Honda Tune-up & Repair. Ed. by Kalton C. Lahue. LC 78-60488. (Tune-up & Repair Ser.). (Illus.). 1978. pap. 4.95 o.p. (ISBN 0-8227-5036-8). Petersen Pub.

Honda XL-XR 250 & 500: '78-'81. Pete Shoemark. 13.50 o.p. (ISBN 0-85696-567-7, 567). Haynes Pubns.

Honda 125 Elsinore & MR175 '73 - '76. Mansur Darlington. (Owners Workshop Manuals Ser.: No. 312). 1979. 13.50 o.p. (ISBN 0-85696-312-7). Haynes Pubns.

Honda 125-300cc Twins. (M320). Clymer Pub.

Honda 1973-84: RTUG. Chilton Automotives Editorial Staff. LC 83-45324. 212p. 1984. pap. 12.50 o.p. (ISBN 0-8019-7489-5). Chilton.

Honda 250 Elsinore '73 - '75. Jeff Clew. (Owners Workshop Manuals Ser.: No. 217). 1979. 13.50 o.p. (ISBN 0-85696-217-1). Haynes Pubns.

Honda 500 & 450 Twins '66 - '78. George Collett & John Witcomb. (Owners Workshop Manuals Ser.: No. 211). 1980. 13.50 o.p. (ISBN 0-85696-211-2). Haynes Pubns.

Honest Andrew. Gloria Skurzynski. LC 79-23516. (Let Me Read Ser.). (Illus.). 32p. (gr. k-3). 1980. 5.95 o.p. (ISBN 0-15-235672-X, HJ). HarBraceJ.

Honest Andrew. Gloria Skurzynski. (Let-Me-Read Ser.). (Illus.). (gr. k-3). 1980. pap. 1.95 o.p. (ISBN 0-15-642152-6, VoyB). HarBraceJ.

Honestly, I Love You, Douglas County. Robert L. Whatley. (Illus.). 256p. 1983. 12.50 o.p. (ISBN 0-932298-33-8). Tri-State Pr Corp.

Honey Feast. Gene Opton & Nancie Hughes. 1979. pap. 4.95 o.p. (ISBN 0-913668-27-3). Ten Speed Pr.

Honey Kitchen: The Best Honey Recipes in the World. Dadant & Sons, Inc., Staff. (Illus.). 192p. 1982. 12.95 o.p. (ISBN 0-684-17489-8, ScribT). Scribner.

Honey of a Chimp. Norma Klein. (gr. 5-7). 1982. pap. 2.25 o.p. (ISBN 0-671-49614-X). Archway.

Honeymoon Caper. James Pattinson. 207p. 1986. pap. 2.95 o.p. (ISBN 0-931773-89-X). Critics Choice Paper.

Honeymoon House. Phoebe Matthews. 1979. pap. 1.75 o.p. (ISBN 0-380-45153-0, 45153). Avon.

Honeymooners Illustrated Trivia. Bob Columbe. (Illus.). 1986. 4.95 o.p. (ISBN 0-399-51308-6, Perigee). Putnam Pub Group.

Hong Kong. (Post Guides Ser.). (Illus.). 144p. (Orig.). 1987. pap. 8.95 o.p. (ISBN 962-10-0014-9). Hunter Pub NY.

Hong Kong by Night. Roger Boschmann. (Asia by Night Ser.). (Illus.). 64p. (Orig.). 1981. pap. 4.95 o.p. (ISBN 962-7031-07-0, Pub. by CFW Pubns Hong Kong). C E Tuttle.

Hong Kong in Focus. Ed. by Derek Maitland. ("In Focus" Ser.). (Illus.). 64p. (Orig.). 1981. pap. 5.95 o.p. (ISBN 962-7031-14-3, Pub. by CFW Pubns, Hong Kong). C E Tuttle.

Hong Kong, Macau & Canton-A Travel Survival Kit. 4th ed. Carol Clewlow. (Illus.). 256p. (Orig.). 1986. pap. 7.95 o.p. (ISBN 0-908086-74-1). Lonely Planet.

Hong Kong's Textile Fabrics Market. (Illus.). 62p. (Orig.). 1987. pap. 3.25 o.p. (S/N 003-009-00511-6). USGPO.

Honkytonk Gelato: Travels through Texas. Stephen Brook. LC 85-47593. 320p. 1985. 12.95 o.p. (ISBN 0-689-11639-X, Atheneum). Macmillan.

Honolulu Then & Now. Roland Morgan. (Illus., Orig.). 1978. pap. 6.95 o.p. (ISBN 0-88875-003-X). Altarinda Bks.

Honor & Dignity of the Profession: A History of the Mississippi State Bar, 1906-1976. Michael deL. Landon. LC 79-4317. (Illus.). 1979. text ed. 17.00x o.p. (ISBN 0-87805-101-5). U Pr of Miss.

Honor Thy Father. Meridel Rawlings. Ed. by Bill Keith. LC 86-81133. (Orig.). 1986. pap. 6.95 o.p. (ISBN 0-910311-39-0). Huntington Hse Inc.

Honorable Ancestor. Hannah Gibson. 192p. (Orig.). 1981. pap. 1.95 o.p. (ISBN 0-8439-0975-7, Pub. by Leisure Bks CT). Dorchester Pub Co.

Honorable Intentions: The Manners of Courtship in the Eighties. Cheryl Merser. LC 82-45180. 256p. 1983. 13.95 o.p. (ISBN 0-689-11311-0, Atheneum). Macmillan.

Honorable Intentions: The Manners of Courtship in the 80's. Cheryl Merser. 272p. 1984. pap. 7.95 o.p. (ISBN 0-03-000082-3, Owl Bks). H Holt & Co.

Honorable Men. Louis Auchincloss. LC 85-20844. 382p. 1985. Repr. of 1985 ed. 16.95 o.p. (ISBN 0-89621-670-5). Thorndike Pr.

Honorine: Avec: Albert Savarus, La Fausse Maitresse. Honore De Balzac. 9.95 o.p. (ISBN 0-686-53880-3). French & Eur.

Honour & Offer. Henry Livings. 1981. pap. 6.95 o.p. (ISBN 0-416-15880-3, NO. 6477). Routledge Chapman & Hall.

Hood. David Scannell. 288p. 1984. pap. 2.95 o.p. (ISBN 0-380-86009-0, 86009). Avon.

Hoodoo Medicine. Faith Mitchell. 1978. pap. 4.95 o.s.i. (ISBN 0-918408-06-7). Reed & Cannon.

Hoods of Manor Grove. Otis Dunbar Richardson. 1976. 10.00 o.p. (ISBN 0-682-48492-X). Exposition-Phoenix.

Hoodwinking of Mrs. Elmo. Date not set. (ISBN 0-385-29577-4). Delacorte.

Hoodwinking of Mrs. Elmo. Robert Kraus. LC 86-32750. 112p. (ps-3). 1987. pap. 12.95 o.p. (ISBN 0-385-29577-4). Delacorte.

Hoof Beats North & South: Horses & Horsemen of the Civil War. Sue Cottrell. 1975. 7.50 o.p. (ISBN 0-682-48280-3, University). Exposition-Phoenix.

Hoofbeats to Harness: Adventures of Jesse Beery, Horse Trainer. Marjorie L. Hoffer. 144p. 1986. 8.95 o.p. (ISBN 0-8062-2785-0). Carlton.

Hoofing on Broadway: A History of Show Dancing. Richard Kislan. (Illus.). 208p. 1987. 19.45 o.p. (ISBN 0-13-809484-5). P-H.

Hook, Line, & Sinker: The Complete Angler's Guide to Terminal Tackle. Gary Soucie. LC 81-20251. (Illus.). 480p. 1983. 22.50 o.p. (ISBN 0-03-048261-5). H Holt & Co.

Hooked on Horses: Bits of This & That about People & Horses after 21 Years in the Racing Game. Howard A. Jones. (Illus.). 144p. 1982. 12.50 o.p. (ISBN 0-682-49792-4, Banner). Exposition-Phoenix.

Hooked on Horses: Bits of This & That about People & Horses after 21 Years in the Racing Game. Howard A. Jones. (Illus.). 256p. 1982. 12.50 o.p. (ISBN 0-682-49791-6, Banner). Exposition-Phoenix.

Hooked on Prescription Drugs. Sue B. Jackson. Ed. by Mary H. Wallace. 112p. (Orig.). 1981. pap. 2.95 o.p. (ISBN 0-912315-33-4). Word Aflame.

Hooked Rug. William W. Kent. LC 78-172437. (Tower Bks). (Illus.). 228p. 1971. Repr. of 1941 ed. 40.00x o.p. (ISBN 0-8103-3914-5). Gale.

Hooked Rugs: A Historical Collector's Guide - How to Make Your Own. William C. Ketchum, Jr. LC 76-13880. 1976. 14.95 o.p. (ISBN 0-15-142168-4). HarBraceJ.

Hook'em Horns: A Story of Texas Football. Denne H. Freeman. LC 74-84329. (College Sports Ser.). Orig. Title: Texas Football. 1980. 9.95 o.p. (ISBN 0-87397-054-3). Strode.

Hooligans Abroad: The Behaviour & Control of English Fans at Continental Football Matches. John Williams & Eric Dunning. 200p. (Orig.). 1984. pap. 19.95x o.p. (ISBN 0-7102-0143-5). Routledge Chapman & Hall.

Hooper's Voluntary Liquidation. 5th ed. G. Auger. 1983. 45.00 o.p. (ISBN 0-85258-163-7). Van Nos Reinhold.

Hoops! Confessions of a College Basketball Analyst. Billy Packer & Roland Lazenby. 192p. 1986. pap. 7.95 o.p. (ISBN 0-8092-5304-6). Contemp Bks.

Hooray for Captain Spaulding. Richard J. Anobile. (Illus.). 1975. pap. 5.45 o.p. (ISBN 0-380-00458-5, 25882-X). Avon.

Hooray for Homicide. James Anderson. (Murder She Wrote Ser.: No. 2). 1985. pap. 2.95 o.p. (ISBN 0-380-89937-X). Avon.

Hooray for Pig! Carla Stevens. LC 73-17074. (Illus.). 48p. (ps-3). 1979. 5.95 o.p. (ISBN 0-395-28824-X, Clarion). HM.

Hooray for Us. Sandol S. Warburg. LC 76-115452. (Illus.). 48p. (gr. 1-3). 1970. 1.95 o.p. (ISBN 0-395-10927-2); Dolphin bdg. 2.20 o.p. (ISBN 0-395-10928-0). HM.

Hoorays & Hosannas. Bernadette M. Snyder. LC 80-66937. (Illus.). 56p. (Orig.). (gr. k-8). 1980. pap. 3.95 o.p. (ISBN 0-87793-205-0). Ave Maria.

Hoosier Farmboy in Lincoln's Army. Ed. by Nancy N. Baxter. 72p. (YA) (gr. 8-12). Date not set. 8.95 o.s.i. (ISBN 0-317-69478-2). Guild Pr IN.

Hoover Dam. (Illus.). 56p. (Orig.). 1985. pap. 2.25 o.p. (ISBN 0-318-18771-X, S/N 024-003-00159-7). USGPO.

Hoover's Dominican Diplomacy & the Origins of the Good Neighbor Policy. E. R. Curry. Ed. by Frank Freidel. LC 78-62379. (Modern American History Ser.: Vol. 5). 1979. lib. bdg. 36.00 o.p. (ISBN 0-8240-3629-8). Garland Pub.

Hope Against Hope: From Moltmann to Merton in One Theological Decade. Walter H. Capps. LC 75-36456. 192p. 1976. 4.75 o.p. (ISBN 0-8006-1436-4, Fortress). Augsburg Fortress.

Hope & the Future of Man. Ed. by Ewert H. Cousins. LC 72-75647. 160p. 1972. pap. 1.50x o.p. (ISBN 0-8006-0540-3, 1-140, Fortress). Augsburg Fortress.

Hope Diamond Refuses. Iris Owens. LC 83-48886. 172p. 1984. 13.45 o.s.i. (ISBN 0-394-51830-6). Knopf.

Hope for Poetry. Cecil Day-Lewis. LC 76-7980. 1976. Repr. of 1939 ed. lib. bdg. 35.00x o.p. (ISBN 0-8371-8847-4, LEHFP). Greenwood.

Hope Hanley's Patterns for Needlepoint. Hope Hanley. LC 75-25627. (Encore Edition). (Illus.). 96p. 1976. 6.95 o.p. (ISBN 0-684-15947-3, ScribT). Scribner.

Hope Leslie: Or, Early Times in the Massachuetts. Catherine M. Sedgwick. 1972. Repr. of 1827 ed. lib. bdg. 29.50 o.p. (ISBN 0-8422-8107-X). Irvington.

Hopes for Great Happenings: Alternatives in Education & Theatre. Albert Hunt. LC 77-76569. (Illus.). 1977. 7.95 o.s.i. (ISBN 0-8008-3927-7). Taplinger.

Hopes Fulfilled. Dorothy Martin. (Peggy Ser.: No. 5). (gr. 7). pap. 3.50 o.p. (ISBN 0-8024-8305-4). Moody.

Hopf Algebras & Galois Theory Two. U. Chase & M. E. Sweedler. LC 75-84143. (Lecture Notes in Mathematics: Vol. 97). (Orig.). 1969. pap. 10.70 o.p. (ISBN 0-387-04616-X). Springer-Verlag.

Hopf Spaces. A. Zabrodsky. LC 76-54352. (Mathematics Studies: Vol. 22). 1976. pap. 26.50 o.p. (ISBN 0-7204-0553-X, North-Holland). Elsevier.

Hopfellow. Jenny Partridge. LC 81-7070. (Oakapple Wood Stories Ser.). 32p. (gr. k-2). 1982. 4.95 o.p. (ISBN 0-03-061512-7). H Holt & Co.

Hopi Voices: Recollections, Traditions, & Narratives of the Hopi Indians. Ed. by Harold Courlander. LC 82-8413. 296p. 1982. 17.50 o.p. (ISBN 0-8263-0612-8). U of NM Pr.

Hopper's Places. Gail Levin. LC 85-40039. (Illus.). 94p. 1985. 18.45 o.p. (ISBN 0-394-54414-5); pap. 14.95 o.p. (ISBN 0-394-72978-1). Knopf.

Hopscotch. Julio Cortazar. 1982. pap. 4.95 o.p. (ISBN 0-380-00372-4, 69825-0, Bard). Avon.

Horace Bushnell's Theory of Language: In the Context of Other Nineteenth-Century Philosophies of Language. Donald A. Crosby. (Studies in Philosophy: No. 22). 300p. 1975. text ed. 33.60x o.p. (ISBN 90-2793-044-9). Mouton.

Horace Mann & the Common School Revival in the U. S. Burke A. Hinsdale. LC 72-78748. 1898. Repr. 39.00x o.p. (ISBN 0-403-08928-X). Somerset Pub.

Horace, Odes & Epodes: A Study in Poetic Word-Order. Henry D. Naylor. (Latin Poetry Ser.: Vol. 9). (LC 77-070832). 1978. Repr. of 1922 ed. lib. bdg. 40.00 o.p. (ISBN 0-8240-2958-5). Garland Pub.

Horace: Satires & Epistles. Ed. by Edward P. Morris. 1980. pap. 12.95x o.p. (ISBN 0-8061-1177-1). U of Okla Pr.

Horace Tabor: His Life & the Legend. Duane A. Smith. (Illus.). 412p. 1981. pap. 9.95 o.p. (ISBN 0-87108-594-1). Pruett.

Horace's Compromise: The Dilemma of the American High School. Theodore R. Sizer. 240p. 1984. 16.45 o.s.i. (ISBN 0-395-34423-9). HM.

Horace's Satires & Epistles. Tr. by Jacob Fuchs. 1977. 9.95 o.p. (ISBN 0-393-04479-3). Norton.

Horary Astrology & Judgment of Events. Barbara Watters. LC 73-78387. 232p. 1982. pap. 10.70 o.p. (ISBN 0-86690-168-X, W1487-024, Valhalla Publ.). Am Fed Astrologers.

Horizon Book of Ancient Rome see Ancient Rome.

Horizons. Norman Bel Geddes. (Illus.). 16.50 o.p. (ISBN 0-8446-5554-6). Peter Smith.

Horizons: An Introduction to French Language & Culture. Dominique Bennett et al. 1984. text ed. 27.95 o.p. (ISBN 0-03-062496-7). HR&W.

Horizons: Exploring the Universe. 1987 ed. Michael A. Seeds. 484p. 1987. pap. text ed. (ISBN 0-534-07926-1). Wadsworth Pub.

Horizons of Anthropology. 2nd ed. Ed. by Sol Tax & Leslie G. Freeman. LC 76-46247. (Illus.). 391p. 1977. text ed. 41.95x o.p. (ISBN 0-202-01157-7); pap. text ed. 19.95x o.p. (ISBN 0-202-01158-5). Aldine de Gruyter.

Horizons of Assent: Modernism, Postmodernism, & the Ironic Imagination. Alan Wilde. LC 80-22576. 224p. 1981. text ed. 18.50x o.p. (ISBN 0-8018-2449-4). Johns Hopkins.

Horizons of Bioenergetics: Proceedings of the Symposium, Bloomington, Oct. 1970. Symposium, Bloomington Staff. Ed. by Anthony San Pietro & Howard Gest. 1972. 43.50 o.p. (ISBN 0-12-618940-4). Acad Pr.

Horizontal Boring. 2nd ed. Ed. by J. R. Beaton et al. (Engineering Craftsmen: No. H28/2). (Illus.). 1976. spiral bdg. 39.95x o.p. (ISBN 0-85083-307-8). Trans-Atl Phila.

Horizontal Man. Helen Eustis. LC 75-44970. (Crime Fiction Ser). 1976. Repr. of 1946 ed. lib. bdg. 21.00 o.p. (ISBN 0-8240-2365-X). Garland Pub.

Horkheimer's Critical Sociology of Religion: The Relative & the Transcendent. Rudolf J. Siebert. LC 78-66280. 1979. pap. text ed. 10.00 o.p. (ISBN 0-8191-0688-7). U Pr of Amer.

Hormonal Contraceptives, Estrogens & Human Welfare. Ed. by Marian C. Diamond & Carol C. Korenbrot. 1978. 25.50 o.p. (ISBN 0-12-214750-2). Acad Pr.

Hormonal Proteins & Peptides: Gonadotropic Hormones, Vol. XI. Ed. by Choh Hao Li. LC 82-22770. 1983. 56.50 o.p. (ISBN 0-12-447211-7). Acad Pr.

Hormonal Proteins & Peptides: Prolactin, Vol. 8. Ed. by Choh Hao Li. LC 80-11061. 1980. 62.50 o.p. (ISBN 0-12-447208-7). Acad Pr.

Hormonal Regulation in Plant Growth & Development. Harald Kaldewey & Yusuf Vardar. LC 72-86049. (Illus.). 535p. 1972. 55.90x o.p. (ISBN 3-527-25436-6). VCH Pubs.

Hormonal Regulation of Sodium Excretion. Ed. by R. Lichardus et al. (Developments in Endocrinology Ser.: Vol. 10). 1981. 81.75 o.p. (ISBN 0-444-80289-4). Elsevier.

Hormonal Steroids, Biochemistry, Pharmacology, Therapeutics, 2 Vols. Ed. by L. Martini & A. Pecile. 1965. Vol. 1. 92.00 o.p. (ISBN 0-12-475301-9); Vol. 2. 92.00 o.p. (ISBN 0-12-475302-7). Acad Pr.

Hormonal Steroids: Proceedings of the Fourth International Congress. Ed. by V. H. James & J. R. Pasqualini. 1976. 235.00 o.p. (ISBN 0-08-019682-9). Pergamon.

Hormone Action. A. M. Malkinson. (Outline Studies in Biology Ser.). 1975. pap. 8.50 o.p. (ISBN 0-412-13070-X, 6185, Pub. by Chapman & Hall). Routledge Chapman & Hall.

Hormone Action, Vol. 2. Ed. by Bert W. O'Malley. 1978. 92.50 o.p. (ISBN 0-12-526302-3). Acad Pr.

Hormone Receptor Interaction: Molecular Aspects. Gerald S. Levey. (Modern Pharmacology-Toxicology Ser.: Vol. 9). 488p. 1976. 89.75 o.p. (ISBN 0-8247-6438-2). Dekker.

Hormone Receptors in the Brain. Junzo Kato et al. (Illus.). 220p. 1973. text ed. 26.50x o.p. (ISBN 0-8422-7078-7). Irvington.

Hormone Research I: Proceedings of the Annual Symposium, 1st, 1974. Annual Hormone Research Symposium Staff. Ed. by M. Norvell & T. Shellenberger. (Illus.). 142p. 1976. text ed. 39.95 o.p. (ISBN 0-89116-009-4). Hemisphere Pub.

Hormone Research II: Proceedings of the Annual Symposium, 2nd, 1975. Annual Hormone Research Symposium Staff. Ed. by M. J. Norvell & T. E. Shellenberger. (Illus.). 266p. 1976. text ed. 34.50 o.p. (ISBN 0-89116-039-6). Hemisphere Pub.

Hormone Research III: Proceedings of the Annual Symposium, 3rd, 1976. new ed. Annual Hormone Research Symposium Staff. Ed. by M. J. Norvell & T. E. Shellenberger. (Illus.). 372p. 1977. text ed. 37.25 o.p. (ISBN 0-89116-070-1). Hemisphere Pub.

Hormones & Atherosclerosis: Proceedings. Ed. by Gregory Pincus. 1959. 67.50 o.p. (ISBN 0-12-557050-3). Acad Pr.

Hormones & Behavior. Seymour Levine. 1972. 50.00 o.p. (ISBN 0-12-445450-X). Acad Pr.

Hormones & Brain Development. Ed. by G. Dorner & M. Kawakami. LC 78-25863. (Developments in Endocrinology Ser.: Vol. 3). 1979. 84.25 o.p. (ISBN 0-444-80091-3, Biomedical Pr). Elsevier.

Hormones & Brain Differentiation. G. Dorner. 1976. 81.75 o.p. (ISBN 0-444-41477-0, North Holland). Elsevier.

Hormones & Cancer. K. W. McKerns. 1974. 85.00 o.p. (ISBN 0-12-485350-1). Acad Pr.

Hormones & Cell Regulation, Vol. 5. Ed. by J. Dumont & J. Nunez. 1981. 68.00 o.p. (ISBN 0-444-80322-X). Elsevier.

Hormones in Blood, 2 Vols. 2nd ed. Ed. by Charles H. Gray & Alfred L. Bacharach. Vol. 1, 1967. 44.50 o.p. (ISBN 0-12-296101-3); Vol. 2, 1968. 48.50 o.p. (ISBN 0-12-296102-1). Acad Pr.

Hormones in Human Reproduction. George W. Corner. LC 42-51440. (Illus.). 1963. pap. 1.65 o.p. (ISBN 0-689-70051-2, 16, Atheneum). Macmillan.

Hormones, Lipoproteins & Atherosclerosis: Proceedings of a Satelite Symposium of the 28th International Congress of Physiological Sciences, Bratislava, Czechoslovakia, 1980. M. Palkovic. LC 80-41926. (Advances in Physiological Sciences Ser.: Vol. 35). (Illus.). 300p. 1981. 57.00 o.p. (ISBN 0-08-027357-2). Pergamon.

Horn: A Comprehensive Guide to the Modern Instrument & Its Music. Robin Gregory. 410p. Repr. of 1969 ed. lib. bdg. 59.00 o.p. (Pub. by Am Repr Serv). Reprint Servs.

Horn: Music Criticisms. Eduard Hanslick. 312p. Repr. of 1963 ed. lib. bdg. 49.00 o.p. (Pub. by Am Repr Serv). Reprint Servs.

Horn of Africa. Ed. by Michael A. Samuels. (Orig.). 1978. pap. 3.95 o.p. (ISBN 0-87855-719-9). Transaction Pubs.

Hornby Gauge O System. Chris Graebe & Julie Graebe. (Hornby Companion Ser. V). (Illus.). 312p. 1985. 55.00 o.s.i. (ISBN 0-904568-35-0, Pub. by New Cavendish England). Schiffer.

Horns & Antlers. Wilfrid S. Bronson. LC 42-7882. (Illus.). (gr. 3-7). 1942. 4.95 o.p. (ISBN 0-15-235942-7, HJ). HarBraceJ.

Horoscopes for Dogs. Jeane Dixon. 1979. 5.95 o.p. (ISBN 0-395-27453-2). HM.

Horowitz: A Biography of Vladimir Horowitz. Glenn Plaskin. LC 82-14275. (Illus.). 640p. 1983. 19.95 o.p. (ISBN 0-688-01616-2). Morrow.

Horrible, Impossible, Bad Witch Child. Barbara Williams. (Illus.). 32p. (ps-3). 1982. pap. 1.95 o.p. (ISBN 0-380-80283-X, 60000-5, Camelot). Avon.

Horrocks: The General Who Lead from the Front. Philip Warner. 224p. 1984. 29.95 o.p. (ISBN 0-241-11312-1, Pub. by Hamish Hamilton England). David & Charles.

Horror Films. CineBooks Staff. LC 89-60764. (Home Library Ser.). 336p. (Orig.). 1989. pap. 11.95 o.p. (ISBN 0-933997-23-X). CineBooks.

Horror Hotel. Hilary Milton. Ed. by Betty Schwartz et al. (Plot-Your-Own Horror Stories Ser.: No. 4). (Illus.). 128p. (gr. 3-7). 1983. pap. 2.85 o.s.i. (ISBN 0-671-49249-7). Wanderer Bks.

Horror in the Movies. Daniel Cohen. (Illus.). 96p. (gr. 3 up). 1982. 10.00 o.p. (ISBN 0-89919-074-X, Clarion). HM.

Horror in the Museum & Other Revisions. H. P. Lovecraft et al. Ed. by August Derleth. 1970. 14.95 o.p. (ISBN 0-87054-031-9). Arkham.

Horror of Life. Roger L. Williams. LC 79-26641. 1980. lib. bdg. 22.50 o.s.i. (ISBN 0-226-89918-7). U of Chicago Pr.

Horror Story. Oliver McNab. 1979. 9.95 o.p. (ISBN 0-395-27765-5). HM.

Horror Wears Blue. Lin Carter. LC 87-13453. (Science Fiction Ser.). 192p. 1987. 12.95 o.p. (ISBN 0-385-12504-6). Doubleday.

Horrors: From Screen to Scream! Ed Naha. 1981. pap. 5.45 o.p. (ISBN 0-380-00499-2, 38653). Avon.

Horrors of Love. Jean Dutourd. Tr. by Robin Chancellor from Fr. LC 75-3991. 1976. Repr. of 1967 ed. lib. bdg. 41.50x o.p. (ISBN 0-8371-7481-3, DUHL). Greenwood.

Hors d'Oeuvre Book. rev. ed. Coralie Castle. LC 85-15448. Orig. Title: Hors d'Oeuvre Etc. (Illus.). 248p. 1985. pap. 10.95 o.p. (ISBN 0-89286-258-0, TX740C316, One Hund One Prods). Ortho.

Hors d'oeuvre, Etc. Coralie Castle & Barbara Lawrence. LC 73-81084. (Illus.). 192p. 1973. pap. 5.95 o.p. (ISBN 0-912238-40-2, One Hund One Prods). Ortho.

Hors d'Oeuvre Etc. see Hors d'Oeuvre Book.

Hors d'Oeuvres Artistry. Julia Weinberg. LC 82-61584. (Illus.). 176p. (Orig.). 1982. pap. 10.95 o.s.i. (ISBN 0-8329-0251-9). New Century.

Horse. 3rd ed. John M. Kays. LC 82-11496. (Illus.). 416p. 1982. 19.95 o.p. (ISBN 0-668-05469-7). Arco.

Horse & Buggy Age in New England. Edwin V. Mitchell. LC 74-7066. 240p. 1974. Repr. of 1937 ed. 35.00x o.p. (ISBN 0-8103-3657-X). Gale.

Horse & His Boy. C. S. Lewis. (Chronicles of Narnia Ser.: Vol. 5). 282p. 1986. cloth 13.95 o.p. (ISBN 0-8161-4093-6, Large Print Bks). G K Hall.

Horse, Bird, & Man: The Origins of Greek Painting. J. L. Benson. Date not set. price not set o.p. U of Mass Pr.

Horse Breeding & Schooling. Date not set. (ISBN 0-87605-853-5). Howell Bk.

Horse-Breeding Farm. Larryann C. Willis. LC 72-5179. (Illus.). 480p. 1973. 17.50 o.p. (ISBN 0-498-01164-X); pap. 9.95 o.p. (ISBN 0-498-01977-2). A S Barnes.

Horse Called Pete. Eliza Bialk. (Illus.). (gr. 4-6). 1948. 6.95 o.p. (ISBN 0-395-06631-X). HM.

Horse Comes First. Mary Calhoun. LC 73-84822. (Illus.). 192p. (gr. 4-6). 1974. 6.95 o.p. (ISBN 0-689-30132-4, Atheneum). Macmillan.

Horse Feeding & Nutrition. Date not set. (ISBN 0-87605-850-0). Howell Bk.

Horse Goddess. Morgan Llywelyn. 1982. 15.45 o.p. (ISBN 0-395-32514-5). HM.

Horse in the Furrow. George E. Evans. 292p. 1986. pap. 11.95 o.p. (ISBN 0-571-08164-9). Faber & Faber.

Horse in Your Backyard? Virginia P. Clemens. LC 77-7394. (Illus.). 154p. (gr. 7-10). 1977. 8.50 o.s.i. (ISBN 0-664-32616-1, Westminster). Westminster John Knox.

Horse Management. John Hickman. (Comparative Medicine & Animal Health Ser.). 1984. 34.50 o.p. (ISBN 0-12-347220-2). Acad Pr.

Horse of Air. Lucy Rees. 216p. (gr. 9 up). 1980. 8.95 o.p. (ISBN 0-416-30741-8, NO. 0207). Routledge Chapman & Hall.

Horse Story Collection. Ed. by Suzanne LeVert. (Illus.). (gr. 3 up). 1985. 6.95 o.s.i. (ISBN 0-671-52591-3, Little Simon). S&S.

Horse That Came to Breakfast. Marilyn D. Anderson. (Illus.). 96p. (gr. 3-5). 1987. 1.95 o.s.i. (ISBN 0-87406-198-9). Willowisp Pr.

Horse That Played Center Field. Hal Higdon. (gr. 3-7). 1979. pap. 0.95 o.p. (ISBN 0-380-01255-3, 39495, Camelot). Avon.

Horse Thief Trail. J. D. Harkleroad. 1980. pap. 1.75 o.p. (ISBN 0-8439-0716-9, Pub. by Leisure Bks CT). Dorchester Pub Co.

Horse Traders. Steven Crist. 1986. 16.45 o.p. (ISBN 0-393-02300-1). Norton.

Horse with Eight Hands. Joan Phipson. LC 74-76280. 208p. (gr. 5-9). 1974. 7.50 o.s.i. (ISBN 0-689-50013-0, M K McElderry). Macmillan.

Horse with the Pink Mane. V. Astafiev. 336p. 1978. pap. 3.95 o.p. (ISBN 0-8285-0943-3, Pub. by Progress Pubs USSR). Imported Pubns.

Horseback Across Three Americas. Verne Albright. (Illus.). 204p. 1974. 10.00 o.p. (ISBN 0-912830-17-4). Printed Horse.

Horselover's Handbook: An Introduction to Owning, Caring for, & Riding Horses. Leda Blumberg. 112p. (Orig.). (gr. 2-6). 1984. pap. 2.95 o.p. (ISBN 0-380-89326-6, Camelot). Avon.

Horseman's Bible. Jack Coggins. LC 66-17921. (Outdoor Bible Ser.). 1966. pap. 4.95 o.p. (ISBN 0-385-03167-X). Doubleday.

Horseman's Catalog. 1979. text ed. 24.95 o.p. (ISBN 0-07-047135-5). McGraw.

Horseman's Etiquette Book. Marcia S. Copper. LC 76-880. (Encore Edition). (Illus.). 160p. 1976. 1.95 o.p. (ISBN 0-684-16187-7, ScribT). Scribner.

Horseman's International Book of Reference. Jean Froissard & Lilly P. Froissard. (Illus.). 416p. 1980. 45.00 o.p. (ISBN 0-09-132400-9, NO. 0217, Pub. by Hutchinson England). Routledge Chapman & Hall.

Horsemanship: A Guide to Information Sources. Ed. by Ellen B. Wells. LC 79-16046. (Sports, Games, & Pastimes Information Guide Ser.: Vol. 4). 152p. 1979. 68.00x o.p. (ISBN 0-8103-1444-4). Gale.

Horsemanship: Basics for Intermediate Riders. Evelyn Pervier. LC 83-12170. (Illus.). 96p. (gr. 7 up). 1983. lib. bdg. 9.29 o.p. (ISBN 0-671-49564-X). Messner.

Horsemanship in Pictures. Susan E. Harris. 1975. pap. 4.95 o.p. (ISBN 0-684-14337-2, SL598, ScribT). Scribner.

Horsepower Tables for Agitator Impellers. L. T. Advani. LC 76-2964. 175p. 1976. 37.00x o.p. (ISBN 0-87201-368-5). Gulf Pub.

Horses & Riding. (Fact Bks.). (Illus.). 96p. (gr. 4-7). 1987. pap. 3.50 o.p. (ISBN 0-528-87177-3, Checkerboard Pr). Macmillan.

Horses in Suburbia. Joyce Taylor. (Illus.). 3.25 o.p. (ISBN 0-85131-085-0, NL51, Pub. by J A Allen U K). S R Smith Sporting Bks.

Horse's Neck. Pete Townshend. 144p. 1985. 12.70 o.p. (ISBN 0-395-38348-X). HM.

Horseshoe: A Romance in Four Acts. Mathilde Waelty. 1979. 5.00 o.p. (ISBN 0-682-49258-2). Exposition-Phoenix.

Horseshoe Hill. Pamela Reynolds. (Illus.). (gr. 4-6). 1965. 10.25 o.p. (ISBN 0-688-41056-1). Lothrop.

Horsethief. Will Benton. 1986. 12.95 o.p. (ISBN 0-8166-0279-4, Large Print Bks). G K Hall.

Horsethief Canyon. Jerry Brucker. 1981. pap. 1.95 o.p. (ISBN 0-8439-0911-0, Pub. by Leisure Bks CT). Dorchester Pub Co.

Horsewhip the Doctor: Tales from Our Medical Past. Ross Patrick. LC 85-1015. (Illus.). 239p. 1986. text ed. 27.50x o.p. (ISBN 0-7022-1867-7). U of Queensland Pr.

Hortense, Couche-toi: Avec: La Conversion d'Alceste, Monsieur Badinet, Les Boulingrin. Georges Courteline. 160p. 1975. 8.95 o.p. (ISBN 0-686-54632-6). French & Eur.

Hortense Is a Star. David N. Bruskin. (Story Bus Subseries: Camp Bus). (Illus.). 10p. (ps-2). 1988. bds. 14.95 o.p. (ISBN 1-55929-010-2). Bound Fun Inc.

Horticultural Reviews, Vol. 1. Ed. by Jules Janick. (Horticultural Reviews Ser.). (Illus.). 1979. 54.95 o.p. (ISBN 0-87055-314-3). AVI.

Horticultural Reviews, Vol. 2. Ed. by Jules Janick. (Illus.). 1980. 54.95 o.p. (ISBN 0-87055-352-6). AVI.

Hosea: An Israelite Prophet in Judean Perspective. Grace I. Emmerson. (JSOT Supplement Ser.: No. 28). 224p. pap. text ed. 11.95x o.s.i. (Pub. by JSOT Pr England). Eisenbrauns.

Hosea Globe & the Fantastical Peg-Legged Chu. Graydon Beeks. LC 74-19269. (Illus.). 192p. (gr. 4-6). 1975. PLB 6.95 o.p. (ISBN 0-689-30464-1, Atheneum). Macmillan.

Hosea-Malachi, Vol. V. Beacon Bible Commentary Staff. 15.95 o.p. (ISBN 0-8010-0692-9). Baker Bk.

Hosea's Heartbreak. Jack R. Riggs. 1984. pap. 5.95 o.p. (ISBN 0-87213-724-4). Loizeaux.

Hosiery & Legwear: Men's, Women's, Boy's & Girl's. 6th ed. Fairchild Market Research Division Staff. (Farichild Fact Files). (Illus.). 50p. 1986. pap. 20.00 o.p. (ISBN 0-87005-551-8). Fairchild.

Hosiery-Legwear: (Men's, Women's, Children's) Fairchild Market Research Division Staff. (Fact File Ser.). (Illus.). 55p. 1984. pap. 17.50 o.p. (ISBN 0-87005-481-3). Fairchild.

Hospice: The Living Idea. Cicely Saunders & Dorothy Summers. (Illus.). 198p. 1981. (ISBN 0-7216-7931-5). Saunders.

Hospital Accreditation Program Scoring Guidelines: Medical Staff Standards. 86p. 1987. pap. 40.00 o.s.i. (ISBN 0-86688-118-2). Joint Comm Hlthcare.

Hospital-Acquired Infection: Principles & Prevention. G. A. Ayliffe & L. J. Taylor. (Illus.). 160p. 1982. pap. 7.50 o.p. (ISBN 0-901144-14-2). Year Bk Med.

Hospital Associated Infections in the Compromised Host. Bodey & Rodriquez. (Handbook on Hospital-Associated Infection Ser.: Vol. 2). 1979. 69.75 o.p. (ISBN 0-8247-6785-3). Dekker.

Hospital Associated Infections in the General Hospital Populations & Specific Measures of Control. Groschel. (Handbook on Hospital-Associated Infections Ser.: Vol. 3). 208p. 1979. 55.00 o.p. (ISBN 0-8247-6815-9). Dekker.

Hospital Budgeting: A Case Study Approach. Charles J. Pendola. 1976. 10.00 o.p. (ISBN 0-682-48411-3). Exposition-Phoenix.

Hospital Cost Containment through Productivity Management. Steven Gray & Wilbert Steffy. 256p. 1982. 27.95 o.p. (ISBN 0-442-22921-6). Van Nos Reinhold.

Hospital Costs in Massachusetts: An Econometric Study. Mary L. Ingbar & Lester D. Taylor. LC 68-14258. (Wertheim Publications in Industrial Relations Ser). (Illus.). 1968. 16.00x o.s.i. (ISBN 0-674-40700-8). Harvard U Pr.

Hospital Crisis Management: A Casebook. A. Brent Garber et al. LC 79-25691. 180p. 1979. text ed. 35.95 o.p. (ISBN 0-89443-079-3). Aspen Pub.

Hospital Dental Practice: A Manual. Raymond F. Zambito. 1978. spiral 22.75 o.p. (ISBN 0-87488-994-4). Med Exam.

Hospital Engineering Handbook. 3rd ed. American Society for Hospital Engineering of the American Hospital Association Staff. LC 80-17346. (Illus.). 348p. 1980. pap. 35.00 o.p. (ISBN 0-939450-74-7, 055120). AHPI.

Hospital Financial Accounting Theory & Practice. 2nd ed. L. Seawell. 722p. instr's. manual 43.95 o.p. (ISBN 0-8403-4062-1). Healthcare Fin Mgmt Assn.

Hospital Humor Cartoons. 2nd ed. William Armstrong. (Armstrong Cartoon Ser.). (Illus.). 48p. (Orig.). (ps up). 1972. pap. 1.00 o.p. (ISBN 0-913452-06-8). Jesuit Bks.

Hospital Infection Control: Principles & Practices. Mary Castle. LC 80-13424. 251p. 1980. 30.00x o.p. (ISBN 0-471-05395-3). Wiley.

Hospital Labor Relations. Richard U. Miller. (Wisconsin Business Monographs: No. 11). (Illus.). 104p. 1980. 7.50 o.p. (ISBN 0-86603-003-4). Bur Busn Wis.

Hospital Medical Racket & You. Rex J. Dye. LC 74-34511. 1975. 6.50 o.p. (ISBN 0-682-48236-6, Banner). Exposition-Phoenix.

Hospital Ministry. Lawrence Holst. Intro. by Martin E. Marty. 256p. 1985. 19.95x o.p. (ISBN 0-8245-0697-9). Crossroad NY.

Hospital on the Move: The Story of an Army Nurse. Marilyn G. Cook. 64p. 1987. 8.95 o.p. (ISBN 0-8062-2831-8). Carlton.

Hospital Patience. Norma Larson. 128p. 1986. 5.95 o.p. (ISBN 0-8007-5216-3). Revell.

Hospital Patient Feeding Systems. National Research Council Advisory Board on Military Personnel Supplies. 1982. pap. text ed. 15.50x o.p. (ISBN 0-309-03296-2). Natl Acad Pr.

Hospital Pharmacy Computer Systems: Report 1986. 1986. 20.00 o.p. (ISBN 0-930530-59-4). Am Soc Hosp Pharm.

Hospital Phone Book 1987-88 Edition. Ed. by Stanley Alperin. 1986. 39.95 o.p. (ISBN 0-916524-26-4, 702). US Direct Serv.

Hospital Salary Survey Report 1984-85. Zabka, John R., Associates Inc. Staff. (Fourteenth Annual Report Ser.). 105.00 o.p. (ISBN 0-939326-14-0). Hosp Compensation.

Hospital Sketches. Louisa May Alcott. 1986. Repr. 9.95 o.p. (ISBN 0-918222-71-0). Morrow.

Hospital: The Hidden Lives of a Medical Center Staff. Michael Medved. 384p. 1983. 15.50 o.p. (ISBN 0-671-42442-4). S&S.

Hospital Use by Children in the United States & Canada. 67p. 1984. pap. 2.75 o.p. (ISBN 0-318-11789-4, S/N 017-022-00845-9). USGPO.

Hospitality Industry-the World of Food Service. Joseph A. Villella. LC 74-31467. (Illus.). 352p. 1975. text ed. 34.95 o.p. (ISBN 0-07-067450-7). McGraw.

Hospitality Management Account. 2nd ed. M. Coltman. 1983. pap. instr's. manual o.p. (ISBN 0-8436-0875-7). Van Nos Reinhold.

Hospitality Management Accounting. 2nd ed. Michael M. Coltman. 400p. 1983. 21.95 o.p. (ISBN 0-8436-0866-8). Van Nos Reinhold.

Hospitality Personnel Management. W. Morgan. 1983. pap. instr's. manual o.p. (ISBN 0-8436-2143-5). Van Nos Reinhold.

Hospitals & Health Care Facilities. 2nd ed. Architectural Record Magazine Editors. 1978. text ed. 49.50 o.p. (ISBN 0-07-002338-7). McGraw.

Hospitals & the Long-Stay Patient. D. Norton. 1967. 28.00 o.p. (ISBN 0-08-011053-3); pap. 13.00 o.p. (ISBN 0-08-011052-5). Pergamon.

Hospitals (Architecture) R. Aloi & C. Bassi. (Illus.). 1972. 50.00 o.p. E J Brill USA.

Hospitals in Today's Health Care Marketplace, Vol. 351. Practising Law Institute Staff. 219p. 1985. pap. 40.00 o.p. (ISBN 0-317-27442-2, A4-4116). PLI.

Host Defenses to Intracellular Pathogens. Ed. by Toby K. Eisenstein et al. LC 82-25957. (Advances In Experimental Medicine & Biology Ser.: Vol. 162). 554p. 1983. 85.00x o.p. (ISBN 0-306-41259-4, Plenum Pr). Plenum Pub.

Host-Parasite Interfaces. Ed. by Brent B. Nickol. 1979. 30.00 o.p. (ISBN 0-12-518750-5). Acad Pr.

Host State & the Transnational Corporation. Juha Kuusi. 200p. 1979. text ed. 37.95 o.p. (ISBN 0-566-00249-3). Gower Pub Co.

Hostage Taking: Preparation, Avoidance, & Survival. rev. ed. (Department of Foreign Foreign Service Ser.: No. 390). (Illus.). 38p. (Orig.). 1984. pap. 1.25 o.p. (ISBN 0-318-19947-5, S/N 044-000-02105-6). USGPO.

Hostages to Fortune. Caroline Moorehead. LC 79-51398. 1980. 12.95 o.p. (ISBN 0-689-11005-7, Atheneum). Macmillan.

Hosteling, U. S. A. The Official American Youth Hostels Handbook. 4th, rev. ed. American Youth Hostels Staff. (Illus.). 208p. 1985. pap. (ISBN 0-88742-019-2). Globe Pequot.

Hostos el Sembrador. Juan Bosch. (Norte Ser.). 208p. 1976. pap. 5.95 o.p. (ISBN 0-940238-19-5). Ediciones Huracan.

Hot Car. Lou Cameron. 208p. (Orig.). 1981. pap. 2.25 o.p. (ISBN 0-380-78949-3, 78949). Avon.

Hot Cross Buns & Other Old Street Cries. John Langstaff. LC 77-14426. (Illus.). 32p. (gr. 3 up). 1978. 7.95 o.p. (ISBN 0-689-50103-X, Atheneum). Macmillan.

Hot Dog! Robert Fischer. LC 80-201. (Illus.). 64p. (gr. 4 up). 1980. lib. bdg. 8.29 o.s.i. (ISBN 0-671-33045-4). Messner.

Hot Dog Chicago: A Native's Dining Guide. Rich Bowen & Dick Fay. 150p. 1983. pap. 3.95 o.p. (ISBN 0-914091-27-1). Chicago Review.

Hot Electrons in Semiconductors: Proceedings of the International Conference, Denton, TX, July 6-8, 1977. International Conference on Hot Electrons in Semiconductors Staff. Ed. by W. Crawford Dunlap. 1978. pap. 46.00 o.p. (ISBN 0-08-022692-2). Pergamon.

Hot Gates & Other Occasional Pieces. William G. Golding. LC 66-12363. 1967. pap. 3.95 o.p. (ISBN 0-15-642180-1, Harv). HarBraceJ.

Hot Licks. Compiled by Guitar Player Magazine Editors. 128p. (Orig.). 1988. pap. 14.95 o.p. (ISBN 0-88188-910-5, 00183313). H Leonard Pub Corp.

Hot Money: Peekaboo Finance & the Politics of Debt. Thomas Naylor. 400p. 1987. 18.45 o.s.i. (ISBN 0-671-62319-2, Linden Pr). S&S.

Hot Stuff: A Cookbook in Praise of the Piquant. Jessica B. Harris. LC 84-45047. (Illus.). 256p. 1985. 16.95 o.p. (ISBN 0-689-11483-4, Atheneum). Macmillan.

Hot Summer, Cold Murder. Gaylord Dold. 176p. 1987. pap. 2.95 o.p. (ISBN 0-380-75058-9). Avon.

Hot Tubs, Spas & Home Saunas. Sunset Editors. LC 78-70274. (Illus.). 80p. 1979. pap. 4.95 o.p. (ISBN 0-376-01242-0). Sunset-Lane.

Hot Tubs, Spas & Home Saunas. Sunset Magazine & Books Editors. LC 78-70274. (Illus.). 80p. 1979. pap. 5.95 o.p. (ISBN 0-376-01244-7, Sunset Bks). Sunset-Lane.

Hot Wire. James Brown. 237p. 1985. 15.95 o.p. (ISBN 0-87795-630-8, Arbor Hse). Morrow.

Hot Working & Forming Processes. 290p. 1980. text ed. 30.00x o.p. (ISBN 0-904357-28-7, Pub. by Inst Metals). Gower Pub Co.

Hotel & Catering French: A New Approach for Advanced Students & Practitioners. David Atkinson. (Illus.). 1980. 55.00 o.p. (ISBN 0-08-023731-2); pap. text ed. 15.50 o.p. (ISBN 0-08-023730-4). Pergamon.

Hotel & Motel Development. Laventhol & Horwath. 224p. 1984. 56.00 o.p. (ISBN 0-87420-629-4, HD1). Urban Land.

Hotel & Motel Security Management. Walter J. Buzby & David Paine. LC 76-12555. 256p. 1976. text ed. 29.95 o.p. (ISBN 0-913708-24-0). Butterworth.

Hotel & Restaurant Business. 3rd ed. Donald E. Lundberg. LC 79-207. 1983. pap. 15.95 o.p. (ISBN 0-8436-2175-3). Van Nos Reinhold.

Hotel & Restaurant Design. Douglas Smith. 137p. 1979. 23.00x o.p. (ISBN 0-435-86501-3, Pub. by Design Council Pub). Intl Spec Bk.

Hotel Architecture & the Work of Morris Lapidus: A Selected Bibliography. Bibliographic Research Library Staff. (Architecture Ser.: A 1402). 8p. 1985. 2.00 o.p. (ISBN 0-89028-432-6). Vance Biblios.

Hotel for Dogs. Lois Duncan. (Illus.). (gr. 1-3). 1980. pap. 1.75 o.p. (ISBN 0-380-01258-8, 62133-9, Camelot). Avon.

Hotel Guide: The Country Hotel Tradition. French Government Tourist Office Staff. 1985. pap. 7.95 o.p. (ISBN 2-904394-04-4). Faber & Faber.

Hotel-Motel (Architecture) G. Aloi. (Illus.). 1970. 40.00 o.s.i. (ISBN 0-685-12023-6). E J Brill USA.

Hotel, Restaurant & Travel Law. 2nd ed. Norman G. Cournoyer & Anthony G. Marshall. 675p. 1988. text ed. 35.95 o.p. (ISBN 0-8273-2700-5). Delmar.

Hotel Security Officer. Ed Ellis. (Illus.). 133p. (Orig.). 1987. pap. 100.00 o.p. (ISBN 0-938481-46-0). Camelot Consult.

Hotel Tacloban. Douglas Valentine. 192p. 1986. pap. 3.50 o.p. (ISBN 0-380-70095-6). Avon.

Hotels & Restaurants in Britain. Date not set. (ISBN 0-86145-771-4, Pub. by Auto Assn England). Salem Hse Pubs.

Hotels & Restaurants in Britain 1983. British Hotels, Restaurants, & Caterers Association. (Illus.). 550p. 1983. pap. 12.95 o.p. (ISBN 0-13-394916-8). P-H.

Hotels & Restaurants in Britain, 1986. (Illus.). 548p. 1986. pap. 10.95 o.p. (ISBN 0-13-394941-9). P-H.

Hotels & Restaurants in Britain, 1987. rev. ed. (Illus.). 564p. 1987. pap. 12.95 o.p. (ISBN 0-13-394966-4). P-H.

Hotels & Restaurants of Britain, 1988. rev. ed. The British Hotels, Restaurants & Caterers Association Staff. (Illus.). 1988. pap. 12.95 o.p. (ISBN 0-13-394958-3). Prentice Hall Pr.

Hotels for Tourism Development. Jagmohan Negi. 1984. 60.00 o.p. (ISBN 0-935638-08-3). Travel & Tourism.

Hothouse. Harold Pinter. 1980. pap. 4.95 o.s.i. (ISBN 0-394-17675-8, E764, Ever); 12.50 o.s.i. (ISBN 0-394-51395-9). Grove.

Hots Springs & Spas of California. Patricia Cooper & Laurel Cook. LC 78-10665. (Illus.). 1978. pap. 3.95 o.s.i. (ISBN 0-89286-145-2, One Hund One Prods). Ortho.

Houghton Mifflin Travel Guides, Vol. 1: The United States. Steve Birnbaum. 1978. 15.00 o.p. (ISBN 0-395-26620-3); pap. 9.95 o.p. (ISBN 0-395-27215-7). HM.

Houghton Mifflin Travel Guides, Vol. 2: Mexico. Steve Birnbaum. 1978. 15.00 o.p. (ISBN 0-395-27079-0); pap. 9.95 o.p. (ISBN 0-395-27214-9). HM.

Houghton Mifflin Travel Guides, Vol. 3: The Caribbean. Steve Birnbaum. 1978. 15.00 o.p. (ISBN 0-395-27105-3); pap. 9.95 o.p. (ISBN 0-395-27213-0). HM.

Hound of Heaven. Glover Wright. LC 85-15797. 1986. 15.95 o.p. (ISBN 0-87795-767-3). Morrow.

Hound of the Baskervilles see Study in Scarlet.

Hounds of Hell: Stories of Canine Horror & Fantasy. Michel Parry. LC 73-16635. 192p. (gr. 9-12). 1974. 7.95 o.s.i. (ISBN 0-8008-3945-5). Taplinger.

Hounds of Summer & Other Stories. Mary McCarthy. 240p. 1981. pap. 3.50 o.p. (ISBN 0-380-78196-4, 78196-4, Bard). Avon.

Hour, American Council Against Nazi Propoganda, Nos. 1-153. 1970. Repr. of 1943 ed. Set. lib. bdg. 65.00x o.p. (ISBN 0-8371-9177-7, HO00). Greenwood.

Hour Is Forever. Ethel Blackledge. 1977. pap. 1.50 o.p. (ISBN 0-380-01682-6, 33530). Avon.

Hour Magazine Cookbook. Gary Collins. LC 85-16692. (Illus.). 200p. 1985. 14.95 o.p. (ISBN 0-399-13083-7). Putnam Pub Group.

Hour Magazine Cookbook. Gary Collins. (Illus.). 192p. 1986. pap. 8.95 o.p. (ISBN 0-399-51282-9, Perigee). Putnam Pub Group.

Hour of Gold, Hour of Lead. Anne M. Lindbergh. LC 72-88792. 1973. 7.95 o.s.i. (ISBN 0-15-142176-5). HarBraceJ.

Hour of the Lily. John Kruse. 524p. 1988. pap. 3.95 o.p. (ISBN 1-55547-250-8). Critics Choice Paper.

Hour of the Unexpected. John Shea. LC 77-73648. 1977. pap. 5.95 o.p. (ISBN 0-913592-85-4). Tabor Pub.

Hourglass Man. Carl Tiktin. 1977. 7.95 o.p. (ISBN 0-87795-161-6, Arbor Hse). Morrow.

Hours of Catherine of Cleves. Intro. by John Plummer. LC 66-23096. (Illus.). 360p. 1975. 50.00 o.p. (ISBN 0-8076-0379-1). Braziller.

Hours with Art & Artists. G. W. Sheldon. Ed. by H. Barbara Weinberg. LC 75-28873. (Art Experience in Late 19th Century America Ser.: Vol. 9). (Illus.). 1978. Repr. of 1882 ed. lib. bdg. 70.00 o.p. (ISBN 0-8240-2233-5). Garland Pub.

House. David Halliwell. 1981. pap. 4.95 o.p. (ISBN 0-413-47030-X). Heinemann Ed.

House above Hollywood. Velda Johnston. (General Ser.). 315p. 1986. lib. bdg. 16.95x o.p. (ISBN 0-8161-4033-2, Large Print Bks). G K Hall.

House at Sandalwood. Virginia Coffman. LC 73-90734. 1974. 7.95 o.p. (ISBN 0-87795-075-X, Arbor Hse). Morrow.

House Between the Worlds. Marion Zimmer Bradley. LC 79-7800. (Science Fiction Ser.). 1980. 10.00 o.p. (ISBN 0-385-12936-X). Doubleday.

House by the Sea. 2nd ed. Penny Harter. (Xtra Ser.: No. 4). 40p. (Orig.). 1981. pap. 2.50 o.s.i. (ISBN 0-89120-021-5). From Here.

House by the Sea: A Journal. May Sarton. (Illus.). 1977. 12.95 o.p. (ISBN 0-393-07518-4). Norton.

House Construction Details. 7th ed. Nelson L. Burbank & Arnold B. Romney. 1981. encore ed. 8.95 o.p. (ISBN 0-684-16824-3, ScribT). Scribner.

House Divided. Ben A. Williams. 17.95 o.p. (ISBN 0-395-08329-X). HM.

House Fever: Buying, Selling, Remodeling, Decorating & Agonizing over Your Home. Michael Braunstein. LC 79-2959. 1980. 6.95 o.p. (ISBN 0-15-142182-X). HarBraceJ.

House for Jonnie O. Blossom Elfman. 1977. 8.95 o.p. (ISBN 0-395-24901-5). HM.

House Full of Kids: Running a Successful Day Care Business in Your Own Home. Karen Murphy. LC 82-73961. 320p. (Orig.). 1984. 16.95x o.p. (ISBN 0-8070-2302-7); pap. 9.95 o.p. (ISBN 0-8070-2303-5, BP653). Beacon Pr.

House Full of Mice. Ruth Link. (gr. 2-5). 1970. PLB 4.25 o.p. (ISBN 0-689-20605-4, Atheneum). Macmillan.

House Full of Prayers. Marian Bennett. (Surprise Bks.). (Illus.). 14p. (Orig.). (ps-3). 1982. pap. 4.95 o.p. (ISBN 0-87239-563-4, 2709). Standard Pub.

House in My Head. Dorothy Rodgers. LC 67-25491. (Photos). 1967. 10.00 o.p. (ISBN 0-689-10230-5, Atheneum). Macmillan.

House: Living at Chatsworth. Duchess of Devonshire. (Illus.). 1982. 30.00 o.p. (ISBN 0-03-062428-2). H Holt & Co.

House Mottoes & Inscriptions. Sophia F. Caulfield. LC 68-21758. 160p. 1968. Repr. of 1908 ed. 35.00x o.p. (ISBN 0-8103-3322-8). Gale.

House Next Door. Anne R. Siddons. 1984. pap. 2.95 o.s.i. (ISBN 0-345-32333-5). Ballantine.

House Next Door. Anne R. Siddons. 1978. 9.95 o.p. (ISBN 0-671-24018-8). S&S.

House of a Thousand Lanterns. Victoria Holt. 384p. 1983. pap. 2.95 o.p. (ISBN 0-449-20498-7, Crest). Fawcett.

House of Another Kind. William Fritts. (Orig.). 1981. pap. 2.25 o.p. (ISBN 0-505-51669-1, Pub. by Tower Bks). Dorchester Pub Co.

House of Cain. Arthur W. Upfield. Intro. by Philip Jose Farmer. (Illus.). 296p. 1983. Repr. of 1928 ed. 20.00 o.p. (ISBN 0-9609986-0-8). D McMillan.

House of Games: Screenplay. David Mamet. LC 86-32013. 160p. 1987. 14.95 o.p. (ISBN 0-394-56189-9); pap. 7.95 o.p. (ISBN 0-394-62382-7, Ever). Grove.

House of Getty. Miller. pap. 4.95 o.s.i. (ISBN 0-8050-0323-1). H Holt & Co.

House of Getty. Russell Miller. (Illus.). 416p. 1986. 17.95 o.s.i. (ISBN 0-8050-0023-2). H Holt & Co.

House of Illusions. Caroline Farr. Bd. with Secret of the Chateau. 1982. pap. 2.50 o.p. (AE1691, Sig). NAL.

House of Kanze. Nobuko Albery. 320p. 1986. 17.45 o.p. (ISBN 0-671-60520-8). S&S.

House of Life: Rachel Carson at Work. Paul Brooks. (Nonfiction Ser.). 368p. 1985. pap. 9.95 o.p. (ISBN 0-8398-2866-7, Gregg). G K Hall.

House of Lords in the Eighteenth Century. Arthur S. Turberville. 1971. Repr. of 1927 ed. lib. bdg. 35.00x o.p. (ISBN 0-8371-4557-0, TUHL). Greenwood.

House of Lords in the Reign of William Third. Arthur S. Turberville. LC 77-110877. vi, 264p. 1970. Repr. of 1913 ed. lib. bdg. 35.00x o.p. (ISBN 0-8371-4558-9, TULW). Greenwood.

House of Pain. Monique Von Cleef & William Waterman. LC 70-188802. (Maurice Gerodius Bk.). 224p. 1973. 7.95 o.p. (ISBN 0-8184-0163-X). Carol Pub Group.

House of Saud: The Rise & Rule of the Most Powerful Dynasty in the Arab World. David Holden & Richard Johns. LC 81-47474. (Illus.). 464p. 1981. 19.95 o.s.i. (ISBN 0-03-043731-8). H Holt & Co.

House of Shadows. Andre Norton & Phyllis Miller. 256p. (Orig.). 1987. text ed. 2.95 o.p. (ISBN 0-317-57989-4, Dist. by St Martin's Pr & Warner Pub Servs). Tor Bks.

House of the Brandersons. Raymond Rudorff. LC 73-82187. 1973. 7.95 o.p. (ISBN 0-87795-067-9, Arbor Hse). Morrow.

House of the Seven Gables. Nathaniel Hawthorne. (Riverside Bookshelf). (Illus.). (gr. 9 up). 1952. 7.95 o.p. (ISBN 0-395-07072-4). HM.

House of the Seven Gables. Nathaniel Hawthorne. LC 85-71903. (Illus.). 304p. 1985. 12.95 o.p. (ISBN 0-89577-219-1). RD Assn.

House of the Seven Gables. Nathaniel Hawthorne. 48p. (Orig.). 1988. pap. 9.95 o.p. (ISBN 1-55651-379-8); write for info. o.p. (ISBN 1-55651-380-1). Cram Cassettes.

House of Thunder. Leigh Nichols. (Orig.). 1982. pap. (ISBN 0-671-43266-4). PB.

House of Wisdom. John Dunne. LC 84-48767. 224p. 1985. 15.45 o.p. HarpR.

House of Young. Alice B. Grenwell. 272p. 1982. 11.00 o.p. (ISBN 0-682-49835-1); pap. 5.95 o.p. (ISBN 0-682-49836-X). Exposition-Phoenix.

House on College Avenue: The Comptons at Wooster, 1891-1913. James R. Blackwood. 1968. pap. 7.95x o.p. (ISBN 0-262-52026-5). MIT Pr.

House on Liberty Street. Mary H. Weik. LC 72-86950. 80p. (gr. 5 up). 1972. 4.50 o.p. (ISBN 0-689-30098-0, Atheneum). Macmillan.

House on Moon Lake. Francesca Duranti. Tr. by Stephen Sartarelli from Ital. LC 86-6548. 192p. 1986. 15.95 o.p. (ISBN 0-394-55037-4). Random.

House on Mount Vernon Street. W. E. Ross. 1974. pap. 0.95 o.p. (ISBN 0-380-01262-6, 18036). Avon.

House on Parchment Street. Patricia A. McKillip. LC 72-86941. (Illus.). 192p. (gr. 3-7). 1978. pap. 1.95 o.s.i. (ISBN 0-689-70451-8, Aladdin). Macmillan.

House on the Quai Notre-Dame. Georges Simenon. Tr. by Alastair Hamilton. LC 75-9682. (Helen Kurt Wolff Bk.). 160p. 1975. 6.95 o.p. (ISBN 0-15-142181-1). HarBraceJ.

House on the Strand. Daphne Du Maurier. 1976. pap. 3.95 o.p. (ISBN 0-380-00643-X, 60317-9). Avon.

House Physician's Handbook. 5th ed. C. Allan Birch et al. (Illus.). 336p. 1980. pap. text ed. 13.75 o.p. (ISBN 0-443-02117-1). Churchill.

House Plants: A Color Guide. Luciano Cretti & Gina B. Bosisio. (Color Guides Ser.). (Illus.). 196p. 1984. 12.95 o.p. (ISBN 0-88254-922-7). Hippocrene Bks.

House Plants for the Purple Thumb. Maggie Baylis. LC 72-94894. (Illus.). 192p. (Orig.). 1973. pap. write for info. o.p. (One Hund One Prods); pap. write for info. o.p. Ortho.

House Plants: How to Grow. 3rd ed. Sunset Editors. LC 76-7660. (Illus.). 80p. 1976. pap. 4.95 o.p. (ISBN 0-376-03336-3, Sunset Bks). Sunset-Lane.

House Prices & Inflation. Ed. by John Tuccillo & Kevin Villani. LC 81-53062. 175p. 1981. pap. text ed. 23.50 o.p. (ISBN 0-87766-306-8). Urban Inst.

House Style Book: New Directions in Design & Decorating for Every Room in the House. Ed. by Deyan Sudjic. 1985. 39.95 o.p. (ISBN 0-03-002888-4). H Holt & Co.

House That Jack Built: A Picture Book in Two Languages. Antonio Frasconi. LC 58-8625. (Illus.). (gr. k-4). 1958. 6.50 o.p. (ISBN 0-15-236300-9, HJ). HarBraceJ.

House Warming. Charles Wing. (Illus.). 264p. 1983. 24.45i o.p. (ISBN 0-316-94668-0); pap. 16.95 o.p. (ISBN 0-316-94669-9). Little.

House Wiring. 5th ed. Roland E. Palmquist. LC 78-50216. 9.95 o.p. (ISBN 0-672-23364-9). G K Hall.

House Wiring Simplified. Floyd M. Mix. (Illus.). 176p. 1984. 9.20 o.p. (ISBN 0-87006-490-8). Goodheart.

House Wittgenstein Built. Paul Wijdeveld. (Illus.). 144p. (Orig.). pap. (Dist. by Kampmann & Co.); (ISBN 0-918825-34-2). Moyer Bell Limited.

Houseboating on Lake Powell. Bob Hirsch. (Illus.). 90p. 1988. pap. 6.95 o.p. (ISBN 0-935810-39-0). Primer Pubs.

Housebuilding Book. Dan Browne. (Illus.). 192p. 1974. text ed. 17.95 o.p. (ISBN 0-07-008486-6); pap. 6.95 o.p. (ISBN 0-07-008487-4). McGraw.

Housebuilding, Planning & Community Action: The Production & Negotiation of the Built Environment. John Short et al. 352p. 1987. text ed. 87.50 o.p. (ISBN 0-7102-0723-9, Pub. by Routledge UK). Routledge Chapman & Hall.

Housebuying Checklist. Don Smith & Jo-An Smith. 1975. pap. 4.45 o.p. (ISBN 0-380-00315-5, 24042, Flare). Avon.

Household after-Tax Income: 1985. 6th ed. (Current Population Reports Series P-23, Special Studies: No. 151). (Illus.). 55p. 1987. pap. 2.75 o.p. (S/N 803-005-10004-9). USGPO.

Household & Family Characteristics: March 1985. Annual ed. (Current Population Reports Series P-20, Population Characteristics: No. 411). (Illus.). 131p. 1986. pap. 6.00 o.p. (S/N 803-005-00003-6). USGPO.

Household & Family Characteristics: Mar. 1986. (Current Population Reports Series P-20, Population Characteristics: No. 419). 157p. 1987. pap. 8.00 o.p. (S/N 803-005-00012-5). USGPO.

Household & Kin. Amy Swerdlow et al. (Women's Lives - Women's Work Ser.). (Illus.). 208p. (Orig.). (gr. 11 up). 1981. pap. 14.95 o. p. o.p. (ISBN 0-912670-91-6). Feminist Pr.

Household Equipment. 8th ed. Leslie J. Peet et al. LC 78-11749. 1979. write for info. o.p. (ISBN 0-02-393390-9); pap. write for info. o.p. Macmillan.

Household Equipment: Selection & Management. Patricia P. Wilson. LC 75-31023. (Illus.). 384p. 1976. text ed. 29.50 o.p. (ISBN 0-395-20596-4). HM.

Household Saints. Francine Prose. (Hall Fiction Ser.). 240p. 1986. pap. 5.95 o.p. (ISBN 0-8398-2894-2). G K Hall.

Household Waste Management in Europe. A. Bridgewater & H. Lidgren. 1981. 34.95 o.p. (ISBN 0-442-30464-1). Van Nos Reinhold.

Househusbands: Men & Housework in American Families. William R. Beer. 176p. 1982. 24.95x o.p. (ISBN 0-03-059978-4); pap. 12.95 o.p. (ISBN 0-89789-046-9). Bergin & Garvey.

Housekeeping Handbook for Institutions, Business & Industry. rev. ed. Edwin B. Feldman. LC 75-83312. 502p. 1979. 29.95 o.p. (ISBN 0-8119-0072-X); members 22.00 o.p. Fell.

Housekeeping Management for Health Care Facilities. rev. ed. Mildred L. Chase. LC 78-23436. 1978. pap. 11.00 o.p. (ISBN 0-87125-045-4). Cath Health.

Houseman's Land of Lost Content: A Critical Study of "A Shropshire Lad" B. J. Leggett. LC 71-100407. 172p. 1970. 17.95x o.p. (ISBN 0-87049-106-7). U of Tenn Pr.

Housemates: How to Find Them, Screen Them, & Live with Them. L. H. Sintetos. LC 84-28670. 168p. (Orig.). 1985. pap. 6.95 o.p. (ISBN 0-571-12536-0). Faber & Faber.

Houses. Joel Oppenheimer. 79p. 1988. Repr. of 1981 ed. 8.00 o.p. (ISBN 0-934834-22-9). White Pine.

Houses of Belgrade. Borislav Pekic. Tr. by Bernard Johnson. LC 78-4988. 1978. 9.95 o.p. (ISBN 0-15-142183-8). HarBraceJ.

Houses of Children. Coleman Dowell. LC 86-15678. 208p. 1987. 15.95 o.s.i. (ISBN 1-55584-043-4). Weidenfeld.

Houses of Horror. Hans Holzer. 192p. 1982. pap. 2.25 o.p. (ISBN 0-8439-1143-3, Pub. by Leisure Bks CT). Dorchester Pub Co.
Houses of New England. Peter Mallary. LC 83-51864. (Illus.). 1984. 35.00f o.p. (ISBN 0-500-01336-5). Thames Hudson.
Houses: Shelters from Prehistoric Times to Today. Anne Siberell. LC 78-14097. (Illus.). (gr. 2-5). 1979. 6.95 o.s.i. (ISBN 0-03-044656-2). H Holt & Co.
Housesitter. Lee Karr. 1980. pap. 2.25 o.p. (ISBN 0-380-76364-8, 76364-8). Avon.
Housewiring Simplified. Floyd M. Mix. LC 80-21122. (Illus.). 176p. 1981. 9.20 o.p. (ISBN 0-87006-309-X). Goodheart.
Housing. Ed. by O. H. Koenigsberger. 140p. 1980. pap. 39.00 o.p. (ISBN 0-08-026082-9). Pergamon.
Housing: A Bibliography 1960-1972. Ed. by Virginia Paulus. 339p. 1974. 25.00 o.p. Transaction Pubs.
Housing Adaptations for Disabled People. Terence Lockhart. 144p. (Orig.). 1982. pap. 27.50 o.p. (ISBN 0-89397-115-4). Nichols Pub.
Housing Allowances in Kansas City & Wilmington: An Appraisal. John D. Heinberg et al. write for info o.p. Urban Inst.
Housing America--The Challenges Ahead: The Long Range Planning Report of the National Association of Home Builders. National Association of Home Builders Staff. 152p. 1985. pap. 25.00 o.p. (ISBN 0-86718-241-5). Nat Assn H Build.
Housing: An Anthology. Ed. by George Sternlieb. 498p. 1974. (ISBN 0-404-10402-9). Transaction Pubs.
Housing & Community Development: Recent Writings, 1980-1983. Dale E. Casper. (Architecture Ser.: Bibliography A 1347). 1985. pap. 2.00 o.p. (ISBN 0-89028-317-6). Vance Biblios.
Housing & Investment in an Inflationary World: Theory & Evidence. John Tuccillo. (Illus.). 55p. (Orig.). 1980. pap. text ed. 6.50 o.p. (ISBN 0-87766-281-9). Urban Inst.
Housing & Public Policy. Stewart Lansley. 246p. 1979. 32.00 o.p. (ISBN 0-7099-0052-X, Pub. by Croom Held Ltd). Routledge Chapman & Hall.
Housing & Young Families in East London. Anthea Holme. (Reports of the Institute of Community Studies). 224p. 1985. 25.00x o.p. (ISBN 0-7102-0362-4). Routledge Chapman & Hall.
Housing Conservation in Older Urban Areas: A Mortgage Insurance Approach. Kenneth F. Phillips & Michael B. Teitz. LC 78-181. (Research Report Ser.: No. 78-2). 39p. 1978. pap. 3.50x o.p. (ISBN 0-87772-254-4). UCB IGS.
Housing Discrimination Law. Robert G. Schwemm. 496p. 1983. text ed. 55.00 o.p. (ISBN 0-87179-389-X, 0389). BNA.
Housing Discrimination Law: 1986 Supplement. Robert G. Schwemm. 160p. 1986. pap. text ed. 20.00 o.p. (ISBN 0-87179-511-6, 0511). BNA.
Housing Economics & Public Policy. Ray Robinson. LC 79-18974. 1979. 26.50 o.p. (ISBN 0-8419-5059-8). Holmes & Meier.
Housing for Special Groups: Proceedings. United Nations Economic Commission for Europe. 1977. pap. 50.00 o.p. (ISBN 0-08-021985-3). Pergamon.
Housing for the Aged: A Bibliography. Mary Vance. (Architecture Ser.: A 1438). 32p. 1985. 4.50 o.p. (ISBN 0-89028-508-X). Vance Biblios.
Housing in Great Britain & Ireland. S. M. Farthing & M. C. Fleming. (Sources of Statistical Information Ser.). 232p. 1977. 22.00 o.p. (ISBN 0-08-022454-7). Pergamon.
Housing in New York: Study of a City. Ed. by Michael A. Stegman. 259p. (Orig.). 1985. pap. text ed. 19.95x o.p. (ISBN 0-88285-110-1). Transaction Pubs.
Housing Land Policy: A Study of the Housebuilding Industry & the Planning System. Yvonne Rydin. 150p. 1986. text ed. 31.95x o.p. (ISBN 0-566-05072-2). Gower Pub Co.
Housing Perspectives: Individuals & Families. 2nd ed. Carol Wedin & Gertrude L. Nygren. LC 79-83677. 291p. (Orig.). 1979. pap. text ed. 13.95x o.p. (ISBN 0-8087-2387-1, Feffer & Simons). Burgess MN Intl.
Housing Policies for the Urban Poor. Raymond J. Struyk et al. 153p. 1978. pap. 8.50 o.p. (ISBN 0-87766-230-4, 23500). Urban Inst.
Housing Policy & Economic Power: The Political Economy of Owner Occupation. Michael Ball. LC 83-13070. 1983. pap. 17.95 o.p. (ISBN 0-416-35280-4, NO. 3967). Routledge Chapman & Hall.
Housing Policy for the Nineteen Eighties. Emory West. (National Urban League Bk.). 192p. pap. 8.95 o.p. (ISBN 0-87855-895-0). Transaction Pubs.
Housing Policy in Britain. A. E. Holmans. 496p. 1986. 55.00 o.p. (ISBN 0-7099-3789-X, Pub. by Croom Helm Ltd). Routledge Chapman & Hall.
Housing Rehabilitation: An Updated Bibliography. Steven L. Best. (Architecture Ser.: A 1476). 48p. 1985. pap. 7.50 o.p. (ISBN 0-89028-606-X). Vance Biblios.
Housing, States & Localities. Peter Dickens et al. 320p. 1985. text ed. 56.00 o.p. (ISBN 0-416-73780-3, 9551). Routledge Chapman & Hall.
Housing Strategy for the City of Detroit: Policy Perspectives Based on Economic Analysis. David W. Rasmussen & Raymond J. Struyk. LC 81-51874. (Illus.). 81p. (Orig.). 1981. pap. text ed. 6.00 o.p. (ISBN 0-87766-300-9, URI 32500). Urban Inst.
Housing the Family. Design Bulletins. 272p. 1983. 25.95 o.p. (ISBN 0-8436-0129-9). Van Nos Reinhold.
Housing Vouchers for the Poor: Lessons from a National Experiment. Ed. by Raymond J. Struyk & Marc Bendick, Jr. 424p. 1981. 26.25 o.p. (ISBN 0-87766-280-0). Urban Inst.
Housing 1970-1971: An Anthology. Ed. by George Sternlieb & Lynee B. Sagalyn. 572p. 1972. Transaction Pubs.
Housing 1973-1974: An Anthology. Ed. by George Sternlieb et al. 461p. 1976. Transaction Pubs.
Houston Astros. rev. ed. Hinz. LC 82-12699. (Baseball Today Ser.). 48p. (gr. 4 up). 1982. PLB 11.45 o.p. (ISBN 0-87191-861-7). Creative Ed.
Houston Home & Garden's Complete Guide to Houston Gardening. John Kriegel. 425p. 1983. 24.95 o.s.i. (ISBN 0-940672-08-1). Shearer Pub.
Houston Oilers. Jim Rothaus. (NFL Today Ser.). (gr. 3-12). 1980. PLB 10.45 o.p. (ISBN 0-87191-796-3); pap. 4.25 o.p. (ISBN 0-89812-248-1). Creative Ed.
Houston Rockets. Jim Moore. (NBA Today Ser.). (Illus.). 48p. (gr. 4 up). 1984. PLB 10.45 o.p. (ISBN 0-87191-978-8). Creative Ed.
How a Market Economy Works. Marc Rosenblum. LC 71-84414. (Real World of Economics Ser.). Orig. Title: Economics. (Illus.). (gr. 5-11). 1970. PLB 4.95 o.p. (ISBN 0-8225-0611-4). Lerner Pubns.
How a Weirdo & a Ghost. Date not set. (ISBN 0-385-29479-4). Delacorte.
How a Weirdo & a Ghost Can Change Your Entire Life. Patricia Windsor. LC 86-1984. (Illus.). 128p. (gr. 4-6). 1986. pap. 13.95 o.p. (ISBN 0-385-29479-4). Delacorte.
How about a Career in Real Estate? Jack Gale. 34p. (Orig.). 1979. pap. 1.95 o.p. (ISBN 0-88462-374-2, 1977-01, Real Estate Ed). Longman Finan.
How & Why? Ask You & I: The Communities Business. Johnnie Trapp. 1979. 4.00 o.p. (ISBN 0-682-49273-6). Exposition-Phoenix.
How & Why Not to Have That Baby. David Van Vleck. LC 70-170319. 1972. 5.00 o.p. (ISBN 0-8397-3364-X); pap. 2.95 o.p. (ISBN 0-8397-3365-8). Eriksson.
How & Why of Growing. Lorus Milne & Margery Milne. (Illus.). (gr. 4-6). 1972. 4.95 o.p. (ISBN 0-689-30033-6, Atheneum). Macmillan.
How & Why: The General Strike. Sarah Harris. (Weighing Up the Evidence Ser.). (Illus.). 64p. (gr. 7-12). 1986. 14.95 o.p. (ISBN 0-317-38887-8, Pub. by Batsford England). David & Charles.
How & Why: The Russian Revolution. Elizabeth Campling. (Weighing Up the Evidence Ser.). (Illus.). 64p. (gr. 6-8). 1987. 17.95 o.p. (ISBN 0-85219-660-1, Pub. by Batsford England). David & Charles.
How Architects Get Work. Golzen. 1987. pap. 24.95 o.p. (ISBN 0-946228-04-3). Van Nos Reinhold.
How Are You Praying? Donald Demaray. 176p. (Orig.). 1985. pap. 7.95 o.p. (ISBN 0-310-23841-2, 6801P). Zondervan.
How Baby Grows. Festus Adebonojo et al. 1985. pap. 8.95 o.p. (ISBN 0-87795-695-2, Arbor Hse). Morrow.
How Behavior Means. Albert Scheflen. LC 74-18605. 240p. 1975. 25.00x o.p. (ISBN 0-87668-188-7). Aronson.
How Big Is a Foot? Rolf Myller. (Illus.). 36p. (gr. 1-3). 1962. 6.95 o.s.i. (ISBN 0-689-20298-9, A-9, Atheneum's Children Bk); pap. 0.95 o.s.i. (ISBN 0-689-70306-6). Macmillan.
How Can I Encourage My Primary Grade Child to Read? Molly Ransbury. (Micromonograph Ser.). 1972. 1.50 o.p. (ISBN 0-87207-875-2). Intl Reading.
How Can I Get My Teenager to Read? Rosemary Winebrenner. (Micromonograph Ser.). 1971. 1.50 o.p. (ISBN 0-87207-871-X). Intl Reading.
How Can I Help My Child Get Ready to Read? Norma Rogers. (Micromonograph Ser.). 1972. 1.50 o.p. (ISBN 0-87207-876-0). Intl Reading.
How Can I Keep from Singing: Pete Seeger. D. Dunaway. 1986. pap. 24.75X o.p. (ISBN 0-245-54261-2, Pub. by Harrap Ltd England). State Mutual Bk.
How Can I Keep from Singing: Pete Seeger. David K. Dunaway. 1981. text ed. 14.95 o.p. (ISBN 0-07-018150-0). McGraw.
How Can I Keep from Singing: Pete Seeger. David K. Dunaway. (Illus.). 1982. pap. text ed. 9.95 o.p. (ISBN 0-07-018151-9). McGraw.
How Can We Be Sure? Joan Solomon. (Science in a Social Context Ser.). 1986. pap. text ed. 6.95x o.p. (ISBN 0-631-91970-8). Basil Blackwell.
How Can We Know? An Essay on the Christian Religion. A. N. Wilson. LC 84-45709. 128p. 1985. 10.95 o.p. (ISBN 0-689-11569-5, Atheneum). Macmillan.
How Children Learn Science: Conceptual Development & Implications for Teaching. Ronald G. Good. (Illus.). 1977. text ed. write for info. o.p. (ISBN 0-02-344640-4). Macmillan.
How Children Learn to Speak. Maurice Sklar. LC 77-95254. (Illus.). 53p. (Orig.). 1969. pap. 6.50x o.p. (ISBN 0-87424-111-1). Western Psych.
How Children See Our World. Jella Lepman. (Illus.). 1975. pap. 4.45 o.p. (ISBN 0-380-00529-8, 17327). Avon.
How Christmas Came to the Sunday-Schools: The Observance of Christmas in the Protestant Church Schools of the United States. Katharine L. Richards. LC 70-159860. 304p. 1971. Repr. of 1934 ed. 40.00x o.p. (ISBN 0-8103-3793-2). Gale.
How Church-Related Are Church-Related Colleges? Answers Based on a Comprehensive Survey of Supporting Constituencies of 18 LCA Colleges. Richard W. Solberg & Merton P. Strommen. LC 80-13833. 96p. (Orig.). 1980. pap. 3.95 o.p. (ISBN 0-8006-1388-0, 1-1388, Fortress). Augsburg Fortress.
How Cities Work: An Introduction. D. Barrie Needham. 1977. 37.00 o.p. (ISBN 0-08-020529-1); pap. 17.50 o.p. (ISBN 0-08-020528-3). Pergamon.
How Come. (Illus.). 48p. (gr. 1-7). 1978. 5.95 o.p. (ISBN 0-448-47484-0, G&D); PLB 6.95 o.p. (ISBN 0-448-13031-9, G&D). Putnam Pub Group.
How Come? Glenda Y. Peterson. 64p. 1981. 5.00 o.p. (ISBN 0-682-49783-5). Exposition-Phoenix.
How Deep the Cup. Jessyca R. Gaver. (Orig.). 1975. pap. 1.50 o.p. (ISBN 0-685-53125-2, LB280DK, Pub. by Leisure Bks CT). Dorchester Pub Co.
How Democracy Failed. Ellen Switzer. LC 74-19461. (gr. 5 up). 1975. 7.95 o.p. (ISBN 0-689-30459-5, Atheneum). Macmillan.
How Did We Find Out about Antarctica? Isaac Asimov. (Illus.). 64p. (gr. 2-7). 1981. pap. 1.95 o.p. (ISBN 0-380-53421-5, Camelot). Avon.
How Did We Find Out about Atoms? Isaac Asimov. 64p. (gr. 9-12). 1982. pap. 1.95 o.p. (ISBN 0-380-59576-1, 59576-1, Camelot). Avon.
How Did We Find Out about Comets? Isaac Asimov. (Illus.). 64p. (gr. 2-7). 1981. pap. 2.50 o.p. (ISBN 0-380-53454-1, Camelot). Avon.
How Did We Find Out about Dinosaurs? Isaac Asimov. 64p. (gr. 5-7). 1982. pap. 1.95 o.p. (ISBN 0-380-59584-2, 59584-2, Camelot). Avon.
How Did We Find Out about Earthquakes? Isaac Asimov. (Illus.). 64p. (gr. 3-7). 1981. pap. 1.95 o.p. (ISBN 0-380-53462-2, 53462-2, Camelot). Avon.
How Did We Find Out about Energy? Isaac Asimov. (Illus.). 64p. (gr. 5-7). 1981. pap. 1.95 o.p. (ISBN 0-380-53447-9, 53447-9, Camelot). Avon.
How Did We Find Out about Germs? Isaac Asimov. (Illus.). 64p. (gr. 4-7). 1981. pap. 1.95 o.p. (ISBN 0-380-53439-8, 53439-8, Camelot). Avon.
How did We Find Out about Life in the Deep Sea? Isaac Asimov. 64p. (gr. 2-7). 1982. pap. 1.95 o.p. (ISBN 0-380-59592-3, 59592-3, Camelot). Avon.
How Did We Find Out about Our Human Roots? Isaac Asimov. (Illus.). 64p. (gr. 9-12). 1982. pap. 1.95 o.p. (ISBN 0-380-59600-8, 59600-8, Camelot). Avon.
How Did We Find Out about Outer Space? Isaac Asimov. (Illus.). 64p. (gr. 9-12). 1981. pap. 1.95 o.p. (ISBN 0-380-53413-4, 53413-4, Camelot). Avon.
How Did We Find Out about Solar Power? Isaac Asimov. 64p. (gr. 2-7). 1982. pap. 1.95 o.p. (ISBN 0-380-59618-0, 59618-0, Camelot). Avon.
How Did We Get Clocks & Calendars? Claypool et al. (Little Question Bks.). (Illus.). 32p. Date not set. PLB 8.95 o.p. Creative Ed.
How Did We Get Clocks & Calendars? Susan Perry. (Creative's Questions & Answers Library). (Illus.). 32p. (ps-4). 1981. PLB 8.95 o.p. (ISBN 0-87191-746-7). Creative Ed.
How Do I Teach Reading? Robert C. Aukerman & Louise R. Aukerman. LC 80-23380. 543p. 1981. text ed. (ISBN 0-02-304970-7). Macmillan.
How Do They Build It? George Sullivan. (Illus.). 112p. (gr. 5 up). 1972. 5.95 o.s.i. (ISBN 0-664-32512-2, Westminster). Westminster John Knox.
How Do They Cope with It? Suzanne Hilton. LC 72-123399. (Illus.). 368p. (gr. 5 up). 1970. 5.25 o.s.i. (ISBN 0-664-32481-9, Westminster). Westminster John Knox.
How Do They Find It? George Sullivan. LC 74-26713. (Illus.). (gr. 5 up). 1975. 7.50 o.s.i. (ISBN 0-664-32567-X, Westminster). Westminster John Knox.
How Do We Eat It? Deborah Vanderniet. LC 82-1420. 54p. 1982. pap. 3.95 o.p. (ISBN 0-87747-905-4). Deseret Bk.
How Do We Know There Is a God? John W. Montgomery. LC 73-16882. 96p. 1973. pap. 3.50 o.p. (ISBN 0-87123-221-9, 200221). Bethany Hse.
How Do We Smell? Pat Blakely. (Creative's Little Question Bks.). (Illus.). 32p. (ps-4). 1982. PLB 8.95 o.p. (ISBN 0-87191-880-3). Creative Ed.
How Do We Smell? Claypool et al. (Little Question Bks.). (Illus.). 32p. Date not set. PLB 8.95 o.p. Creative Ed.
How Do We Talk? Claypool et al. (Little Question Bks.). (Illus.). 32p. Date not set. PLB 8.95 o.p. Creative Ed.
How Do We Talk? Redfern. (Little Question Bks.). 32p. (ps-4). 1982. PLB 7.95 o.p. (ISBN 0-87191-882-X). Creative Ed.
How Do You Do- & Why? Donald W. Shriver, Jr. (Illus., Orig.). (gr. 9-11). 1967. pap. 3.45 o.p. (ISBN 0-8042-9280-9, John knox). Westminster John Knox.
How Do You Do, Mr. Birdsteps? Morse Hamilton. (Illus.). 32p. (ps-3). 1983. pap. 2.25 o.p. (ISBN 0-380-82875-8, 82875-8, Camelot). Avon.
How Do You Know Who's a Stranger? Book & Cassette. Margaret Holland & Jan Demers. (Illus.). 24p. (ps-2). 1987. 4.95 o.s.i. (ISBN 0-87406-193-8). Willowisp Pr.
How Do You Spell TV. Bruce Mosher & Dottie Mosher. (Illus., Orig.). (gr. 1-3). 1970. pap. 1.95 o.p. (ISBN 0-377-00751-X). Friendship Pr.
How Enjoy Your Life & Your Job. Dale Carnegie. 1986. pap. 3.95 o.s.i. (ISBN 0-671-61827-X). PB.
How Evil the Word. Helen G. Farrar. 1974. pap. 0.95 o.p. (ISBN 0-380-00155-1, 21329). Avon.
How Far Is Berkeley? Helen Chetin. LC 77-76435. 122p. (gr. 4-7). 1977. 6.95 o.p. (ISBN 0-15-236750-0, HJ). HarBraceJ.
How Far She Went. Mary Hood. (Southern Writers Ser.). 144p. 1986. pap. 3.95 o.p. (ISBN 0-380-69972-9). Avon.
How Four: A Handbook for Office Workers. James L. Clark & Lyn R. Clark. PWS-Kent Pub.
How God Created. John Dunne. pap. 2.00 o.p. (ISBN 0-268-00120-0). U of Notre Dame Pr.
How Great Will Be Your Joy! Gary J. Coleman. 1977. 3.95 o.p. (ISBN 0-89036-086-3). Hawkes Pub Inc.
How Healthy Is Your School. 1986. 11.95 o.p. AAHPERD.
How Housing Allowances Work: Integrated Findings to Date from the Experimental Housing Allowance Program. David B. Carlson & John D. Heinberg. 95p. 1978. pap. 10.00 o.p. (ISBN 0-87766-215-0, 21300). Urban Inst.
How I Came to Be a Writer. Phyllis R. Naylor. LC 77-23919. (Illus.). (gr. 4 up). 1978. 6.95 o.p. (ISBN 0-689-30625-3, Atheneum). Macmillan.
How I Changed My Mind. Karl Barth. (Illus.). 1966. 3.95 o.p. (ISBN 0-8042-0608-2, John Knox). Westminster John Knox.
How I Committed Suicide: A Reverie. C. L. Sulzberger. LC 81-14555. 224p. 1982. 11.95 o.p. (ISBN 0-89919-054-5). Ticknor & Fields.
How I Conquered Agoraphobia: My Story. Georgia Farnsworth. cancelled o.s.i. (ISBN 0-912216-26-3); pap. 24.95 o.s.i. (ISBN 0-912216-29-8). Angel Pr.
How I Found Freedom in an Unfree World. Harry Browne. 1982. pap. 4.50 o.p. (ISBN 0-380-00423-2, 60119-2). Avon.
How I Got Faith. Willis M. Brown. 199p. 2.00 o.p. (ISBN 0-686-29117-4). Faith Pub Hse.
How I Grow African Violets. Ednah Daw. (Illus.). 108p. (Orig.). 1983. pap. 7.95 o.p. (ISBN 0-85091-164-8, Pub. by Lothian). Intl Spec Bk.
How I Overcame Inoperable Cancer. Hon Sun Wong. 1975. 6.00 o.p. (ISBN 0-682-48284-6, Banner). Exposition-Phoenix.
How I Planned to Plant the White House Vegetable Garden. Derek Fell. LC 75-46348. 1976. 8.50 o.p. (ISBN 0-682-48516-0, Banner). Exposition-Phoenix.

How I Raised Almost Perfect Children. Zahava Haenosh. 64p. 1986. 7.50 o.p. (ISBN 0-317-60860-6). Carlton.
How I Raised Myself from Failure to Success in Selling. Frank Bettger. 1958. 8.95 o.p. (ISBN 0-13-399402-3). P-H.
How I Raised Myself from Failure to Success in Selling. Frank Bettger. 192p. 1983. pap. 7.95 o.p. (ISBN 0-13-423970-9). P-H.
How I Saved the World. Philip Slater. 336p. 1986. pap. 3.95 o.s.i. (ISBN 0-394-62323-1, BC). Grove.
How I Saved the World on Purpose. Susan Shreve. LC 84-25154. (Illus.). 80p. (gr. 3-5). 1985. 10.95 o.s.i. (ISBN 0-03-070456-1). H Holt & Co.
How I Survived to Be Ninety-Five. Robert L. Nellis. (Illus.). 112p. (Orig.). 1984. pap. 6.00 o.p. (ISBN 0-682-40125-0). Exposition-Phoenix.
How I Wrote Certain of My Books. 2nd rev. ed. Raymond Roussel. Tr. by Trevor Winkfield & Kenneth Koch. LC 77-3630. 1977. pap. 7.00 o.p. (ISBN 0-915342-05-7). SUN.
How Indians Use Wild Plants for Food, Medicine & Crafts. Frances Densmore. Orig. Title: Use of Plants by the Chippewa Indians. (Illus.). 14.25 o.p. (ISBN 0-8446-5029-3). Peter Smith.
How Intelligent Are You? Victor Serebriakoff. 128p. 1985. pap. 2.50 o.p. (ISBN 0-451-13335-8, Sig). NAL.
How It Feels When a Parent Dies. Jill Krementz. LC 80-8808. (Illus.). 128p. (gr. 4-9). 1981. 12.95 o.p. (ISBN 0-394-51911-6). Knopf.
How It Is. Samuel Beckett. Tr. by Samuel Beckett from Fr. 1965. pap. 8.95 o.p. (ISBN 0-394-17248-5, E388, Ever). Grove.
How Jesus Became God. Conrad H. Hoehlman. 1960. (ISBN 0-8022-1131-3). Philos Lib.
How Life Begins: A Look at Birth & Care in the Animal World. Chrissy Rankin. LC 84-42786. (Illus.). 64p. 1985. 11.95 o.p. (ISBN 0-399-21199-3, Putnam). Putnam Pub Group.
How Little Is Enough? Salt & Security in the Long Run. Francis P. Hoeber. (NSIC Strategy Paper Ser.: No. 35). 80p. 1981. pap. text ed. 5.95x o.p. (ISBN 0-8448-1383-4, Pub. by Crane Russak & Co). Taylor & Francis.
How Long Have We Got? Ritchie Calder. LC 72-80883. (Beatty Memorial Lectures Series). 1972. pap. 3.25 o.p. (ISBN 0-7735-0150-9, McGill Canada). U of Toronto Pr.
How Long Must I Hide. Mary K. Carey. 240p. 1983. 12.95 o.p. (ISBN 0-89015-412-0). Eakin Pr.
How Long Should They Serve? Limiting Terms for the President & the Congress. John C. Daly et al. 25p. 1980. pap. 5.00 o.p. (ISBN 0-8447-2183-2). Am Enterprise.
How Long? To Go, To Grow, To Know. Ross R. Olney & Patricia J. Olney. LC 83-13392. 40p. (gr. 1-5). 1984. 10.25 o.p. (ISBN 0-688-02773-3); PLB 10.88 o.p. (ISBN 0-688-02774-1). Morrow.
How Managers Make Things Happen. 2nd ed. George S. Odiorne. 288p. 1981. 17.95 o.p. (ISBN 0-13-400549-X). P-H.
How Men Feel: Their Response to Women's Demands for Independence, Equality & Power. Anthony Astrachan. LC 85-22944. 456p. 1986. 19.95 o.s.i. (ISBN 0-385-23333-7, Anchor Pr). Doubleday.
How Mr. Pan Weathered the Storm. Ye Shentao. Tr. by Wenxue & Simen Johnstone. (Orig.). 1987. pap. 4.95 o.p. (ISBN 0-8351-1604-2). China Bks.
How Modern Should Theology Be? Helmut Thielicke. Tr. by H. George Anderson from Ger. LC 69-14620. 96p. 1969. 3.50 o.p. (ISBN 0-8006-0287-0, 1-287, Fortress). Augsburg Fortress.
How Much Do You Tip the Whipper? Harriet Kahn. 104p. 1986. pap. 4.95 o.s.i. (ISBN 0-9614038-0-2). Academy Chi Pubs.
How NATO Weakens the West. Melvyn Krauss. 304p. 1986. 18.45 o.p. (ISBN 0-671-54455-1). S&S.
How Not to Kill Your Houseplants: The Foolproof Guide to Lush, Healthy Plants. Ann Pregosin. (Illus.). 192p. 1986. pap. 9.95 o.p. (ISBN 0-02-081180-2, Collier). Macmillan.
How Old Is the Earth? Patrick M. Hurley. LC 78-25843. (Illus.). 1979. Repr. of 1959 ed. lib. bdg. 35.00x o.p. (ISBN 0-313-20776-3, HUHO). Greenwood.
How OSHA Enforces the Law. Sophie Weber. 82p. 1981. pap. 15.00x o.p. (ISBN 0-918780-21-7). INFORM.
How Ought Science Be Taught. Paul A. Taylor & Ronald K. Gibbs. LC 72-6342. 1972. 29.00x o.p. (ISBN 0-8422-5018-2); pap. text ed. 8.50x o.p. (ISBN 0-8422-0153-X). Irvington.
How Our Grandfathers Lived. Albert B. Hart & Annie B. Chapman. LC 78-164331. 390p. 1971. Repr. of 1921 ed. 43.00x o.p. (ISBN 0-8103-3795-9). Gale.
How People Get Power: Organizing Oppressed Communities for Action. S. Kahn. 1970. pap. text ed. 3.95 o.p. (ISBN 0-07-033198-7). McGraw.
How Plants Are Pollinated. Joan E. Rahn. LC 75-9526. (Illus.). 144p. (gr. 3-7). 1975. 8.95 o.p. (ISBN 0-689-30482-X, Atheneum). Macmillan.
How Plants Travel. Joan E. Rahn. LC 73-76332. (Illus.). 64p. (gr. 4-6). 1973. pap. 4.95 o.p. (ISBN 0-689-30118-9, Atheneum). Macmillan.
How Safe Is Safe? The Design of Policy on Drugs & Food Additives. LC 74-5981. (Academy Forum Ser). 250p. 1974. pap. 10.25x o.p. (ISBN 0-309-02222-3). Natl Acad Pr.
How Schools Can Help Combat Student Suicide. Patricia Williams Boyd. (Combat Ser.). write for info. o.s.i. NEA.
How Schools Work. Rebecca Barr & Robert Dreeben. LC 83-6904. 208p. 1983. 22.50x o.s.i. (ISBN 0-226-03811-4). U of Chicago Pr.
How Secondary School Graduates Perform in the Labor Market: A Study of Indonesia. David H. Clark. (Working Paper Ser.: No. 615). 88p. 1983. 5.00 o.p. (ISBN 0-8213-0260-4, WP 0615). World Bank.
How Shall We Collect the Garbage? A Study in Economic Organization. Dennis R. Young. 83p. 1972. pap. 6.00x o.p. (ISBN 0-87766-051-4, 10008). Urban Inst.
How Should I Love You? Dwight H. Small. LC 78-20588. 1979. 7.95i o.p. (ISBN 0-06-067398-2). HarpR.
How Silly Can You Be? A Book of Jokes. Compiled by William Wiesner. LC 74-4044. (gr. 2-6). 1979. 6.95 o.p. (ISBN 0-395-28830-4, Clarion). HM.
How States Can Opt Out of the Federal Medicare DRG System: A Summary of Legal Issues. (State Legal Initiatives-Legal Development Report: No. 1). 1984. 30.00 o.p. (ISBN 0-317-60393-0). Am Hospital.
How Strong Is Strong. Jamesetta Smith. 160p. 1987. 9.95 o.p. (ISBN 0-8062-3052-5). Carlton.
How the Appacorn Came to Be. Beverly D. Hammes. (Illus.). 64p. (YA) (gr. 7-12). 1987. 6.75 o.p. (ISBN 0-8062-2861-X). Carlton.
How the Birds Got Their Colors. 2nd ed. Retold by & illus. by Pamela Lofts. (Dreamtime Ser.). (Illus.). 32p. (gr. 1-6). 1985. pap. 3.95 o.p. (ISBN 0-915391-08-2, Pub. by Mad Hatter Bks). Slawson Comm.
How the Children Stopped the Wars. Jan Wahl. (Illus.). 96p. (gr. 3-6). 1979. pap. 1.25 o.p. (ISBN 0-380-01271-5, 45815-2, Camelot). Avon.
How the City Works: An Introduction to Its Financial Markets. W. M. Clarke. (Illus.). 112p. 1986. pap. 10.00 o.p. (ISBN 0-08-039235-0, L125, Pub. by WAT). Pergamon.
How the City Works: The Professions. Ed. by W. M. Clarke. (How the City Works Ser.). 1983. 14.75 o.p. (ISBN 0-08-039149-4), Pergamon.
How the IRS Seizes Your Dollars & How to Fight Back. George Hansen & Larry Anderson. 1981. pap. 6.95 o.p. (ISBN 0-671-42795-4, Fireside). S&S.
How the Rabbit Stole the Moon. Louise Moeri. LC 77-3158. (Illus.). 40p. (gr. k-3). 1977. 7.95 o.p. (ISBN 0-395-25765-4). HM.
How the Racers Ski. Warren Witherell. (Illus.). 206p. 1972. 12.95 o.p. (ISBN 0-393-08429-9). Norton.
How the Rooted Travel. Shelley Ehrlich. (Juniper Bk.: No. 42). 1983. pap. 5.00 o.p. (ISBN 1-55780-022-7, JB41). Juniper Pr WI.
How the Settlers Lived. George Laycock. (gr. 6 up). 1980. 8.95 o.s.i. (ISBN 0-679-20684-1). McKay.
How the Sun Was Brought Back to the Sky: Adapted from a Slovenian Folk Tale. Mirra Ginsburg. LC 74-19060. (Illus.). 32p. (ps-2). 1975. 8.95 o.s.i. (ISBN 0-02-735750-3). Macmillan.
How the Swans Came to the Lake: A Narrative History of Buddhism in America. rev. ed. Rick Fields. LC 85-27806. 430p. 1986. 14.95 o.s.i. (ISBN 0-87773-354-6, 74419-5). Shambhala Pubns.
How the World Began: Man in the First Chapters of the Bible. Helmut Thielicke. Tr. by John W. Doberstein from Ger. LC 61-6756. 324p. 1961. pap. 6.95 o.p. (ISBN 0-8006-1894-7, 1-1894, Fortress). Augsburg Fortress.
How the World Looks to a Georgian. Jimmy Morgan. 1978. 5.50 o.p. (ISBN 0-682-49062-8). Exposition-Phoenix.
How the World Works: A Critical Introduction to International Relations. Gary L. Olson. 1984. pap. text ed. write for info. o.p. (ISBN 0-673-15614-1). Scott F.
How They Do It. Robert Wallace. (Illus.). 1980. 9.95 o.p. (ISBN 0-688-03718-6). Morrow.
How Things Get Done: The Nitty-Gritty of Parliamentary Procedure. Dena C. Bank. LC 79-1287. (Citizens' Handbook Ser.). 94p. 1984. 10.95 o.p. (ISBN 0-87249-378-4). U of SC Pr.
How Things Work. Neil Ardley. (Illus.). 127p. 1984. lib. bdg. 11.79 o.p. Messner.
How Things Work in Your Home (and What to Do When They Don't) Time-Life Books Editors. LC 84-25261. (Illus.). 368p. 1985. 25.00 o.s.i. (ISBN 0-03-003672-0). H Holt & Co.
How Thinking Is Written: An Analytic Approach to Writing. Laurence S. Hall. LC 73-21176. (Illus.). 312p. 1975. Repr. of 1963 ed. lib. bdg. 24.75x o.p. (ISBN 0-8371-6059-6, HATW). Greenwood.
How Three: A Handbook for Office Workers. 3rd ed. James L. Clark & Lyn R. Clark. 297p. 1982. 11.95x o.p. (ISBN 0-534-01116-0). PWS-Kent Pub.
How to Achieve Complete Financial Freedom. Richard P. Halverson. 488p. 1985. 18.95 o.p. (ISBN 0-8253-0290-0); pap. 10.95 o.p. (ISBN 0-8253-0291-9). Kampmann.
How to Achieve Mastery in Painting & Drawing: An Illustrated Guide to the Fundamental Principles & Techniques of Art. Maurice Schmidt. LC 73-82092. 1974. 6.00 o.p. (ISBN 0-682-47770-2, Banner). Exposition-Phoenix.
How to Analyse Fiction. William Kenney. (YA) (gr. 9-12). 1982. lib. bdg. 8.29 o.s.i. (ISBN 0-671-45465-X). Messner.
How to Analyze Drama. Christopher R. Reaske. 1984. pap. 5.95 o.s.i. (ISBN 0-671-50426-6). Monarch Pr.
How to Analyze Fiction. William Kenney. (Orig.). 1975. pap. 4.95 o.s.i. (ISBN 0-671-18746-5). Monarch Pr.
How to Analyze Poetry. Christopher Reaske. (How to Ser.). 1975. pap. 5.95 o.s.i. (ISBN 0-671-18747-3). Monarch Pr.
How to Analyze Poetry. Christopher R. Reaske. (gr. 9 up). 1982. PLB 8.29 o.p. (ISBN 0-671-45464-1); pap. 4.95 o.p. Messner.
How to Arrange for Solo Guitar. (Illus.). pap. 4.50 o.p. (ISBN 0-686-09071-3, Pub. by Peer-Southern). CPP Belwin.
How to Assess Maturation & Paleotemp. (Short Course Notes Ser.). 289p. 1982. 10.00 o.p. (ISBN 0-918985-39-0, 7); members 8.00 o.p. SEPM.
How to Assess Your Managerial Style. Charles Margerison. 160p. 1981. 14.95 o.p. (ISBN 0-8144-5632-4); pap. 6.95 o.p. (ISBN 0-8144-7589-2). AMACOM.
How to Automate Your Office. Chau Dang-Tan & Hau Dang-Tan. LC 84-45793. 250p. 1985. 85.00 o.p. (ISBN 0-8144-5803-3). AMACOM.
How to Avoid a Cesarean Section. Christopher Norwood. 192p. 1984. 14.50 o.p. (ISBN 0-671-46916-9). S&S.
How to Avoid a Cesarean Section. Christopher Norwood. 1985. pap. 8.95 o.p. (ISBN 0-671-55454-9, Fireside). S&S.
How to Avoid Divorce. Luciano L'Abate & Bess L'Abate. LC 76-12389. 1976. pap. 4.95 o.p. (ISBN 0-8042-1118-3, John Knox). Westminster John Knox.
How to Avoid Lawyers: A Step by Step Guide to Being Your Own Lawyer in Almost Every Situation. Don Biggs. LC 84-18636. 1000p. (Orig.). 1985. pap. 26.00 o.s.i. (ISBN 0-8240-7284-7). Garland Pub.
How to Avoid Probate. Norman F. Dacey. 608p. 1983. pap. 19.95 o.p. (ISBN 0-517-55150-0). Crown.
How to Avoid Probate: Updated! Norman F. Dacey. 608p. 1980. 19.95 o.p. (ISBN 0-517-53933-0, Michelman Books); pap. 14.95 o.p. (ISBN 0-517-53934-9). Crown.
How to Avoid Products Liability: A Management Guide. Stanley J. Klein. LC 80-20809. (Illus.). 209p. 1980. 79.50 o.p. (ISBN 0-87624-205-0, Inst Busn Plan). P-H.
How to Be a Better Manager. Michael Armstrong. 252p. 1984. 26.50 o.p. (ISBN 0-89397-180-4). Nichols Pub.
How to Be a Better Manager in Ten Easy Steps. George T. Doran. 128p. 1983. 6.95 o.p. (ISBN 0-671-49388-4). Monarch Pr.
How to Be a Christian in an Unchristian World. rev. ed. Fritz Ridenour. LC 72-169603. 192p. (Orig.). 1972. pap. 4.95 o.s.i. (ISBN 0-8307-0611-9, S123150). Regal.
How to Be a Disc Jockey. Dan Ramsey. (Illus.). 224p. 1981. 19.95 o.p. (ISBN 0-8306-9661-X, 1263); pap. 8.95 o.p. (ISBN 0-8306-1263-7, 1263). TAB Bks.
How to Be a Gifted Parent: Realize Your Child's Full Potential. David Lewis. 1981. 14.95 o.p. (ISBN 0-393-01394-4). Norton.
How to Be a Good Corporate Citizen. David Clutterbuck. 254p. 1981. text ed. 36.50 o.p. (ISBN 0-07-084560-3). McGraw.
How to Be a Happy & Successful Investor. Claude B. Goulet. 1977. 4.00 o.p. (ISBN 0-682-48804-6). Exposition-Phoenix.
How to Be a Legal Secretary Without a Computer: Shortcuts to Ignorance. Kathleen C. Steele. (Illus.). 20p. 1987. pap. 1.95x o.p. (ISBN 0-915433-13-3). Packrat WA.
How to Be a Retail Advertising Pro. 18.00 o.p. (ISBN 0-87102-061-0, 60-7660). Natl Ret Merch.
How to Be a Retail Advertising Pro. (Illus.). 304p. 1987. 18.00 o.p. (ISBN 0-317-65507-8, 60-7660); instr's. wkbk. 4.00 o.p. (ISBN 0-317-65508-6). Natl Ret Merch.
How to Be a Successful Failure. Ernest A. Fitzgerald. LC 77-13463. 1978. 6.95 o.p. (ISBN 0-689-10842-7, Atheneum). Macmillan.
How to Be a Successful Inventor: Patenting, Protecting, Marketing & Selling Your Invention. Clarence R. Taylor. 1972. 6.50 o.p. (ISBN 0-682-47473-8, Banner). Exposition-Phoenix.
How to Be a Successful Song Leader. Shockley Flick. 32p. 1986. pap. 2.95 o.p. (ISBN 0-87403-079-X, 3199). Standard Pub.
How to Be a Super Cartoonist. Peter Maddocks. (Illus.). 96p. 1987. pap. 14.95 o.p. (ISBN 0-241-11898-0, Pub. by Hamish Hamilton England). David & Charles.
How to Be a Very Important Person. James C. Humes. LC 78-10724. 1979. pap. text ed. 2.95 o.p. (ISBN 0-07-031158-7). McGraw.
How to Be a Yogi. 6th ed. Swami Abhedananda. 64p. pap. 7.95 o.s.i. (ISBN 0-88697-040-7). Life Science.
How to Be an Effective Advocate. 63p. 1981. 4.75 o.p. (ISBN 0-318-15049-2). NASBE.
How to Be an Effective Bible Teacher. George M. Bowman. 1982. pap. 3.95 o.p. (ISBN 0-87552-120-7). Presby & Reformed.
How to Be an Effective Trainer: Skills for Managers & New Trainers. Barry J. Smith & Brian L. Delahaye. LC 83-1272. (Professional Development Programs). 306p. 1983. 74.95x o.p. (ISBN 0-471-89015-4). Wiley.
How to Be Born Again. Billy Graham. LC 77-76057. 1977. 3.99 o.p. (ISBN 0-8499-4119-9). Word Bks.
How to Be Happy. 192p. (Orig.). 1985. pap. 5.95 o.p. (ISBN 1-85063-025-9, Ark Paperbks). Routledge Chapman & Hall.
How to Be Happy No Matter What. Tom Watson, Jr. LC 77-73559. 160p. 1978. pap. 3.95 o.s.i. (ISBN 0-8307-0465-5, S103125). Regal.
How to Be Modern Art. Ron Padgett. (Morning Coffee Chapbook Ser.). (Illus.). 16p. (Orig.). 1984. pap. 7.50 o.p. (ISBN 0-918273-03-X). Coffee Hse.
How to Be Seventy. George Mikes. 256p. 1982. 19.95 o.s.i. (ISBN 0-233-97453-9, Pub. by A Deutsch England). David & Charles.
How to Be Successful in the Antique Business. rev. ed. Ronald S. Barlow. (Illus.). 192p. 1981. 12.95 o.s.i. (ISBN 0-684-16985-1, ScribT). Scribner.
How to Be Successful in the Antique Business. Ronald S. Barlow. (Illus.). 192p. 1982. pap. 7.95 o.s.i. (ISBN 0-684-17821-4, ScribT). Scribner.
How to Be Sure of Immortality. Fred T. Koepke. 1985. 6.95 o.p. (ISBN 0-533-06491-0). Vantage.
How to Be the Life of the Podium. Sylvia H. Simmons. LC 81-69358. (Illus.). 320p. 1982. 15.95 o.p. (ISBN 0-8144-5740-1); pap. 8.95 o.p. (ISBN 0-8144-7565-5). AMACOM.
How to Be Wrinkle-Free: Look Younger Longer Without Plastic Surgery. Carlotta K. Jacobson & Catherine Ettlinger. (Illus.). 196p. 1986. 24.95 o.p. (ISBN 0-399-13097-7). Putnam Pub Group.
How to Be Young at Sixty: The Fountain of Youth. Cecil Edward Duke. 1975. 5.00 o.p. (ISBN 0-682-48315-X). Exposition-Phoenix.
How to Be Your Own Architect. Murray Goddard. (Illus.). 1977. 11.95 o.p. (ISBN 0-8306-7988-X); pap. 8.95 o.p. (ISBN 0-8306-6988-4, 988). TAB Bks.
How to Be Your Own Contractor. Paul Rauch. 96p. 1984. 6.95 o.p. (ISBN 0-931790-69-7). Brick Hse Pub.
How to Be Your Own Doctor (Sometimes) rev. ed. Keith W. Sehnert & Howard Eisenberg. LC 81-47701. 368p. 1981. pap. 7.95 o.s.i. (ISBN 0-448-12027-5, G&D). Putnam Pub Group.
How to Be Your Own Doctor Sometimes: 10th Anniversary Edition. Howard Eisenberg & Keith W. Sehnert. 1986. pap. 9.95 o.p. (ISBN 0-399-51190-3, G&D). Putnam Pub Group.
How to Be Your Own Phone Company. Alexander G. Gellert. (Illus.). 96p. (Orig.). 1985. pap. 5.70 o.p. (ISBN 0-8306-1869-4, 1869P). TAB Bks.
How to Beat Fatigue. Linda Pembrook. 1976. pap. 1.75 o.p. (ISBN 0-380-00671-5, 29371). Avon.
How to Beat the High Cost Of Travel: 1984 Edition. 4.95 o.p. (ISBN 0-671-49362-0). Prentice Hall Pr.
How to Beat the Market with High-Performance Generic Stocks: Your Broker Won't Tell You about. Avner Arbel. LC 85-2886. 224p. 1985. 16.95 o.p. (ISBN 0-688-04371-2). Morrow.
How to Beat the Stock Market Rip-off. John Sullivan. (Illus.). 140p. pap. 2.95 o.p. (ISBN 0-89036-065-0). Hawkes Pub Inc.

How to Beat the System: The Student's Guide to Good Grades. rev. ed. Kathy Crafts & Brenda Hauther. LC 81-47643. 192p. 1981. 3.95 o.s.i. (ISBN 0-394-17740-1, B-442, BC). Grove.

How to Beat Wall Street. Myron Kandel. LC 85-14975. 216p. 1985. 50.00 o.p. (ISBN 0-932648-66-5). Boardroom.

How to Beat Workers' Compensation Before It Beats You. Robert J. Will. 225p. (Orig.). Date not set. pap. 29.95 o.p. Rate Consults.

How to Beat Your Power Company at Their Own Game. Kalliana R. Krishman. LC 82-91168. 81p. 1984. 6.95 o.p. (ISBN 0-533-05708-6). Vantage.

How to Become a Bestselling Author. Stanley J. Corwin. LC 84-5285. (Illus.). 252p. 1984. 14.95 o.p. (ISBN 0-89879-129-4). Writers Digest.

How to Become a Complete Golfer. Bob Toski et al. LC 77-92909. (Illus.). 288p. 1978. 15.50 o.p. (ISBN 0-914178-15-6, 24169). Golf Digest.

How to Become a Pilot: The Step-by-Step Guide to Flying. Federal Aviation Administration Staff. (Illus.). 257p. 1987. pap. 12.95 o.p. (ISBN 0-8069-6522-3). Sterling.

How to Become a Police Officer. write for info. o.p. Looseleaf Law.

How to Become a Skilled Intercessor. Barbara Shull. 32p. 1978. pap. 2.00 o.p. (ISBN 0-930756-35-5, 533001). Aglow Pubns.

How to Become a Successful Private Eye. Moore E. Kinchum. pap. 6.95 o.p. (ISBN 0-8306-1408-7, 1408). TAB Bks.

How to Become a United States Citizen: Como Hacerse Ciudadano de Los Estados Unidos. 2nd ed. Sally A. Abel. Tr. by Martha Oberti. LC 83-62116. (Illus.). 160p. (Eng. & Span.). 1986. pap. 9.95 o.p. (ISBN 0-87337-031-7). Nolo Pr.

How to Become a U. S. Citizen. Sally Abel. LC 83-62116. 158p. 1983. pap. 9.95 o.p. (ISBN 0-917316-60-6). Nolo Pr.

How to Become an Effective Supervisor: A Survival Manual for the Man in the Middle. E. N. Uhles. 1971. 5.00 o.p. (ISBN 0-682-47303-0, Banner). Exposition-Phoenix.

How to Become Financially Independent by Investing in Real Estate. Albert J. Lowry. (Illus.). 1977. 15.95 o.p. (ISBN 0-671-22693-2). S&S.

How to Become Financially Independent Before You're 35. Jeffrey A. Stern. 1986. pap. 12.95 o.p. (ISBN 0-316-81290-0). Little.

How to Become Great in the Kingdom of God. Bob Yandian. 143p. (Orig.). 1983. pap. text ed. 4.95 o.s.i. (ISBN 0-914307-02-9, Dist. by Harrison Hse). R Tilton Ministries.

How to Become Happily Employed: A Simple Guide to the Nitty Gritty of Finding the Job That Is Right for You. Barbara B. Vinitsky & Janice Y. Benjamin. LC 84-70522. 208p. (Orig.). 1984. pap. 8.95 ea. o.p. (Dist. by Talman Co). Kansas City Job Hunter's Resource Guide (ISBN 0-9613630-0-2). San Francisco Bay Area Job Hunter's Resource Guide (ISBN 0-9613630-2-9). Career Manage Pr.

How to Become the Person You Want to Be. Norman E. Hankins. LC 78-21596. 256p. 1979. 19.95 o.s.i. (ISBN 0-88229-297-8); pap. 7.95 o.p. (ISBN 0-88229-647-7). Nelson-Hall.

How to Believe Again. Helmut Thielicke. Tr. by H. George Anderson from Ger. LC 72-75656. 224p. 1972. pap. 4.95 o.p. (ISBN 0-8006-0123-8, 1-123, Fortress). Augsburg Fortress.

How to Borrow Money. Oliver G. Wood, Jr. & William C. Barksdale. 144p. 1981. 21.95 o.p. (ISBN 0-442-25204-8). Van Nos Reinhold.

How to Borrow Money Below Prime. Nelson Brestoff. LC 84-23534. 256p. 1985. 15.45 o.p. (ISBN 0-671-49439-2). S&S.

How to Break into Motion Pictures, Television Commercials & Modeling. Nina Blanchard. 1980. pap. 2.50 o.p. (ISBN 0-380-47118-3, 47118). Avon.

How to Break Ninety Before You Reach It. 3rd ed. Steve Brody. LC 80-10704. 1980. pap. 6.95 o.p. (ISBN 0-88427-040-8). North River.

How to Break Your Addiction to a Person. Howard M. Halpern. LC 81-20740. 272p. 1982. text ed. 12.95 o.p. (ISBN 0-07-025627-6). McGraw.

How to Bring Men to Christ. R. A. Torrey. LC 76-57111. 128p. 1977. pap. 3.50 o.p. (ISBN 0-87123-230-8, 200230). Bethany Hse.

How to Bring up a Good Child. Richard Krebs. LC 79-54125. 126p. (Orig.). 1980. pap. 4.50 o.p. (ISBN 0-8066-1760-8, 10-3176, Augsburg). Augsburg Fortress.

How to Build a Microcomputer & Really Understand It. Sam Creason. Ed. by Jeffrey D. DeTray. 114p. 1979. pap. 9.95 o.p. (ISBN 0-88006-021-2, BK 7325). Wayne Green Ent.

How to Build a One Hundred Million Dollar Agency in Five Years or Less. Norman G. Levine. LC 79-54234. 1979. 14.95 o.s.i. (ISBN 0-87863-203-4, Farnsworth Pub Co). Longman Finan.

How to Build a One Hundred Thousand Dollar Law Practice. Joseph T. Karcher. LC 75-39133. 1976. 25.00 o.p. (ISBN 0-87624-207-7, Inst Busn Plan). P-H.

How to Build a Street Rod. Lee Kelley. LC 78-55567. (Illus.). 1978. pap. 4.95 o.p. (ISBN 0-8227-5035-X). Petersen Pub.

How to Build & Use Electronic Devices Without Frustration, Panic, Mountains of Money, or an Engineering Degree. 2nd ed. Stuart A. Hoenig. 1980. pap. 18.50 o.p. (ISBN 0-316-36808-3). Little.

How to Build Gulfweed. John Hanna. (Illus.). 28p. 1948. pap. 2.00 o.p. (ISBN 0-915160-09-9). Seven Seas.

How to Build Outdoor Furniture. Donald R. Brann. LC 76-14045. 1983. pap. 7.95 o.p. (ISBN 0-87733-754-3). Easi-Bild.

How to Build Sailboards: Step-by-Step Custom-Made Designs. Hans Fichtner & Michael Garff. LC 82-10532. (Illus.). 128p. 1983. pap. 10.00 o.p. (ISBN 0-915160-28-5). Seven Seas.

How to Build Workbenches. Donald R. Brann. LC 66-30452. 1979. pap. 9.95 o.p. (ISBN 0-87733-672-5). Easi-Bild.

How to Build Your Own Underground Home. Ray G. Scott. (Illus.). 1979. 15.95 o.p. (ISBN 0-8306-9744-6); pap. 8.95 o.p. (ISBN 0-8306-1172-X, 1172). TAB Bks.

How to Build Your Own Underground Home. 2nd ed. Ray G. Scott. LC 84-16417. (Illus.). 256p. 1985. 19.95 o.p. (ISBN 0-8306-0792-7); pap. 11.60 o.p. (ISBN 0-8306-1792-2, 1792). TAB Bks.

How to Buy & Manage Rental Properties: A Simple Guide to Real Estate Management for the Small Investor. Mike Milin & Irene Milin. 220p. 1986. 19.45 o.s.i. (ISBN 0-671-60701-4). S&S.

How to Buy (& Survive!) Your First Computer: A Guide for Small Business Success. Carolee N. Kolve. LC 83-795. (Illus.). 256p. 1983. pap. text ed. 14.95 o.p. (ISBN 0-07-035130-9, BYTE Bks). McGraw.

How to Buy the Right Personal Computer. Herman Holtz. (Illus.). 192p. pap. 10.95 o.p. (ISBN 0-87196-852-5). Facts on File.

How to Buy U. S. Government Surplus. Warren Weagant. 1981. pap. write for info. o.s.i. (ISBN 0-933132-06-9). Command Prods.

How to Calculate Statistics. Carol T. Fitz-Gibbon & Lynn L. Morris. LC 78-58659. (Program Evaluation Kit: Vol. 7). 142p. 1978. pap. 9.95 o.p. (ISBN 0-8039-1072-X). Sage.

How to Carve Meat, Game & Poultry. M. O. Cullen. 12.50 o.p. (ISBN 0-8446-5480-9). Peter Smith.

How to Catch Trout Between the Hatches. Jerry Meyer. (Illus.). 160p. 1982. encore ed. 4.50 o.p. (ISBN 0-684-17467-7, ScribT). Scribner.

How to Change Attitudes & Emotions. Mark Thurston. Orig. Title: A Course in Practical Spirituality. 147p. 1986. wkbk., text, 4 cassettes 29.95 o.p. (ISBN 0-87604-181-0). ARE Pr.

How to Cheat on College Exams & Get Away with It. Butch Cavendish. 1983. pap. 4.95 o.p. (ISBN 0-317-03305-0). Loompanics.

How to Choose & Use Your Doctor. Marvin S. Belsky & Leonard Gross. LC 75-11146. (Priam Ser.). 1979. pap. 4.95 o.p. (ISBN 0-87795-242-6, Arbor Hse). Morrow.

How to Choose the Diet That's Right for You. Steve Waldstein. LC 84-4228. 240p. 1984. 19.95 o.p. (ISBN 0-89594-127-9); pap. 8.95 o.p. (ISBN 0-89594-126-0). Crossing Pr.

How to Choose the Wrong Marriage Partner & Live Unhappily Ever After. Robert L. Mason & Carrie Jacobs. LC 78-52452. 1979. pap. 2.99 o.p. (ISBN 0-8042-2093-X, John Knox). Westminster John Knox.

How to Choose Your Doctor. Marvin S. Belsky & Leonard Gross. LC 75-11146. 1975. 7.95 o.p. (ISBN 0-87795-112-8, Arbor Hse). Morrow.

How to Clean Everything. Alma C. Moore. 1978. 9.95 o.p. (ISBN 0-671-22705-X, Fireside). S&S.

How to Clean Everything. Alma C. Moore. 1979. pap. 6.95 o.p. (ISBN 0-671-22881-1, Fireside). S&S.

How to Coach, Manage & Play Little League Baseball. Charles Einstein. LC 68-12167. 1986. pap. 5.95 o.s.i. (ISBN 0-671-20291-X, Fireside). S&S.

How to Collect More on Your Insurance Claims. Benjamin Lipson. 1985. 15.45 o.p. (ISBN 0-671-54460-8). S&S.

How to Collect More on Your Insurance Claims. Benjamin Lipson. 336p. 1986. pap. 7.95 o.p. (ISBN 0-671-62802-X, Fireside). S&S.

How to Collect Unemployment. Date not set. pap. (ISBN 0-8052-0490-3). Random.

How to Collect Unemployment Insurance: Even If You're Not Eligible. 1981. pap. 4.95 o.p. (ISBN 0-686-30632-5). Loompanics.

How to Communicate with the Learner. Roger Lewis & Nigel Paine. (Orig.). 1985. pap. text ed. 18.95x o.p. (ISBN 0-86184-150-6). Trans Atl Phila.

How to Compete Successfully in Real Estate Investing: A Guide to Exploring & Understanding the Factors That Affect Values. Gordon J. Anderson. LC 72-90059. 1973. 7.50 o.p. (ISBN 0-682-47586-6, Banner). Exposition-Phoenix.

How to Conduct a Client Follow-up Study. 2nd ed. Dorothy F. Beck & Mary Ann Jones. LC 73-94027. 1980. pap. 14.00 with 1979 & 1980 supplements o.s.i. (ISBN 0-87304-181-X). Family Serv.

How to Conduct & Analyze Real Estate Market & Feasibility Studies. G. Vincent Barrett & John P. Blair. 352p. 1981. 32.95 o.p. (ISBN 0-442-22568-7). Van Nos Reinhold.

How to Conduct Association Surveys. American Society of Association Executives Staff. 64p. 1988. pap. text ed. 30.00 o.p. (ISBN 0-88034-031-2). Am Soc Assn Execs.

How to Conquer Fear. Don Gossett. Orig. Title: How You Can Rise Above Fear. 160p. 1981. pap. 2.95 o.p. (ISBN 0-88368-092-0). Whitaker Hse.

How To Conquer Loneliness. A. Kosten. 1961. 13.95x o.p. New Coll U Pr.

How to Conquer the Fear of Public Speaking: And Other Coronary Threats. Max D. Isaacson. 200p. 1984. 12.95 o.p. (ISBN 0-87863-221-2, Farnsworth Pub Co). Longman Finan.

How to Conquer Your Addiction Through Group Therapy: A Practical Guide to Changing Your Addiction Habits with Group Help. Philip J. Flores. LC 87-7595. 528p. (Orig.). pap. text ed. cancelled o.s.i. (ISBN 0-918393-40-X). Harrington Pk.

How to Control & Reduce Inventory. rev. ed. Burton E. Lipman. LC 72-4485. (Illus.). 197p. 1983. pap. 49.50x o.p. (ISBN 0-943064-02-3). Bell Pub.

How to Convert Your Car, Van or Pickup to Diesel. Paul Dempsey. (Illus.). 1978. pap. 7.95 o.p. (ISBN 0-8306-7968-5, 968). TAB Bks.

How to Convert Your Favorite Hobby, Sport, Pastime or Idea to Cash. Al Riolo. LC 83-20886. 208p. (Orig.). 1983. pap. 12.00 o.p. (ISBN 0-87961-139-1). Naturegraph.

How to Cook His Goose: And Other Wild Games. Karen Green & Betty Black. LC 83-61149. 1977. pap. 10.95 o.p. (ISBN 0-8329-2293-5, Pub. by Winchester Pr). New Century.

How to Cope When You Can't: A How to Manual to Help You Cope with the Stress of Modern Living. Don Gossett. LC 85-82556. 176p. 1986. pap. 6.95 o.p. (ISBN 0-910311-35-8). Huntington Hse Inc.

How to Cope with Dangerous Sea Life. Edwin S. Iversen & Renate Skinner. LC 77-81166. (Illus.). 1977. pap. 4.50 o.p. (ISBN 0-89317-017-8). Windward Pub.

How to Cope with Depression Psychically. Rochelle L. Holt. 1985. 2.00 o.p. (ISBN 0-934536-26-0). Merging Media.

How to Cope with Your Child's Teacher. Lorring Madden. 1976. pap. 3.95 o.p. (ISBN 0-89019-057-7). Norwalk Pr.

How to Copyright Software. 2nd., rev. ed. M. J. Salone. 190p. 1987. pap. 24.95 o.p. (ISBN 0-87337-039-2). Nolo Pr.

How to Create a Super Boxer. Champ Thomas. LC 76-19210. 1976. pap. 5.50 o.p. (ISBN 0-682-48578-0). Exposition-Phoenix.

How to Create Super Slide Shows. Burt E. Close. LC 84-5102. 233p. 1984. pap. 10.95 o.p. (ISBN 0-89879-133-2). Writers Digest.

How to Create Your Own Computer Bulletin Board. Larry L. Myers. 214p. 1985. pap. 12.95 o.p. (ISBN 0-317-66420-4). TAB Bks.

How to Crochet a High Fashion Wardrobe. Lucy Somers. 1978. 12.50 o.p. (ISBN 0-682-49027-X). Exposition-Phoenix.

How to Date with Confidence. Barbara Siegel & Scott Siegel. (YA) (gr. 7 up). pap. 2.25 o.p. (ISBN 0-671-60161-X). Archway.

How to Deal with Goals & Objectives. rev. ed. Lynn L. Morris & Carol T. Fitz-Gibbon. LC 78-57012. (Program Evaluation Kit Ser.: Vol. 2). (Illus.). 78p. 1978. pap. 4.95 o.p. (ISBN 0-8039-1065-7). Sage.

How to Decipher & Study Old Documents: Being a Guide to the Reading of Ancient Manuscripts, the Key to the Family Deed Chest. 2nd ed. Emma E. Cope. LC 73-18446. 170p. 1974. Repr. of 1903 ed. 43.00x o.p. (ISBN 0-8103-3701-0). Gale.

How to Defend a Drunk Driving Case: A Guide to Practical, Procedural, & Legal Aspects. John H. Hingson. LC 86-215646. (Criminal Law Ser.). 259p. 1986. pap. 55.00 o.p. (ISBN 0-87632-517-7). Clark Boardman.

How to Defend Yourself Against the I.R.S. Sandor Frankel & Robert S. Fink. 1985. 16.45 o.s.i. (ISBN 0-671-55513-8). S&S.

How to Design a Program Evaluation. Carol T. Fitz-Gibbon & Lynn L. Morris. LC 78-57011. (Program Evaluation Kit: Vol. 3). 1978. pap. 8.50 o.p. (ISBN 0-8039-1068-1). Sage.

How to Design an Effective Graphics Presentation, Vol. 17. Laboratory for Computer Graphics & Spatial Analysis, Harvard University Graduate School of Design Staff. (Harvard Library of Computer Graphics, Mapping Collection). (Illus.). 86p. 1981. pap. 15.95 o.p. (ISBN 0-8122-1197-9). U of Pa Pr.

How To Design, Build & Program Your Own Advanced Working Computer System. Robert P. Haviland. (Illus.). 322p. 1979. 16.95 o.p. (ISBN 0-8306-0022-1); pap. 11.95 o.p. (ISBN 0-8306-1332-3, 1332). TAB Bks.

How to Design, Build & Program Your Own Working Computer System. Robert P. Haviland. 1979. pap. 9.95 o.p. (ISBN 0-8306-9773-X, 1111P). TAB Bks.

How to Develop Your ESP Power. Jane Roberts. Orig. Title: Coming of Seth. 1985. pap. 3.50 o.s.i. (ISBN 0-671-55744-0). PB.

How to Develop Your GMP QC Manual. John J. Riordan & William Cotliar. 96p. pap. cancelled o.s.i. (ISBN 0-914176-20-X); pap. cancelled o.s.i. Wash Busn Info.

How to Divorce Your Wife. Furden Athearn. 1977. pap. 1.95 o.p. (ISBN 0-8439-0503-4, LB503, Pub. by Leisure Bks CT). Dorchester Pub Co.

How to Divorce Your Wife. Furden Athearn. 1977. pap. 1.75 o.p. (ISBN 0-8439-0467-4, Pub. by Leisure Bks CT). Dorchester Pub Co.

How to Do All Things: Your Use of Divine Power. Mark-Age Staff. LC 72-121118. 144p. 1970. pap. 5.00 o.p. (ISBN 0-912322-01-2). Mark-Age.

How to Do Everything Right & Live to Regret It: Confessions of a Harried Housewife. Fay Angus. LC 82-48425. 192p. 1983. 10.45 o.p. (ISBN 0-06-060236-8). HarpR.

How-To-Do-It Encyclopedia of Painting & Wallcovering. Bob Percival. (Illus.). 272p. (Orig.). 1982. 18.95 o.p. (ISBN 0-8306-2460-0, 1460); pap. 12.95 o.p. (ISBN 0-8306-1460-5). TAB Bks.

How to Do Practical Construction Cost Estimates. Arnold Acker. Ed. by J. N. Howell. LC 84-72825. 165p. 1984. pap. 52.00 o.p. (ISBN 0-932223-00-1). Churchill PC.

How to Do Your Own Divorce in California. 13th, rev. ed. Charles E. Sherman. LC 80-117985. 184p. 1986. pap. 12.95 o.p. (ISBN 0-87337-009-0). Nolo Pr.

How to Do Your Own Divorce in Texas. Charles E. Sherman & Jim Simons. LC 80-18479. 125p. 1983. pap. 12.95 o.p. (ISBN 0-917316-71-1). Nolo Pr.

How To Do Your Own Professional Picture Framing. Raymond D. Brown. (Illus.). 160p. 1981. 11.95 o.p. (ISBN 0-8306-9650-4, 1238); pap. 8.70 o.p. (ISBN 0-8306-1238-6). TAB Bks.

How to Draft Estate Documents. Pennsylvania Bar Institute Staff. 341p. 1985. 50.00 o.p. (ISBN 0-318-19049-4, 304). PA Bar Inst.

How to Draw Donald Duck. Disney, Walt, Productions Staff. Ed. by Kate Klimo. (Mickey's Drawing Class Ser.). (Illus.). 64p. 1983. pap. 3.95 o.s.i. (ISBN 0-671-44494-8, Little Simon). S&S.

How to Draw Goofy. Disney, Walt, Productions Staff. Ed. by Kate Klimo. (Mickey's Drawing Class Ser.). (Illus.). 64p. 1983. pap. 3.95 o.s.i. (ISBN 0-671-44495-6, Little Simon). S&S.

How to Draw Mickey Mouse. Disney, Walt, Productions Staff. Ed. by Kate Klimo. (Mickey's Drawing Class Ser.). (Illus.). 64p. 1983. pap. 3.95 o.s.i. (ISBN 0-671-44493-X, Little Simon). S&S.

How to Draw Pluto. Disney, Walt, Productions Staff. Ed. by Kate Klimo. (Mickey's Drawing Class Ser.). 64p. 1983. pap. 3.95 o.s.i. (ISBN 0-671-44496-4, Little Simon). S&S.

How to Draw Robots & Spaceships. Larry Evans. (Illus., Orig.). 1982. pap. 4.50 o.p. (ISBN 0-8431-4004-6). Troubador Pr.

How to Dress an Old-Fashioned Doll. Mary H. Morgan. (Illus.). (gr. 5 up). 11.00 o.p. (ISBN 0-8446-4784-5). Peter Smith.

How to Dress Rich. Dale Gody & Monique Ross. 128p. 1983. pap. 6.75 o.p. (ISBN 0-671-45334-3, Fireside). S&S.

How to Drive & Survive. Rudolf Rikal. 1977. 6.50 o.p. (ISBN 0-682-48852-6). Exposition-Phoenix.

How to Eat a Slug & Other Poems. Frank R. Maloney. 64p. (Orig.). 1975. pap. 5.00 o.p. (ISBN 0-914742-14-0). Copper Canyon.

How to Eat & Drink Your Way Through a French or Italian Menu. James Beard. LC 70-108820. 1971. pap. 2.95 o.p. (ISBN 0-689-70332-5, 190, Atheneum). Macmillan.

How to Enjoy Opera Without Really Trying. John Cargher. (Illus.). 176p. 1987. pap. 12.95 o.p. (ISBN 0-87905-274-0). Gibbs Smith Pub.

How to Enjoy Your Life & Your Job. rev. ed. Dale Carnegie. 1985. 15.45 o.p. (ISBN 0-671-54644-9). S&S.

How to Entertain Children with Magic You Can Do. Merlini the Great. 1971. pap. 2.95 o.p. (ISBN 0-671-21056-4, Fireside). S&S.

How to Evaluate & Improve Your COBOL Programming Methods. Paul Noll & Mike Murach. Ed. by Judy Taylor. LC 85-62606. 71p. 1985. pap. 5.00 o.p. (ISBN 0-911625-28-3). M Murach & Assoc.

How to Evaluate Changes in Credit Policy. Credit Research Foundation. 16p. 1987. 40.00 o.p. (ISBN 0-939050-52-8). Credit Res NYS.

How to Evaluate People in Business: The Track-Record Method of Making Correct Judgments. Charles A. Dailey & Ann M. Madsen. LC 82-16233. 240p. 1983. pap. text ed. 10.95 o.p. (ISBN 0-07-015087-7). McGraw.

How to Evaluate Your Net Worth: Making Financial Statements Work for You. Robert J. Wiley. LC 85-17954. 248p. 1986. 19.95 o.p. (ISBN 0-471-88147-3). Wiley.

How to Evict a Tenant. 12th, rev. ed. Alvin Baranov. (Illus.). 147p. 1987. 14.95 o.p. Wolcotts.

How to Evict a Tenant. 12th ed. Alvin B. Baranov. LC 77-79957. (Illus.). 147p. 1985. Repr. of 1978 ed. 14.95 o.p. (ISBN 0-910531-04-8). Wolcotts.

How to Examine Your Breasts: A Guide to Breast Health Care. Judith Tetzleff & Prabharathie G. Nama. (Illus.). 1986. pap. 1.00 o.p. (ISBN 0-686-84300-2). Budlong.

How to Expand Your S. I. Q. (Social Intelligence Quotient) Dane Archer. LC 79-19568. (Illus.). 176p. 1980. 9.95 o.p. (ISBN 0-87131-286-7); pap. 5.95 o.p. (ISBN 0-87131-296-4). M Evans.

How to Fall Out of Love. Debora Phillips & Robert Judd. 1978. 6.95 o.p. (ISBN 0-395-27116-9). HM.

How to Fight Fair with Your Kids...& Win! Luree Nicholson & Laura Torbet. LC 79-1837. 350p. 1980. 12.95 o.p. (ISBN 0-15-142191-9); pap. 7.95 o.p. (ISBN 0-15-642191-7, Harv). HarBraceJ.

How to Finance Your Company. Cyril Aydon. 206p. 1976. text ed. 19.50x o.p. (ISBN 0-220-66309-2, Pub. by Busn Bks England). Gower Pub Co.

How to Find & Land Your First Full-Time Job. Leonard Gorwen. LC 82-6742. 144p. 1983. lib. bdg. 9.95 o.p. (ISBN 0-668-05458-1); pap. 4.95 o.p. (ISBN 0-668-05463-8). Arco.

How to Find Business Intelligence in Washington. VIII ed. (Business Research Ser.: Vol. 4). 350p. 1986. pap. 95.00 o.p. (ISBN 0-934940-31-2). Wash Res Pub.

How to Find Company Intelligence in Federal Documents. 2nd ed. Washington Researchers Publishing Staff. (Briefcase Ser.: Bk. 5). 1988. pap. 50.00 o.p. (ISBN 0-934940-59-2). Wash Res Pub.

How to Find Company Intelligence in Federal Documents, Vol. 5. Washington Researchers Staff. (Briefcase Ser.). 90p. (Orig.). 1986. pap. 50.00 o.p. (ISBN 0-934940-37-1). Wash Res Pub.

How to Find Company Intelligence in Libraries. 2nd ed. Washington Researchers Publishing Staff. (Briefcase Ser.: Bk. 7). 1988. pap. 40.00 o.p. (ISBN 0-934940-61-4). Wash Res Pub.

How to Find Company Intelligence in Libraries. Washington Researchers Staff. (Briefcase Ser.: Vol. 7). 30p. (Orig.). 1986. pap. 40.00 o.p. (ISBN 0-934940-39-8). Wash Res Pub.

How to Find Company Intelligence in State Documents. 9th ed. Washington Researchers Publishing Staff. (Briefcase Ser.). 170p. 1987. pap. 50.00 o.p. (ISBN 0-934940-60-6). Wash Res Pub.

How to Find Company Intelligence in State Documents. 10th ed. Washington Researchers Publishing Staff. (Briefcase Ser.: Bk. 6). 1988. pap. 50.00 o.p. (ISBN 0-934940-67-3). Wash Res Pub.

How to Find Company Intelligence in State Documents. VIII ed. Washington Researchers Staff. (Briefcase Ser.: Vol. 6). 98p. (Orig.). 1986. pap. 50.00 o.p. (ISBN 0-934940-38-X). Wash Res Pub.

How to Find Company Intelligence On-Line. 2nd ed. Washington Researchers Publishing Staff. (Briefcase Ser.: Bk. 8). 1988. pap. 50.00 o.p. (ISBN 0-934940-62-2). Wash Res Pub.

How to Find Company Intelligence On-line. Washington Researchers Staff. (Briefcase Ser.: Vol. 8). 40p. (Orig.). 1986. pap. 50.00 o.p. (ISBN 0-934940-40-1). Wash Res Pub.

How to Find Health Through Prayer. Glenn Clark. LC 77-7830. 1977. pap. 2.95i o.p. (ISBN 0-06-061391-2, RD 242). HarpR.

How to Find Information about Acquisition Candidates. Washington Researchers Publishing Staff. LC 86-51570. (Executive Reports). 79p. (Orig.). 1987. pap. 85.00 o.p. (ISBN 0-934940-45-2). Wash Res Pub.

How to Find Information about Companies: The Corporate Intelligence Source Book. V ed. Washington Researchers Staff. (Business Research Ser.: Vol. 3). 353p. 1987. pap. 125.00 o.p. (ISBN 0-934940-42-8). Wash Res Pub.

How to Find Information about Executives. Washington Researchers Publishing Staff. LC 86-51569. (Executive Reports). 72p. (Orig.). 1987. pap. 60.00 o.p. (ISBN 0-934940-44-4). Wash Res Pub.

How to Find Information about Foreign Firms. Washington Researchers Publishing Staff. LC 86-51568. (Executive Reports). 93p. (Orig.). 1987. pap. 75.00 o.p. (ISBN 0-934940-46-0). Wash Res Pub.

How to Find Information about Private Companies. Washington Researchers Publishing Staff. LC 86-51566. (Executive Reports). 149p. (Orig.). 1987. pap. 95.00 o.p. (ISBN 0-934940-47-9). Wash Res Pub.

How to Find Information about Service Companies. Washington Researchers Publishing Staff. LC 86-51567. (Executive Reports). 156p. (Orig.). 1987. pap. 95.00 o.p. (ISBN 0-934940-52-5). Wash Res Pub.

How to Find Information on Telecommunications. 150.00 o.p. (ISBN 0-686-33029-3). Info Gatekeepers.

How to Find Out about Children's Literature. 3rd ed. Alec Ellis. 1977. 36.00 o.p. (ISBN 0-08-016970-8); pap. text ed. 11.25 o.p. (ISBN 0-08-018230-5). Pergamon.

How to Find Out about Economics. S. A. Parsons. 242p. 1972. text ed. 19.50 o.p. (ISBN 0-08-016694-6). Pergamon.

How to Find Out about Iron & Steel. D. White. 1970. text ed. 21.00 o.p. (ISBN 0-08-015790-4); pap. text ed. 9.50 o.p. (ISBN 0-08-015789-0). Pergamon.

How to Find Out about Italy. F. S. Stych. LC 70-123271. 1970. 34.00 o.p. (ISBN 0-08-015810-2). Pergamon.

How to Find Out about Local Government. W. H. Snape. 1969. text ed. 16.50 o.p. (ISBN 0-08-013957-4); pap. text ed. 7.75 o.p. (ISBN 0-08-013956-6). Pergamon.

How to Find Out about Patents. F. Newby. 1967. pap. 15.75 o.p. (ISBN 0-08-012332-5). Pergamon.

How to Find Out about Statistics. Gillian Burrington. 160p. 1972. 21.00 o.p. (ISBN 0-08-016963-5). Pergamon.

How to Find Out about the Chemical Industry. R. Brown & G. A. Campbell. 1969. pap. text ed. 14.00 o.p. (ISBN 0-08-013050-X). Pergamon.

How to Find Out about the Social Sciences. Gillian Burrington. LC 75-5809. 148p. 1975. 23.00 o.p. (ISBN 0-08-018289-5). Pergamon.

How to Find Out about the United Kingdom Cotton Industry. B. Yates. 1967. 19.75 o.p. (ISBN 0-08-012360-0); pap. text ed. 6.25 o.p. (ISBN 0-08-012361-9). Pergamon.

How to Find Out about the Victorian Period. L. Madden. LC 74-116777. 1970. 29.00 o.p. (ISBN 0-08-015834-X); pap. 14.25 o.p. (ISBN 0-08-015833-1). Pergamon.

How to Find Out about the Wool Textile Industry. H. Lemon. 1968. 37.00 o.p. (ISBN 0-08-012984-6); pap. 18.75 o.p. (ISBN 0-08-012983-8). Pergamon.

How to Find Out in Banking & Investment. N. Burgess. 1969. pap. 14.25 flexi-cover o.p. (ISBN 0-08-013045-3). Pergamon.

How to Find Out in Chemistry. 2nd ed. C. R. Burman. LC 67-549. 1967. text ed. 19.75 o.p. (ISBN 0-08-011881-X); pap. text ed. 9.25 o.p. (ISBN 0-08-011880-1). Pergamon.

How to Find Out in History. H. Hepworth. (How to Find Out Series). (Illus.). 1966. text ed. 17.25 o.p. (ISBN 0-08-011482-2). Pergamon.

How to Find Out in Mathematics. 2nd ed. J. E. Pemberton. 1969. text ed. 24.00 o.p. (ISBN 0-08-006824-3); pap. text ed. 10.75 o.p. (ISBN 0-08-006823-5). Pergamon.

How to Find Out in Philosophy & Psychology. D. H. Borchardt. 1968. text ed. 12.00 o.p. (ISBN 0-08-012596-4); pap. 5.75 o.p. (ISBN 0-08-012595-6). Pergamon.

How to Find Out in Psychiatry: A Guide to Sources of Mental Health Information. Ed. by Bette Greenberg. LC 78-16005. 1979. 24.00 o.p. (ISBN 0-08-021860-1). Pergamon.

How to Find Romance after Forty. Julia Grice. LC 85-15947. 300p. 1985. 14.95 o.p. (ISBN 0-87131-461-4). M Evans.

How to Find Your Wonderful Someone. Phyllis R. Naylor. LC 79-171503. 96p. (Orig.). 1972. pap. 0.50 o.p. (ISBN 0-8006-0107-6, Fortress). Augsburg Fortress.

How to Fix It. Morton J. Schultz. 1971. text ed. 19.50 o.p. (ISBN 0-07-055653-9). McGraw.

How to Fix What's Wrong with Our Schools: A Toolkit for Concerned Parents. Bertha Davis & Dorothy Arnof. LC 83-5102. 216p. 1983. 14.45 o.p. (ISBN 0-89919-193-2); pap. 6.70 o.p. (ISBN 0-89919-216-5). Ticknor & Fields.

How to Fly. Gordon Baxter. (Illus.). 224p. 1981. 13.70 o.s.i. (ISBN 0-671-44801-3). Summit Bks.

How to Fly Lightplanes. Robert T. Smith. (Illus.). 1979. 8.95 o.p. (ISBN 0-8306-9780-2, 2260H); pap. 4.95 o.p. (ISBN 0-8306-2260-8, 2260). TAB Bks.

How to Forecast Interest Rates: A Guide to Profits for Consumers, Managers & Investors. Martin J. Pring. 192p. 1981. text ed. 26.50 o.p. (ISBN 0-07-050865-8). McGraw.

How to Forecast Weather. Dan Ramsey. (Illus.). 224p. (Orig.). 1983. 16.95 o.p. (ISBN 0-8306-0268-2, 1568H); pap. 11.15 o.p. (ISBN 0-8306-0168-6, 1568). TAB Bks.

How to Form Your Own California Corporation. 6th ed. Anthony Mancuso. Ed. by Ralph Warner. LC 80-118046. (Illus.). 200p. 1985. pap. 24.95 o.p. (ISBN 0-917316-83-5). Nolo Pr.

How to Form Your Own New York Corporation. Anthony Mancuso & Lewis Rosenbluth. LC 84-60605. 180p. (Orig.). 1984. pap. 19.95 o.p. (ISBN 0-917316-74-6). Nolo Pr.

How to Form Your Own Texas Corporation. 3rd ed. Anthony Mancuso. LC 82-27047. 210p. 1984. pap. 21.95 o.p. (ISBN 0-917316-72-X, Dist. by Publishers Group). Nolo Pr.

How to Gain a Testimony of the Gospel of Jesus Christ. John J. Stewart. LC 78-52122. 74p. 1978. 5.50 o.p. (ISBN 0-88290-097-8). Horizon Utah.

How to Get a Better Job Quicker. rev. ed. Richard A. Payne. LC 78-2106. 1979. 12.95 o.p. (ISBN 0-8008-3964-1). Taplinger.

How to Get a Career Job. Vertie Lee Carter. 1978. pap. 4.00 o.p. (ISBN 0-682-49159-4). Exposition-Phoenix.

How to Get a Grant for Your Own Special Project. Ulysses V. Spiva. 73p. 1980. pap. text ed. 9.50x o.p. (ISBN 0-89917-301-2). TIS Inc.

How to Get a Job in Boston, or Anywhere Else. rev, 4th ed. Renee Levine. LC 83-48192. 176p. pap. 7.95 o.p. (ISBN 0-87106-918-0). Globe Pequot.

How to Get a Job in Dallas, Fort Worth: The Insider's Guide. rev., 2nd ed. Thomas M. Camden & Nancy Bishop. LC 86-30123. (Illus.). 504p. (Orig.). 1987. pap. 14.95 o.p. (ISBN 0-9609516-9-5). Surrey Bks.

How to Get a Job in Dallas-Ft. Worth: The Insider's Guide. Thomas M. Camden & Nancy Bishop. LC 83-18137. (Illus.). 443p. (Orig.). 1984. pap. 13.95 o.p. (ISBN 0-9609516-1-X, Dist. by Publishers Group). Surrey Bks.

How to Get a Job in New York: The Insider's Guide. Thomas M. Camden & Susan Fleming-Holland. LC 85-20773. (Illus.). 462p. (Orig.). 1986. pap. 13.95 o.p. (ISBN 0-9609516-7-9). Surrey Bks.

How to Get a Loan from Your Bank, Credit Union, or Finance Company. J. Knox McConnell. 1975. 4.00 o.p. (ISBN 0-682-48442-3, Banner). Exposition-Phoenix.

How to Get a Manuscript Published. Ed. by Strode Publishers Staff. 48p. (Orig.). 1983. pap. 1.95 o.p. (ISBN 0-87397-254-6). Strode.

How to Get a Summer Job. Jack Rudman. (Career Examination Ser.: CS-41). (Cloth bdg. avail. on request). pap. 2.00 o.p. (ISBN 0-8373-4002-0). Natl Learning.

How to Get & Keep!--Good Industrial Customers Through Effective Direct Mail. Henry Lavin. (Illus.). 1980. 14.95 o.p. (ISBN 0-682-49609-X, Banner). Exposition-Phoenix.

How to Get Children to Do What You Want Them to Do. Paul E. Wood & Bernard Schwartz. LC 76-54846. 1979. pap. 5.95 o.p. (ISBN 0-13-409821-8). P-H.

How to Get Everything You Want Out of Life. Joyce Brothers. 1979. 9.95 o.p. (ISBN 0-671-22659-2). S&S.

How to Get Free Press: A Do It Yourself Guide to Promote Your Interests, Organization or Business. Toni Delacorte et al. 240p. 1981. 12.95 o.p. Kampmann.

How to Get Free Press: The Step-By-Step Guide to Successful Media Coverage for Your Business, Organization, or Political Campaign. Toni Delacorte et al. 240p. 1984. pap. 6.95 o.p. (ISBN 0-380-68189-7, 68189-7). Avon.

How to Get from the Airport to the City. Norman Crampton. 160p. 1988. pap. 4.95 o.p. (ISBN 0-87131-536-X). M Evans.

How to Get I. D. in Canada. 2nd ed. Ronald G. Eriksen. LC 84-81635. (Illus.). 1984. pap. 7.95 o.p. (ISBN 0-915179-13-X). Loompanics.

How to Get in Shape. Argie W. Post. (Illus.). 1977. 4.50 o.p. (ISBN 0-682-48548-9). Exposition-Phoenix.

How to Get into an Ivy League School. Barbara J. Stahl & Patrick McQuaid. 128p. 1985. pap. 6.95 o.p. (ISBN 0-671-52783-5). Monarch Pr.

How to Get it Built. Werner R. Hashagen. Ed. by Sunny Gibbs. LC 81-90234. (Illus.). 240p. (Orig.). 1982. pap. 18.00 o.p. (ISBN 0-942514-00-9). Azure Coast.

How to Get Lost & Found in Fiji. J. McDermott. 205p. (Orig.). 1987. pap. 9.95 o.s.i. (ISBN 1-55650-017-3). Hunter Pub NY.

How to Get More Out of the Mass. Joseph T. McGloin. LC 74-80938. 1974. pap. 3.50 o.p. (ISBN 0-89243-011-7, 41230). Liguori Pubns.

How to Get More Sales from Your Advertising. Edmund J. Gross. (Illus.). 48p. 1968. pap. 4.00 o.p. (ISBN 0-912256-03-6). Halls of Ivy.

How to Get on the Barter Bandwagon. Mark E. Fournier. Ed. by Jane Fournier & Boye De Mente. (Illus.). 64p. 1980. pap. 6.00 o.p. (ISBN 0-914778-32-3). Phoenix Bks.

How to Get Ready to Sleep, How to Get Ready for Surgery, & How to Get Ready to Die: A Thanatology. Paul Bussard. 1978. 4.00 o.p. (ISBN 0-682-49107-1). Exposition-Phoenix.

How to Get Rich, Fall in Love, Lose Weight, & Solve All Your Problems by Saying "No" Cathy Guisewite. LC 82-72412. (Illus.). 60p. (Orig.). 1983. pap. 2.95 o.p. (ISBN 0-8362-1986-4). Andrews & McMeel.

How to Get Rich with Your Microcomputer. Edwin L. Simpson. 109p. (Orig.). 1984. pap. 12.00 o.p. (ISBN 0-915665-03-4). Premier Publishers.

How to Get Started As a Manufacturers' Representative. William H. Krause. 256p. 1980. 15.95 o.p. (ISBN 0-8144-5584-0). AMACOM.

How to Get Started As a Manufacturer's Representative. William H. Krause. 1982. 8.95 o.p. (ISBN 0-8144-7574-4). AMACOM.

How to Get Started in Video. Daniel Cohen & Susan Cohen. LC 86-7751. 128p. (gr. 7-12). 1986. PLB 11.40 o.p. (ISBN 0-531-10250-5). Watts.

How to Get Started in Your Own Franchise Business. rev. ed. David Seltz. LC 79-27945. 1980. 19.95 o.s.i. (ISBN 0-87863-172-0, Farnsworth Pub Co). Longman Finan.

How to Get Started When You Don't Know Where to Begin. Patricia Hoyt. LC 79-3762. (Illus.). 209p. 1980. 8.95 o.p. (ISBN 0-15-232263-9, HJ). HarBraceJ.

How to Get the Best Buy from Your Car Dealer: An Inside View of What to Watch for in Buying a New or Used Car. W. P. Mann. (ISBN 0-682-49324-4). Exposition-Phoenix.

How to Get the Degree You Want: Bear's Guide to Non-Traditional College Degrees. 8th ed. John Bear. LC 82-905. 273p. (Orig.). 1982. pap. 9.95 o.p. (ISBN 0-89815-080-9). Ten Speed Pr.

How to Get the Job You Want. Meyer Donaho. 1976. 12.95 o.p. (ISBN 0-13-407254-5); pap. 5.95 o.p. (ISBN 0-13-407247-2). P-H.

How to Get the Most Out of Your Social Security & Monthly Benefits. Carl Sciacca. 1974. 4.50 o.p. (ISBN 0-682-47927-6). Exposition-Phoenix.

How to Get the Upper Hand. Ralph Charell. 1979. pap. 2.25 o.p. (ISBN 0-380-42796-6, 42796-6). Avon.

How to Get What You Pray For. Bill Austin. LC 83-50970. 160p. 1984. pap. 4.95 o.p. (ISBN 0-8423-1473-3). Tyndale.

How to Get What You Want in Your Life Today. Bryan Bruno. 48p. 1988. pap. 10.00 o.p. (ISBN 0-944750-00-1). Success Group.

How to Get Your Child into Modeling & Commercials. Cheri Fein. 1986. pap. 9.95 o.p. (ISBN 0-671-60092-3, Fireside). S&S.

How to Get Your Own Trademark. 160p. 1988. 24.95 o.p. Enterprise Del.

How to Get Your Share of Business Insurance. Millard A. Samuel. 6.50 o.p. (ISBN 0-686-31050-0, 29062). Rough Notes.

How to Give Away Your Faith. Paul E. Little. LC 66-20710. 1966. pap. 5.95 o.p. (ISBN 0-87784-553-0). Inter-Varsity.

How to Grow a Young Reader: A Parent's Guide to Kids & Books. John Lindskoog & Kathryn Lindskoog. 1978. pap. 3.95 o.p. (ISBN 0-89191-115-4). Cook.

How to Grow Fruits & Berries. Lorelie M. Mintz. LC 79-28753. (Illus.). 96p. (gr. 4-6). 1980. lib. bdg. 7.29 o.s.i. (ISBN 0-671-33086-1). Messner.

How to Grow Today's Children: A Guide for Modern Parents. James R. Jacobson. 1975. 6.00 o.p. (ISBN 0-682-48363-X, Banner). Exposition-Phoenix.

How to Handle Customer Complaints. Chris Moore. 140p. 1975. text ed. 32.00x o.p. (ISBN 0-7161-0263-3). Gower Pub Co.

How to Handle Debt Collection Matters: Before & After Judgement. Massachusetts Continuing Legal Education, Inc. Staff. LC 84-61756. (Illus.). 170p. 1985. 35.00 o.p. Mass CLE.

How to Handle Grievances. 1974. 7.50 o.p. (ISBN 0-8144-6950-7). AMACOM.

How to Have a Creative Crisis. Norman Wright. 176p. 1986. 10.95 o.p. (ISBN 0-8499-0540-0). Word Bks.

How to Have Air-Conditioning & Still Be Comfortable. Herbert L. Laube. LC 73-172957. (Illus.). 254p. 12.95 o.p. (ISBN 0-912524-04-9). Busn News.

How to Have All the Energy You Need Every Day. Pat King. (Living Books Ser.). 160p. 1986. 3.50 o.p. (ISBN 0-8423-1465-2). Tyndale.

How To Have Fun with Your Body. Michael Lester & Susan Subtle. (Illus.). 128p. (Orig.). 1986. pap. 5.70 o.s.i. (ISBN 0-395-37934-2). HM.

How to Have Powerful Daily Devotions. James Stone. (How To Ser.). 81p. (Orig.). 1983. pap. 2.50 o.s.i. (ISBN 0-934942-33-1). White Wing Pub.

How to Help Handicapped Children Get an Education: A Success Story. Children's Defense Fund Staff. 28p. (Orig.). 1981. pap. 2.20 o.s.i. (ISBN 0-938008-18-8). Children's Defense.

How to Help Your Business Clients Penetrate Foreign Markets. 268p. 1984. 35.00 o.p. (ISBN 0-318-03923-0, 271). PA Bar Inst.

How to Hold on to Your Job. S. Eric Wachtel. LC 83-16408. 180p. 1983. pap. 6.95 o.p. (ISBN 0-87131-419-3, 0674-210). M Evans.

How to Improve Adult Education in Your Church. Jerold W. Apps. LC 72-78560. 128p. (Orig.). 1972. pap. 4.50 o.p. (ISBN 0-8066-1226-6, 10-3180, Augsburg). Augsburg Fortress.

How to Improve Customer Service. E. P. Birsner. 1987. 55.00 o.p. (ISBN 0-317-63376-7). AMACOM.

How to Improve Writing Skills. Desk Top Seminar Staff. (Professional Development Programs Ser.). 208p. 1983. Trainer's Guide. 145.00 o.p. (ISBN 0-471-88931-8); 95.00 o.p. (ISBN 0-471-88932-6). Wiley.

How to Improve Your Memory & Concentration. Michael C. Kellett. 176p. 1983. 5.95 o.p. (ISBN 0-671-49237-3). Monarch Pr.

How to Improve Your Mind. 96p. (ISBN 0-8022-1621-8). Philos Lib.

How to Improve Your Reading Comprehension Skills. Idell Holburt. 224p. (Orig.). 1981. pap. 7.95 o.p. (ISBN 0-671-09260-X). Monarch Pr.

How to Improve Your Test-Taking Skills. 3rd ed. Sara J. Coffman. 1982. pap. text ed. 4.50x o.p. (ISBN 0-89917-373-X). TIS Inc.

How to Increase Your Faith. Steve Ost. (Cornerstone Ser.). 32p. 1981. pap. 2.00 o.p. (ISBN 0-930756-61-4, 533003). Aglow Pubns.

How to Increase Your Money-Making Power in the 80's. 4th rev. ed. John A. Appleman. LC 81-66409. 320p. 1981. 12.95 o.p. (ISBN 0-8119-0433-4). Fell.

How to Increase Your Speed & Agility. Frederick C. Hagerman. (Illus.). 1986. pap. 8.95 o.p. (ISBN 0-399-51236-5). Putnam Pub Group.

How to Insulate Your Home & Save Fuel. U. S. Department of Housing & Urban Development Staff. LC 77-74565. (Illus.). 1977. pap. 3.50 o.p. (ISBN 0-486-23521-1). Dover.

How to Insulate Your Home & Save Fuel. United States Department of Housing & Urban Development Staff. 11.75 o.p. (ISBN 0-8446-5619-4). Peter Smith.

How to Interpret Visual Resources. Harry Stein. (Social Studies Skills Ser.). 96p. (YA) (gr. 7 up). 1983. lib. bdg. 11.90 o.p. (ISBN 0-531-04670-2). Watts.

How to Invest in Bonds. Hugh C. Sherwood. LC 74-81543. 176p. 1976. pap. text ed. 5.95 o.p. (ISBN 0-07-056685-2). McGraw.

How to Invest in Real Estate. Maurice A. Unger. 160p. (Orig.). 1975. pap. text ed. 4.95 o.p. (ISBN 0-07-065915-X). McGraw.

How to Involve Parents in Early Childhood Education. Ed. by Brigham Young University Press Staff. 200p. (Orig.). 1982. pap. text ed. 9.95x o.p. (ISBN 0-8425-2089-9). Brigham.

How to Keep Going When the Storms Keep Coming. Ross Campbell & Randall Gray. 288p. (Orig.). 1986. pap. 6.95 o.p. (ISBN 0-8423-1376-1). Tyndale.

How to Keep Snakes in Captivity. rev. ed. Ross Allen. LC 76-184098. pap. 2.95 o.p. (ISBN 0-8200-0304-2). Great Outdoors.

How to Keep the Heart Healthy Fit. 11th ed. Paul C. Bragg & Patricia Bragg. pap. 4.95 o.p. (ISBN 0-87790-004-3). Health Sci.

How to Keep the Home Fires Burning: Have An Affair with Your Spouse. Ann P. Hinton. (Orig.). 1985. pap. 5.95 o.p. (ISBN 0-671-55255-4, Pub. by Fireside). S&S.

How to Keep Your Honda ATC Alive: A Manual of Step by Step Procedures Anyone Can Understand. Richard Sealey & David Old. (Illus.). 240p. 1986. pap. 14.95 o.p. (ISBN 0-912528-45-1). John Muir.

How to Keep Your Honda Car Alive: A Manual of Step by Step Procedures for the Compleat Idiot. Fred Cisin & Jack Parvin. (Illus.). 272p. (Orig.). 1983. 17.95 o.p. (ISBN 0-912528-25-7). John Muir.

How to Keep Your Lawyer Honest. Ted King. 1986. 8.50 o.p. (ISBN 0-8062-2499-1). Carlton.

How to Keep Your Subaru Alive: Easy Step by Step Repair & Maintenance Procedures. Larry Owens. (Illus.). 424p. (Orig.). 1986. pap. 17.95 o.p. (ISBN 0-912528-49-4). John Muir.

How to Keep Your Volkswagen Alive. 11th ed. John Muir. 418p. 1988. pap. 17.95 o.p. (ISBN 0-945465-12-2). John Muir.

How to Keep Your Volkswagen Alive: A Manual of Step by Step Procedures for the Compleat Idiot. 32nd ed. John Muir & Tosh Gregg. LC 79-63486. (Illus.). 384p. (Span., Ger., & Eng.). 1986. pap. 17.95 o.p. (ISBN 0-912528-50-8). John Muir.

How to Know Everthing about Anyone Through Handwriting. Anne Conway. LC 87-7072. (Illus.). 224p. 1987. 14.95 o.p. (ISBN 0-8069-6590-8). Sterling.

How to Know the Fullness of the Spirit. Gerald Rowlands. (Cornerstone Ser.). (Illus.). 32p. 1982. pap. 2.00 o.p. (ISBN 0-930756-68-1, 533005). Aglow Pubns.

How to Know the Mites & Ticks. Burruss McDaniel. (Pictured Key Nature Ser.). 350p. 1979. wire coil o.p. (ISBN 0-697-04757-1); pap. text ed. write for info. o.p. (ISBN 0-697-04756-3). Wm C Brown.

How to Launder Money. John Gregg. 1982. pap. 8.00 o.p. (ISBN 0-317-03306-9). Loompanics.

How to Learn Astrology. Marc E. Jones. LC 76-55119. (Illus.). 190p. 1977. pap. 4.95 o.p. (ISBN 0-87773-098-9). Shambhala Pubns.

How to Learn from a Course in Miracles. rev. ed. Tara Singh. LC 85-24790. (Orig.). 1985. 8.95 o.p. (ISBN 1-55531-000-1); pap. 4.50 o.p. (ISBN 1-55531-001-X). Life Action Pr.

How to Live Better on Less: A Guide for Waste Watchers. Barbara Jurgensen. LC 74-77677. (Illus.). 144p. (Orig.). 1974. pap. 5.95 o.p. (ISBN 0-8066-1427-7, 10-3181, Augsburg). Augsburg Fortress.

How to Live Forever: The Science & Practice. Harry Gaze. 205p. 1963. pap. 8.95 o.s.i. (ISBN 0-88697-033-4). Life Science.

How to Live in the Circle of Prayer & Make Your Dreams Come True. Stella T. Mann. (Illus.). 180p. 1975. pap. 4.95 o.p. (ISBN 0-87516-206-1). DeVorss.

How to Live Life to the Fullest: A Handbook for Seasoned Citizens. Mary L. Coakley. LC 83-63167. 168p. 1984. pap. 2.45 o.p. (ISBN 0-87973-628-3, 628). Our Sunday Visitor.

How to Live Tax-Free & Rent-Free Now & into the 1990's, Vol. 3. Jim Anderson. LC 78-113752. 376p. (One $10 real estate study tape free with book purchase see notice inside book). 1987. lib. bdg. 25.00 o.p. (ISBN 0-932574-02-5); text ed. 15.00 o.p. (ISBN 0-932574-03-3). Brun Pr.

How to Live Tax-Free-Legally & Rent-Free-Now & Into the 1990's, Vol. 3. Jim Anderson. 1987. lib. bdg. 25.00 o.p. (ISBN 0-317-64396-7); text ed. 15.00 o.p. (ISBN 0-317-64397-5). Brun Pr.

How to Live to Be One Hundred - or More: The Ultimate Diet, Sex & Exercise Book. George Burns. 1985. 12.95 o.p. (ISBN 0-8161-3911-3, Large Print Bks). G K Hall.

How to Live with a Problem Drinker & Survive. Gary Forrest. LC 79-55620. 1980. 8.95 o.s.i. (ISBN 0-689-11038-3, Atheneum). Macmillan.

How to Live with & Overcome the Problems of Mental Retardation. Rasmee Hasitavej. LC 73-82088. 1973. 5.50 o.p. (ISBN 0-682-47767-2, Banner). Exposition-Phoenix.

How to Live with Another Person. David Viscott. LC 74-80711. 148p. 1974. 6.95 o.p. (ISBN 0-87795-092-X, Arbor Hse). Morrow.

How to Live with Another Person. David S. Viscott. LC 74-80711. (Priam Ser.). 1979. pap. 4.50 o.p. (ISBN 0-87795-241-8, Arbor Hse). Morrow.

How to Live with Schizophrenia. rev. ed. Abram Hoffer & Humphry Osmond. 1974. 8.95 o.s.i. (ISBN 0-8216-0004-4, Pub. by Univ Bks). Carol Pub Group.

How to Look Terrific in a Bathing Suit. Ellington Darden. 96p. 1986. pap. 7.70 o.p. (ISBN 0-671-50492-4, Fireside). S&S.

How to Lose One Hundred Million Dollars & Other Valuable Advice. Royal Little. LC 79-11628. (Illus.). 1979. 12.95 o.p. (ISBN 0-316-52786-6). Little.

How to Love Yankees with a Clear Conscious. Bo Whaley. 1988. pap. 5.95 o.p. (ISBN 0-934395-87-X). Rutledge Hill Pr.

How to Maintain & Repair Five, Ten, & Fifteen Speed Bicycles. Derailleur. (Illus.). 1978. pap. text ed. 5.95 o.p. (ISBN 0-07-072230-7). McGraw.

How to Maintain & Service Your Small Computer. John G. Stephenson & Bob Cahill. LC 83-60157. 224p. 1983. pap. 17.95 o.p. (ISBN 0-672-22016-4, 22016). Sams.

How to Make a Million Dowsing & Drilling for Oil. Earl Pyle. 1977. 6.50 o.p. (ISBN 0-682-48782-1). Exposition-Phoenix.

How to Make a Professional Demo Tape. George J. Williams, III. (Illus., Orig.). 1982. pap. 7.95x o.p. Tree by River.

How to Make an Adding Machine: That Even Adds Roman Numerals. Lee Goeller. LC 79-87516. (Illus.). (gr. 2-5). 1979. 7.95 o.p. (ISBN 0-15-236834-5, HJ). HarBraceJ.

How to Make an L.D.S. Quiet Book. Ann F. Pritt. 38p. 1976. pap. 3.95 o.p. (ISBN 0-87747-116-9). Deseret Bk.

How to Make & Cook with Gourmet Vinegars. Marsha P. Johnson. 64p. 1986. pap. 4.95 o.p. (ISBN 0-914667-05-X). Culinary Arts.

How to Make Bamboo Fly Rods. George W. Barnes. LC 77-6738. 1977. 14.95 o.s.i. (ISBN 0-8329-2374-5, Pub. by Winchester Pr). New Century.

How to Make Basic Hospital Equipment. Compiled by Roger England. (Illus.). 86p. (Orig.). 1979. pap. 7.75x o.p. (ISBN 0-903031-60-4, Pub. by Intermed Tech England). Intermediate Tech.

How to Make Baskets. Mary White. LC 72-162523. 206p. Repr. of 1902 ed. 35.00x o.p. (ISBN 0-8103-3064-4). Gale.

How to Make Better QSLs. Jack Janicke. 54p. 1977. pap. 4.95 o.p. (ISBN 0-88006-006-9). Wayne Green Ent.

How to Make Big Money Selling Commercial & Industrial Property. Weldon Girard. 1977. 24.95 o.p. (ISBN 0-13-417956-0, Busn). P-H.

How to Make Braided Rugs. Sally C. Carty. LC 76-49513. (Illus.). 1977. 10.95 o.p. (ISBN 0-07-010195-7); pap. text ed. 6.95 o.p. (ISBN 0-07-010196-5). McGraw.

How to Make Built-in Furniture. 2nd ed. Dalfabbro. 1974. text ed. 22.95 o.p. (ISBN 0-07-015181-4). McGraw.

How to Make Children's Furniture & Play Equipment. 2nd ed. Mario Dal Fabbro. (Illus.). 192p. 1975. text ed. 34.50 o.p. (ISBN 0-07-015186-5). McGraw.

How to Make Cities Liveable: Design Guidelines for Urban Homesteading. Environmental Design Press Staff. Ed. by Gary O. Robinette. 149p. 1984. 28.95 o.p. (ISBN 0-442-22203-3). Van Nos Reinhold.

How to Make Ends Meet: Fifty-Five Special Job-Hunting Strategies for Retirees. Joyce S. Mitchell. 192p. 1986. pap. 7.95 o.p. (ISBN 0-13-417908-0). P-H.

How to Make It When You're Cash Poor. A. Hollis Norton. 256p. 1985. 15.45 o.s.i. (ISBN 0-671-54079-3). S&S.

How to Make Lifetime Friends with Peers & Parents. William F. O'Dell. 1978. 5.50 o.p. (ISBN 0-682-49093-8, Banner). Exposition-Phoenix.

How to Make Love to the Same Person for the Rest of Your Life: And Still Love It. Dagmar O'Connor. LC 85-6869. 240p. 1985. 12.95 o.p. (ISBN 0-385-19854-X). Doubleday.

How to Make Miniature Furniture. John Davenport. (Illus.). 168p. 1988. 19.95 o.p.; pap. 12.95 o.p. Wynwood Pr.

How to Make Mission Style Lamps & Shades. Popular Mechanics Co. Staff. 10.50 o.p. (ISBN 0-8446-5928-2). Peter Smith.

How to Make Money in the Antiques-&-Collectibles Business. Elyse Sommer. 1979. 10.95 o.p. (ISBN 0-395-27758-2). HM.

How to Make Money with Stock Options. L. G. McMillan. 1975. 6.00 o.p. (ISBN 0-682-48171-8, Banner). Exposition-Phoenix.

How to Make Money with Your Camera. Ted Schwarz. LC 74-82517. (Illus.). 220p. 1974. pap. 7.95 o.p. (ISBN 0-912656-30-1). Price Stern.

How to Make Money Writing Fillers. Connie Emerson. LC 86-3623. 266p. (Orig.). 1985. pap. 8.95 o.p. (ISBN 0-89879-196-0, 1389). Writers Digest.

How to Make Nineteen Kinds of American Folk Art from Maska to TV Commercials. Jean Kinney & Cle Kinney. LC 73-91014. (Illus.). 128p. (gr. 5 up). 1974. 7.95 o.p. (ISBN 0-689-30400-5, Atheneum). Macmillan.

How to Make Nuclear Weapons Obsolete. Robert Jastrow. 224p. 1985. 15.45i o.p. (ISBN 0-316-45828-7). Little.

How to Make over Eighty Thousand Dollars a Year on CICS Command Level Programming. David L. Shyh-Yuan. 280p. 1983. perfect binding 38.50 o.p. (ISBN 0-9611810-0-1). CCD Online Syst.

How to Make People Like You When You Know They Don't. Bob Donahue & Marilyn Donahue. 1982. pap. 4.95 o.p. (ISBN 0-8423-1531-4). Tyndale.

How to Make Possum's Honey Bread. Carla Stevens. LC 75-28183. 40p. (gr. 2-6). 1979. 6.50 o.p. (ISBN 0-395-28882-7, Clarion). HM.

How to Make Sunday School Fun for Everyone. Evelyn Witter. Ed. by Dolores Ronaldson. LC 82-62793. (Illus.). 82p. 1983. pap. text ed. 6.95 o.p. (ISBN 0-916260-22-4). Meriwether Pub.

How to Make Sure Your Baby Is Well-& Stays That Way. H. A. Haessler. 368p. 1985. pap. 7.95 o.p. (ISBN 0-380-69924-9). Avon.

How to Make War: A Comprehensive Guide to Modern Warfare. James F. Dunnigan. (Illus.). 416p. 1982. 14.50 o.p. (ISBN 0-688-00780-5). Morrow.

How to Make Working Decoys. George R. Starr, Jr. LC 82-26595. (Illus.). 1978. 21.95 o.p. (ISBN 0-8329-2609-4, Pub. by Winchester Pr). New Century.

How to Make Your Advertising Twice As Effective at Half the Cost. Herschell G. Lewis. LC 85-9573. 273p. 1986. 27.95 o.p. (ISBN 0-13-417882-3, Busn); pap. 10.95 o.p. (ISBN 0-13-417874-2). P-H.

How to Make Your Backyard More Interesting Than TV. Glenwood J. Beckwith. (McGraw-Hill Paperbacks). (Illus., Orig.). 1980. pap. text ed. 6.95 o.p. (ISBN 0-07-004266-7). McGraw.

How to Make Your Car Last a Lifetime. Bob Fendell. LC 80-19759. (Illus.). 216p. 1981. 14.95 o.s.i. (ISBN 0-03-053661-8); pap. 7.95 o.s.i. (ISBN 0-03-053656-1). H Holt & Co.

How to Make Your IRA Grow: Investing under the New Tax Law. Priscilla Meyer. LC 85-45937. 192p. 1986. pap. 3.95 o.p. (ISBN 0-394-62174-3, BC). Grove.

How to Make Your Life Work, or Why Aren't You Happy? Ken Keyes, Jr. & Bruce T. Burkan. LC 74-76803. (Illus.). 192p. 1974. pap. 2.95 o.p. (ISBN 0-9600688-5-6). Love Line Bks.

How to Make Your Own Alcohol Fuels. 2nd ed. Larry W. Carley. (Modern Automotive Ser.). (Illus.). 182p. 1983. 13.95 o.p.; pap. 7.95 o.p. (ISBN 0-8306-2084-2, 2084). TAB Bks.

How to Make Your Own Herbal Cosmetics. Liz Sanderson. LC 78-65301. (Illus.). 1979. pap. 4.95 o.p. (ISBN 0-87983-190-1). Keats.

How to Make Your Own Liqueurs. Campbell, Arthur, Inc. Staff. (Illus., Orig.). 1982. pap. 2.95 o.p. (ISBN 0-932775-02-0). Campbell Inc.

How to Make Your Own Picture Frames. 3rd ed. Hal Rogers & Ed Reinhardt. (Illus.). 144p. (gr. 9-12). 1964. text ed. 17.50 o.p. (ISBN 0-8230-2451-2). Watson-Guptill.

How to Make Your Own Trail Wines. Frank Alexander. (Illus.). 1978. pap. 1.95 o.p. (ISBN 0-916956-02-4, Kokono). Front Row.

How to Make Your Own TV Show. Thad Mumford & Michaela Muntean. Ed. by Doris Duenewald. LC 78-58211. (Elephant Books Ser.). (Illus.). 1978. pap. 2.95 o.p. (ISBN 0-448-16401-9, G&D). Putnam Pub Group.

How to Make Your Science Project Scientific. Thomas Moorman. LC 74-75568. (Illus.). 104p. (gr. 5 up). 1974. 9.95 o.p. (ISBN 0-689-30436-6, Atheneum). Macmillan.

How to Manage a Repressed Economy. Ronald I. McKinnon & Donald J. Mathieson. LC 81-20283. (Essays in International Finance Ser.: No. 145). 1981. pap. text ed. 4.50x o.p. (ISBN 0-88165-052-8). Princeton U Int Finan Econ.

How to Manage By Results. 4th. ed. Dale D. McConkey. LC 83-10547. 301p. 1985. pap. 12.95 o.p. (ISBN 0-8144-7636-8). AMACOM.

How to Manage Structured Programming. Edward Yourdon. (Illus.). 1976. 15.00 o.p. (ISBN 0-917072-02-2, Yourdon). P-H.

How to Manage with a Union, Bks. 1 & 2. Jules J. Justin. 1979. 50.00 set o.p. (ISBN 0-442-23380-9). Van Nos Reinhold.

How to Master the Art of Closing Sales. S. Massimino. 1983. pap. 9.95 o.p. (ISBN 0-8144-7593-0). AMACOM.

How to Maximize Your Advertising Investment. Philip M. Johnson. LC 80-10997. 224p. 1983. 27.95 o.p. (ISBN 0-8436-0769-6). Van Nos Reinhold.

How to Measure Achievement. rev. ed. Lynn L. Morris & Carol T. Fitz-Gibbon. LC 78-58656. (Program Evaluation Kit Ser.: Vol. 6). (Illus.). 159p. 1978. pap. 8.50 o.p. (ISBN 0-8039-1067-3). Sage.

How to Measure Attitudes. Marlene E. Henerson et al. LC 78-57010. (Program Evaluation Kit: Vol. 5). 184p. 1978. pap. 8.95 o.p. (ISBN 0-8039-1070-3). Sage.

How to Measure Program Implementation. Lynn L. Morris & Carol T. Fitz-Gibbon. LC 78-58655. (Program Evaluation Kit Ser.: Vol. 4). (Illus.). 80p. 1978. pap. 7.95 o.p. (ISBN 0-8039-1066-5). Sage.

How to Measure Programmer Productivity. Girish Parikh. LC 82-60955. (Illus.). 95p. 1981. pap. 15.00 o.s.i. (ISBN 0-89435-059-5). QED Info Sci.

How to Meditate: A Practical Guide. Kathleen McDonald. Ed. by Robina Courtin. (Wisdom Basic Book, Orange Ser.). (Illus.). 227p. (Orig.). pap. cancelled o.s.i. (ISBN 0-86171-009-6). Wisdom MA.

How to Meet the Challenge of Life & Death. Hyman J. Schachtel. 50p. 1979. 6.95x o.p. (ISBN 0-87201-102-X). Gulf Pub.

How to Modernize a Basement. rev. ed. Donald R. Brann. LC 66-22941. 98p. 1978. lib. bdg. 5.95 o.p. (ISBN 0-87733-015-8); pap. 5.95 o.p. (ISBN 0-87733-615-6). Easi-Bild.

How To Modify & Collect Child Support. 1987. 17.95 o.p. (ISBN 0-87337-013-9). Nolo Pr.

How to Motivate Your Child Toward Success. William S. McBirnie. 1979. pap. 3.95 o.p. (ISBN 0-8423-1528-4). Tyndale.

How to Multiply Top Executive Effectiveness. H. W. Koch. 1970. pap. text ed. 39.50 o.p. (ISBN 0-13-424275-0). P-H.

Titles

How to Multiply Your Baby's Intelligence. Glenn Doman. LC 83-9026. (Illus.). 336p. 1984. 15.95 o.s.i. (ISBN 0-385-18880-3). Doubleday.
How to Negotiate Successfully in Real Estate. Tony Hoffman. 1984. 16.45 o.s.i. (ISBN 0-671-49775-8). S&S.
How-to of Collective Bargaining see Issues in the Public Employee Relations Library: Series 1.
How to Open a Small Sophisticated Restaurant & What Everyone Should Know about Dining Out. Patrick A. Tracey, Jr. (Illus.). 112p. 1984. 7.95 o.p. (ISBN 0-682-40128-5). Exposition-Phoenix.
How to Open a Small Sophisticated Restaurant & What Everyone Should Know about Dining Out. Patrick A. Tracey, Jr. 7.95 o.p. (ISBN 0-317-04552-0). Exposition-Phoenix.
How to Organize & Maintain an Efficient Hospital Housekeeping Department. Charles B. Miller. LC 80-29176. (Illus.). 144p. (Orig.). 1981. pap. 22.50 o.p. (ISBN 0-939450-29-1, 085140). AHPI.
How to Overcome a Bad Back. James R. Sherman. LC 79-90870. (Illus., Orig.). 1980. pap. 5.95 o.p. (ISBN 0-935538-00-3). Pathway Bks.
How to Participate in a Group. Judith E. Greenberg & Helen Carey. (Social Studies Skills Ser.). 96p. (YA) (gr. 7 up). lib. bdg. 11.90 o.p. (ISBN 0-531-04671-0). Watts.
How to Pass the California Real Estate Exam. National Real Estate Institute Staff. 350p. (Orig.). 1982. wkbk 29.95x o.p. (ISBN 0-915799-03-0). Natl Real Estate Inst.
How to Pay for College 1987-88. 7th ed. Don Betterton. 13p. (Orig.). 1986. pap. 1.25 o.p. (ISBN 0-87866-533-1). Petersons Guides.
How to Pay for College 1988-89. 8th ed. Don Betterton. 13p. (Orig.). 1987. pap. 1.50 o.p. (ISBN 0-87866-676-1). Petersons Guides.
How to Pay Zero Taxes: Over One Hundred Fifty Ways to Reduce Your Taxes- to Nothing! 4th ed. Jeff A. Schnepper. LC 85-111832. 417p. 1985. 9.95 o.p. (ISBN 0-201-16448-5). Addison-Wesley.
How to Photograph a Woman. George Adams. 1979. pap. 5.95 o.p. (ISBN 0-380-43117-3, 43117-3). Avon.
How to Pick up Two Girls. Ed. by Robert Singer. 256p. 1985. pap. 6.95 o.p. (ISBN 0-380-89682-6). Avon.
How to Plan & Conduct Productive Business Meetings. Donald L. Kirpatrick. 1976. 57.95 o.p. (ISBN 0-85013-085-9). Dartnell Corp.
How to Plan Your Succesful Retirement. 128p. 1988. pap. 9.95 o.p. (ISBN 0-318-23708-3). Am Assn Retire.
How to Play Bebop, Vol. 1: The Bebop Scales & Other Scales in Common Use. David Baker. 48p. 1985. pap. text ed. 7.95 o.p. (ISBN 0-89917-459-0). Tichenor Pub.
How to Play Better Baseball. Bud Harrelson & Joel H. Cohen. LC 70-190402. (Illus.). 192p. 1972. 5.95 o.p. (ISBN 0-689-10501-0, Atheneum). Macmillan.
How to Play Girls' Softball. Arnold Madison. LC 81-479. (Illus.). 128p. (gr. 4-6). 1981. lib. bdg. 9.79 o.p. (ISBN 0-671-33051-9). Messner.
How to Play Piano from Chord Symbols: A Guide to Playing More Notes Without Reading More Notes. Duane Shinn. 1978. pap. 6.95 o.p. (ISBN 0-912732-43-1). Duane Shinn.
How to Play Platform Tennis. new, rev. ed. Dick Squires. (McGraw-Hill Paperbacks). 1977. pap. text ed. 3.95 o.p. (ISBN 0-07-060530-0). McGraw.
How to Play Power Tennis with Ease. Sally M. Huss. (Illus.). (gr. 6 up). 1979. pap. 6.95 spiral bound o.p. (ISBN 0-15-236836-1, HJ). HarBraceJ.
How to Play Slo-Pitch Softball. Richard L. Critchfield. 1979. 5.95 o.p. (ISBN 0-533-03724-7). Vantage.
How to Play with Your Baby. Athina Aston. LC 83-48037. (Your Learning Child Ser.: Vol. 1). (Illus.). 120p. 1983. pap. 7.95 o.p. (ISBN 0-914788-73-6). Globe Pequot.
How to Play with Your Timex Sinclair 1000. Bob Albrecht et al. 124p. 1983. 12.95 o.p. (ISBN 0-395-34926-5); pap. 7.95 cancelled o.p. (ISBN 0-395-34919-2). HM.
How to Play Your Best Tennis All the Time. Jack Kramer & Larry Sheehan. LC 76-53402. (Illus.). 1978. pap. 6.95 o.p. (ISBN 0-689-70576-X, Atheneum). Macmillan.
How to Pray Effectively. Wayne Mack. (Christian Growth Ser.). 1977. pap. 2.95 o.p. (ISBN 0-87552-331-5). Presby & Reformed.
How to Prepare a Marketing Plan. 3rd ed. John Stapleton. 304p. 1982. text ed. 59.95x o.p. (ISBN 0-566-02288-5). Gower Pub Co.
How to Prepare & Present a Business Plan. Joseph R. Mancuso. (Illus.). 316p. 1983. 19.95 o.p. (ISBN 0-13-430629-5); pap. 10.95 o.p. (ISBN 0-13-430611-2). P-H.
How to Prepare & Write Your Employee Handbook. E. Anson. 1984. 75.00 o.p. (ISBN 0-8144-1140-1). AMACOM.
How to Prepare for High School Entrance Examinations: Including SSAT & CO-OP. 5th ed. Peters et al. 544p. 1985. pap. 8.95 o.p. (ISBN 0-8120-3586-0). Barron.
How to Prepare for the Advanced Placement Exam in American History. 2nd ed. 1983. pap. 8.95 o.p. (ISBN 0-8120-2378-1). Barron.
How to Prepare for the American College Test: ACT. Prescott Evarts, Jr. (Orig.). 1980. pap. text ed. 5.95 o.p. (ISBN 0-07-019767-9). McGraw.
How to Prepare for the American College Testing Program (ACT) 4th ed. M. Shapiro & F. Obrecht. 608p. 1982. pap. 7.95 o.p. (ISBN 0-8120-2495-8). Barron.
How to Prepare for the CBEST (California Basic Education Skills Test) 1988. pap. 9.95 o.p. (ISBN 0-8120-3954-8). Barron.
How to Prepare for the College Board Achievement Test - Biology. 8th ed. Maurice Bleifeld. LC 81-3892. 352p. 1981. 9.50 o.p. (ISBN 0-8120-5416-4); pap. 8.95 o.p. (ISBN 0-8120-2766-3). Barron.
How to Prepare for the College Board Achievement Test - English. 5th ed. Jerome Shostak. 224p. (gr. 11-12). 1984. pap. text ed. 8.95 o.p. (ISBN 0-8120-2767-1). Barron.
How to Prepare for the College Board Achievement Test - Mathematics Level II. Howard Dodge. LC 78-8655. 1984. pap. 8.95 o.p. (ISBN 0-8120-2769-8). Barron.
How to Prepare for the High School Competency & Proficiency Tests. Morton Selub & Morris Bramson. (Books for Professionals Ser.). 407p. 1983. pap. 7.95 o.p. (ISBN 0-15-600026-1, BFP). HarBraceJ.
How to Prepare for the High School Equivalency Exam (GED) 6th ed. Rockowitz et al. (Test Preparation Ser.). 1984. pap. 8.95 o.p. (ISBN 0-8120-2763-9). Barron.
How to Prepare for the Law School Admission Test (LSAT) 3rd ed. Jerry Bobrow. 1985. text ed. 23.95 o.p. (ISBN 0-8120-5555-1); pap. 8.95 o.p. (ISBN 0-8120-2790-6). Barron.
How to Prepare for the Miller Analogies Test (MAT) Phyllis Cash. (McGraw-Hill Paperbacks). (Orig.). 1979. pap. text ed. 5.95 o.p. (ISBN 0-07-010222-8). McGraw.
How to Prepare for the New High School Equivalency Examination. C. Jenkins et al. (Illus.). 1978. pap. 7.95 o.p. (ISBN 0-07-032350-X). McGraw.
How to Prepare for the Police Officer Entrance Examination. Donald Schroeder & Frank Lombardo. LC 82-18472. 256p. 1982. pap. 7.95 o.p. (ISBN 0-8120-2593-8). Barron.
How to Prepare for the Police Officer Examination (Including Transit & Housing Officer) Donald J. Schroeder & Frank A. Lombardo. LC 85-26740. 1986. 8.95 o.p. (ISBN 0-8120-3666-2). Barron.
How to Prepare for the Postal Clerk Carrier Examination. Philip Barkus. LC 82-24296. 256p. 1982. pap. 8.95 o.p. (ISBN 0-8120-2524-5). Barron.
How to Prepare for the Reading Skills Test. 2nd ed. Roger B. Goodman & William Ince. 1983. pap. text ed. 5.95 o.p. (ISBN 0-07-023799-9). McGraw.
How to Prepare for the Real Estate Licensing Exam. M. A. Hines. 1983. pap. 9.95 o.p. (ISBN 0-15-600075-X, BFP). HarBraceJ.
How to Prepare for the SAT College Entrance Examinations. 13th ed. Samuel C. Brownstein et al. 608p. 1986. 23.95 o.p. (ISBN 0-8120-5763-5); pap. 8.95 o.p. (ISBN 0-8120-3723-5). Barron.
How to Prepare for the Texas Real Estate Exam: A Study Manual for Brokers & Salespeople. 3rd ed. David F. Distelhorst. LC 84-2138. 252p. (Orig.). 1984. pap. 19.95 o.p. (ISBN 0-88462-496-X, 1970-03, Real Estate Ed). Longman Finan.
How to Prepare for the Texas Real Estate Exam. 2nd ed. David F. Distelhorst. 248p. (Orig.). 1980. pap. 14.95 o.p. (ISBN 0-88462-270-3, 1970-03, Real Estate Ed). Longman Finan.
How to Prepare for the Uniform Certified Public Accountant Examination. Person Wolinsky Associates Inc. 531p. 1983. pap. 13.95 o.s.i. (ISBN 0-8120-2648-9). Barron.
How to Prepare Your Child for School. National Education Association Staff. 1983. pap. 1.95 o.p. (ISBN 0-380-82255-5, 82255). Avon.
How to Prepare Your Own Mail Order Catalog (Without Merchandise & for Pennies) Premier Publishers, Inc. Staff. 1986. Set. pap. 10.00 o.p. (ISBN 0-915665-11-5). Premier Publishers.
How to Present an Evaluation Report. rev. ed. Lynn L. Morris & Carol T. Fitz-Gibbon. LC 78-58657. (Program Evaluation Kit Ser.: Vol. 8). (Illus.). 80p. 1978. pap. 4.95 o.p. (ISBN 0-8039-1069-X). Sage.
How to Probate an Estate: A Handbook for Executors & Administrators. Williams J. Moody. LC 86-4748. 1986. pap. 5.95 o.p. (ISBN 0-671-62880-1). S&S.
How to Probate an Estate: California. 2nd, rev. ed. Julia Nissley. LC 85-63248. 325p. 1987. pap. 24.95 o.p. (ISBN 0-87337-052-X). Nolo Pr.
How to Produce a Good-Looking Book Fast & Cheap. Carole Marsh. (Podunk Publishing Ser.). 50p. (gr. 4 up). 1986. pap. 7.95 o.p. Gallopade Pub Group.
How to Profit from Seasonal Commodity Spreads: A Complete Guide. Jacob Bernstein. LC 82-13543. 537p. 1983. 72.50 o.p. (ISBN 0-471-86432-3). Wiley.
How to Profit from the Coming Oil Crisis. Kurt Wulff & Bill Bruns. 1988. 17.95 o.p. (ISBN 0-553-05287-X). Bantam.
How to Profit on the Real Estate Roller Coaster: An Investor's Guide to Avoiding Big Mistakes. Marvin T. Levin & Barbara Nichols. LC 85-30125. 224p. 1986. text ed. 17.95 o.p. (ISBN 0-13-766320-X). P-H.
How to Prosper During the Coming Bad Years. Howard Ruff. 384p. 1980. pap. 4.95 o.s.i. (ISBN 0-446-32497-3). Warner Bks.
How to Prosper in the Underground Economy. Larry Burkett & William Proctor. LC 81-14172. (Illus.). 288p. 1982. 11.50 o.p. (ISBN 0-688-00778-3). Morrow.
How to Protect Your Business. Council of Better Business Bureaus, Inc. Staff. 200p. 1985. pap. 8.95 o.p. (ISBN 0-13-430539-6). P-H.
How to Protect Your Faith. Norvel Hayes. 70p. (Orig.). 1983. pap. 3.95 o.p. (ISBN 0-89274-279-8). Harrison Hse.
How to Publish a Church Newsletter. Walter W. Knight. LC 83-70372. (Orig.). 1983. pap. 6.95 o.p. (ISBN 0-8054-3108-X). Broadman.
How to Raise a Healthy Child: In Spite of Your Doctor. Robert S. Mendelsohn. 288p. 1986. pap. 8.95 o.p. (ISBN 0-8092-4995-2). Contemp Bks.
How to Raise & Train a Golden Retriever. Evelyn Miller. (Illus.). pap. 2.95 o.p. (ISBN 0-87666-306-4, DS-1018). TFH Pubns.
How to Raise & Train a Pomeranian. Arthur Liebers & Georgie M. Sheppard. (Illus.). pap. 2.95 o.p. (ISBN 0-87666-352-8, DS-1029). TFH Pubns.
How to Raise Capital. Gregory I. Kravitt & Jeffrey E. Grossman. LC 82-73630. 250p. 1984. 40.00 o.p. (ISBN 0-87094-380-4). Dow Jones-Irwin.
How to Raise Confident Children. Richard L. Strauss. 156p. 1984. pap. 4.95 o.p. (ISBN 0-8010-8239-0). Baker Bk.
How to Raise Money to Make Money. IBP Research & Editorial Staff. LC 80-26568. (Illus.). 432p. 1980. 99.50 o.p. (ISBN 0-87624-214-X, Inst Busn Plan). P-H.
How to Raise Venture Capital. Venture Capital Editors & Stanley Pratt. 288p. 1982. 17.95 o.s.i. (ISBN 0-684-17444-8, ScribT). Scribner.
How to Raise Your Man: The Problems of a New Style Woman in Love with an Old Style Man. Rose DeWolf. 192p. 1983. 11.95 o.p. (ISBN 0-531-09808-7). Watts.
How to Read a Newspaper. Helen Carey & Judith E. Greenberg. (Social Studies Skills Ser.). 96p. (YA) (gr. 7 up). 1983. lib. bdg. 11.90 o.p. (ISBN 0-531-04672-9). Watts.
How to Read a Play. Ronald Hayman. LC 77-2455. 1977. pap. 4.95 o.p. (ISBN 0-394-17022-9, E695, Ever). Grove.
How to Read an ECG. 3rd ed. Margaret G. Blowers & Roberta S. Sims. (Illus.). 70p. 1983. pap. 16.95 spiral bdg. o.p. (ISBN 0-87489-307-0). Med Economics.
How to Read & Profit from Financial News. Gerald Krefetz. LC 84-2046. 224p. 1984. 16.45 o.p. (ISBN 0-89919-262-9). Ticknor & Fields.
How to Read & Profit from Financial News. Gerald Krefetz. LC 84-2046. 240p. 1985. pap. 7.70 o.p. (ISBN 0-89919-404-4). Ticknor & Fields.
How to Read & Understand Blueprints. John A. Nelson. 304p. 1982. 32.95 o.s.i. (ISBN 0-442-26188-8). Van Nos Reinhold.
How to Read Faster & Better. Franklin J. Agardy. 1981. 11.95 o.s.i. (ISBN 0-671-24690-9). S&S.
How to Read German. Marie H. Law. 1966. pap. 4.95x o.p. (ISBN 0-393-04144-1, NortonC). Norton.
How to Read Palms. Litzkah R. Gibson. Ed. by Sherri Adelman. (Illus.). 184p. (YA) (gr. 10-12). 1989. pap. 8.95 o.p. (ISBN 0-8119-0033-9). Fell.
How to Read the Greek New Testament. Guy N. Woods. 5.00 o.p. (ISBN 0-89225-103-4). Gospel Advocate.
How to Reduce Interest Rates & Poverty. Arthur Dahlberg. LC 82-22029. (Illus.). 598p. 1984. pap. 12.95 o.p. Cobble Hill Pr.
How to Repair & Maintain Your IBM Computer. Gene B. Williams. LC 84-45156. 208p. 1986. 12.50 o.p. (ISBN 0-8019-7537-9). Chilton.
How to Repair CB Radios. Lawrence Schultz. Ed. by Mark Haas. (Electro Skills Ser.). (Illus.). 176p. 1980. pap. text ed. 11.30 o.p. (ISBN 0-07-055638-5). McGraw.
How to Repair Diesel Engines. Paul Dempsey. LC 75-20847. (Illus.). 308p. 1975. 15.95 o.p. (ISBN 0-8306-5817-3); pap. 10.60 o.p. (ISBN 0-8306-4817-8, 817). TAB Bks.
How to Repair Home Laundry Appliances. 2nd ed. Ben Gaddis. (Illus.). 176p. 1986. 21.95 o.p. (ISBN 0-8306-9562-1, 2662); pap. 14.60 o.p. (ISBN 0-8306-0662-9, 2662P). Tab Bks.
How to Repair the Wrong You've Done. Ken Wilson. (Living As a Christian Ser.). 80p. 1982. pap. 3.50 o.p. (ISBN 0-89283-116-2). Servant.
How to Respond to a Skeptic. Lewis A. Drummond & Paul R. Baxter. (Orig.). 1986. pap. 5.95 o.p. (ISBN 0-8024-7703-8). Moody.
How to Restore & Improve Your Victorian House. Alan Johnson. (Illus.). 160p. 1983. 32.95 o.p. (ISBN 0-7153-8334-5). David & Charles.
How to Restore & Repair Practically Everything. L. Johnson. 208p. 1985. text ed. 19.95 o.p. (ISBN 0-07-032607-X). McGraw.
How to Restore the Model a Ford. Leslie R. Henry. Ed. by Clymer Publications. (Illus.). pap. 5.00 o.p. (ISBN 0-89287-262-4, H522). Clymer Pub.
How to Retain & Regain Your Health & Your Youth. Ida Alter. LC 86-91874. 80p. (Orig.). 1987. pap. text ed. 8.00 o.p. (ISBN 0-682-40336-9). Exposition-Phoenix.
How to Ride a Tiger. Norma Farber. LC 83-4289. (Illus.). 32p. (gr. k-3). 1983. 9.70 o.s.i. (ISBN 0-395-34553-7). HM.
How to Run a Growing Company. W. Delaney. 1983. pap. 6.95 o.p. (ISBN 0-8144-7590-6). AMACOM.
How to Run a Public Relations Campaign. M. Williams-Thompson. 1969. pap. text ed. 3.50 o.p. (ISBN 0-08-013424-6). Pergamon.
How to Run a Small Business. 4th ed. Jacob K. Lasser. 306p. 1974. text ed. 24.95 o.p. (ISBN 0-07-036565-2, P&RB). McGraw.
How to Run a Traditional Jewish Household. Blu Greenberg. 1983. 19.25 o.s.i. (ISBN 0-671-41700-2). S&S.
How to Sail. Carl D. Lane. (Illus.). 1947. 14.95 o.p. (ISBN 0-393-03118-7). Norton.
How to Save a Million. Jonathan Place. LC 82-82315. 156p. (Orig.). 1982. pap. 4.95 o.p. (ISBN 0-448-16807-3, G&D). Putnam Pub Group.
How to Save Lots of Money on Your Phone Bill. Howard Strange. 128p. (Orig.). 1981. pap. 4.95 o.s.i. (ISBN 0-345-29654-0). Ballantine.
How to Save Tax Dollars When You Sell Your House. 4th ed. Rich Robinson. 1980. pap. 1.95 o.s.i. (ISBN 0-88462-372-6, 1968-01, Real Estate Ed). Longman Finan.
How to Save the World. Robert Allen. (Illus.). 150p. 1980. 14.95 o.p. (IUCN79, IUCN); pap. 7.50 o.p. (IUCN120). UNIPUB.
How to Save the World: A Fourth World Guide to the Politics of Scale. Ed. by Nicholas Alberry. 192p. 1984. pap. 9.95 o.p. (ISBN 0-85500-209-3). Newcastle Pub.
How to Save Your Hair: A Complete Guide to the Prevention & Treatment of Baldness. Suzanne K. Flynn. LC 84-12453. (Orig.). 1984. pap. 6.95 o.p. (ISBN 0-87795-579-4, Arbor Hse). Morrow.
How to Save Your Life. Earl Ubell. LC 73-7520. 1973. 7.50 o.p. (ISBN 0-15-142179-X). HarBraceJ.
How to Seek a New & Better Job. 3rd ed. Ed. by James H. Kennedy. 1984. pap. 5.00 o.p. (ISBN 0-916654-31-1). Consultants News.
How to Select & Place Your Parents in a Nursing Home. Marg Lamitie. 1985. 10.00 o.p. (ISBN 0-682-40265-6). Exposition-Phoenix.
How to Select & Use an Executive Search Firm. A. Robert Taylor. 160p. 1984. text ed. 29.95 o.p. (ISBN 0-07-062959-5). McGraw.
How to Select & Use Management Consultants. Rev. ed. LC 9-73027. 33p. 1974. 3.00 o.p. (ISBN 0-939199-02-5). ACME.
How to Select Your Own Computer. William Constandse. 132p. 1983. 12.95 o.p. (ISBN 0-8119-0596-9). Fell.
How to Select Your Small Computer Without Frustration. Hillel Segal & Jess Burst. (Illus.). 208p. 1983. pap. 16.95 o.p. (ISBN 0-13-431320-8); pap. 14.95 o.p. P-H.
How to Self Create an Internal-Unity Existence: Essence, Phase One Pursuits One Through Fourteen. James L. Hubbard. 1979. 7.50 o.p. (ISBN 0-682-49331-7). Exposition-Phoenix.
How to Sell a Dealership. Elmer H. West. 64p. (Orig.). 1980. pap. 7.95 o.p. (ISBN 0-682-49645-6). Exposition-Phoenix.
How to Sell Anything to Anybody. Joe Girard & Stanley H. Brown. 1978. 8.95 o.p. (ISBN 0-671-22651-7). S&S.

How to Sell Every Magazine Article You Write. Lisa C. Cool. LC 86-15864. (No.8). 136p. 1986. 15.95 o.p. (ISBN 0-89879-236-3). Writers Digest.
How to Sell New Homes & Condominiums. David Stone. LC 75-15546. 1977. text ed. 42.50 o.p. (ISBN 0-07-061735-X). McGraw.
How to Sell to the People's Republic of China. S. Massimino. 1980. 24.95 o.p. (ISBN 0-442-88010-3). Van Nos Reinhold.
How to Sell Your Arts & Crafts. Loretta Holz. LC 76-25904. (Encore Edition). (Illus.). 4.95 o.p. (ISBN 0-684-16206-7, ScribT). Scribner.
How to Sell Your Ideas. J. Nirenberg. 272p. 1984. text ed. 15.95 o.p. (ISBN 0-07-046577-0). McGraw.
How to Sell Your Own Home Without a Real Estate Agent & Save Thousands of Dollars. Joseph M. Gardner, Jr. 1975. 6.50 o.p. (ISBN 0-682-48180-7, Banner). Exposition-Phoenix.
How to Sell Yourself. Joe Girard. 1980. 10.95 o.p. (ISBN 0-671-25038-8). S&S.
How to Sell Yourself on an Interview. Arthur R. Pell. 192p. (Orig.). 1982. pap. 6.95 o.p. (ISBN 0-671-43147-1). Monarch Pr.
How to Serve on a Jury. P. J. Callahan. LC 53-5766. (Legal Almanac Ser.: No. 31). 80p. 1953. (ISBN 0-379-11031-8). Oceana.
How to Set Up a Business Office: The Complete Guide to Locating, Outfitting & Staffing. Norma A. Morris. (Illus.). 210p. 1981. 15.95 o.p. (ISBN 0-913864-62-5). Enterprise Del.
How to Set up for a Mah-Jongg Game & Other Lost Arts. Carol E. Rinzler & Joan Gelman. (Illus.). 176p. 1987. 12.70 o.s.i. (ISBN 0-671-55428-X). S&S.
How to Set up Your Own Small Business, Vols. I & II. Max Fallek. 1989. Set. lib. bdg. 149.95 o.p. (ISBN 0-939069-05-9); Set. 3-ring binder 149.95 o.p. (ISBN 0-939069-00-8). Amer Inst Small Bus.
How to Set up Your Own Small Business, Vols. I & II. Max Fallek. 1988. Set. lib. bdg. 149.95 3-ring binder o.p. (ISBN 0-939069-21-0). Amer Inst Small Bus.
How to Share Your Faith Without Being Offensive. Joyce Neville. 160p. (Orig.). 1983. pap. 6.95 o.p. (ISBN 0-8164-2228-1). HarpR.
How to Shoot an Amateur Naturalist. Gerald Durrell. (Illus.). 205p. 1985. 15.95 o.p. (ISBN 0-316-19717-3). Little.
How To Sleep Without Drugs. Jeffrey Sussman. 224p. 1986. 9.95 o.p. (ISBN 0-87052-313-9). Hippocrene Bks.
How to Solarize Your House. Thomas Dean & Jay Hedden. (Illus.). 176p. 1982. 5.95 o.p. (ISBN 0-684-16295-4, ScribT); pap. 3.50 o.p. (ISBN 0-684-17425-1). Scribner.
How to Solve Your Decorating Problems. Barbara Taylor Bradford. 1976. 14.95 o.s.i. (ISBN 0-671-22202-3). S&S.
How To Solve Your Small Business Advertising Problems: The All Media Guide To Effective Advertising. William K. Witcher. (Illus.). 212p. 1986. pap. 17.95 o.p. (ISBN 0-937769-50-9). Mark Inc CA.
How to Stand Up for Your Rights & Win! Roy M. Cohn. 336p. 1982. pap. 8.50 o.p. (ISBN 0-671-25342-5, Fireside). S&S.
How to Start a Family Business & Make It Work. Jerome Goldstein. LC 84-3995. 168p. 1984. 9.95 o.p. (ISBN 0-87131-435-5). M Evans.
How to Start a Small Business. Larry Lackey. LC 78-126370. 1971. 6.95 o.p. (ISBN 0-682-47147-X, Banner). Exposition-Phoenix.
How to Start & Manage Your Own Small Business. Gardiner C. Greene. 243p. 1975. text ed. 25.95 o.p. (ISBN 0-07-024350-6). McGraw.
How to Start & Operate a Mail Order Business. 3rd. ed. Julian L. Simon. LC 80-13807. (Illus.). 544p. 1981. text ed. 34.50 o.p. (ISBN 0-07-057417-0). McGraw.
How to Start & Run a Successful Home Typing Business. 2nd rev. ed. Peggy Glenn. LC 80-81400. (Illus.). 116p. (Orig.). 1980. pap. 14.95 perfect bdg. o.p. (ISBN 0-936930-00-4); pap. 14.95 spiral bdg. o.p. (ISBN 0-936930-01-2). Aames-Allen.
How to Start, Finance & Manage Your Own Small Business. Joseph R. Mancuso. LC 77-14303. (Illus.). 1978. 18.95 o.p. (ISBN 0-13-434928-8); pap. 10.95 o.p. (ISBN 0-13-434910-5). P-H.
How to Start, Finance & Manage Your Own Small Business. rev. ed. Joseph R. Mancuso. 432p. 1984. 19.95 o.p. (ISBN 0-13-434879-6); pap. 12.95 o.p. (ISBN 0-13-434861-3). P-H.
How to Start Your Own Business & Succeed. Arthur H. Kuriloff & John M. Hemphill. 1978. text ed. 60.00 o.p. (ISBN 0-07-035648-3). McGraw.
How to Stay Ahead Financially. Philip Gordis. 1977. 10.95 o.p. (ISBN 0-393-08794-8). Norton.
How to Stay Out of Court. Robert Coulson. LC 83-73660. 199p. 1984. pap. 7.95 o.p. (ISBN 0-943001-04-8). Am Arbitration.
How to Stock a Quality Home Library Inexpensively. Jane A. Williams. 20p. (Orig.). 1987. pap. 3.50 o.p. (ISBN 0-942617-00-2). Blstckng Pr.
How to Stop a War: Lessons of Two Hundred Years of War & Peace. James F. Dunnigan & William Martel. LC 87-5278. (Illus.). 312p. 1987. 18.95 o.p. (ISBN 0-385-24009-0). Doubleday.
How to Stop Smoking. Marilyn S. Halper. LC 80-10897. (Strang Ser.). 160p. 1981. 12.95 o.s.i. (ISBN 0-03-048301-8); pap. 6.95 o.s.i. (ISBN 0-03-048296-8). H Holt & Co.
How to Stop Worrying about Your Kids. J. D. Sanderson. 1978. 8.95 o.p. (ISBN 0-393-08808-1). Norton.
How to Stop Worrying & Start Living. Dale Carnegie. 1977. pap. 3.95 o.s.i. (ISBN 0-671-53267-7). PB.
How to Stop Worrying & Start Living. Dale Carnegie. 1948. 9.95 o.s.i. (ISBN 0-671-34900-7). S&S.
How to Stop Worrying & Start Living. rev. ed. Dale Carnegie. 1985. pap. 4.50 o.s.i. (ISBN 0-671-62394-X). PB.
How to Study. 2nd ed. Arthur W. Kornhauser. LC 37-2272. 1937. pap. text ed. 1.25x o.s.i. (ISBN 0-226-45115-1). U of Chicago Pr.
How to Study Acts. Joseph M. Gettys. 219p. 1976. pap. 5.00s o.p. (ISBN 0-87921-028-1). Attic Pr.
How to Study in College. 2nd ed. Walter Pauk. LC 72-7923. 1974. pap. 13.95 o.p. (ISBN 0-395-17815-0). HM.
How to Succeed in Company Politics. 2nd ed. Edward J. Hegarty. 1976. text ed. 37.50 o.p. (ISBN 0-07-027847-4). McGraw.
How to Succeed in Life Insurance Selling. Hugh S. Bell. 4.50 o.p. (ISBN 0-686-31052-7, 29705). Rough Notes.
How to Successfully Manage Real Estate in Your Spare Time. Albert J. Lowry. 1979. 29.95 o.s.i. (ISBN 0-671-24829-4). S&S.
How to Survive a Tax Audit. 1974. pap. 2.00 o.p. (ISBN 0-918734-19-3). Reymont.
How to Survive & Market Yourself in Management. new ed. Andrew Pleninger. LC 77-1409. 1977. 12.95 o.p. (ISBN 0-8144-5436-4). AMACOM.
How to Survive & Market Yourself in Management. Andrew Pleninger. LC 77-1409. 256p. 1981. 6.95 o.p. (ISBN 0-8144-7542-6). AMACOM.
How to Survive & Prosper As an Artist. Caroll Michels. LC 82-21192. 169p. 1983. 14.95 o.p. (ISBN 0-03-061572-0, Owl Bks.). H Holt & Co.
How to Survive at College. 5th ed. Sara J. Coffman. 1984. pap. text ed. 14.95x o.p. (ISBN 0-89917-485-X). TIS Inc.
How to Survive in Your Native Land. James Herndon. 1977. pap. 9.95 o.p. (ISBN 0-671-23027-1, Touchstone Bks). S&S.
How to Survive Medical School. Toni Martin. LC 82-2551. 185p. 1983. 13.95 o.s.i. (ISBN 0-03-062539-4). H Holt & Co.
How to Survive on Fifty Thousand to One Hundred Fifty Thousand Dollars a Year. Stanley J. Cohen & Robert Wool. 224p. 1984. 13.45 o.p. (ISBN 0-395-35298-3). HM.
How to Survive Probate & Minimize the Attorney's Fee. Barbara R. Stock. (Illus.). 176p. (Orig.). 1987. 16.95 o.p. (ISBN 0-913455-07-5). Linch Pub.
How to Survive Without a Salary. rev. ed. Charles Long. (Illus.). 232p. (Orig.). 1986. pap. 8.95 o.p. (ISBN 0-920197-03-5, Pub. by Summerhill CN). Sterling.
How to Survive Your Adolescent's Adolescence. Robert C. Kolodny et al. 420p. 1984. 17.95 o.p. (ISBN 0-316-50158-1). Little.
How to Survive Your First Six Months in Florida. rev. ed. Robert Tolf. Date not set. 3.95 o.p. Trend Bk Div.
How to Switch Careers. Bob Weinstein. 224p. (Orig.). 1985. pap. 6.95 o.p. (ISBN 0-671-53064-X, Pub. by Fireside). S&S.
How to Take & Pass Simple Tests for Civil Service Jobs. Solomon Wiener. 224p. (Orig.). 1981. pap. 9.95 o.p. (ISBN 0-671-42777-6). Monarch Pr.
How to Take Charge of Your Life. Mildred Newman & Bernard Berkowitz. LC 76-55147. 1977. 5.95 o.p. (ISBN 0-15-142192-7). HarBraceJ.
How to Take Great Photos from Airplanes. Frank K. Smith. (Modern Aircraft Ser). (Illus.). 1978. 8.95 o.p. (ISBN 0-8306-9879-5); pap. 8.70 o.p. (ISBN 0-8306-2251-9, 2251). TAB Bks.
How to Take the Hassle Out of Homemaking. Rena Stronach. (Living Books). 176p. 1986. 3.50 o.p. (ISBN 0-8423-1375-3). Tyndale.
How to Take Twenty Pounds Off Your Man. Suzy Kalter. 256p. 1985. 12.70 o.p. (ISBN 0-671-50618-8). S&S.
How to Talk to Christians about Money. W. A. Poovey. LC 82-70958. 136p. (Orig.). 1982. pap. 6.95 o.p. (ISBN 0-8066-1933-3, 10-3179, Augsburg). Augsburg Fortress.
How to Talk to the Birds & the Beasts. Jacques LeComte & Dorothee Koechlin-Schwartz. LC 79-54013. (Illus.). 1980. 9.95 o.p. (ISBN 0-87795-252-3, Arbor Hse). Morrow.
How to Talk to Your Animals. Jean C. George. LC 85-5476. (Illus.). 320p. 1985. 15.95 o.p. (ISBN 0-15-142200-1). HarBraceJ.
How to Tap into Your Own Genius. Thomas D. Cowan. 192p. 1984. pap. 6.95 o.p. (ISBN 0-671-53071-2, Fireside). S&S.
How to Teach a Demonstration-Type Subject. Florence Nelson. 10p. 1981. handbk. 3.50 o.s.i. (ISBN 0-918328-03-9); pap. 3.50 o.s.i. (ISBN 0-686-96688-0). Carma.
How to Teach a Lecture-Type Subject. Florence Nelson. 12p. 1980. pap. 3.50 handbk. o.s.i. (ISBN 0-918328-06-3). Carma.
How to Teach Flying. Albert J. Taylor. (Illus.). 304p. 1984. pap. 12.15 o.p. (ISBN 0-8306-2343-4, 2343P). TAB Bks.
How to Teach Junior Highs. Barbara Smith. 1965. 3.95 o.s.i. (ISBN 0-664-20617-4, Westminster). Westminster John Knox.
How to Teach Origins. John N. Moore. 1987. pap. 14.95 o.p. (ISBN 0-8010-6219-5). Baker Bk.
How to Teach Your Children about Sex. Stan Berenstain & Janice Berenstain. 1984. pap. 2.95 o.p. (ISBN 0-345-29458-0). Ballantine.
How to Teach Your Dog to Play Frisbee. Karen Pryor. 1985. pap. 4.95 o.p. (ISBN 0-671-55552-9). S&S.
How to Telecommunicate: A Personal Computer User's Guide. Corey Sandler. LC 85-27019. (Illus.). 224p. 1986. pap. 17.95 o.p. (ISBN 0-03-005522-9, Owl Bks). H Holt & Co.
How to Tell Your Friends from the Apes. Will Cuppy. 1945. 4.50 o.p. (ISBN 0-87140-953-4). Liveright.
How to Tour China. 1988. 9.95 o.p. (ISBN 0-317-67720-9). China Bks.
How to Train Your Own Gun Dog. Charles S. Goodall. LC 77-92420. (Illus.). 160p. 1977. 12.95 o.p. (ISBN 0-87605-561-7). Howell Bk.
How to Travel & Stay Healthy. Duff H. Pfanner. 1979. pap. 5.00 o.p. (ISBN 0-682-49440-2). Exposition-Phoenix.
How to Treasure Hunt in the City. G. Howard Poteet. Ed. by Bettye Nelson. LC 76-40846. (Illus., Orig.). pap. write for info. o.p. (ISBN 0-915920-27-1). Ram Pub.
How to Trim, Groom & Show Your Dog. Date not set. (ISBN 0-87605-563-3). Howell Bk.
How to Trim Your Hips & Shape Your Thighs. Jim Everroad & Lonna Moscow. (Illus., Orig.). 1979. pap. 1.95 o.p. (ISBN 0-8431-0668-9). Price Stern.
How to Try a Criminal Case. Stephen Hrones. 1982. text ed. 34.50 o.p. (ISBN 0-13-435610-1, Busn). P-H.
How to Tune Your Car. 6th rev. ed. Ed. by Spence Murray. LC 72-15282. (Basic Repair & Maintenance Ser.). (Illus.). 1979. pap. 5.95 o.p. (ISBN 0-8227-5049-X). Petersen Pub.
How to Tune Your Car. 7th ed. Petersen Publishing Co. Staff. (Petersen's Basic Auto Repair Ser.). (Illus.). 1000p. 1983. pap. 7.95 o.p. Petersen Pub.
How to Turn Lemons into Money. Louise Armstrong. LC 75-43785. (Illus.). (gr. 3-6). 1976. 5.50 o.p. (ISBN 0-15-237250-4, HJ). HarBraceJ.
How to Turn Lemons into Money. Louise Armstrong. LC 75-43785. (Illus.). (gr. 3-6). 1976. pap. 2.95 o.p. (ISBN 0-15-237251-2, VoyB). HarBraceJ.
How to Turn Minuses into Pluses. Nancy L. Van Pelt. Ed. by Richard W. Coffen. (Better Living Ser.). 32p. (Orig.). 1985. pap. 1.25 o.s.i. (ISBN 0-8280-0303-3). Review & Herald.
How to Turn up into Down into Up: A Child's Guide to Inflation, Depression, & Economic Recovery. Louise Armstrong. LC 77-13278. (Illus.). (gr. 3-6). 1978. 4.95 o.p. (ISBN 0-15-236838-8, HJ); pap. 1.95 o.p. (ISBN 0-15-642204-2, VoyB). HarBraceJ.
How to Turn War into Peace: A Child's Guide to Conflict Resolution. Louise Armstrong. LC 79-11797. (Let Me Read Ser.). (Illus.). (gr. 3-6). 1979. 4.95 o.p. (ISBN 0-15-236840-X, HJ). HarBraceJ.
How to Turn War into Peace: A Child's Guide to Conflict Resolution. Louise Armstrong. LC 79-11797. (Let-Me-Read Ser.). (Illus.). 32p. (ps-3). 1979. pap. 1.95 o.p. (ISBN 0-15-642206-9, VoyB). HarBraceJ.
How to Tutor. 2nd ed. 304p. 1987. pap. 11.95 o.p. (ISBN 0-941995-01-1). Paradigm ID.
How to Tutor in an Open-Learning Scheme: Group-Study Version. Roger Lewis. (Orig.). 1981. pap. text ed. 32.00x o.p. (ISBN 0-86184-051-8). Trans Atl Phila.
How to Tutor in an Open-Learning Scheme: Self-Study Version. Roger Lewis. (Orig.). 1981. pap. text ed. 23.95x o.p. (ISBN 0-318-21730-9). Trans Atl Phila.
How to Understand & Influence People & Organizations: Practical Psychology for Goal Achievement. Michael R. Perlson. 256p. 1982. 16.95 o.p. (ISBN 0-8144-5684-7). AMACOM.
How to Understand & Negotiate a Book Contract or Magazine Agreement. Richard Balkin. LC 85-14435. 156p. 1985. 11.95 o.p. (ISBN 0-89879-190-1). Writers Digest.
How to Understand & Survive the Coming Tax Reforms. Donald B. Susswein. LC 85-1442. (Management Briefing Ser.). 1985. write for info. o.p. (ISBN 0-8144-2315-9). AMACOM.
How to Understand the Law. Anthony D'Amato. 180p. 1988. 25.00 o.p. (ISBN 0-941320-55-3). Transnatl Pubs.
How to Use a Medical Library. 6th rev. ed. Leslie T. Morton. 1979. pap. 15.00 o.p. (ISBN 0-433-22451-7). E J Brill USA.
How to Use Adding & Calculating Machines. 3rd ed. Arthur L. Walker et al. 1967. text ed. 15.56 o.p. (ISBN 0-07-067823-5, G). McGraw.
How to Use Astral Power: Key to a Miraculous New Life. MacNitt. 1976. 14.95 o.p. (ISBN 0-13-436139-3, Parker). P-H.
How to Use Business Machines. 3rd ed. H. D. Fasnacht et al. 1969. text ed. 11.92 o.p. (ISBN 0-07-019972-8). McGraw.
How to Use Computers as a Resource. Richard Diem. (Social Studies Skills Ser.). 96p. (YA) (gr. 7 up). 1983. lib. bdg. 11.90 o.p. (ISBN 0-531-04676-1). Watts.
How to Use Financial Statements. 2nd ed. I. Kellogg. 1979. pap. text ed. 70.00 o.p. (ISBN 0-07-033520-6). McGraw.
How to Use Role Playing. (Leadership Pamphlet Ser.: No. 6). 1955. 1.40 o.p. (ISBN 0-88379-019-X). A A A C E.
How to Use SuperCalc. Deborrah Smithy-Willis et al. (Illus.). 256p. 1983. 25.95 o.p. (ISBN 0-8306-1522-9, 1522). TAB Bks.
How to Use SuperCalc. Debra Smithy-Willis & Jerry Willis. 200p. 1982. pap. 9.95 o.p. (ISBN 0-88056-095-9, Dist. by Weber Systems); with software 19.95 o.p. Weber Systems.
How to Use Tax Shelters Today. rev. ed. Ed. by Irving Schreiber & Joseph P. Sullivan. LC 81-80022. 600p. 1980. 98.00 o.p. (ISBN 0-916592-37-5). Panel Pubs.
How to Use the Basic Seven Professional Teaching Techniques. Florence Nelson. 8p. 1978. handbook 3.00 o.s.i. (ISBN 0-918328-09-8). Carma.
How to Use the Freedom of Information Act. Washington Researchers Staff. (Briefcase Ser.: Vol. 2). 50p. (Orig.). 1988. pap. 40.00 o.p. (ISBN 0-934940-64-9). Wash Res Pub.
How to Use the HP12C. Robert E. Gallaher, Jr. (Illus.). 60p. (Orig.). 1985. pap. text ed. 10.00 o.s.i. (ISBN 0-913652-58-X). Realtors Natl.
How to Use the IBM PC. Jerry Willis & William Manning. (How to Use Ser.). (Illus.). 128p. 1984. pap. 5.95 o.p. (ISBN 0-88056-308-7, Dist. by Weber Systems). Weber Systems.
How to Use the Macintosh. Jerry Willis. (How to Use Ser.). (Illus.). 128p. 1984. pap. 3.95 o.p. (ISBN 0-88056-307-9, Dist. by Weber Systems). Weber Systems.
How to Use the Power of Mind in Everyday Life. Craig Carter. 96p. 1976. pap. 4.50 o.p. (ISBN 0-911336-65-6). Sci of Mind.
How to Use the Sixteen Charts which Helped Jesse Livermore Make Three Times a Fortune in the Stock Market. Horace H. Welsingford. (Illus.). 97p. 1984. 117.75 o.p. (ISBN 0-86654-115-2). Inst Econ Finan.
How to Use Your Bible. Wanda Milner. (Illus.). 24p. (Orig.). 1983. pap. 2.95 o.p. (ISBN 0-87239-690-8, 3200). Standard Pub.
How to Use Your Time to Get Things Done. Edwin B. Feldman. LC 68-18138. 273p. 1968. 12.95 o.p. (ISBN 0-8119-0110-6). Fell.
How to Wake a Sleeping Beauty. Kevin Scally. (Magic Road Bks.). (Illus.). 32p. (ps-3). 1984. 3.95 o.p. (ISBN 0-448-11128-4, G&D). Putnam Pub Group.
How to Watch a Football Game. Frank Barrett & Lynn Barrett. LC 79-3448. (Illus.). 256p. (Orig.). 1980. pap. 7.95 o.p. (ISBN 0-03-056958-3). H Holt & Co.
How to Watch Football on TV. Chris Schenkel. Penguin USA.
How to Win. rev. ed. Mike Goodman. 1983. pap. 3.95 o.p. (ISBN 0-87067-617-2, BR617). Holloway.
How to Win an Argument. Michael A. Gilbert. 1979. pap. text ed. 4.95 o.p. (ISBN 0-07-023215-6). McGraw.
How to Win at Duplicate Bridge. Marshall Miles. 1957. 7.50 o.p. (ISBN 0-682-40066-1, Banner). Exposition-Phoenix.
How to Win at Gin Rummy. Oswald Jacoby. (Illus.). 1978. pap. 4.95 o.s.i. (ISBN 0-03-042886-6). H Holt & Co.
How to Win at Othello. Goro Hasegawa & Maxine Brady. LC 77-5259. (Illus.). 1977. pap. 2.95 o.p. (ISBN 0-15-642215-8, Harv). HarBraceJ.
How to Win at Trivial Pursuit. Robert J. Heller. 128p. 1984. pap. 3.95 o.p. (ISBN 0-03-000347-4, Owl Bks). H Holt & Co.
How to Win at Video Games. Consumer Guide Editors. 1984. spiral bdg. 1.00 o.p. (ISBN 0-517-42470-3). Outlet Bk Co.

How to Win Friends & Influence People. Dale Carnegie. 1937. 9.95 o.s.i. (ISBN 0-671-35500-7). S&S.
How to Win in a Crisis. Creath Davis. 224p. 1987. pap. 7.95 o.p. (ISBN 0-310-23191-4, 6323P). Zondervan.
How to Win Votes: The Politics of Nineteen Eighty. Edward N. Costikyan. LC 79-3892. 1980. 12.95 o.p. (ISBN 0-15-142221-4). HarBraceJ.
How to Witness to a Jehovah's Witness. William J. Schnell. Orig. Title: Christians, Awake! 160p. 1975. pap. 4.95 o.p. (ISBN 0-8010-8283-8). Baker Bk.
How to Work in Stained Glass. 2nd ed. Anita Isenberg & Seymour Isenberg. LC 82-73537. (Illus.). 372p. 1983. 16.95 o.p. (ISBN 0-8019-7354-6); pap. 17.95 o.p. (ISBN 0-8019-7355-4). Chilton.
How to Work Toward Agreement. Thomas Moorman. LC 78-11260. (gr. 6 up). 1979. 7.95 o.p. (ISBN 0-689-30661-X, Atheneum). Macmillan.
How to Write. Gertrude Stein. 14.75 o.p. (ISBN 0-8446-5250-4). Peter Smith.
How to Write a Book. Cecil Hunt. 1952. (ISBN 0-8022-0761-8). Philos Lib.
How to Write a Children's Book & Get It Published. Barbara Seuling. 208p. 1984. 14.95 o.s.i. (ISBN 0-684-18055-3, ScribT). Scribner.
How to Write a Lesson Plan for Adult Classes. rev. ed. Florence Nelson. 6p. 1978. 5.00 o.s.i. (ISBN 0-918328-10-1). Carma.
How to Write a Love Letter. Marc L'Heureux. 1966. pap. 2.00 o.p. (ISBN 0-8065-0119-7, Pub. by Citadel Pr). Carol Pub Group.
How to Write a Million Dollar Memo. Cheryl Reimold. (Clear & Simple Ser.). (Orig.). 1984. pap. 4.95 o.p. (ISBN 0-440-53782-7, Dell Trade Pbks). Dell.
How to Write a Report. Gerald Newman. (gr. 7 up). 1980. PLB 9.90 o.p. (ISBN 0-531-04135-2). Watts.
How to Write a Research Paper. R. Berry. 1974. pap. 35.00 o.p. (ISBN 0-08-006392-6). Pergamon.
How to Write a Research Paper. Phyllis Cash. (How to Ser.). 128p. (Orig.). 1983. pap. 5.95 o.s.i. (ISBN 0-671-47093-0). Monarch Pr.
How to Write a Winning Business Plan. Joseph Mancuso. (Illus.). 320p. 1985. 19.95 o.p. (ISBN 0-13-441569-8); pap. 12.95 o.p. (ISBN 0-13-441551-5). P H.
How to Write & Market Your Own Educational Materials. Lois Roets. 64p. (Orig.). 1986. pap. text ed. 10.00 o.p. (ISBN 0-911943-08-0). Leadership Pub.
How to Write & Sell Your Sense of Humor. Gene Perret. 281p. 1986. pap. 9.95 o.p. (ISBN 0-89879-240-1). Writers Digest.
How to Write Better Business Letters. 4th ed. Earle A. Buckley. (Illus.). 1971. 10.95 o.p. (ISBN 0-07-008778-4); pap. text ed. 4.95 o.p. (ISBN 0-07-008779-2). McGraw.
How to Write Computer Manuals for Users. Susan Grimm. 211p. 1982. 23.00 o.p. (ISBN 0-534-97941-6). Van Nos Reinhold.
How to Write Lyrics That Make Sense & Dollars. Hy Glaser. 1977. 9.95 o.p. (ISBN 0-682-48764-3, Banner). Exposition-Phoenix.
How to Write Mac Software. Scott Knaster. 510p. 1986. pap. 27.95 o.p. (ISBN 0-8104-6564-7). Sams.
How to Write Nursing Care Plans. Annita Watson & Marlene Mayers. (Illus.). 102p. (Orig.). 1976. pap. text ed. 6.95 o.p. (ISBN 0-318-20018-X). Markham McKenzie.
How to Write Off Your Down Payment. Nelson E. Brestoff. 192p. 1986. 15.95 o.p. (ISBN 0-399-13058-6). Putnam Pub Group.
How to Write Puts & Calls. Lyle T. Alverson. LC 68-16643. 1968. 7.50 o.p. (ISBN 0-682-46790-1, Banner). Exposition-Phoenix.
How to Write Romance Novels that Sell. Marilyn M. Lowery. LC 81-42695. 256p. 1983. 12.95 o.p. (ISBN 0-89256-224-2); pap. 8.95 o.p. (ISBN 0-89256-239-0). Rawson Assocs.
How to Write Short Stories that Sell. Louis Boggess. LC 79-26010. 212p. 1984. pap. 7.95 o.p. (ISBN 0-89879-139-1). Writers Digest.
How to Write the History of a Family: A Guide for the Genealogist. W. P. Phillimore. LC 70-179653. (Illus.). viii, 214p. 1972. Repr. of 1876 ed. 43.00x o.p. (ISBN 0-8103-3117-9). Gale.
How to Write Themes for English & Humanities. Helen Mallonee. 1978. pap. text ed. 12.95x o.p. (ISBN 0-89917-003-X). TIS Inc.
How to Write Yourself Up. rev. ed. John D. Wool. 1983. pap. 3.75 o.p. (ISBN 0-88323-187-5, 225). Pendergrass Pub.
How Two: Handbook for Office Workers. 2nd ed. James L. Clark & Lyn R. Clark. (Business Ser.). 280p. 1979. pap. text ed. 8.95x o.p. (ISBN 0-534-00635-3). PWS-Kent Pub.
How Wars Begin. A. J. Taylor. LC 79-84236. 1979. 10.95 o.p. (ISBN 0-689-10982-2, Atheneum). Macmillan.
How Wars End. Ed. by V. Sevrok. 336p. 1974. 6.45 o.p. (ISBN 0-8285-0478-4, Pub. by Progress Pubs USSR). Imported Pubns.
How We Came to the Fifth World: Como Vinimos al Quinto Mundo. Harriet Rohmer & Graciela C. De Lopez. LC 76-7240. (Fifth World Tales Ser.). (Illus.). (gr. k-6). pap. 4.95 spanish bilingual ed. o.p. (ISBN 0-89239-004-2, Imprenta de Libros Infantiles). Childrens Book Pr.
How We Discommunicate. Philip Lesly. (Illus.). 1979. 13.95 o.p. (ISBN 0-8144-5532-8). AMACOM.
How We Got the Bible. Neil R. Lightfoot. 1962. 7.95 o.p. (ISBN 0-8010-5502-4). Baker Bk.
How We Live: Then & Now. (Illus.). 39p. (Orig.). 1987. pap. 3.50 o.p. (ISBN 0-318-22903-X, S/N 003-024-06253-4). USGPO.
How We Play the Game: Why Sports Dominate American Life. Richard Lipsky. LC 80-66074. (Illus.). 256p. 1980. 14.95x o.p. (ISBN 0-8070-3224-7). Beacon Pr.
How We Started Students on Successful Foodservice Careers. Herman A. Breithaupt. LC 72-75296. 256p. 1983. 16.95 o.p. (ISBN 0-8436-0544-8). Van Nos Reinhold.
How, When, & Where to Go Public with a Small Company. E. Wilson Roberts. LC 72-94571. 1972. 10.00 o.p. (ISBN 0-682-47648-X, Banner). Exposition-Phoenix.
How, Why, When, Where Book, Vol. 3. William Coleman. 23p. (gr. 1-6). 1985. pap. 3.50 o.p. (ISBN 0-89191-927-9, 59279, Chariot Bks). Cook.
How, Why, When, Where Book, Vol. 4. William Coleman. 23p. (gr. 1-6). 1985. pap. 3.50 o.p. (ISBN 0-89191-929-5, 59295, Chariot Bks). Cook.
How Winners Do It: High Impact People Skills for Your Career Success. Michael W. Mercer. LC 88-5460. (Illus.). 224p. 1988. 17.95 o.p. (ISBN 0-938901-13-3). Wllngtn Pubs.
How You Can Appear in TV Commercials. rev. ed. Ron Millkie & Ray Carlson. LC 73-12796. 40p. 1980. pap. 2.95 o.p. (ISBN 0-87576-045-7). Pilot Bks.
How You Can Be a Peacemaker. Mary E. Jegen. 128p. 1985. pap. 2.95 o.p. (ISBN 0-89243-231-4). Liguori Pubns.
How You Can Become Financially Independent by Investing in Real Estate. Albert J. Lowry. 1982. 18.45 o.s.i. (ISBN 0-671-44959-1). S&S.
How You Can Go from Broke to Broker in Real Estate. Margaret Brower & Scott Brower. 256p. 1981. 10.00 o.p. (ISBN 0-682-49744-4, Banner). Exposition-Phoenix.
How You Can Manage Your Money: A Christian's Guide to Personal & Family Financial Decision Making. John W. Johnson. LC 80-67798. 248p. (Orig.). 1981. pap. 7.95 o.p. (ISBN 0-8066-1860-4, 10-3182, Augsburg). Augsburg Fortress.
How You Can Pray with Power & Get Results. Lowell Lundstrom. 272p. 1984. pap. text ed. 3.95 o.p. (ISBN 0-88368-151-X). Whitaker Hse.
How You Can Profit from the New Tax Laws. Rev. & updated ed. The J. K. Lasser Tax Institute Staff. 208p. 1987. pap. 6.95 o.p. (ISBN 0-13-444050-1). P-H.
How You Can Rise Above Fear see How to Conquer Fear.
How You Can Stop Smoking Now As I Did After 33 Years. James A. Michaelsen. 1979. 6.00 o.p. (ISBN 0-682-49091-1). Exposition-Phoenix.
How You Feeling CPL. Date not set. (ISBN 0-07-374625-8). McGraw.
How Your Mother & Father Met. Tobi Tobias. (Illus.). (gr. k-5). 1978. text ed. 6.95 o.p. (ISBN 0-07-064957-X). McGraw.
Howard Baker's Washington. Howard Baker. (Illus.). 1982. 14.98 o.p. (ISBN 0-393-01562-9). Norton.
Howard Hawks. Rev. ed. Robin Wood. (British Film Institute Bks.). (Illus.). 216p. 1981. pap. 9.95 o.p. (ISBN 0-85170-111-6). U of Ill Pr.
Howard Hodgkin: Forty Paintings. David Sylvester & John McEwen. (Illus.). 128p. 1985. text ed. 25.00 o.p. (ISBN 0-8076-1106-9). Braziller.
Howard Hughes. Jerry Bell. 1977. pap. 2.95 o.p. (ISBN 0-89036-069-3). Hawkes Pub Inc.
Howard Jones. Philip Kamin. (Illus.). 32p. (gr. 3 up). 1985. pap. 4.95 o.p. (ISBN 0-88188-412-X, 00183317, Robus Bks). H Leonard Pub Corp.
Howard Nemerov. Ross LaBrie. (United States Authors Ser.). 1980. lib. bdg. 13.50 o.p. (ISBN 0-8057-7298-7, Twayne). G K Hall.
Howard the Duck--The Movie Storybook. Adapted by Michael J. Pellowski. (Illus.). (gr. 3 up). 1986. pap. 4.95 o.p. (ISBN 0-448-48605-9, Pub. by Playvalue). Putnam Pub Group.
Howard's Monster. Penny Porter. (gr. k-3). 1978. 4.50 o.p. (ISBN 0-682-49144-6). Exposition-Phoenix.
Howells: A Century of Criticism. Ed. by Kenneth E. Eble. LC 62-13275. 260p. 1970. Repr. of 1962 ed. 15.95x o.p. (ISBN 0-87074-050-4). SMU Press.
Howling III. Gary Brandner. 256p. 1985. pap. 3.50 o.s.i. (ISBN 0-449-12834-2, GM). Fawcett.
Howling in the Woods. Velda Johnston. (Red Badge Mysteries Ser.). 1984. pap. 3.50 o.p. (ISBN 0-396-08446-X). Dodd.
How'm I Doing? The Wit & Wisdom of Ed Koch. (Orig.). 1985. pap. 2.95 o.p. (ISBN 0-440-03728-X, Bryans). Dell.
How's Your Family? Jerry M. Lewis. LC 78-11820. 1979. 20.00 o.p. (ISBN 0-87630-181-2). Brunner-Mazel.
Hoyle's Card Games. Edmund Hoyle. 1979. pap. 11.95 o.p. (ISBN 0-7100-0115-0). Routledge Chapman & Hall.
HPI Market Data Handbook (1986) rev. ed. (Illus.). 52p. (Orig.). 1986. pap. 5.00x o.p. (ISBN 0-87201-409-6). Gulf Pub.
HPI Market Data Handbook, 1987. (Illus.). 44p. pap. 5.00 o.p. (ISBN 0-87201-435-5). Gulf Pub.
HPLC in Food Analysis. R. Macrae. 1983. 67.50 o.p. (ISBN 0-12-464780-4). Acad Pr.
HRD Professional's Bibliography of Resources & References. Ed. by Homer H. Johnson. LC 86-40394. 56p. (Orig.). 1986. pap. text ed. 8.95 o.p. (ISBN 0-88390-203-6, 432). Univ Assocs.
HRH: The Man Who Will Be King. LC 78-73860. 1979. 11.95 o.p. (ISBN 0-87795-212-4, Arbor Hse). Morrow.
HRIS Development: A Project Team Guide to Building an Effective Information System. Alfred J. Walker. 256p. 1982. 37.95 o.p. (ISBN 0-442-29003-9). Van Nos Reinhold.
Hrotsvitha: The Theatricality of Her Lays. Mary M. Butler. LC 60-13637. 256p. 1960. (ISBN 0-8022-0205-5). Philos Lib.
Hsi K'ang & His Poetical Essay on the Lute. R. H. Van Gulik. LC 68-58913. 1969. 15.00 o.p. (ISBN 0-8048-0868-6). C E Tuttle.
HSLA Steels - Technology & Applications: Proceedings of 1983 Conference. 1173p. 91.00 o.p. (6226L). ASM.
HTST Pasteurizer Operation Manual. Oregon Association of Milk, Food, & Environment Sanitarians, Inc., Education & Training Committee. (Illus.). 6.50 o.s.i. (ISBN 0-88246-057-9). Oreg St U Bkstrs.
Hualcan: Life in the Highlands of Peru. William W. Stein. LC 75-26221. (Cornell Studies in Anthropology). (Illus.). 383p. 1975. Repr. of 1961 ed. lib. bdg. 35.00x o.p. (ISBN 0-8371-8406-1, STHU). Greenwood.
Huancavelica Mercury Mine: A Contribution to the History of the Bourbon Renaissance in the Spanish Empire. Arthur P. Whitaker. 1972. Repr. of 1941 ed. lib. bdg. 22.50x o.p. (ISBN 0-8371-5240-2, WHHM). Greenwood.
Huck Embroidery. Ondori Publishing Company Staff. LC 82-81056. (Illus.). 120p. 1982. pap. 7.50 o.p. (ISBN 0-87040-519-5). Japan Pubns USA.
Huckleberry Finn see Graded Readers for Students of English As a Second Language.
Hudson: A Survey of Historic Structures. Lois G. Newkirk. (Illus.). 320p. 1988. 24.95 o.p. (ISBN 0-938936-77-8). Daring Bks.
Hudson County: The Left Bank. Joan F. Doherty. LC 86-1566. (Illus.). 168p. 1986. 22.95 o.p. (ISBN 0-89781-172-0). Windsor Pubns Inc.
Hudson-Mohawk Gateway: An Illustrated History. Thomas Phelan. 192p. 1985. 22.95 o.s.i. (ISBN 0-89781-118-6). Windsor Pubns Inc.
Hudson River Basin, Vol. 2. Ralph W. Richardson. 1979. 29.95 o.p. (ISBN 0-12-588402-8). Acad Pr.
Hudson River Basin: Environmental Problems & Instititional Response, Vol. 1. Ralph W. Richardson. 1979. 29.95 o.p. (ISBN 0-12-588401-X). Acad Pr.
Hudson Valley Paintings, 1700-1750. Janet R. MacFarlane. (Illus.). pap. text ed. 3.50 o.p. (ISBN 0-686-32415-3). Albany Hist & Art.
Huey, Dewey, & Louie. Frwd. by Carl Barks. (Walt Disney Best Comics Ser.). (Illus.). 1988. 25.00 o.p. (ISBN 0-89659-878-0). Abbeville Pr.
Huey Lewis & the News. Jay Byrd. (Illus.). 32p. (gr. 4-12). 1985. 4.95 o.p. (ISBN 0-88188-328-X, Robus Books). H Leonard Pub Corp.
Huggables: How to Make Large Stuffed Animals. Janet Weaver & Alice Weaver. 1977. pap. 6.95 o.p. (ISBN 0-89328-004-6). Lorenz Corp.
Huggy Bear & Other Plays: Huggy Bear, The Arcata Promise, A Superstition. David Mercer. 1981. pap. 6.95 o.p. (ISBN 0-413-38320-2, NO. 2624). Heinemann Ed.
Hugh Gaitskell: A Political Biography. Philip M. Williams. (Illus.). 1007p. 1979. 49.50x o.p. (ISBN 0-389-20032-8). B&N Imports.
Hugh Johnson's Cellar Book. Hugh Johnson. 224p. 1986. 25.00 o.s.i. (ISBN 0-671-62896-8). S&S.
Hugh Johnson's Modern Encyclopedia of Wine. Hugh Johnson. LC 82-3203. (Illus.). 544p. 1983. 29.95 o.p. (ISBN 0-671-45134-0). S&S.
Hugh Johnson's Pocket Encyclopedia of Wine, 1984. Rev. ed. Hugh Johnson. 1984. 8.95 o.p. (ISBN 0-671-49667-0). S&S.
Hugh Johnson's Pocket Encyclopedia of Wine, 1985. Hugh Johnson. 184p. 1985. 8.95 o.s.i. (ISBN 0-671-52740-1). S&S.
Hugh Johnson's Pocket Encyclopedia of Wine 1986. Hugh Johnson. 1986. 8.95 o.p. (ISBN 0-671-61179-8). S&S.
Hugh Johnson's Pocket Encyclopedia of Wine: 1982 Edition. Hugh Johnson. 1982. pap. 5.95 o.p. (ISBN 0-671-43995-2). S&S.
Hugh MacDiarmid Anthology: Poems in Scots & English. Hugh MacDiarmid. Ed. by Michael Grieve & Alexander Scott. (The Scottish Ser). 1972. 18.95 o.p. (ISBN 0-7100-7432-8). Routledge Chapman & Hall.
Hugh MacDiarmid: The Terrible Crystal. Alan Bold. 256p. 1986. pap. 12.50 o.p. (ISBN 0-7102-0881-2, 08812). Routledge Chapman & Hall.
Hugo Black & the Bill of Rights: Proceedings of the First Hugo Black Symposium in American History on the Bill of Rights & American Democracy. Ed. by Virginia V. Hamilton. LC 77-24689. 136p. 1978. 9.75 o.p. (ISBN 0-8173-9309-9). U of Ala Pr.
Hugo Black: The Alabama Years. Virginia Hamilton. LC 75-181566. (Illus.). 352p. 1982. pap. text ed. 12.50 o.p. (ISBN 0-8173-0128-3). U of Ala Pr.
Hugo the Hippo. Thomas Baum. LC 76-14354. (Illus.). 64p. (ps-3). 1976. 5.95 o.p. (ISBN 0-15-237300-4, HJ). HarBraceJ.
Hugo Wolf: A Biography. Frank Walker. 522p. Repr. of 1968 ed. lib. bdg. 69.00 o.p. (Pub. by Am Repr Serv). Reprint Servs.
Hugoliad, or The Grotesque & Tragic Life of Victor Hugo. Eugene Ionesco. Tr. by Yara Milos from Fr. LC 86-48460. 128p. 1987. 15.95 o.s.i. (ISBN 0-394-56092-2). Grove.
Huguenots, 2 vols. Giacomo Meyerbeer. Ed. by Charles Rosen & Philip Gossett. LC 76-49196. (Early Romantic Opera Ser.: Vol. 20). 1979. lib. bdg. 180.00 o.p. (ISBN 0-8240-2919-4). Garland Pub.
Hukbalahap Insurrection: A Case Study of a Successful Anti-Insurgency Operation in the Philippines, 1946-1955. Lawrence M. Greenberg. LC 87-600597. (Center for Military History Publication. Historical Analysis Ser.: No. 93-8). (Illus.). 171p. 1987. pap. 8.50 o.p. (ISBN 0-318-23829-2, S/N 008-029-00162-4). USGPO.
Hulk, No. 3. Marvel Comics Staff & Stan Lee. (Illus.). 224p. 1982. pap. 1.95 o.s.i. (ISBN 0-448-16837-5, Pub. by Tempo). Ace Bks.
Hulk Hogan: Battle of the Bands. Jill Wolf. (Collector Sticker Bks). (Illus.). 24p. (gr. 2-3). 1986. pap. 1.95 o.p. (ISBN 0-89954-539-4). Antioch Pub Co.
Human Action: Conceptual & Empirical Issues. Ed. by Theodore Mischel. 1969. 29.95 o.p. (ISBN 0-12-498650-1). Acad Pr.
Human Action of Forgiving: A Critical Application of the Metaphysics of Alfred North Whitehead. Jean C. Lambert. (Illus.). 300p. (Orig.). 1985. lib. bdg. 27.50 o.p. (ISBN 0-8191-4596-3); pap. text ed. 15.25 o.p. (ISBN 0-8191-4597-1). U Pr of Amer.
Human Anatomy. Kent M. Van De Graaff. 736p. 1984. text ed. write for info o.p. (ISBN 0-697-04743-1); instr's manual avail. o.p. (ISBN 0-697-04744-X); lab manual avail. o.p. (ISBN 0-697-04789-X); transparencies avail. o.p. (ISBN 0-697-00255-1). Wm C Brown.
Human Anatomy & Physiology. Robert Carola et al. LC 85-81849. 928p. 1988. text ed. (ISBN 0-395-35188-X). HM.
Human Anatomy & Physiology. 3rd ed. John W. Hole, Jr. 1000p. 1984. text ed. write for info o.p. (ISBN 0-697-04790-3). Wm C Brown.
Human Anatomy & Physiology: A Laboratory Manual of, Vol. 2. 3rd ed. Donald R. Ferruzzi. (Illus.). 243p. 1986. 18.95 o.p. (ISBN 0-9609098-4-2). Biomat Pub Co.
Human Anatomy & Physiology: Cat Version see Human Anatomy & Physiology Laboratory Manual.
Human Anatomy & Physiology Laboratory Manual: The Pig Version see Human Anatomy & Physiology Laboratory Manual.
Human Anatomy & Physiology Laboratory Manual. 3rd ed. Elaine N. Marieb. Incl. Human Anatomy & Physiology Laboratory Manual: The Pig Version. Elaine N. Marieb. (Illus.). 700p. pap. text ed. 24.95; instr's guide 9.95; transparencies avail.; Human Anatomy & Physiology: Cat Version. pap. text ed. 24.95. (Illus.). 700p. 1989. pap. text ed. instr's. guide o.p.; transparencies avail. o.p. Benjamin-Cummings.
Human Anatomy Atlas. Charles N. Berry & Christian A. Hovde. (Illus.). 36p. (Orig.). 1960. pap. 2.95x o.p. (ISBN 0-8437-9083-0). Hammond Inc.

Human Anatomy, Physiology & Pathophysiology. G. E. Thews et al. 784p. 1985. Reference Edition 284.75 o.p. (ISBN 0-444-80544-3); student edition 89.50 o.p. (ISBN 0-444-80704-7). Elsevier.
Human & National Nutrition. Ed. by Geoffrey H. Bourne. 282p. 1983. 139.95x o.p. (ISBN 3-8055-3591-0). Transaction Pubs.
Human Animal. Phil Donahue. 234p. 1985. 19.45 o.p. (ISBN 0-671-54696-1). S&S.
Human Anti-Human Gammaglobulins: Their Specificity & Function. R. Grubb & G. Samuelsson. 240p. 1971. 65.00 o.p. (ISBN 0-08-016451-X). Pergamon.
Human Antiparasitic Drugs: Pharmacology & Usage. D. M. James & H. M. Gilles. LC 84-13110. 289p. 1985. 32.50 o.p. (ISBN 0-471-90253-5, Dist. by A R Liss). Wiley.
Human Apes. Dale Carlson. LC 72-86755. 176p. (gr. 5-9). 1973. 5.95 o.p. (ISBN 0-689-30079-4, Atheneum). Macmillan.
Human Aspects of Economics: A Human Treatise of Unemployment, Inflation & World Poverty. C. A. Cannegieter. (Illus.). 224p. 1982. 12.50 o.p. (ISBN 0-682-49751-7, University). Exposition-Phoenix.
Human Aspects of Management: A Case Study Approach. J. W. Chilver. 1976. text ed. 17.75 o.p. (ISBN 0-08-021048-1); pap. text ed. 7.75 o.p. (ISBN 0-08-021047-3). Pergamon.
Human Behavior: An Inventory of Scientific Findings Shorter Ed. Bernard Berelson & Gary A. Steiner. (Illus., Orig.). 1967. pap. text ed. 9.74 o.p. (ISBN 0-15-539790-7, HC). HarBraceJ.
Human Behavior & Environment, Vol. 1. Ed. by Irwin Altman & J. F. Wohlwill. (Illus.). 316p. 1976. 42.50x o.p. (ISBN 0-306-33301-5, Plenum Pr). Plenum Pub.
Human Behavior & Environment, Vol. 2. Ed. by Irwin Altman & J. F. Wohlwill. (Illus.). 358p. 1977. 42.50x o.p. (ISBN 0-306-33302-3, Plenum Pr). Plenum Pub.
Human Behavior & Environment, Vol. 3: Children & the Environment. Ed. by Irwin Altman & J. F. Wohlwill. (Illus.). 316p. 1978. 42.50x o.p. (ISBN 0-306-40090-1, Plenum Pr). Plenum Pub.
Human Behavior at Work. 6th ed. Keith Davis. (Management Ser.). (Illus.). 576p. 1981. text ed. 36.95 o.p. (ISBN 0-07-015516-X). McGraw.
Human Behavior: Biological, Psychological & Sociological. Ed. by Alfred M. Freedman & Harold I. Kaplan. LC 75-178073. (Studies in Human Behavior Ser). 1972. pap. text ed. 5.95x o.p. (ISBN 0-689-70284-1, HB3, Atheneum). Macmillan.
Human Behavior in Daily Life. Leon Merkin. 187p. 1984. 10.95 o.p. (ISBN 0-682-40135-8). Exposition-Phoenix.
Human Behavior: Prediction & Control in Modern Society. Ed. by Thomas G. Bever & Herbert S. Terrace. LC 73-7253. 163p. 1974. pap. text ed. 6.95x o.p. (ISBN 0-8422-9104-0). Irvington.
Human Behavior: Towards a Practical Understanding. Jill Ford. (Library of Social Work Ser.). 160p. 1983. pap. 8.95x o.p. (ISBN 0-7100-9218-0). Routledge Chapman & Hall.
Human Biochemical Genetics. R. Ananthakrishnan et al. LC 73-645. 147p. 1973. text ed. 22.50x o.p. (ISBN 0-8422-7095-7). Irvington.
Human Biochemistry. 10th ed. James M. Orten & Otto W. Neuhaus. LC 81-14089. (Illus.). 993p. 1982. 37.95 o.p. (ISBN 0-8016-3730-9). Mosby.
Human Blood Coagulation: Proceedings. Ed. by H. C. Hemker. (Boerhaave Ser. for Postgraduate Medical Education, Vol. 1). (Illus.). 1970. 24.00 o.p. (ISBN 0-387-91060-3). Springer-Verlag.
Human Body. Isaac Asimov. (Illus.). (gr. 7 up). 1963. 11.95 o.p. (ISBN 0-395-07350-2). HM.
Human Body. Ed. by Monks of Solesmes Staff. (Papal Teaching Ser.). 1960. 6.50 o.s.i. (ISBN 0-8198-3309-6). Dghtrs St Paul.
Human Body in Equipment Design. Albert Damon et al. LC 65-22067. (Illus.). 1966. 27.00x o.s.i. (ISBN 0-674-41450-0). Harvard U Pr.
Human Brain. Isaac Asimov. (Illus.). 1964. 10.00 o.p. (ISBN 0-395-07353-7). HM.
Human Brain: An Introduction to Its Functional Anatomy. John Nolte. LC 81-38337. (Illus.). 331p. 1981. pap. text ed. 26.95 o.p. (ISBN 0-8016-3702-3). Mosby.
Human Brain & Human Learning. Leslie A. Hart. LC 82-12650. 256p. 1983. text ed. 20.00x o.p. (ISBN 0-582-28380-9); pap. text ed. 16.95 o.p. (ISBN 0-582-28379-5). Longman.
Human Brain in Dissection. Donald G. Montemurro & J. Edward Bruni. 1981. text ed. write for info. o.p. (ISBN 0-7216-6438-5). Saunders.
Human Capital: The Cultural Sources of America's Economic Decline - & Rebirth. James Fallows. LC 87-42659. 320p. 1988. 19.95 o.p. (ISBN 0-394-56498-7). Random.
Human Carcinogenesis: Symposium. Ed. by Curtis C. Harris & Herman N. Autrup. LC 83-3827. 1983. 93.50 o.p. (ISBN 0-12-327660-8). Acad Pr.
Human Center: Moral Agency in the Social World. Howard L. Harrod. LC 80-2392. 160p. 1981. 3.50 o.p. (ISBN 0-8006-0657-4, 1-657, Fortress). Augsburg Fortress.
Human Chain for Divine Grace: Lutheran Sermons for Evangelical Outreach. Ed. by Ronald J. Lavin. LC 77-15236. (Orig.). 1978. pap. 3.25 o.p. (ISBN 0-8006-1333-3, Fortress). Augsburg Fortress.
Human Chlamydial Infections. Julius Schachter & Chandler Dawson. LC 75-12032. (Illus.). 286p. 1978. 41.50 o.p. (ISBN 0-88416-043-2). Year Bk Med.
Human Circulation. Eric Neil. Ed. by J. J. Head. LC 78-66621. (Carolina Biology Readers Ser.: No. 82). (Illus.). 16p. (gr. 10 up). 1979. pap. 1.80 o.p. (ISBN 0-89278-282-X, 45-9682). Carolina Biological.
Human Color Vision. new ed. Robert Boynton. LC 78-26443. 1979. text ed. 38.95 o.p. (ISBN 0-03-084682-X, HoltC). HR&W.
Human Comedy. rev. ed. William Saroyan. LC 43-51036. (Illus.). 246p. 1943. 10.95 o.p. (ISBN 0-15-142299-0). HarBraceJ.
Human Communication. Ed. by Nancy L. Harper. 396p. 1974. 24.00x o.p. (ISBN 0-8422-5190-1); pap. text ed. 12.95x o.p. (ISBN 0-8422-0445-8). Irvington.
Human Communication: A Symbolic Interactionist Perspective. Julia T. Wood. 1982. pap. text ed. 22.95 o.p. (ISBN 0-03-051071-6). HR&W.
Human-Computer Interaction. Ed. by E. D. Megaw & E. J. Lloyd. (Ergonomics Special Issue Ser.: Vol. 16, No. 1). 170p. 1984. pap. 47.00x o.p. (ISBN 0-85066-993-6). Taylor & Francis.
Human Condition. Clayton Brusch. LC 86-913650. 1987. pap. 8.00 o.p. (ISBN 0-682-40321-0). Exposition-Phoenix.
Human Condition. Joel Rudinger. (Anthology of the Arts Ser.). 1976. pap. 3.00x o.p. (ISBN 0-918342-00-7). Cambric.
Human Conduct: Problems of Ethics. shorter ed. John Hospers. 1972. 13.95 o.p. (ISBN 0-15-540093-2). HarbraceJ.
Human Connection. Ashley Montagu & Floyd Matson. 228p. 1980. pap. text ed. 4.95 o.p. (ISBN 0-07-042842-5). McGraw.
Human Connection. Ashley Montagu & Floyd Matson. 1979. text ed. 10.95 o.p. (ISBN 0-07-042840-9). McGraw.
Human Connection. Ashley-Montagu & Floyd Matson. 1983. 12.50 o.p. (ISBN 0-8446-6054-X). Peter Smith.
Human Cytogenetics: Proceedings of the ICN-UCLA Symposia on Molecular & Cellular Biology, Vol. 7. ICN-UCLA Symposia Staff. Ed. by Robert S. Sparkes et al. (ICN-UCLA Symposia on Molecular & Cellular Biology Ser.). 1977. 54.50 o.p. (ISBN 0-12-656350-0). Acad Pr.
Human Design: Molecular, Cellular & Systematic Physiology. William S. Beck. (Illus.). 1971. text ed. 29.95 o.p. (ISBN 0-15-539815-6, HC). HarBraceJ.
Human Development. 4th ed. Grace J. Craig. (Illus.). 608p. 1986. text ed. (ISBN 0-13-445065-5). P-H.
Human Development: A Social Work Perspective. Riva Specht & Grace J. Craig. (Illus.). 384p. 1982. text ed. (ISBN 0-13-444778-6). P-H.
Human Development: An Emergent Science. 3rd ed. Justin Pikunas. (Illus.). 1976. text ed. 32.95 o.p. (ISBN 0-07-050015-0). McGraw.
Human Development: An Introduction to the Psychodynamics of Growth, Maturity & Aging. 3rd ed. Eric Raynor. (National Institute of Social Services Library: No. 22). 240p. 1986. pap. text ed. 17.95x o.p. (ISBN 0-04-155010-2). Unwin Hyman.
Human Development Program for Institutionalized Teenagers. Compiled by John Jensen. 1974. 11.95 o.p. (ISBN 0-86584-034-2). Palomares & Assoc.
Human Development 1988-89. 16th, rev. ed. Ed. by Michael G. Walraven & Hiram Fitzgerald. LC 72-91973. (Annual Editions Ser.). (Illus.). 288p. 1988. pap. 9.95x o.p. (ISBN 0-87967-710-4). Dushkin Pub.
Human Energy. Pierre Teilhard De Chardin. LC 79-139231. (Helen & Kurt Wolff Bk.). 1971. 5.95 o.p. (ISBN 0-15-142390-3). HarBraceJ.
Human Energy. Pierre Teilhard De Chardin. LC 79-139231. Orig. Title: Energie Humaine. 191p. 1972. pap. 3.95 o.p. (ISBN 0-15-642300-6, HB234, Harv). HarBraceJ.
Human Energy: The Critical Factor for Individuals & Organizations. John D. Ingalls. 285p. 1979. text ed. 18.95 o.p. (ISBN 0-89384-055-6). Univ Assocs.
Human Engineering: Marvel or Menace? John Langone. (gr. 7 up). 1978. 12.95 o.p. (ISBN 0-316-51427-6). Little.
Human Environment. Michael Treshow. (Population Biology Ser.). 1976. text ed. 29.95 o.p. (ISBN 0-07-065136-1). McGraw.
Human Equation. Clell Edgar Bowman. 1976. 8.00 o.p. (ISBN 0-682-48437-7). Exposition-Phoenix.
Human Evoked Potentials: Applications & Problems. Ed. by Dietrich Lehmann & Enoch Callaway. LC 79-4320. (NATO Conference Series III, Human Factors: Vol. 9). 512p. 1979. 79.50x o.p. (ISBN 0-306-40160-6, Plenum Pr). Plenum Pub.
Human Evolution. 3rd ed. J. B. Birdsell. 1981. text ed. 31.50 o.p. (ISBN 0-395-30784-8). HM.
Human Evolution. B. A. Wood. (Outline Studies in Biology). 1978. pap. 8.50 o.p. (ISBN 0-412-15600-8, NO. 6325, Pub. by Chapman & Hall). Routledge Chapman & Hall.
Human Existence: Contradiction & Hope. Walter Strolz. Orig. Title: Widerspruch und Hoffnung Des Daseins. 1967. 14.95 o.p. (ISBN 0-268-00122-7). U of Notre Dame Pr.
Human Experimentation. Ed. by Robert L. Bogomolny. LC 76-10649. 212p. 1976. pap. 9.95x o.p. (ISBN 0-87074-155-1). SMU Press.
Human Factor. Graham Greene. 1979. pap. 2.95 o.p. (ISBN 0-380-41491-0, 69799-8). Avon.
Human Factor: Biomedicine in the Manned Space Program to 1980. John A. Pitts. LC 85-21526. (NASA SP-4213. NASA History Ser.). (Illus.). 404p. 1985. 23.00 o.p. (ISBN 0-318-20418-5, S/N 033-000-00977-1). USGPO.
Human Factors in Long-Duration Space Flight. National Research Council, Space Science Board Staff. LC 70-189063. (Illus.). 288p. 1972. pap. 8.25 o.p. (ISBN 0-309-01947-8). Natl Acad Pr.
Human Factors in Mechanized Warfare. R. E. Simpkin. (Brasseys Ser.). (Illus.). 191p. 1983. 45.00 o.p. (ISBN 0-08-028340-3). Pergamon.
Human Factors in Telecommunications International Symposium, 4th. VDE Berlin Staff. 1968. 75.00 o.s.i. (ISBN 0-686-37974-8). Info Gatekeepers.
Human Factors in Telecommunications International Symposium, 5th. Post Office Research Dept. London, England Staff. 1970. 75.00 o.s.i. (ISBN 0-686-37975-6). Info Gatekeepers.
Human Factors in Telecommunications International Symposium, 6th. Swedish Telecommunications Administration Staff & LM Ericson Telephone Company Staff. 1972. 75.00 o.s.i. (ISBN 0-686-37978-0). Info Gatekeepers.
Human Factors in Telephone Communications International Symposium, 3rd. Het PTT-BEDRIJF, the Netherlands Staff. 1967. pap. 75.00 o.s.i. (ISBN 0-686-37973-X). Info-Gatekeepers.
Human Family Systems: An Evolutionary View. P. L. Van Den Berghe. 350p. 1979. pap. 21.25 o.p. (ISBN 0-444-99064-X). Elsevier.
Human Fantasy. Edward Echols. 64p. (Orig.). 1980. pap. 3.00 o.p. (ISBN 0-682-49652-9). Exposition-Phoenix.
Human Fertilization. Ed. by H. Ludwig & P. F. Tauber. LC 77-99146. (Illus.). 300p. 1978. 36.00 o.p. (ISBN 0-88416-245-1). Year Bk Med.
Human Genetic Variation in Response to Medical & Environmental Agents: Pharmacogenetics & Ecogenetics. Ed. by A. G. Motulsky et al. (Human Genetics Ser.: Supplement 1). (Illus.). 1979. pap. 26.00 o.p. (ISBN 0-387-09175-0). Springer-Verlag.
Human Genetics. S. Armendares & R. Lisker. (International Congress Ser.: No. 411). 1978. 116.00 o.p. (ISBN 0-444-15252-0, Excerpta Medica). Elsevier.
Human Genetics. J. H. Edwards. 1978. pap. 6.95 o.p. (ISBN 0-412-13170-6, NO. 6097, Pub. by Chapman & Hall). Routledge Chapman & Hall.
Human Genetics. 2nd ed. Edward Novitski. 1982. write for info. o.p. (ISBN 0-02-388570-X). Macmillan.
Human Genetics: A Selection of Insights. Ed. by W. J. Schull & R. Chakraborty. LC 78-13701. (Benchmark Papers in Genetics: Vol. 10). 359p. 1982. 51.95 o.p. (ISBN 0-87933-321-9). Van Nos Reinhold.
Human Genetics & Social Problems. Ed. by Thomas Mertens & Sandra K. Robinson. 212p. 1973. text ed. 29.00x o.p. (ISBN 0-8422-5090-5); pap. text ed. 12.95x o.p. (ISBN 0-8422-0230-7). Irvington.
Human Genetics 1984. Ed. by Emanuel Hackel. LC 85-6186. (Illus.). 105p. 1985. text ed. 9.00 o.p. (ISBN 0-915355-04-3). Am Assn Blood.
Human Geography & Ecology in the Sinu Country of Columbia. B. Le Roy Gordon. LC 77-4433. (Ibero-Americana: No. 39). 1977. Repr. of 1957 ed. lib. bdg. 35.00x o.p. (ISBN 0-8371-9047-9, GOHU). Greenwood.
Human Growth: The Story of How Life Begins & Goes On. Lester F. Beck. LC 77-75011. (Illus.). 120p. 1969. 6.95 o.p. (ISBN 0-15-142577-9). HarBraceJ.
Human Health & Disease. Ed. by Philip L. Faseb & Dorothy D. Katz. LC 76-53166. (Biological Handbks: Vol. 2). (Illus.). 1983. 84.00 o.p. (ISBN 0-08-030072-3). Pergamon.
Human Heart & Circulation. V. Navarantham. 1975. 22.00 o.p. (ISBN 0-12-514750-3). Acad Pr.
Human Helplessness: Theory & Applications. Ed. by Judy Garber & Martin E. Seligman. LC 79-6773. 1980. 37.50 o.p. (ISBN 0-12-275050-0). Acad Pr.
Human Hemoglobin Variants & Their Characteristics. Ed. by H. Lehmann & P. A. Kynoch. 242p. 1976. 79.00 o.p. (ISBN 0-7204-0585-8, Biomedical Pr). Elsevier.
Human Immune System: The New Frontier in Medicine. Steven B. Mizel & Peter Jaret. 1986. pap. 8.95 o.p. (ISBN 0-671-62332-X, Fireside). S&S.
Human in the Photo-Optical System: Proceedings, Vol. 5. Society of Photo-Optical Instrumentation Engineers Staff. 28.00 o.p. (ISBN 0-89252-007-8). SPIE.
Human Infection with Fungi, Actinomycetes & Algae. Roger D. Baker et al. LC 72-160588. (Illus.). 1971. 230.60 o.p. (ISBN 0-387-05378-6). Springer-Verlag.
Human Intestinal Flora. D. R. Drasar & M. J. Hill. 1975. 94.00 o.p. (ISBN 0-12-221750-0). Acad Pr.
Human Life: A Biblical Perspective for Bioethics. J. Robert Nelson. LC 83-48140. 208p. 1984. pap. 10.95 o.p. (ISBN 0-8006-1754-1, 1-1754, Fortress). Augsburg Fortress.
Human Life Is Sacred. Irish Bishop's Pastoral Staff. 1977. pap. 1.50 o.s.i. (ISBN 0-8198-0416-9). Dghtrs St Paul.
Human Lymphocyte Differentiation: Its Application to Cancer. B. Serrou & C. Rosenfeld. (Inserm Symposium Ser.: No. 8). 1978. 116.00 o.p. (ISBN 0-7204-0664-1, North Holland). Elsevier.
Human Lymphokines. Ed. by Amanullah Khan & Norwood Hill. 1982. 39.95 o.p. (ISBN 0-12-406080-3). Acad Pr.
Human Machine: A View of Intelligent Mechanisms. Igor Aleksander. (Illus.). 1978. pap. text ed. 9.95x o.p. (ISBN 2-604-00023-7). Gower Pub Co.
Human Medicine: Ethical Perspective on New Medical Issues. James B. Nelson. LC 73-78258. 1973. 7.50 o.p. (ISBN 0-8066-1323-8, 10-3183, Augsburg). Augsburg Fortress.
Human Memory. Vernon H. Gregg. (Essential Psychology Ser.). 1975. pap. 4.50x o.p. (ISBN 0-416-81980-X, NO. 2737). Routledge Chapman & Hall.
Human Memory: Theory, Research & Individual Differences, Vol. 22. Michael W. Eysenck. 1977. 28.00 o.p. (ISBN 0-08-020405-8). Pergamon.
Human Microscopic Anatomy. Seong S. Han. (Illus.). 1980. text ed. 31.95x o.p. (ISBN 0-07-025961-5). McGraw.
Human Motivation: Physiological, Behavioral & Social Approaches. Russell G. Geen et al. 1984. text ed. 44.00 o.p. (ISBN 0-205-08114-2, 798114). Allyn.
Human Nature & Conduct. John Dewey. LC 30-19598. 306p. 1935. 5.95 o.p. (ISBN 0-394-60439-3). Modern Lib.
Human Nature in Politics. Sugwon Kang. 1980. 39.95 o.p. (ISBN 0-87855-430-0). Transaction Pubs.
Human Nature of Organizations. J. Douglas Brown. LC 73-85862. 180p. 1979. pap. 3.95 o.p. (ISBN 0-8144-7514-0). AMACOM.
Human Nature under Fire: The Political Philosophy of Hannah Arendt. Gordon J. Tolle. LC 81-43723. 180p. (Orig.). 1982. lib. bdg. 29.25 o.p. (ISBN 0-8191-2560-1); pap. text ed. 12.25 o.p. (ISBN 0-8191-2561-X). U Pr of Amer.
Human Nutrition in Tropical Africa. 2nd, Rev. ed. M. C. Latham. (Food & Nutrition Papers: No. 11). 306p. 1980. pap. 22.00 o.p. (ISBN 92-5-100412-9, F2049, FAO). UNIPUB.
Human Operator in Complex Systems. Ed. by W. T. Singleton. 267p. 1971. 22.50x o.p. (ISBN 0-85066-008-4). Taylor & Francis.
Human Organ Transplantation & Public Policy. Carolyn H. Thompson. (Public Administration Ser.: P 1787). 12p. 1985. 2.00 o.p. (ISBN 0-89028-587-X). Vance Biblios.
Human Organism. 5th ed. R. De Coursey. 1980. text ed. 41.95 o.p. (ISBN 0-07-016275-1). McGraw.
Human Organism. 4th ed. Russell M. DeCoursey. (Illus.). 672p. 1974. text ed. 35.95 o.p. (ISBN 0-07-016234-4, C). McGraw.
Human Osteology: A Laboratory & Field Manual of the Human Skeleton. 2nd ed. William M. Bass. Ed. by David R. Evans. LC 77-172091. (Special Publications Ser.: No. 2). (Illus.). 288p. (Orig.). 1971. pap. 9.00 o.p. (ISBN 0-943414-07-5). MO Arch Soc.

Human Pedigree. Anthony Smith. (McGraw-Hill Paperback). 320p. 1976. pap. text ed. 3.95 o.p. (ISBN 0-07-059045-1). McGraw.
Human Physical Growth & Maturation: Methodologies & Factors. Ed. by F. E. Johnston et al. LC 79-27633. (NATO ASI Series A, Life Sciences: Vol. 30). 376p. 1980. 69.50x o.p. (ISBN 0-306-40420-6, Plenum Pr). Plenum Pub.
Human Placenta: Proteins & Hormones. Ed. by A. Klopper et al. (Serono Symposia Ser.: No. 35). 1981. 94.50 o.p. (ISBN 0-12-416150-2). Acad Pr.
Human Placental Villitides: A Review of Chronic Intrauterine Infection see Aortic Alterations in Rabbits Following Sheathing with Silastic & Polyethylene Tubes.
Human Poisoning from Native & Cultivated Plants. rev. exp. ed. James W. Hardin & James W. Arena. LC 73-76174. (Illus.). xii, 192p. 1973. 16.95 o.p. (ISBN 0-8223-0303-5). Duke.
Human Population Genetics. Aravinda Chakravarti. 1984. 41.95 o.p. (ISBN 0-442-21745-5). Van Nos Reinhold.
Human Possibilities. W. Paul Kiley. LC 63-18055. 104p. 1963. (ISBN 0-8022-0855-X). Philos Lib.
Human Potential: An Essay on Its Cultivation. William T. Couch. LC 72-97940. xii, 410p. 1974. 31.50 o.p. (ISBN 0-8223-0300-0). Duke.
Human Predicament in Hardy's Novels. J. Dave. 224p. 1985. text ed. 39.95x o.p. (ISBN 0-391-03340-9). Humanities.
Human Puzzle: Psychological Research & Christian Belief. David C. Myers. LC 77-15873. 1978. pap. 8.95x o.p. (ISBN 0-06-065558-5, RD 265). HarpR.
Human Race. Terence Dixon & Martin Lucas. LC 82-14280. (New Press Ser.). 256p. 1982. text ed. 24.95 o.p. (ISBN 0-07-017080-0). McGraw.
Human Reflex: Behavioral Psychology in Biblical Perspective. Rodger K. Bufford. LC 80-8900. (Illus.). 256p. 1981. 14.95i o.p. (ISBN 0-06-061165-0). HarpR.
Human Relations & Your Career: A Guide to Interpersonal Skills. David W. Johnson. (Illus.). 1978. pap. text ed. (ISBN 0-13-445601-7). P-H.
Human Relations: Power & Politics. Albert Mueller-Deham. 436p. 1958. (ISBN 0-8022-1167-4). Philos Lib.
Human Reproduction & Development. James L. Mariner. (Illus.). 155p. (Orig.). (gr. 9-12). 1979. pap. text ed. 5.25x o.p. (ISBN 0-88334-118-2). Ind Sch Pr.
Human Resource Accounting. Gary Blau. (Studies in Productivity: Highlights of the Literature Ser.: Vol. 6). 55p. 1978. pap. 35.00 o.p. (ISBN 0-08-029487-1). Work in Amer.
Human Resource Accounting. Ed. by A. G. Hopwood. 1977. pap. 35.00 o.p. (ISBN 0-08-021419-3). Pergamon.
Human Resource Dynamics Administration & Policy: A Bibliography. Barbara J. Ray. (Public Adiministration Series: Bibliography P 1775). 76p. 1985. pap. 11.25 o.p. (ISBN 0-89028-575-6). Vance Biblios.
Human Resources: Cases & Concepts. Leon C. Megginson. (Harbrace Business & Economics Ser.). (Orig.). 1968. pap. text ed. 10.95 o.p. (ISBN 0-15-540401-6, HC). HarBraceJ.
Human Resources Development in the Organization: A Guide to Information Sources. Ed. by Jerome L. Franklin. LC 76-28289. (Management Information Guide Ser.: No. 35). 192p. 1978. 68.00x o.p. (ISBN 0-8103-0835-5). Gale.
Human Resources in Psychology. Ed. by Gary R. VandenBos et al. (Special Issue, American Psychologist: Vol. 36, No. 11). 1981. pap. 16.00 o.p. (ISBN 1-55798-002-0, 4013611). Am Psychol.
Human Resources Management: Text & Cases. Fred K. Foulkes & E. Robert Livernash. (Illus.). 456p. 1982. text ed. 27.95 o.p. (ISBN 0-13-446310-2); pap. text ed. (ISBN 0-13-446302-1). P-H.
Human Resources, 1988-89. Ed. by Fred Maidment. (Annual Editions Ser.). (Illus.). 256p. 1988. pap. text ed. 9.95 o.p. (ISBN 0-87967-771-6). Dushkin Pub.
Human Responses to Environmental Odors. Ed. by Amos Turk & James Johnston, Jr. 1974. 61.00 o.p. (ISBN 0-12-703860-4). Acad Pr.
Human Rights. Ed. by A. I. Melden. 152p. 1970. pap. text ed. (ISBN 0-534-00220-X). Wadsworth Pub.
Human Rights. David Owen. 1978. 8.95 o.p. (ISBN 0-393-01186-0). Norton.
Human Rights: A Compilation of International Instruments. 15.00 o.p. (ISBN 92-1-154024-0, E.81.XIV.1). UN.
Human Rights & Foreign Policy. E. Luard. LC 80-41774. 32p. 1981. pap. 9.00 o.p. (ISBN 0-08-027405-6). Pergamon.
Human Rights & Freedoms in the U. S. S. R. F. Medvedev & G. Kulikov. 256p. 1981. 4.00 o.p. (ISBN 0-8285-2114-X, Pub. by Progress Pubs U. S. S. R.). Imported Pubns.
Human Rights & the South African Legal Order. John Dugard. LC 77-85536. 1978. text ed. 50.50 o.p. (ISBN 0-691-09236-2); pap. 20.00x LPE o.p. (ISBN 0-691-10060-8). Princeton U Pr.
Human Rights & U. S. Foreign Policy: Principles & Applications. Ed. by Peter G. Brown & Douglas MacLean. 1979. pap. 15.00x o.p. (ISBN 0-669-04326-5). Lexington Bks.
Human Rights Begin with Breakfast. J. Madeley. 34p. 1982. pap. 9.00 o.p. (ISBN 0-08-028926-6). Pergamon.
Human Rights Book. Milton Meltzer. LC 79-13017. 272p. (gr. 6 up). 1979. 11.95 o.p. (ISBN 0-374-33514-1). FS&G.
Human Rights in American & Russian Political Thought. Arpad Kadarkay. LC 81-43910. (Illus.). 252p. (Orig.). 1982. PLB 32.25 o.p. (ISBN 0-8191-2481-8); pap. text ed. 13.25 o.p. (ISBN 0-8191-2482-6). U Pr of Amer.
Human Rights Issues in Counselor Training & Supervision: Bibliography. 1983. 1.00 o.p. (ISBN 0-317-59908-9, 72182C). Am Assn Coun Dev.
Human Rights: Rhetoric or Reality. Ed. by George W. Forell & William H. Lazareth. LC 77-20537. (Justice Bks). 64p. 1978. pap. 0.95 o.p. (ISBN 0-8006-1553-0, 1-1553, Fortress). Augsburg Fortress.
Human Rights, the Helsinki Accords & the United States, 3 vols in 9. Ed. by Igor I. Kavaas & Jacqueline P. Granier. LC 82-81319. 1982. Set. lib. bdg. 395.00 o.p. (ISBN 0-89941-152-5). W S Hein.
Human Rights Training Manual: ACES. 1982. 6.00 o.p. (ISBN 0-317-59907-0, 72181C). Am Assn Coun Dev.
Human Season. Edward L. Wallant. LC 60-10923. 192p. 1973. pap. 1.65 o.p. (ISBN 0-15-642330-8, Harv). HarBraceJ.
Human Season: Selected Poems, 1926-1972. Archibald MacLeish. 1972. 6.00 o.p. (ISBN 0-395-13943-0). HM.
Human Service Practice with the Elderly. Marion L. Beaver. (Illus.). 256p. 1983. text ed. 32.00 o.p. (ISBN 0-13-447482-1). P-H.
Human Services in Industry. Dale A. Masi. 272p. 1981. 37.00x o.p. (ISBN 0-669-05104-7). Lexington Bks.
Human Services Management: Analysis & Applications. Myron E. Weiner. 640p. 1982. text ed. (ISBN 0-534-10885-7). Wadsworth Pub.
Human Services Professional Development: Future Directions. Joann Chennault & J. F. Burnford. 1978. text ed. 22.95 o.p. (ISBN 0-07-010732-7). McGraw.
Human Settlements & Energy: A Seminar of the United Nations Economic Commission for Europe. Ed. by C. I. Jackson. 1978. 31.00 o.p. (ISBN 0-08-022427-X); pap. 17.75 o.p. (ISBN 0-08-022411-3). Pergamon.
Human Settlements in Europe: Post-War Trends & Policies. pap. 7.00 o.p. (ISBN 0-686-94570-0, UN76/2E9, UN). UNIPUB.
Human Sex & Sexuality. Edwin B. Steen & James H. Price. 338p. 1977. pap. text ed. write for info. o.p. (ISBN 0-02-416260-4). Macmillan.
Human Sex Differences: A Primatologist's Perspective. G. Mitchell. 256p. 1981. 29.95 o.p. (ISBN 0-442-23865-7). Van Nos Reinhold.
Human Sexual Expression. Benjamin A. Kogan. LC 73-75179. 385p. 1973. pap. text ed. 10.95 o.p. (ISBN 0-15-540426-1, HC). HarBraceJ.
Human Sexuality. 4th ed. James L. McCary & Stephen P. McCary. 589p. 1982. text ed. (ISBN 0-534-01108-X); (ISBN 0-534-01109-8). Wadsworth Pub.
Human Sexuality. William H. Masters et al. 1982. text ed. 24.95 o.p. (ISBN 0-316-54990-8). Little.
Human Sexuality. 2nd ed. William H. Masters et al. 1984. text ed. write for info. o.p. (ISBN 0-673-39524-3). Scott F.
Human Sexuality. Raymond Rosen & Linda R. Rosen. 576p. 1981. text ed. 22.00 o.p. (ISBN 0-394-32028-X, RanC). Random.
Human Sexuality. 2nd ed. David A. Schulz. (Illus.). 432p. 1984. pap. text ed. (ISBN 0-13-447615-8). P-H.
Human Sexuality: A Preliminary Study - the United Church of Christ. LC 77-25398. 1977. pap. 5.95 o.p. (ISBN 0-8298-0341-6). Pilgrim NY.
Human Sexuality & Its Problems. John Bancroft. LC 82-14719. 447p. 1983. pap. text ed. 33.50 o.p. (ISBN 0-443-01659-3). Churchill.
Human Sexuality: Brief Edition. Herant Katchadourian et al. LC 79-705. 1979. pap. text ed. 22.95 o.p. (ISBN 0-03-045051-9, HoltC). HR&W.
Human Sexuality in Nursing Care. Jean Glover. LC 84-19881. 160p. (Orig.). 1984. pap. 11.95 o.p. (ISBN 0-7099-1141-6, Pub. by Croom Held Ltd). Routledge Chapman & Hall.
Human Sexuality: Study Guide. 1977. pap. 1.75 o.p. (ISBN 0-8298-0339-4). Pilgrim NY.
Human Sexuality 1988-89. 13th, rev. ed. Ed. by Ollie Pocs. LC 75-20756. (Annual Editions Ser.). (Illus.). 256p. 1988. pap. text ed. 9.95x o.p. (ISBN 0-87967-716-3). Dushkin Pub.
Human Side of Mergers & Acquisitions: Managing Collisions Between People, Cultures, & Organizations. Anthony F. Buono & James L. Bowditch. LC 88-7853. (Management Ser.). 344p. 1989. text ed. 26.95x o.p. (ISBN 1-55542-135-0). Jossey-Bass.
Human Side of Music. Charles W. Hughes. (ISBN 0-8022-0755-3). Philos Lib.
Human Side of Statistical Consulting. James R. Boen & Douglas A. Zahn. (Research Methods Ser.). 196p. 1982. 23.95 o.p. (ISBN 0-534-97949-1, Lifetime Learn). Van Nos Reinhold.
Human Side of the Game: Lives in Bowling. Emily Simone. 1977. 6.00 o.p. (ISBN 0-682-48903-4). Exposition-Phoenix.
Human Society in Ethics & Politics. Bertrand Russell. 1954. text ed. 35.00x o.p. (ISBN 0-04-172004-0). Unwin Hyman.
Human Stress & Cognition: An Information Processing Approach. Ed. by Vernon Hamilton & David M. Warburton. LC 78-31691. 502p. 1979. 122.00 o.p. (ISBN 0-471-27572-7, Pub. by Wiley-Interscience). Wiley.
Human Subjects in Medical Experimentation: A Sociological Study of the Conduct & Regulation of Clinical Research. Bradford H. Gray. LC 80-11612. 316p. 1981. Repr. of 1975 ed. lib. bdg. 26.50 o.p. (ISBN 0-89874-134-3). Krieger.
Human Track. Sherry Brannan. 80p. 1986. 6.75 o.p. (ISBN 0-8062-2780-X). Carlton.
Human Tumors: Histology, Diagnosis, & Technique. Pierre Masson. Tr. by Sidney D. Kobernick from Fr. LC 70-83489. (Illus.). 1430p. 1970. text ed. 75.00x o.p. (ISBN 0-8143-1405-8). Wayne St U Pr.
Human Tumour in Short Term Culture: Techniques & Clinical Applications. Ed. by P. Dendy. 1976. 91.00 o.p. (ISBN 0-12-209850-1). Acad Pr.
Human Understanding, Vol. 1: The Collective Use & Evolution of Concepts. Stephen Toulmin. LC 73-166391. 500p. 1972. 47.00 o.p. (ISBN 0-691-07185-3); pap. 14.95 o.p. (ISBN 0-691-01996-7). Princeton U Pr.
Human Use of Human Beings: Cybernetics & Society. Norbert Weiner. 1986. pap. 1.95 o.p. (ISBN 0-380-01273-1, 50682-3, Discus). Avon.
Human Values. Ed. by Godfrey Vesey. (No. 16). 1978. text ed. 32.50x o.p. (ISBN 0-391-00894-3). Humanities.
Human Values & Science, Art & Mathematics. Hugh G. Lieber & Lillian R. Lieber. (Illus.). 1961. 3.95 o.p. (ISBN 0-393-06339-9). Norton.
Human Variation & Human Microevolution. Jane H. Underwood. (Illus.). 1978. pap. text ed. (ISBN 0-13-447573-9). P-H.
Human Variation: The Biopsychology of Age, Race, & Sex. Ed. by R. T. Osborne et al. 1978. 47.00 o.p. (ISBN 0-12-529050-0). Acad Pr.
Human Way. Maurice Friedman. LC 81-8011. (Religion & Human Experience Ser.). 168p. 1982. 13.95 o.p. (ISBN 0-89012-025-0). Anima Pubns.
Human Way: Readings in Anthropology. H. Russell Bernard. 1975. pap. write for info. o.p. (ISBN 0-02-308920-2, 30892). Macmillan.
Human Zoo. Desmond Morris. 204p. 1970. pap. 2.25 o.p. (ISBN 0-440-33913-8). Dell.
Humaniora Islamica: An Annual Publication of Islamic Studies & the Humanities, Vol. 1. Ed. by Herbert W. Mason et al. 1973. pap. text ed. 32.00x o.p. (ISBN 0-686-31749-1). Mouton.
Humanising the Workplace: New Proposals & Perspectives. Richard N. Ottoway. 176p. 1977. 25.00 o.p. (ISBN 0-85664-345-9, Pub. by Croom Helm Ltd). Routledge Chapman & Hall.
Humanism & Behaviorism: Dialogue & Growth. Abraham Wandersman et al. 400p. 1976. 110.00 o.p. (ISBN 0-08-019589-X); pap. 17.00 o.p. (ISBN 0-08-019588-1). Pergamon.
Humanism: Its Philosophical, Ethical & Sociological Aspects. M. Petrosyan. 307p. 1972. 4.45 o.p. (ISBN 0-8285-0196-3, Pub. by Progress Pubs USSR). Imported Pubns.
Humanism: Philosophical Essays. Ferdinand C. Schiller. Repr. of 1912 ed. lib. bdg. 35.00x o.p. (ISBN 0-8371-2837-4, SCHU). Greenwood.
Humanism, Psychology & Education. Hirsch L. Silverman. 90p. 1969. pap. text ed. 4.95x o.p. (ISBN 0-8290-0643-5). Irvington.
Humanist Tradition in the West. Alan Bullock. (Illus.). 208p. 1985. 24.45 o.p. (ISBN 0-393-02237-4). Norton.
Humanistic Delivery of Services to Families in a Changing & Technological Age. Ed. by Jacquelyn A. Kegley. LC 81-43815. 270p. (Orig.). 1982. lib. bdg. 32.00 o.p. (ISBN 0-8191-2497-4); pap. text ed. 14.00 o.p. (ISBN 0-8191-2498-2). U Pr of Amer.
Humanistic Education: Objectives & Assessment. Arthur W. Combs et al. 1978. pap. 4.75 o.s.i. (ISBN 0-87120-089-9, 611-78136). Assn Supervision.
Humanistic Geography. David Ley & M. Samuels. 1978. 18.95x o.p. (ISBN 0-416-60101-4, NO. 2862). Routledge Chapman & Hall.
Humanistic View of Religion. 65-27460 ed. Sonja Biersted. 160p. 1966. (ISBN 0-8022-0126-1). Philos Lib.
Humanistic Viewpoint in the Social Sciences. Henry Winthrop. LC 72-8660. 144p. 1972. 24.00x o.p. (ISBN 0-8422-5062-X); pap. text ed. 9.75x o.p. (ISBN 0-8422-0269-2). Irvington.
Humanities: A Selective Guide to Information Sources. 2nd ed. A. Robert Rogers. LC 79-25335. (Library Science Text Ser.). 355p. 1979. 33.00x o.p. (ISBN 0-87287-206-8); pap. text ed. 21.00x o.p. (ISBN 0-87287-222-X). Libs Unl.
Humanities & the Theatre, 2 vols. 118p. 1983. Set. pap. text ed. 8.75 o.p. (ISBN 0-8191-3533-X, Co-pub. by Am Theat Assn). U Pr of Amer.
Humanity & Culture: An Introduction to Anthropology. Oriol Pi-Sunyer & Zdenek Salzmann. LC 77-76336. (Illus.). 1978. text ed. 32.50 o.p. (ISBN 0-395-25051-X). HM.
Humanity's Search for the Meaning of Life: A Brief Survey of History, Philosophy, Religion, Art, Music, & Architecture. June Stephenson. 178p. (Orig.). 1986. pap. 10.00 o.p. (ISBN 0-941138-03-8). Diemer-Smith.
Humanizing College Learning: A Taste of Hemlock. Charles A. Brownfield. LC 73-79214. 1973. 10.00 o.p. (ISBN 0-682-47717-6, University). Exposition-Phoenix.
Humankind. Peter Farb. LC 77-9083. 1978. 15.95 o.p. (ISBN 0-395-25710-7). HM.
Humankind Emerging. 4th ed. Bernard G. Campbell. 1985. pap. text ed. write for info. o.p. (ISBN 0-673-39000-4). Scott F.
Humanoid Touch. Jack Williamson. LC 80-13817. 228p. 1980. 10.95 o.p. (ISBN 0-03-056052-7). H Holt & Co.
Humans. Mike Dowdall & Pat Welch. (Illus.). 128p. 1984. 15.45 o.p. (ISBN 0-671-53257-X). S&S.
Humble Romance & Other Stories. Mary E. Wilkins Freeman. 1887. 11.00 o.p. (ISBN 0-403-04108-2). Somerset Pub.
Hume: A Collection of Critical Essays. Ed. by V. C. Chappell. 429p. 1974. pap. 9.95x o.p. (ISBN 0-268-00560-5). U of Notre Dame Pr.
Hume's Moral Theory. J. L. Mackie. (International Library of Philosophy & Scientific Method). 1980. 26.95x o.p. (ISBN 0-7100-0524-5); pap. 10.95x o.p. (ISBN 0-7100-0525-3). Routledge Chapman & Hall.
Hume's Philosophy of Human Nature. John Laird. LC 82-48344. (Philosophy of David Hume Ser.). 323p. 1983. lib. bdg. 42.00 o.p. (ISBN 0-8240-5414-8). Garland Pub.
Humiliations Follow'd with Deliverances...with a Narrative, of a Notable Deliverance Lately Received by Some English Captives, from the Hands of Cruel Indians see True History of the Captivity & Restoration of Mrs. Mary Rowlandson.
Humility of God. John Macquarrie. LC 77-18707. 96p. 1978. pap. 4.65 o.s.i. (ISBN 0-664-24200-6, Westminster). Westminster John Knox.
Humility: The Beauty of Holiness. Andrew Murray. 75p. 1987. pap. 2.95 o.p. (ISBN 0-310-55092-0, 19009P). Zondervan.
Hummel Art Two with Prices. John F. Hotchkiss. 156p. 12.95 o.p. (ISBN 0-87069-284-4). Wallace-Homestead.
Hummel Figurines & Plates: A Collectors Identification & Value Guide. 5th ed. Carl F. Lucky. (Illus.). 370p. 1983. pap. 9.95 o.p. (ISBN 0-89689-042-2). Bks Americana.
Hummy & the Wax Castle. Elizabeth Earnst. LC 84-80074. (Illus.). 1984. pap. 3.95 o.s.i. (Inst Creation). Master Bks.
Humor in American Song. Arthur Loesser. LC 79-181804. (Illus.). 318p. 1975. Repr. of 1942 ed. 40.00x o.p. (ISBN 0-8103-4040-2). Gale.
Humor in Human Quirks in Paintings & Rhyme. Victor R. Griffin. 1977. 5.00 o.p. (ISBN 0-682-48989-1). Exposition-Phoenix.
Humoral Factors in Host Defense: Symposium. Ed. by Y. Yamamura et al. LC 83-12317. 1983. 41.50 o.p. (ISBN 0-12-768220-1). Acad Pr.
Humorous & Dramatic Poetry. Selma S. Markstein. 1985. 5.75 o.p. (ISBN 0-8062-2520-3). Carlton.
Humorous Stories & Anecdotes. M. F. Gogulan & L. F. Kusemchenko. 159p. 1986. pap. 2.95 o.p. (ISBN 0-8285-3247-8, Pub. by Rus Lang Pubs USSR). Imported Pubns.

Humorous Verse of Lewis Carroll. Lewis Carroll. (Illus.). 14.25 o.p. (ISBN 0-8446-1814-4). Peter Smith.

Humour, Wit & Satire of the Seventeenth Century. John Ashton. LC 67-24350. (Social History Reference Ser.). 466p. 1968. Repr. of 1883 ed. 30.00x o.p. (ISBN 0-8103-3251-5). Gale.

Humpty Dumpty. Ray Marshall & Korky Paul. Ed. by Kate Klimo. (Chubby Pop-Ups Ser.). (Illus.). 10p. 1983. 3.80 o.s.i. (ISBN 0-671-46236-9, Little Simon). S&S.

Humpty Dumpty & Other Favorite Nursery Rhymes. Jane Longmore. 12p. (gr. k). 4.95 o.p. (ISBN 0-531-03552-2). Watts.

Hundertwasser: The Complete Graphic Work 1951-1986. Walter Koschatzky. LC 85-43481. (Illus.). 216p. 1986. 85.00 o.p. (ISBN 0-8478-0698-7). Rizzoli Intl.

Hundestammvater und Kerberos, 2 vols. Freda Kretschmar. Repr. of 1938 ed. Set. 37.00 o.p. (ISBN 0-384-30430-3). Johnson Repr.

Hundred Great Indians Through the Ages. H. N. Verma & A. Verma. 1976. 15.00 o.p. E J Brill USA.

Hundred Years Eating: Food, Drink, & the Daily Diet in Britain Since the Late Nineteenth Century. James P. Johnston. (Illus.). 1977. 9.95 o.p. (ISBN 0-7735-0306-4, McGill Canada). U of Toronto Pr.

Hundredth Dove. Jane Yolen. LC 80-13635. (Illus.). 80p. 1980. pap. 7.95 o.s.i. (ISBN 0-8052-0659-0). Schocken.

Hung Gar Kung-Fu Chinese Art of Self-Defense. Bucksam Kong & Eugene H. Ho. Ed. by John Scurra. LC 73-75551. (Ser. 310). 1973. pap. text ed. 9.95x o.p. (ISBN 0-89750-038-5, Dist. by Wehman). Ohara Pubns.

Hungarian Concise Dictionary: Hungarian-English, Vol. 2. 7th ed. Laszlo Orszagh. 1983. 30.00x o.p. (ISBN 96-305-3031-7, H268). Vanous.

Hungarian Deluxe Dictionary: English-Hungarian, Vol. 1. 6th ed. L. Orszagh. 1988. 95.00x o.p. (ISBN 96-305-0554-1, H-331). Vanous.

Hungarian Deluxe Dictionary: Hungarian-English, Vol. 2. 6th ed. L. Orszagh. 1988. 95.00x o.p. (ISBN 96-305-0067-1, H-330). Vanous.

Hungarian-English-English-Hungarian Dictionary, 2 vols. 11th, rev. ed. Laszlo Orszagh. 1977. Set. 15.00 o.p. (ISBN 0-686-68937-2). Vol. 1, Hung.-Eng., 464pp (ISBN 963-05-1255-6). Vol. 2, Eng.-Hung., 608pp (ISBN 963-05-1256-4). E J Brill USA.

Hungarian-English, English-Hungarian Pocket Dictionary. (Hungarian & Eng.). pap. 6.95 o.p. E J Brill USA.

Hungarian Little Dictionary, 2 vols. 12th ed. (Hungarian & Eng.). Set. 15.00 o.p. (ISBN 0-685-12024-4). Vol. 1, Hungarian-English (ISBN 9-6305-2019-2). Vol. 2, English-Hungarian (ISBN 9-6305-2018-4). E J Brill USA.

Hungarian Perspectives on Questions of International Law. H. S. Bokor. 1986. (ISBN 9-02-473293-X). E J Brill USA.

Hungarian Pocket Dictionary: English-Hungarian, Vol. 1. 15th ed. Laszlo Orszagh. 606p. 1987. 8.50x o.p. (ISBN 963-05-4487-3, H272). Vanous.

Hungarian Pocket Dictionary: Hungarian-English, Vol. 2. 15th ed. Laszlo Orszagh. 462p. 1987. 8.50x o.p. (ISBN 96-305-1256-4, H273). Vanous.

Hungarians in America 1583-1974: A Chronology & Fact Book. Joseph Szeplaki. LC 75-11505. (Ethnic Chronology Ser.: No. 18). 152p. 1975. text ed. 8.50 o.p. (ISBN 0-379-00514-X). Oceana.

Hungarians in the United States. Glen Dawson. 13p. 1972. imitation vellum 15.00 o.p. (ISBN 0-317-11651-7). Dawsons.

Hungary. Zoltan Halasz. (Illus.). 1982. 35.00 o.p. (ISBN 0-318-00235-3). E J Brill USA.

Hungary: A Decade of Economic Reform. Ed. by Paul Hare et al. (Illus.). 272p. 1981. text ed. 34.95x o.p. (ISBN 0-04-339021-8). Unwin Hyman.

Hungary, Nineteen Fifty-Six Revisited: The Message of a Revolution a Quarter of a Century After. Ferenc Feher & Agnes Heller. 192p. 1983. text ed. 37.95x o.p. (ISBN 0-04-321031-7). Unwin Hyman.

Hunger. Knut Hamsun. 1980. pap. 1.75 o.p. (ISBN 0-380-00556-5, 42028, Bard). Avon.

Hunger & Thirst & Other Plays. Eugene Ionesco. Tr. by Donald Watson from Fr. Incl. Picture; Anger; Salutations. 1969. pap. 3.95 o.p. (ISBN 0-394-17316-3, E506, Ever). Grove.

Hunger Fighter in Burma: The Story of Brayton Case. Robert F. Cramer. (Orig.). 1968. pap. 0.95 o.p. (ISBN 0-377-84111-0). Friendship Pr.

Hunger Fighters. Paul De Kruif. LC 67-32084. 372p. (gr. 7-12). 1967. pap. 0.95 o.s.i. (ISBN 0-15-642430-4, Harv). HarBraceJ.

Hunger for Salt: An Anthropological, Physiological, & Medical Analysis. D. A. Denton. (Illus.). 665p. 1982. 165.00 o.p. (ISBN 0-387-11286-3). Springer-Verlag.

Hunger in a Land of Plenty. George Schuyler. 252p. 1980. 15.95 o.p.; pap. 8.95 o.p. Transaction Pubs.

Hunger of Memory: The Education of Richard Rodriguez, An Autobiography. Richard Rodriguez. LC 81-81810. 208p. 1981. 14.95 o.s.i. (ISBN 0-87923-418-0). Godine.

Hunger Strike: The Anorectic's Struggle for Survival As a Metaphor for Our Age. Susie Orbach. 1986. 15.45 o.p. (ISBN 0-393-02278-1). Norton.

Hunger, Technology & Limits to Growth: Christian Responsibility for Three Ethical Issues. Robert L. Stivers. LC 83-72120. 176p. (Orig.). 1984. pap. 9.95 o.p. (ISBN 0-8066-2064-1, 10-3184, Augsburg). Augsburg Fortress.

Hunger: The World Food Crisis, An NSTA Environmental Materials Guide. Kathryn M. Fowler. 1977. pap. 1.00 o.p. (ISBN 0-87355-005-6). Natl Sci Tchrs.

Hunger: Understanding the Crisis Through Games, Dramas, & Songs. Patricia H. Sprinkle. LC 78-52451. 112p. (Orig.). 1980. pap. 7.95 o.s.i. (ISBN 0-8042-1312-7, John Knox). Westminster John Knox.

Hungry Angel. Roger Vadim. Tr. by William Attwood. LC 83-45087. 288p. 1983. 14.95 o.s.i. (ISBN 0-689-11413-3, Atheneum). Macmillan.

Hungry Bird Book: How to Make Your Garden Their Haven on Earth. Robert Arbib & Tony Soper. LC 75-122251. (Illus.). 1970. 8.95 o.s.i. (ISBN 0-8008-4020-8). Taplinger.

Hungry for God. Ralph Martin. 1976. pap. (ISBN 0-515-09587-7). Jove Pubns.

Hungry Forties: Life Under the Bread Tax. J. C. Unwin. (Development of Industrial Society Ser.). (Illus.). 274p. 1971. Repr. of 1904 ed. 32.50x o.p. (ISBN 0-7165-1769-8, BBA 04704, Pub. by Irish Academic Pr). Biblio Dist.

Hungry Tigress & Other Traditional Asian Tales. Rafe Martin. LC 83-20278. (Illus.). 150p. 1984. 6.95 o.p. (ISBN 0-87773-261-2); pap. 6.95 o.p. (ISBN 0-394-72339-2). Shambhala Pubns.

Hunt for Life's Extras, the Story of Archibald Rutledge. Idella F. Bodie. LC 80-50789. (Illus.). 176p. 1982. Clothbound 11.95 o.p. (ISBN 0-87844-046-1). Sandlapper Pub Co.

Hunted. Charles Manyoky-Nemeth. Tr. by Alex Falconer. 1979. 5.50 o.p. (ISBN 0-682-49355-4). Exposition-Phoenix.

Hunted Heart. Barbara Doyle. (Velvet Glove Ser.: No. 9). 192p. (Orig.). 1984. pap. 2.25 o.p. (ISBN 0-380-89458-0). Avon.

Hunter. Eric Sauter. 192p. 1983. pap. 2.95 o.p. (ISBN 0-380-84475-3, 84475). Avon.

Hunter. Richard Stark. 1981. lib. bdg. 11.50 o.p. (ISBN 0-8398-2706-7, Gregg). G K Hall.

Hunter-Killer. J. D. Macdonnell. (WWII Men in Action Ser.). 1979. pap. (ISBN 0-8439-0684-7, Pub. by Leisure Bks CT). Dorchester Pub Co.

Hunter: Tales of a Different Papa. Christopher Keane. LC 76-8644. 1976. 8.95 o.p. (ISBN 0-87795-135-7, Arbor Hse). Morrow.

Hunters. Phillip Whitfield. (Illus.). 1978. 14.95 o.p. (ISBN 0-671-24398-5). S&S.

Hunter's Book of the Pronghorn Antelope. Bert Popowski & Wilf E. Pyle. LC 81-16331. 356p. 1982. 18.95 o.p. (ISBN 0-8329-3605-7, Pub. by Winchester Pr). New Century.

Hunters in the Snow: A Collection of Short Stories. David Kranes. LC 78-70705. 1979. pap. 9.95 o.p. (ISBN 0-87480-146-X). U of Utah Pr.

Hunters of Karinhall. Carl H. Wijkmark. 1976. pap. 1.75 o.p. (ISBN 0-380-00612-X, 27680). Avon.

Hunters of the Black Swamp. Lloyd C. Harnishfeger. LC 70-128803. (Real Life Bks.). (Illus.). (gr. 5-11). 1971. PLB 5.95 o.p. (ISBN 0-8225-0701-3). Lerner Pubns.

Hunter's Orange. William Dieter. LC 82-73280. 256p. 1983. 13.95 o.s.i. (ISBN 0-689-11379-X, Atheneum). Macmillan.

Hunter's Orange. William Dieter. 256p. 1984. pap. 2.95 o.p. (ISBN 0-380-68684-8). Avon.

Hunting & Fishing. Currier & Ives Portfolios. (Chronicles of America Ser.). (Illus.). 32p. pap. 2.95 o.p. (ISBN 0-8437-2980-5). Hammond Inc.

Hunting Hypothesis: A Personal Conclusion Concerning the Evolutionary Nature of Man. Robert Ardrey. LC 75-37781. 256p. 1976. 10.00 o.p. (ISBN 0-689-10672-6, Atheneum). Macmillan.

Hunting in Ireland. Collin A. Lewis. (Illus.). 17.95 o.p. (ISBN 0-85131-213-6, NL51, Pub. by J A Allen U K). S R Smith Sporting Bks.

Hunting of Cain: A True Story of Money, Greed & Fratricide. Dan E. Moldea. LC 82-73032. 320p. 1983. 15.95 o.s.i. (ISBN 0-689-11357-9, Atheneum). Macmillan.

Hunting of the Hare. Ed. by Lionel R. Woolner. (Illus.). 6.10 o.p. (ISBN 0-85131-122-9, Pub. by J A Allen U K). S R Smith Sporting Bks.

Hunting Rabbits & Hares: The Complete Guide to North America's Favorite Small Game. Richard P. Smith. (Illus.). 160p. (Orig.). 1986. pap. 12.95 o.p. (ISBN 0-8117-2056-X). Stackpole.

Hunting Rifle: Gun Digest Book. Jack Lewis. LC 83-70142. (Illus.). 256p. (Orig.). 1983. pap. 12.95 o.p. (ISBN 0-910676-56-9). DBI.

Hunting Season. John Coyne. 320p. 1987. 15.95 o.p. (ISBN 0-02-528590-4). Macmillan.

Hunting Season. J. K. Mayo. LC 85-21925. 256p. 1986. 15.95 o.p. (ISBN 0-03-008002-9). H Holt & Co.

Hunting Shack. Gunnard Landers. LC 78-72918. 1979. 8.95 o.p. (ISBN 0-87795-207-8, Arbor Hse). Morrow.

Hunting the Bismarck. C. S. Forester. 118p. 1983. pap. 2.95 o.p. (ISBN 0-583-10388-X, Pub. by Granada England). Academy Chi Pubs.

Hunting Trips of a Ranchman: Sketches of Sport on the Northern Cattle Plains. Theodore Roosevelt. LC 75-104553. (Illus.). 362p. Repr. of 1885 ed. lib. bdg. 39.50 o.p. (ISBN 0-8398-1763-0). Irvington.

Hunting We Will Go. Michael Clayton. (ISBN 0-85131-178-4, NL51, Pub. by J A Allen U K). S R Smith Sporting Bks.

Huntington: An Illustrated History. James E. Casto. LC 85-5318. 160p. 1985. 22.95 o.p. (ISBN 0-89781-101-1). Windsor Pubns Inc.

Huntsville Breakout. Tom Cutter. (Tracker Ser.: No. 7). 144p. 1985. pap. 2.25 o.p. (ISBN 0-380-89584-6). Avon.

Hurdles: The Admissions Dilemma in American Education. Ed. by Herbert S. Sacks. LC 77-15350. 1978. 13.95 o.p. (ISBN 0-689-10857-5, Atheneum). Macmillan.

Hurrah for Alexander! Jeri Marsh. LC 77-74013. (Illus.). (gr. k-3). 1977. PLB 4.95 o.p. (ISBN 0-87614-092-4). Carolrhoda Bks.

Hurrah for the Next Man Who Dies. Mark Goodman. LC 84-45048. 288p. 1985. 14.95 o.s.i. (ISBN 0-689-11482-6, Atheneum). Macmillan.

Hurricane. Gardner Fox. 1976. pap. 1.50 o.p. (ISBN 0-685-69510-7, LB375DK, Pub. by Leisure Bks CT). Dorchester Pub Co.

Hurricane Season. Mickey Friedman. 192p. 1984. pap. 2.50 o.s.i. (ISBN 0-345-31548-0). Ballantine.

Hurricanes: Monster Storms from the Sea. Ruth Brindze. LC 72-85915. (Illus.). 112p. (gr. 5-9). 1973. 7.95 o.p. (ISBN 0-689-30423-4, Atheneum). Macmillan.

Hurricanes over Murmansk. John Golley. (Illus.). 224p. 1987. 17.95 o.p. (ISBN 0-85059-832-X, Pub. by PSL P Stephens). Sterling.

Hurry Home Again. Marie M. Hald. 192p. 1984. pap. 6.00 o.p. (ISBN 0-682-40174-9). Exposition-Phoenix.

Hurt & Healing of Divorce. Darlene Petri. LC 75-18647. 192p. (Orig.). 1976. pap. 1.95 o.p. (ISBN 0-912692-79-0). Cook.

Hurting & Healing: How to Cope with Hurt Feelings. Patti Williams. 80p. 1980. 5.00 o.p. (ISBN 0-682-49598-0). Exposition-Phoenix.

Husband Hunting: How to Win at the Mating Game. Jane Carpineto. 1986. pap. 6.95 o.p. (ISBN 0-671-60389-2, Fireside). S&S.

Husbandry, Medicine & Surgery in Captive Reptiles. Fredric Frye. LC 73-77929. (Illus.). text ed. 23.00 o.p. Veterinary Med.

Husbands & Other Men I've Played with. Patricia F. Sheinwold. LC 76-22661. 1976. 7.95 o.p. (ISBN 0-395-24779-9). HM.

Husbands, Lovers & Other Perishables. Chick Wallace. 1978. 5.00 o.p. (ISBN 0-682-49077-6); pap. 4.00 o.p. (ISBN 0-682-49080-6). Exposition-Phoenix.

Husband's Story. Norman Collins. LC 78-3594. 1978. 10.95 o.p. (ISBN 0-689-10898-2, Atheneum). Macmillan.

Hush. David St. John. (New Poetry Ser.). 1976. 6.95 o.p. (ISBN 0-395-24673-3); pap. 3.95 o.p. (ISBN 0-395-24672-5). HM.

Hush Little Baby. Aliki. (Illus.). (ps-1). 1972. 11.95x o.s.i. (ISBN 0-13-448167-4, Pub. by Treehouse); pap. 4.95 o.s.i. (ISBN 0-13-448175-5). P-H.

Hush Up! Jim Aylesworth. LC 79-2137. (Illus.). 32p. (gr. k-2). 1980. 7.95 o.s.i. (ISBN 0-03-054841-1). H Holt & Co.

Husqvarna Competition Models '72 - '75. Mansur Darlington. (Owners Workshop Manuals Ser.: No. 221). 1979. 13.50 o.p. (ISBN 0-85696-221-X). Haynes Pubns.

Husqvarna Service - Repair Handbook: 125-450cc Singles, 1966-1975. Ed. by Jeff Robinson. (Illus.). pap. text ed. 13.95 o.p. (ISBN 0-89287-014-1, M423). Clymer Pub.

Hussard sur le Toit: Roman. Jean Giono. 14.50 o.p. (ISBN 0-685-34168-2). Schoenhof.

Husserl & the Search for Certitude. Leszek Kolakowski. LC 74-29724. 96p. 1987. Repr. of 1975 ed. 8.95 o.p. (ISBN 0-317-60136-9). U of Chicago Pr.

Husserl: Expositions & Appraisals. Ed. by Frederick Elliston & Peter McCormick. LC 75-19882. 370p. 1976. text ed. 28.95 o.p. (ISBN 0-268-01063-3). U of Notre Dame Pr.

Hustle, Sweet Love. Maggie Davis. 1988. pap. 3.95 o.p. (ISBN 0-7701-0922-5). PaperJacks US.

Hustler. Walter Tevis. 1976. pap. 1.50 o.p. (ISBN 0-380-00860-2, 31278). Avon.

Hut Hopping in the Austrian Alps. William E. Reifsnyder. LC 73-77290. pap. 5.95 o.s.i. Sierra.

Hut Six Story: The Story of Breaking the Enigma Codes. Gordon Welchman. 1982. text ed. 12.95 o.p. (ISBN 0-07-069180-0). McGraw.

Huts & Hideaways. David Stiles. 144p. 5.95 o.p. (ISBN 0-8092-7817-0). Contemp Bks.

Hutterian Brethren, Fifteen Twenty-Eight to Nineteen Thirty-One see Principle of Non-Resistance As Held by the Mennonite Church.

HVAC Control Systems. Raymond K. Schneider. LC 80-23588. 358p. 1981. text ed. (ISBN 0-471-05180-2). Wiley.

HVAC Energy Analysis. 20.00 o.p. (ISBN 0-317-65065-3). Am Consul Eng.

H.W. Fowler see Persian Words in English.

Hwa-Rang & Chung-Mu of Tae Kwon Do Hyung. Jhoon Rhee. LC 77-163382. (Korean Arts Ser.). (Illus.). 1971. pap. text ed. 10.95 o.p. (ISBN 0-89750-004-0, 109, Dist. by Wehman). Ohara Pubns.

Hwa Rang Do, Vol. 3. Joo B. Lee. LC 78-52313. (Ser. 408). 1980. pap. 10.95 o.p. (ISBN 0-89750-070-9). Ohara Pubns.

Hyacinth from Limbo & Other Stories. Jean R. Smith. 1958. (ISBN 0-8022-1596-3). Philos Lib.

Hyaluronidase & Cancer. E. Cameron. 1966. 65.00 o.p. (ISBN 0-08-011480-6). Pergamon.

Hybrid Buildings. Joseph Fenton. (Pamphlet Architecture Ser.: No. 11). (Illus.). 46p. 1985. pap. 7.00 o.s.i. (ISBN 0-910413-14-2). Princeton Arch.

Hybrid Microcircuit Reliability Data Compiled by IIT Research Institute, Chicago. Reliability Analysis Center. 200p. 1976. pap. 145.00 o.p. (ISBN 0-08-020535-6). Pergamon.

Hybridization: An Evolutionary Perspective. Ed. by Donald A. Levin. LC 78-10947. (Benchmark Papers in Genetics: Vol. 11). 321p. 1982. 52.95 o.p. (ISBN 0-87933-341-3). Van Nos Reinhold.

Hybridization & the Flora of the British Isles. Ed. by C. A. Stace. 1975. 133.00 o.p. (ISBN 0-12-661650-7). Acad Pr.

Hybridization of Somatic Cells. Boris Ephrussi. LC 79-39783. (Illus.). 192p. 1972. 23.50 o.p. (ISBN 0-691-08114-X); pap. 8.95 o.p. (ISBN 0-691-08117-4). Princeton U Pr.

Hybridomas & Cellular Immortality. Ed. by Baldwin H. Tom & James P. Allison. LC 83-13847. 326p. 1983. 59.50x o.p. (ISBN 0-306-41467-8, Plenum Pr). Plenum Pub.

Hyde & Seek. Benjamin Wolff. 176p. 1984. pap. 2.75 o.p. (ISBN 0-380-88757-6, 88757-6). Avon.

Hyde in Deep Cover. Benjamin Wolff. 144p. 1985. pap. 2.95 o.p. (ISBN 0-380-89648-6). Avon.

Hyde Park Murder. Elliott Roosevelt. 390p. 1986. lib. bdg. 16.95 o.p. (ISBN 0-8161-3991-1, Large Print Bks). G K Hall.

Hyde Place. Virginia Coffman. LC 74-80704. 1974. 7.95 o.p. (ISBN 0-87795-086-5, Arbor Hse). Morrow.

HYDRA-C.mmp: An Experimental Computer System. W. A. Wulf et al. (Advanced Computer Science Ser.). (Illus.). 351p. 1981. text ed. 55.95x o.p. (ISBN 0-07-072120-3). McGraw.

Hydra Conspiracy. Philip Kirk. (Butler Ser.: No. 1). 1979. pap. 1.75 o.p. (ISBN 0-8439-0655-3, Pub. by Leisure Bks CT). Dorchester Pub Co.

Hydra Monster. Lee Falk. 1973. pap. 0.75 o.p. (ISBN 0-380-01275-8, 17061). Avon.

Hydration & Intermolecular Interaction: Infrared Investigations with Polyelectrolyte Membranes. George Zundell. 1970. 79.00 o.p. (ISBN 0-12-782850-8). Acad Pr.

Hydraulic & Excavation Tables. 11th ed. 350p. 1957. pap. 13.00 o.p. (S/N 024-003-00161-9). USGPO.

Hydraulic & Pneumatic Operation of Machines. H. C. Town. (Illus.). 192p. (ISBN 0-8022-1733-8). Philos Lib.

Hydraulic Cement Pastes, Their Structure & Properties: Proceedings of the University of Sheffield Conference, April 8-9, 1976. University of Sheffield Conference Staff. (Illus.). 1976. pap. 32.50x o.p. (ISBN 0-7210-1047-4, Pub. by C & CA London). Scholium Intl.

Hydraulic Control Systems: Design & Analysis of the Dynamics. P. Dransfield. (Lecture Notes in Control & Information Sciences Ser.: Vol. 33). 227p. 1981. pap. 18.00 o.p. (ISBN 0-387-10890-4). Springer-Verlag.

Hydraulic Engineering. Ed. by Robert M. Regan. 1226p. 1987. 92.00x o.p. (ISBN 0-87262-610-5). Am Soc Civil Eng.

Hydraulic Forging Presses. 3rd ed. E. Mueller. (Illus.). 1969. 56.00 o.p. (ISBN 0-387-04286-5). Springer-Verlag.

Hydraulic Mechanisms in Automation. J. Prokes. 334p. 1977. 84.25 o.p. (ISBN 0-444-99829-2). Elsevier.

Hydraulic Problems Solved by Stochastic Methods. Ed. by Peder Hjorth et al. LC 77-78941. 1977. 18.00 o.p. (ISBN 0-918334-22-5). WRP.

Hydraulic Servo-Mechanisms & their Applications. 130p. 1970. 33.75x o.p. (ISBN 0-318-21259-5, Pub. by Trade & Tech England). Gower Pub Co.

Hydraulic Structures, 2 vols. M. Grishin. 732p. 1982. 15.45 o.p. (ISBN 0-8285-2448-3, Pub. by Mir Pubs USSR). Imported Pubns.

Hydraulic Systems Analysis. J. Stringer. LC 75-25885. 173p. 1976. 29.00 o.p. (ISBN 0-470-83377-7, JW). Krieger.

Hydraulic Transport of Solids by Pipelines. A. G. Bain & S. T. Bonnington. 1971. 65.00 o.p. (ISBN 0-08-015778-5). Pergamon.

Hydraulics for Operators. rev. ed. W. Elgar Brown. 145p. 1985. pap. text ed. 19.95 o.p. (ISBN 0-250-40650-0). Butterworth.

Hydrides for Energy Storage: Proceedings of an International Symposium Held in Norway, Aug. 1977. Ed. by A. F. Andresen & A. Maeland. 1978. 140.00 o.p. (ISBN 0-08-022715-5). Pergamon.

Hydrocarbon Control Feasibility: Its Impact on Air Quality. Air Pollution Control Association Specialty Conference, New York, 1977. 160p. 1977. 10.00 o.p. (ISBN 0-318-12261-8, SP-23); members 8.00 o.p. (ISBN 0-318-12262-6). Air & Waste.

Hydrocarbon Fuel Cell Technology: A Symposium. Ed. by Bernard S. Baker. (Illus.). 1966. 98.50 o.p. (ISBN 0-12-074250-0). Acad Pr.

Hydrocarbons & Halogenated Hydrocarbons in the Aquatic Environment. Ed. by B. K. Afghan & D. Mackay. LC 79-26462. (Environmental Science Research Ser.: Vol. 16). 600p. 1980. 95.00x o.p. (ISBN 0-306-40329-3, Plenum Pr). Plenum Pub.

Hydroelectric Engineering for Civil Engineers, Vol. 8. S. Leliavsky. (Illus.). 250p. 1983. 49.95 o.p. (ISBN 0-412-22530-1, NO. 6687, Chapman & Hall). Routledge Chapman & Hall.

Hydroelectricity Prospects in the New Energy Situation: Proceedings of a Symposium of the Committee on Electric Power of the United Nations Commission for Europe, Athens, Greece, Nov. 5-9, 1979. United Nations Economic Commission for Europe, Geneva, Switzerland. LC 80-40819. 530p. 1981. 170.00 o.p. (ISBN 0-08-025702-X). Pergamon.

Hydrogen & Deuterium, 2 Vols. Young. (IUPAC Solubility Data Ser.: Vol. 5 & 6). 670p. 1981. 220.00 o.p. (ISBN 0-08-023927-7). Pergamon.

Hydrogen Bonding by C-H Groups. R. D. Green. LC 74-11310. 207p. 1974. 62.95 o.p. (ISBN 0-470-32478-3). Halsted Pr.

Hydrogen Effects in Metals: Proceedings of a Meeting held at Moran, Wyoming, 1980. Ed. by I. M. Bernstein & Anthony W. Thompson. (Illus.). 1059p. 55.00 o.p. (ISBN 0-89520-378-2); member 32.00 o.p. (ISBN 0-317-36230-5); student members 20.00 o.p. (ISBN 0-317-36231-3). ASM.

Hydrogen Energy Process IV: Proceedings of the World Hydrogen Energy Conference, 4th, Pasadena, CA, June 13-17, 1982. World Hydrogen Energy Conference Staff & T. N. Veziroglu. Ed. by W. D. Van Vorst et al. (Advances in Hydrogen Energy Ser.: No. 3). 2000p. 1982. 515.00 o.p. (ISBN 0-08-028699-2). Pergamon.

Hydrogen Energy Progress: Proceedings of the World Conference, 3rd, Tokyo, Japan, June 23-26, 1980, 4 vols. World Hydrogen Energy Conference Staff et al. Ed. by T. N. Veziroglu et al. LC 80-40559. (Advances in Hydrogen Energy Ser.: 2). (Illus.). 2500p. 1981. 525.00 set o.p. (ISBN 0-08-024729-6). Pergamon.

Hydrogen Energy Progress V: Proceedings of the 5th World Hydrogen Energy Conference, Toronto, Canada, 15-20 July 1984, 4 vols. Ed. by T. N. Veziroglu & J. B. Taylor. (Advances in Hydrogen Energy Ser.: No.4). 1968p. 1984. 480.00 o.p. (ISBN 0-08-030953-4, Intl Assn Hydro Energy). Pergamon.

Hydrogen Energy System: Proceedings of the World Conference, 2nd, Zurich, Aug. 1978, 5 Vols. World Hydrogen Energy Conference Staff. Ed. by T. N. Veziroglu & W. Seifritz. LC 78-40507. 1979. Set. 645.00 o.p. (ISBN 0-08-023224-8). Pergamon.

Hydrogen in Metals, 3 vols. International Association for Hydrogen Energy Staff. 1977. Set. 735.00 o.p. (ISBN 0-08-022108-4). Pergamon.

Hydrogen in Metals I: Basic Properties. Ed. by G. Alefeld & J. Voelkl. (Topics in Applied Physics Ser.: Vol. 28). (Illus.). 1978. 64.00 o.p. (ISBN 0-387-08705-2). Springer-Verlag.

Hydrogen: Proceedings of the World Hydrogen Energy Conference Papers on Today, Tomorrow & Beyond, 4th, CA, June 13-17, 1982. World Hydrogen Energy Conference Staff & T. N. Veziroglu. 132p. 1983. pap. 55.00 o.p. (ISBN 0-08-031139-3). Pergamon.

Hydrogen Systems: Proceedings of the Beijing International Symposium on Hydrogen Systems, Beijing, China, 7-11 May 1985. Ed. by T. N. Veziroglu et al. 1136p. 1986. 280.00 o.p. (ISBN 0-08-033453-9). Pergamon.

Hydrological Techniques for Upstream Conservation. Ed. by S. H. Kunkle & J. L. Thames. (Conservation Guides: No. 2). 145p. (Eng. & Fr., 2nd Printing 1979). 1976. pap. 9.50 o.p. (ISBN 92-5-100115-4, F742, FAO). UNIPUB.

Hydrology. A. J. Raudkivi. 1979. 115.00 o.p. (ISBN 0-08-024261-8). Pergamon.

Hydrology & Water Resources, 1982. 215p. (Orig.). 1982. pap. text ed. 37.50x o.p. (ISBN 0-85825-165-5, Pub. by Inst Engineering Australia). Gower Pub Co.

Hydrology in Practice. Elizabeth M. Shaw. 1983. 48.95 o.p. (ISBN 0-442-30565-6). Van Nos Reinhold.

Hydrometallurgy: Proceedings. Society of Mining Engineers of AIME, 1973. LC 72-88874. 30.00x o.p. (ISBN 0-89520-017-1). SMM&E Inc.

Hydrometallurgy-Research, Development & Plant Practice: Proceedings of the AIME Annual Meeting, Atlanta, 1983. Ed. by K. Osseo-Asare & J. D. Miller. (Illus.). 1020p. 55.00 o.p. (ISBN 0-89520-456-8); members 32.00 o.p. (ISBN 0-317-36306-9); student members 16.00 o.p. (ISBN 0-317-36307-7). ASM.

Hydronautics. Ed. by Herman E. Sheets & Victor T. Boatwright. 1970. 75.50 o.p. (ISBN 0-12-639150-5). Acad Pr.

Hydroponic Food Production: A Definitive Guide to Soilless Culture. 3rd ed. Howard M. Resh. LC 86-32572. (Illus.). 384p. 1987. text ed. 29.95 o.p. (ISBN 0-88007-160-5). Woodbridge Pr.

Hydroponic Gardening: The Magic of Hydroponics for the Home Gardener. Raymond Bridwell. LC 72-86151. (Illus.). 224p. 1972. 8.95 o.p. (ISBN 0-912800-00-3); pap. 7.95 o.p. (ISBN 0-912800-09-7). Woodbridge Pr.

Hydrostatic Tests, Module 26-3. (Nondestructive Examination Techniques I Ser.). (Illus.). 36p. 1979. spiral bdg. 7.00x o.p. (ISBN 0-87683-092-0). GP Pub.

Hygiene Standards of Chrysotile Asbestos Dust. British Occupational Hygiene Society. 1968. pap. 3.05 o.p. (ISBN 0-08-012995-1). Pergamon.

Hyksos Period & the New Kingdom (1675-1080 B.C.) see Scepter of Egypt: A Background for the Study of Egyptian Antiquities in the Metropolitan Museum of Art.

Hymns & Human Life. Eric Routley. 346p. 1953. (ISBN 0-8022-1399-5). Philos Lib.

Hymns for the Drowning: Poems for Vishnu by Nammalvar. Tr. by A. K. Rananujan from Tamil. LC 81-47151. (Princeton Library of Asian Translations). 145p. 1982. 23.50 o.p. (ISBN 0-691-06492-X); pap. 8.00 o.p. (ISBN 0-691-01385-3). Princeton U Pr.

Hymns, How to Sing Them. Ed. by Mandus A. Egge & Janet Moede. (Orig.). 1966. pap. 1.75 o.p. (ISBN 0-8066-0634-7, 11-9204, Augsburg). Augsburg Fortress.

Hymns of Hermes. Hermes Trismegistos. Tr. by G. R. S. Mead from Gr. 84p. (Orig.). 1985. pap. 4.00 o.p. (ISBN 0-933999-57-7). Phanes Pr.

Hymns of Luke's Infancy Narratives: Their Origin, Meaning & Significance. Stephen Farris. (JSoT Supplement Ser.: No. 44). 225p. pap. text ed. 14.95x o.s.i. (Pub. by JSOT Pr England). Eisenbrauns.

Hymns to the Night. 2nd ed. Novalis, pseud. Tr. by Dick Higgins from Ger. LC 84-4402. 56p. 1984. 12.50 o.p. (ISBN 0-914232-67-3); pap. 5.95 o.s.i. (ISBN 0-914232-66-5). McPherson & Co.

Hypatia, Issue No. 2. Ed. by A. Al-Hibri. 100p. 1985. pap. 19.25 o.p. (ISBN 0-08-031851-7). Pergamon.

Hypatia: Essays in Classics, Comparative Literature, & Philosophy. Ed. by Ulrich Goldsmith et al. LC 85-72021. 1985. 25.00x o.p. (ISBN 0-87081-156-8). Univ Pr Colo.

Hypatia; or, New Foes with an Old Face: 1853. Charles Kingsley. Ed. by Robert L. Wolff. (Victorian Fiction Ser.). 1975. lib. bdg. 73.00 o.p. (ISBN 0-8240-1571-1). Garland Pub.

Hyper- & Hypoglycemia. LaDean Griffin. 16p. Date not set. pap. 2.95 o.p. (ISBN 0-913923-27-3). Woodland UT.

Hyperactive Child. Domeena C. Renshaw. 1975. pap. 6.70 o.p. (ISBN 0-316-74030-6). Little.

Hyperactive Child & Stimulant Drugs. James J. Bosco & Stanley S. Robin. LC 76-57934. 1977. lib. bdg. 20.00x o.s.i. (ISBN 0-226-06661-4). U of Chicago Pr.

Hyperactive Children: The Social Ecology of Identification & Treatment. Ed. by Carol K. Whalen & Barbara Henker. LC 80-324. 1980. 29.95 o.p. (ISBN 0-12-745950-2). Acad Pr.

Hyperactivity: Current Issues, Research & Theory. 2nd ed. Dorothea M. Ross & Shella A. Ross. LC 81-19780. (Personality Processes Ser.). 491p. 1982. 48.95 o.p. (ISBN 0-471-06331-2, Pub. by Wiley-Interscience). Wiley.

Hyperbaric Diving Systems & Thermal Protection. Ed. by C. E. Johnson. (OED: Vol. 6). 156p. 1978. 24.00 o.p. (ISBN 0-317-33544-8, H00134); members 12.00 o.p. (ISBN 0-317-33545-6). ASME.

Hypercycle: A Principle of Natural Self-Organization. M. Eigen & P. Schuster. 1979. 14.00 o.p. (ISBN 0-387-09293-5). Springer-Verlag.

Hyperfine Interactions. Arthur J. Freeman & Richard B. Frankel. 1967. 99.50 o.p. (ISBN 0-12-266750-6). Acad Pr.

Hyperfunctions & Theoretical Physics: Proceedings of the Symposium, Nice, 1973. Symposium, Nice Staff. Ed. by F. L. Pham. (Lecture Notes in Mathematics Ser.: Vol. 449). iv, 218p. 1975. pap. 16.00 o.p. (ISBN 0-387-07151-2). Springer-Verlag.

Hypergraphics User's Guide: Apple II Version. Thomas C. Irby & Darrell L. Ward. 1983. pap. text ed. 19.95 o.p. (ISBN 0-07-068143-0). McGraw.

Hyperinflation: How You Can Come Out Ahead & Your Personal Financial Success Program. John Kamin. 32p. 1977. 5.00 o.p. (ISBN 0-911353-04-6). Forecaster Pub.

Hyperinflation Service. McGraw.

Hypersonic Flow Research, PAAS7. Ed. by Frederick R. Riddell. LC 62-11318. (Illus.). 758p. 1962. 69.50 o.p. (ISBN 0-317-36830-3). AIAA.

Hypertension. 2nd ed. Julian T. Hart. (Library of General Practice Ser.). 296p. 1987. text ed. 28.00 o.p. (ISBN 0-443-01665-8). Churchill.

Hypertension. Ed. by Jean Robinson & Barbara McVan. LC 84-1315. (Nursing Now Ser.: Vol. 2). 136p. 1984. text ed. 13.95 o.p. (ISBN 0-916730-77-8). Springhouse Pub.

Hypertension: Mechanisms & Management. Ed. by P. S. Kincaid-Smith & J. A. Whitworth. 200p. 1982. text ed. 18.50 o.p. (Pub by Adis Pr Australia). Year Bk Med.

Hypertension: Physiological Basis & Treatment. Ed. by Helen H. Ong & John C. Lewis. 1984. 45.50 o.p. (ISBN 0-12-526850-5). Acad Pr.

Hypertension Research: Methods & Models. Radzialowski. (Modern Pharmacology-Toxicology Ser.: Vol. 19). 600p. 1982. 85.00 o.p. (ISBN 0-8247-1344-3). Dekker.

Hypertension, Steroid & Mineral Metabolsim: Festschrift to Frederic C. Bartter. Ed. by James C. Chan. (Journal: Nephron: Vol. 23, No. 2). (Illus.). 1979. pap. 24.75 o.p. (ISBN 3-8055-3001-3). S Karger.

Hypertension: The Renal Basis. Ed. by David B. Gordon. LC 79-6598. (Benchmark Papers in Human Physiology Ser.: Vol. 13). 448p. 1982. 61.95 o.p. (ISBN 0-87933-356-1). Van Nos Reinhold.

Hypertensive Disorders in Pregnancy. Ed. by Fritz Beller & Ian MacGillivray. LC 78-24680. (Illus.). 108p. 1979. text ed. 18.50 o.p. (ISBN 0-88416-262-1). Year Bk Med.

Hyperuricaemia & Gout in Clinical Practice. Bryan T. Emmerson. 174p. 1982. text ed. 18.50 o.p. (ISBN 0-86792-006-8). Year Bk Med.

Hypno Weight Control: How to Lose Weight & Discover Yourself Through Self-Hypnosis. Frank Di Tullo. LC 73-91093. 1974. 7.50 o.p. (ISBN 0-682-47853-9, Banner). Exposition-Phoenix.

Hypnos: Massimo Scolari Works 1980-1986. Massimo Scolari et al. LC 86-82944. (Illus.). 100p. (Orig.). 1987. pap. 20.00 o.p. (ISBN 0-8478-0791-6). Rizzoli Intl.

Hypnosex: Sexual Joy Through Self-Hypnosis. Daniel L. Araoz & Robert T. Bleck. 1983. 5.95 o.p. (ISBN 0-87795-466-6, Arbor Hse). Morrow.

Hypnosex: Sexual Joy Through Self-Hypnosis. Daniel L. Araoz & Robert T. Bleek. LC 81-71661. 1982. 12.95 o.p. (ISBN 0-87795-367-8, Arbor Hse). Morrow.

Hypnosis at Its Bicentennial. Ed. by F. H. Frankel & H. Zamansky. LC 78-16605. 320p. 1978. 42.50x o.p. (ISBN 0-306-40029-4, Plenum Pr). Plenum Pub.

Hypnosis in Anaesthesiology: Proceedings. European Congress of Anaesthesiology of the World Federation of Societies of Anaesthesiologists, 1st, Vienna, 1962. Ed. by J. Lassner. (Anaesthesiology & Resuscitation Ser.: Vol. 2). 1964. pap. 14.20 o.p. (ISBN 0-387-03166-9). Springer-Verlag.

Hypnosis, Is It For You? Robert McDermott. (Outreach Ser.). 32p. 1982. pap. 1.25 o.p. (ISBN 0-8163-0481-5). Pacific Pr Pub Assn.

Hypnosis: Its Nature & Therapeutic Uses. H. B. Gibson. LC 77-92821. 1980. 8.95 o.p.; pap. 4.95 o.s.i. (ISBN 0-8008-4043-7). Taplinger.

Hypnosis of Life. Roy Masters. LC 78-78158. 1978. pap. 9.95 o.p. Foun Human Under.

Hypnotic Investigation of Psychodynamic Processes. Ed. by Milton H. Erickson & Ernest Rossi. LC 79-15939. (Collected Papers of Milton H. Erickson on Hypnosis: Vol. 3). 367p. 1980. 31.95x o.p. (ISBN 0-470-26723-2). Halsted Pr.

Hypnotic Suggestion. S. J. Van Pelt. 96p. 1956. (ISBN 0-8022-1764-8). Philos Lib.

Hypnotic Susceptibility. Ernest R. Hilgard. 434p. 1965. text ed. 21.50 o.p. (ISBN 0-15-540523-3, HC). HarBraceJ.

Hypnotic Techniques for Increasing Self Esteem. Ed. by R. A. Steffenhagen. 268p. 1983. text ed. 29.50x o.s.i. (ISBN 0-8290-0775-X). Irvington.

Hypochondria: Toward a Better Understanding. Robert Meister. LC 79-8700. 1980. 12.95 o.s.i. (ISBN 0-8008-4044-5). Taplinger.

Hypoglycaemic Tumors. J. Laurent et al. 1971. 31.50 o.p. (ISBN 90-219-2029-8, Excerpta Medica). Elsevier.

Hypoglycin: Proceedings. Symposium, Kingston, Jamaica Staff. Ed. by Eccleston A. Kean. (PAABS Symposium Ser.). 1976. 60.50 o.p. (ISBN 0-12-404150-7). Acad Pr.

Hypothalamic Control of Lactation. F. G. Sulman. LC 70-125281. (Monographs on Endocrinology: Vol. 3). (Illus.). 1970. 46.00 o.p. (ISBN 0-387-04973-8). Springer-Verlag.

Hypothalamic Hormones: Chemistry, Physiology & Clinical Applications. Derek Gupta & Wolfgang Voelter. (Illus.). 758p. 1978. 75.30x o.p. (ISBN 3-527-25712-8). VCH Pubs.

Hypothalamic Hormones: Chemistry, Physiology, Pharmacology & Clinical Uses. M. Motta et al. (Serono Symposia Ser.). 1976. 65.50 o.p. (ISBN 0-12-509150-8). Acad Pr.

Hypothalamic Hormones: Structure, Synthesis, & Biological Activity. Derek Gupta & Wolfgang Voelter. (Illus.). 328p. 1975. 34.20x o.p. (ISBN 3-527-25589-3). VCH Pubs.

Hypothalamus. Webb Haymaker et al. (Illus.). 820p. 1969. 69.25x o.p. (ISBN 0-398-00810-8). C C Thomas.

Hypothalamus. Ed. by L. Martini et al. 1971. 99.00 o.p. (ISBN 0-12-475550-X). Acad Pr.

Hypothalmic Hormones. Ed. by J. R. Sowers. (Benchmark Papers in Human Physiology Ser.: Vol. 14). 368p. 1982. 52.95 o.p. (ISBN 0-87933-358-8). Van Nos Reinhold.

Hypothermia. Robert S. Pozoz & David O. Born. LC 82-3519. (Illus.). 224p. 1982. 14.95 o.p. (ISBN 0-8329-0127-X). New Century.

Hypothermia for Cardiovascular Surgery. Hitoshi Mohri & David H. Dillard. LC 81-82628. (Illus.). 140p. 1981. text ed. 21.50 o.p. (ISBN 0-89640-060-3). Igaku-Shoin.

Hypothermia in Neurosurgery: Proceedings. European Congress Of Neurosurgery - Rome - 1963. Ed. by P. E. Maspes & B. Hughes. (Illus.). 1963. pap. 55.50 o.p. (ISBN 0-387-80683-0). Springer-Verlag.

Hypothyroidism. John F. Hennessy. (Contemporary Patient Management Ser.). 1978. spiral 14.50 o.p. (ISBN 0-87488-898-0). Med Exam.

Hypoxia: Man at Altitude. Ed. by John R. Sutton & Charles S. Houston. LC 81-84773. (Illus.). 213p. (Orig.). 1982. pap. text ed. 24.95 o.p. (ISBN 0-86577-048-4). Thieme Med Pubs.

Hysterectomy & You. Delthia T. Ricks et al. (Illus.). 40p. 1985. pap. 2.00 o.p. (ISBN 0-317-59869-4). Budlong.

Hysteria Reflex & Instinct. Ernst Kretschmer. LC 60-13651. 176p. 1960. (ISBN 0-8022-0892-4). Philos Lib.

Hysteroscopy. Robert S. Neuwirth. LC 75-296. (Major Problems in Obstetrics & Gynecology Ser., Vol. 8). (Illus.). 116p. 1975. write for info. o.p. (ISBN 0-7216-6762-7). Saunders.

Hyte Maneuver. David Milton. 1989. pap. 3.95 o.p. Pinnacle MO.

I

I A H S International Symposium on Housing Problems, 1976: Proceedings, 2 vols. P. F. Rad. Ed. by P. F. Rad et al. 1977. pap. 125.00 o.p. (ISBN 0-08-022121-1). Pergamon.

I Almost Burned in Hell. Peggy Joan Fontenot. 1978. 5.50 o.p. (ISBN 0-682-49078-4). Exposition-Phoenix.

I Am a Fish. Geoffrey Bull. (Tell-Tale Bks.). (gr. k-2). 1975. 1.95 o.p. (ISBN 0-87508-876-7). Chr Lit.

I Am a Giant. Ivan Sherman. LC 74-22189. (gr. 5-8). 1975. 7.50 o.p. (ISBN 0-15-237983-5, HJ). HarBraceJ.

I Am a Sparrow. Geoffrey Bull. (Tell-Tale Bks.). (gr. k-2). 1975. 1.95 o.p. (ISBN 0-87508-880-5). Chr Lit.

I Am All. James Boulden. (Illus.). 72p. 1982. pap. 2.95 o.p. (ISBN 0-87516-481-1). DeVorss.

I Am an Orthodox Jew. Laura Greene. LC 78-14094. (Illus.). (gr. k-4). 1979. 5.95 o.p. (ISBN 0-03-044661-9). H Holt & Co.

I Am Blind & My Dog Is Dead. Sam Gross. (Illus.). 1978. pap. 3.95 o.p. (ISBN 0-380-40162-2, 57554-X). Avon.

I Am Curious (Yellow) Vilgot Sjoman. 1969. pap. 1.75 o.p. (ISBN 0-394-17133-0, B184, BC). Grove.

I Am Eskimo: Aknik My Name. Paul Green & Abbe Abbott. LC 59-15891. (Illus., Orig.). 1959. pap. 3.95 o.p. (ISBN 0-88240-001-0). Alaska Northwest.

I Am Five! Peter Jarrette & Dorothy Rose. (Birthday Year Bks.). (Illus.). 24p. 1982. 3.80 o.s.i. (ISBN 0-671-44469-7, Little Simon). S&S.

I Am Four! Peter Jarrette & Dorothy Rose. (Birthday Year Bks.). (Illus.). 24p. 1982. 3.80 o.s.i. (ISBN 0-671-44468-9, Little Simon). S&S.

I Am Joseph. Barbara Cohen. LC 79-20001. (Illus.). (gr. 2 up). 1980. 12.95 o.p. (ISBN 0-688-41933-X); PLB 12.88 o.p. (ISBN 0-688-51933-4). Lothrop.

I Am Learning to Live Because You Must Die: A Hospital Diary. Cordula Zickgraf. Tr. by David L. Scheidt from Ger. LC 80-2371. 144p. 1981. pap. 6.95 o.p. (ISBN 0-8006-1434-8, 1-1434, Fortress). Augsburg Fortress.

I Am of the Fourth Gospel: A Study in Johannine Usage & Thought. Philip B. Harner. Ed. by John Reumann. LC 72-123506. (Facet Bks.). 72p. (Orig.). 1970. pap. 1.00 o.p. (ISBN 0-8006-3060-2, 1-3060, Fortress). Augsburg Fortress.

I Am One: Prayers for Singles. Carol Greene. LC 85-23015. 112p. (Orig.). 1985. pap. 6.50 o.p. (ISBN 0-8066-2186-9, 10-3191, Augsburg). Augsburg Fortress.

I Am Somebody. Laura Greene. LC 79-22288. (Social Value Ser.). (Illus.). 32p. (gr. k-3). 1980. PLB 11.27 o.p. (ISBN 0-516-01476-5); pap. 3.95 o.p. (ISBN 0-516-41476-3). Childrens.

I Am Somebody: The True Story of a Black U. S. Navy Frogman. Bernard Waddell. LC 85-60456. (Illus.). 253p. 1986. 17.95 o.p. (ISBN 0-933341-04-0). Quinlan Pr.

I Am the Cat. Ed. by Lee B. Hopkins. LC 81-2609. (Illus.). 40p. (gr. 4 up). 1981. 10.95 o.p. (ISBN 0-15-237987-8, HJ). HarBraceJ.

I Am the Lord Thy Sex: An Interpretation of Genesis & Exodus. Arlen J. Jens. 1975. 5.00 o.p. (ISBN 0-682-48377-X). Exposition-Phoenix.

I Am the Sun. Maurice Kenny. 1979. 1.00 o.p. (ISBN 0-934834-03-2). White Pine.

I Am the Vine. Joel S. Goldsmith. 1972. pap. 1.00 o.p. (ISBN 0-87516-138-3). DeVorss.

I Am Three! Peter Jarrette & Dorothy Rose. (Birthday Year Bks.). (Illus.). 24p. 1982. 3.80 o.s.i. (ISBN 0-671-44467-0, Little Simon). S&S.

I Am Two! Peter Jarrette & Dorothy Rose. (Birthday Year Bks.). (Illus.). 24p. 1982. 3.80 o.s.i. (ISBN 0-671-44466-2, Little Simon). S&S.

I Am Two from Kentucky: The Poetry of J. C. Kirby. J. C. Kirby. 1979. 6.00 o.p. (ISBN 0-682-49188-8). Exposition-Phoenix.

I Am Vidocq. Vincent McConnor. 416p. 1985. 16.95 o.p. (ISBN 0-396-08716-7). Dodd.

I Am Watching. Shirley Gibson. LC 73-75842. (House of Anansi Poetry Ser.: No. 26). 58p. 1973. 2.00 o.p. (ISBN 0-88784-126-0, Pub. by Hse Anansi Pr Canada); pap. 3.95 o.p. (ISBN 0-88784-026-4). U of Toronto Pr.

I Am What I Do: Contemplation & Human Experience. Barbara Doherty. 226p. 1982. pap. 9.95 o.p. (ISBN 0-88347-129-9). Thomas More.

I Am Who I Am. Phyllis Shaughnessy. LC 84-60422. 51p. 1984. pap. 6.95 o.p. (ISBN 0-89390-054-0). Resource Pubns.

I Am Yahweh. Walther Zimmerli. Ed. by Walter Brueggemann. Tr. by Doug Scott from Ger. LC 81-85326. 160p. 1982. 16.95 o.s.i. (ISBN 0-8042-0519-1, John Knox). Westminster John Knox.

I & Thou. Martin Buber. 14.75 o.p. (ISBN 0-8446-6219-4). Peter Smith.

I Ate the Whole Thing. Wm. Armstrong. (Armstrong Cartoon Ser.). (Illus.). 48p. (Orig.). 1973. pap. 1.00 o.p. (ISBN 0-913452-21-1). Jesuit Bks.

I. B. I. Guide Bearings. 9th ed. S. H. Friedman. LC 85-80852. 1440p. 1986. 120.00 o.p. (ISBN 0-916966-17-8). Interchange.

I Became Alone. Judith Thurman. LC 75-9589. (Illus.). 144p. (gr. 7 up). 1975. 6.95 o.p. (ISBN 0-689-30487-0, Atheneum). Macmillan.

I Believe: A Woman's Workshop on Relational Doctrine. Robert E. Webber. (Woman's Workshop Ser.). 160p. 1986. pap. 4.50 o.p. (ISBN 0-310-36701-8, 12214P). Zondervan.

I Believe in Mission. Mariano DiGangi. 1979. pap. 2.95 o.p. (ISBN 0-87552-255-6). Presby & Reformed.

I Believe in Satan's Downfall. Michael Green. (I Believe Ser.). 256p. (Orig.). 1981. pap. 7.95 o.p. (ISBN 0-8028-1892-7). Eerdmans.

I Believe in the Resurrection of the Body. Rubem Alves. Tr. by L. M. McCoy from Ger. & Port. LC 85-16246. 80p. 1986. pap. 4.95 o.p. (ISBN 0-8006-1885-8, 1-1885, Fortress). Augsburg Fortress.

I Believe: The Christian's Creed. Helmut Thielicke. Tr. by H. George Anderson & John W. Doberstein. LC 68-23991. 272p. (Orig.). 1968. pap. 5.50 o.p. (ISBN 0-8006-1027-X, 1-1027, Fortress). Augsburg Fortress.

I-C Test Equipment. Ed. by Rich Force. (Seventy-Three Test Equipment Library: Vol. 4). 136p. 1977. pap. text ed. 4.95 o.p. (ISBN 0-88006-013-1, LB7362). Wayne Green Ent.

I Came to the City: Essays & Comments on the Urban Scene. Michael E. Hurst. 1975. pap. 13.95 o.p. (ISBN 0-395-17016-8). HM.

I Can Be a Machinist. Stella Frederick. Ed. by S. Michele McFadden. (Reach High Career Awareness Ser.). (Illus.). (gr. 1-4). 1979. pap. text ed. 4.95x o.p. (ISBN 0-89262-020-X). Career Pub.

I Can Be a Marine Biologist. Stella Frederick. Ed. by S. Michele McFadden. (Reach High Career Awareness Ser.). (Illus.). (gr. 1-4). 1978. pap. 4.95x o.p. (ISBN 0-89262-018-8). Career Pub.

I Can Count the Petals of a Flower. John Wahl & Stacey Wahl. LC 76-17538. (Illus.). 32p. 1976. pap. 4.50 o.s.i. (ISBN 0-87353-061-6). NCTM.

I Can Get It for You Wholesale. Jerome Weidman. 1984. pap. 7.95 o.p. (ISBN 0-87795-604-9, Arbor Hse). Morrow.

I Can Go Home Again. Arthur G. Powell. LC 84-6935. 324p. 1984. Repr. of 1943 ed. 18.50 o.s.i. (ISBN 0-87152-398-1). Reprint.

I Can Help the Teacher: A Program for Training the Non-Academic Teacher Aide. Leola G. Hayes. 1977. pap. 3.00 o.p. (ISBN 0-682-48943-3). Exposition-Phoenix.

I Can Read Spanish. Penrose Colyer. (I Can Read Ser.). (gr. 2 up). 1981. PLB 9.40 o.p. (ISBN 0-531-04285-5). Watts.

I Can Talk to God Anytime, Anyplace. Jane B. Moncure. LC 82-7245. 32p. (ps-k). 1982. PLB 4.95 o.p. (ISBN 0-89693-205-2). Dandelion Hse.

I Can Tell You Anything, God. Hartwig Lohmann. Tr. by Ingalill H. Hjelm from Ger. LC 77-15237. 64p. 1978. pap. 1.95 o.p. (ISBN 0-8006-1324-4, 1-1324, Fortress). Augsburg Fortress.

I Can, You Can Too! Mamie McCullough. 224p. 1987. 14.95 o.p. (ISBN 0-8407-3068-3). Nelson.

I Can't Stay Long. Laurie Lee. LC 75-31902. 240p. 1976. 6.95 o.p. (ISBN 0-689-10695-5, Atheneum). Macmillan.

I Ching & Its Associations. Diana F. Hook. (Illus.). 1980. 15.95 o.p. (ISBN 0-7100-0506-7); pap. 7.95 o.p. (ISBN 0-7100-0507-5). Routledge Chapman & Hall.

I Ching & Mankind. Diana F. Hook. 1975. 12.95 o.p. (ISBN 0-7100-8058-1). Routledge Chapman & Hall.

I Ching & You. Diana F. Hook. 160p. 1988. pap. 9.95 o.p. (ISBN 1-85063-098-4). Routledge Chapman & Hall.

I Ching & You. Diane F. Hook. 160p. 1985. pap. 8.95 o.p. (ISBN 0-7100-8042-5). Routledge Chapman & Hall.

I Ching: The Oracle. Kerson Huang. 1987. pap. 6.95 o.p. (ISBN 0-317-56868-X). Workman Pub.

I Come As a Thief. Louis Auchincloss. 1972. 6.95 o.p. (ISBN 0-395-13939-2). HM.

I Cook As I Please. Marcand H. Kreish. 1978. 4.00 o.p. (ISBN 0-682-48854-2, Banner). Exposition-Phoenix.

I Could Have Been a Contender, or the Other Book of Lists. Margaret Oberman & Doug Steckler. 1979. pap. 2.95 o.p. (ISBN 0-380-46383-0, 46383). Avon.

I Cry When the Sun Goes Down: The Story of Herman Wrice. Jean H. Berg. LC 75-20387. (Illus.). (gr. 3-6). 1975. 6.95 o.s.i. (ISBN 0-664-32570-X, Westminster). Westminster John Knox.

I. D. B. I. Guide Drive Belts. 4th ed. S. H. Friedman. LC 85-80851. 768p. 1986. 90.00 o.p. (ISBN 0-916966-15-1). Interchange.

I. D. L. I. Guide Drive Lines. S. H. Friedman. LC 85-80850. 736p. 1986. 90.00 o.p. (ISBN 0-916966-14-3). Interchange.

I Dedicate This Song to You. Judith Weber. 133p. 1986. pap. 2.25 o.p. (ISBN 0-671-54351-2). Archway.

I Do Not Like It When My Friend Comes to Visit. Ivan Sherman. LC 73-75326. (gr. k-1). 1973. 8.95 o.p. (ISBN 0-15-238000-0, HJ). HarBraceJ.

I Do Windows. Neal Stanford. 48p. 1982. 6.00 o.p. (ISBN 0-682-49865-3). Exposition-Phoenix.

I Don't Know Where I'm Going, but I Sure Ain't Lost. Jess Lair. 256p. 1983. pap. 3.50 o.p. (ISBN 0-449-20056-6, Crest). Fawcett.

I Don't Need to Know Your Name to Be Your Friend. Conrad Weiser. LC 72-75658. (Center Bks). (Illus.). 129p. 1972. pap. 0.50 o.p. (ISBN 0-8006-0124-6, Fortress). Augsburg Fortress.

I Don't Want to Be Like Her. Marcia Kruchten. 128p. (gr. 5-8). 1986. 2.25 o.s.i. (ISBN 0-87406-064-8). Willowisp Pr.

I, Giorghos: A Novel. William J. Lederer. LC 83-42670. 1984. 12.45 o.p. (ISBN 0-393-01788-5). Norton.

I Gotta Be Free. Ruth Hallman. LC 77-23347. (Hiway Bk.: A High Interest-Low Reading Level Book). 92p. (gr. 7 up). 1977. 8.95 o.s.i. (ISBN 0-664-32619-6, Westminster). Westminster John Knox.

I Gotta Be Me! Tammy Baker & Cliff Dudley. LC 78-64670. 1978. 6.95 o.p. (ISBN 0-89221-048-6). New Leaf.

I Greet the Dawn: Poem of Paul Laurence Dunbar. Ashley Bryan. LC 77-21232. (Illus.). (gr. 6 up). 1978. 7.95 o.p. (ISBN 0-689-30613-X, Atheneum). Macmillan.

I Hate It. Miriam Schlein. Ed. by Caroline Rubin. LC 78-1744. (Self-Starter Bks.). (Illus.). (ps-2). 1978. PLB 9.75 o.p. (ISBN 0-8075-3505-2). A Whitman.

I Hate to Cook Almanack: A Book of Days. Peg Bracken. LC 76-20512. 1976. 8.95 o.p. (ISBN 0-15-144050-6). HarBraceJ.

I Hate Witnessing Leader's Guide. Rob Burkhart. LC 84-18165. 64p. 1985. pap. 3.95 o.s.i. (ISBN 0-8307-1011-6, 6101987). Regal.

I Have Been Before the Judgement Seat of Christ: A Religious Autobiography. Gladys Cuss. 189p. 1980. 7.95 o.p. (ISBN 0-682-49521-2). Exposition-Phoenix.

I Have Chosen You. Shirley Sealy. 192p. (Orig.). (YA) (gr. 11 up). 1982. pap. 5.95 o.p. (ISBN 0-88042-004-9, 8404). Pubs Bk Sales.

I Have Loved You Already. Princess Orelia Benskina. 1975. 3.50 o.p. (ISBN 0-682-47871-7). Exposition-Phoenix.

I Have Seen the Stars. Harold W. Brigham. 64p. 1987. 6.95 o.p. (ISBN 0-8062-2962-4). Carlton.

I Haven't a Thing to Wear! Judith Keith. 320p. 1981. pap. 6.95 o.p. (ISBN 0-380-55574-3, 62604-7). Avon.

I Hear America Talking. Stuart B. Flexner. 1979. pap. 8.95 o.p. (ISBN 0-671-24994-0, Touchstone Bks). S&S.

I Hear Them Calling My Name: A Journey Through the New South. Chet Fuller. 320p. 1981. 12.95 o.p. (ISBN 0-395-30528-4). HM.

I Hear Two Voices, God! Donald Deffner. LC 12-2817. 1983. pap. 2.08 o.p. (ISBN 0-570-03882-0). Concordia.

I Hear You Calling Me. Lily McCormack. LC 75-20980. (Illus.). 201p. 1975. Repr. of 1949 ed. lib. bdg. 22.50x o.p. (ISBN 0-8371-8350-2, MCIH). Greenwood.

I Hear You're in Real Estate! Karl Breckenridge. 144p. (Orig.). 1988. pap. 9.75 o.p. Western Bk Journ.

I Hid in the Reeds. Geoffrey Bull. (Hide & Seek Bks.). (gr. k-2). 1975. 1.95 o.p. (ISBN 0-87508-885-6). Chr Lit.

I Hurried, I Waited: A Belgian Odyssey. Dorothy F. Youngblood. 220p. 1987. text ed. 16.95 o.p. (ISBN 0-682-40323-7). Exposition-Phoenix.

I Hurt Inside: A Christian Psychologist Helps You Understand & Overcome Feelings of Fear, Frustration, & Failure. Ralph C. Underwager. LC 72-90265. (Study of Generations Paperbacks Ser). 104p. 1973. pap. 4.50 o.p. (ISBN 0-8066-1312-2, Augsburg); study guide 00.30 o.p. (10-3186). Augsburg Fortress.

I Hurt Too Much for a Band-Aid. Kenneth J. Olson. Ed. by Helen Lovell. LC 79-6517. 144p. (Orig.). 1980. pap. 4.95 o.p. (ISBN 0-89019-072-0). Norwalk Pr.

I Is the Body of Life. Da Free John. 1982. pap. 12.95 o.s.i. (ISBN 0-913922-60-9). Dawn Horse Pr.

I, Judas. Taylor Caldwell & Jess Stearn. LC 77-5518. 1977. 10.95 o.p. (ISBN 0-689-10806-0, Atheneum). Macmillan.

I Just Saw Jesus, Still Doing Miracles, Still Touching Lives. Paul Eshleman. 224p. (Orig.). 1985. pap. 6.95 o.p. (ISBN 0-89840-100-3). Heres Life.

I Knew Blessed Maximilian. 2nd ed. Juventyn M. Mlodozeniec. pap. cancelled o.s.i. (ISBN 0-911988-09-2). AMI Pr.

I Know a Lot of Things. Ann Rand & Paul Rand. LC 56-5576. (Illus.). (ps-1). 1956. 6.95 o.p. (ISBN 0-15-243281-7, HJ). HarBraceJ.

I Know a Lot of Things. Paul Rand & Ann Rand. LC 56-5576. (Illus.). 32p. (ps-1). 1973. pap. 1.35 o.p. (ISBN 0-15-644400-3, VoyB). HarBraceJ.

I Know God Loves Me. Jill Wolf. (Illus.). 24p. (gr. 2-6). 1984. pap. 1.95 o.p. (ISBN 0-89954-288-3). Antioch Pub Co.

I Know His Touch. Luba Bershadsky & Ada Millington. LC 83-72042. 192p. (Orig.). 1984. pap. 6.95 o.p. (ISBN 0-89107-299-3, Crossway Bks). Good News.

I Know It When I See It: Pornography, Violence, & Public Sensitivity. Michael Leach. LC 75-23017. 1975. 5.95 o.s.i. (ISBN 0-664-20800-2, Westminster). Westminster John Knox.

I Know Some Spinners Weave My End. Caleb Roosevelt. 80p. 1986. 8.95 o.p. (ISBN 0-932020-43-7). Seven Locks Pr.

I, Koch: A Decidedly Unauthorized Biography of the Mayor of New York City. Arthur Browne et al. 384p. 1985. 18.95 o.p. (ISBN 0-396-08647-0). Dodd.

I Launch at Paradise: A Consideration of John Donne, Poet & Preacher. Frederick A. Rowe. LC 65-84641. 1964. 10.00x o.p. A R Allenson.

I Lay Down My Life. Harry Cargas. 1964. 2.50 o.p. (ISBN 0-8198-0063-5); pap. 1.50 o.s.i. (ISBN 0-8198-0064-3). Dghtrs St Paul.

I Learn to Pray. Marian Bennett. (Wipe-Clean Bks.). (Illus.). 12p. (ps). 1985. pap. 1.39 o.p. (ISBN 0-87239-953-2, 3513). Standard Pub.

I Like It Here. Kingsley Amis. 1958. 4.50 o.p. (ISBN 0-15-152097-6). HarBraceJ.

I Like Vegetables. Sharon Lerner. LC 67-15698. (Nature Books for Young Readers). (Illus.). (gr. 3-6). 1967. PLB 5.95 o.p. (ISBN 0-8225-0260-7). Lerner Pubns.

I Live & Move. Dorothy Henderson. 1953. (ISBN 0-8022-0708-1). Philos Lib.

I Live in the World. William J. Fogleman. (Illus., Orig.). (gr. 7-9). 1967. pap. 3.45 o.p. (ISBN 0-8042-9290-6, John Knox). Westminster John Knox.

I Live under a Black Sun: A Novel. Edith Sitwell. LC 70-171419. 326p. 1973. Repr. lib. bdg. 22.50x o.p. (ISBN 0-8371-6260-2, SIBS). Greenwood.

I Look to the Mountain for Strength & Love. Mercita C. Nagle. 1980. 5.00 o.p. (ISBN 0-682-49548-4). Exposition-Phoenix.

I Love Lucy Book. Bart Andrews. LC 84-6033. (Illus.). 448p. 1985. pap. 11.95 o.s.i. (ISBN 0-385-19033-6, Dolp). Doubleday.

I Love My Baby Sister (Most of the Time) Elaine Edelman. LC 83-2563. (Illus.). 32p. (ps-1). 1984. 11.00 o.p. (ISBN 0-688-02245-6); lib. bdg. 11.88 o.p. (ISBN 0-688-02247-2). Lothrop.

I Love My Love. Mary Essex, pseud. 168p. 1988. lib. bdg. 19.95x o.s.i. (ISBN 0-7451-0812-1, Pub. by Chivers Pr UK). G K Hall.

I Love You. Marlee Alex & Ben Alex. 52p. 1983. 9.95 o.p. (ISBN 0-87123-262-6, 230262). Bethany Hse.

I Love You. Remy Charlip. 1981. pap. 1.50 o.p. (ISBN 0-380-53090-2, 53090-2). Avon.

I Love You, Mouse. John Graham. LC 78-6214. (Illus.). (ps-3). 1978. pap. 6.95 o.p. (ISBN 0-15-644106-3, VoyB). HarBraceJ.

I. M. A. Booksnoop's Amazing, Astounding, Astonishing Library Kit. Elaine Prizzi & Jeanne Hoffman. (gr. 5-8). 1982. pap. 10.95 o.p. (ISBN 0-8224-2253-0). D S Lake Pubs.

I, Mark: A Personal Encounter. Carl Walters, Jr. LC 78-52450. (Bible Speaks to Us Today Ser.). 144p. 1980. pap. 7.95 o.p. (ISBN 0-8042-0272-9, John Knox). Westminster John Knox.

I Married a Prince: A Cinderella Story from Hawaii. Myrtle King Kaapu. LC 76-40773. 1977. 10.00 o.p. (ISBN 0-682-48649-3). Exposition-Phoenix.

I Met a Man. John Ciardi. (Illus.). (gr. 2-4). 1961. PLB 8.95 o.p. (ISBN 0-395-18018-X). HM.

I Murdered My Love. Eddie H. Lee & Don Derivaux. 1986. 8.95 o.p. (ISBN 0-533-06893-2). Vantage.

I Never Played the Game. Howard Cosell & Peter Bonventre. 635p. 1986. lib. bdg. 19.95x o.p. (ISBN 0-8161-4110-X, Large Print Bks); pap. 11.95x o.p. (ISBN 0-8161-4111-8). G K Hall.

I Never Played the Game. Howard Cosell & Peter Bonventure. LC 85-11548. 1985. 18.95 o.p. (ISBN 0-688-04481-6). Morrow.

I Never Played the Game. Howard Cosell & Peter Bonvenure. 384p. 1986. pap. 4.50 o.p. (ISBN 0-380-70159-6). Avon.

I Never Promised You a Rose Garden. Hannah Green. LC 64-11018. 1964. 14.95 o.p. (ISBN 0-03-043725-3). H Holt & Co.

I Never Promised You an Apple Orchard. Charles M. Schulz. 1976. 3.95 o.s.i. (ISBN 0-03-017216-0). H Holt & Co.

I Once Knew an Indian Woman. Ebbitt Cutler. (Illus.). 80p. (gr. 7-12). 1973. 3.95 o.p. (ISBN 0-395-16044-8). HM.

I Paint What I See. Gahan Wilson. 1975. pap. 9.50 o.p. (ISBN 0-671-22031-4, Fireside). S&S.

I Paint with Words...Hope You Like My Pictures. Klyde. 1979. 4.00 o.p. (ISBN 0-682-49318-X). Exposition-Phoenix.

I Pittori Ala Corte Angionina Di Napoli, 1266-1414. Ferdinando Bologna, 1st. Ed. by Giuliano Briganti. LC 79-106768. (Saggi E Studi Di Storia Dell'arte). (Illus.). 802p. (Ital.). 1970. 87.50x o.s.i. (ISBN 0-271-00117-8). Pa St U Pr.

I Pledge Allegiance: Patriotism & the Bible. Paul S. Minear. LC 74-31489. 1975. pap. 2.95 o.s.i. (ISBN 0-664-24819-5, Westminster). Westminster John Knox.

I Prayed, He Answered. William L. Vaswig. LC 77-72457. 1977. pap. 6.95 o.p. (ISBN 0-8066-1589-3, 10-3189, Augsburg). Augsburg Fortress.

I. R. A. at War: An Illustrated History 1916 to the Present. Eamonn O'Doherty. (Illus.). 144p. 1986. pap. 21.95 o.p. (ISBN 0-85342-753-4, Pub. by Mercier Pr Ireland). Irish Bks Media.

I Remember Lindbergh. John Grierson. LC 77-76436. (Illus.). 192p. (gr. 7 up). 1977. 8.95 o.p. (ISBN 0-15-238895-8, HJ). HarBraceJ.

I Remember Mama: A Play in Two Acts. John Van Druten. LC 45-35067. 177p. 1945. 10.95 o.p. (ISBN 0-15-176661-4). HarBraceJ.

I Remember My Brother Morris. Irving Klein. 1978. 4.50 o.p. (ISBN 0-682-48992-1). Exposition-Phoenix.

I Remember Tall Ships. F. Brookesmith. (Illus.). 270p. 1982. pap. 20.00 o.p. (ISBN 0-87556-573-5). Saifer.

I, Robot. Isaac Asimov. 1984. pap. 3.50 o.p. (ISBN 0-345-32140-5). Ballantine.

I. S. I. Guide Seals. 6th ed. S. H. Friedman. LC 85-80849. 800p. 1986. 90.00 o.p. (ISBN 0-916966-16-X). Interchange.

I. S. Turgenev: Dvoryanskoye Gnezdo. Ed. by P. Waddington. 1969. 29.00 o.p. (ISBN 0-08-012923-4); pap. 14.25 o.p. (ISBN 0-08-012922-6). Pergamon.

I, Sami: Or Sixty-Five Years on the Road. Samuel Silverman. LC 78-15726. (Illus.). 170p. 1978. 1.95 o.s.i. (ISBN 0-915864-63-0). Academy Chi Pubs.

I Saw It in the Mirror by the Moonbeam. George E. Browne. 1980. 6.00 o.p. (ISBN 0-682-49546-8). Exposition-Phoenix.

I Saw the Holy Shroud. Peter M. Rinaldi. LC 83-71121. (Illus.). 112p. 1983. 4.95 o.s.i. (ISBN 0-89944-072-X); pap. 2.85 o.s.i. (ISBN 0-89944-069-X). Don Bosco Multimedia.

I Saw You from Afar: A Visit to the Bushmen of the Kalahari Desert. Marlin Perkins & Carol M. Perkins. LC 65-10479. (Illus.). (gr. 2-7). 1965. PLB 6.95 o.p. (ISBN 0-689-30011-5, Atheneum). Macmillan.

I See a Long Journey: Three Novellas. Rachel Ingalls. 144p. 1986. 14.70 o.s.i. (ISBN 0-671-62782-1). S&S.

I See Four. Mildred Krentel. (Illus.). (gr. 1-4). 1959. 2.50 o.p. (ISBN 0-87213-470-9). Loizeaux.

I Seek an Island. Karl H. Bolay. (Illus.). 48p. 1982. 5.00 o.p. (ISBN 0-682-49784-3). Exposition-Phoenix.

I Shall Not Be Moved! Sandi H. Querin. 1987. 6.75 o.p. (ISBN 0-8062-3014-2). Carlton.

I Should Care: The Sammy Cahn Story. Sammy Cahn. LC 74-80708. (Illus.). 1974. 8.95 o.p. (ISBN 0-87795-090-3, Arbor Hse). Morrow.

I Should Have Died. Philip Deane. LC 76-25896. 1977. 7.95 o.p. (ISBN 0-689-10766-8, Atheneum). Macmillan.

I Should Have Stayed Home. Horace McCoy. Ed. by Bruce S. Kupelnick. LC 76-52112. (Classics of Film Literature Ser.). 1978. lib. bdg. 21.00 o.p. (ISBN 0-8240-2883-X). Garland Pub.

I Skate! Margaret Faulkner. LC 79-15932. (Illus.). (gr. 3-7). 1979. 14.95 o.p. (ISBN 0-316-26002-9). Little.

I Sold Myself a Dream. Harry Henig. 1977. 10.00 o.p. (ISBN 0-682-48928-X). Exposition-Phoenix.

I Speak Basic to My Apple. 2nd ed. Jones. LC 85-7582. tchr's. manual 18.75 o.p. (ISBN 0-8104-6198-6); 10.95 o.p. (ISBN 0-8104-6199-4). Sams.

I Speak BASIC to My Computer. Jones. 1985. 10.95 o.p. (ISBN 0-8104-6170-6). Sams.

I Speak BASIC to My PET. Aubrey Jones. (I Speak BASIC Ser.). 224p. 1982. pap. text ed. 9.75 o.p. (ISBN 0-8104-6176-5); tchr's. manual 18.75 o.p.; exam set 15.00 o.p.; classroom set (tchr's. manual, 20 student texts & exam set) 200.00 o.p. Sams.

I Speak BASIC to My VIC. Aubrey B. Jones, Jr. (Illus.). 238p. 1983. student 9.75 o.p. (ISBN 0-8104-6169-2, 6169); tchr's manual 18.75 o.p. (ISBN 0-8104-6179-X, 6179); exam set 15.00 o.p.; classroom set (tchr's manual, 20 student texts and exam set) 200.00 o.p. Sams.

I Speak English. Ruth J. Colvin. 103p. 1980. pap. 7.75 o.p. (ISBN 0-930713-28-1). Lit Vol Am.

I Spy with My Little Eye. Lucille Ogle. (Illus.). 1970. text ed. 9.95 o.p. (ISBN 0-07-047548-2). McGraw.

I Stand by the Door. Helen S. Shoemaker. LC 66-20784. 1977. pap. 2.25 o.p. (ISBN 0-8499-4102-4, 4102-4). Word Bks.

I Stand Corrected. William Safire. 480p. 1986. 10.95 o.p. (ISBN 0-380-70049-2). Avon.

I Swear by Apollo. Agatha Young. 1975. pap. 1.50 o.p. (ISBN 0-380-00274-4, 22608). Avon.

I Take Thee, Serenity. Daisy Newman. LC 75-8984. 320p. 1975. 8.95 o.p. (ISBN 0-395-20551-4). HM.

I Take This Land. Richard Powell. 1985. pap. 2.95 o.p. (ISBN 0-89176-038-5, 6038). Mockingbird Bks.

I Thank You, Father: Peace-It's Wonderful. Princess Orelia Benskina. 1976. 4.00 o.p. (ISBN 0-682-48425-3). Exposition-Phoenix.

I, the President. Kenneth C. Walters. 1984. 11.95 o.p. (ISBN 0-533-05950-X). Vantage.

I Think I'm Having a Baby. Caryl Hansen. 112p. 1982. pap. 1.95 o.p. (ISBN 0-380-80564-2, 80564-2, Flare). Avon.

I Think This Is Where We Came in. Phyllis A. Wood. LC 75-33093. (Hiway Bk: A High Interest - Low Reading Level Book). 152p. 1976. 7.95 o.s.i. (ISBN 0-664-32582-3, Westminster). Westminster John Knox.

I Thought I Heard the City. Lilian Moore. LC 69-18964. (Illus.). (gr. 4-7). 1969. PLB 4.95 o.p. (ISBN 0-689-20623-2, Atheneum). Macmillan.

I, Too, Have Heard the Wind. Stephen Zografakis. 40p. 1987. 6.95 o.p. (ISBN 0-8062-2889-X). Carlton.

I, too, Shall Wear Purple. Eva M. Johnson. 288p. 1986. 12.95 o.p. (ISBN 0-8062-2977-2). Carlton.

I Walk & Talk with Angels: A True Life Story. Edward W. Oldring. 1978. 8.00 o.p. (ISBN 0-682-49067-9). Exposition-Phoenix.

I Walked by Night. Ed. by Lilias R. Haggard. (Illus.). 198p. 1981. 15.00 o.p. (ISBN 0-85115-046-2, Pub. by Boydell & Brewer). Longwood Pub Group.

I Walked Through the Valley of the Shadow of Alcoholism. Chester H. Purington. 1985. 6.00 o.p. (ISBN 0-682-40221-4). Exposition-Phoenix.

I Want a Brother or Sister. Astrid Lindgren. Tr. by Barbara Lucas from Swedish. (Illus.). 32p. (ps-3). 1981. 9.95 o.p. (ISBN 0-15-239387-0, HJ). HarBraceJ.

I Want It Now. Kingsley Amis. LC 69-12024. 1969. 9.95 o.p. (ISBN 0-15-145803-0). HarBraceJ.

I Want the Truth. Margaret J. Anderson. 96p. (YA) (gr. 7 up). 1969. pap. 1.25 o.p. (ISBN 0-88243-531-0, 02-0531). Gospel Pub.

I Want to Be in Love Again. Barbara Rex. 1977. 8.95 o.p. (ISBN 0-393-08767-0). Norton.

I Want to Go to London: New Wave & Punk Travel Guide. 1984. 9.95 o.p. (ISBN 0-318-02772-0). Bks Nippan.

I Want to See God - I Am a Daughter of the Church, 2 vols. in 1. P. Marie Eugene. 1216p. Date not set. pap. 39.95 o.s.i. (ISBN 0-87061-134-8). Chr Classics.

I Want to Take Picture. Bill Burke. 1987. 50.00 o.s.i. (ISBN 0-932526-16-0). Nexus Pr.

I Wanted to Be Famous. Joe Ginter. (Illus.). 1981. pap. 5.00 o.p. (ISBN 0-682-49806-8). Exposition-Phoenix.

I Was a High School Drop-In. Cliff Schimmels. (Illus.). 160p. 1985. 10.95 o.p. (ISBN 0-8007-1453-9). Revell.

I Was a Stranger. John W. Hackett. 1978. 8.95 o.p. (ISBN 0-395-27087-1). HM.

I Was Fighting for Peace, but, Lord, There Was Much More. G. P. Johnson. 1979. 5.00 o.p. (ISBN 0-682-49451-8). Exposition-Phoenix.

I Was Once a Tree. Jovan De Rocco. (Illus.). 1979. 6.00 o.p. (ISBN 0-682-49424-0). Exposition-Phoenix.

I Was There! with the Yanks in France. Hilman R. Bankhage & C. Le Roy Baldridge. LC 74-147680. (Library of War & Peace; Artists on War). 1972. lib. bdg. 46.00 o.p. (ISBN 0-8240-0437-X). Garland Pub.

I Will! Emma L. Hayhurst. 1978. 10.00 o.p. (ISBN 0-682-49002-4). Exposition-Phoenix.

I Will Lift up Mine Eyes. Glenn Clark. 1937. pap. 7.95 o.p. (ISBN 0-06-061393-9, RP518). HarpR.

I Will Tell You about God. Hans Froer. Tr. by E. Theodore Bachmann from Ger. LC 78-14666. 80p. (gr. k up). 1979. pap. 0.50 o.p. (ISBN 0-8006-1350-3, 1-1350, Fortress). Augsburg Fortress.

I Wish I Weres: Little Verses for Little Children. William H. Patterson. 1977. 5.00 o.p. (ISBN 0-682-48696-5). Exposition-Phoenix.

I Wish This War Were Over. Diana O'Hehir. LC 83-45502. 288p. 1984. 13.95 o.p. (ISBN 0-689-11442-7, Atheneum). Macmillan.

I Wonder as I Wander: An Autobiographical Journey. Langston Hughes. (Orig.). 1964. pap. 5.95 o.p. (ISBN 0-8090-0068-7, AmCen); 20.00 o.p. Hill & Wang.

I Won't Apologize. S. Prokofieva. 48p. 1985. pap. 3.45 o.p. (ISBN 0-8285-2934-5, Pub. by Raduga Pubs USSR). Imported Pubns.

I Won't Be Crippled When I See Jesus. Everett J. Payton. LC 79-50084. 160p. 1979. pap. 4.95 o.p. (ISBN 0-8066-1716-0, 10-3188, Augsburg). Augsburg Fortress.

I Won't Be Home for Christmas & Other Short Stories. Carrie W. Foster. 57p. 1980. 4.00x o.p. (ISBN 0-682-49662-6). Exposition-Phoenix.

I Would Do It Again. Georgia Moats Casper & Imogene Moats Doden. 1978. 7.00 o.p. (ISBN 0-682-49071-7, Lochinvar). Exposition-Phoenix.

IAEA Laboratory Activity Report One: Primer Informe. (Technical Reports: No. 25). 1964. pap. 6.25 o.p. (IAEA). UNIPUB.

IAEA Safeguards for State's Systems of Accounting & Control of Nuclear Materials. 1980 ed. 28p. pap. 6.50 o.p. (ISBN 0-686-81862-8, ISGINF2, IAEA). UNIPUB.

IAEA Safeguards 1980-1985: A Progress Report. (Yes Ser.). 14p. (Orig.). 1987. pap. text ed. 5.00 o.p. (ISBN 0-317-55617-7, ISP749, IAEA). UNIPUB.

Ian Keown's Caribbean Hideaways with a Special Supplements on Mexico & Charter Yachts. Ian Keown. 1979. 12.95 o.p. (ISBN 0-517-53678-1, Dist. by Crown); pap. 5.95 o.p. (ISBN 0-517-53679-X). Crown.

IAPX 286 Programmer's Reference Manual Numeric Supplement. Intel Staff. 16.95 o.p. (ISBN 0-8359-3054-8, Reston). P-H.

IAPX 88. Intel Staff. 1983. pap. 14.95 o.p. (ISBN 0-8359-3016-5, Reston). P-H.

Iatrogenic Carcinogenesis. D. Schmaehl et al. 1977. soft cover 18.00 o.p. (ISBN 0-387-08200-X). Springer-Verlag.

Iberoamerica. 4th ed. Americo Castro. (Span). (gr. 10-12). 1971. pap. text ed. 16.95 o.p. (ISBN 0-03-069170-2, HoltC). HR&W.

Ibiza & Formentera Travel Guide. Berlitz Editors. (Travel Guides Ser.). 1978. pap. 4.95 o.p. (ISBN 0-317-12106-5, Berlitz). Macmillan.

Ibiza Travel Guide. (Berlitz Travel Guides). (Illus.). 1982. pap. 4.95 o.p. (ISBN 0-02-969240-7, Berlitz). Macmillan.

IBM BASIC from the Ground Up. David E. Simon. 1984. 15.95 o.p. (ISBN 0-317-02352-7, 6350). Sams.

IBM BASIC Handbook. David A. Lien. LC 84-71386. (Illus.). 237p. (Orig.). 1984. pap. 14.95 o.p. (ISBN 0-932760-23-6). CompuSoft.

IBM BASIC Manual. Lynne Mass & Thomas M. Kemnitz. LC 85-418. (Kids Working with Computers Ser.). (Illus.). 48p. (gr. 2 up). 1985. lib. bdg. 11.27 o.p. (ISBN 0-516-08426-7). Childrens.

IBM Business Set. Walden. 1985. pap. 35.90 o.p. (ISBN 0-471-01137-1). Wiley.

IBM CPU & Storage Architecture: System-370-Mode & 370-XA Mode. Joe Leben & Jim Arnold. (Data Processing Training Ser.). 256p. 1984. pap. 59.95 o.p. (ISBN 0-471-80142-9). Wiley.

IBM Displaywriter Simplified. Donald C. Scot. 384p. 1983. 38.95 o.p. (ISBN 0-442-28044-0). Van Nos Reinhold.

IBM Graphics from the Ground Up. Simon. 352p. 1984. 15.95 o.p. (ISBN 0-317-05883-5). Sams.

IBM: Hardware Selection. (Papers- Online Conference, London, 1979). 278p. (Orig.). 1979. pap. text ed. 35.50x o.p. (ISBN 0-903796-50-3, Pub. by Online Conferences England). Gower Pub Co.

IBM I-O Architecture & Virtual Storage Concepts: Systems-370-Mode & 370-XA-Mode Processors. Joe Leben & Jim Arnold. LC 84-7589. (Data Processing Training Ser.). 250p. 1984. spiral-bound 59.95 o.p. (ISBN 0-471-80141-0, 1-615). Wiley.

IBM LOGO Manual. Lynne Mass & Thomas M. Kemnitz. LC 85-5279. (Kids Working with Computers Ser.). (Illus.). 48p. (gr. 2 up). 1985. lib. bdg. 11.27 o.p. (ISBN 0-516-08427-5). Childrens.

IBM MVS. 1979. pap. text ed. 46.25x o.p. (ISBN 0-903796-38-4, Pub. by Online Conferences England). Gower Pub Co.

IBM OS Assembler Language - Subroutines Macros & Tables, Bk. 5. Donna N. Tabler et al. LC 85-17791. (Data Processing Training Ser.: No. 1-615). 355p. 1986. pap. 59.95x o.p. (ISBN 0-471-80718-4). Wiley.

IBM OS Assembler Language-Arithmetic Operations. D. N. Tabler et al. LC 85-2317. (Data Processing Training Ser.). 356p. 1985. pap. 59.95 o.p. (ISBN 0-471-80135-6). Wiley.

IBM OS Assembler Language: Language Basics. Donna Tabler & Ruth Ashley. LC 84-10407. (Data Processing Training Ser.: 1-615). 250p. 1985. pap. text ed. 59.95x o.p. (ISBN 0-471-80134-8). Wiley.

IBM-PC. Mosbysorts. 1984. 250.00 o.p. (ISBN 0-8016-3844-5). Mosby.

IBM PC & PCjr LOGO Programming Primer. Donald Martin et al. LC 84-51654. 24.95 o.p. (ISBN 0-672-22379-1); Book & Software Pack. 24.95 o.p. Sams.

IBM PC & XT User's Handbook. Jeffrey R. Weber. (How to Use Your Personal Computer Ser.). 520p. 1983. pap. 15.95 o.p. (ISBN 0-938862-47-2). Weber Systems.

IBM PC-AT: A Guide for Users & Managers. Corey Sandler. LC 85-8464. (Illus.). 224p. 1986. 17.95 o.p. (ISBN 0-03-005523-7). H Holt & Co.

IBM-PC Conversion Handbook of BASIC. J. Mel Harris & Michael L. Scofield. LC 83-13977. 176p. 1983. pap. 15.95 o.p. (ISBN 0-13-448481-9). P-H.

IBM PC Diskguide. 1983. pap. text ed. 4.00 o.p. (ISBN 0-07-931094-X). McGraw.

IBM PC-DOS Handbook. Richard A. King. LC 83-61387. (Illus.). 296p. 1983. pap. 17.95 o.p. (ISBN 0-89588-103-9). SYBEX.

IBM-PC-DOS Handbook. 2nd ed. Richard A. King. 340p. (Orig.). 1986. pap. 18.95 o.p. (ISBN 0-89588-368-6). Sybex.

IBM PC Expansion & Software Guide. 4th ed. Ed. by Que Corp. 1000p. 1984. pap. 19.95 o.p. (ISBN 0-88022-067-8, 19). Que Corp.

IBM PC Expansion & Software Guide. 2nd ed. Que Corporation. Ed. by Diane Brown & David Noble. (Que's IBM PC Library). (Illus.). 560p. (Orig.). 1983. pap. 16.95 o.p. (ISBN 0-88022-027-9, 15). Que Corp.

IBM-PC for Kids from Eight to Eighty. Francis H. Short & Michael P. Zabinsky. LC 84-50176. 200p. 1984. pap. 15.95 o.p. (ISBN 0-672-22337-6, 22337). Sams.

IBM-PC from the Inside Out. Murray Sargent, III & Richard Shoemaker. 288p. 1983. pap. 18.95 o.p. (ISBN 0-201-06896-6). Addison-Wesley.

IBM-PC in Your Corporation. Jeffrey B. Walden. LC 85-705. (IBM Personal Computer Ser.). 203p. 1985. pap. 17.95 o.p. (ISBN 0-471-80849-0). Wiley.

IBM-PC, MicroMasion: Using Your Computer to Have a Safer, More Convenient Home. David B. Bonynge. (Illus.). 176p. (Orig.). 1985. pap. 11.60 o.p. (ISBN 0-8306-1926-7, 1926). TAB Bks.

IBM-PC Programs. William Barden, Jr. 376p. 1985. pap. text ed. 17.45 o.p. (ISBN 0-03-072017-6, HoltC). HR&W.

IBM-PC Public Domain Software, Vol. 1. Gary Phillips. Ed. by Monet Thomson. 547p. 1983. pap. 24.95 o.p. (ISBN 0-912677-06-6). Tate Pub.

IBM-PC User's Reference Manual. Held. 432p. 1984. 24.95 o.p. (6262). Sams.

IBM-PC: VisiCalc. Robert Crowley. 256p. 1984. pap. 20.45 o.p. (ISBN 0-03-062634-X); pap. 40.45 with diskette o.p. (ISBN 0-03-063982-4). HR&W.

IBM-PCjr Assembler Language. David C. Willen. LC 84-71060. 286p. 1984. pap. 15.95 o.p. (ISBN 0-672-22360-0, 22360). Sams.

IBM-PCjr Encyclopedia. Gary Phillips. 280p. 1985. pap. 19.95 o.p. (NO. 9055, Pub. by Chapman & Hall New York). Routledge Chapman & Hall.

IBM-PCjr Entertainer. Brian Sawyer. 180p. 1984. pap. text ed. 12.95 o.p. (ISBN 0-07-881151-1, 151-7). Osborne-McGraw.

IBM-PCjr Image Maker: Graphics on the IBM-PCjr. Jonathan Erickson & William D. Cramer. 200p. (Orig.). 1984. pap. text ed. 15.95 o.p. (ISBN 0-07-881138-4). Osborne-McGraw.

IBM-PCjr User's Handbook. Weber Systems, Inc. Staff. (User's Handbooks Ser.). 304p. 1984. 9.95 o.p. (ISBN 0-345-31597-9). Ballantine.

IBM-PCjr User's Reference Manual. G. Held. 1984. 24.95 o.p. (ISBN 0-317-05634-4, 6373). Sams.

IBM Personal Computer Directory: Hardware, Software, & Peripherals. Kelly-Grimes Corporation Staff. LC 84-17394. (Kelly-Grimes Buyers Guide Ser.: No. 1-702). 581p. 1985. pap. 26.95 o.p. (ISBN 0-471-87821-9, Pub. by Wiley Pr). Wiley.

IBM Personal Computer Handbook. Louis E. Frenzel, Jr. et al. LC 83-50939. 352p. 1984. pap. 15.95 o.p. (ISBN 0-672-22004-0, 22004). Sams.

IBM Personal Computer Made Easy. Arthur Naiman. 1983. 11.45 o.p. (ISBN 0-395-34413-1); pap. 5.70 o.p. (ISBN 0-395-34933-8). HM.

IBM Personal Computer User's Guide. James E. Kelley, Jr. 352p. 1983. spiral bdg., incl. disk o.p. 29.95 o.p. (ISBN 0-440-03946-0, Banbury). Dell.

IBM Personal Computer: What You Should Know. rev. ed. Adar et al. LC 83-72637. 170p. 1984. pap. 14.95x o.s.i. (ISBN 0-89435-102-8). QED Info Sci.

IBM: Small Systems. 122p. (Orig.). 1979. text ed. 46.25x o.p. (ISBN 0-903796-47-3, Pub. by Online Conferences England); pap. 22.00 o.p. Gower Pub Co.

IBM: Teleprocessing-SNA & Distributed Processing. 1979. pap. text ed. 53.00x o.p. (ISBN 0-903796-40-6, Pub. by Online Conferences England). Gower Pub Co.

IBM: The User's Guide to the Impact of Series H. 167p. 1981. text ed. 43.55x o.p. (ISBN 0-903796-74-0, Pub. by Online Conferences England). Gower Pub Co.

IBM: VM-CMS. (Online Conference London Ser: 1979). 176p. (Orig.). 1979. pap. text ed. 22.00x o.p. (ISBN 0-903796-43-0, Pub. by Online Conferences England). Gower Pub Co.

Ibn Kammuna's Examination of the Three Faiths: A Thirteenth-Century Essay in the Comparative Study of Religion. Ed. & tr. by Moshe Perlmann. LC 73-102659. 1971. 32.00x o.p. (ISBN 0-520-01658-0). U of Cal Pr.

Ibo-Speaking Peoples of Southern Nigeria: A Selected Annotated List of Writings, 1627 to 1970. Joseph C. Anafulu. 321p. 1981. lib. bdg. 55.00 o.p. (ISBN 3-601-00006-7). Kraus Intl.

Ibsen: The Man & His Work. Edward Beyer. LC 79-1917. (Illus.). 1980. 10.95 o.p. (ISBN 0-8008-4055-0); pap. 5.95 o.s.i. (ISBN 0-8008-4056-9). Taplinger.

IC Functional Equivalence Guide. Ed. by Jim Fitzgerald. 480p. 1987. 95.00 o.p. (ISBN 0-317-57572-4). DATA Busn Pub.

IC Generic Source Guide. 560p. 1987. 105.00 o.p. (ISBN 0-317-57573-2). DATA Busn Pub.

IC Timer Handbook with One Hundred Projects & Experiments. Joseph J. Carr. 15.95 o.p. (ISBN 0-8306-0007-8, 1290). TAB Bks.

IC 178 Designs & Applications. Date not set. (ISBN 0-8104-0654-3). Sams.

Icarus. Peter Way. 224p. 1981. pap. 2.50 o.p. (ISBN 0-380-54858-5, 54858-5). Avon.

Icarus Seal. Christopher Hyde. 320p. 1982. 12.45 o.p. (ISBN 0-395-32044-5). HM.

Icarus Threat. Hugh McLeave. 1985. 13.95 o.p. (ISBN 0-8166-0222-0, Large Print Bks). G K Hall.

ICCH Commodities & Financial Futures Yearbook, 1983-84. Ed. by M. J. Atkin. 424p. 1983. 52.50 o.p. (ISBN 0-7099-0536-X, Pub. by Croom Helm Ltd). Routledge Chapman & Hall.

Ice. Tristan Jones. 1980. pap. 3.50 o.p. (ISBN 0-380-50757-9, 63248-9). Avon.

Ice. Ed McBain. 305p. 1983. 15.50 o.p. (ISBN 0-87795-468-2, Arbor Hse). Morrow.

Ice: A Novel. Anna Kavan. 158p. 1985. 14.45 o.p. (ISBN 0-393-02273-0); pap. 5.70 o.p. (ISBN 0-393-30256-3). Norton.

Ice Age in Britain. B. W. Sparks & R. G. West. (Methuen Library Reprint Ser.). (Illus.). 320p. 1981. 49.95x o.p. (ISBN 0-416-32160-7, 3583). Routledge Chapman & Hall.

Ice Age of Elizabethans see Plymouth: A New History.

Ice & Fire. Andrea Dworkin. LC 86-13141. 192p. 1987. 14.95 o.s.i. (ISBN 1-55584-025-6). Weidenfeld.

Ice Bird. David Lewis. (Illus.). 1976. 8.50 o.p. (ISBN 0-393-03185-3). Norton.

Ice Brothers. Sloan Wilson. LC 79-52252. 1979. 11.95 o.p. (ISBN 0-87795-232-9, Arbor Hse). Morrow.

Ice Castle. Elizabeth Wolfe. 256p. (Orig.). 1982. pap. 2.50 o.p. (ISBN 0-8439-1040-2, Pub. by Leisure Bks CT). Dorchester Pub Co.

Ice Cathedral. George Leonard. 224p. 1984. 14.70 o.p. (ISBN 0-671-49676-X). S&S.

Ice-Core Drilling. Ed. by John F. Splettstoesser. LC 76-3219. (Illus.). x, 189p. 1976. pap. 11.95x o.p. (ISBN 0-8032-5843-7). U of Nebr Pr.

Ice Cream. 3rd ed. Wendell S. Arbuckle. (Illus.). 1977. 42.95 o.p. (ISBN 0-87055-256-2). AVI.

Ice Cream. Hilary Walden. 1985. pap. 12.95 o.p. (ISBN 0-671-60094-X, Fireside). S&S.

Ice Cream & Ices. Nancy Arum. Ed. by Margery Stein. LC 81-68842. (Great American Cooking Schools Ser.). (Illus.). 84p. 1981. pap. 5.95 o.p. (ISBN 0-941034-07-0). I Chalmers.

Ice Cream Ocean: & Other Delectable Poems of the Sea. Ed. & illus. by Susan Russo. LC 83-16195. (Illus.). 40p. (gr. k-3). 1984. 10.25 o.p. (ISBN 0-688-02122-0); PLB 10.88 o.p. (ISBN 0-688-02123-9). Lothrop.

Ice Cubes Replacement. 1968. 13.60 o.p. (ISBN 0-07-521130-0). McGraw.

Ice Dancing. Amelie La Tourette. 224p. 18.95 o.p. (ISBN 0-317-47453-7, 8098X, Pandora Pr); pap. 7.95 o.p. (ISBN 0-86358-110-2, 81102, Pandora Pr). Routledge Chapman & Hall.

Ice Futures. Thomas Johnson. 52p. (Orig.). 1977. 15.00 o.p. (ISBN 0-685-67091-0); pap. 5.00 o.p. (ISBN 0-914742-21-3). Copper Canyon.

Ice Ghosts Mystery. Jane L. Curry. LC 74-190552. (gr. 5-9). 1972. 7.95 o.p. (ISBN 0-689-30302-5, Atheneum). Macmillan.

Ice Is Also Great. L. L. Smith. 1977. 7.50 o.p. (ISBN 0-682-48839-9). Exposition-Phoenix.

Ice Is Coming. Patricia Wrightson. LC 76-45438. 228p. (gr. 7 up). 1977. 5.95 o.p. (ISBN 0-689-50081-5, Atheneum). Macmillan.

Ice Trail. Anne E. Crompton. 128p. (gr. 3-7). 1980. 9.50 o.p. (ISBN 0-416-30691-8, NO. 0191). Routledge Chapman & Hall.

Ice World. Hal Clemeny. 1981. pap. 2.25 o.s.i. (ISBN 0-345-30082-3, Del Rey). Ballantine.

Iceberg Utilization: Proceedings of the First International Iceberg Utilization Conference, Ames, Iowa. Ed. by A. A. Husseiny. LC 78-5119. (Illus.). 780p. 1978. 110.00 o.p. (ISBN 0-08-022916-6); pap. 67.00 o.p. (ISBN 0-08-022915-8). Pergamon.

Iced Delights. Shona C. Poole. LC 86-16547. (Illus.). 80p. 1987. pap. 9.95 o.p. (ISBN 0-385-23814-2). Doubleday.

Icehouse Bottom Site. Jefferson Chapman. (Illus.). 146p. 1975. pap. 9.95x o.p. (ISBN 0-87049-179-2, Pub. by U of Tenn Dept of Anthropology). U of Tenn Pr.

Iceland. (Visitor's Guides Ser.). (Illus.). 192p. (Orig.). 1986. pap. 10.95 o.p. (ISBN 0-935161-50-3). Hunter Pub NY.

Iceland, Eighteen Seventy Four to Nineteen Seventy-Four: A Handbook. Ed. by J. Nordal & V. Kristinsson. (Illus.). 1975. 25.00 o.s.i. (ISBN 0-685-65373-0). E J Brill USA.

Iceland: Reluctant Ally. Donald E. Nuechterlein. LC 75-3868. (Illus.). 213p. 1975. lib. bdg. 22.50x o.p. (ISBN 0-8371-8096-1, NUIC). Greenwood.

Icelandic-English Dictionary. 3rd ed. A. Sigurdsson. (Icelandic & Eng.). 80.00 o.s.i. (ISBN 0-686-64772-6). E J Brill USA.

Icelandic Sagas & Manuscripts. rev. & updated ed. Jonas Kristjansson. (Illus.). 1980. 25.00 o.p. E J Brill USA.

Ich Lausche Dem Leben. Ed. by Hildegard R. Boeninger & D. Pietschmann. (Orig., Ger.). 1963. pap. 6.95x o.p. (ISBN 0-393-09558-4, NortonC). Norton.

Ichnology: Trace Fossils in Sedimentology & Stratigraphy. A. A. Ekdale et al. (Short Course Notes Ser.: No. 15). 317p. 1984. pap. 25.00 o.p. (ISBN 0-918985-42-0). SEPM.

ICHPER Book of Worldwide Games & Dances. International Council on Health, Physical Education & Recreation Staff. (Illus.). 1967. pap. 9.40x o.p. (ISBN 0-88314-102-7, 245-07144). AAHPERD.

ICIAM '87: Proceedings of the First International Conference on Industrial & Applied Mathematics. James McKenna. (SIAM Proceedings). 504p. cancelled o.s.i. Soc Indus-Appl Math.

Icicle & the Sun. William Sansom. LC 75-31691. (Illus.). 159p. 1975. Repr. of 1959 ed. lib. bdg. 15.00x o.p. (ISBN 0-8371-8442-8, SAICS). Greenwood.

Icky Bug Alphabet Book. Jerry Pallotta. (Illus.). 32p. (ps-1). 10.95 o.p. (ISBN 0-933341-95-4); pap. 4.95 o.p. (ISBN 0-933341-66-0). Quinlan Pr.

Iconography of Religions: An Introduction. Albert C. Moore. LC 76-62598. 344p. 1977. 12.00 o.p. (ISBN 0-8006-0488-1, 1-489, Fortress). Augsburg Fortress.

Iconography of the Conversion of Saint Paul. Thomas Martone. Ed. by S. J. Freedberg. (Outstanding Dissertations in Fine Arts Ser.). (Illus.). 325p. 1985. Repr. of 1978 ed. 45.00 o.p. (ISBN 0-8240-6882-3). Garland Pub.

Iconography of the Facade of Saint-Gilles-Du-Gard. Carra F. O'Meara. LC 76-23668. (Outstanding Dissertations in the Fine Arts - Medieval). (Illus.). 352p. 1977. Repr. of 1975 ed. lib. bdg. 63.00 o.p. (ISBN 0-8240-2717-5). Garland Pub.

Iconologia. Cesare Ripa. LC 75-27865. (Renaissance & the Gods Ser.: Vol. 21). (Illus.). 581p. 1976. Repr. of 1611 ed. lib. bdg. 88.00 o.p. (ISBN 0-8240-2070-7). Garland Pub.

Iconology: Image, Text, Ideology. W. J. Mitchell. LC 85-1177. x, 226p. 1986. 20.00x o.s.i. (ISBN 0-226-53228-3). U of Chicago Pr.

ICP Software Directory, 7 vols. International Computer Programs, Inc. Staff. Ed. by Dennis L. Hamilton. 1985. Set. softcover 550.00 o.p. (ISBN 0-88094-041-7). Intl Computer.

ICP Software Directory, 10 vols. 58th ed. International Computer Programs, Inc. Ed. by Dennis L. Hamilton & Monika A. Keesling. 1987. Set. pap. 934.00 o.p. (ISBN 0-88094-094-8). Intl Computer.

ICP Software Directory. International Computer Programs, Inc. Ed. by Dennis L. Hamilton & Monika A. Keesling. (Minicomputer Ser. Industry Specific Applications: Vol. 6). pap. 125.00 o.p. (ISBN 0-88094-115-4). Intl Computer.

ICP Software Directory. International Computer Programs, Inc. Ed. by Dennis L. Hamilton & Monika A. Keesling. (Microcomputer Systems & Utilities Ser.: Vol. 1). 75.00 o.p. (ISBN 0-88094-116-2). Intl Computer.

ICP Software Directory, 4 vols. 59th ed. International Computer Programs, Inc. Ed. by Dennis L. Hamilton & Monika A. Keesling. (Microcomputer Ser.). 1988. Set. 295.00 o.p. (ISBN 0-88094-109-X). Intl Computer.

ICP Software Directory, 6 vols. 59th ed. International Computer Programs, Inc. Ed. by Dennis L. Hamilton & Monika A. Keesling. (Mainfram-Minicomputer Ser.). 1988. 639.00 o.p. (ISBN 0-88094-108-1). Intl Computer.

ICP Software Directory, 10 vols. 59th ed. International Computer Programs, Inc. Ed. by Dennis L. Hamilton & Monika A. Keesling. 1988. Set. 934.00 o.p. (ISBN 0-88094-107-3). Intl Computer.

ICP Software Directory, 10 vols. 57th ed. Ed. by International Computer Programs, Inc. Staff & Dennis L. Hamilton. 1987. softcover 934.00 o.p. (ISBN 0-88094-081-6). Intl Computer.

ICP Software Directory, 6 vols. 57th ed. Ed. by International Computer Programs, Inc. Staff & Dennis L. Hamilton. (Mainframe - Minicomputer Ser.). 1987. softcover 639.00 o.p. (ISBN 0-88094-082-4). Intl Computer.

ICP Software Directory, 4 vols. 57th ed. Ed. by International Computer Programs, Inc. Staff & Dennis L. Hamilton. (Microcomputer Ser.). 1987. softcover 295.00 o.p. (ISBN 0-88094-083-2). Intl Computer.

ICP Software Directory: Banking, Insurance & Finance. 58th ed. International Computer Programs, Inc. Ed. by Dennis L. Hamilton & Monika A. Keesling. (Mainframe-Minicomputer Ser.: Vol. 4). 1987. pap. 125.00 o.p. (ISBN 0-88094-100-6). Intl Computer.

ICP Software Directory: Banking, Insurance & Finance. International Computer Programs, Inc. Ed. by Dennis L. Hamilton & Monika A. Keesling. (Mainframe-Minicomputer Ser.: Vol. 4). 125.00 o.p. (ISBN 0-88094-113-8). Intl Computer.

ICP Software Directory: Banking, Insurance & Finance. 57th ed. Ed. by International Computer Programs, Inc. & Dennis L. Hamilton. (Mainframe - Minicomputer Ser.: Vol. 4). 1987. softcover 125.00 o.p. (ISBN 0-88094-087-5). Intl Computer.

ICP Software Directory: Banking, Insurance & Finance, 6 vols, Vol. 4. 56th ed. International Computer Programs, Inc. Staff. Ed. by Dennis L. Hamilton & Monika A. Keesling. (Mainframe-Minicomputer Ser.). 1986. Set. 125.00 o.s.i. (ISBN 0-88094-074-3). Intl Computer.

ICP Software Directory: Cross Industry Applications. International Computer Programs, Inc. Staff. Ed. by Richard J. Spangler. 1983. 150.00 o.p. (ISBN 0-88094-020-4). Intl Computer.

ICP Software Directory: General Accounting. 58th ed. International Computer Programs, Inc. Ed. by Dennis L. Hamilton & Monika A. Keesling. (Mainframe-Minicomputer Ser.: Vol. 2). 1987. pap. 125.00 o.p. (ISBN 0-88094-098-0). Intl Computer.

ICP Software Directory: General Accounting. 58th ed. International Computer Programs, Inc. Ed. by Dennis L. Hamilton & Monika A. Keesling. (Microcomputer Ser.: Vol. 2). 1987. pap. 75.00 o.p. (ISBN 0-88094-104-9). Intl Computer.

ICP Software Directory: General Accounting. 59th ed. International Computer Programs, Inc. Ed. by Dennis L. Hamilton & Monika A. Keesling. (Mainframe-Minicomputer Ser.: Vol. 2). 1988. 125.00 o.p. (ISBN 0-88094-111-1). Intl Computer.

ICP Software Directory: General Accounting. International Computer Programs, Inc. Ed. by Dennis L. Hamilton & Monika A. Keesling. (Microcomputer Ser.: Vol. 2). 75.00 o.p. (ISBN 0-88094-117-0). Intl Computer.

ICP Software Directory: General Accounting. 57th ed. Ed. by International Computer Programs, Inc. Staff & Dennis L. Hamilton. (Mainframe - Minicomputer Ser.: Vol. 2). 1987. softcover 125.00 o.p. (ISBN 0-88094-085-9). Intl Computer.

ICP Software Directory: General Accounting. 57th ed. Ed. by International Computer Programs, Inc. Staff & Dennis L. Hamilton. (Microcomputer Ser.: Vol. 2). 1987. softcover 75.00 o.p. (ISBN 0-317-57523-6). Intl Computer.

ICP Software Directory: General Accounting, 4 vols, Vol. 2. 56th ed. International Computer Programs, Inc. Staff. Ed. by Dennis L. Hamilton & Monika A. Keesling. (Microcomputer Ser.). 1986. Set. 75.00 o.s.i. (ISBN 0-88094-078-6). Intl Computer.

ICP Software Directory: General Accounting, 6 vols, Vol. 2. 56th ed. International Computer Programs, Inc. Staff. Ed. by Dennis L. Hamilton & Monika A. Keesling. (Mainframe-Minicomputer Ser.). 1986. Set. 125.00 o.s.i. (ISBN 0-88094-072-7). Intl Computer.

ICP Software Directory: Industry Specific Applications. 58th ed. International Computer Programs, Inc. Ed. by Dennis L. Hamilton & Monika A. Keesling. (Mainframe-Minicomputer Ser.: Vol. 6). 1987. pap. 125.00 o.p. (ISBN 0-88094-102-2). Intl Computer.

ICP Software Directory: Industry Specific Applications. 58th ed. International Computer Programs, Inc. Ed. by Dennis L. Hamilton & Monika A. Keesling. (Microcomputer Ser.: Vol. 4). 1987. pap. 150.00 o.p. (ISBN 0-88094-106-5). Intl Computer.

ICP Software Directory: Industry Specific Applications. International Computer Programs, Inc. Ed. by Dennis L. Hamilton & Monika A. Keesling. (Microcomputer Ser.: Vol. 4). 150.00 o.p. (ISBN 0-88094-119-7). Intl Computer.

ICP Software Directory: Industry Specific Applications. 57th ed. Ed. by International Computer Programs, Inc. Staff & Dennis L. Hamilton. (Mainframe - Minicomputer Ser.: Vol. 6). 1987. softcover 125.00 o.p. (ISBN 0-88094-089-1). Intl Computer.

ICP Software Directory: Industry Specific Applications. 57th ed. Ed. by International Computer Programs, Inc. Staff & Dennis L. Hamilton. (Microcomputer Ser.: Vol. 4). 1987. softcover 150.00 o.p. (ISBN 0-88094-093-X). Intl Computer.

ICP Software Directory: Mainframe-Minicomputer Series, 6 vols. 58th ed. International Computer Programs, Inc. Staff. Ed. by Dennis L. Hamilton & Monika A. Keesling. (Mainframe-Minicomputer Ser.). 1987. pap. 639.00 o.p. (ISBN 0-88094-095-6). Intl Computer.

ICP Software Directory: Management & Administration. 57th ed. International Computer Programs, Inc. Ed. by Dennis L. Hamilton & Monika A. Keesling. (Mainframe - Minicomputer Ser.: Vol. 3). 1987. softcover 125.00 o.p. (ISBN 0-88094-086-7). Intl Computer.

ICP Software Directory: Management & Administration. 58th ed. International Computer Programs, Inc. Ed. by Dennis L. Hamilton & Monika A. Keesling. (Mainframe-Minicomputer Ser.: Vol. 3). 1987. 125.00 o.p. (ISBN 0-88094-099-9). Intl Computer.

ICP Software Directory: Management & Administration. International Computer Programs, Inc. Ed. by Dennis L. Hamilton & Monika A. Keesling. (Mainframe-Minicomputer Ser.: Vol. 3). 125.00 o.p. (ISBN 0-88094-112-X). Intl Computer.

ICP Software Directory: Manufacturing & Engineering. 58th ed. International Computer Programs, Inc. Ed. by Dennis L. Hamilton & Monika A. Keesling. (Mainframe-Minicomputer Ser.: Vol. 5). 1987. pap. 125.00 o.p. (ISBN 0-88094-101-4). Intl Computer.

ICP Software Directory: Manufacturing & Engineering. International Computer Programs, Inc. Ed. by Dennis L. Hamilton & Monika A. Keesling. (Mainframe-Minicomputer Ser.: Vol. 5). 125.00 o.p. (ISBN 0-88094-114-6). Intl Computer.

ICP Software Directory: Manufacturing & Engineering. 57th ed. Ed. by International Computer Programs, Inc. & Dennis L. Hamilton. (Mainframe - Minicomputer Ser.: Vol. 5). 1987. softcover 125.00 o.p. (ISBN 0-88094-088-3). Intl Computer.

ICP Software Directory: Microcomputer Series, 4 vols. 58th ed. International Computer Programs, Inc. Ed. by Dennis L. Hamilton & Monika A. Keesling. 1987. Set. pap. 295.00 o.p. (ISBN 0-88094-096-4). Intl Computer.

ICP Software Directory: Office Automation & Business Management. 58th ed. International Computer Programs, Inc. Ed. by Dennis L. Hamilton & Monika A. Keesling. (Microcomputer Ser.: Vol. 3). 1987. pap. 75.00 o.p. (ISBN 0-88094-105-7). Intl Computer.

ICP Software Directory: Office Automation & Business Management. International Computer Programs, Inc. Ed. by Dennis L. Hamilton & Monika A. Keesling. (Microcomputer Ser.: Vol. 3). 75.00 o.p. (ISBN 0-88094-118-9). Intl Computer.

ICP Software Directory: System Software. International Computer Programs, Inc. Staff. Ed. by Richard J. Spangler. 1983. 150.00 o.p. (ISBN 0-686-39679-0). Intl Computer.

ICP Software Directory: Systems & Utilities. 58th ed. International Computer Programs, Inc. Ed. by Dennis L. Hamilton & Monika A. Keesling. (Mainframe-Minicomputer Ser.: Vol. 1). 1987. pap. 175.00 o.p. (ISBN 0-88094-097-2). Intl Computer.

ICP Software Directory: Systems & Utilities. 58th ed. International Computer Programs, Inc. Ed. by Dennis L. Hamilton & Monika A. Keesling. (Microcomputer Ser.: Vol. 1). 1987. pap. 75.00 o.p. (ISBN 0-88094-103-0). Intl Computer.

ICP Software Directory: Systems & Utilities. 59th ed. International Computer Programs, Inc. Ed. by Dennis L. Hamilton & Monika A. Keesling. (Mainframe-Minicomputer Ser.: Vol. 1). 1988. 175.00 o.p. (ISBN 0-88094-110-3). Intl Computer.

ICP Software Directory: Systems & Utilities. 57th ed. Ed. by International Computer Programs, Inc. Staff & Dennis L. Hamilton. (Mainframe - Minicomputer Ser.: Vol. 1). 1987. softcover 175.00 o.p. (ISBN 0-88094-084-0). Intl Computer.

ICP Software Directory: Systems & Utilities. 57th ed. Ed. by International Computer Programs, Inc. Staff & Dennis L. Hamilton. (Microcomputer Ser.: Vol. 1). 1987. softcover 75.00 o.p. (ISBN 0-88094-091-3). Intl Computer.

ICP Software Directory-United Kingdom: Software Products, Services & Suppliers. International Computer Programs, Inc. Staff & Richard J. Spangler. 1983. 125.00 o.p. (ISBN 0-88094-018-2). Intl Computer.

ICP Software Directory, Vol. 1: Systems Software. International Computer Programs, Inc. Staff. Ed. by Dennis L. Hamilton. 1985. softcover 150.00 o.p. (ISBN 0-88094-042-5). Intl Computer.

ICP Software Directory, Vol. 2: General Accounting Systems. International Computer Programs, Inc. Staff. Ed. by Dennis L. Hamilton. 1985. pap. 95.00 o.p. (ISBN 0-88094-043-3). Intl Computer.

ICP Software Directory, Vol. 3: Management & Administration Systems. International Computer Programs, Inc. Staff. Ed. by Dennis L. Hamilton. 1985. pap. 95.00 o.p. (ISBN 0-88094-044-1). Intl Computer.

ICP Software Directory, Vol. 4: Banking, Insurance & Finance Systems. International Computer Programs, Inc. Staff. Ed. by Dennis Hamilton. 1985. pap. 95.00 o.p. (ISBN 0-88094-045-X). Intl Computer.

ICP Software Directory, Vol. 5: Manufacturing & Engineering Systems. International Computer Programs, Inc. Staff. Ed. by Dennis L. Hamilton. 1985. pap. 95.00 o.p. (ISBN 0-88094-046-8). Intl Computer.

ICP Software Directory, Vol. 6: Specialized Industry Systems. International Computer Programs, Inc. Staff. Ed. by Dennis L. Hamilton. 1985. pap. 95.00 o.p. (ISBN 0-88094-047-6). Intl Computer.

ICP Software Directory, Vol. 7: Microcomputer Systems, Specialized Business Applications, Pt. II. International Computer Programs, Inc. Staff. Ed. by Dennis L. Hamilton. 1985. pap. 95.00 o.p. (ISBN 0-88094-049-2). Intl Computer.

ICP Software Directory, Vol. 7: Microcomputer Systems, Systems Software & General Business Applications, Pt. I. International Computer Programs, Inc. Staff. Ed. by Dennis L. Hamilton. 1985. pap. 95.00 o.p. (ISBN 0-88094-048-4). Intl Computer.

ID for Sale in the Mail. Michael Hoy. 80p. (Orig.). 1987. pap. text ed. 14.95 o.p. (ISBN 0-915179-60-1). Loompanics.

I'd Like to See Less of You. Beverly Barr. LC 74-20357. (Illus.). 1975. 7.95 o.p. (ISBN 0-689-10645-9, Atheneum). Macmillan.

I'd Like to Try a Monster' S Eye. Judith Thurman. LC 76-47630. (Illus.). (ps-2). 1977. 6.50 o.p. (ISBN 0-689-30574-5, Atheneum). Macmillan.

I'd Rather Be Forty Than Pregnant. Herbert I. Kavet. (Illus.). 96p. 1984. pap. 3.95 o.p. (ISBN 0-8092-5355-0). Contemp Bks.

I'd Rather Do It Myself, If You Don't Mind. Shirley Schwarzrock & C. Gilbert Wrenn. (Coping with Ser.). (Illus.). 39p. (gr. 7-12). 1970. pap. text ed. 3.00 o.p. (ISBN 0-913476-31-5). Am Guidance.

IDA: A User's Guide to the IDA Interactive Data Analysis & Forecasting System. Robert F. Ling & Harry V. Roberts. 1982. text ed. 18.95 o.p. (ISBN 0-07-037906-8). McGraw.

IDA: Independent Democratic, Amalgamated. John D. Rhymer. 1978. 10.00 o.p. (ISBN 0-682-49041-5). Exposition-Phoenix.

Ida Makes a Movie. Kay Chorao. LC 73-20147. (Illus.). 48p. (ps-3). 1979. 5.95 o.p. (ISBN 0-395-28782-0, Clarion). HM.

Idaho Divorce Book. Susan M. Graham. 1979. pap. 17.95 o.p. (ISBN 0-932722-02-4). Solstice Pr.

Idaho: Gem of the Mountains. Merle Wells & Arthur A. Hart. LC 85-6384. 256p. 1985. 24.95 o.p. (ISBN 0-89781-141-0). Windsor Pubns Inc.

Idaho Industrial Minerals. 1975. 14.50 o.p. (ISBN 0-686-29524-2). Minobras.

Idaho Manufacturing Directory, 1985-86. 204p. 1985. pap. 45.00 o.p. (ISBN 0-318-02861-1). Manufacturers.

Idaho State & Local Government. Sydney Duncombe et al. LC 77-155358. (Illus.). 1971. 3.00 o.p. (ISBN 0-87004-224-6). Caxton.

Idaho Supplement for Modern Real Estate Practice. 4th ed. Idaho Real Estate Commission Staff. LC 84-5. 132p. 1984. pap. text ed. 9.95 o.p. (ISBN 0-88462-503-6, 1510-20, Real Estate Ed). Longman Finan.

Idaho: Trusts. 1983. 8.50 o.p. (ISBN 0-686-90706-X). Am Law Inst.

IDAM File Organizations. James C. French. Ed. by Harold Stone. LC 85-1066. (Computer Science: Distributed Database Systems Ser.: No. 15). 172p. 1985. 44.95 o.p. (ISBN 0-8357-1631-7). UMI Res Pr.

Idea Handbook for Colleges & Universities. 158p. (Orig.). 1979. pap. 10.00 o.p. (ISBN 0-89492-037-5). Acad Educ Dev.

Idea Handbook for Colleges & Universities, 1981: Educational Opportunities for Handicapped Students. S. G. Tickton et al. 123p. (Orig.). 1981. pap. 5.00 o.p. (ISBN 0-89492-055-3). Acad Educ Dev.

Idea Handbook, 1982: Attracting & Retaining Highly Qualified Young Faculty Members at Colleges & Universities. Sidney G. Tickton. 192p. 1982. pap. 12.00 o.p. (ISBN 0-89492-056-1). Acad Educ Dev.

Idea of a Southern Nation: Southern Nationalists & Southern Nationalism, 1830-1860. John M. McCardell, Jr. 1979. 19.95x o.p. (ISBN 0-393-01241-7). Norton.

Idea of I.Q. Russell Marks. LC 81-40166. 320p. (Orig.). 1982. lib. bdg. 30.25 o.p. (ISBN 0-8191-2062-6); pap. text ed. 15.25 o.p. (ISBN 0-8191-2063-4). U Pr of Amer.

Idea of Phenomenology: Husserlian Exemplarism. Andre De Muralt. Tr. by Garry L. Breckon from Fr. LC 73-94433. (Studies in Phenomenology & Existential Philosophy). 1974. text ed. 32.95x o.p. (ISBN 0-8101-0448-2). Northwestern U Pr.

Idea of Principle in Leibnitz & the Evolution of Deductive Theory. Jose Ortega y Gasset. LC 66-18068. 1971. 10.00x o.p. (ISBN 0-393-01086-4). Norton.

Idea of Progress in Recent American Protestant Thought, 1930-1960. Paul A. Carter. Ed. by Richard C. Wolf. LC 69-14621. (Facet Bks). 1969. pap. 0.50 o.p. (ISBN 0-8006-3052-1, 1-3052, Fortress). Augsburg Fortress.

Idea of Social Structure: Papers in Honor of Robert K. Merton. Ed. by Lewis A. Coser. 547p. (Orig.). 1975. text ed. 20.00 o.p. (ISBN 0-15-540548-9, HC). HarBraceJ.

Idea of the Garden in the Renaissance. Terry Comito. 1978. 32.00x o.p. (ISBN 0-8135-0841-X). Rutgers U Pr.

Ideal Book for Children: Freddie & the Ten Commandments. 2nd ed. Barbara L. Williams. 0.95 o.p. (ISBN 0-686-13718-3). Crusade Pubs.

Ideal Cardiac Pacing. A-Haddi Hakki. (Major Problems in Clinical Surgery Ser.: Vol. 31). (Illus.). 290p. 1984. write for info. o.p. (ISBN 0-7216-1251-2). Saunders.

Ideal Home. Fulvio Testa. LC 85-22929. 26p. (gr. 1-4). 1986. 8.95 o.p. (ISBN 0-87226-055-0, Dist. by Har-Row). P Bedrick Bks.

Ideal Horse: How to Train Him & Yourself. Burt Phillips. (Illus.). 251p. 1982. 20.00 o.p. (ISBN 0-682-49896-3, Banner). Exposition-Phoenix.

Ideal Managers Library. Stewart. 1987. pap. 40.85 o.p. (ISBN 0-471-63510-3). Wiley.

Ideal of Rationality. S. Nathanson. LC 84-12790. 192p. 1985. text ed. 27.50x o.p. (ISBN 0-391-03166-X). Humanities.

Ideals & Realities in Russian Literature. P. Kroptkin. 1971. Repr. of 1916 ed. lib. bdg. 35.00x o.p. (ISBN 0-8371-4518-X, KRID). Greenwood.

Ideals Easter. Ideals Staff. 1985. pap. 3.50 o.p. (ISBN 0-8249-1041-9). Ideals.

Ideals Eggs & Cheese Cookbook. Darlene Kronchnabel. 64p. (Orig.). 1982. pap. 3.95 o.p. (ISBN 0-8249-3009-6). Ideals.

Ideas & Concepts. George Santayana. LC 64-16360. 352p. 1954. Philos Lib.

Ideas for Better Church Meetings. Jerold W. Apps. LC 75-2842. 128p. (Orig.). 1975. pap. 4.50 o.p. (ISBN 0-8066-1487-0, 10-3190, Augsburg). Augsburg Fortress.

Ideas for Prayer. Hubert Van Zeller. 1973. pap. 3.95 o.p. (ISBN 0-87243-046-4). Templegate.

Ideas for the Thoughtful Teacher: Bicentennial Edition. 2nd,rev. ed. Charles F. Bevans. 1975. 5.00 o.p. (ISBN 0-682-48366-4, University). Exposition-Phoenix.

Ideas of Chemistry. Martha O. Visscher. (Illus.). 530p. 1978. text ed. 19.95 o.p. (ISBN 0-15-540550-0, HC). HarBraceJ.

Ideas of Richard Wagner: An Examination & Analysis of His Major Aesthetic, Political, Economic, Social, & Religious Thoughts. rev. ed. Alan D. Aberbach. 396p. (Orig.). 1987. lib. bdg. 28.75 o.p. (ISBN 0-8191-4145-3); pap. text ed. 16.75 o.p. (ISBN 0-8191-4146-1). U Pr of Amer.

Ideas on Human Evolution: Selected Essays, 1949-1961. Ed. by William Howells. LC 62-11399. (Illus.). 1967. pap. text ed. 3.95x o.p. (ISBN 0-689-70101-2, 98, Atheneum). Macmillan.

Ideas on Institutions: Analysing the Literature on Long-Term Care & Custody, Vol. I. Kathleen Jones & A. J. Fowles. 250p. (Orig.). 1984. pap. 13.95x o.p. (ISBN 0-7100-9721-2). Routledge Chapman & Hall.

Ideas to Make Your Days Easier: A Potpourri of Helpful Hints. Elenora Strand. 1977. 4.00 o.p. (ISBN 0-682-48813-5). Exposition-Phoenix.

Idee Fixe ou Deux Hommes a la Mer. Paul Valery. (Coll. Idees). pap. 3.95 o.p. (ISBN 0-685-36614-6). Schoenhof.

Identification & Analysis of Organic Pollutants in the Air. Lawrence H. Keith. 1984. 49.95 o.p. (ISBN 0-250-40575-X). Butterworth.

Identification & Police Line-Ups. William E. Ringel. 211p. (Orig.). 1968. pap. 5.00x o.p. (ISBN 0-87526-038-1). Gould.

Identification Methods for Microbiologists, Pt. B. 2nd ed. F. A. Skinner & D. W. Lovelock. LC 79-41203. (Society for Applied Bacteriology Technical Ser.: No.14). 1980. 64.00 o.p. (ISBN 0-12-647750-7). Acad Pr.

Identification of Frost-Susceptible Participles in Concrete Aggregates. (National Cooperative Highway Research Program Report). 58p. 1969. 2.80 o.p. (ISBN 0-317-36087-6, 1740). Transport Res Bd.

Identification of Functional Groups in Organophosphorus Compounds. L. C. Thomas. 1975. 43.50 o.p. (ISBN 0-12-688550-8). Acad Pr.

Identification of Vegetable Fibers. D. M. Catling & J. Graywon. LC 81-18186. 1982. 38.00 o.p. (ISBN 0-412-22300-7, NO. 6683, Pub. by Chapman & Hall). Routledge Chapman & Hall.

Identification of Vibrating Structures. Ed. by H. G. Natke. (CISM - International Centre for Mechanical Sciences Courses & Lectures Ser.: Vol. 272). (Illus.). 510p. 1982. pap. 36.90 o.p. (ISBN 0-387-81651-8). Springer-Verlag.

Identification, Storage, & Handling of Components, Parts, & Materials. (Quality Assurance Practices Ser.: Module 31-4). (Illus.). 34p. 1979. spiral bdg. 6.00x o.p. (ISBN 0-87683-135-8). GP Pub.

Identifying American Furniture. 2nd, rev. ed. Milo M. Nueve. (Illus.). 124p. 1989. pap. 15.00 o.p. (ISBN 0-910050-96-1, 689). AASLH Pr.

Identifying & Estimating the Genetic Impact of Chemical Mutagens. National Research Council, Board on Toxicology & Environmental Health Hazards. 295p. 1983. pap. text ed. 11.50x o.p. (ISBN 0-309-03345-4). Natl Acad Pr.

Identity & Community: A Social Introduction to Religion. L. Shannon Jung. pap. 4.49 o.p. (ISBN 0-8042-0830-1, John Knox). Westminster John Knox.

Identity of Christianity. Stephen Sykes. LC 83-48907. 256p. 1984. 21.95 o.p. (ISBN 0-8006-0720-1, 1-720, Fortress). Augsburg Fortress.

Identity of Jesus Christ: The Hermeneutical Bases of Dogmatic Theology. Hans W. Frei. LC 74-80422. 192p. 1975. 8.95 o.p. (ISBN 0-8006-0292-7, 1-292, Fortress). Augsburg Fortress.

Identity of Man. J. Bronowski. 1988. 16.00 o.p. (ISBN 0-8446-6339-5). Peter Smith.

Identity of Man. Grahame Clark. (Illus.). 224p. 1983. 17.95x o.p. (ISBN 0-416-33550-0, NO. 3773). Routledge Chapman & Hall.

Identity of the Individual in the Psalms. Steven J. Croft. (JSOT Supplement Ser.: No. 44). 280p. pap. text ed. 15.95x o.s.i. (Pub. by JSOT Pr England). Eisenbrauns.

Ideological Revolution in the Middle East. 2nd ed. Leonard Binder. LC 77-24596. 424p. 1979. lib. bdg. 27.50 o.p. (ISBN 0-88275-593-5). Krieger.

Ideologies of Liberation in Black Africa, 1856-1970: Documents on Modern African Political Thought from Colonial Times to the Present. J. Ayo Langley. 858p. 1979. 45.00x o.p. (ISBN 0-8476-6219-5). Rowman.

Ideologies of Planning Law. Patrick McAuslan. (Urban & Regional Planning Ser.: Vol. 22). 1980. 70.00 o.p. (ISBN 0-08-023696-0); pap. 26.00 o.p. (ISBN 0-08-025198-6). Pergamon.

Ideology & Economics: U. S. Relations with the Soviet Union, 1918-1933. Joan H. Wilson. LC 73-89133. 208p. 1974. 23.00x o.p. (ISBN 0-8262-0157-1). U of Mo Pr.

Ideology & the Development of Sociological Theory. 2nd ed. Irving M. Zeitlin. (Series in Sociology). (Illus.). 336p. 1981. text ed. (ISBN 0-13-449769-4). P-H.

Ideology, Culture & the Process of Schooling. Henry A. Giroux. 168p. 1981. 24.95 o.p. (ISBN 0-87722-228-2). Temple U Pr.

Ideology for Survival. George Sommerville. 277p. 1984. text ed. 17.50x o.p. (ISBN 0-86140-185-9). Humanities.

Ideology of Motherhood: A Study of Sydney Suburban Mothers. Betsy Wearing. LC 83-71799. (Studies in Society: No. 21). 242p. 1984. text ed. 30.00 o.s.i. (ISBN 0-86861-135-2); pap. text ed. 13.95 o.p. (ISBN 0-86861-143-3). Unwin Hyman.

Ides of March Conspiracy. Clyde Matthews. LC 78-57331. 1979. 9.95 o.p. (ISBN 0-87795-201-9, Arbor Hse). Morrow.

Idiot. Fyodor Dostoyevsky. Tr. by Constance Garnett. LC 82-42864. (Illus.). 10.95 o.p. (ISBN 0-394-60434-2). Modern Lib.

Idiotypes & Lymphocytes. Constantin Bona. LC 81-10759. (Immunology: An International Series of Monographs & Treatise). 1981. 24.95 o.p. (ISBN 0-12-112950-0). Acad Pr.

Idol for Others. Gordon Merrick. 1977. pap. 3.95 o.p. (ISBN 0-380-00971-4, 84756-6). Avon.

Idol: Rock Hudson; the True Story of an American Film Hero. LC 86-11142. (Illus.). 273p. 1986. 16.45 o.p. (ISBN 0-394-55489-2, Pub. by Villard Bks). Random.

Idols of Our Time. Bob Goudzwaard. Tr. by Mark V. Vennen from Dutch. LC 84-652. 120p. (Orig.). 1984. pap. 6.95 o.p. (ISBN 0-87784-970-6). Inter-Varsity.

IEEE Communications Society's Tutorials in Modern Communication. Ed. by V. B. Lawrence & J. L. LoCicero. LC 82-10599. (Computer Software Engineering Ser.). 348p. 1982. text ed. 44.95 o.p. (ISBN 0-914894-48-X, Computer Sci Pr). W H Freeman.

IEEE Recommended Practice for Protection & Coordination of Industrial & Commercial Power Systems. Institute of Electrical & Electronics Engineers, Inc. (IEEE) Staff. LC 75-27282. 312p. 1976. 19.95x o.p. (ISBN 0-471-01802-3, Pub. by Wiley-Interscience). Wiley.

IEEE Standard 488-1978: IEEE Standard Digital Interface for Programmable Instrumentation. 1978. 13.00 o.p. (ISBN 0-317-03948-2, SHO7260). Inst Electrical.

IEEE Standard 728-1982: IEEE Standard Recommended Practice for Code & Format Conventions for Use with ANSI-IEEE Standard 488-1978, IEEE Standard Digital Interface for Programmable Instrumentation. 1982. 11.00 o.p. (ISBN 0-317-03940-7, SHO8854). Inst Electrical.

IEEE Supplement, No. 802.3. (IEEE Standards Publications). 1988. 35.00 o.p. (ISBN 0-471-61153-0). Wiley.

IEEE Trial Use Guide for Transmission Structure Foundation Design: Standard 691-1985. 216p. 1985. 29.95 o.p. (ISBN 0-471-01075-8). Wiley.

If. Amy W. Carmichael. (Illus.). 64p. 1980. 5.95 o.p. (ISBN 0-310-42202-7, 6885P). Zondervan.

If a Black Were President of the U. S. A. Farghaneh Nejand. 1977. 4.00 o.p. (ISBN 0-682-48853-4). Exposition-Phoenix.

If an Agent Knocks: Federal Investigators & Your Rights. 1.00 o.p. Natl Lawyers Guild.

If at First... Sandra Boynton. (Illus.). 32p. (ps-1). 1980. 12.45 o.p. (ISBN 0-316-10487-6); pap. 3.95 o.p. (ISBN 0-316-10486-8). Little.

If Grandma Had Wheels: Jewish Folk Sayings. Ed. by Ruby G. Strauss. LC 85-7466. (Illus.). 64p. 1985. 8.95 o.s.i. (ISBN 0-689-31156-7, Atheneum Childrens Bks). Macmillan.

If I Can Write, You Can Write. Charlie Shedd. LC 84-13058. 192p. 1984. 12.95 o.p. (ISBN 0-89879-115-4). Writers Digest.

If I Could Change My Mom & Dad. Bill Orr & Erwin Lutzer. 128p. 1983. pap. 3.50 o.p. (ISBN 0-8024-0174-0). Moody.

If I Had a Robot... What to Expect from the Personal Robot. Nelson B. Winkless, III. 247p. (Orig.). 1984. pap. 11.95 o.p. (ISBN 0-317-39386-3). Robot Inst Am.

If I Had Been... Ten Historical Fantasies. Ed. by Daniel Snowman. (Illus.). 233p. 1979. 15.50x o.p. (ISBN 0-8476-6136-9). Rowman.

If I Loved You Wednesday. Jeannette Eyerly. (gr. 7-10). 1982. pap. 2.50 o.p. (ISBN 0-671-61353-7). Archway.

If I Ran the Zoo. Dr. Seuss. LC 50-10185. (Illus.). 64p. (gr. k-3). 1980. pap. 3.95 o.s.i. (ISBN 0-394-84545-5, BYR). Random.

If I Were King of the Universe. Abelson. (Fraggle Rock Bks.). (gr. 2-6). 5.95 o.s.i. (ISBN 0-03-071087-1). H Holt & Co.

If It Please You. Raymond Carver. 25p. 1984. deluxe ed. 50.00 Deluxe Signed Ed. o.s.i. (ISBN 0-935716-28-9). Lord John.

If Life Is a Bowl of Cherries, What Am I Doing in the Pits? Erma Bombeck. 1981. pap. 2.95 o.p. (ISBN 0-449-23894-6, Crest). Fawcett.

If Life Is a Bowl of Cherries-What Am I Doing in the Pits? Erma Bombeck. (General Ser.). 1978. lib. bdg. 12.95 o.p. (ISBN 0-8161-6613-7, Large Print Bks). G K Hall.

If Love Comes. Ann Ashton. LC 86-19963. (Starlight Romance Ser.). 192p. 1987. 12.95 o.p. (ISBN 0-385-23476-7). Doubleday.

If Love Is the Answer, What Is the Question? Uta West. 1977. text ed. 8.95 o.p. (ISBN 0-07-069476-1). McGraw.

If Mice Could Fly. John Cameron. LC 79-4927. (Illus.). (ps-3). 1979. 8.95 o.p. (ISBN 0-689-30731-4, Atheneum). Macmillan.

If Not for Love. Carol Franz. (Orig.). 1981. pap. text ed. 2.50 o.p. (ISBN 0-505-51603-9, Pub. by Tower Bks). Dorchester Pub Co.

If Not for Profit, for What? A Behavioral Theory of the Nonprofit Sector Based on Entrepreneurship. Dennis R. Young. Frwd. by John Simon. LC 82-48482. 192p. 1983. 25.00X o.p. (ISBN 0-669-06154-9). Lexington Bks.

If Not Now, When? Date not set. (ISBN 0-8052-3497-7). Random.

If Not Now, When? A Novel. Primo Levi. Tr. by William Weaver. 384p. 1985. 15.45 o.s.i. (ISBN 0-671-49336-1). Summit Bks.

If on a Winter's Night a Traveler. Italo Calvino. Tr. by William Weaver from Ital. LC 80-8741. (Helen & Kurt Wolff Bk.). 288p. 1981. 12.95 o.p. (ISBN 0-15-143689-4). HarBraceJ.

If Productivity Is the Problem. Kenneth F. Huddleston. 54p. cancelled o.s.i. (ISBN 0-318-22129-2, SN36). Natl Ctr Res Voc Ed.

If Television Didn't Have Censorship. Glenn Gilbert. LC 86-60761. 136p. (Orig.). 1986. pap. 6.95 o.p. (ISBN 0-86666-252-9). Authors Unltd.

If the Earth Falls In. Mavis T. Clark. LC 75-4781. 176p. (gr. 6 up). 1979. 6.95 o.p. (ISBN 0-395-28900-9, Clarion). HM.

If the Old Could. Jane Somers. LC 83-49027. 250p. 1984. 13.95 o.s.i. (ISBN 0-394-53757-2). Knopf.

If the Reaper Ride. Elizabeth Norman. 1978. pap. 1.95 o.p. (ISBN 0-380-01886-1, 37135-9). Avon.

If the Shoe Fits. Andrew L. Von Louth. 1979. 10.00 o.p. (ISBN 0-682-49276-0). Exposition-Phoenix.

If They Ask You, You Can Write a Song. Al Kasha. 1984. pap. 8.95 o.p. (ISBN 0-346-16006-5). Cornerstone.

If We Can Love. Ed. by Vernon Neufeld. LC 82-83885. 340p. 1983. pap. 16.95 o.s.i. (ISBN 0-87303-074-5). Faith & Life.

If We Could Hear the Grass Grow. Eleanor Craig. (Illus.). 1983. 14.50 o.p. (ISBN 0-671-46188-5). S&S.

If Wishes Were Saabs & Other Nursery Rhymes for Modern Times. Tom Darbyshire & Stefan Underhill. 1986. pap. 5.95 o.p. (ISBN 0-316-17281-2). Little.

If Words Could Set Us Free. Gertrude B. Bailey. 1974. 4.00 o.p. (ISBN 0-682-47975-6). Exposition-Phoenix.

If You Believe in Me. Janice Kaplan. 144p. (YA) (gr. 7 up). 1984. pap. 2.25 o.p. (ISBN 0-380-87213-7, Flare). Avon.

If You Can Count to Four. 5th ed. Jim Jones. LC 66-15520. 246p. 1974. pap. 5.95 o.s.i. (ISBN 0-8008-4126-3). Taplinger.

If You Can't Be Good. Ross Thomas. 1986. 17.95 o.p. (ISBN 0-317-53118-2, Large Print Bks). G K Hall.

If You Love Me. Billy Hanks. 108p. 1985. pap. 8.95 o.p. (ISBN 0-8499-3019-7, 3019-7). Word Bks.

If You Love Me, Call Me Dorrie. Bonnie S. Smith. (Pennypinchers Ser.). (gr. 3-6). 1982. pap. 2.95 o.p. (ISBN 0-89191-710-1). Cook.

If You Love Me, Let Me Go. Norma Johnston. LC 78-6711. 168p. (gr. 7 up). 1978. 8.95 o.s.i. (ISBN 0-689-30655-5, Atheneum Childrens Bks). Macmillan.

If You Love Somebody Who Smokes: Confessions of a Nicotine Addict. Cynthia Morgan. LC 87-71061. 96p. 1987. pap. 5.95 o.p. (ISBN 0-317-64320-7). City Miner Bks.

If You Must Write. W. H. Johnson. 100p. 1956. (ISBN 0-8022-0806-1). Philos Lib.

If You Promise Not to Tell Activity Book. Joe Wyman. 48p. (gr. k-8). 1985. wkbk. 5.95 o.p. (ISBN 0-86653-289-7). Good Apple.

If You Rub a Wrinkle. Gail George. 14p. (ps). 1986. 6.95 o.s.i. (ISBN 0-394-88415-9, BYR). Random.

If You Want to Evaluate Your Library... F. W. Lancaster. 208p. 1988. pap. text ed. 48.00x o.p. (ISBN 0-85365-928-1, L928-1, Pub. by Library Assn Pub London). ALA.

If You're Afraid of the Dark Remember the Night Rainbow. Cooper Edens. Date not set. 10.95 o.p. (ISBN 0-310-57060-3, 16106). Zondervan.

Ifigenia in Tauride. Tommaso Traetta. Ed. by Howard M. Brown. LC 76-20982. (Italian Opera 1640-1770 Ser.). 1978. lib. bdg. 77.00 o.p. (ISBN 0-8240-2646-2). Garland Pub.

IFO Report. Thierry J. Sagnier. 336p. 1983. pap. 3.50 o.p. (ISBN 0-380-83337-9, 83337-9). Avon.

Ifugao Law. Roy F. Barton. LC 78-76334. (Illus.). 1969. Repr. of 1919 ed. 26.50x o.p. (ISBN 0-520-01427-8). U of Cal Pr.

Igor Fedorovitch Stravinsky, 1882-1971: A Practical Guide to Publications of His Music. Dominique-Rene De Lerma. LC 74-79152. 150p. 1974. 13.50x o.p. (ISBN 0-87338-158-0). Kent St U Pr.

IIc BASIC Paint: Graphics for the Apple II Family. Bruce Hicks & Sylvia Baron. LC 84-7290. (General Trade Books). 260p. 1985. pap. 16.95 o.p. (ISBN 0-471-80503-3); incl. disk 39.95 o.p. (ISBN 0-471-81506-3). Wiley.

IIE Microsoftware: Economic Analysis. Gary Whitehouse et al. 1981. cancelled 175.00 o.p. (ISBN 0-89806-013-3). Inst Indus Eng.

IIE Microsoftware: Work Measurement. Gary Whitehouse et al. 1982. cancelled 175.00 o.p. (ISBN 0-89806-035-4). Inst Indus Eng.

IISS Commentary Special Reports I: Steel Plants U. S. A., 1960-1980. Ed. by R. L. Deily. 238p. 1982. 50.00 o.p. (ISBN 0-317-34774-8). Iron & Steel.

Ikat of India. Commentary by Martha Longenecker. LC 81-85347. (Illus.). 48p. 1981. 7.95 o.s.i. Mingei Intl Mus.

Ike & Porker. Susan E. Kirby. 160p. (gr. 3-6). 1983. 8.70 o.s.i. (ISBN 0-395-34556-1). HM.

Ikebana & Bonsai, 1989. Shufunmoto Company, Ltd. Staff. (Illus.). 114p. 1988. spiral bdg. with laminated covers 8.95 o.p. (ISBN 4-07-974593-1, Pub. by Shufunotomo Co Ltd, Japan). C E Tuttle.

Ila-Speaking Peoples of Northern Rhodesia, 2 Vols. Edwin W. Smith & A. M. Dale. 1966. 20.00 o.p. (ISBN 0-8216-0097-4, Pub. by Univ Bks). Carol Pub Group.

Iliad of Homer. 48p. (Orig.). 1988. pap. 9.95 o.p. (ISBN 1-55651-425-5); cassette o.p. (ISBN 1-55651-426-3). Cram Cassettes.

Ilion-The Town Remington Made. Warren E. Schulz. 1977. pap. 6.00 o.p. (ISBN 0-682-48731-7). Exposition-Phoenix.

Iljushiny Razgovory. Diana Vinkovetsky. LC 81-20095. (Illus.). 142p. (Rus.). 1981. pap. 7.50 o.s.i. (ISBN 0-938920-08-1). Hermitage.

I'll Be Wearing a White Carnation. Judi Miller. 320p. 1985. pap. 3.50 o.p. (ISBN 0-380-89586-2). Avon.

I'll Buy That! Fifty Small Wonders & Big Deals That Revolutionized the Lives of Consumers. Ed. by Consumer Report Book Editors. 256p. (Orig.). 1986. pap. 20.00 o.s.i. (ISBN 0-89043-032-2); 30.00 o.s.i. (ISBN 0-89043-046-2); ltd. ed. 75.00 o.s.i. (ISBN 0-89043-047-0). Consumer Reports.

I'll Fix Anthony. Judith Viorst. (Illus.). 32p. (ps-3). 1987. pap. 3.95 o.p. (Aladdin). Macmillan.

ILL Met by Moonlight. W. Stanley Moss. (Echoes of War Ser.). 1987. pap. 10.95 o.p. (ISBN 0-907675-46-8, Pub. by Buchan & Enright England). Seven Hills Bk Dists.

Ill Seen Ill Said. Samuel Beckett. LC 81-47695. 64p. 1982. pap. 4.95 o.p. (ISBN 0-394-17953-6, E818, Ever). Grove.

I'll Take Care of the Corcodiles. Stefan Mahlqvist. LC 78-45642. (Illus.). 32p. (gr. 1-4). 1978. 6.95 o.p. (ISBN 0-689-50124-2, Atheneum). Macmillan.

I'll Take Tomorrow: The Story of a Courageous Woman Who Dared to Subject Herself to a Medical Experiment; The First Successful Heart-Lung Transplant. Mary Gohlke & Max Jennings. Ed. by Maureen Heffernen. LC 84-28803. 204p. 12.95 o.p. (ISBN 0-87131-458-4). M Evans.

Illegal Drugs & Alcohol: An Injury to America? Ed. by Mark A. Siegel et al. (Instructional Aides Ser.). 118p. 1983. pap. 14.95 o.p. (ISBN 0-936474-32-7). Info Plus TX.

Illegal Entries. Adele Kenny. 60p. 1984. pap. 5.95 o.p. (ISBN 0-934536-16-3). Merging Media.

Illiac IV: The First Supercomputer. R. Michael Hord. LC 81-19437. (Digital Systems Design ser.). (Illus.). 350p. 1982. text ed. 46.95 o.p. (ISBN 0-914894-71-4, Computer Sci Pr). W H Freeman.

Illinois: Agency. 1983. 8.50 o.p. (ISBN 0-686-90708-6). Am Law Inst.

Illinois Business Directory, 1987-88, 2 vols. rev. ed. American Directory Publishing Co., Inc. Staff. 3079p. 1987. Set. pap. 165.00 o.p. (ISBN 0-944316-06-9). Amer Directory.

Illinois Civil Practice, 1987 & Illinois Criminal Practice, 1987, 2 vols. Michie Company Editorial Staff. 1987. Set. 90.00x o.s.i. (ISBN 0-87473-286-7); Civil Vol. only, 1227 pgs. 60.00x o.s.i. (ISBN 0-87473-284-0); CriminL Vol. only, 915 pgs. 60.00x o.s.i. (ISBN 0-87215-864-0, 73044). Michie Co.

Illinois: Conflict of Laws. 1983. 8.50 o.p. (ISBN 0-686-90715-9). Am Law Inst.

Illinois: Contracts. 1983. 9.50 o.p. (ISBN 0-686-90463-X). Am Law Inst.

Illinois Cook County Marketing Directory: 1988. 1138p. 1988. 195.00 o.p. Manufacturers.

Illinois Dupage County Marketing Directory: 1988. 268p. 1988. 90.00 o.p. Manufacturers.

Illinois Images of the Landscape. Willard Clay. (Illus.). 160p. 1988. cancelled 35.00 o.p. (ISBN 0-942394-83-6). Westcliffe Pubs Inc.

Illinois in the Second World War: Vol. 1, Operation Home Front. Mary Watters. LC 51-3163. 1951. 5.00 o.p. (ISBN 0-912154-18-7). Ill St Hist Lib.

Illinois in the Second World War: Vol. 2, The Production Front. Mary Watters. LC 51-3163. 1952. 5.00 o.p. (ISBN 0-912154-19-5). Ill St Hist Lib.

Illinois Insurance Law: A License Preparation Manual for Life & Health, Property & Casualty. Marshall W. Reavis. LC 83-5437. 174p. 1983. text ed. 15.95 o.p. Longman Finan.

Illinois Lake County Marketing Directory: 1988. 124p. 1988. 60.00 o.p. Manufacturers.

Illinois Manufacturers Directory, 1988. 1504p. 1988. 125.00 o.p. (ISBN 0-318-02862-X, Pub. by Manufacturers' News Inc). Manufacturers.

Illinois: Property, Vols. 1-3. 1983. 9.50 o.p. (ISBN 0-686-90719-1). Am Law Inst.

Illinois Services Directory, 1988. 1416p. 1987. 135.00 o.p. (ISBN 0-318-02863-8). Manufacturers.

Illinois Supplement for Modern Real Estate Practice. 8th ed. Real Estate Education Company Staff. Ed. by John D. Ballou & Thomas H. Bowman, Jr. 176p. (Orig.). 1984. pap. text ed. 9.95 o.p. (ISBN 0-88462-502-8, 1510-03, Real Estate Ed). Longman Finan.

Illinois Tort Law & Practice. Jerome Mirza. LC 88-82172. 1988. 74.50 o.p. Lawyers Co-Op.

Illinois: Trusts. 2nd ed. 1983. 11.50 o.p. (ISBN 0-686-90469-9). Am Law Inst.

Illiteracy in America. Ed. by Gary McCuen. LC 87-9151. (Ideas in Conflict Ser.). (Illus.). 152p. 1988. lib. bdg. 11.95 o.p. (ISBN 0-86596-067-4). GEM McCuen Pubns.

Illiteracy in America: Extent, Causes & Suggested Solutions. Patricia H. Smith. 101p. 1986. pap. 4.75 o.p. (ISBN 0-318-21685-X, S/N 065-000-00253-1). USGPO.

Illiterate America. Jonathan Kozol. LC 84-20487. 288p. 1985. 15.95 o.p. (ISBN 0-385-19536-2, Anchor Pr). Doubleday.

Illiterate Digest. Will Rogers. LC 77-145720. (Illus.). 352p. 1975. Repr. of 1924 ed. 48.00x o.p. (ISBN 0-8103-3975-7). Gale.

Illness As Metaphor. Susan Sontag. 87p. 1988. pap. 5.95 o.p. (ISBN 0-374-52073-9). FS&G.

Illness As Metaphor. Susan Sontag. 87p. 1988. 15.95 o.p. (ISBN 0-374-17446-6); pap. 5.95 o.p. (ISBN 0-317-67507-9). FS&G.

Illness Called Alcoholism. American Medical Association Staff. 20p. (Orig.). 1977. pap. 1.75 o.p. (ISBN 0-89970-274-0, OP-192). AMA.

Illumination, Color, A Contrast Tables: Naturally Illuminated Objects. M. R. Nagel et al. 1978. 69.50 o.p. (ISBN 0-12-513750-8). Acad Pr.

Illumination Engineering for Energy Efficient Luminous Environments. R. Helms. 1980. text ed. 65.00 o.p. (ISBN 0-13-450809-2). P-H.

Illuminations. Janice D. Civen. LC 84-8009. (Illus.). 128p. 1984. 15.95 o.p. (ISBN 0-396-08176-2). Dodd.

Illuminations. Bruce Kaduk. LC 85-51961. 60p. 1986. pap. 5.95 o.p. (ISBN 1-55523-013-X). Winston-Derek.

Illuminations of the Stavelot Bible. Wayne R. Dynes. LC 77-94693. (Outstanding Dissertations in the Fine Arts Ser.). (Illus.). 1978. lib. bdg. 44.00 o.p. (ISBN 0-8240-3225-X). Garland Pub.

Illumines. Gerard de Nerval & Max Milner. 441p. (Folio 848). 1976. 4.50 o.p. (ISBN 0-686-54815-9). Schoenhof.

Illusion. Mignon Warner. (Nightingale Ser.). 363p. 1986. pap. 11.95x o.p. (ISBN 0-8161-4063-4, Large Print Bks). G K Hall.

Illusion & Reality. Christopher Caudwell. LC 48-5327. 370p. 1973. pap. 2.25 o.p. (ISBN 0-7178-0374-0). Intl Pubs Co.

Illusion of Immortality. Corliss Lamont. 320p. 1959. (ISBN 0-8022-0907-6). Philos Lib.

Illusion: Soviet Soldiers in Hitler's Armies. Jurgen Thorwald. Tr. by Richard Winston & Clara Winston. LC 75-14033. (Helen & Kurt Wolff Bks.). (Illus.). 342p. 1975. 12.50 o.p. (ISBN 0-15-144085-9). HarBraceJ.

Illusionist: A Novel. Anita Mason. 1984. 16.95 o.p. (ISBN 0-03-070779-X). H Holt & Co.

Illusions. Charlotte V. Allen. LC 86-25956. 320p. 1987. 16.95 o.p. (ISBN 0-689-11891-0, Atheneum). Macmillan.

Illusory Flame: Chinese Love Stories. Tr. by Howard S. Levy. (Illus.). 1962. 15.00x o.p. (ISBN 0-686-00725-5). Oriental Bk Store.

Illustrated Apple LOGO Book. Robert G. Humphries. (Illustrated Ser.). (Illus.). 183p. (Orig.). 1985. pap. 19.95 o.p. (ISBN 0-915381-72-9). Wordware Pub.

Illustrated AutoCAD Book (2.18) Paul Schlieve & Tom W. Berghauser. (Illustrated Ser.). 333p. (Orig.). 1986. pap. 19.95 o.p. (ISBN 0-915381-82-6). Wordware Pub.

Illustrated Basic Carpentry. Graham Blackburn. LC 77-1669. (Illus.). 1977. pap. 6.70 o.p. (ISBN 0-316-09870-1). Little.

Illustrated Bible Dictionary. M. G. Easton. (Baker's Paperback Reference Library). 760p. 1983. pap. 12.95 o.p. (ISBN 0-8010-3386-1). Baker Bk.

Illustrated Book of the Great Ancient Temples. Lyman Metropulous. (Masterpieces of World Architecture Library). (Illus.). 141p. 1983. 112.50 o.p. (ISBN 0-86650-042-1). Gloucester Art.

Illustrated C Programming Book. Emmett Beam. LC 85-659. (Illus.). 286p. 1985. pap. 19.95 o.p. (ISBN 0-915381-65-6). Wordware Pub.

Illustrated Challenge from Beyond. H. P. Lovecraft & Robert E. Howard. 5.95 o.p. (ISBN 0-686-31234-1). Necronomicon.

Illustrated Corvette Buyer's Guide. Michael Antonick. LC 82-14312. (Buyer's Guide Ser.). (Illus.). 156p. 1983. pap. 13.95 o.p. (ISBN 0-87938-160-4). Motorbooks Intl.

Illustrated Custom Boat Building. R. B. Roberts-Goodson. (Illus.). 192p. (Orig.). pap. 12.95 o.p. (ISBN 0-8227-8029-1). Petersen Pub.

Illustrated dBASE III Book. Russell A. Stultz. (Illustrated Ser.). (Illus.). 320p. (Orig.). 1985. pap. 19.95 o.p. (ISBN 0-915381-75-3). Wordware Pub.

Illustrated Dictionary of Building Materials & Techniques. Paul Bianchina. (Illus.). 270p. 1986. 22.95 o.p. (ISBN 0-8306-0281-X, NO. 2681); pap. 14.60 o.p. (ISBN 0-8306-0481-2). TAB Bks.

Illustrated Dictionary of Electronics. 3rd ed. Rufus P. Turner & Stan Gibilisco. (Illus.). 720p. 1985. 34.95 o.p. (ISBN 0-8306-0866-4, 1866); pap. 21.95 o.p. (ISBN 0-8306-1866-X). TAB Bks.

Illustrated Dictionary of Photography. D. Backhouse et al. (Illus.). 212p. (Orig.). pap. 11.95 o.p. (ISBN 0-85242-668-2, Pub. by Fountain Pr UK). Seven Hills Bk Dists.

Illustrated Dictionary of Place Names: United States & Canada. Ed. by Kelsie B. Harder. 632p. 1986. 21.95 o.p. (ISBN 0-8160-1143-5); pap. 12.95 o.p. (ISBN 0-8160-1048-X). Facts on File.

Illustrated Dictionary of World Religions. Arthur Jones. 1982. text ed. 20.00 o.s.i. (ISBN 0-08-024176-X). Pergamon.

Illustrated Directory of Architects 1986. 2nd ed. Moxley & Woods. 1987. pap. 31.95 o.p. (ISBN 0-85139-725-5). Van Nos Reinhold.

Illustrated Elvis. W. A. Harbinson. (Illus.). 160p. 1987. pap. 9.95 o.p. (ISBN 0-399-51374-4, Perigee Bks). Putnam Pub Group.

Illustrated Emanuelle: Based on the Novel by Emmanuelle Arsan. Guido Crepax. 144p. 1980. pap. 9.95 o.p. (ISBN 0-8021-4316-4, E765, Ever). Grove.

Illustrated Encyclopedia of British Pottery & Porcelain. Geoffrey A. Godden. 360p. 1980. 40.00 o.p. (ISBN 0-214-20692-0, Pub. by Hutchinson Pub UK). Seven Hills Bk Dists.

Illustrated English-Chinese Dictionary for Pupils. Zhao C. Qun. (Illus.). 524p. (gr. 4-10). 1981. pap. 7.95 o.p. (ISBN 0-8351-1280-2). China Bks.

Illustrated Fact Book of Science. Ed. by Michael W. Dempsey. LC 82-16412. (Illus.). 236p. 1983. 9.95 o.p. (ISBN 0-668-05729-7, 5729). Arco.

Illustrated Guide to Allied Fighters of World War II. Bill Gunston. LC 80-70976. (Illustrated Military Guides Ser.). (Illus.). 160p. 1981. 9.95 o.p. (ISBN 0-668-05228-7, 5228). Arco.

Illustrated Guide to Better Fishing. Bob Zwirz. LC 81-70997. 256p. 1982. 9.95 o.p. (ISBN 0-910676-38-0). DBI.

Illustrated Guide to Better Fishing. 2nd ed. Bob Zwirz. LC 81-70997. (Illus.). 256p. (Orig.). 1985. pap. 11.95 o.p. (ISBN 0-910676-85-2). DBI.

Illustrated Guide to Britain. Automobile Association of England Staff. (Illus.). 1986. 27.45 o.p. (ISBN 0-393-01227-1). Norton.

Illustrated Guide to Cat Dissection. Clifford Keeney. (Illus.). 256p. 1982. lab manual 12.95x o.p. (ISBN 0-89582-080-3). Morton Pub.

Illustrated Guide to Eigtheenth Century English Drinking Glasses. 2nd ed. L. M. Bickerton. (Illus.). 431p. 99.50 o.p. (ISBN 0-907462-61-8). Antique Collect.

Illustrated Guide to Foliage Houseplants. P-H.

Illustrated Guide to Food Preparation. 4th ed. Margaret McWilliams. LC 76-13996. (Illus.). 1982. spiral bdg. 15.95x o.p. (ISBN 0-8087-3420-2). Plycon Pr.

Illustrated Guide to German, Italian & Japanese Fighters of World War II. Bill Gunston. LC 80-67627. (Illustrated Military Guides). (Illus.). 160p. 1980. 9.95 o.p. (ISBN 0-668-05093-4, 5093). Arco.

Illustrated Guide to Growing Your Own Orchids. Ed. by Wilma Rittershausen. LC 83-83424. (Illustrated Gardening Guides Ser.). (Illus.). 160p. 1984. 9.95 o.p. (ISBN 0-668-06197-9, 6179-9). Arco.

Illustrated Guide to Home Retrofitting for Energy Savings. Energy Resources Center Staff. Ed. by Knight et al. LC 80-23568. (Illus.). 384p. 1981. text ed. 21.95 o.p. (ISBN 0-07-019490-4). McGraw.

Illustrated Guide to Individualized Kindergarten Instruction. Mary B. Oxley. LC 76-15372. 1976. text ed. 14.95x o.p. (ISBN 0-13-450957-9, Parker). P-H.

Titles

Illustrated Guide to Linear Programming. Saul I. Gass. 1970. text ed. 29.95 o.p. (ISBN 0-07-022960-0). McGraw.

Illustrated Guide to Medical Terminology. Helen R. Strand. 110p. 1968. lib. bdg. 15.00 o.p. (ISBN 0-683-08006-7); pap. 9.50 o.p. (ISBN 0-685-91060-1, Pub. by W & W). Krieger.

Illustrated Guide to Soviet Ground Forces. (Illus.). 1983. 9.95 o.p. (ISBN 0-668-05344-5). Arco.

Illustrated Guide to Textiles. 3rd ed. Marjory Joseph & Audrey Gieseking. (Illus.). 1981. pap. 12.95x o.p. (ISBN 0-8087-3435-0). Plycon Pr.

Illustrated Guide to the Design of Computer Programs. Y. Singh. pap. write for info. o.s.i. Meghan-Kiffer.

Illustrated Guide to the Modern Soviet Navy. John Jordan. LC 81-71939. (Illustrated Military Guides Ser.). (Illus.). 160p. 1983. 9.95 o.p. (ISBN 0-668-05504-9, 5504). Arco.

Illustrated Guide to the Soviet Ground Forces. Ed. by Ray Bonds. LC 81-67085. (Illus.). 160p. 1981. 9.95 o.p. (5344). Arco.

Illustrated Guide to Worcester Porcelain, 1751-1793. Henry Sandon. (Illus.). 96p. 1980. 35.00 o.p. (ISBN 0-09-142110-1, Pub. by Hutchinson Pub UK). Seven Hills Bk Dists.

Illustrated Guide to World War II Tanks & Fighting Vehicles. Ed. by Ray Bonds. LC 80-70975. (Illustrated Military Guides Ser.). (Illus.). 160p. 1981. 9.95 o.p. (ISBN 0-668-05232-5, 5232). Arco.

Illustrated Handbook of Vernacular Architecture. 3rd ed. R. W. Brunskill. (Illus.). 260p. (Orig.). 1987. pap. 12.95 o.p. (ISBN 0-571-13916-7). Faber & Faber.

Illustrated Handbook: The Museum of Fine Arts, Boston. Museum of Fine Arts, Boston Staff. LC 75-21769. (Illus.). 196p. (Orig.). 1970. pap. 13.50 o.p. Mus Fine Arts Boston.

Illustrated Harvard: Harvard University in Wood Engravings & Words. Michael McCurdy. LC 86-316. (Illus.). 64p. 1986. 14.95 o.p. (ISBN 0-87106-896-6). Globe Pequot.

Illustrated Heritage Dictionary & Information Book. 1977. 34.95 o.p. (ISBN 0-395-25441-8). HM.

Illustrated History of English Literature, 3 Vols. Alfred C. Ward. Repr. of 1953 ed. 195.00x o.p. (ISBN 0-403-04110-4). Somerset Pub.

Illustrated Jazz Book. Taylor J. Barton. (Illustrated Ser.). (Illus.). 326p. (Orig.). 1986. pap. 19.95 o.p. (ISBN 0-915381-77-X). Wordware Pub.

Illustrated Justine: Based on the Novel by the Marquis De Sade. Illus. by Guido Crepax. (Illus.). 160p. 1981. pap. 12.50 o.p. (ISBN 0-8021-4358-X, E798, Ever). Grove.

Illustrated Leaves of Grass. Walt Whitman. Ed. by Howard Chapnick. LC 74-123465. (Illus.). 1971. 7.95 o.p. (ISBN 0-448-02074-2, G&D). Putnam Pub Group.

Illustrated Letter. Charles Hamilton. (Illus.). 176p. 1987. 24.95 o.p. (ISBN 0-87663-664-4). Universe.

Illustrated Life of Jesus: From The National Gallery of Art Collection. Richard I. Abrams & Warner Hutchinson. LC 81-17575. (Illus.). 1982. 40.00 o.p. (ISBN 0-687-01356-9); deluxe ed. 75.00 o.p. (ISBN 0-687-01358-5). Abingdon.

Illustrated London Map. (Illus.). Date not set. Salem Hse Pubs.

Illustrated Manual of Sex Therapy. 2nd ed. Helen S. Kaplan. (Illus.). 200p. 1988. pap. 17.95 o.p. (87-18189). Brunner-Mazel.

Illustrated Microsoft Windows 1.03. Robert E. Whitsitt, II & Lana K. Bryan. (Illustrated Ser.). (Illus.). 256p. (Orig.). 1987. pap. 19.95 o.p. (ISBN 0-915381-89-3). Wordware Pub.

Illustrated MS-PC-DOS Book (3.2) Russell A. Stultz. Ed. by Thomas H. Berliner. LC 84-22213. (Illus.). 220p. 1985. pap. 19.95 o.p. (ISBN 0-915381-53-2). WordWare Pub.

Illustrated MultiMate Book. Paula S. Stone. (Illustrated Ser.). (Illus.). 280p. 1985. pap. 19.95 o.p. (ISBN 0-915381-64-8). WordWare Pub.

Illustrated Notebook for Anatomy Students. William Shearer. (Illus.). 230p. 1982. pap. text ed. College-Hill.

Illustrated PageMaker 1.0a. Phyllis S. Moore. (Illustrated Ser.). (Illus.). 256p. (Orig.). 1988. pap. 19.95 o.p. (ISBN 1-55622-051-0). Wordware Pub.

Illustrated Patchwork Crochet: Contemporary Granny Squares for Clothing & Home Decorating. Bella Scharf. LC 82-82220. (Illus.). 1976. pap. 12.95 o.p. (ISBN 0-8329-0185-7). New Century.

Illustrated PC-FOCUS Book. Bart Benne. LC 85-3352. (Illustrated Ser.). (Illus.). 143p. 1985. pap. 19.95 o.p. (ISBN 0-915381-73-7). Wordware Pub.

Illustrated Poems for Children. Robert Baram. (ps up). 1988. pap. 1.75 o.p. (ISBN 0-317-67473-0, CH0445). Dghtrs St Paul.

Illustrated Q & A. Thomas B. Calvert. (Illustrated Ser.). 321p. (Orig.). 1987. pap. 19.95 o.p. (ISBN 0-915381-98-2). Wordware Pub.

Illustrated RM-COBOL Book. Deborah L. Stone. LC 85-658. (Illus.). 240p. 1985. pap. 19.95 o.p. (ISBN 0-915381-60-5). Wordware Pub.

Illustrated Sporting Books. John H. Slater. LC 71-75800. 212p. 1969. Repr. of 1899 ed. 35.00x o.p. (ISBN 0-8103-3889-0). Gale.

Illustrated Stories from Church History, 16 vols. Larry Porter. Ed. by Paul R. Cheesman. (Illus.). cancelled o.s.i. (ISBN 0-911712-21-6). Eagle Mktg Corp.

Illustrated SuperCalc 3 Book. Guy Pegues. LC 85-669. (Illus.). 176p. 1984. pap. 19.95 o.p. (ISBN 0-915381-62-1). Wordware Pub.

Illustrated Technical Dictionary. Maxim Newmark. (ISBN 0-8022-1209-3). Philos Lib.

Illustrated Textbook of Dog Diseases. James Herriot. (Illus.). 284p. 1980. 12.95 o.p. (ISBN 0-87666-733-7, PS-770). TFH Pubns.

Illustrated TK! Solver Book. Thomas H. Berliner, III & Clemens A. Kathman. LC 84-25692. (Illus.). 157p. 1984. pap. 19.95 o.p. (ISBN 0-915381-63-X). Wordware Pub.

Illustrated Touring Atlas of Britain. (Illus.). Date not set. (ISBN 0-86145-196-1, Pub. by Auto Assn England). Salem Hse Pubs.

Illustrated Treasury of Budd Railway Passenger Cars. James W. Kerr. (Railroad & Americana Transportation Ser.). (Illus.). 250p. 1986. 90.00x o.p. (ISBN 0-919295-02-9). Delta Pubns VT.

Illustrated Treasury of Pullman Standard Railway Passenger Cars Since 1945, Vols. I & II. O. M. Kerr. Ed. by James W. Kerr. (Railroad & Americana Transportation Ser.). (Illus.). 270p. (Orig.). 1986. pap. 90.00x o.p. (ISBN 0-919295-03-7). Delta Pubns VT.

Illustrated Treasury of the American Locomotive Company. O. M. Kerr. Ed. by James W. Kerr. (Railroad & Americana Transportation Ser.). (Illus.). 224p. 1987. 90.00 o.p. (ISBN 0-919295-00-2). Delta Pubns VT.

Illustrated Tumor Nomenclature. 2nd ed. H. Hamperl & L. V. Ackermann. (Illus., Eng., Span., Fr. & Rus.). 1969. 44.00 o.p. (ISBN 0-387-04567-8). Springer-Verlag.

Illustrated Turbo Pascal 3.01. Paul L. Schlieve. (Illustrated Ser.). 329p. (Orig.). 1986. pap. 19.95 o.p. (ISBN 0-915381-78-8). Wordware Pub.

Illustrated Ventura 1.1. Robert W. Kerstetter. (Illustrated Ser.). (Illus.). 270p. (Orig.). (YA) (gr. 6 up). 1988. pap. 19.95 o.p. (ISBN 1-55622-052-9). Wordware Pub.

Illustrated VP-Info. 1.2. Mick McAllister. (Illustrated Ser.). (Illus.). 319p. (Orig.). 1987. pap. 19.95 o.p. (ISBN 1-55622-017-0). Wordware Pub.

Illustrated Who's Who of the Cinema. Orbis Editors. LC 83-790. 1983. lib. bdg. 65.00 o.p. Macmillan.

Illustrated World of Thoreau. Henry David Thoreau. Ed. by Howard Chapnick. LC 73-15134. (Illus.). 192p. 1976. pap. 6.95 o.p. (ISBN 0-448-12590-0, G&D). Putnam Pub Group.

Illustrated Yoga. Zorn. pap. 3.00 o.p. (ISBN 0-87980-218-9). Wilshire.

Illustrating Paul's Letter to the Romans. James E. Hightower, Jr. LC 84-7074. 1984. pap. 5.95 o.p. (ISBN 0-8054-2251-X). Broadman.

Illustration & Perspective. E. Mitooka. (Illus.). 140p. (Orig.). 1986. pap. 26.95 o.p. (ISBN 4-766-10212-6, Pub. by Graphic Sha Japan). Bks Nippan.

Illustration of Books: A Manual for the Use of Students. Joseph Pennell. LC 78-146921. 180p. 1971. Repr. of 1896 ed. 40.00x o.p. (ISBN 0-8103-3641-3). Gale.

Illustrations Collection: Its Formation, Classification & Exploitation. Edmund V. Corbett. LC 72-164185. (Illus.). 164p. 1971. Repr. of 1941 ed. 40.00x o.p. (ISBN 0-8103-3786-X). Gale.

Illustrations from the Works of Andreas Vesalius of Brussels. Andreas Vesalius. Ed. by J. B. Saunders & Charles D. O'Malley. 18.00 o.p. (ISBN 0-8446-4830-2). Peter Smith.

Illustrator Illustrated No. 2: North American Edition. (Illus.). 1981. pap. 12.95 o.p. (ISBN 2-88046-009-3). Norton.

Illustrator Illustrated: The Art Directors' Index to Illustration, Graphics & Design, No. 4. (Illus.). 1984. 49.50 o.p. (ISBN 2-88046-035-2, Pub. by Roto-Vision Switzerland). Norton.

Illustrierte Technische Woerterbucher: Maschinenelemente, Vol. 1. A. Schlomann. (Illus., Ger., Eng., Fr., Rus., Span. & Ital., Illustrated dictionary elements of machinery & tools). 1968. 59.95 o.p. (ISBN 0-686-56482-0, M-7469, Pub. by R. Oldenbourg). French & Eur.

Illustriertes Woerterbuch. 3rd ed. (Illus.). 192p. (Ger., Eng., Fr. & Span., Illustrated Dictionary). 1962. 29.95 o.p. (ISBN 3-8036-0250-5, M-7477, Pub. by Gebrueder Weiss). French & Eur.

Ilma Ruth Aho: Worker in His Field. Marjorie T. Whittlesey. (Illus.). 200p. 1985. 15.00 o.p. (ISBN 0-682-40246-X). Exposition-Phoenix.

ILO-Norway African Regional Training Course for Senior Social Security Managers & Administrative Officials. International Labour Office Staff. iii, 333p. (Orig.). 1982. pap. 24.50 o.p. (ISBN 92-2-102857-7). Intl Labour Office.

Ilya Ehrenburg: Selections from People, Years & Life. Ed. by C. Moody. LC 73-128339. 312p. 1972. pap. 80.00 o.p. (ISBN 0-08-006354-3). Pergamon.

Ilyin Oral Interview Test. Donna Ilyin. (Illus.). 1976. test & manual 23.95 o.p. (ISBN 0-88377-057-1); 50 scoring sheets 6.50 o.p. (ISBN 0-685-57363-X). Newbury Hse.

I'm a Good Helper. Ron Klug & Lyn Klug. LC 81-65644. (Illus., Orig.). (ps-1). 1981. pap. 4.95 o.p. (ISBN 0-8066-1880-9, 10-3200, Augsburg). Augsburg Fortress.

I'm a Nigerian. Enewe Eriye. 1979. (ISBN 0-682-49426-7). Exposition-Phoenix.

I'm a Patient, Too. CanSurmount - The Dramatic Support Program for Cancer Patients. Albert F. Hill et al. 160p. 1986. pap. 8.95 o.p. (ISBN 0-941130-22-3). Lyons & Burford.

I'm Alive: An Autobiography. Cecil Williams. LC 79-1783. 224p. 1980. 9.50 o.p. (ISBN 0-06-250950-0). HarpR.

I'm Already Tucked In. Bil Keane. 128p. (Orig.). 1982. pap. 1.95 o.p. (ISBN 0-449-12381-2, GM). Fawcett.

I'm an Endangered Species: The Autobiography of a Free Enterpriser. D. H. Byrd. LC 78-62614. 122p. 1978. 9.00x o.p. (ISBN 0-88415-258-8, Pub. by Pacesetter Pr). Gulf Pub.

I'm an Expert: Motivating Independent Study Projects for Grades 4-6. Mel Cebulash. 1982. pap. 7.95 o.p. (ISBN 0-673-16570-1). Scott F.

I'm Cat. Jan Pienkowski. (Illus.). (gr. 1-4). 1986. 4.95 o.s.i. (ISBN 0-671-61349-9, Little Simon). S&S.

I'm Doing My Best-but It Isn't Enough: Choices & Coping Steps for Personal Dilemmas & Distress. Pat Keating. LC 85-72690. 220p. (Orig.). 1986. pap. 9.95 o.p. (ISBN 0-931494-82-6). Brunswick Pub.

I'm Frog. Jan Pienkowski. (Illus.). (gr. 1-4). 1986. 4.95 o.s.i. (ISBN 0-671-61351-0, Little Simon). S&S.

I'm Glad I'm Little. Kathleen Wulf. LC 76-16535. (Illus.). (ps-2). 1976. 7.45 o.p. (ISBN 0-913778-53-2). Childs World.

I'm Glad You're Open Weekdays: Everyday Prayers to the God Who Works Between Sundays. Betty W. Skold. LC 85-3923. 112p. (Orig.). 1985. pap. 5.95 o.p. (ISBN 0-8066-2129-X, 10-3201, Augsburg). Augsburg Fortress.

I'm Going to Be a Missionary. Virginia B. Carter. (Orig.). (gr. 4-8). 1978. pap. 2.95 o.p. (ISBN 0-89036-103-7). Hawkes Pub Inc.

I'm Gonna Hit Myself a Homerun Today. Michael Yarmosky. LC 79-19178. (Illus.). 32p. (gr. k-2). 1982. 10.95 o.p. (ISBN 0-03-052441-5). H Holt & Co.

I'm Hiding. Myra C. Livingston & Erik Blegvad. LC 61-6119. (Illus.). (gr. k-2). 1961. 4.50 o.p. (ISBN 0-15-238090-6, HJ). HarBraceJ.

I'm in Love with a Mannequin. Frank Alexander. LC 76-8767. (Illus.). 1976. pap. 1.95 o.p. (ISBN 0-916956-00-8, Kokono). Front Row.

I'm Mouse. Jan Pienkowski. (Illus.). (gr. 1-4). 1986. 4.95 o.s.i. (ISBN 0-671-61352-9, Little Simon). S&S.

I'm Nobody! Who Are You? Mary Anderson. LC 73-84818. (gr. 4-6). 1974. 8.95 o.p. (ISBN 0-689-30128-6, Atheneum). Macmillan.

I'm Not a Women's Libber, But... Anne B. Follis. 128p. 1982. pap. 2.25 o.p. (ISBN 0-380-59477-3, 59477-3). Avon.

I'm Not the Same Person I Was Yesterday. Jay C. Rochelle. LC 73-89082. (Center Bk.). (Illus.). 128p. (Orig.). 1974. pap. 4.50 o.p. (ISBN 0-8006-5076-X, Fortress). Augsburg Fortress.

I'm Not Your Other Half. Caroline B. Cooney. LC 84-7768. (Pacer Bks.). 160p. (gr. 7 up). 1984. 10.95 o.p. (ISBN 0-399-21134-9). Putnam Pub Group.

I'm on My Way Running: Women Speak on Coming of Age. Lyn Reese & Jean Wilkinson. 384p. 1983. pap. 4.95 o.p. (ISBN 0-380-83022-1, 83022-1, Discus). Avon.

I'm Only One Person, What Can I Do? J. Harry Haines. (Orig.). 1985. pap. 5.95 o.p. (ISBN 0-8358-0521-2). Upper Room.

I'm Panda. Jan Pienkowski. (Illus.). (gr. 1-4). 1986. 4.95 o.s.i. (ISBN 0-671-61350-2, Little Simon). S&S.

I'm Running Away from Home, but I'm Not Allowed to Cross the Street. Gabrielle Burton. 1975. pap. 1.65 o.p. (ISBN 0-380-01534-X, 21865). Avon.

I'm Still Here Lord! Betty Isler. 1984. pap. 2.08 o.p. (ISBN 0-570-03938-X, 12-2873). Concordia.

I'm Vinny, I'm Me. Bianca Bradbury. (Illus.). 224p. (gr. 5-9). 1977. 6.95 o.p. (ISBN 0-395-25297-0). HM.

I'm Worried about Your Drinking: Feelings of Family & Friends Who Care. Judith Mattison. LC 77-84093. 1978. pap. 4.95 o.p. (ISBN 0-8066-1620-2, 10-3204, Augsburg). Augsburg Fortress.

Image. 2nd ed. Jean De Berg. Tr. by Patsy Southgate. LC 75-32905. (Illus.). 1966. pap. 1.95 o.s.i. (ISBN 0-394-17400-3, B307, BC). Grove.

Image Analysis, Enhancement & Interpretation. D. L. Misell. (Practical Methods in Electron Microscopy: Vol. 7). 1979. pap. 35.50 o.p. (ISBN 0-7204-0666-8, North Nolland). Elsevier.

Image & Likeness: A Play in Three Acts. Nicholas Wenckheim. 1978. 5.50 o.p. (ISBN 0-682-49284-1). Exposition-Phoenix.

Image & Other Stories. Isaac Bashevis Singer. 405p. 1986. lib. bdg. 17.95 o.p. (ISBN 0-8161-4027-8, Large Print Bks). G K Hall.

Image & Other Stories. Isaac Bashevis Singer. 320p. pap. 8.95 o.p. (ISBN 0-374-52079-8). FS&G.

Image Bank: Visual Ideas for the Creative Color Photographer. Ed. by Michael O'Connor. (Illus.). 176p. 1983. 59.50 o.p. (ISBN 0-8230-4007-0, Amphoto). Watson-Guptill.

Image Information Recovery: Proceedings, Vol. 16. Society of Photo-Optical Instrumentation Engineers Staff. 1968. 29.00 o.p. (ISBN 0-89252-019-1). SPIE.

Image Magic. Jim Zuckerman. LC 78-50984. (Photography How-to Ser.). (Illus.). 1978. pap. 3.95 o.p. (ISBN 0-8227-4016-8). Petersen Pub.

Image of Europe in Henry James. Christof Wegelin. LC 58-9271. 212p. 1967. Repr. of 1958 ed. 15.95x o.p. (ISBN 0-87074-122-5). SMU Press.

Image of Evil. William Beechcroft. 228p. 1985. 14.95 o.p. (ISBN 0-396-08558-X). Dodd.

Image of God in Man. David Cairns. 252p. 1953. (ISBN 0-8022-0207-1). Philos Lib.

Image of Ourselves: Women with Disabilities Talking. Ed. by Jo Campling. 160p. 1981. pap. 9.95x o.p. (ISBN 0-7100-0822-8). Routledge Chapman & Hall.

Image of the King: A Biography of Charles I & Charles II. Richard Ollard. LC 79-50965. (Illus.). 1979. 12.95 o.p. (ISBN 0-689-11006-5, Atheneum). Macmillan.

Image of the New World: The American Continent Portrayed in Native Texts. Gordon Brotherston. (Illus.). 1979. 19.95 o.s.i. (ISBN 0-500-01206-7). Thames Hudson.

Image of the New World: The American Continent Portrayed in Native Texts. Gordon Brotherston. (Illus., Orig.). 1982. pap. 10.95 o.s.i. (ISBN 0-500-27232-8). Thames Hudson.

Image One. Milwaukee Team Staff. (Illus.). 38p. (Orig.). 1981. pap. 2.50 o.p. (ISBN 0-936098-03-1). Intl Marriage.

Image Processing & Computer-Aided Design in Electronics: Proceedings of the European Congress on Electron Microscopy, 5th. European Congress on Electron Microscopy Staff. Ed. by P. W. Hawkes. 1973. 83.00 o.p. (ISBN 0-12-333365-2). Acad Pr.

Image Reconstruction from Projections Implementation & Applications. Ed. by G. T. Herman. LC 79-13823. (Topics in Applied Physics Ser.: Vol. 32). (Illus.). 1979. 59.50 o.p. (ISBN 0-387-09417-2). Springer-Verlag.

Imagery in Healing: Shamanism & Modern Medicine. Jeanne Achterberg. 1985. 10.95 o.p. (ISBN 0-394-73031-3). Shambhala Pubns.

Imagery of Art Wolfe. Photos by Art Wolfe. Ed. by Charles Mauzy. (Illus.). 144p. 1985. 40.00 o.p. (ISBN 0-916567-06-0). Arpel Graphic.

Images & Enterprise: Technology & the American Photographic Industry, 1839-1925. Reese V. Jenkins. LC 75-11348. (Studies in the History of Technology). (Illus.). 374p. 1976. 35.00x o.p. (ISBN 0-8018-1588-6). Johns Hopkins.

Images & Shadows: Part of a Life. Iris Origo. LC 79-134574. (Helen & Kurt Wolff Bks.). 1971. 8.50 o.p. (ISBN 0-15-144101-4). HarBraceJ.

Images from the Southwest. David Lavender. LC 86-60517. (Illus.). 144p. 1986. 35.00 o.s.i. (ISBN 0-87358-414-7); pap. 19.95 o.s.i. (ISBN 0-87358-416-3). Northland.

Images, Images, Images: The Book of Programmed Multi-Image Production (S-12) 3rd ed. Ed. by Eastman Kodak Company Staff. (Illus.). 264p. 1983. pap. 24.95 o.p. (ISBN 0-87985-327-1). Eastman Kodak.

Images of a Golden Past: Dutch Genre Painting of the 17th Century. Christopher Brown. LC 84-6257. (Illus.). 240p. 1984. 55.00 o.p. (ISBN 0-89659-439-4). Abbeville Pr.

Images of American Society: A History of the United States, 2 vols. G. D. Lillibridge. LC 75-31017. (Illus.). 736p. 1976. Vol. 1. pap. 17.50 o.p. (ISBN 0-395-21873-X); Vol. 2. pap. 17.50 o.p. (ISBN 0-395-21874-8). HM.

Images of Bahrain. Middle East Economic Digest Staff. (Illus.). 188p. 1985. lib. bdg. 37.50 o.p. (ISBN 0-946510-07-5). Lynne Rienner.

Images of Christmas. Ed. by Eliane Wilson. (Illus.). 128p. 1984. 12.95 o.s.i. (ISBN 0-385-19465-X). Doubleday.

Images of Crisis: Literary Iconology, 1750 to the Present. George P. Landow. 200p. 1982. 30.00x o.p. (ISBN 0-7100-0818-X). Routledge Chapman & Hall.

Images of Development: Egyptian Engineers in Search of Industry. Clement H. Moore. 336p. 1980. text ed. 37.50x o.p. (ISBN 0-262-13161-7). MIT Pr.

Images of Family Life in Magazine Advertising: 1920-1978. B. Brown. 156p. 1981. 31.95 o.p. HR&W.

Images of Libery. Michael Grumet. 1986. 25.00 o.p. (ISBN 0-87795-808-4); pap. 12.95 o.p. (ISBN 0-87795-782-7). Morrow.

Images of Love & Death in Late Medieval & Renaissance Art. Clifton Olds et al. (Illus.). 132p. 1975. pap. 5.50 o.p. (ISBN 0-912303-09-3). Michigan Mus.

Images of Maharashtra: A Regional Profile in India. Ed. by N. K. Wagle. 160p. 1980. pap. text ed. 10.50x o.p. (ISBN 0-7007-0144-3). Humanities.

Images of Man in Psychological Research. John Shotter. (Essential Psychology Ser.). 1975. pap. 4.95 o.p. (ISBN 0-416-81740-8, NO. 2507). Routledge Chapman & Hall.

Images of My Self: Meditation & Self-Exploration Through the Imagery of the Gospels. Jean Gill. 128p. 1982. pap. 3.95 o.p. (ISBN 0-8091-2463-7). Paulist Pr.

Images of Religion in America. Jerald C. Brauer. Ed. by Richard C. Wolf. LC 67-22984. (Facet Bks). 48p. 1967. pap. 0.50 o.p. (ISBN 0-8006-3040-8, 1-3040, Fortress). Augsburg Fortress.

Images of Spain. Mordecai Richler. (Illus.). 1977. 27.50 o.p. (ISBN 0-393-08792-1). Norton.

Images of Sport in Early Canada: Les images du sport dans le Canada d'autrefois. Compiled by Nancy J. Dunbar. (Illus.). 96p. 1976. 14.95 o.p. (ISBN 0-7735-0246-7, McGill Canada); pap. 7.50 o.p. (ISBN 0-7735-0244-0, McGill Canada). U of Toronto Pr.

Images of the Church in the New Testament. Paul S. Minear. LC 60-11331. 294p. 1970. pap. 9.95 o.s.i. (ISBN 0-664-24903-5, Westminster). Westminster John Knox.

Images of the Colorado Plateau, Vol. 50, No. 2. 32p. 1978. pap. 1.50 o.p. (ISBN 0-686-46149-5). Mus Northern Ariz.

Images of Women in Literature. 3rd ed. Mary A. Ferguson. LC 80-82761. (Illus.). 528p. 1980. pap. 18.50 o.p. (ISBN 0-395-29113-5). HM.

Images of Women in Literature. 2nd ed. Mary Ann Ferguson. LC 76-13098. (Illus.). 1977. pap. 10.50 o.p. (ISBN 0-395-24481-1). HM.

Images That Last. Larry W. Brown. 1979. 5.00 o.p. (ISBN 0-682-49460-7). Exposition-Phoenix.

Images: The Photographs of Peter Gasser. Helmut Gernsheim & Kaspar M. Fleischmann. LC 85-47827. (Illus.). 120p. 1985. 60.00 o.p. (ISBN 0-89381-197-1). Aperture.

Imaginary Lands. Ed. by Robin McKinley. 224p. 1985. pap. 2.95 o.s.i. (ISBN 0-441-36694-5). Ace Bks.

Imaginary Magnitude. Stanislaw Lem. Tr. by Marc E. Heine. LC 83-18624. (Helen & Kurt Wolff Bk.). 176p. 1984. Repr. of 1973 ed. 15.95 o.p. (ISBN 0-15-144118-9). HarBraceJ.

Imagination. Clare A. Mangin. 64p. 1986. 6.95 o.p. (ISBN 0-8062-2805-9). Carlton.

Imagination & Me Book. Joe Wayman & Don Mitchell. (gr. k-8). 1976. 6.95 o.p. (ISBN 0-916456-02-1, GA54). Good Apple.

Imagination & Reality. Charles Rycroft. 143p. 1968. text ed. 22.50x o.s.i. (ISBN 0-8236-2520-6). Intl Univs Pr.

Imagination of Spring: The Poetry of Afanasy Fet. Richard F. Gustafson. LC 76-15198. 1976. Repr. lib. bdg. 35.00x o.p. (ISBN 0-8371-8146-1, GUIS). Greenwood.

Imaginative Literature. 3rd ed. Alton C. Morris et al. 1978. 14.95 o.p. (ISBN 0-15-540729-5). HarbraceJ.

Imaginative Literature: Fiction, Drama, Poetry. 2nd ed. Alton C. Morris et al. 1973. text ed. 10.95 o.p. (ISBN 0-15-540727-9, HC). HarBraceJ.

Imagine Me. John Alderman. 40p. 1985. pap. text ed. 1.95 o.s.i. (ISBN 0-914307-45-2). R Tilton Ministries.

Imagineering: How to Profit from Your Creative Powers. Michael LeBoeuf. LC 80-13232. 240p. 1980. text ed. 9.95 o.p. (ISBN 0-07-036952-6). McGraw.

Imagineering: How to Profit from Your Creative Powers. Michael LeBoeuf. (McGraw-Hill Paperback Ser.). 1982. pap. text ed. 6.95 o.p. (ISBN 0-07-036954-2). McGraw.

Imaging in Hepatobiliary Disease. Dooley et al. 1986. 63.00 o.p. (ISBN 0-8016-1418-X). Mosby.

Imaging Saturn. Henry S. Cooper, Jr. LC 83-10. (Illus.). 224p. 1985. pap. 8.95 o.p. (ISBN 0-03-005614-4, Owl Bks.). H Holt & Co.

Imaging Saturn: The Voyager Flights to Saturn. Henry S. Cooper, Jr. LC 83-10. (Illus.). 224p. 1983. 19.95 o.s.i. (ISBN 0-03-061688-3, Owl Bks.). H Holt & Co.

Imagini...Degli Dei. Vincenzo Cartari. LC 75-27855. (Renaissance & the Gods Ser.: Vol. 12). (Illus.). 602p. 1976. Repr. of 1571 ed. lib. bdg. 88.00 o.p. (ISBN 0-8240-2061-8). Garland Pub.

Imagining America. Peter Conrad. 336p. 1982. pap. 3.95 o.p. (ISBN 0-380-59899-X, 59899-X, Discus). Avon.

Imam Ali: Source of Light, Wisdom & Might. Sulayman Kattani. Tr. by I. K. Howard. 148p. 1986. text ed. 25.00 o.p. (ISBN 0-7103-0153-7). Routledge Chapman & Hall.

Imari. Takeshi Nagatake. LC 80-84463. (Famous Ceramics of Japan Ser.: Vol. 6). (Illus.). 40p. 1982. 19.95 o.p. (ISBN 0-87011-487-5). Kodansha.

Imitation. Joel Weinsheimer. (International Library of Phenomenology & Moral Sciences). 280p. 1985. 39.95x o.p. (ISBN 0-7102-0012-9). Routledge Chapman & Hall.

Imitation Game & Other Plays. Ian McEwan. 1982. 11.45 o.p. (ISBN 0-395-32515-3); pap. 6.25 o.p. (ISBN 0-395-32933-7). HM.

Imitation of Christ. Thomas a Kempis. 1973. Repr. of 1960 ed. 8.95x o.p. (ISBN 0-460-00484-0, Evman); pap. 2.95x o.p. (ISBN 0-460-01484-6, DEL-04176). Biblio Dist.

Imitation of Christ. Thomas a Kempis. 1967. 5.95 o.p. (ISBN 0-88088-320-0). Peter Pauper.

Immaculate Deception: A New Look at Childbirth in America. Suzanne Arms. LC 74-28129. (San Francisco Ser.). 336p. 1975. 11.95 o.p. (ISBN 0-395-19893-3); pap. 6.95 o.p. (ISBN 0-395-19973-5). HM.

Immaculate Forrest. W. R. Philipson. 223p. 1952. (ISBN 0-8022-1964-0). Philos Lib.

Immanual Kant (Seventeen Twenty-Four to Eighteen Hundred Four) The British Academy Annual Philosophical Lecture see Study of Kant.

Immediate Critical Reception of Ernest Hemingway. Frank L. Ryan. LC 79-6026. 77p. 1980. text ed. 19.00 o.p. (ISBN 0-8191-0970-3); pap. text ed. 8.75 o.p. (ISBN 0-8191-0971-1). U Pr of Amer.

Immediate Experience: Movies, Comics, Theatre & Other Aspects of Popular Culture. Robert Warshow. LC 62-7694. 1970. pap. text ed. 3.25x o.p. (ISBN 0-689-70227-2, 159, Atheneum). Macmillan.

Immediate Hypersensitivity: Modern Concepts & Developments. Ed. by Michael K. Bach. (Immunology Ser.: Vol. 7). 872p. 1978. 115.00 o.p. (ISBN 0-8247-6602-4). Dekker.

Immigrant Labour in Kuwait. Abdulrasool Al-Moosa & Keith McLachlan. LC 84-29316. 166p. 1985. 29.00 o.p. (ISBN 0-7099-3554-4, Pub. by Croom Helm Ltd). Routledge Chapman & Hall.

Immigrants. Howard Fast. 1977. 12.95 o.s.i. (ISBN 0-395-25699-2). HM.

Immigrants & Emigrants. Hugh Bodey. (History in Focus Ser.). (Illus.). 72p. (gr. 7-10). 1982. 17.95 o.p. (ISBN 0-7134-3564-X, Pub. by Batsford England). David & Charles.

Immigrant's Daughter. Howard Fast. 490p. 1986. lib. bdg. 18.95 o.p. (ISBN 0-8161-3992-X, Large Print Bks). G K Hall.

Immigrants in American Life: Selected Readings. rev. ed. Arthur Mann. LC 73-3055. (Illus.). 262p. (YA) (gr. 7 up). 1974. pap. 11.48 o.p. (ISBN 0-395-17011-7). HM.

Immigrants Speak: The Italian Americans Tell Their Story. Ed. by Salvatore J. LaGumina. LC 79-67388. (Illus.). 209p. 1979. lib. bdg. 14.95 o.s.i. (ISBN 0-913256-37-4); pap. 9.95 o.s.i. (ISBN 0-934733-07-4). Ctr Migration.

Immigrant's Story. Arejas Vitkauskas. 200p. 1956. (ISBN 0-8022-1779-6). Philos Lib.

Immigrating to Canada. Segal. Date not set. price not set o.p. (ISBN 0-88908-626-5). ISC Pr.

Immigration, Aliens & Law: A Selected Bibliography. Dittakavi N. Rao. (Public Admininistration Ser.: Bibliography P 1644). 1985. pap. 6.75 o.p. (ISBN 0-89028-334-6). Vance Biblios.

Immigration & Ethnicity: A Guide to Information Sources. John D. Buenker & Nicholas C. Burckel. LC 74-11515. (American Government & History Information Guide Ser.: Vol. 1). 310p. 1977. 68.00x o.p. (ISBN 0-8103-1202-6). Gale.

Immigration & Illegal Aliens-Burden or Blessing? Ed. by Mark Siegel et al. 78p. 1983. pap. 13.95 o.p. (ISBN 0-936474-31-9). Info Plus TX.

Immigration & Social Policy in Britain. Catherine Jones. 275p. 1980. pap. 13.95x o.p. (ISBN 0-422-74680-0, NO. 6363, Pub. by Tavistock England). Routledge Chapman & Hall.

Immigration Employment Compliance Handbook: How to Comply with Immigration Reporting Requirements When Hiring New Employees. Austin T. Fragomen & Steven C. Bell. 1987. pap. 65.00 o.p. (ISBN 0-87632-551-7). Clark Boardman.

Immigration Law & Defense. National Immigration Project. 75.00 o.p. Natl Lawyers Guild.

Immigration Primer. Austin T. Fragomen, Jr. & Steven C. Bell. 445p. 1985. 50.00 o.p. (H1-2978). PLI.

Immigration Procedures Handbook. Austin T. Fragomen et al. 1987. 85.00 o.p. (ISBN 0-87632-535-5). Clark Boardman.

Immigration Raids on the Workplace. 30.00 o.p. Natl Lawyers Guild.

Immobile. Samuel Beckett. 1976. 59.95 o.p. (ISBN 0-686-51927-2). French & Eur.

Immobilized Enzymes for Industrial Reactors. Ed. by Ralph A. Messing. 1975. 94.50 o.p. (ISBN 0-12-492350-X). Acad Pr.

Immodest Agenda: Rebuilding America Before the 21st Century. A. Etzioni. (New Press Ser.). 464p. 1982. text ed. 26.95 o.p. (ISBN 0-07-019723-7). McGraw.

Immodest Agenda: Rebuilding America Before the 21st Century. A. Etzioni. 432p. 1984. pap. text ed. 9.95 o.p. (ISBN 0-07-019724-5). McGraw.

Immoraliste. Andre Gide. 1958. 9.50 o.p. (ISBN 0-685-11245-4). Schoenhof.

Immortal Dragon of Sylene & Other Faith Tales. Rafael Tilton. (Illus.). 128p. (gr. 8-12). 1982. 9.95 o.p. (ISBN 0-86683-656-X). HarpR.

Immortal Longings. G. T. Bellhouse. 1952. (ISBN 0-8022-0097-4). Philos Lib.

Immortalist. Heathcote Williams. (Orig.). 1980. pap. 3.95 o.p. (ISBN 0-7145-3714-4). Riverrun NY.

Immortality. J. Altasen et al. 733p. 1978. 7.45 o.p. (ISBN 0-8285-0939-5, Pub. by Progress Pubs USSR). Imported Pubns.

Imm's Outline of Entomology. 6th ed. O. W. Richards & R. G. Davies. 1978. 29.95x o.p. (ISBN 0-412-21660-4, NO. 6238, Pub. by Chapman & Hall England); pap. 12.95x o.p. (ISBN 0-412-21670-1, NO. 6239). Routledge Chapman & Hall.

Immunbiologie: Einfuehrung in die allergologischen und immunologischen Grundlagen der klinischen Medizin. R. Schuppli. (Ueberarbeitete Auflage). (Illus.). 1979. pap. 14.00 o.p. (ISBN 3-8055-3000-5). S Karger.

Immune Complexes & Their Role in the Pathogenesis of Various Diseases. Margherita Branca et al. LC 72-10434. (Illus.). 220p. 1973. text ed. 23.50x o.p. (ISBN 0-8422-7058-2). Irvington.

Immune Deficiency. Ed. by M. D. Cooper et al. (Illus.). 1979. pap. 24.00 o.p. (ISBN 0-387-09490-3). Springer-Verlag.

Immune Disorders. Ed. by Helen Hamilton & Minnie B. Rose. (Nurses's Clinical Library). (Illus.). 192p. 1985. text ed. 19.95 o.p. (ISBN 0-916730-76-X). Springhouse Pub.

Immune Mechanisms & Disease. Ed. by D. Bernard Amos et al. LC 79-19241. 1979. 44.00 o.p. (ISBN 0-12-055850-5). Acad Pr.

Immune Recognition: Proceedings of the Leukocyte Culture Conference, 9th. Leukocyte Culture Conference Staff. Ed. by Alan S. Rosenthal. 1975. 75.50 o.p. (ISBN 0-12-597850-2). Acad Pr.

Immune Regulators in Transfer Factor. Ed. by Amanullah Khan et al. LC 79-1464. 1979. 65.50 o.p. (ISBN 0-12-406060-9). Acad Pr.

Immune Response at the Cellular Level. Ed. by Theodore P. Zacharia. (Methods in Molecular Biology Ser: Vol. 6). 256p. 1973. 69.75 o.p. (ISBN 0-8247-6086-7). Dekker.

Immune Surveillance. Ed. by Richard T. Smith & Maurice Landy. LC 73-138439. (Perspectives in Immunology Ser). 1971. 77.00 o.p. (ISBN 0-12-652250-2). Acad Pr.

Immune System: Functions & Therapy of Dysfunction. G. Doria & A. Eshkol. LC 79-41519. (Serono Symposia Ser.: No.27). 1980. 67.50 o.p. (ISBN 0-12-220550-2). Acad Pr.

Immune System: Genes, Receptors, Signals. Ed. by Eli Sercarz et al. 1974. 60.50 o.p. (ISBN 0-12-637150-4). Acad Pr.

Immune System: Proceedings of the Colloquium of the Workshop for Biological Chemistry, Mosbach, Baden, Germany, April 29 - May 1, 1976. Workshop for Biological Chemistry Staff. Ed. by F. Melchers. (Illus.). 1977. 49.00 o.p. (ISBN 0-387-07976-9). Springer-Verlag.

Immunhematology-Immunology, Transplantation Problems, Leukemia, Coagulation see Proceedings of the International Society of Blood Transfusion, 12th Congress, Moscow, 1969.

Immunity & Atherosclerosis. P. Constantinides et al. (Serono Symposia Ser.: No.24). 1980. 61.50 o.p. (ISBN 0-12-186250-X). Acad Pr.

Immunity & Cancer in Man: An Introduction. Arnold E. Reif et al. (Immunology Ser: Vol. 3). 192p. 1975. 45.00 o.p. (ISBN 0-8247-6291-6). Dekker.

Immunity Cancer Chemotherapy. Ed. by Enrico Mihich. 1967. 78.50 o.p. (ISBN 0-12-495750-1). Acad Pr.

Immunity to Infections of the Respiratory System in Man & Animals: Proceedings of the International Symposium. Ed. by R. H. Regamey. (Developments in Biological Standardization: Vol. 28). (Illus.). xi, 659p. 1975. 33.50 o.p. (ISBN 3-8055-2249-5). S Karger.

Immunoassays for Clinical Chemistry. 2nd ed. W. M. Hunter & J. E. T. Corrie. LC 82-17838. (Illus.). 701p. 1983. text ed. 95.00 o.p. (ISBN 0-443-02704-8). Churchill.

Immunobiological & Immunochemical Studies of the Oyster, Crassptrea Virginica. Ronald T. Acton. 144p. 1972. text ed. 29.50x o.p. (ISBN 0-8422-7034-5). Irvington.

Immunobiology of Proteins & Peptides II. Ed. by M. Z. Atassi. (Advances in Experimental Medicine & Biology: Vol. 150). 238p. 1982. 49.50x o.p. (ISBN 0-306-41110-5, Plenum Pr). Plenum Pub.

Immunobiology of the Tumor-Host Relationship: Proceedings. Ed. by Richard T. Smith & Maurice Landy. (Perspectives in Immunology Ser.). 1975. 77.00 o.p. (ISBN 0-12-652260-X). Acad Pr.

Immunobiology of Transfer Factor. Ed. by Charles H. Kirkpatrick & Denis R. Burger. (Symposium). 1983. 47.00 o.p. (ISBN 0-12-409850-9). Acad Pr.

Immunocytochemistry. 3rd ed. Ludwig A. Sternberger. LC 85-9496. 524p. 1985. 52.50 o.p. (ISBN 0-471-86721-7). Wiley.

Immunodiffusion. 2nd ed. Alfred J. Crowle. 1973. 100.50 o.p. (ISBN 0-12-198156-8). Acad Pr.

Immunogenetics: Its Application to Clinical Medicine. Ed. by Takehiko Sasazuki & Tomio Tada. 1984. 33.00 o.p. (ISBN 0-12-619420-3). Acad Pr.

Immunoglobulin Idiotypes. Charles Janeway et al. LC 81-12895. (ICN-UCLA Symposia on Molecular & Cellular Biology Ser.: Vol. 20). 1981. 77.00 o.p. (ISBN 0-12-380380-2). Acad Pr.

Immunoglobulins. Ed. by Gary W. Litman & Robert A. Good. LC 78-1439. (Comprehensive Immunology Ser.: Vol. 5). (Illus.). 398p. 1978. 65.00x o.p. (ISBN 0-306-33105-5, Plenum Med Bk). Plenum Pub.

Immunologic Disorders in Infants & Children. 2nd ed. E. Richard Stiehm & Vincent A. Fulginiti. LC 79-66045. (Illus.). 817p. 1980. text ed. (ISBN 0-7216-8603-6). Saunders.

Immunologic Intervention. Ed. by Jonathan W. Uhr & Maurice Landy. (Perspectives in Immunology Ser.). 1972. 71.50 o.p. (ISBN 0-12-706950-X). Acad Pr.

Immunologic Tolerance & Macrophage Function: Proceedings of the Midwest Autumn Immunology Conference, 7th Meeting, Michigan, November, 1978. Midwest Autumn Immunology Conference Staff. Ed. by R. Baram et al. LC 79-243. (Developments in Immunology Ser.: Vol. 4). 266p. 1979. 65.00 o.p. (ISBN 0-444-00316-9, Biomedical Pr). Elsevier.

Immunological Aspects of Skin Disease. L. Fry & P. Seah. LC 74-4078. 289p. 1974. 28.00 o.p. (ISBN 0-471-28458-0, Pub. by Wiley). Krieger.

Immunological Deficiency Syndromes. Paul J. Edelson et al. LC 73-13446. (Illus.). 220p. 1972. text ed. 24.50x o.p. (ISBN 0-8422-7082-5). Irvington.

Immunological Influence on Human Fertility. Ed. by Barry Boettcher. 370p. 1977. 52.50 o.p. (ISBN 0-12-109950-4). Acad Pr.

Immunological Methods in Endocrinology. Ed. by K. Federlin & K. Federlin. 1971. 16.50 o.p. (ISBN 0-12-250650-2). Acad Pr.

Immunological Methods in the Biological Sciences: Enzymes & Proteins. R. J. Mayer & J. H. Walker. 1980. 52.00 o.p. (ISBN 0-12-480750-X). Acad Pr.

Immunological Parameters of Host - Tumor Relationships, Vol. 4. Ed. by D. W. Weiss. 1977. 58.00 o.p. (ISBN 0-12-743554-9). Acad Pr.

Immunological Parameters of Host-Tumor Relationship, Vol. 5. Ed. by David Weiss. 1979. 43.50 o.p. (ISBN 0-12-743555-7). Acad Pr.

Immunological Tolerance. Ed. by Maurice Landy & W. Braun. (Perspectives in Immunology Ser). 1969. 65.50 o.p. (ISBN 0-12-435650-8). Acad Pr.

Immunological Tolerance: Mechanisms & Potential Therapeutic Applications. Ed. by David Katz & Baruj Benacerraf. 1974. 71.50 o.p. (ISBN 0-12-401650-2). Acad Pr.

Immunology, 2 Pts. Edward S. Golub. LC 80-25794. (Benchmark Papers in Microbiology Ser.: Vol. 16). 1983. Set. 89.95 o.p. (ISBN 0-87933-092-9); Pt. 1, 377pp. 54.95 o.p. (ISBN 0-87933-384-7); Pt. 2, 271pp. 47.95 o.p. (ISBN 0-87933-385-5). Van Nos Reinhold.

Immunology. Roitt et al. 1985. 29.95 o.p. (ISBN 0-8016-4149-7). Mosby.

Immunology: An Introduction. Ian R. Tizard. LC 83-15096. 428p. 1984. text ed. 41.75 o.s.i. (ISBN 0-03-060277-7). SCP.

Immunology & Aging. Ed. by T. Makinodan & Edmond Yunis. LC 76-53755. (Comprehensive Immunology Ser.: Vol. 1). (Illus.). 224p. 1977. 45.00x o.p. (ISBN 0-306-33101-2, Plenum Med Bk). Plenum Pub.

Immunology & Serology. 3rd ed. Philip L. Carpenter. LC 74-31833. (Illus.). 495p. 1975. text ed. 32.95 o.p. (ISBN 0-7216-3422-2). HR&W.

Immunology at a Glance. 3rd ed. Playfair. (Illus.). 80p. 1985. pap. 7.95 o.p. (ISBN 0-632-01322-2, B-39492). Mosby.

Immunomodulation by Bacteria & Their Products. Ed. by Herman Friedman et al. LC 81-17888. 320p. 1982. 59.50x o.p. (ISBN 0-306-40885-6, Plenum Pr). Plenum Pub.

Immunomodulation by Microbial Products & Related Synthetic Compounds. Yuichi Yamamura. (International Congress Ser.: Vol. 563). 1982. 138.50 o.p. (ISBN 0-444-90234-1). Elsevier.

Immunomodulators & Non-Specific Host Defence Mechanisms Microbial Infections: International Symposium, 6-8 May, 1987, West Berlin, FRG. Ed. by K. N. Masihi & W. Lange. (Advances in the Biosciences Ser.: Vol. 68). 480p. 1988. 110.00 o.p. (ISBN 0-08-036138-2). Pergamon.

Immunopathology: Eighth International Symposium. Frank J. Dixon & Peter A. Miescher. 1982. 85.00 o.p. (ISBN 0-12-218320-7). Acad Pr.

Immunopathology: Methods & Techniques. Ed. by Theodore P. Zacharia & S. Breese, Jr. (Immunology Ser: Vol. 2). 280p. 1973. 65.00 o.p. (ISBN 0-8247-6115-4). Dekker.

Immunopathology of Lymphoreticular Neoplasms. Ed. by J. J. Twomey & R. A. Good. LC 77-27315. (Comprehensive Immunology Ser.: Vol. 4). (Illus.). 782p. 1978. 89.50x o.p. (ISBN 0-306-33104-7, Plenum Med Bk). Plenum Pub.

Immunopathology of the Small Intestine. Michael N. Marsh. LC 86-5620. 461p. 1986. (ISBN 0-471-90706-5, Dist. by A R Liss). Wiley.

Immunopathology: Proceedings of the International Symposium, 3rd. International Symposium on Immunopathology Staff. Ed. by Peter A. Miescher & Pierre Graham. (Illus.). 392p. 1964. 85.00 o.p. (ISBN 0-8089-0625-9). Grune.

Immunopharmacology. Ed. by J. W. Hadden et al. LC 77-23915. (Comprehensive Immunology Ser.: Vol. 3). (Illus.). 442p. 1977. 69.50x o.p. (ISBN 0-306-33103-9, Plenum Med Bk). Plenum Pub.

Immunoregulation. Ed. by N. Fabris et al. LC 83-4777. 488p. 1983. 85.00x o.p. (ISBN 0-306-41358-2, Plenum Pr). Plenum Pub.

Immunotherapy: Cellular Transplants & Immunostimulation. E. Richard Stiehm et al. LC 74-591. 233p. 1974. text ed. 23.50x o.p. (ISBN 0-8422-7199-6). Irvington.

Immunotherapy of Human Cancer: Proceedings of the M. D. Anderson Annual Clinical Conference of Cancer, 22nd. M. D. Anderson Annual Clinical Conference of Cancer Staff & M. D. Anderson Hospital & Tumor Institute. LC 77-17701. (Illus.). 437p. 1978. 75.00 o.p. (ISBN 0-89004-263-2). Raven.

Immunotoxicology of Drugs & Chemicals. J. Descotes. 400p. 1986. 138.00 o.p. (ISBN 0-444-90363-1). Elsevier.

Imp. Neiderman. 1985. pap. 3.50 o.s.i. (ISBN 0-671-50786-9). PB.

Impact American Beer Market Review & Forecast: 1983. 4th ed. Marvin R. Shanken. (Illus.). 65p. pap. 150.00 o.p. (ISBN 0-918076-21-8). M Shanken Comm.

Impact American Beer Market Review & Forecast: 1982 Edition. 3rd ed. Marvin R. Shanken. (Illus.). 55p. 1982. pap. 150.00 o.p. (ISBN 0-918076-19-6). M Shanken Comm.

IMPACT American Beer Market Review & Forecast: 1986 Edition. 7th ed. Marvin R. Shanken. (Illus.). 1986. pap. 225.00 o.p. (ISBN 0-918076-42-0). M Shanken Comm.

IMPACT American Beer Market Review & Forecast: 1987 Edition. Marvin R. Shanken. (Illus.). 60p. 1987. pap. 325.00 o.p. (ISBN 0-918076-51-X). M Shanken Comm.

Impact American Beer Market Review & Forecast. 2nd ed. Marvin R. Shanken. (Illus.). 41p. 1981. pap. 100.00 o.p. (ISBN 0-918076-15-3). M Shanken Comm.

Impact American Beer Market Review & Forecast. Marvin R. Shanken. (Illus.). 1980. pap. 75.00 o.p. (ISBN 0-918076-09-9). M Shanken Comm.

Impact American Beer Market Review & Forecast. 5th ed. Marvin R. Shanken. (Illus.). 80p. 1984. pap. 175.00 o.p. (ISBN 0-918076-27-7). M Shanken Comm.

IMPACT American Beer Market Review & Forecast. 6th ed. Marvin R. Shanken. (Illus.). 76p. 1985. pap. 195.00 o.p. (ISBN 0-918076-34-X). M Shanken Comm.

Impact American Distilled Spirits Market Review & Forecast. 4th ed. Marvin R. Shanken. (Illus.). 1979. pap. 75.00 o.p. (ISBN 0-918076-04-8). M Shanken Comm.

Impact American Distilled Spirits Market Review & Forecast. 6th ed. Marvin R. Shanken. (Illus.). 45p. 1981. pap. 100.00 o.p. (ISBN 0-918076-14-5). M Shanken Comm.

Impact American Distilled Spirits Market Review & Forecast. 5th ed. Marvin R. Shanken. (Illus.). 1980. pap. 75.00 o.p. (ISBN 0-918076-08-0). M Shanken Comm.

Impact American Distilled Spirits Market Review & Forecast. 7th ed. Marvin R. Shanken. (Illus.). 64p. 1982. pap. 150.00 o.p. (ISBN 0-918076-18-8). M Shanken Comm.

IMPACT American Distilled Spirits Market Review & Forecast. 8th ed. Marvin R. Shanken. (Illus.). 78p. 1983. pap. 150.00 o.p. (ISBN 0-918076-22-6). M Shanken Comm.

Impact American Distilled Spirits Market Review & Forecast. 9th ed. Marvin R. Shanken. (Illus.). 86p. 1984. pap. 175.00 o.p. (ISBN 0-918076-28-5). M Shanken Comm.

IMPACT American Distilled Spirits Market Review & Forecast. 10th ed. Marvin R. Shanken. (Illus.). 91p. 1985. pap. 195.00 o.p. (ISBN 0-918076-33-1). M Shanken Comm.

IMPACT American Distilled Spirits Market Review & Forecast. 11th ed. Marvin R. Shanken. (Illus.). 1986. pap. 225.00 o.p. (ISBN 0-918076-41-2). M Shanken Comm.

IMPACT American Distilled Spirits Market Review & Forecast. 11th ed. Marvin R. Shanken. (Illus.). 70p. 1987. pap. 325.00 o.p. (ISBN 0-918076-50-1). M Shanken Comm.

Impact American Distilled Spirits Market Review & Forecast. Ed. by Marvin R. Shanken. (Illus.). 1976. 75.00 o.p. (ISBN 0-918076-10-2). M Shanken Comm.

Impact American Distilled Spirits Market Review & Forecast. 2nd ed. Ed. by Marvin R. Shanken. (Illus.). 1977. 75.00 o.p. (ISBN 0-918076-05-6). M Shanken Comm.

Impact American Distilled Spirits Review & Forecast. 3rd ed. Marvin R. Shanken. 1978. 75.00 o.p. (ISBN 0-918076-02-1). M Shanken Comm.

IMPACT American Wine Market Review & Forecast: 1983. 9th ed. Marvin R. Shanken. (Illus.). 73p. 1983. pap. 150.00 o.p. (ISBN 0-918076-23-4). M Shanken Comm.

Impact American Wine Market Review & Forecast. Marvin R. Shanken. (Illus.). 1975. 75.00 o.p. (ISBN 0-918076-12-9). M Shanken Comm.

Impact American Wine Market Review & Forecast. 7th ed. Marvin R. Shanken. (Illus.). 55p. 1981. pap. 100.00 o.p. (ISBN 0-918076-13-7). M Shanken Comm.

Impact American Wine Market Review & Forecast. 4th ed. Marvin R. Shanken. 1978. 75.00 o.p. (ISBN 0-918076-00-5). M Shanken Comm.

Impact American Wine Market Review & Forecast. 5th ed. Marvin R. Shanken. (Illus.). 1979. pap. 75.00 o.p. (ISBN 0-918076-03-X). M Shanken Comm.

Impact American Wine Market Review & Forecast. 8th ed. Marvin R. Shanken. (Illus.). 72p. 1982. pap. 150.00 o.p. (ISBN 0-918076-17-X). M Shanken Comm.

IMPACT American Wine Market Review & Forecast. 10th ed. Marvin R. Shanken. (Illus.). 100p. 1984. pap. 175.00 o.p. (ISBN 0-918076-29-3). M Shanken Comm.

IMPACT American Wine Market Review & Forecast. 11th ed. Marvin R. Shanken. (Illus.). 103p. 1985. pap. 195.00 o.p. (ISBN 0-918076-32-3). M Shanken Comm.

IMPACT American Wine Market Review & Forecast. 12th ed. Marvin R. Shanken. (Illus.). 1986. pap. 225.00 o.p. (ISBN 0-918076-40-4). M Shanken Comm.

IMPACT American Wine Market Review & Forecast. 13th ed. Marvin R. Shanken. (Illus.). 80p. 1987. pap. 325.00 o.p. (ISBN 0-918076-49-8). M Shanken Comm.

Impact American Wine Market Review & Forecast. 2nd ed. Ed. by Marvin R. Shanken. (Illus.). 1976. 75.00 o.p. (ISBN 0-918076-11-0). M Shanken Comm.

Impact American Wine Market Review & Forecast. 3rd ed. Ed. by Marvin R. Shanken. (Illus.). 1977. 75.00 o.p. (ISBN 0-918076-06-4). M Shanken Comm.

Impact & Improvement of School Testing Programs. Ed. by Warren G. Findley. LC 63-5289. (National Society for the Study of Education Yearbooks Ser: No. 62, Pt. 2). 1963. lib. bdg. 6.50x o.s.i. (ISBN 0-226-60071-8). U of Chicago Pr.

IMPACT Beverage Trends in America Review & Forecast. 2nd ed. Marvin R. Shanken. (Illus.). 1986. pap. 695.00 o.p. (ISBN 0-918076-43-9). M Shanken Comm.

IMPACT Beverage Trends in America Review & Forecast. 3rd ed. Marvin R. Shanken. (Illus.). 90p. 1987. pap. 595.00 o.p. (ISBN 0-918076-48-X). M Shanken Comm.

IMPACT Beverage Trends in American Review & Forecast. Marvin R. Shanken. (Illus.). 95p. 1985. pap. 395.00 o.p. (ISBN 0-918076-35-8). M Shanken Comm.

Impact Crashworthiness: First International Symposium on Structural Crashworthiness, University of Liverpool, September 14-16, 1983. Ed. by N. Jones. 120p. 1983. pap. 18.25 o.p. (ISBN 0-08-031121-0, 11/1, 11). Pergamon.

Impact Management: Personal Power Strategies for Success. George J. Lumsden. 1982. 6.95 o.p. (ISBN 0-8144-7575-2). AMACOM.

Impact of Aerospace Technology on Studies of the Earth's Atmosphere. A. K. Oppenheim. LC 74-5410. 1974. 34.00 o.p. (ISBN 0-08-018131-7). Pergamon.

Impact of Agricultural Extension: A Case Study of the Training & Visit Systems in Haryana, India. Gershon Feder et al. (Working Paper Ser.: No. 756). 104p. 1985. 5.00 o.p. (ISBN 0-8213-0646-4, WP 0756). World Bank.

Impact of Collective Bargaining on Management. Sumner H. Slichter et al. LC 60-53058. 982p. 1960. 31.95 o.p. (ISBN 0-8157-7984-4). Brookings.

Impact of Cybernation Technology on Black Automotive Workers in the U. S. Samuel D. James. Ed. by Richard Farmer. LC 85-16500. (Research for Business Decisions Ser.: No. 84). 138p. 1985. 39.95 o.p. (ISBN 0-8357-1719-4). UMI Res Pr.

Impact of Decentralization on Curriculum: Selected Viewpoints. I. Ezra Staples et al. LC 75-10830. 64p. 1975. pap. text ed. 3.75 o.s.i. (ISBN 0-87120-070-8, 611-75050). Assn Supervision.

Impact of Environmental Regulations on Business Transactions: Real Property Transfers & Mergers & Acquisitions. 610p. 1986. 45.00 o.p. (ISBN 0-317-60062-1, N4-4466). PLI.

Impact of Environmental Regulations on Business Transactions: Real Property Transfers & Mergers & Acquisitions. 384p. 1988. write for info. o.p. (N4-4496). PLI.

Impact of High Speed & VLSI Technology on Communication Systems: Related Conference Proceedings. Ed. by J. E. Flood & C. J. Hughes. (IEE Conference Publication: No. 230). 113p. 1983. pap. 56.00 o.s.i. (ISBN 0-85296-287-8, IC230). Inst Elect Eng.

Impact of Insulin on Metabolic Pathways. Ed. by E. Shafrir. 1972. 65.50 o.p. (ISBN 0-12-638050-3). Acad Pr.

Impact of Mass Media. Ray Hiebert & Carol Reuss. LC 84-21333. 378p. (Orig.). 1985. pap. text ed. 17.95x o.p. (ISBN 0-582-28555-0). Longman.

Impact of Microprocessors on British Business. National Computing Centre, Ltd. Staff. LC 80-478324. 72p. (Orig.). 1979. pap. 15.00x o.s.i. (ISBN 0-85012-232-5). Intl Pubns Serv.

Impact of Modern Communication Technology: Australia. (New Communication Order Ser.: No. 1). 122p. 1982. pap. 13.00 o.p. (ISBN 0-686-95476-9, UPB119, UPB). UNIPUB.

Impact of Noise Pollution: A Socio-Technological Introduction. George Bugliarello et al. 475p. 1976. 59.00 o.p. (ISBN 0-08-018166-X). Pergamon.

Impact of North Sea Hydrocarbons. Ed. by David K. Jones. (Illus.). 1977. pap. 32.00 o.p. (ISBN 0-08-022263-3). Pergamon.

Impact of Oil on the Marine Environment. (GESAMP Reports & Studies: No. 6). 1977. pap. 17.50 o.p. (ISBN 92-5-100219-3, F934, FAO). UNIPUB.

Impact of Product Liability on International Trade. 1980. pap. 5.00 o.p. (ISBN 0-918734-07-X). Reymont.

Impact of Protein Chemistry on the Biomedical Sciences. Alan N. Schechter & Ann Dean. 1984. 65.50 o.p. (ISBN 0-12-622780-2). Acad Pr.

Impact of Public Employee Unions on City Budgeting & Employee Remuneration: A Case Study of San Francisco. Harry C. Katz. LC 70-52690. (Outstanding Dissertations in Economics Ser.). 1984. lib. bdg. 31.00 o.p. (ISBN 0-8240-4153-4). Garland Pub.

Impact of Recession: On Industry, Employment & the Regions, 1976-1981. Alan R. Townsend. (Illus.). 224p. 1983. 30.00 o.p. (ISBN 0-7099-2417-8, Pub. by Croom Helm Ltd); pap. 10.95 o.p. (ISBN 0-7099-2433-X, Pub. by Croom Helm Ltd). Routledge Chapman & Hall.

Impact of Social Policy. Vic George & Paul Wilding. (Radical Social Policy Ser.). 288p. (Orig.). 1984. pap. 14.95x o.p. (ISBN 0-7100-9670-4). Routledge Chapman & Hall.

Impact of South Africa-Related Divestment on Equity Portfolio Performance. 50p. 1985. 50.00 o.p. (ISBN 0-317-52532-8). IRRC Inc DC.

Impact of Soviet Policies in Armenia, Nineteen Twenty to Nineteen Thirty-Six: A Study of Planned Cultural Transformation. Mary A. Matossian. LC 79-2910. 239p. 1981. Repr. of 1962 ed. 23.50 o.p. (ISBN 0-8305-0081-2). Hyperion Conn.

Impact of Taxes on Real Estate Transactions in New York State. LC 85-62766. (Real Estate & Law Practice Handbook Ser.: No. 266). 1985. 45.00 o.p. (N4-4446). PLI.

Impact of Taxes on U.S. Citizens Working Abroad. Ernest R. Larkins. Ed. by Richard N. Farmer. LC 83-9201. (Research for Business Decisions Ser.: No. 66). 144p. 1983. 42.95 o.p. (ISBN 0-8357-1487-X). UMI Res Pr.

Impact of Technology on Production. Ed. by T. M. Husband. 136p. 1984. pap. 36.00 o.p. (ISBN 0-08-031823-1). Pergamon.

Impact of the Media on Collective Bargaining. American Arbitration Association Staff. Ed. by Linda Miller. LC 80-65636. 82p. 1980. pap. 4.00 o.p. (ISBN 0-943001-16-1). Am Arbitration.

Impact of the Microelectronics Industry on the Structure of the Canadian Economy. J. Michael McLean. 50p. 1979. pap. text ed. 3.00x o.p. (ISBN 0-920380-22-0, Pub. by Inst Res Pub Canada). Gower Pub Co.

Impact of the States: The President's 1988 Budget. (State-Federal Relations Ser.). 59p. 1987. pap. 35.00 o.p. (ISBN 1-55516-835-3). Natl Conf State Legis.

Impact of Town Centre Shopping Schemes in Britain: Their Impact on Traditional Retail Environments. R. L. Bennison. (Progress in Planning Ser.: Vol. 14, Part 1). (Illus.). 104p. 1980. pap. 16.25 o.p. (ISBN 0-08-026789-0). Pergamon.

Impact of Toxiology on Food Processing. Ed. by John C. Ayres & John C. Kirschman. (Institute of Food Technologists Basic Symposia Ser.). (Illus.). 1981. 59.95 o.p. (ISBN 0-87055-387-9). AVI.

Impact of United States Forces in Korea. Suk B. Lee. LC 87-7915. (Illus.). 119p. (Orig.). 1987. pap. 3.50 o.p. (ISBN 0-318-23439-4, S/N 008-020-01096-1). USGPO.

Impact of Victorian Children's Fiction. J. S. Bratton. 230p. 1981. 27.50x o.p. (ISBN 0-389-20210-X, 06992). B&N Imports.

Impact on Consumers of a Restructured Personal Federal Tax. John H. Green. Ed. by Richard Farmer. LC 85-20980. (Research for Business Decisions: No. 88). 164p. 1985. 44.95 o.p. (ISBN 0-8357-1724-0). UMI Res Pr.

Impact Yearbook. 4th ed. Marvin Shanken. (1988 Ed.). 1988. pap. 105.00 o.p. (ISBN 0-918076-55-2). M Shanken Comm.

Impact Yearbook: 1985 Edition. Marvin R. Shanken. (Illus.). 180p. 1985. pap. 105.00 o.p. (ISBN 0-918076-31-5). M Shanken Comm.

IMPACT Yearbook, 1986. 2nd ed. Marvin R. Shanken. (Illus.). 227p. 1985. pap. 105.00 o.p. (ISBN 0-918076-37-4). M Shanken Comm.

IMPACT Yearbook, 1987. 3rd ed. Marvin R. Shanken. (Illus.). 1987. pap. 105.00 o.p. (ISBN 0-918076-45-5). M Shanken Comm.

Impacts & Influences. Ed. by James Curran & Anthony Smith. 320p. 1987. 37.50 o.p. (ISBN 0-416-00602-7); pap. 15.95 o.p. (ISBN 0-416-00612-4). Routledge Chapman & Hall.

Impacts of Federal Grant Requirements on Transit Agencies: National Cooperative Transit Research & Development Program Report 2. Transportation Consulting Division, Booz, Allen & Hamilton Inc. Staff et al. LC 82-74270. (Illus.). 73p. 1982. 7.60 o.p. (ISBN 0-309-03572-4). Natl Res Coun.

Impacts of Mexican Oil Policy on Economic & Political Development. Jesus-Augustin Velasco. LC 82-47787. 256p. 1983. 30.00x o.p. (ISBN 0-669-05592-1). Lexington Bks.

Impacts of Microcomputers on Operations Research. Ed. by S. I. Gass et al. (Publications in Operations Research: Vol. 5). 288p. 1986. 62.50 o.p. (ISBN 0-444-01088-2). Elsevier.

Impaired Vision in Childhood: Proceedings of the Jerusalem Conference, May 1977. Jerusalem Conference on Impaired Vison in Childhood Staff. Ed. by I. Nawratzki & S. Merin. (Illus.). 1979. pap. 100.00 o.p. (ISBN 0-08-024416-5). Pergamon.

Impasse Resolution in Public Sector interest Disputes. Ed. by James Gallagher. 254p. 1977. pap. 10.00 o.p. (ISBN 0-89215-069-6). U Cal LA Indus Rel.

Imperfect Therapist: Learning from Failure in Therapeutic Practice. Jeffrey A. Kottler & Diane S. Blau. LC 88-46083. (Social & Behavioral Science Ser.). 208p. 1989. text ed. 19.95x o.p. (ISBN 1-55542-145-8). Jossey-Bass.
Imperial Age of Venice. Chambers. 1971. 6.95 o.p. (ISBN 0-15-144230-4). HarBraceJ.
Imperial Age of Venice: 1380-1580. D. S. Chambers. (History of European Civilization Library). (Illus.). 1970. pap. text ed. 6.95 o.p. (ISBN 0-15-540891-7, HC). HarBraceJ.
Imperial Civil Service of Rome. Harold Mattingly. LC 79-1638. 1981. Repr. of 1910 ed. 18.00 o.p. (ISBN 0-88355-940-4). Hyperion Conn.
Imperial Earth. Arthur C. Clarke. LC 75-30595. 303p. 1976. 7.95 o.s.i. (ISBN 0-15-144233-9). HarBraceJ.
Imperial Gardens of Japan. Teiji Itoh. (Illus.). 292p. 85.00 o.p. (ISBN 0-317-54979-0). Apollo.
Imperial Presidency. Arthur M. Schlesinger, Jr. 1973. 16.95 o.p. (ISBN 0-395-17713-8). HM.
Imperial Science & National Survival. David Montgomery. LC 80-70692. 1981. 2.50x o.p. (ISBN 0-87081-094-4). Univ Pr Colo.
Imperial Theme: Further Interpretations of Shakespeare's Tragedies Including the Roman Play. 3rd ed. G. Wilson Knight. 1965. pap. 13.95x o.p. (ISBN 0-416-68740-7, NO. 2274). Routledge Chapman & Hall.
Imperial War Museum Review. (No.1). 112p. 1987. 9.95 o.p. (ISBN 0-901627-37-2). Janes Info Group.
Imperialism & Chinese Nationalism: Germany in Shantung. John E. Schrecker. LC 73-129119. (East Asian Ser: No. 58). (Illus.). 1971. 24.50x o.s.i. (ISBN 0-674-44520-1). Harvard U Pr.
Imperialism & Nationalism in the Middle East: The Anglo-Egyptian Experience 1882-1982. Ed. by Keith M. Wilson. 192p. 1983. 32.00x o.p. (ISBN 0-7201-1682-1). Mansell.
Imperialism & the Anti-Imperialist Mind. Lewis Feuer. LC 86-42575. 265p. 1986. 23.95 o.p. Prometheus Bks.
Imperialism, Colonialism, & Hunger: East & Central Africa. Robert I. Rotberg. LC 82-48009. 288p. 1982. 32.00x o.p. (ISBN 0-669-05871-8). Lexington Bks.
Imperialismo, Fase Superior Del Capitalismo. Vladimir I. Lenin. 131p. (Span.). 1979. pap. 1.45 o.p. (ISBN 0-8285-1376-7, Pub. by Progress Pubs USSR). Imported Pubns.
Implantation: The Role of Proteinases, & Blockage of Implantation Through Proteinase Inhibitors. H. W. Denker. (Advances in Anatomy, Embryology & Cell Biology: Vol. 53, Pt. 5). (Illus.). 1977. pap. 31.00 o.p. (ISBN 0-387-08479-7). Springer-Verlag.
Implementation, Change, & the Federal Bureaucracy: School Desegregation Policy in HEW, 1964-1968. Beryl Radin. LC 76-58320. 1977. pap. text ed. 12.95x o.p. (ISBN 0-8077-2522-6). Tchrs Coll.
Implementation of Health Fitness Exercise Programs. 1986. 11.95 o.p. AAHPERD.
Implementing Curriculum Change: Proceedings. UNESCO Staff. 1978. pap. 5.50 o.p. (ISBN 0-685-20397-2, UB62, UB). UNIPUB.
Implementing Indexation of the Tax Laws. (Statement of Tax Policy Ser.: No. 9). 1981. pap. 9.50 o.p. (ISBN 0-686-84301-0). Am Inst CPA.
Implementing Pastoral Care in Schools. Jeanette Raymond. LC 85-14978. 304p. 1985. 33.00 o.p. (ISBN 0-7099-2273-6, Pub. by Croom Helm Ltd); pap. 14.95 o.p. (ISBN 0-7099-4211-7). Routledge Chapman & Hall.
Implementing Public Policy. Ruth Levitt. 256p. 1980. 30.00 o.p. (ISBN 0-7099-0068-6, Pub. by Croom Helm Ltd). Routledge Chapman & Hall.
Implementing the AT&T Settlement: The New Telecommunications Era. Practising Law Institute Staff & Herbert E. Forrest. LC 84-100988. (Patents, Copyrights, Trademarks, & Literary Property Course Handbook Ser.: No. 172). 1983. 45.00 o.p. PLI.
Implementing the Electronic Office. John Whitehead. (Information Technology Ser.). 224p. 1986. 34.50 o.p. (ISBN 0-7099-3674-5, Pub. by Croom Helm Ltd). Routledge Chapman & Hall.
Implementing Urologic Procedures. Ed. by Jean Robinson & Barbara McVan. LC 81-2939. (Nursing Photobook Ser.). (Illus.). 160p. 1981. text ed. 17.95 o.p. (ISBN 0-916730-32-8). Springhouse Pub.
Implications of Commission Recommendations That Doses Be Kept As Low As Readily Achievable. International Commission on Radiological Protection. LC 73-10384. (ICRP Publication Ser.: No. 37). 1973. pap. 15.25 o.p. (ISBN 0-08-017694-1). Pergamon.
Implications of Continental Drift to the Earth Sciences, Vol. 2. Ed. by D. H. Tarling & S. K. Runcorn. 1973. 115.00 o.p. (ISBN 0-12-683702-3). Acad Pr.
Importance of Crocus. Roger Duvoisin. LC 81-5030. (Illus.). (ps). 1981. 9.95 o.s.i. (ISBN 0-394-84957-4); lib. bdg. 9.99 o.s.i. (ISBN 0-394-94957-9). Knopf.
Important Family. Dorothy Eden. 352p. 1983. pap. 3.50 o.p. (ISBN 0-380-63297-7, 63297-7). Avon.
Important Thing About. Joy T. Friedman. LC 80-83936. (Illus.). 96p. (gr. k-2). 1981. pap. 3.99 o.p. (ISBN 0-448-13947-2, G&D). Putnam Pub Group.
Importing: A Practical Manual for Coping with Canadian Customs. 2nd ed. Ernest Y. Maitland. 401p. 1981. 21.95 o.p. (ISBN 0-88908-085-2). ISC Pr.
Impossible Possibilities. Louis Pauwels & Jacques Bergier. 1973. pap. 1.25 o.p. (ISBN 0-380-01278-2, 15255). Avon.
Impossible Possum. Ellen Conford. (Illus.). (gr. 1-3). 1971. 10.45i o.p. (ISBN 0-316-15297-8). Little.
Imposters. George V. Higgins. LC 85-30599. 480p. 1986. pap. 16.95 o.p. (ISBN 0-03-008014-2). H Holt & Co.
Imposters. George V. Higgins. 1986. 16.95 o.p. (ISBN 0-317-44817-X). H Holt & Co.
Impostor Phenomenon: Overcoming the Fear That Haunts Your Success. Pauline R. Clance. LC 85-60596. 224p. 1985. 14.95 o.p. (ISBN 0-931948-77-0). Peachtree Pubs.
Impressionism. Ed. by Theodore Reff. (Modern Art in Paris 1855 to 1900 Ser.). 157p. 1981. lib. bdg. 53.00 o.p. (ISBN 0-8240-4723-0). Garland Pub.
Impressionist Painting. Albert Chatelet. (Color Slide Program of Art Enjoyment Ser.). (Illus.). 1962. text ed. 24.95 o.p. (ISBN 0-07-010710-6). McGraw.
Impressionists in England: The Critical Reception. Kate Flint. (Schools of Art Ser.). (Illus.). 400p. 1984. 29.95 o.p. (ISBN 0-7100-9470-1). Routledge Chapman & Hall.
Impressionists: Portraits & Confidences. Pascal Bonafoux. 1987. 60.00 o.p. (ISBN 0-8478-0732-0). Rizzoli Intl.
Impressions: A Trip to the German Democratic Republic. Julia Singer. LC 78-11299. (Illus.). (gr. 4-6). 1979. 8.95 o.p. (ISBN 0-689-30696-2, Atheneum). Macmillan.
Impressions of Russia. G. Brandes. 7.75 o.p. (ISBN 0-8446-1728-8). Peter Smith.
Imprint Catalog in the Rare Book Division, 21 vols. New York Public Library, Research Libraries, Rare Division Staff. 1979. Set. lib. bdg. 1925.00 o.p. (ISBN 0-8161-0092-6, Hall Library). G K Hall.
Imprinting: Early Experience in the Developmental Psychology. Eckhard H. Hess. LC 72-14437. 488p. 1973. 29.50 o.p. (ISBN 0-442-23391-4, VN). Krieger.
Imprints: The Life Long Effects of the Birth Experience. Arthur Janov. 1984. pap. 8.95 o.p. (ISBN 0-399-51086-9, Wideview). Putnam Pub Group.
Imprisoned Mind: Guru Shisya Tradition in Indian Culture. Akhileshwar Jha. 1980. 18.50x o.p. (ISBN 0-8364-0665-6, Pub. by Ambika India). South Asia Bks.
Improbable Book of Records. Quentin Blake & John Yeoman. LC 76-4466. (Illus.). 32p. (gr. 2-6). 1976. 6.95 o.p. (ISBN 0-689-30535-4, Atheneum). Macmillan.
Improbable Triumvirate: Kennedy-Khrushchev-Pope John, an Asterisk to the History of a Hopeful Year, 1962-3. Norman Cousins. 171p. 1972. 5.95 o.p. (ISBN 0-393-05396-2). Norton.
Improbable World of Veteran Outdoorsman. McManus. pap. 8.95 o.p. (ISBN 0-8050-0436-X). H Holt & Co.
Impromptu Du Palais Royal. Jean Cocteau. 80p. 1962. 8.95 o.p. (ISBN 0-686-54530-3). French & Eur.
Improve Your Health & Save Money at the Same Time. Albert B. Bartlett. 1977. pap. 3.50 o.p. (ISBN 0-89036-077-4). Hawkes Pub Inc.
Improved Criteria for Traffic Signal Systems in Urban Networks. (National Cooperative Highway Research Project Report). 86p. 1971. 4.80 o.p. (ISBN 0-309-02004-2). Transport Res Bd.
Improved Criteria for Traffic Signal Systems on Urban Arterials. (National Cooperative Highway Research Program Report). 55p. 1969. 2.80 o.p. (ISBN 0-317-36088-4, 1748). Transport Res Bd.
Improved Feeding of Cattle & Sheep. P. N. Wilson & T. D. Brigstocke. 238p. 1981. pap. text ed. 24.50 o.p. (Pub. by Granada England). Gower Pub Co.
Improved Indicators of Science & Mathematics in Grades 1-12. National Research Council. Ed. by Richard J. Murnane & Senta A. Raizen. 216p. 1987. pap. text ed. 17.50x o.p. (ISBN 0-309-03740-9). Natl Acad Pr.
Improved Pavement Shoulder Joint Design. (National Cooperative Highway Research Program Report). 103p. 1979. 7.20 o.p. (ISBN 0-309-02908-2). Transport Res Bd.
Improved Village Technology for Women's Activities: A Manual for West Africa. vi, 292p. (Orig.). 1984. pap. 19.25 o.p. (ISBN 92-2-103818-1). Intl Labour Office.
Improvement of Reading. 4th ed. Ruth Strang et al. (Curriculum & Methods in Education Ser.). 1967. text ed. 26.00 o.p. (ISBN 0-07-061995-6, C). McGraw.
Improvement of Working Conditions & Working Environments in the Iron & Steel Industry: Proceedings of the International Labour Office, Iron & Steel Committee, 10th Session, Geneva, 1981. International Labour Office, Iron & Steel Committee. v, 86p. (Orig.). 1981. pap. 8.55 o.p. (ISBN 92-2-102688-4). Intl Labour Office.
Improving Articulation & Transfer Relationships. Ed. by Frederick C. Kintzer. LC 81-48567. (Community College Ser.: No. 39). 1982. 12.95x o.p. (ISBN 0-87589-885-8). Jossey-Bass.
Improving Assessment of Schoolchildren: A Guide to Evaluating Cognitive, Emotional & Physical Problems. Carol S. Lidz. LC 80-26130. (Social & Behavioral Science Ser.). 1981. text ed. 26.95x o.p. (ISBN 0-87589-488-7). Jossey-Bass.
Improving Bank Profits: How to Decrease Operating Expenses & Increase Income. Paul F. Jannott. LC 83-25853. 239p. 1984. text ed. 47.00 o.p. (ISBN 0-87267-046-5). Bank Admin Inst.
Improving CAI in BASIC. Sharon Burrowes & Ted Burrowes. 88p. 1985. 6.00 o.p. (ISBN 0-924667-08-7). Intl Council Comp.
Improving Children's Competence: Advances in Child Behavioral Analysis & Therapy, Vol. I. Ed. by Paul Karoly & John J. Steffen. LC 82-47798. (Advances in Child Behavior Analysis & Therapy Ser.). 336p. 1982. 32.00x o.p. (ISBN 0-669-05640-5). Lexington Bks.
Improving College Information for Prospective Students. Ed. by David W. Chapman. 128p. 1980. pap. 14.50 o.p. (ISBN 0-89964-162-8). Coun Adv & Supp Ed.
Improving College Reading. 2nd ed. Lee A. Jacobus. 312p. 1972. pap. text ed. 8.95 o.p. (ISBN 0-15-540928-X, HC, HC). HarBraceJ.
Improving College Reading. 3rd ed. Lee A. Jacobus. 340p. 1978. pap. text ed. 12.95 o.p. (ISBN 0-15-540930-1, HC). HarBraceJ.
Improving College Reading. 4th. ed. Lee A. Jacobus. 386p. 1983. pap. text ed. 13.00 o.p. (ISBN 0-15-540932-8, HC). HarBraceJ.
Improving Discussion Leadership. Ronald Hyman. 154p. (Orig.). 1980. pap. 11.95x o.p. (ISBN 0-8077-2610-9). Tchrs Coll.
Improving Education for Disadvantaged Children: Some Belgian Studies. P. Osterrieth et al. LC 79-4086. 1979. 44.00 o.p. (ISBN 0-08-024265-0). Pergamon.
Improving Employee Productivity: A Case Study see Issues in the Public Employee Relations Library: Series 5.
Improving Employee Safety & Health Performance: A Managerial Guide. Kingsley Hendrick. 1982. 37.50 o.p. (ISBN 0-8240-7269-3). Garland Pub.
Improving Energy Demand Analysis. National Research Council. 136p. 1984. pap. text ed. 13.50x o.p. (ISBN 0-309-03477-9). Natl Acad Pr.
Improving Guidance Programs. N. Gysbers & Earl J. Moore. 1981. text ed. 22.33 o.p. (ISBN 0-13-452656-2). P-H.
Improving Industrial Relations: The Advisory Role of ACAS. Eric Armstrong & Rosemary Lucas. LC 85-6638. 230p. 1985. 29.00 o.p. (ISBN 0-7099-0554-8, Pub. by Croom Helm Ltd). Routledge Chapman & Hall.
Improving Management Performance in Health Care Institutions: A Total Systems Approach. Addison C. Bennett. LC 78-8010. (Illus.). 256p. (Orig.). 1978. write for info. o.p.; pap. 25.00 o.p. (ISBN 0-939450-69-0, 001104). AHPI.
Improving Marking & Reporting in Classroom Instruction. Norman E. Gronlund. (Illus.). 64p. 1974. text ed. write for info. o.p. (ISBN 0-02-348140-4, 34814). Macmillan.
Improving Performance in Tax-Supported Agencies. 1981. pap. 5.00 o.p. (ISBN 0-918734-31-2). Reymont.
Improving Plant Power Reliability: Proceedings, American Nuclear Society Executive Conference, Hot Springs VA, 27-29 September 1976. 200p. pap. 22.00 softcover o.p. (ISBN 0-89448-300-5, 650002). Am Nuclear Soc.
Improving Problem-Solving Participation: The Case of Local Transnational Voluntary Organizations. Chimezie A. Osigweh. (Illus.). 280p. (Orig.). 1983. lib. bdg. 30.00 o.p. (ISBN 0-8191-3439-2); pap. text ed. 14.25 o.p. (ISBN 0-8191-3440-6). U Pr of Amer.
Improving Productivity & Effectiveness. Marvin E. Mundell. (Illus.). 512p. 1983. text ed. 49.00 o.p. (ISBN 0-13-452805-0). P-H.
Improving Productivity Through Advanced Office Controls. Robert E. Nolan et al. 432p. 1981. 29.95 o.p. (ISBN 0-8144-5617-0). AMACOM.
Improving Programs for the Gifted. Philadelphia Suburban School Study Council, Group A Staff. LC 65-27076. 136p. 1965. pap. text ed. 3.00x o.p. (ISBN 0-8134-0852-0, 852). Inter Print Pubs.
Improving Public Health: Ethical Dilemmas. Ed. by Spyros Doxiadis. LC 86-24573. 234p. 1987. 36.70 o.p. (ISBN 0-471-91313-8, Dist. by A R Liss). Wiley.
Improving Reading & Study Skills. Ed. by Ann S. Algier & Keith W. Algier. LC 81-48565. (College Learning Assistance Ser.: No. 8). 1982. 13.95x o.p. (ISBN 0-87589-880-7). Jossey-Bass.
Improving Reading in Every Class: A Sourcebook for Teachers. 3rd ed. Ellen L. Thomas & H. Alan Robinson. 480p. 1981. text ed. 32.00 abr. ed. o.s.i. (ISBN 0-205-07365-4, 237365); pap. 30.00 abr. ed. o.s.i. (ISBN 0-205-07730-7, 237730); duplicator masters 27.15 o.s.i. (ISBN 0-205-06447-7). Allyn.
Improving Reading in the Secondary Schools. 2nd ed. Lawrence E. Hafner. 1974. pap. write for info. o.p. (ISBN 0-02-348680-5, 34868). Macmillan.
Improving the Accountability of Career Education Programs: Evaluation Guidelines & Checklists. Kay Angana Adams & Jerry Walker. 103p. 1979. 6.75 o.p. (ISBN 0-318-15488-9, RD 168). Natl Ctr Res Voc Ed.
Improving Today's Curriculum for Tomorrow's Challenges. Philadelphia Suburban School Study Council Staff. LC 64-20044. 76p. 1964. pap. text ed. 1.50x o.p. (ISBN 0-8134-0064-3, 64). Inter Print Pubs.
Improving Traffic Operations & Safety at Exit Gore Areas. (National Cooperation Highway Research Program Report). 120p. 1973. 6.00 o.p. (ISBN 0-309-02201-0). Transport Res Bd.
Improving Transportation Services for the Elderly, the Handicapped & the Disadvantaged. (Transportation Research Report Ser.). 49p. 1977. 3.40 o.p. (ISBN 0-309-02689-X). Transport Res Bd.
Improving Vocational Education Curriculum. ERIC Clearinghouse on Adult, Career, & Vocational Education Staff. 56p. 1983. 4.95 o.p. (ISBN 0-318-22130-6, BB70). Natl Ctr Res Voc Ed.
Improving Voice & Articulation. 2nd ed. Hilda B. Fisher. 1975. text ed. 27.95 o.p. (ISBN 0-395-19232-3). HM.
Improving Your Health with Vitamin A. Ruth Adams & Frank Murray. (Illus.). 128p. (Orig.). 1978. pap. 1.25 o.s.i. (ISBN 0-915962-24-1). Comm Channels.
Improving Your Memory. Laird S. Cermak. 123p. 1976. 3.95 o.p. (ISBN 0-393-01124-0). Norton.
Improving Your Serve. Chuck Swindoll. 1986. deluxe ed. 9.95 o.p. (ISBN 0-8499-3851-1). Word Bks.
Improving Your Speech. John A. Grasham & Glenn G. Gooder. (Illus.). 326p. (Orig.). 1960. pap. text ed. 12.95 o.p. (ISBN 0-15-541260-4, HC). HarBraceJ.
Improvisation. John Hodgson & Ernest Richards. LC 79-52093. 224p. 1979. pap. 4.95 o.p. (ISBN 0-394-17099-7, E734, Ever). Grove.
Improvised Munitions Black Book, 3 vols. Set. lib. bdg. cancelled o.s.i. (ISBN 0-8490-3549-X). Gordon Pr.
Improvised Munitions Systems. James J. Glackin. LC 76-13258. 80p. 1976. pap. 8.00 o.p. (ISBN 0-87364-057-8). Paladin Pr.
Improvising Rock Guitar. Straw Dog. LC 72-92915. (Green Note Music Publications Ser.). (Illus.). 1975. 14.95 o.s.i. (ISBN 0-02-871280-3); pap. 5.95 o.s.i. (ISBN 0-02-870970-5). Schirmer Bks.
Impulse. Kenneth B. Young. LC 84-91285. 139p. 1985. 10.95 o.p. (ISBN 0-533-06365-5). Vantage.
IMS Programming Techniques: A Guide to Using DL-1. Dan Kapp & Joseph F. Leben. (Illus.). 320p. 1978. 21.95 o.p. (ISBN 0-442-80505-5). Van Nos Reinhold.
In a Certain Light. Karen Brownstein. 276p. 1985. 17.95 o.p. (ISBN 0-399-13084-5). Putnam Pub Group.
In a Class By Herself. Ivy Ruckman. LC 82-48759. 208p. (gr. 7 up). 1983. 12.95 o.p. (ISBN 0-15-238242-9, HJ). HarBraceJ.
In a Class of Their Own. new ed. Ed. by Barbara Ireson. 148p. (gr. 5-9). 1985. 12.95 o.p. (ISBN 0-571-13474-2). Faber & Faber.
In a Glamorous Fashion. Paul La Vine. (Illus.). 224p. 1980. 25.00 o.s.i. (ISBN 0-684-16610-0, ScribT). Scribner.
In a High Place. Joanne Meschery. 1981. 15.95 o.p. (ISBN 0-671-43024-6). S&S.
In a Meadow, Two Hares Hide. Jennifer Bartoli. Ed. by Kathy Pacini. LC 78-15221. (Illus.). (gr. k-2). 1978. PLB 10.75 o.p. (ISBN 0-8075-3628-8). A Whitman.

In a Minor Key: Negro Youth in Story & Fact. Ira D. Reid. LC 73-160450. (Illus.). 134p. 1971. Repr. of 1940 ed. lib. bdg. 35.00x o.p. (ISBN 0-8371-3346-7, RENY). Greenwood.

In a Promise. Herbert Brokering. LC 68-25801. (Illus.). 1968. 7.50 o.p. (ISBN 0-8066-0818-8, 10-3205, Augsburg). Augsburg Fortress.

In a Shallow Grave. James Purdy. LC 75-30399. 1976. 7.50 o.p. (ISBN 0-87795-124-1, Arbor Hse); pap. 3.95 o.p. (ISBN 0-87795-176-4). Morrow.

In a Shallow Grave. James Purdy. 1984. pap. 5.95 o.p. (ISBN 0-87795-605-7, Arbor Hse). Morrow.

In a Strange Land. Vladimir Korolenko. Tr. by Gregory Zilboorg. LC 74-14354. 214p. 1975. Repr. of 1925 ed. lib. bdg. 35.00x o.p. (ISBN 0-8371-7801-0, KOSL). Greenwood.

In a Time Between Wars. Milton Kaplan. 96p. 1973. pap. 1.95 o.p. (ISBN 0-393-04219-7). Norton.

In a Year of Our Lord: A Memoir of American Innocence. John Mullen. LC 76-48772. 1977. 8.95 o.p. (ISBN 0-87795-160-8, Arbor Hse). Morrow.

In Africa. Marc Bernheim & Evelyne Bernheim. LC 72-85913. 48p. (ps-4). 1973. 8.95 o.p. (ISBN 0-689-30315-7, Atheneum). Macmillan.

In America & in Need: Immigrant, Refugee & Entrant Women. Abby Spero. 175p. (Orig.). 1985. pap. 35.00 o.p. (ISBN 0-87117-143-0). Am Assn Comm Jr Coll.

In & About Hartford: Tours & Tales. Marion H. Grant. (Illus.). 360p. 1977. 2.50x o.p. (ISBN 0-940748-26-6); pap. 1.00x o.p. (ISBN 0-686-26746-X). Conn Hist Soc.

In & Around Paris. Philippe Gloaguen & Pierre Josse. (Collier World Traveler Ser.). (Illus.). 224p. 1986. pap. 8.95 o.p. (ISBN 0-02-097690-9, Collier). Macmillan.

In Another Land. Jane Sorenson. (Jennifer Bks.). 144p. (gr. 5-8). 1985. 2.95 o.p. (ISBN 0-87239-934-6, 2984). Standard Pub.

In Between Advents: Biblical & Spiritual Arrivals. Dennis E. Groh. LC 86-45199. (Bible for Christian Life Ser.). 64p. 1986. pap. 3.95 o.p. (ISBN 0-8006-2025-9, 1-2025, Fortress). Augsburg Fortress.

In Broken Country. David Wagoner. LC 79-13364. 1979. 8.95 o.p. (ISBN 0-316-91704-4, Pub. by Atlantic-Little Brown); pap. 5.95 o.p. (ISBN 0-316-91703-6, Pub. by Atlantic-Little Brown). Little.

In But Still Out: Women in the Church. Elizabeth H. Verdesi. LC 75-34365. 218p. 1976. pap. 3.95 o.s.i. (ISBN 0-664-24788-1, Westminster). Westminster John Knox.

In Caps & Gowns: The Story of the McGill School for Graduate Nurses, 1920-1964. Barbara L. Tunis. 154p. 1966. 6.00 o.p. (ISBN 0-7735-9067-6, McGill Canada). U of Toronto Pr.

In Care & into Work. Charles Burgess. LC 80-42289. (Residential Social Work Ser.). 160p. 1981. 21.00x o.p. (ISBN 0-422-77640-8, NO. 3465, Pub by Tavistock England). Routledge Chapman & Hall.

In Celebration of Babies. Carol Tannenhauser & Cheryl Moch. 1987. lib. bdg. 20.00 o.p. Ballantine.

In Celebration of Children: An Interfaith Religious Action Kit. Children's Defense Fund Staff et al. LC 83-71460. 90p. (Orig.). (gr. 12 up). 1983. pap. 6.50 o.p. (ISBN 0-938008-07-2). Children's Defense.

In Celebration of Louisville. Martin E. Beimer. Ed. by Karl Stull. (Illus.). 368p. (YA) (gr. 7 up). 1988. 39.95 o.s.i. (ISBN 0-89781-239-5). Windsor Pubns Inc.

In Celebration of Texas. Archie P. McDonald. Ed. by Susan Wells. LC 86-5651. (Illus.). 488p. 1986. 29.95 o.p. (ISBN 0-89781-165-8). Windsor Pubns Inc.

In Celebration of the Book: Literary New Mexico. Ed. by Dwight Myers & Carol Myers. 226p. 1982. deluxe ed. 200.00 o.p. (ISBN 0-89016-063-5). Lightning Tree.

In Celebration of the Discovery of the Abandoned Star Factory. David Horton. 1982. 125.00 o.p. (ISBN 0-932526-06-3). Nexus Pr.

In Christ, My Lord. Barbara O. Webb. 1982. pap. 4.95 o.p. (ISBN 0-570-03852-9, 12YY2807). Concordia.

In Clover. Myra Scovel. LC 79-24882. 120p. 1980. 8.95 o.s.i. (ISBN 0-664-21366-9, Westminster). Westminster John Knox.

In Command of Tomorrow: Resource and Environmental Strategies for Americans. Sterling Brubaker. LC 74-24401. (Resources for the Future). 192p. 1975. pap. 14.50x o.p. (ISBN 0-8018-1700-5). Johns Hopkins.

In Common Cause. rev. ed. John W. Gardner. 1975. pap. 2.95 o.p. (ISBN 0-393-00787-1). Norton.

In Condor Country. David Darlington. 1987. 15.45 o.s.i. (ISBN 0-395-40798-2). HM.

In Conflict & Order: Understanding Society. 3rd ed. D. Stanley Eitzen. 520p. 1984. pap. text ed. write for info. o.p. (ISBN 0-205-08273-4, 818273); write for info. o.p. (ISBN 0-205-08275-0, 818275). Allyn.

In Deacon's Orders, 1895. Walter Besant. Ed. by Robert L. Wolff. Bd. with Red Pottage, 1899. Mary Cholmondely. LC 75-1541. (Victorian Fiction Ser). 1976. lib. bdg. 16.50 o.p. (ISBN 0-8240-1612-2). Garland Pub.

In Deep Water. Jerry Jenkins. (Bradford Family Adventures Ser.). (Illus.). 128p. (gr. 3-6). 1986. 2.95 o.p. (ISBN 0-87403-091-9, 2921). Standard Pub.

In Defence of Canada, Vol. II: Appeasement & Rearmament. James Eayrs. LC 66-3834. (Studies in the Structure of Power). 1965. 17.50x o.p. (ISBN 0-8020-1485-2); pap. 10.00 o.p. U of Toronto Pr.

In Defence of Canada, Vol. III: Peacemaking & Deterrence. James Eayrs. LC 68-3834. (Studies in the Structure of Power). 1977. 30.00x o.p. (ISBN 0-8020-1907-2); pap. 10.95 o.p. (ISBN 0-8020-6328-4). U of Toronto Pr.

In Defence of Dagon. H. P. Lovecraft. Intro. by S. T. Joshi. 42p. (Orig.). 1985. pap. 4.95 o.p. (ISBN 0-318-04716-0). Necronomicon.

In Defence of Fantasy: A Study of the Genre in English & American Literature since 1945. Ann Swinfen. LC 83-11164. 253p. (Orig.). 1984. pap. 13.95x o.p. (ISBN 0-7100-9525-2). Routledge Chapman & Hall.

In Defense of Animals. J. J. McCoy. LC 76-58508. (Illus.). 192p. (gr. 6 up). 1979. 8.95 o.p. (ISBN 0-395-28864-9, Clarion). HM.

In Defense of Animals. Ed. by Peter Singer. 224p. 1985. 29.95x o.p. (ISBN 0-631-14327-0). Basil Blackwell.

In Defense of Decadent Europe. Raymond Aron. 308p. 1984. pap. text ed. 11.25 o.p. (ISBN 0-8191-3316-7). U Pr of Amer.

In Defense of Fascism: A New Critical Evaluation of the Fascist Experience in Modern History. Harrison Osborne. (Science of Man Library Bk.). 1978. 127.75 o.p. (ISBN 0-89266-128-3). Am Classical Coll Pr.

In Defense of Practical Reason. Konstantin Kolenda. (Rice University Studies: Vol. 55, No. 1). 107p. 1969. pap. 10.00x o.p. (ISBN 0-89263-199-6). Rice Univ.

In Defense of Welfare. Ed. by Phillip Bean et al. 250p. 1986. pap. 17.95 o.p. (ISBN 0-422-79090-7, 9634, Pub. by Tavistock England). Routledge Chapman & Hall.

In Disregard for the Law. A. Artsibasov. Tr. by Vadim Kuleshov. 268p. 1982. pap. 2.95 o.p. (ISBN 0-8285-2997-3, 132154, Pub. by Progress Pubs USSR). Imported Pubns.

In Due Season. Herbert F. Brokering. LC 66-22563. (Illus.). 1966. 6.50 o.p. (ISBN 0-8066-0620-7, 10-3209, Augsburg). Augsburg Fortress.

In Epistolam Ad Corinthios Iam et Iiam, Ad Galatas et Ad Ephesios see Commentarius Cantabrigiensis in Epistolas Pauli e Schola Petri Abaelardi.

In Epistolam ad Philippenses, ad Colossenses, ad Thessalonicenses Primam et Secundam, ed Timotheam Priman et Secundam, ad Titum et Philemonem see Commentarius Cantabrigiensis in Epistolas Pauli e Schola Petri Abaelardi.

In Epistolam Ad Romanos see Commentarius Cantabrigiensis in Epistolas Pauli e Schola Petri Abaelardi.

In First Gear: The French Automobile Industry to 1914. James M. Laux. 256p. 1976. lib. bdg. 22.50x o.p. (ISBN 0-7735-0264-5, McGill Canada). U of Toronto Pr.

In Freedom's Cause. (Guild Books Classic Illustrated Ser.). (Illus.). pap. 0.59 o.p. (ISBN 0-685-74104-4, 168). Guild Bks.

In Front of the Table & Behind It. Shirley Schwarzrock & C. Gilbert Wrenn. (Coping with Ser.). (Illus.). 41p. (gr. 7-12). 1971. pap. text ed. 3.00 o.p. (ISBN 0-913476-24-2). Am Guidance.

In Front of Your Nose: Nineteen Forty-Five to Nineteen Fifty see Collected Essays, Journalism, & Letters of George Orwell.

In Germany. Ernst Haas. 1977. 35.00 o.p. (Studio). Penguin USA.

In Ghurka Company. J. P. Cross. (Illus.). 204p. 1987. 24.95 o.p. (ISBN 0-85368-865-6, Pub. by Arms & Armour). Sterling.

In God We Trust: Creation's Mysteries Revealed. Bro. Ignatius. 1977. 5.50 o.p. (ISBN 0-682-48752-X). Exposition-Phoenix.

In God's Great Way. Jennie Davis. LC 82-7446. (Illus.). 32p. (gr. 1-2). 1982. lib. bdg. 4.95 o.p. Dandelion Hse.

In Good Spirits. David J. Ludwig. LC 82-70944. (Orig.). 1982. pap. 6.95 o.p. (ISBN 0-8066-1919-8, 10-3208, Augsburg). Augsburg Fortress.

In Granny's Garden. Sarah Harrison. LC 79-28585. (Hlus.). 32p. (gr. k-3). 1980. 7.95 o.s.i. (ISBN 0-03-050876-2). H Holt & Co.

In Hard Times: Reformers among the Late Victorians. Herman Ausubel. LC 72-9826. 403p. 1973. Repr. of 1960 ed. lib. bdg. 35.00x o.p. (ISBN 0-8371-6600-4, AUHT). Greenwood.

In Harm's Way: A RNVR Officer at War, 1940-44. Geoffrey Hobday. (Illus.). 1985. 16.95 o.s.i. (ISBN 0-901627-30-5). Janes Info Group.

In Heart & Home: A Woman's Workshop on Worship. Robert E. Webber. (Woman's Workshop Ser.). 112p. (Orig.). 1985. pap. 2.95 o.p. (ISBN 0-310-36681-X, 12209P). Zondervan.

In Heavenly Places. Albert B. Simpson. pap. 3.95 o.p. (ISBN 0-87509-021-4). Chr Pubns.

In Her Father's Footsteps. Bianca Bradbury. LC 75-43891. (Illus.). 176p. (gr. 5-9). 1976. 6.95 o.p. (ISBN 0-395-24381-5). HM.

In Her Own Image: Women Working in the Arts. Ed. by Elaine Hedges & Ingrid Wendt. (Women's Lives-Women's Work Ser.). (Illus.). 336p. (gr. 11 up). 1980. o. p. 17.95 o.s.i.; pap. 9.95 o.s.i. (ISBN 0-912670-62-2); teaching guide, 64 p. 5.00 o.s.i. (ISBN 0-912670-76-2). Feminist Pr.

In Hieremiam Prophetam Libri 6. Saint Hieronymus. (Corpus Scriptorum Ecclesiasticorum Latinorum Ser: Vol. 59). 1913. 40.00 o.p. (ISBN 0-384-23040-7). Johnson Repr.

In Him Was Life. Caroline Glyn. LC 76-26492. 1977. softcover 5.95 o.s.i. (ISBN 0-664-24118-2, Westminster). Westminster John Knox.

In His Garden: The Anatomy of a Murderer. Leo Damore. LC 79-54008. (Illus.). 1981. 14.95 o.p. (ISBN 0-87795-250-7, Arbor Hse). Morrow.

In His Image: The Jewish Philosophy of Man As Expressed in Rabbinic Tradition. Samuel Belkin. LC 78-10192. 1979. Repr. of 1960 ed. lib. bdg. 27.50x o.p. (ISBN 0-313-21234-1, BEIH). Greenwood.

In His Name. Kirkie Morissey. 132p. 1985. pap. 4.95 o.p. (ISBN 0-89109-056-8). NavPress.

In His Steps. Charles Sheldon. 1970. pap. 4.95 o.p. (ISBN 0-310-32791-1, 9058P). Zondervan.

In His Steps. Charles M. Sheldon. 1982. gift ed. 7.95 o.s.i. (ISBN 0-915720-66-3). Brownlow Pub Co.

In Honor Bound: A Novel. Gerald Seymour. 1984. 14.45 o.p. (ISBN 0-393-01859-8). Norton.

In-House Training Programs on Quantitative Techniques: A Collection of Case Studies. American Hospital Association Clearinghouse for Hospital Management Engineering Staff. LC 82-11654. 148p. 1982. pap. text ed. 18.75 o.p. (ISBN 0-87258-369-4, AHA-133200). Am Hospital.

In Joy Still Felt: Autobiography of Isaac Asimov 1954-1978. Isaac Asimov. 1981. pap. 9.95 o.p. (ISBN 0-380-53025-2, 53025-2). Avon.

In-Laws & Outlaws: Kingship & Marriage in England, 1800-1980. Sybil Wolfram & Margaret Hall. 240p. 1987. 43.00 o.p. (ISBN 0-7099-2796-7, Pub. by Croom Helm UK). Routledge Chapman & Hall.

In Love & Anger. Anne Holden. LC 86-913960. 256p. 1986. text ed. 14.95 o.p. (ISBN 0-682-40316-4). Exposition-Phoenix.

In Love & Friendship. Date not set. (ISBN 0-385-29505-7). Delacorte.

In Love & Friendship. Hilary Norman. 528p. 1987. pap. 17.95 o.p. (ISBN 0-385-29505-7). Delacorte.

In Love & in Trouble. Laurel Trivelpiece. (gr. 7 up). 1981. pap. 2.25 o.p. (ISBN 0-671-50443-6). Archway.

In Love & Trouble: Stories of Black Women. Alice Walker. LC 73-7607. 1973. 6.50 o.p. (ISBN 0-15-144405-6). HarBraceJ.

In Love's Fury. Robin Tolivar. 320p. 1985. pap. 2.95 o.p. (ISBN 0-380-89539-0). Avon.

In Malaysia. Walls & Martin. 148p. (Orig.). 1986. pap. 10.95 o.p. (ISBN 0-946983-03-8, Pub. by Bradt Prodns UK). Bradt Ent.

In Man We Trust: The Neglected Side of Biblical Faith. Walter Brueggemann. LC 72-1761. 144p. 1972. 7.95 o.p. (ISBN 0-8042-0199-4, John Knox). Westminster John Knox.

In Meiner Seele Bin Ich Frei. Brad Steiger. 242p. (Orig., Ger.). 1983. pap. 5.95 o.p. (ISBN 0-88155-018-3). Illum Way Pub.

In Memory of H. L. Meerwein. (Topics in Current Chemistry: Vol. 80). (Illus.). 1979. 81.00 o.p. (ISBN 0-387-09309-5). Springer-Verlag.

In Memory of Her: A Feminist Theological Reconstruction of Christian Origins. Elisabeth S. Fiorenza. LC 82-19896. 275p. 1983. 22.50 o.p. (ISBN 0-8245-0493-3). Crossroad NY.

In Memory Yet Green: The Autobiography of Isaac Asimov, 1920-1954, Vol. 1. Isaac Asimov. 1980. pap. 7.95 o.p. (ISBN 0-380-75432-0, 75432-0). Avon.

In Miners' Mirage Land. Idah M. Strobridge. (Nevada Classics Ser.). (Illus.). 136p. 1982. pap. 15.95 o.p. (ISBN 0-936332-12-3). Falcon Hill Pr.

In My Father's House. Corrie Ten Boom. (General Ser.). 1977. lib. bdg. 11.50 o.p. (ISBN 0-8161-6412-6, Large Print Bks). G K Hall.

In My Father's House. Min S. Yee & Thomas N. Layton. 384p. 1981. 13.95 o.p. (ISBN 0-03-053396-1). H Holt & Co.

In My Mother's House. Kim Chernin. LC 82-19514. 307p. (gr. 7 up). 1983. 14.45 o.p. (ISBN 0-89919-167-3). Ticknor & Fields.

In My Own Key. Elisabeth Soderstrom. (Illus.). 102p. 1980. 19.95 o.p. (ISBN 0-241-10318-5, Pub. by Hamish Hamilton England). David & Charles.

In My Soul I Am Free. Brad Steiger. 206p. 1968. pap. 2.95 o.p. (ISBN 0-914766-11-2). Illum Way Pub.

In My Understanding. George Simms. LC 81-70555. 160p. 1982. 9.95 o.p. (ISBN 0-8006-0674-4, 1-674, Fortress). Augsburg Fortress.

In Old Hollywood: The Movies During Their Golden Years. Clyde O. Jackson. 1977. 6.50 o.p. (ISBN 0-682-48971-9). Exposition-Phoenix.

In Olde Connecticut. Charles B. Todd. LC 68-26612. 256p. 1968. Repr. of 1906 ed. 35.00x o.p. (ISBN 0-8103-3540-9). Gale.

In Olde Massachusetts: Sketches of Old Times & Places During the Early Days of the Commonwealth. Charles B. Todd. LC 77-99060. 266p. 1971. Repr. of 1907 ed. 35.00x o.p. (ISBN 0-8103-3775-4). Gale.

In One Barn: Efficient Livestock Housing & Management Under One Roof. Lee Pelley. LC 83-25219. (Illus.). 166p. (Orig.). 1984. pap. 11.95 o.s.i. (ISBN 0-88150-006-2). Countryman.

In Orbit. Wright Morris. LC 75-14359. 153p. 1976. 11.95x o.p. (ISBN 0-8032-0882-0); pap. 5.95 o.p. (ISBN 0-8032-5830-5, BB 612, Bison). U of Nebr Pr.

In Our Grandmothers' Footsteps: A Walking Tour of London. Jennifer Clarke. LC 85-47598. 176p. (Orig.). 1985. pap. 7.95 o.p. (ISBN 0-689-11623-3, Atheneum). Macmillan.

In Our Time: Socialism & the Rise of Labor, 1885-1905. Verity Burgmann. 236p. 1985. text ed. 29.95x o.p. (ISBN 0-86861-529-3). Unwin Hyman.

In Our Times. 2nd ed. Norman L. Rosenberg & Emily S. Rosenberg. (Illus.). 336p. 1982. pap. text ed. (ISBN 0-13-453787-4). P-H.

In Parables. John Crossan. LC 73-7067. 160p. 1973. 12.95xi o.p. (ISBN 0-06-061606-7). HarpR.

In Patagonia. Bruce Chatwin. LC 78-885. 1980. 9.95 o.s.i. (ISBN 0-671-40045-2); pap. 7.95 o.s.i. (ISBN 0-671-44857-9). Summit Bks.

In Person: The Great Entertainers. Martin Gottfried. (Illus.). 256p. 1985. 49.50 o.p. (ISBN 0-8109-1613-4). Abrams.

In Person: The Prince & Princess of Wales. Alastair Burnet. 1985. 14.95 o.s.i. (ISBN 0-671-62217-X). Summit Bks.

In Place & Out. Michael Tarachow. (Illus., Orig.). 1982. pap. 17.50 o.p. (ISBN 0-915316-98-6). Pentagram.

In Plain Sight: Photographs by Beaumont Newhall. Photos by Beaumont Newhall. LC 83-14892. (Illus.). 84p. 1984. 27.50 o.p. (ISBN 0-87905-078-0, Peregrine Smith); limited edition 300.00 o.p. (ISBN 0-87905-086-1). Gibbs Smith Pub.

In Praise of Adam. Reuel Denney. LC 61-18887. (Phoenix Poets Ser). 1962. pap. 1.50 o.s.i. (ISBN 0-226-14301-5, PP3, Phoen). U of Chicago Pr.

In Praise of Ale, or Songs, Ballads, Epigrams & Anecdotes Relating to Beer Malt, & Hops. W. T. Marchant. LC 68-22038. 640p. 1968. Repr. of 1888 ed. 48.00x o.p. (ISBN 0-8103-3511-5). Gale.

In Praise of God: Loving Thanks from a Grateful Daughter. Sharlotte Rae. 1979. 4.00 o.p. (ISBN 0-682-49271-X). Exposition-Phoenix.

In Praise of Love. Date not set. (ISBN 0-8052-3808-5); pap. (ISBN 0-8052-0715-5). Random.

In Praise of More Folly. David I. Naglee. 208p. 1982. 10.00 o.p. (ISBN 0-682-49803-3, Banner). Exposition-Phoenix.

In Praise of Practical Fertilizer: Thoughts from Near New Burlington. John Baskin. (Illus.). 223p. 1982. 14.95 o.p. (ISBN 0-393-01563-7). Norton.

In Praise of Wild Herbs: Remedies & Recipies From Old Provence. Ludo Chardenon. Tr. by Susan Kinnell & John Frederick. LC 83-24069. (Illus.). 112p. 1984. pap. 7.95 o.p. (ISBN 0-88496-208-3). Capra Pr.

In Private, in Public: The Prince & Princess of Wales. 160p. 1986. 15.95 o.s.i. (ISBN 0-671-63304-X). Summit Bks.

In Pursuit of Antiquity. Roderick Whitfield. LC 70-86877. (140 Illus). 1969. 12.50 o.p. (ISBN 0-8048-0746-9). C E Tuttle.

In Pursuit of Equality of Educational Opportunity: A Selective Bibliography & Guide to the Research Literature. Richard H. Quay. LC 76-52691. 200p. 1977. lib. bdg. 28.00 o.p. (ISBN 0-8240-9872-2). Garland Pub.

In Pursuit of Religion. Reynold Borzaga. pap. 4.95 o.p. (ISBN 0-941850-01-3). Liturgical Pubns.

In Pursuit of the American Dream. Bob Dotson. LC 85-47600. (Illus.). 320p. 1985. 14.95 o.p. (ISBN 0-689-11628-4, Atheneum). Macmillan.

In Pursuit of the Past: Decoding the Archaeological Record. Lewis R. Binford. LC 82-50816. (Illus.). 1983. 18.95f o.p. (ISBN 0-500-05042-2). Thames Hudson.

In Pursuit of Truth: Essays on the Philosophy of Karl Popper on the Occasion of His 80th Birthday. Ed. by Paul Levinson. 304p. 1982. text ed. 25.00x o.p. (ISBN 0-391-02609-7). Humanities.

In Pursuit of Youth: Everyday Nutrition for Everyone over 35. Betty Kamen & Si Kamen. 384p. 1984. 17.95 o.p. (ISBN 0-396-08364-1). Dodd.

In Quest of Man. P. Alsberg. 1970. text ed. 15.50 o.p. (ISBN 0-08-015680-0). Pergamon.

In Quest of the Truth: A Survey of Medieval Jewish Thought. Israel Kane. LC 84-90191. 77p. 1985. 8.95 o.p. (ISBN 0-533-06243-8). Vantage.

In Quest of Treasure: New Poems for Young People with Study Guides. Irma G. Rhodes. (YA) 1971. 4.00 o.p. (ISBN 0-682-47321-9). Exposition-Phoenix.

In Re Alger Hiss, Vol. I. Ed. by Edith Tiger. (American Century Ser.). 438p. 1979. 17.50 o.p. (ISBN 0-8090-5808-1, Am Century); pap. 8.95 o.p. (ISBN 0-8090-0143-8). Hill & Wang.

In Real Life I'm Just Kate. Barbara Morgenroth. LC 81-1421. 180p. (gr. 5-9). 1981. 9.95 o.s.i. (ISBN 0-689-30851-5, Atheneum Childrens Bks). Macmillan.

In Red Man's Land: A Study of the American Indian. Francis E. Leupp. LC 76-44529. (Beautiful Rio Grande Classics Ser.). 170p. 1976. Repr. of 1914 ed. lib. bdg. 12.00 o.p. (ISBN 0-87380-115-6). Rio Grande.

In Rem Foreclosures: The U. S. Supreme Court Imposes Additional Notice Requirements. William A. Campbell. LC 85-623125. 1983. 1.00 o.p. Institute Government.

In Remembrance of Rose: A Lennox Kemp Mystery. M. R. Meek. LC 86-29771. 1987. 14.95 o.p. (ISBN 0-684-18832-5). Scribner.

In Response to Aggression: Methods of Control & Prosocial Alternatives. rev. ed. Arnold P. Goldstein et al. (Pergamon General Psychology Ser.: No. 98). (Illus.). 576p. 1981. 79.00 o.p. (ISBN 0-08-025580-9); pap. 28.00 o.p. (ISBN 0-08-025579-5). Pergamon.

In Response to God: How Christians Make Ethical Decisions. Isabel Rogers. pap. 4.95 o.p. (ISBN 0-8042-9080-6, John Knox). Westminster John Knox.

In Retrospect: The History of a Historian. Arthur M. Schlesinger. LC 63-15318. 1963. 4.50 o.p. (ISBN 0-15-144490-0). HarBraceJ.

In Return For... Alpha De Monte. 240p. 1983. 11.00 o.p. (ISBN 0-682-49934-X, Banner). Exposition-Phoenix.

In Savage Times: Leonard Woolf on Peace & War. Leonard Woolf. Incl. Fear & Politics: a Debate at the Zoo; The Way of Peace; The League & Abyssinia; The International Postwar Settlement. LC 72-148378. (Library of War & Peace; the Character & Causes of War). 1973. lib. bdg. 46.00 o.p. (ISBN 0-8240-0466-3). Garland Pub.

In Search of a Faith That Works. Earl Palmer. LC 85-18421. (In Search of Ser.). 140p. 1985. 10.95 o.p. (ISBN 0-8307-0889-8, 5110509). Regal.

In Search of a Meaningful Past. Ed. by Arthur N. Gilbert. LC 77-169903. (New Perspectives in History Ser). (Orig.). 1972. pap. 6.75 o.p. (ISBN 0-395-12567-7). HM.

In Search of a Past: The Rearing of an English Gentleman 1933-45. Ronald Fraser. LC 84-45049. 192p. 1984. 12.95 o.p. (ISBN 0-689-11480-X, Atheneum). Macmillan.

In Search of a Responsible World Society: The Social Teachings of the World Council of Churches. Paul Bock. LC 74-9986. 252p. 1974. 10.00 o.s.i. (ISBN 0-664-20708-1, Westminster). Westminster John Knox.

In Search of a Small Business Definition: An Exploration of the Small-Business Definitions of the U. S., the U. K., Israel, & the People's Republic of China. Leah Hertz. LC 81-40926. 482p. 1982. lib. bdg. 39.50 o.p. (ISBN 0-8191-2308-0); pap. text ed. 20.50 o.p. (ISBN 0-8191-2309-9). U Pr of Amer.

In Search of Billy Cole. Jack Newcombe. 198p. 1984. 14.95 o.p. (ISBN 0-87795-608-1, Arbor Hse). Morrow.

In Search of Deity. John Maquarrie. 288p. 14.95x o.p. (ISBN 0-8245-0682-0). Crossroad NY.

In Search of Early Christian Unity. Peter Roberts. 1985. 18.00 o.p. (ISBN 0-533-05859-7). Vantage.

In Search of Enemies: A CIA Story. John Stockwell. 1978. 12.95 o.p. (ISBN 0-393-05705-4). Norton.

In Search of Excellence. Needham, Richard, & Associates Staff & John Swaim. 52p. 1984. 5.95 o.p. (ISBN 0-318-17733-1). Natl Middle Schl.

In Search of God. Marietta Moskin. LC 79-10493. (Illus.). 160p. (gr. 6 up). 1979. 10.95 o.s.i. (ISBN 0-689-30719-5, Atheneum). Macmillan.

In Search of God. Peter Ritchie, Jr. 1978. 4.00 o.p. (ISBN 0-682-49111-X). Exposition-Phoenix.

In Search of God & Self: Renaissance & Reformation Thought. Donald J. Wilcox. 1975. pap. 18.95 o.p. (ISBN 0-395-17178-4). HM.

In Search of Graphics: Adventures in Computer Art. Sandra Markle & William Markle. LC 84-25108. (Illus.). 136p. (gr. 4 up). 1984. PLB 11.88 o.p. (ISBN 0-688-04989-3); pap. 10.20 o.p. (ISBN 0-688-04988-5). Lothrop.

In Search of Jerusalem: Religion & Ethics in the Writings of A. M. Klein. Gretl Fischer. 288p. 1976. 14.95x o.p. (ISBN 0-7735-0227-0, McGill Canada). U of Toronto Pr.

In Search of L. L. Bean. M. R. Montgomery. 288p. 1984. 16.95 o.p. (ISBN 0-316-57864-9). Little.

In Search of Peace. Ed. by Waris Shere. 1980. 12.50 o.p. (ISBN 0-682-49551-4, University). Exposition-Phoenix.

In Search of Self: An Exploration of the Role of the School in Promoting Self-Understanding. Arthur T. Jersild. 1952. pap. text ed. 5.95x o.p. (ISBN 0-8077-1569-7). Tchrs Coll.

In Search of Spanish Painting. R. Scott Stevenson. 1954. 5.95 o.p. (ISBN 0-8022-1642-0). Philos Lib.

In Search of Spiritual Leadership. Ken Hanna. 144p. 1987. pap. 5.95 o.p. (ISBN 0-89693-246-X). Victor Bks.

In Search of the Constitution: Reflections on State & Society in Britain. Nevil Johnson. LC 76-43316. 1977. 34.00 o.p. (ISBN 0-08-021379-0). Pergamon.

In Search of the Monkey Girl. Spalding Gray. (Illus.). 80p. 1982. 25.00 o.p.; ltd. ed. 300.00 o.p. (ISBN 0-89381-097-5). Aperture.

In Search of the Past: An Introduction to Archaelogy. John Bower. 484p. 1986. text ed. (ISBN 0-534-10992-6). Wadsworth Pub.

In Search of the Primitive. Stanley Diamond. LC 72-82195. 387p. 1981. 0.00 o.p. (ISBN 0-87855-045-3). Transaction Pubs.

In Search of the Scrounger. Alan Deacon. 110p. 1976. pap. text ed. 7.50x o.p. (ISBN 0-7135-1992-4, Pub. by Bedford England). Gower Pub Co.

In Search of Theatre. Eric Bentley. LC 74-18333. (Illus.). 1975. pap. text ed. 4.95x o.p. (ISBN 0-689-70522-0, 212, Atheneum). Macmillan.

In Search of Truth. John E. Bragg. LC 85-90162. 1986. 15.00 o.p. (ISBN 0-682-40285-0). Exposition-Phoenix.

In Season & Out. Bruce Clanton. LC 80-54272. (Illus.). 84p. 1981. pap. 7.95 o.p. (ISBN 0-89390-025-7). Resource Pubns.

In Season, Out of Season: An Introduction to the Thought of Jacques Ellul. Jacques Ellul. LC 82-47743. 160p. (Orig.). 1982. pap. 7.64i o.p. (ISBN 0-06-062239-3, RD/397). HarpR.

In Self-Defense. Steven B. Mizel & Peter Jaret. LC 84-12906. 256p. 1985. 15.95 o.p. (ISBN 0-15-144552-4). HarBraceJ.

In Sepia. Jon Anderson. LC 73-13310. (Pitt Poetry Ser). 1974. 15.95x o.p. (ISBN 0-8229-3278-4); pap. 6.95 o.p. (ISBN 0-8229-5245-9). U of Pittsburgh Pr.

In-Service Handbook for Mathematics Education. Ed. by Alan Osborne. LC 77-7287. 260p. 1977. pap. 5.00 o.s.i. (ISBN 0-87353-119-1). NCTM.

In-Service Primary Teacher Education in Asia: Report of the APEID Finalization Meeting on the Joint Innovation Project, New Delhi, India, 3-12 December 1981. (APEID Ser.). 100p. 1982. pap. 5.00 o.p. (ISBN 0-686-82542-X, UB105, UB). UNIPUB.

In-Service: The Teacher & the School. Carol Donoughue et al. 220p. 1981. 25.00 o.p. (ISBN 0-89397-109-X). Nichols Pub.

In-Service Training & Educational Development: An International Survey. David Hopkins. 368p. 1985. 34.50 o.p. (ISBN 0-7099-3710-5, Pub. by Croom Helm Ltd). Routledge Chapman & Hall.

In-Service Training & Staff Development for the Paraprofessional in Libraries: A Selective Bibliography. Lorna Peterson. (Public Administration Ser.: P 1727). 7p. 1985. 2.00 o.p. (ISBN 0-89028-497-0). Vance Biblios.

In Sight of Sever: Essays from Harvard. David T. McCord. LC 63-19143. 1963. 19.50x o.s.i. (ISBN 0-674-44701-8). Harvard U Pr.

In Small Doses. Phyllis R. Naylor. LC 78-72978. 1979. 8.95 o.p. (ISBN 0-689-10962-8, Atheneum). Macmillan.

In Southern Light: Treks Through Brazil & Africa. Alex Shoumatoff. 272p. 1986. 17.45 o.p. (ISBN 0-671-49441-4). S&S.

In Spirit & in Truth: A Guide to Praying. Martha G. Rowlett. LC 82-50944. 112p. 1983. pap. 5.95 o.p. (ISBN 0-8358-0448-8). Upper Room.

In Spite Of. John C. Powys. 320p. 1953. (ISBN 0-8022-2008-8). Philos Lib.

In Such Dark Places. Joseph Caldwell. 230p. 1978. 8.95 o.p. (ISBN 0-374-17648-5). FS&G.

In Such Dark Places. Joseph Caldwell. 1984. pap. 6.95 o.p. (ISBN 0-932870-54-6). Alyson Pubns.

In the Active Voice. Mary Douglas. 280p. 1982. 26.95x o.p. (ISBN 0-7100-9065-X). Routledge Chapman & Hall.

In the Bank...or up the Chimney? A Dollars & Cents Guide to Energy-Saving Home Improvements. Allan D. Ackerman et al. (Illus.). 1975. pap. 1.25x o.p. (ISBN 0-89011-477-3, ECR-107). Abt Bks.

In the Beginning: An Introduction to Archaeology. 5th ed. Brian M. Fagan. LC 84-7887. 1984. text ed. write for info. o.p. (ISBN 0-673-39002-0). Scott F.

In the Beginning God: Jottings from Genesis. William Hartley. 96p. 1975. pap. 1.45 o.p. (ISBN 0-8010-4132-5). Baker Bk.

In the Beginning There Were the Parents: Discussion Guide. Dolores Curran. 1980. pap. 2.95 o.p. (ISBN 0-03-056978-8). HarpR.

In the Beginning There Were the Parents. Dolores Curran. 1978. pap. 4.95 o.p. (ISBN 0-03-042766-5). HarpR.

In the Boom Boom Room. David Rabe. 112p. pap. 8.95 o.s.i. (ISBN 0-394-62205-7, Ever). Grove.

In the Castle of the Bear. Steve Senn. LC 85-7951. 156p. (gr. 5-8). 1985. 11.95 o.s.i. (ISBN 0-689-31167-2, Atheneum Childrens Bks). Macmillan.

In the Cattle Country: History of Potter County, 1887-1966. Della T. Key. 14.95 o.p. (ISBN 0-89015-021-4). Eakin Pr.

In the Cause of Architecture. Ed. by Frederick Gutheim. (Illus.). 246p. 1975. text ed. 39.95 o.p. (ISBN 0-07-025350-1). McGraw.

In the Center: The Story of a Retreat. Barbara Rogers. LC 82-84468. 145p. (Orig.). 1983. pap. 4.95 o.p. (ISBN 0-87793-267-0). Ave Maria.

In the City of Paris. Hannah Green. LC 81-43649. (Illus.). 32p. (ps-3). 1985. 11.95 o.p. (ISBN 0-385-15692-8); lib. bdg. 11.95 o.p. (ISBN 0-385-15693-6). Doubleday.

In the Claws of the KGB: Memoirs of a Double Agent. Rupert Sigl. 248p. 1978. 7.95 o.p. (ISBN 0-8059-2520-1). Dorrance.

In the Clear Light. Fiona Kidman. 208p. 1985. 13.45 o.p. (ISBN 0-393-01987-X). Norton.

In the Clearing. Robert Frost. 1962. 10.95 o.p. (ISBN 0-8050-0625-7); pap. 5.95 o.p. (ISBN 0-8050-0624-9). H Holt & Co.

In the Company of Others. Jory Graham. LC 78-22252. 288p. 1982. 10.95 o.p. (ISBN 0-15-144642-3). HarBraceJ.

In the Dark. R. M. Lamming. LC 85-47642. 240p. 1986. 13.95 o.p. (ISBN 0-689-11629-2, Atheneum). Macmillan.

In the Dead of the Night. Rachel Scott. (Velvet Glove Ser.: No. 6). 320p. (Orig.). 1984. pap. 2.25 o.p. (ISBN 0-380-88278-7, 88278-7). Avon.

In the Deserts of This Earth. Uwe George. Tr. by Richard Winston & Clara Winston. LC 78-23672. (Helen & Kurt Wolff Bks). (Illus.). 309p. 1979. pap. 7.95 o.p. (ISBN 0-15-644435-6, Harv). HarBraceJ.

In the Empire of Ice. Olga Cabral. LC 80-53808. (Illus.). 88p. (Orig.). 1980. pap. 3.25 o.p. (ISBN 0-931122-19-8). West End.

In the Eye of the Typhoon. Ruth E. Lo & Katherine S. Kinderman. LC 80-7937. (Illus.). 288p. 1980. 12.95 o.p. (ISBN 0-15-144374-2). HarBraceJ.

In the Flesh. Clive Barker. 224p. 1987. 12.70 o.s.i. (ISBN 0-671-62687-6, Poseidon). PB.

In the Footsteps of Boswell & Johnson. Israel Shenker. 320p. 1982. 13.95 o.p. (ISBN 0-395-31856-4). HM.

In the Footsteps of the Abominable Snowman: Stories of Science & Fantasy see Lost Face: Best Science Fiction from Czechoslovakia.

In the Fullness of Time: The Memoirs of Paul H. Douglas. Paul H. Douglas. LC 74-182327. 1972. 13.50 o.p. (ISBN 0-15-144376-9). HarBraceJ.

In the Grip of Terror. Andrei. Grachev. 150p. 1984. pap. 2.95 o.p. (ISBN 0-8285-2399-1, Pub. by Progress Pubs USSR). Imported Pubns.

In the Guiana Forest: Studies of Nature in Relations to the Struggle for Life. James Rodway. LC 69-18997. (Illus.). 1970. Repr. of 1894 ed. 25.00 o.p. (ISBN 0-8371-1027-0, ROG&). Greenwood.

In the Heart of Bantuland. Dugald Campbell. LC 70-79271. 1969. Repr. of 1922 ed. 35.00x o.p. (ISBN 0-8371-4835-9, CAB&, Pub. by Negro U Pr). Greenwood.

In the Heart of Pennsylvania: Nineteenth & Twentieth Century Quiltmaking Traditions. Jeannette Lasansky. LC 84-29585. (Illus.). 104p. pap. 16.95 o.p. (ISBN 0-8122-0975-3). U of Pa Pr.

In the Heart of Pennsylvania: Pieced by Mother. Jeannette Lasansky. (Illus.). 120p. (Orig.). 1987. pap. 19.95 o.p. (ISBN 0-8122-0977-X). U of Pa Pr.

In the Heart of Pennsylvania: Symposium Papers. Jeannette Lasansky. LC 86-823. (Illus.). 96p. pap. 15.95 o.p. (ISBN 0-8122-0976-1). U of Pa Pr.

In the Heat of the Summer. John Katzenbach. LC 81-69158. 1982. 13.95 o.p. (ISBN 0-689-11269-6, Atheneum). Macmillan.

In the Hell of Auschwitz. Judith Sternberg Newman. 1964. pap. 4.00 o.p. (ISBN 0-682-41172-8). Exposition-Phoenix.

In the Hollow of His Hand. James Purdy. LC 86-5462. 256p. 1986. 16.95 o.s.i. (ISBN 1-55584-002-7). Weidenfeld.

In the House of Stone & Light: A Human History of Grand Canyon. J. Donald Hughes. (Illus.). 137p. text ed. 12.00 o.p. (ISBN 0-938216-28-7). GCNHA.

In the Jaws of History. Bui Diem & David Chanoff. 1987. 18.45 o.s.i. (ISBN 0-395-42637-5). HM.

In the Labyrinth. John D. Morley. Ed. by Upton Brady. LC 86-3409. 212p. 1986. 15.95 o.p. (ISBN 0-87113-070-X). Atlantic Monthly.

In the Labyrinth. Alain Robbe-Grillet. Tr. by Richard Howard from Fr. LC 77-92785. 1978. pap. 2.95 o.s.i. (ISBN 0-394-17032-6, B408, BC). Grove.

In the Land of Israel. Amos Oz. Tr. by Maurie Goldberg-Bartura. LC 83-12940. (Helen & Kurt Wolff Bks.). 272p. 1983. 12.95 o.p. (ISBN 0-15-144644-X). HarBraceJ.

In the Land of Light: Israel, a Portrait of Its People. Rodney Smith. LC 83-6130. (Illus.). 1983. 39.00 o.p. (ISBN 0-395-34425-5). HM.

In the Land of the Living: Wartime Letters by Confederates from the Chattahoochee Valley of Alabama & Georgia. Ray Mathis. LC 81-84420. (Illus.). 148p. 1982. 21.50x o.p. (ISBN 0-916624-35-8). Troy State Univ.

In the Land of the Mind. Karen Rose. LC 74-19195. (gr. 7 up). 1975. 7.95 o.p. (ISBN 0-689-30456-0, Atheneum). Macmillan.

In the Last Analysis. Adam E. Armstrong. 1956. (ISBN 0-8022-0038-9). Philos Lib.

In the Last Analysis. Amanda Cross. Ed. by J. Barzun & W. H. Taylor. LC 81-47350. (Crime Fiction 1950-1975 Ser.). 187p. 1983. lib. bdg. 18.00 o.p. (ISBN 0-8240-4960-8). Garland Pub.

In the Life of a Romany Gypsy. Manfri F. Wood. Ed. by J. A. Brune. (Illus.). 1979. pap. 8.95x o.p. (ISBN 0-7100-0197-5). Routledge Chapman & Hall.

In the Life of Floyd Wells. Floyd Wells. 1986. text ed. 25.00 o.p. (ISBN 0-682-40317-2). Exposition-Phoenix.

In the Light of the Sun: From Sunspots to Solar Energy. Mark Washburn. LC 80-8762. 1981. 14.95 o.p. (ISBN 0-15-186737-2). HarBraceJ.

In the Midst of Death. Lawrence Block. pap. 2.95 o.p. (Arbor Hse). Morrow.

In the Name of God. Ida Krangel. 1956. (ISBN 0-8022-0889-4). Philos Lib.

In the Name of Jesus Christ. Albert A. Iacobucci. 129p. 1985. 10.95 o.p. (ISBN 0-533-06419-8). Vantage.

In the Name of Money: A Professional's Guide to the Federal Reserve, Interest Rates & Money. Paul DeRosa & Gary H. Stern. (Illus.). 192p. 1981. text ed. 24.95 o.p. (ISBN 0-07-016521-1). McGraw.

In the Name of Sanity. Lewis Mumford. LC 73-6214. 244p. 1973. Repr. of 1954 ed. lib. bdg. 22.50x o.p. (ISBN 0-8371-6891-0, MUNS). Greenwood.

In the Name of the Working Class: The Former Police Chief of Budapest Reveals the Inside Story of the Hungarian Revolution of 1956. Sandor Kopacsi. Tr. by Daniel Staffman & Judy Staffman. 320p. 1987. 17.95 o.s.i. (ISBN 0-8021-0010-4). Grove.

In the Orchard. 2nd ed. Charles W. Pratt. LC 85-51420. (Illus.). 64p. 1986. 22.00 o.p. (ISBN 0-930954-23-8); pap. 12.95 o.s.i. (ISBN 0-930954-27-0). Tidal Pr.

In the Palm House. Tony Sullivan. 236p. 1988. 18.95 o.p. (ISBN 0-233-98019-9, Pub. by A Deutsch England). David & Charles.

In the Potter's Hand. Gretchen Quie & Karen M. Hess. LC 81-65648. 256p. (Orig.). 1982. pap. 7.95 o.p. (ISBN 0-8066-1884-1, 10-3247, Augsburg). Augsburg Fortress.

In the Purely Pagan Sense. John Lehmann. (Gay Modern Classics Ser.). 264p. 1985. 18.95 o.p. (ISBN 0-907040-56-X, Pub. by GMP England); pap. 7.50 o.p. (ISBN 0-907040-55-1). Alyson Pubns.

In the Ring of the Rise. Vincent Marinaro. (ISBN 0-8329-0244-6). Lyons & Burford.

In the Running: The New Woman Candidate. Ruth B. Mandel. LC 80-24190. 304p. 1981. 12.95 o.p. (ISBN 0-89919-027-8). Ticknor & Fields.

In the Running: The New Woman Candidate. Ruth B. Mandel. LC 83-70746. 312p. 1983. pap. 10.95x o.p. (ISBN 0-8070-6715-6, BP 663). Beacon Pr.

In the Service of the Peacock Throne. Parviz C. Radji. 352p. 1984. 29.95 o.p. (ISBN 0-241-10960-4, Pub. by Hamish Hamilton England). David & Charles.

In the Shadow of a Rainbow: The True Story of a Friendship Between Man & Wolf. Robert F. Leslie. 192p. 1974. 6.95 o.p. (ISBN 0-393-08697-6). Norton.

In the Shadow of FDR: From Harry Truman to Ronald Reagan. William E. Leuchtenburg. LC 83-45147. (Orig.). 1983, 400p. 31.95 o.p. (ISBN 0-8014-1387-7); Paperback Ser. pap. 8.95 1985, 360p. o.p. (ISBN 0-8014-9303-X). Cornell U Pr.

In the Shadow of His Wings. Carol Schuller. LC 86-5287. 192p. 1986. 12.95 o.p. (ISBN 0-8407-5941-X). Nelson.

In the Shadow of Man. Jane Van Lawick-Goodall. 1971. 12.95 o.p. (ISBN 0-395-12726-2). HM.

In the Shadow of Powers: Dantes Bellegarde in Haitian Social Thought. P. Bellegarde-Smith. (American Institute for Marxist Studies, Historical Ser.: No. 11). 264p. 1985. text ed. 29.95x o.p. (ISBN 0-391-03214-3). Humanities.

In the Shadow of the Bush. Percy A. Talbot. LC 73-79821. (Illus.). 1970. Repr. of 1912 ed. lib. bdg. 35.00x o.p. (ISBN 0-8371-1468-3, TAI&, Pub. by Negro U Pr). Greenwood.

In the Shadow of the Cat. Wendy England. 1980. pap. 2.25 o.p. (ISBN 0-8439-0803-3, Pub. by Leisure Bks CT). Dorchester Pub Co.

In the Shadow of the Sun. Marion Belle. LC 84-91307. 104p. 1985. 8.95 o.p. (ISBN 0-533-06394-9). Vantage.

In the Shadow of the White Rose. Wanda Luttrell. (Living Bks.). 176p. 1986. pap. 3.50 o.p. (ISBN 0-8423-1602-7). Tyndale.

In the Skin. Karl Harter. 1981. pap. 2.75 o.p. (ISBN 0-380-78485-8, 78485-8). Avon.

In the Spirit of Stonewall. 85p. 2.00 o.p. (ISBN 0-89567-033-X). World View Forum.

In the States: Wisconsin, Arizona, New York. Julia Braithwaite & Christine Gorder. 130p. 1985. pap. text ed. 11.95 o.p. (ISBN 0-03-070293-3, HoltC). HR&W.

In the Steps of St. Patrick. Brian De Breffny. (Illus.). 1982. 9.98 o.s.i. (ISBN 0-500-24110-4). Thames Hudson.

In the Storm of the Eye: A Lifetime at CBS. Bill Leonard. (Illus.). 256p. 1987. 18.95 o.p. (ISBN 0-399-13255-4, Putnam). Putnam Pub Group.

In the Suicide Mountains. John Gardner. 1980. 5.95 o.p. (ISBN 0-395-29468-1). HM.

In the Teeth of the Evidence. Dorothy L. Sayers. 1976. pap. 2.50 o.p. (ISBN 0-380-01280-4, 62943-7). Avon.

In the Tennessee Mountains. Mary N. Murfree. LC 68-20019. (Americans in Fiction Ser.). (Illus.). 322p. lib. bdg. 14.95 o.p. (ISBN 0-8398-1270-1); pap. text ed. 9.95x o.p. (ISBN 0-89197-793-7). Irvington.

In the Throne Room of the Mountain Gods. Galen Rowell. LC 76-21248. (Illus.). 336p. 1977. 18.50 o.s.i. (ISBN 0-87156-184-0). Sierra.

In the Twilight of the Revolution: The Political Theory of Amilcar Cabral. J. McCulloch. 200p. (Orig.). 1982. pap. 12.95 o.p. (ISBN 0-7100-9411-6). Routledge Chapman & Hall.

In the Vanguard: Six American Women in Public Life. Peggy Lamson. 1979. 9.95 o.p. (ISBN 0-395-27608-X). HM.

In the Vatican. Peter Hebblethwaite. LC 86-7927. 214p. 1986. 16.95 o.p. (ISBN 0-917561-24-4). Adler & Adler.

In the Village. Hilde Heyduck-Huth. LC 72-57808. Orig. Title: Thomas in Dorf. (Illus.). (ps-1). 1971. 3.50 o.p. (ISBN 0-15-238751-X, HJ). HarBraceJ.

In the Wake of Diaghilev. Richard Buckle. LC 82-12096. (Illus.). 367p. 1983. 19.95 o.p. (ISBN 0-03-062493-2). H Holt & Co.

In the Way of the Whale: The Whaling Journal of John F. Martin, 1841 to 1844. John F. Martin. Ed. by Kenneth R. Martin. LC 80-66462. (Illus.). 224p. 1987. 25.00 o.p. (ISBN 0-87923-350-8). Godine.

In the Western World. John N. Miller. LC 79-65811. 1979. pap. 3.00 o.p. (ISBN 0-933180-03-9). Spoon Riv Poetry.

In the Wink of an Eye. Kelly Cherry. 320p. 1983. 15.95 o.p. (ISBN 0-15-144656-3). HarBraceJ.

In the Woods & Fields of Concord: Selections from the Journals of Henry David Thoreau. Henry David Thoreau. Ed. by Walter Harding. LC 82-10563. (Illus.). 176p. 1982. pap. 6.95 o.p. (ISBN 0-87905-090-X, Peregrine Smith). Gibbs Smith Pub.

In Their Wisdom. C. P. Snow. LC 74-12273. 486p. 1974. encore ed. 2.95 o.p. (ISBN 0-684-17725-0). Scribner.

In These Last Days see Word Studies in the Greek New Testament, for the English Reader.

In These Mountains. Peter Sacks. LC 85-29898. 64p. 1986. 17.95 o.p. (ISBN 0-02-606660-2). Macmillan.

In This Evening Light. Clyde O. Jackson. 1979. 8.00 o.p. (ISBN 0-682-49479-8). Exposition-Phoenix.

In This Sign. Joanne Greenberg. 288p. 1978. pap. 1.95 o.p. (ISBN 0-380-00941-2, 52712-X). Avon.

In This Sign. Joanne Greenberg. 288p. 1984. pap. 6.95 o.p. (ISBN 0-8050-0722-9, Owl Bks). H Holt & Co.

In Transition: How Feminism, Sexual Liberation, & the Search for Self-Fulfillment Have Altered America. Judith Bardwick. LC 78-14168. 17.95 o.p. (ISBN 0-03-043061-5, HoltC). HR&W.

In Tune with the Infinite. Ralph W. Trine. (Pivot Family Reader Ser.). 176p. 1973. pap. 1.25 o.p. (ISBN 0-87983-052-2). Keats.

In Vitro Aspects of Erythropoiesis. Ed. by M. J. Murphy, Jr. LC 78-16104. (Illus.). 1978. 54.50 o.p. (ISBN 0-387-90320-8). Springer-Verlag.

In Vitro Fertilization & Embryo Transfer: Proceedings of the World Conference, Kiel, West Germany, September 24-27, 1980. World Conference on Embryo Transfer in Vitro Fertilization & Instrumental Insemination Staff. Ed. by E. S. Hafez & K. Semm. LC 81-20853. 408p. 1982. 58.00 o.p. (ISBN 0-8451-3005-6). A R Liss.

In Vitro Methods in Cell-Mediated & Tumor Immunity. Ed. by Barry R. Bloom & John R. David. 1976. 88.50 o.p. (ISBN 0-12-107760-8). Acad Pr.

In Vitro Methods in Cell-Mediated Immunity. Ed. by Barry R. Bloom & Philip R. Glade. 1971. 78.00 o.p. (ISBN 0-12-107750-0). Acad Pr.

In Vitro Toxicity Testing of Environmental Agents, Current & Future Possibilities: Part A; Survey of Test Systems - Part B-Development of Risk Assessment Guidelines, 2 vols. Ed. by Alan R. Kolber et al. (NATO Conference Series I, Ecology: Vol. 5A & 5B). 1983. Pt. A, 572p. 89.50x o.p. (ISBN 0-306-41123-7, Plenum Pr); Pt. B, 564p. 89.50x o.p. (ISBN 0-306-41124-5, Plenum Pr); Set. 150.00 o.p. (Plenum Pr). Plenum Pub.

In Vivo Immunology: Histophysiology of the Lymphoid System. Ed. by Paul Nieuwenhuis et al. (Advances in Experimental Medicine & Biology: Vol. 149). 872p. 1982. 125.00x o.p. (ISBN 0-306-41039-7, Plenum Pr). Plenum Pub.

In Wartime: The State of Children in Lebanon. Ed. by Jennifer W. Bryce & Haroutune K. Armenian. (Books From the American University of Beirut Press). (Illus.). 220p. 1988. text ed. 30.00x o.p. (ISBN 0-8156-6081-2, Pub. by Am U Beirut). Syracuse U Pr.

In Wildness Is the Preservation of the World. Eliot Porter. LC 62-20527. (Exhibit Format Ser.). (Illus.). 168p. 1962. 32.50 o.s.i. (ISBN 0-87156-000-3). Sierra.

In Winter. Michael K. Ryan. LC 80-19799. (National Poetry Ser.). 64p. 1981. 9.95 o.p. (ISBN 0-03-058942-8); pap. 5.95 o.p. (ISBN 0-03-058941-X). H Holt & Co.

In Winter's Shadow. Gillian Bradshaw. 1982. 15.95 o.p. (ISBN 0-671-43512-4). S&S.

In Worlds Apart-Professionals & Their Clients in the Welfare State. Tim Robinson. 87p. 1978. pap. text ed. 5.00x o.p. (ISBN 0-7199-0942-2, Pub. by Bedford England). Gower Pub Co.

In Your Eye, Andy Capp. Reginald Smythe. (Andy Capp Ser.). (Illus.). 1981. pap. 1.50 o.p. (ISBN 0-449-13590-X, GM). Fawcett.

Inability to Mourn: Principles of Collective Behavior. Alexander Mitscherlich & Margarete Mitscherlich. 1975. pap. 22.00 o.p. (ISBN 0-686-51232-4, ST00020, Ever). Grove.

Inability to Mourn: Principles of Collective Behavior. Alexander Mitscherlich & Margarete Mitscherlich. 1984. pap. 9.95 o.p. (ISBN 0-394-62170-0, E918, Ever). Grove.

Inactivation of Peroxidase, Pectinesterase & Alkaline Phosphatase in Polymers as a Model for Irradiation of Dried Foodstuffs. (Agricultural Research Reports: No. 113). 1972. pap. 4.00 o.p. (ISBN 90-220-0383-3, PDC188, PUDOC). UNIPUB.

Inangaro: The Legend of the Coconut, 4 bks. Date not set. Boxed Set. 600.00 o.p. Ohio St U Pr.

Inaugural Addresses of the Presidents of Liberia: From Joseph Jenkins Roberts to William Richard Tolbert, 1848-1976. Ed. & compiled by Joseph S. Guannu. 1980. 20.00 o.p. (ISBN 0-682-49444-5, University). Exposition-Phoenix.

Inborn Disorders of Sphingolipid Metabolism. Ed. by S. M. Aronson & B. W. Volk. 1967. 95.00 o.p. (ISBN 0-08-012038-5). Pergamon.

Inborn Errors of Specific Immunity: Proceedings of the New York State Department of Health on Birth Defects, 9th Symposium. New York State Department of Health Staff. Ed. by Bernard Pollara et al. LC 79-23179. (Birth Defects Institute Ser.). 1980. 54.50 o.p. (ISBN 0-12-559650-2). Acad Pr.

Inbred & Genetically Defined Strains of Laboratory Animals 1 & 2. Faseb. 1983. 140.00 o.p. (ISBN 0-08-030075-8). Pergamon.

Incantations. Charles Bound. LC 77-92531. 96p. 1978. 6.95 o.p. (ISBN 0-15-144367-X). HarBraceJ.

Incas. Garcilasco De La Vega. 448p. 1964. pap. 3.50 o.p. (ISBN 0-380-01269-3, 45542-0, Discus). Avon.

Incendiary Fellowship. Elton Trueblood. LC 67-11508. 1978. pap. 4.95i o.p. (ISBN 0-06-068641-3, RD 284). HarpR.

Incense Tree. Jacqueline La Tourette. (Orig.). 1986. pap. 3.95 o.s.i. (ISBN 0-449-12611-0, GM). Fawcett.

Incentive, Achievement & Community: An Analysis of Black Viewpoints on Issues Relating to Black Australian Education. Roberta B. Sykes. 152p. 1986. pap. 9.95 o.p. (00833277, Pub. by Sydney Pr). Intl Spec Bk.

Incentives for Resource Allocation: A Case Study of Sudan. Shankar N. Acharya. (Working Paper: No. 367). iii, 113p. 1979. 5.00 o.p. (ISBN 0-686-36088-5, WP0367). World Bank.

Incest: A Biosocial View. Joseph Shepher. 1985. lib. bdg. 24.50 o.p. (ISBN 0-8240-7260-X). Garland Pub.

Inchworm, Inchworm: Persistent Problems in Reading Education. Ed. by Constance M. McCullough. 278p. (Orig.). 1980. pap. text ed. 9.00 o.p. (ISBN 0-87207-937-6). Intl Reading.

Incidents in My Life. D. D. Home. 1973. 7.95 o.p. (ISBN 0-8216-0208-X, Pub. by Univ Bks). Carol Pub Group.

Incineration Systems: Selection & Design. Calvin R. Brunner. LC 83-26124. (Illus.). 417p. 1984. 56.95 o.p. (ISBN 0-442-21192-9). Van Nos Reinhold.

Incineration Systems Seminar Notebook. 2nd ed. Calvin R. Brunner. 477p. 1985. Wkbk. 97.00 o.p. (ISBN 0-86587-592-8). Gov Insts.

Incinerator & Solid Waste Technology, 1962-1975. Ed. by J. W. Stephenson et al. 415p. 1975. pap. text ed. 60.00 o.p. (ISBN 0-685-62568-0, I00092). ASME.

Inclusive-Language Lectionary: Readings for Year A. LC 83-16779. 192p. 1983. pap. 7.95 o.s.i. (ISBN 0-664-24506-4, Westminster). Westminster John Knox.

Inclusive-Language Lectionary: Readings for Year C. LC 85-12100. 270p. 1985. pap. 9.95 o.p. (ISBN 0-664-24565-X, Westminster). Westminster John Knox.

Inclusive Language Lectionary: Year C. 9.95 o.p. (ISBN 0-8298-0730-6). Pilgrim NY.

Income, Consumption & Poverty in Thailand, 1962-63 to 1975-76. Oey Astra Meesook. (Working Paper: No. 364). 97p. 1979. 5.00 o.p. (ISBN 0-686-36147-4, WP-0364). World Bank.

Income Distribution, Growth & Basic Needs in India. R. Sinha et al. 175p. 1979. 24.00 o.p. (ISBN 0-85664-968-6, Pub. by Croom Helm Ltd). Routledge Chapman & Hall.

Income Distribution: The Limits to Redistribution. Martin Slater & Richard Lecomber. Ed. by David Collard. 267p. 1981. 47.95x o.p. (ISBN 0-470-27099-3). Halsted Pr.

Income, Employment & Urban Residential Location. Larry L. Orr. (Institute for Research on Poverty Monograph Ser). 1975. 17.50 o.p. (ISBN 0-12-528440-3). Acad Pr.

Income-Expense Analysis: Apartments. Ed. by Kenneth Anderson. 1978. pap. 22.50 o.p. (ISBN 0-912104-32-5). Inst Real Estate.

Income-Expense Analysis: Apartments. Ed. by Kenneth Anderson. 1979. pap. 22.50 o.p. (ISBN 0-912104-39-2). Inst Real Estate.

Income-Expense Analysis: Apartments. Ed. by Kenneth R. Anderson & Stacey L. Ruiz. 224p. (Orig.). 1982. pap. 59.00 o.p. (ISBN 0-912104-64-3). Inst Real Estate.

Income-Expense Analysis: Apartments. (Orig.). 1980. pap. 24.50 o.p. (ISBN 0-912104-51-1). Inst Real Estate.

Income-Expense Analysis: Apartments Condominums & Cooperatives, 1977. Ed. by Kenneth Anderson. 1977. pap. 17.50 o.p. (ISBN 0-912104-27-9). Inst Real Estate.

Income-Expense Analysis: Apartments, 1981. 220p. 1981. pap. text ed. 24.50 o.p. (ISBN 0-912104-55-4). Inst Real Estate.

Income-Expense Analysis: Apartments, 1983. Ed. by Kenneth R. Anderson & Stacey L. Ruiz. 224p. (Orig.). 1983. pap. 61.95 o.p. (ISBN 0-912104-72-4, 85503). Inst Real Estate.

Income-Expense Analysis: Apartments, 1984. Ed. by Kenneth Anderson & Stacey Ruiz. 224p. (Orig.). 1984. pap. 75.50 o.p. (ISBN 0-912104-77-5). Inst Real Estate.

Income-Expense Analysis: Conventional Apartments. Institute for Real Estate Management Staff. (Illus.). 216p. 1986. pap. 79.00 o.p. (ISBN 0-317-56228-2). Inst Real Estate.

Income-Expense Analysis: Conventional Apartments, No. 85506. 216p. 1986. pap. 79.00 o.p. (ISBN 0-317-57162-1). Inst Real Estate.

Income-Expense Analysis: Office Buildings Downtown & Suburban, No. 84206. 248p. 1986. pap. 79.00 o.p. (ISBN 0-317-57154-0). Inst Real Estate.

Income-Expense Analysis: Office Buildings (Downtown & Suburban), 1984. Ed. by Kenneth Anderson & Stacey Ruiz. 224p. (Orig.). 1984. pap. 75.50 o.p. (ISBN 0-912104-78-3). Inst Real Estate.

Income-Expense Analysis: Office Buildings. Ed. by Kenneth R. Anderson & Stacey L. Ruiz. 200p. (Orig.). 1982. pap. 29.50 o.p. (ISBN 0-912104-65-1). Inst Real Estate.

Income-Expense Analysis: Office Buildings. Institute of Real Estate Management Staff. (Illus.). 248p. 1986. pap. 79.00 o.p. (ISBN 0-317-56233-9). Inst Real Estate.

Income-Expense Analysis: Office Buildings, 1983 Edition. Ed. by Kenneth R. Anderson & Stacey L. Ruiz. 224p. 1983. pap. 61.95 o.p. (ISBN 0-912104-73-2, 84203). Inst Real Estate.

Income-Expense Analysis: Suburban Office Buildings, - 1981. 175p. 1981. pap. text ed. 17.50 o.p. (ISBN 0-912104-56-2). Inst Real Estate.

Income-Expense Analysis: Suburban Office Buildings, 1977. Ed. by Kenneth Anderson. 1977. pap. 7.50 o.p. (ISBN 0-912104-28-7). Inst Real Estate.

Income-Expense Analysis: Suburban Office Buildings. Ed. by Kenneth Anderson. 1978. pap. 10.00 o.p. (ISBN 0-912104-34-1). Inst Real Estate.

Income-Expense Analysis: Suburban Office Buildings. Ed. by Kenneth Anderson. 1979. lib. bdg. 15.00 o.p. (ISBN 0-912104-40-6). Inst Real Estate.

Income-Expense Analysis: Suburban Office Buildings. (Orig.). 1980. pap. 17.50 o.p. (ISBN 0-912104-52-X). Inst Real Estate.

Income Maintenance: Interdiciplinary Approaches to Research. Larry L. Orr et al. 1971. 24.50 o.p. (ISBN 0-12-528450-0). Acad Pr.

Income Opportunities Magazine Guide to Family Finance. Income Opportunities Editors. 240p. 1986. pap. 9.95 o.p. (ISBN 0-13-536392-6). P-H.

Income-Property Development, Financing, & Investment. Mary A. Hines. LC 82-49254. (Illus.). 336p. 1983. 37.00x o.p. (ISBN 0-669-06440-8). Lexington Bks.

Income Redistribution & the Social Security Program. Nancy Wolff. Ed. by Fred Bateman. LC 87-10791. (Research in Business Economics & Public Policy Ser.: No. 12). 190p. 1987. 49.95 o.p. (ISBN 0-8357-1807-7). UMI Res Pr.

Income Redistribution & the Welfare State. Adrian L. Webb. 125p. 1971. pap. text ed. 6.25x o.p. (ISBN 0-7135-1806-5, Pub. by Bedford England). Gower Pub Co.

Income Redistribution Theories & Programs: Cases, Commentary & Analyses. Barbara E. Brudno. 481p. 1976. 32.95 o.p. (ISBN 0-314-31909-3). West Pub.

Income Tax Guide for Teachers: NEA Federal. John C. Arch. pap. 6.95 o.p. (ISBN 0-8106-1386-7). NEA.

Income Tax Law & Practice. 5th, rev. ed. B. B. Lal. xi, 854p. 1983. text ed. 45.00x o.p. (ISBN 0-7069-2022-8, Pub. by Vikas India). Advent NY.

Income Tax Law for Ministers & Religious Workers: 1988 Edition. B. J. Worth. 96p. 1987. pap. 5.95 o.p. (ISBN 0-8010-9683-9). Baker Bk.

Income Taxation of Estates & Trusts. 349p. 1983. 8.00 o.p. (ISBN 0-318-02400-4). ICLE Georgia.

Income Taxation of Estates & Trusts, 1981. 628p. 1981. 25.00 o.p. (ISBN 0-686-96098-X, D4-5136). PLI.

Income Taxation of Estates & Trusts 1986. 646p. 1986. pap. 15.00 o.p. (D4-5183). PLI.

Income Taxation of Estates & Trusts, 1984. Practising Law Institute Staff & Arthur D. Sederbaum. LC 84-122357. (Tax Law & Estate Planning Ser.). (Illus.). 1984. 35.00 o.p. PLI.

Incompatability in Fungi: Proceedings of the International Congress of Botany, Edinburgh, 1964. International Congress of Botany Staff. Ed. by J. R. Raper & K. Esser. (Illus.). viii, 124p. 1966. pap. 32.00 o.p. (ISBN 0-387-03334-3). Springer Verlag.

Incomplete Bibliography of Works Relating to Marketing for Public Sector & Nonprofit Organizations. 3rd ed. Michael L. Rothschild. (Monograph: No. 12). 178p. 1981. 7.50 o.p. (ISBN 0-86603-011-5). Bur Busn Wis.

Incompris see Fils De Personne.

Incorporated Wife. Ed. by Hilary Callan & Shirley Ardener. LC 84-12743. 224p. 1984. 26.50 o.p. (ISBN 0-7099-0521-1, Pub. by Croom Helm Ltd); pap. 13.50 o.p. (ISBN 0-7099-0556-4). Routledge Chapman & Hall.

Incorporating a Law Firm. 237p. 1982. 9.00 o.p. (ISBN 0-318-02384-9). ICLE Georgia.

Incorporating the Professional Practice. 2nd ed. George E. Ray. (Illus.). 1978. text ed. 32.95 o.p. (ISBN 0-13-455923-1, Busn). P-H.

Incorporating the Professional Practice. 3rd ed. George E. Ray. LC 82-513. 264p. 1982. text ed. 39.95 o.p. (ISBN 0-13-455931-2, Busn); pap. 32.95 o.p. P-H.

Incorporating Your Talents: A Guide to the One-Person Corporation, or How to Lead a Sheltered Life. Robert A. Esperti & Renno L. Peterson. LC 82-14860. 243p. 1984. text ed. 23.95 o.p. (ISBN 0-07-019669-9). McGraw.

Incorrigibles. Harold McGowan. 1978. 10.00 o.p. (ISBN 0-682-48980-8). Exposition-Phoenix.

Increased Intracranial Pressure in Children. 2nd ed. William E. Bell & William F. McCormick. (Major Problems in Clinical Pediatrics Ser.: Vol. 8). (Illus.). 485p. 1978. (ISBN 0-7216-1708-5). Saunders.

Increasing Agricultural Productivity: Proceedings of the Agricultural Sector Symposium, 3rd. Agricultural Sector Symposium Staff. Ed. by Ted J. Davis. 307p. 1982. 15.00 o.p. (ISBN 0-8213-0099-7). World Bank.

Increasing Forest Productivity: Proceedings of the SAF National Convention, 1981. SAF National Convention Staff. LC 82-50328. (Illus.). 368p. (Orig.). 1982. pap. 19.00 o.p. (ISBN 0-939970-13-9, SAF 82-01). Soc Am Foresters.

Increasing Guidance Effectiveness Through School-Community Cooperation: A Guide to Developing Cooperative Relationships Between Schools & Business, Industry & Labor in Rural Communities. Walter M. Stein et al. 581p. 1978. 25.50 o.p. (ISBN 0-318-15492-7, SN19). Natl Ctr Res Voc Ed.

Increasing Your Sales Through Customer Services: A Critical Function in Transition. Ed. by Fred S. Rosenau & Leslie R. Chase. LC 83-83399. 100p. 1984. pap. 39.95 o.p. (ISBN 0-942774-15-9). Info Indus.

Increasing Your Wealth: A Professional Portfolio Manager Tells You How To. Eugene Lerner & Richard Koff. LC 86-82241. 160p. pap. 8.95 o.p. (ISBN 0-89586-516-5). Price Stern.

Incredible Charlie Brown. Charles M. Schulz. (Illus., Fr., For, Language Fr). 1971. pap. 1.50 o.s.i. (ISBN 0-03-086014-8). H Holt & Co.

Incredible Detectives. Don Caulfield & Joan Caulfield. (Illus.). (gr. 4-6). 1983. pap. 0.95 o.p. (ISBN 0-380-01282-0, 50443, Camelot). Avon.

Incredible Hulk: The Secret Story of Marvel's Gamma-Powered Goliath. David A. Kraft. LC 81-10021. (Secret Stories of the Sensational Super Heroes Ser.). (Illus.). 64p. (gr. 3 up). 1981. PLB 13.27 o.p. (ISBN 0-516-02413-2). Childrens.

Incredible Miles & Other Poems. Miriam C. Bragg. 1979. 5.00 o.p. (ISBN 0-682-49380-5). Exposition-Phoenix.

Incredible Schloch Homes. Robert L. Fish. 1976. pap. 2.95 o.p. (ISBN 0-380-00636-7). Avon.

Incredible Tide. Alexander Key. LC 70-100952. (gr. 7 up). 1970. 4.25 o.s.i. (ISBN 0-664-32470-3, Westminster). Westminster John Knox.

Incredible Voyage. Tristan Jones. 1980. pap. 4.50 o.p. (ISBN 0-380-49999-1, 68106-4). Avon.

Incredible Will of H. R. Heartman. Jean Harmeling. LC 82-73656. 128p. (gr. 5-9). 1983. pap. 4.95 o.p. (ISBN 0-89107-279-9, Crossway Bks). Good News.

Increible Historia de una Bella Joven. Albert Pavlic. 1979. 6.50 o.p. (ISBN 0-682-49325-2). Exposition-Phoenix.

Incubus in English Literature: Provenance & Progeny. Nicolas Kiessling. (Illus.). 104p. 1977. pap. 8.95 o.p. (ISBN 0-87422-006-8). Wash St U Pr.

Incunabula in American Libraries: A Supplement to the Third Census of Fifteenth-Century Books Recorded in North American Collections (1964) Frederick R. Goff. LC 72-76024. xii, 104p. 1972. 10.00x o.p. (ISBN 0-8139-0939-2, Bibliographical Society of America). U Pr of Va.

Incursion. Dirk Hanson. 1987. 16.95 o.p. (ISBN 0-316-34374-9). Little.

Ind Rev Book. (Our Nations Heritage Ser.). Date not set. (ISBN 0-07-375424-2). McGraw.

Indaba: Let's Talk. Ed. by Sheila Bruton. Brian Bassingthwaighte & Janet Hooper. Ed. by Athol Eugard. 1976. pap. 1.95 o.p. (ISBN 0-377-00052-3). Friendship Pr.

Indecent Deception. R. H. Doty. LC 84-90095. 158p. 1985. 10.00 o.p. (ISBN 0-533-06169-5). Vantage.

Indefinite Nights: And Other Stories. Patricia Ferguson. 196p. 1988. 18.95 o.p. (ISBN 0-233-98103-9, Pub. by A Deutsch England). David & Charles.

Indeh: An Apache Odyssey. Eve Ball. LC 80-13186. (Illus.). 1980. 15.95 o.p. (ISBN 0-8425-1789-8). Brigham.

Indentured Labour in the British Empire, 1840 to 1920. Ed. by Kay Saunders. (Illus.). 336p. 1983. 38.00 o.p. (ISBN 0-7099-2321-X, Pub. by Croom Helm Ltd). Routledge Chapman & Hall.

Independence Day. B. A. Ecker. 208p. (YA) (gr. 7 up). 1983. pap. 2.25 o.p. (ISBN 0-380-82990-8, 82990-8, Flare). Avon.

Independence in All Things, Neutrality in Nothing. Elizabeth Wright. LC 73-88669. (Illus.). 1973. 10.00 o.p. (ISBN 0-87930-023-X). Miller Freeman.

Independence Movements in Africa, Pt. 1 see Tarikh.

Independence Movements in Africa, Pt. 2 see Tarikh.

Independent Activities for Learning Centers. Ed. by Thelma J. Gomez & Elizabeth Simpson. 1971. pap. 4.75x o.p. (ISBN 0-8422-0145-9). Irvington.

Independent Language Arts Activities: Seatwork for the Primary Grades. 2nd ed. Bernice M. Chappel. LC 66-26670. (gr. 1-3). 1973. pap. 4.95 o.p. (ISBN 0-8224-4215-9). D S Lake Pubs.

Independent Living & Disability Policy in the Netherlands: Three Models of Residential Care & Independent Living. Gerben DeJong. 94p. 1984. write for info. o.p. World Rehab Fund.

Independent Living for the Handicapped & the Elderly. Elizabeth E. May et al. 1974. text ed. 29.95 o.p. (ISBN 0-395-18108-9). HM.

Independent Living: Getting Started. Denise Y. Guynn. Ed. by David Pozzi-Johnson. LC 79-730911. (Illus.). 1979. pap. 159.00 o.s.i. (ISBN 0-89290-150-0, A581-SATC). Soc for Visual.

Independent Living Skills for the Severely Handicapped Deaf Person Preparing to Enter Gainful Employment. University of Tennessee, 1979, Knoxville, Tenn. Staff. Ed. by Sue E. Ouellette & Glenn T. Lloyd. (Monograph: No. 5). (Illus.). 103p. (Orig.). 1980. pap. text ed. 5.00 o.s.i. (ISBN 0-914494-06-6). Am Deaf & Rehab.

Independent People: An Epic. Halldor Laxness. Tr. by J. A. Thompson from Icelandic. LC 76-7973. 1976. Repr. of 1946 ed. lib. bdg. 37.50x o.p. (ISBN 0-8371-8872-5, LAIP). Greenwood.

Independent Spirits: Spiritualism & English Plebians 1850-1910. Logie Barrow. (History Workshop Ser.). 304p. 1986. lib. bdg. 34.95 o.p. (ISBN 0-7100-9883-9); pap. text ed. 17.95 o.p. (ISBN 0-7102-0815-4). Routledge Chapman & Hall.

Independent Study & Research in Literature. Bryan Gillespie. LC 75-2175. 1975. 3.50 o.p. (ISBN 0-912112-07-7). Everett-Edwards.

Indespensable Shopping Guide. Ed. by Leona Bowman. Jo-An Jenkins. Ed. by Patricia McColl. LC 79-55613. 1980. pap. 8.95 o.p. (ISBN 0-689-11030-8, Atheneum). Macmillan.

Index Africanus. new ed. J. O. Asamani. LC 76-187266. (Bibliographical Ser., No. 53). 452p. 1975. 30.00x o.p. (ISBN 0-8179-2531-7). Hoover Inst Pr.

Index Card of Figures & Tables for Civil Engineering Reference Manual. (Engineering Review Manual Ser.). 2p. 1986. pap. 2.85 o.p. (ISBN 0-932276-66-0). Prof Pubns CA.

Index Card of Figures & Tables for the Engineer-in-Training Review Manual. (Engineering Review Manual Ser.). 2p. (Orig.). 1985. pap. 2.85 o.p. (ISBN 0-932276-60-1). Prof Pubns CA.

Index Card of Figures & Tables for the Mechanical Engineering Review Manual. (Engineering Review Manual Ser.). 2p. (Orig.). 1985. pap. 2.85 o.p. (ISBN 0-932276-58-X). Prof Pubns CA.

Index in Xenophontis Memorabilia. Mary K. Lander. Repr. of 1900 ed. 12.00 o.p. (ISBN 0-384-31186-5). Johnson Repr.

Index Islamicus: First Supplement 1956-1960. Compiled by J. D. Pearson & Wolfgang Behn. 344p. 1978. Repr. of 1962 ed. 53.00x o.p. (ISBN 0-7201-0381-9). Mansell.

Index Libycus: A Cumlative Index to Bibliography of Libya, 1915-1975. Hans Schuter. 1981. 29.00 o.s.i. (ISBN 0-8161-8534-4, Hall Reference). G K Hall.

Index Libycus: Supplement I, Nineteen Seventy to Nineteen Seventy-five. Hans Schluter et al. 1979. lib. bdg. 29.00 o.s.i. (ISBN 0-8161-8076-8, Hall Reference). G K Hall.

Index of Computer Hardware & Software in Use in North Carolina Local Governments. 280p. 1986. 13.00 o.p. (ISBN 0-686-39424-0). Institute Government.

Index of Japanese Painters. Ed. by Society of Friends of Eastern Art Staff. LC 58-9985. 1958. 7.95 o.p. (ISBN 0-8048-0262-9). C E Tuttle.

Index of Legislation: 1982 General Assembly of North Carolina. 51p. 1982. 5.00 o.p. (ISBN 0-686-39450-X). Institute Government.

Index of Majors, 1984-85. 7th ed. College Board Staff. 620p. (Orig.). 1984. pap. 11.95 o.p. (ISBN 0-87447-186-9, 001869). College Bd.

Index of Majors, 1987-88. 782p. (Orig.). 1987. pap. 12.95 o.p. College Bd.

Index of Majors,1987-88. 10th ed. 782p. (Orig.). 1987. pap. 12.95 o.p. (ISBN 0-87447-287-3). College Bd.

Index of Musical Wind-Instrument Makers, Vol. 28. 6th, rev. & enl. ed. L. G. Langwill. (Illus.). 1980. 125.00 o.s.i. (ISBN 90-247-2599-2). E J Brill USA.

Index of Obituaries in Boston Newspapers, 1704-1800, 3 Vols. Boston Athenaeum Staff. 1970. Set. 156.00 o.p. (ISBN 0-8161-0761-0, Hall Library). G K Hall.

Index of Paramedical Vocabulary. J. E. Schmidt. (Illus.). 324p. 1974. spiral bdg. 13.25 o.p. (ISBN 0-398-02833-8). C C Thomas.

Index of Post-Nineteen Thirty Seven European Manuscript Accessions. India Office Library. Commonwealth Relations Office, Great Britain Staff. 1970. 100.00 o.p. (ISBN 0-8161-0687-8, Hall Library). G K Hall.

Index of the Recorded Anthology of American Music. Ed. by New World Records Staff. 10p. 1980. 2.00 o.p. (ISBN 0-686-47570-4). Inst Am Music.

Index to American Genealogies: With Supplement. 5th ed. 1966. Repr. of 1908 ed. 60.00x o.p. (ISBN 0-8103-3127-6). Gale.

Index to American Jewish Archives I-XXIV. White. Date not set. 25.00 o.p. Ktav.

Index to Anthologies of Latin American Literature in English Translation. Juan R. Freudenthal & Jeffrey Katz. 1978. lib. bdg. 22.00 o.p. (ISBN 0-8161-7861-5, Hall Reference). G K Hall.

Index to Anthropological Subject Headings. 2nd, rev. ed. 1981. lib. bdg. 100.00 o.p. (ISBN 0-8161-0405-0, Hall Library). G K Hall.

Index to Architecture Series: Bibliography A 637-A 876 (January 1982-December 1982) Vance Bibliographies Staff. (Arch. Ser.: No. A877). 1983. pap. 10.50 o.p. (ISBN 0-88066-327-8, A 877). Vance Biblios.

Index to Architecture Series Bibliography No. A 1297 to A 1416 (January, 1985-June, 1985) (Architecture Ser.: A 1417). 38p. 1985. 6.00 o.p. (ISBN 0-89028-467-9). Vance Biblios.

Index to Architecture Series: Bibliography No. A-877 to A-1296 (January 1983-December 1984) Vance Bibliographies Staff. (Architecture Ser.: Bibliography A-1297). 130p. 1985. pap. 16.50 o.p. (ISBN 0-89028-227-7). Vance Biblios.

Index to Art Periodicals, 11 Vols. Art Institute of Chicago, Ryerson Library Editors. 1970. Set. 920.00 o.p. (ISBN 0-8161-0627-4, Hall Library). G K Hall.

Index to Art Periodicals, 1st Supplement. Art Institute of Chicago, Ryerson Library Staff. 1974. lib. bdg. 110.00 o.p. (ISBN 0-8161-0727-0, Hall Library). G K Hall.

Index to Best American Short Stories & O. Henry Prize Stories. Ray L. White. LC 87-28112. (G. K. Hall Reference Bks.). 224p. 1988. 35.00x o.s.i. (ISBN 0-8161-8955-2). G K Hall.

Index to Birthplaces of American Authors. Richard Newman & R. Glenn Wright. 1979. lib. bdg. 22.00 o.p. (ISBN 0-8161-8230-2, Hall Reference). G K Hall.

Index to Birthplaces of United Kingdom Authors. Mark Harris & R. Glenn Wright. 1979. lib. bdg. 18.00 o.p. (ISBN 0-8161-8273-6, Hall Reference). G K Hall.

Index to Black Periodicals: 1984. Ed. by Central State University Staff & Hallie Q. Brown Memorial Library Staff. 200p. 1988. 95.00 o.p. (ISBN 0-8161-0454-9, Hall Library). G K Hall.

Index to Black Periodicals: 1985. G. K. Hall Library Catalogs Staff. 180p. 1988. 90.00 o.p. (ISBN 0-8161-0465-4, Hall Library). G K Hall.

Index to Black Periodicals: 1986. G. K. Hall Library Catalogs Staff. 180p. 1988. 90.00 o.p. (ISBN 0-8161-0471-9, Hall Library). G K Hall.

Index to Black Periodicals: 1987. G. K. Hall Library Catalogs Staff. 180p. 1988. 90.00 o.p. (ISBN 0-8161-0472-7, Hall Library). G K Hall.

Index to Changes of Name. William P. Phillimore & E. A. Fry. LC 68-27180. 392p. 1969. Repr. of 1905 ed. 34.00x o.p. (ISBN 0-8103-3132-2). Gale.

Index to Children's Literature in English Before 1900: Catalog of the Baldwin Library of the University of Florida at Gainesville. University of Florida, Gainesville, Baldwin Library of Childrens Literature Editors. (Supplements). 1981. lib. bdg. 340.00 o.p. (ISBN 0-8161-0370-4, Hall Library). G K Hall.

Index to Collective Biographies for Young Readers. 3rd ed. Compiled by Judith Silverman. LC 79-472. 1979. 29.95 o.p. (ISBN 0-8352-1132-0). Bowker.

Index to Franklin Co., Ohio Guardianships & Estates: 1803-1850. W. Louis Phillips. (Orig.). 1984. pap. 6.50 o.p. (ISBN 0-917890-45-0). Heritage Bk.

Index to Genealogical Periodical Literature, 1960-1977. Kip Sperry. LC 79-9407. (Genealogy & Local History Ser.: Vol. 9). 192p. 1979. 68.00x o.p. (ISBN 0-8103-1403-7). Gale.

Index to Genealogical Periodicals. Rev. ed. Donald L. Jacobus & Carl Boyer, III. LC 83-71407. 373p. 1983. 20.00 o.p. (ISBN 0-936124-07-5). C Boyer.

Index to Grass Species, 3 Vols. Smithsonian Institution, Washington, D. C. Staff. Ed. by Agnes Chase & Cornelia D. Niles. 1970. Set. 300.00 o.p. (ISBN 0-8161-0445-X, Hall Library). G K Hall.

Index to Hayden's Virginia Genealogies. Virginia Genealogical Society Staff. 208p. 1977. 15.00 o.s.i. (ISBN 0-686-47791-X, VA 31). Southern Hist Pr.

Index to Latin American Legislation, Third Supplement. 1978. 120.00 o.p. (ISBN 0-8161-0094-2, Hall Library). G K Hall.

Index to Latin American Legislation, 1950-1960, 2 Vols. Library of Congress Staff. 1970. Set. 195.00 o.p. (ISBN 0-8161-0594-4, Hall Library). G K Hall.

Index to Latin American Periodical Literature, 1929-1960, 8 Vols. Organization of American States Editors. 1970. Set. 540.00 o.p. (ISBN 0-8161-0501-4, Hall Library). G K Hall.

Index to Latin American Periodical Literature 1966-1970. Organization of American States Editors. 1980. lib. bdg. 198.00 o.p. (ISBN 0-8161-0314-3, Hall Library). G K Hall.

Index to Learned Chinese Periodicals. Columbia University, East Asian Library Staff. 1970. lib. bdg. 78.00 o.p. (ISBN 0-8161-0644-4, Hall Library). G K Hall.

Index to Literature on Race Relations in South Africa, 1910-1975. P. J. Potgieter. 1979. lib. bdg. 56.00 o.p. (ISBN 0-8161-8295-7, Hall Reference). G K Hall.

Index to Manuscripts, 2 vols. Edinburgh University Library Staff. 1980. Set. 175.00 o.p. (ISBN 0-8161-0706-8, Hall Library). G K Hall.

Index to Maps in Books & Periodicals, Third Supplement. American Geographical Society Staff. (Library Catalogs-Supplements Ser.). 676p. 1987. lib. bdg. 175.00 o.s.i. (ISBN 0-8161-0458-1, Hall Library). G K Hall.

Index to Marquis Who's Who Books, 1986. 500p. 1986. 62.00 o.p. (ISBN 0-8379-1423-X). Marquis.

Index to Marquis Who's Who Books, 1987. 500p. 1987. 62.00 o.p. (ISBN 0-8379-1424-8). Marquis.

Index to Medical Socioeconomic Literature, 1962-1970, 4 vols. American Medical Association, Division of Library & Archival Services Staff. 1980. lib. bdg. 310.00 o.p. (ISBN 0-8161-0338-0, Hall Library). G K Hall.

Index to Musical Festchriften & Similar Publications. Walter Gerboth. 188p. Repr. of 1969 ed. lib. bdg. 39.00 o.p. (Pub. by Am Repr Serv). Reprint Servs.

Index to Parachuting, Nineteen Hundred to Nineteen Seventy-Five: An Annotated Bibliography. Michael Horan. LC 76-24773. (Reference Library of Science & Technology Ser.: Vol. 6). 1977. lib. bdg. 25.00 o.p. (ISBN 0-8240-9904-4). Garland Pub.

Index to Periodical Articles by & about Negroes, Decennial Cumulation, 1950-1959. Central State University Ohio Editors. 1970. 68.00 o.p. (ISBN 0-8161-0503-0, Hall Library). G K Hall.

Index to Periodical Articles by & About Negroes, 1977. Central State University Ohio Editors. lib. bdg. 68.00 o.s.i. (ISBN 0-8161-0869-2, Hall Library). G K Hall.

Index to Periodical Articles on South African Political & Social History Since 1902: Vol. 3- Bibliographies on South African Political History. Ed. by P. W. Coetzer & J. H. Le Roux. 1982. lib. bdg. 110.00 o.s.i. (ISBN 0-8161-8518-2, Hall Reference). G K Hall.

Titles

Titles

Index to Periodical Articles Related to Law, Five Year Cumulation, 1969-73, Vols. 11-15. Ed. by Roy M. Mersky et al. LC 65-29677. 1974. 35.00 o.p. (ISBN 0-87802-051-9). Glanville.

Index to Periodical Articles, 1950-1964, 2 Vols. Ed. by Royal Institute of International Affairs, London Staff. 1970. Set. 225.00 o.p. (ISBN 0-8161-0711-4, Hall Library). G K Hall.

Index to Post-1944 Periodical Articles on Political Economic & Social Problems - Tenth Supplement see Bibliographie Courante D'Articles de Periodiques Posterieurs a 1944 Sur les Problems Politiques, Economiques et Sociaux: Dixieme Supplement.

Index to Printed Maps. Bancroft Library, University of California, Berkeley Editors. 1964. lib. bdg. 79.00 o.p. (ISBN 0-8161-0704-1, Hall Library). G K Hall.

Index to Public Administration Series: Bibliography No. P 1597 - P 1716 (January 1985-June 1985) (Public Administration Ser.: P 1717). 43p. 1985. 6.75 o.p. (ISBN 0-89028-487-3). Vance Biblios.

Index to Public Administration Series: Bibliography No. P-1117 to P 1596 (January 1983-December-1984) Vance Bibliographies Staff. (Public Administration Ser.: Bibliography P-1597). 158p. 1985. pap. 18.25 o.p. (ISBN 0-89028-247-1). Vance Biblios.

Index to Public Administration Series: Bibliography P 877- P 1116 (January 1982-December 1982) Vance Bibliographies Staff. (Public Administration Ser.: Bibliography P 1117). 78p. 1983. pap. 12.00 o.p. (ISBN 0-88066-347-2). Vance Biblios.

Index to Record & Tape Reviews: A Classical Music Buying Guide Nineteen Eighty-Two. Antoinette O. Maleady. LC 72-3355. 1983. 60.00 o.p. (ISBN 0-917600-08-8). Chulainn Press.

Index to Record & Tape Reviews: A Classical Music Buying Guide 1980. Antoinette O. Maleady. LC 72-3355. (Annual Ser.). 1981. 55.00x o.p. (ISBN 0-917600-06-1). Chulainn Press.

Index to Record & Tape Reviews: A Classical Music Buying Guide, 1977. Antoinette O. Maleady. LC 72-3355. 1978. 42.50 o.p. (ISBN 0-917600-03-7). Chulainn Press.

Index to Record & Tape Reviews: A Classical Music Buying Guide, 1979. Antoinette O. Maleady. 1980. 52.50 o.p. (ISBN 0-917600-05-3). Chulainn Press.

Index to Record & Tape Reviews: A Classical Music Buying Guide, 1975. Antoinette O. Maleady. LC 72-3355. 1976. 35.00 o.p. (ISBN 0-917600-01-0). Chulainn Press.

Index to Record & Tape Reviews: A Classical Music Buying Guide, 1978. Antoinette O. Maleady. LC 72-3344. 1979. 47.50 o.p. (ISBN 0-917600-04-5). Chulainn Press.

Index to Record & Tape Reviews: A Classical Music Buying Guide, 1976. Antoinette O. Maleady. LC 72-3355. 1977. 37.50 o.p. (ISBN 0-917600-02-9). Chulainn Press.

Index to Record & Tape Reviews: A Classical Music Buying Guide, 1981. Antoinette O. Maleady. LC 72-3355. 57.50x o.p. (ISBN 0-917600-07-X). Chulainn Press.

Index to Reviews of Bibliographical Publications, 1978, Vol. 3. Bibliographic Society of Northern Illinois Staff. Ed. by Terry Oggel. 1979. lib. bdg. 27.50 o.p. (ISBN 0-8161-8477-1, Hall Reference). G K Hall.

Index to S. T. Wiley's History of Monongalia County (1883) Norman B. Shively. 1976. 5.00 o.p. (ISBN 0-87012-253-3). McClain.

Index to Southeast Asian Journals, 1975-1979: A Guide to Articles, Book Reviews, & Composite Works. Donald C. Johnson. 1982. lib. bdg. 44.00 o.p. (ISBN 0-8161-8564-6, Hall Reference). G K Hall.

Index to Spanish American Collective Biography: The Andean Countries, Vol. I. Ed. by Sara de Mundo Lo. 496p. 1981. 62.50 o.p. (ISBN 0-8161-8181-0). G K Hall.

Index to Spanish American Collective Biography: Vol. 2-Mexico. Sara De Mundo Lo. 1982. lib. bdg. 68.00 o.p. (ISBN 0-8161-8529-8, Hall Reference). G K Hall.

Index to Speech, Language & Hearing Journal Titles, 1954-1978. Paul H. Ptacek et al. LC 79-20058. 328p. text ed. 52.50 o.s.i. College-Hill.

Index to the Biographees in Nineteenth Century California County Histories. Ed. by J. Carlyle Parker. LC 79-11900. (Genealogy & Local History Ser.: Vol. 7). 304p. 1979. 68.00x o.p. (ISBN 0-8103-1406-1). Gale.

Index to the Contemporary Scene, Vol. 1. Ed. by David W. Brunton. LC 73-645955. 122p. 1973. 50.00x o.p. (ISBN 0-8103-1056-2). Gale.

Index to the Contemporary Scene, Vol. 2. Ed. by David W. Brunton. xiv, 136p. 1975. 50.00x o.p. (ISBN 0-8103-1057-0). Gale.

Index to the Evangelist & the Christian. Dennis Gulledge & David McWhirter. LC 83-70079. 160p. (Orig.). 1983. pap. 3.95 o.p. (ISBN 0-89900-231-5). College Pr Pub.

Index to the Louisiana Historical Quarterly, Vol. 1-33. Boyd Cruise. 1956. slip case 50.00 o.p. (ISBN 0-911116-05-2). Pelican.

Index to the Proceedings of the Lunar & Planetary Science Conferences, Houston, Texas, 1970-1978. Ed. by Amanda R. Masterson. LC 79-20109. (Illus.). 325p. 1979. 54.00 o.p. (ISBN 0-08-024620-6). Pergamon.

Index to the United States Patent Classification. Ed. by Alice B. Aderholt. 248p. 1986. pap. 12.00 o.p. (ISBN 0-318-22612-X, S/N 903-006-00007-2). USGPO.

Index to the United States Patent Classification, December 1987. Ed. by Alice B. Aderholt. 246p. 1987. pap. 12.00 o.p. (S/N 903-006-00010-2). USGPO.

Index to Tracts I-XIX see Metaphor.

Index to Tracts XXI-XXIX see Needed Words.

Index to Women of the World from Ancient to Modern Times: Biographies & Portraits. Norma O. Ireland. LC 75-120841. (Useful Reference Ser. of Library Bks: Vol. 97). 1970. lib. bdg. 16.00x o.p. (ISBN 0-87305-097-5). Faxon.

Index to Yankee Magazine, 1935-1978. Ed. by Susan Mahnke. LC 79-66743. 304p. 1979. 10.00 o.p. (ISBN 0-911658-98-X). Yankee Bks.

Index Translationium, Vol. 6. Incl. Index Translationium. (Vol. 16). pap. 73.00 (U302). UNIPUB; Index Translationium: International Biography of Translations. (Vol. 25). 931p. 1976. pap. text ed. 83.50 (ISBN 92-3-001174-6, U309). UNIPUB; Index Translationium: International Bibliography of Translations. (Vol. 26). 1977. 89.25 (ISBN 92-3-001255-6, U749). UNIPUB; Index Translationium. (Vol. 27). 1979. 89.25 (ISBN 92-3-001414-1, U878). UNIPUB; Index Translationium. (Vol. 28). 1979. 93.00 (ISBN 92-3-001464-8, U921). UNIPUB; Index Translationium: International Bibliography of Translations. (Vol. 30, 1977). 1024p. 1981. pap. 111.50 (ISBN 92-3-001911-9, U1104). UNIPUB; Index Translationium: International Bibliography of Translations. (Vol. 31, 1978). 1122p. (Eng., Fr. & Span.). 1984. pap. 119.00 (ISBN 92-3-001912-7, U1189). UNIPUB. pap. 1.00 o.p. (U300, UNESCO). UNIPUB.

Index Translationium see Index Translationium.

Index Translationium: International Biography of Translations see Index Translationium.

Index Translationium: International Bibliography of Translations see Index Translationium.

Indexation of the Tax Laws for Inflation. (Statement of Tax Policy Ser.: No. 6). 1980. pap. 9.50 o.p. (ISBN 0-686-70238-7). Am Inst CPA.

Indexed Categories & Their Application. P. T. Johnstone et al. (Lecture Notes in Mathematics: Vol. 661). (Illus.). 1978. pap. 17.00 o.p. (ISBN 0-387-08914-4). Springer-Verlag.

Indexes of Edgefield County, South Carolina Vol. 1: Probate Records. Lee C. Hendrix. 160p. 1979. 20.00 o.s.i. (ISBN 0-317-39987-X). Southern Hist Pr.

Indexing & Abstracting: An International Bibliography. Hans H. Wellisch. LC 80-11907. 308p. 1980. 32.50 o.p. (ISBN 0-87436-300-4). ABC-Clio.

Indexing & Abstracting, 1977-1981: An International Bibliography. Hans H. Wellisch. LC 84-3064. 277p. 1984. lib. bdg. 45.00 o.p. (ISBN 0-87436-398-5). ABC-Clio.

India. rev. ed. T. A. Raman. LC 83-80052. (World Cultures Ser). (Illus.). (gr. 6 up). 1983. text ed. 13.70 ea. 1-4 copies o.p. (ISBN 0-88296-128-4); text ed. 10.96 ea. 5 or more copies o.p. (ISBN 0-88296-393-7); tchr's. guide 8.96 o.p. (ISBN 0-88296-393-7). Gateway Pr MI.

India. Time-Life Books Editors. (Library of Nations). (Illus.). 160p. (YA) (gr. 7 up). 1986. lib. bdg. 23.93 o.p. (ISBN 0-8094-5315-0). Time-Life.

India: A Guide for the Quality-Conscious Traveler. Louise Nicholson. Ed. by Joyce Johnson. LC 85-71410. (Illus.). 270p. 1985. 19.95 o.p. (ISBN 0-87113-047-5). Atlantic Monthly.

India: A Practical Guide. J. Leak. 240p. (Orig.). 1982. pap. 11.95 o.p. (ISBN 0-933982-29-1, Lascelles). Bradt Ent.

India: A Travel Survival Kit. 2nd ed. Geoff Crowther et al. (Illus.). 792p. (Orig.). 1984. pap. 14.95 o.p. (ISBN 0-908086-54-7). Lonely Planet.

India: An Uncommitted Society. J. C. Kapur. 240p. 1982. text ed. 22.50x o.p. (ISBN 0-7069-1878-9, Pub. by Vikas India). Advent NY.

India & Britain, 1947-1968. K. Banerjee. 1977. 14.00x o.p. (ISBN 0-88386-903-9). South Asia Bks.

India & China. P. C. Bagchi. 176p. 1951. (ISBN 0-8022-0049-4). Philos Lib.

India & Southeast Asia. T. A. Raman et al. LC 74-75937. (World Cultures Ser). (Illus.). (gr. 6 up). 1974. text ed. 12.43 1-4 copies o.p. (ISBN 0-88296-159-4); text ed. 9.94 5 or more o.p. (ISBN 0-88296-159-4); tchr's guide skills manual incl. 8.94 o.p. (ISBN 0-686-85961-8). Gateway Pr MI.

India & the Communist Countries: Documents 1979. J. A. Naik. 224p. 1982. text ed. 35.00x o.p. (ISBN 0-391-02573-2, 90404). Humanities.

India & the Indian Ocean: New Horizons. Maharaj K. Chopra. 280p. 1982. text ed. 15.00x o.p. (ISBN 0-391-02770-0). Humanities.

India & the Passing of Empire. George Dunbar. 1952. (ISBN 0-8022-0424-4). Philos Lib.

India & the West: Documents 1976-78. Ed. by J. A. Naik. 482p. 1981. text ed. 39.95x o.p. (ISBN 0-391-02157-5). Humanities.

India & the West: Documents, 1979. J. A. Naik. 231p. 1982. text ed. 35.00x o.p. (ISBN 0-391-02572-4, 90402). Humanities.

India: Art & Culture, 1300-1900. Stuart C. Welch. 496p. 1985. 65.00 o.p. (ISBN 0-03-006114-8). H Holt & Co.

India Britannica. Geoffrey Moorhouse. (Illus.). 207p. 1987. pap. 8.95 o.s.i. (ISBN 0-89733-289-X, Pub. by Granada England). Academy Chi Pubs.

India: Cradle of Cultures. Chaman Lal. (Illus.). 346p. 1980. text ed. 32.50x o.p. (ISBN 0-391-01872-8). Humanities.

India: Emergent Power? Stephen P. Cohen & Richard L. Park. LC 78-50920. (Strategy Paper Ser.: No. 33). 95p. 1978. pap. 9.00 o.p. (ISBN 0-8448-1353-2, Pub. by Crane Russak & Co). Taylor & Francis.

India: Government & Politics in a Developing Nation. 2nd ed. Robert L. Hardgrave, Jr. 250p. (Orig.). 1975. text ed. 8.95 o.p. (ISBN 0-15-541351-1, HC). HarBraceJ.

India: Government & Politics in a Developing Nation. 3rd ed. Robert L. Hardgrave, Jr. 285p. 1980. pap. text ed. 10.50 o.p. (ISBN 0-15-541352-X, HC). HarBraceJ.

India in Asia & Africa: Documents, 1976-78. Ed. by J. A. Naik. 673p. 1981. text ed. 45.00x o.p. (ISBN 0-391-02167-2). Humanities.

India in Asia & Africa: Documents, 1979. Ed. by J. A. Naik. 247p. 1982. text ed. 29.95x o.p. Humanities.

India in Soviet Global Strategy. J. Banerjee. 1977. 12.50x o.p. (ISBN 0-88386-908-X). South Asia Bks.

India in the Mind of Germany: Schelling, Schopenhauer & Their Times. Jean W. Sedlar. LC 81-40842. 270p. (Orig.). 1982. lib. bdg. 30.50 o.p. (ISBN 0-8191-2191-6); pap. text ed. 13.25 o. p. o.p. (ISBN 0-8191-2192-4). U Pr of Amer.

India on Fifteen & Twenty-Five Dollars a Day. Jan Aaron. 358p. 1985. pap. 9.95 o.p. (ISBN 0-671-49903-3). Prentice Hall Pr.

India: Resources & Development. B. L. Johnson. LC 78-15402. (Illus.). 211p. 1979. text ed. 28.50x o.p. (ISBN 0-06-493348-2). B&N Imports.

India: Selected Readings. rev. ed. Hyman Kublin. LC 72-7637. (World Regional Studies). 230p. (gr. 9-12). 1973. pap. 8.28 o.p. (ISBN 0-395-13929-5). HM.

India Song. Marguerite Duras. Tr. by Barbara Bray from Fr. LC 75-16763. (Orig.). 1976. pap. 3.95 o.p. (ISBN 0-394-17893-9, E647, Ever). Grove.

India: Studies in State Finances. Christine Wallich. LC 82-11087. (World Bank Staff Working Papers: No. 523). 186p. (Orig.). 1982. pap. 8.00 o.p. (ISBN 0-8213-0013-X, WP2523). World Bank.

India Who's Who, 1985. 56.00 o.p. (ISBN 0-8002-3846-X). Intl Pubns Serv.

India Who's Who: 1986. 485p. 68.00 o.p. (ISBN 0-8002-4087-1). Intl Pubns Serv.

India Widow. Sarah Woodhouse. 240p. 1986. text ed. 15.95 o.p. (ISBN 0-07-071675-7). McGraw.

Indian Agents of the Old Frontier. Flora W. Seymour. 1973. lib. bdg. 27.50x o.p. (ISBN 0-374-97290-7, Octagon). Hippocrene Bks.

Indian Alchemy or Rasayana: In the Light of Asceticism & Geriatrics. S. Mahdihassan. 1979. text ed. 15.95x o.p. (ISBN 0-7069-0769-8, Pub. by Vikas India). Advent NY.

Indian & Pioner Settlement in the Nooksack Lowland to 1890. Tremaine. (Occasional Papers: No. 4). pap. WWU CPNS.

Indian & the White Man in New England. Chandler Whipple. LC 73-93961. (First Encounter Ser.). (Illus., Orig.). 1976. 12.00 o.s.i. (ISBN 0-912944-41-2); pap. 8.00 o.s.i. (ISBN 0-912944-38-2). Berkshire Traveller.

Indian Art. Richard Winstedt. (ISBN 0-8022-1907-1). Philos Lib.

Indian Art of the Americas. Frederick J. Dockstader. LC 73-89979. (Illus., Orig.). 1973. 5.00x o.p. (ISBN 0-934490-09-0). Mus Am Ind.

Indian Arts & Crafts Board: An Aspect of New Deal Indian Policy. Robert F. Schrader. LC 83-5816. (Illus.). 376p. 1983. 19.95x o.p. (ISBN 0-8263-0669-1). U of NM Pr.

Indian Arts in North America. George C. Vaillant. LC 72-97071. (Illus.). 63p. 1973. Repr. of 1939 ed. lib. bdg. 30.00x o.p. (ISBN 0-8154-0469-7). Cooper Sq.

Indian Attachment. Sarah Lloyd. Ed. by Pat Golbitz. LC 84-62000. (Illus.). 244p. 1984. 12.95 o.p. (ISBN 0-688-03027-0). Morrow.

Indian Ballet Dancing. Projesh Banerjee. (Illus.). 170p. 1983. text ed. 45.00x o.p. (ISBN 0-391-02716-6). Humanities.

Indian Boy's Days: The Indian Then & Now-His Presence & Influence on Our Life-style. Allan Hulsizer. (Illus.). 64p. 1983. 7.50 o.p. (ISBN 0-682-49959-5). Exposition-Phoenix.

Indian Children's Books. H. Gilliland. 1980. write for info. o.p. (ISBN 0-89992-502-2); pap. 7.95 o.p. (ISBN 0-89992-503-0). Coun India Ed.

Indian Cinema, Nineteen Eighty-Seven. 140p. 1988. text ed. 25.00x o.p. (ISBN 0-7069-4018-0, Pub. by Vikas India). Advent NY.

Indian Cinema Superbazaar. Ed. by Aruna A. Vasudev & Philippe Lenglet. 1983. text ed. 40.00x o.p. (ISBN 0-7069-2226-3, Pub. by Vikas India). Advent NY.

Indian Country. League of Women Voters Education Fund. LC 76-21579. 1976. pap. 2.95, 5 for 10.00 o.p. (ISBN 0-89959-104-3, 605). LWV US.

Indian Crafts. D. N. Saraf. (Illus.). 60.00x o.p. (ISBN 0-7069-0735-3, Pub. by Vikas India). Advent NY.

Indian Economic Development: Retrospect & Prospect. Shrinivas Y. Thakur. 236p. 1984. text ed. 25.00x o.p. (ISBN 0-86590-169-4, Pub. by Sterling Pubs India). Apt Bks.

Indian Economy: Problems of Development & Planning. 11th & rev. ed. A. N. Agrawal. 680p. 1985. text ed. 45.00x o.p. (ISBN 0-7069-2855-5, Pub. by Vikas India). Advent NY.

Indian-English Literature: A Survey. Elena J. Kalinnikova. 248p. 1981. text ed. 15.25x o.p. (ISBN 0-391-02539-2). Humanities.

Indian Family in Transition. John S. Augustin. 256p. 1982. text ed. 20.00x o.p. (ISBN 0-7069-1970-X, Pub. by Vikas India). Advent NY.

Indian Fan. Victoria Holt. 1988. 18.95 o.p. Doubleday.

Indian Financial System. M. Y. Khan. LC 80-904855. 464p. 1980. text ed. 35.00x o.p. (ISBN 0-7069-1101-6, Pub. by Vikas India). Advent NY.

Indian Freedom Movement & Thought, 1919-1929. Lal Bahadur. Ed. by J. C. Johari. 1983. text ed. 40.00x o.p. (ISBN 0-86590-158-9, Pub. by Sterling Pubs India). Apt Bks.

Indian Freedom Movement & Thought, 1930-1947. R. C. Gupta & J. C. Johari. 1983. text ed. 40.00x o.p. (ISBN 0-86590-159-7, Pub. by Sterling Pubs India). Apt Bks.

Indian Gymnosperms in Time & Space. C. G. Ramanujam. (Illus.). 50p. 1976. Repr. 8.00 o.p. (ISBN 0-88065-178-4, Pub. by Messers Today & Tomorrow Printers & Publishers). Scholarly Pubns.

Indian How Book. Arthur C. Parker. (Illus.). 13.50 o.p. (ISBN 0-8446-5234-2). Peter Smith.

Indian Insect Life: A Manual of the Insects of the Plains (Tropical India) H. Maxwell Lefroy. xii, 786p. 1986. Repr. of 1909 ed. 150.00 o.p. (ISBN 0-88065-150-4, Pub. by Messers Today & Tomorrow Printers & Publishers). Scholarly Pubns.

Indian Insect Pests. H. Maxwell Lefroy. xii, 318p. 1971. Repr. of 1906 ed. 15.00 o.p. (ISBN 0-88065-149-0, Pub. by Messers Today & Tomorrow Printers & Publishers). Scholarly Pubns.

Indian Left: Critical Appraisals. Ed. by Bipan Chandra. 1983. text ed. 45.00x o.p. (ISBN 0-7069-2103-8, Pub. by Vikas India). Advent NY.

Indian Legacy: Native American Influences on World Life & Culture. Hermina Poatgieter. LC 81-14171. (Illus.). 192p. (gr. 7 up). 1981. lib. bdg. 10.79 o.s.i. (ISBN 0-671-41703-7). Messner.

Indian Librarianship. Ravinder N. Sharma. 333p. 1981. 19.95 o.p. Asia Bk Corp.

Indian Life on the Northwest Coast of North America As Seen by the Early Explorers & Fur Traders During the Last Decade of the 18th Century. Erna Gunther. LC 72-188822. 320p. 1972. 15.00x o.s.i. (ISBN 0-226-31088-4). U of Chicago Pr.

Indian Linguistic Families of America North of Mexico see Introduction to Handbook of American Indian Languages.

Indian Mushroom Science I: Proceedings of the Survey & Cultivation of Edible Mushrooms in India National Symposium, 1st, Srinagar, 1976. Survey & Cultivation of Edible Mushrooms in India, National Symposium Staff. Ed. by C. K. Atal et al. (Current Trends in Life Sciences Ser.: Vol. 2). xxii, 532p. 1978. 25.00 o.p. (ISBN 0-88065-021-4, Pub. by Messers Today & Tomorrow Printers & Publishers). Scholarly Pubns.

Indian Muslims. M. Mujeeb. 590p. 1967. 14.00x o.p. (ISBN 0-7735-0021-9, McGill Canada). U of Toronto Pr.

Indian Nationalism: An Historical Analysis. R. Suntharalingam. 1983. text ed. 37.50x o.p. (ISBN 0-7069-2106-2, Pub. by Vikas India). Advent NY.

Indian Paths of Pennsylvania. Paul A. W. Wallace. LC 66-4482. 1971. 9.50 o.p. (ISBN 0-685-19109-5). Pa Hist & Mus.

Indian Poetry in English: A Literary History & Anthology. Ed. by A. N. Dwivedi. 159p. 1983. 9.75 o.s.i. (ISBN 0-86578-012-9). Ind-US Inc.

Indian Religions. S. Radhakrishnan. 1979. 7.00x o.p. (ISBN 0-8364-0367-3). South Asia Bks.

Indian Stories from the Pueblos: Tales of New Mexico & Arizona. Frank G. Applegate. (Beautiful Rio Grande Classics Ser.). 198p. 12.00 o.p. (ISBN 0-87380-076-1); pap. 4.00 o.p. (ISBN 0-87380-138-5). Rio Grande.

Indian Summer & More. Robert E. Witt. 64p. 1980. 5.00 o.p. (ISBN 0-682-49668-5). Exposition-Phoenix.

Indian Summer of the Heart. Daisy Newman. 1982. 14.45 o.p. (ISBN 0-395-32517-X). HM.

Indian Sweets & Desserts. Aroona Reejhsinghani. 136p. 1983. pap. 2.50 o.s.i. (ISBN 0-86578-228-8). Ind-US Inc.

Indian Sword Strikes in East Pakistan. Lachhman Singh. (Illus.). 1979. 20.00x o.p. (ISBN 0-7069-0742-6, Pub. by Vikas India). Advent NY.

Indian Tales of North America: An Anthology for the Adult Reader. Ed. by Tristram P. Coffin. LC 61-11866. (American Folklore Soc. Bibliographical & Special Ser.: No. 13). 175p. 1961. pap. 6.95 o.p. (ISBN 0-292-73506-5). U of Tex Pr.

Indian Theogony: Comparative Study of Indian Mythology from the Vedas to the Puranas. rev. ed. Sukumari Bhattacharji. 1978. Repr. of 1970 ed. 18.50x o.p. (ISBN 0-8364-0160-3). South Asia Bks.

Indian Treasure on Rockhouse Creek. William N. McElrath. LC 84-9527. (gr. 5-8). 1984. pap. 5.95 o.p. (ISBN 0-8054-4517-X, 4245-17). Broadman.

Indian Way. Ranjee Shahani. 1951. (ISBN 0-8022-1540-8). Philos Lib.

Indian Witchcraft. R. N. Saletore. 216p. 1981. text ed. 17.50x o.p. (ISBN 0-391-02480-9). Humanities.

Indian Women. Ed. by D. Jain. 1975. pap. 10.00 o.s.i. (ISBN 0-685-79106-8). E J Brill USA.

Indian Women Through the Ages (1976) H. N. Verma & Amrit Verma. 1977. 12.50 o.s.i. (ISBN 0-685-80305-8). E J Brill USA.

Indiana. Georges Sand. 358p. 1976. 37.50 o.p. (ISBN 0-686-54952-X). Schoenhof.

Indiana: Agency. 1983. 8.50 o.p. (ISBN 0-686-90723-X). Am Law Inst.

Indiana Alcoholic Beverage Laws: Annotated. Michie Company Editorial Staff. (State Practice Publications Ser.). 350p. 1984. pap. 10.00 o.p. (ISBN 0-87215-787-3, 24223). Michie Co.

Indiana: An Illustrated History. Patrick J. Furlong. LC 85-20205. 232p. 1985. 24.95 o.p. (ISBN 0-89781-152-6). Windsor Pubns Inc.

Indiana Business Directory, 1987-88. American Directory Publishing Co., Inc. Staff. 1552p. (Orig.). 1987. pap. 85.00 o.p. (ISBN 0-944316-01-8). Amer Directory.

Indiana College Scholarship Guide: The Most Comprehensive Source to over 100 Million Dollars Scholarships for Indiana College Students. LC 87-20860. 168p. (Orig.). 1987. pap. 9.95 o.p. (ISBN 0-944369-00-6). Brackemyre Pub.

Indiana: Conflict of Laws. 1983. 6.00 o.p. Am Law Inst.

Indiana: Contracts. 1983. 9.50 o.p. (ISBN 0-686-90726-4); 7.00 o.p. (ISBN 0-686-90727-2). Am Law Inst.

Indiana Jones & the Eye of the Fates. Richard Wenk. LC 84-90847. (Find Your Adventure Fate Ser.: No. 4). 128p. (Orig.). 1984. pap. 1.95 o.s.i. (ISBN 0-345-31716-5). Ballantine.

Indiana Judicial System. National Center for State Courts Staff. 37p. (On loan through the NCSC Library). 1974. (NCRO-073). Natl Ctr St Courts.

Indiana Manufacturers Directory, 1988. 629p. 1988. 89.00 o.p. (ISBN 0-318-02878-6). Manufacturers.

Indiana Media Directory, 1988: The Most Up-to-Date, Detailed Listing of All Indiana Newspapers & Radio & TV Stations. 152p. (Orig.). 1987. pap. 23.00 o.p. (ISBN 0-944369-01-4). Brackemyre Pub.

Indiana: Off the Beaten Path, A Guide to Unique Places. Bill Thomas & Phyllis Thomas. LC 84-48889. (Illus.). 168p. (Orig.). 1985. pap. 8.95 o.s.i. (ISBN 0-88742-024-9). Globe Pequot.

Indiana Pacers. Jim Moore. (NBA Today Ser.). (Illus.). 48p. (gr. 4 up). 1984. PLB 10.45 o.p. (ISBN 0-87191-979-6). Creative Ed.

Indiana Politics during the Civil War. Kenneth M. Stampp. LC 77-23629. 320p. 1978. 15.00x o.p. (ISBN 0-253-37022-1). Ind U Pr.

Indiana: Restitution. 1983. 8.50 o.p. (ISBN 0-686-90731-0). Am Law Inst.

Indiana: Trusts, Vols. 1 & 2. 1983. 8.50 o.p. (ISBN 0-686-90476-1). Am Law Inst.

Indianapolis Dining. Reid Duffy. LC 87-6643. 160p. (Orig.). 1987. pap. 4.95 o.p. (ISBN 1-55652-008-5). Chicago Review.

Indianapolis Five Hundred Yearbook: 1969-1972. Ed. by John Mahoney & Carl Hungness. (Illus.). 304p. lib. bdg. 100.00 o.p. (ISBN 0-915088-22-3). C Hungness.

Indians. Robin May. (Illus.). 160p. 1982. 10.95 o.p. (ISBN 0-8119-0458-X, Pub. by Bison Bks.). Fell.

Indians Before Columbus: Twenty Thousand Years of North American History Revealed by Archaeology. Paul S. Martin et al. LC 47-1434. (Illus.). 1947. lib. bdg. 27.50x o.s.i. (ISBN 0-226-50781-5). U of Chicago Pr.

Indians Before Columbus: Twenty Thousand Years of North American History Revealed by Archaeology. Paul S. Martin et al. LC 47-1434. (Illus.). xxiv, 582p. 1975. pap. text ed. 6.95x o.s.i. (ISBN 0-226-50782-3, P630, Phoen). U of Chicago Pr.

Indians in New Zealand: Studies in a Sub-Culture. Ed. by Kapil Tiwarni. 20.00x o.p. (ISBN 0-686-43916-3, Pub. by Price Milburn). South Asia Bks.

Indians of Cape Flattery. facs. ed. James G. Swan. (Shorey Indian Ser.). (Illus.). 108p. pap. 8.95 o.s.i. (ISBN 0-8466-0024-2, S24). Shorey.

Indians of South America. Paul Radin. 1969. Repr. of 1942 ed. lib. bdg. 22.50 o.p. (ISBN 0-8371-1123-4, RAIS). Greenwood.

Indians of the Great Plains. Norman Bancroft-Hunt & Forman Werner. LC 81-85585. (Illus.). 128p. 1982. 25.00 o.p. (ISBN 0-688-01215-9). Morrow.

Indians of the Northwest Coast. 2nd ed. Pliny E. Goddard. LC 72-81191. (Handbook Ser.: No. 10). (Illus.). 175p. 1972. Repr. of 1934 ed. lib. bdg. 25.00x o.p. (ISBN 0-8154-0428-X). Cooper Sq.

Indians of Yoknapatawpha: A Study in Literature & History. Lewis M. Dabney. LC 73-77659. x, 163p. 1974. 20.00 o.p. (ISBN 0-8071-0058-7). La State U Pr.

Indian's Ruby. Timothy C. Davis. LC 85-7368. 196p. (Orig.). 1986. pap. 6.95 o.p. (ISBN 0-89636-198-5). Accent Bks.

India's Demography: Essays on the Contemporary Population. Ed. by T. Dyson & N. Crook. 235p. 1984. text ed. 17.50x o.p. (ISBN 0-391-03108-2). Humanities.

India's Educated Women. Rhoda L. Blumberg & Leela Dwarkai. 1982. 16.00x o.p. (ISBN 0-8364-0834-9, Pub. by Hindustan). South Asia Bks.

India's Foreign Policy: Studies in Continuity & Change. Ed. by Bimal Prasad. 1979. text ed. 40.00x o.p. (ISBN 0-7069-0818-X, Pub. by Vikas India). Advent NY.

India's Green Revolution. Francine R. Frankel. LC 74-132237. (Center of International Studies Ser.). 1971. 28.00 o.p. (ISBN 0-691-07536-0). Princeton U Pr.

India's Historical Demography, Vol. II: Studies in Famine, Disease & Social Change. Ed. by T. Dyson. (London Studies on South Asia (Centre of South Asian Studies, School of Oriental & African Studies, University of London): No. 8). (Illus.). 280p. 1989. 37.00 o.p. (ISBN 0-913215-43-0). Riverdale Co.

India's Political Economy. Balraj Mehta. 1983. 11.00x o.p. (ISBN 0-8364-1026-2, Pub. by Avishkar Prakashan India). South Asia Bks.

India's Religious Art: Ideas & Ideals. K. V. Rajan. (Illus.). 1982. text ed. 45.00x o.p. (ISBN 0-391-02916-9). Humanities.

Indicators of Environmental Quality. Ed. by William A. Thomas. LC 72-86142. (Environmental Science Research Ser.: Vol. 1). 286p. 1972. 45.00x o.p. (ISBN 0-306-36301-1, Plenum Pr); pap. 9.95 o.p. (ISBN 0-306-20011-2). Plenum Pub.

Indicators of Suicide & Depression Among Drug Abusers: 1979-1981. Margaret Allison. (National Institute on Drug Abuse Treatment Research Monograph Ser.). 75p. 1985. pap. 2.75 o.p. (ISBN 0-318-19946-7, S/N 017-024-01272-6). USGPO.

Indicia...A Romance. Kathleen Burch. (Illus.). 1988. special ed. 75.00 o.p. (ISBN 0-936050-06-3). Burning Bks.

Indifferent Mean: Adiaphorism in the English Reformation to 1554. Bernard J. Verkamp. Ed. by Robert C. Walton & Philip N. Bebb. LC 77-13672. (Studies in the Reformation: Vol. I). 160p. 1978. text ed. 19.95x o.p. (ISBN 0-8143-1583-6). Wayne St U Pr.

Indigenous Architecture Worldwide: A Guide to Information Sources. Ed. by Lawrence Wodehouse. LC 79-26580. (Art & Architecture Information Guide Ser.: Vol. 12). 408p. 1980. 68.00x o.p. (ISBN 0-8103-1450-9). Gale.

Indigenous Economics: A Cultural Approach. Chinyamata Chipeta. (Illus.). 280p. 1981. 12.50x o.p. (ISBN 0-682-49657-X). Exposition-Phoenix.

Indigent Rich: A Theory of General Equilibrium in a Keynesian System. J. W. Cumes. 224p. 1972. 55.00 o.p. (ISBN 0-08-017534-1). Pergamon.

Indignant Eye: The Artist As a Social Critic in Prints & Drawings from the 15th Century to Picasso. Ralph E. Shikes. LC 69-14604. (Illus.). 1976. pap. 12.95x o.p. (ISBN 0-8070-6671-0, BP543). Beacon Pr.

Indignant Heart: A Black Worker's Journal. Charles Denby. LC 78-65368. 300p. 1978. 20.00 o.p. (ISBN 0-89608-093-5); pap. 7.50 o.p. (ISBN 0-89608-092-7). South End Pr.

Indira Gandhi Speaks on Democracy, Socialism & Third World Non-Alignment. Ed. by Henry M. Christman. LC 72-6611. 160p. 1975. 8.95 o.s.i. (ISBN 0-8008-4180-8). Taplinger.

Indirect & Direct Wallerian Degeneration in the Intramedullary Root Fibers of the Hypoglossal Nerve: An Electron Microscopal Study in the Kitten. H. Aldskogius. LC 74-10068. (Advances in Anatomy, Embryology and Cell Biology Ser.: Vol. 50, Pt. 1). (Illus.). 80p. (Orig.). 1974. pap. 23.60 o.p. (ISBN 0-387-06750-7). Springer-Verlag.

Indirect Rule in British Africa see Tarikh.

Indirections: Shakespeare & the Art of Illusion. Anthony B. Dawson. LC 78-6016. 1978. 25.00x o.p. (ISBN 0-8020-5413-7). U of Toronto Pr.

Individual & the Community. Liao Wen-Kuei. LC 73-14035. (International Library of Psychology, Philosophy & Scientific Method Ser). 314p. 1974. Repr. of 1933 ed. lib. bdg. 35.00x o.p. (ISBN 0-8371-7142-3, LIIN). Greenwood.

Individual & the Microenvironment. Y. Sychev. 165p. 1978. 6.45 o.p. (ISBN 0-8285-3302-4, Pub. by Progress Pubs USSR). Imported Pubns.

Individual & the State see Is Conscience a Crime?.

Individual Annuities As a Source of Retirement Income. rev. ed. S. Travis Pritchett & John E. Stinton. (FLMI Insurance Education Program Ser.). 94p. 1982. pap. text ed. 9.00 o.p. (ISBN 0-915322-50-1). LOMA.

Individual Creations: The Grand Tour, Vol. 3. Flavio Conti. Tr. by Patrick Creagh. LC 77-94394. 1979. 15.95 o.p. (ISBN 0-15-144368-8). HarBraceJ.

Individual Differences. V. J. Shackleton & C. A. Fletcher. 194p. 1984. pap. 5.95 o.p. (ISBN 0-416-33760-0, NO. 9179). Routledge Chapman & Hall.

Individual Differences in Language Ability & Language Behavior. Ed. by Charles F. Fillmore et al. LC 78-20044. (Perspectives in Neurolinguistics & Psycholinguistics Ser.). 1979. 33.00 o.p. (ISBN 0-12-255950-9). Acad Pr.

Individual Income Tax Returns, 1984: Returns Filed, Sources of Income, Exemptions, Itemized Deductions, & Tax Computations. 2nd, Annual ed. (Internal Revenue Service Publication 1304 Ser.). (Illus.). 176p. 1986. pap. 8.50 o.p. (S/N 048-004-01936-1). USGPO.

Individual Income Tax, 1989. James Pratt et al. 45.00 o.p. (ISBN 0-256-06725-2); study guide 13.50 o.p. (ISBN 0-256-06731-7). Irwin.

Individual Inventor: What He Should Know about the U. S. Patent System. Philip McGran. 24p. 1982. 5.00 o.p. (ISBN 0-682-49905-6). Exposition-Phoenix.

Individual Investor's Guide to Investment Publications. International Publishing Corporation, Inc. Staff. 1988. pap. 19.95 o.p. (ISBN 0-942641-07-8). Longman.

Individual Investor's Guide to No-Load Mutual Funds. 7th ed. American Association of Individual Investors Staff. 400p. (Orig.). 1988. pap. 19.95 o.p. (ISBN 0-942641-05-1). Intl Pub IL.

Individual Investor's Guide to No-Load Mutual Funds. 5th, rev. ed. Ed. by Barbara G. Craig. (American Association of Individual Investors Financial Planning Library). 320p. 1986. pap. 19.95 o.p. (ISBN 0-930369-16-5). Invest Info.

Individual Investor's Guide to No-Load Mutual Funds. 4th rev. ed. G. W Perritt & L. Kay Shannon. (American Association of Individual Investors Financial Planning Library). 350p. 1985. pap. 19.95 o.p. (ISBN 0-930369-11-4). Invest Info.

Individual Investor's Microcomputer Resource Guide. 6th ed. American Association of Individual Investors Staff. 400p. 1988. pap. 15.95 o.p. (ISBN 0-942641-06-X). Intl Pub Il.

Individual Investor's Microcomputer Resource Guide. 3rd, rev., & enl. ed. Norm Nicholson. (AAII Library of Financial Planning). 236p. 1985. pap. 11.95 o.p. (ISBN 0-930369-13-0). Invest Info.

Individual Open Salts Illustrated: The 1976 Annual. Allan B. Smith & Helen B. Smith. (Illus.). 1976. pap. 7.00 o.p. (ISBN 0-940554-01-1). Country Hse.

Individual Open Salts Illustrated: The 1978 Annual. Allan B. Smith & Helen B. Smith. (Illus.). 1978. pap. 8.50 o.p. (ISBN 0-940554-03-8). Country Hse.

Individual Retirement Accounts Handbook. Jere J. Knoles. LC 78-63394. 1978. 29.95 o.p. (ISBN 0-87624-256-5, Inst Busn Plan); pap. 19.50 o.p. (ISBN 0-87624-255-7). P-H.

Individual Retirement Plans. 48p. 1985. 6.00 o.p. (21); members 3.00 o.p. Am Consul Eng.

Individual Rights in Constitutional Law: 1986 Supplement 4th Edition see Constitutional Law: 1986 Case Supplement to 11th Edition.

Individual Rights in the Corporation: A Reader on Employee Rights. Ala F. Westin & Stephan Salisbury. 1981. pap. 8.95 o.p. (ISBN 0-394-74803-4). Pantheon.

Individual Society & Health Behavior. Andie L. Knutson. 534p. 1982. pap. 6.95x o.p. (ISBN 0-87855-685-0). Transaction Pubs.

Individual Taxation, 1988. James W. Pratt et al. 1988. 40.95 o.p.; Study Guide 12.95 o.p. (ISBN 0-256-06469-5). Irwin.

Individual, the Enterprise & the State. Ed. by R. I. Tricker. LC 77-78350. 169p. 1977. 26.95x o.p. (ISBN 0-470-99211-5). Halsted Pr.

Individualized Education Programs (IEP's) A Handbook for Vocational Educators. L. Allen Phelps & Laurie J. Batchelor. 38p. 1979. 2.80 o.p. (ISBN 0-318-22132-2, IN188). Natl Ctr Res Voc Ed.

Individualized Health Incentive Program Modules For Physically Disabled Students, 5 Vols. Kathryn Reggio & Josephine Davidson. Ed. by Danna Shooltz. Incl. Vol. 1. Safety & Survival Education. 336p. 1976; Vol. 2. Environmental & Community Health. 62p; Vol. 3. Sociological Health Problems. 56p. 1977; Vol. 4. Mental Health & Family Life Education. (Illus.). 138p. 1977; Vol. 5. Physical Health. (Illus.). 138p. 1977. 4.50 ea. o.p.; 17.50 set o.p. (ISBN 0-686-38806-2). Human Res Ctr.

Individualized Learning Program for the Profoundly Retarded. M. Susan De Vore. (Illus.). 256p. 1978. 32.25x o.p. (ISBN 0-398-03728-0). C C Thomas.

Individualized Reading. Sam Duker. 288p. 1971. 27.25x o.p. (ISBN 0-398-02274-7). C C Thomas.

Individualized Student Teaching: A Systematic Approach. Richard Steiner. 105p. 1970. pap. text ed. 4.00x o.p. (ISBN 0-8422-0171-8). Irvington.

Individualizing Instruction. Fred T. Tyler. LC 62-2192. (National Society for the Study of Education Yearbooks Ser: No. 61, Pt. 1). 1962. lib. bdg. 6.50x o.s.i. (ISBN 0-226-60063-7). U of Chicago Pr.

Individualizing Language Instruction: Strategies & Methods. Renee S. Disick. 242p. (Orig.). 1975. pap. text ed. 8.00 o.p. (ISBN 0-15-541404-6, HC). HarBraceJ.

Individuals & World Politics. Robert A. Isaak. 1975. pap. (ISBN 0-87872-094-4). Brooks-Cole.

Individuated Hobbit: Jung, Tolkien & the Archetypes of Middle-Earth. Timothy R. O'Neill. 1979. 8.95 o.p. (ISBN 0-395-28208-X). HM.

Indivisible Island: The Story of the Partition of Ireland. Frank Gallagher. LC 74-5772. (Illus.). 316p. 1974. Repr. of 1957 ed. lib. bdg. 35.00x o.p. (ISBN 0-8371-7515-1, GAII). Greenwood.

Indo-English Literature: A Collection of Critical Essays on Indian Creative Writers in English. Ed. by K. K. Sharma. 273p. 1977. text ed. 15.00x o.p. (ISBN 0-391-02534-1). Humanities.

Indochinese Students in U. S. Schools: A Guide for Administrators. Language & Orientation Resource Center Staff. LC 81-15554. (Language in Education Ser.: No. 42). 1981. 19.95x o.p. (ISBN 0-15-599112-4); pap. 9.50 o.p. (ISBN 0-15-599113-2). Ctr Appl Ling.

Indoles, Vol. 25, Pt. 1. Ed. by William Houlihan. 587p. 1966. 77.00 o.p. (ISBN 0-471-37500-4). Krieger.

Indoles, Vol. 25, pt. 3. Ed. by William J. Houlihan. LC 76-154323. (Chemistry of Heterocyclic Compounds, a Series of Monographs). 586p. 1979. 196.95 o.p. (ISBN 0-471-05132-2, Pub. by Wiley-Interscience). Krieger.

Indonesia. (Hildebrand's Travel Guides Ser.). (Illus.). 208p. pap. 11.95 o.p. (ISBN 0-87052-020-2). Hippocrene Bks.

Indonesia. (Post Guides Ser.). (Illus.). 144p. (Orig.). 1987. pap. 8.95 o.p. (ISBN 962-10-0027-0). Hunter Pub NY.

Indonesia Handbook. rev. 3rd. ed. Bill Dalton. Ed. by Castleman Deke. (Illus.). 600p. (Orig.). pap. 12.95 o.p. (ISBN 0-918373-04-2). Moon Pubns CA.

Indonesia: Innovation in the Management of Primary School Construction. (Educational Building Reports: No. 8). 1978. pap. 5.25 o.p. (ISBN 0-685-65232-7, UB67, UB). UNIPUB.

Indonesia: Post Report. rev. ed. (Department of Foreign Service Ser.: No. 248). (Illus.). 35p. 1986. pap. 1.50 o.p. (ISBN 0-318-19945-9, S/N 044-000-02106-4). USGPO.

Indonesian Cooking: Slamat Makan. Ina D. Hartog. 1981. pap. 15.00 o.s.i. (ISBN 0-911268-39-1). E J Brill USA.

Indonesian-English Dictionary. 2nd ed. John M. Echols & Hassan Shadily. 431p. 1963. 39.50x o.p. (ISBN 0-8014-0112-7). Cornell U Pr.

Indonesian Kitchen. Copeland Marks & Mintari Soeharjo. LC 80-69385. 1981. 12.95 o.p. (ISBN 0-689-11142-8, Atheneum). Macmillan.

Indonesian: The Development & Use of a National Language. Khaidir Anwar. (Illus.). viii, 205p. 1980. pap. 9.50x o.p. (ISBN 0-8214-0770-8). Ohio U Pr.

Indoor Cycling. John Krausz & Vera Van der Reis Krausz. LC 86-11436. 1987. pap. 11.95 o.p. (ISBN 0-385-27931-0). Doubleday.

Indoor-Outdoor Highest Quality Marijuana Grower's Guide. rev. ed. Mel Frank & Ed Rosenthal. LC 81-10942. (Illus.). 96p. 1982. pap. 5.95 o.p. (ISBN 0-915904-59-4). And-Or Pr.

Indoor Photography. Bruce Pinkard. (Illus.). 168p. 1986. 35.95 o.p. (ISBN 0-7134-4160-7, Pub. by Batsford England). David & Charles.

Indoor Plants & How to Grow Them. A. Bertrand. (Illus.). 96p. 1955. (ISBN 0-8022-0118-0). Philos Lib.

Indoor Pollutants. National Research Council Assembly of Life Sciences. 1981. pap. text ed. 16.25x o.p. (ISBN 0-309-03188-5). Natl Acad Pr.

Indroduction to CP-M Assembly Language. 3rd ed. Jon Lindsay. 1985. write for info. o.p. (ISBN 0-8104-5210-3). Sams.

Induced Mutagenesis: Molecular Mechanisms & Their Implications for Environmental Protection. Ed. by Christopher W. Lawrence. LC 82-16706. (Basic Life Sciences Ser.: Vol. 23). 442p. 1983. 75.00x o.p. (ISBN 0-306-41163-6, Plenum Pr). Plenum Pub.

Induced Representations & Banach-Algebraic Bundles. J. M Fell et al. (Lecture Notes in Mathematics: Vol. 582). 1977. soft cover 21.00 o.p. (ISBN 0-387-08147-X). Springer-Verlag.

Induction Heating Handbook. E. J. Davies & P. G. Simpson. 460p. 1978. text ed. 39.95 o.p. (ISBN 0-07-084515-8). McGraw.

Induction Heating Practice. D. Warburton-Brown. (Illus.). 200p. 1956. (ISBN 0-8022-1808-3). Philos Lib.

Induction in Elizabethan Drama. Thelma N. Greenfield. LC 74-11155. 1970. 6.00 o.p. (ISBN 0-87114-053-5). U of Oreg Bks.

Induction in Geometry. L. Golovina & I. Yaglom. 133p. 1979. pap. 2.95 o.p. (ISBN 0-8285-1534-4, Pub. by Mir Pubs USSR). Imported Pubns.

Indus Valley Civilization: A Bibliographic Essay. Ashim K. Roy & N. W. Gidwani. 264p. 1982. text ed. 22.50 o.p. (ISBN 0-391-02562-7). Humanities.

Industrial Abrasive Materials & Compositions. Ed. by M. J. Collie. LC 81-38326. (Chem. Tech. Rev. Ser. 190). (Illus.). 351p. 1981. 45.00 o.p. (ISBN 0-8155-0851-4). Noyes.

Industrial Accident Prevention. 4th ed. Herbert W. Heinrich. 1959. text ed. 29.95 o.p. (ISBN 0-07-028058-4). McGraw.

Industrial Administration & Management. 4th ed. J. Batty et al. (Illus.). 592p. 1979. pap. 28.50x o.p. (ISBN 0-7121-0954-4, Pub. by Macdonald & Evans England). Trans-Atl Phila.

Industrial & Commercial Heat Recovery Systems. Sydney Reiter. 256p. 1983. 31.95 o.p. (ISBN 0-442-27943-4). Van Nos Reinhold.

Industrial & Labor Relations Terms: A Glossary. 4th rev. ed. Robert E. Doherty. LC 79-18839. (ILR Bulletin: No. 44). 40p. 1979. pap. 2.50 o.p. (ISBN 0-87546-075-5). ILR Pr.

Industrial & Manufacturing Chemistry, 3 vols. G. W. Martin & W. Francis. (Illus.). 800p. 1955. (ISBN 0-8022-1068-6). Philos Lib.

Industrial & Organizational Psychology. 4th ed. B. V. Gilmer & Edward L. Deci. (M-H Series in Psychology). (Illus.). 1976. text ed. 32.95 o.p. (ISBN 0-07-023289-X). McGraw.

Industrial Applications of Radioisotopes & Radiation. S. M. Rao et al. 362p. 1986. 29.95 o.p. (ISBN 0-470-20255-6). Halsted Pr.

Industrial Applications of Radioisotopes & Radiation in Czechoslovakia, France, the Soviet Union & the United Kingdom. (Proceedings Ser.). (Illus.). 595p. 1967. pap. 75.75 o.p. (ISBN 92-0-167067-2, ISP598, IAEA). UNIPUB.

Industrial Archaeology: An Historical Survey. Arthur Raistrick. (Illus.). 1972. text ed. 19.95x o.p. (ISBN 0-413-28050-0, NO. 2398, Pub. by Eyre Methuen England). Heinemann Ed.

Industrial Behavior Modification: A Management Handbook. Ed. by Richard O'Brien & Alyce M. Dickinson. 480p. 35.00 o.p. (ISBN 0-686-84781-4). Work in Amer.

Industrial Buying Behavior: Concepts, Issues, & Applications. Rowland T. Moriarty. (Illus.). 208p. 1983. 37.00x o.p. (ISBN 0-669-06212-X). Lexington Bks.

Industrial Capacity & Defense Planning: Sustained Conflict & Surge Capability in the 1980s. Lee D. Olvey & Henry A. Leonard. LC 82-48595. 192p. 1983. 27.00x o.p. (ISBN 0-669-06331-2). Lexington Bks.

Industrial Capital & Chinese Peasants: A Study of the Livelihood of Chinese Tobacco Cultivators. Han-Seng A. Chen. Ed. by Ramon H. Myers. 1980. lib. bdg. 48.00 o.p. (ISBN 0-8240-4266-2). Garland Pub.

Industrial Ceramics. F. Singer. Ed. by S. Singer. 1963. 99.00x o.p. (ISBN 0-412-06610-6, NO. 6582, Pub. by Chapman & Hall England). Routledge Chapman & Hall.

Industrial Change in Advanced Economies: Spatial Perspectives. Ed. by F. E. Hamilton. 336p. 1986. 50.00 o.p. (ISBN 0-7099-3828-4, Pub. by Croom Helm UK). Routledge Chapman & Hall.

Industrial Chemical Exposure: Guidelines for Biological Monitoring. Roberts R. Lauwerys. LC 82-70668. (Illus.). 160p. 1983. text ed. 20.00 o.p. (ISBN 0-931890-10-1, Biomed Pubns). Year Bk Med.

Industrial-Commercial Refrigeration Maintenance. Ed. by C. Brady et al. (Illus.). 226p. 1982. spiral bdg. 45.00x o.p. (ISBN 0-85083-528-3). Trans-Atl Phila.

Industrial Companies. Ed. by Financial Times Staff. 1986. 105.00 o.p.; Standing Order. 94.50 o.p. St James Pr.

Industrial Cooperation Between East & West. Friedrich Levcik & Jan Stankovsky. LC 78-73222. 304p. 1979. 35.00 o.p. (ISBN 0-87332-126-X). M E Sharpe.

Industrial Cooperation Between Poland & the West. John Garland. Ed. by Richard Farmer. LC 84-28070. (Research for Business Decisions Ser: No.71). 216p. 1985. 34.95 o.p. (ISBN 0-8357-1619-8). UMI Res Pr.

Industrial Crafts. Ed. by Richard A. Vorndran. LC 77-73248. 64p. (gr. 7-9). pap. text ed. cancelled o.s.i. (ISBN 0-02-820330-5). Glencoe.

Industrial Democracy & Labour Market Policy in Sweden. John A. Fry. 1979. 46.00 o.p. (ISBN 0-08-022462-8); pap. 25.00 o.p. (ISBN 0-08-022498-9). Pergamon.

Industrial Design. Raymond Loewy. (Illus.). 250p. 1989. pap. 35.00 o.p. Overlook Pr.

Industrial Development Bond Financing 1985, 2 vols, Vol. 220 & 221. Practising Law Institute Staff. 1267p. 1985. pap. 45.00 o.p. (ISBN 0-317-27526-7, J4-3560). PLI.

Industrial Development Bonds: The Fundamental Impact of TEFRA. 346p. 1982. 15.00 o.p. (ISBN 0-318-02439-X). ICLE Georgia.

Industrial Development Handbook. Donald C. Lochmoeller. Ed. by Frank H. Spink, Jr. Dorothy A. Muncy & Oakleigh H. Thorne. LC 75-37218. (Community Builders Handbook Ser.). (Illus.). 256p. 1975. 50.00 o.p. (ISBN 0-87420-562-X, I02); members 37.50 o.p. Urban Land.

Industrial Development of Bengal, 1900-1939. A. Z. Iftikhar-Ul-Awwal. 268p. 1982. text ed. 32.50x o.p. (ISBN 0-7069-1579-8, Pub. by Vikas India). Advent NY.

Industrial Digital Control Systems. Ed. by K. Warwick & D. Rees. (IEE Control Engineering Ser.: NO. 29). 456p. 1986. 60.00 o.p. (ISBN 0-86341-081-2). Inst Elect Eng.

Industrial Electrochemistry. Derek Pletcher. (Illus.). 332p. 1984. 29.00 o.p. (ISBN 0-412-16500-7, NO. 6654, Pub. by Chapman & Hall); pap. 29.95 o.p. (ISBN 0-412-26530-3, NO. 9160, Pub. by Chapman & Hall). Routledge Chapman & Hall.

Industrial Electronics: A Text-Lab Manual. 2nd ed. Paul B. Zbar & Peter Orne. 1951. text ed. 13.70 o.p. (ISBN 0-07-072740-6). McGraw.

Industrial Electronics Handbook. Kretsmann. (Illus.). 192p. 1957. (ISBN 0-8022-0893-2). Philos Lib.

Industrial Energy Conservation: A Selected Bibliography. Anthony G. White. (Architecture Ser.: A 1365). 5p. 1985. 2.00 o.p. (ISBN 0-89028-355-9). Vance Biblios.

Industrial Engineering Manual: For the Textile Industry. 2nd ed. Norbert L. Enrick. LC 77-15461. 270p. 1978. lib. bdg. 26.00 o.p. (ISBN 0-88275-631-1). Krieger.

Industrial Engineering Plant Audit. Wilbert Steffy & Leonard Hawley. (Illus.). 83p. 1977. 12.00 o.p. (ISBN 0-938654-18-7, AUDIT). Indus Dev Inst Sci.

Industrial English. T. C. Jupp & Sue Hodlin. 1975. text ed. 21.00x o.p. (ISBN 0-435-28400-2); pap. text ed. 17.50x o.p. (ISBN 0-435-28401-0). Heinemann Ed.

Industrial Enzymology. T. Godfrey & J. Reichelt. LC 82-14461. 582p. 1982. 100.00 o.p. (ISBN 0-943818-00-1, Stockton Pr). Groves Dict Music.

Industrial Explosion Prevention & Protection. Frank T. Bodurtha. (Illus.). 1980. text ed. 44.00 o.p. (ISBN 0-07-006359-1). McGraw.

Industrial Fasteners Handbook. Ed. by Trade & Technical Press, Ltd. Staff. (Illus.). 175.00x o.p. (ISBN 0-85461-062-6). Trans-Atl Phila.

Industrial Gas Cleaning. 2nd, rev. ed. Werner Strauss. LC 74-8066. 632p. 1976. 155.00 o.p. (ISBN 0-08-017004-8); pap. 155.00 o.p. (ISBN 0-08-019933-X). Pergamon.

Industrial Gases. Norman Booth. LC 72-10293. 1973. pap. 35.00 o.p. (ISBN 0-08-016860-4). Pergamon.

Industrial Golden Egg Goose: One Man's Struggle Against Pollution & Unethical Practices. Robert V. Sherer. 1979. 10.00 o.p. (ISBN 0-682-49304-X). Exposition-Phoenix.

Industrial Groupings in Japan: 1986-87. 7th ed. 590p. 1986. pap. 500.00 o.p. (ISBN 0-8002-4095-2). Intl Pubns Serv.

Industrial Heat Exchangers: Proceedings of 1985 Conference. 423p. 80.00 o.p. (6076L). ASM.

Industrial Housing Systems, an Evaluation: Proceedings of the IAHS Cairo Workshop, 1976. A. Fareed & M. El-Hifnawi. (Illus.). 1979. 60.00 o.p.; pap. 85.00 o.p. (ISBN 0-08-024236-7). Pergamon.

Industrial Innovation & Regional Economic Development. Ed. by J. B. Goddard. 120p. 1980. pap. 19.00 o.p. (ISBN 0-08-026102-7). Pergamon.

Industrial Landscape. David Plowden. LC 85-309. (Illus.). 1985. 39.45 o.p. (ISBN 0-393-01992-6). Norton.

Industrial Laser Annual Handbook. Morris Levitt & David Belforte. 350p. 1987. 125.00 o.p. (ISBN 0-87814-320-3). PennWell Bks.

Industrial Laser Materials Processing Bibliography, 5 vols. 4th ed. Ed. by David A. Belforte. 500p. 1985. pap. text ed. 145.00 o.p. (ISBN 0-916389-05-7). Belforte Assoc.

Industrial Lighting Systems. John P. Frier & Mary E. Frier. (Illus.). 336p. 1980. text ed. 33.50 o.p. (ISBN 0-07-022457-9). McGraw.

Industrial Location Policy: The Indian Experience. Uday Sekhar. (Working Paper Ser.: No. 620). 117p. 1983. 5.00 o.p. (ISBN 0-8213-0273-6, WP 0620). World Bank.

Industrial Management: A Bibliography. Marian Dworaczek. (Public Administration Ser.: P 1790). 58p. 1985. pap. 9.00 o.p. (ISBN 0-89028-590-X). Vance Biblios.

Industrial Management in the Soviet Union: The Role of the CPSU in Industrial Decision-Making, 1917-1970. William J. Conyngham. LC 74-170206. (Publications Ser.: No. 116). 389p. 1973. 12.95x o.p. (ISBN 0-8179-6161-5). Hoover Inst Pr.

Industrial Management Services. H. Beeley. (Illus.). 316p. 1981. pap. 15.95x o.p. (ISBN 0-7121-0942-0). Trans-Atl Phila.

Industrial Marketing & Sales Management in the Computer Age. Robert F. Kelleher. 180p. 1983. 23.95 o.p. (ISBN 0-8436-0867-6). Van Nos Reinhold.

Industrial Marketing Management. 2nd ed. Robert W. Haas. 464p. 1982. text ed. write for info. o.p. (ISBN 0-534-01084-9). PWS-Kent Pub.

Industrial Marketing Management. Michael D. Hutt & Thomas W. Speh. LC 80-65803. 656p. 1981. text ed. 31.95x o.p. (ISBN 0-03-052656-6); Instr's manual 20.00 o.p. (ISBN 0-03-052661-2). Dryden Pr.

Industrial Metric Conversion. Russell F. Jerd. 92p. (Orig.). 1983. pap. text ed. 9.95x o.p. (ISBN 0-89917-391-8). Tichenor Pub.

Industrial Microbiology. Ed. by R. W. Thoma. (Benchmark Papers in Microbiology: Vol. 12). 1982. 59.95 o.p. (ISBN 0-87933-251-4). Van Nos Reinhold.

Industrial Minerals & Rocks. 4th ed. LC 73-85689. 1975. 40.00x o.p. (ISBN 0-89520-028-7). SMM&E Inc.

Industrial Model Building. Gary Lamit. (Illus.). 528p. 1981. text ed. 40.33 o.p. (ISBN 0-13-461566-2). P-H.

Industrial Movement & Regional Development: The British Case. M. E. Sant. 268p. 1975. 34.00 o.p. (ISBN 0-08-017965-7). Pergamon.

Industrial Organic Chemicals in Perspective. Harold A. Wittcoff & Bryan G. Reuben. (2 Pts.). 1983. Set. 105.00 o.p. (ISBN 0-471-80560-2). Wiley.

Industrial Organic Chemicals in Perspective, Part 2: Technology, Formulation & Use. Harold Wittcoff & Bryan G. Reuben. LC 79-19581. 502p. 1980. 84.00 o.p. (ISBN 0-471-05780-0, Pub. by Wiley-Interscience). Wiley.

Industrial Organic Coatings: Update. Business Communications Staff. 230p. 1987. 1750.00 o.p. (C-017R). BCC.

Industrial Organization & Prices. 2nd ed. James V. Koch. (Illus.). 1980. text ed. (ISBN 0-13-462481-5). P-H.

Industrial Organization & Regulation Exams, Puzzles & Problems, Vol. 8. Compiled by Edward Tower. 214p. 1985. 14.00 o.p. (ISBN 0-88024-208-6). Eno River Pr.

Industrial Organization & Regulation Reading Lists, Vol. 7. Compiled by Edward Tower. 206p. 1985. 14.00 o.p. (ISBN 0-88024-207-8). Eno River Pr.

Industrial-Organizational Psychology: 1980 Overview, Vol. 11, No. 3. Ed. by H. Meltzer & Ross Stagner. (Special Issue, Professional Psychology). (Professional Psychology). 16.00 o.p. (ISBN 0-912704-51-9, 2151103). Am Psychol.

Industrial Parks: A Bibliography & Geographical Introduction. Raymond J. Towse. (Public Administration Ser.: P 1793). 29p. 1985. 4.50 o.p. (ISBN 0-89028-593-4). Vance Biblios.

Industrial Policies - Strategy Debate since 1970: General, International & United States, a Selected Bibliography. Ontario Ministry of Treasury & Economics, Library Services Staff. (Public Administration Ser.: P 1806). 17p. 1985. 2.25 o.p. (ISBN 0-89028-636-1). Vance Biblios.

Industrial Policies & Technology Transfers Between East & West. Ed. by C. T. Saunders. (East-West European Economic Interaction, Workshop Paper: Vol 3). (Illus.). 1978. pap. 33.70 o.p. (ISBN 0-387-81456-6). Springer-Verlag.

Industrial Policy: A Bibliography. Joseph J. Galin. (Public Administration Ser.: Bibliography P 1648). 1985. pap. 2.00 o.p. (ISBN 0-89028-338-9). Vance Biblios.

Industrial Pollution Control Handbook. H. F. Lund. 1971. text ed. 86.50 o.p. (ISBN 0-07-039095-9). McGraw.

Industrial Pollution Control: Issues & Techniques. Nancy J. Sell. (Environmental Engineering Ser.). 384p. 1980. 29.95 o.p. (ISBN 0-442-20398-5). Van Nos Reinhold.

Industrial Progress & Human Welfare: The Rise of the Factory System in 19th Century Lancaster. Thomas R. Winpenny. LC 82-10995. 142p. (Orig.). 1982. lib. bdg. 25.25 o.p. (ISBN 0-8191-2628-4); pap. 9.75 o.p. (ISBN 0-8191-2629-2). U Pr of Amer.

Industrial Purchasing Controls for the Small & Medium Sized Firm. Wilbert Steffy et al. (Illus.). 170p. 1980. 12.00 o.p. (ISBN 0-938654-24-1, IND P). Indus Dev Inst Sci.

Industrial Real Estate. 3rd ed. 668p. 25.00 o.s.i. (ISBN 0-317-35671-2, BK 132); members 22.50 o.s.i. (ISBN 0-317-35672-0). Realtors Natl.

Industrial Real Estate. 3rd ed. Society of Industrial Realtors Staff et al. 718p. 23.75 o.p. (ISBN 0-318-15184-7, 35-1003). Natl Assoc Realtors.

Industrial Relations. Michael P. Jackson. 281p. 1977. text ed. 25.00 o.p. (ISBN 0-85664-194-4, Pub. by Croom Helm Ltd). Routledge Chapman & Hall.

Industrial Relations. rev. ed. Michael P. Jackson. 288p. 1982. pap. 10.95 o.p. (ISBN 0-7099-1417-2, Pub. by Croom Helm Ltd). Routledge Chapman & Hall.

Industrial Relations: A Textbook. 3rd ed. Michael P. Jackson. LC 85-14991. 288p. (Orig.). 1985. pap. 14.95 o.p. (ISBN 0-7099-1474-1, Pub. by Croom Helm Ltd). Routledge Chapman & Hall.

Industrial Relations & New Technology. Annette Davies. LC 85-28052. 272p. 1985. 34.50 o.p. (ISBN 0-7099-0882-2, Pub. by Croom Helm Ltd). Routledge Chapman & Hall.

Industrial Relations in Construction. W. S. Hilton. 1968. 29.00 o.p. (ISBN 0-08-013040-2); pap. 14.25 o.p. (ISBN 0-08-013039-9). Pergamon.

Industrial Relations in Europe: The Imperatives of Change. Ed. by B. C. Roberts. LC 85-21321. 288p. 1985. 43.00 o.p. (ISBN 0-7099-4212-5, Pub. by Croom Helm Ltd). Routledge Chapman & Hall.

Industrial Relations in the Future. Ed. by Michael Poole. 180p. (Orig.). 1984. pap. 16.95x o.p. (ISBN 0-7102-0145-1). Routledge Chapman & Hall.

Industrial Relations of Occupational Health & Saftey. Ed. by Breen Creighton & Neil Gunningham. 240p. 1985. 24.95 o.p. (ISBN 0-949614-10-6, Pub. by Croom Helm Ltd). Routledge Chapman & Hall.

Industrial Relations Practices of Foreign-Owned Firms in Britain. Peter J. Buckley & Peter Enderwick. 160p. 1985. 33.00x o.p. (ISBN 0-8448-1478-4, Pub. by Crane Russak & Co). Taylor & Francis.

Industrial Research & Technological Innovation. Ed. by Edwin Mansfield. (Illus.). 1968. 12.95x o.p. (ISBN 0-393-09724-2, NortonC). Norton.

Industrial Research in the United Kingdom. 11th ed. 575p. 1986. 220.00X o.p. (Pub. by Longman). Gale.

Industrial Revolution in France, 1815-1848. Arthur L. Dunham. 1955. 10.00 o.p. (ISBN 0-682-47037-6, University). Exposition-Phoenix.

Industrial Robot Specifications. Andre Cugy & Kogan Page. Ed. by Adrian Ioannou. LC 84-14660. 367p. 1984. text ed. 175.00 o.p. (ISBN 0-8144-7628-7). AMACOM.

Industrial Robots. 2nd, rev. ed. 785p. (Orig.). 1985. pap. 48.00 o.p. (ISBN 0-317-39382-0). Robot Inst Am.

Industrial Robots, Vol. 2. P. Lammineur & O. Cornillie. (EPO Applied Technology Ser.: Vol. 2). (Illus.). 164p. 1984. 65.00 o.p. (ISBN 0-08-031143-1). Pergamon.

Industrial Robots: A Summary & Forecast. 2nd ed. Tech Tran Corporation Staff. (Illus.). 247p. 1983. spiral bound 50.00 o.p. (ISBN 0-918989-04-3). Tech Tran Consult.

Industrial Robots: A Survey of Domestic & Foreign Patents (1969-1983), Vol. 6 (Robotics & Artificial Intelligence Applications Series. Ed. by Justin A. Bereny. LC 85-71672. 250p. (Orig.). 1985. pap. 89.50x o.p. (ISBN 0-89934-230-2, BT021). Busn Tech Info Serv.

Industrial Robots & Robotics. Edward Kafrissen & Mark Stephans. 396p. 1984. 30.95 o.p. (ISBN 0-317-18044-4). Robot Inst Am.

Industrial Robots Symposium, 14th International: Proceedings. 738p. 1984. 126.00 o.p. (ISBN 0-317-18023-1). Robot Inst Am.

Industrial Scheduling Abstracts: 1950-1966. S. Eilon & J. R. King. 1967. 11.75 o.p. (ISBN 0-934454-50-7). Lubrecht & Cramer.

Industrial Sealing Technology. H. H. Buchter. LC 78-2421. 441p. 1979. 64.50 o.p. (ISBN 0-471-03184-4, EM20, Pub. by Wiley-Interscience). Wiley.

Industrial Solid State Electronics: Devices & Systems. Timothy J. Maloney. (Illus.). 1979. text ed. 37.33 o.p. (ISBN 0-13-463406-3). P-H.

Industrial Spying & Espionage. Joseph L. Cook & Earleen H. Cook. (Public Administration Ser.: P-1707). 49p. 1985. pap. 7.50 o.p. (ISBN 0-89028-457-1). Vance Biblios.

Industrial Statistics Yearbook, 1984: Commodity Production Statistics 1975-1984, Vol. II. 815p. 1987. 50.00 o.p. (ISBN 0-317-58057-4, E/F.86.XVII.19). UN.

Industrial Statistics Yearbook, 1984: General Industrial Statistics, Vol. I. 643p. 1987. 50.00 o.p. (ISBN 92-1-061116-0, E.86.XVII.18). UN.

Industrial Systems Engineering & Management in Developing Countries: Proceedings of the International Conference, 3-6 November 1980, Asian Institute of Technology, Bangkok, Thailand. Ed. by M. T. Tabucanon & P. Abdulbhan. Incl. Fracture & Society, Vol. 4: Fracture & Society. 1978. 71.00 o.p. (ISBN 0-08-022146-7). (Illus.). 928p. 1981. 185.00 o.p. (ISBN 0-08-027611-3). Pergamon.

Industrial Technological Development: A Network Approach. Hakan Hakansson. 240p. 1986. 43.00 o.p. (ISBN 0-7099-3763-6, Pub. by Croom Helm Ltd). Routledge Chapman & Hall.

Industrial Toxicology. 3rd rev. ed. Alice Hamilton & Harriet L. Hardy. LC 73-91922. 584p. 1974. 30.00 o.p. (ISBN 0-88416-029-7). Year Bk Med.

Industrial Union Bulletin (Industrial Workers of the World, 2 vols, No. 31. Industrial Workers of the World Staff. 1970. Repr. of 1909 ed. Set. lib. bdg. 160.00x o.p. (ISBN 0-8371-9180-7, IB00). Greenwood.

Industrial Unionist, 2 vols. I.W.W., EmergencyProgram Branches Staff. 1970. Repr. Set. lib. bdg. 155.00x o.p. (ISBN 0-8371-9165-3, IN00). Greenwood.

Industrial Waste Water & Wastes II. Ed. by B. Goransson. 1977. 75.00 o.p. (ISBN 0-08-020954-8). Pergamon.

Industrial Wastewater Management Handbook. Hardam S. Azad. 1976. text ed. 65.00 o.p. (ISBN 0-07-002661-0). McGraw.

Industrial Water Economy. Institution of Chemical Engineers. 1982. 52.50 o.s.i. (ISBN 0-08-028765-4). Pergamon.

Industrial Wood Energy Handbook. Georgia Technical Research Institute Staff & S. Drucker. 272p. 1983. 43.95 o.p. (ISBN 0-442-22085-5). Van Nos Reinhold.

Industrialised Embayments & Their Environmental Problems - a Case Study of Swansea Bay: Proceedings of an Interdisciplinary Symposium Held at University College, Swansea, 26-28 Sept. 1979. Ed. by M. B. Collins et al. LC 80-40507. (Illus.). 608p. 1980. 120.00 o.p. (ISBN 0-08-023992-7). Pergamon.

Industrialization: A New Concept for Housing. C. A. Grubb & M. I. Phares. (Special Studies in U. S. Economic, Social & Political Issues). 1984. pap. text ed. 9.95x o.p. (ISBN 0-8290-1561-2). Irvington.

Industrialization & Growth - The Experience of Large Countries. Hollis Chenery. (Working Paper: No. 539). 38p. 1982. pap. 5.95 o.p. (ISBN 0-8213-0097-0). World Bank.

Industrialization in the Building Industry. Barry J. Sullivan. 280p. 1980. 36.95 o.p. (ISBN 0-442-27941-8). Van Nos Reinhold.

Industrialization of Developing Countries. V. L. Tyagunenko. 363p. 1973. 5.95 o.p. (ISBN 0-8285-0306-0, Pub. by Progress Pubs USSR). Imported Pubns.

Industry, Prices & Markets. W. D. Reekie. 176p. 1979. text ed. 25.00x o.p. (ISBN 0-86003-505-0, Pub. by Philip Allan UK); pap. text ed. 12.50x o.p. (ISBN 0-86003-605-7, Pub. by Philip Allan IK). Humanities.

Industry's Role in Development of Fusion Power: Set of Papers. Atomic Industrial Forum Staff. (Technical & Economic Reports: Fusion). 1984. 375.00 o.p. (ISBN 0-318-02241-9). US Coun Energy Awareness.

Indy 500. Jim Murphy. LC 83-2093. (Illus.). 96p. (gr. 4up). 1983. 11.45 o.s.i. (ISBN 0-89919-151-7, Clarion). HM.

Inelastic Behavior of Composite Materials AMD, Vol. 13. Ed. by Carl T. Herakovich. 212p. 1975. pap. 20.00 o.p. (ISBN 0-685-78343-X, I00093). ASME.

Inelastic Behavior of Pressure Vessel & Piping Components, PVP-PB-028. Ed. by T. Y. Chang & F. Krempl. (Pressure Vessel & Piping Division Ser.: Bk. No. G00136). 1978. 20.00 o.p. (ISBN 0-685-37568-4). ASME.

Inequalities: Proceedings, 3 vols. Ed. by Oved Shisha. Vol. 1, 1967. 54.50 o.p. (ISBN 0-12-640350-3); Vol. 2, 1970. 95.50 o.p. (ISBN 0-12-640302-3); Vol. 3, 1972. 82.50 o.p. (ISBN 0-12-640303-1). Acad Pr.

Inequality: Social Stratification Reconsidered. Lloyd A. Fallers. LC 73-78665. xi, 330p. 1974. pap. text ed. 3.95x o.s.i. (ISBN 0-226-23684-6, P578, Phoen). U of Chicago Pr.

Inerrancy & the Church. Ed. by John Hannah. (Orig.). 1984. pap. 14.95 o.p. (ISBN 0-8024-0327-1). Moody.

Inertia of the Vacuum: A New Foundation for Theoretical Physics. Donald R. McGregor. (Illus.). 96p. 1981. 6.00 o.p. (ISBN 0-682-49722-3, University). Exposition-Phoenix.

Inevitable. Nick H. Edwards. (Illus.). 1980. 5.00 o.p. (ISBN 0-682-49523-9). Exposition-Phoenix.

Inevitable Peace. Carl J. Friedrich. Repr. of 1948 ed. lib. bdg. 35.00x o.p. (ISBN 0-8371-2397-6, FRIN). Greenwood.

Inevitable Revolution. Leo Tolstoy. Tr. by Ronald Sampson. 30p. 1981. lib. bdg. 12.95 o.p. (ISBN 0-88286-140-9); pap. 2.50 o.p. (ISBN 0-88286-115-8). C H Kerr.

Infallibility: The Crossroads of Doctrine. Peter Chirico. LC 82-84593. (Theology & Life Ser.: Vol. 1). pap. 9.95 o.p. (ISBN 0-89453-296-0). M Glazier.

Infancy. Michael E. Lamb & Joseph J. Campos. 272p. 1982. pap. text ed. 10.00 o.p. (ISBN 0-394-32287-8, RanC). Random.

Infancy & Caregiving. Janet Gonzalez-Mena & Dianne W. Eyer. LC 79-91838. (Illus.). 163p. 1980. pap. 10.95 o.p. (ISBN 0-87484-515-7). Mayfield Pub.

Infant & Child Mortality As a Determinant of Fertility: The Policy Implications. Susan H. Cochrane & K. C. Zachariah. (Staff Working Paper: No. 556). 44p. 1983. 3.50 o.p. (ISBN 0-8213-0147-0, WP 0556). World Bank.

Infant Baptism & Adult Conversion. O. Hallesby. 1964. pap. 5.50 o.p. (ISBN 0-8066-0400-X, 10-3346, Augsburg). Augsburg Fortress.

Infant Care: Abstracts of the Literature--Supplement. Tannis M. Williams. 75p. 1974. 6.25 o.p. (ISBN 0-87868-996-6, 9966). Child Welfare.

Infant Colic: What It Is & What You Can Do About It. Christopher Farran. 106p. 1982. 10.95 o.s.i. (ISBN 0-684-17779-X, ScribT). Scribner.

Infant Colic: What It Is & What You Can Do About It. Christopher Farran. 144p. 1984. pap. 5.95 o.p. (ISBN 0-684-18153-3, ScribT). Scribner.

Infant Development: From Theory to Practice. Judith S. Musick & Joanne Householder. 374p. 1986. pap. text ed. (ISBN 0-534-05562-1). Wadsworth Pub.

Infant Nutrition. Ed. by D. H. Merritt. (Benchmark Papers in Human Physiology: Vol. 7). 1976. 69.50 o.p. (ISBN 0-12-787070-9). Acad Pr.

Infant Temperament & Its Relationship to Child Abuse with the First Two Years of Life. Vicki B. Owsley. iii, 51p. 1984. pap. text ed. 6.95x o.p. (ISBN 0-932269-04-4). Wyndham Hall.

Infant-Toddler Growth & Development: A Guide for Training Child Care Workers. rev. ed. Ed. by Audrey Robertson. 26p. (Orig.). 1984. pap. text ed. 10.50 o.p. (ISBN 0-934140-10-3). Toys N Things.

Infanticide. Maria W. Piers. 1978. 7.95 o.p. (ISBN 0-393-01169-0). Norton.

Infanticide & the Handicapped Newborn. Ed. by Dennis J. Horan & Melinda Oelahoyde. 250p. (Orig.). 1982. pap. 7.95 o.p. (ISBN 0-8425-2053-8). Brigham.

Infantile Psychosis & Other Papers: Selected Papers of Margaret Mahler. LC 79-51915. 1979. 40.00x o.p. (ISBN 0-685-22268-3); Vol. 2. (ISBN 0-87668-345-6). Aronson.

Infantry Brigade in Combat: First Brigade, 25th Infantry Division ("Tropic Lightning") in the Third Viet Cong-North Vietnamese Army Offensive, August 1968. Duquesne A. Wolf. (Illus.). 49p. 1984. pap. text ed. 10.00x o.p. (ISBN 0-89745-053-1). Sunflower U Pr.

Infantry in Vietnam. Albert N. Garland. (Vietnam Ser.: No. 1). (Illus.). 319p. 1984. Repr. of 1967 ed. 18.95 o.p. (ISBN 0-89839-065-6). Battery Pr.

Infantryman's Guide to Urban Combat. lib. bdg. cancelled o.s.i. (ISBN 0-8490-3682-8). Gordon Pr.

Infants & Mothers. T. Berry Brazelton. 234p. 1972. pap. 9.95 o.s.i. (ISBN 0-440-54076-3, Delta). Dell.

Infants', Toddlers', Boys' & Girls' Wear. Fairchild Market Research Division Staff. (Fairchild Fact Files Ser.). (Illus.). 55p. 1985. pap. 17.50 o.p. (ISBN 0-87005-522-4). Fairchild.

Infection & the Surgical Patient. Ed. by Hiram C. Polk, Jr. LC 82-4460. (Clinical Surgery International Ser.: Vol. 4). (Illus.). 219p. 1982. text ed. 48.00 o.p. (ISBN 0-443-02517-7). Churchill.

Infection Control: An Integrated Approach. Karen Axnick & Mary Yarbrough. LC 82-24933. (Illus.). 578p. 1983. text ed. 35.95 o.p. (ISBN 0-8016-0411-7). Mosby.

Infection Control & Drug & Antibiotic Review: QRB Special Edition. 80p. 1979. pap. 20.00 o.s.i. (ISBN 0-86688-039-9). Joint Comm Hlthcare.

Infection in Joint Replacement Surgery: Prevention & Management. Nas Ser Eftekhar. (Illus.). 416p. 1983. cloth 70.00 o.p. (ISBN 0-8016-1505-4). Mosby.

Infection in Surgery: Basic & Clinical Aspects. J. McK. Watts et al. (Symposium Ser.). (Illus.). 488p. 1981. text ed. 81.50 o.p. (ISBN 0-443-02246-1). Churchill.

Infection-Prone Hospital Patient. John F. Burke & Gavin Y. Hildick-Smith. 1978. text ed. 22.50 o.p. (ISBN 0-316-11680-7). Little.

Infections & Pregnancy. C. R. Coid. 1978. 128.00 o.p. (ISBN 0-12-179350-8). Acad Pr.

Infectious Blood Diseases of Man & Animals, 2 Vols. David Weinman & Miodrag Ristic. LC 68-18685. 1968. Vol. 1. 98.50 o.p. (ISBN 0-12-742501-2); Vol. 2. 104.00 o.p. (ISBN 0-12-742502-0). Acad Pr.

Infectious Diseases: Epidemiology & Clinical Practice. 3rd ed. A. B. Christie. (Illus.). 1981. text ed. 98.00 o.p. (ISBN 0-443-02263-1). Churchill.

Infectious Diseases in Emergency Medicine. Michael Rolnick & James C. Kane. Date not set. text ed. Appleton & Lange.

Infernal Grove. Malcolm Muggeridge. LC 81-17718. (Chronicles of Wasted Time, Chronicle 2). 1982. 7.25 o.p. (ISBN 0-688-00953-0, Quill NY). Morrow.

Inferno. Dante Alighieri. 48p. (Orig.). 1988. pap. 9.95 o.p. (ISBN 1-55651-427-1); audiocassette tape incl. o.p. (ISBN 1-55651-428-X). Cram Cassettes.

Inferno. Larry Niven & Jerry Pournelle. 1979. lib. bdg. 13.50 o.p. (ISBN 0-8398-2450-5, Gregg). G K Hall.

Infertility: A Common-Sense Guide for the Childless. Andrew Stanway. 224p. (Orig.). 1987. pap. 8.99 o.p. (ISBN 0-7225-1404-2, Pub. by Thorsons (England)). Sterling.

Infertility: A Common-Sense Guide for the Childless. Andrew Stanway. LC 88-34110. 224p. 1988. Repr. lib. bdg. 22.95x o.p. (ISBN 0-8095-7050-5). Borgo Pr.

Infertility: A Couple's Guide to Its Causes & Treatments. Mary Harrison. 1979. 7.95 o.p. (ISBN 0-395-25375-6); pap. 3.95 o.p. (ISBN 0-395-27699-3). HM.

Infidelities. Freda Bright. LC 86-47673. 384p. 1986. 17.95 o.p. (ISBN 0-689-11797-3, Atheneum). Macmillan.

Infill: A Selective Bibliography. Mary E. Huls. (Architecture Ser.: A 1473). 10p. 1985. 2.00 o.p. (ISBN 0-89028-603-5). Vance Biblios.

Infinite & Final Cause of Creation. Emmanuel Swedenborg. Tr. by J. J. Wilkinson from Lat. 235p. Repr. of 1847 ed. cancelled o.s.i. (ISBN 0-915221-12-8). Swedenborg Sci Assn.

Infinite Dimensional Lie Transformation Groups. H. Omori. LC 74-23625. (Lecture Notes in Mathematics: Vol. 427). xi, 149p. 1975. pap. 14.00 o.p. (ISBN 0-387-07013-3). Springer-Verlag.

Infinite Dimensional Linear Systems Theory. R. F. Curtain & A. J. Pritchard. (Lecture Notes in Control & Information Science: Vol. 8). 1978. pap. 19.00 o.p. (ISBN 0-387-08961-6). Springer-Verlag.

Infinite Dreams. Joe W. Haldeman. 1979. pap. 2.25 o.p. (ISBN 0-380-47605-3, 47605-3). Avon.

Infinite Power for Richer Living. Joseph Murphy. 1974. pap. 5.95 o.p. (ISBN 0-13-464396-8, Reward). P-H.

Infinite Riches. Leo Rosten. 1979. text ed. 14.95 o.p. (ISBN 0-07-053983-9). McGraw.

Infinite Thought Projections of Jesus. Alton E. Carpenter. 1975. 10.00 o.p. (ISBN 0-682-48356-7). Exposition-Phoenix.

Infinite Vistas: New Tools for Astronomy. Ed. by James Cornell & John Carr. 256p. 1985. 18.95 o.p. (ISBN 0-684-18287-4, ScribT). Scribner.

Infinite Woman. Edison Marshall. 1976. pap. 1.75 o.p. (ISBN 0-380-00667-7, 29330). Avon.

Infinite Worlds of Giordano Bruno. Antoinette M. Paterson. (Illus.). 240p. 1970. spiral bdg. 29.00x o.p. (ISBN 0-398-01452-3). C C Thomas.

Infinity Concerto. Greg Bear. 352p. 1984. pap. 3.50 o.s.i. (ISBN 0-425-09536-3). Berkley Pub.

Infirmaties of Genius. W. R. Bett. 1952. (ISBN 0-8022-0121-0). Philos Lib.

Inflammation: Mechanisms & Control. Irwin H. Lepow & Peter A. Ward. 1972. 71.50 o.p. (ISBN 0-12-444050-9). Acad Pr.

Inflammatory Bowel Diseases. Ed. by Burton I. Korelitz. (Illus.). 248p. 1982. 36.50 o.p. (ISBN 0-88416-310-5). Year Bk Med.

Inflammatory Process. 2nd ed. Ed. by Benjamin W. Zweifach et al. Vol. 1, 1974. 105.00 o.p. (ISBN 0-12-783401-X); Vol. 2, 1973. 85.00 o.p. (ISBN 0-12-783402-8); Vol. 3, 1974. 89.00 o.p. (ISBN 0-12-783403-6). Acad Pr.

Inflated Self: Human Illusions & the Bibical Call to Hope. David G. Myers. 176p. 1980. 12.95 o.p. (ISBN 0-8164-0459-3); pap. 5.95 o.p. (ISBN 0-8164-2326-1). HarpR.

Inflation: A Study in Stability. J. W. Cumes. 202p. 1975. 50.00 o.p. (ISBN 0-08-018167-8). Pergamon.

Inflation: A World-Wide Disaster. 2nd ed. Irving S. Friedman. 320p. 1980. 12.95 o.p. (ISBN 0-395-30064-9); pap. 6.95 o.p. (ISBN 0-395-29847-4). HM.

Inflation Accounting. Elwood Miller. 240p. 1980. 24.95 o.p. (ISBN 0-442-21909-1). Van Nos Reinhold.

Inflation & Unemployment: Theory, Experience & Policy-Making. Ed. by Victor Argy & John Nevile. (Illus.). 320p. 1985. text ed. 39.95 o.p. Unwin Hyman.

Inflation: Causes, Consequences, & Cures. George W. Wilson. LC 81-47830. (Midland Bks: No. 277). (Illus.). 192p. 1982. 20.00x o.p. (ISBN 0-253-33008-4); pap. 7.50x o.p. (ISBN 0-253-20277-9). Ind U Pr.

Inflation, Deflation, Reflation: Managemnent & Accounting in Economic Uncertainty. J. P. Wilson. 345p. 1980. text ed. 41.00x o.p. (ISBN 0-220-67015-3, Pub. by Busn Bks England). Gower Pub Co.

Inflation, Policy & Unemployment Theory. Edmund S. Phelps. (Illus.). 1972. 15.95x o.p. (ISBN 0-393-09395-6). Norton.

Inflation: The Rising Cost of Living on a Small Planet. Robert Fuller. LC 79-57383. (Worldwatch Papers). 1980. pap. 4.00 o.p. (ISBN 0-916468-33-X). Worldwatch Inst.

Inflation-Wise: How to Do Almost Everything for Less. Christopher A. McLachlan. 1981. pap. 4.95 o.p. (ISBN 0-380-76836-4, 76836-4). Avon.

Inflected English see Fate of French-E in English: The Plural of Nouns Ending in-th.

Influence. Robert B. Cialdini. 1985. pap. write for info. o.p. (ISBN 0-673-15514-5). Scott F.

Influence: How & Why People Agree to Do Things. Robert B. Cialdini. LC 83-21963. 290p. 1985. 15.95 o.p. (ISBN 0-688-01560-3, Guill); pap. 7.95 o.p. Morrow.

Influence of Darwin on Philosophy & Other Essays. John Dewey. 11.50 o.p. (ISBN 0-8446-1153-0). Peter Smith.

Influence of Microstructure on the Properties of Case: Carburized Components. G. Parrish. 1980. 75.00 o.p. (ISBN 0-87170-090-5). ASM.

Influence of Ocular Light Perception on Metabolism in Man & Animal. F. Hollwich. LC 78-17076. (Topics in Environmental Physiology & Medicine Ser.). (Illus.). 1979. 69.50 o.p. (ISBN 0-387-90315-1). Springer-Verlag.

Influence of Photography on American Landscape Painting, 1839-1880. Elizabeth Lindquist-Cock. LC 76-23608. (Outstanding Dissertations in the Fine Arts - 2nd Series - American). (Illus.). 1977. Repr. of 1967 ed. lib. bdg. 58.00 o.p. (ISBN 0-8240-2680-2). Garland Pub.

Influence of the Holy Spirit: The Popular View of the Apostolic Age & the Teaching of the Apostle Paul. Hermann Gunkel. Tr. by Roy A. Harrisville & Philip A. Quanbeck, II. LC 78-20022. 144p. 1979. 3.00 o.p. (ISBN 0-8006-0544-6, 1-544, Fortress). Augsburg Fortress.

Influence of the Mongols of Russia: A Dimensional History. Paul Harrison Silfen. LC 74-76040. 1974. 7.00 o.p. (ISBN 0-682-47969-1, University). Exposition-Phoenix.

Influence of the Sea on the Political History of Japan. George A. Ballard. 312p. 1972. Repr. of 1921 ed. 37.50x o.p. (ISBN 0-7165-2049-4, BBA 02212, Pub. by Irish Academic Pr Ireland). Biblio Dist.

Influence Surfaces of Orthogonal Anisotropic Plates. S. Krug & P. Stein. Tr. by H. Juhl. (Illus., Eng. & Ger.). 1961. 71.50 o.p. (ISBN 0-387-02711-4). Springer-Verlag.

Influence: What It Is & How to Use It. Kenneth L. Higbee & Larry C. Jensen. LC 77-12933. (Illus.). 1978. pap. 0.90 o.p. (ISBN 0-8425-0748-5). Brigham.

Influences on Childbearing Intentions Across the Fertility Career: Demographic & Socioeconomic Factors & the Value of Children. Rodolfo A. Bulatao & James T. Fawcett. Ed. by Sandra E. Ward. LC 83-11693. (Papers of the East-West Population Institute: No. 60-F). x, 152p. (Orig.). 1983. pap. text ed. 3.00 o.p. (ISBN 0-86638-043-4). EW Ctr HI.

Influential Theologians on Wo-Man. William E. Phipps. LC 79-5431. 1980. lib. bdg. 24.25 o.p. (ISBN 0-8191-1383-2); pap. text ed. 10.00 o.p. (ISBN 0-8191-0880-4). U Pr of Amer.

Influentials in Two Border Cities: A Study in Community Decision-Making. William V. D'Antonio & William H. Form. 1965. 22.95 o.p. (ISBN 0-268-00135-9). U of Notre Dame Pr.

Influenza: The Viruses & the Disease. Charles H. Stuart-Harris. LC 76-26808. (Illus.). 252p. 1976. 24.50 o.p. (ISBN 0-88416-124-2). Year Bk Med.

Influenza: Virus Vaccines & Strategy. Ed. by P. Selby. 1976. 40.50 o.p. (ISBN 0-12-635950-4). Acad Pr.

Influenza Viruses & Influenza. Ed. by Edwin D. Kilbourne. 1975. 94.50 o.p. (ISBN 0-12-407050-7). Acad Pr.

Informal "Diplomatic Relations" The Case of Japan & the Republic of China, 1972-1974. David N. Rowe. (Foreign Area Studies: No. 15). 82p. 1975. pap. 15.00 o.p. (ISBN 0-208-09509-8, Archon). Shoe String.

Informal Learning in Elementary Schools. Danny G. Fulks. LC 78-61303. 1978. pap. text ed. 10.00 o.p. (ISBN 0-8191-0606-2). U Pr of Amer.

Informal Logic Examples & Exercises. Malcolm Acock. 263p. 1985. pap. text ed. (ISBN 0-534-04494-8). Wadsworth Pub.

Informal Reading Assessment. Paul C. Burns & Betty D. Roe. 1980. pap. 11.50 o.p. (ISBN 0-395-30574-8). HM.

Informal Sector Employment in Egypt: Employment Opportunities & Equity in Egypt, 7 papers. Mahmoud Abdel-Fadil. Ed. by International Labour Office. (Technical Papers: No. 1). viii, 39p. (Orig.). 1983. Set. pap. 17.50 o.p. (ISBN 92-2-102997-2). Intl Labour Office.

Information & Computer Science. Gerald W. Kimble. LC 74-3316. (Illus.). 1975. text ed. 17.95x o.p. (ISBN 0-03-082833-3). Irvington.

Information & Skill. David Legge & Paul J. Barber. (Essential Psychology Ser.). 1976. pap. 4.50x o.p. (ISBN 0-416-84070-1, NO. 2295). Routledge Chapman & Hall.

Information for Science & Technology: The International Scene. Scott Adams. (Occasional Papers: No. 109). 45p. 1973. pap. 2.00 o.p. (ISBN 0-317-58903-2). U of Ill Lib Info SCi.

Information Linkage Between Applied Mathematics & Industry. Ed. by Peter C. Wang et al. 1979. 65.50 o.p. (ISBN 0-12-734250-8). Acad Pr.

Information Linkage Between Applied Mathematics & Industry II. Ed. by A. L. Schoenstadt et al. LC 80-17975. 1980. 32.00 o.p. (ISBN 0-12-628750-3). Acad Pr.

Information Machine: The United States Information Agency & American Foreign Policy. Robert E. Elder. LC 68-14105. 1968. 15.95x o.p. (ISBN 0-8156-2118-3). Syracuse U Pr.

Information Machines: Their Impact on Man & the Media. Ben H. Bagdikian. 13.25 o.p. (ISBN 0-8446-5845-6). Peter Smith.

Information Management in the Nuclear Industry. Ed. by E. L. Zebroski & R. L. Simard. (Illus.). 94p. 1984. pap. 44.00 o.p. (ISBN 0-08-031483-X). Pergamon.

Information Mechanics. Frederick W. Kantor. LC 77-6747. 397p. 1977. 44.95x o.p. (ISBN 0-471-02968-8, Pub. by Wiley-Interscience). Wiley.

Information-Organization-Power: Management in a Knowledge Society. Dale Zand. Ed. by William R. Newton. (Illus.). 224p. 1981. text ed. 20.95 o.p. (ISBN 0-07-072743-0). McGraw.

Information Please Almana, 1986. 1985. 9.95 o.p. (ISBN 0-395-39461-9); pap. 5.70 o.p. (ISBN 0-395-39462-7). HM.

Information Please Almanac: Atlas & Yearbook 1987. 1986. pap. 5.70 o.p. (ISBN 0-395-42503-4). HM.

Information Please Almanac, 1985. (Illus.). 1984. 9.70 o.p. (ISBN 0-395-36698-4); pap. 5.70 o.p. (ISBN 0-395-36699-2). HM.

Information Policy Primer see Understanding U. S. Information Policy.

Information Processing in Children. Ed. by Sylvia Farnham-Diggory. 1972. 22.00 o.p. (ISBN 0-12-249550-0). Acad Pr.

Information Processing in Motor Skills. R. G. Marteniuk. LC 75-43982. 1976. text ed. 25.95 o.p. (ISBN 0-03-006091-5, HoltC). HR&W.

Information Processing in the Visual Systems of Arthropods. Ed. by R. Wehner. LC 72-91887. 340p. 1973. pap. 32.00 o.p. (ISBN 0-387-06020-0). Springer-Verlag.

Information Processing Management. 2nd ed. Ralph A. Szweda. LC 78-56964. 407p. 1978. text ed. 19.95x o.p. PWS-Kent Pub.

Information Processing Systems for Management. 2nd ed. Donna Hussain & K. M. Hussain. 1985. 39.95x o.p. (ISBN 0-256-03209-2). Irwin.

Information Resources in the Environmental Sciences. Ed. by George S. Bonn. LC 73-75784. (Allerton Park Institute Ser.: No. 18). 238p. 1973. 7.00x o.p. (ISBN 0-87845-037-8). U of Ill Lib Info Sci.

Information Revolution. Ed. by Donald M. Lamberton & Richard D. Lambert. LC 73-89781. (Annals of the American Academy of Political & Social Science: No. 412). 300p. 1974. pap. 7.95 o.p. (ISBN 0-87761-175-0). Am Acad Pol Soc Sci.

Information Sources in Biotechnology. Anita Crafts-Lighty. LC 83-17479. 306p. 1983. 80.00 o.p. (ISBN 0-943818-04-4, Pub by Stockton Pr). Groves Dict Music.

Information Sources on Bioconversion of Agricultural Wastes. (UNIDO Guides to Information Sources: No.33). 84p. 1980. pap. 4.00 o.p. (ISBN 0-686-70500-9, UNID228, UN). UNIPUB.

Information Sources on the Pesticides Industry. 1st Rev. ed. (Guides to Information Sources: No. 10). pap. 5.00 o.p. (UNID280, UNIDO). UNIPUB.

Information Sources, 1985. Ed. by Leslie R. Chase & Faye Henderson. 1984. 59.75 o.p. (ISBN 0-317-16325-6). Info Indus.

Information Sources, 1986. Ed. by Leslie R. Chase & Patti Tuttle. 1985. pap. write for info. o.p. (ISBN 0-942774-22-1). Info Indus.

Information Sources 1988. Ed. by Barbara Van Gorder & Ann Ellis. 1988. 89.95 o.p. (ISBN 0-942774-25-6). Info Indus.

Information Systems Architecture: A System Developer's Primer. William H. Inmon. (Illus.). 288p. 1986. text ed. 48.00 o.p. (ISBN 0-13-464694-0). P-H.

Information Systems Developement: A Systematic Approach. M. Sundburg & G. Goldkuhl. 1981. text ed. 46.67 o.p. (ISBN 0-13-464677-0). P-H.

Information Systems for Planning & Control: Concepts & Cases. J. C. Higgins. 1976. 37.50x o.p. (ISBN 0-7131-3375-9); pap. 23.95x o.p. (ISBN 0-7131-3376-7). Trans-Atl Phila.

Information Technology & Industrial Policy. Jill Hills. 290p. 1984. 30.00 o.p. (ISBN 0-7099-3701-6, Pub. by Croom Helm Ltd). Routledge Chapman & Hall.

Information Technology in a Democracy. Ed. by Alan F. Westin. LC 72-143233. (Studies in Technology & Society). 1971. 32.00x o.s.i. (ISBN 0-674-45435-9). Harvard U Pr.

Information Technology in Health Science Education. Ed. by E. C. De Land. LC 78-7201. 624p. 1978. 95.00x o.p. (ISBN 0-306-31113-5, Plenum Pr). Plenum Pub.

Information Technology: Practice, Potential, Limitations & Effects on the Profession: Proceedings of the 55th Aslib Annual Conference. Ed. by Heather Taylor. 124p. 1983. pap. 19.00 o.p. (ISBN 0-85142-170-9). Learned Info.

Information Technology Research & Development: Critical Trends & Issues. Office of Technology Assessment, Congress of the United States Staff. (Illus.). 368p. 1985. 91.00 o.p. (ISBN 0-08-033648-5, Pub. by PPI). Pergamon.

Information Technology Serving Society, 2 vols. R. L. Chartrand. 1979. Set which also incl. Computers in the Service of Society. 77.00 o.p. (ISBN 0-08-024106-9, PBL). Pergamon.

Information Theory & Reliable Communication. CISM (International Center for Mechanical Sciences), Dept. of Automation & Information, Cambridge, 1970. Ed. by R. Gallager. (CISM Pubns. Ser.: No. 30). (Illus.). 115p. 1973. pap. 12.90 o.p. (ISBN 0-387-81145-1). Springer-Verlag.

Information Theory for Systems Engineers. rev ed. L. P. Hyvaerinen. (Lecture Notes in Operations Research & Mathematical Systems: Vol. 5). 1968. pap. 14.70 o.p. (ISBN 0-387-04254-7). Springer-Verlag.

Information Theory with New Applications. Silviu Guiasu. (Illus.). 1977. text ed. 65.00 o.p. (ISBN 0-07-025109-6). McGraw.

Information to Authors: Editorial Guidelines Reprinted from 246 Medical Journals. Ed. by Harriet Meiss & Doris Jaeger. LC 80-19712. 702p. 1980. pap. 26.00 o.p. (ISBN 0-8067-1251-1). Urban & S.

Information Transfer: ISO Standards Handbook I. International Organization for Standardization Staff. 1979. pap. 15.00 o.p. (ISBN 92-67-10017-3, UM40, UNESCO). UNIPUB.

Information Transmission in the Nervous System. A. M. Uttley. 1979. 34.00 o.p. (ISBN 0-12-709750-3). Acad Pr.

Information U. S. A. Matthew Lesko. LC 82-11080. 990p. 1983. 52.00 o.s.i. (ISBN 0-670-39823-3, Dist. by Penguin). Penguin USA.

Informational Macromolecules: Proceedings of the Symposium, Rutgers University, 1962. Informational Macromolecules Symposium Staff. Ed. by Henry J. Vogel et al. 1963. 77.00 o.p. (ISBN 0-12-722550-1). Acad Pr.

Informe Anual Del Secretario General 1980. OAS, General Secretariat. (Documentos Oficiales de la OEA Ser.: OEA Ser. D III.31). 76p. (Span.). 1980. pap. 20.00 o.p. (ISBN 0-8270-1317-5). OAS.

Informed Argument: A Multi Disciplinary Reader & Guide. Robert K. Miller. 598p. 1986. pap. text ed. 13.00 net o.p. (ISBN 0-15-541460-7, Pub. by HC). HarBraceJ.

Informed Heart. Bruno Bettelheim. 1976. pap. 3.95 o.p. (ISBN 0-380-01302-9, 60049-8, Discus). Avon.

Informed Performer's Directory of Instruction for the Performing Arts. Kat Smith. 320p. 1985. pap. 9.95 o.p. (ISBN 0-380-89804-7). Avon.

Informed Vision: Essays on Learning & Human Nature. David Hawkins. LC 74-81796. 256p. 1974. 8.95x o.p. (ISBN 0-87586-041-9). Agathon.

Informed Writer. Charles Bazerman. LC 80-68140. 320p. 1980. pap. 14.95 o.p. (ISBN 0-395-29715-X). HM.

Infrared Absorption Spectra, 2 vols. Herbert M. Hershenson. Incl. Index for 1945-57. 1959. 43.50 (ISBN 0-12-343250-2). Acad Pr.

Infrared & Raman Spectra of Crystals. G. Turrell. 1972. 91.50 o.p. (ISBN 0-12-705050-7). Acad Pr.

Infrared & Raman Spectra of Polyatomic Molecules see Molecular Spectra & Molecular Structure.

Infrared & Raman Spectroscopy, Pt. A. Edward Brame & Jeanette Graselli. (Practical Spectroscopy Ser.: Vol. 1). 1976. 75.00 o.p. (ISBN 0-8247-6392-0). Dekker.

Infrared Application Manual. 1983. 9.00 o.p. (ISBN 0-318-18019-7, HE 3-1983). Natl Elec Mfrs.

Infrared Detectors. U. S. Specialty Group on Infrared Detectors. Ed. by T. S. Moss & W. L. Wolfe. 1976. 35.00 o.p. (ISBN 0-08-020548-8). Pergamon.

Infrared Physics Three: Papers from the Third International Conference (CIRP 3) Held in Zurich, Switzerland, 23-27 July 1984. Ed. by F. K. Kneubuhl & T. S. Moss. 550p. 1985. pap. 76.00 o.p. (ISBN 0-08-031442-2, Pub. by Aberdeen Scotland). Pergamon.

Infrared Radiation: A Handbook for Applications. M. A. Bramson. LC 66-26812. (Optical Physics & Engineering Ser.). 624p. 1968. 110.00x o.p. (ISBN 0-306-30274-8, Plenum Pr). Plenum Pub.

Infrared Spectra of Labelled Compounds. S. Pinchas & I. Laulicht. 1971. 65.50 o.p. (ISBN 0-12-556650-6). Acad Pr.

Infrared Spectroscopy. Carl D. Slater et al. 1974. write for info. o.p. (ISBN 0-87150-706-4, WG 4091, Pub. by Willard Grant Pr). PWS-Kent Pub.

Infrared Spectroscopy: Experimental Methods & Techniques. J. E. Stewart. 1970. 99.75 o.p. (ISBN 0-8247-1643-4). Dekker.

Infrared Spectroscopy of High Polymers. Rudolph Zbinden. 1964. 67.00 o.p. (ISBN 0-12-776950-1). Acad Pr.

Infrastructure: A Bibliography. Mary E. Huls. (Public Administration Ser.: P 1804). 9p. 1985. 2.00 o.p. (ISBN 0-89028-634-5). Vance Biblios.

Infundibular Cerebrospinal-Fluid Contacting Neurons. I. Vigh-Teichmann & B. Vigh. (Advances in Anatomy, Embryology, & Cell Biology: Vol. 50, Pt. 2). (Illus.). 91p. 1974. pap. 28.40 o.p. (ISBN 0-387-06979-8). Springer-Verlag.

Ingenious Dr. Franklin: Selected Scientific Letters of Benjamin Franklin. Ed. by Nathan G. Goodman. LC 74-81751. 256p. 1974. 24.95x o.p. (ISBN 0-8122-7680-9); pap. 9.95 o.p. (ISBN 0-8122-1067-0). U of Pa Pr.

Ingenue among the Lions: The Letters of Emily Clark to Joseph Hergesheimer. Emily Clark. Ed. by Gerald Langford. 245p. 1965. 13.50x o.p. (ISBN 0-292-73274-0). U of Tex Pr.

Ingmar Bergman: A Critical Biography. Peter Cowie. (Illus.). 352p. 1982. 19.95 o.s.i. (ISBN 0-684-17771-4, ScribT). Scribner.

Ingmar Bergman: A Critical Biography. Peter Cowie. (Illus.). 416p. 1983. pap. 9.95 o.s.i. (ISBN 0-684-18032-4, ScribT). Scribner.

Ingmar Bergman Directs: A Visual Analysis by Halcyon. John Simon. LC 73-12895. (Illus.). 315p. 1974. pap. 4.95 o.p. (ISBN 0-15-644360-0, Harv). HarBraceJ.

Ingredient Substitution Recipe, Bk. 1. A. C. Doyle. 30p. 1984. pap. 4.95 o.p. (ISBN 0-318-00206-X, Pub. by Cookbk Consort). Prosperity & Profits.

Ingredient X. L. C. Schroeter. 1970. 22.00 o.p. (ISBN 0-08-015866-8). Pergamon.

Ingres. Robert Rosenblum & Jean A. Ingres. (Library of Great Painters). (Illus.). 176p. 1985. 45.00 o.p. (ISBN 0-8109-0195-1). Abrams.

Ingres' Sculptural Sytle: A Group of Unknown Drawings see Exhibition Catalogues from the Fogg Art Museum.

Ingrid Bergman: Legends. Sheridan Morley. 14.95 o.p. (ISBN 0-316-58370-7). Little.

Inhabitants of New Hampshire: 1776. Emily S. Wilson. 124p. 1983. pap. 7.95 o.p. (ISBN 0-912606-13-4). Hunterdon Hse.

Inherit the Earth. Irma Walker. LC 81-2856. 276p. (gr. 6 up). 1981. PLB 12.95 o.p. (ISBN 0-689-30834-5, Atheneum). Macmillan.

Inheritance & Natural History. R. J. Berry. (New Natural Ser.). (Illus.). 1978. 14.95 o.s.i. (ISBN 0-8008-4195-6). Taplinger.

Inheritance of Poetry. Gladys L. Adshead & Annis Duff. (Illus.). 424p. (gr. 7-9). 1948. 14.95 o.p. (ISBN 0-395-06537-2). HM.

Inheritors of Alexander the Great. G. Nicholas Tantzos. LC 86-70661. (Illus.). 288p. 1987. 29.95 o.p. (ISBN 0-938311-00-X). Atlantic Intl Pubns.

Inhibition & Destruction of the Microbial Cell. Ed. by W. B. Hugo. 1971. 119.50 o.p. (ISBN 0-12-361150-4). Acad Pr.

Inhibition & Inactivation of Vegetative Microbes. Ed. by F. A. Skinner & W. B. Hugo. (Society of Applied Bacteriology Symposia Ser.: Vol. 1). 1977. 95.50 o.p. (ISBN 0-12-648065-6). Acad Pr.

Inhibition & Learning. R. A. Boakes & M. S. Halliday. 1972. 87.00 o.p. (ISBN 0-12-108050-1). Acad Pr.

Inhibitors of Nucleic Acid Synthesis: Biophysical & Biochemical Aspects. H. Kersten & W. Kersten. (Molecular Biology Biochemistry & Biophysics Ser.: Vol. 18). (Illus.). ix, 184p. 1975. 38.00 o.p. (ISBN 0-387-06825-2). Springer-Verlag.

Inhibitors: Tools in Cell Research Proceedings. Gesellschaft Fuer Biologische Chemie, 20th Colloquium, Mossbach-Baden, 1969. Ed. by T. Buecher & H. Sies. LC 72-100694. 1970. 39.00 o.p. (ISBN 0-387-04441-8). Springer-Verlag.

Inhomogeneous Optical Waveguides. M. S. Sodha & A. K. Ghatak. LC 76-49643. (Optical Physics & Engineering Ser.). (Illus.). 282p. 1977. 65.00x o.p. (ISBN 0-306-30916-5, Plenum Pr). Plenum Pub.

Inhuman Condition. Clive Barker. 192p. 1986. 12.70 o.s.i. (ISBN 0-671-62686-8, Poseidon Pr). S&S.

Inhuman Condition. Clive Barker. 256p. pap. 3.95 o.p. (ISBN 0-671-61270-0). Archway.

INIS: Authority List for Journal Titles. 305p. (Orig.). pap. text ed. 26.00 o.p. (ISBN 92-0-178186-5, IN1114, IAEA). UNIPUB.

INIS: Character Set Representation & Coding Rules. (INIS Reference Ser.: No. 7, Rev. 2). (Illus.). 25p. 1983. pap. text ed. 5.00 o.p. (ISBN 92-0-178282-9, IN7/R2, IAEA). UNIPUB.

INIS: Magnetic Tape Specifications & Record Format. 3rd Rev. ed. (INIS Reference Ser.: No. 9). 29p. 1980. pap. 5.50 o.p. (ISBN 92-0-178380-9, IN9R3, IAEA). UNIPUB.
INIS Reference Series, 16 vols. International Atomic Energy Agency Staff. (Illus.). 1100p. (Orig.). 1969-1974. pap. 72.25 o.p. (ISBN 0-685-02939-5, IAEA). UNIPUB.
Initial Effects of Ionizing Radiations on Cells. Ed. by Robert J. Harris. 1963. 55.00 o.p. (ISBN 0-12-327162-2). Acad Pr.
Initial Graphics Exchange Specification (IGES) Version 3.0. 1986. 55.00 o.p. (ISBN 0-317-52545-X, SP686). Soc Auto Engineers.
Initial Report & Preliminary Recommendations of the National Commission on Nursing. 80p. 1981. 9.00 o.p. (C-654100). Am Hospital.
Initial Value Methods for Boundary Value Problems: Theory & Applications of Invariant Imbedding. Gunther H. Meyer. (Mathematics in Science & Engineering Ser.). 1973. 65.50 o.p. (ISBN 0-12-492950-8). Acad Pr.
Initials & Pseudonyms: A Dictionary of Literary Disguises, 2 Vols. William Cushing. 928p. 1982. Repr. of 1888 ed. Set. 80.00x o.p. (ISBN 0-8103-3962-5). Gale.
Initiates. Paul Virdell. LC 80-70225. 288p. 1981. 11.95 o.p. (ISBN 0-87795-314-7, Arbor Hse). Morrow.
Initiation a la Compatibilite Financiere et Administrative. 3rd canadienne francaise ed. William W. Pyle et al. 1985. 45.95x o.p. (ISBN 0-256-03199-1); 14.95 o.p. (ISBN 0-256-03200-9); 12.95 o.p. (ISBN 0-256-03201-7). Irwin.
Initiation: Stories & Short Novels on Three Themes. Ed. by David Thorburn. 1971. pap. text ed. 7.95 o.p. (ISBN 0-15-541511-5, HC). HarBraceJ.
Injection Molding of Plastics. 2nd ed. (Illus.). 198p. 1984. pap. 36.00 o.p. (ISBN 0-938648-00-4). T-C Pubns CA.
Injection Moulding. Ed. by E. Calvert et al. (E.I.T.B. Instruction Manuals Ser.). (Illus.). 163p. 1982. pap. 39.95x spiral bdg. o.p. (ISBN 0-85083-553-4). Trans-Atl Phila.
Injured on the Job: A Handbook for Massachusetts Workers. 4th rev. ed. MassCOSH Legal Committee. Ed. by Robert M. Schwartz. LC 82-81398. (Illus.). 256p. (Orig.). 1982. pap. 7.00 o.p. (ISBN 0-9608416-3-6). Mass Coalition.
Injuries of the Ligaments & Their Repair: Hand-Knee-Foot. Ed. by George Chapchal. LC 77-76624. (Illus.). 252p. 1977. 36.00 o.p. (ISBN 0-88416-133-1). Year Bk Med.
Injuries to the Major Branches of the Peripheral Nerves of the Forearm. 2nd ed. Morton Spinner. (Illus.). 278p. 1978. write for info. o.p. (ISBN 0-7216-8524-2). Saunders.
Injury Fact Book. Susan P. Baker et al. LC 82-49194. (Insurance Institute for Highway Safety Bk.). 352p. 1984. 37.00x o.p. (ISBN 0-669-06426-2). Lexington Bks.
Injury to Insult: Unemployment, Class, & Political Response. Kay L. Schlozman & Sidney Verba. (Illus.). 1979. 29.50x o.p. (ISBN 0-674-45441-3). Harvard U Pr.
Ink Bottles & Inkwells. William E. Covill, Jr. LC 72-165308. (Illus.). 71. lib. bdg. 22.50x o.p. (ISBN 0-88492-004-6). W S Sullwold.
Ink-Line Sketching. Paul Laseau. LC 86-7743. (Illus.). 160p. 1986. pap. 20.95 o.p. (ISBN 0-442-25968-9). Van Nos Reinhold.
Ink-Stone: A P. G. Wodehouse Haiku Book. Harold J. Isaacson. LC 83-90815. 163p. 1986. 10.00 o.p. (ISBN 0-533-05826-0). Vantage.
Inkle Weaving. Helene Bress. LC 74-8426. (Illus.). 214p. 1974. pap. 11.95 o.s.i. (ISBN 0-684-16732-8). Scribner.
Inkle Weaving: A Comprehensive Manual. Lavinia Bradley. (Illus.). 90p. 1983. pap. 7.95 o.p. (ISBN 0-7100-9086-2). Routledge Chapman & Hall.
Inklings: C. S. Lewis & His Friends. Humphrey Carpenter. 1979. 10.95 o.p. (ISBN 0-395-27628-4). HM.
Inklings: C. S. Lewis, J. R. R. Tolkien & Their Friends. Humphrey Carpenter. 256p. 1981. pap. 3.50 o.s.i. (ISBN 0-345-29552-8). Ballantine.
Inland Waters of Latin America. R. Zeisler & G. D. Ardizzone. (Commission for Inland Fisheries of Latin America (COPESCAL): Technical Papers: No. 1). 179p. (Eng. & Span.). 1979. pap. 12.25 o.p. (ISBN 92-5-000780-9, F1831, FAO). UNIPUB.
Inland Waterways of the Netherlands, 3 vols. E. E. Benest. (Illus.). 1966-71. 40.00 set o.s.i. (ISBN 0-685-36177-2). E J Brill USA.
Inlays, Crowns & Bridges. 3rd ed. Kantorowicz. 220p. 1985. 31.00 o.p. (ISBN 0-7236-0499-1, Pub. by John Wright UK). Butterworth.
Inmarypraise. Gunter Grass. Tr. by Christopher Middleton from Ger. (Helen & Kurt Wolff Bk.). (Illus.). 88p. 1974. 15.00 o.s.i. (ISBN 0-15-144406-4). HarBraceJ.
Inmates. John Powys. 1952. (ISBN 0-8022-2007-X). Philos Lib.
Innards & Other Variety Meats. Jana Allen & Margaret Gin. LC 73-91942. (Illus.). 144p. 1974. 7.95 o.s.i. (ISBN 0-912238-49-6, One Hund One Prods); pap. 4.95 o.p. (ISBN 0-912238-48-8). Ortho.
Inner City Regeneration. Robert K. Home. (Illus.). 208p. 1982. 33.00 o.p. (ISBN 0-419-12150-1, NO. 3684, Pub. by E & FN Spon); pap. 13.95 o.p. (ISBN 0-419-12160-9, NO. 3685). Routledge Chapman & Hall.
Inner-City Schools: Children, Teachers & Parents. C. Turney et al. 1979. pap. 17.00x o.p. (ISBN 0-424-00052-0, Pub. by Sydney U Pr). Intl Spec Bk.
Inner City Teaching. C. Turney & C. Ryan. 1979. pap. 14.00x o.p. (ISBN 0-424-00053-9, Pub. by Sydney U Pr). Intl Spec Bk.
Inner Eye of Alfred Stieglitz. Robert E. Haines. LC 82-13641. (Illus.). 170p. (Orig.). 1983. lib. bdg. 29.25 o.p. (ISBN 0-8191-2717-5); pap. text ed. 12.25 o.p. (ISBN 0-8191-2718-3). U Pr of Amer.
Inner Game of Skiing. W. Timothy Gallwey & Robert Kriegel. 1979. pap. 4.50 o.p. (ISBN 0-553-25752-8). Bantam.
Inner House. 199p. 1986. 15.00 o.p. (ISBN 0-947898-25-5). Kraus Repr.
Inner I. Terry L. Temes. 48p. (Orig.). 1983. pap. 4.00 o.p. (ISBN 0-682-49936-6). Exposition-Phoenix.
Inner Landscape. Michael Gilbert. 5.50 o.p. (ISBN 0-317-52041-5). Jelm Mtn.
Inner Landscapes: The Theater of Sam Shepard. Ron Mottram. LC 84-50795. 184p. 1985. pap. 8.95 o.p. (ISBN 0-8262-0452-X). U of Mo Pr.
Inner Life. Andrew Murray. 144p. 1984. pap. 4.95 o.p. (ISBN 0-310-29751-6, 10364P). Zondervan.
Inner Limits of Mankind: Heretical Reflections on Today's Values, Culture & Politics. Ervin Laszlo. LC 77-30732. 1978. 31.00 o.p. (ISBN 0-08-023013-X); pap. 13.00 o.p. (ISBN 0-08-023012-1). Pergamon.
Inner Man. Martin Walser. Tr. by Leila Vennewitz from Ger. LC 84-672. 288p. 1985. 15.95 o.p. (ISBN 0-03-059373-5). H Holt & Co.
Inner Parent: Raising Ourselves, Raising Our Children. Susan Isaacs & Marti Keller. 1979. 9.95 o.p. (ISBN 0-15-144423-4). HarBraceJ.
Inner Path from Where You Are to Where You Want to Be: A Spiritual Odyssey. Terry Cole-Whittaker. LC 84-42930. 239p. 1986. 14.95 o.p. (ISBN 0-89256-283-8). Rawson Assocs.
Inner Paths. Himalayan International Institute Staff. 110p. pap. 3.95 o.p. (ISBN 0-89389-049-9). Himalayan Pubs.
Inner Planets. Clark R. Chapman. LC 76-58914. (Illus.). 1977. encore ed. 3.95 o.p. (ISBN 0-684-14898-6, ScribT). Scribner.
Inner Sanctuary. Charles Ross. 1967. pap. 3.95 o.p. (ISBN 0-85151-042-6). Banner of Truth.
Inner-Shell & X-Ray Physics of Atoms & Solids. Ed. by Derek J. Fabian et al. LC 81-11945. (Physics of Atoms & Molecules Ser.). 976p. 1981. 145.00x o.p. (ISBN 0-306-40819-8, Plenum Pr). Plenum Pub.
Inner Source: Exploring Hypnosis with Dr. Herbert Spiegel. Donald S. Connery. 1982. 15.50 o.s.i. (ISBN 0-03-046496-X). H Holt & Co.
Inner Source: Exploring Hypnosis with Dr. Herbert Spiegel. Donald S. Connery. 1984. pap. 7.95 o.s.i. (ISBN 0-03-000439-X, Owl Bks). H Holt & Co.
Inner Space: The Wonder of You. Judith Geller. (Student Scientist Ser.). (gr. 7-12). 1978. PLB 10.97 o.p. (ISBN 0-8239-0445-8). Rosen Group.
Inner Speech & Thought. A. N. Sokolov. LC 69-17679. (Illus.). 294p. 1972. 50.00x o.p. (ISBN 0-306-30529-1, Plenum Pr); pap. 14.95x o.p. (ISBN 0-306-20013-9). Plenum Pub.
Inner Speech & Thought. A. N. Sokolov. LC 74-26701. 294p. 1975. pap. text ed. 14.95x o.p. (ISBN 0-306-20013-9, Plenum Pr). Plenum Pub.
Inner World. Gopi Krishna. 12p. 1978. pap. 3.95 o.p. (ISBN 0-88697-001-6). Life Science.
Inner World of Reading. Dan Ungaro & Michele Borba. 110p. (Orig.). 1987. pap. text ed. 11.50x o.p. (ISBN 0-87562-090-6). Spec Child.
Inner World of the Middle-Aged Man. Peter Chew. 1977. pap. 4.95 o.p. (ISBN 0-395-25857-X). HM.
Innocence. Harriet Daimler. LC 82-84627. 152p. 1983. pap. 3.50 o.s.i. (ISBN 0-394-62436-X, B490, BC). Grove.
Innocent Blood. P. D. James. 1980. 10.95 o.s.i. (ISBN 0-684-16591-0, ScribT). Scribner.
Innocent Eye: Childhood in Mark Twain's Imagination. Albert E. Stone. LC 79-103991. xi, 289p. 1970. Repr. of 1961 ed. 27.50 o.p. (ISBN 0-208-00820-9, Archon). Shoe String.
Innocent Killers. Jane Van Lawick-Goodall & Hugo Van Lawick-Goodall. 1973. 12.95 o.p. (ISBN 0-395-12109-4). HM.
Innocent Millionaire. Stephen Vizinczey. LC 84-45816. 370p. 1985. 17.95 o.p. (ISBN 0-87113-015-7). Atlantic Monthly.
Innocent Three, Church Defender. Charles E. Smith. LC 79-88939. 1971. Repr. of 1951 ed. lib. bdg. 59.50x o.p. (ISBN 0-8371-3145-6, SMIN). Greenwood.
Innocents. Georges Simenon. LC 73-16004. (Helen & Kurt Wolff Bk.). 1974. 6.50 o.p. (ISBN 0-15-144430-7). HarBraceJ.
Innocents. Carolyn Slaughter. 256p. 1986. 16.95 o.p. (ISBN 0-684-18643-8). Scribner.
Innovation & Australian Industrial Relations. Chris Fisher. 226p. 1983. 24.95 o.p. (ISBN 0-949614-00-9, Pub. by Croom Helm Ltd); pap. 12.95 o.p. (ISBN 0-949614-01-7). Routledge Chapman & Hall.
Innovation & Change in Reading Instruction. Ed. by Helen M. Robinson. LC 68-4728. (National Society for the Study of Education Yearbooks Ser: No. 67, Pt. 2). 1968. lib. bdg. 8.00x o.s.i. (ISBN 0-226-60092-0). U of Chicago Pr.
Innovation & Employment. David Foster. 1980. 35.00 o.p. (ISBN 0-08-022500-4); pap. 16.00 o.p. (ISBN 0-08-022499-7). Pergamon.
Innovation, Competition & Government Policy in the Semiconductor Industry. Robert W. Wilson et al. LC 80-8317. 240p. 1980. 27.00x o.p. (ISBN 0-669-03995-0). Lexington Bks.
Innovation Diffusion: A New Perspective. Lawrence A. Brown. LC 80-49706. 375p. 1981. 25.00 o.p. (ISBN 0-416-74270-X, NO. 3469). Routledge Chapman & Hall.
Innovation in Teacher Education. Ed. by C. Turney. 1977. pap. 27.00x o.p. (ISBN 0-424-00032-6, Pub. by Sydney U Pr). Intl Spec Bk.
Innovation Through Recession: SRHE Annual Conference, 1982. Ed. by Geoffrey Squires. 125p. 1983. 24.00x o.p. (ISBN 0-900868-98-8, Open Univ Pr). Taylor & Francis.
Innovations & Organizations. Gerald Zaltman et al. LC 84-797. 224p. 1984. Repr. of 1973 ed. 21.50 o.p. (ISBN 0-89874-719-8). Krieger.
Innovations in Banking: Business Strategies & Employee Relations. Timothy Morris. 176p. 1986. 43.00 o.p. (ISBN 0-7099-4607-4, Pub. by Croom Helm Ltd). Routledge Chapman & Hall.
Innovations in Client-Centered Therapy. David A. Wexler & Laura N. Rice. LC 74-10538. (Personality Processes Ser.). 517p. 1974. 61.95x o.p. (ISBN 0-471-93715-0, Pub. by Wiley-Interscience). Wiley.
Innovations in Construction & Maintenance of Transportation Facilities. (Special Report). 175p. 1974. 7.40 o.p. (ISBN 0-309-02297-5). Transport Res Bd.
Innovations in Diagnostic Radiology. Alexander R. Margulis & Charles A. Gooding. (Continuing Medical Education Ser.). 1981. 90.00 o.p. (ISBN 0-12-788491-2). Acad Pr.
Innovations in Education: Reformers & Their Critics. 4th ed. John M. Rich. 400p. 1984. pap. text ed. write for info. o.p. (ISBN 0-205-08206-8, 238206). Allyn.
Innovations in Helping Chronic Patients: College Students in a Mental Institution. Julian Rappaport et al. 1971. 49.00 o.p. (ISBN 0-12-581150-0). Acad Pr.
Innovations in Mental Health Services to Disaster Victims. Ed. by Mary Lystak. (DHHS Publication Ser.: No. ADM 85-1390). (Illus.). 187p. 1985. pap. 4.00 o.p. (ISBN 0-318-19944-0, S/N 017-024-01269-6). USGPO.
Innovations in Patient Care: An Action Research Study of Change in a Psychiatric Hospital. Ed. by David Towell & Clive Harries. 228p. 1979. 25.00 o.p. (ISBN 0-85664-692-X, Pub. by Croom Helm Ltd). Routledge Chapman & Hall.
Innovations in Policing. Mollie Weatheritt. 256p. 1986. 29.00 o.p. (ISBN 0-7099-4044-0, Pub. by Croom Helm Ltd). Routledge Chapman & Hall.
Innovations in Subsurface Exploration of Soils: Five Reports. (Transportation Research Report Ser.). 85p. 1976. 2.40 o.p. (ISBN 0-309-02495-1). Transport Res Bd.
Innovations in Tax Policy & Other Essays. C. Lowell Harriss. LC 72-81472. 1972. pap. 3.50 o.s.i. (ISBN 0-686-05016-9). Lincoln Inst Land.
Innovations In Telecommunications. Ed. by Jamal T. Manassah. LC 81-20608. (International Symposium on the Kuwait Foundation Ser.). 1982. Pt. A. 69.50 o.p. (ISBN 0-12-467401-1); Pt. B. 77.00 o.p. (ISBN 0-12-467402-X). Acad Pr.
Innovations in the Care of the Elderly. Ed. by Bernard Isaacs & Helen Evers. LC 84-45554. 192p. 1984. 28.00 o.p. (ISBN 0-7099-1310-9, Pub. by Croom Helm Ltd); pap. 15.00 o.p. (ISBN 0-7099-1317-6). Routledge Chapman & Hall.
Innovations in the Water & Wastewater Fields. Ed. by E. A. Glysson et al. (Illus.). 240p. 1984. text ed. 44.95 o.p. (ISBN 0-250-40645-4). Butterworth.
Innovations in Transportation System Planning: Seven Reports. (Transportation Research Record Ser.). 85p. 1976. 3.80 o.p. (ISBN 0-309-02496-X). Transport Res Bd.
Innovative Approaches to Mined Land Reclamation. Ed. by Claire L. Carlson & James H. Swisher. (Illus.). 768p. 1987. text ed. 50.00x o.p. (ISBN 0-8093-1381-2). S Ill U Pr.
Innovative Computer Developments & Their Impact on Organizations. Ed. by H. F. Wedde. 1986. pap. 18.50 o.p. (ISBN 0-08-034068-7, Pub. by PPL). Pergamon.
Innovative Counseling: A Handbook of Readings. 1986. pap. text ed. 16.00 o.p. (ISBN 0-911547-98-3). Am Assn Coun Dev.
Innovative Electric Rates: Issues in Cost-Benefit Analysis. Sanford V. Berg. LC 82-47751. 352p. 1983. 38.00x o.p. (ISBN 0-669-04835-6). Lexington Bks.
Innovative Reporting in Foreign Currency Translation. Denise M. Guithues. Ed. by Richard Farmer. LC 85-22757. (Research for Business Decisions: No. 85). 140p. 1985. 39.95 o.p. (ISBN 0-8357-1720-8). UMI Res Pr.
Innovative Therapies in the Care of the Terminally Ill & Bereaved. Judith M. Stillion. (Death Education, Aging & Health Care Ser.). 225p. cancelled o.s.i. (ISBN 0-89116-629-7). Hemisphere Pub.
Innovative Work Practices. Robert H. Guest. (Work in America Institute Studies in Productivity: No. 21). 56p. 1982. pap. 39.00 o.s.i. (ISBN 0-08-029502-9, L120). Pergamon.
Inoculate! Neil Bayne. 1979. pap. 2.25 o.p. (ISBN 0-8439-0664-2, Pub. by Leisure Bks CT). Dorchester Pub Co.
Inorganic & Analytical Chemistry. Ed. by F. Boschke. LC 51-5497. (Topics in Current Chemistry: Vol. 26). (Illus.). 125p. 1972. pap. 26.70 o.p. (ISBN 0-387-05589-4). Springer-Verlag.
Inorganic & Analytical Chemistry. Ed. by F. Boschke et al. LC 51-5497. (Topics in Current Chemistry: Vol. 14, Pt. 1). (Illus.). 1970. pap. 27.20 o.p. (ISBN 0-387-04816-2). Springer-Verlag.
Inorganic & Nuclear Chemistry: H. H. Hyman Memorial Volume. Ed. by J. J. Katz. 1976. 95.00 o.p. (ISBN 0-08-020637-9). Pergamon.
Inorganic Biochemistry. E. T. Degens et al. LC 76-2616. (Topics in Current Chemistry: Vol. 64). 1976. 42.00 o.p. (ISBN 0-387-07636-0). Springer-Verlag.
Inorganic Biological Crystal Growth. Ed. by B. Pamplin. (Illus.). 284p. 1981. 73.00 o.p. (ISBN 0-08-028420-5, C999, H210, H999). Pergamon.
Inorganic Chemistry. Ed. by J. D. Dunitz et al. (Structure & Bonding Ser.: Vol. 14). (Illus.). iii, 176p. 1973. pap. 38.00 o.p. (ISBN 0-387-06162-2). Springer-Verlag.
Inorganic Chemistry. E. Fluck et al. Ed. by F. Boschke. LC 51-5497. (Topics in Current Chemistry: Vol. 35). (Illus.). 129p. 1973. pap. 24.30 o.p. (ISBN 0-387-06080-4). Springer-Verlag.
Inorganic Chemistry in Nonaqueous Solvents. A. K. Holliday & A. G. Massey. 1965. text ed. 17.75 o.p. (ISBN 0-08-011335-4); pap. text ed. 7.75 o.p. (ISBN 0-08-011334-6). Pergamon.
Inorganic Chemistry of Vitamin B1120. J. M. Pratt. 1972. 66.00 o.p. (ISBN 0-12-564050-1). Acad Pr.
Inorganic Determinations Including Photometric Methods. (Illus.). 1972. Repr. of 1959 ed. 41.50 o.p. (ISBN 0-317-59531-8). Krieger.
Inorganic Hydrides. B. L. Shaw. 1967. 35.00 o.p. (ISBN 0-08-012110-1); pap. 35.00 o.p. (ISBN 0-08-012109-8). Pergamon.
Inorganic Plant Nutrition. Hugh G. Gauch. LC 72-76542. 488p. 1982. 55.95 o.p. (ISBN 0-87933-003-1). Van Nos Reinhold.
Inorganic Polymers. Business Communications Staff. 1988. 1950.00 o.p. (ISBN 0-89336-556-4, C-051). BCC.
Inorganic Reaction Chemistry: Reactions of the Elements & Their Compounds, Vol. 2A. D. T. Burns & A. Townshend. Ed. by A. H. Carter. LC 80-42049. (Ellis Horwood Series in Analytical Chemistry). 300p. 1981. 90.00x o.p. (ISBN 0-470-27105-1). Halsted Pr.
Inorganic Reaction Chemistry: Systematic Chemical Separation, Vol. 1. D. T. Burns et al. (Analytical Chemistry Ser.). 248p. 1981. pap. 31.95 o.p. (ISBN 0-470-27237-6). Halsted Pr.
Inorganic Sulphur Chemistry. Ed. by Graham Nickless. 770p. 1969. 179.00 o.p. (ISBN 0-444-40684-0). Elsevier.
Inorganic Syntheses, Vol. 18. Ed. by Brodie E. Douglas. LC 39-23015. (Inorganic Syntheses Ser.). 238p. 1977. 45.95x o.p. (ISBN 0-471-03393-6, Pub. by Wiley-Interscience). Wiley.
Inpatient Utilization of Short-Stay Hospitals by Diagnosis, United States, 1984. Edmund J. Graves. LC 83-600256. (DHHS Publication PHS 87 Ser.: No. 1750). (Illus.). 85p. 1987. pap. 4.50 o.p. (ISBN 0-318-22907-2, S/N 017-022-00996-0). USGPO.
Input-Output. Bates. (Infotech Computer State of the Art Reports). 524p. 1975. 61.00 o.p. (ISBN 0-08-028499-X). Pergamon.

Titles

Input-Output Analysis & the Structure of Income Distribution. K. Miyazawa. (Lecture Notes in Economics & Math Systems: Vol. 116). 150p. 1976. pap. 13.00 o.p. (ISBN 0-387-07613-1). Springer-Verlag.

Input-Output Approaches in Global Modeling: Proceedings of the Fifth IIASA Symposium on Global Modeling, Sept. 26-29,1977. Ed. by G. Bruckmann. (IIASA Proceedings: Vol. 9). (Illus.). 518p. 1980. 140.00 o.p. (ISBN 0-08-025663-5). Pergamon.

Inquiries into Child Language. Diane N. Bryen. 400p. 1982. text ed. 39.00 o.p. (ISBN 0-205-07642-4, 2476428). Allyn.

Inquiring Man. 3rd ed. Don Bannister & Fay Fransella. LC 85-22410. 224p. 1986. 29.00 o.p. (ISBN 0-7099-3950-7, Pub. by Croom Helm Ltd); pap. 13.50 o.p. (ISBN 0-7099-3951-5). Routledge Chapman & Hall.

Inquiring Mind: An Introduction to Epistemology. George Boas. LC 58-6815. (Paul Carus Lectures Ser.). 437p. 1959. 14.95 o.p. (ISBN 0-87548-099-3). Open Court.

Inquiry into Life. 4th ed. Sylvia S. Mader. 864p. 1985. text ed. write for info. o.p. (ISBN 0-697-04798-9). Wm C Brown.

Inquiry into the Human Prospect. Robert L. Heilbroner. LC 73-21879. 150p. 1974. pap. 2.95x expanded ed. o.p. (ISBN 0-393-09217-8). Norton.

Inquiry into the Human Prospect. Robert L. Heilbroner. 1979. 10.95 o.p. (ISBN 0-393-01256-5, Pub. by Roto-Vision Switzerland). Norton.

Inquiry into the Nature & Progress of Rent & the Principles by Which It Is Regulated: A Greenwood Archival Edition. Thomas R. Malthus. 1970. Repr. of 1915 ed. lib. bdg. 35.00x o.p. (ISBN 0-8371-2362-3, MANR). Greenwood.

Inquisition: The Hammer of Heresy. Edward Burman. 256p. 1984. 15.00 o.p. (ISBN 0-85030-377-X, Pub. by Thorsons UK). Weiser.

Inquisitors. Jerzy Andrzejewski. Tr. by Konrad Syrop from Polish. LC 76-6896. 1976. Repr. of 1960 ed. lib. bdg. 22.50x o.p. (ISBN 0-8371-8868-7, ANIN). Greenwood.

Ins & Outs & Wins of Contract Bridge. Ira Martin. 1977. 6.00 o.p. (ISBN 0-682-48900-X). Exposition-Phoenix.

Ins & Outs of On-Track & Off-Track Horse Race Betting. Kaplan & Loughrey. 1971. 5.00x o.p. (ISBN 0-87526-084-5). Gould.

Ins & Outs of Ups & Downs. Ira L. Fox. LC 82-90730. 1983. 10.95 o.p. (ISBN 0-87212-170-4). Libra.

Ins, Outs & Ups of Venture Capital. Howard S. Kossak. LC 86-914010. 96p. 1986. text ed. 16.00 o.p. (ISBN 0-682-40310-5). Exposition-Phoenix.

Inscape & Landscape: The Human Perception of Environment. Pierre Dansereau. LC 75-9990. 118p. 1975. 21.00x o.p. (ISBN 0-231-03991-3); pap. 14.00x o.p. (ISBN 0-231-03992-1). Columbia U Pr.

Inscription in Fifteenth-Century Florentine Painting. Dario A. Covi. Ed. by S. J. Freedberg. (Outstanding Dissertations in Fine Arts Ser.). (Illus.). 800p. 1985. Repr. of 1958 ed. lib. bdg. 95.00 o.p. (ISBN 0-8240-6853-X). Garland Pub.

Inscripts. Samuel Hazo. LC 75-14553. xiv, 140p. 1975. 10.00x o.p. (ISBN 0-8214-0199-8); pap. 6.00 o.p. (ISBN 0-8214-0205-6, 82-82055). Ohio U Pr.

Inscrutable Earth: Explorations into the Science of Earth. Ronald B. Parker. 240p. 1984. 14.95 o.s.i. (ISBN 0-684-18173-8, ScribT). Scribner.

Insearch: Discovering the Real You. Frances Coe & Ivan Coe. 112p. 1981. 6.50 o.p. (ISBN 0-682-49713-4, Testament). Exposition-Phoenix.

Insect & Plant Viruses: An Atlas. Ed. by Karl Maramorosch. 1978. 77.00 o.p. (ISBN 0-12-470275-9). Acad Pr.

Insect Development. P. A. Lawrence. LC 76-8196. (Royal Entomological Society of London Symposium Ser.). 230p. 1976. 26.75 o.p. (ISBN 0-470-15098-X, John Wiley). Krieger.

Insect Diseases, Vol. 1. Ed. by George Cantwell. LC 73-90772. 326p. 1974. 69.75 o.p. (ISBN 0-8247-6117-0). Dekker.

Insect Ecology. Rev. ed. E. G. Matthews & R. L. Kitching. LC 83-7015. (Australian Ecology Ser.). (Illus.). 212p. 1984. pap. text ed. 15.95x o.p. (ISBN 0-7022-1812-X). U of Queensland Pr.

Insect Friends & Enemies. Margaret M. Anderson. (Illus.). 64p. 1981. 7.50 o.p. (ISBN 0-682-49689-8). Exposition-Phoenix.

Insect-Fungus Symbiosis: Nutrition, Mutualism & Commensalism. Ed. by Lekh R. Batra. LC 78-20640. (Illus.). 276p. 1979. text ed. 47.95x o.p. (ISBN 0-470-26671-6). Halsted Pr.

Insect Herbivory. I. D. Hodkinson & M. K. Hughes. LC 82-9525. (Outline Studies in Ecology). (Illus.). 80p. 1982. pap. 8.50 o.p. (ISBN 0-412-23870-5, NO. 6751, Pub. by Chapman & Hall). Routledge Chapman & Hall.

Insect Hormones. 2nd ed. J. Vladimir Novak. 1975. 65.00 o.p. (ISBN 0-412-11630-8, NO. 6211, Pub. by Chapman & Hall). Routledge Chapman & Hall.

Insect Hormones & Bioanalogues. K. Slama et al. LC 72-94418. (Illus.). 500p. 1974. pap. 69.00 o.p. (ISBN 0-387-81112-5). Springer-Verlag.

Insect Juvenile Hormones: Chemistry & Action, Proceedings of the Symposium, Washington, D.C., 1971. Chemistry & Action of Insect Juvenile Hormones Symposium Staff. Ed. by Julius J. Menn & Morton Beroza. 1972. 61.00 o.p. (ISBN 0-12-490950-7). Acad Pr.

Insect Muscle. P. N. Usherwood. 1975. 138.00 o.p. (ISBN 0-12-709450-4). Acad Pr.

Insect Phylogeny. Willi Hennig. LC 80-40853. 514p. 1981. 118.00 o.p. (ISBN 0-471-27848-3). Wiley.

Insecticide, Herbicide, Fungicide Quick Guide, 1988. rev. ed. B. G. Page & W. T. Thomson. 180p. 1988. perfect bdg. 14.50 o.p. Thomson Pubns.

Insects: A Selection. Susan Peters. 1971. pap. 7.00 o.s.i. (ISBN 0-686-02017-0). Turtles Quill.

Insects All Around Us. Richard Armour & P. Galdone. 1981. text ed. 9.95 o.p. (ISBN 0-07-002266-6). McGraw.

Insects & Diseases of Vegetables in the Home Garden. William W. Cantelo & Raymond E. Webb. 56p. 1980. pap. 4.25 o.p. (ISBN 0-318-11794-0, S/N 001-000-04019-7). USGPO.

Insects & Mites: Techniques for Collection & Preservation. George C. Steyskal et al. (Agriculture Dept. Miscellaneous Publication Series 1443). (Illus.). 107p. 1986. 4.75 o.p. (ISBN 0-318-22609-X, S/N 001-000-04466-4). USGPO.

Insects & Plants. Pierre Jolivet. LC 85-16109. (Handbook Ser.: No. 2). (Illus.). 208p. (Orig.). 1986. pap. 19.95 o.p. (ISBN 0-916846-25-3). Flora & Fauna.

Insects & Plants: The Amazing Partnership. Elizabeth K. Cooper. LC 63-7893. (Illus.). (gr. 4-6). 1963. 4.95 o.p. (ISBN 0-15-238701-3, HJ). HarBraceJ.

Insects & Spiders. C. P. Friedlander. 124p. 1956. (ISBN 0-8022-0545-3). Philos Lib.

Insects in Perspectives. Michael D. Atkins. (Illus.). 1978. text ed. write for info. o.p. (ISBN 0-02-304500-0). Macmillan.

Insects on Grain Legumes in Northern Australia: A Survey of Potential Pests & Their Enemies. Merle Shepard & R. J. Lawn. LC 82-13463. (Illus.). 89p. 1983. pap. 9.95 o.p. (ISBN 0-7022-1802-2). U of Queensland Pr.

Insects That Feed on Trees & Shrubs: An Illustrated Practical Guide. Warren T. Johnson & H. H. Lyon. (A Comstock Bk Ser). (Illus.). 464p. 1976. 49.50x o.p. (ISBN 0-8014-0956-X). Cornell U Pr.

Insects You Have Seen. Lloyd Eighme. LC 79-24141. (Review & Herald Crown Ser.). (gr. 6 up). 1980. pap. 6.50 o.p. (ISBN 0-8127-0259-X). Review & Herald.

Inservice Data Reporting & Analysis: PVP-Vol. 35, Vol. 11. Ed. by J. T. Fong. 236p. 1979. 30.00 o.p. (ISBN 0-317-33550-2, H00149); members 15.00 o.p. (ISBN 0-317-33551-0). ASME.

Inshore Fishing: Its Skills, Risks, Rewards. Stan Judd. (Illus.). 144p. 17.50 o.p. (ISBN 0-85238-096-8, FN55, FNB). UNIPUB.

Inshore Squadrons. Alexander Kent. 256p. 1985. pap. 3.50 o.s.i. (ISBN 0-515-07984-7). Jove Pubns.

Inside a Mormon Mission. Jack S. Bailey. 190p. pap. 3.95 o.p. (ISBN 0-89036-076-6). Hawkes Pub Inc.

Inside a Sand Castle & Other Secrets. Mary L. Cuneo. (Illus.). (gr. k-3). 1979. reinforced bdg. 6.95 o.p. (ISBN 0-395-27805-8). HM.

Inside a Sensitivity Training Group. Irving R. Weschler & Jerome Reisel. (Monograph & Research Ser.: No. 4). 133p. 1959. 5.00 o.p. (ISBN 0-89215-006-8). U Cal LA Indus Rel.

Inside American Ballet Theatre. Clive Barnes. (Quality Paperbacks Ser.). (Illus.). 192p. 1983. pap. 11.95 o.p. (ISBN 0-306-80192-2). Da Capo.

Inside Buchmanism. Geoffrey Williamson. 266p. 1955. (ISBN 0-8022-1891-1). Philos Lib.

Inside China Today: A Western View. E. Grey Dimond. 1983. 16.00 o.p. (ISBN 0-393-01711-7). Norton.

Inside Congress. Ed. by Bruce F. Norton. 184p. 1971. pap. text ed. 6.00x o.p. (ISBN 0-8422-0176-9). Irvington.

Inside Corner: Talks with Tom Seaver. Ed. by Joel H. Cohen. LC 73-91636. 1974. 7.95 o.p. (ISBN 0-689-10600-9, Atheneum). Macmillan.

Inside CP-M Plus. David E. Cortesi. 1984. 17.95 o.p. (ISBN 0-03-070671-8). HR&W.

Inside CP-M-86. David E. Cortesi. 1984. 16.95 o.p. (ISBN 0-03-062656-0). HR&W.

Inside dBASE III. National Training Systems Staff. 1985. 49.95 o.p. (ISBN 0-8104-7380-1). Sams.

Inside Death Valley. rev. 3rd ed. Chuck Gebhardt. LC 80-83123. (Illus.). 166p. 1980. pap. 5.95 o.p. (ISBN 0-9601410-1-4). C Gebhardt.

Inside Football. Ed. by John Walsh. 224p. (Orig.). 1983. pap. 4.95 o.p. (ISBN 0-449-90103-3, Columbine). Fawcett.

Inside Football, 1984. Ed. by Massillon Society Staff & John Walsh. (Orig.). 1984. pap. 5.95 o.p. (ISBN 0-449-90129-7, Columbine). Fawcett.

Inside Framework. 1985. 49.95 o.p. (ISBN 0-8104-7306-2). Sams.

Inside Home Box Office: The Billion-Dollar War Between HBO, Hollywood, & the Home Video Revolution. George Mair. (Illus.). 224p. 1988. 17.95 o.p. (ISBN 0-396-08420-6). Dodd.

Inside Investment Banking. Ernest Bloch. 350p. 1986. 39.95 o.p. (ISBN 0-87094-899-7). Dow Jones-Irwin.

Inside Karsrilevke. Date not set. (ISBN 0-8052-0173-4). Random.

Inside Kensington Palace. Andrew Morton. 232p. 1988. lib. bdg. 19.95x o.s.i. (ISBN 0-7451-0786-9, Pub. by Chivers Pr UK). G K Hall.

Inside Mao Tse-Tung's Thought: An Analytical Blueprint of His Actions by a Former Top Chinese Communist Leader. Yeh Ch'ing. Ed. by Stephen Pan. Tr. by T. H. Tsuan & Ralph Mortensen. 1975. 12.50 o.p. (ISBN 0-682-48339-7). Exposition-Phoenix.

Inside One, Two, Three. 1985. 49.95 o.p. (ISBN 0-8104-7375-5). Sams.

Inside Out. Kathleen Brady. 1979. 8.95 o.p. (ISBN 0-393-08843-X). Norton.

Inside Out: Developmental Strategies for Teaching Writing. Dan Kirby & Tom Liner. LC 81-10073. 256p. (Orig.). 1981. pap. text ed. 12.50x o.p. (ISBN 0-86709-007-3). Boynton Cook Pubs.

Inside Outlets: The Best Bargain Shopping in New England. Naomi R. Rosenberg & Marianne W. Sekulow. (Illus.). 224p. (Orig.). 1985. pap. 8.95 o.p. (ISBN 0-916782-66-2). Harvard Common Pr.

Inside Outside. Deirdra Baldwin & Gene Davis. 40p. 1983. pap. 35.00 spec. signed ed. o.s.i. (ISBN 0-915380-17-X); unsigned 10.00 o.s.i. Word Works.

Inside Outside. Philip Jose Farmer. 1980. lib. bdg. 12.50 o.p. (ISBN 0-8398-2622-2, Gregg). G K Hall.

Inside Outside. Ruth Ray. LC 86-50603. 100p. 1986. 6.95 o.p. (ISBN 1-55523-030-X). Winston-Derek.

Inside Secrets of Wordstar 2000 & 2000 Plus. David D. Busch. (Illus.). 192p. (Orig.). 1985. 21.95 o.p. (ISBN 0-8306-0993-8, 1993); pap. 14.60 o.p. (ISBN 0-8306-1993-3). Tab Bks.

Inside Spinal Tap. Peter Occhiogrosso. 129p. 1985. 12.95 o.p. (ISBN 0-87795-697-9, Arbor Hse). Morrow.

Inside Stories of the Forbidden City. Er Si et al. Tr. by Zhao Shuhan & Er Si. (Illus.). 165p. 1986. pap. 3.95 o.p. (ISBN 0-8351-1664-6). China Bks.

Inside Story: Creative Home Decorating. Annette Stramesi. LC 77-71482. 144p. 1977. 7.95 o.p. (ISBN 0-916752-14-3). Longman Trade.

Inside Story of Metal. Norman F. Smith. LC 77-10768. (Illus.). 192p. (gr. 7 up). 1977. lib. bdg. 8.79 o.s.i. (ISBN 0-671-32860-3). Messner.

Inside Symphony. National Training Systems Staff. 1985. 49.95 o.p. (ISBN 0-8104-7378-X). Sams.

Inside the Amiga with C. John Berry & Waite Group. 440p. 1986. pap. 22.95 o.p. (ISBN 0-672-22468-2). Sams.

Inside the Apple IIGS. Gary Bond. 449p. (Orig.). 1987. pap. 19.95 o.p. (ISBN 0-89588-365-1). Sybex.

Inside the Bauhaus. Howard Dearstyne. Ed. by David Spaeth. LC 85-43483. (Illus.). 280p. 1986. 40.00 o.p. (ISBN 0-8478-0699-5); pap. 22.50 o.p. (ISBN 0-8478-0702-9). Rizzoli Intl.

Inside the Cell. Maya Pines. LC 79-22746. (Illus.). 96p. 1980. 13.95x o.p. (ISBN 0-89490-031-5). Enslow Pubs.

Inside the Cuban Revolution. Adolfo Gilly. Tr. by Felix Gutierrez. LC 74-1780. 83p. 1976. Repr. of 1964 ed. lib. bdg. 15.00x o.p. (ISBN 0-8371-7399-X, GICR). Greenwood.

Inside the Cyclist. Ed Burke et al. Ed. by Velo-News. (Illus.). 128p. (Orig.). 1981. pap. 7.95 o.p. (ISBN 0-941950-00-X). Vitesse Pr.

Inside the Cyclist. rev. ed. Ed Burke et al. Ed. by Velo-News Staff. LC 84-50852. (Illus.). 160p. 1984. pap. 9.95 o.p. (ISBN 0-941950-06-9). Vitesse Pr.

Inside the Gate. Mildred Lawrence. LC 68-25187. (gr. 7 up). 1968. 5.95 o.p. (ISBN 0-15-238728-5, HJ). HarBraceJ.

Inside the Haveli. Rama Mehta. 208p. 1977. pap. 4.25 o.s.i. (ISBN 0-86578-059-5). Ind-US Inc.

Inside the Haveli. Rama Mehta. 208p. 1977. 12.00 o.s.i. (ISBN 0-86578-256-3). Ind-US Inc.

Inside the Middle East. D. Hiro. 1982. text ed. 19.95 o.p. (ISBN 0-07-029055-5); pap. text ed. 8.95 o.p. (ISBN 0-07-029056-3). McGraw.

Inside the Private Office: Memoirs of the Secretary to British Foreign Ministers. Nicholas Henderson. (Illus.). 152p. 1987. 15.95 o.p. (ISBN 0-89733-219-9). Academy Chi Pubs.

Inside the SAS. Tony Geraghty. (Elite Unit Ser.: No. 2). (Illus.). 249p. 1981. 17.95 o.p. (ISBN 0-89839-039-7). Battery Pr.

Inside the Whale: Ten Personal Accounts of Social Research. Ed. by Colin Bell & Sol Encel. 1978. text ed. 22.00 o.p. (ISBN 0-08-022244-7); pap. text ed. 16.75 o.p. (ISBN 0-08-022243-9). Pergamon.

Inside the World of Miniatures & Dollhouses: A Comprehensive Guide to Collecting & Creating. Bernard Rosner & Jay Beckerman. LC 76-16458. (Illus.). 256p. 1976. pap. 9.95 o.p. (ISBN 0-679-50620-9). McKay.

Inside Today's Home. 4th ed. Ray Faulkner & Sarah Faulkner. LC 74-11832. (Illus.). 1975. text ed. 31.95 o.p. (ISBN 0-03-089480-8, HoltC). HR&W.

Inside Today's Home. 1982. 28.50 o.p. (ISBN 0-03-089714-9). HR&W.

Inside Track: A Successful Job Search Method. William Lareau. LC 85-25823. 224p. 1985. 12.95 o.p. (ISBN 0-8329-0408-2). New Century.

Inside Wall Street: Continuity & Change in the Financial District. Robert Sobel. 1977. 12.95 o.p. (ISBN 0-393-05643-0). Norton.

Inside Your Computer. Ian R. Sinclair. (Illus.). 108p. 1983. pap. 12.95 o.p. (ISBN 0-88006-058-1, BK7390). Wayne Green Ent.

Insider Trading Handbook 1987. Donald C. Langevoort. (Securities Law Ser.). 1987. 85.00 o.p. (ISBN 0-87632-539-8). Clark Boardman.

Insider's England. Date not set. (ISBN 0-7117-0307-8). Salem Hse Pubs.

Insider's Guide to Florida Restaurants. Harold W. Stayman, Jr. & Norma H. Stayman. 64p. (Orig.). 1988. pap. 4.95 o.p. (ISBN 0-8069-6812-5). Sterling.

Insider's Guide to Franchising. Bryce Webster. 320p. 1986. 17.95 o.p. AMACOM.

Insider's Guide to Japan. Peter Popham. (Illus.). 208p. (Orig.). 1984. pap. 12.95 o.p. (ISBN 0-87011-661-4). Kodansha.

Insider's Guide to Owning Land in Subdivisions: How to Buy, Appraise & Get Rid of Your Lot. Patricia A. Simko. 39p. 1980. pap. 1.50x o.p. (ISBN 0-918780-17-9). INFORM.

Insider's Guide to the Colleges. 9th ed. Ed. by Yale Daily News Staff. LC 73-161129. 496p. 1983. pap. 9.95 o.p. (ISBN 0-312-92330-9). Congdon & Weed.

Insider's Guide to the Colleges: 1984-85. 10th ed. Yale Daily News Staff & Margaret Waters. LC 73-161139. 496p. 1984. pap. 9.95 o.p. (ISBN 0-312-92331-7). Congdon & Weed.

Insiders' Guide to the Outer Banks of North Carolina, 1986-87. Monty Joynes & Dave Poyer. (Insiders' Guides Ser.). (Illus.). 400p. 1986. pap. 5.95 o.p. (ISBN 0-912367-11-3). Insiders Guide.

Insider's Guide to the Outer Banks, 1985-86. Monty Joynes & Dave Poyer. LC 84-52541. (Insider's Guides Ser.). (Illus.). 392p. 1985. pap. 5.95 o.p. (ISBN 0-912367-03-2). Insiders Guide.

Insiders' Guide to the Triangle of North Carolina: Raleigh, Cary, Durham, Chapel Hill. Dee Reid & J. Barlow Herget. (Insiders' Guide Ser.). (Illus.). 712p. 1986. 7.95 o.p. (ISBN 0-912367-13-X). Insiders Guide.

Insiders' Guide to Williamsburg, Virginia. Susan Bruno & Donna Quaresima. LC 83-51606. (Insiders' Guides Ser.). (Illus.). 250p. 1984. pap. 4.95 o.p. (ISBN 0-912367-06-7). Insiders Guide.

Insiders: The Truth Behind the Scandal Rocking Wall Street. Mark Stevens. 224p. 1987. 18.95 o.p. (ISBN 0-399-13266-X, Putnam). Putnam Pub Group.

Insight. Bernard Lonergan. 1957. pap. 15.95 o.p. (ISBN 0-8022-0994-7). Philos Lib.

Insight & Vision: The Problem of Communism in Marx's Thought. R. N. Berki. 218p. 1984. Repr. of 1974 ed. 21.95x o.p. (ISBN 0-460-10172-2, Pub. by Evman England); pap. 9.95X o.p. (ISBN 0-460-11172-8, Pub. by Evman England). Biblio Dist.

Insight Guides: Pacific Northwest. Ed. by Hans J. Hoefer. (Insight Guides Ser.). (Illus.). 330p. (Orig.). 1986. pap. 15.95 o.s.i. (ISBN 0-932575-22-6). Gr Arts Ctr Pub.

Insight into Relativity. Marvin G. Moore. 144p. 1987. 10.95 o.p. (ISBN 0-8062-3056-8). Carlton.

Insights into English Structure: A Programmed Course. Russell N. Campbell & Judith W. Lindfors. 1969. pap. text ed. (ISBN 0-13-467571-1). P-H.

Insights into Prehistory. Michael Baran. 128p. 1982. 8.00 o.p. (ISBN 0-682-49876-9). Exposition-Phoenix.

Insights into the Beyond. Paul B. Zacharias. LC 76-6756. pap. 1.00 o.s.i. (ISBN 0-87785-156-5). Swedenborg.

Insights: Readings in Children's Literature. Ed. by William J. Curtis et al. 74p. 1970. pap. text ed. 4.50x o.p. (ISBN 0-8290-2400-X). Irvington.

Insights: Self-Portraits by Women. Compiled by Joyce T. Cohen. LC 78-58501. (Illus.). 144p. 1978. 20.00x o.s.i. (ISBN 0-87923-246-3); pap. 9.95 o.s.i. (ISBN 0-87923-247-1). Godine.

Insights Training. 2nd ed. Carlsen. Date not set. (ISBN 0-07-009909-X). McGraw.

Insignia Guide. pap. cancelled o.s.i. (ISBN 0-8395-3064-1, SL3064). BSA.

Insignia of the Notitia Dignitatum: A Contribution to the Study of Late Antique Illustrated Manuscripts. Pamela C. Berger. LC 79-57511. (Outstanding Dissertations in Fine Arts Ser.: No. 5). 375p. 1981. lib. bdg. 53.00 o.p. (ISBN 0-8240-3927-0). Garland Pub.

Insinuation: The Tactics of English Satire. James W. Nichols. LC 72-159467. (De Proprietatibus Litterarum, Ser. Major: No. 22). 142p. 1971. text ed. 9.60x o.p. (ISBN 0-686-22495-7). Mouton.

Insolubilized Enzymes. Ed. by M. Salmona et al. 1974. 29.50 o.p. (ISBN 0-7204-7527-9). Elsevier.

Insolvency Accounting. R. Wiener & R. Christian. 1977. text ed. 38.50 o.p. (ISBN 0-07-070135-0). McGraw.

Inspection & Measurement. Ed. by S. Booth et al. (Engineering Craftsmen: No. H26). (Illus.). 1969. spiral bdg. 39.95x o.p. (ISBN 0-89563-008-7). Trans-Atl Phila.

Inspection, Gaging & Testing. Society of Manufacturing Engineers Staff. (Productivity Equipment Ser.). 696p. 1984. 47.00 o.p. (ISBN 0-87263-170-2). SME.

Inspection, Maintenance & Rehabilitation of Old Dams. Compiled by American Society of Civil Engineers Staff. 956p. 1974. pap. 34.00x o.p. (ISBN 0-87262-061-1). Am Soc Civil Eng.

Inspection Manual. 76p. 3.50 o.p. (ISBN 0-318-12813-6, AITC 200). Am Inst Timber.

Inspection of Construction Operations. (Civil-Structural Inspection Ser.: Module 29-1). (Illus.). 62p. 1979. spiral bdg. 8.00x o.p. (ISBN 0-87683-116-1). GP Pub.

Inspection of Fracture Critical Bridge Members: Supplement to the Bridge Inspector's Training Manual. James W. Harland. (FHWA Implementation Package 86-26 Ser.). (Illus.). 233p. (Orig.). 1986. pap. 11.00 o.p. (S/N 050-001-00302-3). USGPO.

Inspector General. Nikolai Gogol. Ed. by Henry Popkin. Tr. by Andrew MacAndrew. 1976. pap. 0.95 o.p. (ISBN 0-380-00585-9, 28878, Bard). Avon.

Inspector-General: Sir Jeremiah Fitzpatrick & the Politics of Social Reform 1783-1802. Oliver MacDonagh. 344p. 1982. 29.95 o.p. (ISBN 0-85664-421-8, Pub. by Croom Helm). Routledge Chapman & Hall.

Inspector Mouse. Steadman. 1981. 9.95 o.s.i. (ISBN 0-03-059113-9). H Holt & Co.

Inspector Smart Gets the Message! Richard Fowler. LC 82-82623. (Illus.). 16p. (gr. 1-3). 1983. 7.95i o.p. (ISBN 0-316-28983-3). Little.

Inspiration for Embroidery. Constance Howard. 240p. 1967. 27.50 o.p. (ISBN 0-8231-4017-2); pap. 15.50 o.s.i. Branford.

Inspiration Three, Vol. 3: Three Famous Classics in One Book - Wisdom of Luther, Calvin & Wesley. Compiled by David Poling. LC 73-80032. (Pivot Family Reader Ser). 1973. pap. 1.25 o.p. (ISBN 0-87983-043-3). Keats.

Inspiration Three, Vol. 5: Three Famous Classics in One Book. O. Henry et al. LC 73-80032. (Pivot Family Reader Ser.). 1973. pap. 1.25 o.p. (ISBN 0-87983-045-X). Keats.

Inspirational & Other Poems. JoAnn C. Paro. LC 85-51409. 54p. 1986. 5.95 o.p. (ISBN 0-938232-89-4, Dist. by Baker & Taylor Co.). Winston-Derek.

Inspirational Announcements & Letterheads. (Easy-to-Make Photocopier Bks.). (Orig.). 1984. pap. 14.95 o.p. (ISBN 0-87280-042-3, Asher-Gallant). Caddylak Systs.

Inspirational Poems to Touch the Heart. Carolyn K. Chapman. 48p. 1987. 6.50 o.p. Carlton.

Inspirational Posters. (Easy-to-Make Photocopier Bks.). (Orig.). 1983. pap. 14.95 o.p. (ISBN 0-87280-030-X, Asher-Gallant). Caddylak Systs.

Inspirations from the Olde Dover House. Michael Henderson. 1977. 4.00 o.p. (ISBN 0-682-48985-9). Exposition-Phoenix.

Inspired Letters. Frank C. Laubach. 220p. 1972. 2.95 o.p. (ISBN 0-317-35468-X). New Readers.

Inspiring Parenthood. Janice Presser. 1986. 10.45 o.p. (ISBN 0-345-33334-9, Pub. by Ballantine Ephiphany). Ballantine.

Instabilities of a Homogeneous Plasma see Theory of Plasma Instabilities.

Instabilities of an Inhomogeneous Plasma see Theory of Plasma Instabilities.

Installation Guidelines for Solar DHW Systems in One & Two Family Dwellings. 107p. 1979. pap. 5.50 o.p. (ISBN 0-318-11795-9, S/N 023-000-00520-4). USGPO.

Installation of Instrumentation & Process Control Systems. (EEUA Handbook Ser.: No. 34). (Illus.). 1977. text ed. 9.00 o.p. (ISBN 0-09-458880-5). Syentek.

Installing Heat Pumps. Jack Johnson & Wayne Hammock. (Illus.). 304p. (Orig.). 1983. 18.95 o.p. (ISBN 0-8306-0263-1); pap. 13.60 o.p. (ISBN 0-8306-0163-5, 1563P). TAB Bks.

Installment Sales Tax Reporting. Stephen R. Mettling. (Residential Financing Resource Library). 13p. (Orig.). 1982. pap. 6.50 o.s.i. (ISBN 0-88462-142-1, 1905-25, Real Estate Ed). Longman Finan.

Instant Answer Book of Countries. Warender & Tyler. (People of the World Ser.). (gr. 4-9). 1978. 7.95 o.s.i. (ISBN 0-86020-211-9, Usborne-Hayes); PLB 12.95 o.p. (ISBN 0-88110-118-4); pap. 4.95 o.p. (ISBN 0-86020-190-2). EDC.

Instant Chef: Shortcut Magic to Gourmet Cooking for the Working Person. A. K. Newmon. 1980. 8.95 o.p. (ISBN 0-682-49374-0). Exposition-Phoenix.

Instant Evolution: We'd Better Get Good at It. Thomas P. Carney. LC 79-17835. 1980. text ed. 13.95x o.p. (ISBN 0-268-01145-1). U of Notre Dame Pr.

Instant Facts see World Book Desk Reference Set.

Instant Guide to Healthy Cacti. Ed. by David Longman. LC 84-40639. (Complete Plant Doctor Ser.). 88p. 1985. 5.95 o.s.i. (ISBN 0-8129-1179-2). Times Bks.

Instant Guide to Healthy Flowering Houseplants. Ed. by David Longman. LC 84-40633. (Complete Plant Doctor Ser.). (Illus.). 80p. (Orig.). 1985. 5.95 o.p. (ISBN 0-8129-1172-5). Times Bks.

Instant Guide to Healthy Flowering Houseplants. Ed. by David Longman. LC 84-40633. (Complete Plant Doctor Ser.). (Illus.). 88p. 1986. 5.95 o.p. (ISBN 0-8129-1171-7, Dist. by Random House). Times Bks.

Instant Guide to Healthy Foliage Houseplants. Ed. by David Longman. LC 84-40634. (Complete Plant Doctor Ser.). (Illus.). 80p. (Orig.). 1985. 5.95 o.p. (ISBN 0-8129-1173-3). Times Bks.

Instant Guide to Healthy Foliage Houseplants, Vol. II. Ed. by David Longman. LC 84-40634. (Complete Plant Doctor Ser.). (Illus.). 88p. 1986. 5.95 o.p. (ISBN 0-8129-1174-1, Dist. by Random House). Times Bks.

Instant Guide to Healthy Indoor Bulbs & Annuals. Ed. by David Longman. LC 84-40636. (Complete Plant Doctor Ser.). 88p. 1985. 5.95 o.p. (ISBN 0-8129-1176-8). Times Bks.

Instant Guide to Healthy Palms & Ferns. Ed. by David Longman. LC 84-40637. (Complete Plant Doctor Ser.). (Illus.). 80p. (Orig.). 1985. 5.95 o.s.i. (ISBN 0-8129-1177-6). Times Bks.

Instant Guide to Healthy Succulents. Ed. by David Longman. LC 84-40635. (Complete Plant Doctor Ser.). (Illus.). 88p. 1985. 5.95 o.p. (ISBN 0-8129-1175-X). Times Bks.

Instant Japanese. Masahiro Watanabe & Kei Nagashima. (Illus.). 188p. 1981. pap. 4.95 o.p. (ISBN 0-89346-182-2). Heian Intl.

Instead of Death: New & Expanded Edition. rev. ed. William Stringfellow. 1976. pap. 3.95 o.p. (ISBN 0-8164-2120-X). HarpR.

Instead of Regulation: Alternatives to Federal Regulatory Agencies. Ed. by Robert W. Poole, Jr. 416p. 1981. o. p. 28.50 o.p. (ISBN 0-669-04585-3); pap. 17.00x o.p. (ISBN 0-669-06168-9). Lexington Bks.

Instincts of the Herd in Peace & War. 2nd ed. Wilfred Trotter. LC 74-19217. 264p. 1975. Repr. of 1923 ed. 34.00x o.p. (ISBN 0-8103-4090-9). Gale.

Institutes. 3rd ed. Rudolph Sohm. LC 72-118812. 1970. Repr. of 1907 ed. 45.00x o.p. (ISBN 0-678-04542-9). Kelley.

Institutes of Moral Philosophy. 2nd rev. ed. Adam Ferguson. LC 75-11219. (British Philosophers & Theologians of the 17th & 18th Centuries Ser.: Vol. 22). 1978. Repr. of 1773 ed. lib. bdg. 51.00 o.p. (ISBN 0-8240-1773-0). Garland Pub.

Institution of the Christian Religion Embracing Almost the Whole Sum of Piety, & Whatever Is Necessary to Know the Doctrine of Salvation. John Calvin. Ed. by Ford L. Battles. LC 74-3718. 416p. 1975. pap. 9.95 o.p. (ISBN 0-8042-0489-6). Westminster John Knox.

Institutional Adjustment: A Challenge to a Changing Economy. Ed. by Carey C. Thompson. 194p. 1967. 13.95x o.p. (ISBN 0-292-73678-9). U of Tex Pr.

Institutional Buildings: Architecture of the Controlled Environment. Architectural Record Magazine Editors. (Illus.). 182p. 1980. text ed. 39.50 o.p. (ISBN 0-07-002343-3). McGraw.

Institutional Care & the Mentally Handicapped: The Mental Handicap Hospital. Andy Alaszewski. LC 85-22025. 224p. 1985. 27.50 o.p. (ISBN 0-7099-0564-5, Pub. by Croom Helm Ltd). Routledge Chapman & Hall.

Institutional Drive: A Study in Pluralistic Democracy. Carl G. Gustavson. LC 66-14029. xviii, 199p. 1966. 15.00x o.p. (ISBN 0-8214-0019-3). Ohio U Pr.

Institutional Framework of the European Communities. David Freestone & Scott Harrison. 192p. 1987. 42.50 o.p. (ISBN 0-317-64383-5, Pub. by Croom Helm UK). Routledge Chapman & Hall.

Institutional Impacts on Campus, Community, & Business Constituencies. Ed. by Richard L. Alfred. LC 81-48566. (Community Colleges Ser.: No. 38). 1982. 12.95x o.p. (ISBN 0-87589-884-X). Jossey-Bass.

Institutiones Mathematicae: Linear Differential Equations & Control, Vol. 1. R. Conti. 1977. 45.00 o.p. (ISBN 0-12-363601-9). Acad Pr.

Institutions & Processes of American National Government. Ed. by Carl Lieberman. LC 83-1128. 408p. (Orig.). 1983. lib. bdg. 32.50 o.p. (ISBN 0-8191-3071-0); pap. text ed. 15.25 o.p. (ISBN 0-8191-3072-9). U Pr of Amer.

Institutions of American Government. George L. Davis & Samuel H. Shannon. LC 73-621. 145p. 1973. 20.00x o.p. (ISBN 0-8422-5087-5); pap. text ed. 4.75x o.p. (ISBN 0-8422-0295-1). Irvington.

Instruccion Publica in la URSS. N. Kuzin et al. 212p. (Span.). 1977. 4.45 o.p. (ISBN 0-8285-1480-1, Pub. by Progress Pubs USSR). Imported Pubns.

Instructed Conscience: The Shaping of the American National Ethic. Donald H. Meyer. LC 76-175512. (Illus.). 1972. 18.95x o.p. (ISBN 0-8122-7651-5); pap. 11.95x o.p. (ISBN 0-8122-1066-2). U of Pa Pr.

Instruction in Christian Love. Martin Bucer. o.p. (John Knox). Westminster John Knox.

Instructional Aids in Mathematics, 34th Yearbk. National Council of Teachers of Mathematics Staff. LC 76-189323. (Illus.). 442p. 1973. 21.00 o.p. (ISBN 0-87353-014-4). NCTM.

Instructional Computing: An Action Guide for Educators. J. Richard Dennis & Robert Kansky. 1984. pap. write for info. o.p. (ISBN 0-673-16606-6). Scott F.

Instructional Course Lectures, Vol. 34. American Academy of Orthopaedic Surgeons Staff. 1985. text ed. 63.50 o.p. (ISBN 0-8016-0106-1). Mosby.

Instructional Materials for Exceptional Children: Selection, Management & Adaptation. Joseph J. Stowitschek et al. LC 80-11730. 393p. 1980. text ed. 35.00 o.p. (ISBN 0-89443-277-X). Aspen Pub.

Instructional Strategies for Physical Education. Joyce M. Harrison. 560p. 1983. pap. text ed. write for info. o.p. (ISBN 0-697-07205-3). Wm C Brown.

Instructional Technology & Programmed Instruction. Paul Saettler. 93p. 1969. pap. text ed. 6.95x o.p. (ISBN 0-8290-1112-9). Irvington.

Instructional Technology: Selected Proceedings of the Fourth Canadian Symposium, Winnipeg, Canada, October 1983. Ed. by P. R. Smith. 180p. 1985. pap. 36.00 o.p. (ISBN 0-08-031847-9). Pergamon.

Instructions. Diane Vreuls. 1971. pap. 5.00 o.p. (ISBN 0-87711-046-8). Story Line.

Instructions for Authors: Biomedical Journals. Marshall D. Stein & Jo L. Smith. 1986. pap. 38.00 o.p. (ISBN 0-12-664220-6). Acad Pr.

Instructions for Monitoring the Impact of General Revenue Sharing at the Local Level. League of Women Voters Education Fund. 113p. 1976. 3.00 o.p. (ISBN 0-89959-036-5, 626). LWV US.

Instructions for the Preparation of Specifications, Standards & Technical Manuals, 2 vols. Ed. by Jerome H. Lieblich. 788p. Set. loose-leaf 119.50 o.p. (ISBN 0-912702-12-5). Global Eng.

Instructions for Undressing the Human Race. Fernando Alegria. (Illus., Orig., Span.). 1968. pap. 5.00 o.p. (ISBN 0-685-13650-7). Story Line.

Instructions to the Double. Tess Gallagher. LC 76-378309. 76p. 1975. o. p. 12.00 o.p. (ISBN 0-915308-04-5); pap. 5.00 o.p. (ISBN 0-915308-03-7). Graywolf.

Instructors & Their Jobs. 3rd ed. W. R. Miller & H. C. Rose. (Illus.). 298p. 1975. 20.96 o.p. (ISBN 0-8269-4162-1). Am Technical.

Instructor's Guide. Mary Lou Conlin. 1975. pap. 4.50 o.p. (ISBN 0-395-19228-5). HM.

Instructor's Guide: Understanding Aging & Human Needs. 379p. 37.50 o.p. (ISBN 0-318-12745-8, 90100607); members 22.50 o.p. (ISBN 0-318-12746-6, 901-00606). Am Health Care Assn.

Instructors' Handbook. British Horse Society & Pony Club Staff. LC 76-55317. 1977. 9.95 o.p. (ISBN 0-8120-5125-4). Barron.

Instructor's Manual for en Route: Introduction au Francais: Et au Monde Francophone. Albert Valdman & Marva A. Barnett. 187p. 1986. pap. gratis avail. o.p. (ISBN 0-02-422310-7). Macmillan.

Instructor's Manual for Psychology. Richard M. Lerner & Phillip C. Kendall. 288p. 1986. write for info. instr's. manual o.p. (ISBN 0-02-369920-5). Macmillan.

Instructor's Manual with Transparency Masters: Computer-Based Information Systems: A Managerial Approach. 2nd ed. Donald W. Kroeber & Hugh J. Watson. 243p. 1986. pap. price not set o.p. (ISBN 0-02-366880-6). Macmillan.

Instrument Fitting. Ed. by J. Barr et al. (Engineering Craftsmen: No. H24). (Illus.). 1969. spiral bdg. 39.95x o.p. Trans-Atl Phila.

Instrument Flying. Jeff W. Griffin. pap. 10.95 o.s.i. (ISBN 0-8306-2293-4, 2293). TAB Bks.

Instrument Flying Handbook. rev. ed. Federal Aviation Administration Staff. 268p. pap. text ed. cancelled o.s.i. (ISBN 0-939158-07-8). Flightshops.

Instrument Flying Handbook: Ac 61-27c. Federal Aviation Administration Staff. (Illus.). 1980. pap. 8.50 o.p. (ISBN 0-86677-005-4, Pub. by Cooper). Aviation.

Instrument Maintenance Management, Vol. 13: Proceedings of the 13th Instrument Maintenance Management Symposium, Vol. 13. Instrument Maintenance Management Symposium Staff. LC 67-13017. 70p. 1979. pap. text ed. 12.50x o.p. (ISBN 0-87664-448-5). Instru Soc.

Instrument Pilot's Guide. 2nd ed. L. W. Reithmaier. LC 74-30480. (Illus.). 206p. 1974. pap. 2.95 o.p. (ISBN 0-8168-7305-4, 27305SP, TAB-Aero). TAB Bks.

Instrument Rating Practical Test Standards, Airplane-Helicopter. rev. ed. Federal Aviation Administration Staff. 23p. 1976. pap. text ed. 1.75 o.p. (ISBN 0-939158-11-6). Flightshops.

Instrument Rating Question Book. (FAA-T-8080-7A Ser.). 239p. 1986. pap. 9.00 o.p. (ISBN 0-318-20119-4, S/N 050-007-00732-9). USGPO.

Instrument Rating-Written Test Guide. rev. ed. Federal Aviation Administration Staff. 200p. 1977. pap. text ed. 4.25 o.p. (ISBN 0-939158-04-3). Flightshops.

Instrument Repairer. Educational Research Council of America Staff. Ed. by Theodore N. Ferris & John P. Marchak. (Real People at Work Ser.: Series O). (Illus.). 36p. (Orig.). (gr. 5). 1976. pap. text ed. 2.70 o.p. (ISBN 0-89247-110-7, 9537). Changing Times.

Instrumental Inorganic Chemistry. Ed. by F. L. Boschke. LC 79-14180. (Topics in Current Chemistry: Vol. 85). (Illus.). 1979. 58.00 o.p. (ISBN 0-387-09338-9). Springer-Verlag.

Instrumental Methods Analysis. 6th ed. Willard. Watts.

Instrumental Music Guide. A. Harold Goodman. LC 77-7923. 1977. pap. 2.40 o.p. (ISBN 0-8425-1525-9). Brigham.

Instrumental Music in Worship. M. C. Kurfees. 10.95 o.p. (ISBN 0-89225-106-9). Gospel Advocate.

Instrumental Music of Carl Philipp Emanuel Bach. David Schulenberg. Ed. by George Buelow. LC 84-244. (Studies in Musicology: No. 77). 202p. 1984. 42.95 o.p. (ISBN 0-8357-1564-7). UMI Res Pr.

Instrumental Organic Elemental Analysis. Ed. by R. Belcher. 1978. 82.50 o.p. (ISBN 0-12-085950-5). Acad Pr.

Instrumental Techniques for Food Analysis. Robert E. Van Atta. 1979. pap. text ed. 14.95x o.p. (ISBN 0-89917-008-0). TIS Inc.

Instrumentation & Control for Water & Wastewater Treatment & Transport Systems. S. H. Jenkins. 1978. pap. 110.00 flexi-cover o.p. (ISBN 0-08-022098-3). Pergamon.

Instrumentation & Control in the 80's: Proceedings of the 1984 Joint Symposium. Instrument Society of America Staff. 356p. 1984. pap. text ed. 47.50x o.p. (ISBN 0-87664-815-4). Instru Soc.

Instrumentation & Control of Water & Wastewater Treatment & Transport Systems: Proceedings of the IAWPRC Workshop, 4th, Houston & Denver, April 27 - May 4, 1985. Ed. by R. A. Drake. (Advances in Water Pollution Control Ser.). (Illus.). 766p. 1985. 190.00 o.p. (ISBN 0-08-032591-2, Pub. by P P L). Pergamon.

Instrumentation for Measurement of Moisture: Literature Review & Recommended Reserch. (National Cooperative Highway Research Program Report). 60p. 1973. 4.00 o.p. (ISBN 0-309-02023-9). Transport Res Bd.

Instrumentation in Amino Acid Sequence Analysis. Ed. by Richard Perham. 1976. 46.00 o.p. (ISBN 0-12-551250-3). Acad Pr.

Instrumentation in the Aerospace Industry & Advances in Test Measurement: Tutorial Proceedings of the International Instrumentation Symposium, 26th, 2 Pts, Vol. 26 & Vol. 17. International Instrumentation Symposium Staff. LC 69-59467. 440p. 1980. Set. pap. text ed. 96.00x o.p. (ISBN 0-87664-649-6); pap. text ed. 54.00x ea. o.p. Pt. 1, 440 Pp (ISBN 0-87664-473-6). Pt. 2, 404 Pp (ISBN 0-87664-654-2). Instru Soc.

Instrumentation in the Aerospace Industry & Advances in Test Measurement: Proceedings of the International Instrumentation Symposium, 26th, 2 Pts, Vol. 27 & Vol. 18. International Instrumentation Symposium Staff. LC 69-59467. 1981. Set. pap. text ed. 96.00x o.p. (ISBN 0-87664-528-7); Pt. 1, 408 Pp. pap. text ed. 54.00x o.p. (ISBN 0-87664-515-5); Pt. 2, 408 Pp. pap. text ed. 54.00x o.p. (ISBN 0-87664-527-9). Instru Soc.

Instrumentation in the Aerospace Industry & Advances in Test Measurement: Proceedings of the International Instrumentation Symposium, 28th, 2 Vols, Vol. 28 & Vol. 19. International Instrumentation Symposium Staff. LC 69-59467. 1982. Set. pap. text ed. 149.00x o.p. (ISBN 0-87664-691-7); Pt. 1, 524 p. pap. text ed. 80.00x o.p. (ISBN 0-87664-689-5); Pt. 2, 516 p. pap. text ed. 80.00x o.p. (ISBN 0-87664-690-9). Instru Soc.

Instrumentation in the Aerospace Industry, Vol. 30: Proceedings of the International Instrumentation Symposium, 30th, 1984. International Instrumentation Symposium Staff. Bd. with Vol. 21. Advances in Test Measurement. LC 69-59467. 692p. pap. text ed. 80.00x o.p. (ISBN 0-87664-806-5). Instru Soc.

Instrumentation in the Mining & Metallurgy Industries, Vol. 7: Proceedings of the 8th Mining & Metallurgy Instrumentation Symposium. Mining & Metallurgy Instrumentation Symposium Staff. LC 73-82889. 180p. 1980. text ed. 30.00x o.p. (ISBN 0-87664-470-1). Instru Soc.

Instrumentation in the Mining & Metallurgy Industries, Vol. 8: Proceedings of the 9th Mining & Metallurgy Instrumentation Symposium. Mining & Metallurgy Instrumentation Symposium. LC 73-82889. 150p. 1982. pap. text ed. 25.00x o.p. (ISBN 0-87664-519-8). Instru Soc.

Instrumentation in the Mining & Metallurgy Industries, Vol. 9. Mining & Metallurgy Instrumentation Symposium Staff. LC 73-83889. 212p. 1982. pap. text ed. 30.00x o.p. (ISBN 0-87664-729-8). Instru Soc.

Instrumentation in the Power Industry, Vol. 23: Proceedings of the 23rd Power Instrumentation Symposium. Instrument Society of America Staff. LC 62-52679. 150p. 1980. pap. text ed. 30.00x o.p. (ISBN 0-87664-476-0). Instru Soc.

Instrumentation in the Power Industry, Vol. 24: Proceedings of the 24th Power Instrumentation Symposium. Power Instrumentation Symposium Staff. LC 62-52679. 200p. 1981. pap. text ed. 35.00x o.p. (ISBN 0-87664-520-1). Instru Soc.

Instrumentation in the Power Industry, Vol. 26: Proceedings of the Power Instrumentation Symposium. Power Instrumentation Symposium Staff. LC 62-52679. 248p. 1983. pap. text ed. 40.00x o.p. (ISBN 0-87664-770-0). Instru Soc.

Instrumentation in the Pulp & Paper Industry, Vol. 19: Proceedings of the Pulp & Paper Instrumentation Symposium. Pulp & Paper Instrumentation Symposium Staff. LC 73-82889. 52p. 1981. pap. text ed. 15.00x o.p. (ISBN 0-87664-517-1). Instru Soc.

Instrumentation in the Pulp & Paper Industry, Vol. 18: Proceedings of the Pulp & Paper Instrumentation Symposium. Pulp & Paper Instrumentation Symposium Staff. LC 73-82889. 71p. 1980. pap. text ed. 15.00x o.p. (ISBN 0-87664-475-2). Instru Soc.

Instrumentation Symposium for the Process Industries, Vol. 35: Proceedings of the Annual Instrumentation Symposium for the Process Industries. Instrumentation Symposium Staff. 118p. 1980. pap. text ed. 20.00x o.p. (ISBN 0-87664-487-6). Instru Soc.

Instrumentation Symposium for the Process Industries, Vol. 34: Proceedings of the Annual Instrumentation Symposium for the Process Industries. Instrumentation Symposium Staff. 118p. 1979. pap. text ed. 20.00x o.p. (ISBN 0-87664-446-9). Instru Soc.

Instrumentation-82: Proceedings of the 1982 Pacific Northwest Section Conference & Exhibit. Pacific Northwest Section Conference & Exhibit Staff. 114p. 1982. pap. text ed. 17.95x o.p. (ISBN 0-87664-679-8). Instru Soc.

Instruments of America's Foreign Policy. H. Bradford Westerfield. LC 79-25848. (Illus.). xvii, 538p. 1980. Repr. of 1963 ed. lib. bdg. 42.50x o.p. (ISBN 0-313-22271-1, WEIN). Greenwood.

Instruments of Communication. P. Meredith. 1966. 160.00 o.p. (ISBN 0-08-010663-3). Pergamon.

Instruments of Darkness. T. Ernesto Bethancourt. LC 78-11133. 160p. (YA) (gr. 7 up). 1979. 7.95 o.p. (ISBN 0-8234-0346-7). Holiday.

Instruments of Darkness: The History of Electronic Warfare. Alfred Price. (Illus.). 1978. 12.95 o.p. (ISBN 0-684-15806-X, ScribT); encore ed. 4.95 o.p. (ISBN 0-684-17249-6). Scribner.

Insubstantial Pageant: Ceremony & Confusion at Queen Victoria's Court. Jeffrey L. Lant. LC 80-17749. 278p. 1980. 12.95 o.s.i. (ISBN 0-8008-4191-3). Taplinger.

Insular Possession. Timothy Mo. LC 86-27983. 608p. 1987. 19.45 o.s.i. (ISBN 0-394-55430-2). Random.

Insularismo e Ideologia Burguesa. Juan Flores. 128p. 1980. pap. 4.95 o.p. (ISBN 0-940238-20-9). Ediciones Huracan.

Insulation - Materials & Processes for Aerospace & Hydrospace Applications: Proceedings, Symposium, San Francisco, 25-28 May 1965. (Science of Advanced Materials & Process Engineering Ser., Vol. 8). 880p. pap. 8.00 o.p. (ISBN 0-938994-08-5). SAMPE.

Insulin Treatment in Psychiatry. Max Rinkel. 1959. (ISBN 0-8022-1350-2). Philos Lib.

Insurance & Risk Management for Small Business. Mark R. Greene. (Starting & Managing Ser.: Vol. 30). 97p. 1986. pap. 3.00 o.p. (ISBN 0-318-22403-8, S/N 045-000-00235-7). USGPO.

Insurance & Third-Party-Payable Claims see Doctors' Administrative Program.

Insurance, Excess, & Reinsurance Coverage Disputes 1984. Practising Law Institute Staff & Barry R. Ostrager. LC 83-62212. (Litigation & Administrative Practice Ser.: No. 256). 1984. 40.00 o.p. PLI.

Insurance for Computers: A Checklist. Lorna Peterson. (Public Administration Ser.: P 1748). 6p. 1985. 2.00 o.p. (ISBN 0-89028-528-4). Vance Biblios.

Insurance Guide for Savings Institutions. 116p. 1983. 74.95 o.p. (ISBN 0-929097-19-X, 17210). US League Savi Inst.

Insurance Information Sources. Ed. by Roy Thomas. LC 75-137575. (Management Information Guide Ser.: No. 24). 340p. 1971. 68.00x o.p. (ISBN 0-8103-0824-X). Gale.

Insurance Law. 265p. 1981. 5.00 o.p. (ISBN 0-318-02408-X). ICLE Georgia.

Insurance Law Cases, Materials & Problems. Kenneth H. York & John W. Whelan. LC 82-10964. (American Casebook Ser.). 715p. 1982. text ed. 29.95 o.p. (ISBN 0-314-67596-5). West Pub.

Insurance Law Institute. 473p. 1982. 16.00 o.p. (ISBN 0-318-02410-1). ICLE Georgia.

Insurance Law Institute. 411p. 1983. 17.00 o.p. (ISBN 0-318-02411-X). ICLE Georgia.

Insurance Practice & Litigation. Pennsylvania Bar Institute Staff. 137p. 1984. 25.00 o.p. (ISBN 0-318-02198-6, 255). PA Bar Inst.

Insurance Primer: Fire & Casuality. 13th rev ed. George R. Fessler & Ray D. Westcott. 172p. 1984. pap. text ed. 7.95 o.p. (ISBN 0-935810-10-2, Dist by Medtech). Primer Pubs.

Insurance Producer's Handbook, 2 vols. Alfred I. Jaffe. 689p. 1980. Set. 125.00 o.p. (ISBN 0-686-73129-8, Inst Busn Plan). P-H.

Insurance Producer's Handbook: Vol. 1-Personal Lines. Alfred I. Jaffe. LC 78-58728. 207p. 1978. 49.50 o.p. (ISBN 0-87624-253-0, Inst Busn Plan). P-H.

Insurance Producer's Handbook: Vol. 2-Commercial Lines. Alfred I. Jaffe. LC 78-58728. 1980. 69.50 o.p. (ISBN 0-87624-254-9, Inst Busn Plan). P-H.

Insurance Products under the Securities Laws 1985: New Regulatory Initiatives: A Course Handbook. Gary E. Hughes & Paul J. Mason. 320p. 1985. pap. 15.00 o.p. (B4-6726). PLI.

Insurance: What Do You Need? How Much Is Enough? David W. Kennedy. LC 86-82236. 276p. 1987. 19.95 o.p. (ISBN 0-89586-568-8); pap. 9.95 o.p. (ISBN 0-89586-436-3). Price Stern.

Insuring Business Risks in Canada: How to Get the Most for Your Money. 1st ed. Geoffrey Bromwich. 103p. 1978. 3.50 o.p. (ISBN 0-88908-037-2). ISC Pr.

Insuring Your Home: How to Choose the Right Policy & Get the Most Benefit from Your Claim. Stephen Mink. 224p. (Orig.). 1986. pap. 7.95 o.p. (ISBN 0-86553-153-6). Congdon & Weed.

Insurrection in Dublin. James Stephens. 1979. text ed. 13.00x o. p. o.p. (ISBN 0-391-00942-7); pap. text ed. 6.50x o.p. (ISBN 0-391-00943-5). Humanities.

InTech Index: A Cumulative Index of Technical Articles Appearing in Instrumentation Technology (now InTech) 1954-1979. Compiled by Information Concepts, Inc. (ICON) Staff. LC 80-83406. 144p. 1980. pap. text ed. 29.95x o.p. (ISBN 0-87664-490-6). Instru Soc.

Integer & Non-Linear Programming. Ed. by J. Abadie. 544p. 1970. 123.75 o.p. (ISBN 0-7204-2036-9). Elsevier.

Integer Programming. Harold Greenberg. (Mathematics in Science & Engineering Ser.: Vol. 76). 1971. 47.50 o.p. (ISBN 0-12-299450-7). Acad Pr.

Integer Programming & Related Areas: A Classified Bibliography 1976 - 1978. Compiled at the Institute Fuer Oekonometrie und Operations Research, Univ of Bonn. Ed. by D. Hausmann. LC 78-18918. (Lecture Notes in Economics & Mathematical Systems: Vol. 160). 1978. pap. 20.00 o.p. (ISBN 0-387-08939-X). Springer-Verlag.

Integral Calculus. Walter Ledermann. (Library of Mathematics). 1967. pap. 5.00x o.p. (ISBN 0-7100-4355-4). Routledge Chapman & Hall.

Integral Operators in the Theory of Linear Partial Differential Equations. Stefan Bergman. LC 68-57393. (Ergenbisse der Mathematik und Grenzgebiete: Vol. 23). (Illus.). 1969. 29.00 o.p. (ISBN 0-387-04468-X). Springer-Verlag.

Integral Representations. I. Reiner & K. W. Roggenkamp. (Lecture Notes in Mathematics: Vol. 744). 1979. pap. 19.00 o.p. (ISBN 0-387-09546-2). Springer-Verlag.

Integral Yoga-Hatha. Date not set. pap. 12.95 o.p. (ISBN 0-8050-1042-4). H Holt & Co.

Integrated Approach to Foreign Bank Analysis. Morris, Robert, Associates Staff. LC 81-84671. (Illus.). 48p. (Orig.). 1981. pap. 15.00 o.s.i. (ISBN 0-936742-04-6). Robt Morris Assocs.

Integrated Atlas of Gastric Diseases. Klaus Krentz. LC 75-16099. (Illus.). 212p. 1976. 25.00 o.p. (ISBN 0-88416-058-0). Year Bk Med.

Integrated Automation Practice. L. Pun et al. LC 74-81330. 368p. 1976. 42.00 o.p. (ISBN 0-444-10709-6, North-Holland). Elsevier.

Integrated Circuit Fabrication Technology. D. J. Elliott. 1982. text ed. 49.95 o.p. (ISBN 0-07-019238-3). McGraw.

Integrated Circuits: A Basic Course for Engineers & Technicians. Robert G. Hibbard. (Texas Instruments Electronics Ser.). 1969. text ed. 49.50 o.p. (ISBN 0-07-028651-5). McGraw.

Integrated Desk-Top Environments: Symphony, Framework, Visi-On & DesQ. P. B. Seybold & R. T. Marshak. 208p. 1985. pap. pap. text ed. 16.95 o.p. (ISBN 0-07-056324-1). McGraw.

Integrated Devices in Digital Circuit Design. Gordon S. Hope. LC 80-17152. 368p. 1981. 45.50x o.p. (ISBN 0-471-07920-0). Wiley.

Integrated Environment in Building Design. Ed. by A. F. Sherratt. LC 74-22250. 281p. 1975. 62.95x o.p. (ISBN 0-470-78575-6). Halsted Pr.

Integrated Environmental Control for Coal-Fired Power Plants. Ed. by H. E. Hesketh. 158p. 1981. 30.00 o.p. (ISBN 0-686-34498-7, H00181). ASME.

Integrated Injection Logic. Ed. by J. E. Smith. 421p. 1980. 42.95x o.p. (ISBN 0-471-08675-4, Pub. by Wiley-Interscience); pap. 22.00x o.p. (ISBN 0-471-08676-2). Wiley.

Integrated Models in Geography. Ed. by Richard J. Chorley. Peter Haggett. 1969. pap. 12.50x o.p. (ISBN 0-416-29840-0, NO. 2132). Routledge Chapman & Hall.

Integrated Optics & Optical Communications. Ed. by Gray Ward. 1974. pap. 12.95x o.p. (ISBN 0-8422-0402-4). Irvington.

Integrated Optics: Related Conference Proceedings. Ed. by J. R. Wait et al. (IEE Conference Publication: No. 227). 158p. 1983. pap. 60.00 o.s.i. (ISBN 0-85296-281-9). Inst Elect Eng.

Integrated Pest Management. Ed. by J. Lawrence Apple & Ray F. Smith. LC 76-17549. (Illus.). 214p. 1976. 39.50x o.p. (ISBN 0-306-30929-7, Plenum Pr). Plenum Pub.

Integrated Photoelasticity. Hillar Aben. (Illus.). 1979. text ed. 48.00x o.p. (ISBN 0-07-000043-3). McGraw.

Integrated Principles of Zoology. 7th ed. Cleveland P. Hickman & Larry S. Roberts. (Illus.). 1168p. 1983. 42.95 o.p. (ISBN 0-8016-2173-9). Mosby.

Integrated Renewable Resources Management for United States Insular Areas. LC 86-600595. (OTA-F: No. 325). 447p. (Orig.). 1987. pap. 18.00 o.p. (ISBN 0-317-62862-3, S-N 052-003-01055-1). USGPO.

Integrated Rural Development in Latin America. Richard L. Lacroix. (Working Paper Ser.: No. 716). 98p. 1985. 5.00 o.p. (ISBN 0-8213-0494-1, WP 0716). World Bank.

Integrated Rural Development in the Third World: Its Concepts, Problems & Prospects. Edet M. Abasiekong. (Illus.). 144p. 1982. 7.50 o.p. (ISBN 0-682-49750-9, University). Exposition-Phoenix.

Integrated Services Digital Networks (ISDN) William Stallings. LC 85-80548. 325p. 1985. 39.00 o.p. (ISBN 0-8186-0625-8, Q625). IEEE Comp Soc.

Integrated Software for Microcomputer Systems. Lynne S. Rosenthal. (National Bureau of Standards Special Publication. Computer Science & Technology: No. 500-135). 38p. (Orig.). 1986. pap. 1.75 o.p. (ISBN 0-318-22405-4, S/N 003-003-02711-1). USGPO.

Integrated Studies in Patient Care. Marion Glass & Evelyn Atchison. LC 76-46127. 1978. pap. text ed. 19.95 o.p. (ISBN 0-8273-1608-9); instr's. guide 7.00 o.p. (ISBN 0-8273-1609-7). Delmar.

Integrated Studies in Patient Care. Marion Glass & Evelyn Atchison. 1978. 23.95 o.p. (ISBN 0-442-22699-3). Van Nos Reinhold.

Integrated Transformational Grammar of the English Language. Garland Cannon. (Costerus New Ser.: No. 8). 1978. pap. text ed. 35.00x o.p. (ISBN 90-6203-400-4). Humanities.

Integrated Urban Models. Stephen H. Putman. (Research in Planning & Design Ser.). 310p. 1983. 30.00 o.p. (ISBN 0-85086-098-9, 5057, Pub. by Pion). Routledge Chapman & Hall.

Integrated Voice-Data Terminals. International Resource Development, Inc. Staff. 215p. 1984. 1850.00x o.p. (ISBN 0-88694-585-2). Intl Res Dev.

Integrating College Study Skills: Reasoning in Reading, Listening, & Writing. Peter E. Sotiriou. 352p. 1984. pap. text ed. (ISBN 0-534-02823-3). Wadsworth Pub.

Integrating Jerusalem Schools. Zev Klein. (Quantitative Studies in Social Relations Ser.). 1980. 29.50 o.p. (ISBN 0-12-413250-2). Acad Pr.

Integrating Nutrition into Agricultural & Rural Development Projects: A Manual. (Nutrition in Agriculture Ser.: No. 1). 63p. 1982. pap. 7.50 o.p. (ISBN 92-5-101305-5, F2414, FAO). UNIPUB.

Integrating Population Education in Rural Development Programmes. 29p. 1977. pap. 7.50 o.p. (ISBN 92-5-100321-1, F933, FAO). UNIPUB.

Integration & Development in Israel. Samuel N. Eisenstadt & Rivkah Bar-Yosef. 720p. 1971. casebound 24.95x o.p. (ISBN 0-87855-178-6). Transaction Pubs.

Integration & Excision of DNA Molecules. Ed. by P. H. Hofschneider & P. Starlinger. (Colloquium der Gesellschaft Fur Biologische Chemie: Vol 28). (Illus.). 1978. 30.00 o.p. (ISBN 0-387-08560-2). Springer-Verlag.

Integration Theory: With Special Attention to Vector Measures. K. Bichteler. LC 72-97636. (Lecture Notes in Mathematics: Vol. 315). 357p. 1973. pap. 16.00 o.p. (ISBN 0-387-06158-4). Springer-Verlag.

Integrity of Being. Peter Ralston. 236p. (Orig.). 1983. pap. 13.50 o.p. (ISBN 0-317-47156-2, Dist. by Bookpeople). C Hsin Pr.

Integrity of Mission: The Inner Life & Outreach of the Church. Orlando E. Costas. LC 79-1759. 1979. pap. 5.95 o.p. (ISBN 0-06-061586-9, RD 235). HarpR.

Integrity of the Body. Frank M. Burnet. LC 62-8180. (Illus.). 1966. pap. 1.75 o.p. (ISBN 0-689-70029-6, 85, Atheneum). Macmillan.

Intellectual & Manual Labour: A Critique of Epistemology. Alfred Sohn-Rethel. LC 77-12975. (Critical Social Studies). 1978. text ed. 26.50x o.p. (ISBN 0-391-00774-2); pap. text ed. 15.00x o.p. (ISBN 0-333-23046-9). Humanities.

Intellectual Crisis in English Catholicism: Liberal Catholics, Modernists, & the Vatican in the Late Nineteenth & Early Twentieth Centuries. William J. Schoenl. Ed. by Peter Stanmsky & Leslie Hume. LC 81-48368. 360p. 1982. lib. bdg. 52.00 o.p. (ISBN 0-8240-5164-5). Garland Pub.

Intellectual Experiments of the Greek Enlightenment. Friedrich Solmsen. LC 74-25629. 296p. 1975. 34.00 o.p. (ISBN 0-691-07201-9). Princeton U Pr.

Intellectual Follies: A Memoir of the Literary Venture in New York & Paris. Lionel Abel. 384p. 1984. 17.45 o.p. (ISBN 0-393-01841-5). Norton.

Intellectual Follies: A Memoir of the Literary Venture in New York & Paris. Lionel Abel. 304p. 1987. pap. 7.70 o.p. (ISBN 0-393-30379-9). Norton.

Intellectual Foundations of Library Education. Ed. by Don R. Swanson. LC 65-2702. (University of Chicago Studies in Library Science Ser). 1965. lib. bdg. 5.75x o.s.i. (ISBN 0-226-78467-3). U of Chicago Pr.

Intellectual Giftedness in Disabled Persons. Joanne R. Whitmore & C. June Maker. 268p. 1985. 36.00 o.p. (ISBN 0-87189-236-7). Aspen Pub.

Intellectual Primer. Jay C. Knode. 1955. (ISBN 0-8022-0873-8). Philos Lib.

Intellectual Property Law Review, 1986. Ed. by Barry Kramer. LC 79-88703. (Intellectual Property Library Ser.). 450p. 1986. 69.95 o.p. (ISBN 0-87632-507-X). Clark Boardman.

Intellectual Property Rights in an Age of Electronics & Information. LC 86-600522. (OTA-CIT-302). (Illus.). 316p. (Orig.). 1986. pap. 15.00 o.p. (ISBN 0-318-20408-8, S/N 052-003-01036-4). USGPO.

Intellectual Versus the City: From Thomas Jefferson to Frank Lloyd Wright. Morton White & Lucia White. LC 81-1755. xiv, 270p. 1981. Repr. of 1977 ed. lib. bdg. 35.00x o.p. (ISBN 0-313-22786-1, WHIV). Greenwood.

Intellectualized Emotions & the Art of James Joyce. Agwonorobo E. Eruvbetine. 1980. 7.50 o.p. (ISBN 0-682-49530-1, University). Exposition-Phoenix.

Intellectuals & the Powers: And Other Essays. Edward Shils. LC 79-178196. 388p. 1983. pap. text ed. 25.00x o.s.i. (ISBN 0-226-75334-4, Midway Reprint). U of Chicago Pr.

Intellectuals in Politics in the Greek World: From Early Times to the Hellenistic Age. Frank L. Vatai. LC 84-15589. 184p. 1984. 32.00 o.p. (ISBN 0-7099-2613-8, Pub. by Croom Helm Ltd). Routledge Chapman & Hall.

Intellectuals on the Road to Class Power: A Sociological Study of the Role of the Intelligentsia in Socialism. George Konrad & Ivan Szelenyi. Tr. by Andrew Arato & Richard E. Allen. LC 77-92547. 256p. 1979. 10.00 o.s.i. (ISBN 0-15-177860-4). HarBraceJ.

Intelligence: An Introduction. David W. Pyle. (Illus.). 1979. 19.95x o.p. (ISBN 0-7100-0306-4); pap. 8.95x o.p. (ISBN 0-7100-0307-2). Routledge Chapman & Hall.

Intelligence & Experience. J. M. Hunt. (Illus.). 416p. 1961. 35.95x o.p. (ISBN 0-471-06907-8). Wiley.

Intelligence in the War of Independence. Ed. by Hale, Nathan, Institute Staff. 1985. Repr. of 1976 ed. write for info. o.p. (ISBN 0-935067-07-8). Nathan Hale Inst.

Intelligence: Its Organization & Development. Michael Cunningham. 1972. 27.50 o.p. (ISBN 0-12-199150-4). Acad Pr.

Intelligence Men: Makers of the I.Q. Controversy. Raymond E. Fancher. LC 84-27381. (Illus.). 1985. 18.45 o.p. (ISBN 0-393-01982-9). Norton.

Intelligent Eye. Richard L. Gregory. 1971. pap. text ed. 3.95 o.p. (ISBN 0-07-024664-5). McGraw.

Intelligent Instrumentation: Microprocessor Applications in Measurement & Control. George C. Barney. (Illus.). 528p. 1985. text ed. 52.00 o.p. (ISBN 0-13-468943-7). P-H.

Intelligent Investing: Profit-Making Moves in the Stock Market. George S. Brunson. 1971. 7.50 o.p. (ISBN 0-682-47252-2, Banner). Exposition-Phoenix.

Intelligent Investor's Guide to IRAs & Keogh Plans. Nigel Littlejohn. LC 83-45214. 224p. 1984. 19.95 o.p. (ISBN 0-8144-5777-0); pap. 9.95 o.p. (ISBN 0-8144-7606-6). AMACOM.

Intelligent Investor's Guide to Real Estate. David W. Walters. LC 80-17718. (Wiley Series in California Real Estate). 364p. 1980. 24.95 o.p. (ISBN 0-471-07874-3). Wiley.

Intelligent Man's Way to Prevent War. Ed. by Leonard Woolf. LC 70-148372. (Library of War & Peace; the Character & Causes of War). 1973. lib. bdg. 46.00 o.p. (ISBN 0-8240-0464-7). Garland Pub.

Intelligent Universe: A New View of Creation & Evolution. Fred Hoyle. 1984. 18.95 o.s.i. (ISBN 0-03-070083-3). H Holt & Co.

Intelligible World: Metaphysics & Value. Wilbur M. Urban. LC 76-51208. 1977. Repr. of 1929 ed. lib. bdg. 35.00x o.p. (ISBN 0-8371-9437-7, URIW). Greenwood.

Intemperate Zone: The Third World Challenge to U. S. Foreign Policy. Richard E. Feinberg. 216p. 1983. 17.00 o.p. (ISBN 0-393-01712-5). Norton.

Intensional & Higher Order Modal Logic PPR. D. Gallin. (MSS Ser.: Vol. 19). 1987. 49.00 o.p. (ISBN 0-317-65933-2). Elsevier.

Intensive Care & Emergency Medicine: Proceedings of the Fourth International Symposium. Ed. by J. L. Vincent. (Anaesthesiologie & Intensivemedizin. Anaesthesiology & Intensive Care Medicine: Band 167). (Illus.). xiii, 190p. 1984. pap. 21.70 o.p. (ISBN 0-387-13412-3). Springer Verlag.

Intensive Care of Newborn Infants: A Practical Manual. Theodore R. Thompson. LC 83-10454. (Illus.). 388p. 1983. spiral bdg. 29.50x o.p. (ISBN 0-8166-1095-9). U of Minn Pr.

Intensive Course in Bengali. Krishna Bhattacharya. 1984. 14.00x o.p. (ISBN 0-8364-1229-X, Pub. by Ctrl Inst). South Asia Bks.

Intensive Course in English: English Language Services, 3 vols. 1969. Vol. 1. pap. 4.50 o.p. (ISBN 0-87789-003-X); Vol. 2. pap. 4.95 o.p. (ISBN 0-87789-004-8). Vol. 3 (ISBN 0-87789-005-6). ELS Educ Servs.

Intensive Gardening Round the Year. Paul Doscher et al. LC 80-21921. (Illus.). 224p. 1981. pap. 10.95 o.s.i. (ISBN 0-8289-0399-9). Greene.

Intensive Group Experience: The New Pietism. Thomas C. Oden. 1972. pap. 3.45 o.s.i. (ISBN 0-664-24951-5, Westminster). Westminster John Knox.

Intensivhaltung von Nutztieren aus ethischer, rechtlicher und ethologischer Sicht. Ed. by Gotthard M. Teutsch & Eisenhart Von Loeper. (Tierhaltung-Animal Management: No. 8). 228p. (Ger.). 1979. pap. 20.95x o.p. (ISBN 0-8176-1119-3). Birkhauser.

Intentional Interviewing & Counseling. Allen E. Ivey. LC 82-14689. (Counseling Ser.). 320p. 1982. pap. text ed. 14.25 pub net o.p. (ISBN 0-534-01331-7). Brooks-Cole.

Inter-Act: Using Interpersonal Communication Skills. 4th ed. Kathleen S. Verderber & Rudolph F. Verderber. 323p. 1986. pap. text ed. (ISBN 0-534-05478-1). Wadsworth Pub.

Inter-American Bank Index of Periodical Articles on the Economics of Latin America. Inter-American Development Bank, Washington, D. C. Staff. 2016p. 1983. lib. bdg. 620.00 o.p. (ISBN 0-8161-0416-6, Hall Library). G K Hall.

Inter-Ethnic Death Rate Differential in Florida. James H. Boykin. Date not set. 5.00 o.p. (ISBN 0-9603342-5-4); pap. 3.75x o.p. Boykin.

Inter Ice Age Four. Kobo Abe. Tr. by E. Dale Saunders from Japanese. (Perigee Japanese Library). 240p. 1981. pap. 4.95 o.p. (ISBN 0-399-50519-9, Perigee). Putnam Pub Group.

Inter-Noise '85: Proceedings, 2 vols. International Conference on Noise Control Engineering Staff. Ed. by H. Steinhardt. 1985. Set. 85.00 o.p. Noise Control.

Inter-Racial Marriages in London: A Comparative Study. C. T. Kannan. 1972. 12.50 o.s.i. E J Brill USA.

Interact in Spanish. Melvyn C. Resnick. 1985. pap. text ed. 11.00 o.p. (ISBN 0-88377-420-8); tchr's. ed. 13.25 o.p. (ISBN 0-88377-450-X). Newbury Hse.

Interacting Bose-Fermi Systems in Nuclei. Ed. by F. Iachello. LC 81-4319. (Ettore Majorana International Science Series, Physical Sciences: Vol. 10). 412p. 1981. 85.00x o.p. (ISBN 0-306-40733-7, Plenum Pr). Plenum Pub.

Interacting Systems in Development. 2nd ed. James D. Ebert & Ian M. Sussex. LC 78-100552. (Modern Biology Ser.). 338p. 1970. pap. text ed. 18.95x o.p. (ISBN 0-03-081306-9, HoltC). HR&W.

Interaction Between Science & Philosophy: Sambursky Festschrift. Ed. by Yehuda Elkana. 1972. text ed. 17.50x o.p. (ISBN 0-391-00255-4). Humanities.

Interaction of Gases with Solid Surfaces. William A. Steele. LC 73-21747. 356p. 1974. 95.00 o.p. (ISBN 0-08-017724-7). Pergamon.

Interaction of High-Energy Particles with Nuclei. Ed. by T. E. Ericson. (Italian Physical Society: Course 38). 1967. 77.00 o.p. (ISBN 0-12-368838-8). Acad Pr.

Interaction of Metals & Gases, Vol. 1. Thermodynamics & Phase Relations. Johan D. Fast. 1965. 70.50 o.p. (ISBN 0-12-249801-1). Acad Pr.

Interaction of Radiation & Anti-Tumor Drugs: Proceedings of the Stanford Code Memorial Symposium, Royal Institute, London, Sept., 1976. Stanford Cade Memorial Symposium Staff. Ed. by Kurt Hellmann. (International Journal of Radiation Oncology, Biology, Physics: Vol. 4, No. 1-2 78--Special Issue). (Illus.). 1978. pap. 58.00 o.p. (ISBN 0-08-022666-3). Pergamon.

Interaction Studies in Nuclei. H. Jochim & B. Ziegler. LC 75-23218. 1975. 92.00 o.p. (ISBN 0-444-10963-3, North-Holland). Elsevier.

Interaction Within the Brain-Pituitary Adrenocortical System. Ed. by Mortyn Jones et al. 1979. 76.00 o.p. (ISBN 0-12-389150-7). Acad Pr.

Interactional Psychotherapy. Benjamin B. Wolman. 224p. 1984. 31.95 o.p. (ISBN 0-442-20831-6). Van Nos Reinhold.

Interactions Between Electromagnetic Fields & Matter. Karl-Heinz Steiner. LC 73-2931. xvi, 351p. 1973. 44.00 o.p. (ISBN 0-08-017292-X). Pergamon.

Interactions of Selected Drugs & Nutrients in Patients: Handbook. 3rd ed. Daphne A. Roe. 152p. 1982. pap. 22.75 o.p. (ISBN 0-88091-004-6). Am Dietetic Assn.

Interactions on Metal Surfaces, Vol. 4. Ed. by R. Gomer. LC 75-1281. (Topics in Applied Physics Ser). (Illus.). 340p. 1975. 46.00 o.p. (ISBN 0-387-07094-X). Springer-Verlag.

Interactive Data Analysis: A Practical Primer. Donald R. McNeil. LC 76-46571. (Probability & Mathematical Ser.). 186p. 1977. pap. 24.95x o.p. (ISBN 0-471-02631-X, Pub. by Wiley-Interscience). Wiley.

Interactive-Fluid-Structural Dynamic Problems in Power Engineering. Ed. by M. K. Au-Yang & F. J. Moody. (PVP Ser.: vol. 46). 177p. 1981. 30.00 o.p. (ISBN 0-686-34516-9, H00182). ASME.

Interactive Layout System Comparison Charts: 1985 Edition. Harold Durbin. 1985. write for info. o.s.i. (ISBN 0-936786-09-4). Durbin Assoc.

Interactive Systems for Experimental Applied Mathematics. Ed. by Melvin Klerer & Juris Reinfelds. 1968. 75.50 o.p. (ISBN 0-12-414650-3). Acad Pr.

Interactive Systems: Proceedings of the IBM Informatik Symposium, 6th, Bad Homburg, Germany, Sept., 1976. IBM Informatik Symposium Staff. Ed. by A. Blaser & C. Hackl. (Lecture Notes in Computer Science: Vol. 49). 1977. 21.00 o.s.i. (ISBN 0-387-08141-0). Springer-Verlag.

Interactive Video in Special & General Education: A Development Manual. Patti Zembrosky-Barkin & Gary Nave. 68p. 1985. (ISBN 0-924667-25-7). Intl Council Comp.

Interactive Video Systems & Services. International Resource Development, Inc. Staff. 217p. 1983. 1450.00x o.p. (ISBN 0-88694-564-X). Intl Res Dev.

Interagency & Interstate Cooperation in Criminal Justice: A Select Bibliography. Mary E. Huls. 1985. pap. 2.00 o.p. (ISBN 0-89028-382-6). Vance Biblios.

Interatomic Potentials. Ian M. Torrens. 1972. 64.50 o.p. (ISBN 0-12-695850-5). Acad Pr.

Interatomic Potentials & Crystalline Defects: Proceedings of the TMS-AIME Fall Meeting, Pittsburgh, 1980. Ed. by Jong K. Lee. (Illus.). 380p. 30.00 o.p. (ISBN 0-89520-377-4); members 18.00 o.p. (ISBN 0-317-36243-7); student members 10.00 o.p. (ISBN 0-317-36244-5). ASM.

Interavia ABC Aerospace Directory, 1987. 35th ed. 1987. 175.00 o.p. (ISBN 0-8002-4155-X). Intl Pubns Serv.

Intercambios: An Activities Manual. Ronald G. Freeman. 209p. 1980. pap. text ed. 9.00 o.p. (ISBN 0-394-32425-0, RanC). Random.

Intercellular Communication in Plants: Studies on Plasmodesmata. Ed. by B. E. Gunning & A. W. Robards. (Illus.). 300p. 1976. 46.00 o.p. (ISBN 0-387-07570-4). Springer-Verlag.

Intercellular Junctions & Synapses see Queues: Receptors & Recognition Series B.

Interchange Drive Belt Guide. 780p. 1989. 115.00 o.p. (ISBN 0-916966-19-4). Interchange.

Intercom: Readings in Organizational Communication. Stewart Ferguson & Sherry D. Ferguson. 412p. 1980. pap. text ed. 14.95x o.p. (ISBN 0-8104-5127-1). Transaction Pubs.

Intercomparison of Stratospheric-Mesospheric Data: Proceedings of the Topical Meeting of the COSPAR Interdisciplinary Scientific Commission A (Meeting A1) of the COSPAR 25th Plenary Meeting, Graz, Austria, 25 June-7 July 1984. Ed. by A Ghazi & R. T. Watson. (Illus.). 148p. 1985. pap. 54.00 o.p. (ISBN 0-08-032734-6, Pub. by PPL). Pergamon.

Interconnect: Why & How. RAK Associates Staff & Dick Kuehn. 75p. 1982. 15.00 o.p. (ISBN 0-686-98038-7). Telecom Lib.

Interconnection Glossary. 25.00 o.p. (ISBN 0-686-32974-0). Info Gatekeepers.

Interconnection Networks for Large-Scale Parallel Processing: Theory & Case Studies. Howard J. Siegel. LC 79-6015. 288p. 1985. 42.00x o.p. (ISBN 0-669-03594-7). Lexington Bks.

Intercultural Communication. L. E. Sarbaugh. 148p. 1979. pap. text ed. 9.95x o.p. (ISBN 0-8104-6090-4). Transaction Pubs.

Intercultural Education in the Two-Year College: A Handbook on Strategies for Change. Ed. by Jorge M. Perez Ponce. 90p. (Orig.). 1976. pap. 4.00x o.p. (ISBN 0-936876-11-5). LRIS.

Interdependent Development. Harold Brookfield. LC 74-18752. 248p. 1975. 11.95x o.p. (ISBN 0-8229-1118-3); pap. text ed. 11.95x o.p. (ISBN 0-416-78070-9). U of Pittsburgh Pr.

Interdisciplinary Surface Science: Proceedings of the ISSC6 Conference, Warwick, U. K., April 18-21, 1983, Vol. VI. Ed. by P. J. Dobson. 250p. 1984. pap. 45.00 o.p. (ISBN 0-08-031146-6). Pergamon.

Interdisciplinary Surface Science: Proceedings of the 5th Interdisciplinary Surface Science Conference, (ISSC), April 6-9, 1981, University of Liverpool, U. K. Ed. by R. H. Williams et al. 260p. 1983. pap. 36.00 o.p. (ISBN 0-08-029318-2, A145, C125). Pergamon.

Interdisciplinary Team: A Handbook for the Education of Exceptional Children. Anne K. Golin & Alex J. Ducanis. LC 81-738. 206p. 1981. text ed. 32.00 o.p. (ISBN 0-89443-346-6). Aspen Pub.

Interest-Bearing Corporate Demand Deposit Accounts: Their Impact on Financial Institutions. 109p. 1985. 60.00 o.p. (ISBN 0-318-04774-8, 635). Bank Admin Inst.

Interest Group Politics. Allan Cigler & Burdett Loomis. LC 82-22208. 373p. 1983. pap. 13.95 o.p. (ISBN 0-87187-247-1). Congr Quarterly.

Interest Group Society. Jeffrey M. Berry. 1984. pap. text ed. write for info. o.p. (ISBN 0-673-39422-0). Scott F.

Interest Rate Policies in Selected Developing Countries, 1970-1982. James A. Hanson & Craig R. Neal. (Working Paper: No. 753). 188p. 1985. 8.00 o.p. (ISBN 0-8213-0608-1, WP 0753). World Bank.

Interests & the Growth of Knowledge. Barry Barnes. (Direct Editions Ser.). (Orig.). 1977. pap. 11.95x o.p. (ISBN 0-7100-8669-5). Routledge Chapman & Hall.

Interface. Joe Gores. LC 73-91882. 216p. 1974. 5.95 o.p. (ISBN 0-87131-146-1). M Evans.

Interface Assignment. William Rayner. LC 77-4493. 7.95 o.p. (ISBN 0-689-10804-4, Atheneum). Macmillan.

Interface: Calculus & the Computer. David A. Smith. LC 75-25016. (Illus.). 288p. 1976. pap. 14.95 o.p. (ISBN 0-395-21875-6). HM.

Interface Data Book for Word Processing Typesetting. Ronald A. Labuz & Paul Altimonte. 195p. 1984. pap. 29.95 o.p. (ISBN 0-8352-1908-9). Bowker.

Interface Discontinued Devices. 1987. 70.00 o.p. DATA Busn Pub.

INTERFACE Eighty-One (G-135) Proceedings of the Kodak Microelectronics Seminar. (Illus.). 118p. 1982. pap. 6.50 o.p. (ISBN 0-87985-307-7). Eastman Kodak.

Interface for Murder. Lloyd Biggle, Jr. LC 87-9028. (Crime Club Ser.). 192p. 1987. 12.95 o.p. (ISBN 0-385-24310-3). Doubleday.

Interface in Retrospect: 1978-1980. Ed. by Molly M. Jellison. 1980. 7.50 o.p. (1027). Am Assn Comm Jr Coll.

Interface: The Painter & the Mask. Francoise Gilot. LC 83-61745. Orig. Title: Le Regard et Son Masque. (Illus.). 200p. 1983. 18.95 o.p. (ISBN 0-912201-02-9); pap. 9.95 o.p. (ISBN 0-912201-03-7). CSU Pr Fresno.

Interfaces in Metal Matrix Composites. Ed. by A. K. Dhingra & S. G. Fishman. LC 86-20106. (Illus.). 257p. 1986. 69.00 o.p. (ISBN 0-87339-051-2). Minerals Metals.

Interfacing Test Circuits with Single-Board Computers. Robert H. Luetzow. (Illus.). 256p. (Orig.). 1983. 19.95 o.p. (ISBN 0-8306-0183-X); pap. 13.50 o.p. (ISBN 0-8306-0583-5, 1583P). TAB Bks.

Interfacing to the S-100 Microcomputers. S. Libes & M. Garetz. 1981. pap. text ed. 16.95 o.p. (ISBN 0-07-931037-0). McGraw.

Interfacing Your Microcomputer to Virtually Anything. Joseph J. Carr. LC 84-8709. (Illus.). 336p. (Orig.). 1984. 21.95 o.p. (ISBN 0-8306-0890-7, 1890H); pap. 13.60 o.p. (ISBN 0-8306-1890-2, 1890). TAB Bks.

Interferon & Nonspecific Resistance. Alexander Yabrov. LC 80-13677. 374p. 1980. 44.95 o.p. (ISBN 0-87705-497-5). Human Sci Pr.

Interferons, 2 vols. Incl. Vol. 1. Edward Dubovi et al (ISBN 0-8422-7247-X); Vol. 2. Page S. Morahan et al (ISBN 0-8422-7248-8). 1977. text ed. 34.50x ea. o.p. Irvington.

Interferons. Ed. by G. Rita. LC 68-23504. 1968. 65.00 o.p. (ISBN 0-12-589050-8). Acad Pr.

Interferons: Symposium. Ed. by Thomas C. Merigan & Robert M. Friedman. 481p. 1982. 56.50 o.p. (ISBN 0-12-491220-6). Acad Pr.

Interflow Eighty. Institution of Chemical Engineers Staff. 1982. 58.00 o.s.i. (ISBN 0-08-028758-1). Pergamon.

Intergovernmental Fiscal Relations During the First Reagan Administration: A Bibliography. Jacqueline Mundell. (Public Administration Ser.: P 1715). 17p. 1985. 2.25 o.p. (ISBN 0-89028-465-2). Vance Biblios.

Intergovernmental Organizations & the Ocean. (UNITAR, agency). pap. 8.50 o.p. (UTR2, UNITAR). UNIPUB.

Intergovernmental Relations in the United States. William V. Holloway. LC 72-7472. 182p. 1972. 29.50x o.p. (ISBN 0-8422-5054-9); pap. text ed. 6.95x o.p. (ISBN 0-8422-0257-9). Irvington.

Intergrated Electronic Circuits & System. King. 1983. 37.95 o.p. (ISBN 0-442-30562-1). Van Nos Reinhold.

Intergrated Medicine. Ed. by Stacey B. Day. (Companion to the Life Sciences Ser.: Vol. 2). 625p. 1980. 41.95 o.p. (ISBN 0-442-25163-7). Van Nos Reinhold.

Intergration in the Nervous System. Ed. & pref. by Hiroshi Asanuma. LC 79-84783. (Illus.). 357p. 1979. 52.50 o.p. (ISBN 0-89640-033-6). Igaku-Shoin.

Interim Materials on Highway Capacity. (Transportation Research Circular). 276p. 1980. 10.00 o.p. (ISBN 0-317-36090-6). Transport Res Bd.

Interim Results of the Middle Atmosphere Program: A Selection of Invited Papers from the Symposium Jointly Sponsored by the IAGA & IAMAP at the XVIII General Assembly of the IUGG, Hamburg, Federal Republic of Germany, August 1985. Ed. by R. G. Roper. 112p. 1985. pap. 36.00 o.p. (ISBN 0-08-032594-7). Pergamon.

Interior Best Selection II. Ed. by Graphic-Sha Staff & Orange Book Co. Staff. 288p. 1986. 69.95 o.s.i. (ISBN 4-766-10386-6, Pub. by Graphic Sha Japan). Bks Nippan.

Interior Cost Data, 1986. 3rd ed. Means, R. S., Company, Inc. Staff. Ed. by Kornelis Smit. (Illus.). 400p. 1985. pap. 40.95 o.p. (ISBN 0-87629-008-X). R S Means.

Interior Design of Stores: A Bibliography. Mary Vance. (Architecture Ser.: A 1439). 15p. 1985. 2.25 o.p. (ISBN 0-89028-509-8). Vance Biblios.

Interior Designers Handbook on Plants. David L. Hamilton. 256p. 1987. 42.00 o.p. (ISBN 0-939129-54-X). Hamiltons Pub.

Interior Lighting. J. B. DeBoer & D. Fischer. (Philips Technical Library). (Illus.). 1978. text ed. 85.00x o.p. (ISBN 0-333-25670-0, Pub. by Macmillan England). Scholium Intl.

Interior of the Earth: Its Structure, Constitution & Evolution. 2nd ed. M. H. Bott. 404p. 1982. 47.25 o.p. (ISBN 0-444-00723-7). Elsevier.

Interior Planting Design File. Susan Van Gieson & Regina Kurtz. LC 80-70578. (Illus.). 96p. 1984. pap. 18.95 o.s.i. (ISBN 0-442-22344-7). Van Nos Reinhold.

Interior Plantscapes: Installation Maintenance & Management. George H. Manaker. 1981. pap. text ed. 34.67 o.p. (ISBN 0-13-469312-4). P-H.

Interior: S. Kitahara's Modernism. S. Kitahara. (Illus.). 120p. 1986. 32.95 o.s.i. (ISBN 4-897-37054-X, Pub. by Rikuyo-Sha Japan). Bks Nippan.

Interlibrary Loan. Systems & Procedures Exchange Center Staff. (SPEC Kit & Flyer Ser.: No. 92). 98p. 1983. 20.00 o.p. (ISBN 0-318-03463-8). Assn Res Lib.

Interlinear Greek-English New Testament: Numerically Coded to Strong's Exhaustive Concordance. 1187p. (Orig.). 1981. pap. 19.95 o.p. (ISBN 0-8010-5034-0). Baker Bk.

Interlingual Critic: Interpreting Chinese Poetry. James J. Liu. LC 81-47010. 160p. 1982. 17.95x o.p. (ISBN 0-253-33030-0). Ind U Pr.

Interlude & Other Poems. Ottys Sanders & Ruth Sanders. Ed. by Nortex Press Staff. 104p. 1988. text ed. 14.95 o.p. Eakin Pr.

Intermediate Accounting. Paul P. Danos & Eugene A. Imhoff, Jr. (Illus.). 1088p. 1983. text ed. 42.67 o.p. (ISBN 0-13-469338-8); practice set 12.95 o.p. (ISBN 0-13-469619-0). P-H.

Intermediate Accounting. James D. Edwards et al. 1981. text ed. 34.50x o.p. (ISBN 0-256-02427-8); study guide 8.25 o.p. (ISBN 0-256-02581-9); study guide, vol. 1 8.25 o.p.; working papers, vol. 2 11.25 o.p. (ISBN 0-256-02553-3); Practice set 6.95 o.p. (ISBN 0-256-02555-X); CPA Exam Supplement 11.25 o.p. (ISBN 0-256-02729-3). Irwin.

Intermediate Accounting. 2nd ed. Loren A. Nikolai et al. 1232p. 1982. text ed. 38.95x o.p. (ISBN 0-534-01349-X). PWS-Kent Pub.

Intermediate Accounting. Loren A. Nikolai et al. 1120p. 1980. text ed. 28.95x o.p. (ISBN 0-534-00786-4, Kent Pub.); study guide 8.95x o.p. (ISBN 0-534-00821-6); working papers 12.95x o.p. (ISBN 0-534-00830-5). PWS-Kent Pub.

Intermediate Accounting. Glenn A. Welsch et al. (Fourth Canadian edition). 1986. 47.95x o.p. (ISBN 0-256-03331-5). Irwin.

Intermediate Accounting. 7th ed. Glenn A. Welsch et al. (Illus.). 1986. 46.95x o.p. (ISBN 0-256-03328-5); Vol. 1. pap. 14.95x work papers o.p. (ISBN 0-256-03330-7); Vol. II. pap. 14.95x o.p. (ISBN 0-256-03460-5); Vol. I. study guide 12.95x o.p. (ISBN 0-256-03329-3); Vol. II. study guide 12.95 o.p. (ISBN 0-256-03459-1). Irwin.

Intermediate Accounting. Jan R. Williams & Keith G. Stanga. 1328p. 1984. text ed. 31.25 o.p. (ISBN 0-15-541514-X, HC). HarBraceJ.

Intermediate Accounting: Concepts, Methods & Uses. 4th ed. Sidney Davidson et al. LC 84-24672. 1376p. 1985. text ed. 40.95x o.s.i. (ISBN 0-03-058923-1); study guide 13.95x o.s.i. (ISBN 0-03-058926-6); instr's. manual 19.95 o.s.i. (ISBN 0-03-058924-X); test bank 100.00 o.s.i. (ISBN 0-03-058928-2). Dryden Pr.

Intermediate Alegebra with Applications. Terry Wesner & Harry L. Nustad. 816p. 1985. text ed. write for info. o.p. (ISBN 0-697-00117-2). Wm C Brown.

Intermediate Algebra. Jack Barker et al. 1983. pap. text ed. 28.95 o.p. (ISBN 0-03-058959-2). HR&W.

Intermediate Algebra. Linda Gilbert & Jimmie Gilbert. (Illus.). 512p. 1983. text ed. (ISBN 0-13-469536-4). P-H.

Intermediate Algebra. 2nd ed. Alfonse Gobran. 1979. text ed. write for info. o.p. (ISBN 0-87150-230-5, PWS 1841, Prindle). PWS-Kent Pub.

Intermediate Algebra. Herbert J. Greenburg & Charlotte W. Murphy. 512p. 1982. text ed. write for info. o.p. (ISBN 0-87150-324-7, 33L 2581, Prindle). PWS-Kent Pub.

Intermediate Algebra. L. Murphy Johnson & Arnold R. Steffensen. 1985. text ed. write for info. o.p. (ISBN 0-673-15632-X). Scott F.

Intermediate Algebra. Steven Kahan. 588p. 1981. text ed. 20.95 o.p. (ISBN 0-15-541530-1, HC). HarBraceJ.

Intermediate Algebra. Jerome E. Kaufmann. 550p. 1982. text ed. write for info. o.p. (ISBN 0-87150-340-9, 2721, Prindle). PWS-Kent Pub.

Intermediate Algebra. 4th ed. Margaret L. Lial & Charles D. Miller. 1984. text ed. write for info. o.p. (ISBN 0-673-15891-8). Scott F.

Intermediate Algebra. Martin M. Zuckerman. (Illus.). 550p. 1976. text ed. 16.95x o.p. (ISBN 0-393-09207-0). Norton.

Intermediate Algebra: A Text Workbook. Marion W. Keller. LC 74-171526. 1972. pap. 29.95 o.p. (ISBN 0-395-12643-6). HM.

Intermediate Algebra: Alternate Edition. Martin M. Zuckerman. 1980. 15.95x o.p. (ISBN 0-393-95127-8). Norton.

Intermediate Algebra: An Applied Approach. Richard N. Aufmann & Vernon C. Barker. LC 82-84332. 512p. 1983. pap. 28.95 o.p. (ISBN 0-395-34061-6). HM.

Intermediate Algebra: An Individual Learning System. rev. ed. Richard B. Thompson. 1976. pap. text ed. write for info. o.p. (ISBN 0-87150-216-X, PWS 1723, Prindle). PWS-Kent Pub.

Intermediate Algebra for College Students. Mary P. Dolciani et al. LC 71-146721. 1971. text ed. 28.50 o.p. (ISBN 0-395-12072-1). HM.

Intermediate Analysis: An Introduction to Theory of Functions of One Real Variable. John M. Olmsted. LC 56-5844. (Illus.). 1981. Repr. of 1956 ed. 29.50x o.p. (ISBN 0-89197-796-1). Irvington.

Intermediate Calculus. James Hurley. 1980. text ed. 41.95 o.p. (ISBN 0-03-056783-1, CBS C). SCP.

Intermediate Conversational French. 3rd ed. Julian Harris & Andre Leveque. LC 79-172937. 1972. text ed. 27.95 o.p. (ISBN 0-03-088063-7, HoltC). HR&W.

Intermediate Financial Management. Eugene F. Brigham & Louis J. Gapenski. 1040p. 1985. text ed. 36.95x o.s.i. (ISBN 0-03-063848-8); instr's. manual 19.95 o.s.i. (ISBN 0-03-063849-6). Dryden Pr.

Intermediate Microeconomics. 2nd ed. Roger L. Miller. 1982. text ed. 37.95x o.p. (ISBN 0-07-042159-5). McGraw.

Intermediate Microeconomics. Solberg. 1982. text ed. 29.95 o.p. (ISBN 0-256-02710-2). Irwin.

Intermediate Microeconomics & Its Applications. 3rd ed. Walter Nicholson. LC 82-72178. 699p. 1983. text ed. 32.95x o.s.i. (ISBN 0-03-062363-4). Dryden Pr.

Intermediate Perspective. Victor R. Lalli. 1959. text ed. 6.00 o.p. (ISBN 0-682-40056-4, University). Exposition-Phoenix.

Intermediate Physics for Medicine & Biology. Russell K. Hobbie. LC 77-27293. 557p. 1978. text ed. 43.50 o.p. (ISBN 0-471-03212-3). Wiley.

Intermediate Quantum Mechanics. 2nd ed. Hans A. Bethe & Roman W. Jackiw. LC 68-24363. (Lecture Notes & Supplements in Physics Ser.: No. 9). 1968. pap. write for info. o.p. (ISBN 0-8053-0755-9, Adv Bk Prog MSP). Addison-Wesley.

Intermediate-Range Nuclear Forces in Europe: Issue & Approaches. Ed. by Gloria Duffy. (Special Report of the Arms Control & Disarmament Program, Stanford University). 89p. 1982. pap. 7.00 o.p. (ISBN 0-935371-04-4). ISIS.

Intermediate Spanish: Civilizacion y Cultura. 2nd ed. John G. Copeland et al. (Span.). 1981. pap. text ed. 14.96 o.p. (ISBN 0-03-057606-7). HR&W.

Intermediate Spanish: Conversacion y Repaso. 2nd ed. John G. Copeland et al. (Span.). 1981. pap. text ed. 18.95 o.p. (ISBN 0-03-057601-6); lab manual 11.95 o.p. (ISBN 0-03-057603-2); tapes 150.00 o.p. (ISBN 0-03-057602-4). HR&W.

Intermediate Statistical Methods. G. Barrie Wetherill. 1981. 25.00x o.p. (ISBN 0-412-16440-X, 2045, Pub. by Chapman & Hall). Routledge Chapman & Hall.

Intermediate Statistical Methods: Worked Solutions. G. Barrie Wetherill. 1981. pap. 2.00x o.p. (ISBN 0-412-23520-X, 6555, Pub. by Chapman & Hall). Routledge Chapman & Hall.

Intermediate Transfer Methods for Eliminating goto's from C Language Programs. abr. ed. Algo Publishing Staff. 52p. 1987. pap. 14.95 o.p. (ISBN 0-945473-27-3). Algo Pub.

Intermediate Treatment & Social Work. R. Jones & A. Kerslake. Ed. by Martin Davies. LC 80-670035. (Orig.). 1980. pap. text ed. 6.50x o.p. (ISBN 0-435-82483-X). Gower Pub Co.

Intermediate Two Bids in Bridge: A Modern Alternative for Standard American Bidders. Don Gold. (Illus.). 1981. 7.95 o.p. (ISBN 0-682-49579-4). Exposition-Phoenix.

Intermetallic Semiconducting Films. H. H. Wieder. LC 76-80293. 1970. 95.00 o.p. (ISBN 0-08-013367-3). Pergamon.

Intermolecular Interactions: From Diatomics to Biopolymers. Bernard Pullman. LC 77-24278. (Perspectives in Quantum Chemistry Ser.). 447p. 1978. 152.95 o.p. (ISBN 0-471-99507-X). Wiley.

Internal Accountability: An International Emphasis. Wagdy M. Abdallah. Ed. by Richard Farmer. LC 84-2662. (Research for Business Decisions Ser.: No. 68). 130p. 1984. 37.95 o.p. (ISBN 0-8357-1555-8). UMI Res Pr.

Internal Audit Manual. 150p. 1980. 150.00 o.p. (ISBN 0-318-14109-4); members 90.00 o.p. (ISBN 0-318-14110-8). Finan Mgrs Soc.

Internal Audit of the Budget Process. Richard S. Savich. 56p. 1976. 13.50 o.p. (ISBN 0-317-12383-1, 401.11A). Inst Inter Aud.

Internal Audit Training Program: How to Organize & Administer a Continuing Education Plan for Your Internal Audit Team. William E. Fergusson. (Research Report: No. 23). (Illus.). 1980. pap. text ed. 10.00 o.p. (ISBN 0-89413-084-6, 474). Inst Inter Aud.

Internal Auditing: Directions & Opportunities. Robert K. Mautz et al. Ed. by Richard Holman. (Illus.). 271p. 1984. text ed. 47.00 o.p. (ISBN 0-89413-122-2). Inst Inter Aud.

Internal Auditor's Information Security Handbook. Barry Wilkins. (Illus.). 1979. pap. text ed. 13.50 o.p. (ISBN 0-89413-080-3). Inst Inter Aud.

Internal Combustion Engines, 2 vols. Rowland S. Benson & N. D. Whitehouse. LC 79-40359. (Thermodynamics & Fluid Mechanics for Mechanical Engineers). (Illus.). 1984. Vol. 1. pap. 21.00 o.p. (ISBN 0-08-022718-X); Set. pap. text ed. 36.00 set o.p. (ISBN 0-08-031630-1); Vol. 2. pap. text ed. 21.00 o.p. (ISBN 0-08-022720-1). Pergamon.

Internal Consultant. Dennis J. Lovelace. 64p. 1982. 5.00 o.p. (ISBN 0-682-49879-3). Exposition-Phoenix.

Internal Conversion Processes. Ed. by Joseph H. Hamilton. 1966. 55.50 o.p. (ISBN 0-12-321850-0). Acad Pr.

Internal Fixation: Basic Principles, Modern Means, Biomechanics. M. Allgower & S. M. Perren. (Illus.). 1976. with slides 160.00 o.p. (ISBN 0-387-92106-0). Springer-Verlag.

Internal Gravity Waves in the Ocean. Jo Roberts. (Marine Science Ser.: Vol.2). 288p. 1975. 79.75 o.p. (ISBN 0-8247-6226-6). Dekker.

Internal Medicine. 2nd ed. Jay H. Stein. (Illus.). 2338p. 1987. text ed. 85.00 o.p. Little.

Internal Medicine: Medical Examination Manual. Manuel M. Villaverde. 1979. pap. 21.95 o.p. (ISBN 0-442-25094-0). Van Nos Reinhold.

Internal Revenue Acts of the United States: 1950-1951 Legislative Histories, Laws & Administrative Documents, 7 vols. Ed. by Bernard D. Reams, Jr. LC 82-81278. 1982. Set. lib. bdg. 450.00 o.p. (ISBN 0-89941-155-X). W S Hein.

Internal Revenue Cumulative Bulletin 1986-2, July-Dec. 813p. 1987. 37.00 o.p. (ISBN 0-318-23557-9, S/N 048-004-01939-6). USGPO.

Internal Revenue Service Practice & Procedure Deskbook. Ira L. Shafiroff. 611p. 1985. text ed. 15.00 o.p. (ISBN 0-317-18469-5, J1-1454). PLI.

Internal Revenue Service, 1986 Annual Report. (IRS Publications: N0.55). Orig. Title: Annual Report of the Commisioner & Chief Counsel of the Internal Revenue Service. (Illus.). 76p. 1987. pap. 3.50 o.p. (ISBN 0-317-62865-8, S-N 048-004-01948-5). USGPO.

Internatioanl Nifedipine Adalat Symposium, 2nd. W. Lochner et al. (Illus.). 400p. 1975. pap. 27.20 o.p. (ISBN 0-387-07471-6). Springer-Verlag.

International Adjustment in the 1980's. Vijay Joshi. (Working Paper: No. 485). 57p. 1982. pap. 3.50 o.p. (ISBN 0-8213-0062-8). World Bank.

International Aerospace Review, AAS6. Ed. by Jerry Grey & Lawrence A. Hamdan. LC 82-3883. (Illus.). 313p. 1982. 20.00 o.p. (ISBN 0-915928-63-9). AIAA.

International Affairs: Cumulative Index 1922-1976 (Volumes 1-52) 1983. 30.00 o.p. (ISBN 0-317-01048-4). Learned Info.

International Airline Phrase Book. J. W. Bator. 236p. 1983. pap. 6.95 o.p. (ISBN 0-8351-1246-2). China Bks.

International Album of Wine: Your Personal Record of Wine Labels & Tastes. Steven J. Schneider & Paul Bacon. LC 75-21474. 1977. 16.95 o.s.i. (ISBN 0-03-014641-0). H Holt & Co.

International & English-Language Collections: A Survey of Holdings at the Hoover Institution on War, Revolution & Peace. Kenneth M. Glazier & James R. Hobson. LC 77-142946. (Library Survey Ser.: No. 3). 20p. 1971. pap. 2.00x o.p. (ISBN 0-8179-5032-X). Hoover Inst Pr.

International & U. S. Programs Solar Flux see Sharing the Sun.

International Arms Review, Vol. II. Tr. by Lionel Seaton. (Illus.). 1979. 6.95 o.p. (ISBN 0-89149-029-9). Jolex.

International Arms Review, Vol. I. Lionel Seaton. (Illus.). 1977. 6.95 o.p. (ISBN 0-89149-008-6). Jolex.

International Art & Antiques Yearbook Nineteen Seventy-Nine to Nineteen Eighty. Ed. by Marcelle d'Argy Smith. 1979. 50.00x o.p. (ISBN 0-900305-21-5, National Magazine Co., Ltd.). Gale.

International Aspects of U. S. Income Taxation: Cases & Materials, Vol. I, Pts. 1 & 2. Elisabeth A Owens. LC 80-18605. 418p. 1980. pap. text ed. 12.50x o.p. (ISBN 0-915506-23-8). Harvard Law Intl Tax.

International Aspects of U. S. Income Taxation: Cases & Materials, Vol. II, Pt. 3. William C. Gifford & Elisabeth A. Owens. LC 80-18605. 760p. (Orig.). 1982. pap. text ed. 25.00x o.p. (ISBN 0-915506-26-2). Harvard Law Intl Tax.

International Association of Cooking Schools Cookbook. International Association of Cooking Schools Members Staff. Ed. by Helen S. Harman. LC 81-70440. 200p. 1981. pap. 10.95 o.p. (ISBN 0-941034-14-3). I Chalmers.

International Atlas: World Latitudes, Longitudes, & Time Changes. Compiled by Thomas Shanks. 448p. 1985. 29.95 o.p. (ISBN 0-917086-57-0). A C S Pubns Inc.

International Auction Records: Volume 22-1988. E. Mayer. (Illus.). 1600p. 1988. 202.00 o.p. (ISBN 3-906985-01-6). Editions Pub.

International Banking: The Foreign Activities of the Banks of Principal Industrial Countries (1976) rev. ed. U. Steuber. Tr. by R. Pringle & R. Pringle. Repr. of 1974 ed. 47.50 o.s.i. (ISBN 90-286-0375-1). E J Brill USA.

International Benefits Seminar Proceedings, Oct. 21-24, 1981, Montreal. Ed. by Mary E. Brennan. 115p. (Orig.). 1982. pap. 10.00 o.p. (ISBN 0-89154-174-8). Intl Found Employ.

International Benefits, 1983. Ed. by Becky A. Wright. 198p. (Orig.). 1984. pap. text ed. 15.00 o.p. (ISBN 0-89154-216-7). Intl Found Employ.

International Bibliography of Air Law, 1900-1971. Wybo P. Heere. LC 72-86857. 595p. 1972. 40.00 o.p. (ISBN 0-379-00010-5). Oceana.

International Bibliography of Economics - Bibliographie Internationale de Science Economique, Vol. 29. Ed. by International Committee for Social Science Information & Documentation. LC 55-2317. (International Bibliography of the Social Sciences Ser. - Bibliographie Internationale des Sciences Sociales). 502p. 1981. 108.00x o.s.i. Intl Pubns Serv.

International Bibliography of Economics, 1978, Vol. 27. Ed. by International Committee for Social Science Information & Documentation. LC 55-2317. (International Bibliography of the Social Sciences Ser.). 526p. 1980. 90.00x o.p. (ISBN 0-422-80890-3). Intl Pubns Serv.

International Bibliography of Jewish History & Thought. Ed. by Jonathan Kaplan. 483p. 1984. lib. bdg. 41.00 o.p. (ISBN 3-598-07503-0). K G Saur.

International Bibliography of Political Science - Bibliographie Internation ale de Science Politique, Vol. 28. Ed. by International Committee for Social Science Information & Documentation. LC 54-14355. (International Bibliogarphy of the Social Science Ser.). 451p. 1981. 90.00x o.s.i. (ISBN 0-422-80920-9). Intl Pubns Serv.

International Bibliography of Political Science 1977, Vol. 26. Ed. by International Committee for Social Science Information & Documentation. LC 54-14355. (International Bibliography of the Social Sciences Ser.). 1979. 90.00x o.s.i. Intl Pubns Serv.

International Bibliography of Political Science, 1978, Vol. 27. Ed. by International Committee for Social Science Information & Documentation. LC 54-14355. (International Bibliography of the Social Sciences Ser.). 405p. 1980. 85.00x o.s.i. Intl Pubns Serv.

International Biotechnology Directory 1984: Products, Companies, Research & Organizations. Jim Coombs. LC 83-12138. 426p. 1983. 100.00 o.p. (ISBN 0-943818-03-6, Pub by Stockton Pr). Groves Dict Music.

International Book of Honor. 1st ed. Ed. by J. M. Evans. LC 83-70200. (Illus.). 700p. 1985. 75.00 o.s.i. (ISBN 0-934544-24-7). Am Biog Inst.

International Books in Print, 1987: English Language Titles Published Outside the United States & the U. K, 2 vols. 6th ed. Ed. by Barbara Venel. xx, 2187p. 1987. Pt. 1: Author-Title. lib. bdg. 250.00 o.p. (ISBN 3-598-20591-0). K G Saur.

International Books in Print, 1987: English Language Titles Published Outside the United States & the U. K, 2 vols, Pt. II. 1987. Subject Guide. lib. bdg. 250.00 set o.p. (ISBN 3-598-20592-9). K G Saur.

International Borrowing by Developing Countries. Marilyn J. Seiber. (Pergamon Policy Studies on Business & Economics). 220p. 1982. 50.00 o.p. (ISBN 0-08-026332-1). Pergamon.

International Business. 3rd ed. Donald A. Ball et al. 1988. 40.95 o.p. (ISBN 0-256-05825-3); study guide 13.95 o.p. (ISBN 0-256-06156-4). Irwin.

International Business, Vol. 4. Compiled by James W. Dean & Richard Schwindt. 145p. 1985. 14.00 o.p. (ISBN 0-88024-104-7). Eno River Pr.

International Business & Multinational Enterprises. 3rd ed. Stefan H. Robock et al. 1983. 39.95x o.p. (ISBN 0-256-02514-2). Irwin.

International Business Bibliography. International Business Unit, Department of Management Science, University of Manchester Institute of Science & Technology Staff. LC 76-27166. (Reference Library of Social Science Ser.: Vol. 36). 1977. lib. bdg. 57.00 o.p. (ISBN 0-8240-9899-4). Garland Pub.

International Business Dictionary. Frank Gaynor. (ISBN 0-8022-0573-9). Philos Lib.

International Business Transactions in Nutshell. 2nd ed. Donald T. Wilson. LC 83-21669. (Nutshell Ser.). 476p. 1983. text ed. 11.95 o.p. (ISBN 0-314-77619-2). West Pub.

International Business Travel & Relocation Directory. 5th ed. 1028p. 1987. 385.00x o.p. (ISBN 0-8103-2517-9). Gale.

International CAD-CAM Software Directory. Philip C. Flora. (Illus.). 190p. (Orig.). 1985. pap. text ed. 35.00 o.p. (ISBN 0-910747-06-7, Co-pub TAB Bks & TAB-TPR). Tech Data TX.

International Capital Markets. 2nd ed. 188p. 1982. 120.00 o.p. (ISBN 0-8002-3427-8). Intl Pubns Serv.

International Catalogue of Films, Filmstrips & Slides. International Union Against Cancer Staff. pap. text ed. 38.00 o.p. CJ Hogrefe Pubs.

International Chamber of Commerce Arbitration. W. Lawrence Craig & William W. Park. LC 84-7466. 500p. 1984. lib. bdg. 75.00 o.p. (ISBN 0-379-10161-0). Oceana.

International Class Struggle, Nos. 1-3. 1969. Repr. of 1937 ed. lib. bdg. 11.75x o.p. (ISBN 0-8371-9151-3, IC00). Greenwood.

International Classification of Diseases: Clinical Modification, 3 vols. 9th rev. ed. (DHHS Publication Ser.: Nos. 80-126). 2634p. 1980. 40.00 o.p. (ISBN 0-318-21340-0, S/N 017-022-00714-2); pap. text ed. 29.00 o.p. (ISBN 0-318-21341-9, S/N 017-022-00715-1); pap. 29.00 o.p. USGPO.

International Classification of Goods & Services for the Purposes of the Registration of Marks under the Nice Agreement. 99p. (Orig.). 1984. pap. 49.50 o.p. (ISBN 92-805-0088-0, WIPO75, WIPO). UNIPUB.

International Classification of Goods & Services for the Purpose of the Registration of Marks, Pt. 1. 135p. 1983. pap. text ed. 49.50 o.p. (ISBN 92-805-0087-2, WIPO72, WIPO). UNIPUB.

International Codata Conference on Generation, Compilation, Evaluation & Dissemination of Data for Science & Technology, 4th: Proceedings. Ed. by M. Bertrand Dreyfus. 160p. 1975. pap. 65.00 o.p. (ISBN 0-08-019850-3). Pergamon.

International Codata Conference, 6th Biennial, Santa Flavia, Italy, 1978: Proceedings. Ed. by Bertrand Dreyfus. (Illus.). 400p. 1979. 230.00 o.p. (ISBN 0-08-023371-6). Pergamon.

International Code of Botanical Nomenclature. Ed. by Frans A. Stafleu. (Regnum Vegetabile: Vol. 111). 472p. 1983. lib. bdg. 71.50x o.p. (ISBN 0-318-11898-X). Lubrecht & Cramer.

International Code of Nomenclature of Bacteria. Ed. by S. P. Lapage et al. LC 75-20730. 152p. 1975. 7.50 o.p. (ISBN 0-914826-04-2). Am Soc Microbio.

International Colloquium on the Law of Outer Space, No. XXVI: Proceedings, 1984. 351p. 1984. 38.00 o.p. (ISBN 0-915928-71-X). AIAA.

International Commercial Banking Management. James L. Kammert. 336p. 1981. 24.95 o.p. (ISBN 0-8144-5680-4). AMACOM.

International Communications Glossary. Media Institute Staff & Timothy G. Brown. LC 84-62298. 114p. (Orig.). 1984. pap. 12.95 o.p. (ISBN 0-937790-27-3). Media Inst.

International Communism & World Revolution: History & Methods. Gunther Nollau. LC 75-14702. 357p. 1975. Repr. of 1961 ed. lib. bdg. 22.50x o.p. (ISBN 0-8371-8232-8, NOIC). Greenwood.

International Comparative Research: Social Structure & Public Institutions in Eastern & Western Europe. M. Niessen et al. LC 82-16519. (Vienna Centre Ser.). 184p. 1984. 42.00 o.p. (ISBN 0-08-031334-5). Pergamon.

International Competition in Services: Banking Building, Software, Know-How. LC 87-619820. (OTA-ITA Ser.: No. 328). (Illus., Orig.). 1987. pap. 16.00 o.p. (S/N 052-003-01067-4). USGPO.

International Conference of Parallel Processing, 14th 1985. 868p. 1985. 80.00 o.p. (ISBN 0-8186-0637-1, Q637); microfiche 80.00 o.p. (ISBN 0-8186-4637-3). IEEE Comp Soc.

International Conference on Composite Materials Five (ICCM V) Ed. by W. C. Harrigan et al. LC 85-13827. 1741p. 1985. 95.00 o.p. (ISBN 0-87339-000-8). Minerals Metals.

International Conference on Entity-Relationship Approach, 4th 1985: Proceedings. 327p. 1985. 45.00 o.p. (ISBN 0-8186-0645-2, Q645); microfiche 45.00 o.p. (ISBN 0-8186-4645-4). IEEE Comp Soc.

International Conference on Five per Cent Fluorouracil Ointment in Dermatology. Ed. by F. Serri. (Dermatologica: Vol. 140, Suppl. 1). 1970. pap. 38.75 o.p. (ISBN 3-8055-0836-0). S Karger.

International Conference on Infrared Physics, 2nd, (CIRP 2), Zurich, 1979. Ed. by Fritz Kneubuhl. 264p. 1980. pap. 48.00 o.p. (ISBN 0-08-025055-6). Pergamon.

International Conference on Input-Output Techniques, Seventh: Proceedings. (UNIDO Ser.). 472p. 1985. pap. 33.00 o.p. (UN84/2B9 5071, UN). UNIPUB.

International Conference on Laboratory Astrophysics. Ed. by J. Rosenberg. 1969. 19.25 o.p. (ISBN 0-7204-0193-3, North Holland). Elsevier.

International Conference on Magnetic Alloys & Oxides: Haifa, Israel, August 1977. Ed. by A. J. Freeman et al. 1978. 110.75 o.p. (ISBN 0-444-85162-3, North-Holland). Elsevier.

International Conference on Nonimaging Concentrators, Vol. 441. Ed. by M. C. Ruda. 116p. 42.00 o.p. (ISBN 0-89252-476-6). SPIE.

International Conference on Social Science & Medicine, 6th, Amsterdam, 1979: Second Special Conference Issue. Ed. by Peter J. McEwan. 80p. 1981. pap. 17.25 o.p. (ISBN 0-08-026763-7). Pergamon.

International Conference on Solid-Solid Phase Transformations: Proceedings, Pittsburgh, 1981. Ed. by Hubert I. Aaronson & David E. Laughlin. (Illus.). 1610p. 1983. 70.00 o.p. (ISBN 0-89520-452-5); members 45.00 o.p. (ISBN 0-317-36279-8); student members 25.00 o.p. (ISBN 0-317-36280-1). ASM.

International Conference on Supercomputing Systems 1st 1985. LC 85-62322. 718p. 1985. 70.00 o.p. (ISBN 0-8186-0654-1, Q654). IEEE Comp Soc.

International Conference on the Future Supply of Nature-Made Petroleum & Gas: Proceedings. United Nations Institute for Training & Research Staff. 1977. 99.00 o.p. (ISBN 0-08-021734-6); pap. 77.00 o.p. (ISBN 0-08-021735-4). Pergamon.

International Conference on Trends in Industrial & Labor Relations. Ed. by Charles M. Rehmus et al. (Orig.). 1974. pap. text ed. 9.95x o.p. (ISBN 0-87855-660-5). Transaction Pubs.

International Conflict. Anne T. Feraru. (CISE Learning Package Ser.: No. 5). 67p. (Orig.). 1974. pap. text ed. 3.00x o.p. (ISBN 0-936876-22-0). LRIS.

International Conflict Resolution: Theory & Practice. Ed. by Edward E. Azar & John W. Burton. LC 85-30040. 176p. 1986. lib. bdg. 30.00x o.p. (ISBN 0-931477-71-9). Lynne Rienner.

International Congress of International Union for Study of Social Insects, Eighth, Wageningen, Netherlands, September 5-10, 1977: Proceedings. 1977. pap. 18.00 o.p. (ISBN 90-220-0640-9, PDC69, PUDOC). UNIPUB.

International Congress of Pharmacology, 6th, Helsinki, 1975: Pharmacological Abstracts. 1977. 170.00 o.p. (ISBN 0-08-021308-1). Pergamon.

International Congress of Pharmacology, 7th, Paris, 1978: Abstracts. Ed. by J. R. Boissier et al. 1979. 230.00 o.p. (ISBN 0-08-023768-1). Pergamon.

International Congress of Pure & Applied Chemistry, 23rd, Boston, 1971. Proceedings Special Lectures Supplement. International Union of Pure & Applied Chemistry. 1976. Vol. 1. 105.00 o.p. (ISBN 0-08-020762-6); Vol. 2. 85.00 o.p. (ISBN 0-08-020763-4); Vol. 3. 35.00 o.p. (ISBN 0-08-020764-2); Vol. 4. 135.00 o.p. (ISBN 0-08-020765-0); Vol. 5. 35.00 o.p. (ISBN 0-08-020766-9); Vol. 6. 75.00 o.p. (ISBN 0-08-020767-7); Vol. 7. 70.00 o.p. (ISBN 0-08-020768-5); Vol. 8. 80.00 o.p. (ISBN 0-08-020769-3). Pergamon.

International Congress on Pharmacy: Proceedings, 2nd, Boston, 17-20 July 1980. LC 80-70866. 1980. 6.00 o.p. (ISBN 0-686-73989-2). AACP Alexandria.

International Cook's Catalogue. James Beard et al. (Illus.). 1983. 19.95 o.p. (ISBN 0-394-41768-2). Random.

International Cooperation & Competition in Civilian Space Activities. Intro. by John H. Gibbons. LC 84-601087. (OTA ISC-329). (Illus.). 482p. (Orig.). 1985. pap. 17.00 o.p. (ISBN 0-318-18774-4, S/N 052-003-00958-7). USGPO.

International Cotton Market Prospects. M. Elton Thigpen & Maw-Cheng Yang. (Working Paper: No. 2). v, 67p. 1978. 5.00 o.p. (ISBN 0-686-36096-6, BK-1970). World Bank.

International Countertrade: A Guide for Managers & Executives. Pompiliu Verzariu. 100p. (Orig.). 1984. pap. 3.75 o.p. (ISBN 0-318-22407-0, S/N 003-009-00435-7). USGPO.

International Court of Justice. G. Elian. 1971. 12.50 o.s.i. (ISBN 0-685-47309-0). E J Brill USA.

International Court of Justice: A Selected Bibliography of Law Review Articles. Jim Milles. (Public Administration Ser.: Bibliography P 1618). 1985. pap. 2.25 o.p. (ISBN 0-89028-288-X). Vance Biblios.

International Cub Scout Book. LC 81-2931. (Illus.). 116p. (gr. 3-6). 1981. 11.95 o.p. (ISBN 0-8437-3385-3). Hammond Inc.

International Cultivator's Handbook. William Drake. (Illus.). 144p. 1987. 14.95 o.p. (ISBN 0-914171-13-5). Ronin Pub.

International Debt Problem: Lessons for the Future. Herber Giersch. 210p. 1985. lib. bdg. 57.50x o.p. (ISBN 3-16-345085-7, Pub. by J C B Mohr BRD). Coronet Bks.

International Development Research Centre Projects: 1970-1981. IDRC, Ottawa Staff. 384p. (Eng., Fr. & Span.). 1982. pap. write for info. o.p. (ISBN 0-88936-308-0, IDRC180, IDRC). UNIPUB.

International Development 1964 Motivations: Methods in Development: Foreign Aid. Society for International Development Staff. LC 64-8541. 152p. o.p. Oceana.

International Dictionary. Otto Jesperson. (Ger., Fr. & Eng.). 1930. 9.95 o.p. (ISBN 3-533-01130-5, M-7480, Pub. by Carl Winter). French & Eur.

International Dictionary of Films & Filmmakers, Vol. II: Directors - Filmakers. Ed. by Christopher Lyon. 1986. pap. 18.95 o.s.i. (ISBN 0-399-51229-2). Putnam Pub Group.

International Dictionary of Medicine & Biology, 3 vols. Sidney I. Landau. LC 85-16867. 3200p. Set. 395.00 o.p. (ISBN 0-471-01849-X). Wiley.

International Dictionary of Metallurgy, Mineralogy, Geology & the Mining & Oil Industries. A. Gagnacci-Schwicker & Schwicker. 1530p. (Eng., Fr., Ger. & Ital.). 1970. 88.00 o.p. (ISBN 3-7625-0751-1, M-7482, Pub. by Bauverlag). French & Eur.

International Dimensions of Human Rights, 2 vols. Karel Vasek. Ed. by Philip Alston. LC 81-22566. 755p. (Co-published with Greenwood Press, Inc., Westport, CT). 1984. Set. pap. 78.75 o.p. (ISBN 92-3-101477-3, U1257, UNESCO). UNIPUB.

International Dimensions of Industrial Relations. Duane Kujawa. Ed. by David A. Ricks. (International Dimensions of Business Ser.). 200p. text ed. (ISBN 0-534-01391-0). PWS-Kent Pub.

International Dinner Party Cookbook. Jan Bilton. LC 86-14321. 1987. 18.95 o.p. (ISBN 0-8050-0133-6). H Holt & Co.

International Directory of Business Information Sources & Services, 1986. 400p. 1987. pap. 70.00 o.p. (ISBN 0-946653-18-6, Pub. by Europa Eng). Intl Pubns Serv.

International Directory of Corporate Affiliations. National Register Publising Co. Staff. LC 67-22770. 1984. 347.00 o.p. (ISBN 0-87217-050-0). Natl. Register.

International Directory of Discontinued ICs & Discrete Semiconductors. Ed. by Jim Fitzgerald. 320p. 1987. 75.00 o.p. (ISBN 0-317-57575-9). DATA Busn Pub.

International Directory of Executive Recruiters. 4th ed. Ed. by James H. Kennedy. LC 73-91011. 1984. pap. 27.95 o.p. (ISBN 0-916654-29-X). Consultants News.

International Directory of Fish Technology Institutes. (Fisheries Technical Papers: No. 152, Rev. 1). 114p. 1980. pap. 8.25 o.p. (ISBN 92-5-101002-1, F2031, FAO). UNIPUB.

International Directory of Mountaineering Clubs & Organizations. George Pokorny et al. LC 79-1890. 162p. 1979. pap. 5.00 o.p. (ISBN 0-87842-112-2). Mountain Pr.

International Directory of Musical Instrument Collections. Ed. by Jean Jenkins. 1977. pap. 25.00 o.s.i. (ISBN 0-685-01107-0). E J Brill USA.

International Directory of Sex Research & Related Fields, 2 vols. Indiana University, Institute for Sex Research Staff. 1976. Set. lib. bdg. 150.00 o.p. (ISBN 0-8161-0043-8, Hall Library). G K Hall.

International Directory of Vacuum Equipment, Manufacturers & Suppliers. Ed. by B. Halliday. 48p. 1983. pap. 18.75 o.p. (ISBN 0-08-031117-2, 11, 17, 16). Pergamon.

International Disaster Relief: Toward a Responsive System. S. Green. 1977. 14.95 o.p. (ISBN 0-07-024287-9); pap. text ed. 3.95 o.p. (ISBN 0-07-024288-7). McGraw.

International Distributor Locator. A. Palmisano. LC 77-82718. 1977. pap. 35.00 o.p. (ISBN 0-917408-03-9). Bergano Bk Co.

International Economic Law of Belligerent Occupation. Ernst H. Feilchenfeld. xii, 181p. Repr. of 1942 ed. 28.00 o.p. (ISBN 0-384-15413-1). Johnson Repr.

International Economic Order. Orlando Letelier & Michael Moffitt. 100p. 1977. pap. (ISBN 0-87855-666-4). Transaction Pubs.

International Economic Problems. 3rd ed. James C. Ingram. LC 77-11139. (Introduction to Economics Ser.). 174p. 1978. pap. text ed. (ISBN 0-471-02182-2). Wiley.

International Economics. 2nd ed. Robert J. Carbaugh. 349p. 1985. text ed. (ISBN 0-534-03831-X). Wadsworth Pub.

International Economics: A Policy Approach. 2nd ed. Mordechai E. Kreinin. (Illus.). 1975. text ed. 20.95 o.p. (ISBN 0-15-541545-X, HC). HarBraceJ.

International Economics: A Policy Approach. 4th ed. Mordechai E. Kreinin. 432p. 1983. text ed. 22.50 o.p. (ISBN 0-15-541537-9, HC). HarBraceJ.

International Economics Exams, Puzzles & Problems, Vol. 10. Compiled by Edward Tower. 213p. 1985. 14.00 o.p. (ISBN 0-88024-210-8). Eno River Pr.

International Economics Reading Lists, Vol. 9. Compiled by Edward Tower. 215p. 1985. 14.00 o.p. (ISBN 0-88024-209-4). Eno River Pr.

International Encyclopedia of Dogs. Date not set. (ISBN 0-87605-623-0). Howell Bk.

International Encyclopedia of Sociology. Ed. by Michael Mann. LC 83-15340. 434p. 1983. 34.50x o.p. (ISBN 0-8264-0238-0). Continuum.

International Energy Studies. Ed. by R. K. Pachauri. LC 80-25976. 534p. 1980. 65.00 o.p. (ISBN 0-317-54710-0). Krieger.

International Engineering-Scientific Software Directory. Philip C. Flora. (Illus.). 200p. (Orig.). 1985. pap. text ed. 35.00 o.p. (ISBN 0-910747-05-9, Co-pub TAB Bks & TAB-TPR). Tech Data TX.

International English. Virginia Haley. LC 75-28718. (Illus.). 1975. pap. 7.95 o.p. (ISBN 0-8048-1151-2). C E Tuttle.

International Essays for Business Decision Makers, Vol. IV. Ed. by Mark B. Winchester. 1980. 17.95 o.p. (ISBN 0-8144-5608-1). AMACOM.

International Essays for Business Decision Makers, Vol. VI. Ed. by Mark B. Winchester. 1982. 21.95 o.p. AMACOM.

International Essays for Business Decision Makers 1977. Ed. by Mark B. Winchester. LC 77-89595. 247p. (Orig.). 1977. pap. 10.00x o.p. (ISBN 0-87201-269-7). Gulf Pub.

International Essays I. LC 86-12439. (Illus.). 195p. (Orig.). 1986. pap. 6.00 o.p. (S/N 008-020-01076-6). USGPO.

International Essays II. Egon Reinisch et al. LC 87-12286. (Illus.). 289p. (Orig.). 1987. pap. 8.50 o.p. (ISBN 0-318-22909-9, S/N 008-020-01109-6). USGPO.

International Exchange of Tax Information: Recent Developments. Practising Law Institute Staff et al. LC 85-61436. (Tax Law & Estate Planning Ser.). 1985. 15.00 o.p. (J43566). PLI.

International Extradition: U. S. Law & Practice, Releases 1 & 2. Ed. by M. C. Bassiouni. LC 82-22373. 1983. Set. looseleaf 170.00 o.p. (ISBN 0-379-20746-X). Oceana.

International Fiction of Henry James. J. N. Sharma. 1980. text ed. 15.00x o.p. (ISBN 0-333-90300-5). Humanities.

International Financial Flows: A Statistical Handbook. G. E. Dennis. LC 83-25557. 376p. 1984. 32.00x o.p. (ISBN 0-669-07788-7). Lexington Bks.

International Financial Integration: The Limits of Sovereignty. David T. Llewellyn. LC 80-11699. (Problems of Economic Integration Ser.). 215p. 1981. 45.95x o.p. (ISBN 0-470-26960-X). Halsted Pr.

International Financial Law, 2 vols. R. Rendell. 319p. 1983. 120.00 o.p. (ISBN 0-8002-3421-9). Intl Pubns Serv.

International Financial Markets Institute, 2 vols, Vols. 481 & 482. Practising Law Institute Staff. 1108p. 1985. pap. 40.00 o.p. (ISBN 0-317-27483-X, #B4-6716). PLI.

International Financial Offerings. Practising Law Institute Staff & Alan L. Beller. (Corporate Law & Practice Course Handbook Ser.: No. 504). 360p. 1985. 15.00 o.p. (B4-6724). PLI.

International Financial Statistics, Yearbook 1987: Bureau of Statistics. 744p. 25.00 o.s.i. (ISBN 1-55775-075-0). Intl Monetary.

International Fish Cookery. Lou S. Pappas. LC 79-11572. (Illus.). 1979. pap. 6.95 o.p. (ISBN 0-89286-148-7, One Hund One Prods). Ortho.

International Fish Trade of Southeast Asian Nations. Jesse M. Floyd. LC 84-10168. (East-West Environment & Policy Institute Research Report Ser.: No. 16). 66p. 1984. pap. text ed. 3.00 o.p. (ISBN 0-318-03783-1). EW Ctr HI.

International Foundation Directory. 2nd ed. Ed. by Henry V. Hodson. LC 73-90303. 378p. 1979. 65.00 o.p. (ISBN 0-905118-41-3). Intl Pubns Serv.

International Franchise Association Presents "Cultivating the Franchise Relationship," A Play in Three Acts: Official Transcript of Proceedings. Legal & Government Affairs Symposium & International Transcript of Proceedings. LC 84-189403. write for info. o.p. Intl Franchise.

International Franchise Association Presents "Management & Law," A Play in Three Acts: Official Transcript of Proceedings. Legal & Government Affairs Symposium & International Franchise Association. LC 84-193018. write for info. o.p. Intl Franchise.

International Garage Sale. Stefan Kanfer. 1985. 13.45 o.p. (ISBN 0-393-01986-1). Norton.

International Gas Chromatography Symposium, Third. Ed. by N. Brenner. 1962. 120.00 o.p. (ISBN 0-12-131650-5). Acad Pr.

International Geographic Encyclopedia & Atlas. 1979. 7.95 o.p. (ISBN 0-395-27170-3). HM.

International Geography - 76, 12 vols. Ed. by I. P. Gerasimov. Incl. Vol. 1. Geomorphology & Paleography. 1978. pap. 57.00 o.p. (ISBN 0-08-023141-1); Vol. 2. Climatology, Hydrology, Glaciology. 1978. pap. 57.00 o.p. (ISBN 0-08-023142-X); Vol. 3. Geography of the Ocean. 1978. pap. 37.00 o.p. (ISBN 0-08-023143-8); Vol. 4. Biogeography & Soil Geography. 1978. pap. 37.00 o.p. (ISBN 0-08-023144-6); Vol. 5. General Physical Geography. 1978. pap. 37.00 o.p. (ISBN 0-08-023145-4); Vol. 6. General Economic Geography. 1978. pap. 57.00 o.p. (ISBN 0-08-023146-2); Vol. 7. Geography of Population. 1978. pap. 57.00 o.p. (ISBN 0-08-023147-0); Vol. 8. Regional Geography. 1978. pap. 57.00 o.p. (ISBN 0-08-023148-9); Vol. 9. Historical Geography. 1978. pap. 37.00 o.p. (ISBN 0-08-023149-7); Vol. 10. Geographical Education, Geographical Literature & Dissemination of Geographical Knowledge. 1978. pap. 37.00 o.p. (ISBN 0-08-023150-0); Vol. 11. General Problems of Geography & Geosystems Modelling. 1978. pap. 37.00 o.p. (ISBN 0-08-023151-9); Vol. 12. Additional Volume Including Author Index. 1978. pap. 57.00 o.p. (ISBN 0-08-023152-7). LC 78-40224. 1978. pap. 465.00 set o.p. (ISBN 0-08-023154-3). Pergamon.

International Geography 1972: Proceedings of the International Geographical Congress, 22nd, Canada, 2 vols. International Geographical Congress Staff. Ed. by W. Peter Adams & Frederick M. Helleiner. Set. 125.00x o.p. (ISBN 0-8020-3298-2). U of Toronto Pr.

International Gold Problem. Royal Institute of International Affairs Staff. (Social Economic History Ser.). Repr. of 1931 ed. 25.00 o.p. (ISBN 0-384-52280-7). Johnson Repr.

International Great Meals in Minutes. Ed. by Time-Life Books Editors. 1986. 24.95 o.p. (ISBN 0-316-85091-8). Little.

International Guide to Qualifications in Education. National Equivalence Information Center Staff. LC 84-17083. 675p. 1984. 90.00x o.p. (ISBN 0-7201-1716-X). Mansell.

International Guide to the Relais et Chateaux, 1985. Relais et Chateaux Staff. 200p. (Orig.). 1985. pap. 10.00 o.p. (ISBN 2-905421-00-2). Faber & Faber.

International Halley Watch Amateur Observers' Manual for Scientific Comet Studies. Stephen J. Edberg. LC 83-20591. (Illus.). 192p. 1983. pap. 9.95 o.p. (ISBN 0-89490-102-8). Enslow Pubs.

International Hallmarks on Gold & Platinum. 21.00 o.p. (ISBN 0-911403-07-8, Pub. by Tardy FR). Seven Hills Bk Dists.

International Hallmarks on Silver Collected by Tardy. English ed. Tardy. (Illus.). 550p. (Orig.). 1981. pap. 30.00 o.s.i. (ISBN 0-911403-07-8, 2390169, Pub. by Tardy FR). Seven Hills Bk Dists.

International Handbook of Education Systems: Asia, Australasia & Latin America, Vol. 3. Ed. by Robert Cowen & Martin McLean. LC 82-17375. (International Handbook of Educational Systems Ser.: 1-670). 844p. 1984. 85.00x o.p. (ISBN 0-471-90214-4, Pub. by Wiley-Interscience). Wiley.

International Handbook of Education Systems: Europe & Canada, Vol. 1. Ed. by Brian Holmes. (International Handbook of Educational Systems Ser.). 729p. 1983. 81.95x o.p. (ISBN 0-471-90078-8, Pub. by Wiley-Interscience). Wiley.

International Handbook of Education Systems: Sub-Saharan Africa - North Africa & the Middle East. Ed. by John Cameron & Paul Hurst. (International Handbook of Educational Systems Ser.). 896p. 1983. 81.95 o.p. (ISBN 0-471-90079-6). Wiley.

International Handbook of Universities. 10th ed. International Association of Universities Staff. Ed. by D. J. Aitken & A. Taylor. 1300p. 1987. 140.00x o.p. (ISBN 0-935859-04-7, Stockton Pr). Groves Dict Music.

International Herald Tribune Guide to Business Travel & Entertainment in Europe. Peter Graham. LC 83-82526. 224p. 1984. pap. 9.95 o.p. (ISBN 0-03-070772-2). H Holt & Co.

International Human Resource Management. Bigoness. Date not set. 19.95 o.p. (ISBN 0-256-05799-0). Irwin.

International Image Market: In Search of an Alternative Perspective. Armand Mattelart et al. Tr. by Nicholas Garnham from Fr. (Comedia Ser.). 180p. 1987. 18.00 o.p. (ISBN 0-906890-68-3, Dist. by Kampmann); pap. 7.90 o.p. (ISBN 0-906890-67-5). M Boyars Pubs.

International Immigration Policies & Programmes: World Survey. United Nations Staff. (Population Studies: No. 80). iii, 111p. 1982. 10.00 o.p. (ISBN 92-1-151091-0, E.82.XIII.4). UN.

International Indebtedness & the Developing Countries. George C. Abbott. LC 79-5070. 310p. 1979. 35.00 o.p. (ISBN 0-87332-149-9). M E Sharpe.

International Industrial Sensor Directory. Philip C. Flora. (Illus.). 200p. (Orig.). 1986. pap. text ed. 45.00 o.p. (ISBN 0-910747-19-9, Co-pub TAB Bks & TAP-TPR). Tech Data TX.

International Institute of Agriculture. Asher Hobson. 1931. 32.00 o.p. (ISBN 0-384-23740-1); pap. 26.00 o.p. (ISBN 0-384-23730-4). Johnson Repr.

International Interactions: Events-Data Analysis Applied to the Middle East. Thomas J. Sloan. (CISE Learning Package Ser.: No. 12). (Illus.). 49p. (Orig.). 1975. pap. text ed. 3.00x o.p. (ISBN 0-936876-27-1). LRIS.

International-Intercultural Education in the Four-Year College: A Handbook on Strategies for Change. Ed. by Marvin Williamsen & Cynthia T. Morehouse. (FAMC Occasional Publication Ser.: No.22). 88p. (Orig.). 1977. pap. text ed. 4.00x o.p. (ISBN 0-936876-07-7). LRIS.

International Investment in South Africa. Alison Cooper & Micheline Tusenius. 189p. (Orig.). 1987. text ed. 125.00 o.p. (ISBN 0-931035-19-8). IRRC Inc DC.

International Jobs - Where They Are, How to Get Them. Eric Kocher. (Illus.). 1979. 11.95 o.p. (ISBN 0-201-03898-6); pap. 6.95 o.p. (ISBN 0-201-03899-4). Addison-Wesley.

International Journal of Lifelong Education, Vol. 4. 1985. institutions 80.00 o.p. (ISBN 0-317-31529-3); individuals 40.00 o.p. (ISBN 0-317-31530-7). Taylor & Francis.

International Journal of Psychoanalytic Psychotherapy, No. 6. Ed. by Robert Langs. LC 75-648853. 498p. 1977. 23.00 o.p. (ISBN 0-87668-282-4). Aronson.

International Journal of Psychoanalytic Psychotherapy, 1983-84, Vol. 10. Ed. by Robert Langs. LC 75-648853. 639p. 1984. 50.00x o.s.i. (ISBN 0-87668-633-1). Aronson.

International Labour Documentation, Cumulative Edition, 1965-1969, 8 vols. International Labour Office, Central Library, Geneva Staff. 5334p. 1970. Set. lib. bdg. 875.00 o.p. (ISBN 0-8161-0902-8, Hall Library). G K Hall.

International Labour Standards. 1978. pap. 10.50 o.p. (ISBN 92-2-101861-X, ILO77, ILO). UNIPUB.

International Law. Prakash Chandra. 1986. text ed. 20.00x o.p. (ISBN 0-7069-2826-1, Pub. by Vikas India). Advent NY.

International Law & Aboriginal Rights. Ed. by Barbara Hocking. 288p. 1987. 39.00 o.p. (ISBN 0-949614-35-1, Pub. by Croom Helm UK). Routledge Chapman & Hall.

International Law & Practice in Ancient India. Ed. by H. S. Bhatia. 1977. text ed. 15.00x o.p. (ISBN 0-391-01081-6). Humanities.

International Law for Seagoing Officers. 4th ed. Burdick H. Brittin. (Illus.). 624p. 1981. 24.95 o.p. (ISBN 0-87021-304-0); bulk rates avail. o.p. Naval Inst Pr.

International Legal Process (1968, 3 vols. Chayes. 1985. Set. text ed. 31.00 o.p. (ISBN 0-316-13829-0); Volume 1. text ed. 15.00 o.p. (ISBN 0-316-13830-4); Volume 2. text ed. 15.00 o.p. (ISBN 0-316-13831-2); Documents Volume. text ed. 9.95 o.p. (ISBN 0-316-13832-0). Little.

International Lending, Risk & the Euromarkets. Anthony Angelini et al. LC 79-10712. 213p. 1979. 31.95x o.p. (ISBN 0-470-26653-8). Halsted Pr.

International Library & Information Programmes: Proceedings. ICLG Conference, 1977 & D. Burnett. 1979. 12.00 o.p. (ISBN 0-85365-591-X). Nichols Pub.

International List of Articles on the History of Education Published in Non-Educational Serials, 1965-1974. Joseph M. McCarthy. LC 76-24769. (Reference Library of Social Science Ser.: Vol. 33). 1977. lib. bdg. 33.00 o.p. (ISBN 0-8240-9909-5). Garland Pub.

International Literary Market Place, 1987-1988. 575p. 1987. 110.00 o.p. (ISBN 0-8352-2341-8). Bowker.

International Mail Order Gourmet: A Sourcebook of Selected Delicacies from Around the World. Ed. by Jamie Harrison & Shelley Boris. (Illus.). 112p. (Orig.). 1987. lib. bdg. 24.80 o.p. (ISBN 0-89471-578-X); pap. 12.95 o.p. (ISBN 0-89471-536-4). Running Pr.

International Management & Business Policy. Michael Z. Brooke & H. Lee Remmers. LC 78-69612. (Illus.). 1978. Repr. of 1977 ed. text ed. 31.50 o.p. (ISBN 0-395-26505-3). HM.

International Maritime Dictionary. 2nd ed. Rene De Kerchove. 1961. 44.95 o.p. (ISBN 0-442-02062-7). Van Nos Reinhold.

International Maritime Organisation. Ed. by Samir Mankabady. 378p. 1984. 49.50 o.p. (ISBN 0-7099-1749-X, Pub. by Croom Helm Ltd). Routledge Chapman & Hall.

International Maritime Organisation: Accidents at Sea, Vol. 2. Samir Mankabady. 350p. 1986. 60.00 o.p. (ISBN 0-7099-4640-6, Pub. by Croom Helm UK). Routledge Chapman & Hall.

International Maritime Organisation: International Shipping Rules, Vol. 1. 2nd ed. Samir Mankbady. 368p. 1986. 76.50 o.p. (ISBN 0-7099-3591-9, Pub. by Croom Helm UK). Routledge Chapman & Hall.

International Marketing. 3rd ed. Vern Terpstra. 624p. 1983. 36.95x o.p. (ISBN 0-03-062734-6). Dryden Pr.

International Marketing. K. A. Yarker. 178p. 1976. text ed. 23.50x o.p. (ISBN 0-220-66298-3, Pub. by Busn Bks England). Gower Pub Co.

International Marketing Data & Statistics, 1985. 10th ed. 400p. 1985. 160.00x o.p. (ISBN 0-86338-087-5, Pub. by Euromonitor Pubns). Gale.

International Marketing Data & Statistics 1987. 12th ed. 380p. 1987. 180.00x o.p. (ISBN 0-86338-087-5). Gale.

International Marketing Data & Statistics 1987-1988. 12th ed. 400p. 1987. 180.00x o.s.i. (Pub. by Euromonitor Pubns). Gale.

International Marketing Handbook, Nineteen Eighty-Five. 2nd ed. Ed. by Frank E. Bair. 3672p. 1985. 220.00x o.p. (ISBN 0-8103-2057-6). Gale.

International Marketing Handbook Supplement. 2nd ed. Ed. by Frank E. Bair. 1200p. 1986. 100.00X o.p. (ISBN 0-8103-0546-1). Gale.

International Marketing: Managerial Perspectives. Subhash C. Jain & Lewis R. Tucker. LC 78-31876. 518p. 1979. pap. text ed. 17.25 o.p. (ISBN 0-8436-0903-6). PWS-Kent Pub.

International Meeting on Computer Applications for Nuclear Power Plant Operations: Proceedings in Pasc, WA September 8-12, 1985. 864p. 1985. 90.00 o.p. (ISBN 0-89448-127-4, 700114). Am Nuclear Soc.

International Menu Diabetic Cookbook. Betty Marks & Lucille H. Schechter. 320p. 1985. 14.95 o.p. (ISBN 0-8092-5390-9). Contemp Bks.

International Mergers & Acquisitions. Terence E. Cooke. 296p. 1986. text ed. 65.00x o.p. (ISBN 0-631-14747-0). Basil Blackwell.

International Metallic Materials Cross Reference. 2nd ed. 432p. 1983. pap. write for info. o.p. (ISBN 0-931690-16-1). Genium Pub.

International Migration & Economic Development. Brinley Thomas. LC 82-48325. (World Economy Ser.). 85p. 1983. lib. bdg. 17.00 o.p. (ISBN 0-8240-5380-X). Garland Pub.

International Migration Law. R. Plender. 1972. 50.000 o.s.i. (ISBN 9-0286-0162-7). E J Brill USA.

International Migration, 1945-1957. 414p. 1959. 10.50 o.p. (ISBN 92-2-100201-2). Intl Labour Office.

International Monetary Fund & Low-Income Countries. Bela Mukhoti. (Foreign Agricultural Economic Reports: No. 224). 48p. 1987. pap. 2.50 o.p. (ISBN 0-318-22910-2, S/N 001-019-00465-7). USGPO.

International Monetary Tangle: Myths & Realities. Guillaume Guindey. Tr. by Michael L. Hoffman. LC 77-77797. 128p. (Fr.). 1977. 35.00 o.p. (ISBN 0-87332-108-1). M E Sharpe.

International Money: Issues & Analysis. Andrew D. Crockett. 1978. 24.50 o.p. (ISBN 0-12-195750-0). Acad Pr.

International Monopolies & the Developing Countries. E. Nukhovich. 1980. 7.95 o.p. (ISBN 0-8285-1801-7, Pub. by Progress Pubs USSR). Imported Pubns.

International Mortality Statistics. Michael Alderson. 380p. 1981. 65.00x o.p. (ISBN 0-87196-514-3). Facts on File.

International Mutual Assistance in Administrative Matters. E. Loebenstein. LC 72-96054. (Osterreichische Zeitschrift Fuer Offentliches Recht: Suppl. 2). 93p. 1972. pap. 24.80 o.p. (ISBN 0-387-81120-6). Springer-Verlag.

International Naturist Guide. 400p. 16.95 o.p. (ISBN 90-215-1282-3, INF). Elysium.

International Needlework Designs. Mira Silverstein. LC 77-21189. (Encore Edition). (Illus.). 1978. 6.95 o.p. (ISBN 0-684-16925-8, ScribT). Scribner.

International News Agencies. Oliver Boyd-Barrett. LC 80-51779. (Constable Communication & Society Ser.: Vol. 13). (Illus.). 284p. 1980. 29.95 o.p. (ISBN 0-8039-1511-X); pap. 14.95 o.p. (ISBN 0-8039-1512-8). Sage.

International Nuclear Commerce: Proceedings, American Nuclear Society Executive Conference. 360p. pap. 40.00 o.p. (ISBN 0-89448-306-4, 650009). Am Nuclear Soc.

International Occupational Safety & Health Resource Catalogue. Jane H. Ives. 320p. 1981. 47.95 o.p. (ISBN 0-03-060299-8). H Holt & Co.

International Offshore Mechanics & Arctic Engineering Symposium, 3rd: Proceedings. 1983. pap. text ed. (IX0161). ASME.

International Oil Market. Alessandro Roncaglia. Ed. by J. A. Kregel. LC 84-5555. 1985. 39.95 o.p. (ISBN 0-87332-282-7); pap. 15.95 o.p. (ISBN 0-87332-290-8). M E Sharpe.

International Organization: An Interdisciplinary Bibliography. Michael Haas. LC 68-28099. (Bibliographical Ser.: No. 41). 944p. 1971. 35.00x o.p. (ISBN 0-8179-2411-6). Hoover Inst Pr.

International Organization Documents for Translation from French. Ed. by J. Coveney. 93p. 1972. 25.00 o.p. (ISBN 0-08-016287-8). Pergamon.

International Organizations: A Guide to Information Sources. Ed. by Alexine L. Atherton. LC 73-17502. (International Relations Guide Ser.: Vol. 1). 384p. 1976. 68.00x o.s.i. (ISBN 0-8103-1324-3). Gale.

International Organizations: Principles & Issues. 3rd ed. A. LeRoy Bennett. (Illus.). 544p. 1984. pap. text ed. (ISBN 0-13-473496-3). P-H.

International Organizations: 1988. Ed. by Karin Koek. (Encyclopedia of Associations Ser.: Vol. 4). 1987. 195.00x o.p. (ISBN 0-8103-1845-8). Gale.

International Organizations, 1988: Supplement to Vol. 4 of the Encyclopedia of Associations. Ed. by Karin Koek. 1988. pap. text ed. 135.00x o.p. (ISBN 0-8103-2518-7). Gale.

International Parliamentary Conference: Proceedings, 69th, Rome, 1982, 2 vols. Inter-Parliamentary Union Staff. 1982. Vol. 1. Vol. 2. write for info. o.p. UN.

International Pasta Cookbook. Joan Nathan. LC 77-12259. 1977. pap. 8.95 o.p. (ISBN 0-916752-25-9). Longman Trade.

International Patent Classifications, 1984, 9 vols. 4th ed. 1984. 482.00 o.p. (ISBN 3-4521-9413-2). Intl Pubns Serv.

International Perspectives in Health Economics: Selected Papers from the World Congress in Health Economics, Leiden, the Netherlands, September 1980. Gavin H. Mooney. (Journal of Social Science & Medicine Ser.: No. 15). 72p. 1981. pap. 18.00 o.p. (ISBN 0-08-028131-1). Pergamon.

International Perspectives on Family Violence. Richard J. Gelles & Claire P. Cornell. LC 82-48524. 176p. 1983. 22.00x o.p. (ISBN 0-669-06199-9); pap. 17.00x o.p. (ISBN 0-669-06198-0). Lexington Bks.

International Perspectives on Neglected Sexually Transmitted Diseases: Impact on Venereology, Infertility, & Maternal & Infant Health. King K. Holmes & Per-Anders Mardh. (Illus.). 352p. 1983. text ed. 50.00 o.p. (ISBN 0-07-029676-6). McGraw.

International Perspectives on Voluntary Action Research. Ed. by David H. Smith & John Van Til. LC 82-20090. 430p. (Orig.). 1983. lib. bdg. 48.25 o.p. (ISBN 0-8191-2862-7); pap. text ed. 25.50 o.p. (ISBN 0-8191-2863-5). U Pr of Amer.

International Petroleum Encyclopedia, 1988. Ed. by Oil & Gas Journal Staff. 400p. 1988. 95.00 o.p. (ISBN 0-87814-327-0, I8801). PennWell Bks.

International Photography Index: 1979. Ed. by William S. Johnson & Susan E. Cohen. 230p. (gr. 10-12). 1983. lib. bdg. 110.00 o.s.i. (ISBN 0-8161-8536-0, Hall Reference). G K Hall.

International Photography Index: 1981. Ed. by William S. Johnson & Susan E. Cohen. 299p. 1984. lib. bdg. 105.00 o.s.i. (ISBN 0-8161-8640-5, Hall Reference). G K Hall.

International Politics: A Framework for Analysis. 4th ed. K. J. Holsti. (Illus.). 512p. 1983. text ed. (ISBN 0-13-473322-3). P-H.

International Politics: Major Contemporary Trends & Issues. Anam Jailtly. 326p. 1987. text ed. 35.00x o.p. (Pub. by Sterling Pubs India). Apt Bks.

International Politics of Surplus Capacity: Competition for Market Shares in the World Recession. Ed. by Susan Strange & Roger Tooze. (Illus.). 1981. text ed. 29.95x o.p. (ISBN 0-04-382034-4). Unwin Hyman.

International Population Assistance: the First Decade. Rafael M. Salas. 1979. 58.00 o.p. (ISBN 0-08-024701-6); pap. 28.00 o.p. (ISBN 0-08-024700-8). Pergamon.

International Population Census Bibliography: 1945-1977. rev. ed. Doreen S. Goyer. LC 79-25890. (Studies in Population). 1980. 33.00 o.p. (ISBN 0-12-294380-5). Acad Pr.

International Port of Call: An Illustrated Maritime History of the Golden Gate. Robert J. Schwendinger. LC 84-25733. (Illus.). 176p. 1984. 22.95 o.p. (ISBN 0-89781-122-4). Windsor Pubns Inc.

International Production & the Multinational Enterprise. John H. Dunning. (Illus.). 416p. 1981. text ed. 40.00x o.p. (ISBN 0-04-330319-6); pap. text ed. 19.95x o.p. (ISBN 0-04-330320-X). Unwin Hyman.

International Race Car Drivers. Mark Dillon & Frank Haigh. LC 73-22514. (Superwheels & Thrill Sports Bks.). (Illus.). 52p. (gr. 5-10). 1974. PLB 9.95 o.p. (ISBN 0-8225-0413-8). Lerner Pubns.

International Redistribution of Wealth & Power: A Study of the Charter of Economic Rights & Duties of States. Robert F. Meagher. (Pergamon Policy Studies). 1981. 58.00 o.p. (ISBN 0-08-022478-4); pap. 23.00 o.p. (ISBN 0-08-027557-5). Pergamon.

International Reference Ionosphere - Status 1985-86: Proceedings of the URSI-COSPAR Workshop on the International Reference Ionosphere Held in Louvain-la-Neuve, Belgium, 25 October - 1st November. Ed. by K. Rawer & Y. V. Ramanamurty. 138p. 1986. pap. 52.00 o.p. (ISBN 0-08-034026-1, PBL). Pergamon.

International Regional Organizations: Constitutional Foundations. Ed. by Ruth C. Lawson. LC 74-10016. 387p. 1975. Repr. of 1962 ed. lib. bdg. 26.00x o.p. (ISBN 0-8371-7655-7, LARO). Greenwood.

International Registration Plan. American Association of Motor Vehicle Administrators, & American Trucking Association, State Laws. 32p. 1987. pap. text ed. 7.00 o.s.i. (ISBN 0-88711-084-3). Am Trucking Assns.

International Regulatory Aspects for Pesticide Chemicals. G. Vettorazzi. 232p. 1979. 82.00 o.p. (ISBN 0-8493-5607-5). CRC Pr.

International Relations. Prakash Chandra. 306p. 1986. text ed. 25.00x o.p. (ISBN 0-7069-2368-5, Pub. by Vikas India). Advent NY.

International Relations: A Handbook of Current Theory. Ed. by Margot Light & A. J. R. Groom. LC 85-10734. 245p. 1985. lib. bdg. 27.50x o.p. (ISBN 0-931477-12-3). Lynne Rienner.

International Relations Dictionary. 3rd ed. Jack C. Plano & Roy Olton. LC 82-3996. (Clio Dictionaries in Political Science Ser.: No. 2). 488p. 1982. lib. bdg. 37.50 o.p. (ISBN 0-87436-332-2); pap. 18.00 o.p. (ISBN 0-87436-336-5). ABC-Clio.

International Relations of Eastern Europe: A Guide to Information Sources. Ed. by Robin A. Remington. LC 73-17512. (International Relations Information Guide Ser.: Vol. 8). 296p. 1978. 68.00x o.p. (ISBN 0-8103-1320-0). Gale.

International Relations Research & Training in the People's Republic of China. Douglas P. Murray. (Special Report of the Northeast Asia-United States Forum on International Policy, Stanford University). 56p. 1982. pap. 5.00 o.p. (ISBN 0-935371-05-2). ISIS.

International Relations: Theories & Evidence. Michael P. Sullivan. (Illus.). 400p. 1976. text ed. (ISBN 0-13-473470-X). P-H.

International Relations: Understanding the Behavior of Nations. Close Up Foundation Staff. (Illus.). 70p. (YA) (gr. 11-12). 1988. pap. text ed. 8.00 o.p. (ISBN 0-932765-20-3); tchr's. guide & video set avail. o.p. Close Up Foun.

International Relations: Vol. 1, Law. Jack E. Vincent. LC 83-3541. (International Relations Ser.). 80p. (Orig.). 1983. pap. text ed. 9.25 o.p. (ISBN 0-8191-3160-1). U Pr of Amer.

International Review, 4 vols, No. 1. 1969. Repr. of 1939 ed. Set. lib. bdg. 36.00x o.p. (ISBN 0-8371-9185-8, IROO). Greenwood.

International Review of Cytology, Vol. 81. Ed. by Geoggrey H. Bourne & James F. Danielli. 1983. 80.00 o.p. (ISBN 0-12-364481-X). Acad Pr.

International Review of Cytology Supplement, No. 16. G. H. Bourne & J. F. Danielli. (Serial Publication). 1983. 29.95 o.p. (ISBN 0-12-364377-5). Acad Pr.

International Review of Forestry Research, Vols. 1-3. Ed. by J. A. Romberger & P. Mikola. write for info. o.p. Vol. 1, 1964 (ISBN 0-12-365501-3). Vol. 3, 1970. write for info. o.p. (ISBN 0-12-365503-X). Acad Pr.

International Review of General & Experimental Zoology, 4 vols. Ed. by William J. Felts & Richard J. Harrison. Vol. 1, 1964. 77.00 o.p. (ISBN 0-12-368101-4); Vol. 2. 55.50 o.p. (ISBN 0-12-368102-2); Vol. 3, 1968. 77.00 o.p. (ISBN 0-12-368103-0); Vol. 4, 1970. 77.00 o.p. (ISBN 0-12-368104-9); Set. 178.50 o.p. Acad Pr.

International Review of Halogen Chemistry, 3 Vols. Ed. by Viktor Gutmann. LC 66-30147. (Illus.). Vol. 1, 1967. 123.50 o.p. (ISBN 0-12-310901-9); Vol. 2, 1967. 123.50 o.p. (ISBN 0-12-310902-7); Vol. 3, 1968. 123.50 o.p. (ISBN 0-12-310903-5). Acad Pr.

International Review of Sport Sociology: A Quarterly Edited by the Committee for Sociology of Sport of the International Council of Sport & Physical Education (UNESCO) & of the International Sociological Association, Vol. 13, No. 2. UNESCO Staff & Polish Scientific Publications Staff. 115p. 1982. pap. 10.00 o.p. (ISBN 0-686-81424-X, UM56, UNESCO). UNIPUB.

International Review of Sport Sociology, Vol. 12. 1978. Set Of 4 Vols. pap. 26.50 o.p. (ISBN 0-685-65233-5, UM37, UNESCO). UNIPUB.

International Review of Unemployment Insurance Schemes. Saul J. Blaustein & Isabel Craig. (Studies in Unemployment Insurance). 1977. pap. 1.00 o.p. (ISBN 0-911558-22-5). W E Upjohn.

International Safe Travel Guide. Robert C. Downes & William J. Bartman. LC 87-6392. 144p. (Orig.). 1987. pap. 6.95 o.p. (ISBN 0-932620-78-7). Betterway Pubns.

International School on Electro & Photonuclear Reactions I: Proceedings of the International School on Electro & Photonuclear Reactions, 1st Course, Erice, Italy, June 2-17, 1976. International School on Electro & Photonuclear Reactions Staff. Ed. by C. Schaerf. (Lecture Notes in Physics: Vol. 61). 1977. soft cover 32.00 o.s.i. (ISBN 3-540-08139-9). Springer-Verlag.

International Schools & Their Role in the Field of International Education. R. J. Leach. 1969. 29.00 o.p. (ISBN 0-08-013037-2); pap. 14.25 o.p. (ISBN 0-08-013036-4). Pergamon.

International Securities Markets. (Corporate Law & Practice Ser.). 439p. 1987. 45.00 o.p. (B4-6802). PLI.

International Security in the Southeast Asian & Southwest Pacific Region. Ed. by T. B. Millar. LC 83-5937. (Illus.). 317p. 1984. text ed. 32.50 o.p. (ISBN 0-7022-1973-8). U of Queensland Pr.

International Seminar on Land Taxation, Land Tenure & Land Reform in Developing Countries. Ed. by A. M. Woodruff et al. LC 67-30788. (Orig.). 1966. pap. text ed. 3.65 o.s.i. (ISBN 0-686-00917-7). Lincoln Inst Land.

International Sherlock Holmes: A Companion Volume to the World Bibliography of Sherlock Holmes & Dr. Watson. Ronald B. De Waal. LC 79-24533. 621p. 1980. 62.50 o.p. (ISBN 0-208-01777-1, Archon). Shoe String.

International Social Welfare: A Selected Bibliography. Daniel S. Sanders & Richard J. Estes. Date not set. 5.00 o.s.i. (84-500-04). Coun Soc WK Ed.

International Socialist Review, Vols. 1-24. Socialist Workers Party. Incl. Vols. 1 & 2. lib. bdg. 30.00 (ISBN 0-313-21677-0, I201); Vol. 3. lib. bdg. 30.00 (ISBN 0-313-21678-9, I203); Vol. 4. lib. bdg. 30.00 (ISBN 0-313-21679-7, I204); Vol. 5. lib. bdg. 30.00 (ISBN 0-313-21680-0, I205); Vol. 6. lib. bdg. 30.00 (ISBN 0-313-21681-9, I206); Vol. 7. lib. bdg. 30.00 (ISBN 0-313-21682-7, I207); Vol. 8. lib. bdg. 30.00 (ISBN 0-313-21683-5, I208); Vols. 9 & 10. lib. bdg. 30.00 (ISBN 0-313-21684-3, I209); Vols. 11 & 12. lib. bdg. 30.00 (ISBN 0-313-21686-X, I211); Vols. 13 & 14. lib. bdg. 30.00 (ISBN 0-313-21687-8, I213); Vols. 15-17. lib. bdg. 30.00 (ISBN 0-313-21688-6, I215); Vols. 18-20. lib. bdg. 30.00 (ISBN 0-313-21689-4, I218); Vols. 21-24. lib. bdg. 39.00 (ISBN 0-313-21690-8, I221). 1968. Repr. of 1943 ed. Set. lib. bdg. 365.00x o.p. (ISBN 0-8371-9241-2, I200). Greenwood.

International Socialist Review, Vols. 1-18, No. 8. Socialist Workers Party. Incl. Vol. 1. lib. bdg. 40.00 (ISBN 0-313-21659-2, I101); Vol. 2. lib. bdg. 40.00 (ISBN 0-313-21660-6, I102); Vol. 3. lib. bdg. 40.00 (ISBN 0-313-21661-4, I103); Vol. 4. lib. bdg. 40.00 (ISBN 0-313-21662-2, I104); Vol. 5. lib. bdg. 40.00 (ISBN 0-313-21663-0, I105); Vol. 6. lib. bdg. 40.00 (ISBN 0-313-21664-9, I106); Vol. 7. lib. bdg. 40.00 (ISBN 0-313-21665-7, I107); Vol. 8. lib. bdg. 40.00 (ISBN 0-313-21666-5, I108); Vol. 9. lib. bdg. 40.00 (ISBN 0-313-21667-3, I109); Vol. 10. lib. bdg. 40.00 (ISBN 0-313-21668-1, I110); Vol. 11. lib. bdg. 40.00 (ISBN 0-313-21669-X, I111); Vol. 12. lib. bdg. 40.00 (ISBN 0-313-21670-3, I112); Vol. 13. lib. bdg. 40.00 (ISBN 0-313-21671-1, I113); Vol. 14. lib. bdg. 40.00 (ISBN 0-313-21672-X, I114); Vol. 15. lib. bdg. 40.00 (ISBN 0-313-21673-8, I115); Vol. 16. lib. bdg. 40.00 (ISBN 0-313-21674-6, I116); Vol. 17. lib. bdg. 40.00 (ISBN 0-313-21675-4, I117); Vol. 18. lib. bdg. 40.00 (ISBN 0-313-21676-2, I118). 1968. Repr. of 1918 ed. Set. lib. bdg. 655.00x o.p. (ISBN 0-8371-9186-6, I100). Greenwood.

International Solidarity with the Spanish Republic 1936-1939. D. Ibarruri et al. 390p. 1975. pap. 3.95 o.p. (ISBN 0-8285-0480-6, Pub. by Progress Pubs USSR). Imported Pubns.

International Stock Exchange Official Yearbook 1987-88. The London Stock Exchange Staff. 1100p. 1988. 230.00 o.p. (ISBN 0-935859-29-2, Stockton Pr). Groves Dict Music.

International Stockman's School Handbooks, 1984. Ed. by Frank H. Baker. Incl. Vol. 20. Beef Cattle Science Handbook. 1000p. 1983. 58.50x (ISBN 0-86531-672-4); Vol. 16. Dairy Science Handbook. 500p. 1983. 47.50x (ISBN 0-86531-673-2); Vol. iv. Sheep & Goat Handbook. 500p. 1983. 39.50x (ISBN 0-86531-674-0). Westview.

International Survey of Recent Painting & Sculpture. Kynaston McShine. (Illus.). 384p. (Orig.). 1984. pap. 25.00 o.p. (ISBN 0-87070-391-9). Museum Mod Art.

International Survey: Structured Programming, 3 vols. Infotech Staff. (Infotech Computer State of the Art Reports). 466p. 1978. Set. 920.00x o.p. (ISBN 0-08-028532-5). Pergamon.

International Surveys: Exhibitions of Modern European Art. Ed. by Theodore Reff. (Modern Art in Paris 1855 to 1900 Ser.). 500p. 1981. lib. bdg. 53.00 o.p. (ISBN 0-8240-4725-7). Garland Pub.

International Symposium Digest, Beverly Hills: May 1976. 180p. 40.00 o.p. (ISBN 0-318-16486-8); members 30.00 o.p. (ISBN 0-318-16487-6). SID.

International Symposium Digest, Chicago: May 1979. 150p. 40.00 o.p. (ISBN 0-318-16490-6); members 30.00 o.p. (ISBN 0-318-16491-4). SID.

International Symposium on Cavitation Inception. Ed. by W. B. Morgan & B. R. Parkin. 238p. 1979. 30.00 o.p. (ISBN 0-686-59662-5, G00156). ASME.

International Symposium on Food Toxiology: A Special Issue of Food Addictives & Contaminants, Vol. 1. Ed. by R. Walker & M. E. Knowles. (No. 2). 164p. 1984. 22.00x o.p. (ISBN 0-85066-996-0). Taylor & Francis.

International Symposium on Hepatotoxicity. Ed. by M. Eliakim. 1974. 39.50 o.p. (ISBN 0-12-237850-4). Acad Pr.

International Symposium on Labeled & Unlabeled Antibody in Cancer Diagnosis & Therapy. Ed. by Anne McCarthy & Florence I. Gregoric. (NCI Monographs 3, 1987). (Illus.). 189p. 1987. pap. 9.50 o.p. (ISBN 0-318-22608-1, S/N 017-042-00194-3). USGPO.

International Symposium on Magnetic Resonance, 4th, Rehovot-Jerusalem, 1971: Proceedings. Ed. by D. Fiat. 360p. 1976. 89.00 o.p. (ISBN 0-08-020791-X). Pergamon.

International Symposium on Polyvinylchloride, 2nd: Proceedings. Ed. by A. Guyot. LC 77-73904. 1977. 55.00 o.p. (ISBN 0-08-021203-4). Pergamon.

International Symposium on Shipboard Acoustics: Proceedings, 1976. International Symposium on Shipboard Acoustics. Ed. by J. H. Janssen. 1977. 105.25 o.p. (ISBN 0-444-41650-1). Elsevier.

International Symposium on Subsurface Injection of Liquid Wastes: Proceedings. LC 86-8523. 1986. 43.75 o.p. (ISBN 0-318-22996-X). Natl Water Well.

International Symposium on Vaginal Mycoses Vienna, September 1981. (Journal: Chemotherapy: Suppl. 1, Vol. 28). (Illus.). 112p. 1983. pap. 24.00 o.p. (ISBN 3-8055-3638-0). S Karger.

International Syndicated Loans. 1984. 88.00 o.p. (ISBN 0-8002-3167-8). Intl Pubns Serv.

International System & the Third World. S. P. Verma. 1988. text ed. 40.00x o.p. (ISBN 0-7069-4016-4, Pub. by VikaS India). Advent NY.

International Tax Summaries 1987: A Guide for Planning & Decisions. Jon D. Jacobs. (Professional Accounting & Business Ser.). 1088p. 1987. 75.00 o.p. (ISBN 0-471-85975-3). Wiley.

International Taxation after the Tax Reform Act of 1984: Fifteenth Annual Institute on Internation Taxation, Vol. 214. Practising Law Institute Staff. 449p. 1984. pap. 40.00 o.p. (ISBN 0-317-27515-1, J4-3555). PLI.

International Technology & Transfer: Major Issues & Policy Responses. Tagi Sagafi-Nejad & Farok J. Contractor. LC 82-47904. cancelled o.s.i. (ISBN 0-669-05687-1). Lexington Bks.

International Technology for the Nonferrous Smelting Industry. T. K. Corwin et al. LC 82-3434. (Chemical Tech. Rev. 205, Pollution Tech Rev. 90). (Illus.). 413p. 1982. 36.00 o.p. (ISBN 0-8155-0894-8). Noyes.

International Telecommunications Standards: Issues & Implications for the 1980's. 1983. 75.00 o.p. (ISBN 0-317-11967-2). Info Gatekeepers.

International Terrorism & the CIA. V. Syrokomsky. 264p. 1983. pap. 3.95 o.p. (ISBN 0-8285-2653-2, Pub. by Progress Pubs USSR). Imported Pubns.

International Test Conference 1985: Proceedings. 988p. 1985. 80.00 o.p. (ISBN 0-8186-0641-X); microfiche 80.00 o.p. (ISBN 0-8186-4641-1). IEEE Comp Soc.

International Textbook of Cardiology. Ed. by T. O. Cheng. 1328p. 1986. 125.00 o.s.i. (ISBN 0-08-034310-4, H215, Pub. by PPI). Pergamon.

International Textile Directory. Textile Institute Staff. 400p. 1987. 160.00cancelled o.p. (ISBN 0-943818-90-7, Stockton Pr). Groves Dict Music.

International Trade. annual Incl. 1952. pap. o.p. (ISBN 0-685-48323-1, G2). UNIPUB; 1957-58. pap. 1.50 o.p. (ISBN 0-685-48324-X, G114). UNIPUB; 1959. pap. 2.00 o.p. (ISBN 0-685-48325-8, G115). UNIPUB; 1960. pap. 5.00 (ISBN 0-685-48326-6, G4). UNIPUB; 1961. pap. 5.00 (ISBN 0-685-48327-4, G5). UNIPUB; 1962. (Eng., Fr. & Span.). pap. 5.50 (ISBN 0-685-48328-2, G6). UNIPUB; 1963. pap. 5.50 (ISBN 0-685-48329-0, G116). UNIPUB; 1964. pap. 5.50 (ISBN 0-685-48330-4, G7). UNIPUB; 1965. pap. 6.50 (ISBN 0-685-48331-2, G8). UNIPUB; 1966. pap. 9.50 (ISBN 0-685-48332-0, G10). UNIPUB; 1967. pap. 13.00 (ISBN 0-685-48333-9, G9). UNIPUB; 1968. pap. 13.75 (ISBN 0-685-48334-7, G11). UNIPUB; 1969. pap. 13.00 (ISBN 0-685-48335-5, G12). UNIPUB; 1970. pap. 13.00 (ISBN 0-685-48336-3, G13). UNIPUB; 1971. pap. 15.00 (ISBN 0-685-48337-1, G14). UNIPUB; 1972. pap. 16.50 (ISBN 0-685-48338-X, G15). UNIPUB. (Reports On International Trade Ser.). (Illus., Orig., Eng., Fr. & Span.). pap. (GATT). UNIPUB.

International Trade. I. F. Pearce. 1970. text ed. 17.95x o.p. (ISBN 0-393-09948-2, NortonC). Norton.

International Trade. Kenneth H. Smith. LC 70-84419. (Real World of Economics Ser.). (Illus.). (gr. 5-11). 1970. PLB 4.95 o.p. (ISBN 0-8225-0616-5). Lerner Pubns.

International Trade & Investment: Two Perspectives. Marina v. N. Whitman. LC 81-6326. (Essays in International Finance Ser.: No. 143). 1981. pap. text ed. 4.50x o.p. (ISBN 0-88165-050-1). Princeton U Int Finan Econ.

International Trade: Contemporary Viewpoints. Ed. by Marie S. Ensign & Laurie Adler. (Dynamic Organization Ser.). 234p. 1986. lib. bdg. 39.00 o.p. (ISBN 0-87436-461-2). ABC-Clio.

International Trade in Armaments Prior to World War II. Incl. Bloody Traffic. A. Fenner Brockway. LC 78-147551; Report of the First Subcommittee of the Temporary Mixed Commission on Armaments of the League of Nations. Report A.81. LC 75-147553; Secret International: Armament Firms at Work. Union of Democratic Control. LC 71-147552. (Library of War & Peace; Control & Limitation of Arms). 1972. lib. bdg. 46.00 o.p. (ISBN 0-8240-0331-4). Garland Pub.

International Trade in Art. Paul M. Bator. LC 82-17405. viii, 108p. 1983. lib. bdg. 16.00x o.s.i. (ISBN 0-226-03909-9); pap. text ed. 6.95x o.s.i. (ISBN 0-226-03910-2). U of Chicago Pr.

International Trade, Investment & Payments. H. Peter Gray. LC 78-69573. (Illus.). 1979. text ed. 31.95 o.p. (ISBN 0-395-26659-9). HM.

International Trade: Law & Practice. Ed. by J. Lew & C. Stanbrook. 213p. 1984. 120.00 o.p. (ISBN 0-8002-3168-6). Intl Pubns Serv.

International Trade: Theory & Empirical Evidence. 2nd ed. R. Heller. 1973. pap. text ed. (ISBN 0-13-473918-3). P-H.

International Trademark Design: A Handbook of Marks of Identity. Peter Wildbur. 135p. 1982. pap. 17.95 o.p. (ISBN 0-442-29306-2). Van Nos Reinhold.

Titles

International Traveler's Phrasebook. (Illus.). 96p. Date not set. pap. 6.95 o.p. (ISBN 0-8442-9495-0, Passport Bks). Natl Textbk.

International Tune-up-Maintenance, Scouts, Wagons, Pickups, Through 1980. (Illus.). pap. 9.95 o.p. (ISBN 0-89287-137-7, A233). Clymer Pub.

International Values Databooks. Ed. by Gordan Heald. 480p. 172.00 o.p. (ISBN 0-317-52869-6, Pub. by Croom Helm UK). U. S. A (ISBN 0-7099-4715-1). Great Britain (ISBN 0-7099-4716-X). France (ISBN 0-7099-4717-8). West Germany (ISBN 0-7099-4718-6). Routledge Chapman & Hall.

International Vegetarian Cook Book. Sunset Magazine & Books Editors. LC 82-83218. (Illus.). 96p. 1983. pap. 5.95 o.p. (ISBN 0-376-02921-8, Sunset Bks). Sunset-Lane.

International War Resistance Through World War II. Larra Gara & Charles Chatfield. (Garland Library of War & Peace). 1975. lib. bdg. 46.00 o.p. (ISBN 0-8240-0449-3). Garland Pub.

International Whole Meals: International Cuisines-the Wholefood Way. Gai Stern. (Illus.). 200p. (Orig.). 1987. pap. 9.95 o.p. (ISBN 0-907061-93-1, Pub. Prism Pr). Avery Pub.

International Who's Who in Engineering. 1st ed. 1983. 132.00x o.p. (ISBN 0-900332-71-9). Intl Pubns Serv.

International Who's Who In Music & Musicans Directory. 10th ed. Ed. by Douglas M. Scott. 900p. 1985. 85.00x o.p. (ISBN 0-8103-0424-4). Gale.

International Who's Who 1985-86. 1676p. 1986. 130.00 o.p. (ISBN 0-946653-07-0, EUR51, EUR). UNIPUB.

International Who's Who 1986-87. 50th ed. 1783p. (Orig.). 1986. 145.00 o.p. (ISBN 0-318-21268-4, EUR58, EUR). UNIPUB.

International Who's Who 1987-88. 1800p. 1987. 165.00x o.p. (ISBN 0-946653-33-X, Pub. by Europa England). Gale.

International Workshop on Software Specification & Design, 3rd 1985: Proceedings. 259p. 1985. 44.00 o.p. (ISBN 0-8186-0638-X, Q638); microfiche 44.00 o.p. (ISBN 0-8186-4638-1). IEEE Comp Soc.

International Writers' & Artists Yearbook 1984. 77th ed. 530p. 1983. pap. 10.95 o.p. (ISBN 0-7136-2377-2, Pub by A & C Black England). Writers Digest.

International Writers' & Artists' Yearbook 1985. 78th ed. 530p. (Orig.). 1984. pap. 11.95 o.p. (ISBN 0-7136-2594-5, 1450). Writers Digest.

International Writers' & Artists' Yearbook 1987. 530p. (Orig.). 1986. pap. 12.95 o.p. (ISBN 0-7136-2836-7, Pub. by A & C Black England). Writers Digest.

International Writers' & Artists' Yearbook, 1988. 81st annual ed. Ed. by Christine Robinson. 530p. (Orig.). 1987. pap. 14.95 o.p. (ISBN 0-7136-2952-5, Pub. by A & C Black). Writers Digest.

International Yearbook & Statesmen's Who's Who, 1986. 34th ed. 1986. 180.00 o.p. (ISBN 0-611-00689-8). Intl Pubns Serv.

International Yearbook of Educational & Instructional Technology 1984-85. Ed. by C. W. Osborne. 450p. 1984. 37.50x o.p. (ISBN 0-89397-188-X). Taylor & Francis.

International Yearbook of Educational & Instructional Technology 1986-1987. Ed. by Chris Osborne. (IYEIT Ser.). 200p. 1986. 39.50 o.p. (ISBN 0-89397-239-8). Nichols Pub.

International Yearbook of Serials Librarianship, Vol. I. David P. Woodworth. (Illus.). 225p. 1988. text ed. 34.95 o.s.i. (ISBN 0-86656-844-1). Haworth Pr.

International Youth in Achievement. Ed. by J. S. Thomson. 946p. 1981. 45.00 o.s.i. (ISBN 0-934544-10-7). Am Biog Inst.

International Zoo Yearbook, 1981, Vol. 21. Ed. by P. J. Olney. LC 63-28248. (Illus.). 404p. 1981. 65.00x o.p. (ISBN 0-8002-2966-5). Intl Pubns Serv.

International Zoo Yearbook, 1982, Vol. 22. LC 63-28248. 404p. 1982. 78.00x o.p. (ISBN 0-8002-3090-6). Intl Pubns Serv.

International Zoo Yearbook, 1984, Vol. 23. 85.00 o.p. (ISBN 0-8002-3617-3). Intl Pubns Serv.

International 85. Ed. by ISES Staff. (Illus.). 3000p. 1986. 495.00 o.s.i. (ISBN 0-08-033176-9, B000, B115, Pub. by PPI). Pergamon.

Internationale Beschrankung der Rustungen. Hans Wehberg. LC 72-147563. (Library of War & Peace; Control & Limitation of Arms). 1973. lib. bdg. 46.00 o.p. (ISBN 0-8240-0337-3). Garland Pub.

Internationale Bibliographie der rechtssoziologischen Literatur. 2nd ed. Manfred Rehbinder. x, 73p. 1977. 36.25x o.p. (ISBN 3-8059-0488-6). De Gruyter.

Internationale Germanistische Bibliographie. Ed. by Hans-Albrecht Koch & Uta Koch. Vol. 1980, xiv, 851. 75.00 o.p. (ISBN 3-598-10405-7); Vol. 1982, lxvii, 1398. 100.00 o.p. (ISBN 3-598-21182-1). K G Saur.

Internationaler Riechstoff Kodex. 4th ed. Arno Mueller. (Ger., Eng. & Fr., International codex of perfumes). 1968. 56.00 o.p. (ISBN 3-7785-0035-X, M-7483, Pub. by Huethig). French & Eur.

Internationalism in Nineteenth Century Europe. Ed. by Sandi Cooper. LC 74-147743. (Library of War & Peace; Documentary Anthologies). 1976. lib. bdg. 46.00 o.p. (ISBN 0-8240-0505-8). Garland Pub.

Internationalization of Business: An Introduction. Richard D. Robinson. 384p. 1984. text ed. 31.95x o.p. (ISBN 0-03-060301-3). Dryden Pr.

Internationalizing Japan's Financial System. Eric W. Hayden. (Occasional Paper of the Northeast Asia-United States Forum on International Policy, Stanford University). 29p. 1980. pap. 4.00 o.p. (ISBN 0-935371-03-6). ISIS.

Internistische Krebstherapie. Ed. by K. W. Brunner & G. A. Nagel. (Illus.). 450p. 1975. 40.80 o.p. (ISBN 0-387-07455-4). Springer-Verlag.

Internment in Concentration Camps & Its Consequences. P. Matussek. Tr. by D. Jordan from Ger. LC 74-32362. (Illus.). 300p. 1975. 21.00 o.p. (ISBN 0-387-07123-7). Springer-Verlag.

Intern's Tale. Colin Douglas. LC 82-47995. 192p. 1982. pap. 7.95 o.p. (ISBN 0-394-17996-X, E831, Ever). Grove.

Internships Nineteen Eighty-Eight. Ed. by Katherine Jobst. 350p. (Orig.). 1987. pap. 18.95 o.p. (ISBN 0-89879-279-7). Writers Digest.

Internships, Nineteen Eighty-Seven. Ed. by Katherine Jobst. 350p. (Orig.). 1987. pap. 18.95 o.p. (ISBN 0-89879-225-8). Writers Digest.

Internships 1985. 5th ed. Ed. by Lisa S. Hulse. 384p. (Orig.). 1985. pap. 12.95 o.p. (ISBN 0-89879-157-X, 3042). Writers Digest.

Internships 1986. Ed. by Lisa S. Hulse. 444p. (Orig.). 1985. pap. 14.95 o.p. (ISBN 0-89879-204-5). Writers Digest.

Interpersonal & Organizational Communications in a Records Management Environment. 122p. 1981. 17.00 o.p. (ISBN 0-933887-05-1). Assn Recs Mgrs & Admin.

Interpersonal Communication. Kurt Danziger. 250p. 1976. 70.00 o.p. (ISBN 0-08-018757-9); pap. 70.00 o.p. (ISBN 0-08-018756-0). Pergamon.

Interpersonal Communication. 2nd ed. Stewart L. Tubbs & Sylvia Moss. 299p. 1981. pap. text ed. 13.00 o.p. (ISBN 0-394-32684-9, RanC). Random.

Interpersonal Communication: A Question of Needs. Michael D. Scott & William G. Powers. LC 77-76342. (Illus.). 1978. text ed. 25.95 o.p. (ISBN 0-395-25055-2). HM.

Interpersonal Communication: Essays in Phenomenology & Hermeneutics. Ed. by Joseph J. Pilotta. LC 82-40211. (Current Continental Research Ser.: No. 2). 196p. (Orig.). 1982. PLB 26.75 o.p. (ISBN 0-8191-2475-3); pap. text ed. 10.50 o.p. (ISBN 0-8191-2476-1). U Pr of Amer.

Interpersonal Communication in Organizations. Craig Aronoff & Otis W. Baskin. 1979. text ed. write for info. o.p. (ISBN 0-673-16090-4); pap. text ed. 14.70x o.p. (ISBN 0-673-16091-2). Scott F.

Interpersonal Communication Journal. Lynn Phelps & Sue Dewine. LC 76-3576. (Illus.). 200p. 1976. pap. text ed. 15.95 o.p. (ISBN 0-8299-0102-7); instr's. manual avail. o.p. (ISBN 0-8299-0566-9). West Pub.

Interpersonal Conflict Resolution. Alan C. Filley. 180p. 1975. pap. write for info. o.p. (ISBN 0-673-07589-3). Scott F.

Interpersonal Interaction in Nursing. Virgil Parsons & Nancy Sanford. 1978. 12.95 o.p. (ISBN 0-201-05551-1, 05551, Hlth-Sci). Addison-Wesley.

Interpersonal Processes: Introductory Readings. Gerald Goodman & David Dooley. 117p. 1972. pap. text ed. 9.50x o.p. (ISBN 0-8422-0197-1). Irvington.

Interpersonal Psychotherapy. Arthur Burton. LC 74-29379. 172p. 1975. Repr. of 1972 ed. 10.00x o.p. (ISBN 0-87668-192-5). Aronson.

Interpersonal Sexuality. David F. Shope. LC 74-6692. (Illus.). 344p. 1975. pap. 14.95 o.p. (ISBN 0-7216-8253-7). HR&W.

Interpersonal Skills for the Manager. James M. Daily. LC 82-73405. 275p. 1982. ringed binder 29.95x o.p. (ISBN 0-87094-350-2). Dow Jones-Irwin.

Interpersonal Skills in Nursing: Research & Applications. Ed. by Carolyn Kagan. LC 85-9627. 304p. (Orig.). 1985. pap. 15.50 o.p. (ISBN 0-7099-1552-7, Pub. by Croom Helm Ltd). Routledge Chapman & Hall.

Interplanetary Dust & Zodiacal Light. Ed. by H. Elsaesser & H. Fechtig. LC 78-2597. 1976. pap. 23.00 o.p. (ISBN 0-387-07615-8). Springer-Verlag.

Interplay: A Theory of Religion & Education. Gabriel Moran. LC 80-53203. 172p. (Orig.). 1981. pap. 8.95 o.p. (ISBN 0-88489-125-9). St Mary's.

Interpol: International Crime Fighter. Iris Noble. LC 74-24323. (Illus.). (gr. 5 up). 1975. 6.25 o.p. (ISBN 0-15-238733-1, HJ). HarBraceJ.

Interpolation Theory: Function Spaces, Differential Operators. H. Triebel. (North-Holland Mathematical Library: Vol. 18). 528p. 1978. 131.75 o.p. (ISBN 0-7204-0710-9, North-Holland). Elsevier.

Interpretation des Examens de Laboratoire. Ed. by G. Siest et al. (Illus.). 428p. 1981. pap. 96.75 o.p. (ISBN 3-8055-2756-X). S Karger.

Interpretation des Examens de Laboratoire see Interpretation of Clinical Laboratory Tests.

Interpretation of Analytical Chemical Data by the Use of Cluster Analysis. D. Luc Massart & Leonard Kaufman. LC 82-20117. (Chemical Analysis Ser.: Monographs on Analytical Chemistry & Its Applications). 237p. 1983. 68.00x o.p. (ISBN 0-471-07861-1, Pub. by Wiley Interscience). Wiley.

Interpretation of Clinical Chemistry Laboratory Data. Fraser. 1986. 14.50 o.p. (ISBN 0-8016-1684-0). Mosby.

Interpretation of Clinical Laboratory Tests. Ed. by G. Siest et al. LC 83-70684. Orig. Title: Interpretation des Examens de Laboratoire. (Illus.). 500p. 1985. text ed. 59.50 o.p. (ISBN 0-931890-11-X, Biomed Pubns). Year Bk Med.

Interpretation of Early Music. Robert Donington. 766p. 1982. Repr. 31.95 o.p. (ISBN 0-571-04789-0). Faber & Faber.

Interpretation of History. Ed. by Joseph R. Strayer. LC 83-1762. 186p. 1983. Repr. of 1943 ed. lib. bdg. 35.00x o.p. (ISBN 0-313-23971-1, STIH). Greenwood.

Interpretation of Infrared Spectra: A Programmed Introduction. R. R. Hill & D. A. Rendell. 208p. 1975. 48.95 o.p. (ISBN 0-471-25771-0, Wiley Heyden). Wiley.

Interpretation of Language. rev. ed. Theodore Thass-Thienemann. Incl. Vol. 1. Understanding the Symbolic Meaning of Language. 512p. (ISBN 0-87668-087-2); Vol. 2. Understanding the Unconscious Meaning of Language. 488p (ISBN 0-87668-088-0). LC 73-79984. 1973. 40.00x ea. o.p. Aronson.

Interpretation of Mark. Ed. by William R. Telford. LC 84-18708. (Issues in Religion & Theology Ser.). 176p. 1985. pap. 7.95 o.p. (ISBN 0-8006-1772-X, 1-1772, Fortress). Augsburg Fortress.

Interpretation of Mass Spectra of Organic Compounds. Mynard C. Hamming & Norman G. Foster. 1972. 112.00 o.p. (ISBN 0-12-322150-1). Acad Pr.

Interpretation of Matthew. Ed. by Graham Stanton. LC 83-5508. (Issues in Religion & Theology Ser.). 176p. 1983. pap. 2.50 o.p. (ISBN 0-8006-1766-5, 1-1766, Fortress). Augsburg Fortress.

Interpretation of Plainchant: A Preliminary Study. Alec Robertson. 1970. Repr. of 1937 ed. lib. bdg. 35.00x o.p. (ISBN 0-8371-4322-5, ROPL). Greenwood.

Interpretation of Universal History. Jose Ortega y Gasset. Tr. by Mildred Adams from Span. 304p. 1973. 8.95x o.p. (ISBN 0-393-05478-0). Norton.

Interpretation: The Poetry of Meaning. Ed. by Stanley R. Hopper & David L. Miller. LC 67-13470. (Orig.). 1967. pap. 2.25 o.p. (ISBN 0-15-644880-7, Harv). HarBraceJ.

Interpretation Theory in Applied Geophysics. F. S. Grant & G. F. West. (Illus.). 1965. text ed. 69.95 o.p. (ISBN 0-07-024100-7). McGraw.

Interpretations & Forecasts Nineteen Twenty-Two to Nineteen Seventy-Two. Lewis Mumford. LC 72-88793. 1973. 12.95 o.p. (ISBN 0-15-167680-1). HarBraceJ.

Interpretations of Fascism. Renzo De Felice. Tr. by Brenda H. Everett. 1977. 18.50x o.s.i. (ISBN 0-674-45962-8). Harvard U Pr.

Interpretations of Federal Reserve Policy in the Speeches of Benjamin Strong, Governor of the Federal Reserve Bank of New York. W. Randolph Burgess. LC 82-48177. (Gold, Money, Inflation & Deflation Ser.). 352p. 1983. lib. bdg. 44.00 o.p. (ISBN 0-8240-5227-7). Garland Pub.

Interpretations of History: Confucius to Toynbee. Alban G. Widgery. LC 81-2116. 260p. 1981. Repr. of 1961 ed. lib. bdg. 35.00 o.p. (ISBN 0-313-23041-2, WIIN). Greenwood.

Interpretations of Plato: A Swarthmore Symposium. Ed. by Helen F. North. (Supplement Mnemosyne: No. 50). viii, 112p. 1980. text ed. 25.00x o.p. (ISBN 0-391-01138-3). Humanities.

Interpretative Account of Creativity in Childhood, Adolescence & Adulthood see Creativity in the Life Cycle.

Interpreter's Handbook: How to Become a Conference Interpreter. 2nd. & rev ed. J. Herbert. 1968. pap. 15.00 o.s.i. (ISBN 0-686-46741-8). E J Brill USA.

Interpreting Automotive Systems. Harry G. Hill. LC 75-19527. 1977. pap. 18.95 o.p. (ISBN 0-8273-1057-9); 6.00 o.p. instr's. guide (ISBN 0-8273-1058-7). Delmar.

Interpreting Engineering Drawings. 3rd ed. Cecil H. Jensen & Raymond D. Hines. LC 80-65469. (Blueprint Reading Ser.). 352p. 1984. pap. text ed. 18.95 o.p. (ISBN 0-8273-1936-3). Delmar.

Interpreting Financial Statements of Life & Health Insurance Companies. H. Ray Eanes. (FLMI Insurance Education Program Ser.). 1983. pap. text ed. 3.00 o.p. (ISBN 0-915322-61-7). LOMA.

Interpreting Lacan. Intro. by Joseph H. Smith & William Kerrigan. (Psychiatry & the Humanities Ser.: Vol. 6). 1988. pap. 11.95x o.p. (ISBN 0-317-59961-5). Yale U Pr.

Interpreting Literature: Preliminaries to Literary Judgment. 6th ed. K. L. Knickerbocker & H. W. Reninger. LC 77-24453. 1978. text ed. 20.95 o.p. (ISBN 0-03-020331-7, HoltC). HR&W.

Interpreting Machines: Architecture & Programming of the B1700-1800 Series. E. I. Organick & J. A. Hinds. (Operating & Programming Systems Ser.: Vol. 5). 316p. 1978. text ed. 49.00 o.p. (ISBN 0-444-00241-3, North-Holland); pap. text ed. 17.75 o.p. (ISBN 0-444-00242-1). Elsevier.

Interpreting Mozart on the Keyboard. Eva Badura-Skoda. 319p. Repr. of 1962 ed. lib. bdg. 49.00 o.p. (Pub. by Am Repr Serv). Reprint Servs.

Interpreting Personality: A Survey of Twentieth-Century Views. Ed. by Alfred M. Freedman & Harold I. Kaplan. LC 71-178072. (Studies in Human Behavior Ser). 1972. pap. text ed. 4.95x o.p. (ISBN 0-689-70283-3, HB2, Atheneum). Macmillan.

Interpreting Politics: An Introduction to Political Science. Peter C. Sederberg. LC 77-1657. (Chandler & Sharp Publications in Political Science). 378p. 1977. pap. text ed. 11.95x o.s.i. (ISBN 0-88316-529-5). Chandler & Sharp.

Interpreting the Bible. J. C. Von Hofmann. Tr. by Christian Preus. LC 59-12029. 1959. pap. 4.25 o.p. (ISBN 0-8066-0185-X, 10-3350, Augsburg). Augsburg Fortress.

Interpreting the Earth. Robert R. Compton. 544p. 1977. text ed. 17.50 o.p. (ISBN 0-15-541547-6, HC). HarBraceJ.

Interpreting the Gospels. Ed. by James L. Mays. LC 80-8057. 324p. 1981. pap. 13.95 o.p. (ISBN 0-8006-1439-9, 1-1439, Fortress). Augsburg Fortress.

Interpreting the Gospels for Preaching. D. Moody Smith. LC 79-8900. 128p. (Orig.). 1980. pap. 4.95 o.p. (ISBN 0-8006-1381-3, 1-1381, Fortress). Augsburg Fortress.

Interpreting the Indian: Twentieth-Century Poets & the Native American. Michael Castro. LC 83-14539. 224p. 1983. 22.50x o.p. (ISBN 0-8263-0672-1). U of NM Pr.

Interpreting the Landscape: Landscape Archaeology. Michael Aston. (Illus.). 144p. 1986. 45.00 o.p. (ISBN 0-7134-3649-2, Pub. by Batsford England); pap. 24.95 o.p. (ISBN 0-7134-3650-6, Pub. by Batsford England). David & Charles.

Interpreting the Southern California Sensory Integration Tests. A. Jean Ayres. LC 76-46889. 58p. 1976. pap. 14.50x o.p. (ISBN 0-87424-130-8). Western Psych.

Interpreting Transference. Nathan Leites. 1979. 10.95x o.p. (ISBN 0-393-01180-1). Norton.

Interpretive Surface Marker Analysis. David F. Keren. LC 87-31918. 200p. 1989. write for info. o.p. (ISBN 0-89189-274-5). Am Soc Clinical.

Interpretive Techniques for Microstructural Analysis. Ed. by J. L. McCall & P. M. French. LC 77-2333. 308p. 1977. 59.50x o.p. (ISBN 0-306-31036-8, Plenum Pr). Plenum Pub.

Interregional & International Trade. rev. ed. Bertil Ohlin. LC 67-17317. (Economic Studies: No. 39). (Illus.). 1967. 22.50x o.p. (ISBN 0-674-46000-6). Harvard U Pr.

Interregional Movements & Regional Growth. Ed. by William C. Wheaton. (Papers on Public Economics Ser.: Vol. 2). 253p. (Orig.). 1980. pap. 12.00x o.p. (ISBN 0-87766-257-6, 26600). Urban Inst.

Interregional Water Transfers: Projects & Problems: Proceedings of the Task Force Meeting, International Institute for Applied Systems Analysis, Laxenburg, Austria, Oct. 1977. Ed. by G. N. Golubev & A. K. Biswas. 1979. 42.00 o.p. (ISBN 0-08-022430-X). Pergamon.

Interrelationships of Fishes: Supplement No. 1 to the Zoological Journal of the Linnean Society, Vol. 53, 1973. Ed. by P. H. Greenwood et al. 1974. 73.50 o.p. (ISBN 0-12-300850-6). Acad Pr.

Interreligious Dialogue: Facing the Next Frontier. Ed. by Richard W. Rousseau. LC 81-52035. (Modern Theological Themes Ser.: Selection from the Literature: Vol. I). 234p. (Orig.). 1981. pap. 13.50 o.p. (ISBN 0-940866-00-5). U Scranton Pr.

Interrogating the Oracle: A History of the London Browning Society. William S. Peterson. LC 69-15916. (Illus.). xii, 276p. 1969. 16.00x o.p. (ISBN 0-8214-0056-8, Dist. by Wedgestone). Ohio U Pr.

Interscholastic Coach. Irvin A. Keller. 400p. 1982. text ed. (ISBN 0-13-475707-6). P-H.

Intersexuality in the Animal Kingdom. R. Reinboth. (Illus.). 510p. 1975. 59.00 o.p. (ISBN 0-387-07118-0). Springer-Verlag.

Interstate Commerce Commission: 1986 Annual Report. 100th, annual ed. (Illus.). 1987. pap. 4.00 o.p. (ISBN 0-318-22750-9, S/N 026-000-01256-2). USGPO.

Interstate Gourmet: California & Pacific Northwest. rev. ed. Neal O. Weiner & David M. Schwartz. 256p. 1986. pap. 6.95 o.s.i. (ISBN 0-671-62835-6). Summit Bks.

Interstate Gourmet: California & the Pacific Northwest, Vol. 3. Neal O. Weiner & David M. Schwartz. LC 83-656. (Illus.). 288p. 1983. pap. 5.75 o.s.i. (ISBN 0-671-44994-X). Summit Bks.

Interstate Gourmet: Mid Atlantic. rev. ed. Neal O. Weiner & David M. Schwartz. 1986. pap. 6.95 o.s.i. (ISBN 0-671-62834-8). Summit Bks.

Interstate Gourmet: Mid-Atlantic States, Vol. 2. Neal O. Weiner & David M. Schwartz. LC 83-380. (Illus.). 256p. 1983. pap. 5.75 o.s.i. (ISBN 0-671-44993-1). Summit Bks.

Interstate Gourmet: New England, Vol. 1. Neal O. Weiner & David M. Schwartz. LC 82-19399. 1983. pap. 5.75 o.s.i. (ISBN 0-671-44992-3). Summit Bks.

Interstate Gourmet: Routes 91 & 89. Neal O. Weiner & David M. Schwartz. 64p. (Orig.). 1982. pap. 3.80 o.s.i. (ISBN 0-671-45228-2). Summit Bks.

Interstate Gourmet: Southeast. Neil Weiner & David Schwartz. 1985. 6.95 o.s.i. (ISBN 0-671-52336-8). Summit Bks.

Interstate Gourmet: Texas & the Southwest. Barbara Rodriguez & Tom Miller. 1986. pap. 6.95 o.s.i. (ISBN 0-671-52334-1). Summit Bks.

Interstate Railroad. Jerry Marlette. (Illus.). 1986. Transport Res Bd.

Interstate Variations in Employers' Cost of Workmen's Compensation: Effect on Plant Location Exemplified in Michigan. John F. Burton. 75p. 1966. pap. 0.50 o.p. (ISBN 0-911558-57-8). W E Upjohn.

Interstellar Communication: Scientific Perspectives. Ed. by Cyril Ponnamperuma & A. G. Cameron. (Illus.). 272p. 1974. pap. 18.50 o.p. (ISBN 0-395-17809-6). HM.

Interstellar Travel: Past, Present & Future. John W. Macvey. 1978. pap. 2.25 o.p. (ISBN 0-380-41368-X, 41368). Avon.

Intertec Publishing Corporation Staff: 87-88 Season. 22nd ed. Intertec Publishing Corporation Staff. 60p. 1987. pap. 12.95 o.p. (ISBN 0-87288-274-8, SMG-22). Intertec Pub.

Interval Mathematics: Proceedings of the International Symposium, Karlsruhe, West Germany, May 20-24, 1975. Ed. by K. Nickel. (Lecture Notes in Computer Science Ser.: Vol. 29). vi, 331p. 1975. pap. 20.00 o.p. (ISBN 0-387-07170-9). Springer-Verlag.

Interval Mathematics: 1980. Karl L. Nickel. LC 80-25009. 1980. 47.00 o.p. (ISBN 0-12-518850-1). Acad Pr.

Interventional Neuroradiology. Cahan et al. (Illus.). 300p. 1989. 90.00 o.p. (ISBN 0-8016-0528-8). Mosby.

Interventional Radiology. Christos A. Athanasoulis et al. LC 77-11329. (Illus.). 806p. 1982. text ed. 140.00 o.p. (ISBN 0-7216-1448-5). Saunders.

Interview Guide for Supervisors. Ed. by Ronald A. Bouchard et al. 6.00 o.p. (ISBN 0-910402-70-1); 3.00 o.p. Coll & U Personnel.

Interview, Nineteen Seventeen - Nineteen Twenty, Conducted by William O. Inglis. John D. Rockefeller. Ed. by David F. Hawke. 48p. (Incl. Index & 19 Microfiche). 1984. lib. bdg. 87.00x o.p. (ISBN 0-88736-007-6). Meckler Corp.

Interview with Israel Regardie: His Final Thoughts & Views. Ed. by Christopher S. Hyatt. 176p. (Orig.). 1985. pap. 7.95 o.p. (ISBN 0-941404-31-5). Falcon Pr Az.

Interviewer's Manual. Henry H. Morgan. 55p. 1973. pap. text ed. 8.70 o.p. (ISBN 0-15-816860-7, Psych Corp). HarBraceJ.

Interviewing for Managers: A Complete Guide to Employment Interviewing. Rev. ed. John D. Drake. 1982. 19.95 o.p. (ISBN 0-8144-5737-1). AMACOM.

Interviewing Principles & Practices: A Project Text. 2nd ed. Charles J. Stewart. 112p. 1982. 9.95 o.p. (ISBN 0-8403-2914-8). Kendall-Hunt.

Interviewing Principles & Practices: A Project Text. 3rd ed. Charles J. Stewart. 128p. 1985. pap. 10.95 o.p. (ISBN 0-8403-3602-0). Kendall-Hunt.

Interviewing: Principles & Practices. 4th ed. Charles J. Stewart & William B. Cash, Jr. 384p. 1985. pap. text ed. write for info. o.p. (ISBN 0-697-04258-8); instrs.' manual avail. o.p. (ISBN 0-697-00465-1). Wm C Brown.

Interviewing Skills for Family Assistance Workers. David Kurtz & Eldon Marshall. 121p. 1980. Set. write for info. o.p. (ISBN 0-89695-023-9); instr's manual 7.50 o.p. (ISBN 0-89695-024-7); trainee's manual 7.50 o.p. (ISBN 0-89695-025-5). U Tenn CSW.

Interviews That Get Results. Suzee Vlk. 128p. (Orig.). 1984. pap. text ed. 7.95 o.p. (ISBN 0-671-50457-6). Monarch Pr.

Interviews W. C. Williams: Speaking Straight Ahead. William Carlos Williams. Ed. by Linda Wagner. LC 76-14797. 1976. 8.50 o.p. (ISBN 0-8112-0620-3); pap. 2.95 o.p. (ISBN 0-8112-0621-1, NDP421). New Directions.

Interviews with Film Directors. Ed. by Andrew Sarris. 1969. pap. 1.95 o.p. (ISBN 0-380-01303-7, 21568, Bard). Avon.

Interviews with Francis Bacon. rev., enl. ed. David Sylvester. (Illus.). 176p. 1981. pap. 9.95 o.s.i. (ISBN 0-500-27196-8). Thames Hudson.

Interviews with Robert Frost. Ed. by Edward C. Lathem. LC 66-11570. 1966. 7.50 o.p. (ISBN 0-03-054600-1). H Holt & Co.

Intestinal Absorption of Metal Ions, Trace Elements & Radionuclides. S. C. Skoryna et al. 448p. 1971. 110.00 o.p. (ISBN 0-08-015721-1). Pergamon.

Intestinal Permeation: Proceedings of the Fourth Workshop Conference, Oct. 1975. Ed. by M. Kramer & F. Lauterbach. (International Congress Ser.: No. 391). 1977. 109.00 o.p. (ISBN 90-219-0321-0, Excerpta Medica). Elsevier.

Intimacy. Edward Stark. 1978. pap. 1.95 o.p. (ISBN 0-8439-0524-7, Pub. by Leisure Bks CT). Dorchester Pub Co.

Intimacy, Family, & Society. Arlene S. Skolnick & Jerome H. Skolnick. 1974. pap. 13.95 o.p. (ISBN 0-316-79719-7). Little.

Intimacy: Strategies for Successful Relationships. C. Edward Crowther & Gayle Stone. 260p. (Orig.). 1987. 16.95 o.p. (ISBN 0-88496-255-5). Capra Pr.

Intimate Architecture: Contemporary Clothing Design. Susan Sidlaukas. (Illus.). 52p. (Orig.). 1982. pap. 7.00 o.p. (ISBN 0-938437-03-8). MIT List Visual Arts.

Intimate Circle: The Sexual Dynamics of Family Life. Miriam Ehrenberg & Otto Ehrenberg. 1988. 18.45 o.s.i. (ISBN 0-671-64455-6). S&S.

Intimate Gospel: Studies in John. Earl F. Palmer. 1978. pap. 5.95 o.p. (ISBN 0-8499-2941-5). Word Bks.

Intimate Grand: Inside Arizona's Grand Canyon. Dowling Campbell. LC 84-62425. (Western Horizons Bks.). (Illus.). 84p. (Orig.). 1984. pap. 11.95 o.p. (ISBN 0-87358-373-6). Northland.

Intimate Life. Norval Geldenhuys. (ISBN 0-8022-0575-5). Philos Lib.

Intimate Male: Candid Discussions About Women, Sex & Relationships. Linda Levine & Lonnie Barbach. LC 83-6420. 384p. 1983. 16.95 o.p. (ISBN 0-385-17612-0, Anchor Pr). Doubleday.

Intimate Partners: Hidden Patterns in Love Relationships. Clifford J. Sager & Bernice Hunt. 1979. text ed. 8.95 o.p. (ISBN 0-07-054427-1). McGraw.

Intimate Persuasion. Alice Bowen. (Candlelight Ecstasy Ser.: No. 501). (Orig.). 1987. pap. 2.25 o.p. (ISBN 0-440-14120-6). Dell.

Intimate Secrets: Which to Keep & Which to Tell. Karen Blaker. 1986. 16.95 o.p. (ISBN 0-316-09948-1). Little.

Intimate Strangers. Thelma Olshakers. 336p. 1983. pap. 3.50 o.s.i. (ISBN 0-345-30695-3). Ballantine.

Intimations of Christianity Among the Ancient Greeks. Simone Weil. 1976. 12.50 o.p. (ISBN 0-7100-8524-9). Routledge Chapman & Hall.

Into Passion's Dawn. Michele DuBarry. (Loves of Angela Carlyle Ser.: No. 1). 1981. pap. 2.50 o.p. (ISBN 0-8439-0902-1, Pub. by Leisure Bks CT). Dorchester Pub Co.

Into Television. Ed. by G. Moir. LC 68-8870. 1969. pap. 9.75 o.p. (ISBN 0-08-013032-1). Pergamon.

Into the Back Country. Maurice L'Heureux. 160p. 1983. pap. 2.75 o.p. (ISBN 0-380-81588-5, 81588-5). Avon.

Into the Beyond: A Dramatic Romance in Four Acts. Franco Silvestro Buono. 1977. 7.50 o.p. (ISBN 0-682-48478-4). Exposition-Phoenix.

Into the Dark: A Beginner's Guide to Developing & Printing Black & White Negatives. Edward E. Davis. LC 78-11284. (Illus.). 224p. (gr. 5 up). 1979. 9.95 o.s.i. (ISBN 0-689-30676-8, Atheneum). Macmillan.

Into the Painted Bear Lair. Pamela Stearns. (Illus.). (gr. 3-7). 1976. 6.95 o.p. (ISBN 0-395-24736-5). HM.

Into the Third Century: A Profile of America. Nancy R. Jacobs et al. (Information Aids Ser.). 144p. 1986. pap. 17.95 o.p. (ISBN 0-936474-57-2). Info Plus TX.

Into the Third Century: Where Do We Stand? Rev. ed. Ed. by Mark A. Siegel & Nancy R. Jacobs. (Information Aids Ser.). 144p. 1986. pap. text ed. 17.95 o.p. (ISBN 0-936474-57-2). Info Plus TX.

Into the Wilderness: Dialogue Meditations on the Temptations of Jesus. Hubert F. Beck & Robert L. Otterstad. LC 74-80417. 96p. 1974. pap. 0.50x o.p. (ISBN 0-8006-1082-2, Fortress). Augsburg Fortress.

Into Winter: Discovering a Season. William P. Nestor. LC 82-9232. (Illus.). 192p. (gr. 5-8). 1982. 9.70 o.s.i. (ISBN 0-395-32866-7). HM.

Intolerable Burden. Teresa Waugh. 192p. 1989. 19.95 o.p. (ISBN 0-241-12352-6, Pub. by Hamish Hamilton). David & Charles.

Intonation in North Indian Music. Mark Levy. 1982. 23.50x o.p. (ISBN 0-8364-0860-8, Pub by Biblia Impex). South Asia Bks.

Intonation Studies for Band. Wesley Pearce. LC 77-8522. (Illus.). 238p. 1977. 11.95 o.p. (ISBN 0-87421-093-3). Utah St U Pr.

Intra-Abdominal Infection. S. E. Wilson et al. 1981. text ed. 50.00x o.p. (ISBN 0-07-070815-0). McGraw.

Intracellular Parasitic Protozoa. Masamichi Aikawa & Charles R. Sterling. 1974. 29.50 o.p. (ISBN 0-12-045350-9). Acad Pr.

Intracellular Protein Turnover. Ed. by Robert T. Schimke & Nobuhiko Katunuma. 1975. 49.50 o.p. (ISBN 0-12-625550-4). Acad Pr.

Intracellular Staining in Neurobiology. Ed. by S. B. Kater & C. Nicholson. LC 73-77837. (Illus.). 332p. 1973. 60.00 o.p. (ISBN 0-387-06261-0). Springer-Verlag.

Intracellular Transport. International Society for Cell Biology Staff. Ed. by Katherine B. Warren. (Proceedings: Vol. 5). 1967. 74.50 o.p. (ISBN 0-12-611905-8). Acad Pr.

Intracoastal Waterway. Jan Moeller & Bill Moeller. LC 79-66981. (Illus.). 1979. 14.95 o.p. (ISBN 0-915160-88-9). Seven Seas.

Intractable Pain. Mark Mehta. LC 72-97913. (Major Problems in Anaesthesia Ser.: Vol. 2). (Illus.). 290p. 1973. text ed. write for info. o.p. (ISBN 0-7216-6262-5). Saunders.

Intraocular Lens Implantation. Rosen & Haining. 1983. 75.00 o.p. (ISBN 0-8016-4168-3). Mosby.

Intraocular Lens Implantation: Techniques & Complications. Henry M. Clayman et al. LC 82-8267. (Illus.). 300p. 1982. text ed. 70.00 o.p. (ISBN 0-8016-1080-X). Mosby.

Intraovarian Control Mechanisms. Ed. by Cornelia C. Channing & Sheldon J. Segal. LC 82-9849. (Advances in Experimental Medicine & Biology Ser.: Vol. 147). 402p. 1982. 75.00x o.p. (ISBN 0-306-41030-3, Plenum Pr). Plenum Pub.

Intrauterine Devices: Development, Evaluation, & Program Implementation. Ed. by Robert G. Wheeler et al. 1974. 53.00 o.p. (ISBN 0-12-745550-7). Acad Pr.

Intrauterine Exposure to Diethylstilbestrol in the Human. 1977. 3.00 o.p. Am Coll Obstetric.

Intravenous Medications: A Handbook for Nurses & Other Allied Health Personnel. 4th ed. Betty L. Gahart. 268p. 1984. pap. text ed. 21.95 o.p. (ISBN 0-8016-1746-4). Mosby.

Intricate Music: A Biography of John Steinbeck. Thomas Kiernan. LC 79-12595. 1979. 12.95 o.p. (ISBN 0-316-49202-7). Little.

Intrinsic Bases of Adaptation: A Collection of Readings. Ed. by Harold R. Strang. 149p. 1975. pap. text ed. 6.95x o.p. (ISBN 0-8290-0661-3). Irvington.

Intrinsic Neuronal Organization of the Vestibular Nuclear Complex in the Cat: A Golgi Study. E. Hauglie-Hanssen. LC 64-20582. (Advances in Anatomy, Embryology & Cell Biology: Vol. 40, Pt. 5). (Illus.). 1968. pap. 25.40 o.p. (ISBN 0-387-04089-7). Springer-Verlag.

Introduced Birds of the World. John L. Long. LC 81-50625. (Illus.). 528p. 1981. text ed. 50.00x o.p. (ISBN 0-87663-318-1). Universe.

Introducing CAL: A Practical Guide to Writing Computer Assisted Learning Programs. Keith Hudson. 200p. 1984. 39.95 o.p. (ISBN 0-412-26230-4, NO. 9315, Pub. by Chapman & Hall); pap. 19.95 o.p. (ISBN 0-412-26240-1, NO. 9190, Pub. by Chapman & Hall). Routledge Chapman & Hall.

Introducing Communications Protocols. Logica, Ltd. Staff. (Illus.). 83p. (Orig.). 1978. pap. 16.75x o.s.i. (ISBN 0-85012-208-2). Intl Pubns Serv.

Introducing Computerized Telephone Switchboards (PABXs) National Computing Centre, Ltd. Staff. (Illus.). 92p. (Orig.). 1982. 15.00x o.p. (ISBN 0-85012-364-X). Intl Pubns Serv.

Introducing Computers. Malcolm Peltu. (Illus.). 326p. (Orig.). 1983. pap. text ed. 20.00x o.p. (ISBN 0-85012-321-6). Intl Pubns Serv.

Introducing Corporate Planning. 2nd ed. D. E. Hussey. (Pergamon International Library). 1979. pap. text ed. 14.00 o.p. (ISBN 0-08-022485-7). Pergamon.

Introducing Culture. 3rd, ref. ed. Ernest L. Schusky & T. Patrick Culbert. (P-H Anthropology Ser.). (Illus.). 1978. pap. text ed. (ISBN 0-13-477240-7). P-H.

Introducing Data Processing. National Computing Centre, Ltd. Staff. 237p. (Orig.). 1980. pap. 18.50x o.s.i. (ISBN 0-85012-245-7). Intl Pubns Serv.

Introducing dBASE III. Lan Barnes. 304p. 1985. pap. text ed. 24.95 o.p. (ISBN 0-07-003777-9, BYTE Bks). McGraw.

Introducing Macrobiotic Cooking. Wendy Esko. LC 79-1957. (Illus.). 1979. pap. 9.95 o.p. (ISBN 0-87040-458-X). Japan Pubns USA.

Introducing Microcom. Burton. 1984. 38.95 o.p. (ISBN 0-442-30599-0). Van Nos Reinhold.

Introducing New Testament Theology. Archibald M. Hunter. 1958. 4.95 o.s.i. (ISBN 0-664-20230-6, Westminster). Westminster John Knox.

Introducing Pascal. Seymour V. Pollack. LC 83-10756. 371p. 1984. pap. text ed. 20.95 o.p. (ISBN 0-03-060563-6). HR&W.

Introducing Philosophy: A Text with Readings. 3rd ed. Robert C. Solomon. 650p. 1985. pap. text ed. 17.00 net o.p. (ISBN 0-15-541560-3, HC). HarBraceJ.

Introducing Philosophy: Problems & Perspectives. 2nd ed. Robert C. Solomon. 560p. 1981. pap. text ed. 12.75 o.p. (ISBN 0-15-541559-X, HC). HarBraceJ.

Introducing Philosophy: Problems & Perspectives. Robert C. Solomon. 1977. 13.95 o.p. (ISBN 0-15-541558-1). HarbraceJ.

Introducing Prehistory. Avraham Ronen. LC 72-10803. (Archaeology Ser.). (Illus.). (gr. 5 up). 1976. PLB 8.95 o.p. (ISBN 0-8225-0833-8). Lerner Pubns.

Introducing ProDOS. G. Mainis. 192p. 1985. pap. text ed. 17.95 o.p. (ISBN 0-07-039716-3). McGraw.

Introducing Shakespeare. George B. Harrison. Repr. of 1939 ed. 39.00x o.p. (ISBN 0-403-08926-3). Somerset Pub.

Introducing Sociology. Ed. by Peter Worsley et al. (Education Ser.). 608p. (Orig.). 1970. pap. 7.95 o.p. (ISBN 0-14-080187-1). Penguin.

Introducing Structures. A. J. Francis. (International Series in Structure & Solid Body Mechanics). 1980. 50.00 o.p. (ISBN 0-08-022701-5); pap. 16.00 o.p. (ISBN 0-08-022702-3). Pergamon.

Introducing the Bible. Alice Parmalee. (Epiphany Ser.). 128p. 1983. pap. 2.25 o.s.i. (ISBN 0-345-30575-2). Ballantine.

Introducing the GDR. Collets Staff. 320p. 1976. pap. 12.50x o.p. (ISBN 0-317-53876-4, Pub. by Collets (UK)). State Mutual Bk.

Introducing the Macintosh. C. Duff. 1984. pap. text ed. 14.95 o.p. (ISBN 0-07-018024-5, BYTE Bks). McGraw.

Introducing the Macintosh Office. Keith Thompson. 1985. pap. 19.95 o.p. (ISBN 0-912677-58-9). Tate Pub.

Introducing the Young Child to the Social World. Huber M. Walsh. (Illus.). 1980. text ed. write for info. o.p. (ISBN 0-02-424200-4). Macmillan.

Introducing Underwater Archaeology. Elisha Linder & Avner Raban. LC 72-10801. (Archaeology Ser.). (gr. 5 up). 1976. PLB 8.95 o.p. (ISBN 0-8225-0834-6). Lerner Pubns.

Introducing Your Kids to the Outdoors. rev. ed. Joan Dorsey. LC 82-80135. (Illus.). 156p. 1982. pap. 8.95 o.s.i. (ISBN 0-913276-34-0). Stone Wall Pr.

Introduction a la Methode de Leonardo da Vinci. Paul Valery. (Coll. Idees). pap. 3.95 o.p. (ISBN 0-685-36615-4). Schoenhof.

Introduction & Methodology to the Study of Police Assaults in the South Central United States. Chapman et al. (Criminal Justice Policy & Administration Research Ser: No. 1). 30p. 1974. pap. 1.00 o.p. (ISBN 0-686-20784-X). Univ OK Gov Res.

Introduction Au Francais Actuel. Robert E. Helbling & A. Barnett. LC 72-84085. (gr. 9-12). 1973. text ed. 16.95 o.p. (ISBN 0-03-086737-1, HoltC); instr's manual 19.95 o.p. (ISBN 0-03-086738-X); lab. manual 8.95 o.p. (ISBN 0-03-086739-8); tapes 315.00 o.p. (ISBN 0-03-086740-1). HR&W.

Introduction in Ordinary Differential Equations. Zane C. Motteler. 1972. write for info. o.p. (ISBN 0-87150-136-8, PWS 1041, Prindle). PWS-Kent Pub.

Introduction of an Alpha-Functional Carbon Chain & Special Condensation Reactions: Formation of C-C Bonds, Vol. 3. Jean Mathieu & Jean Weill-Raynal. LC 73-361113. 564p. (Orig.). 1979. 130.00 o.p. (ISBN 0-88416-098-X). Year Bk Med.

Titles

Introduction on-Deut see Mastering Old Testament Facts.

Introduction on Environmental Issues. Jon Luoma. 1984. text ed. write for info. o.p. (ISBN 0-02-372810-8). Macmillan.

Introduction to a Philosophy of Religion. Alice J. Von Hildebrand. LC 79-139972. 1971. 6.95 o.p. (ISBN 0-8199-0426-0). Franciscan Herald.

Introduction to a Theological Theory of Language. Gerhard Ebeling. Tr. by R. A. Wilson from Ger. LC 72-87057. 224p. 1973. 6.50 o.p. (ISBN 0-8006-0256-0, 1-256, Fortress). Augsburg Fortress.

Introduction to Abstract Mathematics. T. A. Bick. 1971. text ed. 21.50 o.p. (ISBN 0-12-095850-3). Acad Pr.

Introduction to Accounting: Selected Readings. Ed. by Richard C. Walker. LC 72-86363. 93p. 1972. pap. text ed. 3.50x o.p. (ISBN 0-8422-0233-1). Irvington.

Introduction to Ada. David Price. 1984. text ed. 32.00 o.p. (ISBN 0-13-477653-4); pap. 27.95 o.p. (ISBN 0-13-477646-1). P-H.

Introduction to Advanced Field Theory, Vol. 22. G. Barton. LC 63-22253. 163p. 1963. text ed. 9.50 o.p. (ISBN 0-470-05497-2, Pub. by Wiley). Krieger.

Introduction to African Civilization. John G. Jackson. 384p. 1970. 10.00 o.p. (ISBN 0-8216-0099-0, Pub. by Univ Bks). Carol Pub Group.

Introduction to Agricultural Economics. Donald J. Epp & John W. Malone, Jr. 1981. text ed. write for info. o.p. (ISBN 0-02-333940-3). Macmillan.

Introduction to AI & Expert Systems One: Their Application & Consequences, Vol. I. Randall Davis & Patrick Winston. (Illus.). 80p. 1988. pap. text ed. 12.00 o.p. (ISBN 0-929280-26-1). Amer Artificial.

Introduction to AI & Expert Systems, Vol. II. Avron Barr & Dina Barr. (Illus.). 100p. 1988. pap. text ed. 12.00 o.p. (ISBN 0-929280-21-0). Amer Artificial.

Introduction to Air Chemistry. Samuel S. Butcher & Robert J. Charlson. 1972. 28.00 o.p. (ISBN 0-12-148250-2). Acad Pr.

Introduction to Algebraic K-Theory. John Milnor. LC 74-161197. (Annals of Mathematics Studies: No. 72). 220p. 1971. 25.00 o.p. (ISBN 0-691-08101-8). Princeton U Pr.

Introduction to American Archaeology, Vol. 1: North & Middle America. Gordon R. Willey. 1966. text ed. 56.00 o.p. (ISBN 0-13-477836-7). P-H.

Introduction to American Studies. Ed. by Malcolm Bradbury & Howard Temperley. LC 79-42620. (Illus.). 352p. (Orig.). 1981. text ed. 30.00x o.p. (ISBN 0-582-48903-2); pap. text ed. 15.95 o.p. (ISBN 0-582-48904-0). Longman.

Introduction to Analysis. W. Vance Underhill. LC 80-5584. 432p. 1980. pap. text ed. 16.75 o.p. (ISBN 0-8191-1205-4). U Pr of Amer.

Introduction to Animal Biology. Claude A. Villee & Warren F. Walker, Jr. 1979. text ed. 35.95 o.p. (ISBN 0-7216-9026-2, CBS C). SCP.

Introduction to Animal Physiology & Physiological Genetics. E. M. Pantelouris. 1967. text ed. 29.00 o.p. (ISBN 0-08-011722-8); pap. text ed. 22.00 o.p. (ISBN 0-08-018981-4). Pergamon.

Introduction to Anthropology. Joseph B. Aceves & H. Gill King. LC 79-66304. 1979. text ed. 18.00 o.p. (ISBN 0-394-33288-1, RanC). Random.

Introduction to Apple Keyboarding. Peter Mears. 1984. 39.95 o.p. (ISBN 0-03-064131-4); with diskette 40.45 o.p. (ISBN 0-03-064129-2). HR&W.

Introduction to Apple Keyboarding. Peter Mears. 1984. pap. 40.45 incl. disk o.p. (ISBN 0-03-064138-1). HR&W.

Introduction to Applied Solid State Physics: Topics on the Applications of Semiconductors, Superconductors, & the Nonlinear Optical Properties of Solids. Richard Dalven. LC 79-21902. (Illus.). 346p. 1980. 35.00x o.p. (ISBN 0-306-40385-4, Plenum Pr). Plenum Pub.

Introduction to Archaeology. 2nd ed. James J. Hester & James Grady. LC 75-1410. 1982. text ed. 30.95 o.p. (ISBN 0-03-046291-6, HoltC). HR&W.

Introduction to Asian Music Nineteen Sixty Six: Asia Society Guides. William L. Purcell. 44.00 o.p. (10753). Ayer Co Pubs.

Introduction to Astronautics, 2 vols. Harry O. Ruppe. 1967-68. 98.00 ea. o.p. Vol. 1 (ISBN 0-12-603101-0). Vol. 2 (ISBN 0-12-603102-9). Set. 164.00 o.p. (ISBN 0-686-57486-9). Acad Pr.

Introduction to Astronomy. William Starbird & Ronald Oriti. 1977. text ed. write for info. o.p. (ISBN 0-02-478560-1). Macmillan.

Introduction to Attribution Processes. Kelly G. Shaver. (Orig.). 1975. pap. text ed. 8.95 o.p. (ISBN 0-316-78327-7). Little.

Introduction to Automation for Librarians. William Saffady. LC 83-7164. (Illus.). viii, 304p. 1983. 35.00x o.p. (ISBN 0-8389-0386-X). ALA.

Introduction to Automotive Solid State Electronics. LC 81-52155. 96p. 1981. pap. 9.95 o.p. (ISBN 0-672-21825-9). Sams.

Introduction to Ayurveda: The Science of Life. rev. ed. Chandrasehekhar Thakkur. LC 74-75522. 1974. 8.95 o.p. (ISBN 0-88231-057-7). ASI Pubs Inc.

Introduction to Backgammon: A Step-by-Step Guide. Paul Magriel. LC 77-7727. (Illus.). 1978. 10.35 o.p. (ISBN 0-8129-0735-3). Times Bks.

Introduction to BASIC. Edward J. Coburn. (Structured Programming for Microcomputers Ser.). 384p. 1986. pap. 17.95 o.p. (ISBN 0-8273-2478-2, 2478-2); instr's. guide 10.60 o.p. Delmar.

Introduction to BASIC: A Structured Approach. Chris Siragusa. 250p. 1980. write for info. o.p. (ISBN 0-87150-289-5, 2282, Prindle). PWS-Kent Pub.

Introduction to BASIC Programming: A Structured Approach. Peter B. Worland. LC 78-56436. (Illus.). 1979. pap. 20.95 o.p. (ISBN 0-395-26775-7). HM.

Introduction to Battlefield Weapons Systems & Technology. R. G. Lee. (Illus.). 160p. 1981. text ed. 29.50 o.p. (ISBN 0-08-027043-3); pap. text ed. 15.00 o.p. (ISBN 0-08-027044-1). Pergamon.

Introduction to Behavioural Ecology. 2nd ed. John R. Krebs & Nicholas B. Davies. (Illus.). 340p. pap. text ed. 22.95x cancelled o.s.i. (ISBN 0-87893-428-6). Sinauer Assocs.

Introduction to Benefit-Cost Analysis for Evaluating Public Programs. T. R. Durham. (Learning Packages in the Policy Sciences Ser.: No. 14). (Illus.). 70p. 1979. pap. text ed. 3.75x o.p. (ISBN 0-936826-03-7). PS Assocs Croton.

Introduction to Biblical Hebrew Syntax. Bruce K. Waltke. 1988. text ed. 30.00x o.p. (ISBN 0-931464-31-5). Eisenbrauns.

Introduction to Biblical Literature. 2nd ed. O. B. Davis. 1988. pap. text ed. 13.50x o.p. Boynton Cook Pubs.

Introduction to Bibliographical & Textual Studies. William P. Williams & Craig S. Abbott. 106p. 1985. 30.00x o.p. (ISBN 0-87352-133-1); pap. 14.50x o.p. (ISBN 0-87352-134-X). Modern Lang.

Introduction to Biochemistry. 4th ed. William R. Fearon. Ed. by William J. Jessop. 1961. text ed. 12.95 o.p. (ISBN 0-12-250550-6). Acad Pr.

Introduction to Biochemistry. 2nd ed. Joseph I. Routh. LC 76-28945. (Illus.). 1978. pap. text ed. 22.95 o.p. HR&W.

Introduction to Biochemistry. 2nd ed. Joseph I. Routh et al. 1978. pap. text ed. 20.95 o.p. (CBS C). SCP.

Introduction to Biological Psychology. 2nd ed. Philip M. Groves & Kurt Schlesinger. 752p. 1982. pap. text ed. write for info. o.p. (ISBN 0-697-06644-4). Wm C Brown.

Introduction to Biological Rhythms. John D. Palmer. 1976. 48.50 o.p. (ISBN 0-12-544450-8). Acad Pr.

Introduction to Biology. Fred W. Rabe. 208p. 1986. pap. text ed. 14.95 o.p. (ISBN 0-8403-4080-X). Kendall-Hunt.

Introduction to Biomedical Instrumentation. 2nd ed. D. J. Dewhurst. 288p. 1975. 72.00 o.p. (ISBN 0-08-018755-2); pap. 70.00 o.p. (ISBN 0-08-018884-2). Pergamon.

Introduction to Bivariate & Multivariate Analysis. Richard Lindeman et al. 1980. text ed. write for info. o.p. (ISBN 0-673-15099-2). Scott F.

Introduction to Black Sociology. R. Staples. 1976. text ed. 33.95 o.p. (ISBN 0-07-060840-7). McGraw.

Introduction to Breadcraft. Marna E. Kern. LC 77-24981. 1978. 11.95 o.p. (ISBN 0-395-25770-0); pap. 5.95 o.p. (ISBN 0-395-25951-7). HM.

Introduction to Budgeting. Wanat. LC 77-14937. 1978. pap. (ISBN 0-87872-149-5). Brooks-Cole.

Introduction to Business. 2nd ed. Paul G. Hastings. (Illus.). 640p. 1974. text ed. 40.95 o.p. (ISBN 0-07-027020-1). McGraw.

Introduction to Business. Joseph T. Straub & Stan Kossen. 672p. 1983. text ed. 24.95x o.p. (ISBN 0-534-01353-8). PWS-Kent Pub.

Introduction to Business: A Societal Approach. 3rd ed. Walter W. Perlick & Raymond V. Lesikar. 1979. 16.95x o.p. (ISBN 0-256-02086-8). Irwin.

Introduction to Business Accounting for Managers. 3rd ed. W. C. Hartley. 1980. text ed. 36.00 o.p. (ISBN 0-08-024061-5); pap. text ed. 12.00 o.p. (ISBN 0-08-024062-3). Pergamon.

Introduction to Business & Office Careers. Grady Kimbrall. (gr. 7-10). 1975. pap. text ed. 7.33 activity ed. o.p. (ISBN 0-87345-181-3). Glencoe.

Introduction to Business Communication. Zane K. Quible et al. (Illus.). 496p. 1981. text ed. (ISBN 0-13-479055-3). P-H.

Introduction to Business Mathematics. Robert Ochs & James Gray. 1981. pap. text ed. 23.95 o.p. (HoltC). HR&W.

Introduction to Business Programming & Systems Analysis. Keith Lohmuller. (Illus.). 238p. (Orig.). 1983. 18.95 o.p. (ISBN 0-8306-0437-5, 1437); pap. 13.15 o.p. (ISBN 0-8306-1437-0). TAB Bks.

Introduction to Business: Workbook. 3rd ed. David P. Alexander & Walter W. Perlick. 1979. pap. 6.50x o.p. (ISBN 0-256-01691-7). Irwin.

Introduction to Calculus. 2nd ed. K. Kuratowski. 1969. 85.00 o.p. (ISBN 0-08-012850-5). Pergamon.

Introduction to Calculus One & Two. Alfred B. Willcox et al. 1972. text ed. 40.95 o.p. (ISBN 0-395-05543-1). HM.

Introduction to Camp Counseling. Richard Kraus & Margery Scanlin. (Illus.). 352p. 1983. pap. text ed. (ISBN 0-13-479188-6). P-H.

Introduction to Cataloging, Vol. 2: Entry Headings with Emphasis on Cataloging Process & Personal Names. new ed. John J. Boll. (Library Education Ser). (Illus.). 448p. 1974. text ed. 37.95 o.p. (ISBN 0-07-006412-1). McGraw.

Introduction to Chemical Analysis. Walter E. Harris & Byron Kratochvil. 1981. text ed. 36.95x o.s.i. (ISBN 0-03-056882-X, CBS C); instr's manual 9.95 o.s.i. (ISBN 0-03-058101-X). SCP.

Introduction to Chemical Metallurgy: In SI-Metric Units. 2nd ed. R. H. Parker. 1978. 91.00 o.p. (ISBN 0-08-022125-4); pap. 25.00 o.p. (ISBN 0-08-022126-2). Pergamon.

Introduction to Chemistry of Life. Peter Berlow. 1982. text ed. 42.75 o.s.i. (ISBN 0-03-058516-3, CBS C); instr's manual 4.95 o.s.i. (ISBN 0-03-058517-1); lab manual 18.95 o.s.i. (ISBN 0-03-058519-8); overheads 400.00 o.s.i. (ISBN 0-03-060583-0). SCP.

Introduction to Children's Literature. Joan Glazer & Gurney Williams, III. (Illus.). 736p. 1979. text ed. 31.95 o.p. (ISBN 0-07-023380-2). McGraw.

Introduction to Children's Literature. Mary J. Lickteig. 448p. text ed. (ISBN 0-675-08716-3). Merrill.

Introduction to Christian Theology Today. Stephen Sykes. LC 73-16911. 1974. pap. 3.95 o.p. (ISBN 0-8042-0474-8, John Knox). Westminster John Knox.

Introduction to Christianity: A Case Method Approach. Alice F. Evans & Robert A. Evans. pap. 7.95 o.p. (ISBN 0-8042-1314-3, John Knox). Westminster John Knox.

Introduction to Clinical Allergy. Ben F. Feingold. (Illus.). 408p. 1973. 40.75 o.p. (ISBN 0-398-02797-8). C C Thomas.

Introduction to Clinical Psychology. Douglas A. Bernstein & Michael T. Nietzel. (Psychology Ser.). (Illus.). 1980. text ed. 38.95 o.p. (ISBN 0-07-005016-3). McGraw.

Introduction to Co-Operatives. Trevor Bottomley. 67p. (Orig.). 1979. pap. 4.50x o.p. (ISBN 0-903031-63-9, Pub. by Intermed Tech England). Intermediate Tech.

Introduction to COBOL. John A. Bonno & Kent T. Fields. 1982. pap. 20.95 o.p. (ISBN 0-256-02287-9). Irwin.

Introduction to Colloid Science. W. J. Popiel. 1978. 25.00 o.p. (ISBN 0-682-48737-6, University). Exposition-Phoenix.

Introduction to Color Photographic Processing. Ed. by Eastman Kodak Company. 56p. 1978. pap. 5.75 o.p. (ISBN 0-87985-216-X, J-3). Eastman Kodak.

Introduction to Color Process Monitoring. 1980. pap. 2.99 o.p. (ISBN 0-87985-348-4, Z-99). Eastman Kodak.

Introduction to Communication Studies. Waldhart-Applegate. 288p. 1985. pap. text ed. 16.50 o.p. (ISBN 0-8403-3695-0). Kendall-Hunt.

Introduction to Communications Careers. Hauenstein & Bachmeyer. (gr. 9-10). 1975. pap. text ed. 7.33 activity ed. o.p. (ISBN 0-87345-183-X). Glencoe.

Introduction to Comparative Mysticism. De Marquette. (ISBN 0-8022-0375-2). Philos Lib.

Introduction to Comparative Pathology: A Consideration of Some Reactions of Humans & Animal Tissues to Injurious Agents. Geoffrey A. Gresham & A. R. Jennings. 1962. 70.00 o.p. (ISBN 0-12-301950-8). Acad Pr.

Introduction to Comparative Physiology. Leon Goldstein. LC 76-26009. 1977. text ed. 31.95 o.p. (ISBN 0-03-012411-5, HoltC). HR&W.

Introduction to Comparative Politics: Comparing Political System Performance in Three Worlds. John D. Nagle. LC 84-8215. 360p. 1984. pap. text ed. 18.95x o.p. (ISBN 0-8304-1042-2). Nelson-Hall.

Introduction to Competitive Bidding. Charles H. Goren & Ronald P. Von der Porten. LC 83-25396. 192p. 1984. pap. 7.95 o.p. (ISBN 0-385-18892-7). Doubleday.

Introduction to Complex Variables. Edward A. Grove & Gerasimbs E. Ladas. 1974. text ed. 25.95 o.p. (ISBN 0-395-17087-7). HM.

Introduction to Computer Data Processing. Margaret S. Wu. (Illus.). 576p. 1975. text ed. 16.95 o.p. (ISBN 0-15-541631-6, HC). HarBraceJ.

Introduction to Computer Data Processing. 2nd ed. Margaret S. Wu. 521p. 1979. text ed. 22.95 o.p. (ISBN 0-15-541635-9, HC). HarBraceJ.

Introduction to Computer Data Processing with BASIC. Margaret S. Wu. 468p. 1980. text ed. 22.95 o.p. (ISBN 0-15-541638-3, HC). HarBraceJ.

Introduction to Computer Graphics. John T. Demel & Michael J. Miller. 425p. 1984. solutions manual o.p. PWS-Kent Pub.

Introduction to Computer Organization & Data Structures. Harold Stone. (Computer Science Ser.). 1971. text ed. 42.95 o.p. (ISBN 0-07-061726-0). McGraw.

Introduction to Computer Programming. F. H. George. (Illus.). 1968. text ed. 12.10 o.p. (ISBN 0-08-012394-5); pap. text ed. 5.50 o.p. (ISBN 0-08-012393-7). Pergamon.

Introduction to Computer Science. Thomas C. Bartee. 1974. text ed. 38.95 o.p. (ISBN 0-07-003880-5). McGraw.

Introduction to Computers. 5th ed. Keith London. 300p. 1986. pap. 15.95 o.p. (ISBN 0-571-13381-9). Faber & Faber.

Introduction to Computers & Data Processing. Harry Katzan, Jr. LC 78-65051. 580p. 1979. text ed. 19.95x o.p. PWS-Kent Pub.

Introduction to Computers & Information Systems Without Basic. Thomas H. Athey & Robert W. Zmud. 1986. text ed. write for info. o.p. (ISBN 0-673-15961-2). Scott F.

Introduction to Computers & Information Systems with BASIC. Thomas H. Athey & Robert W. Zmud. 1986. text ed. write for info. o.p. (ISBN 0-673-18185-5). Scott F.

Introduction to Computers Basic. International ed. Frederick Harold. (Illus.). 615p. 1984. 25.00 o.p. (ISBN 0-314-77918-3). West Pub.

Introduction to Computing. Peter Lafferty. (Clear & Simple Home Computer Ser.: Vol. I). (Illus.). 192p. 1984. pap. 9.50 o.p. (ISBN 0-671-49442-2, Fireside). S&S.

Introduction to Computing: Content for a High School Course. rev. ed. Jean Rogers. 48p. 1982. 2.50 o.p. (ISBN 0-317-59964-X). Intl Council Comp.

Introduction to Computing with BASIC. John R. Rice. LC 73-2438. 1973. text ed. 17.95 o.p. (ISBN 0-03-086300-7, HoltC). HR&W.

Introduction to Construction Careers. Don Lux. (gr. 7-10). 1975. pap. text ed. 7.33 activity ed. o.p. (ISBN 0-87345-187-2). Glencoe.

Introduction to Contemporary Business. 2nd ed. William Rudelius. (Illus.). 1976. text ed. 19.95 o.p. (ISBN 0-15-541648-0, HC); pap. 7.95 study guide o.p. (ISBN 0-15-541649-9). HarBraceJ.

Introduction to Contemporary Business. 3rd ed. William Rudelius et al. 560p. 1981. text ed. 24.95 o.p. (ISBN 0-15-541655-3, HC). HarBraceJ.

Introduction to Contemporary Linguistic Semantics. George L. Dillon. LC 76-4183. 1977. pap. text ed. (ISBN 0-13-479469-9). P-H.

Introduction to Contemporary Music. Joseph Machlis. (Illus.). 1961. 13.95x o.p. (ISBN 0-393-09546-0, NortonC). Norton.

Introduction to Contemporary Statistics. Lambert H. Koopmans. 624p. 1981. text ed. write for info. o.p. (ISBN 0-87872-292-0, Duxbury Pr). PWS-Kent Pub.

Introduction to Continuum Mechanics. W. M. Lai et al. LC 72-10904. 1978. text ed. 76.00 o.p. (ISBN 0-08-022698-1). Pergamon.

Introduction to Control System Analysis & Design. Francis J. Hale. (Illus.). 400p. 1973. text ed. (ISBN 0-13-479824-4). P-H.

Introduction to Control Systems Design. Virgil Eveleigh. (Electrical & Electronic Engineering Ser.). 1972. text ed. 52.95 o.p. (ISBN 0-07-019773-3). McGraw.

Introduction to Control Systems Performance Measurements. K. C. Garner. 1968. 55.00 o.p. (ISBN 0-08-012499-2); pap. 55.00 o.p. (ISBN 0-08-012498-4). Pergamon.

Introduction to Convergence. S. C. Malik. LC 84-3701. 210p. 1984. text ed. 26.95x o.p. (ISBN 0-470-20070-7). Halsted Pr.

Introduction to Counseling. 2nd ed. Gary S. Belkin. 624p. 1984. pap. text ed. write for info o.p. (ISBN 0-697-06070-5). Wm C Brown.

Introduction to Crime & Justice. Ed. by John W. Silva. LC 72-86200. 1973. 29.00x o.p. (ISBN 0-8422-5049-2); pap. text ed. 9.50x o.p. (ISBN 0-8422-0223-4). Irvington.

Introduction to Criminal Justice. Tiber Farkas. 1977. pap. text ed. 17.50 o.p. (ISBN 0-8191-0184-2). U Pr of Amer.

Introduction to Criminal Justice. 3rd ed. Joseph J. Senna & Larry J. Siegel. (Illus.). 515p. 1983. text ed. 35.00 o.p. (ISBN 0-314-77791-1). West Pub.

Introduction to Crop Husbandry. 5th ed. J. A. Lockhart & A. J. Wiseman. (Illus.). 300p. 1983. text ed. 48.00 o.p. (ISBN 0-08-029793-5); pap. text ed. 19.25 o.p. (ISBN 0-08-029792-7). Pergamon.

Introduction to Cultural & Social Anthropology. Peter B. Hammond. 1978. text ed. write for info. o.p. (ISBN 0-02-349790-4, 34979). Macmillan.

Introduction to Cultural Anthropology. A. K. Islam. 1973. 21.00x o.p. (ISBN 0-8422-5042-5); pap. text ed. 6.95x o.p. (ISBN 0-8422-0214-5). Irvington.

Introduction to Cultural Geography. Henry M. Kendall et al. 449p. 1976. text ed. 22.00 net o.p. (ISBN 0-15-541670-7, HC). HarBraceJ.

Introduction to Data Analysis & Statistical Inference. Carl Morris & John Rolph. (Illus.). 416p. 1981. pap. text ed. 44.67 o.p. (ISBN 0-13-480582-8). P-H.

Introduction to Data-Base Management in Business. James Bradley. 642p. 1983. text ed. 37.95 o.p. (ISBN 0-03-061693-X). HR&W.

Introduction to Data Processing. Northwest Regional Educational Laboratory Staff. (gr. 10-12). 1977. 14.40 o.p. (ISBN 0-02-831030-6); tchr's guide 5.20 o.p. (ISBN 0-02-831050-0); student guide 4.00 o.p. (ISBN 0-02-831040-3). Glencoe.

Introduction to Data Processing. Gary S. Popkin & Arthur M. Pike. LC 76-10893. (Illus.). 1977. text ed. 17.95 o.p. (ISBN 0-395-20628-6). HM.

Introduction to Data Processing. 2nd ed. Beryl Robichaud et al. Orig. Title: Understanding Modern Business Data Processing. (Illus.). (gr. 9-12). 1977. text ed. 20.48 o.p. (ISBN 0-07-053190-0). McGraw.

Introduction to Data Structures & Non-Numeric Computation. Doron J. Cohen & Peter C. Brillinger. (Illus.). 656p. 1972. text ed. 37.33 ref. ed. o.p. (ISBN 0-13-479899-6). P-H.

Introduction to Debate. Carolyn B. Keefe et al. 1982. text ed. (ISBN 0-02-362430-2). Macmillan.

Introduction to Decision Analysis. Baird. LC 77-13570. 1978. 18.95 o.p. (ISBN 0-87872-144-4). PWS-Kent Pub.

Introduction to DECsystem 20 Assembly Programming. Stephen A. Longo. LC 83-7414. (Computer Science Ser.). 224p. 1983. pap. text ed. 17.00 pub net o.p. (ISBN 0-534-02942-6). Brooks-Cole.

Introduction to Dental Anatomy. 9th ed. James H. Scott & Norman Symons. (Dental Ser.). (Illus.). 1983. pap. text ed. 29.50 o.p. (ISBN 0-443-02561-4). Churchill.

Introduction to Design & Culture in the Twentieth Century. Penny Sparke. (Illus.). 192p. 1986. 37.95 o.p. (ISBN 0-04-701014-2); pap. text ed. 14.95x o.p. (ISBN 0-04-701015-0). Unwin Hyman.

Introduction to Differentiable Manifolds & Riemannian Geometry. William M. Boothby. (Pure & Applied Mathematics Ser.). 424p. 1975. 48.00 o.p. (ISBN 0-12-116050-5). Acad Pr.

Introduction to Differential Equations. William E. Boyce & Richard C. DiPrima. 310p. 1970. (ISBN 0-471-09338-6). Wiley.

Introduction to Differential Equations. R. Creighton Buck & Ellen Buck. LC 75-25009. (Illus.). 416p. 1976. text ed. 31.50 o.p. (ISBN 0-395-20654-5). HM.

Introduction to Digital Computer Design. 2nd ed. V. Rajaraman & T. Radhakrishnan. (Illus.). 416p. 1982. pap. text ed. (ISBN 0-13-480657-3). P-H.

Introduction to Digital Computing. F. H. George. 1966. pap. text ed. 10.25 o.p. (ISBN 0-08-011280-3). Pergamon.

Introduction to Digital Filtering. Ed. by R. E. Bogner & A. G. Constantinides. LC 74-4924. 198p. 1975. 59.95 o.p. (ISBN 0-471-08590-1, Pub. by Wiley-Interscience). Wiley.

Introduction to Digital Signal Processing. John Karl. 420p. pap. cancelled o.s.i. (ISBN 0-12-398420-3). Acad Pr.

Introduction to Dinghy Sailing. Nicolette M. Walker. (Illus.). 104p. 1981. 15.95 o.p. (ISBN 0-7153-8022-2). David & Charles.

Introduction to Divine & Human Readings. Cassiodorus Senator. Tr. by Leslie W. Jones. (Columbia University Records of Civilization Ser). 1969. pap. 5.95x o.p. (ISBN 0-393-09856-7, NortonC). Norton.

Introduction to Dutch. 5th, rev. ed. W. Z. Shetter. 1984. pap. 15.00 o.p. (ISBN 9-0247-9978-3). E J Brill USA.

Introduction to Dynamic Morphology. Edmund Mayer. 1963. 84.50 o.p. (ISBN 0-12-480650-3). Acad Pr.

Introduction to Dynamics & Control. Henry M. Power & Robert J. Simpson. (Illus.). 1978. text ed. 40.95 o.p. (ISBN 0-07-084081-4). McGraw.

Introduction to Dynamics & Control. R. J. Richards. 320p. 1979. pap. 24.95 o.p. (ISBN 0-470-20577-6, Co-Pub. with Longman). Wiley.

Introduction to Ecological Biochemistry. J. B. Harborne. 1977. 20.00 o.p. (ISBN 0-12-324670-9). Acad Pr.

Introduction to Ecological Biochemistry. 2nd ed. J. B. Harborne. 1982. 44.00 o.p. (ISBN 0-12-324680-6); pap. 18.00 o.p. (ISBN 0-12-324682-2). Acad Pr.

Introduction to Ecology. J. C. Emberlin. (Illus.). 304p. 1983. pap. text ed. 22.50x o.p. (ISBN 0-7121-0965-X). Trans-Atl Phila.

Introduction to Ecology Laboratory Manual. 2nd Ed. ed. James F. Reynolds & Thomas R. Wentworth. 1981. lab manual 8.95 o.p. (ISBN 0-89459-135-5). Hunter Textbks.

Introduction to Econometric Forecasting & Forecasting Models. Ed. by Lawrence R. Klein & Richard M. Young. LC 79-1542. (Wharton Econometric Forecasting Studies: No. 3). 176p. 1980. 29.00x o.p. (ISBN 0-669-02896-7). Lexington Bks.

Introduction to Econometrics. A. A. Walters. 1970. text ed. 12.95x o.p. (ISBN 0-393-09931-8, NortonC). Norton.

Introduction to Economic Cybernetics. Oskar Lange. Ed. by Antoni Banasinski. Tr. by Jozef Stadler. LC 73-106449. (Illus.). 200p. 1970. 31.00 o.p. (ISBN 0-08-006652-6). Pergamon.

Introduction to Educational Administration in Nigeria. D. A. Edem. 233p. 1986. pap. 18.95 o.p. (ISBN 0-471-27984-6). Wiley.

Introduction to Educational Gerontology. new ed. Ed. by R. H. Sherron & D. B. Lumsden. LC 78-13292. (Illus.). 1978. pap. text ed. 19.50 o.p. (ISBN 0-89116-101-5). Hemisphere Pub.

Introduction to Educational Measurement. 4th ed. Victor H. Noll et al. LC 78-69587. (Illus.). 1979. text ed. 38.36 o.p. (ISBN 0-395-26871-0). HM.

Introduction to Eighteenth Century Drama, 1700-1780. Frederick S. Boas. LC 77-27612. 1978. Repr. of 1953 ed. lib. bdg. 27.50x o.p. (ISBN 0-313-20193-5, BOEC). Greenwood.

Introduction to Electric Circuits. 5th ed. Herbert W. Jackson. (Illus.). 736p. 1981. text ed. 37.33 o.p. (ISBN 0-13-481432-0). P-H.

Introduction to Electric Circuits. 6th ed. Herbert W. Jackson. (Illus.). 800p. 1986. text ed. 44.00 o.p. (ISBN 0-13-481425-8). P-H.

Introduction to Electrical Applied Physics. Astbury. (Illus.). 241p. 1957. (ISBN 0-8022-0042-7). Philos Lib.

Introduction to Electronic Speech Synthesis. Neil Sclater. 112p. 1982. pap. 9.95 o.p. (ISBN 0-672-21896-8, 21896). Sams.

Introduction to Electronics. William G. Oldham & Steven E. Schwartz. LC 70-179870. 629p. 1972. text ed. 32.95 o.p. (ISBN 0-03-086075-X, HoltC). HR&W.

Introduction to Electronics for Technologists. John P. Hoffman. LC 77-74381. (Illus.). 1978. text ed. 29.50 o.p. (ISBN 0-395-25115-X). HM.

Introduction to Elementary Particle Theory. Yuri V. Novozhilov. Tr. by Jonathon L. Rosner. 1975. 100.00 o.p. (ISBN 0-08-017954-1). Pergamon.

Introduction to Elementary Particles. 2nd ed. W. S. Williams. LC 73-84251. (Pure & Applied Physics Ser.: Vol. 12). 1971. 82.00 o.p. (ISBN 0-12-756756-9). Acad Pr.

Introduction to Elementary Reading: Selected Materials. Ronald G. Noland et al. Ed. by Jone P. Wright & Elizabeth Allen. 246p. 1971. pap. text ed. 7.25x o.p. (ISBN 0-8422-0172-6). Irvington.

Introduction to Energy Technology. V. A. Vanikov & E. V. Putyatin. 304p. 1981. 8.80 o.p. (ISBN 0-8285-1965-X, Pub. by Mir Pubs USSR). Imported Pubns.

Introduction to Engineering Design with Graphics & Design Projects. T. Shoup et al. 1981. pap. text ed. 35.00 o.p. (ISBN 0-13-482364-8). P-H.

Introduction to Engineering Materials. L. M. Gourd. 192p. 1982. pap. text ed. 19.95x o.p. (ISBN 0-7131-3444-5). Trans-Atl Phila.

Introduction to Engineering Measurements. A. Richard Graham. (Illus.). 224p. 1975. text ed. 33.00 ref. ed o.p. (ISBN 0-13-482406-7). P-H.

Introduction to Engineering: Methods, Concepts & Issues. Edward V. Krick. LC 75-41432. 358p. 1976. pap. text ed. 27.95x o.p. (ISBN 0-471-50750-4). Wiley.

Introduction to Engineering Systems. Samuel Seely. 548p. 1972. 135.00 o.p. (ISBN 0-08-016821-3); pap. text ed. 135.00 o.p. (ISBN 0-08-018998-9). Pergamon.

Introduction to Environmental Conflict Management: Proceedings of a Seminar, Vols. I & II. 1984. Vol. 1. 7.50 o.p. (ISBN 1-55516-437-4); Vol. 2. 7.50 o.p. (ISBN 1-55516-407-2); Set. 12.00 o.s.i. (ISBN 1-55516-408-0). Natl Conf State Legis.

Introduction to Environmental Design. Anthony C. Antoniades. LC 76-20696. (Illus.). 360p. 1976. pap. text ed. 8.95x o.p. (ISBN 0-8422-0543-8). Irvington.

Introduction to Environmental Engineering. Davis & Cornwell. 1985. text ed. write for info. o.p. (ISBN 0-534-04137-X, 21R4300, Pub. by PWS Engineering). PWS-Kent Pub.

Introduction to Environmental Studies. 2nd ed. Jonathan Turk. 368p. 1985. pap. text ed. 29.50 o.s.i. (ISBN 0-03-064233-7, CBS C); instr's manual 14.00 o.s.i. (ISBN 0-03-064234-5). SCP.

Introduction to Enzymology. Alan H. Mehler. 1957. 65.50 o.p. (ISBN 0-12-487750-8). Acad Pr.

Introduction to Epidemiology. Michael Alderson. LC 77-9247. (Illus.). 240p. 1978. pap. 20.00 o.p. (ISBN 0-88416-203-6). Year Bk Med.

Introduction to Ergodic Theory. Y. G. Sinai. Tr. by V. Scheffer from Rus. LC 76-3030. (Mathematical Notes Ser.: No. 18). 150p. 1976. pap. 20.50 o.p. (ISBN 0-691-08182-4). Princeton U Pr.

Introduction to Estate Planning. Chris J. Prestopino. LC 86-80989. (Irwin Series in Financial Planning & Insurance). 418p. 1987. 34.95 o.p. (ISBN 0-256-03467-2). Irwin.

Introduction to Ethics: A Philosophical Orientation. Ed. by Thomas R. Koenig. 187p. 1974. pap. text ed. 8.95x o.p. (ISBN 0-8422-0444-X). Irvington.

Introduction to Experimental Psychology. Eva E. Conrad & Terry Maul. LC 81-1647. 542p. 1981. pap. (ISBN 0-471-06005-4). Wiley.

Introduction to Exploration Economics. 2nd ed. R. E. Megill. LC 75-153985. 180p. 1979. 49.95 o.p. (ISBN 0-87814-115-4, P-4214). Pennwell Bks.

Introduction to Extrusion. P. N. Richardson. Tr. by Luis E. Mendoza. (SPE Processing Ser.). (Illus.). 90p. (Span.). pap. 26.50 o.p. (ISBN 0-686-48175-5, 1101). T-C Pubns CA.

Introduction to Farm Organization & Managements. M. Buckett. (Illus.). 280p. 1981. text ed. 65.00 o.p. (ISBN 0-08-024433-5); pap. 19.95 o.p. (ISBN 0-08-024432-7). Pergamon.

Introduction to Federal Taxation: 1988 Edition. William L. Raby & Victor H. Tidwell. (Illus.). 544p. 1987. text ed. 39.33 o.p. (ISBN 0-13-483646-4). P-H.

Introduction to Feynman Diagrams. S. M. Bilenky. LC 73-21657. 1974. text ed. 53.00 o.p. (ISBN 0-08-017799-9). Pergamon.

Introduction to Field Quantization. Y. Takahashi. 1969. 75.00 o.p. (ISBN 0-08-012824-6). Pergamon.

Introduction to Film Assembly. 48p. 1980. 16.00 o.p. (ISBN 0-88362-025-1, 0411). Graphic Arts Tech Found.

Introduction to Financial Accounting. H. Paul Hooper. 679p. 1982. text ed. 42.75 o.p. (ISBN 0-8299-0387-9). West Pub.

Introduction to Financial Management. Howard Lanser & John A. Halloran. 1985. text ed. write for info. o.p. (ISBN 0-673-16556-6); write for info. study guide o.p. (ISBN 0-673-16643-0). Scott F.

Introduction to Financial Management. Lawrence D. Schall & Charles W. Haley. (Finance Ser.). (Illus.). 1977. text ed. 31.50 o.p. (ISBN 0-07-055097-2, C). McGraw.

Introduction to Finite Element Analysis. D. H. Norrie & G. De Vries. 1978. 41.50 o.p. (ISBN 0-12-521660-2). Acad Pr.

Introduction to Finite Markov Processes: Continuous Time Finite Markow Processes. S. R. Adke & Shri S. Manjunath. LC 84-19272. 310p. 1984. 28.95x o.p. (ISBN 0-470-27457-3). Halsted Pr.

Introduction to Fishery Sciences. William F. Royce. 351p. 1972. text ed. 53.00 o.p. (ISBN 0-12-600950-3). Acad Pr.

Introduction to Fixed Appliances. 2nd ed. Isaacson & Williams. 168p. 1978. 16.50 o.p. (ISBN 0-7236-0480-0, Pub. by John Wright UK). Butterworth.

Introduction to Flight: Its Engineering & History. John D. Anderson, Jr. (Illus.). 1978. text ed. 43.00 o.p. (ISBN 0-07-001637-2). McGraw.

Introduction to Fluid & Particle Mechanics. S. J. Michell. 1970. 90.00 o.p. (ISBN 0-08-013313-4); pap. 90.00 o.p. (ISBN 0-08-013312-6). Pergamon.

Introduction to Fluid Mechanics. 2nd ed. James E. John & William L. Haberman. 1980. text ed. (ISBN 0-13-483941-2). P-H.

Introduction to Forensic Toxicology. Ed. by Robert H. Cravey & Randall C. Baselt. LC 79-56929. (Illus.). 300p. 1981. text ed. 74.00 o.p. (ISBN 0-931890-06-3, Biomed Pubns). Year Bk Med.

Introduction to FORTRAN IV Programming: A Self-Paced Approach. G. W. Dickson & H. R. Smith. LC 74-189809. 1972. pap. text ed. 17.95 o.p. (ISBN 0-03-088088-2, HoltC). HR&W.

Introduction to Foundations of American Education. 6th ed. James A. Johnson et al. 1984. text ed. write for info. o.p. (ISBN 0-205-08322-6, 238322). Allyn.

Introduction to French Classical Tragedy. C. J. Gossip. 204p. 1981. 28.50x o.p. (ISBN 0-389-20163-4). B&N Imports.

Introduction to Functional Occlusion. Major M. Ash, Jr. & Sigurd P. Ramfjord. LC 81-5275. (Illus.). 240p. 1982. write for info. o.p. (ISBN 0-7216-1428-0). Saunders.

Introduction to Gas Discharges. 2nd ed. A. M. Howatson. 261p. 1976. 65.00 o.p. (ISBN 0-08-020575-5); pap. 10.75 o.p. (ISBN 0-08-020574-7). Pergamon.

Introduction to Gas-Liquid Chromatography. R. A. Jones. 1970. 39.50 o.p. (ISBN 0-12-389850-1). Acad Pr.

Introduction to General, Organic & Biochemistry. Frederick A. Bettelheim & Jerry March. LC 83-20124. 708p. 1984. text ed. 42.75 o.s.i. (ISBN 0-03-061548-8); study guide 16.00 o.s.i. (ISBN 0-03-064122-5). SCP.

Introduction to General Pathology. 2nd ed. V. G. Spector. (Churchill Livingstone Medical Text). (Illus.). 320p. 1981. pap. text ed. 18.00 o.p. (ISBN 0-443-01970-3). Churchill.

Introduction to General Relativity. 2nd ed. R. Adler. 1975. text ed. 51.95 o.p. (ISBN 0-07-000423-4). McGraw.

Introduction to General Relativity. H. A. Atwater. LC 73-16251. 1975. 60.00 o.p. (ISBN 0-08-017692-5); pap. 60.00 o.p. (ISBN 0-08-017718-2). Pergamon.

Introduction to Genetics. David J. Merrell. 750p. 1975. text ed. 17.95x o.p. (ISBN 0-393-09247-X). Norton.

Introduction to Geography. 5th ed. Henry M. Kendall et al. (Illus.). 810p. 1976. text ed. 23.00 o.p. (ISBN 0-15-542152-2, HC). HarBraceJ.

Introduction to Geological Maps. 2nd rev ed. J. A. Thomas. (Illus.). 1977. pap. text ed. 6.95x o.p. (ISBN 0-04-550024-X). Unwin Hyman.

Introduction to Geometrical & Physical Optics. Joseph Morgan. LC 77-13033. 462p. 1978. Repr. of 1953 ed. lib. bdg. 29.50 o.p. (ISBN 0-88275-620-6). Krieger.

Introduction to Geometry. G. A. Dickinson. (Illus.). 192p. (ISBN 0-8022-0397-3). Philos Lib.

Introduction to Georgian Architecture. Albert E. Richardson. LC 50-749. 256p. 1949. Repr. 39.00x o.p. (ISBN 0-403-07235-2). Somerset Pub.

Introduction to Grain Marketing. 1st ed. Walter J. Wills. LC 74-155289. 198p. 1972. 16.65 o.p. (ISBN 0-8134-1299-4, 1299); text ed. 12.50x o.p. Inter Print Pubs.

Introduction to Grothendieck Duality Theory. A. Altmann & S. Kleiman. LC 77-132180. (Lecture Notes in Mathematics: Vol. 146). 1970. pap. 11.00 o.p. (ISBN 0-387-04935-5). Springer-Verlag.

Introduction to Group Representation Theory. R. Keown. (Mathematics in Science & Engineering Ser.). 1975. 70.50 o.p. (ISBN 0-12-404250-3). Acad Pr.

Introduction to Group Theory with Applications. Gerald Burns. (Material Science & Technology Ser.). 1977. 54.50 o.p. (ISBN 0-12-145750-8). Acad Pr.

Introduction to Guidance: The Professional Counselor. 2nd ed. Ed. by E. L. Tolbert. 1982. text ed. (ISBN 0-673-39183-3). Scott F.

Introduction to Handbook of American Indian Languages. Franz Boas. Ed. by Preston Holder. Bd. with Indian Linguistic Families of America North of Mexico. J. W. Powell. LC 65-19467. xii, 221p. 1966. pap. 5.50x o.p. (ISBN 0-8032-5017-7, BB 301, Bison). U of Nebr Pr.

Introduction to Health Careers. Mary E. Kimbrall. (gr. 7-10). 1975. pap. text ed. 7.33 activity ed o.p. (ISBN 0-87345-179-1). Glencoe.

Introduction to Health Services. 2nd ed. Ed. by Stephen J. Williams & Paul R. Torrens. (Health Services Ser.). 498p. 1984. 29.95 o.p. (ISBN 0-471-86900-7). Wiley.

Introduction to Higher Algebra. J. Mostowski & M. Stark. 1964. 82.00 o.p. (ISBN 0-08-010152-6). Pergamon.

Introduction to Historical Geology. Fred Keller et al. (Illus.). 1979. lab manual 8.95x o.p. (ISBN 0-89459-194-0). Hunter Textbks.

Introduction to Hospitality: Recreation Careers. Judi Evert. (gr. 7-10). 1975. pap. text ed. 7.33 activity ed. o.p. (ISBN 0-87345-185-6). Glencoe.

Introduction to Hotel & Restaurant Management: A Book of Readings. 4th ed. Robert A. Brymer. 1984. pap. text ed. 14.95 o.p. (ISBN 0-8403-3283-1, 40328301). Kendall-Hunt.

Introduction to Housing Layout. (Greater London Council Study). 186p. 1978. pap. 23.50 o.p. (ISBN 0-85139-298-9). Nichols Pub.

Titles

Introduction to HUD-Subsidized Housing Programs: A Handbook for the Legal Services Advocate. Fred Fuchs. 164p. cancelled o.s.i. (33,843B). NCLS Inc.

Introduction to Human Behavior. John S. Wodarski. LC 84-17924. 270p. 1985. pap. 19.00x o.p. (ISBN 0-936104-51-1, 1282). Pro Ed.

Introduction to Human Genetics. 3rd ed. H. Eldon Sutton. 1980. text ed. 34.95 o.p. (ISBN 0-03-043081-X, CBS C). SCP.

Introduction to Hunting. John Williams. (Illus.). pap. 5.25 o.p. (ISBN 0-85131-200-4, Pub. by J A Allen U K). S R Smith Sporting Bks.

Introduction to Hydrodynamics & Water Waves. B. Le Mehante. LC 75-18631. (Illus.). 512p. 1976. text ed. 44.00 o.p. (ISBN 0-387-07232-2). Springer-Verlag.

Introduction to Hypersonic Flow. G. G. Chernyi. Ed. by Ronald F. Probstein. 1961. 65.50 o.p. (ISBN 0-12-170650-8). Acad Pr.

Introduction to Indonesian Law. Sudargo Gautama & Robert N. Hornick. xiii, 192p. 1974. pap. 7.50x o.p. (ISBN 0-8377-0603-3, Pub. by Alumni Press). Rothman.

Introduction to Industrial & Systems Engineering. reference ed. Wayne C. Turner et al. (P-H Ser. in Industrial & Systems Engineering). (Illus.). 1978. pap. text ed. 42.00 o.p. (ISBN 0-13-484543-9). P-H.

Introduction to Industrial Drying Operations. R. B. Keey. LC 77-30467. 396p. 1978. 93.00 o.p. (ISBN 0-08-020594-1); pap. 28.00 o.p. (ISBN 0-08-020593-3). Pergamon.

Introduction to Industrial Economics. 4th ed. P. J. Devine et al. (Illus.). 500p. 1985. pap. text ed. 24.95x o.p. (ISBN 0-04-338124-3). Unwin Hyman.

Introduction to Industrial Management. F. Folts. LC 77-22994. 686p. 1979. Repr. of 1963 ed. 37.50 o.p. (ISBN 0-88275-566-8). Krieger.

Introduction to Injection Molding. C. I. Weir. Tr. by Luis E. Mendoza. (SPE Processing Ser.). (Illus.). 92p. (Span.). 26.50 o.p. (ISBN 0-686-48174-7, 1102). T-C Pubns CA.

Introduction to Insect Biology & Diversity. Howell V. Daly et al. (Illus.). 1978. text ed. 44.95 o.p. (ISBN 0-07-015208-X). McGraw.

Introduction to Insect Physiology. F. Bursell. 1971. 76.00 o.p. (ISBN 0-12-146650-7). Acad Pr.

Introduction to Insurance. 2nd ed. Mark S. Dorfman. (P-H Series in Security & Insurance). (Illus.). 496p. 1982. pap. text ed. (ISBN 0-13-485367-9). P-H.

Introduction to Interactive Computer Graphics. Joan E. Scott. LC 81-7621. (Illus.). 255p. 1982. 18.95 o.p. (ISBN 0-471-05773-8); pap. 18.95x o.p. (ISBN 0-471-86623-7). Wiley.

Introduction to International Law. Ronald B. Kirkemo. (Quality Paperback Ser.: No. 312). 235p. 1975. pap. 4.95 o.p. (ISBN 0-8226-0312-8). Littlefield.

Introduction to International Relations: The Global Condition in the Late Twentieth Century. Frederic S. Pearson & J. Martin Rochester. 624p. 1984. text ed. 22.00 o.p. (ISBN 0-394-34933-4, RanC). Random.

Introduction to International Taxation. (Tax Law & Estate Planning Course Handbook Ser.: Vol. 202). 429p. 1984. 45.00 o.p. (ISBN 0-317-11444-1, J4-3549). PLI.

Introduction to Investment Management. C. Ronald Sprecher. 1975. text ed. 31.50 o.p. (ISBN 0-395-18706-0). HM.

Introduction to Ionospheric Physics. Henry Risbeth & O. K. Garriott. (International Geophysics Ser.: Vol. 14). 1969. 49.50 o.p. (ISBN 0-12-588940-2). Acad Pr.

Introduction to Jazz History. Donald D. Megill & Richard Demory. (Illus.). 200p. 1984. pap. text ed. 28.00 o.p. (ISBN 0-13-485441-1). P-H.

Introduction to Jesuit Life: The Constitutions & History Through 435 Years. Thomas H. Clancy. Ed. by George E. Ganss. LC 75-46080. (Study Aids on Jesuit Topics Ser.: No. 3). 422p. 1976. 12.00 o.s.i. (ISBN 0-912422-15-7); pap. 5.50 o.s.i. (ISBN 0-912422-12-2). Inst Jesuit.

Introduction to Jesus of Nazareth. Eric W. Johnson. (Illus.). 512p. (Orig.). 1981. pap. 11.95x o.p. (ISBN 0-88334-146-8). Ind Sch Pr.

Introduction to Judaism. Joseph Kalir. LC 79-6758. 170p. 1980. text ed. 26.25 o.p. (ISBN 0-8191-0948-7); pap. text ed. 11.50 o.p. (ISBN 0-8191-0949-5). U Pr of Amer.

Introduction to Kinetic Theory. T. Koga. LC 76-93474. 1970. 130.00 o.p. (ISBN 0-08-006538-4); pap. text ed. 29.00 o.p. (ISBN 0-08-018993-8). Pergamon.

Introduction to Language & Language Teaching. C. J. Brumfit & J. T. Roberts. 224p. (Orig.). 1983. pap. 22.95 o.p. (ISBN 0-7134-1599-1, Pub. by Batsford England). David & Charles.

Introduction to Latent Variable Models. B. S. Everett. LC 84-12677. (Monographs on Statistics & Applied Probability). 150p. 1984. text ed. 22.00 o.p. (ISBN 0-412-25310-0, 9196, Pub. by Chapman & Hall England). Routledge Chapman & Hall.

Introduction to Law. 2nd ed. Phil Harris. (Law in Context Ser.). xix, 434p. 1984. text ed. 22.50x o.p. (ISBN 0-297-78459-5, Pub. by Weidenfeld & Nicolson England). Rothman.

Introduction to Law & the Legal System. 2nd ed. Harold J. Grilliot. LC 78-69579. (Illus.). 1979. text ed. 23.50 o.p. (ISBN 0-395-26866-4). HM.

Introduction to Library Services for Library Technicians. Barbara E. Chernik. LC 81-15663. (Library Science Text Ser.). (Illus.). 187p. 1982. text ed. 28.00 o.p. (ISBN 0-87287-275-0); 20.00 o.p. (ISBN 0-87287-282-3); pap. 20.00 o.p. Libs Unl.

Introduction to Linear Algebra. Philip W. Gillett. 1975. text ed. 25.50 o.p. (ISBN 0-395-18574-2). HM.

Introduction to Linear Algebra. Roger C. McCann. 419p. 1984. text ed. 30.00 net o.p. (ISBN 0-15-543001-7, HC). HarBraceJ.

Introduction to Linear Models & the Design & Analysis of Experiments. William Mendenhall. 1968. write for info. o.p. (ISBN 0-685-21739-6). PWS-Kent Pub.

Introduction to Linear Programming & Game Theory. Paul R. Thie. LC 78-15328. 335p. 1979. text ed. 36.95 o.p. (ISBN 0-471-04248-X). Wiley.

Introduction to Linear Programming & Matrix Game Theory. M. J. Fryer. LC 77-13371. 121p. 1978. pap. text ed. 15.95x o.p. (ISBN 0-470-99327-8). Halsted Pr.

Introduction to Literature: Fiction, Poetry, Drama. 8th ed. Sylvan Barnet et al. 1985. pap. text ed. write for info. o.p. (ISBN 0-673-39193-0). Scott F.

Introduction to Local Area Computer Networks. K. C. Gee. 150p. 1984. pap. 19.50 o.p. (ISBN 0-471-80036-8). Wiley.

Introduction to Logic. 63-11481 ed. Immanuel Kant. Tr. by Thomas K. Abbot. 104p. 1963. (ISBN 0-8022-0823-1). Philos Lib.

Introduction to Macroeconomic Policy. H. Vane & J. Thompson. 317p. 1982. text ed. 27.50x o.p. (ISBN 0-7108-0130-0, Pub. by Harvester Pr UK). Humanities.

Introduction to Macroeconomics. Paul W. Barkley. (Illus.). 418p. 1977. pap. text ed. 12.00 o.p. (ISBN 0-15-518816-X, HC). HarBraceJ.

Introduction to Macroeconomics. 2nd ed. Paul Wonnacott & Ron Wonnacott. 1982. text ed. 21.95x o.p. (ISBN 0-07-071582-3). McGraw.

Introduction to Management. Warren R. Plunkett & Raymond F. Attner. LC 82-18698. 544p. 1983. text ed. write for info. o.p. (ISBN 0-534-01298-1). PWS-Kent Pub.

Introduction to Management: A Contingency Approach. Fred Luthans. 1975. text ed. 32.95x o.p. (ISBN 0-07-039125-4). McGraw.

Introduction to Management in the Hospitality Industry. 2nd ed. Thomas F. Powers. LC 83-21765. (Management Ser.). 469p. 1984. (ISBN 0-471-06046-1). Wiley.

Introduction to Management: Principles, Practices, & Processes. David Schwartz. 649p. 1980. text ed. 22.95 o.p. (ISBN 0-15-543423-3, HC). HarBraceJ.

Introduction to Management Science. Sang M. Lee. 736p. 1983. text ed. 36.95x o.p. (ISBN 0-03-059183-X); instr's. manual 19.95 o.p. (ISBN 0-03-059184-8); study guide 14.95x o.p. (ISBN 0-03-059186-4). Dryden Pr.

Introduction to Management Science. 2nd ed. Bernard W. Taylor, III. 816p. 1986. 41.00 o.s.i. (ISBN 0-205-11534-9, H1534-0); study guide 15.00 o.s.i. (ISBN 0-205-11535-7, H1535-7); instr's. manual avail. o.s.i. (ISBN 0-205-11536-5, H1536-5); test bank avail. o.s.i. (ISBN 0-205-11537-3, H1537-3). Allyn.

Introduction to Management Science. Nesa L. Wu & Jack A. Wu. 1980. text ed. 31.95 o.p. (ISBN 0-395-30774-0); 2.50 o.p. HM.

Introduction to Management Science: Quantitative Approaches to Decision Making. 4th ed. David R. Anderson et al. (Illus.). 758p. 1985. text ed. 41.75 o.p. (ISBN 0-314-85214-X). West Pub.

Introduction to Manufacturing Careers. Willis Ray. (gr. 7-10). 1975. pap. text ed. 7.33 activity ed. o.p. (ISBN 0-87345-177-5). Glencoe.

Introduction to Map Projections. McDonnel. 184p. 1979. 35.00 o.p. (ISBN 0-8247-6830-2). Dekker.

Introduction to Marine Ecology. R. S. Barnes & R. N. Hughes. (Illus.). 348p. 1982. pap. text ed. 23.95x o.p. (ISBN 0-632-00892-X). Blackwell Sci.

Introduction to Marketing Management. 5th ed. James D. Scott et al. 1985. 39.95 o.p. (ISBN 0-256-03236-X). Irwin.

Introduction to Mass Communication. Jay Black & Frederick C. Whitney. 496p. 1983. pap. text ed. write for info o.p. (ISBN 0-697-04355-X); instr's. manual avail. o.p. (ISBN 0-697-04360-6). Wm C Brown.

Introduction to Materials Engineering. Frank L. Bouquet. (Illus.). 70p. (Orig.). 1986. text ed. 75.00 o.p. (ISBN 0-937041-05-X); pap. text ed. 50.00 o.p. (ISBN 0-937041-06-8). Systems Co.

Introduction to Mathematical Biology. S. I. Rubinow. LC 75-12520. 386p. 1975. 54.95 o.p. (ISBN 0-471-74446-8, Pub. by Wiley-Interscience). Wiley.

Introduction to Mathematical Economics. M. Casson. 1973. pap. 20.95 o.p. (ISBN 0-442-30718-7). Van Nos Reinhold.

Introduction to Mathematical Economics. Anthony L. Ostrosky, Jr. & James V. Koch. LC 78-69569. (Illus.). 1979. text ed. 37.50 o.p. (ISBN 0-395-27052-9). HM.

Introduction to Mathematical Modelling: A Summer School at Stanford 1985. H. Sieburg. 300p. 1988. 48.00 o.p. (ISBN 9971-50-308-5); pap. 32.00 o.p. (ISBN 9971-50-348-4). World Scientific Pub.

Introduction to Mathematical Patterns of Cultural Diffusion. Robert L. Hamblin & Jerry L. Miller. (CISE Learning Package Ser.: No. 20). (Illus.). 39p. (Orig.). 1976. pap. text ed. 3.00x o.p. (ISBN 0-936876-32-8). LRIS.

Introduction to Mathematical Philosophy. Bertrand Russell. 1971. pap. 9.95 o.s.i. (ISBN 0-671-20927-2, Touchstone Bks). S&S.

Introduction to Mathematics. R. A. Good. 1966. text ed. 15.95 o.p. (ISBN 0-15-543480-2, HC). HarBraceJ.

Introduction to Mathematics. 5th ed. Bruce E. Meserve & Max Sobel. (Illus.). 512p. 1984. text ed. (ISBN 0-13-487348-3). P-H.

Introduction to Mechanical Properties of Materials: An Ecological Approach. Melvin M. Eisenstadt. 1971. text ed. write for info. o.p. (ISBN 0-02-332140-7, 33214). Macmillan.

Introduction to Medical Microbiology. Marcus M. Jensen & Donald N. Wright. (Illus.). 464p. 1985. text ed. 48.00 o.p. (ISBN 0-13-487380-7). P-H.

Introduction to Medicine. Crapo et al. (Illus.). 1986. 39.00 o.p. (ISBN 0-8016-1280-2). Mosby.

Introduction to Mental Retardation. Robert M. Smith. 1971. text ed. 33.95 o.p. (ISBN 0-07-058903-8). McGraw.

Introduction to Metallurgical Analysis: Chemical & Instrumental. S. K. Jain. 472p. 1986. text ed. 40.00x o.p. (ISBN 0-7069-1894-0, Pub. by Vikas India). Advent NY.

Introduction to Metallurgical Laboratory Techniques. P. G. Ormandy. LC 68-18530. 1968. text ed. 12.00 o.p. (ISBN 0-08-012560-3). Pergamon.

Introduction to Meteorology. 3rd ed. Sverre Petterssen. LC 68-15476. 1968. text ed. 57.95 o.p. (ISBN 0-07-049720-6). McGraw.

Introduction to Microcomputers. Erik L. Dagless & David Aspinall. LC 81-5437. 233p. 1982. text ed. 25.95 o.p. (ISBN 0-914894-25-0, Computer Sci Pr). W H Freeman.

Introduction to Microcomputers. 1979. pap. text ed. 42.00x o.p. (ISBN 0-903796-44-9, Pub. by Online Conferences England). Gower Pub Co.

Introduction to Microeconomics. Paul W. Barkley. (Illus.). 327p. 1977. pap. text ed. 12.00 o.p. (ISBN 0-15-518817-8, HC). HarBraceJ.

Introduction to Microeconomics. 2nd ed. David Laidler. LC 81-6626. 330p. 1981. pap. 26.95x o.p. (ISBN 0-470-27243-0). Halsted Pr.

Introduction to Micrographics. rev. ed. Association for Information & Image Management Staff. Ed. by Ellen T. Meyer. (Consumer Ser.). 1980. pap. 4.50 o.p. (ISBN 0-89258-069-0, C101); pap. 4.00 member o.p. Assn Inform & Image Mgmt.

Introduction to Microprocessors. Ed. by David Aspinall & Erik Dagless. 1977. 39.50 o.p. (ISBN 0-12-064550-5). Acad Pr.

Introduction to Mineralogy: Crystallography & Petrology. C. W. Correns et al. Tr. by W. D. Johns. LC 72-460063. (Illus.). 1969. 27.00 o.p. (ISBN 0-387-04443-4). Springer-Verlag.

Introduction to Mini & Microcomputers. F. C. Monds & R. A. McLaughlin. 144p. 1981. 33.00 o.p. (ISBN 0-906048-48-6, NS006). Inst Elect Eng.

Introduction to Modern American Spiritualism. E. Hardinge. 12.50 o.p. (ISBN 0-8216-0100-8, Pub. by Univ Bks). Carol Pub Group.

Introduction to Modern Business. 9th ed. Vernon A. Musselman & John H. Jackson. (Illus.). 656p. 1984. text ed. (ISBN 0-13-488312-8). P-H.

Introduction to Modern Philosophy: Examining the Human Condition. 4th ed. Alburey Castell. 656p. 1983. text ed. write for info. o.p. (ISBN 0-02-320080-4). Macmillan.

Introduction to Modern Physics. 2nd ed. John D. McGervey. 1984. pap. text ed. 20.00 o.p. (ISBN 0-12-483562-7). Acad Pr.

Introduction to Modern Psychology. O. L. Zangwill. 1951. Philos Lib.

Introduction to Modern Theories of Economic Growth. Jones. 1975. pap. 31.95 o.p. (ISBN 0-442-30719-5). Van Nos Reinhold.

Introduction to Modern Virology. S. B. Primrose & N. J. Dimmock. (Illus.). 246p. 1980. pap. text ed. 15.00x o.p. (ISBN 0-632-00463-0). Blackwell Sci.

Introduction to Molecular Biological Techniques. reference ed. L. Jack Bradshaw. 1966. pap. text ed. 24.00 o.p. (ISBN 0-13-489187-2). P-H.

Introduction to Molecular Biology. S. E. Bresler. 1970. 82.00 o.p. (ISBN 0-12-132550-4). Acad Pr.

Introduction to Molecular Embryology. J. Brachet. LC 73-12632. (Heidelberg Science Library: Vol. 19). (Illus.). 180p. 1974. pap. 10.00 o.p. (ISBN 0-387-90077-2). Springer-Verlag.

Introduction to Money & Banking. Oliver G. Wood, Jr. LC 79-65818. 420p. 1980. text ed. 22.95x o.p. PWS-Kent Pub.

Introduction to Monopulse. Donald Rhodes. (Illus.). 119p. 1980. Repr. of 1959 ed. 25.00 o.p. (ISBN 0-89006-091-6). Artech Hse.

Introduction to Music: Selected Readings. rev ed. Ed. by Walter Gerboth et al. (Orig.). 1969. pap. text ed. 5.95x o.p. (ISBN 0-393-09790-0, NortonC). Norton.

Introduction to Neurophysiology. J. F. Stein. (Illus.). 384p. 1982. pap. text ed. 19.95 o.p. (ISBN 0-632-00582-3, B 4781-9). Mosby.

Introduction to Neutron Kinetics of Nuclear Power Reactors. J. G. Tyror & R. I. Vaughan. LC 76-94936. 1970. text ed. 27.00 o.p. (ISBN 0-08-006667-4). Pergamon.

Introduction to Nonlinear Laser Spectroscopy. Marc Levenson. LC 81-17608. (Quantum Electronics: Principles & Applications Ser.). 1982. 39.00 o.p. (ISBN 0-12-444720-1). Acad Pr.

Introduction to Nonlinear Optimization. Wismer. (System Science & Engineering Ser.: Vol. 1). 396p. 1977. 42.25 o.p. (ISBN 0-444-00234-0, North-Holland). Elsevier.

Introduction to Nonprofit Organization Accounting. Emerson O. Henke. (Business Ser.). 500p. 1980. text ed. 30.95x o.p. (ISBN 0-534-00742-2). PWS-Kent Pub.

Introduction to Nuclear Theory. I. E. McCarthy. LC 68-19781. 555p. 1968. text ed. 29.50 o.p. (ISBN 0-471-58140-2, Pub. by Wiley). Krieger.

Introduction to Numerical Computations. James S. Vandergraft. (Computer Science & Applied Mathematics Ser.). 1978. 39.50 o.p. (ISBN 0-12-711350-9). Acad Pr.

Introduction to Numerical Mathematics. E. L. Stiefel. Tr. by W. C. Rheinboldt. 1963. 35.00 o.p. (ISBN 0-12-671150-X). Acad Pr.

Introduction to Nursing Care. R. Winifred Johnson & Douglass W. Johnson. 1976. text ed. 24.90 o.p. (ISBN 0-07-032595-2). McGraw.

Introduction to Oceanography. 3rd ed. David A. Ross. (Illus.). 528p. 1982. text ed. (ISBN 0-13-491357-4). P-H.

Introduction to Old Javanese Language & Literature: A Kawi Prose Anthology. Mary S. Zurbuchen. LC 76-16235. (Michigan Papers in South & Southeast Asian Languages & Linguistics: No. 3). xii, 150p. 1976. pap. 7.00 o.p. (ISBN 0-89148-053-6). Ctr S&SE Asian.

Introduction to Old Testament Poetic Books. C. Hassell Bullock. 1979. 11.95 o.p. (ISBN 0-8024-4143-2). Moody.

Introduction to On-Line Systems. National Computing Centre, Ltd. Staff. Ed. by J. A. Pritchard. LC 72-97131. (Computers & the Professional Ser.). 120p. 1973. 21.00x o.s.i. (ISBN 0-85012-088-8). Intl Pubns Serv.

Introduction to Optical Electronics. 2nd ed. Amnon Yariv. LC 76-11773. 1976. text ed. 39.95 o.p. (ISBN 0-03-089892-7, HoltC). HR&W.

Introduction to Optical Waveguides. M. J. Adams. LC 80-42059. 401p. 1981. 81.95x o.p. (ISBN 0-471-27969-2). Wiley.

Introduction to Optimization Theory in a Hilbert Space. A. V. Balakrishnan. LC 77-155591. (Lecture Notes in Operations Research & Mathematical Systems: Vol. 42). 1971. pap. 10.70 o.p. (ISBN 0-387-05416-2). Springer-Verlag.

Introduction to Organic & Biochemistry. 4th ed. William H. Brown. 1979. write for info. o.p. (ISBN 0-87150-719-6, WG 4191, Pub. by Willard Grant Pr); write for info. study guide 1976 o.p. (ISBN 0-87150-720-X, WG 4196). PWS-Kent Pub.

Introduction to Organic & Biological Chemistry. Antony Wilbraham & Michael Matta. 1984. 35.95 o.p. (ISBN 0-8053-9651-9); instr's. guide 9.95 o.p. (ISBN 0-8053-9652-7); study guide by Staley 14.95 o.p. (ISBN 0-8053-9654-3). Benjamin-Cummings.

Introduction to Organic Chemistry. H. Lowther. 1964. text ed. 12.00 o.p. (ISBN 0-08-010819-9); pap. 40.00 o.p. (ISBN 0-08-010818-0). Pergamon.

Introduction to Organic Lab Techniques. 2nd ed. Donald Pavia. 1982. text ed. 46.75x o.s.i. (ISBN 0-03-058424-8, CBS C); instr's manual 12.00 o.s.i. (ISBN 0-03-058426-4). SCP.

Introduction to Organizational Behavior. 2nd ed. Richard M. Steers. 1984. pap. text ed. write for info. o.p. (ISBN 0-673-16630-9). Scott F.

Introduction to Organizational Behavior: Text & Readings. L. L. Cummings & Randall B. Dunham. 1980. pap. 22.50x o.p. (ISBN 0-256-02043-4). Irwin.

Introduction to Particle Production in Hadron Physics. S. Humble. 1974. 52.50 o.p. (ISBN 0-12-361450-3). Acad Pr.

Introduction to Pascal & Computer Applications. Richard M. Jones. 460p. 1983. pap. write for info. o.p. (ISBN 0-697-06839-0). Wm C Brown.

Introduction to Pascal: Including Turbo Pascal. Rodnay Zaks. LC 85-63778. 464p. (Orig.). 1986. pap. 21.95 o.p. (ISBN 0-89588-319-8). Sybex.

Introduction to Personality. Desmond S. Cartwright. 1974. text ed. 28.95 o.p. (ISBN 0-395-30788-0). HM.

Introduction to Personality. Lawrence A. Fehr. 576p. 1983. text ed. write for info. o.p. (ISBN 0-02-336700-8). Macmillan.

Introduction to Personality. 3rd ed. Walter Mischel. LC 80-29201. 1981. text ed. 33.95 o.s.i. (ISBN 0-03-056998-2, HoltC). HR&W.

Introduction to Personality. E. Jerry Phares. 1984. Repr. text ed. write for info. o.p. (ISBN 0-673-18662-8). Scott F.

Introduction to Personality & Psychotherapy. Joseph F. Rychlak. LC 72-6887. 600p. 1973. text ed. 19.95 o.p. (ISBN 0-395-14056-0). HM.

Introduction to Pharmaceutical Dosage Forms. 4th ed. Howard C. Ansel. LC 84-9732. (Illus.). 405p. 1985. text ed. 32.50 o.p. (ISBN 0-8121-0956-2). Lea & Febiger.

Introduction to Philosophical Analysis. 2nd ed. John Hospers. 1967. pap. text ed. (ISBN 0-13-491688-3). P-H.

Introduction to Philosophical Logic. A. C. Grayling. LC 82-6854. 300p. 1982. text ed. 29.50x o.p. (ISBN 0-389-20299-1); pap. text ed. 9.95x o.p. (ISBN 0-389-20300-9). B&N Imports.

Introduction to Philosophy. Max Rosenberg. 1955. (ISBN 0-8022-1373-1). Philos Lib.

Introduction to Philosophy: From Wonder to World View. Donald Scherer et al. (Illus.). 1979. text ed. (ISBN 0-13-491860-6). P-H.

Introduction to Philosophy of Education. 2nd ed. R. G. Woods & R. St. Barrow. 200p. 1982. 21.00 o.p. (ISBN 0-416-30330-7, NO.3745); pap. 11.95 o.p. (ISBN 0-416-30340-4, NO.3746). Routledge Chapman & Hall.

Introduction to Photography: A Self Directing Approach. 2nd ed. M. J. Rosen. LC 81-82564. 1982. pap. 25.95 o.p. (ISBN 0-395-29765-6). HM.

Introduction to Physical Anthropology. 3rd ed. Harry Nelson & Robert Jurmain. (Illus.). 609p. 1985. pap. text ed. 32.00 o.p. (ISBN 0-314-85282-4). West Pub.

Introduction to Physical Education. 9th ed. John Nixon & Ann Jewett. 1980. text ed. 27.95 o.p. (ISBN 0-03-056778-5, CBS C). SCP.

Introduction to Physical Geography. 2nd ed. Henry M. Kendall et al. (Illus.). 423p. 1974. text ed. 20.00 o.p. (ISBN 0-15-544004-7, HC). HarBraceJ.

Introduction to Physical Geology. 3rd ed. Otto C. Kopp. (Illus.). 144p. 1980. 8.95x o.p. (ISBN 0-89459-103-7). Hunter Textbks.

Introduction to Physical Hydrology. Ed. by Richard J. Chorley. 1971. pap. 14.95 o.p. (ISBN 0-416-68810-1, NO.2135). Routledge Chapman & Hall.

Introduction to Physical Methods of Treatment in Psychiatry. Ed. by William Sargant & Eliot Slater. LC 72-91423. 336p. 1973. 30.00x o.s.i. (ISBN 0-87668-062-7). Aronson.

Introduction to Physical Signs. Richard Thompson. (Illus.). 240p. 1981. pap. text ed. 19.95 o.p. (ISBN 0-632-00054-6, B 4943-9). Mosby.

Introduction to Physics, Vol. 1: Mechanics, Hydrodynamics, Thermodynamics. P. Frauenfelder & P. Huber. 1966. 145.00 o.p. (ISBN 0-08-011603-5); pap. 145.00 o.p. (ISBN 0-08-013521-8). Pergamon.

Introduction to Piecewise-Linear Topology. C. P. Rourke & B. J. Sanderson. LC 72-85229. (Ergebnisse der Mathematik und Ihrer Grenzgebiete: Vol. 69). (Illus.). 140p. 1972. 17.60 o.p. (ISBN 0-387-05800-1). Springer-Verlag.

Introduction to Plane Geometry. H. F. Baker. LC 70-141879. 1971. text ed. 22.50 o.p. (ISBN 0-8284-0247-7). Chelsea Pub.

Introduction to Plant Taxonomy. George H. Lawrence. (Illus.). 1955. text ed. write for info. o.p. (ISBN 0-02-368120-9). Macmillan.

Introduction to Plasma Physics. 2nd ed. William B. Thompson. 1964. text ed. 27.00 o.p. (ISBN 0-08-011180-7). Pergamon.

Introduction to Political Analysis. David E. Apter. 1977. text ed. 26.25 o.p. Scott F.

Introduction to Political Philosophy. A. R. Murray. 1954. (ISBN 0-8022-1176-3). Philos Lib.

Introduction to Political Research. Richard L. Cole. (Illus.). 1980. pap. text ed. write for info. o.p. (ISBN 0-02-323350-8). Macmillan.

Introduction to Political Science. 3rd ed. Carlton C. Rodee et al. 1975. text ed. 20.95x o.p. (ISBN 0-07-053376-8). McGraw.

Introduction to Polymer Chemistry. D. Margerison & G. C. East. 1967. text ed. 33.00 o.p. (ISBN 0-08-011891-7); pap. text ed. 12.75 o.p. (ISBN 0-08-011890-9). Pergamon.

Introduction to Population. Kenneth C. Kammeyer & Helen L. Ginn. 336p. 1986. text ed. (ISBN 0-534-10618-8). Wadsworth Pub.

Introduction to Powder Metallurgy. Joel S. Hirchorn. LC 76-83260. 341p. 1969. Metal Powder.

Introduction to Powder Metallurgy. Joel S. Hirschhorn. 341p. 1969. 15.00 o.p. (ISBN 0-317-34849-3); members 12.00 o.p. (ISBN 0-317-34850-7). Metal Powder.

Introduction to Practical High Resolution Nuclear Magnetic Resonance Spectroscopy. Dennis Chapman & P. D. Magnus. 1966. pap. 69.00 o.p. (ISBN 0-12-168550-0). Acad Pr.

Introduction to Printing: The Craft of Letterpress. Herbert Simon. (Illus.). 128p. 1980. pap. 7.50 o.p. (ISBN 0-571-11528-4). Faber & Faber.

Introduction to Private Security. Karen M. Hess. Ed. by Henry M. Wrobleski. (Criminal Justice Ser.). (Illus.). 337p. 1982. text ed. 33.50 o.p. (ISBN 0-314-63252-2). West Pub.

Introduction to Probabilistic Automata. Azaria Paz. LC 74-137627. (Computer Science & Applied Mathematics Ser). 1971. 66.00 o.p. (ISBN 0-12-547650-7). Acad Pr.

Introduction to Probability: Theory & Applications. R. L. Scheaffer & Wm. Mendenhall. LC 75-3562. 1975. text ed. write for info. o.p. (ISBN 0-87872-084-7, Duxbury Pr). PWS-Kent Pub.

Introduction to Professional Food Service. rev. ed. James P. Coffman. 322p. 1983. pap. 18.95 o.p. (ISBN 0-8436-2056-0). Van Nos Reinhold.

Introduction to Programming: A BASIC Approach. Van C. Hare, Jr. 1970. text ed. 18.95 o.p. (ISBN 0-15-543600-7, HC). HarBraceJ.

Introduction to Programming BASIC: A Structured Approach. 2nd ed. Chris R. Siragusa. 340p. 1983. pap. text ed. write for info. o.p. (ISBN 0-87150-386-7, 8020). PWS-Kent Pub.

Introduction to Protein Sequence Analysis. L. R. Croft. LC 79-41488. 157p. 1980. pap. 31.95 o.p. (ISBN 0-471-27710-X). Wiley.

Introduction to Psychiatry. Kurt Kolle. LC 62-12825. 96p. 1963. (ISBN 0-8022-0881-9). Philos Lib.

Introduction to Psychoanalytic Theory of Motivation. W. Toman. 1976. text ed. 20.00 o.p. (ISBN 0-08-009485-6). Pergamon.

Introduction to Psychology. 8th ed. Rita L. Atkinson et al. 701p. 1983. text ed. 24.00 o.p. (ISBN 0-15-543677-5, HC). HarBraceJ.

Introduction to Psychology. 5th ed. Rita L. Atkinson et al. 1971. 15.95 o.p. (ISBN 0-15-543647-3). HarbraceJ.

Introduction to Psychology. 4th ed. L. Dodge Fernald & Peter S. Fernald. LC 77-78911. (Illus.). 1978. text ed. 25.95 o.p. (ISBN 0-395-25815-4). HM.

Introduction to Psychology. 6th ed. Ernest R. Hilgard et al. (Illus.). 1975. text ed. 20.95 o.p. (ISBN 0-15-543657-0, HC). HarBraceJ.

Introduction to Psychology. 7th ed. Ernest R. Hilgard et al. 653p. 1979. text ed. 22.95 o.p. (ISBN 0-15-543668-6, HC). HarBraceJ.

Introduction to Psychology. 6th ed. Clifford T. Morgan et al. (Illus.). 704p. 1979. text ed. 38.95 o.p. (ISBN 0-07-043205-8). McGraw.

Introduction to Psychology: Selected Readings. Ludy T. Benjamin, Jr. & Robert J. Warwick. 93p. 1971. pap. text ed. 5.95x o.p. (ISBN 0-8422-0152-1). Irvington.

Introduction to Psychology: Selected Readings. Ed. by O. Desiderato. 1970. pap. text ed. 8.95x o.p. (ISBN 0-8422-0096-7). Irvington.

Introduction to Psychology: Student's Workbook. 3rd ed. James O. Whittaker. 256p. 1976. 10.95 o.p. (ISBN 0-7216-9322-9). HR&W.

Introduction to Public Health. 7th ed. Daniel M. Wilner et al. (Illus.). 470p. 1978. (ISBN 0-02-428190-5, 42819). Macmillan.

Introduction to Qualified Pension & Profit Sharing Plans 1984: The tax reform act of 1986, Vol 247. (Tax Law & Estate Planning Ser.). 512p. 1986. 45.00 o.p. (ISBN 0-686-80157-1, J4-3589). PLI.

Introduction to Quantitative Cytochemistry. George Wied. 1966. 99.00 o.p. (ISBN 0-12-748850-2). Acad Pr.

Introduction to Quantitative Cytochemistry, 2. George Wied & Gunter F. Bahr. 1970. 95.50 o.p. (ISBN 0-12-748852-9). Acad Pr.

Introduction to Quantitative Ultramicroanalysis. I. M. Korenman. 1965. 65.50 o.p. (ISBN 0-12-420550-X). Acad Pr.

Introduction to Quantum Electronics. H. G. Unger. LC 76-86534. 1970. 31.00 o.p. (ISBN 0-08-006368-3). Pergamon.

Introduction to Queueing Theory. B. V. Gnedenko & I. N. Kovalenko. 296p. 1968. text ed. 58.00x o.p. (ISBN 0-7065-0602-2, Pub. by Keter Pub Jerusalem). Coronet Bks.

Introduction to Radio Frequency Design. W. H. Hayward. (Illus.). 384p. 1982. text ed. 41.00 o.p. (ISBN 0-13-494021-0). P-H.

Introduction to Radiographic Cephalometry. Ed. by Alex Jacobson & Page Caufield. LC 84-27838. (Illus.). 137p. 1985. text ed. 45.00. o.p. (ISBN 0-8121-0963-5). Lea & Febiger.

Introduction to Real Analysis. Derek S. Ball. LC 72-84200. (Mathematical Topics). (Illus.). 324p. 1973. 80.00 o.p. (ISBN 0-08-016936-8); pap. text ed. 80.00 o.p. (ISBN 0-08-016937-6). Pergamon.

Introduction to Real Estate Law. 2nd ed. Charles S. Coit. 328p. (Orig.). 1985. pap. text ed. 24.95 o.p. (ISBN 0-88462-508-7, 1594-01, Real Estate Ed). Longman Finan.

Introduction to Real Estate Law. Institute for Paralegal Training Staff. Ed. by Russell C. Bellavance & Caroline S. Laden. LC 78-7930. (Paralegal Ser.). 466p. 1978. text ed. 21.95 o.p. (ISBN 0-8299-2006-4). West Pub.

Introduction to Real Property. Cornelius J. Moynihan. (Text Ser.). 254p. 1962. 12.95 o.p. (ISBN 0-317-00038-1). West Pub.

Introduction to Regency Architecture. Paul Reilly. LC 48-10921. 98p. 1948. Repr. 29.00x o.p. (ISBN 0-403-07234-4). Somerset Pub.

Introduction to Research in Speech. John J. Auer. LC 77-5311. 1977. Repr. of 1959 ed. lib. bdg. 24.75x o.p. (ISBN 0-8371-9581-0, AUIR). Greenwood.

Introduction to Research in the Health Sciences. Polgar & Thomas. 1988. (ISBN 0-443-03607-1). Churchill.

Introduction to Satellite TV. Chris Bowick & Tim Kearney. LC 83-60159. 142p. 1983. pap. text ed. 9.95 o.p. (ISBN 0-672-21978-6). Sams.

Introduction to Scientific Research. Edgar B. Wilson. 1962. pap. text ed. 5.95 o.p. (ISBN 0-07-070846-0). McGraw.

Introduction to Scientific Research in Librarianship. Herbert Goldhor. LC 79-631732. (Monograph: No. 12). 201p. 1972. 5.00x o.p. (ISBN 0-87845-036-X). U of Ill Lib Info Sci.

Introduction to Sedimentology. 2nd ed. R. C. Selley. 1982. 25.00 o.p.; pap. (ISBN 0-12-636362-5). Acad Pr.

Introduction to Selling. An Experiential Approach to Skill Development. Richard D. Nordstrom. 350p. 1981. pap. text ed. (ISBN 0-02-388200-X). Macmillan.

Introduction to Semiconductor Theory. A. Anselm. (Illus.). 646p. 1982. text ed. 63.00 o.p. (ISBN 0-13-496034-3). P-H.

Introduction to Set Theory & Topology. 2nd, rev. ed. K. Kuratowski. 356p. 1972. text ed. 21.00 o.p. (ISBN 0-08-016160-X). Pergamon.

Introduction to Social Psychology. John T. Doby. (Illus.). 1966. 24.50x o.p. (ISBN 0-89197-245-5). Irvington.

Introduction to Social Security: A Workers Education Manual. 2nd ed. 1984. 14.00 o.p. (ISBN 92-2-103638-3). Intl Labour Office.

Introduction to Social Welfare & Social Work: Structure, Function, & Process. Beulah R. Compton. 598p. 1980. text ed. (ISBN 0-534-10506-8). Wadsworth Pub.

Introduction to Social Work. 3rd ed. Rex A. Skidmore & Milton G. Thackeray. (Illus.). 448p. 1982. text ed. (ISBN 0-13-497040-3). P-H.

Introduction to Sociology. Lewis A. Coser et al. 540p. 1983. 22.50 o.p. (ISBN 0-15-545910-4, HC). HarBraceJ.

Introduction to Sociology. B. S. Green & E. A. Johns. 1967. 14.50 o.p. (ISBN 0-08-012155-1); pap. 8.50 o.p. (ISBN 0-08-012154-3). Pergamon.

Introduction to Sociology. 2nd ed. James B. McKee. LC 73-5200. 545p. 1974. text ed. 25.00 o.p. (ISBN 0-03-091557-0, HoltC). HR&W.

Introduction to Sociology. 4th ed. Jerry D. Rose. 1980. pap. 22.95 o.p. (ISBN 0-395-30714-7). HM.

Introduction to Sociology. 3rd ed. Elbert W. Stewart & James A. Glynn. (Illus.). 1979. pap. text ed. 22.95 o.p. (ISBN 0-07-061371-0). McGraw.

Introduction to Sociology. Henry L. Tischler et al. LC 81-7091. 1983. text ed. 30.95 o.p. (ISBN 0-03-056093-4). HR&W.

Introduction to Sociology. 2nd ed. Henry L. Tischler et al. 624p. 1986. text ed. 30.95 o.p. (ISBN 0-03-002707-1, HoltC). HR&W.

Introduction to Software Quality Control. Chin-Kuei Cho. LC 80-15244. (Business Data Processing Ser.). 445p. 1980. 49.95 o.p. (ISBN 0-471-04704-X, Pub. by Wiley-Interscience). Wiley.

Introduction to Solid Mechanics. Irving H. Shames. (Illus.). 688p. 1975. text ed. 58.00 o.p. (ISBN 0-13-497503-0). P-H.

Introduction to Solid State Electronics. F. F. Wang. LC 79-188. 266p. 1979. 33.75 o.p. (ISBN 0-444-85237-9, North Holland). Elsevier.

Introduction to Spectroscopic Methods for the Identification of Organic Compounds, Vol. 1. F. Scheinmann. LC 76-99991. 1970. 55.00 o.p. (ISBN 0-08-006661-5); pap. 55.00 o.p. (ISBN 0-08-006662-3). Pergamon.

Introduction to Standard COBOL Programming. Fredric Stuart. 239p. 1974. pap. text ed. 14.95 o.p. (ISBN 0-15-545963-5, HC). HarBraceJ.

Introduction to Statics. Helen Plants & Wallace Venable. LC 74-32425. (Illus.). 1045p. 1975. text ed. 41.75 o.p. (ISBN 0-8299-0023-3). West Pub.

Introduction to Statistical Ideas for Social Scientists. G. Kalton. 58p. 1966. pap. 5.95x o.p. (ISBN 0-412-08460-0, NO. 6624, Pub. by Chapman & Hall England). Routledge Chapman & Hall.

Introduction to Statistics: A Nonparametric Approach. 2nd ed. Gottfried E. Noether. LC 75-19532. (Illus.). 336p. 1976. text ed. 30.50 o.p. (ISBN 0-395-18578-5). HM.

Introduction to Steroid Chemistry. J. R. Hanson. 1968. 35.00 o.p. (ISBN 0-08-012809-2); pap. 7.75 o.p. (ISBN 0-08-012808-4). Pergamon.

Introduction to Stochastic Integration. K. L. Chung & Ruth Williams. (Progress in Probability & Statistics Ser.: Vol. 4). 217p. 1983. text ed. 24.95 o.p. (ISBN 0-8176-3117-8). Birkhauser.

Introduction to Stochastic Processes. Paul Hoel et al. LC 79-105035. (Illus.). 1972. text ed. 35.95 o.p. (ISBN 0-395-12076-4). HM.

Introduction to Stratificational Linguistics. David G. Lockwood. 369p. 1972. pap. text ed. 12.95 o.p. (ISBN 0-15-546213-X, HC). HarBraceJ.

Introduction to Structural Psychology. Roger Mucchielli. Tr. by Charles L. Markmann. 272p. 1972. pap. 3.95 o.p. (ISBN 0-380-01283-9, 13268). Avon.

Introduction to Structured BASIC for the Cromemco C-10. Wayne T. Watson. 256p. 1984. pap. text ed. write for info. o.p. (ISBN 0-02-424580-1). Macmillan.

Introduction to Structured COBOL: With Business Applications. Thomas R. McCalla. 500p. 1984. write for info. tchr's manual o.p. Brooks-Cole.

Introduction to Structured Programming Using BASIC. Coleman Barnett. 520p. 1984. pap. text ed. 25.00x o.p. (ISBN 0-89787-402-1). Gorsuch Scarisbrick.

Introduction to Structured Programming with Pascal. Milton Underkoffler. 376p. 1983. pap. text ed. write for info. o.p. (ISBN 0-87150-394-8, 8040). PWS-Kent Pub.

Introduction to Structured Programming with PL-1 & PL-C. Milton Underkoffler. 1980. write for info. o.p. (ISBN 0-87150-292-5, 2302, Prindle). PWS-Kent Pub.

Introduction to Synthetic Array & Imaging Radars. Shahan A. Hovanessian. LC 79-27922. (Illus.). 156p. 1980. 45.00x o.p. (ISBN 0-89006-082-7). Artech Hse.

Introduction to System Safety Engineering. William P. Rodgers. LC 80-12545. 144p. 1980. Repr. of 1971 ed. lib. bdg. 17.50 o.p. (ISBN 0-89874-180-7). Krieger.

Introduction to Taxation. 10th ed. Ray M. Sommerfeld & Hershel M. Anderson. 700p. 1984. text ed. 26.00 o.p. (ISBN 0-15-546329-2, HC). HarBraceJ.

Introduction to Taxation. 2nd ed. Ray M. Sommerfeld et al. (Harbrace Business & Economics Ser.). 607p. 1972. text ed. 17.95 o.p. (ISBN 0-15-546303-9, HC). HarBraceJ.

Introduction to Taxation Advanced Topics. 2nd ed. Ray M. Sommerfeld & Hershel M. Anderson. 608p. 1982. text ed. 24.00 o.p. (ISBN 0-15-546321-7, HC). HarBraceJ.

Introduction to Taxation: Advanced Topics. Ray M. Sommerfeld et al. (Illus.). 592p. 1980. text ed. 21.95 o.p. (ISBN 0-15-546315-2, HC). HarBraceJ.

Introduction to Taxation: 1983 Edition. Ray M. Sommerfeld et al. 1982. text ed. 24.95 o.p. (ISBN 0-15-546319-5, HC); instr's. manual o.p. HarBraceJ.

Introduction to Taxation: 1983-1984 Supplement. Ray M. Sommerfeld et al. 63p. 1983. 1.95 o.p. (ISBN 0-15-546328-4, HC). HarBraceJ.

Introduction to Taxation 1986. rev. ed. James E. Parker. (Illus.). 910p. 1985. text ed. 47.25 o.p. (ISBN 0-314-85284-0). West Pub.

Introduction to Taxation, 1989. Ray M. Sommerfeld et al. 700p. 1987. text ed. write for info. o.p.; pap. text ed. 2.20 o.p. (ISBN 0-15-546332-2). HarBraceJ.

Introduction to Teaching & Learning. Denis Lawton. (Studies in Teaching & Learning). 142p. (Orig.). 1981. pap. text ed. 14.95 o.s.i. (ISBN 0-340-26077-7). Princeton Bk Co.

Introduction to Technical Drawing: Metric Edition. Norman Stirling. LC 79-56653. 370p. 1981. pap. text ed. 22.95 o.p. (ISBN 0-8273-1928-2). Delmar.

Introduction to the American Business Enterprise. 6th ed. Jerry B. Poe. 1986. 34.95x o.p. (ISBN 0-256-03361-7); review guide & wkbk. 13.95x o.p. (ISBN 0-256-03362-5). Irwin.

Introduction to the Art Song. Barbara Meister. LC 79-66640. 1980. 11.95 o.s.i. (ISBN 0-8008-4203-0, Crescendo). Taplinger.

Introduction to the Ashley Library Catalog 1922-30. Thomas J. Wise. 64p. 1985. pap. 10.00 o.p. Saifer.

Introduction to the Australian Economy. Ron Hefford et al. (Illus.). 261p. 1980. text ed. 32.50x o.p. (ISBN 0-7022-1495-7); pap. text ed. 12.00x o.p. (ISBN 0-7022-1496-5). U of Queensland Pr.

Introduction to the BIA Affairs. Jack Allen & Dennis Moristo. (American Indian Treaties Publications Ser.). 27p. 1971. pap. 2.00 o.p. (ISBN 0-935626-22-0). U Cal AISC.

Introduction to the Bible. Stanley A. Cook. LC 78-12762. 1979. Repr. of 1945 ed. lib. bdg. 35.00x o.p. (ISBN 0-313-21028-4, COIB). Greenwood.

Introduction to the Bible. Henry J. Flanders, Jr. et al. 588p. 1973. text ed. 25.75 o.p. (ISBN 0-394-34416-2, RandC). Random.

Introduction to the Biological Basis of Feeding: Essential Biological Ideas Necessary to a Study of Living Beings from the Evolutionary Standpoint. Faustino Cordon. LC 79-40933. (Illus.). 250p. 1980. pap. 41.00 o.p. (ISBN 0-08-025484-5). Pergamon.

Introduction to the Biology of Marine Life. 3rd ed. James L. Sumich. 400p. 1984. pap. text ed. write for info o.p. (ISBN 0-697-04795-4). Wm C Brown.

Introduction to the Books of the Bible. C. F. Drewes. 1929. 5.95 o.p. (ISBN 0-570-03185-0, 12-2110). Concordia.

Introduction to the Chemistry of Benzenoid Components. M. Tomlinson. 1971. 55.00 o.p. (ISBN 0-08-015659-2); pap. 55.00 o.p. (ISBN 0-08-016921-X). Pergamon.

Introduction to the Classical Guitar: An Ensemble Approach for the Classroom. Donald L. Hamann. LC 82-16100. (Illus.). 148p. (Orig.). 1983. lib. bdg. 26.25 o.p. (ISBN 0-8191-2758-2); pap. text ed. 10.00 o.p. (ISBN 0-8191-2759-0). U Pr of Amer.

Introduction to the Computer: An Integrative Approach. 2nd ed. Jeffrey E. Frates & William Molrup. (Illus.). 496p. 1984. text ed. (ISBN 0-13-480319-1). P-H.

Introduction to the Constitution of India. 10th, rev. ed. Durga D. Basu. 1984. pap. 9.00x o.p. (ISBN 0-8364-1097-1, Pub. by P-H India). South Asia Bks.

Introduction to the Cornish Language: Holeugh an Lergh. pap. 4.95 o.p. (ISBN 0-89979-022-4). British Am Bks.

Introduction to the DEC System Ten Assembler Language Programming. Michael Singer. LC 78-8586. 160p. 1978. pap. 23.45 o.p. (ISBN 0-471-03458-4, JW). Krieger.

Introduction to the Electron Theory of Solids. J. Stringer. 1967. 65.00 o.p. (ISBN 0-08-012219-1); pap. 65.00 o.p. (ISBN 0-08-012220-5). Pergamon.

Introduction to the Electron Theory of Small Molecules. A. C. Hurley. 1977. 82.50 o.p. (ISBN 0-12-362460-6). Acad Pr.

Introduction to the Fine Structure of Plant Cells. M. C. Ledbetter & K. Porter. LC 70-134021. (Illus.). 1970. 36.00 o.p. (ISBN 0-387-05195-3). Springer-Verlag.

Introduction to the Finite Element Method Using BASIC Programs. D. K. Brown. 196p. 1984. pap. 16.95 o.p. (ISBN 0-412-00581-6, NO. 9021, Pub. by Chapman & Hall); 34.00 o.p. (ISBN 0-412-00571-9, NO. 9020). Routledge Chapman & Hall.

Introduction to the Foundations of Education. 2nd ed. Allan C. Ornstein & Daniel U. Levine. 1981. text ed. 26.95 o.p. (ISBN 0-395-30690-6). HM.

Introduction to the Geometry of Numbers. 2nd ed. J. W. S. Cassels. LC 75-154801. (Grundlehren der Mathematischen Wissenschaften: Vol. 99). (Illus.). 1971. 47.00 o.p. (ISBN 0-387-02397-6). Springer-Verlag.

Introduction to the Global Society: Interdisciplinary Perspectives. Kenneth E. Boulding & Elise Boulding. (CISE Learning Package Ser.: No. 1). (Illus.). 43p. (Orig.). 1977. pap. text ed. 3.00x o.p. (ISBN 0-936876-20-4). LRIS.

Introduction to the Graphical Kernel System-GKS. Frank R. Hopgood et al. (APIC Studies in Data Processing Ser.: No. 19). 1983. 26.50 o.p. (ISBN 0-12-355570-1). Acad Pr.

Introduction to the Handbook of American Indian Languages. Franz Boas. LC 63-21768. 70p. 1963. pap. 3.95 o.p. (ISBN 0-87840-150-4). Georgetown U Pr.

Introduction to the History of Education. Richard Aldrich. (Studies in Teaching & Learning). 188p. (Orig.). 1982. pap. text ed. 16.95 o.s.i. (ISBN 0-340-26293-1). Princeton Bk Co.

Introduction to the History of Sociology. Ed. by Harry E. Barnes. LC 47-12522. 1948. lib. bdg. 30.00x o.s.i. (ISBN 0-226-03723-1). U of Chicago Pr.

Introduction to the Human Services: Developing Knowledge, Skills, & Sensitivity. Charlotte Epstein. (Illus.). 368p. 1981. text ed. (ISBN 0-13-484501-3). P-H.

Introduction to the IAPX 286: Concepts & Architecture. Intel Staff. 1984. pap. text ed. 19.95 o.p. (ISBN 0-8359-3219-2, Reston). P-H.

Introduction to the IBM Personal Computer: Keyboarding. Peter Mears. 1984. with diskette 40.45 o.p. (ISBN 0-03-064134-9). HR&W.

Introduction to the Law of Carriage of Goods by Sea. C. J. Hill. 1974. 12.50 o.s.i. (ISBN 0-540-07374-1). E J Brill USA.

Introduction to the Law of Future Interests. Ashbel G. Gulliver. 87p. 1959. pap. 4.50 o.p. (ISBN 0-314-28209-2). West Pub.

Introduction to the Liquid State. Ed. by Peter A. Egelstaff. 1967. 81.50 o.p. (ISBN 0-12-232940-6). Acad Pr.

Introduction to the Liturgy of the Lord's Supper. David E. Babin. LC 68-19700. (Orig.). 1968. pap. 1.95 o.p. (ISBN 0-8192-1000-5). Morehouse Pub.

Introduction to the Longitudinal Static Stability of Low-Speed Aircraft. F. G. Irving. 1966. 40.00 o.p. (ISBN 0-08-010741-9). Pergamon.

Introduction to the Mass Media. Fred Fedler. (Illus.). 429p. 1978. pap. text ed. 14.95 o.p. (ISBN 0-15-543470-5, HC). HarBraceJ.

Introduction to the Mathematical Theory of Coding. Ian F. Blake & Ronald C. Mullin. 1976. 32.50 o.p. (ISBN 0-12-103560-3). Acad Pr.

Introduction to the Mathematics of Finance. rev. ed. A. H. Pollard. 1978. pap. text ed. 11.00 o.p. (ISBN 0-08-021796-6). Pergamon.

Introduction to the Mechanics of Viscous Fluids. Lu. 440p. 1977. 46.00 o.p. (ISBN 0-89116-498-7). Hemisphere Pub.

Introduction to the Mechanics of Viscous Fluids. P. Lu. LC 77-3428. (Thermal & Fluids Engineering Ser.). (Illus.). 1977. Repr. of 1973 ed. text ed. 42.00 o.p. (ISBN 0-07-038907-1). McGraw.

Introduction to the Methods of Optical Crystallography. F. D. Bloss. LC 61-6759. 1961. text ed. 38.95 o.p. (ISBN 0-03-010220-0, HoltC). HR&W.

Introduction to the Microcomputer & Its Applications: PC-DOS, Wordstar, Lotus, 1-2-3 & dBASE. Chao C. Chien. (Information Systems Ser.). 1988. pap. text ed. 30.95 o.p. (ISBN 0-256-05768-0). Irwin.

Introduction to the Mocktail. 1988. 5.95 o.p. Am Bartenders.

Introduction to the New Economics. Bernard L. Cohen. 192p. 1959. (ISBN 0-8022-0276-4). Philos Lib.

Introduction to the New Testament. Edward W. Bauman. LC 61-10616. 1961. pap. 5.00 o.s.i. (ISBN 0-664-20365-5, Westminster). Westminster John Knox.

Introduction to the New Testament. Edward W. Bauman. LC 61-10616. 190p. 1979. pap. 5.95 o.s.i. (ISBN 0-664-24279-0, Westminster). Westminster John Knox.

Introduction to the New Testament. Raymond F. Collins. LC 82-45070. (Illus.). 480p. 1983. 24.95 o.s.i. (ISBN 0-385-18126-4). Doubleday.

Introduction to the New Testament: An Approach to Its Problems. Willi Marxsen. Tr. by G. Buswell from Ger. LC 68-15419. 304p. 1968. pap. 8.50 o.p. (ISBN 0-8006-1181-0, 1-1181, Fortress). Augsburg Fortress.

Introduction to the New Testament: History & Literature of Early Christianity, Vol. II. Helmut Koester. LC 82-71828. (Foundations & Facets Ser.). 400p. 1982. 22.95 o.p. (ISBN 0-8006-2101-8, 1-2101, Fortress). Augsburg Fortress.

Introduction to the New Testament: History, Culture, & Religion of the Hellenistic Age, Vol. I. Helmut Koester. LC 82-71828. (Foundations & Facets Ser.). 448p. 1982. 24.95 o.p. (ISBN 0-8006-2100-X, 1-2100, Fortress). Augsburg Fortress.

Introduction to the New Zealand Economy. Brian Easton & Norman Thomson. LC 81-19737. (Illus.). 339p. 1983. text ed. 29.50x o.p. (ISBN 0-7022-1920-7); pap. 13.50x o.p. (ISBN 0-7022-1940-1). U of Queensland Pr.

Introduction to the Numerical Solutions of Differential Equations. Douglas A. Quinney. LC 85-11842. 283p. 1985. 34.95 o.p. (ISBN 0-471-90849-5). Wiley.

Introduction to the Old Testament: A Presentation of Its Results & Problems. Otto Kaiser. Tr. by John Sturdy from Ger. LC 73-82220. 1977. pap. 14.95 o.p. (ISBN 0-8066-1575-3, 10-3386, Augsburg). Augsburg Fortress.

Introduction to the Petroleum Geology of the North Sea. Ed. by K. W. Glennie. 236p. 1984. pap. text ed. 31.00x o.p. (ISBN 0-632-01268-4, Pub. by Blackwell Sci UK). Blackwell Sci.

Introduction to the Phenomenological Theory of Ferroelectricity. J. Grindlay. LC 72-90455. 1970. 70.00 o.p. (ISBN 0-08-006362-4). Pergamon.

Introduction to the Philosophy of Education. D. J. O'Connor. 155p. 1975. 6.95 o.p. (ISBN 0-8022-1238-7). Philos Lib.

Introduction to the Philosophy of Science. rev. 2nd ed. Karel Lambert & Gordon G. Brittan, Jr. 1979. lib. bdg. 27.00 o.p. (ISBN 0-917930-37-1); pap. text ed. 9.40 o.p. (ISBN 0-917930-17-7). Ridgeview.

Introduction to the Physical Landscape: Watersheds & Fluvial Systems. Edwin D. Ongley. (CISE Learning Package Ser.: No. 21). (Illus.). 52p. (Orig.). 1976. pap. text ed. 3.00x o.p. (ISBN 0-936876-33-6). LRIS.

Introduction to the Physics of Electroweak Interactions. S. M. Bilenky. LC 81-15839. (Illus.). 250p. 1982. 87.00 o.p. (ISBN 0-08-026502-3). Pergamon.

Introduction to the Physiology of Hearing. J. O. Pickles. 1982. 21.00 o.p. (ISBN 0-12-554750-1); pap. 19.50 o.p. (ISBN 0-12-554752-8). Acad Pr.

Introduction to the Principles of Disease. 2nd ed. John B. Walter. (Illus.). 686p. 1983. write for info. o.p. (ISBN 0-7216-9121-8); write for info. study guide o.p. (ISBN 0-7216-9118-8). Saunders.

Introduction to the Principles of Drug Design. H. J. Smith & H. Williams. (Illus.). 384p. 1983. pap. 28.00 o.p. (ISBN 0-7236-0672-2). Butterworth.

Introduction to the Principles of Morals & Legislation. Jeremy Bentham & H. L. Hart. 385p. 1982. 14.95x o.p. (ISBN 0-416-31910-6, NO. 3710). Routledge Chapman & Hall.

Introduction to the Principles of Plant Physiology. 3rd ed. W. Stiles. 633p. 1969. 45.00x o.p. (ISBN 0-416-41850-3, NO.6275). Routledge Chapman & Hall.

Introduction to the Properties of Crystal Surfaces. Jack Blakely. 1973. 24.00 o.p. (ISBN 0-08-017641-0). Pergamon.

Introduction to the Psychology of Language. Peter Herriott. 1976. pap. 8.50x o.p. (ISBN 0-416-85500-8, NO.2750). Routledge Chapman & Hall.

Introduction to the Raj Quartet. Janis Tedesco & Janet Popham. LC 85-623. 296p. (Orig.). 1985. lib. bdg. 30.25 o.p. (ISBN 0-8191-4570-X); pap. text ed. 14.50 o.p. (ISBN 0-8191-4571-8). U Pr of Amer.

Introduction to the Reformed Tradition: A Way of Being the Christian Community. John H. Leith. 1977. 10.00 o.p. (ISBN 0-8042-0471-3, John Knox). Westminster John Knox.

Introduction to the Regenerative Method for Simulation Analysis. A. Crane & J. Lemoine. (Lecture Notes in Control & Information Sciences: Vol. 4). 1977. pap. text ed. 9.70 o.p. (ISBN 0-387-08408-8). Springer-Verlag.

Introduction to the Relativistic String Theory. B. M. Barbashov & V. V. Nesterenko. Tr. by T. Y. Dumbrajs. 300p. 1989. 46.00 o.p. (ISBN 9971-50-687-4). World Scientific Pub.

Introduction to the Science of Missions. J. H. Bavinck. 1977. pap. 8.95 o.p. (ISBN 0-8010-0600-7). Baker Bk.

Introduction to the Science of Sociology. abr. ed. Robert W. Park & Ernest W. Burgess. Ed. by Morris Janowitz. LC 71-126075. 1970. pap. text ed. 4.75 o.s.i. (ISBN 0-226-64606-8, P380, Phoen). U of Chicago Pr.

Introduction to the Sociology of Learning. Sarane S. Boocock. LC 72-7924. (Illus.). 1972. text ed. 17.50 o.p. (ISBN 0-395-12565-0, 3-04930). HM.

Introduction to the Sources of European Economic History, 1500-1800. Ed. by Charles Wilson & Geoffrey Parker. LC 76-55851. (World Economic History Ser.). (Illus.). 296p. 1978. 32.50x o.p. (ISBN 0-8014-1109-2). Cornell U Pr.

Introduction to the Spectroscopy of Biological Polymers. Ed. by D. W. Jones. 1977. 82.50 o.p. (ISBN 0-12-389250-3). Acad Pr.

Introduction to the Statistical Analysis of Data. Theodore W. Anderson & Stanley L. Sclove. LC 77-78890. (Illus.). 1978. text ed. 30.50 o.p. (ISBN 0-395-15045-0). HM.

Introduction to the Statistical Theory of Classical Simple Dense Fluids. G. H. Cole. 1967. 75.00 o.p. (ISBN 0-08-010397-9). Pergamon.

Introduction to the Study of Fabrics of Geological Bodies. B. Sander. 1970. 145.00 o.p. (ISBN 0-08-006660-7). Pergamon.

Introduction to the Study of Society. Albion Small & George Vincent. (Reprint in Sociology Ser.). (Illus.). 1982. pap. text ed. 7.95 o.p. (ISBN 0-8290-1204-4). Irvington.

Introduction to the Technology of Pottery. P. Rado. LC 79-90454. 1969. text ed. 33.00 o.p. (ISBN 0-08-006458-2); pap. text ed. 11.25 o.p. (ISBN 0-08-006457-4). Pergamon.

Introduction to the Theology of Rudolf Bultmann. Walter Schmithals. Tr. by John Bowden. 1968. 6.50 o.p. (ISBN 0-8066-0816-1, 10-3390, Augsburg). Augsburg Fortress.

Introduction to the Theory & Context of Accounting. 2nd ed. R. Sidebotham. 1970. pap. text ed. 9.50 o.p. (ISBN 0-08-015619-3). Pergamon.

Introduction to the Theory & Practice of Econometrics. George G. Judge et al. LC 81-16249. (Probability & Mathematical Statistics Ser.). 839p. 1982. 46.95 o.p. (ISBN 0-471-08277-5). Wiley.

Introduction to the Theory of Algebraic Numbers & Functions. Martin Eichler. (Pure & Applied Mathematics: Vol. 23). 1966. 76.00 o.p. (ISBN 0-12-233650-X). Acad Pr.

Introduction to the Theory of Analytic Spaces. R. Narasimhan. (Lecture Notes in Mathematics: Vol. 25). 1966. pap. 10.70 o.p. (ISBN 0-387-03608-3). Springer-Verlag.

Introduction to the Theory of Atomic Spectra. I. I. Sobel'man. 632p. 1972. 155.00 o.p. (ISBN 0-08-016166-9). Pergamon.

Introduction to the Theory of Computation. Erwin Engeler. (Computer Science & Applied Mathematics Ser). 1973. text ed. 19.25 o.p. (ISBN 0-12-239250-7). Acad Pr.

Introduction to the Theory of Diffraction. C. J. Ball. 1971. text ed. 30.00 o.p. (ISBN 0-08-015787-4); pap. text ed. 12.75 o.p. (ISBN 0-08-015786-6). Pergamon.

Introduction to the Theory of Economic Growth. R. Ramanathan. (Lecture Notes in Economics & Mathematical Systems: Vol. 205). (Illus.). 347p. 1982. pap. 32.50 o.p. (ISBN 0-387-11943-4). Springer-Verlag.

Introduction to the Theory of Experimental Design. David J. Finney. LC 60-8126. (Midway Reprint Ser.). 1975. pap. text ed. 9.00x o.s.i. (ISBN 0-226-25000-8). U of Chicago Pr.

Introduction to the Theory of Flight of Artificial Earth Satellites. P. E. El'yasberg. 356p. 1967. text ed. 70.00 o.p. (ISBN 0-7065-0477-1, Pub. by Keter Pub Jerusalem). Coronet Bks.

Introduction to the Theory of Heavy-Ion Collisions. W. Norenberg & H. A. Weidenmuller. (Lecture Notes in Physics: Vol. 51). (Illus.). 1980. soft cover 23.00 o.p. (ISBN 0-387-09753-8). Springer-Verlag.

Introduction to the Theory of Kinetic Equations. Richard L. Liboff. LC 76-30383. (Illus.). 410p. 1979. Repr. of 1969 ed. lib. bdg. 26.00 o.p. (ISBN 0-88275-496-3). Krieger.

Introduction to the Theory of Magnetism. D. Wagner. 290p. 1972. 75.00 o.p. (ISBN 0-08-016595-8). Pergamon.

Introduction to the Theory of Matroids. R. Von Randow. (Lecture Notes Economics & Mathematics System Ser.: Vol. 109). ix, 102p. 1975. pap. 11.00 o.p. (ISBN 0-387-07177-6). Springer-Verlag.

Introduction to the Theory of Music. Howard Boatwright. (Illus.). 1956. 16.95x o.p. (ISBN 0-393-02057-6, NortonC). Norton.

Introduction to the Theory of Plasma Turbulence. V. N. Tsytovich. 142p. 1972. text ed. 32.00 o.p. (ISBN 0-08-016587-7). Pergamon.

Introduction to the Theory of Shells. Clive L. Dym. LC 73-13563. 172p. 1973. text ed. 32.00 o.p. (ISBN 0-08-017784-0); pap. text ed. 17.50 o.p. (ISBN 0-08-017785-9). Pergamon.

Introduction to the Theory of Similarity. A. A. Gukhman. 1965. 33.50 o.p. (ISBN 0-12-305450-8). Acad Pr.

Introduction to the Therapeutic Process. Jack E. Hokanson. (Illus.). 416p. 1983. text ed. 19.00 o.p. (ISBN 0-394-34788-9, RanC). Random.

Introduction to the UCSD p-System. Charles W. Grant & Jon Butah. LC 81-50655. (Illus.). 300p. 1982. pap. 19.95 o.p. (ISBN 0-89588-061-X, P370). SYBEX.

Introduction to the Use of Computers in Law. Mary Ann Mason. LC 83-27743. 223p. 1984. pap. text ed. 11.95 o.p. (ISBN 0-314-80352-1). West Pub.

Introduction to Theology: An Invitation to Reflection Upon the Christian Mythos. Theodore W. Jennings, Jr. LC 76-7867. 192p. 1976. pap. 3.00 o.p. (ISBN 0-8006-1234-5, 1-1234, Fortress). Augsburg Fortress.

Introduction to Theories of Learning. 2nd ed. B. R. Hergenhahn. 512p. 1982. text ed. (ISBN 0-13-498725-X). P-H.

Introduction to Theories of Personality. Robert B. Ewen. 1980. 22.25i o.p. (ISBN 0-12-245150-3). Acad Pr.

Introduction to Theories of Personality. 2nd ed. Robert B. Ewen. 595p. 1985. text ed. 26.00 net o.p. (ISBN 0-15-546360-8, EWEN2, HC, HC). HarBraceJ.

Introduction to Topology. Yu. Borisovich et al. 316p. 1985. 9.95 o.p. (ISBN 0-8285-3376-8, Pub. by Mir Pubs USSR). Imported Pubns.

Introduction to Trade-Mark Law in the Benelux. W. Mak & H. Molijn. 140p. pap. write for info. o.p. (ISBN 90-6544-021-6). Kluwer Academic.

Introduction to Transportation. Donald J. Bowersox et al. 1981. text ed. write for info. o.p. (ISBN 0-02-313030-X). Macmillan.

Introduction to TRS-80 Data Files. John D. Adams. 102p. (Orig.). 1984. spiral binding 24.95 o.p. (ISBN 0-88006-066-2, CC7398). Wayne Green Ent.

Introduction to Tudor Architecture. John H. Harvey. LC 50-621. 1949. Repr. 39.00x o.p. (ISBN 0-403-07232-8). Somerset Pub.

Introduction to Tudor Drama. Frederick S. Boas. LC 76-50079. (Illus.). 1977. Repr. of 1933 ed. lib. bdg. 24.75x o.p. (ISBN 0-8371-9073-8, BOIT). Greenwood.

Introduction to Turbo Pascal. Douglas S. Stivison. LC 85-71778. 268p. 1985. pap. 16.95 o.p. (ISBN 0-89588-269-8). SYBEX.

Introduction to Turbo Pascal. 2nd ed. Douglas S. Stivison. 386p. (Orig.). 1987. pap. 19.95 o.p. (ISBN 0-89588-414-3). Sybex.

Introduction to Turbo Prolog. Carl Townsend. 315p. (Orig.). 1986. pap. 21.95 o.p. (ISBN 0-89588-359-7). Sybex.

Introduction to UNIX System V. R. A. Byers. 1985. pap. text ed. 17.95 o.p. (ISBN 0-07-912629-4). McGraw.

Introduction to Variational Methods in Control Engineering. A. R. Noton. 1965. 11.75 o.p. (ISBN 0-08-011365-6); pap. text ed. 8.25 o.p. (ISBN 0-08-013584-6). Pergamon.

Introduction to Vector Analysis. 6th ed. B. Hague. 1970. pap. 6.95x o.p. (ISBN 0-412-20730-3, NO.6137, Pub. by Chapman & Hall). Routledge Chapman & Hall.

Introduction to Virology. K. M. Smith & D. A. Ritchie. 250p. 1980. 18.95x o.p. (ISBN 0-412-21960-3, NO.2888, Pub by Chapman & Hall England); pap. 18.95x o.p. (ISBN 0-412-21970-0, NO.2889). Routledge Chapman & Hall.

Introduction to Viscous Flow. William F. Hughes. LC 78-14471. (Illus.). 1979. text ed. 45.95 o.p. (ISBN 0-07-031130-7). McGraw.

Introduction to West African Economics. H. W. Ord & I. Livingstone. 1969. pap. text ed. 13.00x o.p. (ISBN 0-435-97430-0). Heinemann Ed.

Introduction to Word Processing. Hal Glatzer. LC 81-84004. (Illus.). 205p. 1981. pap. 9.95 o.p. (ISBN 0-89588-076-8, W101). SYBEX.

Introduction to WordStar. Arthur Naiman. 1982. pap. 11.95 o.p. (ISBN 0-89588-077-6). Sybex.

Introduction to Yoga Principles & Practices. Sachindra K. Majumdar. (Illus.). 1965. 7.50 o.p. (ISBN 0-8216-0101-6, Pub. by Univ Bks). CArol Pub Group.

Introduction to Zen Buddhism. D. T. Suzuki. 1964. pap. 4.50 o.p. (ISBN 0-394-17474-7, B341, BC). Grove.

Introduction to Zen Buddhism. D. T. Suzuki. 1952. (ISBN 0-8022-1677-3). Philos Lib.

Introduction to Zoology. T. H. Savory. 230p. 1968. (ISBN 0-8022-2261-7). Philos Lib.

Introductions to Shakespeare. Peter Alexander. (Orig.). 1964. pap. 1.25 o.p. (ISBN 0-393-00216-0, Norton Lib). Norton.

Introductory Algebra. D. Franklin Wright & Bill New. 1978. text ed. write for info. o.p. (ISBN 0-87150-245-3, PWS 1991, Prindle). PWS-Kent Pub.

Introductory Algebra: An Applied Approach. Richard N. Aufmann & Vernon C. Barker. LC 82-82886. 512p. 1984. pap. 28.95 o.p. (ISBN 0-395-32593-5). HM.

Introductory Astronomy. Sidgwick. (ISBN 0-8022-1567-X). Philos Lib.

Introductory Astronomy & Astrophysics. Elske P. Smith & Kenneth C. Jacobs. LC 72-88853. (Illus.). 480p. 1973. text ed. 36.95 o.p. (ISBN 0-7216-8387-8). HR&W.

Introductory Atlas: Economics, Commerce & Administration, a Visual Analysis, Vol. 1. N. Skene Smith. 1966. 45.00 o.p. (ISBN 0-08-010966-7). Pergamon.

Introductory Business Management Simulation: Guide for Participants. 2nd ed. M. Archer & C. Dakin. 144p. 1983. text ed. 10.95 o.p. (ISBN 0-07-548540-0). McGraw.

Introductory Calculus with Applications. 2nd ed. Jogindar Ratti & Manoug Manougian. LC 76-13096. (Illus.). 1977. text ed. 20.50 o.p. (ISBN 0-395-24545-1). HM.

Introductory Chemistry for Health Professionals. Ken Liska & Lucy T. Pryde. 1983. text ed. write for info. o.p. (ISBN 0-02-370980-4). Macmillan.

Introductory Chemistry Laboratory Manual. Anthony V. Guzzo. 192p. wire coil 17.95 o.p. (ISBN 0-8403-3657-8). Kendall-Hunt.

Introductory College Mathematics: Consumer Mathematics. Robert D. Hackworth & Joseph Howland. LC 75-23617. 67p. 1976. pap. text ed. 10.95 o.p. (ISBN 0-7216-4410-4). HR&W.

Introductory College Mathematics: Probability. Robert D. Hackworth & Joseph Howland. LC 75-23624. 80p. 1976. pap. text ed. 11.95 o.p. (ISBN 0-7216-4417-1). HR&W.

Introductory College Mathematics: Tables & Graphs. Robert D. Hackworth & Joseph Howland. LC 75-23628. (Illus.). 62p. 1976. pap. text ed. 10.95 o.p. (ISBN 0-7216-4421-X). HR&W.

Introductory Course in Teaching & Training Methods for Management Development. 277p. 1981. 26.95x o.p. (ISBN 9-2210-1006-6). Intl Pubns Serv.

Introductory Course on Theory & Practice of Mechanical Vibrations. J. S. Rao & K. Gupta. LC 84-5225. 395p. 1985. 44.95 o.p. (ISBN 0-470-20076-6). Wiley.

Introductory Economics. Ed. by Michael Veseth. LC 81-166410. 1981. 32.40i o.p. (ISBN 0-12-719565-3). Acad Pr.

Introductory Foods: A Laboratory Manual of Food Preparation & Evaluation. 3rd ed. Mary L. Morr & Theodore F. Irmiter. (Illus.). 1980. pap. text ed. write for info. o.p. (ISBN 0-02-384120-6). Macmillan.

Introductory Group Theory & Its Applications to Molecular Structure. 2nd ed. John R. Ferraro & Joseph S. Ziomek. LC 75-33752. 292p. 1975. 39.50x o.p. (ISBN 0-306-30768-5, Plenum Pr). Plenum Pub.

Introductory Horticulture. H. Edward Reiley & Carroll L. Shry, Jr. LC 77-81006. 1979. pap. text ed. 27.95 o.p. (ISBN 0-8273-1893-6); instr's. guide 6.16 o.p. (ISBN 0-8273-1645-3). Delmar.

Introductory Horticulture. 2nd ed. H. Edward Reiley & Carroll L. Shry, Jr. LC 82-73367. 640p. 1983. text ed. 24.95 o.p. (ISBN 0-8273-2198-8). Delmar.

Introductory Language Essays. Ed. by Dudley Bailey. 1965. pap. 3.95x o.p. (ISBN 0-393-09643-2, NortonC). Norton.

Introductory Lectures on Psychoanalysis. Sigmund Freud. Tr. by James Strachey. 1979. 13.98 o.p. (ISBN 0-87140-637-3). Liveright.

Introductory Management Science. Gary D. Eppen & Floyd J. Gould. (Illus.). 736p. 1984. pap. text ed. (ISBN 0-13-501973-7). P-H.

Introductory Mathematics for the Clinical Laboratory. Kanai L. Mukherjee. LC 78-10915. (Illus.). 139p. 1979. pap. text ed. 12.00 o.p. (ISBN 0-89189-069-6, 45-9-006-00). Am Soc Clinical.

Introductory Methods of Numerical Analysis. 2nd ed. S. S. Sastry. (Illus.). 212p. 1985. pap. text ed. 22.33 o.p. (ISBN 0-13-501503-0). P-H.

Introductory Microeconomics. Michael Veseth. 362p. 1981. pap. text ed. 19.00 net o.p. (ISBN 0-15-543472-1, VMIC2, HC). HarBraceJ.

Introductory Musicianship: A Workbook. Theodore A. Lynn. 246p. 1979. pap. 14.95 text-wkbk. o.p. (ISBN 0-15-543551-5, HC). HarBraceJ.

Introductory Musicianship: A Workbook. 2nd ed. Theodore A. Lynn. 250p. 1984. pap. text ed. 16.00 o.p. (ISBN 0-15-543552-3, HC). HarBraceJ.

Introductory Nuclear Reactor Statics. Karl O. Ott & Winfred A. Bezella. LC 83-15466. 1983. 48.00 o.p. (ISBN 0-89448-026-X, 350009). Am Nuclear Soc.

Introductory Nutrition. 6th ed. Guthrie. 1986. 39.95 o.p. (ISBN 0-8016-2038-4). Mosby.

Introductory Organic Chemistry. J. T. Gerig. 1974. 19.00 o.p. (ISBN 0-12-280750-2). Acad Pr.

Introductory Phototypesetting. Leslie G. Heath & Ian Faux. (Illus.). 230p. 1980. 40.00 o.p. (ISBN 0-88362-063-4, 1519). Graphic Arts Tech Found.

Introductory Physics: A Problem-Solving Approach. Jesse D. Wall. 1977. text ed. 26.00 o.p. (ISBN 0-669-00188-0). Heath.

Introductory Plant Biology. 3rd ed. Kingsley Stern. 672p. 1985. write for info. o.p. (ISBN 0-697-00737-5); pap. text ed. write for info. o.p. (ISBN 0-697-05024-6); instr's. manual avail. o.p. (ISBN 0-697-05117-X); lab manual avail. o.p. (ISBN 0-697-04930-2); transparencies avail. o.p. (ISBN 0-697-04943-4). Wm C Brown.

Introductory Psychology. 3rd ed. Walter M. Vernon. 1980. text ed. 33.50 o.p. (ISBN 0-395-30845-3). HM.

Introductory Psychology: The Modern View. 2nd ed. Douglas W. Matheson. LC 81-2204. (Illus.). 416p. 1982. pap. text ed. 18.95x o.s.i. (ISBN 0-88295-213-7). Harlan Davidson.

Introductory Psychology Through Science Fiction. 2nd ed. Harvey A. Katz & Patricia Warrick. 1977. pap. 16.95 o.p. (ISBN 0-395-30816-X). HM.

Introductory Readings in Educational Measurement. Ed. by Victor H. Noll et al. LC 73-169902. (Illus., Orig.). 1972. pap. 10.95 o.p. (ISBN 0-395-05005-7, 3-41295). HM.

Introductory Readings on Language. 4th ed. Ed. by W. L. Anderson & Norman C. Stageberg. LC 74-16229. 1975. pap. text ed. 17.95 o.p. (ISBN 0-03-089578-2, HoltC). HR&W.

Introductory Soil Science: A Laboratory Manual. R. H. Beck et al. (Illus.). 276p. 1984. 10.80x o.p. (ISBN 0-87563-222-X). Stipes.

Introductory Soil Science: A Study Guide & Laboratory Manual. Leon J. Johnson. (Illus.). 1979. pap. text ed. write for info. o.p. (ISBN 0-02-361120-0). Macmillan.

Introductory Soils Laboratory Handbook. Orton C. Butler. 1979. 8.00 o.p. (ISBN 0-682-49169-1, University). Exposition-Phoenix.

Introductory Spanish. Donald D. Walsh. 1946. 5.95x o.p. (ISBN 0-393-09454-5, NortonC). Norton.

Introductory Spatial Analysis. David Unwin. (Illus.). 1982. 32.00x o.p. (ISBN 0-416-72190-7, NO. 3576); pap. 13.95x o.p. (ISBN 0-416-72200-8, NO. 3575). Routledge Chapman & Hall.

Introductory Statistical Analysis. Theodore W. Anderson & Stanley L. Sclove. (Illus.). 512p. 1974. text ed. 18.50 o.p. (ISBN 0-395-14015-3). HM.

Introductory Statistics. 2nd ed. M. H. Quenouille. 1950. pap. 15.25 o.p. (ISBN 0-08-013783-0). Pergamon.

Introductory Statistics: A Microcomputer Approach. Freeman F. Elzey. LC 84-12722. (Statistics Ser.). 260p. 1984. pap. text ed. 27.00 pub net o.p. (ISBN 0-534-03280-X). Brooks-Cole.

Introductory Statistics: A Service Course. A. H. Pollard. 1973. pap. 65.00 o.p. (ISBN 0-08-017352-7). Pergamon.

Introductory Statistics for Psychology. Thorne. LC 79-10613. 1980. text ed. write for info. o.p. (ISBN 0-87872-222-X, Duxbury Pr). PWS-Kent Pub.

Introductory Statistics for Psychology: The Logic & the Methods. Gustav Levine. LC 80-81254. 1981. 27.00i o.p. (ISBN 0-12-445480-1). Acad Pr.

Introductory Statistics with Applications. Wayne W. Daniel. LC 76-10897. (Illus.). 1977. text ed. 42.76 o.p. (ISBN 0-395-24430-7). HM.

Introductory Structured COBOL Programming. Gary S. Popkin. LC 80-51061. 471p. 1981. pap. text ed. 19.95x o.p. (ISBN 0-534-23166-7). PWS-Kent Pub.

Introductory Textile Manual. June Grossbart et al. LC 81-40721. (Illus.). 110p. (Orig.). 1982. pap. text ed. 11.00 o.p. (ISBN 0-8191-1897-4). U Pr of Amer.

Introductory Theological Wordbook. Iris V. Cully & Kendig B. Cully. 1964. pap. 2.25 o.s.i. (ISBN 0-664-24475-0, Westminster). Westminster John Knox.

Intruders: The Incredible Visitations at Copley Woods. Budd Hopkins. LC 86-29806. (Illus.). 288p. 1987. 17.45 o.s.i. (ISBN 0-394-56076-0). Random.

Intuition Through the Ages. Helene A. Gerling. 1972. 3.00 o.p. (ISBN 0-682-47410-X). Exposition-Phoenix.

Intuitive Manager. Roy Rowan. 1986. 15.95 o.p. (ISBN 0-316-75974-0). Little.

Inuit Youth: Growth & Change in the Canadian Arctic, Vol. 1. Richard Condon. (Adolescents Ser.). 275p. 1987. text ed. 32.00 o.p. (ISBN 0-8135-1212-3). Rutgers U Pr.

Invaders from Dark Land. Lynn Beach. (Wizards, Warriors & You Ser.: No. 15). 112p. 1986. pap. 2.95 o.p. (ISBN 0-380-75043-0). Avon.

Invariant Manifolds. M. W. Hirsch et al. (Lecture Notes in Mathematics: Vol. 583). 1977. soft cover 13.00 o.p. (ISBN 0-387-08148-8). Springer-Verlag.

Invariant Theory. T. A. Springer. LC 77-5890. (Lecture Notes in Mathematics: Vol. 585). 1980. pap. 13.00 o.p. (ISBN 0-387-08242-5). Springer-Verlag.

Invariant Wave Equations: Proceedings of the International School of Mathematical Physics, Erice, Italy, June 27-July 9, 1977. International School of Mathematical Physics Staff. Ed. by G. Velo & A. S. Wightman. (Lecture Notes in Physics Ser.: Vol. 73). 1978. pap. 25.00 o.s.i. (ISBN 0-387-08655-2). Springer-Verlag.

Invasion. Frank McLynn. 224p. 1987. 39.95 o.p. (ISBN 0-7102-0736-0, Pub. by Routledge UK). Routledge Chapman & Hall.

Invasion from the East. Howard A. Wilson. LC 78-52203. 1978. pap. 5.95 o.p. (ISBN 0-8066-1671-7, 10-3393, Augsburg). Augsburg Fortress.

Invasion of the Creepy Crawlies. (Danger Mouse Lift-the-Flap Bks.). 16p. (gr. k-3). 1986. 5.70i o.p. (ISBN 0-316-14713-3). Little.

Invasion of the Mutants. Caroline Cooney. (Which Way Bk.: No. 17). (gr. 6 up). 23.95 o.p. Archway.

Invasion of the Mutants. Stephen Mooser. (Which Way Bk.: No. 17). (Orig.). (gr. 3-6). 1985. pap. 1.95 o.p. (ISBN 0-671-52634-0). Archway.

Invented Lives: The Marriage of F. Scott & Zelda Fitzgerald. James R. Mellow. (Illus.). 569p. 1984. 22.00 o.s.i. (ISBN 0-395-34412-3). HM.

Inventing Ivanov. Roberta Smoodin. LC 84-45035. 320p. 1985. 15.95 o.s.i. (ISBN 0-689-11495-8, Atheneum). Macmillan.

Invention & Economic Growth. Jacob Schmookler. LC 66-14453. 1966. 24.50x o.s.i. (ISBN 0-674-46400-1). Harvard U Pr.

Invention of Morel & Other Stories. Adolfo Bioy Casares. 1964. pap. (ISBN 0-292-73280-5). U of Tex Pr.

Invention of the World. Hodgins. 1978. 8.95 o.p. (ISBN 0-15-145281-4). HarBraceJ.

Invention Protection for Practicing Engineers. Tom Arnold & Frank S. Vaden. LC 73-133266. 1983. 21.95 o.p. (ISBN 0-8436-0312-7); pap. 15.95 o.p. (ISBN 0-8436-0313-5). Van Nos Reinhold.

Inventive Universe. K. G. Denbigh. LC 75-13561. 220p. 1975. 8.95 o.p. (ISBN 0-8076-0802-5). Braziller.

Inventories & Foreign Currency Translation Requirements. Kathleen R. Bindon. Ed. by Richard N. Farmer. LC 82-21729. (Research for Business Decisions: No. 56). 158p. 1983. 42.95 o.p. (ISBN 0-8357-1391-1). Univ Microfilms.

Inventors Behind the Inventor. Roger Burlingame. LC 47-31023. (gr. 7 up). 1965. 4.95 o.p. (ISBN 0-15-238806-0, HJ); pap. 0.60 o.p. (ISBN 0-15-645326-6). HarBraceJ.

Inventory & Production Decisions. Mansfield W. Williams. Ed. by Fred Bateman. LC 83-18179. (Research in Business Economics & Public Policy Ser.: No. 7). 196p. 1984. 42.95 o.p. (ISBN 0-8357-1446-2). UMI Res Pr.

Inventory Control Abstracts: 1953-1965. S. Eilon & W. Lampkin. 1968. 14.70 o.p. (ISBN 0-934454-53-1). Lubrecht & Cramer.

Inventory Design & Analysis. Ed. by W. E. Frayer et al. (Illus.). 368p. 1974. pap. 6.50 o.p. (ISBN 0-939970-11-2). Soc Am Foresters.

Inventory Management Factomatic-A Portfolio of Successful Forms, Reports, Records & Procedures. Robert S. Kuehne & R. Jerry Baker. (Illus.). 1978. text ed. 54.95 o.p. (ISBN 0-13-502369-6, Busn). P-H.

Inventory of Educational Innovations in Asia & the Pacific: EIA, Nos. 131-144. 62p. 1983. pap. 6.50 o.p. (ISBN 0-686-44009-9, UB116, UB). UNIPUB.

Inventory of Educational Innovations in Asia & the Pacific: EIA, Nos. 145-172. 150p. 1981. pap. 8.75 o.p. (ISBN 0-686-44011-0, UB118, UB). UNIPUB.

Inverse Problems in Quantum Scattering Theory. K. Chadan & P. C. Sabatier. (Texts & Monographs in Physics). (Illus.). 1977. 53.90 o.p. (ISBN 0-387-08092-9). Springer-Verlag.

Inversions: A Catalog of Calligraphic Cartwheels. Scott Kim. 125p. 1985. pap. 9.95 o.p. (ISBN 0-262-61041-8, 00277216, Pub. by Bradford). MIT Pr.

Invertebrate Cell Culture Applications. Ed. by Karl Maramorosch & Jun Mitsuhashi. 245p. 1982. 35.00 o.p. (ISBN 0-12-470290-2). Acad Pr.

Invertebrate Endocrinology & Hormonal Heterophylly. Ed. by W. J. Burdette. (Illus.). 438p. 1974. 39.00 o.p. (ISBN 0-387-06594-6). Springer-Verlag.

Invertebrate Immune Defense Mechanisms. Ronald T. Acton et al. 1973. 23.50x o.p. (ISBN 0-8422-7054-X). Irvington.

Invertebrate Immunity: Mechanisms of Invertebrate Vector-Parasite Relations. Ed. by Karl Maramorosch. 1975. 65.50 o.p. (ISBN 0-12-470265-1). Acad Pr.

Invertebrate Neurons & Behavior. Ed. by C. A. Wiersma. 100p. 1976. pap. text ed. 8.95x o.p. (ISBN 0-262-73045-6). MIT Pr.

Invertebrate Oogenesis, Vol. 2. Meredith Gould et al. 300p. 1972. 32.50x o.p. (ISBN 0-8422-7030-2). Irvington.

Invertebrate Oogenesis, Vol. 1: Interactions Between Oocytes & Their Accessory Cells. Robert King et al. 277p. 1972. text ed. 32.50x o.p. (ISBN 0-8422-7015-9). Irvington.

Invertebrate Pathology: Noncommunicable Diseases. Albert K. Sparks. 1972. 74.00 o.p. (ISBN 0-12-656450-7). Acad Pr.

Invertebrate Photoreceptors: A Comparative Analysis. Jerome J. Wolken. 1971. 39.50 o.p. (ISBN 0-12-762350-7). Acad Pr.

Invertebrate Tissue Culture. C. Vago. 1971-72. Vol. 1. 68.00 o.p. (ISBN 0-12-709901-8); Vol. 2, 1972. 68.00 o.p. (ISBN 0-12-709902-6). Acad Pr.

Invertebrate Tissue Culture: Applications in Medicine, Biology & Agriculture. Ed. by Edouard Kurstak & Karl Marqmorosch. 1976. 65.50 o.p. (ISBN 0-12-429740-4). Acad Pr.

Invertebrate Zoology. 4th ed. Robert D. Barnes. 1980. text ed. 48.00 o.s.i. (CBS C). SCP.

Invertebrate Zoology. 4th ed. Robert L. Barnes. LC 77-16997. (Illus.). 1090p. 1980. 41.95 o.p. HR&W.

Invertebrate Zoology. 3rd ed. Joseph G. Engemann & Robert W. Hegner. 1981. text ed. write for info. o.p. (ISBN 0-02-333780-X). Macmillan.

Invest in Yourself: A Woman's Guide to Starting Her Own Business. Peg Moran. LC 82-45967. (Illus.). 208p. 1984. pap. 9.95 o.p. (ISBN 0-385-18798-X). Doubleday.

Investigating Crimes: An Introduction. Alfred R. Stone & Stuart M. Deluca. LC 79-88446. (Illus.). 1980. text ed. 30.50 o.p. (ISBN 0-395-28525-9). HM.

Investigating Graphs. Ed Catherall. LC 82-19886. (Investigating Mathematics Ser.). (Illus.). 32p. (gr. 3-6). PLB 11.67 o.p. (ISBN 0-516-02281-4). Childrens.

Investigating Rape: A New Approach for Police. Ian Blair. LC 84-23802. 110p. 1985. 26.00 o.p. (ISBN 0-7099-2098-9, Pub. by Croom Helm Ltd). Routledge Chapman & Hall.

Investigating Your Health. new ed. Benjamin F. Miller et al. LC 74-111257. (Illus.). 564p. 1974. text ed. 28.36 o.p. (ISBN 0-395-17078-8). HM.

Investigation, Findings & Recommendations: Special Commission on Social Security Disability in the Commonwealth of Massachusetts. Special Commission on Social Security Disability. 84p. cancelled o.s.i. (36,068). NCLS Inc.

Investigation of Fire & Explosion Accidents in the Chemical, Mining, & Fuel-Related Industries. Joseph M. Kuchta. LC 85-600188. (Illus.). 90p. 1986. pap. 4.50 o.p. (ISBN 0-318-21342-7, S/N 024-004-02167-5). USGPO.

Investigation of Fires. Charles L. Roblee & Al McKechnie. 1981. pap. text ed. 33.00 o.p. (ISBN 0-13-503169-9). P-H.

Investigation of Nuclear Structure by Scattering Processes at High Energies: Proceedings. International School of Nuclear Physics, Sept 23-30, 1974. Ed. by H. Schopper. 360p. 1975. 42.00 o.p. (ISBN 0-444-10887-4, North-Holland). Elsevier.

Investigation of Oncogenic Viruses, Vol. 1. George J. Todaro et al. 234p. 1974. text ed. 29.50x o.p. (ISBN 0-8422-7234-8). Irvington.

Investigation of Oncogenic Viruses, Vol. 2. Martin S. Hirsch et al. 272p. 1974. text ed. 32.50x o.p. (ISBN 0-8422-7235-6). Irvington.

Investigation of Ralph Nader. Thomas Whiteside. LC 72-79452. Orig. Title: Ralph Nader. 1972. 7.95 o.p. (ISBN 0-87795-034-2, Arbor Hse). Morrow.

Investigation of Rate & Mechanisms of Reactions, Vol. 6, Pt. 2. 3rd ed. Gordon G. Hammes. LC 73-8850. (Techniques of Chemistry Ser.). 665p. 1974. 100.95 o.p. (ISBN 0-471-93127-6, Pub. by Wiley-Interscience). Wiley.

Investigation of Rates & Mechanisms of Reactions, Vol. 6, Pt. 1. 3rd ed. Ed. by Edward S. Lewis. LC 74-8850. 852p. 1974. 71.50 o.p. (ISBN 0-471-93095-4, John Wiley). Krieger.

Investigation of the Bottom Three Hundred Meter Layer of the Atmosphere. N. L. Byzova. 120p. 1965. text ed. 28.00x o.p. (ISBN 0-7065-0379-1, Pub. by Keter Pub Jerusalem). Coronet Bks.

Investigation of the Laws of Thought. George Boole. 16.00 o.p. (ISBN 0-8446-1699-0). Peter Smith.

Investigations of Microteaching. D. McIntyre et al. 256p. 1977. 24.50 o.p. (ISBN 0-85664-537-0, Pub. by Croom Helm Ltd). Routledge Chapman & Hall.

Investigative Photography. Elliott R. Berrin. 1983. 4.65 o.p. (ISBN 0-686-40876-4, TR-83-1). Society Fire Protect.

Investing at the Race Track. William L. Scott. 1982. 18.45 o.p. (ISBN 0-671-43152-8). S&S.

Investing in Classic Automobiles for Profit & Capital Gain. Richard H. Rush. 1984. 21.45 o.p. (ISBN 0-671-47324-7, Linden Pr). S&S.

Investing in Old Buildings. Ed. by Sally E. Nielsen. (Illus.). 1980. pap. 3.95 o.s.i. (ISBN 0-686-70221-2). Greater Portland.

Investing in the Eighties: What to Buy & When. Patricia Beadle. LC 81-47297. (Illus.). 224p. 1981. 12.95 o.p. (ISBN 0-15-145284-9). HarBraceJ.

Investing in Zero's Coupon Bonds: All About Cats, Strips, Tigers, Lions, TR & TBRs. Lawrence Rosen. LC 86-9262. 264p. 1986. 19.95 o.p. (ISBN 0-471-84707-0). Wiley.

Investing Money: The Facts about Stocks & Bonds. Ruth Brindze. LC 68-28801. (Illus.). (gr. 7 up). 1968. 5.50 o.p. (ISBN 0-15-238828-1, HJ). HarBraceJ.

Investment Analysis & Portfolio Management. Sid Mittra & Chris Gassen. 857p. 1981. text ed. 26.00 o.p. (ISBN 0-15-546882-0, HC). HarBraceJ.

Investment Analysis for Real Estate Decisions. Gaylon E. Greer & Michael D. Farrell. 604p. 1984. text ed. 34.95x o.p. (ISBN 0-03-061247-0); instr's. manual incl. supplementary material 19.95 o.p. (ISBN 0-03-061248-9); newsletter avail. o.p. Dryden Pr.

Investment Banking. Financial Consulting Staff. 1985. 295.00 o.p. (ISBN 0-938124-07-2). Rubicon.

Investment Banking, 1988. 104p. 1988. 24.95 o.p. (ISBN 0-87584-189-9). Harvard Busn.

Investment Behaviour of British Life Insurance Companies. J. C. Dodds. 193p. 1979. 50.00 o.p. (ISBN 0-7099-0058-9, Pub. by Croom Helm Ltd). Routledge Chapman & Hall.

Investment Companies: Industry Responses to New Contexts & Concepts, Vol. 477. Practising Law Institute Staff. 802p. 1985. pap. 40.00 o.p. (ISBN 0-317-27473-2, #B4-6709). PLI.

Investment Demand in a Developing Country: The Nigerian Case. Harold G. Osuagwu. LC 80-8183. (Illus.). 430p. (Orig.). 1982. lib. bdg. 35.50 o.p. (ISBN 0-8191-2048-0); pap. text ed. 18.75 o.p. (ISBN 0-8191-2049-9). U Pr of Amer.

Investment Efficiency in a Socialist Economy. H. Fiszel. 1966. 21.00 o.p. (ISBN 0-08-011760-0). Pergamon.

Investment in Education: The Equity-Efficiency Quandary. Ed. by Theodore W. Schultz. LC 72-84408. 296p. 1972. lib. bdg. 20.00x o.s.i. (ISBN 0-226-74080-3). U of Chicago Pr.

Investment in Indian Education: Uneconomic? Stephen P. Heyneman. (Working Paper: No. 327). 56p. 1979. 3.50 o.p. (ISBN 0-686-36040-0, WP-0327). World Bank.

Investment in International Agricultural Research: Some Economic Dimensions. Grant M. Scobie. (Working Paper: No. 361). iv, 98p. 1979. 5.00 o.p. (ISBN 0-686-36067-2, WP-0361). World Bank.

Investment Limited Partnerships Handbook. Robert J. Haft & Peter M. Fass. LC 87-13210. (Securities Law Ser.: No. 4). 1987. 85.00 o.p. (ISBN 0-87632-558-4). Clark Boardman.

Investment Regulation Around the World. Ed. by Richard M. Hammer et al. LC 83-12479. (Tax & Business Guides for Professionals Ser.). 331p. 1983. 68.50x o.p. (ISBN 0-471-88131-7). Wiley.

Investment Regulation Around the World: 1984 Supplement. R. M. Hammer et al. (Tax & Business Guides for Professionals Ser.). 128p. 1984. pap. 28.50 o.p. (ISBN 0-471-81677-9). Wiley.

Investment Return & Property-Liability Insurance Ratemaking. Robert W. Cooper. 1974. 12.95x o.p. (ISBN 0-256-01605-4). Irwin.

Investment Trust Yearbook & Who's Who 1986. U. K. Association of Investment Trust Cos. Staff. 512p. 1986. 90.00x o.p. (ISBN 0-935859-02-0, Stockton Pr). Groves Dict Music.

Investments. 5th ed. Frederick Amling. (Illus.). 704p. 1984. text ed. 46.00 o.p. (ISBN 0-13-504324-7). P-H.

Investments. Bodie & Kane. (Illus.). 928p. 1989. text ed. 41.95 o.p. (ISBN 0-8016-0523-7). Mosby.

Investments. Robert W. Kolb. 1986. text ed. write for info. o.p. (ISBN 0-673-15977-9). Scott F.

Investments. Frank K. Reilly. 656p. 1982. text ed. 32.95x o.s.i. (ISBN 0-03-056712-2); study guide 13.95 o.s.i. (ISBN 0-03-060136-3); instr's. manual 20.00 o.s.i. (ISBN 0-03-056713-0). Dryden Pr.

Investments: An Introduction. Herbert B. Mayo. 640p. 1984. text ed. 32.95x o.s.i. (ISBN 0-03-063792-9); instr's. manual with test bank 19.95 o.s.i. (ISBN 0-03-063793-7). Dryden Pr.

Investments: Analysis & Management. Charles P. Jones. LC 84-19594. 681p. 1985. (ISBN 0-471-88228-3). Wiley.

Investor Relations that Work. Arthur R. Roalman. 320p. 1981. 34.95 o.p. (ISBN 0-8144-5620-0). AMACOM.

Investor's Annual, 1985. Chet Currier & Associated Press Staff. 1986. pap. 9.95 o.p. (ISBN 0-531-15504-8). Watts.

Investor's Encyclopedia. Associated Press & Chet Currier. 480p. 1985. 24.95 o.p. (ISBN 0-531-09586-X). Watts.

Investor's Guide to High Technology Corporations, 1983-84. Ed. by American Investor Information Services Staff. (Hi-Tech Investmesnt Profiles Ser.). (Illus.). 400p. 1983. ring binder 295.00x o.p. (ISBN 0-89563-051-6). Coronet Bks.

Investor's Guide to the Military Industry: Fiscal Year 1987. Ed. by Albert Donnay. 778p. (Orig.). 1988. pap. 950.00 ring binder o.p. (ISBN 0-9621396-0-2). Nuclear Free Am.

Invisibility Factor. Josepha Sherman. (Transformers Find Your Fate Ser.: No. 9). (Orig.). 1986. pap. 2.50 o.p. (ISBN 0-345-33391-8, Pub. by Ballantine Trade). Ballantine.

Invisible Bankers: Everything the Insurance Industry Never Wanted You to Know. Andrew Tobias. LC 81-18564. 1982. 15.50 o.p. (ISBN 0-671-22849-8, Linden Pr). S&S.

Invisible Bankers: Everything You Always Wanted to Know About Insurance But Were Afraid to Ask. Andrew Tobias. 1983. pap. 3.95 o.p. (ISBN 0-671-46181-8). PB.

Invisible Billionaire, Daniel Ludwig. Jerry Shields. 1986. 19.45 o.p. (ISBN 0-395-35402-1). HM.

Invisible Castle. Lee Martin. Ed. by Stephanie Spinner. LC 85-19649. (Thundercats Thriller Series). (Illus.). 64p. (gr. 2-6). 1986. pap. 1.95 o.s.i. (ISBN 0-394-87878-7). Random.

Invisible Colleges: Diffusion of Knowledge in Scientific Communities. Diana Crane. LC 77-182088. 1972. lib. bdg. 10.50x o.s.i. (ISBN 0-226-11857-6). U of Chicago Pr.

Invisible Decade: U. K. Women in the United Nations Decade 1976-1985. Georgina Ashworth & Lucy Bonnerjea. 220p. (Orig.). 1985. pap. text ed. 32.95 o.p. (ISBN 0-566-00895-5). Gower Pub Co.

Invisible Empires: Multinational Companies & the Modern World. Louis Turner. LC 79-134582. 1971. 6.95 o.p. (ISBN 0-15-145301-2). HarBraceJ.

Invisible Estate. Peter Balakian & Bruce Smith. (Illus.). 56p. 1984. 85.00 o.p. (ISBN 0-916375-01-3). Press Alley.

Invisible Hand in Economics & Politics. Milton Friedman. (Orig.). 1981. pap. text ed. 7.50x o.p. (ISBN 9971-902-22-2, Pub. by Inst Southeast Asian Stud). Gower Pub Co.

Invisible Hand: The Marijuana Business. Roger Warner. LC 85-29823. 320p. 1986. 17.95 o.p. (ISBN 0-688-05095-6, Pub. by Beech Tree Bks). Morrow.

Invisible Hunters. Harriet Rohmer. Date not set. 10.95 o.p. (ISBN 0-317-70121-5). Childrens.

Invisible Intruder. Carolyn Keene. (Nancy Drew Ser.: Vol. 46). (Illus.). (gr. 4-7). 1969. 4.50 o.p. (ISBN 0-448-09546-7, G&D); PLB 3.29 o.p. (ISBN 0-448-19546-1). Putnam Pub Group.

Invisible Man's Literary Heritage: Benito Cereno & Moby Dick. Valeria B. Gray. (Costerus New Ser.: No. XII). 1978. pap. text ed. 17.50x o.p. (ISBN 90-6203-652-X). Humanities.

Invisible Men: Life in Baseball's Negro Leagues. Donn Rogosin. LC 82-73026. (Illus.). 320p. 1983. 14.95 o.p. (ISBN 0-689-11363-3, Atheneum). Macmillan.

Invisible Pyramid. Loren Eiseley. 1983. 14.25 o.p. (ISBN 0-8446-5980-0). Peter Smith.

Invisible Residents. Ivan T. Sanderson. 1973. pap. 0.95 o.p. (ISBN 0-380-01304-5, 15511). Avon.

Invisible Rival. TSR Inc. Staff. LC 87-90082. (LAZER TAG Adventure Ser.: No. 3). 128p. (Orig.). (gr. 4 up). 1987. pap. 2.95 o.p. (ISBN 0-88038-516-2). TSR Inc.

Invisible Universe: The Story of Radio Astronomy. G. L. Verschuur. LC 73-22202. (Heidelberg Science Library: Vol. 20). (Illus.). 160p. 1974. pap. 12.95 o.p. (ISBN 0-387-90078-0). Springer-Verlag.

Invisible Victory. Richard Gordon. LC 77-21368. 1978. 8.95 o.p. (ISBN 0-689-10836-2, Atheneum). Macmillan.

Invisible Walls: A German Family under the Nuremberg Laws. Ingeborg Hecht. Tr. by J. Maxwell Brownjohn from Ger. LC 85-5870. 144p. 1985. 13.95 o.p. (ISBN 0-15-145317-9). HarBraceJ.

Invisible Way. Reshad Feild. LC 78-19501. 1979. 7.64i o.p. (ISBN 0-06-062587-2). HarpR.

Invisible Women: The Schooling Scandal. Dale Spender. 179p. 1983. 5.95 o.p. (ISBN 0-906495-94-6). Norton.

Invisible World: Sights Too Fast, Too Slow, Too Far, Too Small for the Naked Eye to See. Alex Pomasanoff. LC 81-2105. (Illus.). 160p. 1981. 25.00 o.p. (ISBN 0-395-31326-0). HM.

Invitacion: Spanish for Communication & Cultural Awareness. Angela Labarca & Elmer A. Rodriguez. 1983. text ed. 30.95 o.p. (ISBN 0-03-059606-8). HR&W.

Invitation: French Communication & Cultural Awareness. 2nd ed. Gilbert A. Jarvis. (Fr.). 1984. text ed. 31.95 o.p. (ISBN 0-03-069271-7). HR&W.

Invitation to Action: The Lutheran-Reformed Dialogue, Ser. III, 1981-1983; A Study of Ministry, Sacraments & Recognition. James E. Andrews & Joseph A. Burgess. LC 84-47885. 144p. 1984. pap. 2.00 o.p. (ISBN 0-8006-1818-1, 1-1818, Fortress). Augsburg Fortress.

Invitation to Fly: Basics for the Private Pilot. 2nd ed. Dennis Glaeser et al. 619p. 1985. text ed. (ISBN 0-534-04800-5). Wadsworth Pub.

Invitation to German. Margarita Madrigal & Ursula Meyer. (Illus.). 1978. pap. 5.75 o.p. (ISBN 0-671-24234-2, Fireside). S&S.

Invitation to Goethe's Faust. H. G. Haile. LC 77-7461. (No. 21). 244p. 1978. 16.75 o.p. (ISBN 0-8173-7326-8). U of Ala Pr.

Invitation to Health. 3rd ed. Dianne R. Hales & Brian K. Williams. (Illus.). 704p. 1986. pap. text ed. 29.95 o.p. (ISBN 0-8053-2294-9). testing program 9.95 o.p. (ISBN 0-8053-2298-1); classroom resource manual 9.95 o.p. (ISBN 0-8053-2295-7). Benjamin-Cummings.

Invitation to Indian Architecture. K. V. Rajan. (Heritage India Ser.). (Illus.). 100p. 1984. text ed. 15.00x o.p. (ISBN 0-391-02735-2). Humanities.

Invitation to Italian. Margarita Madrigal. 1965. pap. 5.75 o.p. (ISBN 0-671-38121-0, Fireside). S&S.

Invitation to Japanese Civilization. Elwood. Watts.

Invitation to Law & Social Science: Deserts, Disputes, & Distribution. Richard O. Lempert & Joseph Sanders. LC 85-12899. 1986. 40.50 o.p. (ISBN 0-582-28495-3); pap. 23.45 o.p. (ISBN 0-582-28496-1). Longman.

Invitation to Learning & Memory. John F. Hall. 320p. 1982. text ed. 38.00 o.p. (ISBN 0-205-07608-4, 7976089); tchr's ed. free o.p. (ISBN 0-205-07609-2, 7976097). Allyn.

Invitation to Listening. 2nd ed. Richard L. Wink & Lois Williams. LC 75-31007. (Illus.). 352p. 1976. text ed. 24.50 o.p. (ISBN 0-395-18651-X). HM.

Invitation to Philosophical Thinking. Monroe C. Beardsley & Elizabeth L. Beardsley. 178p. 1972. pap. text ed. 10.95 o.p. (ISBN 0-15-546902-9, HC). HarBraceJ.

Invitation to Physics. Ken Greider. (Illus.). 1973. text ed. 14.95 o.p. (ISBN 0-15-546907-X, HC). HarBraceJ.

Invitation to Psychology. John P. Houston & Victor Benassi. 741p. 1979. text ed. 25.00 o.p. (ISBN 0-12-356860-9); instrs'. manual 3.50 o.p. (ISBN 0-12-356862-5); study guide 10.00 o.p. (ISBN 0-12-356864-1); test blank 3.50 o.p. (ISBN 0-12-356861-7); test bklt. 3.50 o.p. (ISBN 0-12-356863-3). Acad Pr.

Invitation to Spanish. new ed. Margarita Madrigal & Ezequias Madrigal. 1971. pap. 5.95 o.p. (ISBN 0-671-21222-2, Fireside). S&S.

Invitation to the Theatre. George R. Kernodle. (Illus.). 1967. text ed. 14.95 o.p. (ISBN 0-15-546921-5, HC). HarBraceJ.

Invitation to the Theatre. 2nd, abr. ed. George R. Kernodle & Portia Kernodle. (Illus.). 370p. 1978. pap. text ed. 14.50 o.p. (ISBN 0-15-546923-1, HC). HarBraceJ.

Invitation to the Theatre. George R. Kernodle & Portia Kernodle. (Illus., Brief ed.). 1971. pap. text ed. 11.95 o.p. (ISBN 0-15-546922-3, HC). HarBraceJ.

Invitation to the Waltz. Rosamond Lehmann. LC 75-5990. 189p. 1975. pap. 2.95 o.p. (ISBN 0-15-645384-3, HB316, Harv). HarBraceJ.

Invitation to Think. LC 64-22623. 72p. 1965. (ISBN 0-8022-1182-8). Philos Lib.

Invitations to Investigate: An Introduction to Scientific Exploration. Paul F. Brandwein & Hy Ruchlis. LC 77-102440. (Illus.). (gr. 7 up). 1970. 5.95 o.p. (ISBN 0-15-238835-4, HJ). HarBraceJ.

Invite a Bird to Dinner: Simple Feeders You Can Make. Beverly C. Crook. LC 78-8657. (Illus.). (gr. 3-7). 1978. 10.25 o.p. (ISBN 0-688-41849-X); PLB 10.88 o.p. (ISBN 0-688-51849-4). Lothrop.

Involuntary Journey to Siberia, Russian Edition. Andrei Amalrik. LC 75-118829. 294p. (Rus). 1970. 10.00 o.p. (ISBN 0-15-145503-1). HarBraceJ.

Involved. Wilfred M. Hillock. LC 77-78102. (Anvil Ser.). 1977. pap. 8.95 o.p. (ISBN 0-8127-0140-2). Review & Herald.

Involvement with Music: Essential Skills & Concepts. Alfred B. Balkin & Jack A. Taylor. 448p. 1975. pap. 13.75 o.p. (ISBN 0-395-16989-5). HM.

Involving Volunteers in Your Advancement Programs. Ed. by Virginia C. Smith & Patricia L. Alberger. 112p. 1983. 14.50 o.p. (ISBN 0-89964-210-1). Coun Adv & Supp Ed.

Inward Journey. Joseph F. Doherty & William Stephenson. 1973. pap. text ed. 10.95 o.p. (ISBN 0-15-546945-2, HC). HarBraceJ.

Inward Pilgrimage: Spiritual Classics from Augustine to Bonhoeffer. Bernhard M. Christensen. LC 75-22725. 144p. 1975. pap. 8.50 o.p. (ISBN 0-8066-1510-9, 10-3400, Augsburg). Augsburg Fortress.

Inyo-Sierra Passage. Jack Rowe. 248p. 1987. pap. 3.50 o.p. (ISBN 1-55547-172-2). Critics Choice Paper.

Iolaus: An Anthology of Friendship. 3rd ed. Edward Carpenter. LC 76-174018. 248p. 1971. Repr. of 1920 ed. 30.00x o.p. (ISBN 0-8103-3790-8). Gale.

Ion Caraion: Poems. Ion Caraion. Tr. by Marguerite Dorian & Elliott B. Urdang. LC 81-4847. vii, 112p. 1981. 17.95x o.p. (ISBN 0-8214-0608-6); pap. 8.95 o.p. (ISBN 0-8214-0620-5). Ohio U Pr.

Ion-Exchange Chromatography. Ed. by H. F. Walton. LC 75-31610. (Benchmark Papers in Analytical Chemistry Ser.: Vol. 1). 400p. 1976. 83.00 o.p. (ISBN 0-12-787725-8). Acad Pr.

Ion Exchange Equilibrium Constants, Vol. 10. Y. Marcus & D. G. Howery. 1976. pap. 10.75 o.p. (ISBN 0-08-020992-0). Pergamon.

Ion Exchange in Analytical Chemistry. W. Rieman & H. Walton. LC 74-105870. 1970. 75.00 o.p. (ISBN 0-08-015511-1). Pergamon.

Ion Exchange Membranes. Ed. by D. S. Flett. LC 83-4343. 210p. 1983. 56.95 o.p. (ISBN 0-470-27452-2). Halsted Pr.

Ion Exchange Resins. Robert Kunin. LC 58-6078. 518p. 1972. Repr. of 1958 ed. 32.50 o.p. (ISBN 0-88275-065-8). Krieger.

Ion Homeostasis of the Brain: Proceedings of The Alfred Benzon Symposium, 3rd, Copenhagen & Lund, 1970. Benzon, Alfred, Symposium et al. Ed. by B. K. Siesjo & S. C. Sorensen. 1971. 93.50 o.p. (ISBN 0-12-642850-6). Acad Pr.

Ion Implantation & Ion Beam Analysis Techniques in Corrosion Studies. Ed. by J. C. Scully. 1977. pap. 19.25 o.p. (ISBN 0-08-021420-7). Pergamon.

Ion Implantation & Ion Beam Processing of Materials: Proceedings of the 3rd Symposium on Ion Implantation & Ion Beam Processing of Materials, Boston, MA, Nov. 1983. Ed. by G. K. Hubler et al. (Materials Research Society Symposia Ser.: Vol. 27). 800p. 1984. 120.00 o.p. (ISBN 0-444-00869-1, North Holland). Elsevier.

Ion Implantation Metallurgy: Proceedings of the Annual Meeting of the Materials Research Society, Cambridge, 1979. Annual Meeting of the Materials Research Society Staff. Ed. by Carolyn M. Preece & J. K. Hirvoen. (Illus.). 197p. 26.00 o.p. (ISBN 0-89520-364-2); members 16.00 o.p. (ISBN 0-317-34880-9); student members 9.00 o.p. (ISBN 0-317-34881-7). ASM.

Ion Implantation: Science & Technology. Ed. by James F. Ziegler. 1984. 65.50 o.p. (ISBN 0-12-780620-2). Acad Pr.

Ion Implementation & Ion Beam Analysis Techniques in Corrosion: Selected Papers Presented at the Conference at the Corrosion & Protection Centre, UMIST, Manchester, 28-30 June 1978. Ed. by J. C. Scully. 148p. 1981. pap. 19.25 o.p. (ISBN 0-08-026135-3). Pergamon.

Ion-Molecule Reactions, 2 Pts. J. L. Franklin. LC 78-16358. (Benchmark Papers in Physical Chemistry & Chemical Physics: 3). 1983. Set. 118.95 o.p. (ISBN 0-87933-091-0); Pt. 1: Kinetics, 399p. 65.95 o.p. (ISBN 0-87933-331-6); Pt. 2: Elevated Pressure, 379p. 65.95 o.p. (ISBN 0-87933-337-5). Van Nos Reinhold.

Ion Selective Electrode Methodology, 2 vols. Ed. by A. K. Covington. 1979. Vol. 1, 272 pgs. 81.50 o.p. (ISBN 0-8493-5247-9); Vol. 2, 144 pgs. 68.00 o.p. (ISBN 0-8493-5248-7). CRC Pr.

Ion-Selective Electrode Reviews, Vol. 1. J. D. Thomas. (Illus.). 280p. 1980. 52.00 o.p. (ISBN 0-08-026044-6). Pergamon.

Ion-Selective Electrode Reviews, Vol. 2, No. 2. Ed. by J. D. Thomas. (Illus.). 146p. 1981. pap. 34.00 o.p. (ISBN 0-08-027128-6). Pergamon.

Ion-Selective Electrode Reviews, Vol. 2. J. D. R. Thomas. 1981. 68.00 o.p. (ISBN 0-08-028434-5). Pergamon.

Ion-Selective Electrode Reviews, Vol. 3. Ed. by J. D. Thomas. (Illus.). 248p. 1982. 68.00 o.p. (ISBN 0-08-029692-0). Pergamon.

Ion-Selective Electrode Reviews, Vol. 4. Ed. by J. D. Thomas. (Illus.). 286p. 1983. 92.00 o.p. (ISBN 0-08-030414-1). Pergamon.

Ion-Selective Electrode Reviews, Vol. 5. Ed. by J. D. Thomas. (Illus.). 298p. 1984. 92.00 o.p. (ISBN 0-08-031492-9). Pergamon.

Ion-Selective Electrode Reviews, Vol. 6. Ed. by J. D. Thomas. (Illus.). 278p. 1985. 105.00 o.p. (ISBN 0-08-033201-3, Pub. by PPL). Pergamon.

Ion-Selective Microelectrodes & Their Use in Excitable Tissues. Ed. by Eva Sykova et al. LC 81-1625. 380p. 1981. 59.50x o.p. (ISBN 0-306-40723-X, Plenum Pr). Plenum Pub.

Ion-Sensitive Intracellular Micro-Electrodes: How to Make & Use Them. R. C. Thomas. (Biological Techniques Ser.). 1979. 42.00 o.p. (ISBN 0-12-688750-0). Acad Pr.

Ion Transport in Plants. Ed. by W. P. Anderson. 1973. 104.00 o.p. (ISBN 0-12-058250-3). Acad Pr.

Ion Transport Through Biological Membranes: An Integrated Theoretical Approach. M. C. Mackey. (Lecture Notes in Biomathematics Ser.: Vol. 7). 256p. 1976. pap. 17.00 o.p. (ISBN 0-387-07532-1). Springer-Verlag.

Ionic Equilibria. J. E. Prue. 1966. 35.00 o.p. (ISBN 0-08-011344-3). Pergamon.

Ionic Interactions: From Dilute Solutions to Fused Salts. Ed. by S. Petrucci. (Physical Chemistry Ser.: Vol. 22). 1971. Vol. 1. 80.00 o.p. (ISBN 0-12-553001-3); Vol. 2. 77.00 o.p. (ISBN 0-12-553002-1). Acad Pr.

Ionization in High-Temperature Gases, PAAS12. Ed. by K. E. Shuler & J. B. Fenn. LC 63-23423. (Illus.). 409p. 1963. 39.50 o.p. (ISBN 0-317-36824-9). AIAA.

Ionization of Carbon Acids. J. R. Jones. 1974. 43.50 o.p. (ISBN 0-12-389750-5). Acad Pr.

Ionization Potentials: Some Variations, Implications & Applications. L. H. Ahrens. (Illus.). 100p. 1983. 39.00 o.p. (ISBN 0-08-025274-5). Pergamon.

Ionizing Radiation: Levels & Effects, 2 vols. 448p. 1982. 12.50x o.p. Intl Pubns Serv.

Ionizing Radiation Sources & Biological Effects: 1982 Report of the General Assembly, with Annexes. United Nations Scientific Committee on the Effects of Atomic Radiation. 63.00 o.s.i. (ISBN 92-1-142050-4, E.82.IX.8). UN.

Ions, Cell Proliferation & Cancer. Ed. by Alton L. Boynton & Wallace L. McKeehan. LC 82-20786. 1982. 59.50 o.p. (ISBN 0-12-123050-3). Acad Pr.

Iowa Business Directory, 1987-88. rev. ed. American Directory Publishing Co., Inc. Staff. 1047p. 1987. pap. 85.00 o.p. (ISBN 0-944316-04-2). Amer Directory.

Iowa Legal Forms, 10 Vols. 1984. looseleaf 295.00 o.p. (ISBN 0-86678-100-5). Butterworth MN.

Iowa Manufacturers Register, 1988. 320p. 1988. 50.00 o.p. (ISBN 0-318-02879-4). Manufacturers.

Iowa Writers' Workshop Cookbook. Ed. by Connie Brothers. 1986. pap. 9.95 o.p. (ISBN 0-317-53643-5). Fell.

IPA Thesaurus & Frequency List. 3rd ed. Ed. by Dwight R. Tousignaut. (Subject Terms Ser.). 172p. 1985. pap. text ed. 20.00 o.p. (ISBN 0-930530-55-1). Am Soc Hosp Pharm.

Iphigene: My Life & The New York Times, the Memoirs of Iphigene Ochs Sulzberger. Susan W. Dryfoos. (Illus.). 320p. 1987. 22.50 o.p. (ISBN 0-317-63087-3). Times Bks.

Iqbal, Jinnah, & Pakistan: The Vision & the Reality. Ed. by C. M. Naim. LC 79-25477. (Foreign & Comparative Studies Program, South Asian Ser.: No. 5). 216p. (Orig.). 1979. pap. text ed. 8.00x o.p. (ISBN 0-915984-81-4). Syracuse U Foreign Comp.

Ir Genes & Ia Antigens (Symposium) (MS-Repro) Ed. by Hugh O. McDevitt. 1978. 54.50 o.p. (ISBN 0-12-483260-1). Acad Pr.

IRA Book: The Complete Guide to IRA's & Retirement Planning. Center for the Study of Services Staff & Robert Krughoff. 1984. 6.95 o.p. (ISBN 0-686-40868-3). Ctr Study Serv.

Iran. Fredick E. Lockyear. (World Education Ser.). (Illus.). 64p. (Orig.). 31.50 o.p. (ISBN 0-317-65052-1); 25.80xerographic o.p. (ISBN 0-317-65053-X). Am Assn Coll Registrars.

Iran. Banri Namikawa. LC 73-79762. (This Beautiful World Ser.: Vol. 45). (Illus.). 130p. (Orig.). 1973. pap. 4.95 o.p. (ISBN 0-87011-213-9). Kodansha.

Iran Bastan Museum, Teheran. Firouz Bagherzadeh et al. LC 80-82645. (Oriental Ceramics Ser.: Vol. IV). (Illus.). 166p. 1981. 65.00 o.p. (ISBN 0-87011-443-3). Kodansha.

Iran Bastan Museum, Teheran see Oriental Ceramics: The World's Great Collections.

Iran: Economic Development Under Dualistic Conditions. Jahangir Amuzegar & M. Ali Fekrat. LC 79-153044. (Publications of the Center for Middle Eastern Studies Ser.: No. 7). 1971. lib. bdg. 13.00x o.s.i. (ISBN 0-226-01754-0). U of Chicago Pr.

Iranxe: Notas Gramaticais e Lista Vocabular. Robert E. Meader. 193p. 1967. pap. 2.00x o.p. (ISBN 0-88312-777-6); microfiche (2) 4.00 o.p. (ISBN 0-88312-397-5). Summer Inst Ling.

Iraq: A Country Study. 3rd ed. Ed. by Richard F. Nyrop. LC 79-24184. (Area Handbook Ser.: DA Pam 550-31). (Illus.). 320p. 1979. 11.00 o.p. (ISBN 0-318-21865-8, S/N 008-020-00818-4). USGPO.

Ireland. Derek A. C. Davies. LC 72-77797. (This Beautiful World Ser.: Vol. 37). (Illus.). 118p. (Orig.). 1972. pap. 4.95 o.p. (ISBN 0-87011-180-9). Kodansha.

Ireland. rev.__1986 ed. John Harrison & Shirley Harrison. (Pocket Guides Ser.). pap. 5.95 o.p. (ISBN 0-528-84840-2). Rand McNally.

Ireland. (Ordnance Survey Leisure Guides Ser.). 176p. 1987. 26.95 o.p. (ISBN 0-86145-375-1, Pub. by British Tour); pap. 19.95 o.p. (ISBN 0-86145-357-3). Salem Hse Pubs.

Ireland. Ian Robertson. (Blue Guides Ser.). (Illus.). 1984. 24.95 o.p. (ISBN 0-393-01541-6); pap. 14.95 o.p. (ISBN 0-393-00094-X). Norton.

Ireland: A Dictionary for 1985. Ed. by James O'Donnell. 400p. 1985. 65.00x o.p. (Pub. by Inst of Public Admin Dublin). Gale.

Ireland: A Directory 1985. Ed. by James O'Donnell. 384p. 1985. 65.00x o.p. (ISBN 0-906980-39-9). Gale.

Ireland: A Picture Book to Remember Her By. rev. ed. (Illus.). 1978. 5.98 o.s.i. (ISBN 0-517-24616-3). Crown.

Ireland & Irish-Australia: Studies in Cultural & Political History. Ed. by Oliver MacDonagh & W. F. Mandle. 288p. 1986. 52.50 o.p. (ISBN 0-7099-4617-1, Pub. by Croom Helm Ltd). Routledge Chapman & Hall.

Ireland & the Classical Tradition. new ed. W. B. Stanford. 272p. 1984. pap. 22.50x o.p. (ISBN 0-7165-2361-2, Pub. by Irish Academic Pr Ireland). Biblio Dist.

Ireland in Eighteen Hundred & Four. 2nd ed. Ed. by Seamus Grimes. (Illus.). 64p. 1980. Repr. of 1806 ed. 12.50x o.p. (ISBN 0-906127-24-6, BBA 03843, Pub. by Irish Academic Pr Ireland). Biblio Dist.

Ireland in the New Century. Horace Plunkett. (Cooperative Studies). 360p. 1983. Repr. of 1982 ed. 17.50x o.p. (ISBN 0-7165-0294-1, BBA 04859, Pub. by Irish Academic Pr Ireland). Biblio Dist.

Ireland in the Nineteenth Century: A Breviate of Official Publications. Arthur Maltby & Jean Maltby. (Guides to Official Publications Ser.: Vol. 4). (Illus.). 1979. 79.00 o.p. (ISBN 0-08-023688-X). Pergamon.

Ireland: Land of Mist & Magic. Kathleen A. Meyer. LC 82-14668. (Discovering Our Heritage Ser.). (Illus.). 144p. (gr. 5 up). 1983. PLB 12.95 o.p. (ISBN 0-87518-228-3). Dillon.

Ireland on Twenty-Five Dollars a Day. Susan Poole. 396p. 1985. pap. 9.95 o.p. (ISBN 0-671-52472-0). Prentice Hall Pr.

Ireland on Twenty-Five Dollars a Day, 1983-84. 308p. 1982. pap. 7.95 o.p. (ISBN 0-671-45382-3). Prentice Hall Pr.

Ireland Revisited. Jill Uris. LC 81-43402. (Illus.). 160p. 1982. 35.00 o.s.i. (ISBN 0-385-17616-3). Doubleday.

Ireland's Field Day. The Field Day Theatre Company. LC 85-52220. 120p. 1986. pap. text ed. 9.95x o.p. (ISBN 0-268-01160-5). U of Notre Dame Pr.

Irene. Albert de Routisie. 1970. pap. 0.95 o.p. (ISBN 0-394-17404-6, B237, BC). Grove.

Irene Emery Roundtable on Museum Textiles: 1974 Proceedings. Archaeological Textiles Staff. Ed. by Patricia Fiske. LC 75-21585. (Illus.). 312p. 1975. pap. 37.50 o.p. (ISBN 0-87405-005-7). Textile Mus.

Iridion. Zygmunt Krasinski. Ed. by George R. Noyes. Tr. by Florence Noyes from Pol. LC 74-30841. 281p. 1975. Repr. of 1927 ed. lib. bdg. 35.00x o.p. (ISBN 0-8371-7937-8, KRIR). Greenwood.

Iris Book. Molly Price. 1983. 13.50 o.p. (ISBN 0-8446-6024-8). Peter Smith.

Iris de Suse: Roman. Jean Giono. (Coll. Soleil). 12.50 o.p. (ISBN 0-685-34169-0). Schoenhof.

Iris Murdoch. Richard Todd. 96p. 1984. pap. 5.95 o.p. (ISBN 0-416-35420-3, NO. 3819). Routledge Chapman & Hall.

Irish-American Experience: A Guide to the Literature. Seamus P. Metress. LC 80-69050. 226p. (Orig.). 1981. lib. bdg. 28.25 o.p. (ISBN 0-8191-1694-7); pap. text ed. 12.50 o.p. (ISBN 0-8191-1695-5). U Pr of Amer.

Irish & Anglo-Irish Landed Gentry When Cromwell Came to Ireland. J. O'Hart. 804p. 1968. Repr. of 1884 ed. 45.00x o.p. (ISBN 0-7165-0038-8, BBA 02220, Pub. by Irish Academic Pr Ireland). Biblio Dist.

Irish Booksellers & English Writers: 1740-1800. Richard C. Cole. 288p. 1986. 39.95x o.p. (ISBN 0-391-03432-4). Humanities.

Irish Commune: The Experiment of Ralahine, County Clare 1831-1833. E. T. Craig. (Co-Operative Studies). 226p. 1983. pap. 12.50x o.p. (ISBN 0-7165-2349-3, Pub. by Irish Academic Pr Ireland). Biblio Dist.

Irish Donkey. Averil Swinfen. (Illus.). pap. 5.25 o.p. (ISBN 0-85131-239-X, NL51, Pub. by J A Allen U K). S R Smith Sporting Bks.

Irish Glass: Waterford, Cork, Belfast in the Age of Exuberance. 2nd rev. ed. Phelps Warren. (Faber Monographs on Glass). (Illus.). 280p. 1981. 53.95 o.p. (ISBN 0-571-18028-0). Faber & Faber.

Irish Gypsy. Virginia Henley. 304p. 1982. pap. 2.75 o.p. (ISBN 0-380-80598-7). Avon.

Irish History & Culture: Aspects of a People's Heritage. Ed. by Harold Orel. LC 75-35532. (Illus.). x, 390p. 1976. 14.00 o.p. (ISBN 0-7006-0136-8); pap. 12.95x o.p. (ISBN 0-7006-0137-6). U Pr of Ks.

Irish in America. rev. ed. James E. Johnson. LC 66-10148. (In America Bks.). (Illus.). (gr. 5 up). 1976. PLB 8.95 o.p. (ISBN 0-8225-0203-8); pap. 3.95 o.p. (ISBN 0-8225-1012-X). Lerner Pubns.

Irish in the Victorian City. Ed. by Roger Swift & Sheridan Gilley. LC 85-19484. 320p. 1985. 32.50 o.p. (ISBN 0-7099-3333-9, Pub. by Croom Helm Ltd). Routledge Chapman & Hall.

Irish Land League Crisis. Norman D. Palmer. 340p. 1976. Repr. of 1940 ed. lib. bdg. 20.50x o.p. (ISBN 0-374-96196-4, Octagon). Hippocrene Bks.

Irish Language: An Annotated Bibliography. Edwards. 1983. lib. bdg. 43.00 o.p. (ISBN 0-8240-9294-5). Garland Pub.

Irish Literature in English: The Romantic Period (1789-1850, Vol. I, Pts. 1, 2 & 3. Patrick Rafroidi. (Illus.). 1980. text ed. 70.00x o.p. (ISBN 0-391-01032-8). Humanities.

Irish Literature in English: The Romantic Period, (1789-1850), Vol. 11, pt 4 Bibliography. Patrick Rafroidi. 1980. text ed. 70.00x o.p. (ISBN 0-391-01033-6). Humanities.

Irish Mythology: A Dictionary. Peter Kavanagh. (Illus.). 150p. (Hand Set & Printed). 100.00 o.p. (ISBN 0-914612-00-X). Kavanagh.

Irish Narrow Gauge Railway. John Prideaux. LC 80-85510. (Illus.). 96p. 1981. 19.95 o.p. (ISBN 0-7153-8071-0). David & Charles.

Irish Neutrality & the U. S. A. 1939-1947. T. Ryle Dwyer. 241p. 1977. 22.50x o.s.i. (ISBN 0-87471-994-1). Rowman.

Irish Official Publications: A Guide to Republic of Ireland Papers, with a Breviate of Reports 1922-1972. Arthur Maltby & Brian McKenna. LC 80-40873. (Guides to Official Publications Ser.: Vol. 7). 388p. 1980. 77.00 o.p. (ISBN 0-08-023703-7). Pergamon.

Irish People: An Illustrated History. Kenneth Neill. (Illus.). 238p. 1985. pap. 12.95 o.p. (Pub. by Gill & MacMillan). Seven Hills Bk Dists.

Irish Plays & Playwrights. Cornelius Weygandt. LC 79-17616. (Illus.). 1979. Repr. of 1913 ed. lib. bdg. 35.00x o.p. (ISBN 0-313-22040-9, WEIP). Greenwood.

Irish Poetry after Yeats: Seven Poets. Ed. by Maurice Harmon. 1981. 15.45i o.p. (ISBN 0-316-34686-1); pap. 9.95 o.p. (ISBN 0-316-34688-8). Little.

Irish Priests in Penal Times. William P. Burke. 508p. 1968. Repr. of 1914 ed. 32.50x o.p. (ISBN 0-7165-0034-5, Pub. by Irish Academic Pr Ireland). Biblio Dist.

Irish Question. Schools Council History 13-16 Project Staff. (Modern World Problems Ser.). (Illus.). 1979. lib. bdg. 12.95 o.p. (ISBN 0-912616-72-5); pap. text ed. 6.95 o.p. (ISBN 0-912616-71-7). Greenhaven.

Irish Standard Gauge Railways. Tom Middlemass. LC 80-68690. (Illus.). 96p. 1981. 19.95 o.p. (ISBN 0-7153-8007-9). David & Charles.

Irish Village. Robin Morrison & Christopher Fitz-Simon. (Illus.). 160p. 1986. 19.95 o.p. (ISBN 0-8050-0056-9). H Holt & Co.

Irish Women: Image & Achievement. Noirin N. Riain et al. Ed. & intro. by Eilean N. Chuilleanain. (Arlen House Ser.). 192p. 15.00 o.p. (ISBN 0-905223-61-6, Dist. by Kampmann). M Boyars Pubs.

Irma & Jerry. George Selden. (Illus.). 208p. (gr. 3 up). 1982. pap. 2.50 o.p. (ISBN 0-380-80978-8, 80978-8, Camelot). Avon.

Iron Age in Italy. David Randall-Maciver. LC 74-9221. (Illus.). 243p. 1975. Repr. of 1927 ed. lib. bdg. 27.00x o.p. (ISBN 0-8371-7633-6, RAIA). Greenwood.

Iron Age in Lowland Britain. D. W. Harding. (Illus.). 260p. 1985. 14.95 o.p. (ISBN 0-7102-0683-6). Routledge Chapman & Hall.

Iron & Steel. 260p. 1980. 27.00 o.p. (ISBN 0-89883-404-X, HS-30). Soc Auto Engineers.

Iron & Steel Industry in Nineteen Eighty-Three. OECD Staff. 50p. (Orig., Eng. & Fr.). 1985. pap. 10.00x o.p. (ISBN 92-64-02670-3). OECD.

Iron & Steel Works of the World. 8th ed. 1983. 162.50 o.p. Intl Pubns Serv.

Iron Blast Furnace: Theory & Practice. J. G. Peacey & W. G. Davenport. 1979. text ed. 44.00 o.p. (ISBN 0-08-023218-3); pap. text ed. 16.25 o.p. (ISBN 0-08-023258-2). Pergamon.

Iron Dream. Norman Spinrad. (Science Fiction Rediscovery Ser.). 1977. pap. 2.25 o.p. (ISBN 0-380-00200-0, 22947). Avon.

Iron Duke. John R. Tunis. LC 38-27108. (Illus.). 1938. 4.95 o.p. (ISBN 0-15-238985-7, HJ). HarBraceJ.

Iron Gates. Margaret Millar. 1974. pap. 0.95 o.p. (ISBN 0-380-00015-6, 19158). Avon.

Iron Horses to Promontory Railroad: Central Pacific-Union Pacific. Gerald M. Best. LC 69-20447. (Illus.). 1969. 26.95 o.p. (ISBN 0-87095-001-0). Gldn West Bks.

Iron in Biochemistry & Medicine. Ed. by A. Jacobs & M. Worwood. 1974. 130.50 o.p. (ISBN 0-12-379150-2). Acad Pr.

Iron in the Pines: The Story of New Jersey's Ghost Towns & Bog Iron. Arthur D. Pierce. (Illus.). 1966. pap. 9.95x o.p. (ISBN 0-8135-0514-3). Rutgers U Pr.

Iron Jehu. Ray Hogan. (Nightingale Paperbacks Ser.). 219p. 1987. pap. 11.95 o.p. (ISBN 0-8161-4333-1, Large Print Bks). G K Hall.

Iron Laws of the Historical Inevitabilities. C. M. Flumiani. (Illus.). 1977. 117.45 o.p. (ISBN 0-89266-081-3). Am Classical Coll Pr.

Iron Man of the Hoh. Nelson B. Bentley. 69p. (Orig.). 1976. 12.00 o.p.; pap. 5.00 o.p. (ISBN 0-914742-17-5). Copper Canyon.

Iron Pirate. Douglas Reeman. 304p. 1987. 17.95 o.p. (ISBN 0-399-13281-3, Putnam). Putnam Pub Group.

Iron Stallions. Max Hennessy. LC 81-69132. (Illus.). 320p. 1982. 10.95 o.p. (ISBN 0-689-11245-9, Atheneum). Macmillan.

Iron-Sulfur Proteins. Thomas G. Spiro. LC 82-2599. (Metal Ions in Biology Ser.). 434p. 1982. 117.50 o.p. (ISBN 0-471-07738-0, Pub. by Wiley-Interscience). Wiley.

Iron Will of Jefferson Davis. Cass Canfield. LC 78-53908. (Illus.). 1978. 7.95 o.p. (ISBN 0-15-145642-9). HarBraceJ.

Ironic Vision: A Study of the Fiction of R. K. Narayan. M. K. Naik. (Illus.). 163p. 1983. 16.95 o.s.i. (ISBN 0-86578-177-X). Ind-US Inc.

Ironmaking Conference: Proceedings of the Forty-Second Conference. LC 77-613444. 728p. 1983. 60.00 o.p. (ISBN 0-89520-156-9). Iron & Steel.

Ironmaking Conference: Proceedings of the Forty-Third Conference. Ironmaking Conference Staff. LC 77-613444. 524p. 1984. 60.00 o.p. (ISBN 0-89520-163-1). Iron & Steel.

Iroquois Indians, Vol. 2. Incl. Historical Report on the Niagara River to 1759. Donald H. Kent; Findings of Fact, & Opinion. Indian Claims Commission. (American Indian Ethnohistory Ser: North Central & Northeastern Indians). (Illus.). 1979. lib. bdg. 51.00 o.p. (ISBN 0-8240-0769-7). Garland Pub.

Iroquois Restoration: Iroquois Diplomacy on the Colonial Frontier, 1701-1754. Richard Aguila. LC 82-135390. (Illus.). 286p. 1982. 25.00x o.p. (ISBN 0-8143-1717-0). Wayne St U Pr.

Irradiation Effects in Fissile Materials. J. Leteurtre & Y. Quere. (Defects in Crystalline Solids Ser.: Vol. 6). 1972. 26.50 o.p. (ISBN 0-444-10382-1, North-Holland). Elsevier.

Irradiation Effects in Nuclear Fuels. J. A. Robertson. LC 67-26575. 309p. 1969. 19.00 o.p. (ISBN 0-685-58270-1, 450012). Am Nuclear Soc.

Irreconcilables: The Fight Against the League of Nations. Ralph Stone. 224p. 1973. pap. 2.75x o.p. (ISBN 0-393-00671-9). Norton.

Irredeemable America: The Indians' Estate & Land Claims. Ed. by Imre Sutton et al. LC 85-1108. (History Series: Native American Studies, UNM: No. 1). (Illus.). 444p. 1986. 27.50x o.p. (ISBN 0-8263-0806-6). U of NM Pr.

Irregular People. Joyce Landorf. 1982. 9.95 o.p. (ISBN 0-8499-0291-6). Word Bks.

Irregular Serials & Annuals, 1987. Ed. by Bowker, R. R., Staff. 1900p. 1987. 159.95 o.p. (ISBN 0-8352-2382-5); microfiche-combined with Ulrich's 650.00 o.p. (ISBN 0-8352-2423-6). Bowker.

Irresistible Desserts. (Step-by-Step Cooking Ser.). (Illus.). 160p. 10.95 o.p. (ISBN 0-8120-5680-9). Barron.

Irreversible Aspects of Continuum Mechanics & Transfer of Physical Characteristics in Moving Fluids: Proceedings. International Union of Theoretical & Applied Mechanics Symposium Vienna 1966. Ed. by H. Parkus & L. I. Sedov. LC 68-11180. (Illus.). 1968. 70.80 o.p. (ISBN 0-387-80869-8). Springer-Verlag.

Irreversible Thermodynamics. Science Press Staff. 1981. 42.95 o.p. (ISBN 0-442-20074-9). Van Nos Reinhold.

Irrigation & Agricultural Development. S. S. Johl & C. De Clerq. LC 80-40435. (Illus.). 386p. 1980. 89.00 o.p. (ISBN 0-08-025675-9). Pergamon.

Irrigation & Society in Medieval Valencia. Thomas F. Glick. LC 79-95923. (Illus.). 1970. 29.50x o.s.i. (ISBN 0-674-46675-6, Belknap Pr). Harvard U Pr.

Irrigation: International Guide to Organizations & Institutions. Ed. by International Irrigation Information Center, Bet Dagan, Israel Staff. LC 80-49935. 165p. 1980. 71.00 o.p. (ISBN 0-08-026363-1). Pergamon.

Irrigation Managament in Japan: A Critical Review of Japanese Social Science Research. William W. Kelly. (Occasional Paper Ser.: No. 12). 85p. 1982. 7.35 o.p. (ISBN 0-317-56267-3). Cornell CIS RDC.

Irrigation of Field & Orchard Crops Under Semi-Arid Conditions. Ed. by J. Shalhevet et al. (Illus.). 110p. 1980. pap. text ed. 13.75 o.p. (ISBN 0-08-025511-6). Pergamon.

Irritation Testing of Skin & Mucous Membranes: Proceedings of a Workshop Held at the Karthhaus-Ittingen, near Frauenfeld, Switzerland, April 1984. Ed. by C. Reinhart et al. (Illus.). 180p. 1985. pap. 41.00 o.p. (ISBN 0-08-032004-X, Pub. by PPL). Pergamon.

Irvin S. Cobb. Wayne Chatterton. (Twayne's United States Authors Ser.: 493). 192p. 1986. lib. bdg. 18.95x o.p. (ISBN 0-8057-7452-1, Twayne). G K Hall.

Irving Berlin: Master Composer of Twentieth Century Songs. Barbara Salsini. Ed. by D. Steve Rahmas. (Outstanding Personalities Ser.: No. 15). 32p. (Orig.). (YA) (gr. 7-12). 1972. lib. bdg. 3.75 incl. catalog cards o.p. (ISBN 0-87157-515-9); pap. 2.50 vinyl laminated covers o.p. (ISBN 0-87157-015-7). SamHar Pr.

Irving Norman: The Human Condition Paintings, 1965-1985. Alternative Museum Staff. LC 85-73713. (Illus.). 1986. pap. 5.00 o.p. (ISBN 0-932075-06-1). Alternative Mus.

Irving Solution. Leonard Simon. LC 76-39719. 1977. 7.95 o.p. (ISBN 0-87795-158-6, Arbor Hse). Morrow.

Irving Solution. Leonard Simon. 1978. pap. 1.75 o.p. (ISBN 0-380-01928-0, 37770). Avon.

Irving's Delight. Art Buchwald. 1976. pap. 1.50 o.p. (ISBN 0-380-00678-2, 29660). Avon.

Is Any Among You Sick? The Dynamics of a Healing Ministry. Gene G. Day. 1979. pap. 3.95 o.p. (ISBN 0-682-49494-1). Exposition-Phoenix.

Is Anyone There? Una Leavy. LC 86-3434. 32p. (ps-2). 1986. 11.95 o.p. (ISBN 0-87226-083-6, Bedrick Blackie). P Bedrick Bks.

Is Chelsea Going Blind? Alida E. Young. 160p. (gr. 5-8). 1986. 2.50 o.p. (ISBN 0-87406-134-2). Willowisp Pr.

Is Conscience a Crime? Norman Thomas. Bd. with War's Heretics: A Plan for the Conscientious Objector. Norman Thomas; Individual & the State. Roger Baldwin. LC 71-147658. (Library of War & Peace; Conscrip. & Cons. Object.). 1973. lib. bdg. 46.00 o.p. (ISBN 0-8240-0421-3). Garland Pub.

Is Divorce the Answer? An Examination of No-Fault Divorce Against the Background of the Irish Debate. William Binchy. 116p. 1984. pap. 10.00x o.p. (ISBN 0-7165-0314-X, BBA 04861, Pub. by Irish Academic Pr Ireland). Biblio Dist.

Is God Cruel? Jackie M. Smith. (Illus., Orig.). (gr. 11-12). 1965. pap. 1.25 o.p. (ISBN 0-8042-9345-7, John Knox). Westminster John Knox.

Is God Dead Within You? Shirley O. Crawford. 112p. 1981. 6.50 o.p. (ISBN 0-682-49789-4). Exposition-Phoenix.

Is God Really Fair? Dick Dowsett. 1985. pap. 3.95 o.p. (ISBN 0-8024-3277-8). Moody.

Is God Still Here: Q-Book No. 15. C. Alton Robertson. (Orig.). 1968. pap. 0.75 o.p. (ISBN 0-377-86371-8). Friendship Pr.

Is Inflation Ending? Are You Ready? A. G. Shilling & Kiril Sokoloff. LC 82-23962. (Illus.). 288p. 1983. text ed. 18.95 o.p. (ISBN 0-07-056879-0). McGraw.

Is It Really Only Monday? PlanBook. David Sipress. (gr. k-6). 1981. pap. 4.95 o.p. (ISBN 0-8224-3829-1). D S Lake Pubs.

Is It Really So? A Guide to Clear Thinking. Dwight J. Ingle. LC 75-28253. 1976. softcover 3.50 o.s.i. (ISBN 0-664-24783-0, Westminster). Westminster John Knox.

Is It True What They Say About Edgar Cayce? Lytle W. Robinson. 192p. 1981. pap. 2.95 o.s.i. (ISBN 0-425-06754-8). Berkley Pub.

Is It Worth Remembering. Jesse T. McLeod. 1988. 18.95 o.p. (ISBN 0-938936-69-7). Daring Bks.

Is Man the Phoenix? A Study of Immortality. Bruce Reichenbach. LC 82-21905. 198p. 1983. pap. text ed. 11.50 o.p. (ISBN 0-8191-2672-1). U Pr of Amer.

Is President John F. Kennedy Alive... & Well? Beranrd M. Bane. LC 88-116961. 189p. 1988. pap. 9.00 o.p. (ISBN 0-930924-29-0). BMB Pub Co.

Is President John F. Kennedy Alive... & Well? Bernard M. Bane. LC 76-21807. 161p. 1981. pap. 7.50 o.s.i. (ISBN 0-930924-08-8). BMB Pub Co.

Is Salami & Eggs Better Than Sex? Memoirs of a Happy Eater. Alan King & Mimi Sheraton. 176p. 1985. 15.95 o.p. (ISBN 0-316-49365-1). Little.

Is That All There Is? Overcoming Disappointment in an Age of Diminished Expectations. David Brandt. 1984. 14.50 o.s.i. (ISBN 0-671-45892-2, Poseidon). PB.

Is That It? Bob Geldof. (Illus.). 360p. 1987. 18.95 o.s.i. (ISBN 1-55584-115-5). Weidenfeld.

Is That What People Do? Robert Sheckley. 409p. 1984. 19.95 o.p. (ISBN 0-03-063707-4). H Holt & Co.

Is That What People Do? Robert Sheckley. LC 83-12908. 19.45 o.p. HR&W.

Is the Cat Dreaming Your Dream. Margaret O. Hyde. LC 79-22684. (gr. 7-9). 1980. text ed. 8.95 o.p. (ISBN 0-07-031594-9). McGraw.

Is There a Fortune Waiting for You? Theodore W. Roth. 256p. 1974. 6.95 o.p. (ISBN 0-8065-0434-X, Pub. by Citadel Pr). Carol Pub Group.

Is There Life after Death? Robert Kastenbaum. (Illus.). 208p. (Orig.). 1986. pap. 7.95 o.p. (ISBN 0-668-06524-9). P-H.

Is There Life after Housework? Don A. Aslett. LC 81-11666. (Illus.). 134p. 1981. pap. 6.95 o.p. (ISBN 0-89879-067-0). Writers Digest.

Is There Life in Outer Space? Robert Kraske. LC 76-929. (Illus.). 86p. (gr. 5 up). 1976. 7.95 o.p. (ISBN 0-15-239190-8, HJ). HarBraceJ.

Is There Sex after Marriage? Carol Botwin. 320p. 1985. 16.95 o.p. (ISBN 0-316-10350-0). Little.

Is This a Put-on? Lee Finks. LC 85-90999. 120p. 1985. 3.00 o.p. (ISBN 0-682-40233-8). Exposition-Phoenix.

Is United States Military Intervention in Central America Illegal? Jules Lobel & Michael Ratner. 1.00 o.p. Natl Lawyers Guild.

Is Your God Big Enough? Mildred Tengbom. LC 72-90261. 128p. (Orig.). 1973. pap. 2.95 o.p. (ISBN 0-8066-1308-4, 10-3403, Augsburg). Augsburg Fortress.

Isaac Asimov: A Checklist of Works Published in the United States. Marjorie M. Miller. LC 72-76948. (Serif Ser.: No. 25). 111p. 1972. 11.00x o.p. (ISBN 0-87338-126-2). Kent St U Pr.

Isaac Asimov's Fantasy. Isaac Asimov. Ed. by Shawna McCarthy. LC 78-60795. 348p. 1985. 12.95 o.p. (ISBN 0-385-23017-6, Dial). Doubleday.

Isaac Asimov's Near Futures & Far. Isaac Asimov. (Illus.). 288p. 1981. 10.95 o.s.i. (ISBN 0-385-27205-7, Dial). Doubleday.

Isaac Babel, Russian Master of the Short Story. James E. Falen. Date not set. write for info. o.p. U of Tenn Pr.

Isaac I. Stevens: Young Man in a Hurry. Kent D. Richards. LC 79-13637. (Illus.). 1979. 5.95x o.p. (ISBN 0-8425-1697-2). Brigham.

Isaac Israeli: A Neoplatonic Philosopher of the Early Tenth Century. Isaac Israeli. Compiled by A. Altmann & S. M. Stern. LC 78-26529. 1979. Repr. of 1958 ed. lib. bdg. 35.00x o.p. (ISBN 0-313-20844-1, ISNP). Greenwood.

Isabel's Double. Kenneth Lillington. LC 83-25317. 128p. (gr. 6 up). 1984. 11.95 o.p. (ISBN 0-571-13197-2). Faber & Faber.

Isadora Duncan: The Russian Years. Ilya I. Schneider. Tr. by David Magarshack. LC 69-14517. (Helen & Kurt Wolff Bk.). (Illus.). 1969. 6.95 o.p. (ISBN 0-15-145740-9). HarBraceJ.

Isaiah-Daniel, Vol. IV. Beacon Bible Commentary Staff. 15.95 o.p. (ISBN 0-8010-0691-0). Baker Bk.

ISAM-GENT Nineteen Eighty-One. Ed. by F. D. Stott et al. 672p. 1982. 96.00 o.p. (ISBN 0-12-672360-5). Acad Pr.

ISAM Nineteen Seventy-Seven. Ed. by F. D. Stott. 1978. 72.00 o.p. (ISBN 0-12-672350-8). Acad Pr.

Isamu Noguchi: A Study of the Sculpture. Nancy Grove. Ed. by S. J. Freedberg. (Outstanding Dissertations in Fine Arts Ser.). (Illus.). 310p. 1985. Repr. of 1983 ed. 55.00 o.p. (ISBN 0-8240-6866-1). Garland Pub.

ISBN, ISSN: A Book's Fingerprints. Florencio O. Garcia. 18p. 1986. write for info. o.s.i. (ISBN 0-9616535-1-5). Fog Pubns.

Iscariot. Bertil Gartner. Ed. by John Reumann. Tr. by Victor I. Gruhn from Ger. LC 73-157544. (Facet Bks.). 64p. (Orig.). 1971. pap. 0.50 o.p. (ISBN 0-8006-3065-3, 1-3065, Fortress). Augsburg Fortress.

ISCEBS Continuing Education Course (1983-1984) Answers to the Questions on Subject Matter for the Learning Guide (Study Aid, Vol. 1. 1984. spiral bd. 12.00 o.p. (ISBN 0-911731-06-7). Intl Soc Emp.

ISDN & Its Impact on Information Technology: Related Conference Proceedings. Ed. by J. E. Flood & C. J. Hughes. (IEE Conference Publication: No. 244). 150p. 1985. pap. 70.00 o.s.i. (ISBN 0-85296-309-2, IC244). Inst Elect Eng.

ISDN: Concepts, Methods, & Systems. Peter Bocker. 250p. 1988. text ed. 66.00 o.s.i. (ISBN 0-89006-275-7). Artech Hse.

ISDN: Technology, Applications & Standards. William Stallings. 352p. 1988. 34.95 o.p. (ISBN 0-02-948074-4). Macmillan.

Ish River. Robert Sund. LC 82-73721. 80p. (Orig.). 1983. pap. 7.50 o.p. (ISBN 0-86547-102-9). N Point Pr.

Ishi, Last of His Tribe. Theodora Kroeber. LC 64-19401. (Illus.). (gr. 4 up). 1964. 7.95 o.p. (ISBN 0-395-27716-7, Pub. by Parnassus). HM.

Ishkabibble! Dorothy Crayder. LC 75-30862. (Illus.). (gr. 4-6). 1976. 5.95 o.p. (ISBN 0-689-30499-4, Atheneum). Macmillan.

Ishmael My Brother. Compiled by Anne Cooper. pap. 5.95 o.s.i. (ISBN 0-912552-47-6). Missions Adv Res Com Ctr.

Ishmael Reed: A Primary & Secondary Bibliography. Elizabeth A. Settle & Thomas A. Settle. 155p. 1982. lib. bdg. 29.00 o.s.i. (ISBN 0-8161-8514-X, Hall Reference). G K Hall.

Isidore of Seville on the Pagan Gods. Katherine N. MacFarlane. LC 79-54274. (Transactions Ser: Vol. 70, pt. 3). 1980. 10.00 o.p. (ISBN 0-87169-703-3). Am Philos.

Islam at a Glance. Ed. by Hakeem A. Hameed. 125p. 1981. text ed. 15.00x o.p. (ISBN 0-7069-1313-2, Pub. by Vikas India); pap. 4.95x o.p. (ISBN 0-7069-1413-9). Advent NY.

Islam in Africa South of the Sahara: A Select Bibliographic Guide. Patrick E. Ofori. 223p. 1977. lib. bdg. 42.00 o.p. (ISBN 3-262-00003-5). Kraus Intl.

Islam in Asia. Rafi Israeli. 350p. 1979. 24.95 o.p. (ISBN 0-87855-367-3). Transaction Pubs.

Islam in the Modern World. Elie Kedourie. 336p. 1981. 17.95 o.p. (ISBN 0-03-059213-5). H Holt & Co.

Islam Reconsidered: A Brief Historical Background to the Religion & Thought of the Moslem World. Kenneth Oster. 1979. 7.50 o.p. (ISBN 0-682-49189-6, University). Exposition-Phoenix.

Islam: The Way of Submission. Solomon Nigosian. 208p. pap. cancelled o.s.i. (ISBN 0-317-57150-8). Inner Tradit.

Islamic Art & Architecture. LC 76-14076. (Garland Library of the History of Art: XIII). 1977. lib. bdg. 61.00 o.p. (ISBN 0-8240-2423-0). Garland Pub.

Islamic Carpets & Textiles. Friedrich Spuhler. Tr. by George Wingfield Digby & Cornelia Wingfield Digby. (Illus.). 251p. 1978. 75.00 o.p. (ISBN 0-571-09783-9). Faber & Faber.

Islamic Cosmology. Anton M. Heinen. 366p. (Orig.). 1982. pap. text ed. 63.50x o.p. (ISBN 3-515-03177-4, Pub. by Franz Steiner). Coronet Bks.

Islamic Jesus: An Annotated Bibliography of Sources in English & French. Don Wismer. LC 76-24737. (Reference Library of the Humanities Ser.: Vol. 58). 1977. lib. bdg. 40.00 o.p. (ISBN 0-8240-9940-0). Garland Pub.

Islamic Medicine. Muhammad S. Khan. (Illus.). 102p. Date not set. lib. bdg. 24.95 o.p. (ISBN 0-7102-0329-2). Routledge Chapman & Hall.

Islamic Metalwork in the Freer Gallery of Art. Esin Atil et al. (Illus.). 273p. (Orig.). 1985. pap. 14.00 o.p. (ISBN 0-318-18776-0, S/N 047-001-00161-3). USGPO.

Islamic Patterns: An Analytical & Cosmological Approach. Keith Critchlow. LC 82-74543. (Illus.). 192p. 1984. pap. 12.95f o.s.i. (ISBN 0-500-27071-6). Thames Hudson.

Islamic State. Asgar Ali Engineer. 192p. 1981. text ed. 20.00x o.p. (ISBN 0-89891-002-1, Pub. by Vikas India). Advent NY.

Islamic Tradition. World Religions Development Center. (Illus.). 144p. 1987. pap. 8.95 o.p. (ISBN 0-89505-009-9); pap. 3.75 guide Bk. o.p. Tabor Pub.

Islamization among the Upper Pokomo. 2nd ed. Robert L. Bunger. LC 80-242. (Foreign & Comparative Studies-African Ser.: No. 33). 128p. (Orig.). 1979. pap. 7.00x o.p. (ISBN 0-915984-55-5). Syracuse U Foreign Comp.

Island. Thomas Perry. 320p. 1989. pap. 3.95 o.p. (ISBN 0-380-70663-6). Avon.

Island. Neal Travis. 528p. 1986. pap. 4.50 o.p. (ISBN 0-380-75089-9). Avon.

Island: A Native History of America's Coastal Islands. Bill Thomas. (Illus.). 1980. 29.95 o.p. (ISBN 0-393-01373-1). Norton.

Island Biogeography of Mammals. Ed. by L. R. Heaney & B. D. Patterson. 256p. 1986. pap. text ed. 27.00 o.p. (ISBN 0-12-335735-7). Acad Pr.

Island Called California: An Ecological Introduction to Its Natural Communities. Elna Bakker. LC 70-107657. (Illus.). 1971. 15.95 o.p. (ISBN 0-520-01682-3); pap. 4.95 o.p. (ISBN 0-520-02159-2, CAL244). U of Cal Pr.

Island Cruising Club Book of Ropework for Yachtsmen. Robert Dearn. 128p. 1987. 22.95 o.p. (ISBN 0-7153-8937-8). David & Charles.

Island Ecosystems: Biological Organization in Selected Hawaiian Communities. Ed. by Dieter Mueller-Dombois. Kent W. Bridges & Hampton L. Carson. LC 80-27650. (U. S. - IBP Synthesis Ser.: Vol. 15). 608p. 1982. 42.95 o.p. (ISBN 0-87933-381-2). Van Nos Reinhold.

Island Flame. Karen Robards. 352p. (Orig.). 1983. pap. 3.50 o.s.i. (ISBN 0-8439-2046-7, Pub. by Leisure Bks CT). Dorchester Pub Co.

Island in Time: A Memoir of Childhood. Olga Carlisle. LC 79-9434. (Illus.). 240p. 1980. 12.95 o.p. (ISBN 0-03-053326-0). H Holt & Co.

Island Intrigue. Preston MacAdams. (Michael Sheriff: The Shield Ser.: No. 3). 208p. 1985. pap. 2.95 o.p. (ISBN 0-380-89689-3). Avon.

Island of Bute. Ian S. Munro. (Islands Ser). (Illus.). 208p. 1973. 19.95 o.p. (ISBN 0-7153-6081-7). David & Charles.

Island of Crimea. Vassily Aksyonov. Tr. by Michael H. Heim. 1983. 16.45 o.p. (ISBN 0-394-52431-4). Random.

Island of Dogs. Lee Falk. (Phantom Ser.: No. 13). (Orig.). 1975. pap. 0.95 o.p. (ISBN 0-380-00243-4, 23085). Avon.

Island of Flowers. Nora Roberts. (Silhouette Romances Ser.). 1984. lib. bdg. 8.95 o.p. (ISBN 0-8398-2819-5, Gregg). G K Hall.

Island of Nightmares. Leota A. Grady. 112p. 1987. 8.75 o.p. (ISBN 0-8062-3050-9). Carlton.
Island of Silence. 3rd ed. Carolyn B. Norris. LC 83-71342. (Illus.). 240p. 1983. pap. 4.50 o.p. (ISBN 0-933076-03-7). Alinda Pr.
Island on the Edge of the World: The Story of St. Kilda. Charles Maclean. LC 79-63116. (Illus.). 176p. 1980. 8.95 o.s.i. (ISBN 0-8008-4263-4). Taplinger.
Island Paradise. Patricia Pickney. 1976. pap. 1.50 o.p. (ISBN 0-380-01306-1, 15388). Avon.
Island Race. Winston S. Churchill. (Illus.). 320p. 1985. 24.95 o.s.i. (ISBN 0-396-08750-7). Dodd.
Island Rogue. Linda R. Wisdom. (Nightingale Ser.). 347p. 1986. pap. 10.95x o.p. (ISBN 0-8161-4044-8, Large Print Bks). G K Hall.
Island Sunrise: Prehistoric Culture in the British Isles. Jill P. Walsh. LC 75-4666. (Illus.). 128p. (gr. 6 up). 1979. 8.95 o.p. (ISBN 0-395-28928-9, Clarion). HM.
Island to Island. Alistair Campbell. 120p. 1986. 16.95 o.p. (ISBN 0-7233-0735-0, Pub. by Whitcoulls NZ). Intl Spec Bk.
Island Voices: Stories from the West Indies. new ed. V. S. Naipaul et al. Ed. by Andrew Salkey. 1970. pap. 4.95 o.p. (ISBN 0-87140-229-7). Liveright.
Island Within. Ludwig Lewisohn. LC 79-14091. (Jewish Legacy Ser.). 1979. pap. 5.95x o.p. (ISBN 0-87441-318-4). Behrman.
Islands. Bill Robinson. (Illus.). 216p. 1985. 22.95 o.p. Dodd.
Islands, Capes, & Sounds: The North Carolina Coast. Thomas J. Schoenbaum. LC 81-21557. (Illus.). 352p. 1982. 22.50 o.p. (ISBN 0-89587-021-5). Blair.
Islands of Experience. Dean Nichols. 1972. 5.00 o.p. (ISBN 0-682-47549-1). Exposition-Phoenix.
Islands of History. Marshall Sahlins. LC 84-8820. (Illus.). 224p. 1985. 22.50x o.s.i. (ISBN 0-226-73357-2). U of Chicago Pr.
Islands of Ireland. Kenneth McNally. (Illus.). 1979. 17.95 o.p. (ISBN 0-393-04509-9). Norton.
Islands of Terror. R. G. Austin. (Which Way Bks.: No. 18). (Illus., Orig.). (gr. 3-6). 1985. pap. 1.95 o.p. (ISBN 0-671-52636-7). Archway.
Islands of the West: From Baja to Vancouver. Page Stegner. LC 85-2164. (Illus.). 152p. 1985. 35.00 o.p. (ISBN 0-87156-844-6). Sierra.
Islands Out of Time: A Memoir of the Last Days of Atlantis. William I. Thompson. LC 85-1478. 240p. 1985. 16.95 o.p. (ISBN 0-385-19571-0, Dial). Doubleday.
Isle of Man: A Book About the Manx. Christopher Killip. (Illus.). 96p. 1980. 25.00 o.s.i. (ISBN 0-7287-0187-1); pap. 12.95 o.s.i. (ISBN 0-7287-0186-3). Eastview.
Isle of Palms: Sketches of Hainan. American Presbyterian Mission Staff. LC 78-74354. (Modern Chinese Economy Ser.: Vol. 21). 141p. 1980. lib. bdg. 20.00 o.p. (ISBN 0-8240-4269-7). Garland Pub.
Isle of the Shapeshifters. Otto Coontz. 224p. (gr. 5up). 1983. 6.70 o.p. (ISBN 0-395-34552-9). HM.
Isles & Continents. Maurice L. Draper. (Orig.). 1982. pap. 14.00 o.p. (ISBN 0-8309-0343-7). Herald Hse.
Isms & Ologies. Atnold Kellett. 160p. 1966. (ISBN 0-8022-0841-X). Philos Lib.
Isoelectric Focusing. Ed. by Nicholas Catsimpoolas. 1976. 60.50 o.p. (ISBN 0-12-163950-9). Acad Pr.
Isoenzymes. D. W. Moss. (Illus.). 224p. 1982. 44.00 o.p. (ISBN 0-412-22200-0, NO. 6722, Pub. by Chapman & Hall England). Routledge Chapman & Hall.
Isolated Schools. C. Turney et al. 152p. 1980. pap. 17.00x o.p. (ISBN 0-424-00068-7, Pub. by Sydney U Pr Australia). Intl Spec Bk.
Isolated Splendor: Put-in-Bay & South Bass Island. Robert J. Dodge. (YA) 1975. 12.50 o.p. (ISBN 0-682-48233-1, Lochinvar). Exposition-Phoenix.
Isolation & Protest. R. K. Sharma. 182p. 1983. text ed. 17.50x o.p. (ISBN 0-391-02949-5). Humanities.
Isolation & Purification of Hormones. Melvin Weisbart et al. (Illus.). 220p. 1973. text ed. 20.00x o.p. (ISBN 0-8422-7107-4). Irvington.
Isoquinoline Alkaloids: Chemistry & Pharmacology. Maurice Shamma. 1972. 43.50 o.p. (ISBN 0-12-638250-6). Acad Pr.
Isotope Dilution Analysis. J. Tolgyessy et al. 196p. 1972. 50.00 o.p. (ISBN 0-08-015856-0). Pergamon.
Isotopic Gas Analysis for Biochemists. Raymond Glascock. 1954. 26.00 o.p. (ISBN 0-12-286150-7). Acad Pr.
Isotopic Tracers in Biology: An Introduction to Tracer Methodology. 3rd ed. Martin D. Kamen. (Organic & Biological Chemistry, Vol. 1). 1957. 79.50 o.p. (ISBN 0-12-394862-2). Acad Pr.
ISPRS Commission IV, 1982 Symposium on Cartographic & Data Bank Applications of Photogrammetry & Remote Sensing. 579p. 1983. 17.00 o.p. (ISBN 0-937294-45-4). ASP & RS.
Israel. Fred Feldman. (Orig.). 1984. pap. 3.95 o.p. (ISBN 0-440-03842-1). Dell.
Israel. Time-Life Books Editors. (Library of Nations). (Illus.). 160p. (YA) (gr. 7 up). 1986. lib. bdg. 23.93 o.p. Time-Life.
Israel: A First View. Snowdon. (Illus.). 1986. 19.95 o.p. (ISBN 0-316-80226-3). Little.
Israel: A History of the Jewish People. Israel Goldberg. LC 72-162629. 715p. 1972. Repr. lib. bdg. 29.50x o.p. (ISBN 0-8371-6196-7, GOIS). Greenwood.
Israel after Begin. Daniel Gavron. 240p. 1984. 13.45 o.p. (ISBN 0-395-35320-3). HM.
Israel after the Exile: Sixth & Fifth Centuries B. C. William F. Lofthouse. LC 78-10629. (Illus.). 1979. Repr. of 1928 ed. lib. bdg. 35.00x o.p. (ISBN 0-313-21008-X, LOIS). Greenwood.
Israel & South Africa: The Progression of a Relationship. LC 76-47719. 1978. Repr. pap. 8.00 o.p. (ISBN 0-911026-03-7). New World Press NY.
Israel & the Creation of a Palestinian State: A European Perspective. Joseph Weiler. LC 85-5929. 160p. 1985. 27.50 o.p. (ISBN 0-7099-3605-2, Pub. by Croom Helm Ltd). Routledge Chapman & Hall.
Israel & the Dead Sea Scrolls. Edmund Wilson. 416p. 1978. pap. 9.25 o.p. (ISBN 0-374-51341-4). FS&G.
Israel & the Holy Land. Dymphna Byrne. (Rand McNally Pocket Guide). (Illus.). 95p. 1985. pap. 5.95 o.p. (ISBN 0-528-84874-7). Rand McNally.
Israel & the Holy Land. (Phaidon Cultural Guides Ser.). (Illus.). 1987. 17.95 o.p. (ISBN 0-13-506320-5). P-H.
Israel & the Occupied Territories. Lynne R. Franks. LC 87-18817. (World Education Ser.). (Illus.). 288p. (Orig.). 1987. pap. 15.00 o.p. (ISBN 0-910054-87-8). Am Assn Coll Registrars.
Israel Defence Forces Insignia. M. Furlan. 70p. 1986. pap. 7.00 o.p. WW Milit Exch.
Israel for Christians. A. James Rudin. LC 82-7241. 160p. (Orig.). 1983. pap. 8.95 o.p. (ISBN 0-8006-1643-X, 1-1643). Augsburg Fortress.
Israel: Heroes & Hustlers, Hard Hats & Holy Men. Ze'ev Chafets. 288p. 1986. 17.95 o.p. (ISBN 0-688-04337-2). Morrow.
Israel in America: A Too-Comfortable Exile? Jacob Neusner. LC 84-45719. 160p. 1985. 14.95 o.p. (ISBN 0-8070-3602-1). Beacon Pr.
Israel in America: A Too-Comfortable Exile? Jacob Neusner. LC 84-45719. 212p. 1986. pap. 8.95 o.p. (ISBN 0-8070-3603-X, BP719). Beacon Pr.
Israel in Revolution, 6-74 C.E. A Political History Based on the Writings of Josephus. David M. Rhoads. LC 75-36452. 208p. 1976. 5.00 o.p. (ISBN 0-8006-0442-3, 1-442); pap. 3.00 o.p. (ISBN 0-8006-1442-9, 1-1442, Fortress). Augsburg Fortress.
Israel on Thirty & Thirty Five Dollars a Day, 1984-85. (Dollar a Day Guides). 354p. 1983. 9.95 o.p. (ISBN 0-671-47594-0). Prentice Hall Pr.
Israel: The Changing National Agenda. Avraham Schweitzer. 192p. 1986. 34.50 o.p. (ISBN 0-7099-3382-7, Pub. by Croom Helm UK). Routledge Chapman & Hall.
Israel, the Korean War & China. Michael Brecher. (Shiloah Ser.). 1974. text ed. 6.95 o.p. (ISBN 0-87855-233-2). Transaction Pubs.
Israel: The Partitioned State. Amos Perlmutter. (Illus.). 384p. 1985. 19.95 o.p. (ISBN 0-684-18396-X, ScribT). Scribner.
Israel Yearbook, 1985. 41st ed. 1986. 45.00 o.p. (ISBN 0-8002-3980-6). Intl Pubns Serv.
Israeli Communist Party. Moshe M. Czudnowski & Jacob M. Landau. LC 65-19765. (Studies Ser.: No. 9). 1965. pap. 5.95x o.p. (ISBN 0-8179-3092-2). Hoover Inst Pr.
Israeli Film: Social & Cultural Influences 1912-1973. O. G. Arzooni. Ed. by Garth S. Jowett. LC 81-48345. (Dissertations on Film Ser.). 387p. 1983. lib. bdg. 55.00 o.p. (ISBN 0-8240-5102-5). Garland Pub.
Israeli Occupation: International Law & Political Realities. Donald E. George. 1980. 12.50 o.p. (ISBN 0-682-49439-9). Exposition-Phoenix.
Israeli Secret Service. 2nd ed ed. Richard Deacon. LC 78-5685. (Illus.). 326p. 1985. pap. 3.95 o.s.i. (ISBN 0-8008-4268-5). Taplinger.
Israeli Tanks & Combat Vehicles. Steven J. Zaloga. (Tanks Illustrated Ser.: Vol. 3). (Illus.). 64p. (Orig.). 1985. pap. 9.95 o.p. (ISBN 0-85368-580-0, Pub. by Arms & Armour). Sterling.
Israeli Vacuum Congress, Fourth: Proceedings. Ed. by J. Yarwood. 1977. pap. 26.00 o.p. (ISBN 0-08-021284-0). Pergamon.
Israelite & Judaean History. Ed. by John H. Hayes & J. Maxwell Miller. LC 76-41913. (Old Testament Library). (Illus.). 768p. 1977. 27.50 o.s.i. (ISBN 0-664-21291-3, Westminster). Westminster John Knox.
Israelite Religion. Helmer Ringgren. Tr. by David E. Green from Ger. LC 66-10757. 408p. 1975. pap. 7.95 o.p. (ISBN 0-8006-1121-7, 1-1121, Fortress). Augsburg Fortress.
Israelitische Pfingstfest und der Plejadenkult. Hubert Grimme. 1907. pap. 12.00 o.p. (ISBN 0-384-20060-5). Johnson Repr.
Israel's Apostasy & Restoration in Prophetic Thought: Essays in Honor of Roland Kenneth Harrison. Ed. by Avraham Gileadi. 336p. 1987. 26.95 o.p. (ISBN 0-8407-7532-6). Nelson.
Israel's Lebanon War. Ze'ev Schiff & Ehud Ya'ari. Tr. by Ina Friedman. 340p. 1984. 18.45 o.p. (ISBN 0-671-47991-1). S&S.
ISRM List of Members, 1980. ISRM Staff. 250p. 1981. pap. 51.00 o.p. (ISBN 0-08-027587-7). Pergamon.
Issue in Literary Criticism. Myron F. Brightfield. LC 68-23278. 1968. Repr. of 1932 ed. lib. bdg. 35.00x o.p. (ISBN 0-8371-0029-1, BRLC). Greenwood.
Issue of Small Versus Large in the Indian Textile Industry: An Analytical & Historical Survey. Dipak Mazumdar. (World Bank Staff Working Papers: No. 645). 112p. 1985. 5.00 o.p. (ISBN 0-8213-0364-3). World Bank.
Issue Voting & Party Realignment. Donald S. Strong. LC 77-1087. 128p. 1977. 12.95 o.p. (ISBN 0-8173-4836-0); pap. 6.95 o.p. (ISBN 0-8173-4837-9). U of Ala Pr.
Issues & Trends in Contemporary Politics. rev. ed. Ed. by William O. Peterfi. LC 81-43762. (Illus.). 1983. pap. text ed. 10.00 o.p. (ISBN 0-8191-2667-5). U Pr of Amer.
Issues Before the Thirty-Seventh General Assembly of the United Nations. United Nations Association of the U. S. A. Staff. Ed. by Donald J. Puchala. 168p. 1982. 18.00x o.p. (ISBN 0-669-06398-3). Lexington Bks.
Issues Before the 38th General Assembly of the United Nations. United Nations Association Staff. 180p. 1983. 19.00x o.p. (ISBN 0-669-07391-1). Lexington Bks.
Issues Before the 41st General Assembly of the United Nations. Ed. by John Tessitore. LC 86-45595. 208p. 1986. 25.00x o.p. (ISBN 0-669-14013-9); pap. text ed. 14.95x o.p. (ISBN 0-669-14012-0). Lexington Bks.
Issues in Acoustics Signal-Image Processing & Recognition. Ed. by C. H. Chen. (NATO ASI Series, F: Computer & System Sciences: Vol. 1). 333p. 1983. 48.80 o.p. (ISBN 0-387-12192-7). Springer-Verlag.
Issues in Adult Basic Education & Other Adult Education: An Annotated Bibliography & Guide to Research. Darlene F. Russ-Eft et al. LC 80-16926. (Garland Bibliographies in Contemporary Education, Vol. 1; Garland Reference Library of Social Science). 200p. 1980. 31.00 o.p. (ISBN 0-8240-9551-0). Garland Pub.
Issues in Aggregation. Ed. by Karlene H. Roberts & Leigh Burstein. LC 80-81900. (Methodology of Social & Behavioral Science Ser.: No. 6). 1980. pap. text ed. 13.95x o.p. (ISBN 0-87589-850-5). Jossey-Bass.
Issues in Business & Society. 3rd ed. William T. Greenwood. LC 76-12021. (Illus.). 576p. 1977. pap. 14.75 o.p. (ISBN 0-395-21410-6). HM.
Issues in Canadian Economics. Lawrence H. Officer & Lawrence B. Smith. LC 73-21373. 424p. 1975. pap. text ed. 9.95 o.p. (ISBN 0-07-077447-1). McGraw.
Issues in Canadian-U. S. Transborder Computer Data Flows. W. E. Cundiff & Mado Reid. 89p. 1979. pap. text ed. 6.50x o.s.i. (ISBN 0-920380-12-3, Pub. by Inst Res Pub Canada). Gower Pub Co.
Issues in Caribbean International Relations. Ed. by Basil A. Ince et al. LC 82-21733. 360p. (Orig.). 1983. lib. bdg. 33.00 o.p. (ISBN 0-8191-2913-5, Co-pub. by Inst Intl Rel); pap. text ed. 16.50 o.p. (ISBN 0-8191-2914-3). U Pr of Amer.
Issues in Childhood Social Development. Ed. by Harry McGurk. (Psychology in Progress Ser.). 1979. 25.00x o.p. (ISBN 0-416-70560-X, NO.2343); pap. 12.95x o.p. (ISBN 0-416-71500-1, NO.2344). Routledge Chapman & Hall.
Issues in Cognition: Proceedings of a Joint Conference in Psychology. Chinese Academy of Sciences Staff. Ed. by National Academy of Sciences Staff. 475p. (Orig.). 1985. pap. 20.00 o.p. (ISBN 0-912704-98-5, 4060010). Am Psychol.
Issues in Cultural Anthropology: Selected Readings. Ed. by David W. McCurdy & James P. Spradley. 1979. pap. text ed. 15.25 o.p. (ISBN 0-316-55526-6). Little.
Issues in Evaluation & Accountability. Ed. by Colin Lacey & Denis Lawton. LC 81-16925. 1982. 28.00x o.p. (ISBN 0-416-74740-X, NO. 3591); pap. 12.95x o.p. (ISBN 0-416-74750-7, NO. 3592). Routledge Chapman & Hall.
Issues in Foundations of Education. Ed. by Robert B. Primack. 240p. 1970. pap. text ed. 8.95x o.p. (ISBN 0-8290-1109-9). Irvington.
Issues in Income Distribution. Stephen O. Bender et al. Ed. by Ronald Soligo & Fred R. Von der Mehden. (Rice University Studies: Vol. 61, No. 4). (Illus.). 176p. (Orig.). 1976. pap. 10.00x o.p. (ISBN 0-89263-226-7). Rice Univ.
Issues in International Economics. Ed. by Peter Oppenheimer. (Oxford International Symposia). 300p. 1980. 40.00x o.p. (ISBN 0-85362-186-1, Oriel). Routledge Chapman & Hall.
Issues in Italian Syntax. Luigi Rizzi. 202p. 1981. 32.50 o.p. (ISBN 90-70176-33-5); pap. 22.50 o.p. Foris Pubns.
Issues in Personal Perception. Ed. by Mark Cook. (Psychology in Progress Ser.). 280p. 1984. 33.00 o.p. (ISBN 0-416-32450-9, NO. 4173); pap. 12.95 o.p. (ISBN 0-416-32460-6, NO. 4170). Routledge Chapman & Hall.
Issues in Phonological Theory: Proceedings of the Urbana Conference on Phonology, University of Illinois, 1971. Urbana Conference on Phonology Staff. Ed. by Michael J. Kenstowicz & Charles W. Kisseberth. (Janua Linguarum Ser.: No. 74). 1973. 27.20x o.p. (ISBN 90-2792-498-8). Mouton.
Issues in Rock Mechanics: Twenty-Third Symposium. Ed. by Richard E. Goodman & Francios E. Hueze. LC 82-71989. (Illus.). 1133p. 1982. 45.00x o.p. (ISBN 0-89520-297-2). SMM&E Inc.
Issues in Social Policy. 2nd ed. Kathleen Jones & John Brown. 208p. 1983. pap. 10.95x o.p. (ISBN 0-7100-9440-X). Routledge Chapman & Hall.
Issues in Sociological Theory: Another Look at the "Old Masters" James T. Duke. LC 83-14631. 408p. 1983. lib. bdg. 38.25 o.p. (ISBN 0-8191-3455-4); pap. text ed. 18.75 o.p. (ISBN 0-8191-3456-2). U Pr of Amer.
Issues in the Management of Microcomputer Systems. John Barkley & Lynne S. Rosenthal. LC 85-600583. (NBS Special Publication Computer Science & Technology Ser.: No. 500-125). (Illus.). 54p. (Orig.). 1985. pap. 2.25 o.p. (S/N 003-003-02678-6). USGPO.
Issues in the Public Employee Relations Library: Series 1, Vols. 1-10. Incl. Vol. 1. Rethinking the Philosophy of Employee Relations in the Public Service; Vol. 2. Handling Employee Grievances; Vol. 3. How-to of Collective Bargaining; Vol. 4. Pioneer Collective Bargaining Laws for Public Employees; Vol. 5. When School Districts Bargain; Vol. 6. Canadian Trailblazer: The New Collective Bargaining Law; Vol. 7. Strikes & Solutions; Vol. 8. Labor Contract Clauses; Vol. 9. Counseling Employees; Vol. 10. Right to Meet & Confer: Legislative Enactments. 12.00 ea. o.p. Intl Personnel Mgmt.
Issues in the Public Employee Relations Library: Series 2, Vols. 11-20. Incl. Vol. 11. Anatomy of a Comprehensive Employee Relations Program; Vol. 12. Upgrading the Supervisor's Labor Relations Skill; Vol. 13. Drafting the Public Sector Labor Agreement; Vol. 14. Making the Collective Bargaining Agreement Work; Vol. 15. Employee Relations in the Academic Setting; Vol. 16. Getting Ready to Bargain; Vol. 17. New Challenge: The Disadvantaged; Vol. 18. Police Collective Bargaining; Vol. 19. Pricing Employee Benefits; Vol. 20. Six Strike Stories. 12.00 ea. o.p. Intl Personnel Mgmt.
Issues in the Public Employee Relations Library: Series 3, Vols. 21-30. Incl. Vol. 21. Public Personnel Administration: Critique & Credo; Vol. 22. Behavioral Science Approaches to Employee Relations; Vol. 23. New Roles for Public Officials in Labor Relations; Vol. 24. Common Law of the Shop; Vol. 25. Negotiated Grievance Procedures in Public Employment; Vol. 26. Union View of Public Management's Responsibilities in Collective Bargaining; Vol. 27. Collective Public Employee Relations in Australia; Vol. 28. New Horizons in Public Employee Bargaining; Vol. 29. Fact-Finding in the Public Sector: A Case Study; Vol. 30. Labor Relations Source Book. 12.00 ea. o.p. Intl Personnel Mgmt.
Issues in the Public Employee Relations Library: Series 4, Vols. 31-35. Incl. Vol. 31. Day-to-Day Union-Management Relationships; Vol. 32. Collective Public Employee Relations Abroad: Some Foreign Answers to American Questions; Vol. 33. Scope of Collective Bargaining in the Public Sector. o.p.; Vol. 34. Collective Bargaining & Public Administration; Vol. 35. Employee Relations Policy in Local Government. 1971. 12.00 ea. o.p. Intl Personnel Mgmt.

Issues in the Public Employee Relations Library: Series 5, Vols. 36-40. Incl. Vol. 36. Alternate Language for Public: Sector Labor Contracts; Vol. 37. Compulsory Arbitration in Public Employment; Vol. 38. Grievance Arbitration in the Public Sector; Vol. 39. Improving Employee Productivity: A Case Study; Vol. 40. Disciplinary Policies & Practices. 12.00 ea. o.p. Intl Personnel Mgmt.

Issues in Urban Education, Vol. I. Ed. by Earl J. Ogletree. 410p. 1976. pap. text ed. 12.00x o.p. (ISBN 0-8422-0520-9). Irvington.

Issues of Organizational Design: A Mathematical Programming View of Organizations. Borge Obel. (Illus.). 273p. 1981. 42.00 o.p. (ISBN 0-08-025837-9). Pergamon.

Issues, Perspectives, & Definitions: Selected Readings. Ed. by Magdalene M. Carney. LC 74-31130. 197p. 1976. 12.00x o.p. (ISBN 0-8422-5237-1); pap. 6.00x o.p. (ISBN 0-8422-0438-5). Irvington.

Istanbul. John Freely. (Blue Guides Ser.). (Illus.). 400p. 1983. 25.95 o.p. (ISBN 0-393-01558-0); 14.95 o.p. Norton.

Istanbul Boy: Boyle Gelmis Boyle Gitmez (That's How It Was But Not How It's Going to Be) The Autobiography of Aziz Nesin, Pt. 1. Aziz Nesin. Tr. by Joseph S. Jacobson. (Middle East Monographs: No. 3). 239p. 1977. 11.95x o.p. (ISBN 0-292-73810-2, Pub. by Ctr Mid East Stud); pap. 6.95x o.p. (ISBN 0-292-73809-9). U of Tex Pr.

Istanbul: Strolling Through Istanbul. 2nd ed. H. Sumner-Boyd & J. Freely. (Illus.). 1973. pap. 25.00 o.p. (ISBN 0-88431-146-5). E J Brill USA.

Istria Croatian Coast Travel Guide. Berlitz Editors. (Travel Guides Ser.). 1977. pap. 4.95 o.p. (ISBN 0-317-12104-9, Berlitz). Macmillan.

It Ain't Necessarily So: An Autobiography. Larry Adler. LC 86-33485. (Illus.). 256p. 1987. 17.95 o.s.i. (ISBN 0-394-55757-3). Grove.

It All Depends: A Pragmatic Approach to Organization. Harvey Sherman. LC 66-25021. 218p. 1966. pap. 7.50 o.p. (ISBN 0-8173-4833-6). U of Ala Pr.

It All Started with Marx. Richard Armour. 1958. pap. text ed. 5.95 o.p. (ISBN 0-07-002254-2). McGraw.

It Came from the Swamp: Your Federal Government at Work. Susan Trausch. 227p. 1986. 15.45 o.p. (ISBN 0-395-38466-4). HM.

It Came to Pass in the San Juan Islands. Roderic M. Olzendam & Gordon Keith. LC 78-73807. 1978. 7.95 o.p. (ISBN 0-8323-0318-6); pap. 4.95 o.p. (ISBN 0-8323-0319-4). Binford-Metropolitan.

It Can Happen to You. Beatrice. (Illus.). 75p. 1983. 12.00 o.p. (ISBN 0-682-49960-9). Exposition-Phoenix.

It Can't Be Helped. Benjamin Lee. LC 79-1183. 152p. (gr. 7 up). 1979. 7.95 o.p. (ISBN 0-374-33648-2). FS&G.

It Changed My Life: Writings on the Women's Movement. Betty Friedan. 416p. 1985. Repr. of 1985 ed. 7.70 o.p. (ISBN 0-393-30243-1). Norton.

It Did Happen. Maurits Boas. 128p. 1984. 12.95 o.p. (ISBN 0-8119-0530-6). Fell.

It Doesn't Always Have to Rhyme. Eve Merriam. (Illus.). (gr. 5 up). 1964. PLB 5.95 o.p. (ISBN 0-689-20671-2, Atheneum). Macmillan.

It Happened at Mackey's Point. Jane B. Moncure. LC 84-7039. (Illus.). 32p. (gr. 2-3). 1984. lib. bdg. 4.95 o.p. Dandelion Hse.

It Happened in Chichipica. Francis Kalnay. LC 74-158004. (Illus.). 127p. (gr. 4-6). 1971. 4.95 o.p. (ISBN 0-15-239340-4, HJ). HarBraceJ.

It Happened in Our Lifetime: A Memoir in Words & Pictures. John Phillips. 1985. 24.95 o.p. (ISBN 0-316-70609-4). Little.

It Isn't Easy Being Special - Let's Help Special Needs Learners: A Resource Guide for Vocational Education Teachers. Denie Denniston et al. 44p. 1980. 3.25 o.p. (ISBN 0-318-22135-7, RD184). Natl Ctr Res Voc Ed.

It Looked Like for Ever. 1979 ed. Mark Harris. LC 79-14423. 1979. text ed. 9.95 o.p. (ISBN 0-07-026720-0). McGraw.

It Never Rains in Los Angeles. Charles Flowers. 1973. pap. 1.25 o.p. (ISBN 0-380-01308-8, 16766). Avon.

It Pays to Be a Man: Pay Equity Information Packet. Women's Legal Defense Fund Staff. 14p. 1986. 4.00 o.p. (ISBN 0-317-67864-7). Women's Legal Defense.

It Seemed Like Nothing Happened: The Tragedy & Promise in America of the 1970s. Peter N. Carroll. 1982. 19.95 o.p. (ISBN 0-03-058319-5). H Holt & Co.

It Seemed Like Nothing Happened: The Tragedy & Promise of America in the 1970s. Peter N. Carroll. 1984. pap. 9.95 o.s.i. (ISBN 0-03-071057-X). H Holt & Co.

It Seems Like Magic: A Picture-Word Book. (Learning Curves Bks.). (Illus.). 16p. (ps-1). 1987. pap. 4.95 o.p. (ISBN 0-553-18360-5). Bantam.

It Sounds Like Fun: How to Use & Enjoy Your Tape Recorder & Stereo. Edward F. Dolan, Jr. LC 81-296. (Illus.). 192p. (gr. 7 up). 1981. lib. bdg. 9.79 o.s.i. (ISBN 0-671-34053-0). Messner.

It Takes Brains. Eiveen Weiman. LC 81-10805. 276p. (gr. 3-7). 1982. PLB 10.95 o.p. (ISBN 0-689-30896-5, Atheneum). Macmillan.

It Takes More Than Excellence. William S. Appleton. 192p. 1987. 13.70 o.p. (ISBN 0-671-60025-7). P-H.

It Was a Pretty Good Year. Jane Flory. LC 77-21782. (gr. 3-7). 1977. 6.95 o.p. (ISBN 0-395-25835-9). HM.

It Will Be Worth It All: A Study in the Believer's Rewards. Woodrow M. Kroll. LC 76-30438. 1977. pap. 2.50 o.s.i. (ISBN 0-87213-475-X). Loizeaux.

Italian-American Catalog. Joseph Giordano. LC 85-4556. (Illus.). 256p. 1986. 14.95 o.p. (ISBN 0-385-19375-0, Dolp). Doubleday.

Italian-Americans. rev. ed. Luciano J. Iorizzo & Salvatore Mondello. (Immigrant Heritage of America Ser.). 1980. lib. bdg. 20.95 o.s.i. (ISBN 0-8057-8416-0, Twayne). G K Hall.

Italian Armor for Princely Courts. Leonid Tarassuk. (Illus.). 24p. 1986. pap. 5.00 o.p. (ISBN 0-86559-080-X). Art Inst Chi.

Italian Art: Fourteen Hundred to Fifteen Hundred. C. Gilbert. 1980. pap. text ed. (ISBN 0-13-507947-0). P-H.

Italian Ceramics. Giuseppe Liverani. Ed. by Robert J. Charleston. LC 78-55079. (Masterpieces of Western & Near Eastern Ceramics Ser.: Vol. V). (Illus.). 308p. 1981. 250.00 o.p. (ISBN 0-87011-346-1). Kodansha.

Italian Commercial Policies in the 1970's. Enzo R. Grilli. (Working Paper: No. 428). 47p. 1980. pap. 5.00 o.p. (ISBN 0-686-39767-3, WP-0428). World Bank.

Italian Cooking Class Cookbook. Consumer Guide Staff. 1988. pap. 4.98 o.p. (ISBN 0-517-38115-X). Crown.

Italian Cooking in the Grand Tradition. Jo Bettoja & Anna M. Cornetto. LC 82-4979. (Illus.). 320p. 1982. 24.95 o.p. (ISBN 0-385-27424-6, Dial). Doubleday.

Italian Country Inns & Villas. Karen Brown & Clare Brown. (Karen Brown's European Country Inns Ser.). (Illus.). 224p. (Orig.). 1985. pap. text ed. 9.95 o.p. (ISBN 0-930328-07-8). Travel Pr.

Italian Crafts: Inspirations from Folk Art. Alex D'Amato & Janet D'Amato. LC 76-30523. (Illus.). 160p. 1977. 7.95 o.p. (ISBN 0-87131-227-1). M Evans.

Italian Design: Descendants of Leonardo da Vinci. Ed. by Matteo Thun & F. Shimizu. 304p. 1988. 79.95 o.p. (ISBN 4-766-10430-7). Bks Nippan.

Italian Drawings, 1780-1890. Roberta J. M. Olson. LC 79-9648. (Illus.). 248p. 1980. 29.95x o.p. (ISBN 0-253-11963-4). Ind U Pr.

Italian-English, English-Italian Technical Dictionary. 11th, enl. ed. G. Marolli. (Illus., Ital. & Eng.). 135.00 o.p. (ISBN 8-8005-1040-X). E J Brill USA.

Italian Experience in Texas. Cavaliere V. Belfiglio. (Illus.). 264p. 1983. 12.95 o.p. (ISBN 0-89015-380-9). Eakin Pr.

Italian Favorites. Bon Appetit Magazine Editors. LC 87-2599. (Cooking with Bon Appetit Ser.). 1987. 12.95 o.p. (ISBN 0-89535-184-6). Knapp Pr.

Italian for Commerce. J. Popescu. 1968. text ed. 26.00 o.p. (ISBN 0-08-012454-2); pap. text ed. 10.25 o.p. (ISBN 0-08-012453-4). Pergamon.

Italian Glass, Nineteen Fifty to Nineteen Sixty. Waltraud Neuwirth. (Illus.). 300p. (Eng., Fr., Ger. & Ital.). 1988. 55.00 o.p. (ISBN 3-900282-28-5, Pub. by Waltraud Neuwirth). Seven Hills Bk Dists.

Italian Interior. Fumio Shimizu et al. 260p. 1988. 79.95 o.p. (ISBN 4-7661-0480-3, Pub. by Graphic Sha Japan). Bks Nippan.

Italian Islands. Dana Facaros & Michael Pauls. LC 86-22816. (Cadogan Guides Ser.). (Illus.). 344p. 1987. pap. 12.95 o.s.i. (ISBN 0-87106-829-X). Globe Pequot.

Italian Jokes. Joe Bonfanti. 1976. pap. 1.25 o.p. (ISBN 0-685-69147-0, LB356ZK, Pub. by Leisure Bks CT). Dorchester Pub Co.

Italian Majolica Tile. A. Pica. (Illus.). 1969. 50.00 o.s.i. (ISBN 0-685-36166-7). E J Brill USA.

Italian Merchant in the Middle Ages. Armando Sapori. 1970. pap. text ed. 3.95x o.p. (ISBN 0-393-09956-3, NortonC). Norton.

Italian New Wave Design - Memphis & the Recent Work of Ettore Sottsass, Jr. A Bibliography. Carole Cable. (Architecture Ser.: A 1495). 5p. 1985. 2.00 o.p. (ISBN 0-89028-625-6). Vance Biblios.

Italian Plays, 1500-1700, in the University of Illinois Library. Compiled by Marvin T. Herrick. LC 66-17248. 92p. 1966. pap. 10.00 o.p. (ISBN 0-252-72743-6). U of Ill Pr.

Italian Popular Tales. Thomas F. Crane. LC 68-21762. 424p. 1968. Repr. of 1885 ed. 37.00x o.p. (ISBN 0-8103-3462-3). Gale.

Italian Provincial Cookery. Bea Lazzaro & Lotte Mendelsohn. Ed. by Neysa Hebbard. LC 85-51876. (Illus.). 352p. 1986. 16.95 o.p. (ISBN 0-89909-089-3). Yankee Bks.

Italian Public Enterprises. M. V. Posner & Stuart J. Woolf. LC 67-4204. 1967. 15.00x o.s.i. (ISBN 0-674-46951-8). Harvard U Pr.

Italian Repatriation from the United States, 1900-1914. Betty B. Caroli. LC 77-89343. (Illus.). 160p. 1977. pap. 9.95x o.s.i. (ISBN 0-913256-10-2). Ctr Migration.

Italian Road to Socialism: An Interview with Giorgio Napolitano of the Italian Communist Party. Eric Hobsbawm. Tr. by John Cammett & Victoria DeGrazia. LC 77-83770. 132p. 1977. pap. 3.95 o.p. (ISBN 0-88208-089-X). Chicago Review.

Italian Romanesque Sculpture: An Annotated Bibliography. Dorothy F. Glass. 1983. lib. bdg. 49.00 o.p. (ISBN 0-8161-8331-7, Hall Reference). G K Hall.

Italian Sculpture of the Renaissance: The Charles Eliot Norton Lectures for the Years 1927-1928. Eric R. Maclagan. LC 70-110272. (Illus.). 1971. Repr. of 1935 ed. lib. bdg. 35.00x o.p. (ISBN 0-8371-4498-1, MAIS). Greenwood.

Italian Stage: From Goldoni to D'Annunzio. Marvin Carlson. LC 80-10554. 239p. 1981. lib. bdg. 21.95x o.p. (ISBN 0-89950-000-5). McFarland & Co.

Italian Textbook: Ci Divertiamo con la Famiglia Tatasure. Carmen P. Malandrino. LC 76-20046. (Illus.). 1977. text ed. 8.50 o.p. (ISBN 0-682-48608-6, University). Exposition-Phoenix.

Italian Travel Guide. Berlitz Editors. (Travel Guides Ser.). 1978. pap. 4.95 o.p. (ISBN 0-317-12109-X, Berlitz). Macmillan.

Italians. Ernest Tremblay. (Orig.). 1984. pap. 3.95 o.p. (ISBN 0-440-04180-5, Emerald). Dell.

Italic Copybook: The Cantaneo Manuscript. Stephen Harvard. LC 81-50465. 64p. 1981. 20.00 o.s.i. (ISBN 0-8008-4286-3, Pentalic). Taplinger.

Italic Handwriting. Tom Gourdie. 1976. pap. 3.50 o.s.i. (ISBN 0-8008-4288-X, Pentalic). Taplinger.

Italo-American Diplomatic Relations, Eighteen Sixty-One to Eighteen Eighty-Two: The Mission of George Perkins Marsh, First American Minister to the Kingdom of Italy. Mary P. Trauth. LC 79-25192. 190p. 1980. Repr. of 1958 ed. lib. bdg. 35.00x o.p. (ISBN 0-313-22143-X, TRIA). Greenwood.

Italy. Dorothy Daly. LC 79-89187. (Rand McNally Pocket Guide). (Illus., Orig.). 1980. pap. 5.95 o.p. (ISBN 0-528-84877-1). Rand McNally.

Italy. Philippe Gloaguen & Pierre Josse. (Collier World Traveler Ser.). (Illus.). 192p. 1986. pap. 6.95 o.p. (ISBN 0-02-097720-4, Collier). Macmillan.

Italy. (Berlitz Country Guides). (Illus.). 256p. 1988. 9.95 o.p. (ISBN 0-02-969640-2, Berlitz). Macmillan.

Italy. Time-Life Books Editors. (Library of Nations). (Illus.). 160p. (YA) (gr. 7 up). 1986. lib. bdg. 23.93 o.p. Time-Life.

Italy: A Cultural Guide. Ernest Hauser. LC 81-65998. 1981. 14.95 o.p. (ISBN 0-689-11175-4, Atheneum); pap. 9.95 o.p. (ISBN 0-689-11233-5, Atheneum). Macmillan.

Italy & Spain: 1600-1750. reference ed. Robert Enggass & Jonathan Brown. (Sources & Documents in the History of Art Ser.). 1970. pap. text ed. 22.33 o.p. (ISBN 0-13-508101-7). P-H.

Italy: Balanced on the Edge of Time. Anthony DiFranco. LC 82-17722. (Discovering Our Heritage Ser.). (Illus.). 112p. (gr. 5 up). 1983. PLB 12.95 o.p. (ISBN 0-87518-229-1). Dillon.

Italy from Unification to 1919: Growth & Decay of a Liberal Regime. Salvatore Saladino. LC 75-101945. (Europe Since 1500 Ser.). 1970. pap. text ed. 9.95x o.s.i. (ISBN 0-88295-762-7). Harlan Davidson.

Italy Nineteen Eighty-Seven. Steve Birnbaum. (Illus.). 768p. 1987. pap. 12.70 o.s.i. (ISBN 0-395-42333-3). HM.

Italy: Society in Crisis-Society in Transformation. John Fraser. 288p. 1981. 27.50x o.p. (ISBN 0-7100-0771-X). Routledge Chapman & Hall.

Italyon Cultural Guide: A Phaidon Cultural Guide. Phaidon Press Limited Staff. (Illus.). 832p. 1985. 16.95 o.p. (ISBN 0-13-506734-0). P-H.

Itations of Jamaica & I Rastafari. Millard Faristzaddi. LC 82-82460. (Illus.). 192p. (Orig.). 1982. pap. 9.95 o.p. (ISBN 0-394-62435-1, E836, Ever). Grove.

Item from the Late News. Thea Astley. LC 82-11177. 200p. 1983. 17.95 o.p. (ISBN 0-7022-1702-6). U of Queensland Pr.

Items from Our Catalog. Alfred Gingold. 80p. 1982. pap. 4.95 o.p. (ISBN 0-380-81695-4, 81695). Avon.

Iterates of Maps on an Interval. C. Preston. (Lecture notes in Mathematics: Vol. 999). 205p. 1983. pap. 13.00 o.p. (ISBN 0-387-12322-9). Springer-Verlag.

Itinerary of Benjamin of Tudela. Adler. Tr. by Marcus N. Adler. LC 68-9344. 1964. 25.00 o.p. (ISBN 0-87306-033-4). Feldheim.

ITPA: Clinical Interpretation & Remediation. Thomas P. Lombardi & Estelle J. Lombardi. LC 77-78605. (Illus.). 184p. 1977. pap. 9.00x o.p. (ISBN 0-87562-058-2). Spec Child.

It's a Dog's Life. Mark Stern. LC 77-25494. (Illus.). (ps-3). 1978. 7.95 o.p. (ISBN 0-689-30643-1, Atheneum). Macmillan.

It's a Funny Thing Humour: The International Conference on Humor & Laughter. Antony J. Chapman & Hugh C. Foot. LC 76-53731. 400p. 1977. 100.00 o.p. (ISBN 0-08-021376-6). Pergamon.

It's a Girl's Game Too. Alice Siegel & Margo McLoone. LC 79-9422. (Illus.). 128p. (gr. 5 up). 1980. 9.95 o.p. (ISBN 0-03-046526-5). H Holt & Co.

It's a Lovely Day, Outside. Pamela La Fane. 160p. 1981. 19.95 o.p. (ISBN 0-575-03014-3, Pub. by Gollancz England). David & Charles.

It's a Mile from Here to Glory. Robert C. Lee. (gr. 5 up). 1972. 12.95 o.p. (ISBN 0-316-51949-9). Little.

It's a Model World. Suzanne Hilton. LC 72-76435. (Illus.). 128p. (gr. 5 up). 1972. 5.95 o.s.i. (ISBN 0-664-32515-7, Westminster). Westminster John Knox.

It's a Pig World Out There. Phyllis Demong. 1983. pap. 4.95 o.p. (ISBN 0-380-53082-1, 53082-1). Avon.

It's about Love. rev. ed. Ginilou DeMarco. (Living Bk.). 160p. 1987. pap. 3.95 o.p. (ISBN 0-8423-1815-1). Tyndale.

It's about Time: A Practical Guide to Managing Your Most Important Resource. Stewart L. Stokes, Jr. 160p. (Orig.). 1983. pap. 11.95 o.p. (ISBN 0-8436-0878-1); bk. & cassette 24.95 o.p. Van Nos Reinhold.

It's Alive! the Classic Cinema Saga of Frankenstein. Gregory W. Mank. LC 80-26625. (Illus.). 196p. 1982. pap. 12.95 o.s.i. (ISBN 0-498-02592-6). A S Barnes.

It's All Due to Leprechauns. Greg Branson. (Playwright's Press). 1987. pap. 6.95 o.p. (ISBN 0-948553-05-7, 1167). Routledge Chapman & Hall.

It's All Relative: Einstein's Theory of Relativity. Necia H. Apfel. LC 80-28188. (Illus.). 144p. (gr. 5 up). 1981. 12.25 o.p. (ISBN 0-688-41981-X); PLB 11.88 o.s.i. (ISBN 0-688-51981-4); pap. 7.25 o.s.i. Lothrop.

It's BASIC. Shelley Lipson. LC 81-20027. (Illus.). (gr. 4-6). pap. 3.95 o.s.i. (ISBN 0-03-000754-2). H Holt & Co.

It's BASIC: The ABC's of Computer Programming. Shelley Lipson. LC 81-20027. (Illus.). 48p. (gr. 4-6). 1982. 8.95 o.s.i. (ISBN 0-03-061592-5); pap. 3.95 o.s.i. H Holt & Co.

It's Different When You Manage. Raymond J. Winters. LC 83-47500. 272p. 1983. 23.00x o.p. (ISBN 0-669-06679-6). Lexington Bks.

Its Economic Life see America Rediscovered.

Its Foreign Affairs see America Rediscovered.

It's Fun to Bake & Decorate. Harriet Chelmo. 1961. 2.95 o.p. (ISBN 0-685-09359-X). Exposition-Phoenix.

It's Fun to Be in Love with an Older Man. Fadila Klicic. 1977. 4.00 o.p. (ISBN 0-682-48683-3). Exposition-Phoenix.

It's Fun to Teach. Victor Hoag. (Orig.). 1951. pap. 1.00 o.p. (ISBN 0-8192-1043-9). Morehouse Pub.

It's Going to Rain. Ada B. Litchfield. LC 80-12732. (Illus.). 32p. (ps-2). 1980. 8.95 o.p. (ISBN 0-689-30779-9, Atheneum). Macmillan.

It's Going to Sting Me: A Coward's Guide to the Great Outdoors. Ronald Rood. (McGraw-Hill Paperbacks). 1977. pap. text ed. 3.95 o.p. (ISBN 0-07-053579-5). McGraw.

It's Great to Pray. Kathryn W. Orso. LC 74-80379. (Illus.). 96p. 1974. 4.95 o.p. (ISBN 0-8192-1177-X). Morehouse Pub.

It's Hard to Leave While the Music's Playing. I. S. Cooper. 1977. 9.95 o.p. (ISBN 0-393-08756-5). Norton.

It's Hard to Tell You How I Feel: Helping Children Express & Understand Their Feelings. Richard L. Krebs. LC 81-65646. 128p. (Orig.). 1981. pap. 5.50 o.p. (ISBN 0-8066-1882-5, 10-3453, Augsburg). Augsburg Fortress.

It's How You Play the Game. Chad Klinger. 148p. 1982. pap. text ed. 4.95x o.p. (ISBN 0-88334-154-9). Ind Sch Pr.

It's Never Too Late to Start Over. Jo Danna. LC 83-63268. 331p. 1984. pap. 6.00 o.p. (ISBN 0-9610036-1-8). Palomino Pr.

It's Okay, God, We Can Take It. Bo Newhaus. (Illus.). 140p. 1986. 9.95 o.p. (ISBN 0-89015-576-3). Eakin Pr.

It's Only Rock & Roll. Bruce Pollock. (gr. 7 up). 1980. 7.95 o.p. (ISBN 0-395-29182-8). HM.

Its People see America Rediscovered.

It's Perfectly True: And Other Stories. Hans Christian Andersen. Tr. by Paul Leyssac. LC 38-27263. (Illus.). (gr. 1 up). 1938. 7.50 o.p. (ISBN 0-15-239343-9, HJ). HarBraceJ.

Its Political Life see America Rediscovered.

It's Raining Said John Twaining: Danish Nursery Rhymes. N. M. Bodecker. LC 72-85912. (Illus.). 32p. (ps-3). 1973. 6.95 o.p. (ISBN 0-689-30316-5, Atheneum); pap. 1.95 o.p. (ISBN 0-689-70437-2). Macmillan.

It's Real. Mary H. Wallace. (Illus.). 224p. (Orig.). 1981. pap. 5.95 o.p. (ISBN 0-912315-17-2). Word Aflame.

It's Smart to Use a Dummy. Suzanne Hilton. LC 78-155902. (A Junior Literary Guild Selection). (Illus.). 124p. (gr. 5 up). 1971. 5.50 o.s.i. (ISBN 0-664-32500-9, Westminster). Westminster John Knox.

It's Sunday Night Again? Donna Gladman. Ed. by Arthur L. Zapel. LC 79-84726. (Illus.). 1979. pap. text ed. 4.95 o.p. (ISBN 0-916260-04-6). Meriwether Pub.

It's Time to Backdate. V. Harvey Mortensen. 107p. 1983. pap. 2.00 o.p. (ISBN 0-89036-149-5). Hawkes Pub Inc.

It's Up to You. Ernest Holmes. Ed. by Willis H. Kinnear. 94p. 1968. pap. 4.50 o.p. (ISBN 0-911336-34-6). Sci of Mind.

It's What You Learn After You Know It All That Counts: The Autobiography of Earl Weaver. Rev. ed. Earl Weaver & Berry Stainback. (Illus.). 1986. pap. 8.50 o.p. (ISBN 0-671-47239-9, Fireside). S&S.

It's Women's Work, Too! Walter Oleksy. LC 80-10879. (Illus.). 192p. (gr. 7 up). 1980. lib. bdg. 9.29 o.s.i. (ISBN 0-671-33041-1). Messner.

It's Your Body. Lawrence Elson. (Illus.). 576p. 1974. text ed. 45.95 o.p. (ISBN 0-07-019299-5). McGraw.

It's Your Business to Decide. Gordon P. Miller. 145p. 1983. pap. 14.95 o.p. (ISBN 0-8436-0862-5). Van Nos Reinhold.

It's Your Time - Use It or Lose It. Mitchell Tucker. 1975. 6.50 o.p. (ISBN 0-682-48259-5, Banner). Exposition-Phoenix.

It's Your Wedding: How to Plan & Enjoy it. Marjorie B. Woods. 208p. 1985. pap. 3.50 o.p. (ISBN 0-515-07921-9). Jove Pubns.

It's Your World. Claudia Blocksom. (Illus.). 40p. (gr. 1-8). 1971. pap. 2.95 o.p. (ISBN 0-8431-1749-4). Troubador Pr.

ITU in a Changing World. 2nd, rev. ed. George Codding, Jr. & Anthony M. Rutkowski. 1988. text ed. 20.00 o.p. (ISBN 0-89006-257-9). Artech Hse.

Iturbide of Mexico. William S. Robertson. LC 68-23321. (Illus.). 1968. Repr. of 1952 ed. lib. bdg. 22.50x o.p. (ISBN 0-8371-0203-0, ROIM). Greenwood.

IV Therapy. Shirley L. McGill & Jean R. Smith. LC 83-3849. (Illus.). 166p. 1983. pap. 14.95 o.p. (ISBN 0-89303-277-8). Appleton & Lange.

Ivan Albright: A Retrospective Exhibition. 2nd ed. Frederick A. Sweet. LC 64-25439. (Illus.). 59p. 1974. pap. 1.50x o.p. (ISBN 0-86559-005-2). Art Inst Chi.

Ivan & the Daring Escape. Myrna Grant. (Ivan Ser.). (gr. 3-8). 1976. pap. 3.50 o.p. (ISBN 0-8423-1847-X). Tyndale.

Ivan & the Hidden Bible. Myrna Grant. (Ivan Ser.). (gr. 3-8). 1975. pap. 3.50 o.p. (ISBN 0-8423-1848-8). Tyndale.

Ivan & the Informer. Myrna Grant. (Ivan Ser.). (gr. 3-9). 1977. pap. 3.50 o.p. (ISBN 0-8423-1846-1). Tyndale.

Ivan & the Secret in the Suitcase. Myrna Grant. (Ivan Ser.). (gr. 3-8). 1975. pap. 3.50 o.p. (ISBN 0-8423-1849-6). Tyndale.

Ivan Lendl's Power Tennis. Eugene Scott. 144p. 1983. pap. 9.95 o.p. (ISBN 0-671-45908-2, Fireside). S&S.

Ivanhoe. Walter Scott. 48p. (Orig.). 1989. pap. 9.95 o.p. (ISBN 1-55651-429-8); audiocassette tape incl. o.p. (ISBN 1-55651-430-1). Cram Cassettes.

Ivatan Syntax. Lawrence A. Reid. (Oceanic Linguistics Special Publication Ser.: No. 2). (Orig.). 1966. pap. text ed. 8.00x o.p. (ISBN 0-87022-690-8). UH Pr.

I've Always Done It My Way. Ruth Stout. 1975. 7.50 o.p. (ISBN 0-682-48355-9). Exposition-Phoenix.

I've Got Me & I'm Glad. Cherrie Farnette et al. LC 77-83654. (Kids & Careers Ser.). (Illus.). 104p. (gr. 2-6). 1977. pap. text ed. 6.95 o.p. (ISBN 0-913916-52-8, IP 52-8). Incentive Pubns.

I've Got to Talk to Somebody, God. 15th, anniversary ed. Marjorie Holmes. LC 84-28724. 144p. 1985. pap. 5.95 o.s.i. (ISBN 0-385-19751-9, Galilee). Doubleday.

I've Met Them All. Walter H. Marshall. LC 82-91157. (Illus.). 186p. (Orig.). 1983. 12.95 o.p. (ISBN 0-934318-10-7); pap. 8.95 o.p. (ISBN 0-934318-09-3). Falcon Pr MT.

I've Never Told Anyone, but... Joyce Hagelthorn & Marilyn Ruben. 161p. 1987. pap. 9.95 o.p. (ISBN 0-939644-27-4). Media Prods & Mktg.

I've Served My Time in Hell. David Dingle. 1977. 5.00 o.p. (ISBN 0-682-48789-9). Exposition-Phoenix.

Ivoires. Tardy & M. L'Abbe Bidault. (Illus.). 287p. (Orig., Fr.). Vol. 1. pap. 85.00 o.p. (ISBN 0-911403-04-3, 2390119, Pub. by Tardy FR); Vol. 2. pap. 125.00 o.p. (ISBN 2-901622-00-3). Seven Hills Bk Dists.

Ivor Roberts-Jones. Peter Cannon-Brookes. (Illus.). 128p. 1987. pap. 12.95 o.p. (ISBN 0-86294-042-7, Pub. by Trefoil Bks Ltd UK). Seven Hills Bk Dists.

Ivory & Ebony Towers: Race Relations & Higher Education. Charles V. Willie. LC 80-8946. 192p. 1981. 29.00x o.p. (ISBN 0-669-04479-2). Lexington Bks.

Ivory Fan. Valerie Bradstreet. 160p. (Orig.). 1982. pap. 2.25 o.p. (ISBN 0-380-79244-3, 79244-3). Avon.

Ivory Palaces. Ruth E. Wheeler. LC 85-90988. 96p. 1985. 10.00 o.p. (ISBN 0-682-40275-3). Exposition-Phoenix.

Izbrannaia Proza. Vladislav Khodasevich. LC 82-60843. 320p. (Rus.). 1982. pap. 9.95 o.p. (ISBN 0-89830-063-0). Russica Pubs.

Izbrannye Rasskazy Shestidesyatykh. Intro. by Marc Altshuller. LC 84-28696. 348p. 1985. pap. 13.50 o.s.i. (ISBN 0-938920-52-9). Hermitage.

Izvenite za Vnimanie: Collection of Poems & Stories. Alexand Baskov. 1980. 3.95 o.s.i. RWCPH.

Izzy Manheim's Reunion. Myers. 1978. 10.00 o.p. (ISBN 0-15-145890-1). HarBraceJ.

J

J. B. Priestley: An Annotated Bibliography. Alan E. Day. LC 78-68251. (Garland Reference Library of the Humanities). 350p. 1980. lib. bdg. 48.00 o.p. (ISBN 0-8240-9798-X). Garland Pub.

J. Bracken Lee: The Taxpayer's Champion. George B. Russell. 4.95 o.p. (ISBN 0-8315-0037-9). Speller.

J. B.'s Daughter. Sherlock. 1981. text ed. 11.95 o.p. (ISBN 0-07-056750-6). McGraw.

J. D. Salinger. 2nd rev. ed. Warren French. (United States Author Ser.). 1976. lib. bdg. 15.95 o.s.i. (ISBN 0-8057-7163-8, Twayne). G K Hall.

J. D. Salinger. Warren French. (United States Authors Ser.). 1985. pap. 8.95 o.s.i. (ISBN 0-8057-7447-5, Twayne). G K Hall.

J. E. Buttersworth, 19th-Century Marine Painter. Rudolph J. Schaefer. LC 74-82666. (Illus.). xxvi, 276p. 1975. 75.00 o.s.i. (ISBN 0-913372-12-9). Mystic Seaport.

J. E. Spingarn & the Rise of the NAACP. B. Joyce Ross. LC 78-139326. (Studies in American Negro Life). 1972. 10.00 o.s.i. (ISBN 0-689-10531-2, Atheneum); pap. text ed. 3.95x o.s.i. (ISBN 0-689-70337-6, NL32, Atheneum). Macmillan.

J. Hardin & Son. Brand Whitlock. Ed. by Paul W. Miller. LC 82-2240. xl, 465p. 1982. lib. bdg. 18.95 o.p. (ISBN 0-8214-0640-X); pap. 9.95 o.p. (ISBN 0-8214-0641-8). Ohio U Pr.

J. J. O'Malley Goes Hollywood. Crockett Johnson. 224p. 1986. pap. 2.95 o.s.i. (ISBN 0-345-32882-5, Del Rey). Ballantine.

J. J.'s Bluff: Or the Theory of Business Relativity. J. J. Anthony. 112p. 1981. 6.50 o.p. (ISBN 0-682-49707-X). Exposition-Phoenix.

J. K. Lasser's All You Should Know about IRA, Keogh, & Other Retirement Plans. 160p. 1983. pap. 5.75 o.s.i. (ISBN 0-671-45978-3, Fireside). S&S.

J. K. Lasser's Business Tax Deduction Master Guide 1988. W. Murray Bradford & Glenn B. Davis. LC 84-24815. 1987. 29.95 o.p. (ISBN 0-13-510323-1); pap. 18.95 o.p. (ISBN 0-13-510315-0). S&S.

J. K. Lasser's Managing Your Family Finances. Lasser Institute. 1976. 14.95 o.s.i. (ISBN 0-671-22306-2). S&S.

J. K. Lasser's Official Tax Guide for Small Business 1988. 394p. 1988. 29.95 o.p. (ISBN 0-13-510414-9); pap. 18.95 o.p. (ISBN 0-13-510406-8). Prentice Hall Pr.

J. K. Lasser's One Hundred One Plans to Pay Less Taxes. 208p. 1983. pap. 5.75 o.s.i. (ISBN 0-671-45977-5, Fireside). S&S.

J. K. Lasser's One Hundred One Plans to Pay Less Taxes: 1986. Lasser, J. K., Tax Institute Staff. 210p. 1986. pap. 6.95 o.p. (ISBN 0-671-60293-4). S&S.

J. K. Lasser's Personal Finance Planner 1988. J. K. Lasser Tax Institute Staff. (Illus.). 512p. (Orig.). 1988. pap. 14.95 o.p. (ISBN 0-13-510504-8). Prentice Hall Pr.

J. K. Lasser's Quick & Easy Taxes 1988. The J. K. Lasser Tax Institute Staff. 96p. 1988. pap. 3.95 o.p. (ISBN 0-13-510281-2). P-H.

J. K. Lasser's Retirement Plan Handbook 1988. The J. K. Lasser Tax Institute Staff. (The IRAs Four-Hundred One KEOGHs & Other Pension Plans Ser.). (Orig.). 1988. pap. 8.95 o.p. (ISBN 0-13-510331-2). Prentice Hall Pr.

J. K. Lasser's Smart Money Management. 240p. 5.95 o.s.i. (ISBN 0-671-45979-1, Fireside). S&S.

J. K. Lasser's Smart Money Management. 1985. pap. 5.95 o.p. (ISBN 0-671-55639-8). S&S.

J. K. Lasser's the Professional Edition of Your Income Tax, 1985. J. K. Lasser. 500p. 1984. 29.95 o.p. (ISBN 0-671-52888-2). S&S.

J. K. Lasser's Tri-State Guide, 1988: New York, New Jersey, Connecticut. J. K. Lasser Tax Institute Staff. (Orig.). 1988. pap. 5.95 o.p. (ISBN 0-13-510512-9). S&S.

J. K. Lasser's Your Income Tax. rev. ed. The J. K. Lasser Tax Institute Staff. Ed. by Bernard Greisman. 368p. 1987. pap. 8.95 o.p. (ISBN 0-13-510422-X). P-H.

J. K. Lasser's Your Income Tax. 1984 ed. 332p. 1983. pap. 6.95 o.s.i. (ISBN 0-671-49501-1, Fireside). S&S.

J. K. Lasser's Your Income Tax, 1985. 332p. 1984. pap. 6.95 o.p. (ISBN 0-671-52887-4). S&S.

J. K. Lasser's Your Income Tax, 1986. Lasser, J. K., Tax Institute Staff. 1986. pap. 7.95 o.p. (ISBN 0-671-60284-5). S&S.

J. K. Lasser's Your Income Tax, 1987. updated ed. The J. K. Lasser Tax Institute Staff. 368p. 1986. pap. 8.95 o.p. (ISBN 0-13-509746-0). P-H.

J. M. Synge. Eugene Benson. (Grove Press Modern Dramatists Ser.). (Illus.). 224p. (Orig.). 1983. pap. 9.95 o.p. (ISBN 0-394-62432-7, E833, Ever). Grove.

J. Paul Getty Museum Journal: (Including Aquisitions-1985, No. 14. write for info. o.p. J P Getty Trust.

J. R. McCulloch (1789-1864) Treatise or Taxation? Ed. by B. P. O'Brien. 1974. 30.00x o.p. (ISBN 0-7073-0189-0, Pub. by Scot Acad Pr). Longwood Pub Group.

J. R. R. Tolkien. D. Rodgers & I. A. Rodgers. 249p. 1982. pap. 6.95 o.p. (ISBN 0-88254-704-6). Hippocrene Bks.

J. Robert Oppenheimer: Shatterer of Worlds. Peter J. Goodchild. 1981. 15.00 o.p. (ISBN 0-395-30530-6). HM.

J. S. Bach: The Modern Composer. Augusta Rubin. LC 75-44620. (Illus.). 1977. 60.00 o.s.i. (ISBN 0-8008-4297-9, Crescendo). Taplinger.

J. V. Foix. Patricia J. Boehne. (World Authors Ser.). 1980. 16.95 o.p. (ISBN 0-8057-6412-7, Twayne). G K Hall.

J'accuse. Emile Zola. 1958. 3.95 o.p. (ISBN 0-686-55783-2). French & Eur.

Jack & Jill. Ray Marshall & Korky Paul. Ed. by Kate Klimo. (Illus.). 10p. 1983. 3.80 o.s.i. (ISBN 0-671-46238-5, Little Simon). S&S.

Jack & Jill & Other Favorite Rhymes. Illus. by Blanche F. Wright. (Real Mother Goose Pop-Ups Ser.). (Illus.). 12p. (ps-1). 1985. 3.95 o.p. (ISBN 0-528-82601-8, Checkerboard Pr). Macmillan.

Jack & Jill & Other Nursery Rhymes. Illus. by Jane Longmore. (Illus.). (gr. k). 1984. 4.95 o.p. (ISBN 0-531-03553-0). Watts.

Jack & the Beanstalk. Ed McBain. 1984. pap. 14.95 o.p. (ISBN 0-03-062197-6). H Holt & Co.

Jack Dempsey: The Manassa Mauler. Randy Roberts. LC 80-992. (Illus.). 320p. 1980. pap. 6.95 o.p. (ISBN 0-394-17660-X, E759, Ever). Grove.

Jack-in-the-Box Planet. Robert Hoskins. LC 77-21134. 156p. 1978. 7.95 o.s.i. (ISBN 0-664-32625-0, Westminster). Westminster John Knox.

Jack Jump Under the Candlestick. Donna L. Pape. Ed. by Ann Fay. LC 82-1918. (Self-Starter Bks.). (Illus.). (ps-1). 1982. PLB 9.75 o.p. (ISBN 0-8075-3753-5). A Whitman.

Jack Kerouac. Tom Clark. (Illus.). 1984. 22.95 o.p. (ISBN 0-15-145932-0). HarBraceJ.

Jack Kerouac. Tom Clark. LC 83-22628. 320p. 1984. pap. 10.95 o.p. (ISBN 0-15-645662-1, Harv). HarBraceJ.

Jack Kerouac. Harry R. Huebel. LC 79-53652. (Western Writers Ser.: No. 39). (Illus.). 48p. (Orig.). 1979. pap. 2.95x o.p. (ISBN 0-88430-063-3). Boise St Univ.

Jack London & the Klondike: The Genesis of an American Writer. Franklin Walker. LC 66-20412. (Illus.). 288p. 1978. pap. 14.95 o.p. (ISBN 0-87328-022-9). Huntington Lib.

Jack London First Editions. James E. Sisson & Robert W. Martens. LC 78-63374. (Illus.). 1978. 49.50 o.p. (ISBN 0-932458-00-9). Star Rover.

Jack London Series II. Ed. by C. Booss & P. Horowitz. (Avenel Readers Library). (Illus.). 720p. 1982. jacketed ed. 6.98 o.s.i. (ISBN 0-517-38581-3, Avenel). Outlet Bk Co.

Jack London Stories. Jack London. (gr. 3 up). 1978. 6.95 o.p. (ISBN 0-448-41103-2, G&D); PLB 6.99 o.p. (ISBN 0-448-13044-0). Putnam Pub Group.

Jack London's Klondike Tales. Jack London. 224p. (Orig.). pap. 2.25 o.p. (ISBN 0-505-51797-3, Pub. by Tower Bks). Dorchester Pub Co.

Jack London's The Call of the Wild see Graded Readers for Students of English As a Second Language.

Jack Nicklaus' the Full Swing. Jack Nicklaus & Ken Bowden. LC 84-80308. (Illus.). 208p. 1984. 22.95 o.p. (ISBN 0-914178-68-7). Golf Digest.

Jack-Roller at Seventy. Jack-Roller & Jon Snodrass. LC 81-47825. 192p. 1982. 22.00x o.p. (ISBN 0-669-04912-3); pap. 12.00x o.p. (ISBN 0-669-09778-0). Lexington Bks.

Jack Smith's L.A. Jack Smith. LC 80-13127. 224p. 1980. text ed. 9.95 o.p. (ISBN 0-07-058471-0). McGraw.

Jack Sprat's Legacy: The Science & Politics of Fat & Cholesterol. Patricia Hausman. 288p. 1982. 3.95 o.p. (ISBN 0-399-90111-6, Pub. by Richard Marek). Ctr Sci Public.

Jack Tars & Commodores: The American Navy, 1783-1815. William M. Fowler, Jr. (Illus.). 310p. 1984. 17.45 o.p. (ISBN 0-395-35314-9). HM.

Jack the Giantkiller. Tony Ross. (Illus.). 32p. (gr. k-3). 1987. 12.95 o.p. (ISBN 0-86264-060-1, Pub. by Century Hutchinson). David & Charles.

Jack the Ripper. Richard Gordon. LC 80-66000. 1980. 9.95 o.p. (ISBN 0-689-11101-0, Atheneum). Macmillan.

Jack the Ripper: One Hundred Years of Mystery. Peter Underwood. (Illus.). 208p. 1988. 19.95 o.p. (ISBN 0-7137-1954-0, Pub. by Blandford Pr England). Sterling.

Jack Vance. Ed. by Tim Underhill & Chuck Miller. LC 79-57353. (Writers of the 21st Century Ser.). 1981. 12.95 o.s.i. (ISBN 0-8008-4294-4); pap. 5.95 o.s.i. (ISBN 0-8008-4295-2). Taplinger.

Jack Williamson: A Primary & Secondary Bibliography. Robert E. Myers. 1979. lib. bdg. 15.00 o.p. (ISBN 0-8161-8158-6, Hall Reference). G K Hall.

Jackeen J. O'Malley for Congress. Crockett Johnson. 224p. (Orig.). 1985. pap. 2.95 o.s.i. (ISBN 0-345-32981-3, Pub. by Del Rey). Ballantine.

Jacki Sorenson's Aerobic Lifestyle Book. Jacki Sorenson & Bill Bruns. (Illus.). 1983. 15.50 o.s.i. (ISBN 0-671-45616-4, Poseidon). PB.

Jacki Sorenson's Aerobic Lifestyle Book. Jacki Sorenson & Bill Bruns. (Illus.). 1985. pap. 9.95 o.s.i. (ISBN 0-671-54361-X, +004). S&S.

Jackie. Luevester Lewis. (Illus.). (gr. k-5). 1970. pap. 1.00 o.p. Third World.

Jackie Mason's America. Jackie Mason. 192p. 1983. 12.00 o.p. (ISBN 0-8184-0338-1). Carol Pub Group.

Jackie Winsor. Ellen H. Johnson. (Illus.). 1979. pap. 4.00 o.p. (ISBN 0-87070-637-3). Museum Mod Art.

Jackie Zeman's Beauty on the Go. Jacklyn Zeman & Dianna Whitley. 224p. 1986. pap. 9.95 o.p. (ISBN 0-671-54326-1). S&S.

Jackie's Kitchen Charts. Jacqueline Hostage. LC 82-14680. (Illus.). 128p. (Orig.). 1982. pap. 5.95 plastic comb bdg o.p. (ISBN 0-932620-16-7). Betterway Pubns.

Jacko. John S. Goodall. LC 72-149750. (Illus.). (ps-3). 1972. 7.95 o.p. (ISBN 0-15-239493-1, HJ). HarBraceJ.

Jacko. John S. Goodall. LC 72-149750. (Illus.). 60p. (ps-3). 1984. pap. 3.95 o.p. (ISBN 0-15-239494-X, VoyB). HarBraceJ.

Jackrabbit Goalie. Matt Christopher. LC 78-5438. (Illus.). (gr. 1-3). 1978. 10.45i o.p. (ISBN 0-316-13975-0). Little.

Jackson Browne, Neil Diamond & Elton John: An Analysis of Nineteenth Century Musical Thought. Nathaniel R. Gorham. (Illus.). 352p. (Orig.). Date not set. 29.50 o.p. (ISBN 0-939303-09-4); pap. 7.95 o.p. (ISBN 0-939303-10-8). Educ Lrn Syst.

Jackson Pollock: Drawing into Painting. Bernice Rose. LC 79-92490. (Illus.). 96p. 1980. 17.50 o.p. (ISBN 0-87070-516-4); pap. 8.95 o.p. (ISBN 0-87070-517-2). Museum Mod Art.

Jacksonian Democracy. 2nd ed. J. L. Bugg, Jr. & P. C. Stewart. LC 75-36667. 1976. pap. text ed. 7.95 o.p. (ISBN 0-03-014151-6, HoltC). HR&W.

Jacksonian Democracy & the Historians. Alfred A. Cave. LC 80-13384. (University of Florida Monographs, Social Sciences: No. 22). 86p. 1980. Repr. of 1964 ed. lib. bdg. 35.00x o.p. (ISBN 0-313-22418-8, CAJA). Greenwood.

Jaclyn Smith Beauty Book. Jaclyn Smith. (Illus.). 160p. 1985. 17.45 o.p. (ISBN 0-671-50172-0). S&S.

Jacob the Liar. Jurek Becker. Tr. by Melvin Kornfeld. LC 75-19184. (Helen & Kurt Wolff Bks.). 256p. 1975. 7.95 o.p. (ISBN 0-15-145975-4). HarBraceJ.

Jacobean City Comedy. 2nd ed. Brian Gibbons. 1981. 26.00x o.p. (ISBN 0-416-73450-2, NO. 2041); pap. 14.95x o.p. (ISBN 0-416-73460-X, NO. 2040). Routledge Chapman & Hall.

Titles

Jacobean Drama: An Anthology. Ed. by Richard C. Harrier. Incl. Every Man in His Humour. Ben Jonson. 544p; Malcontent. John Marston; White Devil. John Webster; Bussy d'Ambois. George Chapman. (Seventeenth Century Ser). Orig. Title: Anchor Anthology of Jacobean Drama. 1968. Vol. 1. pap. 4.95x o.p. (ISBN 0-393-00559-3); Vol. 2. pap. (ISBN 0-393-00560-7). Norton.

Jacobean Pageant: The Court of King James First. George P. Akrigg. LC 62-5508. (Illus.). 1967. pap. text ed. 6.95x o.p. (ISBN 0-689-70003-2, 103, Atheneum). Macmillan.

Jacobite Narrative of the War in Ireland, 1688-1691. John T. Gilbert. 358p. 1969. Repr. of 1892 ed. text ed. 27.50x o.p. (ISBN 0-7165-0050-7, BBA 02165, Pub. by Irish Academic Pr. Ireland). Biblio Dist.

Jacobite Risings in Britain 1689-1746. Bruce Lenman. 1980. 34.50 o.p. (ISBN 0-8419-7004-1). Holmes & Meier.

Jacob's Well: A Novel. Stephen Harrigan. 288p. 1984. 15.45 o.p. (ISBN 0-671-44945-1). S&S.

Jacoby, Ohio Civil Practice: A Guide to Civil Practice in Ohio Under the Rules of Civil Procedure, 2 vols. Sidney B. Jacoby. (Baldwin's Ohio Practice Ser.). 3220p. 1970. Set, annual cum supp. bdrs. 135.00 o.p. (ISBN 0-8322-0005-0). Banks-Baldwin.

Jacoby's First Case. J. C. Smith. LC 79-55604. 1980. 9.95 o.p. (ISBN 0-689-11057-X, Atheneum). Macmillan.

Jacques Joseph: Surgical Sculptor. Paul Natvig. (Illus.). 284p. 1982. write for info. o.p. (ISBN 0-7216-6679-5). Saunders.

Jacques Lacan: An Annotated Bibliography. Michael Clark. (Garland Reference Library of the Humanities). 1032p. 1988. lib. bdg. 54.00 o.p. Garland Pub.

Jacques Lipschitz & Cubism. Deborah A. Stott. LC 77-94717. (Outstanding Dissertations in the Fine Arts Ser.). 1978. lib. bdg. 40.00 o.p. (ISBN 0-8240-3251-9). Garland Pub.

Jacques Offenbach. Alexander Faris. 1981. 25.00 o.s.i. (ISBN 0-684-16797-2, ScribT). Scribner.

Jade Unicorn. Jay Halpern. 448p. 1980. pap. 2.50 o.p. (ISBN 0-380-50708-0, 50708-0). Avon.

Jaguar. 2th ed. Lord Montague. LC 80-27039. (Illus.). 240p. 1981. 25.00 o.s.i. (ISBN 0-498-02547-0). A S Barnes.

Jaguar. Morris Simon. LC 85-51043. (Amazing Stories Ser.). 220p. (Orig.). 1985. pap. 2.95 o.p. (ISBN 0-88038-256-2). TSR Inc.

Jaguar Service - Repair Handbook: All 3.8 & 4.2 E-Types. Ed. by Jeff Robinson. (Illus.). pap. text ed. 12.95 o.p. (ISBN 0-89287-055-9, A225). Clymer Pub.

Jaguar XK: Collectors Guide. Paul Skilleter. (Collector's Guide Series). (Illus.). 125p. 1982. 29.95 o.p. (ISBN 0-900549-49-1, Pub. by Motor Racing England). Motorbooks Intl.

Jailhouse Lawyers Manual. Prison Committee of NLG SF. 1982. 10.00 o.p. Natl Lawyers Guild.

Jake & Katie. Brad Solomon. 304p. 1980. pap. 2.50 o.p. (ISBN 0-380-52969-6, 52969). Avon.

Jake McGee & His Feet. Mary Waldorf. (Illus.). 96p. (gr. 3-6). 1980. 5.95 o.p. (ISBN 0-395-29066-X). HM.

Jake O'Shawnasey. Stephen Cosgrove. (Serendipity Bks.). (Illus.). 32p. (gr. 1-6). 1975. pap. 1.95 o.s.i. (ISBN 0-8431-0558-5). Price Stern.

Jalousie. Alain Robbe-Grillet. Ed. by Germaine Bree & Eric Schoenfeld. (Orig., Fr.). 1963. pap. text ed. write for info. o.p. (ISBN 0-02-401880-5). Macmillan.

Jamaa: A Charismatic Movement in Katanga. Johannes Fabian. 296p. 1971. 22.95x o.p. (ISBN 0-8101-0339-7). Northwestern U Pr.

Jamaica. Amanda H. Douglass. (Inflation Fighter Ser.). 208p. 1982. pap. 1.50 o.p. (ISBN 0-8439-1147-6, Pub. by Leisure Bks CT). Dorchester Pub Co.

Jamaica. Hildebrand Editorial Staff. (Hildebrand Travel Guides Ser.). (Illus.). 127p. 1985. pap. 8.95 o.p. (ISBN 0-87052-016-4, Pub. by Hildebrand). Hippocrene Bks.

Jamaica, As It Was, As It Is, & As It May Be. Bernard M. Senior. LC 78-82321. 1969. Repr. of 1835 ed. 35.00x o.p. (ISBN 0-8371-1654-6, SEJ&, Pub. by Negro U Pr). Greenwood.

Jamaica: Beautiful Jamaica. 4th, rev. ed. E. Blake. (Illus.). 1980. 35.00 o.s.i. (ISBN 0-686-77960-6). E J Brill USA.

Jamaica: Beautiful Jamaica. 4th rev. ed. E. Blake. (Illus.). 1974. 25.00 o.s.i. (ISBN 0-685-58565-4). E J Brill USA.

Jamaica Travel Guide. Berlitz Editors. (Travel Guides Ser.). 1981. pap. 4.95 o.p. (ISBN 0-317-12276-2, Berlitz). Macmillan.

Jamaican Midnight. Sherryl Woods. (Velvet Glove Ser.: No. 21). 208p. 1985. pap. 2.25 o.p. (ISBN 0-380-89788-1). Avon.

Jambeaux. Laurence Gonzales. LC 79-1824. 1979. 9.95 o.p. (ISBN 0-15-146038-8). HarBraceJ.

Jambees. Marcel Ayme. 1967. pap. 9.95 o.p. (ISBN 0-686-50131-4). French & Eur.

James: A Good News Commentary. Peter H. Davids. LC 83-47720. (Good News Commentary Ser.). 176p. (Orig.). 1983. pap. 7.95 o.p. (ISBN 0-06-061697-0, RD-499). HarpR.

James Anthony Froude: A Bibliography of Studies. Robert Goetzman. LC 75-24080. (Reference Library of the Humanities: Vol. 27). 1976. lib. bdg. 28.00 o.p. (ISBN 0-8240-9985-0). Garland Pub.

James Beard: The Fireside Cookbook. James A. Beard. 320p. 1982. pap. 9.95 o.p. (ISBN 0-671-44774-2, Fireside). S&S.

James Bond & Moonraker. Christopher Wood. (Orig.). 1979. pap. 2.95 o.s.i. (ISBN 0-425-07656-3). Jove Pubns.

James Bond Bedside Companion. Raymond Benson. (Illus.). 385p. 1984. 19.95 o.p. (ISBN 0-396-08383-8). Dodd.

James Bond Cookbook. Homer Goodall. (Illus.). 72p. (Orig.). pap. cancelled o.s.i. (ISBN 0-939427-50-8, 02032). Alpha Pubns OH.

James Bond: The Authorized Biography of 007. John Pearson. LC 85-45544. 328p. pap. 3.95 o.s.i. (ISBN 0-394-62140-9, BC). Grove.

James Bond Trivia Quiz Book: From Odd Job to Money Penny... Everything You Always Wanted to Know about Agent 007. Phillip Gurin. 1984. pap. 4.95 o.p. (ISBN 0-87795-580-8, Arbor Hse); (10-copy prepack) 49.50 o.p. (ISBN 0-87795-615-4). Morrow.

James Branch Cabell: A Reference Guide. Maurice Duke. 1979. lib. bdg. 18.00 o.p. (ISBN 0-8161-7838-0, Hall Reference). G K Hall.

James Brown: The Godfather of Soul. James Brown & Bruce Tucker. (Illus.). 352p. 1986. 18.95 o.p. (ISBN 0-02-517430-4). Macmillan.

James Cagney: A Celebration. Richard Schickel. 19.95 o.p. (ISBN 0-316-77309-3). Little.

James Clerk Maxwell: A Biography. Ivan Tolstoy. LC 82-13605. (Illus.). viii, 192p. 1983. lib. bdg. 17.00x o.s.i. (ISBN 0-226-80785-1); pap. text ed. 6.95 o.s.i. (ISBN 0-226-80787-8). U of Chicago Pr.

James Connolly: Selected Political Writings. Bernard Ransom & Owen D. Edwards. 1974. pap. 4.95 o.s.i. (ISBN 0-394-17874-2, E630, Ever). Grove.

James Dickey: The Expansive Imagination. Ed. by Richard J. Calhoun. LC 72-90914. 1973. lib. bdg. 25.00 o.p. (ISBN 0-912112-00-X). Everett-Edwards.

James Franklin Gilman: Nineteenth Century Painter. Adele G. Dawson. LC 75-20929. 168p. 1975. 15.00 o.p. (ISBN 0-914016-20-2). Phoenix Pub.

James Gandon: Vitruvius Hibernicus. Edward McParland. Ed. by John Harris & Alastair Laing. (Studies in Architecture: No. XXIV). (Illus.). 224p. 1986. 125.00 o.p. (ISBN 0-302-02576-6, Pub. by Zwemmer Bks UK). Sotheby Pubns.

James Gould Cozzens: A Life Apart. Matthew J. Bruccoli. LC 82-23312. 368p. 1983. 15.95 o.p. (ISBN 0-15-146048-5). HarBraceJ.

James Harrington's Republic. W. Calvin Dickinson. LC 82-24749. 126p. (Orig.). 1983. lib. bdg. 24.75 o.p. (ISBN 0-8191-3019-2); pap. text ed. 10.00 o.p. (ISBN 0-8191-3020-6). U Pr of Amer.

James Howe, 3 vols. 1985. Boxed Set. pap. 7.50 o.p. (ISBN 0-380-89989-2). Avon.

James Hutton's Medical Dissertation. Arthur Donovan & Joseph Prentiss. LC 80-65850. (Transaction Ser.: Vol. 70, Pt. 6). 1980. 10.00 o.p. (ISBN 0-87169-706-8). Am Philos.

James I & the Politics of Literature: Jonson, Shakespeare, Donne, & Their Contemporaries. Jonathan Goldberg. LC 82-21325. 312p. 1983. text ed. 34.50x o.p. (ISBN 0-8018-2971-2). Johns Hopkins.

James Jones. George Garrett. LC 83-18665. (Album Biographies Ser.). (Illus.). 256p. 1984. 18.95 o.p. (ISBN 0-15-146049-3). HarBraceJ.

James Jones. George Garrett. LC 83-18665. 256p. 1984. pap. 10.95 o.p. (ISBN 0-15-645955-8, Harv). HarBraceJ.

James Joyce: A Student's Guide. Matthew Hodgart. 1978. 19.95x o.p. (ISBN 0-7100-8817-5); pap. 8.95 o.p. (ISBN 0-7100-8943-0). Routledge Chapman & Hall.

James Joyce & the German Novel, 1922-1933. Breon Mitchell. LC 75-36980. xvi, 194p. 1976. 15.00x o.p. (ISBN 0-8214-0192-0). Ohio U Pr.

James Joyce's Aesthetic Theory: Its Development & Application. Dolf Sorenson. 1977. pap. text ed. 15.00x o.p. (ISBN 90-6203-200-1). Humanities.

James Joyce's Odyssey: A Guide to the Dublin of Ulysses. Frank Delaney & Jorge Lewinski. LC 81-83276. (Illus.). 224p. 1982. 19.95 o.p. (ISBN 0-03-060457-5). H Holt & Co.

James M. Comley Papers: An Inventory to the Microfilm Edition. Andrea D. Lentz. 24p. 1973. 2.50 o.p. (ISBN 0-318-03196-5). Ohio Hist Soc.

James MacArthur: Colonial Conservative 1798-1867. John M. Ward. 345p. 1982. 43.00x o.p. (ISBN 0-424-00087-3, Pub. by Sydney U Pr). Intl Spec Bk.

James Mill & the Art of Revolution. Joseph Hamburger. LC 77-8124. (Yale Studies in Political Science: No. 8). 1977. Repr. of 1963 ed. lib. bdg. 35.00x o.p. (ISBN 0-8371-9675-2, HAJM). Greenwood.

James Russell Lowell: His Life & Work. Ferris Greenslet. LC 77-77162. 324p. 1969. Repr. of 1905 ed. 36.00x o.p. (ISBN 0-8103-3893-9). Gale.

James Shirley: A Reference Guide. Ruth K. Zimmer. 1980. lib. bdg. 25.00 o.p. (ISBN 0-8161-7974-3, Hall Reference). G K Hall.

James Stewart. Allan Hunter. (Film Stars Ser.). (Illus.). 96p. 1985. 7.95 o.p. (ISBN 0-87052-123-3). Hippocrene Bks.

James Stirling: A Select Bibliography. Valerie J. Nurcombe. (Architecture Ser.: A 1403). 32p. 1985. 4.50 o.p. (ISBN 0-89028-433-4). Vance Biblios.

James T. Fields: Biographical Notes & Personal Sketches with Unpublished Fragments & Tributes from Men & Women of Letters. Ed. by Annie Fields. LC 73-157501. 282p. 1971. Repr. of 1881 ed. 43.00x o.p. (ISBN 0-8103-3724-X). Gale.

James Thomson: An Annotated Bibliography of Selected Writings & the Important Criticism. Hilbert H. Campbell. LC 75-24092. (Reference Library of the Humanities: Vol. 33). 158p. 1976. lib. bdg. 31.00 o.p. (ISBN 0-8240-9979-6). Garland Pub.

James Tissot. Ed. by Krystyna Matyjaszkiewicz. LC 84-18542. (Illus.). 144p. 1985. 45.00 o.p. (ISBN 0-89659-516-1). Abbeville Pr.

James Wallace, 3 vols. Robert Bage. Ed. by Ronald Paulson. LC 78-60847. (Novel 1720-1805 Ser.: Vol. 11). 1979. 112.00 o.p. (ISBN 0-8240-3660-3). Garland Pub.

James Watt & the Steam Revolution, a Documentary History. Compiled by Eric H. Robinson & James Musson. LC 71-96795. (Illus.). 1969. lib. bdg. 29.50x o.p. (ISBN 0-678-07756-8). Kelley.

James Weldon Johnson & Arna Wendell Bontemps: A Reference Guide. Ed. by Robert E. Fleming. 1978. lib. bdg. 19.00 o.p. (ISBN 0-8161-7932-8, Hall Reference). G K Hall.

James Weldon Johnson: Black Leader, Black Voice. Eugene Levy. Ed. by John H. Franklin. LC 72-95134. (Negro American Biographies & Autobiographies Ser). 1973. lib. bdg. 20.00x o.s.i. (ISBN 0-226-47603-0). U of Chicago Pr.

James Weldon Johnson: Black Leader, Black Voice. Eugene Levy. Ed. by John H. Franklin. LC 72-95134. (Negro-American Biographies & Autobiographies Ser.). (Illus.). 1976. pap. text ed. 5.95x o.s.i. (ISBN 0-226-47604-9, P700, Phoen). U of Chicago Pr.

James Whatman, Father & Son. Thomas Balston. Ed. by John Bidwell. LC 78-74386. (Nineteenth-Century Book Arts & Printing History Ser.: Vol. 1). (Illus.). 1979. lib. bdg. 26.00 o.p. (ISBN 0-8240-3875-4). Garland Pub.

James White. Virgil Robinson. LC 75-16921. (Illus.). 1976. 9.95 o.p. (ISBN 0-8280-0049-2). Review & Herald.

James Wilson, Founding Father: 1742-1798. Charles Page Smith. LC 73-7077. (Illus.). 426p. 1973. Repr. of 1956 ed. lib. bdg. 22.50x o.p. (ISBN 0-8371-6908-9, SMJW). Greenwood.

Jamie Reid. Gordon Ogilvie. 448p. 1981. pap. 2.75 o.p. (ISBN 0-380-76737-6, 76737-6). Avon.

Jamie Wyeth. Jamie Wyeth. (Illus.). 1982. pap. 12.45 o.s.i. (ISBN 0-395-32529-3). HM.

Jamie's Tiger. Jan Wahl. LC 77-88969. (Illus.). (ps-2). 1978. 7.95 o.p. (ISBN 0-15-239500-8, HJ). HarBraceJ.

Jammu Fox: A Biography of Maharaja Gulab Singh of Kashmir, 1792-1857. Bawa S. Singh. LC 73-23023. (Illus.). 291p. 1974. 15.00x o.p. (ISBN 0-8093-0652-2). S Ill U Pr.

Jan Both: Paintings, Drawings & Prints. James D. Burke. LC 75-23783. (Outstanding Dissertations in the Fine Arts - 17th Century). (Illus.). 1976. lib. bdg. 55.00 o.p. (ISBN 0-8240-1980-6). Garland Pub.

Jan Groover. Susan Kismaric. (Illus.). 64p. (Orig.). 1987. pap. 18.50 o.p. (ISBN 0-87070-309-9). Museum Mod Art.

Jan Masaryk. Bruce Lockhart. 1951. (ISBN 0-8022-0987-4). Philos Lib.

Jan Saudek-Photographs. RotoVision. 40.00 o.p. (ISBN 2-88046-028-X). Norton.

Janacek: Leaves from His Life. Leos Janacek. Tr. by Vilem Tausky & Margaret Tausky. LC 81-52424. (Illus.). 160p. 1982. 11.95 o.s.i. (ISBN 0-8008-4299-5, Crescendo). Taplinger.

Janacek's Tragic Operas. Michael Ewans. LC 77-93894. 288p. 1978. 22.50x o.p. (ISBN 0-253-37504-5). Ind U Pr.

Jane. Dee Wells. 1978. pap. 1.75 o.p. (ISBN 0-380-00222-1, 38356-X). Avon.

Jane Addams on Peace & Freedom, 1914-1935. Allen Davis. LC 71-147761. (Library of War & Peace: Documentary Anthologies). 1976. lib. bdg. 38.00 o.p. (ISBN 0-8240-0501-5). Garland Pub.

Jane & May Morris: A Biographical Story 1839-1938. Jan Marsh. 1987. pap. 10.95 o.p. (ISBN 0-86358-026-2). Routledge Chapman & Hall.

Jane & Prudence. Barbara Pym. 1985. lib. bdg. 15.95 o.p. (ISBN 0-8161-3861-3, Large Print Bks). G K Hall.

Jane Austen, Feminism & Fiction. Margaret Kirkham. 206p. 1986. pap. 10.95 o.p. (ISBN 0-416-01181-0, 9665). Routledge Chapman & Hall.

Jane Austen: Her Concept of Social Life. Sushila Singh. 1981. text ed. 18.00x o.p. Coronet Bks.

Jane Austen Library Vol. I: Lady Susan. Jane Austen. Ed. by R. W. Chapman. LC 83-40456. 200p. 1987. 20.00x o.s.i. (ISBN 0-8052-3894-8). Schocken.

Jane Eyre. Charlotte Bronte. LC 84-61675. (Illus.). 480p. 1984. 12.95 o.p. (ISBN 0-89577-200-0). RD Assn.

Jane Eyre. Charlotte Bronte. (Movieworld Ser.). (Illus.). 32p. 1985. pap. text ed. 5.95 o.p. (ISBN 0-582-33152-8). Longman.

Jane Eyre. 2nd ed. Charlotte Bronte. Ed. by Richard J. Dunn. (Critical Edition Ser.). 1987. 24.95 o.p. (ISBN 0-393-02424-5). Norton.

Jane Fonda's Workout Book. Jane Fonda. LC 81-13553. 256p. 1981. 19.95 o.s.i. (ISBN 0-671-43217-6). S&S.

Jane Fonda's Year of Fitness & Health 1984. Jane Fonda. 1983. pap. 8.95 o.p. (ISBN 0-671-46998-3). S&S.

Jane Fonda's Year of Fitness, Health & Nutrition, 1985. Jane Fonda. 1984. pap. 9.95 o.p. (ISBN 0-671-47649-1). S&S.

Jane Grigson's British Cookery. Jane Grigson. LC 84-48442. (Illus.). 256p. 1985. 24.95 o.p. (ISBN 0-689-11524-5, Atheneum). Macmillan.

Jane Grigson's Fruit Book. Jane Grigson. LC 82-45168. (Illus.). 528p. 1982. 19.95 o.p. (ISBN 0-689-11305-6, Atheneum). Macmillan.

Jane Grigson's Vegetable Book. Jane Grigson. LC 79-2038. 1979. 19.95 o.p. (ISBN 0-689-10994-6, Atheneum). Macmillan.

Jane Wyman - The Actress & the Woman: An Illustrated Biography. Lawrence J. Quirk. LC 85-25284. (Illus.). 1986. 19.95 o.p. (ISBN 0-934878-68-4). Dembner Bks.

Jane Wyman: A Biography. Joe Morella & Edward Z. Epstein. (Illus.). 240p. 1985. 15.95 o.p. (ISBN 0-385-29402-6). Delacorte.

Jane Wyman: A Biography. Joe Morella & Edward Z. Epstein. (General Ser.). 350p. 1986. lib. bdg. 18.95x o.p. (ISBN 0-8161-4065-0, Large Print Bks). G K Hall.

Jane Wyman: The Actress & the Woman. Lawrence J. Quirk. LC 85-25284. (Illus.). 224p. 1987. pap. 10.95 o.p. (ISBN 0-934878-90-0). Dembner Bks.

Jane's Aerospace Dictionary. 2nd ed. Bill Gunston. 565p. 1986. 39.95 o.p. (ISBN 0-7106-0365-7). Janes Info Group.

Jane's Airport & Handling Agents - Central & Latin America Including the Caribbean. Ed. by Paul Portnoi. 600p. 1988. 3-ring binder 150.00x o.p. (ISBN 0-7106-0554-4). Janes Info Group.

Jane's Airport Equipment 1986-87. 5th ed. Ed. by David F. Rider. (Illus.). 800p. 1986. 137.50x o.p. (ISBN 0-7106-0831-4). Janes Info Group.

Jane's Airports & Handling Agents - Far East, Asia, Australasia Region. Ed. by Paul Portnoi. 1988. 3-ring binder 150.00x o.p. (ISBN 0-7106-0553-6). Janes Info Group.

Jane's Airports & Handling Agents - United States, Canada Region. 1685p. 1988. 3-ring binder 150.00x o.p. (ISBN 0-7106-0552-8). Janes Info Group.

Jane's Airports & Handling Agents: Europe. 1987. 150.00 o.p. (ISBN 0-7106-0532-3). Janes Info Group.

Jane's Airports & Handling Agents: Middle East, Asia. 1988. 150.00 o.p. (ISBN 0-7106-0533-1). Janes Info Group.

Jane's All the World's Aircraft 1986-87. Ed. by John W. Taylor. (Illus.). 970p. 1986. 141.50x o.p. (ISBN 0-7106-0835-7). Janes Info Group.

Jane's Armour & Artillery 1986-87. 7th ed. Ed. by Christopher F. Foss. (Illus.). 930p. 137.50 o.p. (ISBN 0-7106-0833-0). Janes Info Group.

Jane's Armoured Personnel Carriers. Ed. by Christopher F. Foss. (Illus.). 208p. 1986. 22.00 o.p. (ISBN 0-7106-0354-1). Janes Info Group.

Jane's Aviation Review. 5th ed. Ed. by Michael J. Taylor. (Illus.). 176p. 1986. 16.95 o.p. (ISBN 0-7106-0368-1). Janes Info Group.

Jane's Aviation Review. 6th ed. Ed. by Michael J. Taylor. 176p. 1987. 16.95 o.p. (ISBN 0-7106-0446-7). Janes Info Group.

Jane's Avionics 1986-87. 5th ed. Ed. by Stephen R. Broadbent. (Illus.). 550p. 1986. 112.00x o.p. (ISBN 0-7106-0830-6). Janes Info Group.

Jane's Battlefield Air Defence, 1988-89. Christopher Foss & Tony Cullen. (Illus.). 400p. 1988. pap. 90.00x o.p. (ISBN 0-7106-0865-9). Janes Info Group.
Jane's Career. H. G. DeLisser. (Caribbean Writers Ser.). 1972. pap. text ed. 7.00 o.p. (ISBN 0-435-98540-X). Heinemann Ed.
Jane's Fighting Ships 1986-87. Ed. by John Moore. 800p. 1986. 135.00x o.p. (ISBN 0-7106-0828-4). Janes Info Group.
Jane's Freight Containers, 1986. 18th ed. Ed. by Patrick Finlay. (Illus.). 660p. 1986. 137.50x o.p. (ISBN 0-7106-0822-5). Janes Info Group.
Jane's High Speed Marine Craft & Air Cushion Vehicles, 1986. 19th ed. Ed. by Robert L. Trillo. (Illus.). 400p. 1986. 125.00x o.p. (ISBN 0-7106-0823-3). Janes Info Group.
Jane's Infantry Weapons 1986-87. Ed. by Ian V. Hogg. 950p. 1986. 136.00x o.p. (ISBN 0-7106-0829-2). Janes Info Group.
Jane's Main Battle Tanks. Christopher F. Foss. (Illus.). 205p. 1984. 18.95 o.p. (ISBN 0-7106-0277-4). Janes Info Group.
Jane's Main Battle Tanks. 2nd ed. Christopher F. Foss. 205p. 1986. 22.00 o.p. (ISBN 0-7106-0372-X). Janes Info Group.
Jane's Military Communications, 1986. 7th ed. Ed. by R. J. Raggett. (Illus.). 910p. 1986. 140.00 o.p. (ISBN 0-7106-0824-1). Janes Info Group.
Jane's Military Review. 5th ed. Ed. by Ian V. Hogg. (Illus.). 176p. 1986. 16.95x o.p. (ISBN 0-7106-0369-X). Janes Info Group.
Jane's Military Review. 6th ed. 176p. 1987. 16.95x o.p. (ISBN 0-7106-0447-5). Janes Info Group.
Jane's Military Vehicles & Ground Support Equipment, 1986. 7th ed. Ed. by Christopher Foss & Terry Gander. (Illus.). 910p. 1986. 137.50x o.p. (ISBN 0-7106-0825-X). Janes Info Group.
Jane's NATO Warships Handbook. Ed. by John Moore. 480p. 1987. pap. 13.95 o.p. (ISBN 0-7106-0377-0). Janes Info Group.
Jane's Naval Review. 5th ed. Ed. by John Moore. (Illus.). 176p. 1986. 16.95x o.p. (ISBN 0-7106-0370-3). Janes Info Group.
Jane's Naval Review. 6th ed. Ed. by John Moore. 176p. 1987. 16.95 o.p. (ISBN 0-7106-0448-3). Janes Info Group.
Jane's Spaceflight Directory, 1986. Ed. by Reginald Turnill. (Illus.). 430p. 1986. 120.00x o.p. (ISBN 0-7106-0367-3). Janes Info Group.
Jane's Urban Transport Systems, 1986. 5th ed. Ed. by Chris Bushell & Peter Stonham. (Illus.). 570p. 1986. 125.00 o.p. (ISBN 0-7106-0826-8). Janes Info Group.
Jane's Warsaw Pact Merchant Ships Recognition Handbook. David Greenman & E. C. Talbot-Booth. (Illus.). 192p. (Orig.). 1987. pap. 16.95 o.p. (ISBN 0-7106-0455-6). Janes Info Group.
Jane's Weapon System, 1982-1983. Ed. by Ronald T. Pretty. (Jane's Yearbooks). (Illus.). 1000p. 1982. 140.00 o.p. (ISBN 0-86720-619-5). Janes Info Group.
Jane's Weapon Systems, 1983-1984. 14th ed. Ed. by Ronald T. Pretty. (Jane's Yearbooks). (Illus.). 1000p. 1983. 125.00x o.p. (ISBN 0-7106-0786-5). Janes Info Group.
Jane's Weapon Systems 1984-85. Ed. by Ronald T. Pretty. (Jane's Yearbooks). (Illus.). 1000p. 1984. 125.00 o.p. (ISBN 0-7106-0799-7). Janes Info Group.
Jane's Weapon Systems, 1985-1986. 16th ed. Ed. by Ronald T. Pretty. (Jane's Yearbooks). (Illus.). 1000p. 1985. 125.00x o.p. (ISBN 0-7106-0819-5). Janes Info Group.
Jane's Weapon Systems 1986-87. 17th ed. Ed. by Ronald T. Pretty. (Illus.). 1060p. 1986. 145.00 o.p. (ISBN 0-7106-0832-2). Janes Info Group.
Jane's World Aircraft Recognition Handbook. Derek Wood. (Illus.). 512p. 1982. 12.95 o.p. (ISBN 0-86720-636-5). Janes Info Group.
Jane's World Railways, 1982-1983. (Jane's Yearbooks). (Illus.). 550p. 140.00 o.p. (ISBN 0-86720-606-3). Janes Info Group.
Jane's World Railways, 1983-1984. Ed. by Geoffrey F. Allen. (Jane's Yearbooks). (Illus.). 550p. 1983. 125.00x o.p. (ISBN 0-7106-0787-3). Janes Info Group.
Jane's World Railways 1984-85. Ed. by Geoffrey F. Allen. (Illus.). 800p. 1984. 125.00x o.p. (ISBN 0-7106-0802-0). Janes Info Group.
Jane's World Railways, 1985-1986. 27th ed. Ed. by Geoffrey F. Allen. (Jane's Yearbooks). (Illus.). 800p. 1985. 125.00x o.p. (ISBN 0-7106-0818-7). Janes Info Group.
Jane's World Railways 1986-87. Ed. by Geoffrey F. Allen. (Illus.). 870p. 1986. 140.00x o.p. (ISBN 0-7106-0834-9). Janes Info Group.
Janet Flanner's World: Uncollected Writing's 1932-1975. Janet Flanner. Ed. by Irving Drutman. LC 79-1820. 1979. 12.95 o.p. (ISBN 0-15-146154-6). HarBraceJ.
Janet Reachfar & Chickabird. Jane Duncan. LC 77-12709. (ps-3). 1979. 7.95 o.p. (ISBN 0-395-28788-X, Clarion). HM.
Janey. Roy J. Campbell. 192p. 1982. 9.00 o.p. (ISBN 0-682-49875-0). Exposition-Phoenix.
Janni's Stork. Rosemary Harris. LC 83-15796. (Illus.). 32p. (gr. 3-7). 1984. 10.95 o.p. (ISBN 0-911745-20-3, Bedrick Blackie). P Bedrick Bks.
Janus: The Conquest of War, a Psychological Enquiry. Williams McDougall. LC 79-148369. (Library of War & Peace; the Character & Causes of War). 1972. lib. bdg. 46.00 o.p. (ISBN 0-8240-0462-0). Garland Pub.
Japan. (Post Guides Ser.). (Illus.). 144p. (Orig.). 1987. pap. 8.95 o.p. (ISBN 962-10-0015-7). Hunter Pub NY.
Japan. Time-Life Books Editors. (Library of Nations). (Illus.). 160p. (YA) (gr. 7 up). 1985. lib. bdg. 23.93 o.p. Time-Life.
Japan: A Comparative View. Ed. by Albert M. Craig. LC 78-70285. 1979. 40.00 o.p. (ISBN 0-691-05271-9). Princeton U Pr.
Japan: A Partnership in Progress. Nobuhiko Ushiba & Gerald L. Curtis. Trilateral Comm.
Japan-A Travel Survival Kit. 2nd ed. Ian McQueen. (Illus.). 520p. (Orig.). 1989. pap. 12.95 o.p. (ISBN 0-908086-70-9). Lonely Planet.
Japan & America: A Comparative Study in Language & Culture. Bernice Goldstein & Kyoko Tamura. LC 74-81653. 1975. 7.50 o.p. (ISBN 0-8048-1109-1). C E Tuttle.
Japan & the East. Earl Speneer. (Illus.). 231p. 1987. 34.95 o.p. (ISBN 0-9511652-0-8, Pub. by Hove Foto Bks). Seven Hills Bk Dists.
Japan & the Japanese. new ed. Mainichi Newspapers Staff. LC 72-95973. 240p. 1974. 7.95 o.p. (ISBN 0-87040-223-4); pap. 4.95 o.p. (ISBN 0-87040-227-7). Japan Pubns USA.
Japan & the Soviet Union, Pt. 1. Ed. by Donald S. Detwiler & Charles B. Burdick. (War in Asia & the Pacific Ser., 1937 to 1949: Vol. 10). 670p. 1980. lib. bdg. 74.00 o.p. (ISBN 0-8240-3294-2). Garland Pub.
Japan & the Soviet Union, Pt. 2. Ed. by Donald S. Detwiler & Charles B. Burdick. (War in Asia & the Pacific Ser., 1937 to 1949: Vol. 11). 610p. 1980. lib. bdg. 74.00 o.p. (ISBN 0-8240-3295-0). Garland Pub.
Japan & the World Energy Problem. Herbert I. Goodman. (Occasional Paper of the Northeast Asia-United States Forum on International Policy, Stanford University). 66p. 1980. pap. 5.00 o.p. (ISBN 0-935371-02-8). ISIS.
Japan As a Market & Source of Supply. G. C. Allen. 1967. pap. text ed. 10.50 o.p. (ISBN 0-08-012234-5). Pergamon.
Japan at the Brink. Konosuke Matsushita. Tr. by Charles Terry from Japanese. LC 75-30180. 136p. 1975. 8.95 o.p. (ISBN 0-87011-270-8). Kodansha.
Japan Dictionary. Lewis Bush. (Illus.). 224p. 1957. (ISBN 0-8022-0200-4). Philos Lib.
Japan Directory of Professional Associations, 1984-1987. 275.00 o.p. (ISBN 0-8002-3173-2). Intl Pubns Serv.
Japan Directory, 1986. 496.00 o.p. (ISBN 0-8002-3978-4). Intl Pubns Serv.
Japan Directory: 1987. 1800p. 1987. 495.00 o.p. (ISBN 0-8002-4105-3). Intl Pubns Serv.
Japan Electronics Almanac, 1986. 54.00 o.p. (ISBN 0-8002-3983-0). Intl Pubns Serv.
Japan Electronics Buyer's Guide, 1986, 4 vols. 185.00 o.p. (ISBN 0-8002-3982-2). Intl Pubns Serv.
Japan Electronics Buyers' Guide, 1988. 25th ed. 1300p. 1988. 175.00 o.p. (ISBN 0-8002-4215-7). Intl Pubns Serv.
Japan: God's Door to the Far East. Lloyd R. Neve. LC 73-78255. 1973. write for info o.p. (ISBN 0-8066-1321-1, 10-3465, Augsburg). Augsburg Fortress.
Japan in Story & Pictures. Lily Edelman. LC 53-9027. (Illus.). (gr. 4-6). 1953. 4.95 o.p. (ISBN 0-15-239701-9, HJ). HarBraceJ.
Japan Is a Circle. Kenichi Yoshida. LC 75-14731. 149p. 1976. Repr. 8.95x o.p. (ISBN 0-87011-262-7). Kodansha.
Japan: Selected Readings. rev. ed. Hyman Kublin. LC 72-84106. (Illus.). 228p. (gr. 6-9). 1973. pap. 7.52 o.p. (ISBN 0-395-13930-9). HM.
Japan Statistical Yearbook, 1985. 35th ed. 1986. 175.00 o.p. (ISBN 4-8223-0585-6). Intl Pubns Serv.
Japan Statistical Yearbook: 1986. LC 78-58221. 836p. 1986. 180.00 o.p. (ISBN 0-8002-4068-5). Intl Pubns Serv.
Japan: The Beauty of Food. Photos by Reinhart Wolf. (Illus.). 192p. 1987. 50.00 o.p. (ISBN 0-8478-0867-X). Rizzoli Intl.
Japan: The Fragile Superpower. Frank Gibney. 1975. 10.95x o.p. (ISBN 0-393-05530-2). Norton.
Japan: The Fragile Superpower. rev. ed. Frank Gibney. 1979. 12.95 o.p. (ISBN 0-393-05704-6). Norton.
Japan: The Years of Trial 1919-52. Hyoe Murakami. LC 83-80223. (Illus.). 248p. 1983. pap. 5.25 o.p. (ISBN 0-87011-610-X). Kodansha.
Japan Trade Directory 1986-87. 1300p. 1987. 265.00x o.p. (ISBN 4-8224-0324-6, Pub. by Japan External Trade). Gale.
Japan Trade Directory 1987-1988. 1987. 265.00x o.p. (ISBN 0-317-55922-2, Pub. by Japan External Trade). Gale.
Japanese see Glass Children & Other Essays.
Japanese: A Cultural Portrait. Robert S. Ozaki. LC 77-93224. 1978. 15.00 o.p. (ISBN 0-8048-1183-0). C E Tuttle.
Japanese: A Graded Approach to Reading, Writing & Vocabulary Building. Masakazu Watabe & Kent S. Gilbert. 336p. cancelled o.s.i. (ISBN 0-8048-1448-1). C E Tuttle.
Japanese Americans: Evolution of a Subculture. 2nd ed. Harry H. Kitano. (Ethnic Groups in American Life Ser.). 224p. 1976. Ref. Ed. 15.95 o.p. (ISBN 0-13-509430-5); pap. text ed. 17.33 o.p. (ISBN 0-13-509422-4). P-H.
Japanese & the Japanese: Words in Culture. Takao Suzuki. Tr. by Akira Miura. LC 77-15296. 152p. 1978. 12.95x o.p. (ISBN 0-87011-325-9); pap. 4.25 o.p. (ISBN 0-87011-642-8). Kodansha.
Japanese & U. S. Inflation: A Comparative Analysis. Ching-Yuan Lin. LC 83-48723. 192p. 1984. 27.00x o.p. (ISBN 0-669-07399-7). Lexington Bks.
Japanese Antiques: With a Guide to Shops. rev. ed. Patricia Salmon. (Illus.). 256p. 1986. pap. 12.95 o.p. (Pub. by Art Inter Pubs). UH Pr.
Japanese Armed Forces Order of Battle, 1937-1945, Vol. I. Ed. by W. Victor Madej. (Illus.). 1982. 13.95 o.s.i. (ISBN 0-941052-67-2, 77); pap. 9.95 o.s.i. (ISBN 0-941052-04-4, 17). Valor Pub.
Japanese Art & Handicraft. H. L. Joly & K. Tomita. (Illus.). 214p. 70.00 o.s.i. (ISBN 0-317-55119-1). Apollo.
Japanese Art & Handicraft. limited ed. Henri L. Joly & Kumasaku Tomita. LC 76-24135. (Illus.). 1977. Repr. of 1916 ed. 70.00 o.p. (ISBN 0-8048-1205-5). C E Tuttle.
Japanese Brush Painting Techniques: Sumi-e - A Meditation in Ink. Paul Siudzinski. LC 83-9107. (Illus., Orig.). 1983. pap. 7.95 o.p. (ISBN 0-8069-7752-3). Sterling.
Japanese Ceramics. John Ayers. (Baur Collection Ser.). (Illus.). 184p. 1983. 195.00 o.p. (Pub. by Baur Foundation Switzerland). Routledge Chapman & Hall.
Japanese Challenge & the American Response: A Symposium. (Research Papers & Policy Studies: No. 6). 1982. pap. 7.00x o.p. (ISBN 0-912966-49-1). IEAS.
Japanese Character: A Cultural Profile. Nyozekan Hasegawa. Tr. by John Bester from Japanese. LC 66-19819. (Illus.). 157p. 1982. pap. 5.25 o.p. (ISBN 0-87011-517-0). Kodansha.
Japanese Cloisonne: History, Technique & Appreciation. Coben & Ferster. (Illus.). 65.00 o.s.i. (ISBN 0-317-55048-9). Apollo.
Japanese Corpse. Janwillem Van De Wetering. LC 77-5027. 1977. 7.95 o.p. (ISBN 0-395-25777-8). HM.
Japanese Crane: Bird of Happiness. Dorothy Britton. LC 81-82027. (Illus.). 60p. 1982. 19.95 o.s.i. (ISBN 0-87011-484-0). Kodansha.
Japanese Design Motifs: 4260 Illustrations of Heraldic Crests. Matsuya Piece-Goods Store Staff. Tr. & illus. by Fumie Adachi. (Illus.). 15.75 o.p. (ISBN 0-8446-4630-X). Peter Smith.
Japanese Economic Development of Manchuria, 1932-1945. Ramon H. Myers. LC 80-8833. (China During the Interregnum 1911-1949, the Economy & Society). 340p. 1982. lib. bdg. 36.00 o.p. (ISBN 0-8240-4689-7). Garland Pub.
Japanese Fan Paintings From Western Collection. Kurt A. Gitter & Pat Fisher. LC 84-19097. 136p. 1985. 24.95 o.p. (ISBN 0-295-96282-8). U of Wash Pr.
Japanese Film Directors. Audie Bock. LC 84-82294. (Illus.). 380p. 1985. pap. 14.95 o.s.i. (ISBN 0-87011-304-6). Kodansha.
Japanese Finance. Stephen Bronte. 258p. 1982. 88.00 o.p. (ISBN 0-8002-3404-9). Intl Pubns Serv.
Japanese Gothic. Akihisa Ogino. LC 85-90131. 158p. 1985. 11.95 o.p. (ISBN 0-533-06637-9). Vantage.
Japanese IKAT Weaving. Jun Tomita & Noriko Tomita. 11.95 o.s.i. (ISBN 0-318-19566-6). Robin & Russ.
Japanese Industrial Competition to 1990. (Economist Intelligence Unit Ser.). (Illus.). 224p. 1982. text ed. 25.00 o.p. Abt Bks.
Japanese Investment in Manchurian Manufacturing, Mining, Transportation & Communications, 1931-1945. Ann R. Kinney. Ed. by Ramon H. Myers. LC 80-8835. (China During the Interregnum 1911-1949, The Economy & Society Ser.). 172p. 1982. lib. bdg. 24.00 o.p. (ISBN 0-8240-4690-0). Garland Pub.
Japanese Kites. Tal Streeter. 184p. 1980. pap. 9.95 o.s.i. (ISBN 0-317-34796-9); pap. 8.00 members o.s.i. (ISBN 0-317-34797-7). Japan Soc.
Japanese Language. Haruhiko Kindaich. Tr. by Umeyo Hirano. LC 77-93226. 1976. 16.50 o.p. (ISBN 0-8048-1185-7). C E Tuttle.
Japanese Literature: An Introduction for Western Readers. Donald Keene. (YA) (gr. 9 up). 1955. pap. 2.25 o.p. (ISBN 0-394-17200-0, E9, Ever). Grove.
Japanese Marketing System: Adaptations & Innovations. M. Y. Yoshino. 1971. 30.00x o.p. (ISBN 0-262-24012-2). MIT Pr.
Japanese Military Studies Nineteen Thirty-Seven to Nineteen Forty-Nine, Naval Armament Program & Naval Operations: Japanese & Chinese Studies & Documents, Vol. 4. Ed. by Donald S. Detwiler & Charles B. Burdick. (War in Asia & the Pacific Ser., 1937 to 1949). 550p. 1980. Part I. lib. bdg. 74.00 o.p. (ISBN 0-8240-3288-8); lib. bdg. 650.00 set of 15 vols. o.p. (ISBN 0-686-60107-6). Garland Pub.
Japanese Military Studies Nineteen Thirty-Seven to Nineteen Forty-Nine, Naval Armament Program & Naval Operations: Japanese & Chinese Studies & Documents, Vol. 5. Ed. by Donald S. Detwiler & Charles B. Burdick. (War in Asia & the Pacific Ser., 1937 to 1949). 520p. 1980. Part II. lib. bdg. 74.00 o.p. (ISBN 0-8240-3289-6); lib. bdg. 845.00 set 15 vols. o.p. Garland Pub.
Japanese Military Studies: The Southern Area: Japanese & Chinese Studies & Documents, Vol. 7. Ed. by Donald S. Detwiler & Charles B. Burdick. (War in Asia & the Pacific Ser., 1937 to 1949). 420p. 1980. Part II. lib. bdg. 75.00 o.p. (ISBN 0-8240-3291-8). Garland Pub.
Japanese Military Studies 1937-1949: Command, Administration, & Special Operations; Japanese & Chinese Studies & Documents. Ed. by Donald S. Detwiler & Charles B. Burdick. (War in Asia & the Pacific Ser., 1937 to 1949: Vol. 3). 660p. 1980. lib. bdg. 75.00 o.p. (ISBN 0-8240-3287-X). Garland Pub.
Japanese Military Studies 1937-1949: China, Manchuria, & Korea, Pt. 1. Ed. by Donald S. Detwiler & Charles B. Burdick. (War in Asia & the Pacific Ser., 1937 to 1949: Vol. 8). 630p. 1980. lib. bdg. 60.50 o.p. (ISBN 0-8240-3292-6). Garland Pub.
Japanese Military Studies 1937-1949: China, Manchuria, & Korea, Pt. 2. Ed. by Donald S. Detwiler & Charles B. Burdick. (War in Asia & the Pacific Ser., 1937 to 1949: Vol. 9). 650p. 1980. lib. bdg. 60.50 o.p. (ISBN 0-8240-3293-4). Garland Pub.
Japanese Military Studies, 1937-1949: Political Background of the War: Japanese & Chinese Studies & Documents, Vol. 2. Ed. by Donald S. Detwiler & Charles B. Burdick. (War in Asia & the Pacific Ser., 1937 to 1949). 500p. 1980. lib. bdg. 75.00 o.p. (ISBN 0-8240-3286-1). Garland Pub.
Japanese Military Studies, 1937-1949: The Southern Area: Japanese & Chinese Studies & Documents, Vol. 6. Ed. by Donald S. Detwiler & Charles B. Burdick. (War in Asia & the Pacific Ser., 1937 to 1949). 530p. 1980. Part I. lib. bdg. 75.00 o.p. (ISBN 0-8240-3290-X). Garland Pub.
Japanese Military Studies, 1937-1949: The Sino-Japanese & the Chinese Civil Wars, Pt. 1. Ed. by Donald S. Detwiler & Charles B. Burdick. (War in Asia & the Pacific Ser., 1937 to 1949: Vol. 13). 460p. 1980. lib. bdg. 60.50 o.p. (ISBN 0-8240-3297-7). Garland Pub.
Japanese Military Studies, 1937-1949: The Sino-Japanese & the Chinese Civil Wars, Pt. 2. Ed. by Donald S. Detwiler & Charles B. Burdick. (War in Asia & the Pacific Ser., 1937 to 1949: Vol. 14). 610p. 1980. lib. bdg. 60.50 o.p. (ISBN 0-8240-3298-5). Garland Pub.
Japanese Military Studies, 1939-1949: The Sino-Japanese & the Chinese Civil Wars, Pt. 3. Ed. by Donald S. Detwiler & Charles B. Burdick. (War in Asia & the Pacific Ser., 1937 to 1949: Vol. 15). 570p. 1980. lib. bdg. 60.50 o.p. (ISBN 0-8240-3299-3). Garland Pub.
Japanese Mind: The Goliath Explained. Robert Christopher. 352p. 1983. 16.50 o.p. (ISBN 0-671-44947-8, Linden Pr). S&S.
Japanese Money Market. Robert E. Emery. LC 83-48452. 160p. 1984. 29.00x o.p. (ISBN 0-669-07208-7). Lexington Bks.
Japanese Motifs for Needlepoint. Sally Nicoletti. LC 80-22650. (Illus.). 136p. 1981. 15.95 o.p. (ISBN 0-688-00163-7). Morrow.
Japanese Participation in British Industry: Trojan Horse or Catalyst for Growth. John H. Dunning. LC 85-28374. 256p. 1986. 43.00 o.p. (ISBN 0-7099-4500-0, Pub. by Croom Helm Ltd). Routledge Chapman & Hall.
Japanese People & Foreign Policy: A Study of Public Opinion in Post-Treaty Japan. Douglas H. Mendel. LC 74-141277. (Illus.). 1971. Repr. of 1961 ed. lib. bdg. 35.00x o.p. (ISBN 0-8371-5882-6, MEJP). Greenwood.
Japanese: People of the Three Treasures. Robert Newman. (Illus.). (YA) (gr. 7 up). 1964. 4.25 o.p. (ISBN 0-689-20301-2, Atheneum). Macmillan.

Japanese Periodicals & Newspapers in Western Languages. Compiled by G. Raymond Nunn. 264p. 1979. 64.00x o.p. (ISBN 0-7201-0934-5). Mansell.

Japanese Pharmaceutical Related: 1984 to 1986. 2nd ed. 1984. 238.00 o.p. (ISBN 0-8002-3895-8). Intl Pubns Serv.

Japanese Polearms. Ronald Knutsen. 45.00x o.p. (ISBN 0-87556-138-1). Saifer.

Japanese Politics - An Inside View: Readings from Japan. Ed. & tr. by Hiroshi Itoh. LC 72-12407. (Illus.). 248p. 1973. Paperback Ser. 27.50x o.p. (ISBN 0-8014-0735-4); pap. 9.95x o.p. (ISBN 0-8014-9138-X). Cornell U Pr.

Japanese Pottery. Soame Jenyns. 508p. 1971. 49.95 o.p. (ISBN 0-571-08709-4). Faber & Faber.

Japanese Print: Its Evolution & Essence. Muneshige Narazaki. LC 66-12551. (Illus.). 1966. 100.00 o.p. (ISBN 0-87011-031-4). Kodansha.

Japanese Rule in Formosa. Yosaburo Takekoshi. Tr. by George Braithwaite. 1978. Repr. of 1907 ed. 30.00x o.p. (ISBN 0-89986-340-X). Oriental Bk Store.

Japanese Scroll Painting. Kenji Toda. LC 35-4632. (Illus.). 1970. Repr. of 1935 ed. lib. bdg. 24.25x o.p. (ISBN 0-8371-1883-2, TOSP). Greenwood.

Japanese Short Stories. Ryunosuke Akutagawa. Tr. by Takashi Kojima. LC 61-18087. 1970. 5.95 o.p. (ISBN 0-87140-993-3); pap. 3.95 o.p. (ISBN 0-87140-215-7). Liveright.

Japanese Soviet Relations: Interaction of Politics, Economics & National Security. Young C. Kim. (Washington Papers: Vol. II, No. 21). 96p. (Orig.). pap. text ed. 7.95 o.p. (ISBN 0-8191-5977-8, Pub. by CSIS). U Pr of Amer.

Japanese Steel Industry: With an Analysis of the U. S. Steel Import Problem. Kiyoshi Kawahito. LC 70-170470. (Special Studies in International Economics & Development). 1972. 39.50x o.p. (ISBN 0-275-28273-2). Irvington.

Japanese Thought in the Tokugawa Period (1600-1868) Methods & Metaphors. Ed. by Tetsuo Najita & Irwin Scheiner. LC 78-1463. 1978. lib. bdg. 18.50x o.s.i. (ISBN 0-226-56801-6). U of Chicago Pr.

Japanese Tin Toys. (Wonderland of Toys Bks.: Vol. 1). (Illus.). 1984. 16.20 o.p. (ISBN 0-318-02769-0). Bks Nippan.

Japanese Tradition & Western Law: Emperor, State, & Law in the Thought of Hozumi Yatsuka. Richard H. Minear. LC 72-115478. (East Asian Ser: No. 48). 1970. 18.50x o.s.i. (ISBN 0-674-47252-7). Harvard U Pr.

Japanese Youth Confronts Religion: A Sociological Survey. Fernando M. Basabe. LC 67-28418. 1967. 6.00 o.p. (ISBN 0-8048-0324-2). C E Tuttle.

Japan's Best Loved Poetry Classic: Hyakunin Isshu, Vol. 1. 3rd rev. ed. Tr. by Howard S. Levy. (Illus.). 1976. 15.00X o.p. (ISBN 0-89986-257-8); pap. 8.00 o.s.i. Oriental Bk Store.

Japan's Economic Expansion & Foreign Trade, 1955 to 1970. (Studies in International Trade: No. 2). (Orig.). 1971. pap. 7.00 o.p. (ISBN 0-685-02938-7, G93, GATT). UNIPUB.

Japan's Economic Role in East Asia: Implications for U. S. Business. 50p. 1984. 4.00 o.s.i. (ISBN 0-317-06763-X). Japan Soc.

Japan's Political System. 2nd ed. Robert E. Ward. (Illus.). 1978. pap. text ed. 26.00 o.p. (ISBN 0-13-509588-3). P-H.

Japan's Religions, Shinto & Buddhism. Lafcadio Heim. 1966. 10.00 o.p. (ISBN 0-8216-0102-4, Pub. by Univ Bks). Carol Pub Group.

Japan's Reshaping of American Labor Law. William B. Gould. (Illus.). 272p. 1984. text ed. 24.95x o.p. (ISBN 0-262-07091-X). MIT Pr.

Jardin De Kanashima. Pierre Boulle. 320p. 1964. 7.95 o.p. (ISBN 0-686-54103-0); pap. 9.95 o.p. (ISBN 0-686-54104-9). French & Eur.

Jardin De Plaisance et Fleur De Rhetorique, 2 Vols. 1910-25. 67.00 o.p. (ISBN 0-384-26884-6); pap. 55.00 o.p. (ISBN 0-384-26885-4). Johnson Repr.

Jargon of Authenticity. Theodor W. Adorno. Tr. by Knut Tarnowski & Frederick Will. 188p. 1986. pap. 10.95 o.p. (ISBN 0-7102-0870-7, 08707). Routledge Chapman & Hall.

Jargon Signals - Whistle Talk - Signs of the American Railroad: American Railroadiana. Ed. & illus. by Hugo J. Forde. (Illus.). 86p. (Orig.). Date not set. pap. 7.50 o.p. J Chesterfield Bks.

Jasmin. Jan Truss. LC 81-8114. 204p. (gr. 3-7). 1982. PLB 10.95 o.p. (ISBN 0-689-50228-1, Atheneum). Macmillan.

Jasmine Finds Love. Jane Claypool. LC 82-13633. (Hiway-Floweromance Bk.: A High Interest-Low Reading Level Book). 80p. (gr. 7-10). 1982. 8.95 o.s.i. (ISBN 0-664-32699-4, Westminster). Westminster John Knox.

Jasmin's Witch: A Case of Possession in Seventeenth-Century France. Emmanuel L. Ladurie. Tr. by Brian Pearce. (Illus.). (ISBN 0-394-53741-6). Pantheon.

Jason & the Money Tree. Sonia Levitin. LC 73-17939. (gr. 3-7). 1974. 9.95 o.p. (ISBN 0-15-239820-1, HJ). HarBraceJ.

Jason in Outer Space. Kuninori. (Jason & Loriel Ser.). (Illus.). 40p. (Orig.). (gr. 2-4). 1989. PLB cancelled o.s.i. (ISBN 0-943173-15-9); pap. cancelled o.s.i. (ISBN 0-943173-25-6). Harbinger AZ.

Jason Voyage: The Quest of the Golden Fleece. Tim Severin. 288p. 1986. 18.45 o.p. (ISBN 0-671-49813-4). S&S.

Jason's First Quest. Roger E. Moore. LC 84-51003. (Fantasy Forest Bks.). (Illus.). 80p. (Orig.). (ps-5). 1984. pap. text ed. 1.95 o.p. (ISBN 0-88038-170-1). TSR Inc.

Jasper & the Hero Business. Betty Horvath. (Illus.). 32p. (gr. k-3). 1978. pap. 1.25 o.p. (ISBN 0-380-40246-7, 51995-X, Camelot). Avon.

Jasper F. Cropsey, Eighteen Twenty-Three to Nineteen Hundred. William S. Talbot. LC 76-23652. (Outstanding Dissertations in the Fine Arts - American). (Illus.). 1977. Repr. of 1972 ed. lib. bdg. 101.00 o.p. (ISBN 0-8240-2731-0). Garland Pub.

Jataka Tales. Nancy Deroin. LC 74-20981. 96p. (gr. 2-5). 1975. 5.95 o.p. (ISBN 0-395-20281-7). HM.

Jataka Tales from the Ajanta Murals. Anjali Pal. (Illus.). 103p. (gr. 4-6). 1968. 2.00 o.s.i. (ISBN 0-88253-330-4). Ind-US Inc.

Jaundice During Pregnancy: With Special Emphasis on Recurrent Jaundice During Pregnancy & Its Differential Diagnosis. U. P. Haemmerli. 1967. pap. 12.10 o.p. (ISBN 0-387-90001-2). Springer-Verlag.

Javits: The Autobiography of a Public Man. Jacob K. Javits & Rafael Steinberg. (Illus.). 1981. 16.95 o.p. (ISBN 0-395-29912-8). HM.

Jawaharlal Nehru. A. Gorev. 1982. 8.95 o.p. (ISBN 0-8285-2455-6, Pub. by Progress Pubs USSR). Imported Pubns.

Jawaharlal Nehru of India Eighteen Eighty-Nine to Nineteen Sixty-Four. Ian Copland. (Leaders of Asia Ser.). 53p. (Orig.). 1980. pap. 4.95x o.p. (ISBN 0-7022-1506-6). U of Queensland Pr.

Jay J. Armes: Investigator. Ed. by Frederick Nolan. 1977. pap. 1.95 o.p. (ISBN 0-380-01756-3, 34694-X). Avon.

JAZZ! David Bolocan. 1985. 24.95 o.p. (ISBN 0-8306-0978-4, 1978); pap. 17.60 o.p. (ISBN 0-8306-1978-X). TAB Bks.

Jazz. Paul O. Tanner et al. 240p. 1987. write for info. incl. cassette o.p. (ISBN 0-697-03663-4). Wm C Brown.

Jazz: A Photo History. Joachim-Ernst Berendt. LC 79-7629. (Illus.). 1979. 35.00 o.s.i. (ISBN 0-02-870290-5). Schirmer Bks.

Jazz: America's Classical Music. Grover Sales. (Illus.). 240p. 1984. 18.95 o.p. (ISBN 0-13-509126-8); pap. 9.95 o.p. (ISBN 0-13-509118-7). P-H.

Jazz & Blues. Graham Vulliamy. (Routledge Popular Music Ser.). 158p. 1982. 14.95x o.p. (ISBN 0-7100-0894-5). Routledge Chapman & Hall.

Jazz at Work. Sharyn Venit & Diane Burns. LC 85-20294. 256p. 1985. pap. 19.95 o.p. (ISBN 0-471-83188-3). Wiley.

Jazz Book: A Complete Tutorial. Edward M. Baras. (Illus.). 300p. (Orig.). 1986. pap. text ed. 18.95 o.p. (ISBN 0-07-881197-X). Osborne-McGraw.

Jazz Book: From New Orleans to Rock & Free Jazz. rev. ed. Joachim Berendt. Ed. & tr. by Dan Morgenstern. LC 73-81750. 480p. 1975. 12.95 o.p. (ISBN 0-88208-027-X); pap. 8.95 o.p. (ISBN 0-88208-028-8). Chicago Review.

Jazz Dance: An Adult Beginner's Guide. Helene C. Andreu. 184p. 1983. o. p. 15.95 o.p. (ISBN 0-13-509968-4); pap. 7.95 o.p. (ISBN 0-13-509950-1). P-H.

Jazz-Five Easy Pieces. Jean Stein. 200p. (Orig.). 1985. pap. text ed. 17.95 o.p. (ISBN 0-07-881111-2). Osborne-McGraw.

Jazz Improvisation: A Comprehensive Method of Study for All Players. rev. ed. David Baker. 135p. 1983. pap. 21.95 o.p. (ISBN 0-89917-397-7). Tichenor Pub.

Jazz Improvisation & Harmony. Alan Phillips, pseud. (Illus.). 96p. 1973. pap. 6.95 o.p. (ISBN 0-317-01522-2). CPP Belwin.

Jazz Is. Nat Hentoff. 1978. pap. 2.25 o.p. (ISBN 0-380-01858-6, 36558, Discus). Avon.

Jazz: Its Evolution & Essence. rev. ed. Andre Hodeir. Tr. by David Noakes from Fr. LC 79-52101. (Illus.). 1980. pap. 3.95 o.s.i. (ISBN 0-394-17525-5, B436, BC). Grove.

Jazz Man. Mary H. Weik. LC 66-10417. (Illus.). (gr. 2 up). 1966. PLB 6.95 o.p. (ISBN 0-689-30021-2, Atheneum). Macmillan.

Jazz Quiz Book. David Baker & Jeanne Baker. Ed. by Lida Baker. 72p. (Orig.). 1984. pap. 2.95 o.p. (ISBN 0-89917-413-2, Frangipani Pr). TIS Inc.

Jazz Retrospect. Max Harrison. 1977. 11.00 o.s.i. (ISBN 0-8008-4310-X, Crescendo). Taplinger.

Jazz Singer. 7.95 o.s.i. (ISBN 0-89524-130-7). Cherry Lane.

Jazz Text. Charles Nanry. 276p. 1982. pap. text ed. 9.95x o.p. (ISBN 0-442-25908-5). Transaction Pubs.

Jazz Tips & Traps. Dick Andersen. 250p. (Orig.). 1986. pap. text ed. 18.95 o.p. (ISBN 0-07-881189-9). Osborne-McGraw.

Jazzercise Workout Book: Your Customized Fitness Program-for Life. Judi S. Missett. (Illus.). 224p. (Orig.). 1986. pap. 12.95 o.p. (ISBN 0-684-18660-8). Scribner.

Jazzmen. Ed. by Frederic Ramsey, Jr. & Charles E. Smith. LC 77-4215. (Illus.). 1977. pap. 4.95 o.p. (ISBN 0-15-646205-2, Harv). HarBraceJ.

JCAH Guide to Life Safety. 184p. 1984. 35.00 o.s.i. (ISBN 0-86688-068-2, DEP-150). Joint Comm Hlthcare.

JCL & Advanced FORTRAN Programming. H. Ramden. (Methods in Geomathematics Ser.: Vol. 2). 170p. 1976. pap. 73.75 o.p. (ISBN 0-444-41415-0). Elsevier.

JCL in a System-370 Environment. Barry L. Bateman & Gerald N. Pitts. 192p. 1983. pap. 23.95 o.p. (ISBN 0-8436-1606-7). Van Nos Reinhold.

Je Lis Tu Lis, 3 bks. Marie-Anne Hameau. (gr. 4-6). Bk. 1. text ed. 14.95 o.p. (ISBN 0-685-35643-4); Bk. 2. text ed. 14.95 o.p. (ISBN 0-685-35644-2); text ed. 6.50 o.p. (ISBN 0-685-35645-0). Bk. 3. French & Eur.

Je ne T'ai Jamais Promis un Verger de Pommiers. Charles M. Schulz. (Fr.). pap. 5.95 o.s.i. (ISBN 0-03-061644-1). H Holt & Co.

Jealous Child. E. Podolsky. 1954. (ISBN 0-8022-1992-6). Philos Lib.

Jealousy. Eva Eriksson. LC 84-27461. (Victor & Rosalie Bks.). (Illus.). 32p. (ps-3). 1985. PLB 8.95 o.p. (ISBN 0-87614-237-4). Carolrhoda Bks.

Jealousy. Alain Robbe-Grillet. Tr. by Richard Howard from Fr. LC 77-92783. 1978. 4.50 o.s.i. (ISBN 0-394-17031-8, B407, BC). Grove.

Jean Anderson's Processor Cooking. Jean Anderson. LC 78-27880. (Illus.). 1979. 14.95 o.p. (ISBN 0-688-03389-X). Morrow.

Jean Anouilh: Five Plays, Vol. 2. Jean Anouilh. Incl. Ardele; Time Remembered; Mademoiselle Colombe; Restless Heart; Lark. (Mermaid Dramabook Ser.). 302p. (Orig.). 1959. pap. 6.95 o.p. (ISBN 0-8090-0713-4). Hill & Wang.

Jean Arp at the Metropolitan Museum of Art. Intro. by Henry Geldzahler. LC 72-77067. (Illus.). 1972. pap. 1.50 o.p. (ISBN 0-87099-117-5). Metro Mus Art.

Jean-Baptiste Lully, the Founder of French Opera. R. H. Scott. 1977. 6.95 o.s.i. (ISBN 0-8008-4320-7, Crescendo). Taplinger.

Jean-Baptiste Oudry Sixteen Eighty-Six to Seventeen Fifty-Five, 2 vols. Hal N. Opperman. LC 76-23674. (Outstanding Dissertations in the Fine Arts Ser.). 1200p. 1977. lib. bdg. 146.00 o.p. (ISBN 0-8240-2718-3). Garland Pub.

Jean Barois. Roger Martin du Gard. 512p. 1972. 3.95 o.p. (ISBN 0-686-55503-1). Schoenhof.

Jean Cocteau En Verve. Jean Cocteau. 128p. 8.95 o.p. (ISBN 0-686-54532-X). French & Eur.

Jean Dubuffet, Partitions 1980-1981; Psycho-Sites 1981. Carter Ratcliff. LC 82-19018. (Illus.). 44p. (Orig.). 1982. pap. text ed. 16.50 o.p. (ISBN 0-938608-10-X). Pace Pubns.

Jean Genet. Jeannette L. Savona. LC 83-49390. (Modern Dramatists Ser.). 224p. 1984. 19.50 o.s.i. (ISBN 0-394-53858-7, GP 902). Grove.

Jean Genet. Jeannette L. Savona. LC 83-49390. (Modern Dramatists Ser.). 224p. 1984. pap. 9.95 o.s.i. (ISBN 0-394-62045-3, E921, Ever). Grove.

Jean-Louis Ou Lafille Trouvee, 2 vols. facsimile ed. Honore De Balzac. 1961. 50.00 ea. o.p. French & Eur.

Jean-Luc Godard. John F. Kreidl. (Filmmakers Ser.). 1980. lib. bdg. 13.50 o.p. (ISBN 0-8057-9270-8, Twayne). G K Hall.

Jean-Luc Godard: A Guide to References & Resources. Julia Lesage. 1979. lib. bdg. 52.00 o.s.i. (ISBN 0-8161-7925-5, Hall Reference). G K Hall.

Jean-Paul Sartre. Catherine S. Brosman. (World Authors Ser.). 168p. 1984. pap. 5.95 o.p. (ISBN 0-8057-6590-5, Twayne). G K Hall.

Jean Pauls Hesperus. Hans Bach. 27.00 o.p. (ISBN 0-384-02935-3); pap. 22.00 o.p. (ISBN 0-685-02214-5). Johnson Repr.

Jean Piaget: An Interdisciplinary Critique. Ed. by Sohan Modgil & Celia Modgil. (International Library of Psychology). 200p. 1983. 23.95x o.p. (ISBN 0-7100-9451-5). Routledge Chapman & Hall.

Jean Renoir. Andre Bazin. 1986. pap. 9.95 o.p. (ISBN 0-671-62247-1, Touchstone Bks). S&S.

Jean Renoir: Essays, Conversations, Reviews. Penelope Gilliatt. LC 75-6905. (McGraw-Hill Paperbacks). (Illus.). 136p. 1975. (ISBN 0-07-023225-3); pap. text ed. 2.95 o.p. (ISBN 0-07-023224-5). McGraw.

Jean Rhys: The Complete Novels. Jean Rhys. 1985. 24.50 o.p. (ISBN 0-393-02226-9). Norton.

Jean Rhys: Woman in Passage. Helen Nebeker. 250p. (Orig.). 1981. pap. 8.95 o.p. (ISBN 0-920792-04-9). Eden Pr.

Jean Santeuil et Les Plaisirs et les Jours see Oeuvres.

Jean Toomer. Brian J. Benson & Mabel M. Dillard. (United States Authors Ser.). 1980. lib. bdg. 13.50 o.p. (ISBN 0-8057-7322-3, Twayne). G K Hall.

Jeanne & the Men in Her Life. Lorraine Anderson. 48p. 1986. 6.50 o.p. (ISBN 0-8062-2689-7). Carlton.

Jeanne Jones Party Planner & Entertaining Diary. Jeanne Jones. (Illus.). 1979. 5.95 o.s.i. (ISBN 0-89286-156-8, One Hund One Prods). Ortho.

Jeannette's Secret. Seaver. (ISBN 0-8050-0965-5). Seaver Bks.

Jean's Christmas Stocking: Storybook for Young Deaf Children. Carolyn Norris et al. (Illus.). 24p. 1982. pap. 3.25 o.p. (ISBN 0-686-43092-1). Modern Signs.

Jeans French Dictionary. (Langenscheidt Jeans Dictionary Ser.). 224p. 1984. pap. 1.95 o.p. (ISBN 0-88729-252-6). Langenscheidt.

Jeans German Dictionary. (Langenscheidt Jeans Dictionary Ser.). 224p. 1984. pap. 1.95 o.p. Langenscheidt.

Jeans Italian Dictionary. (Langenscheidt Jeans Dictionary Ser.). 224p. 1984. pap. 1.95 o.p. Langenscheidt.

Jeans Spanish Dictionary. (Langenscheidt Jeans Dictionary Ser.). 224p. 1984. pap. 1.95 o.p. (ISBN 0-88729-251-8). Langenscheidt.

Jean's Way: A Love Story. Derek Humphry & Ann Wickett. pap. 6.50 o.p. (ISBN 0-394-62017-8, Ever). Grove.

Jeans Webster Dictionary. (Langenscheidt Jeans Dictionary Ser.). 224p. 1984. pap. 1.95 o.p. (ISBN 0-88729-604-1). Langenscheidt.

Jedi Master's Quizbook. Rusty Miller. (Orig.). 1982. pap. 1.95 o.s.i. (ISBN 0-345-30697-X, Del Rey). Ballantine.

Jeeno, Heloise & Igamor, The Long, Long Horse. Michael De Larrabeiti. (Illus.). 24p. (gr. 1-3). 1984. 10.95 o.p. (ISBN 0-7207-1257-2). Salem Hse Pubs.

Jeep All Models: 1969-1978, 4-Wheel Drive Maintenance. Ed. by Eric Jorgenson. (Illus.). pap. 8.95 o.p. (ISBN 0-89287-291-8, A234). Clymer Pub.

Jeep Service, Repair Handbook: Covers Willy-Overland Model MB & Ford Model GPW. Clymer Publications Staff. (Illus.). pap. 7.95 o.p. (ISBN 0-89287-250-0, A162). Clymer Pub.

Jeep Wagoneer, Cherokee, Commando, Truck 1962-1984. 348p. 1986. 13.50 o.p. (ISBN 0-8019-7516-6). Chilton.

Jeeves, Jeeves, Jeeves. P. G. Wodehouse. 1976. pap. 4.95 o.p. (ISBN 0-380-00627-8, 43794). Avon.

Jeff & Jenny & the Kidnapping. Nellie Frisinger. LC 78-55337. (Jeff & Jenny Adventure Ser.). (Illus.). (gr. 2-6). 1978. pap. 2.95 o.p. (ISBN 0-89636-136-5). Accent Bks.

Jeff & Jenny at Camp Pinecrest. Nellie Frisinger. LC 83-73204. (Jeff & Jenny Adventure Ser.). 128p. (Orig.). (gr. 4-6). 1984. pap. 2.95 o.p. (ISBN 0-89636-121-7). Accent Bks.

Jeff & Jenny on the Chinchilla Ranch. Nellie Frisinger. LC 77-75132. (Jeff & Jenny Adventure Ser.). (Illus.). (gr. 2-6). 1977. pap. 2.95 o.p. (ISBN 0-916406-73-3). Accent Bks.

Jeff & Jenny Winter in Alaska. Nellie Frisinger. LC 77-81775. (Jeff & Jenny Adventure Ser.). (Illus.). (gr. 2-6). 1977. pap. 2.95 o.p. (ISBN 0-916406-82-2). Accent Bks.

Jeff & the Bad Guy. Aleda Renken. LC 73-75863. (gr. 3-7). 1973. pap. 1.00 o.p. (ISBN 0-570-03602-X, 39-1025). Concordia.

Jeff Wall: Transparencies. Els Barents. LC 86-29820. (Illus.). 120p. 1987. pap. 25.00 o.p. (ISBN 0-8478-0792-4). Rizzoli Intl.

Jefferson and-or Mussolini. Ezra Pound. LC 36-3936. 1970. pap. 2.95 o.p. (ISBN 0-87140-213-0). Liveright.

Jefferson Davis: His Rise & Fall. A. Tate. 1929. 30.00 o.p. (ISBN 0-527-89000-6). Kraus Repr.

Jefferson Scandals: A Rebuttal. Virginius Dabney. LC 81-1669. (Illus.). 156p. 1981. 12.95 o.p. (ISBN 0-396-07964-4). Dodd.

Jeffersonian America: Notes on the United States of America Collected in the Years 1805-1807 & 1811-1812. Augustus J. Foster. Ed. by Richard B. Davis. LC 78-17928. 1980. Repr. of 1954 ed. lib. bdg. 35.00x o.p. (ISBN 0-313-22076-X, FOJA). Greenwood.

Jeffersons. Gelfand. (TV & Movie Tie-ins Ser.). (Illus.). 32p. (gr. 4 up). 1985. PLB 8.95 o.p. Creative Ed.

Jefferson's English Crisis, 1803-1809: Commerce, Embargo, & the Republican Revolution. Burton Spivak. LC 78-13110. 250p. 1979. 20.00x o.p. (ISBN 0-8139-0805-1). U Pr of Va.

Jefferson's Nephews: A Frontier Tragedy. Boynton Merrill, Jr. LC 76-3267. 1976. 35.00 o.p. (ISBN 0-691-04640-9). Princeton U Pr.

Jeffrey's Latest Thirteen: More Alabama Ghosts. Kathryn T. Windham. LC 82-50029. (Supernatural Ser.). 1982. 8.95 o.p. (ISBN 0-87397-232-5). Strode.

Jehovah's Jailbreak. Paul Tully. (Lythway Ser.). 168p. 1988. lib. bdg. 17.50 o.p. (ISBN 0-7451-0673-0, Pub. by Chivers Pr UK). G K Hall.

Jehovah's Witness: Not Just Another Denomination. Gordon E. Duggar. (Illus.). 144p. 1982. 8.00 o.p. (ISBN 0-682-49874-2). Exposition-Phoenix.

Jehovah's Witnesses. Royston Pike. 144p. 1954. (ISBN 0-8022-1976-4). Philos Lib.

Jehovah's Witnesses & Prophetic Speculation. Edmond C. Gruss. pap. 5.95 o.p. (ISBN 0-8010-3710-7). Baker Bk.

Jelly. Jack Ansell. LC 75-167745. 1971. 5.95 o.p. (ISBN 0-87795-018-0, Arbor Hse). Morrow.

Jelly Moulds. Sally Kevill-Davies. Ed. by Noel Riley. (Antique Pocket Guides). (Illus.). 64p. (Orig.). 1983. pap. 5.95 o.p. (ISBN 0-7188-2584-5, Pub. by Lutterworth Pr UK). Seven Hills Bk Dists.

Jemimalee. Mary E. Robertson. (Illus.). 1977. lib. bdg. 7.95 o.p. (ISBN 0-07-053163-3); text ed. 6.95 o.p. (ISBN 0-07-053162-5). McGraw.

Jemimalee. Mary E. Robinson. (Illus.). 124p. (gr. 5 up). 1979. pap. 1.50 o.p. (ISBN 0-380-45849-7, 45849-7, Camelot). Avon.

Jemmy. Jon Hassler. LC 79-23091. 180p. (gr. 7 up). 1980. 8.95 o.s.i. (ISBN 0-689-50130-7, Atheneum). Macmillan.

Jenkins. Jean Cassou. (Modern Artists Ser.). (Illus.). 288p. 65.00 o.p. (ISBN 0-8109-0215-X). Abrams.

Jennie & the Black Stockings. Jane B. Moncure. LC 84-7036. (Illus.). 32p. (gr. 1-2). lib. bdg. 6.95 o.p. (ISBN 0-89693-225-7). Dandelion Hse.

Jennifer Grey Mysteries, 6 bks. 2nd ed. Jerry B. Jenkins. 1986. Set. text ed. 11.95 o.p. (ISBN 0-8024-4345-1). Moody.

Jenny Lind Chapel: Pioneer Church at Andover. Erwin Weber. LC 75-316870. (Augustana College Library Occasional Paper: No. 12). 31p. 1975. pap. 1.00x o.p. (ISBN 0-910182-35-3). Augustana Coll.

Jenny Lives with Eric & Martin. Susanne Bosche. (Illus.). 52p. (Orig.). (gr. k-6). 1983. pap. 5.50 o.p. (ISBN 0-907040-22-5, Pub. by GMP England). Alyson Pubns.

Jenny 'n Dad. Gordon Baxter. 1985. 12.70 o.s.i. (ISBN 0-671-46954-1). Summit Bks.

Jenny Saw. Betty J. Speer. 176p. 1987. 8.95 o.p. (ISBN 0-8062-2659-5). Carlton.

Jenny's War. Jack Stonely. 344p. 1985. pap. 3.75 o.p. (ISBN 0-317-66394-1). Critics Choice Paper.

Jeremiah: The Iron Prophet. George T. Dickinson. (Horizon Ser.). 1978. pap. 5.95 o.p. (ISBN 0-8127-0183-6). Review & Herald.

Jeremy Taylor, Seventeen Hundred to Nineteen Seventy-Six: An Annotated Checklist. William P. Williams. LC 78-68302. (Garland Reference Library of the Humanities: No. 177). 96p. 1979. lib. bdg. 14.00 o.p. (ISBN 0-8240-9756-4). Garland Pub.

Jericho. John A. Bartlett. Ed. by Graham I. Davies. (Cities of the Biblical World Ser.). 128p. (Orig.). 1983. pap. 7.95 o.p. (ISBN 0-8028-1033-0). Eerdmans.

Jericho Mosaic. 4th ed. Edward Whittemore. 1987. 16.45 o.p. (ISBN 0-393-02395-8). Norton.

Jerry Brown: Man on the White Horse. J. D. Lorenz. 1978. 8.95 o.p. (ISBN 0-395-25767-0). HM.

Jerry Lewis: In Person. Jerry Lewis & Herb Gluck. LC 81-70109. 320p. 1982. 14.95 o.p. (ISBN 0-689-11290-4, Atheneum). Macmillan.

Jerry Wurf: Labor's Last Angry Man. Joseph Goulden. LC 81-70110. (Illus.). 320p. 1982. 14.95 o.p. (ISBN 0-689-11291-2, Atheneum). Macmillan.

Jersey Blue: An Irreverent Sage of the Making of the New World. Rebecca Singleton. (Orig.). 1982. 16.95 o.s.i. (ISBN 0-671-44584-7, Poseidon); pap. 5.75 o.s.i. (ISBN 0-671-44583-9). PB.

Jersey City: A City in Socio-Economic & Political Change. Matthew F. Amato, Jr. (Illus.). 1979. 5.00 o.p. (ISBN 0-682-49511-5). Exposition-Phoenix.

Jersey Devil Design-Build Book. Michael J. Crosbie. LC 84-26367. 1985. 19.95 o.p. (ISBN 0-87905-188-4). Gibbs Smith Pub.

Jerusalem. G. Frederick Owen. (Illus.). 176p. 1972. 7.95 o.p. (ISBN 0-8341-0215-3). Beacon Hill.

Jerusalem. Trude Weiss-Rosmarin. (ISBN 0-8022-1845-8). Philos Lib.

Jerusalem & Rome: The Problem of Authority in the Early Church: Hans Von Campenhausen & Henry Chadwick. Tr. by G. W. Luetkeholter from Ger. LC 66-24859. (Facet Bks). 34p. 1966. pap. 0.50 o.p. (ISBN 0-8006-3031-9, 1-3031, Fortress). Augsburg Fortress.

Jerusalem, Jerusalem. Lesley Hazleton. Ed. by Joyce Johnson. LC 86-1223. 244p. 1986. 16.95 o.p. (ISBN 0-87113-064-5). Atlantic Monthly.

Jerusalem Poker. Edward Whittemore. 1979. pap. 2.50 o.p. (ISBN 0-380-44305-8, 44305-8). Avon.

Jerusalem Question: 1917-1968. H. Eugene Bovis. LC 73-149796. (Studies Ser.: No. 29). (Illus.). 175p. 1971. 9.95x o.p. (ISBN 0-8179-3291-7). Hoover Inst Pr.

Jerzy Kosinski. Norman Lavers. (United States Authors Ser.). 1982. lib. bdg. 14.50 o.s.i. (ISBN 0-8057-7352-5, Twayne). G K Hall.

Jess: Pasteups Nineteen Fifty-One to Nineteen Eighty-Three. Michael Auping. LC 83-82281. (Illus.). 155p. 1983. 10.00 o.p. (ISBN 0-916758-14-1). Ringling Mus Art.

Jesse Jackson. rev. ed. Eddie Stone. (Orig.). 1984. pap. 2.75 o.p. (ISBN 0-87067-714-4, BH714). Holloway.

Jesse Jackson: I Am Somebody. Paul Westman. LC 80-20521. (Taking Part Ser.). (Illus.). 48p. (gr. 3 up). 1980. PLB 9.95 o.p. (ISBN 0-87518-203-8). Dillon.

Jesse Stuart: A Reference Guide. J. R. LeMaster. 1979. lib. bdg. 30.50 o.p. (ISBN 0-8161-8041-5, Hall Reference). G K Hall.

Jesse: The Biography of an American Writer-Jesse Hilton Stuart. H. Edward Richardson. (Illus.). 592p. 1984. text ed. 21.95 o.p. (ISBN 0-07-062307-4). McGraw.

Jessie White Mario: Risorgimento Revolutionary. Elizabeth A. Daniels. LC 78-158178. (Illus.). vii, 199p. 1972. 14.00 o.p. (ISBN 0-8214-0103-3). Ohio U Pr.

Jesuits & Jacobins: Enlightenment & Enlightened Despotism in Austria. Paul P. Bernard. LC 78-151997. 207p. 1971. 19.95 o.p. (ISBN 0-252-00180-X). U of Ill Pr.

Jesus. Lucas Grollenberg. Tr. by John Bowden. LC 78-13478. 138p. 1979. pap. 4.50 o.s.i. (ISBN 0-664-24232-4, Westminster). Westminster John Knox.

Jesus: A Biography. Ed B. Lorenz. (Illus.). (gr. 3-7). 1977. 4.95 o.p. (ISBN 0-89328-011-9). Lorenz Corp.

Jesus & a Little Girl see What the Bible Tells Us: Third Series.

Jesus & His Adversaries: The Form & Function of the Conflict Stories in the Synoptic Tradition. Arland J. Hultgren. LC 79-50093. 224p. 1979. pap. 9.50 o.p. (ISBN 0-8066-1717-9, 10-3480, Augsburg). Augsburg Fortress.

Jesus & His Friends. Ruth Odor. (Flip-a-Bible-Story Bks.). (Illus.). 16p. (Orig.). (ps-4). 1982. pap. 3.95 o.p. (ISBN 0-87239-560-X, 2734). Standard Pub.

Jesus & the Children: Biblical Resources for Study & Preaching. Hans-Ruedi Weber. LC 79-87754. 1980. pap. 5.95 o.p. (ISBN 0-8042-1316-X, John Knox). Westminster John Knox.

Jesus & the Constraints of History. A. E. Harvey. LC 11-16095. 192p. 1982. 23.00 o.s.i. (ISBN 0-664-21825-3, Westminster). Westminster John Knox.

Jesus & the Future: Unsolved Questions on Eschatology. Richard H. Hiers. LC 80-82189. 1981. 16.50 o.p. (ISBN 0-8042-0341-5, John Knox); pap. 4.99 o.p. (ISBN 0-8042-0340-7). Westminster John Knox.

Jesus & the Gospel. William R. Farmer. LC 81-43078. 320p. 1982. 3.95 o.p. (ISBN 0-8006-0666-3, 1-666, Fortress). Augsburg Fortress.

Jesus & the Gospels. D. R. De Lacey. (Discovering the Bible Ser.). (gr. 8-10). pap. 9.95 o.p. (ISBN 0-7175-1162-6). Dufour.

Jesus & the Hidden Bible. Joseph Krimsky. 1951. (ISBN 0-8022-0896-7). Philos Lib.

Jesus & the Language of the Kingdom: Symbol & Metaphor in New Testament Interpretation. Norman Perrin. LC 80-20822. 240p. 1980. pap. 11.95 o.p. (ISBN 0-8006-1432-1, 1-1432, Fortress). Augsburg Fortress.

Jesus & the Synoptic Gospels: A Bibliographic Study Guide. David E. Aune. Ed. by Mark L. Branson. (TSF - IBR Bibliographic Study Guides Ser.). 99p. (Orig.). 1981. pap. 6.95 o.p. (ISBN 0-8308-5498-3). Inter-Varsity.

Jesus & the Wilderness Community at Qumran. Ethelbert Stauffer. Tr. by Hans Spaltenholz. LC 64-11861. (Facet Bks). 1964. pap. 1.00 o.p. (ISBN 0-8006-3010-6, Fortress). Augsburg Fortress.

Jesus & the World of Judaism. Geza Vermes. LC 83-16535. 224p. 1984. pap. 1.95 o.p. (ISBN 0-8006-1784-3, 1-1784, Fortress). Augsburg Fortress.

Jesus As Precursor. Robert W. Funk. Ed. by William A. Beardslee. LC 75-18949. (Semeia Studies). 184p. 1975. pap. 3.95 o.p. (ISBN 0-8006-1502-6, 1-1502, Fortress). Augsburg Fortress.

Jesus Christ. Robert Hicks & Richard Bewes. (Understanding Bible Truth Ser.). (Orig.). 1981. pap. 0.95 o.p. (ISBN 0-89840-026-0). Heres Life.

Jesus Christ, Disciplemaker. Bill Hull. LC 84-70471. 216p. 1984. 5.95 o.p. (ISBN 0-89109-516-0). NavPress.

Jesus Christ Returns by 1988? Gordon McDowell. LC 83-90836. 66p. 1984. 5.95 o.p. (ISBN 0-533-05838-4). Vantage.

Jesus Christ, Son of God. Mary L. Ellis. (Illus., Orig.). (gr. 5-7). 1967. pap. 3.95 o.p. (ISBN 0-8042-9440-2, John Knox). Westminster John Knox.

Jesus Does Great Things see Bible Pop-O-Rama Books.

Jesus-God & Man. 2d ed. Wolfhart Pannenberg. Tr. by Lewis L. Wilkins & Duane A. Priebe. LC 76-26478. 1977. 12.50 o.s.i. (ISBN 0-664-21289-1, Westminster). Westminster John Knox.

Jesus God's Way of Healing & Power to Promote Health. Wilford H. Reidt & John G. Lake. 171p. 1981. pap. 5.95 o.p. (ISBN 0-89274-197-X). Harrison Hse.

Jesus Goes Away see What the Bible Tells Us: Third Series.

Jesus Grows Up. Rebecca Bennett. (Wipe-Clean Bks.). (Illus.). 12p. (ps). 1985. pap. 1.39 o.p. (ISBN 0-87239-954-0, 3514). Standard Pub.

Jesus in Contemporary Historical Research. Gustaf Aulen. Tr. by Ingalill H. Hjelm from Swedish. LC 75-36451. 176p. 1976. 3.50 o.p. (ISBN 0-8006-0438-5, 1-438, Fortress). Augsburg Fortress.

Jesus in His Time. Ed. by Hans J. Schultz. Tr. by Brian Watchorn from Ger. LC 70-99613. 160p. (Orig.). 1971. pap. 5.50 o.p. (ISBN 0-8006-0163-7, 1-163, Fortress). Augsburg Fortress.

Jesus in History: An Approach to the Study of the Gospels. Howard C. Kee. 1970. pap. text ed. 9.95 o.p. (ISBN 0-15-547381-6, HC). HarBraceJ.

Jesus in the Gospel of John. Jacob Jervell. Tr. by Harry T. Cleven. LC 84-14547. 96p. (Orig.). 1984. pap. 6.95 o.p. (ISBN 0-8066-2089-7, 10-3516, Augsburg). Augsburg Fortress.

Jesus in the Gospels. Ed. by Daughters of St. Paul. (Illus.). 297p. (gr. 1 up). 1988. 12.00 o.p. (ISBN 0-317-67475-7, CH0288). Dghtrs St Paul.

Jesus in the Memory of the Early Church. Nils A. Dahl. LC 76-27072. 1976. pap. 8.95 o.p. (ISBN 0-8066-1561-3, 10-3519, Augsburg). Augsburg Fortress.

Jesus in the Midst: Spiritual Writings. Chiara Lubich. LC 76-18455. 80p. 1976. pap. 2.95 o.p. (ISBN 0-911782-26-5). New City.

Jesus Is Born. (Orig.). (gr. k-3). 1988. pap. 3.50 o.p. (ISBN 0-8054-4001-1). Broadman.

Jesus Is Born. Ed. by Patricia Mahany. (Classroom Activity Bks.). (Illus.). 48p. (Orig.). (ps-k). 1984. pap. 2.95 o.p. (ISBN 0-87239-719-X, 2449). Standard Pub.

Jesus Is Coming. Paul L. Tan. 1982. pap. 2.95 o.p. (ISBN 0-88469-095-4). BMH Bks.

Jesus Is No Secret. Carolyn Nystrom. (Children's Bible Basics Ser.). (Illus.). (gr. 2 up). 1983. pap. 3.95 o.p. (ISBN 0-8024-0193-7). Moody.

Jesus Jewels. Marie M. Hald. 118p. 1983. pap. 5.00 o.p. (ISBN 0-682-49963-3). Exposition-Phoenix.

Jesus Life: A Guide for Young Christians. Alvin N. Rogness. LC 72-90260. 112p. (Orig.). (YA) (gr. 7 up). 1973. pap. 5.95 o.p. (ISBN 0-8066-1307-6, 10-3521, Augsburg). Augsburg Fortress.

Jesus Living the Father's Values. Megan McKenna & Darryl Ducote. LC 78-71530. (Followers of the Way Ser.: Vol. 3). (gr. 9-12). 1979. 22.50 o.p. (ISBN 0-8091-9544-5); cassette 7.50 o.p. (ISBN 0-8091-7668-8). Paulist Pr.

Jesus: Lord for All Times. Donald G. Dawe. 128p. 1975. pap. 3.95 o.p. (ISBN 0-8042-9066-0, John Knox); tchrs' ed 3.95 o.p. (ISBN 0-8042-9067-9). Westminster John Knox.

Jesus' Lost Gospels: The Discovery at Nag Hammadi. Ed. by J. Frank O'Quinn. (Illus.). 48p. 1981. pap. text ed. 6.95 o.s.i. (ISBN 0-9609802-0-2). Life Science.

Jesus Loves Children. Ed. by C. Brusselmans. 5.95 o.p. (ISBN 0-8215-9889-9). Sadlier.

Jesus Loves Me, This I Know: Devotions for Families with Young Children. Rolf E. Aaseng. LC 72-90253. 1977. pap. 5.50 o.p. (ISBN 0-8066-1572-9, 10-3523, Augsburg). Augsburg Fortress.

Jesus Means Freedom. Ernst Kasemann. Tr. by Frank Clarke from Ger. LC 75-94357. 168p. (Orig.). 1972. pap. 6.50 o.p. (ISBN 0-8006-1235-3, 1-1235, Fortress). Augsburg Fortress.

Jesus of Faith: A Study in Christology. Michael L. Cook. LC 80-84510. 192p. (Orig.). pap. 7.95 o.p. (ISBN 0-8091-2349-5). Paulist Pr.

Jesus of Nazareth. William Barclay. pap. 2.95 o.p. (ISBN 0-345-34254-2). Ballantine.

Jesus of Nazareth: The Man & His Time. Herbert Braun. Tr. by Everett R. Kalin from Ger. LC 78-14664. 160p. 1979. 6.95 o.p. (ISBN 0-8006-0531-4, 1-531, Fortress). Augsburg Fortress.

Jesus on Social Institutions. Shailer Mathews. Ed. by Kenneth Cauthen & Leander E. Keck. LC 72-139346. (Lives of Jesus Ser). 240p. 1971. pap. 2.00 o.p. (ISBN 0-8006-0156-4, 1-156, Fortress). Augsburg Fortress.

Jesus on the Mountain: A Study in Matthean Theology. Terence L. Donaldson. (JSNT Supplement Ser.: No. 8). 326p. pap. text ed. 14.95x o.s.i. (Pub. by JSOT Pr England). Eisenbrauns.

Jesus on Trial. A. E. Harvey. LC 77-79588. 1977. Repr. 6.95 o.p. (ISBN 0-8042-0335-0, John Knox). Westminster John Knox.

Jesus on Trial. Gerard S. Sloyan. LC 73-79040. 176p. 1973. pap. 3.75 o.p. (ISBN 0-8006-1033-4, Fortress). Augsburg Fortress.

Jesus, Our Brother. William V. Coleman & Patricia R. Coleman. (Daybreak Ser.). (Illus.). 1977. tchrs. ed. 9.95x o.p. (ISBN 0-89622-044-3). Twenty-Third.

Jesus' Parables & the War of Myths: Essays on Imagination in the Scriptures. Amos N. Wilder. LC 81-43083. 176p. 1982. 3.50 o.p. (ISBN 0-8006-0668-X, 1-668, Fortress). Augsburg Fortress.

Jesus Prayer. Per-Olof Sjogren. Tr. by Sydney Linton from Swedish. LC 75-18789. 96p. 1975. pap. 3.95 o.p. (ISBN 0-8006-1216-7, 1-1216, Fortress). Augsburg Fortress.

Jesus Prayer for Today. Arthur A. Vogel. LC 81-84349. 128p. (Orig.). 1982. pap. 5.95 o.p. (ISBN 0-8091-2413-0). Paulist Pr.

Jesus Prays. L. M. Borchardt. (Learning Awareness Ser.). 16p. (gr. 1-2). pap. 0.78 o.p. (ISBN 0-317-60475-9, 61HH2015). Concordia.

Jesus' Proclamation of the Kingdom of God. Johannes Weiss. Ed. by Leander E. Keck. Tr. by Richard H. Hiers & David L. Holland. LC 79-135267. (Lives of Jesus Ser). 160p. (Orig.). 1971. pap. 1.50 o.p. (ISBN 0-8006-0153-X, 1-153, Fortress). Augsburg Fortress.

Jesus' Promise to the Nations. Joachim Jeremias. LC 81-70553. 96p. 1982. pap. 5.50 o.p. (ISBN 0-8006-1632-4, 1-1632, Fortress). Augsburg Fortress.

Jesus' Saving Questions. Gloria Hutchinson. 118p. (Orig.). 1984. pap. text ed. 4.95 o.p. (ISBN 0-86716-028-4). St Anthony Mess Pr.

Jesus Style. Gayle D. Erwin. 211p. 1985. 9.95 o.p. (ISBN 0-8499-0509-5, 0509-5). Word Bks.

Jesus, Symbol-Maker for the Kingdom. Bernard B. Scott. LC 80-2388. 192p. 1981. 15.95 o.p. (ISBN 0-8006-0654-X, 1-654, Fortress). Augsburg Fortress.

Jesus Tells a Story see Bible Pop-O-Rama Books.

Jesus, the Children's Friend. Miriam J. Hall. 62p. (Orig.). 1983. pap. 1.95 o.p. (ISBN 0-8341-0815-1). Beacon Hill.

Jesus the Jew. Markus Barth. Tr. by Frederick Prussner from Ger. LC 77-15741. 1978. Repr. of 1975 ed. 6.95 o.p. (ISBN -08042-0834-4, John Knox). Westminster John Knox.

Jesus: The Man. Edward W. H. Vick. LC 78-10253. (Anvil Ser.). 1979. pap. 6.95 o.p. (ISBN 0-8127-0220-4). Review & Herald.

Jesus, the Man & the Myth. James P. Mackey. LC 78-61627. 320p. 1979. pap. 10.95 o.p. (ISBN 0-8091-2169-7). Paulist Pr.

Jesus: The Way to Freedom. Donald P. Gray. LC 79-66823. (Illus.). 80p. 1979. pap. text ed. 4.95 o.p. (ISBN 0-88489-112-7). St Mary's.

Jesus Tradition Outside the Gospels. David Wenham. (Gospel Perspectives Ser.: No. 5). 419p. pap. text ed. 14.95x o.s.i. (Pub by JSOT Pr England). Eisenbrauns.

Jesus Went about Doing Good. Jean H. Richards. LC 80-70475. (gr. 1-4). 1983. 5.95 o.p. (ISBN 0-8054-4289-8, 4242-89). Broadman.

Jesus: Word & Presence. Peter C. Hodgson. LC 70-157538. 1971. 9.95 o.p. (ISBN 0-8006-0039-8, Fortress). Augsburg Fortress.

Jesus, Zoroaster, Buddha, Socrates, Muhammad. E. Yamauchi. pap. 0.75 o.p. (ISBN 0-87784-145-4). Inter-Varsity.

Jet. Frank Whittle. (Illus.). 320p. 1955. (ISBN 0-8022-1873-3). Philos Lib.

Jet Engine Manual. E. Mangham & A. Peace. 1962. (ISBN 0-8022-1045-7). Philos Lib.

Jet FBO's. pap. 9.95x o.p. Aviation.

Jet, Rocket, Nuclear, Ion & Electric Propulsion. W. H. Loh. LC 68-26005. (Applied Physics & Engineering Ser.: Vol. 7). 1969. 70.00 o.p. (ISBN 0-387-04053-6). Springer-Verlag.

Jet 88. Ian Hill. (Illus.). Date not set. pap. 9.95 o.p. (ISBN 0-317-56134-0, Pub. by AvCom Intl). Aviation.

Jeune Parque see Poesies.

Jeux de l'Esprit. Pierre Boulle. 256p. 1971. 9.95 o.p. (ISBN 0-686-54105-7). French & Eur.

Jeux de Massacre: Theatre. Eugene Ionesco. (Le Manteau d'Arlequin). pap. 4.50 o.p. (ISBN 0-685-34253-0). Schoenhof.

Jeux de Patience. Bruce Hart & Carole Hart. (Fr.). (gr. 7 up). 1983. pap. 2.50 o.p. (ISBN 0-380-84525-3, 84523, Flare). Avon.

Jeux et Sports. Roger Caillois. (Methodique Ser.). 1848p. 49.95 o.p. (ISBN 0-686-56444-8). French & Eur.

Jew - Hate as a Sociological Problem. Peretz Bernstein. 320p. (ISBN 0-8022-0115-6). Philos Lib.

Jew As Pariah: Jewish Identity & Politics in the Modern Age. Ed. by Ron Feldman. 1978. pap. 6.95 o.p. (ISBN 0-394-17042-3, E711, Ever). Grove.

Jew in American Sports. Harold U. Ribalow & Meir Z. Ribalow. (Illus.). 448p. (gr. 6 up). 1985. 16.95 o.p. (ISBN 0-88254-995-2). Hippocrene Bks.

Jew Suss. Arthur Rawlinson & Dorothy Farnum. Ed. by Bruce S. Kupelnick. LC 76-52125. (Classics of Film Literature Ser.). 1978. lib. bdg. 22.00 o.p. (ISBN 0-8240-2891-0). Garland Pub.

Jewel of Humility. Sri Chinmoy. (Illus.). 56p. (Orig.). 1980. pap. 2.00 o.p. (ISBN 0-88497-493-6). Aum Pubns.

Jewel of Seven Stars. Bram Stoker. 256p. 1989. pap. 3.95 o.p. (ISBN 0-88184-501-9). Carroll & Graf.

Jewel of the Nile. Joan Wilder. 1985. pap. 3.50 o.p. (ISBN 0-380-89984-1). Avon.

Jewel of the Nile. Joan Wilder. 392p. 1986. lib. bdg. 16.95 o.p. (ISBN 0-8161-4125-8, Large Print Bks). G K Hall.

Jeweled Birdcage. Susannah James. (Orig.). 1982. pap. 2.95 o.p. (Sig). NAL.

Jewelry of the Ancient World. Renate Rosenthal. LC 72-10797. (Archaeology Ser.). (gr. 5 up). 1975. PLB 8.95 o.p. (ISBN 0-8225-0830-3). Lerner Pubns.

Jewelry on Display. Mariann Coutchie. (Illus.). 1982. pap. 18.95 o.p. (ISBN 0-911380-56-6). Signs of Times.

Jewels of Elvish. Nancy Berberick. LC 87-51251. (Illus.). 352p. (Orig.). 1989. pap. 3.95 o.p. (ISBN 0-88038-536-7). TSR Inc.

Jewess of Toledo. F. Grillparzer. Tr. by Arthur Burkhard. 5.00x o.p. (ISBN 0-685-57218-8). M S Rosenberg.

Jewish Agricultural Utopias in America, 1880-1910. Uri D. Herscher. LC 81-4620. (Illus.). 214p. 1981. 22.50x o.p. (ISBN 0-8143-1678-6). Wayne St U Pr.

Jewish America. Seymour Kurtz. LC 84-10065. (Illus.). 250p. 1985. text ed. 29.95 o.p. (ISBN 0-07-035655-6). McGraw.

Jewish Americans: Three Generations in a Jewish Community. Sidney Goldstein & Calvin Goldscheider. (Brown Classics in Judaica Ser.). (Illus.). 294p. 1985. pap. text ed. 14.25 o.p. (ISBN 0-8191-4721-4). U Pr of Amer.

Jewish & Christian Self-Definition, Vol. 1: The Shaping of Christianity in the Second & Third Centuries. Ed. by E. P. Sanders. LC 79-7390. 336p. 1980. 5.00 o.p. (ISBN 0-8006-0578-0, 1-578, Fortress). Augsburg Fortress.

Jewish & Christian Self-Definition, Vol. 2: Aspects of Judaism in the Greco-Roman Period. Ed. by E. P. Sanders et al. LC 79-7390. 450p. 1981. 5.00 o.p. (ISBN 0-8006-0660-4, 1-660, Fortress). Augsburg Fortress.

Jewish & Christian Self-Definition, Vol. 3: Self-Definition in the Greco-Roman World. Ed. by Ben F. Meyer & E. P. Sanders. LC 79-7390. 320p. 1983. 24.95 o.p. (ISBN 0-8006-0690-6, 1-690, Fortress). Augsburg Fortress.

Jewish & Female: Choices & Changes in Our Lives Today. Susan W. Schneider. (Illus.). 448p. 1984. 19.45 o.p. (ISBN 0-671-42103-4). S&S.

Jewish & Hebrew Onomastics: A Bibliography. Robert Singerman. (Reference Library of the Humanities: Vol. 92). (LC 76-052684). 1977. lib. bdg. 23.00 o.p. (ISBN 0-8240-9881-1). Garland Pub.

Jewish & Pauline Studies. W. D. Davies. LC 82-48620. 432p. 1983. text ed. 6.95 o.p. (ISBN 0-8006-0694-9, Fortress). Augsburg Fortress.

Jewish Artists of the Nineteenth & Twentieth Centuries. Karl Schwarz. (ISBN 0-8022-1516-5). Philos Lib.

Jewish Baseball Stars. Harld V. Ribalow & Meir Ribalow. (Illus.). 1984. 12.95 o.p. (ISBN 0-88254-898-0). Hippocrene Bks.

Jewish Cookbook for Children. Ronnie Steinkoler. LC 80-17428. (Illus.). 96p. (gr. 4-7). 1980. lib. bdg. 7.79 o.s.i. (ISBN 0-671-33093-4). Messner.

Jewish Face. (Illus.). 1.50 o.p. (ISBN 0-914131-38-9, D44). Torah Umesorah.

Jewish Historical Treasures. Azriel Eisenberg. LC 68-57432. (Illus.). 300p. 1969. 12.50 o.p. (ISBN 0-8197-0076-2). Bloch.

Jewish Holiday Kitchen. Date not set. (ISBN 0-8052-3712-7). Random.

Jewish Holidays. Margery Cuyler. LC 77-10801. (Illus.). (gr. 2-5). 1978. 6.95 o.p. (ISBN 0-03-039936-X). H Holt & Co.

Jewish Identity in an Age of Ideologies. Jacob B. Agus. LC 76-14230. 1978. 25.00 o.p. (ISBN 0-8044-5018-8). Ungar.

Jewish Intellectualism & Russian Marxism. Date not set. (ISBN 0-8052-3685-6). Random.

Jewish Kids Catalog. Chaya Burstein. (Illus.). 224p. 1986. 12.95 o.p. (ISBN 0-317-63290-6). JPS Phila.

Jewish Landmarks of New York: A Travel Guide & History. Bernard Postal & Lionel Koppman. LC 76-27400. (Orig.). 1978. 15.95 o.s.i. (ISBN 0-8303-0153-4). Fleet.

Jewish Life on New York's Lower East Side: Drawings & Paintings, 1912-1962. S. Zagat. Ed. by I. R. Zagat. (Illus.). 1972. 30.00 o.s.i. (ISBN 0-911268-09-X). E J Brill USA.

Jewish Lights: Substitute Teachers Kit. Rabin. 1984. 3.00x o.p. (ISBN 0-940646-28-5). Rossel Bks.

Jewish Marriage Anthology. Ed. by Philip Goodman. Hanna Goodman. LC 65-17045. (Illus.). 1965. 13.95 o.p. (ISBN 0-8276-0145-X, 236). JPS Phila.

Jewish Medical Ethics. Immanual Jakobovitz. 1959. (ISBN 0-8022-0789-8). Philos Lib.

Jewish Meditation. Date not set. (ISBN 0-8052-4006-3). Random.

Jewish Monotheism & Christian Trinitarian Doctrine. Pinchas Lapide & Jurgen Moltmann. Tr. by Leonard Swidler from Ger. LC 80-8058. 96p. 1981. pap. 4.95 o.p. (ISBN 0-8006-1405-4, 1-1405, Fortress). Augsburg Fortress.

Jewish Music in Its Historical Development. Abraham Z. Idelsohn. LC 80-24235. (Illus.). xi, 535p. 1981. Repr. of 1948 ed. lib. bdg. 38.50 o.p. (ISBN 0-313-22749-7, IDJM). Greenwood.

Jewish Mystical Tradition. Bakeer. 9.95 o.p. Pilgrim NY.

Jewish Partisans: A Documentary of Jewish Resistance in the Soviet Union During World War II, Vol. II. Ed. by Jack N. Porter. LC 81-40258. 314p. (Orig.). 1982. lib. bdg. 30.50 o.p. (ISBN 0-8191-2537-7); pap. text ed. 14.25_o.p o.p. (ISBN 0-8191-2538-5). U Pr of Amer.

Jewish Presence: Essays on Identity & History. Lucy Dawidowicz. LC 78-6236. 308p. 1978. pap. 3.95 o.p. (ISBN 0-15-646221-4, Harv). HarBraceJ.

Jewish Return. Date not set. pap. (ISBN 0-8052-0649-3). Random.

Jewish Seat: Antisemitism & the Appointment of Jews to the Supreme Court. Thomas Karfunkel & Thomas W. Ryley. 1978. 7.50 o.p. (ISBN 0-682-49058-X, University). Exposition-Phoenix.

Jewish Sects at the Time of Jesus. Marcel Simon. Tr. by James H. Farley from Fr. LC 66-25265. 192p. 1980. pap. 6.95 o.p. (ISBN 0-8006-0183-1, 1-183, Fortress). Augsburg Fortress.

Jewish Survival. Trude Weiss-Rosmarin. (ISBN 0-8022-1846-6). Philos Lib.

Jewish Symbols. Charles Wengrov. (Illus.). (ps-3). 1960. pap. 0.99 o.p. (ISBN 0-914080-24-5). Shulsinger Sales.

Jewish Tradition. World Religions Delvelopment Center. (Illus.). 200p. 1978. pap. 8.95 o.p. (ISBN 0-89505-011-0); pap. 3.75 guide bk. o.p. (ISBN 0-317-60034-6). Tabor Pub.

Jewish Tradition, Guide. World Religions Development Center. 84p. 1978. pap. 3.75 o.p. (ISBN 0-89505-010-2). Tabor Pub.

Jewish Travel Guide, 1986. Ed. by Sidney Lightman. (Illus.). 296p. (Orig.). 1986. pap. 9.25 o.p. (ISBN 0-900498-94-3, Pub. by Jewish Chronicle Pubns England). Hermon.

Jewish Travel Guide 1988. Ed. by Sidney Lightman. (Illus.). 290p. 1988. pap. 9.50 o.p. (ISBN 1-870216-00-8, Pub. by Jewish Chronicle Pubns England). Hermon.

Jewish Woman in Judaism: The Significance of Women's Status in Religious Culture. Solomon Appleman. 1979. 10.00 o.p. (ISBN 0-682-49431-3). Exposition-Phoenix.

Jewish Word Book. Sidney J. Jacobs. 356p. (Eng. & Hebrew.). 1982. 12.50 o.p. (ISBN 0-8246-0249-8). Jonathan David.

Jewish World in the Time of Jesus. Charles Guignebert. 1959. 6.00 o.p. (ISBN 0-8216-0033-8, Pub. by Univ Bks). Carol Pub Group.

Jews. Alan Unterman. (Library of Religious Beliefs & Practices). 212p. 1986. pap. text ed. 14.95 o.p. (ISBN 0-7100-0842-2). Routledge Chapman & Hall.

Jews & Christians after the Holocaust. Ed. by Abraham J. Peck. LC 81-70665. 128p. 1982. 9.95 o.p. (ISBN 0-8006-0678-7, 1-678, Fortress). Augsburg Fortress.

Jews & Judaism in the United States: A Documentary History. Ed. by Marc L. Raphael. 352p. 1983. pap. text ed. 10.95x o.p. (ISBN 0-87441-347-8). Behrman.

Jews & Modern Capitalism. Werner Sombart. 1981. 39.95 o.p. (ISBN 0-87855-402-5). Transaction Pubs.

Jews & Money: The Myths & the Reality. Gerald Krefetz. LC 82-5639. 280p. 1982. 13.45 o.p. (ISBN 0-89919-129-0). Ticknor & Fields.

Jews & Non-Jews in Eastern Europe, 1918-1945. Ed. by George Mosse & Bela Vago. 1974. 15.95x o.p. (ISBN 0-87855-155-7). Transaction Pubs.

Jews, Greeks & Barbarians: Aspects of the Hellenization of Judaism in the Pre-Christian Period. Martin Hengel. Tr. by John Bowden from Ger. LC 80-8051. 192p. 1980. 2.50 o.p. (ISBN 0-8006-0647-7, 1-647, Fortress). Augsburg Fortress.

Jews in Music. Arthur Holde. 1960. (ISBN 0-8022-0737-5). Philos Lib.

Jews in Spain & Portugal: A Bibliography. Robert Singerman. LC 75-1166. (Reference Library of Social Science: No. 11). 376p. 1975. lib. bdg. 52.00 o.p. (ISBN 0-8240-1089-2). Garland Pub.

Jews in the East, 2 vols. Ludwig A. Frankl. Tr. by P. Beaton. LC 78-97278. 1975. Repr. of 1859 ed. Set. lib. bdg. 28.50x o.p. (ISBN 0-8371-2596-0, FRJE); Vol. 1. lib. bdg. 15.65 o.p. (ISBN 0-8371-2599-5, FRJF); Vol. 2. lib. bdg. 15.65 o.p. (ISBN 0-8371-2600-2, FRJG). Greenwood.

Jews in the Soviet Satellites. Peter Meyer. LC 79-97297. 1971. Repr. of 1953 ed. lib. bdg. 48.50x o.p. (ISBN 0-8371-2621-5, MEJS). Greenwood.

Jews in Weimar Germany. Donald L. Niewyk. LC 79-26234. x, 262p. 1980. 30.00 o.p. (ISBN 0-8071-0661-5). La State U Pr.

Jews of Europe & the Inquisition of Venice, 1550-1670. Brian Pullan. LC 83-7147. 364p. 1983. 32.50x o.p. (ISBN 0-389-20414-5). B&N Imports.

Jews of Rhodes: The History of a Sephardic Community. 2nd ed. Marc D. Angel. LC 77-93661. 1980. 12.50 o.p. Hermon.

Jews of the Middle East (1860-1972) Hayyim J. Cohen. 224p. 1973. casebound 12.95x o.p. (ISBN 0-87855-169-7). Transaction Pubs.

Jews Without Money. Michael Gold. 1981. pap. 0.95 o.p. (ISBN 0-380-01309-6, 29520-2, Bard). Avon.

Ji: Signs & Symbols of Japan. Donald Richie & Mana Maeda. LC 74-29569. (Illus.). 132p. 1975. 29.95 o.p. (ISBN 0-87011-247-3). Kodansha.

Jiang Jie-Shi: 1887-1975. Chiang Kai-Shek & J. S. Gregory. LC 82-199758. (Leaders of Asia Ser.). (Illus.). 40p. 1982. 4.95 o.p. (ISBN 0-7022-1800-6). U of Queensland Pr.

Jig Boring. Ed. by F. T. Bright et al. (Engineering Craftsmen: No. H27). (Illus.). 1969. spiral bdg. 39.95x o.p. Trans-Atl Phila.

Jigsaw. Geoffrey Linden. (Orig.). 1974. pap. 3.45 o.p. (ISBN 0-380-00148-9, 21295). Avon.

Jigsaw Classroom. Elliot Aronson et al. LC 78-583. (Sageview Edition). (Illus.). 197p. 1978. 20.00 o.p. (ISBN 0-8039-0997-7). Sage.

Jigsaw John. Al Martinez. 1976. pap. 1.50 o.p. (ISBN 0-380-00740-1, 29942). Avon.

Jill. Philip Larkin. 1985. 13.95 o.p. (ISBN 0-317-53127-1, Large Print Bks). G K Hall.

Jill the Pill. Julie Castiglia. LC 79-12305. (Illus.). 32p. (gr. 1-5). 1979. 6.95 o.p. (ISBN 0-689-50105-6, Atheneum). Macmillan.

Jim. Ruth Bornstein. LC 77-12712. (Illus.). 32p. (ps-3). 1979. 7.95 o.p. (ISBN 0-395-28772-3, Clarion). HM.

Jim Along, Josie: A Collection of Folk Songs & Singing Games for Young Children. Ed. by Nancy Langstaff & John Langstaff. LC 79-118757. (Illus.). (gr. k up). 1970. 10.95 o.p. (ISBN 0-15-240250-0, HJ). HarBraceJ.

Jim & the Beanstalk. Raymond Briggs. LC 77-111062. (Illus.). (gr. k-3). 1980. PLB 6.99 o.p. (ISBN 0-698-30203-6, Coward); pap. 2.95 o.p. (ISBN 0-698-20510-3, Coward). Putnam Pub Group.

Jim Dine: Recent Work (Hearts) Jim Dine. Ed. by Pace Gallery Publications. (Illus.). 26p. (Orig.). 1981. pap. text ed. 12.00 o.p. (ISBN 0-938608-16-9). Pace Pubns.

Jim Frog. Russell Hoban. LC 83-12586. (Illus.). (gr. k-2). 1984. pap. 6.95 o.s.i. (ISBN 0-03-069501-5). H Holt & Co.

Jim Hart Story. Thomas Barnidge & Douglas Grow. LC 77-12538. (Illus.). 1977. 6.95 o.p. (ISBN 0-8272-1705-6); pap. 4.95 o.p. (ISBN 0-8272-1704-8). CBP.

Jim Henson's Muppets: Very Easy Piano Favorites. Ed. by Milton Okun & Dan Fox. (Illus.). 95p. 1983. pap. 3.95 o.s.i. (ISBN 0-89524-183-8, 2501). Cherry Lane.

Jim Plunkett Story: The Saga of a Man Who Came Back. Jim Plunkett & Dave Newhouse. LC 81-66958. 1981. 12.95 o.p. (ISBN 0-87795-326-0, Arbor Hse). Morrow.

Jimi Hendrix: Note for Note. Richard Daniels. (Orig.). (YA) (gr. 8 up). 1980. pap. 8.95 o.s.i. (ISBN 0-89524-108-0, 5005). Cherry Lane.

Jimmy Carter: In Search of the Great White House. Betty Glad. (Illus.). 1980. 19.95 o.p. (ISBN 0-393-07527-3). Norton.

Jingo Django. Sid Fleischman. (Illus.). 174p. (gr. 4-7). 1987. 14.45 o.p. (ISBN 0-316-28580-3). Little.

JKDIGIT, A Program to Control a Digitizing Board for Geologists, Written in Basic for an IBM Personal Computer. John O. Kork. (Geological Survey Bulletin: 1616). 73p. 1986. pap. 3.75 o.p. (ISBN 0-318-21297-8, S/N 024-001-03548-1). USGPO.

Joan Antida Thouret: When God Hear the voice of the Poor. Gino Lubich & Piero Lazzarin. Tr. by Joel Brody from Ital. LC 84-62540. 1985. pap. 5.95 o.p. (ISBN 0-911782-47-8). New City.

Joan Crawford: Legends. Anna Raeburn. 1986. pap. 14.95 o.p. (ISBN 0-316-50055-0). Little.

Joan Didion: Essays & Conversations. Ed. by Ellen G. Friedman. LC 84-5263. (Ontario Review Press Critical Ser.). 190p. 1984. 17.95 o.p. (ISBN 0-86538-035-X); pap. 9.95 o.p. (ISBN 0-86538-036-8). Ontario Rev NJ.

Joan Miro, Lithographs, Vol. 1. Michael Leiris & Fernand Mourlot. (Illus.). 231p. 1972. 150.00x o.p. (ISBN 0-8148-0494-2, Pub. by Tudor). Hennessey.

Joan of Arc. Sarah L. Loening. 1951. (ISBN 0-8022-0927-0). Philos Lib.

Joan of Arc. Edward Lucie-Smith. (Illus.). 1977. 10.95 o.p. (ISBN 0-393-07520-6). Norton.

Joan Walsh Anglund Sampler. Joan W. Anglund. (Illus.). 1963. 5.50 o.p. (ISBN 0-15-240390-6, HJ). HarBraceJ.

Joanna. Roberta Gellis. (Roselynde Chronicles Ser.). 1984. lib. bdg. 13.95 o.p. (ISBN 0-8398-2862-4, Gregg). G K Hall.

Joanna & Ulysses. May Sarton. (Illus.). (gr. 8 up). 1963. 4.95 o.p. (ISBN 0-393-08494-9). Norton.

Joanna's Husband & David's Wife. Elizabeth F. Hailey. 336p. 1986. 17.95 o.p. (ISBN 0-385-29436-0). Delacorte.

Joanna's Husband & David's Wife. Elizabeth F. Hailey. (Large Print Bks (General Ser.)). 488p. 1986. lib. bdg. 19.95x o.p. (ISBN 0-8161-4131-2). G K Hall.

Job. Myles M. Bourke. (Bible Ser.). Pt. 1. pap. 1.00 o.p. (ISBN 0-8091-5073-5); Pt. 2. pap. 1.00 o.p. (ISBN 0-8091-5074-3). Paulist Pr.

Job: A Comedy of Justice. Robert A. Heinlein. 384p. 1984. 16.95 o.p. (ISBN 0-345-31649-5, Del Rey). Ballantine.

Job at Last see Getting along Series of Skills.

Job Burnout in Public Education: Symptoms, Causes, & Survival Skills. Anthony J. Cedoline. 1982. text ed. 19.95x o.p. (ISBN 0-8077-2694-X). Tchrs Coll.

Job Control & Union Structure. R. Herding. 414p. (Orig.). 1971. pap. text ed. 39.95x o.p. (ISBN 90-237-2232-9). Gower Pub Co.

Job Descriptions in Banking: The Complete Guide to Planning, Writing, & Using Job Descriptions. Frank Oldham, Jr. Ed. by Jeffrey L. Seglin. LC 84-6443. 256p. 1984. 47.00 o.p. (ISBN 0-87267-049-X). Bank Admin Inst.

Job Evaluation. 2nd ed. Jay L. Otis & R. H. Leukart. 1954. text ed. 35.00 ref. ed. o.p. (ISBN 0-13-509562-X). P-H.

Job Evaluation: An Analytical Review. National Research Council. 170p. 1979. pap. 9.95x o.p. (ISBN 0-309-02882-5). Natl Acad Pr.

Job Game: A Career Handbook. Mariann Loniello et al. 128p. (Orig.). 1984. pap. text ed. 15.00x o.p. (ISBN 0-89787-803-5). Gorsuch Scarisbrick.

Job Guides Set, 1989, 2 vols. Date not set. Set. 64.50 o.p. (ISBN 0-87866-815-2); Set. pap. 36.00 o.p. (ISBN 0-87866-814-4). Petersons Guides.

Job: Interviews by Daniel Odier. William S. Burroughs. LC 73-20496. 212p. 1974. pap. 4.95 o.p. (ISBN 0-394-17870-X, E642, Ever). Grove.

Job: Living Patiently. J. Allen Blair. LC 66-25720. 1966. pap. 5.95 o.p. (ISBN 0-87213-051-7). Loizeaux.

Job Loss Survival Manual. Dean B. Peskin. LC 79-13522. 192p. 1981. 5.95 o.p. (ISBN 0-8144-7543-4). AMACOM.

Job Outlook in Brief. William M. Austin. (Illus.). 28p. 1986. pap. 1.50 o.p. (ISBN 0-318-21550-0, S/N 029-001-02908-0). USGPO.

Job Placement: Programs for the Future. Connye M. Barrow. 29p. 1982. 3.75 o.p. (ISBN 0-318-22137-3, IN239). Natl Ctr Res Voc Ed.

Job Satisfaction: A Bibliography. Jacqueline Mundell. (Public Administration Ser.: P 1799). 12p. 1985. 2.00 o.p. (ISBN 0-89028-629-9). Vance Biblios.

Job Satisfaction & Work Adjustment: Implications for Vocational Education. Rene V. Davis & Lloyd H. Lofquist. 30p. 1981. 2.80 o.p. (ISBN 0-318-22139-X, IN218). Natl Ctr Res Voc Ed.

Job Search Workshop for Disabled, Dislocated & Discouraged Workers: Participant Manual. rev. ed. Colleen Ryan. 130p. (Orig.). 1986. spiral bound 12.00 o.p. (ISBN 0-936352-22-1). U of KS Cont Ed.

Job Search Workshop for Disabled, Dislocated & Discouraged Workers: Trainer Manual. rev. ed. Colleen Ryan. 337p. (Orig.). 1986. spiral bound 24.50 o.p. (ISBN 0-936352-21-3). U of KS Cont Ed.

Job-Song of Solomon, Vol. III. Beacon Bible Commentary Staff. 15.95 o.p. (ISBN 0-8010-0690-2). Baker Bk.

Job Speaks to Us Today. John Job. LC 79-19632. (Bible Speaks to Us Today Ser.). 128p. 1980. pap. 4.25 o.p. (ISBN 0-8042-0132-3, John Knox). Westminster John Knox.

Job World Workbook. Ted R. Morford & Shelley M. Mauer. (Job World Ser.). 86p. (Orig.). (gr. 8). 1981. deluxe ed. 6.95 wkbk. o.p. (ISBN 0-940428-01-6); instr's manual 18.65 o.p. (ISBN 0-940428-00-8). Ed Assocs KY.

Jobbing Actor. John Le Mesurier. (Illus.). 192p. 1984. 18.95 o.p. (ISBN 0-241-11063-7, Pub. by Hamish Hamilton England). David & Charles.

Jobs & Earnings for State Citizens: Monitoring the Outcomes of State Economic Development & Employment & Training Programs. Richard E. Winnie et al. 146p. 1977. pap. text ed. 6.50 o.p. (ISBN 0-87766-208-8). Urban Inst.

Jobs, Dollars & EEO: How to Hire More Productive Entry-Level Workers. Richard A. Fear & James F. Ross. LC 82-274. (Illus.). 240p. 1983. text ed. 24.95 o.p. (ISBN 0-07-020199-4). McGraw.

Job's Illness: Loss, Grief & Integration; a Psychological Interpretation. J. H. Kahn. 284p. 1975. 55.00 o.p. (ISBN 0-08-018087-6). Pergamon.

Jobs in Arts & Media Management: What They Are & How to Get One. James Abruzzo. LC 85-16099. 1986. text ed. 32.50 o.p. (ISBN 0-89676-090-1); pap. text ed. 19.95x o.p. (ISBN 0-89676-073-1). Drama Bk.

Jobs in the Arts & Arts Administration. rev. 1984 ed. 11p. 1981. 4.00 o.p. (ISBN 0-686-95193-X). Ctr for Arts Info.

Jobs or Dogma: The Industrial Assistance Commission & Australian Politics. John Warhurst. LC 82-8653. (Policy, Politics, & Administration Ser.). (Illus.). 255p. 1983. text ed. 25.00x o.p. (ISBN 0-7022-1850-2); pap. text ed. 8.50x o.p. (ISBN 0-7022-1982-7). U of Queensland Pr.

Jobs That Suck... And Some That Don't. Andy Kane. (Illus.). 152p. 1984. pap. 10.00 o.p. (ISBN 0-87364-304-6). Paladin Pr.

Job's Year. Joseph Hansen. 269p. 1983. 14.95 o.p. (ISBN 0-03-061689-1). H Holt & Co.

Jobson's Mining Yearbook, 1985. 28th ed. 1985. 265.00 o.p. (ISBN 0-8002-3956-3). Intl Pubns Serv.

Jobson's Mining Yearbook 1987-88. 500p. 1987. text ed. 375.00 o.p. (ISBN 0-317-56547-8). Intl Pubns Serv.

Jobson's Yearbook of Public & Private Companies of Australia & New Zealand 1986-87. 700p. 1986. text ed. 350.00 o.p. (ISBN 0-8002-4092-8). Intl Pubns Serv.

Jocelyn. John Galsworthy. LC 76-29902. 1977. 6.95 o.s.i. (ISBN 0-03-020431-3). H Holt & Co.

Jock Culture, U. S. A. Neil D. Isaacs. 1978. 9.95 o.p. (ISBN 0-393-08807-3). Norton.

Jock Momma. Diane N. Jacko. LC 85-6958. 128p. (Orig.). 1985. pap. 5.95 o.p. (ISBN 0-571-12539-5). Faber & Faber.

Jocks. Scott Cohen. (Illus.). 96p. (Orig.). 1983. pap. 9.50 o.p. (ISBN 0-671-47693-9, Fireside). S&S.

Jodo: Way of the Stick. rev. ed. Michael Finn. (Illus.). 128p. 1985. pap. text ed. 12.00 o.p. (ISBN 0-87364-364-X). Paladin Pr.

Joe Dimaggio: the Yankee Clipper. Irving Gerber. (American Destiny Ser.: Italian Americans). (Illus.). (gr. 4-12). 1979. of 10 12.95 set o.p. (ISBN 0-87594-187-7). Book Lab.

Joe Louis: My Life. Joe Louis et al. LC 77-91341. (Illus.). 288p. 1978. 10.95 o.p. (ISBN 0-15-146375-1). HarBraceJ.

Joe Louis: The Brown Bomber. Bill Libby. LC 80-12372. (Illus.). 224p. (gr. 5 up). 1980. 11.88 o.p.; PLB 11.88 o.p. (ISBN 0-688-51968-7). Lothrop.

Joe Namath's Football Basics. Joe Namath. (Illus.). 224p. 1986. 17.45 o.s.i. (ISBN 0-671-52325-2). S&S.

Joe Orton. Christopher W. Bigsby. (Contemporary Writers Ser.). 96p. 1982. pap. 5.95x o.p. (ISBN 0-416-31690-5, NO. 3558). Routledge Chapman & Hall.

Joe Orton. Maurice Charney. (Modern Dramatists Ser.). 192p. 1984. 22.50 o.p. (ISBN 0-394-54241-X, GP941). Grove.

Joe Orton. Maurice Charney. (Modern Dramatists Ser.). 192p. 1984. pap. 7.95 o.p. (ISBN 0-317-13014-5, Ever). Grove.

Joe Orton. Maurice Charney. (Modern Dramatists Ser.). 192p. (Orig.). Date not set. pap. 7.95 o.p. (ISBN 0-394-62306-1). Grove.

Joe-Pye & Delphinium. Joseph S. Mihina. 64p. 1980. 5.00 o.p. (ISBN 0-682-49593-X). Exposition-Phoenix.

Joe, the First Thirty Years. Joseph Michaels. 1977. 4.50 o.p. (ISBN 0-682-48765-1). Exposition-Phoenix.

Joel Peter Witkin: Photographs. Photos by Joel P. Witkin. (Illus.). 132p. 1985. 50.00x o.p. (ISBN 0-942642-15-5). Twelvetrees Pr.

Joel: The Outpouring of God's Glory. Bob Yandian. (Commentaries for Laymen Ser.). 160p. (Orig.). 1986. pap. 5.95 o.p. (ISBN 0-89274-402-2). Harrison Hse.

Joe's Junk. Susan Russo. LC 81-13228. (Illus.). 32p. (gr. k-2). 1982. 9.95 o.s.i. (ISBN 0-03-061264-0). H Holt & Co.

Joe's World. Muriel Dobbin. LC 83-45060. (Illus.). 128p. 1983. 10.95 o.p. (ISBN 0-689-11426-5, Atheneum). Macmillan.

Joetta Community Library: A Simulation Exercise in Library Administration. Robert E. Brown. (Occasional Papers: No. 118). 78p. 1975. pap. 2.00 o.p. (ISBN 0-317-58931-8). U of Ill Lib Info Sci.

Joey. Wendy Kesselman. LC 72-83434. (Illus.). 64p. (Orig.). (gr. 3-6). 1972. 5.95 o.p. (ISBN 0-88208-005-9); pap. 3.95 o.p. (ISBN 0-88208-031-8). Chicago Review.

Joey & DeVon. James Bruce Eure. 1976. 8.00 o.p. (ISBN 0-682-48414-8). Exposition-Phoenix.

Joey Green Loves Red Balloons. Wanda J. Groves. 32p. 1986. 5.75 o.p. (ISBN 0-8062-2772-9). Carlton.

Joey Runs Away. Jack Kent. LC 85-3673. (Illus.). 32p. (gr. k-3). 1985. 12.95 o.s.i. (ISBN 0-13-510462-9). P-H.

Jogging. William J. Bowerman & W. E. Harris. 1978. pap. text ed. 1.75 o.p. (ISBN 0-441-40560-6). Ace Bks.

Jogging for Health & Fitness. Frank Rosato. 108p. pap. 6.95x o.p. Morton Pub.

Johann Sebastian Bach. Hannsdieter Wohlfarth. Tr. by Albert L. Blackwell. LC 84-47916. (Illus.). 128p. 1985. pap. 14.95 o.p. (ISBN 0-8006-0736-8, 1-736, Fortress). Augsburg Fortress.

Johann Sebastian Bach: Life, Times, Influence. Ed. by B. Schwendowius & W. Domling. (Illus.). 1977. 45.00 o.s.i. (ISBN 3-7618-0589-6). E J Brill USA.

Johanna Lindsey, 4 vols. 1981. Set. pap. 10.45 o.p. (ISBN 0-380-78444-0, 78444). Avon.

Johannesburg Requiem. Sheila Roberts. LC 79-25581. 182p. 1980. 8.95 o.s.i. (ISBN 0-8008-4405-X). Taplinger.

Johannine Christianity: Essays on Its Setting, Sources, & Theology. Moody D. Smith. 233p. 1985. 21.95x o.p. (ISBN 0-87249-449-7). U of SC Pr.

Johannine Circle. Oscar Cullmann. Tr. by John Bowden. LC 75-42249. 1976. 6.95 o.s.i. (ISBN 0-664-20744-8, Westminster). Westminster John Knox.

Johannis Dominici Lucula Noctis. Edmund Hunt. (Mediaeval Studies Ser.: No. 4). 1940. 45.00 o.p. (ISBN 0-268-00146-4). U of Notre Dame Pr.

Johannnes Brahms & Theodor Billroth: Letters From a Musical Friendship. Johannes Brahms. 264p. Repr. of 1957 ed. lib. bdg. 39.00 o.p. (Pub. by Am Repr Serv). Reprint Servs.

John, Vol. IV. Beacon Bible Expositions Staff. 6.95 o.p. (ISBN 0-8010-0777-1). Baker Bk.

John: A Good News Commentary. J. Ramsey Michaels. LC 83-47729. (Good News Commentary Ser.). 288p. (Orig.). 1983. pap. 9.95 o.p. (ISBN 0-06-065575-5, RD-462). HarpR.

John A. Williams. Gilbert H. Muller. (United States Authors Ser.: No. 472). 167p. 1984. lib. bdg. 19.50 o.s.i. (ISBN 0-8057-7413-0, Twayne). G K Hall.

John: Acts, Vol. VII. Beacon Bible Commentary Staff. 15.95 o.p. (ISBN 0-8010-0694-5). Baker Bk.

John Andrews. Lamia Doumato. (Architecture Ser.: A 1454). 9p. 1985. 2.00 o.p. (ISBN 0-89028-544-6). Vance Biblios.

John-Apostle of Love. Earl McQuay. LC 81-70774. (Chosen Messenger Ser.). 128p. (Orig.). 1982. pap. text ed. 3.50 o.p. (ISBN 0-89636-080-6). Accent Bks.

John Arden. Frances Gray. LC 82-47993. (Illus.). 180p. (Orig.). 1982. pap. 9.95 o.p. (ISBN 0-394-62415-7, E820, Ever). Grove.

John Ashbery: A Comprehensive Bibliography. David K. Kermani. LC 75-5138. (Reference Library of the Humanities). (Illus.). 220p. 1976. lib. bdg. 36.00 o.p. (ISBN 0-8240-9997-4). Garland Pub.

John Barth: An Annotated Bibliography. Joseph Weixlmann. LC 75-24076. (Reference Library of the Humanities: Vol. 25). 250p. 1976. lib. bdg. 32.00 o.p. (ISBN 0-8240-9987-7). Garland Pub.

John Barth: An Introduction. David Morrell. LC 75-27284. (Illus.). 256p. 1976. 22.50x o.s.i. (ISBN 0-271-01220-X). Pa St U Pr.

John Barth, Jerzy Kosinski & Thomas Pynchon. Thomas P. Walsh & Cameron Northouse. 1978. lib. bdg. 19.00 o.p. (ISBN 0-8161-7910-7, Hall Reference). G K Hall.

John Berryman: A Reference Guide. Gary Q. Arpin. 1976. lib. bdg. 22.50 o.p. (ISBN 0-8161-7804-6, Hall Reference). G K Hall.

John Bull & the Papists; or, Passages in the Life of an Anglican Rector, 1846. A. H. Edgar. Ed. by Robert L. Wolff. (Victorian Fiction Ser.). 1976. lib. bdg. 73.00 o.p. (ISBN 0-8240-1527-4). Garland Pub.

John Bunyan: Pilgrim's Prayer Book. rev. ed. John Bunyan & Louis G. Parkhurst, Jr. 136p. 1986. pap. 5.95 o.p. (ISBN 0-8423-4933-2). Tyndale.

John Bunyan, (1628-1688) His Life, Times & Work. John Brown. Ed. by Frank M. Harrison. (Illus.). xxiv, 515p. 1969. Repr. of 1928 ed. 39.50 o.p. (ISBN 0-208-00726-1, Archon). Shoe String.

John Burgoyne of Saratoga. James Lunt. LC 75-15699. (Illus.). 369p. 1975. 14.95 o.p. (ISBN 0-15-146402-2). HarBraceJ.

John Burningham's Number Play Series: A Great New Concept in Teaching Math, 6 bks. John Burningham. Incl. Pigs Plus: Learning Addition. LC 82-51283. 1983. 4.95 (ISBN 0-670-55508-8); Ride Off: Learning Subtraction. LC 82-51278. 1983. 4.95 (ISBN 0-670-59798-8); Read One: Numbers as Words. LC 82-51281. 1983. 4.95 (ISBN 0-670-58986-1); Five Down: Numbers as Signs. LC 82-51279. 1983. 4.95 o.p. (ISBN 0-670-31698-9); Count Up: Learning Sets. LC 82-51282. 1983. 4.95 (ISBN 0-670-24410-4); Just Cats: Learning Groups. LC 82-51280. 1983. 4.95 (ISBN 0-670-41094-2). (Illus.). (ps-k). 1983 (Viking Kestrel). Penguin USA.

John Burroughs, Naturalist. Elizabeth B. Kelley. 1959. 7.50 o.p. (ISBN 0-682-40054-8, Banner). Exposition-Phoenix.

John C. Portman, Jr. The Man & His Architecture. Frances Gretes. (Architecture Ser.: A 1395). 10p. 1985. 2.00 o.p. (ISBN 0-89028-405-9). Vance Biblios.

John Calvin: A Biography. T. H. Parker. LC 75-33302. (Illus.). 208p. 1976. 10.95 o.s.i. (ISBN 0-664-20810-X, Westminster). Westminster John Knox.

John Calvin vs. the Westminster Confession. Holmes Rolston, III. LC 75-37422. (Orig.). 1972. pap. 4.95 o.p. (ISBN 0-8042-0488-8, John Knox). Westminster John Knox.

John Calvin's Treatises Against the Anabaptists & Against the Libertines. John Calvin. Tr. by Benjamin W. Farley. 360p. (Orig.). 1982. pap. 16.95 o.p. (ISBN 0-8010-2476-5). Baker Bk.

John Carter of Mars. Edgar Rice Burroughs. LC 64-15790. (Illus.). 12.50 o.p. (ISBN 0-940724-04-9). A E Ryter.

John Chisum: Jinglebob King of the Pecus. Mary W. Clarke. (Illus.). 160p. 1985. 11.95 o.p. (ISBN 0-89015-465-1). Eakin Pr.

John Clancy's Christmas Cookbook. John Clancy. (Illus.). 1982. 17.50 o.p. (ISBN 0-87851-207-1). Hearst Bks.

John Clare Reference Guide. H. O. Dendurent. 1978. 24.00 o.p. (ISBN 0-8161-8071-7, Hall Reference). G K Hall.

John Cobb's Theology in Process. Ed. by David R. Griffin & Thomas J. Altizer. LC 77-23135. 212p. 1977. 17.50 o.s.i. (ISBN 0-664-21292-1, Westminster). Westminster John Knox.

John Coltrane. Bill Cole. LC 76-14289. (Illus.). 1978. pap. 10.95 o.s.i. (ISBN 0-02-870500-9). Schirmer Bks.

John Coltrane. Bill Cole. LC 76-14289. (Illus.). 1976. 14.95 o.s.i. (ISBN 0-02-870660-9). Schirmer Bks.

John Come Down the Backstay. Caroline Tapley. LC 73-84839. (Illus.). 192p. (gr. 4-6). 1974. 6.25 o.p. (ISBN 0-689-30149-9, Atheneum). Macmillan.

John Cougar Mellencamp. (Illus.). 32p. (gr. 4-12). 1985. 4.95 o.p. (ISBN 0-88188-345-X, Pub. by Robus BKs). H Leonard Pub Corp.

John Deere Snowmobile Service-Repair: 1972-1977. David Sales. Ed. by Eric Jorgenson. (Illus.). pap. 8.95 o.p. (ISBN 0-89287-163-6, X950). Clymer Pub.

John Denver. Charles Morse & Ann Morse. LC 74-14551. (Rock 'n Pop Stars Ser.). (Illus.). 32p. (gr. 3-6). 1974. PLB 7.95 o.p. (ISBN 0-87191-392-5); pap. 3.95 o.p. (ISBN 0-89812-104-3). Creative Ed.

John Dewey: Philosopher of Science & Freedom. Ed. by Sidney Hook. LC 76-7567. 1976. Repr. of 1950 ed. lib. bdg. 35.00x o.p. (ISBN 0-8371-8840-7, HOJDP). Greenwood.

John Donne & the New Philosophy. Charles M. Coffin. 1958. Repr. of 1937 ed. text ed. 12.50x o.p. (ISBN 0-391-00444-1). Humanities.

John Donne: Devotions Upon Emergent Occasions. Ed. by Anthony Raspa. 248p. 1976. 20.00x o.p. (ISBN 0-7735-0194-0, McGill Canada). U of Toronto Pr.

John Donne: Language & Style. A. C. Partridge. (Language Library). 259p. 1978. 24.95x o.p. (ISBN 0-233-97030-4). Basil Blackwell.

John Donne: The Critical Heritage. Ed. by A. J. Smith. (Critical Heritage Ser.). 448p. 1975. 40.00x o.p. (ISBN 0-7100-8242-8). Routledge Chapman & Hall.

John Doyle Lee: Zealot, Pioneer Builder, Scapegoat. Juanita Brooks. LC 84-12849. 406p. 1984. pap. 12.50 o.s.i. (ISBN 0-935704-21-3). Howe Brothers.

John Drinkwater: A Comprehensive Bibliography of His Works. Michael Pearce. LC 76-24745. (Reference Library of the Humanities Ser.: Vol. 66). 1977. lib. bdg. 31.00 o.p. (ISBN 0-8240-9932-X). Garland Pub.

John Dunton & the English Book Trade: A Study of His Career with a Checklist of His Publications. Stephen Parks. LC 75-24078. (Reference Library of the Humanities: Vol. 40). 450p. 1976. lib. bdg. 73.00 o.p. (ISBN 0-8240-9965-6). Garland Pub.

John Evelyn & His Times. B. Saunders. 1970. 50.00 o.p. (ISBN 0-08-007118-X). Pergamon.

John F. Kennedy. American. Charles Dollen. (Illus., Orig.). 1965. 5.00 o.p. (ISBN 0-8198-0068-6); pap. 4.00 o.p. (ISBN 0-8198-0069-4). Dghtrs St Paul.

John Fell, the University Press & the Fell Types. Stanley Morison. LC 78-74401. (Nineteenth-Century Book Arts & Printing History Ser.: Vol. 14). 315p. 1980. lib. bdg. 100.00 o.p. (ISBN 0-8240-3888-6). Garland Pub.

John Ford Movie Mystery. Andrew Sarris. LC 75-37286. (Illus.). 192p. 1976. pap. 6.95 o.p. (ISBN 0-253-28515-1). Ind U Pr.

John Fowles: A Reference Guide. Barry N. Olshen & Toni A. Olshen. 1980. lib. bdg. 19.00 o.p. (ISBN 0-8161-8187-X, Hall Reference). G K Hall.

John Foxe. Warren W. Wooden. (English Authors Ser.). 1983. lib. bdg. 18.95 o.p. (ISBN 0-8057-6830-0, Twayne). G K Hall.

John Foxe & the Elizabethan Church. V. Norskov Olsen. 1973. 42.00x o.p. (ISBN 0-520-02075-8). U of Cal Pr.

John Gibson Lockhart: Petter's Letters to His Kinfolk. Ed. by William Ruddick. 1977. 12.50x o.p. (ISBN 0-7073-0135-1, Pub. by Scot Acad Pr). Longwood Pub Group.

John Gielgud: A Celebration. Gielgud Brandeth. LC 83-83217. (Illus.). 186p. 1984. 14.45i o.p. (ISBN 0-316-10634-8). Little.

John Gilley of Baker's Island. Charles W. Eliot. 72p. 1985. pap. text ed. 2.50 o.p. (ISBN 0-934745-03-X). Acadia Pub Co.

John Gould, the Bird Man: A Chronology & Bibliography. Gordon C. Sauer. (Illus.). xxiv, 416p. 1982. 65.00 o.p. (ISBN 0-7006-0230-5). U Pr of KS.

John Halifax, Gentleman. Dinah M. Mulock. 1983. pap. text ed. 5.95x o.p. (ISBN 0-460-11123-X, Evman). Biblio Dist.

John Hawkes. Patrick O'Donnell. (United States Authors Ser.). 1982. lib. bdg. 14.50 o.p. (ISBN 0-8057-7351-7, Twayne). G K Hall.

John Hedgecoe's Complete Course in Photographing Children. John Hedgecoe. (Illus.). 1985. pap. 10.95 o.p. (ISBN 0-671-54278-8). S&S.

John Hedgecoe's Darkroom Techniques. John Hedgecoe. LC 84-5457. (Illus.). 191p. 1985. pap. 10.95 o.s.i. (ISBN 0-671-50890-3). S&S.

John Hedgecoe's Nude Photography. John Hedgecoe. (Illus.). 208p. 1984. 24.45 o.p. (ISBN 0-671-52326-0). S&S.

John Hedgecoe's Photographer's Workbook. John Hedgecoe. (Illus.). 153p. 1985. 9.95 o.p. (ISBN 0-671-50806-7). S&S.

John Hedgecoe's Taking Great Photographs. John Hedgecoe. 1984. 12.95 o.p. (ISBN 0-671-50807-5). S&S.

John Heywood's Works & Miscellaneous Short Poems. John Heywood. Intro. by Burton A. Milligan. LC 80-12408. (Illinois Studies in Language & Literature: Vol. 41). xi, 297p. 1980. Repr. of 1956 ed. lib. bdg. 41.50x o.p. (ISBN 0-8371-9075-4, HEWO). Greenwood.

John Hogan: Irish Neoclassical Sculptor in Rome 1800-1858: A Biography & Catalogue Raisonne. John Turpin. (Illus.). 216p. 1982. text ed. 27.50x o.p. (ISBN 0-7165-0212-7, BBA 04796, Pub by Irish Academic Pr Ireland). Biblio Dist.

John Humphrey Noyes: The Putney Community. Ed. by George W. Noyes. (Illus.). 1931. 30.00x o.p. (ISBN 0-8156-8059-7). Syracuse U Pr.

John Huston: Maker of Magic. Stuart M. Kaminsky. LC 77-17017. 1978. 10.95 o.p. (ISBN 0-395-25716-6). HM.

John J. McCarthy's Secrets of Super Selling. John J. McCarthy. LC 82-9533. 320p. 1982. 50.00 o.p. (ISBN 0-932648-25-8). Boardroom.

John J. Pershing, General of the Armies: A Biography. Frederick Palmer. 1970. Repr. of 1948 ed. lib. bdg. 22.50x o.p. (ISBN 0-8371-2986-9, PAJP). Greenwood.

John James Wettstein, Sixteen Ninety-Three to Seventeen Fifty-Four: An Account of His Life, Work, & Some of His Contemporaries. Charles L. Powell. (Church Historical Society London Ser.: No. 31). Repr. of 1938 ed. 60.00 o.p. (ISBN 0-8115-3155-4). Kraus Repr.

John, Jude, Revelation, Vol. XII. Beacon Bible Expositions Staff. 282p. 1983. text ed. 6.95 o.p. (ISBN 0-8010-0789-5). Baker Bk.

John Keats. John Keats. (Pocket Poets Ser.). 1963. pap. 3.50 o.p. (ISBN 0-289-27745-0). Dufour.

John Keble: Priest, Professor & Poet. Brian W. Martin. 191p. 1976. 25.00 o.p. (ISBN 0-85664-381-5, Pub. by Croom Helm Ltd). Routledge Chapman & Hall.

John Knox. Eustace Percy. LC 65-11937. 1965. 7.95 o.p. (ISBN 0-8042-0924-3, John Knox). Westminster John Knox.

John Knox in Controversy. Hugh Watt. 1951. (ISBN 0-8022-1820-2). Philos Lib.

John Lautner: Bibliography & Building List. Edward H. Teague. (Architecture Ser.: Bibliography A 1345). 1985. pap. 2.00 o.p. (ISBN 0-89028-315-X). Vance Biblios.

John Leech: His Life & Work, 2 Vols. William P. Frith. LC 69-17491. 286p. 1969. Repr. of 1891 ed. Set. 65.00x o.p. (ISBN 0-8103-3831-9). Gale.

John Lennon. Tony Bradman. (Profiles Ser.). (Illus.). 64p. (gr. 5-8). 1986. 9.95 o.p. (ISBN 0-241-11561-2, Pub. by Hamish Hamilton England). David & Charles.

John Lennon & Julian Lennon. Nancy Martin. (Avon Superstar Ser.). 1986. pap. 2.50 o.p. (ISBN 0-380-75083-X). Avon.

John Lennon: One Day at a Time: A Personal Biography of the Seventies. rev. ed. Anthony Fawcett. LC 80-8060. (Illus.). 192p. 1981. pap. 8.95 o.p. (ISBN 0-394-17754-1, E772, Ever). Grove.

John: Living Eternally. J. Allen Blair. LC 77-28529. 1978. pap. 4.95 o.p. (ISBN 0-87213-046-0). Loizeaux.

John Locke. Geraint Parry. (Political Thinkers Ser.). 1978. text ed. 21.00x o.p. (ISBN 0-04-320130-X); pap. text ed. 11.95x o.p. (ISBN 0-04-320131-8). Unwin Hyman.

John Locke: A Reference Guide. John W. Yolton & Jean S. Yolton. (Reference Guides to Literature Ser.). 1985. lib. bdg. 54.50 o.s.i. (ISBN 0-8161-8236-1, Hall Reference). G K Hall.

John Locke & English Literature of the Eighteenth Century. Kenneth MacLean. Ed. by Peter A Schouls. LC 83-48573. (Philosophy of John Locke Ser.: Vol. 9). 184p. 1984. lib. bdg. 25.00 o.p. (ISBN 0-8240-5608-6). Garland Pub.

John Locke & the Doctrine of Majority-Rule. Willmoore Kendall. LC 41-52730. (Studies in Social Science Ser: Vol. 26, No. 2). 141p. 1965. pap. 6.95 o.p. (ISBN 0-252-72499-2). U of Ill Pr.

John Locke, Physician & Philosopher. Kenneth Dewhurst. LC 83-48567. (Philosophy of John Locke Ser.). 343p. 1985. lib. bdg. 40.00 o.p. (ISBN 0-8240-5602-7). Garland Pub.

John M. Synge: A Few Personal Recollections. John Masefield. 48p. 1971. Repr. of 1915 ed. 15.00x o.p. (ISBN 0-7165-1348-X, BBA 02068, Pub. by Cuala Press Ireland). Biblio Dist.

John McLoughlin: Father of Oregon. Robert C. Johnson. LC 58-11483. (Illus.). 330p. 1975. pap. 9.95 o.p. (ISBN 0-8323-0283-X). Binford-Metropolitan.

John Maher of Delancey Street: A Guide for Peaceful Revolution in America. Grover Sales. (Illus.). 176p. 1976. 7.95 o.p. (ISBN 0-393-07499-4). Norton.

John Marshall. Teri Martini. LC 73-11430. (Illus.). (gr. 4-7). 1974. 5.25 o.s.i. (ISBN 0-664-32540-8, Westminster). Westminster John Knox.

John Marston: A Reference Guide. Kenneth Tucker. (RGL Ser.). 1985. lib. bdg. 54.95 o.s.i. (ISBN 0-8161-8355-4). G K Hall.

John Masefield's Letters from the Front 1915-1917. Ed. by Peter Vansittart. LC 84-51644. 307p. 1985. 18.95 o.p. (ISBN 0-531-09776-5). Watts.

John Maynard Keynes: Critical Assessments, 4 vols. Ed. by John C. Wood. (Leading Economists Ser.). 2096p. 1983. Set. 495.00 o.p. (ISBN 0-7099-2729-0, Pub. by Croom Helm Ltd). Routledge Chapman & Hall.

John Merven Carrere: Eighteen Fifty-Eight to Nineteen Eleven. Lamia Doumato. (Architecture Ser.: Bibliography A 1340). 1985. pap. 2.25 o.p. (ISBN 0-89028-310-9). Vance Biblios.

John Nash: Architect to King George the Fourth. John N. Summerson. LC 35-10833. 295p. 1935. Repr. 29.00x o.p. (ISBN 0-403-03876-6). Somerset Pub.

John O. Meusebach: German Colonizer in Texas. Irene M. King. 206p. 1967. pap. 9.95 o.p. (ISBN 0-292-73656-8). U of Tex Pr.

John Osborne: A Reference Guide. Cameron Northouse & Thomas P. Walsh. (Series Seventy: No. 2). 1977. lib. bdg. 19.00 o.p. (ISBN 0-8161-1152-9, Hall Reference). G K Hall.

John Prebble's Scotland. John Prebble. (Illus.). 288p. 1985. 34.95 o.p. (ISBN 0-436-38634-8, Pub. by Secker & Warburg UK). David & Charles.

John Prip: Master Metalsmith. Tim McCreight et al. LC 87-62619. (Illus.). 52p. (Orig.). 1987. pap. 10.00 o.p. (ISBN 0-911517-48-0). Mus of Art RI.

John Quincy Adams & the Foundations of American Foreign Policy. Samuel F. Bemis. (Illus.). 640p. 1973. pap. 4.95 o.p. (ISBN 0-393-00684-0, N684, Norton Lib). Norton.

John Rastell. Albert Geritz & Amos L. Laine. (English Authors Ser.). 135p. 1983. lib. bdg. 18.95 o.p. (ISBN 0-8057-6849-1, Twayne). G K Hall.

John Rawls & His Critics. David T. Mason & J. H. Wellbank. LC 81-43347. 500p. 1982. lib. bdg. 91.00 o.p. (ISBN 0-8240-9285-6). Garland Pub.

John Ross, Cherokee Chief. Gary Moulton. LC 76-1146. 292p. 1978. pap. 17.00x o.p. (ISBN 0-8203-0422-0). U of Ga Pr.

John Ruskin. Frederic Harrison. LC 72-78229. 224p. 1971. Repr. of 1902 ed. 30.00x o.p. (ISBN 0-8103-3719-3). Gale.

John Skelton: The Complete English Poems. John Skelton. Ed. by John Scattergood. LC 82-16075. (Yale English Poets Ser.). 560p. 1983. text ed. 32.50 o.p. (ISBN 0-300-02970-5); pap. text ed. 12.95 o.p. (ISBN 0-300-02971-3). Yale U Pr.

John Stainer. Peter Charlton. (Illus.). 208p. 1984. 39.95 o.s.i. (ISBN 0-7153-8387-6). David & Charles.

John Stainier. Ward Rutherford. LC 75-31326. (Island Ser). (Illus.). 1976. 18.95 o.p. (ISBN 0-7153-7075-8). David & Charles.

John Steinbeck. Warren French. (United States Authors Ser.). 192p. 1984. pap. 7.95 o.s.i. (ISBN 0-8057-7424-6, Twayne). G K Hall.

John Steinbeck: The California Years. Brian St. Pierre. LC 83-17186. (Illus.). 128p. 1984. pap. 7.95 o.p. (ISBN 0-87701-281-4). Chronicle Bks.

John Stuart Mill: Critical Assessments, 4 vols. Ed. by John C. Wood. 1986. 475.00 o.p. (ISBN 0-7099-3686-9, Pub. by Croom Helm UK). Routledge Chapman & Hall.

John Taverner: Part 1. Ed. by P. C. Buck. (Tudor Church Music Ser.: Vol. 1). 1963. Repr. of 1923 ed. Broude.

John Taverner: Part 2. Ed. by P. C. Buck. (Tudor Church Music Ser.: Vol. 3). 1963. Repr. of 1924 ed. 85.00x o.p. Broude.

John Taylor: Mormon Philosopher, Prophet of God. Francis M. Gibbons. LC 84-73532. 312p. 1985. 10.95 o.p. (ISBN 0-87747-714-0). Deseret Bk.

John Travolta: Staying Fit! John Travolta. (Illus.). 1984. 15.45 o.p. (ISBN 0-671-49798-7). S&S.

John W. Foster: Politics & Diplomacy in the Imperial Era, 1873-1917. Michael J. Devine. LC 80-17387. (Illus.). x, 187p. 1981. 18.00x o.p. (ISBN 0-8214-0437-7, 82-83244). Ohio U Pr.

John Webb & Seventeenth Century English Architecture: A Selected Bibliography. Bibliographic Research Library Staff. (Architecture Ser.: A 1388). 6p. 1985. 2.00 o.p. (ISBN 0-89028-398-2). Vance Biblios.

John Wesley's England: A Nineteenth Century Pictorial History Based on an 18th Century Journal. Ed. by Richard Bewes. (Illus.). 128p. (Orig.). 1981. pap. 9.95 o.p. (ISBN 0-8164-2319-9). HarpR.

John Wesley's Journal. Abridged by Nehemiah Crunock. 1951. (ISBN 0-8022-1852-0). Philos Lib.

John Wilhelm's Guide to Mexico. 5th ed. John Wilhelm. 1978. text ed. 13.95 o.p. (ISBN 0-07-070289-6). McGraw.

John Wilmot, Earl of Rochester: His Life & Writings. Johannes Prinz. Repr. of 1927 ed. 59.00x o.p. (ISBN 0-403-04129-5). Somerset Pub.

John Wise, Early American Democrat. George A. Cook. 1967. lib. bdg. 18.50x o.p. (ISBN 0-374-91919-4, Octagon). Hippocrene Bks.

John Witherspoon: Parson, Politician, Patriot. Martha L. Stohlman. LC 88-26132. (Illus.). 1989. 7.95 o.s.i.; pap. 7.95 o.s.i. (ISBN 0-664-24795-4). Westminster John Knox.

John Young: Space Shuttle Commander. Paul Westman. LC 81-15264. (Taking Part Ser.). (Illus.). 48p. (gr. 3 up). 1981. PLB 9.95 o.p. (ISBN 0-87518-223-2). Dillon.

Johnnie Coeur. Romain Gary. pap. 4.95 o.p. (ISBN 0-685-34127-5). Schoenhof.

Johnny Come Lately: A Short History of the Condom. Jeannette Parisot. (Illus.). 144p. (Orig.). 1988. pap. 12.50 o.p. (Journeyman Pr England). Riverrun NY.

Johnny Lincoln & His Three Dogs. Joyce S. Carver. (Illus.). 38p. 1982. 5.50 o.p. (ISBN 0-682-49920-X). Exposition-Phoenix.

Johnny Osage. Janice H. Giles. 1977. pap. 1.75 o.p. (ISBN 0-380-01810-1, 35667). Avon.

Johnny Takes a Reigncheck. David L. Sloan. 272p. 1983. 12.00 o.p. (ISBN 0-682-49986-2). Exposition-Phoenix.

Johnny's Such a Bright Boy, What a Shame He's Retarded. Kate Long. 1978. 10.00 o.p. (ISBN 0-395-25346-2); pap. 4.95 o.p. (ISBN 0-395-27164-9). HM.

John's Choice. Jane B. Moncure. LC 82-7461. (Illus.). 32p. (gr. 3-4). 1982. lib. bdg. 4.95 o.p. Dandelion Hse.

John's Magic: John Bosco. Dolores Ready. LC 77-86595. (Stories About Christian Heroes Ser.). (Illus.). (gr. 1-5). 1977. pap. 1.95 o.p. (ISBN 0-86683-765-5). HarpR.

Johnson J. Hooper. Paul Somers, Jr. (United States Authors Ser.: No. 454). 1984. lib. bdg. 19.95 o.s.i. (ISBN 0-8057-7394-0, Twayne). G K Hall.

Johnson Service-Repair Handbook: 1.5 to 35 Hp, 1965-1983. Clymer Publications. (Illus.). pap. 9.00 o.p. (ISBN 0-89287-230-6, B663). Clymer Pub.

Johnson Service-Repair Handbook: 40-140hp, 1965-1983. Ed. by Eric Jorgensen. (Illus.). pap. 9.00 o.p. (ISBN 0-89287-219-5, B665). Clymer Pub.

Johnson's Wonder-Working Providence, 1638-1651. Ed. by J. Franklin Jameson. (Original Narratives). 284p. 1967. Repr. of 1910 ed. 21.50x o.p. (ISBN 0-06-480428-3). B&N Imports.

Joi Bangla! The Children of Bangladesh. Jason Laure & Ettagale Laure. LC 74-14394. (Illus.). 160p. (gr. 7 up). 1974. 9.95 o.p. (ISBN 0-374-33780-2). FS&G.

Joiner. James Whitehead. 1979. pap. 1.50 o.p. (ISBN 0-380-01284-7, 41707-3, Bard). Avon.

Joining of Materials for Aerospace Systems Symposium: Proceedings, Dayton OH, 15-17 November 1965. (Science of Advanced Materials & Process Engineering Ser., Vol. 9). 525p. pap. 8.00 o.p. (ISBN 0-938994-09-3). SAMPE.

Joining of the Stone. Shirley R. Murphy. 1983. pap. 2.25 o.p. (ISBN 0-380-65201-3, 65201, Flare). Avon.

Joining the Human Race: How to Teach the Humanities. 2nd ed. Fred E. Schroeder. LC 72-90212. 1973. lib. bdg. 15.00 o.p. (ISBN 0-912112-17-4). Everett-Edwards.

Joining Together: Group Theory & Group Skills. 2nd ed. David W. Johnson & Frank P. Johnson. LC 74-23698. 480p. 1982. pap. text ed. 28.00 o.p. (ISBN 0-13-510396-7). P-H.

Joint Acquisitions List of Africana, 1980 (Supplement to Catalog of the Melville J. Herskovits Library of African Studies, Northwestern University Library, 1972) 856p. 1982. lib. bdg. 130.00 o.s.i. (ISBN 0-8161-0411-5, Pub by Hall Library). G K Hall.

Joint Acquisitions List of Africana: 1978. Northwestern University Staff. 1980. lib. bdg. 95.00 o.s.i. (ISBN 0-8161-0329-1, Hall Library). G K Hall.

Joint Economic Report, 1987. (Illus.). 220p. (Orig.). 1987. pap. 5.00 o.p. (ISBN 0-317-62870-4, S-N 052-071-00684-2). USGPO.

Joint Living Trust Forms Kit (Married) Barbara R. Stock. 54p. 1987. wkbk. 49.95 o.p. (ISBN 0-913455-15-6). Linch Pub.

Joint Practice: A Selected Annotated Bibliography. Patricia Harper. LC 84-13826. (Reference Library of Social Science). 224p. 1984. lib. bdg. 32.50 o.p. (ISBN 0-8240-8776-3). Garland Pub.

Joint Property. Alexander A. Bove. LC 82-5497. 224p. 1982. pap. 8.75 o.p. (ISBN 0-671-44967-2, Fireside). S&S.

Joint Treatment of Industrial & Municipal Wastewaters. H. G. Schwartz, Jr. et al. Ed. by Water Pollution Control Federation Staff. LC 65-5192. (Illus.). 34p. 1976. pap. 4.00 o.p. (ISBN 0-943244-15-3, M0021LN). Water Pollution.

Joint Ventures Between Hospitals & Physicians: A Competitive Strategy for the Healthcare Marketplace. Linda A. Burns & Douglas M. Mancino. 250p. 1986. 35.00 o.p. (ISBN 0-87094-710-9). Dow Jones-Irwin.

Joint Ventures in Mexico. Robert J. Radway. LC 82-13773. (AMA Management Briefing). 1984. pap. 10.00 o.p. (ISBN 0-8144-2273-X). AMACOM.

Joints & Synovial Fluid, Vol. 1. L. Sokoloff. Ed. by Leon Sokoloff. 1978. 78.00 o.p. (ISBN 0-12-655101-4). Acad Pr.

Joke of the Century. David Hughes. 224p. 1986. 14.95 o.s.i. (ISBN 0-8008-4419-X). Taplinger.

Jokes & Riddles. Oscar Weigle. (Elephant Activity Bks.). (Illus.). 128p. (gr. k-3). 1975. pap. 1.50 o.p. (ISBN 0-448-11884-X, G&D); PLB 3.49 o.p. (ISBN 0-448-13618-X). Putnam Pub Group.

Jokes: Context Use & Function. Christopher Wilson. (European Monographs in Social Psychology). 1979. 66.00 o.p. (ISBN 0-12-758150-2). Acad Pr.

Jokes, Jokes, Jokes. Ed. by Helen Hoke. (Terrific Triple Titles Ser). (Illus.). (gr. 4-6). 1963. PLB 12.90 o.p. (ISBN 0-531-01704-4). Watts.

Jolly Hares. S. Mikhalkov. 118p. 1969. 4.45 o.p. (ISBN 0-8285-1170-5, Pub. by Progress Pubs USSR). Imported Pubns.

Jonah. LC 76-11275. (Sunshine Bks.). (Illus.). 20p. (ps-1). 1976. pap. 1.50 o.p. (ISBN 0-8006-1577-8, 1-1577, Fortress). Augsburg Fortress.

Jonah. Ellen G. Traylor. 256p. (Orig.). 1987. pap. 6.95 o.p. (ISBN 0-8423-1946-8). Tyndale.

Jonah & the Great Fish. 2nd ed. Ella K. Lindvall. (People of the Bible Ser.). (Illus.). (gr. 2). 1984. 4.95 o.p. (ISBN 0-8024-0398-0). Moody.

Jonah Complex. Andre Lacocque & Pierre Lacocque. LC 80-84649. 1981. 6.99 o.p. (ISBN 0-8042-0091-2, John Knox); pap. 8.95 o.p. (ISBN 0-8042-0092-0). Westminster John Knox.

Jonah Legend: A Suggestion of Interpretation. William Simpson. LC 72-177422. (Illus.). vi, 192p. 1971. Repr. of 1899 ed. 35.00x o.p. (ISBN 0-8103-3820-3). Gale.

Jonah Watch. Jack Cady. 224p. 1983. pap. 2.75 o.p. (ISBN 0-380-62828-7, 62828-7). Avon.

Jonah Watch: A True-Life Ghost Story in the Form of a Novel. Jack Cady. LC 81-66973. 1982. 12.95 o.p. (ISBN 0-87795-342-2, Arbor Hse). Morrow.

Jonathan Down under. Patricia Beatty. (gr. 5-9). 1982. 10.25 o.p. (ISBN 0-688-01467-4). Morrow.

Jonathan Fisher & the Centerfold Caper. Richard Peck. 160p. 1983. pap. 2.25 o.p. (ISBN 0-380-85209-8, 85209-8, Flare). Avon.

Jonathan Swift: Political Writer. J. A. Downie. 352p. 1984. 50.00x o.p. (ISBN 0-7100-9645-3). Routledge Chapman & Hall.

Jonathan Swift: Political Writer. J. A. Downie. 350p. 1986. pap. text ed. 14.95 o.p. (ISBN 0-7102-0769-7). Routledge Chapman & Hall.

Jones' Animal Nursing. 3rd ed. D. R. Lane. (Illus.). 1980. text ed. 74.00 o.p. (ISBN 0-08-024945-0); pap. text ed. 40.00 o.p. (ISBN 0-08-024944-2). Pergamon.

Jones' Animal Nursing. 2nd ed. Ed. by Roger Pinniger. LC 74-188111. 485p. 1972. text ed. 20.00 o.p. (ISBN 0-08-016839-6). Pergamon.

Jones Road Print Shop & Stable 1971-1981: A Catalogue Raisonne. John Loring & David Acton. Ed. by Trent Myers. (Illus.). 54p. (Orig.). 1983. art catalog 11.95 o.p. (ISBN 0-913883-10-7). Madison Art.

Joni Nineteen Eighty-Nine Planner. Joni E. Tada. 1988. pap. 8.95 spiral bd. o.p. (ISBN 0-89066-115-4). World Wide Pubs.

Jons Moor. Date not set. (ISBN 0-8052-3797-6). Random.

Jonsmod Eighty-Two: A Workshop of the Joint North Sea Modelling Group on Mathematical Models of the North Sea & Surrounding Continental Shelf Seas, Heriot-Watt University, Edinburgh, U. K., Sept. 1-3, 1982. Ed. by P. P. Dyke & N. S. Heaps. 136p. 1984. pap. 26.00 o.p. (ISBN 0-08-031425-2). Pergamon.

Jonson's Masque of Gipsies: In the Burley Belvoir & Windsor Versions. W. W. Greg. 246p. 1979. 10.00x o.p. (ISBN 0-686-26937-3). State Mutual Bk.

Jordan. Middle East Economic Digest Staff. Ed. by Trevor Mostyn. (MEED Practical Guides Ser.). (Illus.). 282p. (Orig.). 1985. pap. 16.95x o.p. (ISBN 0-9505211-8-3). Lynne Rienner.

Jordan's Real Food Guide. David Mabey. 288p. 1986. pap. 6.95 o.p. (ISBN 0-907621-35-X, Pub. by Quiller Pr England). Intl Spec Bk.

Jordons. George Bower. 1984. 15.95 o.p. (ISBN 0-87795-523-9, Arbor Hse). Morrow.

Jorinda & Joringel: Large Print. Adapted by & illus. by Angela Koconda-Brons. (Illus.). 17p. (gr. k-3). 1983. 22.95 o.p. (ISBN 0-88010-089-3, Pub. by Walter Keller Switzerland). Anthroposophic.

Jo's Boys. Louisa May Alcott. (Dent's Illustrated Children's Classics Ser.). (Illus.). 335p. (gr. 6 up). 1976. Repr. of 1960 ed. 10.95x o.p. (ISBN 0-460-05044-3, Pub. by J. M. Dent England). Biblio Dist.

Jo's Search. Dorothy Dart. 136p. (Orig.). 1984. pap. 3.95 o.p. (ISBN 0-86760-014-4, Pub. by Albatross Bks). Meyer Stone Bks.

Jose de Espronceda: An Annotated Bibliography, 1834 to 1978. David J. Billick. LC 80-8514. 200p. 1981. lib. bdg. 43.00 o.p. (ISBN 0-8240-9470-0). Garland Pub.

Jose M. Arguedas: Los Rios profundos. Ed. by William Rowe. LC 73-4524. 288p. 1973. 21.00 o.s.i. (ISBN 0-08-017014-5); pap. 12.75 o.s.i. (ISBN 0-08-017015-3). Pergamon.

Josef Hoffmann's Bestecke Fur die Weiner Werkstatte: Josef Hoffmann's Flatware Designs for Wiener Werkstatte. Waltraud Neuwirth. (Illus.). 316p. 1982. pap. 36.00 o.p. (ISBN 3-900282-18-8, Pub. by Waltraud Neuwirth). Seven Hills Bk Dists.

Joseph: A Story of Divine Providence: A Text Theoretical & Textlinguistic Analysis of Gensis 37 & 39-48. Robert E. Longacre. xiv, 324p. 1988. text ed. write for info. o.p. (ISBN 0-931464-42-0). Eisenbrauns.

Joseph & Anna's Time Capsule: A Legacy of Old Jewish Prague. Chaya M. Burstein. (Illus.). 40p. (gr. 4-7). 1984. 8.70 o.s.i. (ISBN 0-671-50712-5). Summit Bks.

Joseph & Koza, or the Sacrifice to the Vistula. Isaac Bashevis Singer. LC 78-106398. (ps-3). 1970. 4.95 o.p. (ISBN 0-374-33795-0). FS&G.
Joseph & the Amazing Technicolor Dreamcoat. Tim Rice & Andrew L. Webber. LC 81-23722. (Illus.). 48p. (gr. k-4). 1982. 11.45 o.p. (ISBN 0-03-061517-8). H Holt & Co.
Joseph Andrews. Henry Fielding. 401p. rag paper 40.00 o.p. (ISBN 0-913720-25-9, Sandstone); leather bound 60.00 o.p. (ISBN 0-913720-24-0). Beil.
Joseph Andrews & Shamela. Henry Fielding. 1975. Repr. of 1973 ed. 8.95x o.p. (ISBN 0-460-00467-0, Evman); pap. 2.95x o.p. (ISBN 0-460-01467-6, Evman). Biblio Dist.
Joseph Campbell: A Critical Biography. Norah Suanders & A. A. Kelly. 192p. 1987. 31.95 o.p. (ISBN 0-86327-151-0, Pub. by Wolfhound Pr Ireland). Irish Bks Media.
Joseph Conrad. Roger Tennant. LC 80-69393. 1981. 16,95 o.p. (ISBN 0-689-11152-5, Atheneum). Macmillan.
Joseph Conrad: A Study in Existential Vision. R. J. Das. 132p. 1980. text ed. 10.50x o.p. (ISBN 0-391-01915-5). Humanities.
Joseph Conrad & Charles Darwin. R. O'Hanlon. 189p. 1984. text ed. 35.00x o.p. (ISBN 0-391-03120-1). Humanities.
Joseph Conrad & the Ethics of Darwinism: The Challenges of Science. Allan Hunter. 259p. 1983. 38.50 o.p. (ISBN 0-7099-1265-X, Pub. by Croom Helm Ltd). Routledge Chapman & Hall.
Joseph Conrad & the Fiction of Autobiography. Edward W. Said. LC 66-18255. 1966. 15.00x o.p. (ISBN 0-674-48350-2). Harvard U Pr.
Joseph Conrad & the West: Signs of Empire. Jacques Darras. 164p. 1982. 28.50x o.p. (ISBN 0-389-20071-9). B&N Imports.
Joseph Conrad: Theme & Treatment of Evil, Vol. 3. R. K. Kapur. (English Language & Literature Ser.). 150p. 1978. 10.50x o.p. (ISBN 0-391-02541-4). Humanities.
Joseph E. Brown & the Confederacy. Louis B. Hill. LC 70-138612. 360p. 1973. Repr. of 1939 ed. lib. bdg. 35.00x o.p. (ISBN 0-8371-5722-6, HIJB). Greenwood.
Joseph Rusling Meeker: Images of the Mississippi. C. R. Brown. LC 81-83078. (Delta Ser.). (Illus.). 40p. (Orig.). 1981. pap. 7.00 o.p. (ISBN 0-89280-018-6). Montgomery Mus.
Joseph Smith & the Beginning of Mormonism. Richard L. Bushman. LC 84-2451. 272p. 1988. pap. 8.95 o.p. (ISBN 0-252-06012-1). U of Ill Pr.
Joseph Smith & World Government. Hyrum L. Andrus. 144p. 1972. pap. 3.95 o.p. (ISBN 0-89036-032-4). Hawkes Pub Inc.
Joseph Urban & American Theater Architecture: A Selected Bibliography. Bibliographic Research Library Staff. (Architecture Ser.: A 1391). 5p. 1985. 2.00 o.p. (ISBN 0-89028-401-6). Vance Biblios.
Joseph Wood Krutch. John S. Margolis. Date not set. write for info. o.p. U of Tenn Pr.
Josephine Clardy Fox. Ruby Burns. LC 73-83925. 1970. 8.00 o.p. (ISBN 0-87404-042-6). Tex Western.
Josephine Herbst: The Story She Could Never Tell. Elinor Langer. (Illus.). 384p. 1984. 19.95 o.p. (ISBN 0-316-51399-7). Little.
Josephine: The Empress & Her Children. Nina Epton. (Illus.). 256p. 1976. 10.95 o.p. (ISBN 0-393-07500-1). Norton.
Josh Carter & the Old Stagecoach Mystery. William C. Odell. (Windrider Ser.). 176p. (gr. 6-8). 1986. 3.50 o.p. (ISBN 0-8423-1964-6). Tyndale.
Josh Lawton. Melvyn Bragg. 208p. 1989. 19.95 o.p. (ISBN 0-340-42329-3, Pub. by Hodder & Stoughton UK). David & Charles.
Joshua, a Model for Leadership. Harold W. Hambley. 72p. 1986. 7.95 o.p. (ISBN 0-8062-2870-9). Carlton.
Joshua-Esther, Vol. II. Beacon Bible Commentary Staff. 15.95 o.p. (ISBN 0-8010-0689-9). Baker Bk.
Joshua-Esther see Mastering Old Testament Facts.
Joshua, Judges, Samuel, Kings. Walter E. Rast. Ed. by Foster R. McCurley. LC 78-54559. (Proclamation Commentaries: the Old Testament Witnesses for Preaching). 132p. 1978. pap. 4.95 o.p. (ISBN 0-8006-0594-2, 1-594, Fortress). Augsburg Fortress.
Joshua Slocum. Walter M. Teller. LC 71-163954. 1971. 30.00 o.p. (ISBN 0-8135-0700-6). Rutgers U Pr.
Joshua, the Czar, & the Chicken Bone Wish. Barbara Girion. LC 78-15012. (Illus.). (gr. 4-6). 1978. 10.95 o.s.i. (ISBN 0-684-15929-5, Pub. by Scribner). Macmillan.
Josiah Wedgewood. Samuel Smiles. LC 71-141603. 322p. 1971. Repr. of 1894 ed. 43.00x o.p. (ISBN 0-8103-3617-0). Gale.
Josiah Willard Gibbs - American Physicist Par Excellance. Raymond J. Seeger. (Men of Physics Ser.). 1974. 51.00 o.p. (ISBN 0-08-018013-2). Pergamon.
Josiah Willard Gibbs: The History of a Great Mind. Lynde P. Wheeler. LC 76-113021. (Illus.). xiii, 270p. 1970. Repr. of 1962 ed. 27.50 o.p. (ISBN 0-208-00826-8, Archon). Shoe String.
Josie's Way. Winifred Wolfe. LC 79-56018. 1980. 9.95 o.p. (ISBN 0-87795-259-0, Arbor Hse). Morrow.
Joslin Diabetes Manual. 11th ed. Ed. by Leo P. Krall. LC 77-29115. (Illus.). 324p. 1978. pap. 8.50 o.p. (ISBN 0-8121-0607-5). Lea & Febiger.
Josquin Des Prez's "Missa Pange Lingua" An Edition, with Notes for Performance & Commentary. Thomas Warburton. LC 76-22703. (Early Musical Masterworks--Critical Editions & Commentaries). ix, 63p. 1977. 22.00x o.p. (ISBN 0-8078-1296-X). U of NC Pr.
Jour de L'Homme see This Day Is Ours.
Journal Intimes. Benjamin Constant. 9.95 o.p. (ISBN 0-686-54611-3). French & Eur.
Journal Nineteen Forty-Two to Nineteen Forty-Nine. Andre Gide. (Fr.). pap. 7.95 o.p. (ISBN 0-685-34149-6). Schoenhof.
Journal, Nineteen Thirty-Nine to Nineteen Forty-Two. Andre Gide. (Fr.). pap. 6.95 o.p. (ISBN 0-685-34148-8). Schoenhof.
Journal of a Residence in the Sandwich Islands, 1823-1825. C. S. Stewart. LC 71-135064. (Sandwich Islands Publications). (Illus.). 1971. Repr. of 1830 ed. text ed. 10.00x o.p. (ISBN 0-87022-772-6). UH Pr.
Journal of a Soul. Pope John XXIII. Tr. by Dorothy White. LC 79-7786. (Illus.). 504p. 1980. pap. 7.95 o.p. (ISBN 0-385-14842-9, Im). Doubleday.
Journal of a Voyage to New York & a Tour in Several of the American Colonies in Sixteen Seventy-Nine to Sixteen Eighty. Jasper Danckaerts & Peter Sluyter. Ed. by Henry C. Murphy. xv, 437p. 1967. Repr. of 1867 ed. 28.00 o.p. (ISBN 0-8398-0351-6). Parnassus Imprints.
Journal of Aircraft, Vol. 24. Ed. by Thomas M. Weeks. 1987. 215.00 o.p. (ISBN 0-317-66156-6). AIAA.
Journal of Eugene Delacroix. Eugene Delacroix. Ed. by Herbert Wellington. Tr. by Lucy Norton. (Landmarks in Art History Ser.). (Illus.). 517p. 1980. Paperback Ser. pap. 14.95 o.p. (ISBN 0-8014-9196-7). Cornell U Pr.
Journal of Guidance, Control, & Dynamics, Vol. 10. Ed. by Donald C. Fraser. (J). 1987. 125.00 o.p. (ISBN 0-317-36784-6). AIAA.
Journal of Jewish Bibliography, 4 vols. Ed. by Bloch. Set. 35.00 o.s.i. (ISBN 0-685-48593-5). Feldheim.
Journal of Madame Giovanni. Alexandre Dumas. Tr. by M. E. Wilbur. (Black & Gold Lib). 1945. 6.95 o.p. (ISBN 0-87140-947-X, Co-Pub with Tudor). Liveright.
Journal of Pastoral Practice, Vol. 1, No. 1 - Winter, 1977. Jay E. Adams. 1977. pap. 3.50 o.p. (ISBN 0-8010-0116-1). Baker Bk.
Journal of Pastoral Practice, Vol. V, No.1. Jay E. Adams. 1981. pap. 5.00 o.p. (ISBN 0-8010-0178-1). Baker Bk.
Journal of Pastoral Practice, Vol. I, No. 2. Jay E. Adams. 1977. pap. 3.50 o.p. (ISBN 0-8010-0125-0). Baker Bk.
Journal of Pastoral Practice, Vol. V, No. 2. Jay E. Adams. 1981. pap. 5.00 o.p. (ISBN 0-8010-0183-8). Baker Bk.
Journal of Pastoral Practice, Vol. IV, No. 2. Ed. by Jay E. Adams. 1980. pap. 5.00 o.p. (ISBN 0-87552-032-4). Presby & Reformed.
Journal of Pastoral Practice, Vol. IV, No. 3. Jay E. Adams. pap. 5.00 o.p. (ISBN 0-8010-0170-6). Baker Bk.
Journal of Pastoral Practice, Vol. V, No 3. Jay E. Adams. 1982. pap. 5.00 o.p. (ISBN 0-8010-0186-2). Baker Bk.
Journal of Pastoral Practice, Vol. IV, No. 4. Jay E. Adams. pap. 5.00 o.p. (ISBN 0-8010-0177-3). Baker Bk.
Journal of Phenomenological Psychology. Ed. by A. Giorgi. (JPP Ser.: Vol. 13-1). 150p. 1982. pap. text ed. 10.00x o.p. Humanities.
Journal of Phenomenological Psychology. Ed. by A. Giorgi. (JPP Spring 1984 Ser.: Vol. 15-1). 106p. 1984. pap. text ed. 10.00x o.p. (ISBN 0-317-13890-1). Humanities.
Journal of Phenomenological Psychology: Fall 1980, Vol. 7, No. 2. Ed. by A. Giorgi. 118p. 1980. pap. text ed. 10.00x o.p. Humanities.
Journal of Phenomenological Psychology: Fall 1977, Vol. 8, No. 1. Ed. by A. Giorgi. 1978. pap. text ed. 10.00x o.p. (ISBN 0-391-01223-1). Humanities.
Journal of Phenomenological Psychology, Fall, 1985, Vol. 16, No. 2. Ed. by A. Giorgi. 104p. 1985. pap. text ed. 15.00x o.p. (ISBN 0-317-38217-9). Humanities.
Journal of Phenomenological Psychology: Studies in the Science of Human Experience & Behavior, Vols. 1-7. Ed. by A. Giorgi et al. (Biannual pub.). 1970. Vols.1-6. pap. 4.50x each issue o.p.; Vol. 7. pap. 10.00x each issue o.p. Humanities.
Journal of Phenomenological Psychology: Spring 1978, Vol. 8, No. 2. Ed. by A. Giorgi. 1978. pap. text ed. 10.00x o.p. (ISBN 0-391-01242-8). Humanities.
Journal of Phenomenological Psychology, Spring, 1985, Vol. 16, No. 1. Ed. by A. Giorgi. 111p. 1985. pap. text ed. 15.00x o.p. (ISBN 0-317-38216-0). Humanities.
Journal of Propulsion & Power, Vol. 3. Ed. by R. H. Waesche. 1987. 180.00 o.p. (ISBN 0-317-66151-5). AIAA.
Journal of Research in Science Teaching, Vol. 20, Issue 5. Ed. by James A. Shymansky & John E. Penick. 136p. 1983. pap. 16.50 o.p. (ISBN 0-471-88187-2). Wiley.
Journal of Social Issues: Cumulative Index 1945-1975 (Volumes 1-31) 1983. 22.00 o.p. (ISBN 0-317-01049-2). Learned Info.
Journal of Spacecraft & Rockets, Vol. 24. Ed. by Frank J. Redd. 96p. (J). 1985. 130.00 o.p. (ISBN 0-317-36786-2). AIAA.
Journal of the Commons House of Assembly, November 20, 1755-July 6, 1757. Ed. by Terry W. Lipscomb. (Colonial Records of South Carolina Ser.). 485p. 1989. text ed. 39.95x o.p. (ISBN 0-87249-948-0). U of SC Pr.
Journal of the Discovery of the Source of the Nile. John H. Speke. 1969. Repr. of 1906 ed. 13.95x o.p. (ISBN 0-460-00050-0, Evman). Biblio Dist.
Journal of the Proceedings of the Friends of Domestic Industry: In General Convention Met at the City of New York, October 26, 1831. Alexander Everett. Ed. by Michael Hudson. Bd. with British Opinions on the Protecting System. (Neglected American Economists Ser.). 1975. lib. bdg. 61.00 o.p. (ISBN 0-8240-1003-5). Garland Pub.
Journal of the Proceedings of the Society which Conducts the Monthly Anthology & Boston Review: Oct. 3, 1805 to July 2, 1811. Boston Athenaeum. (Robert Charles Billings Fund Publication Ser.: No. 4). (Illus.). 344p. 1910. 10.00 o.p. (ISBN 0-934552-10-X). Boston Athenaeum.
Journal of the Waterloo Campaign. 388p. 1985. 25.00 o.p. (ISBN 0-947898-04-2). Kraus Repr.
Journal of Thermophysics & Heat Transfer, Vol. 1. Ed. by A. L. Crosbie. 1987. 120.00 o.p. (ISBN 0-317-66159-0). AIAA.
Journal of Voyage to Australia. Andrew C. Bruening. 62p. 1984. 5.50x o.p. (ISBN 0-86516-034-1). Bolchazy-Carducci.
Journal of William Charles Macready, 1832-1851. J. C. Trewin. (Arcturus Bks.). 358p. 1970. pap. text ed. 2.85 o.p. (ISBN 0-8093-0423-6). S Ill U Pr.
Journal up the Straits: Oct. 11, 1856-May 5, 1857. Herman Melville. Ed. by Raymond Weaver. LC 74-143858. (Illus.). 1971. Repr. of 1935 ed. lib. bdg. 20.00x o.p. (ISBN 0-8154-0383-6). Cooper Sq.
Journal '86. Ed. by Kathleen Courrier. (Illus.). 76p. (Orig.). 1986. pap. text ed. 7.50 o.p. (ISBN 0-915825-13-9). World Resources Inst.
Journalism & Politics. M. Chalapathi Rau. 324p. 1983. text ed. 32.50x o.p. (ISBN 0-7069-2392-8, Pub. by Vikas India). Advent NY.
Journalism's Unofficial Ambassador: A Biography of Edward Price Bell 1869-1943. James D. Startt. LC 79-17071. (Illus.). xiii, 260p. 1980. 18.95x o.p. (ISBN 0-8214-0415-6). Ohio U Pr.
Journalist Biographies Master Index. 1st ed. Ed. by Alan E. Abrams. LC 77-9144. (Biographical Index Ser.: No. 4). 1979. 90.00x o.p. (ISBN 0-8103-1086-4). Gale.
Journals: Early Fifties Early Sixties. Allen Ginsberg. Ed. & intro. by Gordon Ball. LC 76-54581. (Illus.). 1977. pap. 6.95 o.p. (ISBN 0-394-17034-2, E704, Ever). Grove.
Journals in Psychology: A Resource Listing for Authors. Ed. by APA Staff. LC 88-71880. 88p. (Orig.). 1988. pap. 15.00 o.p. (ISBN 1-55798-042-X, 4070020). Am Psychol.
Journals of a Methodist Farmer, 1871 to 1875. Ed. by Jean Stovin. (Illus.). 251p. 1982. 28.50 o.p. (ISBN 0-7099-2324-4, Pub. by Croom Helm Ltd). Routledge Chapman & Hall.
Journals of a Scientician. Piero Modigliani. 1957. (ISBN 0-8022-1130-5). Philos Lib.
Journals of Lewis & Clark. Bernard De Voto. 1973. 22.00 o.p. (ISBN 0-395-07607-2). HM.
Journaux Intimes. Charles Baudelaire. pap. 75.00 o.p. (ISBN 0-686-50132-2). French & Eur.
Journaux Intimes. Benjamin Constant. 1965. 9.95 o.p. (ISBN 0-686-54612-1). French & Eur.
Journey. Ann Cameron. 336p. 1982. pap. 5.95 o.p. (ISBN 0-380-79087-4, 79087-4). Avon.
Journey Across Russia: The Soviet Union Today. Bart McDowell. LC 76-56998. (Illus.). 1977. 12.95 o.p. (ISBN 0-87044-220-1). Natl Geog.
Journey among the Economists. Arrigo Levi. LC 73-83218. 284p. 1974. 9.95 o.p. (ISBN 0-912050-12-8, Library Pr). Open Court.
Journey for Three. Isabelle Holland. LC 74-17382. 112p. (gr. 3-7). 1975. 4.95 o.p. (ISBN 0-395-20213-2). HM.
Journey Home. John Hillaby. LC 84-4580. (Illus.). 320p. 1984. 15.95 o.p. (ISBN 0-03-072008-7). H Holt & Co.
Journey Homeward. Susan Muto. 6.95 o.p. (ISBN 0-87193-001-3). Dimension Bks.
Journey in North America by Alexander Boloni Farkas (Kolozsvar, 1834) Ed. by Theodore Schoenman. Tr. by Helen B. Schoenman. LC 77-2116. (Memoirs Ser.: Vol.120). (Illus.). 1977. 10.00 o.p. (ISBN 0-87169-120-5). Am Philos.
Journey into Light. Ann Ray. LC 76-53174. (Illus.). 304p. (Orig.). 1978. pap. 8.95 o.p. (ISBN 0-916438-06-6). Univ of Trees.
Journey into Light: Lessons of Pain & Joy to Renew Your Energy & Strengthen Your Faith. Doris B. Murdock. 168p. 1984. 13.95 o.p. (ISBN 0-13-511460-8, Spec); 5.95 o.p. (ISBN 0-13-511452-7). P-H.
Journey into Limbo. Scott Michel. 1962. 6.95 o.p. (ISBN 0-87140-801-5). Liveright.
Journey into Terror: The Story of the Riga Ghetto. Gertrude Schneider. 229p. 1981. Repr. of 1979 ed. 19.95 o.p. (ISBN 0-935764-00-3). Irvington.
Journey of a Diabetic. Lawrence M. Pray & Richard Evans. 208p. 1983. 14.50 o.p. (ISBN 0-671-45396-3). S&S.
Journey of a Diabetic. Lawrence M. Pray & Richard Evans, III. 208p. 1986. pap. 6.95 o.p. (ISBN 0-671-61440-1, Fireside). S&S.
Journey of Fray Marcos de Niza, by Cleve Hallenbeck. Tr. by Marco Da Nizza. LC 73-11861. (Illus.). 115p. 1973. Repr. of 1949 ed. lib. bdg. 22.50x o.p. (ISBN 0-8371-7091-5, MAJO). Greenwood.
Journey of Niels Klim to the World Underground. Ludvig Holberg. LC 73-13401. 236p. 1974. Repr. of 1960 ed. lib. bdg. 24.75 o.p. (ISBN 0-8371-7049-4, HONK). Greenwood.
Journey of the Wolf. Douglas Day. LC 76-41224. 1977. 8.95 o.p. (ISBN 0-689-10771-4, Atheneum). Macmillan.
Journey: Spiritual Insights. Chiara Lubich. Tr. by Hugh Moran & William Hartnett. 158p. 1984. pap. 5.95 o.p. (ISBN 0-911782-51-6). New City.
Journey Through Love. John Hillaby. 1977. 8.95 o.p. (ISBN 0-395-24775-6). HM.
Journey Through the Universe: An Introduction to Astronomy. Thomas L. Swihart. LC 77-76343. (Illus.). 1978. text ed. 32.50 o.p. (ISBN 0-395-25518-X). HM.
Journey Thru Earlyland. M. Christal. (Illus.). 96p. (ps-k). 1982. pap. 4.00 o.p. (ISBN 0-682-49925-0). Exposition-Phoenix.
Journey to Boston. Mary E. Chase. 1965. 3.95 o.p. (ISBN 0-393-08476-0). Norton.
Journey to Excellence. Mike Robson. LC 86-4044. 182p. 1986. 24.95 o.p. (ISBN 0-471-99853-2). Wiley.
Journey to Ixtlan. Carlos Castaneda. 1973. pap. 8.50 o.s.i. (ISBN 0-671-21639-2, Touchstone Bks). S&S.
Journey to Jericho. Scott O'Dell. LC 71-82479. (Illus.). (gr. 1-5). 1974. reinforced bdg. 5.95 o.p. (ISBN 0-395-19839-9). HM.
Journey to Kars. Philip Glazebrook. LC 84-45094. 320p. 1984. 12.95 o.p. (ISBN 0-689-11504-0, Atheneum). Macmillan.
Journey to Kars: A Modern Traveller in the Ottoman Lands. Philip Glazebrook. (Illus.). 256p. 1985. pap. 7.95 o.p. (ISBN 0-03-005607-1, Owl Bks.). H Holt & Co.
Journey to Love. David Hutton. 1986. pap. 5.95 o.p. (ISBN 0-936411-00-7). Beyond Words Pub.
Journey to North Korea: Personal Perceptions. Ed. by C. I. Kim & B. C. Koh. (Research Papers & Policy Studies: No. 8). (Illus.). 164p. pap. 10.00x o.p. (ISBN 0-686-46630-6). IEAS.
Journey to the Center of the Crystal Ball (Autobiography, S. D. Stookey) 64p. 1985. 40.00 o.p. (ISBN 0-916094-69-3). Am Ceramic.
Journey to the Frontier: Two Roads to the Spanish Civil War. Peter Stansky & William Abrahams. (Illus.). 1970. pap. 5.95x o.p. (ISBN 0-393-00509-7, Norton Lib). Norton.
Journey to the High Southwest: A Traveler's Guide. Robert L. Casey. (Illus.). 400p. (Orig.). 1983. pap. 16.95 o.p. (ISBN 0-914718-78-9). Pacific Search.
Journey to the High Southwest: A Traveler's Guide. 2nd, rev. ed. Robert L. Casey. LC 84-25366. (Illus.). 400p. 1985. pap. 14.95 o.p. (ISBN 0-914718-96-7). Globe Pequot.
Journey to the Lake District from Cambridge: A Summer Diary, 1779. William Wilberforce. Ed. by C. E. Wrangham. (Illus.). 96p. 1983. 15.95x o.p. (ISBN 0-85362-204-3, Oriel); pap. 8.95 o.p. (ISBN 0-85362-205-1). Routledge Chapman & Hall.
Journey to the Magical City: A Quadriplegic Person's Reflections on Suffering & Love. Robert T. Standhardt. LC 83-80413. 96p. (Orig.). 1983. pap. 4.50 o.p. (ISBN 0-8358-0458-5). Upper Room.

Journey to the West, 3 vols. 1980. Set. silk 46.95 o.p. (ISBN 0-8351-1446-5). China Bks.

Journey to the West, Bk. 1. Wu Cheng'en. Tr. by W. J. F. Jenner from Chinese. (Illus.). 575p. 1982. 16.95 o.p. (ISBN 0-8351-1003-6). China Bks.

Journey to the West, No. 2. Wu Cheng'en. Tr. by W. J. Jenner from Chinese. (Illus.). 638p. 1984. pap. 16.95 o.p. (ISBN 0-8351-1193-8). China Bks.

Journey to the West, Vol. 3. 1986. silk 16.95 o.p. (ISBN 0-8351-1364-7). China Bks.

Journey to Work. Kate K. Liepmann. LC 73-13403. (Illus.). 199p. 1973. Repr. of 1944 ed. lib. bdg. 35.00x o.p. (ISBN 0-8371-7051-6, LIJW). Greenwood.

Journey Toward the Heart: Discourses on the Sufi Way. Bhagwan S. Rajneesh. LC 79-1762. 272p. 1980. pap. 9.57i o.p. (ISBN 0-06-066786-9, RD 313). HarpR.

Journey under the Sea. Raymond A. Montgomery. (Choose Your Own Adventure Ser.). (gr. 3-8). pap. 3.95 o.p. (ISBN 0-553-25911-3). Bantam.

Journey with the Law. Lawrence F. Small. 216p. (Orig.). 1984. 16.95 o.s.i. (ISBN 0-934318-44-1); pap. 9.95 o.s.i. (ISBN 0-317-13807-3). Falcon Pr MT.

Journey Within. Romain Rolland. (ISBN 0-8022-1369-3). Philos Lib.

Journey Without End. Henry Gilfond. 1958. (ISBN 0-8022-0593-3). Philos Lib.

Journeyed. Date not set. (ISBN 0-8052-3756-9). Random.

Journeying Through a Jungle. Sandy F. Ray. LC 79-84787. 1979. 5.95 o.p. (ISBN 0-8054-5169-2). Broadman.

Journeying Through the Days, 1986. 1985. spiral bdg. 10.95 o.p. (ISBN 0-8358-0523-9, Dist. by Abingdon Press). Upper Room.

Journeying Through the Days 1986: A Calendar Journal for Personal Reflection. 1985. spiral bound 4.75 o.p. Upper Room.

Journeying Through the Days, 1987. 272p. (Orig.). 1986. pap. 10.95 o.p. (ISBN 0-8358-0541-7). Upper Room.

Journeying Through the Days, 1988. Upper Room Staff. 272p. (Orig.). 1987. pap. 10.95 o.p. (ISBN 0-8358-0551-4). Upper Room.

Journeying Through the Days 1989. 272p. 1988. pap. 10.95 o.p. (ISBN 0-8358-0573-5). Upper Room.

Journeyman. Alan Brilliant. pap. 3.50 o.p. (ISBN 0-87775-014-9). Unicorn Pr.

Journeys Between Wars. John Dos Passos. 394p. 1980. lib. bdg. 27.50x o.p. (ISBN 0-374-92251-9, Octagon). Hippocrene Bks.

Journeys in Wonderland. Lewis Carroll. 1989. 5.98 o.p. (ISBN 0-8317-5505-9). Smith Pubs.

Journeys into Paintings. Claude Marks. (Illus.). 1988. Metro Mus Art.

Journeys into the Bright World: A Personal Account of the Ketamine Experience. Howard S. Alltounian & Marcia Moore. 1978. pap. 5.95 o.s.i. (ISBN 0-914918-12-5). Whitford Pr.

Journeys with the Senator. Ivo Sparkman. LC 77-79834. 1977. 12.95 o.p. (ISBN 0-87397-129-9). Strode.

Joy & Adventure of Growing Younger. M. Kimbrough. LC 12-2969. 1983. pap. 2.25 o.p. (ISBN 0-570-03876-6). Concordia.

Joy: Expanding Human Awareness. William C. Schutz. 1967. pap. 1.95 o.p. (ISBN 0-394-17255-8, B323, BC). Grove.

Joy in a Woolly Coat. Julie A. Church. LC 86-73130. (Illus.). 100p. (Orig.). 1987. pap. 9.95 o.s.i. (ISBN 0-941171-85-X). Canticle Pub.

Joy in His Presence: Christian Reflections on Everyday Life. Lily M. Gyldenvand. LC 81-67806. 112p. (Orig.). 1981. pap. 4.95 o.p. (ISBN 0-8066-1896-5, 10-3596, Augsburg). Augsburg Fortress.

Joy of Ascension. Randall Weischedel. LC 82-73249. (Illus.). 136p. 1983. 9.95 o.p. (ISBN 0-87516-499-4). DeVorss.

Joy of Bach. Robert E. Lee. LC 79-57201. (Illus.). 136p. (Orig.). 1979. pap. 4.95 o.p. (ISBN 0-8066-1776-4, 10-3598, Augsburg). Augsburg Fortress.

Joy of Baking. Barbara Grunes. 240p. 1986. 22.95 o.p. (ISBN 0-8249-3060-6). Ideals.

Joy of Canvas Painting, Vol. 2. Joyce Beebe. (Illus.). 80p. (Orig.). 1987. pap. write for info. o.p. (ISBN 0-917119-43-6, 45-1071). Priscillas Pubns.

Joy of Flying. Robert J. Traister. (Illus.). 272p. 1982. pap. 11.60 o.p. (ISBN 0-8306-2321-3, 2321). TAB Bks.

Joy of Frogs. Tomi Ungerer. LC 84-73211. (Illus.). 48p. 1985. 9.95 o.s.i. (ISBN 0-394-54922-8, GP976). Grove.

Joy of Mathematics. Theoni Pappas. LC 86-50374. (Illus.). 164p. (Orig.). 1986. pap. 10.95 o.p. (ISBN 0-933174-39-X). Wide World Tetra.

Joy of Music. Leonard Bernstein. (Illus.). (gr. 9 up). 1959. 12.95 o.p. (ISBN 0-671-39720-6). S&S.

Joy of Photographing People. Eastman Kodak Co. Editors. LC 83-12215. 240p. 1983. 29.95 o.p. (ISBN 0-201-11694-4); pap. 14.95 o.p. (ISBN 0-201-11695-2). Addison-Wesley.

Joy of Signing: The New Illustrated Guide for Mastering Sign Language & the Manual Alphabet. Lottie L. Riekehof. LC 77-83947. Orig. Title: Talk to the Deaf. (Illus.). 324p. 1978. 14.95 o.p. (ISBN 0-88243-518-3, 02-0518). Gospel Pub.

Joy of Spinning. Marilyn Kluger. (Illus.). 1978. pap. 6.70 o.p. (ISBN 0-671-24213-X, Fireside). S&S.

Joy of Stress. Peter Hanson. (Illus.). 304p. 1987. pap. 8.95 o.p. (ISBN 0-8362-2412-4). Andrews & McMeel.

Joy of Stuffed Preppies. Randall C. Douglas, III. (Illus.). 1982. pap. 3.95 o.p. (ISBN 0-03-061596-8, Owl Bks). H Holt & Co.

Joy of the Lord. Mary Light. pap. 0.50 o.p. (ISBN 0-910924-67-8). Macalester.

Joy of Wildflowers: A Fieldbook of Familiar Flowers of Rural & Urban Habitats in the Eastern United States. Millie B. House. (Phalarope Bk.). (Illus.). 176p. 1986. pap. 8.95 o.p. (ISBN 0-13-511635-X). P-H.

Joy to the World: An Introduction to Kingdom Evangelism. Robert T. Henderson. LC 80-14597. 207p. (Orig.). 1980. pap. 6.50 o.p. (ISBN 0-8042-2096-4, John Knox). Westminster John Knox.

Joy with Honey. Doris Mech. 135p. 1979. 4.95 o.p. (ISBN 0-930756-46-0, 532002). Aglow Pubns.

Joyce & Dante: The Shaping Imagination. Mary T. Reynolds. LC 80-7550. (Illus.). 369p. 1981. 37.00 o.p. (ISBN 0-691-06446-6). Princeton U Pr.

Joyce Cary: An Existentialist Approach. B. Majumdar. 220p. 1982. text ed. 22.50x o.p. (ISBN 0-391-02807-3). Humanities.

Joyce Cary: His Theme & Technique. K. K. Sharma. 208p. 1976. text ed. 9.95x o.p. (ISBN 0-391-02550-3). Humanities.

Joyce Cary's Trilogies: Pursuit of the Particular Real. Hazard Adams. LC 83-3461. 1983. 20.00 o.p. (ISBN 0-8130-0759-3). U Presses Fla.

Joyce: The Man, the Work, the Reputation. Marvin Magalaner & Richard M. Kain. LC 79-17270. 1980. Repr. of 1956 ed. lib. bdg. 32.50x o.p. (ISBN 0-313-21258-9, MAJY). Greenwood.

Joyce Treiman. Lester D. Longman & Bloch Maurice. Ed. by Denise Solomon. LC 77-14058. (Illus.). 1978. pap. 7.95 o.p. (ISBN 0-912158-81-6). Hennessey.

Joyce's Debt to Rabelais. Ed. by James J. Wilhelm & Richard Saez. (Outstanding Dissertations in Comparative Literature Ser.). 285p. 1988. lib. bdg. 50.00 o.p. (ISBN 0-8240-7490-4). Garland Pub.

Joyce's Ulysses & the Assault upon Character. James H. Maddox, Jr. 1978. 30.00x o.p. (ISBN 0-8135-0851-7). Rutgers U Pr.

Joyful Christian: One Hundred Readings from the Works of C. S. Lewis. C. S. Lewis. LC 77-21685. 1977. 12.95 o.p. (ISBN 0-02-570900-3). Macmillan.

Joyful Community: An Account of the Bruderhof, a Communal Movement Now in Its Third Generation. Benjamin Zablocki. 1980. pap. 5.95 o.s.i. (ISBN 0-226-97749-8, P885, Phoen). U of Chicago Pr.

Joyful Noise. Donald Finkel. LC 66-11396. (Orig.). 1966. pap. 3.95 o.p. (ISBN 0-689-10088-4, Atheneum). Macmillan.

Joyful Sound: Christian Hymnody. 2nd ed. William J. Reynolds & Milburn Price. LC 77-12048. 1978. 26.95 o.p. (ISBN 0-03-040831-8, HoltC). HR&W.

Joyful Stuffed Dolls & Animals. Ondori Publishing Company Staff. (Illus.). 111p. (Orig.). 1985. pap. 7.95 o.p. (ISBN 0-317-14887-7). Japan Pubns USA.

Joyful Waiting. Lois Kikkert. 1.17 o.p. (ISBN 0-8091-9330-2). Paulist Pr.

Joyner's Guide to Official Washington for Doing Business Overseas. Ed. by Nelson T. Joyner, Jr. & Jackie Durham. LC 79-20957. (Pergamon Policy Studies). 400p. 1980. 140.00 o.p. (ISBN 0-08-025108-0). Pergamon.

Joyous Vision: A Sourcebook for Elementary Art Appreciation. Al Hurwitz & Stanley Madeja. (Illus.). 320p. 1977. pap. text ed. 32.33 o.p. (ISBN 0-13-511600-7). P-H.

Joys of Smoking Cigarettes. Jim Fitzgerald. (Illus.). 144p. 1983. pap. 6.95 o.p. (ISBN 0-03-063357-5). H Holt & Co.

Joys of Yiddish. Leo Rosten. 1968. text ed. 19.95 o.p. (ISBN 0-07-053975-8). McGraw.

Joysprick: An Introduction to the Language of James Joyce. Anthony Burgess. LC 74-17009. (Illus.). 187p. 1975. pap. 3.95 o.s.i. (ISBN 0-15-646561-2, Harv). HarBraceJ.

JSP & JSD: The Jackson Approach to Software Development. John Cameron. 257p. 1983. 30.00 o.p. (ISBN 0-8186-8516-6). IEEE Comp Soc.

JTPA & Vocational Education Telephone Directory. 22p. 1987. pap. 1.50 o.s.i. (ISBN 0-937925-39-X). Capitol VA.

Juan Gris. Gaya A. Nuno. LC 85-42874. (Illus.). 128p. 1986. 19.95 o.p. (ISBN 0-8478-0611-1). Rizzoli Intl.

Juan Rulfo. Luis Leal. (World Authors Ser.). 151p. 1983. lib. bdg. 20.50 o.s.i. (ISBN 0-8057-6539-5, Twayne). G K Hall.

Juan Valera: Pepita Jimenez. Ed. by R. E. Lott. 1974. 33.00 o.p. (ISBN 0-08-017918-5); pap. 13.00 o.p. (ISBN 0-08-017919-3). Pergamon.

Juarez, Man of Law. Elizabeth B. De Trevino. LC 74-12012. 160p. (gr. 3 up). 1974. 5.95 o.p. (ISBN 0-374-33950-3). FS&G.

Jubal Sackett. Louis L'Amour. 1985. pap. 16.95 o.p. (ISBN 0-553-05086-9). Bantam.

Jubal Sackett. Louis L'Amour. 495p. 1986. lib. bdg. 17.95 o.p. (ISBN 0-8161-3976-8, Large Print Bks). G K Hall.

Jubilee. Margaret Walker. 1966. 15.95 o.p. (ISBN 0-395-08288-9). HM.

Jubilee Chemical Engineering Symposium: Proceedings of the Symposium Organised by the Institution of Chemical Engineers, Imperial College, London, U. K., April 1982. Institution of Chemical Engineers Staff. (Institution of Chemical Engineers Symposium Ser.: Vol. 73). 678p. 1982. 99.00 o.s.i. (ISBN 0-08-028770-0). Pergamon.

Jubileo en el Zocalo. Ramon Sender. Ed. by Florence H. Sender. LC 64-12388. (Orig., Span.). 1964. pap. text ed. 5.95x o.p. (ISBN 0-89197-254-4). Irvington.

Judaism: A Portrait. Date not set. (ISBN 0-8052-0344-3). Random.

Judaism & American Idea. Date not set. (ISBN 0-8052-0635-3). Random.

Judaism & Christianity: Essays. Leo Baeck. Tr. by Walter Kaufmann. LC 58-5590. (Temple Bk). 1970. pap. 8.95 o.p. (ISBN 0-689-70243-4, T17, Atheneum). Macmillan.

Judaism & Hellenism: Studies in Their Encounter in Palestine During the Early Hellenistic Period. Martin Hengel. Tr. by John Bowden from Ger. LC 83-39574. 672p. 1981. 21.95 o.p. (ISBN 0-8006-1495-X, 1-1495, Fortress). Augsburg Fortress.

Judaism & Its History: In Two Parts. Abraham Geiger. Tr. by Charles Newburgh from Ger. LC 85-9043. (Brown Classics in Judaica Ser.). 414p. 1985. pap. text ed. 18.50 o.p. (ISBN 0-8191-4491-6). U Pr of Amer.

Judaism & Vegetarianism. Richard H. Schwartz. (Illus.). 160p. 1982. 15.00 o.p. (ISBN 0-682-49827-0); pap. 9.00 o.p. (ISBN 0-682-49828-9). Exposition-Phoenix.

Judaism: Fossil or Ferment? Elieser Berkovits. 224p. 1956. (ISBN 0-8022-0110-5). Philos Lib.

Judaism: The Evidence of the Mishnah. Jacob Neusner. LC 80-26080. xx, 420p. 1985. 25.00x o.s.i. (ISBN 0-226-57617-5); pap. 15.95 o.s.i. (ISBN 0-226-57619-1). U of Chicago Pr.

Judaism, Thought & Legend. Meir Meiseles. Tr. by Rebecca Schonfeld-Brand & Aryeh Newman. 1978. pap. 9.95 o.s.i. (ISBN 0-87306-140-3). Feldheim.

Judas Cross. Jeffrey M. Wallman. 1978. pap. 1.50 o.p. (ISBN 0-380-01846-2, 36426). Avon.

Judas Goat. Robert B. Parker. 1978. 7.95 o.p. (ISBN 0-395-26682-3). HM.

Judas Kiss. Victoria Holt. 336p. 1982. pap. 3.95 o.p. (ISBN 0-449-20055-8, Crest). Fawcett.

Judas Priest. (Metal Mania Ser.). (Illus.). 48p. (gr. 4-12). 1984. 6.95 o.p. (ISBN 0-88188-326-3, Robus Books). H Leonard Pub Corp.

Judas the Pious. Francine Prose. (Hall Fiction Paperbacks). 288p. 1986. pap. 5.95 o.p. (ISBN 0-8398-2913-2). G K Hall.

Jude. Betty Burton. 500p. 1987. 17.95 o.s.i. (ISBN 0-684-18722-1). Scribner.

Jude the Obscure. Thomas Hardy. Ed. by Robert C. Slack. LC 67-18704. 1927. 6.95 o.s.i. (ISBN 0-394-60462-8). Modern Lib.

Judge Benjamin: Superdog. Judith W. McInerney. LC 81-85092. (Illus.). 144p. (gr. 3-7). 1982. 10.95 o.p. (ISBN 0-8234-0448-X). Holiday.

Judge Benjamin: The Superdog Rescue. Judith W. McInerney. LC 83-48961. (Illus.). 128p. (gr. 3-7). 1984. 9.95 o.p. (ISBN 0-8234-0515-X). Holiday.

Judge Spencer Dissents. Henry Denker. 320p. 1986. 17.95 o.p. (ISBN 0-688-06386-1). Morrow.

Judgement & Choice: The Psychology of Decision. Robin M. Hogarth. LC 79-42822. 250p. 1980. 24.95x o.p. (ISBN 0-471-27744-4, Pub. by Wiley-Interscience). Wiley.

Judgement Day. James T. Farrell. 464p. 1973. pap. 1.25 o.p. (ISBN 0-380-01311-8, 14282). Avon.

Judgement Day. Penelope Lively. 1986. 13.50 o.p. (ISBN 0-317-53128-X, Large Print Bks). G K Hall.

Judgement of Eve. Edgar Pangborn. (Science Fiction Rediscovery Ser: Vol. 18). 1976. pap. 2.25 o.p. (ISBN 0-380-00757-6, 30387). Avon.

Judges. Matilda Alexander. (Illus.). 35p. (gr. k-4). 1979. pap. text ed. 8.75 o.p. CEF Press.

Judges & Ruth. rev. ed. Samuel Ridout. 415p. 1981. pap. 7.25 o.p. (ISBN 0-87213-720-1). Loizeaux.

Judging Delinquents: Context & Process in Juvenile Court. Robert M. Emerson. LC 70-75047. 307p. 1969. 27.95x o.p. (ISBN 0-202-23001-5). Aldine de Gruyter.

Judging Justice: An Introduction to Contemporary Political Philosophy. Philip Pettit. 192p. 1980. 26.95x o.p. (ISBN 0-7100-0563-6); pap. 11.95x o.p. (ISBN 0-7100-0571-7). Routledge Chapman & Hall.

Judging People: A Guide to Orthodox & Unorthodox Methods of Assessment. D. Mackenzie Davey & Marjorie Harris. (Illus.). 176p. 1982. text ed. 19.95 o.p. (ISBN 0-07-084581-6). McGraw.

Judgment in Blood. Jack D. Hunter. 272p. (Orig.). 1986. pap. 3.50 o.p. (ISBN 0-380-89983-3). Avon.

Judgment in the Gate. Ed. by Richie Martin. LC 86-70285. (Orig.). 1986. pap. 6.95 o.p. (ISBN 0-89107-396-5, Crossway Bks). Good News.

Judgment of History. Marie C. Swabey. 1954. (ISBN 0-8022-1679-X). Philos Lib.

Judicial Maze: The System in New York State. rev. ed. League of Women Voters of New York State Staff. Ed. by Lenore Banks. (Illus.). pap. text ed. 4.00 o.p. (ISBN 0-938588-07-9). LWV NYS.

Judicial Review in Mexico: A Study of the Amparo Suit. Richard D. Baker. (Latin American Monographs, No. 22). 318p. 1971. 13.50x o.p. (ISBN 0-292-70105-5). U of Tex Pr.

Judo. 2nd ed. Daeshik Kim & Kyung Sun Shin. (Physical Education Activities Ser.). 96p. 1977. pap. text ed. write for info. o.p. (ISBN 0-697-07069-7). Wm C Brown.

Judo in Action: Throwing Techniques. Kazuzo Kudo. (Illus.). pap. 6.25 o.p. (ISBN 0-87040-074-6). Japan Pubns USA.

Judo: Sport Techniques for Physical Fitness & Tournament. Bruce Tegner. LC 76-18090. (Illus.). 144p. 1976. pap. 4.95 o.p. (ISBN 0-87407-025-2, T25). Thor.

Judo: The Gentle Way. Alan Fromm & Nicolas Soames. (Illus.). 144p. (Orig.). 1982. pap. 10.95 o.p. (ISBN 0-7100-9025-0). Routledge Chapman & Hall.

Judy Collins Song Book. Judy Collins. (Illus.). 1969. pap. 8.95 o.p. (ISBN 0-448-01918-3, G&D). Putnam Pub Group.

Judy Gorman's Vegetable Cookbook. Judy Gorman. Ed. by Sandra Taylor. LC 86-50093. (Illus.). 416p. 1986. 19.95 o.p. (ISBN 0-89909-099-0). Yankee Bks.

Judy: Portrait of an American Legend. T. J. Watson & Chapman. 160p. 1986. text ed. 24.95 o.p. (ISBN 0-07-068487-1). McGraw.

Judy's Summer Adventure. Sally Scott. LC 60-6211. (Illus.). (gr. 1-5). 1960. 3.95 o.p. (ISBN 0-15-241133-X, HJ). HarBraceJ.

Juel Andersen's Carob Primer. Robin Clute & Sigrid Andersen. 56p. (Orig.). 1983. pap. 3.95 o.p. (ISBN 0-916870-60-X). Creative Arts Bk.

Juel Andersen's Sea Green Primer. Richard Ford & Juel Andersen. (Illus.). 64p. (Orig.). 1983. pap. 3.95 o.p. (ISBN 0-916870-65-0). Creative Arts Bk.

Juel Andersen's Sesame Primer. Juel Andersen. (Illus.). 64p. (Orig.). 1983. pap. 3.95 o.p. (ISBN 0-916870-66-9). Creative Arts Bk.

Juel Andersen's Tempeh Primer. Robin Clute & Juel Andersen. (Illus.). 58p. (Orig.). 1983. pap. 3.95 o.p. Creative Arts Bk.

Juggler. Karl Kopp. (Illus.). 1978. lib. bdg. 18.00 o.p. (ISBN 0-916908-37-2); pap. 3.00 o.p. (ISBN 0-916908-09-7). Place Herons.

Juggling for the Complete Klutz. 2nd ed. John Cassidy & B. C. Rimbeaux. (Illus.). 1980. pap. 9.95 incl. 3 juggling bean bags o.p. (ISBN 0-932592-00-7). Klutz Pr.

Juggling with Jesus & His Two-Thousand Year Legacy to Mankind. Hugh Latymer de Nedham. LC 76-44900. 1977. 10.00 o.p. (ISBN 0-682-48651-5, University). Exposition-Phoenix.

Juilliard Report on Teaching the Literature & Materials of Music. Juilliard School of Music - New York Staff. 1970. Repr. of 1953 ed. lib. bdg. 22.50x o.p. (ISBN 0-8371-3008-5, JURT). Greenwood.

Jules & Jim. Henri-Pierre Roche. 240p. 1980. pap. 2.95 o.p. (ISBN 0-380-00024-5, 52399-X, Bard). Avon.

Jules Fonrobert'che Sammlung Mittel & Sudamerikanischer Munzen & Medaillen. Ed. by Adolph Weyl. LC 73-93474. (Illus.). 608p. 1974. Repr. of 1878 ed. 25.00x o.p. (ISBN 0-88000-034-1). Quarterman.

Julia. Susan Bright. Ed. by Joseph F. Lomax & J. Whitebird. (Illus.). 1977. pap. 3.00 o.p. (ISBN 0-930324-01-3). Wings Pr.

Julia: A Portrait of Julia Strachey. Julia Strachey & Frances Partridge. LC 83-81067. (Illus.). 308p. 1983. 16.45i o.p. (ISBN 0-316-69283-2). Little.

Julia & the Bazooka & Other Stories. Anna Kavan. 157p. 1985. pap. 5.70 o.p. (ISBN 0-393-30284-9). Norton.

Julia Foster's Patchwork: Her Own Ideas for You to Make. Julia Foster. (Illus.). 128p. 1988. 22.95 o.p. (ISBN 0-241-11673-2, Pub. by Hamish Hamilton). David & Charles.

Julia Margaret Cameron: Her Life & Photographic Work. Helmut Gernsheim. LC 73-85258. (Illus.). 204p. 1974. 25.00 o.p. (ISBN 0-912334-50-9); pap. 14.50 o.p. (ISBN 0-912334-51-7). Aperture.

Julian Block's Guide to Year-Round Tax Savings, 1984. Julian Block. 220p. (Orig.). 1984. pap. 9.95 o.p. (ISBN 0-87094-535-1). Dow Jones-Irwin.

Julian Block's Guide to Year-Round Tax Savings, 1985. Julian Block. 220p. 1985. pap. 9.95 o.p. (ISBN 0-87094-576-9). Dow Jones-Irwin.

Julian Messner Book of Dates & Events. Julian Messner. (Illus.). 192p. (gr. 4-8). 1986. lib. bdg. 9.79 o.p. (ISBN 0-671-55034-9). Messner.

Juliana Horatia Ewing & Her Books. Horatia K. Eden. LC 71-77001. (Library of Lives & Letters). (Illus.). 304p. 1969. Repr. of 1896 ed. 40.00x o.p. (ISBN 0-8103-3897-1). Gale.

Julie. Carherine Marshall. 384p. 1985. pap. 4.50 o.p. (ISBN 0-8007-8585-1, Spire Bks). Revell.

Julie. Catherine Marshall. 1984. text ed. 15.95 o.p. (ISBN 0-07-040608-1). McGraw.

Julie. Catherine Marshall. (Hall Large Print Bk.). 1985. lib. bdg. 19.95 o.p. (ISBN 0-8161-3813-3, Large Print Bks). G K Hall.

Juliette. Marquis de Sade. Tr. by Austryn Wainhouse from Fr. 1968. pap. 14.95 o.p. (ISBN 0-394-17131-4, E676, Ever). Grove.

Julio, the Shoeshine Boy. Phyllis B. Goody. (Illus.). (gr. 2-5). 1977. 6.50 o.p. (ISBN 0-682-48790-2). Exposition-Phoenix.

Julius Caesar see also Tragedy of Julius Caesar.

Julius Caesar. William Shakespeare. Ed. by J. H. Walter. (Players' Shakespeare Ser). (YA) (gr. 9 up). 1962. 3.50 o.p. (ISBN 0-8238-0113-6). Plays.

Julius Caesar. William Shakespeare. 48p. (Orig.). 1988. pap. 9.95 o.p. (ISBN 1-55651-479-4); audiocassette tape incl. o.p. (ISBN 1-55651-480-8). Cram Cassettes.

Julius Guttag Collection of Latin American Coins. Edgar H. Adams. LC 74-80921. (Illus.). 532p. 1974. Repr. 35.00x o.p. (ISBN 0-88000-027-9). Quarterman.

Julius Robert Mayer, Prophet of Energy. R. B. Lindsay. LC 72-8045. (Men of Physics Ser.). 1973. 60.00 o.p. (ISBN 0-08-016985-6). Pergamon.

July 1914 - the Outbreak of the First World War: Selected Documents. Ed. by Immanuel Geiss. 400p. 1974. pap. 5.95 o.p. (ISBN 0-393-00722-7, Norton Lib). Norton.

Jumble Book, No. 4. Henri Arnold & Bob Lee. 128p. 1986. pap. 2.25 o.s.i. (ISBN 0-515-08758-0). Berkley Pub.

Jumeau Prince of Dollmakers. Constance E. King. (Illus.). 119p. 1983. 17.95 o.p. (ISBN 0-87588-203-X, 2500). Hobby Hse.

Jument Verte. Marcel Ayme. (Coll. Soleil). 1960. 12.50 o.p. (ISBN 0-685-11282-9). Schoenhof.

Jument Verte. Marcel Ayme. (Illus.). deluxe ed. 61.25 o.p. (ISBN 0-685-37182-4). French & Eur.

Jump off the Cliff Notes: A Parody. Gina Cascone & Annette Cascone. 96p. (Orig.). 1988. pap. 4.95 o.p. (ISBN 1-55785-073-9). Bart Books.

Jumping Bean. Edna Miller. (Illus.). 32p. 1984. pap. 4.95 o.s.i. (ISBN 0-13-512377-1). P-H.

Jumping the Train Tracks with Angela. Paul Durcan. 97p. 1983. pap. 7.95 o.p. (ISBN 0-906897-68-8); 11.95 o.p. (ISBN 0-906897-69-6). Dufour.

June. Grace S. Chu. 53p. 1986. 5.95 o.p. (ISBN 0-533-06932-7). Vantage.

June Twenty-Second, Nineteen Forty-One: Soviet Historians & the German Invasion. Vladimir Petrov. Tr. by Aleksandr M. Nekrich. LC 68-9364. viii, 322p. 1968. 24.95x o.p. (ISBN 0-87249-134-X). U of SC Pr.

Juneteenth at Comanche Crossing. Doris H. Pemberton. (Illus.). 340p. 1983. 19.95 o.p. (ISBN 0-89015-373-6). Eakin Pr.

Jung & Feminism: Liberating the Archetypes. Demaris S. Wehr. LC 86-47864. 144p. 1987. 17.95 o.p. (ISBN 0-8070-6734-2). Beacon Pr.

Jung in Context: Modernity & the Making of a Psychology. Peter Homans. LC 78-27596. 240p. 1982. pap. text ed. 6.95x o.s.i. (ISBN 0-226-35109-2). U of Chicago Pr.

Jung: Man & Myth. Vincent Brome. LC 77-14736. 1978. 11.95 o.p. (ISBN 0-689-10853-2, Atheneum); pap. 6.95 o.p. (ISBN 0-689-70588-3, 262). Macmillan.

Junge Deutsche Prosa. Irmgard Feix & Ernestine Schlant. (Rinehart Editions). 1974. text ed. 14.95 o.p. (ISBN 0-03-080092-7). HR&W.

Jungle. Helen Borten. LC 68-11496. (Illus.). (gr. 2-5). 1968. 5.75 o.p. (ISBN 0-15-241355-3, HJ). HarBraceJ.

Jungle. Upton Sinclair. 48p. (Orig.). 1989. pap. 9.95 o.p. (ISBN 1-55651-481-6); audiocaaette tape incl. o.p. (ISBN 1-55651-482-4). Cram Cassettes.

Jungle Babies. (Animals & Their Babies Ser.). (Illus.). 32p. (ps-3). 1987. pap. 5.95 o.s.i. (ISBN 0-671-63488-7, Little Simon). S&S.

Jungle Cowboy. Stanley E. Brock. LC 79-163885. (Illus.). 1972. 8.95 o.s.i. (ISBN 0-8008-4444-0). Taplinger.

Jungle Doctor Meets Mongoose. Paul White. (Jungle Doctor Picture Fable Ser.). 80p. (gr. k-5). 1986. pap. 22.50 o.p. (ISBN 0-85364-270-2, Pub. by Paternoster UK). Attic Pr.

Jungle Doctor's Fables. Paul White. (Jungle Doctor Picture Fable Ser.). 77p. (gr. 1-7). 1986. pap. 22.50 o.p. (ISBN 0-85364-402-0, Pub. by Paternoster UK). Attic Pr.

Jungle Doctor's Hippo Happenings. Paul White. (Jungle Doctor Picture Fable Ser.). 74p. (gr. 1-7). 1986. pap. 22.50 o.p. (ISBN 0-85364-147-1, Pub. by Paternoster UK). Attic Pr.

Jungle Doctor's Monkey Tales. Paul White. (Jungle Doctor Picture Fable Ser.). 76p. (gr. 1-7). 1986. pap. 22.50 o.p. (ISBN 0-85364-403-9, Pub. by Paternoster UK). Attic Pr.

Jungle Doctor's Rhino Rumblings. Paul White. (Jungle Doctor Picture Fable Ser.). 76p. (gr. 1-7). 1986. Set. pap. 22.50 o.p. (ISBN 0-85364-166-8, Pub. by Paternoster UK). Attic Pr.

Jungle Doctor's Tug-of-War. Paul White. (Jungle Doctor Picture Fable Ser.). 80p. (gr. 1-7). 1986. Set. pap. 22.50 o.p. (ISBN 0-85364-404-7, Pub. by Paternoster UK). Attic Pr.

Jungle People: A Kaingang Tribe of the Highlands of Brazil. Jules Henry. (Orig.). 1964. pap. 1.95 o.s.i. (ISBN 0-394-70521-1, V521, Vin). Random.

Junior Citizen. Louis DeJean. (ISBN 0-8022-0372-8). Philos Lib.

Junior Confirmation Book. J. Tanner. 4.95 o.p. (ISBN 0-317-61057-0, 15-6143, Augsburg). Augsburg Fortress.

Junior Encyclopedia of Israel. Harriet Sirof. (Illus.). 1980. 16.95 o.p. (ISBN 0-8246-0228-5). Jonathan David.

Junior High Freestyle Swimmer. C. Paul Jackson. (Illus.). (gr. 6-9). 1965. 7.95 o.p. (ISBN 0-8038-3706-2). Hastings.

Junior High Ministry: A Guidebook for the Leading & Teaching of Early Adolescents. Wayne Rice. 1978. pap. 6.95 o.p. (ISBN 0-310-34971-0, 10825P). Zondervan.

Junior High School Years. Philadelphia Suburban School Study Council, Group B Staff. LC 65-23203. 64p. 1965. pap. text ed. 1.50x o.p. (ISBN 0-8134-6830-2, 6830). Inter Print Pubs.

Junior Judo, 3 vols. Mick Leigh. (Illus.). 144p. 1983. Set. pap. 23.50x o.p. (ISBN 0-572-01228-4). Trans-Atl Phila.

Junior Karate. Russell Kozuki. (Illus.). (gr. 4-6). 1977. pap. 2.50 o.p. (ISBN 0-671-62489-X). Archway.

Junior Saints: The Rich Rare Humor of Kids in Church. Oren Arnold. LC 75-12108. (Illus.). 128p. 1976. pap. 4.95 o.p. (ISBN 0-8254-2117-9). Kregel.

Junior Soccer. John Jarman. (Illus.). 78p. 1976. 7.95 o.p. (ISBN 0-571-10846-6); pap. 4.95 o.p. (ISBN 0-571-10847-4). Faber & Faber.

Junior Year Abroad. Howard R. Simpson. LC 85-13184. (Crime Club Ser.). 192p. 1986. 12.95 o.p. (ISBN 0-385-23260-8). Doubleday.

Juniper Hill. Dorothy Daniels. (Orig.). 1976. pap. 1.50 o.s.i. (ISBN 0-671-80807-9). PB.

Junk Food Alternative. Linda Burum. LC 80-17799. (Illus.). 168p. (Orig.). 1980. pap. 6.95 o.p. (ISBN 0-89286-163-0, One Hund One Prods). Ortho.

Junk Treasures: A Sourcebook for Using Recycled Materials with Children. Mary J. Cliatt & Jean M. Shaw. (Illus.). 256p. 1981. pap. 16.95 o.p. (ISBN 0-13-512608-8). P-H.

Junkers. Piers P. Read. 256p. 1986. pap. 1.75 o.p. (ISBN 0-380-00542-5, 56937-X, Bard). Avon.

Junkers Bombers, Vol. 1. Manfred Griehl. (Warbirds Illustrated Ser.: No. 43). (Illus.). 68p. (Orig.). 1987. pap. 9.95 o.p. (ISBN 0-85368-783-8, Pub. by Arms & Armour). Sterling.

Junketeers. T. G. Broat. LC 76-49026. 1977. 8.95 o.p. (ISBN 0-689-10777-3, Atheneum). Macmillan.

Juries on Trial: Faces of American Justice. Paula DiPerna. LC 84-9406. 1984. 17.50 o.p. (ISBN 0-934878-43-9, Dist. by Norton). Dembner Bks.

Jurisdiction in a Nutshell. 4th ed. Albert A. Ehrenzweig et al. LC 80-312. (Nutshell Ser.). 232p. 1980. pap. 9.95 o.p. (ISBN 0-8299-2086-2). West Pub.

Jurisdictional Histories for Ohio's 88 Counties, 1788-1985. W. Louis Phillips. 36p. (Orig.). 1986. pap. 5.00 o.p. (ISBN 0-917890-81-7). Heritage Bk.

Jury: History of the Trial Jury. Lloyd Moore. 1973. 00.00 o.p. (ISBN 0-87084-576-4). Anderson Pub C.

Jury Instructions on Damages in Tort Actions. Graham Douthwaite. 554p. 1981. text ed. 37.50x o.p. (ISBN 0-87473-137-2, A Smith Co); Nineteen Eighty-four suppl. only. 12.50x o.p. (ISBN 0-87473-182-8). Michie Co.

Jury Selection: An Attorney's Guide to Jury Law & Selection. V. Hale Starr & Mark McCormick. LC 84-82019. 105p. 1986. write for info. o.p. (ISBN 0-316-81063-0). Little.

Jury: Techniques for the Trial Lawyer. (Litigation & Administrative Practice Course Handbook: Vol. 241). 161p. 1987. 40.00 o.p. (ISBN 0-317-11467-0, H4-4919). PLI.

Jury Trials. 262p. 1984. 25.00 o.p. (ISBN 0-88129-119-6). Wash Bar CLE.

Jury Woman. rev. ed. Mary Timothy. LC 75-24030. 256p. (Orig.). 1975. pap. 4.95 o.p. (ISBN 0-912078-46-4). Volcano Pr.

Just a Face in the Dark. Mark McShane. LC 87-6801. (Crime Club Ser.). 192p. 1987. 12.95 o.s.i. (ISBN 0-385-24308-1). Doubleday.

Just a Lark! Annotations by Jim Flegg. LC 84-45555. (Illus.). 160p. 1984. 15.00 o.p. (ISBN 0-7099-1049-5, Pub. by Croom Helm Ltd). Routledge Chapman & Hall.

Just & the Unjust. James G. Cozzens. LC 42-17992. (Modern Classic Ser.). 434p. 1950. 11.95 o.s.i. (ISBN 0-15-146577-0). HarBraceJ.

Just Another Day in Paradise. Maxwell. 1987. pap. 2.95 o.p. (ISBN 0-553-25789-7). Bantam.

Just Before the Divorce. Alfred Hayes. LC 68-8373. 1968. pap. 1.95 o.p. (ISBN 0-689-10112-0, Atheneum). Macmillan.

Just Between Sisters. Cindy Savage. (Impressions Ser.). 128p. (Orig.). (gr. 5-8). 1987. pap. 2.50 o.s.i. (ISBN 0-87406-260-8). Willowisp Pr.

Just Cleo & Me. Dix Wanamaker. 1979. 5.00 o.p. (ISBN 0-682-49262-0). Exposition-Phoenix.

Just How Stories. Girls of Lady Eden's School, London. (Illus.). 23p. (ps-3). 1981. 9.95 o.p. (ISBN 0-224-01713-6, Pub. by Jonathan Cape). Salem Hse Pubs.

Just Juggle. S. Cohen. 208p. 1983. pap. text ed. 7.95 o.p. (ISBN 0-07-011623-7). McGraw.

Just Like Abraham Lincoln. Bernard Waber. (Illus.). (gr. 1-5). 1974. reinforced bdg. 6.95 o.p. (ISBN 0-395-20107-1). HM.

Just Like Always. Elizabeth-Ann Sachs. LC 81-2289. 180p. (gr. 3-7). 1981. PLB 9.95 o.s.i. (ISBN 0-689-30859-0, Atheneum). Macmillan.

Just Like Daddy. Frank Asch. (ps-3). 1981. 10.95x o.s.i. (ISBN 0-13-514042-0). P-H.

Just Like Daddy. Frank Asch. (Illus.). 32p. (ps-3). 1984. pap. 4.95 o.s.i. (ISBN 0-13-514035-8, Pub. by Treehouse). P-H.

Just Married. Cynthia Blair. 1984. pap. 2.50 o.s.i. (ISBN 0-345-31277-5). Ballantine.

Just Me. Barbara Seuling. LC 81-6893. (Let-Me-Read Ser.). (Illus.). 64p. (gr. 1-5). 1982. 8.95 o.p. (ISBN 0-15-241682-X, HJ). HarBraceJ.

Just Me. Barbara Seuling. LC 81-6893. (Let-Me-Read Ser.). (Illus.). 64p. (gr. 1-5). 1982. pap. 3.95 o.p. (ISBN 0-15-241683-8, VoyB). HarBraceJ.

Just off Fifth. Edith Begner. 352p. 1981. pap. 2.95 o.p. (ISBN 0-380-77321-X, 77321). Avon.

Just One Indian Boy. Elizabeth Witheridge. LC 73-84841. 224p. (gr. 5-9). 1974. 6.25 o.p. (ISBN 0-689-30151-0, Atheneum). Macmillan.

Just Talk to Me: Talking & Listening for a Happier Marriage. Andre Bustanoby & Fay Bustanoby. 192p. (Orig.). 1981. pap. text ed. 7.95 o.p. (ISBN 0-310-22181-1, 9211P). Zondervan.

Just the Two of Them. Mary Anderson. LC 74-75554. (Illus.). 192p. (gr. 4-6). 1974. 6.95 o.p. (ISBN 0-689-30402-1, Atheneum). Macmillan.

Just Wait till You Have Children of Your Own! Erma Bombeck & Bil Keane. 1983. pap. 3.95 o.p. (ISBN 0-449-20834-6, Crest). Fawcett.

Just What the Doctor Ordered. Harriet W. Goodman & Barbar Morse. LC 81-6786. 678p. 1982. 25.00 o.p. (ISBN 0-03-051011-2). H Holt & Co.

Just Writing. 3rd ed. Charles S. Laubheim et al. 1978. pap. text ed. 14.95 o.p. (ISBN 0-8403-2499-5, 40249901). Kendall-Hunt.

Just Writing. Charles S. Laubheim et al. 1986. 19.95 o.p. (ISBN 0-8403-4154-7). Kendall-Hunt.

Just You & Me God. Barbara Paret. LC 73-5351. 64p. 1973. 3.25 o.p. (ISBN 0-8042-2380-7, John Knox). Westminster John Knox.

Justice. Giorgio De Vecchia. 236p. 1954. (ISBN 0-8022-1770-2). Philos Lib.

Justice & Consequences. John P. Conrad. LC 78-348. 192p. 1981. 20.00x o.p. (ISBN 0-669-02190-3). Lexington Bks.

Justice & Equality. reference ed. Hugo A. Bedau. (Central Issues of Philosophy Ser). (Illus.). 1971. pap. text ed. (ISBN 0-13-514125-7). P-H.

Justice As Fairness: Perspectives on the Justice Model. Ed. by David Fogel & Joe Hudson. 300p. 1981. pap. text ed. 17.95 o.p. (ISBN 0-87084-287-0). Anderson Pub Co.

Justice at Iritara. Lawrence Cortesi. 224p. (Orig.). 1982. pap. 2.25 o.p. (ISBN 0-505-51776-0, Pub. by Tower Bks). Dorchester Pub Co.

Justice Church: The New Function of the Church in North American Christianity. Frederick Herzog. LC 80-15091. 176p. (Orig.). 1980. pap. 13.95 o.p. (ISBN 0-88344-249-3). Orbis Bks.

Justice Denied: The Black Man in White America. Ed. by William Chace & Peter Collier. 1970. pap. text ed. 8.95 o.p. (ISBN 0-15-547760-9, HC). HarBraceJ.

Justice in Jerusalem. Date not set. pap. (ISBN 0-8052-5003-4). Random.

Justice in Plato's Republic. Peter Fireman. 1957. (ISBN 0-8022-0503-8). Philos Lib.

Justice League of America. Robert L. Fleming. (Super Powers Which Way Bks.: No. 3). (Illus.). 128p. (Orig.). (gr. 3-6). 1984. pap. 2.50 o.p. (ISBN 0-671-47567-3). Archway.

Justice on Appeal. Paul D. Carrington et al. 263p. 1976. 12.95 o.p. (ISBN 0-314-31933-6). West Pub.

Justice: The Memoirs of Attorney General Richard Kleindienst. Richard G. Kleindienst. LC 85-5182. 260p. 1985. 16.95 o.p. (ISBN 0-915463-15-6, Pub. by Jameson Bks, Dist. by Kampmann). Green Hill.

Justification by Faith: A Matter of Death & Life. Gerhard O. Forde. LC 81-70663. 112p. 1982. pap. 2.95 o.p. (ISBN 0-8006-1634-0, 1-1634, Fortress). Augsburg Fortress.

Justification by Faith in Modern Theology. Henry P. Hamann. 114p. 1957. Concordia Schl Grad Studies.

Justification by Success: The Invisible Captivity of the Church. J. Stanley Glen. LC 78-52446. 1979. 6.95 o.p. (ISBN 0-8042-0835-2, John Knox). Westminster John Knox.

Justification of Knowledge. Robert Reymond. LC 76-43394. 1976. pap. 6.95 o.p. (ISBN 0-87552-406-0). Presby & Reformed.

Justin. Grace L. Parr. 1975. 10.95 o.p. (ISBN 0-89015-143-1). Eakin Pr.

Justin Winsor: Scholar-Librarian. Ed. by Wayne Cutler & Michael H. Harris. LC 80-19310. (Heritage of Librarianship: No. 5). 196p. 1980. lib. bdg. 25.00 o.p. (ISBN 0-87287-200-9). Libs Unl.

Juvenile & Adult Correctional Departments, Institutions, Agencies & Paroling Authorities Directory. (1985). pap. 35.00 o.p. (ISBN 0-942974-51-4); pap. 10.00 o.p. (ISBN 0-942974-62-X). Am Correctional.

Juvenile & Adult Correctional Departments, Institutions, Agencies & Paroling Authorities Directory 1987. rev. ed. Ed. by Diana N. Travisono. (Illus.). 600p. 1987. pap. 35.00 o.p. (ISBN 0-942974-80-8). Am Correctional.

Juvenile Delinquency. 2nd ed. Martin R. Haskell & Lewis Yablonsky. 1980. pap. 17.95 o.p. (ISBN 0-395-30618-3). HM.

Juvenile Delinquency. 3rd ed. Martin R. Haskell & Lewis Yablonsky. LC 81-82668. 1982. pap. 24.50 o.p. (ISBN 0-395-31724-X). HM.

Juvenile Delinquency. Peter C. Kratcoski & Lucille D. Kratcoski. 1979. text ed. 31.00 o.p. (ISBN 0-13-514281-4). P-H.

Juvenile Delinquency. Mary Murrell & David Lester. 1981. pap. write for info. o.p. (ISBN 0-02-478790-6). Macmillan.

Juvenile Delinquency & the Schools. Ruth Strang. LC 48-6850. (National Society for the Study of Education Yearbooks Ser: No. 47, Pt. 1). 1948. lib. bdg. 5.50x o.s.i. (ISBN 0-226-60000-9). U of Chicago Pr.

Juvenile Delinquency & Urban Areas. rev. ed. Clifford R. Shaw & Henry D. McKay. LC 69-14511. 1972. pap. text ed. 3.95x o.s.i. (ISBN 0-226-75127-9, P448, Phoen). U of Chicago Pr.

Juvenile Delinquency: Causes, Patterns, & Reactions. William B. Sanders. LC 80-18550. 1981. text ed. 27.95 o.p. (ISBN 0-03-040776-1, HoltC). HR&W.

Juvenile Delinquency: Concepts & Controls. professional reference ed. Robert C. Trojanowicz & Merry Morash. (Illus.). 448p. 1983. pap. text ed. 35.00 o.p. (ISBN 0-13-514323-3). P-H.

Juvenile Delinquency: Theory, Law & Practice. 2nd ed. Larry J. Siegel & Joseph J. Senna. (Illus.). 568p. 1985. text ed. 36.50 o.p. (ISBN 0-314-85298-0). West Pub.

Juvenile Delinquency Today. Joseph S. Roucek. 1958. (ISBN 0-8022-1389-8). Philos Lib.

Juvenile Justice. Willard A. Heaps. LC 74-4011. 208p. 1979. 7.95 o.p. (ISBN 0-395-28906-8, Clarion). HM.

Juvenile Justice? Allison Morris & Mary McIsaac. LC 79-300710. (Cambridge Studies in Criminology). 1978. text ed. 24.95x o.p. (ISBN 0-435-82601-8). Gower Pub Co.

Juvenile Justice Policy: Analyzing Trends & Outcomes. Academy of Criminal Justice Sciences Staff & Scott H. Decker. LC 83-21187. (Perspectives in Criminal Justice Ser.: No. 7). 1984. 25.00 o.p. (ISBN 0-8039-2197-7); pap. 12.95 o.p. (ISBN 0-8039-2198-5). Sage.

Juvenile Law & Practice. cancelled o.s.i. (37,357J). NCLS Inc.

Juvenile Misconduct & Delinquency. William Arnold & Terrence Brungardt. LC 82-82284. 512p. 1983. pap. 23.95 o.p. (ISBN 0-395-32562-5). HM.

Juvenile Rheumatoid Arthritis. 2nd ed. Earl J. Brewer. LC 78-64701. (Major Problems in Clinical Pediatrics Ser.: Vol. 6). 1982. text ed. write for info. o.p. (ISBN 0-7216-1986-X). Saunders.

Juveniles in the Family Courts. Michael Fabricant. LC 82-47927. 176p. 1982. 26.00x o.p. (ISBN 0-669-05706-1). Lexington Bks.

Juxtaoral Organ: Morphology & Clinical Aspects. W. Zenker. LC 81-23069. (Illus.). 117p. 1982. text ed. 22.50 o.p. (ISBN 0-8067-2221-5). Urban & S.

K Factor in Successful Selling. 120p. (Eng. & Span.). 2.50 ea. o.p. Life Ins Mktg Res.

K

K Factor: Reversing & Preventing High Blood Pressure Without Drugs. Richard D. Moore & George D. Webb. 333p. 1986. 17.95 o.p. (ISBN 0-02-586190-5). Macmillan.

K-Theory & Operator Algebras: Proceedings. Conference on K-Theory & Operator Algebras, University of Georgia, Athens, Ga., Apr. 21-25, 1975. Ed. by B. B. Morrel & I. M. Singer. (Lecture Notes in Mathematics: Vol. 575). 1977. soft cover 13.00 o.p. (ISBN 0-387-08133-X). Springer-Verlag.

Kabbalah. David S. Milton. LC 79-3360. 360p. 1980. 13.95 o.p. (ISBN 0-15-146608-4). HarBraceJ.

Kabul. M. E. Hirsh. LC 85-47633. 512p. 1986. 19.95 o.p. (ISBN 0-689-11598-9, Atheneum). Macmillan.

Kachinas: A Hopi Artist's Documentary. Barton Wright. Bd. with Kachinas of the Zuni. 1986. slipcased 80.00 o.s.i. (ISBN 0-87358-421-X). Northland.

Kachinas of the Zuni see Kachinas: A Hopi Artist's Documentary.

Kagan's Superfecta & Other Stories. Allen Hoffman. LC 81-69912. 304p. 1982. 12.95 o.p. (ISBN 0-89659-234-0); special ltd. ed. 100.00 o.p. (ISBN 0-89659-271-5). Abbeville Pr.

Kago. Christopher Wood. 1986. 16.95 o.s.i. (ISBN 0-8050-0062-3). H Holt & Co.

Kahn Report on Sexual Preferences. Sandra S. Kahn & Jean Davis. 288p. 1982. pap. 3.95 o.p. (ISBN 0-380-58032-2). Avon.

Kahuna Sorcerers of Hawaii, Past & Present: With a Glossary of Ancient Religious Terms & the Books of the Hawaiian Royal Dead. Julius S. Rodman. (Illus.). 1979. 20.00 o.p. (ISBN 0-682-49196-9, Banner). Exposition-Phoenix.

Kaiseki: Zen Tastes in Japanese Cooking. Kaichi Tsuji. LC 72-174218. (Illus.). 207p. 1981. 49.00 o.p. (ISBN 0-87011-173-6). Kodansha.

Kaleidoscope: A Book of Readings. 2nd ed. Kevin Ryan & James M. Cooper. 1975. pap. 9.50 o.p. (ISBN 0-395-18623-4). HM.

Kaleidoscope in Woodcuts. Antonio Frasconi. LC 69-105218. (Illus.). 1968. 4.50 o.p. (ISBN 0-15-146690-4). HarBraceJ.

Kaleidoscope Plus. Rosemary Cobham. 160p. 1980. 14.95 o.p. (ISBN 0-85683-046-1, Pub. by Shepheard-Walwyn UK). Dufour.

Kaleidoscope: Readings in Education. 3rd ed. Kevin Ryan & James M. Cooper. LC 79-90056. (Illus.). 1980. pap. 14.95 o.p. (ISBN 0-395-28498-8). HM.

Kalendarium Manuale Utriusque Ecclesiae Orientalis & Occidentalis. Nicolaus Nilles. 1509p. (Fr.). Date not set. Repr. of 1897 ed. text ed. 310.50x o.p. (ISBN 0-576-99195-3, Pub. by Gregg Intl Pubs England). Gregg Intl.

Kama Sutra of Vatsyayana. Ed. by Mulk R. Anand. 276p. 1981. text ed. 125.00x o.p. (ISBN 0-391-02224-5). Humanities.

Kamen Rider, Vol. 2. (Big Little Bks.: No. 41). (Illus.). 350p. 1984. 6.95 o.p. (ISBN 0-318-02693-7). Bks Nippan.

Kamen Rider, Vol. 3. (Big Little Bks.: No. 62). (Illus.). 350p. 1984. 6.95 o.p. (ISBN 0-318-02703-8). Bks Nippan.

Kamen Rider Super, No. 1. (Big Little Bks.: No. 82). (Illus.). 350p. 1984. 6.95 o.p. (ISBN 0-318-02716-X). Bks Nippan.

Kamikaze. Aero Publishers, Inc., Aeronautical Staff. LC 66-19666. (Aero Ser: Vol. 7). 1966. pap. 5.95 o.p. (ISBN 0-8168-0524-5, 20524, TAB-Aero). TAB Bks.

Kamikazes. Edwin P. Hoyt. (Illus.). 1983. 16.50 o.p. (ISBN 0-87795-496-8, Arbor Hse). Morrow.

Kampuchea: From Tragedy to Rebirth. A. Usvatov et al. 184p. 1979. pap. 5.45 o.p. (ISBN 0-8285-1595-6, Pub. by Progress Pubs USSR). Imported Pubns.

Kanata: The Story of Canada, Bk. 1. Dennis Adair & Janet Rosenstock. 1981. pap. 3.95 o.p. (ISBN 0-380-77826-2). Avon.

Kandinsky: Complete Writings on Art, 2 Vols. Wassily Kandinsky. Ed. by Kenneth C. Lindsay & Peter Vergo. LC 81-12798. (Documents of Twentieth Century Art Ser.). 1982. 62.50 o.p. (ISBN 0-8057-9950-8, Twayne). G K Hall.

Kandinsky Watercolors: A Selection from the Solomon R. Guggenheim Museum & the Hilla von Rebay Foundation. Louise A. Swendsen & Vivian E. Barnett. LC 80-54165. (Illus.). 76p. 1980. soft cover museum catalogue 18.00 o.p. (ISBN 0-89207-027-7). S R Guggenheim.

Kane & Abel. Jeffrey Archer. 540p. 1980. 14.95 o.p. (ISBN 0-671-25121-X). S&S.

K'ang Yu-Wei: A Biography & a Symposium. Jung-Pang Lo. LC 66-20911. (Association for Asian Studies Monograph: No. 23). 541p. 1967. 19.95x o.p. (ISBN 0-8165-0152-1). U of Ariz Pr.

Kangaroo for Christmas. James Flora. LC 62-14243. (Illus.). (gr. k-3). 1962. 5.95 o.p. (ISBN 0-15-242026-6, HJ); 4.95 o.p. (ISBN 0-15-242027-4). HarBraceJ.

Kano Eitoku. Tsuneo Takeda. Tr. by H. Mack Horton & Catherine Kaputa. LC 76-44155. (Japanese Arts Library: Vol. 3). 178p. 1977. 25.00 o.p. (ISBN 0-87011-295-3). Kodansha.

Kansas a Land of Contrast. rev. ed. Robert Richmond. LC 79-53861. 1979. pap. text ed. 18.95x o.p. (ISBN 0-88273-026-6). Forum Pr IL.

Kansas Business Directory, 1987-88. rev. ed. American Directory Publishing Co., Inc. Staff. 950p. 1987. pap. 75.00 o.p. (ISBN 0-944316-00-X). Amer Directory.

Kansas Business Directory, 1988-89. rev. ed. American Directory Publishing Co., Inc. Staff. 867p. 1988. pap. 85.00 o.p. (ISBN 0-944316-18-2). Amer Directory.

Kansas City Chiefs. Julian May. (NFL Today Ser.). (gr. 4-8). 1980. lib. bdg. 10.45 o.p. (ISBN 0-87191-729-7); pap. 4.25 o.p. (ISBN 0-89812-232-5). Creative Ed.

Kansas City Epicure. Clarence Kelley. Ed. by Kathy Champlin & Gretchen Weidenbach. (American Epicure Ser.). 151p. 1986. pap. 7.95 o.p. (ISBN 0-89716-158-0). Peanut Butter.

Kansas City Kings. Jim Moore. (NBA Today Ser.). (Illus.). 48p. (gr. 4 up). 1984. PLB 10.45 o.p. (ISBN 0-87191-980-X). Creative Ed.

Kansas City Kings. Dan Zadra et al. (N.B.A. Today Ser.). (Illus.). 48p. Date not set. PLB 10.45 o.p. Creative Ed.

Kansas City Royals. O ed. Martin. LC 82-13979. (Baseball Today Ser.). (Illus.). 48p. (gr. 4 up). 1982. PLB 11.45 o.p. (ISBN 0-87191-862-5). Creative Ed.

Kansas City: The Spirit, the People, the Promise. Patricia E. Pace. LC 82-50189. 272p. 1987. 29.95 o.s.i. (ISBN 0-89781-211-5). Windsor Pubns Inc.

Kansas Corporation Law & Practice. James K. Logan & Alson R. Martin. LC 79-90448. 1983. Vol.1. 180.00 o.p.; Vol. 2, 1983 Revision. Revision 30.00, o.p. (ISBN 0-942357-16-7). KS Bar CLE.

Kansas in Color: Photographs Selected by Kansas! Magazine. Andrea Glenn. LC 82-60564. (Illus.). 128p. 1982. 14.95 o.p. (ISBN 0-7006-0229-1). U Pr of KS.

Kansas Night Wind. Willard Cheesman. LC 84-91298. 80p. 1985. 6.95 o.p. (ISBN 0-533-06390-6). Vantage.

Kansas: Trusts. 8.50 o.p. (ISBN 0-686-90756-6). Am Law Inst.

Kant. Alexander D. Lindsay. LC 76-109970. 1970. Repr. of 1934 ed. lib. bdg. 22.50x o.p. (ISBN 0-8371-4473-6, LIKA). Greenwood.

Kant. Ralph C. Walker. (Arguments of the Philosophers Ser.). 1978. 26.95x o.p. (ISBN 0-7100-8994-5). Routledge Chapman & Hall.

Kant: Moral Legislation & Two Senses of "Will" Gary M. Hochberg. LC 81-40396. 238p. (Orig.). 1982. lib. bdg. 29.75 o.p. (ISBN 0-8191-2121-5); pap. text ed. 13.25 o.p. (ISBN 0-8191-2122-3). U Pr of Amer.

Kant on History & Religion. Michel Despland. 368p. 1973. text ed. 20.00x o.p. (ISBN 0-7735-0125-8, McGill Canada). U of Toronto Pr.

Kant Studies Today. Ed. by Lewis W. Beck. LC 68-57207. 516p. 1969. 29.95 o.p. (ISBN 0-87548-028-4). Open Court.

Kantian Ethics. A. E. Teale. LC 74-30981. 328p. 1975. Repr. of 1951 ed. lib. bdg. 22.50x o.p. (ISBN 0-8371-7940-8, TEKE). Greenwood.

Kantian Thing in Itself. 160p. 1956. (ISBN 0-8022-1117-8). Philos Lib.

Kantorovich: Essays in Optimal Planning. Intro. by Leon Smolinski. LC 75-46110. 288p. 1976. 39.95 o.p. (ISBN 0-87332-076-X). M E Sharpe.

Kant's Pre-Critical Ethics. 2nd ed. Paul A. Schilpp. Ed. by Lewis W. Beck. LC 75-32043. (Philosophy of Immanuel Kant Ser.: Vol. 6). 1976. Repr. of 1960 ed. lib. bdg. 29.00 o.p. (ISBN 0-8240-2330-7). Garland Pub.

Kant's Theory of Knowledge. H. A. Prichard. Ed. by Lewis W. Beck. LC 75-32042. (Philosophy of Immanuel Kant Ser.: Vol. 5). 1977. Repr. of 1909 ed. lib. bdg. 32.00 o.p. (ISBN 0-8240-2329-3). Garland Pub.

Kant's Transcendental Idealism: An Interpretation & Defense. Henry E. Allison. LC 83-5756. 400p. 1984. text ed. 37.50t o.p. (ISBN 0-300-03002-9). Yale U Pr.

Kapital. Karl Marx. 380p. pap. 9.95 o.p. (ISBN 0-89526-931-7). Regnery Gateway.

Karate. Sin The & Hiang The. LC 82-72608. (Illus.). 200p. (Orig.). 1982. pap. 9.95 o.s.i. (ISBN 0-89708-099-8). And Bks.

Karate: Defence & Attack. rev. ed. K. Enoeda & J. Chisholm. (Illus.). 96p. 1986. pap. text ed. 12.00 o.p. (ISBN 0-87364-378-X). Paladin Pr.

Karel Reisz. Georg M. Gaston. (Filmmakers Ser.). 1980. lib. bdg. 14.50 o.p. (ISBN 0-8057-9277-5, Twayne). G K Hall.

Karen's Choice. Janice Hermansen. (Living Bks.). 224p. 1985. 3.50 o.p. (ISBN 0-8423-2027-X). Tyndale.

Karl Barth. David Mueller. Ed. by Bob E. Patterson. LC 70-188066. (Makers of the Modern Theological Mind Ser). 1972. 8.95 o.p. (ISBN 0-87680-254-4, 80254). Word Bks.

Karl Barth. David L. Mueller. 172p. 1984. pap. text ed. 8.95 o.p. (ISBN 0-8499-3002-2, 3002-2). Word Bks.

Karl Barth & Radical Politics. Ed. by George Hunsinger. LC 76-976. 236p. 1976. softcover 6.45 o.s.i. (ISBN 0-664-24797-0, Westminster). Westminster John Knox.

Karl Barth: His Life from Letters & Autobiographical Texts. Eberhard Busch. Tr. by John Bowden from Ger. LC 76-15881. (Illus.). 592p. 1976. 19.95 o.p. (ISBN 0-8006-0485-7, 1-485, Fortress). Augsburg Fortress.

Karl Kautsky, Eighteen Fifty-Four to Nineteen Thirty-Eight: Marxism in the Classical Years. Gary P. Steenson. LC 78-3701. (Illus.). 1978. 29.95x o.p. (ISBN 0-8229-3377-2). U of Pittsburgh Pr.

Karl Kraus & the Soul-Doctors: A Pioneer Critic & His Criticism of Psychiatry & Psychoanalysis. Thomas Szasz. LC 76-17004. xviii, 180p. 1976. 20.00x o.p. (ISBN 0-8071-0196-6). La State U Pr.

Karl Lark-Horovitz, Pioneer in Solid State Physics. V. A. Johnson. LC 77-91464. (Men of Physics Ser.). 1969. 75.00 o.p. (ISBN 0-08-006581-3); pap. 75.00 o.p. (ISBN 0-08-006580-5). Pergamon.

Karl Marx. Ed. by Tom Bottomore. 200p. 1979. 34.95x o.p. (ISBN 0-631-10961-7); pap. 16.95x o.p. (ISBN 0-631-11061-5). Basil Blackwell.

Karl Marx. Allen Wood. (Arguments of the Philosophers Ser.). 280p. 1981. 26.95x o.p. (ISBN 0-7100-0672-1). Routledge Chapman & Hall.

Karl Marx: A Christian Assessment of His Life & Thought. David Lyon. LC 81-8268. 192p. (Orig.). 1981. pap. 7.95 o.p. (ISBN 0-87784-879-3). Inter-Varsity.

Karl Marx & Friedrich Engels, an Analytical Bibliography. Cecil L. Eubanks. LC 75-24779. (Reference Library of Social Science: Vol. 23). 1977. lib. bdg. 29.00 o.p. (ISBN 0-8240-9957-5). Garland Pub.

Karl Marx: Beacon for Our Times. Gus Hall. LC 83-12841. 96p. (Orig.). 1983. pap. 1.75 o.p. (ISBN 0-7178-0607-3). Intl Pubs Co.

Karl Marx on Freedom of the Press & Censorship. Ed. by Saul K. Padover. LC 78-172260. (Karl Marx Library: Vol. 4). 264p. 1974. text ed. 10.00 o.p. (ISBN 0-07-048077-X). McGraw.

Karl Marx, Romantic Irony & the Proletariat: Studies in the Mythopoetic Origins of Marxism. Leonard P. Wessell. LC 79-12386. xii, 300p. 1979. text ed. 32.50 o.p. (ISBN 0-8071-0587-2). La State U Pr.

Karl Shapiro: A Descriptive Bibliography. Lee Bartlett. LC 78-68245. (Reference Library of Humanities Ser.). 1979. lib. bdg. 28.00 o.p. (ISBN 0-8240-9812-9). Garland Pub.

Karlstadt's Battle with Luther: Documents in a Liberal-Radical Debate. Ed. by Ronald J. Sider. LC 77-78642. 180p. (Orig.). 1978. pap. 5.95 o.p. (ISBN 0-8006-1312-0, 1-1312, Fortress). Augsburg Fortress.

Karma & Destiny in the I Ching. Guy Damian-Knight. 256p. 1987. pap. 12.95 o.p. (ISBN 1-85063-038-0, 30380, Ark Paperbks). Routledge Chapman & Hall.

Karst Geomorphology. Ed. by M. M. Sweeting. LC 81-6558. (Benchmark Papers in Geology Ser.: Vol. 59). 448p. 1982. 63.95 o.p. (ISBN 0-87933-379-0). Van Nos Reinhold.

Kartusch Book Cassette. Stephen Cosgrove. Ed. by Mary H. Manoni. (Serendipity Book Cassettes). (Illus.). 16p. (gr. k-3). pap. 25.95 o.p. (ISBN 0-89290-053-9). Soc for Visual.

Kashmir, Ladakh & Zanskar: A Travel Survival Kit. 2nd ed. Margret Schettler & Rolf Schettler. (Illus.). 204p. (Orig.). 1989. pap. 7.95 o.p. (ISBN 0-908086-63-6). Lonely Planet.

Kashmir Shawl. F. Ames. (Illus.). 1985. 79.50 o.p. Antique Collect.

Kasimir Malevich's Black Square & the Gensis of Suprematism 1907-1915. William S. Simmons. LC 79-57496. (Outstanding Dissertations in the Fine Arts Ser.). (Illus.). 334p. 1981. lib. bdg. 46.00 o.p. (ISBN 0-8240-3942-4). Garland Pub.

Kassandra & the Wolf. Margarita Karapanou. Tr. by N. C. Germanacos. LC 76-229. 132p. 1976. 6.95 o.p. (ISBN 0-15-142174-9). HarBraceJ.

Kastenbaum: Between Life & Death. 192p. 1979. 19.50 o.p. Springer Pub.

Katalog Des Kunsthistorischen Instituts in Florenz, Catalogue of the Institute for the History of Art, Florence, 9 vols. Institute for the History of Art, Florence, Kunsthistorischen Institut - Florence Staff. 1964. Set. 890.00 o.p. (ISBN 0-8161-0696-7, Pub. by Hall Libray); 1st suppl. 2 vols. (1968) 220.00 o.p. (ISBN 0-8161-0763-7); 2nd suppl. 2 vols. (1972) 220.00 o.p. (ISBN 0-8161-0905-2); 3rd suppl, 2 vols. (1976) 230.00 o.p. (ISBN 0-8161-0052-7). G K Hall.

Kataloge der Internationale Jugendbibliothek, (Catalogs of the International Youth Library, 5 pts. Internationalen Jugendbibliothek, (International Youth Library) Staff. Incl. Pt. 1. Alphabetischer Katalog, (Alphabetical, 5 vols. 2634p. 1970. Set. lib. bdg. 495.00 (ISBN 0-8161-0759-9); Pt. 2. Laenderkatalog, (Language Sections Catalog, 4 vols. 2493p. 1970. Set. lib. bdg. 395.00 (ISBN 0-8161-0110-8); Pt. 3. Systematischer Katalog, (Classified, 2 vols. 1140p. 1970. Set. lib. bdg. 198.00 (ISBN 0-8161-0108-6); Pt. 4. Titelkatalog, (Title, 4 vols. 2274p. 1970. Set. lib. bdg. 395.00 (ISBN 0-8161-0111-6); Pt. 5. Illustratorenkatalog, (Catalog of Illustrators, 3 vols. 1487p. Set. 298.00 (ISBN 0-8161-0109-4). 1968. G K Hall.

Kate: A Divorced Mother's Story. Robert F. McGowan. 1983. 13.95 o.p. (ISBN 0-533-05749-3). Vantage.

Kate Alone. Patricia L. Gauch. (gr. 4 up). pap. 1.95 o.p. (ISBN 0-671-43870-0). Archway.

Kate Greenaway Transfer Designs. 96p. 1981. pap. 4.95 o.p. (ISBN 0-87588-171-8, 1248). Hobby Hse.

Kate Quinton's Days. Susan Sheehan. 176p. 1984. 15.45 o.p. (ISBN 0-395-36220-2). HM.

Kate: The Life of Katharine Hepburn. Charles Higham. (Illus.). 244p. 1975. 7.95 o.p. (ISBN 0-393-07486-2). Norton.

Kate's Secret Riddle Book. Sid Fleischman. (Illus.). (gr. k-3). 1978. pap. 1.25 o.p. (ISBN 0-380-40253-X, 51987-9, Camelot). Avon.

Katharine Hepburn. Sheridan Morley. (Illus.). 192p. 1984. 19.95 o.p. (ISBN 0-316-58368-5). Little.

Katharine the Great: The Life of Katharine Graham. Deborah Davis. 1979. 10.00 o.p. (ISBN 0-15-146784-6). HarBraceJ.

Katherine. Anya Seton. 1954. 12.95 o.p. (ISBN 0-395-08173-4). HM.

Katherine Anne Porter. George Hendrick. (United States Authors Ser.: No. 90). 1965. lib. bdg. 14.95 o.s.i. (ISBN 0-8057-0592-9, Twayne). G K Hall.

Katherine Anne Porter: A Life. Joan Givner. 572p. 1984. pap. 10.75 o.p. (ISBN 0-671-50586-6, Touchstone Bks). S&S.

Katherine Anne Porter's Women: The Eye of Her Fiction. Jane K. DeMouy. 238p. 1983. text ed. 25.00x o.p. (ISBN 0-292-79018-X). U of Tex Pr.

Katherine Porter: Works on Paper 1969 to 1979. Katherine Porter. LC 80-65252. (Illus.). 24p. 1980. pap. 2.50 o.p. (ISBN 0-88401-034-1). Fine Arts Mus.

Kathleen Kennedy: Her Life & Times. Lynne McTaggart. LC 83-1979. (Illus.). 264p. 1983. 14.95 o.p. (ISBN 0-385-27415-7, Dial). Doubleday.

Kathleen Kennedy: Her Life & Times. Lynne McTaggart. 288p. 1985. pap. 8.95 o.p. (ISBN 0-03-000478-0, Owl Bks). H Holt & Co.

Kathleen Woodiwiss, 4 vols. 1984. Set. pap. 18.25 o.p. (ISBN 0-380-88708-8, 88708-8). Avon.

Kathryn Klinger's First Book of Beauty. Kathryn Klinger. 256p. 1984. 16.45 o.p. (ISBN 0-671-46283-0). S&S.

Kathy. Barbara Miller & Charles P. Conn. (Illus.). 160p. 1981. 8.95 o.p. (ISBN 0-8007-1093-2); pap. 2.75 o.p. (ISBN 0-8007-8415-4, Spire Bks). Revell.

Kathy Cooks...Naturally. Kathy Hoshijo. 544p. 1981. pap. 15.00 o.p. (ISBN 0-936602-24-4). Kampmann.

Katie. Michael McDowell. 1982. pap. 3.95 o.p. (ISBN 0-380-80184-1, 80184-1). Avon.

Katie & the Smallest Bear. Ruth McCarthy. LC 85-9791. (Illus.). 32p. (ps-1). 1986. 8.95 o.s.i. (ISBN 0-394-87855-8); lib. bdg. 9.99 o.s.i. (ISBN 0-394-97855-2). Knopf.
Katie the Camel. Alice L. Mason & Russ Flint. (Illus.). 16p. (gr. k-6). 1984. pap. 1.50 o.p. (ISBN 0-8249-8066-2). Ideals.
Katie's Magic Glasses. Jane Goodsell. (Illus.). (gr. k-3). 1974. PLB 7.95 reinforced bdg. o.p. (ISBN 0-395-20108-X). HM.
Katie's Magic Glasses. Jane Goodsell. (Illus.). (gr. k-3). 1978. pap. 2.25 o.p. (ISBN 0-395-26690-4). HM.
Katsura: A Princely Retreat. Akira Naito. Tr. by Charles S. Terry from Japanese. LC 75-30183. 182p. 1977. 125.00 o.s.i. (ISBN 0-87011-271-6). Kodansha.
Katsura Villa: The Ambiguity of Its Space. Arata Isozaki & Osamu Sato. LC 86-17686. (Illus.). 280p. 1987. 75.00 o.p. (ISBN 0-8478-0783-5). Rizzoli Intl.
Katy Smith's Winning Workout. Kathy Smith & Judy Jones. Date not set. Running Pr.
Kauai: Hawaii's Garden Island. Robert Wenkam. (Illus.). 144p. 1986. 34.95 o.s.i. (ISBN 0-938379-00-3). Tradewinds Pub.
Kauai: Traveler's Guide. Bill Gleasner & Diana Gleasner. (Illus.). 1978. pap. 4.00 o.p. (ISBN 0-932596-03-7, Pub. by Oriental). Intl Spec Bk.
Kavanaugh's Juvenile Speaker. Mrs. Russell Kavanaugh. LC 78-57859. (Granger Poetry Library). 1978. Repr. of 1877 ed. 16.75x o.p. (ISBN 0-89609-097-3). Roth Pub Inc.
Kaw Valley Landscapes: A Guide to Eastern Kansas. James R. Shortridge. 1977. pap. 8.50x o.p. (ISBN 0-87291-091-1). Coronado Pr.
Kawasaki AE-AR 50 & 80 '81-'84. Chris Rogers. 13.50 o.p. (ISBN 1-85010-007-1, 1007). Haynes Pubns.
Kawasaki Jet Ski 1976-1983 Service-Repair-Maintenance. Anton Vesely & Sydnie Wauson. (Illus., Orig.). 1982. pap. 13.95 o.p. (ISBN 0-89287-354-X, X956). Clymer Pub.
Kawasaki KDX 80-420 Singles 1979-1981. Anton Vesely. Ed. by Eric Jorgensen. (Illus., Orig.). 1981. pap. 13.95 o.p. (ISBN 0-89287-338-8, M446). Clymer Pub.
Kawasaki KX 80-450 Piston Port 1974-1981. (Illus., Orig.). 1981. pap. text ed. 13.95 o.s.i. (ISBN 0-89287-337-X, M445). Clymer Pub.
Kawasaki KZ, Z, & ZX750: 1980-1985 Service Repair Performance. Anton Vesley. Ed. by Sydnie A. Wauson. (Illus., Orig.). 1982. text ed. 13.95 o.p. (ISBN 0-89287-356-6, M450). Clymer Pub.
Kawasaki Snowmobiles Nineteen Seventy-Six to Nineteen Eighty: Service, Repair, Maintenance. Mike Bishop. Ed. by Eric Jorgensen. (Illus.). 152p. (Orig.). 1980. pap. text ed. 8.95 o.p. (ISBN 0-89287-320-5, X995). Clymer Pub.
Kawasaki: 250-750cc Triples 1969-1979--Service, Repair, Maintenance Handbook. 4th ed. Ed. by Eric Jorgensen. (Illus.). pap. 11.95 o.p. (ISBN 0-89287-192-X, M353). Clymer Pub.
Kawasaki 900-1000cc. (M354). Clymer Pub.
Kayak Paddling Strokes. John Pursell & N. Reese. (Lost Arts Ser.). 25p. pap. 2.95 o.p. (ISBN 0-8466-6033-4, U33). Shorey.
Kayak Trips in Puget Sound & the San Juan Islands. Randel Washburne. (Illus.). 150p. (Orig.). 1986. pap. 9.95 o.p. (ISBN 0-931397-05-7). Pacific Search.
KAYPRO Connection-Selecting, Installing & Using Peripherals. Lee F. Ryan & Andrew Townsend. (Illus.). 256p. (Orig.). 1985. 19.95 o.p. (ISBN 0-8306-0880-X, 1880); pap. 14.60 o.p. (ISBN 0-8306-1880-5). TAB Bks.
Kays Gary, Columnist. Frwd. by Pete C. McKnight. LC 81-68572. (Illus.). 185p. 1981. 10.95 o.p. (ISBN 0-914788-43-4). Globe Pequot.
KBG & the United Nations. Lawrence B. Sulc. Ed. by Hale, Nathan, Institute Staff. (Orig.). 1986. pap. 5.00 o.p. (ISBN 0-935067-09-4). Nathan Hale Inst.
K.C. A History of Kansas City, Missouri. A. Theordore Brown & Lyle W. Dorsett. LC 78-14514. (Western Urban History Ser.). (Illus.). 1978. 14.95 o.p. (ISBN 0-87108-526-7); pap. 9.95 o.p. (ISBN 0-87108-563-1). Pruett.
KC's Deals on Wheels. Christine Sprenger et al. 1985. pap. 20.50x IBM o.p. (ISBN 0-256-03148-7); pap. 20.50 Apple o.p. (ISBN 0-256-03149-5). Irwin.
Kean. Giles Playfair. LC 73-10878. (Illus.). 346p. 1973. Repr. of 1939 ed. lib. bdg. 24.75x o.p. (ISBN 0-8371-7047-8, PLKE). Greenwood.
KEANAS. Konrad E. Sadek. 1978. 7.00 o.p. (ISBN 0-682-48913-1). Exposition-Phoenix.
Keaton: The Man Who Wouldn't Lie Down. Tom Dardis. (Illus.). 1979. encore ed. 4.95 o.p. (ISBN 0-684-17177-5, ScribT). Scribner.
Keats. John Keats. (Plain Texts of the Poets Ser). 1968. pap. 2.50x o.p. (ISBN 0-7022-0647-4). U of Queensland Pr.
Keats. Illus. by Patricia Machin. (Pocket Poets Ser.). (Illus.). 52p. 1985. 4.95 o.p. (ISBN 0-86350-047-1). Salem Hse Pubs.
Keats & the Daemon King. Werner W. Beyer. LC 76-86270. 1969. Repr. of 1947 ed. lib. bdg. 27.50x o.p. (ISBN 0-374-90627-0, Octagon). Hippocrene Bks.
Keats: The Critical Heritage. Ed. by G. M. Matthews. 1971. 36.00x o.p. (ISBN 0-7100-7147-7). Routledge Chapman & Hall.
Keelhauled: Unsportsmanlike Conduct & the America's Cup. Douglas Rigg. 1986. 19.45 o.p. (ISBN 0-671-61293-X). S&S.
Keep 'em Rolling. Stephen W. Meader. LC 67-17155. (Illus.). (gr. 7 up). 1967. 4.95 o.p. (ISBN 0-15-242195-5, HJ). HarBraceJ.
Keep It Running. C. Edward Cavert. 1985. pap. text ed. 74.25 o.p. (ISBN 0-07-079272-0). McGraw.
Keep It Running: A Study Guide. C. Edward Cavert et al. (Illus.). 1978. pap. text ed. 19.95 o.p. (ISBN 0-07-009880-8). McGraw.
Keep It Simple. Marian Burros. LC 81-4398. 256p. 1981. 11.95 o.p. (ISBN 0-688-00450-4). Morrow.
Keep the Baby, Faith. Philip DeGrave. LC 86-2127. (Crime Club Ser.). 192p. 1986. 12.95 o.p. (ISBN 0-385-19742-X). Doubleday.
Keep the Baby, Faith. Philip DeGrave. LC 87-510. 336p. 1987. 16.95 o.p. (ISBN 0-385-23989-0, Pub. by GC Large Print). Doubleday.
Keep the Fire Glowing: How a Loving Marriage Builds a Loving Family. Pat Williams & Jill Williams. 160p. 1986. 9.95 o.p. (ISBN 0-8007-1498-9). Revell.
Keep the River on Your Right. Tobias Schneebaum. (Illus.). 1969. pap. 12.50 o.s.i. (ISBN 0-394-62438-6, E838, Ever). Grove.
Keep Young after Forty! Vivienne Lewis. (Lythway Ser.). 168p. 1988. lib. bdg. 17.50x o.s.i. (ISBN 0-7451-0686-2, Pub. by Chivers Pr UK). G K Hall.
Keeper. Audrey Laski. LC 68-28251. 1968. 4.95 o.p. (ISBN 0-393-08568-6). Norton.
Keeper of the Children. William H. Hallahan. 1979. pap. 2.50 o.p. (ISBN 0-380-45203-0, 45203-0). Avon.
Keepers of the Kingdom. Glennita Miller. 1983. 18.25 o.p. (ISBN 0-671-42523-4). S&S.
Keeping a Family Cow. Joann S. Grohman. (Illus.). 192p. 1981. encore ed. 4.95 o.p. (ISBN 0-684-16867-7, ScribT). Scribner.
Keeping America at Work: Strategies for Employing the New Technologies. Robert T. Lund & John A. Hansen. LC 85-17900. 272p. 1986. 19.95 o.p. (ISBN 0-471-81563-2). Wiley.
Keeping Christmas: Activities & Devotions for the Twelve Days of Christmas. Sandra Sorlien. 40p. (Orig.). 1982. pap. 4.95 o.p. (ISBN 0-8066-1940-6, 10-3667, Augsburg). Augsburg Fortress.
Keeping Days. Norma Johnston. LC 73-78727. 256p. (gr. 6 up). 1973. 6.95 o.p. (ISBN 0-689-30110-3, Atheneum). Macmillan.
Keeping Food Fresh. Janet Bailey. LC 84-14924. 384p. 1985. pap. 12.95 o.s.i. (ISBN 0-385-27675-3, Dial). Doubleday.
Keeping Free. Frank Pollard. LC 82-73932. 1983. 4.95 o.p. (ISBN 0-8054-5216-8). Broadman.
Keeping in Touch. Ellen Goodman. 317p. 1985. 16.45 o.s.i. (ISBN 0-671-55376-3). Summit Bks.
Keeping It off: Winning at Weight Loss. Robert Colvin et al. 212p. 1985. 16.45 o.s.i. (ISBN 0-671-53294-4). S&S.
Keeping Love Alive. Elof G. Nelson. LC 77-84088. 1978. pap. 4.50 o.p. (ISBN 0-8066-1613-X, 10-3670, Augsburg). Augsburg Fortress.
Keeping of Animals: Adaptation & Social Relations in Livestock Producing Communities. Ed. by Riva Berleant-Schiller & Eugenia Shanklin. LC 81-65015. (Illus.). 208p. 1983. text ed. 25.95x o.s.i. (ISBN 0-86598-033-0, Pub. by Allanheld). Rowman.
Keeping off the Casualty List. Leroy Eims. 132p. 1986. pap. 5.95 o.p. (ISBN 0-89693-152-8). Victor Bks.
Keeping Our Cities Clean. Ross R. Olney. LC 78-26253. (Illus.). 64p. (gr. 4 up). 1979. lib. bdg. 6.97 o.s.i. (ISBN 0-671-32942-1). Messner.
Keeping Pets, Bk. 1. Eileen Everett. (gr. 3-7). 1973. pap. 1.00 o.p. (ISBN 0-08-016235-5). Pergamon.
Keeping Pets, Bk. 7. Eileen Everett. 1973. pap. 1.00 o.p. (ISBN 0-08-016241-X). Pergamon.
Keeping Shelf. Muriel F. Blackwell. LC 85-5953. 1985. 6.95 o.p. (ISBN 0-8054-5023-8). Broadman.
Keeping the Faith: A Guide to the Christian Message. David G. Truemper & Frederick A. Niedner, Jr. LC 81-43072. 144p. 1981. pap. 3.95 o.p. (ISBN 0-8006-1608-1, 1-1608, Fortress). Augsburg Fortress.
Keeping Track of Teaching: Assessment in the Modern Classroom. Harry Black & Patricia Broadfoot. (Education Bks.). 100p. (Orig.). 1982. pap. 12.95x o.p. (ISBN 0-7100-9017-X). Routledge Chapman & Hall.
Keeping Warm. Mary Gardner. LC 86-47688. 256p. 1987. 17.95 o.p. (ISBN 0-689-11841-4, Atheneum). Macmillan.
Keeping Your Balance. Byrd & Horton. 1986. 6.95 o.p. (ISBN 0-8499-3056-1). Word Bks.
Keeping Your Horse Healthy: The Prevention & Cure of Illness. Pritz Sevelius et al. (Illus.). 176p. 1981. Repr. of 1978 ed. 25.95 o.p. (ISBN 0-7153-7638-1). David & Charles.
Keir Hardie: The Making of a Socialist. Fred Reid. (Social History Ser.). 211p. 1978. 19.00 o.p. (ISBN 0-85664-624-5, Pub. by Croom Helm Ltd). Routledge Chapman & Hall.
Keith Preston: Studies in the Diction of the Sermo Amatorius in Roman Comedy see Bruno Lier: Ad Topica Carminum Amatorium Symbolae.
Keller's Bomb. Lawrence Dunning. 1978. pap. 1.95 o.p. (ISBN 0-380-40873-2, 40873). Avon.
Kelly. David Chandler. LC 81-71684. 320p. 1982. 14.95 o.p. (ISBN 0-87795-395-3, Arbor Hse). Morrow.
Kelly's Business Directory 1987. 1986. text ed. 160.00 o.p. (ISBN 0-610-00586-3). Intl Pubns Serv.
Ken Kern's Homestead Workshop. Ken Kern & Barbara Kern. (Illus.). 160p. 1981. encore ed. 4.95 o.p. (ISBN 0-684-17015-9, ScribT). Scribner.
Ken Kern's Masonry Stove. Barbara Kern & Ken Kern. (Illus.). 1983. 17.95 o.s.i. (ISBN 0-684-17775-7, ScribT). Scribner.
Ken Russell: A Guide to Reference & Resources. Diane Rosenfeldt. 1978. lib. bdg. 20.50 o.p. (ISBN 0-8161-7881-X, Hall Reference). G K Hall.
Ken Tyler-Master Printer-& the American Print Renaissance. Pat Gilmour. LC 85-24905. (Illus.). 160p. 1986. 25.00 o.p. (ISBN 0-933920-16-4, Dist by Rizzoli). Hudson Hills.
Kendo No Kata: Forms of Japanese Kendo. Michael Finn. (Illus.). 64p. 1986. pap. text ed. 10.00 o.p. (ISBN 0-87364-411-5). Paladin Pr.
Kennaway Papers. James Kennaway & Susan Kennaway. LC 81-47454. 144p. 1981. 11.95 o.p. (ISBN 0-03-059578-9). H Holt & Co.
Kennedy. Reg Gadney. LC 83-10802. 1983. 16.95 o.s.i. (ISBN 0-03-069406-X). H Holt & Co.
Kennedy & Roosevelt: The Uneasy Alliance. Michael R. Beschloss. (Illus.). 1980. 14.95 o.p. (ISBN 0-393-01335-9). Norton.
Kennedy & Roosevelt: The Uneasy Alliance. Michael R. Beschloss. (Illus.). 320p. 1981. pap. 5.95 o.p. (ISBN 0-393-00062-1). Norton.
Kennedy in Vietnam: American Vietnam Policy 1960-1963. William J. Rust. Ed. by U. S. News Books Staff. (Illus.). 240p. 1985. 15.95 o.s.i. (ISBN 0-684-18370-6, ScribT). Scribner.
Kennedy Justice. Victor S. Navasky. LC 77-145633. 1977. pap. 5.95 o.p. (ISBN 0-689-70543-3, 231, Atheneum). Macmillan.
Kennedy Round in American Trade Policy: The Twilight of the GATT. John W. Evans. LC 77-139725. (Center for International Affairs Ser). 1971. 27.00x o.s.i. (ISBN 0-674-50275-2). Harvard U Pr.
Kennedy Without Tears: The Man Beneath the Myth. Tom Wicker. (Illus.). 1964. 2.95 o.p. (ISBN 0-688-01934-X). Morrow.
Kennedys: An American Drama. Peter Collier & David Horowitz. LC 84-2502. (Illus.). 608p. 1984. 21.45 o.s.i. (ISBN 0-671-44793-9). Summit Bks.
Kennedy's Revised Latin Primer. Benjamin H. Kennedy. 1962. pap. text ed. 7.50 o.p. (ISBN 0-582-36240-7). Longman.
Kennel Murder Case. S. S. Van Dine. 1980. lib. bdg. 11.50 o.p. (ISBN 0-8398-2558-7, Gregg). G K Hall.
Kennel Murder Case: A Philo Vance Mystery. S. S. Van Dine. 312p. 1984. pap. 3.95 o.s.i. (ISBN 0-684-18248-3, ScribT). Scribner.
Kennet & Avon Canal. Kenneth R. Clew. (Illus.). 240p. 1985. 30.95 o.p. (ISBN 0-7153-8656-5). David & Charles.
Kenneth Clark. Meryle Secrest. (Illus.). 416p. 1985. 18.95 o.p. (ISBN 0-03-054066-6). H Holt & Co.
Kenneth Noland: A Retrospective. Diane Waldman. LC 77-70424. (Illus.). 1981. pap. 12.00 o.p. (ISBN 0-89207-009-9). S R Guggenheim.
Kenny Duncan Is Dead: Reflections on a Teenage Suicide. John-Michael Williams. 96p. (YA) pap. cancelled o.s.i. (ISBN 1-55783-032-0). Applause Theatre Bk Pubs.
Kenny Roger's America. Kenny Rogers. (Illus.). 1986. 24.95 o.p. (ISBN 0-316-75419-6). Little.
Kenny the Kitty. Irene Keller. (Illus.). 16p. (Orig.). (gr. k-6). 1982. pap. 1.50 o.p. (ISBN 0-8249-8989-9). Ideals.
Keno. T. V. Olsen. 176p. 1987. pap. 2.75 o.p. (ISBN 0-380-75292-1). Avon.
Kensei. Steven Schlossstein. 464p. 1984. pap. 3.95 o.p. (ISBN 0-380-69369-0). Avon.
Kensho. Dennis Schmidt. 320p. 1986. pap. 10.95 o.s.i. (ISBN 0-441-43527-0, Pub. by Ace Science Fiction). Ace Bks.
Kent State: What Happened & Why. James A. Michener. (Illus.). 1981. pap. 2.95 o.p. (ISBN 0-449-23869-5, Crest). Fawcett.
Kentuckians. Janice H. Giles. 1953. 7.95 o.p. (ISBN 0-395-07737-0). HM.
Kentucky. Photos by James Archambeault. LC 81-86037. (Illus.). 160p. (Text by Thomas D. Clark). 1982. 35.00 o.s.i. (ISBN 0-912856-74-2). Graphic Arts Ctr.
Kentucky Basketball: Big Blue Machine. Russell Rice. LC 75-32110. (College Sports Ser.). 1982. 12.95 o.p. (ISBN 0-87397-240-6). Strode.
Kentucky Business Directory, 1987-88. rev. ed. American Directory Publishing Co., Inc. Staff. 951p. 1987. pap. 75.00 o.p. (ISBN 0-944316-09-3). Amer Directory.
Kentucky Instructions to Juries: 1975-86, 3 Vols. 3rd ed. John S. Palmore. Vol. I, Criminal. 35.00 o.p.; Vol. II, Civil. 35.00 o.p.; Vol. III. Anderson Pub Co.
Kentucky: Judgments. 1983. 8.50 o.p. (ISBN 0-686-90760-4). Am Law Inst.
Kentucky Manufacturers Register, 1988. 240p. 1987. 46.00 o.p. (ISBN 0-318-02881-6). Manufacturers.
Kentucky Media Directory, 1988: The Most up-to-Date, Detailed Listing of all Kentucky Media. (Illus.). 106p. (Orig.). 1988. pap. 19.00 o.p. (ISBN 0-944369-02-2). Brackemyre Pub.
Kentucky Rules of Court. Michie Company Editorial Staff. (State Practice Publications Ser.). 1030p. 1984. pap. 30.00 o.p. (ISBN 0-87215-748-2, 73809); Nineteen Eighty-five suppl. only. 8.00 o.p. (ISBN 0-87215-906-X, 73811). Michie Co.
Kentucky Supplement to Modern Real Estate Practice. 2nd ed. L. Randolph McGee. 1978. pap. 9.95 o.s.i. (ISBN 0-88462-289-4, 1510-18, Real Estate Ed). Longman Finan.
Kenya. Hildebrand Editorial Staff. (Travel Guide Ser.). (Illus.). 160p. 1986. pap. 9.95 o.s.i. (ISBN 0-87052-224-8, Pub. by Hildebrand). Hippocrene Bks.
Kenya: A Country Study. 3rd ed. Ed. by Harold D. Nelson. LC 84-6420. (Area Handbook Ser.: DA Pam 550-56). (Illus.). 363p. 1984. 13.00 o.p. (ISBN 0-318-21868-2, S/N 008-020-00992-0). USGPO.
Kenya: A Visitor's Guide. Arnold Curtis. (Illus.). 170p. (Orig.). 1987. pap. 12.95 o.p. (ISBN 1-55650-005-X). Hunter Pub NY.
Kenya: The Years of Change. Vivien S. Prince. (Illus.). 144p. 9.50 o.p. (ISBN 0-8062-2787-7). Carlton.
Kept for the Master's Use. Frances Havergel. 120p. 1986. pap. 5.50 o.p. (ISBN 0-89693-279-6). Victor Bks.
Kept in Stitches. Katie Kane. 47p. 1982. pap. 4.00 o.p. (ISBN 0-682-49901-3). Exposition-Phoenix.
Keratinization-a Survey of Vertebrate Epithelia. P. F. Parakkal & Nancy J. Alexander. (Monographs on the Ultrastructure of Cells & Organisms). 1972. 30.00 o.p. (ISBN 0-12-454140-2). Acad Pr.
Kermie, Where Are You? Virginia Holt. LC 85-62008. (Lift-the-Flaps Storybooks). (Illus.). 24p. (ps-k). 1986. 5.95 o.s.i. (ISBN 0-394-87993-7). Random.
Kern County Panorama. Ralph Kreiser & Thomas Hunt. (Illus.). 52p. 1961. pap. 1.50 o.s.i. (ISBN 0-943500-07-9). Kern Historical.
Kerr's Country Kitchen. Don Kerr & Vivian Kerr. (Illus.). 164p. 1981. pap. 6.95 o.p. (ISBN 0-933614-08-X). Peregrine Pr Pubs.
Kerygma & Comedy in the New Testament: A Structuralist Approach to Hermeneutic. Dan O. Via, Jr. LC 74-80425. 192p. 1975. 8.95 o.p. (ISBN 0-8006-0281-1, Fortress). Augsburg Fortress.
Keshub Chunder Sen: A Search for Cultural Synthesis in India. Meredith Borthwick. 1978. 13.50x o.p. (ISBN 0-88386-904-7). South Asia Bks.
Kestner: King of Dollmakers. Jan Foulke. 236p. 1982. 19.95 o.s.i. (ISBN 0-87588-185-8, 1257). Hobby Hse.
Ketone Enolates: Regiospecific Preparation & Synthetic Uses. Jean D'Angelo. 1977. pap. 14.00 o.p. (ISBN 0-08-021587-4). Pergamon.
Ketuba: Jewish Marriage Contracts Through the Ages. 2nd ed. David Davidovitch. (Illus.). 1974. 29.50 o.s.i. (ISBN 0-87203-054-7). Hermon.
Key. Florence P. Heide. (Illus.). (gr. 5-7). 1971. PLB 4.50 o.p. (ISBN 0-689-20656-9, Atheneum). Macmillan.
Key Exchange. Kevin Wade. 96p. 1983. pap. 2.50 o.p. (ISBN 0-380-61119-8, 61119-8, Bard). Avon.
Key into the Language of America. Roger Williams. Ed. by John J. Teunissen & Evelyn J. Hinz. LC 72-6590. 264p. 1973. 25.00x o.p. (ISBN 0-8143-1490-2). Wayne St U Pr.
Key Issues in Criminology. Roger Hood & Richard Sparks. LC 77-90231. (Illus., Orig.). 1970. pap. text ed. 3.95 o.p. (ISBN 0-07-029730-4). McGraw.
Key Issues in Education: Comparative Perspectives. Ed. by Keith Watson. LC 85-14961. 127p. 1985. 23.00 o.p. (ISBN 0-7099-2795-9, Pub. by Croom Helm Ltd). Routledge Chapman & Hall.

Key Issues in Health. Robert A. Burton et al. (Illus.). 369p. 1978. pap. text ed. 11.95 o.p. (ISBN 0-15-548368-4, HC). HarBraceJ.

Key of the Keelson. Eben M. Anderson. LC 84-90213. 55p. 1985. 6.95 o.p. (ISBN 0-533-06266-7). Vantage.

Key Thoughts for Talks. Reed L. Hart. (Orig.). 1978. pap. 3.50 o.p. (ISBN 0-89036-105-3). Hawkes Pub Inc.

Key to a Fourth One Thousand Quilt Patterns. Judy Rehmel. LC 84-90561. (Illus.). 240p. 1983. ring binder 11.00x o.p. (ISBN 0-913731-03-X). J Rehmel.

Key to a Second One Thousand Quilt Patterns. Judy Rehmel. LC 84-90559. (Illus.). 240p. 1979. ring binder 11.00x o.p. (ISBN 0-913731-01-3). J Rehmel.

Key to a Successful Church Library. rev. ed. Erwin E. John. LC 58-13940. (Orig.). 1967. pap. 5.95 o.p. (ISBN 0-8066-0711-4, 10-3684, Augsburg). Augsburg Fortress.

Key to a Third One Thousand Quilt Patterns. Judy Rehmel. LC 84-90560. (Illus.). 240p. 1980. ring binder 11.00x o.p. (ISBN 0-913731-02-1). J Rehmel.

Key to Better Reading. Paul D. Leedy. LC 68-13094. (Illus.). 1969. pap. text ed. 3.95 o.p. (ISBN 0-07-037023-0). McGraw.

Key to Dooyeweerd. S. Wolfe. 1978. pap. 2.95 o.p. (ISBN 0-87552-542-3). Presby & Reformed.

Key to Eckankar. Paul Twitchell. LC 85-81715. 43p. 1985. pap. 4.95 o.p. (ISBN 0-88155-035-3). Illum Way Pub.

Key to Health, Wealth, & Love. Julia Seton-Sears. 32p. 1976. pap. 4.95 o.s.i. (ISBN 0-88697-025-3). Life Science.

Key to Japan's Economic Strength: Human Power. Rosalie L. Tung. LC 82-48172. 240p. 1984. 35.00x o.p. (ISBN 0-669-06039-9). Lexington Bks.

Key to Psychiatry: A Textbook for Students. 3rd ed. M. J. Sainsbury. 426p. 1980. 30.00 o.p. (ISBN 0-471-26009-6, Pub. by Wiley Med). Wiley.

Key to Quality: A Guide to Joint Commission Home Care Accreditation. 45p. pap. cancelled o.s.i. Joint Comm Hlthcare.

Key to the Stars. Woolley. (Illus.). 142p. 1957. (ISBN 0-8022-1934-9). Philos Lib.

Key to the Treasure. Peggy Parish. LC 66-17901. (Illus.). 160p. (gr. 2-5). 1967. 9.95 o.s.i. (ISBN 0-02-769930-7). Macmillan.

Key to the True Quabbalah. 2nd ed. Franz Bardon. Tr. by Peter A. Dimai from Ger. (Illus.). 270p. 1975. 21.00 o.p. (ISBN 0-914732-12-9). Bro Life Inc.

Key to Urania see Mythological Astronomy of the Ancients Demonstrated.

Key to Your Child's Heart. Gary Smalley. 160p. 1984. 10.95 o.p. (ISBN 0-8499-0433-1, 0433-1). Word Bks.

Key Word & Other Mysteries. Isaac Asimov. (Illus.). 56p. (gr. 2-6). 1979. pap. 1.95 o.p. (ISBN 0-380-43224-2, 63776-6, Camelot). Avon.

Key Words to the Fauna & Flora of the British Isles & Northwestern Europe. Ed. by G. J. Kerrich et al. (Systematic Association Special Ser.). 1978. 55.50 o.p. (ISBN 0-12-405550-8). Acad Pr.

Keyboard Harmony. George A. Wedge. 1924. pap. 9.95 o.s.i. (ISBN 0-02-872790-8). Schirmer Bks.

Keyboard Harmony Course, 2 bks. Angela Diller. 1937. pap. 2.95 ea. o.s.i. Bk. I (ISBN 0-02-870730-3). Bk. II (ISBN 0-02-870740-0). Schirmer Bks.

Keyboard Music. Ed. by Denis Matthews. LC 78-58317. (Illus.). 1978. 12.50 o.s.i. (ISBN 0-8008-4455-6, Crescendo); pap. 7.95 o.s.i. (ISBN 0-8008-4456-4, Crescendo). Taplinger.

Keyboard Proficiency. Louise Guhl. 263p. 1979. pap. text ed. 14.95 o.p. (ISBN 0-15-548315-3, HC). HarBraceJ.

Keyboard Works of Felix Maximo Lopez: An Anthology. Ed. by Alma Espinosa. LC 82-24767. (Illus.). 216p. (Orig.). 1983. lib. bdg. 31.25 o.p. (ISBN 0-8191-3038-9); pap. text ed. 13.75 o.p. (ISBN 0-8191-3039-7). U Pr of Amer.

Keynes, Schumpeter & the Effort to Save Capitalism from Total Collapse. Osvald W. Mitchell. (Illus.). 165p. 1989. 127.75 o.p. (ISBN 0-86654-276-0). Inst Econ Finan.

Keynotes. George Egerton. Ed. by Ian Fletcher & John Stokes. LC 76-24384. (Decadent Consciousness Ser.). 1977. lib. bdg. 46.00 o.p. (ISBN 0-8240-2758-2). Garland Pub.

Keys of Power: A Study of Indian Ritual & Belief. John Abbott. 1974. 10.00 o.p. (ISBN 0-8216-0219-5, Pub. by Univ Bks). Carol Pub Group.

Keys to a Powerful Vocabulary: Level I. Minnette Lenier & Janet Maker. (Illus.). 240p. 1982. pap. text ed. (ISBN 0-13-514968-1). P-H.

Keys to American English. Constance Gefvert et al. 396p. (Orig.). 1975. pap. text ed. 10.00 net o.p. (ISBN 0-15-597858-6, HC). HarBraceJ.

Keys to Costal & Chaparral Flowering Plants of Southern California. Barbara J. Collins. 256p. 1985. pap. text ed. 13.95 o.p. (ISBN 0-8403-3731-0). Kendall-Hunt.

Keys to Reading & Study Skills. 2nd ed. Harriet Krantz & Joan Kimmelman. 336p. 1985. pap. text ed. 15.95 o.p. (ISBN 0-03-071093-6, HoltC). HR&W.

Keys to Relationships. 1977. pap. 2.15 o.s.i. (ISBN 0-8395-3032-3, 3032). BSA.

Keys to Soil Taxonomy. U. S. Department of Agriculture, Soil Conservation Service Staff. 1985. pap. text ed. 8.00 o.s.i. (ISBN 0-932865-00-3). Cornell U Dept.

Keys to Successful Color. Foster Caddell. (Illus.). 144p. 1979. 27.50 o.p. (ISBN 0-8230-2580-2). Watson-Guptill.

Keys to the Families & Genera of Queensland. 2nd ed. H. T. Clifford & Gwen Ludlow. (Flowering Plants (Magnoliophyta)). (Illus.). 1979. pap. 25.00x o.p. (ISBN 0-7022-1225-3). U of Queensland Pr.

Keys to the Growth of Neighborhood Development Organizations. N. Mayer. 96p. 1981. pap. text ed. 8.00 o.p. (ISBN 0-87766-299-1). Urban Inst.

Keys to the Kingdom. F. A. Walton. (Illus.). 80p. 1985. 8.00 o.p. (ISBN 0-682-40247-8). Exposition-Phoenix.

Keys to the North American Species of Carex. K. K. Mackenzie. 1960. 6.00x o.p. (ISBN 0-934454-55-8). Lubrecht & Cramer.

Keystone. Peter Lovesey. 1984. pap. 2.95 o.s.i. (ISBN 0-394-72604-9). Pantheon.

Keystorn of the Guitar. Darrel Irving. (Illus.). 96p. 1987. pap. 14.95 o.s.i. (ISBN 0-317-66185-X, Pub. by Calliope Music). Bold Strummer Ltd.

KG Two Hundred. Ed. by P. W. Stahl. (Illus.). 224p. 1981. 19.95 o.p. (ISBN 0-86720-564-4). Janes Info Group.

KGB. Brian Freemantle. LC 81-23205. (Illus.). 192p. 1982. 14.95 o.p. (ISBN 0-03-062458-4); pap. 6.95 o.p. (ISBN 0-03-071059-6). H Holt & Co.

KGB. Don Lawson. LC 83-14619. (Spy Shelf Ser.). 192p. (gr. 4 up). 1984. lib. bdg. 8.79 o.s.i. (ISBN 0-671-50833-4). Messner.

Khajuraho. Eliky Zannas. (Illus.). 1960. 132.00x o.p. (ISBN 0-686-21868-X). Mouton.

Khaki & Gown. Lord Birdwood. 10.00 o.p. (ISBN 0-8315-0041-7). Speller.

Khrushchev of the Ukraine. Victor Alexandrov. 1957. (ISBN 0-8022-0018-4). Philos Lib.

Kiangsi Native Trade & Its Taxation. Stanley Wright. LC 78-74332. (Modern Chinese Economy Ser.). 201p. 1980. lib. bdg. 26.00 o.p. (ISBN 0-8240-4258-1). Garland Pub.

Kiatsu. Koichi Tohei. (Illus.). 180p. 1983. pap. text ed. 16.95 o.p. (ISBN 0-87040-536-5). Japan Pubns USA.

Kibbutz: New Way of Life. D. Leon. 1969. 55.00 o.p. (ISBN 0-08-013357-6); pap. 55.00 o.p. (ISBN 0-08-013356-8). Pergamon.

Kick It! Judy Perlmutter. LC 85-73828. 128p. 1986. 3.95 o.p. (ISBN 0-89586-456-8). Price Stern.

Kick Out the Jams: Detroit's Cass Corridor 1963-1977. Commentary by Jay Belloli & Mary J. Jacob. (Illus.). 148p. 1981. pap. 19.95 o.p. (ISBN 0-89558-082-9). Detroit Inst Arts.

Kicking over Sacred Cows. Charles Capps. 132p. (Orig.). 1984. pap. 4.95 o.s.i. (ISBN 0-914307-18-5, Dist. by Harrison Hse). R Tilton Ministries.

Kicking the Football Soccer Style with Tips on Playing Soccer. Pete Gogolak. Ed. by Ray Siegener. LC 73-190403. (Illus.). 1972. 4.95 o.p. (ISBN 0-689-10502-9, Atheneum). Macmillan.

Kicking the Habit: Four Australian Therapeutic Communities. Charlotte Carr-Gregg. LC 83-26118. 186p. 1985. text ed. 25.00x o.p. (ISBN 0-7022-1748-4). U of Queensland Pr.

Kid Blackie: The Colorado Days of Jack Dempsey. Toby Smith. (Illus.). 1988. 7.95 o.p. (ISBN 0-317-67804-3). Johnson Bks.

Kid Breckenridge. Bernard Palmer. (Breck Western Ser.). 276p. 1984. pap. 3.50 o.p. (ISBN 0-8423-2059-8). Tyndale.

Kid Business: How it Exploits the Children it Should Help. Ronald B. Taylor. 1981. 12.95 o.p. (ISBN 0-395-30515-2). HM.

Kid from Rincon. Arthur Moore. 1979. pap. 1.50 o.s.i. (ISBN 0-449-14181-0, GM). Fawcett.

Kid from Tomkinsville. John R. Tunis. LC 40-27364. (Illus.). 1940. 4.95 o.p. (ISBN 0-15-242565-9, HJ). HarBraceJ.

Kid from Tomkinsville. John R. Tunis. LC 86-27104. 272p. (gr. 2-7). 1987. pap. 4.95 o.p. (ISBN 0-15-200500-5, Gulliver Bks). HarBraceJ.

Kid Gloves. Alan Leonard. (Illus.). 64p. (ps up). Date not set. 10.95 o.p. (ISBN 0-374-34128-1). FS&G.

Kidnapped. Karl Dortzbach & Deborah Dortzbach. LC 74-25708. (Illus.). 1977. pap. 1.95 o.p. (ISBN 0-06-061976-7, HJ 35). HarpR.

Kidnapped. Robert Louis Stevenson. 1977. pap. 2.50x o.p. (ISBN 0-460-01762-4, DEL-04194, Evman). Biblio Dist.

Kidnapped. Robert Louis Stevenson. LC 86-70328. (Illus.). 240p. (gr. 7-12). 1986. 12.95 o.p. (ISBN 0-89577-232-9). RD Assn.

Kidnapped Saint & Other Stories by B. Traven. Ed. by Nina C. Klein & H. Arthur Klein. LC 74-9349. 1977. 8.95 o.s.i. (ISBN 0-88208-049-0); pap. 5.95 o.s.i. (ISBN 0-88208-074-1). Chicago Review.

Kidnapping. Jerry Jenkins. (Bradford Family Adventures Ser.). 128p. (Orig.). (gr. 4-8). 1984. pap. 3.50 o.p. (ISBN 0-87239-794-7, 2944). Standard Pub.

Kidnapping of Anna. Ruth Hooker & Carole Smith. Ed. by Kathy Pacini. LC 78-32051. (High-Low Mysteries Ser.). (Illus.). (gr. 3-8). 1979. PLB 8.95 o.p. (ISBN 0-8075-4176-1). A Whitman.

Kidnapping of Christina Lattimore. Joan L. Nixon. (gr. 7 up). 1979. 8.95 o.p. (ISBN 0-15-242657-4, HJ). HarBraceJ.

Kidney. 2nd ed. Abner Golden. LC 76-30733. 222p. 1977. 21.50 o.p. (ISBN 0-686-74090-4). Krieger.

Kidney: Diagnosis & Management. Ed. by Neal S. Bricker & Michael A. Kirschenbaum. LC 82-24753. 540p. 1984. 37.50x o.p. (ISBN 0-471-09572-9). Wiley.

Kidney Disease Case Studies. 3rd ed. Alvin E. Parrish. 1983. pap. text ed. 22.75 o.p. (ISBN 0-87488-022-X). Med Exam.

Kids & Careers Ser, 4bks. 384p. 1979. 25.95 o.p. (ISBN 0-913916-75-7, IP75-7). Incentive Pubns.

Kids & Cubs. O. Perovskaya. 262p. 1975. 2.10 o.p. (ISBN 0-8285-1172-1, Pub. by Progress Pubs USSR). Imported Pubns.

Kids & the IBM PC & PCjr. rev. ed. Edward H. Carlson. Ed. by Compute! Publications, Inc. Staff. 272p. (Orig.). (ps-7). 1985. pap. 12.95 o.p. (ISBN 0-942386-93-0). Compute Pubns.

Kids Are Gone, Lord, but I'm Still Here: Prayers for Mothers. Betty W. Skold. LC 80-67801. 96p. (Orig.). 1981. pap. 5.95 o.s.i. (ISBN 0-8066-1863-9, 10-3703, Augsburg). Augsburg Fortress.

Kids Ask: Carole Marsh Answers Kids Questions about Writing & Writers. Carole Marsh. (Carole Marsh Bks.). (Illus.). 50p. (Orig.). (gr. 3-12). 1986. pap. 7.95 o.p. (ISBN 0-935326-88-X). Gallopade Pub Group.

Kids' Book about Parents. Fayerweather Street School Staff & Eric E. Rofes. 216p. 1989. 11.45 o.s.i. (ISBN 0-395-35394-7). HM.

Kids' Book of Lists. Margo McLoone-Basta & Alice Siegel. LC 80-13255. (Illus.). 128p. (gr. 4-8). 1980. 9.95 o.p. (ISBN 0-03-056226-0). H Holt & Co.

Kid's Candidate. Jonah Kalb. (Illus.). 128p. (gr. 5-9). 1975. 5.95 o.p. (ISBN 0-395-21893-4). HM.

Kids' Cat Book. Tomie DePaola. LC 79-2090. (Illus.). 32p. (gr. k-3). 1984. pap. 5.95 o.p. (ISBN 0-8234-0534-6). Holiday.

Kids' Chic: Great Looks for Kids & How to Put Them Together. Mary E. McGlone & Gloria G. Mayer. (Illus.). 192p. 1984. pap. 9.95 o.p. (ISBN 0-87131-436-3). M Evans.

Kid's Code & Cipher Book. Nancy Garden. LC 80-10434. (Illus.). 176p. (gr. 5 up). 1981. 10.95 o.s.i. (ISBN 0-03-053856-4); pap. 4.95 o.s.i. (ISBN 0-03-059267-4). H Holt & Co.

Kids, Food, & Diabetes: A Book of Recipes, Menus, & Practical Advice. Gloria Loring. 256p. 1986. 17.95 o.p. (ISBN 0-8092-4956-1). Contemp Bks.

Kids, Food & Diabetes: A Book of Recipes, Menues, & Practical Advice. Gloria Loring. 416p. (Orig.). 1987. pap. 11.95 o.p. (ISBN 0-8092-4955-3). Contemp Bks.

Kids' Fort Book. David Stiles. 56p. (Orig.). (gr. 3 up). 1982. pap. 2.25 o.p. (ISBN 0-380-79277-X, Camelot). Avon.

Kid's Goal-Setting Guide: (For Parents) Lanson Ross. 192p. 1985. pap. 4.95 o.p. (ISBN 0-8423-2061-X). Tyndale.

Kid's Guide to Southern California. (Gulliver Travel Ser.). 160p. (gr. 2 up). 1988. 6.95 o.p. (Gulliver Bks). HarbraceJ.

Kids in Court: The ACLU Defends Their Rights. Samuel Epstein & Beryl Epstein. LC 81-69515. 240p. (gr. 7 up). 1982. 9.95 o.s.i. (ISBN 0-02-733480-5, Four Winds). Macmillan.

Kids' Letters to President Reagan. Compiled by Bill Adler. LC 81-19472. (Illus.). 128p. 1982. 6.95 o.p. (ISBN 0-87131-370-7); pap. 4.95 o.p. (ISBN 0-87131-377-4). M Evans.

Kid's New York. Peter Lawrence. 1982. pap. 6.95 o.p. (ISBN 0-380-81315-7, 81315-7). Avon.

Kids Next Door. Ian Menter. (Illus.). 32p. (gr. k-3). 1985. 9.95 o.p. (ISBN 0-241-11534-5, Pub. by Hamish Hamilton England). David & Charles.

Kids' Stuff Math. Marjorie Frank. LC 74-18907. (Kids' Stuff Set). 313p. (gr. 2-6). 1974. 12.95 o.p. (ISBN 0-913916-12-9, IP 12-9). Incentive Pubns.

Kids' Stuff: Reading & Language Experiences, Intermediate-Jr High. Imogene Forte et al. (Kids' Stuff Set). (Illus.). 362p. (gr. 4-8). 1973. 12.95 o.p. (ISBN 0-913916-02-1, IP 02-1). Incentive Pubns.

Kids' Stuff: Reading & Language Experiences-Primary. Imogene Forte & Joy MacKenzie. LC 74-18905. (Kids' Stuff Set). (Illus.). 310p. (gr. 1-3). 1975. 12.95 o.p. (ISBN 0-913916-01-3, IP 01-3). Incentive Pubns.

Kids Stuff Set, 6 bks. 1980. 75.95 o.p. (ISBN 0-913916-99-4, IP99-4). Incentive Pubns.

Kids T.A.L.K! Teach Articulation & Language to Kids. Mary C. Parker. (Illus.). 496p. (gr. k-6). 1988. 195.00 o.p. Kids TALK.

Kids Very Own Quilt Book. Willow A. Soltow. LC 85-51708. (Illus.). 176p. (Orig.). (gr. k-10). 1986. pap. 14.95 o.p. (ISBN 0-87069-469-3). Wallace-Homestead.

Kids Who Underachieve: Strategies for Understanding & Parenting the Academically Troubled Child. Lawrence J. Greene. 224p. 1986. 16.45 o.s.i. (ISBN 0-671-55235-X). S&S.

Kids Working with Robots: The RB5X. T. M. Kemnitz et al. 1986. 9.95 o.p. (ISBN 0-89824-083-2); Apple Demo Diskette 15.00 o.p. (ISBN 0-89824-123-5). Trillium Pr.

Kids Working with Word Processors: Apple Writer. Lynne Mass. (gr. 4 up). 1987. pap. text ed. 6.00 o.p. (ISBN 0-89824-101-4). Trillium Pr.

Kids Working with Word Processors: Bank Street Writer. Lynne Mass. (gr. 4 up). 1987. pap. text ed. 6.00 o.p. (ISBN 0-89824-100-6). Trillium Pr.

Kids' World Almanac of Records & Facts. Alice Siegel & Margo McLoone-Basta. 288p. (Orig.). (gr. 3-7). 1985. pap. 4.95 o.p. (ISBN 0-345-32660-1). Pharos Bks NY.

Kidsplaces. Lucy E. Haagen & Nancy Metzloff. LC 88-63006. 230p. Date not set. pap. (ISBN 0-89089-356-X). Carolina Acad Pr.

Kierkegaard Handbook. Frederick Sontag. LC 79-87741. 1980. pap. 7.25 o.s.i. (ISBN 0-8042-0654-6, John Knox). Westminster John Knox.

Kierkegaard the Cripple. Theodor Haecker. (ISBN 0-8022-0655-7). Philos Lib.

Kierkegaard, the Melancholy Dane. H. V. Martin. (ISBN 0-8022-1066-X). Philos Lib.

Kierkegaard's Authorship: A Guide to the Writings of Kierkegaard. George E. Arbaugh & George B. Arbaugh. LC 68-2512. (Augustana College Library Ser.: No. 32). 431p. 1968. 6.95x o.p. (ISBN 0-910182-32-9). Augustana Coll.

Kierkegaard's Fear & Trembling: Critical Appraisals. Ed. by Robert L. Perkins. LC 79-16984. xii, 264p. 1981. text ed. 24.75 o.p.; pap. 14.75 o.p. (ISBN 0-8173-0146-1). U of Ala Pr.

Kierkegaard's Thought. Gregor Malantschuk. Tr. by Howard V. Hong & Edna H. Hong. LC 77-155000. 400p. (Eng.). 1972. 38.50 o.p. (ISBN 0-691-07166-7, 317); pap. 10.00 o.p. (ISBN 0-691-01982-7). Princeton U Pr.

Kikiriki: Stories & Poems in English & Spanish for Children. Ed. by Sylvia C. Pena. (Illus.). 116p. (Orig.). (gr. k-6). 1987. pap. 7.50 o.p. (ISBN 0-317-59970-4). Arte Publico.

Kiki's Paris: Artists & Lovers (Nineteen Hundred to Nineteen Thirty) Billy Kliiver & Julie Martin. 1989. write for info. o.p. Abrams.

Kilimanjaro: The White Roof of Africa. Harald Lange. (Illus.). 176p. 1985. 24.95 o.p. (ISBN 0-89886-100-4). Mountaineers.

Kilims: Flat Woven Tapestry Rugs. Yanni Petsopoulos. (Illus.). 394p. 100.00 o.p. (ISBN 0-317-55103-5). Apollo.

Kill All the Lawyers? A User Friendly Guide to Working with a Lawyer. Sloan Bashinsky. 156p. 12.95 o.p. (ISBN 0-671-60468-6). S&S.

Kill & Tell. William X. Kienzle. 250p. 1984. 12.95 o.p. (ISBN 0-8362-6120-8). Andrews & McMeel.

Kill & Tell. William X. Kienzle. (General Ser.). 1984. lib. bdg. 15.95 o.p. (ISBN 0-8161-3779-X, Large Print Bks). G K Hall.

Kill Devil Hill: Discovering the Secret of the Wright Brothers. Harry B. Combs & Martin Caidin. 1979. 16.95 o.p. (ISBN 0-395-28216-0). HM.

Kill Fee. Barbara Paul. 224p. 1985. 13.95 o.s.i. (ISBN 0-684-18426-5, ScribT). Scribner.

Kill-Off. Jim Thompson. 192p. 1987. pap. 3.95 o.p. (ISBN 0-445-40572-4). Mysterious Pr.

Kill the Envious Moon. Arthur DePonceau. 1985. 12.50 o.p. (ISBN 0-682-40213-3). Exposition-Phoenix.

Killashandra. Anne McCaffrey. 384p. 1986. 16.95 o.p. (ISBN 0-345-31599-5, Del Rey); pap. 4.50 o.p. (ISBN 0-345-31600-2). Ballantine.

Killdeer Mountain. Dee Brown. LC 82-15460. 256p. 1983. 14.45 o.p. (ISBN 0-03-040691-9). H Holt & Co.

Killed in Paradise. William L. DeAndrea. LC 87-40384. (Matt Cobb Mystery Ser.). 176p. 1988. pap. 15.45 o.s.i. (ISBN 0-89296-346-8). Mysterious Pr.

Killed on the Ice. William L. DeAndrea. 224p. 1987. pap. 3.50 o.p. (ISBN 0-445-40606-2). Mysterious Pr.
Killeen. Mary Leland. LC 86-7901. 160p. 1986. 12.95 o.p. (ISBN 0-689-11826-0, Atheneum). Macmillan.
Killer Bears. Mike Cramond. (Illus.). 224p. 1981. 7.95 o.s.i. (ISBN 0-684-17285-2, ScribT). Scribner.
Killer in the Rain. Raymond Chandler. 1987. pap. 3.95 o.s.i. (ISBN 0-345-35185-1). Ballantine.
Killer Plants & Other Stories. Gordon Giles et al. Ed. by Roger Elwood. LC 73-21479. (Illus.). 48p. (gr. 4-8). 1974. PLB 3.95g o.p. (ISBN 0-8225-0953-9). Lerner Pubns.
Killer Robot. Seth McEvoy. (Not Quite Human: No. 6). (gr. 5 up). 1987. pap. 2.50 o.p. (ISBN 0-671-62563-2). Archway.
Killer Salt. Marietta Whittlesey. 1978. pap. 2.95 o.p. (ISBN 0-380-39297-6, 62141X). Avon.
Killer Satellites. Philip Kirk. (Butler Ser.: No. 6). (Orig.). 1980. pap. 1.75 o.p. (ISBN 0-8439-0730-4, Pub. by Leisure Bks CT). Dorchester Pub Co.
Killer Swan. Eth Clifford. (gr. 5-8). 1980. 8.95 o.p. (ISBN 0-395-29742-7). HM.
Killer's Town. Lee Falk. (Phantom Ser.: No. 9). 1973. pap. 0.95 o.p. (ISBN 0-380-01312-6, 17731). Avon.
Killey's Fractures of the Middle Third of the Facial Skeleton. 4th ed. P. Banks. (Dental Practioner Handbook: No. 3). (Illus.). 104p. 1981. pap. 16.00 o.p. (ISBN 0-7236-0625-0). Butterworth.
Killing Cup. Peter Van Greenaway. 221p. 1988. 18.95 o.p. (ISBN 0-575-04062-9, Pub. by Gollancz England). David & Charles.
Killing Cure. Evelyn Walker & Perry D. Young. LC 85-24785. 1986. pap. 17.95 o.p. (ISBN 0-03-069906-1). H Holt & Co.
Killing Doll. Ruth Rendell. 1984. 12.45 o.s.i. (ISBN 0-394-53097-7). Pantheon.
Killing Doll. Ruth Rendell. (General Ser.). 1984. lib. bdg. 15.95 o.p. (ISBN 0-8161-3720-X, Large Print Bks). G K Hall.
Killing Floor. Ai. 1979. 7.95 o.p. (ISBN 0-395-27593-8); pap. 3.95 o.p. (ISBN 0-395-27590-3). HM.
Killing Floor. Arthur Lyons. 1982. pap. 3.95 o.p. (ISBN 0-03-060397-8, Owl BKs). H Holt & Co.
Killing in Real Estate. Rudd Brown. Ed. by Nancy Chirich. LC 86-21579. 208p. (Orig.). 1986. pap. 6.95 o.s.i. (ISBN 0-912761-06-7, Cliffhanger Pr). Cliffhanger Pr.
Killing Kindness. Reginald Hill. 1983. 10.95 o.p. (ISBN 0-394-51910-8); pap. 3.95 o.p. (ISBN 0-394-71060-6). Pantheon.
Killing of Billy Jowett. Clay Randall. (Orig.). 1981. pap. 1.95 o.p. (ISBN 0-505-51729-9, Pub. by Tower Bks). Dorchester Pub Co.
Killing of Idi Amin. Leslie Watkins. 1977. pap. 1.75 o.p. (ISBN 0-380-01675-3, 33464). Avon.
Killing of Karen Silkwood. Richard Rashke. 1981. 11.95 o.p. (ISBN 0-395-30233-1). HM.
Killing the Hidden Waters. Charles Bowden. LC 77-5633. (Illus.). 186p. 1977. pap. 11.95 o.p. (ISBN 0-292-76439-1). U of Tex Pr.
Killing Tree. Jay Bennett. (gr. 7 up). 1979. pap. 1.50 o.p. (ISBN 0-380-44289-2, 56259, Flare). Avon.
Killing Waters. Shelby Young & Bob Teets. 112p. 1985. 9.95 o.p. McClain.
Killings. Calvin Trillin. LC 83-9313. 240p. 1984. 14.45 o.p. (ISBN 0-89919-233-5). Ticknor & Fields.
Killsquad No. 1: Counter Attack. Frank Garrett. 192p. 1986. pap. 2.50 o.p. (ISBN 0-380-75151-8). Avon.
Killsquad, No. 10: Mob War. Frank Garrett. 160p. 1988. pap. 2.75 o.p. (ISBN 0-380-75367-7). Avon.
Killsquad No. 2: Mission Revenge. Frank Garrett. 176p. 1986. pap. 2.50 o.p. (ISBN 0-380-75152-6). Avon.
Killsquad No. 4: The Judas Soldiers. Frank Garrett. 176p. 1987. pap. 2.50 o.p. (ISBN 0-380-75154-2). Avon.
Killsquad No. 5: Blood Beach. Frank Garrett. 176p. 1987. pap. 2.50 o.p. (ISBN 0-380-75155-0). Avon.
Killsquad No. 6: The Seventh Whore of Babylon. Frank Garrett. 192p. 1987. pap. 2.50 o.p. (ISBN 0-380-75156-9). Avon.
Killsquad No. 7: Polar Assault. Frank Garrett. 176p. (Orig.). 1987. pap. 2.50 o.p. (ISBN 0-380-75363-4). Avon.
Killsquad, No. 9: Devil's Island. Frank Garrett. 176p. 1987. pap. 2.75 o.p. (ISBN 0-380-75365-0). Avon.
Kilobaud Klassroom: A Course in Digital Electronics. George Young & Peter Stark. Ed. by Chris Crocker et al. 419p. (Orig.). 1982. pap. text ed. 14.95 o.p. (ISBN 0-88006-027-1, BK 7386). Wayne Green Ent.
Kilobyte Kid's Book of Personal Computers. Raymond Spangenburg & Diane Moser. (Illus.). 125p. 1983. pap. (ISBN 0-534-02871-3). Brooks-Cole.
Kiltartan Poetry Book. Lady Gregory. 76p. 1971. Repr. of 1918 ed. 15.00x o.p. (ISBN 0-7165-1353-6, BBA 02059, Pub. by Cuala Press Ireland). Biblio Dist.
Kim Williams' Cookbook & Commentary. Kim Williams. LC 86-82242. 1987. pap. 9.95 o.p. (ISBN 0-89586-518-1). Price Stern.
Kimbell Art Museum: A Catalogue of the Collection. Kimbell Art Museum Staff. LC 73-177945. (Illus.). 336p. 1972. 30.00 o.p. (ISBN 0-912804-00-9). Kimbell Art.
Kime's International Handbook, 1981. (ISBN 0-900503-14-9). Intl Pubns Serv.
Kimura: Paintings & Works on Paper 1968-1984. Denys Sutton. Ed. by Judith Lyon & Jan Lancaster. (Illus.). 130p. 1985. text ed. 25.00 o.p. (ISBN 0-943044-03-0); pap. text ed. 15.00 o.p. (ISBN 0-943044-02-2). Phillips Coll.
Kincaid. Henry Denker. 352p. 1986. pap. 3.95 o.p. (ISBN 0-380-69893-5). Avon.
Kind Words: A Dictionary of Euphemisms. J. S. Neaman & C. G. Silver. 320p. 1984. pap. text ed. 7.95 o.p. (ISBN 0-07-046141-4). McGraw.
Kindergarten. Elzbieta Ettinger. (Hall Fiction Ser.). 320p. 1986. pap. 6.95 o.p. (ISBN 0-8398-2893-4). G K Hall.
Kindergarten Chats. Louis H. Sullivan. (Illus.). 252p. 1986. pap. 9.95 o.p. (ISBN 0-87905-418-2). Gibbs Smith Pub.
Kindergarten Chats & Other Writings. Louis H. Sullivan. 9.95 o.p. (ISBN 0-317-42987-6, Pub. by Peregrine Smith Bks). Gibbs Smith Pub.
Kindergarten: Its Encounter with Educational Thought in America. Evelyn Weber. LC 70-75202. 1969. pap. 9.95x o.p. (ISBN 0-8077-2315-0). Tchrs Coll.
Kindergarten Through Twelth Arts Eudcation in the United States: Present Context, Future Needs. 40p. 1986. 7.50 o.p. (ISBN 0-317-60249-7, 1020A). Music Ed Natl.
Kinderstomatologie 2. rev. ed. Ed. by W. Kuenzel & J. Toman. 1976. 80.75 o.p. (ISBN 3-8055-2407-2). S Karger.
Kindhearted Xiawudong. Mei Ying. (Illus.). 56p. (ps-3). 1984. pap. 2.95 o.p. (ISBN 0-8351-1300-0). China Bks.
Kindness of Dr. Avicenna. John Pearson. 1982. 15.50 o.p. (ISBN 0-03-061932-7). H Holt & Co.
Kindness Weapon. Bruce Wannamaker. LC 84-7038. (Illus.). 32p. (gr. 1-2). lib. bdg. 4.95 o.p. Dandelion Hse.
Kindred & Clan in the Middle Ages & After. Bertha Phillpotts. 1972. lib. bdg. 20.50x o.p. (ISBN 0-374-96433-5, Octagon). Hippocrene Bks.
Kinds of Love. May Sarton. LC 70-125860. 1970. 12.95 o.p. (ISBN 0-393-08620-8). Norton.
Kinesics: The Power of Silent Command. M. Cundiff. 1972. 14.95 o.p. (ISBN 0-13-516245-9, Parker). P-H.
Kinesiology: Workbook & Laboratory Manual. Ruth Harris. (Illus.). 1977. pap. 16.95 o.p. (ISBN 0-395-20668-5). HM.
Kinetic Analysis of Enzyme Reaction: Tentative Guideline, Vol. 2. National Committee for Clinical Laboratory Standards. 1982. 20.00 o.p. (ISBN 0-318-19371-X, C7-T). NAtl Comm Clin Lab Stds.
Kinetic Methods of Analysis. K. B. Yatsimirskii. Tr. by P. J. Harvey. 1966. 45.00 o.p. (ISBN 0-08-011364-8); pap. 45.00 o.p. (ISBN 0-08-013827-6). Pergamon.
Kinetic Parameters of Electrode Reactions of Metallic Compounds, Vol. 1. R. Tamamushi. 1976. pap. 50.00 o.p. (ISBN 0-08-020991-2). Pergamon.
Kinetics & Thermodynamics in Biochemistry. 2nd ed. H. G. Bray & K. White. 1967. 71.00 o.p. (ISBN 0-12-128456-5). Acad Pr.
Kinetics Applied to Organic Reactions. Wiendelt Drenth & Harold Kwart. (Studies in Organic Chemistry Ser.: Vol. 9). 224p. 1980. 29.75 o.p. (ISBN 0-8247-6889-2). Dekker.
Kinetics of Experimental Tumour Processes. N. M. Emanuel. (Illus.). 350p. 1982. 105.00 o.p. (ISBN 0-08-024909-4). Pergamon.
Kinetics of Inorganic Reactions. A. G. Sykes. 1966. 33.00 o.p. (ISBN 0-08-011441-5); pap. 75.00 o.p. (ISBN 0-08-011440-7). Pergamon.
Kinetics of Muscle Contraction. D. C. White & John Thorson. 1975. pap. 15.25 o.p. (ISBN 0-08-018149-X). Pergamon.
Kinetics of Wastewater Treatment, Copenhagen, Denmark, June 1979. S. H. Jenkins. 1980. flexi-cover 63.00x o.p. (ISBN 0-08-024855-1). Pergamon.
Kinfolks: The Wilgus Stories. Gurney Norman. 112p. 1986. pap. 3.50 o.p. (ISBN 0-380-69926-5). Avon.
King: A Biography. 2nd ed. David L. Lewis. LC 78-5261. (Blacks in the New World Ser.). 481p. 1978. 32.50 o.p. (ISBN 0-252-00679-8); pap. 9.95 o.p. (ISBN 0-252-00680-1). U of Ill Pr.
King & Pierce Counties Street Guide & Directory, 1989. Thomas Bros. Maps Staff. (Illus.). 204p. 1988. pap. 19.95 o.p. Thomas Bros Maps.
King & Queen...a Fairy Tale. Renee Catherine. (Illus.). 1979. 5.00 o.p. (ISBN 0-682-49393-7). Exposition-Phoenix.
King & the Kingdom. William Barclay. LC 69-12836. 1969. pap. 3.95 o.s.i. (ISBN 0-664-24843-8, Westminster). Westminster John Knox.
King Arthur & the Knights of the Round Table see New Method Supplementary Readers: Bestseller Pack.
King Arthur's Daughter. Vera Chapman. 1978. pap. 1.75 o.p. (ISBN 0-380-01958-2, 38398). Avon.
King Carlo of Capri. Warren Miller & Edward Sorel. LC 58-1749. (Illus.). (gr. 1-4). 1958. 2.95 o.p. (ISBN 0-15-242744-9, HJ). HarBraceJ.
King Cobra. William C. Matthews. 240p. 1983. pap. 2.75 o.p. (ISBN 0-380-81604-0, 81604-0). Avon.
King Crockett: Nature & Civility on the American Frontier. Catherine L. Albanese. 1979. pap. 3.50x o.p. (ISBN 0-912296-40-2, Dist. by U Pr of Va). Am Antiquarian.
King Devil. Charlotte MacLeod. LC 78-5981. 1978. 8.95 o.p. (ISBN 0-689-30659-8, Atheneum). Macmillan.
King Edward Plot. Robert L. Hall. 1979. text ed. 9.95 o.p. (ISBN 0-07-025609-8). McGraw.
King George V. Harold Nicolson. 1984. pap. 19.95x o.p. (ISBN 0-09-465720-3, Pub. by Constable Pubs UK). Trans-Atl Phila.
King George V. Kenneth Rose. LC 83-48931. (Illus.). 1984. 19.45 o.s.i. (ISBN 0-394-53448-4). Knopf.
King Henry Fifth see also Henry Fifth.
King Henry Fourth, Pt. 1 see also Henry Fourth, Pt. 1.
King Henry Fourth, Pt. 2 see also Henry Fourth, Pt. 2.
King Henry Sixth, Pt. 1 see also Henry Sixth, Pt. 1.
King Henry Sixth, Pt. 2 see also Henry Sixth, Pt. 2.
King Henry Sixth, Pt. 3 see also Henry Sixth, Pt. 3.
King Henry VIII's Mary Rose: Its Fate & Future: the Story of One of the Most Exciting Projects in Marine Archaeology. Alexander McKee. 1978. 10.95 o.p. (ISBN 0-285-62091-6, Pub. by Souvenir Pr). Intl Spec Bk.
King Horn: Poems Written at Montolieu in Old Languedoc, 1969-1981. Ed. by Michael Baldwin. 118p. (Orig.). 1983. pap. 8.95x o.p. (ISBN 0-7100-9494-9). Routledge Chapman & Hall.
King in the Garden. Leon Garfield. LC 84-10064. (Illus.). 32p. (gr. 1-3). 1985. 11.75 o.p. (ISBN 0-688-04106-X). Lothrop.
King Jaguar. Dan Sherman. LC 78-73867. 1979. 9.95 o.p. (ISBN 0-87795-221-3, Arbor Hse). Morrow.
King James Fourth of Scotland: A Brief Survey of His Life & Times. Robert L. Mackie. LC 76-9098. (Illus.). 1976. Repr. of 1958 ed. lib. bdg. 22.50x o.p. (ISBN 0-8371-8145-3, MAKJ). Greenwood.
King John see also Life & Death of King John.
King John & Matilda: A Critical Edition. Robert Davenport. Ed. by Joyce O. Davis. LC 79-54334. (Renaissance Drama Ser.). 200p. 1980. lib. bdg. 26.00 o.p. (ISBN 0-8240-4452-5). Garland Pub.
King Kobold Revived. Christopher Stasheff. 224p. 1986. pap. 2.95 o.s.i. (ISBN 0-441-44490-3, Pub. by Charter Bks). Ace Bks.
King Kong: A Picture Book. LC 76-27269. (Illus.). (gr. 1). 1976. pap. 0.95 o.p. (ISBN 0-448-12789-X, G&D). Putnam Pub Group.
King Kong Joke Book. Jim Simon. 1977. pap. 1.25 o.p. (ISBN 0-505-51124-X, Pub. by Tower Bks). Dorchester Pub Co.
King Lear see also Tragedy of King Lear.
King Lear. Ed. by E. A. Colman. (Challis Shakespeare Ser). 1981. pap. 9.00x o.p. (ISBN 0-424-00082-2, Pub. by Sydney U Pr Australia). Intl Spec Bk.
King Lear by William Shakespeare. 48p. (Orig.). 1988. pap. 9.95 o.p. (ISBN 1-55651-477-8); cassette o.p. (ISBN 1-55651-478-6). Cram Cassettes.
King Lear: Text, Sources, Criticism. William Shakespeare. Ed. by George B. Harrison & Robert F. McDonnell. (Orig.). 1962. pap. text ed. 8.95 o.p. (ISBN 0-15-548500-8, HC). HarBraceJ.
King Lear: TV Edition. William Shakespeare. Ed. by Alfred Harbage. 176p. 1984. pap. 2.25 o.p. (ISBN 0-14-007177-6). Penguin.
King Lion & His Cooks. Louise Brierley. (Illus.). 32p. (gr. k-3). 1982. 10.95 o.s.i. (ISBN 0-03-061218-7). H Holt & Co.
King Moo, the Wordmaker. Pers Crowell. LC 75-21133. (Illus.). (gr. 1-3). 1976. 5.95 o.p. (ISBN 0-87004-253-X). Caxton.
King Oedipus see also Oedipus.
King of Comedy. Mack Sennett. LC 82-49234. (Cinema Classics Ser.). 284p. 1985. lib. bdg. 35.00cancelled o.s.i. (ISBN 0-8240-5777-5). Garland Pub.
King of Creation. Henry M. Morris. LC 80-80558. 1980. pap. 6.95 o.s.i. (ISBN 0-89051-059-8). Master Bks.
King of Hearts. David Slavitt. LC 76-29228. 1976. 8.95 o.p. (ISBN 0-87795-153-5, Arbor Hse). Morrow.
King of Instruments: A History of the Organ. Bernard Sonnaillon. Tr. by Stewart Spencer. LC 84-43041. (Illus.). 260p. 1985. 65.00 o.p. (ISBN 0-8478-0582-4). Rizzoli Intl.
King of Rome. Andre Castelot. LC 74-6778. (Illus.). 396p. 1974. Repr. of 1960 ed. lib. bdg. 35.00x o.p. (ISBN 0-8371-7571-2, CAKR). Greenwood.
King of the Castle, the Making of a Dynasty: Seagram's & the Bronfman Empire. Peter Newman. LC 78-65198. 1979. 11.95 o.p. (ISBN 0-689-10963-6, Atheneum). Macmillan.
King of the Confessors. Thomas Hoving. 352p. 1982. pap. 3.95 o.s.i. (ISBN 0-345-30370-9). Ballantine.
King of the Hermits & Other Stories. Jack Sendak. LC 66-10888. (Illus.). 128p. (gr. 2 up). 1967. 10.95 o.p. (ISBN 0-374-34158-3). FS&G.
King of the Pipers. Peter Elwell. LC 83-22176. (Illus.). 32p. (gr. 1-5). 1984. SBE 10.95 o.s.i. (ISBN 0-02-733460-0). Macmillan.
King of the Zoo. Claire Schumacher. LC 84-1099. (Illus.). 32p. (ps-2). 1985. 11.75 o.p. (ISBN 0-688-04131-0, Morrow Junior Books); PLB 11.88 o.p. (ISBN 0-688-04132-9, Morrow Junior Books). Morrow.
King of Two Sicilies. Andrezej Kusniewicz. Tr. by Celina Wieniewska. LC 80-7935. 228p. 1980. 11.95 o.p. (ISBN 0-15-147271-8). HarBraceJ.
King Philip. Cecile P. Edwards. (gr. 3-8). 1962. pap. 2.20 o.p. (ISBN 0-395-07274-3, Piper). HM.
King-Pierce Counties Street Atlas & Directory, 1989. rev. ed. Thomas Bros. Maps Staff. (Illus.). 207p. 1988. pap. 19.95 o.p. (ISBN 0-88130-300-3). Thomas Bros Maps.
King-Pierce Counties Street Atlas, 1986. Thomas Bros. Maps Staff. (Illus.). 207p. 1986. pap. 19.95 o.p. Thomas Bros Maps.
King-Pierce-Snohomish Counties Street Atlas & Directory, 1987. rev. ed. Thomas Bros. Maps Staff. (Illus.). 307p. 1986. pap. 25.95 o.p. (ISBN 0-88130-196-5). Thomas Bros Maps.
King-Pierce-Snohomish Counties Street Atlas, 1986. Thomas Bros. Maps Staff. (Illus.). 307p. pap. 25.95 o.p. Thomas Bros Maps.
King, Queen, Knave. Vladimir Nabokov. (Rus.). 1969. text ed. 6.95 o.p. (ISBN 0-07-045716-6). McGraw.
King, Queen, Knave. Vladimir Nabokov. 288p. 1987. pap. text ed. 7.95 o.p. (ISBN 0-07-045722-0). McGraw.
King Richard I: The Autobiography of America's Greatest Auto Racer. Richard Petty & William Neely. (Illus.). 256p. 1986. 17.95 o.p. (ISBN 0-02-595910-7). Macmillan.
King Rollo & King Frank. David McKee. (King Rollo Ser.). (Illus.). 32p. (ps up). 1982. PLB 6.95 o.p. (ISBN 0-87191-834-X). Creative Ed.
King Rollo & the Balloons. David McKee. (King Rollo Ser.). (Illus.). 32p. (ps up). 1982. PLB 6.95 o.p. (ISBN 0-87191-830-7). Creative Ed.
King Rollo & the Bath. David McKee. (King Rollo Ser.). (Illus.). 32p. (ps up). 1982. PLB 6.95 o.p. (ISBN 0-87191-833-1). Creative Ed.
King Rollo & the Dishes. David McKee. (King Rollo Ser.). (Illus.). 32p. (ps up). 1982. PLB 6.95 o.p. (ISBN 0-87191-832-3). Creative Ed.
King Rollo & the Dog. David McKee. (King Rollo Ser.). 32p. (ps up). 1982. PLB 6.95 o.p. (ISBN 0-87191-901-X). Creative Ed.
King Rollo & the Masks. David McKee. (King Rollo Ser.). 32p. (ps up). 1982. PLB 6.95 o.p. (ISBN 0-87191-900-1). Creative Ed.
King Rollo & the Playroom. David McKee. (King Rollo Ser.). 32p. (ps up). 1982. PLB 6.95 o.p. (ISBN 0-87191-899-4). Creative Ed.
King Rollo & the Search. David McKee. (King Rollo Ser.). (Illus.). 32p. (ps up). 1982. PLB 6.95 o.p. (ISBN 0-87191-835-8). Creative Ed.
King Rollo & the Tree. David McKee. (King Rollo Ser.). (Illus.). 32p. (ps up). 1982. PLB 6.95 o.p. (ISBN 0-87191-831-5). Creative Ed.
King Season. Kirby L. Wilkins. 199p. 1985. 15.95 o.p. (ISBN 0-87795-714-2, Arbor Hse). Morrow.
King-Snohomish Counties Street Atlas, 1986. Thomas Bros. Maps Staff. (Illus.). 222p. pap. 18.50 o.p. (ISBN 0-88130-143-4). Thomas Bros Maps.
King-Snohomish Counties Street Atlas & Directory, 1987. rev. ed. Thomas Bros. Maps Staff. (Illus.). 222p. 1986. pap. 19.95 o.p. (ISBN 0-88130-195-7). Thomas Bros Maps.
King Solomon's Mines. Illus. by Gino D'Achille. LC 82-3843. (Step-Up Adventures Ser.: No. 5). (Illus.). 96p. (gr. 2-5). 1982. lib. bdg. 4.99 o.p. (ISBN 0-394-95275-8); pap. 1.95 o.p. (ISBN 0-394-85275-3). Random.

King Solomon's Mines. H. Rider Haggard. (Dent's Illustrated Children's Classics Ser.). (Illus.). 223p. (gr. 4 up). 1974. Repr. of 1963 ed. 11.00x o.p. (ISBN 0-460-05060-5, BKA 01600, Pub. by J. M. Dent England). Biblio Dist.

King, the Cat & the Fiddle. Yehudi Menuhin et al. LC 83-112. (Illus.). 32p. (gr. k-3). 1983. 10.95 o.p. (ISBN 0-03-061515-1). H Holt & Co.

King Thrushbeard. Jacob Grimm. LC 74-123890. (Illus.). (gr. k-3). 1970. 5.95 o.p. (ISBN 0-15-242940-9, HJ). HarBraceJ.

King Who Rained. Fred Gwynne. LC 80-12939. (Illus.). 40p. (gr. 4 up). 1987. 11.95 o.s.i. (ISBN 0-13-516212-2); pap. 5.95 o.s.i. (ISBN 0-13-516170-3). Prentice Hall Pr.

Kingdom. L. W. Henderson. 1974. pap. 1.75 o.p. (ISBN 0-380-00000-8, 18978). Avon.

Kingdom: Arabia & the House of Sa'ud. Robert Lacey. LC 81-83741. (Illus.). 656p. 1982. 19.95 o.s.i. (ISBN 0-15-147260-2). HarBraceJ.

Kingdom by the Sea. Paul Theroux. (General Ser.). 1984. lib. bdg. 18.95 o.p. (ISBN 0-8161-3705-6, Large Print Bks). G K Hall.

Kingdom Conflict. Joseph M. Stowell. 156p. 1984. pap. 6.50 o.p. (ISBN 0-89693-376-8). Victor Bks.

Kingdom in Mark: A New Place & a New Time. Werner H. Kelber. LC 73-88353. 190p. 1974. 10.95 o.p. (ISBN 0-8006-0268-4, 1-268, Fortress). Augsburg Fortress.

Kingdom in the Country. James Conaway. (Illus.). 288p. 1987. 17.45 o.s.i. (ISBN 0-395-37775-7). HM.

Kingdom Life in a Fallen World: Living out the Sermon on the Mount. Sinclair B. Ferguson. (Christian Character Library). 224p. 1986. hdbk. 8.95 o.p. (ISBN 0-89109-492-X). NavPress.

Kingdom Lost & Found: A Fable for Everyone. M. Terese Donze, Sr. LC 82-71983. (Illus.). 64p. (Orig.). 1982. pap. 3.95 o.p. (ISBN 0-87793-253-0). Ave Maria.

Kingdom of Evil: A Continuation of the Journal of Fantazius Mallare. Ben Hecht. LC 78-7288. (Illus.). 1978. pap. 3.95 o.p. (ISBN 0-15-647123-X, Harv). HarBraceJ.

Kingdom of Fear. Ed. by Tim Underwood & Chuck Miller. (Series on Stephen King). 256p. 1986. 25.00 o.p. (ISBN 0-88733-018-5). Underwood-Miller.

Kingdom of God in America. rev. ed. Martin E. Marty. xxx, 218p. 1988. 35.00x o.p. (ISBN 0-8195-5212-7); pap. 12.95 o.p. (ISBN 0-8195-6222-X). Wesleyan U Pr.

Kingdom of Heaven. Hilton Hotema. 45p. 1960. pap. 8.95 o.s.i. (ISBN 0-88697-030-X). Life Science.

Kingdom of Jesus. John D. Stoops. 1951. (ISBN 0-8022-1655-2). Philos Lib.

Kingdom of Servants. Dwight L. Dye. 1979. 3.95 o.p. (ISBN 0-87162-218-1, D5050). Warner Pr.

Kingdom of Summer. Gillian Bradshaw. 1981. 12.95 o.p. (ISBN 0-671-25472-3). S&S.

Kingdom of the Wicked. Anthony Burgess. 379p. 1985. 17.95 o.p. (ISBN 0-87795-753-3, Arbor Hse). Morrow.

Kingdom Revisited: An Essay on Christian Social Ethics. Charles L. Kammer, 3rd. LC 81-40045. 188p. (Orig.). 1981. lib. bdg. 27.50 o.p. (ISBN 0-8191-1737-4); pap. text ed. 13.25 o.p. (ISBN 0-8191-1738-2). U Pr of Amer.

Kingdom Within You. Edward F. Grant. 1977. 6.50 o.p. (ISBN 0-682-48874-7). Exposition-Phoenix.

Kings & Councillors: An Essay in the Comparative Anatomy of Human Society. A. M. Hocart. Ed. by Rodney Needham. LC 71-101297. (Classics in Anthropology Ser). 1972. pap. text ed. 3.95x o.s.i. (ISBN 0-226-34568-8, P368, Phoen). U of Chicago Pr.

Kings & Prophets of Israel. Adam C. Welch. 264p. 1953. (ISBN 0-8022-1847-4). Philos Lib.

Kings & Queens of Early Britain. Geoffrey Ashe. 224p. 1984. 16.95 o.p. (ISBN 0-413-47920-X, NO. 9166). Heinemann Ed.

King's Beard. Mary Tozer. (Illus.). (ps-3). 1979. 6.95 o.p. (ISBN 0-15-242924-7, HJ). HarBraceJ.

King's Book. Louise A. Vernon. LC 80-18998. (Illus.). 128p. (gr. 3-8). 1980. pap. 4.50 o.p. (ISBN 0-8361-1933-9). Herald Pr.

King's Book of Kings: The Shah-nameh of Shah Tahmasp. Stuart C. Welch. LC 78-188400. (Illus.). 200p. 1972. 85.00 o.p. (ISBN 0-87099-028-4). Metro Mus Art.

King's Book, or a Necessary Doctrine & Erudition for Any Christian Man, 1543. Ed. by Thomas A. Lacey. (Church Historical Society, London, N.S. Ser.: No. 10). Repr. of 1932 ed. 40.00 o.p. (ISBN 0-8115-3134-1). Kraus Repr.

Kings, Commoners & Colonists. Selma R. Williams. LC 73-84840. (Illus.). 288p. (gr. 7 up). 1974. 7.95 o.p. (ISBN 0-689-30150-2, Atheneum). Macmillan.

King's Damsel. Vera Chapman. 1978. pap. 1.50 o.p. (ISBN 0-380-01916-7, 37606). Avon.

King's Drum & Other African Stories. Harold Courlander. LC 62-14242. (Illus.). (gr. 3-7). 1962. 6.50 o.p. (ISBN 0-15-242925-5, HJ). HarBraceJ.

King's Drum: And Other African Stories. Harold Courlander. LC 62-14242. (Illus.). (gr. 3-7). 1970. pap. 3.95 o.p. (ISBN 0-15-647190-6, VoyB). HarBraceJ.

King's Government & the Common Law, Fourteen Seventy-One to Sixteen Forty-One. Charles Ogilvie. LC 78-6586. vii, 176p. 1978. Repr. of 1958 ed. lib. bdg. 22.50x o.p. (ISBN 0-313-20492-6, OGKG). Greenwood.

Kings in the Counting House. Herbert Mitgang. LC 82-72062. 1983. 14.50 o.p. (ISBN 0-87795-424-0, Arbor Hse). Morrow.

Kings in the Counting House. Herbert Mitgang. 240p. 1984. pap. 2.95 o.s.i. (ISBN 0-345-31506-5). Ballantine.

King's Indian. Ed. by David Levy et al. (Illus.). 136p. 1981. 19.95 o.s.i. (ISBN 0-907352-02-2, Capablanca). Imprint Edns.

King's Indian, 1982. Ed. by David Levy et al. (Illus.). 1982. 19.95 o.s.i. (ISBN 0-907352-12-X, Capablanca). Imprint Edns.

King's Monster. Carolyn Haywood. LC 79-18134. (Illus.). 32p. (gr. k-3). 1980. 11.75 o.p. (ISBN 0-688-22214-5); PLB 11.88 o.p. (ISBN 0-688-32214-X). Morrow.

King's Nurseries. John Field. (Illus.). 144p. 1987. 40.00 o.p. (ISBN 0-907383-01-7). Taylor & Francis.

Kings of Black Magic. I. G. Edmonds. LC 79-19534. 160p. (gr. 4-8). 1981. 12.95 o.p. (ISBN 0-03-051376-6). H Holt & Co.

Kings of Love: The Poetry & History of the Ni'matullahi Sufi Order of Iran. P. L. Wilson & N. Pourjavady. LC 78-62008. 1979. write for info. o.p. (ISBN 0-87773-733-9, Dist. by Bookpeople). Shambhala Pubns.

Kings of San Carlos. James L. Haley. LC 86-32974. (Double D Western Ser.). 192p. 1987. 12.95 o.s.i. (ISBN 0-385-15589-1). Doubleday.

King's Orchard. Agnes S. Turnbull. 1963. 8.95 o.p. (ISBN 0-395-08273-0). HM.

King's Way: The Life of Madame de Maintenon. Francoise Chandernagor. Tr. by Barbara Bray. (Helen & Kurt Wolff Bk.). 512p. 1984. 15.95 o.p. (ISBN 0-15-147274-2). HarBraceJ.

King's White Elephant. Rosemary Harris. (Illus.). 32p. (gr. k-3). 1977. 5.95 o.p. (ISBN 0-571-10302-2); pap. 2.95 o.p. (ISBN 0-571-11133-5). Faber & Faber.

Kingston Fortune. Stephen Longstreet. 1975. pap. 1.95 o.p. (ISBN 0-380-00366-X, 25585). Avon.

Kingston General Hospital: A Social & Institutional History. Margaret Angus. 1973. 10.00 o.p. (ISBN 0-7735-0173-8, McGill Canada). U of Toronto Pr.

Kinins III. Ed. by Hans Fritz et al. (Advances in Experimental Medicine & Biology Ser.: Vol. 156). 1244p. 1983. 165.00x o.p. (ISBN 0-306-41167-9, Plenum Pr). Plenum Pub.

Kink & I: A Psychiatrist's Guide to Untwisted Living. James D. Mallory & Stanley C. Baldwin. LC 73-78688. 224p. 1973. pap. 6.95 o.p. (ISBN 0-89693-289-3). Victor Bks.

Kinks: The Official Biography. Jon Savage. LC 84-26905. (Illus.). 176p. 1985. 19.95 o.p. (ISBN 0-571-13379-7); pap. 9.95 o.p. (ISBN 0-571-13407-6). Faber & Faber.

Kinta Years. Janice H. Giles. 1973. 7.95 o.p. (ISBN 0-395-14011-0). HM.

Kintyre. Alasdair Carmichael. (Island Ser.). 1974. 19.95 o.p. (ISBN 0-7153-6317-4). David & Charles.

Kiowa. Elgin Groseclose. LC 77-78493. 1978. 6.95 o.p. (ISBN 0-89191-114-6); pap. 3.95 o.p. (ISBN 0-89191-113-8). Cook.

Kirby Koala Happy Day Rhymes. Karen Stiles et al. (Kirby Koala Ser.). (Illus.). 22p. (ps-2). 1983. 2.50 o.p. (ISBN 0-89954-210-7). Antioch Pub Co.

Kirby Koala Special Wish Book. (gr. 2-3). 1.95 o.p. (ISBN 0-89954-364-2). Antioch Pub Co.

Kirby Page & the Social Gospel: Pacifist & Socialist Aspects. Charles Chatfield. LC 70-147695. (Library of War & Peace: Documentary Anthologies). 1976. lib. bdg. 46.00 o.p. (ISBN 0-8240-0451-5). Garland Pub.

Kiri Te Kanawa: A Biography. David Fingleton. LC 82-73013. 188p. 1983. 13.95 o.p. (ISBN 0-689-11345-5, Atheneum). Macmillan.

Kirlian Photography: Research & Prospects. L. Gennaro & F. Guzzon. (Illus.). 152p. 1982. 14.95 o.p. (ISBN 0-85692-045-2, Pub. by Salem Hse Ltd). Salem Hse Pubs.

Kirsty Knows Best. Annalena McAfee. LC 87-3359. (Illus.). 32p. (gr. 2-6). 1988. 8.95 o.s.i. (ISBN 0-394-89478-2); lib. bdg. 9.99 o.s.i. (ISBN 0-394-99478-7). Knopf.

Kirsty's Kite. Carol C. Stilz. (Illus.). 40p. (gr. k up). 1988. 11.95 o.p. (ISBN 0-86760-089-6, Pub. by Albatross Bks). Meyer Stone Bks.

Kirtland Economy Revisited: A Market Critique of Sectarian Economics. Marvin S. Hill & C. Keith Rooker. LC 78-3848. (Studies in Mormon History: No. 3). (Illus.). 1977. pap. 4.95 o.p. (ISBN 0-8425-1230-6). Brigham.

Kisling Eighteen Ninety One to Nineteen Fifty-Three, Vol. 2. Henri Troyat. Tr. by Michael Feinberg from Fr. (Illus.). 350p. 1983. 125.00 o.p. (ISBN 0-8390-0327-7). Abner Schram Ltd.

Kiss: A Jambalaya. John F. Nims. 80p. 1982. 11.95 o.p. (ISBN 0-395-31829-7); pap. 6.95 o.p. (ISBN 0-395-31830-0). HM.

Kiss Daddy Goodnight. Louise Armstrong. 1986. pap. 3.95 o.s.i. (ISBN 0-671-60659-X). PB.

Kiss Daddy Goodnight Ten Years Later. Louis Armstrong. 1987. pap. 3.95 o.s.i. (ISBN 0-671-64934-5). PB.

Kiss Me Again, Stranger. Daphne Du Maurier. 1972. pap. 1.25 o.p. (10330). Avon.

Kiss Me Again, Stranger. Daphne Du Maurier. 1987. pap. 3.95 o.p. (ISBN 0-440-14576-7). Dell.

Kiss of Kin: A Novel. Mary L. Settle. (Signature Editions). 184p. 1986. pap. 5.95 o.p. (ISBN 0-684-18715-9). Scribner.

Kiss the Tears Away. Anna Hudson. (Candlelight Ecstasy Ser.: No. 156). (Orig.). 1983. pap. 1.95 o.s.i. (ISBN 0-440-14525-2). Dell.

Kisses That Miss & Other Awkward Moments. Antonia Van der Meer. (YA) (gr. 7 up). pap. 2.25 o.p. (ISBN 0-671-50922-5). Archway.

Kissinger Noodles... or Westward, Mr. Ho: A Novel. Max Wilk. 1976. 7.95 o.p. (ISBN 0-393-08728-X). Norton.

Kissinger Study of Southern Africa: National Security Study Memorandum 39(Secret) Intro. by Mohamed A. El-Khawas & Barry Cohen. LC 76-18043. 192p. 1976. o. p. 6.95 o.p. (ISBN 0-88208-071-7); pap. 5.95 o.p. (ISBN 0-88208-072-5). Chicago Review.

Kit Brandon. Sherwood Anderson. 1985. 6.95 o.p. (ISBN 0-87795-707-X, Arbor Hse). Morrow.

Kit Car Catalog, 1985. Curt Scott. Ed. by Judy Scott. (Illus.). 184p. 1985. pap. 8.95 o.p. (ISBN 0-9614882-0-4, Dist. by Motorbooks Intl). Crown Pub CA.

Kit Cars. Gavin Engen. LC 77-6203. (Superwheels & Thrill Sports Bks.). (Illus.). (gr. 4-9). 1977. PLB 9.95 o.p. (ISBN 0-8225-0417-0). Lerner Pubns.

Kit Carson. Cynthia Klingel & Dan Zadra. (We the People Ser.). (Illus.). 32p. PLB 10.45 o.p. Creative Ed.

Kit Carson's Long Walk & Other True Tales of Old San Diego. Henry Schwartz. LC 80-68570. (Illus.). 112p. (Orig.). 1980. pap. 3.95 o.p. (ISBN 0-933362-03-X). Assoc Creative Writers.

Kit Furniture Book. Lynda Graham-Barber. (Illus.). 1982. pap. 9.95 o.p. (ISBN 0-394-70674-9). Pantheon.

Kit GR 2 Clay Boats. Date not set. (ISBN 0-07-017563-2). McGraw.

Kita Taiheiyo ni Hyoryushita Nihon Nanpasen. Bert Webber. Tr. by Sakyo Adachi from Japanese. (Illus., Orig., Eng.). (YA) (gr. 7-12). pap. cancelled o.s.i. (ISBN 0-936738-25-1). Webb Research.

Kitab Al Tawhid. Muhammad I. Al-Wahhab. 120p. (Orig., Arabic.). 1978. pap. 4.95 o.s.i. (ISBN 0-939830-20-5, Pub. by IIFSO Kuwait). New Era Pubns MI.

Kitchen ABC's: A Dictionary for Cooks. alice H. Regis. 196p. 1988. pap. 9.95 o.p. (ISBN 0-936417-07-2). Axelrod Pub.

Kitchen Bouquets. Bert Greene. 430p. 1986. pap. 9.95 o.p. (ISBN 0-671-62793-7, Fireside). S&S.

Kitchen Bygones: A Collector's Guide. Geoffrey Warren. 128p. 1985. pap. 12.95 o.s.i. (ISBN 0-285-62669-8, Pub. by Souvenir Pr Ltd UK). Seven Hills Bk Dists.

Kitchen Chemistry: Science Experiments to Do at Home. Robert Gardner. LC 82-60639. (Illus.). 128p. (gr. 4 up). 1982. lib. bdg. 9.98 o.s.i. (ISBN 0-671-42102-6). Messner.

Kitchen Communion. Cornelia M. Renfroe. LC 59-11220. (Illus.). 1959. 2.50 o.p. (ISBN 0-8042-2400-5, John Knox). Westminster John Knox.

Kitchen Science: A Compendium of Essential Information for Every Cook. Howard Hillman. (Illus.). 272p. 1981. 11.95 o.p. (ISBN 0-395-30533-0). HM.

Kitchen Tools: Cooking with a Twist & a Flair. Patricia Gentry. LC 85-18795. (Illus.). 144p. (Orig.). 1985. pap. 8.95 o.p. (ISBN 0-89286-257-2, TX656G46, One Hund One Prods). Ortho.

Kitchens: Creative Ideas for Your Home. Home Magazine Editors. LC 84-7883. (Illus.). 308p. 1984. 24.95 o.p. (ISBN 0-89535-137-4). Knapp Pr.

Kitchens: Planning & Remodeling. 5th ed. Sunset Editors. LC 76-7663. (Illus.). 80p. 1976. pap. 3.95 o.p. (ISBN 0-376-01337-0, Sunset Bks.). Sunset-Lane.

Kite Building & Kite Flying Handbook, with 42 Kite Plans. Jack Wiley. (Illus.). 288p. (Orig.). 1984. pap. 15.50 o.p. (ISBN 0-8306-1669-1, 1669). TAB Bks.

Kite Ride. Mary H. Manoni. (Adventures of Raggedy Ann & Raggedy Andy Book Cassettes). (Illus.). 16p. (gr. k-3). 1979. 24.95 o.p. (ISBN 0-89290-059-8); 6 bks. & one cassette incl. o.p. Soc for Visual.

Kite That Won the Revolution. Isaac Asimov. (Illus.). 148p. (gr. 7 up). 1973. pap. 0.95 o.p. (ISBN 0-395-17445-7, Sandpiper). HM.

Kites Will Fly: A Novel. Bhisham Sahni. (Vikas Library of Modern Moien Writing Ser.: No. 9). 200p. 1982. text ed. 18.95x o.p. (ISBN 0-7069-1332-9, Pub. by Vikas India). Advent NY.

Kiteworld. Keith Roberts. LC 85-18601. 288p. 1986. 15.95 o.p. (ISBN 0-87795-790-8). Morrow.

Kits, Cats, Lions & Tigers. Lee B. Hopkins. Ed. by Kathy Pacini. LC 78-11421. (Illus.). (gr. 3-5). 1979. PLB 9.75 o.p. (ISBN 0-8075-4181-8). A Whitman.

Kitsch: The World of Bad Taste. Gillo Dorfles. LC 78-93950. (Illus.). 320p. 1967. pap. 4.95 o.p. (ISBN 0-87663-911-2). Universe.

Kittelsen Theodor. Illus. by Ostby. (Illus.). 200p. 1978. 75.00x o.p. (ISBN 82-090-1227-4, N534). Vanous.

Kitten Is Born. Heiderose Fischer-Nagel & Andreas Fischer-Nagel. (Illus.). (ps-3). 1983. 9.95 o.p. (ISBN 0-399-20961-1, Putnam). Putnam Pub Group.

Kitten Visits the Park. Lin Songying. (Illus.). 18p. (gr. 1-2). 1986. pap. 1.95 o.p. (ISBN 0-8351-1704-9). China Bks.

Kitty the Raccoon. Jamie Stamper. LC 86-50986. (Illus.). 54p. (gr. k-6). 1986. pap. 9.95 o.p. (ISBN 0-932433-21-9). Windswept Hse.

Kittymouse. Sumiko Davies. LC 78-16716. (Illus.). 32p. (gr. k-3). 1979. 7.95 o.p. (ISBN 0-15-243028-8, HJ). HarBraceJ.

Kiviok's Magic Journey: An Eskimo Legend. James Houston. LC 73-75435. (Illus.). (gr. 1-4). 1973. 5.25 o.p. (ISBN 0-689-30419-6, Atheneum). Macmillan.

KKK: The Invisible Empire. David Lowe. (Illus.). 1967. 11.95 o.p. (ISBN 0-393-05307-5). Norton.

Klan Killer. R. L. Mack. 80p. 1982. 5.50 o.p. (ISBN 0-682-49770-3). Exposition-Phoenix.

Klaus Barbie: The Untold Story. Ladislas De Hoyos. Tr. by Nicholas Courtin. LC 85-11326. (Illus.). 336p. 1985. text ed. 17.95 o.p. (ISBN 0-07-016297-2). McGraw.

Kleber Flight. Hans Koning. LC 81-66025. 1981. 12.95 o.p. (ISBN 0-689-11221-1, Atheneum). Macmillan.

Kleines Literarisches Lexikon, Vol. 26. 4th ed. Horst Ruediger. (Ger.). 1972. 19.95 o.p. (ISBN 3-7720-0953-0, M-7695, Pub. by Francke). French & Eur.

Kleines Literarisches Lexikon: Autoren 1, Von Den Anfaengen Bis Zum 19. Jahrhundert, Vol. 1. 4th ed. Horst Ruediger. (Ger.). 1969. 22.95 o.p. (ISBN 3-7720-0601-9, M-7503, Pub. by Francke). French & Eur.

Kleines Literarisches Lexikon: Sachbegriffe, Vol. 4. 4th ed. Horst Ruediger. (Ger.). 1966. 12.95 o.p. (ISBN 0-686-56622-X, M-7505, Pub. by Francke). French & Eur.

Klemperer on Music: Shavings from a Musician's Workbench. Otto Klemperer. 256p. 1986. text ed. 20.00x o.p. (ISBN 0-87663-497-8). Universe.

Klingon Gambit. Robert E. Vardeman. (Star Trek Ser.). 160p. 1984. lib. bdg. 10.95 o.p. (ISBN 0-8398-2834-9, Gregg). G K Hall.

Klondike Letters: The Correspondence of a Gold Seeker in 1898. Ed. by Juliette C. Reinicker. LC 84-21530. (Northern Library History). (Illus.). 64p. (Orig.). 1984. pap. 6.95 o.s.i. (ISBN 0-88240-292-7). Alaska Northwest.

Klondike Lost: A Decade of Photographs by Kinsey & Kinsey. Norm Bolotin. LC 79-25687. (Illus.). 1980. album style 12.95 o.s.i. (ISBN 0-88240-130-0). Alaska Northwest.

Kloppelspitzen. (Second Ser.). (Illus.). 448p. (Ger.). 1981. 48.00x o.p. (ISBN 0-8103-4313-4). Gale.

Kluge & Narrische Welt. S. M. 240p. Repr. of 1723 ed. 29.00 o.p. (ISBN 0-384-52835-X). Johnson Repr.

Klynts Law. Elliott Baker. LC 75-45144. 312p. 1976. 8.95 o.p. (ISBN 0-15-147283-1). HarBraceJ.

KMG Main Hurdman Guide To Preparing Financial Reports. 1987 ed. Ed. by Morton B. Solomon et al. 392p. 1986. pap. (ISBN 0-471-85482-4); Special ed. pap. (ISBN 0-471-85761-0). Wiley.

Knapik Cookbook. new ed. Harold Knapik. LC 70-131271. (Illus.). 1971. 7.95 o.p. (ISBN 0-87140-526-1). Liveright.

Knave & the Game: A Collection of Short Stories. Laurence M. Janifer. LC 79-7689. (Science Fiction Ser.). 192p. 1987. 12.95 o.p. (ISBN 0-385-15238-8). Doubleday.

Knee Arthrography: A Practical Approach. Richard D. Wolfe. (Monographs in Clinical Radiology). (Illus.). 256p. 1984. write for info. o.p. (ISBN 0-7216-9578-7). Saunders.

Knee Braces: Seminar Report. Ed. by David Drez, Jr. (Illus.). 90p. 1985. 15.00 o.p. (ISBN 0-89203-006-2). Amer Acad Ortho Surg.

Knee-Knock Rise. Natalie Babbitt. (gr. 3-6). 1981. pap. 1.25 o.p. (ISBN 0-380-00849-1, 44875, Camelot). Avon.

Knee: Ligament & Articular Cartilage Injuries. Ed. by D. E. Hastings. (Progress in Orthopedic Surgery: Vol. 3). (Illus.). 1978. 26.00 o.p. (ISBN 0-387-08679-X). Springer-Verlag.

Knife Between the Ribs. Jack Scott. (Lythway Ser.). 248p. 1988. lib. bdg. 18.50x o.p. (ISBN 0-7451-0678-1, Pub. by Chivers Pr UK). G K Hall.

Knife for All Seasons. Nancy Elmont. LC 80-70845. (Illus.). 160p. 1981. 11.95 o.p. (ISBN 0-916752-48-8). Longman Trade.

Knife Is Not Enough. Henry H. Kessler. LC 68-20822. (Illus.). 1968. 5.95 o.p. (ISBN 0-393-07416-1). Norton.

Knight Must Fall. Theodora Wender. 160p. 1985. pap. 2.95 o.p. (ISBN 0-380-89520-X). Avon.

Knight of Olmedo (El Caballero de Olmedo) The Spanish Text with a Facing English Translation. Lope de Vega. Tr. by Willard F. King. LC 78-186118. xxviii, 187p. (Eng. & Span.). 1972. 17.95x o.p. (ISBN 0-8032-0500-7). U of Nebr Pr.

Knight of the Swords. Michael Moorcock. 160p. 1986. pap. 2.95 o.s.i. (ISBN 0-425-08533-3). Berkley Pub.

Knight's Castle. Edward Eager. LC 56-5234. (Illus.). (gr. 3-7). 1956. 6.75 o.p. (ISBN 0-15-243102-0, HJ). HarBraceJ.

Knight's Castle. Edward Eager. LC 84-19817. (Illus.). 192p. (gr. 3-6). 1965. pap. 4.95 o.p. (ISBN 0-15-647350-X, VoyB). HarBraceJ.

Knight's Modern Seamanship. 17th ed. Ed. by Noel. 1983. 43.95 o.s.i. (ISBN 0-442-26863-7). Van Nos Reinhold.

Knight's Modern Seamanship. 16th ed. John V. Noel, Jr. & Frank E. Bassett. 1977. text ed. 18.95 o.p. (ISBN 0-442-26049-0). Van Nos Reinhold.

Knights of Illusions. Jane Atkin. (Candlelight Ecstasy Ser.: No. 497). (Orig.). 1987. pap. 2.25 o.p. (ISBN 0-440-14596-1). Dell.

Knights Templar. Stephen Howarth. LC 81-66035. 1982. 18.95 o.p. (ISBN 0-689-11185-1, Atheneum). Macmillan.

Knit with Style. Ferne G. Cone. LC 79-13744. (Connecting Threads Ser.). (Illus.). 1979. pap. 9.95 o.p. (ISBN 0-914842-38-2). Madrona Pubs.

Knitting from the Netherlands. Tellegen Van der Klift. 1984. 13.95 o.p. (ISBN 0-937274-17-8). Dodd.

Knitting from the Top. Barbara G. Walker. (Illus.). 128p. 1982. pap. 10.95 o.s.i. (ISBN 0-684-17669-6, ScribT). Scribner.

Knitting Now! Gabi Tubbs. 264p. 1985. pap. 14.95 o.p. (ISBN 0-684-18379-X). Scribner.

Knitting with Gwen Byrne, 2 bks. 1987. pap. 7.95 ea. o.p. Morrow.

Knives Eighty Five. 5th ed. Ed. by Ken Warner. (Illus.). 256p. (Orig.). pap. 10.95 o.p. (ISBN 0-910676-81-X). DBI.

Knives 1984. Ken Warner. (Illus.). 256p. 1983. pap. 10.95 o.p. (ISBN 0-910676-63-1). DBI.

Knives '88. Ed. by Ken Warner. LC 80-67744. (Illus.). 256p. (Orig.). 1987. pap. 12.95 o.p. (ISBN 0-87349-015-0). DBI.

Knock on a Door. Mary T. Blanton. LC 84-7027. (Illus.). 32p. (ps-k). 1984. lib. bdg. 4.95 o.p. Dandelion Hse.

Knock; or, the Triumph of Medicine: A Comedy in Three Acts. Jules Romains. Tr. by Betty S. Sacks. LC 84-90104. 1984. 7.95 o.p. (ISBN 0-533-06171-7). Vantage.

Knock ou le Triomphe de la Medecine. Jules Romains. (Coll. Soleil). 1958. 12.95 o.p. (ISBN 0-685-11284-5). Schoenhof.

Knock Wood. Candice Bergen. (Illus.). 304p. 1984. 17.45 o.p. (ISBN 0-671-25294-1, Linden Pr). S&S.

Knock Wood. Candice Bergen. (General Ser.). 1984. lib. bdg. 17.95 o.p. (ISBN 0-8161-3764-1, Large Print Bks); pap. 9.95 o.p. (ISBN 0-8161-3776-5). G K Hall.

Knock Wood! Superstition Through the Ages. Daniel Deerforth. LC 79-164220. 208p. 1974. Repr. of 1928 ed. 43.00x o.p. (ISBN 0-8103-3964-1). Gale.

Knockover. Newton Thornburg. 1975. pap. 1.25 o.p. (ISBN 0-380-00303-1, 24174). Avon.

Knot Theory: Proceedings, Plans-Sur-Bex, Switzerland 1977. Ed. by J. C. Hausman. (Lecture Note in Mathematics Ser.: Vol. 685). 1978. 22.00 o.p. (ISBN 0-387-08952-7). Springer-Verlag.

Knots & Crosses. Ian Rankin. LC 87-5342. (Crime Club Ser.). 192p. 1987. 12.95 o.s.i. (ISBN 0-385-24307-3). Doubleday.

Knots & Links. Dale Rolfsen. LC 76-15514. (Mathematics Lecture Ser: No. 7). (Illus.). 439p. 1976. pap. text ed. 20.00 o.p. (ISBN 0-914098-16-0). Publish or Perish.

Knotted Skein. Carla Neggers. (Velvet Glove Ser.: No. 7). 192p. 1984. pap. 2.25 o.p. (ISBN 0-380-89433-5, 89433-5). Avon.

Knott's Handbook for Vegetable Growers. 2nd ed. Oscar A. Lorenz & Donald N. Maynard. LC 79-26840. 390p. 1980. pap. 24.50 o.p. (ISBN 0-471-05322-8). Wiley.

Know about the Armada. Henry Garnett. LC 66-10696. (Illus.). (gr. 7 up). 1967. 14.95 o.p. (ISBN 0-8023-1121-0). Dufour.

Know Africa, 3 Vols. Ralph Uwechue. Incl. Vol. 1. Africa Today; Vol. 3. Makers of Modern Africa; Vol. 3. Africa Who's Who. 3290p. 1981. 325.00x set o.p. (ISBN 0-903274-13-2, Pub. by Africa Journal Limited). Gale.

Know or Listen to Those Who Know. Ed. by John W. Gardner & Francesca G. Reese. 247p. 1975. 7.95 o.p. (ISBN 0-393-08735-2). Norton.

Know Thyself: Jnani Yoga. Omraam M. Aivanhov. (Complete Works: Vol. 17). (Illus.). 271p. 1981. pap. 11.95 o.p. (ISBN 2-85566-162-5). Prosveta USA.

Know Your Ancestors: A Guide to Genealogical Research. Ethel W. Williams. LC 60-15252. 1960. bds. 12.50 o.p. (ISBN 0-8048-0344-7). C E Tuttle.

Know Your Bible. W. Graham Scroggie. 608p. 1965. 22.95 o.p. (ISBN 0-8007-0169-0). Revell.

Know Your Eyes. corrections & updates ed. I. A. Abrahamson, Jr. LC 76-23195. 218p. 1977. Repr. of 1972 ed. 11.50 o.p. (ISBN 0-88275-928-0). Krieger.

Know Your Genes. Aubrey Milunsky. 1977. 9.95 o.p. (ISBN 0-395-25374-8). HM.

Know Your Law. Greville Janner. (Building Your Business Ser.). 229p. 1984. text ed. 17.95x o.p. (ISBN 0-09-151810-5, Pub. by Busn Bks England). Gower Pub Co.

Know Your Merchandise: For Retailers & Consumers. 4th ed. Isabel B. Wingate et al. (Illus.). 544p. 1975. text ed. 23.85 o.p. (ISBN 0-07-070985-8, G). McGraw.

Know Your Oscilloscope. 4th ed. Robert G. Middleton. LC 80-52230. 1980. pap. 11.95 o.p. (ISBN 0-672-21742-2). Sams.

Know Your Signs - Be a Better Driver: Driving Interstate & Superhighways. Eileen L. Corcoran. (Know Your Signs Ser.). 1973. pap. 4.75 o.p. (ISBN 0-88323-112-3, 200). Pendergrass Pub.

Know Your Woods. rev. ed. Albert J. Constantine. 1975. 19.95 o.s.i. (ISBN 0-684-14115-9, ScribT). Scribner.

Know Yourself! Ernest Holmes. Ed. by Willis H. Kinnear. 96p. (Orig.). 1970. pap. 4.50 o.p. (ISBN 0-911336-36-2). Sci of Mind.

Knowin' All Them Things That Ain't So: Managing Today's Public Library. Thomas Ballard. (Occasional Papers: No. 168). 1985. pap. 5.00 o.p. (ISBN 0-317-59020-0). U of Ill Lib Info Sci.

Knowing & Acting: An Invitation to Philosophy. Stephen Toulmin. (Illus.). 256p. 1976. pap. text ed. write for info. o.p. (ISBN 0-02-421020-X). Macmillan.

Knowing & Caring: Philosophical Issues in Social Work. Roberta W. Imre. LC 82-20209. 164p. (Orig.). 1983. lib. bdg. 24.75 o.p. (ISBN 0-8191-2859-7); pap. text ed. 10.25 o.p. (ISBN 0-8191-2860-0). U Pr of Amer.

Knowing Beans about Coffee. Joan Korenblit & Kathie Janger. Ed. by Suzanne Brown. 64p. (Orig.). 1985. pap. write for info. o.p. (KJ102). Am Cooking.

Knowing the Face of God. Tim Stafford. 256p. Date not set. pap. 12.95 o.p. (ISBN 0-310-32851-9, 10836). Zondervan.

Knowing the Face of God: The Search for a Personal Relationship with God. Tim Stafford. 256p. 1986. text ed. 12.95 o.p. (ISBN 0-310-32850-0, 10836). Zondervan.

Knowing the Poor: A Case Study in Textual Reality Construction. Bryan S. Green. (International Library of Phenomology & Moral Sciences). 224p. 1983. 25.95x o.p. (ISBN 0-7100-9282-2). Routledge Chapman & Hall.

Knowing the Unknowable God: Ibn-Sina, Maimonides, Aquinas. David B. Burrell. LC 85-40600. 160p. 1986. text ed. 15.95x o.p. (ISBN 0-268-01225-3, 85-12253). U of Notre Dame Pr.

Knowing Where to Look: The Ultimate Guide to Research. Lois Horowitz. LC 84-20876. 368p. 1984. 18.95 o.p. (ISBN 0-89879-159-6). Writers Digest.

Knowing Your Tefilen & Mezuzos: A Layman's Guide to Understanding & Appreciating Tefilin & Mezuzos. Zeev Rothschild. 80p. (Orig.). 1982. pap. 2.50 o.s.i. (ISBN 0-686-76528-1). Feldheim.

Knowledge Acquisition for Knowledge-Based Systems. John Boose & Brian R. Gaines. (Illus.). 100p. 1988. pap. text ed. 12.00 o.p. (ISBN 0-929280-08-3). Amer Artificial.

Knowledge & Cosmos: Development & Decline of the Medieval Perspective. Robert K. DeKosky. LC 79-66226. 1979. text ed. 27.50 o.p. (ISBN 0-8191-0814-6); pap. text ed. 16.25 o.p. (ISBN 0-8191-0815-4). U Pr of Amer.

Knowledge & Development, Vol. 1: Advances in Research & Theory. Ed. by Willis F. Overton & J. M. Gallagher. LC 76-26163. 276p. 1977. 40.00x o.p. (ISBN 0-306-33201-9, Plenum Pr). Plenum Pub.

Knowledge & Development, Vol. 2: Piaget & Education. Ed. by J. M. Gallagher & J. A. Easley. (Illus.). 314p. 1978. 40.00x o.p. (ISBN 0-306-40089-8, Plenum Pr). Plenum Pub.

Knowledge & Social Imagery. David Bloor. (Routledge Direct Editions). 168p. 1976. 16.95x o.p. (ISBN 0-7100-8377-7). Routledge Chapman & Hall.

Knowledge & Value: Introductory Readings in Philosophy. 2nd ed. Ed. by Elmer Sprague & Paul W. Taylor. 700p. 1967. text ed. 21.95 o.p. (ISBN 0-15-548642-X, HC). HarBraceJ.

Knowledge, Belief & Transcendence: Philosophical Problems in Religion. James H. Hall. 1975. pap. 8.50 o.p. (ISBN 0-395-19502-0). HM.

Knowledge Engineering & Computer Modelling in CAD. (Illus.). 488p. 1986. pap. text ed. 120.00 o.p. (ISBN 0-408-00824-5). Butterworth.

Knowledge in Action. Jurgen Ruesch. LC 75-2489. 332p. 1976. 25.00x o.p. (ISBN 0-87668-201-8). Aronson.

Knowledge Industry Two Hundred: America's Two Hundred Largest Media Companies. 1st ed. Ed. by Judith S. Duke. 500p. 1982. 155.00x o.p. (ISBN 0-8103-1624-2, Pub. by Knowledge Indus). Gale.

Knowledge: Its Creation, Distribution, & Economic Significance, Vol. I, Knowledge & Knowledge Production. Fritz Machlup. LC 80-7544. 264p. 1980. 30.00 o.p. (ISBN 0-691-04226-8). Princeton U Pr.

Knowledge of the Holy. A. W. Tozer. LC 85-42794. 208p. 1985. pap. 12.95 large print o.p. (ISBN 0-06-068413-5). HarpR.

Knowledge Representation: Design Issues. Doug Skuce & John Sowa. (Illus.). 85p. 1988. pap. text ed. 12.00 o.p. (ISBN 0-929280-24-5). Amer Artificial.

Koch: As Time Goes by: Memoirs of a Writer. Howard Koch. LC 78-22260. 1979. 10.95 o.p. (ISBN 0-15-109769-0). HarBraceJ.

KODAK Complete Darkroom DATAGUIDE: Processing & Printing Information for Black-&-White & Color. 5th ed. Eastman Kodak Company. Orig. Title: QSL Adress Book. 58p. (Orig.). 1984. pap. 19.95 o.p. (ISBN 0-87985-355-7). Eastman Kodak.

Kodak Data for Aerial Photography. 4th ed. (Illus.). 1976. pap. 4.95 o.p. (ISBN 0-87985-167-8, M-29). Eastman Kodak.

Kodak Guide to 35 MM Photography. Eastman Kodak Company Staff. LC 79-54310. (Illus.). 286p. (Orig.). 1987. text ed. 19.95 o.p. (ISBN 0-87985-242-9, AC-95H); pap. 9.95 o.p. (ISBN 0-87985-236-4, AC-95S). Eastman Kodak.

Kodak Guide to 35mm Photography (AC-95S) Eastman Kodak Company Staff. LC 83-83259. (Illus.). 286p. 1984. pap. 9.95 o.p. (ISBN 0-87985-347-6). Eastman Kodak.

Kodak: More Joy of Photography. 1981. 24.95 o.p. (ISBN 0-201-04544-3); pap. 14.38 o.p. (ISBN 0-201-04543-5). Addison-Wesley.

Kodak Pocket Guide to Great Picture Taking. 112p. 1984. pap. 5.95 o.p. (ISBN 0-671-54137-4). S&S.

Kodak Pocket Guide to Nature Photography. Eastman Kodak Company Editors. 1985. pap. 5.95 o.p. (ISBN 0-671-50670-6). S&S.

Kodak Pocket Guide to Photographing Cats. Eastman Kodak Company Editors. 1985. pap. 5.95 o.s.i. (ISBN 0-671-50671-4). S&S.

Kodak Pocket Guide to Photographing Dogs. Eastman Kodak Company Editors. 1985. pap. 5.95 o.s.i. (ISBN 0-671-55825-0). S&S.

Kodak Pocket Guide to Sports Photography. 112p. 1984. pap. 5.95 o.s.i. (ISBN 0-671-50668-4). S&S.

Kodak Pocket Guide to Video Cameras. (Illus.). 112p. 1987. pap. 5.95 o.p. (ISBN 0-671-62843-7, Fireside). S&S.

Kolo Moser. Daniele Baroni & Antonio D'Auria. LC 85-43052. (Illus.). 144p. 1985. pap. 19.95 o.p. (ISBN 0-8478-0667-7). Rizzoli Intl.

Kolyma Tales. Varlam Shalamov. Tr. by John Glad. 1980. 9.95 o.p. (ISBN 0-393-01324-3). Norton.

Kommunalplanung Von Neuen Herausfurderungen. Dieter Von Loelhoeffel & Dieter Schimanke. (Stadtforschung Ser.: Vol. 2). 304p. (Ger.). 1983. pap. 14.95 o.p. (ISBN 0-8176-1484-2). Birkhauser.

Kompendium der Inneren Medizin. U. Sprandel & F. Stark. xvi, 426p. 1987. pap. 26.75 o.p. (ISBN 3-8055-3562-7). S Karger.

Komposition Von Vergils Georgica, Mit Vier Beilagen. Magdalena Schmidt. Repr. of 1930 ed. 19.00 o.p. (ISBN 0-384-54070-8). Johnson Repr.

Komsomol: Question & Answers. A. Andreyev et al. 1980. pap. 2.95 o.p. (ISBN 0-8285-1827-0, Pub. by Progress Pubs USSR). Imported Pubns.

Kon-Tiki. Thor Heyerdahl. (Enriched Classics Edition). (gr. 11 up). 1983. pap. 3.95 o.s.i. (ISBN 0-671-49950-5). PB.

Kon-Tiki. rev. ed. Thor Heyerdahl. LC 50-9489. (Illus.). 304p. (gr. 7 up). 1984. 16.95 o.p. Rand McNally.

Kondratieff's Cycles & the Future of the Stock Market in Its Convulsions & Price Gyrations. Institute for Economic & Financial Research Editorial Council Staff. (Illus.). 167p. 1986. 147.75 o.p. (ISBN 0-86654-190-X). Inst Econ Finan.

Konets Prekrasnoi Epokhi. Joseph Brodsky. (Rus.). 1977. pap. 4.50 o.p. (ISBN 0-88233-263-5). Ardis Pubs.

Kongur: China's Elusive Summit. Chris Bonington. (Illus.). 1983. 19.45 o.p. (ISBN 0-393-01762-1). Norton.

Konkordanz zu den Gedichten: Hugo von Hofmannsthals. Steven P. Sondrup & Craig M. Inglis. 1977. text ed. 5.00 o.p. (ISBN 0-8425-0843-0). Brigham.

Konrad. Christine Nostlinger. Tr. by Anthea Bell. (Illus.). 136p. (gr. 2-5). 1983. pap. 2.50 o.p. (ISBN 0-380-62018-9, 60040-4, Camelot). Avon.

Konrad Lorenz: A Bibliography. Alec Nisbett. LC 76-29116. (Helen & Kurt Wolf Book). (Illus.). 1977. 10.00 o.p. (ISBN 0-15-147286-6). HarBraceJ.

Konrad Lorenz: The Man & His Ideas. Richard I. Evans. LC 75-9581. 302p. 1975. 10.00 o.p. (ISBN 0-15-147285-8). HarBraceJ.

Konstantin Paustovskii: Selected Stories. Ed. by P. Henry & P. Henry. 1967. pap. text ed. 6.25 o.p. (ISBN 0-08-011859-3). Pergamon.

Kontaktlinsenvademekum, 1987. 3rd, rev., enl. ed. Ed. by H. Streitenberg. (Illus.). x, 206p. 1987. pap. 22.00 o.p. (ISBN 3-8055-4345-X). S Karger.

Kontinent Four: Contemporary Russian Writers. Ed. by George Bailey. 528p. 1982. pap. 4.95 o.p. (ISBN 0-380-81182-0, 81182-0, Bard). Avon.

Kook Book. Art Budd. 72p. 1979. pap. 2.95 o.p. (ISBN 0-939116-05-7). Frontier WA.

Kora in Hell: Improvisations. William Carlos Williams. LC 57-10122. (Pocket Poets Ser.: No. 7). pap. 2.00 o.s.i. (ISBN 0-87286-053-1). City Lights.

Korea. Philip J. Gannon. LC 85-14210. (World Education Ser.). (Illus.). 152p. (Orig.). 1985. pap. 5.00 o.p. (ISBN 0-910054-81-9). Am Assn Coll Registrars.

Korea & Taiwan-A Travel Survival Kit. 2nd ed. Geoff Crowther. (Illus.). 200p. (Orig.). 1985. pap. 7.95 o.p. (ISBN 0-908086-71-7). Lonely Planet.

Korea & Taiwan Travel Survival. Geoff Crowther. 1983. pap. 6.95 o.p. (ISBN 0-908086-10-5). Lonely Planet.

Korea Directory, 1983. (ISBN 0-8002-2899-5). Intl Pubns Serv.

Korea in the World Today. Ed. by Roger Pearson. 1976. pap. 15.00 o.p. (ISBN 0-930690-01-X). Coun Soc Econ.

Korea: Post Report. (State Department Publication 1979. Department & Foreign Service Ser.: No. 314). (Illus.). 36p. 1986. pap. 2.00 o.p. (ISBN 0-318-20406-1, S/N 044-000-02125-1). USGPO.

Korea Statistical Yearbook, 1983. Intl Pubns Serv.

Korean Immigration to the United States: Its Demographic Pattern & Social Implications for Both Societies. Hagen Koo & Eui-Young Yu. LC 81-12514. (Papers of the East-West Population Institute: No. 74). v, 31p. (Orig.). 1981. pap. text ed. 1.25 o.p. (ISBN 0-86638-017-5). EW Ctr HI.

Korean People's Democratic Republic. Glenn D. Paige. LC 65-27783. (Studies Ser.: No. 11). 1966. pap. 4.95x o.p. (ISBN 0-8179-3112-0). Hoover Inst Pr.

Korean Sex Jokes in Traditional Times: 206 Stories. Tr. by Howard S. Levy. 1972. pap. 15.00x o.p. (ISBN 0-686-01302-6). Oriental Bk Store.

Korean War. Max Hastings. (Illus.). 480p. 1987. 22.45 o.s.i. (ISBN 0-671-52823-8). S&S.

Korrectional Kartoons for the Captive Audience. (Illus.). 32p. (Orig.). 1982. pap. 4.00 o.s.i. (ISBN 0-942974-00-X). Am Correctional.

Kosoy Travel Guide to Canada. Ted Kosoy. 1985. pap. 7.95 o.p. (ISBN 0-531-03897-1). Watts.

Kosoy Travel Guide to Europe. Ted Kosoy. 1985. pap. 7.95 o.p. (ISBN 0-531-03898-X). Watts.

Kostya Ryabtsev's Diary. N. Ognev. 180p. 1978. pap. 5.45 o.p. (ISBN 0-8285-1172-1, Pub. by Progress Pubs Russia). Imported Pubns.

Kovels' Advertising Collectibles Price List. Ralph M. Kovel & Terry H. Kovel. 1986. pap. 11.95 o.p. (ISBN 0-517-55871-8). Crown.

Kovels' Antique & Collectibles Price List. 15th ed. Ralph M. Kovel & Terry H. Kovel. (Illus.). 800p. 1982. 10.95 o.p. (ISBN 0-517-54761-9). Crown.

Kovels' Antique Price List. 11th ed. Ralph M. Kovel & Terry H. Kovel. (Illus.). 1978. pap. 8.95 o.p. (ISBN 0-517-53468-1). Crown.

Kovel's Antique Price List. 12th ed. Ralph M. Kovel & Terry H. Kovel. (Illus., Orig.). 1979. pap. 9.95 o.p. (ISBN 0-517-53879-2). Crown.

Kovels' Antiques & Collectibles Price List. 17th ed. Ralph M. Kovel & Terry H. Kovel. (Illus.). 1984. pap. 9.95 o.p. (ISBN 0-517-55425-9). Crown.

Kovels' Antiques & Collectibles Price List. 18th ed. Ralph M. Kovel & Terry H. Kovel. (Illus.). 800p. 1985. pap. 10.95 o.p. (ISBN 0-517-55809-2). Crown.

Kovels' Antiques & Collectibles Price List. 19th ed. Ralph M. Kovel & Terry H. Kovel. (Illus.). 800p. 1986. pap. 10.95 o.p. (ISBN 0-517-56236-7). Crown.

Kovels' Antiques & Collectibles Price List. 16th ed. pap. 9.95 o.p. (ISBN 0-517-55028-8). Crown.

Kovels' Antiques Price List. 9th ed. Ralph M. Kovel & Terry H. Kovel. (Illus.). flexible bdg. 7.95 o.p. (ISBN 0-517-52738-3). Crown.

Kovels' Antiques Price List. 10th ed. Ralph M. Kovel & Terry H. Kovel. (Illus.). 1977. pap. 8.95 o.p. (ISBN 0-517-53143-7). Crown.

Kovels' Antiques Price List. 8th ed. Ralph M. Kovel & Terry H. Kovel. (Illus.). 624p. 1975. pap. 6.95 o.p. (ISBN 0-517-52402-3). Crown.

Kovels' Antiques Price List, No. 14. Ralph M. Kovel & Terry H. Kovel. (Illus.). 736p. 1981. pap. 9.95 o.p. (ISBN 0-517-54474-1). Crown.

Kovels' Bottle Price List. 6th ed. Ralph M. Kovel & Terry H. Kovel. (Illus.). 224p. 1982. pap. 10.95 o.p. (ISBN 0-517-54587-X). Crown.

Kovels' Bottle Price List. 7th ed. Ralph M. Kovel & Terry H. Kovel. (Illus.). 1984. pap. 10.95 o.p. (ISBN 0-517-55426-7). Crown.

Kovels' Collector's Book of Antique Labels. Ralph M. Kovel & Terry H. Kovel. 1981. pap. 2.98 o.p. (ISBN 0-517-54497-0). Crown.

Kovels' Illustrated Price Guide to Depression Glass & American Dinnerware. Ralph M. Kovel & Terry H. Kovel. (Illus.). 256p. pap. 9.95 o.p. (ISBN 0-517-54023-1). Crown.

Kovels' Illustrated Price Guide to Royal Doulton. Ralph M. Kovel & Terry H. Kovel. (Illus.). 224p. 1980. 9.95 o.p. (ISBN 0-517-54022-3). Crown.

Kovels' Official Bottle Price List. 3rd ed. Ralph M. Kovel & Terry H. Kovel. (Illus.). 256p. pap. 6.95 o.p. (ISBN 0-517-52189-X). Crown.

Kovels' Organizer for Collectors. Ralph M. Kovel & Terry H. Kovel. pap. 8.95 o.p. (ISBN 0-517-53347-2). Crown.

Krankon Ghetto & the Plasjon Camp Remembered. Malvina Graf. 275p. 1988. text ed. 22.00 o.p. U Presses Fla.

Krauter: Die Magischen Heiler. Paul Twitchell. 1978. pap. 3.95 o.p. (ISBN 0-914766-39-2). Illum Way Pub.

Kremlin & the West: A Realistic View of Relations With the Soviet Union. Wolfgang Leonhard. 1986. 17.45 o.p. (ISBN 0-393-02372-9). Norton.

Kremlin Cat & the Bomb. K. G. Babington. 159p. 1983. 14.95x o.p. (ISBN 0-85362-203-5, Oriel). Routledge Chapman & Hall.

Kremlin Contract. James Barwick. 256p. 1987. 17.95 o.p. (ISBN 0-399-13238-4, Putnam). Putnam Pub Group.

Kremlin Since Stalin. Wolfgang Leonhard. Tr. by Elizabeth Wiskemann & Marian Jackson. LC 75-8720. 403p. 1975. Repr. of 1962 ed. lib. bdg. 39.75x o.p. (ISBN 0-8371-8042-2, LEKS). Greenwood.

Kreskin's Mind Power Book. Kreskin. LC 77-24545. (Illus.). 1977. text ed. 8.95 o.p. (ISBN 0-07-035480-4). McGraw.

Krippendorf's Tribe. Frank Parkin. LC 85-47634. 192p. 1986. 13.95 o.p. (ISBN 0-689-11651-9, Atheneum). Macmillan.

Krishna: Devotional Songs of Mirabai. Mirabai & Pritish Nandy. 68p. (Orig.). 1982. pap. text ed. (ISBN 0-7069-1495-3, Pub. by Vikas India); text ed. 5.25x o.p. (ISBN 0-7069-1494-5). Advent NY.

Krishnamurti on Education. J. Krishnamurti. LC 76-62933. (Orig.). 1977. pap. 6.68i o.p. (ISBN 0-06-064794-9, RD 201). HarpR.

Kristen's Choice. Pat Rushford. LC 86-8050. 160p. (Orig.). (YA) (gr. 7-10). 1986. pap. 5.95 o.p. (ISBN 0-8066-2219-9, 10-3724, Augsburg). Augsburg Fortress.

Kristin & Boone. Karen Rose & Lynda Halfyard. LC 83-12580. 224p. (gr. 5up). 1983. 6.70 o.p. (ISBN 0-395-34560-X). HM.

Kristy's Courage. Babbis Friis. Tr. by Lise S. McKinnon. LC 65-18728. (Illus.). (gr. 4-6). 1965. 5.95 o.p. (ISBN 0-15-243370-8, HJ). HarBraceJ.

Kritischer Wissenschafts-Theorie. Ed. by Chr. Hubig & W. Van Rahden. (De Gruyter Studienbuch). 1978. 15.20x o.p. (ISBN 3-11-007079-0). De Gruyter.

Krokodil, Krokodil see Crocodile, Crocodile.

Kronstadt Rebellion. Emanual Pollack. 1960. (ISBN 0-8022-1999-3). Philos Lib.

Kropotkin. Martin A. Miller. LC 75-20885. 1979. pap. text ed. 5.95x o.s.i. (ISBN 0-226-52594-5, P818, Phoen). U of Chicago Pr.

Kropotkin's Revolutionary Pamphlets. Peter Kropotkin. Ed. by Roger Baldwin. 13.25 o.p. (ISBN 0-8446-0748-7). Peter Smith.

Krsna: The Supreme Personality of Godhead, 3 vols. Swami A. C. Bhaktivedanta. LC 74-118081. (Illus.). 1970. Vol. 1. pap. 12.95 o.p.; Vol. 2. pap. 2.95 o.p. (ISBN 0-912776-32-3); Vol. 3. pap. 2.95 o.p. Bhaktivedanta.

Kryptogamenflora Von Deutschland Osterreich und der Schweiz. G. Ludwig Rabenhorst. (Illus.). Set. 2375.00 o.p. (ISBN 0-384-49385-8); Set. pap. 2200.00 o.p. (ISBN 0-685-13484-9). Johnson Repr.

Krypton, Xenon, & Radon: Gas Solubilities. Clever. (Solubility Data Ser.: Vol. 2). 1979. 110.00 o.p. (ISBN 0-08-022352-4). Pergamon.

Kryptonite Kid. Joseph Torchia. LC 79-1078. 192p. 1979. 7.95 o.p. (ISBN 0-03-046676-8). H Holt & Co.

Kryptonite Kid. Joseph Torchia. LC 79-1078. 192p. 1980. pap. 2.95 o.s.i. (ISBN 0-03-057798-5). H Holt & Co.

Ku-Band Satellite TV: Theory, Installation & Repair. Frank Baylin & Brent Gale. 359p. 1986. pap. 22.95 o.p. (ISBN 0-672-22565-4). Sams.

Ku Klux Klan: America's Recurring Nightmare. Fred J. Cook. LC 80-19325. (Illus.). 224p. (YA) (gr. 7 up). 1980. lib. bdg. 9.79 o.s.i. (ISBN 0-671-34055-7). Messner.

Kubrick. Michel Ciment. Tr. by Gilbert Adair from Fr. LC 82-6224. (Illus.). 240p. 1983. 25.00 o.p. (ISBN 0-03-061687-5); pap. 16.95 o.p. (ISBN 0-03-063949-2). H Holt & Co.

Kuesel on Closing Sales. Harry N. Kuesel. 1979. 14.95 o.p. (ISBN 0-13-516849-X); pap. 5.95 o.p. (ISBN 0-13-516864-3). P-H.

Kulturlesebuch Fur Anfanger. 2nd ed. Harry Steinhauer. (Orig., Ger.). 1967. pap. text ed. write for info. o.p. (ISBN 0-02-416850-5). Macmillan.

Kulung-Nepali-English Glossary. Krishna P. Rai et al. 84p. 1975. pap. 2.00x o.s.i. (ISBN 0-88312-780-6). Summer Inst Ling.

Kundalini Yoga-Sadhana Guidelines. LC 85-9918. 107p. 1985. Repr. of 1978 ed. lib. bdg. 19.95x o.p. (ISBN 0-89370-886-0). Borgo Pr.

Kung Fu Butterfly Swords. William Cheung. Ed. by Mike Lee. LC 84-62297. (Weapons Ser.). 224p. (Orig.). 1985. pap. 7.95 o.p. (ISBN 0-89750-125-X, 438). Ohara Pubns.

Kuno: One of the Last of the General Practitioners. Kuno Hammerberg. (Illus.). 1979. 8.50 o.p. (ISBN 0-682-49421-6). Exposition-Phoenix.

Kunstbuchlin: Two Hundred & Ninety-Three Renaissance Woodcuts for Artists & Illustrators. Jost Amman. (Illus.). 10.25 o.p. (ISBN 0-8446-1532-3). Peter Smith.

Kuntu Drama. Ed. by Paul C. Harrison. Incl. A Beast Story. Adrienne Kennedy; Devil's Mask. Lennox Brown; Great Goodness of Life. Imanu Amiri; The Great MacDaddy. Paul C. Harrison; Kabnis. Jean Toomer; Mars. Clav Goss; The Owl Answers. Adrienne Kennedy; A Season in the Congo. Aime Cesaire. pap. 12.50 o.p. (ISBN 0-394-17806-8, E615, Ever). Grove.

Kuomintang: A Sociological Study of Demoralization. Cheng Wang. Ed. by Ramon H. Myers. LC 80-8824. (China During the Interregnum 1911-1949, the Economy & Society Ser.). 179p. 1982. lib. bdg. 24.00 o.p. (ISBN 0-8240-4679-X). Garland Pub.

Kura: Design & Tradition of the Japanese Storehouse. abr. ed. Teiji Itoh. Tr. by Charles S. Terry from Japanese. LC 80-21087. (Illus.). 192p. 1980. pap. 17.50 o.p. (ISBN 0-914842-53-6). Madrona Pubs.

Kuramochi Boundaries of Riemann Surfaces: Proceedings of the Research Institute for Mathematical Sciences Symposium, Kyoto, 1965. Research Institute for Mathematical Sciences Staff. (Lecture Notes in Mathematics: Vol. 58). 1968. pap. 10.90 o.p. (ISBN 0-387-04228-8). Springer-Verlag.

Kurdish Revolt, Nineteen Sixty-One to Nineteen Seventy. Edgar O'Ballance. LC 73-5817. 196p. 1973. 23.00 o.p. (ISBN 0-208-01395-4, Archon). Shoe String.

Kurozumikyo & the New Religions of Japan. Helen Hardacre. 1988. 30.00 o.p.; pap. 12.95 o.p. Princeton U Pr.

Kurt Thomas on Gymnastics. Kurt Thomas & Hannon. 1980. 19.95 o.p. (ISBN 0-671-24798-0, 24798); pap. 8.95 o.p. (ISBN 0-671-25508-8, 25508). S&S.

Kurzes Handbuch der Geschichte der Medizin. 3rd, 4th ed. K. Sudhoff. viii, 534p. (Ger.). 1982. 75.50 o.p. (ISBN 3-8055-3583-X). S Karger.

Kusarigama. Tadashi Yamashita. Ed. by Mike Lee. LC 86-61872. (Weapons Ser.). 144p. 1986. pap. 7.95 o.p. (ISBN 0-89750-108-X, 448). Ohara Pubns.

Kush: Lost Kingdom of the Nile: A Loan Exhibition from the Museum of Fine Arts Boston. Timothy Kendall. LC 82-73157. (Illus.). 64p. (Orig.). 1982. pap. 7.00 o.p.i. (ISBN 0-934358-11-7). Brockton Art Fuller.

Kuwait. Middle East Economic Digest Staff. Ed. by John Whelan. (MEED Practical Guides Ser.). (Illus.). 256p. (Orig.). 1985. pap. 16.95x o.p. (ISBN 0-946510-05-9). Lynne Rienner.

Kuwait: Urban & Medical Ecology, a Geomedical Study. G. E. Ffrench & A. G. Hill. LC 71-156994. (Geomedical Monograph Ser.: Vol. 4). (Illus.). 1971. 34.30 o.p. (ISBN 0-387-05384-0). Springer-Verlag.

Kuyo Chico: Applied Anthropology in an Indian Community. Oscar Nunez Del Prado & William F. Whyte. LC 72-96621. 192p. 1973. lib. bdg. 12.50x o.s.i. (ISBN 0-226-60886-7). U of Chicago Pr.

Kwashiokor. H. C. Trowell. (Nutrition Foundations' Reprint Ser.). 1982. 45.00 o.p. (ISBN 0-12-701150-1). Acad Pr.

KWIC Index of Rock Mechanics Literature: Pt. 1, 1870-1968. E. Hoek & Imperial College of Science & Technology, Rock Mechanics Section. 1977. 248.00 o.p. (ISBN 0-08-022063-0). Pergamon.

KWIC Index of Rock Mechanics Literature: Pt. 2, 1969-1976. Ed. by J. P. Jenkins & E. T. Brown. LC 79-40980. 742p. 1979. 250.00 o.p. (ISBN 0-08-022065-7). Pergamon.

Kyokushin Way. Masutatsu Oyama. LC 79-1961. 1979. 9.50 o.p. (ISBN 0-87040-460-1). Japan Pubns USA.

Kyoto Country Retreats: The Katsura & Shugakuin Palaces. Michio Fujioka. LC 83-47619. (Great Japanese Art Ser.). (Illus.). 48p. 1983. 22.95 o.p. (ISBN 0-87011-602-9). Kodansha.

L

L. A. Robert M. Parker. (Illus.). 192p. 1984. 25.95 o.p. (ISBN 0-15-147300-5). HarBraceJ.

L. A. Robert M. Parker. LC 83-26383. (Illus.). 192p. 1984. pap. 10.95 o.p. (ISBN 0-15-647590-1, Harv). HarBraceJ.

L. A. Eighty-Four. Norman Giller. (Illus.). 192p. 1983. pap. 7.95 o.p. H Holt & Co.

L. A. Lunch - Downtown Dining: A Selective Guide to the Best Luncheon Spots in Downtown Los Angeles. Randi Markowitz & Charles R. Noble, III. LC 84-7745. 170p. (Orig.). 1984. pap. 5.95 o.p. (ISBN 0-87701-308-X). Chronicle Bks.

L. & G. Stickley: Mission Furniture. (Illus.). 192p. 1985. pap. 17.50 o.p. (ISBN 0-87905-410-7). Gibbs Smith Pub.

L. C. Susan Daitch. 284p. 1987. 17.95 o.p. (ISBN 0-15-149280-8). HarBraceJ.

L. D. Landau, Vol. 2. D. Ter Haar. 1969. 17.75 o.p. (ISBN 0-08-006451-5); pap. 50.00 o.p. (ISBN 0-08-006450-7). Pergamon.

L. L. Bean Fly-Fishing Handbook. Dave Whitlock. LC 83-25893. (Illus.). 1984. pap. 8.95 o.p. (ISBN 0-8329-0301-9). Lyons & Burford.

L Systems. Ed. by G. Rozenberg & A. Salomaa. (Lecture Notes in Computer Science: Vol. 15). vi, 338p. 1974. pap. 23.00 o.p. (ISBN 0-387-06867-8). Springer-Verlag.

L-Ten-Eleven Tristar & the Lockheed Story. Douglas J. Ingells. LC 73-83065. (Illus.). 256p. 1973. 13.95 o.p. (ISBN 0-8168-6650-3, 26651P, TAB-Aero); pap. 10.95 o.p. (ISBN 0-8168-6651-1). TAB Bks.

LA-Access. pap. 9.95 o.p. (ISBN 0-671-60337-X). S&S.

La Guardia: A Fighter Against His Times, 1882-1933. Arthur Mann. 1969. pap. text ed. 2.95x o.s.i. (ISBN 0-226-50330-5, P330, Phoen). U of Chicago Pr.

La la Noo. Jack B. Yeats. 68p. 1971. Repr. of 1943 ed. 15.00x o.p. (ISBN 0-7165-1398-6, BBA 02084, Pub. by Cuala Press Ireland). Biblio Dist.

L.A. Picnincs: The Complete Guide to Picnic Sites & Styles in & Around Los Angeles. Ellen Melinkoff. LC 85-428. (Illus.). 160p. 1985. pap. 7.95 o.p. (ISBN 0-87701-329-2). Chronicle Bks.

La Varenne Tour Book. Faye Levy. (Illus.). 171p. 1979. pap. 7.95 o.p. (ISBN 0-89716-057-6). Peanut Butter.

Lab Manual for Anatomy & Physiology. Theresa Page. 1982. spiral bdg. 16.95 o.p. (ISBN 0-317-47204-6). Paladin Hse.

Labeling of Clinical Laboratory Materials: Approved Standard. 2nd ed. National Committee for Clinical Laboratory Standards. 1979. 20.00 o.p. (ISBN 0-318-19385-X, GP1-A2). Natl Comm Clin Lab Stds.

Labeling Regulatory Requirements for Medical Devices. 50p. 1986. pap. 2.75 o.p. (ISBN 0-318-20407-X, S/N 017-012-00327-3). USGPO.

Labels Pres Sens Rol. Date not set. (ISBN 0-07-521093-2). McGraw.

Labor Action, Vols. 4-22, No. 19. Workers Party of the United States. Incl. Vols. 4 & 5. lib. bdg. 185.00 (ISBN 0-313-21691-6, LA01); Vols. 6 & 7. lib. bdg. 185.00 (ISBN 0-313-21692-4, LA02); Vols. 8 & 9. lib. bdg. 185.00 (ISBN 0-313-21693-2, LA03); Vols. 10 & 11. lib. bdg. 195.00 (ISBN 0-313-21694-0, LA04); Vols. 12-14, No. 8. lib. bdg. 125.00 (ISBN 0-313-21695-9, LA05); Vol. 14, Nos. 9-52. lib. bdg. 83.00 (ISBN 0-313-21696-7, LA06); Vol. 15. lib. bdg. 94.00 (ISBN 0-313-21697-5, LA07); Vol. 16. lib. bdg. 94.00 (ISBN 0-313-21698-3, LA08); Vol. 17. lib. bdg. 94.00 (ISBN 0-313-21699-1, LA09); Vol. 18. lib. bdg. 94.00 (ISBN 0-313-21700-9, LA10); Vol. 19. lib. bdg. 94.00 (ISBN 0-313-21701-7, LA11); Vol. 20. lib. bdg. 94.00 (ISBN 0-313-21702-5, LA12); Vols. 21 & 22. lib. bdg. 105.00 (ISBN 0-313-21703-3, LA13). 1969. Repr. of 1958 ed. Set. lib. bdg. 1405.00x o.p. (ISBN 0-8371-9262-5, LAP1). Greenwood.

Labor Age, 22 vols, No. 1. American Workers Party Staff. Incl. Vols. 1-3. lib. bdg. 31.00 (ISBN 0-313-21704-1, LB01); Vols. 4 & 5. lib. bdg. 31.00 (ISBN 0-313-21705-X, LB04); Vols. 6 & 7. lib. bdg. 31.00 (ISBN 0-313-21706-8, LB06); Vol. 8. lib. bdg. 31.00 (ISBN 0-313-21707-6, LB08); Vols. 9 & 10. lib. bdg. 31.00 (ISBN 0-313-21708-4, LB09); Vol. 11. lib. bdg. 27.00 (ISBN 0-313-21709-2, LB11); Vol. 12. lib. bdg. 27.00 (ISBN 0-313-21710-6, LB12); Vol. 13. lib. bdg. 27.00 (ISBN 0-313-21711-4, LB13); Vol. 14. lib. bdg. 27.00 (ISBN 0-313-21712-2, LB14); Vol. 15. lib. bdg. 27.00 (ISBN 0-313-21713-0, LB15); Vol. 16. lib. bdg. 27.00 (ISBN 0-313-21714-9, LB16); Vol. 17. lib. bdg. 27.00 (ISBN 0-313-21715-7, LB17); Vol. 18. lib. bdg. 27.00 (ISBN 0-313-21716-5, LB18); Vol. 19. lib. bdg. 27.00 (ISBN 0-313-21717-3, LB19); Vol. 20. lib. bdg. 27.00 (ISBN 0-313-21718-1, LB20); Vols. 21 & 22. lib. bdg. 27.00 (ISBN 0-313-21719-X, LB21). 1969. Repr. of 1933 ed. Set. lib. bdg. 400.00x o.p. (ISBN 0-8371-9130-0, LB00). Greenwood.

Labor & Inequality. Ed. by Peter Townsend & Nicholas Bosanquet. 304p. 1972. (ISBN 0-7163-4003-8). Transaction Pubs.

Labor & Poverty. Michael Lipton. (Working Paper Ser.: No. 616). 160p. 1983. 8.00 o.p. (ISBN 0-8213-0266-3, WP 0616). World Bank.

Labor & the Law. 3rd ed. Charles O. Gregory & Harold A. Katz. 1979. 35.00 o.p. (ISBN 0-393-01208-5); pap. text ed. 10.95x o.p. (ISBN 0-393-09995-4). Norton.

Labor Arbitration in Health Care. Ed. by Earl R. Baderschneider & Paul F. Miller. 324p. 5.00 o.p. (ISBN 0-318-12383-5); members 7.50 o.p. (ISBN 0-318-12384-3). Am Arbitration.

Labor Arbitration: What You Need to Know. 3rd ed. Robert Coulson. LC 81-66912. 176p. 1986. pap. 8.00 o.p. (ISBN 0-943001-05-6). Am Arbitration.

Labor Baron: A Portrait of John L. Lewis. James A. Wechsler. LC 72-143312. 278p. 1972. Repr. of 1944 ed. lib. bdg. 22.50x o.p. (ISBN 0-8371-5968-7, WELB). Greenwood.

Labor Bulletin, Vols. 1-2, No. 1. Labor Research Front Staff. 1969. Repr. of 1938 ed. lib. bdg. 33.00x o.p. (ISBN 0-8371-9187-4, LP00). Greenwood.

Labor Confronts the Transnationals. Ed. by Labor Research Association Staff. LC 84-10773. 120p. (Orig.). 1984. pap. 3.50 o.p. (ISBN 0-7178-0612-X, New World Paperback). Intl Pubs Co.

Labor Contract Clauses see Issues in the Public Employee Relations Library: Series 1.

Labor Defense Network Operations Manual. Legal Aid Foundation of L.A. Natl Lawyers Guild.

Labor Dictionary. P. H. Casselman. (ISBN 0-8022-0219-5). Philos Lib.

Labor Economics. Morgan. 0.00 o.p. Irwin.

Labor Economics: A Guide to Information Sources. Ross Azevedo. LC 73-17568. (Economics Information Guide Ser.: Vol. 8). 280p. 1978. 68.00x o.p. (ISBN 0-8103-1297-2). Gale.

Labor Economics: Wages, Employment & Trade Unionism. 5th ed. F. Ray Marshall. 1984. 35.95x o.p. (ISBN 0-256-02999-7). Irwin.

Labor Enterprises in Israel: The Cooperative Economy, Vol. 1. Abraham Daniel. 312p. 1976. pap. text ed. 5.95 o.p. (ISBN 0-87855-638-9). Transaction Pubs.

Labor Force, Employment & Productivity in Historical Perspective. Michael R. Darby. (Monograph & Research Ser.: No. 37). 151p. 1984. looseleaf 6.00 o.p. (ISBN 0-89215-121-8). U Cal LA Indus Rel.

Labor Force Participation of Black & White Youth. Donald R. Williams. Ed. by Fred Bateman. LC 87-5868. (Research in Business Economics & Public Policy Ser.: No. 11). 134p. 1987. 49.95 o.p. (ISBN 0-8357-1804-2). UMI Res Pr.

Labor in Power: The Labor Party & Governments in Queensland, Nineteen Fifteen to Nineteen Fifty-Seven. Ed. by D. J. Murphy et al. (Illus.). 583p. 1980. text ed. 42.50x o.p. (ISBN 0-7022-1428-0). U of Queensland Pr.

Labor in Soviet Global Strategy. Roy Godson. LC 83-27116. (NSIC Strategy Paper Ser.: No. 40). 120p. pap. cancelled o.s.i. (ISBN 0-8448-1472-5, Pub. by Crane Russak & Co). Taylor & Francis.

Labor Law. Sidney Fox. 124p. 1968. pap. 4.00x o.p. (ISBN 0-87526-042-X). Gould.

Labor Law. 3rd, rev. ed. Carl Rachlin. LC 61-14008. (Segal Almanac Ser.: No. 7). 97p. 1961. (ISBN 0-379-11007-5). Oceana.

Labor Law Colloquium. Pennsylvania Bar Institute Staff. 59p. 1985. 50.00 o.p. (ISBN 0-318-19055-9, 317). PA Bar Inst.

Labor Law Institute. 119p. 1983. 9.00 o.p. (ISBN 0-318-02414-4). ICLE Georgia.

Labor Law: Twenty-Ninth Annual Institute on Labor Law. Institute of Labor Law Developments Staff. 1983. write for info. o.p. (#352). Bender.

Labor Laws of Korea. (American Chamber of Commerce in Korea Ser.). 1977. 40.00 o.p. A M Newman.

Labor Legislation from an Economic Point of View. Gustavo R. Velasco. Ed. by Benjamin A. Rogge. LC 73-86984. 76p. 1973. 3.00x o.p. (ISBN 0-913966-02-9). Liberty Fund.

Labor Legislation in China. Augusta Wagner. LC 78-22780. (Modern Chinese Economy Ser.). 301p. 1980. lib. bdg. 40.00 o.p. (ISBN 0-8240-4283-2). Garland Pub.

Labor-Management Contracts at Work: Analysis of Awards Reported by the American Arbitration Association. Morris Stone. LC 78-31591. viii, 307p. 1979. Repr. of 1961 ed. lib. bdg. 35.00x o.p. (ISBN 0-313-20966-9, STLW). Greenwood.

Labor-Management Relations. 2nd ed. D. Quinn Mills. (Management Ser.). 656p. 1982. text ed. 33.95x o.p. (ISBN 0-07-042419-5). McGraw.

Labor-Management Relations in Colorado. Harry Seligson & George Bardwell. LC 61-14374. 1961. 12.00 o.p. (ISBN 0-8040-0178-2, SB). Ohio U Pr.

Labor Markets, Urban Systems, & the Urbanization Process in Southeast Asian Countries. Terence G. McGee. LC 82-11633. (Papers of the East-West Population Institute: No. 81). v, 28p. (Orig.). 1982. pap. text ed. 1.00 o.p. (ISBN 0-86638-010-8). EW Ctr HI.

Labor of Love. Barbara Roush. 1982. pap. 2.50 o.p. (ISBN 0-380-80879-X, 80879-X). Avon.

Labor Power, Vols. 1-2. Socialist Workers Party Staff. 1970. Repr. of 1941 ed. lib. bdg. 31.00x o.p. (ISBN 0-8371-9242-0, LC00). Greenwood.

Labor Productivity: A Bibliographical Guide to Productivity, Mathematical Models & Case Studies. Coppa & Avery Consultants Staff. (Public Administration Ser.: P 1791). 11p. 1985. 2.00 o.p. (ISBN 0-89028-591-8). Vance Biblios.

Labor Rates for the Construction Industry, 1986. 13th ed. Means, R. S., Company, Inc. Staff. Ed. by William Mahoney. 336p. 1985. pap. 45.95 o.p. (ISBN 0-87629-010-1). R S Means.

Labor Relations. 5th ed. Arthur A. Sloane & Fred Witney. LC 84-11734. (Illus.). 544p. 1985. text ed. 38.00 o.p. (ISBN 0-13-519562-4). P-H.

Labor Relations: Development, Structure, Process. 3nd ed. John A. Fossum. 1985. 38.95x o.p. (ISBN 0-256-03291-2). Irwin.

Labor Relations in Japan Today. Tadashi Hanami. LC 78-71313. 253p. 1982. pap. 5.25 o.p. (ISBN 0-87011-492-1). Kodansha.

Labor Relations in Japan Today. Tadashi Hanami. LC 78-71313. (Illus.). 253p. 1979. 15.50 o.p. (ISBN 0-87011-374-7). Kodansha.

Labor Relations in Pennsylvania Construction Industry. Pennsylvania Bar Institute Staff. 197p. 1983. 25.00 o.p. (ISBN 0-318-02175-7, 229). PA Bar Inst.

Labor Relations in the Health Professions. William B. Werther & Carol A. Lockhart. 1976. pap. 12.95 o.p. (ISBN 0-316-93100-4). Little.

Labor Relations Law. 4th ed. Benjamin J. Taylor & Fred Whitney. 848p. 1983. pap. text ed. 38.33 o.p. (ISBN 0-13-519652-3). P-H.

Labor Relations Process. 2nd ed. William H. Holley & Kenneth M. Jennings. 672p. 1984. text ed. 33.95x o.p. (ISBN 0-03-062799-0); instr's. manual w/transparency acetates 20.95 o.p. (ISBN 0-03-062801-6). Dryden Pr.

Labor Relations Source Book see Issues in the Public Employee Relations Library: Series 3.

Labor Revolt in Alabama: The Great Strike of 1894. R. D. Ward & W. W. Rogers. LC 65-16386. (Southern Historical Ser: Vol. 9). 176p. 1965. 12.50 o.p. (ISBN 0-8173-5214-7). U of Ala Pr.

Labor Sector. 3rd rev. ed. Neil W. Chamberlain et al. (Illus.). 1980. text ed. 35.95 o.p. (ISBN 0-07-010435-2). McGraw.

Laboratory Anatomy of the Frog. 4th ed. Raymond A. Underhill. (Laboratory Anatomy Ser.). 72p. 1980. write for info. wire coil o.p. (ISBN 0-697-04645-1). Wm C Brown.

Laboratory Anatomy of the Shark. Lawrence M. Ashley & Robert B. Chiasson. 96p. 1987. Wire Coil. write for info. o.p. (ISBN 0-697-05121-8). Wm C Brown.

Laboratory Anatomy of the White Rat. 4th ed. Robert B. Chiasson. (Laboratory Anatomy Ser.). 112p. 1980. wire coil write for info. o.p. (ISBN 0-697-04644-3). Wm C Brown.

Laboratory & Exercise Book for Elementary Italian. (ISBN 0-8191-0095-1). U Pr of Amer.

Laboratory Design. Coppa & Avery Consultants Staff. (Architecture Ser.: Bibliography A 1322). 1985. pap. 2.00 o.p. (ISBN 0-89028-272-2). Vance Biblios.

Laboratory Exercises in Microbiology. 3rd ed. Raymond B. Otero. 288p. 1984. 19.95 o.p. (ISBN 0-8403-3459-1). Kendall-Hunt.

Laboratory Exercises in Respiratory Therapy. 2nd ed. Cynthia A. Shoup. LC 82-12542. (Illus.). 265p. 1982. pap. text ed. 18.95 o.p. (ISBN 0-8016-4594-8). Mosby.

Laboratory Experiments in Microbiology: Brief Edition. Christine Case & Ted Johnson. 1986. 18.95 o.p. (ISBN 0-8053-9316-1); instr's. guide to lab manual 9.95 o.p. (ISBN 0-8053-9309-9). Benjamin-Cummings.

Laboratory Experiments in Motor Learning. 5th ed. 1982. 17.95 o.p. Kendall-Hunt.

Laboratory Experiments in Organic Chemistry. 3rd ed. Jerry R. Mohrig & Douglas C. Neckers. 582p. 1979. text ed. (ISBN 0-534-25471-3). Wadsworth Pub.

Laboratory Experiments in Physical Science. Anton Postl. 1978. 12.95 o.p. (ISBN 0-88246-089-7). Oreg St U Bkstrs.

Laboratory Explorations in General Zoology. 6th ed. Robert D. Burns & Karl A. Stiles. 1977. write for info. o.p. (ISBN 0-02-317160-X, 31716). Macmillan.

Laboratory Guide for Biological Science. William T. Keeton et al. (Orig.). 1968. pap. text ed. 12.95x o.p. (ISBN 0-393-09823-0, NortonC). Norton.

Laboratory Guide to Frog Anatomy. Eli. C. Minkoff. LC 74-22206. 176p. 1975. pap. text ed. 7.75 o.p. (ISBN 0-08-018315-8). Pergamon.

Laboratory Inquiries into Concepts of Biology. 5th ed. William Andresen et al. 1984. pap. text ed. 12.95 o.p. (ISBN 0-8403-3354-4, 40335401). Kendall-Hunt.

Laboratory Investigations in Human Physiology. George K. Russell. (Illus.). 1978. pap. text ed. write for info. o.p. (ISBN 0-02-404680-9). Macmillan.

Laboratory Management. Jack E. Newell. LC 76-155040. (Series in Laboratory Medicine). 250p. 1972. 32.00 o.p. (ISBN 0-316-60451-8). Little.

Laboratory Manual for Chemistry, Man & Society. 2nd ed. Mark M. Jones et al. LC 75-21147. (Illus.). 335p. 1976. lab manual 17.95 o.p. (ISBN 0-7216-5223-9). HR&W.

Laboratory Manual for Entomology & Plant Pathology. 2nd ed. Louis L. Pyenson & Harvey E. Barke. (Illus.). 1981. pap. 17.95 o.s.i. (ISBN 0-87055-393-3). AVI.

Laboratory Manual for Food Canners & Processors, Vol. 2. Analysis, Sanitation & Statistics. 3rd ed. Ed. by National Food Processors Association Staff. (Illus.). 1968. 50.00 o.p. (ISBN 0-87055-028-4). AVI.

Laboratory Manual for General Botany. John McClymont. 1978. wire coil bdg. 7.95 o.p. (ISBN 0-88252-079-2). Paladin Hse.

Laboratory Manual for Introductory Biology. Wendell Wall. coil binding 10.95 o.p. (ISBN 0-88252-101-2). Paladin Hse.

Laboratory Manual for Man & His Environment. Jack S. Griffith. 136p. 1983. pap. 9.95 o.p. (ISBN 0-8403-3146-0). Kendall-Hunt.

Laboratory Manual for Physical Geology. 6th ed. James H. Zumberge & Robert H. Rutford. 200p. 1983. write for info. wire coil o.p. (ISBN 0-697-05043-2); instrs.' manual avail. o.p. (ISBN 0-697-05045-9). Wm C Brown.

Laboratory Manual for Principles of Biology. 2nd ed. Caroline Adams et al. (Illus.). 94p. 1979. pap. 7.95x lab manual o.p. (ISBN 0-89459-147-9). Hunter Textbks.

Laboratory Manual for Schnid's the Chemical Basis of Life. William D. Shulz & Howard B. Powell. 1982. pap. write for info. o.p. (ISBN 0-316-77375-1). Little.

Laboratory Manual in Anatomy & Physiology. Robert Neff & Elinor Plaisted. (Illus.). 106p. 1970. pap. text ed. 6.95x o.p. (ISBN 0-8422-0100-9). Irvington.

Laboratory Manual in Food Preservation. Marion L. Fields. 1977. pap. 10.95 o.p. (ISBN 0-87055-241-4). AVI.

Laboratory Manual in General Zoology. 2nd ed. Grover C. Miller & Melissa Jones. (Illus.). 108p. 1983. lab manual 10.95x o.p. (ISBN 0-89459-204-1). Hunter Textbks.

Laboratory Manual of Human Anatomy & Physiology. 2nd ed. Russell M. DeCoursey. (Illus.). 256p. 1974. text ed. 19.95 o.p. (ISBN 0-07-016239-5). McGraw.

Laboratory Manual of Mammalian Anatomy & Physiology. 4th ed. Sigmund Grollman. (Illus.). 266p. 1978. pap. text ed. write for info. o.p. (ISBN 0-02-348090-4, 34809). Macmillan.

Laboratory Medicine-Urinalysis & Medical Microscopy. 2nd ed. Ed. by James A. Freeman & Myrton F. Beeler. LC 82-17254. (Illus.). 611p. 1983. text ed. 47.50 o.p. (ISBN 0-8121-0822-1). Lea & Febiger.

Laboratory Methods for the Diagnosis of Sexually Transmitted Diseases. Ed. by Berttina B. Wentworth & Franklyn N. Judson. LC 84-20394. 272p. 1984. 25.00x o.p. (ISBN 0-87553-128-8). Am Pub Health.

Laboratory Methods in Antimicrobial Chemotherapy. Ed. by Phillips et al. (Illus.). 1978. text ed. 51.00 o.p. (ISBN 0-443-01664-X). Churchill.

Laboratory Notes on Electrical & Galvano-Magnetic Measurements. H. H. Wieder. (Materials Science Monographs: Vol. 2). 278p. 1979. 76.50 o.p. (ISBN 0-444-41763-X). Elsevier.

Laboratory Physics. Lloyd A. Case. LC 76-7374. (Illus.). 144p. 1976. pap. text ed. 6.00x o.p. (ISBN 0-8422-0535-7). Irvington.

Laboratory Studies in General Zoology. 6th Ed. ed. H. Eugene Lehman. (Illus.). 1981. 12.95 o.p. (ISBN 0-89459-140-1). Hunter Textbks.

Laboratory Studies in Integrated Zoology. 6th ed. Frances M. Hickman & Cleveland P. Hickman. (Illus.). 480p. 1983. pap. 14.95 o.p. (ISBN 0-8016-2178-X). Mosby.

Laboratory Study of Plants. Winston Hackbarth. 80p. (Orig.). 1981. lab manual 6.95x o.p. (ISBN 0-89459-150-9). Hunter Textbks.

Laboratory Techniques for the Detection of Hereditary Metabolic Disorders. Vivian E. Shih. LC 82-8920. 134p. 1982. Repr. of 1973 ed. lib. bdg. 34.95 o.p. (ISBN 0-89874-492-X). Krieger.

Laboratory Techniques in Biochemistry & Molecular Biology: Vol. 9, Sequencing of Proteins & Peptides. Ed. by G. Allen et al. 328p. 1981. 123.25 o.p. (ISBN 0-444-80275-4, Biomedical Pr); pap. 28.50 o.p. (ISBN 0-444-80254-1). Elsevier.

Laboratory Test Handbook with DRG Index. Jacobs & Kasten. 1984. pap. 40.00 o.p. (ISBN 0-8016-2996-9). Mosby.

Laboratory Work in Hydraulics. W. R. Lomax & A. J. Saul. 264p. 1979. pap. text ed. 17.50x o.p. (ISBN 0-258-97088-X, Pub. by Granada England). Gower Pub Co.

Laboratory Work in Soil Mechanics. 2nd ed. Brain Vickers. 170p. 1983. pap. text ed. 19.50x o.p. (ISBN 0-246-22819-9, Pub. by Granada England). Gower Pub Co.

Laboring Class Movements in the United States: Historical Perspectives. Dale E. Casper. (Public Administration Ser.: Bibliography P 1632). 1985. pap. 2.25 o.p. (ISBN 0-89028-302-8). Vance Biblios.

Laboring in the Harvest. LeRoy Eims. 108p. 1985. pap. 4.95 o.p. (ISBN 0-89109-530-6). NavPress.

Labors of Love. R. V. Cassill. LC 79-56020. 1980. 10.95 o.p. (ISBN 0-87795-261-2, Arbor Hse). Morrow.

Labour Circulation & the Labour Process. Ed. by Guy Standing. LC 84-14306. 416p. 1985. 43.00 o.p. (ISBN 0-7099-3342-8, Pub. by Croom Helm Ltd). Routledge Chapman & Hall.

Labour Force Estimates & Projections 1950-2000, 6 vols. Incl. Vol. 1. Asia. pap. 8.55 (ISBN 92-2-001666-4, ILO250). UNIPUB; Vol. 2. Africa. pap. 8.55 (ISBN 92-2-001667-2, ILO251). UNIPUB; Vol. 3. Latin America. pap. 7.15 (ISBN 9-2200-1668-0, ILO252). UNIPUB; Vol. 4. Europe, Northern America, Oceania & U. S. S. R. pap. 8.55 (ISBN 9-2200-1669-9, ILO253). UNIPUB; Vol. 5. World Summary. pap. 7.15 (ISBN 92-2-001670-2, ILO254). UNIPUB; Vol. 6. Methodological Supplement. pap. 10.00 (ISBN 92-2-101671-4, ILO255). UNIPUB. 1977. pap. 45.75 set o.p. (ISBN 92-2-101672-2, ILO95, ILO). UNIPUB.

Labour Force Participation & Development. 1978. pap. 17.10 o.p. (ISBN 92-2-101770-2, ILO87, ILO). UNIPUB.

Labour Force Participation & Development. 2nd ed. Guy Standing. (WEP Study Ser.). xi, 267p. 1982. pap. 17.25 o.p. (ISBN 92-2-102763-5, ILO404, ILO). UNIPUB.

Labour Inspection: Purposes & Practice. 3rd ed. 1985. 14.00 o.p. Intl Labour Office.

Labour into the Eighties. Ed. by David S. Bell. 168p. 1980. 25.00 o.p. (ISBN 0-7099-0443-6, Pub. by Croom Helm Ltd). Routledge Chapman & Hall.

Labour Party's Political Thought: A History. 2nd ed. Geoffrey Foote. 384p. (Orig.). 1986. pap. 17.00 o.p. (ISBN 0-7099-1097-5, Pub. by Croom Helm Ltd). Routledge Chapman & Hall.

Labour Surplus Economy. M. K. Rakshit. 295p. 1982. text ed. 25.00x o.p. (ISBN 0-333-90402-8). Humanities.

LaBrava. Elmore Leonard. 1983. 14.95 o.p. (ISBN 0-87795-527-1, Arbor Hse). Morrow.

Labyrinth. Reza Saberi. 246p. 1982. pap. 7.95 o.p. (ISBN 0-682-49898-X). Exposition-Phoenix.

Labyrinth: A Novel. A. C. Smith. (Illus.). 192p. 1986. pap. 3.95 o.p. (ISBN 0-03-007322-7, Owl Bks). H Holt & Co.

Labyrinth: A Photo Album. Rebecca Grand. (Illus.). 64p. 1986. pap. 5.95 o.p. (ISBN 0-03-007323-5, Owl Bks). H Holt & Co.

Labyrinth: A Storybook Based on the Movie. Louise Gikow. LC 85-17644. (Illus.). 64p. (gr. 1-4). 1986. 6.95 o.p. (ISBN 0-03-007324-3). H Holt & Co.

Labyrinth of Solitude: Life & Thought in Mexico. Octavio Paz. Tr. by Lysander Kemp from Span. (YA) (gr. 9 up). 1962. pap. 5.95 o.s.i. (ISBN 0-394-17242-6, E359, Ever). Grove.

Labyrinth of Solitude, the Other Mexico, & Return to the Labyrinth of Solitude, Mexico & the U. S., & the Philanthropic Ogre. Octavio Paz. Tr. by Lysander Kemp from Span. 408p. 1985. pap. 10.95 o.s.i. (ISBN 0-394-17992-7, E-811, Ever). Grove.

Lace. Shirley Conran. 1982. 16.95 o.p. (ISBN 0-671-44662-2). S&S.

Lace Curtain Murders: A Romance. Sophie Belfort. LC 85-48128. 256p. 1986. 14.95 o.p. (ISBN 0-689-11801-5, Atheneum). Macmillan.

Lace Dictionary: Including Historic & Commercial Terms, Technical Terms, Native & Foreign. Ed. by C. R. Clifford. (Illus.). 160p. 1981. Repr. of 1913 ed. 35.00x o.p. (ISBN 0-8103-4311-8). Gale.

Lace II. Shirley Conran. 515p. 1986. lib. bdg. 18.95 o.p. (ISBN 0-8161-3967-9, Large Print Bks). G K Hall.

Lacht am Besten. Peter Fabrizius. Ed. by Clair H. Bell. LC 57-5200. (Illus., Ger.). 1957. text ed. 14.00x o.p. (ISBN 0-89197-262-5). Irvington.

Lackovic. Ivan Sedej. (Illus.). 136p. 1987. 22.50 o.p. (ISBN 0-87052-395-3). Hippocrene Bks.

Lacquer Lady. F. Tennyson Jesse. (Virago Modern Classics Ser.). 384p. 1981. pap. 5.95 o.p. (ISBN 0-385-27181-6, Virago). Doubleday.

Lacrosse for Beginners. Stuart James. LC 80-27810. (Illus.). 128p. (gr. 7 up). 1981. lib. bdg. 9.29 o.s.i. (ISBN 0-671-34050-6). Messner.

Lactic Acid Bacteria in Beverages & Food: Proceedings. Long Ashton Symposium - Fourth, University of Bristol, September, 1974. Ed. by J. G. Carr et al. 1975. 68.50 o.p. (ISBN 0-12-160650-3). Acad Pr.

Lactic Acid: Properties & Chemistry of Lactic Acid & Derivatives. Stichting ILRA International Research Association Staff. LC 76-163974. (Illus.). 594p. 1971. 79.50x o.p. (ISBN 3-527-25344-0). VCH Pubs.

LACUS Forum, 3rd: Proceedings. Linguistic Association of Canada & the U. S. Staff. Ed. by Robert J. Di Pietro & Edward L. Blansitt, Jr. 1976. pap. text ed. 12.95 o.s.i. (ISBN 0-917496-07-8). Hornbeam Pr.

LACUS Forum, 8th: Proceedings. Linguistic Association of Canada & the U. S. Staff. Ed. by Waldemar Gutwinski & Grace Jolly. 1981. pap. text ed. 12.95 o.s.i. (ISBN 0-917496-22-1). Hornbeam Pr.

Lad & the Lion. Edgar Rice Burroughs. LC 64-15791. (Illus.). 12.50 o.p. (ISBN 0-940724-05-7). A E Ryter.

Ladd: The Life, the Legend, the Legacy of Alan Ladd. Beverly Linet. LC 78-57334. (Illus.). 1979. 10.95 o.p. (ISBN 0-87795-203-5, Arbor Hse). Morrow.

Ladies-in-Waiting: From the Tudors to the Present Day. Anne Somerset. LC 83-48861. (Illus.). 352p. 1984. 18.45 o.s.i. (ISBN 0-394-52000-9). Knopf.

Ladies' Man. Richard Price. 1978. 8.95 o.p. (ISBN 0-395-27082-0). HM.

Ladies of Castine. Miriam A. Bourne. (Illus.). 224p. 1986. 19.50 o.p. (ISBN 0-87795-729-0, Arbor Hse). Morrow.

Ladies of Missalonghi. Colleen McCullough. 268p. 1987. 17.95 o.p. (ISBN 0-8161-4366-8). G K Hall.

Ladies of the Court: A Century of Women at Wimbledon. Virginia Wade. LC 83-46158. (Illus.). 192p. 1984. 16.95 o.s.i. (ISBN 0-689-11468-0, Atheneum). Macmillan.

Ladies of the Sun: Three Modern Comedies Adapted from the Work of Euripides. Lee Morris. 1982. 8.00 o.p. (ISBN 0-682-49912-9). Exposition-Phoenix.

Ladies of the T'ang: 22 Classical Chinese Stories. Elizabeth Te-Chen Wang. 350p. 1973. 15.00 o.p. (ISBN 0-89955-181-5, Pub. by Mei Ya China). Intl Spec Bk.

Ladies of the Valley. Herbert Kastle. LC 78-73874. 1979. 10.95 o.p. (ISBN 0-87795-228-0, Arbor Hse). Morrow.

Ladies Were Not Expected: Abigail Scott Duniway & Women Rights. Dorothy N. Morrison. LC 77-2969. (Illus.). (gr. 4-8). 1977. 6.95 o.p. (ISBN 0-689-30599-0, Atheneum). Macmillan.

Lado English Series, 6 bks. Robert Lado. (gr. 7 up). 1970. pap. text ed. 2.25 ea. o.p.; Bk. 2. (ISBN 0-88345-074-7); Bk. 3. pap. text ed. (ISBN 0-88345-075-5); Bk. 4. pap. text ed. (ISBN 0-88345-076-3). Bk. 5 (ISBN 0-88345-077-1). Bk. 6. pap. text ed. (ISBN 0-88345-078-X); wkbks. 1.25 ea., tchrs' manual, bks. 1-3 2.95,tchrs' manual, bks. 4-6 1.95 ea. o.p.; cassettes 75.00 ea. o.p. Prentice ESL.

Lady, A Champion. Russell Ramsey. (Living Books). 192p. 1985. pap. 2.95 o.p. (ISBN 0-8423-2114-4). Tyndale.

Lady & the Vote. Marion K. Sanders. LC 73-13408. (Illus.). 172p. 1974. Repr. of 1956 ed. lib. bdg. 22.50x o.p. (ISBN 0-8371-7057-5, SALV). Greenwood.

Lady Apprentices. Ruth Pomeranz. 144p. 1973. pap. text ed. 7.50x o.p. (ISBN 0-7135-1868-5, Pub. by Bedford England). Gower Pub Co.

Lady Bought with Rifles. Jeanne Williams. 320p. 1987. pap. 3.95 o.p. (ISBN 0-380-70264-9). Avon.

Lady Cat Lost. Jeanne Dixon. LC 81-2292. 204p. (gr. 4-6). 1981. PLB 9.95 o.p. (ISBN 0-689-30841-8, Atheneum). Macmillan.

Lady Chatterley's Lover. D. H. Lawrence. 1969. pap. 3.95 o.p. (ISBN 0-394-62424-6, B479, BC). Grove.

Lady Chatterley's Lover. 2nd ed. David H. Lawrence. LC 82-42866. 1982. 7.95 o.s.i. (ISBN 0-394-60430-X). Modern Lib.

Lady Darlington. Fred M. Stewart. LC 75-169924. 1971. 6.95 o.p. (ISBN 0-87795-023-7, Arbor Hse). Morrow.

Lady Darlington. Fred M. Stewart. (Large Print Bks.). 470p. 1986. lib. bdg. 17.95x o.p. (ISBN 0-8161-3932-6). G K Hall.

Lady for the Defense. Mary V. Fox. LC 74-27460. 160p. 1975. 6.50 o.p. (ISBN 0-15-243400-3, HJ). HarBraceJ.

Lady from Long Boat Key. Edith B. Dunn. 128p. 1986. 9.95 o.p. (ISBN 0-8062-2578-5). Carlton.

Lady from Maxim's. Georges Feydeau. Tr. by John Mortimer. (National Theatre Plays Ser.). 1977. pap. text ed. 7.50x o.p. (ISBN 0-435-23235-5). Heinemann Ed.

Lady Gregory: The Woman Behind the Irish Renaissance. Mary Lou Kohfeldt. LC 84-45044. (Illus.). 320p. 1985. 19.95 o.s.i. (ISBN 0-689-11486-9, Atheneum). Macmillan.

Lady in Jade Green. H. G. Freeman. 1974. 6.00 o.p. (ISBN 0-682-48061-4). Exposition-Phoenix.

Lady in Kicking Horse Reservoir. Richard Hugo. 96p. 1973. pap. 4.95 o.p. (ISBN 0-393-04225-1). Norton.

Lady in the Lake. Raymond Chandler. (YA) (gr. 9 up). 1976. pap. 3.95 o.p. (ISBN 0-394-72145-4, Vin). Random.

Lady in the Tower. Jean Plaidy. (Queen of England Ser.: Vol. 4). 576p. 1987. 18.95 o.p. (ISBN 0-399-13181-7, Putnam). Putnam Pub Group.

Lady Is the Tiger. Paul Coggins. 192p. 1987. pap. 2.95 o.p. (ISBN 0-380-75224-7). Avon.

Lady Jane. A. C. Smith. LC 85-13181. 192p. 12.95 o.p. (ISBN 0-03-006168-7, Owl Bks); pap. 5.95 o.p. (ISBN 0-03-005968-2, Owl Bks). H Holt & Co.

Lady Jane Grey & the House of Suffolk. Alison Plowden. (Illus.). 201p. 1986. 15.95 o.p. (ISBN 0-531-15000-3). Watts.

Lady L. Romain Gary. (Coll. Soleil). (Fr.). 1963. 11.50 o.p. (ISBN 0-685-11285-3). Schoenhof.

Lady Loved Too Well. Jack Donahue. 1978. pap. text ed. 8.95 o.p. (ISBN 0-07-017541-1). McGraw.

Lady Nobody. Marguerite Zutter. 1979. 4.00 o.p. (ISBN 0-682-49260-4). Exposition-Phoenix.

Lady of Han-Gilen. Judith Tarr. (Avaryan Rising Ser.: Vol. 2). 320p. 1986. cancelled 16.95 o.s.i. (ISBN 0-312-94271-0). Bluejay Bks.

Lady of Independence. Helen Argers. 224p. 1983. pap. 2.75 o.p. (ISBN 0-380-64667-6, 64667). Avon.

Lady of Light & Darkness. Diane L. Parson. 256p. (Orig.). 1982. pap. 8.95 o.p. (ISBN 0-671-45883-3, Timescape). PB.

Lady of Moray. Bonnie C. Copeland. LC 79-51400. 1979. 13.95 o.p. (ISBN 0-689-10996-2, Atheneum). Macmillan.

Lady of Pleasure. James Shirley. Ed. by Marilyn J. Thorensen & Stephen Orgel. LC 79-54328. (Renaissance Drama Second Ser.). 335p. 1980. lib. bdg. 45.00 o.p. (ISBN 0-8240-4478-9). Garland Pub.

Lady of Pleasure & Death. Lionel Gentle. LC 84-90067. 133p. 1985. 8.95 o.p. (ISBN 0-533-06145-8). Vantage.

Lady on My Right & Other Poems. Clarence Gantt. 64p. 1982. 5.00 o.p. (ISBN 0-682-49826-2). Exposition-Phoenix.

Lady on the Burning Deck. Catherine Heath. LC 78-27172. 218p. 1980. pap. 3.95 o.s.i. (ISBN 0-8008-4529-3). Taplinger.

Lady or the Tiger? & Other Stories. Frank Stockton. 1884. 49.00x o.p. (ISBN 0-403-08955-7). Somerset Pub.

Lady Oracle. Margaret Atwood. 1978. pap. 3.95 o.p. (ISBN 0-380-01799-7, Bard). Avon.

Lady Rogue. Carole N. Douglas. (Orig.). 1983. pap. 3.50 o.s.i. (ISBN 0-345-31136-1). Ballantine.

Lady Sackville: A Biography. Susan M. Alsop. 288p. 1983. pap. 3.95 o.p. (ISBN 0-380-63701-4, 63701-4, Discus). Avon.

Lady Who Saw the Good Side of Everything. Pat D. Tapio. LC 75-4610. (Illus.). 32p. (ps-3). 1979. 6.95 o.p. (ISBN 0-395-28826-6, Clarion). HM.

Lady with the Moving Parts. Merrill J. Gerber. LC 78-57322. 1978. 8.95 o.p. (ISBN 0-87795-193-4, Arbor Hse). Morrow.

Ladybird on a Bicycle. Akiko Sueyeshi. LC 83-1501. (Illus.). 40p. (gr. 2-6). 1983. 9.95 o.p. (ISBN 0-571-11802-X). Faber & Faber.

Ladybugs & Lettuce Leaves. Jorie Hunken & John Madama. Ed. by Dorinda Hale & Sandra Hackman. (Illus.). 84p. (gr. 4-8). 1982. pap. text ed. 6.95 o.p. (ISBN 0-89329-096-3); tchr's manual 105 pgs. 8.00 o.p. (ISBN 0-89329-097-1). Ctr Sci Public.

Ladysmead. Jane Gillespie. (Nightingale Paperbacks Ser.). 1984. pap. 9.95 o.p. (ISBN 0-8161-3744-7, Large Print Bks). G K Hall.

Lafayette: Man in the Middle. Sabra Holbrook. LC 77-2553. (gr. 7 up). 1977. 7.95 o.p. (ISBN 0-689-30585-0, Atheneum). Macmillan.

Lafcadio Hearn's American Days. Edward L. Tinker. LC 71-99064. (Library of Lives & Letters). (Illus.). 400p. 1970. Repr. of 1924 ed. 43.00x o.p. (ISBN 0-8103-3366-X). Gale.

LAFCO Spheres of Influence: Effective Planning for the Urban Fringe. John M. Eells. (Working Paper: 77-3). 1977. pap. 5.00x o.p. (ISBN 0-685-87445-1). UCB IGS.

Lagerfeld's Sketchbook: Karl Lagerfeld's Illustrated Fashion Journal of Anna Piaggi. Anna Piaggi. LC 86-11038. (Illus.). 224p. 1986. 50.00 o.s.i. (ISBN 1-55584-019-1). Weidenfeld.

Laghu-Vakya-Vritti. Shankara. (Sanskrit & English). pap. 1.50 o.s.i. (ISBN 0-87481-067-1). Vedanta Pr.

Lagonga: A History of the Marque. Arnold Davye et al. 1979. 39.95 o.p. (ISBN 0-7153-7695-0). David & Charles.

Lagos Consulate, 1851-1861. Robert S. Smith. 1979. 40.00x o.p. (ISBN 0-520-03746-4). U of Cal Pr.

Lair of Ancient Dreams. Asa Drake. 240p. 1982. pap. 2.50 o.p. (ISBN 0-380-80325-9, 80325-9). Avon.

Lake & Reservoir Restoration. G. Dennis Cooke et al. (Illus.). 450p. 1986. text ed. 44.95 o.p. (ISBN 0-250-40643-8). Butterworth.

Lake Balaton. Gy Illyes & Janos Reismann. (Illus.). 4.50x o.p. (ISBN 0-89918-277-1, H277). Vanous.

Lake Champlain: Reflections on Our Past. Intro. by Jennie G. Versteeg. (Illus.). 300p. 1987. pap. text ed. write for info. o.p. (ISBN 0-944277-17-9). U VT Ctr Rsch VT.

Lake District. Brian Spencer. (Vistor's Guide Ser). 144p. 1986. pap. 9.95 o.p. (ISBN 0-317-40338-9). Hunter Pub NY.

Lake District: Ordnance Survey Leisure Guide. British Automobile Association Staff. (British Automobile Association Ordance Survey Leisure Guides). 120p. (Orig.). 1984. pap. 18.95 o.p. (ISBN 0-86145-192-9, Pub. by Automobile Assn Brit). Salem Hse Pubs.

Lake Fear. Ian McMahan. LC 84-42978. (Illus.). 128p. (gr. 4-7). 1985. 11.95 o.s.i. (ISBN 0-02-765580-6). Macmillan.

Lake Management. Ed. by S. E Jorgensen. (Water Development, Supply & Management). 1980. 65.00 o.p. (ISBN 0-08-022432-6). Pergamon.

Lake Mess Monster. Beverly Komoda. LC 80-17569. (Illus.). 48p. (ps-3). 1981. 5.95 o.s.i. (ISBN 0-8193-1033-6); PLB 5.95 o.s.i. (ISBN 0-8193-1034-4). Parents.

Lake Powell in the Eighties. Ken Reinhart & Scott Baker. (Illus.). 72p. 1985. pap. 14.95 o.p. (ISBN 0-935810-25-0). Primer Pubs.

Lake Shore & Michigan Southern. Bill Warrick & Dave McLellan. (Illus.). 1986. Transport Res Bd.

Lakeboat. David Mamet. LC 80-8919. 112p. 1981. 12.50 o.s.i. (ISBN 0-394-51952-3, GP845). Grove.

Lakeboat. David Mamet. 112p. 1981. pap. 4.95 o.p. (ISBN 0-394-17925-0, E778, Ever). Grove.

Lakes: Chemistry, Geology, Physics. Ed. by A. Lerman et al. LC 78-17842. (Illus.). 1978. 55.00 o.p. (ISBN 0-387-90322-4). Springer-Verlag.

Lakes of New York State, Vol. 3: Ecology of the Lakes of East-Central New York. Ed. by Jay A. Bloomfield. 1980. 51.00 o.p. (ISBN 0-12-107303-3). Acad Pr.

Lakeside Lore: Ohio's Chautauqua Vacationland. Eleanor Durr. 1979. 9.00 o.p. (ISBN 0-682-49445-3). Exposition-Phoenix.

Lakestown Rebellion. Kristin Hunter. LC 78-1085. 1978. 9.95 o.p. (ISBN 0-684-15572-9, ScribT). Scribner.

Lala Shri Ram: A Study in Entrepreneurship & Industrial Management. Arun Joshi. LC 75-904545. 1975. 20.00x o.p. (ISBN 0-88386-645-5). South Asia Bks.

Lama: A Story of Tibet. Frederick R. Hyde-Chambers. 480p. 1985. text ed. 16.95 o.p. (ISBN 0-07-031600-7). McGraw.

Lambda-Rings & the Representation Theory of the Symmetric Group. D. Knutson. LC 73-75663. (Lecture Notes in Mathematics: Vol. 308). iv, 203p. 1973. pap. 14.00 o.p. (ISBN 0-387-06184-3). Springer-Verlag.

Lambert's Birds of Shore & Estuary. Terence Lambert. (Encore Edition). (Illus.). 1979. 5.95 o.p. (ISBN 0-684-16906-1, ScribT). Scribner.

Lambeth Conferences & Women Priests: The Historical Background of the Lambeth Conferences & Their Impact on the Episcopal Church in America. Michael M. Marrett. 208p. 1981. 12.50 o.p. (ISBN 0-682-49765-7, Testament). Exposition-Phoenix.

Lambing Time. Jane Miller. LC 78-52384. (Illus.). (gr. 1-4). 1978. 7.95 o.p. (ISBN 0-416-30591-1, NO. 0061). Routledge Chapman & Hall.

Lamborghini Countach. Graham Robson. 1986. 4.98 o.p. (ISBN 0-517-62731-0). Crown.

Lament for Art O'Leary. Frank O'Connor. (Illus.). 32p. 1971. Repr. of 1940 ed. 15.00x o.p. (ISBN 0-7165-1390-0, BBA 02071, Pub. by Cuala Press Ireland). Biblio Dist.

Lament for Lost Lovers. Alanna Knight. 1973. pap. 0.75 o.p. (ISBN 0-380-01316-9, 16576). Avon.

Laminar Flow Forced Convection in Ducts: Supplement 1 to Advances in Heat Transfer. Ramesh Shah & A. L. London. (Supplement I to Advances in Heat Transfer). 1978. 99.50 o.p. (ISBN 0-12-020051-1). Acad Pr.

Lamp for Jonathan. Essie Summers. (Large Print Bks., Nightingale Ser.). 305p. 1987. pap. 11.95x o.p. (ISBN 0-8161-4270-X, Large Print Bks). G K Hall.

Lamp unto My Feet. Doris Wallace. LC 83-91018. 49p. 1985. 5.95 o.p. (ISBN 0-533-06008-7). Vantage.

Lamplighter. Maria Cummins. 1972. Repr. of 1854 ed. 28.50 o.p. (ISBN 0-8422-8031-6). Irvington.

Lamplighter & Son. Craig Skinner. LC 82-82947. 1984. 14.95 o.p. (ISBN 0-8054-5705-4). Broadman.

Lamprey's Legacy. Richard Shaw. 256p. 1983. pap. 2.75 o.p. (ISBN 0-380-61721-8, 61721-8). Avon.

Lancashire & Yorkshire Co-Operator & Useful Classes Advocate, Ser. 1: Nos. 1-6, Ser. 2: Nos. 1-12, Ser. 3: Nos. 1-10. 1970. Repr. lib. bdg. 20.00x o.p. (ISBN 0-8371-9189-0, LY00). Greenwood.

Lancashire Watch Company, Prescott, Lancashire, England 1889-1910. Bede Smith. 1973. 7.50 o.p. (ISBN 0-913602-08-6). K Roberts.

Land & Fresh Water Molluscs of the Azores. W. Backhuys. (Illus.). 1975. pap. 60.00 o.p. (ISBN 90-04-06447-8). E J Brill USA.

Land & Imagination: The Rural Dream in America. Elaine R. Hedges & William L. Hedges. 280p. 1980. pap. text ed. 12.50x o.p. Boynton Cook Pubs.

Land & Labor in China. R. H. Tawney. LC 77-72070. 1978. pap. 9.95 o.p. (ISBN 0-87332-106-5). M E Sharpe.

Land & Liberty: Anarchist Influences in the Mexican Revolution. Ricardo F. Magon. Ed. by David Poole. (Illus.). 156p. 1977. pap. 6.50 o.p. (ISBN 0-904564-16-9). Left Bank.

Land & Life: A Selection from the Writings of Carl Ortwin Sauer. Carl O. Sauer. Ed. by John Leighly. LC 63-21069. 1974. 42.00x o.p. (ISBN 0-520-02633-0); pap. 3.95 o.p. (ISBN 0-520-01124-4, CAL 132). U of Cal Pr.

Land & Water Resources Survey in the Jebel Marra Area, the Sudan: Final Report. (Illus.). 70p. (Orig.). 1968. pap. 23.50 o.p. (ISBN 92-5-101622-4, F253, FAO). UNIPUB.

Land Baron Mirage. Rosalind Earnest Dickenson. 1976. 4.00 o.p. (ISBN 0-682-48582-9). Exposition-Phoenix.

Land Clearance: Alternative Techniques for Removing Trees & Bushes. Compiled by Agriculture Panel of the Intermediate Technology Development Group (London) (Illus.). 65p. (Orig.). 1981. pap. 4.75x o.p. (ISBN 0-903031-77-9, Pub. by Intermed Tech England). Intermediate Tech.

Land Data Systems Now: Proceedings of the North American Conference on Modernization of Land Data Systems, 2nd, Washington, D. C., 1978. North American Conference on Modernization of Land Data Systems, 2nd, Washington, DC, 1978. 283p. 1979. 6.50 o.p. (ISBN 0-317-32459-4, L280). Am Congrs Survey.

Land Development. (Illus.). 336p. 1981. pap. 28.00 o.p. (ISBN 0-86718-297-0). Nat Assn H Build.

Land Divers of Pentecost. Glen Wright. Ed. by Carol Murphy. (Illus.). (gr. 3-6). 1981. PLB 6.95 o.p. (ISBN 0-89868-112-X, Read Res); pap. text ed. 4.95 o.p. (ISBN 0-89868-119-7, Read Res). ARO Pub.

Land Endures. Mary E. Pearce. 1983. pap. 2.95 o.s.i. (ISBN 0-345-30261-3). Ballantine.

Land Fit for Heroes: Life in England after the Great War. Christopher Grayling. (Illus.). 208p. 1987. 29.95 o.p. (ISBN 0-907675-68-9, Pub. by Buchan & Enright UK). Seven Hills Bk Dists.

Land for the Cities of Asia. Ed. by James R. Brown & A. M. Woodruff. LC 77-161842. 416p. 1971. pap. 3.00 o.s.i. (ISBN 0-686-00012-4). Lincoln Inst Land.

Land Full of Possibilities: A History of South Australia's Northern Territory. P. F. Donovan. (Illus.). xxii, 267p. 1982. text ed. 32.50x o.p. (ISBN 0-7022-1606-2). U of Queensland Pr.

Land in Africa: Its Administration, Law, Tenure & Use: A Select Bibliography. Patrick E. Ofori. 199p. 1979. lib. bdg. 40.00 o.p. (ISBN 3-262-00474-X). Kraus Intl.

Land Information Systems: An Annotated Bibliography. D. David Moyer. 195p. 1978. 11.00 o.p. (ISBN 0-317-32460-8, L290). Am Congrs Survey.

Land Management Issues & Development Strategies in Developing Countries. Ed. by Sein Lin & S. Ramakrishnan. (Lincoln Institute Monograph: No. 78-4). (Orig.). 1979. pap. text ed. 4.00 o.s.i. (ISBN 0-686-25118-0). Lincoln Inst Land.

Land Management: New Directions. Ed. by D. Chiddick & A. Spedding. 488p. 1984. 55.00 o.p. (ISBN 0-419-13080-2, 6901, Pub. by E & FN Spon England). Routledge Chapman & Hall.

Land of Canaan. Isaac Asimov. LC 70-155557. (Illus.). (gr. 7 up). 1971. 5.95 o.p. (ISBN 0-395-12572-3). HM.

Land of Christmas. Mary P. Warren. LC 78-58241. (Illus.). 1979. 12.95 o.p. (ISBN 0-8066-1675-X, 10-3725, Augsburg). Augsburg Fortress.

Land of Dreams. Michael Foreman. LC 82-11889. (Illus.). 32p. (gr. k-3). 1982. 11.95 o.p. (ISBN 0-03-062053-8). H Holt & Co.

Land of Jesus. Alvin N. Rogness. LC 76-1389. (Illus.). 1976. 6.95 o.p. (ISBN 0-8066-1531-1, 10-3750, Augsburg). Augsburg Fortress.

Land of Open Doors: Being Letters from Western Canada, 1911-1913. J. Burgon Bickersteth. LC 76-41611. 1976. pap. 7.50 o.p. (ISBN 0-8020-6266-0). U of Toronto Pr.

Land of Opportunity: The Entrepreneurial Spirit in America. Donald Lambro. 1986. 17.95 o.p. (ISBN 0-316-51289-3). Little.

Land of Precious Snow. Thaddeus Tuleja. 1980. pap. 1.95 o.p. (ISBN 0-380-44297-3, 44297). Avon.

Land of Saddle-Bags: A Study of the Mountain People of Appalachia. James W. Raine. LC 70-78223. (Illus.). 272p. 1969. Repr. of 1924 ed. 35.00x o.p. (ISBN 0-8103-0160-1). Gale.

Land of Strangers. Lillian Budd. 1980. pap. 2.25 o.p. (ISBN 0-380-48314-9, 48314). Avon.

Land of the Dacotahs. Bruce Nelson. LC 65-108129. (Illus.). x, 354p. 1964. pap. 7.95 o.p. (ISBN 0-8032-5145-9, BB 176, Bison). U of Nebr Pr.

Land of the Great Sophy. Roger Stevens. LC 78-73476. (Illus.). 1979. 11.95 o.s.i. (ISBN 0-8008-4540-4). Taplinger.

Land of the Hibernating Rivers: Life in the Arctic. T. A. Cheney. LC 68-13814. (Curriculum-Related Bks.). (Illus.). (gr. 5 up). 1969. 4.50 o.p. (ISBN 0-15-243581-6, HJ). HarBraceJ.

Land of the Icy Death: Tierra De la Muerte Glacial. Harriet Rohmer. LC 76-29211. (Fifth World Tales Ser.). (Illus.). (gr. k-6). 1978. pap. 5.95 spanish bilingual ed. o.p. (ISBN 0-89239-009-3, Imprenta de Libros Infantiles). Childrens Book Pr.

Land of the Lakes. Melvyn Bragg. (Illus.). 1984. 24.45 o.p. (ISBN 0-393-01834-2). Norton.

Land of the Long Night. Paul Du Chaillu. LC 75-159938. (Tower Bks.). (Illus.). 288p. (gr. 5 up). 1971. Repr. of 1899 ed. 40.00x o.p. (ISBN 0-8103-3905-6). Gale.

Land of the Soviets in Verse & Prose, Vol. 1. G. Dzyubenko. 398p. 1982. 19.95 o.p. (ISBN 0-8285-2519-6, Pub. by Progress Pubs USSR). Imported Pubns.

Land of the Soviets in Verse & Prose, Vol. 2. Ed. by G. Dzyubenko & A. Kondratovich. 381p. 1982. 19.95 o.p. (ISBN 0-8285-2552-8, Pub. by Progress Pubs USSR). Imported Pubns.

Land of Urban Promise: Continuing the Great Tradition. Julian E. Kulski. 1967. 25.00 o.p. (ISBN 0-268-00150-2). U of Notre Dame Pr.

Land Plants: Origins, Sex & Making a Living. Martin Roeder. 48p. 1983. pap. 6.95 o.p. (ISBN 0-8403-3093-6). Kendall-Hunt.

Land Pooling by Local Government for Planned Urban Development in Perth. R. W. Archer. (Lincoln Institute Monograph: No. 80-4). (Illus.). 69p. 1980. pap. 5.00 o.s.i. (ISBN 0-686-29508-0, Australian Institute of Urban Studies). Lincoln Inst Land.

Land Question & European Society Since 1650. Frank Hugget. (History of European Civilization Library Ser.). 1975. pap. text ed. 9.95 o.p. (ISBN 0-15-549005-2, HC). HarBraceJ.

Land Reform & Development in the Middle East. Doreen Warriner. LC 75-31476. (Illus.). 238p. 1975. Repr. of 1962 ed. lib. bdg. 22.50x o.p. (ISBN 0-8371-8530-0, WALR). Greenwood.

Land Reform Implementation: A Comparative Perspective. Sein Lin. 1974. pap. 3.00 o.s.i. (ISBN 0-686-17292-2). Lincoln Inst Land.

Land Reform in Italy: Achievements and Perspectives. (Agricultural Planning Studies: No. 53). pap. 6.00 o.p. (F252, FAO). UNIPUB.

Land Reform in Japan. Date not set. (ISBN 0-8052-3948-0). Random.

Land Reform: Land Settlement & Cooperatives 1986, No. 1/2. 131p. (Orig.). 1986. pap. text ed. 9.75 o.p. (F3101, FAO). UNIPUB.

Land Remembers. Ben Logan. LC 74-6565. 290p. 1985. pap. 10.95 o.p. (ISBN 0-88361-095-7). Stanton & Lee.

Land Rent, Housing & Urban Planning: A European Perspective. Ed. by Michael Ball et al. LC 84-17497. 228p. 1984. 34.50 o.p. (ISBN 0-7099-3240-5, Pub. by Croom Helm Ltd). Routledge Chapman & Hall.

Land Resource Economics: The Economics of Real Estate. 3rd ed. Raleigh Barlowe. (Illus.). 1978. text ed. 38.33 ref. ed. o.p. (ISBN 0-13-522532-9). P-H.

Land Rover Series III Parts Catalogue. British Leyland Motors. 1988. 35.00 o.p. (ISBN 0-8376-0531-8). Bentley.

Land Rush: The Secret World of Real Estate's Super Brokers & Developers. Mark Stevens. 304p. 1984. text ed. 15.95 o.p. (ISBN 0-07-061273-0). McGraw.

Land Scarcity & Rural Inequality in Tanzania: Some Case Studies from Rungwe District. P. M. Hekken. (Communications: No. 3). (Illus.). 1972. pap. 7.60x o.p. (ISBN 90-2796-984-1). Mouton.

Land Subdivision: Monographs. Mary Vance. (Public Administration Ser.: P 1821). 19p. 1985. 3.00 o.p. (ISBN 0-89028-671-X). Vance Biblios.

Land System of the United States: An Introduction to the History & Practice of Land Use & Land Tenure. Marion Clawson. LC 68-10250. (Illus.). x, 145p. 1968. 13.95x o.p. (ISBN 0-8032-0016-1). U of Nebr Pr.

Land Tenure Center: Its First Three Years: a Cooperative Program of the American Nations, the Agency for International Development, & the University of Wisconsin. University of Wisconsin, Madison, Land Tenure Center Staff. LC 81-169971. write for info. o.p. U of Wis Land.

Land They Fought for. Clifford Dowdey. LC 73-19499. (Mainstream of America Ser). (Illus.). 438p. 1974. Repr. of 1955 ed. lib. bdg. 28.25x o.p. (ISBN 0-8371-7328-0, DOLA). Greenwood.

Land Transactions & Finance. Grant Nelson & Dale Whitman. (Black Letter Ser.). 385p. 1983. pap. text ed. 14.95 o.p. (ISBN 0-314-74081-3). West Pub.

Land Transportation in Japan: Planning for High Speeds. (Training Documents: No. 3). 45p. 1974. pap. 5.00 o.p. (ISBN 0-686-75155-8, CRD006, UNCRD). UNIPUB.

Land Use. Kenneth P. Davis. 1976. text ed. 40.95 o.p. (ISBN 0-07-015534-8). McGraw.

Land Use Allocation: Processes, People, Politics, Professionals. Society of American Foresters Staff. Ed. by H. H. Evans. (SAF Convention Proceedings Ser.). (Illus.). 298p. (Orig.). 1981. pap. 18.00 o.p. (ISBN 0-939970-07-4). Soc Am Foresters.

Land Use & Environment Law Review: 1984. Frederic A. Strom. Incl. 1984 (ISBN 0-87632-116-3); 1976. (ISBN 0-87632-117-1); 1977. (ISBN 0-87632-118-X); 1978. (ISBN 0-87632-119-8); 1979. o. p. (ISBN 0-87632-120-1); 1980 45.00, (ISBN 0-87632-121-X). LC 70-127585. 42.50 ea. o.p. Clark Boardman.

Land Use & Resources: Studies in Applied Geography. Ed. by Dudley Stamp. (Special Publications of the Institute of British Geographers: No. 1). 1980. 28.50 o.p. (ISBN 0-12-663080-1). Acad Pr.

Land Use & Town & Country Planning. Ed. by W. F. Maunder & J. T. Coppock. 1978. 55.00 o.p. (ISBN 0-08-022451-2). Pergamon.

Land Use Control: Interface of Law & Geography. Rutherford H. Platt. Ed. by Salvatore J. Natoli. LC 76-18389. (Resource Papers for College Geography Ser.). (Illus.). 1976. pap. text ed. 5.00 o.p. (ISBN 0-89291-109-3). Assn Am Geographers.

Land Use Law & Litigation. Pennsylvania Bar Institute Staff. 231p. 1985. 30.00 o.p. (ISBN 0-318-19056-7, 289). PA Bar Inst.

Land Water & Power: A History of the Turlock Irrigation District, 1887-1987. Alan M. Paterson. LC 87-70947. (Western Lands & Waters Ser.: Vol. XIV). (Illus.). 420p. 1987. 26.50 o.p. (ISBN 0-87062-177-7). A H Clark.

Land Without Justice. Milovan Djilas. LC 58-8574. 366p. 1972. pap. 8.95 o.s.i. (ISBN 0-15-648117-0, Harv). HarBraceJ.

Land Without Shadow. Michael Mewshaw. 1981. pap. 2.50 o.p. (ISBN 0-380-51516-4, 51516-4). Avon.

Landfall. Julius Horwitz. LC 76-29904. 1977. 7.95 o.s.i. (ISBN 0-03-014926-6). H Holt & Co.

Landfall. Betty Levin. LC 79-12421. 216p. (gr. 7 up). 1979. 8.95 o.p. (ISBN 0-689-50148-X, Atheneum). Macmillan.

Landing & Marketing Facilities at Selected Sea Fishing Ports. (Fisheries Reports: No. 36). 345p. 1966. pap. 21.25 o.p. (ISBN 0-686-92943-8, F1659, FAO). UNIPUB.

Landlording: A Handymanual for Scruplous Landlords & Landladies Who Do It Themselves. 3rd ed. Leigh Robinson. LC 79-57253. 261p. 1983. 15.00 o.p. (ISBN 0-932956-01-7). Express.

Landlord's Law Book - Evictions: California. David Brown. LC 85-61224. (Orig.). 1986. pap. 24.95 o.p. (ISBN 0-87337-018-X). Nolo Pr.

Landman's Encyclopedia. 2nd ed. R. L. Hankinson & R. L. Hankinson, Jr. LC 81-6422. 494p. 1981. 75.00x o.p. (ISBN 0-87201-420-7). Gulf Pub.

Landmark Changes in Divorce Taxation Rules. Massachusetts Continuing Legal Education-New England Law Institute, Inc. Staff. LC 84-61758. 136p. write for info. o.p. Mass CLE.

Landmark Films: The Cinema & Our Century. William Wolf & Lillian K. Wolf. LC 79-1487. 430p. 1986. pap. 8.95 o.p. (ISBN 0-394-62183-2, Ever). Grove.

Landmark Neighborhoods in Chicago. Commission on Chicago Historical & Architectural Landmarks. (Illus.). 64p. (Orig.). 1981. pap. 3.50 o.p. (ISBN 0-934076-02-2). Chicago Review.

Landmarks in History. K. Momjan. 248p. 1980. 5.95 o.p. (ISBN 0-8285-1821-1, Pub. by Progress Pubs USSR). Imported Pubns.

Landmarks in Metrology. LC 81-101402. 240p. 1983. pap. text ed. 33.00x o.p. (ISBN 0-87664-790-5). Instru Soc.

Landmarks in the History of Education. T. R. Jarman. 1952. (ISBN 0-8022-0793-6). Philos Lib.

Landmarks of Irish Drama. Ed. by Brendan Kennelly. 640p. 1988. pap. text ed. 13.95 o.p. Routledge Chapman & Hall.

Landmarks of Liberty. Hammond Incorporated Editors. LC 77-114691. (Hammond Profile Ser.). (Illus.). (gr. 7 up). 1970. 9.95 o.p. (ISBN 0-8437-3078-1). Hammond Inc.

Landmobile & Marine Radio Technology Handbook. Edward M. Noll. 1985. 24.95 o.p. (ISBN 0-672-22427-5, 22427-5). Sams.

Lando Calrissian & the Flamewind of Oseon. L. Neil Smith. 192p. 1983. pap. 2.50 o.s.i. (ISBN 0-345-31163-9, Del Rey). Ballantine.

Lando Calrissian & the Starcave of Thonboka. L. Neil Smith. 192p. 1983. pap. 2.50 o.s.i. (ISBN 0-345-31164-7, Del Rey). Ballantine.

Landrum-Griffin Act: Twenty Years of Federal Protection of Union Members' Rights. Janice R. Bellace. LC 79-2465. (Labor Relations & Public Policy Ser.: No. 19). 363p. 1979. pap. 15.00 o.p. (ISBN 0-89546-014-9). Indus Res Unit-Wharton.

Lands & Peoples, 6 vols. LC 84-22430. (Illus.). 1987. text ed. write for info. o.p. (ISBN 0-7172-8011-X). Grolier Inc.

Land's End. Kevin Starr. LC 78-26795. 1979. text ed. 14.95 o.p. (ISBN 0-07-060880-6). McGraw.

Land's Lord. T. Obinkaram Echewa. LC 76-18327. 160p. 1976. 8.95 o.p. (ISBN 0-88208-069-5); pap. 3.95 o.p. (ISBN 0-88208-070-9). Chicago Review.

Landscape Alphabet. Ed. by Ruth Mortimer. (Illus.). 48p. 1981. pap. 3.00 o.p. (ISBN 0-87391-023-0). Smith Coll.

Landscape & Distance: Contemporary Poets from Virginia. Ed. by Margaret Gibson & Richard McCann. LC 75-2350. 189p. 1975. 10.95x o.p. (ISBN 0-8139-0622-9); pap. 5.95x o.p. (ISBN 0-8139-0656-3). U Pr of Va.

Landscape & Silence. Harold Pinter. (Illus.). 1970. 3.95 o.s.i. (ISBN 0-394-47572-0, GP634). Grove.

Landscape & Silence. Harold Pinter. (Illus.). 1970. pap. 3.95 o.s.i. (ISBN 0-394-17289-2, E555, Ever). Grove.

Landscape Architecture: Monographs Published 1970-1984. Mary Vance. (Architecture Series: Bibliography A 1458). 116p. 1985. pap. 15.75 o.p. (ISBN 0-89028-548-9). Vance Biblios.

Landscape Construction. M. E. Downing. 1977. 28.00x o.p. (ISBN 0-419-10890-4, NO. 6089, Pub. by E & FN Spon). Routledge Chapman & Hall.

Landscape Construction Procedures, Techniques & Design. Floyd Giles. 140p. 1986. text ed. 14.80x o.p. (ISBN 0-87563-277-7). Stipes.

Landscape Drawing. Wendon Blake. (Artist's Painting Library Ser.). (Illus.). 80p. (Orig.). 1981. pap. 8.95 o.p. (ISBN 0-8230-2593-4). Watson-Guptill.

Landscape Garden Designer. William Kent. Ed. by John D. Hunt & Peter Willis. LC 87-50752. (Illus.). 240p. 1988. 95.00 o.p. (ISBN 0-318-23735-0, Pub. by Zwemmer Bks UK). Sotheby Pubns.

Landscape in Pastel. Aubrey Phillips. (Leisure Arts Ser.: No. 23). (Illus.). 32p. (Orig.). 1984. pap. 2.95 o.p. (ISBN 0-89134-087-4). North Light Bks.

Landscape It Yourself. Harold Givens. LC 76-14436. (Illus.). 1977. pap. 12.95 o.p. (ISBN 0-15-147689-6, Harv). HarBraceJ.

Landscape of Britain. Adam Nicolson. LC 84-50007. (Illus.). 1984. 19.95f o.p. (ISBN 0-500-54101-9). Thames Hudson.

Landscape of Industry. Clifford Tandy. LC 75-28033. 314p. 1975. 84.95x o.p. (ISBN 0-470-84440-X). Halsted Pr.

Landscape Painting for Beginners. Joanna Carrington. LC 79-84664. (Start to Paint Ser.). (Illus.). 1979. pap. 3.95 o.s.i. (ISBN 0-8008-4543-9, Pentalic). Taplinger.

Landscape Planning for a New Australian Town. K. McCoy. (Developments in Landscape Management & Urban Planning: Vol. 3). 1976. 47.50 o.p. (ISBN 0-444-41340-5). Elsevier.

Landscape with Traveler: The Pillow Book of Francis Reeves. Barry Gifford. 1982. pap. 6.25 o.s.i. (ISBN 0-03-060604-7, Owl Bks). H Holt & Co.

Landscapes & Documents. Alan Rogers. 85p. 1974. pap. text ed. 3.75x o.p. (ISBN 0-7199-0883-3, Pub. by Bedford England). Gower Pub Co.

Landscapes in Watercolor. Wendon Blake. (Artist's Painting Library). (Illus.). 80p. 1979. pap. 8.95 o.p. (ISBN 0-8230-2621-3). Watson-Guptill.

Landscapes of Bacchus: The Vine in Portugal. Dan Stanislawski. (Illus.). 224p. 1970. 14.50x o.p. (ISBN 0-292-70010-5). U of Tex Pr.

Landscapes of the Night. Christopher Evans. Date not set. 6.95 o.s.i. (ISBN 0-671-55190-6). PB.

Lane. Alan H. Kempner, Jr. 1979. 6.50 o.p. (ISBN 0-682-49373-2). Exposition-Phoenix.

Lane County: An Illustrated History of the Emerald Empire. Dorothy Velasco. LC 85-16864. 168p. 1985. 22.95 o.p. (ISBN 0-89781-140-2). Windsor Pubns Inc.

Lanes One Walks Thru. Lane A. Francom. 19p. 1985. 5.95 o.p. (ISBN 0-533-06247-0). Vantage.

Lange Weg des Lukas B see Long Journey of Lukas B.

Langenscheidt Comprehensive German Dictionary. 1104p. (Ger.). 47.50 o.p. (ISBN 0-340-14967-1). Langenscheidt.

Langenscheidt English-Latin Lilliput Dictionary. 640p. (Eng. & Lat.). plastic 2.00 o.p. (ISBN 3-468-96484-6). Langenscheidt.

Langenscheidt Modern Greek-English Lilliput Dictionary. 640p. (Eng. & Ger.). plastic 2.00 o.p. (ISBN 3-468-96472-2). Langenscheidt.

Langenscheidt Taschenwoerterbuch German Dictionary. 1278p. (Ger.). 12.95 o.p. (ISBN 0-88729-068-X). Langenscheidt.

Langenscheidts Sportwoerterbuch. R. Lembke. 319p. (Ger., Eng., Fr. & Span., Dictionary of Sports). 1971. 9.95 o.p. (ISBN 0-686-56629-7, M-7538, Pub. by Langenscheidt). French & Eur.

Langer of North Dakota: A Study in Isolationism 1940-1959. Glenn H. Smith. Ed. by Frank Freidel. LC 78-62502. (Modern American History Ser.: Vol. 16). 250p. 1979. lib. bdg. 31.00 o.p. (ISBN 0-8240-3639-5). Garland Pub.

Langfristplanung in der Energiewirtschaft. Kurt Schmitz. (Interdisciplinary Systems Research Ser.: No. 65). 274p. (Ger.). 1979. pap. 27.95x o.p. (ISBN 0-8176-1068-5). Birkhauser.

Langston Hughes & Gwendolyn Brooks: A Reference Guide. R. Baxter Miller. 1978. 25.00 o.p. (ISBN 0-8161-7810-0, Hall Reference). G K Hall.

Langston Hughes, Poet of Harlem. Norita D. Larson. Ed. by Ann Redpath. (People to Remember Ser.). (Illus.). 32p. (gr. 4 up). 1981. PLB 8.95 o.p. (ISBN 0-87191-798-X). Creative Ed.

Language Acquisition & Linguistic Theory. Ed. by Susan Tavakolian. (Illus.). 304p. 1981. text ed. 32.50x o.p. (ISBN 0-262-20039-2). MIT Pr.

Language Acquisition: Models & Methods. C. A. S. D. S. Study Group on Mechanisms of Language Development, London, 1968. Ed. by Renira Huxley & Elisabeth Ingram. 1971. 55.00 o.p. (ISBN 0-12-363450-4). Acad Pr.

Language: All About It. Irene B. McDonald. 112p. (Orig.). (gr. 10-12). 1980. pap. text ed. 4.25x o.p. (ISBN 0-88334-140-9). Ind Sch Pr.

Language: An Introduction to the Study of Speech. Sapir. 1980. text ed. 17.50x o.p. (ISBN 0-246-11074-0). Humanities.

Language & Cognition. Adam Schaff. Ed. by Robert S. Cohen. Tr. by Olgierd Wojtasiewicz from Pol. 192p. (Orig.). 1966. pap. text ed. 2.95 o.p. (ISBN 0-07-055081-6). McGraw.

Language & Communication in the Elderly: Clinical, Therapeutic, & Experimental Issues. Loraine K. Obler & Martin L. Albert. LC 80-5348. 240p. 1980. 30.00x o.p. (ISBN 0-669-03868-7). Lexington Bks.

Language & Context: The Acquisition of Pragmatics. E. Bates. (Language, Thought & Culture Ser.). 1976. 34.50 o.p. (ISBN 0-12-081550-8). Acad Pr.

Language & Experience: Descriptions of Living Language in Husserl & Wittgenstein. Harry P. Reeder. LC 84-7588. (Current Continental Research Ser.: CCR 301). 226p. 1984. lib. bdg. 27.00 o.p. (ISBN 0-8191-4009-0); pap. text ed. 13.50 o.p. (ISBN 0-8191-4010-4). U Pr of Amer.

Language & Historical Change. N. S. Baron. (North-Holland Linguistic Ser: Vol. 36). 320p. 1978. 73.75 o.p. (ISBN 0-444-85077-5, North-Holland). Elsevier.

Language & Language Learning: Theory & Practice. 2nd ed. Nelson Brooks. 1964. text ed. 12.95 o.p. (ISBN 0-15-549232-2, HC). HarBraceJ.

Language & Learning in Home & School. Ed. by Alan Davies. xi, 179p. (Orig.). 1982. pap. text ed. 22.50x o.p. (ISBN 0-435-10192-7). Heinemann Ed.

Language & Learning to Read: What Teachers Should Know About Language. R. E. Hodges & E. Hugh Rudorf. LC 70-175170. 1903. pap. 19.95 o.p. (ISBN 0-395-12639-8). HM.

Language & Logic. Milos Prazak. LC 62-9771. 160p. 1963. (ISBN 0-8022-2013-4). Philos Lib.

Language & Man: Anthropological Issues. Ed. by William C. McCormack & Stephen A. Wurm. (World Anthropology Ser.). (Illus.). xiv, 394p. 1976. 43.25 o.p. (ISBN 90-279-7839-5). Mouton.

Language & Mind. enl. ed. Noam Chomsky. LC 70-187121. 194p. 1972. 8.50 o.p. (ISBN 0-15-147810-4). HarBraceJ.

Language & Perception. George A. Miller & Philip N. Johnson-Laird. LC 75-30605. 960p. 1976. 37.00x o.p. (ISBN 0-674-50947-1). Harvard U Pr.

Language & Perception: Essays in the Philosophy of Language. Frank B. Ebersole. LC 79-88305. 1979. pap. text ed. 14.50 o.p. (ISBN 0-8191-0776-X). U Pr of Amer.

Language & Sex. Barrie Thorne. Ed. by Nancy Henley. 328p. 1975. 15.00 o.p. (ISBN 0-88377-043-1). Newbury Hse.

Language & the Brain, 2 vols. William O. Dingwall. LC 80-8491. 1981. lib. bdg. 121.00 o.p. (ISBN 0-8240-9495-6). Garland Pub.

Language & Thought: Anthropological Issues. Ed. by William C. McCormack & Stephen A. Wurm. (World Anthropology Ser.). 1977. text ed. 53.25 o.p. (ISBN 90-279-7540-X). Mouton.

Language & Thought in Schizophrenia. Ed. by J. S. Kasanin. 1964. pap. 2.95 o.p. (ISBN 0-393-00252-7, Norton Lib). Norton.

Language Approach to Open Syllables. Edna C. Young. 57p. 1981. 3-ring binder 29.95 o.p. (ISBN 0-88450-744-0, 2081-B). Communication Skill.

Language Arts Activities for Elementary Schools. Paul C. Burns & Randall K. Bassett. LC 81-82574. 1981. pap. 16.95 o.p. (ISBN 0-395-31688-X). HM.

Titles

Titles

Language Arts Bulletin Boards. Charles L. Thompson & Johnny F. Bell. 1967. pap. 4.95 o.p. (ISBN 0-8224-4200-0). D S Lake Pubs.

Language Arts in Childhood Education. 4th ed. Paul C. Burns & Betty L. Broman. LC 81-80802. (Illus.). 1980. text ed. 21.95 o.p. (ISBN 0-395-30571-3). HM.

Language Arts in Elementary Schools. Wilmer K. Trauger. 1963. text ed. 10.95 o.p. (ISBN 0-07-065139-6). McGraw.

Language Arts: Learning Processes & Teaching Practices. Charles Temple & Jean W. Gillet. 1984. text ed. (ISBN 0-673-39182-5). Scott F.

Language As Ideology. Gunther Kress. 1981. pap. 9.95x o.p. (ISBN 0-7100-0795-7). Routledge Chapman & Hall.

Language as Resource: A Social & Educational Perpective on Language Minorities in the United States. Sandra McKay & Sau-Ling Wong. 300p. 1988. pap. text ed. 16.50 o.p. (ISBN 0-06-632608-7). Newbury Hse.

Language Assessment for Remediation. David J. Muller et al. 170p. 1981. 25.00 o.p. (ISBN 0-7099-1706-6, Pub. by Croom Helm Ltd); pap. 10.75 o.p. (ISBN 0-7099-1707-4). Routledge Chapman & Hall.

Language Bar. Victor Grove. (ISBN 0-8022-0639-5). Philos Lib.

Language by Ear & by Eye: The Relationships Between Speech & Reading. Ed. by James F. Kavanagh & Ignatius G. Mattingly. 1972. 23.00x o.p. (ISBN 0-262-11044-X); pap. 14.95x o.p. (ISBN 0-262-61015-9). MIT Pr.

Language Change & Linguistic Reconstruction. Henry M. Hoenigswald. LC 59-12287. 1965. pap. text ed. 4.50x o.s.i. (ISBN 0-226-34741-9). U of Chicago Pr.

Language, Counter-Memory, Practice: Selected Essays and Interviews. Michel Foucault. Ed. & tr. by Donald F. Bouchard. LC 77-4561. (Illus.). 240p. 1977. 29.95x o.p. (ISBN 0-8014-0979-9). Cornell U Pr.

Language, Culture & Cognition: Readings in Cognitive Anthropology. Ronald W. Casson. 1981. write for info. o.p. (ISBN 0-02-320050-2). Macmillan.

Language Development. Ed. by Andrew Lock & Eunice Fisher. 260p. 1983. pap. 10.95 o.p. (ISBN 0-7099-1932-8, Pub. by Croom Helm Ltd). Routledge Chapman & Hall.

Language Development & Assessment. Joan Reynell. 178p. 1980. text ed. 16.50 o.p. (ISBN 0-88416-377-6). Year Bk Med.

Language Development & Intellectual Functioning. Kevin F. Collis. (APEID Occasional Papers: No. 10). 20p. 1983. pap. 5.00 o.p. (ISBN 0-686-44024-2, UB125, UB). UNIPUB.

Language Disorders & Learning Disabilities, Topics in Language Disorders, Vol. 1, No.1. Katherine G. Butler & Geraldine P. Wallach. LC 82-1665. 118p. 1982. 19.95 o.p. (ISBN 0-89443-688-0). Aspen Pub.

Language Disorders in Adolescents. Donald F. Tibbits. LC 82-71669. (Cliffs Speech & Hearing Ser.). 120p. (Orig.). 1982. pap. text ed. 4.95 o.p. (ISBN 0-8220-1832-2). Cliffs.

Language Disorders in Children: A Resource Book for Speech-Language Pathologists. Merlin J. Mecham & Mary L. Willbrand. (Illus.). 304p. 1979. 37.50x o.p. (ISBN 0-398-03865-1). C C Thomas.

Language Enrichment Activities for the Elementary School. Joseph Crescimbeni. (Illus.). 1979. text ed. 15.95x o.p. (ISBN 0-13-522987-1, Parker). P-H.

Language, Ethnicity & Intergroup Relations. Ed. by H. Giles. (European Monographs in Social Psychology Ser.). 1978. 65.00 o.p. (ISBN 0-12-283740-1). Acad Pr.

Language Experience Approach for Teaching Reading: A Research Perspective. 2nd ed. MaryAnne Hall. 49p. 1978. pap. text ed. 2.25 o.p. (ISBN 0-87207-861-2). Intl Reading.

Language Experiences in Communication. Roach V. Allen. LC 75-31011. (Illus.). 512p. 1976. text ed. 28.95 o.p. (ISBN 0-395-18624-2). HM.

Language in America: A Report on Our Deteriorating Semantic Environment. Neil Postman et al. 1969. pap. text ed. write for info. o.p. (ISBN 0-02-396350-6). Macmillan.

Language in Sign: An International Perspective on Sign Language. Ed. by Jim G. Kyle & Bencie Woll. (Illus.). 304p. 1983. pap. 25.25 o.p. (ISBN 0-7099-1528-4, Pub. by Croom Helm Ltd). Routledge Chapman & Hall.

Language in the Inner City: Studies in the Black English Vernacular. William Labov. LC 72-80376. (Conduct & Communication Ser). 438p. 1973. text ed. 30.00x o.p. (ISBN 0-8122-7658-2); pap. 15.95 o.p. (ISBN 0-8122-1051-4, Pa Paperbks). U of Pa Pr.

Language in Thought & Action. 4th ed. Samuel I. Hayakawa. LC 78-53859. 1978. 10.95 o.p. (ISBN 0-15-148112-1). HarBraceJ.

Language in Thought & Action. 3rd ed. Samuel I. Hayakawa. 1972. pap. text ed. 7.95 o.p. (ISBN 0-15-550118-6, HC, HC). HarBraceJ.

Language Interpretation & Communication. Ed. by D. Gerver & H. W. Sinaiko. LC 78-15195. (NATO Conference Series III, Human Factors: Vol. 6). 438p. 1978. 60.00x o.p. (ISBN 0-306-40051-0, Plenum Pr). Plenum Pub.

Language Learning Disabilities: Diagnosis & Remediation. Ed. by Carol T. Wren et al. 345p. 1983. 35.00 o.p. (ISBN 0-89443-935-9). Aspen Pub.

Language Learning Process: Implications for Management of Disorders. Joan Laughton & Suzanne Hasenstab. 280p. 1986. 35.00 o.p. (ISBN 0-87189-288-X). Aspen Pub.

Language Master, Bk. 1. Barbara Levy. (Language Master Ser.). (Illus.). 48p. (ps-6). 1984. wkbk 5.95 o.p. (ISBN 0-86653-204-8). Good Apple.

Language Master, Bk. 3. Barbara Levy. (Language Master Ser.). (Illus.). (YA) (gr. 8-10). 1984. wkbk 5.95 o.p. (ISBN 0-86653-257-9). Good Apple.

Language Master: CB, Bk. 4. Barbara Levy. (Language Master Ser.). (Illus.). 48p. (YA) (gr. 10-12). 1984. wkbk 4.95 o.p. (ISBN 0-86653-263-3). Good Apple.

Language Not to Be Betrayed: Selected Prose. Edward Thomas. Ed. by Edna Longley. 320p. 1981. 22.50 o.p. (ISBN 0-89255-056-2). Persea Bks.

Language of Anatomy see Preliminary Announcement.

Language of Cats & Other Stories. Spencer Holst. 128p. 1973. pap. 1.65 o.p. (ISBN 0-380-01317-7, 14381, Bard). Avon.

Language of Clothes. Alison Lurie. LC 81-40220. (Illus.). 256p. 1981. 19.50 o.s.i. (ISBN 0-394-51302-9). Random.

Language of Counseling. Jay E. Adams. LC 86-11048. 90p. 1981. pap. 2.45 o.p. (ISBN 0-87552-009-X). Presby & Reformed.

Language of Counseling. Jay E. Adams. 1981. pap. 2.45 o.p. (ISBN 0-8010-0181-1). Baker Bk.

Language of Creative Financing. Stephen R. Mettling. (Residential Financing Resource Library). 26p. (Orig.). 1981. pap. 6.50 o.s.i. (ISBN 0-88462-127-8, 1905-04, Real Estate Ed). Longman Finan.

Language of Decision: An Essay in Prescriptivist Ethical Theory. J. Ibberson. LC 85-27203. 160p. 1986. text ed. 35.00 o.p. (ISBN 0-391-03394-8). Humanities.

Language of Faith. Aaron Bin-Nun. LC 78-65723. 1979. 8.95 o.p. (ISBN 0-88400-061-3). Shengold.

Language of Fiction. David Lodge. 310p. pap. 9.95 o.p. (ISBN 0-7102-0238-5). Routledge Chapman & Hall.

Language of Linguistics: Reflections on Linquistic Terminology, with Particular Reference to Level & Rank. Reinhard R. Hartmann. (Tuebinger Beitraege Zur Linguistik Ser.: No. 44). (Illus.). 180p. (Orig.). 1973. pap. 16.00x o.p. (ISBN 3-87808-044-1). Benjamins North Am.

Language of Love. Gary Smalley. 1988. 12.95 o.p. (ISBN 0-8499-0557-5). Word Bks.

Language of Modern Music. Donald Mitchell. 168p. 1982. pap. 6.95 o.p. (ISBN 0-571-06570-8). Faber & Faber.

Language of Money: An Irreverent Dictionary of Business & Finance. William Davis. 1973. 6.95 o.p. (ISBN 0-395-13999-6). HM.

Language of National Defense in English. Robert W. Nicholson & Ralph R. Williams. (English for Careers Ser.). (gr. 10 up). 1978. pap. text ed. 3.75 o.p. (ISBN 0-88345-327-4). Prentice ESL.

Language of Painting. Charles Johnson. Repr. of 1949 ed. lib. bdg. 35.00x o.p. (ISBN 0-8371-2525-1, JOLP). Greenwood.

Language of Publishing in English. Swinburne. (English for Careers Ser.). (gr. 10 up). 1980. pap. text ed. (ISBN 0-685-78816-4). Prentice ESL.

Language of Real Estate. 2nd ed. John W. Reilly. LC 82-15026. 570p. (Orig.). 1982. pap. 24.95 o.p. (ISBN 0-88462-603-2, 1961-01, Real Estate Ed). Longman Finan.

Language of Silence. J. Allen Boone. LC 72-126035. 1970. 4.95i o.p. (ISBN 0-06-060911-7, RD-182). HarpR.

Language of Stained Glass. Robert Sowers. LC 80-29703. (Illus.). 220p. 1981. 27.50 o.p. (ISBN 0-917304-61-6). Timber.

Language of the Air Force in English. Francis A. Cartier. (English for Careers Ser.). (Illus.). 1976. pap. text ed. 3.95 o.p. (ISBN 0-88345-271-5, 18510). Prentice ESL.

Language of the Army in English. Turner. (English for Careers Ser). (Illus.). 1978. pap. text ed. 3.95 o.p. (ISBN 0-88345-349-5, 18506). Prentice ESL.

Language of the Christian Community. Sara Little. (Illus., Orig.). (gr. 11-12). 1965. pap. 3.45 o.p. (ISBN 0-8042-9240-X, John Knox); tchrs' guide pap. 4.50 o.p. (ISBN 0-686-76882-5). Westminster John Knox.

Language of the Environment in English. (English for Careers Ser.). (gr. 10 up). 1980. pap. text ed. (ISBN 0-88345-353-3). Prentice ESL.

Language of the Navy in English. R. G. Sansom. (English for Careers Ser). (Illus.). (gr. 10 up). 1978. pap. text ed. 6.95 o.p. (ISBN 0-88345-274-X, 18507). Prentice ESL.

Language Origins: A Bibliography Part One A-K Part Two L-Z. Ed. by Gordon W. Hewes. (Approaches to Semiotics Ser.: No. 44). 890p. 1975. text ed. 136.00 o.p. (ISBN 90-2793-401-0). Mouton.

Language Play: An Introduction to Linguistics. Don L. Nilsen & Alleen Nilsen. 1978. pap. text ed. 15.50 o.p. (ISBN 0-88377-102-0). Newbury Hse.

Language Remediation & Expansion: One Hundred Skill-Building Reference Lists. Catharine S. Bush. (Illus.). 216p. 1979. pap. text ed. 18.95 o.p. (ISBN 0-88450-797-1, 3052-B). Communication Skill.

Language Situation & Language Policy in Slovenia. James W. Tollefson. LC 80-5579. 296p. 1981. lib. bdg. 27.50 o.p. (ISBN 0-8191-1570-3); pap. text ed. 12.50 o.p. (ISBN 0-8191-1571-1). U Pr of Amer.

Language Skills for Journalists. R. Thomas Berner. LC 78-69584. 1979. pap. 12.95 o.p. (ISBN 0-395-26789-7). HM.

Language Teaching & the Microcomputer. Rex W. Last. 192p. 1984. pap. 15.95x o.p. (ISBN 0-631-13413-1). Basil Blackwell.

Language Teaching Projects for the Third World. Ed. by C. J. Brumfit. (English Language Teaching Documents Ser.: Vol. 116). 160p. 1983. pap. text ed. 7.50 o.s.i. (ISBN 0-08-030342-0, 667, Dist. by Alemany Pr). Pergamon.

Language: The Social Mirror. Elaine Chaika. 272p. 1982. pap. 16.50 o.p. (ISBN 0-88377-203-5). Newbury Hse.

Language Transfer in Language Learning. Ed. by Susan Gass & Larry Selinker. 392p. 1983. pap. text ed. 24.00 o.p. (ISBN 0-88377-305-8). Newbury Hse.

Language Use & School Performance. Aaron V. Cicourel et al. 1974. 29.95 o.p. (ISBN 0-12-174950-9). Acad Pr.

Languages & Linguistics: An Introduction. Joe E. Pierce. (Janua Linguarum Series Didactica: No. 4). 188p. (Orig.). 1975. pap. text ed. 22.40x o.p. (ISBN 90-2793-371-5). Mouton.

Langue et Langue. 4th ed. Oreste Pucciani & Jacqueline Hamel. (Fr.). 1983. text ed. 28.95 o.p. (ISBN 0-03-062517-3); instr's. manual 19.95 o.p. (ISBN 0-03-062518-1); lab manual 11.95 o.p. (ISBN 0-03-062519-X); tapes avail. o.p. (ISBN 0-03-062521-1). HR&W.

Lanning Roper & His Gardens. Jane Brown. LC 86-22060. (Illus.). 224p. 1987. lib. bdg. 37.50 o.p. (ISBN 0-8478-0787-8). Rizzoli Intl.

Lantern in the Valley. Betty E. Hanna. (Illus.). 64p. 1981. 6.95 o.p. (ISBN 0-89015-276-4). Eakin Pr.

Lantern Keeper's Bedtime Book. Geoffrey Hayes. LC 86-603. (Illus.). 48p. (ps-3). 1986. 6.95 o.s.i. (ISBN 0-394-87288-6, BYR); lib. bdg. 7.99 o.s.i. (ISBN 0-394-97288-0, BYR). Random.

Lao-English Dictionary, 2 vols. Allen Kerr. LC 82-12826. (Publications in the Languages of Asia Ser.: No. 2). 1223p. (Laotian & Eng.). 1973. Set. 49.95 o.p. (ISBN 0-8132-0526-3). Cath U Pr.

Laoithe Fiannuigheachta, 2 vols. Ed. by John O'Daly. 592p. 1859-61. Repr. 21.00 o.p. (ISBN 0-384-42965-3). Johnson Repr.

Laparoscopic Techniques in Studies of Reproductive Physiology. W. Richard Dukelow et al. 1977. text ed. 32.50x o.p. (ISBN 0-8422-7232-1). Irvington.

Laplace Transform for Electrical Engineers. Starkey. 280p. 1955. (ISBN 0-8022-1630-7). Philos Lib.

LaPlace Transforms & Applications. E. Watson. 1981. 24.95 o.p. (ISBN 0-442-30176-6). Van Nos Reinhold.

Laplace Transforms for Electronic Engineers. 2nd ed. J. G. Holbrook. 1966. 90.00 o.p. (ISBN 0-08-011411-3). Pergamon.

Lara in London. Larissa Vassilyeva. Tr. by Olga Franklin. 1978. 16.25 o.p. (ISBN 0-08-023718-5); pap. 8.25 o.p. (ISBN 0-08-023717-7). Pergamon.

Larbi & Leila: A Tale of Two Mice. Harold Berson. LC 73-12378. (Illus.). 32p. (ps-3). 1979. 5.50 o.p. (ISBN 0-395-28766-9, Clarion). HM.

Large Amplitude Motion in Molecules One. Ed. by F. L. Boschke. (Topics in Current Chemistry: Vol. 81). (Illus.). 1979. 58.00 o.p. (ISBN 0-387-09310-9). Springer-Verlag.

Large Bowel Cancer: Clinical Surgery International, Vol. 1. Ed. by Jerome J. DeCosse. (Illus.). 225p. 1981. text ed. 48.00 o.p. (ISBN 0-443-02126-0). Churchill.

Large Families in London. Hilarly Land. 154p. 1969. pap. text ed. 6.25x o.p. (ISBN 0-7135-1577-5, Pub. by Bedford England). Gower Pub Co.

Large Food & Selected Non-Food Containers. Business Communications Staff. 1988. 2450.00 o.p. (ISBN 0-89336-680-3, P-110). BCC.

Large Gardens & Parks: Maintenance, Management & Design. Tom Wright. 194p. (Orig.). 1982. text ed. 35.50x o.p. (ISBN 0-246-11402-9, Pub by Granada England). Gower Pub Co.

Large Ground Movements & Structures. Ed. by James D. Geddes. LC 78-19092. 1064p. 1978. 102.95x o.p. (ISBN 0-470-26460-8). Halsted Pr.

Large Molecules. J. H. Fuhrhop et al. LC 67-11280. (Structure & Bonding Ser.: Vol. 18). (Illus.). 216p. 1974. 45.00 o.p. (ISBN 0-387-06658-6). Springer-Verlag.

Large Rotating Machine Winding. R. T. Anderson et al. (Illus.). 201p. 1981. Repr. of 1969 ed. spiral 52.50x o.p. (ISBN 0-89563-049-4). Trans-Atl Phila.

Large Scale Integration. Electronics Magazine Editors. 1976. text ed. 33.50 o.p. (ISBN 0-07-019187-5). McGraw.

Large-Scale Mamalian Cell Culture. Ed. by Joseph Feder & William R. Tolbert. 1985. 22.50 o.p. (ISBN 0-12-250430-5); pap. 22.50 o.p. (ISBN 0-12-250431-3). Acad Pr.

Large Spare Sets of Linear Equations: Proceedings of the Institute of Mathematics Oxford Conference, April 1970. Institute of Mathematics Staff. Ed. by R. Reid. 1971. 51.50 o.p. (ISBN 0-12-586150-8). Acad Pr.

Large Type Crosswords, No. 3. Ed. by Margaret P. Farrar. 1978. pap. 3.95 o.s.i. (ISBN 0-671-24135-4, Fireside). S&S.

Largemouth, Smallmouth & Close Kin. Dave Bowring. LC 82-1922. 176p. (Orig.). 1982. pap. 12.95 o.p. (ISBN 0-8329-3630-8, Pub. by Winchester Pr). New Century.

Larger Than Life! Herbert H. Hutner. 1979. 7.00 o.p. (ISBN 0-682-49480-1). Exposition-Phoenix.

Larger Trout for the Western Fly Fisherman. Charles E. Brooks. (Illus.). 224p. 1983. pap. 14.95 o.p. (ISBN 0-8329-0329-9). Lyons & Burford.

Lark & the Laurel. Barbara Willard. LC 74-102442. (gr. 7 up). 1970. 5.95 o.p. (ISBN 0-15-243604-9, HJ). HarBraceJ.

Larkin at Sixty. Anthony Thwaite. 144p. 1982. 15.95 o.p. (ISBN 0-571-11878-X). Faber & Faber.

Larks in the Popcorn. H. Allen Smith. LC 74-15560. (Illus.). 256p. 1974. Repr. of 1948 ed. lib. bdg. 24.75x o.p. (ISBN 0-8371-7791-X, SMLP). Greenwood.

Larousse Book of Cocktails. Jacques Salle. LC 85-5851. 160p. 1985. pap. 9.95 o.p. (ISBN 0-03-005604-7). H Holt & Co.

Larousse French-English Dictionary. (Fr. & Eng.). 1981. pap. 3.95 o.p. (ISBN 0-671-47166-X). PB.

Larry Christenson's Financial Record System for Families & Individuals. Larry Christenson. 160p. (Orig.). 1980. spiral bdg. 5.95 o.p. (ISBN 0-87123-344-4, 210344). Bethany Hse.

Larry King. Larry King & Emily Yoffe. 240p. 1982. 14.50 o.p. (ISBN 0-671-41138-1). S&S.

Larry the Lion. Alice L. Mason. (Illus.). 16p. (gr. k-6). 1984. pap. 1.50 o.p. (ISBN 0-8249-8068-9). Ideals.

Larry's Number One. Rodiger. (EDSR Ser.). 14p. 1985. pap. 10.00 o.s.i. (ISBN 0-932582-42-7). Dance Notation.

Larval Serum Proteins of Insects. Klaus Scheller. (Illus.). 190p. 1983. pap. 32.50 o.p. (ISBN 0-86577-140-5). Thieme Med Pubs.

Las Vegas-Access. (Access Travel Guides Ser.). 9.95 o.p. (ISBN 0-671-60335-3). P-H.

Las Vegas-Access. Richard S. Wurman. (Access Guidebooks). (Illus.). 72p. (Orig.). 1985. pap. 7.95 o.p. (ISBN 0-915461-13-7). Access Pr.

Las Vegas Trivia. Morgan White, Jr. LC 85-62728. (Illus.). 200p. 1985. pap. 7.95 o.p. (ISBN 0-933341-20-2). Quinlan Pr.

Las Vegas 1987-1988. (Frommer's City Guides). 224p. 5.95 o.p. (ISBN 0-671-62544-6). Prentice Hall Pr.

Lascivious Scenes from the Convent. LC 83-83190. 144p. 1984. pap. 5.95 o.p. (ISBN 0-394-62203-0, E935, Ever). Grove.

Laser Cinematography of Explosions. CISM (International Center for Mechanical Sciences) Staff. Ed. by A. K. Oppenheim & M. M. Kamel. (CISM Publications: No. 100). (Illus.). 226p. 1974. pap. 26.60 o.p. (ISBN 0-387-81179-6). Springer-Verlag.

Laser-Induced Discharge Phenomena. Ed. by Y. P. Raizer. LC 77-21738. (Illus.). 380p. 1977. 75.00x o.p. (ISBN 0-306-10923-9, Consultants). Plenum Pub.

Laser Industry. Business Communications Staff. 114p. 1986. pap. 1750.00 o.p. (ISBN 0-89336-453-3, GB050N). BCC.

Laser Interaction & Related Plasma Phenomena, Vols. 1-4. Ed. by Helmut J. Schwarz & Heinrich Hora. Incl. Vol. 1. 524p. 1970. 85.00x (ISBN 0-306-37141-3); Vol. 2. 598p. 1972. 85.00x (ISBN 0-306-37142-1); Vol. 3A. 458p. 1974. 85.00x (ISBN 0-306-37143-X); Vol. 3B. 562p. 1974. 85.00x (ISBN 0-306-37150-2); Vol. 4A. 678p. 1977. 95.00x (ISBN 0-306-37144-8); Vol. 4B. 576p. 1977. 95.00x (ISBN 0-306-37154-5). LC 79-135851. (Illus., Plenum Pr). Plenum Pub.

Laser Interaction & Related Plasma Phenomena, Vol. 5. Ed. by H. J. Schwarz et al. LC 79-135851. 864p. 1981. 110.00x o.p. (ISBN 0-306-40545-8, Plenum Pr). Plenum Pub.

Laser Light Scattering. Benjamin Chu. 1974. 89.00 o.p. (ISBN 0-12-174550-3). Acad Pr.

Laser Market Opportunities. International Resource Development, Inc. Staff. 206p. 1984. 1285.00x o.p. (ISBN 0-88694-606-9). Intl Res Dev.

Laser Monitoring of the Atmosphere. Ed. by Hinkley. (Topics in Applied Physics Ser.: Vol. 14). (Illus.). 1976. 60.00 o.p. (ISBN 0-387-07743-X). Springer-Verlag.

Laser Physics. L. V. Tarasov. 208p. 1983. 10.95 o.p. (ISBN 0-8285-2570-6, Pub. by Mir Pubs USSR). Imported Pubns.

Laser Physics: Proceedings on the 2nd New Zealand Summer School in Laser Physics. Ed. by D. F. Walls & J. D Harvey. 287p. 1980. 51.50 o.p. (ISBN 0-12-733280-4). Acad Pr.

Laser Safety Handbook. Alex Mallow & Leon Chabot. 1978. 42.95 o.s.i. (ISBN 0-442-25092-4). Van Nos Reinhold.

Laser Spectroscopy. 2nd ed. W. Demtroeder. LC 51-5497. (Topics in Current Chemistry: Vol. 17). (Illus.). iii, 106p. 1973. 21.30 o.p. (ISBN 0-387-06334-X). Springer-Verlag.

Laser Spectroscopy of Atoms & Molecules. Ed. by H. Walter. (Topics in Applied Physics Ser.: Vol. 2). (Illus.). 340p. 1976. 60.00 o.p. (ISBN 0-387-07324-8). Springer-Verlag.

Laser: Supertool of the Nineteen Eighties. Jeff Hecht & Dick Teresi. LC 81-16608. (Illus.). 272p. 1982. 15.45 o.p. (ISBN 0-89919-082-0). Ticknor & Fields.

LaserJet Unlimited: How to Get the Most from Your Hewlett-Packard LaserJet or LaserJet Plus Printer. Ted Nace & Michael Gardner. (Illus.). 212p. 1986. pap. 24.95 o.p. (ISBN 0-938151-00-2). Peachpit Pr.

Lasers. 2nd ed. Bela A. Lengyel. LC 77-139279. (Series in Pure & Applied Optics). 388p. 1971. 49.95X o.p. (ISBN 0-471-52620-7, Pub. by Wiley-Interscience). Wiley.

Lasers & Hematoporphyrin Derivative in Cancer. Ed. by Yoshihiro Hayata & Thomas J. Dougherty. LC 83-22554. (Illus.). 128p. 1983. text ed. 59.00 o.p. (ISBN 0-89640-095-6). Igaku-Shoin.

Lasers in Cardiovascular Disease. Ed. by Rodney A. White & Warren Grundfest. (Illus.). 200p. 1987. 53.50 o.p. (ISBN 0-8151-9258-4, LIC-1). Year Bk Med.

Lasers in Fluid Mechanics & Plasmdynamics, 1983. Ed. by Charles P. Wang. (Illus.). 176p. 1983. 26.50 o.p. (ISBN 0-317-06660-9). AIAA.

Lasers in Materials Processing. Ed. by E. A. Metzbower. 1983. 63.00 o.p. (ISBN 0-87170-173-1). ASM.

Lasers in Metallurgy. Ed. by Kali Mukherjee & J. Mazumder. LC 81-85419. 301p. 1981. 10.00 o.p. (ISBN 0-89520-385-5). Minerals Metals.

Lasers in Metalworking: A Summary & Forecast. Tech Tran Corporation Staff. (Illus.). 165p. 1983. spiral bdg. 50.00 o.p. (ISBN 0-918989-03-5). Tech Tran Consult.

Lasers: Operation; Equipment; Practical Application; Design. Coherent, Inc., Laser Division Staff. (Illus.). 1980. text ed. 44.00 o.p. (ISBN 0-07-011593-1). McGraw.

Lasers: The Light Wave of the Future. Allan Maurer. LC 81-7939. (Illus.). 192p. 1982. 12.95 o.p. (ISBN 0-668-05298-8, 5298). Arco.

Lashtrow: Nevada Queen High. Roe Richmond. (Lashtrow Ser.). 208p. 1985. pap. 2.25 o.p. (Pub. by Leisure Bks CT). Dorchester Pub Co.

Laska: Adventures with a Wolfdog. Ronald Rood. 1980. 10.95 o.p. (ISBN 0-393-01360-X). Norton.

Lasseter: The Making of a Legend. Billy Marshall-Stoneking. (Illus.). 240p. 1985. 24.95 o.p. (ISBN 0-86861-609-5). Unwin Hyman.

Lasso Your Heart. Betty Cavanna. (gr. 6-9). 1952. 5.50 o.s.i. (ISBN 0-664-32089-9, Westminster). Westminster John Knox.

Last Alien. Steven Charles. (Private School Ser.: No. 6). (YA) (gr. 7 up). 1987. pap. 2.50 o.p. (ISBN 0-671-60331-0). Archway.

Last American Frontier. Frederic L. Paxson. LC 75-115693. (Illus.). 402p. 1970. Repr. of 1910 ed. lib. bdg. 21.50x o.p. (ISBN 0-8154-0324-0). Cooper Sq.

Last American Revolution: Confessions of A Dead Politician. Robert Fox. 260p. 1987. 9.95 o.p. (ISBN 0-317-64475-0). December Pr.

Last Assassin. Daniel Easterman. LC 84-18711. 432p. 1985. 16.95 o.p. (ISBN 0-385-19794-2). Doubleday.

Last Battle. C. S. Lewis. (Chronicles of Narnia Ser.: Vol. 7). 254p. 1986. 13.95 o.p. (ISBN 0-8161-4095-2, Large Print Bks). G K Hall.

Last Beautiful Days of Autumn. John Nichols. 1982. 26.95 o.p. (ISBN 0-03-059254-2); pap. 16.95 o.p. (ISBN 0-03-059253-4, Owl Bks). H Holt & Co.

Last Best Hope. Tauber. 1977. 10.95 o.p. (ISBN 0-15-148377-9). HarBraceJ.

Last Blossom on the Plum Tree. Brooke Astor. LC 84-42511. 224p. 1986. 16.45 o.s.i. (ISBN 0-394-53716-5). Random.

Last Bull Market. Robert Sobel. 1980. 13.95 o.p. (ISBN 0-393-01309-X). Norton.

Last Call. Bill Ransom. (Illus.). 1983. pap. 4.25 o.p. (ISBN 0-911287-03-5). Blue Begonia.

Last Call for H.M.S. Edinburgh. Frank Pearce. LC 81-70059. (Illus.). 256p. 1982. 14.95 o.p. (ISBN 0-689-11277-7, Atheneum). Macmillan.

Last Castle. George MacDonald. 288p. 1986. pap. 5.95 o.p. (ISBN 0-89693-267-2). Victor Bks.

Last Chance: Tombstone's Early Years. John M. Myers. LC 50-5638. (Illus.). 266p. 1973. pap. 6.50 o.p. (ISBN 0-8032-5780-5, BB 569, Bison). U of Nebr Pr.

Last Cold-War Cowboy. James P. Sloan. 272p. 1988. pap. 3.50 o.p. (ISBN 1-55547-252-4). Critics Choice Paper.

Last Corsair. Dan Van Der Vat. (Illus.). 288p. 1985. pap. 5.95 o.p. (ISBN 0-586-06265-3, Pub. by Granada England). Academy Chi Pubs.

Last Crime. John Domatilla. LC 80-20650. 1981. 8.95 o.p. (ISBN 0-689-11121-5, Atheneum). Macmillan.

Last Dalai Lama: A Biography. Michael H. Goodman. LC 85-27906. 364p. 1986. 22.50 o.p. (ISBN 0-87773-355-4, 55246-6). Shambhala Pubns.

Last Days of Alfred Hitchcock. David Freeman. LC 84-42672. (Illus.). 280p. 1984. 18.95 o.p. (ISBN 0-87951-984-3). Overlook Pr.

Last Days of America. Paul E. Erdman. (General Ser.). 1982. lib. bdg. 17.95 o.p. (ISBN 0-8161-3349-2, Large Print Bks). G K Hall.

Last Days of America. Paul E. Erdman. 1981. 13.95 o.p. (ISBN 0-671-24248-2). S&S.

Last Days of Louisiana Red. Ishmael Reed. 1976. pap. 3.50 o.p. (ISBN 0-380-00736-3, 62950-X, Bard). Avon.

Last Days of Mash. Arlene Alda & Alan Alda. (Illus.). 128p. 1984. pap. 9.95 o.p. (ISBN 0-88101-008-1). Unicorn Pub.

Last Days of Shelley & Byron. Morpurgo. (Illus.). 200p. 1952. (ISBN 0-8022-1152-6). Philos Lib.

Last Days of the Farmer: A Personal Account. Gene Logsdon. 320p. 1989. 18.95 o.p. (ISBN 0-86547-377-3). N Point Pr.

Last Deal. Laurence Gonzales. LC 81-66017. 1981. 13.95 o.p. (ISBN 0-689-11199-1, Atheneum). Macmillan.

Last Ditch. Louis MacNiece. 52p. 1971. Repr. of 1940 ed. 15.00x o.p. (ISBN 0-7165-1389-7, BBA 02067, Pub. by Cuala Press Ireland). Biblio Dist.

Last Elegant Bear. Dennis Kyte. (Illus.). 1983. pap. 10.95 o.s.i. (ISBN 0-671-47442-1, Little Simon). S&S.

Last Empire: Photography in British India 1855-1911. Clark Worswick. LC 76-21208. (Illus.). 152p. 1976. 25.00 o.p. (ISBN 0-912334-86-X); pap. 15.00 o.p. (ISBN 0-89381-018-5). Aperture.

Last Entrepreneurs: America's Regional Wars for Jobs & Dollars. Robert Goodman. 350p. pap. 8.00 o.p. (ISBN 0-89608-145-1). South End Pr.

Last European Peace Conference: Paris 1946-Conflict of Values, Vol. 10. Stephen Kertesz. Ed. by Kenneth W. Thompson. (The Credibility of Institions, Policies & Leadership). 204p. (Orig.). 1985. lib. bdg. 26.25 o.p. (ISBN 0-8191-4420-7, Co-pub. by White Miller Center); pap. 12.25 o.p. (ISBN 0-8191-4421-5). U Pr of Amer.

Last Eve. Gail White. LC 85-91011. 160p. 1985. 10.00 o.p. (ISBN 0-682-40244-3). Exposition-Phoenix.

Last Exit to Brooklyn. Hubert Selby, Jr. 1965. pap. 2.95 o.p. (ISBN 0-394-17467-4, B313, BC). Grove.

Last Exit to Brooklyn: A Novel. Hubert Selby, Jr. LC 85-45940. 320p. 1986. pap. 3.95 o.p. (ISBN 0-394-62182-4, BC). Grove.

Last Fall. Bruce Stolbov. LC 86-24398. (Science Fiction Ser.). 192p. 1987. 12.95 o.p. (ISBN 0-385-23028-1). Doubleday.

Last Fix: Dan Russell & the World That Lost Him. Ellen Russell. LC 70-160409. 256p. 1971. 7.95 o.p. (ISBN 0-15-148480-5). HarBraceJ.

Last Flight. Earhart. 1968. pap. 0.75 o.p. (ISBN 0-15-649410-8, Harv). HarBraceJ.

Last Flight. David Hess. 1974. 4.50 o.p. (ISBN 0-682-48067-3). Exposition-Phoenix.

Last Flight. Myrick Land. 160p. 1975. 6.95 o.p. (ISBN 0-393-08717-4). Norton.

Last Free Bird. A. Harris Stone. (Illus.). (ps-3). 1972. 1.50 o.p. (ISBN 0-13-523985-0); PLB 5.95 o.p. (ISBN 0-13-523993-1). P-H.

Last Hero. Leslie Charteris. (Saint Ser.). (Illus.). 317p. 1982. pap. 2.50 o.p. (ISBN 0-441-74917-8). Ace Bks.

Last Immortal. J. O. Jeppson. 1980. 9.95 o.p. (ISBN 0-395-28949-1). HM.

Last James Dean Book. Alighieri Dante. LC 84-60616. (Illus.). 64p. (Orig.). 1984. pap. 12.95 o.p. (ISBN 0-688-03927-8, Quill NY). Morrow.

Last Jews in Berlin. Bernard Gross. 1982. 14.95 o.s.i. (ISBN 0-671-24727-1). S&S.

Last Jews of Radauti. Ayse Gursan-Salzmann & Laurence Salzmann. LC 82-22176. (Illus.). 192p. 1983. 29.95 o.p. (ISBN 0-385-27808-X, Dial). Doubleday.

Last Judgment in Sixteenth Century Northern Europe: a Study of the Relation Between Art & the Reformation. Craig Harbison. LC 75-23793. (Outstanding Dissertations in the Fine Arts - 16th Century). (Illus.). 437p. 1976. lib. bdg. 55.00 o.p. (ISBN 0-8240-1988-1). Garland Pub.

Last Junior Year. Barbara Morgenroth. LC 78-2750. (gr. 5-9). 1978. 6.95 o.p. (ISBN 0-689-30663-6, Atheneum). Macmillan.

Last Laugh. S. J. Perelman. 1982. pap. 4.80 o.p. (ISBN 0-671-42516-1, Touchstone Bks). S&S.

Last Laugh, Mr. Moto. John P. Marquand. 1986. pap. 4.95 o.p. (ISBN 0-316-54705-0). Little.

Last Letters of Resistance: Farewells from the Bonhoeffer Family. Ed. by Eberhard Bethge & Renate Bethge. Tr. by Dennis Slabaugh. LC 85-45504. 128p. 1986. pap. 7.95 o.p. (ISBN 0-8006-1884-X, 1-1884, Fortress). Augsburg Fortress.

Last Little Citadel: American High Schools since 1940. Robert L. Hampel. (Study of High Schools Ser.: Vol. 3). 217p. 1986. 15.45 o.p. (ISBN 0-395-36451-5). HM.

Last Loud Cry. William B. Engle. LC 86-91261. (Illus.). 448p. 1986. text ed. 24.95 o.p. (ISBN 0-682-40305-9, Testament). Exposition-Phoenix.

Last Magic. N. Richard Nash. LC 78-55022. 1978. 10.95 o.p. (ISBN 0-689-10905-9, Atheneum). Macmillan.

Last Man on Earth. Ed. by Isaac Asimov & Martin H. Greenberg. (Orig.). 1982. pap. 2.95 o.p. (ISBN 0-449-24531-4, Crest). Fawcett.

Last Moments of a World. Margaret Gaan. (Illus.). 288p. 1981. pap. 4.95 o.p. (ISBN 0-393-00066-4). Norton.

Last Moments of a World. Margaret Gaan. (Illus.). 1978. 9.95 o.p. (ISBN 0-393-05657-0). Norton.

Last Monster. Jane Annixter & Paul Annixter. LC 80-7978. (gr. 4-6). 1980. 6.95 o.p. (ISBN 0-15-243614-6, HJ). HarBraceJ.

Last Museum. Brion Gysin. 192p. 1986. pap. 7.95 o.s.i. (ISBN 0-394-62263-4, Ever). Grove.

Last Navigator. Stephen D. Thomas. (Illus.). 304p. 1987. 22.95 o.p. (ISBN 0-8050-0096-8). H Holt & Co.

Last Night I Dreamed: Twenty One Short Plays. Richard Urdahl. LC 74-76919. (Open Book Ser). (Illus.). 80p. 1974. pap. 1.00x o.p. (ISBN 0-8006-0159-9, Fortress). Augsburg Fortress.

Last of a Breed: Portrait of Working Cowboys. Ed. by Barbara Rodriguez. (Illus.). 175p. 1983. 35.00 o.p. (ISBN 0-932012-50-7). Texas Month Pr.

Last of a Breed: Portraits of Working Cowboys. Martin H. Schreiber. LC 87-47910. 104p. 1988. pap. 17.95 o.p. (ISBN 0-553-34528-1). Bantam.

Last of the Bohemians: Twenty Years with Leon-Paul Fargue. Andre Beucler. Tr. by Geoffrey Sainsbury. LC 79-108841. 1971. Repr. of 1954 ed. lib. bdg. 35.00x o.p. (ISBN 0-8371-3729-2, BEBO). Greenwood.

Last of the Bush Pilots. Harmon Helmericks. 395p. 1987. pap. text ed. 9.95 o.s.i. (ISBN 0-935704-27-2). Howe Brothers.

Last of the Dragons. E. Nesbit. LC 79-28584. (Illus.). 32p. (gr. k-4). 1980. text ed. 8.95 o.p. (ISBN 0-07-046285-2). McGraw.

Last of the Fathers: Saint Bernard of Clairvaux & the Encyclical Letter, Doctor Mellifluus. Thomas Merton. Repr. of 1954 ed. lib. bdg. 35.00x o.p. (ISBN 0-8371-4434-5, MELF). Greenwood.

Last of the Great Stations. Bill Bradley. Ed. by Jim Walker. LC 79-84387. (Special Ser.: No. 72). (Illus.). 1979. pap. 13.95 o.p. (ISBN 0-916374-36-X). Interurban.

Last of the Mohicans. James Fenimore Cooper. LC 76-13132. (Illus.). (gr. 7 up). 1976. 7.95 o.p. (ISBN 0-679-20372-9). McKay.

Last of the Mohicans. James Fenimore Cooper. (Illus.). 414p. 1984. 12.95 o.s.i. (ISBN 0-396-08260-2). Dodd.

Last of the Mohicans. James Fenimore Cooper. LC 84-61431. (Illus.). 432p. 1984. 12.95 o.p. (ISBN 0-89577-199-3). RD Assn.

Last of the Panzers: German Tanks 1944-1945. William Auerbach. (Illus.). 64p. 1984. pap. 9.95 o.p. (ISBN 0-85368-632-7, Pub. by Arms & Armour Pr). Sterling.

Last of the Sailormen. Bob Roberts. (Illus.). 166p. 1985. pap. 15.00 o.p. (ISBN 0-317-62994-8). Saifer.

Last of the Three Foot Loggers. Allan Kreig. LC 63-2212. (Illus.). 96p. 16.95 o.p. (ISBN 0-87095-014-2). Gldn West Bks.

Last Outlaw. Lawrence Cortesi. (Orig.). 1980. pap. (ISBN 0-505-51560-1, Pub. by Tower Bks). Dorchester Pub Co.

Last President. Michael Kurland & S. W. Barton. 356p. 1988. pap. 3.95 o.p. (ISBN 1-55547-248-6). Critics Choice Paper.

Last Prima Donnas. Lanfranco Rasponi. LC 82-47820. 1982. 22.50 o.s.i. (ISBN 0-394-52153-6). Knopf.

Last Prophet. William T. Whitsitt. 1980. pap. 3.00 o.p. (ISBN 0-937984-00-0). Broadside Pr.

Last Pursuit. George F. Croffoot. LC 86-913440. 1986. 15.00 o.p. (ISBN 0-682-40319-9). Exposition-Phoenix.

Last Quadrant. Meira Chand. LC 81-14400. 204p. 1982. 11.45 o.p. (ISBN 0-89919-079-0). Ticknor & Fields.

Last Resorts: A Novel. Carle Boylan. 288p. 1986. 16.45 o.s.i. (ISBN 0-671-54998-7). Summit Bks.

Last Reveille. David Morrell. 1978. pap. 1.95 o.s.i. (ISBN 0-449-23527-0, Crest). Fawcett.

Last Rites: The Death of William Saroyan. Aram Saroyan. (Illus.). 176p. 1984. pap. text ed. 10.00 o.p. (ISBN 0-688-01262-0, Quill NY); pap. 5.70 o.p. (ISBN 0-688-02146-8). Morrow.

Last Romance. Erica Abeel. 288p. 1985. pap. 6.95 o.p. (ISBN 0-380-89672-9). Avon.

Last Romantic. Martin Birnbaum. 1960. 14.95x o.p. New Coll U Pr.

Last Romantic: A Biography of Queen Marie of Roumania. Hannah Pakula. (Illus.). 536p. 1985. 22.45 o.p. (ISBN 0-671-46364-0). S&S.

Last Seen Alive. Dorothy Simpson. (Luke Thanet Mystery Ser.). 224p. 1985. 13.95 o.s.i. (ISBN 0-684-18435-4, ScribT). Scribner.

Last Sitting. Bert Stern & Pat Golbitz. LC 82-6350. (Illus.). 192p. 1982. 30.00 o.p. (ISBN 0-688-01173-X). Morrow.

Last Spartans. Larry Ferazani. LC 85-71764. (Illus.). 150p. 1985. 14.95 o.p. (ISBN 0-933341-09-1). Quinlan Pr.

Last Stands: Notes from Memory. H. Masters. 216p. 1983. pap. text ed. 6.95 o.p. (ISBN 0-07-040786-X). McGraw.

Last Stuarts: British Royalty in Exile. James Lees-Milne. (Illus.). 256p. 1984. 17.95 o.p. (ISBN 0-684-18147-9, ScribT). Scribner.

Last Summer's Smugglers. Sesyle Joslin. LC 72-88170. (Illus.). 160p. (gr. 4-7). 1973. 4.75 o.p. (ISBN 0-15-243620-0, HJ). HarBraceJ.

Last Temptation: A Novel of Treason. David Mure. 1987. 17.95 o.p. (ISBN 0-907675-16-6, Pub. by Buchan & Enright England). Seven Hills Bk Dists.

Last Things. Robert Hicks & Richard Bewes. (Understanding Bible Truth Ser.). (Orig.). 1981. pap. 1.50 o.p. (ISBN 0-89840-020-1). Heres Life.

Last Town. Norman Marion. 1979. pap. 1.75 o.p. (ISBN 0-8439-0659-6, Pub. by Leisure Bks CT). Dorchester Pub Co.

Last Trail. Zane Grey. 256p. 1981. pap. 2.25 o.p. (ISBN 0-505-51761-2, Pub. by Tower Bks). Dorchester Pub Co.

Last Trial: On the Legend & Lore of the Command to Abraham to Offer Isaac As a Sacrifice - the Akedah. Shalom Spiegel. LC 79-12664. (Jewish Legacy Ser.). 1979. pap. 7.95x o.p. (ISBN 0-87441-290-0). Behrman.

Last Viking: A Fable. Alfred E. Morris. 1977. 4.50 o.p. (ISBN 0-682-48738-4). Exposition-Phoenix.

Last Voyage of Odysseus: A Novel. Karen L. Carey. LC 82-3970. (Illus.). xii, 187p. 1983. text ed. 16.95x o.p. (ISBN 0-8214-0683-3); pap. 9.95 o.p. (ISBN 0-8214-0749-X). Ohio U Pr.

Last Voyage of Thomas Cavendish, 1591-1592. Thomas Cavendish. Ed. by David B. Quinn. LC 74-11619. (Studies in the History of Discoveries Ser). x, 166p. 1976. lib. bdg. 39.95x o.s.i. (ISBN 0-226-09819-2). U of Chicago Pr.

Last Wild Horse. Morris Weeks. LC 77-13392. (Illus.). (gr. 7 up). 1977. 6.95 o.s.i. (ISBN 0-395-25838-3). HM.

Last Wish. Betty Rollin. 1985. 15.45 o.p. (ISBN 0-671-52597-2, Linden Pr). S&S.

Last Wish. Betty Rollin. (General Ser.). 309p. 1986. lib. bdg. 15.95 o.p. (ISBN 0-8161-4062-6, Large Print Bks). G K Hall.

Last Word: Exploring Careers in Contemporary Communication. The Fashion Group Inc., Members & Friends Staff. Ed. by Regina Ovesy. 128p. (gr. 7-12). 1983. lib. bdg. 9.97 o.p. (ISBN 0-8239-0526-8). Rosen Group.

Titles

Last Words of Dutch Schultz. William S. Burroughs. LC 80-54557. (Illus.). 128p. 1981. pap. 4.95 o.p. (ISBN 0-394-17852-1). Seaver Bks.
Last World War & the End of Time. Emmett J. Culligan. (Illus.). 210p. 1981. pap. 6.00 o.s.i. (ISBN 0-89555-034-2). TAN Bks Pubs.
Last Writings, Preliminary Studies for Part Two Philosophical Investigations. Ludwig Wittgenstein. Tr. by C. G. Luckhardt & Maximilian A. E. Aue. LC 82-42549. 256p. 1982. 28.50x o.s.i. (ISBN 0-226-90445-8). U of Chicago Pr.
Last Year at Marienbad: Text for the Film by Alain Resnais. Alain Robbe-Grillet. Tr. by Richard Howard from Fr. (Illus.). 1962. pap. 4.95 o.s.i. (ISBN 0-394-17234-5, E320, Ever). Grove.
Last Year's Nightingale. Claire Lorrimer. 400p. 1988. 22.95 o.p. (ISBN 0-7126-0368-9, Pub. by Century Hutchinson). David & Charles.
Last Years of British Railways Steam: Reflections Ten Years After. O. S. Nock. 1978. 22.95 o.p. (ISBN 0-7153-7583-0). David & Charles.
Last Years of French Louisiana. Marc De Villiers du Terrage. Ed. by Carl A. Brasseaux & Glenn R. Conrad. Tr. by Hosea Phillips. LC 82-73751. 525p. 20.00x o.p. (ISBN 0-940984-05-9). U of SW LA Ctr LA Studies.
Last Years of Napoleon. Ralph Korngold. LC 74-12578. (Illus.). 429p. 1974. Repr. of 1959 ed. lib. bdg. 24.50x o.p. (ISBN 0-8371-7725-1, KONA). Greenwood.
Last Years of Thomas Jefferson, 1809-1826. Esther Wilcox Kuenzli. LC 74-21443. 1974. 5.50 o.p. (ISBN 0-682-48168-8, University). Exposition-Phoenix.
Lasting Words of Jesus. Howard W. Roberts. LC 85-12288. 1986. pap. 4.95 o.p. (ISBN 0-8054-2257-9). Broadman.
Late Baroque Churches of Venice. Douglas Lewis. LC 78-94704. (Outstanding Dissertations in the Fine Arts Ser.). 1979. lib. bdg. 63.00 o.p. (ISBN 0-8240-3236-5). Garland Pub.
Late Bloomer. David A. Kaufelt. pap. 2.50 o.p. (ISBN 0-440-15320-4). Dell.
Late Bloomer. David A. Kaufelt. LC 79-4591. 1979. 8.95 o.p. (ISBN 0-15-148792-8). HarBraceJ.
Late Bloomers: How to Achieve Your Potential at Any Age. Carol Colman & Michael Perelman. 224p. 1985. 15.95 o.p. (ISBN 0-02-527320-5). Macmillan.
Late Gothic to Renaissance Painters. John Canaday. 1972. pap. 4.95 o.p. (ISBN 0-393-00664-6, Norton Lib). Norton.
Late Great Dick Hart. Bernal C. Payne, Jr. LC 86-10537. 144p. (YA) (gr. 5 up). 1986. 12.70 o.s.i. (ISBN 0-395-41453-9). HM.
Late Great Pennsylvania Station. Lorraine B. Diehl. LC 85-3988. (Illus.). 168p. 1985. 19.95 o.p. (ISBN 0-8281-1181-2, Dist. by H M). Am Heritage.
Late Hour. Mark Strand. LC 77-88904. 1978. 6.95 o.p. (ISBN 0-689-10879-6, Atheneum); pap. 6.95 o.s.i. (ISBN 0-689-10977-6, Atheneum). Macmillan.
Late Innings: A New Baseball Companion. Roger Angell. 1982. 17.95 o.p. (ISBN 0-671-42567-6). S&S.
Late Night Thoughts on Listening to Mahler's Ninth Symphony. Lewis Thomas. (General Ser.). 1984. lib. bdg. 13.95 o.p. (ISBN 0-8161-3721-8, Large Print Bks). G K Hall.
Late Saxon & Viking Art. Thomas D. Kendrick. LC 49-4888. 152p. 1949. Repr. 39.00x o.p. (ISBN 0-403-08936-0). Somerset Pub.
Late Seventeenth Century Scientists. Ed. by D. Hutchings. 1969. pap. 13.75 o.p. (ISBN 0-08-013358-4). Pergamon.
Lateinische Osterfeiern und Osterspiele. Ed. by Walther Lipphardt. LC 74-80629. (Ausgaben Deutscher Literatur des XV. bis XVIII Jahrhunderts, Reihe Drama: Vol. 5). 1452p. (Ger.). 1975. 73.60x o.p. (ISBN 3-11-006742-0). De Gruyter.
Lateinische Ubersetzung der Didache. Teaching of the Twelve Apostles Staff. 142p. Repr. of 1913 ed. 12.00 o.p. (ISBN 0-384-59780-7). Johnson Repr.
Latent Image: The Discovery of Photography. Beaumont Newhall. LC 83-10494. 160p. 1983. pap. 10.95x o.p. (ISBN 0-8263-0673-X). U Of NM Pr.
Later Adventures of Tom Jones. Bob Coleman. 1985. 15.45 o.p. (ISBN 0-671-54643-0, Linden Pr). S&S.
Later Criminal Careers. Sheldon S. Glueck & Eleanor T. Glueck. 1937. 23.00 o.p. (ISBN 0-527-34088-X). Kraus Repr.
Later Life. 2nd ed. Lewis R. Aiken. 1982. text ed. 26.95 o.p. (ISBN 0-03-059751-X). HR&W.
Later Life: The Realities of Aging. Harold G. Cox. (Illus.). 480p. 1984. text ed. (ISBN 0-13-524157-X). P-H.
Later Middle Ages: From the Norman Conquest to the Eve of the Reformation. J. C. Dickinson. (Ecclesiastical History of England Ser.). 487p. 1979. text ed. 30.00x o.p. (ISBN 0-06-491678-2). B&N Imports.
Later Renaissance in England: Nondramatic Verse & Prose, 1600-1660. Ed. by Herschel Baker. 1975. text ed. 26.50 o.p. (ISBN 0-395-16038-3). HM.
Later Work of Aubrey Beardsley. Aubrey Beardsley. (Illus.). 14.00 o.p. (ISBN 0-8446-1617-6). Peter Smith.
Lateralisation of Language in the Child: Proceedings of the International Symposium, St. Ode, Belgium, Oct. 1-3, 1979. Ed. by Yvan Lebrun & O. Zangwill. (Neurolinguistics Ser.: Vol. 10). 1981. text ed. 37.25 o.p. (ISBN 90-265-0337-7, Pub. by Swets & Zeitlinger Netherlands). CJ Hogrefe Pubs.
Lathe Operations. Richard R. Kibbe. LC 84-11797. 236p. 1985. pap. 17.95 o.p. (ISBN 0-471-89023-5). Wiley.
Latin: A Historical & Linguistic Handbook. Mason Hammond. 272p. 1976. 24.50x o.s.i. (ISBN 0-674-51290-1); pap. text ed. 8.95x o.s.i. (ISBN 0-674-51289-8). Harvard U Pr.
Latin America. Tad Szulc. LC 65-27528. (New York Times Byline Books). (Orig.). 1966. pap. 2.95 o.p. (ISBN 0-689-10266-6, Atheneum). Macmillan.
Latin America: A Survey of Holdings at the Hoover Institution on War, Revolution & Peace. Joseph W. Bingaman. LC 78-142949. (Library Survey Ser.: No. 5). 96p. 1972. pap. 3.00x o.p. (ISBN 0-8179-5052-4). Hoover Inst Pr.
Latin America & the Caribbean see Developing Areas: A Classed Bibliography of the Joint Bank-Fund Library, World Bank Group & International Monetary Fund.
Latin America in English-Language Reference Books: A Selected, Annotated Bibliography. Ed. by Ann H. Graham & Richard D. Woods. LC 80-28880. 56p. 1981. pap. text ed. 7.75 o.p. (ISBN 0-87111-267-1). SLA.
Latin America in Maps see Historical Atlas of Latin America: Political, Geographic, Economic, Cultural.
Latin America in the Post-Import Substitution Era. Werner Baer & Larry Samuelson. 1977. pap. 25.00 o.p. (ISBN 0-08-021822-9). Pergamon.
Latin America in the Struggle Against Imperialism, for National Independence, Democracy, People's Welfare, Peace & Socialism. 1975. pap. 0.40 o.s.i. (ISBN 0-87898-117-9). New Outlook.
Latin America: Myth & Reality. Peter Nehemkis. LC 77-2958. 1977. Repr. of 1964 ed. lib. bdg. 35.00x o.p. (ISBN 0-8371-9560-8, NELA). Greenwood.
Latin America: Political Culture & Development. 2nd ed. R. Fitzgibbons & J. Fernandez. 1981. pap. text ed. 29.00 o.p. (ISBN 0-13-524348-3). P-H.
Latin America: The Search for a New International Role. R. G. Hellman & H. J. Rosenbaum. LC 75-692. (Latin American International Affairs Ser.: Vol. 1). 297p. 1975. 18.95x o.p. (ISBN 0-470-36917-5). Halsted Pr.
Latin America: World List of Specialized Periodicals. (Eng. & Fr.). 1974. pap. text ed. 14.00x o.p. (ISBN 0-686-22561-9). Mouton.
Latin American Civilization, 2 vols. 3rd ed. Ed. by Benjamin Keen. (Colonial Origins Ser.). 1974. Vol. 1. pap. 14.95 o.p. (ISBN 0-395-17582-8); Vol. 2. pap. 14.95 o.p. (ISBN 0-395-17583-6). HM.
Latin American Culture Studies: Information & Materials for Teaching about Latin America. 3rd ed. Ed. by Edward Glab, Jr. (Latin American Culture Studies Project Ser.). xi, 466p. 1981. pap. text ed. 9.95x o.p. (ISBN 0-86728-001-8). U TX Inst Lat Am Stud.
Latin American Filmography. Susan J. Higgins. (Latin American Culture Studies Project Ser.). 132p. 1978. pap. text ed. 3.95x o.p. (ISBN 0-86728-011-5). U TX Inst Lat Am Stud.
Latin American Policy of the U. S. Samuel F. Bemis. (Illus.). 1967. pap. 3.45 o.p. (ISBN 0-393-00412-0, Norton Lib). Norton.
Latin American Politics & Development. Howard Wiarda & Harvey F. Kline. LC 78-56434. (Illus.). 1979. text ed. 26.50 o.p. (ISBN 0-395-27056-1). HM.
Latin American Populism in Comparative Perspective. Ed. by Michael Conniff. LC 80-54572. 270p. 1985. 24.95 o.p. (ISBN 0-8263-0580-6); pap. 12.95x o.p. (ISBN 0-8263-0581-4). U of NM Pr.
Latin American Research & Publications at the University of Texas at Austin, 1893-1969. Institute of Latin American Studies Staff. (Institute of Latin American Studies Guides & Bibliographies Ser.: No. 3). 197p. 1971. 9.95x o.p. (ISBN 0-292-74600-8); pap. 3.75x o.p. (ISBN 0-292-74601-6). U of Tex Pr.
Latin American Spanish for Travellers. Berlitz Editors. (Travellers Series for English Speakers). 1972. pap. 2.95 o.p. (ISBN 0-02-964130-6, Berlitz); cassettepak 10.95 o.p. (ISBN 0-02-962130-5); 8-track cartridgepak, 1973 10.95 o.p. (ISBN 0-02-968130-8). Macmillan.
Latin Americans: Past & Present. Helen M. Bailey et al. LC 78-174553. (Illus.). 392p. (gr. 9-12). 1972. pap. 9.88 o.p. (ISBN 0-395-13373-4, 2-02850). HM.
Latin Can Be Fun. George Cappellanus. Tr. by Peter Needham. (Lat.). 1977. 7.95x o.p. (ISBN 0-285-62161-0, Pub. by Souvenir Pr). Intl Spec Bk.
Latin Crossword Puzzle Book. John K. Colby. (gr. 9-12). text ed. 2.00x o.p. (ISBN 0-88334-045-3). Ind Sch Pr.
Latin-English Dictionary of St. Thomas Aquinas. Roy J. Deferrari. 1115p. 1988. pap. 17.95 o.p. (ISBN 0-317-67490-0, MS0320). Dghtrs St Paul.
Latin Hexametre Verse. Samuel E. Winbolt. Ed. by Steele Commager. LC 77-70818. (Latin Poetry Ser.). 1978. lib. bdg. 33.00 o.p. (ISBN 0-8240-2982-8). Garland Pub.
Latin Literature. W. A. Laidlaw. 1952. (ISBN 0-8022-0902-5). Philos Lib.
Latino Families in the United States: A Resourcebook for Family Life Education. Ed. by Sally J. Andrade. LC 82-22321. (Illus.). 176p. (Orig., Eng. & Span.). 1983. pap. text ed. 2.00 o.p. (ISBN 0-934586-10-1). Plan Parent.
Latinoamerica: Su Civilizacion y Su Cultura. Eugenio C. Rodriquez. 432p. 1983. pap. text ed. 14.00 o.p. (ISBN 0-88377-300-7). Newbury Hse.
Latinos in the United States: The Sacred & the Political. David T. Abalos. LC 85-41010. 240p. 1987. text ed. 21.95x o.s.i. (ISBN 0-268-01277-6). U of Notre Dame Pr.
Latrobe, Jefferson, & the National Capitol. Paul F. Norton. LC 76-23662. (Outstanding Dissertations in the Fine Arts Ser.). (Illus.). 430p. 1977. lib. bdg. 68.00 o.p. (ISBN 0-8240-2716-7). Garland Pub.
Latter Days. Dorothea Condry. 12p. 1980. pap. 1.00 o.p. (ISBN 0-686-27506-3). Samisdat.
Lattice Theory. T. Donnellan. LC 67-28661. 1968. 75.00 o.p. (ISBN 0-08-012563-8); pap. 75.00 o.p. (ISBN 0-08-012562-X). Pergamon.
Laugh & Love. Milton Hildebrand. (Illus.). 1979. 7.50 o.p. (ISBN 0-682-49237-X). Exposition-Phoenix.
Laugh-It's Good for the Jaws. Ted M. Donald. 1985. 10.95 o.p. (ISBN 0-533-06534-8). Vantage.
Laugh off the Pounds. Lo Linkert. (Illus.). 1980. pap. 4.95 o.p. (ISBN 0-89149-059-0). Jolex.
Laugh with Health. Manfred Koch. 1984. pap. 10.95 o.p. (ISBN 0-03-071308-0). H Holt & Co.
Laugh with Your Teenager. Byron W. Arledge. 128p. 1985. pap. 4.95 o.p. (ISBN 0-8423-2102-0). Tyndale.
Laughing at Gravity: Conversations with Isaac Newton. Elizabeth A. Socolow. LC 87-42846. (Barnard New Women Poets Ser.). 188p. 1988. 22.50 o.p. (ISBN 0-8070-6804-7); pap. 9.95 o.p. (ISBN 0-8070-6805-5, BP 771). Beacon Pr.
Laughing Boy. Oliver La Farge. 1929. 12.95 o.p.; pap. 6.95 o.p. (ISBN 0-395-08383-4, SenEd). HM.
Laughing Last: Alger Hiss. Tony Hiss. 1977. 8.95 o.p. (ISBN 0-395-24899-X). HM.
Laughing Out Loud & Other Religious Experiences. Tom Mullen. 1983. 8.95 o.p. (ISBN 0-8499-0329-7). Word Bks.
Laughter in the Second Act. Donald Sinden. (Illus.). 217p. 1985. 24.95 o.p. (ISBN 0-340-28540-0, Pub. by Hodder & Stoughton UK). David & Charles.
Launching of Linda Bell. William F. Hallstead. LC 81-47531. 156p. (YA) 1981. 10.95 o.p. (ISBN 0-15-243685-5, HJ). HarBraceJ.
Laura. Vera Caspary. 224p. 1981. pap. 1.95 o.p. (ISBN 0-380-00043-1, 51565-1). Avon.
Laura. Vera Caspary. 1977. Repr. of 1943 ed. lib. bdg. 21.95x o.p. (ISBN 0-89244-066-X). Queens Hse-Focus Serv.
Laura, Alice's New Puppy. Philippe Dumas. (Illus.). 64p. (ps-3). 1979. 11.95 o.p. (ISBN 0-575-02568-9, Pub. by Gollancz England). David & Charles.
Laura Ashley: Home Furnishings. Laura Ashley. 1983. pap. 3.00 o.p. (ISBN 0-517-54964-6, Harmony). Crown.
Laura Ashley Home Furnishings Catalog: 1985. Laura Ashley. 1985. pap. 4.00 o.p. (ISBN 0-517-55582-4, Harmony). Crown.
Laura Cereta: Quattrocento Humanist. Albert Rabil, Jr. LC 81-183309. (Medieval & Renaissance Texts & Studies: Vol. 3). 190p. 1981. 14.00 o.p. (ISBN 0-86698-002-4); pap. 10.00 o.p. (ISBN 0-86698-007-5). Medieval & Renaissance NY.
Laura Ingalls Wilder: Pioneer & Author. William Anderson. (Illus.). 54p. 1987. 7.95 o.s.i. Anderson MI.
Laura Jordan. Dennis Higman. 448p. (Orig.). 1982. pap. 3.25 o.p. (ISBN 0-505-51769-8, Pub. by Leisure Bks CT). Dorchester Pub Co.
Laura Riding: A Bibliography. Joyce Wexler. LC 80-8481. 1981. lib. bdg. 39.00 o.p. (ISBN 0-8240-9476-X). Garland Pub.
Laura Z: A Life. Laura Z. Hobson. (Illus.). 420p. 1983. 17.95 o.p. (ISBN 0-87795-524-7, Arbor Hse). Morrow.
Laurel Line: An Anthracite Region Railway. James Henwood & John Muncie. LC 86-909. (Interurbans Special Ser.: No. 103). (Illus.). 208p. 1986. 34.95 o.p. (ISBN 0-916374-72-6). Interurban.
Lauren's Secret Ring. Monica DeBruyn. Ed. by Ann Fay. LC 79-27261. (Albert Whitman Concept Bks.: Level 1). (Illus.). (gr. 1-3). 1980. PLB 10.75 o.p. (ISBN 0-8075-4391-8). A Whitman.
Laurie Anderson: Works from 1969-1983. Janet Kardon et al. (Illus.). 96p. 1983. pap. 18.00 o.p. (ISBN 0-88454-033-2). U of Pa Contemp Art.
Laurie McBain, 3 vols. 1981. Set. pap. 8.85 o.p. (ISBN 0-380-78410-6). Avon.
Lauro Olmo: La Camisa. Ed. by A. K. Ariza & I. F. Ariza. 1968. text ed. 9.75 o.s.i. (ISBN 0-08-012616-2); pap. text ed. 3.50 o.s.i. (ISBN 0-08-012615-4). Pergamon.
Lavalite World. Philip Jose Farmer. (World of Tiers Ser.). 288p. 1982. pap. 2.75 o.s.i. (ISBN 0-441-47422-5). Ace Bks.
Lavandar. Sham Zeyadi. LC 84-91282. 97p. 1985. 10.95 o.p. (ISBN 0-533-06362-0). Vantage.
Lavinia Bat. Russell Hoban. LC 84-680. (Ponders Bks.). (Illus.). (ps-2). 1984. 4.95 o.s.i. (ISBN 0-03-069503-1). H Holt & Co.
Lavinia's Cottage: A Pop-Up Story. John S. Goodall. LC 82-71160. (Illus.). 16p. (gr. 1-4). 1983. 8.95 o.s.i. (ISBN 0-689-50257-5, M K McElderry). Macmillan.
Law & Accounts for Executives. Sherring. 1981. pap. 31.95 o.p. (ISBN 0-85258-195-5). Van Nos Reinhold.
Law & Business Directory of Corporate Counsel: 1983-1984 Edition. rev. & enlg. ed. Ed. by Law & Business Inc. Staff. 1546p. 1983. 125.00 o.p. (ISBN 0-15-100030-1, Pub. by Law & Business). HarBraceJ.
Law & Business Directory of Major U. S. Law Firms, 2 vols. Ed. by Law & Business Inc. Staff. 1983. 175.00 o.p. (ISBN 0-15-100031-X, H42930). HarBraceJ.
Law & Economics. Isidore Silver. LC 71-84422. (Real World of Economics Ser.). (Illus.). (gr. 5-11). 1970. PLB 4.95 o.p. (ISBN 0-8225-0619-X). Lerner Pubns.
Law & Economics: An Introductory Analysis. Werner Z. Hirsch. LC 79-51700. (Mathematical Economics, Econometrics & Economic Theory Ser.). 1979. 24.50 o.p. (ISBN 0-12-349480-X). Acad Pr.
Law & Ethics in Counseling. Dean L. Hummel et al. 1984. 36.95 o.p. (ISBN 0-442-23384-1). Van Nos Reinhold.
Law & Ethics in the Medical Office Including Bioethical Issues. Marcia Lewis & Carol D. Warden. LC 82-9993. 227p. 1983. pap. text ed. 13.95x o.p. (ISBN 0-8036-5616-5). Davis Co.
Law & Gospel. Werner Elert. Ed. by Franklin Sherman. Tr. by Edward H. Schroeder from Ger. LC 66-25263. (Facet Bks). 64p. (Orig.). 1967. pap. 1.50 o.p. (ISBN 0-8006-3035-1, 1-3035, Fortress). Augsburg Fortress.
Law & Gospel: A Study for Integrating Faith & Practice. 2nd ed. John W. Montgomery. (Lawyers' Quest IV Ser.). 50p. (Orig.). 1986. pap. text ed. 8.00 o.s.i. (ISBN 0-944561-12-8). Chr Legal.
Law & Legal Information Directory. 4th ed. Ed. by Steven Wasserman & Jacqueline W. O'Brien. 813p. 1986. 285.00x o.p. (ISBN 0-8103-2341-9). Gale.
Law & Liability: A Guide for Nurses. Janine Fiesta. LC 82-13698. 208p. 1983. 17.95 o.p. (ISBN 0-471-07879-4, Pub. by Wiley Med). Wiley.
Law & Liability in Athletics, Physical Education, & Recreation. James A. Baley & David L. Matthews. LC 83-22492. 430p. 1984. write for info. o.p. (ISBN 0-697-06824-2, Pub. by Longwood Div). Wm C Brown.
Law & Logic: A Critical Account of Legal Argument. J. Horovitz. LC 72-76386. (Library of Exact Philosophy: Vol. 8). 240p. 1972. 28.80 o.p. (ISBN 0-387-81066-8). Springer-Verlag.
Law & Morality. Lev I. Petrazhitskii. Tr. by Hugh W. Babb. xlvi, 335p. Repr. of 1955 ed. 37.00 o.p. (ISBN 0-384-45970-6). Johnson Repr.
Law & Morality. D. Don Welch. LC 86-45195. 192p. 1987. pap. text ed. 14.95 o.p. (ISBN 0-8006-1974-9, 1-1974). Augsburg Fortress.

Law & Morality. Don Welch. LC 86-45195. 1987. 7.95 o.p. (ISBN 0-8006-1776-2, Fortress). Augsburg Fortress.

Law & Order: The Scales of Justice. rev. 2nd. ed. Ed. by Abraham S. Blumberg. LC 72-87667. 188p. 1970. text ed. 0.00o.p. (ISBN 0-87855-050-X); pap. text ed. 6.95x o.p. (ISBN 0-87855-543-9). Transaction Pubs.

Law & Politics in the Middle Ages: An Introduction to the Sources of Medieval Political Ideas. Walter Ullmann. LC 74-19415. (Sources of History Ser.). 320p. 1975. 32.50x o.p. (ISBN 0-8014-0940-3). Cornell U Pr.

Law & Politics of Abortion. Ed. by Carl Schneider & Maris A. Vinovskis. LC 79-3134. 320p. 1980. 22.00x o.p. (ISBN 0-669-03386-3). Lexington Bks.

Law & Practice Relating to Pollution Control in the Member States of the European Communities: Italy. Commission of the European Communities. 1983. 40.00x o.s.i. (ISBN 0-8448-1447-4, Pub. by Crane Russak & Co). Taylor & Francis.

Law & Psychiatry III: Selected Papers Presented at the Fourth International Congress on Law & Psychiatry, Pembroke College, Oxford England, 19-22 July 1979. Ed. by David N. Weisstub. 100p. 1981. pap. 18.25 o.p. (ISBN 0-08-026113-2). Pergamon.

Law & Responsibility in Warfare: The Vietnam Experience. Ed. by Peter D. Trooboff. LC 74-22431. xiv, 280p. 1975. 26.00x o.p. (ISBN 0-8078-1239-0). U of NC Pr.

Law & Science in Collaboration: Resolving Regulatory Issues of Science & Technology. Ed. by J. D. Nyhart & Milton M. Carrow. LC 81-47689. 320p. 1983. 30.00x o.p. (ISBN 0-669-04907-7). Lexington Bks.

Law & Social Change: Civil Rights Laws & Their Consequences. Harrell R. Rodgers & Charles S. Bullock. (Illus.). 160p. 1972. pap. text ed. 25.95 o.p. (ISBN 0-07-053378-4). McGraw.

Law & Society. Steven Vago. (Ser. in Sociology). (Illus.). 352p. 1981. text ed. (ISBN 0-13-526483-9). P-H.

Law & Society: Essays in the Sociology of Law. Leslie Green. 502p. 1975. text ed. 35.00 o.p. (ISBN 0-379-00307-4). Oceana.

Law & Society in Classical Athens. Richard Garner. 192p. 1987. pap. 32.95 o.p. (ISBN 0-7099-3847-0, Pub. by Croom Helm UK). Routledge Chapman & Hall.

Law & the Administration of Justice in the Old Testament & Ancient East. Hans J. Boecker. Tr. by Jeremy Moiser. LC 80-65556. 224p. 1980. pap. 14.95 o.p. (ISBN 0-8066-1801-9, 10-3761, Augsburg). Augsburg Fortress.

Law & the American Future. Ed. by Murray L. Schwartz. 1975. 9.95 o.p.; pap. 4.95 o.p. Am Assembly.

Law & the Citizen-Student in Wisconsin: A Handbook for Secondary Students. James W. Stewart & David R. Zitlow. (Illus.). 225p. 1981. pap. text ed. 6.95 o.p. (ISBN 0-314-63146-1). West Pub.

Law & the College Student: Justice in Evolution. William G. Millington. LC 79-14211. 629p. 1979. text ed. 34.25 o.p. (ISBN 0-8299-2047-1). West Pub.

Law & the Life Insurance Contract. 5th ed. Janice E. Greider & William T. Beadles. (Irwin Series in Insurance & Economic Security). 1984. 27.95x o.p. (ISBN 0-256-02823-0). Irwin.

Law & the Media in the Midwest. John R. Finnegan & Patricia A. Hirl. 1984. pap. 26.00 o.p. Butterworth MN.

Law & the Mentally Handicapped in North Carolina. H. Rutherford Turnbull. 275p. 1980. 10.00 o.p. (ISBN 0-686-39468-2). Institute Government.

Law & the National Labor Policy. Archibald Cox. (Monograph & Research Ser.: No. 5). 111p. 1960. 5.00 o.p. (ISBN 0-89215-007-6). U Cal LA Indus Rel.

Law & the Poor. Edward A. Parry. LC 79-56966. (English Working Class Ser.). 1980. lib. bdg. 40.00 o.p. (ISBN 0-8240-0117-6). Garland Pub.

Law & the Writer. Ed. by Kirk Polking & Leonard S. Meranus. LC 79-19500. 300p. 1985. pap. 10.95 o.p. (ISBN 0-89879-170-7). Writers Digest.

Law As Logic & Experience. Max Radin. LC 70-122408. ix, 171p. 1971. Repr. of 1940 ed. 21.00 o.p. (ISBN 0-208-01048-3, Archon). Shoe String.

Law As Process: An Anthropological Approach. Sally F. Moore. 1978. 25.00x o.p. (ISBN 0-7100-8758-6). Routledge Chapman & Hall.

Law at Harvard: A History of Ideas & Men, 1817-1967. Arthur E. Sutherland. LC 67-17320. (Illus.). 1967. 29.50x o.s.i. (ISBN 0-674-51500-5, Belknap Pr). Harvard U Pr.

Law, Business & Society. 1st ed. McAdams. 1986. 35.95 o.p. (ISBN 0-256-03070-7). Irwin.

Law, Business & Society. 2nd ed. McAdams. 1989. 38.95 o.p. (ISBN 0-256-07374-0). Irwin.

Law, Capitalism & Democracy: A Sociology of Australian Legal Order. Pat O'Malley. 180p. 1983. text ed. 30.00x o.p. (ISBN 0-86861-373-8); pap. text ed. 15.95 o.p. (ISBN 0-86861-381-9). Unwin Hyman.

Law Dictionary. rev. ed. Steven H. Gifis. LC 74-18126. 240p. 1975. pap. 4.95 pocket-sized o.p. (ISBN 0-8120-0543-0). Barron.

Law Dictionary: Fachwoerterbuch der anglo-amerikanischen Rechtssprache, Englisch-Deutsch. 3rd, rev. ed. Ed. by Barbara Jacobs. LC 75-33315. 888p. (Ger.). 1976. pap. 89.00 o.p. (ISBN 3-11-001698-2). De Gruyter.

Law Enforcement & Criminal Justice: An Introduction. Georgette Bennett-Sandler et al. LC 78-69537. (Illus.). 1979. text ed. 26.95 o.p. (ISBN 0-395-27467-2). HM.

Law Enforcement Education in the Middle Grades: Police-Student Relations. Phyllis McDonald. 96p. 1978. pap. 7.95 o.p. (ISBN 0-8106-1710-2). NEA.

Law Enforcement Handbook of Connecticut. Gould Editorial Staff. 200p. looseleaf 7.95 o.p. Gould.

Law Enforcement Handbook of Pennsylvania. Larry E. Holtz. looseleaf 24.95 o.p. Gould.

Law Giveth: Legal Aspects of the Abortion Controversy. Barbara Milbauer & Bert N. Obrentz. LC 82-45184. 320p. 1983. 21.95 o.s.i. (ISBN 0-689-11312-9, Atheneum). Macmillan.

Law in a Changing America. Ed. by Geoffrey C. Hazard, Jr. LC 68-27498. 1968. 5.95 o.p. (ISBN 0-936904-02-X); pap. 2.45 o.s.i. (ISBN 0-936904-27-5). Am Assembly.

Law in Classical Athens. Douglas M. MacDowell. LC 78-54141. (Aspects of Greek & Roman Life Ser.). 280p. 1978. 38.50x o.p. (ISBN 0-8014-1198-X). Cornell U Pr.

Law in Contemporary Society: The Orgain Lectures. Vern Countryman et al. 115p. 1973. 8.95x o.p. (ISBN 0-292-74606-7). U of Tex Pr.

Law in Japan: The Legal Order in a Changing Society. Ed. by Arthur T. Von Mehren. LC 62-19226. 1963. 52.00x o.s.i. (ISBN 0-674-51600-1). Harvard U Pr.

Law in the Curriculum. Murry Nelson. LC 78-50367. (Fastback Ser.: No. 106). 1978. pap. 0.90 o.p. (ISBN 0-87367-106-6). Phi Delta Kappa.

Law, Justice & Social Policy. Rosalind Brooke. 136p. 1979. 20.00 o.p. (ISBN 0-85664-636-9, Pub. by Croom Helm Ltd). Routledge Chapman & Hall.

Law, Lawyers, & Laymen: Making Sense Out of the American Legal System. Bertram Harnett. LC 83-10779. 336p. 1984. 17.95 o.p. (ISBN 0-15-149102-X). HarBraceJ.

Law, Legislation & Liberty: Vol. 3: the Political Order of a Free People. F. A. Hayek. LC 78-25905. 1979. lib. bdg. 18.00x o.s.i. (ISBN 0-226-32087-1). U of Chicago Pr.

Law of Arrest, Search, & Investigation. Douglas R. Gill et al. 95p. 1979. 1.50 o.p. (ISBN 0-686-39461-5). Institute Government.

Law of Bankers' Commercial Credits. 6th ed. Harold C. Gutteridge & Maurice Megrah. 318p. 1979. 22.50x o.p. (ISBN 0-905118-42-1). Intl Pubns Serv.

Law of Christ, 3 vols. Bernard Haring. 646p. Vol. 1. 17.95 o.p. (ISBN 0-8091-0084-3); Vol. 2. 17.95 o.p. (ISBN 0-8091-0085-1); Vol. 3. 17.95 o.p. (ISBN 0-8091-0086-X). Paulist Pr.

Law of Church-State Relations in a Nutshell. Leonard F. Manning. LC 80-22991. (Nutshell Ser.). 305p. 1981. pap. text ed. 11.95 o.p. (ISBN 0-8299-2113-3). West Pub.

Law of Corrections & Prisoners' Rights in a Nutshell. 2nd ed. Sheldon Krantz. LC 83-6852. (Nutshell Ser.). 386p. 1983. pap. text ed. 10.95 o.p. (ISBN 0-314-74111-9). West Pub.

Law of Criminal Procedure: An Analysis & Critique. David A. Jones. 600p. 1981. text ed. 29.75 o.p. (ISBN 0-316-47283-2). Scott F.

Law of Disputed & Forged Documents. J. Newton Baker. (Illus.). 1955. 35.00x o.s.i. (ISBN 0-87215-079-8). Michie Co.

Law of Domestic Relations in West Virginia. William O. Morris. LC 73-84550. 534p. 1973. 35.00x o.p. (ISBN 0-87215-161-1). Michie Co.

Law of Gravity. Johanna Hurwitz. LC 77-13656. (Illus.). (gr. 3-7). 1978. 7.50 o.p. (ISBN 0-688-22142-4); PLB 11.88 o.p. (ISBN 0-688-32142-9). Morrow.

Law of Marriage & Marital Alternatives. William J. O'Donnell & David A. Jones. LC 80-8029. 272p. 1982. 36.00x o.p. (ISBN 0-669-03944-6). Lexington Bks.

Law of Politics: Federal & California Fair Political Practices & Election Laws. Palmer B. Madden et al. LC 75-38488. (Illus.). xv, 934p. 1977. 70.00 o.p. (ISBN 0-318-01444-0). Cal Cont Ed Bar.

Law of Population: A Treatise in Six Books, 2 vols. M. T. Sadler. 1384p. 1971. Repr. of 1830 ed. Set. 75.00x o.p. (ISBN 0-7165-1579-2, BBA 02142, Pub. by Irish Academic Pr Ireland). Biblio Dist.

Law of Premises Liability. Joseph A. Page. LC 76-11993. 325p. 1976. text ed. 49.75 o.p. (ISBN 0-87084-683-3); Suppl. 1985-86. 24.75 o.p. Anderson Pub Co.

Law of Probation & Parole in North Carolina. Stevens H. Clarke. 131p. 1979. 6.50 o.p. (ISBN 0-686-39460-7). Institute Government.

Law of Real Estate Brokers: 1985 Supplement. D. Barlow Burke, Jr. 96p. 1985. pap. 27.50 o.p. (ISBN 0-316-11678-5). Little.

Law of Special Educational Needs: A Guide to the Education Act 1981. Bryan Cox. LC 84-15600. 134p. 1984. 22.50 o.p. (ISBN 0-7099-3429-7, Pub. by Croom Helm Ltd). Routledge Chapman & Hall.

Law of Suspension & Expulsion: An Examination of the Substantive Issues in Controlling Student Conflict. Robert E. Phay. 66p. 1975. 4.95 o.p. (ISBN 0-686-39470-4). Institute Government.

Law of the Ancient Romans. Alan Watson. LC 71-128124. 128p. 1970. 12.95x o.p. (ISBN 0-87074-120-9); pap. 8.95x o.p. (ISBN 0-87074-121-7). SMU Press.

Law of the Gun. J. T. Edson. 192p. 1984. pap. 2.25 o.s.i. (ISBN 0-425-09790-0). Berkley Pub.

Law of the Harvest. Sterling W. Sill. 392p. 1980. 10.95 o.p. (ISBN 0-88290-142-7). Horizon Utah.

Law of the Land: The Evolution of Our Legal System. Charles Rembar. 1981. pap. 7.95 o.p. (ISBN 0-671-43828-X, Touchstone Bks). S&S.

Law of the Rhythmic Breath. Ella A. Fletcher. LC 80-19750. 372p. 1980. Repr. of 1979 ed. lib. bdg. 22.95x o.p. (ISBN 0-89370-644-2). Borgo Pr.

Law of the Sea: A Select Bibliography. 71p. 12.00 o.p. (ISBN 92-1-133335-0, E.85.V.2). UN.

Law of the Sea: Oceanic Resources. Erin B. Jones. LC 72-96510. xiv, 176p. 1972. 13.95x o.p. (ISBN 0-87074-134-9). SMU Press.

Law of Torts Cases & Materials: 1981 Supplement. 2nd ed. Page Keeton et al. (American Casebook Ser.). 144p. 1981. pap. text ed. 4.95 o.p. (ISBN 0-314-61781-7). West Pub.

Law of Tug, Tow, & Pilotage: Supplement. Alex L. Parks. LC 81-9906. 96p. 1984. pap. 15.00x o.p. (ISBN 0-87033-320-8). Cornell Maritime.

Law of War & Peace in Islam: A Study of Moslem International Law. Majid Khadduri. LC 76-147599. (Library of War & Peace; International Law). lib. bdg. 42.00 o.p. (ISBN 0-8240-0360-8). Garland Pub.

Law Office Management 1986. 768p. 1986. 45.00 o.p. (A4-4161). PLI.

Law Officer's Pocket Manual, 1987-88. BNA Editorial Staff. 1987. pap. 7.95 o.p. (ISBN 0-317-65303-2). BNA.

Law or War? Lucia A. Mead. LC 70-147601. (Library of War & Peace; International Law). lib. bdg. 42.00 o.p. (ISBN 0-8240-0362-4). Garland Pub.

Law, Politics, & Birth Control. C. Thomas Dienes. LC 71-182195. 381p. 1972. 29.95 o.p. (ISBN 0-252-00200-8). U of Ill Pr.

Law Practice Management: Pennsylvania Legal Practice Course Materials. Pennsylvania Bar Institute Staff. 185p. 1985. 25.00 o.p. (ISBN 0-318-02176-5, PLP-85). PA Bar Inst.

Law Relating to Activities of Man in Space. S. Houston Lay & Howard J. Taubenfeld. LC 77-102747. 1970. lib. bdg. 32.50x o.s.i. (ISBN 0-226-46964-6). U of Chicago Pr.

Law, Rights & the Welfare State. Ed. by Charles Sampford & D. J. Galligan. 240p. 1986. 43.00 o.p. (ISBN 0-7099-3838-1, Pub. by Croom Helm Ltd). Routledge Chapman & Hall.

Law School Admission Test: Preparation for the New Test. Gino Crocetti & B. M. Clarke. LC 82-1825. 416p. (Orig.). 1982. pap. 7.95 o.p. (ISBN 0-668-05427-1, 5427). Arco.

Law, Society, & Industrial Justice. Philip Selznick & Philippe Nonet. 290p. 1978. pap. text ed. 6.95x o.p. (ISBN 0-87855-610-9). Transaction Pubs.

Law, State & Society. Ed. by Bob Fryer et al. 234p. 1981. 31.00 o.p. (ISBN 0-7099-1004-5, Pub. by Croom Helm Ltd). Routledge Chapman & Hall.

Law Week's Summary & Analysis of Current Law: BNA's Legal Services. write for info. o.p. BNA.

Lawless Liberators. Rosalie Schwarz. 300p. 1989. 37.50 o.p. Duke.

Lawley Road & Other Stories. R. K. Narayan. 159p. 1969. pap. 4.00 o.s.i. (ISBN 0-88253-062-3). Ind-US Inc.

Lawrence, Greene & Lowry: The Fictional Landscape of Mexico. Douglas W. Veitch. 193p. 1978. pap. text ed. 10.55x o.p. (ISBN 0-88920-069-6, Pub. by Wilfrid Laurier Canada). Humanities.

Lawrence Nineteen Twelve: The Bread & Roses Strike. William Cahn. LC 80-10878. (Illus.). 240p. 1982. pap. 7.95 o.p. (ISBN 0-8298-0390-4). Pilgrim NY.

Lawrence of Arabia & His World. Richard P. Graves. LC 76-7183. (Encore Edition). (Illus.). 128p. 1976. 3.95 o.p. (ISBN 0-684-16543-0, ScribT). Scribner.

Lawrence Olivier: Theater & Cinema. Robert L. Daniels. LC 78-75346. (Illus.). 1980. 19.95 o.s.i. (ISBN 0-498-02287-0). A S Barnes.

Laws in the Pentateuch. Martin Noth. 304p. pap. 13.95 o.p. (ISBN 0-317-31484-X, 30-870-259, Fortress). Augsburg Fortress.

Laws of Christian Living: The Commandments. Perry McDonald & William Odell. LC 85-63162. 170p. (Orig.). 1986. pap. 6.95 o.p. (ISBN 0-87973-593-7, 593). Our Sunday Visitor.

Laws of Deuteronomy. Calum M. Carmichael. LC 73-19206. 277p. 1974. 32.50x o.p. (ISBN 0-8014-0824-5). Cornell U Pr.

Lawyer in Society. J. J. Cavanaugh. LC 62-21557. 96p. 1963. (ISBN 0-8022-0224-1). Philos Lib.

Lawyer Looks at Abortion. Lynn D. Wardle & Mary A. Wood. 250p. 1982. 7.95 o.p. (ISBN 0-8425-2054-6). Brigham.

Lawyer Looks at the Constitution. Rex E. Lee. (Illus.). 256p. 1981. 9.95 o.p. (ISBN 0-8425-1904-1). Brigham.

Lawyer Looks at the Equal Rights Amendment. Rex E. Lee. LC 80-22202. (Illus.). 150p. 1980. pap. 7.95 o.p. (ISBN 0-8425-1883-5). Brigham.

Lawyers & Certified Public Accountants: A Study of Interprofessional Relations: Statements on Practice in the Field of Federal Income Taxation & Estate Planning. National Conference of Lawyers & CPA's Staff. LC 82-226568. 19p. 1981. pap. 1.00 o.p. (ISBN 0-317-01766-7). Am Inst CPA.

Lawyers & Creditors Service Directory, 2 vols. Stelter. 1986. Set. pap. 89.00 o.p. (ISBN 0-941161-10-2). Pes Inc WI.

Lawyers & the Pursuit of Legal Right. Joel F. Handler et al. (Poverty Policy Analysis Ser.). 1978. 19.50 o.p. (ISBN 0-12-322860-3); pap. 10.00 o.p. (ISBN 0-12-322866-2). Acad Pr.

Lawyers & the System of Justice. David Mellinkoff. 983p. 1976. 31.95 o.p. (ISBN 0-314-28246-7). West Pub.

Lawyer's Desk Book. 6th ed. IBP Research & Editorial Staff. LC 79-13813. 650p. 1979. 49.50 o.p. (ISBN 0-87624-323-5, Inst Busn Plan). P-H.

Lawyer's Desk Book. 5th ed. IBP Research & Editorial Staff. LC 66-28535. 1978. 29.95 o.p. (ISBN 0-87624-322-7, Inst Busn Plan). P-H.

Lawyer's Desk Book. 7th ed. Institute for Business Planning, Inc. Staff. LC 83-12835. 1984. 59.50 o.p. (ISBN 0-87624-324-3, Inst Busn Plan). P-H.

Lawyers in the Third World: Comparative & Developmental Perspectives. Ed. by C. J. Dias et al. (Studies of Law in Social Change & Development: No. 3). (Illus.). 400p. 1983. 59.50 o.p. (ISBN 0-8419-9750-0, Africana). Holmes & Meier.

Lawyers of Hell. Ron Gorton. LC 78-27011. 225p. 1979. 9.95 o.p. (ISBN 0-8119-0319-2). Fell.

Lawyers' Quest III: Vocation, Work & Calling. Lynn R. Buzzard. (Lawyers' Quest Ser.). 129p. (Orig.). 1985. pap. text ed. 8.00 o.s.i. (ISBN 0-944561-11-X). Chr Legal.

Lawyer's Register by Specialties & Fields of Law. 8th ed. Ed. by Margaret A. Schultz. 1987. 89.50 o.p. (ISBN 0-934607-01-X). Jury Verdict.

Lawyers, the Rule of Law & Liberalism in Modern Egypt. Farhat J. Ziadeh. LC 68-9503. (Publications Ser.: No. 75). 177p. 1968. 10.95x o.p. (ISBN 0-8179-1751-9); pap. 5.95x o.p. (ISBN 0-8179-1752-7). Hoover Inst Pr.

Lay Action: The Church's Third Force. Cameron P. Hall. (Orig.). 1974. pap. 3.50 o.p. (ISBN 0-377-00018-3). Friendship Pr.

Lay Bare the Heart: An Autobiography of the Civil Rights Movement. James Farmer. 362p. 1985. 15.95 o.p. (ISBN 0-87795-624-3, Arbor Hse). Morrow.

Lay Caregiving. Diane Detwiler-Zapp & William C. Dixon. LC 81-66519. (Creative Pastoral Care & Counseling Ser.). 1982. pap. 4.50 o.p. (ISBN 0-8006-0567-5, 1-567, Fortress). Augsburg Fortress.

Lay Ministers Guide to the Book of Common Prayer. Clifford W. Atkinson. 1988. pap. 5.95 o.p. (ISBN 0-8192-1222-9). Morehouse Pub.

Layayoga: An Advanced Method of Concentration. Shyam S. Goswami. (Illus.). 1980. 35.00 o.p. (ISBN 0-7100-0078-2). Routledge Chapman & Hall.

Laying a Watercolour Wash. Leslie Worth. (Leisure Arts Ser.: Bk. 4). (Illus.). 32p. 1984. pap. 2.95 o.p. (ISBN 0-89134-089-0, Pub. by North Light). Writers Digest.

Laying on of Hands. Derek Prince. (Foundation Ser.: Bk. V). 1965-66. pap. 1.95 o.p. (ISBN 0-934920-04-4, B-14). Derek Prince.

Layla & Majnun. Nizami. Ed. & tr. by R. Gelpke. LC 78-58219. 206p. 1979. pap. 8.95 o.p. (ISBN 0-87773-133-0). Shambhala Pubns.

Titles

Titles

Layman in Christian History. Ed. by Stephen C. Neill & Hans-Ruedi Weber. 1963. 7.50 o.s.i. (ISBN 0-664-20469-4, Westminster). Westminster John Knox.
Layman Looks at the Names of Jesus. John Timmerman. 1985. pap. 4.95 o.p. (ISBN 0-8423-2110-1). Tyndale.
Layman's Guide to Applying the Bible. Walter A. Henrichsen. 224p. (Orig.). 1985. pap. 8.95 o.p. (ISBN 0-310-37691-2, 11233P); Set pack. pap. 20.85 o.p. (ISBN 0-310-37698-X, 11238P). Zondervan.
Layman's Guide to Psychiatry & Psychoanalysis. Eric Berne. 1982. pap. 3.50 o.s.i. (ISBN 0-345-30922-7). Ballantine.
Layman's Handbook of Interior Design. Ellen Angell. 1972. 5.00 o.p. (ISBN 0-682-47363-4, Banner). Exposition-Phoenix.
Layman's Introduction to Christian Thought. James Kallas. LC 69-16919. 1969. pap. 3.25 o.s.i. (ISBN 0-664-24854-3, Westminster). Westminster John Knox.
Layout Procedures & Techniques. Resource Systems International Staff. 1982. pap. text ed. 15.00 o.p. (ISBN 0-8359-3955-3, Reston). P-H.
Lazare: Le Miroir des Limbes. Andre Malraux. 264p. 1974. 18.50 o.p. (ISBN 0-686-56328-X). Schoenhof.
Lazarillo de Tormes. Robert L. Fiore. (World Authors Ser.: No. 714). 150p. 1984. lib. bdg. 17.95 o.p. (ISBN 0-8057-6561-1, Twayne). G K Hall.
Lazarillo De Tormes, La Vida Del Buscon. Quevedo. (Span). 4.50x o.s.i. (ISBN 0-686-00067-6). Colton Bk.
Lazarus Effect. Frank Herbert & Bill Ransom. 400p. 1985. pap. 3.50 o.s.i. (ISBN 0-425-07129-4). Berkley Pub.
Lazy Jack & Other Children's Stories. June N. Witherspoon. (Illus.). 64p. (gr. k-2). 1984. pap. 5.50 o.p. (ISBN 0-682-40148-X). Exposition-Phoenix.
Lazy Man's Guide to Relaxation. 3rd, rev. ed. Israel Regardie. LC 83-81835. 84p. 1983. pap. 4.95 o.p. (ISBN 0-941404-28-5). Falcon Pr AZ.
LC Subject Headings Weekly Lists: A Working Cumulation 1987. 800p. 1987. pap. 360.00x o.p. (ISBN 0-8103-0244-6). Gale.
LCGT Technical Guide. Donna Ilyin & Susan Rubin. (Listening Comprehension Group Test Ser.). 24p. 1981. pap. text ed. 6.50 o.p. (ISBN 0-88377-211-6). Newbury Hse.
Le Corbusier. Robert F. Jordan. LC 72-75903. (Illus.). 300p. 1972. 10.00 o.p. (ISBN 0-88208-002-4). Chicago Review.
Le Corbusier: The Machine & the Grand Design. Norma Evenson. LC 60-6079. (Planning & Cities Ser). (Illus., Orig.). 1969. 7.95 o.p. (ISBN 0-8076-0514-X); pap. 5.95 o.p. (ISBN 0-8076-0518-2). Braziller.
Le Regard et Son Masque see Interface: The Painter & the Mask.
Leabhar Na Feinne. J. F. Campbell. 272p. 1972. Repr. of 1872 ed. 40.00x o.p. (ISBN 0-7165-2060-5, Pub. by Irish Academic Pr Ireland). Biblio Dist.
Leachate from Municipal Landfills: Production & Management. James C. Lu et al. LC 84-22746. (Pollution Technology Review Ser.: No. 119). (Illus.). 453p. 1985. 42.00 o.p. (ISBN 0-8155-1021-7). Noyes.
Lead Absorption in Children: Management, Clinical & Environmental Aspects. J. J. Chisolm & D. M. O'Hara. LC 81-16306. (Illus.). 240p. 1982. 32.50 o.p. (ISBN 0-8067-0331-8). Urban & S.
Lead & Lead Alloys: Properties & Technology. W. Hofmann. Tr. by Lead Development Association. (Illus.). 1970. 65.20 o.p. (ISBN 0-387-04880-4). Springer-Verlag.
Lead in Man & the Environment. Jennifer M. Ratcliffe. LC 81-2905. (Ellis Horwood Series in Environmental Sciences). 240p. 1981. 86.95 o.p. (ISBN 0-470-27184-1). Halsted Pr.
Lead Manufacturing in Britain: A History. D. J. Rowe. (Illus.). 427p. 1983. 29.95 o.p. (ISBN 0-7099-2250-7, Pub. by Croom Helm). Routledge Chapman & Hall.
Lead Nineteen Sixty-Eight: Proceedings, International Conference on Lead - 3rd - Venice - 1968. Ed. by A. I. Hughes. LC 66-18688. 1970. 115.00 o.p. (ISBN 0-08-015644-4). Pergamon.
Lead Poisoning in Animal Models. C. F. Simpson et al. 160p. 1976. text ed. 34.50x o.p. (ISBN 0-8422-7268-2). Irvington.
Lead Poisoning in Man & the Environment. E. Jernigan et al. 1973. text ed. 34.50x o.p. (ISBN 0-8422-7105-8). Irvington.
Lead Pollution: Causes & Control. R. M. Harrison & D. P. Laxen. 168p. 1981. 29.95x o.p. (ISBN 0-412-16360-8, NO. 6570, Pub. by Chapman & Hall). Routledge Chapman & Hall.
Lead Soldiers. Uri Orlev. Tr. by Hillel Halkin from Hebrew. LC 79-26348. 234p. 1980. 9.95 o.s.i. (ISBN 0-8008-4576-5). Taplinger.
Lead Time. Garry Wills. LC 82-45372. 408p. 1983. 18.95 o.p. (ISBN 0-385-17695-3). Doubleday.
Lead Toxicity. Ed. by Radhey L. Singhal & John A. Thomas. LC 79-16784. (Illus.). 524p. 1980. text ed. 45.00 o.p. (ISBN 0-8067-1801-3). Urban & S.
Lead Versus Health: Sources & Effects of Low Level Lead Exposure. Michael Rutter & Robin R. Jones. LC 82-16000. 379p. 1983. 67.95 o.p. (ISBN 0-471-90028-1, Dist. by A R Liss). Wiley.
Lead-Zinc-Tin '80: Proceedings of the World Symposium at the AIME Annual Meeting, Las Vegas, 1980. World Symposium at the AIME Annual Meeting Staff. Ed. by T. S. Cigan & T. J. O'Keefe. (Illus.). 1045p. 55.00 o.p. (ISBN 0-89520-358-8); members 32.00 o.p. (ISBN 0-317-34882-5); student members 16.00 o.p. (ISBN 0-317-34883-3). ASM.
Leader: A New Face for American Management. Michael Maccoby. 288p. 1983. pap. 6.95 o.s.i. (ISBN 0-345-30856-5). Ballantine.
Leader: A Political Biography of Gough Whitlam. James Walter. (Illus.). 295p. 1981. text ed. 25.00x o.p. (ISBN 0-7022-1557-0). U of Queensland Pr.
Leader & the Damned. Colin Forbes. LC 84-2883. 480p. 1984. 15.95 o.p. (ISBN 0-689-11469-9, Atheneum). Macmillan.
Leader by Destiny. Jeanette Eaton. LC 38-32981. (Illus.). 1938. 6.95 o.p. (ISBN 0-15-244176-X, HJ). HarBraceJ.
Leaders At Work in Food Service Handbook. 41p. Date not set. 5.95 o.p. (ISBN 0-318-23893-4). Future Home.
Leader's Digest, 3 Vols. (Vols. 1, 2, 3). write for info. 1953 o.p. (ISBN 0-88379-034-3); write for info. 1955 o.p. (ISBN 0-88379-035-1); write for info. 1956 o.p. (ISBN 0-88379-036-X). A A A C E.
Leader's Digest: Blue Book of Basic Documents 1985. 16p. 1985. pap. 0.35 o.p. (ISBN 0-686-88519-8, 26-145). Girl Scouts USA.
Leader's Guide for Mentor Training. 78p. 1988. 7.90 o.p. Northwest Regional.
Leaders Guide for Yearbook: Untold Stories. Bill Wolfe & Martha Wolfe. 80p. (Orig.). 1983. pap. 6.95 o.s.i. (ISBN 0-936664-13-4). Group Pub.
Leader's Guide to the Successful Job Search in Student Development. Wendy Settle & Eric Schlesinger. 1985. 5.00 o.p. (ISBN 1-55620-021-8, 72613C). Am Assn Coun Dev.
Leaders in American Education. Ed. by Robert J. Havighurst. LC 6-16938. (National Society for the Study of Education Yearbooks Ser: No. 70, Pt. 2). 1971. lib. bdg. 8.50x o.s.i. (ISBN 0-226-60107-2). U of Chicago Pr.
Leaders 87. 1987 ed. Marvin R. Shanken. 1987. pap. 5.00 o.p. (ISBN 0-918076-53-6). M Shanken Comm.
Leadership & Group Dynamics in Recreation Services. Douglas H. Sessoms & Jack L. Stevenson. 285p. 1983. 31.95x o.p. (ISBN 0-205-07282-8, EDP 847282, Pub. by Longwood Div). Allyn.
Leadership & Motivation: Essays of Douglas McGregor. Ed. by Warren G. Bennis et al. 1966. pap. 9.95x o.p. (ISBN 0-262-63015-X). MIT Pr.
Leadership Development for Public Service. Barry A. Passett. LC 70-149755. (Building Blocks of Human Potential Ser.). 142p. 1971. 9.95x o.p. (ISBN 0-87201-428-2). Gulf Pub.
Leadership Education: A Source Book. Frank H. Freeman et al. (Special Report Ser.: No. 9). 1986. pap. 40.00 o.p. (ISBN 0-912879-58-0). Ctr Creat Leader.
Leadership in Crisis. Donald Gerig. LC 81-51741. 128p. 1981. pap. 3.95 o.p. (ISBN 0-8307-0797-2, 5415304). Regal.
Leadership in Nineteenth Century Africa see Tarikh.
Leadership in Organizations. Howard T. Prince. (Illus.). 621p. 1985. 28.00 o.p. (ISBN 0-318-18781-7, S/N 008-027-00003-0). USGPO.
Leadership in Organizations. Gary Yukl. (Illus.). 336p. 1981. text ed. 35.00 o.p. (ISBN 0-13-527176-2). P-H.
Leadership in the British Civil Service. Richard A. Chapman. 224p. 1984. 28.00 o.p. (ISBN 0-7099-3402-5, Pub. by Croom Helm Ltd). Routledge Chapman & Hall.
Leadership in the Least Developed Nation: Bangladesh. Zillur R. Khan. LC 83-7922. (Foreign & Comparative Studies Program, South Asian, No. 8). (Illus., Orig.). 1983. pap. 11.00x o.p. (ISBN 0-915984-85-7). Syracuse U Foreign Comp.
Leadership Is an Art. Max De Pree. LC 87-43199. 150p. 1988. 16.00 o.p. (ISBN 0-87013-254-7). Mich St U Pr.
Leadership, Love & Aggression. Allison Davis. LC 82-21342. 272p. 1983. 15.95 o.p. (ISBN 0-15-149348-0). HarBraceJ.
Leadership on the Job: Guides to Good Supervision. Ed. by William K. Fallon. 320p. 1982. 17.95 o.p. (ISBN 0-8144-5727-4). AMACOM.
Leadership Skills for Women. Marilyn Manning. Ed. by Michael G. Crisp. LC 88-72261. (Fifty Minute Ser.). (Illus.). 96p. (Orig.). 1989. pap. 7.95 o.p. Crisp Pubns.
Leadership Training for Directors of Group Seminars Abroad: A Japan Model. Lois V. Edinger & Roland H. Nelson. LC 81-67787. (Occasional Paper Ser.: No. 12). 87p. 1981. 8.00 o.p. (ISBN 0-916994-21-X). Ctr Intl Stud Duke.
Leadership: You Can Have What It Takes. Charles Nieman. 186p. (Orig.). 1983. pap. text ed. 5.50 o.s.i. (ISBN 0-914307-08-8, Dist. by Harrison Hse). R Tilton Ministries.
Leading Constitutional Decisions. 16th ed. Robert F. Cushman. 480p. 1982. pap. text ed. (ISBN 0-13-527374-9). P-H.
Leading Consultants in Technology, 2 vols. 2nd ed. Set. 195.00 o.p. Data Vol (ISBN 0-89235-086-5). Index Vol (ISBN 0-89235-098-9). Res Pubns CT.
Leading Consultants in Technology 1983, 2 vols. 2nd ed. Ed. by Louann Chaudier. 1996p. (Orig.). 1985. Set. 195.00 o.p. (ISBN 0-89235-089-X). Res Pubns CT.
Leading Edge Growth Strategies: New Approaches for Accelerated Business Growth & Premium Profits in the Next Twenty Years. Mack Hanan. LC 83-21274. 207p. 1983. text ed. 59.95 ring binder o.p. (ISBN 0-13-527334-X, Busn). P-H.
Leading Journalists Tell What a Free Press Means to America. Society of Professional Journalists Staff. LC 85-146465. 250p. Date not set. price not set o.p. Soc Pro.
Leading Our Children to God. William Brinkmann & William Ditewig. LC 83-72992. (Illus.). 96p. (Orig.). 1984. pap. 4.95 o.p. (ISBN 0-87793-310-3). Ave Maria.
Leading the First Century Church in the Space Age. F. Dale Simpson. 1972. 8.75 o.p. (ISBN 0-89137-003-X); pap. 5.95 o.p. Quality Pubns.
Leadville. Edwin Booth. (Orig.). 1981. pap. 1.95 o.p. (ISBN 0-505-51643-8, Pub. by Tower Bks). Dorchester Pub Co.
Leadville: Colorado's Magic City. Edward Blair. (Illus.). 1980. price not set o.p. (ISBN 0-87108-544-5). Pruett.
Leaf Beetle Host Plants in Northeastern North America: Coleoptera: Chrysomelidae. John A. Wilcox. 32p. 1979. pap. 4.95x o.p. (ISBN 0-916846-09-1). Flora & Fauna.
Leaf in the Storm. Lin Yutang. 368p. 1980. 5.95 o.p. (ISBN 0-89955-164-5, Pub. by Mei Ya China); pap. 7.45 o.p. (ISBN 0-89955-193-9, Pub. by Mei Ya China). Intl Spec Bk.
Leaf Protein Concentrates. Lehel Telek & Horace D. Graham. (Illus.). 1983. 115.95 o.p. (ISBN 0-87055-412-3). AVI.
Leaf Storm & Other Stories. Gabriel Garcia Marquez. 1978. pap. 1.65 o.p. (ISBN 0-380-01323-1, 35816, Bard). Avon.
Leafy Rivers. Jessamyn West. 1974. pap. 1.25 o.p. (ISBN 0-380-00059-8, 19422). Avon.
Leafy Salad Vegetables. Edward J. Ryder. (Illus.). 1979. 43.95 o.s.i. (ISBN 0-87055-323-2). AVI.
League for Industrial Democracy: New York L. I. D. Monthly, Vols. 1-10, No. 8. 1922-32. Repr. lib. bdg. 52.00x o.p. (ISBN 0-8371-9269-2, LG00). Greenwood.
League of Hawks. Allan Caillou. 192p. (Orig.). 1986. pap. 3.50 o.p. (ISBN 1-55547-105-6). Critics Choice Paper.
League: The Rise & Decline of the NFL. David Harris. LC 86-47575. (Illus.). 672p. (Orig.). 1986. 21.95 o.p. (ISBN 0-553-05167-9). Bantam.
Leah's Journey. Goldreich. 1978. 10.00 o.p. (ISBN 0-15-149451-7). HarBraceJ.
Leakey's Luck: The Life of Louis Seymour Bazett Leakey. Sonia Cole. 448p. 1975. 15.95 o.p. (ISBN 0-15-149456-8). HarBraceJ.
Lean & Green Diet. Susan M. Perry & Lisa Bellini. 112p. 1985. pap. 3.75 o.p. (ISBN 0-380-89878-0). Avon.
Lean Years: A History of the American Worker 1920-1933. Irving Bernstein. 592p. 1972. pap. 5.95 o.p. (ISBN 0-395-13657-1, 73, SenEd). HM.
Lean Years, Happy Years. Angelo Pellegrini. LC 83-13578. 200p. 1983. 12.95 o.p. (ISBN 0-914842-98-6). Madrona Pubs.
Lean Years: Politics in the Age of Scarcity. Richard J. Barnet. 1982. pap. 7.75 o.p. (ISBN 0-671-43829-8, Touchstone Bks). S&S.
Leaning into the Wind: The Wilderness of Widowhood. Betty Bryant. LC 75-13031. 96p. 1975. pap. 0.50x o.p. (ISBN 0-8006-1208-6, Fortress). Augsburg Fortress.
Leaning Tower of Babel. Richard Mitchell. 1987. pap. 7.95 o.s.i. (ISBN 0-671-63926-9, Fireside). S&S.
Leaning Tower of Babel: And Other Outrages from the Underground Grammarian. Richard Mitchell. (Illus.). 256p. 1984. 14.95 o.p. (ISBN 0-316-57509-7). Little.
Leap into Danger. Leif Hamre. Tr. by Evelyn Ramsden. LC 59-12343. 1966. pap. 0.60 o.p. (ISBN 0-15-649483-3, AVB42, VoyB). HarBraceJ.
Leap into Danger. Leif Hamre. 1959. 4.50 o.p. (ISBN 0-15-244355-X, HJ). HarBraceJ.
Leap of Reason. Don Cupitt. LC 75-44180. 1976. 8.50 o.s.i. (ISBN 0-664-20749-9, Westminster). Westminster John Knox.
Leaping into Being. N. Arthur Coulter, Jr. LC 83-50642. (Illus.). 100p. (Orig.). pap. 1.95 o.s.i. (ISBN 0-910217-03-3). Synergetics WV.
Learical Lexicon: A Magnificent Feast of Boshblobberbosh & Fun from the Works of Edward Lear. Myra C. Livingston. LC 84-18635. (Illus.). 64p. (gr. 5 up). 1985. 12.95 o.s.i. (ISBN 0-689-50318-0, M K McElderry). Macmillan.
Learn about Letters. (E.T. Practice Workbooks). (Illus.). 48p. 1983. pap. 2.40 o.s.i. (ISBN 0-671-47679-3, Little Simon). S&S.
Learn about Numbers. (E.T. Practice Workbooks). (Illus.). 48p. 1983. pap. 2.40 o.s.i. (ISBN 0-671-47682-3, Little Simon). S&S.
Learn at Home the Sesame Street Way. Children's Television Workshop Staff & Sara B. Stein. 286p. 1982. pap. 9.50 o.p. (ISBN 0-671-45866-3, Fireside). S&S.
Learn BASIC Programming in Fourteen Days on Your Commodore 64. Gil Schechter. LC 84-50052. 12.95 o.p. (ISBN 0-672-22279-5). Sams.
Learn Chess: A New Way for All, 2 vols. C. H. Alexander & T. J. Beach. 1978. pap. 12.95 o.p. (ISBN 0-08-021055-4). Pergamon.
Learn English for Science. A. R. Bolitho & P. L. Sandler. (English As a Second Language Bk.). 108p. 1977. pap. text ed. 6.95 student bk. o.p. (ISBN 0-582-55247-8). Longman.
Learn Magic. Henry Hay. LC 74-80337. 1975. lib. bdg. 11.50x o.p. (ISBN 0-88307-542-3). Gannon.
Learn That Language: Principles of Language Learning. D. W. Meech. 83p. 1976. pap. 2.00 o.s.i. (ISBN 0-88312-782-2). Summer Inst Ling.
Learn to Improve Your Thinking Skills. Karl Albrecht. 1980. 15.95 o.p. (ISBN 0-13-136325-5, Spec); pap. 8.95 o.p. (ISBN 0-13-136317-4). P-H.
Learn to Talk Old Jack Lang: A Handbook of Australian Rhyming Slang. John Meredith. 64p. (Orig.). 1985. 5.95 o.p. (ISBN 0-86417-003-3, Pub. by Kangaroo Pr). Intl Spec Bk.
Learn to Type Fast. 3rd ed. Barbara Aliaga. 77p. 1987. spiral bdg. 11.50 o.p. (ISBN 0-88908-634-6). ISC Pr.
Learn While You Play. Compiled by Chava Shairo. 20p. 1.50 o.p. (ISBN 0-914131-41-9, B68). Torah Umesorah.
Learn with E.T. Things That Go. (Illus.). 24p. 1983. pap. 1.90 o.s.i. (ISBN 0-671-47728-5, Little Simon). S&S.
Learned Hippopotamus: Poems Conveying Useful Information About Animals, Ordinary & Extraordinary. Gavin Ewart. (Illus.). (gr. 1-4). 1988. 11.95 o.p. (ISBN 0-09-163350-8, Pub. by Century Hutchinson). David & Charles.
Learned Ladies. Tr. by Richard Wilbur. LC 77-85199. 160p. 1978. 8.95 o.p. (ISBN 0-15-149480-0). HarBraceJ.
Learned Societies & Printing Clubs of the United Kingdom. Abraham Hume. LC 66-16418. 108p. 1966. Repr. of 1853 ed. 40.00x o.p. (ISBN 0-8103-3081-4). Gale.
Learning. J. Charles Jones. (Professional Education for Teacher's Ser). (Orig.). 1967. pap. text ed. 6.95 o.p. (ISBN 0-15-550380-4, HC). HarBraceJ.
Learning. 2nd ed. William S. Sahakian. 1976. pap. 16.95 o.p. (ISBN 0-395-30832-1). HM.
Learning about Jesus. rev. ed. Francis Schraff et al. 80p. (gr. 2-4). 1980. pap. 1.95 o.p. (ISBN 0-89243-129-6). Liguori Pubns.
Learning About Love. Jordan Jenkins. LC 78-12381. (Social Values Ser.). (Illus.). 32p. (ps-3). 1979. PLB 11.27 o.p. (ISBN 0-516-02020-X); pap. 3.95 o.p. (ISBN 0-516-42020-8). Childrens.
Learning about Microcomputers: Hardware & Application Software. Edward J. Coburn. 448p. 1986. pap. 25.95 o.p. (ISBN 0-8273-2562-2); instr's. guide 10.00 o.p. (ISBN 0-8273-2563-0). Delmar.
Learning About Sex: A Guide for Children & Their Parents. Jennifer J. Aho & John W. Petras. LC 78-53949. (Illus.). (gr. 4 up). 1978. 7.95 o.p. (ISBN 0-03-045666-5); pap. 6.95 o.p. (ISBN 0-03-043966-3). H Holt & Co.
Learning about Sex: The Contemporary Guide for Young Adults. 3rd ed. Gary Kelly. LC 77-7058. 1977. 10.95 o.p. (ISBN 0-8120-5171-8); pap. 5.95 o.p. (ISBN 0-8120-0890-1). Barron.
Learning Activities & Teaching Ideas for the Special Child in the Regular Classroom. Peggy Glazzard. (Illus.). 368p. 1982. pap. text ed. 22.33 o.p. (ISBN 0-13-527093-6). P-H.
Learning & Behavior. F. J. Stendenbach. (Current Sociology-la Sociologie Contemporaine: No. 14-3). 1967. pap. 10.40x o.p. (ISBN 90-2796-571-4). Mouton.

Learning & Psychosomatic Approach to the Nature & Treatment of Illness: 18th Annual Conference of the Society for Psychosomatic Research. Ed. by Peter Mellett. 1977. pap. 53.00 o.p. (ISBN 0-08-020881-9). Pergamon.

Learning & Review Aid for Statics: To Go with Engineering Mechanics. Bela I. Sandor & A. L. Schlack. 176p. 1983. pap. text ed. (ISBN 0-13-278903-5). P-H.

Learning & Teaching Through the Senses. Kathrene M. Tobey. LC 70-92899. (Illus.). 1970. pap. 3.25 o.s.i. (ISBN 0-664-24874-8, Westminster). Westminster John Knox.

Learning & the Professors. Ed. by Ohmer Milton & Edward J. Shoben, Jr. LC 67-22230. xvii, 216p. 1968. 12.00x o.p. (ISBN 0-8214-0036-3); pap. 5.95x o.p. (ISBN 0-8214-0105-X). Ohio U Pr.

Learning Business Math with Electronic Calculators. 2nd ed. Richard R. McCready. 320p. 1980. pap. text ed. 19.95x o.p. (ISBN 0-534-00741-4). PWS-Kent Pub.

Learning Business Mathematics with Electronic Calculators. Richard R. McCready. 1975. pap. text ed. (ISBN 0-534-00396-6). PWS-Kent Pub.

Learning by Doing BASIC. Sandra Barber & Kianpour Mihankhah. 101p. (Orig.). 1983. pap. text ed. 8.50x o.p. (ISBN 0-89917-393-4). Tichenor Pub.

Learning Centers & Individualized Reading in Behavioral Terms. Alex W. Vlangas & Richard J. Williams. (Illus.). 1973. pap. text ed. 6.95x o.p. (ISBN 0-8422-0292-7). Irvington.

Learning Centers for Young Children. 2nd ed. Georgia B. Houle. (Illus.). 40p. 1985. pap. text ed. 7.50 o.p. (ISBN 0-940139-06-5). Tot Lot Child Care.

Learning Clubs for the Poor. Lea A. Hunter & Magdalen Sienkiewicz. LC 83-82024. (Orig.). 1984. pap. 4.95 o.p. (ISBN 0-8091-2602-8). Paulist Pr.

Learning Commodore 64 BASIC. David A. Lien. LC 84-71389. (CompuSoft Learning Ser.). (Illus.). 346p. (gr. 7 up). 1984. pap. 14.95 o.p. (ISBN 0-932760-22-8). CompuSoft.

Learning Disabilities: A Competency Based Approach. Larry A. Faas. LC 75-31010. (Illus.). 512p. 1976. pap. 16.35 o.p. (ISBN 0-395-20586-7). HM.

Learning Disabilities: A Family Affair. Betty B. Osman. 1980. pap. 3.50 o.s.i. (ISBN 0-446-32786-7). Warner Bks.

Learning Disabilities & Reading Difficulties. Ed. by Robert F. O'Neil & Robert Weinberg. 168p. 1969. pap. text ed. 12.95x o.p. (ISBN 0-8290-1088-2). Irvington.

Learning Disabilities: Selected ACLD Papers. Samuel A. Kirk & Jeanne M. McCarthy. LC 74-20857. 1975. text ed. 23.00 o.p. (ISBN 0-395-20200-0). HM.

Learning Disabilities: Systemizing Teaching & Service Delivery. David Sabatino et al. LC 81-7886. 526p. 1981. text ed. 35.00 o.p. (ISBN 0-89443-361-X). Aspen Pub.

Learning Disabilities: Theories, Diagnosis, & Teaching Strategies. 3rd ed. Janet W. Lerner. LC 80-82975. (Illus.). 560p. 1981. text ed. 28.95 o.p. (ISBN 0-395-29710-9). HM.

Learning Disability: The Unrealized Potential. Alan O. Ross. 1977. text ed. 24.95 o.p. (ISBN 0-07-053875-1). McGraw.

Learning Disabled Adolescent: Learning Success in Content Areas. Delores M. Woodward & Delores Peters. LC 83-2740. 371p. 1983. 35.00 o.p. (ISBN 0-89443-875-1). Aspen Pub.

Learning Disorders in Children: Diagnosis, Medication, Education. Ed. by Lester Tarnopol. 1971. 15.95 o.p. (ISBN 0-316-83200-6). Little.

Learning Electricity & Electronics Through Experiments. J. A. Wilson & Milton Kaufman. LC 78-17723. (Illus.). 1979. pap. text ed. 12.50 o.p. (ISBN 0-07-070675-1). McGraw.

Learning Electrocardiography: A Complete Course. 2nd ed. Jules Constant. (Illus.). 1981. text ed. 40.50 o.p. (ISBN 0-316-15322-2). Little.

Learning English As a Second Language: Level 1, 2, 3, 4, 5, 3 vols, Level 1, 2, 3. Lawrence S. Finkel et al. LC 75-132280. (Learning English Ser). (Illus., Orig.). 1970-76. level 1 5.00 o.p. (ISBN 0-379-14250-3); pap. 3.95 ea. o.p. Oceana.

Learning for Little Kids: Parents' Sourcebook for the Years 3 to 8. Sandy Jones. 1979. 15.95 o.p. (ISBN 0-395-26296-8); pap. 7.95 o.p. (ISBN 0-395-27210-6). HM.

Learning from Atlanta. Robert Brambilla. (Learning from the U. S. A. Ser.). 150p. (Orig.). 1981. pap. text ed. 6.95 o.p. (ISBN 0-87855-835-7). Transaction Pubs.

Learning from Experience: Evaluating Early Childhood Demonstration Programs. National Research Council. 271p. 1982. pap. text ed. 13.50x o.p. (ISBN 0-309-03232-6). Natl Acad Pr.

Learning from Jesus. Rosanna B. Fountain. (Illus., Orig.). (gr. 1-3). 1967. pap. 1.95 o.p. (ISBN 0-8042-9461-5, John Knox). Westminster John Knox.

Learning Golf: The Lyle Way. Sandy Lyle. (Illus.). 189p. 1987. 29.95 o.p. (ISBN 0-340-38319-4, Pub. by Hodder & Stoughton UK). David & Charles.

Learning How to Learn: The English Primary School & American Education. Robert J. Fisher. 270p. 1972. pap. text ed. 6.95 o.p. (ISBN 0-15-550396-0, HC). HarBraceJ.

Learning in Animals. Ed. by Robert Hendersen. LC 81-2247. (Benchmark Papers in Behavior Ser.: Vol. 14). 1982. 53.95 o.p. (ISBN 0-87933-348-0). Van Nos Reinhold.

Learning in Groups. David Jaques. LC 84-45288. 318p. 1984. 32.50 o.p. (ISBN 0-7099-0046-5, Pub. by Croom Helm Ltd); pap. 17.00 o.p. (ISBN 0-7099-1471-7). Routledge Chapman & Hall.

Learning in Two Languages. Ricardo Garcia. LC 76-16879. (Fastback Ser.: No.84). 53p. (Orig., Span.). 1976. pap. 0.90 o.p. (ISBN 0-87367-084-1). Phi Delta Kappa.

Learning, Language, & Cognition: Theory, Research, & Method for the Study of Human Behavior & Its Development. Arthur W. Staats. 1968. 44.50x o.p. (ISBN 0-03-066565-5); pap. text ed. 18.50x o.p. (ISBN 0-8290-0687-7). Irvington.

Learning Language at Home: Level I & II, 2 Vols. Merle B. Karnes. pap. 19.95, 1977 o.p. (ISBN 0-86586-114-5). pap. 19.95, 1978 o.p. (ISBN 0-86586-115-3); pap. 16.96 members o.p. Coun Exc Child.

Learning Lessons: Social Organization in the Classroom. Hugh Mehan. LC 78-24298. (Illus.). 1979. text ed. 18.95 o.p. (ISBN 0-674-52015-7). Harvard U Pr.

Learning Liberation: Women's Response to Men's Education. Jane Thompson. (Radical Forum on Adult Education Ser.). 207p. 1983. 29.00 o.p. (ISBN 0-7099-2414-3, Pub. by Croom Helm Ltd); pap. 14.75 o.p. (ISBN 0-7099-2439-9). Routledge Chapman & Hall.

Learning LISP. Gnosis, Inc. Staff. 192p. 1983. 21.95 o.p. (ISBN 0-13-527821-X); disk o.p. 14.95 o.p.; book & disk 29.95 o.p. (ISBN 0-13-527839-2). P-H.

Learning Mathematical Concepts at Home. Merle B. Karnes. 1980. pap. 19.95 o.p. (ISBN 0-86586-107-2); pap. 16.96 o.p. Coun Exc Child.

Learning More about Phonics. Compiled by Constance McAllister. (Illus., Orig.). (gr. 2-6). 1979. pap. 2.95 o.p. (ISBN 0-87534-174-8). Highlights.

Learning Our Way: Essays in Feminist Education. Ed. by Charlotte Bunch & Sandra Pollack. LC 83-15182. (Crossing Press Feminist Ser.). 334p. (Orig.). 1983. 26.95 o.p. (ISBN 0-89594-112-0); pap. 12.95 o.p. (ISBN 0-89594-111-2). Crossing Pr.

Learning Process for Religious Education. Richard J. Reichert. LC 74-14308. (Orig.). 1974. pap. 3.95 o.p. (ISBN 0-8278-0001-0, Pub. by Pflaum Pr). Pflaum Pr.

Learning Process: How to Pass Examinations. Abdul S. Hassam. 1978. 5.50 o.p. (ISBN 0-682-49117-9, University). Exposition-Phoenix.

Learning Psychology by Doing. Sheldon S. Brown. 1984. pap. text ed. 12.95 o.p. (ISBN 0-8403-3363-3). Kendall-Hunt.

Learning: Psychology Of. K. P. Hillner. 1978. 80.00 o.p. (ISBN 0-08-017864-2); pap. 80.00 o.p. (ISBN 0-08-017865-0). Pergamon.

Learning Statistics: A Common-Sense Approach. James D. Wynne. 1982. text ed. write for info. o.p. (ISBN 0-02-430680-0). Macmillan.

Learning Systems: Decision, Simulation, & Control. Y. M. El-Fattah & C. Foulard. (Lecture Notes in Control & Information Sciences Ser.: Vol. 9). (Illus.). 1978. pap. 14.00 o.p. (ISBN 0-387-09003-7). Springer-Verlag.

Learning the ABC's with Animals. Carmen Fuentes. 1984. 4.95 o.p. (ISBN 0-533-05683-7). Vantage.

Learning the Alphabet. National Education Association Staff. 1983. pap. 1.95 o.p. (ISBN 0-380-82586-4, 82586). Avon.

Learning the Nemeth Braille Code: A Manual for Teachers. Ruth H. Craig. LC 79-15984. (Illus.). 1980. pap. text ed. 1.00x o.p. (ISBN 0-8425-1701-4). Brigham.

Learning the VI Editor. 2nd, rev. ed. Linda Lamb. (Nutshell Handbks. (for Beginning & Advanced UNIX Users)). 1987p. pap. write for info. o.p. (ISBN 0-937175-17-X). O'Reilly & Assocs.

Learning Theory & Behavior Modification. Stephen Walker. Ed. by Peter Herriot. LC 83-19475. (New Essential Psychology Ser.). 192p. 1984. pap. 6.50 o.p. (ISBN 0-416-33810-0, NO. 4065). Routledge Chapman & Hall.

Learning Theory & Mental Development. William K. Estes. 1970. 27.50 o.p. (ISBN 0-12-243550-8). Acad Pr.

Learning Through Dance. Carla De Sola. (Illus.). 252p. pap. 10.95 o.p. (ISBN 0-941500-43-8). Sharing Co.

Learning Through Movement: Activities for the Preschool & Elementary Grades. 2nd, Rev. ed. Betty Rowen. LC 82-3317. 1982. pap. text ed. 8.95x o.p. (ISBN 0-8077-2720-2). Tchrs Coll.

Learning Through Small Group Discussion. Jean Rudduck. 137p. 1978. pap. 16.00 o.p. (ISBN 0-900868-63-5, Open Univ Pr). Taylor & Francis.

Learning Through the Built Environment: An Ecological Approach to Child Development. Sharon E. Sutton. LC 84-6740. (Illus.). 1985. text ed. 39.50x o.s.i. (ISBN 0-8290-1351-2). Irvington.

Learning to Apply New Concepts to Casework Practice. Ed. by Gertrude Einstein. LC 68-59388. 1969. pap. 7.00 o.p. (ISBN 0-87304-015-5). Family Serv.

Learning to Believe: A Meditation on the Christian Creed. Carroll E. Simcox. LC 80-2372. 112p. 1981. pap. 5.95 o.p. (ISBN 0-8006-1497-6, 1-1497, Fortress). Augsburg Fortress.

Learning to Care: The Training of Staff for Residential Social Work with Young People. Spencer M. Bullock & Kenneth Hosie. 136p. 1980. text ed. 28.00x o.p. (ISBN 0-566-00400-3). Gower Pub Co.

Learning to Change: Report of a Regional Training Workshop on Systems Approach for Education - Teacher In-Service Programme (SAFE-TIP) 121p. 1980. pap. 6.50 o.p. (ISBN 0-686-60078-9, UB78, UB). UNIPUB.

Learning to Compose. Larry Austin & Thomas Clark. 240p. 1988. text ed. write for info. o.p. (ISBN 0-697-03495-X). Wm C Brown.

Learning to Compute, 2 bks. Wilmer L. Jones. 1978. Bk. 1. pap. text ed. 4.68 o.p. (ISBN 0-15-550402-9, HC); Bk. 2. pap. text ed. 5.07 o.p. (ISBN 0-15-550403-7). HarBraceJ.

Learning to Die, Learning to Live. Robert M. Herhold. LC 76-7861. (Illus.). 96p. 1976. pap. 2.95 o.p. (ISBN 0-8006-1232-9, Fortress). Augsburg Fortress.

Learning to Help: Basic Skills Exercises. Philip Priestley & James McGuire. LC 82-18860. (Illus.). 200p. 1983. 28.00 o.p. (ISBN 0-422-77470-7, NO. 3786, Pub. by Tavistock); pap. 12.50 o.p. (ISBN 0-422-77480-4, NO. 3787). Routledge Chapman & Hall.

Learning to Labour: How Working Class Kids Get Working Class Jobs. Paul E. Willis. (Illus.). 216p. 1977. 24.00x o.p. (ISBN 0-566-00150-0, 00730-7, Pub. by Saxon Hse England). Lexington Bks.

Learning to Learn in Higher Education. Jean Wright. 199p. 1982. 28.00 o.p. (ISBN 0-7099-2744-4, Pub. by Croom Helm Ltd). Routledge Chapman & Hall.

Learning to Live Again: My Triumph over Cancer. Joel Solkoff. LC 82-18743. 220p. 1983. 16.95 o.s.i. (ISBN 0-03-057647-4). H Holt & Co.

Learning to Live from Within: A Glimpse of Jesus As Healer. George F. Freemesser. 1985. 8.95 o.p. (ISBN 0-87193-242-3). Dimension Bks.

Learning to Live with the Love of Your Life. Dorothy Greenwald & Robert Greenwald. LC 79-1825. 1979. 7.95 o.p. (ISBN 0-15-149482-7). HarBraceJ.

Learning to Live Without Violence: A Handbook for Men. rev. ed. Daniel J. Sonkin & Michael Durphy. LC 85-20388. 176p. (Orig.). 1985. pap. 10.00 o.p. (ISBN 0-912078-76-6). Volcano Pr.

Learning to Look: A Handbook for the Visual Arts. 2nd ed. Joshua C. Taylor. LC 80-26251. 086p. 1981. lib. bdg. 15.00x o.s.i. (ISBN 0-226-79152-1). U of Chicago Pr.

Learning to Nurse: Integrating Theory & Practice. Margaret F. Alexander. LC 82-9568. (Studies in Nursing). (Illus.). 259p. 1983. pap. text ed. 14.00 o.p. (ISBN 0-443-02623-8). Churchill.

Learning to Philosophize. E. R. Emmet. 1965. 4.75 o.p. (ISBN 0-8022-0456-2). Philos Lib.

Learning to Program. Howard Johnston. (Illus.). 464p. 1985. pap. text ed. 29.00 o.p. (ISBN 0-13-527754-X). P-H.

Learning to Read the Language of Americans: Sounds & Symbols. Walter N. Watts & Etheldra M. Watts. 210p. 1972. pap. 6.95x o.p. (ISBN 0-8422-0241-2). Irvington.

Learning to Spell Correctly. Barbara Gregorvich & Mary H. Manoni. LC 78-730054. (Illus.). 1978. pap. text ed. 159.00 o.s.i. (ISBN 0-89290-127-6, 331-SATC). Soc for Visual.

Learning to Swim & Other Stories. Graham Swift. 1985. 14.70 o.s.i. (ISBN 0-671-54613-9, Poseidon). S&S.

Learning to Talk Is Child's Play. Carolyn Ausberger & Margaret J. Martin. 120p. 1982. pap. text ed. 7.95 o.p. (ISBN 0-88450-826-9, 3000-B). Communication Skill.

Learning Together & Alone: Cooperation, Competition, & Individualization. David W. Johnson & Roger T. Johnson. (Illus.). 224p. 1975. pap. text ed. (ISBN 0-13-527945-3). P-H.

Learning Together in the Christian Fellowship. Sara Little. LC 56-9220. (Orig.). 1956. pap. 2.25 o.p. (ISBN 0-8042-1320-8, John Knox). Westminster John Knox.

Learning Tree. Gordon Parks. 1981. pap. 2.50 o.p. (ISBN 0-449-23855-5, Crest). Fawcett.

Learning Vacations. 4th ed. Gerson G. Eisenberg. LC 81-21002. 273p. 1981. pap. 7.95 o.p. (ISBN 0-87866-175-1). Petersons Guides.

Learning with Commodore LOGO. Daniel Watt. (Illus.). 320p. 1985. pap. text ed. 21.95 o.p. (ISBN 0-07-068581-9, BYTE Bks). McGraw.

Learning with Puppets. David Currell. 208p. 1980. 15.95 o.p. (ISBN 0-8238-0250-7). Plays.

Learning with TI LOGO. Daniel Watt. (Illus.). 336p. 1986. pap. text ed. 21.95 o.p. (ISBN 0-07-068580-0, BYTE Bks). McGraw.

Learning with Your Home Computer. Ray Curnow & Susan Curran. (Clear & Simple Home Computer Ser.: Vol. IV). (Illus.). 128p. 1984. pap. 9.50 o.p. (ISBN 0-671-49445-7, Fireside). S&S.

Learning Word Processing Concepts Using AppleWriter. LeRoy Finkel. (Illus.). 80p. 1983. text ed. 12.00 o.p. (ISBN 0-07-020986-3). McGraw.

Learning Z-BASIC on the Heath-Zenith Z-100. University of Kansas Academic Computing Services Staff. (Illus.). 304p. 1985. pap. 17.95 o.p. (ISBN 0-89303-621-8). Brady Bks.

Least You Should Know about English, Form A. 3rd, rev. ed. Teresa F. Glazier. 304p. 1985. pap. text ed. 16.95 o.p. (ISBN 0-03-069779-4, HoltC). HR&W.

Least You Should Know About English, Form A. 2nd ed. Teresa F. Glazier. 208p. 1985. pap. text ed. 12.95 o.p. (ISBN 0-03-070694-7, HoltC). HR&W.

Least You Should Know about English, Form B. 3rd ed. Teresa F. Glazier. 312p. 1986. pap. text ed. 16.95 o.p. (ISBN 0-03-002607-5, HoltC). HR&W.

Leather Boots. Gershon Kranzler. saddle-stitched 5.00 o.p. (ISBN 0-87559-130-2). Shalom.

Leather Guide, 1979-80. (ISBN 0-317-12201-0). Intl Pubns Serv.

Leatherman. Dick Gackenbach. LC 77-2584. (Illus.). 48p. (gr. 2-5). 1979. 6.95 o.p. (ISBN 0-395-28855-X, Clarion). HM.

Leatherstocking Saga. James Fenimore Cooper. Ed. by Allan Nevins. 840p. 1982. pap. 8.95 o.p. (ISBN 0-380-58453-0, 58453-0). Avon.

Leave of Absence. Ralph McInerny. LC 85-48150. 256p. 1986. 14.95 o.p. (ISBN 0-689-11783-3, Atheneum). Macmillan.

Leave of Absence: A Novel. Theodore Morrison. 1981. 12.95 o.p. (ISBN 0-393-01439-8). Norton.

Leave Well Enough Alone. Rosemary Wells. (gr. 7-9). 1980. pap. 1.95 o.p. (ISBN 0-671-42687-7). Archway.

Leaves from Conjurors' Scrap Books, or, Modern Magicians & Their Works. Hardin J. Burlingame. LC 74-148349. 280p. 1971. Repr. of 1891 ed. 40.00x o.p. (ISBN 0-8103-3371-6). Gale.

Leaves of Autumn. Devi Mitra. 64p. 1986. 6.95 o.p. (ISBN 0-8062-2838-5). Carlton.

Leaves of Grass. Walt Whitman. 1968. 5.95 o.p. (ISBN 0-88088-574-2). Peter Pauper.

Leaves of Grass: Comprehensive Reader's Edition. Walt Whitman. Ed. by Sculley Bradley et al. 1968. pap. 6.95 o.p. (ISBN 0-393-00430-9, Norton Lib). Norton.

Leaves Still Talk. David Kalugin. (Illus.). 1979. pap. 4.95 o.p. (ISBN 0-933586-04-3). Book Promo Pr.

Leaves Turn Autumn. Lea. (Illus.). 160p. 1983. 8.50 o.p. (ISBN 0-682-49984-6). Exposition-Phoenix.

Leaving Home. Evelyn Bence. 144p. 1986. pap. 4.95 o.p. (ISBN 0-8423-2129-2). Tyndale.

Leaving Home. Arlene K. Richards & Irene Willis. LC 80-12721. 192p. (gr. 7 up). 1980. 8.95 o.s.i. (ISBN 0-689-30757-8, Atheneum). Macmillan.

Leaving School & Starting Work. E. Venables. 1968. text ed. 6.05 o.p. (ISBN 0-08-012954-4); pap. text ed. 3.30 o.p. (ISBN 0-08-012953-6). Pergamon.

Leaving the Hospital: Discharge Planning for Total Patient Care. Bascom W. Ratliff. 204p. 1981. 25.50 o.p. (ISBN 0-398-04146-6). C C Thomas.

LeBaron Secret. Stephen Birmingham. 1986. 17.95 o.p. (ISBN 0-316-09649-0). Little.

Leben des Bischofs Benno der Zweiter von Osnabruck. Norbert. Bd. with Ausfuehrliches Namenregister und Sachregister Mit Genauem Inhalsverzeichnis der Seither Erschienene Baende 1-90. (Geschichtschreiber der Deutschen Vorzeit Ser: Vol. 91). (Ger.). 12.00 o.p. (ISBN 0-384-41895-3). Johnson Repr.

Leben Des Heiligen Severin. 3rd ed. Eugippius. Tr. by C. Rodenbery. (Ger.). Repr. of 1912 ed. 12.00 o.p. (ISBN 0-384-14820-4). Johnson Repr.

Lebendige Literatur: Deutsches Lesebuch Fur Anfanger. 2nd ed. Frank G. Ryder & E. Allen McCormick. 1974. pap. 16.95 o.p. (ISBN 0-395-13826-4). HM.

Lebendiges Rio. Harriet Greenberg & Arnold L. Greenberg. 1979. pap. 3.50 o.p. (ISBN 0-935572-07-4). Alive Pubns.

Lebesgue Measure & Intergral. B. D. Craven. 240p. 1982. 39.95 o.p. (ISBN 0-470-20448-6, Co-Pub. with Longman). Wiley.

Lecciones para el aprendizaje del Idioma Shipibo-Conibo. Norma Faust. (Documento del Trabajo (Peru) Ser.: No. 1). 160p. 1973. pap. 6.00x o.s.i. (ISBN 0-88312-783-0); microfiche (2) 4.00 o.s.i. (ISBN 0-88312-353-3). Summer Inst Ling.

Lecherous Professor: Sexual Harassment on Campus. Billie W. Dziech & Linda Weiner. LC 82-73960. 228p. 1984. 16.95x o.p. (ISBN 0-8070-3100-3); pap. 8.95 o.p. (ISBN 0-8070-3101-1, BP 690). Beacon Pr.

Lectura y Lengua: Curso Intermedio. Laurel A. Briscoe. LC 77-83324. (Illus.). 1978. text ed. 27.95 o.p. (ISBN 0-395-25545-7). HM.

Lecturas Basicas: A Cultural Reader. 2nd ed. Helen Aguera & Modesto Diaz. 1981. pap. text ed. 13.00 o.p. (ISBN 0-03-058109-5). HR&W.

Lecturas Basicas: A Literary Reader. 2nd ed. Guillermo I. Castillo-Feliu & Edward J. Mullen. (Span.). 1981. pap. text ed. 11.95 o.p. (ISBN 0-03-058108-7). HR&W.

Lecturas Basicas Literaturas: A Literary Reader. 3rd ed. Guillermo I. Castillo-Feliu & Edward J. Mullen. 96p. (Span.). 1985. pap. text ed. 11.95 o.p. (ISBN 0-03-071031-6). HR&W.

Lecture Hall Design: A Bibliography. Mary E. Huls. (Architecture Ser.: A 1488). 6p. 1985. 2.00 o.p. (ISBN 0-89028-618-3). Vance Biblios.

Lecture Notes in Computer Science, Vol. 1: Proceedings of the Gesellschaft fuer Informatik Symposium, 3 Jahrestagung, Hamburg, 1973. Ed. by W. Bauer. xi, 508p. 1973. pap. 21.00 o.p. (ISBN 0-387-06473-7). Springer Verlag.

Lecture Notes on Anaesthetics. 3rd ed. Lunn. 1986. 14.25 o.p. (ISBN 0-8016-3063-0). Mosby.

Lecture Notes on Clinical Medicine. 3rd ed. D. Rubenstein & D. Wayne. (Illus.). 448p. 1985. pap. text ed. 14.50 o.p. (ISBN 0-632-01254-4, B4239-6). Mosby.

Lecture Notes on Opthalmology. 7th ed. Trevor & Roper. 1986. pap. 12.75 o.p. (ISBN 0-8016-5161-1). Mosby.

Lecture Notes on the Infectious Diseases. 4th ed. Mandal & Mayon. (Illus.). 288p. 1984. pap. 40.00 o.p. (ISBN 0-632-01168-8, B-3156-4). Mosby.

Lecture Notes on Vertebrate Zoology. Ronald Pearson & John N. Ball. LC 80-29672. 225p. 1981. pap. 31.95x o.p. (ISBN 0-470-27143-4). Halsted Pr.

Lectures & Essays. William K. Clifford. write for info. o.p. (ISBN 0-685-50585-5). Chelsea Pub.

Lectures et Fantaisies. Marie E. Galanti. 1979. pap. 15.50 o.p. (ISBN 0-395-30979-4). HM.

Lectures Held at the Third Plansee Seminar. Plansee Seminar De Re Metallica - 3rd - Reutte - 1958. Ed. by F. Benesovsky. (Illus.). 465p. 1959. pap. 29.00 o.p. (ISBN 0-387-80520-6). Springer Verlag.

Lectures in Dynamic Psychiatry. Ed. by Milton Kurian & Morton H. Hand. LC 63-21524. 144p. 1963. text ed. 20.00x o.s.i. (ISBN 0-8236-2960-0). Intl Univs Pr.

Lectures in Isotope Geology. E. Jaeger. Ed. by J. C. Hunziker. (Illus.). 1979. 31.00 o.p. (ISBN 0-387-09158-0). Springer-Verlag.

Lectures in Modern Analysis & Applications - Two. J. Glimm et al. Ed. by C. T. Taam. LC 76-94096. (Lecture Notes in Mathematics: Vol. 140). 1970. pap. 10.70 o.p. (ISBN 0-387-04929-0). Springer-Verlag.

Lectures in Modern Analysis & Applications, No. 3. R. M. Dudley. Ed. by C. T. Taam. LC 64-54683. (Lecture Notes in Mathematics Ser.: Vol. 170). 1970. pap. 14.00 o.p. (ISBN 0-387-05284-4). Springer-Verlag.

Lectures in Plasma Physics: The Magnetohydrodynamic Approach to the Problem of Plasma Confinement in Closed Magnetic Configurations. Ed. by C. Mercier & H. Luc. 1975. pap. 18.15 o.p. (ISBN 0-08-020456-2). Pergamon.

Lectures in Scattering Theory. A. G. Sitenko. Ed. & tr. by P. J. Shepherd. 280p. 1971. 51.00 o.p. (ISBN 0-08-016574-5). Pergamon.

Lectures in Set Theory with Particular Emphasis on the Method of Forcing. T. J. Jech. (Lecture Notes in Mathematics: Vol. 217). 1971. pap. 5.70 o.p. (ISBN 0-387-05564-9). Springer-Verlag.

Lectures in Statistical Physics. R. Balescu et al. LC 78-155594. (Lecture Notes in Physics: Vol. 7). 1971. pap. 10.70 o.p. (ISBN 0-387-05418-9). Springer-Verlag.

Lectures in Theoretical Physics, Vol. 14 B: Mathematical Methods in Theoretical Physics. Ed. by Asim O. Barut & W. Brittin. LC 59-13034. (Illus.). 520p. 1973. 32.50 o.p. (ISBN 0-87081-047-2). Univ Pr Colo.

Lectures in Theoretical Physics Vol. 13: Desitter & Conformal Groups & Their Applications. Ed. by Asim O. Barut & Wesley E. Brittin. LC 59-13034. 1971. 32.50x o.p. (ISBN 0-87081-014-6); pap. text ed. 10.00x o.p. (ISBN 0-87081-039-1). Univ Pr Colo.

Lectures in Theoretical Physics, Vol. 14A: Topics in Strong Interactions. Ed. by A. O. Barut & Wesley E. Brittin. LC 59-13034. (Illus.). 455p. 1972. text ed. 32.50x o.p. (ISBN 0-87081-043-X). Univ Pr Colo.

Lectures libres. Rebecca M. Valette. (Orig., Fr.). 1969. pap. text ed. 7.95 o.p. (ISBN 0-15-550460-6, HC). HarBraceJ.

Lectures on Algebraic & Differential Topology: Delivered at the II. ELAM. R. Bott et al. LC 72-86695. (Lecture Notes in Mathematics: Vol. 279). v, 174p. 1972. pap. 7.00 o.p. (ISBN 0-387-05944-X). Springer-Verlag.

Lectures on Boolean Algebras. P. R. Halmos. 150p. 1974. pap. 13.50 o.p. (ISBN 0-387-90094-2). Springer-Verlag.

Lectures on Current Algebra & Its Applications. Sam B. Treiman & Roman Jackiw. LC 70-181519. (Princeton Series in Physics). 280p. 1972. 24.50 o.p. (ISBN 0-691-08118-2); pap. 6.95 o.p. (ISBN 0-691-08107-7). Princeton U Pr.

Lectures on Density Wave Theory. K. Rohlfs. LC 77-20939. (Lecture Notes in Physics: Vol. 69). 1977. pap. text ed. 12.00 o.p. (ISBN 0-387-08448-7). Springer-Verlag.

Lectures on Differential Equations. S. Lefschetz. (Annals of Math Studies). 1946. 16.00 o.p. (ISBN 0-527-02730-8). Kraus Repr.

Lectures on Don Quixote. Vladimir Nabokov. Ed. by Fredson Bowers. LC 82-47665. 256p. 1983. 17.95 o.p. (ISBN 0-15-149595-5). HarBraceJ.

Lectures on Ergodic Theory. P. R. Halmos. LC 60-8964. 10.95 o.p. (ISBN 0-8284-0142-X). Chelsea Pub.

Lectures on Field Theory & the Many-Body Problem. Ed. by E. R. Caianiello. (Spring School Lectures, 1961). 1961. 40.50 o.p. (ISBN 0-12-154556-3). Acad Pr.

Lectures on Forms of Higher Degree. J. I. Igusa. (Tata Institute Lecture Notes Ser.). 1979. pap. 15.00 o.p. (ISBN 0-387-08944-6). Springer-Verlag.

Lectures on Geometric Quantization. D. J. Simms. Ed. by J. Ehlers et al. (Lecture Notes in Physics: Vol. 53). 1976. soft cover 12.00 o.p. (ISBN 0-387-07860-6). Springer-Verlag.

Lectures on Gerontology, 2 vols. Ed. by A. Viidik. 1982. Vol. 1. 44.00 o.p. (ISBN 0-12-721601-4); Vol. 2. (ISBN 0-12-721602-2). Acad Pr.

Lectures on Gleason Parts. H. S. Bear. (Lecture Notes in Mathematics: Vol. 121). 1970. 10.70 o.p. (ISBN 0-387-04910-X). Springer-Verlag.

Lectures on Integration of the Equations of Motion of a Rigid Body about a Fixed Point. V. V. Golubev. 240p. 1953. text ed. 49.00x o.p. (Pub. by Keter Pub Jerusalem). Coronet Bks.

Lectures on Introduction to Moduli Problems & Orbit Spaces. P. E. Newstead. (Tata Institute Lecture Notes). 1979. pap. 12.00 o.p. (ISBN 0-387-08851-2). Springer-Verlag.

Lectures on Linear Least-Squares Estimation. T. Kailath. (CISM International Centre for Mechanical Sciences: Vol. 140). (Illus.). 1978. pap. 17.20 o.p. (ISBN 0-387-81386-1). Springer-Verlag.

Lectures on Linear Sequential Machines. M. A. Harrison. 1970. 52.50 o.p. (ISBN 0-12-327750-7). Acad Pr.

Lectures on Macroeconomic Planning, 2 pts. L. Johansen. 1977. Pt. 1: General Aspects. 35.00 o.p. (ISBN 0-7204-0565-3, North-Holland); Pt. 2: Centralization, Decentralization & Planning Under Uncertainty. 47.00 o.p. (ISBN 0-444-85119-4). Elsevier.

Lectures on Mathematical Theory of Extremum Problems. I. V. Girsanov. Tr. by D. Louvish from Rus. LC 72-80360. (Lecture Notes in Economics & Mathematical Systems: Vol. 67). (Illus.). 139p. 1979. pap. 11.00 o.p. (ISBN 0-387-05857-5). Springer-Verlag.

Lectures on Metaphysics & Logic, 4 Vols. William Hamilton. Repr. of 1861 ed. Set. cancelled o.s.i. (ISBN 3-7728-0170-6). Adlers Foreign Bks.

Lectures on Operator Algebras: Tulane University Ring & Operator Theory Year, 1970-71, Vol. 2. Ed. by K. H. Hofmann. (Lecture Notes in Mathematics: Vol. 247). 786p. 1972. pap. 19.00 o.p. (ISBN 0-387-05729-3). Springer-Verlag.

Lectures on Optimization: Theory & Algorithms. J. Cea & M. K. Murthy. (Tata Institute Lectures on Mathematics Ser.). 1979. pap. 14.00 o.p. (ISBN 0-387-08850-4). Springer-Verlag.

Lectures on Ordinary Differential Equations: A Symposium Vol. Ed. by Robert McKelvey. 1970. 70.50 o.p. (ISBN 0-12-485150-9). Acad Pr.

Lectures on Partial & Pfaffian Differential Equations. W. Haack & W. Wendland. 1972. 140.00 o.p. (ISBN 0-08-016553-2); pap. 27.00 o.p. (ISBN 0-08-018997-0). Pergamon.

Lectures on Radiating Gasdynamics: General Equations & Boundary Conditions. CISM (International Center for Mechanical Sciences) Staff. Ed. by C. Ferrari. (CISM Publications: No. 146). (Illus.). 83p. 1975. pap. 12.40 o.p. (ISBN 0-387-81204-0). Springer-Verlag.

Lectures on Rings & Modules Vol. 1: Tulane University Ring & Operator Theory Year, 1970-71, Vol. 1. K. H. Hofmann. (Lecture Notes in Mathematics Ser.: Vol. 246). 661p. 1972. pap. 19.00 o.p. (ISBN 0-387-05760-9). Springer-Verlag.

Lectures on Russian Literature. Vladimir Nabokov. Ed. by Fredson Bowers. LC 81-47315. 416p. 1981. 19.95 o.p. (ISBN 0-15-149599-8). HarBraceJ.

Lectures on Selected Topics in Equilibrium & Non-Equilibrium Statistical Mechanics. D. Ter-Haar & F. Henin. LC 77-8300. 1977. 33.00 o.p. (ISBN 0-08-017937-1). Pergamon.

Lectures on Solid State Physics. G. Busch & D. Schade. 1977. text ed. 69.00 o.p. (ISBN 0-08-016894-9); pap. text ed. 31.00 o.p. (ISBN 0-08-021653-6). Pergamon.

Lectures on Stochastic Differential Equations & Malliavin Calculus. S. Watanabe. (Tata Institute Lectures on Mathematics Ser.). viii, 118p. 1984. pap. 15.00 o.p. (ISBN 0-387-12897-2). Springer-Verlag.

Lectures on Structure & Significance of Science. H. Mohr. (Illus.). 1977. 33.90 o.p. (ISBN 0-387-08091-0). Springer-Verlag.

Lectures on Summability. A. Peyerimhoff. LC 79-97995. (Lecture Notes in Mathematics: Vol. 107). 1969. pap. 10.70 o.p. (ISBN 0-387-04626-7). Springer-Verlag.

Lectures on the Philosophy of Religion, 3 vols. Georg W. Hegel. Tr. by E. B. Speirs & J. B. Sanderson. 1968. Repr. of 1895 ed. Set. text ed. 80.00x o.p. (ISBN 0-7100-6080-7). Humanities.

Lectures on the Theory of Algebraic Functions of One Variable. M. Deuring. LC 72-97679. (Lecture Notes in Mathematics Ser.: Vol. 314). 151p. 1973. pap. 12.00 o.p. (ISBN 0-387-06152-5). Springer-Verlag.

Lectures on the Theory of Functions of a Complex Variable. George W. Mackey. LC 76-58264. 274p. 1977. Repr. of 1967 ed. 20.50 o.p. (ISBN 0-88275-531-5). Krieger.

Lectures on the Theory of Functions of Several Complex Variables. B. Malgrange. (Tata Institute Lectures on Mathematics Ser.). iii, 132p. 1984. pap. 7.10 o.p. (ISBN 0-387-12875-1). Springer-Verlag.

Lectures on Torus Embeddings & Applications. T. Oda. (Tata Institute Lecture Notes Ser.). 1979. pap. 14.00 o.p. (ISBN 0-387-08852-0). Springer-Verlag.

Lectures on Transcendental Numbers. K. Mahler. Ed. by B. Divis & W. J. Le Veque. 1976. 17.00 o.p. (ISBN 0-387-07986-6). Springer-Verlag.

Lectures on Wave Propagation. G. B. Whitman. (Tata Institute Lectures on Mathematics). (Illus.). 151p. 1980. pap. 9.00 o.p. (ISBN 0-387-08945-4). Springer-Verlag.

Led Zeppelin. Philip Kamin. (Robus Bks.). (Illus.). 32p. (Orig.). (gr. 3 up). 1986. pap. 4.95 o.p. (ISBN 0-88188-424-3, HL00183438). H Leonard Pub Corp.

Lee Krasner, Solstice. Barbara Novak. (Illus.). 24p. (Orig.). 1981. pap. 9.00 o.p. (ISBN 0-938608-02-9). Pace Pubns.

Lee's Lieutenants, 3 vols. Douglas S. Freeman. 1942-1944. Set. lib. rep. ed. 90.00 o.s.i. (ISBN 0-684-17926-1, ScribT). Scribner.

Lee's Meadow Country. John Hunt. (Lythway Ser.). 168p. 1988. lib. bdg. 17.50x o.p. (ISBN 0-7451-0635-8, Pub. by Chiver Pr UK). G K Hall.

Leeson Park & Belsize Square. Peter Straub. 1984. 11.95 o.p. (ISBN 0-934438-91-9); deluxe ed. 30.00 signed o.p. (ISBN 0-934438-90-0). Underwood-Miller.

Left & Right. Li Zigan. (Illus.). 23p. (gr. k-2). 1984. pap. 2.50 o.p. (ISBN 0-8351-1404-X). China Bks.

Left at the Post. Evan Jones. LC 83-23262. 56p. 1984. 10.95 o.p. (ISBN 0-7022-1717-4); pap. 5.95 o.p. (ISBN 0-7022-1718-2). U of Queensland Pr.

Left Bank Celebrity Cookbook. Luc Meyer. 187p. (Orig.). 1982. pap. 8.95 o.s.i. (ISBN 0-89716-064-9). Peanut Butter.

Left Bank: Writers, Artists, & Politics from the Popular Front to the Cold War. Herbert R. Lottman. LC 81-13276. 352p. 1982. 15.95 o.p. (ISBN 0-395-31322-8). HM.

Left Foot, Right Foot March Album for Piano (for School & Lodge) 2.50 o.p. (ISBN 0-913650-58-7). CPP Belwin.

Left Hand of God: Essays on Discipleship & Patriotism. Ed. by William H. Lazareth et al. LC 75-36457. (Confrontation Bks). 176p. 1976. pap. 1.00x o.p. (ISBN 0-8006-1452-6, Fortress). Augsburg Fortress.

Left-Handed Woman. Peter Handke. Tr. by Ralph Manheim from Ger. 87p. 1978. 7.95 o.p. (ISBN 0-374-18497-6). FS&G.

Left, Right, Left, Right. Muriel Stanek. LC 79-79548. (Albert Whitman Concept Bks.). (Illus.). 40p. (gr. k-2). 1969. PLB 11.25 o.p. (ISBN 0-8075-4421-3). A Whitman.

Left, the Right & the Jews. W. D. Rubinstein. LC 82-8614. 256p. 1982. 20.00x o.p. (ISBN 0-87663-400-5). Universe.

Left Ventricular Performance. (Landmark Ser.). 1979. 22.50x o.p. (ISBN 0-8422-4122-1). Irvington.

Leftovers. Coralie Castle. LC 83-17203. (Illus.). 192p. (Orig.). 1983. pap. 8.95 o.p. (ISBN 0-89286-218-1, One Hund One Prods). Ortho.

Leg Length Discrepancy: The Injured Knee. Ed. by D. S. Hungerford. 1977. 24.00 o.p. (ISBN 0-387-08037-6). Springer-Verlag.

Leg to Stand On. Oliver Sacks. 256p. 1984. 14.70 o.s.i. (ISBN 0-671-46780-8). Summit Bks.

Legacy. Florence Hurd. 1977. pap. 1.95 o.p. (ISBN 0-380-01677-X, 33480). Avon.

Legacy of a Gunfighter. W. F. Bragg. 1980. pap. 1.75 o.s.i. (ISBN 0-8439-0790-8, Pub. by Leisure Bks CT). Dorchester Pub Co.

Legacy of Chopin. Jan Holzman. 1954. (ISBN 0-8022-0736-7). Philos Lib.

Legacy of Drennan's Crossing. Wanda Luttrell. 400p. 1985. 4.50 o.p. (ISBN 0-8423-2112-8). Tyndale.

Legacy of Eve: Women of the Bible. Nancy Tischler. LC 76-44971. 1977. pap. 3.95 o.p. (ISBN 0-8042-0074-2, John Knox). Westminster John Knox.

Legacy of Ladysmith. John K. Crane. 1986. 17.45 o.p. (ISBN 0-671-60586-0, Linden Pr). S&S.

Legacy of Loneliness. Sharon B. Wagner. 1974. pap. 0.95 o.p. (ISBN 0-380-01324-X, 18531). Avon.

Legacy of Maimonides. Ben Z. Bokser. (ISBN 0-8022-0149-0). Philos Lib.

Legacy of Minneapolis: Preservation Amid Change. John R. Borchert et al. (Illus.). 195p. 1983. pap. 14.95 o.p. (ISBN 0-89658-047-4). Voyageur Pr.

Legacy of the Desert: Understanding the Arabs. Jules Archer. (gr. 7-12). 1976. 8.95 o.p. (ISBN 0-316-04965-4). Little.

Legacy of the Holocaust: Psychohistorical Themes in the Second Generation. Robert M. Prince. Ed. by Peter E. Nathan. LC 84-24036. (Research in Clinical Psychology Ser.: No. 12). 240p. 1985. 39.95 o.p. (ISBN 0-8357-1627-9). UMI Res Pr.

Legacy of the Lake. Michael A. Smith. 1980. pap. 2.25 o.p. (ISBN 0-380-75879-2, 75879-2). Avon.

Legacy of Womanhood. Elizabeth M. Mantis. 64p. 1985. 7.50 o.p. (ISBN 0-682-40207-9). Exposition-Phoenix.

Legacy to Lebanon. Grace D. Guthrie. (Illus.). 154p. 1984. pap. 8.00 o.p. (ISBN 0-89410-550-7, Pub. by G D Guthrie). Three Continents.

Legal Abortion: The English Experience. A. Hordern. 1971. 85.00 o.p. (ISBN 0-08-016567-2). Pergamon.

Legal Accountability in the Nursing Process. 2nd ed. Irene Murchison et al. LC 81-16956. (Illus.). 188p. 1982. pap. text ed. 19.95 o.p. (ISBN 0-8016-3604-3). Mosby.

Legal Aid in the United States: A Study of the Availability of Lawyers' Services for Persons Unable to Pay Fees. Emery A. Brownell. LC 77-141417. (Illus.). xxiv, 114p. 1971. Repr. of 1951 ed. lib. bdg. 35.00x o.p. (ISBN 0-8371-4859-5, BRLE). Greenwood.

Legal & Business Aspects of the Magazine Industry, 1984, Vol 397. Stephen H. Gross & Edward L. Smith. LC 79-88392. (Patents, Copyrights, Trademarks, & Literary Property Course Handbook Ser.: 1983-1984). 1984. 15.00 o.p. (ISBN 0-686-59549-1, G43745). PLI.

Legal & Business Problems of the Advertising Industry 1984. (Patents, Copyrights, Trademarks, & Literary Property Course Handbook Ser.). 300p. 1984. 15.00 o.p. (ISBN 0-686-79966-6, G4-3746). PLI.

Legal & Ethical Issues in Cancer Care in the United States. Dennis A. Robbins. 176p. 1983. 25.50 o.p. (ISBN 0-398-04841-X). C C Thomas.

Legal Aspects of Certification & Accreditation. Donald G. Langsley. LC 83-72022. 308p. 1983. 34.95 o.p. Am Bd Med Spec.

Legal Aspects of Chemical Testing for Intoxication. 2nd ed. James C. Drennan. LC 83-621587. (Administration of Justice Memoranda Ser.). 34p. 1982. 3.00 o.p. Institute Government.

Legal Aspects of Doing Business in Japan, 1983. Practising Law Institute Staff et al. LC 82-62774. (Commercial Law & Practice Course Handbook Ser.: No. 295). (Illus.). 512p. 1983. 40.00 o.p. PLI.

Legal Aspects of Doing Business with Japan. (Commercial Law & Practice Ser.). 222p. 1985. 30.00 o.p. (ISBN 0-686-80119-9, A4-3099). PLI.

Legal Aspects of Educating the Developmentally Disabled. H. Rutherford Turnbull. 50p. 1975. 4.95 o.p. (ISBN 0-686-39469-0). Institute Government.

Legal Aspects of Evidence. Robert W. Ferguson & Allan H. Stokke. (HBJ Criminal Justice Ser.). 139p. 1979. pap. text ed. 10.95 o.p. (ISBN 0-15-550490-8, HC). HarBraceJ.

Legal Aspects of Health Care Administration. 2nd ed. George D. Pozgar. LC 82-22663. 265p. 1983. 29.50 o.p. (ISBN 0-89443-810-7). Aspen Pub.

Legal Aspects of Marketing. Marshall C. Howard. 1964. pap. text ed. 19.95 o.p. (ISBN 0-07-030531-5). McGraw.

Legal Aspects of Medical Practice. 3rd ed. Bernard Knight. (Illus.). 1982. pap. text ed. 17.50 o.p. (ISBN 0-443-02558-4). Churchill.

Legal Aspects of Private Security. Arthur J. Bilek et al. LC 79-55202. 287p. 1981. text ed. 16.95 o.p. (ISBN 0-87084-488-1). Anderson Pub Co.

Legal Aspects of Real Estate Timesharing. Practising Law Institute Staff & William B. Ingersoll. LC 82-60440. (Real Estate Law & Practice Course Ser.: No. 220). (Illus.). 1982. 40.00 o.p. (N4-4391). PLI.

Legal Aspects of the Hospital's Role in Obtaining Organs for Transplantation. Jane E. Baluses. LC 84-621642. (Health Law Bulletin Ser.: No. 65). 1983. 2.00 o.p. Institute Government.

Legal Aspects of Travel Agency Operation. Jeffrey Miller. LC 81-84033. (Travel Management Library). 208p. 1982. 21.95 o.p. (ISBN 0-916032-14-0). Delmar.

Legal Aspects of Zoning Practices: A Checklist, 1980-1984. Dale E. Casper. (Public Administration Ser.: P 1823). 15p. 1985. 2.25 o.p. (ISBN 0-89028-673-6). Vance Biblios.

Legal Assassination of a Sheriff. A. Eugene Hoag. LC 84-90119. 199p. 1985. 12.95 o.p. (ISBN 0-533-06198-9). Vantage.

Legal Assistant's Handbook. Thomas W. Brunner et al. 225p. 1982. 20.00 o.p. (ISBN 0-87179-368-7); pap. 27.00 o.p. (ISBN 0-87179-369-5, 0369). BNA.

Legal Boundaries of California Nursing Practice. 3rd ed. Robert D. Anderson. 221p. 1984. text ed. 35.00 home study course o.p.; pap. 15.00 reference book o.p. (ISBN 0-942028-11-2). R D Anderson.

Legal Care for Your Software. Daniel Remer. (Illus.). 248p. 1983. pap. 24.95 o.p. (ISBN 0-917316-58-4). Nolo Pr.

Legal Care for Your Software. 2nd ed. Daniel Remer. LC 82-1822. 247p. 1984. pap. 24.95 o.p. (ISBN 0-917316-85-1). Nolo Pr.

Legal Controls of International Conflict, 2 vols. Julius Stone. LC 79-147739. (Library of War & Peace; International Law). lib. bdg. 38.00 ea. o.p. Garland Pub.

Legal Dictionary. E. A. Geissler & Lise Wolff. 200p. 1980. 45.00x o.p. (ISBN 0-686-44720-4, Pub. by Collets (UK)). State Mutual Bk.

Legal Economics. 329p. 1983. 12.00 o.p. (ISBN 0-318-02416-0). ICLE Georgia.

Legal Education & Lawyer Competency. E. Gordon Gee & Donald W. Jackson. 370p. (Orig.). 1982. (ISBN 0-8425-2059-7). Brigham.

Legal Environment of Business. Rate A. Howell et al. LC 83-16329. 690p. 1984. text ed. 32.95x o.p. (ISBN 0-03-061809-6); instr's. manual with test bank 19.95 o.p. (ISBN 0-03-061811-8); study guide 12.95x o.p. (ISBN 0-03-061812-6). Dryden Pr.

Legal Environment of Business. 2nd ed. Roger E. Meiners & Al H. Ringleb. (Illus.). 715p. 1985. text ed. 41.75 o.p. (ISBN 0-314-85278-6). West Pub.

Legal Environment of Business: Public & Private Laws. 3rd. ed. Michael P. Litka & James E. Inman. LC 87-12754. 544p. 32.95 o.p. (ISBN 0-317-60069-9); text ed. 29.95 o.p. (ISBN 0-317-60070-2). Pub Horizons.

Legal, Ethical & Management Aspects of the Dental Care System. 2nd ed. Irene R. Woodall. LC 82-8198. (Illus.). 300p. 1982. pap. text ed. 21.95 o.p. (ISBN 0-8016-5683-4). Mosby.

Legal Ethics. Henry S. Drinker. LC 80-11445. (Legal Studies of the William Nelson Cromwell Foundation). xxii, 448p. 1980. Repr. of 1953 ed. lib. bdg. 42.50x o.p. (ISBN 0-313-22321-1, DRLG). Greenwood.

Legal Ethics Problems. Mortimer D. Schwartz & Richard C. Wydick. (American Casebook Ser.). 210p. 1983. pap. text ed. write for info. Tchr's. manual o.p. (ISBN 0-314-80558-3). West Pub.

Legal Ethics Problems. Mortimer O. Schwartz & Richard C. Wydick. LC 83-14630. (American Casebook Ser.). 285p. 1983. text ed. 17.95 o.p. (ISBN 0-314-75956-5). West Pub.

Legal Ethics, Professional Responsibility: A Selected Bibliography of Articles. Dittakavi Nagakansara Rao. LC 85-184600. (Public Administration Ser.). 18p. 1985. 3.00 o.p. (ISBN 0-89028-414-8, P 1684). Vance Biblios.

Legal Foundations of Land Use Planning. Jerome G. Rose. 561p. 1979. 17.95 o.p. Transaction Pubs.

Legal Guide for Lesbian & Gay Couples. 4th ed. Denis Clifford & Hayden Curry. Ed. by Ralph Warner. LC 80-18278. (Illus.). 300p. 1986. pap. 17.95 o.p. (ISBN 0-87337-021-X). Nolo Pr.

Legal Guide for North Carolina School Board Members. Ann M. Dellinger. 70p. 1978. 2.50 o.p. (ISBN 0-686-39471-2). Institute Government.

Legal Guide for the Family. Donald Very & Eugene F. Keefe. 370p. 1988. deluxe ed. write for info. o.p. (ISBN 0-89434-091-3). Ferguson.

Legal Guide for the Visual Artist. Tad Crawford. 208p. 1985. pap. 16.95 o.p. (ISBN 0-942604-08-3). Madison Square.

Legal Handbook for Architects, Engineers & Contractors, Vol. 2. Ed. by Albert Dib & James K. Grant. 270p. 1986. 45.00 o.p. (ISBN 0-87632-486-3). Clark Boardman.

Legal Handbook for Small Business. Marc J. Lane. LC 77-13774. 1978. 15.95 o.p. (ISBN 0-8144-5452-6). AMACOM.

Legal Instruments Embodying the Results of the 1964-1967 Trade Conference, 5 vols. General Agreement on Tariffs & Trade Staff. (Orig.). 1967. Set. pap. 122.00 o.p. (ISBN 0-685-11722-7, G22, GATT). UNIPUB.

Legal Issues for Library & Information Managers. Ed. by William Z. Nasri & John R. Rizzo. 145p. 1987. 24.95 o.s.i. (ISBN 0-86656-591-4). Haworth Pr.

Legal Issues in Pension Investment 1985. 483p. 1985. 45.00 o.p. (J4-3577). PLI.

Legal Issues of Female Inmates. Katherine Gabel et al. LC 83-110559. (Illus.). 1982. 6.00 o.p. (ISBN 0-317-04103-7). Smith Coll.

Legal Limits of Journalism. H. Lloyd. 1968. pap. text ed. 4.20 o.p. (ISBN 0-08-012914-5). Pergamon.

Legal Limits on the Use of Chemical & Biological Weapons. Ann V. Thomas & A. J. Thomas, Jr. LC 78-128123. 344p. 1970. 17.95x o.p. (ISBN 0-87074-111-X). SMU Press.

Legal Malpractice. 2nd ed. Ronald E. Mallen. 191p. 1985. (ISBN 0-314-91272-X). West Pub.

Legal Medicine with Special Reference to Diagnostic Imaging. Ed. by A. Everette James. LC 79-19277. (Illus.). 412p. 1980. text ed. 35.00 o.p. (ISBN 0-8067-0951-0). Urban & S.

Legal Papers of John Adams, 3 vols. Ed. by Lyman H. Butterfield et al. LC 65-13855. (Adams Papers Ser). (Illus.). 1968. 3.95 ea. o.p. (Atheneum). Vol. 1 (ISBN 0-689-70040-7, TAP 9). Vol. 2 (ISBN 0-689-70041-5, TAP 10). Vol. 3 (ISBN 0-689-70042-3, TAP 11). Macmillan.

Legal Pitfalls in Architecture, Engineering & Building Construction. N. Walker et al. 1978. text ed. 29.50 o.p. (ISBN 0-07-067851-0). McGraw.

Legal Problems of the Poor: Cases & Materials. Arthur L. Berney et al. 1440p. 1975. 25.50 o.p. (ISBN 0-316-09189-8). Little.

Legal Process & International Order see United States & the World Court.

Legal Protection for Microbiology & Genetic Engineering Inventions. R. Saliwanchik. Ed. by J. E. Davies. (Biotechnology Ser.: No. 1). 1982. text ed. 49.95 o.p. (ISBN 0-201-10938-7). Benjamin-Cummings.

Legal Psychology: Eyewitness Testimony - Jury Behavior. L. Craig Parker, Jr. 196p. 1980. 28.00x o.p. (ISBN 0-398-04054-0). C C Thomas.

Legal Realism & Justice. Edwin N. Garlan. xii, 161p. 1981. Repr. of 1941 ed. lib. bdg. 20.00x o.p. (ISBN 0-8377-0614-9). Rothman.

Legal Regulation of Consumer Credit. Stanley Morganstern. LC 72-4364. (Legal Almanac Ser.: No. 70). 128p. 1972. 6.95 o.p. (ISBN 0-379-11083-0). Oceana.

Legal Remedies for Sexual Harassment. Women's Legal Defense Fund Staff. 16p. 1983. pap. 5.00 o.p. (ISBN 0-932689-09-4). Women's Legal Defense.

Legal Research. Charles P. Nemeth. (Illus.). 256p. 1987. pap. text ed. 25.00 o.p. (ISBN 0-13-528175-X). P-H.

Legal Research: A Self-Teaching Guide to the Law Library. W. William Hodes. 184p. 1983. 15.00 o.p. (ISBN 1-55681-046-6); tchr's. manual 2.50 o.p. (ISBN 1-55681-047-4). Natl Inst Trial Ad.

Legal Research Manual: A Game Plan for Legal Research & Analysis. Christopher G. Wren & Jill R. Wren. LC 83-9955. (Illus.). 197p. (Orig.). 1983. pap. text ed. 8.95 o.p. (ISBN 0-916951-15-4). Adams & Ambrose.

Legal Responsibilities of the Local Zoning Administrator in North Carolina. Phillip P. Green. 102p. 1982. 5.00 o.p. (ISBN 0-686-39444-5). Institute Government.

Legal Responsibility & Moral Responsibility. Walter Moberly. Ed. by Franklin Sherman. LC 65-21820. (Facet Bks). 64p. (Orig.). 1965. pap. 1.00 o.p. (ISBN 0-8006-3020-3, 1-3020, Fortress). Augsburg Fortress.

Legal Rights & Responsibilities of Indiana Teachers. 4th ed. Ed. by Fred Swalls et al. 1980. pap. text ed. 8.95x o.p. (ISBN 0-8134-2152-7, 2152). Inter Print Pubs.

Legal Rights of Nonsmokers. Alvan Brody & Betty Brody. 1977. pap. 1.75 o.p. (ISBN 0-380-01771-7, 35048). Avon.

Legal Secretarial Procedures. Joyce Morton. LC 78-23892. 1979. pap. text ed. (ISBN 0-13-528489-9). P-H.

Legal Secretary's Encyclopedic Dictionary. 3rd ed. Ed. by Prentice-Hall Editorial Staff. Mary A. DeVries. LC 81-8700. 445p. 1982. 24.95 o.p. (ISBN 0-13-528869-X, Busn). P-H.

Legal Structure of Defense Organization Memorandum Prepared for the President's Blue Ribbon Commission on Defense Management. 187p. 1986. pap. 9.00 o.p. (ISBN 0-318-21298-6, S/N 040-000-00502-1). USGPO.

Legal Systems. Bernadine Meyer & Blair J. Kolasa. (Illus.). 1978. text ed. (ISBN 0-13-529404-5). P-H.

Legal Systems & Social Systems. Ed. by Adam Podgorecki et al. LC 85-14920. 288p. 1985. 32.95 o.p. (ISBN 0-7099-2075-X, Pub. by Croom Helm Ltd). Routledge Chapman & Hall.

Legal Terminology English & German. Ruediger Renner & Jeffery Tooth. (Eng. & Ger.). cancelled o.s.i. Adlers Foreign Bks.

Legal Terminology Handbook. David Garrett & Bryn Henderson. 228p. 1986. pap. 25.00 o.p. (ISBN 0-941161-04-8). Pes Inc WI.

Legal Times of Washington D. C. Circuit Handbook. Ed. by Law & Business Inc. Staff. 1061p. Date not set. Supplement avail. 55.00 o.p. (ISBN 0-15-100017-4, #H39867, Pub. by Law & Business). HarBraceJ.

Legal-Wise: Self-Help Legal Forms Guide. Carl W. Battle. 116p. 1985. 9.95 o.p. (ISBN 0-533-06355-8). Vantage.

Legal Word Book. Frank S. Gordon & Thomas Hemnes. 1978. 7.95 o.p. (ISBN 0-395-26662-9). HM.

Legal Writing: Sense & Nonsense. David Mellinkoff. 272p. (Orig.). 1981. pap. text ed. 11.95 o.p. (ISBN 0-314-63275-1). West Pub.

Legend. Peter J. Laucks. 64p. 1983. 6.50 o.p. (ISBN 0-682-40122-6). Exposition-Phoenix.

Legend & the Storm. Cal Roy. LC 75-17931. (Illus.). 224p. (gr. 7 up). 1975. 6.95 o.p. (ISBN 0-374-34367-5). FS&G.

Legend in Blue Steel. Spider Page. (Blue Steel: No. 1). 1978. pap. 1.50 o.p. (ISBN 0-89300-002-7). Blazing Pubns.

Legend of Arthur in the Middle Ages. Ed. by P. B. Grout et al. (Arthurian Studies: VII). 254p. 1983. 51.00 o.p. (ISBN 0-85991-132-2, Pub. by Boydell & Brewer). Longwood Pub Group.

Legend of Bear Bryant. Mickey Herskowitz. (Illus.). 1986. text ed. 17.95 o.p. (ISBN 0-07-028398-2). McGraw.

Legend of Good Women: Written in Praise of Women Faithful in Love by Geoffrey Chaucer. Florence H. Anastasas. 1976. 10.00 o.p. (ISBN 0-682-48385-0, University). Exposition-Phoenix.

Legend of Henry Ford. Keith Sward. LC 68-16412. 1968. pap. text ed. 5.95x o.p. (ISBN 0-689-70191-8, 129, Atheneum). Macmillan.

Legend of New Amsterdam. Peter Spier. LC 78-6032. (Illus.). 32p. (ps-3). 1979. PLB 7.95a o.s.i. (ISBN 0-385-13180-1). Doubleday.

Legend of Salome. H. G. Zagona. 146p. (Orig.). 1959. pap. text ed. 18.00x o.p. (ISBN 0-317-55992-3, Pub. by Droz Switzerland). Coronet Bks.

Legend of Sleepy Hollow & Other Tales. Washington Irving. LC 86-62660. (Illus.). 248p. (gr. 6-12). 1987. 12.95 o.p. (ISBN 0-89577-255-8). RD Assn.

Legend of the American Rabbit. Stewart Moskowitz. Ed. by Kate Klimo. (Moskowitz Bks.). (Illus.). 32p. 1983. 4.80 o.s.i. (ISBN 0-671-45544-3, Little Simon). S&S.

Legend of the American Rabbit. Stewart Moskowitz. LC 82-7930. (Illus.). 48p. (ps-2). 1982. lib. bdg. 8.79 o.s.i. (ISBN 0-671-45885-X). Messner.

Legend of the Doozer Who Didn't. Louise Gikow. LC 84-66623. (Fraggle Rock Bks.). (Illus.). 32p. (ps-2). 1984. 5.95 o.s.i. (ISBN 0-03-000717-8); pap. 1.95 o.s.i. (ISBN 0-03-004563-0). H Holt & Co.

Legend of the Milky Way. Lee. (gr. 2-6). 11.50 o.s.i. (ISBN 0-03-060439-7). H Holt & Co.

Legend of the Sons of God: A Fantasy. T. C. Lethbridge. (Illus.). 126p. 1983. pap. 5.95 o.p. (ISBN 0-7100-9500-7). Routledge Chapman & Hall.

Legend of the Truant Tree. Jovan DeRocco. (Illus.). 112p. 1982. 6.50 o.p. (ISBN 0-682-49804-1). Exposition-Phoenix.

Legendary Fictions of the Irish Celts. Patrick Kennedy. LC 68-25518. 368p. 1968. Repr. of 1866 ed. 34.00x o.p. (ISBN 0-8103-3467-4). Gale.

Legendary Lore of the Holy Wells of England. Robert C. Hope. LC 68-21775. (Illus.). 254p. 1968. Repr. of 1893 ed. 35.00x o.p. (ISBN 0-8103-3445-3). Gale.

Legends from the Future. Ewald Bash. (Illus., Orig.). 1972. pap. 1.75 o.p. (ISBN 0-377-02101-6). Friendship Pr.

Legends in the Mahabharata. S. A. Dange. 1969. 9.95 o.p. (ISBN 8-1208-0202-0). Orient Bk Dist.

Legends of Florence, 2 Vols. Charles G. Leland. LC 68-27173. 1969. Repr. of 1895 ed. 35.00x ea. o.p. Vol. 1, First Ser (ISBN 0-8103-3843-2). Vol. 2, Second Ser. (ISBN 0-8103-3844-0); set o.p. (ISBN 0-8103-3899-8). Gale.

Legends of Flowers. Paolo Mantegazza. Tr. by Mrs. Alexander Kennedy. LC 73-180973. (Illus.). 192p. 1975. Repr. of 1927 ed. 35.00x o.p. (ISBN 0-8103-4051-8). Gale.

Legends of Highwaymen & Others. Richard Blakeborough. LC 75-154493. (Illus.). 276p. 1971. Repr. of 1924 ed. 40.00x o.p. (ISBN 0-8103-3373-2). Gale.

Legends of Our Time. Elie Wiesel. 1980. pap. 1.75 o.p. (ISBN 0-380-00931-5, 49429, Bard). Avon.

Legends of the Earth. Dorothy B. Vitriano. 1976. pap. 4.95 o.p. (ISBN 0-8065-0534-6, Pub. by Citadel Pr). Carol Pub Group.

Legends of the Madonna, As Represented in the Fine Arts. Anna B. Jameson. LC 70-89273. (Tower Bks.). (Illus.). 426p. 1972. Repr. of 1890 ed. 42.00x o.p. (ISBN 0-8103-3114-4). Gale.

Legends of the North. Olivia Coolidge. (Illus.). (gr. 7 up). 1951. 13.45 o.p. (ISBN 0-395-06726-X). HM.

Legends of the Saints, in the Scottish Dialect of the Fourteenth Century, 3 Vols. Ed. by W. M. Metcalfe. 1896. Set. 140.00 o.p. (ISBN 0-384-32090-2). Johnson Repr.

Legion. William P. Blatty. 256p. 1983. 14.50 o.p. (ISBN 0-671-47045-0). S&S.

Legion of the Dark. Tom C. Liliom. Ed. by Lois Penoi & Jon Penoi. LC 85-62370. (Illus.). 338p. 1985. pap. 3.95 o.p. (ISBN 0-942316-11-8). Pueblo Pub Pr.

Legions of the Mist. Amanda Cockrell. LC 79-51353. 1979. 12.95 o.p. (ISBN 0-689-10989-X, Atheneum). Macmillan.

Legislation in the U. S. S. R. P. P. Gureyev & P. I. Sedugin. 269p. 1977. 3.95 o.p. (ISBN 0-8285-0338-9, Pub. by Progress Pubs USSR). Imported Pubns.

Legislative Acts of the U. S. S. R., 1977-1979. Ed. by L. N. Smirnov. 381p. 1983. 7.95 o.p. (ISBN 0-8285-2235-9, 831996, Pub by Progress Pubs USSR). Imported Pubns.

Legislative Attitudes Toward State Constitutional Revision: The Oklahoma Case. David R. Morgan. (Legislative Research Ser: No. 1). 1971. pap. 1.00 o.p. (ISBN 0-686-20785-8). Univ OK Gov Res.

Legislative Decision-Making & the Politics of Tax Reform: The Oklahoma Senate. E. Lee Bernick. (Legislative Research Ser: No. 9). 35p. 1973. pap. 2.50 o.p. (ISBN 0-686-20786-6). Univ OK Gov Res.

Legislative Drafting. F. Reed Dickerson. LC 77-8391. 149p. 1977. Repr. of 1954 ed. lib. bdg. 25.00x o.p. (ISBN 0-8371-9688-4, DILD). Greenwood.

Legislative Elite in an Indian State: Rajasthan. Lata Puri Shashi. 1978. 12.50x o.p. (ISBN 0-8364-0261-8). South Asia Bks.

Legislative History of the Securities Act of 1933 & Securities Exchange Act of 1934, 11 vols. Compiled by J. S. Ellenberger & Ellen P. Mahar. 1973. Set. 350.00x o.p. (ISBN 0-8377-0802-8); microfilm avail. o.p. Rothman.

Legislative Origins of American Foreign Policy, 5 vols. Ed. by Richard D. Challener. Incl. Vol. 1. Proceedings, April 7, 1913 to March 7, 1923. 415p. lib. bdg. 53.00 (ISBN 0-8240-3030-3); Vol. 2. Proceedings, December 3, 1923 to March 3, 1933. 279p. lib. bdg. 37.00 (ISBN 0-8240-3031-1); Vol. 3. Legislative Origins of the Truman Doctrine, March to April, 1947. 235p. 30.00 (ISBN 0-8240-3032-X); Vol. 4. Foreign Relief Aid, 1947. 401p. lib. bdg. 48.00 (ISBN 0-8240-3033-8); Vol. 5. Foreign Relief Assistance Act of 1948. 809p. lib. bdg. 86.00 (ISBN 0-8240-3034-6). (Senate Foreign Relations Committee's Historical Ser.). 1979. Garland Pub.

Legislative Process in Canada: The Need for Reform. W. A. Neilson & J. C. MacPherson. 328p. 1978. pap. text ed. 12.95x o.p. (ISBN 0-920380-11-5, Pub. by Inst Res Pub Canada). Gower Pub Co.

Legislative Role Structures, Power Bases & Behavior Patterns: An Empirical Examination of the U. S. Senate. Samuel A. Kirkpatrick & Lawrence K. Pettit. (Legislative Research Ser.: No. 6). 1973. pap. 2.50 o.p. (ISBN 0-686-18646-X). Univ OK Gov Res.

Legislative Roll-Call Analysis. Lee F. Anderson et al. (Handbooks for Research in Political Behavior). 1966. 12.95 o.s.i. (ISBN 0-8101-0052-5). Northwestern U Pr.

Legislative Systems in Developing Countries. G. R. Boynton & Chong Lim Kim. LC 75-13342. 288p. 1975. 27.75 o.p. (ISBN 0-8223-0344-2). Duke.

Legislative Voting Patterns & Partisan Cohesion in a One-Party Dominant Legislature. E. Lee Bernick. (Legislative Research Ser: No. 3). 26p. 1973. pap. 1.00 o.p. (ISBN 0-686-20788-2). Univ OK Gov Res.

Legislators & Patronage in Oklahoma. Jean G. McDonald. (Legislative Research Ser: No. 10). 1975. 2.50 o.p. (ISBN 0-686-18648-6). Univ OK Gov Res.

Legitimacy in the Modern State. John H. Schaar. 341p. 1981. 26.95 o.p. (ISBN 0-87855-337-1). Transaction Pubs.

Legs! Super Legs in Six Weeks. Gayle Olinekova. (Illus.). 128p. 1983. pap. 8.50 o.p. (ISBN 0-671-47241-0, Fireside). S&S.

Lehmann Toys. Jurgen Cieslik & Marianne Cieslik. (Illus.). 220p. 24.95 o.s.i. (ISBN 0-904568-40-7, Pub. by New Cavendish England). Schiffer.

Lehrbuch der Linearen Algebra. 2nd rev. ed. W. Nef. (Mathematische Reihe Ser.: No.31). 276p. (Ger.). 1977. 37.95x o.p. (ISBN 0-8176-0960-1). Birkhauser.

Lehrbuch der speziellen pathologischen Anatomie, 3 vols. incl. supplement. 11th & 12th ed. E. Kaufmann. Ed. by Staemmler. 1955-1972. Set. write for info. o.p. (ISBN 0-685-24750-3). De Gruyter.

Lehrerhandbuch, Pt. 2. write for info. o.p. (ISBN 3-468-49927-2). Langenscheidt.

Lehrerheft I see Deutsch X 3.

Lehrerheft II see Deutsch X 3.

Lehrerheft III see Deutsch X 3.

Leibniz-Clarke Correspondence. H. G. Alexander. 200p. 1957. (ISBN 0-8022-0017-6). Philos Lib.

Leibniz Philosophical Writings. Gottfried W. Leibniz. Ed. by G. H. Parkinson. Tr. by Mary Morris. 294p. 1983. pap. 7.95x o.p. (ISBN 0-460-11905-2, Pub. by Evman England). Biblio Dist.

Leibniz Philosophical Writings. Gottfried W. Leibniz & G. H. Parkinson. Tr. by Mary Morris from Ger. (Rowman & Littlefield University Library). 270p. 1973. 13.50x o.p. (ISBN 0-87471-659-4); pap. 7.00x o.p. (ISBN 0-87471-660-8). Rowman.

Leica Accessory Guide: Pocket Books. D. H. Laney. (Illus.). 124p. 1984. flexible leather-textured binding 11.95 o.p. (ISBN 0-906447-28-3, Pub. by Hove Foto Bks). Seven Hills Bk Dists.

Leica Advertising 1925-1950. Friedrich W. Ruttinger. (Illus.). 159p. (Ger. & Eng.). 1987. pap. 19.95 o.p. (ISBN 3-88984-018-3, Pub. by Hove Foto Bks). Seven Hills Bk Dists.

Leica CL. Theo Kisselbach. (Illus.). 136p. 1987. 22.95 o.p. (ISBN 0-317-61778-8, Pub. by Hove Foto Bks). Seven Hills Bk Dists.

Leica International Price Guide, 1986-87. 3rd ed. Ed. by D. R. Grossmark. 95p. (Orig.). 1986. pap. 7.95 o.p. (ISBN 0-906447-34-8, Pub. by Hove Foto Bks). Seven Hills Bk Dists.

Leica Pocket Book. 2nd ed. B. Tompkins & D. H. Laney. (Illus.). 130p. leather textured binding 11.95 o.p. (ISBN 0-906447-26-7). Seven Hills Bk Dists.

Leica Price Guide, 1984-85: Pocket Book. D. R. Grossmark. 84p. 1984. pap. 7.95 o.p. (ISBN 0-906447-29-1, Pub. by Hove Foto Bks). Seven Hills Bk Dists.

Leica R-3 & R-3 MOT Reflex Manual. Heinz Von Lichem. (Illus.). 135p. 1979. 22.95 o.p. (ISBN 0-906447-06-2, Pub. by Hove Foto Bks). Seven Hills Bk Dists.

Leica R-4 Reflex Manual. Theo Kisselbach. (Illus.). 152p. 22.95 o.p. (ISBN 0-906447-12-7). Seven Hills Bk Dists.

Leica, the First Sixty Years. rev. ed. Gianni Rogliatti. (Illus.). 200p. 1986. 26.95 o.p. (ISBN 0-906447-32-1, Pub. by Hove Foto Bks). Seven Hills Bk Dists.

Leigh Wiener: Memoir of a Master Photojournalist. Leigh Wiener. (Illus.). 250p. 1987. 34.95 o.p. (ISBN 0-916567-13-3). Arpel Graphic.

Leipziger Semitische Studien, 7 vols in 5. Set. 380.00 o.p. (ISBN 0-384-32150-X). Johnson Repr.

Leisure. Kenneth Roberts. (Aspects of Modern Sociology, the Social Structure of Modern Britain Ser). 1970. pap. text ed. 9.95x o.p. (ISBN 0-582-48807-9). Humanities.

Leisure & Recreation Management. G. Torkildsen. (Illus.). 1983. pap. 33.00x o.p. (ISBN 0-419-11740-7, NO. 6681, Pub. by E & FN Spon). Routledge Chapman & Hall.

Leisure & the American Dream. Compton & Ellis. (Illus.). 425p. 1988. 22.95 o.p. (ISBN 0-8016-1028-1). Mosby.

Leisure Counseling: An Aspect of Leisure Education. Arlin Epperson et al. (Illus.). 392p. 1977. 37.50x o.p. (ISBN 0-398-03619-5). C C Thomas.

Leisure Crisis. John Oswalt. 168p. 1987. pap. 6.95 o.p. (ISBN 0-89693-241-9). Victor Bks.

Leisure Fun, No. 17: Find-a-Word. Norman Goldfind. 128p. (Orig.). 1988. pap. 2.50 o.s.i. (ISBN 1-55785-028-3). Bart Books.

Leisure: Integrating a Neglected Component in Life Planning. Carl McDaniels. 54p. cancelled o.s.i. (ISBN 0-318-22142-X, IN245). Natl Ctr Res Voc Ed.

Leisure Leadership: Working with People in Recreation & Park Settings. E. William Niepath. (Illus.). 416p. 1983. text ed. (ISBN 0-13-530071-1). P-H.

Leisure, Recreation & Tourism. Ed. by John Goddard. (Journal of Regional Studies: No. 15). (Illus.). 96p. 1981. pap. 18.75 o.p. (ISBN 0-08-028945-2). Pergamon.

Leisure, Recreation & Tourism Abstracts Word List. 53p. 1983. pap. 15.00 o.p. CAB Intl.

Lekachmacher Family. Carol Richman. LC 76-23409. (Illus.). 1976. 8.95 o.p. (ISBN 0-914842-14-5). Madrona Pubs.

Lemegetton: A Medieval Manual of Solomonic Magic. Ed. by Kevin Wilby. (Illus.). 137p. (Orig.). 1987. pap. 18.00 o.p. (ISBN 0-933999-05-4). Phanes Pr.

Lemniscatory Ruled Surface in Space & Counterspace. George Adams. Tr. by Stephen Eberhart from Ger. & Eng. (Illus.). 83p. 1979. pap. 9.95x o.s.i. (Pub. by Steinerbooks). Anthroposophic.

Lemon & a Star. Elizabeth C. Spykman. LC 55-7614. (gr. 5 up). 1955. 5.95 o.p. (ISBN 0-15-244713-X, HJ). HarBraceJ.

Lemon Book. Ralph Nader et al. (Illus.). 300p. (Orig.). 1980. pap. 7.95 o.p. (ISBN 0-89803-039-0, Dist. by Kampmann). Green Hill.

Lempriere's Classical Dictionary Writ Large. Rev. ed. J. Lempriere. 700p. 1984. 27.95 o.p. (ISBN 0-7102-0068-4). Routledge Chapman & Hall.

Lending Packages for Small & Medium-Sized Enterprises. Malcolm Robbie et al. (Illus.). 193p. 1983. 31.00 o.p. (ISBN 0-7099-2229-9, Pub. by Croom Helm Ltd); pap. 11.50 o.p. Routledge Chapman & Hall.

Lending to Agricultural Enterprises. Thomas L. Frey & Robert H. Behrens. LC 81-12874. 498p. 1981. 44.00 o.p. (ISBN 0-87267-037-6). Bank Admin Inst.

Lending Transactions & the Bankruptcy Act 1985: Volumes 342-434, 2 vols. 1297p. 1985. pap. 40.00 o.p. (ISBN 0-317-27430-9, #A4-4109). PLI.

Lengthening Shadow of a Woman: A Biography of Charlotte Hawkins Brown. Constance H. Marteena. 1977. 6.50 o.p. (ISBN 0-682-48597-7). Exposition-Phoenix.

Lengua y Lectura: Un Repaso y una Continuacion. Matilde O. Castells & Phyllis Z. Boring. 430p. 1970. text ed. 14.95 o.p. (ISBN 0-15-550553-X, HC). HarBraceJ.

Lenin & Ghandi. Rene Fulop-Miller. LC 79-147617. (Library of War & Peace: Non-Resistance & Non-Violence). 1972. lib. bdg. 46.00 o.p. (ISBN 0-8240-0374-8). Garland Pub.

Lenin & the World Revolutionary Process. B. Ponomarev. 525p. 1980. 11.00 o.p. (ISBN 0-8285-1661-8, Pub. by Progress Pubs USSR). Imported Pubns.

Lenin in Zurich. Alexander Solzhenitsyn. Tr. by H. T. Willetts from Rus. 309p. 1976. 8.95 o.p. (ISBN 0-374-18501-8). FS&G.

Lenin on Language. V. I. Lenin. Ed. by P. N. Denisov & N. A. Kondrashov. 293p. 1983. 5.95 o.p. (ISBN 0-8285-2588-9, Pub. by Raduga Pubs USSR). Imported Pubns.

Lenin the Revolutionary. V. P. Filatov et al. 1980. 4.00 o.p. (ISBN 0-8285-1849-1, Pub. by Progress Pubs USSR). Imported Pubns.

Leningrad-Art & Architecture. V. Schwarz. 312p. 1981. 8.95 o.p. (ISBN 0-8285-2354-1, Pub. by Progress Pubs USSR). Imported Pubns.

Leningrad Watercolors, 2 vols. Maria S. Merian. LC 76-4690. (Helen & Kurt Wolff Bk.). (Illus.). 1975. Set. 900.00 o.p. (ISBN 0-15-149837-7). HarBraceJ.

Leninism & the Agrarian & Peasant Question, 2 vols. S. P. Trapeznikov. 1114p. 1981. Set. 15.95 o.p. (ISBN 0-8285-2491-2, Pub. by Progress Pubs USSR). Imported Pubns.

Leninism: Selected Writings. Joseph Stalin. LC 74-27668. 479p. 1975. Repr. of 1942 ed. lib. bdg. 45.00x o.p. (ISBN 0-8371-7907-6, STLSW). Greenwood.

Lenin's Boyhood & Adolescence. A. I. Ulyanova. 31p. 1972. pap. 0.79 o.p. (ISBN 0-8285-1177-2, Pub. by Progress Pubs USSR). Imported Pubns.

Lenin's Doctrine on National Liberation Revolutions & the Modern World. V. Zotov. 151p. 1982. pap. 1.45 o.p. (ISBN 0-8285-2385-1, Pub. by Progress Pubs USSR). Imported Pubns.

Lenin's Political Thought, Vols. 1 & 2. Neil Harding. 550p. 1982. pap. text ed. 19.95x o.p. (ISBN 0-391-02698-4). Humanities.

Lent. Elisabeth S. Fiorenza & Urban T. Holmes. Ed. by Elizabeth Achtemeier & Gerhard Krodel. LC 79-7377. (Proclamation 2: Aids for Interpreting the Lessons of the Church Year, Ser. B). 64p. 1981. pap. 3.75 o.p. (ISBN 0-8006-4070-5, 1-4070, Fortress). Augsburg Fortress.

Lent. Peter Gomes. LC 84-18756. (Proclamation 3 C Ser.). 64p. 1985. pap. 3.75 o.p. (ISBN 0-8006-4127-2, Fortress). Augsburg Fortress.

Lent. William Hordern & John Otwell. LC 74-24901. (Proclamation 1: Aids for Interpreting the Lessons of the Church Year Ser. B). 64p. 1974. pap. 2.95 o.p. (ISBN 0-8006-4073-X, 1-4073). Augsburg Fortress.

Lent. Jack D. Kingsbury & Chester Pennington. Ed. by Elizabeth Achtemeier et al. LC 79-7377. (Proclamation 2: Aids for Interpreting the Lessons of the Church Year, Ser. A). 64p. (Orig.). 1980. pap. 3.75 o.p. (ISBN 0-8006-4093-4, 1-4093, Fortress). Augsburg Fortress.

Lent. Marianne H. Micks & Thomas E. Ridenhour. Ed. by Elizabeth Achtemeier et al. LC 79-7377. (Proclamation 2: Aids for Interpreting the Lessons of the Church Year Ser. C). 64p. 1979. pap. 3.75 o.p. (ISBN 0-8006-4082-9, 1-4082, Fortress). Augsburg Fortress.

Lent. Charles W. Smith & Helmut Koester. LC 74-76925. (Proclamation 1: Aids for Interpreting the Lessons of the Church Year, Ser. A). 64p. 1974. pap. 2.95 o.p. (ISBN 0-8006-4063-2, 1-4063, Fortress). Augsburg Fortress.

Lent. Herman G. Stuempfle, Jr. & Peter J. Kearney. LC 73-79350. (Proclmation 1: Aids for Interpreting the Lessons of the Church Year Ser. C). 64p. 1973. pap. 2.95 o.p. (ISBN 0-8006-4053-5, 1-4053, Fortress). Augsburg Fortress.

Lenten Chancel Dramas. William A. Poovey. LC 68-13421. 1968. pap. 1.95 o.p. (ISBN 0-8066-0801-3, 10-3816, Augsburg). Augsburg Fortress.

Lenten Pastoral Letter. Bernard J. Flanagan. 1976. pap. 0.50 o.p. (ISBN 0-685-77497-X). Franciscan Herald.

Leo Possessed. Dilys Owen. (Illus.). (gr. 5 up). 1979. 7.95 o.p. (ISBN 0-15-244897-7, HJ). HarBraceJ.

Leon Bloy: The Pauper Prophet. Emmanuela Polimeni. 1951. (ISBN 0-8022-1997-7). Philos Lib.

Leon Krier: Bibliography & Building List. Edward H. Teague. (Architecture Ser.: A 1435). 5p. 1985. 2.00 o.p. (ISBN 0-89028-485-7). Vance Biblios.

Leonard B. Willeke: Excellence in Architecture & Design. Thomas W. Brunk. (Illus.). 225p. 1986. 45.00x o.p. (ISBN 0-8143-2222-0, Dist. for the University of Detroit Press). Wayne St U Pr.

Leonardo: A Study in Chronology & Style. Carlo Pedretti. 1982. 24.95 o.p. (ISBN 0-384-45281-7); pap. 14.95 o.p. (ISBN 0-384-45280-9). Johnson Repr.

Leonardo, Architect. Carlo Pedretti. LC 85-45954. (Illus.). 363p. 1985. 75.00 o.p. (ISBN 0-8478-0646-4). Rizzoli Intl.

Leonardo Da Vinci. Jack Wasserman. LC 74-13112. (Library of Great Painters). (Illus.). 160p. 1975. 45.00 o.p. (ISBN 0-8109-0262-1). Abrams.

Leonardo Da Vinci: Anatomical Drawings from the Royal Library, Windsor Castle. Kenneth Keele & Jane Roberts. (Illus.). 168p. 1983. 4.95 o.p. (ISBN 0-87099-362-3). Metro Mus Art.

Leonardo da Vinci: The Marvelous Works of Nature & Man. Martin Kemp. 368p. 1981. 70.00x o.p. (ISBN 0-460-04354-4, Pub. by Dent Australia). State Mutual Bk.

Leonardo to Van Gogh: Master Drawings from Budapest. Terez Gerszi et al. LC 84-22370. (Illus.). 224p. (Orig.). 1985. pap. 24.95 o.p. (ISBN 0-86559-064-8). Art Inst Chi.

Leonard's Annual Price Index of Art Auctions: 1985-1986 Auction Season, Vol. 6. Susan Theran. 550p. 1986. 175.00 o.p. (ISBN 0-918819-05-9). Auction Index.

Leonard's Annual Price Index of Art Auctions, 1986-1987 Auction Seasons, Vol. 7. Susan Theran. (Books on Auction Records Ser.). 600p. 1987. 195.00 o.p. (ISBN 0-918819-06-7). Auction Index.

Leonie. Elizabeth Adler. 1985. 18.45 o.p. (ISBN 0-394-54700-4, Pub. by Villard Bks). Random.

Leon's Prize. Jerry Smath. (Illus.). 40p. (ps-3). 1987. 5.95 o.p. (ISBN 0-8193-1169-3). Parents.

Leopard. Cecil Bodker. Tr. by Gunnar Poulsen from Danish. LC 74-19314. 192p. (gr. 4-6). 1975. PLB 7.95 o.p. (ISBN 0-689-30444-7, Atheneum). Macmillan.

Leopard. Giuseppe Di Lampedusa. Tr. by A. Colquhoun. LC 60-6794. 1960. 13.50 o.p. (ISBN 0-394-43291-6). Pantheon.

Leopard's Tooth. William Kotzwinkle. LC 75-25504. (Illus.). 96p. (gr. 3-6). 1979. 6.95 o.p. (ISBN 0-395-28862-2, Clarion). HM.

Leopold, the See-Through Crumbpicker. James Flora. LC 61-6114. (Illus.). (gr. k-3). 1961. 6.95 o.p. (ISBN 0-15-244892-6, HJ). HarBraceJ.

Leper & Other Stories. Milovan Djilas. Tr. by Lovett F. Edwards. LC 64-14641. 1964. 9.95 o.s.i. (ISBN 0-15-149859-8). HarBraceJ.

Lepidoptera Genetics. Roy Robinson. 1971. 113.00 o.p. (ISBN 0-08-006659-3). Pergamon.

Leprosy. Ed. by Robert C. Hastings. (Medicine in the Tropics Ser.). (Illus.). 331p. 1986. text ed. 120.00 o.p. (ISBN 0-443-02893-1). Churchill.

Leprosy in Five Young Men. George J. Hill. LC 79-125621. (Illus.). 1971. 19.50x o.p. (ISBN 0-87081-003-0). Univ Pr Colo.

Lernbuch I see Deutsch X 3.

Lernbuch II see Deutsch X 3.

Lernbuch III see Deutsch X 3.

Leroy & the Old Man. William E. Butterworth. LC 79-6553. 160p. (gr. 7 up). 1980. 8.95 o.s.i. (ISBN 0-02-716210-9, Four Winds). Macmillan.

Lertfaden Zur Kriegsschuldfrage see Case for the Central Powers.

Les Miserables see also Miserables.

Lesage ou le Metier de Romancier. Laufer. (Bibliotheque des Idees). 24.40 o.p. (ISBN 0-685-34041-4). French & Eur.

Lesbian & Gay Parents' Legal Guide to Child Custody. 5.00 o.p. Natl Lawyers Guild.

Lesbian Nation: The Feminist Solution. Jill Johnston. 1974. pap. 9.50 o.p. (ISBN 0-671-21729-1, Touchstone Bks). S&S.

Lesbian Path. Margaret Cruikshank. 1980. pap. 6.95 o.p. (ISBN 0-912216-20-4). Angel Pr.

Lesbian Peoples. Monique Wittig & Sande Zeig. 1979. pap. 5.95 o.p. (ISBN 0-380-46441-1, 46441-1). Avon.

Lesbian-Woman. Del Martin & Phyllis Lyon. LC 72-76532. 350p. 1972. 3.95 o.s.i. (ISBN 0-553-23597-4). Volcano Pr.

Leseheft I mit Uebungen, "Aktuell und interessant" see Deutsch X 3.

Leseheft II mit Uebungen, "Aktuell und interessant" Die Laender der Bundesrepublik Deutschland see Deutsch X 3.

Leseheft III, "Aktuell und interessant" Die wichtigsten Staedte in den deutsch sprachigen Laendern see Deutsch X 3.

Leslie Wilkinson: A Practical Idealist. Max Dupain & Peter Johnson. (Illus.). 128p. 1983. 30.00 o.p. (ISBN 0-04-729002-1). Unwin Hyman.

Less Stress. David Congo & Janet Congo. LC 85-18306. 1985. pap. 6.95 o.s.i. (ISBN 0-8307-0968-1, 5418240). Regal.

Less Than Angels. Barbara Pym. 400p. 1986. lib. bdg. 15.95x o.p. (ISBN 0-8161-3842-7, Large Print Bks). G K Hall.

Less Than Human. Robert Clarke. 208p. 1986. pap. 2.95 o.p. (ISBN 0-380-89992-2). Avon.

Less Than Zero: A Novel. Bret E. Ellis. 1985. 15.45 o.p. (ISBN 0-671-54329-6). S&S.

Less Than-4-Year Awards in Institutions of Higher Education: 1983-85, CS 87-373. Elaine Kroe. (Education Department Publication Ser.). (Illus.). 72p. 1987. pap. 3.50 o.p. (ISBN 0-318-23559-5, 065-000-00307-4). USGPO.

Lesser Festivals, Vols. 1 & 2. Philip Pfatteicher. LC 74-24917. (Proclamation 1: Aids for Interpreting the Lessons of the Church Year Ser.). 64p. 1975. pap. 2.95 ea. o.p. (1-1309, Fortress); Vol. 1. pap. (ISBN 0-8006-1309-0, 1-1310); Vol. 2. pap. (ISBN 0-8006-1310-4). Augsburg Fortress.

Lesser Festivals 1: Saints' Days & Special Occasions. Richard L. Thulin. Ed. by Elizabeth Achtemeier et al. LC 79-7377. (Proclamation 2: Aids for Interpreting the Lessons of the Church Year). 64p. (Orig.). 1980. pap. 3.75 o.p. (ISBN 0-8006-1393-7, 1-1393, Fortress). Augsburg Fortress.

Lesser Festivals 2: Saints' Days & Special Occasions. John B. Trotti. Ed. by Elizabeth Achtemeier et al. LC 79-7377. (Proclamation 2: Aids for Interpreting Thee Lessons of the Church Year). 64p. (Orig.). 1980. pap. 3.75 o.p. (ISBN 0-8006-1394-5, 1-1394, Fortress). Augsburg Fortress.
Lesser Festivals 3: Saints' Days & Special Occasions. Richard Reid & Milton Crum, Jr. Ed. by Elizabeth Achtemeier et al. LC 79-7377. (Proclamation 2: Aids for Interpreting the Lessons of the Church Year). 64p. (Orig.). 1981. pap. 3.75 o.p. (ISBN 0-8006-1395-3, 1-1395, Fortress). Augsburg Fortress.
Lesser Festivals 4: Saints' Days & Special Occasions. Lorenz Nieting. Ed. by Elizabeth Achtemeier et al. LC 79-7377. (Proclamation Two Ser.: Aids for Interpreting the Lessons of the Church Year). 64p. (Orig.). 1981. pap. 3.75 o.p. (ISBN 0-8006-1396-1, 1-1396, Fortress). Augsburg Fortress.
Lesson Is Murder. Joanne Hoppe. LC 76-46787. 1977. 6.95 o.p. (ISBN 0-15-244899-3, HJ). HarBraceJ.
Lesson of the Scaffold: The Public Execution Controversy in Victorian England. David D. Cooper. LC 73-92901. (Illus.). xi, 212p. 1974. 13.95x o.p. (ISBN 0-8214-0148-3). Ohio U Pr.
Lesson Plans & the Teacher. 4.21 o.p. (ISBN 0-912126-13-2, 1262-00). Keystone Pubns.
Lesson Plans in Accounting. Donald Musselman & Vernon Musselman. LC 77-87606. 1978. pap. text ed. 6.75x o.p. (ISBN 0-8134-1980-8, 1980). Inter Print Pubs.
Lessons. Lee Zacharias. 1981. 12.95 o.p. (ISBN 0-395-30546-2). HM.
Lessons from a Sheepdog. W. Phillip Keller. 1983. 8.95 o.p. (ISBN 0-8499-0335-1). Word Bks.
Lessons from an Unconventional War: Reassessing U. S. Strategies for Future Conflicts. Ed. by Richard A. Hunt & Richard H. Shultz, Jr. (Pergamon Policy Studies on International Politics Ser.). 250p. 1981. 34.00 o.p. (ISBN 0-08-027186-3). Pergamon.
Lessons from Great Lives. Sterling W. Sill. LC 80-84567. 300p. 1981. 9.95 o.p. (ISBN 0-88290-172-9, 2049). Horizon Utah.
Lessons from History: The Tokushi Yoron. Arai Hakuseki. Tr. by Joyce Ackroyd from Japanese. LC 81-11707. 417p. 1982. text ed. 37.50x o.p. (ISBN 0-7022-1485-X). U of Queensland Pr.
Lessons from the Past: From Dief to Mulroney. Heward Grafftey. (Illus.). 256p. 1987. cloth 24.95 o.p. (ISBN 0-920792-77-4). Eden Pr.
Lessons in EKG Interpretation: A Basic Self-Instructional Guide. Charles P. Summerall. LC 84-21025. 208p. 1985. pap. 19.95 o.p. (ISBN 0-471-88232-1). Wiley.
Lessons of Grenada. (Department of State Publication Ser.: No. 9457). (Illus.). 25p. (Orig.). 1986. pap. 1.25 o.p. (ISBN 0-318-20453-3, SN/044-000-02109-9). USGPO.
Lessons of History. William Smyth. 1955. 6.00 o.p. S&S.
Lessons of Recent Wars in the Third World: Approaches & Case Studies, Vol. 1. Ed. by Robert E. Harkavy & Stephanie G. Neuman. LC 83-47912. 320p. 1985. 40.00x o.p. (ISBN 0-669-06765-2). Lexington Bks.
Lessons on New Testament Evidences. Wallace Wartick. 250p. 1980. pap. 4.95 cancelled o.p. (ISBN 0-89900-141-6). College Pr Pub.
Lessons on Security & Disarmament from the History of the League of Nations. James T. Shotwell & Marina Salvin. LC 74-15557. 149p. 1975. Repr. of 1949 ed. lib. bdg. 35.00x o.p. (ISBN 0-8371-7824-X, SHSD). Greenwood.
Lester's Turn. Jan Slepian. LC 80-29467. 144p. (gr. 6-10). 1981. PLB 8.95 o.s.i. (ISBN 0-02-782940-5). Macmillan.
Let a River Be. Betty S. Cummings. LC 77-22647. 216p. (gr. 7 up). 1978. 8.95 o.p. (ISBN 0-689-30635-0, Atheneum). Macmillan.
Let God Arise. Richard Holloway. 4.95 o.p. (ISBN 0-8192-1136-2). Morehouse Pub.
Let God Love You. Lloyd Ogilvie. 1978. pap. 7.95 o.p. (ISBN 0-8499-2831-1, 2831-1). Word Bks.
Let Herbs Do It. Virginia W. Bentley. (Illus.). 1973. pap. 6.95 o.p. (ISBN 0-395-15478-2). HM.
Let It Begin in Me. R. Earl Allen. LC 84-19934. 1985. pap. 4.25 o.p. (ISBN 0-8054-5005-X). Broadman.
Let It Go. Marilyn Halvorson. LC 86-2017. 224p. (gr. 7 up). 1986. pap. 14.95 o.p. (ISBN 0-385-29484-0). Delacorte.
Let It Go. Date not set. (ISBN 0-385-29484-0). Delacorte.
Let It Grow: Your Church Can Chart a New Course. Marvin G. Rickard. LC 84-22733. 1985. pap. 5.95 o.p. (ISBN 0-88070-074-2). Multnomah.
Let Justice Be Done: The Foreign Policy of Dr. H. V. Evatt. Alan Renouf. LC 83-5534. 314p. 1984. text ed. 25.00 o.p. (ISBN 0-7022-1893-6). U of Queensland Pr.
Let Me Be a Free Man: A Documentary History of Indian Resistance. Ed. by Jane B. Katz. LC 74-11910. (Voices of the American Indian Ser.). (Illus.). 184p. (gr. 6 up). 1975. PLB 8.95 o.p. (ISBN 0-8225-0640-8). Lerner Pubns.
Let Me Be Me. Nicholas Vacc & Joseph Wittmer. LC 80-66710. 318p. 1980. pap. text ed. 15.45x o.p. (ISBN 0-915202-23-9). Accel Devel.
Let Me Fall before I Fly. Barbara Wersba. LC 78-157312. 1971p. (gr. 4up). pap. 5.25 o.p. (ISBN 0-689-30001-8, Atheneum). Macmillan.
Let Me Hear the Music. Carol Barford. LC 78-23966. 128p. (gr. 6 up). 1979. 7.95 o.p. (ISBN 0-395-28959-9, Clarion). HM.
Let Me Speak: Learning Games for the Retarded Child. Dorothy Jeffree & Roy McConkey. LC 77-73825. (Illus.). 1977. 7.95 o.s.i. (ISBN 0-8008-4646-X). Taplinger.
Let My People Go. Tom Hess. 144p. (Orig.). 1987. pap. text ed. 15.00 o.p. (ISBN 0-936369-16-7). Son-Rise Pubns.
Let Out the Sunshine. Regina R. Barnett. 144p. (Orig.). (YA) (gr. k up). 1981. pap. text ed. 12.00 o.p. (ISBN 0-697-01762-1). Wm C Brown.
Let Peas Be with You: Food Poems. Ronald L. Smith. LC 82-72607. (Illus.). 106p. (Orig.). 1982. pap. 4.95 o.s.i. (ISBN 0-89708-108-0). And Bks.
Let the Band Play Dixie. Lawrence Wells. LC 86-32816. 336p. 1987. 17.95 o.p. (ISBN 0-385-23467-8). Doubleday.
Let the Bastards Freeze in the Dark. Diane Simmons. 1980. 11.95 o.p. (ISBN 0-671-61004-X, Wyndham). S&S.
Let the Children Come. Elizabeth B. Jones. 112p. 1980. pap. 2.95 o.p. (ISBN 0-8010-5102-9). Baker Bk.
Let the Emperor Speak: A Novel of Caesar Augustus. Allan Massie. LC 87-9107. 352p. 1987. 18.95 o.p. (ISBN 0-385-24156-9). Doubleday.
Let the Glory Out. Albert Gore. Penguin USA.
Let the Good Times Roll: The Complete Cajun Handbook. Andy Edmunds. 224p. 1984. pap. 7.95 o.p. (ISBN 0-380-88377-5, 883775). Avon.
Let the Lion Eat Straw. Ellease Southerland. LC 78-21021. 1979. 7.95 o.s.i. (ISBN 0-684-16070-6, ScribT). Scribner.
Let the Rail-Splitter Awake. Pablo Neruda. (Orig., Span. & Eng.). pap. 4.50 o.p. (ISBN 0-904526-61-5, Pub. by Journeyman Pr London). Riverrun NY.
Let the Record Show. Clyde O. Jackson. (Illus.). 111p. 1983. 7.50 o.p. (ISBN 0-682-49985-4). Exposition-Phoenix.
Let the Record Show: Memoirs of a Parole Board Member. Margie Sturgis. 1977. 5.50 o.p. (ISBN 0-682-48991-3). Exposition-Phoenix.
Let There Be Clothes. Lynn Schnurnberger. (Illus.). 1988. pap. 16.95 o.p. (ISBN 0-317-66703-3). Workman Pub.
Let There Be Clothes: Forty Thousand Years of Fashion Unveiled. Lynn Schnurnberger. (Illus.). 224p. (Orig.). 1987. pap. 15.95 o.p. (ISBN 0-89480-833-8). Workman Pub.
Let There Be Light. Bernice Dittmer. LC 87-603822. 240p. 1988. write for info. o.p. (ISBN 0-930208-23-4). Mangan Bks.
Let There Be Light. Ida Dunbar. 1978. 5.50 o.p. (ISBN 0-682-49076-8). Exposition-Phoenix.
Let There Be Love: Sex & the Handicapped. Gunnel Enby. LC 74-21696. 84p. 1975. 7.50 o.s.i. (ISBN 0-8008-4652-4). Taplinger.
Let Us Adore Him: Dramas & Meditations for Advent, Christmas, Epiphany. W. A. Poovey. LC 72-78563. 128p. 1972. 3.50 o.p. (ISBN 0-8066-1229-0, 10-3820, Augsburg); pap. 1.95 o.p. (ISBN 0-8066-1230-4, 10-3821). Augsburg Fortress.
Let Us Love. Dale E. Rogers. 1982. 8.95 o.p. (ISBN 0-8499-0298-3). Word Bks.
Let Us Now Praise Famous Men. James Agee & Walker Evans. 496p. 1980. pap. 11.70 o.s.i. (ISBN 0-395-29696-X). HM.
Let Us Now Praise Famous Women: Women Photographers for the U. S. Government, 1935 to 1944. Andrea Fisher. 1987. 18.95 o.p. (ISBN 0-86358-123-4, Pandora Pr). Routledge Chapman & Hall.
Let Us Now Praise Famous Women: Women Photographers for the U. S. Government, 1935 to 1944. Andrea Fisher. (Illus.). 160p. 1987. 39.95 o.p. (ISBN 0-86358-122-6, A0829, Pandora Pr); pap. 15.95 o.p. (ISBN 0-317-60672-7, A0833, Pandora Pr). Routledge Chapman & Hall.
Let Us Now Praise Obscure Women: A Comparative Study of Publicly Supported Unmarried Mothers in Government Housing in the United States & Britain. Rachel Z. Forman. LC 82-17579. 240p. (Orig.). 1983. lib. bdg. 27.75_o.p o.p. (ISBN 0-8191-2813-9); pap. text ed. 13.25 o.p. (ISBN 0-8191-2814-7). U Pr of Amer.
Let Us Worship God: An Interpretation for Families. John F. Jansen. (Orig.). 1967. pap. 2.95 o.p. (ISBN 0-8042-9622-7, John Knox). Westminster John Knox.
Let Yourself Go: Try Creative Sunday School. Charlotte W. Edwards. LC 77-88121. (Orig.). 1969. pap. 3.25 o.p. (ISBN 0-8192-1099-4). Morehouse Pub.
Letarouilly on Renaissance Rome: An American Student Edition. abr. ed. Paul Letarouilly. Ed. by John B. Bayley. (Classical America Series in Art & Architecture). (Illus.). xiv, 158p. 1984. text ed. write for info. o.p. (ISBN 0-8038-0076-2); pap. text ed. 14.95 o.p.; 14.95 o.p. (ISBN 0-8038-9250-0). Architectural.
Let'er Buck: A Story of the Passing of the Old West. Charles W. Furlong. LC 77-159961. 284p. 1971. Repr. of 1921 ed. 40.00 o.p. (ISBN 0-8103-3405-4). Gale.
Lethal Orders. James Pattinson. 208p. 1986. pap. 2.95 o.p. (ISBN 0-931773-76-8). Critics Choice Paper.
Let's Celebrate. Pasadena Art Alliance Staff. (Orig.). 1980. pap. 5.95 o.p. (ISBN 0-937042-03-X). Pasadena Art.
Let's Choose Executors. Sara Woods. (Anthony Maitland Detective Ser.). 224p. 1986. pap. 2.95 o.p. (ISBN 0-380-69860-9). Avon.
Let's Cook It Right. rev. ed. Adelle Davis. LC 62-9440. (Illus.). 1962. 6.95 o.s.i. (ISBN 0-15-150166-1). HarBraceJ.
Let's Cook It Right. Adelle Davis. LC 62-9440. pap. 4.50x o.p. (ISBN 0-451-11161-3). NAL.
Let's Count. Marilyn McAuley. (Peek & Find Bks.). (Illus.). 28p. (gr. 1-3). 1984. bds. 3.95 o.p. (ISBN 0-89191-879-5, 58792). Cook.
Let's Discuss. Irene Brauza. 1979. 5.00 o.p. (ISBN 0-682-49363-5). Exposition-Phoenix.
Let's Eat Right to Keep Fit. rev. ed. Adelle Davis. LC 75-134581. 334p. 1970. 8.95 o.p. (ISBN 0-15-150304-4). HarBraceJ.
Let's Eat Right to Keep Fit. Adelle Davis. LC 71-128463. pap. 3.95x o.p. (ISBN 0-451-09644-4). NAL.
Let's Face It. Christine Piff. 128p. 1986. 16.95 o.p. (ISBN 0-575-03533-1, Pub. by Gollancz England). David & Charles.
Let's Get Well. Adelle Davis. LC 65-19054. 1972. pap. 3.50 o.p. (ISBN 0-451-09852-8). NAL.
Let's Get Well. Adelle Davis. LC 65-19054. 580p. 1965. 16.95 o.s.i. (ISBN 0-15-150372-9). HarBraceJ.
Let's Go Outdoors with Children: Administrative Guide for Grades 1-4. Richard Purchase & Betty Purchase. (CPA Christian Education Ser. Book). 32p. 1972. pap. 1.50 o.s.i. (ISBN 0-664-29763-3, Westminster). Westminster John Knox.
Let's Go! Piggety Pig. Harriet Ziefert. (ps-k). 2.95 o.p. (ISBN 0-316-98760-3). Little.
Let's Go Visiting. Jay Stauter. (Illus.). 48p. 1983. 5.50 o.p. (ISBN 0-682-40119-6). Exposition-Phoenix.
Let's Grow! Children's Gardening Fun Kit. Linda Tilgner. (ps-5). 1988. pap. 19.95 plus enclosures o.p. (ISBN 0-88266-537-5, Garden Way Pub). Storey Comm Inc.
Let's Have a Conference. Elizabeth Lowry-Corry. 160p. 1987. 25.50 o.p. (ISBN 0-85142-209-8). Learned Info.
Let's Have a Party: 101 Mix & Match a Party Ideas for the Jewish Holidays. Ruth E. Brinn & Judyth R. Saypol. (Illus.). 80p. (ps-4). 1981. pap. 4.95 o.p. (ISBN 0-930494-10-5). Kar Ben.
Let's Have Music. Sheldon R. Shepard. 128p. 1987. 8.95 o.p. (ISBN 0-8062-2827-X). Carlton.
Let's Learn Astrology: The First Astrology Workbook for Beginners. rev. ed. Patricia G. Crossley. LC 73-90470. 1973. 8.95 o.p. (ISBN 0-682-47727-3, Banner). Exposition-Phoenix.
Let's Live. William H Stacy. LC 75-3833. 1975. pap. text ed. 4.95x o.p. (ISBN 0-8134-1720-1, 1720). Inter Print Pubs.
Let's Look at Indonesia. David Ellis. 1973. pap. 1.25 o.p. (ISBN 0-85363-077-1). OMF Bks.
Let's Look for Colors. Bill Gillham & Susan Hulme. LC 83-24047. (Let's Look Bks.). (Illus.). 24p. (ps-1). 1984. 4.95 o.p. (ISBN 0-698-20612-6, Coward). Putnam Pub Group.
Let's Love One Another. Bessie Dean. LC 77-74492. (Books for LDS Children). (Illus.). 64p. (ps-3). 1978. pap. 3.95 o.p. (ISBN 0-88290-077-3). Horizon Utah.
Let's Make It Happen! Girl Scouts of the U. S. A. Staff. 72p. (YA) (gr. 9-12). 1979. 3.50 o.p. (ISBN 0-88441-322-5, 20-815). Girl Scouts USA.
Let's Make It Happen: Leaders' Guide. 26p. 1979. pap. 2.00 o.p. (ISBN 0-88441-323-3, 20-816). Girl Scouts USA.
Let's Make Rabbits. Leo Lionni. LC 81-18713. (Illus.). 32p. (ps-2). 1982. 9.95 o.s.i. (ISBN 0-394-85196-X); lib. bdg. 11.99 o.s.i. (ISBN 0-394-95196-4). Pantheon.
Let's Marry Said the Cherry: & Other Nonsense Poems. N. M. Bodecker. LC 74-76271. (Illus.). 80p. (gr. 4 up). 1974. 7.95 o.p. (ISBN 0-689-50004-1, Atheneum). Macmillan.
Let's Play. Carla Dijs & Kees Moerbeek. LC 86-80650. (Revolving Board Bks.). (Illus.). 10p. (ps-k). 1986. bds. 4.95 o.p. (ISBN 0-8050-0135-2). H Holt & Co.
Let's Pretend. Julie Hagstrom. 1986. pap. 3.95 o.s.i. (ISBN 0-671-61919-5). PB.
Let's Pretend with the Muppet Babies. Illus. by Manhar Chauhan. LC 85-63346. (Gatefold Bks.). (Illus.). 16p. (ps-1). 1986. 3.95 o.s.i. (ISBN 0-394-88143-5, BYR). Random.
Let's Salute Andy Capp. Reginald Smythe. 1985. pap. 2.25 o.s.i. (ISBN 0-449-12655-2, GM). Fawcett.
Let's Sing & Play Animals: A Sing & Play Book & Cassette. (Learning Curves Bks.). (Illus.). 24p. (ps-1). 1987. pap. 6.95 incl. cassette o.p. (ISBN 0-553-45904-X). Bantam.
Let's Sing & Play People at Work: A Sing & Play Book & Cassette. (Learning Curves Bks.). (Illus.). 24p. (ps-1). 1987. pap. 6.95 o.p. (ISBN 0-553-45905-8). Bantam.
Let's Stay Healthy: A Guide to Lifelong Nutrition. Adelle Davis. Ed. by Ann Gildroy. LC 80-8744. 320p. 1982. 12.95 o.s.i. (ISBN 0-15-150443-1). HarBraceJ.
Let's Talk. Mary Finocchiaro. (gr. 9 up). 1970. pap. text ed. 3.95 o.p. (ISBN 0-88345-094-1, 17743). Prentice ESL.
Let's Talk About Food. Ed. by Philip White & Nancy Selvey. LC 73-85401. 1974. 7.50 o.p. (ISBN 0-88416-008-4). Year Bk Med.
Let's Talk about God: Devotions for Families with Young Children. Gertrude A. Priester. LC 67-11494. (Illus.). 272p. 1967. 3.95 o.s.i. (ISBN 0-664-20750-2, Westminster). Westminster John Knox.
Let's Talk it Over God! Hattie Smith. LC 84-50077. 105p. 1984. 5.95 o.p. (ISBN 0-938232-46-0). Winston-Derek.
Let's Worship God Alone. H. L. Shrake. 1954. (ISBN 0-8022-1566-1). Philos Lib.
Letter Does Not Blush. Nicholas Parsons. 1987. 26.95 o.p. (ISBN 0-907675-21-2, Pub. by Buchan & Enright England). Seven Hills Bk Dists.
Letter for Johanna: Memories of a Massachusetts Boyhood. John Knowlton. 1978. 13.50 o.p. (ISBN 0-682-49099-7). Exposition-Phoenix.
Letter Killeth... Roy Masters. Ed. by Dorothy Baker. 213p. (Orig.). 1988. pap. 9.95 o.p. (ISBN 0-933900-14-7). Foun Human Under.
Letter Mastery. Judith M. Smith. Ed. by Donald E. Smith. (Michigan Tracking Program). 1976. pap. 1.95x o.p. (ISBN 0-914004-45-X). Ulrich.
Letter of Credit. Lennart Bruce. (Illus.). 1973. pap. 8.00 o.p. (ISBN 0-87711-051-4). Story Line.
Letter of Porphyry the Neo-Platonist. Tr. by Alice Zimmern. 1984. pap. 4.95 o.p. (ISBN 0-916411-87-7, Pub. by Alexandrian Pr). Holmes Pub.
Letter Perfect. Charles P. Crawford. 176p. (gr. 7-10). 1984. pap. text ed. 1.95 o.p. Archway.
Letter Perfect: A Handbook of Model Letters for Managers & Executives. Dianna Booher. 512p. 1988. 59.95 o.p. (ISBN 0-669-16819-X). Lexington Bks.
Letter to a Younger Son. Christopher Leach. LC 81-47556. (Helen & Kurt Wolff Bk.). 156p. 1982. 9.95 o.p. (ISBN 0-15-150444-X). HarBraceJ.
Letter to Anywhere. Al Hine & John Alcorn. LC 65-10961. (Illus.). (gr. 2-5). 1965. 4.95 o.p. (ISBN 0-15-245071-8, HJ). HarBraceJ.
Letter to Jeanie: Highlights of Sixty Years with Social Work Professionals & Volunteers. Clare M. Tousley. LC 76-16430. 74p. 1976. 3.50 o.p. (ISBN 0-87304-144-5). Family Serv.
Letter to Lord Liszt. Martin Walser. Tr. by Lelia Vennewitz. 149p. Date not set. 13.95 o.p. (ISBN 0-317-53083-6). HR&W.
Letter to My Mother. Georges Simenon. Tr. by Ralph Manheim. LC 75-28383. (Helen Kurt Wolff Bk.). 96p. 1976. 5.95 o.p. (ISBN 0-15-150445-8). HarBraceJ.
Letter to the Colossians: A Commentary. Edward Schweizer. Tr. by Andrew Chester. LC 81-65657. 352p. (Orig.). 1982. pap. 15.95 o.p. (ISBN 0-8066-1893-0, 10-3823, Augsburg). Augsburg Fortress.
Letter Tracking: Reusable Edition. Ed. by W. Edwards & S. Edwards. (Large Type Tracking Ser.). (gr. k-1). 1973. wkbk. 5.00 o.p. (ISBN 0-89039-019-3). Ann Arbor Pubs.
Lettering. Graily Hewitt. LC 76-26844. (Illus.). 336p. 1981. pap. 9.95 o.s.i. (ISBN 0-8008-4728-8, Pentalic). Taplinger.
Lettering & Calligraphy. Joan Freeman. (Illus.). 128p. 1984. 12.95 o.p. (ISBN 0-668-06193-6, 6193-6). Arco.
Lettering & Design: A Practical Approach Through Handwriting. Carol Vincent. (Illus.). 96p. (Orig.). 1986. pap. 9.95 o.p. (ISBN 0-7137-1638-X, Pub. by Blandford Pr England). Sterling.
Lettering for Architects & Designers. Martha Sutherland. LC 83-21569. (Illus.). 96p. 1984. pap. 16.95 o.p. (ISBN 0-442-28181-1). Van Nos Reinhold.

Letters, 2 vols. Abigail Adams. LC 72-78635. Repr. Set. cancelled o.s.i. (ISBN 0-403-01935-4). Somerset Pub.

Letters. Joseph Addison. Repr. of 1941 ed. cancelled o.s.i. (ISBN 0-403-07201-8). Somerset Pub.

Letters, 2 vols. James Boswell. Repr. of 1924 ed. Set. 59.00x o.p. (ISBN 0-403-04137-6). Somerset Pub.

Letters. Gustave Flaubert. 1951. (ISBN 0-8022-0511-9). Philos Lib.

Letters. Maxim Gorky. 199p. 1973. 4.95 o.p. (ISBN 0-8285-1085-7, Pub. by Progress Pubs USSR). Imported Pubns.

Letters. Arnold Schonberg. 309p. Repr. of 1965 ed. lib. bdg. 49.00 o.p. (Pub. by Am Repr Serv). Reprint Servs.

Letters & Journals: Judge William Edmond, Judge Holbrook Curtis, Judge William Edmond Curtis, & Dr. Holbrook Curtis. 1926. plus three separate pamplhets 5.00 set o.p. (ISBN 0-940748-29-0). Conn Hist Soc.

Letters & Journals of Thomas Wentworth Higginson: 1846-1906. Thomas W. Higginson. Ed. by Mary T. Higginson. LC 73-88435. (Illus.). 358p. 1970. Repr. of 1921 ed. 35.00x o.p. (ISBN 0-8371-1843-3, HIH&, Pub. by Negro U Pr). Greenwood.

Letters & Numbers for Needlepoint. Elinor Parker. LC 77-16711. (Illus.). 1978. pap. 11.95 o.p. (ISBN 0-684-15527-3, ScribT). Scribner.

Letters & Poems of Mary Stuart. Clifford Bax. (ISBN 0-8022-0085-0). Philos Lib.

Letters Concerning Mythology. Thomas Blackwell. LC 75-27887. (Renaissance & the Gods Ser.: Vol. 42). (Illus.). 1976. Repr. of 1748 ed. lib. bdg. 88.00 o.p. (ISBN 0-8240-2091-X). Garland Pub.

Letters for Everyday Use. Angelica W. Cass. pap. (ISBN 0-671-09224-3). Monarch Pr.

Letters for My Children: One Mother's Quest for Answers about the Nuclear Threat. Deirdre Rhys-Thomas. 180p. 1987. 14.95 o.p. (ISBN 0-86358-181-1, AO171, Pandora Pr). Routledge Chapman & Hall.

Letters, Friends & Family. Date not set. (ISBN 0-8052-0429-6). Random.

Letters from a Faint-Hearted Feminist. Jill Tweedie. LC 83-61274. (Illus.). 144p. 1984. 9.95 o.p. (ISBN 0-88186-226-6). Parkwest Pubns.

Letters from Amelia: An Intimate Portrait of Amelia Earhart. Ed. by Jean L. Backus. LC 81-68356. (Illus.). 262p. 1982. pap. 10.95 o.p. (ISBN 0-8070-6703-2, BP 644). Beacon Pr.

Letters from Carrie. Janet Harder. LC 80-83940. (Illus.). 152p. (gr. 6 up). 1980. 10.95 o.p. (ISBN 0-932052-23-1). North Country.

Letters from England. Eca de Queiroz. Tr. by Ann Stevens from Port. LC 70-123109. 192p. 1970. 12.00x o.p. (ISBN 0-8214-0080-0). Ohio U Pr.

Letters from Father: The Truman Family's Personal Correspondence. Margaret Truman. LC 80-70224. (Illus.). 256p. 1981. 12.95 o.p. (ISBN 0-87795-313-9, Arbor Hse). Morrow.

Letters from Mesopotamia: Official, Business, & Private Letters on Clay Tablets from Two Millennia. A. Leo Oppenheim. LC 67-20576. 1967. lib. bdg. 14.00x o.s.i. (ISBN 0-226-63190-7). U of Chicago Pr.

Letters from Nantucket & Martha's Vineyard. J. Hector St. John de Crevecoeur. 1986. pap. 5.95 o.p. Morrow.

Letters from New England: The Massachusetts Bay Colony, 1629-1638. Ed. by Everett Emerson & Winfred E. Bernhard. LC 75-32484. (Commonwealth Ser.: Vol. 2). 286p. 1976. 22.50x o.p. (ISBN 0-87023-209-6). U of Mass Pr.

Letters from Nicaragua. Rebecca Gordon. LC 86-62136. 220p. 1986. pap. 8.95 o.p. (ISBN 0-933216-22-X). Spinsters Aunt Lute.

Letters from Prison & Other Essays. Adam Michnik. Tr. by Maya Latynski. (Society & Culture in East-Central Europe: No. 2). 393p. 1987. pap. 10.95 o.p. (ISBN 0-520-06175-6). U of Cal Pr.

Letters from Russia, 1919. P. D. Ouspensky. 1978. pap. 5.00 o.p. (ISBN 0-7100-0077-4). Routledge Chapman & Hall.

Letters from Sachiko. James Trager. LC 82-43512. 224p. 1982. 12.95 o.p. (ISBN 0-689-11337-4, Atheneum). Macmillan.

Letters from SDA Pastors to Pearl. Pearl Brians. pap. write for info. o.p. (ISBN 0-914009-78-8). VHI Library.

Letters from the Dead. Campbell Black. pap. 3.50 o.s.i. (ISBN 0-671-61921-7). PB.

Letters from the Grand Tour. Joseph Spence. Ed. by Slava Klima. 452p. 1975. 25.00x o.p. (ISBN 0-7735-0090-1, McGill Canada). U of Toronto Pr.

Letters from the Promised Land: Swedes in America 1840-1914. H. Arnold Barton. 344p. 1975. 22.50 o.p. (ISBN 0-318-16617-8); pap. 9.95 o.p. (ISBN 0-318-16618-6). Swedish-Am.

Letters from the Promised Land: Swedes in America, 1840-1914. Ed. by H. Arnold Barton. LC 74-22843. (Illus.). 350p. 1975. 22.50 o.p. (ISBN 0-8166-0740-0); pap. 10.95 o.p. (ISBN 0-8166-1009-6). U of Minn Pr.

Letters from the Saints. C. Williamson. 220p. 1958. (ISBN 0-8022-1890-3). Philos Lib.

Letters from Westerbork. Etty Hillesum. Tr. by Arnold Pomerans. LC 86-42625. 160p. (Dutch.). 1986. 14.45 o.s.i. (ISBN 0-394-55350-0). Pantheon.

Letters Home. Harry S. Truman & Monte M. Poen. LC 84-10953. (General Ser.). 1984. 17.95 o.p. (ISBN 0-8161-3748-X, Large Print Bks). G K Hall.

Letters, Numbers, & Colors. Amery & Hindley. (Younger Bks.). (gr. k-2). 1979. 10.95 o.p. (Usborne-Hayes). EDC.

Letters of a Javanese Princess. Raden A. Kartini. 1964. pap. 3.95 o.p. (ISBN 0-393-00207-1, Norton Lib). Norton.

Letters of an Irish Publican. John B. Keane. 88p. 1974. pap. 7.95 o.p. (ISBN 0-85342-390-3, Pub. by Mercier Pr Ireland). Irish Bks Media.

Letters of Cicero: A Selection in Translation. Marcus T. Cicero. Ed. & tr. by L. P. Wilkinson. 1968. pap. 3.95 o.p. (ISBN 0-393-00454-6, Norton Lib). Norton.

Letters of Composers Through Six Centuries. Piero Weiss. 1986. 49.00 o.p. (Pub. by Am Repr Serv). Reprint Servs.

Letters of Credit & Bankers' Acceptances 1984. Practising Law Institute Staff & Reade H. Ryan. LC 83-207729. (Commercial Law & Practice Course Handbook Ser.: No. 331). (Illus.). 630p. 1984. 40.00 o.p. PLI.

Letters of David Hume, 2 vols. David Hume. Ed. by J. Y. Greig. LC 82-48348. (Philosophy of David Hume Ser.). 1064p. 1983. lib. bdg. 121.00 o.p. (ISBN 0-8240-5407-5). Garland Pub.

Letters of Evelyn Waugh. Evelyn Waugh. Ed. by Mark Amory. LC 80-17818. 684p. 1980. 25.00 o.p. (ISBN 0-89919-021-9). Ticknor & Fields.

Letters of George Gissing to Eduard Bertz: 1887-1903. George R. Gissing. Ed. by Arthur C. Young. LC 80-12936. xl, 337p. 1980. Repr. of 1961 ed. lib. bdg. 37.50x o.p. (ISBN 0-313-22454-4, GILE). Greenwood.

Letters of J. R. R. Tolkien. Ed. by Humphrey Carpenter & Christopher Tolkien. 464p. 1981. 16.95 o.p. (ISBN 0-395-31555-7). HM.

Letters of James Joyce, 3 vols. James Joyce. Incl. Vol. 1. reissue ed. Ed. by Stuart Gilbert. (Illus.). 444p. 1966. 20.00 (ISBN 0-670-42638-5); Vol. 2. Ed. by Richard Ellmann. (Illus.). 1966. 20.00 (ISBN 0-670-42667-9); Vol. 3. Ed. by Richard Ellmann. (Illus.). 1966. 20.00 (ISBN 0-670-42723-3). 1966. boxed set 60.00 o.p. (ISBN 0-670-42639-3); banded, vols. 2 & 3 40.00 o.p. (ISBN 0-670-42695-4). Penguin USA.

Letters of Lafayette to Washington, 1777-1799. 2nd rev. ed. Ed. by Louis Gottschalk & Shirley Bill. LC 76-8599. (Memoirs Ser.: Vol. 115). 1976. 15.00 o.p. (ISBN 0-87169-115-9). Am Philos.

Letters of Lord Nelson. Horatio Nelson. 1960. 11.95x o.p. (ISBN 0-460-00244-9, Evman). Biblio Dist.

Letters of Mary Wordsworth, Eighteen Hundred to Eighteen Fifty-Five. Mary Wordsworth. Ed. by Mary E. Burton. LC 78-14345. 1979. Repr. of 1958 ed. lib. bdg. 35.00 o.p. (ISBN 0-313-20632-5, WOLO). Greenwood.

Letters of Paul: Conversations in Context. Calvin J. Roetzel. LC 74-21901. (Biblical Foundations Ser.). 160p. (Orig.). 1975. pap. 5.95 o.p. (ISBN 0-8042-0208-7, John Knox). Westminster John Knox.

Letters of Robert G. Ingersoll. Eva I. Wakefield. (ISBN 0-8022-1792-3). Philos Lib.

Letters of Saint Athanasius. C. R. Shapland. 1952. (ISBN 0-8022-1542-4). Philos Lib.

Letters of St. Boniface. Boniface. Tr. by Ephraim Emerton from Lat. LC 76-18847. (Columbia University Records of Civilization Ser.). 204p. 1976. pap. 5.95x o.p. (ISBN 0-393-09147-3). Norton.

Letters of Samuel Pepys & His Family Circle. Ed. by Helen T. Heath. LC 78-10795. 1979. Repr. of 1955 ed. lib. bdg. 35.00x o.p. (ISBN 0-313-20656-2, HELE). Greenwood.

Letters of Sigmund Freud & Arnold Zweig. Ed. by Ernst L. Freud. LC 74-95859. 1971. pap. 2.35 o.p. (ISBN 0-15-650680-7, HB196, Harv). HarBraceJ.

Letters of Stephen Gardiner. Stephen Gardiner. Ed. by James A. Muller. Repr. of 1933 ed. lib. bdg. 35.00x o.p. (ISBN 0-8371-4223-7, GALE). Greenwood.

Letters of Thomas Attwood Digges (1742-1821) Ed. by Robert H. Elias & Eugene D. Finch. LC 81-16450. 666p. 1982. lib. bdg. 34.95x o.p. (ISBN 0-87249-412-8). U of SC Pr.

Letters of Thomas Carlyle to His Brother Alexander, with Related Family Letters. Thomas Carlyle. Ed. by Edwin W. Marrs, Jr. LC 68-21978. (Illus.). 47.00x o.s.i. (ISBN 0-674-52612-0). Harvard U Pr.

Letters of Virginia Woolf, Vol. V. Virginia Woolf. LC 75-25538. 1979. 14.95 o.s.i. (ISBN 0-15-150928-X). HarBraceJ.

Letters of Virginia Woolf: 1888-1912, Vol. I. Ed. by Nigel Nicolson & Joanne Trautmann. LC 75-25538. (Illus.). 531p. 1975. 14.95 o.s.i. (ISBN 0-15-150924-7). HarBraceJ.

Letters of Virginia Woolf: 1912-1922, Vol. II. Ed. by Nigel Nicolson & Joanne Trautmann. LC 75-25538. (Illus.). 1976. 14.95 o.s.i. (ISBN 0-15-150925-5). HarBraceJ.

Letters of Virginia Woolf, 1929-1931, Vol. IV. Virginia Woolf. 1979. 14.95 o.s.i. (ISBN 0-15-150927-1). HarBraceJ.

Letters of Virginia Woolf: 1936-1941, Vol. VI. Virginia Woolf. Ed. by Nigel Nicholson & Joanne Trautmann. LC 75-25538. 576p. 1980. 19.95 o.s.i. (ISBN 0-15-150929-8). HarBraceJ.

Letters of Vita Sackville-West to Virgina Woolf. Ed. by Louise Desalve & Mitchell A. Leaska. LC 85-16903. (Illus.). 400p. 1986. pap. 8.95 o.p. (ISBN 0-688-06271-7, Quill). Morrow.

Letters of Vita Sackville-West to Virginia Woolf. Ed. by Louise DeSalvo & Mitchell A. Leaska. LC 84-60758. (Illus.). 400p. 1984. 17.95 o.p. (ISBN 0-688-03963-4). Morrow.

Letters on Art & Literature. Francois Mauriac. 1953. (ISBN 0-8022-1091-0). Philos Lib.

Letters on Slavery from the Old World. James Williams. LC 71-97445. Repr. of 1861 ed. 35.00x o.p. (ISBN 0-8371-2718-1, WIO&, Pub. by Negro U Pr). Greenwood.

Letters on the Healing Ministry. Albert E. Day & James K. Wagner. 144p. 1986. pap. 6.95 incl. study guide o.p. (ISBN 0-317-30215-9, ICN 606462, Dist. by Abingdon Pr). Upper Room.

Letters Rogatory. Ed. by Bernard A. Grossman. 97p. 1956. 8.00 o.p. (ISBN 0-87945-015-0). Fed Legal Pubn.

Letters That Get Action. C. L. Keyworth. LC 83-21344. 192p. 1984. 10.95 o.p. (ISBN 0-668-05694-0); pap. 6.95 o.p. (ISBN 0-668-05700-9). Arco.

Letters to a Young Bride. Ruth H. Calkin. 112p. 1985. 10.95 o.p. (ISBN 0-8423-2134-9). Tyndale.

Letters to a Young Doctor. Philip Rhodes. 127p. 1983. pap. 14.00x o.p. (ISBN 0-7279-0165-6, Pub. by British Med Assoc UK). Taylor & Francis.

Letters to Alice: On First Reading Jane Austen. Fay Weldon. LC 84-24077. 128p. 1985. 14.95 o.s.i. (ISBN 0-8008-4743-1). Taplinger.

Letters to Alice: On First Reading Jane Austen. Fay Weldon. LC 86-221. 128p. 1986. pap. 4.95 o.s.i. (ISBN 0-15-650981-4, Harv). HarBraceJ.

Letters to an Unknown Generation. David G. Yuengling. 1979. 6.00 o.p. (ISBN 0-682-49389-9). Exposition-Phoenix.

Letters to Benvenuta. Rainer M. Rilke. 1951. (ISBN 0-8022-1348-0). Philos Lib.

Letters to Dr. Kugelmann. Karl Marx. LC 73-10876. 148p. 1973. Repr. of 1934 ed. lib. bdg. 35.00x o.p. (ISBN 0-8371-7045-1, MALK). Greenwood.

Letters to John. Pam Prater. 1988. 10.00 o.p. Jelm Mtn.

Letters to My Daughter. Dagobert D. Runes. 131p. 1954. (ISBN 0-8022-1439-8). Philos Lib.

Letters to My Son. Dagobert D Runes. 92p. 1949. (ISBN 0-8022-1441-X). Philos Lib.

Letters to Ottla. Date not set. (ISBN 0-8052-3372-5). Random.

Letters to the Modern Church. Wayne Hoffman. LC 79-88401. 1979. pap. 3.75 o.p. (ISBN 0-933350-23-6). Morse Pr.

Letters to the Seven Churches of Asia in Their Local Setting. C. J. Hemer. (JSoT Supplement Ser.: No. 11). 375p. pap. text ed. 15.95x o.s.i. (Pub. by JSOT Pr England). Eisenbrauns.

Letters to Thelma: From One Christian Science Sunday School Teacher to Another. Estelle F. Jackson. 1976. 5.00 o.p. (ISBN 0-682-48622-1). Exposition-Phoenix.

Letters: Volume II, 1823-1838. Ed. by Ralph M. Aderman et al. (Critical Editions Program Ser.). 1979. 36.50 o.p. (ISBN 0-8057-8523-X, Twayne). G K Hall.

Letters Written by a Peruvian Princess, 1748. Francoise Graffigny. Ed. by Michael F. Shugrue. LC 74-16070. (Novel in England, 1700-1775 Ser.). 1975. lib. bdg. 61.00 o.p. (ISBN 0-8240-1121-X). Garland Pub.

Lettland Zwischen Demokratie und Diktatur. Jurgen Von Hehn. 1957. pap. 8.00 o.p. (ISBN 0-384-22080-0). Johnson Repr.

Lettre a la N. R. F. Marcel Proust. (Cahiers Marcel Proust). pap. 5.95 o.p. (ISBN 0-685-37067-4). Schoenhof.

Lettre Aux Communistes Espagnols. Fernando Arrabal. 176p. 1978. 9.95 o.p. (ISBN 0-686-54446-3). French & Eur.

Lettres a Andre Gide: Avec: Responses d'Andre Gide. Jean Cocteau. 224p. 1970. 15.95 o.p. (ISBN 0-686-54537-0). French & Eur.

Lettres a Helene Picard. Colette. 240p. 1958. 8.95 o.p. (ISBN 0-686-54579-6). French & Eur.

Lettres a Madame Hanska, 4 vols. Honore De Balzac & Roger Pierrot. (Edition critique). 1968-71. Vol. 1. 49.95 o.p. (ISBN 0-686-53885-4); Vol. 2, 1841-1845. 24.95 o.p. (ISBN 0-686-53886-2); Vol. 3, 1845-1847. 49.95 o.p. (ISBN 0-686-53887-0); Vol. 4, 1847-1850. 49.95 o.p. (ISBN 0-686-53888-9). French & Eur.

Lettres a Madame Recamier. Rene de Chateaubriand. 576p. 1951. 9.95 o.p. (ISBN 0-686-54366-1). French & Eur.

Lettres a Marguerite Moreno. Colette. 360p. 1959. 14.95 o.p. (ISBN 0-686-54580-X). French & Eur.

Lettres a un Ami: Cent Onze Lettres Inedites a Claude Hochet. Benjamin Constant et al. 256p. 1949. 11.95 o.p. (ISBN 0-686-54613-X). French & Eur.

Lettres Au Petit Corsaire. Colette. 160p. 1963. 7.95 o.p. (ISBN 0-686-54582-6). French & Eur.

Lettres et Manuscripts (Illustre) Nombres Lettres Inedites de Chateaubriand a Benjamin Constant, a Armand Carrel, au Sculpteur Emoyne, Vol. 19. Rene de Chateaubriand. (Illus.). 96p. 1976. 35.00 o.p. (ISBN 0-686-54367-X). French & Eur.

Lettres Inedites aux Siens. Charles Baudelaire. 1966. 19.95 o.p. (ISBN 0-686-51924-8). French & Eur.

Letty Fox: Her Luck. Christina Stead. LC 78-23847. 517p. 1979. pap. 5.95 o.p. (ISBN 0-15-650885-0, Harv). HarBraceJ.

Letzte Sommer. Ricarda Huch. Ed. by Dieter Cunz. (Ger.). 1963. pap. 2.95x o.p. (ISBN 0-393-09603-3, NortonC). Norton.

Leukemia: Recent Developments in Diagnosis & Therapy. Ed. by E. Thiel & S. Thierfelder. (Recent Results in Cancer Research Ser.: Vol. 93). (Illus.). 340p. 1984. 75.00 o.p. (ISBN 0-387-13289-9). Springer-Verlag.

Leukemic Cell. Daniel Catovsky. (Methods in Hematology: Vol. 2). (Illus.). 230p. 1981. text ed. 55.50 o.p. (ISBN 0-443-01911-8). Churchill.

Leukotrienes & Prostacyclin. Ed. by F. Berti & G. Folco. (NATO ASI Series A, Life Sciences: Vol. 154). 306p. 59.50x o.p. (ISBN 0-306-41173-3, Plenum Pr). Plenum Pub.

Leutebuch: Ein Leichtes Lesebuch. Albrecht Holschuh. LC 77-76512. (Illus.). 178p. (Orig., Ger.). 1977. pap. text ed. 11.00 net o.p. (ISBN 0-15-550601-3, HC). HarBraceJ.

Levanter. Eric Ambler. LC 81-70069. 1982. pap. 7.95 o.p. (ISBN 0-689-70618-9, 277, Atheneum). Macmillan.

Levantine. Peter Delacorte. LC 84-14744. 1985. 15.45 o.p. (ISBN 0-393-01881-4). Norton.

Level Five. Duff Hart-Davis. LC 81-69145. 1982. 13.95 o.p. (ISBN 0-689-11257-2, Atheneum). Macmillan.

Level II ROMs. Mark D. Goodwin. (Illus.). 532p. 1983. 24.95 o.p. (ISBN 0-8306-0275-5, 1575); pap. 17.15 o.p. (ISBN 0-8306-0175-9). TAB Bks.

Levels of Personality. Mark Cook. LC 88-47779. 208p. 1984. pap. 16.95 o.p. (ISBN 0-275-91601-4, B1601). Praeger.

Leveraged Acquisitions: Private & Public 1985, Vol. 472. Practising Law Institute Staff. 625p. 1985. pap. 15.00 o.p. (ISBN 0-317-27463-5, B4-6706). PLI.

Leveraged Finance: How to Raise & Invest Cash. Mark Stevens. 1982. pap. 5.95 o.p. (ISBN 0-13-535096-4, Reward). P-H.

Leveraged Leasing 1984, Vol. 324. (Commercial Law & Practice Course Handbook Ser.). 478p. 1987. 15.00 o.p. (A4-4086). PLI.

Levi Coffin & the Underground Railroad. Charles Ludwig. LC 75-12583. 176p. 1975. 7.95 o.p. (ISBN 0-8361-1770-0). Herald Pr.

Levin H.S. (Illus.). 64p. 1984. 16.95 o.p. (ISBN 0-317-62021-5). H L Levin.

Levi's. Ed Cray. 1978. 9.95 o.p. (ISBN 0-395-26477-4). HM.

Levitan. T. Yurova. 235p. 1981. 38.00 o.p. (ISBN 0-8285-2028-3, Pub. by Aurora Pubs USSR). Imported Pubns.

Leviticus: A Commentary. Martin Noth. LC 77-7654. (Old Testament Library). 208p. 1977. 15.95 o.s.i. (ISBN 0-664-20774-X, Westminster). Westminster John Knox.

Lewes Workshop on Solutions in Nuclear & Elementary Particle Physics: Proceedings, Delaware University, June 1984. Ed. by A. Chodos et al. 320p. 1984. 44.00 o.p. (ISBN 9971-966-89-1). World Scientific Pub.

Lewis & Clark College: Eighteen Sixty-Seven to Nineteen Sixty-Seven. Martha F. Montague. LC 68-28925. (Illus.). 1968. 8.95 o.p. (ISBN 0-8323-0037-3). Binford-Metropolitan.

Lewis & Lewis: The Life & Times of a Victorian Solicitor. John Juxon. LC 83-24198. (Illus.). 320p. 1984. 18.45 o.p. (ISBN 0-89919-277-7). Ticknor & Fields.

Lewis Carroll. Beverly L. Clark. Ed. by Roger C. Schlobin. (Reader's Guides to Contemporary Science Fiction & Fantasy Authors Ser.: Vol. 47). (Orig.). 1988. 17.95x o.p. (ISBN 1-55742-031-9); pap. 9.95x o.p. (ISBN 1-55742-030-0). Starmont Hse.
Lewis Carroll's Bedside Book. Ed. by Edgar Cuthwillis. (Illus.). 1979. 4.95 o.p. (ISBN 0-395-28596-8). HM.
Lewis Hine in Europe, 1918-1919: The Lost Photographs. Daile Kaplan. (Illus.). 240p. 1988. 49.95 o.p. (ISBN 0-89659-745-8). Abbeville Pr.
Lewis Morris, Anglo-American Statesman, ca 1613-1691. Samuel S. Smith. 136p. 1983. text ed. 15.00 o.p. (ISBN 0-391-02767-0). Humanities.
Lewis Mumford Reader. Ed. by Donald Miller. LC 86-42617. 416p. 1986. 23.45 o.p. (ISBN 0-394-55526-0); pap. 14.95 o.p. (ISBN 0-394-74630-9). Pantheon.
Lewis Perry of Exeter. William G. Saltonstall. LC 79-55586. (Illus.). 1980. 7.95 o.p. (ISBN 0-689-11056-1, Atheneum). Macmillan.
Lewis Said, Lewis Did. Harriet Ziefert. LC 86-61789. (Great Big Board Bks.). (Illus.). 14p. (ps). 1987. 3.95 o.s.i. (ISBN 0-394-88690-9, BYR). Random.
Lewis Tappan & the Evangelical War Against Slavery. Bertram Wyatt-Brown. LC 68-19228. (Studies in American Negro Life). 1971. pap. text ed. 3.95x o.p. (ISBN 0-689-70257-4, NL27, Atheneum). Macmillan.
Lexical Basis of Russian: An Integrated Students Dictionary. Ed. by V. V. Morovskin. 1165p. 1985. 15.95 o.p. (ISBN 0-8285-3352-0, Pub. by Rus Lang Pubs USSR). Imported Pubns.
Lexicon. Stephen M. Sechi et al. (Atlantean Trilogy Ser.). (Illus.). 160p. 1985. 14.00 o.p. (ISBN 0-9610770-4-2). Bard Games.
Lexicon Medicum. Boleslaw Zlotnickiego. 1604p. (Eng., Rus., Fr., Ger., Lat. & Pol.). 1976. 95.00 o.p. (ISBN 0-686-57263-7, M-6576). French & Eur.
Lexicon Universal Encyclopedia, 21 vols. rev. ed. LC 85-27032. (Illus.). 1987. text ed. write for info. o.p. (ISBN 0-7172-2021-4). Grolier Inc.
Lexikon Allergologicum. K. Wilken-Jensen. 1965. 31.00 o.p. (ISBN 0-08-011838-0). Pergamon.
Lexikon der Genetik der Hundekrankheiten. E. Wiesner & S. Willer. (Illus.). 352p. (Ger.). 1983. 27.50 o.p. (ISBN 3-8055-3616-X). S. Karger.
Lexikon 2000, Vol. 2. (Ger.). 1970. 86.00 o.p. (ISBN 3-8075-1002-8, M-7188, Pub. by Wissen). French & Eur.
Lexikon 2000, Vol. 3. (Ger.). 1971. 86.00 o.p. (ISBN 3-8075-1003-6, M-7187, Pub. by Wissen). French & Eur.
Lexikon 2000, Vol. 4. (Ger.). 1971. 86.00 o.p. (ISBN 3-8075-1004-4, M-7186, Pub. by Wissen). French & Eur.
Lexikon 2000, Vol. 5. (Ger.). 1971. 86.00 o.p. (ISBN 3-8075-1005-2, M-7185, Pub. by Wissen). French & Eur.
Lexikon 2000, Vol. 6. (Ger.). 1971. 86.00 o.p. (ISBN 3-8075-1006-0, M-7184, Pub. by Wissen). French & Eur.
Lexikon 2000, Vol. 7. (Ger.). 1972. 86.00 o.p. (ISBN 3-8075-1007-9, M-7183, Pub. by Wissen). French & Eur.
Lexikon 2000, Vol. 8. (Ger.). 1972. 86.00 o.p. (ISBN 3-8075-1008-7, M-7182, Pub. by Wissen). French & Eur.
Lexikon 2000, Vol. 9. (Ger.). 1972. 86.00 o.p. (ISBN 3-8075-1009-5, M-7181, Pub. by Wissen). French & Eur.
Lexikon 2000, Vol. 10. (Ger.). 1972. 86.00 o.p. (ISBN 3-8075-1010-9, M-7180, Pub. by Wissen). French & Eur.
Lexikon 2000, Vol. 11. (Ger.). 1973. 86.00 o.p. (ISBN 3-8075-1011-7, M-7179, Pub. by Wissen). French & Eur.
Lexikon 2000, Vol. 12. (Ger.). 1973. 86.00 o.p. (ISBN 3-8075-1012-5, M-7178, Pub. by Wissen). French & Eur.
Lexikon 2000, Vol. 13. (Ger.). 1973. 86.00 o.p. (ISBN 3-8075-1013-3, M-7177, Pub. by Wissen). French & Eur.
Lexique Anglais-Francais des Appareils de Mesures Electriques. Jean Mercier. 44p. (Eng. & Fr.). 1973. pap. 1.95 o.p. (ISBN 0-686-57044-8, M-6405). French & Eur.
Lexique Anglais-Francais des Termes Appartenant Aux Technques En Usage I.G.N, 2 vols, Pt. 1. Thuillier. 464p. (Fr. & Eng., English-French Lexicon of Terms Pertaining to Techniques Used at I.G.N.). 1958. pap. 14.95 o.p. (ISBN 0-686-56781-1, M-6357). French & Eur.
Lexique Anglais-Francais des Termes Appartenant Aux Techniques En Usage a I.G.N, Pt.2. Ed. by Brommer. 122p. (Fr. & Eng., English-French Lexicon of Terms Pertaining to Techniques Used at I.G.N). 1958. pap. 7.95 o.p. (ISBN 0-686-56778-1, M-6356). French & Eur.
Lexique de L'Anglais des Affaires. Ivan de Renty. 352p. (Eng. & Fr.). 1977. pap. 5.95 o.p. (ISBN 0-686-57286-6, M-4761). French & Eur.
Lexique Francais-Anglais et Anglais-Francais des Termes d'usage Courant en Machines Outils et Machines Similaires. 56p. (Fr., French-English, English-French Lexicon of Commonly Used Terms in Machine Tools and Similar Machines). 1960. pap. 6.95 o.p. (ISBN 0-686-56794-3, M-6365). French & Eur.
Lexique Informatique. Maurice Balay. 128p. (Fr.). 1971. pap. 9.95 o.p. (ISBN 0-686-56908-3, M-6021). French & Eur.
Li Chih: His Life Works. Hok-Lam Chan. LC 79-57496. 250p. 1980. 35.00 o.p. (ISBN 0-87332-160-X). M E Sharpe.
Li-Prophylaxis of Depression. (Landmark Ser.). 1979. 22.50x o.p. (ISBN 0-8422-4113-2). Irvington.
Li Ta-Chao & the Origins of Chinese Marxism. Maurice Meisner. LC 67-10904. 1970. pap. text ed. 6.95x o.s.i. (ISBN 0-689-70221-3, 154, Atheneum). Macmillan.
Liability in Trans-European Road Transport. Ed. by G. R. Cyriax. 90p. 1980. pap. 65.00x o.p. (ISBN 0-566-03018-7). Gower Pub Co.
Liability Insurance Coverage Principles. 1984. 25.00 o.p. (ISBN 0-88129-140-4). Wash Bar CLE.
Liability of Corporate Officers & Directors with 1985 Supplement. William E. Knepper & Dan A. Bailey. 846p. 1978. pap. text ed. 50.00x o.p. (ISBN 0-87473-118-6, A Smith Co); Suppl. 1985. 20.00x o.p. (ISBN 0-87473-195-X). Michie Co.
Liang Ch'i-Ch'ao & Intellectual Transition in China, 1890-1907. Hao Chang. LC 75-162635. (East Asian Ser: No. 64). 1971. 24.50x o.s.i. (ISBN 0-674-53009-8). Harvard U Pr.
Liar, Liar. Laurence Yep. LC 83-5432. 160p. (gr. 7 up). 1983. 10.25 o.p. (ISBN 0-688-02417-3). Morrow.
Liar, Liar. Laurence Yep. 176p. (YA) (gr. 7 up). 1985. pap. 2.50 o.p. (ISBN 0-380-69844-7, Flare). Avon.
Liars. Peter Hill. 1978. 6.95 o.p. (ISBN 0-395-26383-2). HM.
Liars in Love. Date not set. pap. (ISBN 0-385-28552-3). Delacorte.
Liars in Love. Richard Yates. 256p. 1982. pap. 9.95 o.p. (ISBN 0-385-28552-3, Delta). Dell.
Libby. Milt Machlin. (Orig.). 1980. pap. 2.75 o.p. (ISBN 0-505-51533-4, Pub. by Tower Bks). Dorchester Pub Co.
Libby Holman: Body & Soul. Hamilton D. Perry. (Illus.). 288p. 1983. 16.45i o.p. (ISBN 0-316-70014-2). Little.
Libby Shadows a Lady. Catherine Woolley. LC 74-2029. (Illus.). 192p. (gr. 3-7). 1974. lib. bdg. 11.88 o.p. (ISBN 0-688-31787-1). Morrow.
Liber Amicorum Presented to Prof. Dr. Wm. Penn. Ed. by H. O. Thijssen. (Journal: Diagnostic Imaging: Vol. 52, No. 2-3). (Illus.). 132p. 1983. pap. 60.00 o.p. (ISBN 3-8055-3671-2). S Karger.
Liberal Christianity at the Crossroads. John B. Cobb, Jr. LC 73-9738. 128p. 1973. 4.95 o.s.i. (ISBN 0-664-20977-7, Westminster). Westminster John Knox.
Liberal Crackup. R. Emmett Tyrrell, Jr. 288p. 1984. 16.45 o.p. (ISBN 0-671-52735-5). S&S.
Liberal Education at Yale: The Yale College Course of Study 1945-1978. Daniel Catlin, Jr. LC 82-17576. 264p. (Orig.). 1983. lib. bdg. 32.00 o.p. (ISBN 0-8191-2796-5); pap. text ed. 14.25 o.p. (ISBN 0-8191-2797-3). U Pr of Amer.
Liberal International Economic Order: The International Monetary System & Economic Development. Deepak Lal. LC 80-22523. (Essays in International Finance Ser.: No. 139). 1980. pap. text ed. 4.50x o.p. (ISBN 0-88165-046-3). Princeton U Int Finan Econ.
Liberal Party Politics in Britain. Arthur I. Cyr. LC 76-702. 350p. 1977. text ed. 12.95 o.p. (ISBN 0-87855-145-X). Transaction Pubs.
Liberal Socialism: The Pure Welfare Economics of a Liberal Socialist Economy. 2nd rev. ed. Burnham P. Beckwith. 1974. text ed. 20.00 o.p. (ISBN 0-682-47785-0, University). Exposition-Phoenix.
Liberal Studies: An Outline Course, 2 Vols. N. C. Dexter & E. G. Rayner. 1964. Vol. 1. pap. text ed. 7.00 o.p. (ISBN 0-08-010451-7); Vol. 2. pap. text ed. 6.25 o.p. (ISBN 0-08-010453-3). Pergamon.
Liberal Thought in Modern America. Dwight D. Murphey. 482p. (Orig.). lib. bdg. 36.75 o.p. (ISBN 0-8191-5756-2); pap. text ed. 22.50 o.p. (ISBN 0-8191-5757-0). U Pr of Amer.
Liberalism & the Social Problem. Winston S. Churchill. LC 72-3299. (British History Ser., No. 30). 1972. Repr. of 1909 ed. lib. bdg. 75.00x o.p. (ISBN 0-8383-1528-3). Haskell.
Liberalism, Nationalism & the German Intellectuals, 1822-1847. R. Hinton Thomas. LC 75-11803. 148p. 1975. Repr. of 1951 ed. lib. bdg. 22.50x o.p. (ISBN 0-8371-8140-2, THLI). Greenwood.
Liberalization with Stabilization in the Southern Cone of Latin. V. Corbo & J. De Melo. 1985. pap. 26.00 o.p. (ISBN 0-08-033412-1, Pub. by PPL). Pergamon.
Liberating Bond: Covenants Biblical & Contemporary. Wolfgang Roth & Rosemary R. Ruether. (Orig.). 1978. pap. 2.95 o.p. (ISBN 0-377-00076-0). Friendship Pr.
Liberating Faith: Bonhoeffer's Message for Today. Geffrey B. Kelly. LC 84-15863. 208p. (Orig.). 1984. pap. 11.95 o.p. (ISBN 0-8066-2092-7, 10-3832, Augsburg). Augsburg Fortress.
Liberating Our White Ghetto. Joseph R. Barndt. LC 70-176477. 1972. pap. 2.95 o.p. (ISBN 0-8066-1206-1, 10-3835, Augsburg). Augsburg Fortress.
Liberation & Change. Gustavo Gutierrez & Richard Shaull. LC 76-44970. 1977. pap. 5.50 o.p. (ISBN 0-8042-0661-9, John Knox). Westminster John Knox.
Liberation & Freedom in an Urban Learning Community. Walter N. Watts. 1973. 29.75x o.p. (ISBN 0-8422-5137-5); pap. 6.95x o.p. (ISBN 0-8422-0360-5). Irvington.
Liberation of Clementine Tipton. Jane Flory. LC 74-8180. (Illus.). 224p. (gr. 3-7). 1974. 5.95 o.p. (ISBN 0-395-19493-8). HM.
Liberation of One: The Autobiography of Romuald Spasowski, Polish Ambassador to the Unites States. Romuald Spasowski. Tr. by Richard Lourie. LC 85-24899. (Illus.). 720p. 1986. 24.95 o.p. (ISBN 0-15-151276-0). HarBraceJ.
Liberation of the Riviera. Peter Leslie. 1986. 12.95 o.p. (ISBN 0-671-61048-1, Wyndham Bks). S&S.
Liberation Theology. Ed. by Ronald H. Nash. 1986. text ed. 15.95 o.p. (ISBN 0-8010-6745-6). Baker Bk.
Liberation Theology. Ed. by Ronald H. Nash. 268p. 1988. pap. 12.95 o.p. (ISBN 0-8010-6781-2). Baker Bk.
Liberation Theology. Emilio Nunez. 1985. text ed. 15.95 o.p. (ISBN 0-8024-4893-3). Moody.
Liberation Theology: An Evangelical View from the Third World. J. Andrew Kirk. LC 79-5212. (New Foundations Theological Library). 246p. (Peter Toon & Ralph Martin series editor). 1980. 12.95 o.p. (ISBN 0-8042-3704-2, John Knox). Westminster John Knox.
Liberation Theology in Latin America. James V. Schall. LC 80-82266. 411p. (Orig.). 1982. pap. 13.95 o.s.i. (ISBN 0-89870-006-X). Ignatius Pr.
Liberator, Eleutherios. Da Free John. (Illus.). 114p. 1982. 19.95 o.s.i. (ISBN 0-913922-66-8); pap. 10.95 o.s.i. (ISBN 0-913922-67-6). Dawn Horse Pr.
Liberator of the Nations: Biblical Blueprints on Political Action. Dennis Peacocke. cancelled o.s.i. (ISBN 0-930462-14-9). Am Bur Eco Res.
Liberators: My Life in the Soviet Army. Viktor Suvorov. LC 83-42685. 1983. 13.45 o.p. (ISBN 0-393-01759-1). Norton.
Liberators of Latin America. Bob Young & Jan Young. LC 70-120166. (Illus.). (gr. 7-12). 1970. PLB 10.88 o.p. (ISBN 0-688-51030-2). Lothrop.
Liberia, 2 vols. Harry H. Johnston. LC 71-78372. (Illus.). 1970. Repr. of 1906 ed. Set. 76.00x o.p. (ISBN 0-8371-3897-3, JOL&, Pub. by Negro U Pr); Vol. 1. 42.00 o.p. (ISBN 0-8371-1347-4, JOM&, Pub. by Negro U Pr); Vol. 2. 42.00 o.p. (ISBN 0-8371-1348-2, JON&, Pub. by Negro U Pr). Greenwood.
Liberia: A Country Study. Ed. by Harold D. Nelson. LC 85-7393. (Army Department Pamphlet 550-38. Area Handbook Ser.). (Illus.). 371p. 1985. 12.00 o.p. (ISBN 0-318-18782-5, S/N 008-020-01041-3). USGPO.
Liberian History Before Eighteen Fifty-Seven: A Reference for Elementary Pupils. Joseph S. Guannu. 1977. 6.00 o.p. (ISBN 0-682-48868-2). Exposition-Phoenix.
Libertine in Love. Caroline Courtney. 352p. 1986. pap. 10.95x o.p. (ISBN 0-8161-3946-6, Large Prints Bks). G K Hall.
Liberty & Equality. Ed. by Ellen F. Paul. 176p. 1985. pap. 14.95x o.p. (ISBN 0-631-13718-1). Basil Blackwell.
Liberty & Union, 2 vols. 2nd ed. Martin Ridge et al. (Illus.). 525p. (YA) (gr. 7-12). 1973. Vol. 2. text ed. 31.00 o.p. (ISBN 0-395-14379-9). HM.
Liberty Cap. Enid Davis. LC 77-17208. (Illus.). 225p. 1978. pap. 1.00 o.p. (ISBN 0-915864-15-0). Academy Chi Pubs.
Liberty, Equality, & Law. Ed. by Sterling M. McMurrin. LC 86-28300. 225p. 1987. pap. 8.95 o.p. (ISBN 0-87480-271-7). U of Utah Pr.
Liberty, Equality, Sisterhood: On the Emancipation of Women in Church & Society. Elisabeth Moltmann-Wendel. Tr. by Ruth C. Gritsch from Ger. LC 77-15240. 96p. 1978. pap. 0.50 o.p. (ISBN 0-8006-1325-2, 1-1325, Fortress). Augsburg Fortress.
Liberty Sword. Gardner F. Fox. 1976. pap. 1.25 o.p. (ISBN 0-685-69145-4, LB358ZK, Pub. by Leisure Bks CT). Dorchester Pub Co.
Liberty to the Captives. George E. Ogle. LC 76-48578. 1977. 5.95 o.p. (ISBN 0-8042-1494-8, John Knox). Westminster John Knox.
Liberty's Grandson: An Unconventional Autobiography. Roderic M. Olzendam & Gordon Keith. 1977. 7.50 o.p. (ISBN 0-682-48894-1). Exposition-Phoenix.
Librarian & the Machine. Paul Wasserman. LC 65-25320. 170p. 1965. 30.00x o.p. (ISBN 0-8103-0164-4). Gale.
Librarian Authors: A Biobibliography. Rudolf Engelbarts. LC 80-28035. 282p. 1981. lib. bdg. 25.00x o.p. (ISBN 0-89950-007-2). McFarland & Co.
Librarian-Educator Interdependence. John T. Corrigan. 1976. 3.00 o.p. (ISBN 0-87507-002-7). Cath Lib Assn.
Librarians As Professionals: The Occupation's Impact on Library Work Arrangements. William J. Reeves. LC 79-2389. (Illus.). 192p. 1980. 24.50x o.p. (ISBN 0-669-03163-1). Lexington Bks.
Librarian's Hints for Students. Christine R. Wyandt. 1979. 5.50 o.p. (ISBN 0-682-49487-9). Exposition-Phoenix.
Librarian's Manual: A Treatise on Bibliography, Comprising a Select & Descriptive List of Bibliographical Works; to Which Are Added, Sketches of Public Libraries. Reuben A. Guild. LC 70-174942. (Illus.). x, 318p. 1972. Repr. of 1858 ed. 46.00x o.p. (ISBN 0-8103-3811-4). Gale.
Librarianship: A Definition. J. G. Meijer. (Occasional Papers: No. 155). 40p. 1982. pap. 3.00 o.p. (ISBN 0-317-59002-2). U of Ill Lib Info Sci.
Librarianship & the Third World. A. M. Abdul Huq & Mohammed M. Aman. LC 76-30916. (Reference Library of Social Science Ser.: Vol. 40). 1977. lib. bdg. 55.00 o.p. (ISBN 0-8240-9897-8). Garland Pub.
Libraries & Data Processing--Where Do We Stand? John S. Melin. (Occasional Papers: No. 72). 45p. 1964. pap. 1.00 o.p. (ISBN 0-317-58853-2). U of Ill Lib Info Sci.
Libraries & Neighborhood Information Centers. Ed. by Carol L. Kronus & Linda Crowe. LC 78-81002. (Allerton Park Institutes: No. 17). 142p. 1972. 6.00x o.p. (ISBN 0-87845-034-3). U of Ill Lib Info Sci.
Libraries in Schools. Eric Leyland. 143p. 1965. (ISBN 0-8022-0971-8). Philos Lib.
Libraries in the East: An International & Comparative Study. George Chandler. (International Bibliographical & Library Ser.). 214p. 1971. 48.00 o.p. (ISBN 0-12-785104-6). Acad Pr.
Libraries in West Africa. Ed. by Helen Davies. 199p. 1982. lib. bdg. 23.00 o.p. (ISBN 3-598-10440-5). K G Saur.
Libraries, Information Centers & Databases in Science & Technology: A World Guide. Helga Lengenfelder. 561p. 1985. 100.00x o.p. (ISBN 3-598-10533-9). K G Saur.
Libraries Serving Youth - YSS: Proceedings from Mohont Conference. 1987. write for info. o.p. (ISBN 0-931658-12-8). NY Lib Assn.
Libraries Serving Youth: Directions for Service in the 1990's. Ed. & intro. by Judith Rovenger. 80p. (Orig.). 1987. pap. 10.00 o.p. (ISBN 0-317-61036-8). NY Lib Assn.
Library Acquisitions Special Reports. Ed. by Scott R. Bullard. 115p. 1981. pap. 31.00 o.p. (ISBN 0-08-026112-4). Pergamon.
Library & Manuscripts of Piero Di Cosimo De'Medici. Francis Ames-Lewis. LC 83-48687. (Theses from the Courtauld Institute of Art Ser.). (Illus.). 655p. 1984. lib. bdg. 80.00 o.p. (ISBN 0-8240-5975-1). Garland Pub.
Library Assistance to Readers. Robert L. Collison. (Illus.). 147p. 1963. 5.95 o.p. (ISBN 0-8022-0284-5). Philos Lib.
Library Automation: A Current Review. Peter Gillman & Silvina Peniston. 72p. 1984. pap. 19.00 o.p. (ISBN 0-85142-188-1). Learned Info.
Library Automation As a Source of Management Information: Proceedings of the Clinic on Library Applications of Data Processing, 1982. Ed. by F. W. Lancaster. LC 83-9110. 200p. 1983. 15.00 o.p. (ISBN 0-87845-068-8). U of Ill Lib Info Sci.
Library Bibliographies & Indexes: A Subject Guide to Resource Material Available from Libraries, Information Centers, Library Schools, & Library Associations in the U. S. & Canada. Ed. by Paul Wasserman & Esther Herman. LC 74-26741. xii, 314p. 1975. 88.00x o.p. (ISBN 0-8103-0390-6). Gale.
Library Buildings, Innovation for Changing Needs: Proceedings. Ed. by Alphonse F. Trezza. LC 73-39011. (Illus.). 302p. 1972. pap. 12.00x o.p. (ISBN 0-8389-3132-4). ALA.
Library Catalog of the Conservation Center of the Institute of Fine Arts. New York University Editors. 1980. lib. bdg. 100.00 o.p. (Hall Library). G K Hall.

Library Catalog of the International Museum of Photography at George Eastman House, 4 vols. International Museum of Photography, George Eastman House Staff. 1982. Set. lib. bdg. 365.00 o.p. (ISBN 0-8161-0294-5, Hall Library). G K Hall.

Library Catalog of the Martin P. Catherwood Library of the New York State School of Industrial & Labor Relations, 12 vols. Cornell University, New York State School of Industrial & Labor Relations Staff. 1970. Set. lib. bdg. 1190.00 o.p. (ISBN 0-8161-0757-2, Hall Library). G K Hall.

Library Catalog of the Martin P. Catherwood Library of the New York State School of Industrial & Labor Relations, First Supplement. Cornell University, New York State School of Industrial & Labor Relations Staff. 873p. 1970. lib. bdg. 115.00 o.p. (ISBN 0-8161-0772-6, Hall Library). G K Hall.

Library Catalog of the Martin P. Catherwood Library of the New York State School of Industrial & Labor Relations: Fifth Supplement, 3 vols. 1905p. 1982. Set. lib. bdg. 295.00 o.s.i. (ISBN 0-8161-0362-3, Hall Library). G K Hall.

Library Catalog of the Metropolitan Museum of Art, New York, 25 vols. Ed. by Metropolitan Museum of Art, New York Staff. 1960. Set. lib. bdg. 2050.00 o.p. (ISBN 0-8161-0496-4, Hall Library); Suppls. 1-5. 120.00 ea. o.p. First Suppl. 1962 (ISBN 0-8161-0579-0). Second Suppl. 1965 (ISBN 0-8161-0670-3). Third Suppl. 1968 (ISBN 0-8161-0748-3). Fourth Suppl. 1970 (ISBN 0-8161-0846-3). Fifth Suppl (ISBN 0-8161-0936-2). G K Hall.

Library Catalog of The Metropolitan Museum of Art (New York), Suppl. 6. Ed. by Metropolitan Museum of Art, New York Staff. 1975. lib. bdg. 120.00 o.p. (ISBN 0-8161-1126-X); lib. bdg. 220.00 suppl. 7, 1977 o.p. (ISBN 0-8161-0028-4). G K Hall.

Library Catalog of the Metropolitan Museum of Art, 1983-1986: Third Supplement, 3 vols. 2nd ed. (Library Catalogs). 1800p. 1987. lib. bdg. 600.00 o.s.i. (ISBN 0-8161-0417-4, Hall Library). G K Hall.

Library Catalog of the Metropolitan Museum of Art, 48 vols. 2nd, rev. & enl. ed. Ed. by Metropolitan Museum of Art, New York Staff. 1980. Set. lib. bdg. 4835.00 o.p. (ISBN 0-8161-0295-3, Hall Library). G K Hall.

Library Catalogue of the Radzinowicz Library, 6 vols. Institute of Criminology, University of Cambridge, England Staff. Ed. by R. Perry. (Bib.Guides). 1979. Set. lib. bdg. 595.00 o.p. (ISBN 0-8161-0242-2, Hall Library). G K Hall.

Library Catalogue of the School of Oriental & African Studies, 28 Vols. University of London - School of Oriental & African Studies Staff. 1970. Set. 2665.00 o.p. (ISBN 0-8161-0635-5, Hall Library); First Suppl. 1970 16 Vols. 1750.00 o.p. (ISBN 0-8161-0734-3). G K Hall.

Library Catalogue of the School of Oriental & African Studies: Third Supplement, 19 vols. University of London, School of Oriental & African Studies Staff. 1979. Set. lib. bdg. 2070.00 o.p. (ISBN 0-8161-0261-9, Hall Library). G K Hall.

Library Catalogue of the School of Oriental & African Studies: 2nd Supplement, 16 vols. University of London - School of Oriental & African Studies Staff. 1973. Set. lib. bdg. 1750.00 o.p. (ISBN 0-8161-0841-2, Hall Library). G K Hall.

Library Display Ideas. Linda C. Franklin. LC 80-17036. (Illus.). 244p. 1980. lib. bdg. 13.95x o.p. (ISBN 0-89950-008-0); pap. 9.95x o.p. (ISBN 0-89950-009-9). McFarland & Co.

Library Education: 2000 A.D. & After. Ed. by Larry Barr. 38p. 1977. 5.00x o.p. (ISBN 0-931510-05-8). Hi Willow.

Library Effectiveness: State of the Arts. Library Administration & Management Association Preconference Staff. 414p. 1980. 25.00 o.p. (ISBN 0-8389-6836-8); members 20.00 o.p. (ISBN 0-317-32215-X). ALA.

Library Interior Layout & Design. Ed. by Rolf Fuhlrott & Michael Dewe. (IFLA Publication: No. 24). 145p. 1982. lib. bdg. 26.00 o.p. (ISBN 3-598-20386-1). K G Saur.

Library of Congress Classification Schedules: A Cumulation of Additions & Changes Through 1985. Ed. by Helen Savage. 1986. pap. 2200.00 o.p. (ISBN 0-8103-2450-4). Gale.

Library of Congress Classification Schedules: A Cumulation of Additions & Changes Through 1986. Ed. by Helen Savage. 1987. pap. text ed. 2275.00x o.p. (ISBN 0-8103-2650-7). Gale.

Library of Congress Classification Schedules: Complete Schedule plus Additions & Changes Through 1986. Ed. by Helen Savage. 1987. pap. text ed. 4500.00 o.p. (ISBN 0-8103-2600-0). Gale.

Library of Congress Subject Headings for Judaica. 2nd ed. Daniel D. Stuhlman. 1986. 12.00 o.p. (ISBN 0-934402-21-3); MS DOS disk 12.00 o.p. (ISBN 0-934402-22-1); 100.00 o.p. (ISBN 0-934402-20-5). BYLS Pr.

Library of Japanese Art: Kaigetsudo. Richard Lane. Ed. by Takahashi Seiichiro. LC 59-6633. (Illus.). 88p. 1959. 2.50 o.p. (ISBN 0-8048-1362-0). C E Tuttle.

Library of Japanese Art: Kokei. Kobayashi Kokei & Michiaki Kawakita. LC 57-12495. 1957. pap. 1.25 o.p. (ISBN 0-8048-0378-1). C E Tuttle.

Library of Japanese Art: Sotatsu. Tawaraya Sotatsu. Ed. by Ichimatsu Tanaka. LC 56-8491. (Illus.). 1956. pap. 1.25 o.p. (ISBN 0-8048-0363-3). C E Tuttle.

Library School Teaching Methods: Courses in the Selection of Adult Materials. Ed. by Larry E. Bone. LC 77-625419. 137p. 1969. 5.00x o.p. (ISBN 0-87845-022-X). U of Ill Lib Info Sci.

Library Science Dissertations, Nineteen Seventy-Three to Nineteen Eighty-One: An Annotated Bibliography. Gail Schlachter & Dennis Thomison. LC 82-17172. (Research Studies in Library Science: No. 18). 414p. 1982. 50.00 o.p. (ISBN 0-87287-299-8). Libs Unl.

Library Services for Adults. Gene Martin. LC 84-6228. (Small Library Publication Library Administration & Management Association: No. 9). 8p. 1984. pap. 2.50x o.p. (ISBN 0-8389-5660-2). ALA.

Library Services for Handicapped People: An Annotated Bibliography of British Material 1970-1981. Wendy Hay. 34p. 1982. pap. 10.00x o.p. (ISBN 0-85365-824-2, Pub. by Library Assn Pub London). ALA.

Library Services for Young People in England & Wales, 1830-1970. Alec Ellis. 1971. 42.00 o.p. (ISBN 0-08-016586-9). Pergamon.

Library Services in Theory & Context. Michael K. Buckland. 250p. 1983. text ed. 39.00 o.p. (ISBN 0-08-030134-7); pap. text ed. 15.75 o.p. (ISBN 0-08-030133-9). Pergamon.

Library Statistics of Colleges & Universities, 1976 Institutional Data (Libgis II, Hegis XI) Richard M. Beazley. (Monograph: No. 16). 184p. 1979. pap. 5.00x o.p. (ISBN 0-87845-061-0, NCES 78-234). U of Ill Lib Info Sci.

Library Structures & Staffing Systems. Malcolm Tunley. (Library Association Management). 1979. 10.75x o.p. (ISBN 0-85365-771-8). Nichols Pub.

Library Use Instruction in Selected American Colleges. Stuart W. Miller. (Occasional Papers: No. 134). 47p. 1978. pap. 2.00 o.p. (ISBN 0-317-58973-3). U of Ill Lib Info Sci.

Library: What's in It for You? Sherry Gwin. 1973. text ed. 1.00x o.p. (ISBN 0-8134-1579-9, 1579). Inter Print Pubs.

Libro de Buen Amor. Juan Ruiz. LC 77-181876. 536p. 1972. 60.50 o.p. (ISBN 0-691-06086-X); pap. 11.50x o.p. (ISBN 0-691-10002-0). Princeton U Pr.

Libros en Espanol: An Annotated List of Children's Books in Spanish. 52p. (Span.). 1978. 2.50 o.p. (ISBN 0-87104-628-8, Branch Lib). NY Pub Lib.

Libya: A Country Study. 3rd ed. Ed. by Harold D. Nelson. LC 79-14183. (Area Handbook Ser.: DA Pam 550-85). (Illus.). 350p. 1979. 11.00 o.p. (ISBN 0-318-21869-0, S/N 008-020-00817-6). USGPO.

Libyan Kill. Will O'Neil. 1980. 10.95 o.p. (ISBN 0-393-01319-7). Norton.

Libyan: Libya. H. Kanter. (Geomedical Monograph Ser.: Vol. 1). (Illus., Eng. & Ger.). 1967. 31.30 o.p. (ISBN 0-387-03925-2). Springer-Verlag.

License to Rape: Sexual Abuse of Wives. David Finkelhor & Kersti Yllo. 1985. 16.45 o.p. (ISBN 0-03-059474-X). H Holt & Co.

License to Steal: Secrets of Acquiring Distress Property. rev. ed. Ed. by Patricia McCarthy. 248p. (Orig.). 1984. pap. text ed. write for info. o.p. (ISBN 0-9603818-4-8). C R Leonard & Assocs.

Licensed Architect: Building Design Examination Primer. Ken Zinns et al. LC 85-70871. (Illus.). 350p. (Orig.). 1986. pap. 38.00 o.p. (ISBN 0-933885-03-2). Arcade Pubs.

Licensed to Live. John B. Coker & John P. Martin. 256p. 1985. 34.95x o.p. (ISBN 0-631-14165-0). Basil Blackwell.

Licensing & Certification of Psychologists & Counselors: A Guide to Current Policies, Procedures, & Legislation. Bruce R. Fretz & David H. Mills. LC 80-8011. (Social & Behavioral Science Ser.). 1980. text ed. 25.95x o.p. (ISBN 0-87589-470-4). Jossey-Bass.

Lichens of Ohio, Pt. II: Fruticose & Cladoniform. Conan J. Taylor. 1968. 4.00 o.p. (ISBN 0-86727-056-X). Ohio Bio Survey.

Lichtstreifen. P. Willig. 141p. 1973. pap. 35.00 o.p. (ISBN 0-08-016281-9); pap. 3.80 o.p. (ISBN 0-08-017826-X). Pergamon.

Lid off a Daffodil. John Pool. (Illus.). 1985. pap. 5.95 o.p. (ISBN 0-03-004427-8, Owl Bks). H Holt & Co.

L'Idalma Overo Chi la Dura la Vince. Bernardo Pasquini. Ed. by Howard M. Brown. LC 76-20996. (Italian Opera 1640-1770 Ser.). 1978. lib. bdg. 77.00 o.p. (ISBN 0-8240-2610-1). Garland Pub.

Lie Algebras. I. N. Stewart. LC 73-117720. (Lecture Notes in Mathematics: Vol. 127). 1970. pap. 10.70 o.p. (ISBN 0-387-04916-9). Springer-Verlag.

Lie down with Lions. Ken Follett. (G K Hall Large Print Books). 537p. 1986. lib. bdg. 19.95 o.p. (ISBN 0-8161-4167-3, Large Print Bks); pap. 11.95 o.p. (ISBN 0-8161-4168-1). G K Hall.

Lied: The Unfolding of Its Style. Anneliese Landau. LC 79-6725. 1980. text ed. 23.25 o.p. (ISBN 0-8191-0935-5); pap. text ed. 10.25 o.p. (ISBN 0-8191-0936-3). U Pr of Amer.

Lieder Line by Line. Lois Phillips. 1980. 12.95 o.p. (ISBN 0-684-16442-6, ScribT); encore ed. 12.95 o.p. (ISBN 0-684-17553-3). Scribner.

Lieutenant Zagoskin's Travels in Russian America, 1842-1844: The First Ethnographic & Geographic Investigations in the Yukon & Kuskokwim Valleys of Alaska. Ed. by Henry N. Michael. LC 67-2141. (Illus.). 1967. 25.00x o.p. (ISBN 0-8020-3164-1). U of Toronto Pr.

Life. William Purves & Gordon Orians. 1000p. 1983. text ed. write for info. o.p. (ISBN 0-87150-768-4, 4521, Pub. by Willard Grant Pr). PWS-Kent Pub.

Life above the Jungle Floor: A Biologist Explores a Strange & Hidden Tree Top World. Donald Perry. 1986. 16.45 o.s.i. (ISBN 0-671-54454-3). S&S.

Life After Death. S. Ralph Harlow. 160p. 1982. pap. 8.95 o.s.i. (ISBN 0-914918-40-0). Whitford Pr.

Life After Death. T. A. Kantonen. LC 62-8205. 1975. pap. 1.50 o.p. (ISBN 0-8006-2010-0, Fortress). Augsburg Fortress.

Life after Doomsday: A Survivalist Guide to Nuclear War & Other Disasters. Bruce D. Clayton. (Illus.). 192p. 1981. 14.95 o.p. (ISBN 0-385-27148-4, Dial). Doubleday.

Life after Youth: Female, 40, What Next? Ruth H. Jacobs. LC 78-73854. 1979. 12.50x o.p. (ISBN 0-8070-3790-7); pap. 6.95 o.p. (ISBN 0-8070-3791-5, BP-605). Beacon Pr.

Life Against Death: The Psychoanalytical Meaning of History. 2nd ed. Norman O. Brown. xxx, 366p. 1985. 25.00x o.p. (ISBN 0-8195-5148-1); pap. 9.95 o.p. (ISBN 0-8195-6144-4). Wesleyan U Pr.

Life: An Enigma, a Precious Jewel. Daisaku Ikeda. LC 81-84836. 256p. 1982. 15.95x o.p. (ISBN 0-87011-433-6); pap. 5.25 o.p. (ISBN 0-87011-618-5). Kodansha.

Life: An Introduction to Biology. George G. Simpson & William S. Beck. (Illus.). 546p. (Shorter ed.). 1969. text ed. 15.00 o.p. (ISBN 0-15-550716-8, HC). HarBraceJ.

Life & Adventures of Captain John Avery, the Famous English Pirate... Now in Possession of Madagascar see Perfidious P.

Life & Adventures of Common Sense, 1769, 2 vols. in 1. Herbert Lawrence. LC 74-23918. (Novel in England, 1700-1775 Ser). 1975. lib. bdg. 61.00 o.p. (ISBN 0-8240-1187-2). Garland Pub.

Life & Adventures of Joe Thompson, 1750, 2 vols. in 1. Edward Kimber. LC 74-17302. (Novel in England, 1700-1775 Ser). 1975. lib. bdg. 61.00 o.p. (ISBN 0-8240-1130-9). Garland Pub.

Life & Adventures of John Muir. new ed. James M. Clarke. LC 79-64178. (Illus.). 1979. 14.95 o.p. (ISBN 0-932238-01-7, Pub. by Avant Bks). Slawson Comm.

Life & Adventures of John Muir. James M. Clarke. LC 79-64178. (Sierra Club Paperback Library Ser.). (Illus.). 338p. 1980. pap. 7.95 o.s.i. (ISBN 0-87156-241-3). Sierra.

Life & Adventures of Robinson Crusoe see also Robinson Crusoe.

Life & Adventures of Santa Claus. L. Frank Baum. (Illus.). (gr. k-2). 1971. 6.95 o.p. (ISBN 0-682-47386-3, Classic). Exposition-Phoenix.

Life & Crimes of Agatha Cristie. Charles Osborne. (Rainbow Bks.). (Illus.). 256p. 1983. 17.95 o.s.i. (ISBN 0-03-062784-2). H Holt & Co.

Life & Death in Psychoanalysis. Jean Laplanche. Tr. by Jeffrey Mehlman. LC 75-36928. (Illus.). 160p. 1976. pap. 12.50x o.p. (ISBN 0-8018-1637-8). Johns Hopkins.

Life & Death of a Brave Bull. Maia Wojciechowska. LC 77-181537. (Illus.). 48p. (gr. 3 up). 1972. 6.50 o.p. (ISBN 0-15-245200-1, HJ). HarBraceJ.

Life & Death of King John see also King John.

Life & Death of Mary Wollstonecraft. Claire Tomalin. LC 74-14816. (Illus.). 316p. 1975. 8.95 o.p. (ISBN 0-15-151539-5). HarBraceJ.

Life & Death of St. Thomas More. Nicholas Harpsfield. Repr. of 1932 ed. 69.00x o.p. (ISBN 0-403-04140-6). Somerset Pub.

Life & Death of the Press Barons. Piers Brendon. LC 82-73017. (Illus.). 288p. 1983. 14.95 o.p. (ISBN 0-689-11341-2, Atheneum). Macmillan.

Life & Death on the Corporate Battlefield. Paul Solman & Thomas Friedman. 1983. 13.50 o.p. (ISBN 0-671-25564-9). S&S.

Life & Dreams of You & Me. Homer L. Dyer, III. 1979. 4.00 o.p. (ISBN 0-682-49347-3). Exposition-Phoenix.

Life & Energy. Isaac Asimov. 384p. 1976. pap. 4.50 o.p. (ISBN 0-380-00942-0, 60007-2, Discus). Avon.

Life & Labors of David Livingstone. J. E. Chambliss. LC 76-132642. (Illus.). 1971. Repr. of 1875 ed. lib. bdg. 36.00x o.p. (ISBN 0-8371-3636-9, CDL&, Pub. by Negro U Pr). Greenwood.

Life & Letters of Captain John Brown. Ed. by Richard D. Webb. LC 71-82085. (Illus.). 1972. Repr. of 1861 ed. lib. bdg. 25.00x o.p. (ISBN 0-8371-1560-4, WJB&, Pub. by Negro U Pr). Greenwood.

Life & Letters of Charles Inglis: His Ministry in America & Consecration As First Colonial Bishop from 1759 to 1787. John W. Lydekker. (Church Historical Society London N. S. Ser.: No. 20). Repr. of 1936 ed. 50.00 o.p. (ISBN 0-8115-3144-9). Kraus Repr.

Life & Letters of John Keats. Richard M. Houghton. 1969. Repr. of 1927 ed. 11.95x o.p. (ISBN 0-460-00801-3, Evman). Biblio Dist.

Life & Letters of John Locke, with Extracts from His Journals & Common-Place Books. Peter King. LC 83-48569. (Philosophy of John Locke Ser.). 1984. lib. bdg. 60.00 o.p. (ISBN 0-8240-5605-1). Garland Pub.

Life & Letters of Robert Browning. Alexandra L. Orr. LC 74-136942. (Illus.). 431p. 1973. Repr. of 1908 ed. lib. bdg. 24.75x o.p. (ISBN 0-8371-5416-2, ORRB). Greenwood.

Life & Letters of Washington Irving, 4 vols. Pierre M. Irving. LC 67-23893. 1832p. 1967. Repr. of 1863 ed. 85.00x set o.p. (ISBN 0-8103-3044-X). Gale.

Life & Loves of Gable. Jack Scagnetti. LC 75-43842. (Illus.). 160p. 1976. 12.95 o.p. (ISBN 0-8246-0205-6). Jonathan David.

Life & Loves of Gable. Jack Scagnetti. 1982. pap. 8.95 o.p. (ISBN 0-8246-0279-X). Jonathan David.

Life & Loves of Hattie. Yvonne T. Errickson. 1985. 11.95 o.p. (ISBN 0-533-06470-8). Vantage.

Life & Opinions of Tristram Shandy, Gentleman, 3 vols. Laurence Sterne. Ed. by Melvyn New. (Florida Edition of the Works of Laurence Sterne). 75.00x o.p. (ISBN 0-8130-0819-0). U Presses Fla.

Life & Reign of the Emperor Lucius Septimius Severus. Maurice Platnauer. 1970. Repr. of 1918 ed. lib. bdg. 22.50x o.p. (ISBN 0-8371-4313-6, PLLS). Greenwood.

Life & Religion of Muhammad. Muhammad B. Al-Majilisi. Tr. by James Merrick. 463p. 1987. pap. 19.95 o.p. (ISBN 0-7103-0216-9, 02169, Kegan Paul). Routledge Chapman & Hall.

Life & Society: A Meditation on the Social Thought of Jose Ortega y Gassett. Andrew J. Weigert. 250p. 1983. text ed. 29.95x o.s.i. (ISBN 0-8290-1278-8). Irvington.

Life & Songs of Carl Michael Bellman. P. B. Austin. 1967. 12.95x o.p. (ISBN 0-89067-048-X). Am Scandinavian.

Life & Teaching of the Masters of the Far East, 5 Vols. Baird T. Spalding. 5.00 ea. o.p.; Vol. 1. o.p. (ISBN 0-87516-084-0); (ISBN 0-87516-085-9); Vol. 3. Vol. 4. (ISBN 0-87516-087-5); Vol. 5. (ISBN 0-87516-088-3). DeVorss.

Life & Thought of Ordinary Chinese: Collected Essays. Wolfram Eberhard. (East Asian Folklore & Social Life Monographs: Vol. 106). 230p. 1982. 22.00x o.p. (ISBN 0-89986-337-X). Oriental Bk Store.

Life & Times of a Killer. A. Goff Bedford. 1980. 12.50 o.p. (ISBN 0-682-49370-8). Exposition-Phoenix.

Life & Times of Cavour, 2 Vols. William R. Thayer. LC 68-9634. (Illus.). 1971. Repr. of 1911 ed. 42.50x o.p. (ISBN 0-86527-117-8). Fertig.

Life & Times of Cleopatra. Carlo M. Franzero. (Illus.). 300p. 1958. (ISBN 0-8022-0529-1). Philos Lib.

Life & Times of Henry Clay, 2 vols. Calvin Colton. (Neglected American Economists Ser.). 1975. Set. lib. bdg. 121.00 o.p. (ISBN 0-8240-1008-6); lib. bdg. 110.00 o.p. Garland Pub.

Life & Times of Jehuda Halevi. Rudolf Kayser. (ISBN 0-8022-0832-0). Philos Lib.

Life & Times of King Cotton. David L. Cohn. LC 73-11996. 286p. 1974. Repr. of 1956 ed. lib. bdg. 22.50x o.p. (ISBN 0-8371-7115-6, COKC). Greenwood.

Life & Times of Lord Mountbatten. John Terraine. LC 79-3740. (Illus.). 288p. (Orig.). 1980. 4.95 o.p. (ISBN 0-03-056899-4). H Holt & Co.

Life & Times of Los Angeles: A Newspaper, a Family & a City. Marshall Berges. LC 83-9243. (Illus.). 304p. 1984. 17.95 o.p. (ISBN 0-689-11427-3, Atheneum). Macmillan.

Life & Times of Nero. Carolo M. Franzero. (Illus.). 340p. 1956. (ISBN 0-8022-0530-5). Philos Lib.

Life & Work of Albert Carrier-Belleuse. June E. Hargrove. LC 76-23625. (Outstanding Dissertations in the Fine Arts - 19th Century). (Illus.). 1977. Repr. lib. bdg. 85.00 o.p. (ISBN 0-8240-2695-0). Garland Pub.

Life & Work of George Inness. Nicolai Cikovsky, Jr. LC 76-23605. (Outstanding Dissertations in the Fine Arts - American). (Illus.). 1977. Repr. of 1965 ed. lib. bdg. 85.00 o.p. (ISBN 0-8240-2679-9). Garland Pub.

Life & Work of John Nash, Architect. John Summerson. (Illus.). 288p. 1980. 47.50x o.p. (ISBN 0-262-19190-3). MIT Pr.

Life & Work of the Minister. Daniel D. Preston. 1968. 5.95 o.s.i. (ISBN 0-934942-11-0). White Wing Pub.

Life & Work of Thomas Chippendale. Christopher Gilbert. Ed. by Geoffrey Beard. (Illus.). 638p. 1986. 60.00 o.p. (ISBN 0-86294-038-9, Pub by Trefoil Bks Ltd Uk). Seven Hills Bk Dists.

Life & Work of Vincent Van Gogh. Carl Nordenfalk. 1953. (ISBN 0-8022-1226-3). Philos Lib.

Life & Work of Wilhelm Reich. Michel Cattier. 1979. pap. 1.65 o.p. (ISBN 0-380-01327-4, 14928). Avon.

Life & Works of Eugenio D'Ors. Pilar Saenz. 1984. 15.50x o.p. (ISBN 0-936968-06-0). Intl Bk Ctr.

Life & Works of Mr. Anonymous. Willard R. Espy. 1979. pap. 2.75 o.p. (ISBN 0-380-45047-X, 45047-X). Avon.

Life As Laughter: Following Bhagwan Shree Rajneesh. Bob Mullan. (Illus.). 204p. 1984. 26.95x o.p. (ISBN 0-7102-0141-9); pap. 12.95 o.p. (ISBN 0-7102-0043-9). Routledge Chapman & Hall.

Life as Revealed by the Microscope. J. LeRoy Conel. LC 78-92736. (Illus.). 262p. 1970. (ISBN 0-8022-2310-9). Philos Lib.

Life As Theater: A Dramaturgical Sourcebook. Dennis Brissett & Charles Edgley. LC 74-82604. 1975. text ed. 32.95x o.p. (ISBN 0-202-30277-6). Aldine de Gruyter.

Life at the Dakota: New York's Most Unusual Address. Stephen Birmingham. LC 79-4800. (Illus.). 1979. 12.50 o.p. (ISBN 0-394-41079-3). Random.

Life at the Sea's Frontiers. Richard Perry. LC 73-3969. (Many Worlds of Wildlife Ser.). (Illus.). 320p. 1974. 7.95 o.s.i. (ISBN 0-8008-4795-4). Taplinger.

Life Before Man. Margaret Atwood. 1980. 11.95 o.p. (ISBN 0-671-25115-5). S&S.

Life Before Man. Margaret Atwood. 384p. 1987. pap. 4.95 o.p. (ISBN 0-449-21377-3). HR&W.

Life Between the Questions. Carolyn Huffman & Lu Ann Barrow. 80p. 1985. 8.95 o.p. (ISBN 0-8499-0446-3, 0446-3). Word Bks.

Life Can Begin Again: Sermons on the Sermon on the Mount. Helmut Thielicke. Tr. by John W. Doberstein from Ger. LC 63-12535. 240p. 1963. pap. 5.95 o.p. (ISBN 0-8006-1934-X, 1-1934, Fortress). Augsburg Fortress.

Life-Career Manual for Leaders. rev. ed. Compiled by Robert W. Rozzelle & Vivian McCoy. 143p. 1977. spiral 16.50 o.p. (ISBN 0-936352-16-7). U of KS Cont Ed.

Life-Career Manual for Participants. rev. ed. Compiled by Robert W. Rozzelle & Vivian McCoy. 111p. 1977. spiral bound 9.50 o.p. (ISBN 0-936352-17-5). U of KS Cont Ed.

Life Chances: Approaches to Social & Political Theory. Ralf Dahrendorf. LC 79-18685. 1980. lib. bdg. 15.00x o.s.i. (ISBN 0-226-13408-3). U of Chicago Pr.

Life Choices: Applying Sociology. Robert E. Kennedy. 208p. 1986. pap. text ed. 9.95 o.p. (ISBN 0-03-069634-8, HoltC). HR&W.

Life Choices: Confronting the Life & Death Decisions Created by Modern Medicine. Howard Levine. 304p. 1986. 17.45 o.p. (ISBN 0-671-55385-2). S&S.

Life Company Operations. Ed. by Life Office Management Association Staff. LC 74-83846. (FLMI Insurance Education Program Ser.). 540p. 1974. pap. text ed. 12.00 o.p. (ISBN 0-915322-10-2). LOMA.

Life Cycle Cost Analysis Handbook. Ralph Aikman & Rachel Schwartz. 1977. pap. 25.00x o.p. (ISBN 0-89011-509-5, HMD-128). Abt Bks.

Life Cycle Cost Data. Alphonse Dell'Isola & Stephen J. Kirk. (Illus.). 160p. 1983. text ed. 39.95 o.p. (ISBN 0-07-016282-4). McGraw.

Life Cycle Investing: Investing for the Time of Your Life. Donald R. Nichols. 300p. 1985. 17.95 o.p. (ISBN 0-87094-614-5). Dow Jones-Irwin.

Life Cycle Theory & Pastoral Care. Donald Capps. LC 83-5585. (Theology & Pastoral Care Ser.). 128p. 1983. pap. 7.95 o.p. (ISBN 0-8006-1726-6, 1-1726, Fortress). Augsburg Fortress.

Life Divine. Sri Aurobindo. 1112p. 1980. 19.50 o.p. (ISBN 0-89071-290-5, Pub. by Sri Aurobindo Ashram India); pap. 15.00 o.p. (ISBN 0-89071-289-1). Aurobindo Assn.

Life Education in the Workplace: How to Design, Lead & Market Employee Seminars. Kathryn Apgar & Donald P. Riley. 184p. 1982. 19.95 o.s.i. (ISBN 0-87304-197-6). Family Serv.

Life-Extending Technologies: A Technology Assessment. Theodore J. Gordon. 1980. 65.00 o.p. (ISBN 0-08-023132-2). Pergamon.

Life Financial Reports. rev. ed. Ed. by Price Gaines. 786p. 1987. pap. 40.95 o.p. (ISBN 0-87218-057-3). Natl Underwriter.

Life for Death. Michael Mewshaw. 1983. pap. 3.95 o.p. (ISBN 0-380-54593-4, 65243-9). Avon.

Life Full of Holes. Larbi Layachi, pseud. LC 81-47638. 128p. 1982. pap. 3.50 o.s.i. (ISBN 0-394-17946-3, B481, BC). Grove.

Life, Health & Other Benefit Programs: Answers to the Questions on Subject Matter for the Learning Guide, CEBS Course 1. 4th ed. 1986. pap. 15.00 o.p. (ISBN 0-89154-312-0). Intl Found Employ.

Life, Health & Other Group Benefit Programs Learning Guide: CEBS Course 1. 4th ed. 1986. spiral bound 18.00 o.p. (ISBN 0-89154-311-2). Intl Found Employ.

Life History & the Historical Moment. Erik H. Erikson. 1977. 14.95x o.p. (ISBN 0-393-01103-8, N860); pap. 3.95 o.p. (ISBN 0-393-00860-6). Norton.

Life I Really Lived. Jessamyn West. Ed. by Julian P. Muller. LC 79-1853. 1979. 11.95 o.s.i. (ISBN 0-15-151562-X). HarBraceJ.

Life in a Crystal Palace. Alan Harrington. 1976. pap. 1.65 o.p. (ISBN 0-380-01326-6, 15784, Discus). Avon.

Life in America, 2 vols. Marshall Davidson. LC 74-10940. 1104p. 1974. Set. 25.00 o.p. (ISBN 0-395-17214-4). HM.

Life in Forest & Jungle. Richard Perry. LC 74-21573. (Many Worlds of Wildlife Ser). (Illus.). 256p. 1975. 9.95 o.s.i. (ISBN 0-8008-4799-7). Taplinger.

Life in Large Families: Views of Mormon Women. Howard M. Bahr et al. LC 82-45005. 264p. (Orig.). 1982. lib. bdg. 30.75 o.p. (ISBN 0-8191-2551-2); pap. text ed. 14.00 o.p. (ISBN 0-8191-2552-0). U Pr of Amer.

Life in Lesu. Hortense Powdermaker. (Illus.). 1971. pap. 2.95x o.p. (ISBN 0-393-00566-6, Norton Lib). Norton.

Life in Modern China. 90p. (Orig.). 1984. pap. 2.95 o.p. (ISBN 0-8351-1271-3). China Bks.

Life in Pictures. John Betjeman. Compiled by Bevis Hiller. (Illus.). 160p. 1987. 19.45 o.s.i. (ISBN 0-8052-6003-X, Pub. by J Murray Bk-D Herbert UK). Schocken.

Life in Rural America. Ed. by National Geographic Society Staff. LC 74-1562. (Special Publications Series 9: No. 1). (Illus.). 208p. 1974. 7.95, avail. only from Natl. Geog. o.p. (ISBN 0-87044-146-9). Natl Geog.

Life in Sanchi Sculptures. A. L. Srivastava. (Illus.). 163p. 1983. text ed. 80.00 o.p. (ISBN 0-391-02717-4). Humanities.

Life in Space. LC 83-4840. (Single Title Ser.). 1983. 39.95 o.p. (ISBN 0-8094-4900-5). Time-Life.

Life in the Castle in Medieval England. John Burke. (Illus.). 120p. 1978. 14.50x o.p. (ISBN 0-8476-6069-9). Rowman.

Life in the Fifth Dimension. Bonnie B. O'Brien & Dorothy E. Sample. 1984. pap. 6.50 o.p. (ISBN 0-8054-5214-1). Broadman.

Life in the Retirement Bed of Roses. Georgia B. Watson. LC 81-84831. (Illus.). 104p. (Orig.). 1982. 6.50x o.p. (ISBN 0-935834-06-0). Rainbow Books.

Life in the Sea. Gunner Thorson. LC 73-118405. (World University Library). (Illus., Orig.). 1971. pap. text ed. 3.95 o.p. (ISBN 0-07-064543-4). McGraw.

Life in the Spirit & Mary. Christopher O'Donnell. (Mary Library). 160p. (Orig.). 1981. pap. 7.95 o.p. (ISBN 0-89453-261-8). M Glazier.

Life in the Theatre. David Mamet. LC 77-91884. 1978. pap. 9.95 o.p. (ISBN 0-394-17040-7, E709, Ever). Grove.

Life in Western Mining Camps: Social & Legal Aspects, 1848-1872. Darlene Mucibabich. 1977. 5.00 o.p. (ISBN 0-682-48882-8, Lochinvar). Exposition-Phoenix.

Life Insurance. 10th ed. Kenneth Black, Jr. & S. S. Huebner. (Illus.). 784p. 1982. pap. text ed. 36.33 o.p. (ISBN 0-13-535799-3). P-H.

Life Insurance. Kenneth Black, Jr. & Harold Skipper, Jr. (Illus.). 768p. 1987. text ed. 41.00 o.p. (ISBN 0-13-535881-7). P-H.

Life Insurance. 9th ed. S. S. Huebner & Kenneth Black. (Illus.). 608p. 1976. 22.95 o.p. (ISBN 0-13-535781-0). P-H.

Life Insurance Fundamentals: To Prepare for the Life Insurance Agents' License Examination. Prudential Insurance Company of America Staff. LC 76-17652. 314p. 1976. pap. text ed. 11.50 o.p. Krieger.

Life Insurance Game. Ronald Kessler. LC 84-6642. 320p. 1985. 16.95 o.s.i. (ISBN 0-03-070507-X). H Holt & Co.

Life Insurance Investment in Commercial Real Estate. H. Wayne Snider. 1956. 9.00x o.p. (ISBN 0-256-00679-2). Irwin.

Life Insurance Investments: Readings. Ed. by Life Office Management Association Staff. (FLMI Insurance Education Program Ser.). 1982. pap. text ed. 10.00 o.p. (ISBN 0-915322-48-X). LOMA.

Life Insurance: Its Rate of Return. William D. Brownlie. LC 83-61584. (Illus.). 201p. (Orig.). 1983. pap. 13.75 o.p. (ISBN 0-87218-033-6). Natl Underwriter.

Life Insurance: Theory & Practice. rev. ed. Robert I. Mehr. 1977. 19.95x o.p. (ISBN 0-256-01938-X). Irwin.

Life Is Goodbye-Life Is Hello: Grieving Well Through All Kinds of Loss. Alla Bozarth-Campbell. LC 82-8064. (Illus.). 160p. 1982. 10.95 o.p. (ISBN 0-89638-060-2); pap. 8.95 o.p. (ISBN 0-89638-061-0). CompCare.

Life Is No Yuk for the Yak. T. Hart et al. 371p. 1976. 60.00 o.p. (ISBN 84-252-0611-1, S-50271, French & Eur). French & Eur.

Life Its Ownself: The Semi-Tougher Adventures of Billy Clyde Puckett. Dan Jenkins. 288p. 1984. 15.45 o.p. (ISBN 0-671-46024-2). S&S.

Life Itself. Francis Crick. 1982. pap. 7.95 o.s.i. (ISBN 0-671-25563-0, Touchstone Bks). S&S.

Life I've Lived. Shepard B. Clough. LC 80-5503. 297p. 1981. lib. bdg. 29.00 o.p. (ISBN 0-8191-1116-3); pap. text ed. 14.00 o.p. (ISBN 0-8191-1117-1). U Pr of Amer.

Life Journeys. C. R. Barber. (Illus.). 100p. 1981. 21.00 o.p. (ISBN 0-08-027396-3); pap. 12.00 o.p. (ISBN 0-08-026420-4). Pergamon.

Life, Law & Letters: Essays & Sketches. Louis Auchincloss. 1979. 8.95 o.p. (ISBN 0-395-28151-2). HM.

Life, Liberty & the Pursuit of Happiness. Mary Ann Kearny & James Baker. (Readers Ser.: Stage 6). 168p. 1978. pap. text ed. 9.25 o.p. (ISBN 0-88377-111-X). Newbury Hse.

Life of a Photograph: Archival Processing, Matting, Framing & Storage. Laurence E. Keefe, Jr. & Dennis Inch. (Illus.). 331p. 1983. 24.95 o.p.; pap. 22.95 o.p. (ISBN 0-240-80005-2). Focal Pr.

Life of a Prig. Thomas de Longueville. Ed. by Robert L. Wolff. (Victorian Fiction Ser.). 1975. Repr. of 1885 ed. lib. bdg. 73.00 o.p. (ISBN 0-8240-1538-X). Garland Pub.

Life of Baptists in the Life of the World. Ed. by Walter B. Shurden. LC 85-1401. 1985. pap. 7.95 o.p. (ISBN 0-8054-6582-0). Broadman.

Life of Beans & Peas. 2nd ed. Elementary Science Study Staff. 1975. 11.76 o.p. (ISBN 0-07-018581-6). McGraw.

Life of Beethoven. Anton Schindler. Tr. by Ignace Moscheles. (Illus.). 1966. Repr. 12.50 o.p. (ISBN 0-910648-01-8). Gamut Music.

Life of Birds. 3rd ed. Carl Welty. 1982. text ed. 39.95 o.s.i. (ISBN 0-03-057917-1, CBS C). SCP.

Life of Bret Harte, with Some Account of the California Pioneers. Henry C. Merwin. LC 67-23887. 380p. 1967. Repr. of 1911 ed. 39.00x o.p. (ISBN 0-8103-3042-3). Gale.

Life of Buffalo Bill. William Cody. 1976. pap. 1.25 o.p. (ISBN 0-685-73456-0, L*B399, Pub. by Leisure Bks CT). Dorchester Pub Co.

Life of Byron Jaynes. James H. Kunstler. LC 82-14267. 1983. 16.00 o.p. (ISBN 0-393-01721-4); pap. 7.70 o.p. (ISBN 0-393-30116-8). Norton.

Life of Christ. F. W. Farrar. 750p. lib. bdg. 24.95 o.p. (ISBN 0-8254-5110-8). Kregel.

Life of D. H. Lawrence. Keith M. Sagar. (Illus.). 1980. 17.95 o.p. (ISBN 0-394-50953-6). Pantheon.

Life of Franklin Pierce. Nathaniel Hawthorne. LC 72-78731. 1852. Repr. 39.00x o.p. (ISBN 0-403-04146-5). Somerset Pub.

Life of Henry Eighth see also Henry Eighth.

Life of Henry Fifth see also Henry Fifth.

Life of Her Own. Marc Brandel. 468p. 1985. 17.45 o.p. (ISBN 0-395-37724-2). HM.

Life of Jackson Emerson. Ellen T. Emerson. Ed. by Hall G. K. Staff. LC 80-14908. (Twayne's American Literary Manuscript Ser.). (Illus.). 269p. 1981. 26.00 o.p. (ISBN 0-8057-9651-7, Twayne). G K Hall.

Life of Jesus. Illus. by Napoli. LC 78-132901. (Illus.). (ps-2). 1971. pap. 3.50 o.p. (ISBN 0-8066-1110-3, 10-3840, Augsburg). Augsburg Fortress.

Life of Jesus. Friedrich Schleiermacher. Ed. by Jack C. Verheyden & Leander E. Keck. Tr. by Gilmour MacLean from Ger. LC 72-87056. (Lives of Jesus Ser.). 542p. 1975. pap. 4.50 o.p. (ISBN 0-8006-1272-8, 1-1073, Fortress). Augsburg Fortress.

Life of Jesus Critically Examined. David F. Strauss. Ed. by Peter C. Hodgson & Leander E. Keck. LC 72-75655. (The Lives of Jesus Ser.). 832p. 1972. pap. 4.00 o.p. (ISBN 0-8006-1271-X, 1-1271, Fortress). Augsburg Fortress.

Life of Jesus for Everyman. William Barclay. LC 75-12282. 96p. 1975. pap. 5.72 o.p. (ISBN 0-06-060404-2, RD 319). HarpR.

Life of John Berryman. John Haffenden. 451p. 1984. pap. 7.95 o.p. (ISBN 0-7448-0004-8, Ark Paperbks). Routledge Chapman & Hall.

Life of John Japanese: Working in Japan. Patrick Graupp. 1984. 8.95 o.p. (ISBN 0-533-06044-3). Vantage.

Life of John Paul II. Mieczyslaw Malinski & Steven Grant. 64p. 1.50 o.p. (NCR461). Paulist Pr.

Life of Liszt. Louis Nohl. LC 70-140402. 204p. 1970. Repr. of 1889 ed. 40.00x o.p. (ISBN 0-8103-3610-3). Gale.

Life of Mathilda of Canossa. 180p. 400.00 o.p. (ISBN 0-8115-0902-8). Kraus Repr.

Life of Maxim Gorky. Alexander Roskin. (ISBN 0-8022-1379-0). Philos Lib.

Life of Miguel De Cervantes. Henry E. Watts. LC 79-141743. 216p. 1971. Repr. of 1891 ed. 35.00x o.p. (ISBN 0-8103-3631-6). Gale.

Life of One Doctor & His Patients. C. C. Huntley. 96p. (Orig.). 1984. pap. 4.95 o.s.i. (ISBN 0-934318-38-7). Falcon Pr MT.

Life of Our Lord in Art: With Some Account of the Artistic Treatment of the Life of St. John the Baptist. Estelle M. Hurll. LC 76-89272. 392p. 1969. Repr. of 1898 ed. 31.00 o.p. (ISBN 0-8103-3137-3). Gale.

Life of Paul. 2nd ed. Benjamin W. Robinson. LC 18-19810. (Midway Reprint Ser). 1973. pap. text ed. 16.00x o.s.i. (ISBN 0-226-72261-9). U of Chicago Pr.

Life of Prayer. A. B. Simpson. 122p. 1975. pap. 3.95 o.p. (ISBN 0-87509-164-4). Chr Pubns.

Life of Raymond Chandler. Frank MacShane. (Hall Non-Fiction Ser.). (Illus.). 320p. 1986. pap. 8.95 o.p. (ISBN 0-8398-2905-1). G K Hall.

Life of Robert Burns. Catherine Carswell. LC 78-164157. (Illus.). 428p. 1971. Repr. of 1931 ed. 42.00x o.p. (ISBN 0-8103-3788-6). Gale.

Life of Roger Brooke Taney, Chief Justice of the United States Supreme Court. Bernard C. Steiner. 1971. Repr. of 1922 ed. lib. bdg. 35.00x o.p. (ISBN 0-8371-4344-6, STRT). Greenwood.

Life of Saint Catherine of Siena. Raymond of Cupua. LC 80-84466. 30.00 o.p. (ISBN 0-89453-151-4). M Glazier.

Life of Sir Edwin Lutyens. Christopher Hussey. (Illus.). 602p. 1985. 49.50 o.p. (ISBN 0-907462-59-6). Apollo.

Life of Sir Humphrey Gilbert, England's First Empire Builder. William G. Gosling. LC 76-109737. 1970. Repr. of 1911 ed. lib. bdg. 35.00x o.p. (ISBN 0-8371-4227-X, GOHG). Greenwood.

Life of Stephen F. Austin, Founder of Texas, 1793-1836: A Chapter in the Westward Movement of the Anglo-American People. Eugene C. Barker. 1949. 19.95 o.p. (ISBN 0-87611-002-2). Tex St Hist Assn.

Life of the Cave. Charles E. Mohr & T. Poulson. (Our Living World of Nature Ser.). 1966. text ed. 16.95 o.p. (ISBN 0-07-042651-1). McGraw.

Life of the Marquis of Dalhousie, 2 vols. William Lee-Warner. (Illus.). 952p. 1972. Repr. of 1904 ed. Set. 75.00x o.p. (ISBN 0-7165-2139-3, BBA 03082, Pub. by Irish Academic Pr). Biblio Dist.

Life of the Marsh. W. A. Niering. 1966. text ed. 13.95 o.p. (ISBN 0-07-046555-X). McGraw.

Life of the Party. Maureen Freely. 416p. 1985. 17.45 o.p. (ISBN 0-671-50614-5). S&S.

Life of the Reverend Mr. George Trosse. Ed. by A. W. Brink. 148p. 1974. 9.75x o.p. (ISBN 0-7735-0153-3, McGill Canada). U of Toronto Pr.

Life of the Virgin Mary. Rainer M. Rilke. 1952. (ISBN 0-8022-1349-9). Philos Lib.

Life of Timon of Athens see also Timon of Athens.

Life of Titus Andronicus see also Titus Andronicus.

Life of W. T. Stead, 2 vols. Frederic Whyte. LC 77-147461. (Library of War & Peace; Peace Leaders: Biographies & Memoirs). 1972. Set. lib. bdg. 92.00 o.p. (ISBN 0-8240-0320-9). Garland Pub.

Life of William Blake. Alexander Gilchrist. Ed. by Ruthven Todd. (Illus.). 432p. 1982. pap. text ed. 8.95x o.p. (ISBN 0-460-01971-6, Pub. by Evman England). Biblio Dist.

Life on a Cool Plastic Ice Floe. K. Follis Cheatham. LC 78-6430. 180p. 1978. 7.95 o.s.i. (ISBN 0-664-32632-3, Westminster). Westminster John Knox.

Life on Board a Yacht. LC 83-83191. (Classics of the Victorian Imagination Ser.). 160p. 1984. 12.50 o.p. (ISBN 0-394-53880-3, GP 917). Grove.

Life on the Highest Plane, 3 Vols. Ruth Paxson. 512p. 1983. Repr. of 1928 ed. 15.95 o.p. (ISBN 0-8010-7074-0). Baker Bk.

Life on the Mississippi. Mark Twain. LC 87-61681. (Illus.). 384p. 1987. 12.95 o.p. (ISBN 0-89577-275-2). RD Assn.

Titles

Life on the Planet Earth. Harold J. Morowitz & Lucille S. Morowitz. (Illus.). 400p. 1974. text ed. 14.95x o.p. (ISBN 0-393-09269-0). Norton.

Life out of Death: Meditations on the Easter Mystery. Hans U. Von Balthasar. LC 84-48704. 64p. 1985. pap. 3.50 o.p. (ISBN 0-8006-1821-1, 1-1821, Fortress). Augsburg Fortress.

Life Partially Relived in Vignettes. Laura Robinson. 1977. 10.00 o.p. (ISBN 0-682-48817-8). Exposition-Phoenix.

Life Penalty. Joy Fielding. LC 84-4062. 336p. 1984. 15.95 o.p. (ISBN 0-385-18871-4). Doubleday.

Life Planning. Kirk E. Farnsworth & Wendell H. Lawhead. 96p. (Orig.). 1981. pap. 7.95 o.p. (ISBN 0-87784-840-8). Inter-Varsity.

Life Planning Workbook for Guidance in Planning & Personal Goal Setting see Planning Your Future: A Workbook for Personal Goal Setting.

Life Plans: Looking Forward to Retirement. Grace Weinstein. LC 78-12310. 1979. 9.95 o.p. (ISBN 0-03-039691-3); pap. 4.95 o.p. (ISBN 0-03-039696-4). H Holt & Co.

Life Rates & Data, 1987. Ed. by Price Gaines. 660p. 1987. pap. 19.00 o.p. (ISBN 0-87218-054-9). Natl Underwriter.

Life Science Monograph, No. 2. Ed. by G. Raspe. Tr. by J. Long et al. 221p. 1972. 52.00 o.p. (ISBN 0-08-017596-1). Pergamon.

Life Sciences & Space Research, Vol. 2. Ed. by M. Florkin & A. Dollfus. (Cospar Ser.). 1964. 47.50 o.p. (ISBN 0-444-10198-5, North-Holland). Elsevier.

Life Sciences & Space Research XXI (1) Proceedings of the Topical Meeting of the COSPAR Interdisciplinary Scientific Commission F (Meetings F4 & F8) of the COSPAR 25th Plenary Meeting held in Graz, Austria 25 June-7 July 1984. Ed. by H. P. Klein & G. Korneck. (Illus.). 300p. 1985. pap. 54.00 o.p. (ISBN 0-08-032746-X, Pub. by PPL). Pergamon.

Life Sciences & Space Research XXI (2) Proceedings of Workshops VII & XI & of the COSPAR Interdisciplinary Scientific Commission F (Meetings F1, F3, F5, F6, F7, & F9) of the COSPAR 25th Plenary Meeting Held in Graz, Austria, 25 June - 7 July 1984. Ed. by H. Oser et al. (Illus.). 334p. 1985. pap. 54.00 o.p. (ISBN 0-08-032752-4, Pub by PPL). Pergamon.

Life Smiles Back: More Than Two Hundred Classic Photos From the Famous Back Page of America's Favorite Magazine. Ed. by Philip B. Kunhardt, Jr. (Illus.). 224p. 1987. 17.45 o.s.i. (ISBN 0-671-64399-1). S&S.

Life Span Developmental Psychology: Personality & Socialization. Ed. by Paul B. Baltes & K. Warner Schaie. 1973. 47.00 o.p. (ISBN 0-12-077150-0). Acad Pr.

Life Span: The Hastings Center Report on Values & Life-Extending Technologies. Ed. by Robert M. Veatch. LC 78-3354. 1979. 12.95 o.p. (ISBN 0-06-250908-X). HarpR.

Life Spans: Or, How Long Things Last. Frank Kendig & Richard Hutton. LC 79-15952. 288p. (Orig.). 1980. 12.95 o.p. (ISBN 0-03-053261-2); pap. 5.95 o.p. (ISBN 0-03-040876-8). H Holt & Co.

Life Spent for Ireland. W. J. Daunt. 440p. 1972. Repr. of 1896 ed. 25.00x o.p. (ISBN 0-7165-0025-6, BBA 02157, Pub. by Irish Academic Pr Ireland). Biblio Dist.

Life Steps In. Ruby M. Ayres. (Lythway Ser.). 1987. lib. bdg. 17.50x o.p. (ISBN 0-7451-0573-4, Pub. by Chivers Pr UK). G K Hall.

Life-Stories Interview: Creating Portraits on Tape. Paul Friedman. 99p. (Orig.). 1985. pap. text ed. 22.50 o.p. (ISBN 0-936352-24-8). U of KS Cont Ed.

Life Story. Virginia L. Burton. (gr. k-3). 1977. pap. 4.50 o.p. (ISBN 0-395-26071-X). HM.

Life Story of an Old Rebel. John Denvir. 306p. 1972. Repr. of 1910 ed. 25.00x o.p. (ISBN 0-7165-0012-4, BBA 02159, Pub. by Irish Academic Pr Ireland). Biblio Dist.

Life Stress. Ed. by Stacey B. Day. (Companion to the Life Sciences Ser.: Vol. III). 416p. 1982. 42.95 o.p. (ISBN 0-442-26294-9). Van Nos Reinhold.

Life Styles in the Black Ghetto. William McCord et al. 1969. pap. text ed. 3.65 o.p. (ISBN 0-393-09857-5, NortonC). Norton.

Life-Time. Jane F. Rittmayer. 1979. 7.50 o.p. (ISBN 0-682-49253-1). Exposition-Phoenix.

Life-Time Furniture: Cloister Styles. (Illus.). 112p. 1985. pap. 8.95 o.p. (ISBN 0-87905-415-8). Gibbs Smith Pub.

Life to Come & Other Stories. E. M. Forster. 1976. pap. 2.50 o.p. (ISBN 0-380-00870-X, 48611-3, Bard). Avon.

Life to Live: A Novel. Yvonne Burgess. LC 80-17914. 183p. 1981. 8.95 o.s.i. (ISBN 0-8008-4816-0). Taplinger.

Life Transitions Reader. 124p. (Orig.). 1980. pap. text ed. 14.00 o.p. (ISBN 0-936352-10-8). U of KS Cont Ed.

Life Was Meant to Be Lived: A Centenary Portrait of Eleanor Roosevelt. Joseph P. Lash. LC 84-1589. (Illus.). 163p. 1984. 24.50 o.p. (ISBN 0-393-01877-6). Norton.

Life Wasn't Meant to Be Easy. Donna M. Hill. LC 83-90807. 99p. 1985. 7.95 o.p. (ISBN 0-533-05815-5). Vantage.

Life Wish. Jill Ireland. (Illus.). 1987. 17.95 o.p. (ISBN 0-316-10926-6). Little.

Life with Elvis. David Stanley. (Illus.). 1986. 13.95 o.p. (ISBN 0-8007-1490-3). Revell.

Life with Father. Clarence Day. (General Ser.). 1984. lib. bdg. 13.95 o.p. (ISBN 0-8161-3755-2, Large Print Bks). G K Hall.

Life with Grover. Alexander C. Brown. LC 62-18217. (Illus.). 80p. 1962. pap. 4.00 o.p. (ISBN 0-87033-271-6). Tidewater.

Life with Lindsay & Crouse. Cornelia Otis Skinner. (Illus.). 1976. 10.00 o.p. (ISBN 0-395-24511-7). HM.

Life with Rose Kennedy. Caroline Latham. 325p. 1986. 16.95 o.p. (ISBN 0-317-52557-3). Thorndike Pr.

Life with Spice Resource Manual. Daisy Hepburn. 1984. 7.95 o.s.i. (ISBN 0-8307-0936-3, 5203006). Regal.

Life with the Mentally Sick Child. P. R. Lacey. LC 71-97950. 1970. text ed. 14.50 o.p. (ISBN 0-08-006978-9); pap. text ed. 5.75 o.p. (ISBN 0-08-006977-0). Pergamon.

Life with Two Languages: An Introduction to Bilingualism. Francois Grosjean. (Illus.). 1982. text ed. 27.00x o.p. (ISBN 0-674-53091-8). Harvard U Pr.

Life with Wine: A Self-Portrait of the Wine Business in the Napa & Sonoma Valleys Plus 100 Recipes That Go with the Product. Nancy Chirich. Ed. by Gretchen Stengel. LC 83-16556. (Illus.). 196p. (Orig.). 1984. pap. 7.95 o.p. (ISBN 0-912761-00-8). Cliffhanger Pr.

Life with Working Parents: Practical Hints for Everyday Situations. Esther Hautzig. LC 76-15223. (Illus.). 128p. (gr. 5 up). 1976. 10.95 o.s.i. (ISBN 0-02-743500-8). Macmillan.

Life Without Compromise. John R. Bisagno. LC 81-71253. 1983. 3.95 o.p. (ISBN 0-8054-1503-3). Broadman.

Life, Work, & Rebellion in the Coal Fields: Southern West Virginia Miners, 1880-1920. David A. Corbin. LC 80-25493. (Working Class in American History). (Illus.). 282p. 1981. 24.95 o.p. (ISBN 0-252-00850-2); pap. text ed. 12.50 o.p. (ISBN 0-252-00895-2). U of Ill Pr.

Lifeboat Ethics: The Moral Dilemma of World Hunger. Ed. by George R. Lucas, Jr. & Thomas W. Ogletree. LC 76-10002. 192p. 1976. 8.95i o.p. (ISBN 0-06-065308-6); pap. 4.95x o.p. (ISBN 0-06-065309-4, RD170, HarpR). HarpR.

Lifeboat: The Story of Coxwain Dick Evans & His Many Rescues. Ian Skidmore. LC 78-66965. 1979. 16.95 o.p. (ISBN 0-7153-7691-8). David & Charles.

Lifeline: The Story of Your Circulatory System. Leo Schneider. LC 58-11561. (Illus.). (gr. 7 up). 1958. 6.95 o.p. (ISBN 0-15-245250-8, HJ). HarBraceJ.

Lifelines: The Stacey Letters, 1836-1858. Ed. by Jane Vansittart. LC 76-362. (Illus.). 1976. 8.95 o.s.i. (ISBN 0-8008-4841-1). Taplinger.

Lifelines: The Ten Commandments for Today. Edith Schaeffer. 1983. pap. 2.50 o.s.i. (ISBN 0-345-31154-X). Ballantine.

Lifelong Education & International Relations. Ettore Gelpi. LC 85-14982. (International Adult Education Ser.). 206p. 1985. 31.00 o.p. (ISBN 0-7099-1186-6, Pub. by Croom Helm Ltd). Routledge Chapman & Hall.

Lifelong Education & the Training of Teachers. Ed. by A. J. Cropley & H Ravindra. 1978. 65.00 o.p. (ISBN 0-08-022987-5); pap. 65.00 o.p. (ISBN 0-08-023008-3). Pergamon.

Lifelong Learning. ERIC Clearinghouse on Adult, Career, & Vocational Education Staff. 46p. 1983. 4.95 o.p. (ISBN 0-318-22143-8, BB67). Natl Ctr Res Voc Ed.

Lifelong Learning. Ed. by F. W. Jessup. 1969. 18.75 o.p. (ISBN 0-08-013407-6); pap. 45.00 o.p. (ISBN 0-08-013406-8). Pergamon.

Lifelong Learning: Formal, Nonformal, Informal, & Self-Directed. Donald W. Mocker & George E. Spear. 31p. 1982. 3.75 o.p. (ISBN 0-318-22144-6, IN241). Natl Ctr Res Voc Ed.

Lifelong Lover. Marvin B. Brooks & Sally W. Brooks. LC 84-25926. 240p. 1985. pap. 8.95 o.p. (ISBN 0-385-17713-5). Doubleday.

Lifelong Sexual Vigor: How to Avoid & Overcome Impotence. Marvin B. Brooks & Sally W. Brooks. LC 81-43115. 264p. 1981. 12.95 o.p. (ISBN 0-385-17712-7). Doubleday.

Lifeprints: New Patterns of Love & Work for Today's Women. G. Baruch & R. Barnett. 368p. 1983. text ed. 14.95 o.p. (ISBN 0-07-052981-7). McGraw.

Lifer. Ted Winters & Al Janssen. (Living Books). 320p. 1985. pap. 3.95 o.p. (ISBN 0-8423-2142-X). Tyndale.

Life's Byways: Poetry & Prose. Fred Keagle. 1979. 4.00 o.p. (ISBN 0-682-49335-X). Exposition-Phoenix.

Life's Little Ironies. Thomas Hardy. 256p. 1985. pap. 4.95 o.p. (ISBN 0-86299-069-6, Pub. by A Sutton Pub England). Academy Chi Pubs.

Life's Morning. George Gissing. Ed. by Pierre Coustillas. 408p. (Orig.). 1985. pap. 8.95 o.p. (ISBN 0-416-01091-1, NO. 9282). Routledge Chapman & Hall.

Life's Work. Date not set. (ISBN 0-385-29503-0). Delacorte.

Life's Work: A Harry Stoner Novel. Jonathan Valin. 240p. 1986. pap. 14.95 o.p. (ISBN 0-385-29503-0). Delacorte.

Lifespan. 2nd ed. Guy R. Lefrancois. Ed. by Ken King. 640p. 1984. text ed. write for info. o.p. (ISBN 0-534-02969-8). Wadsworth Pub.

Lifestyle Counseling for Adjustment to Disability. Warren R. Rule. LC 83-15777. 372p. 1984. 36.00 o.p. (ISBN 0-89443-895-6). Aspen Pub.

Lifestyles of Library Users & Nonusers. Michael Madden. (Occasional Papers: No. 137). 43p. 1979. pap. 2.00 o.p. (ISBN 0-317-58978-4). U of Ill Lib Info Sci.

Lifetime of Happiness. Stephen Parker. (Illus.). 72p. 1970. 5.00 o.p. Kayak.

Lifetime-Value Packagetion Package. Ed. by John Flint. LC 87-82976. 1987. 48.50 o.p. (ISBN 0-911752-54-4). I & O Pub.

Lifnim Meshurat Hadin. Kirschenblaum. 1989. price not set o.p. Ktav.

Lift (Elevator) Erection. Ed. by L. B. Chiles et al. (Engineering Craftsmen: No. J26). (Illus.). 1978. spiral bdg. 39.95x o.p. Trans-Atl Phila.

Lift (Elevator) Practice. Ed. by L. B. Chiles et al. (Engineering Craftsmen Ser.: No. J5). (Illus.). 203p. 1979. spiral bdg. 49.95x o.p. Trans-Atl Phila.

Lift (Elevator) Servicing & Maintenance. Ed. by L. B. Chiles et al. (Engineering Craftsmen: No. J25). (Illus.). 1974. spiral bdg. 39.95x o.p. Trans-Atl Phila.

Lift My Spirits, Lord: Prayers of a Struggling Christian. Bryan J. Leech. LC 84-9351. 128p. (Orig.). 1984. pap. 6.95 o.p. (ISBN 0-8066-2090-0, 10-3850, Augsburg). Augsburg Fortress.

Lift up Your Face! Helen Peabody. (Illus.). 128p. 1975. 8.95 o.p. (ISBN 0-8158-0315-X). Chris Mass.

Lift up Your Life. Morris Goldstein. LC 60-13644. 208p. 1961. (ISBN 0-8022-0605-0). Philos Lib.

Lifting the Curse. Beryl Kingston. 1980. 17.50x o.p. (ISBN 0-85223-176-8, Pub. by Ebury Pr England). State Mutual Bk.

Ligand Field Energy Diagrams. E. Konig & S. Kremer. LC 76-45670. (Illus.). 454p. 1977. 75.00x o.p. (ISBN 0-306-30946-7, Plenum Pr). Plenum Pub.

Light, 3 vols. 3rd. ed. R. W. Ditchburn. 1977. pap. 25.00 o.p. (ISBN 0-12-218101-8); Vol. 2, 1976. pap. 38.00 o.p. (ISBN 0-12-218102-6); Vol. 3. 95.00 o.p. (ISBN 0-12-218150-6). Acad Pr.

Light & Electron Microscopy of Cells & Tissues: An Atlas for Students in Biology & Medicine. E. B. Sandborn. 1972. 32.50 o.p. (ISBN 0-12-617950-6). Acad Pr.

Light & Life. L. O. Bjorn. LC 76-27618. 247p. 1976. pap. 13.00x o.p. (ISBN 0-8448-1006-1, Pub. by Crane Russak & Co). Taylor & Francis.

Light & Shadows. 2nd ed. Elementary Science Study Staff. 1975. tchr's. guide 13.32 o.p. (ISBN 0-07-018582-4). McGraw.

Light at Eventide: Devotions for the Autumn. Johan Lunde. Tr. by Palmer Loken. 1977. pap. 4.95 o.p. (ISBN 0-8066-1574-5, 10-3861, Augsburg). Augsburg Fortress.

Light, Color, & Environment. rev. ed. Faber Birren. 112p. 1982. pap. 20.95 o.p. (ISBN 0-442-21270-4). Van Nos Reinhold.

Light Company. Millie Budd. (Illus.). 585p. 1987. 24.50 o.p. (ISBN 0-88415-436-X). Gulf Pub.

Light Desserts. Bon Appetit Magazine Editors. (Cooking with Appetit Ser.). (Illus.). 144p. 1984. 12.95 o.p. (ISBN 0-89535-135-8). Knapp Pr.

Light for My Life. Desmond B. Hills. Ed. by Bobbie J. Van Dolson. 384p. (gr. 3-8). 1981. 8.50 o.p. (ISBN 0-8280-0041-7). Review & Herald.

Light for the Gentiles: Paul & the Growing Church. Leland Jamison. 1962. 1.50 o.s.i. (ISBN 0-664-21408-8, Westminster). Westminster John Knox.

Light from Many Lamps. Lillian E. Watson. 1951. 15.45 o.s.i. (ISBN 0-671-42300-2). S&S.

Light from the Darkness: Paintings by Peter Birkhauser. Kaspar Birkhauser. Ed. by Eva Wertenschlag. (Illus.). 80p. (Eng. & Ger.). 1980. pap. 23.95x o.p. (ISBN 0-8176-1190-8, Dist. by Sigo Pr). Birkhauser.

Light in August. William Faulkner. 512p. (YA) 1972. pap. 4.95 o.p. (ISBN 0-394-71189-0, V189, Vin). Random.

Light in August. William Faulkner. 48p. (Orig.). 1989. pap. 9.95 o.p. (ISBN 1-55651-527-8); audiocassette tape incl. o.p. (ISBN 1-55651-528-6). Cram Cassettes.

Light in the Jungle. Cass Falden. 280p. 1989. pap. 11.95 o.p. (ISBN 0-932727-19-0). Hope Pub Hse.

Light in the Swamp. Velda Johnston. (Large Print Bks., Nightingale Ser.). 292p. 1987. pap. 11.95x o.p. (ISBN 0-8161-4268-8, Large Print Bks). G K Hall.

Light List, V. 6, Pacific Coast & Pacific Islands, Eleventh, Twelfth, Thirteenth, Fourteenth, & Seventeenth Coast Guard Districts: Commandant Instruction M 16502.6 Ser. Annual ed. (Illus.). 345p. 1987. pap. 16.00 o.p. (S/N 050-012-00230-4). USGPO.

Light List, Vol. 1: Atlantic Coast, from St. Croix River, Maine, to Toms River, New Jersey, First Coast Guard District. (Commandant Instruction Ser.: No. M 16502.1). (Illus.). 402p. (Orig.). 1988. pap. 20.00 o.p. (S/N 050-012-00241-0). USGPO.

Light List, Vol. 2: Atlantic Coast, from Ocean City Inlet, Maryland to Little River, South Carolina, Fifth Coast Guard District. (Commandant Instruction Ser.: No. M 16502.2). (Illus.). 313p. 1987. pap. 16.00 o.p. (ISBN 0-318-22392-9, S/N 050-012-00227-4). USGPO.

Light List, Vol. 2: Toms River, New Jersey to Little River, South Carolina, Fifth Coast Guard District. (Commandant Instruction Ser.: No. 16502.2). (Illus.). 378p. (Orig.). 1988. pap. 19.00 o.p. (S/N 050-012-00240-1). USGPO.

Light List, Vol. 4: Gulf of Mexico, from Ecofina River, Florida, to Rio Grande, Texas, Eighth Coast Guard District. (Commandant Instruction Ser.: No. M16502.4). (Illus.). 383p. (Orig.). 1987. pap. 19.00 o.p. (ISBN 0-318-22412-7, S/N 050-012-00229-1). USGPO.

Light List, Vol. 4: Gulf of Mexico, from Econfina River, Florida, to Rio Grande, Texas, Eighth Coast Guard District. (Commandant Instruction: No. M 16502.4). (Illus.). 389p. (Orig.). 1987. pap. 20.00 o.p. (S/N 050-012-00239-8). USGPO.

Light Metal, 1985. Ed. by H. O. Bohner. LC 84-29479. 1525p. 1985. 80.00 o.p. (ISBN 0-89520-488-6). Minerals Metals.

Light Metals 1979: Proceedings. AIME Annual Meeting, New Orleans, 1979. Ed. by Warren S. Peterson. (Illus.). 977p. 55.00 o.p. (ISBN 0-89520-145-3); members 32.00 o.p. (ISBN 0-317-36296-8); student members 16.00 o.p. (ISBN 0-317-36297-6). ASM.

Light Metals 1980: Proceedings. AIME Annual Meeting, Las Vegas, 1980. Ed. by Curtis J. McMinn. (Illus.). 1029p. 15.00 o.p.; members 32.00 o.p. (ISBN 0-89520-359-6); student members 16.00 o.p. (ISBN 0-317-36295-X). ASM.

Light Metals 1981: Proceedings. AIME Annual Meeting, Chicago, 1981. Ed. by Gordon M. Bell. (Illus.). 1060p. 55.00 o.p.; members 32.00 o.p. (ISBN 0-317-36292-5); student members 16.00 o.p. (ISBN 0-317-36293-3). ASM.

Light 'N Easy Cooking: Recipes for a Trimmer Slimmer Lifestyle. Brenda Wood & Clara Jones. LC 85-71871. 192p. 1985. spiral 7.95 o.p. (ISBN 0-89636-188-8). Accent Bks.

Light of Asia. Edwin Arnold. LC 79-4436. 1969. pap. 4.50 o.s.i. (ISBN 0-8356-0405-5, Quest). Theos Pub Hse.

Light of Asia & the Indian Song of Songs: Gita Govinda. Tr. by Edwin Arnold. 1949. pap. 2.00 o.p. (ISBN 0-88253-115-8). Ind-US Inc.

Light of Asia: Buddha Sakyamuni in Asian Art. Pratapaditya Pal et al. (Illus.). 332p. 1984. 35.00 o.p. (ISBN 0-87587-116-X); pap. 16.95 o.p. LA Co Art Mus.

Light of Asia or, the Great Renunciation (Mahabhinishkramana) Being the Life & Teaching of Gautama, Prince of India, Founder of Buddhism. Edwin Arnold. x, 176p. 1972. pap. 5.00 o.p. (ISBN 0-7100-7006-3). Routledge Chapman & Hall.

Light of Christ. Pope John Paul II. 256p. 1987. pap. 9.95 o.p. (ISBN 0-8245-0820-3). Crossroad NY.

Light of Christ. Evelyn Underhill. LC 82-80475. (Treasures from the Spiritual Classics Ser.). 64p. 1982. pap. 2.95 o.p. (ISBN 0-8192-1312-8). Morehouse Pub.

Light of Christ: Meditations for Every Day of the Year. Ed. by Tony Castle. pap. 9.95 o.p. Crossroad NY.

Light of Dark. Themba Hlongwane. 1978. 4.00 o.p. (ISBN 0-682-49074-1). Exposition-Phoenix.

Light of Distant Skies: 1760-1835. James T. Flexner. LC 68-54703. (Illus.). 1969. pap. 5.95 o.p. (ISBN 0-486-22179-2). Dover.

Light of Iman from the House of 'Imran. Surat A. Imran. (Zahra Publications). 240p. 1987. pap. 13.95 o.p. (ISBN 0-7103-0267-3, Pub. by Routledge UK). Routledge Chapman & Hall.

Light of Lost Suns. Amir Gilboa. Tr. by Shirley Kaufman from Hebrew. LC 78-61062. (Persea Ser. of Poetry in Translation). 1979. 10.00 o.p. (ISBN 0-89255-037-6); pap. 4.95 o.p. (ISBN 0-89255-038-4). Persea Bks.

Light of the Bhagavat. Bhaktivedanta Swami. 1985. 12.95 o.p. (ISBN 0-89213-135-7). Bhaktivedanta.

Light of Truth Beaming on the Human Race. Nadine Dawson. 1980. 9.00 o.s.i. (ISBN 0-682-49576-X). Exposition-Phoenix.

Light on C. S. Lewis. Ed. by Jocelyn Gibb. LC 66-12361. (Illus.). 1966. 4.95 o.p. (ISBN 0-15-151981-1). HarBraceJ.

Light: Physical & Biological Action. Howard H. Seliger & W. D. McElroy. (U. S. Atomic Energy Commission Monographs). 1965. 23.50 o.p. (ISBN 0-12-635850-8). Acad Pr.

Light Scattering by Phonon Polaritons. R. Claus et al. (Springer Tracts in Modern Physics Ser.: Vol. 75). (Illus.). 240p. 1975. 34.20 o.p. (ISBN 0-387-07423-6). Springer-Verlag.

Light Scattering from Polymer Solutions. Ed. by M. B. Huglin. (Physical Chemistry Ser.: Vol. 27). 1972. 121.50 o.p. (ISBN 0-12-361050-8). Acad Pr.

Light Scattering in Planetary Atmospheres. V. V. Sobolev. Tr. by W. M. Irvine. 1975. 71.00 o.p. (ISBN 0-08-017934-7). Pergamon.

Light: The Complete Handbook of Lighting Design. Susan S. Szenasy. (Illus.). 144p. 1986. 24.95 o.p. (ISBN 0-89471-391-4); pap. 14.95 o.p. (ISBN 0-89471-392-2). Running Pr.

Light Transmission Optics. 2nd ed. Dietrich Marcuse. 500p. 1982. 39.95 o.p. (ISBN 0-442-26309-0). Van Nos Reinhold.

Light upon the Path: Poems & Prose & Points. Georgia O. Borland. 1984. 8.95 o.p. (ISBN 0-533-06050-8). Vantage.

Light Vehicle Fitting. Ed. by R. Aylen et al. (Engineering Craftsmen Ser.: No. H32). (Illus.). 261p. 1981. wire-bound 52.50x o.p. Trans-Atl Phila.

Light Within You: Looking at Life Through New Eyes. John Claypool. 1983. 9.95 o.p. (ISBN 0-8499-0273-8). Word Bks.

Light Years. James Salter. 1977. pap. 1.75 o.p. (ISBN 0-380-01644-3, 33027). Avon.

Lighten Our Darkness: Toward an Indigenous Theology of the Cross. Douglas J. Hall. LC 75-38963. 1976. 10.95 o.s.i. (ISBN 0-664-20808-8, Westminster). Westminster John Knox.

Lighthouse. Tony Parker. LC 76-11056. 1976. 8.95 o.p. (ISBN 0-8008-4853-5). Taplinger.

Lighthouse Keeper's Lunch. Ronda Armitage. (Illus.). (ps-2). 1979. 9.95 o.p. (ISBN 0-233-96868-7). Andre Deutsch.

Lighthouse of Langdon: Presenting 20th Century Jehovah to Doomsday Man. Rohen Langdon. 207p. 1980. 9.00 o.p. (ISBN 0-682-49637-5). Exposition-Phoenix.

Lighthouses & Lifeboats on the Redwood Coast. Ralph C. Shanks, Jr. LC 77-93457. (Illus.). 1978. 32.00 o.s.i. (ISBN 0-930268-04-0); pap. 8.95 o.p. (ISBN 0-930268-03-2). Costano.

Lighting Fittings, Performance & Design. A. R. Bean & R. H. Simons. (International Series in Electrical Engineering: Vol. 1). 1969. 85.00 o.p. (ISBN 0-08-012594-8). Pergamon.

Lighting System Noise Criterion (LS-NC) Ratings. 1980. 5.00 o.p. (ISBN 0-318-18023-5, LE 2-1974). Natl Elec Mfrs.

Lighting, Visibility & Railroad-Highway Grade Crossings. (Transportation Research Record Ser.). 56p. 1977. 2.40 o.p. (ISBN 0-309-02653-9). Transport Res Bd.

Lightning. Ed McBain. (General Ser.). 1985. lib. bdg. 16.95 o.p. (ISBN 0-8161-3829-X, Large Print Bks). G K Hall.

Lightning: An Eighty-Seventh Precinct Novel. Ed McBain. 1984. 15.95 o.p. (ISBN 0-87795-581-6, Arbor Hse). Morrow.

Lightning & Power Systems. (IEE Conference Publications Ser.: No. 236). 209p. 1984. pap. 78.00 o.s.i. (ISBN 0-85296-293-2, IC236). Inst Elect Eng.

Lightning Bugs & Other Reconnaissance Drones. William Wagner. LC 81-71064. 220p. 1982. 6.95x o.p. (ISBN 0-8168-6654-6, 26654, TAB-Aero). TAB Bks.

Lightning Forward: A History of the 25th Infantry Division (Tropic Lightning) 1941-1978. Melvin Walthall. 1979. 10.00 o.p. (ISBN 0-686-67704-8). Exposition-Phoenix.

Lightning Time. Gregory Maguire. LC 78-18771. 256p. (gr. 5 up). 1978. 11.95 o.p. (ISBN 0-374-34458-2). FS&G.

Lightplane Propeller Design, Selection, Maintenance & Repair. William A. Welch. (Modern Aviation Ser.). (Illus.). 1979. 8.95 o.p. (ISBN 0-8306-9765-9, 2269); pap. 4.95 o.p. (ISBN 0-8306-2269-1). TAB Bks.

Lights! Action! Camera! Learn! William H. Blazier. LC 74-80347. 1974. 10.00 o.p. (ISBN 0-686-10561-3). Allison Pubs.

Lights & Tides of the World, 2 vols. & 2 supplements. rev. ed. F. N. Hopkins. 1973. Set. 90.00 o.s.i. (ISBN 0-686-77975-4). E J Brill USA.

Lights & Tides of the World, 2 vols. F. N. Hopkins. 1973. Set. 70.00 o.s.i. (ISBN 0-685-58570-0); 2 suppls. incl. o.s.i. (ISBN 0-685-58571-9). E J Brill USA.

Lights, Camera, Cats! Judith E. Weber. (Illus.). (gr. 3-7). 1978. 10.25 o.p. (ISBN 0-688-41867-8); PLB 10.88 o.p. (ISBN 0-688-51867-2). Lothrop.

Lights Out! Kids Talk about Summer Camp. Eric H. Arnold & Jeffrey Loeb. (Illus.). (gr. 3 up). 1985. 13.45 o.p. (ISBN 0-316-05184-5); pap. 4.95 o.p. (ISBN 0-316-05183-7). Little.

Lightworks: Interpreted from the Original Hebrew Book of Isaiah. David Rosenberg. LC 78-3356. 78p. 1978. 6.00 o.p. (ISBN 0-686-81738-9). SUN.

Lignin Biochemistry. Walter J. Schubert. 1965. 37.50 o.p. (ISBN 0-12-630950-7). Acad Pr.

Like a Field Riddled. Myra Sklarew. LC 87-16961. (Lost Roads Ser.: No. 32). 112p. (Orig.). 1987. pap. 7.95 o.p. (ISBN 0-317-64478-5). Lost Roads.

Like a Lamb to Slaughter. Lawrence Block. LC 84-9324. 256p. 1984. 15.95 o.p. (ISBN 0-87795-526-3, Arbor Hse). Morrow.

Like a Lover. Lynn Michaels. (Velvet Glove Ser.: No. 8). 192p. 1984. pap. 2.25 o.p. (ISBN 0-380-89441-6, 89441-6). Avon.

Like a Mantle, the Sea. Stella Shepherd. LC 73-85450. (Illus.). 184p. 1971. 9.50x o.p. (ISBN 0-8214-0133-5). Ohio U Pr.

Like a Mighty Wind. Mel Tari & Cliff Dudley. LC 76-182854. 1978. 3.95 o.p. (ISBN 0-89221-121-0); pap. 2.95 o.p. (ISBN 0-89221-049-4). New Leaf.

Like a Promise. Phyllis C. Gobbell. LC 83-71490. 1983. 8.95 o.p. (ISBN 0-8054-7319-X). Broadman.

Like a Winter Cloud. Atlanta G. Hardy. LC 84-91386. 141p. 1985. 10.95 o.p. (ISBN 0-533-06471-6). Vantage.

Like Father, Like Sons (And Daughter Too) Thom Hunter. (Illus.). 160p. 1987. 8.95 o.p. (ISBN 0-8007-1517-9). Revell.

Like, Love, Lust: A View of Sex & Sexuality. John Langone. 144p. 1981. pap. 2.25 o.p. (ISBN 0-380-54189-0, 54189-0, Flare). Avon.

Like, Love, Lust: A View of Sex & Sexuality. John Langone. 204p. (gr. 7 up). 1980. 9.95 o.p. (ISBN 0-316-51429-2). Little.

Like Me. Alan Brightman. (Illus.). 48p. (gr. k-3). 1976. PLB 12.45 o.p. (ISBN 0-316-10808-1); pap. 6.95 o.p. (ISBN 0-316-10807-3). Little.

Like Normal People. Robert Meyers. (Illus.). 1978. text ed. 9.95 o.p. (ISBN 0-07-041761-X). McGraw.

Like the One You Love: Intimacy & Equality in Modern Marriage. Samuel Southard. LC 73-21966. 128p. 1974. pap. 2.75 o.s.i. (ISBN 0-664-24986-8, Westminster). Westminster John Knox.

Like Your Style, Andy Capp. Reginald Smythe. 128p. 1984. pap. 1.95 o.s.i. (ISBN 0-449-12572-6, GM). Fawcett.

Likrat Shabbat. Sidney Greenberg. LC 72-97593. 10.00x o.p. (ISBN 0-87677-076-6). Hartmore.

Lilias, Yoga & Your Life. Lilias Folan. (Illus.). 192p. 1981. pap. 10.95 o.p. (ISBN 0-02-080060-6, Collier). Macmillan.

Lilies & Other Stories. Ru Zhijuan. 205p. 1985. text ed. 4.95 o.p. (ISBN 0-8351-1332-9). China Bks.

Lilika Nakos. Deborah Tannen. (World Authors Ser.). 1983. lib. bdg. 24.95 o.s.i. (ISBN 0-8057-6524-7, Twayne). G K Hall.

Lillian Hellman: An Annotated Bibliography. Steven H. Bills. LC 78-68282. 248p. 1979. lib. bdg. 31.00 o.p. (ISBN 0-8240-9803-X). Garland Pub.

Lillian Hellman: The Woman Who Made the Legend. William Wright. (Illus.). 400p. 1986. 18.45 o.s.i. (ISBN 0-671-52687-1). S&S.

Lilliput Goes to War. Ed. by Kaye Webb. (Illus.). 288p. 1986. 24.95 o.p. (ISBN 0-09-161760-X, Pub. by Century Hutchinson). David & Charles.

Lilly, Willy & the Mail-Order Witch. Othello Bach. LC 83-7422. (Illus.). 48p. (ps-4). PLB 13.45 o.s.i. (B0489). Caedmon.

Lilt of the Irish-An Encyclopedia of Irish Humor & Lore. Henry D. Spalding. LC 77-24307. 1978. 16.95 o.p. (ISBN 0-8246-0218-8). Jonathan David.

Lily & the Bull. Moyra Caldecott. 192p. 1979. 9.95 o.p. (ISBN 0-8090-6572-X). Hill & Wang.

Lily Goes to the Playground. Jill Krementz. LC 85-62037. (Great Big Board Bks.). (Illus.). 14p. (ps). 1986. bds. 3.95 o.s.i. (ISBN 0-394-87999-6). Random.

Limb of Your Tree: The Story of an Adopted Twin's Search for Her Roots. Doris D. Smith. 176p. 1984. 10.00 o.p. (ISBN 0-682-40132-3). Exposition-Phoenix.

Limb Prosthetics. 5th ed. A. Bennet Wilson, Jr. LC 75-44350. 104p. 1976. 7.50 o.p. (ISBN 0-88275-944-2). Krieger.

Limbert Furniture, Nos. 112 & 119. (Illus.). 128p. 1985. pap. 9.95 o.p. (ISBN 0-87905-411-5). Gibbs Smith Pub.

Limbic Mechanisms: The Continuing Evolution of the Limbic System Concept. Ed. by K. E. Livingston & O. Hornykiewicz. LC 78-1542. 558p. 1978. 75.00x o.p. (ISBN 0-306-31135-6, Plenum Pr). Plenum Pub.

Limbo. Joel Hammil. LC 79-54011. 1980. 9.95 o.p. (ISBN 0-87795-254-X, Arbor Hse). Morrow.

Lime-Fly Ash-Stabilized Base & Substances. (National Cooperative Highway Research Program Synthesis of Highway Practice). 66p. 1976. 4.80 o.p. (ISBN 0-309-02510-9). Transport Res Bd.

Limelight. Terence Feeley. 320p. 1986. pap. 3.95 o.p. (ISBN 0-931773-85-7). Critics Choice Paper.

Limit Design for Reinforced Concrete Structures. M. Z. Cohn. (Bibliography: No. 8). 1970. pap. 36.25 o.p. (ISBN 0-685-85146-X, B-8) (ISBN 0-685-85147-8). ACI.

Limit State Theory for Reinforced Concrete Design. 2nd ed. B. P. Hughes. (Illus.). 1977. 26.95x o.p. (ISBN 0-8464-0572-5); pap. text ed. 17.50x o.p. (ISBN 0-8464-0573-3). Beekman Pubs.

Limited Liability & the Corporation. Ed. by Tony Orhnial. (Illus.). 224p. 1982. 28.00 o.p. (ISBN 0-7099-1919-0, Pub. by Croom Helm Ltd). Routledge Chapman & Hall.

Limited Master, Mate & Operator License Study Course, 4 vols. Ed. by Richard A. Block et al. (Illus.). 1986. Set. pap. 65.00 o.p. Bk. 1: 475 p (ISBN 0-934114-72-2). Bk. 2: 475 p (ISBN 0-934114-73-0). Bk. 3: 335 p (ISBN 0-934114-74-9). Bk. 4: 368 p (ISBN 0-934114-75-7). 3-ring plastic binder 67.00 o.p. (ISBN 0-934114-77-3). Marine Educ.

Limited Offerings Exemptions: Regulation D. J. Hicks. 1986. 75.00 o.p. (ISBN 0-87632-504-5). Clark Boardman.

Limiting Conventional Forces in Europe: An Alternative to the Mutual & Balanced Force Reduction Negotiations. William R. Bowman. LC 85-600617. (National Security Affairs Monograph). 99p. (Orig.). 1985. pap. 2.00 o.p. (ISBN 0-318-19938-6, S/N 008-020-01050-2). USGPO.

Limiting State Spending: The Legislature or the Electorate. Frank M. Bowen & Eugene C. Lee. LC 79-10327. (Research Report: No. 79-4). 1979. pap. 5.00x o.p. (ISBN 0-87772-265-X). UCB IGS.

Limitless Sky: The Work of Charles M. Russell. Ginger Renner. LC 85-60941. (Illus.). 144p. 1986. 35.00 o.p. (ISBN 0-87358-384-1); ltd. ed. 200.00 o.p. (ISBN 0-87358-385-X). Northland.

Limits: A Transition to Calculus. O. Lexton Buchanan, Jr. Ed. by Albert E. Meder, Jr. (Modern Mathematics Ser). (gr. 9 up). 1966. pap. 8.60 o.p. (ISBN 0-395-17941-6). HM.

Limits of National Liberation: Problems of Economic Management in the Democratic Republic of Vietnam, with a Statistical Appendix. Adam Fforde & Suzanne H. Paine. 192p. 1987. lib. bdg. 55.00x o.p. (ISBN 0-317-64430-0, Pub. by Croom Helm UK). Routledge Chapman & Hall.

Limits of Religious Thought. 5th ed. H. L. Mansel. 1986. Repr. of 1870 ed. lib. bdg. 25.00X o.p. (ISBN 0-935005-46-3). Ibis Pub VA.

Limits of Scientific Inquiry. Ed. by Gerald Holton & Robert S. Morison. 1979. 19.95x o.p. (ISBN 0-393-01212-3); pap. 5.95x o.p. (ISBN 0-393-95056-5). Norton.

Limits of Story. George Aichele, Jr. LC 84-48726. (Semeia Studies). 160p. 1985. pap. 1.95 o.p. (ISBN 0-8006-1513-1, 1-1513, Fortress). Augsburg Fortress.

Limits of the Earth. Fairfield Osborn. LC 76-148640. 1971. Repr. of 1953 ed. lib. bdg. 35.00x o.p. (ISBN 0-8371-6005-7, OSLE). Greenwood.

Limits of the Novel: Evolutions of a Form from Chaucer to Robbe-Grillet. David I. Grossvogel. (Paperback Ser.). 357p. 1971. pap. 8.95x o.p. (ISBN 0-8014-9115-0). Cornell U Pr.

Limits to Capital. David Harvey. LC 82-40322. 452p. 1982. lib. bdg. 30.00x o.s.i. (ISBN 0-226-31952-0). U of Chicago Pr.

Limits to Capital. David Harvey. LC 82-40322. 496p. 1984. pap. text ed. 12.95x o.s.i. (ISBN 0-226-31953-9). U of Chicago Pr.

Limits to Solar & Biomass Energy Growth. Yale M. Schiffman & Gregory J. D'Alessio. LC 81-48071. 320p. 1983. 32.00x o.p. (ISBN 0-669-05253-1). Lexington Bks.

Limnological Analyses. Robert G. Wetzel & Gene E. Likens. 1979. pap. text ed. 24.95 o.p. (ISBN 0-7216-9243-5, CBS C). SCP.

Limnology of Tundra Ponds: Barrow, Alaska. Ed. by J. E. Hobbie. LC 80-26373. (US-IBP Synthesis Ser.: Vol. 13). 514p. 1982. 44.95 o.p. (ISBN 0-87933-386-3). Van Nos Reinhold.

Limo. Dan Jenkins & Edwin Shrake. LC 76-11576. 1976. 8.95 o.p. (ISBN 0-689-10734-X, Atheneum). Macmillan.

Limuria: The Lesser Dependencies of Maritius. Sir Robert Scott. LC 75-3741. (Illus.). 1976. Repr. of 1961 ed. lib. bdg. 35.00x o.p. (ISBN 0-8371-8058-9, SCLIM). Greenwood.

Lincoln & Kennedy: Medical & Ballistic Comparisons of Their Assassinations. John K. Lattimer. LC 80-7963. 1980. 19.95 o.p. (ISBN 0-15-152281-2). HarBraceJ.

Lincoln Calendar. Ed. by John Schildt. (Illus.). 32p. (Orig.). 1985. pap. 5.95 o.p. (ISBN 0-932751-02-4). Beidel Printing Hse.

Lincoln Center Story. Alan Rich. LC 84-6441. (American Heritage Bks.). (Illus.). 128p. 1984. 19.45 o.p. (ISBN 0-8281-1169-3). HM.

Lincoln County. Tom Cutter. (Tracker Ser.: No. 2). 160p. 1983. pap. 2.25 o.p. (ISBN 0-380-84152-5, 84152-5). Avon.

Lincoln Library of Essential Information, 2 vols. 43rd ed. Frontier Press Company Staff. LC 82-645884. (Illus.). (gr. 5 up). 1985. Set. 149.50 o.s.i. (ISBN 0-912168-12-9). Frontier Pr Co.

Lincoln Library of Sports Champions, 20 vols. 4th ed. Frontier Press Company Staff. LC 84-81800. (Illus.). 2560p. (gr. 4 up). 1985. Set. 349.50 o.p. (ISBN 0-912168-11-0). Frontier Pr Co.

Lincoln Papers: The Story of the Collection with Selections to July 4, 1861, 2 Vols in 1. U. S. National Archives Staff. LC 48-9019. 1968. Repr. of 1948 ed. 26.00 o.p. (ISBN 0-527-62580-9). Kraus Repr.

Lincoln: The Prairie Capital. James L. McKee. (Illus.). 192p. 1984. 24.95 o.s.i. (ISBN 0-89781-109-7). Windsor Pubns Inc.

Lincoln's Negro Policy. Earnest S. Cox. 1968. 3.00 o.p. (ISBN 0-911038-13-2); pap. 2.00 o.p. (ISBN 0-911038-12-4). Noontide.

Lincoln's Religion. William J. Wolf. LC 70-123035. Orig. Title: Almost Chosen People. 1970. pap. 2.25 o.p. (ISBN 0-8298-0181-2). Pilgrim NY.

Lincoln's Youth: Indiana Years, Seven to Twenty-One, 1816-1830. Louis A. Warren. LC 75-26223. (Illus.). 298p. 1976. Repr. of 1959 ed. lib. bdg. 22.75x o.p. (ISBN 0-8371-8408-8, WALY). Greenwood.

Linda Mason's Sun-Sign Makeovers. Linda Mason. 128p. 1985. 25.00 o.p. (ISBN 0-374-18766-5); pap. 14.95 o.p. (ISBN 0-374-51939-0). FS&G.

Lindbergh Alone. Brendan Gill. LC 76-54288. (Illus.). 224p. 1977. 11.95 o.p. (ISBN 0-15-152401-7). HarBraceJ.

Lindbergh of Minnesota: A Political Biography. Bruce L. Larson. LC 73-6596. 1973. 14.50 o.s.i. (ISBN 0-15-152400-9). HarBraceJ.

Linden Hills. Gloria Naylor. LC 84-16222. 320p. 1985. 16.95 o.s.i. (ISBN 0-89919-357-9). Ticknor & Fields.

Lindi the Leopard. Georgeanne Irvine. (Zoo Babies Ser.). (Illus.). 16p. (Orig.). (gr. k-6). 1983. pap. 1.25 o.p. (ISBN 0-8249-8054-9). Ideals.

Lindisfarne Gospels. Janet Backhouse. LC 81-65990. (Cornell Phaidon Bks.). (Illus.). 96p. 1981. 29.95 o.p. (ISBN 0-8014-1354-0). Cornell U Pr.

Lindisfarne: The Cradle Island. Magnus Magnusson. (Illus.). 224p. 1985. pap. 15.00 o.p. (ISBN 0-85362-223-X, Oriel Press). Routledge Chapman & Hall.

Line in Water. Amrita Pritam. Tr. by Krishna Gorowara from Punjabi. (Mayfair Paperbacks). 141p. 1975. 5.95 o.s.i. (ISBN 0-89253-012-X); pap. 2.50 o.s.i. (ISBN 0-89253-023-5). Ind-US Inc.

Lineage of Lady Meed: The Development of Mediaeval Venality-Satire. John A. Yunck. (Mediaeval Studies Ser.: No. 17). 1963. 35.00 o.p. (ISBN 0-268-00157-X). U of Notre Dame Pr.

Linear Algebra. Norman J. Bloch & John G. Michaels. (Illus.). 1977. text ed. 38.95 o.p. (ISBN 0-07-005906-3). McGraw.

Linear Algebra. A. H. Lightstone. LC 74-93018. (Century Mathematics Ser.). (Illus.). 1969. 39.00x o.p. (ISBN 0-89197-275-7); pap. text ed. 19.50x o.p. (ISBN 0-89197-824-0). Irvington.

Linear Algebra, Vol. 2A. Michael O'Nan. (Illus.). 1971. text ed. 14.95 o.p. (ISBN 0-15-518558-6, HC). HarBraceJ.

Linear Algebra: A Concrete Approach. Dennis M. Schneider et al. 1982. write for info. o.p. (ISBN 0-02-476810-3). Macmillan.

Linear Algebra & Projective Geometry. Reinhold Baer. (Pure and Applied Mathematics Ser.: Vol. 2). 1952. 65.50 o.p. (ISBN 0-12-072250-X). Acad Pr.

Linear Analysis of Frameworks. Tom R. Graves-Smith. (Ellis Horwood Series in Engineering Science). (Illus.). 451p. 1983. 68.95 o.p. (ISBN 0-470-27449-2). Halsted Pr.

Titles

Titles

Linear & Regular Celestial Mechanics: Perturbed Two-Body Motion, Numerical Methods, Canonical Theory. E. L. Stiefel & G. Scheifele. LC 72-133369. (Grundlehren der Mathematischen Wissenschaften: Vol. 174). 1971. 54.00 o.p. (ISBN 0-387-05119-8). Springer-Verlag.

Linear Determinants with Applications to Picard Scheme of a Family of Algebraic Groups. B. Iversen. (Lecture Notes in Mathematics: Vol. 174). 1971. pap. 11.00 o.p. (ISBN 0-387-05301-8). Springer-Verlag.

Linear Differential Equations. Kenneth S. Miller. 1963. 10.95x o.p. (ISBN 0-393-09599-1, NortonC). Norton.

Linear Discontinued Devices. 1987. 70.00 o.p. DATA Busn Pub.

Linear Engineering Systems: Tools & Techniques. Michael P. Smyth. 386p. 1972. 44.00 o.p. (ISBN 0-08-016324-6). Pergamon.

Linear Geometry. 2nd ed. K. W. Gruenberg. LC 76-27693. (Graduate Texts in Mathematics Ser.). (Illus.). 1977. 25.00 o.p. (ISBN 0-387-90227-9). Springer-Verlag.

Linear Integrated Circuits. Thomas Young. LC 80-22791. (Electronic Technology Ser.). 495p. 1981. (ISBN 0-471-97941-4); pap. (ISBN 0-471-86270-3). Wiley.

Linear Integrated Networks: Fundamentals. George Moschytz. 1974. 29.95 o.p. (ISBN 0-442-25581-0). Van Nos Reinhold.

Linear Motor & Its Application to Tracked Hovercraft. E. R. Laithwaite. 12p. 1971. pap. 2.25x o.p. (ISBN 0-317-03988-1). Am Soc Civil Eng.

Linear Multiobjective Programming. M. Zeleny. LC 73-22577. (Lecture Notes in Economics & Mathematical Systems: Vol. 95). (Illus.). x, 220p. 1974. pap. 12.00 o.p. (ISBN 0-387-06639-X). Springer-Verlag.

Linear Multivariable Systems. W. A. Wolovich. (Applied Mathematical Sciences Ser.: Vol. 11). (Illus.). 370p. 1974. pap. 16.50 o.p. (ISBN 0-387-90101-9). Springer-Verlag.

Linear Operators, 3 pts. Nelson Dunford & Jacob T. Schwartz. Incl. Pt. 1. General Theory. LC 79-8185. 872p. 1958. 77.95x o.p. (ISBN 0-470-22605-6); Pt. 2. Spectral Theory, Self Adjoint Operators in Hilbert Space. 1072p. 1963. 110.00 o.p. (ISBN 0-470-22638-2); Pt. 3. Spectral Operators. 667p. 1971. 95.00x o.p. (ISBN 0-471-22639-4). LC 57-10545. (Pure & Applied Mathematics Ser.). 1982. Set. 225.00 o.p. (ISBN 0-471-86913-9, Pub. by Wiley-Interscience). Wiley.

Linear Operators & Systems: Operator Theory, Mathematical Systems Theory, Control Process. P. A. Fuhrmann. 1981. text ed. 61.95 o.p. (ISBN 0-07-022589-3). McGraw.

Linear Programming. 4th ed. Saul I. Gass. (Illus.). 480p. 1975. text ed. 39.95 o.p. (ISBN 0-07-022968-6). McGraw.

Linear Programming: Algorithms & Applications. S. Vajda. 1981. pap. 12.95x o.p. (ISBN 0-412-16430-2, NO. 2231, Pub. by Chapman & Hall). Routledge Chapman & Hall.

Linear Systems. Ralph Schwarz & B. Friedland. (Electronic & Electrical Engineering Ser.). 1965. text ed. 49.95 o.p. (ISBN 0-07-055778-0). McGraw.

Linear Systems Analysis. Chung L. Liu & J. W. Liu. (Illus.). 416p. 1975. text ed. 44.00 o.p. (ISBN 0-07-038120-8). McGraw.

Linear Systems of Ordinary Differential Equations. Nikolai P. Erugin. (Mathematics in Science & Engineering: Vol. 28). 1966. 84.50 o.p. (ISBN 0-12-241850-6). Acad Pr.

Linear Topological Spaces. J. Kelly & I. Namioka LC 75-41498. (Graduate Texts in Mathematics: Vol. 36). 270p. 1976. 22.00 o.p. (ISBN 0-387-90169-8). Springer-Verlag.

Linearized Analysis of One-Dimensional Magnetohydrodynamic Flows. Roy M. Gundersen. (Springer Tracts in Natural Philosophy: Vol. 1). (Illus.). 1965. 21.00 o.p. (ISBN 0-387-03216-9). Springer-Verlag.

Lineman's & Cableman's Handbook. 6th ed. Edwin B. Kurtz & Thomas M. Shoemaker. 768p. 1982. text ed. 61.00 o.p. (ISBN 0-07-035678-5). McGraw.

Liner Shipping Conferences: An Annotated Bibliography. Charles H. MacKenzie et al. LC 84-47869. (Dalhousie Ocean Studies Programme Bk.). 160p. 1984. 29.00x o.p. (ISBN 0-669-08660-6). Lexington Bks.

Lines & Shadows. Joseph Wambaugh. LC 83-13313. 383p. 1984. 15.95 o.p. (ISBN 0-688-02619-2). Morrow.

Lines from Beyond. Verna S. Winstead. 64p. 1984. 8.00 o.p. (ISBN 0-682-40191-9). Exposition-Phoenix.

Lines from the O. U. Mathematics Letter. Ed. by Josephine P. Andree. Incl. Vol. 1. Number Extensions. pap. 1.60 o.p. (ISBN 0-685-39271-6); Vol. 2. Theory of Games. pap. 0.95 o.p. (ISBN 0-685-39272-4); Vol. 3. Geometric Extensions. pap. 1.60 o.p. (ISBN 0-685-39273-2). (gr. 9-12). 1971. Vol. 1, Number Expressions, 102p, 1.60. pap. o.p. Vol. 2, Theory of Games, 42p, .95. Vol. 3, Geometric Extensions, 102p, 1.60. o.p. NCTM.

Lines of Destiny: How To Read Faces, & Hands the Chinese Way. Kwok Man Ho et al. LC 86-11838. (Illus.). 190p. 1986. 9.95 o.s.i. (ISBN 0-87773-365-1). Shambhala Pubns.

Lingering Summer. Wyn Richards. (Lythway Ser.). 208p. 1988. lib. bdg. 18.50x o.s.i. (ISBN 0-7451-0718-4, Pub. by Chivers Pr UK). G K Hall.

Linguet: Eighteenth-Century Intellectual Heretic of France. Benjamin Paskoff. 1983. 8.00 o.p. (ISBN 0-682-49961-7, University). Exposition-Phoenix.

Linguistic Approach to Buddhist Thought. Genjun H. Sasaki. x, 194p. 1986. 22.00x o.p. (ISBN 81-208-0038-9, Pub. by Motilal Banarsidass India). South Asia Bks.

Linguistic Aspects of Science. Leonard Bloomfield. (Foundations of the Unity of Science Ser: Vol. 1, No. 4). 1939. pap. text ed. 1.95x o.s.i. (ISBN 0-226-57579-9, P403, Phoen). U of Chicago Pr.

Linguistic Atlas of Scotland: Scots Section, Vol. 1. Ed. by J. Y. Mather et al. (Illus.). 429p. 1975. 128.50 o.p. (ISBN 0-85664-160-X, Pub. by Croom Helm Ltd). Routledge Chapman & Hall.

Linguistic Atlas of Scotland: Scots Section, Vol. 2. Ed. by J. Y. Mather et al. (Illus.). 292p. 1977. 128.50 o.p. (ISBN 0-85664-111-1, Pub. by Croom Helm Ltd). Routledge Chapman & Hall.

Linguistic Atlas of Scotland: Scots Section, Vol. III, Phonology. Ed. by J. Y. Mather & H. H. Speitel. LC 76-369611. (Illus.). 418p. 1986. 302.00 o.p. (ISBN 0-85664-716-0, Pub. by Croom Helm Ltd). Routledge Chapman & Hall.

Linguistic Atlas of the Upper Midwest, 3 vols. Harold B. Allen. 450p. Vol. 1, 450 p., 1973. 50.00x o.p. (ISBN 0-8166-0686-2); Vol. 2, 100p., 1975. 50.00x o.p. (ISBN 0-8166-0756-7); Vol. 3, 376p., 1976. 50.00x o.p. (ISBN 0-8166-0789-3). Gale.

Linguistic Atlas of the Upper Midwest, Vol. 1. Harold B. Allen. LC 72-96716. (Illus.). 448p. 1973. 25.00x o.p. (ISBN 0-8166-0686-2). U of Minn Pr.

Linguistic Atlas of the Upper Midwest, Vol. 2. Harold B. Allen. LC 72-96716. vi, 92p. 1975. 25.00x o.p. (ISBN 0-8166-0756-7). U of Minn Pr.

Linguistic Atlas of the Upper Midwest, Vol. 3. Harold B. Allen. LC 72-96716. (Illus.). 362p. 1976. 25.00x o.p. (ISBN 0-8166-0789-3). U of Minn Pr.

Linguistic Communication & Speech Acts. Kent Bach & Robert M. Harnish. (Illus.). 1979. text ed. 30.00x o.p. (ISBN 0-262-02136-6). MIT Pr.

Linguistic Convergence: An Ethnography of Speaking at Fort Chipewyan, Alberta. Ronald Scollon & Suzanne B. Scollon. (Language, Thought & Culture Ser.). 1979. 43.50 o.p. (ISBN 0-12-633380-7). Acad Pr.

Linguistic Diversity & Language Belief in Kenya: The Special Position of Swahili. John Rhoades. LC 77-20016. (Foreign & Comparative Studies Program, African Ser.: No. 26). 127p. 1977. pap. text ed. 6.00x o.p. (ISBN 0-915984-23-7). Syracuse U Foreign Comp.

Linguistic Ecumenism: A Barthian Road Back from Babel. William J. Ellos. LC 83-12484. 116p. (Orig.). 1983. lib. bdg. 24.75 o.p. (ISBN 0-8191-3422-8); pap. text ed. 10.00 o.p. (ISBN 0-8191-3423-6). U Pr of Amer.

Linguistic Self-Criticism see Persian Words in English.

Linguistic Structures of Native America. Harry Hoijer et al. Ed. by Cornelius Osgood. Repr. of 1946 ed. 29.00 o.p. Johnson Repr.

Linguistic Style & Persuasion. Rolph Sandell. 1977. 76.00 o.p. (ISBN 0-12-618150-0). Acad Pr.

Linguistic Theory & Structural Stylistics. Talbot J. Taylor. (Language & Communication Library: Vol. 2). 140p. 1981. 35.00 o.p. (ISBN 0-08-025821-2). Pergamon.

Linguistic Theory in America: The First Quarter Century of Transformational Generative Grammar. Frederick J. Newmeyer. LC 79-27195. 1980. 31.00 o.p. (ISBN 0-12-517150-1). Acad Pr.

Linguistic Turn: Recent Essays in Philosophical Method. Ed. by Richard Rorty. LC 67-13811. 1971. pap. 12.00x o.p. (ISBN 0-226-72566-9, P421, Phoen). U of Chicago Pr.

Linguistics. Peter H. Salus. LC 69-13632. (Speech Communication Ser). 1969. pap. write for info. o.p. (ISBN 0-02-405290-6, SC14). Macmillan.

Linguistics & Literary Theory. Karl D. Uitti. 264p. 1974. pap. text ed. 5.95x o.p. (ISBN 0-393-09293-3). Norton.

Linguistics & the Teacher. Ed. by Ronald Carter. (Language, Education & Society Ser.). 208p. (Orig.). 1983. pap. 12.95x o.p. (ISBN 0-7100-9193-1). Routledge Chapman & Hall.

Linguistics in Philosophy. Zeno Vendler. LC 67-18221. 214p. 1967. 26.50x o.p. (ISBN 0-8014-0436-3). Cornell U Pr.

Linguistics in School Programs. Ed. by Albert H. Marckwardt. LC 76-13494. (National Society for the Study of Education Yearbooks Ser: No. 69, Pt. 2). 1970. lib. bdg. 8.00x o.s.i. (ISBN 0-226-60102-1). U of Chicago Pr.

Linguistics in the Netherlands 1977-1979. Ed. by W. Zonneveld & F. Weerman. (Publications in Language Sciences: No. 1). 483p. 1980. pap. text ed. Humanities.

Linguistique-Linguistics: Catalogues et Inventaires. (Maison des Sciences de l'homme, Service d'Echange d'Information Scientifiques, Publications Serie C: No. 4). 1971. pap. 14.00 o.p. (ISBN 0-686-21807-8). Mouton.

Lining Up. Richard Howard. LC 83-45121. 88p. 1984. 13.95 o.p. (ISBN 0-689-11420-6, Atheneum); pap. 7.95 o.p. (ISBN 0-689-11421-4, Atheneum). Macmillan.

Link & the Promise. Virginia Haven. LC 83-80407. 97p. 1983. 6.95 o.p. (ISBN 0-88290-211-3). Horizon-Utah.

Link Boys. Constance Fecher. LC 75-149219. (Illus.). 192p. (gr. 4 up). 1971. 4.50 o.p. (ISBN 0-374-34497-3). FS&G.

Linked Lives. Gertrude Douglas. Ed. by Robert L. Wolff. (Victorian Fiction Ser.). 1976. Repr. of 1876 ed. lib. bdg. 73.00 o.p. (ISBN 0-8240-1537-1). Garland Pub.

Linking Developmental Assessment & Curricula: Prescriptions for Early Intervention. Stephen J. Bagnato & John T. Neisworth. LC 81-3468. 368p. 1981. text ed. 36.00 o.p. (ISBN 0-89443-367-9). Aspen Pub.

Linking Philosophy & Practice. Ed. by Sharon Merriam. LC 81-48476. (Continuing Education Ser.: No. 15). 1982. pap. text ed. 11.95x o.p. (ISBN 0-87589-889-0). Jossey-Bass.

Linking Science Education to the Rural Environment: Some Experiences. 77p. 1980. pap. 5.00 o.p. (ISBN 0-686-63001-7, UB83, UB). UNIPUB.

Linking the Human Life Issues. Ed. by F. Russell Hittinger. 233p. (Orig.). 1986. pap. 7.95 o.p. (ISBN 0-89526-801-9). Regnery Gateway.

Links. Charles Panati. 1978. 8.95 o.p. (ISBN 0-395-26293-3). HM.

Links Between Judaism & Christianity. 66-18489 ed. Samuel Umen. 168p. 1967. (ISBN 0-8022-1749-4). Philos Lib.

Links with Space. David Spangler. pap. 1.50 o.p. (ISBN 0-87516-284-3). DeVorss.

Linnaeus: Progress & Prospects in Linnaean Research. Ed. by G. Broberg. (Illus.). 318p. 1980. 49.50x o.p. (ISBN 0-913196-31-2). Hunt Inst Botanical.

Linnaeus's Oland & Gotland Journey, 1741: Casebound Edition of Biological Journal of the Linnean Society, Vol. 5, No's 1 & 2. Ed. by M. Asberg & W. T. Stern. 1974. 58.00 o.p. (ISBN 0-12-064750-8). Acad Pr.

Linotte: The Early Diary of Anais Nin 1914-1920, Vol. 1. Anais Nin. Tr. by Jean Sherman. LC 77-20314. (Illus.). 1978. 14.95 o.p. (ISBN 0-15-152488-2). HarBraceJ.

Linottes. Georges Courteline. 192p. 1966. 8.95 o.p. (ISBN 0-686-54633-4). French & Eur.

Linz Tattoo. Nicholas Guild. 352p. 1985. text ed. 16.95 o.p. (ISBN 0-07-025112-6). McGraw.

Lion & Dragon in Northern China. R. F. Johnston. 1977. 30.00x o.p. (ISBN 0-89986-002-8). Oriental Bk Store.

Lion & the Dragon. Christopher Cook. (Illus.). 192p. 1985. 30.95 o.p. (ISBN 0-241-11411-X, Pub. by Hamish Hamilton England). David & Charles.

Lion at Sea. Max Hennessy. LC 77-20779. 1978. 8.95 o.p. (ISBN 0-689-10845-1, Atheneum). Macmillan.

Lion Country. Frederick Buechner. LC 70-135569. 1971. 5.95 o.p. (ISBN 0-689-10382-4, Atheneum). Macmillan.

Lion Encyclopedia of the Bible. 2nd ed. Ed. by Pat Alexander. (Illus.). 352p. pap. write for info. o.s.i. (ISBN 0-7459-1576-0). Lion USA.

Lion in Egypt. Peter Danielson. (Children of the Lion Ser.: Bk. 4). 1985. lib. bdg. 12.95 o.p. (ISBN 0-8398-2872-1, Gregg). G K Hall.

Lion in Love. Shelagh Delaney. 104p. 1961. pap. 6.95 o.p. (ISBN 0-413-38330-X, NO. 2999). Heinemann Ed.

Lion in the Sky. Jerry Scutts. (Illus.). 152p. 1987. 19.95 o.p. (ISBN 0-85059-788-9, Pub. by PSL P Stephens). Sterling.

Lion in the Valley. Elizabeth Peters. LC 86-5968. 508p. 1986. Repr. of 1986 ed. 16.95 o.p. (ISBN 0-89621-730-2). Thorndike Pr.

Lion in the Valley: An Amelia Peabody Mystery. Elizabeth Peters. LC 85-48126. 288p. 1986. 14.95 o.p. (ISBN 0-689-11619-5, Atheneum). Macmillan.

Lion Is Down in the Dumps. Richard Hefter. LC 77-7256. (Sweet Pickles Ser.). (Illus.). (gr. k-2). 1977. 2.95 o.p. (ISBN 0-03-021441-6). H Holt & Co.

Lion of Comarre. Arthur C. Clarke. Bd. with Against the Fall of Night. LC 68-28816. 214p. 1968. 5.75 o.s.i. (ISBN 0-15-152524-2). HarBraceJ.

Lion of Freedom: Feargus O'Connor & the Chartist Movement, 1832-1842. James Epstein. (Illus.). 327p. 1982. 33.00 o.p. (ISBN 0-85664-922-8, Pub. by Croom Helm Ltd). Routledge Chapman & Hall.

Lion of the Valley: Saint Louis, Missouri. James N. Primm. LC 81-8627. (Western Urban History Ser.: Vol. III). (Illus.). 1981. 22.95 o.p. (ISBN 0-87108-546-1); pap. 16.95 o.p. (ISBN 0-87108-713-8). Pruett.

Lion on the Mountain. Paige Dixon. LC 72-75268. (Illus.). (gr. 4-6). 1972. 6.95 o.p. (ISBN 0-689-30050-6, Atheneum). Macmillan.

Lion Unannounced: Twelve Stories & a Fable. Leonard Casper. LC 75-128125. (Illus.). 228p. 1971. 15.95x o.p. (ISBN 0-87074-028-8). SMU Press.

Lionel: A Collector's Guide & History: Advertising & Art, Vol. VI. Tom McComas & James Tuohy. (Lionel Collector Ser.). (Illus.). 166p. 1982. 24.95 o.s.i. (ISBN 0-937522-02-3). TM Bks.

Lionel: A Collector's Guide & History: Standard Guage. Tom McComas & James Tuohy. (Lionel Collector's Ser.: Vol. III). (Illus.). 30.00 o.s.i. (ISBN 0-317-40987-5). TM Bks.

Lionel Richie: An Illustrated Biography. D. Nathan. 128p. 1985. pap. text ed. 9.95 o.p. (ISBN 0-07-046030-2). McGraw.

Lionors. Barbara F. Johnson. 1975. pap. 1.95 o.p. (ISBN 0-380-00408-9, 36111). Avon.

Lions Share. Jeannette Hanby. 1982. 16.45 o.p. (ISBN 0-395-32043-7). HM.

Lion's Share: A History of Arkansas Enterprises for the Blind. Roy Kumpe & Jim Lester. LC 83-61324. 1983. 11.50 o.p. (ISBN 0-914546-45-7). Rose Pub.

Lion's Tail. Douglas F. Davis. LC 79-23293. (Illus.). 32p. (gr. 2-5). 1980. 8.95 o.p. (ISBN 0-689-50153-6, Atheneum). Macmillan.

Lion's Way. Lewis Orde. LC 80-66493. 1981. 13.95 o.p. (ISBN 0-87795-268-X, Arbor Hse). Morrow.

Lipid Metabolism, Vol. 1. Ed. by Salih J. Wakil. 1970. 94.50 o.p. (ISBN 0-12-730950-0). Acad Pr.

Lipid Metabolism in Mammals, 2 vols. Ed. by Fred Snyder. Incl. Vol. 1. 420p (ISBN 0-306-35802-6); Vol. 2. 408p (ISBN 0-306-35803-4). LC 77-913. (Monographs in Lipid Research). (Illus.). 1977. 55.00x ea. o.p. (Plenum Pr). Plenum Pub.

Lipid Metabolism, Obesity & Diabetes Mellitis. Ed. by R. Levine & E. F. Pfeiffer. 1974. 28.50 o.p. (ISBN 0-12-445350-3). Acad Pr.

Lipid Pharmacology, Vol. 2. Ed. by Rodolfo Paoletti & Charles J. Gueck. 1976. 71.50 o.p. (ISBN 0-12-544952-6). Acad Pr.

Lipid Storage Diseases: Enzymatic Defects & Clinical Implications. Ed. by Joseph Bernsohn & Herbert J. Grossman. LC 70-137623. 1971. 66.00 o.p. (ISBN 0-12-092850-7). Acad Pr.

Lipids & Lipidoses. Ed. by G. Schettler. LC 65-26055. (Illus.). 1967. 81.80 o.p. (ISBN 0-387-03921-X). Springer-Verlag.

Lipoprotein Metabolism. Ed. by H. Greten. (Illus.). 180p. 1976. pap. 17.00 o.p. (ISBN 0-387-07635-2). Springer-Verlag.

Lipoprotein Metabolism & Endocrine Regulation. Ed. by L. W. Hessel & J. M. Krans. (Developments in Endocrinology: Vol. 4). 1979. 86.00 o.p. (ISBN 0-444-80102-2, Biomedical Pr). Elsevier.

Liquid Chromatography in the Biomedical Sciences: Invited Papers from the 15th International Symposium Held in Ronneby, Sweden, 18-21 June 1984. Ed. by S. Eksborg et al. 200p. 1985. pap. 28.00 o.p. (ISBN 0-08-032600-5). Pergamon.

Liquid Crystal Polymers I. Ed. by M. Gordon. (Advances in Polymer Science, Fortschritte der Hochpolymerenforschung: Vol. 59). (Illus.). 180p. 1984. 41.00 o.p. (ISBN 0-387-12818-2). Springer Verlag.

Liquid Crystal Polymers II-III. Ed. by M. Gordon & N. A. Plate. (Advances in Polymer Science Ser.: Vol. 60-61). (Illus.). 1984. 54.00 o.p. (ISBN 0-387-12994-4). Springer-Verlag.

Liquid Crystals & Ordered Fluids. Ed. by Julian Johnson & Roger Porter. Incl. Vol. 1. LC 76-110760. 494p. 1970. 85.00x (ISBN 0-306-30466-X); Vol. 2. LC 74-1269. 784p. 1974. 105.00x (ISBN 0-306-35182-X); Vol. 3. LC 74-1269. 560p. 1978. 95.00x (ISBN 0-306-35183-8). Plenum Pr). Plenum Pub.

Liquid Filtration. Ed. by Nicholas P. Cheremisinoff & David S. Azbel. LC 82-46063. (Illus.). 400p. 1983. text ed. 64.95 o.p. (ISBN 0-250-40600-4). Butterworth.

Liquid Fuels. D. A. Williams & G. Jones. 1963. pap. 9.75 o.p. (ISBN 0-08-010385-5). Pergamon.

Liquid Gas Carrier Register 1986. 21st ed. 1986. text ed. 175.00 o.p. (ISBN 0-8002-4026-X). Intl Pubns Serv.

Liquid Helium. Ed. by G. Careri. (Italian Physical Society: Course 21). 1964. 93.50 o.p. (ISBN 0-12-368821-3). Acad Pr.

Liquid Metals. Norman H. March. 1968. 41.00 o.p. (ISBN 0-08-012331-7). Pergamon.

Liquid Metals: An Introduction to the Physics & Chemistry of Metals in the Liquid State. Mitsuo Shimoji. 1978. 118.00 o.p. (ISBN 0-12-641550-1). Acad Pr.

Liquid Scintillation Counting: Recent Developments. Ed. by Philip E. Stanley & Bruce Scoggins. 1974. 63.50 o.p. (ISBN 0-12-663850-0). Acad Pr.

Liquid Scintillation: Science & Technology. Ed. by A. A. Noujaim et al. 1976. 49.50 o.p. (ISBN 0-12-522350-1). Acad Pr.

Liquid Semiconductors. Melvin Cutler. 1977. 65.00 o.p. (ISBN 0-12-196650-X). Acad Pr.

Liquified Petroleum Gas Tanker Practice. T. W. Woolcott. 125p. 1977. 35.00x o.p. Sheridan.

Liquor Offenses: Arrest Warrant Forms. University of North Carolina, Institute of Government, Chapel Hill Staff & Ann L. Sawyer. LC 84-62164. 1984. 4.00 o.p. Institute Government.

Lisa Connection. Mesa Research Staff. 1984. pap. 19.95 o.p. (ISBN 0-8359-4088-8, Reston). P-H.

Lisbon, Madrid & Costa del Sol 1987-1988. (Frommer's City Guides). 224p. 5.95 o.p. (ISBN 0-671-62339-7). Prentice Hall Pr.

Lisbon Travel Guide. (Berlitz Travel Guides). (Illus.). 1982. pap. 6.95 o.p. (ISBN 0-02-969200-8, Berlitz). Macmillan.

List of Books on the History of Industry & the Industrial Arts. John Crerar Library Staff. LC 67-14030. 1966. Repr. of 1915 ed. 46.00x o.p. (ISBN 0-8103-3104-7). Gale.

List of French Doctoral Dissertations on Africa, 1884-1961. Boston University Libraries Staff. 1970. 69.00 o.p. (ISBN 0-8161-0742-4, Hall Library). G K Hall.

List of Professional Genealogists & Related Services 1985. (Illus.). 96p. 1987. pap. text ed. 4.00 o.p. (ISBN 0-318-16977-0). Assn Prof Genealogists.

List of Proprietary Substances & Nonfood Compounds, Authorized for Use Under USDA Inspection & Grading Programs, Effective As of Jan. 1, 1987. (Agriculture Dept. Miscellaneous Publication Series 1419). 472p. 1987. pap. 22.00 o.p. (ISBN 0-318-22607-3, S/N 001-000-04491-5). USGPO.

List of Proprietary Substances & Nonfood Compounds Authorized for Use under USDA Inspection & Grading Programs, Effective As of Jan. 1, 1988. (Miscellaneous Publication Ser.: No. 1419). 478p. 1988. pap. 22.00 o.p. (S/N 001-000-04513-0). USGPO.

List of Standard Abbreviations, (Symbols) for Synthetic Polymers & Polymeric Materials: Basic Definitions of Terms Relating to Polymers. new ed. Ed. by K. L. Loening. 1978. pap. 35.00 o.p. (ISBN 0-08-022371-0). Pergamon.

Listen, Children, Listen: An Anthology of Poems for the Very Young. Ed. by Myra C. Livingston. LC 70-167836. (Illus.). 96p. (gr. k-4). 1972. 9.95 o.p. (ISBN 0-15-245570-1, HJ). HarBraceJ.

Listen! Jesus Is Praying. Warren W. Wiersbe. 1982. pap. 4.95 o.p. (ISBN 0-8423-2167-5). Tyndale.

Listen! Listen! Ann Rand & Paul Rand. LC 70-91011. (Illus.). (ps-3). 1970. 5.95 o.p. (ISBN 0-15-245580-9, HJ). HarBraceJ.

Listen, Listen. Kate Wilhelm. 320p. 1981. 13.95 o.p. (ISBN 0-395-31269-8). HM.

Listen Metaphysics. Frank S. Merritt. LC 73-77404. (Illus.). 1974. (ISBN 0-8022-2118-1). Philos Lib.

Listen! Piggety Pig: A Book of Animal Noises. Harriet Ziefert. (Piggety Pig Bks.). (Illus.). (ps-k). 2.95 o.p. (ISBN 0-316-98761-1). Little.

Listen! Techniques for Improving Communication Skills. Thomas E. Anastasi, Jr. 122p. 1983. pap. 13.95 o.s.i. (ISBN 0-8436-0864-1). Van Nos Reinhold.

Listen the Lord. Seven Who Hear Staff. pap. 4.95 o.p. (ISBN 0-685-19950-9). Rydal.

Listen! The Wind. Anne M. Lindbergh. LC 38-27808. (Illus.). 1940. 9.95 o.s.i. (ISBN 0-15-152649-4). HarBraceJ.

Listen to a Shadow. Compiled by Mary Zuverink & Georgette Haskin. (Orig.). (gr. k-3). 1976. pap. 2.95 o.p. (ISBN 0-377-00046-9); 1.95 o.p. tchr's guide (ISBN 0-685-68741-4, 00047). Friendship Pr.

Listen to a Shape. Marcia Brown. (Marcia Brown Concept Library). (gr. 1-4). 1979. 4.95 o.p. (ISBN 0-531-02383-4); PLB 8.90 s&l o.p. (ISBN 0-531-02930-1). Watts.

Listen to Light: Haiku. Raymond Roseliep. LC 80-39854. (Illus.). 128p. 1980. 10.00x o.p. (ISBN 0-934184-05-4); pap. 5.00 o.p. (ISBN 0-934184-06-2). Alembic Pr.

Listen to the Children. Harlem Youth Group Staff. 1985. 5.95 o.p. (ISBN 0-8062-2446-0). Carlton.

Listen to Your Body: A Gynecologist Answers Women's Most Intimate Questions. Niels Lauersen & Eileen Stukane. LC 82-16989. 540p. (Orig.). 1986. pap. 9.50 o.p. (ISBN 0-671-43648-1, Fireside). S&S.

Listen to Yourself; Think Everything Over, Vol 1. Tripitaka Master Hua. Tr. by Buddhist Text Translation Society Staff. (Illus.). 153p. (Orig.). 1978. pap. 7.00 o.p. (ISBN 0-917512-24-3). Buddhist Text.

Listeners. James E. Gunn. 240p. 1985. pap. 2.95 o.s.i. (ISBN 0-345-30036-X, Del Rey). Ballantine.

Listening. Norman Wakefield. 120p. 1981. pap. 6.95 o.p. (ISBN 0-8499-2920-2). Word Bks.

Listening. 2nd ed. Andrew D. Wolvin & Carolyn G. Coakley. 352p. 1985. pap. text ed. write for info. o.p. (ISBN 0-697-00286-1); write for info. instr's manual o.p. (ISBN 0-697-00524-0). Wm C Brown.

Listening: A Programmed Approach. 2nd ed. E. A. Erway. 1979. pap. text ed. 21.95 o.p. (ISBN 0-07-019660-5). McGraw.

Listening Comprehension Group Test: Examiner's Test Manual. Donna Ilyin. (Listening Comprehension Group Test Ser.). 32p. 1981. pap. text ed. 5.50 o.p. (ISBN 0-88377-212-4); LCWT answer sheets (50) 6.50 o.p. (ISBN 0-88377-214-0); keys LCPT 6.50 o.p. (ISBN 0-88377-213-2). Newbury Hse.

Listening Heart. Joyce M. Smith. 1981. pap. 2.95 o.p. (ISBN 0-8423-2375-9). Tyndale.

Listening: It Can Change Your Life. Lyman K. Steil et al. 1985. pap. text ed. 6.95 o.p. (ISBN 0-07-060937-3). McGraw.

Listening Made Easy: How to Improve Listening on the Job, at Home & in the Community. Robert L. Montgomery. 128p. 1981. 11.95 o.p. (ISBN 0-8144-5650-2). AMACOM.

Listening to America. Stuart B. Flexner. 1982. 24.00 o.p. (ISBN 0-671-24895-2). S&S.

Listening to America: An Illustrated History of Words & Phrases from Our Lively & Splendid Past. Stuart B. Flexner. 592p. 1984. pap. 13.95 o.p. (ISBN 0-671-52798-3, Touchstone Bks). S&S.

Listening to Life. Ray Owen. Ed. by Mary Penoi & Kay Condit. 124p. (Orig.). 1987. pap. 5.95 o.p. (ISBN 0-942316-14-2). Pueblo Pub Pr.

Listening to Music. rev. ed. Douglas Moore. (Illus.). 1963. pap. 5.45 o.p. (ISBN 0-393-00130-X, Norton Lib). Norton.

Listening to Our Bodies: The Rebirth of Feminine Wisdom. Stephanie Demetrakopoulos. LC 81-70489. 256p. 1983. 16.95x o.p. (ISBN 0-8070-6704-0). Beacon Pr.

Listening Valley. D. E. Stevenson. LC 77-71379. 1978. 7.95x o.s.i. (ISBN 0-03-020446-1). H Holt & Co.

Listening Walls. Margaret Millar. 1975. pap. 1.25 o.p. (ISBN 0-380-00414-3, 25536). Avon.

Listing of Cartoons on Architectural Subjects Within Selected Anthologies, Including Brief Descriptions with Subject & Building Type Indexing. Carole Cable. (Architecture Ser.: A 1482). 13p. 1985. 2.00 o.p. (ISBN 0-89028-612-4). Vance Biblios.

Listing of Service Companies: The Conference of Franchise Suppliers Registry. 31p. 1987. 2.95 o.p. (ISBN 0-317-66123-X). Intl Franchise Assn.

Liszt. Sacheverell Sitwell. (Illus.). 400p. 1956. (ISBN 0-8022-1580-7). Philos Lib.

Litany of Friends: New & Selected Poems. Dudley Randall. LC 80-85234. 101p. 1981. 10.00 o.p. (ISBN 0-916418-33-2); pap. 6.00 o.p. (ISBN 0-916418-29-4). Lotus.

Lite Flight. Christine Sprenger et al. 1984. IBM. 19.50x o.p. (ISBN 0-256-03150-9); Apple. 19.50 o.p. (ISBN 0-256-03151-7). Irwin.

Liter. William J. Shimek. LC 74-11895. (Early Metric Ser.). (Illus.). 32p. (gr. 2-5). 1975. PLB 4.95 o.p. (ISBN 0-8225-0587-8). Lerner Pubns.

Literacy As a Human Problem. Ed. by James C. Raymond. LC 81-19757. xi, 206p. 1982. 16.50 o.p. (ISBN 0-8173-0108-9); pap. 8.95 o.p. (ISBN 0-8173-0110-0). U of Ala Pr.

Literal Interpretation of the Bible. Paul L. Tan. 114p. 1979. pap. 3.95 o.p. (ISBN 0-88469-098-9). BMH Bks.

Literarische Mord. Fritz Woelcken. Ed. by E. F. Bleiler. LC 78-60827. (Fiction of Popular Culture Ser.: Vol. 19). 1979. lib. bdg. 46.00 o.p. (ISBN 0-8240-9649-5). Garland Pub.

Literarische Polemik zu Beginn des grossen Abendlaendischen Schismas. Franz P. Bliemetzrieder. (Illus.). 14.00 o.p. (ISBN 0-384-04715-7). Johnson Repr.

Literary Art of Edward Gibbon. Harold L. Bond. LC 75-4977. 167p. 1975. Repr. of 1960 ed. lib. bdg. 22.50x o.p. (ISBN 0-8371-8050-3, BOLA). Greenwood.

Literary Atlas & Gazetteer of the British Isles. Michael Hardwick. LC 73-7185. (Illus.). 216p. 1973. 40.00x o.p. (ISBN 0-8103-2004-5). Gale.

Literary Blunders. Henry B. Wheatley. LC 68-30616. 240p. 1969. Repr. of 1893 ed. 34.00x o.p. (ISBN 0-8103-3317-1). Gale.

Literary Britain & Ireland. Ian Ousby. (Blue Guides Ser.). (Illus.). 462p. 1985. pap. 14.95 o.p. (ISBN 0-393-30077-3). Norton.

Literary Criticism for New Testament Critics. Norman R. Petersen. Ed. by Dan O. Via, Jr. LC 77-15241. (Guides to Biblical Scholarship: New Testament Ser.). 96p. (Orig.). 1978. pap. 4.50 o.p. (ISBN 0-8006-0465-2, 1-465, Fortress). Augsburg Fortress.

Literary Criticism of D. H. Lawrence. Tajindar Singh. 167p. 1984. text ed. 18.95x o.p. (ISBN 0-86590-270-4, Pub. by Sterling Pubs India). Apt Bks.

Literary Criticism of the New Testament. William A. Beardslee. Ed. by Dan O. Via, Jr. LC 77-94817. (Guides to Biblical Scholarship: New Testament Ser.). 96p. (Orig.). 1970. pap. 4.50 o.p. (ISBN 0-8006-0185-8, 1-185, Fortress). Augsburg Fortress.

Literary Dissent in Communist China. Merle R. Goldman. LC 67-17311. 1971. pap. text ed. 3.75x o.s.i. (ISBN 0-689-70260-4, 168, Atheneum). Macmillan.

Literary Dublin: A History. Herbert A. Kenny. LC 72-6626. (Illus.). 1974. 12.00 o.s.i. (ISBN 0-8008-4921-3). Taplinger.

Literary Enterprise in Eighteenth Century France. Remy G. Saisselin. LC 78-112530. 208p. 1979. 21.50x o.p. (ISBN 0-8143-1618-2). Wayne St U Pr.

Literary Essays. Daiches. 225p. 1957. (ISBN 0-8022-0335-3). Philos Lib.

Literary Forgeries. James A. Farrer. LC 68-23156. 308p. 1969. Repr. of 1907 ed. 30.00x o.p. (ISBN 0-8103-3305-8). Gale.

Literary Guide to Ireland. Susan Cahill & Thomas Cahill. 352p. 1979. 13.95 o.p. (ISBN 0-905473-35-3, Pub. by Wolfhound Pr Ireland); pap. 5.95 o.p. (ISBN 0-905473-36-1, Pub. by Wolfhound Pr Ireland). Irish Bks Media.

Literary History of Philadelphia. Ellis P. Oberholtzer. LC 72-81510. 454p. 1969. Repr. of 1906 ed. 48.00x o.p. (ISBN 0-8103-3563-8). Gale.

Literary Impact of the Authorized Version. C. S. Lewis. Ed. by John Reumann. LC 63-17883. (Facet Bks). 48p. (Orig.). 1963. pap. 2.50 o.p. (ISBN 0-8006-3003-3, 1-3003, Fortress). Augsburg Fortress.

Literary Legacy of C. S. Lewis. Chad Walsh. 1979. 10.95 o.p. (ISBN 0-15-152725-3). HarBraceJ.

Literary Lodgings. Elaine Borish. 1984. 22.00x o.p. (ISBN 0-09-465180-9, Pub. by Constable Pubs UK). Trans-Atl Phila.

Literary Manuscripts of Harold Frederic: A Catalogue. Noel Polk. LC 79-17452. 123p. 1980. lib. bdg. 28.00 o.p. (ISBN 0-8240-9544-8). Garland Pub.

Literary Market Place, 1988. Ed. by Bowker, R. R., Staff. 1181p. 1987. pap. 85.00 o.p. (ISBN 0-8352-2391-4). Bowker.

Literary San Francisco: A Pictoral History from the Beginnings to the Present. Lawrence Ferlinghetti & Nancy J. Peters. LC 79-3598. 224p. 1981. pap. 9.57 o.p. (ISBN 0-06-250326-X, CN4016). HarpR.

Literary Style & Music. Herbert Spencer. 1951. (ISBN 0-8022-1616-1). Philos Lib.

Literate Revolution in Greece & Its Cultural Consequences. Eric A. Havelock. LC 81-47133. 328p. 1982. 29.00 o.p. (ISBN 0-691-09396-2); pap. 12.95 o.p. (ISBN 0-691-00026-3). Princeton U Pr.

Literature: A College Anthology. Patrick W. Shaw. LC 76-19905. (Illus.). 1977. text ed. 21.95 o.p. (ISBN 0-395-24841-8). HM.

Literature & Ideas in America: Essays in Memory of Harry Hayden Clark. Ed. by Robert Falk. xi, 243p. 1975. 15.00x o.p. (ISBN 0-8214-0180-7). Ohio U Pr.

Literature & Method: Towards a Critique of I. A. Richards, T. S. Eliot & F. R. Leavis. Pamela McCallum. (Literature & Society Ser.). 288p. 1982. text ed. 45.00x o.p. (ISBN 0-391-02795-6). Humanities.

Literature & National Identity: Nineteenth-Century Russian Critical Essays. Ed. by Paul Debreczeny & Jesse Zeldin. LC 77-109598. xxvi, 188p. 1970. 17.95x o.p. (ISBN 0-8032-0748-4). U of Nebr Pr.

Literature & Philosophy: An Analysis of the Philosophical Novel. Stephen D. Ross. LC 69-11284. (Century Philosophy Ser.). (Orig.). 1969. pap. text ed. 12.95x o.p. (ISBN 0-89197-278-1). Irvington.

Literature & the Child. Bernice E. Cullinan et al. 594p. 1981. text ed. 26.00 net o.p. (ISBN 0-15-551110-6, HC). HarBraceJ.

Literature & the Left in France. J. E. Flower. 240p. 1985. pap. text ed. 11.95 o.p. (ISBN 0-416-39640-2, 9488). Routledge Chapman & Hall.

Literature & the Social Order in Eighteenth Century England. Stephen Copley. LC 84-14940. (World & Word Ser.). 204p. 1984. 31.00 o.p. (ISBN 0-7099-0755-9, Pub. by Croom Helm Ltd); pap. 15.50 o.p. (ISBN 0-7099-3400-9). Routledge Chapman & Hall.

Literature as Social Discourse: The Practice of Linguistic Criticism. Roger Fowler. LC 81-47761. 216p. 1982. 17.50x o.p. (ISBN 0-253-33511-6). Ind U Pr.

Literature del Siglo XX. 2nd ed. Ernesto G. DaCal & Margarita Ucelay. (Span.). 1968. pap. text ed. 27.95 o.p. (ISBN 0-03-055585-X). HR&W.

Literature for Composition: Essays, Fiction, Poetry, & Drama. Ed. by Sylvan Barnet et al. 1984. write for info. o.p. (ISBN 0-673-39188-4). Scott F.

Literature for Today's Young Adults. 2nd ed. Alleen Pace Nilsen & Kenneth L. Donelson. 1985. text ed. write for info. o.p. (ISBN 0-673-15933-7). Scott F.

Literature in Protestant England: 1560-1660. Alan Sinfield. LC 82-18408. 168p. 1983. text ed. 26.50x o.p. (ISBN 0-389-20341-6, 07185). B&N Imports.

Literature in the Marketplace. Per Gedin. LC 77-76566. 208p. 1977. 12.95 o.s.i. (ISBN 0-87951-066-8). Overlook Pr.

Literature of American Wilderness, 5 vols. 1984. Set. 19.95 o.p. (ISBN 0-87905-238-4, Peregrine Smith). Gibbs Smith Pub.

Literature of Fantasy: An Annotated Bibliography of Modern Fantasy Fiction. Roger C. Schlobin. LC 78-68287. (Garland Reference Library of the Humanities: No. 176). 1979. lib. bdg. 48.00 o.p. (ISBN 0-8240-9757-2). Garland Pub.

Literature of Slang. William J. Burke. LC 67-982. 190p. 1965. Repr. of 1939 ed. 35.00x o.p. (ISBN 0-8103-3243-4). Gale.

Literature of Sports. Tom Dodge. 1980. pap. text ed. 17.00 o.p. (ISBN 0-669-02744-8). Heath.

Literature of the American Indian. Thomas E. Sanders & Walter W. Peek. LC 72-89050. 480p. 1973. text ed. write for info. o.p. (ISBN 0-02-477640-8). Macmillan.

Literature of the American Indian. abridged ed. Thomas E. Sanders & Walter W. Peek. 1976. pap. write for info. o.p. (ISBN 0-02-477650-5). Macmillan.

Literature of the American People. Ed. by Arthur H. Quinn. 1172p. 1951. 137.50x o.p. (ISBN 0-89197-279-X). Irvington.

Literature of the American West. Ed. by J. Golden Taylor. LC 71-132448. 1971. pap. 22.95 o.p. (ISBN 0-395-05458-3). HM.

Literature of the Rebellion. John R. Bartlett. LC 77-109311. 1970. Repr. of 1866 ed. 35.00x o.p. (ISBN 0-8371-3568-0, BLR&, Pub. by Negro U Pr). Greenwood.

Literature of Unemployment: A Checklist, 1980-1984. Dale E. Casper. (Public Administration Ser.: P 1810). 12p. 1985. 2.00 o.p. (ISBN 0-89028-640-X). Vance Biblios.

Literature: Structure, Sound & Sense. 2nd ed. Laurence Perrine. 1450p. 1974. text ed. 15.95 o.p. (ISBN 0-15-551102-5, HC). HarBraceJ.

Literature: Structure, Sound & Sense. 3rd ed. Laurence Perrine. 1525p. 1978. text ed. 16.95 o.p. (ISBN 0-15-551104-1, HC). HarBraceJ.

Literature: Structure, Sound & Sense. 4th ed. Laurence Perrine & Thomas R. Arp. 1492p. 1983. text ed. 20.00 o.p. (ISBN 0-15-551106-8, HC). HarBraceJ.

Literature Through Performance: "Shakespeare's Mirror" & "A Canterbury Caper" Katherine H. Burkman. LC 76-25615. (Illus.). xxviii, 104p. 1978. 10.00x o.p. (ISBN 0-8214-0365-6); pap. 3.95x o.p. (ISBN 0-8214-0384-2). Ohio U Pr.

Literatures of the World in English. Ed. by Bruce King. 238p. 1985. pap. 9.95x o.p. (ISBN 0-7100-7903-6). Routledge Chapman & Hall.

Lithium Research & Therapy. F. N. Johnson. 1975. 89.00 o.p. (ISBN 0-12-386550-6). Acad Pr.

Lithium Treatment of Manic-Depressive Illness. M. Schou. (Illus.). x, 50p. 1985. pap. 10.00 o.p. (ISBN 3-8055-4255-0). S Karger.

Lithographers Manual. 7th ed. LC 83-80279. (Illus.). 590p. 1983. 54.50 o.p. (ISBN 0-88362-048-0, 1407). Graphic Arts Tech Found.

Lithographic Pressman's Handbook. 2nd ed. Abrahim Lavi & George W. Jorgensen. LC 77-4641. (Illus.). 168p. 1977. 48.00 o.p. (ISBN 0-88362-016-2, 1524). Graphic Arts Tech Found.

Lithographic Presswork. A. S. Porter. (Illus.). 320p. 1980. 40.00 o.p. (ISBN 0-88362-060-X, 1511). Graphic Arts Tech Found.

Lithographs of Thomas Hart Benton. new ed. Ed. by Creekmore Fath. LC 78-70912. (Illus.). 245p. 1979. 35.00 o.p. (ISBN 0-292-74621-0). U of Tex Pr.

Titles

Lithography & Silkscreen Art & Technique. Fritz Eichenberg. (Illus.). 154p. pap. 25.00 o.p. (ISBN 0-317-54921-9). Apollo.
Lithuania Calling Collect: An Exploration of the Roads to Love. Elbert Rynberg. 160p. 1983. 8.50 o.p. (ISBN 0-682-49970-6). Exposition-Phoenix.
Lithuania: Encyclopedic Survey. J. Zinkus. 432p. 1988. 13.95 o.s.i. (ISBN 0-8285-3796-8, Pub. by Encyclopedia Pubs USSR). Imported Pubns.
Lithuanian Cemetery. Ed. by A. Kezys. LC 75-21496. 1977. 19.95 o.p. (ISBN 0-8294-0279-9). Loyola.
Lithuanian Dialectology. Alfred Senn. pap. 8.00 o.p. (ISBN 0-384-54870-9). Johnson Repr.
Litigating Copyright, Trademark, & Unfair Competition Cases 1985. 442p. 1985. 15.00 o.p. (H4-4979). PLI.
Litigating International Law. Anthony D'Amato. 240p. lib. bdg. cancelled o.s.i. (ISBN 0-941320-40-5). Transnatl Pubs.
Litigating Medical Malpractice Claims: ALI-ABA Course of Study Materials. Massachusetts Continuing Legal Education-New England Law Institute, Inc. Staff & American Law Institute-American Bar Association Committee on Continuing Professional Education. LC 85-62205. Date not set. price not set o.p. Am Law Inst.
Litigating Psychological Injury Claims. Eric H. Marcus & William A. Barton. 190p. 1988. 35.00 o.p. PES Inc WI.
Litigation Management. 1984. (ISBN 0-88129-149-8). Wash Bar CLE.
Litigation Strategies in Draft Resistance Cases. 6.00 o.p. Natl Lawyers Guild.
Litigation Under the Federal Freedom of Informaton Act & Privacy Act: 1987. 12th ed. Ed. by Allan Adler. 376p. 1987. pap. 40.00 o.p. (ISBN 0-86566-041-7). ACLU DC.
Lito the Shoeshine Boy. David Mangurian. LC 74-26826. (Illus.). 64p. (gr. 3 up). 1975. 8.95 o.s.i. (ISBN 0-02-762250-9, Four Winds). Macmillan.
Litter Abatement Measures. James E. Kundell. 74p. (Orig.). 1979. pap. 3.25 o.p. (ISBN 0-89854-062-3). U of GA Inst Govt.
Little Al's Beautiful Dream. Ines Warren. (Illus.). 57p. (gr. 2 up). 1985. 5.95 o.p. (ISBN 0-533-06261-6). Vantage.
Little America. Rob Swigart. 1977. 7.95 o.p. (ISBN 0-395-25172-9); pap. 3.95 o.p. (ISBN 0-395-25443-4). HM.
Little Angel Who Would Not Obey. Eleanor S. Thompson. (Illus.). (ps-3). 1979. 4.50 o.p. (ISBN 0-682-49250-7). Exposition-Phoenix.
Little Angel with the Pink Wings. Venzi. (gr. 2-3). plastic bdg. 2.00 o.s.i. (ISBN 0-8198-0077-5); pap. 1.25 o.s.i. (ISBN 0-8198-0078-3). Dghtrs St Paul.
Little Anthology of Modern Irish Verse. Compiled by Lennox Robinson. 52p. 1971. Repr. of 1928 ed. 15.00x o.p. (ISBN 0-7165-1368-4, BBA 02078, Pub. by Cuala Press Ireland). Biblio Dist.
Little Ark. Jan De Hartog. LC 53-11959. (Illus.). 1970. Repr. of 1953 ed. 5.95 o.p. (ISBN 0-689-10373-5, Atheneum). Macmillan.
Little Baby Carriage: Baby's Toys, Baby's Family, Going to Bed. Suzanne Green. (Little Bookmobile Ser.). (Illus.). 14p. (ps). 1987. 8.95 o.p. (ISBN 0-385-23929-7). Doubleday.
Little Big Man. Thomas Berger. 448p. 1981. pap. 3.75 o.p. (ISBN 0-449-23854-7, Crest). Fawcett.
Little Big Rig. Illus. by Marc Arceneaux. (Beep Beep Board Bks.). (Illus.). 14p. 1984. 2.85 o.s.i. (ISBN 0-671-47339-5, Little Simon). S&S.
Little Birds, Big Birds. (Animals & Their Babies Ser.). (Illus.). 32p. (ps-3). 1987. pap. 5.95 o.s.i. (ISBN 0-671-63491-7, Little Simon). S&S.
Little Birds: Erotica. Anais Nin. LC 78-22267. 1979. 8.95 o.s.i. (ISBN 0-15-152761-X). HarBraceJ.
Little Birds: Erotica. Anais Nin. 168p. 1986. pap. 4.95 o.p. (ISBN 0-15-652798-7, Harv). HarBraceJ.
Little Bit Different. St. John's Episcopal Church Staff & Michel Deloache. 296p. 1975. pap. 9.50 o.p. (ISBN 0-939114-61-5). Wimmer Bks.
Little Black Book of Atomic War. Marc I. Barasch. (Illus.). 112p. (Orig.). 1983. pap. 3.95 o.p. (ISBN 0-440-54703-2, Dell Trade Pbks). Dell.
Little Black Fish. Samuel Bahrang. LC 74-128812. (Illus.). (gr. k-4). 1971. PLB 3.95 o.p. (ISBN 0-87614-013-4). Carolrhoda Bks.
Little Blue Brontosaurus. Byron Preiss & William Stout. LC 83-7424. (Illus.). 48p. (ps-3). PLB 10.45 o.s.i. Caedmon.
Little Blue Heaven. Hertha Dial & Catherine Richter. 1972. 4.50 o.p. (ISBN 0-87516-111-1). DeVorss.
Little Boat. Michel Gay. LC 84-42985. (Illus.). 32p. (ps-k). 1985. bds. 3.95 o.s.i. (ISBN 0-02-737550-1); PLB 7.95 o.s.i. (ISBN 0-02-737540-4). Macmillan.
Little Book Cliff Railway: The Life & Times of a Colorado Narrow Gauge. Robert W. McLeod & Lyndon J. Lampert. LC 82-20485. 1984. 24.95 o.p. (ISBN 0-87108-638-7). Pruett.
Little Book of Computer Music Instruments. Dexter Morrill. Date not set. price not set o.p. W Kaufmann.
Little Book of Famous Insults. 1964. 5.95 o.p. (ISBN 0-88088-366-9). Peter Pauper.
Little Book of Inspiration: Seven Famous Classics, 1 vol. 290p. Date not set. pap. (ISBN 0-87983-424-2). Keats.
Little Boy Who Loved Dirt & Almost Became a Superslob. Judith Vigna. LC 74-14519. (Illus.). 32p. (ps-1). 1975. PLB 11.25 o.p. (ISBN 0-8075-0865-9). A Whitman.
Little Britches. Ralph Moody. (Illus.). (gr. 10 up). 1962. 10.95 o.p. (ISBN 0-393-07421-8). Norton.
Little Brother & Little Sister. Barbara Cooney. LC 81-43058. (Illus.). 48p. (gr. 2-3). 1982. pap. 10.95 o.p. (ISBN 0-385-14584-5). Doubleday.
Little, Brown Handbook. 3rd ed. Little, Brown Editors & H. Ramsey Fowler. 1986. text ed. write for info. o.p. (ISBN 0-673-39209-0); write for info. o.p. (ISBN 0-673-39210-4). Scott F.
Little, Brown Reader. 4th ed. Ed. by Marcia Stubbs & Sylvan Barnet. 1986. pap. text ed. (ISBN 0-673-39239-2). Scott F.
Little Brute Family. Russell Hoban. (Snuggle & Read Story Bks.). (Illus.). 32p. (ps-2). 1980. pap. 2.25 o.p. (ISBN 0-380-51151-7, 63792-8, Camelot). Avon.
Little Brute Family. Russell Hoban. LC 66-16102. (Illus.). 32p. (gr. k-2). 1966. 9.95 o.s.i. (ISBN 0-02-744110-5). Macmillan.
Little Bulldog. Mimi Skandalakis. (Illus.). 304p. (ps-2). 1986. 24.95 o.p.; pap. 5.00 o.s.i. (ISBN 0-935265-09-0). Agee Pub.
Little Cement Mixer. Illus. by Marc Arceneaux. (Beep Beep Board Bks.). (Illus.). 14p. 1984. 2.85 o.s.i. (ISBN 0-671-47340-9, Little Simon). S&S.
Little Chen & the Dragon Brothers. 1980. pap. 2.50 o.p. (ISBN 0-8351-0731-0). China Bks.
Little Clay Hut. 78p. 1975. 2.95 o.p. (ISBN 0-8285-1186-1, Pub. by Progress Pubs USSR). Imported Pubns.
Little Community. Robert Redfield. Bd. with Peasant Society & Culture. 266p. 1960. pap. text ed. 5.00x o.s.i. (ISBN 0-226-70664-8, P53, Phoen). U of Chicago Pr.
Little Critics: Essays, Satires & Sketches on China. Yu-T'Ang Lin. LC 79-2831. (First Series: 1930-1932). 299p. 1988. Repr. of 1939 ed. 28.00 o.p. Hyperion Conn.
Little Critics: Essays, Satires, Sketches on China. Yu-T'Ang Lin. LC 79-2832. (Second Series: 1933-1935). 258p. 1988. Repr. of 1939 ed. 26.00 o.p. Hyperion Conn.
Little Destiny. Vera Cleaver & Bill Cleaver. LC 79-10322. (gr. 5 up). 1979. 11.75 o.p. (ISBN 0-688-41904-6); PLB 11.88 o.p. (ISBN 0-688-51904-0). Lothrop.
Little Doctor. Georges Simenon. Tr. by Jean Stewart from Fr. LC 80-7942. (Helen & Kurt Wolff Bk.). 1981. 10.95 o.p. (ISBN 0-15-152768-7). HarBraceJ.
Little Drummer Boy. Ezra J. Keats. LC 68-25714. (gr. k-3). 1972. pap. 4.95 o.s.i. (ISBN 0-02-044090-1, Collier). Macmillan.
Little Eva, Baby Doll, & Blondy Ryan: Sports Trivia, Nicknames & Real First Names, Bk. I. Vic Maestri. (Orig.). pap. 4.50 o.p. (ISBN 0-682-49710-X). Exposition-Phoenix.
Little Fellow. Peter Coates & Thelms Niklaus. (ISBN 0-8022-0307-8). Philos Lib.
Little Fellow: The Life & Work of Charles Chaplin. Peter Cotes & Thelma Niklaus. 1966. pap. 1.95 o.p. (ISBN 0-8065-0104-9, 204, Pub. by Citadel Pr). Carol Pub Group.
Little Fire Engine. Illus. by Marc Arceneaux. (Beep Beep Board Bks.). (Illus.). 14p. 1984. 2.85 o.s.i. (ISBN 0-671-47338-7, Little Simon). S&S.
Little Fishes. Erik C. Haugaard. (Illus.). (gr. 6-8). 1967. 6.95 o.p. (ISBN 0-395-06802-9). HM.
Little Fly. Marilyn Davis. (Illus.). (ps-2). 1977. pap. 3.00 o.p. (ISBN 0-682-48739-2). Exposition-Phoenix.
Little Forecaster. Mary H. Ellyson. 64p. 1986. 6.95 o.p. (ISBN 0-8062-2876-8). Carlton.
Little French Pantry. The Vaness-Ann Collection Staff. Ed. by Margaret Marti. (Illus.). 96p. 1983. pap. text ed. 8.95 o.p. (ISBN 0-686-88958-4). Vanessa-Ann Collec.
Little Frog Flies & Falls. 1986. 1.50 o.p. (ISBN 0-8351-1708-1). China Bks.
Little Fur in the Meringue Never Really Hurts the Filling. Cherie Blanton. 6.00 o.p. (ISBN 0-918544-90-4). Wimmer Bks.
Little Garbage Truck. Illus. by Marc Arceneaux. (Beep Beep Board Bks.). (Illus.). 14p. 1984. 2.85 o.s.i. (ISBN 0-671-47341-7, Little Simon). S&S.
Little Giant: The Life of I. K. Brunel, A Novel. Alan Buck. 320p. 1986. 32.95 o.p. (ISBN 0-7153-8793-6). David & Charles.
Little Girl Lost. Lee Templeton. 82p. (gr. 4-9). 1983. 6.95 o.p. (ISBN 0-89015-368-X). Eakin Pr.
Little Green Monster: Story Book For Young Children in Sign Language. Sue Johnson. (Talking Fingers Bks.). (Illus.). 36p. 1985. pap. 4.25 o.p. (ISBN 0-317-42758-X). Modern Signs.
Little Hatchy Hen. James Flora. LC 69-18624. (Illus.). (gr. 1-4). 1969. 7.95 o.p. (ISBN 0-15-245765-8, HJ). HarBraceJ.
Little Hill. Harry Behn. LC 49-10198. (Illus.). (gr. k-3). 1949. 4.50 o.p. (ISBN 0-15-245966-9, HJ). HarBraceJ.
Little Hotel. Christina Stead. 1980. pap. 2.50 o.p. (ISBN 0-380-48389-0, 48389, Bard). Avon.
Little House. (Fun Time Pop-Up Ser.). (Illus.). (ps-1). 2.49 o.p. (ISBN 0-517-48303-3); pap. 2.49 o.p. (ISBN 0-517-46820-4). Outlet Bk Co.
Little Humpbacked Horse. P. Yershov. 104p. 1980. 4.45 o.p. (ISBN 0-8285-1189-6, Pub. by Progress Pubs USSR). Imported Pubns.
Little Igloo. Lorraine Beim & Jerrold Beim. LC 41-15460. (Illus.). (ps-3). 1941. 5.95 o.p. (ISBN 0-15-246145-0, HJ). HarBraceJ.
Little Inventions That Made Big Money: Children's Version. Richard E. Paige. 100p. 3.50 o.p. (ISBN 0-318-16900-2). Mindsight Pub.
Little Joe's Italian Cookbook: Specialty Recipes from San Francisco's Favorite North Beach Restaurant. Franco Montarello. LC 85-7063. (Illus.). 128p. (Orig.). 1985. pap. 7.95 o.p. (ISBN 0-87701-356-X). Chronicle Bks.
Little Kid's Craft Book. Jackie Vermeer & Marian Lariviere. (Illus.). 128p. (gr. 3-6). 1981. pap. 3.45 o.p. (ISBN 0-380-00147-0, 20990). Avon.
Little League Baseball Leader. S. C. Lee. LC 74-77738. (Super Star Ser.). 1974. 4.95 o.p. (ISBN 0-87397-046-2). Strode.
Little Leftover Witch. Florence Laughlin. LC 60-11815. (Illus.). 116p. (gr. 2-5). 1971. 10.95 o.s.i. (ISBN 0-02-754560-1); pap. 2.95x o.s.i. (ISBN 0-02-044300-5). Macmillan.
Little Leftover Witch. Florence Laughlin. LC 60-11815. (Illus.). (gr. 2-5). 1973. pap. 3.95 o.s.i. (ISBN 0-02-044180-0, Collier). Macmillan.
Little Lives. John H. Spyker. 1980. pap. 2.25 o.p. (ISBN 0-380-48322-X, 48322). Avon.
Little Local Murder. Robert Banard. (Nightingale Large Print Ser.). 1985. pap. 9.95 o.p. (ISBN 0-8161-3798-6, Large Print Bks). G K Hall.
Little Local Murder. Robert Barnard. 192p. 1983. 11.95 o.s.i. (ISBN 0-684-17882-6, ScribT). Scribner.
Little Luv Angel. Toby Bluth. (Illus.). 48p. (gr. k-6). 1985. 5.95 o.p. (ISBN 0-8249-8093-X). Ideals.
Little Mermaid. (ps). 1985. 1.95 o.s.i. (ISBN 0-671-55663-0, Little Simon). S&S.
Little Millard Mustardseed. Darrell Nelson. LC 78-72834. (Illus.). (gr. k-3). 1979. pap. 2.95 o.p. (ISBN 0-89191-063-8). Cook.
Little Miss Helpful Plans a Party: A Pop-Up Book. Roger Hargreaves. (Mr. Men & Little Miss Pop-Up Bks.). 12p. (ps-k). 1983. pop-up 4.95 o.s.i. (ISBN 0-8431-0833-9). Price Stern.
Little Moscows: Communism & Working Class Militancy in Inter-War Britain. Stuart Macintyre. 216p. 1980. 30.00 o.p. (ISBN 0-7099-0083-X, Pub. by Croom Helm Ltd). Routledge Chapman & Hall.
Little Mouse ABC. Katherine Holabird & Linda Craig. (Little Mouse Learning Bks.). (Illus.). 32p. 1983. 4.80 o.s.i. (ISBN 0-671-47733-1, Little Simon). S&S.
Little Mouse on the Prairie. Stephen Cosgrove. Ed. by Mary H. Manoni. (Serendipity Book Cassettes). (Illus.). (gr. 1-3). 1979. pap. text ed. 24.95 o.p. (ISBN 0-89290-068-7). Soc for Visual.
Little Mouse One Two Three. Katherine Holabird. (Little Mouse Learning Bks.). (Illus.). 32p. 1983. 4.80 o.s.i. (ISBN 0-671-47732-3, Little Simon). S&S.
Little Nasty. Ruth Tomalin. (Illus.). 79p. (gr. 2-5). 1985. 10.95 o.p. (ISBN 0-571-13420-3). Faber & Faber.
Little Novels of Sicily. Giovanni Verga. Tr. by D. H. Lawrence. LC 75-11483. 226p. 1975. Repr. of 1953 ed. lib. bdg. 22.50x o.p. (ISBN 0-8371-8199-2, VENS). Greenwood.
Little Nursery Rhymes. Zokeisha. (Puppet Story Board Bks.). (Illus.). 12p. (ps-2). 1981. 2.95 o.s.i. (ISBN 0-671-42642-7, Little Simon). S&S.
Little Octopus. (ps). 1985. 1.95 o.s.i. (ISBN 0-671-55662-2, Little Simon). S&S.
Little Oleg. Margaret Cort. LC 77-103606. (Illus.). (gr. k-4). 1971. PLB 3.95 o.p. (ISBN 0-87614-007-X). Carolrhoda Bks.
Little Original Sin: The Life & Work of Jane Bowles. Millicent Dillon. LC 80-25879. (Illus.). 480p. 1981. 18.95 o.s.i. (ISBN 0-03-058317-9). H Holt & Co.
Little Original Sin: The Life & Work of Jane Bowles. Millicent Dillon. 1982. pap. 9.95 o.s.i. (ISBN 0-03-062027-9, Owl Bks). H Holt & Co.
Little Owl: An Eightfold Buddhist Admonition. Janwillem Van De Wetering. 1978. 6.95 o.p. (ISBN 0-395-26456-1). HM.
Little Painter. Ralph Marchant & Jill Marchant. LC 72-170148. (Illus.). (gr. k-4). 1971. PLB 5.95 o.p. (ISBN 0-87614-029-0). Carolrhoda Bks.
Little Pear. Eleanor F. Lattimore. LC 31-22069. (Illus.). (gr. 2-5). 1931. 7.50 o.p. (ISBN 0-15-246682-7, HJ). HarBraceJ.
Little Pear & His Friends. Eleanor F. Lattimore. LC 34-27286. (Illus.). (gr. k-3). 1934. 5.95 o.p. (ISBN 0-15-246861-7, HJ). HarBraceJ.
Little People's Book of Baby Animals. Susan Jeffers. LC 80-50178. (Illus.). 30p. (ps-1). 1980. 2.50 o.p. (ISBN 0-394-84570-6). Random.
Little Pilgrimages Among Old New England Inns: Being an Account of Little Journeys to Various Quaint Inns & Hostelries of Colonial New England. Mary C. Crawford. LC 76-107629. (Illus.). 400p. 1970. Repr. of 1907 ed. 40.00x o.p. (ISBN 0-8103-3536-0). Gale.
Little Plane. Michel Gay. LC 84-42986. (Illus.). 32p. (ps-k). 1985. bds. 3.95 o.s.i. (ISBN 0-02-737510-2); PLB 7.95 o.s.i. (ISBN 0-02-737500-5). Macmillan.
Little Pretty Pocket-Book. facsim. ed. John Newbery. LC 67-4962. (Illus.). 1967. 4.95 o.p. (ISBN 0-15-246890-0, HJ). HarBraceJ.
Little Rabbit's Garden. Marie Wabbes. (Illus.). (ps). 1987. pap. 4.95 o.s.i. (ISBN 0-87113-126-9, Joy St Bks). Little.
Little Rabbit's Merry Christmas. J. P. Miller. LC 82-80385. (Sniffy Bks.). (Illus.). 24p. (ps-1). 1982. pap. 3.95 spiral plastic o.s.i. (ISBN 0-394-85427-6). Random.
Little Raw on Monday Mornings. Robert Cormier. 176p. 1980. pap. 1.95 o.p. (ISBN 0-380-51490-7, 51490-7). Avon.
Little Red Cap. Jacob Grimm & Wilhelm K. Grimm. LC 83-61776. (Illus.). 22p. (gr. 1 up). 1983. pap. 5.95 o.p. (ISBN 0-907234-48-8). Picture Bk Studio.
Little Red Phone. Henry Kane. LC 81-71669. 220p. 1982. 12.95 o.p. (ISBN 0-87795-375-9, Arbor Hse). Morrow.
Little Red Riding Hood. Retold by B. G. Ford. (Illus.). 8p. (gr. k-1). 1985. 8.95 o.p. (ISBN 0-448-18969-0, G&D). Putnam Pub Group.
Little Red Riding Hood. Jacob Grimm & Wilhelm K. Grimm. Ed. & illus. by Harriet Pincus. LC 68-11505. (Illus.). (gr. k-3). 1968. 6.95 o.p. (ISBN 0-15-247132-4, HJ). HarBraceJ.
Little Red Riding Hood. Jacob Grimm & Wilhelm K. Grimm. LC 82-7700. (Illus.). 32p. (ps-3). 1987. pap. 5.95 o.p. (ISBN 0-8234-0653-9). Holiday.
Little Red Riding Hood. (Signed English Ser.). 32p. 1980. pap. 5.50 o.p. (ISBN 0-913580-05-8, Clerc Bks). Gallaudet Univ Pr.
Little Red Riding Hood with Benjy & Bubbles. Ruth L. Perle. LC 78-55627. (Read with Me Ser.). (Illus.). (gr. k-3). 1979. 2.95 o.p. (ISBN 0-03-044961-8). H Holt & Co.
Little Revenge: Benjamin Franklin & His Son. Willard Randall. (Illus.). 416p. 1985. 22.50 o.p. (ISBN 0-316-73364-4). Little.
Little Rhetoric. Edward P. Corbett. LC 76-45081. 1977. pap. text ed. write for info. o.p. (ISBN 0-673-15663-X). Scott F.
Little Round Bun. Tr. by I. Zheleznova. 18p. (ps-4). 1980. pap. 2.45 o.p. (ISBN 0-8285-1906-4, Pub. by Malysh Pubs USSR). Imported Pubns.
Little Sailor's Biglet. Ziner Fennie. (Illus.). 1957. 4.95 o.p. (ISBN 0-395-27668-3). HM.
Little Shepard of Kingdom Come. John Fox, Jr. 1973. pap. 1.25 o.p. (ISBN 0-380-01330-4, 17707). Avon.
Little Ship Astro-Navigation. M. J. Rantzen. 1952. (ISBN 0-8022-1311-1). Philos Lib.
Little Shop of Horrors. (Illus.). 1987. pap. 6.95 o.p. (ISBN 0-399-51319-1, Perigee). Putnam Pub Group.
Little Simon ABC. Ed. by Kate Klimo. (Illus.). 40p. (ps). 1982. 5.75 o.s.i. (ISBN 0-671-45037-9, Little Simon). S&S.
Little Simon Jokes & Riddles. Mik Brown & Lynn Offerman. (Animal Fun Jokes & Riddles Ser.). (Illus.). 40p. (gr. k-3). 1984. 5.95 o.s.i. (ISBN 0-671-52814-9, Little Simon). S&S.
Little Simon One Two Three. Vanessa Mermaid. (Illus.). 40p. (ps). 1982. 5.75 o.s.i. (ISBN 0-671-45045-X, Little Simon). S&S.
Little Sins. Meredith Rich. LC 82-45604. 456p. 1985. 16.95 o.p. (ISBN 0-385-18424-7). Doubleday.
Little Sister Rabbit. Ulf Nilsson. Ed. by Melanie Kroupa. LC 84-72595. (Illus.). 32p. (gr. 1-3). 1985. 12.95 o.p. (ISBN 0-87113-009-2, 607533, Pub. by Atlantic-Little, Brown). Little.
Little Snake. Edda Reinl. LC 82-60894. (Illus.). 28p. (ps-2). 1982. 13.95 o.p. (ISBN 0-907234-15-1). Picture Bk Studio.

Little Spotted Fish. Jane H. Yolen. LC 74-14819. 32p. (ps-4). 1979. 7.95 o.p. (ISBN 0-395-28835-5, Clarion). HM.
Little Stories about God. Mary R. McDonald. (Illus.). (gr. k-1). 1964. 5.50 o.s.i. (ISBN 0-8198-0080-5). pap. 4.50 o.s.i. (ISBN 0-8198-0081-3). Dghtrs St Paul.
Little Stories from the Screen. William A. Lathrop. Ed. by Bruce S. Kupelnick. LC 76-52110. (Classics of Film Literature Ser.). 1978. lib. bdg. 22.00 o.p. (ISBN 0-8240-2881-3). Garland Pub.
Little Tales of Mysogyny. Patricia Highsmith. 160p. 1987. pap. 8.95 o.p. (ISBN 0-89296-917-2). Mysterious Pr.
Little Things. Anne Laurin. LC 77-23868. (Illus.). (ps-3). 1978. 6.95 o.p. (ISBN 0-689-30623-7, Atheneum). Macmillan.
Little Tiny Rooster. William Lipkind & Nicolas Mordvinoff. LC 60-12309. (Illus.). 32p. (gr. k-3). 1960. 6.50 o.p. (ISBN 0-15-247577-X, HJ). HarBraceJ.
Little Tours of Hell: Tall Tails of Food & Holidays. Josephine Saxton. 192p. 1986. 19.95 o.p. (ISBN 0-86358-094-7, 80947); pap. 7.95 o.p. (ISBN 0-86358-095-5, 89055). Routledge Chapman & Hall.
Little Treasury of Familiar Prose. Raymond Lister. (Little Treasury Ser.). 1964. 3.95 o.p. (ISBN 0-212-35942-8). Dufour.
Little Truck. Michael Gay. LC 84-42983. 32p. (ps-1). 1985. lib. bdg. 7.95 o.s.i. (ISBN 0-02-737520-X); pap. 3.95 o.s.i. (ISBN 0-02-737530-7). Macmillan.
Little Weaver of Thai-Yen Village: Bilingual in Vietnamese & English. Tran-Khanh-Tuyet & Nancy Hom. LC 77-78105. (Fifth World Tales Ser.). (Illus.). (gr. k-6). pap. 4.95 o.p. (ISBN 0-89239-013-1, Imprenta de Libros Infantiles). Childrens Book Pr.
Little Wee Tyke. Marcia Sewall. LC 79-11853. (Illus.). (ps-2). 1979. 7.95 o.p. (ISBN 0-689-30724-1, Atheneum). Macmillan.
Little White Hood. B. Battistella. 1980. pap. 1.50 o.p. (ISBN 0-8198-4405-5). Dghtrs St Paul.
Little White Horse. Elizabeth Goudge. (YA) (gr. 7 up). 1978. pap. 1.75 o.p. (ISBN 0-380-01875-6, 52050). Avon.
Little Wilson & Big God: The Autobiography. Anthony Burgess. 480p. 1987. 22.50 o.s.i. (ISBN 1-55584-100-7). Weidenfeld.
Little Witch's Carnival Books. Linda Glovach. (Illus.). 48p. (gr. 1-4). 1982. 7.95 o.s.i. (ISBN 0-13-538074-X). P-H.
Little Women. Louisa May Alcott. LC 84-63128. (Illus.). 432p. (gr. 4-12). 1985. 12.95 o.p. (ISBN 0-89577-209-4). RD Assn.
Little Wrinkle & the Baby. Anna Ford. LC 86-42918. (Mini-Storybooks). (Illus.). 32p. (ps-3). 1987. pap. 1.25 o.s.i. (ISBN 0-394-88684-4, BYR). Random.
Littles. John Peterson. (Illus.). (gr. 4-6). 1970. pap. 1.95 o.p. (ISBN 0-590-32006-8). Scholastic Inc.
Littlest Angel. Date not set. bds. 8.95 incl. cassette o.p. Ideals.
Littlest Angel - Newest Angel. Date not set. 6.95 o.p. Ideals.
Littlest Angel: A Pop-Up Book. Ron Kidd. (Illus.). 12p. (gr. k-6). 1985. 10.95 o.p. (ISBN 0-8249-8098-0). Ideals.
Littlest Angel Earns His Halo. Date not set. 5.95 o.p. Ideals.
Littlest Pine Cone. Delta Waters. (gr. 3-6). 1975. 4.00 o.p. (ISBN 0-682-48406-7). Exposition-Phoenix.
Liturgical & Mystical Theology of Nicolas Cabasilas. 2nd ed. Constance N. Tsirpanlis. 103p. 1979. pap. 6.99 o.p. (ISBN 0-686-36328-0). EO Pr.
Liturgy As Dance & the Liturgical Dancer. Carolyn Deitering. (Illus.). 144p. 1984. pap. 8.95 o.p. (ISBN 0-8245-0654-5). Crossroad NY.
Liturgy: Celebrating with Children. Ed. by Rachel Reeder. (Liturgy, the Quarterly Journal of the Liturgical Conference: Vol. 1, No. 3). (Illus.). 80p. 1981. pap. 7.95 o.p. (ISBN 0-918208-02-5). Liturgical Conf.
Liturgy: Easter's Fifty Days. Ed. by Rachel Reeder. (Journal of The Liturgical Conference: Vol. 3, No. 1). (Illus.). 72p. 1982. pap. text ed. 7.95 o.p. (ISBN 0-918208-29-7). Liturgical Conf.
Liturgy of the Word for Children. Sr. Jan Ihli. LC 79-90003. 176p. 1979. pap. 9.95 o.p. (ISBN 0-8091-2176-X). Paulist Pr.
Liturgy: One Hundred Sixty-Nine Pronouncements from Benedict Fourteenth to John Twenty-Third. Ed. by Monks of Solesmes Staff. (Papal Teaching Ser.). 5.00 o.s.i. (ISBN 0-8198-0083-X). Dghtrs St Paul.
Liu Shao-chi: Mao's First Heir-Apparent. Tien-Min Li. LC 72-152427. (Special Project). 223p. 1975. 11.95x o.p. (ISBN 0-8179-4141-X). Hoover Inst Pr.
Livable Cities: A Grass-Roots Guide to Rebuilding Urban America. Robert Cassidy. LC 79-3446. (Illus.). 412p. (Orig.). 1980. 16.95 o.p. (ISBN 0-03-042951-X); pap. 8.95 o.p. (ISBN 0-03-056291-0). H Holt & Co.
Live & Let Live. Chesser. 128p. 1958. (ISBN 0-8022-0237-3). Philos Lib.
Live Bait. Frank Tuohy. LC 78-4689. 1979. 7.95 o.p. (ISBN 0-03-043636-2). H Holt & Co.
Live in Child Care: Complete Guide. Barbara Binswanger & Betsy Ryan. LC 86-13520. 144p. 1986. 15.95 o.p. (ISBN 0-385-23680-8, Dolp); pap. 8.95 o.p. (ISBN 0-385-23681-6, Dolp). Doubleday.
Live It up Andy Capp. Reginald Smythe. (Andy Capp Ser.). (Illus.). 1982. pap. 1.75 o.s.i. (ISBN 0-449-12534-3, GM). Fawcett.
Live or Die. Anne Sexton. 1966. 8.95 o.p. (ISBN 0-395-08181-5); pap. 4.50 o.p. (ISBN 0-395-08180-7). HM.
Live Smart, Die Smarter. DeWitt M. Shy. LC 78-53620. 1978. 7.95 o.p. (ISBN 0-87397-136-1). Strode.
Live Theatre: An Introduction to the History & Practice of the Stage. Hugh Hunt. LC 78-17037. (Illus.). 1978. Repr. of 1962 ed. lib. bdg. 24.75x o.p. (ISBN 0-313-20570-1, HULT). Greenwood.
Live with Jesus. Alexander Campbell & Gerry Haff. 90p. (Orig.). (gr. 1-6). 1984. pap. 12.95 o.p. (ISBN 0-940754-20-7). Ed Ministries.
Lived-In Architecture: Le Corbusier's Pessac Revisited. Philippe Boudon. Tr. by Gerald Onn. (Illus.). 1972. pap. 8.95x o.p. (ISBN 0-262-52053-2). MIT Pr.
Liver Biopsy Interpretation. 3rd ed. P. Scheuer. 1980. text ed. write for info. o.p. (ISBN 0-7216-0761-6). Saunders.
Liver Carcinogenesis. Ed. by Karoly Lapis & Jan V. Johannessen. LC 79-134. (Illus.). 413p. 1979. text ed. 80.50 o.p. (ISBN 0-89116-149-X). Hemisphere Pub.
Liver: Morphology, Biochemistry, Physiology, 2 vols. Ed. by C. Rouiller. 1963-64. Vol. 1. 97.00 o.p. (ISBN 0-12-598901-6); Vol. 2. 97.00 o.p. (ISBN 0-12-598902-4). Acad Pr.
Liver: Normal & Abnormal Functions, 2 pts. Ed. by Frederick F. Becker. (Biochemistry of Disease Ser.: Vol. 5). 472p. 1975. Part A. 95.00 o.p. (ISBN 0-8247-6205-3); Part B. 85.00 o.p. (ISBN 0-8247-6214-2). Dekker.
Liver Regeneration, No. 1. Leonard I. Malkin et al. (Illus.). 200p. 1973. text ed. 24.00x o.p. (ISBN 0-8422-7079-5). Irvington.
Liver Regeneration, No. 2. Nelson Fausto et al. LC 72-13504. (Illus.). 220p. 1973. text ed. 24.00x o.p. (ISBN 0-8422-7080-9). Irvington.
Liverpool Town Planning & Housing Exhibition: Transactions of Conference Held March 9-13, 1914 at Liberty Buildings Liverpool. Liverpool Town Planning & Housing Exhibition Staff. Ed. by S. D. Adshead et al. LC 84-48725. (Rise of Urban Britain Ser.). 1985. Repr. of 1914 ed. lib. bdg. 35.00 o.p. (ISBN 0-317-17765-6). Garland Pub.
Lives & Letters from Kiester House. Donna K. Gibson. 184p. 1987. pap. text ed. write for info. o.p. (ISBN 0-933227-94-9). Closson Pr.
Lives at Stake: The Science & Politics of Environmental Health. Laurence Pringle. LC 80-14272. (Science for Survival Ser.). (Illus.). 144p. (gr. 6 up). 1980. PLB 9.95 o.s.i. (ISBN 0-02-775410-3). Macmillan.
Lives: Chinese Working Women. Ed. by Mary Sheridan & Janet W. Salaff. LC 83-48401. (Midland Bks: No. 319). 272p. 1984. 20.00x o.p. (ISBN 0-253-33604-X); pap. 8.95x o.p. (ISBN 0-253-20319-8). Ind U Pr.
Lives of Famous Romans. Olivia Coolidge. (Illus.). (gr. 7 up). 1965. 6.95 o.p. (ISBN 0-395-06730-8). HM.
Lives of Jean Toomer: A Hunger for Wholeness. Cynthia E. Kerman & Richard Eldridge. LC 86-27622. (Illus.). 448p. 1987. text ed. 29.95 o.p. (ISBN 0-8071-1354-9). La State U Pr.
Lives of Labor-Lives of Love: Fragments of Friendly Autobiographies. Sheldon Glueck. LC 76-24259. (Illus.). 1977. 8.50 o.p. (ISBN 0-682-48632-9, Banner). Exposition-Phoenix.
Lives of Lee Miller. Antony Penrose. LC 85-5878. 208p. 1985. 29.95 o.s.i. (ISBN 0-03-005833-3). H Holt & Co.
Lives of Talleyrand. Crane Brinton. 1963. pap. 4.95 o.p. (ISBN 0-393-00188-1, Norton Lib). Norton.
Lives of the English Poets: Selection. Samuel Johnson. 1980. 12.95x o.p. (ISBN 0-460-00770-5, Evman); pap. 9.95x o.p. (ISBN 0-460-01770-5, Evman). Biblio Dist.
Lives of the Georgian Age: 1714-1837. Laurence Urdang. Ed. by William Gould & Patrick Hanks. LC 77-2684. (Lives of the... Age Ser). (Illus.). 516p. 1978. 27.50x o.p. (ISBN 0-06-494332-1). B&N Imports.
Lives of the Great Composers. Harold C. Schonberg. LC 73-116112. (Illus.). 1970. 19.95 o.p. (ISBN 0-393-02146-7). Norton.
Lives of the Great Twentieth Century Artists. Edward Lucie-Smith. LC 86-3195. (Illus.). 360p. 1986. 45.00 o.p. (ISBN 0-8478-0722-3). Rizzoli Intl.
Lives of the Poets: Six Stories & a Novella. E. L. Doctorow. 1986. pap. 3.95 o.p. (ISBN 0-380-69996-6). Avon.
Lives of the Tudor Age, 1485 to 1603. Ann Hoffmann. LC 76-15685. (Lives of the...Age Ser.). (Illus.). 500p. 1977. text ed. 27.50x o.p. (ISBN 0-06-494331-3). B&N Imports.
Lives on the Mend. Florence Littauer. 1985. pap. 9.95 o.p. Word Bks.
Livestock & Equality in East Africa: The Economic Basis for Social Structure. Harold K. Schneider. LC 78-20400. (Illus.). 304p. 1980. 17.50x o.p. (ISBN 0-253-19565-9). Ind U Pr.
Livestock & Meat Marketing. 2nd ed. John H. McCoy. (Illus.). 1979. 32.95 o.p. (ISBN 0-87055-321-6). AVI.
Livestock Health Encyclopedia. 3rd ed. Rudolph Seiden. Ed. by W. James Gough. LC 68-8793. (Illus.). 628p. 1968. text ed. 31.50 o.p. (ISBN 0-8261-0003-1). Springer Pub.
Livestock Husbandry Techniques. J. I. McNitt. (Illus.). 256p. (Orig.). 1982. pap. text ed. 12.25x o.p. (ISBN 0-246-11871-7, Pub. by Granada England). Gower Pub Co.
Livestock Management in the Arid Zone. Ed. by V. Squires. 271p. 1981. 50.70 o.p. (ISBN 0-909605-23-8). CAB Intl.
Livestock of China. George E. Taylor. LC 78-74304. (Modern Chinese Economy Ser.). 174p. 1980. lib. bdg. 26.00 o.p. (ISBN 0-8240-4286-7). Garland Pub.
Living a Day at a Time. Jacob S. List. LC 62-18541. 104p. 1962. (ISBN 0-8022-0983-1). Philos Lib.
Living Abroad & Sailing. Paul A. Crick. 128p. 1981. 8.00 o.p. (ISBN 0-682-49808-4, Banner). Exposition-Phoenix.
Living Alone. Beryl Cross. 160p. 1957. (ISBN 0-8022-0318-3). Philos Lib.
Living Alone. John Givens. LC 80-69366. 1981. 11.95 o.p. (ISBN 0-689-11147-9). Macmillan.
Living among the Bedouin Arabs. Alex R. Johnson. 1985. 8.95 o.p. (ISBN 0-533-06472-4). Vantage.
Living: An Interpretive Approach to Biology. Melissa Stanley & George Andrykovitch. 204p. 1982. Instrs' Manual 3.50 o.p. (ISBN 0-201-07174-6); Study Guide 9.95 o.p. (ISBN 0-201-07175-4). Addison-Wesley.
Living & Dying: An Inquiry into the Enigma of Death & After-Life. Vidya Dehejia. 1979. 8.95x o.p. (ISBN 0-7069-0815-5, Pub. by Vikas India). Advent NY.
Living & Learning in Two Languages: Bilingual-Bicultural Education in the U. S. F. Von Maltitz. 1975. text ed. 19.95 o.p. (ISBN 0-07-067609-7). McGraw.
Living & the Dead. Konstantin M. Simonov. Tr. by R. Ainsztein. LC 68-54438. (Illus.). 1969. Repr. of 1962 ed. lib. bdg. 45.00x o.p. (ISBN 0-8371-0657-5, SILD). Greenwood.
Living Animals of the Bible. Walter W. Ferguson. (Encore Editions). 1974. 3.95 o.p. (ISBN 0-684-15245-2, ScribT). Scribner.
Living As a Christian Study Guide. 52p. Date not set. pap. 3.00 o.p. (ISBN 0-89283-276-2). Servant.
Living As Disciples. Henrietta T. Wilkinson. (Illus., Orig.). (gr. 5-7). 1965. pap. 2.95 o.p. (ISBN 0-8042-9411-9, John Knox). Westminster John Knox.
Living Beyond Fear: A Tool for Transformation. rev. ed. Jeanne Segal. 140p. 1987. pap. 9.95 o.p. (ISBN 0-87877-073-9); cassette 9.95 o.p. (ISBN 0-87877-074-7). Newcastle Pub.
Living Brain. W. Grey Walter. (Illus.). 1963. pap. 2.95 o.p. (ISBN 0-393-00153-9, Norton Lib). Norton.
Living Chemistry. David Ucko. 1977. text ed. 33.75 o.p. (ISBN 0-12-705950-4). Acad Pr.
Living Country Blues. Harry Oster. LC 69-20397. (Illus.). 480p. 1969. 51.00x o.p. (ISBN 0-8103-5026-2). Gale.
Living Crafts. G. Bernard Hughes. (Illus.). 200p. 1954. (ISBN 0-8022-0756-1). Philos Lib.
Living, Dealing, Learning & Growing with Your Children. Dudley E. Morgan. 1983. 7.95 o.p. (ISBN 0-8062-2146-1). Carlton.
Living Earth Manual of Peng-Shui: Chinese Geomancy. Stephen Skinner. (Illus.). 160p. (Orig.). 1982. pap. 9.95 o.p. (ISBN 0-7100-9077-3). Routledge Chapman & Hall.
Living Faith. Jacques Ellul. LC 82-48928. 288p. 1985. pap. 15.34 o.p. (ISBN 0-06-062236-9). HarpR.
Living Faith: Mastectomy or Partial? Ask Jesus. Margaret H. Johnson. 1980. 5.00 o.p. (ISBN 0-682-49554-9). Exposition-Phoenix.
Living for Justice: A Study Guide to Hunger for Justice: the Politics of Food & Faith. CALC Staff. 28p. (Orig.). 1982. pap. 1.00 o.p. Orbis Bks.
Living Free. Joy Adamson. LC 61-15810. (Helen & Kurt Wolff Bk.). (Illus.). 161p. 1961. 15.95 o.p. (ISBN 0-15-152925-6). HarBraceJ.
Living Garden: The 400-Year History of an English Garden. George Ordish. (Illus.). 272p. 1985. 17.45 o.p. (ISBN 0-395-38780-9). HM.
Living God's Joy. Douglas Cooper. LC 78-71158. (Redwood Ser.). 1979. pap. 4.95 o.p. (ISBN 0-8163-0241-3). Pacific Pr Pub Assn.
Living Hope: A Commentary on I & II Peter. Robert Mounce. 1982. pap. 5.95 o.p. (ISBN 0-8028-1915-X). Eerdmans.
Living in Christ. Ralph M. Riggs. LC 67-25874. 1967. pap. 1.50 o.p. (ISBN 0-88243-538-8, 02-0538). Gospel Pub.
Living in Christian Community. Arthur G. Gish. LC 79-11848. 384p. 1979. pap. 9.95 o.p. (ISBN 0-8361-1887-1). Herald Pr.
Living in Cities: Urbanism & Society in Metropolitan Australia. Ed. by Ian Burnley & James Forrest. (Illus.). 280p. 1985. text ed. 25.00x o.p. (ISBN 0-86861-502-1). Unwin Hyman.
Living in Covenant with God. Mary B. Rudolph. (Illus., Orig.). (gr. 3-5). 1965. pap. 2.45 o.p. (ISBN 0-8042-9422-4, John Knox). Westminster John Knox.
Living in Light of Eternity. Christian Character Library Staff & Stacy P. Rinehart. 176p. 1986. hdbk. 8.95 o.p. (ISBN 0-89109-551-9). NavPress.
Living in Taiwan: A Handbook for Housewives. Helen Freytag. 289p. 1980. 16.90 o.p. (ISBN 0-89955-149-1, Pub. by Mei Ya China). Intl Spec Bk.
Living in Taiwan: 1985 Edition. 162p. (Orig.). 1986. pap. write for info. o.p. (Augsburg). Augsburg Fortress.
Living in the Eye of the Storm. John A. Lynn. 164p. 1983. pap. 3.95 o.p. (ISBN 0-910068-50-X). Am Christian.
Living in the Presence of God. Eugene B. Hines. LC 84-24305. 1985. pap. 4.95 o.p. (ISBN 0-8054-5229-X). Broadman.
Living in Troubled Lands: The Complete Guide to Personal Security Abroad. Patrick Collins. LC 85-130273. 200p. 1981. 17.95 o.p. (ISBN 0-87364-205-8). Paladin Pr.
Living in Two Cultures: The Socio-Cultural Situation of Migrant Workers & Their Families. (Illus.). 325p. (Co-published with Gower Publishing Co. Ltd.). 1982. pap. 25.50 o.p. (ISBN 92-3-101869-8, U1204, UNESCO). UNIPUB.
Living Insects. R. D. Hughes. LC 74-12549. (Australian Naturalist Library). (Illus.). 304p. 1975. 14.95 o.s.i. (ISBN 0-8008-4929-9). Taplinger.
Living Isles: A Natural History of Britain & Ireland. Peter Crawford. 1987. 24.95 o.p. (ISBN 0-684-18801-5). Scribner.
Living It Up: A Guide to the Named Apartment Houses of New York. Thomas Norton & Jerry Patterson. LC 83-45508. (Illus.). 256p. 1984. 25.00 o.p. (ISBN 0-689-11436-2, Atheneum). Macmillan.
Living Japanese Style. 191p. 1984. pap. 10.00 o.p. (ISBN 0-318-20229-8, Pub.by Japan Travel Bureau Tokyo). A M Newman.
Living Lean & Loving It: Classic Flavors Without the Fat. Carla M. Ennis & Eve Lowry. (Illus.). 288p. 1987. 19.95 o.p. (ISBN 0-8016-3215-3). Mosby.
Living, Loving & Learning. Leo F. Buscaglia. 288p. 1983. pap. 5.95 o.p. (ISBN 0-449-90024-X, Columbine). Fawcett.
Living Metals. P. Schwarzkopf. (Illus.). 1962. 25.00 o.s.i. E J Brill USA.
Living New England Artists: Biographical Sketches. Frank T. Robinson. Ed. by H. Barbara Weinberg. LC 75-28880. (Art Experience in Late 19th Century America Ser.: Vol. 14). (Illus.). 1977. Repr. of 1888 ed. lib. bdg. 53.00 o.p. (ISBN 0-8240-2238-6). Garland Pub.
Living on a Few Acres: Yearbook of Agriculture, 1978. 432p. 1978. 13.00 o.p. (ISBN 0-318-11797-5, S/N 001-000-03809-5). USGPO.
Living on a Shoestring: A Scrounge Manual for the Hobbyist. George M. Ewing. (Illus.). 1983. pap. 7.97 o.p. (ISBN 0-88006-059-X, BK7393). Wayne Green Ent.
Living on the Edge: The Winter Ascent of Kanchenjunga. Cherie Bremer-Kamp. (Illus.). 216p. 1987. 19.95 o.p. (ISBN 0-87905-271-6). Gibbs Smith Pub.
Living Past: Fifteen Historic Places in Minnesota. rev. ed. Nancy Eubank. (Minnesota Historic Sites Pamphlet Ser.: No. 7). (Illus.). 32p. 1978. pap. 2.75 o.p. (ISBN 0-87351-077-1). Minn Hist.
Living Past of Montreal: Le Passe Vivant de Montreal. rev. ed. Eric McLean & R. D Wilson. (Illus.). 128p. 1976. 9.95 o.p.; pap. 5.95 o.p. (ISBN 0-7735-0259-9, McGill Canada). U of Toronto Pr.
Living Past: Western Historiographical Traditions. Alfred J. Andrea & Wolfe W. Schmokel. LC 81-20878. 314p. 1982. Repr. of 1975 ed. 19.50 o.p. (ISBN 0-89874-152-1). Krieger.

Living Portraits from the Old Testament. Paul Culbertson. 192p. 1978. pap. 2.95 o.p. (ISBN 0-8341-0507-1). Beacon Hill.

Living Proof. Hank Williams, Jr. 1983. pap. 3.95 o.p. (ISBN 0-440-05213-0). Dell.

Living Resources of the Southern Ocean. I. Everson. (Southern Ocean Fisheries Survey Programmes: No. 77-1). 160p. (Eng. & Span.). 1977. pap. 10.00 o.p. (ISBN 92-5-100428-5, F1321, FAO). UNIPUB.

Living Rocks. Geoffrey Grigson. 96p. 1957. (ISBN 0-8022-0630-1). Philos Lib.

Living Room. Sol Stein. LC 73-91499. 1974. 7.95 o.p. (ISBN 0-87795-077-6, Arbor Hse). Morrow.

Living Roots of Reformation. Jan Lochman. LC 78-66954. 1979. pap. 3.50 o.p. (ISBN 0-8066-1686-5, 10-3978, Augsburg). Augsburg Fortress.

Living Saints Witness at Work. T. Edward Barlow. 1976. 6.00 o.p. (ISBN 0-8309-0153-1). Herald Hse.

Living Simply. Daisy Hepburn. LC 84-3360. (Life with Spice Bible Study Ser.). 1984. 2.95 o.s.i. (ISBN 0-8307-0947-9, 6101848). Regal.

Living Spanish: Cassette Edition. 1969. 15.95 o.p. (ISBN 0-517-00897-1); cassettes, manual & dictionary incl. o.p. Crown.

Living Stage: A History of the World Theatre. Kenneth MacGowen & W. Melnitz. 1955. text ed. (ISBN 0-13-538942-9). P-H.

Living State. Ed. by R. K. Mishra. LC 84-555. 450p. 1984. 34.95 o.p. (ISBN 0-470-20027-8). Halsted Pr.

Living State with Remarks on Cancer. Albert Szent-Gyorgyi. 1972. 30.00 o.p. (ISBN 0-12-680960-7). Acad Pr.

Living Temple: A Practical Theology of the Body & the Foods of the Earth. Carl E. Braaten & LaVonne Braaten. LC 75-36746. 128p. 1976. pap. 2.95 o.p. (ISBN 0-06-061044-1, RD-147). HarpR.

Living the Friendly Way. 2.00 o.p. (ISBN 0-936672-39-0). Aerial Photo.

Living the Good News: An Introduction to Moral Theology. Nicholas Lohkamp. 170p. (Orig.). 1982. pap. text ed. 4.50 o.p. (ISBN 0-86716-016-0). St Anthony Mess Pr.

Living the Gospel: A Study of One Peter. Joseph M. Gettys. (Orig.). 1970. pap. 1.25 o.p. (ISBN 0-8042-9029-6, John Knox). Westminster John Knox.

Living the Richness of the Cross. John Dalrymple. LC 83-70945. 128p. (Orig.). 1983. pap. 3.95 o.p. (ISBN 0-87793-274-3). Ave Maria.

Living the Sacraments: A Call to Conversion. David M. Knight. LC 85-60888. 140p. (Orig.). 1985. pap. 6.50 o.p. (ISBN 0-87973-815-4, 815). Our Sunday Visitor.

Living the Sky: The Cosmos of the American Indian. Ray A. Williamson. (Illus.). 300p. 1984. 19.45 o.p. (ISBN 0-395-35414-5). HM.

Living Theatre. Pierre Biner. (Illus.). 1973. pap. 1.65 o.p. (ISBN 0-380-01331-2, 17640, Discus). Avon.

Living Through the Twentieth Century. Olive K. Gilliam. 4.95 o.p. (ISBN 0-533-00341-5). Vantage.

Living Together. Grace Walker. (Illus.). 1979. 5.00 o.p. (ISBN 0-682-49509-3). Exposition-Phoenix.

Living Together: A Guide to the Law for Unmarried Couples. Barbara Hirsch. 1976. 7.95 o.p. (ISBN 0-395-24780-2); pap. 3.95 o.p. (ISBN 0-395-24977-5). HM.

Living Together Alone: The New American Monasticism. Charles A. Fracchia. LC 78-3362. (Illus., Orig.). 1979. pap. 5.95i o.p. (ISBN 0-06-063011-6, RD 272). HarpR.

Living Together in the Sea. Leon P. Zann. (Illus.). 416p. 1980. 29.95 o.p. (ISBN 0-87666-500-8, H-990). TFH Pubns.

Living Together Kit. 4th ed. Toni Ihara & Ralph Warner. (Illus.). 224p. 1984. pap. 14.95 o.p. (ISBN 0-917316-73-8). Nolo Pr.

Living Tradition of Maria Martinez. Susan Peterson. LC 77-75373. (Illus.). 240p. 1977. 45.00 o.p. (ISBN 0-87011-319-4). Kodansha.

Living Treasures: An Odyssey Through China's Extraordinary Nature Reserves. Tang Xiyang. LC 87-47583. 208p. 1987. 29.95 o.p. (ISBN 0-553-05236-5). Bantam.

Living True. Coleen Evans. 132p. 1985. pap. 4.95 o.p. (ISBN 0-89693-321-0). Victor Bks.

Living Trust Forms Kit (Individual--Married) Barbara R. Stock. 54p. 1987. wkbk. 29.95 o.p. (ISBN 0-913455-16-4). Linch Pub.

Living Trust Forms Kit (Single) Barbara R. Stock. 54p. 1987. wkbk. 29.95 o.p. (ISBN 0-913455-14-8). Linch Pub.

Living Upcountry: A Pilgrim's Progress. Don Mitchell. Ed. by Dennis Dinan. LC 86-50091. 192p. 1986. 12.95 o.p. (ISBN 0-89909-100-8). Yankee Bks.

Living Victoriously with Illness & Death: Suggestions for Family & Friends. David E. Cook. LC 86-70141. 90p. (Orig.). (YA) (gr. 9-12). 1986. pap. 4.95 o.p. (ISBN 0-931494-93-1). Brunswick Pub.

Living Well Naturally. Anthony J. Sattilaro & Tom Monte. LC 83-22623. 236p. 1984. 13.45 o.p. (ISBN 0-395-34422-0). HM.

Living We've Just Begun. Douglas Cooper. (Redwood Ser.). 96p. 1983. pap. 4.95 o.p. (ISBN 0-8163-0505-6). Pacific Pr Pub Assn.

Living When a Loved One Has Died. Earl Grollman. 1979. pap. 6.95 o.p. (ISBN 0-8070-2741-3). Beacon Pr.

Living Wild: The Secrets of Animal Survival. David F. Robinson. Ed. by Alma D. MacConomy. LC 80-80702. (Illus.). 208p. 1980. 14.95 o.p. (ISBN 0-912186-37-2). Natl Wildlife.

Living Wilderness. Ruthford G. Montgomery. LC 64-20648. (Illus.). 249p. (gr. 8-12). 1969. Repr. of 1964 ed. 6.95 o.s.i. (ISBN 0-87004-131-2). Caxton.

Living with Art. rev. ed. William McCarter & Rita Gilbert. 448p. 1985. pap. text ed. 23.00 o.p. (ISBN 0-394-35500-8, KnopfC). Knopf.

Living with Beautiful Crochet. Nihon Vogue Staff. (Illus.). 82p. 1987. pap. 9.95 o.p. (ISBN 0-87040-740-6). Japan Pubns USA.

Living with Chronic Neurologic Disease: A Handbook for Patient & Family. I. S. Cooper. 1976. 8.95 o.p. (ISBN 0-393-06409-3); pap. 4.95 o.p. (ISBN 0-393-06416-6). Norton.

Living with Computers. McKeown. 640p. 1986. text ed. 26.00 o.p. (ISBN 0-15-551133-5, Pub. by HC); text ed. 34.95 includes disk o.p. (ISBN 0-317-42734-2); software o.p. (ISBN 0-15-551140-8). HarBraceJ.

Living with Differences. Shirley Schwarzrock & C. Gilbert Wrenn. (Coping with Ser.). (gr. 7-12). 1973. pap. text ed. 3.00 o.p. (ISBN 0-913476-19-6). Am Guidance.

Living with Environmental Law. Massachusetts Continuing Legal Education, Inc. Staff. LC 84-229088. (Illus.). 1984. 25.00 o.p. Mass CLE.

Living with Fear: You As a Therapist. Isaac M. Marks. 1978. text ed. 27.50 o.p. (ISBN 0-07-040395-3). McGraw.

Living with Mirrors: Two Books of Poetry. Lauren Lawrence & David Lawrence. 1979. 5.00 o.p. (ISBN 0-682-49412-7). Exposition-Phoenix.

Living with Modern Sculpture: The John P. Putnam, Jr. Memorial Collection at Princeton. Patrick J. Kelleher. LC 81-80639. (Illus.). 144p. 1981. 24.00x o.p. (ISBN 0-691-03897-X). Princeton U Pr.

Living with Myself. William Hulme. LC 64-10164. 1971. pap. 4.50 o.p. (ISBN 0-8066-1129-4, 10-3990, Augsburg). Augsburg Fortress.

Living with Mysterious Epilepsy: My 48-Year Victory Over Fear. Ruth C. Adam. Ed. by Walter C. Alvarez. LC 73-92057. 1974. 6.00 o.p. (ISBN 0-682-47906-3, Banner). Exposition-Phoenix.

Living with Nature in Hawaii. rev. ed. Jan Moon. 136p. 1979. pap. 5.95 o.p. (ISBN 0-912180-06-4). Petroglyph.

Living with Pain. Barbara Wolf. 1977. 10.95 o.p. (ISBN 0-8164-9328-6). Phoenix Soc.

Living with Paraplegia. Michael A. Rogers. 200p. (Orig.). 1986. pap. 13.95 o.p. (ISBN 0-571-13951-5). Faber & Faber.

Living with Preschoolers. Williard Abraham. (Illus.). 160p. 1976. pap. 3.95 o.p. (ISBN 0-89019-055-0). Norwalk Pr.

Living with Surgery: Before & After. Paul J. Melluzzo & Eleanor Nealon. LC 80-51388. 320p. (Orig.). 1981. pap. 6.95 o.s.i. (ISBN 0-03-059081-7). H Holt & Co.

Living with Surgery, Before & After. Paul J. Melluzzo & Eleanor Nealon. LC 81-1265. pap. cancelled o.s.i. (ISBN 0-317-26116-9, 2024998). Bks Demand UMI.

Living with Teens: A Parent's Handbook. Howard R. Bingham. LC 83-72479. 71p. 1983. 6.95 o.p. (ISBN 0-87747-956-9). Deseret Bk.

Living with the Kennedys: The Joan Kennedy Story. Marcia Chellis. 240p. 1985. 17.45 o.p. (ISBN 0-671-50152-6). S&S.

Living with the Kennedys: The Joan Kennedy Story. Marcia Chellis. (General Ser.). 1986. lib. bdg. 19.95 o.p. (ISBN 0-8161-4058-8, Large Print Bks.). G K Hall.

Living with Your Teenage Daughter & Liking it. Meryl Fishman & Kathleen Horwich. 1983. pap. 8.50 o.p. (ISBN 0-671-46880-4, Fireside). S&S.

Living Without Guilt & or Blame: Conscience, Superego & Psychotherapy. Ben N. Ard, Jr. 137p. 1983. 8.00 o.p. (ISBN 0-682-40127-7). Exposition-Phoenix.

Living Wonders: Mysteries & Curiosities of the Animal World. John Michell & Robert J. Rickard. LC 82-50859. (Illus., Orig.). 1983. pap. 9.95 o.s.i. (ISBN 0-500-27263-8). Thames Hudson.

Living Word: Scripture & Myth, Vol. 1. William J. O'Malley. LC 80-80534. 180p. (Orig.). (gr. 9-12). 1980. pap. text ed. 4.95 o.p. (ISBN 0-8091-9558-5). Paulist Pr.

Living Word Vocabulary: A 44,000 Word Vocabulary Inventory. Edgar Dale & J. O'Rourke. 704p. 1981. 49.95 o.p. (ISBN 0-7166-3115-6). World Bk.

Living Worldwide. (Multinational Business Guides). 1980. pap. 60.00 o.p. (ISBN 0-931000-11-4). Suburban Pub CT.

Living Zen. Robert Linssen. Tr. by Diana Abrahams-Curiel. 1971. pap. 12.50 o.p. (ISBN 0-394-17391-0, E578, Ever). Grove.

Livre de Seyntz Medicines. Henry Duke of Lancaster. Ed. by E. J. Arnould. 1967. Repr. of 1940 ed. 19.00 o.p. (ISBN 0-384-22400-8). Johnson Repr.

Livy: The Composition of His History. T. J. Luce. LC 77-72126. 1977. 36.00 o.p. (ISBN 0-691-03552-0). Princeton U Pr.

Lizard Ecology: A Symposium. Ed. by William W. Milstead. LC 66-17955. 312p. 1967. 31.00x o.p. (ISBN 0-8262-0058-3). U of Mo Pr.

Lizzie. Evan Hunter. LC 83-15642. 430p. 1984. 16.95 o.p. (ISBN 0-87795-570-0, Arbor Hse). Morrow.

Llegaron los Hippies. Manuel Abreu. 112p. 1978. pap. 3.95 o.p. (ISBN 0-940238-24-1). Ediciones Huracan.

Llewellyn's Moon Sign Book, 1984. Ed. by Terry Buske & Carl L. Weschcke. LC 13-1677. (Annual Ser.). (Illus.). 512p. 1983. pap. 3.95 o.p. (ISBN 0-87542-413-9, L-413). Llewellyn Pubns.

Llewellyn's Sun Sign Book, Annual 1987. 4th ed. Llewellyn Publications Staff. Ed. by Terry Buske. 400p. 1986. pap. 3.95 o.p. (ISBN 0-87542-432-5). Llewellyn Pubns.

Llewellyn's Sun Sign Book, 1984. Ed. by Mitt Wood. (Annual Ser.). (Illus.). 500p. 1983. pap. 3.95 o.p. (ISBN 0-87542-416-3). Llewellyn Pubns.

Llewellyn's Sun Sign Book, 1985. 2nd ed. Llewellyn Publications Staff. Ed. by Matthew Wood. 400p. pap. 3.95 o.p. (ISBN 0-87542-428-7, L-420). Llewellyn Pubns.

Llewellyn's 1987: Astrological Calendar. 57th ed. Llewellyn Publications Staff. Ed. by Terry Buske. (Llewellyn Annual). (Illus.). 56p. 1986. pap. 6.95 o.p. (ISBN 0-87542-430-9). Llewellyn Pubns.

Llewellyn's 1987: Daily Planetary Guide & Astrologer's Date Book. 10th ed. Llewellyn Publications Staff. Ed. by Terry Buske. 160p. 1986. pap. 5.95 o.p. (ISBN 0-87542-431-7). Llewellyn Pubns.

Llewellyn's 1987: Moon Sign Book. 82nd ed. Llewellyn Publications Staff. Ed. by Terry Buske. LC 13-1677. (Llewellyn Annual). 400p. 1986. mass market size 3.95 o.p. (ISBN 0-87542-429-5). Llewellyn Pubns.

LLoyd's Maritime Directory, 1986. 5th ed. 750p. 148.00 o.p. (ISBN 0-8002-4027-8). Intl Pubns Serv.

Lloyd's of London: A Portrait. Hugh Cockerell. LC 84-70597. 150p. 1984. 27.50 o.p. (ISBN 0-87094-570-X). Dow Jones-Irwin.

Lloyd's Ship Manager Marine Equipment Guide 1987. 400p. 1986. pap. 95.00 o.p. (ISBN 1-85044-086-7). Intl Pubns Serv.

LO! Charles Fort. Ed. by Lester Del Rey. LC 75-407. (Library of Science Fiction). 1975. lib. bdg. 21.00 o.p. (ISBN 0-8240-1412-X). Garland Pub.

Lo Linkert's Golftoons. 3rd ed. Lo Linkert. (Illus.). 1980. 4.95 o.p. (ISBN 0-89149-037-X). Jolex.

Load-Bearing Wall Panels: Design & Application. (PCI Journal Reprints Ser.). 16p. pap. 5.00 o.p. (ISBN 0-686-40039-9, JR106). P-PCI.

Loaded & Rollin' Trucks & Their Drivers. rev. ed. John Lynott. (Encore Edition). (Illus.). 1979. pap. 1.95 o.p. (ISBN 0-684-16911-8, SL856, ScribT). Scribner.

Loan Officers Handbook. 795p. 1986. 60.00 o.p. (ISBN 0-317-66139-6, 128). Bank Admin Inst.

Loan Review: A Guide. 2nd., rev ed. 96p. 1987. 48.00 o.p. (230). Bank Admin Inst.

Loba. Diane Di Prima. LC 78-50779. (Illus.). 1978. 15.00 o.p. (ISBN 0-914728-21-0); pap. 5.00 o.p. (ISBN 0-914728-20-2); signed ed. 15.95 o.p. (ISBN 0-914728-22-9). Wingbow Pr.

Lobbying: A Constitutionally Protected Right. Hope Eastman. LC 77-85166. 35p. 1977. pap. 5.00 o.p. (ISBN 0-8447-3267-2). Am Enterprise.

Loblolly Book: Omnibus Edition. Thad Sitton & Lincoln King. (Loblolly Ser.). (Illus.). 512p. (gr. 3-6). 1986. Set. 24.95 o.p. (ISBN 0-87719-059-3). Texas Month Pr.

Local Anaesthetic. Gunter Grass. Tr. by Ralph Manheim. LC 78-100501. (Helen & Kurt Wolff Bks.). 1970. 6.95 o.s.i. (ISBN 0-15-152957-4). HarBraceJ.

Local Analgesia in Dentistry. 2nd ed. D. Roberts & Sowray. (Illus.). 168p. 1979. pap. 24.00 o.p. (ISBN 0-7236-0507-6, Pub. by John Wright UK). Butterworth.

Local Analgesia in Dentistry. D. H. Roberts & J. H. Sowray. (Illus.). 192p. 1987. pap. 27.50 o.p. (ISBN 0-7236-0954-3). Butterworth.

Local Area Networking Directory. 3rd ed. Phillips Publishing, Inc. Staff. Ed. by Mark Kimmel. 275p. 1983. pap. 127.00 o.p. (ISBN 0-934960-11-9). Phillips Pub Inc.

Local Area Networks: A User's Guide for Business Professionals. James H. Green. (Illus.). 275p. 1985. pap. 17.95 o.p. (ISBN 0-673-18065-4). Scott F.

Local Area Networks: Applications, Technologies & Opportunities. International Resource Development, Inc. Staff. 215p. 1984. 1650.00x o.p. (ISBN 0-88694-592-5). Intl Res Dev.

Local Area Networks in Large Organzitions. Madron. 1984. 16.95 o.p. (ISBN 0-8104-6205-2). Sams.

Local Area Personal Income, 1979-84: Summary. Annual ed. (Local Area Personal Income Ser.: Vol. 1). (Illus.). 161p. 1986. pap. 8.00 o.p. (ISBN 0-318-21624-8, 003-010-00165-8). USGPO.

Local Coalitions in Europe. Ed. by Colin Mellors & Bert Pijnenburg. 256p. 1988. lib. bdg. 57.50 o.p. (ISBN 0-415-01271-6). Routledge Chapman & Hall.

Local Cohomology: A Seminar Given by A. Grothendieck at Harvard University, 1961. A. Grothendieck. Ed. by Hartshorne. (Lecture Notes in Mathematics Ser.: Vol. 41). 1967. pap. 10.70 o.p. (ISBN 0-387-03912-0). Springer-Verlag.

Local Control in Education: Three Demonstration School Districts in New York City. Marilyn Gittell et al. LC 73-185779. (Special Studies in U. S. Economic, Social & Political Issues). 1972. 27.50x o.p. (ISBN 0-89197-827-5); pap. text ed. 12.50x o.p. (ISBN 0-89197-828-3). Irvington.

Local Currents & Their Applications. Ed. by A. S. Wightman & D. H. Sharp. LC 73-77075. 160p. 1975. pap. 18.50 o.p. (ISBN 0-444-10521-2, North-Holland). Elsevier.

Local Government. Howard Elcock. 288p. 1982. 29.95x o.p. (ISBN 0-416-85750-7, NO. 3682); pap. 12.50x o.p. (ISBN 0-416-33170-X, NO. 3683). Routledge Chapman & Hall.

Local Government & Public Employees: Journal Articles, 1974-1984. Dale E. Casper. (Public Administration Ser.: P 1741). 13p. 1985. 2.00 o.p. (ISBN 0-89028-521-7). Vance Biblios.

Local Government & Rural Development in the Philippines. Santiago S. Simpas et al. (Special Series on Rural Local Government: No. 12). (Illus.). 109p. (Orig.). 1974. pap. text ed. 3.50 o.p. (ISBN 0-86731-098-7). Cornell CIS RDC.

Local Government Auditing: A Manual for Public Officials. Ed. by Peter F. Rousmaniere et al. Arnold Olenick & Vincent Pirnicory. 90p. 1979. pap. 14.95 o.p. (ISBN 0-916450-27-9). Nat Civic League.

Local Government in China under the Ch'ing. Ch'u T'ung-tsu. LC 62-11396. (East Asian Ser: No. 9). 1962. 27.00x o.p. (ISBN 0-674-53675-4). Harvard U Pr.

Local Government: Is It Manageable? Gordon Bayley. 1979. 23.00 o.p. (ISBN 0-08-024279-0). Pergamon.

Local Heroines: A Women's History Gazetteer to England, Scotland & Wales. Jane Legget. (Illus.). 470p. 1988. text ed. (ISBN 0-86358-037-8, Pub. by Pandora Pr); pap. text ed. (Pub. by Pandora Pr). Routledge Chapman & Hall.

Local History & Genealogy Resources of the California State Library & Its Sutro Branch. 44p. 1983. write for info. o.p. CA State Library Fndtn.

Local Income Taxes: Economic Effects & Equity. R. Stafford Smith. LC 77-633802. (Illus.). 220p. (Orig.). 1972. pap. 4.50x o.p. (ISBN 0-87772-076-2). UCB IGS.

Local Institutional Development for Primary Health Care. Rebecca M. Doan et al. (Special Series on Local Institutional Development: No. 4). 61p. 1985. pap. text ed. 6.50 o.p. (ISBN 0-86731-111-8). Cornell CIS RDC.

Local Institutions & Rural Development in Malaysia. Stephen Chee. 112p. 1974. pap. 3.50 o.p. (ISBN 0-317-56349-1). Cornell CIS RDC.

Local Institutions & Rural Development in South Korea. Ronald Aqua. 82p. 1974. pap. 3.50 o.p. (ISBN 0-86731-099-5). Cornell CIS RDC.

Local Mechanisms Controlling Blood Vessels. W. R. Keatinge & M. Clare Harman. (Monographs of the Physiological Society: No. 37). 1980. 50.50 o.p. (ISBN 0-12-402850-0). Acad Pr.

Local Network Handbook. George R. Davis. (Illus.). 260p. 1983. pap. text ed. 32.50 o.p. (ISBN 0-07-015823-1). McGraw.

Local Plan Inquiry: The Role in Local Plan Preparation, Vol. 19/2. Ed. by G. Marsh. (Illus.). 80p. 1983. pap. 22.00 o.p. (ISBN 0-08-030442-7). Pergamon.

Local Politics in Britain. rev. ed. John Gyford. 192p. (Orig.). 1984. pap. 13.50 o.p. (ISBN 0-7099-1168-8, Pub. by Croom Helm Ltd). Routledge Chapman & Hall.

Local Public Schools: How to Pay for Them? Dorothy C. Tompkins. LC 72-4083. (Public Policy Bibliographies: No. 2). 102p. (Orig.). 1972. pap. 3.50x o.p. (ISBN 0-87772-152-1). UCB IGS.
Local Quantum Theory. R. Jost. (Italian Physical Society: Course 45). 1970. 77.00 o.p. (ISBN 0-12-368845-0). Acad Pr.
Local Telecommunications: Into the Digital Era. Ed. by J. M. Griffiths. (Telecommunications Ser.). 304p. 1986. 55.00 o.s.i. (ISBN 0-86341-080-4, TE017). Inst Elect Eng.
Locating Computer Software. Ted Kruse. 110p. 1985. lib. bdg. 17.00 o.p. (ISBN 0-8240-8719-4). Garland Pub.
Locating Language in Time & Space, Vol. I. Ed. by William Labov. LC 80-757. (Quantitative Analysis of Linguistic Structure Ser.). 1980. 44.50 o.p. (ISBN 0-12-432060-0). Acad Pr.
Location of Immigrant Industry Within a U. K. Assisted Area: The Scottish Experience. Henderson. (Progress in Planning Ser.: Vol. 14, Part 2). (Illus.). 121p. 1980. pap. 16.25 o.p. (ISBN 0-08-026807-2). Pergamon.
Locations. Jim Harrison. LC 68-21703. 1968. 4.95 o.p. (ISBN 0-393-04257-X). Norton.
Loch Ness Monster: The Evidence. Steuart Campbell. (Illus.). 160p. (Orig.). 1986. pap. 8.95 o.p. (ISBN 0-85030-451-2, Pub. by Aquarian Pr England). Sterling.
Locked-Wheel Pavement Skid Tester Correlation & Calibration Techniques. (National Cooperative Highway Research Project Report). 100p. 1974. 6.00 o.p. (ISBN 0-309-02302-5). Transport Res Bd.
Locke's Essay Concerning Human Understanding, Bks. II & IV. John Locke. 405p. 1962. Repr. of 1905 ed. 4.95 o.p. (ISBN 0-87548-033-0). Open Court.
Locke's Travels in France, Sixteen Seventy-Five to Sixteen Seventy-Nine: As Related in His Journals, Correspondence & Other Papers. John Lough. LC 83-48572. (Philosophy of John Locke Ser.). 375p. 1984. lib. bdg. 45.00 o.p. (ISBN 0-8240-5607-8). Garland Pub.
Lockheed Hercules. Francis K. Mason. (Illus.). 242p. 1985. 19.95 o.p. (ISBN 0-85059-698-X, Pub. by PSL P Stephens England). Sterling.
Loco the Burro & Ali the Jungle Beasts: A Story Poem for Children. J. Russ Whitman. (Illus.). (gr. 2-5). 1979. 5.00 o.p. (ISBN 0-682-49255-8). Exposition-Phoenix.
Locomotion & Energetics in Anthropods. Ed. by Clyde F. Herreid, II & Charles R. Fourtner. LC 81-13779. 554p. 1981. 89.50x o.p. (ISBN 0-306-40830-9, Plenum Pr). Plenum Pub.
Locomotion of Animals. R. McNeill Alexander. (Tertiary Level Biology Ser.). 192p. 1982. 39.95x o.p. (ISBN 0-412-00001-6, NO.5001, Pub. by Chapman & Hall); pap. 18.95x o.p. (ISBN 0-412-00011-3, NO. 5002). Routledge Chapman & Hall.
Locomotive Boiler Explosions. C. H. Hewison. (Illus.). 144p. 1983. 22.95 o.p. (ISBN 0-7153-8305-1). David & Charles.
Locomotives of the Rio Grande: Colorado Railroad Museum. LC 80-24685. (Illus.). 96p. 1981. 9.95 o.p. (ISBN 0-918654-25-4). Co RR Mus.
Loess: Lithology & Genesis. Ed. by I. J. Smalley. LC 75-30690. (Benchmark Papers in Geology: Vol. 26). 448p. 1975. 80.50 o.p. (ISBN 0-12-787472-0). Acad Pr.
Loesungsheft I see Deutsch X 3.
Loesungsheft II see Deutsch X 3.
Loesungsheft III see Deutsch X 3.
Loetz Austria 1900 Glass-Glass-Verre-Vetri. Waltraud Neuwirth. (Illus.). 320p. (Eng., Ger., Fr. & Ital.). 1987. 55.00 o.p. (ISBN 3-900282-26-9, Pub. by Waltraud Neuwirth). Seven Hills Bk Dists.
Loetz Austria 1905-1918, Glass. Waltraud Neuwirth. (Illus.). 400p. (Eng., Fr., Ger. & Ital.). 1987. 55.00 o.p. (ISBN 3-900282-27-7, Pub. by Waltraud Neuwirth). Seven Hills Bk Dists.
Loffelchen: Eine Erzahlung. Albrecht Goes. Ed. by Christoph E. Schweitzer. LC 68-13150. (Orig., Ger.). 1968. pap. text ed. 2.50x o.p. (ISBN 0-89197-280-3). Irvington.
Log & Trig Tables. Lyman M. Kells et al. 1955. pap. text ed. 2.95 o.p. (ISBN 0-07-033601-6). McGraw.
Log Buildings. facs. ed. S. A. Witzel. (Shorey Lost Arts Ser.). pap. 3.95 o.s.i. (ISBN 0-8466-6043-1, U43). Shorey.
Log of Baker Abel. Paul Strotman. 32p. 1988. 6.50 o.p. (ISBN 0-8062-3083-5). Carlton.
Log Scaling & Timber Cruising. J. R. Dilworth. 1984. pap. text ed. 11.90x o.p. (ISBN 0-88246-031-5). Oreg St U Bkstrs.
Logan Turner's Diseases of the Nose, Throat & Ear. 9th ed. Birrell. 26.00 o.p. (ISBN 0-7236-0617-X). Butterworth.
Logging & Lumbering. Kathleen Abrams & Lawrence Abrams. LC 80-19473. (Illus.). 96p. (gr. 4 up). 1980. lib. bdg. 9.29 o.s.i. (ISBN 0-671-34007-7). Messner.
Logging Railroads of the White Mountains. C. Francis Belcher. (Illus.). 256p. 1981. pap. 14.95 o.s.i. (ISBN 0-910146-32-2). AMC Books.
Logic, 2 vols. Hermann Lotze. Ed. by Maurice Natanson. LC 78-66738. (Phenomenology Background, Foreground & Influences Ser.: Vol. 8). 1980. Set. lib. bdg. 94.00 o.p. (ISBN 0-8240-9562-6). Garland Pub.
Logic & Grammar see Metaphor.
Logic & Knowledge: 1901-1950. Bertrand Russell. Ed. by Robert C. Marsh. 398p. 1977. text ed. 27.95x o.p. (ISBN 0-04-164001-2). Unwin Hyman.
Logic & Language. A. G. Flew. 1953. (ISBN 0-8022-0515-1). Philos Lib.
Logic & Language of Education. George F. Kneller. LC 66-17627. 242p. 1966. text ed. 14.50 o.p. (ISBN 0-471-49518-2, Pub. by Wiley). Krieger.
Logic & Philosophy: Selected Readings. Ed. by Gary Iseminger. (Century Philosophy Ser). 1980. text ed. 18.95x o. p. o.s.i. (ISBN 0-89197-829-1); pap. text ed. 14.95x o.s.i. (ISBN 0-89197-830-5). Irvington.
Logic & the Nature of Reality. 2nd ed. L. O. Kattsoff. 1967. pap. 12.50 o.p. (ISBN 0-685-25490-9). E J Brill USA.
Logic, Automata & Algorithms. Mark A. Aiserman et al. (Mathematics in Science & Engineering Ser). (Rus). 1971. 89.00 o.p. (ISBN 0-12-046350-4). Acad Pr.
Logic Colloquium 1980: Papers Intended for the European Meeting of the Association for Symbolic Logic. Ed. by D. Van Dalen & D. Lascar. (Studies in Logic & the Foundations of Mathematics: Vol. 108). 342p. 1982. 73.75 o.p. (ISBN 0-444-86465-2, I-319-82, North Holland). Elsevier.
Logic Design of Digital Systems. 2nd ed. Dietmeyer. 1978. text ed. write for info. o.p. (ISBN 0-205-05960-0, EDP 285960). Allyn.
Logic for Living. Henry H. Williams. Ed. by Mary J. Hammer. 1951. (ISBN 0-8022-1887-3). Philos Lib.
Logic for Mathematicians. 2nd ed. John B. Rosser. LC 77-7663. 1978. text ed. 19.95 o.p. (ISBN 0-8284-0294-9). Chelsea Pub.
Logic for Problem Solving. R. Kowalski. (Artificial Intelligence Ser.: Vol. 7). 295p. 1979. 36.50 o.p. (ISBN 0-444-00365-7, North Holland); pap. 23.00 o.p. (ISBN 0-444-00368-1). Elsevier.
Logic for the Labyrinth: A Guide to Critical Thinking. Garth L. Hallett. 240p. 1984. lib. bdg. 26.75 o.p. (ISBN 0-8191-3802-9); pap. text ed. 11.25 o.p. (ISBN 0-8191-3803-7). U Pr of Amer.
Logic for the Millions. A. E. Mander. (ISBN 0-8022-1044-9). Philos Lib.
Logic, Induction & Ontology. P. K. Sen. (Jadavpur Studies in Philosophy: Vol. 2). 241p. 1982. text ed. 12.50x o.p. (ISBN 0-391-02491-4). Humanities.
Logic, Laws, & Life: Some Philosophical Complications. Ed. by Robert G. Colodny. LC 76-50886. (Philosophy of Science Ser.). 1977. 24.95x o.p. (ISBN 0-8229-3346-2). U of Pittsburgh Pr.
Logic of Images in International Relations. Robert Jervis. LC 79-90951. 1970. 31.50 o.p. (ISBN 0-691-07532-8). Princeton U Pr.
Logic of Inconsistency: A Study in Nonstandard Possible-World Semantics & Ontology. Nicholas Rescher & Robert Brandom. LC 80-11338. (American Philosophical Quarterly Library of Philosophy). 174p. 1979. 22.50x o.p. (ISBN 0-8476-6248-9). Rowman.
Logic of International Relations. 5th ed. Walter S. Jones. 1984. pap. text ed. 21.00 o.p. (ISBN 0-316-47288-3); tchr's. manual avail. o.p. (ISBN 0-316-47289-1). Scott F.
Logic of Poverty: The Case of the Brazilian Northeast. Simon Mitchell. (Direct Edition Ser.). 200p. (Orig.). 1981. pap. 18.95x o.p. (ISBN 0-7100-0637-3). Routledge Chapman & Hall.
Logic of Promise in Moltmann's Theology. Christopher Morse. LC 78-54556. 192p. 1979. 12.95 o.p. (ISBN 0-8006-0523-3, 1-523, Fortress). Augsburg Fortress.
Logic of Psychology: A Dynamic Approach. Reuben Fine. LC 82-21983. 232p. (Orig.). 1983. lib. bdg. 27.25 o.p. (ISBN 0-8191-2891-0); pap. text ed. 12.50 o.p. (ISBN 0-8191-2892-9). U Pr of Amer.
Logic of Social Action: An Introduction to Sociological Analysis. Raymond Boudon. Tr. by David Silverman from Fr. 208p. 1981. 21.95X o.p. (ISBN 0-7100-0857-0); pap. 9.95x o.p. (ISBN 0-7100-0858-9). Routledge Chapman & Hall.
Logic of Subjectivity: Kierkegaard's Philosophy of Religion. Louis P. Pojman. LC 83-1053. 174p. 1984. 17.50x o.p. (ISBN 0-8173-0166-6). U of Ala Pr.
Logic of the Scientific Method. Donald Brady. LC 73-15697. 92p. 1973. pap. text ed. 6.95x o.p. (ISBN 0-8422-0361-3). Irvington.
Logic: Or, the Right Use of Reason in the Enquiry after Truth, with a Variety of Rules to Guard Against Error, in the Affairs of Religion & Human Life as Well as the Sciences. Isaac Watts. LC 83-48579. (Philosophy of John Locke Ser.). 365p. 1984. lib. bdg. 44.00 o.p. (ISBN 0-8240-5615-9). Garland Pub.
Logic Programming Techniques. Steven Hardy & Leon Sterling. (Illus.). 75p. 1988. pap. text ed. 12.00 o.p. (ISBN 0-929280-17-2). Amer Artificial.
Logic, Science, & Dialectic: Collected Papers in Greek Philosophy. G. E. Owen. LC 85-17479. 394p. 42.50 o.p. (ISBN 0-8014-9359-5); pap. 19.95 o.p. (ISBN 0-317-64880-2). Cornell U Pr.
Logic: Techniques of Formal Reasoning. Donald Kalish & Richard Montague. 1964. text ed. 18.95 o.p. (ISBN 0-15-551180-7, HC). HarBraceJ.
Logica Modernorum, 2 vol. set, Pts. 1 & 2, Vol. 2. Lambertus M. De Rijk. (Philosophical Texts & Studies: Vol. 16). 1967. text ed. 110.00x o.p. Humanities.
Logical Analysis of Quantum Mechanics. E. Scheibe. 1973. 71.00 o.p. (ISBN 0-08-017158-3). Pergamon.
Logical Answers to Difficult Questions. Richard K. Suffern. 64p. 1984. 5.50 o.p. (ISBN 0-682-40197-8). Exposition-Phoenix.
Logical Data Base Design. Robert M. Curtice & Paul E. Jones, Jr. (Van Nos Reinhold Data Processing Ser.). 272p. 1982. 36.95 o.p. (ISBN 0-442-24501-7). Van Nos Reinhold.
Logical Design of Operating Systems. Alan C. Shaw. (Illus.). 304p. 1974. text ed. 46.00 o.p. (ISBN 0-13-540112-7). P-H.
Logical Self Defense. 2nd ed. R. H. Johnson & J. A. Blair. 1983. text ed. 13.95 o.p. (ISBN 0-07-548588-5). McGraw.
Logico-Linguistic Papers. P. F. Strawson. 1974. pap. 14.95x o.p. (ISBN 0-416-70300-3, NO. 2537). Routledge Chapman & Hall.
Logistics & Benefits of Using Mathematical Models of Hydrologic & Water Resource Systems: Selected Papers from an International Symposium, IIASA Laxenburg, Austria. Ed. by A. J. Askew et al. 270p. 1981. 67.00 o.p. (ISBN 0-08-025662-7). Pergamon.
LOGO Activities for the Computer: A Beginner's Guide. Jane Hyman & Pat Ruane. (gr. 3 up). 1984. pap. 8.95 o.s.i. (ISBN 0-671-49923-8). Wanderer Bks.
Logos. Winston. Date not set. 15.00 o.p. Ktav.
Loin de Rueil. Raymond Queneau. 234p. 1944. 9.95 o.p. (ISBN 0-686-54677-6). Schoenhof.
Loire: Phaidon Cultural Guides. 1986. 14.95 o.p. (ISBN 0-13-540121-6). P-H.
Loire Valley, Normandy, Brittany. Ian Robertson. (Blue Guides Ser.). (Illus.). 24.95 o.p. (ISBN 0-393-01542-4); pap. 15.95 o.p. (ISBN 0-393-00095-8). Norton.
Loire Valley Travel Guide. (Berlitz Travel Guides). (Illus.). 1982. pap. 4.95 o.p. (ISBN 0-02-969310-1, Berlitz). Macmillan.
Lokaneyya-Pakarana. Padmanabh S. Jaini. (Pali Text Society Ser.: No. 175). 336p. 1986. 29.95 o.p. (ISBN 0-86013-150-5, 31505, Pali Text). Routledge Chapman & Hall.
Lola: A Novel. Delacorta, pseud. 1985. 9.70 o.s.i. (ISBN 0-671-47752-8). Summit Bks.
Lolita. Vladimir Nabokov. (Rus.). pap. 8.00 o.p. (ISBN 0-88233-228-7). Ardis Pubs.
Lolita: A Screenplay. Vladimir Nabokov. LC 73-15918. 228p. 1983. pap. text ed. 6.95 o.p. (ISBN 0-07-045768-9). McGraw.
Lollipop Books Ser. (A Lollipop Is Best, Eating Lollipops, Find the Lollipops, We Like Lollipops.). (Illus.). 8p. (ps-2). 1987. pap. 3.95 ea. o.p. (ISBN 0-02-688523-9, Pub. by Checkerboard Pr). Macmillan.
Lollipop Lexicon. Lois Johnson. 1979. 4.50 o.p. (ISBN 0-682-49348-3). Exposition-Phoenix.
Lollipops & Parachutes: One Hundred & Twenty Stimulating Learning Activities for Children of Active, Caring Adults. Donna Stiscak. (Illus.). 112p. 1984. text ed. 10.95 o.p. (ISBN 0-07-061503-9). McGraw.
Lomas. Ed. by Frederic A. Engel. LC 81-42219. (Prehistoric Andean Ecology: Man Settlement & the Environment in the Andes Ser.: Vol. 5). (Illus.). 188p. 1987. text ed. cancelled o.s.i. (ISBN 0-391-03388-3). Humanities.
Lombard Cavalcade. Virginia Coffman. LC 81-67523. 464p. 1982. 15.50 o.p. (ISBN 0-87795-355-4, Arbor Hse). Morrow.
Lombard Heiress. Virginia Coffman. LC 82-72071. 304p. 1982. 14.95 o.p. (ISBN 0-87795-434-8, Arbor Hse). Morrow.
Lonaconing Journals: The Founding of a Coal & Iron Community, 1837-1840. Katherine A. Harvey. LC 76-50177. (Transactions Ser.: Vol. 67, Pt. 2). (Illus.). 1977. pap. 10.00 o.p. (ISBN 0-87169-672-X). Am Philos.
London. 12th ed. Ylva French. (Blue Guide). 1986. pap. 15.95 o.p. (ISBN 0-393-30081-1). Norton.
London. rev. ed. F. George Kay. LC 79-89188. (Rand McNally Pocket Guide). (Illus., Orig.). 1984. pap. 5.95 o.p. (ISBN 0-528-84293-5). Rand McNally.
London. (AA-OS Leisure Guides). 120p. 1988. 24.95 o.p. (ISBN 0-86145-504-5, Pub. by British Tour); pap. 19.95 o.p. (ISBN 0-86145-503-7, Pub. by British Tour). Salem Hse Pubs.
London. Stuart Rossiter. (Blue Guides Ser.). (Illus.). 1984. 24.95 o.p. (ISBN 0-393-01543-2); pap. 12.95 o.p. (ISBN 0-393-00096-6). Norton.
London Affair. Anthony Stuart. LC 80-66500. 1981. 9.95 o.p. (ISBN 0-87795-275-2, Arbor Hse). Morrow.
London Album: 1840-1915. Roger Whitehouse. (Illus.). 192p. 1982. 31.50 o.p. (ISBN 0-436-57090-4, Pub. by Secker & Warburg UK); pap. 29.95 o.p. (ISBN 0-436-57091-2, Pub. by Secker & Warburg UK). David & Charles.
London Bibliography of Social Sciences, Ninth Supplement: 1974, Vol. 32. D. A. Clarke. 461p. 1975. 64.00 o.p. (ISBN 0-7201-0524-2). Mansell.
London Bibliography of Social Sciences, Tenth Supplement: 1975, Vol. 33. D. A. Clarke. 418p. 1976. 64.00 o.p. (ISBN 0-7201-0634-6). Mansell.
London Bibliography of the Social Sciences: Eleventh Supplement, 1976, Vol. 34. D. A. Clarke. LC 31-9970. 458p. 1977. lib. bdg. 64.00 o.p. (ISBN 0-7201-0721-0). Mansell.
London Bibliography of the Social Sciences: Eighth Supplement, 1972-1973, Vols. 29-31. D. A. Clarke. 1768p. 1975. 191.00x o.p. (ISBN 0-7201-0454-8). Mansell.
London Bibliography of the Social Sciences: Fourteenth Supplement, 1979, Vol. 37. Ed. by D. A. Clarke. 400p. 1980. lib. bdg. 80.00 o.p. (ISBN 0-7201-1594-9). Mansell.
London Bibliography of the Social Sciences, Twelfth Supplement, 1977, Vol. 35. Ed. by D. A. Clarke. 402p. 1978. lib. bdg. 48.00x o.p. (ISBN 0-7201-0829-2). Mansell.
London Bibliography of the Social Sciences: Thirteenth Supplement, 1978, Vol. 36. Ed. by D. A. Clarke. 416p. 1979. lib. bdg. 69.00 o.p. (ISBN 0-7201-0929-9). Mansell.
London by Bus & Tube. Date not set. Salem Hse Pubs.
London Churches at the Reformation: With an Account of Their Contents. Henry B. Walters. (Church Historical Society London N. S. Ser.: No. 37). Repr. of 1939 ed. 95.00 o.p. (ISBN 0-8115-3160-0). Kraus Repr.
London Guide. Date not set. (ISBN 0-905522-68-0). Salem Hse Pubs.
London in Your Pocket. Fairgrieve. (City in Your Pocket Ser.). 1984. pap. 2.95 o.p. (ISBN 0-8120-2973-9). Barron.
London Life. Henry James. LC 57-6531. 1979. pap. 3.25 o.p. (ISBN 0-394-17076-8, B419, BC). Grove.
London Missionary Society's Report of the Proceedings Against the Late Rev. J. Smith of Demerara, Who Was Tried Under Martial Law & Condemned to Death, on a Charge of Aiding & Assisting in a Rebellion of Negro Slaves. London Missionary Society Staff. LC 78-79809. 1970. Repr. of 1824 ed. 35.00x o.p. (ISBN 0-8371-1506-X, LMS&, Pub. by Negro U Pr). Greenwood.
London Plenary Meeting of the Trilateral Commission. Trilateral Comm.
London Police in the Nineteenth Century. John Wilkes. (Cambridge Topic Bks.). (Illus.). 52p. (gr. 5-10). 1984. PLB 8.95 o.p. (ISBN 0-8225-1233-5). Lerner Pubns.
London Shopping Guide & Streetfinder. Date not set. Salem Hse Pubs.
London Signs & Inscriptions. Philip Norman. LC 68-22039. (Camden Library Ser). (Illus.). 258p. 1968. Repr. of 1893 ed. 35.00x o.p. (ISBN 0-8103-3496-8). Gale.
London Snow. Paul Theroux. (gr. k-10). 1980. 6.95 o.p. (ISBN 0-395-29458-4). HM.
London Street Games. 2nd ed. Norman Douglas. LC 68-31089. 114p. 1968. Repr. of 1931 ed. 30.00x o.p. (ISBN 0-8103-3477-1). Gale.
London Theatre Today: A Guide for Travelers. Mildred Fischer. (Illus.). 144p. (Orig.). 1981. pap. 4.50 o.p. (ISBN 0-914846-09-4). Golden West Pub.
London Transports. Maeve Binchy. 1986. pap. 3.95 o.p. (ISBN 0-440-14870-7). Dell.
London: Where to Go, What to Do. (Illus.). 128p. 1988. pap. 12.95 o.p. (ISBN 0-86145-480-4, Pub. by British Tour). Salem Hse Pubs.
London Yankees: Portraits of American Writers & Artists in England, 1894-1914. Stanley Weintraub. Tr. by Eileen Ellenbogen. LC 78-22276. 1979. 14.95 o.p. (ISBN 0-15-152978-7). HarBraceJ.
London's Homeless. John Greve. 76p. 1964. pap. text ed. 3.75x o.p. (ISBN 0-686-70849-0, Pub. by Bedford England). Gower Pub Co.
London's Lost Route to Basing-Stoke: The Story of the Basinstoke Canal. Paul A. Vine. LC 68-23819. (Illus.). 1968. 24.95x o.p. (ISBN 0-678-05641-2). Kelley.

Titles

London's Lost Route to the Sea: An Historical Account of the Inland Navigations Which Linked the Thames to the English Channel. 3rd ed. P. A. Vine. (Inland Waterways Histories Ser.). (Illus.). 328p. 1987. Repr. of 1973 ed. 35.95 o.p. (ISBN 0-7153-8778-2). David & Charles.

London's Secret History. Peter Bushell. 1983. 27.50x o.p. (ISBN 0-09-464730-5, Pub. by Constable Pubs UK). Trans-Atl-Phila.

Lone Hunt. William O. Steele. LC 56-10074. (Illus.). (gr. 4-6). 1956. 6.75 o.p. (ISBN 0-15-248293-8, HJ). HarBraceJ.

Lone Hunt. William O. Steele. LC 75-29489. (Illus.). 176p. (gr. 4-6). 1976. pap. 1.75 o.p. (ISBN 0-15-652983-1, VoyB). HarBraceJ.

Lone Journey: The Life of Roger Williams. Jeanette Eaton. LC 44-8239. (gr. 7 up). 1944. 5.95 o.p. (ISBN 0-15-248472-8, HJ). HarBraceJ.

Lone Journey: The Life of Roger Williams. Jeanette Eaton. LC 44-8239. (Illus.). 1966. pap. 0.75 o.p. (ISBN 0-15-652985-8, VoyB). HarBraceJ.

Lone Star & the Renegade Comanches, No. 10. Wesley Ellis. 192p. 1983. pap. 2.25 o.p. (ISBN 0-515-06235-9). Jove Pubns.

Lone Star Ranger. Zane Grey. (Large Print Bks.). 399p. 1986. lib. bdg. 16.95x o.p. (ISBN 0-8161-4123-1, Large Print Bks). G K Hall.

Lone Star Regionalism: The Dallas Nine & Their Circle. Ed. by Patrick Stewart. (Illus.). 224p. 1985. 29.95 o.p. (ISBN 0-87719-014-3); pap. 19.95 o.p. (ISBN 0-87719-015-1). Texas Month Pr.

Lone Woman & Others. Constance Urdang. LC 80-5261. (Pitt Poetry Ser.). 1980. 15.95x o.p. (ISBN 0-8229-3430-2); pap. 6.95 o.p. (ISBN 0-8229-5320-X). U of Pittsburgh Pr.

Loneliness. Irma Kurtz. 126p. 1984. 4.95x o.p. (ISBN 0-631-12578-7). Basil Blackwell.

Loneliness & Existential Freedom. James Park. (Existential Freedom Ser.: No. 4). 1974. pap. 5.00x o.p. (ISBN 0-89231-004-9). Existential Bks.

Loneliness Is Not a Disease. Tim Timmons. (Epiphany Bks.). 1983. pap. 2.25 o.s.i. (ISBN 0-345-30509-4). Ballantine.

Loneliness of Dying. Norbert Elias. 100p. 1985. text ed. 15.95x o.p. (ISBN 0-631-13902-8). Basil Blackwell.

Lonely African. Colin M. Turnbull. 1968. pap. 10.95 o.s.i. (ISBN 0-671-20069-0, Touchstone Bks). S&S.

Lonely God, Lonely Man. Dean Turner. LC 60-13363. 1961. (ISBN 0-8022-1741-9). Philos Lib.

Lonely Tower: Studies in the Poetry of W. B. Yeats. 2nd ed. T. R. Henn. (Library Reprints Ser.). xxiv, 412p. 1979. 59.95x o.p. (ISBN 0-416-72490-6, 2821). Routledge Chapman & Hall.

Loner. Bianca Bradbury. LC 75-105246. (Illus.). (gr. 3-7). 1970. 6.95 o.p. (ISBN 0-395-06655-7). HM.

Loner. Paige Dixon. LC 78-6843. (Illus.). (gr. 4-6). 1978. 6.95 o.p. (ISBN 0-689-30651-2, Atheneum). Macmillan.

Loners. Nancy Garden. 1974. pap. 0.95 o.p. (ISBN 0-380-00104-7, 20230). Avon.

Lone's Christmas Boots & Other Tales from the Mother Lode. Billy D. Edson. (Illus.). 95p. 1983. pap. 4.50 o.p. (ISBN 0-682-49916-1). Exposition-Phoenix.

Lonesome Traveler. Jack Kerouac. 1970. pap. 3.95 o.p. (ISBN 0-394-17171-3, B253, BC). Grove.

Lonesome Walls: An Odyssey Through Ghost Towns of the Old West. Tom Barkdull. LC 79-159490. 1971. 7.50 o.p. (ISBN 0-682-47298-0, Lochinvar). Exposition-Phoenix.

Lonesome Whistle. Dee Brown. LC 79-17990. (Illus.). 144p. (gr. 4-8). 1980. 8.95 o.s.i. (ISBN 0-03-050666-2). H Holt & Co.

Long Ago. Cyndy Szekeres. LC 76-56113. (Illus.). 1977. text ed. 9.95 o.p. (ISBN 0-07-062665-0). McGraw.

Long & Happy Life. Reynolds Price. 1983. pap. 2.25 o.p. (ISBN 0-380-01399-1, 59279-7, Bard). Avon.

Long Christmas Dinner & Other Plays in One Act. Thornton Wilder. 1980. pap. 2.50 o.p. (ISBN 0-380-50245-3, 50245-3, Bard). Avon.

Long Desire. Evan S. Connell. LC 78-14175. 288p. 1980. 10.95 o.s.i. (ISBN 0-03-046161-8); pap. 4.95 o.s.i. (ISBN 0-03-057793-4). H Holt & Co.

Long Distance Message Telephone Rates. 140p. 1987. loose-leaf 15.00 o.p. NARUC.

Long Distance Runner's Guide to Training & Racing: Build Your Endurance, Strength & Efficiency. Ken Sparks & Gary Bjorkland. 288p. 1984. 18.95 o.p. (ISBN 0-13-540229-8); pap. 9.95 o.p. (ISBN 0-13-540211-5). P-H.

Long Distance Swimming. Forsberg. 1957. (ISBN 0-8022-0519-4). Philos Lib.

Long Dive. Ray Smith & Catriona Smith. LC 78-66614. (Illus.). 1979. 8.95 o.p. (ISBN 0-689-30672-5, Atheneum). Macmillan.

Long Feud: Selected Poems. Louis Untermeyer. LC 62-9446. 1962. 9.95 o.p. (ISBN 0-15-152999-X). HarBraceJ.

Long Fuse. Alan White. LC 74-3340. 1974. 5.95 o.p. (ISBN 0-15-153000-9). HarBraceJ.

Long Goodbye. Raymond Chandler. 1987. pap. 3.95 o.s.i. (ISBN 0-345-34938-5). Ballantine.

Long-Haired Boy. Christopher Matthew. LC 79-55594. 1980. 9.95 o.p. (ISBN 0-689-11051-0, Atheneum). Macmillan.

Long Haired Maiden. Ding Yuzhen. (Illus.). 34p. (gr. 2). 1987. pap. 2.95 o.p. (ISBN 0-8351-1463-5). China Bks.

Long Island Heritage. Ron Ziel. (Railroad Heritage Ser.: RH5). (Illus.). 1979. pap. 6.00 o.p. (ISBN 0-931584-05-1). Carstens Pubns.

Long Island Railroad. Fred Kramer & John Krause. 1978. pap. text ed. 14.95 o.p. (ISBN 0-911868-34-8). Carstens Pubns.

Long Journey. Barbara Corcoran. (Illus.). (gr. 3-7). 1970. PLB 5.50 o.p. (ISBN 0-689-20596-1, Atheneum). Macmillan.

Long Journey: Literary Themes of French Canada. Jack Warwick. LC 68-117293. (Romance Ser.). 1968. 20.00x o.p. (ISBN 0-8020-5198-7). U of Toronto Pr.

Long Journey of Lukas B. Willi Fahrmann. Tr. by Anthea Bell from Ger. LC 84-6100. Orig. Title: Lange Weg des Lukas B. 288p. (gr. 7 up). 1985. 12.95 o.s.i. (ISBN 0-02-734330-8). Bradbury Pr.

Long Lance. Tom Martin. (Lythway Ser.). 1987. lib. bdg. 15.95x o.p. (ISBN 0-7451-0592-0, Pub. by Chivers Pr UK). G K Hall.

Long Lavender Look. John D. MacDonald. (General Ser.). 363p. 1986. lib. bdg. 15.95x o.p. (ISBN 0-8161-4007-3, Large Print Bks). G K Hall.

Long Life Gourmet Cookbook. Barry Herman & Bill Lawren. 384p. 1984. 15.50 o.p. (ISBN 0-671-47000-0). S&S.

Long Life to You: Modern Medicine at Work. Leo Schneider. LC 68-25195. (Illus.). (gr. 7 up). 1968. 4.95 o.p. (ISBN 0-15-248632-1, HJ). HarBraceJ.

Long Live the Spy. Charles M. Russell. LC 87-9054. (Crime Club Ser.). 192p. 1987. 12.95 o.s.i. (ISBN 0-385-24312-X). Doubleday.

Long Lives: Chinese Elderly & the Communist Revolution. Deborah Davis-Friedmann. (Harvard East Asian Ser.: No. 100). (Illus.). 160p. 1983. text ed. 21.00x o.p. (ISBN 0-674-53860-9). Harvard U Pr.

Long May: I Have Come a Long Way; I Have a Long Way to Go. Sef Al-Jundi. LC 84-91284. 84p. 1985. 6.95 o.p. (ISBN 0-533-06354-X). Vantage.

Long Midnight. Alan White. LC 73-13952. 1974. 5.95 o.p. (ISBN 0-15-153075-0). HarBraceJ.

Long Path, A New York Hiking Trail. New York-New Jersey Trail Conference Staff. 56p. 1982. pap. 5.95 o.p. (ISBN 0-9603966-1-6). NY-NJ Trail Confer.

Long Range Energetic Resources & Growth see Towards a Plan of Actions for Mankind.

Long Range Mineral Resources & Growth see Towards a Plan of Actions for Mankind.

Long Range Planning Cumulative Index, Vols. 1-17. Ed. by B. Taylor. 1986. pap. 28.00 o.p. (ISBN 0-08-032664-1, Pub. by PPL). Pergamon.

Long Range Population Projects for Minor Civil Divisions: Computer Programs & Users Manual. Michael R. Greenber. 140p. 1973. pap. 7.00 o.p. (ISBN 0-87855-589-7). Transaction Pubns.

Long Ride Home. James L. Summers. LC 66-10140. (gr. 9 up). 1966. 3.50 o.s.i. (ISBN 0-664-32389-8, Westminster). Westminster John Knox.

Long Riders. Steven P. Smith. 192p. 1980. pap. 2.25 o.p. (ISBN 0-380-76174-2, 76174). Avon.

Long Road: Sino-Russian Economic Contacts from Ancient Times to 1917. M. I. Sladkovsky. 302p. 1981. 7.00 o.p. (ISBN 0-8285-2126-3, Pub. by Progress Pubs USSR). Imported Pubns.

Long Shadow. Anna Gilbert. 301p. 1986. pap. 3.95 o.p. (ISBN 0-931773-80-6). Critics Choice Paper.

Long Shadow. Denise Robins. (Large Print Bks., Nightingale Ser.). 399p. 1987. pap. 12.95x o.p. (ISBN 0-8161-4281-5, Large Print Bks). G K Hall.

Long Shadows. Laurence Snelling. 224p. 1976. 7.95 o.p. (ISBN 0-393-08738-7). Norton.

Long Slide. Ray Smith & Catriona Smith. LC 77-449. (ps-1). 1977. 7.95 o.p. (ISBN 0-689-30576-1, Atheneum). Macmillan.

Long Term Care: Challenges & Opportunities. Healthcare Financial Management Association Staff. (Illus.). 120p. 1985. pap. text ed. 12.00 o.p. (ISBN 0-930228-27-8). Healthcare Fin Man Assn.

Long-Term Care: Current Experience & a Framework for Analysis. William Scanlon et al. (Health Policy & the Elderly Ser.). 162p. 1979. pap. 7.95x o.p. (ISBN 0-87766-246-0, 25300). Urban Inst.

Long Term Care: Options in an Expanding Market. Susan Hughes. 250p. 1986. 35.00 o.p. (ISBN 0-87094-497-5). Dow Jones-Irwin.

Long Term Care Standards Manual: 1986. 142p. 1985. pap. 25.00 o.s.i. (ISBN 0-86688-091-7, LTC-205). Joint Comm Hlthcare.

Long Term Care Survey Guide. 58p. pap. cancelled o.s.i. (ISBN 0-86688-149-2). Joint Comm Hlthcare.

Long Term Marriage. Floyd Thatcher & Harriett Thatcher. 1981. 5.95 o.p. (ISBN 0-8499-2963-6). Word Bks.

Long Term Study with Co. Dergocrine Mesylate (Hydergine) in Healthy Pensioners: Results after Three Years. Ed. by S. Koeberle & R. Spiegel. (Journal: Gerontology: Vol. 30, Suppl. 1). (Illus.). 52p. 1984. pap. 25.50 o.p. (ISBN 3-8055-3891-X). S Karger.

Long Thirst: Prohibition in America 1920-1933. Thomas M. Coffey. 346p. 1975. 9.95 o.p. (ISBN 0-393-05557-4). Norton.

Long Time Dying. Olga Masters. 272p. 1986. pap. 17.95 o.p. (ISBN 0-7022-1888-X). U of Queensland Pr.

Long Time Dying. Olga Masters. LC 85-8522. 330p. 1987. pap. 8.95 o.p. (ISBN 0-7022-2024-8). U of Queensland Pr.

Long Time Sleeping. Michael Sinclair. 1976. 7.95 o.p. (ISBN 0-393-08739-5). Norton.

Long Time to Hate. Willo D. Roberts. 240p. (Orig.). 1982. pap. 2.50 o.p. (ISBN 0-380-79319-9, 79319-9). Avon.

Long Tunnel. Mead Arble. LC 76-11526. 1976. 8.95 o.p. (ISBN 0-689-10738-2, Atheneum). Macmillan.

Long Walks in France. Adam Nicolson et al. (Illus.). 1983. 17.95 o.p. (ISBN 0-517-55043-1). Crown.

Long Way Home. Margot Benary-Isbert. LC 59-7519. (gr. 7 up). 1959. 5.95 o.p. (ISBN 0-15-248830-8, HJ). HarBraceJ.

Long Way Together: A Personal View of NCTE's First Sixty-Seven Years. J. Nicholas Hook. LC 79-22732. (Illus.). 303p. (Orig.). 1979. pap. 10.00 o.p. (ISBN 0-8141-3021-6). NCTE.

Longarm & the Boot Hillers. Tabor Evans. (Longarm Ser.: No. 34). 208p. (Orig.). 1981. pap. 2.25 o.p. (ISBN 0-515-06584-6). Jove Pubns.

Longarm on the Nevada Line, No. 76. Tabor Evans. 192p. 1985. pap. 2.50 o.p. (ISBN 0-515-08173-6). Jove Pubns.

Longcase Clock. Eric Bruton. (Illus.). 1977. 29.95x o.p. (ISBN 0-8464-0578-4). Beekman Pubs.

Longer Poems of Velimir Khlebnikov. Vladimir Markov. LC 75-16851. (Univ. of California Publications in Modern Philology: Vol. 62). (Illus.). 273p. 1975. Repr. of 1962 ed. lib. bdg. 27.50x o.p. (ISBN 0-8371-8265-4, MAVK). Greenwood.

Longer the Thread. Emma Lathen. 192p. pap. 3.50 o.p. (ISBN 0-671-65053-X). Archway.

Longest Battle: The War at Sea 1939-1945. Richard Hough. Ed. by Howard Cady. LC 86-23632. (Illus.). 371p. 1987. Repr. of 1986 ed. 19.95 o.p. (ISBN 0-688-04310-0). Morrow.

Longest Living Snowflake: A Story in Verse for Children. Helen H. Combs. (Illus.). (ps-k). 1979. 4.00 o.p. (ISBN 0-682-49290-6). Exposition-Phoenix.

Longest Race. Hal Roth. (Illus.). 1983. 19.45 o.p. (ISBN 0-393-03278-7). Norton.

Longest War: Northern Ireland & the IRA. Kevin Kelley. LC 82-25840. 384p. 1983. 9.95 o.p. (ISBN 0-88208-148-9); pap. 9.95 o.p. (ISBN 0-88208-149-7). Chicago Review.

Longest War: Sex Differences in Perspective. Carol Tavris & Carole W. Offir. (Illus.). 333p. (Orig.). 1977. pap. text ed. 14.95 o.p. (ISBN 0-15-551182-3, HC). HarBraceJ.

Longevity of Athletes. Anthony P. Polednak. (Illus.). 284p. 1979. 36.25 o.p. (ISBN 0-398-03867-8). C C Thomas.

Longing. Maria Espinosa. LC 85-71393. 301p. (Orig.). 1986. pap. 10.00 perfect o.p. (ISBN 0-933529-01-5). Cayuse Pr.

Longing for Darkness: Kamante's Tales from Out of Africa. Ed. by Peter Beard. LC 74-19092. (Illus.). 242p. 1975. 19.95 o.p. (ISBN 0-15-153080-7). HarBraceJ.

Longing in the Land. Date not set. (ISBN 0-8052-3834-4). Random.

Longitude Zero Eighteen Eighty-Four to Nineteen Eighty-Four: Proceedings of an International Symposium held at the National Maritime Museum, Greenwich, London, 9-13 July 1984 to Mark the Centenary of the Adoption of the Greenwich Meridian. Ed. by P. Beer et al. (Illus.). 408p. 1985. pap. 89.00 o.p. (ISBN 0-08-032726-5, Pub. by PPL). Pergamon.

Longitudinal Leisure Skills for Severely Handicapped Learners: The Ho'onanea Curriculum Component. Bonnie B. Wuerch & Luanna M. Voeltz. LC 82-4343. (Illus.). 254p. (Orig.). 1982. pap. text ed. 17.95 o.p. (ISBN 0-933716-26-5, 265). P H Brookes.

Longitudinal Studies on the Class of 1961: The Graduate Science Students. Alan S. Berger. (Report Ser: No. 107). 1967. 3.00x o.p. (ISBN 0-932132-07-3). NORC.

Longman Concise Dictionary of Business English. J. H. Adam. 404p. 1985. pap. 9.95x o.p. (ISBN 0-582-84221-2). Longman.

Longman Dictionary of Business English. Ed. by J. H. Adam. 528p. 1982. 19.95 o.p. (ISBN 0-582-55552-3). Longman.

Longman Dictionary of Scientific Usage. A. Godman & E. M. F. Payne. (Illus.). 1979. pap. text ed. 16.95x o.p. (ISBN 0-582-52587-X). Longman.

Longman Guide to Shakespeare Quotations. Date not set. (ISBN 0-582-55575-2). Longman.

Longobardischen Koenigin Rosemundae, Wahrhaffte Lebens & Liebesgeschicht. Damirus. 690p. Repr. of 1729 ed. 75.00 o.p. (ISBN 0-384-10760-5). Johnson Repr.

Longtime Californ' A Documentary Study of an American Chinatown. Victor G. Nee & Brett De Barry. LC 72-12389. (Illus.). 448p. 1974. pap. 4.75 o.p. (ISBN 0-395-19845-3, 82, SenEd). HM.

Longue Marche: Essai Sur la Chine. Simone de Beauvoir. 368p. 1957. 9.95 o.p. (ISBN 0-686-54090-5). Schoenhof.

Loo Sanction. Trevanian. 1976. pap. 2.50 o.p. (ISBN 0-380-00175-6, 65383-4). Avon.

Look-alikes. Henrik Drescher. LC 85-225. (Illus.). 32p. (gr. k-3). 1985. 13.00 o.p. (ISBN 0-688-05816-7); PLB 12.88 o.p. (ISBN 0-688-05817-5). Lothrop.

Look Around & Listen see Sounds All Around.

Look at Alcoholism. Rebecca Anders. LC 77-12981. (Lerner Awareness Bks.). (Illus.). (gr. 3-6). 1977. PLB 4.95 o.p. (ISBN 0-8225-1311-0). Lerner Pubns.

Look at Boulder: From Settlement to City. Phyllis Smith. 1981. price not set o.p. (ISBN 0-87108-590-9). Pruett.

Look at Death. Rebecca Anders. LC 77-14182. (Lerner Awareness Bks.). (gr. 3-6). 1977. PLB 4.95 o.p. (ISBN 0-8225-1308-0). Lerner Pubns.

Look at Fourth Way Work: A System of Esoteric Exercises Based on the Work of Gurdjieff. Nicholas Tereshchenko. 1987. pap. 15.00 o.p. (ISBN 0-317-57174-5). Phanes Pr.

Look at Kids. Leila Berg. lib. bdg. 11.50x o.p. (ISBN 0-88307-308-0). Gannon.

Look at Norway. A. Beskow. (Illus.). 1981. 45.00 o.p. (ISBN 82-05-13081-7). E J Brill USA.

Look at Physical Handicaps. Margaret S. Pursell. LC 75-38468. (Lerner Awareness Bks.). (Illus.). 36p. (gr. 3-6). 1976. PLB 4.95 o.p. (ISBN 0-8225-1305-6). Lerner Pubns.

Look at Plants. (Wonders of Learning Kits Ser.). (gr. 3-6). 1980. incl. cass. & tchrs. guide 28.95 o.p. (ISBN 0-686-74406-3, 04970). Natl Geog.

Look at Plants with E.T. Ed. by Kate Klimo. (Illus.). 14p. 1983. 3.80 o.s.i. (ISBN 0-671-46435-3, Little). S&S.

Look at the Environment. Margaret S. Pursell. LC 75-38465. (Lerner Awareness Bks.). (Illus.). 36p. (gr. 3-6). 1976. PLB 4.95 o.p. (ISBN 0-8225-1302-1). Lerner Pubns.

Look at the Harlequins. Vladimir Nabokov. (McGraw-Hill Paperback Ser.). 1981. pap. text ed. 5.95 o.p. (ISBN 0-07-045717-4). McGraw.

Look at the Harlequins. Vladimir Nabokov. LC 74-10677. 262p. 1974. text ed. 7.95 o.p. (ISBN 0-07-045738-7). McGraw.

Look Behind You, Thomas Wolfe: Ghosts of a Common Tribal Heritage. Elaine Westall Gould. 1976. 7.00 o.p. (ISBN 0-682-48431-8, University). Exposition-Phoenix.

Look Down That Winding River: An Informal Profile of the Mississippi. Ben L. Burman. LC 72-6610. (Illus.). 1973. 7.95 o.s.i. (ISBN 0-8008-4960-4). Taplinger.

Look for the Living: The Corporate Nature of Resurrection Faith. Peter Selby. LC 76-15884. 224p. 1976. pap. 5.95 o.p. (ISBN 0-8006-1245-0, Fortress). Augsburg Fortress.

Look Good - Feel Good Through Yoga. Joy Abrams et al. LC 78-4288. (Illus.). (gr. 6 up). 1978. 7.95 o.s.i. (ISBN 0-03-019436-9). H Holt & Co.

Look How Many People Wear Glasses: The Magic of Lenses. Ruth Brindze. LC 75-8947. (gr. 5-9). 1975. 7.95 o.p. (ISBN 0-689-50028-9, Atheneum). Macmillan.

Look-I'm Flat Again. Violeta Centeno-Beltran. 1985. 10.95 o.p. (ISBN 0-533-06520-8). Vantage.

Look Kitten. Emanuel Schongut. Ed. by Kate Klimo. (Kitten Board Bks.). 14p. 1983. 3.80 o.s.i. (ISBN 0-671-46388-8, Little Simon). S&S.

Look, Listen & Learn: A Primary Class Activity Packet on the Americas. Mildred Schell. (gr. 1-6). 1973. pap. text ed. 5.95 o.p. (ISBN 0-377-58079-1). Friendship Pr.

Look of Eagles. John T. Foote. (Illus.). 14.95 o.p. (ISBN 0-85131-019-2, NL51, Pub. by J A Allen U K). S R Smith Sporting Bks.

Look of Eagles: Racing Story. John T. Foote. 1970. 12.50x o.p. (ISBN 0-87556-090-3). Saifer.

Look of Love. Karen Hayden. (Illus.). 96p. (Orig.). 1981. pap. 1.95 o.p. (ISBN 0-380-78774-1, 78774). Avon.

Look of Paradise: A Pictorial History of Northampton, Mass. Jacqueline Van Voris. LC 84-16704. (Illus.). 160p. 1984. 22.50 o.p. (ISBN 0-914659-07-3). Phoenix Pub.

Look to the Harbour. Will Pringle. 240p. 1987. 10.95 o.p. (ISBN 0-8062-2674-9). Carlton.

Look to This Day for Tomorrow. Dorothy Henderson. 1975. 6.00 o.p. (ISBN 0-682-48384-2). Exposition-Phoenix.

Look Who's Coming. Richard E. Orchard. LC 74-33870. 128p. 1975. pap. 1.25 o.p. (ISBN 0-88243-541-8, 02-0541). Gospel Pub.

Look Younger, Feel Healthier: A Safe, Professional, Step-by-Step Guide to Total Nutritional Health. Carlton Fredericks. 320p. 1982. pap. 6.75 o.p. (ISBN 0-671-44948-6, Fredericks). S&S.

Look Younger, Think Clearer, Live Longer. Edwin Flatto. 1978. pap. 2.95 o.p. (ISBN 0-935540-04-0). Plymouth Pr.

Look, You're a Leader. Daisy Hepburn. LC 85-19637. 284p. 1985. pap. 7.95 o.s.i. (ISBN 0-8307-1098-1, 5418647); resource manual avail. o.s.i. (ISBN 0-8307-1074-4, 5203023). Regal.

Looking Ahead: The Vision of Science Fiction. Dick Allen & Lori Allen. 408p. (Orig.). 1975. pap. text ed. 8.00 o.p. (ISBN 0-15-551184-X, HC). HarBraceJ.

Looking at Astrology. Liz Greene. LC 77-83149. (Illus.). 30p. (gr. 1-8). 1981. pap. 7.50 o.p. (ISBN 0-916360-13-X). CRCS Pubns CA.

Looking at BASIC. Penny Holland. LC 84-13834. (Easy-Read Computer Activity Bk.). (Illus.). 32p. (gr. k-3). 1985. lib. bdg. 10.40 o.p. (ISBN 0-531-04893-4). Watts.

Looking at Christmas from the Inside. Ralph K. Bates. LC 82-50304. 80p. (Orig.). 1982. pap. 3.95 o.p. (ISBN 0-8358-0432-1). Upper Room.

Looking at Computer Graphics. Penny Holland. (Easy-Read Computer Activity Bk.). (Illus.). 32p. (gr. k-3). 1985. lib. bdg. 10.40 o.p. (ISBN 0-531-04895-0). Watts.

Looking at Computer Programming. Penny Holland. LC 84-7549. (Easy-Read Computer Activity Bk.). (Illus.). 32p. (gr. 3-6). 1984. 10.40 o.p. (ISBN 0-531-04876-4). Watts.

Looking at Houses. Audrey Gee. (History in Focus Ser.). (Illus.). 72p. (gr. 7-12). 1983. 19.95 o.p. (ISBN 0-7134-0845-6, Batsford England). David & Charles.

Looking at Law School: A Student Guide from the Society of American Law Teachers. Ed. by Stephen Gillers. LC 76-53301. 1977. 9.95 o.s.i. (ISBN 0-8008-4966-3). Taplinger.

Looking at LOGO. Penny Holland. LC 84-7593. (Easy-Read Computer Activity Ser.). (Illus.). 32p. (gr. 3-6). 1984. PLB 10.40 o.p. (ISBN 0-531-04875-6). Watts.

Looking at Modern Painting. Ed. by Leonard Freedman. (Illus., Orig.). 1961. pap. 8.50x o.p. (ISBN 0-393-09534-7, NortonC). Norton.

Looking at Sails. Bruce Banks & Dick Kenny. (Illus.). 1980. 12.95 o.p. (ISBN 0-393-03251-5). Norton.

Looking at Schools: Good, Bad, & Indifferent. Edward A. Wynne. LC 79-2798. 272p. 1980. 35.00x o.p. (ISBN 0-669-03292-1). Lexington Bks.

Looking at the Stars. Michael W. Ovenden. (Illus.). 192p. 1958. (ISBN 0-8022-1254-9). Philos Lib.

Looking Backward: A Reintroduction to American History. Lloyd C. Gardner & William L. O'Neill. (Illus.). 544p. 1974. Vol. 1. text ed. 26.95 o.p. (ISBN 0-07-022842-6); Vol. 2. pap. (ISBN 0-07-022841-8). McGraw.

Looking Beyond. Jeffrey A. Watson. 132p. 1986. pap. 5.50 o.p. (ISBN 0-89693-155-2). Victor Bks.

Looking for a Kidnapper. Cornel I. Hammons. 6.95 o.p. (ISBN 0-533-06011-7). Vantage.

Looking for Ifugao Mountain: Bilingual, Pilipino & English. Al Robles. LC 77-78104. (Fifth World Tales Ser.). (Illus.). 24p. (gr. k-6). 1977. pap. 5.95 o.p. (ISBN 0-89239-012-3, Imprenta de Libros Infantiles). Childrens Book Pr.

Looking for Laforgue: An Informal Biography of Jules Laforgue. David Arkell. LC 79-89449. 1979. 20.00 o.p. (ISBN 0-89255-042-2). Persea Bks.

Looking for Mr. Goodbar. Judith Rossner. LC 75-2317. 1975. 7.95 o.p. (ISBN 0-671-22025-X). S&S.

Looking for Santa Claus. Henrik Drescher. LC 84-4419. (Illus.). 32p. (ps-1). 1984. 12.50 o.p. (ISBN 0-688-02997-3); lib. bdg. 11.47 o.p. (ISBN 0-688-02999-X). Lothrop.

Looking for Work in the New Economy. Robert Wegmann & Miriam Johnson. 303p. 1988. pap. 14.95 o.p. (ISBN 0-942784-19-7). Am Assn Coun Dev.

Looking for Zippy. Pete Kersten & Rick Kersten. LC 86-80461. (Kersten Brother's Critter Tales Sturdi-Flap Bks.). 12p. (ps-3). 1986. 4.95 o.p. (ISBN 0-316-49002-4). Little.

Looking Forward. Gillian Tindall. 1985. 14.95 o.p. (ISBN 0-87795-669-3, Arbor Hse). Morrow.

Looking Glass. Michael Sutton & Cynthia Mandelberg. (Illus.). 96p. 1983. pap. 4.00 o.p. (ISBN 0-88145-002-2). Broadway Play.

Looking Glass War. John Le Carre. 385p. 1986. 17.95 o.p. (ISBN 0-8161-4040-5, Large Print Bks); pap. 10.95 o.p. (ISBN 0-8161-4041-3). G K Hall.

Looking Glasse for London & England by Thomas Lodge & Robert Greene: A Critical Edition. George A. Clugston. Ed. by Stephen Orgel. LC 79-3098. (Renaissance Drama Second Ser.). 300p. 1980. lib. bdg. 40.00 o.p. (ISBN 0-8240-4482-7). Garland Pub.

Looking Good, Feeling Beautiful. Avon Products. 1981. 14.95 o.p. (ISBN 0-671-25224-0). S&S.

Looking Good in London. Date not set. Salem Hse Pubs.

Looking into Degas. Eunice Lipton. 1988. pap. 14.95x o.p. (ISBN 0-520-06340-6). U of Cal Pr.

Looking into Teaching. Allan C. Ornstein & Harry L. Miller. 1980. text ed. 36.36 o.p. (ISBN 0-395-30692-2). HM.

Looking into the Future: An Occupational Worktext. Ellen Glasser. 1975. pap. 2.75x o.p. (ISBN 0-88323-118-2, 206). Pendergrass Pub.

Looking Toward the 1980's. National Association for Women Deans, Administrators & Counselors. 1978. pap. 3.00 o.p. (ISBN 0-686-00405-1). Natl Assn Women.

Loon Feather. Iola Fuller. LC 40-27210. 1940. 9.50 o.p. (ISBN 0-15-153201-X). HarBraceJ.

Loon Lake. E. L. Doctorow. 304p. 1981. pap. 3.50 o.s.i. (ISBN 0-553-20027-5). Bantam.

Looniest Limerick Book in the World. Joseph Rosenbloom. LC 81-85034. (Illus.). 128p. (gr. 3 up). 1982. 10.05 o.p. (ISBN 0-8069-4660-1); PLB 13.29 o.p. (ISBN 0-8069-4661-X); pap. 3.95 o.p. (ISBN 0-8069-7920-8). Sterling.

Loop's Progress. Chuck Rosenthal. LC 86-4131. 240p. 1986. 15.95 o.s.i. (ISBN 1-55584-001-9). Weidenfeld.

Loosening the Grip: A Handbook of Alcohol Information. 2nd ed. Jean Kinney & Gwen Leaton. LC 82-6319. (Illus.). 353p. 1982. pap. text ed. 17.95 o.p. (ISBN 0-8016-2688-9). Mosby.

Lope de Vega: El Castigo sin Venganza. Ed. by C. A. Jones. 1966. 35.00 o.p. (ISBN 0-08-011775-9); pap. 35.00 o.p. (ISBN 0-08-011774-0). Pergamon.

Lope de Vega Los Celos de Rodamonte, Edicion Critica. Sabatino G. Maglione. LC 84-29156. 158p. (Orig.). 1985. lib. bdg. 25.25 o.p. (ISBN 0-8191-4557-2); pap. text ed. 11.50 o.p. (ISBN 0-8191-4558-0). U Pr of Amer.

Loper Longears. Prudence P. McGowan. 64p. 1986. 6.95 o.p. (ISBN 0-8062-2907-1). Carlton.

Lopsided World. Barbara Ward. 1968. 3.95 o.p. (ISBN 0-393-05360-1, NortonC); pap. 1.95 o.p. (ISBN 0-393-09805-2). Norton.

Lorca: The Poet & His People. Arturo Barea. LC 72-92121. xv, 176p. 1973. Repr. of 1949 ed. lib. bdg. 18.50x o.p. (ISBN 0-8154-0447-6). Cooper Sq.

Lord Acton: Historian of Liberty. Robert Schuettinger. LC 74-20792. 263p. 1974. 19.95 o.p. (ISBN 0-87548-294-5). Open Court.

Lord Alfred Douglas: A Biography. H. Montgomery Hyde. (Illus.). 400p. 1985. 19.95 o.p. (ISBN 0-396-08693-4). Dodd.

Lord & Me: A Personal Testimony. Jim Eksten. 1977. 4.00 o.p. (ISBN 0-682-48908-5). Exposition-Phoenix.

Lord Elgin's Lady. Theodore Vrettos. 352p. 1982. 12.95 o.p. (ISBN 0-395-31333-3). HM.

Lord Gauranga: Love Incarnate. 2.00 o.p. (ISBN 0-685-61441-7). Aum Pubns.

Lord, I Can Resist Anything but Temptation. Harold Bussell. (Orig.). 1985. pap. 4.95 o.p. (ISBN 0-310-37271-2, 12389P). Zondervan.

Lord Jim. Joseph Conrad. 1974. pap. 1.95x o.p. (ISBN 0-460-01925-2, Evman). Biblio Dist.

Lord Jim. Joseph Conrad. 48p. (Orig.). 1989. pap. 9.95 o.p. (ISBN 1-55651-529-4); audiocassette tape incl. o.p. (ISBN 1-55651-530-8). Cram Cassettes.

Lord Kalvan of Otherwhen. H. Beam Piper. Ed. by Lester Del Rey. LC 75-421. (Library of Science Fiction). 1975. lib. bdg. 21.00 o.p. (ISBN 0-8240-1426-X). Garland Pub.

Lord Lobster. Neil Rolde. (Illus.). (gr. 5-8). write for info. o.p. (ISBN 0-88448-035-6); pap. write for info. o.p. (ISBN 0-88448-034-8). Harpswell Pr.

Lord, Make My Life Count. Raymond C. Ortlund. LC 75-6188. 144p. (gr. 11). 1975. pap. 3.95 o.s.i. (ISBN 0-8307-0348-9, S112175). Regal.

Lord Novgorod the Great Essays in the History & Culture of a Medieval City State, Pt. 1: The Historical Background. Henrik Birnbaum. (UCLA Slavic Studies: Vol. 2). (Illus.). 170p. (Orig.). 1981. pap. 12.95 o.p. (ISBN 0-89357-088-5). Slavica.

Lord of Darkness. Robert Silverberg. 575p. 1983. 15.95 o.p. (ISBN 0-87795-443-7, Arbor Hse). Morrow.

Lord of Parables: Instructor Edition. LeRoy Lawson. LC 83-12640. 128p. (Orig.). 1984. pap. 2.95 o.p. (ISBN 0-87239-706-8, 39980); pap. 2.50 student edition o.p. (ISBN 0-87239-707-6, 39981). Standard Pub.

Lord of the Dance. Andrew M. Greeley. (Hall Large Print Bk.). lib. bdg. 18.95 o.p. (ISBN 0-8161-3797-8, Large Print Bks); pap. text ed. 11.95 o.s.i. (ISBN 0-8161-3807-9). G K Hall.

Lord of the Dance: The Beauty of the Disciplined Life. Deidre Bobgan. LC 86-62979. 160p. (Orig.). 1987. pap. 5.95 o.p. (ISBN 0-89081-583-6). Harvest Hse.

Lord of the Flies. William Golding. 48p. (Orig.). 1988. pap. 9.95 o.p. (ISBN 1-55651-525-1); audiocassette tape incl. o.p. (ISBN 1-55651-526-X). Cram Cassettes.

Lord of the Mohawks: A Biography of Sir William Johnson. rev. ed. James T. Flexner. LC 77-13877. 1979. 16.95 o.p. (ISBN 0-316-28609-5). Little.

Lord of the Morning. Frank Topping. LC 77-78646. 64p. 1978. pap. 0.75 o.p. (ISBN 0-8006-1313-9, 1-1313, Fortress). Augsburg Fortress.

Lord of the Mountain: Messages for Lent & Easter. James R. Bjorge. LC 78-66941. 1979. pap. 3.75 o.p. (ISBN 0-8066-1687-3, 10-4110, Augsburg). Augsburg Fortress.

Lord of the Seasons. Peter Firth. LC 78-71047. 1979. pap. 4.95 o.p. (ISBN 0-8042-2408-0, John Knox). Westminster John Knox.

Lord Peter. Dorothy L. Sayers. 1976. pap. 6.95 o.p. (ISBN 0-380-01694-X, 59683-0). Avon.

Lord Peter Views the Body. Dorothy L. Sayers. 1976. pap. 2.50 o.p. (ISBN 0-380-00946-3, 63503-8). Avon.

Lord Peter Wimsey Companion. Stephen Clarke. (Illus.). 49.95 o.p. FS&G.

Lord Peter Wimsey Cookbook. Elizabeth B. Ryan & William J. Eakins. LC 80-39544. (Joan Kahn Bk). (Illus.). 160p. 1981. 10.45 o.p. (ISBN 0-89919-032-4). Ticknor & Fields.

Lord Rayleigh, the Man & His Work. R. B. Lindsay. LC 79-94934. (Men of Physics Ser.). 1970. 65.00 o.p. (ISBN 0-08-006821-9); pap. 65.00 o.p. (ISBN 0-08-006820-0). Pergamon.

Lord, Teach Me Wisdom. Carole Mayhall. LC 78-78013. 180p. 1979. pap. 5.95 o.p. (ISBN 0-89109-432-6). NavPress.

Lord, Teach Us to Pray. Norman P. Madsen. LC 83-61890. 96p. (Orig.). 1983. pap. 2.00 o.p. (ISBN 0-87973-611-9, 611). Our Sunday Visitor.

Lord, the People Have Driven Me On. Benjamin E. Mays. 1981. 7.95 o.p. (ISBN 0-533-04503-7). Vantage.

Lord Won't Mind. Gordon Merrick. 1981. pap. 4.50 o.p. (ISBN 0-380-01404-1, 60027-7). Avon.

Lords & Commons. Frank O'Connor. 56p. 1971. Repr. of 1938 ed. 15.00x o.p. (ISBN 0-7165-1386-2, BBA 02072, Pub. by Cuala Press Ireland). Biblio Dist.

Lord's Hidden Message in Money. Jovah. 1986. 5.75 o.p. (ISBN 0-8062-2404-5). Carlton.

Lords, Ladies, & Gentlemen: A Memoir. Clifton Daniel. (Illus.). 1984. 16.95 o.p. (ISBN 0-87795-598-0, Arbor Hse). Morrow.

Lords of Discipline. Pat Conroy. 544p. 1980. 12.95 o.p. (ISBN 0-395-29462-2). HM.

Lords of the Khyber: The Story of the North West Frontier. Andre Singer. LC 84-8078. (Illus.). 240p. 1984. 22.95 o.p. (ISBN 0-571-11796-1). Faber & Faber.

Lord's Oysters. Gilbert Byron. LC 74-9246. xiv, 344p. 1967. Repr. of 1957 ed. 30.00x o.s.i. (ISBN 0-8103-5032-7). Gale.

Lord's Prayer. L. M. Borchardt. (Learning Awareness Ser.). 16p. (gr. 1-2). pap. 0.78 o.p. (ISBN 0-570-04350-6, 61HH2014). Concordia.

Lord's Prayer. Ronald E. Cottle. 48p. 1980. 0.95 o.p. (ISBN 0-88243-566-3, 02-0566). Gospel Pub.

Lord's Prayer. Oswald Hoffman. LC 81-47834. 128p. 1982. 10.53 o.p. (ISBN 0-06-063999-7). HarpR.

Lord's Prayer. Joachim Jeremias. Ed. & tr. by John Reumann. LC 64-11859. (Facet Bks.). 56p. 1964. pap. 0.95 o.p. (ISBN 0-8006-3008-4, 1-3008, Fortress). Augsburg Fortress.

Lord's Prayer. St. Cyprian of Carthage. Ed. by Edmond Bonin. 112p. (Orig.). 1983. pap. 6.95 o.p. (ISBN 0-87061-076-7). Chr Classics.

Lord's Prayer: A Way of Life. Donald W. Shriver, Jr. LC 83-9843. 108p. (Orig.). 1983. pap. 4.95 o.s.i. (ISBN 0-8042-2409-9, John Knox). Westminster John Knox.

Lord's Presence. Alton H. McEachern. LC 85-29055. 1986. pap. 4.95 o.p. (ISBN 0-8054-2314-1). Broadman.

Lord's Supper As a Christological Problem. Willi Marxsen. Ed. by John Reumann. Tr. by Lorenz Nieting from Ger. LC 79-81528. (Facet Bks.). 64p. 1970. pap. 1.00 o.p. (ISBN 0-8006-3059-9, 1-3059, Fortress). Augsburg Fortress.

Lore & Science in Ancient Pythagoreanism. Walter Burkert. Tr. by Edwin L. Minar, Jr. from Ger. LC 70-162856. (Illus.). 512p. 1972. 37.00x o.p. (ISBN 0-674-53918-4). Harvard U Pr.

Loren D. Adams: A Retrospective Exhibition. Norton (R. W.) Art Gallery Staff. LC 79-83531. (Comtemporary Realists Ser.). (Illus.). 1979. pap. 6.50x o.p. (ISBN 0-913060-16-X). Norton Art.

Lorenzino. Arvin Upton. 1977. 7.95 o.p. (ISBN 0-393-08762-X). Norton.

Lorenzo Ghiberti. R. Krautheimer. (Monographs in Art & Archaeology: No. 31). 1970. Repr. 90.00x o.p. (ISBN 0-691-03820-1). Princeton U Pr.

Lorenzo the Magnificent: The Story of an Orphaned Blue Jay. Robert F. Leslie. LC 84-20719. (Illus.). 188p. 1985. 12.45 o.p. (ISBN 0-393-01974-8). Norton.

Loretta Lynn. Robert K. Krishef. LC 77-90155. (Country Music Bks.). (Illus.). 64p. (gr. 5 up). 1978. 5.95 o.p. (ISBN 0-8225-1401-X). Lerner Pubns.

Loretta Young. Date not set. (ISBN 0-385-29397-6). Delacorte.

Loretta Young: An Extraordinary Life. Joe Morella & Edward Z. Epstein. (Illus.). 288p. 1986. pap. 16.95 o.p. (ISBN 0-385-29397-6). Delacorte.

Los Alamos Experience. Phyllis K. Fisher. (Illus.). 240p. 1985. 12.95 o.p. (ISBN 0-87040-623-X, Dist. by Harper & Row). Japan Pubns USA.

Los Alamos: The First Forty Years. Los Alamos Historical Society Staff. Ed. by Fern Lyon & Jacob Evans. LC 84-20088. (Illus.). 176p. 1984. pap. 12.95 o.p. Los Alamos Hist Soc.

Los Angeles-Access. rev. ed. Richard S. Wurman. (Access Guidebooks). (Illus.). 144p. 1985. pap. 9.95 o.p. (ISBN 0-915461-08-0). Access Pr.

Los Angeles & Ventura Counties Thomas Guide, 1988. Thomas Bros. Maps Staff. (Illus.). 387p. 1988. pap. 19.95 o.p. (ISBN 0-88130-275-9). Thomas Bros Maps.

Los Angeles County Museum of Art Report, July 1, 1977-June 30, 1979. Los Angeles County Museum of Art Curatorial Staff. LC 80-641019. (Illus.). 84p. (Orig.). 1980. pap. 2.00 o.p. (ISBN 0-87587-093-7). LA Co Art Mus.

Los Angeles County Museum of Art Report, July 1, 1981-June 30, 1983. Los Angeles County Museum of Art Staff. (Illus.). 128p. 1984. pap. 5.00 o.p. (ISBN 0-87587-117-8). LA Co Art Mus.

Los Angeles County Public Schools: How Are They Doing? (1984) Lillian S. Clancy. (How Are They Doing Ser.). 360p. 1984. pap. 17.95 o.p. (ISBN 0-939580-12-8). CA Schl Surveys.

Los Angeles County Public Schools: How Are They Doing? 1985. Lillian S. Clancy. (California Public Schools: How Are They Doing? 1985 Ser.: Vol. 2). 420p. (Orig.). 1984. pap. 23.95 o.p. (ISBN 0-939580-20-9). CA Schl Surveys.

Los Angeles County Public Schools, 1986, Vol. 2. Lillian S. Clancy. (California Public Schools Ser.: How Are They Doing?). 400p. (Orig.). 1985. pap. 24.95 o.p. (ISBN 0-939580-29-2). CA Schl Surveys.

Los Angeles County Public Schools, 1987. Lillian S. Clancy. (California Public Schools: How Are They Doing? Ser.). 400p. (Orig.). 1987. pap. 24.95 o.p. (ISBN 0-939580-38-1). CA Schl Surveys.

Los Angeles County Public Schools, 1988, Vol. 2. Lillian S. Clancy. (California Public Schools: How Are They Doing? Ser.). 400p. (Orig.). 1987. pap. 29.95 o.p. (ISBN 0-939580-46-2). CA Schl Surveys.

Los Angeles County Street Atlas, 1984. Thomas Brothers Maps. (Illus.). 288p. 1983. pap. 10.50 o.p. (ISBN 0-88130-048-9). Thomas Bros Maps.

Los Angeles County Street Atlas, 1985. Thomas Bros.Maps. (Illus.). 288p. 1985. pap. 10.95 o.p. (ISBN 0-88130-098-5). Thomas Bros Maps.

Los Angeles County Street Atlas, 1986. Thomas Bros. Maps Staff. (Illus.). 288p. 1986. pap. 11.95 o.p. (ISBN 0-88130-166-3). Thomas Bros Maps.

Los Angeles County Street Atlas 1987. Thomas Bros Maps, Staff. LC 86-14011. (Illus.). 288p. 1987. pap. 12.95 o.p. (ISBN 0-88130-218-X). Thomas Bros Maps.

Los Angeles County Street Guide & Directory Zip Code Edition 1988. Thomas Bros. Maps Staff. (Illus.). 292p. 1988. 17.95 o.p. (ISBN 0-88130-262-7). Thomas Bros Maps.

Los Angeles Dodgers. rev. ed. Brannon. LC 82-12730. (Baseball Today Ser.). 48p. (gr. 4 up). 1982. PLB 11.45 o.p. (ISBN 0-87191-863-3). Creative Ed.

Los Angeles in Fiction: A Collection of Original Essays. Ed. by David Fine. LC 84-10430. 269p. (Orig.). 1984. 24.95x o.p. (ISBN 0-8263-0759-0); pap. 9.95 o.p. (ISBN 0-8263-0760-4). U of NM Pr.

Los Angeles in Your Pocket. 2nd ed. Baca. (Barron's City in Your Pocket Ser.). 1984. pap. 2.95 o.p. (ISBN 0-8120-2746-9). Barron.

Los Angeles Lakers. rev. ed. Jim Moore. (NBA Today Ser.). (Illus.). 48p. (gr. 4 up). 1984. PLB 11.45 o.p. (ISBN 0-87191-981-8). Creative Ed.

Los Angeles-Orange Counties Street Atlas, 1986. Thomas Bros. Maps Staff. (Illus.). 432p. 1986. pap. 19.95 o.p. (ISBN 0-88130-167-1). Thomas Bros Maps.

Los Angeles-Orange Counties Street Atlas 1987. Thomas Bros Maps, Staff. (Illus.). 434p. 1987. pap. 21.95 o.p. (ISBN 0-88130-219-8). Thomas Bros Maps.

Los Angeles-Orange Counties Street Atlas, 1984. Thomas Brothers Maps. (Illus.). 432p. 1983. pap. 18.00 o.p. (ISBN 0-88130-050-0). Thomas Bros Maps.

Los Angeles-Orange Counties Street Atlas, 1985. Thomas Brothers Maps. (Illus.). 432p. 1984. pap. 18.00 o.p. (ISBN 0-88130-093-4). Thomas Bros Maps.

Los Angeles-Orange Counties Zip Code Street Atlas, 1986. Thomas Bros. Maps Staff. (Illus.). 436p. 1986. pap. 25.95 o.p. (ISBN 0-88130-165-5). Thomas Bros Maps.

Los Angeles-Orange Counties Zip Code Street Atlas 1987. Thomas Bros Maps, Staff. (Illus.). 434p. 1987. pap. 27.95 o.p. (ISBN 0-88130-217-1). Thomas Bros Maps.

Los Angeles Prints: 1883-1980. Ebria Feinblatt & Bruce Davis. (Illus.). 112p. (Orig.). 1980. pap. 10.00x o.p. (ISBN 0-87587-097-X). LA Co Art Mus.

Los Angeles Rams. Julian May. (NFL Today Ser.). (Illus.). (gr. 3-6). 1977. PLB 10.95 o.p. (ISBN 0-87191-596-0); pap. 4.25 o.p. (ISBN 0-686-67473-1). Creative Ed.

Los Angeles Times Book of the 1984 Olympic Games. Los Angeles Times Sports Staff. Ed. by Bill Dwyre. (Illus.). 224p. 1984. 30.00 o.p. (ISBN 0-8109-1284-8). Abrams.

Los Angeles Times California Cookbook. Los Angeles Times Food Staff. (Illus.). 400p. 1981. 25.00 o.p. (ISBN 0-8109-1277-5). Abrams.

Los Angeles-Ventura Counties Street Atlas 1987. Thomas Bros Maps, Staff. (Illus.). 382p. 1987. pap. 19.95 o.p. (ISBN 0-88130-211-2). Thomas Bros Maps.

Los Angeles: Winter Vacation Guide, 1989. (Illus.). cancelled o.s.i. Wrld Travel.

Los Angeles Zip Code Street Atlas, 1986. Thomas Bros. Maps Staff. (Illus.). 290p. 1986. pap. 14.95 o.p. (ISBN 0-88130-174-4). Thomas Bros Maps.

Los Angeles Zip Code Street Atlas 1987. Thomas Bros Maps, Staff. (Illus.). 288p. 1987. pap. 16.95 o.p. Thomas Bros Maps.

Los Angeles 1987-1988. (Frommer's City Guides). 224p. 5.95 o.p. (ISBN 0-671-62542-X). Prentice Hall Pr.

Loser. George Konrad. Tr. by Ivan Sanders from Hungarian. LC 82-47669. (Helen & Kurt Wolff Bk.). 320p. 1982. 14.95 o.p. (ISBN 0-15-153442-X). HarBraceJ.

Losing Time. John Hopkins. (Illus.). 152p. 1983. pap. 4.00 o.p. (ISBN 0-88145-005-7). Broadway Play.

Loss & How to Cope with It. Joanne E. Bernstein. LC 76-50027. (gr. 6 up). 1979. 8.95 o.s.i. (ISBN 0-395-28891-6, Clarion). HM.

Loss Control Safety Guidebook for Trades & Services. George Matwes & Helen Matwes. 1975. pap. 14.95 o.p. (ISBN 0-442-25194-7). Van Nos Reinhold.

Loss-Free Benchmark Investing. Frank R. Anderson. (Illus.). 100p. 1986. pap. 15.00 o.p. (ISBN 0-937257-03-6). Benchmark Winnetka.

Loss of Heart. Robert McCrum. 288p. 1983. pap. 2.95 o.p. (ISBN 0-380-64634-X, 64634-X). Avon.

Loss Prevention & Control. BNA's Environment & Safety Services Staff. (Policy & Practice Ser.). 416.00 o.p. (ISBN 0-87179-919-7). BNA.

Loss Prevention & Safety Promotion in the Process Industries: Chemical Process Hazards, 3 Vols. Institution of Chemical Engineers Staff. (Institution of Chemical Engineers Symposium Ser.: Vol. 82). 1983. Set. 140.00 o.s.i. (ISBN 0-08-031396-5, 1902, 1903, 1100); Vol. 1. 79.00 o.s.i. (ISBN 0-08-030291-2); Vol. 2. 40.00 o.s.i. (ISBN 0-08-030292-0); Vol. 3. 40.00 o.s.i. (ISBN 0-08-030293-9). Pergamon.

Loss Prevention for Smaller Banks. Bank Administration Institute. 27p. 1964. 8.00 o.p. (207). Bank Admin Inst.

Lost. Sonia O. Lisker. LC 74-22281. (Illus.). 48p. 1975. 6.75 o.p. (ISBN 0-15-249363-8, HJ). HarBraceJ.

Lost. Thomas Thompson. 1977. pap. 2.50 o.p. (ISBN 0-440-15089-2). Dell.

Lost & Found. Elaine Livermore. LC 74-20753. (Illus.). 48p. (gr. k-3). 1975. PLB 5.95 o.p. (ISBN 0-395-20279-5). HM.

Lost & Found. Judith Thurman. LC 77-21037. (Illus.). (ps-2). 1978. 7.95 o.p. (ISBN 0-689-30611-3, Atheneum). Macmillan.

Lost & Found Princess. Jane Flory. (gr. 2-5). 1979. PLB 5.95 o.p. (ISBN 0-395-27808-2). HM.

Lost Art of Disciple Making. LeRoy Eims. LC 78-17227. 176p. (Orig.). 1978. pap. 5.95 o.p. (ISBN 0-89109-472-5). NavPress.

Lost Body. Aime Cesaire & Pablo Picasso. 1986. 14.95 o.p. Braziller.

Lost Boston. Jane H. Kay. (Illus.). 320p. 1980. 24.95 o.p. (ISBN 0-395-27609-8). HM.

Lost Boundaries. William L. White. LC 48-6112. 1948. 5.95 o.p. (ISBN 0-15-153477-2). HarBraceJ.

Lost Boundaries. William L. White. LC 48-6112. (YA) (gr. 7 up). 1967. pap. 0.50 o.p. (ISBN 0-15-653610-2, VoyB). HarBraceJ.

Lost Chicago. David Lowe. LC 75-19181. 1975. 20.00 o.p. (ISBN 0-395-20726-6). HM.

Lost Chicago. David Lowe. 1978. pap. 8.95 o.p. (ISBN 0-395-26468-5). HM.

Lost Christmas. Howard Knotts. LC 78-1903. (Let Me Read Ser.). (Illus.). (gr. k-4). 1978. pap. 1.75 o.p. (ISBN 0-15-653648-X, VoyB). HarBraceJ.

Lost Colony Colorbook. Carole M. Longmeyer. (Lost Colony Collection). (Illus.). 60p. (Orig.). (gr. 6 up). 1983. pap. 6.00 o.p. (ISBN 0-935326-40-5). Gallopade Pub Group.

Lost Colony Cookbook. Carole M. Longmeyer. (Lost Colony Collection Ser.). (Illus.). 200p. (Orig.). 1983. pap. 14.95 o.p. (ISBN 0-935326-39-1). Gallopade Pub Group.

Lost Colony Garden Book. Carole M. Longmeyer. (Lost Colony Collection Ser.). (Illus.). 200p. (Orig.). 1983. pap. 7.95 o.p. (ISBN 0-935326-46-4). Gallopade Pub Group.

Lost Colony of the Confederacy. Eugene C. Harter. LC 85-9129. (Illus.). 1985. 14.95 o.p. (ISBN 0-87805-259-3). U Pr of Miss.

Lost Elementary Schools of Victorian England: The People's Education. Philip W. Gardner. LC 84-9503. 320p. 1984. 38.50 o.p. (ISBN 0-7099-1156-4, Pub. by Croom Helm Ltd). Routledge Chapman & Hall.

Lost Face: Best Science Fiction from Czechoslovakia. Josef Nesvadba. LC 71-126982. Orig. Title: In the Footsteps of the Abominable Snowman: Stories of Science & Fantasy. 1971. 5.95 o.s.i. (ISBN 0-8008-5020-3). Taplinger.

Lost Farm. Jane L. Curry. LC 73-85320. (Illus.). 138p. (gr. 3-7). 1974. 5.95 o.s.i. (ISBN 0-689-30427-7, Atheneum). Macmillan.

Lost Flying Boat. Alan Sillitoe. LC 84-80841. 287p. 1984. 15.95 o.p. (ISBN 0-316-79105-9). Little.

Lost Frontier. Ellsworth T. Chamberlain. 96p. 1986. 7.95 o.p. (ISBN 0-8062-2949-7). Carlton.

Lost Frontier: The Marketing of Alaska. John D. Hanrahan & Peter Gruenstein. (Illus.). 1977. 10.95 o.p. (ISBN 0-393-08804-9). Norton.

Lost God. Virginia Crider. 1968. pap. 1.10 o.p. (ISBN 0-686-05590-X). Rod & Staff.

Lost Goddesses of Early Greece: A Collection of Pre-Hellenic Mythology. Charlene Spretnak. LC 80-68169. (Illus.). 132p. 1981. pap. 6.95 o.p. (ISBN 0-8070-1345-5, BP 682). Beacon Pr.

Lost Goods & Stray Beasts. Peter Sharpe. LC 83-62341. (Chapbook Ser.: No. 5). 64p. (Orig.). 1983. pap. 5.95 o.p. (ISBN 0-937672-14-9). Rowan Tree.

Lost Gospel of the Ages: Key to Immortality & Companion to the Holy Bible. Ed. by John C. Androgeus. (Illus.). 979p. 1978. pap. text ed. 95.00 o.s.i. (ISBN 0-9609802-3-7). Life Science.

Lost Half-Hour: A Collection of Stories. Ed. by Eulalie S. Ross. LC 65-23537. (Illus.). (gr. 4-6). 1963. 5.95 o.p. (ISBN 0-15-249360-3, HJ). HarBraceJ.

Lost Hero: The Mystery of Raoul Wallenberg. Frederick E. Werbell & Thurston Clarke. (Illus.). 1981. text ed. 12.95 o.p. (ISBN 0-07-069410-9). McGraw.

Lost Home. J. Avyzius. 544p. 1974. 7.45 o.p. (ISBN 0-8285-0945-X, Pub. by Progress Pubs USSR). Imported Pubns.

Lost Honor of Katharina Blum. Heinrich Boll. 1975. text ed. 7.95 o.p. (ISBN 0-07-006425-3). McGraw.

Lost in America. Isaac Bashevis Singer. (Illus.). 1981. ltd. ed. 75.00 o.p. (ISBN 0-385-17717-8). Doubleday.

Lost in America. Isaac Bashevis Singer. LC 79-6037. 1981. 17.95 o.p. (ISBN 0-385-15756-8). Doubleday.

Lost in the Jungle. Paul Du Chaillu. LC 79-159939. 262p. 1971. Repr. of 1872 ed. 40.00x o.p. (ISBN 0-8103-3766-5). Gale.

Lost in the Store. Larry Bograd. LC 81-4038. (Illus.). 32p. (gr. k-3). 1981. 9.95 o.s.i. (ISBN 0-02-710980-1). Macmillan.

Lost in the Zoo. Devorah-Leah. (Illus.). 30p. (ps-1). 1983. 7.95 o.p. (ISBN 0-910818-56-8); pap. 5.95 o.p. (ISBN 0-910818-57-6). Judaica Pr.

Lost Lady. Jude Deveraux. (Large Print Books (General Ser.)). 371p. 1985. lib. bdg. 14.95 o.p. (ISBN 0-8161-3950-4). G K Hall.

Lost Legend of Finn. Mary Tannen. 154p. (gr. 4-7). 1983. pap. 2.25 o.p. (ISBN 0-380-63354-X, 63354-X, Camelot). Avon.

Lost Literature of Medieval England. R. M. Wilson. 1952. (ISBN 0-8022-1895-4). Philos Lib.

Lost Love, Last Love. Rosemary Rogers. 1984. pap. 9.95 o.p. (ISBN 0-8161-3714-5, Large Print Bks). G K Hall.

Lost New Orleans. Mary Cable. 256p. 1980. 21.95 o.p. (ISBN 0-395-27623-3). HM.

Lost on Both Sides, Dante Gabriel Rossetti: Critic & Poet. Robert M. Cooper. LC 71-91957. 268p. 1970. 15.50x o.p. (ISBN 0-8214-0069-X, 82-80752). Ohio U Pr.

Lost Ones. Samuel Beckett. 1972. pap. 6.95 o.p. (ISBN 0-394-17786-X, E587, Ever). Grove.

Lost Pharoahs. Leonard Cottrell. 1951. (ISBN 0-8022-0308-6). Philos Lib.

Lost Princess. George Macdonald. (Macdonald Fairy Tales Ser.). 1979. pap. 1.50 o.p. (ISBN 0-89191-163-4). Cook.

Lost Profits. Theo V. Elmore. 64p. 1982. 5.00 o.p. (ISBN 0-682-49845-9). Exposition-Phoenix.

Lost Skiff. Wetzel. 1969. 4.75 o.p. (ISBN 0-15-153608-2). HarBraceJ.

Lost Sophocles. Akiko Kiso. 1984. 11.95 o.p. (ISBN 0-533-05903-8). Vantage.

Lost Souls. George Martin. 40p. 1986. 6.95 o.p. (ISBN 0-8062-2877-6). Carlton.

Lost Star. H. M. Hoover. 160p. 1980. pap. 1.75 o.p. (ISBN 0-380-49635-6). Avon.

Lost Steps. Alejo Carpentier. 1979. pap. 2.50 o.p. (ISBN 0-380-46177-3, 46177-3, Bard). Avon.

Lost String Quartet. N. M. Bodecker. LC 80-1106. (Illus.). 32p. (gr. 1 up). 1981. 9.95 o.p. (ISBN 0-689-50200-1, Atheneum). Macmillan.

Lost Tales of Appalachia. H. B. Lee. 1977. 8.00 o.p. (ISBN 0-87012-193-6). McClain.

Lost Traveller's Dream. Kelly Cherry. LC 83-22590. 256p. 1984. 13.95 o.p. (ISBN 0-15-153617-1). HarBraceJ.

Lost Treasures of Louis Comfort Tiffany. Hugh F. McKean. LC 76-2796. (Illus.). 320p. 1980. pap. 24.95 o.p. (ISBN 0-385-09585-6). Doubleday.

Lost Tribes: History Doctrine, Prophecies & Theories About Israel's Lost Ten Tribes. R. Clayton Brough. LC 79-89351. 1979. 7.95 o.p. (ISBN 0-88290-123-0). Horizon Utah.

Lost Umbrella of Kim Chu. Eleanor Estes. LC 78-59156. (Illus.). 96p. (gr. 4-7). 1978. 7.95 o.p. (ISBN 0-689-50111-0, Atheneum). Macmillan.

Lost Undercover: An FBI Agent's True Story. Ron LaBrecque. (Orig.). 1987. pap. 3.95 o.s.i. (ISBN 0-440-16914-3). Dell.

Lost Victim. Thomas A. Waters. 144p. 1986. pap. 2.95 o.p. (ISBN 1-55547-103-X). Critics Choice Paper.

Lost Villages of England. Maurice Beresford. 360p. 1955. (ISBN 0-8022-0102-4). Philos Lib.

Lost Years: Mural Painting in New York City Under the Works Progress Administration's Federal Art Project 1935-1943. Greta Berman. LC 77-94687. (Outstanding Dissertations in the Fine Arts Ser.). 436p. 1978. lib. bdg. 55.00 o.p. (ISBN 0-8240-3216-0). Garland Pub.

Lots & Lots of Candy. Carolyn Meyer. LC 76-12483. (Illus.). (gr. k-2). 1976. 5.95 o.p. (ISBN 0-15-249400-6, HJ). HarBraceJ.

Lots of Boys. Gelman. (Follow Your Heart Ser.: No. 8). 1985. pap. 2.25 o.p. (ISBN 0-671-53158-1). Archway.

Lottery Book: For People Who Play to Win. Bill Adler. LC 86-5068. 160p. 1986. pap. 5.95 o.p. (ISBN 0-688-05809-4, Quill). Morrow.

Lottery Players Magazine Official Traveler's Guide to Lotteries 1983. Ed. by Samuel W. Valenza, Jr. (LOMAP Ser.: Vol. 1). (Illus.). 24p. saddle stitch 3.50 o.p. (ISBN 0-936918-04-7). Intergalactic NJ.

Lottery Rose. Irene Hunt. 192p. (gr. 7-12). 1981. pap. 2.50 o.s.i. (ISBN 0-441-49518-4, Pub. by Tempo). Ace Bks.

Lottery Rose. Irene Hunt. 1980. pap. 1.95 o.p. (ISBN 0-448-17257-7). Platt.

Lotte's Locket. Virginia Sorensen. LC 64-17087. (Illus.). (gr. 4-6). 1964. 5.95 o.p. (ISBN 0-15-249457-X, HJ). HarBraceJ.

Lottie. Davenport A. Reade. 1977. 7.00 o.p. (ISBN 0-682-48743-0). Exposition-Phoenix.

Lotus Crew. Stewart Meyer. LC 84-48111. 224p. 1984. 12.95 o.p. (ISBN 0-394-54140-5, GP940). Grove.

Lotus Data Matrix. Benson P. Shapiro. 1986. 10.95 o.p. (ISBN 0-256-03724-8). Irwin.

Lotus Flowers: Poems. Ellen B. Voigt. 1987. 13.45 o.p. (ISBN 0-393-02445-8). Norton.

Lotus Guide to Learning Symphony. 400p. 1985. pap. 22.95 o.p. (ISBN 0-201-16686-0). Addison-Wesley.

Lotus 1-2-3 Desktop Companion. Date not set. (ISBN 0-89588-385-6). Sybex.

Lotus 1-2-3 Mastery: A Business Guide to 1-2-3 Productivity. Daniel Harris. 256p. 1984. incl. disk 39.95 o.p. (ISBN 0-13-540741-9). P-H.

Lotus 1-2-3 Models. Gilbert Held. LC 85-701. 250p. 1985. pap. text ed. 17.95 o.p. (ISBN 0-938862-29-4). Weber Systems.

Lotus 1-2-3 Simplified. David Bolocan. (Illus.). 128p. 1984. 16.95 o.p. (ISBN 0-8306-0748-X, 1748); pap. 10.95 o.p. (ISBN 0-8306-1748-5). TAB Bks.

Lotus 1-2-3 User's Handbook. 1984. pap. 12.95 o.p. (ISBN 0-938862-33-2). Weber Systems.

Lou Gehrig's Disease. Lydia G. Sullivan. 32p. 1987. 6.50 o.p. (ISBN 0-8062-2999-3). Carlton.

Lou in the Limelight. Kristin Hunter. LC 81-9264. 192p. (gr. 7 up). 1981. 12.95 o.s.i. (ISBN 0-684-16880-4, Pub. by Scribner). Macmillan.

Loud & Clear: A Guide to Effective Communication. Sy Lazarus. LC 75-4925. 152p. 1975. 10.95 o.p. (ISBN 0-8144-5375-9). AMACOM.

Louder Please: The Autobiography of a Deaf Man. Earnest E. Calkins. LC 74-164148. 276p. 1971. Repr. of 1924 ed. 40.00x o.p. (ISBN 0-8103-3792-4). Gale.

Louder Than Words. Jill Posener. (Illus.). 96p. 1986. pap. 8.95 o.p. (ISBN 0-86358-086-6, 80866, Pandora Pr). Routledge Chapman & Hall.

Louis C. Tiffany's Glass, Bronzes & Lamps: A Complete Collector's Guide. Robert Koch. (Illus.). 1971. 19.95 o.p. (ISBN 0-517-50556-8). Crown.

Louis Comfort Tiffany, 1848-1933. Mary Vance. (Architecture Ser.: A 1399). 8p. 1985. 2.00 o.p. (ISBN 0-89028-429-6). Vance Biblios.

Louis James Hates School. Bill Morrison. (Illus.). (gr. k-3). 1978. 6.95 o.p. (ISBN 0-395-27156-8). HM.

Louis Napoleon & the Second Empire. James M. Thompson. (Illus.). 1967. pap. 2.95 o.p. (ISBN 0-393-00403-1, Norton Lib). Norton.

Louis Simpson: A Reference Guide. William H. Roberson. 1980. lib. bdg. 23.00 o.p. (ISBN 0-8161-8494-1, Hall Reference). G K Hall.

Louis Sullivan: Prophet of Modern Architecture. Hugh Morrison. (Illus.). 1958. 13.25 o.p. (ISBN 0-8446-1317-7). Peter Smith.

Louis the Fourteenth of France: John B. Wolf. LC 67-20618. (Illus., Orig.). 1974. pap. 7.95x o.p. (ISBN 0-393-00753-7, Norton Lib). Norton.

Louis: The Louis Armstrong Story 1900-1971. Max Jones. 256p. Repr. of 1971 ed. lib. bdg. 39.00 o.p. (Pub. by Am Repr Serv). Reprint Servs.

Louis the Seventeenth: The Unsolved Mystery. H. G. Francq. (Illus.). 1970. 25.00 o.s.i. (ISBN 0-685-25488-7). E J Brill USA.

Louis XVI Furniture. Francis Watson. (Illus.). 96p. 1960. (ISBN 0-8022-1818-0). Philos Lib.

Louisa May. Martha Saxton. 1978. pap. 2.95 o.p. (ISBN 0-380-40881-3, 48868-X, Discus). Avon.

Louisa May: A Modern Biography of Louisa May Alcott. Martha Saxton. 1977. 14.95 o.p. (ISBN 0-395-25720-4). HM.

Louisa May Alcott: A Reference Guide. Alma J. Payne. (Reference Bks.). 1980. 19.50 o.p. (ISBN 0-8161-8032-6). G K Hall.

Louise Bourgeois. Deborah Wye. LC 82-60847. (Illus.). 116p. 1982. pap. 12.50 o.p. (ISBN 0-87070-257-2). Museum Mod Art.

Louise Nevelson: Iconography & Sources. Laurie Wilson. LC 79-57492. (Outstanding Dissertations in the Fine Arts Ser.: No. 5). 340p. 1981. lib. bdg. 46.00 o.p. (ISBN 0-8240-3946-7). Garland Pub.

Louisiana! Dana F. Ross. 423p. 1986. 16.95 o.p. (ISBN 0-8161-4112-6, Large Print Bks). G K Hall.

Louisiana Almanac 1968. Ed. by Hodding Carter. (Illus.). 1968. pap. 11.95 o.p. (ISBN 0-911116-48-6). Pelican.

Louisiana Almanac, 1969. Ed. by Hodding Carter. 1969. pap. 11.95 o.p. (ISBN 0-911116-49-4). Pelican.

Louisiana Almanac, 1975-76 Ed. Ed. by James Calhoun & Helen Kempe. (Illus.). 496p. 1975. pap. 11.95 o.p. (ISBN 0-88289-039-5). Pelican.

Louisiana Almanac 1979-80. 10th ed. James Calhoun & Helen Kempe. (Illus.). 1979. 11.95 o.p. (ISBN 0-88289-181-2); pap. 11.95 o.p. (ISBN 0-88289-182-0). Pelican.

Louisiana Almanac, 1984-85 Edition. Ed. by Lucy Core & David Calhoun. (Illus.). 496p. (Orig.). 1984. pap. 11.95 o.p. (ISBN 0-88289-297-5). Pelican.

Louisiana Business Directory,1988-1989. American Directory Publishing Co., Inc. Staff. 1450p. (Orig.). 1988. pap. 110.00 o.p. (ISBN 0-944316-35-2). Amer Directory.

Louisiana: Conflict of Laws. 1983. 8.50 o.p. (ISBN 0-686-90498-2). Am Law Inst.

Louisiana Gothic. Ed. by Glenn R. Conrad & Vaughan B. Baker. LC 83-7000732. (Illus.). 150p. 1984. 25.00 o.p. (ISBN 0-940984-19-9). U of SW LA Ctr LA Studies.

Louisiana Images, 1880-1920: A Photographic Essay, by George Francois Mugnier. George F. Mugnier. Ed. by John R. Kemp & Linda O. King. LC 74-27199. (Illus.). 144p. 1975. pap. 14.95 o.p. (ISBN 0-8071-0151-6). La State U Pr.

Louisiana Purchase: America's Best Buy. John Chase. 4.95 o.p. (ISBN 0-911116-24-9); pap. 1.50 o.p. (ISBN 0-911116-68-0). Pelican.

Louisiana Supplement to Modern Real Estate Practice. John Doiron & Cornelius J. Hyde, III. 96p. (Orig.). 1982. pap. text ed. 9.95 o.s.i. (ISBN 0-88462-293-2, 1510-40, Real Estate Ed). Longman Finan.

Louisiana: Torts, Vols. 1-2. 1983. 12.50 o.p. (ISBN 0-686-90501-6). Am Law Inst.

Louisiane Au Jourd' Hui. Michel Tauriac. (Illus.). 240p. 1981. 19.95 o.p. (ISBN 0-88289-341-6, Pub by Les Editions France). Pelican.

Louvre Dialogues. Pierre Schneider. Tr. by Patsy Southgate from Fr. LC 72-135572. (Illus.). 1971. 10.00 o.p. (ISBN 0-689-10386-7, Atheneum). Macmillan.

Love. Ernesto Cardenal. 160p. 1981. pap. 4.95 o.p. (ISBN 0-8245-0043-1). Crossroad NY.

Love, Acceptance & Forgiveness: Leader's Guide. Margaret Parker. LC 79-63763. 128p. 1984. pap. 3.95 o.s.i. (ISBN 0-8307-0989-4, 6101895). Regal.

Love Against Hate. Karl A. Menninger & Jeanetta L. Menninger. LC 42-50183. 1942. 10.75 o.p. (ISBN 0-15-153891-3). HarBraceJ.

Love, Altruism, & World Crisis: The Challenge of Pitirim Sorokin. Joseph A. Matter. (Quality Paperback: No. 311). 313p. 1975. pap. 3.95 o.p. (ISBN 0-8226-0311-X). Littlefield.

Love, Anarchy & Emma Goldman. Candace Falk. LC 83-18405. 500p. 1984. 25.00 o.p. (ISBN 0-03-043626-5). H Holt & Co.

Love & Addiction. Stanton Peele & Archie Brodsky. LC 74-5818. 1975. 9.95 o.s.i. (ISBN 0-8008-5041-6). Taplinger.

Love & Be Loved: A How-To Book. John Tamiazzo. 176p. 1986. pap. 7.95 o.p. (ISBN 0-87877-087-9, Greenbriar Books). Newcastle Pub.

Love & Discipline. Bank Street College of Education Staff & Barbara Brenner. LC 82-90851. 224p. (Orig.). 1983. pap. 5.95 o.p. (ISBN 0-345-30520-5). Ballantine.

Love & Exile: A Memoir. Isaac Bashevis Singer. LC 79-7211. (Illus.). 384p. 1984. 17.95 o.p. (ISBN 0-385-14060-6). Doubleday.

Love & Exile: A Memoir. Isaac Bashevis Singer. LC 79-7211. 384p. 1985. ltd. ed. 50.00 o.p. (ISBN 0-385-19111-1). Doubleday.

Love & Friendship. Alison Lurie. 304p. 1986. pap. 4.50 o.p. (ISBN 0-380-70071-9). Avon.

Love & Glory: A Novel. Jeane Westin. 528p. 1986. 17.45 o.p. (ISBN 0-671-55667-3). S&S.

Love & Hate: The Natural History of Behavior Patterns. Irenaus Eibl-Eibesfeldt. LC 74-10145. (Illus.). xii, 276p. 1987. pap. 7.95 o.s.i. (ISBN 0-8052-0459-8). Schocken.

Love & Joy. Walter James. 64p. 1982. 5.00 o.p. (ISBN 0-682-49786-X). Exposition-Phoenix.

Love & Living Together. Dale Robb. LC 77-15242. 96p. (Orig.). 1978. pap. 0.50 o.p. (ISBN 0-8006-1326-0, 1-1326). Augsburg Fortress.

Love & Marriage. Herbert Katz. LC 75-11147. 1975. 7.95 o.p. (ISBN 0-87795-110-1, Arbor Hse). Morrow.

Love & Marriage: A Guide for Young People. Curtis E. Avery & Theodore B. Johannis, Jr. LC 73-151027. (Curriculum Related Bks.). (Illus.). 170p. 1971. 5.95 o.p. (ISBN 0-15-249531-2, HJ). HarBraceJ.

Love & Mathematics: Sofya Kovalevskaya. P. Kochina. 340p. 1985. 7.95 o.p. (ISBN 0-8285-3373-3, Pub. by Mir Pubs USSR). Imported Pubns.

Love & Money. Sylvia Porter. Ed. by Jennifer Williams. LC 85-11536. 243p. 1985. 14.95 o.p. (ISBN 0-688-06056-0). Morrow.

Love & Other Natural Disasters. Allen Hannay. 224p. (gr. 9 up). 1982. 14.45 o.p. (ISBN 0-316-34362-5, Pub. by Atlantic Monthly Pr). Little.

Love & Politics: Radical Feminist Theories. C. A. Douglas. (Athene Ser.). 250p. 1988. 25.91 o.p. (ISBN 0-08-034236-1, PBI); pap. 12.51 o.p. (ISBN 0-08-034235-3). Pergamon.

Love & Rage: Entries in a Prison Diary. Carl Harp. 73p. 1981. pap. 3.95 o.p. (ISBN 0-88978-091-9). Left Bank.

Love & Sex: A Modern Jewish Perspective. Robert Gordis. 290p. 1978. 8.95 o.p. (ISBN 0-374-19252-9). FS&G.

Love & Struggle in Mao's Thought. Raymond Whitehead. LC 76-41902. 196p. 1977. write for info. o.p. (ISBN 0-88344-289-2); pap. 2.48 o.p. (ISBN 0-88344-290-6). Orbis Bks.

Love & the Illusion of Love. John F. Gardner. 1976. pap. 1.50 o.p. (ISBN 0-913098-12-4). Myrin Institute.

Love Be Our Light. John J. Sweeney. 160p. 1981. 8.00 o.p. (ISBN 0-682-49762-2). Exposition-Phoenix.

Love Before the Fall. William D. Dean. LC 75-42226. 1976. pap. 4.25 o.s.i. (ISBN 0-664-24792-X, Westminster). Westminster John Knox.

Love Birds: A Book of Poems. Athol J. Ridgway. 80p. 1985. 6.95 o.p. (ISBN 0-533-06576-3). Vantage.

Love Bites. Freda Garmaise. 1981. 11.95 o.p. (ISBN 0-671-42036-4). S&S.

Love Boat: Voyage of Love. William Rotsler. Ed. by Wendy Barish. (Plot-Your-Own-Adventure Stories: No. 1). 128p. (Orig.). (gr. 3-7). 1983. pap. 3.80 o.s.i. (ISBN 0-671-49802-9). Wanderer Bks.

Love Can Be Found. Arieti et al. 1977. 8.95 o.p. (ISBN 0-15-154722-X). HarBraceJ.

Love Can Say No. Lillian Pohlmann. LC 66-10140. (gr. 7-10). 1966. 5.50 o.s.i. (ISBN 0-664-32365-0, Westminster). Westminster John Knox.

Love Comes Softly. Janette Oke. (Nightingale Paperbacks Ser.). 332p. 1987. pap. 12.95 o.p. (ISBN 0-8161-4344-7, Large Print Bks). G K Hall.

Love Comes to Eunice K. O'Herlihy. Gail Hamilton. LC 77-1580. (gr. 5-8). 1977. 5.95 o.p. (ISBN 0-689-30584-2, Atheneum). Macmillan.

Love, Death & the Ladies' Drill Team. Jessamyn West. LC 55-10809. 1968. pap. 0.95 o.s.i. (ISBN 0-15-653905-5, Harv). HarBraceJ.

Love Despite Hate. Date not set. (ISBN 0-8052-3801-8). Random.

Love Divine. Reuben R. Brown. 1979. 5.50 o.p. (ISBN 0-682-49299-X). Exposition-Phoenix.

Love Etc. Bel Kaufman. 1981. pap. 2.75 o.p. (ISBN 0-380-53629-3, 53629-3). Avon.

Love Exchange. Lawrence Kersten & Karen K. Kersten. LC 81-65745. 372p. 1981. 15.95 o.p. (ISBN 0-8119-0426-1). Fell.

Love Feast. Frederick Buechner. LC 74-77839. 1974. 7.95 o.p. (ISBN 0-689-10612-2, Atheneum). Macmillan.

Love for Love. William Congreve. Ed. by Emmett L. Avery. LC 66-20827. (Regents Restoration Drama Ser). xviii, 147p. 1966. 14.50x o.p. (ISBN 0-8032-0353-5); pap. 3.95x o.p. (ISBN 0-8032-5353-2, BB 259, Bison). U of Nebr Pr.

Love for the Taking. Beth Christopher. (Finding Mr. Right Ser.). 208p. 1983. pap. 2.75 o.p. (ISBN 0-380-83311-5, 83311-5). Avon.

Love: From Black Men to Black Women. Ed. by Frances Johnson Barnes. 1976. 5.00 o.p. (ISBN 0-682-48569-1). Exposition-Phoenix.

Love: From Black Women to Black Men. Ed. by Frances J. Barnes. 1977. 5.00 o.p. (ISBN 0-682-48855-0). Exposition-Phoenix.

Love-Girl & the Innocent. Alexander Solzhenitsyn. Tr. by Nicholas Bethell & David Burg. LC 72-97614. 131p. 1970. 5.95 o.p. (ISBN 0-374-19296-0); pap. 2.95 o.p. (ISBN 0-374-50840-2). FS&G.

Love-God's Greatest Gift. Douglas R. Benn. (Illus.). 1981. pap. 4.00 o.p. (ISBN 0-682-49736-3). Exposition-Phoenix.

Love: How to Understand & Enjoy It. Leo Madow. 192p. 10.95 o.s.i. (ISBN 0-684-17341-7, ScribT). Scribner.

Love: How to Understand & Enjoy It. Leo Madow. 192p. 1982. pap. 4.95 o.s.i. (ISBN 0-684-17828-1, ScribT). Scribner.

Love in All Its Disguises. Norman Rosten. LC 81-65135. 192p. 1981. 11.95 o.p. (ISBN 0-87795-324-4, Arbor Hse). Morrow.

Love in Ancient Greece. Robert Flaceliere. Tr. by James Cleugh. LC 72-13866. (Illus.). 224p. 1973. Repr. of 1962 ed. lib. bdg. 22.50x o.p. (ISBN 0-8371-6758-2, FLLA). Greenwood.

Love in Shadow. John R. Boettiger. (Illus.). 1978. 10.95 o.p. (ISBN 0-393-07530-3). Norton.

Love in the Afternoon Cookbook. Jones. 12.95 o.p. (ISBN 0-87131-426-6). M Evans.

Love in the Afternoon Cookbook: Recipes from Your Favorite ABC-TV Soap Operas- Ryan's Hope, One Life to Live, All My Children, General Hospital. Jeanne Jones & Donna Swajeski. LC 83-5685. (Illus.). 160p. 1983. pap. 7.95 o.p. (ISBN 0-87131-405-3). M Evans.

Love in the Afternoon: Recipes from Your Favorite ABC-TV Soap Operas: Ryans Hope, All My Children, One Life to Life, General Hospital. Jane Jones & Donna Swajeski. LC 83-5685. (Illus.). 160p. Date not set. pap. 12.95 o.p. (ISBN 0-317-65062-9). M Evans.

Love in the Middle Ages: A Novel. Helen Barolini. Ed. by Pat Golbitz. LC 85-31021. 320p. 1986. 17.95 o.p. (ISBN 0-688-06387-X). Morrow.

Love in the Ruins. Walker Percy. 384p. 1978. pap. 4.95 o.p. (ISBN 0-380-38984-3). Avon.

Love Is a Happy Cat. Michael W. Fox. LC 82-14216. (Illus.). 112p. 1983. 7.95 o.p. (ISBN 0-937858-16-1); pap. 3.95 o.p. (ISBN 0-937858-34-X). Newmarket.

Love Is a Special Way of Feeling. Joan W. Anglund. LC 60-6224. (Illus.). (gr. 1 up). 1960. 4.95 o.p. (ISBN 0-15-249725-0, HJ). HarBraceJ.

Love Is Always. Michael Miles. 416p. 1988. pap. 4.50 o.p. (ISBN 0-380-70431-5). Avon.

Love Is Better. Alvin E. Peck. LC 83-91499. 223p. 1985. 11.95 o.p. (ISBN 0-533-06089-3). Vantage.

Love Is for Tomorrow. Hope Traver. 271p. 1978. pap. 3.95 o.p. (ISBN 0-930756-37-1, 531006). Aglow Pubns.

Love Is Like Peanuts. Betty Bates. (gr. 7-9). 1981. pap. 1.95 o.p. (ISBN 0-671-47272-0). Archway.

Love Is Like Peanuts. Betty Bates. LC 79-21686. 128p. (gr. 6 up). 1980. 7.95 o.p. (ISBN 0-8234-0402-1). Holiday.

Love Is Like the Sunlight. Mary A. Vandermey. 1985. pap. 5.95 o.p. (ISBN 0-8010-9294-9). Baker Bk.

Love Is No Luxury. rev. ed. Marjory L. Bracher. LC 68-12331. (Orig.). 1968. pap. 0.50 o.p. (ISBN 0-8006-1714-2, Fortress). Augsburg Fortress.

Love Is Not Enough. Bruno Bettelheim. 1971. pap. 2.95 o.p. (ISBN 0-380-01405-X, 56846-2, Discus). Avon.

Love Is Not Enough. Bob Shanks. 320p. 1982. 12.95 o.p. (ISBN 0-393-01586-6). Norton.

Love Is So Much More, Lord. Ruth H. Calkin. LC 79-51739. 1979. pap. 2.50 o.p. (ISBN 0-89191-187-1). Cook.

Love Is the Answer. Robert V. Ozment. 160p. 1986. pap. 5.95 o.p. (ISBN 0-8007-5227-9). Revell.

Love Is the Heart of Everything: Correspondence Between Vladimir Mayakovsky & Lili Brik 1915-1930. Ed. by Bengt Jangfeldt. Tr. by Julian Graffy. 1987. 24.95 o.p. (ISBN 0-394-55569-4). Grove.

Love Knots. Wanda V. Smith. 144p. (gr. 6-8). 1987. 2.25 o.s.i. (ISBN 0-87406-144-X). Willowisp Pr.

Love Knows No Limit. Elisabeth Elliot. 1982. pap. 1.25 o.p. (ISBN 0-89107-270-5). Good News.

Love, Laurie. Betty Cavanna. (gr. 5-9). 1953. 5.50 o.s.i. (ISBN 0-664-32101-1, Westminster). Westminster John Knox.

Love Lessons: A Wartime Diary. Joan Wyndham. 256p. 1985. 14.45i o.p. (ISBN 0-316-96251-1). Little.

Love Lives Here. Mary A. Forehand. (Orig.). (gr. 1-3). 1975. pap. 1.95 o.p. (ISBN 0-377-00028-0). Friendship Pr.

Love Making "Two" 192p. (Orig.). 1982. pap. 2.25 o.p. (ISBN 0-8439-1058-5, Pub. by Leisure Bks CT). Dorchester Pub Co.

Love, Marriage & Romance in Old London. C. J. Thompson. LC 70-76076. (Illus.). 262p. 1971. Repr. of 1936 ed. 40.00x o.p. (ISBN 0-8103-3211-6). Gale.

Love Me, Love Me Not: How to Survive Infidelity. Daniel J. Dolesh & Sherelynn Lehman. 208p. 1985. text ed. 16.95 o.p. (ISBN 0-07-017394-X). McGraw.

Love Me, Love My Teddy Bear. Sam Gross. (Illus.). 1986. pap. 4.95 o.p. (ISBN 0-399-51230-6, Perigee). Putnam Pub Group.

Love Me, Marietta. Jennifer Wilde. (Gregg Hardcovers Ser.). 1985. lib. bdg. 14.95 o.p. (ISBN 0-8398-2876-4, Gregg). G K Hall.

Love Me No More. Denise Robins. 1976. pap. 1.25 o.p. (ISBN 0-380-00825-4, 30916). Avon.

Love Me, Somebody. D. J. LeBeaux. LC 84-90293. 116p. 1985. 9.95 o.p. (ISBN 0-533-06316-7). Vantage.

Love Me to Death. Philip Kirk. (Butler Ser.). 224p. 1984. pap. 2.50 o.p. (ISBN 0-8439-2079-3, Pub. by Leisure Bks CT). Dorchester Pub Co.

Love Me When I'm Most Unlovable: Guide to the Middle School Years. Robert Ricken. (Illus.). 64p. 1984. pap. 6.00 o.p. (ISBN 0-682-40151-X). Exposition-Phoenix.

Love Medicine. Louise Erdrich. (Large Print Bks.). 370p. 1986. lib. bdg. 17.95x o.p. (ISBN 0-8161-3957-1). G K Hall.

Love Needs No Reason. Shirley Dowling. 368p. 1985. pap. 3.50 o.p. (ISBN 0-380-89500-5). Avon.

Love Never Ends. Joyce G. Rice. pap. 4.95 o.p. (ISBN 0-89036-147-9). Hawkes Pub Inc.

Love Never Fails: The Autobiography of Philotheos Zikas, a Christian Pastor in Northern Greece. Philotheos Zikas. 1979. 10.00 o.p. (ISBN 0-682-49020-2, Testament). Exposition-Phoenix.

Love Notes: A Compleat Parenting Kit. Angie Rose. LC 81-83049. 227p. (Orig.). (ps-2). 1981. pap. 19.95 o.p. (ISBN 0-89334-068-5). Humanics Ltd.

Love of Elspeth Baker. Myron S. Kaufmann. LC 81-71681. 680p. 1982. 16.95 o.p. (ISBN 0-87795-390-2, Arbor Hse). Morrow.

Love of Enemies: The Way to Peace. William Klassen. LC 84-47927. (Overtures to Biblical Theology Ser.). 176p. 1984. pap. 2.50 o.p. (ISBN 0-8006-1539-5, 1-1539, Fortress). Augsburg Fortress.

Love of Liberty: The Rule of President William V. S. Tubman in Liberia 1944-1971. Tuan Wreh. LC 76-17361. (Illus.). 1976. 12.00x o.p. (ISBN 0-87663-275-4). Universe.

Love of Life. Jack London. (Illus.). 266p. 1988. pap. 7.95 o.s.i. (ISBN 0-932458-38-6). Star Rover.

Love of Rich Women. William Hamilton. 216p. 1981. 11.95 o.p. (ISBN 0-395-31559-X). HM.

Love of the Two-Armed Form. Da Free John. LC 78-57090. 475p. 1978. 17.95 o.s.i. (ISBN 0-913922-37-4). Dawn Horse Pr.

Love on Any Terms. Nell Kincaid. (Candlelight Ecstasy Ser.: No. 129). (Orig.). 1983. pap. 1.95 o.p. (ISBN 0-440-11927-8). Dell.

Love on the Dole. Walter Greenwood. (Penguin Fiction Ser.). 256p. 1985. pap. 5.95 o.p. (ISBN 0-14-002827-7). Penguin.

Love on the Range. Eileen E. Powers. (Swept Away Ser.: No. 3). 208p. (Orig.). (YA) (gr. 6-9). 1986. pap. 2.50 o.p. (ISBN 0-380-75130-5). Avon.

Love Once Again. Jo A. Simon. 400p. 1983. pap. 3.95 o.p. (ISBN 0-380-83345-X, 83345-X). Avon.

Love Only Once. Johanna Lindsey. (Large Print Bks (General Ser.)). 338p. 1986. lib. bdg. 17.95 o.p. (ISBN 0-8161-4122-3). G K Hall.

Love or Glory. Created by Rosemary Joyce. (Dream Girls Ser.: No. 2). (YA) (gr. 7 up). pap. 2.50 o.p. (ISBN 0-671-62111-4). Archway.

Love Pact: A Layman's Complete Guide to Legal Living Together Agreements. Bernard E. Clair & R. Anthony Daniele. LC 79-6158. 224p. (Orig.). 1980. pap. 6.95 o.p. (ISBN 0-394-17652-9, E753, Ever). Grove.

Love Play. Rosemary Rogers. (General Ser.). 1984. lib. bdg. 13.95 o.p. (ISBN 0-8161-3674-2, Large Print Bks). G K Hall.

Love Poems. Anne Sexton. LC 69-12444. 1973. pap. 4.80 o.p. (ISBN 0-395-08183-1). HM.

Love Poems & Others. Emily Dickinson. (Classics Ser.). 1982. 9.95 o.p. (ISBN 0-88088-907-1). Peter Pauper.

Love Poems by Invadelle. Mary I. Ribaudo. 1985. 7.95 o.p. (ISBN 0-317-28901-2). Vantage.

Love Poems of Ancient Egypt. Tr. by Ezra Pound & Noel Stock. LC 62-16925. 1962. pap. 2.95 o.s.i. (ISBN 0-8112-0158-9, NDP178). New Directions.

Love Poems of Tagore. Rabindranath Tagore. Tr. by Rabindra N. Choudhury from Bengali. (Illus.). 213p. 1983. pap. 5.50 o.s.i. (ISBN 0-89253-062-6). Ind-US Inc.

Love, Poetry & Psychotherapy. E. Lakin Phillips. 1985. 29.95x o.s.i. (ISBN 0-8290-0418-1). Irvington.

Love Polynesian Flying: The Big Birds of Don Don Island-a Fantasy. J. H. Reinburg. 1979. 7.00 o.p. (ISBN 0-682-49454-2). Exposition-Phoenix.

Love Potions. Harry E. Wedeck. LC 62-18549. (Illus.). 1963. (ISBN 0-8022-1836-9). Philos Lib.

Love Road to Calvary: Sermons for Lent & Easter on 1 Corinthians 13. James R. Bjorge. LC 81-52268. 96p. (Orig.). 1982. pap. 3.95 o.p. (ISBN 0-8066-1900-7, 10-4120, Augsburg). Augsburg Fortress.

Love, Sex & Marriage Through the Ages. Bernard I. Murstein. LC 73-92201. 651p. 1974. pap. text ed. 17.95 o.p. (ISBN 0-8261-1461-X); 26.95 o.p. (ISBN 0-8261-1460-1). Springer Pub.

Love Song. Isabel Santana. (Illus.). 96p. 1981. pap. 1.95 o.p. (ISBN 0-380-76893-3, 76893-3). Avon.

Love Songs for an Age of Anxiety. Bradley R. Strahan. (Black Buzzard Illustrated Poetry Chapbook Ser.). (Illus.). 20p. (Orig.). 1981. pap. 2.50 o.p. (ISBN 0-938872-00-1). Black Buzzard.

Love Songs of Arnhem Land. Ronald M. Berndt. LC 77-83828. (Illus.). 1978. 22.50x o.s.i. (ISBN 0-226-04389-4). U of Chicago Pr.

Love Songs of Connacht. Douglas Hyde. 1971. Repr. of 1904 ed. 13.00x o.p. (ISBN 0-7165-1329-3, Pub. by Cuala Press Ireland). Biblio Dist.

Love Stories by New Women. Ed. by Charleen Swansea & Barbara Campbell. 1979. pap. 2.75 o.p. (ISBN 0-380-48058-1, 48058-1, Bard). Avon.

Love Stories for Children. Vern Kennerson. (gr. 4-9). 1977. 6.50 o.p. (ISBN 0-682-48788-0). Exposition-Phoenix.

Love Story. Erich Segal. (YA) (gr. 9-12). 1978. pap. 3.50 o.p. (ISBN 0-380-01760-1). Avon.

Love Story. Erich Segal. (Arabic.). pap. 8.95x o.p. (ISBN 0-86685-261-1). Intl Bk Ctr.

Love Story of Lisa & Snowball, Two Beloved Pets. Carmelina Apostoliti. (Illus.). 64p. 1981. 5.00 o.p. (ISBN 0-682-49815-7). Exposition-Phoenix.

Love Story of Thomas Davis. Ed. by Joseph Hone. 48p. 1971. Repr. of 1945 ed. 15.00x o.p. (ISBN 0-7165-1402-8, BBA 02062, Pub. by Cuala Press Ireland). Biblio Dist.

Love Story Take Three. Date not set. (ISBN 0-385-29445-X). Delacorte.

Love Story, Take Three. Gloria D. Miklowitz. LC 85-16183. (gr. 7 up). 1986. pap. 14.95 o.p. (ISBN 0-385-29445-X). Delacorte.

Love Tested. Gunter Grass. Tr. by Michael Hamburger. (Helen & Kurt Wolff Bk.). (Illus.). 1975. 600.00 o.p. (ISBN 0-15-154728-9). HarbraceJ.

Titles

Love Them In: The Proclamation Theology of D. L. Moody. Stanley N. Gundry. 252p. 1982. pap. 8.95 o.p. (ISBN 0-8010-3783-2). Baker Bk.

Love, Therapy & Politics: Issues in Radical Therapy - The First Year. Ed. by Hogie Wyckoff. LC 75-42899. 1976. pap. 4.95 o.p. (ISBN 0-394-17906-4, E673, Ever). Grove.

Love Thing. Burt Hirschfeld. 320p. pap. 2.95 o.p. (ISBN 0-440-04952-0). Dell.

Love Thy Neighbor. Pierette Evans. 128p. 1987. 8.95 o.p. (ISBN 0-8062-2939-X). Carlton.

Love Unspoken. Mary R. Myers. 224p. (Orig.). 1985. pap. 2.95 o.s.i. (ISBN 0-345-31278-3). Ballantine.

Love Until It Hurts: The Work of Mother Teresa & Her Missionaries of Charity. Daphne Rae. LC 81-47424. (Illus., Orig.). 1981. pap. 9.95 o.p. (ISBN 0-06-066729-X, RD 368). HarpR.

Love, Vanity & the Mirage. Joyanne Griffin. 32p. 1984. pap. 5.50 o.p. (ISBN 0-682-40166-8). Exposition-Phoenix.

Love Victorian Style: III. Grove Press Victorian Library Staff. 1983. Boxed Set. pap. 15.80 o.p. (ISBN 0-394-62010-0, B497, BC). Grove.

Love, Vol. I. Denise Robins. 1979. pap. 2.50 o.s.i. (ISBN 0-345-28515-8). Ballantine.

Love, Vol. IV. Denise Robins. 608p. 1980. pap. 2.50 o.p. (ISBN 0-345-28518-2). Ballantine.

Love Wounds & Multiple Fractures: Poems. Carolanne Ely. 1975. pap. 3.00 o.p. (ISBN 0-915342-02-2). SUN.

Love You Make: An Insider's Story of the Beatles. Peter Brown & Steven Gaines. 1983. text ed. 14.95 o.p. (ISBN 0-07-008159-X). McGraw.

Love Your Neighbour: A Woman's Workshop on Fellowship. Lawrence O. Richards. (Woman's Workshop Ser.). 160p. (Orig.). 1986. pap. 2.95 o.p. (ISBN 0-310-43451-3, 18139P). Zondervan.

Lovefire. Julia Grice. 1977. pap. 3.50 o.p. (ISBN 0-380-01741-5, 84863-5). Avon.

Lovejoy's College Guide. 16th ed. Lovejoy. 1983. 19.95 o.p. (ISBN 0-671-47201-1); pap. 14.95 o.p. (ISBN 0-671-47170-8). Monarch Pr.

Lovejoy's Guide for the Learning Disabled. Charles T. Straughn & Marvelle S. Colby. 1985. 9.95 o.p. (ISBN 0-317-26515-6). Monarch Pr.

Lovejoy's Guide to Graduate Business Schools. Arline Glotzer & Bruce Sheiman. (Orig.). 1983. pap. 14.95 o.p. (ISBN 0-671-44884-6). Monarch Pr.

Lovejoy's Math Review for the SAT. P-H.

Lovejoy's Math Review for the SAT. Richard Rosenberg. (Exam Preparation Guides). (Orig.). 1983. pap. 8.95 o.p. (ISBN 0-671-47150-3). Monarch Pr.

Lovejoy's Preparation for the GED. Idell Holburt. 352p. 1984. pap. 8.95 o.p. (ISBN 0-671-49296-9). Monarch Pr.

Lovejoy's Preparation for the GRE. Patricia O. Jana. 352p. 1984. pap. 8.95 o.p. (ISBN 0-671-47499-5). Monarch Pr.

Lovejoy's Preparation for the PSAT. Richard Rosenberg & John D. Kelly. 352p. 1984. pap. 8.95 o.p. (ISBN 0-671-50337-5). Monarch Pr.

Lovejoy's Shortcuts & Strategies for the LSAT Revised. David Tajgman. (Shortcuts Ser.). 160p. (Orig.). 1985. pap. 7.95 o.p. (ISBN 0-671-55369-0). Monarch Pr.

Lovelace Medical Center: Pioneer in American Health Care. Jake W. Spidle, Jr. LC 87-10250. (Illus.). 229p. 1987. 27.50 o.p. (ISBN 0-8263-1007-9). U of NM Pr.

Lovelaw: Love, Sex, & Marriage Around the World. Anthony Clare. (Illus.). 200p. 1988. pap. 12.95 o.p. (ISBN 0-563-20412-5, Pub. by BBC). Parkwest Pubns.

Lovelock. James McNeish. 399p. 1988. 19.95 o.p. (ISBN 0-340-36430-0, Pub. by Hodder & Stoughton UK). David & Charles.

Lovely in Eyes Not His: Homilies for an Imaging of Christ. Walter J. Burghardt. 224p. (Orig.). 1988. pap. 10.95 o.p. Paulist Pr.

Lovely Time Was Had by All. Ruth D. MacDougall. LC 82-71056. 320p. 1982. 13.95 o.p. (ISBN 0-689-11276-9, Atheneum). Macmillan.

Lovely Vassilisa. Retold by Barbara Cohen. LC 80-12494. (Illus.). 48p. (ps-4). 1980. 9.95 o.p. (ISBN 0-689-30773-X, Atheneum). Macmillan.

Lover. Marguerite Duras. 122p. 1986. lib. bdg. 13.95 o.p. (ISBN 0-8161-4052-9, Large Print Bks). G K Hall.

Lover Man: A Mystery Introducing Artie Deemer. Dallas Murphy. 1987. 14.95 o.p. (ISBN 0-684-18757-4). Scribner.

Loveroot. Erica Jong. LC 74-15483. 128p. 1975. 4.95 o.p. (ISBN 0-03-014046-3); pap. 3.95 o.p. (ISBN 0-03-014051-X). H Holt & Co.

Lovers & Other Killers. James Anderson. (Murder She Wrote Ser.: No. 3). 1986. pap. 2.95 o.p. (ISBN 0-380-89938-8). Avon.

Lover's Familiar. James McMichael. LC 77-94115. (Third Godine Poetry Chapbook Ser.). 1978. 5.00 o.s.i. (ISBN 0-87923-175-0). Godine.

Lover's Gift. Lynn Michaels. (Velvet Glove Ser.: No. 20). 208p. 1985. pap. 2.25 o.p. (ISBN 0-380-89786-5). Avon.

Lovers Guide to Palmistry. Mary E. Anderson. (Illus.). 144p. (Orig.). 1987. pap. 5.95 o.p. (ISBN 0-7137-1711-4, Pub. by Javelin England). Sterling.

Lovers in Evolution. Carolyn M. Kleefeld. LC 83-82753. 81p. (Orig.). 1983. pap. 4.95 o.p. (ISBN 0-9602214-0-9). Jalmar Pr.

Lover's Language Guide to Japan. Richard Crownover. 1976. pap. 3.00 o.p. (ISBN 0-914778-17-X). Phoenix Bks.

Lovers of the African Night. William Duggan. 224p. 1987. pap. 17.95 o.p. (ISBN 0-385-29540-5). Delacorte.

Lovers of the African Night. Date not set. (ISBN 0-385-29540-5). Delacorte.

Lovers: Story of Two Men. Michael Denneny. 1979. pap. 4.95 o.p. (ISBN 0-380-43091-6, 43091-6). Avon.

Love's Answer from Eternity. Guy Chester Belt. 1973. 4.00 o.p. (ISBN 0-682-47696-X). Exposition-Phoenix.

Love's Bitter Sweet. Tr. by Robin Flower. 52p. 1971. Repr. of 1925 ed. 15.00x o.p. (ISBN 0-7165-1363-3, BBA 02052, Pub. by Cuala Press Ireland). Biblio Dist.

Love's Choice. Rosie Thomas. (Avon Romance Ser.). 352p. 1982. pap. 2.95 o.p. (ISBN 0-380-61713-7, 61713-7). Avon.

Love's Cruelty: Edited from the Quarto of 1640 with Introduction & Notes. James Shirley. Ed. by Stephen Orgel. LC 79-54354. (Renaissance Drama Second Ser.). 220p. 1980. lib. bdg. 29.00 o.p. (ISBN 0-8240-4471-1). Garland Pub.

Love's Duet. Patricia Veryan. 320p. 1980. pap. 1.75 o.p. (ISBN 0-449-50050-0, Coventry). Fawcett.

Love's Far Horizon. Lee Roddy. (Chime Ser.). (Illus.). 1981. pap. 2.50 o.p. (ISBN 0-89191-540-0, 55400). Cook.

Love's Perplexing Obsession, Experienced by Two Geniuses: Heinrich Heine & Percy Bysshe Shelley. D. Elaine Stanberry. 1981. 8.95 o.p. (ISBN 0-533-04826-5). Vantage.

Love's Pirate. Mary R. Daheim. 592p. 1983. pap. 4.75 o.p. (ISBN 0-380-83840-0, 83840-0). Avon.

Love's Proud Masquerade. Nomi Berger. 512p. (Orig.). 1982. pap. 3.50 o.p. (ISBN 0-8439-1055-0, Pub. by Leisure Bks CT). Dorchester Pub Co.

Love's Raging Torment. Alma Ashley. 1978. pap. 2.25 o.p. (ISBN 0-505-51250-5, Pub. by Tower Bks). Dorchester Pub Co.

Love's Reply. Cajetan Esser & E. Grau. 1963. 4.95 o.p. (ISBN 0-685-10969-0, L38405); pap. 3.95 o.p. (ISBN 0-8199-0067-2, L38406). Franciscan Herald.

Love's Suspect. Betty Henrichs. (Velvet Glove Ser.: No. 3). 176p. 1984. pap. 2.25 o.p. (ISBN 0-380-88013-X, 88013-X). Avon.

Love's Tender Fury. Jennifer Wilde. (Gregg Hardcovers Ser.). 1985. lib. bdg. 14.95 o.p. (ISBN 0-8398-2875-6, Gregg). G K Hall.

Love's Wine. Patricia Hagan. 336p. 1985. pap. 3.95 o.p. (ISBN 0-380-89534-X). Avon.

Lovestorm. Barbara Benedict. 496p. 1984. pap. 3.75 o.p. (ISBN 0-8439-2062-9). Dorchester Pub Co.

Loving. Marian Bennett. (Wipe-Clean Bks.). (Illus.). 12p. (ps). 1985. pap. 1.39 o.p. (ISBN 0-87239-955-9, 3515). Standard Pub.

Loving. Jean C. Lipke. LC 72-104894. (Being Together Bks.). Orig. Title: Getting Ready for Marriage. (YA) (gr. 7-12). 1971. PLB 5.95 o.p. (ISBN 0-8225-0593-2). Lerner Pubns.

Loving. Danielle Steel. 1981. 9.95 o.p. (ISBN 0-8161-3279-8, Large Print Bks). G K Hall.

Loving a Younger Man: How Women Are Finding & Enjoying a Better Relationship. Victoria Houston. 288p. 1987. 17.95 o.p. (ISBN 0-8092-4730-5). Contemp Bks.

Loving & Learning: Interacting with Your Child from Birth to Three. Norma J. McDiarmid et al. LC 76-40330. 306p. 1977. pap. 7.95 o.p. (ISBN 0-15-654200-5, Harv). HarBraceJ.

Loving & Learning: Interacting with Your Child from Birth to Three. Norma J. McDiarmid et al. LC 74-19395. (Illus.). 306p. 1975. 8.95 o.p. (ISBN 0-15-154730-0). HarBraceJ.

Loving Arrangement. Diana Blayne. (Candlelight Ecstacy Ser.: No. 113). (Orig.). 1983. pap. 1.95 o.p. (ISBN 0-440-15026-4). Dell.

Loving Daughters. Olga Masters. LC 84-3695. 319p. 1986. 15.95 o.p. (ISBN 0-7022-1758-1); pap. 8.95 o.p. (ISBN 0-7022-1877-4). U of Queensland Pr.

Loving Friends: A Portrait of Bloomsbury. David Gadd. LC 74-26596. 1976. pap. 3.45 o.p. (ISBN 0-15-654300-1, Harv). HarBraceJ.

Loving God's Family. Roy Matheson. 160p. 1985. pap. 2.95 o.p. (ISBN 0-89693-524-8). Victor Bks.

Loving Her. Ann A. Shockley. 1978. pap. 1.75 o.p. (ISBN 0-380-38935-5, 38935). Avon.

Loving John: The Untold Story. May Pang & Henry Edwards. (Illus.). 336p. (Orig.). 1983. pap. 8.95 o.s.i. (ISBN 0-446-37916-6). Warner Bks.

Loving Ourselves. Ray Ashford. LC 76-62604. (Orig.). 1977. pap. 3.50 o.p. (ISBN 0-8006-1255-8, Fortress). Augsburg Fortress.

Loving Season. Rebecca Burton. 1979. pap. 2.25 o.p. (ISBN 0-505-51413-3, Pub. by Tower Bk). Dorchester Pub Co.

Loving Seasons. Elizabeth N. Walker. 336p. (Orig.). 1983. pap. 3.95 o.p. (ISBN 0-440-14879-0). Dell.

Loving Spirit. Daphne Du Maurier. 1982. pap. 1.25 o.p. (ISBN 0-380-01337-1, 10686). Avon.

Loving to Be Loved. John F. Cody. 46p. 1980. 5.00 o.p. (ISBN 0-682-49620-0). Exposition-Phoenix.

Loving Upward. Mary Richie. 1976. pap. 1.75 o.p. (ISBN 0-380-00801-7, 30593). Avon.

Lovingly: Poems for All Seasons. Helen S. Rice. 96p. 1970. 8.95 o.p. (ISBN 0-8007-0408-8). Revell.

Low & Slow: An Insider's History of Agricultural Aviation. Mabry I. Anderson. (Illus.). 160p. 1986. pap. text ed. 12.50 o.p. (ISBN 0-936815-00-0). CA Farmer Pub.

Low Angles: A Stoney Winston Mystery. Jim Stinson. 240p. 1986. 13.95 o.s.i. (ISBN 0-684-18626-8). Scribner.

Low Back Pain Syndrome. 3rd ed. Rene Cailliet. LC 80-15815. (Pain Ser.). (Illus.). 230p. 1981. pap. text ed. 12.95x o.p. (ISBN 0-8036-1605-8). Davis Co.

Low Birth Weight: A Medical, Psychological & Social Study. Ed. by Raymond Illsley & Ross G. Mitchell. 272p. 1984. 52.00x o.p. (ISBN 0-471-90355-8, Dist. by A R Liss). Wiley.

Low Blood Sugar: A Doctor's Guide to Its Effective Control. J. Frank Hurdle. Orig. Title: Low Blood Sugar: How to Control This Hidden Menace to Your Health & Vitality. 1971. 12.95 o.p. (ISBN 0-13-541086-X, Reward); pap. 4.95 o.p. (ISBN 0-13-541078-9). P-H.

Low Blood Sugar & You. Carlton Fredericks & Herman Goodman. 1969. pap. 4.95 o.p. (ISBN 0-399-51043-5, G&D); PLB 13.50 o.p. (ISBN 0-448-13341-5, Today Press). Putnam Pub Group.

Low Blood Sugar: How to Control This Hidden Menace to Your Health & Vitality see Low Blood Sugar: A Doctor's Guide to Its Effective Control.

Low Cost Costing: Product Costing with Your Microcomputer. Thomas S. Fiske. (Illus.). 94p. (Orig.). 1984. pap. 24.95 spiral bound o.p. (ISBN 0-88006-084-0); Apple II, II Plus, IIe. spiral bound incl. disk 24.95 o.p. (ISBN 0-88006-067-0, CC7399); IBM-PC. spiral bound incl. disk 24.95 o.p. (ISBN 0-88006-071-9, CC7402); TRS-80 Model I, Model III. spiral bound incl. disk 24.95 o.p. (ISBN 0-88006-072-7, CC7403); spiral bound incl. disk 24.95 o.p. (ISBN 0-88006-092-1, CC7421). Wayne Green Ent.

Low-Cost Housing Technology: An East-West Perspective. Ed. by L. J. Goodman et al. (Illus.). 500p. 1980. 90.00 o.p. (ISBN 0-08-023250-7). Pergamon.

Low-Cost Passive Solar Greenhouses: A Design & Construction Guide. Ron Alward & Andy Shapiro. (Illus.). 176p. 1982. pap. 10.95 o.p. (ISBN 0-684-17503-7, ScribT). Scribner.

Low Cost Rural Health Care & Health Manpower Training: An Annotated Bibliography with Special Emphasis on Developing Countries, 4 vols. Incl. Vol. 1. 165p. 1975 (ISBN 0-88936-051-0, IDRC42). UNIPUB; Vol. 2. 182p. 1976 (ISBN 0-88936-093-6, IDRC69). UNIPUB; Vol. 3. F. M. Delaney. 187p. 1977 (ISBN 0-88936-138-X, IDRC93). UNIPUB; Vol. 4. F. M. Delaney. 186p. 1979 (ISBN 0-88936-201-7, IDRC125). UNIPUB. pap. 10.00 o.p. (IDRC). UNIPUB.

Low Cost Solar Heaters for Your Home. Tom W. Rentz. (Orig.). 1978. pap. 2.95 o.p. (ISBN 0-89036-104-5). Hawkes Pub Inc.

Low Country Liar. Janet Dailey. (Nightingale Paperbacks Ser.). 214p. 1987. pap. 11.95 o.s.i. (ISBN 0-8161-4303-X, Large Print Bks). G K Hall.

Low Energy Ion Beams: Proceedings of the LEIB Conference, 3rd, Loughborough, U. K., March 28-31, 1983. Ed. by W. A. Grant. 120p. 1984. pap. 30.00 o.p. (ISBN 0-08-030553-9). Pergamon.

Low-Income Housing in the Developing World: The Role of Sites & Services & Settlement Upgrading. Geoffrey K. Payne. LC 83-14488. (Public Administration in Developing Countries Ser.). (Illus.). 271p. 1984. 84.95 o.p. (ISBN 0-471-90212-8, 1-625, Pub. by Wiley-Interscience). Wiley.

Low Income Housing: Technology & Policy: Proceedings of the International Conference, Bangkok, June 1977, 3 vols. Ed. by R. P. Pama et al. 1978. 290.00 o.p. (ISBN 0-08-023241-8). Pergamon.

Low Risk Profits in High Risk Times. Robert Kinsman. LC 84-71125. 220p. 1985. 25.00 o.p. (ISBN 0-87094-379-0). Dow Jones-Irwin.

Low Salt Diet & Recipe Book. Beverly Barbour. (Illus.). 1985. pap. 5.95 o.p. (ISBN 0-671-55745-9, Fireside). S&S.

Low Salt Diet Counter. Corinne T. Netzer. (Orig.). 1982. pap. 2.95 o.p. (ISBN 0-440-18501-7). Dell.

Low Speed Marine Diesel Engines. John B. Woodward. LC 80-39635. (Ocean Engineering Ser.). 271p. 1981. 48.50 o.p. (ISBN 0-471-06335-5, Pub. by Wiley-Interscience). Krieger.

Low-Stress Fitness: The-Low Stress Way to Get in Shape. Millie Brown. LC 85-80119. (Illus.). 160p. 1985. pap. 8.95 o.p. (ISBN 0-89586-355-3). Price Stern.

Low Temperature Biology of Foodstuffs. Ed. by J. Hawthorne & E. J. Rolfe. 1969. 115.00 o.p. (ISBN 0-08-013294-4). Pergamon.

Low-Temperature Properties of Polymers. I. I. Perepechko. 272p. 1981. 55.00 o.p. (ISBN 0-08-025301-6). Pergamon.

Low-Volume Roads: Second International Conference. (Transportation Research Record Ser.). 341p. 1979. 18.00 o.p. (ISBN 0-309-02843-4). Transport Res Bd.

Lowenfeld World Technique: Studies in Personality. R. Bowyer. 1969. text ed. 29.00 o.p. (ISBN 0-08-013029-1); pap. 15.00 o.p. (ISBN 0-08-013028-3). Pergamon.

Lower Animals. Martin Wells. LC 68-13140. 1968. pap. text ed. 2.95 o.p. (ISBN 0-07-069255-6). McGraw.

Lower Depths. Maxim Gorky. Ed. by Jacques Chwat. 1974. pap. 0.75 o.p. (ISBN 0-380-00092-X, 18630, Bard). Avon.

Lower Palaeozoic Rocks of the World: Lower Palaeozoic of the Middle East, Eastern & Southern Africa & Antartica, Vol. 3. C. H. Holland. LC 80-41688. (Lower Palaeozoic Rocks of the World Ser.). 331p. 1981. 159.95 o.p. (ISBN 0-471-27945-5, Pub. by Wiley-Interscience). Wiley.

Lower Zuni Sequence in the Southwestern United States. P. L. Kehler. LC 74-31296. (Institute for the Study of Earth & Man: Reports of Investigations, No. 1). 32p. 1975. pap. 1.95x o.p. (ISBN 0-87074-148-9). SMU Press.

Lowestoft Porcelains. G. A. Godden. (Illus.). 1985. 59.50 o.s.i. (ISBN 0-907462-64-2). Antique Collect.

Low's Autobiography. David Low. 1957. 5.00 o.p. S&S.

Loyalists & Redcoats: A Study in British Revolutionary Policy. Paul H. Smith. 1972. pap. 3.95x o.p. (ISBN 0-393-00628-X, Norton Lib). Norton.

Loyalists in Revolutionary America 1760-1781. Robert M. Calhoon. LC 73-8835. (Founding of the American Republic Ser.). 1973. 17.50 o.p. (ISBN 0-15-154745-9). HarBraceJ.

Loyalists in the American Revolution. Claude H. Van Tyne. 12.75 o.p. (ISBN 0-8446-1458-0). Peter Smith.

Loyalty Islands: History of Culture Contacts, 1840-1900. K. R. Howe. LC 76-50009. 1977. 15.00x o.p. (ISBN 0-8248-0451-1). UH Pr.

LSD Psychotherapy. Stanislav Grof. LC 86-23256. 352p. 1986. Repr. lib. bdg. 29.95x o.p. (ISBN 0-8095-6300-2). Borgo Pr.

LSITT. Arthur Herzog. 1983. 14.95 o.p. (ISBN 0-87795-470-4, Arbor Hse). Morrow.

LSU Basketball Organizational Handbook. LC 81-85626. (Illus.). 192p. (Orig.). 1983. spiral 15.95 o.p. (ISBN 0-918438-87-X, PBRO0087). Leisure Pr.

Lu Ban Learns Carpentry. 1981. 2.95 o.p. (ISBN 0-8351-0936-4). China Bks.

Lualda. Melvin Shavelson. LC 74-80709. 1975. 7.95 o.p. (ISBN 0-87795-088-1, Arbor Hse). Morrow.

Lubyanka. James Burch. LC 82-73022. 256p. 1983. 13.95 o.p. (ISBN 0-689-11342-0, Atheneum). Macmillan.

Luca della Robbia. John Pope-Hennessy. LC 79-13566. (Illus.). 282p. 1980. 125.00x o.p. (ISBN 0-8014-1256-0). Cornell U Pr.

Lucas Samaras, Chair Transformations. Ed. by Pace Gallery Publications Staff. LC 79-138435. (Illus.). 64p. (Orig.). 1970. pap. text ed. 12.00 o.p. (ISBN 0-938608-34-7). Pace Pubns.

Lucas Samaras: Sittings. Carter Ratcliff. Ed. by Pace Gallery Publications Staff. (Illus.). 48p. (Orig.). 1980. pap. text ed. 12.00 o.p. (ISBN 0-938608-14-2). Pace Pubns.

Luce & His Empire: A Biography. W. A. Swanberg. LC 73-162778. (Illus.). 448p. 1975. encore ed. 5.95 o.p. (ISBN 0-684-12592-7, ScribT). Scribner.

Luces y Sombras de un Destierro. Bibi Armas de Arenas. 166p. 1979. pap. 6.95 o.p. (ISBN 0-686-65594-X). Ediciones.

Lucia di Lammermoor. Gaetano Donizetti. Tr. by Ellen H. Bleiler. (Illus.). 6.25 o.p. (ISBN 0-8446-4541-9). Peter Smith.

Lucian, Satirist & Artist. Francis G. Allinson. LC 63-10286. (Our Debt to Greece & Rome Ser). Repr. of 1930 ed. 15.00x o.p. (ISBN 0-8154-0010-1). Cooper Sq.

Luciana Avedon's Body Book. Luciana Avedon & Jeanne Molli. LC 76-15189. (Illus.). 208p. 1976. 12.95 o.p. (ISBN 0-87131-211-5). M Evans.

Lucid Exposition of the Middle Way: The Essential Chapters from the Prasannapada of Candrakirti. Tr. by Mervyn Sprung et al from Sanskrit. LC 79-13033. 1979. write for info. o.p. (ISBN 0-87773-711-8, Prajna). Shambhala Pubns.

Lucien Kroll: Buildings & Projects. Wolfgang Pehnt. LC 87-45547. (Illus.). 160p. 1987. pap. 29.95 o.p. (ISBN 0-8478-0866-1). Rizzoli Intl.

Lucifer Mask. Kathleen Rich. 1977. pap. 1.50 o.p. (ISBN 0-505-51186-X, Pub. by Tower Bks). Dorchester Pub Co.

Luck, Chance, & Coincidence. Steve Richards. 160p. 1985. pap. 8.95 o.p. (ISBN 0-85030-401-6). Newcastle Pub.

Luck of Brin's Five. Cherry Wilder. LC 77-1590. (gr. 7 up). 1977. 7.95 o.p. (ISBN 0-689-30601-6, Atheneum). Macmillan.

Luck of Pokey Bloom. Ellen Conford. (Illus.). (gr. 4-6). 1983. 1.95 o.p. (ISBN 0-671-44233-3). Archway.

Luck of the Linscotts: A Novel of Great New England Dynasty. Ann Pinchot. LC 81-71675. 1982. 14.95 o.p. (ISBN 0-87795-381-3, Arbor Hse). Morrow.

Luckiest Man in the World. Randall Silvis. 224p. 1987. pap. 4.50 o.p. (ISBN 0-380-69936-2, Bard). Avon.

Lucks & Talismans: A Chapter of Popular Superstition. Charles R. Beard. LC 74-174903. 280p. Repr. of 1934 ed. 40.00x o.p. (ISBN 0-8103-3871-8). Gale.

Lucky: A Novel. Jackie Collins. 1985. 17.45 o.p. (ISBN 0-671-52493-3). S&S.

Lucky Ghost Shirt. Teri Martini. LC 70-128642. (Illus.). 112p. (gr. 3-6). 1971. 4.50 o.s.i. (ISBN 0-664-32484-3, Westminster). Westminster John Knox.

Lucky Kristoffer. Martin A. Hansen. Tr. by John J. Egglishaw from Danish. LC 73-9298. (Library of Scandinavian Literature Ser: Vol. 25). 377p. 1974. lib. bdg. 8.50x o.p. (ISBN 0-89067-023-4). Am Scandinavian.

Lucky Life. Gerald Stern. LC 77-8541. (New Poetry Ser.). 1977. pap. 6.70 o.p. (ISBN 0-395-25809-X). HM.

Lucky Luciano: His Amazing Trial & Wild Witnesses. Hickman Powell. 338p. 1975. Repr. of 1939 ed. 7.95 o.p. (ISBN 0-8065-0493-5, Pub. by Citadel Pr). Carol Pub Group.

Lucky Man. Mary B. Christian. LC 79-11024. (Ready-to-Read Ser.). (Illus.). 64p. (gr. 1-4). 1979. 7.95 o.s.i. (ISBN 0-02-718270-3). Macmillan.

Lucky Yak. Annetta Lawson. (Illus.). (gr. k-3). 1980. 6.95 o.p. (ISBN 0-395-29523-8, Pub. by Parnassus). HM.

Lucretius & His Influence. George D. Hadzsits. LC 63-10292. (Our Debt to Greece & Rome Ser). 1963. Repr. of 1930 ed. 28.50x o.p. (ISBN 0-8154-0106-X). Cooper Sq.

Lucy & Tom's Day. Shirley Hughes. (ps-1). 1960. 13.95 o.p. (ISBN 0-575-00362-6, Pub. by Gollancz England). David & Charles.

Lucy Atwell's ABC One, Two, Three Pop-Up Book. (Pop-Ups Bks.). (Illus.). (ps-1). 1.98 o.p. (ISBN 0-517-43885-2). Outlet Bk Co.

Lucy Larcom: Life, Letters & Diary. Daniel D. Addison. LC 75-99065. (Library of Lives & Letters). 306p. 1970. Repr. of 1894 ed. 40.00x o.p. (ISBN 0-8103-3611-1). Gale.

Lucy Makes It Big. Sue Dreamer. (Ringling Bros. & Barnum & Bailey Circus Bks.). (Illus.). 32p. (gr. k-3). 1986. 7.95 o.p. (ISBN 0-316-19202-3). Little.

Lucy's Bag Book. Lucy Mackall. 1978. 12.95 o.p. (ISBN 0-395-26302-6); pap. 6.95 o.p. (ISBN 0-395-26473-1). HM.

Ludlow Laughs. Jon Agee. (Illus.). 3.95 o.p. (ISBN 0-317-65307-5). FS&G.

Ludmila Zhivkova: Her Many Worlds-New Culture & Beauty-Concepts & Action. Ed. by L. Zhivkova. 300p. 1982. 16.50 o.p. (ISBN 0-08-028171-0). Pergamon.

Ludovisi Goddess: The Life of Louisa Lady Ashburton. Virginia Surtees. (Illus.). xiv, 210p. 1984. 15.00x o.s.i. (ISBN 0-85955-105-9). Wedgestone Pr.

Ludus Patronymicus: Or, the Etymology of Curious Surnames. Richard S. Charnock. LC 68-23141. 188p. 1968. Repr. of 1868 ed. 35.00x o.p. (ISBN 0-8103-3122-5). Gale.

Ludwig Karl Hilberseimer: An Annotated Bibliography & Chronology. David Spaeth. LC 81-47449. 116p. 1981. lib. bdg. 24.00 o.p. (ISBN 0-8240-9344-5). Garland Pub.

Ludwig Van Beethoven. Eric Roseberry. LC 60-51399. (Great Masters Ser.). 43p. 1960. pap. 3.75 o.p. Boosey & Hawkes.

Ludwig Wittgenstein & the Vienna Circle: Conversations Recorded by Friedrich Waismann. Friedrich Waismann. Ed. by Brian McGuinness. Tr. by Joachim Schulte & B. McGuiness. LC 78-6452. (Illus.). 266p. 1979. text ed. 28.50x o.p. (ISBN 0-06-497310-7). B&N Imports.

Luftwaffe Aircraft & Aces. Edward T. Maloney. (Illus.). 1969. pap. 6.95 o.p. (ISBN 0-911721-74-6, Pub. by WW). Aviation.

Luftwaffe Handbook. Alfred Price. (Encore Editions). (Illus.). 1977. 3.95 o.p. (ISBN 0-684-16691-7, ScribT). Scribner.

Luftwaffe Test Pilot. Hans-Werner Lerche. (Illus.). 158p. 1981. 19.95 o.p. (ISBN 0-86720-583-0). Janes Info Group.

Lug Zelenyi: Kniga Statei. Boris N. Bugaev. 1967. Repr. of 1910 ed. 30.00 o.p. (ISBN 0-384-06245-8). Johnson Repr.

Luganda-English Dictionary. John D. Murphy. LC 72-6860. (Publications in the Languages of Africa Ser.: No. 2). 651p. (Luganda & Eng.). 1973. 36.95 o.p. (ISBN 0-8132-0525-5). Cath U Pr.

Luger Tips. Michael Reese, II. 1976. 6.95 o.s.i. (ISBN 0-913150-36-3). Pioneer Pr.

Lugols Iodine Stain. Date not set. (ISBN 0-07-521053-3). McGraw.

Luigi Colani Design Series. Ed. by San'ei Shobo Publishing Co. Staff. 119p. 32.95 o.s.i. (ISBN 0-317-67598-2). Bks Nippan.

Luigi Pirandello. Susan Bassnett-McGuire. LC 83-47990. (Modern Dramatists Ser.). (Illus.). 108p. 1983. pap. 9.95 o.p. (ISBN 0-394-62410-6, E865, Ever). Grove.

Luis. John Getsinger. LC 75-17658. (Illus.). 48p. (Eng. & Span.). (gr. 3-7). 1976. 7.50 o.p. (ISBN 0-88468-004-5). Ethridge.

Lukacs' Last Autocriticism: The Ontology. Ernest Joos. 149p. 1983. text ed. 15.00x o.p. (ISBN 0-391-02589-9). Humanities.

Luke, Vol. III. Beacon Bible Expositions Staff. 6.95 o.p. (ISBN 0-8010-0678-3). Baker Bk.

Luke. Frederick W. Danker. Ed. by Gerhard Krodel. LC 76-5954. (Proclamation Commentaries: the New Testament Witnesses for Preaching Ser.). 128p. 1976. pap. 4.95 o.p. (ISBN 0-8006-0583-7, 1-583, Fortress). Augsburg Fortress.

Luke: A Challenge to Present Theology. Eduard Schwizer. LC 81-85332. 144p. 1982. pap. 10.50 o.s.i. (ISBN 0-8042-0686-4, John Knox). Westminster John Knox.

Luke & Angela. Christine Nostlinger. Tr. by Anthea Bell. LC 80-8804. 144p. (gr. 7 up). 1981. 8.95 o.p. (ISBN 0-15-249902-4, HJ). HarBraceJ.

Luke & the People of God: A New Look at Luke-Acts. Jacob Jervell. LC 72-78565. 208p. 1979. pap. 10.95 o.p. (ISBN 0-8066-1730-6, 10-4136, Augsburg). Augsburg Fortress.

Luke & the People of God: A New Look at Luke-Acts. Jacob Jervell. LC 72-78565. 208p. 1972. 8.50 o.p. (ISBN 0-8066-1232-0, 10-4135, Augsburg). Augsburg Fortress.

Luke Short's Best of the West. Luke Short. 320p. 1983. 14.95 o.p. (ISBN 0-87795-471-2, Arbor Hse). Morrow.

Luke Sutton: Hired Gun. Leo P. Kelley. LC 87-624. (Double D Western Ser.). 192p. 1987. 12.95 o.s.i. (ISBN 0-385-23787-1). Doubleday.

Lullaby. Oakley Hall. LC 81-66038. 278p. 1982. 13.95 o.p. (ISBN 0-689-11210-6, Atheneum). Macmillan.

Lullaby of Murder. Dorothy S. Davis. 224p. 1984. 12.95 o.p. (ISBN 0-684-18086-3, ScribT). Scribner.

Lum: Urusei Yatsura, Vol. 1. Rumiko Takahashi. Ed. by Seiji Horibuchi. Tr. by Gerard Jones & Satoru Fujii. (Illus.). 48p. (Orig.). 1989. pap. 2.95 o.p. (ISBN 0-929279-29-8). Viz Commns Inc.

Lum: Urusei Yatsura, Vol. 2. Rumiko Takahashi. Ed. by Seiji Horibuchi. Tr. by Gerard Jones & Satoru Fujii. (Illus.). 48p. (Orig.). 1989. pap. 2.95 o.p. (ISBN 0-929279-30-1). Viz Commns Inc.

Lum: Urusei Yatsura, Vol. 3. Rumiko Takahashi. Ed. by Seiji Horibuchi. Tr. by Gerard Jones & Satoru Fujii. (Illus.). 48p. (Orig.). 1989. pap. 2.95 o.p. (ISBN 0-929279-31-X). Viz Commns Inc.

Lum: Urusei Yatsura, Vol. 4. Rumiko Takahashi. Ed. by Seiji Horibuchi. Tr. by Gerard Jones & Satoru Fujii. (Illus.). 48p. (Orig.). 1989. pap. 2.95 o.p. (ISBN 0-929279-32-8). Viz Commns Inc.

Lum: Urusei Yatsura, Vol. 5. Rumiko Takahashi. Ed. by Seiji Horibuchi. Tr. by Gerard Jones & Satoru Fujii. (Illus.). 48p. (Orig.). 1989. pap. 2.95 o.p. (ISBN 0-929279-33-6). Viz Commns Inc.

Lum: Urusei Yatsura, Vol. 6. Rumiko Takahashi. Ed. by Seiji Horibuchi. Tr. by Gerard Jones & Satoru Fujii. (Illus.). 48p. (Orig.). 1989. pap. 2.95 o.p. (ISBN 0-929279-34-4). Viz Commns Inc.

Lum: Urusei Yatsura, Vol. 7. Rumiko Takahashi. Ed. by Seiji Horibuchi. Tr. by Gerard Jones & Satoru Fujii. (Illus.). 48p. (Orig.). 1989. pap. 2.95 o.p. (ISBN 0-929279-35-2). Viz Commns Inc.

Lum: Urusei Yatsura, Vol. 8. Rumiko Takahashi. Ed. by Seiji Horibuchi. Tr. by Gerard Jones & Satoru Fujii. (Illus.). 48p. (Orig.). 1989. pap. 2.95 o.p. (ISBN 0-929279-36-0). Viz Commns Inc.

Lumber Camp Life in Michigan: An Autobiographical Account. Rex J. Dye & Jacob Dye. 1975. 5.00 o.p. (ISBN 0-682-48102-5, Lochinvar). Exposition-Phoenix.

Lumberjack. William Kurelek. LC 74-9377. (Illus.). 48p. (gr. 1 up). 1974. 8.95 o.p. (ISBN 0-395-19922-0). HM.

Lumberjack. William Kurelek. 48p. (gr. 5 up). Repr. text ed. 17.95 o.p. (ISBN 0-88776-052-X, Dist. by U of Toronto Pr); pap. 6.95 o.p. (ISBN 0-88776-082-1). Tundra Bks.

Lumberjack. Stephen W. Meader. LC 34-31292. (Illus.). (gr. 7 up). 1934. 4.95 o.p. (ISBN 0-15-249904-0, HJ). HarBraceJ.

Luminescence & the Light Emitting Diode. E. W. Williams & R. Hall. LC 77-4427. 1978. 65.00 o.p. (ISBN 0-08-020442-2); pap. 60.00 o.p. (ISBN 0-08-020441-4). Pergamon.

Luminescence of Inorganic Solids. Paul Goldberg. 1966. 145.50 o.p. (ISBN 0-12-287550-8). Acad Pr.

Lummis in the Pueblos. Patrick Houlihan. LC 86-60515. (Illus.). 160p. (Orig.). 1986. 29.95 o.p. (ISBN 0-87358-417-1, Entrada Bks); pap. 19.95 o.p. (ISBN 0-87358-407-4, Entrada Bks). Northland.

Lumped & Distributed Passive Networks: A Generalized & Advanced Viewpoint. Ronald W. Wohlers. (Electrical Science Monographs). 1969. 29.50 o.p. (ISBN 0-12-761450-8). Acad Pr.

Lumpy: A Baseball Fable. Tug McGraw. LC 81-10658. (Illus.). 40p. (Orig.). (gr. 5-12). 1981. lib. bdg. 12.90 o.p. (ISBN 0-89471-151-2); pap. 4.95 o.p. (ISBN 0-89471-150-4). Running Pr.

Luna. Delacorta, pseud. Tr. by Victoria Reiter. (Gorodish-Alba Ser.). 128p. 1984. 9.70 o.s.i. (ISBN 0-671-49379-5). Summit Bks.

Lunar Astrology. rev. ed. Alexander Volguine. LC 74-75523. (French Astrology Ser.). 1974. 8.95 o.s.i. (ISBN 0-88231-004-6). ASI Pubs Inc.

Lunar Panorama: A Photographic Guide to the Geology of the Moon. P. D. Lowman, Jr. (Illus.). 1969. 60.00 o.p. E J Brill USA.

Lunar Surface Layer: Materials & Characteristics: Proceedings. Ed. by John W. Salisbury & Peter E. Glaser. 1964. 52.50 o.p. (ISBN 0-12-615450-3). Acad Pr.

Lunatic & Lover: A Play about Strindberg. Michael Meyer. 60p. 1982. pap. 4.95 o.p. (ISBN 0-413-49390-3, NO. 3632). Heinemann Ed.

Lunation Process. Leyla Rael Rudhyar. pap. 3.95 o.p. (ISBN 0-943358-15-9). Aurora Press.

Lunch Box Book. Anne Gilbar. (Orig.). 1984. pap. 3.70 o.p. (ISBN 0-671-50069-4). S&S.

Luncheon & Supper Dishes for Foodservice Menu Planning. Eulalia C. Blair. LC 72-92379. (Foodservice Menu Planning Ser.). 1983. 19.95 o.p. (ISBN 0-8436-0559-6). Van Nos Reinhold.

Luncheon Guest: Talks with College Men & Women about a Search for God. Franklin F. Thomas. (Illus.). 1979. pap. 3.95 o.p. (ISBN 0-682-49402-X). Exposition-Phoenix.

Lung Air Sac System of Birds. H. R. Duncker. LC 75-181322. (Advances in Anatomy, Embryology & Cell Biology: Vol. 45, Pt. 6). (Illus.). 150p. 1972. pap. 60.20 o.p. (ISBN 0-387-05659-9). Springer-Verlag.

Lung Cancer Diagnosis. Ed. by Yoshihiro Hayata. LC 82-3093. (Illus.). 280p. 1982. monograph 78.00 o.p. (ISBN 0-89640-073-5). Igaku-Shoin.

Lung Cancer, 1980: Post-Graduate Course II. Ed. by H. H. Hansen & M. Roth. (International Congress Ser.: Vol. 525). 1981. 48.50 o.p. (ISBN 0-444-90160-4). Elsevier.

Lung Development: Biological & Clinical Perspectives, 2 vols. Ed. by Philip Farrell. LC 82-1616. 1982. Vol. 1: Biochemistry & Physiology. 72.50 o.p. (ISBN 0-12-249701-5); Vol. 2: Neonatal Respiratory Distress. 58.00 o.p. (ISBN 0-12-249702-3). Acad Pr.

Lung Metabolism: Proteolysis & Antiproteolysis, Biochemical Pharmacology, Handling of Bioactive Substances. Ed. by Alain F. Junod & Rodolphe DeHaller. 1976. 71.50 o.p. (ISBN 0-12-392250-X). Acad Pr.

Lurchers & Longdogs. 3rd ed. E. G. Walsh. (Illus.). 1984. 22.00 o.p. (ISBN 0-85115-402-6, Pub. by Boydell & Brewer). Longwood Pub Group.

Lure & Romance of Alchemy. C. J. Thompson. LC 76-167224. (Illus.). vi, 286p. 1975. Repr. of 1932 ed. 40.00x o.p. (ISBN 0-8103-4000-3). Gale.

Lure for Feeling. Wyman. 208p. 1960. (ISBN 0-8022-1940-3). Philos Lib.

Lure of God: A Biblical Background for Process Theism. Lewis S. Ford. LC 77-15230. 160p. 1978. 10.95 o.p. (ISBN 0-8006-0516-0, 1-516, Fortress). Augsburg Fortress.

Lure of Politics. Krishan K. Channan. 68p. 1980. 6.00 o.p. (ISBN 0-682-49641-3). Exposition-Phoenix.

Lure of Sweet Death. Sarah Kemp. LC 87-20114. (Crime Club Ser.). 312p. 1987. 16.95 o.s.i. (ISBN 0-385-23990-4, GC Large Print). Doubleday.

Lure of the Dolphin. Robin Brown. (YA) (gr. 7 up). 1979. pap. 3.95 o.p. (ISBN 0-380-43158-0, 43158). Avon.

Lurking Fear & Other Stories. H. P. Lovecraft. 1982. pap. 2.25 o.p. (ISBN 0-345-30229-X, Del Rey). Ballantine.

Lurking Keats. Geraldine Pederson-Krag. LC 83-25923. 98p. (Orig.). 1984. lib. bdg. 22.00 o.p. (ISBN 0-8191-3788-X); pap. text ed. 8.75 o.p. (ISBN 0-8191-3789-8). U Pr of Amer.

Luscher Color Test. Max Luscher. Ed. & tr. by Ian Scott. 196p. 1980. pap. 3.95 o.s.i. (ISBN 0-671-49177-6). WSP.

Luscombe Story. John C. Swick. (Illus.). 216p. 1987. 29.95 o.p. Aviation.

Lushai Girl. Roberta Forrest. 332p. 1988. 19.95 o.p. (ISBN 0-7181-2678-5, Pub. by Michael Joseph). David & Charles.

Lust Market. Harold H. Cross. 1963. pap. 1.75 o.p. (ISBN 0-8065-0101-4, 140, Pub. by Citadel Pr). Carol Pub Group.

Lust Motif in the Plays of Thomas Middleton. Barbara J. Baines. (Salzburg Studies in English Literature, Jacobean Drama Studies: No. 29). 160p. 1973. pap. text ed. 25.00x o.p. (ISBN 0-391-01306-8). Humanities.

Lutheal Phase. S. L. Jeffcoate. (Wiley Series on Current Topics In Reproductive Endocrinology). 126p. 1985. 44.00 o.p. (ISBN 0-471-90612-3, Dist. by A R Liss). Wiley.

Luther: A Life. John Todd. 416p. 1982. 17.50x o.p. (ISBN 0-8245-0479-8). Crossroad NY.

Luther: A Reformer for the Churches; An Ecumenical Study Guide. Mark Edwards & George H. Tavard. LC 83-48005. 96p. 1983. pap. 5.50 o.p. (ISBN 0-8006-1718-5, 1-1718, Fortress). Augsburg Fortress.

Luther: An Introduction to His Thought. Gerhard Ebeling. Tr. by R. A. Wilson from Ger. LC 77-99612. 288p. 1970. pap. 6.95 o.p. (ISBN 0-8006-1162-4, 1-1162). Augsburg Fortress.

Luther & His Mother. Ian Siggins. LC 80-2386. 96p. (Orig.). 1981. pap. 5.95 o.p. (ISBN 0-8006-1498-4, 1-1498, Fortress). Augsburg Fortress.

Luther & Late Medieval Thomism: A Study in Theological Anthropology. Denis Janz. 191p. 1984. text ed. 25.00x o.p. (ISBN 0-88920-132-3). Humanities.

Luther & the Mystics: A Re-Examination of Luther's Spiritual Experience & His Relationship to the Mystics. Bengt R. Hoffman. LC 75-22724. 264p. 1976. 14.95 o.p. (ISBN 0-8066-1514-1, 10-4140, Augsburg). Augsburg Fortress.

Luther & the Papacy: Stages in a Reformation Conflict. Scott H. Hendrix. LC 80-2393. 224p. 1981. 15.95 o.p. (ISBN 0-8006-0658-2, 1-658, Fortress). Augsburg Fortress.

Luther & the Peasants' War. Hubert Kirchner. Ed. by Charles S. Anderson. Tr. by Darrell Jodock from Ger. LC 73-171507. (Facet Bks.). 48p. (Orig.). 1972. pap. 1.00 o.p. (ISBN 0-8006-3068-8, 1-3068, Fortress). Augsburg Fortress.

Luther & the Peasants' War: Luther's Actions & Reactions. Robert N. Crossley. LC 73-92849. 1974. 8.00 o.p. (ISBN 0-682-47890-3, University). Exposition-Phoenix.

Luther: Early Theological Works. Ed. by James Atkinson. LC 62-12358. (Library of Christian Classics). 376p. 1980. pap. 9.95 o.s.i. (ISBN 0-664-24166-2, Westminster). Westminster John Knox.

Luther Legacy: An Introduction to Luther's Life & Thought for Today. George W. Forell. LC 83-72106. 80p. 1983. pap. 5.95 o.p. (ISBN 0-8066-2050-1, 10-4142, Augsburg). Augsburg Fortress.

Luther on Ministerial Office & Congregational Function. Gert Haendler. Ed. by Eric W. Gritsch. Tr. by Ruth C. Gritsch from Ger. LC 81-43075. 112p. 1981. 9.95 o.p. (ISBN 0-8006-0665-5, 1-665, Fortress). Augsburg Fortress.

Luther: Right or Wrong. Harry J. McSorley, Jr. LC 68-59159. 1969. 9.95 o.p. (ISBN 0-8066-0903-6, 10-4145, Augsburg). Augsburg Fortress.

Luther: Selected Political Writings. Ed. by J. M. Porter. LC 74-76931. 160p. (Orig.). 1974. pap. 1.50 o.p. (ISBN 0-8006-1079-2, 1-1079, Fortress). Augsburg Fortress.

Luther the Preacher. Fred W. Meuser. LC 83-72107. 80p. 1983. pap. 5.95 o.p. (ISBN 0-8066-2051-X, 10-4147, Augsburg). Augsburg Fortress.

Titles

Luther the Reformer: The Story of the Man & His Career. James M. Kittelson. LC 86-17266. (Illus.). 320p. 1986. text ed. 24.95 o.p. (ISBN 0-8066-2315-2, 10-4148, Augsburg); pap. 8.95 o.p. (10-4151). Augsburg Fortress.

Luther: Witness to Jesus Christ: Stages & Themes of the Reformer's Christology. Marc Lienhard. Tr. by Edwin H. Robertson. LC 81-52285. 432p. 1982. text ed. 24.95 o.p. (ISBN 0-8066-1917-1, 10-4149, Augsburg). Augsburg Fortress.

Lutheran Chorale - Its Basic Traditions. Johannes Riedel. 1967. pap. 5.95 spiral bdg. o.p. (ISBN 0-8066-0729-7, 11-9289, Augsburg). Augsburg Fortress.

Lutheran Church among Norwegian Americans, 2 Vols. Clifford Nelson & Eugene L. Fevold. LC 60-6438. 1960. Set. boxed 15.00 o.p. (ISBN 0-8066-0019-5, 10-4150, Augsburg). Augsburg Fortress.

Lutheran Church: Past & Present. Ed. by Vilmos Vajta. LC 76-46120. 1977. pap. 11.50 o.p. (ISBN 0-8066-1573-7, 10-4160, Augsburg). Augsburg Fortress.

Lutheran Higher Education in North America. Richard W. Solberg. LC 85-28757. 400p. (Orig.). 1985. pap. 11.95 o.p. (ISBN 0-8066-2187-7, 10-4168, Augsburg). Augsburg Fortress.

Lutheran Liturgy. rev. ed. Ed. by Luther D. Reed. LC 60-15401. 1960. 14.95 o.p. (ISBN 0-8006-0496-2, Fortress). Augsburg Fortress.

Lutheran Reformers Against Anabaptists. J. S. Oyer. 1964. pap. 12.50 o.s.i. (ISBN 0-685-12029-5). E J Brill USA.

Lutherans & Catholics in Dialogue: Personal Notes for a Study. Paul C. Empie. LC 80-69754. (Orig.). 1981. pap. 4.50 o.p. (ISBN 0-8006-1449-6, 1-1449, Fortress). Augsburg Fortress.

Lutherans in the U. S. A. rev. ed. Willmar Thorkelson. LC 77-84812. 1978. pap. 2.95 o.p. (ISBN 0-8066-1688-1, 10-4200, Augsburg). Augsburg Fortress.

Luther's Got Class. Brumsic Brandon, Jr. LC 75-16502. (Illus.). 96p. 1976. pap. 3.95 o.p. (ISBN 0-8397-5668-2). Eriksson.

Luther's Large Catechism. Martin Luther. Tr. by J. M. Lenker. 1967. flexible bdg. 7.95 o.p. (ISBN 0-8066-0720-3, 10-4211, Augsburg). Augsburg Fortress.

Luther's Theology of the Cross. Regin Prenter. Ed. by Charles S. Anderson. LC 71-152368. (Facet Bks.). 32p. 1971. pap. 2.50 o.p. (ISBN 0-8006-3062-9, 1-3062, Fortress). Augsburg Fortress.

Luther's Theology of the Cross. Walter Von Loewenich. Tr. by Herbert J. Bouman. LC 75-2845. 224p. (Orig.). 1982. pap. 12.95 o.p. (ISBN 0-8066-1490-0, 10-4233, Augsburg). Augsburg Fortress.

Luttes entre les Societies Humaines et Leurs Phases Successives, 2 vols. Jacques Novicow. LC 71-147481. (Library of War & Peace; the Character & Causes of War). 1972. Set. lib. bdg. 92.00 o.p. (ISBN 0-8240-0273-3). Garland Pub.

Luxury Designs for Apartment Living. Barbara Taylor Bradford. LC 77-16899. (Illus.). 352p. 1981. pap. 29.95 o.p. (ISBN 0-385-12769-3). Doubleday.

Luxury Home Plans. Heritage Home Plans, Inc. LC 79-2769. (Illus.). 1980. pap. 7.95 o.p. (ISBN 0-15-654309-5, Harv). HarBraceJ.

Luxury Liner Row-Passenger Ships at New York. William Miller, Jr. 1981. pap. 9.50 o.p. (ISBN 0-915276-27-5). Quadrant Pr.

Luxury Yachts. Time-Life Books Editors & John Rousmaniere. (Seafarers Ser.). (Illus.). 176p. 1982. 13.95 o.p. (ISBN 0-8094-2734-6). Time-Life.

LX. Vane Ivanovic. LC 76-27414. (Illus.). 1977. 14.95 o.s.i. (ISBN 0-15-154797-1). HarBraceJ.

Lyautey in Morocco: Protectorate Administration, 1912-1925. Alan Scham. LC 74-92680. 1970. 42.00x o.p. (ISBN 0-520-01602-5). U of Cal Pr.

Lycian Turkey: An Archaeological Guide. George L. Bean. (Illus.). 1978. 15.95x o.p. (ISBN 0-393-05708-9). Norton.

Lying in Bed. Mark Harris. 192p. 1984. text ed. 14.95 o.p. (ISBN 0-07-026844-4). McGraw.

Lying...Not a Very Fun Thing. Gloria G. Morrell. (gr. 1-3). 1986. pap. 3.95 o.p. (ISBN 0-8054-4338-X). Broadman.

Lyle Official Antiques Review, 1984. (Illus.). 670p. (Orig.). 1983. 24.95 o.p. (ISBN 0-399-50923-2, Perigee). Putnam Pub Group.

Lyle Official Antiques Review, 1985. Compiled by Anthony Curtis. (Illus.). 672p. 1984. pap. 9.95 o.p. (ISBN 0-399-51088-5, Perigee). Putnam Pub Group.

Lyle Official Antiques Review 1986. Anthony Curtis. (Illus.). 672p. 1985. pap. 10.95 o.p. (ISBN 0-399-51179-2, Perigee). Putnam Pub Group.

Lyle Official Arms & Armour Review, 1983. Tony Curtis. (Illus.). 416p. 24.95 o.p. (ISBN 0-686-47037-0). Apollo.

Lyle Official Arms & Armour Review, 1982. Ed. by Tony Curtis. (Illus.). 1980. 24.95 o.p. (ISBN 0-8256-9687-9). Apollo.

Lyle Official Books Review, 1982. Ed. by Tony Curtis. (Illus.). 1980. 24.95 o.p. (ISBN 0-8256-9685-2). Apollo.

Lyman Pierson Powell. Charles S. Macfarland. (ISBN 0-8022-1027-9). Philos Lib.

Lymphatics in Cancer. Cushman D. Haagensen et al. LC 76-126454. (Illus.). 583p. 1972. write for info. o.p. (ISBN 0-7216-4443-0). Saunders.

Lymphatics, Lymph & the Lymphomyelard Complex. J. M. Yoffey & F. C. Coortice. 1971. 158.00 o.p. (ISBN 0-12-772050-2). Acad Pr.

Lymphocyte Differentiation, Recognition & Regulation. D. H. Katz. 1977. 93.50 o.p. (ISBN 0-12-401640-5). Acad Pr.

Lymphocyte Hybridomas: Second Workshop on "Functional Properties of Tumors of T & B Lymphocytes" Sponsored by the National Cancer Institute (NIH) April 3-5, 1978, Bethesda, MD, Ed. by F. Melchers & M. Potter. (Current Topics in Microbiology & Immunology: Vol. 81). (Illus.). 1978. 35.00 o.p. (ISBN 0-387-08810-5). Springer-Verlag.

Lymphocyte Recognition & Effector Mechanisms. Ed. by Lindahl & David Osaba. 1974. 78.50 o.p. (ISBN 0-12-450250-4). Acad Pr.

Lymphocyte Stimulation. rev. 2nd ed. Ed. by N. R. Ling & J. E. Kay. LC 74-83274. 397p. 1975. 154.75 o.p. (ISBN 0-444-10701-0, North-Holland). Elsevier.

Lymphocyte: Structure & Function, Pt. 1. Ed. by John J. Marchalonis. (Immunology Ser.: Vol. 5). 1977. 75.00 o.p. (ISBN 0-8247-6418-8). Dekker.

Lymphocyte: Structure & Function, Pt. 2. Ed. by John J. Marchalonis. (Immunology Ser.: Vol. 5). 1977. 75.00 o.p. (ISBN 0-8247-6419-6). Dekker.

Lymphology: Proceedings of the Sixth International Conference. Ed. by P. Malek & V. Bartos. LC 78-24681. (Illus.). 532p. 1979. text ed. 49.50 o.p. (ISBN 0-88416-280-X). Year Bk Med.

Lyotropic Liquid Crystals. C. L. Khetrapal. (NMR (Nuclear Magnetic Resonance) Ser.). (Illus.). 180p. 1975. 25.00 o.p. (ISBN 0-387-07303-5). Springer-Verlag.

Lyric. David Lindley. (Critical Idiom Ser.: No. 44). 145p. 1985. 15.95 o.p. (ISBN 0-416-31430-9, 9475); pap. 5.50 o.p. (ISBN 0-416-31440-6, 9476). Routledge Chapman & Hall.

Lyric & Polemic: The Literary Personality of Roy Campbell. Rowland Smith. 190p. 1972. 13.75 o.p. (ISBN 0-7735-0121-5, McGill Canada). U of Toronto Pr.

Lyrical & the Epic: Studies of Modern Chinese Literature. Jaroslav Prusek. Ed. by Leo Ou-fan Lee. LC 80-7491. (Studies in Chinese Literature & Society). 320p. 1980. 22.50x o.p. (ISBN 0-253-10283-9). Ind U Pr.

Lyrical Novel: Studies in Hermann Hesse, Andre Gide, & Virginia Woolf. Ralph Freedman. 1963. 19.00 o.p. (ISBN 0-691-06071-1); pap. 12.50 o.p. (ISBN 0-691-01267-9). Princeton U Pr.

Lyrics & Satires from Tom Moore. Thomas Moore. Ed. by Sean O'Faolain. (Illus.). 72p. 1971. Repr. of 1929 ed. 15.00x o.p. (ISBN 0-7165-1370-6, BBA 02070, Pub. by Cuala Press Ireland). Biblio Dist.

Lys Rouge see Romans et Contes.

Lysippos. Franklin P. Johnson. LC 68-29743. (Illus.). 1968. Repr. of 1927 ed. lib. bdg. 35.00x o.p. (ISBN 0-8371-0119-0, JOLY). Greenwood.

Lysistrata, Thesmophoriazusae, Ecclesiazusae, Plutus see Works.

Lysistratha, Empress of the Planet Lustra. Ruth Norman. 450p. 1989. text ed. 15.95 o.p. (ISBN 0-932642-92-6). Unarius Pubns.

Lysosomes & Storage Diseases. Ed. by H. G. Hers & F. Van Hoof. 1973. 123.50 o.p. (ISBN 0-12-342850-5). Acad Pr.

Lytton Strachey. Michael Holroyd. LC 79-88847. (Illus.). 1152p. 1980. pap. 8.95 o.p. (ISBN 0-03-055191-9). H Holt & Co.

Lytton Strachey: A Bibliography. Michael Edmonds. LC 80-8493. (Illus.). 175p. 1981. lib. bdg. 36.00 o.p. (ISBN 0-8240-9494-8). Garland Pub.

M

M. John Sack. (Vietnam Ser.). 224p. 1985. pap. 2.75 o.p. (ISBN 0-380-69866-8). Avon.

M. A. C. Crystallographic Laboratory Manual: Mineralogical Association of Canada, Montreal 1984. Ed. by Gabrielle Donnay & J. D. Donnay. Date not set. pap. price not set o.p. (ISBN 0-317-43254-0). Polycrystal Bk Serv.

M H D Stability & Thermonuclear Containment. Ed. by Alan Jeffrey & T. Taniuti. (Perspectives in Physics Ser.). 1966. 49.50 o.p. (ISBN 0-12-382550-4). Acad Pr.

M O S, Special-Purpose Bipolar Integrated-Circuits & R-F Power Transistor Circuit Design. Texas Instruments Inc. (Illus.). 1976. text ed. 35.00 o.p. (ISBN 0-07-063751-2). McGraw.

M. O. S. T. Integrated-Circuit Engineering. J. Mavor. 72p. 1973. pap. 17.50 o.p. (ISBN 0-901223-49-2, NS002, Pub. by Peregrinus London). Inst Elect Eng.

M R N A: Current Research, 2 vols. G. Guthrie et al. (Illus.). 220p. 1972. Vol. 1. text ed. 27.50x o.p. (ISBN 0-8422-7049-3); Vol. 2. text ed. 27.50x o.p. (ISBN 0-8422-7050-7). Irvington.

M. S. Nurnberg: Memoirs of a Danube River Boatman During the Second World War. Josef Schweiss. (Illus.). 312p. 1981. 12.50 o.p. (ISBN 0-682-49629-4). Exposition-Phoenix.

M. Tomchuk, Graphic Work. Franz Geierhaas. (Illus.). 170p. 1989. 24.00 o.p. M Tomchuk.

Ma alim fi at-Tariq. Sayyid Qutb. 186p. (Orig., Arabic.). 1978. pap. 3.75x o.s.i. (ISBN 0-939830-17-5, Pub. by IIFSO Kuwait). New Era Pubns MI.

Ma 'n Me 'n Hockey. Miles W. Watson. 1979. 4.00 o.p. (ISBN 0-682-49244-2). Exposition-Phoenix.

Maalesh: Journal d'une Tournee de Theatre. Jean Cocteau. 240p. 1950. 8.95 o.p. (ISBN 0-686-54539-7). French & Eur.

Mabel. Betty H. Fussell. LC 81-23286. (Illus.). 256p. 1982. 15.95 o.p. (ISBN 0-89919-090-1). Ticknor & Fields.

Mabel Dodge Luhan: New Woman, New Worlds. Lois P. Rudnick. LC 84-7415. (Illus.). 400p. 1984. 19.95 o.p. (ISBN 0-8263-0763-9). U of NM Pr.

Mabinogion. Gwyn Jones. Tr. by Thomas Jones. (Illus.). 352p. 1976. 22.50x o.p. (ISBN 0-460-04228-9, Pub. by J. M. Dent England). Biblio Dist.

Mabon & the Mysteries of Britain. Caitlin Matthews. 256p. 1987. pap. 11.95 o.p. (ISBN 1-85063-052-6, 30526, Ark Paperbks). Routledge Chapman & Hall.

Mac Access: Information in Motion. Dean Gengle & Steven Smith. 277p. 1987. pap. 21.95 o.p. Sams.

Mac Harshberger: Art Deco Americain. Karin Breuer. LC 86-82729. (Illus.). 32p. 1986. pap. 3.50 o.p. (ISBN 0-88401-051-1). Fine Arts Mus.

Mac Multiplan. Ramsay & Lasselle. (Mac Library). 224p. 1984. 18.95 o.p. (ISBN 0-317-05878-9, 6555). Sams.

Mac Multiplan. Linda K. Woods. Ed. by Lenfest. LC 84-8796. 224p. (Orig.). 1984. 22.95 o.p. (ISBN 0-8306-0851-6, 1851); pap. 16.60 o.p. (ISBN 0-8306-1851-1). TAB Bks.

Mac Revealed: Programming with the Macintosh Toolbox. Chernicoff. 256p. 1984. 19.95 o.p. (ISBN 0-317-06578-5, 6551). Sams.

Macaca Mulatta Enzyme Histochemistry of the Nervous System. S. L. Manocha et al. 1970. 66.00 o.p. (ISBN 0-12-469350-4). Acad Pr.

Macaca Mulatta: Management of a Laboratory Breeding Colony. D. A. Valerio et al. 1969. pap. 27.00 o.p. (ISBN 0-12-710056-3). Acad Pr.

Macaques: Studies in Ecology, Behavior & Evolution. Donald G. Lindburg. (Primate Behavior & Development Ser.). 400p. 1980. 33.95 o.p. (ISBN 0-442-24817-2). Van Nos Reinhold.

Macario. B. Traven. Ed. by S. R. Wilson. (Span.). 1971. pap. 9.32 o.p. (ISBN 0-395-12427-1). HM.

MacArthur. 1977. pap. 1.95 o.s.i. (ISBN 0-671-81200-9). PB.

McBain Brief. Ed McBain. 259p. 1983. 14.95 o.p. (ISBN 0-87795-530-1, Arbor Hse). Morrow.

Macbeth see also Tragedy of Macbeth.

Macbeth. Ed. by A. P. Riemer. 1980. pap. 9.00x o.p. (ISBN 0-424-00081-4, Pub. by Sydney U Pr Australia). Intl Spec Bk.

Macbeth. William Shakespeare. Ed. by George B. Harrison. LC 62-21851. 1963. pap. 1.45 o.p. (ISBN 0-15-654998-0, Harv). HarBraceJ.

Macbeth. William Shakespeare. 48p. (Orig.). 1988. pap. 9.95 o.p. (ISBN 1-55651-575-8); cassette o.p. (ISBN 1-55651-576-6). Cram Cassettes.

Macbeth: Monarch Quick & Easy Notes. 1985. pap. 2.50 o.p. (ISBN 0-671-52881-5). Monarch Pr.

Macbett. Eugene Ionesco. Tr. by Charles Marowitz from Fr. LC 73-6644. 1973. pap. 5.95 o.p. (ISBN 0-394-17805-X, E614, Ever). Grove.

MacBook. Naiman. 1985. 16.95 o.p. (ISBN 0-8104-6560-4). Sams.

McBroom the Rainmaker. Sid Fleischman. (Illus.). 48p. (gr. 3 up). 1982. 12.45i o.p. (ISBN 0-316-28541-2, Pub. by Atlantic Monthly Pr); pap. 3.95 o.p. (ISBN 0-316-28542-0). Little.

McBroom's Ear. Sid Fleischman. LC 81-15636. (Illus.). (gr. 3 up). 1982. 12.45i o.p. (ISBN 0-316-28539-0, Pub. by Atlantic Monthly Pr); pap. 3.95 o.p. (ISBN 0-316-28540-4). Little.

McBroom's Ghost. Sid Fleischman. LC 81-1118. (Illus.). 48p. (gr. 3-7). 1981. 12.45i o.p. (ISBN 0-316-28547-1, Pub. by Atlantic Monthly Pr); pap. 3.95 o.p. (ISBN 0-316-28549-8). Little.

McBroom's Zoo. Sid Fleischman. (Illus.). 48p. (gr. 3 up). 1982. 12.95 o.p. (ISBN 0-316-28536-6, Joy St Bks); pap. 3.95 o.p. (ISBN 0-316-28538-2). Little.

Maccabees, Zealots & Josephus. William R. Farmer. LC 73-15052. 239p. 1974. Repr. of 1956 ed. lib. bdg. 79.50x o.p. (ISBN 0-8371-7152-0, AEFAMA). Greenwood.

McCall's Big Book of Christmas Knit & Crochet. Ed. by McCall's Editors. LC 82-70538. 304p. (Orig.). 1983. pap. 14.95 o.p. (ISBN 0-8019-7252-3). Chilton.

McCall's Big Book of Country Needlecrafts. McCall's Editors. LC 82-73538. (Illus.). 312p. 1983. pap. 14.95 o.p. (ISBN 0-8019-7364-3). Chilton.

McCall's Big Book of Cross Stitch. McCall's Editors. LC 82-73539. (Illus.). 272p. 1983. pap. 14.95 o.p. (ISBN 0-8019-7363-5). Chilton.

McCall's Big Book of Knit Crochet. Ed. by McCall's Editors. LC 82-70538. (Illus.). 304p. (Orig.). 1982. pap. 14.95 o.p. (ISBN 0-8019-7253-1). Chilton.

McCall's Book of Quilts. McCall's Pattern Company Staff. (Illus.). 160p. 1977. pap. 9.50 o.s.i. (ISBN 0-671-22787-4, Fireside). S&S.

McCormick of Chicago. Frank C. Waldrop. LC 74-1782. (Illus.). 328p. 1975. Repr. of 1966 ed. lib. bdg. 27.50x o.p. (ISBN 0-8371-7401-5, WAMO). Greenwood.

McCracken's Removable Partial Prosthodontics. 7th ed. Davis Henderson. (Illus.). 477p. 1984. 52.50 o.p. (ISBN 0-8016-2171-2). Mosby.

McCutcheon's Emulsifiers & Detergents North American & International: 1988. rev. ed. The MC Publishing Company Staff. Ed. by Michael Allured. LC 82-644576. 858p. 1988. 115.00 o.p. (ISBN 0-944254-01-2). MC Pub Co NJ.

MacDiarmid: The Terrible Crystal. Alan Bold. LC 83-3075. 252p. 1984. 22.50x o.p. (ISBN 0-7100-9493-0). Routledge Chapman & Hall.

Macdonald Fairy Tales Gift Set. George Macdonald. (Macdonald Fairy Tales Ser.). 1979. boxed gift set 4.95 o.p. (ISBN 0-89191-172-3). Cook.

MacDonald Trilogy. George MacDonald. 1985. pap. 16.95 boxed set o.p. (ISBN 0-89693-609-0). Victor Bks.

McDonogh Fifteen: Becoming a School. Lucianne B. Carmichael. 208p. 1981. pap. 2.95 o.p. (ISBN 0-380-77594-8, 77594-8, Discus). Avon.

McDouall's Chartist Journal & Trades Advocate, Nos. 1-27. 1969. Repr. lib. bdg. 13.25 o.p. (ISBN 0-8371-9194-7, MC00). Greenwood.

McDougall's Medicine: A Challenging Second Opinion. John A. McDougall. LC 85-21686. 320p. 1985. 14.95 o.p. (ISBN 0-8329-0407-4). New Century.

McDowell's Ghost. Jack Cady. LC 81-66974. 256p. 1981. 14.50 o.p. (ISBN 0-87795-343-0, Arbor Hse). Morrow.

Mace. James Grant. 235p. 1986. pap. 2.95 o.p. (ISBN 1-55547-110-2). Critics Choice Paper.

Macedonian-English, English-Macedonian Dictionary, 2 vols. (Macedonian & Eng.). 1978. Set. 20.00 o.p. (ISBN 0-686-70675-7). Macedonian-English 476pp. English-Macedonian 422pp. E J Brill USA.

Macedonian Greece. John Crossland & Diana Constance. (Illus.). 1982. 19.95 o.p. (ISBN 0-393-01652-8). Norton.

McElroy. Marvin R. O'Connell. 1980. 11.95 o.p. (ISBN 0-393-01358-8). Norton.

MacFonts. D. Leserman. 176p. 1986. pap. text ed. 16.95 o.p. (ISBN 0-07-037400-7). McGraw.

McGarr & the Sienese Conspiracy. Bartholomew Gill. LC 77-24570. 1977. 7.95 o.s.i. (ISBN 0-684-15185-5, ScribT). Scribner.

McGill Hume Studies. Ed. by D. F. Norton & N. Capaldi. LC 78-10398. (Studies in Hume & Scottish Philosophy). 1979. 22.50x o.p. (ISBN 0-89690-000-2); pap. 8.95x o.p. (ISBN 0-89690-001-0). Austin Hill Pr.

McGill Report on Male Intimacy. Michael McGill. 1984. 16.95 o.p. H Holt & Co.

McGill University Report. (Collection Analysis Project Reports Ser.). 73p. 1982. 10.00 o.p. (ISBN 0-318-03482-4). Assn Res Lib.

McGraw-Hill Course in Effective Interviewing. Richard A. Fear. 1973. text ed. 52.50 o.p. (ISBN 0-07-079484-7). McGraw.

McGraw-Hill Encyclopedia of Science & Technology, 15 vols. 5th ed. McGraw-Hill Editors. (Illus.). 12715p. 1982. Set. text ed. 1100.00 o.p. (ISBN 0-07-079280-1). McGraw.

McGraw-Hill Encyclopedia of Science & Technology. 4th ed. McGraw-Hill Encyclopedia of Science & Technology Editors. 1977. text ed. 497.00 o.p. (ISBN 0-07-079590-8, P&RB). McGraw.

McGraw-Hill Guide for Preparing Students for the New High School Equivalency Examination (GED) Theodore Silveira. 1979. pap. text ed. 6.95 o.p. (ISBN 0-07-057447-2). McGraw.

McGraw-Hill Handbook of Business Letters. Roy W. Poe. LC 82-18017. (Illus.). 304p. 1983. text ed. 41.95 o.p. (ISBN 0-07-050367-2). McGraw.

McGraw-Hill Hazardous Waste Monitor: A Quarterly RCRA Update, Vol. 1, No. 1. David J. Lennett. 64p. 1988. pap. text ed. 195.00 o.p. (ISBN 0-07-037168-7). McGraw.

McGraw-Hill Management Awareness Program No. 8. McGraw-Hill Management Awareness Program Editors. 1976. text ed. 8.00 o.p. (ISBN 0-07-045188-5). McGraw.

McGraw-Hill Management Awareness Program No. 7. McGraw-Hill Management Awareness Program Editors. 1976. text ed. 8.00 o.p. (ISBN 0-07-045187-7). McGraw.

McGraw-Hill Yearbook of Science & Technology 1984. McGraw-Hill Editors. (Illus.). 520p. 1983. text ed. 46.00 o.p. (ISBN 0-07-045492-2). McGraw.

McGraw-Hill Yearbook of Science & Technology, 1982-83: Annual Supplement. McGraw Hill Editors. LC 62-12028. (Illus.). 500p. 1982. text ed. 42.00 o.p. (ISBN 0-07-045489-2). McGraw.

McGraw-Hill's Handbook of Clinical Nursing. Margaret E. Armstrong et al. (Illus.). 1979. text ed. 40.95 o.p. (ISBN 0-07-045020-X). McGraw.

McGraw-Hill's National Electrical Code Handbook. 18th ed. Joseph F. McPartland. 1984. text ed. 35.00 o.p. (ISBN 0-07-045700-X). McGraw.

McGregor Solution for Managing the Pains of Fitness. Rob R. McGregor & Stephen E. Devereux. (Illus.). 352p. 1982. 15.95 o.p. (ISBN 0-395-32042-9). HM.

McGuffey Display Carton Six Address Book Set. McGuffey. 1980. 41.95 o.p. (ISBN 0-442-21267-4). Van Nos Reinhold.

McGuffin. John Bowen. LC 84-45817. 156p. 1985. 13.95 o.p. (ISBN 0-87113-018-1). Atlantic Monthly.

McGurk Gets Good & Mad. E. W. Hildick. LC 81-20698. (McGurk Mystery Ser.). (Illus.). 144p. (gr. 3-6). 1982. 9.95 o.p. (ISBN 0-02-743890-2). Macmillan.

MACH-TECH: Proceedings of the International High Technology Machine Tool & Production Engineering Conference, 1st, 13 papers. International High Technology Machine Tool & Production Engineering Conference Staff. 1983. Set. 45.50 o.p. (ISBN 0-317-06842-3, 809). SME.

Machame Anaesthesia Notebook for Medical Auxiliaries: With Special Emphasis on the Developing Countries. G. Kamm & Baumann T. Grof. (Illus.). 160p. 1983. pap. 8.10 o.p. (ISBN 0-387-09055-X). Springer-Verlag.

Macheteros: The Violent Struggle for Puerto Rican Independence. Ronald Fernandez. 1987. 17.95 o.p. (ISBN 0-13-950056-1). P-H.

Machiavelli & His Times. Dorothy E. Muir. LC 74-30928. (Illus.). 262p. 1977. Repr. of 1936 ed. lib. bdg. 22.75x o.p. (ISBN 0-8371-7889-4, MUMA). Greenwood.

Machiavelli & the Nature of Political Thought. Ed. by Martin Fleisher. LC 79-181461. 1972. pap. text ed. 4.95x o.p. (ISBN 0-689-70329-5, 189, Atheneum). Macmillan.

Machiavelli's New Modes & Orders: A Study of the Discourses on Livy. Harvey C. Mansfield, Jr. LC 79-12380. 464p. 1979. 47.50x o.p. (ISBN 0-8014-1182-3). Cornell U Pr.

Machina Coelestis, 2 pts. in 3 vols. Johannes Hevelius. (Lat). 1969. Repr. of 1673 ed. Set. 295.00 o.p. (ISBN 0-384-22800-3). Johnson Repr.

Machinability of Engineering Materials. Ed. by Robert W. Thompson. 1983. 68.00 o.p. (ISBN 0-87170-160-X). ASM.

Machinability Testing & Utilization of Machining Data. 1979. 57.00 o.p. (ISBN 0-87170-085-9). ASM.

Machine a Ecrire see Theatre.

Machine Design Problem Solver. Research & Education Association Staff. (Illus.). 1988. pap. text ed. 28.85 o.p. (ISBN 0-87891-605-9). Res & Educ.

Machine Embroidery with Style. D. Bennett. LC 80-13914. (Connecting Threads Ser.). (Illus.). 100p. 1980. pap. 9.95 o.p. (ISBN 0-914842-45-5). Madrona Pubs.

Machine Independent Organic Software Tools. 2nd ed. M. D. Godfrey. 1983. 30.00 o.p. (ISBN 0-12-286982-6). Acad Pr.

Machine: Independent Organic Software Tools. M. D. Godfrey et al. 1980. 35.00 o.p. (ISBN 0-12-286980-X). Acad Pr.

Machine Language Subroutines for the Color Computer. David D. McLeod. 212p. (Orig.). 1984. 29.95 o.p. (ISBN 0-88006-070-0, CC7404). Wayne Green Ent.

Machine Learning. Pat Langley & Jaime Carbonell. (Illus.). 100p. 1988. pap. text ed. 12.00 o.p. (ISBN 0-929280-22-9). Amer Artificial.

Machine Plays Chess. A. G. Bell. 1978. text ed. 21.00 o.p. (ISBN 0-08-021221-2); pap. text ed. 8.95 o.p. (ISBN 0-08-021222-0). Pergamon.

Machine Robot. (Illus.). 1984. 5.30 o.p. (ISBN 0-318-02681-3). Bks Nippan.

Machine Tool Metalworking. 2nd ed. John L. Feirer. Ed. by D. E. Gilmore. LC 72-10166. (Illus.). 568p. (gr. 10-12). 1973. text ed. 33.45 o.p. (ISBN 0-07-020369-5). McGraw.

Machine Tool Structures, Vol. 1. F. Koenigsberger & J. Tlusty. LC 79-84073. 1970. 140.00 o.p. (ISBN 0-08-013405-X). Pergamon.

Machine Vision: Nineteen Eighty-Four. 388p. 1985. pap. text ed. 45.00 o.p. (ISBN 0-317-18016-9). Robot Inst Am.

Machine Woodworking. rev. ed. Robert E. Smith. (Illus.). (gr. 9-10). 1958. text ed. 13.28 o.p. (ISBN 0-87345-010-8). Glencoe.

Machineries of Joy. Ray Bradbury. 1963. 6.95 o.p. (ISBN 0-671-43830-1). S&S.

Machinery Acoustics. George M. Diehl. LC 73-12980. 204p. 1973. 39.95 o.p. (ISBN 0-471-21360-8, Pub. by Wiley-Interscience). Wiley.

Machinery of Destruction. P-H.

Machinery of Nature. Paul R. Ehrlich. 1986. 18.45 o.p. (ISBN 0-671-49288-8). S&S.

Machinery of the Brain. Dean E. Wooldridge. 1963. pap. text ed. 2.95 o.p. (ISBN 0-07-071841-5). McGraw.

Machinery's Handbook. 21st rev. ed. Erik Oberg et al. Ed. by Paul B. Schubert. LC 72-622276. (Illus.). 2482p. 1979. 40.00x o.p. (ISBN 0-8311-1129-1); guide to tables & formulas 8.95 o.p. Indus Pr.

Machinery's Handbook. 22nd ed. Erik Oberg et al. Ed. by Henry H. Ryffel. LC 72-622276. (Illus.). 2482p. 1984. text ed. 48.00x o.p. (ISBN 0-8311-1155-0); guide to tables & Formulas 9.95 o.p. Indus Pr.

Machines & the Man: A Sourcebook on Automation. Ed. by Robert P. Weeks. LC 61-6338. (Illus., Orig.). 1961. pap. text ed. 5.95x o.p. (ISBN 0-89197-282-X). Irvington.

Machines That Think. Isaac Asimov. 22.95 o.p. (ISBN 0-8050-0623-0). H Holt & Co.

Machines That Think: The Best Science Fiction Stories about Robots & Computers. Ed. by Isaac Asimov et al. LC 83-245. 562p. 1983. 22.95 o.p. (ISBN 0-03-061498-8). H Holt & Co.

Machining for Toolmaking & Experimental Work, 3 vols. 2nd ed. Ed. by P. Heritage et al. (Engineering Craftsmen: No. H1). (Illus.). 1977. Set. spiral bdg. 75.00x o.p. Trans-Atl Phila.

Machining of Plastics. Akira Kobayashi. LC 79-20877. 300p. 1981. Repr. of 1967 ed. lib. bdg. 26.50 o.p. (ISBN 0-89874-007-X). Krieger.

Machining Science & Applications. M. Kronenberg. 1966. 110.00 o.p. (ISBN 0-08-011627-2). Pergamon.

Machining with Abrasives. Richard L. McKee. 320p. 1982. 27.95 o.p. (ISBN 0-442-25281-1). Van Nos Reinhold.

Machinist Dictionary. F. H. Colvin. (Illus.). 500p. (ISBN 0-8022-0286-1). Philos Lib.

Machinists' Ready Reference. rev., enl. ed. Compiled by C. Weingartner. LC 81-81329. (Illus.). 1981. wire bdg. 8.50x o.p. (ISBN 0-911168-50-8). Prakken.

Macht als Gefahr beim Helfer. 4th ed. A. Guggenbuehl-Craig. (Psychologische Praxis: Vol. 45). vi, 106p. 1982. pap. 12.75 o.p. (ISBN 3-8055-3664-X). S Karger.

Machzorim-Rosh Hashana & Yom Kippur. 1982. 9.00 o.s.i. (ISBN 0-686-76540-0). Feldheim.

Macintosh Bible. Dale Coleman & Arthur Naiman. (Illus.). 432p. (Orig.). 1987. pap. 21.00 o.p. (ISBN 0-940235-00-5). Goldstein & Blair.

Macintosh Desktop Design: Second in a Series on Macintosh Desktop Publishing. John Baxter. (Orig.). 1986. pap. 15.95 o.p. (ISBN 0-938949-02-0). Baxter Group.

Macintosh Desktop Typography: First in a Series on Macintosh Desktop Publishing. rev. ed. John Baxter. 1986. pap. 16.95 o.p. (ISBN 0-938949-04-7). Baxter Group.

Macintosh Expansion Guide. Gary Phillips. (Illus.). 320p. (Orig.). 1986. 22.95 o.p. (ISBN 0-8306-0401-4, 2601); pap. 16.60 o.p. (ISBN 0-8306-0301-8). Tab Bks.

Macintosh Game Animation. Ron Person. 280p. (Orig.). 1985. pap. text ed. 15.95 o.p. (ISBN 0-07-881127-9). Osborne-McGraw.

Macintosh Graphics & Sound: Programming in Microsoft Basic. David Kater. 350p. (Orig.). 1985. pap. text ed. 17.95 o.p. (ISBN 0-07-881177-5). Osborne-McGraw.

Macintosh Midnight Madness: Games, Utilities & Other Diversions In Microsoft BASIC for the Apple Macintosh. Waite Group Staff et al. 448p. 1985. pap. 18.95 o.p. (ISBN 0-914845-30-6). Microsoft.

Macintosh Paperwork: Integrating Microsoft Products. Paul Hoffman. 200p. (Orig.). 1985. pap. text ed. 16.95 o.p. (ISBN 0-07-881191-0). Osborne-McGraw.

Macintosh Program Factory. George Stewart. 350p. (Orig.). 1985. pap. text ed. 14.95 o.p. (ISBN 0-07-881175-9). Osborne-McGraw.

Macintosh Revealed: Programming with the Macintosh Toolbox. Chernicott. (Mac Library). 256p. 1984. 19.95 o.p. (ISBN 0-317-05879-7). Sams.

Macintosh Revealed, Vol. I: Unlocking the Toolbox. Stephen Chernicoff. 384p. 1985. 24.95 o.p. (ISBN 0-8104-6551-5). Sams.

Macintosh Revealed, Vol. II: Programming with the Toolbox. Stephen Chernicoff. 544p. 1985. 29.95 o.p. (ISBN 0-8104-6561-2). Sams.

Macintosh Spreadsheets: Using Microsoft Multiplan, Chart, & File. Robert Flast & Lauren Flast. 200p. (Orig.). 1985. pap. text ed. 16.95 o.p. (ISBN 0-07-881187-2). Osborne-McGraw.

Macintosh: The Definitive User's Guide. John M. Allswang. LC 84-24226. (Illus.). 256p. 1985. pap. 15.95 o.p. (ISBN 0-89303-649-8). Brady Bks.

McKeever. Vina Delmar. LC 76-18210. 1976. 8.95 o.p. (ISBN 0-15-158320-X). HarBraceJ.

Mackenzie King Record, 4 vols. Ed. by J. W. Pickersgill. Incl. Vol. 1. 1939-1944. 1960. o.p. (ISBN 0-8020-1129-2); Vol. 2. 1944-1945. Ed. by D. F. Forster. 1968. 30.00x o.p. (ISBN 0-8020-1525-5); Vol. 3. 1945-1946. Ed. by D. F. Forster. 1970. 30.00x o.p. (ISBN 0-8020-1655-3); Vol. 4. 1947-1948. Ed. by D. F. Forster. 1970. 30.00x o.p. (ISBN 0-8020-1686-3). U of Toronto Pr.

Mackinac Island & Saulte St. Marie. Stanley D. Newton. LC 76-4405. (Illus.). 1976. pap. 8.00 o.s.i. (ISBN 0-912382-19-8). Black Letter.

Mackinac National Park, 1875-1895. Keith R. Widder. Ed. by David A. Armour. (Reports in Mackinac History & Archaeology Ser: No. 4). (Illus.). 48p. (Orig.). 1975. pap. 3.00 o.p. (ISBN 0-911872-20-5). Mackinac Island.

Mackinaws Down the Missouri. John Anderson. Ed. by Glenn Barrett. LC 73-79903. (Western Text Society Ser.). 105p. 1973. 7.50 o.p. (ISBN 0-87421-059-3); pap. 5.50 o.p. (ISBN 0-87421-090-9). Utah St U Pr.

Mackintosh Textile Designs. Roger Billcliffe. LC 82-60358. (Illus.). 80p. 1982. 25.00 o.s.i. (ISBN 0-8008-5059-9). Taplinger.

Macknight on the Epistles. James Macknight. 784p. 1984. Repr. of 1966 ed. 24.95 o.p. (ISBN 0-8010-6031-1). Baker Bk.

MacLaren's Men. Robert W. Marsh. 192p. 1982. pap. 2.25 o.p. (ISBN 0-8439-1131-X, Pub. by Leisure Bks CT). Dorchester Pub Co.

McLaren's Men. Robert W. Marsh. 1979. pap. 1.75 o.p. (ISBN 0-505-51435-4, Pub. by Tower Bks). Dorchester Pub Co.

McMath: The Now of Our Human Destiny. Date not set. 12.95 o.p. Chris Mass.

Macmillan Book of Berry Gardening. Helmut Loose. (Gardening Guides Ser.). (Illus.). 128p. 1986. pap. 6.95 o.p. (ISBN 0-02-063360-2, Collier). Macmillan.

Macmillan Book of Ornamental Gardening. Otto Hahn. (Illus.). 128p. 1986. pap. 6.95 o.p. (ISBN 0-02-063130-8). Macmillan.

Macmillan Dictionary for Children. rev. ed. Macmillan Publishing Company Staff. (Illus.). (gr. 2 up). 1977. 12.95 o.s.i. (ISBN 0-02-578750-0). Macmillan.

Macmillan Learning Window Books: First Letters, First Sentences, First Story, & First Words. Peter K. Shreck. (Illus.). (ps-k). 1982. 24-copy prepack 190.80 o.s.i. (ISBN 0-02-782660-0). Macmillan.

Macno. Andrea De Carlo. Tr. by William Weaver. 224p. 1987. 14.95 o.p. (ISBN 0-15-154899-4). HarBraceJ.

MacPascal Programming. Drew Berentes. 1985. 22.95 o.p. (ISBN 0-8306-0891-5, 1891); pap. 16.60 o.p. (ISBN 0-8306-1891-0). TAB Bks.

MCQ's for MRCP, Pt. 1. Ed. by Michael J. Ford & E. Fiona Nicol. LC 85-24258. 215p. (Orig.). 1986. pap. 10.00 o.p. (ISBN 0-443-03531-8). Churchill.

MCQ's in Geriatric Medicine. Rose A. Kenny. 189p. 1985. pap. text ed. 14.00 o.p. (ISBN 0-443-03174-6). Churchill.

MCQs in Obstetrics & Gynaecology. John Studd & D. M. Gibb. LC 82-14694. 310p. 1983. pap. text ed. 13.95 o.p. (ISBN 0-443-02283-6). Churchill.

MCQs in Radiological Physics. T. H. E. Bryant & J. Lovell. LC 82-4478. 135p. 1983. pap. text ed. 11.00 o.p. (ISBN 0-443-02225-9). Churchill.

MCQ's in Undergraduate Obstetrics & Gynaecology. Ian Johnson. LC 84-21411. 151p. 1985. pap. text ed. 10.00 o.p. (ISBN 0-443-03079-0). Churchill.

McQuillin Municipal Corporations: 1967, 22 vols. 3rd ed. LC 49-3779. 1175.00 o.p. (ISBN 0-317-12010-7). Callaghan.

Macrame Book. Helene Bress. LC 79-37222. (Illus.). 224p. 1972. 6.95 o.p. (ISBN 0-684-12756-3, ScribT). Scribner.

Macro & Monetary Economics Exams, Puzzles & Problems, Vol. 4. Compiled by Edward Tower. 203p. 1985. 14.00 o.p. (ISBN 0-88024-204-3). Eno River Pr.

Macro-Engineering: The Rich Potential. Ed. by Robert Salkeld & Frank P. Davidson. LC 81-20535. (Illus.). 176p. 1981. 24.00 o.p. (ISBN 0-915928-58-2). AIAA.

Macroanalytical Procedures Manual. rev. ed. Food & Drug Administration Staff. (FDA Technical Bulletin Ser.: No. 5). (Illus.). 176p. 1984. three hole drill with binder 29.00 o.s.i. (ISBN 0-935584-28-5); foreign 30.50 o.s.i. Assoc Official.

Macrobiotic Shiatsu. David Sergel. LC 86-81327. (Illus.). 272p. 1987. pap. 15.95 o.p. (ISBN 0-87040-671-X). Japan Pubns USA.

Macrobiotics & Oriental Medicine: An Introduction. Michio Kushi & Phillip Janetta. LC 85-81366. 192p. (Orig.). 1986. pap. 13.95 o.p. (ISBN 0-87040-659-0). Japan Pubns USA.

Macrodynamic Economics: Growth, Employment & Prices. Howard J. Sherman. LC 64-13699. (Illus.). 1964. 29.50x o.p. (ISBN 0-89197-283-8); pap. text ed. 8.95x o.p. (ISBN 0-89197-635-3). Irvington.

Macroeconomic Analysis. 3rd ed. Edward Shapiro. 1974. text ed. 15.95 o.p. (ISBN 0-15-551209-9, HC). HarBraceJ.

Macroeconomic Analysis. 5th ed. Edward Shapiro. 632p. 1982. text ed. 26.00 net o.p. (ISBN 0-15-551215-3, HC). HarBraceJ.

Macroeconomic Analysis: Essays in Macroeconomics & Econometrics. Ed. by D. Currie et al. (Illus.). 491p. 1981. 44.00 o.p. (ISBN 0-7099-0311-1, Pub. by Croom Helm Ltd). Routledge Chapman & Hall.

Macroeconomic Implications of Factor Substitution in Industrial Processes. Howard Pack. (Working Paper: No. 377). vii, 60p. 1980. 5.00 o.p. (ISBN 0-686-36185-7, WP-0377). World Bank.

Macroeconomic Policy: New Cambridge, Keynesian & Monetarist Controversies. Keith Cuthbertson. LC 79-12195. (New Studies in Economic). 209p. 1979. 42.95x o.p. (ISBN 0-470-26740-2). Halsted Pr.

Macroeconomic Theory. Thomas Sargent. LC 78-4803. (Economic Theory, Econometrics & Mathematical Economics Ser.). 1979. 36.50 o.p. (ISBN 0-12-619750-4). Acad Pr.

Macroeconomics. Robert Barro. LC 83-21692. 580p. 1984. text ed. 35.95 o.p. (ISBN 0-471-87407-8). Wiley.

Macroeconomics. 3rd ed. William J. Baumol & Alan S. Blinder. 474p. 1986. pap. text ed. 20.00 o.p. (ISBN 0-15-518849-6, Pub. by HC). HarBraceJ.

Macroeconomics. 3rd ed. Ralph T. Byrns & Gerald W. Jr. Stone. 1987. pap. text ed. write for info. o.p. (ISBN 0-673-16684-8). Scott F.

Macroeconomics. Robert L. Crouch. (Harbrace Business & Economics Ser.). (Illus.). 425p. 1972. text ed. 15.95 o.p. (ISBN 0-15-551255-2, HC). HarBraceJ.

Macroeconomics. 4th ed. Edwin G. Dolan. 608p. 1986. pap. text ed. 19.95 o.s.i. (ISBN 0-03-005463-X); wkbk. 8.95 o.s.i. (ISBN 0-03-005474-5). Dryden Pr.

Macroeconomics. Robert B. Ekelund & Robert D. Tollison. 1986. pap. text ed. write for info. o.p. (ISBN 0-673-39124-8). Scott F.

Macroeconomics. Samuel A. Morley. 576p. 1984. text ed. 33.95x o.p. (ISBN 0-03-059301-8); instr's. manual 19.95 o.p. (ISBN 0-03-059302-6). Dryden Pr.

Macroeconomics. 2nd ed. J. Carl Poindexter, Jr. LC 79-51107. 560p. 1981. text ed. 31.95 o.p. (ISBN 0-03-050271-3); instr's. manual 19.95 o.p. (ISBN 0-03-050276-4). Dryden Pr.

Macroeconomics. Truett. 1987. text ed. 24.95 o.p. (ISBN 0-8016-5158-1). Mosby.

Macroeconomics. Lila F. Truett & Dale B. Truett. (Illus.). 513p. 1982. pap. text ed. 23.00 o.p. (ISBN 0-314-63302-2). West Pub.

Macroeconomics. Jack Vernon. 464p. 1980. text ed. 31.95 o.p. (ISBN 0-03-042336-8); instr's. manual 10.00 o.p. (ISBN 0-03-052271-4). Dryden Pr.

Macroeconomics: Analysis & Applications. 2nd ed. George L. Bach. 1980. pap. text ed. (ISBN 0-13-542712-6). P-H.

Macroeconomics for Africa. Charles Harvey. LC 78-321332. (Studies in the Economics of Africa). 1978. pap. text ed. 2.50 plastic o.p. (ISBN 0-435-97201-4). Heinemann Ed.

Macroeconomics: The Theory of Income, Employment & the Price Level. M. R. Darby. 1976. text ed. 39.95 o.p. (ISBN 0-07-015346-9). McGraw.

Macroeconomics: Theory & Policy. Anthony S. Campagna. 512p. 1974. text ed. 16.25 o.p. (ISBN 0-395-17085-0). HM.

Macroeconomics: Theory & Policy. 2nd ed. Michael R. Edgmand. (Illus.). 576p. 1983. pap. text ed. (ISBN 0-13-542688-X). P-H.

Titles

Macroeconomics: Theory & Policy. Fred R. Glahe. 1973. text ed. 14.95 o.p. (ISBN 0-15-551264-1, HC). HarBraceJ.

Macroeconomics: Theory & Policy. 2nd ed. Fred R. Glahe. (Illus.). 404p. 1977. text ed. 23.95 o.p. (ISBN 0-15-551266-8, HC). HarBraceJ.

Macroeconomics: Theory, Evidence & Policy. 2nd ed. Frank C. Wykoff. (Illus.). 640p. 1981. text ed. (ISBN 0-13-543967-1). P-H.

Macroeconomics, 1987-88. 6th ed. John Pisciotta & Mark Vaughan. LC 75-20753. (Annual Editions Ser.). (Illus.). 256p. 1987. pap. text ed. 9.95 o.p. (ISBN 0-87967-666-3). Dushkin Pub.

Macroeconomics 1988-89. 7th, rev. ed. Ed. by John Pisciotta. LC 75-20753. (Annuals Editions Ser.). (Illus.). 256p. 1988. pap. text ed. 9.95x o.p. (ISBN 0-87967-730-9). Dushkin Pub.

Macromolecular Physics: Crystals, Structure, Morphology & Defects, 2 vols. Berhard Wunderlich. 1973. Vol. 1, 1973. 87.00 o.p. (ISBN 0-12-765601-4); Vol. 2, 1976. 103.00 o.p. (ISBN 0-12-765602-2). Acad Pr.

Macromolecules Regulating Growth & Development. Ed. by Elizabeth D. Hay et al. 1974. 57.50 o.p. (ISBN 0-12-612973-8). Acad Pr.

Macrophage Regulation of Immunity. Ed. by Emil R. Unanue & Alan S. Rosenthal. LC 79-24609. 1980. 53.50 o.p. (ISBN 0-12-708550-5). Acad Pr.

Macrophysics. 2nd ed. Donald E. DeGraaf. LC 80-70717. (Illus.). 618p. 1981. pap. text ed. 17.00x o.p. (ISBN 0-930402-07-3). Crystal MI.

Macroprocessors & Techniques for Portable Software. P. J. Brown. LC 3-17597. (Computing Ser.). 244p. 1974. 73.95 o.p. (ISBN 0-471-11005-1, Pub. by Wiley-Interscience). Wiley.

Macroscope. Piers Anthony. 480p. 1985. lib. bdg. 14.95 o.p. (ISBN 0-8398-2899-3, Gregg). G K Hall.

Macroscopic Electromagnetism. F. M. Robinson. LC 73-4280. 256p. 1973. text ed. 40.00 o.p. (ISBN 0-08-017647-X). Pergamon.

Macross Perfect Memory. (Illus.). 260p. 1984. deluxe ed. 29.95 o.p. (ISBN 0-318-02746-1). Bks Nippan.

Macross Plastic Model Book. (Illus.). 1984. 3.95 o.s.i. (ISBN 0-318-02676-7). Bks Nippan.

Macrurous Crustacea, Pts. 1-7. H. Woods. 65.00 o.p. (ISBN 0-384-69198-6). Johnson Repr.

MacTelecommunications. Jonathan Erickson & William D. Cramer. 180p. (Orig.). 1984. pap. text ed. 17.95 o.p. (ISBN 0-07-881155-4). Osborne-McGraw.

Macumba: The Teachings of Maria-Jose, Mother of the Gods. Serge Bramly. 1979. pap. 2.25 o.p. (ISBN 0-380-42317-0, 42317-0). Avon.

McWhinney's Jaunt. Robert Lawson. (Illus.). 78p. (gr. 3-6). 1985. pap. 4.95 o.p. (ISBN 0-316-51751-8). Little.

MacWork MacPlay: Creative Ideas for Fun & Profit on Your Apple Macintosh. Lon Poole. 448p. 1984. pap. 18.95 o.p. (ISBN 0-914845-22-5). Microsoft.

MacWrite: Guide for Students & Business Professionals. Alan Neibauer. LC 84-25238. 320p. 1985. FPT 17.95 o.p. (ISBN 0-03-002129-4). HR&W.

MacWrite Made Easy. Robert Wolenik. LC 84-19781. 210p. 1985. pap. 16.95 o.p. (ISBN 0-03-001763-7). HR&W.

MC68020 32-Bit Microprocessor: User's Manual. Motorola, Inc. Staff. (Illus.). 464p. 1985. pap. 21.95 o.p. (ISBN 0-13-566860-3). P-H.

MC6809 Cookbook. Carl D. Warren. (Illus.). 176p. 11.95 o.p. (ISBN 0-8306-9683-0, 1209); pap. 7.95 o.p. (ISBN 0-8306-1209-2). TAB Bks.

Mad about the Boy: The Life & Times of Boy George & Culture Club. Anton Gill. 1985. pap. 9.95 o.p. (ISBN 0-03-003003-X, Owl Bks). H Holt & Co.

Mad Couple Well Match'd. Richard Brome. Ed. by Steen H. Spove & Stephen Orgel. LC 78-13873. (Renaissance Drama Ser.). 1979. lib. bdg. 37.00 o.p. (ISBN 0-8240-9730-0). Garland Pub.

Mad Peck Studios: A Twenty Year Retrospective. Mad Peck. LC 86-24023. (Illus.). 96p. 1987. pap. 7.95 o.p. (ISBN 0-385-23908-4, Dolp). Doubleday.

Mad Philosopher, Auguste Comte. Boris Sokoloff. LC 75-8827. 186p. 1975. Repr. of 1961 ed. lib. bdg. 22.50x o.p. (ISBN 0-8371-8110-0, SOMAP). Greenwood.

Mad Scientist: Riddle-Jokes-Fun. Joseph Rosenbloom. LC 82-50555. (Illus.). 128p. (gr. 5 up). 1982. 10.95 o.p. (ISBN 0-8069-4662-8); PLB 12.49 o.p. (ISBN 0-8069-4663-6). Sterling.

Madagascar: Recent Economic Development & Future Prospects. P. C. Joshi. iii, 304p. (Eng. & Fr.). 1980. pap. 17.95 o.p. (ISBN 0-8213-9157-7). World Bank.

Madagascar Rediscovered: A History from Early Times to Independence. Mervyn Brown. LC 79-13593. (Illus.). x, 310p. 1979. 29.00 o.p. (ISBN 0-208-01828-X, Archon). Shoe String.

Madam President. Sharinne S. Weiller. LC 84-91352. 177p. 1985. 13.95 o.p. (ISBN 0-533-06449-X). Vantage.

Madam Sarah. Cornelia Otis Skinner. (Illus.). 1967. 6.95 o.p. (ISBN 0-395-08196-3). HM.

Madam Secretary: Frances Perkins. George Martin. 1976. 16.95 o.p. (ISBN 0-395-24293-2). HM.

Madam Varnish & the Golden Era. Henry James. (Illus.). 1979. 7.95 o.p. (ISBN 0-682-49311-2). Exposition-Phoenix.

Madame Bovary. Gustave Flaubert. 48p. (Orig.). 1989. pap. 9.95 o.p. (ISBN 1-55651-579-0); audiocassette tape incl. o.p. (ISBN 1-55651-580-4). Cram Cassettes.

Madame Dacier, Scholar & Humanist. Fern Farnham. LC 73-93075. softcover 7.95 o.p. (ISBN 0-912216-12-3). Angel Pr.

Madame de Sade. Yukio Mishima. Tr. by Donald Keene from Japanese. LC 67-19616. 1967. pap. 4.95 o.p. (ISBN 0-394-17304-X, E463, Ever). Grove.

Madame Maigret's Recipes. Robert J. Courtine. LC 75-6540. (Helen & Kurt Wolff Bk.). (Illus.). 183p. 1975. 8.95 o.p. (ISBN 0-15-154990-7). HarBraceJ.

Madame Maigret's Recipes. Robert J. Courtine. Tr. by Mary Manheim. 1987. pap. 5.95 o.p. (ISBN 0-15-650172-4, Harv). HarBraceJ.

Madame Pastry & Meow. Evelyn W. Minshull. LC 75-11998. (Illus.). 176p. (gr. 4-8). 1975. 5.95 o.s.i. (ISBN 0-664-32573-4, Westminster). Westminster John Knox.

Madan Lal Dhingra & the Revolutionary Movement. V. N. Datta. 115p. 1978. text ed. 12.50x o.p. (ISBN 0-7069-0657-8, Pub. by Vikas India). Advent NY.

Madcap Mystery. Karin Anckarsvard. Tr. by Annabelle MacMillan. LC 62-8343. (Illus.). (gr. 5 up). 1962. 5.95 o.p. (ISBN 0-15-250175-4, HJ). HarBraceJ.

Madcap Mystery. Karin Anckarsvard. Tr. by Annabelle MacMillan from Swedish. LC 62-8343. (gr. 4-7). 1970. pap. 2.75 o.p. (ISBN 0-15-655108-X, VoyB). HarBraceJ.

Madcaps, Millionaires & Mose. John Underwood. (Illus.). 144p. 18.95 o.p. (ISBN 0-911834-16-8). Aviation.

Maddy's Song. Margaret Dickson. 310p. 1985. 15.45 o.p. (ISBN 0-395-36077-3). HM.

Made for Television: Euston Films Limited. Manuel Alvarado & John Stewart. (Orig.). 1985. pap. 11.95 o.p. (ISBN 0-85170-172-8, 9374). Routledge Chapman & Hall.

Made in America. Susan Smith. LC 71-145708. (Illus.). 104p. 1971. Repr. of 1929 ed. 35.00x o.p. (ISBN 0-8103-3396-1). Gale.

Made in America: A Consumer's Guide to More Than 12000 Products Made in America, for Americans & 100 Per Cent by Americans. Ed. by Jerome Rosow. 268p. 1984. 14.95x o.p. (ISBN 0-87196-294-2); pap. 7.95x o.p. (ISBN 0-87196-884-3). Facts on File.

Made in God's Image. Del Olsen. 128p. (Orig.). 1986. pap. 3.95 o.p. (ISBN 0-310-46381-5, 18382P). Zondervan.

Mademoiselle du Vissard. Honore De Balzac. 96p. 1950. 15.95 o.p. (ISBN 0-686-53891-9). French & Eur.

Mademoiselle, Mademoiselle. Jeff Dunas. LC 82-48005. 112p. 1982. 27.95 o.p. (ISBN 0-394-52832-8, GP856). Grove.

Mademoiselle, Mademoiselle! Jeff Dunas. LC 83-61058. (Illus.). 112p. 1984. pap. 14.95 o.p. (ISBN 0-394-62262-6, E962, Ever). Grove.

Madha Khasira al-Alam bi-Inhtat al-Muslimin. 4th ed. Abul H. Nadawi. 432p. (Orig., Arabic.). 1978. pap. 8.50x o.s.i. (ISBN 0-939830-14-0, Pub. by IIFSO Kuwait). New Era Pubns MI.

Madhouses, Mad-Doctors, & Madmen: The Social History of Psychiatry in the Victorian Era. Ed. by Andrew Scull. LC 81-3365. (Illus.). 388p. (Orig.). 1981. 39.95x o.p. (ISBN 0-8122-7801-1); pap. 16.95 o.p. (ISBN 0-8122-1119-7). U of Pa Pr.

Madhres...or Survival. Guido H. Bothma. 222p. 1985. 12.95 o.p. (ISBN 0-533-06309-4). Vantage.

Madhu: Recent Researches in Indian Archaeology & Art History. Nagaraja M. Rao. (Illus.). 339p. 1982. text ed. 120.00x o.p. (ISBN 0-391-02667-4). Humanities.

Madison Avenue Handbook. 22nd ed. Ed. by Peter Glenn. (Illus.). 1979. spiral bdg. 11.95 o.p. (ISBN 0-87314-009-5). Peter Glenn.

Madison Avenue Handbook 1980. 1980. spiral bdg. 13.95 o.p. (ISBN 0-87314-010-9). Peter Glenn.

Madison, Wisconsin. (Panel Advisory Service Report Ser.). 88p. 1981. pap. 10.00 o.p. (ISBN 0-317-06736-2, M-17). Urban Land.

Madman at My Door. Hillary Waugh. 1980. pap. 2.25 o.p. (ISBN 0-380-47159-0, 47159-0). Avon.

Madmen of History. Donald D. Hook. LC 75-14215. 240p. 1975. 9.95 o.p. (ISBN 0-8246-0202-1). Jonathan David.

Madness. Katherine Hale. 1984. pap. 2.95 o.s.i. (ISBN 0-345-31144-2). Ballantine.

Madness & the Brain. Solomon H. Snyder. LC 73-7763. 304p. 1975. pap. text ed. 5.95 o.p. (ISBN 0-07-059521-6). McGraw.

Madonna. Philip Kamin. (Illus.). 32p. (gr. 3 up). 1985. pap. 4.95 o.p. (ISBN 0-88188-404-9, Pub. by Robus Bks). H Leonard Pub Corp.

Madonna. Ed Kelleher & Harriette Vidal. 384p. (Orig.). 1985. pap. 3.75 o.p. (ISBN 0-8439-2215-X, Pub. by Leisure Bks CT). Dorchester Pub Co.

Madonna: Lucky Star. Michael McKenzie. (Illus.). 96p. 1985. pap. 6.95 o.p. (ISBN 0-8092-5233-3). Contemp Bks.

Madrid Travel Guide. Berlitz Editors. (Travel Guides Ser.). 1977. pap. 4.95 o.p. (ISBN 0-317-12111-1, Berlitz). Macmillan.

Mae West Is Dead: Recent Lesbian & Gay Fiction. Ed. by Adam Mars-Jones. 296p. 1983. 19.95 o.p. (ISBN 0-571-13022-4); pap. 6.95 o.p. (ISBN 0-571-13188-3). Faber & Faber.

Magazine. Diane Watson. (Orig.). 1981. pap. 2.50 o.p. (ISBN 0-505-51662-4, Pub. by Tower Bks). Dorchester Pub Co.

Magazine Industry Market Place, 1987. 1987. pap. text ed. 69.95 o.p. (ISBN 0-8352-2269-1). Bowker.

Magazine Publishing Career Directory 1986: 24 Top Industry Leaders. Intro. by John M. Carter. (Career Directory Ser.: Vol. 2). 324p. (Orig.). 1986. pap. 24.95 o.p. (ISBN 0-934829-01-2). Career Pr Inc.

Magazine Publishing Management. Ed. by Folio Magazine Editors. 1977. loose leaf ed. 49.95 o.p. (ISBN 0-918110-01-7). Hanson Pub Grp.

Magazines Career Directory: 1987. rev. ed. Ed. by Ron Fry. (Career Directory Ser.). 300p. 1987. text ed. 34.95 o.p. (ISBN 0-934829-17-9); pap. text ed. 26.95 o.p. (ISBN 0-934829-11-X); Special Bookstore Edition Distributed by Williamson Publishing Co. pap. 17.95 o.p. (ISBN 0-934829-06-3). Career Pr Inc.

Magdalene & Other Poems. W. G. Hughes. 1979. 8.00 o.p. (ISBN 0-682-49229-9). Exposition-Phoenix.

Magga Birds of Ranatan. Herbert L. McClelland. Ed. by May Davenport. Bd. with Why Do We Not See Little People, Miss Wintergreen? Nathan Zimelman; Spots & Splashes & a Million Butterflies. Joyce Deedy. LC 82-70226. 80p. (Orig.). (gr. 5-12). 1984. pap. 3.50x o.p. (ISBN 0-943864-10-0). Davenport.

Maggie. Jennie Tremaine. 192p. 1986. pap. 2.95 o.p. (ISBN 0-931773-37-7). Critics Choice Paper.

Maggie Cassidy. Jack Kerouac. 1978. pap. text ed. 4.95 o.p. (ISBN 0-07-034203-2). McGraw.

Maggie Lane's Oriental Patchwork: Elegant Designs for Easy Living. Maggie Lane. LC 78-7957. (Encore Edition). (Illus.). 1978. 3.95 o.p. (ISBN 0-684-16907-X, ScribT). Scribner.

Maggie the Mink. Alice L. Mason. (Illus.). 16p. (gr. k-6). 1984. pap. 1.50 o.p. (ISBN 0-8249-8067-0). Ideals.

Maggie's Wish. Marilyn D. Anderson. (Treetop Tales Ser.). (Illus.). 96p. (Orig.). (gr. 3-5). 1987. pap. 2.25 o.s.i. (ISBN 0-87406-262-4). Willowisp Pr.

Maggiorino, the Little Apostle of the Good Press. S. Lamera. (gr. 1 up). 1988. pap. 1.75 o.p. (ISBN 0-317-67478-1, CH0340). Dghtrs St Paul.

Maggot. Mary A. Walker. LC 80-12238. 156p. (gr. 5-9). 1980. 9.95 o.p. (ISBN 0-689-30789-6, Atheneum). Macmillan.

Magic Amulet. William O. Steele. LC 78-20573. (gr. 5 up). 1979. 6.95 o.p. (ISBN 0-15-250427-3, HJ). HarBraceJ.

Magic & Healing. C. J. Thompson. LC 73-2850. (Illus.). 190p. 1973. Repr. of 1947 ed. 40.00x o.p. (ISBN 0-8103-3275-2). Gale.

Magic & Mystery in Tibet. Alexandra David-Neel. (Illus.). 1965. 7.50 o.p. (ISBN 0-8216-0110-5, Pub. by Univ Bks). Carol Pub Group.

Magic & Showmanship: A Handbook for Conjurers. Henning Nelms. (Illus.). 14.75 o.p. (ISBN 0-8446-0818-1). Peter Smith.

Magic Apple Tree: A Country Year. Susan Hill. 208p. 1983. 16.95 o.s.i. (ISBN 0-03-063399-0, Owl Bks). H Holt & Co.

Magic Barrel. Bernard Malamud. 1980. pap. 4.50 o.p. (ISBN 0-380-49973-8, Bard). Avon.

Magic Bird. Max Bolliger & Jan Lenica. (Illus.). 32p. (gr. k-3). 1988. 13.95 o.p. (ISBN 0-86264-146-2, Pub. by Century Hutchinson). David & Charles.

Magic Book: A Beginner's Guide to Anytime, Anywhere, Sleight-of-Hand Magic. H. Lorayne. 1983. pap. text ed. 6.95 o.p. (ISBN 0-07-038744-3). McGraw.

Magic Circle: Stories & People in Poetry. Ed. by Louis Untermeyer. LC 52-6912. (Illus.). (gr. 7 up). 1952. 7.95 o.p. (ISBN 0-15-250620-9, HJ). HarBraceJ.

Magic Cooking Pot. Faith M. Towle. LC 74-20761. (Illus.). 48p. (gr. k-3). 1975. reinforced bdg. 6.95 o.p. (ISBN 0-395-20273-6). HM.

Magic Cup. Andrew M. Greeley. LC 79-16720. 1979. text ed. 10.95 o.p. (ISBN 0-07-024250-X). McGraw.

Magic Deer. Illus. by Mei Ying & Mei Ying. (Illus.). 56p. (Orig.). (gr. 3-6). 1983. pap. 3.95 o.p. (ISBN 0-8351-1259-4). China Bks.

Magic Diplomatic Summary: A Chronological Finding Aid. Alexander S. Cochran, Jr. 1982. lib. bdg. 36.00 o.p. (ISBN 0-8240-4325-1). Garland Pub.

Magic Door. Howard Fast. (Illus.). 80p. (gr. 3-7). 1980. pap. 1.95 o.p. (ISBN 0-380-51193-2, 51193-2, Camelot). Avon.

Magic Eye for Ida. Kay Chorao. LC 72-85337. (Illus.). 48p. (ps-3). 1979. 6.95 o.p. (ISBN 0-395-28783-9, Clarion). HM.

Magic Fish. Freya Littledale. Orig. Title: Fisherman & His Wife. (gr. k-3). 1969. pap. 1.95 o.p. (ISBN 0-590-33779-3). Scholastic Inc.

Magic in Frosting. John McNamara. LC 72-79676. 1972. 10.95 o.p. (ISBN 0-686-60806-2). Exposition-Phoenix.

Magic in Names & in Other Things. Edward Clodd. LC 67-23906. 248p. 1968. Repr. of 1920 ed. 30.00x o.p. (ISBN 0-8103-3024-5). Gale.

Magic Island. Madye L. Chastain. LC 64-22271. (Illus.). (gr. 3-7). 1964. 4.50 o.p. (ISBN 0-15-250871-6, HJ). HarBraceJ.

Magic Johnson Larry Bird. Bruce Weber. 1986. pap. 2.50 o.p. (ISBN 0-380-75095-3, Camelot). Avon.

Magic Journey. John Treadwell Nichols. 1978. 11.95 o.p. (ISBN 0-03-015356-5); pap. 7.95 o.s.i. (ISBN 0-03-042866-1). H Holt & Co.

Magic Listening Cap: More Folk Tales from Japan. Yoshiko Uchida. LC 55-5240. (Illus.). (gr. 4-6). 1955. 6.75 o.p. (ISBN 0-15-250978-X, HJ). HarBraceJ.

Magic Listening Cap: More Folk Tales from Japan. Yoshiko Uchida. LC 55-5240. (Illus.). (gr. 4-6). 1955. pap. 1.95 o.p. (ISBN 0-15-655119-5, VoyB). HarBraceJ.

Magic Maize. Mary Buff & Conrad Buff. (Illus.). (gr. 4-6). 1953. Dolphin bdg. 3.57 o.p. (ISBN 0-395-06666-2). HM.

Magic Makers. David Carroll. LC 73-91503. 1974. 8.95 o.p. (ISBN 0-87795-080-6, Arbor Hse). Morrow.

Magic Meadow. Alexander Key. LC 74-19194. (gr. 4-7). 1975. 5.50 o.s.i. (ISBN 0-664-32561-0, Westminster). Westminster John Knox.

Magic Mind Power: Make It Work for You! 2nd ed. Leslie M. LeCron. 176p. 1982. pap. 4.95 o.s.i. (ISBN 0-87516-496-X). DeVorss.

Magic Moments. Joyce S. Whitcomb. 1980. 5.00 o.p. (ISBN 0-682-49619-7). Exposition-Phoenix.

Magic Moments of a Poet. Bobby Jackson. LC 85-50600. 62p. 1984. 3.95 o.p. (ISBN 0-938232-37-1). Winston-Derek.

Magic Mommas, Trembling Sisters, Puritans & Perverts: Feminist Essays. Joanna Russ. LC 85-4147. (Feminist Ser.). 128p. (Orig.). 1985. 17.95 o.p. (ISBN 0-89594-164-3); pap. 6.95 o.p. (ISBN 0-89594-163-5). Crossing Pr.

Magic Moth. Virginia Lee. (Illus.). 64p. (gr. 3-6). 1980. pap. 2.95 o.p. (ISBN 0-395-30008-8, Clarion). HM.

Magic, Myth & Medicine. John Camp. LC 73-18793. 200p. 1974. 8.50 o.s.i. (ISBN 0-8008-5046-7). Taplinger.

Magic of Believing. Claude Bristol. 245p. 1982. pap. 4.95 o.p. (ISBN 0-13-543884-5). P-H.

Magic of ESOPs & LBOs: The Definitive Guide to Employee Stock Ownership Plans & Leveraged Buyouts. Robert A. Frisch. LC 85-80623. (Illus.). 1985. 34.95 o.p. (ISBN 0-87863-244-1, Farnsworth Pub Co). Longman Finan.

Magic of Ham Radio. Ed. by Jerold Swank & Emily Gibbs. 155p. 1980. pap. 4.95 o.p. (ISBN 0-88006-004-2, BK 7312). Wayne Green Ent.

Magic of Honey. Dorothy Perlman. 1978. pap. 1.95 o.p. (ISBN 0-380-00029-6, 39099). Avon.

Magic of Kirigami: Happenings with Paper & Scissors. Florence Temko & Toshie Takahama. (Illus.). 1978. 13.75 o.p. (ISBN 0-87040-434-2). Japan Pubns USA.

Magic of Origami. Alice Gray & Kunihiko Kasahara. LC 77-74654. (Illus.). 1977. 13.75 o.p. (ISBN 0-87040-390-7). Japan Pubns USA.

Magic of Rapport: How You Can Increase Your Communication Skills to Gain Personal Power in Any Situation. Jerry Richardson & Joel Margulis. 176p. 1981. 11.95 o.p. (ISBN 0-936602-26-0). Kampmann.

Magic of Rapport: The Business of Negotiation. Jerry Richardson & Joel Margulis. 208p. 1984. pap. 6.95 o.p. (ISBN 0-380-68205-2, 68205-2). Avon.

Magic of Soccer. Jerry Trecker. LC 81-66004. 1982. 10.95 o.p. (ISBN 0-689-11144-4, Atheneum). Macmillan.

Magic of the Horseshoe. Robert M. Lawrence. LC 68-22034. 350p. 1968. Repr. of 1898 ed. 40.00x o.p. (ISBN 0-8103-3452-6). Gale.
Magic of Tone & the Art of Music. Dane Rudhyar. LC 81-84323. 250p. (Orig.). 1982. pap. 8.95 o.p. (ISBN 0-87773-220-5). Shambhala Pubns.
Magic or Not. Edward Eager. LC 59-5628. (Illus.). (gr. 4-6). 1959. 5.95 o.p. (ISBN 0-15-251157-1, HJ). HarBraceJ.
Magic or Not? Edward Eager. LC 78-71152. (Illus.). 192p. (gr. 3-6). 1979. pap. 4.95 o.p. (ISBN 0-15-655121-7, VoyB). HarBraceJ.
Magic Power of Self-Image Psychology. Maxwell Maltz. 1984. pap. 3.95 o.s.i. (ISBN 0-671-55595-2). PB.
Magic Ring & Other Russian Folktales. Tr. by Robert Chandler. (Illus.). 112p. (gr. 3 up). 1979. 7.50 o.p. (ISBN 0-571-11338-9); pap. 3.95 o.p. (ISBN 0-571-13006-2). Faber & Faber.
Magic Show in a Box. Shari Lewis. (gr. 4-6). 1981. pap. 1.95 o.s.i. H Holt & Co.
Magic, Stage Illusions, Special Effects & Trick Photography. Albert A. Hopkins. 12.00 o.p. (ISBN 0-8446-5478-7). Peter Smith.
Magic Tarot: Vehicle of Eternal Wisdom. Frederic Lionel. Tr. by Marilyn W. Gadzuk. (Illus.). 160p. 1982. 17.95 o.p. (ISBN 0-7100-9416-7). Routledge Chapman & Hall.
Magic: The Western Tradition. Francis King. (Illus.). 1975. pap. 5.95 o.p. (ISBN 0-380-20727-3, 20727). Avon.
Magic Worlds of Fantasy. David D. Duncan. LC 78-1470. (Helen & Kurt Wolff Bks.). (Illus.). 1978. 14.95 o.p. (ISBN 0-15-155102-2). HarBraceJ.
Magical Calendar: A Synthesis of Magical Symbolism from the Seventeenth Centry Renaissance of Medieval Occultism. Ed. by Adam Mclean. (Magnum Opus Hermetic Sourceworks Ser.: No. 1). (Illus.). 109p. (Orig.). 1987. pap. 15.00 o.p. (ISBN 0-933999-04-6). Phanes Pr.
Magical Cupboard. Jane L. Curry. LC 75-43892. (Illus.). 144p. (gr. 3-7). 1976. 6.95 o.p. (ISBN 0-689-50059-9, Atheneum). Macmillan.
Magical Jewels of the Middle Ages & the Renaissance. Joan Evans. 15.50 o.p. (ISBN 0-8446-5572-4). Peter Smith.
Magical Jewels of the Middle Ages & the Renaissance Particularly in England. Joan Evans. LC 75-26288. (Illus.). 288p. 1976. pap. 5.95 o.p. (ISBN 0-486-23367-7). Dover.
Magical Mason. R. A. Gilbert. 320p. Date not set. pap. 13.95 o.p. (ISBN 0-85030-373-7, Pub. by Thorsons UK). Weiser.
Magical Menagerie. Janet McCumsey. (Illus.). 64p. (gr. 2-8). 1983. wkbk. 6.95 o.p. (ISBN 0-86653-106-8, GA 473). Good Apple.
Magical Realm of Sallie Middleton. Sallie Middleton & Celestine Sibley. LC 80-80974. 112p. 1980. 19.95 o.p. (ISBN 0-8487-0503-3). Oxmoor Hse.
Magician & the Balloon. David McKee. LC 86-8058. (Illus.). 26p. (gr. k-3). 1986. 10.95 o.p. (ISBN 0-87226-087-9, Bedrick Blackie). P Bedrick Bks.
Magician & the Petnapping. David McKee. (Illus.). (gr. k-3). 1977. 5.95 o.p. (ISBN 0-395-24916-3). HM.
Magician of Lublin. Isaac Bashevis Singer. Tr. by Elaine Gottlieb & Joseph Singer. 1960. 9.95 o.p. (ISBN 0-374-19633-8). FS&G.
Magill Surveys - American Literature: Colonial Age to 1890. Ed. by Frank N. Magill. LC 80-54246. 413p. 1980. pap. 7.95 o.p. (ISBN 0-89356-304-8). Salem Pr.
Magill Surveys - American Literature: Realism to 1945. Ed. by Frank N. Magill. LC 81-51767. 688p. 1981. pap. 7.95 o.p. (ISBN 0-89356-310-2). Salem Pr.
Magill Surveys - English Literature: Middle Ages to 1800. Ed. by Frank N. Magill. LC 80-54243. 776p. 1980. pap. 7.95 o.p. (ISBN 0-89356-303-X). Salem Pr.
Magill's Bibliography of Literary Criticism. Ed. by Frank N. Magill. LC 79-63017. 2416p. 1979. Set. 200.00x o.p. (ISBN 0-89356-188-6). Salem Pr.
Magistrate. Ernest K. Gann. LC 81-66970. 304p. 1982. 14.50 o.p. (ISBN 0-87795-339-2, Arbor Hse). Morrow.
Magnesium in Health & Disease. Ed. by Marc Cantin & Mildred S. Seelig. LC 78-13181. (Monographs of the Am College of Nutrition: Vol. 4). (Illus.). 1154p. 1980. 225.00 o.p. (ISBN 0-89335-055-9). PMA Pub Corp.
Magnet Schools: Legal & Practical Implications. Ed. by Nolan Estes & Donald R. Waldrip. 1978. 8.95 o.p. (ISBN 0-8329-0001-X). New Century.
Magnetic Atoms & Molecules. W. Weltner. 1983. 47.95 o.p. (ISBN 0-442-29206-6). Van Nos Reinhold.
Magnetic Blueprint of Life. Albert R. Davis & Walter C. Rawls, Jr. 1979. 12.50 o.p. (ISBN 0-682-49215-9). Exposition-Phoenix.
Magnetic Bubbles. T. H. O'Dell. LC 74-12048. 159p. 1975. 45.95x o.p. (ISBN 0-470-65259-4). Halsted Pr.
Magnetic Cure for Common Diseases. H. L. Bansal & R. S. Bansal. 176p. 1983. pap. 5.00 o.s.i. (ISBN 0-86578-223-7). Ind-US Inc.
Magnetic Domains & Techniques for Their Observation. Roy Carey & E. D. Isaac. 1966. 58.00 o.p. (ISBN 0-12-159550-1). Acad Pr.
Magnetic Effect. Albert R. Davis & Walter C. Rawls, Jr. 1975. 10.00 o.p. (ISBN 0-682-48312-5). Exposition-Phoenix.
Magnetic Materials in Industry. P. R. Bardell. (Illus.). 300p. (ISBN 0-8022-0059-1). Philos Lib.
Magnetic Monopoles. Ed. by Richard A. Carrigan & W. Peter Trower. (NATO ASI Series B, Physics: Vol. 102). 348p. 1983. 59.50x o.p. (ISBN 0-306-41399-X, Plenum Pr). Plenum Pub.
Magnetic Properties of Transition Metal Compounds. R. L. Carlin & A. J. Van Duyneveldt. LC 77-18002. (Inorganic Chemistry Concepts: Vol. 2). 1977. 29.00 o.p. (ISBN 0-387-08584-X). Springer-Verlag.
Magnetic Resonance & Related Phenomena. E. Kundla et al. 606p. 1980. 21.30 o.p. (ISBN 0-387-09380-X). Springer-Verlag.
Magnetic Resonance in Chemistry & Biology. Ed. by J. N. Herak & K. J. Adamic. 576p. 1975. 105.00 o.p. (ISBN 0-8247-6119-7). Dekker.
Magnetic Resonance of Phase Transitions. Ed. by Frank J. Owens et al. LC 78-67881. 1979. 71.50 o.p. (ISBN 0-12-531450-7). Acad Pr.
Magnetic Stratigraphy of Sediments. Ed. by James P. Kennett. LC 79-13662. (Benchmark Papers in Geology Ser.: Vol. 54). 464p. 1982. 54.95 o.p. (ISBN 0-87933-354-5). Van Nos Reinhold.
Magnetism see Physics Programs.
Magnetism & Metallurgy, 2 Vols. Ed. by A. E. Berkowitz & E. Kneller. Vol. 1, 1970. 61.00 o.p. (ISBN 0-12-091701-7); Vol. 2, 1969. 72.00 o.p. (ISBN 0-12-091702-5); Set. 49.00 o.p. Acad Pr.
Magneto & Iono Plas: ASR Vo514 Proceedings of Symposium Nine & the COSPAR Interdisciplinary Scientific Commission D of the COSPAR Twenty-fifth Plenary Meeting Held in Graz, Austria, 25 June-7 July 1984. Ed. by E. R. Schmerling et al. LC 83-645550. (Illus.). 434p. 1985. pap. 54.00 o.p. (ISBN 0-08-033193-9, Pub. by PPL). Pergamon.
Magneto-Thermoelasticity: Proceedings of CISM, Department of Mechanics of Solids, Vienna, 1972. CISM (International Center for Mechanical Sciences), Department of Mechanics of Solids Staff. Ed. by H. Parkus. (CISM Publications: No. 118). 61p. 1973. pap. 9.80 o.p. (ISBN 0-387-81134-6). Springer-Verlag.
Magnetofluid Dynamics for Engineers & Applied Physicists. Kenneth R. Cramer & Shi I. Pai. (Illus.). 360p. 1973. text ed. 45.00 o.p. (ISBN 0-07-013425-1). McGraw.
Magnetohydrodynamic Flows in Ducts. H. Branover. 220p. 1978. text ed. 45.00 o.p. (ISBN 0-7065-1581-1, Pub. by Keter Pub Jerusalem). Coronet Bks.
Magnificent Ambersons. Booth Tarkington. 1986. write for info. o.p. (ISBN 0-87795-795-9). Morrow.
Magnificent Charter: The Origin & Role of the Morrill Land-Grant Colleges & Universities. J. B. Edmond. 1978. 12.00 o.p. (ISBN 0-682-49079-2, University); pap. 5.50 o.p. (ISBN 0-682-49081-4). Exposition-Phoenix.
Magnificent Dream. Day Taylor. 496p. (Orig.). 1984. pap. 3.95 o.p. (ISBN 0-440-15424-3). Dell.
Magnificent Foragers: Smithsonian Explorations in the Natural Sciences. LC 78-61066. (Illus.). 223p. 1978. 16.95 o.p. (ISBN 0-89599-001-6, Dist. by Norton). Smithsonian Bks.
Magnificent Microbes. Bernard Dixon. LC 75-14678. 1979. pap. 4.95 o.p. (ISBN 0-689-70589-1, 250, Atheneum). Macmillan.
Magnificent Mind. Gary R. Collins. 224p. 1985. 9.95 o.p. (ISBN 0-8499-0385-8, 0385-8). Word Bks.
Magnificent Moo. Victoria Forrester. LC 82-13781. (Illus.). 40p. (gr. k-1). 1983. 10.95 o.s.i. (ISBN 0-689-30954-6, Atheneum Childrens Bks). Macmillan.
Magnificent Spinster. May Sarton. (Large Print Bks). 522p. 1987. lib. bdg. 19.95 o.p. (ISBN 0-8161-4096-0, Large Print Bk). G K Hall.
Magnificent West: Yosemite. Milton Goldstein. LC 72-85054. 224p. 1976. 35.00 o.p. (ISBN 0-385-03296-X). Doubleday.
Magnum, P. I. Number One: Maui Mystery. William Rotsler. Ed. by Wendy Barish. (Plot-It-Yourself Adventure Stories Ser.). 128p. 1983. pap. 3.80 o.s.i. (ISBN 0-671-49607-7). Wanderer Bks.
Magus of Strovolos: The Extraordinary World of a Spiritual Healer. Kyriacos C. Markides. 288p. (Orig.). 1985. pap. 7.95 o.p. (ISBN 1-85063-027-5, Ark Paperbks). Routledge Chapman & Hall.
Mahabharata. P. Lal. 352p. 1980. text ed. 25.00x o.p. (ISBN 0-7069-1033-8, Pub. by Vikas India); pap. 14.50x o.p. (ISBN 0-686-77530-9). Advent NY.
Mahabharata. Ed. by S. C. Nott. (Illus.). 200p. 1956. (ISBN 0-8022-1230-1). Philos Lib.
Mahadevan Volume: A Collection of Geological Papers in Commeration of the Sixty-First Birthday of Pr. C. Mahadevan. C. Mahadeuan. Ed. by M. S. Krishman. (Illus.). 1961. 5.00x o.p. (ISBN 0-934454-59-0). Lubrecht & Cramer.
Mahamudra: The Quintessance of Mind & Meditation. Takpo Tashi Namgyal. Tr. by Lobsang P. Lhalungpa from Tibetan. LC 85-27963. (Orig.). 1987. pap. 25.00 o.p. (ISBN 0-87773-360-0). Shambhala Pubns.
Maharaja Ranjit Singh As Patron of the Arts. 1982. 29.00x o.p. (ISBN 0-8364-0865-9, Pub. by Marg). South Asia Bks.
Mahatma Gandhi & Comparative Religion. K. L. Rao. 1979. 15.00x o.p. (ISBN 0-89684-034-4). South Asia Bks.
Mahjong Made Easy: Standard Chinese Rules Simplified. Willie Lim. (Illus.). 32p. 1982. 6.00 o.p. (ISBN 0-682-49852-1). Exposition-Phoenix.
Mahler. Michael Kennedy. (Master Musicians Ser.). (Illus.). 208p. 1974. 17.95x o.p. (ISBN 0-460-03141-4, Pub. by J. M. Dent, England). Biblio Dist.
Mahler: The Man & His Music. Egon Gartenberg. LC 77-70274. (Illus.). 1979. pap. 6.95 o.s.i. (ISBN 0-02-871540-3). Schirmer Bks.
Mahler: The Man & His Music. Egon Gartenberg. LC 77-70274. (Illus.). 1978. 16.95 o.s.i. (ISBN 0-02-870840-7). Schirmer Bks.
Mai-Dun see Crows of War.
Maid of Buttermere. Melvyn Bragg. 384p. 1987. 18.95 o.p. (ISBN 0-399-13225-2, Putnam). Putnam Pub Group.
Maid of Honor. Charlotte MacLeod. LC 83-15653. 168p. (gr. 7 up). 1984. 10.95 o.s.i. (ISBN 0-689-31019-6, Atheneum Childrens Bks). Macmillan.
Maid, the Man, & the Fans: Elvis Is the Man. Mae Gutter & Nancy Rooks. 1984. 6.95 o.p. (ISBN 0-533-06053-2). Vantage.
Maiden Crown. Meghan R. Collins. (gr. 7 up). 1979. 8.95 o.p. (ISBN 0-395-28639-5). HM.
Maigret Afraid. Georges Simenon. Tr. by Margaret Duff from Fr. LC 82-23233. 176p. 1983. 13.95 o.s.i. (ISBN 0-15-155560-5). HarBraceJ.
Maigret & the Apparition. Georges Simenon. Tr. by Eileen Ellenbogen. LC 76-14382. (Helen Kurt Wolff Bk.). 1976. 6.95 o.p. (ISBN 0-15-155125-1). HarBraceJ.
Maigret & the Black Sheep. Georges Simenon. Tr. by Helen Thompson. LC 75-20384. (Helen Kurt Wolff Bk.). 168p. 1976. 6.95 o.p. (ISBN 0-15-155146-4). HarBraceJ.
Maigret & the Informer. Georges Simenon. LC 72-91839. 1973. 5.95 o.p. (ISBN 0-15-155140-5). HarBraceJ.
Maigret & the Man on the Bench. Georges Simenon. Tr. by Eileen Ellenbogen. LC 78-13304. (Helen & Kurt Wolff Bk.). 1975. 9.95 o.p. (ISBN 0-15-155145-6). HarBraceJ.
Maigret & the Millionaires. Georges Simenon. Tr. by Jean Stewart from Fr. LC 74-7009. (Helen & Kurt Wolff Bk.). 168p. 1974. 5.95 o.p. (ISBN 0-15-155143-X). HarBraceJ.
Maigret & the Nahour Case. Georges Simenon. LC 82-47661. (Helen & Kurt Wolff Bk.). 168p. 1983. 10.95 o.p. (ISBN 0-15-155559-1). HarBraceJ.
Maigret & the Spinster. Georges Simenon. Tr. by Eileen Ellenbogen. LC 76-27416. (Helen & Kurt Wolff Bk.). 1977. Repr. 6.95 o.p. (ISBN 0-15-155550-8). HarBraceJ.
Maigret & the Toy Village. Georges Simenon. Tr. by Eileen Ellenbogen. LC 79-1843. (Helen & Kurt Wolff Bk.). 1979. 7.95 o.p. (ISBN 0-15-155554-0). HarBraceJ.
Maigret at the Coroner's. Georges Simenon. Tr. by Frances Keene. LC 80-81491. (Helen & Kurt Wolff Bk.). 180p. 1980. Repr. 8.95 o.p. (ISBN 0-15-155556-7). HarBraceJ.
Maigret at the Coroner's. Georges Simenon. Tr. by Frances Keene. (Helen & Kurt Wolff Bk.). 182p. 1984. pap. 3.95 o.s.i. (ISBN 0-15-655143-8, Harv). HarBraceJ.
Maigret Bides His Time. Georges Simenon. Tr. by Alastair Hamilton from Fr. LC 84-25134. (Helen & Kurt Wolff Bk.). 160p. 1985. 12.95 o.p. (ISBN 0-15-155563-X). HarBraceJ.
Maigret et les braves gens: Student Edition. Georges Simenon. Ed. by Rene Daudon. (Orig., Fr.). 1969. pap. text ed. 4.95 o.p. (ISBN 0-15-551287-0, HC). HarBraceJ.
Maigret Has Doubts. Georges Simenon. Tr. by Lyn Moir. LC 78-13771. 144p. 1982. 10.95 o.p. (ISBN 0-15-155558-3). HarBraceJ.
Maigret in Court. Georges Simenon. Tr. by Robert Brain. LC 83-4341. (Helen & Kurt Wolff Bk.). 160p. 1983. Repr. of 1960 ed. 11.95 o.s.i. (ISBN 0-15-155561-3). HarBraceJ.
Maigret in Exile. Georges Simenon. Tr. by Eileen Ellenbogen. LC 78-13771. (Helen & Kurt Wolff Bk.). 1979. 7.95 o.p. (ISBN 0-15-155147-2). HarBraceJ.
Maigret on the Defensive. Georges Simenon. Tr. by Alastair Hamilton. LC 81-47576. (Helen & Kurt Wolff Bk.). 144p. 1981. 10.95 o.p. (ISBN 0-15-155557-5). HarBraceJ.
Maigret's Boyhood Friend. Georges Simenon. LC 79-124825. (Helen & Kurt Wolff Bk.). 1970. 4.95 o.p. (ISBN 0-15-155135-9). HarBraceJ.
Maigret's Christmas: Nine Short Stories. Georges Simenon. LC 77-1724. (Helen & Kurt Wolff Bks). 1977. 8.95 o.p. (ISBN 0-15-155551-6). HarBraceJ.
Maigret's Pipe. Georges Simenon. Tr. by Jean Stewart. LC 78-4169. (Helen & Kurt Wolff Bks.). 1978. 8.95 o.p. (ISBN 0-15-155553-2). HarBraceJ.
Maigret's Rival. Georges Simenon. Tr. by Helen Thomson. LC 79-3362. (Helen & Kurt Wolff Bk.). 180p. 1980. Repr. of 1944 ed. 7.95 o.p. (ISBN 0-15-155555-9). HarBraceJ.
Maigret's Rival. Georges Simenon. (Nightingale Ser.). 244p. 1988. pap. 12.95x o.p. (ISBN 0-8161-4426-5). G K Hall.
Maigret's War of Nerves. Georges Simenon. Tr. by Geoffrey Sainsbury. 216p. 1987. pap. 10.95 o.p. (ISBN 0-8161-4309-9). G K Hall.
Mail Drops. CWL. (Security & Survival Ser.). 48p. (Orig.). 1985. pap. 10.00 o.p. (ISBN 0-939856-45-X). Tech Group.
Mail Handler, U.S. Postal Service. Hy Hammer. 1981. pap. 6.00 o.p. (ISBN 0-668-05247-3). Arco.
Mail Order Dealer's Advertising Rate Manual. 6th ed. Alfred Stern. 83p. 1986. pap. 10.00 o.p. (ISBN 0-915665-12-3). Premier Publishers.
Mailbox Trick. Scott Corbett. (Trick Ser.). (Illus.). (gr. 4-6). 1961. 9.70 o.p. (ISBN 0-316-15701-5, Pub. by Atlantic Monthly Pr). Little.
Mailer: His Life & Times. Peter Manso. (Illus.). 645p. 1985. 19.45 o.p. (ISBN 0-671-44264-3). S&S.
Maillard Reactions in Food: Proceedings of the International Symposium, Uddevalla, Sweden, September 1979. C. Ericksson. (Progress in Food & Nutrition Science Ser.: Vol. 5). (Illus.). 500p. 1982. 170.00 o.p. (ISBN 0-08-025496-9). Pergamon.
Maillol Woodcuts: Three Hundred & Three Great Book Illustrations. Aristide Maillol. (Illus.). 13.25 o.p. (ISBN 0-8446-5790-5). Peter Smith.
Main. Trevanian. LC 76-24896. 1976. 8.95 o.p. (ISBN 0-15-155549-4). HarBraceJ.
Main Currents in American Thought, Vol. 1: The Colonial Mind, 1620-1800. Vernon L. Parrington. 420p. 1955. pap. 6.95 o.p. (ISBN 0-15-655134-9, Harv). HarBraceJ.
Main Currents in American Thought, Vol. 2: The Romantic Revolution in America, 1800-1860. Vernon L. Parrington. 486p. 1955. pap. 6.95 o.p. (ISBN 0-15-655135-7, Harv). HarBraceJ.
Main Currents in American Thought, Vol. 3: Beginnings of Critical Realism in America, 1860-1920. Vernon L. Parrington. LC 56-58467. 429p. 1963. pap. 6.95 o.p. (ISBN 0-15-611677-4, Harv). HarBraceJ.
Main Currents in Indian Sociology: Social & Cultural Context of Medicine in India, Vol. IV. Ed. by Giri Raj Gupta. 1982. text ed. 35.00x o.p. (Pub. by Vikas India). Advent NY.
Main Events. Dan Ivins. LC 82-70869. (Orig.). (YA) (gr. 7-12). 1983. pap. 4.50 o.p. (ISBN 0-8054-5339-3, 4253-39). Broadman.
Main Problems in American History, 2 vols. 4th ed. Ed. by Howard H. Quint et al. 1978. Vol. 1, 367p. pap. text ed. (ISBN 0-534-11247-1); Vol. 2, 417p. pap. text ed. Wadsworth Pub.
Main Street America & the Third World. John M. Hamilton. 208p. (Orig.). 1986. pap. 9.95 o.p. (ISBN 0-932020-39-9). Seven Locks Pr.
Main Street America & the Third World. rev. ed. John M. Hamilton. 228p. 1989. pap. 9.95 o.p. (ISBN 0-932020-64-X). Seven Locks Pr.
Main Trends in Modern Linguistics. Maurice Leroy. Tr. by Glanville Price from Fr. LC 81-20302. xi, 155p. 1982. Repr. of 1967 ed. lib. bdg. 35.00x o.p. (ISBN 0-313-23407-8, LEMAT). Greenwood.
Main Trends of Research in the Social & Human Sciences, Pt. 2: Anthropological & Historical Sciences, Aesthetics & the Sciences of Art, Legal Science, Philosophy, 2 vols. 159p. 1979. Set. 76.50 o.p. (ISBN 92-3-101013-1, U873, UNESCO). UNIPUB.
Mainder the Buttercup. Autumn Stanley. (Illus.). 1977. pap. 3.95 o.p. (ISBN 0-931832-13-6). Fithian Pr.
Maine. William Berchen. (Illus.). 1973. 10.95 o.p. (ISBN 0-395-15457-X). HM.
Maine: An Explorer's Guide. Rev. ed. Christina Tree. (Illus.). 160p. 1984. pap. 9.95 o.p. (ISBN 0-88150-024-0). Countryman.

Maine: An Explorer's Guide. 3rd, rev. & expanded ed. Christina Tree & Mimi E. Steadman. (Explorer's Guides Ser.). (Illus.). 400p. (Orig.). 1987. pap. 13.95 o.s.i. (ISBN 0-88150-083-6). Countryman.

Maine Bar Directory, 1987. Ed. by Tower Publishing Company Staff. 430p. 1987. 3-ring binder 26.25 o.p. (ISBN 0-89442-073-9). Tower Pub Co.

Maine Bar Directory, 1988. Ed. by Tower Staff. 430p. 1988. 28.00 o.p. (ISBN 0-89442-086-0). Tower Pub Co.

Maine Coast: A Nature Lover's Guide. Dorcas S. Miller. LC 79-10290. (Illus.). 192p. 1978. pap. 8.95 o.p. (ISBN 0-914788-12-4). Globe Pequot.

Maine Deeper In: Washington & Aroostook Counties. Martin Brown. LC 81-66264. (Illus.). 128p. 1982. pap. 10.95 o.p. (ISBN 0-89272-127-8). Down East.

Maine: Fifty Years of Change 1940-1990. Ed. by Allen Pease & Wilfred Richard. 194p. (Orig.). 1983. pap. text ed. 5.95x o.p. (ISBN 0-89101-054-8). U Maine Pr.

Maine Is Many Things: A Coloring & Game Book. 2nd ed. Paula Lane. (Maine Geographic Ser.). (Illus.). 48p. (Orig.). (gr. 3-6). 1983. pap. 2.95 o.p. (ISBN 0-89933-014-2). DeLorme Map.

Maine Manufacturing Directory, 1986. 626p. 1986. pap. 27.50 o.p. (ISBN 0-318-02883-2). Manufacturers.

Maine Massacre. Janwillem Van De Wetering. 1978. 8.95 o.p. (ISBN 0-395-27395-1). HM.

Maine Mountain Guide. The Appalachian Mountain Club. 280p. 1976. pap. 6.95 o.p. (ISBN 0-317-33374-7) (ISBN 0-317-33375-5). AMC Books.

Maine Scenic Route. H. Temple Crittenden. 1966. 12.50 o.p. (ISBN 0-87012-060-3). McClain.

Maine: Trusts. 1983. 8.50 o.p. (ISBN 0-686-90504-0). Am Law Inst.

Maine, Vermont, New Hampshire Directory of Manufacturers, 1987-88. 200p. 1987. pap. 52.50 o.p. (ISBN 0-318-02884-0, Pub. by Commerce Register, Inc). Manufacturers.

Maine Woods. Henry David Thoreau. Ed. by Dudley C. Lunt. (Masterworks of Literature Ser). (Illus.). 1950. pap. 3.95x o.p. (ISBN 0-8084-0205-6, M6). New Coll U Pr.

Maine Workers' Compensation Act: Practice & Procedure. Charles D. Devoe. 200p. 1983. poster binder 35.00 o.p. Tower Pub Co.

Mainland: A Novel. Susan F. Schaeffer. 1985. 14.70 o.p. (ISBN 0-671-55717-3, Linden Pr). S&S.

Mainline Churches & the Evangelicals. Richard G. Hutcheson, Jr. LC 80-84648. 192p. (Orig.). 1981. pap. 9.95 o.s.i. (ISBN 0-8042-1502-2, John Knox). Westminster John Knox.

Mains Sales: Piece en 7 Tableaux. Jean-Paul Sartre. 245p. 1976. 3.95 o.p. (ISBN 0-686-54983-X). Schoenhof.

Mainsteam of Civilization: Since 1500. 2nd ed. Joseph R. Strayer et al. (Incl. Chapter 16 through Epilogue from 3-vol.ed of same title). 1974. pap. text ed. 16.95 o.p. (ISBN 0-15-551561-6, HC). HarBraceJ.

Mainstream of Algebra & Trigonometry. A. W. Goodman. LC 72-5241. 475p. 1973. text ed. 17.95 o.p. (ISBN 0-395-16004-9, 3-19075). HM.

Mainstream of Algebra & Trigonometry. 2nd ed. A. W. Goodman et al. LC 79-90059. (Illus.). 1980. text ed. 39.96 o.p. (ISBN 0-395-26765-X). HM.

Mainstream of Civilization. 2nd ed. Joseph R. Strayer. (Illus.). 1974. One-vol. Ed. text ed. 17.95 o.p. (ISBN 0-15-551554-3, HC); Vol. 1. To 1715. pap. text ed. 14.95 o.p. (ISBN 0-15-551556-X, HC); Vol. 2. Since 1660. pap. text ed. 14.95 o.p. (ISBN 0-15-551557-8); Vol. 1. Vol. 1. To 1500. pap. text ed. 12.95 o.p. (ISBN 0-15-551558-6); Vol. 2. 1350-1815. pap. text ed. 12.95 o.p. (ISBN 0-15-551559-4, HC); Vol. 3. Since 1789. pap. text ed. 10.50 o.p. (ISBN 0-15-551560-8). HarBraceJ.

Mainstream of Civilization. 3rd ed. Joseph R. Strayer & Hans W. Gatzke. 864p. 1979. text ed. 25.95 o.p. (ISBN 0-15-551562-4, HC). HarBraceJ.

Mainstream of Civilization: Since 1500. 3rd ed. Joseph R. Strayer & Hans W. Gatzke. 495p. (Incl. chapters 16 through Epilogue of one-vol. ed. of same title). 1979. pap. text ed. 20.95 o.p. (ISBN 0-15-551569-1, HC). HarBraceJ.

Mainstreaming in the Social Studies. John G. Herlihy & Myra T. Herlihy. 1986. 26.00 o.p. (ISBN 0-317-57530-9, 2027730). Nat Coun Soc Studies.

Mainstreaming Language Arts & Social Studies: Special Activities for the Whole Class. Charles Coble & Paul Hounshell. LC 76-13164. (Illus.). 1977. 11.95 o.p. (ISBN 0-673-16388-1). Scott F.

Mainstreaming the Educable Mentally Retarded. new ed. Marjorie Watson. LC 75-12964. (Developments in Classroom Instruction Ser.). 56p. 1977. pap. text ed. 6.95 o.p. (ISBN 0-8106-1800-1). NEA.

Mainstreaming the Learning Disabled Adolescent: A Manual of Strategies & Materials. Dolores M. Woodward. LC 80-19566. 249p. 1981. text ed. 35.00 o.p. (ISBN 0-89443-299-0). Aspen Pub.

Maintaining & Overhauling Lycoming Engines. 2nd, rev. & enl. ed. Joe Christy. (Illus.). 160p. 1986. pap. 13.60 o.p. (ISBN 0-8306-2427-9, 2427). TAB Bks.

Maintaining & Repairing Videocassette Recorders. Robert L. Goodman. (Illus.). 416p. 1983. 22.95 o.p. (ISBN 0-8306-0103-1); pap. 16.60 o.p. (ISBN 0-8306-1503-2, 1503). TAB Bks.

Maintenance Decision Making & Energy Use, Roadside & Pavement Management, & Preferential Bridge Icing. (Transportation Research Record Ser.). 67p. 1978. 4.00 o.p. (ISBN 0-309-02814-0). Transport Res Bd.

Maintenance, Economics, Management, & Pavements. (Transportation Research Record Ser.). 56p. 1979. 3.40 o.p. (ISBN 0-309-02980-5). Transport Res Bd.

Maintenance Engineering Handbook. 3rd ed. Lindley R. Higgins & L. C. Morrow. 1977. text ed. 86.00 o.p. (ISBN 0-07-028755-4). McGraw.

Maintenance Management Techniques. A. S. Corder. 1976. text ed. 22.50 o.p. (ISBN 0-07-084459-3). McGraw.

Maintenance Management, the Federal Role, Unionization, Pavement Maintenance & Ice Control. (Transportation Research Record Ser.). 57p. 1976. 2.60 o.p. Transport Res Bd.

Maintenance of Factory Services: Part Two, 2 vols. Ed. by J. Vaughan et al. (Engineering Craftsmen Ser.: No. J23). (Illus.). 1969. Set. spiral bdg. 65.00x o.p. (ISBN 0-89563-010-9). Trans-Atl Phila.

Maintenance of Factory Services: Part One. Ed. by J. Vaughan et al. (Engineering Craftsmen Ser.: No. J3). (Illus.). 1968. spiral bdg. 45.00x o.p. Trans-Atl Phila.

Maintenance of Numerically Controlled Machine Tools, 2 vols. 2nd ed. Ed. by C. Brothwell et al. (Engineering Craftsmen Ser.: No. J27). (Illus.). 1973. Set. sprial bdg. 75.00x o.p. Trans-Atl Phila.

Maintenance Turns to the Computer. James K. Hildebrand. LC 75-109095. 176p. 1983. 18.95 o.p. (ISBN 0-8436-0808-0). Van Nos Reinhold.

Maison de Claudine. Sidonie G. Colette. (Illus.). 256p. 1976. 12.95 o.p. (ISBN 0-686-54583-4). French & Eur.

Maison de Rendez-vous. Alain Robbe-Grillet. Tr. by Richard Howard from Fr. 1982. pap. 6.95 o.p. (ISBN 0-394-62441-6, E840, BC). Grove.

Maison Jennie. Julie Ellis. 293p. 1984. 15.95 o.p. (ISBN 0-87795-572-7, Arbor Hse). Morrow.

Maistre Nicole Oresme: Le Livre de Politiques D'Aristote. Albert D. Menut. LC 71-131554. (Transactions Ser.: Vol. 60, Pt. 6). (Illus.). 1970. pap. 10.00 o.p. (ISBN 0-87169-606-1). Am Philos.

Maistre Nicole Oresme: Le Livre De Yconomique D'Aristote. Albert D. Menut. LC 57-12783. (Transactions Ser.: Vol. 47, Pt. 5). (Illus.). 1957. pap. 10.00 o.p. (ISBN 0-87169-475-1). Am Philos.

Maitre de Santiago. Henry De Montherlant. 1962. 13.25 o.p. (ISBN 0-685-11334-5). Schoenhof.

Maize. Gil Ott. (Illus.). 1980. ltd. signed ed. o.p. 30.00 o.p. (ISBN 0-915316-70-6); pap. 7.50 o.p. (ISBN 0-915316-69-2). Pentagram.

Majendie's Cat. Frank Fowlkes. 272p. 1987. pap. 3.95 o.p. (ISBN 0-380-70408-0). Avon.

Majesty. Robert Lacey. 1978. pap. 4.95 o.p. (ISBN 0-380-01842-X, 65995-6). Avon.

Majesty at Sea: The Four-Stackers. John H. Shaum, Jr. & William H. Flayhart, III. (Illus.). 1981. 29.95 o.p. (ISBN 0-393-01527-0). Norton.

Majesty: Elizabeth II & the House of Windsor. Robert Lacey. LC 76-27424. 1977. 12.95 o.p. (ISBN 0-15-155684-9). HarBraceJ.

Majesty in Flight: Nature's Birds of Prey in Three Dimensions. Ron Van der Meer. (Illus.). 1984. 14.95 o.p. (ISBN 0-89659-502-1). Abbeville Pr.

Majesty! The God You Should Know. J. Sidlow Baxter. LC 84-47805. 228p. 1984. 12.95 o.s.i. (ISBN 0-89840-070-8). Heres Life.

Majipoor Chronicles. Robert Silverberg. LC 81-67589. 304p. 1982. 12.95 o.p. (ISBN 0-87795-358-9, Arbor Hse); pap. 5.95 o.p. (ISBN 0-87795-359-7). Morrow.

Majistyka: A Case of Mental Rape. Laura M. Boyd. LC 86-62385. 168p. 1987. pap. 14.50 o.p. (ISBN 0-935834-57-5). Rainbow Books.

Major Appliances. Time-Life Books Editors. (Fix-It-Yourself Ser.). 144p. 1987. 17.27 o.p.; lib. bdg. 21.27 o.p. (ISBN 0-8094-6205-2). Time-Life.

Major Appliances & Electric Housewares. Fairchild Market Research Division Staff. (Fairchild Fact Files Ser.). (Illus.). 55p. 1985. pap. 17.50 o.p. (ISBN 0-87005-528-3). Fairchild.

Major British Writers. George B. Harrison. (Shorter ed.). 1967. text ed. 17.53 o.p. (ISBN 0-15-552776-2, HC). HarBraceJ.

Major British Writers, 2 vols. enl. ed. Ed. by George B. Harrison. 1871p. 1959. Vol. 1. text ed. 15.95 o.p. (ISBN 0-15-552774-6, HC); Vol. 2. text ed. 15.00 o.p. (ISBN 0-15-552775-4, HC). HarBraceJ.

Major Classification Systems: The Dewey Centennial. Ed. by Kathryn L. Henderson. (Allerton Park Instituite Ser.: No. 21). 182p. (LC 76-026331). 1976. 8.00x o.p. (ISBN 0-87845-044-0). U of Ill Lib Info Sci.

Major Companies of Europe 1986: Austria, Finland, Liechtenstein, Norway, Sweden, Switzerland, Vol. 3. Ed. by R. M. Whiteside. 250p. 1986. 131.00 o.p. (ISBN 0-86010-804-X); pap. 114.00 o.p. (ISBN 0-86010-803-1). Graham & Trotman.

Major Companies of Europe 1986: Belgium, Denmark, Erie, France, Germany, Greece, Italy, Luxembourg, the Netherlands, Portugal, Spain, Vol. 1. Ed. by R. M. Whiteside. 750p. 1986. 238.00 o.p. (ISBN 0-86010-800-7); pap. 211.00 o.p. (ISBN 0-86010-799-X). Graham & Trotman.

Major Companies of Europe 1986: United Kingdom, Vol. 2. Ed. by R. M. Whiteside. 350p. 1986. 149.00 o.p. (ISBN 0-86010-802-3); pap. 131.00 o.p. (ISBN 0-86010-801-5). Graham & Trotman.

Major Companies of Scandinavia 1985. Ed. by R. Whiteside. 150p. 1985. pap. 79.00 o.p. (ISBN 0-86010-635-7). Graham & Trotman.

Major Companies of the Far East 1986: East Asia-Peoples' Republic of China, Hong Kong, Japan, Republic of Korea, Taiwan, Vol. 2. Ed. by J. Carr. 450p. 1986. 149.00 o.p. (ISBN 0-86010-698-5); pap. 131.00 o.p. (ISBN 0-86010-699-3). Graham & Trotman.

Major Companies of the Far East 1986: South East Asia-Brunei, Indonesia, Malaysia, The Philippines, Singapore, Thailand, Vol. 1. Ed. by J. Carr. 350p. 1986. 149.00 o.p. (ISBN 0-86010-696-9); pap. 131.00 o.p. (ISBN 0-86010-697-7). Graham & Trotman.

Major Companies of U. S. A. 1986. Ed. by A. Wilson. 1400p. 1986. 348.00 o.p. (ISBN 0-86010-778-7); pap. 324.00 o.p. (ISBN 0-86010-797-3). Graham & Trotman.

Major Criminal Justice Systems. Ed. by George F. Cole et al. LC 81-9211. (Sage Focus Editions: Vol. 32). 300p. 1981. 35.00 o.p. (ISBN 0-8039-1671-X); pap. 16.95 o.p. (ISBN 0-8039-1672-8). Sage.

Major Crises in American History: Documentary Problems, Vol. 2. Ed. by Leonard W. Levy & Merrill D. Peterson. 1962. pap. text ed. 5.95 o.p. (ISBN 0-15-553666-4, HC). HarBraceJ.

Major Dobsa und Andere Erzahlungen. Friedrich G. Junger. Ed. by Robert L. Kahn. (Ger). 1965. pap. 2.95x o.p. (ISBN 0-393-09500-2, NortonC). Norton.

Major Energy Companies of Western Europe 1985. Ed. by R. Whiteside. 96p. 1985. pap. 96.00 o.p. (ISBN 0-86010-712-4). Graham & Trotman.

Major Feasts & Seasons: Christmastime. Gabe Huck. (Major Feasts & Seasons Ser.: Vol. 2, No. 1). 1976. 8.95 o.p. (ISBN 0-918208-86-6). Liturgical Conf.

Major Feasts & Seasons: Eastertime. Gabe Huck. (Major Feasts & Seasons Ser.: Vol. 2, No. 2). 1976. 8.95 o.p. (ISBN 0-918208-85-8). Liturgical Conf.

Major Financial Institutions of Continental Europe 1985. Ed. by R. Whiteside. 96p. 1985. pap. 79.00 o.p. (ISBN 0-86010-711-6). Graham & Trotman.

Major Histocompatibility System: The Gorer Symposium. Medawar. (Illus.). 128p. 1985. 24.00 o.p. (ISBN 0-632-01358-3, B-3187-4). Mosby.

Major Ideologies: An Interpretative Survey of Democracy, Socialism & Nationalism. Alexander J. Groth. LC 74-168636. 244p. 1971. pap. 11.50 o.p. (ISBN 0-471-32895-2). Krieger.

Major Issues in Special Education. Ed. by John P. Glavin. 1973. 29.50x o.p. (ISBN 0-8422-5109-X). Irvington.

Major League Baseball Manual. Milwaukee Brewers Staff. LC 80-2562. (Illus.). 192p. 1982. pap. 9.95 o.p. (ISBN 0-385-17515-9, Dolp). Doubleday.

Major Mental Handicap: Methods & Costs of Prevention. Ciba Foundation Staff. (Ciba Symposium Ser.: No. 59). 1978. 36.00 o.p. (ISBN 0-444-90033-0). Elsevier.

Major Ordeals of the Mind & the Countless Minor Ones. Henri Michaux. Tr. by Richard Howard from Fr. LC 73-16237. Orig. Title: Grandes Epreuves De l'Esprit. 192p. 1974. pap. 2.95 o.p. (ISBN 0-15-655250-7, Harv). HarBraceJ.

Major Poems. Gerald M. Hopkins. 1979. 9.95x o.p. (ISBN 0-460-10929-4, Evman); pap. 2.75x o.p. (ISBN 0-460-11929-X, Evman). Biblio Dist.

Major Principles of Media Law. Wayne Overbeck & Rick D. Pullen. LC 81-20174. 359p. 1982. text ed. 26.95 o.p. (ISBN 0-03-058293-8). HR&W.

Major Ternary Structure Families. O. Muller & R. Roy. LC 73-11536. (Crystal Chemistry Ser.: Vol. 4). (Illus.). 487p. 1974. 47.00 o.p. (ISBN 0-387-06430-3). Springer-Verlag.

Major Themes in Northern Black Religious Thought, 1800-1860. Monroe Fordham. LC 75-10618. 1975. 8.50 o.p. (ISBN 0-682-48256-0, University). Exposition-Phoenix.

Major Topics & Issues in Psychology: Scientific Studies in Behavioral Development. Ed. by Hsien Lu. 97p. 1972. 14.95x o.p. (ISBN 0-8422-0165-3). Irvington.

Major Topics & Issues in Psychology. Ed. by Lu Hsien. 97p. 1972. pap. text ed. 6.95x o.p. (ISBN 0-8290-1086-6). Irvington.

Major Writers of America, Vol. 2. Ed. by Perry Miller. 1962. 13.50 o.p. (ISBN 0-15-554601-5). HarbraceJ.

Major Writers of the World. Isaac A. Langnas & Jacob S. List. (Quality Paperback Ser.: No. 148). 1963. pap. 4.95 o.p. (ISBN 0-8226-0148-6). Littlefield.

Majorca Travel Guide. Berlitz Editors. (Travel Guides Ser.). 1976. pap. 4.95 o.p. (ISBN 0-317-12112-X, Berlitz). Macmillan.

Majority-Minority Relations. John E. Farley. (Illus.). 384p. 1982. text ed. (ISBN 0-13-545574-X). P-H.

Major's Physical Diagnosis. 9th ed. Ed. by Mahlon H. Delp & Robert T. Manning. LC 74-9430. (Illus.). 690p. 1975. text ed. write for info. o.p. (ISBN 0-7216-3012-X). Saunders.

Mak. Belle Coates. (gr. 5 up). 1981. 8.95 o.p. (ISBN 0-395-31603-0, Pub. by Parnassus). HM.

Make a Witch, Make a Goblin: A Book of Halloween Crafts. Arnold Dobrin. LC 77-177. (Illus.). 128p. (gr. 2-5). 1977. 8.95 o.s.i. (ISBN 0-02-729950-3, Four Winds). Macmillan.

Make-Ahead Entertaining. Mable Hoffman & Gar Hoffman. LC 85-80246. 159p. 1985. pap. 8.95 o.p. (ISBN 0-89586-362-6). Price Stern.

Make-Believe Bride. Nancy John. (Silhouette Romances Ser.). 1984. lib. bdg. 10.95 o.p. (ISBN 0-8398-2820-9, Gregg). G K Hall.

Make-Believers. Berry Fleming. LC 77-121887. 428p. 1972. 7.95 o.p. (ISBN 0-911116-81-8). Pelican.

Make Eugenicus & the Council of Florence: A Historical Re-evaluation of His Personality. Constance N. Tsirpanlis. 125p. 1979. pap. 9.95 o.p. (ISBN 0-686-36329-9). EO Pr.

Make Hay While the Sun Shines. Alison M. Abel. (Illus.). 48p. (gr. k-3). 1977. 7.95 o.p. (ISBN 0-571-11006-1). Faber & Faber.

Make It & Ride It. C. J. Maginley. LC 49-11081. (Illus.). (gr. 7 up). 1949. 5.95 o.p. (ISBN 0-15-251336-1, HJ). HarBraceJ.

Make It in Denim. Hazel Todhunter. LC 77-76478. (Illus.). 1977. 7.95 o.s.i. (ISBN 0-8008-5051-3). Taplinger.

Make Me a Map of the Valley: The Civil War Journal of Stonewall Jackson's Topographer. Ed. by Archie P. McDonald. LC 73-82036. (Bicentennial Series in American Studies: No. 1). (Illus.). 1973. 19.95 o.p. (ISBN 0-87074-137-3). SMU Press.

Make Money By Moonlighting: Own Your Own Low-Risk Business. Jack Lander. Ed. by Patti Cleary. LC 82-83244. 300p. 1983. 14.95 o.p. (ISBN 0-913864-72-2); pap. 9.95 o.p. (ISBN 0-913864-76-5). Enterprise Del.

Make No Sound. Barbara Corcoran. LC 77-2001. (gr. 5-8). 1977. 6.95 o.p. (ISBN 0-689-30580-X, Atheneum). Macmillan.

Make Room for Rags. Laura Bannon. (Illus.). (gr. k-3). 1964. reinforced bdg. 5.95 o.p. (ISBN 0-395-15496-0). HM.

Make That Story Live! Ruth S. Ensign. (Orig.). (gr. 7-9). 1965. pap. 2.25 o.p. (ISBN 0-8042-9317-1, John Knox). Westminster John Knox.

Make the Bible Your Own. Ruth D. See. (Orig.). 1961. pap. 1.95 o.p. (ISBN 0-8042-1344-5, John Knox). Westminster John Knox.

Make the Eagle Mount Up. Fred E. Gabbard. 1978. 12.00 o.p. (ISBN 0-682-48763-5). Exposition-Phoenix.

Make the Most of Your Best. Dorothy Sarnoff. LC 82-11927. 240p. 1983. pap. 7.95 o.p. (ISBN 0-03-062376-6). H Holt & Co.

Make Things Sailors Made. Marjorie Stapleton. LC 74-33171. (Illus.). 64p. 1975. 6.95 o.s.i. (ISBN 0-8008-5053-X). Taplinger.

Make up Your Mind see Art of Decision-Making: Seven Steps to Achieving More Effective Results.

Make up Your Mind! The Seven Building Blocks to Better Decisions. John D. Arnold. LC 78-16253. (Illus.). 1979. 13.95 o.p. (ISBN 0-8144-5479-8). AMACOM.

Make Your Illness Count: A Hospital Chaplain Shows How God's Healing Power Can Be Released in Your Life. Vernon J. Bittner. LC 76-3862. 128p. (Orig.). 1976. pap. 6.95 o.p. (ISBN 0-8066-1532-X, 10-4260, Augsburg). Augsburg Fortress.

Make Your Life Worthwhile. Emmet Fox. 1946. 9.95i o.p. (ISBN 0-06-062910-X). HarpR.

Make Your Money Grow. rev. ed. Ed. by Theodore J. Miller. 384p. 1984. pap. 8.95 o.p. (ISBN 0-440-05193-2). Dell.

Make Your Own Change. Nancy M. Wright. LC 84-73467. (Illus.). 176p. 1985. pap. 7.95 o.p. (ISBN 0-89272-211-8). Down East.

Make Your Own Classical Guitar. Date not set. (ISBN 0-8052-3833-6). Random.

Make Your Own Miniature Rooms. Estelle A. Worrell. Ed. by Clare Blau. (Illus.). 1978. pap. 5.37 o.p. (ISBN 0-87588-139-4, 1439). Hobby Hse.

Make Your Own Noah's Arc. Rosemary Lowndes & Claude Kailer. (Illus.). 96p. (gr. 3 up). 1984. pap. 12.45i o.p. (ISBN 0-316-53399-8, Pub. by Atlantic-Little, Brown). Little.

Maker & the Myth: Faulkner & Yoknapatawpha, 1977. Ed. by Evans Harrington & Ann J. Abadie. LC 78-60158. (Faulkner & Yoknapatawpha Ser.). 1978. 9.95x o.p. (ISBN 0-87805-049-3); pap. 4.95 o.p. (ISBN 0-87805-075-2). U Pr of Miss.

Maker of Universes. Philip Jose Farmer. Ed. by Lester Del Rey. LC 75-403. (Library of Science Fiction). 1975. lib. bdg. 21.00 o.p. (ISBN 0-8240-1408-1). Garland Pub.

Makers of Black Basaltes. M. Grant. (Illus.). 400p. 1967. 60.00 o.p. (ISBN 0-317-62985-9). Saifer.

Makers of Civilization. L. A. Waddell. 646p. 1986. 20.00 o.p. (ISBN 0-317-53274-X). Noontide.

Makers of Modern Africa see Know Africa.

Makers of Modern Britain. Richard Tames. (Illus.). 168p. (gr. 7-10). 1982. 22.95 o.p. (ISBN 0-7134-4055-4, Pub. by Batsford England). David & Charles.

Makers of Modern Strategy: Military Thought from Machiavelli to Hitler. Ed. by Edward M. Earle. 1943. 58.00x o.p. (ISBN 0-691-06907-7); pap. 12.95 o.s.i. (ISBN 0-691-01853-7). Princeton U Pr.

Makers of the United Studies. Ed. by John L. Frisbee. LC 87-600206. (USAF Warrior Studies Ser.). (Illus.). 362p. 1987. pap. 13.00 o.p. (ISBN 0-318-23561-7, 008-070-00593-0). USGPO.

Makeup on Empty Space. Anne Waldman. LC 83-18128. 96p. 1983. 40.00 o.p. (Pub. by Toothpaste); pap. 8.50 o.p. (ISBN 0-915124-83-1); signed cloth 40.00 o.p. (ISBN 0-915124-84-X). Coffee Hse.

Makin' Free: African-Americans in the Northwest Territory. Reginald R. Larrie. (Illus.). 1981. 7.95 o.p. (ISBN 0-87917-072-7). Ethridge.

Makin' Things for Kids. Ed Baldwin. LC 78-73845. 1980. soft cover 8.95 o.p. (ISBN 0-916752-33-X). Longman Trade.

Making a Book. Ruth Thomson. (Making Ser.). (Illus.). 32p. (gr. 1). 1988. 9.90 o.p. Watts.

Making a Difference: A Catechist's Guide to Successful Classroom Management. Thomas P Walters & Rita T. Walters. LC 85-62390. 94p. (Orig.). 1986. pap. 4.95 o.p. (ISBN 0-934134-61-8). Sheed & Ward MO.

Making a Difference: The Peace Corps at Twenty-Five. Ed. by Milton Viorst. LC 86-9055. 224p. 1986. 16.95 o.s.i. (ISBN 1-55584-010-8). Weidenfeld.

Making a Difference: There's a Lot More to Living Than Money & Success. Whitney N. Seymour, Jr. LC 83-19416. 224p. 1984. 11.95 o.s.i. (ISBN 0-688-02652-4). Morrow.

Making a Film. Lindsay Anderson. LC 76-52087. (Classics of Film Literature Ser.: Vol. 1). (Illus.). 1977. Repr. of 1952 ed. lib. bdg. 22.00 o.p. (ISBN 0-8240-2863-5). Garland Pub.

Making a Go of It: A Study of Stepfamilies in Sheffield. Jacqueline Burgoyne & David Clark. 300p. 1984. 39.95x o.p. (ISBN 0-7102-0318-7). Routledge Chapman & Hall.

Making a Living in Family Law. 274p. 1984. 25.00 o.p. (ISBN 0-88129-122-6). Wash Bar CLE.

Making Action Toys in Wood. Anthony Peduzzi & Judy Peduzzi. LC 85-12674. (Illus.). 120p. (Orig.). 1985. pap. 8.95 o.p. (ISBN 0-8069-1224-3). Sterling.

Making & Repairing Wooden Clock Cases. Vic Taylor & Harold Babb. (Illus.). 192p. 1987. 34.95 o.p. (ISBN 0-7153-8727-8). David & Charles.

Making & Using Inexpensive Classroom Media. Betty J. Wagner & E. Arthur Stunard. LC 76-29236. (Learning Handbooks Ser.). 1976. pap. 5.95 o.p. (ISBN 0-8224-1907-6). D S Lake Pubs.

Making & Using Your Own Tools & Workshop Accessories. pap. 12.95 o.p. (ISBN 0-8306-1360-9, 1360). TAB Bks.

Making Babies in the 80's: The New Parents Baby Book. Renee R. Shield. 160p. 1986. pap. 3.95 o.p. (ISBN 0-380-70088-3). Avon.

Making Babies: The New Science & Ethics of Conception. Peter Singer & Deane Wells. 240p. 1985. 14.95 o.p. (ISBN 0-684-18371-4, ScribT). Scribner.

Making Baskets. Maryanne Gillooly. (Illus.). 32p. 1986. pap. 1.95 o.p. (ISBN 0-88266-341-0, Garden Way Pub). Storey Comm Inc.

Making Bead Flowers & Bouquets. Virginia Nathanson. (Illus.). 192p. 1983. pap. 4.95 o.p. (ISBN 0-486-24464-4). Dover.

Making Cars: A History of Car-Making at Cowley by the People Who Make the Cars. Television History Workshop Staff. (History Workshop Ser.). (Illus.). 160p. (Orig.). 1985. pap. 12.95x o.p. (ISBN 0-7102-0272-5). Routledge Chapman & Hall.

Making Church More Enjoyable. David Mains. (Chapel Talks Ser.). 64p. 0.95 o.p. (ISBN 0-89191-256-8, 52563). Cook.

Making Clothes in Leather. Ben Morris & Elizabeth Morris. LC 75-21619. (Illus.). 95p. 1976. 10.95 o.s.i. (ISBN 0-8008-5063-7). Taplinger.

Making College Pay: How to Earn Money While You're Still in School. Jonathan E. Carson. LC 83-11903. 1983. pap. (ISBN 0-201-10820-8). Addison-Wesley.

Making Computers Work. Trevor J. Bentley. 158p. 1984. 22.00X o.p. (ISBN 0-8448-1485-7, Pub. by Crane Russak & Co). Taylor & Francis.

Making Decisions: Cases for Moral Discussion. Nancy F. Sizer. 166p. 1984. pap. text ed. 7.95 o.p. (ISBN 0-88334-176-X). Ind Sch Pr.

Making Decorative Planters: From Practically Anything. Jackie Vermeer & Marian L. Frew. LC 77-92755. 1978. 9.95 o.p.; pap. 4.95 o.s.i. (ISBN 0-8008-5066-1). Taplinger.

Making Desegregation Work. Mark A. Chesler et al. (Sage Human Services Guides Ser.: Vol. 23). 160p. 1981. 9.95 o.p. (ISBN 0-8039-1725-2). Sage.

Making Dolls. Carol Nicklaus. (Easy-Read Activity Bks.). (Illus.). 32p. (gr. 1-3). 1981. lib. bdg. 9.40 o.p. (ISBN 0-531-04309-6). Watts.

Making Ethical Decisions. Howard C. Kee. (Layman's Theological Library). 1957. pap. 1.45 o.s.i. (ISBN 0-664-24008-9, Westminster). Westminster John Knox.

Making Evaluations Useful to Congress. Ed. by Leonard Saxe. LC 81-48578. (Program Evaluation Ser.: No. 14). 1982. pap. text ed. 12.95x o.p. (ISBN 0-87589-916-1). Jossey-Bass.

Making Evangelism Personal, Pt. 1. G. Michael Cocoris. 56p. (Orig.). 1984. pap. text ed. 1.00 o.p. (ISBN 0-935729-16-X). Church Open Door.

Making Evangelsim Personal, Pt. 2. G. Michael Cocoris. 41p. (Orig.). 1984. pap. text ed. 1.00 o.p. (ISBN 0-935729-17-8). Church Open Door.

Making Experience Pay: Management Success Through Effective Learning. Alan Mumford. 184p. 1981. text ed. 29.95 o.p. (ISBN 0-07-084536-0). McGraw.

Making Experience Work: The Grid Approach to Critique. Robert R. Blake & Jane S. Mouton. (Illus.). 1977. text ed. 21.50 o.p. (ISBN 0-07-005675-7). McGraw.

Making Floral Designs. Pamela Woods. (Illus.). 120p. 1984. 24.95 o.p. (ISBN 0-7134-4225-5, Pub. by Batsford England). David & Charles.

Making Friends: Ways of Encouraging Social Development in Young Children. Don Adcock & Marilyn Segal. (Illus.). 192p. 1983. 14.95 o.p. (ISBN 0-13-547174-5); pap. 6.95 o.p. (ISBN 0-13-547166-4). P-H.

Making Friends with AppleWriter II. Ellen Thro. (Illus.). 160p. 1984. pap. 16.95 o.p. (ISBN 0-13-547183-4). P-H.

Making Game: An Essay on Woodcock. Guy De la Valdene. (Illus.). 204p. 1985. 20.00 o.s.i. (ISBN 0-932558-26-7). Willow Creek Pr.

Making Gifts with Food. Sonia Allison. (Illus.). 64p. 1982. 9.95 o.p. (ISBN 0-7153-8264-0). David & Charles.

Making Happiness Happen. Leith Anderson. 132p. 1987. pap. 5.95 o.p. (ISBN 0-89693-776-3). Victor Bks.

Making High Profits in Uncertain Times: Successful Investing in Inflation & Depression. Robert M. Barnes. 208p. 1982. 29.95 o.p. (ISBN 0-442-21299-2). Van Nos Reinhold.

Making It Big in the City: A Woman's Guide to Living, Loving, & Working There. Peggy Schmidt. (Paperbacks Ser.). 288p. 1984. pap. text ed. 6.95 o.p. (ISBN 0-07-055357-2). McGraw.

Making It in America: Life & Times of Rocky Aoki, Benihana's Pioneer. Jack McCallum. (Illus.). 208p. 1985. 15.95 o.p. (ISBN 0-396-08560-1). Dodd.

Making It in Cable TV: Career Opportunities in Today's Fastest-Growing Media Industry. Joshua Sapan. 128p. 1984. 14.95 o.p. (ISBN 0-399-51030-3, Perigee); pap. 7.95 o.p. (ISBN 0-399-50836-8). Putnam Pub Group.

Making It Legal: A Law Primer for the Craftmaker, Visual Artist, & Writer. Marion Davidson & Martha Blue. (Illus.). 1979. pap. text ed. 8.95 o.p. (ISBN 0-07-015431-7). McGraw.

Making It New. Ed. by John Metcalf. (Contemporary Canadian Stories Ser.). 272p. 1983. pap. 13.95 o.p. (ISBN 0-458-95470-5, NO. 3891). Routledge Chapman & Hall.

Making It on Your First Job: When You're Young, Inexperienced & Ambitious. Peggy J. Schmidt. 272p. 1985. pap. 5.95 o.p. (ISBN 0-380-89519-6). Avon.

Making It on Your Own: The American Dream. S. Norman Feingold & Leonard Perlman. 225p. 1981. 12.50 o.p. (ISBN 0-87491-287-3); pap. 6.95 o.p. (ISBN 0-87491-288-1). Acropolis.

Making It Through Middle Age: Notes While in Transit. William Attwood. LC 81-69157. (Illus.). 256p. 1982. 12.95 o.s.i. (ISBN 0-689-11268-8, Atheneum). Macmillan.

Making It Together: As a Career Couple. Morton H. Shaevitz & Marjorie H. Shaevitz. 1980. 8.95 o.p. (ISBN 0-395-28592-5). HM.

Making Jewelry & Sculpture Through Unit Construction. Patricia Meyerowitz. 11.25 o.p. (ISBN 0-8446-5794-8). Peter Smith.

Making Lampshades. Jim Crowhurst. 36p. (Orig.). 1985. pap. 5.95 o.p. (ISBN 0-86417-013-0, Pub. by Kangaroo Pr). Intl Spec Bk.

Making Love Work. John Button. 160p. 1985. pap. 7.95 o.p. (ISBN 0-85500-206-9). Newcastle Pub.

Making Match Play Pay Off. rev. ed. Lon W. Ramsey. LC 87-2550. (Illus.). 40p. 1987. pap. text ed. 3.95 o.p. Pilot Bks.

Making Mead (Honey Wine) History, Recipes, Methods. Roger A. Morse. (Illus.). 128p. 3.95 o.s.i. (ISBN 0-684-17330-1, ScribT). Scribner.

Making Medical Choices: Ethics & Medicine in a Technological Age. Jane J. Stein. 1978. 10.95 o.p. (ISBN 0-395-27086-3). HM.

Making Miniature Toys & Dolls. Jean Greenhowe. (Illus.). 120p. 1985. pap. 15.95 o.p. (ISBN 0-7134-0799-9, Pub. by Batsford England). David & Charles.

Making Money. Howard Ruff. 904p. 1986. pap. 8.95 o.p. (ISBN 0-671-61441-X, Fireside). S&S.

Making Money: Rogues & Rascals Who Made Their Own. Edward C. Rochette. LC 86-22120. (Illus.). 150p. (Orig.). 1986. pap. 9.95 o.p. (ISBN 0-939650-25-8). R H Pub.

Making Money: Winning the Battle for Middle-Class Financial Success. Howard Ruff. 1984. 17.45 o.p. (ISBN 0-671-50398-7). S&S.

Making Money with Your Home Computer. Dana K. Cassell. LC 84-15329. 128p. 1984. pap. 5.95 o.p. (ISBN 0-396-08448-6). Dodd.

Making Money with Your Microcomputer. 2nd ed. Howard Parmington. (Illus.). 208p. (Orig.). 1985. 16.95 o.p. (ISBN 0-8306-0969-5, 1969); pap. 10.60 o.p. (ISBN 0-8306-1969-0). Tab Bks.

Making Movies: From Script to Screen. Lee R. Bobker. 304p. 1973. pap. text ed. 14.95 o.p. (ISBN 0-15-554630-9, HC). HarBraceJ.

Making Music: An Introduction to Theory. Alvin Etler. (Illus.). 216p. 1974. pap. text ed. 10.95 o.p. (ISBN 0-15-554635-X, HC). HarBraceJ.

Making Music: The Guide to Writing, Performing & Recording. Ed. by George Martin. (Illus.). 352p. 1983. 17.95 o.p. (ISBN 0-688-01465-8). Morrow.

Making News. Martin Mayer. LC 86-19887. 360p. 1987. 18.95 o.p. (ISBN 0-385-18983-4). Doubleday.

Making of a Coast Guard Officer. Joseph H. Hughes, Jr. LC 65-26682. 412p. 1966. (ISBN 0-8022-0757-X). Philos Lib.

Making of a Cowboy. Vern C. Mortensen. LC 84-90172. 158p. 1985. 11.95 o.p. (ISBN 0-533-06233-0). Vantage.

Making of a Dance. Thomas Victor. 1976. 15.00 o.p. (ISBN 0-03-016866-X); pap. 8.95 o.p. (ISBN 0-03-016861-9). H Holt & Co.

Making of a Don. Frederick M. Notarianni. 159p. 1981. 9.00 o.p. (ISBN 0-682-49685-5). Exposition-Phoenix.

Making of a Midsummer Night's Dream: An Eye-Witness Account of Peter Brook's Production from First Rehearsal to First Night. Ed. by David Selbourne. (Illus.). 327p. 1983. 29.95 o.p. (ISBN 0-413-49720-8, NO. 3828). Heinemann Ed.

Making of a Model Citizen in Communist China. Charles P. Ridley et al. LC 73-170203. (Publications Ser.: No. 103). (Illus.). 403p. 1971. 12.95x o.p. (ISBN 0-8179-6031-7). Hoover Inst Pr.

Making of a Pilot. Ed. by Richter. (Illus.). 1966. 3.75 o.s.i. (ISBN 0-664-32378-2, Westminster). Westminster John Knox.

Making of a Prophet. Lindsay Curtis. 1974. pap. 3.95 o.p. (ISBN 0-89036-035-9). Hawkes Pub Inc.

Making of a Psychiatrist. David Viscott. LC 72-8210. 1972. 8.95 o.p. (ISBN 0-87795-049-0, Arbor Hse). Morrow.

Making of a Psychiatrist. David Viscott. LC 72-8210. (Priam Ser.). 1979. pap. 9.95 o.p. (ISBN 0-87795-240-X, Arbor Hse). Morrow.

Making of a Psychiatrist. David Viscott. 1983. pap. 7.95 cancelled o.p. (ISBN 0-686-47188-1, Arbor Hse). Morrow.

Making of a Public Man. Sol M. Linowitz. 288p. 19.95 o.p. (ISBN 0-316-52689-4). Little.

Making of a Stormtrooper. Peter H. Merkl. LC 79-3223. 1980. 25.00 o.p. (ISBN 0-691-07620-0). Princeton U Pr.

Making of a Woman Veterinarian. Sally Haddock & Kathy Matthews. 1985. 16.45 o.p. (ISBN 0-671-49967-X). S&S.

Making of a Writer: A Christian Writer's Guide. Sherwood E. Wirt. LC 87-1099. 160p. (Orig.). 1987. pap. 8.95 o.p. (ISBN 0-8066-2269-5, 10-4263, Augsburg). Augsburg Fortress.

Making of an American: An Adaptation of Memorable Tales by Charles Sealsfield. Ulrich S. Carrington. LC 74-77736. (No. 2). 224p. 1974. 14.95x o.p. (ISBN 0-87074-143-8). SMU Press.

Making of an Opera. John Higgins. LC 78-55609. (Illus.). 1978. 12.95 o.p. (ISBN 0-689-10906-7, Atheneum). Macmillan.

Making of Black America, 2 vols. Ed. by August Meier & Elliott M. Rudwick. LC 67-25486. (Studies in American Negro Life). (Orig.). 1969. Vol. 1: The Origins Of Black Americans. pap. text ed. 4.95x o.p. (ISBN 0-689-70141-1, NL8A, Atheneum); Vol. 2: The Black Community In Modern America. pap. text ed. 5.95x o.p. (ISBN 0-689-70143-8, NL8B). Macmillan.

Making of Britian: Middle Ages. Date not set. (ISBN 0-8052-3957-X). Random.

Making of Geography. Robert E. Dickinson & O. J. R. Howarth. LC 75-38379. 1976. Repr. of 1933 ed. lib. bdg. 22.50x o.p. (ISBN 0-8371-8669-2, DIMG). Greenwood.

Making of Israel. James Cameron. LC 77-76041. (Illus.). 1977. 7.95 o.s.i. (ISBN 0-8008-5084-X). Taplinger.

Making of Jazz: A Comprehensive History. James L. Collier. 1978. 20.00 o.p. (ISBN 0-395-26286-0). HM.

Making of Man. Kenneth Walker. 1963. 14.95 o.p. (ISBN 0-7100-2248-4). Routledge Chapman & Hall.

Making of Mark Twain. John Lauber. LC 85-6169. (Illus.). 310p. 1985. 17.95 o.p. (ISBN 0-8281-1185-5, Dist. by HM). Am Heritage.

Making of Medieval Spain. Gabriel Jackson. LC 73-151307. (History of European Civilization Library). (Illus.). 216p. 1972. pap. text ed. 6.95 o.p. (ISBN 0-15-554642-2, HC). HarBraceJ.

Making of Modern English Society. Janet Roebuck. 1983. pap. 9.95x o.p. (ISBN 0-7100-0415-X). Routledge Chapman & Hall.

Making of Music. Ralph Vaughan Williams. 61p. Repr. of 1955 ed. lib. bdg. 39.00 o.p. (Pub. by Am Repr Serv). Reprint Servs.

Making of 'No, No, Nanette' Donald H. Dunn. (Illus.). 284p. 1972. 7.95 o.p. (ISBN 0-8065-0265-7, Pub. by Citadel Pr). Carol Pub Group.

Making of Raiders of the Lost Ark. Derek Taylor. 192p. 1981. pap. 2.75 o.s.i. (ISBN 0-345-29725-3). Ballantine.

Making of Superstars: The Artists & Executives of the Rock Music World. Robert S. Spitz. LC 76-56338. 1978. 8.95 o.p. (ISBN 0-385-12413-9, Anchor Pr); pap. 2.95 o.p. (ISBN 0-385-06663-5). Doubleday.

Making of the Dark Crystal. Christopher Finch. (Illus.). 96p. 1983. pap. 10.95 o.p. (ISBN 0-03-063332-X). H Holt & Co.

Making of the Dutch Landscape: An Historical Geography of the Netherlands. A. M. Lambert. LC 70-162378. 424p. 1971. 44.00 o.p. (ISBN 0-12-785450-9). Acad Pr.

Making of the Living Planet. Andrew Langley. (Illus.). 1986. 22.50 o.p. (ISBN 0-316-51405-5). Little.

Making of the Parson Jack Russell Terrier. Jean Jackson & Frank Jackson. 192p. 1986. 22.00 o.p. (ISBN 0-85115-436-0, Pub. by Boydell & Brewer). Longwood Pub Group.

Making of the President Nineteen Sixty. Theodore H. White. LC 79-25849. (gr. 10 up). 1961. 10.00 o.p. (ISBN 0-689-10291-7, Atheneum). Macmillan.

Making of the President Nineteen Sixty-Eight. Theodore H. White. LC 78-81935. 1969. 10.00 o.s.i. (ISBN 0-689-10293-3, Atheneum). Macmillan.

Making of the Return of the Jedi. Ed. by John P. Peecher. 288p. 1983. pap. 3.50 o.s.i. (ISBN 0-345-31235-X, Del Rey). Ballantine.

Making of the Return of the Native. John Paterson. LC 77-18909. (University of California Publications English Ser.: No. 19). 1978. Repr. of 1963 ed. lib. bdg. 24.75x o.p. (ISBN 0-313-20064-5, PAMR). Greenwood.
Making of the South Australian Landscape: A Study in the Historical Geography of South Australia. M. Williams. 1974. 96.00 o.p. (ISBN 0-12-785955-1). Acad Pr.
Making of the Wizard of Oz: Movie Magic & Studio Power in the Prime of MGM & the Miracle of Production No. 1060. Aljean Harmetz. LC 83-27532. (Illus.). 352p. 1984. pap. 12.95 o.p. (ISBN 0-87910-000-1). Limelight Edns.
Making of Tocqueville's "Democracy in America" James T. Schleifer. LC 79-9976. xix, 387p. 1980. 35.00x o.p. (ISBN 0-8078-1372-9). U of NC Pr.
Making of Urban Scotland. Ian H. Adams. (Illus.). 1978. 25.00x o.p. (ISBN 0-7735-0329-3, McGill Canada). U of Toronto Pr.
Making Paragraphs Work. Thomas E. Gaston & Muriel Harris. LC 84-22357. 220p. 1985. pap. text ed. 12.95 o.p. (ISBN 0-03-059312-3, HoltC). HR&W.
Making Peace with Food: A Step-By-Step Guide to Freedom from Diet-Weight Conflict, with Index & Bibliography. Susan Kano. LC 85-71530. 224p. (Orig.). 1985. pap. 14.95 o.p. (ISBN 0-934011-85-0). Amity Pub Co.
Making Peace with Your Past. H. Norman Wright. 1984. 10.95 o.p. (ISBN 0-8007-1228-5). Revell.
Making Performance Appraisals Work for You. 2nd rev. ed. 1976. 10.50 o.p. (ISBN 0-8144-6956-6). AMACOM.
Making Pollution Prevention Pay: Ecology with Economy As Policy. Ed. by Donald Huisingh & Vicki Bailey. 168p. 1982. 40.00 o.p. (ISBN 0-08-029417-0). Pergamon.
Making School-Centered INSET Work: A School of Education Pack for Teachers. Patrick Easen. LC 84-23078. 198p. (Orig.). 1985. pap. 13.50 o.p. (ISBN 0-7099-1945-X, Pub. by Croom Helm). Routledge Chapman & Hall.
Making Science Laboratory Equipment: A Manual for Students & Teachers in Developing Countries. Xavier Carelse. LC 82-8625. 273p. 1983. 42.95 o.p. (ISBN 0-471-10353-5, Pub. by Wiley-Interscience). Wiley.
Making Scripture Yours. David Mains. (Chapel Talks Ser.). 64p. 0.95 o.p. (ISBN 0-89191-272-X, 52720). Cook.
Making Sense of Our World: A Guide to Reading the Bible. Alan Dale. 1972. 3.50 o.p. (ISBN 0-8192-1219-9). Morehouse Pub.
Making Sense of Piaget: The Philosophical Roots. Christine Atkinson. 200p. 1984. 24.95X o.p. (ISBN 0-7100-9580-5). Routledge Chapman & Hall.
Making Sense of Sex. Helen S. Kaplan. 1979. 10.95 o.p. (ISBN 0-671-25131-7). S&S.
Making Seventy-Thousand Dollars a Year As a Self-Employed Manufacturer's Representative. Leigh Silliphant & Sureleigh Silliphant. LC 83-16147. 205p. 1983. 18.95 o.p. (ISBN 0-13-547687-9, Busn); pap. 6.95 o.p. (ISBN 0-13-547679-8). P-H.
Making Silver Jewelry. Peter Edwards. (Illus.). 144p. 1983. 30.95 o.p. (ISBN 0-7134-2580-6, Pub. by Batsford England). David & Charles.
Making Sneakers. Bruce McMillan. (Illus.). (gr. k-3). 1980. pap. 6.95 o.p. (ISBN 0-395-29161-5). HM.
Making Space Grow. Barbara Taylor Bradford. (Illus.). 1979. 14.95 o.s.i. (ISBN 0-671-22473-5). S&S.
Making Successful Presentations. George T. Vardaman. 320p. 1981. 19.95 o.p. (ISBN 0-8144-5694-4). AMACOM.
Making the Best Deal: Your Car. Tony Chiu. 1986. pap. 4.95 o.p. (ISBN 0-671-60675-1, Fireside). S&S.
Making the Best Deal: Your Health & Wealth. Tony Chiu. 1986. pap. 4.95 o.p. (ISBN 0-671-60677-8, Fireside). S&S.
Making the Best Deal: Your Home. Tony Chiu. 1986. pap. 4.95 o.p. (ISBN 0-671-60676-X, Firside). S&S.
Making the Collective Bargaining Agreement Work see Issues in the Public Employee Relations Library: Series 2.
Making the Connections: Essays in Feminist Social Ethics. Beverly W. Harrison. Intro. by Carol S. Robb. LC 84-45718. (Illus.). 352p. 1985. 22.95x o.p. (ISBN 0-8070-1524-5). Beacon Pr.
Making the Future Work: Unleashing Our Powers of Innovation for the Decades Ahead. John Diebold. 470p. 1984. 18.45 o.p. (ISBN 0-671-45657-1). S&S.
Making the Good News Relevant: Keeping the Gospel Distinctive in Any Culture. Morris A. Inch. LC 86-746. 128p. 1986. pap. 8.95 o.p. (ISBN 0-8407-7540-7). Nelson.
Making the Most of Fruit on Foodservice Menus. Ed. by Jule Wilkinson. LC 76-51342. (Foodservice Menu Planning Ser.). (Illus.). 256p. 1983. 19.95 o.p. (ISBN 0-8436-2150-8). Van Nos Reinhold.
Making the Most of Management Consulting Services. Jerome H. Fuchs. LC 74-6808. 224p. 1975. 15.95 o.p. (ISBN 0-8144-5371-6). AMACOM.
Making the Most of Your First Job. Catalyst Staff. 240p. 1982. pap. 2.75 o.s.i. (ISBN 0-345-30160-9). Ballantine.
Making the Most of Your Greenhouse. Ian Walls. LC 77-90053. (Illus.). 1978. pap. 5.95 o.p. (ISBN 0-8120-0869-3). Barron.
Making the Most of Your Mind. Stephen B. Douglass & Lee Roddy. 250p. (Orig.). 1982. pap. 6.95 o.p. (ISBN 0-86605-109-0). Heres Life.
Making the Second Half the Best Half. Edmund W. Janss. LC 83-15779. 192p. (Orig.). 1983. pap. 4.95 o.p. (ISBN 0-87123-404-1, 210404). Bethany Hse.
Making the Words Stand Still: How to Rescue the Learning Disabled Child. Donald E. Lyman. (Illus.). 265p. 1986. 16.45 o.s.i. (ISBN 0-395-36219-9). HM.
Making the World Safe for Pornography. E. J. Mishan. LC 73-83001. 262p. 1973. 1.95 o.p. (ISBN 0-912050-41-1, Library Pr). Open Court.
Making Things, Bk. 2. Ann Wiseman. (Illus.). 176p. (gr. 5 up). 1975. 12.95o.p. (ISBN 0-316-94850-0); pap. 7.95 o.p. (ISBN 0-316-94851-9). Little.
Making Time: The Resourceful Woman's Guide to Delegating Household Tasks. Steve DiAntonio. (Orig.). 1986. pap. 5.95 o.p. (ISBN 0-345-32754-3). Ballantine.
Making Up the Difference: Help for Single Parents with Teenagers. George A. Rekers & Judson J. Swihart. 176p. 1984. pap. 6.95 o.p. (ISBN 0-8010-7726-5). Baker Bk.
Making Waves. A. C. Chandler. (Going For It Ser.: No. 1). 1985. pap. 2.50 o.p. (ISBN 0-380-89899-3). Avon.
Making Wood & Stone Jewelry. Jerry Lee. LC 77-76499. (Illus.). 1978. pap. 9.95 o.s.i. (ISBN 0-8008-5081-5). Taplinger.
Making Work. Nicholas Hinton. 24p. 1980. pap. text ed. 4.00x o.p. (ISBN 0-7199-1051-X, Pub. by Bedford England). Gower Pub Co.
Making Work More Human: Proceedings of the International Labour Office Conference, 60th Session, 1975. 2nd ed. International Labour Office Staff. 1978. 10.00 o.p. (ISBN 92-2-101514-9). Intl Labour Office.
Making Your Lawn & Garden Grow. Elvin McDonald. 1981. write for info. o.p. (ISBN 0-916752-07-0). Longman Trade.
Making Your Marriage Work. Mary Jensen & Andrew Jensen. LC 85-7528. 144p. 1985. pap. 6.95 o.p. (ISBN 0-8066-2124-9, 10-4265, Augsburg). Augsburg Fortress.
Makings of an Olympic Champion: A New Approach to Weight Training & Weight Lifting. Russell Wright. LC 76-22273. 1976. 10.00 o.p. (ISBN 0-682-48579-9, Banner). Exposition-Phoenix.
Makro & Mikro. Skachinsky. 1984. 7.95 o.s.i. RWCPH.
Makrookonomische Input-Output Analysen und Dynamische Modelle zur Erfassung Technischer Entwicklung. Ed. by Jurgen V. Seetzen et al. (Interdisciplinary Systems Research Ser.: No. 69). (Illus.). 314p. (Ger.). 1979. pap. 28.95 o.p. (ISBN 0-8176-1089-8). Birkhauser.
Mal Occhio: The Underside of Vision. Lawrence Di Stasi. LC 81-7. (Illus.). 160p. 1981. 17.50 o.s.i. (ISBN 0-86547-033-2). N Point Pr.
Malachi: Lessons for Today. W. A. Lickley. pap. 3.95 o.p. (ISBN 0-88172-114-X). Believers Bkshelf.
Malady of Death. Marguerite Duras. Tr. by Barbara Bray. LC 83-49427. 62p. 1986. 9.95 o.p. (ISBN 0-394-53866-8). Grove.
Malatesta. Henry De Montherlant. 1965. 13.25 o.p. (ISBN 0-685-11336-1). Schoenhof.
Malay Myths & Legends. Jan Knappert. (Writing in Asia Ser.). (Orig.). 1981. pap. text ed. 8.50x o.p. (ISBN 0-686-72738-X). Heinemann Ed.
Malay Politics in Malaysia: A Study of Umno & Pas. John Funston. 1981. pap. text ed. 13.50x o.p. (ISBN 0-686-31818-8, 00116). Heinemann Ed.
Malay Proverbs. rev. ed. Richard Winstedt. Ed. by Tan C. Kwang. 112p. (Malay & Eng.). 1981. pap. 7.50 o.s.i. (ISBN 9971-947-15-3, Pub. by Graham Brash Singapore). Three Continents.
Malayalam Short Stories: An Anthology. Ed. by K. Ayyappa Paniker. 175p. 1982. text ed. 17.95x o.p. (ISBN 0-7069-1297-7, Pub. by Vikas India). Advent NY.
Malays. Richard Winstedt. (ISBN 0-8022-1908-X). Philos Lib.
Malaysia & Singapore: The Building of New States. Stanley S. Bedlington. Ed. by G. M. Kahin. LC 77-3114. (Politics & International Relations of Southeast Asia Ser.). 304p. 1978. 32.50x o.p. (ISBN 0-8014-0910-1); pap. 10.95x o.p. (ISBN 0-8014-9864-3). Cornell U Pr.
Malaysia: Growth & Equity in a Multiracial Society. Kevin Young et al. LC 79-3677. (World Bank Country Economic Report Ser.). (Illus.). 368p. 1980. text ed. 28.95x o.p. (ISBN 0-8018-2384-6); pap. text ed. 12.95x o.p. (ISBN 0-8018-2385-4). Johns Hopkins.
Malaysia: Quest for Politics or Consensus. Kiran K. Datar. 272p. 1983. text ed. 27.50x o.p. (ISBN 0-7069-1972-6, Pub. by Vikas India). Advent NY.
Malaysia: Search for National Unity & Economic Growth. Sevinc Carlson. (Washington Papers: Vol. III, No. 25). 88p. (Orig.). 1975. pap. text ed. 7.95 o.p. (ISBN 0-8191-5981-6, Pub by CSIS). U Pr of Amer.
Malaysia, Singapore & Brunei-A Travel Survival Kit. 2nd ed. Geoff Crowther & Tony Wheeler. (Illus.). 296p. (Orig.). 1986. pap. 8.95 o.p. (ISBN 0-908086-65-2). Lonely Planet.
Malaysian Short Stories. Ed. by Lloyd Fernando. (Writing in Asia Ser.). xvii, 302p. (Orig.). 1981. pap. text ed. 7.50x o.p. (ISBN 0-686-79034-0, 00264). Heinemann Ed.
Malcolm. Edward A. Albee. LC 66-16352. (Illus.). 1966. 4.95 o.p. (ISBN 0-689-10003-5, Atheneum). Macmillan.
Malcolm Lowry. Ronald Binns. 96p. 1984. pap. 5.95 o.p. (ISBN 0-416-37750-5, NO. 9102). Routledge Chapman & Hall.
Malcolm X: The End of White World Supremacy. Ed. & intro. by Iman B. Karim. LC 83-12598. 160p. 1986. pap. 5.95 o.p. (ISBN 0-8050-0151-4). Seaver Bks.
Maldoror. Comte De Lautreamont & Isidore Ducasse. Tr. by John Rodker, from Fr. (Illus.). 310p. cancelled o.s.i. (ISBN 0-941194-26-4); pap. cancelled o.s.i. (ISBN 0-941194-25-6). Black Swan Pr.
Male Accessory Sex Organs: Structure & Function in Mammals. Ed. by David Brandes. 1974. 91.00 o.p. (ISBN 0-12-125650-2). Acad Pr.
Male & Female under Eighteen. Compiled by Nancy Larrick & Eve Merriam. (YA) (gr. 9-12). 1986. pap. 1.50 o.p. (ISBN 0-380-00711-8, 76448-2, Discus). Avon.
Male Experience. James A. Doyle. 336p. 1982. pap. text ed. write for info. o.p. (ISBN 0-697-06553-7). Wm C Brown.
Male-Female Achievement in Eight Learning Areas. National Assessment of Educational Progress Staff. (Across Learning Areas Ser.). 64p. 1975. 2.00 o.p. (ISBN 0-318-13994-4, ED-117-133, Natl Assessment Ed Progress). Ed Comm States.
Male-Female Continuum: Paths to Colleagueship. Carol Pierce & Bill Page. 52p. 1988. pap. text ed. 10.95 o.p. New Dynam Pubns.
Male: From Infancy to Old Age. Sherman J. Silber. (Illus.). 256p. 1981. encore ed. 2.95 o.p. (ISBN 0-684-17307-7, ScribT). Scribner.
Male: From Infancy to Old Age. Sherman J. Silber. 224p. 1982. pap. 2.95 o.s.i. (ISBN 0-684-17664-5, ScribT). Scribner.
Male Nurse. R. G. Brown. 139p. 1973. pap. text ed. 5.00x o.p. (ISBN 0-7135-1879-0, Pub. by Bedford England). Gower Pub Co.
Male Reproduction. Ed. by Brian P. Setchell. 416p. 1984. 49.95 o.p. (ISBN 0-442-28210-9). Van Nos Reinhold.
Male Sexual Function: Myth, Fantasy, Reality. Richard Milsten. 1979. pap. 2.50 o.p. (ISBN 0-380-44990-0, 44990-0). Avon.
Male Sexuality: A Guide to Sexual Fulfillment. Bernie Zilbergeld & John Ullman. 1978. 16.95 o.p. (ISBN 0-316-98792-1). Little.
Malentendu. Albert Camus. Bd. with Caligula. (Coll. Soleil). 6.95 o.p. (ISBN 0-685-37267-7). Schoenhof.
Malevolent Force. June M. Woodring. 1980. 10.00 o.p. (ISBN 0-682-49600-6). Exposition-Phoenix.
Malformed Fetus & Stillbirth: A Diagnostic Approach. Robin M. Winter et al. 1988. (ISBN 0-471-90946-7). Wiley.
Mali: A Handbook of Historical Statistics. Pascal J. Imperato & Eleanor M. Imperato. 1982. lib. bdg. 86.00 o.s.i. (ISBN 0-8161-8147-0, Hall Reference). G K Hall.
Malibu Summer. Stuart Buchan. 1986. pap. 4.50 o.s.i. (ISBN 0-671-55673-8). PB.
Malice in Blunderland. Thomas L. Martin, Jr. (McGraw-Hill Paperbacks Ser.). 156p. 1980. pap. text ed. 3.95 o.p. (ISBN 0-07-040634-0). McGraw.
Malice in Blunderland. Thomas L. Martin, Jr. LC 73-4376. 156p. 1973. text ed. 9.95 o.p. (ISBN 0-07-040617-0). McGraw.
Malignant Disease of the Vulva. Stanley Way. (Illus.). 83p. 1982. 27.75 o.p. (ISBN 0-443-02366-2). Churchill.
Malignant Transformation by Viruses. Ed. by W. H. Kirsten. (Recent Results in Cancer Research Ser.: Vol. 6). (Illus.). 1966. 35.95 o.p. (ISBN 0-387-03645-8). Springer-Verlag.
Malinowski in Mexico: The Economics of a Mexican Market System. Bronislaw Malinowski. Ed. by Susan Drucker-Brown & Julio De La Fuente. (International Library of Anthropology). 260p. 1982. 26.95x o.p. (ISBN 0-7100-9197-4). Routledge Chapman & Hall.
Mallory's Gambit. L. Christian Balling. LC 85-47785. 288p. 1985. 15.95 o.p. (ISBN 0-87113-024-6). Atlantic Monthly.
Malloy's Subway. R. Wright Campbell. LC 81-66021. 1981. 12.95 o.p. (ISBN 0-689-11181-9, Atheneum). Macmillan.
Malnutrition & Endemic Diseases: Their Effects on Education in the Developing Countries. Ed. by K. F. Smart. (Educational Research & Practice Ser.: No. 2). (Illus.). 135p. (Orig.). 1972. pap. 7.50 o.p. (U364, UNESCO). UNIPUB.
Malnutrition & Intellectual Development. J. D. Lloyd-Still. LC 76-17432. (Illus.). 202p. 1976. 19.50 o.p. (ISBN 0-88416-181-1). Year Bk Med.
Malnutrition & Mental Development in Man, 2 vols. Incl. Vol. 1. Ed. by Harold W. Hermann et al. 164p (ISBN 0-8422-7259-3); Vol. 2. Ed. by David J. Kallen et al. 169p. 1976. text ed. 21.50x ea. o.p. Irvington.
Malone Dies. Samuel Beckett. LC 56-8440. 1956. pap. 5.95 o.p. (ISBN 0-394-17028-8, E39, Ever). Grove.
Malpractice: A Guide to the Legal Rights of Doctors & Patients. Donald J. Flaster. 256p. 1983. 15.95 o.p. (ISBN 0-684-17903-2, ScribT). Scribner.
Malraux: Life & Work. Ed. by Martine Decaurcel. 1976. 12.95 o.p. (ISBN 0-15-156280-6). HarBraceJ.
Malsum. Gerald J. O'Hara. 320p. 1981. pap. 2.50 o.p. (ISBN 0-380-77289-2, 77289). Avon.
Malta. Nina Nelson. 1978. 29.95 o.p. (ISBN 0-7134-0941-X, Pub. by Batsford England). David & Charles.
Malta Travel Guide. (Berlitz Travel Guides). (Illus.). 1982. pap. 4.95 o.p. (ISBN 0-02-969360-8, Berlitz). Macmillan.
Malte, Joyau de la Mediterranee. E. Gerada-Azzopardi. (Illus., Fr.). 40.00 o.p. (ISBN 2-85518-054-6). E J Brill USA.
Maltese-English, English-Maltese Dictionary. P. Bugeja. 1982. pap. 17.50 o.p. E J Brill USA.
Maltese Falcon. Ed. by Richard J. Anobile. (Film Classics Library). (Illus.). 256p. 1974. pap. 5.50 o.p. (ISBN 0-380-01485-8, 19109-1, Flare). Avon.
Maltese Sangweech & Other Heroes. Bill Cardoso. LC 83-45501. 288p. 1984. 15.95 o.p. (ISBN 0-689-11443-5, Atheneum). Macmillan.
Mama. Gregorio M. Sierra. 1937. pap. 2.95x o.p. (ISBN 0-393-09456-1, NortonC). Norton.
Mama Mia Italian Cookbook. Angela Catanzaro. 1955. 5.95 o.p. (ISBN 0-87140-969-0). Liveright.
Mama's Italian Cooking. Gloria Cicciarella. 64p. 1985. 8.95 o.p. (ISBN 0-533-06596-8). Vantage.
Mammakarzinom. Ed. by C. Herfarth & M. Betzler. (Beitraege zur Onkologie: Contributions to Oncology: Vol. 22). (Illus.). viii, 142p. 1985. 33.50 o.p. (ISBN 3-8055-4035-3). S Karger.
Mammal Ecology. M. J. Delany. (Tertiary Level Biology Ser.). 1982. pap. 17.95 o.p. (ISBN 0-412-00091-1, NO. 5014, Pub. by Chapman & Hall England). Routledge Chapman & Hall.
Mammal Photography & Observation: A Practical Guide. L. J. Warner. 1979. 34.00 o.p. (ISBN 0-12-735650-9). Acad Pr.
Mammal Species of the World: A Taxonomic & Geographic Reference. Ed. by James H. Honacki & Kenneth E. Kinman. (Orig.). 1982. pap. 55.00 o.p. (ISBN 0-942924-00-2). Assn Syst Coll.
Mammalian Cell Hybridization I. A. Westerveld & G. Marin. (Illus.). 220p. 1973. text ed. 25.50x o.p. (ISBN 0-8422-7096-5). Irvington.
Mammalian Cell Hybridization, II. J. A. Lucy et al. (Illus.). 220p. 1973. text ed. 25.50x o.p. (ISBN 0-8422-7102-3). Irvington.
Mammalian Metabolism of Plant Xenobiotics. R. R. Scheline. 1979. 114.00 o.p. (ISBN 0-12-623350-0). Acad Pr.
Mammalian Mitochondrial Respiratory Chain. Walter W. Wainio. (Molecular Biology Ser.). 1971. 88.00 o.p. (ISBN 0-12-730650-1). Acad Pr.
Mammalian Olfaction: Reproductive Processes, & Behavior. Ed. by Richard L. Doty. 1976. 72.50 o.p. (ISBN 0-12-221250-9). Acad Pr.
Mammalian Oogenesis. Hannah Peters et al. 169p. 1972. text ed. 32.50x o.p. (ISBN 0-8422-7042-6). Irvington.
Mammalian Radiation Lethality: A Disturbance in Cellular Kinetics. Ed. by Victor P. Bond et al. 1965. 21.00 o.p. (ISBN 0-12-114150-0). Acad Pr.

Mammalian Sexual Behavior. D. Dewsbury. 1982. 55.95 o.p. (ISBN 0-87933-396-0). Van Nos Reinhold.

Mammals, Amphibians, & Reptiles of the Northeastern United States. Kenneth Chambers. LC 79-4338. (Illus.). 248p. 1979. 22.50 o.p. (ISBN 0-8018-2207-6). Johns Hopkins.

Mammals in Wyoming. Tim W. Clark & Mark S. Stromberg. Ed. by Joseph T. Collins. LC 86-33210. (Museum of Natural History Public Education Ser.: No. 10). (Illus.). xii, 308p. 1987. 25.00x o.p. (ISBN 0-89338-026-1); pap. 12.95 o.p. (ISBN 0-89338-025-3). U Pr of KS.

Mammals of the Eastern United States. 2nd ed. William J. Hamilton, Jr. & John O. Whitaker, Jr. LC 79-12920. (Handbooks of American History Ser.). (Illus.). 368p. 1979. 29.95x o.p. (ISBN 0-8014-1254-4). Cornell U Pr.

Mammals of the Southwest. E. Lendell Cockrum. LC 81-21834. 176p. 1982. 11.95 o.p. (ISBN 0-8165-0760-0); pap. 5.95 o.p. (ISBN 0-8165-0759-7). U of Ariz Pr.

Mammoth Wash Project, Hunter-Gatherer Adaptation in the Mountain Region of West-Central Arizona. (Research Ser.). 140p. pap. 5.00 o.p. (RS-34). Mus Northern Ariz.

Man. Robert Hicks & Richard Bewes. (Understanding Bible Truth Ser.). (Orig.). 1981. pap. 0.95 o.p. (ISBN 0-89840-025-2). Heres Life.

Man. A. DeSilva Mello. 736p. 1956. (ISBN 0-8022-1098-8). Philos Lib.

Man: A Journal of the Anarchist Ideal & Movement, Vols. 1-8, No. 4. 1970. Repr. of 1940 ed. lib. bdg. 140.00x o.p. (ISBN 0-8371-9195-5, MA00). Greenwood.

Man Against Himself. Karl A. Menninger. LC 38-5962. 1938. 15.00 o.p. (ISBN 0-15-156513-9). HarBraceJ.

Man Against the Mountain. Jim Hunter & Marshall Shelley. 1978. pap. 1.95 o.p. (ISBN 0-89191-143-X). Cook.

Man Alive! Dressing the Free Way. Charles Hix. 208p. 1984. 17.45 o.p. (ISBN 0-671-50085-6). S&S.

Man & Animals: Living, Working & Changing Together. David Anthony et al. LC 84-19501. (Univ. of Pennsylvania Museum Ser.). (Illus.). 80p. 1984. pap. 16.95 o.p. (ISBN 0-8122-0953-2). U of Pa Pr.

Man & Biologically Active Substances: Introduction to the Pharmacology of Health. 2nd ed. I. I. Brekhman. 90p. 1980. 23.00 o.p. (ISBN 0-08-023169-1); pap. 7.75 o.p. (ISBN 0-08-025524-8). Pergamon.

Man & Environment. W. Manshard & O. E. Fischnich. 108p. 1975. pap. 23.00 o.p. (ISBN 0-08-019673-X). Pergamon.

Man & Environment. Philip Sauvain. (Practical Geography Ser.: Bk. 3). (Illus.). 150p. 12.95 o.p. (ISBN 0-7175-0487-5). Dufour.

Man & Environmental Processes. K. J. Gregory & D. E. Walling. (Illus.). 300p. 1980. pap. text ed. 29.95 o.p. (ISBN 0-408-10740-5). Butterworth.

Man & Food. Magnus Pyke. 1970. pap. text ed. 3.95 o.p. (ISBN 0-07-050990-5). McGraw.

Man & Forest: A New Dimension in the Himalaya. K. M. Gupta. 349p. 1979. 15.00 o.p. (ISBN 0-88065-094-X, Pub. by Messers Today & Tomorrow Printers & Publishers). Scholarly Pubns.

Man & His Approach to God in John Duns Scotus. B. M. Bonansea. 258p. (Orig.). 1983. lib. bdg. 31.25 o.p. (ISBN 0-8191-3299-3); pap. text ed. 13.50 o.p. (ISBN 0-8191-3300-0). U Pr of Amer.

Man & His Environment: Proceedings of the Third International Banff Conference, May 1980, Vol. 3. M. F. Mohtadi. 1980. 69.00 o.p. (ISBN 0-08-025792-5). Pergamon.

Man & His Environment, Vol. 2: Proceedings of the Second Banff Conference. Ed. by M. F. Mohtadi. 216p. 1976. 57.00 o.p. (ISBN 0-08-019922-4). Pergamon.

Man & His Fictions: An Introduction to Fiction-Making, Its Forms & Uses. Alvin B. Kernan et al. 1973. pap. text ed. 10.95 o.p. (ISBN 0-15-554716-X, HC). HarBraceJ.

Man & His Technology. Engineering Concepts Curriculum Project, State University of New York Staff. (Illus.). 256p. 1973. text ed. 25.95 o.p. (ISBN 0-07-019510-2). McGraw.

Man & His Tragic Life. Laszlo Vatai. Tr. by Laszlo Keskemethy. 224p. 1955. Philos Lib.

Man & Me, M. D. Robert M. Lee. 1977. 12.50 o.p. (ISBN 0-682-48927-1). Exposition-Phoenix.

Man & Nature: An Anthropological Essay in Human Ecology. Richard A. Watson & Patty J. Watson. (Orig.). 1969. pap. text ed. 7.95 o.p. (ISBN 0-15-554725-9, HC). HarBraceJ.

Man & Number. Donald Smeltzer. (Illus.). (gr. 9 up). 1958. 10.95 o.s.i. (ISBN 0-87523-107-1). Emerson.

Man & Sea Warfare. Ed. by V. M. Grishanov. 226p. 1978. pap. 5.45 o.p. (ISBN 0-8285-0417-2, Pub. by Progress Pubs USSR). Imported Pubns.

Man & Socialism in Cuba: The Great Debate. Ed. by Bertram Silverman. LC 71-139327. 1971. pap. text ed. 3.75x o.p. (ISBN 0-689-70339-2, 195, Atheneum). Macmillan.

Man & Society in an Age of Reconstruction. Karl Mannheim. LC 40-13509. 1967. pap. 3.85 o.p. (ISBN 0-15-656920-5, HB119, Harv). HarBraceJ.

Man & Society in Iran. A. R. Arasteh. 1970. 35.00 o.p. (ISBN 90-04-00107-7). E J Brill USA.

Man & Technics. Oswald Spengler. 104p. Date not set. pap. 3.00 o.p. (ISBN 0-317-53256-1). Noontide.

Man & the Australian Environment. W. S. Hanley & M. J. Cooper. 362p. 1983. text ed. 22.00 o.p. (ISBN 0-07-072952-2). McGraw.

Man & the Environment. 2nd ed. Arthur S. Boughey. (Illus.). 480p. 1975. pap. text ed. write for info. o.p. (ISBN 0-02-312770-8, 31277). Macmillan.

Man & the Horse: An Illustrated History of Equestrian Apparel. Alexander McKay-Smith et al. (Illus.). 1985. 19.45 o.p. (ISBN 0-671-55520-0). S&S.

Man & the Living World. Karl Von Frisch. Tr. by Elsa B. Lowenstein. LC 62-16734. (Helen & Kurt Wolff Bk.). (Illus.). 1963. 8.95 o.p. (ISBN 0-15-156520-1). HarBraceJ.

Man & the Living World. Karl Von Frisch. Tr. by Elsa B. Lowenstein. LC 62-16734. (Illus.). 1965. pap. 1.65 o.p. (ISBN 0-15-656521-8, Harv). HarBraceJ.

Man & the Natural World: An Introduction to Life Science. 2nd ed. Coleman J. Goin & Olive B. Goin. (Illus.). 672p. 1975. text ed. write for info. o.p. (ISBN 0-02-344240-9, 34424). Macmillan.

Man & the Winds. De la Rue. (Illus.). 180p. 1956. (ISBN 0-8022-1408-8). Philos Lib.

Man & This Mysterious Universe. Brynjolf Bjorset. 1953. (ISBN 0-8022-0136-9). Philos Lib.

Man & Two Women. Doris Lessing. 320p. 1984. pap. 9.95 o.s.i. (ISBN 0-671-54190-0, Touchstone Bks). S&S.

Man & Woman: Inside Homo Sapiens. Gabrielle Edwards. 116p. (gr. 7-12). 10.97 o.p. (ISBN 0-8239-0445-8). Rosen Group.

Man & Woman: The Basics of Sex & Marriage. Karl H. Wrage. Tr. by Stanley S. Gilder. LC 72-84540. (Prog. Bk.). 1969. 1.00 o.p. (ISBN 0-8006-0297-8, Fortress). Augsburg Fortress.

Man & World in the Light of Anthroposophy. Rev. ed. Stewart C. Easton. 536p. 1982. pap. 18.00 o.p. (ISBN 0-88010-006-0). Anthroposophic.

Man & World in the Light of Anthroposophy. 2nd ed. Stewart C. Easton. 543p. 1982. pap. 21.00 o.p. (ISBN 0-88010-077-X). Anthroposophic.

Man Answers Death. Corliss Lamont. 1952. (ISBN 0-8022-0908-4). Philos Lib.

Man: Ape or Image. rev. ed. John Rendel-Short. LC 84-60864. 1984. pap. 7.95 o.p. (ISBN 0-89051-110-1). Master Bks.

Man As Art. Malcolm Kirk. (Illus.). 120p. (Orig.). 1987. pap. 16.95 o.p. (ISBN 0-317-56518-4). Parkwest Pubns.

Man As Big As the West: The Ralph Hubbard Story. Nellie S. Yost. LC 79-20068. 1979. 11.95 o.p. (ISBN 0-87108-543-7). Pruett.

Man As He Is, 4 vols. Robert Bage & Ronald Paulson. LC 78-60853. (Novel 1720-1805 Ser.: Vol. 12). 1979. Set. lib. bdg. 150.00 o.p. (ISBN 0-8240-3661-1). Garland Pub.

Man at His Best: The Esquire Guide to Style. Esquire Magazine Editors. (Illus.). 1985. 24.95 o.p. (ISBN 0-201-11989-7). Addison-Wesley.

Man at Work. L. Blyakhman & O. Shkaratan. 306p. 1977. 4.95 o.p. (ISBN 0-8285-0242-0, Pub. by Progress Pubs USSR). Imported Pubns.

Man Born to Be King. Dorothy L. Sayers. 343p. 1983. 19.95 o.p. (ISBN 0-575-00366-9, Pub. by Gollancz England). David & Charles.

Man Called Dundee. Leo P. Kelly. (Double D Western Ser.). 192p. 1988. 12.95 o.s.i. (ISBN 0-385-24182-8). Doubleday.

Man Called Intrepid: The Secret War. William Stevenson. Tr. by John Moore. LC 75-30730. (Illus.). 486p. 1976. 15.95 o.p. (ISBN 0-15-156795-6). HarBraceJ.

Man, Cancer & Immunity. Alister Cochran. 1978. 46.00 o.p. (ISBN 0-12-177550-X). Acad Pr.

Man: Christian Anthropology in the Conflicts of the Present. Jurgen Moltmann. Tr. by John Sturdy from Ger. LC 73-88350. 136p. (Orig.). 1974. pap. 3.50 o.p. (ISBN 0-8006-1066-0, 1-1066, Fortress). Augsburg Fortress.

Man-Computer Communication, 2 vols. Shackel. (Infotech Computer State of the Art Reports Ser.). 600p. 1979. Set. 61.00x o.p. (ISBN 0-08-028522-8). Pergamon.

Man Descending. Guy Vanderhaeghe. LC 85-2758. 240p. 1985. pap. 7.70 o.s.i. (ISBN 0-89919-385-4, Dist. by HM). Ticknor & Fields.

Man East & West: Essays in East-West Philosophy. Howard L. Parsons. (Philosophical Currents Ser: No. 8). 211p. 1975. pap. text ed. 22.50x o.p. (ISBN 90-6032-020-4). Humanities.

Man-Food Equation. Ed. by F. Steele & A. Bourne. 1976. 68.00 o.p. (ISBN 0-12-664850-6). Acad Pr.

Man for Others: Maximilian Kolbe in the Words of Those Who Knew Him. Patricia Treece. LC 82-48404. (Illus.). 192p. 1983. 12.45i o.p. (ISBN 0-06-067069-X). HarpR.

Man Friday & Mind Your Head. Adrian Mitchell. 1981. pap. 6.95 o.p. (ISBN 0-413-31820-6, NO. 6479). Heinemann Ed.

Man from Himself: An Inquiry into the Psychology of Ethics. Erich Fromm. 1947. 7.95 o.p. (ISBN 0-03-025530-9); pap. 4.95 o.p. (ISBN 0-03-018431-2). H Holt & Co.

Man From Nowhere. T. V. Olsen. 144p. 1987. pap. 2.75 o.p. (ISBN 0-380-75293-X). Avon.

Man from the U. S. S. R. & Other Plays. Vladimir Nabokov. Tr. by Dmitri Nabokov. LC 84-10862. (HBJ-Bruccoli Clark Bk.). 352p. 1984. 24.95 o.p. (ISBN 0-15-156882-0). HarBraceJ.

Man from the Valley: Memoirs of a Twentieth Century Virginian. Francis P. Miller. LC 71-132255. xviii, 253p. 1971. 10.95x o.p. (ISBN 0-8078-1161-0). U of NC Pr.

Man, God, & Civilization. John G. Jackson. 1972. 10.00 o.p. (ISBN 0-8216-0113-X, Pub. by Univ Bks). Carol Pub Group.

Man in a Wire Cage. Mark Perakh. 520p. (Orig.). 1988. pap. 4.50 o.p. (ISBN 1-55547-257-5). Critics Choice Paper.

Man in Africa: From the Earliest Beginnings to the Coming of Metal see Tarikh.

Man in Aspic. Constantine FitzGibbon. 1977. 8.95 o.p. (ISBN 0-393-08769-7). Norton.

Man in Ecological Perspective. Ed. by James Metress. 1972. 29.50x o.p. (ISBN 0-8422-5022-0); pap. text ed. 12.50x o.p. (ISBN 0-8422-0125-4). Irvington.

Man in His Prime. Z. Skujins. 288p. 1981. 6.00 o.p. (Pub. by Progress Pubs USSR). Imported Pubns.

Man in Nature & His Behavior. J. N. Martinez. 1951. Philos Lib.

Man in Qur'an & the Meaning of Furqan. Shaykh F. Haeri. 210p. 1987. pap. 18.95 o.p. (ISBN 0-7103-0223-1, Pub. by Routledge UK). Routledge Chapman & Hall.

Man in Search of Immortality. C. R. Salit. 192p. 1958. (ISBN 0-8022-1471-1). Philos Lib.

Man in the Black Coat Turns. Robert Bly. LC 81-3153. 1981. 10.95 o.p. (ISBN 0-385-27186-7, Dial). Doubleday.

Man in the Blue Vest: And Other Stories. W. Gunther Plaut. LC 79-23762. 157p. 1980. 8.95 o.s.i. (ISBN 0-8008-5983-9). Taplinger.

Man in the Cage. Jack Vance. 200p. 1983. lib. bdg. 15.00 o.p. (ISBN 0-934438-82-X). Underwood-Miller.

Man in the Gray Flannel Suit. Sloan Wilson. LC 83-70463. 356p. 1983. 16.95 o.p. (ISBN 0-87795-474-7, Arbor Hse); pap. 8.95 o.p. (ISBN 0-87795-553-0). Morrow.

Man in the Holocene. Max Frisch. Tr. by Geoffrey Skelton. LC 79-3351. (Helen & Kurt Wolff Bk.). 120p. 1980. 9.95 o.p. (ISBN 0-15-156931-2). HarBraceJ.

Man in the Leather Hat. Paul B. Long. 128p. 1986. text ed. 9.95 o.p. (ISBN 0-8010-5631-4). Baker Bk.

Man in the Maze. Robert Silverberg. 192p. 1978. pap. 2.50 o.p. (ISBN 0-380-00198-5). Avon.

Man in the Natural World. Ed. by Irwin Ting. 1973. 29.50x o.p. (ISBN 0-8422-5135-9); pap. text ed. 9.95x o.p. (ISBN 0-8422-0315-X). Irvington.

Man Inside... Landry, Bob St. John. 1981. pap. 2.75 o.p. (ISBN 0-380-56481-5, 56481-5). Avon.

Man into Superman: The Startling Potential of Human Evolution... & How to Be a Part of It. R. C. Ettinger. 1974. pap. 1.50 o.p. (ISBN 0-380-00047-4, 19588). Avon.

Man into Wolf. Robert Eisler. 1952. (ISBN 0-8022-0443-0). Philos Lib.

Man Jumps Out of An Airplane. Barry Yourgrau. 1984. 7.00 o.p. (ISBN 0-915342-46-4). Sun.

Man-Machine Systems: Proceedings of the International Conference, Manchester, UK, July 1982. International Conference on Man-Machine Systems Staff. (IEE Conference Publications: No. 212). 280p. 1982. pap. 70.00 o.p. (ISBN 0-85296-264-9, IC212). Inst Elect Eng.

Man-Made Fibers: Science & Technology, Vols. 2 & 3. H. F. Mark et al. LC 67-13954. 1968p. 1968. 44.50 o.p. (ISBN 0-89874-521-7); Vol. 2, 504 pp. 44.50 o.p.; Vol. 3, 718pp. 64.50 o.p.; Vol. 4. 44.50 o.p. (ISBN 0-89874-524-1); Vol 5. 44.50 o.p. (ISBN 0-89874-525-X). Krieger.

Man-Made Gemstones. Dennis Elwell. LC 78-41291. 191p. 1979. 79.95x o.p. (ISBN 0-470-26606-6). Halsted Pr.

Man-Made Landscape. Ed. by W. Tietze. 100p. 1975. pap. 23.00 o.p. (ISBN 0-08-019667-5). Pergamon.

Man Made Language. 2nd ed. Dale Spender. 264p. 1985. 19.95x o.p. (ISBN 0-7102-0605-4); pap. 9.95 o.p. (ISBN 0-7102-0315-2). Routledge Chapman & Hall.

Man-Made Radio Noise. Edward N. Skomal. 1978. 39.95 o.p. (ISBN 0-442-27648-6). Van Nos Reinhold.

Man-Made Sun: The Quest for Fusion Power. T. A. Heppenheimer. (Illus.). 320p. 1984. 19.45 o.p. (ISBN 0-316-35793-6, 357936). Little.

Man Meets Grizzly: Encounters in the Wild from Lewis & Clark to Modern Times. Coralie M. Beyers. Ed. by F. M. Young. 1980. 10.95 o.p. (ISBN 0-395-29194-1). HM.

Man Named East: And Other New Poems. Peter Redgrove. 160p. (Orig.). 1985. pap. 9.95 o.p. (ISBN 0-7102-0014-5). Routledge Chapman & Hall.

Man Named Tony. Stuart Brown. (Illus.). 1976. 8.95 o.p. (ISBN 0-393-08707-7). Norton.

Man, Nature & Art. R. Wheeler. 1968. 35.00 o.p. (ISBN 0-08-012690-1); pap. 9.25 o.p. (ISBN 0-08-012689-8). Pergamon.

Man of Fire: J. C. Orozco, an Interpretive Memoir. MacKinley Helm. LC 79-106689. (Illus.). 1971. Repr. of 1953 ed. lib. bdg. 23.50x o.p. (ISBN 0-8371-3361-0, HEJO). Greenwood.

Man of Galilee. Clifford Stevens. LC 79-88086. (gr. 6-10). 1979. pap. 1.25 o.p. (ISBN 0-87973-302-0). Our Sunday Visitor.

Man of Glass. Donald Zochert. LC 81-47466. (Nick Caine Adventure Ser.). 264p. 1982. 12.95 o.p. (ISBN 0-03-056222-8). H Holt & Co.

Man of Honor: The Autobiography of Joseph Bonanno. Joseph Bonanno & Sergeo Lalli. 416p. 1983. 17.25 o.p. (ISBN 0-671-46747-6). S&S.

Man of Middle Age. Patricia Zelver. LC 79-1929. 228p. 1980. 12.95 o.p. (ISBN 0-03-048986-5). H Holt & Co.

Man of Nazareth. Anthony Burgess. 1979. text ed. 10.95 o.p. (ISBN 0-07-008962-0). McGraw.

Man of Property. D. S. Mayleas. 1983. text ed. 16.95 o.p. (ISBN 0-07-041208-1). McGraw.

Man of the Desert. Grace L. Hill. 296p. 1986. pap. 10.95 o.p. (ISBN 0-8161-3961-X). G K Hall.

Man of the Family. Ralph Moody. (Illus.). 1978. 8.95 o.p. (ISBN 0-393-07536-2, Norton Lib); pap. 3.95 o.p. (ISBN 0-393-00902-5). Norton.

Man of Two Revolutions: The Story of Justo Gonzales. Floyd Shacklock. 1969. pap. 0.95 o.p. (ISBN 0-377-84161-7). Friendship Pr.

Man of Two Worlds. Frank Herbert & Brian Herbert. 408p. 1986. 18.95 o.p. (ISBN 0-399-13132-9). Putnam Pub Group.

Man on a Donkey. H. F. Prescott. 640p. 1981. pap. 9.95 o.p. (ISBN 0-02-023830-4, Collier). Macmillan.

Man on the Bench in the Barn. Georges Simenon. Tr. by Moura Budberg. LC 73-78875. (Helen & Kurt Wolff Bk.). 188p. 1970. 5.95 o.p. (ISBN 0-15-156928-2). HarBraceJ.

Man Outside Himself: The Facts of Astral Projection. H. Prevost Battersby. LC 69-16354. (Library of Mystic Arts Ser). 160p. 1969. 4.95 o.p. (ISBN 0-8216-0114-8, Pub. by Univ Bks). Carol Pub Group.

Man Ray. Gruppo Editoriale Fabbri Staff. (Great Photographer's Ser.). Date not set. price not set o.p. P-H.

Man, Society & the Environment. Ed. by I. P. Gerasimov. 340p. 1975. 5.45 o.p. (ISBN 0-8285-0432-6, Pub. by Progress Pubs USSR). Imported Pubns.

Man Suddenly Sees to the Edge of the Universe. Richard Casement. 204p. 1984. 12.95 o.p. (ISBN 0-87548-418-2). Open Court.

Man the Engineer: Nature's Copycat. Theodore W. Munch. LC 74-8823. (Franklin Institute Bk). (Illus.). (gr. 6 up). 1974. 6.50 o.s.i. (ISBN 0-664-32555-6, Westminster); pap. 4.50 o.s.i. (ISBN 0-664-34007-5, Westminster). Westminster John Knox.

Man Through the Ages. John Bowle. LC 76-30532. 1977. 13.95 o.p. (ISBN 0-689-10797-8, Atheneum). Macmillan.

Man to Man: Gay Couples in America. Charles Silverstein. LC 80-23566. 384p. 1981. 12.95 o.p. (ISBN 0-688-00041-X). Morrow.

Man Who Came Back. John Rossiter. 1979. 8.95 o.p. (ISBN 0-395-27216-5). HM.

Man Who Changed His Name. Eric Wright. (Large Print Bks., Nightingale Ser.). 288p. 1987. pap. 11.95x o.p. (ISBN 0-8161-4285-8, Large Print Bks). G K Hall.

Man Who Changed His Name: An Inspector Charlie Salter Mystery. Eric Wright. 211p. 1986. 13.95 o.s.i. (ISBN 0-684-18635-7). Scribner.

Man Who Could Do No Wrong. Charles Blair & John Sherrill. 1982. pap. 3.50 o.p. (ISBN 0-8423-4002-5). Tyndale.

Man Who Could Make Things Vanish. Jack Cady. LC 82-72074. 288p. 1983. 14.95 o.p. (ISBN 0-87795-428-3, Arbor Hse). Morrow.

Man Who Fell in Love with His Wife. Ted Whitehead. 94p. (Orig.). 1984. pap. 8.95 o.p. (ISBN 0-571-13376-2). Faber & Faber.

Man Who Fell to Earth. Walter Tevis. 1976. pap. 1.50 o.p. (ISBN 0-380-00493-3, 27276). Avon.

Man Who Had His Hair Cut Short. Johan Daisne, pseud. Tr. by S. J. N Sackett from Flemish. LC 75-5001. 224p. 1976. Repr. of 1965 ed. lib. bdg. 35.00x o.p. (ISBN 0-8371-7426-0, THMW). Greenwood.

Man Who Liked to Look at Himself & a Fix Like This. K. C. Constantine. LC 83-47507. (Double Detective Ser.: No. 3). 160p. (Orig.). 1987. pap. 8.95 o.p. (ISBN 0-87923-468-7); pap. 3.95 o.s.i. (ISBN 0-87923-663-9). Godine.

Man Who Loved Cat Dancing. Marilyn Durham. LC 72-75415. 1972. 7.95 o.p. (ISBN 0-15-156940-1). HarBraceJ.

Man Who Loved Children. Christina Stead. 1979. pap. 1.95 o.p. (ISBN 0-380-01408-4, 40618, Bard). Avon.

Man Who Loved Children. Christina Stead. LC 65-10128. 576p. 1980. 12.95 o.p. (ISBN 0-03-047265-2); pap. 7.95 o.p. (ISBN 0-03-057642-3). H Holt & Co.

Man Who Loved Mata Hari. Dan Sherman. LC 86-80233. 352p. 1986. pap. 3.95 o.s.i. (ISBN 0-394-62244-8, BC). Grove.

Man Who Mistook His Wife for a Hat & Other Clinical Tales. Oliver Sacks. 1986. 16.45 o.s.i. (ISBN 0-671-55471-9). Summit Bks.

Man Who Must Not Die. Kenneth Kay & Marshall Goldberg. 336p. (Orig.). 1982. pap. 3.50 o.p. (ISBN 0-8439-1174-3, Pub. by Leisure Bks CT). Dorchester Pub Co.

Man Who Owned New York. John J. Osborne, Jr. 1981. 10.95 o.p. (ISBN 0-395-30511-X). HM.

Man Who Pulled Down the Sky. John Barnes. (Isaac Asimov Presents Series A Landmark in Science Fiction Publishing). 288p. 1987. 15.95 o.p. (ISBN 0-86553-185-4). Congdon & Weed.

Man Who Rode Midnight. Elmer Kelton. LC 87-528. 264p. 1987. 16.95 o.s.i. (ISBN 0-385-24020-1). Doubleday.

Man Who Shook the World see Apostle.

Man Who Slept Through a Sermon. Evelyn Marxhausen. (Arch Bks.). (Illus.). (gr. k-4). 1979. 0.50 o.p. (ISBN 0-570-06128-8, 59-1246). Concordia.

Man Who Stole the Atlantic Ocean. Louis Phillips. (Illus.). 64p. (gr. 1-5). 1976. pap. 1.25 o.p. (ISBN 0-380-00766-5, 61317-4, Camelot). Avon.

Man Who Wanted to Play Center Field for the New York Yankees. Gary Morgenstein. LC 82-73020. 288p. 1983. 14.95 o.p. (ISBN 0-689-11358-7, Atheneum). Macmillan.

Man Who Was Not with It. Herbert Gold. 1969. pap. 1.65 o.p. (ISBN 0-380-01487-4, 19356, Bard). Avon.

Man Who Wrestled with God: Light from the Old Testament on the Psychology of Individuation. John A. Sanford. LC 80-84829. 128p. 1981. pap. 7.95 o.p. (ISBN 0-8091-2367-3). Paulist Pr.

Man with Bogart's Face. Andrew J. Fenady. 184p. 1978. pap. 1.95 o.p. (ISBN 0-380-01849-7, 49015). Avon.

Man With the Getaway Face. Richard Stark. 1981. lib. bdg. 11.50 o.p. (ISBN 0-8398-2707-5, Gregg). G K Hall.

Man with the Silver Eyes. William O. Steele. LC 76-18850. (gr. 5 up). 1976. 5.95 o.p. (ISBN 0-15-251720-0, HJ). HarBraceJ.

Man with the White Horse. Einar Leistad. 1979. 5.50 o.p. (ISBN 0-682-49285-X). Exposition-Phoenix.

Man with White Slacks. Pilar De Vicente-Gella. 1985. 6.95 o.p. (ISBN 0-533-06395-7). Vantage.

Man Without God: An Introduction to Unbelief. John P. Reid. LC 72-110420. (Theological Resources Ser). 1971. 9.95 o.s.i. (ISBN 0-664-20910-6, Westminster). Westminster John Knox.

Mana Taboo. John U. Fohner. 1980. 10.00 o.p. (ISBN 0-682-49517-4). Exposition-Phoenix.

Manage More by Doing Less. R. O. Loen. 1970. text ed. 34.95 o.p. (ISBN 0-07-038370-7). McGraw.

Manage Your Own Baseball Team: Make the Playoffs! Blues vs. Sharks. George Shea. Ed. by Betty Schwartz. (Manage Your Own Baseball Team Ser.: No. 1). 128p. (Orig.). (gr. 8-12). 1983. pap. 3.40 o.s.i. (ISBN 0-671-47609-2). Wanderer Bks.

Manage Your Plant for Profit & Your Promotion. Richard W. Ogden. 1978. 14.95 o.p. (ISBN 0-8144-5466-6). AMACOM.

Management. Arthur G. Bedeian. 688p. 1986. text ed. 32.95 o.p. (ISBN 0-03-003757-3). Dryden Pr.

Management. 3rd ed. Arthur G. Bedeian & William F. Glueck. 672p. 1983. text ed. 31.95x o.p. (ISBN 0-03-061239-X); study guide 12.95 o.p. (ISBN 0-03-061242-X). Dryden Pr.

Management. 4th ed. Theodore Haimann et al. LC 81-82568. 1982. text ed. 31.50 o.p. (ISBN 0-395-31719-3). HM.

Management. Richard M. Hodgetts. 636p. 1984. text ed. 28.00 o.p. (ISBN 0-15-554643-0, HODGE, HC, HC, HC, HC, HC). HarBraceJ.

Management. 7th, rev. ed. Harold D. Koontz et al. (Illus.). 1980. text ed. 35.50 o.p. (ISBN 0-07-035377-8). McGraw.

Management. 3rd ed. Robert L. Trewatha & M. Gene Newport. 1982. text ed. 39.95x o.p. (ISBN 0-256-02713-7); wkbk. 12.95 o.p. (ISBN 0-256-02754-4). Irwin.

Management: A Middle Management Approach. Kenneth H. Killen. LC 76-13088. (Illus.). 1977. text ed. 20.50 o.p. (ISBN 0-395-16980-1). HM.

Management: A Problem-Solving Process. Robert Kreitner. LC 79-88719. (Illus.). 1981. text ed. 23.95 o.p. (ISBN 0-395-28490-2). HM.

Management: A Systems Approach. David I. Cleland & William R. King. (Management Ser.). (Illus.). 456p. 1972. text ed. 31.95 o.p. (ISBN 0-07-011314-9). McGraw.

Management Accounting. 3rd ed. Anthony. (Plaid Ser.). 1980. 10.95 o.p. (ISBN 0-256-01277-6). Dow Jones-Irwin.

Management Accounting: A Decision Emphasis. 3rd ed. Don T. Decoster & Eldon L. Schafer. Incl. Study Guide to Accompany Management Accounting. 197p. 1983. pap. 16.95 o.p. (ISBN 0-471-89010-3). LC 81-19740. 720p. 1982. pap. (ISBN 0-471-09811-6). Wiley.

Management Accounting (Cost & Management Accounting, Vol. 2. W. M. Harper. 250p. 1982. pap. text ed. 16.95x o.p. (ISBN 0-7121-0469-0). Trans-Atl Phila.

Management, Analysis & Display of Geoscience Data: Proceedings of the First Annual Conference, Golden, CO, January 27-29, 1982. Ed. by D. F. Merriam. 60p. 1983. pap. 57.00 o.p. (ISBN 0-08-030248-3). Pergamon.

Management & Administration of Drug & Alcohol Programs. Marvin D. Feit. (Illus.). 152p. 1979. 22.75x o.p. (ISBN 0-398-03873-2). C C Thomas.

Management & Computers: 1985. Rubicon Consulting Staff. 1985. 295.00 o.p. (ISBN 0-938124-05-6). Rubicon.

Management & Conservation of Resources: Proceedings of the Conference Organised by the Institution of Chemical Engineers at the University of Salford, U. K., April 1982. Institution of Chemical Engineers Staff. (Institution of Chemical Engineers Symposium Ser.: No. 72). 206p. 1982. 50.00 o.s.i. (ISBN 0-08-028769-7). Pergamon.

Management & Control in Large Systems. Ed. by A. A. Voronov. 320p. 1986. 12.95 o.p. (ISBN 0-8285-3447-0, Pub. by Mir Pubs USSR). Imported Pubns.

Management & Cost Accounting. Drury. 1985. pap. 41.95 o.p. (ISBN 0-442-30637-7). Van Nos Reinhold.

Management & Cost Accounting: Student Manual. Drury. 1985. pap. 41.95 o.p. (ISBN 0-442-30638-5). Van Nos Reinhold.

Management & Cost Accounting: Teacher's Manual. Drury. 1985. pap. 33.95 o.p. (ISBN 0-442-30639-3). Van Nos Reinhold.

Management & Economics Journals: An International Selection. Ed. by Vasile G. Tega. LC 76-4578. (Management Information Guide Ser.: No. 33). 400p. 1977. 68.00x o.p. (ISBN 0-8103-0833-9). Gale.

Management & Feeding of Buffaloes. 2nd ed. S. K. Ranjhan & N. N. Pathak. 397p. 1986. text ed. 37.50x o.p. (ISBN 0-7069-0778-7, Pub. by Vikas India); text ed. 37.50 o.p. (ISBN 0-7069-2321-9). Advent NY.

Management & Morale. Fritz J. Roethlisberger. LC 41-4302. 1941. 15.95x o.s.i. (ISBN 0-674-54650-4). Harvard U Pr.

Management & Organizations. E. Frank Harrison. LC 77-75476. (Illus.). 1978. text ed. 28.50 o.p. (ISBN 0-395-25481-7). HM.

Management & Performance. 2nd ed. Andrew D. Szilagyi, Jr. 1984. text ed. write for info. o.p. (ISBN 0-673-16604-X). Scott F.

Management & Staff Development. 37p. 1982. 10.00 o.p. (ISBN 0-8389-6735-3). Assn Coll & Res Libs.

Management & Technology: An Anglo-American Exchange of Views. Ed. by A. G. Mencher. 96p. 1972. 35.00 o.p. (ISBN 0-08-018748-X). Pergamon.

Management & the Law. Samuel Fox. LC 66-20469. 1980. pap. text ed. 7.95x o.p. (ISBN 0-89197-288-9). Irvington.

Management Audit: Maximizing Your Company's Efficiency & Effectiveness. John Nolan. LC 84-45356. (Alexander Hamilton Institute Bk.). 200p. (Orig.). 1984. 35.00 o.p. (ISBN 0-8019-7557-3); pap. 19.95 o.p. (ISBN 0-8019-7558-1). Chilton.

Management: Basic Concepts & Decisions. 2nd ed. Robert Kreitner. LC 82-83364. 656p. 1983. text ed. 31.95 o.p. (ISBN 0-395-32620-6). HM.

Management Budgeting for CETA. Jack C. Bailes. (Papers in Manpower Studies & Education: No. 1). 1975. pap. 2.00x o.p. (ISBN 0-87071-327-2). Oreg St U Pr.

Management Buy-Outs. John Coyne & Mike Wright. 256p. 1985. 31.00 o.p. (ISBN 0-7099-3616-8, Pub. by Croom Helm Ltd). Routledge Chapman & Hall.

Management by Compulsion: The Corporate Urge to Grow. Rolf H. Wild. 1978. 10.00 o.p. (ISBN 0-395-26467-7). HM.

Management by Design: Library Management, Vol. II. Ed. by Shirley Loo. 72p. 1982. pap. 13.00 o.p. (ISBN 0-87111-301-5). SLA.

Management by Menu. 2nd ed. National Institute for Food Service Industry Staff & Kotschevar Lendal H. 380p. 1986. write for info. o.p. (ISBN 0-697-05453-5). Wm C Brown.

Management Classics. 2nd ed. John M. Ivancevich & Michael Matteson. 1981. pap. text ed. write for info. o.p. (ISBN 0-673-16102-1). Scott F.

Management Classics. 3rd ed. Michael Matteson & John M. Ivancevich. 1986. 19.95 o.p. (ISBN 0-256-03449-4). Irwin.

Management: Concepts & Practices. Stephen P. Robbins. (Illus.). 608p. 1984. text ed. (ISBN 0-13-548065-5). P-H.

Management Consulting: A Guide to the Profession. Ed. by Milan Kubr. 369p. 1980. 31.50 o.p. (ISBN 92-2-101165-8). Intl Labour Office.

Management Consulting, 1988. 132p. 1988. 24.95 o.p. (ISBN 0-87584-188-0). Harvard Busn.

Management Control in Airframe Subcontracting. N. E. Harlan. 1956. 65.00 o.p. (ISBN 0-08-018741-2). Pergamon.

Management Control in Government. Alan W. Steiss. LC 81-47027. (Illus.). 368p. 1982. 37.00x o.p. (ISBN 0-669-05375-9). Lexington Bks.

Management Control in Nonprofit Organizations. 3rd ed. Robert Anthony & David Young. 1984. 39.95 o.p. (ISBN 0-256-02960-1). Irwin.

Management Control Systems. 5th ed. Robert Anthony et al. 1984. 41.95x o.p. (ISBN 0-256-02961-X). Irwin.

Management Control Systems for Small & Medium-Sized Firms. Wilbert Steffy et al. (Illus.). 84p. 1980. 12.00 o.p. (ISBN 0-938654-21-7, MGT C). Indus Dev Inst Sci.

Management Decision Methods: For Managers of Engineering & Research. William E. Souder. 352p. 1980. 29.95 o.p. (ISBN 0-442-27888-8). Van Nos Reinhold.

Management Education: Issues in Theory, Research & Practice. Richard D. Freedman & Cary L. Cooper. LC 81-14666. 278p. 1982. text ed. 54.95 o.p. (ISBN 0-471-10078-1). Wiley.

Management Essentials. William F. Glueck. 312p. 1979. 21.95x o.p. (ISBN 0-03-045416-6); instr's. manual 10.00 o.p. (ISBN 0-03-045501-4). Dryden Pr.

Management for Enterpreneurs. Ted Nicholas. 160p. 1988. 29.95 o.p. Enterprise Del.

Management for Research in U. S. Universities. Raymond J. Woodrow. Ed. by Abbott Wainwright. LC 77-27085. 1978. 20.00 o.p. (ISBN 0-915164-05-1). NACUBO.

Management for the Christian Leader. Olan Hendrix. 1986. text ed. 7.95 o.p. (ISBN 0-8010-4313-1). Baker Bk.

Management: Foundations & Practices. 5th ed. Dalton E. McFarland. 1979. text ed. write for info. o.p. (ISBN 0-02-378890-9); instr's. manual avail. o.p. Macmillan.

Management Fumbles & Union Recoveries. W. Kerby Bowling & Waldon Loving. 232p. 1982. pap. text ed. 17.95 o.p. (ISBN 0-8403-2775-7). Kendall-Hunt.

Management Fundamentals. Richard M. Hodgetts. LC 80-65800. 464p. 1981. text ed. 30.95x o.p. (ISBN 0-03-058104-4); study guide 12.95x o.p. (ISBN 0-03-058107-9). Dryden Pr.

Management in Family Living. 5th ed. Paulena Nickell et al. LC 75-41398. 475p. 1976. text ed. write for info. o.p. (ISBN 0-02-387380-9). Macmillan.

Management in Human Service Organizations. Marc L. Miringoff. (Illus.). 1980. text ed. write for info. o.p. (ISBN 0-02-381780-1). Macmillan.

Management in Post-Mao China: An Insider's View. Joseph Y. Battat. Ed. by Richard Farmer. LC 86-6957. (Research for Business Decisions Ser.: No. 76). 198p. 1986. 49.95 o.p. (ISBN 0-8357-1663-5). UMI Res Pr.

Management in the Construction Industry: A Bibliography. Mary Vance. (Architecture Ser.: Bibliography A-1314). 30p. 1985. pap. 4.50 o.p. (ISBN 0-89028-244-7). Vance Biblios.

Management Information Systems. Boon. (Infotech Computer State of the Art Reports). 661p. 1974. 310.00x o.p. (ISBN 0-08-028554-6). Pergamon.

Management Information Systems. Schulteis & Sumner. (Illus.). 640p. 1989. 41.95 o.p. (ISBN 0-8016-4360-0). Mosby.

Management Information Systems & Organizational Behavior. Pat A. Federico et al. Ed. by Kim Brun & Douglas B. McCalla. LC 80-15174. 204p. 1980. lib. bdg. 31.95 o.p. (ISBN 0-275-90477-6, C0477). Praeger.

Management Information Systems Bibliography. Christine E. Thompson. (Public Administration Ser.: P 1705). 9p. 1985. 2.00 o.p. (ISBN 0-89028-455-5). Vance Biblios.

Management: Making Organizations Perform. Hugh J. Smith et al. (Illus.). 1980. text ed. write for info. o.p. (ISBN 0-02-412500-8). Macmillan.

Management: Managing for Results. Martin J. Gannon. 720p. 1988. text ed. write for info. o.p. (ISBN 0-697-00759-6). Wm C Brown.

Management Manual for the Small-Volume Home Builder. National Association of Home Builders Staff. (Illus.). 119p. 1979. pap. 13.00 o.p. (ISBN 0-86718-065-X). Nat Assn H Build.

Management of Advanced Melanoma. Ed. by Larry Nathanson. (Contemporary Issues in Clinical Oncology: Vol. 7). (Illus.). 272p. 1986. text ed. 39.50 o.p. (ISBN 0-317-60721-9). Churchill.

Management of Aid Agencies. G. Cunningham. 220p. 1975. 22.50 o.p. (ISBN 0-85664-029-8, Pub. by Croom Helm). Routledge Chapman & Hall.

Management of Anterior Traumatized Teeth of Children. 2nd ed. Hargreaves et al. 1981. 42.00 o.p. (ISBN 0-443-01716-6). Churchill.

Management of Behavioral & Psychiatric Emergencies. Edwin Robbins et al. (Saunders Blue Book Ser.). (Illus.). 400p. (ISBN 0-7216-1081-1). Saunders.

Management of Business Logistics. 3rd ed. John J. Coyle & Edward J. Bardi. (Illus.). 522p. 1984. text ed. 36.50 o.p. (ISBN 0-314-77875-6). West Pub.

Management of Change. Douglas Basil & Curtis W. Cook. 1974. text ed. 37.50 o.p. (ISBN 0-07-084440-2). McGraw.

Management of Commercial Finance. 3rd ed. J. Samuels & F. Wilkes. 1982. 49.95 o.p. (ISBN 0-442-30724-1). Van Nos Reinhold.

Management of Common Problems in Obstetrics & Gynecology. Ed. by Daniel R. Mishell & Paul F. Brenner. 544p. 1983. pap. 42.95 o.p. (ISBN 0-87489-306-2). Med Economics.

Management of Company Finance. Samuels. 1980. pap. 19.95 o.p. (ISBN 0-442-30723-3). Van Nos Reinhold.

Management of Dental Behavior in Children. Ed. by Louis Ripa & James Barenie. LC 75-35309. (Illus.). 272p. 1979. 31.00 o.p. (ISBN 0-88416-150-1). Year Bk Med.

Management of Disruptive Pupil Behavior in Schools. Ed. by Delwyn P. Tattum. LC 85-29580. 267p. 1986. 44.95 o.p. (ISBN 0-471-90752-9). Wiley.

Management of Educational Personnel. Louis G. Romano et al. LC 73-2953. 1973. 29.75x o.p. (ISBN 0-8422-5093-X); pap. text ed. 9.75x o.p. (ISBN 0-8422-0299-4). Irvington.

Management of Employee Health Benefits: A Selective Bibliography. Lorna Peterson. (Public Administration Ser.: P 1722). 7p. 1985. 2.00 o.p. (ISBN 0-89028-492-X). Vance Biblios.

Management of Epidural Analgesia in Childbirth. 2nd ed. B. A. Waldron. LC 82-4337. (Illus.). 86p. 1983. pap. text ed. 8.00 o.p. (ISBN 0-443-02299-2). Churchill.

Management of Epilepsy. Manfred Sakel. 240p. 1958. (ISBN 0-8022-1467-3). Philos Lib.

Management of Financial Institutions. Benton E. Gup. LC 83-81686. 608p. 1984. pap. 37.95 o.p. (ISBN 0-395-34243-0). HM.

Management of Foreign Exchange Risk. Ed. by Richard Ensor & Boris Antl. 265p. 1982. 120.00 o.p. (ISBN 0-8002-3416-2). Intl Pubns Serv.

Management of Hospitality. Ed. by E. Cassee & R. Reuland. LC 82-18610. (International Series in Hospitality Management). (Illus.). 236p. 1983. 55.00 o.p. (ISBN 0-08-028107-9). Pergamon.

Management of Human Resources: Newer Approaches. Edwin Miller et al. (Illus.). 1980. pap. text ed. 22.33 o.p. (ISBN 0-13-549410-9). P-H.

Management of Human Resources: Personnel Text & Current Issues. Andrew F. Sikula & John F. McKenna. (Management Ser.: 1-309). 465p. 1984. text ed. (ISBN 0-471-86081-6, 1-309). Wiley.

Management of Hypertension. 2nd ed. Norman M. Kaplan. 1987. 8.65 o.p. (ISBN 0-917634-25-X). Creative Infomatics.

Management of Industrial Wastewater in Developing Countries: Proceedings of the International Symposium Held in Alexandria, Egypt, March 28-31, 1981. Ed. by D. C. Stuckey. LC 82-7671. (Illus.). 510p. 1982. 105.00 o.p. (ISBN 0-08-026286-4). Pergamon.

Management of Innovation. Tom Burns & G. M. Stalker. (Orig.). 1961. pap. 13.95x o.p. (ISBN 0-422-72050-X, NO. 2118, Pub. by Tavistock England). Routledge Chapman & Hall.
Management of Insect Pests with Semiochemicals: Concepts & Practice. Ed. by Everett R. Mitchell. LC 81-570. 530p. 1981. 85.00x o.p. (ISBN 0-306-40630-6, Plenum Pr). Plenum Pub.
Management of Learning see Competency Based Learning: Management, Technology, & Design.
Management of Low Back Pain. Harold Carron & Robert E. McLaughlin. (Illus.). 258p. 1982. 36.00 o.p. (ISBN 0-7236-7001-3). Butterworth.
Management of Medical Cost. W. Bryan Latham. LC 85-47668. 350p. 1986. 55.00 o.p. (ISBN 0-8144-5604-9). AMACOM.
Management of Motivation & Remuneration. D. A. Whitmore & J. Ibbetson. 230p. 1977. text ed. 36.75x o.p. (ISBN 0-220-66319-X, Pub. by Busn Bks England). Gower Pub Co.
Management of Organization Design, 2 vols. Ralph H. Kilmann et al. LC 76-23404. 1976. (North Holland); Vol. 1: Strategic Implementation. 49.50 o.p. (ISBN 0-444-00188-3); Vol. 2: Research & Methodology. 53.00 o.p. (ISBN 0-444-00189-1). Elsevier.
Management of Organizational Behavior: Utilizing Human Resources. 4th ed. Paul Hersey & Kenneth H. Blanchard. (Illus.). 368p. 1982. pap. text ed. 31.00 o.p. (ISBN 0-13-549618-7); pap. text ed. (ISBN 0-13-549600-4). P-H.
Management of Peer-Group Learning: Syndicate Methods in Higher Education. Ed. by Gerald Collier. 129p. 1983. 26.00x o.p. (ISBN 0-900868-96-1, Open Univ Pr). Taylor & Francis.
Management of Physical Distribution & Transportation. 7th ed. Charles A. Taff. 1984. 35.95x o.p. (ISBN 0-256-03022-7). Irwin.
Management of Retail Enterprises. Robert F. Lusch. LC 81-17201. 656p. 1982. text ed. 32.25 o.p. (ISBN 0-534-01072-5). PWS-Kent Pub.
Management of Sports Injuries for Women. Marjorie J. Albohm. (Illus.). 350p. 1988. pap. price not set o.p. (ISBN 0-936157-13-5). Benchmark Pr.
Management of the Burned Child. P. P. Rickham & W. C. Hecker. LC 80-29571. (Progress in Pediatric Surgery Ser.: Vol. 14). (Illus.). 250p. 1981. text ed. 29.50 o.p. (ISBN 0-8067-1514-6). Urban & S.
Management of the Diabetic Foot. Irwin Faris. LC 82-4127. (Illus.). 131p. 1983. pap. 21.00 o.p. (ISBN 0-443-02315-8). Churchill.
Management of the Electric Energy Business. Edwin Vennard. LC 79-696. (Illus.). 1979. text ed. 44.50 o.p. (ISBN 0-07-067402-7). McGraw.
Management of the Mind. Milton Harrington. (ISBN 0-8022-0684-0). Philos Lib.
Management of the Patient with Cancer. 2nd ed. Ed. by Thomas F. Nealon. LC 75-12491. (Illus.). 1976. text ed. (ISBN 0-7216-6702-3). Saunders.
Management of the United States Government, Fiscal Year 1987. 138p. 1986. pap. 2.50 o.p. (ISBN 0-318-19937-8, S/N 041-001-00303-7). USGPO.
Management of Toxic & Hazardous Wastes. H. G. Bhatt et al. LC 85-10180. (Illus.). 489p. 1985. 54.95 o.p. (ISBN 0-87371-023-1). Lewis Pubs Inc.
Management of Transportation & Environmental Review Functions. (Transportation Research Record Ser.). 56p. 1976. 3.00 o.p. (ISBN 0-309-02573-7). Transport Res Bd.
Management of Wilderness & Environmental Emergencies. Auerbach & Geehr. 1986. 72.00 o.p. (ISBN 0-8016-0384-6). Mosby.
Management of Wilderness & Environmental Emergencies. Ed. by Paul S. Auerbach & Edward C. Geehr. 1983. write for info. o.p. (ISBN 0-02-304630-9). Macmillan.
Management of Working Capital. N. K. Agarwal. 192p. 1984. text ed. 27.50x o.p. (ISBN 0-86590-183-X, Pub. by Sterling Pubs India). Apt Bks.
Management, Operational Research & the Micro. Ed. by Alan Clementson & A. J. Clewett. 96p. 1981. pap. 17.00 o.p. (ISBN 0-08-025842-5). Pergamon.
Management Organization. Albert K. Wickesberg. (Illus., Orig.). 1966. pap. text ed. 8.95x o.p. (ISBN 0-89197-290-0). Irvington.
Management Overview of Software Reuse. William Wong. LC 86-600581. (National Bureau of Standards Special Publication: No. 500-142). 22p. (Orig.). 1986. pap. 1.50 o.p. (ISBN 0-318-21641-8, S/N 003-003-02757-0). USGPO.
Management Planning: A Systems Approach. Norbert L. Enrick. LC 67-27823. 240p. 1967. 27.50 o.p. (ISBN 0-686-74219-2). Krieger.
Management Policy. 2nd ed. Melvin J. Stanford. (Illus.). 656p. 1983. text ed. (ISBN 0-13-549287-4). P-H.
Management Principle for Finance in the Multinational. David B. Zenoff. 260p. 1980. 120.00 o.p. (ISBN 0-8002-3419-7). Intl Pubns Serv.
Management Principles & Practice: A Guide to Information Sources. Ed. by K. G. Bakewell. LC 76-16127. (Management Information Guide Ser.: No. 32). 544p. 1977. 68.00x o.p. (ISBN 0-8103-0832-0). Gale.
Management Principles: Answers to Questions on Subject Matter, CEBS Course 4. 3rd ed. 1984. pap. 15.00 o.p. (ISBN 0-89154-250-7). Intl Found Employ.
Management Principles: Learning Guide CEBS Course 4. 3rd ed. 1984. Spiral bdg. 18.00 o.p. (ISBN 0-89154-249-3). Intl Found Employ.
Management Process: Cases & Readings. 2nd ed. Stephen J. Carroll, Jr. & Frank T. Paine. 448p. 1977. pap. text ed. write for info. o.p. (ISBN 0-02-319520-7, 31952). Macmillan.
Management Process: Theory, Research, & Practice. 2nd ed. John B. Miner. (Illus.). 1978. text ed. write for info. o.p. (ISBN 0-02-381650-3). Macmillan.
Management Profession. Louis A. Allen. (Management Ser.). 1964. text ed. 39.95 o.p. (ISBN 0-07-001375-6). McGraw.
Management Report, 2 vols. Infotech Staff. (Infotech Structured Prog. Reports). 402p. 1978. 615.00x o.p. (ISBN 0-08-028546-5). Pergamon.
Management Reporting Manual for Colleges. rev. ed. K. Scott Hughes et al. Ed. by Jeanne Nevin. LC 80-12101. 63p. 1980. pap. text ed. 20.00 o.p. (ISBN 0-915164-10-8). NACUBO.
Management Review of the Rhode Island Judicial Systems & Sciences (RIJSS) Department. 42p. 1987. manuscript 3.00 o.s.i. (ISBN 0-317-59077-4, NERO-203). Natl Ctr St Courts.
Management Science. Larry M. Austin & James R. Burns. 608p. 1985. text ed. write for info. o.p. (ISBN 0-02-304840-9). Macmillan.
Management Science for Energy Policy. J. E. Samouilidis. 1982. pap. 35.00 o.p. (ISBN 0-08-028172-9). Pergamon.
Management Science in Defence. Ed. by K. C. Bowen. 105p. 1985. pap. 39.00 o.p. (ISBN 0-08-032658-7, Pub. by Aberdeen Scotland). Pergamon.
Management Science in Life Companies. Charles H. Cissley. LC 75-32898. (FLMI Insurance Education Program Ser.). 1975. pap. text ed. 6.00 o.p. (ISBN 0-915322-15-3). LOMA.
Management Science in Sports. Ed. by R. E. Machol et al. (TIMS Studies in the Management Sciences: Vol. 4). 164p. 1977. pap. 32.50 o.p. (ISBN 0-7204-0507-6, North-Holland). Elsevier.
Management Science Models & the Microcomputer. James R. Burns & Larry M. Austin. 400p. 1985. pap. write for info. o.p. (ISBN 0-02-317300-9). Macmillan.
Management Science-Operations Research: Cases & Readings. James S. Dyer & Roy D. Shapiro. LC 81-19703. 388p. 1982. pap. text ed. 38.95 o.p. (ISBN 0-471-09757-8) (ISBN 0-471-86554-0). Wiley.
Management Science: Quantitative Approaches to Resource Allocation & Decision Making. James C. Hsiao & David S. Cleaver. LC 80-80960. (Illus.). 584p. 1982. text ed. 45.16 o.p. (ISBN 0-395-29488-6); instr's. manual 3.96 o.p. (ISBN 0-395-29489-4). HM.
Management: Skills, Functions & Organization Performance. Carl R. Anderson. 784p. 1984. net 27.75 o.p. (ISBN 0-205-11529-2, H1529-0); net wkbk. 10.75 o.p. (ISBN 0-205-11530-6, H1530-8); instr's. manual avail. o.p. (ISBN 0-205-11531-4, H1531-6); transparencies avail. o.p. (ISBN 0-205-11532-2, H1532-4); test item file avail. o.p. (ISBN 0-205-11533-0, H1533-2). Allyn.
Management: Skills, Functions & Organization Performance. 2nd ed. Carl R. Anderson. 752p. 1988. text ed. write for info. o.p. (ISBN 0-697-00684-0). Instr's Manual (ISBN 0-697-00685-9). Wkbk. & Study Guide (ISBN 0-697-00686-7). Test Item File (ISBN 0-697-00688-3). Wm C Brown.
Management Skills in Marketing. Stephen Morse. (Illus.). 176p. 1982. text ed. 25.95 o.p. (ISBN 0-07-084577-8). McGraw.
Management Standards for Data Processing. Dick H. Brandon. 413p. 1963. 22.50 o.p. (Pub. by Van Nos Reinhold). Krieger.
Management Standards for Developing Information Systems. Norman L. Enger. 1980. pap. 5.95 o.p. (ISBN 0-8144-7527-2). AMACOM.
Management Strategies for Women: Self-Tests, Helpful Hints, Wit & Wisdom & Superb Management Strategies for Woman. Ann M. Thompson & Marcia D. Wood. 1982. pap. 7.70 o.p. (ISBN 0-671-25477-4, Touchstone Bks). S&S.
Management Studies: Questions & Answers. 2nd ed. C. Deverell. 1979. pap. 17.95 o.p. (ISBN 0-85258-177-7). Van Nos Reinhold.
Management System Dynamics. R. G. Coyle. LC 76-40144. 463p. 1977. 108.00x o.p. (ISBN 0-471-99444-8); pap. 48.95 o.p. (ISBN 0-471-99451-0). Wiley.
Management System for Personalizing Reading Instruction see Diagnostic Prescriptive Reading Program.
Management Systems. 2nd ed. Burton Grad et al. 504p. 1979. text ed. 33.95x o.p. (ISBN 0-03-047541-4); instr's. manual 10.00 o.p. (ISBN 0-03-047546-5). Dryden Pr.
Management Systems. August W. Smith. 600p. 1982. text ed. 35.95x o.p. (ISBN 0-03-056731-9); instr's manual 20.95 o.p. (ISBN 0-03-056732-7). Dryden Pr.
Management Systems: Conceptual Considerations. rev. ed. Peter P. Schoderbek et al. 1980. pap. 11.95x o.p. (ISBN 0-256-02275-5). Irwin.
Management Systems for Profit & Growth. 2nd ed. Richard F. Neuschel. 1976. text ed. 39.95 o.p. (ISBN 0-07-046323-9). McGraw.
Management Tactician: Executive Tactics for Getting Results. Edward C. Schleh. (Illus.). 288p. 1974. text ed. 26.95 o.p. (ISBN 0-07-055293-2). McGraw.
Management Techniques Applied to the Construction Industry. 3rd ed. R. Oxley & J. Poskitt. 298p. 1980. text ed. 17.00x o.p. (ISBN 0-246-11341-3, Pub. by Granada England). Gower Pub Co.
Management Techniques for Top Executives. Frederick Parker. LC 85-91009. (Illus.). 1985. 10.00 o.p. (ISBN 0-682-40194-3). Exposition-Phoenix.
Management Techniques in Surgery: Bedside Care of the Surgical Patient. Ed. by Edward E. Etheredge. LC 85-17819. 596p. 1986. pap. 23.00 o.p. (ISBN 0-471-87914-2). Wiley.
Management: Theory & Application. 4th ed. Leslie W. Rue & Lloyd L. Byars. 1986. 36.95x o.p. (ISBN 0-256-03364-1). Irwin.
Management: Theory, Process & Practice. 3rd ed. Richard M. Hodgetts. 546p. 1982. text ed. 33.95x o.p. (ISBN 0-03-059881-8); instr's manual 20.00 o.p. (ISBN 0-03-059882-6). study guide 12.95 o.p. (ISBN 0-03-059883-4). Dryden Pr.
Management Today: Managing Work in Organizations. Thomas J. Atchison & Winston W. Hill. 575p. 1978. text ed. 24.95 o.p. (ISBN 0-15-554780-1, HC). HarBraceJ.
Management's Rights under Public Sector Collective Bargaining. Frank Zeidler. (Public Employee Relations Library: No. 59). 1980. pap. 14.00 o.p. (ISBN 0-686-81157-7). Intl Personnel Mgmt.
Management's Use of Computer Graphics, Vol. 12. Laboratory for Computer Graphics & Spatial Analysis, Harvard University Graduate School of Design Staff. (Harvard Library of Computer Graphics, Mapping Collection). (Illus.). 128p. 1981. pap. 15.95 o.p. (ISBN 0-8122-1192-8). U of Pa Pr.
Management's Use of Maps: Commercial & Political Applications, Vol. 1. Laboratory for Computer Graphics & Spatial Analysis, Harvard University Graduate School of Design Staff. (Harvard Library of Computer Graphics, Mapping Collection). (Illus.). 64p. 1979. pap. 14.50 o.p. (ISBN 0-8122-1181-2). U of Pa Pr.
Management's Use of Maps: Including an Introduction to Computer Mapping for Executives, Vol. 7. Laboratory for Computer Graphics & Spatial Analysis, Harvard University Graduate School of Design Staff. (Harvard Library of Computer Graphics, Mapping Collection). (Illus.). 103p. 1980. pap. 15.95 o.p. (ISBN 0-8122-1187-1). U of Pa Pr.
Manager & Industrial Relations. Trevor Owen. 1979. 51.00 o.p. (ISBN 0-08-022471-7); pap. 17.00 o.p. (ISBN 0-08-022472-5). Pergamon.
Manager & the Man: A Cross-Cultural Study of Personal Values. George W. England et al. LC 74-11582. 97p. 1974. 9.50x o.p. (ISBN 0-87338-161-0, Pub. by Comp. Adm. Research Inst.). Kent St U Pr.
Manager & the Modern Internal Auditor. Lawrence B. Sawyer. (Illus.). 1979. 24.95 o.p. (ISBN 0-8144-5515-8). AMACOM.
Manager As an Editor: Reviewing Memos, Letters & Reports. Louis J. Visco. 175p. 1983. pap. 14.95 o.p. (ISBN 0-8436-0852-8). Van Nos Reinhold.
Manager at Large. V. V. Prabhu. 1979. 9.00x o.p. (ISBN 0-7069-0767-1, Pub. by Vikas India). Advent NY.
Manager in the International Economy. 4th ed. Louis T. Wells & Raymond Vernon. (Illus.). 1981. pap. text ed. 31.00 o.p. (ISBN 0-13-549550-4). P-H.
Manager Manpower Planning: A Professional Management System. Lawrence A. Appley & Keith L. Irons. 128p. 1981. 16.95 o.p. (ISBN 0-8144-5707-X). AMACOM.
Managerial Accounting. 6th ed. Arthur J. Francia et al. LC 83-72203. 601p. 1987. 36.95x o.p. (ISBN 0-87393-042-8); study guide 11.95x o.p. (ISBN 0-87393-081-9); working papers 10.95x o.p. (ISBN 0-87393-082-7). Dame Pubns.
Managerial Accounting. 4th ed ed. Ray H. Garrison. 1985. 38.95x o.p. (ISBN 0-256-03261-0); study guide 12.95x o.p. (ISBN 0-256-03262-9); working papers 12.95 o.p. (ISBN 0-256-03680-2); Microcomputer exercises, IBM Lotus 19.95 o.p. (ISBN 0-256-03504-0); IBM Visicale 19.95 o.p. (ISBN 0-256-03505-9). Irwin.
Managerial Accounting. 3rd ed. Joseph G. Louderback & Geraldine F. Dominiak. 784p. 1982. text ed. 30.95x o.p. (ISBN 0-534-01113-6). PWS-Kent Pub.
Managerial Accounting. 2nd ed. Joseph G. Louderback, 3rd & Geraldine F. Dominiak. 1978. text ed. (ISBN 0-534-00556-X); (ISBN 0-534-00603-5). PWS-Kent Pub.
Managerial Accounting: An Introduction. Pierre L. Titard. 704p. 1983. text ed. 35.95x o.p. (ISBN 0-03-061556-9); instr's manual 19.95 o.p. (ISBN 0-03-061557-7); study guide 14.95x o.p. (ISBN 0-03-061558-5); test bank 100.00 o.p. (ISBN 0-03-062203-4). Dryden Pr.
Managerial Accounting & Control Techniques for the Non-Accountant. Mary M. Fleming. 392p. 1984. 38.95 o.p. (ISBN 0-442-22573-3). Van Nos Reinhold.
Managerial & Cost Accountant's Handbook. Ed. by Homer A. Black & James D. Edwards. LC 78-61201. 1979. 60.00 o.p. (ISBN 0-87094-173-9). Dow Jones-Irwin.
Managerial Behavior: Administration in Complex Organizations. 2nd ed. Leonard R. Sayles. LC 78-31454. 312p. 1979. lib. bdg. 24.50 o.p. (ISBN 0-88275-854-3). Krieger.
Managerial Breakthroughs: Action Techniques for Strategic Change. James R. Emshoff. (Illus.). 1980. 15.95 o.p. (ISBN 0-8144-5612-X). AMACOM.
Managerial Decision Making Process. E. Frank Harrison. 1975. text ed. 21.35 o.p. (ISBN 0-395-18865-2). HM.
Managerial Economics. Samuel C. Webb. LC 75-31039. (Illus.). 608p. 1976. text ed. 37.50 o.p. (ISBN 0-395-20589-1). HM.
Managerial Economics: Analysis & Cases. 5th ed. Thomas J. Coyne. 1984. 34.95 o.p. (ISBN 0-256-02698-X). Irwin.
Managerial Economics: Analysis & Cases. 4th ed. William R. Henry & Warren W. Haynes. 1978. 19.95x o.p. (ISBN 0-256-02079-5). Irwin.
Managerial Economics & Operations Research. rev. ed. Ed. by Edwin Mansfield. LC 70-95540. 1970. pap. text ed. 4.50x o.p. (ISBN 0-393-09919-9). Norton.
Managerial Economics & Operations Research. 3rd ed. Ed. by Edwin Mansfield. 1975. pap. 6.95x o.p. (ISBN 0-393-09297-6). Norton.
Managerial Economics & Operations Research. 4th ed. Ed. by Edwin Mansfield. 1980. 24.95 o.p. (ISBN 0-393-01271-9); pap. text ed. 10.95x o.p. (ISBN 0-393-95060-3). Norton.
Managerial Economics: Text & Cases. Chester R. Wasson. LC 66-11425. (Illus.). 1966. 19.95x o.p. (ISBN 0-89197-291-9); pap. text ed. 8.95x o.p. (ISBN 0-89197-834-8). Irvington.
Managerial Economics: Theory, Practice, & Problems. 2nd ed. Evan J. Douglas. (Illus.). 544p. 1983. text ed. (ISBN 0-13-550210-1). P-H.
Managerial Effectiveness. W. J. Reddin. 1970. text ed. 38.95 o.p. (ISBN 0-07-051358-9). McGraw.
Managerial Experience: Cases, Exercises & Readings. Lawrence R. Jauch et al. 470p. 1983. pap. text ed. 16.95x o.p. (ISBN 0-03-061237-3). Dryden Pr.
Managerial Experience with the IBM PC. Jensen. 1989. (ISBN 0-256-03146-0). Irwin.
Managerial Finance. 7th ed. J. Fred Weston & Eugene F. Brigham. LC 80-65811. 1088p. 1981. text ed. 41.95x o.p. (ISBN 0-03-058186-9); study guide 14.95x o.p. (ISBN 0-03-058188-5). Dryden Pr.
Managerial Finance: A Systems Approach. Eugene M. Lerner. (Harbrace Business & Economics Ser.). (Illus.). 1971. text ed. 16.95 o.p. (ISBN 0-15-554705-4, HC). HarBraceJ.
Managerial Finance for the Seventies. Thomas C. Committe et al. (Finance Ser.). 1972. text ed. 37.95 o.p. (ISBN 0-07-012371-3). McGraw.
Managerial Finance: Principles & Practice. Steven E. Bolten. LC 75-31036. (Illus.). 896p. 1976. text ed. 32.50 o.p. (ISBN 0-395-20462-3). HM.
Managerial Prerogative & the Question of Control. John Storey. (Direct Edition Ser.). 180p. (Orig.). 1983. pap. 19.95x o.p. (ISBN 0-7100-9203-2). Routledge Chapman & Hall.
Managerial Revolution. James Burnham. LC 60-8308. (Midland Bks.: No. 23). 300p. 1960. pap. 4.95x o.p. (ISBN 0-253-20023-7). Ind U Pr.
Managerial Revolution in Higher Education. Francis E. Rourke & Glenn E. Brooks. 184p. 1966. 20.00x o.p. (ISBN 0-8018-0563-5). Johns Hopkins.
Managerial Statistics: A Unified Approach. Chris A. Theodore. LC 81-14321. 499p. 1982. write for info. o.p. (ISBN 0-534-01093-8). PWS-Kent Pub.

Managerial Use of Accounting Data. Emerson O. Henke et al. LC 77-88600. 291p. 1978. 19.00x o.p. (ISBN 0-87201-001-5); wkbk. text ed. 9.00x o.p. (ISBN 0-87201-003-1). Gulf Pub.

Managers: Corporate Life in America. Diane R. Margolis. LC 79-13274. 1979. 10.95 o.p. (ISBN 0-688-03537-X). Morrow.

Manager's Digest: A Handbook for Decision-Making. Lloyd M. Smith. LC 74-21447. 1975. 15.00 o.p. (ISBN 0-682-48187-4, Banner); pap. 8.00 o.p. (ISBN 0-682-48188-2). Exposition-Phoenix.

Manager's Guide to Change. Elmer H. Burack & Florence Torda. LC 79-15537. 235p. 1982. pap. 11.95 o.p. (ISBN 0-534-97995-5, Lifetime Learn). Van Nos Reinhold.

Manager's Guide to Copying & Duplicating. Richard E. Hanson. (Illus.). 1980. text ed. 29.95 o.p. (ISBN 0-07-026080-X). McGraw.

Manager's Guide to Industrial Robots. Ken Susnjara. 186p. 1982. pap. text ed. 9.95 o.p. (ISBN 0-317-18020-7). Robot Inst Am.

Manager's Guide to Profitable Computers. Norman Sanders. LC 78-23624. 224p. 1979. 14.95 o.p. (ISBN 0-8144-5495-X). AMACOM.

Manager's Guide to Small Computers. Charles W. Bradley. 352p. 1984. pap. text ed. 20.45 o.p. (ISBN 0-03-059538-X, HoltC). HR&W.

Manager's Guide to the Antitrust Laws. Edward A. Matto. 192p. 1980. 14.95 o.p. (ISBN 0-8144-5541-7). AMACOM.

Managing. Harold Geneen & Alvin Moscow. LC 84-12731. 312p. 1984. 17.95 o.p. (ISBN 0-385-17496-9). Doubleday.

Managing a Defense Company: For Growth & Profit. Grayson Merrill. 1972. 10.00 o.p. (ISBN 0-682-47493-2, Banner). Exposition-Phoenix.

Managing a Management Development Institution, 1982. 19.95 o.p. (ISBN 9-221-02955-7). Intl Pubns Serv.

Managing a Real Estate Team. Hall Institute of Real Estate. 1980. 22.95x o.p. (ISBN 0-03-056788-2). Dryden Pr.

Managing an Apartment House Profitably. Jerry B. German. LC 73-86543. 1973. 5.00 o.p. (ISBN 0-682-47781-8, Banner). Exposition-Phoenix.

Managing: An Introduction. Joseph T. Straub. LC 83-18789. 608p. 1984. text ed. write for info. o.p. (ISBN 0-534-03114-5). PWS-Kent Pub.

Managing an Organization. Caplow. 19.95 o.s.i. (ISBN 0-03-058578-3). H Holt & Co.

Managing & Accounting for Inventories: Control, Income Recognition, & Tax Strategy. 3rd ed. C. Paul Jannis et al. LC 78-31481. (Ronald Series in Professional Accounting & Business). 458p. 1980. 62.95 o.p. (ISBN 0-471-05016-4, Pub by Ronald Pr). Wiley.

Managing & Developing New Forms of Work Organization. Nitish De et al. (Management Development Ser.: No. 16). (Illus.). 158p. (Orig.). 1980. pap. 17.50 o.p. (ISBN 92-2-102145-9). Intl Labour Office.

Managing & Developing New Forms of Work Organization. (Management Development Ser.: No. 16). 158p. 1981. pap. 17.50 o.p. (ISBN 92-2-102145-9, ILO166, ILO). UNIPUB.

Managing As a Performing Art: New Ideas for a World of Chaotic Change. Peter B. Vaill. LC 88-32842. (Management Ser.). 1989. text ed. 20.95x o.p. (ISBN 1-55542-140-7). Jossey-Bass.

Managing Beyond the Quick Fix: A Completely Integrated Program for Creating & Maintaining Organizational Success. Ralph H. Kilmann. LC 88-46084. (Management Ser.). 1989. text ed. 20.95x o.p. (ISBN 1-55542-132-6). Jossey-Bass.

Managing Business-Government Relationships. J. Ronald Fox. 1982. 33.95x o.p. (ISBN 0-256-02900-8). Irwin.

Managing by Negotiations. Earl Brooks & George S. Odiorne. 1984. 33.95 o.s.i. (ISBN 0-442-20962-2). Van Nos Reinhold.

Managing Career Development. Marilyn A. Morgan. LC 79-66118. 285p. 1980. pap. text ed. 14.95x o.p. (ISBN 0-442-26238-8). PWS-Kent Pub.

Managing Change. Donald L. Kirkpatrick. write for info. o.p. (ISBN 0-8144-5786-X). AMACOM.

Managing Change in the Church. Douglas W. Johnson. (Orig.). 1974. pap. 3.50 o.p. (ISBN 0-377-00017-5). Friendship Pr.

Managing Children's Behavior: A Guide for Parents, Teachers, Counselors, Coaches & All Others Who Work with Children. Rainer Twiford. 144p. 1984. 14.95 o.p. (ISBN 0-13-550633-6); pap. 5.95 o.p. (ISBN 0-13-550625-5). P-H.

Managing Communication in Organizations: An Introduction. H. Wayland Cummings et al. 361p. 1982. pap. text ed. 20.00x o.p. (ISBN 0-89787-314-9). Gorsuch Scarisbrick.

Managing Compensation: Developing & Administering the Total Compensation Program. new ed. J. Gary Berg. LC 76-9809. (Illus.). 320p. 1976. 14.95 o.p. (ISBN 0-8144-5418-6). AMACOM.

Managing Corporate Benefit Plans 1983. Mary E. Brennan. 121p. 1983. pap. text ed. 15.00 o.p. (ISBN 0-89154-221-3). Intl Found Employ.

Managing Costs & Improving Cash Flow. Frank C. Wilson. LC 83-73090. 300p. 1984. 50.00 o.p. (ISBN 0-87094-450-9). Dow Jones-Irwin.

Managing Creation: The Challenge of Building a New Organization. Dennis N. Perkins et al. LC 82-17548. (Organizational Assessment & Change Ser.). 279p. 1983. 34.95 o.p. (ISBN 0-471-05204-3, Pub. by Ronald Pr). Wiley.

Managing Creatively. 2nd ed. Ted Pollock. 285p. 1983. 18.95 o.p. (ISBN 0-8436-0861-7). Van Nos Reinhold.

Managing Cultural Differences. 2nd ed. Philip R. Harris & Robert T. Moran. 610p. 1987. 29.95 o.s.i. (ISBN 0-87201-161-5). Gulf Pub.

Managing Development Through Public-Private Negotiations. Ed. by Rachelle Levitt & John Kirlin. LC 85-51328. 135p. 1985. pap. 36.00 o.p. (ISBN 0-87420-642-1, M21). Urban Land.

Managing Diabetes Properly. 2nd ed. Ed. by Patti Urosevich & Barbara McVann. (New Nursing Skillbook Ser.). (Illus.). 222p. 1985. text ed. 14.95 o.p. (ISBN 0-916730-69-7). Springhouse Pub.

Managing Director. George Copeman. 256p. 1978. text ed. 24.50 o.p. (Pub. by Busn Bks England). Gower Pub Co.

Managing Distributed Systems. National Computing Centre, Ltd. Staff. Ed. by K. C. Gee. (Illus.). 128p. (Orig.). 1980. pap. 27.50x o.s.i. (ISBN 0-85012-229-5). Intl Pubns Serv.

Managing Doctors. Alan Sheldon. 250p. 1986. 35.00 o.p. (ISBN 0-87094-646-3). Dow Jones-Irwin.

Managing Drug Supply in Selection, Procurement, Distribution & Use of Pharmaceuticals in Primary Health Care see Suministro de Medicamentos: La Seleccion, Adquisicion, Distribucion y Uso de Productos Farmaceuticos en la Atencion Primaria de Salud.

Managing Drug Supply: The Selection, Procurement, Distribution, & Use of Pharmaceuticals in Primary Health Care. Management Sciences for Health Staff et al. Ed. by Jonathan D. Quick & Margaret L. Hume. (Illus.). 592p. (Orig.). 1981. pap. text ed. 18.50 o.p. (ISBN 0-913723-06-1). Mgmt Sci Health.

Managing Elephant Depredation in Agricultural & Forestry Projects. John Seidensticker. (Technical Paper Ser.: No. 16). 50p. 1984. 5.00 o.p. (ISBN 0-318-02824-7). World Bank.

Managing Employee Health Benefits: A Guide to Cost Control. Jay Wolfson & Peter J. Levin. LC 84-71570. 1985. 30.00 o.p. (ISBN 0-87094-506-8). Dow Jones-Irwin.

Managing Employee Turnover: A Positive Approach. Edward Roseman. 272p. 1981. 17.95 o.p. (ISBN 0-8144-5585-9). AMACOM.

Managing End User Computing In Information Organizations. William H. Inmon. 325p. 1986. 30.00 o.p. (ISBN 0-87094-941-1). Dow Jones-Irwin.

Managing Expert Systems Projects. Gary Kahn & Neil Jacobstein. (Illus.). 100p. 1988. pap. text ed. 5.00x o.p. (ISBN 0-929280-09-1). Amer Artificial.

Managing Export Distribution. Gary Davies. (Illus.). 192p. 1985. pap. 22.95 o.p. (ISBN 0-434-90298-5, Pub. by W Heinemann Ltd). David & Charles.

Managing Federalism: Studies in Intergovernmental Relations. Arnold M. Howitt. LC 83-15046. 321p. 1984. 14.95 o.p. (ISBN 0-87187-277-3). Congr Quarterly.

Managing for Organizational Effectiveness: An Experiential Approach. F. E. Finch et al. (Management Ser.). 1975. text ed. 35.95 o.p. (ISBN 0-07-020899-9). McGraw.

Managing for Perfomance. 2nd ed. John M. Ivancevich et al. 1983. 31.95x o.p. (ISBN 0-256-02913-X); wkbk 10.95x o.p. (ISBN 0-256-02914-8). Irwin.

Managing for Profit. P. Mills. 160p. 1982. text ed. 22.00 o.p. (ISBN 0-07-084575-1). McGraw.

Managing for Profits. Harvey C. Krentzman. 165p. 1981. pap. 5.50 o.p. (ISBN 0-318-11798-3, S/N 045-000-00206-3). USGPO.

Managing for Success: The Farnsworth Formula. Terry Farnsworth. 192p. 1981. text ed. 19.95 o.p. (ISBN 0-07-084547-6). McGraw.

Managing God's Organization: The Catholic Church in Society. Scott R. Safranski. Ed. by Richard Farmer. LC 85-16540. (Research for Business Decisions: No. 79). 200p. 1985. 44.95 o.p. (ISBN 0-8357-1669-4). UMI Res Pr.

Managing Growing Organizations: A New Approach. Theodore D. Weinshall & Yael-Anna Raveh. LC 82-21967. 412p. 1984. 59.95x o.p. (ISBN 0-471-90116-4, Pub. by Wiley-Interscience). Wiley.

Managing Health Promotion in the Workplace: Guidelines for Implementation & Evaluation. Parkinson, Rebecca S., & Associates Staff. LC 81-84693. 314p. 1982. 26.95 o.p. (ISBN 0-87484-567-X). Mayfield Pub.

Managing Hypertension: The Complete Program Developed by the Cleveland Clinic. James V. Warren & Genell J. Subak-Sharpe. LC 85-15968. 192p. 1986. 14.95 o.s.i. (ISBN 0-385-18768-8). Doubleday.

Managing Incompetency. William P. Anthony. 256p. 1982. 17.95 o.p. (ISBN 0-8144-5672-3). AMACOM.

Managing Induced Rural Development. Jon R. Moris. 1981. pap. 12.50 o.p. (ISBN 0-89249-033-0). Intl Development.

Managing Industrial Relations. M. Marchington. 208p. 1982. text ed. 19.00 o.p. (ISBN 0-07-084580-8). McGraw.

Managing Innovation for Profit. 2nd rev. ed. LC 85-51289. (Illus.). 195p. 1985. spiral bound, plastic 245.00 o.p. (ISBN 0-914993-20-8). Tech Insights.

Managing Innovation: The Social Dimensions of Creativity, Invention & Technology. Ed. by Sven B. Lundstedt, Ohio State University & Colglazier E. William, JFK School of Government, Harvard University. LC 82-293. (Pergamon Policy Studies on Business & Economics Ser.). (Illus.). 280p. 1982. 45.00 o.p. (ISBN 0-08-028815-4, L120). Pergamon.

Managing Insurance Claims in the Dental Office. Ann Ehrlich. (Illus.). 1987. 5.50 o.p. (ISBN 0-940012-12-X). Colwell Syst.

Managing Intergroup Conflict in Industry. Robert R. Blake et al. LC 64-8696. 210p. 1964. 19.00x o.p. (ISBN 0-87201-375-8). Gulf Pub.

Managing International Markets: A Survey of Training Practices & Emerging Trends. A. Kapoor & Robert J. McKay. LC 79-161052. 1971. pap. text ed. 3.95x o.p. (ISBN 0-87850-003-0). Darwin Pr.

Managing IV Therapy. Ed. by Richard West & Barbara McVan. LC 79-28050. (Nursing Photobook Ser.). (Illus.). 1983. pap. 19.95 o.p. (ISBN 0-87434-149-3). Springhouse Pub.

Managing Livestock Wastes. James A. Merkel. (Illus.). 1981. 35.95 o.p. (ISBN 0-87055-373-9). AVI.

Managing Marketing Information. Nigel Piercy & Martin J. Evans. (Illus.). 224p. 1983. 38.90 o.p. (ISBN 0-7099-2025-3, Pub. by Croom Helm Ltd); pap. 12.95 o.p. (ISBN 0-7099-2026-1). Routledge Chapman & Hall.

Managing Money with Your Commodore 64. Amihai Glazer. (Illus.). 144p. 1985. pap. 22.95 o.p. (ISBN 0-13-550641-7). P-H.

Managing Money with Your VIC-20. Amihai Glazer. LC 84-18233. (P-H Personal Computing Ser.). (Illus.). 180p. 1985. pap. 13.95 o.p. (ISBN 0-13-550682-4). P-H.

Managing Multiple Activities in Industrial Education. George H. Silvius & Estell H. Curry. 1971. text ed. 19.35 o.p. (ISBN 0-87345-456-1). Glencoe.

Managing Negotiations: A Guide for Managers, Labor Workers, & Everyone Else Who Wants to Win. Gavin Kennedy et al. (Illus.). 170p. 1982. 12.95 o.p. (ISBN 0-13-550558-5); 5.95 o.p. (ISBN 0-13-550541-0). P-H.

Managing Non-Profit Organizations. Ed. by Patrick H. Montana & Diane Borst. 1979. pap. 5.95 o.p. (ISBN 0-8144-7512-4). AMACOM.

Managing Organizational Behavior. 2nd ed. John R. Schermerhorn, Jr. et al. (Management Ser.). 760p. 1985. write for info. o.p. (ISBN 0-471-87141-9); tchr's. ed. avail. o.p. (ISBN 0-471-81821-6). Wiley.

Managing Organizational Transitions. John R. Kimberly & Robert E. Quinn. 1984. 18.95x o.p. (ISBN 0-256-03136-3). Irwin.

Managing Organizations. William D. Brinckloe & Mary T. Coughlin. 1977. text ed. write for info. o.p. (ISBN 0-02-471200-0). Macmillan.

Managing OS-2: Profiting from Changing Standards. Mike Edelhart & David Strom. 1988. pap. 24.95 o.p. (ISBN 0-13-642893-2). Brady Bks.

Managing Patients with IntrauterineDevices: A Clinic Manual. Elizabeth Connell-Tatum & Howard J. Tatum. LC 84-71601. 1985. 8.65 o.p. (ISBN 0-917634-11-X). Creative Infomatics.

Managing People at Work. J. W. Hunt. 1979. text ed. 28.95 o.p. (ISBN 0-07-084530-1). McGraw.

Managing People at Work: Readings in Personnel. 3rd ed. Dale S. Beach. (Illus.). 1980. pap. text ed. write for info. o.p. (ISBN 0-02-307030-7). Macmillan.

Managing People in Public Agencies: Personnel & Labor Relations. Jonathan Brock. 1984. 24.25 o.p. (ISBN 0-673-39017-9). Scott F.

Managing Performance. Lloyd Baid. LC 85-3301. (St. Clair Series in Management & Organizational Behavior). 167p. 1985. (ISBN 0-471-06243-X). Wiley.

Managing Personal Computer Workstations: A Corporate Resource. Donald R. Woodwell. LC 84-70602. 270p. 1984. 27.50 o.p. (ISBN 0-87094-512-2). Dow Jones-Irwin.

Managing Personal Finance. H. Ulbrich & Bruce Yandle. 1979. 24.95x o.p. (ISBN 0-256-02208-9). Irwin.

Managing Police Organizations. David A. Tanzik & James F. Elliott. LC 80-15788. 278p. (Orig.). 1981. pap. 15.00 o.p. (ISBN 0-87872-275-0). Krieger.

Managing Police Work: Issues & Analysis. Ed. by Jack R. Greene. (Perspectives in Criminal Justice: Vol. 4). (Illus.). 176p. 1982. 22.00 o.p. (ISBN 0-8039-1787-2); pap. 10.95 o.s.i. (ISBN 0-8039-1788-0). Sage.

Managing Research & Development. John E. Gibson. LC 81-2033. 367p. 1981. 48.95x o.p. (ISBN 0-471-08799-8, Pub. by Wiley-Interscience). Wiley.

Managing Return on Investment: Implications for Pricing, Volume, & Funds Flow. George E. Manners, Jr. & Joseph G. Louderback. LC 80-8817. 192p. 1981. 28.00x o.p. (ISBN 0-669-04383-4). Lexington Bks.

Managing Spatial Conflict: The Planning System in Switzerland. P. Gresch. (Illus.). 94p. 1985. pap. 22.00 o.p. (ISBN 0-08-032731-1, Pub. by PPL). Pergamon.

Managing Staff Reductions in Corporations. Clifford E. Harrison. Ed. by Richard Farmer. LC 86-11223. (Research for Business Decisions Ser.: No. 91). 144p. 1986. 39.95 o.p. (ISBN 0-8357-1758-5). UMI Res Pr.

Managing Stress: A Businessperson's Guide. Jere E. Yates. (Illus.). 1980. 12.95 o.p. (ISBN 0-8144-5543-3). AMACOM.

Managing Technological Accidents: Two Blowouts in the North Sea: Proceedings of an IIASA Workshop on Blowout Management. Ed. by D. W. Fischer. (IIASA Proceedings Ser.: Vol. 16). (Illus.). 242p. 1982. 73.00 o.p. (ISBN 0-08-029346-8). Pergamon.

Managing Technological Innovation & Entrepreneurship. J. C. Martin. 340p. 1984. 29.95 o.p. (ISBN 0-317-18033-9). Robot Inst Am.

Managing the Consultant: A Corporate Guide. John J. McGonagle, Jr. LC 80-68271. 320p. 1981. 23.50 o.p. (ISBN 0-8019-7016-4). Chilton.

Managing the Critically Ill Effectively. Ed. by Margaret Van Meter. (Illus.). 250p. 1982. pap. 21.95 o.p. (ISBN 0-87489-274-0). Med Economics.

Managing the Data Center. Allan F. Froehlich. 298p. 1982. 34.95 o.p. Van Nos Reinhold.

Managing the Demand for Fashion Items. Rajendra R. Bhat. Ed. by Richard Farmer. LC 85-1039. (Research for Business Decisions Ser.: No. 73). 138p. 1985. 34.95 o.p. (ISBN 0-8357-1618-X). UMI Res Pr.

Managing the Dollar: From the Plaza to the Louvre. 2nd ed. Yoichi Funabashi. LC 88-9239. 307p. (Orig.). 1988. pap. 19.95 o.p. (ISBN 0-88132-071-4). Inst Intl Eco.

Managing the Drugs in Your Life: A Commonsense Personal & Family Guide. Stephen J. Levy. 1983. text ed. 16.95 o.p. (ISBN 0-07-037411-2). McGraw.

Managing the Dynamic Small Firm: Readings. Lawrence Klatt. 1970. pap. (ISBN 0-534-00669-8). PWS-Kent Pub.

Managing the Employee Benefits Program. rev. ed. Robert M. McCaffery. 256p. 1983. 29.95 o.p. (ISBN 0-8144-5760-6). Amacom.

Managing the Family Forest in the South. Hamlin L. Williston. 90p. 1982. pap. 2.75 o.p. (ISBN 0-318-11799-1, S/N 001-001-00591-6). USGPO.

Managing the Information Systems Audit: A Case Study-Policies, Procedures, & Guidelines. Billy E. Smith. (Illus.). 65p. 1980. Set. pap. text ed. 12.00 o.p. (ISBN 0-89413-086-2); avail. wkbk. o.p. (ISBN 0-89413-087-0). Inst Inter Aud.

Managing the Learning Process. Philip Waterhouse. (Illus.). 191p. 1983. pap. 16.95 o.p. (ISBN 0-07-084136-5). Nichols Pub.

Managing the Medical Enterprise: A Study of Physician Managers. Carol L. Betson. Ed. by Richard Farmer. LC 85-31834. (Research for Business Decisions: No. 89). 206p. 1986. 45.95 o.p. (ISBN 0-8357-1735-6). UMI Res Pr.

Managing the Mind: A Study of Medical Psychology in Early 19th-Century Britain. Michael Donnelly. LC 83-4748. 200p. 1983. 23.00 o.p. (ISBN 0-422-78380-3, NO. 3809). Routledge Chapman & Hall.

Managing the Mobile Employee. Patricia C. Nida. 192p. 1983. pap. text ed. 11.95 o.p. (ISBN 0-8403-3160-6). Kendall-Hunt.

Managing the Modern Organization. 3rd ed. Theodore Haimann et al. LC 77-75879. (Illus.). 1978. text ed. 22.95 o.p. (ISBN 0-395-25512-0). HM.
Managing the Police Organization: Selected Readings. Larry K. Gaines & Truett A. Ricks. (Criminal Justice Ser.). (Illus.). 527p. 1978. pap. text ed. 32.50 o.p. (ISBN 0-8299-0163-9). West Pub.
Managing the Primary School. Joan Dean. 224p. 1986. 29.00 o.p. (ISBN 0-7099-4520-5, Pub. by Croom Helm UK); pap. 13.50 o.p. (ISBN 0-7099-4525-6, Pub. by Croom Helm UK). Routledge Chapman & Hall.
Managing the Primary School. Joan Dean. 256p. 1987. lib. bdg. 40.00x o.p. (ISBN 0-317-64360-6, Pub. by Croom Helm UK). Routledge Chapman & Hall.
Managing the Problem Employee. Edward Roseman. 224p. 1982. 16.95 o.p. (ISBN 0-8144-5714-2). AMACOM.
Managing the Sales Function. Thomas F. Stroh. (Marketing Ser.). (Illus.). 1978. text ed. 31.50 o.p. (ISBN 0-07-062219-1). McGraw.
Managing the Small Business. 3rd ed. John B. Kline et al. 1982. 33.95x o.p. (ISBN 0-256-02508-8). Irwin.
Managing the Troubled Employee. M. Douglas Clark. LC 79-91188. (Illus.). 77p. 1979. Incl. transparency masters. 69.50 o.p. (ISBN 0-88061-009-3). Inst Pub ILCI.
Managing Time. Norman Kobert. LC 80-13891. 140p. 1980. flexible cover 50.00 o.p. (ISBN 0-932648-11-8). Boardroom.
Managing to Survive: How to Outsmart the One-Minute Manager. James Skivington. 128p. (Orig.). 1988. pap. 5.95 o.p. (ISBN 0-7137-1986-9, Pub. by Javelin England). Sterling.
Managing Today & Tomorrow with On-Line Information. Linda G. Christie. 275p. 1985. 27.50 o.p. (ISBN 0-87094-666-8). Dow Jones-Irwin.
Managing: Toward Accountability for Performance. 3rd ed. Robert Albanese. 1981. 33.95x o.p. (ISBN 0-256-02505-3). Irwin.
Managing Training & Training Managers in Public Enterprises in Developing Countries. Ed. by Aubry Armstrong & Stane Mozine. (ICPE Books). 284p. 1980. pap. 20.00x o.p. Kumarian Pr.
Managing Urban Government Services: Strategies, Tools, & Techniques for the Eighties. James L. Mercer et al. 240p. 1981. 21.95 o.p. (ISBN 0-8144-5725-8). AMACOM.
Managing UUCP & USENET. rev., 4th ed. O'Reilly Tim & Grace Todins. Ed. by Dale Dougherty. (Nutshell Handbks. (for Beginning & Advanced UNIX Users)). 242p. 1987. pap. 18.00 o.p. (ISBN 0-937175-09-9). O'Reilly & Assocs.
Managing with Micros: Management Uses of Microcomputers. 2nd ed. Colin Lewis. 208p. 1984. 24.95x o.p. (ISBN 0-631-13136-1); pap. 10.95x o.p. (ISBN 0-631-13642-8). Basil Blackwell.
Managing with Micros: Management Uses of Microcomputers. 3rd ed. Colin Lewis. 232p. 1987. text ed. 34.95x o.p. (ISBN 0-631-15276-8); pap. text ed. 17.95x o.p. (ISBN 0-631-15277-6). Basil Blackwell.
Managing Without a Union. Jules J. Justin. 1979. 36.95 o.p. (ISBN 0-442-23381-7). Van Nos Reinhold.
Managing Your Business with Multiplan: How to Use Microsoft's Award-Winning Electronic Spreadsheet on Your IBM PC. Ruth K. Witkin. (Illus.). 432p. 1984. 17.95 o.s.i. (ISBN 0-914845-06-3). Microsoft.
Managing Your Hard Disk. Don Berliner. LC 86-61154. 560p. (Orig.). 1986. pap. 19.95 o.p. (ISBN 0-88022-265-4, 67). Que Corp.
Managing Your Human Resources: A Partnership Approach. Louis V. Imundo & Martin P. Eisert. 240p. 1982. 15.95 o.p. (ISBN 0-8144-5708-8). AMACOM.
Managing Your Investment Manager: The Complete Guide to Selection, Measurement, & Control. Arthur Williams. LC 79-56084. 210p. 1980. 35.00 o.p. (ISBN 0-87094-187-9). Dow Jones-Irwin.
Managing Your Maternity Leave. Meg Wheatly & Marcie S. Hirsch. LC 82-21389. 225p. 1983. 13.45 o.p. (ISBN 0-395-33128-5); pap. 7.70 o.p. (ISBN 0-395-34032-2). HM.
Managing Your Megabytes: Take Full Advantage of Hard Disks,the Streaming Tapes, Bernoulli Box, Hardboards & Optical Devices. Bernadette M. Olson et al. (Power User Ser.). 176p. (Orig.). 1986. pap. 24.95 o.p. (ISBN 0-915381-84-2); book-diskette 34.95 o.p. (ISBN 0-915381-87-7); diskette 10.00 o.p. (ISBN 0-915381-86-9). Wordware Pub.
Managing Your Money. Nancy G. Miller. 64p. 1979. 2.25 o.p. (ISBN 0-317-35473-6); workbook 0.80 o.p. (ISBN 0-317-35474-4). New Readers.
Managing Your Money with Managing Your Money. Jim Bartimo. LC 86-2187. 336p. (Orig.). 1987. pap. 16.95 o.p. (ISBN 0-914845-93-4). Microsoft.
Managing Your Office Records & Files. 199p. 1984. 14.95 o.p. (ISBN 0-88908-588-9). ISC Pr.
Managing Your Personal Finances, 3 vols. Joyce M. Pitts. (Home & Garden Bulletin Ser.: No. 245). 100p. 1986. Repr. looseleaf 6.00 o.p. (S/N 001-000-04484-2). USGPO.
Managing Your Private Trucking Operation. Thomas R. Henke. LC 76-10120. (Illus.). 1976. pap. text ed. 8.00 o.p. (ISBN 0-87408-005-3). Intl Thom Trans Pr.
Managing Your Time. Ted W. Engstrom & Alex MacKenzie. LC 67-17239. (Orig.). 1968. pap. 3.95 o.p. (ISBN 0-310-24262-2, 9572P). Zondervan.
Manana Is Now. Alberta Eiseman. LC 72-86933. 176p. (gr. 5-9). 1973. 6.95 o.p. (ISBN 0-689-30100-6, Atheneum). Macmillan.
Manchester in 1844: It's Present Condition & Future Prospects. L. Faucher. Ed. by J. P. Culverwell. 152p. 1969. 24.00x o.p. (ISBN 0-7146-1392-4, F Cass Co). Biblio Dist.
Manchu Delta. Ric Bridwell. 144p. (Orig.). 1986. pap. 7.95 o.s.i. (ISBN 0-934318-75-1). Falcon Pr Mt.
Manchuria: A Survey of Its Economic Development. Baron Y. Sakatani. LC 78-74315. (Modern Chinese Economy Ser.). 305p. 1980. lib. bdg. 40.00 o.p. (ISBN 0-8240-4279-4). Garland Pub.
Manchuria: Its People, Resources & Recent History, London, 1904. Alexander Hosie. LC 78-74311. (Modern Chinese Economy Ser.: Vol. 24). 326p. 1980. lib. bdg. 46.00 o.p. (ISBN 0-8240-4272-7). Garland Pub.
Mandarin. Robert Elegant. 544p. 1983. 17.25 o.p. (ISBN 0-671-45173-1). S&S.
Mandarins: Roman. Simone De Beauvoir. (Coll. Blanche). 1961. 13.95 o.p. (ISBN 0-685-11340-X). Schoenhof.
Mandela's Children. Ora Mendels. 1987. 16.95 o.p. (ISBN 0-316-54506-6). Little.
Mandingo. abr. ed. Kyle Onstott. (Falconhurst Ser). 1983. pap. 2.95 o.p. (ISBN 0-449-20280-1, Crest). Fawcett.
Mandrake the Magician Cartoon. King Features Staff. (Illus.). 1978. pap. 1.25 o.s.i. (ISBN 0-448-16473-6, Pub. by Tempo). Ace Bks.
Mandrake's Book. Howard Pearlstein. LC 74-84450. 164p. (Orig.). 1974. pap. 3.00 o.p. (ISBN 0-912528-09-5). John Muir.
Mandschu-Sprachkunde in Korea. Hiu Lie. (Uralic & Altaic Ser.: No. 114). (Illus.). 276p. 1973. pap. text ed. 42.50x o.p. (ISBN 0-686-27752-X). Mouton.
Mandy the Monkey. Margaret S. Pursell. Tr. by Dyan Hammarberg from Fr. LC 77-41410. (Animal Friends Books). (Illus.). (gr. k-4). 1977. PLB 5.95 o.p. (ISBN 0-87614-082-7). Carolrhoda Bks.
Manet & His Critics. George H. Hamilton. 1969. pap. 3.95 o.p. (ISBN 0-393-00372-8, Norton Lib). Norton.
Manet & the Nude, a Study in Iconography in the Second Empire. Beatrice Farwell. LC 79-57509. (Outstanding Dissertations in the Fine Arts Ser.: No. 5). 290p. 1981. lib. bdg. 61.00 o.p. (ISBN 0-8240-3929-7). Garland Pub.
Manet's Complete Paintings, 2 vols. Denis Rouart & Daniel Wildenstein. (Illus., Fr.). 1988. Set. 625.00 o.p. (ISBN 1-55660-011-9); Vol. 1, 308 p. Vol. 2, 275 p. A Wofsy Fine Arts.
Manfred Selig Collection of European Drawings & Prints. Wallace Weston. LC 82-81589. (Illus.). 72p. 1982. 11.95 o.p. (ISBN 0-935558-08-X). Henry Art.
Manganese. Medical Sciences Division Staff. LC 73-18174. (Medical & Biologic Effects of Environmental Pollutants Ser.). 192p. 1974. pap. 10.50 o.p. (ISBN 0-309-02143-X). Natl Acad Pr.
Manganese Compounds As Oxidizing Agents in Organic Chemistry. Diether Arndt. Ed. by Donald G. Lee. Tr. by Chester Claff, Jr. from Ger. 344p. 1981. 18.95 o.p. (ISBN 0-87548-355-0). Open Court.
Manhattan As a Second Language & Other Poems. Jana Harris. LC 81-47851. 96p. 1982. 10.53i o.p. (ISBN 0-06-250383-9, CN4029); pap. 5.72 o.p. (ISBN 0-06-250384-7). HarpR.
Manhattan Country Doctor: A Memoir. Milton J. Slocum. 272p. 1986. 16.95 o.p. (ISBN 0-684-18694-2). Scribner.
Manhattan Is Missing. E. W. Hildick. (Illus.). 192p. (gr. 3). 1982. pap. 1.25 o.p. (ISBN 0-380-01488-2, 55012-1, Camelot). Avon.
Manhattan Moves Uptown: An Illustrated History. Charles Lockwood. 1976. 17.50 o.p. (ISBN 0-395-24674-1). HM.
Manhattan Project. David Bischoff. 1986. pap. 2.95 o.p. (ISBN 0-380-75125-9). Avon.
Manhattan Transients. Sharon Fusselman Mizener. LC 76-50294. 1977. 4.50 o.p. (ISBN 0-682-48734-1, University). Exposition-Phoenix.
Maniac in the Cellar: Sensation Novels of the Eighteen Sixties. Winifred Hughes. LC 80-7530. 232p. 1980. 25.00 o.p. (ISBN 0-691-06441-5). Princeton U Pr.
Manic D Sampler. Ed. by Jennifer Joseph. (Illus.). 48p. (Orig.). 1987. pap. 5.00 o.p. (ISBN 0-916397-02-5). Manic D Pr.
Manichean Aesthetics: The Politics of Literature in Colonial Africa. Abdul R. JanMohamed. LC 83-5808. 328p. 1988. pap. 12.95 o.p. (ISBN 0-87023-651-2). U of Mass Pr.
Manila Espionage. Claire Phillips. (Illus.). 1947. 7.95 o.p. (ISBN 0-8323-0071-3). Binford-Metropolitan.
Manila Goodbye. Robin Prising. LC 74-28236. 224p. 1975. 7.95 o.p. (ISBN 0-395-20432-1). HM.
Manipulating Parents: Tactics Used by Children of All Ages & Ways Parents Can Turn the Tables. Paul W. Robinson et al. 274p. 1981. 14.95 o.p. (ISBN 0-13-552166-1); 7.95 o.p. (ISBN 0-13-552158-0). P-H.
Manipulating the Machine: Changing the Pattern of Ministerial Departments, 1960-83. Christopher Pollitt. 296p. 1984. text ed. 34.95x o.p. (ISBN 0-04-351064-7). Unwin Hyman.
Manipulation of the Immune Response in Cancer. Ed. by N. Avrion Mitchison. (Perspectives in Immunology Ser.). 1979. 54.00 o.p. (ISBN 0-12-500250-5). Acad Pr.
Manipulative Activities & Games in the Mathematics Classroom. Ed. by Lee E. Vochko. 112p. 1979. pap. 8.95 o.p. (ISBN 0-8106-1706-4). NEA.
Manipulator. Jeffrey M. Wallmann. 368p. 1982. pap. 3.25 o.p. (ISBN 0-380-81166-9, 81166-9). Avon.
Manipulus Vocabulorum: A Dictionary of English & Latin Words, Arranged in the Alphabetical Order of the Last Syllables. Peter Levens. Repr. of 1867 ed. 37.00 o.p. (ISBN 0-384-32410-X). Johnson Repr.
Manko Goes to New York & Becomes Famous see **Manko of Mankoland.**
Manko of Mankoland, 3 vols. Joseph Buttinger. Incl. Vol. 1. Adventures of Young & Impressionable Manko As He Meets His Jungle Friends (ISBN 0-682-48898-4); Vol. 2. Further Adventures of Manko-Delights & Frights (ISBN 0-682-48906-9); Vol. 3. Manko Goes to New York & Becomes Famous (ISBN 0-682-48907-7). (Illus.). (gr. 1-6). 1977. 5.00 ea. o.p. Exposition-Phoenix.
Manna: True Stories of Life in the United States, 1900 to 1940 & the Utopia of Manna. John H. Vassos. 64p. 1982. 8.00x o.p. (ISBN 0-682-49655-3). Exposition-Phoenix.
Manned Spaceflight Log. Tim Furniss. (Illus.). 128p. 1983. 10.95 o.p. (ISBN 0-86720-631-4). Janes Info Group.
Manned Spacelight Log. 6th ed. Tim Furniss. 160p. 1987. pap. 14.95 o.p. (ISBN 0-7106-0402-5). Janes Info Group.
Manned Systems Design: Methods, Equipment, & Applications. Ed. by J. Moraal & F. K. Kraiss. LC 81-10732. (NATO Conference Series III, Human Factors: Vol. 17). 498p. 1981. 79.50x o.p. (ISBN 0-306-40804-X, Plenum Pr). Plenum Pub.
Mannequin d'Osier see **Romans et Contes.**
Manner & Method: A Translation of the French Reformed Church's Liturgy. Blair Reynolds. 85p. (Orig.). 1985. pap. 9.95x o.p. (ISBN 0-932269-40-0). Wyndham Hall.
Mannerism on Space Communication: Some Methods & Some Reflections. Anthony L. Coundakis. 194p. 1981. 12.50 o.p. (ISBN 0-682-49734-7). Exposition-Phoenix.
Manners & Customs of the Police. Donald Black. 1980. 36.50 o.p. (ISBN 0-12-102880-1); pap. 17.50 o.p. (ISBN 0-12-102882-8). Acad Pr.
Manners & Morals of the Nineteen Twenties: A Survey of the Religious Press. Mary P. Thaman. LC 77-8129. 1977. Repr. of 1954 ed. lib. bdg. 35.00x o.p. (ISBN 0-8371-9679-5, THMM). Greenwood.
Manning Clark & Australian History: 1915-1963. Stephen Holt. LC 81-11663. (Illus.). 207p. 1982. text ed. 17.50x o.p. (ISBN 0-7022-1590-2). U of Queensland Pr.
Mannings. Fred M. Stewart. LC 72-82173. 1973. 8.95 o.p. (ISBN 0-87795-053-9, Arbor Hse). Morrow.
Manny: A Criminal-Addict's Story. Richard P. Rettig et al. 1977. pap. 17.50 o.p. (ISBN 0-395-24838-8). HM.
Manor. Isaac Bashevis Singer. 1967. 6.95 o.p. (ISBN 0-374-20224-9). FS&G.
Manor incl. the Estate. Isaac Bashevis Singer. LC 67-2596. 818p. 1979. 15.00 o.p. (ISBN 0-374-20225-7). FS&G.
Manpower Planning & Organization Design. Ed. by D. Bryant & R. Niehaus. LC 78-4623. (NATO Conference Series II, Systems Science: Vol. 7). 804p. 1978. 115.00x o.p. (ISBN 0-306-40006-5, Plenum Pr). Plenum Pub.
Manpower Planning in a Free Society. Richard A. Lester. 244p. 1966. 28.00 o.p. (ISBN 0-691-04143-1); pap. 9.50 o.p. (ISBN 0-691-00355-6). Princeton U Pr.
Manpower Planning in Fisheries Development Programs. (Fisheries Technical Papers: No. 65). 40p. 1967. pap. 7.50 o.p. (ISBN 0-686-93246-3, F1730, FAO). UNIPUB.
Manpower Policies for the Use of Science & Technology in Development. Charles V. Kidd. (Policy Studies). 1980. 50.00 o.p. (ISBN 0-08-025124-2). Pergamon.
Manpower Policy for Primary Health Care. Institute of Medicine Staff. LC 78-56907. 1978. 7.75 o.p. (ISBN 0-309-02764-0). Natl Acad Pr.
Manpower Resources & Population under Socialism. V. A. Aperyan. 198p. 1979. 4.95 o.p. (ISBN 0-8285-1607-3, Pub. by Progress Pubs USSR). Imported Pubns.
Man's Book. Ed. by James Wagenvoord. 1978. pap. 7.95 o.p. (ISBN 0-380-01899-3, 76034-7). Avon.
Man's Choice. 3rd, rev. ed. Frank R. Wallace. LC 70-11935. 1970. 12.50 o.p. (ISBN 0-911752-02-1). I & O Pub.
Man's Crown of Glory. Jerry Savelle. 96p. (Orig.). 1983. pap. 2.75 o.p. (ISBN 0-89274-169-4, HH-169). Harrison Hse.
Man's Cultural Dimension. G. Nickerson. 1970. pap. text ed. 9.95x o.p. (ISBN 0-8422-0097-5). Irvington.
Man's Discovery of His Past. Robert F. Heizer. 1969. pap. text ed. 12.95 o.p. (ISBN 0-917962-14-1). T H Peek.
Man's Hope. Andre Malraux. Tr. by Stuart Gilbert & Alastair MacDonald. LC 79-2333. 1979. pap. 12.50 o.s.i. (ISBN 0-394-17093-8, E740, Ever). Grove.
Man's Journey Through Time. L. S. Palmer. (Illus.). 192p. 1959. (ISBN 0-8022-1258-1). Philos Lib.
Man's Life: An Autobiography. Roger Wilkins. 1982. 17.25 o.p. (ISBN 0-671-22673-8). S&S.
Man's Life: An Autobiography. Roger Wilkins. 384p. 1984. pap. 7.75 o.p. (ISBN 0-671-49268-3, Touchstone). S&S.
Man's Lot. Walter Kaufmann. (Illus.). 1978. text ed. 60.00 o.p. (ISBN 0-07-033314-9). McGraw.
Man's Only Hope: A Study of the Life & Ministry of Jesus Christ. Stanley N. Collins. 1978. 6.00 o.p. (ISBN 0-682-49175-6). Exposition-Phoenix.
Man's Physical Environment. A. Faniran & Oyediran Oje. (Orig.). 1980. pap. text ed. 22.50x o.p. (ISBN 0-435-95042-8). Heinemann Ed.
Man's Picture of His World. Roger E. Money-Kyrle. 190p. 1961. text ed. 25.00x o.s.i. (ISBN 0-8236-3140-0). Intl Univs Pr.
Man's Place in Nature. Max Scheler. Tr. by Hans Meyerhoff from Ger. 105p. 1962. pap. 5.25 o.p. (ISBN 0-374-50252-8). FS&G.
Man's Plague? Insects & Agriculture. V. G. Dethier. LC 75-15216. (Illus.). 237p. (Orig.). 1976. 9.95 o.p. (ISBN 0-87850-026-X). Darwin Pr.
Man's Quest for God: Studies in Prayer & Symbolism. Abraham J. Heschel. LC 54-10371. 1954. 5.95 o.s.i. (ISBN 0-684-13582-5, ScribT). Scribner.
Man's Rise to Civilization, As Shown by the Indians of North America from Primeval Times to the Coming of the Industrial State. Peter Farb. 1976. pap. 1.95 o.p. (ISBN 0-380-01409-2, 21576, Discus). Avon.
Man's Search for Himself. Rollo May. 1953. 16.95 o.p. (ISBN 0-393-06290-2). Norton.
Man's Search for Meaning: An Introduction to Logotherapy. Victor E. Frankl. 1970. pap. 6.75 o.s.i. (ISBN 0-671-20782-2, Touchstone Bks). S&S.
Man's Storm: A Novel of Crime Set in London...1703. Keith Heller. 196p. 1986. 13.95 o.s.i. (ISBN 0-684-18653-5). Scribner.
Mansfield Park. Jane Austen. 1980. 14.95x o.p. (ISBN 0-460-00023-3, Evman); pap. 3.75x o.p. (ISBN 0-460-01023-9, Evman). Biblio Dist.
Manshare: A Novel. Maxine Paetro. 288p. 1986. 15.95 o.p. (ISBN 0-87131-472-X). M Evans.
Mansion on Turtle Creek Cookbook. Dean Fearing. LC 87-21535. (Illus.). 256p. 1987. 25.00 o.s.i. (ISBN 1-55584-176-7). Weidenfeld.
Mansions. Neal Travis. 352p. 1984. pap. 4.75 o.p. (ISBN 0-380-88419-4, 88419-4). Avon.
Manson in His Own Words. Nuel Emmons. 288p. 1987. 16.95 o.p. (ISBN 0-8021-0045-7). Grove.
Manston's Travel Key--Europe '88: How to Make a Phone Call, Do Your Laundry, Find a Toilet, Get Around Easily & Much More. Peter B. Manston. (Illus.). 432p. 1988. pap. 10.95 o.p. (ISBN 0-931367-09-3). Travel Keys.
Manston's Travel Key Europe. 2nd ed. Peter B. Manston. LC 86-30907. (Illus.). 430p. 1987. pap. 9.95 o.p. (ISBN 0-931367-07-7, Co-pub. by Prima Pub.). Travel Keys.
Mantle & Core in Planetary Physics. Ed. by J. Coulomb & M. Caputo. (Italian Physical Society: Course 50). 1972. 82.50 o.p. (ISBN 0-12-368850-7). Acad Pr.

Titles

Titles

Mantle & the Prophet: Learning & Power in Modern Iran. Roy Mottahedeh. 1985. 17.45 o.p. (ISBN 0-671-55197-3). S&S.
Mantle of Christ: A History of the Sydney Central Methodist Mission. Don Wright. (Illus.). 179p. 1985. text ed. 25.00x o.p. U of Queensland Pr.
Mantram Handbook. Eknath Easwaran. 264p. 1989. 22.00 o.p. (ISBN 0-915132-49-4); pap. 12.00 o.p. (ISBN 0-915132-48-6). Nilgiri Pr.
Mantrap Garden: A Celia Grant Mystery. John Sherwood. 224p. 1986. 13.95 o.s.i. (ISBN 0-684-18726-4). Scribner.
Manual & Resource Book for Popular Participation Training, 4 vols. Vol. 1. pap. 2.50 o.p. (ISBN 92-1-130089-4, E.78.IV.4); Vol. 2. pap. 2.00 o.p. (ISBN 92-1-130062-2, E.78.IV.5); Vol. 3. pap. 2.50 o.p. (ISBN 92-1-130052-5, E.78.IV.6); Vol. 4. pap. 3.50 o.p. (ISBN 92-1-130058-4, E.78.IV.7). UN.
Manual Art: A Practical Guide to Drawing & Painting. Frank Rosenow. (Illus.). 1980. 9.95 o.p. (ISBN 0-393-01398-7). Norton.
Manual De Fisica Para Ingenieros y Estudiantes. B. M. Yavorski & A. A. Detlaf. 961p. (Span.). 1977. 11.20 o.p. (ISBN 0-8285-1688-X, Pub. by Mir Pubs USSR). Imported Pubns.
Manual de Normas Vicentes en Materia de Derechos Humanos. OAS, General Secretariat, Inter-American Commission of Human Rights. (Human Rights Ser.). 153p. 1980. text ed. 6.00 o.p. (ISBN 0-8270-1153-9). OAS.
Manual de Normas Vigentes en Materia de Direitos Humanos: Actualizado en Julho de 1980. OAS, General Secretariat. (Human Rights Ser.). 149p. (Port.). 1980. pap. text ed. 4.00 o.p. (ISBN 0-8270-1203-9). OAS.
Manual de Prevencion de Accidentes Para Operaciones Industriales. 1649p. 99.00 o.p. (ISBN 0-318-18006-5). Inter-Am Safety.
Manual for Bertie. James Moor & Jack Nelson. 1979. pap. text ed. 4.95 o.p. (ISBN 0-933694-06-7). COMPress.
Manual for Classroom Teachers: How to Recognize & Help Children with Mental & Emotional Disorders. Ed. by Harold L. Gilbert. (Illus.). 194p. 1969. pap. text ed. 8.95x o.p. (ISBN 0-8422-0003-7). Irvington.
Manual for Histologic Technicians. 3rd ed. Ann Preece. 300p. 1972. 22.50 o.p. (ISBN 0-316-71765-7). Little.
Manual for Legal Assistants. National Association of Legal Assistants, Inc. Staff. Ed. by William R. Park. LC 79-18552. 529p. 1979. text ed. 21.95 o.s.i. (ISBN 0-8299-2059-5). West Pub.
Manual for Missionaries on Furlough. Marjorie A. Collins. LC 72-92747. 151p. 1978. pap. 4.45 o.p. (ISBN 0-87808-119-4). William Carey Lib.
Manual for Practical Grammars. Doris Bartholomew. 44p. 1976. pap. 2.50 o.p. (ISBN 0-88312-839-X); microfiche 2.00 o.p. (ISBN 0-88312-330-4). Summer Inst Ling.
Manual for Predicting Chemical Process Design Data: Chapter 9: Thermal Conductivity. Ed. by Ronald P. Danner & Thomas E. Daubert. 1985. pap. 25.00 o.p. (ISBN 0-317-58819-2, X-98C). Am Inst Chem Eng.
Manual for Process Engineering Calculations. 2nd ed. Loyal Clarke & Robert L. Davidson. (Chemical Engineering Ser). 1962. text ed. 49.50 o.p. (ISBN 0-07-011249-5). McGraw.
Manual for Repertory Grid Technique. F. Fransella & D. Bannister. 1977. 46.50 o.p. (ISBN 0-12-265450-1); pap. 26.00 o.p. (ISBN 0-12-265456-0). Acad Pr.
Manual for the Care of Wild Birds. Billie C. Sheaffer. (Illus.). 64p. 1980. 5.00 o.p. (ISBN 0-682-49617-0). Exposition-Phoenix.
Manual for the Department of Social Service. Providence Medical Center Staff. LC 77-73334. 1977. pap. 5.00 o.p. (ISBN 0-87125-037-3). Cath Health.
Manual for the Employment of Aliens. Robert W. Herrington, Jr. & Samuel M. Tidwell. 1987. 25.00 o.p. (ISBN 0-910402-78-7). Coll & U Personnel.
Manual Metal-Arc Welding. Ed. by N. C. Balchin. (Engineering Craftsmen: No. F24). (Illus.). 1977. 39.50x o.p. (ISBN 0-85083-395-7). Trans-Atl Phila.
Manual of AACR 2 Examples for Microcomputer Software. 2nd ed. Nancy B. Olson. Ed. by Edward Swanson. (Illus.). 110p. 1986. pap. text ed. 17.50 o.p. (ISBN 0-936996-20-X). Soldier Creek.
Manual of Accident & Emergency Resuscitation. Ed. by Colin Robertson & Keith Little. LC 83-1290. 181p. 1983. pap. 12.00 o.p. (ISBN 0-471-90154-7, Dist. by A R Liss). Wiley.
Manual of Acute Toxicity: Interpretation & Data Base for 410 Chemicals & 66 Species of Fresh Water Animals. Foster L. Mayer, Jr. & Mark R. Ellersieck. (Fish & Wildlife Service Resource Publication 160). 512p. 1986. pap. 21.00 o.p. (ISBN 0-318-21371-0, S/N 024-010-00668-4). USGPO.
Manual of Admitting Orders & Therapeutics. Eric Larson & Mickey Eisenberg. (Saunders Blue Book Ser.). 237p. 1981. pap. write for info. spiral bdg. o.p. (ISBN 0-7216-3352-8). Saunders.
Manual of Adverse Drug Interactions. 2nd ed. Griffin & D'Arcy. 416p. 1979. pap. 21.50 o.p. (ISBN 0-7236-0508-4, Pub. by John Wright UK). Butterworth.
Manual of Adverse Drug Interactions. 3rd ed. J. Griffin. (Illus.). 433p. 1984. 67.00 o.p. (ISBN 0-7236-0726-5). Butterworth.
Manual of Ambulatory Pediatrics. Rose W. Boynton et al. (Little, Brown Spiral Manual Ser.). 1988. write for info. o.p. Scott F.
Manual of Ambulatory Pediatrics. 2nd ed. Rose W. Boynton et al. 1988. pap. text ed. write for info. o.p. (ISBN 0-673-39787-4). Scott F.
Manual of Anatomy & Physiology Laboratory Animal: The Cat. 3rd ed. Anne B. Donnersberger et al. (Illus.). 455p. 1985. pap. text ed. 21.50 o.p. (ISBN 0-669-07502-7); instr's guide 2.00 o.p. (ISBN 0-669-07503-5). Heath.
Manual of Articulatory Phonetics. William A. Smalley. LC 73-14763. (Applied Cultural Anthropology Ser.). (Illus.). 522p. 1973. pap. text ed. 12.95x o.p. (ISBN 0-87808-139-9). William Carey Lib.
Manual of Avionics: An Introduction to the Electronics of Civil Aviation. Brian Kendal. 276p. 1979. text ed. 38.00x o.p. (ISBN 0-246-11168-2, Pub. by Granada England). Gower Pub Co.
Manual of Bedside Oncology. Dennis A. Casciato & Lowitz Barry B. Bennet. (SPIRAL Manual Ser.). 699p. 1983. spiralbound 19.50 o.p. (ISBN 0-316-13068-0). Little.
Manual of Built-up Roof Systems. American Institute of Architects Staff & C. W. Griffin. 1970. text ed. 41.95 o.p. (ISBN 0-07-001489-2). McGraw.
Manual of Burn Therapeutics: An Interdisciplinary Approach. Roger E. Salisbury & Nancy Newman. (Little, Brown SPIRAL Manual Series). 1983. 18.00 o.p. (ISBN 0-316-76958-4). Little.
Manual of Chest Medicine. John E. Stark et al. LC 85-11008. (Illus.). 255p. (Orig.). 1986. pap. text ed. 16.50 o.p. (ISBN 0-443-02737-4). Churchill.
Manual of Child Psychopathology. Ed. by Benjamin B. Wolman. (Illus.). 1392p. 1971. text ed. 165.95 o.p. (ISBN 0-07-071545-9). McGraw.
Manual of Clinical Gastroenterology. Gail Bongiovanni. 598p. 1983. text ed. 19.95 o.p. (ISBN 0-07-006471-7). McGraw.
Manual of Clinical Problems in Pediatrics. Kenneth B. Roberts. 1979. spiral bdg. 19.50 o.p. (ISBN 0-316-74984-2). Little.
Manual of Cloisonne & Champleve Enameling. J. Patrick Strolsahl et al. (Illus.). 264p. 1981. 14.95 o.s.i. (ISBN 0-684-16822-7, ScribT). Scribner.
Manual of Contact Dermatitis. Sigfrid Fregert. 1981. 22.50 o.p. (ISBN 0-8151-3282-4). Year Bk Med.
Manual of Cryptography. Luigi Sacco. (Cryptographic Ser.). 1977. Repr. of 1935 ed. 20.80 o.p. (ISBN 0-89412-016-6); lib. bdg. 28.80 o.p. (ISBN 0-89412-110-3). Aegean Park Pr.
Manual of Echocardiographic Techniques. Betty J. Phillips. LC 79-3921. (Illus.). 276p. 1980. text ed. write for info. o.p. (ISBN 0-7216-7219-1). Saunders.
Manual of Economic Analysis of Chemical Processes. Institut Francais de Pertrole Staff. Tr. by Ryle Miller & Ethel B. Miller. (Illus.). 1981. text ed. 56.50 o.p. (ISBN 0-07-031745-3). McGraw.
Manual of Field Biology & Ecology. 5th ed. Allen H. Benton & William E. Werner, Jr. 400p. 1972. spiral 9.95x o.p. (ISBN 0-8087-0217-3, Feffer & Simons). Burgess MN Intl.
Manual of Forensic Quotations. Leon Mead & Gilbert F. Newell. LC 68-26591. 226p. 1968. Repr. of 1903 ed. 35.00x o.p. (ISBN 0-8103-3188-8). Gale.
Manual of Fracture Bracing. A. Y. Hall & R. W. Stenner. LC 84-4980. (Illus.). 61p. 1985. text ed. 32.50 o.p. (ISBN 0-443-02691-2). Churchill.
Manual of Freshman English. rev. ed. University of Washington Staff. (Orig.). 1967. pap. 1.25x o.p. (ISBN 0-87015-156-8). Pacific Bks.
Manual of Guitar Technology. Franz Jahnel. (Illus.). 240p. 1981. Repr. of 1963 ed. 110.00 o.p. (ISBN 0-686-74791-7). Bold Strummer Ltd.
Manual of Hematology. C. Sultan et al. LC 83-26071. 380p. 1985. pap. 24.95x o.p. (ISBN 0-471-06002-X). Wiley.
Manual of Hemotherapy. Harold B. Anstall & Paul M. Urie. LC 85-31590. 468p. 1986. pap. 27.50 o.p. (ISBN 0-471-88689-0). Wiley.
Manual of Historic Ornament: Treating Upon the Evolution, Tradition & Development of Architecture & the Applied Arts. 5th ed. Richard Glazier. LC 70-163174. (Tower Bks.). (Illus.). vi, 200p. 1972. Repr. of 1933 ed. 48.00x o.p. (ISBN 0-8103-3937-4). Gale.
Manual of Historic Ornaments. 4th ed. Richard Glazier. 192p. 1983. pap. 12.95 o.p. (ISBN 0-442-22999-2). Van Nos Reinhold.
Manual of Horsemanship. Harold Black. 1978. pap. 5.00 o.p. (ISBN 0-87980-359-2). Wilshire.
Manual of Horsemanship. British Horse Society & Pony Club Staff. (Illus.). Repr. of 1950 ed. text ed. 9.95 o.p. (ISBN 0-8120-5462-8). Barron.
Manual of Horsemanship. 1982. 10.95 o.p. (ISBN 0-8120-5613-2). Barron.
Manual of Industrial Radiation Protection, 6 pts. Incl. Pt 1. Convention & Recommendation Concerning the Protection of Workers Against Ionising Radiations. 1963. 0.70 o.s.i. (ISBN 92-2-100944-0); Pt 2. Model Code of Safety Regulations (Ionising Radiations) 1965. 1.70 o.s.i. (ISBN 92-2-100945-9); Pt 3. General Guide on Protection Against Ionising Radiations. (Illus.). 1963. 2.85 o.s.i. (ISBN 92-2-100946-7); Pt 4. Guide on Protection Against Ionising Radiations in Industrial Radiography & Fluoroscopy. (Illus.). 1965. 2.30 o.s.i. (ISBN 92-2-100947-5); Pt 5. Guide on Protection Against Ionising Radiations in the Application of Luminous Compounds. (Illus.). 1964. 2.30 o.s.i. (ISBN 92-2-100948-3); Pt 6. Radiation Protection in the Mining & Milling of Radioactive Ores. 1968. 4.55 o.s.i. (ISBN 92-2-100949-1). Intl Labour Office.
Manual of Infection Control in Respiratory Care. Arthur J. McLaughlin. 179p. 1983. pap. text ed. 15.50 o.p. Little.
Manual of Instructions for the Survey of the Public Lands of the United States. U. S. Department of the Interior Staff. (BLM Technical Bulletin: No. 6). 333p. 1973. 12.00 o.s.i. (ISBN 0-317-32461-6, S210). Am Congrs Survey.
Manual of Intensional Logic. 2nd ed. Johan Van Benthem. (Center for the Study of Language & Information, Lecture Notes: No. 1). 80p. (Orig.). 1988. pap. 12.95 o.p. (ISBN 0-937073-19-9). Ctr Study Language.
Manual of International Law. 6th ed. Georg Schwarzenberger & E. D. Brown. lix, 612p. 1976. text ed. 40.00x o.p. (ISBN 0-903486-26-1, Pub. by Professional Bks. Ltd.). Rothman.
Manual of Male Photography. Michael Busselle. 1986. 19.95 o.p. (ISBN 0-671-60558-5, Fireside); pap. 9.95 o.p. (ISBN 0-671-60556-9). S&S.
Manual of Methods for General Bacteriology. Ed. by Philipp Gerhardt et al. (Illus.). 524p. 1981. text ed. 37.00 o.p. (ISBN 0-914826-29-8); pap. 29.00 o.p. (ISBN 0-914826-30-1). Am Soc Microbio.
Manual of Non-Fermenting Gram-Negative Bacteria. Thomas R. Oberhofer. LC 84-21965. 154p. 1985. spiral bd. 22.95 o.p. (ISBN 0-471-80544-0, Pub. by Wiley Med.). Wiley.
Manual of Nursing Procedures. Ed. by Massachusetts General Hospital Department of Nursing et al. 1980. text ed. write for info. o.p. Little.
Manual of Nutritional Therapeutics. David H. Alpers et al. (Little, Brown Spiral Manual Ser.). 457p. 1983. Spiral bdg. 18.50 o.p. (ISBN 0-316-03509-2). Little.
Manual of Oncology Therapeutics. Kay See-Lasley & Robert Ignoffo. LC 81-1998. (Illus.). 475p. 1981. pap. text ed. 28.95 o.p. (ISBN 0-8016-4448-8). Mosby.
Manual of Operating Room Management. J. W. Cordner. 1982. pap. 18.95 o.p. (ISBN 0-87489-260-0). Med Economics.
Manual of Ophthalmic Terminology. Harold A. Stein et al. LC 81-14136. (Illus.). 269p. 1982. pap. text ed. 19.95 o.p. (ISBN 0-8016-4769-X). Mosby.
Manual of Outdoor Conservation Education. 96p. 3.00 o.p. (ISBN 0-317-35026-9, B3). Natl Audubon.
Manual of Pack Transportation. H. W. Daley. (Illus.). 224p. pap. 13.00 o.p. (ISBN 0-318-01796-2). Am Donkey.
Manual of Patient Care in Plastic Surgery. Ed. by Bernard M. Barrett. (Spiral Manual Ser.). 1982. spiralbound 18.95 o.p. (ISBN 0-316-08217-1). Little.
Manual of Patient Care in Vascular Surgery. John W. Hallett, Jr. & David C. Brewster. (Spiral Manual Ser.). 262p. 1982. spiralbound 18.50 o.p. (ISBN 0-316-34050-2). Little.
Manual of Pediatric Parenteral Nutrition. Ed. by John A. Kerner. LC 82-20264. 365p. 1983. 42.50 o.p. (ISBN 0-471-09291-6). Wiley.
Manual of Photography. 7th ed. Ed. by R. E. Jacobson et al. (Illus.). 682p. 1978. pap. 29.95 o.p. (ISBN 0-240-51239-1). Focal Pr.
Manual of Plant Names. C. Chichely Plowden. 260p. 1969. (ISBN 0-8022-1990-X). Philos Lib.
Manual of Practical Medical Microbiology & Parasitology. Thomas R. Oberhofer. 499p. 1985. pap. text ed. 29.95 o.p. (ISBN 0-471-80543-2, Pub. by Wiley Med). Wiley.
Manual of Practical Orthodontics. 3rd ed. Tulley & Campbell. 308p. 1970. 22.00 o.p. (ISBN 0-7236-0265-4, Pub. by John Wright UK). Butterworth.
Manual of Psychiatric Emergencies. Steven E. Hyman. (Spiral Manual Ser.). 288p. 1984. 18.50 o.p. (ISBN 0-316-38717-7). Little.
Manual of Psychiatric Nursing Care Plans. Judithm. Schultz & Sheila L. Dark. (Little, Brown Spiral Manual Ser. Nursing). 1982. 15.95 o.p. (ISBN 0-316-77516-9). Little.
Manual of Psychiatric Peer Review. 2nd ed. Ed. by Peer Review Committee of the American Psychiatric Assn. et al. LC 80-69213. 160p. 1981. spiral bdg. 12.00x o.p. (ISBN 0-89042-116-1, 42-116-1). Am Psychiatric.
Manual of Public Health & Community Medicine. 3rd ed. Essex-Cater. 740p. 1979. 79.00 o.p. (ISBN 0-7236-0477-0, Pub. by John Wright UK). Butterworth.
Manual of Renal Disease. Colin B. Brown. LC 84-17582. (Illus.). 227p. 1985. pap. text ed. 16.50 o.p. (ISBN 0-443-02875-3). Churchill.
Manual of Simple Nursing Procedures. 5th ed. Mary J. Leake. LC 71-139430. (Illus.). 1971. pap. write for info. o.p. (ISBN 0-7216-5662-5). Saunders.
Manual of Small Animal Surgical Therapeutics. Ed. by C. W. Betts & Stephen W. Crane. (Illus.). 424p. 1986. pap. text ed. 34.00 o.p. (ISBN 0-443-08327-4). Churchill.
Manual of Structural Kinesiology. 10th ed. Thompsom. 1984. 19.95 o.p. (ISBN 0-8016-4952-8). Mosby.
Manual of Surgical Therapeutics. 6th ed. Robert E. Condon & Lloyd M. Nyhus. (Little, Brown Spiral Manual Ser.). 1981. spiral bdg. 19.50 o.p. (ISBN 0-316-15263-3). Little.
Manual of Symbols & Terminology for Physicochemical Quantities & Units: Part 2 - Heterogeneous Catalysis. Robert L. Burwell, Jr. 1976. pap. 16.00 o.p. (ISBN 0-08-021360-X). Pergamon.
Manual of the Agromyzidae (Diptera) of the United States. Kenneth A. Spencer & George C. Steyskal. (Illus.). 484p. 1986. pap. 22.00 o.p. (S/N 001-000-04462-1). USGPO.
Manual of the Art of Bookbinding Containing Full Instructions in the Different Branches of Forwarding, Gilding & Finishing. James B. Nicholson. Ed. by John Bidwell. LC 78-74391. (Nineteenth-Century Book Arts & Printing History Ser.: Vol. 6). (Illus.). 1980. lib. bdg. 40.00 o.p. (ISBN 0-8240-3880-0). Garland Pub.
Manual of the Professional Cook. M. Pouget. 29.95 o.p. (ISBN 0-911202-21-8). Radio City.
Manual of Traditional Wood Carving with 1,146 Working Drawings & Photographic Illustrations. Ed. by Paul N. Hasluck. (Illus.). 15.75 o.p. (ISBN 0-8446-5583-X). Peter Smith.
Manual of Underwater Photography. T. Glover et al. 1977. 39.50 o.p. (ISBN 0-12-286750-5). Acad Pr.
Manual of Veterinary Surgery. M. Plakhotin. 447p. 1982. 11.95 o.p. (ISBN 0-8285-2316-9, Pub. by Mir Pubs USSR). Imported Pubns.
Manual of Woodcut Printmaking. Walter Chamberlain. (Illus.). 1978. encore ed. 3.95 o.p. (ISBN 0-684-16349-7, ScribT). Scribner.
Manual on Building Maintenance: Management, Vol. 1. Derek Miles. (Illus.). 78p. (Orig.). 1976. pap. 7.75x o.p. (ISBN 0-903031-28-0, Pub. by Intermed Tech England). Intermediate Tech.
Manual on Building Maintenance: Methods, Vol. 2. rev. ed. Derek Miles. (Illus.). 110p. (Orig.). 1979. pap. 7.75x o.p. (ISBN 0-903031-61-2, Pub. by Intermed Tech England). Intermediate Tech.
Manual on Design & Manufacture of Coned Disk Springs or Belleville Springs. 14.00 o.p. (ISBN 0-89883-359-0, HS63). Soc Auto Engineers.
Manual on Employment Discrimination & Civil Rights Actions in the Federal Courts, Attorneys' ed. Charles R. Richey. LC 85-7566. 628p. 1985. looseleaf 75.00 o.p. (ISBN 0-930273-50-8). Michie Co.
Manual on Employment Discrimination & Civil Rights Actions in the Federal Courts: Attorney's Edition. rev. ed. Charles R. Richey. LC 87-3672. 827p. 1987. looseleaf 80.00 o.p. (ISBN 0-930273-35-4). Michie Co.
Manual on Fishermen's Cooperatives. 124p. (Orig.). 1971. pap. 8.75 o.p. (ISBN 0-685-30137-0, F264, FAO). UNIPUB.
Manual on Insurance. Center for Research in Ambulatory Health Care Administration. 142p. 1974. 6.00 o.p. (ISBN 0-317-34837-X, 13-0000-909); members 3.00 o.p. (ISBN 0-317-34838-8); corresp. subscr. 4.80 o.p. (ISBN 0-317-34839-6). Med Group Mgmt.

Manual on Medical Literature for Law Librarians: A Handbook & Annotated Bibliography. Roy M. Mersky & D. Kronick. LC 73-7475. 170p. 1973. 35.00x o.p. (ISBN 0-87802-101-9, Dist. by Oceana). Glanville.

Manual on the Identification & Preparation of Fishery Investment Projects. (Fisheries Technical Papers: No. 149). 1976. pap. 7.50 o.p. (ISBN 0-685-71575-2, F882, FAO). UNIPUB.

Manuale ad usum percelebris ecclesie Sarisburensis. A. J. Collins. (Henry Bradshaw Society Publications: No. 91). 1960. 27.00 o.p. (Pub. by Boydell & Brewer). Longwood Pub Group.

Manuale Typografia, 2 Vols. Giambattista Bodoni. 1960. 200.00x o.p. (ISBN 0-87556-035-0). Saifer.

Manuals on Mayhem: An Annotated Bibliography of Books on Combat Martial Arts & Self-Defense. Bradley J. Steiner. 1979. pap. 6.00 o.p. (ISBN 0-686-26031-7). Loompanics.

Manuel Illustre D'histoire De La Litterature Francaise. Lanson & Tuffrau. (Illus.). 13.95 o.p. (ISBN 0-685-11351-5). French & Eur.

Manufactured Carbon. H. W. Davidson et al. 1968. 23.00 o.p. (ISBN 0-08-012667-7); pap. 9.25 o.p. (ISBN 0-08-012666-9). Pergamon.

Manufacturing & Machine Tool Operations. 2nd ed. Herman W. Pollack. (Illus.). 1979. pap. text ed. 39.33 ref. o.p. (ISBN 0-13-555771-2). P-H.

Manufacturing Controls: How the Manufacturing Manager Can Improve Profitability. Martin R. Smith. 192p. 1981. 26.95 o.p. (ISBN 0-442-21942-3). Van Nos Reinhold.

Manufacturing in Space. (PED Ser.: Vol. 11). 224p. 1983. pap. text ed. 40.00 o.p. (ISBN 0-317-02629-1, H00286). ASME.

Manufacturing: Materials & Processes. 3rd ed. H. D. Moore & D. R. Kibbey. LC 81-4261. 783p. 1982. 45.95 o.p. (ISBN 0-471-87689-5). Wiley.

Manufacturing Organization & Management. 4th ed. Harold T. Amrine & John A. Ritchey. (Illus.). 576p. 1982. pap. text ed. 42.67 o.p. (ISBN 0-13-555748-8). P-H.

Manufacturing Planning & Control Systems. Thomas E. Vollman & D. Clay Whybark. LC 83-70917. 400p. 1984. 40.00 o.p. (ISBN 0-87094-452-5). Dow Jones-Irwin.

Manufacturing Processes. 7th ed. B. H. Amstead et al. LC 78-16185. 739p. 1977. SI Version. text ed. 46.50x o.p. (ISBN 0-471-03575-0); (ISBN 0-471-06245-6). Wiley.

Manufacturing Science & Technology of the Future. Ed. by N. P. Suh. 230p. 1986. pap. 55.00 o.p. (ISBN 0-08-033451-2, Pub. by PPL). Pergamon.

Manufacturing Solutions Based on Engineering Sciences. Ed. by L. Kops. (PED Ser.: Vol. 3). 207p. 1981. 40.00 o.p. (ISBN 0-686-34503-7, H00209). ASME.

Manufacturing Technology for Level-2 Technicians. Bruce J. Black. (Illus.). 183p. 1983. pap. text ed. 20.00x o.p. (ISBN 0-7131-3485-2). Trans-Atl Phila.

Manufacturing Technology for Level-3 Technicians. Bruce J. Black. 224p. 1981. pap. 22.95x o.p. (ISBN 0-7131-3430-5). Trans-Atl Phila.

Manuscript Sources for the History of Irish Civilisation, 11 Vols. National Library of Ireland Staff, Dublin. 1970. Set. lib. bdg. 1090.00 o.p. (ISBN 0-8161-0662-2, Hall Library). G K Hall.

Manuscript Sources for the History of Irish Civilisation: First Supplement, 3 vols. National Library of Ireland Staff. Ed. by Alf MacLochlainn. 1979. Set. lib. bdg. 390.00 o.p. (ISBN 0-8161-0248-1, Hall Library). G K Hall.

Manuscript Tracking: Reusable Edition. Ed. by W. Edwards & S. Edwards. (Large Type Tracking Ser.). (gr. k-1). 1975. 5.00 o.p. (ISBN 0-89039-017-7). Ann Arbor Pubs.

Manuscripts & Readers in Fifteenth-Century England: The Literary Implications of Manuscript Study Essays from the Conference at the University of York. Ed. by Derek Pearsall. LC 83-9223. (Illus.). 144p. 1983. 45.00 o.p. (ISBN 0-85991-148-9, Pub. by Boydell & Brewer). Longwood Pub Group.

Manuscripts Inventory & the Catalogs of Manuscripts, Books & Pictures, 3 vols. Radcliffe College, the Arthur & Elizabeth Schlesinger Library on the History of Women in America Staff. 1973. lib. bdg. 300.00 book catalog o.p. (ISBN 0-8161-1053-0, Hall Library). G K Hall.

Manuscripts of the American Revolution in the Boston Public Library: A Descriptive Catalog. Boston Public Library Staff. 1968. 69.00 o.p. (ISBN 0-8161-0825-0, Hall Library). G K Hall.

Many a Green Isle. Agnes S. Turnbull. (Large Print Bks.). 1985. lib. bdg. 14.95 o.p. (ISBN 0-8161-3645-9). G K Hall.

Many & One: A Social History of the United States. Robert Cruden. (Illus.). 1980. pap. text ed. (ISBN 0-13-555714-3). P-H.

Many-Body Description of Nuclear Structure & Reactions. Ed. by C. Bloch. (Italian Physical Society: Course 36). 1967. 88.00 o.p. (ISBN 0-12-368836-1). Acad Pr.

Many-Body Problem, Vol. 2. Ed. by E. R. Caianiello. (Spring Lectures, 1963). 1964. 32.00 o.p. (ISBN 0-12-154574-1). Acad Pr.

Many Dimensions of Family Practice: Proceedings. North American Symposium on Family Practice Staff. LC 80-14847. 340p. 1980. pap. 15.95 o.p. (ISBN 0-87304-179-8). Family Serv.

Many Islands. William Goodreau. LC 61-9255. (Orig.). 1961. pap. 1.65 o.p. (ISBN 0-689-10100-7, Atheneum). Macmillan.

Many Lives of Benjamin Franklin. Aliki. 1988. price not set o.p. Prentice Hall Pr.

Many Mansions. Donald L. Kimball. 1981. 12.50 o.p. (ISBN 0-682-49514-X). Exposition-Phoenix.

Many Peoples, Many Faiths. 2nd ed. Robert S. Ellwood, Jr. (Illus.). 416p. 1982. pap. text ed. 29.67 o.p. (ISBN 0-13-556001-2). P-H.

Many Powerful Methods of Natural Healing. Franklin Hall. LC 84-90494. 62p. 1985. 7.95 o.p. (ISBN 0-533-06375-2). Vantage.

Many-Valued Logics. J. Barkley Rosser & Atwell R. Turquette. LC 77-405. (Studies in Logic & the Foundations of Mathematics). 1977. Repr. of 1952 ed. lib. bdg. 24.75x o.p. (ISBN 0-8371-9449-0, ROMV). Greenwood.

Many Voices: Bilingualism, Culture & Education. Jane Miller. 250p. 1983. 25.00x o.p. (ISBN 0-7100-9331-4); pap. 11.95x o.p. (ISBN 0-7100-9341-1). Routledge Chapman & Hall.

Many Winters. Nancy Wood. LC 84-81031. (Illus.). 1984. pap. 8.95 o.p. (ISBN 0-88307-662-4). Gannon.

Many Worlds, One God. Kenneth J. Delano. 1977. 7.00 o.p. (ISBN 0-682-48644-2). Exposition-Phoenix.

Manya's Story. Bettyanne Gray. LC 77-92305. (Books for Adults & Young Adults). (Illus.). (gr. 5 up). 1978. PLB 7.95 o.p. (ISBN 0-8225-0762-5). Lerner Pubns.

Mao-Tse-Tung: An Ideological & Psychological Portrait. F. Burlatsky. 396p. 1980. 8.95 o.p. (ISBN 0-8285-1712-6, Pub. by Progress Pubs USSR). Imported Pubns.

Mao Tse Tung on Literature & Art. 1967. 4.95 o.p. (ISBN 0-8351-0456-7). China Bks.

Mao Zedong. Paul Rule. (Leaders of Asia Ser.). 1984. pap. 4.95 o.p. (ISBN 0-318-12093-3). U of Queensland Pr.

Maori Art. A. Hamilton. (Illus.). 75.00x o.p. (ISBN 0-87556-539-5). Saifer.

Maori Songs of New Zealand. Ed. by Viking Seven Seas, Ltd. Staff. 160p. 1967. pap. 5.50 o.p. (ISBN 0-85467-031-9, Pub. by Viking New Zealand). Intl Spec Bk.

Mao's Betrayal. W. Ming. 278p. 1979. 8.45 o.p. (ISBN 0-8285-0404-0, Pub. by Progress Pubs USSR). Imported Pubns.

Mao's China: A Nation in Transition. Ram K. Vepa. 1980. 14.00x o.p. (ISBN 0-8364-0591-9, Pub. by Abhina India). South Asia Bks.

MAP: A Market Anti-Inflation Plan. Abba P. Lerner & David C. Colander. 128p. 1980. pap. text ed. 9.00 o.p. (ISBN 0-15-555060-8, HC). HarBraceJ.

Map Classification: A Comparison of Schemes, with Special Reference to the Continent of Africa. Christopher E. Merrett. (Occasional Papers: No. 154). 1982. 3.00 o.p. U of Ill Lib Info Sci.

Map of Great Britain. (Illus.). Date not set. (ISBN 0-86145-000-0, Pub. by Auto Assn England). Salem Hse Pubs.

Map of London. (Illus.). Date not set. (ISBN 0-86145-069-8, Pub. by Auto Assn England). Salem Hse Pubs.

Map Workbook for Our United States. Victoria W. Reitz. (Social Studies Ser.). 64p. (gr. 7-12). 1984. wkbk. 2.70 o.p. (ISBN 0-88336-492-1). New Readers.

Maphaeus Vegius & His Thirteenth Book of the "Aeneid" Anna C. Brinton. Ed. by Steele Commager. LC 77-70765. (Latin Poetry Ser.). 1978. lib. bdg. 26.00 o.p. (ISBN 0-8240-2963-1). Garland Pub.

Maple Street. Nan H. Agle. LC 78-97034. (gr. 3-7). 1979. 6.95 o.p. (ISBN 0-395-28838-X, Clarion). HM.

Mapping Information. Howard Fisher. 1982. text ed. 45.00 o.s.i. (ISBN 0-89011-571-0). Abt Bks.

Mapping of Australia. R. V. Tooley. 650p. 1980. 75.00 o.p. (ISBN 0-87556-705-3). Saifer.

Mapping Software & Cartographic Data Bases, Vol. 2. Laboratory for Computer Graphics & Spatial Analysis, Harvard University Graduate School of Design Staff. (Harvard Library of Computer Graphics, Mapping Collection). (Illus.). 240p. 1979. pap. 15.95 o.p. (ISBN 0-8122-1182-0). U of Pa Pr.

Mapping the Commodore 64. Sheldon Leemon. 268p. (Orig.). 1984. pap. 15.95 o.p. (ISBN 0-942386-23-X). Compute Pubns.

Maps. Howard McCord. 1971. pap. 5.00 o.p. (ISBN 0-87711-040-9). Story Line.

Maps. (Easy-to-Make Photocopier Bks.). 1982. pap. 14.95 o.p. (ISBN 0-87280-045-8, Asher-Gallant). Caddylak Systs.

Maps & Charts Published in America Before 1800. J. Wheat. 215p. 55.00 o.p. (ISBN 0-87556-685-5). Saifer.

Maps & Surveys of the Pueblo Lands of Los Angeles. Neal Harlow. LC 75-43213. (Illus.). xvii, 169p. 1976. 150.00 o.p. (ISBN 0-87093-173-3). Dawsons.

Maps for America: Cartographic Products of the United States Geological Survey & Others. Morris M. Thompson. LC 81-607878. (Illus.). 279p. 1981. 15.00 o.p. (ISBN 0-317-62871-2, S-N 024-001-03449-2). USGPO.

Maps for the Local Historian- a Guide to the British Sources. J. B. Harley. 86p. 1972. pap. text ed. 6.25x o.p. (ISBN 0-7199-0834-5, Pub. by Bedford England). Gower Pub Co.

Maps of the Roads of Ireland. George Taylor & Andrew Skinner. (Illus.). 328p. 1983. Repr. of 1783 ed. text ed. 40.00x o.p. (ISBN 0-7165-0063-9, BBA 02190, Pub. by Irish Academic Pr Ireland). Biblio Dist.

Maqamat of Badi Al-Zaman Al-Hamadhani. 2nd ed. William J. Prendergast. 204p. 1973. Repr. of 1915 ed. text ed. 9.95x o.p. (ISBN 0-7007-0029-3). Humanities.

Maquiladoras & Migration: Workers in the Mexico-U.S. Border Program. Mitchell A. Seligson & Edward J. Williams. (Mexico-United States Border Development Program Ser.). 220p. 1982. pap. 12.50x o.p. (ISBN 0-292-75072-2). U of Tex Pr.

Mara. Tova Reich. 256p. 1978. 8.95 o.p. (ISBN 0-374-20286-9). FS&G.

Mara Simba: The African Lion. Roger Caras. 215p. 1985. 15.95 o.p. (ISBN 0-03-016611-X). H Holt & Co.

Mara's Way. Diana Stainforth. 592p. 1987. pap. 4.95 o.p. (ISBN 0-380-70333-5). Avon.

Marathon Groups: Reality & Symbol. Elizabeth E. Mintz. LC 73-157796. (Century Psychology Ser.). 1971. 29.50x o.p. (ISBN 0-89197-293-5); pap. text ed. 7.95x o.p. (ISBN 0-89197-294-3). Irvington.

Marathon Made Easier. Cliff Temple. LC 82-71258. 192p. 1982. 12.95 o.p. (ISBN 0-689-11336-6, Atheneum). Macmillan.

Marathon Mom: The Wife & Mother Running Book. Linda Schreiber & JoAnne Stang. 1980. 9.95 o.p. (ISBN 0-395-29135-6); pap. 5.95 o.p. (ISBN 0-395-29136-4). HM.

Marathon Runners. Thomas Barrett & Robert Morrissey, Jr. LC 81-11204. (Illus.). 160p. (gr. 7 up). 1981. lib. bdg. 9.79 o.s.i. (ISBN 0-671-34019-0). Messner.

Marathon Running: A Medical Science Handbook. William N. Taylor. LC 82-17274. (Illus.). 112p. (Orig.). 1982. pap. 12.95x o.p. (ISBN 0-89950-054-4). McFarland & Co.

Marathon: What It Takes to Go the Distance. Marc Bloom. LC 80-18859. (Illus.). 304p. 1981. 15.95 o.p. (ISBN 0-03-052476-8); pap. 7.95 o.p. (ISBN 0-03-059153-8). H Holt & Co.

Marathoning. rev. ed. Bill Rodgers & Joe Concannon. 352p. 1982. pap. 9.50 o.p. (ISBN 0-671-25088-4, Fireside). S&S.

Marbacka. Selma Lagerlof. Tr. by Velma S. Howard. LC 70-167024. (Illus.). viii, 296p. 1974. Repr. of 1926 ed. 34.00x o.p. (ISBN 0-8103-4031-3). Gale.

Marble Dance. Lygia F. Telles. 192p. 1986. pap. 3.95 o.p. (ISBN 0-380-89628-1, Bard). Avon.

Marble Queen. Henri Cole. LC 85-48123. 80p. 1986. 15.00 o.p. (ISBN 0-689-11779-5, Atheneum); pap. 8.95 o.p. (ISBN 0-689-11796-5, Atheneum). Macmillan.

Marbling: A History & Bibliography. Phoebe J. Easton. (Illus.). xiii, 190p. 1983. 100.00 o.p. (ISBN 0-87093-180-6). Dawsons.

Marburg Virus Disease. Ed. by G. A. Martini & R. Siegert. LC 77-142386. (Illus.). 1971. 53.30 o.p. (ISBN 0-387-05199-6). Springer-Verlag.

Marc Chagall. Isaac Kloomok. 1951. (ISBN 0-8022-0870-3). Philos Lib.

Marcel Dube & French-Canadian Drama. Edwin Hamblet. LC 78-114059. 1970. 7.50 o.p. (ISBN 0-682-47054-6). Exposition-Phoenix.

Marcel Duchamp. Octavio Paz. Tr. by Rachel Phillips & Donald Gardner. LC 81-51527. (Illus.). 206p. 1981. Repr. of 1976 ed. 14.95 o.p. (ISBN 0-394-51815-2). Seaver Bks.

Marcel Proust. Roger Shattuck. LC 81-47990. 179p. 1982. 25.50 o.p. (ISBN 0-691-06513-6); pap. 9.95x o.p. (ISBN 0-691-01391-8). Princeton U Pr.

Marcel Proust & Deliverance from Time. Germaine Bree. Tr. by R. J. Richards & A. D. Truitt. LC 81-13256. vii, 252p. 1982. Repr. of 1969 ed. lib. bdg. 35.00x o.p. (ISBN 0-313-23184-2, BRPT). Greenwood.

March Hare Murders. Elizabeth Ferrars. (Black Dagger Crime Ser.). 192p. 1987. text ed. 14.95x o.p. (ISBN 0-86220-708-8, Pub. by Firecrest Pub Ltd). Prescott Pr Nh.

March Inland: Origins of the ILWU Warehouse Division, 1934-1938. Harvey Schwartz. (Monograph Ser: No. 19). 1978. 7.50 o.p. (ISBN 0-89215-090-4). U Cal LA Indus Rel.

March of Empire: Frontier Defense in the Southwest, 1848-1860. Averam B. Bender. LC 69-13819. (Illus.). Repr. of 1952 ed. lib. bdg. 35.00x o.p. (ISBN 0-8371-0306-1, BEMA). Greenwood.

March of Folly: From Troy to Vietnam. Barbara W. Tuchman. (General Ser.). 1984. lib. bdg. 19.95 o.p. (ISBN 0-8161-3761-7, Large Print Bks). G K Hall.

March of Journalism. Harold Herd. LC 73-722. (Illus.). 352p. 1973. Repr. of 1952 ed. lib. bdg. 22.50x o.p. (ISBN 0-8371-6788-4, HEMG). Greenwood.

March of Militant. Michael Crick. 1986. pap. 11.95 o.p. (ISBN 0-571-14643-0). Faber & Faber.

March Toward Matter. John M. McPartland. 1952. (ISBN 0-8022-1032-5). Philos Lib.

Marching On: Daily Readings for Younger People. William Barclay. Ed. by Denis Duncan. LC 74-30053. 1975. pap. 3.25 o.s.i. (ISBN 0-664-24827-6, Westminster). Westminster John Knox.

Marching Orders: Daily Readings for Younger People. William Barclay. LC 74-26601. 1975. pap. 2.95 o.s.i. (ISBN 0-664-24826-8, Westminster). Westminster John Knox.

Marching to Glory: The History of the Salvation Army in the United States, 1880 to 1980. Edward H. McKinley. LC 79-2997. (Illus.). 224p. 1980. 8.95 o.p. (ISBN 0-06-065538-0). HarpR.

Marco see Heinemann Guided Readers.

Marcovaldo or The Seasons in the City: 01027514x. Italo Calvino. Tr. by William Weaver from Ital. LC 83-4372. (Helen & Kurt Wolff Bk.). 121p. 1983. Repr. of 1963 ed. 9.95 o.p. (ISBN 0-15-157081-7). HarBraceJ.

Marcus Crassus & the Late Roman Republic. Allen M. Ward. LC 76-56794. 320p. 1977. 33.00x o.p. (ISBN 0-8262-0216-0). U of Mo Pr.

Mare Crisium: The View from Luna Twenty-Four, Houston, Texas. Ed. by Lunar & Planetary Institute Staff. 733p. 1979. 65.00 o.p. (ISBN 0-08-022965-4). Pergamon.

Margaret Anna Cusack: One Woman's Campaign for Women's Rights. Irene F. Eager. (Arlen House Ser.). 256p. pap. 7.95 o.p. (ISBN 0-905223-11-X, Dist. by Scribner). M Boyars Pubs.

Margaret Bourke-White. Genie Iverson. (People to Remember Ser.). (Illus.). 32p. (gr. 4 up). 1980. PLB 8.95 o.p. Creative Ed.

Margaret Boyles Book of Needle Art. Margaret Boyles. LC 77-73064. (Illus.). 1978. pap. 9.95 o.p. (ISBN 0-15-657964-2, Harv). HarBraceJ.

Margaret Boyles' Designs for Babies. Margaret Boyles. 1983. 17.25 o.p. (ISBN 0-671-43902-2). S&S.

Margaret Boyles' Designs for Babies. Margaret Boyles. 144p. 1984. pap. 8.95 o.p. (ISBN 0-671-53028-3, Fireside). S&S.

Margaret Cole, 1893-1980: A Political Biography. Betty D. Vernon. 240p. 1986. 34.50 o.p. (ISBN 0-7099-2611-1, Pub. by Croom Helm Ltd). Routledge Chapman & Hall.

Margaret Drabble. Joanne V. Creighton. (Contemporary Writers Ser.). 127p. 1985. pap. 5.95 o.p. (ISBN 0-416-38390-4, 9469). Routledge Chapman & Hall.

Margaret Drabble. Nora Stovel. Ed. by Dale Salwak. (Contemporary Writers Ser.: Vol. 2). 1988. 19.95x o.p. (ISBN 1-55742-035-1); pap. 10.95x o.p. (ISBN 1-55742-034-3). Starmont Hse.

Margaret Fuller: Bluestocking, Romantic, Revolutionary. Ellen Wilson. LC 77-381. (Illus.). 192p. (gr. 7 up). 1977. 10.95 o.p. (ISBN 0-374-34807-3). FS&G.

Margaret Mead: A Life. Jane Howard. (Illus.). 416p. 1984. 19.45 o.p. (ISBN 0-671-25225-9). S&S.

Margaret Mitchell: A Dynamo Going to Waste (Letters to Allen Edee 1919-1921) Margaret Mitchell. Ed. by Jane B. Peacock. LC 85-60337. (Illus.). 192p. 1985. 12.95 o.p. (ISBN 0-931948-70-3). Peachtree Pubs.

Margaret Mitchell of Atlanta. Finis Farr. 1976. pap. 1.75 o.p. (ISBN 0-380-00810-6, 20594). Avon.

Margaret Sanger, an Autobiography see Works.

Margaret Thatcher. rev. ed. Russell Lewis. 250p. 1984. 17.95x o.p. (ISBN 0-7102-0258-X). Routledge Chapman & Hall.

Margaret: The Tragic Princess. James Brough. 1979. pap. 2.25 o.p. (ISBN 0-380-44206-X, 44206). Avon.

Margeurite Tanner. Elizabeth N. Dubus. 304p. (Orig.). 1982. pap. 2.95 o.p. (ISBN 0-8439-1037-2, Pub. by Leisure Bks CT). Dorchester Pub Co.
Margie & Me. Beverly Wirth. LC 82-21075. (Illus.). 48p. (gr. k-3). 1983. 8.95 o.s.i. (ISBN 0-02-793110-2, Four Winds). Macmillan.
Margin of Hope: An Intellectual Autobiography. Irving Howe. LC 82-47921. (Illus.). 368p. 1982. 14.95 o.p. (ISBN 0-15-157138-4). HarBraceJ.
Marginal Aspects of Contemporary American Culture. Henry Winthrop. LC 72-8860. 138p. 1972. 22.00x o.p. (ISBN 0-8422-5070-0); pap. text ed. 8.95x o.p. (ISBN 0-8422-0271-4). Irvington.
Marginal Basin Geology: Volcanic & Associated Sedimentary & Tectonic Processes in Modern & Ancient Marginal Basins. Ed. by B. P. Kokelaar & Malcolm Howells. (Illus.). 328p. 1984. text ed. 70.00x o.p. (ISBN 0-632-01073-8). Blackwell Sci.
Marginal Manager: The Changing Role of Supervisors in Australia. Peter Gilmour & Russell D. Lansbury. (Illus.). 179p. 1985. text ed. 30.00x o.p. (ISBN 0-7022-1686-0). U of Queensland Pr.
Marguerite. Gail Haley. (Illus.). 48p. (ps-2). 1988. pap. 12.95 o.p. (ISBN 0-87460-331-5). Lion Bks.
Mari at Fifty: Studies in Honor of the 50th Anniversary of the Discovery of Tell Hariri-Mari. Ed. by Gordon D. Young. 1988. text ed. price not set o.p. (ISBN 0-931464-28-5). Eisenbrauns.
Maria. Isaacs. (Span). 4.00x o.s.i. (ISBN 0-686-00875-8). Colton Bk.
Maria. Maria Von Trapp. 1980. pap. 2.25 o.p. (ISBN 0-380-00783-5, 56267). Avon.
Maria Callas: The Woman Behind the Legend. Arianna Stassinopoulos. 1981. 16.95 o.p. (ISBN 0-671-25583-5). S&S.
Maria Canossa. Sandra Paretti. 288p. 1982. pap. 2.50 o.p. (ISBN 0-380-60277-6, 60277-6). Avon.
Maria: Cuando la Muerte Canta. LC 81-67052. (Coleccion Espejo De Paciencia Ser.). (Illus.). 127p. (Orig., Span.). 1981. pap. 5.95 o.p. (ISBN 0-89729-295-2). Ediciones.
Maria Looney & the Cosmic Circus. Jerome Beatty, Jr. (Illus.). 144p. (Orig.). (gr. 3-7). 1978. pap. 1.95 o.p. (ISBN 0-380-40311-0, 77040-7, Camelot). Avon.
Maria Looney & the Remarkable Robot. Jerome Beatty, Jr. (Illus.). 144p. (Orig.). (gr. 3-7). 1979. pap. 1.95 o.p. (ISBN 0-380-43232-3, 78626-5, Camelot). Avon.
Maria Looney on the Red Planet. Jerome Beatty, Jr. (Illus.). (gr. 3-7). 1977. pap. 1.50 o.p. (ISBN 0-380-01729-6, 75523, Camelot). Avon.
Maria, Maria, Look! Ralph Cintron. 1982. 1.50 o.s.i. (ISBN 0-942582-04-7). Erie St Pr.
Maria Montessori: A Biography. Rita Kramer. LC 83-5124. 1983. pap. 12.50 o.s.i. (ISBN 0-226-45236-0). U of Chicago Pr.
Maria Poppina AB ad ZA. Pamela L. Travers. Tr. by G. M. Lyne. LC 68-12894. (Illus., Latin.). (gr. 6 up). 1968. 4.95 o.p. (ISBN 0-15-252087-2, HJ). HarBraceJ.
Maria Sabina & Her Mazatec Mushroom Velada. R. Gordon Wasson et al. LC 74-964. 1975. limited ed 82.50 o.p. (ISBN 0-15-157202-X); 250.00 o.p. (ISBN 0-15-157204-6). HarBraceJ.
Maria: The Genuine Memoirs of a Young Lady of Rank & Fortune, 1765, 2 vols. in 1. Edward Kimber. LC 74-16057. (Novel in England, 1700-1775 Ser). 1975. lib. bdg. 61.00 o.p. (ISBN 0-8240-1171-6). Garland Pub.
Marian Anderson: Lady from Philadelphia. Shirlee P. Newman. (Illus.). (gr. 5-11). 1966. 5.50 o.s.i. (ISBN 0-664-32370-7, Westminster). Westminster John Knox.
Marian Studies: Proceedings, Vol. 34. Mariological Society of America. North Palm Beach, Fla. Convention, 1983. 160p. 10.00 o.p. (ISBN 0-318-17249-6). Mariological Soc.
Marian Studies: Proceedings of the Mariological Society of America, Atlanta Convention, 1975, Vol. 26. Mariological Society of America Staff. 271p. 10.00 o.p. (ISBN 0-318-14793-9). Mariological Soc.
Marian Studies: Proceedings of the Mariological Society of America, Dayton Convention, 1985. Mariological Society of America Staff. 10.00 o.p. (ISBN 0-318-17886-9). Mariological Soc.
Marian Studies: Proceedings of the Mariological Society of America, Detroit Convention, 1960, Vol. 11. Mariological Society of America Staff. 184p. 10.00 o.p. (ISBN 0-318-14797-1). Mariological Soc.
Marian Studies: Proceedings of the Mariological Society of America, Dayton Convention, 1968, Vol. 19. Mariological Society of America Staff. 128p. 10.00 o.p. (ISBN 0-318-14796-3). Mariological Soc.
Marian Studies: Proceedings of the Mariological Society of America, Kansas City, MO. Convention, 1964, Vol. 15. Mariological Society of America Staff. 184p. 10.00 o.p. (ISBN 0-318-14798-X). Mariological Soc.
Marian Studies: Proceedings of the Mariological Society of America, North Palm Beach Convention, 1967, Vol. 18. Mariological Society of America Staff. 158p. 10.00 o.p. (ISBN 0-318-14791-2). Mariological Soc.
Marian Studies: Proceedings of the Mariological Society of America, San Antonio, Texas, Convention, 1982, Vol. 33. Mariological Society of America Staff. 204p. 10.00 o.p. (ISBN 0-318-17248-8). Mariological Soc.
Mariana. Karen S. Dean. 176p. (YA) (gr. 7 up). 1981. pap. 1.95 o.p. (ISBN 0-380-78345-2, 84269-6, Flare). Avon.
Mariani's Coast-To-Coast Dining Guide. John F. Mariani. LC 84-41003. 704p. (Orig.). 1986. pap. 12.95 o.s.i. (ISBN 0-8129-1309-4, Dist. by Random House). Times Bks.
Mariano Medina: Colorado Mountain Man. Zethyl Gates. (Illus.). 112p. 1981. pap. 5.95 o.p. (ISBN 0-933472-51-X). Johnson Bks.
Maria's House. Jean Merrill. LC 74-75565. (Illus.). 64p. (gr. 3-5). 1974. 4.95 o.p. (ISBN 0-689-30433-1, Atheneum). Macmillan.
Marie & Bruce. Wallace Shawn. LC 80-991. 160p. 1980. pap. 4.95 o.s.i. (ISBN 0-394-17661-8, E-757, Ever). Grove.
Marie Bonaparte: A Life. Celia Bertin. LC 82-47679. (Helen & Kurt Wolff Bk.). (Illus.). 304p. 1982. 17.95 o.p. (ISBN 0-15-157252-6). HarBraceJ.
Maries de la Tour Eiffel see Theatre.
Marihuana: Chemistry, Biochemistry, & Cellular Efffects. Ed. by G. G. Nahas. 400p. 1976. 38.50 o.p. (ISBN 0-387-07554-2). Springer-Verlag.
Marihuana Reconsidered. rev. ed. Lester Grinspoon. LC 77-76767. 1977. 25.00x o.p. (ISBN 0-674-54833-7); pap. 9.95 o.p. (ISBN 0-674-54834-5). Harvard U Pr.
Marihuana: The First Twelve Thousand Years. E. L. Abel. 1982. pap. text ed. 6.95 o.p. (ISBN 0-07-000047-6). McGraw.
Marihuana Today: A Compilation of Medical Findings for the Layman. 3rd, rev. ed. G. K. Russell. LC 77-79477. (Illus.). 80p. 1979. pap. 3.70 o.p. (ISBN 0-08-025509-4). Pergamon.
Marijuana: Biochemical, Physiological, & Pathological Effects. Peter B. Dews et al. (Illus.). 220p. 1973. text ed. 32.50x o.p. (ISBN 0-8422-7094-9). Irvington.
Marijuana Food: A Handbook of Marijuana Extract Cooking. William Drake. (Illus.). 160p. 1987. 9.95 o.p. (ISBN 0-914171-15-1). Ronin Pub.
Marijuana: Medical Uses. 1984. pap. 0.25 o.p. (ISBN 0-89230-159-7). Do it Now.
Marijuana Potency. Michael Starks. LC 77-82454. 1977. pap. 10.95 o.p. (ISBN 0-915904-27-6). And-Or Pr.
Marijuana: Report of the Indian Hemp Drug Commission 1893-1894. 30.00 o.p. Anderson Pub Co.
Marijuana Techniques & Politics. Ed Rosenthal & Mel Frank. 320p. 1985. 12.95 o.p. (ISBN 0-915904-78-0). And-Or Pr.
Marika. Darwin Porter. LC 77-79538. 1977. 8.95 o.p. (ISBN 0-87795-175-6, Arbor Hse). Morrow.
Marilyn. Gloria Steinem. LC 86-19442. (Illus.). 224p. 1986. 24.95 o.p. (ISBN 0-8050-0060-7). H Holt & Co.
Marilyn the Wild. Jerome Charyn. LC 75-31072. 1976. 8.95 o.p. (ISBN 0-87795-129-2, Arbor Hse). Morrow.
Marilyn Wood's Wonderful Weekends. Marilyn Wood. 1984. 9.95 o.p. (ISBN 0-671-47041-8). S&S.
Marin County Street Atlas & Directory, 1986. rev. ed. Thomas Bros. Maps Staff. (Illus.). 72p. 1987. pap. 10.95 o.p. Thomas Bros Maps.
Marin County Street Atlas, 1985. Thomas Bros. Maps Staff. (Illus.). 72p. 1987. pap. 10.95 o.p. (ISBN 0-88130-204-X). Thomas Bros Maps.
Marin County Street Guide & Directory 1988. Thomas Bros. Maps Staff. (Illus.). 74p. 1988. pap. 10.95 o.p. (ISBN 0-88130-276-7). Thomas Bros Maps.
Marin de Gibraltar. Marguerite Duras. (Coll. Soleil). 1952. 13.25 o.p. (ISBN 0-685-11352-3). Schoenhof.
Marin-the Place, the People: Profile of a California County. Jane Futcher. LC 84-22418. (Illus.). 192p. 1985. pap. 14.95 o.s.i. (ISBN 0-15-657304-0, Harv). HarBraceJ.
Marin-the Place, the People: Profile of a California County. Jane Futcher & Robert Conover. LC 80-27986. 1981. 24.95 o.p. (ISBN 0-03-057472-2). H Holt & Co.
Marine Algae of New Zealand: Phaeophyceae, Vol. 2. Ed. by V. J. Chapman. 1961. pap. 24.00x o.p. (ISBN 3-7682-0077-9). Lubrecht & Cramer.
Marine Algae of Virginia. Harold J. Humm. LC 78-16319. (Virginia Institute of Marine Science, Special Papers in Marine Science Ser.: No. 3). (Illus.). 263p. 1979. 17.95x o.p. (ISBN 0-8139-0701-2). U Pr of Va.
Marine & Estuarine Geochemistry. Ed. by Anne C. Sigleo & Akihiko Hattori. LC 85-13127. (Illus.). 340p. 1985. 39.00 o.p. (ISBN 0-87371-007-X). Lewis Pubs Inc.
Marine Applications for Fuel Cell Technology: A Technical Memorandum. (CTA-TM-0-37 Ser.). (Illus.). 39p. (Orig.). 1986. pap. 1.50 o.p. (ISBN 0-318-19936-X, S/N 052-003-01021-6). USGPO.
Marine Chemistry, Vol. 2: Theory & Applications. Dean F. Martin. 464p. 1970. 49.75 o.p. (ISBN 0-8247-1458-X). Dekker.
Marine Corrosion: Causes & Prevention. Francis L. Laque. LC 75-16307. (Corrosion Monograph). 332p. 1975. 59.95x o.p. (ISBN 0-471-51745-3, Pub. by Wiley-Interscience). Wiley.
Marine Diesel Standard Practices. 229p. 5.00 o.p. (ISBN 0-318-13960-X). Diesel Engine.
Marine Electrical Practice. G. O. Watson. (Illus.). 320p. 1957. (ISBN 0-8022-1819-9). Philos Lib.
Marine Geology & Oceanography of Arabian Sea & Coastal Pakistan. Ed. by Bilal U. Haq & John D. Milliman. 384p. 1985. 19.95 o.p. (ISBN 0-442-23216-0). Van Nos Reinhold.
Marine Geology & Oceanography of the Arctic Seas. Ed. by Y. Herman. LC 73-22236. (Illus.). 416p. 1974. 71.50 o.p. (ISBN 0-387-06628-4). Springer-Verlag.
Marine Invertebrates. National Research Council Assembly of Life Sciences. 1981. pap. 19.25x o.p. (ISBN 0-309-03134-6). Natl Acad Pr.
Marine Life: An Illustrated Encyclopedia of Invertebrates in the Sea. J. David George & Jennifer George. LC 79-10976. 288p. 1979. 79.00 o.p. (ISBN 0-471-05675-8, Pub. by Wiley-Interscience). Wiley.
Marine Microbiology. C. D. Litchfield. (Benchmark Papers in Microbiology: Vol. 11). 1976. 84.00 o.p. (ISBN 0-12-786975-1). Acad Pr.
Marine Mysteries & Dramatic Disasters of New England. Edward R. Snow. LC 76-28985. 1976. 9.95 o.s.i. (ISBN 0-396-07378-6). Dodd.
Marine Natural Products. Ed. by R. H. Thomson. 1977. 35.00 o.p. (ISBN 0-08-021242-5). Pergamon.
Marine Organisms: Genetics, Ecology, & Evolution. Ed. by Bruno Battaglia & John A. Beardmore. LC 78-9715. (NATO Conference Series IV, Marine Science: Vol. 2). 768p. 1978. 115.00x o.p. (ISBN 0-306-40020-0, Plenum Pr). Plenum Pub.
Marine Pharmacology. Morris H. Baslow. LC 76-57213. (Illus.). 342p. 1977. pap. text ed. 11.50 with suppl. o.p. (ISBN 0-88275-470-X). Krieger.
Marine Plankton & Sediments: Kiel Symposium. Ed. by W. R. Riedel & T. Saito. (Micropaleontology Special Publications Ser.: No. 3). 235p. 1980. 20.00 o.p. (ISBN 0-686-84254-5). Am Mus Natl Hist.
Marine Plankton Ecology. Ed. by P. Bougis. 1976. 131.75 o.p. (ISBN 0-444-11033-X, North-Holland). Elsevier.
Marine Pollution. Ed. by R. Johnston. 1977. 130.50 o.p. (ISBN 0-12-387650-8). Acad Pr.
Marine Pollution & Marine Waste Disposal. E. A. Pearson & E. De Fraga Frangipane. 1975. pap. 180.00x o.p. (ISBN 0-08-019730-2). Pergamon.
Marine Pollution: Monographs. Mary Vance. (Public Administration Series: Bibliography P 1758). 51p. 1985. pap. 7.50 o.p. (ISBN 0-89028-558-6). Vance Biblios.
Marine Propulsion: Principles & Evolution. Robert Taggart. LC 79-75731. 368p. 1969. 29.00x o.p. (ISBN 0-87201-497-5). Gulf Pub.
Marine Regionalism in the Southeast Asian Seas. Lewis M. Alexander. LC 82-18216. (East-West Environment & Policy Institute Research Report: No. 11). v, 85p. (Orig.). 1982. pap. text ed. 3.00 o.p. (ISBN 0-86638-033-7). EW Ctr HI.
Marine Resources of Kuwait: Their Role in the Development of Non-Oil Resources. Fatimah H. Al-Abdul-Razzak. (Illus.). 300p. 1985. 55.00x o.p. (ISBN 0-7103-0069-7, Kegan Paul). Routledge Chapman & Hall.
Mariner Outboard Shop Manual 2-48 HP, 1976-1984 (Includes Electric Motors) 351p. 1984. pap. 24.95 o.p. (ISBN 0-89287-400-7, B712). Clymer Pub.
Mariner Outboard Shop Manual 50-200Hp, 1976-1984. Kalton Lahue. (Illus.). 341p. 1984. pap. 24.95 o.p. (ISBN 0-89287-401-5, B716). Clymer Pub.
Mariner's Catalog, Vol. 2. Ed. by David R. Getchell et al. LC 73-88647. 1974. pap. 2.00 o.p. (ISBN 0-87742-046-7). Intl Marine.
Mariner's Catalog, Vol. 3. Ed. by George Putz & Peter H. Spectre. LC 73-88647. (Illus.). 192p. 1975. pap. 2.00 o.p. (ISBN 0-87742-058-0). Intl Marine.
Mariner's Catalog, Vol. 6. Ed. by George Putz & Peter Spectre. LC 73-88647. (Illus.). 1978. pap. 2.00 o.p. (ISBN 0-87742-109-9). Intl Marine.
Mariner's Pocket Companion, 1986. Wallace E. Tobin, III. 224p. 1985. pap. 6.95 o.p. (ISBN 0-87021-407-1). Naval Inst Pr.
Mariner's Pocket Companion 1987. Wallace E. Tobin, III. 393p. 1986. 6.95 o.p. (ISBN 0-87021-413-6). Naval Inst Pr.
Mariner's Pocket Companion 1988. Wallace E. Tobin, III. 224p. 1987. flexible bdg. 6.95 o.p. (ISBN 0-87021-421-7). Naval Inst Pr.
Marion Watches Price Guide. Roy Ehrhardt. Ed. by William F. Meggers. (Orig.). 1987. pap. 15.00 o.p. (ISBN 0-913902-54-3). Heart Am Pr.
Marital Arts. Arthur Hoppe. 206p. 1985. 12.95 o.p. (ISBN 0-87795-676-6, Arbor Hse). Morrow.
Marital Choices: Forecasting, Assessing & Improving a Relationship. William J. Lederer. (Illus.). 1981. 12.95 o.p. (ISBN 0-393-01412-6). Norton.
Marital Puzzle. Norman L. Paul & Betty B. Paul. 302p. 1975. 12.95 o.p. (ISBN 0-393-01116-X). Norton.
Marital Rites. Margaret Forster. LC 81-69152. 1982. 9.95 o.p. (ISBN 0-689-11263-7, Atheneum). Macmillan.
Marital Status & Living Arrangements: March, 1985. (Current Population Reports Series P-20, Population Characteristics: No. 410). 95p. 1986. pap. 4.50 o.p. (S/N 803-005-00002-8). USGPO.
Marital Status & Living Arrangements: Mar. 1986. (Current Population Reports Series P-20, Population Characteristics: No. 418). (Illus.). 93p. 1987. pap. 4.50 o.p. (S/N 803-005-00011-7). USGPO.
Marital Violence. Ed. by Norman Johnson. (Sociological Review Monograph: No. 31). 194p. 1985. pap. 14.95x o.p. (ISBN 0-7102-0448-5). Routledge Chapman & Hall.
Marital Violence: The Community Responses. M. Borowski & M. Murch. 1983. pap. 14.95 o.p. (ISBN 0-422-78130-4, NO. 3777, Pub. by Tavistock). Routledge Chapman & Hall.
Maritime Adaptations: Essays on Contemporary Fishing Communities. Ed. by Alexander Spoehr. LC 79-22486. 1980. 15.95x o.p. (ISBN 0-8229-1139-6). U of Pittsburgh Pr.
Maritime Antiques. Alan Major. LC 80-29624. 1981. 12.95 o.s.i. (ISBN 0-498-02496-2). A S Barnes.
Maritime Arts by William Gilkerson. William Gilkerson. (Illus.). 100p. (Orig.). 1981. pap. 12.95 o.p. (ISBN 0-87577-061-4). Peabody Mus Salem.
Maritime Boundaries & Ocean Resources. Ed. by Gerald Blake. 304p. 1988. lib. bdg. 59.95 o.p. (ISBN 0-7099-3974-4, Pub. by Croom Helm UK). Routledge Chapman & Hall.
Maritime Boundary Delimitation: An Annotated Bibliography. Ted L. McDorman & Kenneth P. Beauchamp. 224p. 1983. 27.00x o.p. (ISBN 0-669-06146-8). Lexington Bks.
Maritime Dimension. Ed. by R. P. Barston & Patricia Birnie. (Illus.). 272p. 1981. text ed. 27.50x o.p. (ISBN 0-04-341015-4); pap. text ed. 16.95x o.p. (ISBN 0-04-341016-2). Unwin Hyman.
Maritime Jurisdiction in Southeast Asia: A Commentary & Map. J. R. Prescott. LC 81-2415. (East-West Environment & Policy Institute Research Report: No. 2). v, 60p. (Orig.). 1981. pap. text ed. 3.00 o.s.i. (ISBN 0-86638-024-8). EW Ctr HI.
Maritime Labour Conventions & Recommendations. viii, 224p. 1983. pap. 12.25 o.p. (ISBN 92-2-103096-2). Intl Labour Office.
Maritime Law, Vol. 1: Arrest of Vessels. Ed. by Lennart Hagberg. xvi, 92p. 1976. text ed. 12.00x o.p. Rothman.
Maritime Provinces Prehistory. James A. Tuck. (Canadian Prehistory Ser.). (Illus.). 128p. 1985. pap. 14.95 o.s.i. (ISBN 0-226-56427-4, 56427-4, Pub. by Natl Mus Canada). U of Chicago Pr.
Maritime South Africa: A Pictorial History. Brian Ingpen & Robert Pabst. (Illus.). 176p. 1985. 32.50x o.p. (ISBN 0-7106-0351-7). Janes Info Group.
Maritime Transport: The Evolution of International Marine Policy & Shipping Law. Edgar Gold. LC 80-8641. (Illus.). 448p. 1981. 40.00x o.p. (ISBN 0-669-04338-9). Lexington Bks.
Marjorie Kinnan Rawlings: Sojourner at Cross Creek. Elizabeth Silverthorne. 375p. 1989. 19.95 o.p. (ISBN 0-87951-320-9). Overlook Pr.
Mark, Vol. II. Beacon Bible Expositions Staff. 6.95 o.p. (ISBN 0-8010-0755-0). Baker Bk.
Mark see Word Studies in the Greek New Testament, for the English Reader.
Mark: A Good News Commentary. Larry Hurtado. LC 82-48930. 288p. (Orig.). 1983. pap. 9.95 o.p. (ISBN 0-06-064085-5, RD/447). HarpR.
Mark Adams: A Retrospective. Paul Mills & Robert F. Johnson. LC 85-16630. (Illus.). 112p. 1985. pap. 16.95 o.s.i. (ISBN 0-87701-365-9). Chronicle Bks.

Mark: Good News for Hard Times. George T. Montague. 200p. (Orig.). 1981. pap. 6.95 o.p. (ISBN 0-89283-096-4). Servant.
Mark Gruner's Numbers of Life: An Introduction to Numerology. Mark Gruner & Christopher K. Brown. LC 78-57560. 1979. 9.95 o.s.i. (ISBN 0-8008-5639-2); pap. 3.95 o.s.i. (ISBN 0-08-805640-6). Taplinger.
Mark My Words: Letters of a Businessman to His Son. J. Kingsley Ward. LC 85-30047. (Illus.). 240p. 1986. 15.95 o.p. (ISBN 0-13-531518-2). P-H.
Mark Rothko: The Surrealist Years. Intro. by Robert Rosenblum. (Illus.). 40p. 1981. 15.00 o.p. (ISBN 0-938608-03-7). Pace Pubns.
Mark Skousen's Guide to Financial Privacy. Mark Skousen. 1983. 16.50 o.p. (ISBN 0-671-47060-4). S&S.
Mark-Traditions in Conflict. Theodore J. Weeden, Sr. LC 79-7394. 192p. 1979. pap. 7.95 o.p. (ISBN 0-8006-1371-6, 1-1371, Fortress). Augsburg Fortress.
Mark Twain: An American Prophet. abr. ed. Maxwell Geismar. 352p. 1973. pap. text ed. 2.95 o.p. (ISBN 0-07-023081-1). McGraw.
Mark Twain, an American Voice. Patricia D. Frevert. Ed. by Ann Redpath. (People to Remember Ser.). (Illus.). 32p. (gr. 4 up). 1981. PLB 8.95 o.p. (ISBN 0-87191-802-1). Creative Ed.
Mark Twain As a Literary Comedian. David E. Sloane. LC 78-11125. (Southern Literary Studies Ser.). xiv, 221p. 1979. 25.00x o.p. (ISBN 0-8071-0460-4). La State U Pr.
Mark Twain at His Best. Ed. & intro. by Charles Neider. LC 85-29328. (Illus.). 456p. 1986. pap. 17.95 o.p. (ISBN 0-385-19836-1). Doubleday.
Mark Twain-Howells Letters: The Correspondence of Samuel L. Clemens & William D. Howells, 1872-1910, 2 vols. Samuel L. Clemens. Ed. by Henry N. Smith & William M. Gibson. LC 60-5397. 1960. 70.00x set o.p. (ISBN 0-674-54900-7, Belknap Pr). Harvard U Pr.
Mark Twain in Love. Albert G. Miller. LC 73-5243. (gr. 7 up). 1973. 5.95 o.p. (ISBN 0-15-230295-6, HJ). HarBraceJ.
Mark Twain in the Virginia Evening Bulletin & Gold Hill Daily News. Ed. by Dave Basso. (Great Basin Abstracts Ser.). 44p. 1983. pap. text ed. 18.95 o.p. (ISBN 0-936332-18-2). Falcon Hill Pr.
Mark Twain: Social Critic. Philip S. Foner. LC 58-11505. 440p. 1972. pap. 2.25 o.s.i. (ISBN 0-7178-0356-2). Intl Pubs Co.
Mark Twain: The Development of a Writer. Henry N. Smith. LC 62-19224. 1967. pap. text ed. 3.95x o.p. (ISBN 0-689-70184-5, 99, Atheneum). Macmillan.
Mark Twain? What Kind of a Name Is That? A Story of Samuel Langhorne Clemens. Robert Quackenbush. (Illus.). 32p. 1984. 10.95 o.s.i. (ISBN 0-13-557000-X). P-H.
Mark Twain's Tom Sawyer. Toby Bluth. (Illus.). 48p. (gr. k-6). 1985. 5.95 o.p. (ISBN 0-8249-8097-2). Ideals.
Marked to Die. Michael Brown. (Illus.). 352p. 1984. 16.50 o.p. (ISBN 0-671-45090-5). S&S.
Markers of Biological Individuality: The Transplantation Antigens Immunology. Ed. by Barry D. Kahan & Ralph A. Reisfeld. (Immunology Ser, Vol. 2). 1972. 93.50 o.p. (ISBN 0-12-394350-7). Acad Pr.
Market Assistant. Thomas F. De Voe. LC 72-174033. (Illus.). 456p. 1975. Repr. of 1867 ed. 65.00x o.p. (ISBN 0-8103-4117-4). Gale.
Market for Add-On Boards, Systems & Services for the IBM PC. International Resource Development, Inc. Staff. 241p. 1984. 1850.00x o.p. (ISBN 0-88694-603-4). Intl Res Dev.
Market for Executive Talent. Edward Kaufman. 1978. 11.00 o.p. (ISBN 0-07-033421-8). McGraw.
Market for Frozen Small Pelagic Fish. E. Matton. (Fisheries Technical Papers: No. 221). 138p. (Eng. & Fr.). 1982. pap. 9.50 o.p. (ISBN 92-5-101194-X, F2280, FAO). UNIPUB.
Market in History. Ed. by B. L. Anderson & A. J. Latham. 256p. 1986. 39.00 o.p. (ISBN 0-7099-4120-X, Pub. by Croom Helm Ltd). Routledge Chapman & Hall.
Market Notebook. Pamela Sovold et al. LC 80-16856. 230p. 1980. pap. 7.95 o.p. (ISBN 0-914842-44-7). Madrona Pubs.
Market Reforms in Health Care: Current Issues, New Directions, Strategic Decisions. Ed. by Jack A. Meyer. 331p. 1983. 25.00 o.p. (ISBN 0-8447-2242-1); pap. 10.95 o.p. (ISBN 0-8447-2236-7). Am Enterprise.
Market Research & Analysis. 2nd ed. Donald R. Lehmann. 1985. 39.95x o.p. (ISBN 0-256-03084-7). Irwin.
Market Scope. rev. ed. 1984. 175.00 o.p. (ISBN 0-911790-23-3). Prog Grocers Trade.
Market Scope, 1985: The Desk Top Data Bank of Supermarket Distribution. rev. ed. 1985. 190.00 o.p. (ISBN 0-911790-47-0). Prog Grocers Trade.
Market Structure, Conduct, & Foodgrain Pricing Efficiency: An Indian Case Study. S. Holmes. 1971. pap. text ed. 4.75x o.p. (ISBN 0-8422-0150-5). Irvington.
Market Survey for Nuclear Power in Developing Countries. 1974. pap. 16.00 o.p. (ISP395, IAEA). UNIPUB.
Market Timing with No-Load Mutual Funds. Paul A. Merriman et al. LC 84-28380. (Illus.). 252p. (Orig.). 1985. pap. 12.95 o.p. (ISBN 0-913539-01-5). Backwater Corp.
Market Watch Creative Adbook. 1987 ed. Marvin R. Shanken. 1987. pap. write for info. o.p. (ISBN 0-918076-54-4). M Shanken Comm.
Marketing. Berkowitz et al. (Illus.). 784p. 1985. 34.95 o.p. (ISBN 0-8016-0602-0). Mosby.
Marketing. 2nd ed. Berkowitz et al. (Illus.). 800p. 1988. text ed. 42.95 o.p. (ISBN 0-8016-2759-1); test bank 100.00 o.p. (ISBN 0-8016-2760-5). Mosby.
Marketing. 2nd ed. David L. Kurtz & Louis E. Boone. 720p. 1984. text ed. 33.95x o.s.i. (ISBN 0-03-064087-3); instr's. manual 19.95 o.s.i. (ISBN 0-03-064088-1); study guide 13.95x o.s.i. (ISBN 0-03-064089-X). Dryden Pr.
Marketing. 2nd ed. Maurice I. Mandell & L. Rosenberg. 1981. text ed. (ISBN 0-13-556225-2). P-H.
Marketing. Frederick A. Russ & Charles A. Kirkpatrick. 1982. 30.75 o.p. (ISBN 0-316-76272-5); tchr's. manual avail. o.p. (ISBN 0-316-76273-3). transparency masters avail. o.p. (ISBN 0-316-76271-7); test bank avail. o.p. (ISBN 0-316-76274-1). Little.
Marketing, Advertising & Sales Checklists. (Checklists Bks.). (Orig.). 1984. pap. 14.95 o.s.i. (ISBN 0-87280-128-4, Asher-Gallant). Caddylak Systs.
Marketing & Distributive Education Curriculum. ERIC Clearinghouse on Adult, Career, & Vocational Education Staff. 53p. 1983. 4.95 o.p. (ISBN 0-318-22149-7, BB61). Natl Ctr Res Voc Ed.
Marketing & Economics. R. R. Whitelaw. 1969. text ed. 31.00 o.p. (ISBN 0-08-006583-X); pap. text ed. 11.25 o.p. (ISBN 0-08-006582-1). Pergamon.
Marketing & Financial Control. A. S. Johnson. 1967. 60.00 o.p. (ISBN 0-08-012614-6); pap. 60.00 o.p. (ISBN 0-08-012613-8). Pergamon.
Marketing & PR Media Planning. F. W. Jefkins. LC 74-618347. 1974. 70.00 o.p. (ISBN 0-08-018086-8); pap. text ed. 55.00 o.p. (ISBN 0-08-018085-X). Pergamon.
Marketing & Sales Career Directory, 1987. Ed. by Ron Fry. (Career Directory Ser.). 350p. (Orig.). 1987. text ed. 34.95 o.p. (ISBN 0-934829-20-9); pap. text ed. 26.95 o.p. (ISBN 0-934829-14-4); Special Bookstore Edition Distributed by Williamson Publishing Co. pap. 17.95 o.p. (ISBN 0-934829-08-X). Career Pr Inc.
Marketing & Sales Forecasting. F. Keay. 132p. 1972. pap. text ed. 17.00 o.p. (ISBN 0-08-016738-1). Pergamon.
Marketing & Society: Selected Readings. R. Peterson. 1970. pap. text ed. 5.75x o.p. (ISBN 0-8422-0104-1). Irvington.
Marketing & Strategic Planning for Professional Service Firms. Stanley G. Webb. 304p. 1982. 24.95 o.p. (ISBN 0-8144-5687-1). AMACOM.
Marketing & the Brand Manager. G. Medcalf. 1967. 70.00 o.p. (ISBN 0-08-012602-2); pap. 70.00 o.p. (ISBN 0-08-012601-4). Pergamon.
Marketing & the Computer. I. S. Hugo. 1967. 33.00 o.p. (ISBN 0-08-012606-5); pap. 17.50 o.p. (ISBN 0-08-012605-7). Pergamon.
Marketing & the Sales Manager. F. H. Elsby. 1969. 33.00 o.p. (ISBN 0-08-006537-6); pap. 17.50 o.p. (ISBN 0-08-006536-8). Pergamon.
Marketing & the Small Design Firm: A Selected Checklist of Resources. Jamie W. Coniglio. (Architecture Ser.: A 1449). 5p. 1985. 2.00 o.p. (ISBN 0-89028-539-X). Vance Biblios.
Marketing Architectural & Engineering Services. 2nd ed. Weld Coxe. 1982. 32.95 o.s.i. (ISBN 0-442-22011-1). Van Nos Reinhold.
Marketing Bank Services in Business. A. R. Krachenberg. (Illus.). 107p. 1979. 12.00 o.p. (ISBN 0-938654-07-1, BANK). Indus Dev Inst Sci.
Marketing: Basic Concepts & Decisions. William M. Pride & O. C. Ferrell. LC 76-10892. (Illus.). 1977. text ed. 17.50 o.p. (ISBN 0-395-24529-X). HM.
Marketing: Basic Concepts & Decisions. 3rd ed. William M. Pride & O. C. Ferrell. LC 82-83363. 784p. (Write for info. re computerized ancellaries). 1983. text ed. 32.95 o.p. (ISBN 0-395-32816-0). HM.
Marketing: Basic Concepts & Decisions. 2nd ed. William M. Pride & O. C. Perrell. LC 79-88040. 1980. text ed. 24.95 o.p. (ISBN 0-395-28059-1). HM.
Marketing Behaviour: Issues in Managerial & Buyer Decision Making. Gordon Foxall. 200p. 1981. text ed. 35.50x o.p. (ISBN 0-566-00434-8). Gower Pub Co.
Marketing Bhutan's Potatoes. Gregory J. Scott. 80p. (Orig.). 1983. pap. text ed. 6.50x o.s.i. (ISBN 0-318-22573-5, Pub. by Intl Potato Ctr Peru). Agribookstore.
Marketing Cases. F. H. Elsby. LC 70-122006. 1970. 36.00 o.p. (ISBN 0-08-015784-X); pap. 17.50 o.p. (ISBN 0-08-015783-1). Pergamon.
Marketing: Cases for Analysis. Charles W. Lamb, Jr. LC 82-81740. 512p. 1983. pap. 16.50 o.p. (ISBN 0-395-32636-2). HM.
Marketing Channel: A Conceptual Viewpoint. Bruce E. Mallen. LC 67-17344. 308p. 1967. 19.50 o.p. (ISBN 0-471-56580-6, Pub. by Wiley). Krieger.
Marketing Channels. 2nd ed. Louis E. Boone & James C. Johnson. 578p. 1977. pap. text ed. write for info. o.p. (ISBN 0-02-312150-5). Macmillan.
Marketing Channels. 2nd ed. Bert Rosenbloom. 512p. 1983. 35.95x o.p. (ISBN 0-03-058996-7); instr's. manual 20.00 o.p. (ISBN 0-03-058994-0). Dryden Pr.
Marketing Channels. 2nd ed. Louis W. Stern & Adel I. El-Ansary. (International Management Ser.). (Illus.). 672p. 1982. text ed. 41.00 o.p. (ISBN 0-13-557173-1). P-H.
Marketing Checklist for the Development of a Single-Family Residential Community. William E. Becker. 31p. 1965. pap. 6.50 o.p. (ISBN 0-86718-047-1). Nat Assn H Build.
Marketing Classics: A Selection of Influential Articles. 5th ed. Enis & Cox. 1985. 26.00 o.p. (ISBN 0-205-08341-2, 138341). Allyn.
Marketing Compuprobs with IBM disk. Cosenza & Boone. 1988. pap. 21.95 o.p. (ISBN 0-256-05609-9). Irwin.
Marketing: Concepts & Strategy. 3rd ed. Martin L. Bell. LC 78-69572. (Illus.). 1979. text ed. 29.95 o.p. (ISBN 0-395-26503-7). HM.
Marketing: Contemporary Concepts & Practices. 2nd ed. Schoell. 1985. 29.25 o.p. (ISBN 0-205-08264-5, 138264); 9.00 o.p. (ISBN 0-205-08268-8, 138268). Allyn.
Marketing: Contemporary Dimensions. 3rd ed. Robert A. Robicheaux. LC 82-82470. 432p. 1983. pap. 17.95 o.p. (ISBN 0-395-33166-8). HM.
Marketing: Contemporary Dimensions. 2nd ed. Robert A. Robicheaux & William M. Pride. LC 79-89125. 1980. pap. 12.50 o.p. (ISBN 0-395-28500-3). HM.
Marketing: Contemporary Dimensions. 4th ed. Robert A. Robicheaux et al. LC 84-82501. 448p. 1984. pap. 23.96 o.p. (ISBN 0-395-36493-0). HM.
Marketing Dictionary. Stanley Strand. LC 61-5251. 1962. (ISBN 0-8022-1665-X). Philos Lib.
Marketing Essentials: Student Guide. Lana S. Kendig. (FLMI Insurance Education Program Ser.). 1985. 7.00 o.p. (ISBN 0-915322-69-2). LOMA.
Marketing for Nonprofit Organizations. 2nd ed. Philip Kotler. (Illus.). 592p. 1982. pap. text ed. 39.33 o.p. (ISBN 0-13-556142-6). P-H.
Marketing for the Non-Marketing Executive. Houston G. Elam & Norton Paley. (Illus.). 1978. 15.95 o.p. (ISBN 0-8144-5465-8). AMACOM.
Marketing Guidebook: Blue Book of Grocery Distribution. rev. ed. LC 68-126162. 1985. 225.00 o.p. (ISBN 0-911790-24-1). Prog Grocers Trade.
Marketing Handbook, 2 vols. Edwin E. Bobrow & Mark D. Bobrow. LC 85-70439. 1985. 50.00 ea. o.p. Vol. I: Marketing Practices (ISBN 0-87094-523-8). Vol. II: Marketing Management (ISBN 0-87094-524-6). Dow Jones-Irwin.
Marketing Hotels into the 90's: A Systematic Approach to Increasing Sales. Melvyn Greene. (Illus.). 1982. 24.95 o.p. (ISBN 0-87055-475-1). AVI.
Marketing in a Consumer-Oriented Society. John R. Stuteville. 1975. (ISBN 0-534-00359-1). PWS-Kent Pub.
Marketing in Nonprofit Organizations. new ed. Ed. by Patrick J. Montana. 1978. 13.95 o.p. (ISBN 0-8144-5494-1). AMACOM.
Marketing in the Construction Industry. Ed. by Institute of Marketing Staff. 1974. pap. 17.95x o.p. (ISBN 0-434-90845-2). Trans-Atl Phila.
Marketing in the Developing World. Siro P. Padolecchia. 190p. 1979. 22.50x o.p. (ISBN 0-7069-0667-5, Pub. by Vikas India). Advent NY.
Marketing in the Hospitality Industry. Ronald A. Nykiel. (Illus.). 240p. 1983. 23.95 o.p. (ISBN 0-8436-0886-2). Van Nos Reinhold.
Marketing Interaction. Stephen K. Keiser & Max E. Lupul. 1977. pap. text ed. write for info. o.p. (ISBN 0-02-362800-6). Macmillan.
Marketing: International Edition. 2nd ed. Berkowitz. 1988. 42.95 o.p. (ISBN 0-8016-0399-4). Mosby.
Marketing Is Everybody's Business. 3rd ed. Betsy Gelb & Gabriel Gelb. 1980. pap. text ed. write for info. o.p. (ISBN 0-673-16112-9). Scott F.
Marketing Law. Joe L. Welch. 168p. 1980. text ed. write for info. o.p. (ISBN 0-02-425330-8). Macmillan.
Marketing Life & Health Insurance. Ed. by Nancy E. Strickler. LC 81-83848. (FLMI Insurance Education Program Ser.). 471p. 1981. text ed. 24.00 o.p. (ISBN 0-915322-47-1). LOMA.
Marketing Life & Health Insurance: Student Guide. Richard Bailey. (FLMI Insurance Education Program Ser.). 1986. wkbk. 7.00 o.p. (ISBN 0-915322-87-0). LOMA.
Marketing Management. Boyd & Walker. 1989. 36.95 o.p. (ISBN 0-256-05827-X). Irwin.
Marketing Management. Harper W. Boyd, Jr. & William F. Massy. (Illus.). 618p. 1972. text ed. 18.95 o.p. (ISBN 0-15-555112-4, HC). HarBraceJ.
Marketing Management. Peter & Donnelly. 1986. 37.95 o.p. (ISBN 0-256-03073-1). Irwin.
Marketing Management: Analysis, Planning & Control. 5th ed. Philip Kotler. 768p. 1984. text ed. 42.00 o.p. (ISBN 0-13-557927-9). P-H.
Marketing Management & Administrative Action. 4th ed. Stewart H. Britt & Harper W. Boyd. (Illus.). 1978. text ed. 25.95 o.p. (ISBN 0-07-007923-4, C). McGraw.
Marketing Management: Concepts, Practice & Cases. Haas & Wotruba. 1983. 39.95 o.p. (ISBN 0-256-02956-3). Irwin.
Marketing Management: Foundations & Practices. William Lazer & James Culley. LC 82-84160. 820p. 1983. text ed. 45.96 o.p. (ISBN 0-395-32716-4). HM.
Marketing Management: Text & Cases. Bonoma & Hall. (Illus.). 1088p. 1989. text ed. 42.95 o.p. (ISBN 0-8016-0148-7). Mosby.
Marketing Parks & Recreation. National Park Service Staff & John Crompton. (New Directions in Leisure Ser.). (Illus.). 170p. 15.95 o.p. (ISBN 0-317-30659-6). Venture Pub PA.
Marketing Plan: How to Prepare & Implement It. William M. Luther. 192p. 1982. 22.95 o.p. (ISBN 0-8144-5669-3). AMACOM.
Marketing Principles. 3rd ed. Ben Enis. 1980. write for info. o.p. (ISBN 0-673-16110-2). write for info. study guide o.p. (ISBN 0-673-16111-0). Scott F.
Marketing Problems & Improvement Programs. J. C. Abbott. (Marketing Guides: No. 1). 220p. (Orig., 5th Printing 1975). 1958. pap. 12.50 o.p. (ISBN 92-5-101669-0, F273, FAO). UNIPUB.
Marketing Research. 3rd ed. Gilbert A. Churchill. 704p. 1983. text ed. 37.95x o.p. (ISBN 0-03-060608-X); instr's. manual 20.00 o.p. (ISBN 0-03-060609-8). Dryden Pr.
Marketing Research. 6th ed. David J. Luck et al. (Illus.). 624p. 1982. pap. text ed. (ISBN 0-13-557652-0). P-H.
Marketing Research in a Marketing Environment. William Dillon et al. 816p. 1987. 43.95 o.p. (ISBN 0-8016-1303-5). Irwin.
Marketing Research in Europe ("Esomar") 1978. 135.00 o.p. (ISBN 0-685-58572-7). E J Brill USA.
Marketing Research: Text & Cases. 6th ed. Harper W. Boyd, Jr. et al. 1985. 38.95x o.p. (ISBN 0-256-03183-5). Irwin.
Marketing Strategy & Management. James A. Constantin et al. 1976. text ed. 19.95x o.p. (ISBN 0-256-01694-1). Irwin.
Marketing Strategy & Structure: Study Guide. David J. Rachman & Barry Berman. (Illus.). 160p. 1975. pap. 4.95 o.p. (ISBN 0-13-558320-9). P-H.
Marketing the Arts. Ed. by Michael P. Mokwa et al. 304p. 23.80 o.p. (ISBN 0-318-13411-X); members 19.40 o.p. (ISBN 0-318-13412-8). Assn Perf Arts Presenters.
Marketing: The Uses of Advertising. D. Lowndes. LC 72-97953. 1969. text ed. 19.50 o.p. (ISBN 0-08-006935-5); pap. text ed. 9.75 o.p. (ISBN 0-08-006934-7). Pergamon.
Marketing Theory: The Philosophy of Marketing Science. Shelby D. Hunt. 1983. 36.95x o.p. (ISBN 0-256-02847-8). Irwin.
Marketing Through Measurement. F. Keay & G. F. Wensley. 1970. text ed. 29.00 o.p. (ISBN 0-08-015765-3); pap. text ed. 14.00 o.p. (ISBN 0-08-015764-5). Pergamon.
Marketing Through Research. G. Wills. 1967. 36.00 o.p. (ISBN 0-08-012620-0); pap. 19.25 o.p. (ISBN 0-08-012619-7). Pergamon.
Marketing Today. David J. Rachman. 672p. 1985. text ed. 31.95 o.s.i. (ISBN 0-03-071036-7). Dryden Pr.
Marketing Today: A Basic Approach. David J. Schwartz. (Illus., Orig.). 1973. text ed. 15.95 o.p. (ISBN 0-15-555081-0, HC). HarBraceJ.
Marketing Today: A Basic Approach. 2nd ed. David J. Schwartz. (Illus.). 1977. text ed. 20.95 o.p. (ISBN 0-15-555086-1, HC). HarBraceJ.
Marketing Today: A Basic Approach. 3rd ed. David J. Schwartz. 630p. 1981. text ed. 20.00 o.p. (ISBN 0-15-555089-6). HarBraceJ.

Marketing Workbench: Using Computers for Better Performance. John M. McCann. 250p. 1986. pap. 25.00 o.p. (ISBN 0-87094-763-X). Dow Jones-Irwin.
Marketing Your Law Firm's Services. Pennsylvania Bar Institute Staff. 107p. 1984. 20.00 o.p. (ISBN 0-318-02177-3, 245). PA Bar Inst.
Marketing, 1988. 80p. 1988. 12.95 o.p. (ISBN 0-87584-198-8). Harvard Busn.
Marketing 1988-89. 10th, rev. ed. Ed. by John E. Richardson. LC 73-78578. (Annual Editions Ser.). (Illus.). 256p. 1988. pap. text ed. 9.95x o.p. (ISBN 0-87967-720-1). Dushkin Pub.
Marketplaces of the World. Hiroshi Isogai & Shunjiro Matsushima. LC 72-184665. (This Beautiful World Ser.: Vol. 35). (Illus.). 130p. (Orig.). 1972. pap. 4.95 o.p. (ISBN 0-87011-165-5). Kodansha.
Markets & Merchants: Economic Diversification in Colonial Virginia, 1700-1775. Peter V. Bergstrom. Ed. by Stuart Bruchey. LC 84-45426. (American Economic History Ser.). 270p. 1985. lib. bdg. 40.00 o.p. (ISBN 0-8240-6670-7). Garland Pub.
Markets & Morals. Ed. by Gerald Dworkin et al. LC 66-51111. 206p. 1977. 39.95 o.p. (ISBN 0-470-99169-0). Hemisphere Pub.
Markets in Oaxaca. Ed. by Scott Cook & Martin Diskin. (Institute of Latin American Studies-Special Publication). (Illus.). 349p. 1975. 17.50x o.p. (ISBN 0-292-75014-5). U of Tex Pr.
Markets of Asia-Pacific, 12 Vols. Survey Research Group Staff. Incl. Singapore (ISBN 0-87196-584-4); Malaysia (ISBN 0-87196-585-2); Thailand (ISBN 0-87196-586-0); Indonesia (ISBN 0-87196-587-9); Hong Kong & Macau (ISBN 0-87196-588-7); Philippines (ISBN 0-87196-590-9); Taiwan. 1982 (ISBN 0-87196-589-5); South Korea. 1982 (ISBN 0-87196-591-7); Australia. 1982 (ISBN 0-87196-592-5); cancelled (ISBN 0-87196-593-3); Japan. 1982. cancelled (ISBN 0-87196-594-1); China. 1982 (ISBN 0-87196-595-X). 75.00x ea. o.p.; Set. 499.50 o.p. (ISBN 0-686-92678-1). Facts on File.
Markoff Women: A Novel. June F. Singer. 384p. 1986. 16.95 o.p. (ISBN 0-87131-464-9). M Evans.
Markov Chains: Theory & Applications. Dean L. Isaacson & Richard W. Madsen. LC 84-27792. 270p. 1985. Repr. of 1976 ed. lib. bdg. 43.50 o.p. (ISBN 0-89874-834-8). Krieger.
Markov Processes, 2 vols. E. B. Dynkin. Tr. by J. Fabius et al. (Grundlehren der Mathematischen Wissenschaften: Vols. 121 & 122). 1965. Set. 77.90 o.p. (ISBN 0-387-03301-7). Springer-Verlag.
Markov Processes & Potential Theory. Robert M. Blumenthal. LC 68-18659. (Pure & Applied Mathematics Ser.: Vol. 29). 1968. 75.50 o.p. (ISBN 0-12-107850-7). Acad Pr.
Markova Remembers. Alicia Markova. 1986. 24.95 o.p. (ISBN 0-316-54625-9). Little.
Markrich Sportsworld, Inc. An Audit Practice Case. 2nd ed ed. Holley. 1985. 25.50x o.p. (ISBN 0-256-03309-9). Irwin.
Marks & Monograms of the Modern Movement: 1875-1930. Malcolm Haslam. (Illus.). 1977. 25.00 o.p. (ISBN 0-7188-2291-9, Pub. by Lutterworth Pr UK). Seven Hills Bk Dists.
Marks' Standard Handbook for Mechanical Engineers. 8th ed. Theodore Baumeister. (Illus.). 1978. text ed. 89.00 o.p. (ISBN 0-07-004123-7). McGraw.
Mark's Story of Jesus. Werner H. Kelber. LC 78-14668. 96p. 1979. pap. 4.95 o.p. (ISBN 0-8006-1355-4, 1-1355, Fortress). Augsburg Fortress.
Markus Lupertz. (Illus.). 116p. 1988. pap. 20.00 o.p. (ISBN 90-6918-010-3); 30.00 o.p. Moyer Bell Limited.
Marlborough: A Survey of Panegyrics, Satires & Biographical Writings, 1688-1788. Robert D. Horn. LC 74-14647. (Reference Library of the Humanities: No. 2). (Illus.). 612p. 1975. lib. bdg. 79.00 o.p. (ISBN 0-8240-1054-X). Garland Pub.
Marlborough Street. Richard Bowker. LC 86-16840. (Doubleday Science Fiction Ser.). 192p. (YA) 1987. 12.95 o.s.i. (ISBN 0-385-19753-5). Doubleday.
Marlene Dietrich: Portraits 1926-1960. Klaus-Jurgen Sembach. Tr. by Arthur S. Wensinger & Richard H. Wood. LC 84-51370. (Illus.). 269p. 1985. 49.95 o.s.i. (ISBN 0-394-54264-9, GP948). Grove.
Marlene: The Life of Marlene Dietrich. Charles Higham. (Illus.). 1977. 9.95 o.p. (ISBN 0-393-07515-X). Norton.
Marlowe, Tamburlaine, & Magic. James R. Howe. LC 75-36978. x, 220p. 1976. 15.00x o.p. (ISBN 0-8214-0200-5). Ohio U Pr.
Marmac Guide to Houston. Dale Young. Ed. by Susan H. Smith. (Marmac Guidebook Ser.). 266p. (Orig.). 1984. pap. 7.95 o.p. (ISBN 0-939944-03-0, Dist. by Pelican). Marmac Pub.
Marmac Guide to Houston. 2nd ed. Dale Young. Ed. by Elizabeth Spear. (Marmac City Guidebook Ser.). (Illus.). 272p. (Orig.). cancelled o.s.i. (ISBN 0-317-14925-3). Marmac Pub.
Marmaduke Multiply's Merry Method. pap. 3.00 o.p. (ISBN 0-486-20171-6). Dover.
Marmalade's Picnic. Cindy Wheeler. LC 81-20792. (Illus.). 24p. (ps-1). 1983. 5.95 o.s.i. (ISBN 0-394-85023-8); lib. bdg. 9.99 o.s.i. (ISBN 0-394-95023-2). Knopf.
Marnie. Marion M. Brown. (gr. 5-9). 1971. 4.95 o.s.i. (ISBN 0-664-32491-6, Westminster); pap. 6.50 o.s.i. (ISBN 0-664-20930-0, Westminster). Westminster John Knox.
Maroon Bulldogs: Mississippi State Football. William W. Sorrels. LC 75-30454. (College Sports Ser.). 1975. 10.95 o.p. (ISBN 0-87397-076-4). Strode.
Marooned in Fraggle Rock. David Young. LC 84-6670. (Fraggle Rock Bks.). (Illus.). 48p. (gr. 1-4). 1984. 6.95 o.s.i. (ISBN 0-03-000719-4). H Holt & Co.
Marques Johnson: Nobody Does it Better. Bert Rosenthal. LC 82-4459. (Sports Stars Ser.). (Illus.). (gr. 2-8). 1982. PLB 9.25g o.p. (ISBN 0-516-04325-0); pap. 2.95 o.p. (ISBN 0-516-44325-9). Childrens.
Marquis Who's Who of American Women, 1985-1986. 14th ed. 898p. 1984. 165.00 o.s.i. (ISBN 0-8379-0414-5). Marquis.
Marquis Who's Who Publications: Index to All Books, 1985. LC 74-175407. 1985. 55.00 o.s.i. (ISBN 0-8379-1419-1, 030403). Marquis.
Marrakesh One-Two. Richard Grenier. LC 82-15818. 350p. 1983. 14.45 o.p. (ISBN 0-395-33099-8). HM.
Marriage. Gwen Davis. LC 81-66966. 288p. 1981. 12.95 o.p. (ISBN 0-87795-335-X, Arbor Hse). Morrow.
Marriage. Jean Lipke. LC 70-104896. (Being Together Bks.). Orig. Title: Sex Outside of Marriage. (Illus.). (YA) (gr. 7-12). 1971. PLB 5.95 o.p. (ISBN 0-8225-0598-3). Lerner Pubns.
Marriage among Christians: A Curious Tradition. James T. Burtchaell et al. LC 77-81396. (Illus.). 192p. 1977. pap. 3.50 o.p. (ISBN 0-87793-139-9). Ave Maria.
Marriage & Death Notices from Alabama Newspapers & Family Record 1819 to 1890. Helen S. Foley. 200p. 1981. 25.00 o.s.i. (ISBN 0-89308-208-2). Southern Hist Pr.
Marriage & Divorce in Comparative Conflict of Laws. L. Palsson. 1974. 60.00 o.s.i. (ISBN 90-286-0423-5). E J Brill USA.
Marriage & Divorce, Nineteen Sixteen, Nineteen Twenty-Two to Thirty-Two, 12 vols. in one. U. S. Bureau of the Census Staff. LC 78-24170. 1979. Repr. of 1919 ed. lib. bdg. (ISBN 0-313-20694-5, USMA). Greenwood.
Marriage & Families. Essie E. Lee. LC 77-26962. 224p. (YA) (gr. 7 up). 1978. lib. bdg. 8.79 o.s.i. (ISBN 0-671-32854-9). Messner.
Marriage & Family Counseling: Bibliography. 7.50 o.p. (ISBN 0-317-59909-7, 72506C). Am Assn Coun Dev.
Marriage & Family Law Agreements. Samuel Green & John V. Long. 1984. write for info. o.p. Shepards-McGraw.
Marriage & Family Law in Washington. Mary Weschler. 176p. 1987. 7.95 o.p. (ISBN 0-88908-732-6). ISC Pr.
Marriage & Family, 1988-89. 14th, rev. ed. Ed. by Robert Walsh & Ollie Pocs. LC 74-84596. (Annual Editions Ser.). (Illus.). 256p. 1988. pap. text ed. 9.95x o.p. (ISBN 0-87967-731-7). Dushkin Pub.
Marriage & Remarriage in Populations of the Past. Ed. by J. Dupaquier et al. (Population & Social Structure Ser.). 1981. 131.00 o.p. (ISBN 0-12-224660-8). Acad Pr.
Marriage & Sexuality in Islam: A Translation of al-Ghazali's Book on the Etiquette of Marriage from the Ihya' Madelain Farah. 192p. 1984. 20.00 o.p. (ISBN 0-87480-231-8). U of Utah Pr.
Marriage & the Family. 2nd ed. Carlfred B. Broderick. (Illus.). 448p. 1984. text ed. (ISBN 0-13-559138-4). P-H.
Marriage & the Family. Victor Callan & Patricia Noller. 240p. 1987. 43.00 o.p. (ISBN 0-949614-37-8, Pub. by Croom Helm UK); pap. 22.50 o.p. (ISBN 0-949614-38-6, Pub. by Croom Helm UK). Routledge Chapman & Hall.
Marriage & the Family. Eric Golanty & Barbara Harris. LC 81-82013. (Illus.). 480p. 1982. pap. 25.95 o.p. (ISBN 0-395-28721-9). HM.
Marriage & the Family. Diane I. Levande & Joanne B. Koch. LC 82-81562. 496p. 1983. pap. 24.95 o.p. (ISBN 0-395-33162-5). HM.
Marriage & the Family. 2nd ed. Gilbert D. Nass & Gerald W. McDonald. (Sociology Ser.). (Illus.), 640p. 1982. text ed. 23.00 o.p. (ISBN 0-394-34864-8, RanC). Random.
Marriage & the Family Under Challenge: An Outline of Issues, Trends, & Alternatives. Dorothy F. Beck. LC 76-26307. 101p. 1976. 5.00 o.p. (ISBN 0-87304-145-3). Family Serv.
Marriage & the Jewish Tradition. Stanley R. Brav. 1951. (ISBN 0-8022-0170-9). Philos Lib.
Marriage & the Memo Method. Paul A. Hauck & Edmund S. Kean. LC 75-23291. 128p. 1975. pap. 2.75 o.s.i. (ISBN 0-664-24781-4, Westminster). Westminster John Knox.
Marriage As a Trade. Cicely M. Hamilton. LC 71-149782. 272p. 1971. Repr. of 1909 ed. 35.00x o.p. (ISBN 0-8103-3394-5). Gale.
Marriage Bonds of Tryon & Lincoln Counties, North Carolina. Curtis Bynum. 184p. 1982. Repr. of 1962 ed. 20.00 o.s.i. (ISBN 0-89308-316-X). Southern Hist Pr.
Marriage Counselling in the Community. W. L. Herbert & F. J. Jarvis. 1970. text ed. 8.75 o.p. (ISBN 0-08-006911-8); pap. 6.25 o.p. (ISBN 0-08-006910-X). Pergamon.
Marriage Covenant. John C. Reid. LC 67-11305. (Orig.). 1967. pap. 2.95 o.p. (ISBN 0-8042-1710-6, John Knox). Westminster John Knox.
Marriage Dialogue. Lynn A. Scorseby. LC 76-45150. (Illus.). 189p. 1977. text ed. 10.50 o.p. (ISBN 0-394-34853-2, RanC). Random.
Marriage, Divorce & Adoption: New York. Eugene R. Canudo. 1979. pap. 5.50x o.p. (ISBN 0-87526-222-8). Gould.
Marriage Enrichment: Resource Manual. rev. ed. Marriage Encounter Communities Staff. (Illus.). 152p. 1981. pap. 4.95 o.p. (ISBN 0-936098-00-7). Intl Marriage.
Marriage, Family & Intimate Relationships. Gary S. Belkin & N. Goodman. 1980. pap. 37.16 o.p. (ISBN 0-395-30560-8). HM.
Marriage: Fielding's Mirror of Morality. Murial B. Williams. LC 73-56. (Studies in the Humanities Ser.: No. 1). 160p. 1973. pap. 3.75 o.p. (ISBN 0-8173-7312-8). U of Ala Pr.
Marriage: For Better or for Worse? Robert H. Loeb, Jr. (YA) (gr. 9 up). 1980. PLB 8.90 o.p. (ISBN 0-531-02879-8, G25). Watts.
Marriage Gap. Stanley Rosner & Laura Hobe. 1978. pap. text ed. 3.95 o.p. (ISBN 0-07-053808-5). McGraw.
Marriage Happens to the Nicest People. Rita W. Kramer. (Illus.). 103p. 1983. 6.00 o.p. (ISBN 0-682-49949-8, Banner). Exposition-Phoenix.
Marriage: Ideals & Realizations. William F. Wunsch. 155p. 1973. 1.75 o.p. (ISBN 0-87785-122-0). Swedenborg.
Marriage in Islam: A Manual. Muhammed Abdul-Rauf. LC 75-186483. 1972. 8.50 o.p. (ISBN 0-682-47431-2, Banner). Exposition-Phoenix.
Marriage Is a Gift. Elisabeth Elliot. 1982. pap. 1.25 o.p. (ISBN 0-89107-269-1). Good News.
Marriage is for Two: How to Build a Marriage That Lasts & Works. Omar Stuenkel. LC 81-65640. 96p. (Orig.). 1981. pap. 5.95 o.p. (ISBN 0-8066-1876-0, 10-4290, Augsburg). Augsburg Fortress.
Marriage is Not for Weaklings. Ludwig S. Sondashi. 1977. pap. 4.00 o.p. (ISBN 0-682-48859-3). Exposition-Phoenix.
Marriage Manual. rev. & enl. ed. Hannah Stone & Abraham Stone. Ed. by Gloria S. Aitken & Acquiles Sobrero. (Illus.). 1968. 8.95 o.p. (ISBN 0-671-45101-4). S&S.
Marriage Map: Understanding & Surviving the Stages of Marriage. Maxine Rock. 288p. 1986. 14.95 o.p. (ISBN 0-931948-89-4). Peachtree Pubs.
Marriage Means Encounter. 2nd ed. George Roleder. 281p. 1979. pap. text ed. write for info. o.p. (ISBN 0-697-07590-7). Wm C Brown.
Marriage, Morals, & Sex in America: A History of Ideas. Sidney Ditzion. 1978. pap. 6.95 o.p. (ISBN 0-393-00890-8, Norton Lib). Norton.
Marriage of Heaven & Earth: The Philosophy of Astrology. Gregory Szanto. (Illus., Orig.). 1985. pap. 8.95 o.p. (ISBN 1-85063-021-6, Ark Paperbks). Routledge Chapman & Hall.
Marriage of True Minds: An Intimate Portrait of Leonard & Virginia Woolf. George Spater & Ian Parsons. LC 77-73062. (Illus.). 1977. 12.95 o.p. (ISBN 0-15-157449-9). HarBraceJ.
Marriage of True Minds: An Intimate Portrait of Leonard & Virginia Woolf. George Spater & Ian Parsons. LC 78-14914. (Illus.). 1979. pap. 5.95 o.p. (ISBN 0-15-657299-0, Harv). HarBraceJ.
Marriage Puzzle. Shirley Cook. 128p. (Orig.). 1985. pap. 4.95 o.p. (ISBN 0-310-33611-2, 11718P). Zondervan.
Marriage, the Family, & Society: Toward a Sociology of Marriage & the Family. 2nd ed. Mildred W. Weil. LC 76-50685. 1977. pap. 6.95x o.p. (ISBN 0-8134-1897-6, 1897). Inter Print Pubs.
Marriage to a Difficult Man: The Uncommon Union of Jonathan & Sarah Edwards. Elizabeth D. Dodds. 1971. 6.95 o.s.i. (ISBN 0-664-20900-9, Westminster). Westminster John Knox.
Marriages in Trouble: The Process of Seeking Help. Julia Brannen & Jean Collard. 320p. 1982. 28.00 o.p. (ISBN 0-422-78100-2, NO. 3788, Pub. by Tavistock England). Routledge Chapman & Hall.
Marriages of Middlesex County, Virginia, 1740-1852. Virginia Genealogical Society Staff. 124p. 1976. pap. 15.00 o.p. (ISBN 0-89308-265-1). Southern Hist Pr.
Marriages of Patrick County, Virginia, 1791-1850. Lela C. Adams. 165p. 1972. pap. 20.00 o.p. (ISBN 0-89308-357-7, VA 46). Southern Hist Pr.
Married & Gay: An Intimate Look at a Different Relationship. Brenda Maddox. LC 81-47311. 268p. 1982. 12.95 o.p. (ISBN 0-15-157459-6). HarBraceJ.
Married & Mobile: Making a Move That's Right for You. Kathy Haueisen. LC 84-20521. 128p. (Orig.). 1984. pap. 5.95 o.p. (ISBN 0-8066-2088-9, 10-4293, Augsburg). Augsburg Fortress.
Married Man. Piers P. Read. 272p. 1981. pap. 2.95 o.p. (ISBN 0-380-55103-9, 67967-1). Avon.
Married to Medicine: An Intimate Portrait of Doctor's Wives. Carla Fine. LC 80-69372. 1981. 12.95 o.p. (ISBN 0-689-11128-2, Atheneum). Macmillan.
Married Women's Work: Being the Report of an Inquiry Undertaken by the Women's Industrial Council. Clementina Black. LC 79-56947. (Englishworking Class Ser.). 1980. lib. bdg. 33.00 o.p. (ISBN 0-8240-0102-8). Garland Pub.
Married Working Woman: A Study, London, 1911 see Working Women & Divorce: An Account of Evidence Given on Behalf of the Women's Co-operative Guild Before the Royal Commission on Divorce, London, 1911.
Marriner S. Eccles: Private Entrepreneur & Public Servant. Sidney Hyman. LC 76-46152. (Illus.). 1977. lib. bdg. 15.00x o.s.i. (ISBN 0-226-36410-0, Dist. by U of Chicago Press for Stanford U. Grad School). U of Chicago Pr.
Marrow of the World. Ruth Nichols. LC 76-190558. (gr. 4-7). 1972. 6.95 o.p. (ISBN 0-689-30309-2, Atheneum). Macmillan.
Marry Me, Marybeth. Jeanne Jordan. Ed. by Raymond Woolsey. 96p. 1987. pap. 6.95 o.p. (ISBN 0-8280-0379-3). Review & Herald.
Marrying Off Mother. Christine Nostlinger. Tr. by Anthea Bell. LC 82-47938. 132p. (gr. 4-6). 1982. 10.95 o.p. (ISBN 0-15-252138-0, HJ). HarBraceJ.
Mars & Its Satellites: A Detailed Commentary on the Nomenclature. 2nd ed. Jurgen Blunck. (Illus.). 1982. 10.00 o.p. (ISBN 0-682-49777-0, University). Exposition-Phoenix.
Mars & Its Satellites: A Detailed Commentary on the Nomenclature. Jurgen Blunck. 1977. 10.00 o.p. (ISBN 0-682-48676-0, University). Exposition-Phoenix.
Mars Reference Atmosphere, Vol. 2, Pt. 2. Ed. by A. Kliore. (Illus.). 107p. 1982. pap. 43.00 o.p. (ISBN 0-08-029126-0). Pergamon.
Marsanne. Virginia Coffman. LC 76-150633. 1976. 8.95 o.p. (ISBN 0-87795-138-1, Arbor Hse). Morrow.
Marsh: A Century of Cranberries. Lela P. Winn. 144p. 1981. 7.50 o.p. (ISBN 0-682-49697-9). Exposition-Phoenix.
Marshall Loeb's Money Guide 1986. Marshall Loeb. 24.95 o.p. (ISBN 0-316-53053-0); pap. 12.95 o.p. (ISBN 0-316-53054-9). Little.
Marshall Loeb's 1987 Money Guide. Marshall Loeb. 1986. pap. 12.95 o.p. (ISBN 0-316-53056-5). Little.
Marshall Loeb's 1988 Money Guide. Marshall Loeb. 512p. 1987. 24.95 o.p. (ISBN 0-316-53061-1); pap. 12.95 o.p. (ISBN 0-316-53063-8). Little.
Marshall Miles Teaches Logical Bridge. Marshall Miles. 1967. 6.50 o.p. (ISBN 0-682-45735-3, Banner). Exposition-Phoenix.
Marshall Plan. Charles L. Mee, Jr. 1984. 16.45 o.p. (ISBN 0-671-42149-2). S&S.
Marshall Plan for Lifelong Weight Control. Edward M. Marshall. 1980. 7.95 o.p. (ISBN 0-395-29476-2). HM.
Marshall's Physiology of Reproduction, Vol. 1: Reproductive Cycles of Vertebrates. 4th ed. Ed. by G. E. Lamming. (Illus.). 842p. 1984. text ed. 120.00 o.p. (ISBN 0-443-01968-1). Churchill.
Marshmellowterra: The Land of Marshmallow People & Whimsical Animals. Boris Draznin. (Illus.). 96p. (gr. 7-12). 1982. 6.50 o.p. (ISBN 0-682-49914-5). Exposition-Phoenix.
Marsh's California Corporation Law, 3 vols. Harold Marsh, Jr. 2200p. 1981. 175.00 o.p. (ISBN 0-15-100036-0, Pub. by Law & Business). HarBraceJ.
Marsupials & Politics: Two Comedies. Barry Oakley. 86p. 1982. text ed. 17.50 o.p. (ISBN 0-7022-1608-9); pap. 7.50 o.p. (ISBN 0-7022-1609-7). U of Queensland Pr.
Martereau. Nathalie Sarraute. pap. 7.95 o.p. (ISBN 0-685-11353-1). Schoenhof.
Martha Ann & the Mother Store. Nathaniel Charnley & Betty J. Charney. LC 73-5237. (Illus.). 32p. (gr. k-3). 1973. 5.50 o.p. (ISBN 0-15-252150-X, HJ). HarBraceJ.

Martha Armstrong-Hand's Living Dolls. David Hand. 1983. 14.95 o.p. (ISBN 0-87588-199-8, 2499). Hobby Hse.
Martha W. Griffiths. Ed. by Emily George. LC 81-40922. 302p. (Orig.). 1982. lib. bdg. 32.00 o.p. (ISBN 0-8191-2347-1); pap. text ed. 14.25 o.p. (ISBN 0-8191-2348-X). U Pr of Amer.
Martha Wesley. Franklin Wilder. 1976. 6.50 o.p. (ISBN 0-682-48488-1). Exposition-Phoenix.
Marthe. Tr. by Donald M. Frame. LC 84-1092. (Helen & Kurt Wolff Bk.). 352p. 1984. 19.95 o.p. (ISBN 0-15-157550-9). HarBraceJ.
Martial Arts & the Law. Karl J. Duff. Ed. by Mike Lee. LC 84-62295. (Ser. 439). 96p. (Orig.). 1985. pap. 6.95 o.p. (ISBN 0-89750-126-8). Ohara Pubns.
Martial Arts for Young Athletes. Michael DePasquale, Jr. Ed. by Betty Schwartz. 128p. (Orig.). (gr. 3 up). 1984. pap. 7.95 o.s.i. (ISBN 0-671-50733-8). Wanderer Bks.
Martial Arts: Judo & Karate. Harvey Frommer. LC 78-55205. (Illus.). 1978. 7.95 o.p. (ISBN 0-689-10908-3, Atheneum). Macmillan.
Martial Deduction Planning After ERTA. Massachusetts Continuing Legal Education-New England Law Institute, Inc. Staff. LC 83-63429. write for info. o.p. Mass CLE.
Martial Law: Theory & Practice. H. S. Bhatia. 1979. text ed. 11.50x o.p. (ISBN 0-391-01039-5). Humanities.
Martin - God's Court Jester: Luther in Retrospect. Eric W. Gritsch. LC 83-48004. 304p. 1983. pap. 15.95 o.p. (ISBN 0-8006-1753-3, 1-1753, Fortress). Augsburg Fortress.
Martin Buber. Stephen M. Panko. Ed. by Bob E. Patterson. LC 76-2869. (Markers of the Modern Theological Mind Ser.). 1976. 8.95 o.p. (ISBN 0-87680-470-9, 80470). Word Bks.
Martin Buber. Ronald G. Smith. LC 67-10206. (Makers of Contemporary Theology Ser.). 1967. pap. 3.45 o.p. (ISBN 0-8042-0697-X, John Knox). Westminster John Knox.
Martin Buber & His Critics: An Annotated Bibliography of Writings in English through 1978. Willard Moonan. LC 78-68278. 258p. 1981. lib. bdg. 44.00 o.p. (ISBN 0-8240-9779-3). Garland Pub.
Martin Buber: Jewish Existentialist. Malcolm L. Diamond. 1968. lib. bdg. 17.50x o.p. (ISBN 0-88307-077-4). Gannon.
Martin by Himself. Gloria Skurzynski. (Illus.). (gr. k-3). 1979. PLB 6.95 o.p. (ISBN 0-395-28271-3). HM.
Martin De Porres, Hero. Claire H. Bishop. (Illus.). (gr. 4-6). 1954. 4.25 o.p. (ISBN 0-395-06634-4). HM.
Martin De Porres, Hero. new ed. Claire H. Bishop. (Illus.). 120p. (gr. 5 up). 1973. pap. 0.95 o.p. (ISBN 0-395-17704-9, Sandpiper). HM.
Martin Eden. Jack London. (Literature Ser.). (gr. 7-12). 1969. pap. text ed. 7.17 o.p. (ISBN 0-87720-709-7). AMSCO Sch.
Martin Gardner's New Mathematical Diversions from Scientific American. Martin Gardner. 1966. 9.95 o.p. (ISBN 0-671-45240-1). S&S.
Martin Heidegger. John Macquarrie. LC 68-11970. (Makers of Contemporary Theology Ser.). 1968. pap. 3.95 o.p. (ISBN 0-8042-0659-7, John Knox). Westminster John Knox.
Martin Heidegger: An Illustrated Study. Walter Biemel. Tr. by J. L. Mehta. LC 76-21253. 1976. pap. 6.95 o.p. (ISBN 0-15-657301-6, Harv). HarBraceJ.
Martin Luther Easter Book. Roland Bainton. LC 82-15996. 88p. 1983. pap. 3.95 o.p. (ISBN 0-8006-1685-5, 1-1685, Fortress). Augsburg Fortress.
Martin Luther Had a Wife. William J. Petersen. 1983. pap. 3.95 o.p. (ISBN 0-8423-4104-8). Tyndale.
Martin Luther: His Life & Teachings. James A. Nestingen. LC 82-71829. 80p. 1982. pap. 4.50 o.p. (ISBN 0-8006-1642-1, 1-1642, Fortress). Augsburg Fortress.
Martin Luther: Portfolio Of Letters & Translations from Aesop. 126p. 150.00 o.p. (ISBN 0-8115-0906-0). Kraus Repr.
Martin Van Buren & the Making of the Democratic Party. Robert V. Remini. 1970. pap. 2.25 o.p. (ISBN 0-393-00527-5, Norton Lib). Norton.
Martingales & Stochastic Integrals I. P. A. Meyer. LC 72-88111. (Lecture Notes in Mathematics Ser.: Vol. 284). vi, 89p. 1972. pap. 7.00 o.p. (ISBN 0-387-05983-0). Springer-Verlag.
Martini-Henry Modification. Barrie Hughes. 1979. 8.95 o.p. (ISBN 0-393-08840-5). Norton.
Marty Mann Answers Your Questions about Drinking & Alcoholism. Marty Mann. 128p. 1981. 10.95 o.p. (ISBN 0-03-081857-5); pap. 3.95 o.s.i. (ISBN 0-03-059156-2). H Holt & Co.
Martyrology Pronouncing Dictionary. Anthony I. Russo-Alesi. LC 79-167151. 196p. 1973. Repr. of 1939 ed. 35.00x o.p. (ISBN 0-8103-3272-8). Gale.
Marvel Comics Illustrated Version of Star Wars. Intro. by Stan Lee. 1977. pap. 1.50 o.s.i. (ISBN 0-345-27492-X, Del Rey). Ballantine.
Marvella: A Personal Journey. Marvella Bayh & Mary L. Kotz. LC 80-25195. 1981. pap. 4.95 o.p. (ISBN 0-15-657402-0, Harv). HarbraceJ.
Marvella: A Personal Journey. Marvella Bayh & Mary L. Kotz. LC 79-1809. (Illus.). 1979. 11.95 o.p. (ISBN 0-15-157557-6). HarBraceJ.
Marvelous Inventions of Alvin Fernald. Clifford B. Hicks. LC 60-6055. (Illus.). 120p. (gr. 4-6). 1960. reinforced bdg. 5.95 o.p. (ISBN 0-03-089893-5). H Holt & Co.
Marvelous Land of Oz. L. Frank Baum. 13.50 o.p. (ISBN 0-8446-6197-X). Peter Smith.
Marvelous Macadamia Nut. Rebecca Buyers. LC 82-73616. (Illus.). 84p. (Orig.). 1982. pap. 12.95 o.p. (ISBN 0-941034-74-7). I Chalmers.
Marvelous Mess. Joan Drescher. (Illus.). (gr. k-3). 1980. PLB 7.95 o.p. (ISBN 0-395-29160-7). HM.
Marvels & Mysteries of the World Around Us. Reader's Digest Editors. LC 72-77610. (Illus.). 320p. 1972. 15.99 o.p. (ISBN 0-89577-012-1). RD Assn.
Marwaris: From Traders to Industrialists. Thomas A. Timberg. 1979. text ed. 20.00x o.p. (ISBN 0-7069-0528-8, Pub. by Vikas India). Advent NY.
Marx & Contemporary Scientific Thought. International Council for Philosophy & Humanistic Studies Staff & International Social Science Council Staff. LC 70-101066. (International Social Science Council Publications Ser: No. 13). (Fr). 1969. text ed. 36.00x o.p. (ISBN 0-686-22417-5). Mouton.
Marx & Engels Today: A Modern Dialogue on Philosophy & History. Kenneth N. Cameron. LC 76-5098. 1976. 5.00 o.p. (ISBN 0-682-48512-8, University). Exposition-Phoenix.
Marx As Politician. David Felix. LC 82-10507. 320p. 1983. 27.50x o.p. (ISBN 0-8093-1073-2). S Ill U Pr.
Marx Beyond Marx: Lessons on the Grundrisse. Antonio Negri. Ed. by James Fleming. Tr. by Harry Cleaver & Michael Ryan. Orig. Title: Marx Oltre Marx. 280p. 1984. 39.95 o.s.i. (ISBN 0-89789-018-3). Bergin & Garvey.
Marx-Engels Reader. Ed. by Robert C. Tucker. LC 79-141585. 1971. pap. 4.95x o.p. (ISBN 0-393-09965-2). Norton.
Marx, Freud, & the Critique of Everyday Life: Toward a Permanent Cultural Revolution. Bruce Brown. LC 72-93460. 192p. 1973. pap. 4.95 o.p. (ISBN 0-85345-306-3). Monthly Rev.
Marx Oltre Marx see Marx Beyond Marx: Lessons on the Grundrisse.
Marx on Economics. Ed. by Robert Freedman. LC 61-7691. (Orig.). 1961. pap. 4.95 o.p. (ISBN 0-15-657479-9, Harv). HarBraceJ.
Marxian, Nos. 1-2. 1970. Repr. of 1921 ed. lib. bdg. 12.25x o.p. (ISBN 0-8371-9197-1, MN00). Greenwood.
Marxian Socialism in the U. S. Daniel Bell. (Princeton Studies in American Civilization). 1952. pap. 10.50x o.p. (ISBN 0-691-02155-4). Princeton U Pr.
Marximo y Cristianismo Frente Al Hombre Nuevo see New Creation: Marxist & Christian?.
Marxism & Aesthetics: A Selective Annotated Bibliography. Ed. by Lee Baxandall. LC 68-28865. 1978. text ed. 17.50x o.p. (ISBN 0-391-00298-8). Humanities.
Marxism & Indology. Debiprasad Chattopadhyaya. 273p. 1982. Repr. of 1981 ed. text ed. 19.95x o.p. (ISBN 0-391-02512-0). Humanities.
Marxism & Materialism. rev. ed. David Ruben. (Marxist Theory & Contemporary Capitalism Ser.). 1978. text ed. 27.50x o.p. (ISBN 0-391-00966-4); pap. text ed. 11.00x o.p. (ISBN 0-391-00965-6). Humanities.
Marxism & the Muslim World. Maxime Rodinson. LC 81-81695. 416p. 1982. pap. 8.50 o.s.i. (ISBN 0-85345-586-4). Monthly Rev.
Marxism & the Philosophy of Science- A Critical History: Vol. 1: The First Hundred Years. H. Sheehan. 446p. 1985. text ed. 45.00 o.p. (ISBN 0-391-02998-3). Humanities.
Marxism, Fascism, Cold War: Essays & Lectures 1974-1976. Ernst Nolte. Tr. by Lawrence Krader from Ger. 380p. 1982. text ed. 25.00x o.p. (ISBN 0-391-02565-1). Humanities.
Marxism in Our Time. Isaac Deutscher. Ed. by Tamara Deutscher. LC 79-158915. 312p. 1971. 7.95 o.p. (ISBN 0-87867-006-8). Ramparts.
Marxism: The View from America. Clinton Rossiter. LC 60-10916. 1965. pap. 1.75 o.p. (ISBN 0-15-657618-X, HB95, Harv). HarBraceJ.
Marxist, Nos. 1-4. Workers Educational Institute Staff. 1925-27. Repr. lib. bdg. 33.00x o.p. (ISBN 0-8371-9198-X, MT00). Greenwood.
Marxist Aesthetics: The Foundations Within Everyday Life for an Emancipated Consciousness. Pauline Johnson. 192p. 1984. 25.00x o.p. (ISBN 0-7100-9927-4). Routledge Chapman & Hall.
Marxist Economic Theory, 2 vols. Ernest Mandel. Tr. by Brian Pearce from Fr. LC 68-13658. 800p. 1969. Set. pap. 13.00 o.p. (ISBN 0-85345-166-4). Monthly Rev.
Marxist Literary Thought & China: A Conceptual Framework. Paul Pickowicz. LC 79-620064. (Current Chinese Language Project; Studies in Chinese Terminology Ser.). 69p. 1980. pap. 1.00x o.p. (ISBN 0-912966-22-X). IEAS.
Marxist Looks at Jesus. Milan Machovec. LC 76-10053. 240p. 1976. pap. 6.50 o.p. (ISBN 0-8006-1244-2, Fortress). Augsburg Fortress.
Marxist Quarterly, Nos. 1-3. 1968. Repr. of 1937 ed. lib. bdg. 23.75x o.p. (ISBN 0-8371-9199-8, MX00). Greenwood.
Marxist Review, Vols. 1-3. Marxist-Worker's Party Staff. 1970. Repr. of 1940 ed. lib. bdg. 61.00x o.p. (ISBN 0-8371-9200-5, MV00). Greenwood.
Marxist Social Thought. Ed. by Robert Freedman. LC 68-13362. (Orig.). 1968. pap. 4.95 o.p. (ISBN 0-15-657650-3, HB137, Harv). HarBraceJ.
Marxistische Klassenanalyse Oder Spatburgerliche Mythen see Anti-Communist Myths in Left Disguise.
Marx's Capital. Ben Fine. (Macmillan Studies in Economics). 71p. 1975. pap. text ed. 9.95x o.p. (ISBN 0-333-17845-9). Humanities.
Marx's Capital. 2nd ed. Ben Fine. (Macmillan Studies in Economics). 1984. pap. text ed. 9.95x o.p. (ISBN 0-333-37536-X). Humanities.
Marx's Construction of Social Theory. J. M. Barbalet. 240p. 1983. 26.95x o.p. (ISBN 0-7100-9540-6). Routledge Chapman & Hall.
Marx's Critique of Political Economy: Intellectual Sources & Evolution, 1861-1863, Vol. II. Allen Oakley. 302p. 1985. 32.50x o.p. (ISBN 0-7100-9945-2). Routledge Chapman & Hall.
Marx's Critique of Political Economy: Intellectual Sources & Evolution, Vol. 1. Allen Oakley. (International Library of Economics). 225p. 1984. 30.00x o.p. (ISBN 0-7100-9944-4). Routledge Chapman & Hall.
Marx's Economic Predictions. Fred M. Gottheil. 1967. 15.95 o.p. (ISBN 0-8101-0105-X). Northwestern U Pr.
Marx's Ethics of Freedom. George G. Brenkert. 360p. 1983. 29.95x o.p. (ISBN 0-7100-9461-2). Routledge Chapman & Hall.
Mary. Vladimir Nabokov. 1981. pap. text ed. 4.95 o.p. (ISBN 0-07-045698-4). McGraw.
Mary. Jaroslav Pelikan et al. LC 85-45489. (Illus.). 128p. 1986. 19.95 o.p. (ISBN 0-8006-0765-1, Fortress). Augsburg Fortress.
Mary Andrews: Companion of Sorrow. Carolyn Byers. Ed. by Gerald Wheeler. LC 83-21121. (Banner Bks.). (Illus.). 91p. (Orig.). (gr. 5 up). 1984. pap. 6.95 o.p. (ISBN 0-8280-0212-6). Review & Herald.
Mary Austin Holley: A Biography. Rebecca S. Lee. 1962. pap. write for info. o.p. (ISBN 0-292-73297-X). U of Tex Pr.
Mary Baker Eddy: The Years of Authority. Robert Peel. LC 66-14855. 544p. 1980. pap. 7.95 o.p. (ISBN 0-03-056709-2). H Holt & Co.
Mary Barnes. David Edgar. 87p. 1984. pap. 6.95 o.p. (ISBN 0-413-54860-0, 4110). Heinemann Ed.
Mary Berenson: A Self Portrait from Her Letters & Diaries. Barbara Strachey & Jayne Samuels. (Illus.). 1984. 18.45 o.p. (ISBN 0-393-01827-X). Norton.
Mary Bethune & Her Somedays. Jan Johnson. (Stories About Christian Heroes Ser.). (Illus.). (gr. 1-5). 1979. pap. 1.95 o.p. (ISBN 0-03-049421-4). HarpR.
Mary Gilliatt's Mix-&-Match Decorating Book. Mary Gilliatt. LC 83-42811. (Illus.). 1984. spiral bd. 18.45 o.p. (ISBN 0-394-42128-0). Pantheon.
Mary, Handmaid of the Lord. Joan Jungerman. 1.50 o.p. (ISBN 0-8091-9332-9). Paulist Pr.
Mary in the New Testament: A Collaborative Assessment by Protestant & Roman Catholic Scholars. Ed. by Raymond E. Brown et al. LC 78-8797. 336p. 1978. pap. 6.95 o.p. (ISBN 0-8006-1345-7, 1-1345, Fortress). Augsburg Fortress.
Mary Jemison: Seneca Captive. Jeanne L. Gardner. LC 66-23287. (Illus.). (gr. 5-7). 1966. 5.50 o.p. (ISBN 0-15-252190-9, HJ). HarBraceJ.
Mary McCarthy: A Bibliography. Sherli E. Goldman. LC 68-12574. 80p. 1968. 4.50 o.s.i. (ISBN 0-15-157775-7). HarBraceJ.
Mary, Michael, & Lucifer: Folk Catholicism in Central Mexico. John M. Ingham. (Latin American Monographs: No. 69). (Illus.). 228p. 1986. text ed. 25.00x o.p. (ISBN 0-292-75089-7). U of Tex Pr.
Mary Montgomery, Rebel. Helen F. Daringer. LC 48-6025. (Illus.). (gr. 7 up). 1948. 4.95 o.p. (ISBN 0-15-252231-X, HJ). HarBraceJ.
Mary Myth: On the Femininity of God. Andrew M. Greeley. 240p. 1977. 9.95 o.p. (ISBN 0-8164-0333-3). HarpR.
Mary Olivier: A Life. May Sinclair. LC 82-1549. (Virago Modern Classic Ser.). 392p. 1982. pap. 8.95 o.p. (ISBN 0-385-27653-2, Dial). Doubleday.
Mary Pickford & Douglas Fairbanks: The Most Popular Couple the World Has Known. Booton Herndon. (Illus.). 1977. 9.95 o.p. (ISBN 0-393-07508-7). Norton.
Mary Play: From the N. Town Manuscript. Ed. by Peter Meredith. LC 85-19851. (Illus.). 196p. 1987. pap. text ed. 13.95 o.p. (ISBN 0-582-49078-2). Longman.
Mary Poppins. P. L. Travers. 1972. 9.95 o.p. (ISBN 0-15-252410-X, HJ); pap. 2.25 o.p. (ISBN 0-15-657680-5, VoyB). HarBraceJ.
Mary Poppins & Mary Poppins Comes Back. Pamela L. Travers. LC 37-38860. (Illus.). (gr. 4-6). 1964. 7.50 o.p. (ISBN 0-15-252415-0, HJ). HarBraceJ.
Mary Poppins & Myth. Staffan Bergsten. (Illus.). 1978. text ed. 15.00x o.p. (ISBN 91-22-00127-1). Humanities.
Mary Poppins in Cherry Tree Lane. Pamela L. Travers. (Illus.). 96p. (gr. 3-7). pap. 1.95 o.s.i. (ISBN 0-440-45793-9, YB). Dell.
Mary Poppins in the Kitchen: A Cookery Book with a Story. P. L. Travers & Maurice Moore-Betty. LC 75-10131. (Illus.). 128p. (gr. k up). 1975. 6.95 o.s.i. (ISBN 0-15-252898-9, HJ). HarBraceJ.
Mary Shelley: An Annotated Bibliography. W. H. Lyles. LC 75-17713. (Reference Library of the Humanities: Vol. 22). 320p. 1975. lib. bdg. 45.00 o.p. (ISBN 0-8240-9993-1). Garland Pub.
Mary Shelley's Monster: The Story of Frankenstein. Martin Tropp. 1977. 7.95 o.p. (ISBN 0-686-57866-X); pap. 4.95 o.p. (ISBN 0-395-25337-3). HM.
Mary Stuart. Stephen Spender. LC 79-25615. 104p. 1980. 8.95 o.p. (ISBN 0-89919-008-1); pap. 4.95 o.p. (ISBN 0-89919-013-8). Ticknor & Fields.
Mary Stuart. Friedrich Von Schiller. Tr. by Sophie Wilkins from Ger. 1959. pap. text ed. 5.95 o.p. (ISBN 0-8120-0132-X). Barron.
Mary Wilkins Freeman. Perry Westbrook. (Twayne's United States Author Ser.). 1967. pap. 10.95 o.p. (ISBN 0-8084-0217-X, T122, Twayne). New Coll U Pr.
Mary Wollstonecraft: An Annotated Bibliography of Her Works & Criticism. Janet M. Todd. LC 75-24095. (Reference Library of the Humanities: Vol. 36). 100p. 1976. lib. bdg. 25.00 o.p. (ISBN 0-8240-9976-1). Garland Pub.
Maryland. Carl Bode. 1983. 29.50 o.p. (ISBN 0-912856-83-1). Gr Arts Ctr Pub.
Maryland: A History. Ed. by Richard Walsh & William L. Fox. (Illus.). 1983. 17.00 o.p. (ISBN 0-942370-10-4); pap. 12.50 o.p. (ISBN 0-942370-11-2). MD St Archives.
Maryland Business Kit for Starting & Existing Businesses. Lawless J. Barrientos. LC 85-105171. (Illus.). 1983. pap. 14.95 o.p. (ISBN 0-671-49214-4). S&S.
Maryland: Conflict of Laws. 8.50 o.p. (ISBN 0-686-90788-4). Am Law Inst.
Maryland Criminal Jury Instructions & Commentary. David E. Aaronson. LC 75-2870. 453p. 1975. 25.00x o.p. (ISBN 0-87215-165-4). Michie Co.
Maryland in Africa: The Maryland State Colonization Society, 1831-1857. Penelope Campbell. LC 75-131058. 270p. 1971. 24.95 o.p. (ISBN 0-252-00133-8). U of Ill Pr.
Maryland: Old Line to New Prosperity. Joseph L. Arnold. LC 85-6416. 256p. 1985. 24.95 o.p. (ISBN 0-89781-147-X). Windsor Pubns Inc.
Maryland: Property, Vols. 1-2. 8.50 o.p. Am Law Inst.
Maryland: Property, Vol. 3. 1983. 8.50 o.p. (ISBN 0-686-90508-3). Am Law Inst.
Maryland: Property, Vol. 4. 1983. 8.50 o.p. (ISBN 0-686-90510-5). Am Law Inst.
Maryland Rules, 2 vols. Michie Company Editorial Staff. 1985. 35.00 o.p. (ISBN 0-87215-872-1). Michie Co.
Maryland Supplement for Modern Real Estate Practice. 4th ed. H. Warren Crawford & John F. Rodgers. LC 84-27749. 192p. (Orig.). 1985. pap. text ed. 10.95 o.p. (ISBN 0-88462-511-7, 1510-08, Real Estate Ed). Longman Finan.
Maryland: Trusts. 1983. 8.50 o.p. (ISBN 0-686-90512-1). Am Law Inst.
Mary's Bread Basket & Soup Kettle. Mary Gubser. LC 75-18826. (Illus.). 320p. 1975. 12.95 o.p. (ISBN 0-688-02975-2). Morrow.
Mary's Mirror. Jim Aylesworth. LC 81-6917. (Illus.). 32p. (gr. k-2). 1982. 9.95 o.s.i. (ISBN 0-03-060392-7). H Holt & Co.
Mas Alla de los Paralelos. Antonio Ambrosi. 1977. 7.50 o.p. (ISBN 0-682-48809-7). Exposition-Phoenix.
MASA: Medical Acronyms, Symbols & Abbreviations. Barbara Guidos & Betty Hamilton. LC 83-4191. 186p. 1984. lib. bdg. 45.00 o.p. (ISBN 0-918212-72-3). Neal-Schuman.

MASA: Medical Acronyms, Symbols, & Abbreviations. Betty Hamilton & Barbara Guidos. 260p. 1987. 49.95 o.p. (ISBN 0-317-61452-5). Neal-Schuman.

Masai: Ethnographische Monographie Eines Ostafrikanischen Semitenvolkes. M. Merker. (Landmarks in Anthropology Ser). (Ger). 1968. Repr. of 1910 ed. 46.00 o.p. (ISBN 0-384-38185-5). Johnson Repr.

Masculine Cross & Ancient Sex Worship. Sha Rocco. (Illus.). 65p. 1873. pap. 7.95 o.s.i. (ISBN 0-88697-014-8). Life Science.

Masculine Focus in Home Economics. B. Greenwood & J. Dowell. LC 75-10815. 1975. pap. 2.50 o.p. (ISBN 0-686-14990-4, 261-08422). Home Econ Educ.

Masculinity & Femininity. Benjamin F. Miller et al. LC 75-134861. (Illus.). 120p. (gr. 7 up). 1972. pap. 5.20 o.p. (ISBN 0-395-03243-1, 2-37390). HM.

Masha Nikiforova's Days. V. Voskoboinokov. 85p. 1978. pap. 2.95 o.p. (ISBN 0-8285-1203-5, Pub. by Progress Pubs USSR). Imported Pubns.

Mask. Frank DiFiore. 336p. 1986. pap. 3.95 o.p. (ISBN 0-380-89987-6). Avon.

Mask Magic. Carolyn Meyer. LC 77-14080. (Illus.). (gr. 4-7). 1978. 7.95 o.p. (ISBN 0-15-253107-6, HJ). HarBraceJ.

Mask of Death. Anita Bachelin. (Orig.). 1981. pap. 1.95 o.p. (ISBN 0-8439-8048-6). Dorchester Pub Co.

Mask of Glory. Date not set. pap. (ISBN 0-8052-6004-8). Random.

Mask of Sanity. Hervey Cleckley. LC 82-2124. (Mosby Medical Library). 285p. 1982. pap. 8.95 o.p. (ISBN 0-452-25341-1, 1158-X, Plume). NAL.

Masked Marvels: Baseball's Great Catchers. Associated Features Inc. Editors. LC 81-12182. (Random House Sports Library). (Illus.). 144p. (gr. 5-9). 1982. pap. 1.95 o.p. (ISBN 0-394-85013-0). Random.

Maskengestalten der Guro, Elfenbeinkuste see Masks in Guro Culture, Ivory Coast.

Masks. Fumiko Enchi. LC 83-48033. (Library of Contemporary World Literature). 160p. 1983. pap. 7.95 o.s.i. (ISBN 0-394-72218-3, Vin). Random.

Masks & Mirrors: Essays in Criticism. Marius Bewley. LC 76-101396. 1970. pap. text ed. 3.25x o.p. (ISBN 0-689-70512-3, 203, Atheneum). Macmillan.

Masks & Puppets. Illus. by Louise Nevett. (Make-It-Yourself Ser.). (Illus.). 32p. (gr. k-3). 1984. lib. bdg. 11.90 o.p. (ISBN 0-531-04771-7). Watts.

Masks in Guro Culture, Ivory Coast. Eberhard Fischer & Lorenz Homberger. Ed. by Jeanne Mullin et al. Tr. by Cornelia Lauf & Andrea Isler. Orig. Title: Maskengestalten der Guro, Elfenbeinkuste. (Illus.). 32p. 1986. pap. 4.95 o.p. (ISBN 0-9614587-0-4). Center African Art.

Masks of the World: To Cut Out & Wear. Deborah R. Horner. (gr. 2 up). 1977. pap. 7.95 o.s.i. (ISBN 0-684-14929-X, ScribJ). Scribner.

Maso Di Banco, A Florentine Artist of the Early Trecentine. David G. Wilkins. Ed. by S. J. Freedberg. (Outstanding Dissertations in Fine Arts Ser.). (Illus.). 335p. 1985. Repr. of 1969 ed. 35.00 o.p. (ISBN 0-8240-6871-8). Garland Pub.

Mason Codex. Jo Bannister. LC 87-32046. 192p. 1988. 12.95 o.p. (ISBN 0-385-24330-8). Doubleday.

Mason Porcelain & Ironstone, Seventeen Ninety-Six to Eighteen Fifty-Three. Reginald Haggar & Elizabeth Adams. (Illus.). 222p. 1977. 35.00 o.p. (ISBN 0-571-10945-4). Faber & Faber.

Masonary Construction: The Trowel Worker's Bible. J. M. Nickey. (Illus.). 256p. 1982. 15.95 o.p. (ISBN 0-8306-0062-0); pap. 8.95 o.p. (ISBN 0-8306-1280-7, 1280). TAB Bks.

Masonic Dictionary. C. Bruce Hunter. LC 86-62666. 96p. 1986. pap. 5.00 o.p. (ISBN 0-88053-083-9, M329). Macoy Pub.

Masonry Design & Detailing: For Architects, Engineers & Builders. Christine Beall. (Illus.). 448p. 1984. text ed. 50.00 o.p. (ISBN 0-13-559153-8). P-H.

Masonry Glossary. International Masonry Institute Staff. 100p. 1983. 18.95 o.p. (ISBN 0-8436-0134-5). Van Nos Reinhold.

Masonry in Architecture. Louis G. Redstone. 1984. text ed. 49.50 o.p. (ISBN 0-07-051387-2). McGraw.

Masque of Chameleons. Joan Van E. Frost. 384p. 1981. pap. 2.95 o.s.i. (ISBN 0-449-24472-5, Crest). Fawcett.

Masque of Surgery. Andrew Glaze. 1974. saddlestitched in wrappers 1.60 o.p. (ISBN 0-685-78977-2, Pub. by Menard Pr). Small Pr Dist.

Masquerading Heart. Caroline Courtney. (Nightingale Ser.). 312p. 1986. pap. 11.95 o.p. (ISBN 0-8161-4031-6, Large Print Bks). G K Hall.

Masques. Bill Pronzini. LC 80-70219. 288p. 1981. 12.50 o.p. (ISBN 0-87795-308-2, Arbor Hse). Morrow.

Mass. Jack Fuller. LC 85-61488. 272p. 1985. 16.95 o.p. (ISBN 0-688-04685-1). Morrow.

Mass Appeal. Bill C. Davis. 80p. 1981. pap. 2.50 o.p. (ISBN 0-380-77396-1, 77396-1, Bard). Avon.

Mass Communication: An Introduction. 3rd ed. John R. Bittner. (Illus.). 496p. 1983. pap. text ed. 22.95 o.p. (ISBN 0-13-559286-0). P-H.

Mass Communication: An Introduction. 4th ed. John R. Bittner. (Illus.). 528p. 1986. pap. text ed. (ISBN 0-13-559246-1). P-H.

Mass Communication & Human Interaction. Robert D. Murphy. LC 76-19906. (Illus.). 1977. text ed. 26.50 o.p. (ISBN 0-395-24433-1). HM.

Mass Communications Law in a Nutshell. 2nd ed. Harvey L. Zuckman & Martin J. Gaynes. LC 82-20029. (Nutshell Ser.). 473p. 1983. pap. text ed. 10.95 o.p. (ISBN 0-314-69869-8). West Pub.

Mass for the Dead. William Gibson. LC 67-25481. 1968. pap. 6.95 o.p. (ISBN 0-689-70542-5, Atheneum, 226). Macmillan.

Mass Media & American Politics. 2nd ed. Doris Graber. 385p. 1984. pap. 14.95 o.p. (ISBN 0-87187-320-6). Congr Quarterly.

Mass Media & Democracy. Harry M. Clor. 1974. pap. 10.50 o.p. (ISBN 0-395-30789-9). HM.

Mass Media & the Law. Ed. by David G. Clark & Earl R. Hutchinson. LC 76-115653. 478p. 1970. 32.50 o.p. (ISBN 0-471-15851-8, Pub. by Wiley). Krieger.

Mass Media Christianity: Televangelism & the Great Commission. Jerry D. Cardwell. 234p. (Orig.). 1985. lib. bdg. 26.75 o.p. (ISBN 0-8191-4323-5); pap. text ed. 11.50 o.p. (ISBN 0-8191-4324-3). U Pr of Amer.

Mass Media: Forces in Our Society. 3rd ed. Francis H. Voelker & Ludmila A. Voelker. (Illus.). 470p. 1978. pap. text ed. 12.95 o.p. (ISBN 0-15-555122-1, HC). HarBraceJ.

Mass Media: Forces in Our Society. 2nd ed. Ed. by Francis H. Voelker & Ludmila A. Voelker. (Illus.). 1975. pap. text ed. 10.95 o.p. (ISBN 0-15-555120-5, HC). HarBraceJ.

Mass Media in Australia: Second Edition. 2nd ed. J. S. Western & Colin A. Hughes. LC 82-2685. (Illus.). 209p. 1983. text ed. 22.50x o.p. (ISBN 0-7022-1682-8); pap. text ed. 14.50x o.p. (ISBN 0-7022-1692-5). U of Queensland Pr.

Mass Media IV. Ray Hiebert et al. LC 84-19459. 608p. 1985. pap. text ed. 20.95x o.p. (ISBN 0-582-28535-6). Longman.

Mass Production Justice & the Constitutional Ideal. Ed. by Charles H. Whitebread, 2nd. xxv, 236p. 1970. 14.95x o.p. (ISBN 0-8139-0499-4, Virginia Legal Studies). U Pr of Va.

Mass Society, Social Organizations, & Democracy. Sidney Willmuth. LC 75-4167. 104p. 1976. (ISBN 0-8022-2180-7). Philos Lib.

Mass Transport in Solids. Ed. by F. Beniere & C. R. Catlow. LC 83-8142. (NATO ASI Series B, Physics: Vol. 97). (Illus.). 610p. 1983. 95.00x o.p. (ISBN 0-306-41365-5, Plenum Pr). Plenum Pub.

Mass Unemployment. Edmond Malinvaud. 140p. 1985. 19.95x o.p. (ISBN 0-631-13704-1). Basil Blackwell.

Massachusetts: A Pictorial History. Walter M. Whitehill & Norman Kotker. (Illus.). 400p. 1981. pap. 5.95 o.s.i. (ISBN 0-684-17288-7, ScribT). Scribner.

Massachusetts: A Pictorial History. Walter M. Whitehill & Norman Kotker. LC 76-28586. (Encore Edition). (Illus.). 356p. 1976. 9.95 o.p. (ISBN 0-684-15962-7, ScribT). Scribner.

Massachusetts: A Scenic Discovery. Steve Dunwell. Ed. by James B. Patrick. (Scenic Discovery Ser.). (Illus.). 118p. 1985. Repr. of 1979 ed. 30.00 o.p. (ISBN 0-89909-051-6). Yankee Bks.

Massachusetts: Agency. 1983. 8.50 o.p. (ISBN 0-686-90798-1). Am Law Inst.

Massachusetts & Rhode Island Trail Guide. 5th ed. (Illus.). 460p. 1982. pap. 9.95 o.p. (ISBN 0-317-33376-3) (ISBN 0-317-33377-1). AMC Books.

Massachusetts, Colony to Commonwealth: Documents on the Formation of Its Constitution, 1775-1780. Ed. by Robert J. Taylor. (Documentary Problems in Early American History Ser.). 1972. pap. text ed. 3.95x o.p. (ISBN 0-393-09396-4). Norton.

Massachusetts: Conflict of Laws. 1983. 8.50 o.p. (ISBN 0-686-90804-X). Am Law Inst.

Massachusetts: Contracts. 1983. 9.50 o.p. (ISBN 0-686-90517-2). Am Law Inst.

Massachusetts Corporate Tax Manual. 2nd ed. Ed. by Massachusetts Bar Association Staff. 1986. (ISBN 0-88063-055-8). Butterworth Legal Pubs.

Massachusetts Directory of Manufacturers, 1987-88. 390p. 1987. pap. 62.50 o.p. (ISBN 0-318-02888-3). Manufacturers.

Massachusetts General Hospital Department of Nursing Operating Room Procedure Manual. Massachusetts General Hospital Department of Nursing Staff. 1981. text ed. 19.95 o.p. (ISBN 0-8359-4252-X). Appleton & Lange.

Massachusetts Motor Vehicle Laws. Gould Editorial Staff. (Supplemented annually). looseleaf 17.00x o.p. (ISBN 0-87526-231-7). Gould.

Massachusetts People & Politics, 1919-1933. J. Joseph Huthmacher. LC 59-9276. (Illus.). 1969. pap. text ed. 3.95x o.p. (ISBN 0-689-70103-9, 140, Atheneum). Macmillan.

Massachusetts: Property, Vols. 1-2. 8.50 o.p. (ISBN 0-686-90807-4). Am Law Inst.

Massachusetts Rules of Court State & Federal. 672p. 1986. pap. 18.50 o.p. (ISBN 0-314-23715-1). West Pub.

Massachusetts Tax Valuation List of, 1171. Ed. by Bettye Pruitt. 1978. lib. bdg. 95.00 o.s.i. (ISBN 0-8161-0245-7, Hall Library). G K Hall.

Massachusetts: Trusts. 1983. 9.50 o.p. (ISBN 0-686-90520-2). Am Law Inst.

Massacre at Fall Creek. Jessamyn West. LC 74-30377. 1975. 14.95 o.s.i. (ISBN 0-15-157820-6). HarBraceJ.

Massage, Manipulation & Traction. Ed. by Sidney Licht. LC 76-7959. 292p. 1976. Repr. of 1960 ed. 23.50 o.p. (ISBN 0-88275-415-7). Krieger.

Masses with Young People. Donal Neary. 128p. 1986. Repr. of 1985 ed. 19.95 o.p. (ISBN 0-89622-295-0). Twenty-Third.

Master. Max Brod. 1951. (ISBN 0-8022-0180-6). Philos Lib.

Master: A Life of Jesus. John Pollack. 240p. 1985. 12.95 o.p. (ISBN 0-89693-315-6). Victor Bks.

Master Alcuin, Liturgist. Gerald Ellard. LC 56-8943. (Jesuit Studies). 1956. 2.95 o.p. (ISBN 0-8294-0027-3). Loyola.

Master & Margarita. Mikhail Bulgakov. Tr. by Mirra Ginsburg from Rus. 1970. pap. 5.95 o.p. (ISBN 0-394-17439-9, B147, BC). Grove.

Master Cornhill. Eloise J. McGraw. LC 72-85920. 256p. (gr. 5-9). 1973. 6.25 o.p. (ISBN 0-689-30320-3, Atheneum). Macmillan.

Master Craftsman's Illustrated Woodworking Manual with Projects. Lewis H. Hodges. 21.95 o.p. (ISBN 0-8306-0035-3, 1315); pap. 12.95 o.p. (ISBN 0-8306-1315-3). TAB Bks.

Master Dictionary of Food & Cookery & Menu Translator. Henry Smith. (ISBN 0-8022-1591-2). Philos Lib.

Master Drawings of the Roman Baroque. Dieter Graf. (Illus.). 320p. (Orig.). 1984. pap. 10.95 o.p. (ISBN 0-901486-56-6, Pub. by Victoria & Albert Mus UK). Faber & Faber.

Master Handbook of Acoustics. F. Alton Everest. (Illus.). 352p. 1983. 18.95 o.p.; pap. 14.95 o.p. (ISBN 0-8306-1296-3, 1296). TAB Bks.

Master Handbook of Electronic Tables & Formulas. 3rd ed. Martin Clifford. (Illus.). 322p. 1980. 16.95 o.p. (ISBN 0-8306-9943-0); pap. 9.95 o.p. (ISBN 0-8306-1225-4, 1225). TAB Bks.

Master Handbook of One Thousand & One Practical Electronic Circuits. Ed. by Ken Sessions. LC 75-31458. 602p. 1975. 15.95 o.p. (ISBN 0-8306-5800-9); pap. 19.95 o.p. (ISBN 0-8306-4800-3, 800). TAB Bks.

Master Handbook of Woodworking Techniques. 2nd ed. Percy W. Blandford. (Illus.). 384p. 1987. 25.95 o.p. (ISBN 0-8306-0244-5, NO. 2744); pap. 15.60 o.p. (ISBN 0-8306-2744-8). TAB Bks.

Master-Key to Riches. Napoleon Hill. 1982. pap. 3.50 o.p. (ISBN 0-449-20075-2, Crest). Fawcett.

Master Mariner: Darken Ship. Nicholas Monsarrat. LC 80-20222. (Illus.). 192p. 1981. 9.95 o.p. (ISBN 0-688-00017-7). Morrow.

Master Mechanic. I. G. Broat. LC 78-14510. 1979. 10.95 o.p. (ISBN 0-689-10935-0, Atheneum). Macmillan.

Master of Cape Horn: W. A. Nelson 1839-1929. Hugh Falkus. (Illus.). 1982. 32.95 o.p. (ISBN 0-575-03089-5, Pub. by Gollancz England). David & Charles.

Master of His Fate. J. Maclaren Cobban. 256p. 1987. 15.00 o.p. (ISBN 0-947898-56-5). Kraus Repr.

Master of Jalna. Mazo De La Roche. (Jalna Ser.). 1979. pap. 1.95 o.s.i. (ISBN 0-449-23932-2, Crest). Fawcett.

Master of Light: A Biography of Albert A. Michelson. Dorothy M. Livingston. LC 72-1178. (Illus.). 1979. pap. text ed. 6.95x o.s.i. (ISBN 0-226-48711-3, P813, Phoen). U of Chicago Pr.

Master of Mackenzie Station. Kathleen Yapp. (Orig.). pap. 2.50 o.p. (ISBN 0-89191-373-4, 53736). Cook.

Master of Middle-Earth: The Fiction of J. R. R. Tolkien. Paul H. Kocher. 1973. 9.95 o.p. (ISBN 0-395-14097-8); pap. 3.95 o.p. (ISBN 0-395-17701-4). HM.

Master of the Battlefield: Monty's War Years, 1942-1944. Nigel Hamilton. (Illus.). 864p. 1984. text ed. 25.95 o.p. (ISBN 0-07-025806-6). McGraw.

Master of the Moor. Ruth Rendell. 224p. 1982. 11.45 o.s.i. (ISBN 0-394-52215-X). Pantheon.

Master Plan. Clifton Bullock. 1978. 6.00 o.p. (ISBN 0-682-48273-0). Exposition-Phoenix.

Master Prints from the Fifteenth Through Eighteenth Centuries. Ed. by Diane J. Gingold. LC 77-84545. (Illus.). 1977. pap. 9.00 o.p. (ISBN 0-89280-007-0). Montgomery Mus.

Master Rabbit Leaves Home. (Oak Tree Tales Ser.). (Illus.). (ps-1). 1.98 o.s.i. (ISBN 0-517-45738-5). Outlet Bk Co.

Master Recipes. Stephen Schmidt. (Orig.). 1987. 24.95 o.p. (ISBN 0-449-90259-5, Columbine). Ballantine.

Master Sculptor. Pershing Tousley. LC 81-7189. 1981. pap. 10.00 o.p. (ISBN 0-8309-0316-X). Herald Hse.

Master Semiconductor Replacement Handbook: Listed by Industry Standard Number. TAB Editorial Staff. 684p. 1982. 25.95 o.p. (ISBN 0-8306-1470-2, 1470). TAB Bks.

Master Speaks. Joel Goldsmith. 6.00 o.p. (ISBN 0-8216-0049-4, Pub. by Univ Bks). Carol Pub Group.

Master Theme of the Bible, Pt. I: The Doctrine of the Lamb. J. Sidlow Baxter. (Living Studies). 160p. 1985. pap. 5.95 o.p. (ISBN 0-8423-4187-0). Tyndale.

Master Theses in the Pure & Applied Sciences--Accepted by Colleges & Universities of the United States & Canada, Vol. 29. Ed. by Wade H. Shafer. 412p. 1986. 95.00x o.p. (ISBN 0-306-42385-5, Plenum Pr.). Plenum Pub.

Master Trust: Simplifying Employee Benefits Trust Fund Administration. Michael L. Costa. 288p. 1980. 19.95 o.p. (ISBN 0-8144-5622-7). AMACOM.

Mastera: The Artists. Bella Ezerskaya. 1982. 5.95 o.s.i. RWCPH.

Mastering AppleWorks. Elna Tymes. LC 84-51794. 201p. 1984. pap. 15.95 o.p. (ISBN 0-89588-240-X). SYBEX.

Mastering AutoCAD. George Omura. 645p. (Orig.). 1987. pap. 29.95 o.p. (ISBN 0-89588-378-3). Sybex.

Mastering AutoCAD. 2nd ed. George Omura. 739p. 1988. pap. 29.95 o.p. (ISBN 0-89588-502-6). Sybex.

Mastering Change. Leon Martel. LC 85-24980. 336p. 1986. 18.45 o.p. (ISBN 0-671-47746-3). S&S.

Mastering Color Photography. (Kodak Library of Creative Photography). 1988. 11.95 o.p. (ISBN 0-86706-242-8). Time-Life.

Mastering CP-M. Alan R. Miller. LC 82-62006. (Illus.). 398p. 1983. pap. 18.95 o.p. (ISBN 0-89588-068-7, C302). SYBEX.

Mastering Disk Operations on the Commodore 128. Alan R. Miller. 238p. (Orig.). 1986. pap. 15.95 o.p. (ISBN 0-89588-357-0). Sybex.

Mastering DisplayWrite 3. Michael McCarthy. 447p. (Orig.). 1986. pap. 19.95 o.p. (ISBN 0-89588-340-6). Sybex.

Mastering Excel. Carl Townsend. LC 85-62540. 454p. 1985. pap. 22.95 o.p. (ISBN 0-89588-306-6). Sybex.

Mastering Framework. Douglas Hergert. LC 84-51981. 435p. 1985. pap. 21.95 o.p. (ISBN 0-89588-248-5). SYBEX.

Mastering Golf. Lou Graham & John Bibb. LC 77-91155. 1978. 9.95 o.p. (ISBN 0-8092-7763-8); pap. 8.95 o.p. (ISBN 0-8092-7761-1). Contemp Bks.

Mastering Guitar. David Alzofon. LC 80-24682. 1981. pap. 11.95 o.p. (ISBN 0-671-25421-9, Fireside). S&S.

Mastering Household Electrical Wiring. 2nd ed. James L. Kittle. (Illus.). 304p. (Orig.). 1988. 13.95 o.p. (ISBN 0-8306-0587-8). TAB Bks.

Mastering Medical Language. Anthony L. Spatola. (Illus.). 464p. 1981. 22.95 o.p. (ISBN 0-13-560151-7). Appleton & Lange.

Mastering Microsoft WORD. 2nd ed. Matthew Holtz. 479p. (Orig.). 1987. pap. 21.95 o.p. (ISBN 0-89588-410-0). Sybex.

Mastering MS Word. Matthew Holtz. LC 85-71779. 365p. (Orig.). 1985. pap. 19.95 o.p. (ISBN 0-89588-285-X). Sybex.

Mastering MultiMate Advantage. Charles Ackerman. 349p. (Orig.). 1987. pap. 19.95 o.p. (ISBN 0-89588-380-5). Sybex.

Mastering New Testament Facts, 4 bks. Madeline H. Beck & Lamar Williamson, Jr. Incl. Bk. 1. Introduction & Synoptic Gospels (ISBN 0-8042-0326-1); Bk. 2. The Fourth Gospel & Acts (ISBN 0-8042-0327-X); Bk. 3. Pauline Letters (ISBN 0-8042-0328-8); Bk. 4. The General Letters & Revelation (ISBN 0-8042-0329-6). (Illus., Orig.). 1973. pap. 4.95 ea. o.s.i. (John Knox); pap. 9.95 set o.s.i. Westminster John Knox.

Mastering Old Testament Facts, 4 bks. Madeline H. Beck & Lamar Williamson, Jr. Incl. Bk. 1. Introduction on-Deut. 1979 (ISBN 0-8042-0134-X); Bk. 2. Joshua-Esther. 1979 (ISBN 0-8042-0135-8). (Illus., Orig.). pap. text ed. 4.95 ea. o.s.i. (John Knox); pap. text ed. 9.95 set o.s.i. Westminster John Knox.

Mastering Old Testament Facts, Bk. 4: Isaiah-Malachi. Madeline H. Beck & Lamar Williamson, Jr. (Mastering Old Testament Facts Ser.). (Illus.). 112p. (Orig.). (gr. 9-12). 1981. pap. 4.95 o.s.i. (ISBN 0-8042-0137-4, John Knox). Westminster John Knox.

Mastering Omnis Three. Steven Muller. (Illus.). 224p. 1986. 24.95 o.p. (ISBN 0-8306-0374-3, 2674); pap. 17.60 o.p. (ISBN 0-8306-0474-X). Tab Bks.

Mastering Organic Chemistry: A Problem Solving Approach. Gerald W. Gibson. LC 77-78569. 1979. pap. text ed. 18.95 o.s.i. (ISBN 0-7216-4111-3, CBS C). SCP.

Mastering Paradox. Alan Simpson. 411p. (Orig.). 1986. pap. 24.95 o.p. (ISBN 0-89588-334-1). Sybex.

Mastering Paradox. 2nd ed. Alan Simpson. 463p. 1985. pap. 19.95 o.p. (ISBN 0-89588-375-9). Sybex.

Mastering ProDOS. Timothy Rice & Karen Rice. 260p. (Orig.). 1986. pap. 19.95 o.p. (ISBN 0-89588-315-5). Sybex.

Mastering Q & A. Greg Harvey. 399p. 1986. pap. 21.95 o.p. (ISBN 0-89588-356-2). Sybex.

Mastering Reflex. Robert Ericson & Ann Moskol. 336p. (Orig.). 1986. pap. 19.95 o.p. (ISBN 0-89588-348-1). Sybex.

Mastering Rubik's Cube. Don Taylor. 1981. 1.95 o.p. (ISBN 0-03-059941-5, Owl Bks). H Holt & Co.

Mastering SAMNA Word IV. Ann M. Draper. 425p. (Orig.). 1987. pap. 22.95 o.p. (ISBN 0-89588-376-7). Sybex.

Mastering Sound & Music on the Atari ST. Tim Knight. 280p. (Orig.). 1986. pap. 16.95 o.p. (ISBN 0-89588-391-0). Sybex.

Mastering SuperCalc 3. Greg Harvey. 276p. (Orig.). 1986. pap. 19.95 o.p. (ISBN 0-89588-312-0). Sybex.

Mastering Symphony. Douglas Cobb. LC 84-51746. (Illus.). 763p. 1985. 24.95 o.p. (ISBN 0-89588-244-2). SYBEX.

Mastering Symphony. rev., 2nd ed. Douglas Cobb. LC 85-63786. 817p. (Orig.). 1986. pap. 24.95 o.p. (ISBN 0-89588-341-4). Sybex.

Mastering the Art of Chinese Cooking. Charmaine Solomon. (Illus.). 152p. 1984. text ed. 19.95 o.p. (ISBN 0-07-059655-7). McGraw.

Mastering the International Phonetic Alphabet. Donald M. Decker. 1970. pap. text ed. 2.25 o.p. (ISBN 0-88345-099-2, 17757). Prentice ESL.

Mastering the Tandy 2000. Dan Keen & Dave Dischert. (Illus.). 128p. (Orig.). 1984. 16.95 o.p. (ISBN 0-8306-0829-X); pap. 10.60 o.p. (ISBN 0-8306-1829-5, 1829). TAB Bks.

Mastering ThinkTank of the IBM PC. Jonathan Kamin. LC 85-63324. 350p. (Orig.). 1985. pap. 19.95 o.p. (ISBN 0-89588-327-9). Sybex.

Mastering ThinkTank on the 512k Macintosh. Jonathan Kamin. LC 85-62544. 264p. (Orig.). 1985. pap. 18.95 o.p. (ISBN 0-89588-305-8). Sybex.

Mastering Turbo C. Stan Kelly-Bootle. 578p. (Orig.). 1988. pap. 21.95 o.p. (ISBN 0-89588-462-3). Sybex.

Mastering Typing. Speedwriting Institute. 1976. pap. 4.95 o.p. (ISBN 0-671-18139-4). Monarch Pr.

Mastering Underwater Photography. Carl Roessler. LC 84-6541. (Illus.). 112p. (gr. 9 up). 1984. 12.50 o.p. (ISBN 0-688-03881-6, Morrow Junior Books); pap. 9.95 o.p. (ISBN 0-688-03882-4). Morrow.

Mastering Ventura. Matthew Holtz. 547p. (Orig.). 1987. pap. 22.95 o.p. (ISBN 0-89588-427-5). Sybex.

Mastering WordStar on the IBM-PC. Arthur Naiman. 208p. 1986. pap. 18.95 o.p. (ISBN 0-89588-250-7). Sybex.

Mastering 1-2-3. Carolyn Jorgensen. LC 86-61237. 466p. (Orig.). 1986. pap. 21.95 o.p. (ISBN 0-89588-337-6). Sybex.

Masterpak. James Campbell et al. (Themepaks Ser.). 1976. 6.95 o.p. (ISBN 0-8042-1454-9, John Knox). Westminster John Knox.

Masterpiece. Thomas Hoving. 336p. 1986. 17.45 o.s.i. (ISBN 0-671-61099-6). S&S.

Masterpiece Affair. Kenneth Royce. 1974. pap. 1.25 o.p. (ISBN 0-380-00106-3, 20420). Avon.

Masterpiece in Progress. Jeff Steinberg & James C. Hefley. 288p. 1986. 11.95 o.p. (ISBN 0-8423-4194-3). Tyndale.

Masterpieces from the House of Faberge. Alexander Von Solodkoff et al. Ed. by Christopher Forbes. (Illus.). 192p. 1984. 45.00 o.p. (ISBN 0-8109-0933-2). Abrams.

Masterpieces of Christian Literature, 2 vols. 1203p. 1963. Set. 60.00x o.p. (ISBN 0-89356-150-9). Salem Pr.

Masterpieces of Fantasy Art. Illus. by Vallejo Frazetta et al. (Illus.). 96p. (Orig.). 1987. pap. 7.95 o.p. (ISBN 3-89268-008-6). Parkwest Pubns.

Masterpieces of Furniture. Verna C. Salomonsky. (Illus.). 15.25 o.p. (ISBN 0-8446-2856-5). Peter Smith.

Masterpieces of Medical Photography. Ed. by Joel-Peter Witkin. (Illus.). 96p. 1987. 45.00 o.p. (ISBN 0-942642-21-X). Twelvetrees Pr.

Masterplayers. Michael Sinclair. 1978. 7.95 o.p. (ISBN 0-393-08820-0). Norton.

Masters Affair. Burt Hirschfeld. LC 70-139296. 1971. 6.50 o.p. (ISBN 0-87795-012-1, Arbor Hse). Morrow.

Masters & Johnson on Sex & Human Loving. William H. Masters et al. 1986. 24.95 o.p. (ISBN 0-316-54998-3). Little.

Masters & Statesmen: The Political Culture of American Slavery. Kenneth S. Greenberg. LC 85-9786. (New Studies in American Intellectual & Cultural History Ser.). 208p. 1986. text ed. 22.50x o.p. (ISBN 0-8018-2762-0). Johns Hopkins.

Masters Connection. David Chandler. LC 80-70213. 384p. 1981. 12.95 o.p. (ISBN 0-87795-302-3, Arbor Hse). Morrow.

Masters of British Drama. John Allen. (Illus., Orig.). 1968. pap. 2.25 o.p. (ISBN 0-8065-0099-9, C278, Pub. by Citadel Pr). Carol Pub Group.

Masters of Business. Richard Whitley et al. LC 81-13999. (Illus.). 1982. 28.00x o.p. (ISBN 0-422-76500-7, NO. 3574, Pub. by Tavistock). Routledge Chapman & Hall.

Masters of Equitation. W. Sidney Felton. (Illus.). 7.95 o.p. (ISBN 0-85131-091-5, BL2345, Pub. by J A Allen U K). S R Smith Sporting Bks.

Masters of European Drama. John Allen. (Illus., Orig.). 1968. pap. 2.25 o.p. (ISBN 0-8065-0098-0, C277, Pub. by Citadel Pr). Carol Pub Group.

Masters of Sociological Thought: Ideas in Historical & Social Context. Lewis A. Coser. (Illus.). 1971. text ed. 16.95 o.p. (ISBN 0-15-555128-0, HC). HarBraceJ.

Masters of the Modern Short Story. Ed. by Walter E. Havighurst. LC 45-3743. 1955. 9.50 o.p. (ISBN 0-15-157893-1). HarBraceJ.

Masters or Servants? A Study of Selected English Painters & Their Patrons of the Late 18th & Early 19th Centuries. Josephine Gear. LC 76-23619. (Outstanding Dissertations in the Fine Arts Ser.-18th Century). (Illus.). 453p. 1977. Repr. lib. bdg. 68.00 o.p. (ISBN 0-8240-2690-X). Garland Pub.

Masterworks of Philosophy, Vol. 3. S. E. Frost. (Masterworks Ser.). 192p. 1972. Pts. 1-2. pap. text ed. 2.45 o.p. (ISBN 0-07-040803-3). McGraw.

Masterworks of World Literature, 2 vols. 3rd ed. Ed. by Calvin Brown et al. Incl. Vol. 1. Homer to Cervantes. text ed. 49.50x (ISBN 0-8290-0130-1); Vol. II. Shakespeare to Sartre. text ed. 49.50x (ISBN 0-8290-0131-X). LC 75-92884. 1970. Irvington.

Mastication & Swallowing: Biological & Clinical Correlates. Ed. by Barry J. Sessle & Alan G. Hannam. LC 75-38957. (Illus.). 1975. 35.00x o.p. (ISBN 0-8020-2207-3). U of Toronto Pr.

MATCH Microcomputer Software Program. Learning Achievement Corp. Staff. 1981. text ed. 450.00 o.p. (ISBN 0-07-037117-2, G). McGraw.

Matching Gift Details 1988. Compiled by Elizabeth S. Hall & Jerilyn D. Pope. 150p. 1988. 72.00 o.p. (ISBN 0-89964-258-6). Coun Adv & Supp Ed.

Matching the Gun to the Game. Claire Rees. LC 82-13775. (Illus.). 272p. 1982. 17.95 o.p. (ISBN 0-8329-3672-3, Pub. by Winchester Pr). New Century.

Matchmaking: Science Technology & Manufacturing. Christopher Finch & Srinivasa Ramachandran. LC 82-18687. 236p. 1983. 74.95 o.p. (ISBN 0-470-27371-2). Halsted Pr.

Mate in Three. Bernice Rubens. 256p. 1987. 19.95 o.p. (ISBN 0-241-12124-8, Pub. by Hamish Hamilton). David & Charles.

Mate in Two Moves: The Two-Move Chess Problem Made Easy. Brian Harley. 1970. pap. 3.50 o.p. (ISBN 0-486-22434-1). Dover.

Materia Medica of Ayurveda. Ed. by V. Dash & L. Kashyap. 1980. text ed. 45.00x o.p. (ISBN 0-391-01813-2). Humanities.

Material Behavior & Physical Chemistry in Liquid Metal Systems. Ed. by H. V. Borgstedt. LC 82-3680. 562p. 1982. 89.50x o.p. (ISBN 0-306-40917-8, Plenum Pr). Plenum Pub.

Material-Environment Interactions in Structural & Pressure Containment Devices. Ed. by George V. Smith. (MPC: No. 15). 160p. 1980. 30.00 o.p. (ISBN 0-686-69854-1, G00188). ASME.

Material Requirements for Fiber Optics. Business Communications Staff. 198p. 1985. 1750.00 o.p. (ISBN 0-89336-363-4, GB-073). BCC.

Material Requirements for Fiber Optics. Business Communications Staff. 1988. 2450.00 o.p. (ISBN 0-89336-666-8, GB-073R). BCC.

Material Specifications: Ferrous Materials, 3 pts, Pt. A. (Boiler & Pressure Vessel Code Ser.: Sec II). 1980. 125.00 o.p. (ISBN 0-686-70388-X, P0002A); loose-leaf 175.00 o.p. (ISBN 0-686-70389-8, V0002A). ASME.

Material Specifications: Nonferrous Materials, 3 pts, Pt. B. (Boiler & Pressure Vessel Code Ser.: Sec. II). 1980. 110.00 o.p. (ISBN 0-686-70436-3, P0002B); loose-leaf 150.00 o.p. (ISBN 0-686-70437-1, V0002B). ASME.

Material Specifications: Welding Rods, Electrodes & Filler Metals. (Boiler & Pressure Vessel Code Ser.: Sec II). 1980. 55.00 o.p. (ISBN 0-686-70390-1, P0002C); pap. 70.00 loose-leaf o.p. (ISBN 0-686-70391-X, V0002C). ASME.

Material Specifications: Welding Rods, Electrodes & Filler Metals, 3 pts, Pt. C. (Boiler & Pressure Vessel Code Ser.: Sec. II). 1980. loose leaf 70.00 o.p. (ISBN 0-686-70439-8, V0002C); pap. 55.00 bound o.p. (ISBN 0-686-70440-1, P0002C). ASME.

Material Specifications: Welding Rods, Electrodes & Filler Metals, 3 pts, Pt. C. (Boiler & Pressure Vessel Code Ser.: Sec. II). 1977. 35.00 o.p. (ISBN 0-685-76796-5, R0002C); pap. 50.00 loose-leaf o.p. (ISBN 0-685-76797-3, W0002C). ASME.

Material 4 Drops STR. Date not set. (ISBN 0-07-017693-0). McGraw.

Materialism & the Mind-Body Problem. reference ed. David Rosenthal. LC 77-157186. (Central Issues in Philosophy Ser.). (Illus.). 1971. pap. text ed. (ISBN 0-13-560177-0). P-H.

Materials & Craft of the Scenic Model. Darwin R. Payne. LC 76-15230. (Illus.). 128p. 1976. pap. text ed. 11.95x o.p. (ISBN 0-8093-0783-9). S Ill U Pr.

Materials & Fabrication, Vol. III. Ed. by R. Robert. 603p. 1976. 50.00 o.p. (ISBN 0-317-33562-6, G00100); members 25.00 o.p. (ISBN 0-317-33563-4). ASME.

Materials & Processes of Electron Devices. Max Knoll. (Illus.). 1959. 53.10 o.p. (ISBN 0-387-02430-1). Springer-Verlag.

Materials Book for Reading Games for Middle & Upper Grades. Flora C. Fowler. LC 74-8367. (Illus.). 100p. 1974. pap. text ed. 4.95x o.p. (ISBN 0-8422-0430-X). Irvington.

Materials for Civil & Highway Engineers. Kenneth N. Derucher & Conrad Heins. (Illus.). 416p. 1981. text ed. 48.00 o.p. (ISBN 0-13-560490-7). P-H.

Materials for Metric Instruction. Gary G. Bitter & Charles Geer. 90p. 1975. pap. 2.50 o.s.i. (ISBN 0-317-35361-6, 78). NCTM.

Materials Handbook. 11th ed. G. S. Brady & Henry Clauser. 1977. text ed. 57.50 o.p. (ISBN 0-07-007069-5). McGraw.

Materials Handling in the Printing Industry. M. C. Fairley. 1971. pap. 15.25 o.p. (ISBN 0-08-016448-X). Pergamon.

Materials Nineteen Eighty, Vol. 12. Intro. by Morton Kushner. (National SAMPE Technical Conference Ser.). (Illus.). 1980. 60.00 o.p. (ISBN 0-938994-06-9). SAMPE.

Materials of Construction of Fluid Machinery & Their Relationship to Design & Performance. Ed. by R. C. Cherry et al. 104p. 1981. 24.00 o.p. (ISBN 0-686-34499-5, H00208). ASME.

Materials of the Artist: And Their Use in Painting with Notes on the Techniques of the Old Masters. rev. ed. Max Doerner. Tr. by Eugen Neuhaus. (Illus.). 1949. 15.00 o.p. (ISBN 0-15-158169-X). HarBraceJ.

Materials on the Move: Proceedings, 6th National SAMPE Technical Conference, Clayton, Ohio. 461p. 1974. 30.00 o.p. (ISBN 0-318-16528-7); members 20.00 o.p. (ISBN 0-318-16529-5). SAMPE.

Materials Relating to Legal Aspects of Dental Practice. Compiled by Ben F. Loeb. 122p. 1977. pap. 3.00 o.p. (ISBN 0-686-05735-X). Institute Government.

Materials Research: Scientific Opportunities. 200p. 1988. 32.50 o.p. (ISBN 0-309-03932-0); pap. 22.50 o.p. (ISBN 0-309-03898-7). Natl Acad Pr.

Materials Review Seventy-Five: Proceedings, 7th National SAMPE Technical Conference, New Mexico, October 1975. 532p. 20.00 o.p. (ISBN 0-318-16530-9) (ISBN 0-318-16531-7). SAMPE.

Materials Science & Engineering: Summary. 200p. 1988. 32.50 o.p. (ISBN 0-309-03928-2); pap. 22.50 o.p. (ISBN 0-309-03894-4). Natl Acad Pr.

Materials Science & Manufacturing Processes. Dharmenora Kumar & S. K. Jain. Ed. by A. K. Shargava. 410p. 1983. text ed. 37.50x o.p. (ISBN 0-7069-2145-3, Pub. by Vikas India). Advent NY.

Materials Science in Energy Technology. Ed. by G. G. Libowitz & M. S. Whittingham. LC 78-51235. (Materials Science & Technology Ser.). 1979. 96.00 o.p. (ISBN 0-12-447550-7). Acad Pr.

Materials Science in Space. Ed. by A. Bewersdorff. (Advances in Space Research Ser.: Vol. 1, No. 5). (Illus.). 171p. 1981. pap. 25.00 o.p. (ISBN 0-08-027161-8). Pergamon.

Materials Science in Space: Proceedings of the Topical Meeting of the COSPAR Interdisciplinary Scientific Commission G (Meeting G1) of the COSPAR Twenty-Fifth Plenary Meeting Held in Graz, Austria, 25th June - 7th July 1984. Ed. by A. Bewersdorff. (Illus.). 116p. 1985. pap. 54.00 o.p. (ISBN 0-08-032733-8, Pub. by Aberdeen Scotland). Pergamon.

Materials Science Progress: Anniversary Vol. - Progress in Materials Science. Ed. by J. W. Christian et al. (Illus.). 330p. 1981. 61.00 o.p. (ISBN 0-08-027147-2). Pergamon.

Materials Sciences for the Future. Society for the Advancement of Material & Process Engineering Staff. (Science of Advanced Materials & Process Engineering Ser.). (Illus.). 1986. 60.00 o.p. (ISBN 0-938994-30-1). SAMPE.

Materials Selection for Mineral Industry: Short Course. (Illus.). 76p. pap. 25.00 o.p. (ISBN 0-317-32922-7). SMM&E Inc.

Materials Standard for P-M Structure Parts, 1984-1985. rev. ed. (Illus.). pap. 5.00 o.p. (ISBN 0-318-04233-9). Metal Powder.

Materials Synergisms. (National SAMPE Technical Conference Ser.). (Illus.). 1978. 40.00 o.p. (ISBN 0-686-02630-6). SAMPE.

Maternal & Child Health Data Book: The Health of America's Children. Dana Hughes et al. 302p. (Orig.). 1986. pap. 9.95 o.s.i. (ISBN 0-938008-49-8). Children's Defense.

Maternal & Child Health in Rural Kenya. Ed. by J. K. Van Ginneken & A. S. Muller. 374p. 1984. 26.50 o.p. (ISBN 0-7099-2608-1, Pub. by Croom Helm Ltd). Routledge Chapman & Hall.

Maternal & Child Health Nursing. 5th ed. A. Joy Ingalls & M. Constance Salerno. LC 82-14160. (Illus.). 820p. 1983. 29.95 o.p. (ISBN 0-8016-2324-3); study guide 3rd ed 13.95 o.p. (ISBN 0-8016-2323-5). Mosby.

Maternal-Fetal Medicine: Principles & Practice. Robert K. Creasy & Robert Resnik. (Illus.). 1147p. 1984. 120.00 o.p. (ISBN 0-7216-2749-8). Saunders.

Maternal Nutrition. Barbara Luke. 1980. text ed. 13.00 o.p. (ISBN 0-316-53610-5). Little.

Maternal Nutrition & the Course of Pregnancy. Food & Nutrition Board - Division of Biology & Agriculture Staff. LC 72-605179. (Illus., Orig.). 1970. pap. text ed. 9.95x o.p. (ISBN 0-309-01761-0). Natl Acad Pr.

Maternity & Gynecologic Care: The Nurse & the Family. 3rd ed. Margaret D. Jensen & Irene M. Bobak. (Illus.). 1497p. 1985. 41.95 o.p. (ISBN 0-8016-2494-0). Mosby.

Maternity: Letters from Working Women. Ed. by Margaret L. Davies. 1979. pap. 3.95 o.p. (ISBN 0-393-00894-0, Norton Lib). Norton.

Maternity Nursing. 3rd ed. Arlyne Friesner. Ed. by Beverly Raff. LC 77-80106. (Nursing Outline Ser.). 1982. pap. 16.50 o.p. (ISBN 0-87488-377-6). Med Exam.

Maternity Nursing: Theory to Practice. Glenda F. Butnarescu & Delight M. Tillotson. LC 82-17614. 798p. 1983. 32.00 o.p. (ISBN 0-471-07793-3, Pub. by Wiley Med); write for info tm o.p. (ISBN 0-471-87070-6). Wiley.

Math Activities with a Porpoise. Runelle Konsler & Lauren Mirabella. 1980. pap. 9.95 o.p. (ISBN 0-673-16394-6). Scott F.

Math Entertainer. Philip Heafford. LC 59-11797. (Illus.). 176p. (gr. 7-12). 1983. 12.95 o.p. (ISBN 0-87523-109-8). Enslow Pubs.

Math Entertainer. Philip Heafford. 1959. pap. 12.95 o.s.i. (ISBN 0-317-65152-8). Emerson.

Math for Computer Graphics. Roy A. Liming. LC 79-65814. 1979. 12.95 o.p. (ISBN 0-8168-6751-8, 26751, TAB-Aero). TAB Bks.

Math for the Layman. T. H. Hill. 256p. 1958. (ISBN 0-8022-0723-5). Philos Lib.

Math Games & Activities, Vol. 1. Paul Shoecraft. (Math Games & Activities Ser.). (Illus.). 462p. (gr. k-5). 1984. Vol. 1. tchr's. resource 24.90 o.p. (ISBN 0-941530-01-9). Set (ISBN 0-941530-00-0). R in R.

Math Is Fun. Joseph Degrazia. (Illus.). 159p. (gr. 7-12). 1976. 13.95 o.p. (ISBN 0-89490-111-7). Enslow Pubs.

Math Made Fun for the Young Child. Cleatus Moorehead. LC 78-73458. (ps). 1979. spiral bound 8.95 o.p. (ISBN 0-8054-4922-1, 4249-22). Broadman.

Math Readiness Workbook: Math Readiness Pretest Manual. Kitty Wehrli. (Michigan Arithmetic Program Ser.). (Illus.). (gr. k-3). 1978. 1.50 o.p. (ISBN 0-89039-241-2); 1.00 o.p. (ISBN 0-89039-238-2). Ann Arbor Pubs.

Math Review for the GMAT. Gary R. Gruber. 288p. (Orig.). 1982. pap. 8.95 Softcover o.p. (ISBN 0-671-43985-5). Monarch Pr.

Math Tables & Formulae. F. J. Camm. 144p. 1958. (ISBN 0-8022-0210-1). Philos Lib.

Math Without Tears. Roy Hartkopf. (Nonfiction Ser.). 1985. pap. 7.95 o.p. (ISBN 0-8398-2857-8). G K Hall.

Math Workbook for Foodservice-Lodging. 2nd ed. H. W. Crawford & Milton C. McDowell. 240p. 1983. 11.95 o.p. (ISBN 0-8436-0534-0); pap. 19.95 o.p. (ISBN 0-8436-2197-4). Van Nos Reinhold.

Math Zingo Wrap Box. Date not set. (ISBN 0-07-376794-8). McGraw.

Mathematic Refresher. Kurt Wolter. 96p. 1959. (ISBN 0-8022-1921-7). Philos Lib.

Mathematical Analysis: A Special Course. G. Y. Shilov. 1965. 125.00 o.p. (ISBN 0-08-010796-6); pap. 125.00 o.p. (ISBN 0-08-013616-8). Pergamon.

Mathematical Analysis, Advanced Topics, Pt. 1: Functional Series & Their Application. A. V. Efimov. 360p. 1985. 7.95 o.s.i. (ISBN 0-8285-3069-6, Pub. by Mir Pubs USSR). Imported Pubns.

Mathematical Analysis, Advanced Topics, Pt. 2: Application of Some Methods of Mathematical & Functional Analysis. A. V. Efimov. 371p. 1985. 11.95 o.s.i. (ISBN 0-8285-3070-X, Pub. by Mir Pubs USSR). Imported Pubns.

Mathematical Analysis of Logic. George Boole. (ISBN 0-8022-0154-7). Philos Lib.

Mathematical & Computational Methods in Physiology: Proceedings of a Satellite Symposium of the 28th International Congress of Physiological Sciences, Budapest, Hungary, 1980. Ed. by L. Fedina et al. LC 80-42253. (Advances in Physiological Sciences Ser.: Vol. 34). (Illus.). 400p. 1981. 71.00 o.p. (ISBN 0-08-027356-4). Pergamon.

Mathematical & Education. Wain. 1978. 26.95x o.p. (ISBN 0-442-30141-3). Van Nos Reinhold.

Mathematical Aspects of Finite Elements in Partial Differential Equations. Ed. by Carl De Boor. 1974. 29.95 o.p. (ISBN 0-12-208350-4). Acad Pr.

Mathematical Aspects of Finite Element Methods: Proceedings of the Conference Held in Rome, Dec.10-22, 1975. Ed. by I. Galligani & E. Magenes. (Lecture Notes in Mathematics Ser.: Vol. 606). 1977. pap. text ed. 18.30 o.p. (ISBN 0-387-08432-0). Springer-Verlag.

Mathematical Aspects of Marine Traffic. Ed. by S. H. Hollingdale. (Institute of Mathematics & Its Application Ser.). 1979. 75.00 o.p. (ISBN 0-12-352450-4). Acad Pr.

Mathematical Astronomy for Amateurs. E. A. Beet. (Illus.). 145p. 1972. 7.95x o.p. (ISBN 0-393-06388-7). Norton.

Mathematical Basis of the Arts. Joseph Schillinger. 706p. 1955. (ISBN 0-8022-1501-7). Philos Lib.

Mathematical Biology-a Conference on Theoretical Aspects of Molecular Science: Proceedings of a Conference Held at Southern Illinois University at Carbondale, May 27-28, 1980. Ed. by T. A. Burton. (Illus.). 241p. 1981. 65.00 o.p. (ISBN 0-08-026348-8). Pergamon.

Mathematical Buds. Mu Alpha Theta Staff. (Illus.). 126p. 1978. pap. 3.15 o.s.i. (ISBN 0-317-35362-4). NCTM.

Mathematical Economics & Operations Research: A Guide to Information Sources. Ed. by Joseph Zaremba. LC 73-17586. (Economics Information Guide Ser.: Vol. 10). 624p. 1978. 68.00x o.p. (ISBN 0-8103-1298-0). Gale.

Mathematical Enterprises for Schools. A. J. Cameron. 1966. 11.50 o.p. (ISBN 0-08-011833-X). Pergamon.

Mathematical Essays Dedicated to A. J. MacIntyre. Ed. by Hari Shankar. LC 68-20937. xvi, 377p. 1970. 22.50x o.p. (ISBN 0-8214-0061-4). Ohio U Pr.

Mathematical Fallacies & Paradoxes. Bryan Bunch. 1982. 19.95 o.p. (ISBN 0-442-24905-5). Van Nos Reinhold.

Mathematical Foundations of Computer Science: Proceedings of the Symposium, 3rd, Jadwisin, June 17-22, 1974. Mathematical Foundations of Computer Science Symposium Staff. Ed. by A. Blikle. (Lecture Notes in Computer Science Ser.: Vol. 28). viii, 484p. 1975. pap. 24.00 o.p. (ISBN 0-387-07162-8). Springer-Verlag.

Mathematical Foundations of Computer Science 1979: Proceedings, 8th Symposium, Olomouc, Czechoslovakia, September 3-7, 1979. Ed. by J. Becvar. (Lecture Notes in Computer Science Ser.: Vol. 74). 1979. pap. 32.00 o.p. (ISBN 0-387-09526-8). Springer-Verlag.

Mathematical Foundations of the Finite Element Method with Applications to Partial Differential Equations. Ed. by A. K. Aziz. 1972. 99.50 o.p. (ISBN 0-12-068650-3). Acad Pr.

Mathematical Gardner. Ed. by David A. Klarner. 1980. write for info. o.p. (ISBN 0-87150-294-1, 2321, Prindle). PWS-Kent Pub.

Mathematical Gardner. Ed. by David A. Klarner. 382p. 1982. 28.95 o.p. (ISBN 0-442-25336-2). Van Nos Reinhold.

Mathematical Logic. J. D. Monk. LC 75-42416. (Graduate Texts in Mathematics Ser.: Vol. 37). 1976. 30.95 o.p. (ISBN 0-387-90170-1). Springer-Verlag.

Mathematical Methods for Introductory Physics with Calculus. 2nd ed. Ronald C. Davidson & Jerry B. Marion. LC 79-19656. 232p. 1980. pap. text ed. 18.95x o.p. (ISBN 0-7216-2919-9). SCP.

Mathematical Methods for Social & Management Scientists. T. Marll McDonald. 544p. 1974. text ed. 26.50 o.p. (ISBN 0-395-17089-3). HM.

Mathematical Methods in Clinical Practice. Ed. by G. I. Marchuk & N. I. Nisevich. (Illus.). 150p. 1980. 91.00 o.p. (ISBN 0-08-025493-4). Pergamon.

Mathematical Methods in Finance & Economics. S. J. Khoury & T. D. Parsons. 296p. 1981. 61.75 o.p. (ISBN 0-444-00425-4, North-Holland). Elsevier.

Mathematical Methods in Nuclear Reactor Dynamics. Ziya Akcasu et al. (Nuclear Science & Technology Ser.: Vol. 7). 1971. 80.00 o.p. (ISBN 0-12-047150-7). Acad Pr.

Mathematical Methods in Queueing Theory: Proceedings. Ed. by A. B. Clarke & A. B. Clarke. LC 74-5921. (Lecture Notes in Economics & Mathematical Systems: Vol. 98). 374p. 1974. pap. 14.50 o.p. (ISBN 0-387-06763-9). Springer-Verlag.

Mathematical Methods in Social Science. David J. Bartholomew. LC 80-41593. (Handbook of Applicable Mathematics Ser.). 153p. 1981. 48.95 o.p. (ISBN 0-471-27932-3, Pub. by Wiley-Interscience); pap. 27.00 o.p. (ISBN 0-471-27933-1, Pub. by Wiley-Interscience). Wiley.

Mathematical Methods in the Physical Sciences. Merle C. Potter. (Illus.). 1978. pap. text ed. (ISBN 0-13-561134-2). P-H.

Mathematical Methods of the Theory of Elasticity, Vol. 1. V. Z. Parton & P. I. Perlin. 317p. 1984. 10.00 o.s.i. (ISBN 0-8285-2931-0, Pub. by Mir Pubs USSR). Imported Pubns.

Mathematical Model for Handling in a Warehouse. E. Kay. LC 68-21104. 1968. pap. 35.00 o.p. (ISBN 0-08-012831-9). Pergamon.

Mathematical Modeling. Research & Education Association Staff. LC 82-80745. (Illus.). 384p. (Orig.). 1982. pap. text ed. 13.30 o.s.i. (ISBN 0-87891-538-9). Res & Educ.

Mathematical Modeling & Digital Simulation for Engineers & Scientists. Jon M. Smith. LC 76-52419. 332p. 1977. 40.50x o.p. (ISBN 0-471-80344-8, Pub. by Wiley-Interscience). Wiley.

Mathematical Modeling for Industrial Processes. L. P. Hyvaerinen. LC 70-111899. (Lecture Notes in Operations Research & Mathematical Systems Ser.: Vol. 19). (Illus.). 1970. pap. 10.70 o.p. (ISBN 0-387-04943-6). Springer-Verlag.

Mathematical Modelling of Estuarine Physics: Proceedings. Ed. by J. Suendermann & K. P. Holz. (Lecture Notes on Coastal & Estaurine Studies: Vol. 1). (Illus.). 265p. 1980. 20.00 o.p. (ISBN 0-387-09750-3). Springer-Verlag.

Mathematical Modelling Workbook for Students of Ecology. Clark Jeffries. 224p. 1988. 38.00 o.p. (ISBN 9971-50-713-7). World Scientific Pub.

Mathematical Models & Simulation in Solar Energy Research for Buildings. Ed. by A. V. Sebald. 237p. 1980. pap. 36.00 o.p. (ISBN 0-08-025453-5). Pergamon.

Mathematical Models for Planning & Controlling Air Quality: Proceedings, Vol. 17. Ed. by G. Fronza. 255p. 1982. 73.00 o.p. (ISBN 0-08-029950-4). Pergamon.

Mathematical Models for the Analysis & Optimization of Elastoplastic Structures. A. A. Cyras. (Series in Civil & Mechanical Engineering: 1-622). 121p. 1984. text ed. 42.95x o.p. (ISBN 0-470-20020-0). Halsted Pr.

Mathematical Models in Marketing: A Collection of Abstracts. Ed. by U. H. Funke. 1976. soft cover 23.00 o.p. (ISBN 0-387-07869-X). Springer-Verlag.

Mathematical Models in the Earth Sciences: Proceedings of the 7th Geochautauqua, Syracuse University, Oct. 1978. Ed. by J. M. Cubitt. 90p. 1980. pap. 50.00 o.p. (ISBN 0-08-025305-9). Pergamon.

Mathematical Neurobiology: An Introduction to the Mathematics of the Nervous System. J. S. Griffith. 162p. 1971. 46.00 o.p. (ISBN 0-12-303050-1). Acad Pr.

Mathematical Problems in Theoretical Physics: International Conference, Held in Rome, June 6-15, 1977. Ed. by G. Dell'Antonio et al. (Lecture Notes in Physics: Vol. 80). 1978. pap. 23.00 o.p. (ISBN 0-387-08853-9). Springer-Verlag.

Mathematical Programming & Control Theory. B. D. Craven. (Mathematics Ser.). 1978. pap. 15.95 o.p. (ISBN 0-412-15500-1, NO. 6070, Pub. by Chapman & Hall). Routledge Chapman & Hall.

Mathematical Programming for Management & Business. G. Hayhurst. 1976. pap. 22.50x o.p. (ISBN 0-7131-3355-4). Trans-Atl Phila.

Mathematical Programming: Structures & Algorithms. Jeremy F. Shapiro. LC 79-4478. 388p. 1979. 45.50x o.p. (ISBN 0-471-77886-9, Pub by Wiley-Interscience). Wiley.

Mathematical Programming with Parameters & Multi-Level Constraints. J. E. Falk & A. V. Fiacco. 100p. 1981. pap. 46.00 o.p. (ISBN 0-08-023621-9). Pergamon.

Mathematical Questions from the Classroom. Richard Crouse & Clifford Sloyer. 1977. pap. text ed. write for info. o.p. (ISBN 0-87150-219-4, PWS 1782, Prindle). PWS-Kent Pub.

Mathematical Relationships in Business & Economics. William E. Beatty. LC 70-83261. 1970. pap. text ed. write for info. o.p. (ISBN 0-685-52540-6, PWS 1762, Prindle). PWS-Kent Pub.

Mathematical Sciences: A Collection of Essays. Ed. by COSRIMS Staff. 1969. pap. 10.95x o.p. (ISBN 0-262-53008-2). MIT Pr.

Mathematical Sciences Professional Directory. 196p. 1987. Annual. pap. 24.00 o.p. (ISBN 0-8218-0106-6). Am Math.

Mathematical Statistics. 3rd ed. John E. Freund & Ronald E. Walpole. 1980. text ed. (ISBN 0-13-562066-X). P-H.

Mathematical Statistics with Applications. 2nd ed. William Mendenhall & Richard L. Scheaffer. 1981. pap. write for info. o.p. (ISBN 0-87150-410-3, Duxbury Pr). PWS-Kent Pub.

Mathematical Structure of Finite Random Cybernetic Systems. CISM (International Center for Mechanical Sciences), Department of Automation & Information Staff. Ed. by S. Quiasu. (CISM Pubnlications: No. 86). (Illus.). 215p. 1974. pap. 21.00 o.p. (ISBN 0-387-81174-5). Springer-Verlag.

Mathematical Support Modelling. 5.00 o.p. (ISBN 0-317-65071-8). Am Consul Eng.

Mathematical Systems Theory. Ed. by G. Marchesini & S. K. Mitter. (Lecture Notes in Economics & Mathematical Systems: Vol. 131). 1976. 23.00 o.p. (ISBN 0-387-07798-7). Springer-Verlag.

Mathematical Techniques & Physical Applications. J. Killingbeck & G. H. Cole. 1971. text ed. 25.00 o.p. (ISBN 0-12-406850-2). Acad Pr.

Mathematical Theory of Control: Proceedings. Ed. by A. V. Balakrishna & Lucien W. Neustadt. 1967. 77.00 o.p. (ISBN 0-12-076956-5). Acad Pr.

Mathematical Theory of Elastic Equilibrium. G. Grioli. (Ergebnisse der Angewandten Mathematik: Vol. 7). 1962. pap. 26.60 o.p. (ISBN 0-387-02804-8). Springer-Verlag.

Mathematical Theory of Feynman Path Integrals. S. A. Albeverio & R. J. Hoegh-Krohn. (Lecture Notes in Mathematics: Vol. 523). 1976. soft cover 8.20 o.p. (ISBN 0-387-07785-5). Springer-Verlag.

Mathematical Theory of Program Correctness. M. De Bakker. 1980. text ed. 55.33 o.p. (ISBN 0-13-562132-1). P-H.

Mathematical Topics in Population Genetics. Ed. by Ken-Ichi Kojima. LC 78-103329. (Biomathematics Ser.: Vol. 1). (Illus.). 1970. 52.00 o.p. (ISBN 0-387-05054-X). Springer-Verlag.

Mathematically Speaking. Morton Davis. 484p. 1980. text ed. 20.95 o.p. (ISBN 0-15-555190-6, HC). HarBraceJ.

Mathematico-Deductive Theory of Rote Learning: A Study in Scientific Methodology. Clark L. Hull et al. 1970. Repr. of 1940 ed. lib. bdg. 22.50x o.p. (ISBN 0-8371-3126-X, HURL). Greenwood.

Mathematics. (Easy Way Ser.). 1982. 8.95 o.p. (ISBN 0-8120-2503-2). Barron.

Mathematics. Date not set. (ISBN 0-8052-4035-7). Random.

Mathematics. David Smith. LC 63-10294. (Our Debt to Greece & Rome Ser.). Repr. of 1930 ed. 17.50x o.p. (ISBN 0-8154-0207-4). Cooper Sq.

Mathematics: A Good Beginning. 2nd ed. Andria P. Troutman & Betty K. Lichtenberg. LC 81-17997. (Mathematics Ser.). 1982. pap. text ed. 21.00 pub net o.p. (ISBN 0-8185-0492-7). Brooks-Cole.

Mathematics: A Liberal Arts Approach. Malcolm Graham. 1973. text ed. 13.95 o.p. (ISBN 0-15-555235-X, HC). HarBraceJ.

Mathematics: A Liberal Arts Approach with Basic. 2nd. ed. Irving A. Dodes. LC 79-131. 464p. 1980. lib. bdg. 24.00 o.p. (ISBN 0-88275-892-6). Krieger.

Mathematics Activity Curriculum for Early Childhood & Special Education. Lloyd I. Richardson et al. (Illus.). 1980. pap. text ed. write for info. o.p. (ISBN 0-02-399710-9). Macmillan.

Mathematics: An Appreciation. Michael Bernkopf. 1975. text ed. 16.25 o.p. (ISBN 0-395-18583-1). HM.

Mathematics: An Everyday Experience. 2nd ed. Charles D. Miller & Vern E. Heeren. 1980. text ed. write for info. o.p. (ISBN 0-673-15279-0). Scott F.

Mathematics: An Informal Approach. 2nd ed. Bennett & Nelson. 1985. 24.00 o.p. (ISBN 0-205-08305-6, 568305). Wm C Brown.

Mathematics & Calculus with Applications. 2nd ed. Margaret L. Lial & Charles D. Miller. 1985. text ed. write for info. o.p. (ISBN 0-673-15896-9). Scott F.

Mathematics Applied to Business Problems, 1981. Dorothy W. McPherson. 1982. pap. 16.95 o.p. (ISBN 0-256-02565-7). Irwin.

Mathematics at Work: Algebra. Bertrand B. Singer. (Illus.). (gr. 9-12). 1977. text ed. 32.95x o.p. (ISBN 0-07-057491-X). McGraw.

Mathematics at Work: Decimals. Bertrand B. Singer. (gr. 9-12). 1977. text ed. 32.95 o.p. (ISBN 0-07-057489-8). McGraw.

Mathematics at Work: Fractions. Bertrand B. Singer. (Illus.). (gr. 9-12). 1977. text ed. 32.95 o.p. (ISBN 0-07-057487-1). McGraw.

Mathematics Bulletin Boards. Barbara S. Swabb & Mary E. Thomason. (gr. k-6). 1971. pap. 4.95 o.p. (ISBN 0-8224-4420-8). D S Lake Pubs.

Mathematics for Business & Consumers. 3rd ed. Mason et al. 1984. 24.95 o.p. (ISBN 0-256-03071-5). Irwin.

Mathematics for Consumer Survival. Marvin L. Bittinger et al. (Illus.). 640p. text ed. (ISBN 0-87150-501-0, Prindle); tchr's manual 5.00 o.p. (ISBN 0-686-64028-4); wkbk 4.00 o.p. (ISBN 0-686-64029-2). PWS-Kent Pub.

Mathematics for Electronic Technology. D. P. Howson. 280p. 1975. 37.00 o.p. (ISBN 0-08-018219-4); pap. 23.00 o.p. (ISBN 0-08-018218-6). Pergamon.

Mathematics for Engineering Technology & Computing. H. G. Martin. 1970. text ed. 21.00 o.p. (ISBN 0-08-013961-2); pap. 9.75 o.p. (ISBN 0-08-013960-4). Pergamon.

Mathematics for Everyman: From Simple Numbers to Calculus. Egmont Colerus. LC 57-5817. (Illus.). 255p. 1983. 13.95 o.p. (ISBN 0-89490-110-9). Enslow Pubs.

Mathematics for Everyone. Fred Klinger. 1967. pap. 1.95 o.p. (ISBN 0-8065-0097-2, C253, Pub. by Citadel Pr). Carol Pub Group.

Mathematics for Financial Analysis. Michael Gartenberg & Barry Shaw. 240p. 1976. 55.00 o.p. (ISBN 0-08-019599-7). Pergamon.

Mathematics for Level-Three Technicians. David Smethurst. (Illus.). 282p. 1979. pap. 20.00x o.p. (ISBN 0-7131-3415-1). Trans-Atl Phila.

Mathematics for Level-Two Technicians. C. W. Schofield & D. Smethurst. (Illus.). 1979. pap. text ed. 20.00x o.p. (ISBN 0-7131-3385-6). Trans-Atl Phila.

Mathematics for Operations Research. W. H. Marlow. LC 78-534. 483p. 1978. 58.95x o.p. (ISBN 0-471-57233-0, Pub. by Wiley-Interscience). Wiley.

Mathematics for Pre-College Students. I. Baronov et al. 376p. 1985. 9.95 o.p. (ISBN 0-8285-3043-2, Pub. by Mir Pubs USSR). Imported Pubns.

Mathematics for the Managerial, Social & Life Sciences. F. Lane Hardy & Bevan K. Youse. 903p. 1984. instr's manual 40.00 o.p. (ISBN 0-314-77906-X). West Pub.

Mathematics for the Managerial, Social, & Life Sciences. Lane F. Hardy & Bevan K. Youse. (Illus.). 750p. 1984. text ed. 38.75 o.p. (ISBN 0-314-77905-1). West Pub.

Mathematics for the Technologies. Lawrence M. Clar & James A. Hart. (Illus.). 1978. text ed. (ISBN 0-13-565200-6). P-H.

Mathematics for Today & Tomorrow. 2nd ed. D. Dottori. 1975. text ed. 12.20 o.p. (ISBN 0-07-082244-1). McGraw.

Mathematics for Welding Trades. John Goritz. (Illus.). 336p. 1987. pap. text ed. 20.33 o.p. (ISBN 0-13-563321-4). P-H.

Mathematics: Fundamentals for Managerial Decision-Making. 3rd ed. Michael L. Kovacic. 1979. Repr. text ed. write for info. o.p. (ISBN 0-87150-246-1, PWS 2001, Prindle). PWS-Kent Pub.

Mathematics: Ideas & Applications. Daniel D. Benice. 1978. 22.00 o.p. (ISBN 0-12-088250-7); instr's. ed. 5.00 o.p. (ISBN 0-12-088252-3). Acad Pr.

Mathematics Illustrated Dictionary: Facts, Figures & People, Including the New Math. Jeanne Bendick & Marcia Levin. (Illus.). (gr. 7 up). 1965. text ed. 10.95 o.p. (ISBN 0-07-004460-0). McGraw.

Mathematics in Aristotle. Thomas Heath. LC 78-66593. (Ancient Philosophy Ser.). 305p. 1980. lib. bdg. 36.00 o.p. (ISBN 0-8240-9595-2). Garland Pub.

Mathematics in Biology: Calculus & Related Topics, Preliminary Edition. Duane J. Clow & N. Scott Urguhart. (Illus.). 727p. 1974. pap. text ed. 13.95x o.p. (ISBN 0-393-09280-1). Norton.
Mathematics Is... 2nd ed. Jerome E. Kaufmann. LC 80-39984. 504p. 1981. text ed. 25.00 o.p. (ISBN 0-87150-313-1, 33L 2501, Prindle). PWS-Kent Pub.
Mathematics Laboratory: Theory to Practice. Robert E. Reys & Thomas R. Post. 297p. 1973. text ed. write for info. o.p. (ISBN 0-87150-161-9, PWS1271, Prindle). PWS-Kent Pub.
Mathematics Library: Elementary & Junior High School. 5th ed. Ed. by Margariete M. Wheeler. 1986. pap. 6.75 o.s.i. (ISBN 0-87353-228-7). NCTM.
Mathematics Library for the Practical Worker, 5 Vols. J. E. Thompson. 1982. Set. 37.95 o.p. (ISBN 0-442-28270-2). Van Nos Reinhold.
Mathematics of Contemporary Physics. Ed. by R. F. Streater. (London Mathematical Society Symposia Ser.). 1973. 60.00 o.p. (ISBN 0-12-673150-0). Acad Pr.
Mathematics of Finance. 6th ed. Helen Cissell et al. 1982. text ed. 29.95 o.p. (ISBN 0-395-31692-8). HM.
Mathematics of Finance. 5th ed. Robert Cissell et al. LC 77-73993. (Illus.). 1978. text ed. 22.95 o.p. (ISBN 0-395-25807-3). HM.
Mathematics of Finance. 3rd ed. Hummel & Seebeck. 1970. text ed. 32.95 o.p. (ISBN 0-07-031161-7). McGraw.
Mathematics of Investment. 5th ed. William L. Hart. 448p. 1975. text ed. 20.00 o.p. (ISBN 0-669-93690-1). Heath.
Mathematics of Manpower Planning. S. Vajda. LC 77-26104. 206p. 1978. 76.95 o.p. (ISBN 0-471-99627-0). Wiley.
Mathematics of Multi Objective Optimization. P. Serafini. (CISM International Centre for Mechanical Sciences Ser.: Vol. 289). (Illus.). vii, 441p. 1985. pap. 26.60 o.p. (ISBN 0-387-81860-X). Springer-Verlag.
Mathematics Projects Handbook. 2nd ed. Adrien L. Hess. LC 82-2084. 48p. 1982. pap. 3.75 o.p. (ISBN 0-87353-191-4). NCTM.
Mathematics Response Sheets & Prescription Sheets. William E. Lockhart. (Michigan Prescriptive Program, High School Equivalency-GED Ser.). (gr. 10). 1975. 2.00x o.p. (ISBN 0-89039-165-3). Ann Arbor Pubs.
Mathematics Revealed. Elizabeth Berman. 546p. 1979. 16.00 o.p. (ISBN 0-12-092450-1); instrs'. manual 2.50 o.p. (ISBN 0-12-092452-8). Acad Pr.
Mathematics, Statistics & Systems for Health. Norman T. Bailey. LC 77-1307. (Wiley Series Probability & Mathematical Statistics: Applied Probability & Statistics). 222p. 1978. 63.95x o.p. (ISBN 0-471-99500-2, Pub. by Wiley-Interscience). Wiley.
Mathematics Study Material: High School Equivalency-GED. William E. Lockhart. (Michigan Prescriptive Program Ser.). (gr. 10). 1975. pap. text ed. 7.00 o.p. (ISBN 0-89039-120-3). Ann Arbor Pubs.
Mathematics Teaching Today: Perspectives from Three National Surveys. James T. Fey. 30p. 1981. pap. 3.00 o.p. (ISBN 0-87353-186-8). NCTM.
Mathematics: With Applications. William C. Stewart. 1979. 16.95x o.p. (ISBN 0-256-02114-7). Irwin.
Mathematics with Applications to Business, Economics & Social Sciences. Richard Bouldin. LC 84-10562. 784p. 1985. text ed. 31.95 o.s.i. (ISBN 0-03-062164-X). SCP.
Mathematiques pour la Question de l'Environment. Jean-Claude Rochat. (Interdisciplinary Systems Research Ser.: No. 74). (Illus.). 413p. (Fr.). 1980. pap. 45.95x o.p. (ISBN 0-8176-1126-6). Birkhauser.
Mathematische Auswahl-Funktionen und Gesellschaftliche Entscheidungen. A. Bellen. (Interdisciplinary Systems Research Ser.: No. 14). (Illus.). 343p. (Ger.). 1976. 37.95x o.p. (ISBN 0-8176-0814-1). Birkhauser.
Mathematische Grundlagen Fur Die Organisation der Elektronishen Rechenmaschine der Eidgenossis Chen Technischen Hochschule. J. R. Stock. (ETH Zurich Ser.: No. 6). (Illus.). 74p. (Ger.). 1967. pap. 16.95x o.p. (ISBN 0-8176-0370-0). Birkhauser.
Mathmatters. Randall Souviney & Sarver. LC 78-3535. 1978. 14.95 o.p. (ISBN 0-673-16396-2); pap. 12.95 o.p. (ISBN 0-673-16395-4). Scott F.
Mathu of Kenya: A Political Study. Jack R. Roelker. LC 76-20294. (Publication Ser.: No. 157). 1976. 11.95x o.p. (ISBN 0-8179-6571-8). Hoover Inst Pr.
Matiere des Reves. Michel Butor. 1975. pap. 15.95 o.p. (ISBN 0-686-51943-4). Schoenhof.
Matilda Hippo Has a Big Mouth. Dennis Panek. LC 80-13260. (Illus.). 32p. (ps-2). 1980. 10.95 o.s.i. (ISBN 0-02-769810-6). Bradbury Pr.
Matilda Investigates. Mary Anderson. LC 72-86924. 176p. (gr. 4-6). 1973. 5.95 o.p. (ISBN 0-689-30077-8, Atheneum). Macmillan.
Matilda, My Darling. Nigel Krauth. LC 84-29135. 240p. 1985. 15.95 o.p. (ISBN 0-531-09782-X). Watts.
Matinaux: Avec: La Parole en Archipel. Rene Char. 218p. 1969. 4.95 o.p. (ISBN 0-686-54160-X). Schoenhof.
Matinee Idol. Ron Base. LC 85-15991. 320p. 1986. 16.95 o.p. (ISBN 0-385-25006-1). Doubleday.
Matinee Idols. David Carroll. LC 72-184882. (Illus.). 160p. 1972. 10.00 o.p. (ISBN 0-87795-031-8, A4320, Arbor Hse); pap. 4.95 o.p. (ISBN 0-87795-060-1, A4320P). Morrow.
Mating Dance. Rona Randall. 1980. pap. 2.75 o.p. (ISBN 0-380-50591-6, 50591). Avon.
Mating Reflexes. Norman T. Adler et al. LC 74-9523. 148p. 1975. text ed. 26.50x o.p. (ISBN 0-8422-7236-4). Irvington.
Mating Season. Janet Dailey. (Nightingale Paperbacks Ser.). 248p. 1987. pap. 11.95 o.p. (ISBN 0-8161-4304-8, Large Print Bks). G K Hall.
Mating Trade. Bob Mullan. 307p. 1984. 24.95x o.p.; pap. 13.95 o.p. (ISBN 0-7100-9967-3). Routledge Chapman & Hall.
Matisse, No. 46-47. (Derriere le Miroir Ser.). (Fr.). 1977. pap. 19.95 o.p. (ISBN 0-8120-2435-4). Barron.
Matriarch: Queen Mary & the House of Windsor. Anne Edwards. LC 84-60447. (Illus.). 512p. 1984. 18.95 o.p. (ISBN 0-688-03511-6). Morrow.
Matrices for Engineers. Allan D. Kraus. 270p. 1987. 60.00 o.p. (ISBN 0-317-57937-1). Hemisphere Pub.
Matrimony: One Hundred & Thirty-Eight Pronouncements from Benedict Fourteenth to John Twenty-Third. Ed. by Monks of Solesmes Staff. (Papal Teaching Ser.). 5.50 o.s.i. (ISBN 0-8198-0098-8); pap. 4.50 o.s.i. (ISBN 0-8198-0099-6). Dghtrs St Paul.
Matrix Analysis of Discrete Elastic Systems: Proceedings of CISM, Department of Mechanics of Solids, 1972. CISM (International Center for Mechanical Sciences), Department of Mechanics of Solids Staff. Ed. by H. Kardestuncer. (CISM International Centre for Mechanical Sciences Ser.: No. 179). (Illus.). 47p. 1974. pap. 5.80 o.p. (ISBN 0-387-81235-0). Springer-Verlag.
Matrix Analysis of Electrical Machinery. 2nd ed. Norman N. Hancock. LC 74-3286. 1974. 90.00 o.p. (ISBN 0-08-017898-7); pap. text ed. 13.25 o.p. (ISBN 0-08-017899-5). Pergamon.
Matrix Methods of Structural Analysis. 2nd ed. R. K. Livesley. 208p. 1975. 75.00 o.p. (ISBN 0-08-018888-5); pap. 75.00 o.p. (ISBN 0-08-018887-7). Pergamon.
Matrix Structural Analysis. J. J. Azar. 1972. 55.00 o.p. (ISBN 0-08-016781-0). Pergamon.
Matrix Theory. reference ed. Joel N. Franklin. 1968. text ed. 51.00 o.p. (ISBN 0-13-565648-6). P-H.
Matrix Theory & Applications for Engineers & Mathematicians. Alexander Graham. LC 79-40988. (Mathematics & Its Applications Ser.). 295p. 1980. pap. 42.95x o.p. (ISBN 0-470-27072-1). Halsted Pr.
Matsyendranath & Gorakshanath: Two Spiritual Lions. Sri Chinmoy. 64p. (Orig.). 1974. pap. 2.00 o.p. (ISBN 0-88497-093-0). Aum Pubns.
Matt Gargan's Boy. Alfred Slote. (gr. 3-7). 1977. pap. 1.95 o.p. (ISBN 0-380-01730-X, 53678-1, Camelot). Avon.
Matter-Energy Mechanics. Jakob Mandelker. 1954. (ISBN 0-8022-1040-6). Philos Lib.
Matter, Mind & Man: The Biology of Human Nature. Edmund W. Sinnott. LC 56-13282. 1962. pap. text ed. 2.75x o.p. (ISBN 0-689-70182-9, 9, Atheneum). Macmillan.
Matter of Choice. Angela R. Carl. LC 84-7040. (Illus.). 32p. (gr. 2-3). 1984. lib. bdg. 4.95 o.p. (ISBN 0-89693-223-0). Dandelion Hse.
Matter of Choice: An Essential Guide to Every Aspect of Abortion. Myron K. Denney. 192p. (Orig.). 1983. pap. 9.95 o.p. (ISBN 0-671-46372-1, Fireside). S&S.
Matter of Choosing. Eda Lord. 1963. 3.95 o.p. (45660). S&S.
Matter of Crime: New Stories from the Masters of Mystery & Suspense. Ed. by Matthew J. Bruccoli & Richard Layman. 1987. Volume 1. pap. 6.95 o.p. (ISBN 0-15-657719-4, Harv); Volume 2. pap. 6.95 o.p. (ISBN 0-15-657720-8). HarBraceJ.
Matter of Fear: Portrait of an Argentinian Exile. Andrew Graham-Yooll. LC 82-2959. 144p. 1982. 12.95 o.p. (ISBN 0-88208-144-6); pap. 7.95 o.p. (ISBN 0-88208-145-4). Chicago Review.
Matter of Honor. Jeffrey Archer. 1986. 18.45 o.s.i. (ISBN 0-671-62434-2, Linden Pr). S&S.
Matter of Honor. Jeffrey Archer. 568p. 1987. lib. bdg. 21.95x o.p. (ISBN 0-8161-4248-3, Large Print Bks); pap. 13.95 o.p. (ISBN 0-8161-4267-X, Large Print Bks). G K Hall.
Matter of Honor. William P. McGivern. 1984. 15.95 o.p. (ISBN 0-87795-492-5, Arbor Hse). Morrow.
Matter of Immortality. Jess Stearn. LC 76-11543. 1976. 9.95 o.p. (ISBN 0-689-10721-8, Atheneum). Macmillan.
Matter of Life & Death. Basilea Schlink. LC 73-10827. 96p. 1973. pap. 1.75 o.p. (ISBN 0-87123-359-2, 200359). Bethany Hse.
Matter of Life & Death: Vital Biographical Facts About Selected American Artists. Arnold Schwab. (Reference Library of the Humanities: Vol. 90). (LC 76-052694). 1977. lib. bdg. 19.00 o.p. (ISBN 0-8240-9883-8). Garland Pub.
Matter of Pride. Emily Crofford. LC 81-387. (Illus.). 48p. (gr. 2-6). 1981. PLB 8.95 o.p. (ISBN 0-87614-171-8, AACR2). Carolrhoda Bks.
Matter of Record. Malcolm Gray. LC 87-6792. (Crime Club Ser.). 192p. 1987. 12.95 o.s.i. (ISBN 0-385-24309-X). Doubleday.
Matter of Records: Fred Gaisberg & Golden Era of the Gramophone. Jerrold N. Moore. LC 76-53300. (Illus.). 1977. 10.95 o.s.i. (ISBN 0-8008-5176-5). Taplinger.
Matters Gray & White: A Neurologist, His Patients, & the Mysteries of the Brain. Russell Martin. LC 86-4725. 384p. 1987. 18.95 o.s.i. (ISBN 0-8050-0087-9). H Holt & Co.
Matters of Justice. Michael W. Jackson. 256p. 1986. 39.00 o.p. (ISBN 0-7099-1470-9, Pub. by Croom Helm Ltd). Routledge Chapman & Hall.
Matthew, Vol. I. Beacon Bible Expositions Staff. 6.95 o.p. (ISBN 0-8010-0676-7). Baker Bk.
Matthew. Jack D. Kingsbury. Ed. by Gerhard Krodel. LC 76-46732. (Proclamation Commentaries: the New Testament Witnesses for Preaching Ser.). 132p. (Orig.). 1977. pap. 4.50 o.p. (ISBN 0-8006-0586-1, 1-586, Fortress). Augsburg Fortress.
Matthew: A Good News Commentary. Robert H. Mounce. LC 84-48775. (Good News Commentary Ser.). 288p. (Orig.). 1985. pap. 9.95 o.p. (ISBN 0-06-066032-5). HarpR.
Matthew & His Dad. Arlene Alda. (Illus.). 48p. 1983. 7.75 o.s.i. (ISBN 0-671-45158-8, Little Simon). S&S.
Matthew Arnold: A Life. Park Honan. LC 80-26131. (Illus.). 544p. 1981. text ed. 19.95 o.p. (ISBN 0-07-029697-9). McGraw.
Matthew Arnold & His Critics: A Study of Arnold's Controversies. Sidney Coulling. LC 74-82498. xiv, 351p. 1974. 20.00x o.p. (ISBN 0-8214-0161-0). Ohio U Pr.
Matthew As Story. Jack D. Kingsbury. LC 85-16204. 160p. 1986. pap. 9.95 o.p. (ISBN 0-8006-1891-2, Fortress). Augsburg Fortress.
Matthew Brady's Portrait of an Era. Roy Meredith. (Illus.). 1982. 25.95 o.p. (ISBN 0-393-01395-2). Norton.
Matthew Looney, 4 vols. Jerome Beatty, Jr. Incl. Matthew Looney & the Space Pirates. 1980. Vol. 1. pap. 1.50 o.p. (ISBN 0-380-00848-3, 55905-6); Matthew Looney in the Outback. Jerome Beatty, Jr. 1979. Vol. 2. pap. 1.95 o.p. (ISBN 0-380-00847-5, 57497-7, Camelot); Matthew Looney's Invasion of the Earth. Jerome Beatty, Jr. 1976. Vol. 3. pap. 1.50 o.p. (ISBN 0-380-01493-9, Camelot); Matthew Looney's Voyage to the Earth. 1976. Vol. 4. pap. 1.95 o.p. (ISBN 0-380-01494-7, 53660-9). (gr. 8 up). 1978. pap. 5.25 boxed set o.p. (ISBN 0-380-39693-9, 39693-9, Camelot). Avon.
Matthew Looney in the Outback see Matthew Looney.
Matthew Looney's Invasion of the Earth see Matthew Looney.
Matthew-Luke, Vol. VI. Beacon Bible Commentary Staff. 15.95 o.p. (ISBN 0-8010-0693-7). Baker Bk.
Matthew: Structure, Christology, Kingdom. Jack D. Kingsbury. LC 75-13043. 192p. 1975. 11.95 o.p. (ISBN 0-8006-0434-2, 1-434, Fortress). Augsburg Fortress.
Mattie. Judy Alter. (Double D Western Ser.). 192p. 1988. 12.95 o.s.i. (ISBN 0-385-24167-4). Doubleday.
Mature Judaism: A Programmatic Outline. Yehudi Adam. LC 74-76018. 1974. 5.00 o.p. (ISBN 0-682-47965-9). Exposition-Phoenix.
Mature Mind. 10th anniversary ed. Harry A. Overstreet. 1959. 6.95 o.p. (ISBN 0-393-06308-9). Norton.
Maturing a Christian Conscience. John Carmody. 160p. (Orig.). 1985. pap. 6.95 o.p. (ISBN 0-8358-0510-7). Upper Room.
Maturing Sun: An Army Nurse in India, 1942-45. Angela Bolton. 224p. 1987. 18.95 o.s.i. (ISBN 0-901627-36-4). Janes Info Group.
Maud Gone. Kathleen R. Lawrence. LC 85-48142. 320p. 1986. 16.95 o.p. (ISBN 0-689-11643-8, Atheneum). Macmillan.
Maud: The Illustrated Diary of a Victorian Woman. Maud Berkeley. LC 86-30988. (Illus.). 192p. 1987. 19.95 o.p. (ISBN 0-87701-429-9). Chronicle Bks.
Maugham: A Reappraisal. John Whitehead. 224p. 1987. 28.50 o.p. (ISBN 0-389-20761-6, N 8320). B&N Imports.
Maui see Exploring Hawaii.
Maui the Demigod: An Epic Novel of Mythical Hawaii. Steven Goldsberry. (Illus.). 400p. 1984. 18.45 o.s.i. (ISBN 0-671-47788-9, Pub. by Poseidon). S&S.
Maui: Traveler's Guide. Bill Gleasner & Diana Gleasner. (Illus.). 69p. (Orig.). 1978. pap. 4.00 o.p. (ISBN 0-932596-08-8, Pub. by Oriental). Intl Spec Bk.
Maurice Chevalier: His Life, 1888-1972. James Harding. (Illus.). 240p. 1983. 24.95 o.p. (ISBN 0-436-19107-5, Pub. by Secker & Warburg UK). David & Charles.
Maurice Maeterlinck: A Study of His Life & Thought. W. D. Halls. LC 78-16379. 1978. Repr. of 1960 ed. lib. bdg. 35.00x o.p. (ISBN 0-313-20574-4, HAMM). Greenwood.
Maurice Merleau-Ponty & His Critics: An International Bibliography (1942-1976) Including a Bibliography of His Writings. Francois H. Lapointe & Claire C. Lapointe. LC 75-42885. (Reference Library in the Humanities: No. 51). 1976. lib. bdg. 25.00 o.p. (ISBN 0-8240-9949-4). Garland Pub.
Maurice Moore-Betty Cooking School Book of Fine Cooking. Maurice Moore. LC 73-82185. 1973. 8.95 o.p. (ISBN 0-87795-071-7, Arbor Hse). Morrow.
Maurice Prendergast Water-Color Sketchbook: 1899. Maurice Prendergast. LC 60-16755. (Illus.). 1960. boxed 17.50x o.s.i. (ISBN 0-674-81080-5). Harvard U Pr.
Maurice Ravel Variations on His Life & Work. Hans H. Stuckenschmidt. 271p. Repr. of 1968 ed. lib. bdg. 39.00 o.p. (Pub. by Am Repr Serv). Reprint Servs.
Mauryan India. G. M. Bongard-Levin. (Rus.). 1986. text ed. 50.00x o.p. (ISBN 0-86590-826-5, Pub. by Sterling Pubs India). Apt Bks.
Maverick Guide to Australia, 1983. 4th ed. Robert W. Bone. (Maverick Guide Ser.). (Illus.). 324p. (Orig.). 1982. 10.95 o.p. (ISBN 0-88289-337-8). Pelican.
Maverick Guide to Australia: 1984-1985. Robert W. Bone. (Maverick Guide Ser.). 336p. (Orig.). 1984. pap. 10.95 o.p. (ISBN 0-88289-435-8). Pelican.
Maverick Guide to Australia, 1986-87. Robert W. Bone. (Maverick Guide Ser.). 336p. 1985. pap. 11.95 o.p. (ISBN 0-88289-492-7). Pelican.
Maverick Guide to Hawaii: 1983. 7th. ed. Robert W. Bone. (Maverick Guide Ser.). (Illus.). 437p. (Orig.). 1983. pap. 9.95 o.p. (ISBN 0-88289-371-8). Pelican.
Maverick Guide to Hawaii, 1985. Robert W. Bone. (Maverick Guide Ser.). 456p. 1985. pap. 10.95 o.p. (ISBN 0-88289-469-2). Pelican.
Maverick Guide to Hawaii, 1986. Robert W. Bone. (Maverick Guide Ser.). 448p. (Orig.). 1985. pap. 10.95 o.p. (ISBN 0-88289-491-9). Pelican.
Maverick Guide to Hawaii, 1987. 11th ed. Robert W. Bone. 450p. (Orig.). 1987. pap. 11.95 o.p. (ISBN 0-88289-632-6). Pelican.
Maverick Guide to New Zealand, 1983. Robert W. Bone. (Maverick Guide Ser.). (Illus.). 305p. (Orig.). 1984. pap. 10.95 o.p. (ISBN 0-88289-370-X). Pelican.
Maverick Guide to New Zealand, 1985-1986. Robert W. Bone. (Maverick Guide Ser.). 320p. (Orig.). 1985. pap. 11.95 o.p. (ISBN 0-88289-470-6). Pelican.
Maverick: Succeeding As a Freelance Entrepreneur. Geoffrey Bailey. 224p. 1982. 13.95 o.p. (ISBN 0-531-09869-9). Watts.
Mavericks. Jack Schaefer. LC 67-23312. (Illus.). (gr. 5-8). 1967. 6.95 o.p. (ISBN 0-395-07089-9). HM.
Mawson's Will. Lennard Bickel. 1978. pap. 2.95 o.p. (ISBN 0-380-39131-7, 52076-1, Discus). Avon.
Max: A Biography of Max Beerbohm. David Cecil. LC 84-45637. (Illus.). 528p. 1985. pap. 12.95 o.p. (ISBN 0-689-70683-9, 323, Atheneum). Macmillan.
Max: A Play. Gunter Grass. Tr. by Leslie A. Wilson. Ralph Manheim. 122p. 1972. pap. 3.25 o.s.i. (ISBN 0-15-657782-8). HarBraceJ.
Max & Crystal Eastman on Peace, Revolution & War. Blanche Cook. Ed. by Charles Chatfield & Sandi Cooper. (Library of War & Peace). 1976. lib. bdg. 46.00 o.p. (ISBN 0-8240-0502-3). Garland Pub.
Max Beckmann: Memories of a Friendship. Stephan Lackner. LC 75-81622. (Illus.). 1969. 7.95x o.p. (ISBN 0-87024-120-6). U of Miami Pr.
Max Beerbohm in Perspective. Bohun Lynch. LC 74-13999. (Illus.). xx, 270p. 1975. Repr. of 1922 ed. 40.00x o.p. (ISBN 0-8103-4065-8). Gale.
Max Brand's Best Western Short Stories, Vol. II. Ed. by William F. Nolan. (General Ser.). 305p. 1986. lib. bdg. 15.95 o.p. (ISBN 0-8161-4011-1, Large Print Bks). G K Hall.

Titles

Titles

Max Ernst Loplop: The Artist in the Third Person. Werner Spies. Tr. by J. W. Gabriel from Ger. LC 83-45032. (Illus.). 187p. 1983. 45.00 o.p. (ISBN 0-8076-1065-8). Braziller.
Max Flips Out. Marilyn Kaye. (Out of This World Ser.: No. 4). (YA) (gr. 7 up). pap. 2.50 o.p. (ISBN 0-671-60268-3). Archway.
Max Goes Bad. Marilyn Kaye. (Out of This World Ser.: No. 5). (YA) (gr. 7 up). 1986. pap. 2.75 o.p. (ISBN 0-671-62448-2). Archway.
Max Jamison. Wilfrid Sheed. 260p. 1986. pap. 5.95 o.p. (ISBN 0-87795-836-X). Morrow.
Max on Earth. Marilyn Kaye. (Orig.). (gr. k up). 1986. pap. 2.75 o.p. (ISBN 0-671-60265-9). Archway.
Max on Fire. Marilyn Kaye. (Out of This World Ser.: No. 3). (YA) (gr. 7 up). pap. 2.75 o.p. (ISBN 0-671-60267-5). Archway.
Max Weber & the Destiny of Reason. Franco Ferrarotti. LC 80-5457. Orig. Title: Max Weber e il Destino Ragione. 160p. 1982. 14.95 o.p. (ISBN 0-87332-170-7). M E Sharpe.
Max Weber & the Dispute over Reason & Value: A Study of Philosophy, Ethics & Politics. Stephen Turner & Regis Factor. (International Library of Sociology Ser.). 300p. 1984. 29.95x o.p. (ISBN 0-7100-9889-8). Routledge Chapman & Hall.
Max Weber e il Destino Ragione see Max Weber & the Destiny of Reason.
Max Weber's Theory of Concept Formation: History, Laws, & Ideal Types. Thomas Burger. LC 74-31592. 1976. pap. 16.25 o.p. (ISBN 0-8223-0332-9). Duke.
Maxillary Sinus. 2nd ed. McGowan. 1987. price not set o.p. Year Bk Med.
Maxillofacial Orthopaedics: Clinical Approach for the Growing Child. Ahlin et al. (Illus.). 300p. 1984. text ed. 92.00 o.p. (ISBN 0-86715-150-1). Quint Pub Co.
Maximilian & Charlotte of Mexico, 2 vols. Egon C. Corti. lib. bdg. cancelled o.s.i. (ISBN 0-8490-0595-7). Gordon Pr.
Maximilien Robespierre: Nationalist Dictator. James M. Eagan. 1972. lib. bdg. 20.00x o.p. (ISBN 0-374-92440-6, Octagon). Hippocrene Bks.
Maximillian I, Fourteen Fifty-Nine to Fifteen Nineteen. Gerhard Benecke. (Illus.). 224p. 1982. 26.95x o.p. (ISBN 0-7100-9023-4). Routledge Chapman & Hall.
Maximizing Leadership Effectiveness: Impact of Administrative Style on Faculty & Students. Alexander W. Astin & Rita A. Scherrei. LC 79-9665. (Higher Education Ser.). 1980. text ed. 24.95x o.p. (ISBN 0-87589-454-2). Jossey-Bass.
Maximizing Tax Benefits in Business Construction. Donald E. Swanton. LC 85-29578. 537p. 1986. 72.00 o.p. (ISBN 0-471-88299-2). Wiley.
Maximizing Treatment Gains: Transfer Enhancement in Psychotherapy. Ed. by A. P. Goldstein & Frederick H. Kanfer. LC 78-31265. 1979. 57.50 o.p. (ISBN 0-12-288050-1). Acad Pr.
Maxims of Management: Working Smart to Increase Profits. Martin Smith. LC 86-5202. 1986. 14.95 o.p. (ISBN 0-8329-0419-8). New Century.
Maxims of the Civil Law: Essays in the Evolution of Law. Walter S. Johnson. LC 74-26294. 252p. 1973. Repr. of 1929 ed. lib. bdg. 25.00x o.p. (ISBN 0-912004-10-X). W W Gaunt.
Maximum Concentrations at the Workplace & Biological Tolerance Values for Working Materials 1983. Commission for Investigation of Health Hazards of Chemical Compounds in the Work Area Staff. 75p. 1983. pap. text ed. 10.00x o.p. (ISBN 0-89573-202-5). VCH Pubs.
Maximum Concentrations at the Workplace & Biological Tolerance Values for Working Materials, 1984. 94p. 1984. lab manual 10.50 o.p. (ISBN 0-89573-379-X). VCH Pubs.
Maximum Immunity. Michael A. Weiner & Kathleen Gross. LC 85-18033. 325p. 1986. 16.45 o.s.i. (ISBN 0-395-37910-5). HM.
Maximum Performance with Lotus 1-2-3, Versions 1.0 & 2.0. Robin Stark & Stuart Leitner. (Illus.). 250p. 1986. 25.95 o.p. (ISBN 0-8306-0771-4, 2771); pap. 17.60 o.p. (ISBN 0-8306-2771-5). TAB Bks.
Maximum Probability Estimators & Related Topics. L. Weiss & J. Wolfowitz. (Lecture Notes in Mathematics Ser.: Vol. 424). v, 106p. 1974. pap. 11.00 o.p. (ISBN 0-387-06970-4). Springer-Verlag.
Maximum Security Ward & Other Poems. Ramon Guthrie. Ed. by Sally M. Gall. (Lamplighter Ser.). 216p. 1984. 20.00 o.p. (ISBN 0-89255-079-1); pap. 9.95 o.p. (ISBN 0-89255-080-5). Persea Bks.
Maxine Cheshire, Reporter. Maxine Cheshire & John Greenya. 1978. 10.95 o.p. (ISBN 0-395-26303-4). HM.
Maxwell. Tom Bowers. (Illus.). 300p. Date not set. price not set o.p. Wynwood Pr.
Maxwell Anderson & S. N. Behrman: A Reference Guide. William Klink. 1977. lib. bdg. 17.50 o.p. (ISBN 0-8161-7824-0, Hall Reference). G K Hall.
Maxwell's Ghost. R. B. Frere. 1976. 29.95 o.p. (ISBN 0-575-02044-X, Pub. by Gollancz England). David & Charles.
Maya. rev. ed. Michael D. Coe. (Ancient People & Places Ser.). (Illus.). 180p. 1980. 19.95 o.p. (ISBN 0-500-02097-3); pap. 9.95 o.p. (ISBN 0-500-27195-X). Thames Hudson.
Maya Rulers of Time: A Study of Architectural Sculpture at Tikal, Guatemala. Arthur Miller. (Illus.). 129p. (Eng. & Span.). 1986. pap. 26.95 o.p. (ISBN 0-934718-79-2). Univ Mus of U PA.
Mayan Architecture: A Selected Bibliography. Anthony G. White. (Architecture Ser.: Bibliography A-1306). 5p. 1985. pap. 2.00 o.p. (ISBN 0-89028-236-6). Vance Biblios.
Mayan Poems. James Schevill. (Illus., Orig.). 1978. pap. 4.50 o.p. (ISBN 0-914278-16-9). Copper Beech.
Mayan Sculpture. cancelled o.s.i. Braziller.
Maybe a Miracle. Lee P. Huntington. (Illus.). 80p. (gr. 3-7). 1984. 9.95 o.p. (ISBN 0-698-20602-9, Coward). Putnam Pub Group.
Maybe: A Story. Lillian Hellman. 1980. 13.45 o.p. (ISBN 0-316-35512-7). Little.
Maybe: A Story. Lillian Hellman. 1982. pap. 7.70 o.p. (ISBN 0-316-35509-7). Little.
Maybe You Should Fly a Jet! Maybe You Should Be a Vet! Theodore Le Sieg. LC 80-5084. (Illus.). 48p. (ps-3). 1980. 4.95 o.p.; PLB 6.99 o.p. Beginner.
Maybelle, the Cable Car. Virginia L. Burton. (Illus.). (gr. k-3). 1976. 7.95 o.p. (ISBN 0-395-24905-8); Dolphin bdg. 4.23 o.p. (ISBN 0-395-06679-4). HM.
Maydays. David Edgar. 56p. 1984. pap. 4.95 o.p. (ISBN 0-413-54180-0, NO. 4161). Heinemann Ed.
Mayflies, the Angler, & the Trout. Fred L. Arbona, Jr. LC 79-14092. (Illus.). 224p. 1980. 27.95 o.p. (ISBN 0-8329-2994-8, Pub. by Winchester Pr). New Century.
Mayflower. J. C. Nothim. 1985. 6.95 o.p. (ISBN 0-533-06277-2). Vantage.
Mayflower Miracle. Jonathan King. (Illus.). 164p. 1987. 19.95 o.p. (ISBN 0-7153-9013-9). David & Charles.
Mayonnaise & the Origin of Life: Thoughts of Minds & Molecules. Harold J. Morowitz. 256p. 1985. 15.95 o.p. (ISBN 0-684-18444-3, ScribT). Scribner.
Mayor: An Autobiography. Edward I. Koch & William Rauch. (Illus.). 364p. 1984. 17.45 o.p. (ISBN 0-671-49536-4). S&S.
Mayor of Casterbridge. Thomas Hardy. 48p. (Orig.). 1989. pap. 9.95 o.p. (ISBN 1-55651-581-2); audiocassette tape incl. o.p. (ISBN 1-55651-582-0). Cram Cassettes.
Mayor of Prairieville. Arlene E. Williamson. (Illus.). 32p. 1987. 6.75 o.p. (ISBN 0-8062-3001-0). Carlton.
Mayor of Zalamea: Or the Best Garroting Ever Done. Pedro Calderon de la Barca. 110p. 1983. pap. 7.95 o.p. (ISBN 0-907540-12-0, NO. 4051, Pub. by Salamander Press). Routledge Chapman & Hall.
Maypoles & Wood Demons: The Meaning of Trees. Elizabeth S. Helfman. LC 72-75706. (Illus.). 128p. (gr. 3-7). 1979. 7.95 o.p. (ISBN 0-395-28859-2, Clarion). HM.
Mazda GLC Rearwheel Drive Shop Manual: 1977-1980. Ed. by Eric Jorgensen. (Illus.). pap. 12.95 o.p. (ISBN 0-89287-288-8, A262). Clymer Pub.
Mazda RX2 & RX3 Service Repair Handbook. Ed. by Eric Jorgensen. (RX-2 & RX-3, 1971-1977). (Illus.). pap. 12.95 o.p. (ISBN 0-89287-236-5, A164). Clymer Pub.
Maze. A. H. Garnet. LC 82-5878. 324p. 1982. 14.00 o.p. (ISBN 0-89919-091-X). Ticknor & Fields.
Maze. A. Likhanov. 288p. 1977. 4.95 o.p. (ISBN 0-8285-1206-X, Pub. by Progress Pubs USSR). Imported Pubns.
Maze Puzzles. The Diagram Group Staff. 96p. (Orig.). 1983. pap. 1.75 o.s.i. (ISBN 0-345-30477-2). Ballantine.
Maze Stone. Eileen Dunlop. LC 82-22232. (gr. 6 up). 1983. 10.95 o.p. (ISBN 0-698-20587-1, Coward). Putnam Pub Group.
Mazes & Labyrinths. W. H. Matthews. LC 70-75946. 274p. 1969. Repr. of 1922 ed. 34.00x o.p. (ISBN 0-8103-3839-4). Gale.
Mazzini's Letters. Giuseppe Mazzini. Tr. by Alice Jervis. LC 78-59031. 1979. Repr. of 1930 ed. 18.00 o.p. (ISBN 0-88355-703-7). Hyperion Conn.
M.B.A. Degree. Eppen et al. LC 79-55484. 1979. pap. 5.95 o.p. (ISBN 0-914090-81-X). Chicago Review.
Me. (Feelings & Growth Development Coloring Bks.). (Illus.). (ps-k). 0.75 o.p. (ISBN 0-8091-6546-5). Paulist Pr.
Me: A Book of Poems. Ed. by Lee B. Hopkins. LC 72-115782. (Illus.). 32p. (ps-3). 1979. 7.95 o.p. (ISBN 0-395-28815-0, Clarion). HM.
Me & Dirty Arnie. R. Conrad Stein. LC 81-84216. 132p. (YA) (gr. 8-12). 1982. 9.95 o.p. (ISBN 0-15-253141-6, HJ). HarBraceJ.
Me & Gallagher. Jack Farris. 1982. 13.50 o.p. (ISBN 0-671-45697-0). S&S.
Me & Jim Luke. Robbie Branscum. (YA) (gr. 8-10). 1984. pap. 0.95 o.p. (ISBN 0-380-00354-6, 52688-3). Avon.
Me & My Life. Maria Lindroos. 1980. 7.50 o.p. (ISBN 0-682-49558-1). Exposition-Phoenix.
Me & the Terrible Two. Ellen Conford. (Illus.). (gr. 3-6). 1987. pap. 2.50 o.p. (ISBN 0-671-63666-9). Archway.
Me & the Weirdos. Jane Sutton. (Illus.). (gr. 2-5). 1981. 6.95 o.p. (ISBN 0-395-30447-4). HM.
Me & You & a Dog Named Blue. Barbara Corcoran. LC 78-13746. (gr. 5-9). 1979. 8.95 o.p. (ISBN 0-689-30675-X, Atheneum). Macmillan.
Me De Villedieu's Les Desordres Del L'amour: History, Literature & the Nouvelle Historique. Arthur Flannigan. LC 81-43835. 206p. 1983. lib. bdg. 30.00 o.p. (ISBN 0-8191-2696-9); pap. text ed. 13.25 o.p. (ISBN 0-8191-2697-7). U Pr of Amer.
Me, Minsky, & Max. Bruce Pollock. (gr. 7 up). 1978. 7.95 o.p. (ISBN 0-395-26455-3). HM.
Me Nobody Knows: Children's Voices from the Ghetto. Ed. by Stephen M. Joseph. 144p. 1982. pap. 2.50 o.p. (ISBN 0-380-01339-8, 80663-0). Avon.
Me Spik English. Milly L. Donnelly. 31p. soft bdg. 1.95 o.p. (ISBN 0-930492-08-0). Hawaiian Serv.
Me Too, Iguana. Jacquelyn Reinach. LC 76-43090. (Sweet Pickles Ser.). (Illus.). (gr. k-2). 1977. 2.95 o.p. (ISBN 0-03-018071-6). H Holt & Co.
Meadowlark. Meadowlark Lemon & Jerry Jenkins. LC 87-5751. 224p. 1987. 15.95 o.p. (ISBN 0-8407-4220-7). Nelson.
Meal Management: Laboratory Manual. Glenna W. Harrison. 121p. 1984. pap. text ed. 9.95 o.p. (ISBN 0-89917-410-8, Pub. by College Town Pr). Tichenor Pub.
Meal Planning for People with Kidney Disease. Sachiko St. Jeor et al. LC 77-72580. (Illus.). 1977. pap. 1.25 o.p. (ISBN 0-87480-118-4). U of Utah Pr.
Mealtime. Walker Books Staff. (Time to Talk Ser.). (Illus.). 32p. (ps-2). 1983. 1.50 o.s.i. (ISBN 0-671-47108-2, Little Simon). S&S.
Mean-Field Magnetohydrodynamics & Dynamo Theory. F. Krause & K-H. Radler. (Illus.). 270p. 1981. 50.00 o.p. (ISBN 0-08-025041-6). Pergamon.
Mean Streets. W. C. Armintrout. LC 86-91767. (Car Wars Adventure Gamebook Ser: No. 6). 192p. (Orig.). 1987. pap. 2.95 o.p. (ISBN 0-88038-446-8). TSR Inc.
Meanarthal Remains from Krapina. Fred H. Smith. Date not set. write for info. o.p. U of Tenn Pr.
Meanest Man in Texas. Don Umphrey. LC 84-3383. 288p. 1984. pap. 6.95 o.p. (ISBN 0-8407-5870-7). Nelson.
Meaning & Argument: Elements of Logic. Robert G. Olson. 1969. text ed. 11.95 o.p. (ISBN 0-15-555658-4, HC). HarBraceJ.
Meaning & Behaviour in the Built Environment. Ed. by Geoffrey Broadbent et al. LC 79-41490. 372p. 1980. 100.00x o.p. (ISBN 0-471-27708-8). Wiley.
Meaning & Necessity: A Study in Semantics & Modal Logic. 2nd ed. Rudolf Carnap. LC 56-9132. 1958. pap. text ed. 4.95 o.s.i. (ISBN 0-226-09346-8, P30, Phoen). U of Chicago Pr.
Meaning & the Moral Sciences. Hilary Putnam. (International Library of Philosophy). 1979. pap. 7.95x o.p. (ISBN 0-7100-0437-0). Routledge Chapman & Hall.
Meaning & the Moral Sciences. Hilary Putnam. (International Library of Philosophy & Scientific Method). 1978. 23.95x o.p. (ISBN 0-7100-8754-3). Routledge Chapman & Hall.
Meaning & the Structure of Language. Wallace L. Chafe. LC 79-114855. 1971. lib. bdg. 20.00x o.s.i. (ISBN 0-226-10055-3). U of Chicago Pr.
Meaning for Man. Rollin Chambliss. LC 66-20215. 1967. (ISBN 0-8022-0230-6). Philos Lib.
Meaning in Star Trek. Karin Blair. LC 77-7438. (Illus.). 1977. 9.95 o.p. (ISBN 0-89012-010-2). Anima Pubns.
Meaning in Texts: The Historical Shaping of a Narrative Hermeneutics. Edgar V. McKnight. LC 77-15238. 348p. 1978. 19.95 o.p. (ISBN 0-8006-0518-7, 1-518, Fortress). Augsburg Fortress.
Meaning in the Urban Environment. Martin Krampen. (Research in Planning & Design Ser.). 365p. 1979. 33.00x o.p. (ISBN 0-85086-067-9, NO. 6379, Pub. by Pion England). Routledge Chapman & Hall.
Meaning of Anxiety. Rollo May. 1977. 14.95 o.p. (ISBN 0-393-01136-4). Norton.
Meaning of Commercial Television. Ed. by Stanley T. Donner. 171p. 1967. pap. 4.95x o.p. (ISBN 0-292-73181-7). U of Tex Pr.
Meaning of Company Accounts. 3rd ed. Walter Reid & D. R. Myddleton. 368p. 1982. text ed. 47.50x o.p. (ISBN 0-566-02284-2). Gower Pub Co.
Meaning of Gifts. Paul Tournier. LC 63-19122. 1976. 5.95 o.s.i. (ISBN 0-8042-2124-3, John Knox); pap. 1.25 o.p. Westminster John Knox.
Meaning of Global Apartheid. Gernot Kohler. 32p. 1978. pap. 2.00 o.p. (ISBN 0-87855-761-X). Transaction Pubs.
Meaning of God. Robert H. King. LC 73-80635. 176p. 1973. pap. 6.95 o.p. (ISBN 0-8006-0257-9, Fortress). Augsburg Fortress.
Meaning of Hope: A Biblical Exposition with Concordance. C. F. Moule. Ed. by John Reumann. LC 63-17881. (Facet Bks.). 72p. (Orig.). 1963. pap. 0.50 o.p. (ISBN 0-8006-3001-7, 1-3001, Fortress). Augsburg Fortress.
Meaning of Human Existence. Leslie A. Paul. LC 73-148642. 1971. Repr. of 1949 ed. lib. bdg. 35.00x o.p. (ISBN 0-8371-6008-1, PAHE). Greenwood.
Meaning of Human Nutrition. M. W. Lamb & M. L. Harden. 1975. 24.00 o.p. (ISBN 0-08-017078-1); pap. 13.75 o.p. (ISBN 0-08-017079-X). Pergamon.
Meaning of Jesus Christ. William M. Ramsay. (Orig.). 1964. pap. 3.95 o.p. (ISBN 0-8042-9220-5, John Knox); tchrs' guide pap. 2.60 o.p. (ISBN 0-686-76883-3). Westminster John Knox.
Meaning of Life. Monty Python. LC 83-80495. (Illus.). 128p. 1983. pap. 10.95 o.s.i. (ISBN 0-394-62474-2, E860, Ever). Grove.
Meaning of Shakespeare. Harold C. Goddard. LC 51-2288. 1951. lib. bdg. 33.00x o.s.i. (ISBN 0-226-30040-4). U of Chicago Pr.
Meaning of the Covenant. Haldon Ferris. 1987. 6.75 o.p. (ISBN 0-8062-2841-5). Carlton.
Meaning of the Renaissance & Reformation. Richard L. Demolen et al. 440p. 1974. pap. 11.50 o.p. (ISBN 0-395-12632-0). HM.
Meaning of Truth: A Sequel to Pragmatism. William James. Ed. by Frederick Burkhardt et al. (Works of William James Ser.: Vol. 2). 400p. 1976. text ed. 27.00x o.p. (ISBN 0-674-55861-8). Harvard U Pr.
Meaning, Quantification, Necessity. Martin Davies. (International Library of Philosophy). 260p. 1981. 34.95x o.p. (ISBN 0-7100-0759-0). Routledge Chapman & Hall.
Meaningful Living: Logotherapy Guide to Health. Elisabeth Lukas. Tr. by Joseph B. Fabry. LC 86-228. 140p. 1986. pap. 8.95 o.s.i. (ISBN 0-394-62166-2, Ever). Grove.
Meanings of Deviance. Ed. by Charles M. Vivona. 1973. 29.50x o.p. (ISBN 0-8422-5111-1); pap. text ed. 9.95x o.p. (ISBN 0-8422-0320-6). Irvington.
Means Assemblies Cost Data, 1986. 11th ed. Means, R. S., Company, Inc. Staff. Ed. by William Horsley. (Illus.). 525p. 1985. pap. 44.95 o.p. (ISBN 0-87629-005-5). R S Means.
Means Assemblies Cost Data, 1988. 13th ed. R. S. Means Company, Inc. Staff. (Professional Cost Guides). (Illus.). 1987. pap. 77.95 o.p. (ISBN 0-87629-077-2). R S Means.
Means Concrete Cost Data, 1988. 6th ed. R. S. Means Company, Inc. Staff. (Professional Cost Guides). 1987. pap. 48.95 o.p. (ISBN 0-87629-081-0). R S Means.
Means Electrical Cost Data, 1986. 9th ed. Means, R. S., Company, Inc. Staff. Ed. by William Mahoney. (Illus.). 386p. 1985. pap. 41.95 o.p. (ISBN 0-87629-002-0). R S Means.
Means Electrical Cost Data, 1988. 11th ed. R. S. Means Company, Inc. Staff. (Professional Cost Guides). (Illus.). 1987. pap. 49.95 o.p. (ISBN 0-87629-074-8). R S Means.
Means Facilities Cost Data, 1988. 3rd ed. R. S. Means Company, Inc. Staff. (Professional Cost Guides). 900p. 1987. pap. 141.95 o.p. (ISBN 0-87629-087-X). R S Means.
Means Heavy Construction Cost Data, 1988. R. S. Means Company, Inc. Staff. (Professional Cost Guides). 1987. pap. 51.95 o.p. (ISBN 0-87629-084-5). R S Means.
Means Historical Cost Indexes, 1988. 8th ed. R. S. Means Company, Inc. Staff. Ed. by William F. Mahoney. 20p. 1988. pap. text ed. 27.95 o.p. (ISBN 0-87629-083-7, 60138). R S Means.
Means Interior Cost Data, 1988. 5th ed. R. S. Means Company, Inc. Staff. (Professional Cost Guides). 1987. pap. 48.95 o.p. (ISBN 0-87629-080-2). R S Means.
Means Labor Rates for the Construction Industry, 1988. 15th ed. R. S. Means Company, Inc. Staff. 1987. pap. 120.00 o.p. (ISBN 0-87629-082-9). R S Means.
Means Landscape Cost Data 1988. R. S. Means Company, Inc. Staff. Ed. by William Mahoney. (Illus.). 325p. 1988. pap. 51.95 o.p. (ISBN 0-87629-108-6, 60198). R S Means.
Means Light Commercial Cost Data, 1988. 7th ed. R. S. Means Company, Inc. Staff. (Illus.). 400p. 1987. pap. 48.95 o.p. (ISBN 0-317-69374-3, 60188). R S Means.

Means Light Commerical Cost Data, 1988. 7th ed. R. S. Means Company, Inc. Staff. (Professional Cost Guides). 1987. pap. 48.95 o.p. (ISBN 0-87629-085-3). R S Means.

Means Man-Hour Standards. 1st ed. Robert S. Godfrey. 576p. 1983. text ed. 89.95 o.p. (ISBN 0-911950-60-5). R S Means.

Means Mechanical Cost Data, 1986. 9th ed. Means, R. S., Company, Inc. Staff. Ed. by Melville Mossman. (Illus.). 464p. 1985. pap. 41.95 o.p. (ISBN 0-87629-001-2). R S Means.

Means Mechanical Cost Data, 1988. 11th ed. R. S. Means Company, Inc. Staff. (Professional Cost Guides). 1987. pap. 49.95 o.p. (ISBN 0-87629-073-X). R S Means.

Means Mechanical Cost Data, 1989. 47th ed. (Professional Cost Guide Ser.). 1988. 52.95 o.p. (ISBN 0-87629-113-2). R S Means.

Means Open Shop Building Construction Cost Data, 1988. 4th ed. R. S. Means Company, Inc. Staff. (Professional Cost Guides). 1987. pap. 59.95 o.p. (ISBN 0-87629-086-1). R S Means.

Means Repair & Remodeling Cost Data, 1988. 9th ed. R. S. Means Company, Inc. Staff. (Professional Cost Guides). 1987. pap. 49.95 o.p. (ISBN 0-87629-075-6). R S Means.

Means Residential Cost Data, 1988. 7th ed. R. S. Means Company, Inc. Staff. (Professional Cost Guides). (Illus.). 1987. pap. 48.95 o.p. (ISBN 0-87629-079-9). R S Means.

Means Scheduling Manual. F. W. Horsley. (Illus.). 200p. 1981. pap. 22.75 o.p. (ISBN 0-911950-36-2). R S Means.

Means Site Work Cost Data Annual, 1986. 5th ed. Means, R. S., Company, Inc. Staff. Ed. by Kornelis Smit. (Illus.). 448p. 1985. pap. 41.95 o.p. (ISBN 0-87629-006-3). R S Means.

Means Site Work Cost Data, 1988. 7th ed. R. S. Means Company, Inc. Staff. (Professional Cost Guides). 1987. pap. 49.95 o.p. (ISBN 0-87629-078-0). R S Means.

Means Square Foot Costs, 1986. 7th ed. Means, R. S., Company, Inc. Staff. Ed. by William Mahoney. (Illus.). 425p. 1985. pap. 42.95 o.p. (ISBN 0-87629-004-7). R S Means.

Means Square Foot Costs, 1988. 9th ed. R. S. Means Company, Inc. Staff. (Professional Cost Guides). (Illus.). 1987. pap. 55.95 o.p. (ISBN 0-87629-076-4). R S Means.

Meanwhile Back at the Henhouse: A Novel. Thomas Bledsoe. LC 82-71306. 185p. 1966. 4.95 o.p. (ISBN 0-8040-0197-9, Pub by Swallow). Ohio U Pr.

Measure & Design in American Painting, 1760-1860. Lisa F. Andrus. LC 76-23601. (Outstanding Dissertations in the Fine Arts-American). (Illus.). 1977. Repr. lib. bdg. 68.00 o.p. (ISBN 0-8240-2675-6). Garland Pub.

Measure for Measure. William Shakespeare. Ed. by Louis B. Wright & Virginia A. LaMar. (Folger Library). (Illus.). 288p. (gr. 12 up). pap. text ed. 2.95 o.s.i. (ISBN 0-671-49612-3). WSP.

Measure for Measure: An Old-Spelling & Old-Meaning Edition. William Shakespeare. Ed. by Ernst Leisi. 23p. pap. cancelled o.s.i. (ISBN 3-533-01476-2). Adlers Foreign Bks.

Measure for Measure As Dialectical Art. William B. Bache. LC 69-16057. 70p. (Orig.). 1969. pap. 2.50 o.p. (ISBN 0-911198-18-0). Purdue U Pr.

Measure of a Man. Gene A. Getz. LC 74-175983. 224p. (Orig.). 1974. pap. 4.95 o.p. (ISBN 0-8307-1031-0, 5012104). Regal.

Measure of a Woman. Sarah Fryman. LC 77-74533. (Measure of... Ser.). 64p. 1985. pap. 3.95 o.p. (ISBN 0-8307-0988-6, 6101888). Regal.

Measure of Justice: An Empirical Study of Changes in the California Penal Code, 1955-1971. Ed. by Richard A. Berk et al. (Quantitative Studies in Social Relations). 1977. 43.50 o.p. (ISBN 0-12-091550-2). Acad Pr.

Measure of Light. James Minor. (Haiku Ser.: No. 17). 1985. pap. 2.50 o.p. (ISBN 1-55780-086-3). Juniper Pr WI.

Measure of Sliding Sand. Ira Glackens. LC 76-18450. 1977. 8.95 o.p. (ISBN 0-8397-5740-9). Eriksson.

Measure Theory: Proceedings of the Conference Held at Oberwolfach, 15-21 June, 1975. Ed. by A. Bellow & D. Kolzow. LC 76-26664. (Lecture Notes in Mathematics Ser.: Vol. 541). 1976. pap. 23.00 o.p. (ISBN 0-387-07861-4). Springer-Verlag.

Measured Drawings for Architects. Robert Chitham. (Illus.). 128p. 1980. 32.50x o.p. (ISBN 0-85139-391-8); pap. 17.50x o.p. (ISBN 0-85139-392-6). Nichols Pub.

Measurement & Analysis of Internal Migration: Testing Models with Korean Data. Wen L. Li. LC 83-6883. (Illus.). 172p. (Orig.). 1983. lib. bdg. 27.75 o.p. (ISBN 0-8191-3218-7); pap. text ed. 12.25 o.p. (ISBN 0-8191-3219-5). U Pr of Amer.

Measurement & Detection of Radiation. Nicholas Tsoulfanidis. (Illus.). 571p. 1983. text ed. 49.95 o.p. (ISBN 0-07-065397-6). McGraw.

Measurement & Evaluation in the Schools. Donald L. Beggs & Ernest L. Lewis. 1975. text ed. 20.95 o.p. (ISBN 0-395-18609-9). HM.

Measurement & Evaluation in the School. 2nd ed. Louis J. Karmel. (Illus.). 1978. text ed. write for info. o.p. (ISBN 0-02-362000-5, 36200). Macmillan.

Measurement & Evaluation of Reading. Roger Farr. 1970. pap. text ed. 8.95 o.p. (ISBN 0-15-557550-3, HC). HarBraceJ.

Measurement & Modelling Methods for Computer Systems Performance Studies. Michael F. Barnes. 177p. 1979. pap. 44.50x o.p. (ISBN 0-905897-18-8). Gower Pub Co.

Measurement Error & Banks' Reported Earnings. Reed H. McKnight. Ed. by Richard N. Farmer. LC 83-1393. (Research for Business Decisions Ser.: No. 61). 128p. 1983. 42.95 o.p. (ISBN 0-8357-1411-X). UMI Res Pr.

Measurement, Guidance, & Program Improvement. Ed. by William B. Schrader. LC 81-48491. (Testing & Measurement Ser.: No. 13). 1982. pap. text ed. 13.95x o.p. (ISBN 0-87589-927-7). Jossey-Bass.

Measurement in Physical Education. 5th ed. Donald K. Mathews. LC 77-24002. (Illus.). 1978. text ed. 26.95 o.p. (ISBN 0-7216-6178-5). HR&W.

Measurement of Air Flow: In SI-Metric Units. 5th ed. Ernest Ower & F. C. Pankhurst. 1977. 59.00 o.p. (ISBN 0-08-021282-4); pap. 28.00 o.p. (ISBN 0-08-021281-6). Pergamon.

Measurement of Appearance. Richard S. Hunter. LC 75-20429. 348p. 1975. 58.00 o.p. (ISBN 0-471-42141-3, Pub. by Wiley-Interscience). Wiley.

Measurement of Civil Engineering Work. G. J. Reynolds. 132p. 1980. pap. text ed. 14.50x o.p. (ISBN 0-246-11376-6, Pub. by Granada England). Gower Pub Co.

Measurement of Dissolved Oxygen. Michael L. Hitchman. LC 86-141. 88p. 1988. Repr. of 1978 ed. text ed. price not set. o.p. (ISBN 0-89874-928-X). Krieger.

Measurement of Employment & Unemployment by the Bureau of the Census in Its Current Population Survey. U. S. Department of Commerce, Special Advisory Committee on Employment Statistics. LC 78-11657. 1979. Repr. of 1954 ed. lib. bdg. (ISBN 0-313-20691-0, USME). Greenwood.

Measurement of Neutron Flux & Spectra for Physical & Biological Applications. 1960. 7.00 o.p. NCRP Pubns.

Measurement of Psychological States Through the Content Analysis of Verbal Behavior. Louis A. Gottschalk & Goldine C. Gleser. 1979. Repr. of 1969 ed. 30.00x o.p. (ISBN 0-520-03813-4). U of Cal Pr.

Measurement of Risks. Ed. by George G. Berg & H. David Maillie. LC 81-13969. (Environmental Science Research Ser.: Vol. 21). 560p. 1981. 89.50x o.p. (ISBN 0-306-40818-X, Plenum Pr). Plenum Pub.

Measurement of Safety Performance. William E. Tarrants. LC 79-19208. 400p. 1980. lib. bdg. 47.00 o.p. (ISBN 0-8240-7170-0). Garland Pub.

Measurements & Control Applications. 2nd rev. & enl. ed. Joel O. Hougen. LC 78-55480. (Illus.). 448p. 1979. text ed. 24.98x o.p. (ISBN 0-87664-401-9). Instru Soc.

Measurements in High-Voltage Test Circuits. G. W. Bowdler. LC 72-86488. 192p. 1973. text ed. 45.00 o.p. (ISBN 0-08-016838-8). Pergamon.

Measurements of High Energetic Auroral Radiations with Balloon-Borne Detectors in 1962 & 1963, 2 Vols. Ed. by G. Pfotzer & A. Ehmert. 1965. Set. pap. 10.70 o.p. (ISBN 0-387-03358-0). Springer-Verlag.

Measurements of the Impacts of Materials Substitution: A Case Study in the Automobile Industry. Ed. by A. Bleiloch. 1978. 8.00 o.p. (ISBN 0-685-66804-5, H00131). ASME.

Measurements of Time Reversal in Objective Quantum Theory. F. J. Belinfante. 1975. 45.00 o.p. (ISBN 0-08-018152-X). Pergamon.

Measures of Effectiveness, Railroad-Highway Grade Crossings, & Visibility: Nine Reports. (Transportation Research Record Ser.). 106p. 1976. 7.00 o.p. (ISBN 0-309-02472-2). Transport Res Bd.

Measures on Topological Semi-Groups: Convolution Products & Random Walks. A. Mukherjea & N. A. Tserpes. (Lecture Notes in Mathematics: Vol. 547). 1976. 17.00 o.p. (ISBN 0-387-07987-4). Springer-Verlag.

Measuring & Evaluating School Learning. Lou Carey. 512p. 1988. pap. text ed. 26.25 net o.p. Allyn.

Measuring & Forecasting Engineering Personnel Requirements. 1979. 50.00x o.p. (126-79). AAES.

Measuring Charleston's Overseas Commerce, 1717-1767: Statistics from the Port's Naval Lists. Converse D. Clowse. LC 81-40640. (Illus.). 170p. (Orig.). 1982. lib. bdg. 29.25 o.p. (ISBN 0-8191-2055-3); pap. text ed. 12.50 o.p. (ISBN 0-8191-2056-1). U Pr of Amer.

Measuring Community Performance: A Handbook of Indicators. Joseph W. Whorton, Jr. & David R. Morgan. 78p. 1975. 3.50 o.p. (ISBN 0-686-32068-9). Univ OK Gov Res.

Measuring Disability. Sally Sainsbury. 125p. 1973. pap. text ed. 6.25x o.p. (ISBN 0-7135-1899-5, Pub. by Bedford England). Gower Pub Co.

Measuring Educational Outcomes: Fundamentals of Testing. Bruce W. Tuckman. (Illus.). 576p. 1975. text ed. 19.95 o.p. (ISBN 0-15-557692-5, HC). HarBraceJ.

Measuring Health Status. Sonja M. Hunt et al. 200p. 1986. 34.50 o.p. (ISBN 0-7099-3584-6, Pub. by Croom Helm Ltd). Routledge Chapman & Hall.

Measuring Outcomes of College: Fifty Years of Findings & Recommendations for the Future. C. Robert Pace. LC 79-88774. (Higher Education Ser.). 1979. text ed. 23.95x o.p. (ISBN 0-87589-438-0). Jossey-Bass.

Measuring Performance in Human Service Systems: Planning, Organization & Control. James F. Budde. (Illus.). 1980. 16.95 o.p. (ISBN 0-8144-5551-4). AMACOM.

Measuring Productivity: Trends & Comparisons from the 1st International Productivity Symposium. Solomon Fabricant. 250p. 1984. pap. 46.50 o.p. (ISBN 0-89059-035-4, UPB133 6011, UPB). UNIPUB.

Measuring Project Impact: Monitoring & Evaluation in the PIDER Rural Development Project - Mexico. Michael M. Cernea. (Working Paper: No. 332). vi, 131p. 1979. 5.00 o.p. (ISBN 0-686-36071-0, WP-0332). World Bank.

Measuring Pupil Achievement & Aptitude. 2nd ed. C. Mauritz Lindvall & Anthony J. Nitko. (Orig.). 1975. pap. text ed. 9.95 o.p. (ISBN 0-15-557792-1, HC). HarBraceJ.

Measuring Spoken Language Proficiency. Ed. by James R. Frith. 69p. (Orig.). 1980. pap. text ed. 4.95 o.p. (ISBN 0-87840-188-1). Georgetown U Pr.

Measuring the Impact of Employment Related Social Programs: A Primer on the Evaluation of Employment & Training, Vocational Education, Vocational Rehabilitation, Other Job Oriented Programs. Michael E. Borus. LC 79-13151. 1979. pap. text ed. 7.95 o.p. (ISBN 0-911558-63-2). W E Upjohn.

Measuring the Universe: Cosmic Dimensions from Aristarchus to Halley. Albert Van Helden. LC 84-16397. (Illus.). vii, 204p. 1985. 30.00x o.s.i. (ISBN 0-226-84881-7). U of Chicago Pr.

Measuring Thinking Skills in the Classroom. Richard J. Stiggins & Evelyn Rubel. 32p. 1986. 6.95 o.p. (ISBN 0-8106-0686-0). NEA.

Meat. Leon Lobel & Stanley Lobel. LC 78-5939. 1978. pap. 3.95 o.p. (ISBN 0-15-658549-9, Harv). HarBraceJ.

Meat & Memory. Deborah Pintonelli. (Orig.). 1987. pap. 5.00 o.p. (ISBN 0-942582-13-6). Erie St Pr.

Meat & Poultry Entrees for Foodservice Menu Planning. Eulalia C. Blair. LC 78-9126. (Foodservice Menu Planning Ser.). (Illus.). 256p. 1983. 19.95 o.p. (ISBN 0-8436-2152-4). Van Nos Reinhold.

Meat Balances in OECD Countries, 1977-1983. Organization for Economic Cooperation & Development Staff. 156p. (Orig., Eng. & Fr.). 1985. pap. 15.00x o.p. (ISBN 92-64-02666-5). OECD.

Meat Industry Safety Guidelines. 2nd ed. National Safety Council. LC 78-52082. 112p. 1978. pap. 16.55 o.p. (ISBN 0-87912-044-4, 129.51). Natl Safety Coun.

Meat Makes the Meal. Margaret D. Murphy. LC 77-71479. (Illus.). 144p. 1977. 7.95 o.p. (ISBN 0-916752-11-9). Longman Trade.

Meat Science. 3rd ed. R. A. Lawrie. 1979. text ed. 62.00 o.p. (ISBN 0-08-023173-X); pap. text ed. 21.00 o.p. (ISBN 0-08-023172-1). Pergamon.

Meatman. Mike Mallowe. 1989. pap. 3.95 o.p. Pinnacle MO.

Mecanica De Construccion En Ejemplos y Problemas. V. A. Kiseliov et al. (Illus.). 391p. (Span.). 1973. 8.45 o.p. (ISBN 0-8285-1457-7, Pub. by Mir Pubs USSR). Imported Pubns.

Mecanografia: Metodo Racional. 2nd ed. Rupert P. Sorelle et al. 1962. text ed. 5.95 o.p. (ISBN 0-07-059650-6). McGraw.

Mecca, the Pilgrimage City: A Study of Pilgrim Accomodation. Ghazy A. Makky. (Illus.). 95p. 1978. 28.00 o.p. (ISBN 0-85664-591-5, Pub. by Croom Helm Ltd). Routledge Chapman & Hall.

Mechanical Ability Tests. Ed. by Hy Hammer. 320p. (Orig.). 1984. pap. 8.00 o.p. (ISBN 0-668-05769-6, 5769). Arco.

Mechanical Baby: A Popular History of Writings on the Theory & Practice of Child Care. Daniel Beekman. LC 76-18055. (Illus.). 288p. 1977. 12.95 o.p. (ISBN 0-88208-073-3). Chicago Review.

Mechanical Behaviour of Engineering Materials. W. D. Biggs. 1966. 50.00 o.p. (ISBN 0-08-011415-6); pap. text ed. 50.00 o.p. (ISBN 0-08-011414-8). Pergamon.

Mechanical Behaviour of Materials. K. J. Miller & R. F. Smith. 1980. 415.00 o.p. (ISBN 0-08-024739-3). Pergamon.

Mechanical Behaviour of Materials: Proceedings of the Fourth International Conference on Mechanical Behaviour of Materials, Stockholm, Sweden, August 15-19, 1983, 2 Vols, No. IV. Ed. by J. Carlsson. (International Series on Strength & Fracture of Materials & Structures). (Illus.). 1175p. 1984. 305.00 o.p. (ISBN 0-08-029340-9). Pergamon.

Mechanical Doll. Pamela Stearns. (Illus.). (gr. 5-9). 1979. 6.95 o.p. (ISBN 0-395-27809-0). HM.

Mechanical Drawing: Dimensioning. Resource Systems International Staff. 1982. pap. text ed. 15.00 o.p. (ISBN 0-8359-4304-6, Reston). P-H.

Mechanical Drawing: Field Sketching. Resource Systems International Staff. 1982. pap. text ed. 15.00 o.p. (ISBN 0-8359-4305-4, Reston). P-H.

Mechanical Drawing: Isometric & Obilique. Resource Systems International Staff. 1982. pap. text ed. 15.00 o.p. (ISBN 0-8359-4307-0, Reston). P-H.

Mechanical Drawing: Orthographic. Resource Systems International Staff. 1982. pap. text ed. 15.00 o.p. (ISBN 0-8359-4308-9, Reston). P-H.

Mechanical Drawing: Tools & Lettering. Resource Systems International Staff. 1982. pap. text ed. 15.00 o.p. (ISBN 0-8359-4309-7, Reston). P-H.

Mechanical Engineering for Professional Engineers' Examinations. 3rd ed. J. D. Constance. 1981. pap. text ed. 19.95 o.p. (ISBN 0-07-012457-4). McGraw.

Mechanical Engineers in America Born Prior to 1861: A Biographical Dictionary. 330p. 1980. 20.00 o.p. (ISBN 0-686-69855-X, H00176). ASME.

Mechanical Equipment for Buildings: A Bibliography. Mary Vance. (Architecture Ser.: Bibliography A 1331). 1985. pap. 3.00 o.p. (ISBN 0-89028-281-1). Vance Biblios.

Mechanical Fault Diagnosis & Condition Monitoring. R. A. Collacott. 1977. 81.00x o.p. (ISBN 0-412-12930-2, NO. 3005, Pub. by Chapman & Hall). Routledge Chapman & Hall.

Mechanical Fitting, Vol. 1. Ed. by T. Briggs et al. (Engineering Craftsmen: No. H3). 1968. spiral bdg. 37.50x o.p. (ISBN 0-85083-012-5). Trans-Atl Phila.

Mechanical Fitting, Vol. 2. 2nd ed. Ed. by G. Barnet et al. (Engineering Craftsmen: No. H25). (Illus.). 1973. spiral bdg. 39.95x o.p. (ISBN 0-85083-186-5). Trans-Atl Phila.

Mechanical Giants. Roland Berry. (Illus.). 40p. (gr. 3-6). 1982. 12.95 o.p. (ISBN 0-241-10765-2, Pub. by Hamish Hamilton England). David & Charles.

Mechanical Hands Illustrated. Ichiro Kato. Ed. by Kuni Sadamoto. (Illus.). 214p. (Orig.). 1983. pap. text ed. 34.00 o.p. (ISBN 0-89116-378-6). Hemisphere Pub.

Mechanical Inventions of Emanuel Swedenborg. Emanuel Swedenborg. Ed. & tr. by Alfred Acton. (Illus.). 51p. 1939. pap. 1.00 o.p. (ISBN 0-915221-03-9). Swedenborg Sci Assn.

Mechanical Maintenance, Pt. I. Ed. by A. Baugh et al. (Engineering Craftsmen: No. J1). (Illus.). 1978. spiral bdg. 43.50x o.p. (ISBN 0-85083-016-8). Trans-Atl Phila.

Mechanical Maintenance (& Installation) II, 2 vols. Ed. by J. Vaughan et al. (Engineering Craftsmen Ser.: No. J21). (Illus.). 342p. 1970. Set. 59.95x o.p. (ISBN 0-85083-080-X). Trans-Atl Phila.

Mechanical Maintenance & Installation: Supplementary Training Manual. Ed. by A. T. Gamlin et al. (Engineering Craftsmen: No. J21S). (Illus.). 1976. 59.95x o.p. (ISBN 0-85083-332-9). Trans-Atl Phila.

Mechanical Plumbing Acoustics. 8.00 o.p. (ISBN 0-317-65072-6). Am Consul Eng.

Mechanical Properties of BCC Metals: Proceedings of a Meeting at Honolulu, HI, 1981. Ed. by M. Meshii. (Illus.). 265p. 40.00 o.p. (ISBN 0-89520-391-X); members 25.00 o.p. (ISBN 0-317-36245-3); student members 14.00 o.p. (ISBN 0-317-36246-1). ASM.

Mechanical Properties of Bone. Ed. by S. C. Cowin. (AMD Ser.: Vol. 45). 238p. 1981. 20.00 o.p. (ISBN 0-686-34477-4, G00203). ASME.

Mechanical Stress, Functional Adaptation & the Variation Structure of the Human Femur Diaphysis. E. Amtmann. LC 78-167680. (Advances in Anatomy Ser.: Vol. 44, Pt. 3). (Illus.). 1971. pap. 30.70 o.p. (ISBN 0-387-05464-2). Springer-Verlag.

Mechanical, Thermal & Chemical Storage of Energy. Ed. by W. V. Hassenzahl. LC 81-6485. (Benchmark Papers on Energy Ser.: Vol. 9). 379p. 1982. 57.95 o.p. (ISBN 0-87933-392-8). Van Nos Reinhold.

Mechanical Waves in Solids. Ed. by J. Mandel & L. Brun. (CISM-International Center for Mechanical Sciences Courses & Lectures Ser.: Vol. 222). (Illus.). 1978. pap. 29.00 o.p. (ISBN 0-387-81398-5). Springer-Verlag.

Mechanical Working & Steel Processing Proceedings, Vol. XXIV. Work for Hire Staff. LC 75-17963. 300p. 1987. 60.00 o.p. (ISBN 0-932897-16-9). Iron & Steel.

Mechanics. S. Strelkov. 560p. 1978. 12.50 o.p. (ISBN 0-8285-0791-0, Pub. by Mir Pubs USSR). Imported Pubns.

Mechanics: A Laboratory Manual. 2nd ed. Mohamad Habibi & Robert Warisila. (Illus.). 160p. 1980. pap. text ed. 10.95x o.p. (ISBN 0-89529-043-X). Avery Pub.

Mechanics & Energetics of Biological Transport. E. Heinz. (Molecular Biology, Biochemistry & Biophysics: Vol. 29). (Illus.). 1978. 36.00 o.p. (ISBN 0-387-08905-5). Springer-Verlag.

Mechanics & Materials: An Individualized Approach - Reference Manual-Study Guide. Hornsey et al. LC 76-18470. (Illus.). 1977. pap. 32.50 o.p. (ISBN 0-395-24993-7). HM.

Mechanics Applied to the Transport of Bulk Materials AMD, Vol. 31, Bk. No. G00146. Ed. by S. C. Cowin. 140p. 1979. 20.00 o.p. (ISBN 0-686-58131-8). ASME.

Mechanics Guide to Front Wheel Drive. Larry W. Carley. (Illus.). 240p. 1983. pap. text ed. 28.67 o.p. (ISBN 0-13-569822-7). P-H.

Mechanics of Composite Materials. Robert M. Jones. (Illus.). 350p. 1975. text ed. 50.95 o.p. (ISBN 0-07-032790-4). McGraw.

Mechanics of Composite Materials: International Conference on the Mechanics & Chemistry & Solid Propellants. Ed. by F. W. Wendt et al. 1970. 225.00 o.p. (ISBN 0-08-006421-3). Pergamon.

Mechanics of Composite Materials: Recent Advances. Proceedings of the International Union of Theoretical & Applied Mechanics Symposium, August 16-19, 1982, Blacksburg, Virginia, U. S. A. Zvi Hashin & Carl T. Herakovich. (Illus.). 450p. 1983. 125.00 o.p. (ISBN 0-08-029384-0, A145). Pergamon.

Mechanics of Elastic Structures. 2nd ed. John T. Oden & Eugene A. Ripperger. LC 79-25261. (Illus.). 480p. 1981. text ed. 46.95 o.p. (ISBN 0-07-047507-5). McGraw.

Mechanics of Engineering Soils: SI Version. 6th ed. P. L. Capper & W. F. Cassie. 1976. pap. 15.95 o.p. (ISBN 0-419-10990-0, NO. 6052, Pub. by E & FN Spon). Routledge Chapman & Hall.

Mechanics of Erosion. M. A. Carson. (Monographs in Spatial & Environmental Systems Analysis). (Illus.). 174p. 1971. 16.95x o.p. (ISBN 0-85086-029-6, NO. 2946, Pub. by Pion England). Routledge Chapman & Hall.

Mechanics of Fibre Composites. V. K. Tewary. LC 77-29117. 288p. 1978. 24.95x o.p. (ISBN 0-470-99240-9). Halsted Pr.

Mechanics of Fluids. 5th ed. B. Massey. 1984. pap. 23.95 o.p. (ISBN 0-442-30552-4); pap. 12.95 o.p. (ISBN 0-442-30611-3). Van Nos Reinhold.

Mechanics of Fracture & Fatigue: An Introduction. A. P. Parker. 1981. 33.00x o.p. (ISBN 0-419-11460-2, NO. 6495, Pub. by E & FN Spon); pap. 16.95x o.p. (ISBN 0-419-11470-X, NO. 6494). Routledge Chapman & Hall.

Mechanics of Generalized Continua: Proceedings of the Generalized Cosserat Continuum & the Continuum Theory of Dislocations with Applications, Freudenstadt & Stuttgart, 1967. Generalized Cosserat Continuum & the Continuum Theory of Dislocations with Applications Symposium Staff. Ed. by E. Kroener. LC 68-22401. 1968. 61.00 o.p. (ISBN 0-387-04264-4). Springer-Verlag.

Mechanics of Healing: Spinology. Parnell Bradbury. 1967. 10.00 o.p. (ISBN 0-87556-038-5). Saifer.

Mechanics of Materials. E. J. Hearn. 730p. 1977. text ed. 89.00 o.p. (ISBN 0-08-020618-2); Part 1. pap. text ed. 26.00 o.p. (ISBN 0-08-018749-8); Part 2. pap. text ed. 19.75 o.p. (ISBN 0-08-020617-4). Pergamon.

Mechanics of Materials: Set SI Version. 3rd ed. Archie Higdon et al. LC 77-7069. 752p. 1978. 45.95 o.p. (ISBN 0-471-02379-5). Wiley.

Mechanics of Non-Newtonian Fluids. William R. Schowalter. LC 76-51440. 1978. 75.00 o.p. (ISBN 0-08-021778-8). Pergamon.

Mechanics of Patent Claim Drafting. 2nd ed. John L. Landis. 549p. 1974. 50.00 o.p. (ISBN 0-685-85387-X, G1-0633). PLI.

Mechanics of Porous & Fractured Media: W.S. Series in Theorical & Applied Mechanics. V. N. Nikolaeuskij. (Vol.8). 600p. 1989. 85.00 o.p. (ISBN 9971-50-383-2). World Scientific Pub.

Mechanics of Sediment Transport. 2nd ed. Mehmet S. Yalin. 1977. 90.00 o.p. (ISBN 0-08-021162-3). Pergamon.

Mechanics of Solids, Vol. 2: Linear Theories of Elasticity & Thermoelasticity, Linear & Nonlinear Theories of Rods, Plates, & Shells. Ed. by C. Truesdell. (Illus.). 760p. 1984. pap. 48.00 o.p. (ISBN 0-387-13161-2). Springer-Verlag.

Mechanics of Superconducting Structurés. Ed. by F. C. Moon. (AMD: No. 41). 137p. 1980. 24.00 o.p. (ISBN 0-686-69856-8, G00174). ASME.

Mechanics of Track Support, Piles, & Geotechnical Data. (Transportation Research Record Ser.). 108p. 1979. 5.80 o.p. (ISBN 0-309-02988-0). Transport Res Bd.

Mechanics of Transportation Suspension Systems, AMD Vol. 15. Ed. by B. Paul. 110p. 1975. pap. text ed. 12.00 o.p. (ISBN 0-685-62563-X, I00095). ASME.

Mechanics of Underwriting 1986. 679p. 1986. 15.00 o.p. (B4-6740). PLI.

Mechanics of Wave Forces on Offshore Structures. Turgut Sarpkaya & Michael Isaacson. 624p. 1981. 51.95 o.p. (ISBN 0-442-25402-4). Van Nos Reinhold.

Mechanising Vegetable Production. John Robertson. (Illus.). 196p. 16.95 o.p. (ISBN 0-85236-088-6, Pub. by Farming Pr UK). Diamond Farm Bk.

Mechanism & Application of Leao's Spreading Depression of Electroencephalographic Activity. Jan Bures et al. 1974. 87.50 o.p. (ISBN 0-12-142960-1). Acad Pr.

Mechanism of Drug Action: Symposium. Ed. by Thomas P. Singer et al. LC 83-22362. 1984. 52.50 o.p. (ISBN 0-12-646680-7). Acad Pr.

Mechanism of Epoxidation of Olefins by Pelacids. V. G. Dryuk. 1977. pap. 32.00 o.p. (ISBN 0-08-021586-6). Pergamon.

Mechanism of the Linotype. John S. Thompson. Ed. by John Bidwell. Bd. with History of Composing Machines. LC 78-74413. (Nineteenth Century Book Arts & Printing History Ser.: Vol. 23). (Illus.). 1980. lib. bdg. 46.00 o.p. (ISBN 0-8240-3897-5). Garland Pub.

Mechanism of Toxic Action on Some Target Organs. Ed. by P. L. Chambers & P. Guenze. (Archives of Toxicology: Supplements Vol. 2). (Illus.). 1979. pap. 58.00 o.p. (ISBN 0-387-09305-2). Springer-Verlag.

Mechanisms & Control of Cell Division. Ed. by Thomas L. Rost & Ernest M. Gifford. 1977. 61.00 o.p. (ISBN 0-12-787370-8). Acad Pr.

Mechanisms & Treatment of Cardiac Arrhythmias: Relevance of Basic Studies to Clinical Management. Ed. by H. Joseph Reiser & Leonard Horowitz. (Illus.). 386p. 1984. text ed. 47.50 o.p. (ISBN 0-8067-1621-5). Urban & S.

Mechanisms in Allergy: Reagin-Mediated Hypersensitivity. Ed. by L. Goodfriend et al. (Immunology Ser: Vol. 1). 608p. 1973. 95.00 o.p. (ISBN 0-8247-6074-3). Dekker.

Mechanisms in Bioenergetics. Ed. by G. F. Azzone. 1973. 77.00 o.p. (ISBN 0-12-068960-X). Acad Pr.

Mechanisms in Modern Engineering Design, Vol. II. I. Artobolevsky. (Illus.). 1059p. 1979. 15.00 o.p. (ISBN 0-8285-0687-6, Pub. by Mir Pubs USSR). Imported Pubns.

Mechanisms in Modern Engineering Design, Vol. IV. I. Artobolevsky. (Illus.). 663p. 1977. 9.45 o.p. (ISBN 0-8285-0689-2, Pub. by Mir Pubs USSR). Imported Pubns.

Mechanisms in Modern Engineering Design, Vol. V; Pt. 2. I. I. Artobolevsky. (Illus.). 1980. 9.95 o.p. (ISBN 0-8285-1791-6, Pub. by Mir Pubs USSR). Imported Pubns.

Mechanisms of Animal Discrimination & Learning. N. S. Sutherland & N. J. MacKintosh. LC 79-127705. 1971. 81.00 o.p. (ISBN 0-12-677750-0). Acad Pr.

Mechanisms of Cell-Mediated Cytotoxicity. Ed. by William R. Clark & Pierre Golstein. LC 82-5312. (Advances in Experimental Medicine & Biology: Vol. 146). 610p. 1982. 95.00x o.p. (ISBN 0-306-41012-5, Plenum Pr). Plenum Pub.

Mechanisms of Cognitive Development. Ed. by Robert J. Sternberg. (Illus.). 224p. 1984. text ed. 21.95 o.p. (ISBN 0-7167-1596-1); pap. text ed. 13.95 o.p. (ISBN 0-7167-1597-X). W H Freeman.

Mechanisms of Color Vision. W. S. Stiles. 1978. 82.00 o.p. (ISBN 0-12-671350-2). Acad Pr.

Mechanisms of Deformation & Fracture: Proceedings of the Interdisciplinary Conference, Held at the University of Lulea-Sweden, 20-22, September 1978. Ed. by K. Easterling. (Strength & Fracture of Materials & Structures). 1979. 140.00 o.p. (ISBN 0-08-024258-8). Pergamon.

Mechanisms of Immunity to Virus-Induced Tumors. Blasecki. (Immunology Ser.: Vol. 12). 376p. 1981. 69.75 o.p. (ISBN 0-8247-1162-9). Dekker.

Mechanisms of Immunological Tolerance: Proceedings. Ed. by Milan Hasek et al. 1963. 85.00 o.p. (ISBN 0-12-330250-1). Acad Pr.

Mechanisms of Invasion in Cancer. Ed. by Pierre Denoix. (UICC Monograph Ser.: Vol. 6). (Illus.). 1967. 34.30 o.p. (ISBN 0-387-04008-0). Springer-Verlag.

Mechanisms of Memory. E. Roy John. 1967. text ed. 24.00 o.p. (ISBN 0-12-385850-X). Acad Pr.

Mechanisms of Mineralization in the Invertebrates & Plants. Ed. by Norimitsu Watabe & Karl M. Wilbur. LC 76-43986. (Belle W. Baruch Library in Marine Science: No. 5). xiv, 462p. 1976. 42.95x o.p. (ISBN 0-87249-351-2). U of SC Pr.

Mechanisms of Neurological Disease. Anthony J. Lewis. 1976. 39.00 o.p. (ISBN 0-316-52336-4). Little.

Mechanisms of Polyreactions - Polymer Characterization. J. P. Kennedy et al. (Advances in Polymer Science Ser.: Vol. 21). (Illus.). 1976. 40.00 o.p. (ISBN 0-387-07727-8). Springer-Verlag.

Mechanisms of Release of Biogenic Amines. Ed. by U. S. Von Euler et al. 1966. 120.00 o.p. (ISBN 0-08-011698-1). Pergamon.

Mechanisms of Saccharide Polymerization & Depolymerization. Ed. by J. John Marshall. LC 80-16155. 1980. 52.50 o.p. (ISBN 0-12-474150-9). Acad Pr.

Mechanisms of Speech Recognitions. W. A. Ainsworth. (International Ser. in Natural Philosophy). (Illus.). 140p. 1976. 40.00 o.p. (ISBN 0-08-020395-7); pap. text ed. 23.00 o.p. (ISBN 0-08-020394-9). Pergamon.

Mechanisms of Toxicity & Metabolism: Proceedings of the 6th International Congress of Pharmacology, Helsinki, 1975, Vol. 6. Ed. by N. Karki. 240p. 1976. 100.00 o.p. (ISBN 0-08-020544-5). Pergamon.

Mechanistic Studies of DNA Replication & Genetic Recombination. Ed. by Bruce Alberts & C. Fred Fox. (ICN-UCLA Symposia on Molecular & Cellular Biology Ser.: Vol. XIX). 1980. 44.00 o.p. (ISBN 0-12-048850-7). Acad Pr.

Mechanized Battlefield: A Tactical Analysis. Ed. by John A. English & James Addicott. (Illus.). 202p. 1985. 36.00 o.p. (ISBN 0-08-025405-5). Pergamon.

Mechanoreceptors of the Mammalian Skin: Ultrastructure & Morphological Classification. Z. Halata. (Advances in Anatomy, Embryology & Cell Biology: Vol. 50, Pt. 5). (Illus.). 77p. 1975. pap. 31.90 o.p. (ISBN 0-387-07097-4). Springer-Verlag.

Mechido, Aziza, & Ahmed. Giggy Lezra. LC 69-18969. (Illus.). (gr. 3-7). 1969. lib. bdg. 3.81 o.p. (ISBN 0-689-20233-4, Atheneum). Macmillan.

Medallion Style: A Study in the Origins of Byzantine Taste. James Trilling. Ed. by S. J. Freedberg. (Outstanding Dissertations in Fine Arts Ser.). (Illus.). 140p. 1985. Repr. of 1980 ed. 30.00 o.p. (ISBN 0-8240-6870-X). Garland Pub.

Medallion World Atlas: New Census Edition. rev. ed. Ed. by Martin A. Bacheller. LC 84-675070. (Hammond World Atlas Ser.). (Illus.). 672p. 1986. 65.00 o.p. (ISBN 0-8437-1250-3). Hammond Inc.

Media: A Pocket Guide. Harun Arrasjid & Dorine Arrasjid. 250p. 1972. pap. text ed. 6.95x o.p. (ISBN 0-8422-0255-2). Irvington.

Media & Adult Learning: A Bibliography. John Ohliger & David Gueulette. LC 75-5124. (Reference Library of Humanities: Vol. 18). 486p. 1975. lib. bdg. 64.00 o.p. (ISBN 0-8240-1088-4). Garland Pub.

Media & Kids: Real-World Learning in the Schools. James Morrow & Murray Suid. LC 76-39941. 1977. 9.50x o.p. (ISBN 0-8104-5798-9). Boynton Cook Pubs.

Media & Symbols: The Forms of Expression, Communication, & Education. Ed. by David R. Olson. LC 6-16938. (NSSE 73rd Yearbook: Part 1). 560p. 1974. 10.00x o.s.i. (ISBN 0-226-60114-5). U of Chicago Pr.

Media & the Formation of Public Opinion: A Checklist, 1975-1984. Dale E. Casper. (Public Administration Ser.: P 1687). 17p. 1985. 2.25 o.p. (ISBN 0-89028-417-2). Vance Biblios.

Media Canada: Guidelines for Educators. 2nd rev. ed. Ed. by James D. Miller. 1974. text ed. 4.85 o.p. (ISBN 0-08-016508-7). Pergamon.

Media-Classroom Skills: Games for the Middle School, 2 vols, Vol. 2. Jeanne E. Wieckert & Irene W. Bell. LC 81-2304. (Illus.). 250p. 1981. Vol. 1. lib. bdg. 18.50 o.p. (ISBN 0-87287-227-0); Vol. 2. lib. bdg. write for info. o.p. (ISBN 0-87287-236-X). Libs Unl.

Media Industries: The Production of News & Entertainment. Joseph Turow. LC 83-17519. (Communication Ser.). 288p. 1984. text ed. 36.95 o.p. (ISBN 0-582-28359-0). Longman.

Media Insurance & Risk Management, 1985. Practising Law Institute Staff & John C. Lankenau. LC 85-61644. (Patents, Copyrights, Trademarks, & Literary Property Course Handbks.: No. 205). 544p. 1985. 15.00 o.p. (G43770). PLI.

Media Insurance: Protecting Against High Judgments, Punitive Damages, & Defense Costs. Practising Law Institute Staff & John C. Landenau. LC 83-61575. (Patents, Copyrights, Trademarks, & Literary Property Course Handbook Ser.: No. 162). 520p. 1983. 40.00 o.p. (ISBN 0-317-01782-9). PLI.

Media, Knowledge & Power. Ed. by Oliver Boyd-Barrett & Peter Braham. 368p. 1986. pap. 14.95 o.p. (ISBN 0-7099-5026-8, Pub. by Croom Helm UK). Routledge Chapman & Hall.

Media Law Handbook. 2nd ed. Stuart M. Robertson. 146p. 1983. 6.50 o.p. (ISBN 0-88908-574-9). ISC Pr.

Media Manipulation: A Study of the Press & Bismarck in Imperial Germany. Robert H. Keyserlingk. 1977. pap. text ed. 8.00x o.p. (ISBN 0-685-87413-3). Gower Pub Co.

Media Matter: A Practical Guide to New Zealand Media. John Reynolds. (Illus.). 184p. 1986. pap. 18.95 o.p. (ISBN 0-7233-0700-8, Pub. by Whitcoulls NZ). Intl Spec Bk.

Media Mouse Collection. Jan Grubb. Ed. by Sally Sharpe. (Illus.). 80p. 1988. tchr's ed. 6.95 o.p. (ISBN 0-317-67335-1). Incentive Pubns.

Media Network's Guide to Films on Apartheid & the Southern African Region. 12p. 1986. Repr. of 1985 ed. 2.00 o.p. (ISBN 0-317-56000-X). Africa Fund.

Media Personnel Directory. Ed. by Alan E. Abrams. LC 79-12885. 1979. 80.00x o.p. (ISBN 0-8103-0421-X). Gale.

Media: Perspectives on the People's Right to Know. Close Up Foundation Staff. (Illus.). 30p. 1987. pap. text ed. 6.00x o.p. (ISBN 0-932765-14-9); tchr's. guide avail. o.p. Close Up Foun.

Media Power: Who Is Shaping Your Picture of the World? Robert Stein. Orig. Title: Overexposed Society. 1972. 9.95 o.p. (ISBN 0-395-14006-4). HM.

Media Resources Catalog. Ed. by Southeast Resource Center for Children & Youth Services Staff. 116p. (Orig.). 1984. 5.00 o.p. (ISBN 0-89695-011-5). U Tenn CSW.

Media Unbound: The Impact of Television Journalism on the Public. Stephen Lesher. 270p. 1982. 13.45 o.p. (ISBN 0-395-31827-0). HM.

Media Voices: Debating Critical Issues in Mass Media. George McKenna. LC 81-70655. (Contemporary Focus Paperback Ser.). 228p. 1982. 7.95 o.p. (ISBN 0-87967-245-5). Dushkin Pub.

Media-Wasteland Or Wonderland: Opportunities & Dangers for Christians in the Electronic Age. John W. Bachman. LC 84-24319. 176p. (Orig.). 1984. pap. 7.95 o.p. (ISBN 0-8066-2116-8, 10-4307, Augsburg). Augsburg Fortress.

Media with Microstructures & Wave Propagation: Proceedings of the Conference, Houghton, MI, January 1983. Ed. by E. C. Aifantis & L. Davison. 260p. 1985. pap. 130.00 o.p. (ISBN 0-08-031661-1). Pergamon.

Mediaeval Church. Marshall W. Baldwin. LC 82-2992. (Development of Western Civilization Ser.). xii, 124p. 1982. Repr. of 1953 ed. lib. bdg. 35.00x o.p. (ISBN 0-313-23554-6, BAME). Greenwood.

Mediaeval Islam: A Study in Cultural Orientation. 2nd ed. Ed. by Gustave E. Grunebaum. 1961. pap. 5.95 o.s.i. (ISBN 0-226-31025-6, p69, Phoen). U of Chicago Pr.

Mediaeval Latin Lyrics. Tr. by Helen Waddell. 1977. 12.95x o.p. (ISBN 0-393-04493-9, N873, Norton Lib); pap. 4.95x o.p. (ISBN 0-393-00873-8). Norton.

Mediaeval Society. Sidney Painter. LC 82-2934. (Development of Western Civilization Ser.). x, 109p. 1982. Repr. of 1951 ed. lib. bdg. 35.00x o.p. (ISBN 0-313-23551-1, PAML). Greenwood.

Mediaeval Spanish Allegory. Chandler R. Post. LC 73-137072. (Havard Studies in Comparative Literature: Vol. 4). (Illus.). 331p. 1974. Repr. of 1915 ed. lib. bdg. 22.50x o.p. (ISBN 0-8371-5535-5, POSA). Greenwood.

Mediaeval Statutes of the Faculty of Arts of the University of Freiburgh Im Breisgau. H. Ott & J. M. Fletcher. (Mediaeval Texts & Studies Ser.: No. 10). 1964. pap. 9.95x o.p. (ISBN 0-268-00173-1). U of Notre Dame Pr.

Mediamerica: Form, Content, & Consequence of Mass Communication. updated, 3rd ed. Edward J. Whetmore. 374p. 1987. pap. text ed. (ISBN 0-534-06804-9). Wadsworth Pub.

Mediaspeak: How Television Makes up Your Mind. Donna W. Cross. 288p. 1983. 13.95 o.p. (ISBN 0-698-11131-1, Coward). Putnam Pub Group.

Mediate Your Divorce: A Guide to Cooperative Custody, Property & Support Agreements. Joan Blades. (Illus.). 256p. 1985. pap. 17.95 o.p. (ISBN 0-13-572595-X). P-H.

Mediations: Essays on Brecht, Beckett & the Media. Martin Esslin. LC 81-48547. 256p. 1982. pap. 9.95 o.p. (ISBN 0-394-17970-6, E805, Ever). Grove.

Mediations on the Rosary. Anton Morgenrothy. 136p. 1987. 9.95 o.p. (ISBN 0-937495-01-8). Trinity Comns.

Mediators of Cellular Immunity. Ed. by H. S. Lawrence & M. Landy. (Perspectives in Immunology Ser.). 1969. 65.50 o.p. (ISBN 0-12-439350-0). Acad Pr.

Mediators of the Allergic State: Recent Investigations I. M. Snyderman et al. LC 72-6500. 199p. 1972. 27.50x o.p. (ISBN 0-8422-7032-9). Irvington.

Medicaid Nursing Home Reimbursement in Illinois. Bruce Spitz & Jane Weeks. LC 80-54797. (Illus.). 55p. (Orig.). 1981. pap. text ed. 7.00x o.p. (ISBN 0-87766-288-6). Urban Inst.

Medicaid Nursing Home Reimbursement in Minnesota. Bruce Spitz & Jane Weeks. LC 80-54798. (Illus.). 64p. (Orig.). 1981. pap. text ed. 7.00 o.p. (ISBN 0-87766-398-X). Urban Inst.

Medical Abbreviations & Acronyms. Peter Roody et al. 1976. text ed. 16.95 o.p. (ISBN 0-07-053604-X). McGraw.

Medical-Access. Richard S. Wurman. (Guidebook Ser.). (Illus.). 120p. 1985. pap. 9.95 o.p. (ISBN 0-915461-06-4). Access Pr.

Medical Acronyms & Abbreviations. Marilyn F. DeLong. 276p. 1985. 15.95 o.p. (ISBN 0-87489-392-5). Med Economics.

Medical & Biological Applications of Electrochemical Devices. J. Koryta. LC 79-41212. 331p. 1980. 135.00 o.p. (ISBN 0-471-27678-2). Wiley.

Medical & Biological Applications of Mass Spectroscopy. J. P. Payne et al. 1979. 54.50 o.p. (ISBN 0-12-547950-6). Acad Pr.

Medical & Clinical Aspects of Aging: Proceedings of the International Association of Gerontology, 5th Congress, Vol. 4. International Association of Gerontology Staff. Ed. by H. T. Blumenthal. LC 62-12876. (Aging Around the World Ser.). 690p. 1962. 67.00x o.p. (ISBN 0-231-08952-X). Columbia U Pr.

Medical & Health Care Books & Serials in Print, 1988, 2 vols. Ed. by Bowker, R. R., Staff. 2481p. 1988. Set. 139.95 o.p. (ISBN 0-8352-2470-8). Vol. 1 (ISBN 0-8352-2471-6). Vol. 2 (ISBN 0-8352-2472-4). Bowker.

Medical & Health Encyclopedia, 2 Vols. 756p. 1987. write for info. o.p. (ISBN 0-89434-082-4). Ferguson.

Medical & Health Encyclopedia. Ed. by Richard Waynman. 628p. 1987. (ISBN 0-89434-077-8). Ferguson.

Medical & Health Information Directory, Vol. 3. 3rd ed. Anthony T. Kruzas et al. 767p. 1986. 165.00x o.p. (ISBN 0-8103-0263-2). Gale.

Medical & Health Sciences Word Book. 2nd ed. 1981. 6.95 o.p. (ISBN 0-395-25409-4). HM.

Medical & Legal Professions. Ed. by Walter H. Rubsamen. (Ballad Opera Ser.: Vol. IV). 1974. lib. bdg. 61.00 o.p. (ISBN 0-8240-0903-7). Garland Pub.

Medical Annual 1981-82. Ronald B. Scott & James Fraser. 340p. 1981. text ed. 29.50 o.p. (ISBN 0-7236-0602-1). Butterworth.

Medical Annual 1982-83. Ronald B. Scott & James Fraser. (Illus.). 408p. 1982. pap. text ed. 29.50 o.p. (ISBN 0-7236-0655-2). Butterworth.

Medical Annual 1983. D. J. Gray. (Illus.). 320p. 1983. 35.00 o.p. (ISBN 0-7236-0688-9). Butterworth.

Medical Applications of Microcomputers. Ed. by William A. Corbett. LC 87-2123. 1987. 44.00 o.p. (ISBN 0-471-91499-1, Dist. by A R Liss). Wiley.

Medical Audiology: Disorders of Hearing. Ed. by Frederick N. Martin. (Illus.). 512p. 1981. text ed. (ISBN 0-13-572677-8). P-H.

Medical Care: A Bibliographical Overview of Cost Control. Coppa & Avery Consultants Staff. (Public Administration Ser.: P 1788). 11p. 1985. 2.00 o.p. (ISBN 0-89028-588-8). Vance Biblios.

Medical Care of the Elderly. 2nd ed. M. R. Hall et al. LC 85-22692. 192p. 1986. pap. 20.00 o.p. (ISBN 0-471-90906-8, Dist. by A R Liss). Wiley.

Medical Care Yearbook. Ed. by Prevention Magazine. 224p. 1988. 17.95 o.p. (ISBN 0-87857-748-3). Rodale Pr Inc.

Medical College Admission Test (MCAT) Lawrence Solomon & Morris Bramson. 448p. 1985. pap. 8.95 o.p. (ISBN 0-668-05608-8). Arco.

Medical Complications of Obesity. M. Mancini et al. LC 79-41151. (Serono Symposia Ser.: No. 26). 1980. 82.50 o.p. (ISBN 0-12-467150-0). Acad Pr.

Medical Desk Manual for Law Offices. Carol F. Montgomery. LC 82-71194. (Illus.). 167p. 1967. pap. 15.00 o.p. (ISBN 0-941916-01-4). Assn Trial Ed.

Medical Diagnostic Kits & Products. Business Communications Staff. 211p. 1984. 1500.00 o.p. (ISBN 0-89336-403-7, C-045). BCC.

Medical Directory 143rd Edition. 1987. 125.00 o.p.; Standing Order. 112.50 o.p. St James Pr.

Medical Directory 1986, 2 vols. 142nd ed. 1986. Set. 125.00 o.p. (ISBN 0-912289-73-2); Standing Order. 100.00 o.p. St James Pr.

Medical Doctors Guide to Herbs. John Heinerman. 128p. Date not set. pap. 7.95 o.p. (ISBN 0-913923-39-7). Woodland UT.

Medical Dosage Calculations. Olsen & Ablon. 1983. pap. 13.95 o.p. (ISBN 0-8053-7572-4); instr's. manual 9.95 o.p. (ISBN 0-8053-7573-2). Benjamin-Cummings.

Medical Economics Encyclopedia of Practice & Financial Management. Ed. by Lawrence Farber. 1984. 79.00 o.p. (ISBN 0-87489-343-7). Med Economics.

Medical Education in the United States: A Guide to Information Sources. Ed. by Francesco Cordasco & David N. Alloway. LC 79-24030. (Education Information Guide Ser.: Vol. 8). 426p. 1980. 68.00x o.p. (ISBN 0-8103-1458-4). Gale.

Medical Effects of Nuclear War. British Medical Association's Board of Science & Education Staff. 188p. 1983. pap. 11.95 o.p. (ISBN 0-471-90207-1, Dist. by A R Liss). Wiley.

Medical Electrical Equipment. R. F. Molloy. (Illus.). 320p. 1958. (ISBN 0-8022-1137-2). Philos Lib.

Medical Emergencies in Dentistry: Emergencies in Dental Practice. Abridged ed. Frank M. McCarthy. (Illus.). 422p. 1982. write for info. o.p. (ISBN 0-7216-5879-2). Saunders.

Medical Engineering: Projections for Health Care Delivery. Robert F. Rushmer. 1972. 84.00 o.p. (ISBN 0-12-603650-0). Acad Pr.

Medical Evidence. Joint Working Party of the BMA, the Bar Council, & the Law Society Staff. 1981. pap. 9.50x o.p. (ISBN 0-8002-3871-0, Pub. by British Med Assoc UK). Taylor & Francis.

Medical Examination Review: Nuclear Medicine, Vol. 25. 2nd ed. Nathan A. Solomon. 1984. pap. text ed. 27.75 o.p. Med Exam.

Medical Genetics: Principles & Practice. 2nd ed. James J. Nora & F. Clark Fraser. LC 81-11808. (Illus.). 540p. 1981. text ed. 42.50 o.p. (ISBN 0-8121-0766-7). Lea & Febiger.

Medical Geographic Research in Latin America. Ed. by C. Weil. 100p. 1982. pap. 18.00 o.p. (ISBN 0-08-028895-2). Pergamon.

Medical Geography South & Southeast Asia. Ed. by Ashok K. Dutt. (Illus.). 78p. 1981. pap. 24.00 o.p. (ISBN 0-08-026762-9). Pergamon.

Medical Group Practice Assessment Manual. 87p. 1979. 17.00 o.p. (ISBN 0-933948-08-5, 50-0000-910). Med Group Mgmt.

Medical Group Practice Management. Ed. by Francis F. Manning. 348p. 1977. 27.50 o.p. (ISBN 0-317-34841-8, 400001). Med Group Mgmt.

Medical Groups in the U. S., 1984. Penny L. Havlicek. 126p. 1985. pap. 29.95 o.p. (ISBN 0-89970-203-1, OP-256). AMA.

Medical Handbook for the Layman. Alfred J. Tyrone & C. Cannon-Alfred. 5.95 o.p. (ISBN 0-87505-137-5). Borden.

Medical Hubris: A Reply to Ivan Illich. David Horrobin. LC 80-66836. 146p. 1980. 9.95 o.p. (ISBN 0-88831-080-3); pap. 6.95 o.p. (ISBN 0-88831-086-2). Eden Pr.

Medical Imaging Markets. International Resource Development, Inc. Staff. 166p. 1983. 1285.00x o.p. (ISBN 0-88694-562-3). Intl Res Dev.

Medical Information Sources: A Referral Directory. 5th ed. American Medical Association Staff. 1988. pap. 19.95 o.p. (ISBN 0-89970-320-8). AMA.

Medical Librarian? What's That? Ilona von Magyary-Kossa. LC 74-79293. 1974. 6.00 o.p. (ISBN 0-682-47986-1). Exposition-Phoenix.

Medical Librarianship. John L. Thornton. 168p. (ISBN 0-8022-1722-2). Philos Lib.

Medical Lists for Examinations. Roger Gabriel & Cynthia M. Gabriel. 295p. (Orig.). 1983. pap. text ed. 27.95 o.p. (ISBN 0-407-00233-2). Butterworth.

Medical Malpractice. 250p. 1984. 25.00 o.p. (ISBN 0-88129-121-8). Wash Bar CLE.

Medical Malpractice Law: How Medicine Is Changing the Law. Barbara U. Werthmann. LC 83-49212. 304p. 1984. 38.00x o.p. (ISBN 0-669-07761-5). Lexington Bks.

Medical Malpractice Litigation. Pennsylvania Bar Institute Staff. 205p. 1988. 50.00 o.p. (ISBN 0-318-19060-5, 440). PA Bar Inst.

Medical Malpractice 1984. Ed. by Anne R. Grant. (Trial Annuals Ser.). (Illus.). 72p. (Orig.). 1985. pap. 15.00 o.p. (ISBN 0-941916-19-7). Assn Trial Ed.

Medical Mystery: The Training of Doctors in the United States. Steven Jonas. 1979. 15.00 o.p. (ISBN 0-393-06437-9). Norton.

Medical Negligence & Hospital Liability. Association of Trial Lawyers of America. Education Fund Staff. LC 84-71194. 91p. Date not set. price not set o.p. (ISBN 0-941916-14-6). Assn Trial Ed.

Medical Neurobiology: Neuroanatomical & Neurophysiological Principles Basic to Clinical Neuroscience. 3rd ed. William D. Willis, Jr. & Robert G. Grossman. LC 81-1390. (Illus.). 593p. 1981. text ed. 44.95 o.p. (ISBN 0-8016-5584-6). Mosby.

Medical Obituaries: American Physicans Biographical Notices in Selected Medical Journals before 1907. Lisabeth M. Holloway et al. LC 81-7084. (Garland Reference Library of Social Science: Vol. 104). 513p. 1981. 121.00 o.p. (ISBN 0-8240-9368-2). Garland Pub.

Medical Office Administrative Procedures. Mary A. Frew & David R. Frew. LC 81-17435. (Illus.). 343p. 1983. pap. 14.95x o.p. (ISBN 0-8036-3861-2). Davis Co.

Medical Oncology. Ed. by Lessner. (Fundamental & Clinical Aspects of Internal Medicine Ser.: Vol. 2). 170p. 1978. 37.00 o.p. (ISBN 0-444-00269-3, Biomedical Pr); pap. 27.00 o.p. (ISBN 0-444-00260-X). Elsevier.

Medical Palmistry: Health & Character in the Hand. Marten Steinbach. 1975. 8.95 o.p. (ISBN 0-8216-0222-5, Pub. by Univ Bks). Carol Pub Group.

Medical Parasitology. 3rd ed. J. Walter Beck & John E. Davies. LC 80-25201. (Illus.). 365p. 1981. pap. text ed. 29.95 o.p. (ISBN 0-8016-0552-0). Mosby.

Medical Parasitology: A Self-Instructional Text. 2nd ed. Ruth Leventhal & Russell F. Cheadle. LC 84-14971. (Illus.). 193p. 1985. pap. text ed. 26.95 o.p. (ISBN 0-8036-5597-5). Davis Co.

Medical Pharmacology at a Glance. Neal. 1986. 16.00 o.p. (ISBN 0-8016-3845-3). Mosby.

Medical Pharmacology: Principles & Concepts. 11th ed. Andres Goth & Elliot S. Vesell. (Illus.). 816p. 1984. pap. text ed. 34.95 o.p. (ISBN 0-8016-1962-9). Mosby.

Medical Phrase Index. Jean Lorenzini. 924p. 1978. 35.50 o.s.i. (ISBN 0-87489-198-1); pap. 27.95 o.s.i. Med Economics.

Medical Physiology. Ed. by Arthur M. Brown & Donald W. Stubbs. LC 82-8585. (Illus.). 904p. 1983. 37.95 o.p. (ISBN 0-471-05207-8). Wiley.

Medical Physiology, 2 vols. 14th ed. Vernon B. Mountcastle. LC 79-25943. (Illus.). 2192p. 1979. Set. 75.95 o.p. (ISBN 0-8016-3560-8); Vol. 1. 52.95 o.p. (ISBN 0-8016-3562-4); Vol. 2. 44.50 o.p. (ISBN 0-8016-3566-7). Mosby.

Medical Problems in Dentistry. C. Scully & R. A. Cawson. (Illus.). 528p. 1982. pap. 47.00 o.p. (ISBN 0-7236-0607-2). Butterworth.

Medical Radiation Biology. 2nd ed. Donald J. Pizzarello & Richard L. Witcofski. LC 81-19311. (Illus.). 164p. 1982. text ed. 18.50 o.p. (ISBN 0-8121-0834-5). Lea & Febiger.

Medical Self Care & Assessment. Brent Q. Hafen. (Illus.). 400p. 1983. pap. text ed. 13.95X o.p. Morton Pub.

Medical Sexology, Third International Congress. Ed. by Romano Forleo & Willy Pasini. LC 79-9435. (Illus.). 664p. 1980. 44.50 o.p. (ISBN 0-88416-255-9). Year Bk Med.

Medical Social Work in Action. Zofia Butrym. 128p. 1968. pap. text ed. 5.00x o.p. (ISBN 0-686-70850-4, Pub. by Bedford England). Gower Pub Co.

Medical Sociology. 3rd ed. William C. Cockerham. (Illus.). 380p. 1986. text ed. (ISBN 0-13-573429-0). P-H.

Medical Sociology. John A. Denton. LC 77-94098. (Illus.). 1978. text ed. 29.95 o.p. (ISBN 0-395-25805-7). HM.

Medical Staff: Drug Usage Evaluation. 60p. pap. cancelled o.s.i. (ISBN 0-86688-155-7). Joint Comm Hlthcare.

Medical Staff: Medical Record Function. 62p. pap. cancelled o.s.i. (ISBN 0-86688-157-3). Joint Comm Hlthcare.

Medical Staff: Pharmacy & Therapy. 56p. pap. cancelled o.s.i. (ISBN 0-86688-156-5). Joint Comm Hlthcare.

Medical Staff: Surgical Case Review. 57p. pap. cancelled o.s.i. (ISBN 0-86688-153-0). Joint Comm Hlthcare.

Medical-Surgical Nursing: Common Health Problems of Adults & Children Across the Life Span. Diane M. Billings & Lillian G. Stokes. LC 81-16856. (Illus.). 1450p. 1982. cloth 45.95 o.p. (ISBN 0-8016-0736-1). Mosby.

Medical-Surgical Nursing: Concepts & Clinical Practice. 2nd ed. Wilma J. Phipps et al. LC 82-18886. (Illus.). 2061p. 1983. 49.95 o.p. (ISBN 0-8016-3931-X). Mosby.

Medical-Surgical Nursing: Pretest Self-Assessment & Review. Ed. by Helen Chuan. Margaret Allman. LC 78-50598. (Illus.). 188p. 1978. pap. 13.95 o.p. (ISBN 0-07-051567-0). McGraw-Pretest.

Medical Technician, Medical Assistant, Medical Aide. Ed. by Hy Hammer. LC 81-20647. 176p. (Orig.). 1983. pap. 8.00 o.p. (ISBN 0-668-05370-4, 5370). Arco.

Medical Terminology: A Programmed Text. Phyllis E. Davis. 1976. incl. cassette 76.00 o.p. (ISBN 0-471-80202-6). Wiley.

Medical Terminology: A Programmed Text. 4th ed. Genevieve L. Smith & Phyllis E. Davis. LC 80-17970. 325p. 1981. pap. 18.95 o.p. (ISBN 0-471-05827-0). Wiley.

Medical Terminology for Medical Students. William B. Tyrrell. (Illus.). 176p. 1979. spiral bdg. 23.00 o.p. (ISBN 0-398-03820-1). C C Thomas.

Medical Terms: Their Origin & Construction. 6th, rev., enl. ed. B. Lennox. 1980. pap. 17.50 o.s.i. (ISBN 0-433-19151-1). E J Brill USA.

Medical Testimony in a Worker's Compensation Case. Massachusetts Continuing Legal Education, Inc. Staff. LC 84-61753. (Illus.). 1985. 50.00 o.p. Mass CLE.

Medical Trial Technique Quarterly: 1955-1983, 33 vols. Ed. by Fred Lane. LC 72-135162. 850.00 o.p. Callaghan.

Medical Virology. Frank J. Fenner & David O. White. 1976. 33.00 o.p. (ISBN 0-12-253060-8). Acad Pr.

Medical X-Ray Photo-Optical Systems Evaluation: Proceedings, Vol. 56. Society of Photo-Optical Instrumentation Engineers Staff. (SPIE Seminar Proceedings). 256p. 1975. 16.00 o.p. (ISBN 0-89252-068-X). SPIE.

Medicare & Prepaid Health Plans: New Directions for HMO's. 28p. 1985. pap. 6.00 o.p. (ISBN 0-89970-267-8, OP-196). AMA.

Medicare Directory of Prevailing Charges, 1984. 291p. 1984. pap. 9.00 o.p. (ISBN 0-318-11801-7, S/N 017-060-00161-5). USGPO.

Medicare, Medicaid & the Law. Pennsylvania Bar Institute Staff. 283p. 1983. 30.00 o.p. (ISBN 0-318-02173-0, 240). PA Bar Inst.

Medicare Program Statistics: Health Care Financing Administration, Selected State Data, 1978-1982. 92p. 1984. pap. 4.50 o.p. (ISBN 0-318-11802-5, S/N 017-060-00156-9). USGPO.

Medication Cards for Clinical Use, 1986. Linda C. Skidmore-Roth. 1986. pap. 17.95 o.p. (ISBN 0-8385-6301-5). Appleton & Lange.

Medication Error. Neil M. Davis. 270p. 1981. 15.95 o.p. G F Stickley Co.

Medication Law & Behavior. J. Tyrone Gibson. 429p. 1976. 27.50 o.p. (ISBN 0-471-29760-7, Pub. by John Wiley). Krieger.

Medication Teaching Manual. 3rd ed. 350p. 1983. pap. 20.00 o.p. (ISBN 0-930530-31-4). Am Soc Hosp Pharm.

Medications & Mathematics for the Nurse. 5th ed. Esther Skelley. (Practical Nursing Ser.). (Illus.). 280p. 1982. pap. text ed. 16.95 o.p. (ISBN 0-8273-1923-1); instr's. guide 7.00 o.p. (ISBN 0-8273-1950-9). Delmar.

Medications & Mathematics for the Nurse. Esther Skelley. 1981. 22.95 o.p. (ISBN 0-442-21882-6). Van Nos Reinhold.

Medicinal Chemistry Advances: Proceedings of the International Symposium on Medicinal Chemistry, 7th International Symposium Torremolinos, 2-5 September 1980. Ed. by F. G. de las Heras & S. Vega. LC 81-81913. (Illus.). 528p. 1981. 105.00 o.p. (ISBN 0-08-025297-4). Pergamon.

Medicine: An Illustrated History. Albert S. Lyons & R. Joseph Petrucelli. (Illus.). 1978. 75.00 o.p. (ISBN 0-8109-1054-3). Abrams.

Medicine & Politics Among the Grand River Iroquois: A Study of the Non-Conservatives. Sally M. Weaver. (Illus.). 182p. 1972. pap. text ed. 7.50x o.p. (ISBN 0-660-00059-8, 56431-2, Pub. by Natl Mus Canada). U of Chicago Pr.

Medicine Bow. Lauran Paine. (Lythway Ser.). 176p. 1988. lib. bdg. 17.50x o.p. (ISBN 0-7451-0677-3, Pub. by Chivers Pr UK). G K Hall.

Medicine Cabinet. Byron G. Wels. Ed. by Frank Brady. LC 78-5517. (Illus.). 192p. 1978. 9.95 o.p. (ISBN 0-8437-3407-8); pap. 6.95 o.p. (ISBN 0-8437-3408-6). Hammond Inc.

Medicine for Mountaineering. 2nd ed. Ed. by James A. Wilkerson. LC 75-31059. (Illus.). 350p. 1977. flexible plastic 8.95 o.p. (ISBN 0-916890-06-6). Mountaineers.

Medicine for the Practicing Physician. J. Willis Hurst. 2000p. 1983. text ed. 85.00 o.p. (ISBN 0-409-95031-9). Butterworth.

Medicine for the Soul. Maurice Bassali. 352p. 1986. 14.95 o.p. (ISBN 0-8062-2905-5). Carlton.

Medicine Knife. Don Coldsmith. (Double D Western Ser.). 192p. 1988. pap. 12.95 o.p. (ISBN 0-385-23521-6). Doubleday.

Medicine Man: A Young Doctor on the Brink of the Twenty-First Century. David Black. 192p. 1985. 14.95 o.p. (ISBN 0-531-09702-1). Watts.

Medicine Man of the Early American Indian & His Cultural Background. William T. Corlett. (Illus.). 369p. 1935. 34.50x o.p. (ISBN 0-398-04233-0). C C Thomas.

Medicine: Pre-Test Self-Assessment & Review. 3rd ed. PreTest Service, Inc. Staff & J. M. Dwyer. (Clinical Science Ser.). 272p. 1985. pap. text ed. 13.95 o.p. (ISBN 0-07-051004-0). McGraw.

Medicine, Science & Society: Symposia Celebrating the Harvard Medical School Bicentennial. Ed. by Kurt J. Isselbacher. 746p. 1984. 75.00 o.p. (ISBN 0-471-88882-6). Wiley.

Medicine: The Bare Bones. E. H. Friedman & R. Moshy. LC 85-26619. 1986. (ISBN 0-471-90823-1, Dist. by A R Liss). Wiley.

Medicine Woman. Lynn V. Andrews. LC 81-47546. (Illus.). 288p. 1981. 12.98i o.s.i. (ISBN 0-06-250025-2). HarpR.

Medicines & Drugs: Problems & Risks, Use & Abuse. 2nd ed. Brent Q. Hafen & Brenda Peterson. LC 78-5901. (Illus.). 429p. 1978. pap. 12.75 o.p. (ISBN 0-8121-0637-7). Lea & Febiger.

Medicolegal Handbook: A Guide for Winning Verdicts. Ficarra. 240p. 1983. 49.75 o.p. (ISBN 0-8247-7005-6). Dekker.

Medieval & Renaissance Medicine. B. L. Gordon. 856p. 1960. (ISBN 0-8022-0609-3). Philos Lib.

Medieval Architecture. LC 76-14066. (Garland Library of the History of Art: Vol. IV). 1977. lib. bdg. 61.00 o.p. (ISBN 0-8240-2414-1). Garland Pub.

Medieval Art. LC 76-14067. (Garland Library of the History of Art: Vol. V). 1977. lib. bdg. 61.00 o.p. (ISBN 0-8240-2415-X). Garland Pub.

Medieval Art. Charles R. Morey. (Illus.). 1942. 16.95x o.p. (ISBN 0-393-04170-0, NortonC). Norton.

Medieval Art, Three Hundred Twenty-One to Thirteen Fifty. W. R. Lethaby. (ISBN 0-8022-0960-2). Philos Lib.

Medieval Britain from the Air. Colin Platt. (Illus.). 224p. 1984. 27.95 o.p. (ISBN 0-540-01077-4, Pub. by G Philip UK). Sheridan.

Medieval Contribution to Political Thought: Thomas Aquinas, Marsilius of Padua, Richard Hooker. Alexander P. D'Entreves. 1959. Repr. of 1939 ed. text ed. 12.50x o.p. (ISBN 0-391-00513-8). Humanities.

Medieval Cosmology: Theories of Infinity, Place, Time, Void, & the Plurality of Worlds. Pierre Duhem. Ed. by Roger Ariew. LC 85-8115. 642p. 1986. 35.00x o.s.i. (ISBN 0-226-16922-7). U of Chicago Pr.

Medieval Cultural Tradition in Dante's Comedy. Joseph A. Mazzeo. LC 68-23313. (Illus.). 1968. Repr. of 1960 ed. lib. bdg. 24.75x o.p. (ISBN 0-8371-0166-2, MADC). Greenwood.

Medieval England: A Social History & Archaeology from the Conquest to 1600 A. D. Colin Platt. (Illus.). 1978. encore ed. 9.95 o.p. (ISBN 0-684-17247-X, ScribT). Scribner.

Medieval English Episcopal Registers. Louis A. Haselmayer. (Church Historical Society, London, New Ser.: No. 34). pap. 35.00 o.p. (ISBN 0-8115-3157-0). Kraus Repr.

Medieval Handbooks of Penance. John T. McNeill & Helena M. Gamer. 1965. lib. bdg. 40.00x o.p. (ISBN 0-374-95548-4, Octagon). Hippocrene Bks.

Medieval History & Civilization. Daniel D. McGarry. (Illus.). 896p. 1976. text ed. (ISBN 0-02-379100-4). Macmillan.

Medieval History: Selected Course Outlines & Reading Lists from Leading American Colleges & Universities in History. rev., 3rd ed. Ed. & Penelope D. Johnson. 300p. (Orig.). 1986. pap. text ed. 14.50x o.p. Wiener Pub Inc.

Medieval Humanism: And Other Stories. R. W. Southern. (Illus.). 288p. 1984. pap. 14.95x o.p. (ISBN 0-631-13649-5). Basil Blackwell.

Medieval Humanism: And Other Studies. R. W. Southern. (Illus.). 288p. 1970. 24.95x o.p. (ISBN 0-631-12440-3). Basil Blackwell.

Medieval India. Romila Thapar. (Illus.). 1970. pap. 2.00 o.s.i. (ISBN 0-88253-276-6). Ind-US Inc.

Medieval Islam. Dominique Sourdel. 160p. 1983. 21.95x o.p. (ISBN 0-7100-9453-1). Routledge Chapman & Hall.

Medieval Legacy: A Symposium. Ed. by Andreas Haarder et al. 172p. 1982. pap. text ed. 22.50x o.p. (ISBN 87-7492-393-5). Humanities.

Medieval Lore. Anglicus Bartholomaeus. Ed. by R. Steele. LC 66-23970. (Medieval Library). Repr. of 1926 ed. 18.50x o.p. (ISBN 0-8154-0016-0). Cooper Sq.

Medieval Manuscripts for Mass & Office: A Guide to Their Organization & Terminology. Andrew Hughes. 496p. 1981. 65.00x o.p. (ISBN 0-8020-5467-6). U of Toronto Pr.

Medieval Manuscripts: Part 3 of Biblioteca Pepysiana, a Descriptive Catalogue of the Library of Samuel Pepys. M. R. James. 20.00x o.p. (ISBN 0-87556-471-2). Saifer.

Medieval Panorama: The English Scene from Conquest to Reformation. G. G. Coulton. (Illus.). 816p. 1974. pap. 4.95 o.p. (ISBN 0-393-00708-1, Norton Lib). Norton.

Medieval Philosophy. Frederick C. Copleston. (ISBN 0-8022-0302-7). Philos Lib.

Medieval Political Ideas. Ewart Lewis. LC 73-82907. vii, 661p. 1973. Repr. of 1954 ed. lib. bdg. 42.50x o.p. (ISBN 0-8154-0485-9). Cooper Sq.

Medieval Representative Institutions: Their Origins & Nature. Ed. by Thomas N Bisson. (European Problem Ser.). 154p. 1973. pap. 6.50 o.p. (Pub. by HR&W). Krieger.

Medieval Romance: Themes & Approaches. John Stevens. 256p. 1974. pap. 3.45x o.p. (ISBN 0-393-00715-4, Norton Lib). Norton.

Medieval Slavdom & the Rise of Russia. Frank Nowak. LC 75-110051. xii, 132p. Repr. of 1930 ed. lib. bdg. 35.00x o.p. (ISBN 0-8371-4436-1, NOMS). Greenwood.

Medieval Trade in the Mediterranean World: Illustrative Documents. Ed. by Robert S. Lopez & Irving W. Raymond. (Columbia University Records of Civilization Series). 1967. pap. 5.95x o.p. (ISBN 0-393-09720-X, NortonC). Norton.

Medieval Travellers. Margaret W. Labarge. (Illus.). 1983. 17.00 o.p. (ISBN 0-393-01739-7). Norton.

Medina. Mary McCarthy. LC 72-79919. 88p. 1972. pap. 2.45 o.p. (ISBN 0-15-158530-X, Harv). HarBraceJ.

Medinet Habu - Epigraphic Survey: The Calendar, the Slaughterhouse, & Minor Records of Ramses III, Vol. 3. Harold H. Nelson. LC 30-6904. (Oriental Institute Pubns. Ser: No. 23). 1934. lib. bdg. 70.00x o.s.i. (ISBN 0-226-62119-7, OIP23). U of Chicago Pr.

Medinet Habu Graffiti. Ed. by William F. Edgerton. LC 42-23005. (Oriental Institute Pubns. Ser: No. 36). (Illus.). 1937. lib. bdg. 40.00x o.s.i. (ISBN 0-226-62133-2). U of Chicago Pr.

Meditate Upon These Things. 2nd ed. Compiled by Linda Lee. (Illus.). 160p. 1981. pap. 5.00 o.p. (ISBN 0-87516-463-3). DeVorss.

Meditation: Escape to Reality. Thomas H. Troeger. 1977. pap. 4.95 o.s.i. (ISBN 0-664-24132-8, Westminster). Westminster John Knox.

Meditation for Beginners. Wedgewood. 2.50 o.p. (ISBN 0-8356-5050-2). Theos Pub Hse.

Meditation in Christianity. 2nd ed. Himalayan International Institute Staff. LC 79-92042. 1979. pap. 1.95 o.p. (ISBN 0-89389-063-4). Himalayan Pubs.

Meditation Made Easy. W. P. Petersen & Terry Fehr. (Concise Guides Ser.). (Illus.). (gr. 6 up). 1979. s&l 10.90 o.p. (ISBN 0-531-02894-1). Watts.

Meditation on Emptiness, Pt. VI. Jeffrey Hopkins. Ed. by Elizabeth Napper. (Wisdom Advanced Book: Blue Ser.). (Illus.). 1015p. 1983. 35.00 o.p. (ISBN 0-86171-014-2). Wisdom MA.

Meditations. J. Krishnamurti. LC 79-1784. 1979. gift box 11.95i o.p. (ISBN 0-06-064851-1). HarpR.

Meditations at Ten Thousand Feet: A Scientist in the Mountains. James Trefil. (Illus.). 256p. 1986. 16.95 o.p. (ISBN 0-684-18627-6, Pub. by Scribner). Macmillan.

Meditations for Children. Diane Van Wert. 96p. 1987. 6.95 o.p. (ISBN 0-8062-2886-5). Carlton.

Meditations for Mature Christians. B. C. Schreiber. LC 85-90050. 1985. 13.95 o.p. (ISBN 0-533-06578-X). Vantage.

Meditations for Priests. David M. Knight. 1978. write for info. o.p. (ISBN 0-915488-05-1). Clarity Pub.

Meditations in an Emergency. Frank O'Hara. 1957. pap. 4.95 o.p. (ISBN 0-394-17343-0, E413, Ever). Grove.

Meditations on a Hobby Horse: And Other Essays on the Theory of Art. E. H. Gombrich. LC 84-28112. (Illus.). x, 135p. 1985. pap. 14.95 o.s.i. (ISBN 0-226-30215-6). U of Chicago Pr.

Meditations on Death & Life. Sterling W. Sill. LC 83-80406. 129p. 1983. 7.95 o.p. (ISBN 0-88290-212-1). Horizon-Utah.

Meditations on Freedom & the Spirit. Karl Rahner. 1978. pap. 3.95 o.p. (ISBN 0-8245-0325-2). Crossroad NY.

Meditations on Hope & Love. Karl Rahner. LC 77-76614. 1977. pap. 3.95 o.p. (ISBN 0-8245-0326-0). Crossroad NY.

Meditations on Quixote. Jose Ortega Y Gasset. 1963. pap. 3.95 o.p. (ISBN 0-393-00125-3, Norton Lib). Norton.

Meditations on the Life of Christ: An Illustrated Manuscript of the Fourteenth Century. Ed. by Isa Ragusa & Rosalie B. Green. (Monographs in Art & Archeology: No. 35). (Illus.). 501p. 1975. 52.50x o.p. (ISBN 0-691-03829-5); pap. 11.50 o.p. (ISBN 0-691-10031-4). Princeton U Pr.

Mediterranean Cooking for Everyone. Kay S. Nelson. 11.25 o.p. (ISBN 0-8446-5798-0). Peter Smith.

Mediterranean Diet: Optimal Nutrition for a Long Healthy Life. Carol McConnell & Malcolm McConnell. 1987. 16.45 o.p. (ISBN 0-393-02438-5). Norton.

Mediterranean Europe & the Common Market: Studies of Economic Growth & Integration. Ed. by Eric N. Baklanoff. LC 75-19056. (Mediterranean Europe Ser.: No. 2). 255p. 1976. 20.00 o.p. (ISBN 0-8173-4605-8). U of Ala Pr.

Mediterranean Food. rev. ed. Elizabeth David. (Handbooks Ser). 1956. pap. 5.95 o.p. (ISBN 0-14-046027-6). Penguin.

Mediterranean in the Ancient World. John H. Rose. 1970. Repr. of 1934 ed. lib. bdg. 25.00x o.p. (ISBN 0-8371-1933-2, ROME). Greenwood.

Mediterranean Island Hopping: The Italian Islands, Corsica & Malta. Dana Facaros & Michael Pauls. (Travel Ser.). (Illus.). 500p. 1981. pap. 12.95 o.p. (ISBN 0-88254-589-2, Regnery-Gateway). Hippocrene Bks.

Mediterranean Island Hopping: The Spanish Islands. 2nd ed. Dana Facaros & Michael Pauls. (Handbooks for the Independent Traveller Ser.). (Illus.). 304p. 1982. pap. 12.95 o.p. (ISBN 0-88254-588-4, Regnery-Gateway). Hippocrene Bks.

Mediterranean-Type Ecosystems: Origin & Structure. Ed. by F. DiCastri & H. A. Mooney. LC 72-95688. (Ecological Studies Ser.: Vol. 7). (Illus.). 500p. 1973. 55.00 o.p. (ISBN 0-387-06106-1). Springer-Verlag.

Medium Aevum & the Middle Age see Metaphor.

Medium & High Speed Diesel Engines for Marine Use. S. H. Henshall. 418p. 1972. 27.00 o.p. (ISBN 0-900976-77-2, Pub. by Inst Marine Eng). Intl Spec Bk.

Medium Format Handbook: A Guide to Rollfilm Photography. Roger W. Hicks. (Illus.). 192p. 1986. pap. 22.50 o.p. (ISBN 0-7137-1657-6, Pub. by Blandford Pr England). Sterling.

Mednyanszky. I. Pataky-Brestyanszky. Tr. by Zsuzanna Horn. (Illus.). 1968. pap. 25.00 o.p. (ISBN 0-8283-1121-8). Branden Pub Co.

Medusa Complex. Marvin Albert. LC 81-66972. 320p. 1981. 13.95 o.p. (ISBN 0-87795-341-4, Arbor Hse). Morrow.

Medusa's Hair: An Essay on Personal Symbols & Religious Experiences. Gananath Obeyesekere. LC 80-27372. (Illus.). 252p. 1981. 22.50x o.s.i. (ISBN 0-226-61600-2). U of Chicago Pr.

Meed Index: Le Monde Index. Ed. by Research Publications, Inc. Staff. write for info. o.p. (ISBN 0-903713-79-9). Res Pubns CT.

MEED-TAIC Middle East Financial Directory. 10th ed. Middle East Economic Digest Staff. Ed. by Anna Krajewska. 420p. 1986. lib. bdg. 90.00x o.p. (ISBN 0-946510-16-4). Lynne Rienner.

Meet Andy Capp. Reginald Smythe. (Andy Capp Ser.). (Illus.). 128p. 1979. pap. 1.25 o.s.i. (ISBN 0-449-13716-3, GM). Fawcett.

Meet Baby Animals with E. T. Ed. by Kate Klimo. (Illus.). 14p. 1983. 3.80 o.s.i. (ISBN 0-671-46434-5, Little). S&S.

Meet Me at Tamerlane's Tomb. Barbara Corcoran. LC 74-19351. (Illus.). 160p. (gr. 5-9). 1975. PLB 6.95 o.p. (ISBN 0-689-30446-3, Atheneum). Macmillan.

Meet Me at the Melba. Bronte Woodward. 1978. pap. 1.95 o.s.i. (ISBN 0-440-15355-7). Dell.

Meet Me on the Patio: New Relational Bible Studies for Individuals & Groups. Karl A. Olsson. LC 77-72453. 1977. 7.95 o.p. (ISBN 0-8066-1550-8, 10-4301, Augsburg); pap. 4.50 o.p. (ISBN 0-8066-1590-7, 10-4300). Augsburg Fortress.

Meet the Ancient Greeks. X. L. Messinesi. LC 59-5485. (Illus.). 1959. 5.00 o.p. (ISBN 0-87004-102-9). Caxton.

Meet the Men Who Sailed the Seven Seas. John Dyment. (Step-up Bk). (gr. 2-6). 1966. lib. bdg. 4.99 o.s.i. (ISBN 0-394-90064-2, BYR). Random.

Meet the Muppet Babies. Louise Gikow. (Can You Imagine Ser.). (Illus.). 32p. (ps-2). 1986. pap. 1.95 o.p. (ISBN 0-517-56189-1). Crown.

Meet the Twelve. rev. ed. John H. Baumgaertner. LC 60-6440. (Illus., Orig.). 1960. pap. 4.50 o.p. (ISBN 0-8066-0604-5, 10-4311, Augsburg). Augsburg Fortress.

Meet Your Guru: How to Unlock Your Soul. E. Jorban. 1977. 4.00 o.p. (ISBN 0-682-48836-4). Exposition-Phoenix.

Meeting & Event Planning Guide: Northeast Meeting Sites & Services Directory - Spring, 1989. Ed. by Anne Sage. 100p. (Orig.). 1989. pap. text ed. 7.95 o.p. (ISBN 0-917015-07-X). Control Pub Mktg.

Meeting & Event Planning Guide: Southern Meeting Sites & Services Directory - Fall, 1988. Ed. by Anne Sage. 100p. (Orig.). 1988. pap. text ed. 7.95 o.p. (ISBN 0-917015-06-1). Control Pub Mktg.

Meeting Christ in Handel's Messiah: Lent & Easter Messages Based on Handel's Texts & Music. Roger T. Quillin. 96p. 1984. pap. 4.95 o.p. (ISBN 0-8066-2118-4, 10-4318, Augsburg). Augsburg Fortress.

Meeting Christ in the Sacraments. Colman E. O'Neill. LC 64-20111. 1964. pap. 3.95 o.p. (ISBN 0-8189-0090-3). Alba.

Meeting of European Communist Workers' Parties for Peace & Disarmament. M. Gremetz et al. 205p. 1980. 4.45 o.p. (ISBN 0-8285-1887-4, Pub. by Progress Pubs USSR). Imported Pubns.

Meeting of Extremes in Contemporary Philosophy. B. Bosanquet. Repr. of 1921 ed. 20.00 o.p. (ISBN 0-527-10030-7). Kraus Repr.

Meeting on Gas Chromatographic Determination of Hormonal Steroids. Ed. by Filippo Polvani et al. LC 68-19262. (Illus.). 1968. 66.00 o.p. (ISBN 0-12-561240-0). Acad Pr.

Meeting the Basic Needs of the Rural Poor: The Integrated, Community-Based Approach. Ed. by Philip H. Coombs. LC 80-19838. (Pergamon Policy Studies on International Development). 828p. 1980. 205.00 o.p. (ISBN 0-08-026306-2). Pergamon.

Meeting the Challenge of Supervision. Merle C. Nutt. LC 70-179468. 1972. text ed. 10.00 o.p. (ISBN 0-682-47408-8, University). Exposition-Phoenix.

Meeting the Challenges: Developing Faculty Careers. Michael C. Brookes & Katherine L. German. Ed. & frwd. by Jonathan D. Fife. LC 84-219986. (ASHE-ERIC Higher Education Report Ser.: No. 3, 1983). (Illus.). 47p. (Orig.). 1983. pap. 7.50x o.p. (ISBN 0-913317-02-0). Assn Study Higher Educ.

Meeting the Competitive Challenge: Manufacturing Strategy for U. S. Companies. Elwood S. Buffa. LC 83-73706. 250p. 1984. 22.50 o.p. (ISBN 0-87094-465-7). Dow Jones-Irwin.

Meeting the Competitive Challenge: Manufacturing Strategies for U. S. Companies. Elwood S. Buffa. 1984. pap. 17.95 o.p. (ISBN 0-256-03124-X). Irwin.

Meeting the Costs of Health Care: The Bay Area Experience & the National Issues. Margaret Greenfield. LC 72-5657. 182p. 1972. pap. 6.50x o.p. (ISBN 0-87772-086-X). UCB IGS.

Meetings Between Experts: An Approach to Sharing Ideas in Medical Consultations. David Tuckett et al. 300p. 1986. text ed. 39.95 o.p. (ISBN 0-422-79650-6, 9740, Pub. by Tavistock England); pap. text ed. 16.95 o.p. (ISBN 0-422-79660-3, 9745). Routledge Chapman & Hall.

Meetings with Pasternak: A Memoir. Alexander Gladkov. Tr. by Max Hayward. LC 77-73053. (Helen & Kurt Wolff Bks.). (Illus.). 1977. 8.95 o.p. (ISBN 0-15-158590-3). HarBraceJ.

Meetings with the Master. William G. Jozwiak. LC 84-91374. 118p. 1985. 10.00 o.p. (ISBN 0-533-06459-7). Vantage.

Meg & Mog Birthday Book. Helen Nicoll & Jan Pienkowski. (Meg & Mog Ser.). (Illus.). 32p. (ps-1). 1983. 12.95 o.s.i. (ISBN 0-434-95428-4, Pub. by W Heinemann Ltd). David & Charles.

Megacorp & Oligopoly. Alfred S. Eichner. LC 79-92295. 378p. 1980. pap. 14.95 o.p. (ISBN 0-87332-168-5). M E Sharpe.

Megacycles: Long-Term Episodity in Earth & Planetary History. Ed. by G. E. Williams. LC 79-19908. (Benchmark Papers in Geology: Vol. 57). 448p. 1982. 71.95 o.p. (ISBN 0-87933-366-9). Van Nos Reinhold.

Megagauss Magnetic Field Generation by Explosives & Related Experiments: Proceedings of the EUR-CNEN Association Meetings, Frascati, Italy, 1965. Ed. by H. Knoepfel & F. Herlach. 1976. pap. 29.00 o.p. (ISBN 0-08-020449-X). Pergamon.

Megaliths & Masterminds. Peter L. Brown. (Illus.). 1979. Encore 4.50 o.p. (ISBN 0-684-16891-X, ScribT). Scribner.

Megaliths, Myths & Men: An Introduction to Astro-Archaeology. Peter L. Brown. LC 76-15090. (Illus.). 324p. (YA) (gr. 10 up). 1976. 13.95 o.s.i. (ISBN 0-8008-5187-0). Taplinger.

Megalomania & Mediocrity in the Leadership of Nations: The Meaning for the World. Kenneth G. Rockwell. (Major Currents in Contemporary World History Library). (Illus.). 163p. 1981. 117.75 o.p. (ISBN 0-89266-292-1). Am Classical Coll Pr.

Megastar. Richard Bernstein. LC 84-80883. (Illus.). 96p. (Orig.). 1984. pap. 14.95 o.p. (ISBN 0-394-62305-3, E961, Ever). Grove.

Megastates of America: People, Politics & Power in the Ten Great States. Neal R. Peirce. LC 70-163375. 1972. 14.95 o.p. (ISBN 0-393-05458-6). Norton.

Megatoons: Cartoonists Against Nuclear War. Ed. by David Rosen. 96p. (Orig.). 1984. pap. 7.95 o.p. (ISBN 0-920792-30-8). Eden Pr.

Megatraumas: America at the Year 2000. Richard D. Lamm. LC 85-10692. 256p. 1985. 16.45 o.p. (ISBN 0-395-37912-1). HM.

Megawind Cancellation. Bernard Boucher. LC 78-72977. 1979. 8.95 o.p. (ISBN 0-689-10947-4). Macmillan.

Megiddo. Ed. by Graham I. Davies. (Cities of the Biblical World Ser.). 128p. (Orig.). 1986. pap. 8.95 o.p. (ISBN 0-8028-0247-8). Eerdmans.

Megillon on Sefer Rus - in Hebrew. David Schlossberg. text ed. 1.50 o.p. (ISBN 0-914131-42-7, A31). Torah Umesorah.

Meg's Car. Helen Nicoll & Jan Pienkowski. (Meg & Mog Ser.). (Illus.). 32p. (ps-1). 1983. 12.95 o.s.i. (ISBN 0-434-95426-8, Pub. by W Heinemann Ltd). David & Charles.

Meg's Castle. Helens Nicoll & Jan Pienkowski. (Meg & Mog Ser.). (Illus.). 32p. (ps-1). 1983. 12.95 o.s.i. (ISBN 0-434-95427-6, Pub. by W Heinemann Ltd). David & Charles.

Mehdi: Nothing Is Impossible. Roy Alexander. LC 77-95190. 1978. 10.95 o.p. (ISBN 0-87863-157-7, Farnsworth Pub Co). Longman Finan.

Meher Baba Journal, Vol. 1, No. 11. Meher Baba et al. Ed. by Elizabeth Patterson. (No. 11). (Illus.). 66p. 1974. pap. 2.50x o.p. (ISBN 0-913078-18-2). Sheriar Pr.

Meher Baba Journal, Vol. 1, No. 6. Meher Baba et al. Ed. by Elizabeth C. Patterson. (Illus.). 68p. 1972. pap. 2.50x o.p. (ISBN 0-913078-10-7). Sheriar Pr.

Meher Baba Journal, Vol. 1, No. 7. Meher Baba et al. Ed. by Elizabeth C. Patterson. (Illus.). 68p. 1972. pap. 2.50x o.p. (ISBN 0-913078-11-5). Sheriar Pr.

Meher Baba Journal, Vol. 1, No. 9. Meher Baba et al. Ed. by Elizabeth C. Patterson. (Illus.). 1973. pap. 2.50x o.p. (ISBN 0-913078-13-1). Sheriar Pr.

Meher Baba Journal, Vol. 1, No. 10. Meher Baba et al. Ed. by Elizabeth C. Patterson. (Illus.). 1973. pap. 2.50x o.p. (ISBN 0-913078-14-X). Sheriar Pr.

Mei Foo Sun Chuen, Middle Class Chinese Families in Transition. Sherry Rosen. (Asian Folklore & Social Life Monographs: No. 90). 1976. 18.00x o.p. (ISBN 0-89986-306-X). Oriental Bk Store.

Meiji Japan. Harold Bolitho. LC 80-7448. (Cambridge Topic Bks.). (Illus.). (gr. 5-10). 1980. PLB 8.95 o.p. (ISBN 0-8225-1219-X). Lerner Pubns.

Meiosis: Current Research, Vol. 3. P. L. Melnyk et al. 1972. 24.50x o.p. (ISBN 0-8422-7036-1). Irvington.

Meiosis: Current Research, Vol. 4. M. Callebaut et al. LC 72-6751. 244p. 1972. text ed. 24.50x o.p. (ISBN 0-8422-7041-8). Irvington.

Meiotic Process, I: Pairing, Recombination & Chromosome Movements. Everett Anderson et al. LC 72-6123. (Illus.). 189p. 1972. 29.50x o.p. (ISBN 0-8422-7019-1). Irvington.

Meiotic Process, II: Pairing, Recombination, & Chromosome Movements. Stephen M. Stack et al. LC 72-6123. 208p. 1972. text ed. 29.50x o.p. (ISBN 0-8422-7031-0). Irvington.

Meiotic System. B. John & K. R. Lewis. (Protoplasmatologia: Vol. 6, Pt. F1). (Illus.). 1965. pap. 93.30 o.p. (ISBN 0-387-80733-0). Springer-Verlag.

Meissen Porcelain of the Art Nouveau Period. Johannes Just. LC 84-20239. (Illus.). 164p. 1985. 24.95 o.p. (ISBN 0-911403-06-X). Seven Hills Bk Dists.

Meister. Brod. 1951. Philos Lib.

Meister Eckhart. Steven Smith. 1985. 10.00x o.p. (ISBN 0-317-62190-4, Guild of Pastoral Psych). State Mutual Bk.

Meister Eckhart Speaks. Otto Karrer. 1957. (ISBN 0-8022-0827-4). Philos Lib.

Meistererzahlungen. Ed. by Anna Otten. (Orig., Ger.). 1969. pap. text ed. 17.95 o.p. (ISBN 0-13-574251-X). P-H.

Melancholy Bay: An Odyssey. John Rucker. LC 85-45016. (Illus.). 224p. 1985. 17.95 o.p. (ISBN 0-88742-059-1). Globe Pequot.

Melanchthon on Christian Doctrine: Loci Communes 1555. Philip Melanchthon. Ed. & tr. by Clyde L. Manschreck. (Twin Brooks Ser.). 414p. 1982. pap. 11.95 o.p. (ISBN 0-8010-6143-1). Baker Bk.

Melange. Shyree A. Latham. LC 81-11. (Contemporary American Poets Ser.: Vol. 1). 63p. (Orig.). 1981. 5.95 o.p. (ISBN 0-86663-702-8); deluxe ed. 6.95 o.p. (ISBN 0-86663-704-4); pap. 1.95 o.p. (ISBN 0-86663-703-6). Ide Hse.

Melba the Brain. Ivy Ruckman. LC 79-19326. (Illus.). 132p. (gr. 3-5). 1979. 8.95 o.s.i. (ISBN 0-664-32655-2, Westminster). Westminster John Knox.

Melbourne. David Cecil. LC 76-138583. 1971. Repr. of 1954 ed. lib. bdg. 22.50x o.p. (ISBN 0-8371-5782-X, CEME). Greenwood.

Melbourne. Philip Ziegler. LC 81-70066. 1982. pap. 10.95 o.p. (ISBN 0-689-70623-5, 274, Atheneum). Macmillan.

Melchizedek Truth Principles. Frater Achad. pap. 6.95 o.s.i. (ISBN 0-87516-166-9). DeVorss.

Melinda Takes a Hand. Patricia Beatty. LC 83-7971. 160p. (gr. 5-9). 1983. 10.25 o.p. (ISBN 0-688-02422-X). Morrow.

Melissa. Diane Baumgartner. (Orig.). 1980. pap. 4.95 o.p. (ISBN 0-89191-233-9). Cook.

Melissa's Medley. Sandra Love. LC 77-88965. (gr. 5 up). 1978. 6.95 o.p. (ISBN 0-15-253166-1, HJ). HarBraceJ.

Mellona. Kathalyn Krause. 1979. pap. 2.25 o.p. (ISBN 0-505-51360-9, Pub. by Tower Bks). Dorchester Pub Co.

Mellows: A Chronicle of Unknown Singers. R. Emmet Kennedy. LC 78-32125. (Illus.). 1979. Repr. of 1925 ed. lib. bdg. 25.00x o.p. (ISBN 0-8371-5831-1, KME&, Pub. by Negro U Pr). Greenwood.

Melmoth the Wanderer: A Tale. Charles R. Maturin. LC 61-5561. xxii, 413p. 1961. pap. 6.95x o.p. (ISBN 0-8032-5127-0, BB 114, Bison). U of Nebr Pr.

Melodic, Dyadic & Harmonic Singing: Graded Exercises. 2nd ed. Gene J. Cho. 64p. 1983. pap. text ed. 8.95 o.p. (ISBN 0-8403-2991-1, 40299101). Kendall-Hunt.

Melodic Index to Haydn's Instrumental Music: A Thematic Locator for the Hoboken Thematisch-Bibliographisches Werkverzeichnis, Vols. I & III. Ed. by Gary Chapman & Steven Bryant. LC 81-17727. (Thematic Catalogue Ser.: No. 8). 100p. 1981. lib. bdg. 28.00x o.s.i. (ISBN 0-918728-19-3). Pendragon NY.

Melodrame Entitled "Treason, Stratagems, & Spoils" William L. Adams. Ed. by George N. Belknap. LC 68-56629. 1968. 7.50 o.p. (ISBN 0-87114-084-5). U of Oreg Bks.

Melody Harmonization at the Keyboard. Gene J. Cho. 80p. 1982. pap. text ed. 8.95 o.p. (ISBN 0-8403-2911-3). Kendall-Hunt.

Melquiades, Alchemy & Narrative Theory: The Quest for Gold in 'Cien Anos de Soledad. Chester S. Halka. 1981. 12.00x o.p. (ISBN 0-936968-01-X). Intl Bk Ctr.

Meltdown: The Secret Papers of the Atomic Energy Commission. Daniel F. Ford. 307p. 1986. pap. 6.95 o.s.i. (ISBN 0-671-63449-6, Touchstone Bks). S&S.

Melville. Edward H. Rosenberry. (Illus.). 1979. 21.95x o.p. (ISBN 0-7100-8989-9). Routledge Chapman & Hall.

Melville: A Collection of Critical Essays. Ed. by Richard Chase. (Orig.). 1962. 15.95 o.p. (ISBN 0-13-574293-5, Spec). P-H.

Melville & the Comic Spirit. Edward H. Rosenberry. LC 71-96168. 1970. Repr. of 1955 ed. lib. bdg. 16.50x o.p. (ISBN 0-374-96916-7, Octagon). Hippocrene Bks.

Melville J. Herskovitz. George E. Simpson. LC 73-5966. (Leaders of Modern Anthropology Ser.). 200p. 1973. 26.50x o.p. (ISBN 0-231-03385-0); pap. 15.00x o.p. (ISBN 0-231-03396-6). Columbia U Pr.

Melville: The Critical Heritage. Ed. by Watson G. Branch. (Critical Heritage Ser.). 1985. 38.00x o.p. (ISBN 0-7100-7774-2); 15.00 o.p. (ISBN 0-7102-0513-9). Routledge Chapman & Hall.

Melville's Use of Classical Mythology. Gerard M. Sweeney. (Melville Studies in American Culture: Vol. 5). 169p. (Orig.). 1976. pap. text ed. 12.50x o.p. (ISBN 90-6203-258-3). Humanities.

Melvin Is a Big Cheese. David N. Bruskin. (Story Bus Subseries: City Bus). (Illus.). 10p. (ps-2). 1988. bds. 14.95 o.p. (ISBN 1-55929-011-0). Bound Fun Inc.

MELVYL Catalog Reference Manual University of California. 1987. 25.00 o.p. (ISBN 0-317-03903-2). UCDLA.

MELVYL Reference Manual for the University of California Prototype On-Line Catalog. 1981. 5.00 o.p. (ISBN 0-686-87259-2). UCDLA.

Member of the Family. William E. Butterworth. 176p. (gr. 7 up). 1982. 9.95 o.s.i. (ISBN 0-02-716220-6, Four Winds). Macmillan.

Member of the Family: Strategies for Black Family Continuity. Ann C. Zollar. LC 84-6849. 175p. 1984. lib. bdg. 22.95x o.s.i. (ISBN 0-8304-1031-7). Nelson-Hall.

Member of the Wedding. Carson McCullers. 9.95 o.p. (ISBN 0-395-07979-9). HM.

Members Directory, 1986. Joseph A. Bruno, Jr. & Agnes M. Lotz. 120p. 1986. pap. 20.00 o.p. (ISBN 0-938477-25-0). SSPC.

Members Only. Patricia Welles. LC 80-66495. 1981. 12.95 o.p. (ISBN 0-87795-270-1, Arbor Hse). Morrow.

Membrane Electrodes in Drug-Substances Analysis. V. V. Cosofret. Ed. by J. D. Thomas. (Illus.). 376p. 1981. 87.00 o.p. (ISBN 0-08-026264-3). Pergamon.

Membrane Physiology. Ed. by Thomas E. Andreoli et al. 482p. 1980. pap. text ed. 27.50x o.p. (ISBN 0-306-40432-X, Plenum Pr). Plenum Pub.

Membrane Physiology of Invertebrates. Podesta. 624p. 1982. 125.00 o.p. (ISBN 0-8247-1503-9). Dekker.

Membrane Proteins. Ed. by P. Nicholls et al. LC 77-30604. (Federation of European Biochemical Societies Ser.). 330p. 1978. 93.00 o.p. (ISBN 0-08-022026-6). Pergamon.

Membrane Proteins & Their Interaction with Lipids. Ed. by Roderick A. Capaldi. (Membranes: Structure & Techniques Ser.: Vol. 1). 222p. 1977. 69.75 o.p. (ISBN 0-8247-6595-8). Dekker.

Membrane Receptors. Ed. by P. Cuatrecasas & S. Jacobs. (Receptors & Recognition Ser. B: Vol. 11). 1981. 49.95x o.p. (ISBN 0-412-21740-6, NO. 2156, Pub. by Chapman & Hall). Routledge Chapman & Hall.

Membrane Receptors see Queues: Receptors & Recognition Series B.

Membrane Science & Technology: Industrial, Biological, & Waste Treatment Processes. Ed. by J. E. Flinn. LC 77-118126. 238p. 1970. 49.50x o.p. (ISBN 0-306-30484-8, Plenum Pr). Plenum Pub.

Membrane Structure. D. Branton & D. W. Deamer. Ed. by M. Alfert et al. (Protoplasmatologia: Vol. 2, Pt. E1, 2, 3). (Illus.). 70p. 1972. 24.80 o.p. (ISBN 0-387-81031-5). Springer-Verlag.

Membrane Transformation in Neoplasia. Ed. by Julius Schultz & Ronald E. Black. 1974. 52.50 o.p. (ISBN 0-12-632760-2). Acad Pr.

Membrane Transport in Plants. Ed. by U. Zimmermann & J. Dainty. (Illus.). vi, 473p. 1975. 41.00 o.p. (ISBN 0-387-06989-5). Springer-Verlag.

Membrane Transport in Red Cells. Ed. by J. C. Ellory & V. L. Lew. 1978. 99.00 o.p. (ISBN 0-12-237150-X). Acad Pr.

Membranes & Viruses in Immunopathology: Proceedings. Ed. by S. R. Day & R. A. Good. 1973. 85.00 o.p. (ISBN 0-12-207250-2). Acad Pr.

Membranes: Lipid Bilayers & Biological Membranes: Dynamic Properties, Vol. 3. Ed. by George Eisenman. 536p. 1975. 105.00 o.p. (ISBN 0-8247-6178-2). Dekker.

Membranes, Vol. 2: Lipid Bilayers & Antibiotics. Ed. by George Eisenman. 558p. 1973. 105.00 o.p. (ISBN 0-8247-6049-2). Dekker.

Membranes,Mitochondria, & Connective Tissue see Submicroscopic Cytochemistry.

Memo & Office Forms. (Easy-to-Make Photocopier Bks.). (Orig.). 1980. pap. 14.95 o.p. (ISBN 0-87280-041-5, Asher-Gallant). Caddylak Systs.

Memo from: David O. Selznick. 2nd ed. Ed. by Rudy Behlmer. LC 81-47641. (Illus.). 608p. 1981. pap. 11.95 o.p. (ISBN 0-394-17937-4, E783, Ever). Grove.

Memo from Mercury: Information Technology Is Different. Gordon B. Thompson. 62p. 1979. pap. text ed. 3.00x o.p. (ISBN 0-920380-29-8, Pub. by Inst Res Pub Canada). Gower Pub Co.

Memoir of a Gambler. J. Richardson. 252p. 1982. pap. text ed. 5.95 o.p. (ISBN 0-07-052302-9). McGraw.

Memoir of a Revolutionary. Milovan Djilas. LC 72-91835. 1973. 12.00 o.s.i. (ISBN 0-15-158850-3). HarBraceJ.

Memoir of Central India, Including Malwa, & Adjoining Provinces: With the History, & Copious Illustrations, of the Past & Present Condition of That Country, 2 vols. 3rd ed. John Malcolm. 1144p. 1972. Repr. of 1832 ed. 90.00 set o.p. (ISBN 0-7165-2129-6, BBA 03537, Pub. by Irish Academic Pr). Biblio Dist.

Memoires d'une Jeune Fille Rangee. Simone De Beauvoir. 1958. 8.50 o.p. (ISBN 0-685-11359-0). Schoenhof.

Memoires Interieurs. Gerard Manley Hopkins. Tr. by Francois Mauriac from Fr. 248p. 1961. 4.75 o.p. (ISBN 0-374-20644-9). FS&G.

Memoires pour Servir a l'Histoire des Hommes Illustres. Jean-Pierre Niceron. 18700p. (Fr.). Date not set. Repr. of 1745 ed. text ed. 4554.00x o.p. (ISBN 0-576-72338-X, Pub. by Gregg Intl Pubs England). Gregg Intl.

Memoires sur les Cent Jours. Benjamin Constant. 348p. 14.95 o.p. (ISBN 0-686-54614-8). French & Eur.

Memoirs. Mikhail I. Glinka. Tr. by Richard B. Mudge from Rus. LC 79-27875. (Illus.). xi, 264p. 1980. Repr. of 1963 ed. lib. bdg. 35.00x o.p. (ISBN 0-313-22331-9, GLME). Greenwood.

Memoirs. Robert Houden. Tr. by Wraxall. (Illus.). 8.25 o.p. (ISBN 0-8446-2815-8). Peter Smith.

Memoirs. Charles G. Leland. LC 68-22036. 454p. 1968. Repr. of 1893 ed. 43.00x o.p. (ISBN 0-8103-3533-6). Gale.

Memoirs. Lindley Murray. LC 72-78794. 1827. Repr. 11.00 o.p. (ISBN 0-403-02013-1). Somerset Pub.

Memoirs: From Munich to New War & New Victory. Edward Benes. Tr. by Geoffrey Lias. LC 78-16354. 1978. Repr. of 1954 ed. lib. bdg. 35.00x o.p. (ISBN 0-313-20592-2, BECZ). Greenwood.

Memoirs of a Buccaneer. Louis A. Le Golif. 1954. 3.50 o.p. (ISBN 0-671-46200-8). S&S.

Memoirs of a Cavalier. Daniel Defoe. LC 74-170545. (Novel in England, 1700-1775 Ser). 1972. lib. bdg. 61.00 o.p. (ISBN 0-8240-0546-5). Garland Pub.

Memoirs of a Citizen-Politician. Leroy Owens. 96p. 1984. 6.50 o.p. (ISBN 0-682-40146-3). Exposition-Phoenix.

Memoirs of a Cook: Yesterday & Today. Mildred O. Knopf. LC 86-47680. 320p. 1987. 19.95 o.p. (ISBN 0-689-11749-3, Atheneum). Macmillan.

Memoirs of a Dissident Publisher. Henry Regnery. LC 78-22269. 1979. 12.95 o.p. (ISBN 0-15-173752-5). HarBraceJ.

Memoirs of a Magdalen, or, the History of Louisa Mildmay, 1767, 2 vols. in 1. Hugh Kelly. LC 74-16055. (Novel in England, 1700-1775 Ser). 1975. lib. bdg. 61.00 o.p. (ISBN 0-8240-1175-9). Garland Pub.

Memoirs of a Man: Grenville Clark. Compiled by Mary C. Dimond & J. Garry Clifford. (Illus.). 319p. 1975. 10.00 o.p. (ISBN 0-393-08716-6). Norton.

Memoirs of a Man of Honour, 1747. Antoine Francois. (Novel in England, 1700-1775 Ser). 1975. lib. bdg. 61.00 o.p. (ISBN 0-8240-1119-8). Garland Pub.

Memoirs of a Mathematician Manque. Jagjit Singh. 176p. 1980. text ed. 15.00x o.p. (ISBN 0-7069-1128-8, Pub. by Vikas India). Advent NY.

Memoirs of a Mom. Patricia Johnson. 48p. 1986. 5.95 o.p. (ISBN 0-8062-2795-8). Carlton.

Memoirs of a Russian Lady: Drawings & Tales of Life Before the Revolution. Mariamna Davydoff. Tr. by Olga D. Dax. (Illus.). 160p. 1986. 24.95 o.p. (ISBN 0-8109-0839-5). Abrams.

Memoirs of a Space Traveler: Further Reminiscences of Ijon Tichy. Stanislaw Lem. Tr. by Joel Stern & Maria Swiecicka-Ziemianek. LC 81-47310. (Helen & Kurt Wolff Bk.). 156p. 1982. 9.95 o.p. (ISBN 0-15-158856-2). HarBraceJ.

Memoirs of a Vagrant Soul. Mikhail Naimy. 1952. (ISBN 0-8022-1184-4). Philos Lib.

Memoirs of Alexis Soyer: With Unpublished Receipts & Odds & Ends of Gastronomy. facsimile ed. Ed. by F. Volant & J. R. Warren. 303p. 1986. text ed. 25.00x o.p. (ISBN 0-9510766-0-4, Pub. by Cooks Books UK). U Pr of Va.

Memoirs of an Anti-Zionist Jew. Elmer Berger. 159p. (Orig.). 1978. pap. 5.00x o.p. (ISBN 0-911038-87-6, Inst Hist Rev). Noontide.

Memoirs of an Invisible Man. Harry Saint. LC 85-48144. 320p. 1987. 18.95 o.p. (ISBN 0-689-11735-3, Atheneum). Macmillan.

Memoirs of Arthur Hamilton B. A. A. C. Benson. LC 76-20043. (Decadent Consciousness Ser.: Vol. 4). 1977. Repr. of 1886 ed. lib. bdg. 46.00 o.p. (ISBN 0-8240-2753-1). Garland Pub.

Memoirs of Bartholomew Fair. Henry Morley. LC 67-24348. 414p. 1968. Repr. of 1880 ed. 43.00x o.p. (ISBN 0-8103-3495-X). Gale.

Memoirs of Bryan Perdue, 3 vols. Thomas Holcroft. Ed. by Ronald Paulson. LC 78-60851. (Novel 1720-1805 Ser.: Vol. 15). 1980. Set. lib. bdg. 112.00 o.p. (ISBN 0-8240-3664-6). Garland Pub.

Memoirs of Christopher Columbus. Stephen Marlowe. 1987. 19.95 o.p. (ISBN 0-684-18769-8). Scribner.

Memoirs of Emma Courtney. Mary Hayes. (Mothers of the Novel Ser.). 192p. 1987. pap. 8.95 o.p. (ISBN 0-86358-132-3, 8134X, Pub. by Pandora Pr). Routledge Chapman & Hall.

Memoirs of General Lord Ismay. Lord Ismay. LC 73-22504. (Illus.). 488p. 1974. Repr. of 1960 ed. lib. bdg. 35.00x o.p. (ISBN 0-8371-6280-7, ISMF). Greenwood.

Memoirs of Hector Berlioz. new ed. Hector Berlioz. Tr. by David Cairns from Fr. (Illus.). 672p. 1975. pap. 8.95 o.p. (ISBN 0-393-00698-0, Norton Lib). Norton.

Memoirs of James Second: His Campaigns As Duke of York, 1652-1660. James Second King of Great Britain. Tr. by A. Lytton Sells. LC 71-163544. 301p. 1962. Repr. lib. bdg. 35.00x o.p. (ISBN 0-8371-6209-2, JAME). Greenwood.

Memoirs of Madame De La Tour Du Pin. De la Tour du Pin. (Century Classic Ser.). 1987. pap. 15.95 o.p. (ISBN 0-7126-0866-4, Pub. by Century Hutchinson). David & Charles.

Memoirs of Miles Byrne, 3 vols. in one. Miles Byrne. 1972. Repr. of 1863 ed. 42.50x o.p. (ISBN 0-7165-0027-2, Pub. by Irish Academic Pr). Biblio Dist.

Memoirs of Miss Sidney Bidulph. Frances Sheridan. pap. 9.95 o.p. (ISBN 0-317-65248-6, Pandora Pr). Routledge Chapman & Hall.

Memoirs of My Services in the World War: 1917-1918. George C. Marshall. LC 76-10834. 1976. 10.00 o.p. (ISBN 0-395-20725-8). HM.

Memoirs of Prince Adam Czartoryski & His Correspondence with Alexander First, 2 Vols. in 1. (Russian Ser.: No. 8). 1968. Repr. of 1888 ed. 35.00 o.p. (ISBN 0-87569-005-X). Academic Intl.

Memoirs of the Baron Du Tan, to Which Is Added the Calabrian; or, the History of Charles Brachy, & the Hermit, 1744. Madeleine Angelique Poisson De Gomez. LC 74-16060. (Novel in England, 1700-1775 Ser). 1975. lib. bdg. 61.00 o.p. (ISBN 0-8240-1111-2). Garland Pub.

Memoirs of the Devil. Roger Vadim. Ed. by Daniel Okrent. Tr. by Peter Beglan. LC 76-27428. (Illus.). 1977. 7.95 o.p. (ISBN 0-15-111906-6). HarBraceJ.

Memoirs of the Life of Colonel Hutchinson. Lucy Hutchinson. 1968. pap. 3.25x o.p. (ISBN 0-460-01317-3, Evman). Biblio Dist.

Memoirs of the Life of Sir Samuel Romilly: With a Selection from His Correspondence, 3 vols. Samuel Romilly. (Development of Industrial Societies Ser.). 900p. 1971. Repr. of 1840 ed. 80.00x set o.p. (ISBN 0-7165-1784-1, BBA 03684, Pub. by Irish Academic Pr Ireland). Biblio Dist.

Memoirs of War, 1914-15. Marc Bloch. Tr. by Carole Fink from Fr. LC 79-6849. Orig. Title: Souvenirs De Guerre. (Illus.). 184p. 1980. 27.50x o.p. (ISBN 0-8014-1220-X). Cornell U Pr.

Memorable Memoirs. George Watson. 113p. 1987. 9.95 o.p. (ISBN 0-8062-2888-1). Carlton.

Memorandum of Law on the United States Policy Toward Nicaragua. Theodore Lieverman & Peter Schneider. 4.50 o.p. Natl Lawyers Guild.

Memorandum: On Renewing Schooling & Education. Paul F. Brandwein. Intro. by William Jovanovich. LC 81-47301. 320p. 1982. 14.95 o.s.i. (ISBN 0-15-158857-0). HarBraceJ.

Memorial & Genealogical Record of Southwest Texas. Goodspeed Publishing Company Staff. 661p. 1978. Repr. of 1894 ed. 45.00 o.s.i. (ISBN 0-89308-122-1). Southern Hist Pr.

Memorial: Portrait of a Family. Christopher Isherwood. 1977. pap. 2.25 o.p. (ISBN 0-380-01814-4, 53983-7, Bard). Avon.

Memorials of a Half-Century in Michigan & the Lake Region. Bela Hubbard. LC 75-23322. (Illus.). 608p. 1978. Repr. of 1888 ed. 46.00x o.p. (ISBN 0-8103-4268-5). Gale.

Memorias. L. Brezhnev. 79p. (Span.). 1982. pap. 1.00 o.p. (ISBN 0-8285-2233-2, Pub. by Progress Pubs USSR). Imported Pubns.

Memories. Charlotte V. Allen. 336p. 1984. pap. 3.95 o.s.i. (ISBN 0-425-08988-6). Berkley Pub.

Memories. Mike McQuay. 320p. 1986. pap. 3.95 o.p. (ISBN 0-553-25888-5, Spectra). Bantam.

Memories. Dr. Pietro Montana. 1977. 13.50 o.p. (ISBN 0-682-48841-0). Exposition-Phoenix.

Memories & Meditations. Leon F. Kenney. LC 76-46643. (Illus.). 1977. 5.95 o.s.i. (ISBN 0-664-21290-5, Westminster). Westminster John Knox.

Memories from a Naturalists' Notebook: A Year of Favorite Observations in the World of Nature. Richard Headstrom. (PHalarope Bk.). (Illus.). 240p. 1986. 15.95 o.p. (ISBN 0-13-574377-X). P-H.

Memories-JFK Nineteen Sixty-one to Nineteen Sixty-three-of Cecil Stoughton & Major General Chester V. Clifton. Cecil Stoughton & Chester V. Clifton. (Illus.). 1973. 11.95 o.p. (ISBN 0-393-08682-8). Norton.

Memories of a Catholic Girlhood. Mary McCarthy. LC 57-8842. (Illus.). 245p. 1957. 12.95 o.s.i. (ISBN 0-15-158859-7). HarBraceJ.

Memories of a Country Childhood. Judith Wallace. (Illus.). 1978. 16.95x o.p. (ISBN 0-7022-1067-6); pap. 7.75 o.p. U of Queensland Pr.

Memories of Class. Zygmunt Bauman. (International Library of Sociology). 224p. 1983. 26.95x o.p. (ISBN 0-7100-9196-6). Routledge Chapman & Hall.

Memories of My Childhood: Further Years at Marbacka. Selma O. Lagerloef. Tr. by Velma S. Howard. LC 34-27093. 1975. Repr. of 1934 ed. 35.00 o.p. (ISBN 0-527-54010-2). Kraus Repr.

Memories of Old Cahaba. Anna M. Fry. Repr. 5.00 o.p. (ISBN 0-87397-036-5). Strode.

Memories of Silk & Straw: A Self-Portrait of Small-Town Japan. Junichi Saga. LC 86-45724. (Illus.). 248p. 1987. 22.95 o.p. (ISBN 0-87011-792-0). Kodansha.

Memories of the Future. Paul Horgan. 216p. 1966. 4.95 o.p. (ISBN 0-374-20756-9). FS&G.

Memories of the Past since Snooksie Died. Edwin Mumford. (Orig.). 1980. pap. 6.50 o.p. (ISBN 0-682-49539-5). Exposition-Phoenix.

Memory Babe: A Critical Biography of Jack Kerouac. Gerald Nicosia. Ed. by Fred Jordan. LC 82-24212. (Illus.). 760p. 1983. 22.50 o.s.i. (ISBN 0-394-52270-2, GP865). Grove.

Memory Babe: A Critical Biography of Jack Kerouac. Gerald Nicosia. 768p. 1984. pap. 11.95 o.s.i. (ISBN 0-394-62243-X, E947, Ever). Grove.

Memory Book. Jerry Lucas & Harry Lorayne. 208p. 1985. pap. 2.50 o.p. (ISBN 0-345-33758-1). Ballantine.

Memory Components Handbook, 1988. Intel Staff. 528p. (Orig.). 1988. pap. 18.00 o.p. (ISBN 1-55512-070-9, 210830). Intel Corp.

Memory Discontinued Devices. Ed. by Jim Fitzgerald. 300p. 1987. 70.00 o.p. (ISBN 0-317-57578-3). DATA Busn Pub.

Memory Function Approaches to Stochastic Problems in Condensed Matter. Ed. by M. W. Evans et al. LC 85-5291. (Advances in Chemical Physics Ser.: Pt. 1). 556p. 1985. 84.95 o.p. (ISBN 0-471-80482-7). Krieger.

Memory Is No Stranger. Elizabeth Bartlett. LC 81-1484. xii, 68p. 1981. text ed. 13.95x o.p. (ISBN 0-8214-0602-7); pap. 7.95 o.p. (ISBN 0-8214-0645-0). Ohio U Pr.

Memory, Learning & Higher Function: A Cellular View. Charles D. Woody. (Illus.). 512p. 1983. 89.00 o.p. (ISBN 0-387-90525-1). Springer-Verlag.

Memory Made Easy: The Complete Book of Memory Training. Robert L. Montgomery. (Illus.). 1979. 11.95 o.p. (ISBN 0-8144-5523-9). AMACOM.

Memory of a Girlhood in China. C. Chin-Li. Tr. by Abby Israel from Fr. 1978. text ed. 11.95 o.p. (ISBN 0-07-010818-8). McGraw.

Memory of Departure. Abdulrazak Gurnah. 1988. 15.95 o.s.i. (ISBN 0-8021-1018-5). Grove.

Memory of Old Jack. Wendell Berry. LC 73-15432. 1974. 6.95 o.p. (ISBN 0-15-158865-1). HarBraceJ.

Memory Resident Utilities, Interrupts & Disk Management with MS & PC DOS. Michael Hyman. (MIS-Press Ser.). 373p. (Orig.). 1986. pap. 22.95 o.s.i. (ISBN 0-943518-73-3); book & disk 44.95 o.s.i. MIS Press.

Memory String. Chester G. Osborne. LC 83-15633. 168p. (gr. 4-8). 1984. 11.95 o.s.i. (ISBN 0-689-31020-X, Atheneum Childrens Bks). Macmillan.

Memory Training for Students & Executives. 3rd. ed. Kevin S. Vaz. 1979. pap. 2.95x o.p. (ISBN 0-7069-1581-X, Pub. by Vikas India). Advent NY.

Memos for Management...Leadership. James L. Hayes. 192p. 1983. 14.95 o.p. (ISBN 0-8144-5767-3). AMACOM.

Memos for Management...the Manager's Job. James L. Hayes. 208p. 1983. 14.95 o.p. (ISBN 0-8144-5768-1). AMACOM.

Memphis: Objects, Funiture & Patterns. Richard Horn. 1986. pap. 11.95 o.p. (ISBN 0-671-62011-8, Fireside). S&S.

Memphis: Objects, Furniture, & Patterns. rev. & expanded ed. Richard Horn. (Illus.). 144p. 1986. 19.95 o.p. (ISBN 0-89471-447-3). Running Pr.

Men: A Book for Women. Ed. by James Wagenvoord. 1978. pap. 7.95 o.p. (ISBN 0-380-40212-2, 76026). Avon.

Men Against McCarthy. Richard M. Fried. LC 75-40447. (Contemporary American History Ser.). 428p. 1976. 37.50x o.p. (ISBN 0-231-03872-0); pap. 20.00 o.p. (ISBN 0-231-08360-2). Columbia U Pr.

Men Against the Sea. Charles Nordhoff & James N. Hall. (Illus.). 1934. 16.95 o.p. (ISBN 0-316-61156-5, Pub by Atlantic Monthly Pr.). Little.

Men: An Owner's Manual. Stephanie Brush. 1984. 11.70 o.s.i. (ISBN 0-671-49459-7, Linden Pr). S&S.

Men & Affairs. William Barclay. Ed. by C. L. Rawlins. LC 78-1926. 160p. 1978. pap. 4.95 o.s.i. (ISBN 0-664-24203-0, Westminster). Westminster John Knox.

Men & Angels. Mary Gordon. LC 84-45761. 241p. 1985. 16.45 o.s.i. (ISBN 0-394-52403-9). Random.

Men & Brethren. James G. Cozzens. LC 36-755. (Illus.). 1958. 4.00 o.p. (ISBN 0-15-159135-0). HarBraceJ.

Men & Friendship. Stuart Miller. LC 82-18718. 206p. 1983. 13.45 o.p. (ISBN 0-395-33103-X). HM.

Men & Ideas in the Sixteenth Century. Hans Hillerbrand. 1969. pap. 10.95 o.p. (ISBN 0-395-30628-0). HM.

Men & Machines. Hywel Murrell. (Essential Psychology Ser.). 1976. pap. 4.50x o.p. (ISBN 0-416-82310-6, NO. 2331). Routledge Chapman & Hall.

Men & Marriage: The Changing Role of Husbands. Elizabeth C. Mooney. 224p. 1985. 16.95 o.p. (ISBN 0-531-09703-X). Watts.

Men & Masculinity. Ed. by Joseph H. Pleck & Jack Sawyer. 192p. 1974. 8.95 o.p. (ISBN 0-13-574319-2, Spec); pap. 5.95 o.p. (ISBN 0-13-574301-X, Spec). P-H.

Men & Politics: An Autobiography. Louis Fischer. LC 73-111498. vi, 672p. 1971. Repr. of 1941 ed. lib. bdg. 35.00x o.p. (ISBN 0-8371-4641-0, FIMP). Greenwood.

Men & Sex: A Case Study in "Sexual Politics" Ed. by S. Wise & L. Stanley. 100p. 1984. pap. 19.25 o.p. (ISBN 0-08-031327-2). Pergamon.

Men & the Mountain: Fremont's Fourth Expedition. William Brandon. LC 73-20901. (Illus.). 337p. 1974. Repr. of 1955 ed. lib. bdg. 35.00x o.p. (ISBN 0-8371-5873-7, BRME). Greenwood.

Men & Women & Other Poems. Robert Browning. Ed. by J. W. Harper. 264p. 1984. pap. 5.95x o.p. (ISBN 0-460-11427-1, Evman). Biblio Dist.

Men at War. M. Alexeyev. 413p. 1980. 9.60 o.p. (ISBN 0-8285-2035-6, Pub. by Progress Pubs USSR). Imported Pubns.

Men for Boot Hill. Bruce Thomas. (Lythway Ser.). 160p. 1988. lib. bdg. 17.50 o.p. (ISBN 0-7451-0653-6, Pub. by Chivers Pr UK). G K Hall.

Men from under the Sky: The Arrival of Westerners in Fiji. Stanley Brown. LC 72-96774. (Illus.). 1973. 10.00 o.p. (ISBN 0-8048-1103-2). C E Tuttle.

Men I Hold Great. Francois Mauriac. 1951. (ISBN 0-8022-1092-9). Philos Lib.

Men in Cages. H. U. Triston. LC 70-174122. (Illus.). 258p. 1971. Repr. of 1938 ed. 43.00x o.p. (ISBN 0-8103-3801-7). Gale.

Men in Dark Times. Hannah Arendt. LC 68-24381. 1968. 6.50 o.p. (ISBN 0-15-159147-4). HarBraceJ.

Men in Frocks. Kris Kirk & Ed Heath. (Illus.). 160p. (Orig.). 1984. pap. 9.95 o.p. (ISBN 0-907040-48-9, Pub. by GMP England). Alyson Pubns.

Men in Our Lives: Fathers, Lovers, Husbands, Mentors. Elizabeth Fishel. LC 84-8984. 352p. 1984. 15.95 o.p. (ISBN 0-688-03960-X). Morrow.

Men in the Jungle. Norman Spinrad. 1977. pap. 1.50 o.p. (ISBN 0-8439-0454-2, Pub. by Leisure Bks CT). Dorchester Pub Co.

Men of Cajamarca: A Social & Biographical Study of the First Conquerors of Peru. James Lockhart. LC 72-185236. (Latin American Monographs: No. 27). 514p. 1972. 22.50x o.p. (ISBN 0-292-75001-3). U of Tex Pr.

Men of Company K: The Autobiography of a World War II Rifle Company. Harold P. Leinbaugh & John D. Campbell. LC 85-71977. (Illus.). 288p. 1985. 18.95 o.p. (ISBN 0-688-04421-2). Morrow.

Men of Heart of Red, White & Green: The Italian Antifascists in the Spanish Civil War. Massimo Mangilli-Climpson. 1985. 10.95 o.p. (ISBN 0-533-05835-X). Vantage.

Men of Mathematics. Eric T. Bell. (Illus.). 1937. pap. 10.75 o.s.i. (ISBN 0-671-46401-9, Fireside). S&S.

Men of Metals. Samuel L. Hoyt. 1979. 8.00 o.p. (ISBN 0-87170-059-X). ASM.

Men of Science, Men of God. Henry M. Morris. LC 82-70271. (Illus.). 1982. pap. 2.95 o.p. (ISBN 0-89051-080-6). Master Bks.

Men of the Covenant: The Story of the Scottish Church in the Years of the Persecution. Alexander Smellie. 664p. 1975. Repr. of 1924 ed. 18.95 o.p. (ISBN 0-85151-212-7). Banner of Truth.

Men or Machines: A Philippines Case Study of Labour-Capital Substitution in Road Construction in the Philippines. Deepak Lal & A. Heap. (WEP Study Ser.). xi, 164p. 1978. pap. 17.50 o.p. (ISBN 92-2-101720-6, ILO986, ILO). UNIPUB.

Men Who Control Women's Health. Diane H. Scully. 1980. 10.95 o.p. (ISBN 0-395-29137-2). HM.

Men Who Hate Women & the Women Who Love Them. Susan Forward & Joan Torres. LC 85-48235. 304p. (Orig.). 1986. 16.95 o.p. (ISBN 0-553-05135-0). Bantam.

Men Who Loved Miss Greto Garbo. Alec Ross. 127p. 1987. 8.95 o.p. (ISBN 0-8062-2819-9). Carlton.

Men Who Made Sewanee. Moultrie Guerry. 163p. 1981. 10.00 o.p. (ISBN 0-918769-13-2). Univ South.

Men Who Mastered Time. David Butler. 262p. 1987. 19.95 o.p. (ISBN 0-434-09906-6, Pub. by W Heinemann Ltd). David & Charles.

Men with the Yen. Zavis Zeman. (Illus.). 132p. 1980. pap. text ed. 5.95x o.p. (ISBN 0-686-80423-6, Pub. by Inst Res Pub Canada). Gower Pub Co.

Men, Women, & God. Mace. (John Knox). Westminster John Knox.

Men, Women, & Issues in American History, 2 vols. rev. ed. Ed. by Howard H. Quint & Milton Cantor. 1980. Vol. 1, 304p. pap. text ed. (ISBN 0-534-10789-3); Vol. 2, 311p. pap. text ed. (ISBN 0-534-10792-3). Wadsworth Pub.

Men, Women & Other Anticlimaxes. Anatole Broyard. LC 79-20710. 1980. 9.95 o.p. (ISBN 0-416-00531-4, NO. 0169). Routledge Chapman & Hall.

Menace of Atomic Energy. Ralph Nader & John Abbotts. (Illus.). 1979. pap. 4.95 o.p. (ISBN 0-393-00920-3). Norton.

Menaechmi see also Brothers Menaechmus.

Menaechmi: Plautus. Frank O. Copley. 1956. pap. text ed. write for info. o.p. (ISBN 0-02-325060-7). Macmillan.

Menarche: The Physiological, Psychological & Social Effects of the Onset of Menstruation. Ed. by Sharon Golub. LC 82-48105. 352p. 1983. 35.00x o.p. (ISBN 0-669-05982-X). Lexington Bks.

Mencken Chrestomathy. H. L. Mencken. 1949. 17.95 o.p. (ISBN 0-394-43595-8). Knopf.

Mendelian Inheritance in Man: Catalogs of Autosomal Dominant, Autosomal Recessive, & X-Linked Phenotypes. 7th ed. Victor A. McKusick. 1986. text ed. 75.00X o.p. (ISBN 0-8018-3396-5). Johns Hopkins.

Mendelowitz's Guide to Drawing. 3rd ed. Duane A. Wakeham. 1982. pap. text ed. 26.95 o.p. (ISBN 0-03-057294-0). HR&W.

Mendelssohn. rev. ed. Philip Radcliffe. (Master Musicians Ser.: No. M180). (Illus.). 214p. 1976. pap. 7.95 o.p. (ISBN 0-8226-0715-8). Littlefield.

Mender of Broken Hearts: How Christ Gives Us Courage to Live. Conrad M. Thompson. LC 81-52270. 128p. (Orig.). 1982. pap. 6.95 o.p. (ISBN 0-8066-1902-3, 10-4343, Augsburg). Augsburg Fortress.

Mender's Manual: Repairing & Preserving Garments & Bedding. Estelle Foote. LC 76-12102. 1976. 5.95 o.p. (ISBN 0-15-159150-4). HarBraceJ.

Mendocino Menace. Ruth Macleod. 1973. pap. 0.75 o.p. (ISBN 0-380-01414-9, 15305). Avon.

Mengeles Auschwitz. Nyszli. (ISBN 0-8050-0004-6). Seaver Bks.

Meningiomas Diagnostic & Therapeutic Problems: Proceedings of the International Conference on Numerical Methods in Fluid Dynamics, 4th, University of Colorado, June 24-28, 1974. International Conference on Numerical Methods in Fluid Dynamics Staff. Ed. by R. D. Richtmyer. (Lecture Notes in Physics Ser.: Vol. 35). (Illus.). vi, 457p. 1975. pap. 24.00 o.p. (ISBN 0-387-07139-3). Springer-Verlag.

Menippean Satire: An Annotated Catalogue of Texts & Criticism. Eugene P. Kirk. LC 79-7921. (Garland Reference Library of the Humanities). 1980. lib. bdg. 48.00 o.p. (ISBN 0-8240-9533-2). Garland Pub.

Menlove. James Perrin. (Illus.). 256p. 1985. 34.95 o.p. (ISBN 0-575-03571-4, Pub. by Gollancz England). David & Charles.

Menno Simons: Ein Beitrag zur Geschichte und Theologie der Taufgerinnten. rev. ed. Cornelius Krahn. 192p. (Orig., Ger.). 1984. pap. 12.00 o.p. (ISBN 0-8361-1269-5). Herald Pr.

Meno of Plato. E. Seymer Thompson. LC 78-66555. (Ancient Philosophy Ser.). 385p. 1980. lib. bdg. 45.00 o.p. (ISBN 0-8240-9573-1). Garland Pub.

Menomini Indians. Walter J. Hoffman. (Landmarks in Anthropology Ser). (Illus.). 328p. Repr. of 1896 ed. 46.00 o.p. (ISBN 0-384-23920-X). Johnson Repr.

Menopause. Mary Anderson. LC 82-25303. 128p. 1983. pap. 4.95 o.p. (ISBN 0-571-13071-2). Faber & Faber.

Menopause: A Guide for Women & the Men Who Love Them. Winnifred B. Cutler et al. (Illus.). 1983. 14.50 o.p. (ISBN 0-393-01709-5). Norton.

Menopause: A Time for Positive Change. Judi Fairlie et al. 128p. (Orig.). 1988. pap. 7.95 o.p. (ISBN 0-7137-2055-7, Pub. by Javelin England). Sterling.

Menopause, Naturally: Preparing for the Second Half of Life. Sadja Greenwood. LC 84-7333. (Illus.). 210p. (Orig.). 1984. pap. 10.00 o.p. (ISBN 0-912078-74-X). Volcano Pr.

Men's Changing Roles in the Family. Ed. by Robert A. Lewis & Marvin B. Sussman. LC 86-256. (Marriage & Family Review Ser.: Vol. 9, Nos. 3-4). 288p. 1986. text ed. 29.95 o.s.i. (ISBN 0-86656-501-9); pap. text ed. 24.95 o.s.i. (ISBN 0-86656-502-7). Haworth Pr.

Men's Club. Leonard Michaels. 128p. 1982. pap. 2.95 o.p. (ISBN 0-380-58131-0, 58131-0). Avon.

Men's Furnishings & Work Wear. Fairchild Market Research Division Staff. (Fairchild Fact Files Ser.). 55p. 1985. pap. 17.50 o.p. (ISBN 0-87005-526-7). Fairchild.

Men's Gymnastics. Sho Fukushima & Wrio Russell. (Illus.). 224p. 1980. 25.00 o.p. (ISBN 0-571-11478-4). Faber & Faber.

Men's Outerwear Design. Masaaki Kawashima. LC 77-79658. (Illus.). 1978. text ed. 18.50 o.p. (ISBN 0-87005-196-2). Fairchild.

Men's Sportswear, Casual Wear, Jeans. Fairchild Market Research Division Staff. (Fairchild Fact Files Ser.). (Illus.). 50p. 1986. pap. 20.00 o.p. (ISBN 0-87005-554-2). Fairchild.

Men's Tailored Clothing & Rainwear. Fairchild Market Research Division Staff. (Fairchild Fact Files Ser.). (Illus.). 55p. 1985. pap. 17.50 o.p. (ISBN 0-87005-527-5). Fairchild.

Menstrual Cycle. Rudolf F. Vollman. LC 76-28947. (Major Problems in Obstetrics & Gynecology Ser.: Vol. 7). (Illus.). 1977. text ed. write for info. o.p. (ISBN 0-7216-9075-0). Saunders.

Mental As Physical. Edgar Wilson. (International Library of Philosophy & Scientific Method). 1979. 35.00x o.p. (ISBN 0-7100-0316-1). Routledge Chapman & Hall.

Mental Blocks: The Block Party. Jacklyn Lambert & Jeffrey Samborski. (Illus.). 1985. pap. 17.50 o.p. (ISBN 0-399-51168-7, Perigee). Putnam Pub Group.

Mental Capacity & the Law. 192p. 1982. 8.00 o.p. (ISBN 0-318-02478-0). ICLE Georgia.

Mental Disorder & the Criminal Law. Sheldon S. Glueck. 1925. 29.00 o.p. (ISBN 0-527-34092-8). Kraus Repr.

Mental Evolution & Art. Rodney Chang. (Illus.). 1980. 6.50 o.p. (ISBN 0-682-49481-X, Banner). Exposition-Phoenix.

Mental Gymnastics. Jean M. Shaw & Mary Jo P. Cliatt. (Illus.). 256p. 1984. pap. text ed. 24.00 o.p. (ISBN 0-13-575928-5). P-H.

Mental Health - Psychiatric Nursing: A Holistic Life-Cycle Approach. Cornelia M. Beck & Ruth Parmelee Rawlins. (Illus.). 1534p. 1984. 41.95 o.p. (ISBN 0-8016-0555-5). Mosby.

Mental Health & Black Offenders. Charles E. Owens. LC 78-19588. 208p. 1980. 29.00x o.p. (ISBN 0-669-02645-X). Lexington Bks.

Mental Health & Family Life Education see Individualized Health Incentive Program Modules For Physically Disabled Students.

Mental Health & Social Policy. 2nd ed. David Mechanic. (Series in Social Policy). 1980. pap. text ed. (ISBN 0-13-576025-9). P-H.

Mental Health & the Environment. Ed. by Hugh Freeman. LC 84-9421. (Illus.). 490p. 1985. text ed. 69.00 o.p. (ISBN 0-443-02780-3). Churchill.

Mental Health Care in the European Community. Ed. by Steen P. Mangen. LC 85-6661. 278p. 1985. 29.00 o.p. (ISBN 0-7099-1755-4, Pub. by Croom Helm Ltd). Routledge Chapman & Hall.

Mental Health Concepts. Natalie Kalman & Claire Waughfield. LC 81-70853. (Illus.). 256p. (Orig.). 1983. pap. text ed. 16.95 o.p. (ISBN 0-8273-1706-9); 8.00 o.p. (ISBN 0-8273-1707-7). Delmar.

Mental Health Counsellors at Work. T. M. Magoon et al. 1971. 55.00 o.p. (ISBN 0-08-006422-1). Pergamon.

Mental Health Implications of Life in the Nuclear Age. H. Schweibcl. 1986. pap. 19.95 o.p. (ISBN 0-87332-400-5). M E Sharpe.

Mental Health in Modern Education. Ed. by Paul A. Witty. (National Society for the Study of Education Yearbooks Ser: No. 54, Pt. 2). 1955. pap. text ed. 4.50x o.s.i. (ISBN 0-226-60034-3). U of Chicago Pr.

Mental Health in Primary Care Settings. Ed. by Michael Shepherd et al. 352p. 1986. 39.95 o.p. (ISBN 0-422-80360-X, 9928, Pub. by Tavistock England). Routledge Chapman & Hall.

Mental Health In-Service Training: Some Practical Guidelines for the Psychiatric Consultant. Beulah Parker. LC 68-26388. 132p. 1968. text ed. 20.00x o.s.i. (ISBN 0-8236-3360-8). Intl Univs Pr.

Mental Health Information Systems: Design & Implementation. David J. Kupfer et al. (Library & Information Science Ser.: Vol. 19). 168p. 1976. 49.75 o.p. (ISBN 0-8247-6445-5). Dekker.

Mental Health Interventions for the Aging: Psychotherapeutic Treatment Approaches. Ed. by Arthur M. Horton, Jr. 208p. 1982. 29.95x o.s.i. (ISBN 0-03-061067-2). Bergin & Garvey.

Mental Health Issues & the Urban Poor. Ed. by Dorothy Evans & William Claiborn. LC 73-19708. 1974. 28.00 o.p. (ISBN 0-08-017831-6); pap. 14.25 o.p. (ISBN 0-08-017830-8). Pergamon.

Mental Health Needs of Workers & Management: Expectations & Reality. Ed. by Pasquale A. Carone et al. (Problems of Industrial Psychiatric Medicine Ser.: Vol. XII). 190p. 1988. 19.95 o.p. (ISBN 0-930545-05-2). Maple Hill Pr.

Mental Health Nursing: A Holistic Approach. 2nd ed. Elaine A. Pasquali et al. (Illus.). 723p. 1985. casebound 40.95 o.p. (ISBN 0-8016-3825-9). Mosby.

Mental Health Practices in Primary Care Settings: An Annotated Bibliography. Ed. by Greg Wilkinson. 572p. 1986. 55.00 o.p. (ISBN 0-422-60180-2, 9792, Pub. by Tavistock England). Routledge Chapman & Hall.

Mental Health Professional As Expert Witness: A Bibliography. Frederick Frankena. (Public Administration Ser.: P 1827). 12p. 1985. 2.00 o.p. (ISBN 0-89028-677-9). Vance Biblios.

Mental Health Social Work Observed. Mike Fisher et al. (National Institute Social Services Library: No. 45). 240p. 1983. text ed. 34.95x o.p. (ISBN 0-04-360061-1); pap. text ed. 12.95x o.p. (ISBN 0-04-360062-X). Unwin Hyman.

Mental Health, Vol. 3, (incl. 1984-1987 Supplements) Ed. by Eleanor C. Goldstein. (Social Issues Resources Ser.). 1986. 60.00 o.p. (ISBN 0-89777-078-1). Soc Issues.

Mental Hygiene in Teaching. 2nd ed. Fritz Redl & William Wattenberg. 1959. text ed. 14.95 o.p. (ISBN 0-15-558084-1, HC). HarBraceJ.

Mental Illness & Civil Liberties. Cyril Greenland. 126p. 1970. pap. text ed. 5.00 o.p. (ISBN 0-7135-1826-X, Pub. by Bedford England). Gower Pub Co.

Mental Illness & Health: Its Legacy Tensions, & Changes. Norman J. Finkel. 128p. 1976. pap. text ed. write for info. o.p. (ISBN 0-02-337700-3, 33770). Macmillan.

Mental Illness Programs for Employees. W. B. Goldbeck. (Springer Ser. in Industry & Health Care: Vol. 9). 250p. 1980. pap. 12.00 o.p. (ISBN 0-387-90479-4). Springer-Verlag.

Mental Patient: Studies in the Sociology of Deviance. S. P. Spitzer & Norman K. Denzin. 1968. pap. text ed. 23.95 o.p. (ISBN 0-07-060332-4). McGraw.

Mental Prodigies. Fred Barlow. 1952. (ISBN 0-8022-0061-3). Philos Lib.

Mental Retardation. B. H. Kirman. 1968. pap. text ed. 3.75 o.p. (ISBN 0-08-013371-1). Pergamon.

Mental Retardation in New Zealand. Ed. by Nirbhan N. Sigh & Keri M. Wilton. 308p. 1986. pap. 19.95 o.p. (ISBN 0-7233-0745-8, Pub. by Whitcoulls NZ). Intl Spec Bk.

Mental Retardation: Nature, Needs, & Advocacy. Donald F. Sellin. 1979. text ed. 36.00 o.s.i. (ISBN 0-205-05989-9, 2459892); tests avail. o.s.i. (ISBN 0-205-05990-2, 2459906). Allyn.

Mental Retardation: The Changing Outlook. Robert P. Ingalls. LC 77-23359. 491p. 1978. write for info. o.p. (ISBN 0-02-359660-0); write for info. tchr's. manual o.p. (ISBN 0-02-359670-8). Macmillan.

Mental Robots. Lewis A. Alesen. LC 57-13125. 1957. pap. 1.50 o.p. (ISBN 0-87004-000-6). Caxton.

Mental Tests & Cultural Adaptation. L. J. Cronbach & P. J. Drenth. LC 72-79985. (Psychology Ser.). 1972. pap. text ed. 21.60 o.p. (ISBN 0-686-22640-2). Mouton.

Mentally Abnormal Offender & the Law. H. Rollin. 1969. text ed. 16.25 o.p. (ISBN 0-08-013385-1); pap. text ed. 7.00 o.p. (ISBN 0-08-013384-3). Pergamon.

Mentally Handicapped Adolescent: The Slough Project of the National Society for Mentally Handicapped Children. E. P. Baranyay. 1971. text ed. 24.00 o.p. (ISBN 0-08-016271-1). Pergamon.

Mentally Handicapped Child. Brian H. Kirman. LC 73-6174. 240p. 1973. 7.95 o.s.i. (ISBN 0-8008-5188-9). Taplinger.

Mentor Connection. Michael G. Zey. LC 83-73091. 250p. 1984. 19.95 o.p. (ISBN 0-87094-446-0). Dow Jones-Irwin.

Menu Design. Judi Radice. LC 85-506. (Illus.). 256p. 1985. 49.95 o.p. (ISBN 0-86636-007-7). PBC Intl Inc.

Menu French. David Atkinson. (International Ser. in Hospitality Management). (Illus.). 96p. 1980. text ed. 21.00 o.p. (ISBN 0-08-024309-6); pap. text ed. 9.00 o.p. (ISBN 0-08-024308-8). Pergamon.

Menu Planner. Robert Carrier. (Illus.). 310p. 1985. 29.95 o.p. (ISBN 0-317-28930-6). Little.

Menu Pricing & Strategy. Jack E. Miller. LC 79-25932. (Illus.). 160p. 1983. pap. 18.95 o.p. (ISBN 0-8436-2144-3). Van Nos Reinhold.

Menus for Entertaining. James A. Beard. 1979. pap. 3.95 o.p. (ISBN 0-440-15569-X). Dell.

Mercantilism. Eli F. Heckscher. LC 82-48308. (World Economy Ser.). 927p. 1983. lib. bdg. 110.00 o.p. (ISBN 0-8240-5363-X). Garland Pub.

Mercedes-Benz: A Century of Invention. Automobile Quarterly Staff. LC 85-63588. (Illus.). 112p. 1986. 15.95 o.p. (ISBN 0-915038-48-X, 3-AQ-0050). Auto Quarterly.

Mercedes-Benz Racing Cars. Karl Ludvigsen. (Illus.). 1971. 35.00 o.p. (ISBN 0-393-60014-9). Norton.

Mercedes-Benz Tune-up Maintenance: Gas & Diesel, 1958-1978. Ed. by Eric Jorgensen. (Illus.). pap. 12.95 o.p. (ISBN 0-89287-175-X, A180). Clymer Pub.

Mercedes for the Road. Henry Rasmussen. LC 83-8124. (Survivors Ser.). (Illus.). 130p. (gr. 3-5). Repr. 12.98 o.p. (ISBN 0-87938-191-4). Motorbooks Intl.

Mercenaries for the Crimea: The German, Swiss, & Italian Legions in British Service, 1854-1856. C. C. Bayley. 1977. lib. bdg. 13.50x o.p. (ISBN 0-7735-0273-4, McGill Canada). U of Toronto Pr.

Mercenaries of Tomorrow. Paul Anderson. 256p. 1985. pap. 2.95 o.p. (ISBN 0-317-66395-X). Critics Choice Paper.

Mercenary-Green Hell. Leon DaSilva. 1976. pap. 1.50 o.p. (ISBN 0-685-73458-7, LB388, Pub. by Leisure Bks CT). Dorchester Pub Co.

Mercer Beasley Law Review: 1932-1936, Vols. 1-5. Bound set. 60.00x o.p. (ISBN 0-686-89949-0). Rothman.

Merchandising & Operating Results of Department & Specialty Stores (MOR) 1987. pap. 69.00 o.p. (ISBN 0-87102-121-8, 26-4139). Natl Ret Merch.

Merchandising in Action. Ed. by Lee Dyer. (Illus.). 13.95 o.p. (ISBN 0-911790-07-1). Prog Grocers Trade.

Merchant Marine Deck Examination Illustration Book. (Illus.). 59p. 1987. pap. 3.25 o.p. (ISBN 0-318-23834-9, S/N 050-012-00237-1). USGPO.

Merchant of Prato: Francesco di Marco Datini. Iris Origo. 1979. Repr. lib. bdg. 27.50x o.p. (ISBN 0-374-96149-2, Octagon). Hippocrene Bks.

Merchant of Venice. William Shakespeare. Ed. by J. H. Walter. (Players' Shakespeare Ser). (YA) (gr. 9 up). 1960. 3.50 o.p. (ISBN 0-8238-0116-0). Plays.

Merchant of Venice. William Shakespeare. 48p. (Orig.). 1989. pap. 9.95 o.p. (ISBN 1-55651-583-9); audiocassette tape incl. o.p. (ISBN 1-55651-584-7). Cram Cassettes.

Merchants & Rulers in Gujarat: The Response to the Portuguese in the Sixteenth Century. M. N. Pearson. 1976. 38.50x o.p. (ISBN 0-520-02809-0). U of Cal Pr.

Merchants: The Big Business Families of Saudi Arabia & the Gulf States. Michael Field. LC 84-4386. 384p. 1986. pap. 10.95 o.p. (ISBN 0-87951-226-1). Overlook Pr.

Mercier & Camier. Samuel Beckett. LC 74-21639. 1975. pap. 6.95 o.p. (ISBN 0-394-17835-1, E665, Ever). Grove.

Merck Manual: General Medicine, Vol. I. 14th ed. Ed. by Robert Berkow. 1600p. 1982. pap. 11.95 o.p. (ISBN 0-911910-04-2). Merck.

Merck Manual: Obstetrics, Gynecology, Pediatrics, Genetics, Vol. II. 14th ed. Ed. by Robert Berkow. 600p. 1982. pap. 6.95 o.p. (ISBN 0-911910-05-0). Merck.

Merck Manual of Diagnosis & Therapy. 14th ed. Robert Berkow. LC 1-31760. 1982. 19.75 o.p. (ISBN 0-911910-03-4). Merck.

Mercury Capri. (A288). Clymer Pub.

Mercury Capri Service Repair Handbook All Models, 1970-1976. Ed. by Jeff Robinson. (Illus.). pap. text ed. 12.95 o.p. (ISBN 0-89287-110-5, A143). Clymer Pub.

Mercury Service-Repair Handbook: 4 to 40 Hp, 1964-1982. Ed. by Eric Jorgensen. (Illus.). pap. 9.00 o.p. (ISBN 0-89287-222-5, B650). Clymer Pub.

Mercury Service-Repair Handbook: 50 to 200 Hp, 1964-1982. Clymer Publications & Ray Hoy. (Illus.). pap. 9.00 o.p. (ISBN 0-89287-150-4, B653). Clymer Pub.

Mercury Stern Drive. (B640). Clymer Pub.

Mercy Lord, My Husband's in the Kitchen & Other Equal Opportunity Conversations with God. Toby D. Schwartz. 96p. 1982. pap. 2.95 o.p. (ISBN 0-380-57943-X, 57943-X). Avon.

Mercy of Qur'an & the Advent of Zaman. Shykh F. Haeri. 164p. 1987. pap. 18.95 o.p. (ISBN 0-7103-0224-X, 02231, Kegan Paul). Routledge Chapman & Hall.

Meredith. Ioan Williams. (Critical Heritage Ser.). 424p. 1985. pap. 15.00 o.p. (ISBN 0-7102-0596-1). Routledge Chapman & Hall.

Mereness Calendar: Federal Documents on the Upper Mississippi Valley, 1780-1890, 13 vols. Ed. by University of Illinois at Urbana, University Library, Champaign Staff. 1971. Set. 1530.00 o.p. (ISBN 0-8161-0915-X, Hall Library). G K Hall.

Meres De Gagnants En France Nineteen Forty-One to Nineteen Fifty-Five. pap. 13.50 o.p. (ISBN 0-85131-287-X, Pub. by J A Allen U K). S R Smith Sporting Bks.

Merger Directory. Ed. by Kathleen M. Victory. 500p. 1987. text ed. 189.00 o.p. Cambridge Corp.

Merger, Managers & the Economy. Samuel R. Reid. 1968. text ed. 26.95 o.p. (ISBN 0-07-051787-8). McGraw.

Merger Mania: Arbitrage-Wall Street's Best-Kept Money-Making Secret. Ivan F. Boesky. Ed. by Jeffrey Madrick. LC 84-25193. 242p. 1985. 18.45 o.p. (ISBN 0-03-002602-4). HR&W.

Merger Yearbook. 10th ed. Ed. by Andrew D. Clapp. 512p. 1988. 189.00 o.p. (ISBN 0-939008-11-4). Cambridge Corp.

Mergers & Acquisitions: Current Problems in Perspective. Ed. by Michael Keenan & Lawrence J. White. LC 81-47691. 368p. 1982. 39.00x o.p. (ISBN 0-669-04719-8). Lexington Bks.

MERI Report: Egypt. Middle East Research Institute Staff. LC 85-4136. 211p. 1985. pap. 60.00 lg. format o.p. (ISBN 0-7099-3551-X, Pub. by Croom Helm Ltd). Routledge Chapman & Hall.

MERI Report: Iran. Middle East Research Institute Staff. LC 85-4165. 181p. 1985. pap. 60.00 lg. format o.p. (ISBN 0-7099-3550-1, Pub. by Croom Helm Ltd). Routledge Chapman & Hall.

MERI Report: Israel. Middle East Research Institute Staff. LC 85-4164. 180p. 1985. pap. 60.00 lg. format o.p. (ISBN 0-7099-3548-X, Pub. by Croom Helm Ltd). Routledge Chapman & Hall.

MERI Report: Kuwait. Middle East Research Institute Staff. LC 84-28552. 190p. 1985. pap. 60.00 lg. format o.p. (ISBN 0-7099-3546-3, Pub. by Croom Helm Ltd). Routledge Chapman & Hall.

MERI Report: Saudi Arabia. Middle East Research Institute Staff. LC 84-28553. 190p. 1985. pap. 60.00 lg. format o.p. (ISBN 0-7099-3545-5, Pub. by Croom Helm Ltd). Routledge Chapman & Hall.

MERI Report: Turkey. Middle East Research Institute Staff. LC 84-28554. 182p. 1985. pap. 60.00 lg. format o.p. (ISBN 0-7099-3549-8, Pub. by Croom Helm Ltd). Routledge Chapman & Hall.

MERI Report: United Arab Emirates. Middle East Research Institute Staff. LC 85-4114. 198p 1985. pap. 60.00 lg. format o.p. (ISBN 0-7099-3547-1, Pub. by Croom Helm Ltd). Routledge Chapman & Hall.

MERI Reports on the Middle East: Saudi Arabia, Kuwait, United Arab Emirates, Israel, Turkey, Iran, & Egypt, 7 reports. Middle East Research Institute Staff. 1985. Set. pap. 340.00 lg. format o.p. (ISBN 0-7099-3552-8, Pub. by Croom Helm Ltd). Routledge Chapman & Hall.

Meristems, Growth & Development in Woody Plants: An Analytical Review of Anatomical, Physiological & Morphogenic Aspects. J. A. Romberger. LC 78-51432. (Landmark Reprints in Plant Science Ser.). (Illus.). 224p. 1978. Repr. of 1963 ed. text ed. 15.00x o.s.i. (ISBN 0-86598-005-5, Pub. by Allanheld). Rowman.

Merle Haggard-Memories, Fiddles & Songs. 1975. pap. 5.95 o.p. (ISBN 0-686-10315-7, Pub. by Peer-Southern). CPP Belwin.

Merle: Start of a Dynasty. D. Brian Plummer. (Illus.). 148p. 1982. 18.00 o.p. (ISBN 0-85115-171-X, Pub. by Boydell & Brewer). Longwood Pub Group.

Merleau-Ponty & Marxism: From Terror to Reform. Barry Cooper. LC 78-16829. 1979. 30.00x o.p. (ISBN 0-8020-5435-8). U of Toronto Pr.

Merleau-Ponty: Perception, Structure, Language: a Collection of Essays. Ed. by John Sallis. 172p. 1981. Repr. of 1980 ed. text ed. 15.00x o.p. (ISBN 0-391-02382-9). Humanities.

Merricat's Castle Nursery School Games for Pre-Schoolers. Gretchen Buchenholz & Nursery School Staff. Ed. by Leora M. Sies. 128p. (Orig.). 1984. pap. 8.95 o.p. (ISBN 0-671-47464-2, Fireside). S&S.

Merrie's Secret Wish. Muriel O'Brien. (Illus.). (gr. 3-6). 1980. 5.00 o.p. (ISBN 0-682-49555-7). Exposition-Phoenix.

Merrill's Guide to Computer Performance Evaluation. (Illus.). 1980. SAS Inst.

Merrill's Oregon Rules of Civil Procedure: 1988 Handbook. Fredric R. Merrill. 364p. 1988. pap. 18.50 o.p. Butterworth WA.

Merrily Comes Our Harvest In: Poems for Thanksgiving. Ed. by Lee B. Hopkins. LC 78-52804. (Illus.). (gr. k-3). 1978. 10.95 o.p. (ISBN 0-15-253179-3, HJ). HarBraceJ.

Merrily on High. Colin Stephenson. 192p. 1973. 4.95 o.p. (ISBN 0-8192-1152-4). Morehouse Pub.

Merrily We Roll along. Stephen Sondheim & George Furth. (Illus.). 208p. 1983. pap. (ISBN 0-396-08060-X). Dodd.

Merritt's Textbook of Neurology. 7th ed. Ed. by Lewis P. Rowland. LC 83-19550. 774p. 1984. text ed. 52.50 o.p. (ISBN 0-8121-0893-0). Lea & Febiger.

Merry Gentlemen (& One Lady) J. Bryan, III. LC 84-45610. 283p. 1985. 17.95 o.p. (ISBN 0-689-11533-4, Atheneum). Macmillan.

Merry-Go-Riddle. Ann Bishop. LC 73-7321. (Riddle Bks.). (Illus.). 40p. (gr. 1-3). 1973. PLB 7.75 o.p. (ISBN 0-8075-5072-8). A Whitman.

Merry-Go-Round. Oretta Leigh. LC 84-15731. (Illus.). 32p. (ps-2). 1985. 12.95 o.p. (ISBN 0-8234-0544-3). Holiday.

Merry-Go-Round: A Treasury of Poems. Joan E. Youngblood. 75p. (Orig.). 1985. pap. 6.95x o.p. (ISBN 0-932269-17-6). Wyndham Hall.

Merry-Go-Round in the Sea. Randolph Stow. LC 83-51346. 288p. 1984. Repr. of 1966 ed. 14.95 o.s.i. (ISBN 0-8008-5195-1). Taplinger.

Merry Mix-up: A Finder-Seeker Mystery. Laura Palmer. (Illus.). 32p. (gr. 1-4). 1981. pap. 1.95 o.p. (ISBN 0-380-78071-2, 78071-2, Camelot). Avon.

Merry-Mouse Book of Favorite Poems. Priscilla Hillman. LC 80-2551. (Merry Mouse Bks.). (Illus.). 32p. (ps-3). 1981. 4.95a o.p. (ISBN 0-385-17104-8); PLB o. p. o.p. (ISBN 0-385-17105-6). Doubleday.

Merry-Mouse Book of Prayers & Graces. Illus. by Priscilla Hillman. LC 82-45497. (Balloon Bks.). (Illus.). 32p. (ps-3). 1983. 4.95 o.p. (ISBN 0-385-18337-2). Doubleday.

Merry Mouse Schoolhouse. Priscilla Hillman. LC 81-43137. (Balloon Bks.). (Illus.). 32p. 1982. 4.95a o.p. (ISBN 0-385-17106-4); PLB (ISBN 0-385-17107-2). Doubleday.

Merry Songs & Ballads & Musa Pedestris: Musa Pedestris, 6 vols. John S. Farmer. Repr. of 1896 ed. Set. 85.00x o.p. (ISBN 0-8154-0066-7). Cooper Sq.

Merton: A Biography. Monica Furlong. LC 79-3588. (Illus.). 320p. 1980. 12.95i o.p. (ISBN 0-06-063079-5). HarpR.

Merv. Michael B. Druxman. 1981. pap. 1.95 o.p. (ISBN 0-8439-0883-1, Pub. by Leisure Bks CT). Dorchester Pub Co.

Mescal & Mechanisms of Hallucinations. Heinrich Kluver. LC 66-20593. xviii, 108p. 1966. pap. text ed. 1.50x o.s.i. (ISBN 0-226-44506-2, P531, Phoen). U of Chicago Pr.

Meshugah & Other Stories. Emanuel Fried. Ed. by Joy Walsh. 40p. (Orig.). 1982. pap. 2.95 o.p. (ISBN 0-938838-09-1). Textile Bridge.

Mesmerism & the End of the Enlightenment in France. Robert Darnton. LC 68-25607. (Illus.). 1968. 17.50x o.s.i. (ISBN 0-674-56950-4). Harvard U Pr.

MesoAmerican Archaeology: A Guide to the Literature & Other Information Sources. Susan F. Magee. (Guides & Bibliographics Ser.: No. 12). 81p. 1981. pap. text ed. 5.95x o.p. (ISBN 0-292-75053-6). U of Tex Pr.

Mesolithic Settlement of Northern Europe. John G. Clark. LC 75-95090. 1971. Repr. of 1936 ed. lib. bdg. 22.50x o.p. (ISBN 0-8371-2579-0, CLMS). Greenwood.

Meson & Baryon Spectroscopy. rev. ed. D. B. Lichtenberg. (Illus.). 1965. pap. 13.50 o.p. (ISBN 0-387-90000-4). Springer-Verlag.

Mesonephros of Cat & Sheep. K. Tiedemann. (Advances in Anatomy, Embryology & Cell Biology: Vol. 52, Pt. 3). (Illus.). 1976. soft cover 37.80 o.p. (ISBN 0-387-07779-0). Springer-Verlag.

Mesosphere & Thermosphere. G. Schmidtke & K. S. W. Champion. 1981. pap. 36.00x flexi-cover o.p. (ISBN 0-08-028393-4). Pergamon.

Message & the Sequel. M. E. Mitchell. 1980. 8.50 o.p. (ISBN 0-682-49607-3). Exposition-Phoenix.

Message from Infinity: A Space-Age Correlation of Science & Religion. Gordon N. Patterson. (Illus.). 96p. 1984. 6.50 o.p. (ISBN 0-682-40149-8). Exposition-Phoenix.

Message from Malaga. Helen MacInnes. LC 79-160406. 367p. 1971. 6.95 o.s.i. (ISBN 0-15-159280-2). HarBraceJ.

Message in the Hollow Oak. Carolyn Keene. LC 78-181844. (Nancy Drew Ser.: Vol. 12). (Illus.). 196p. (gr. 4-7). 1935. 4.50 o.p. (ISBN 0-448-09512-2, G&D); PLB 3.29 o.p. (ISBN 0-448-19512-7). Putnam Pub Group.

Message of Exodus. Lester Meyer. LC 83-70519. 176p. (Orig.). 1983. pap. 10.95 o.p. (ISBN 0-8066-2025-0, 10-4347, Augsburg). Augsburg Fortress.

Message of Job: A Theological Commentary. Daniel J. Simundson. LC 86-7893. (Augsburg Old Testament Studies). 160p. (Orig.). 1986. pap. 11.95 o.p. (ISBN 0-8066-2218-0, 10-4349, Augsburg). Augsburg Fortress.

Message of Jonah: A Theological Commentary. Terence E. Fretheim. LC 77-72461. pap. 8.95 o.p. (ISBN 0-8066-1591-5, 10-4350, Augsburg). Augsburg Fortress.

Message of Marienfried: According to Our Lady's Apparitions in 1946. Ami Press Staff. 20p. cancelled o.s.i. (ISBN 0-911988-50-5). AMI Pr.

Message of the Wesleys: A Reader of Instruction & Devotion. Ed. by Philip S. Watson. 270p. 1983. pap. 5.95 o.p. (ISBN 0-310-75031-8, 17027P). Zondervan.

Message to an Aborted Baby Killed by the Cowardice of His Mother & the Venal Complicity of the Attending Physician. Charles Visentin. (Illus.). 1976. 97.75 o.p. (ISBN 0-89266-015-5). Am Classical Coll Pr.

Messages of Love. Samuel Youd. 1961. 4.95 o.p. S&S.

Messenger for Parliament. Erik C. Haugaard. (Illus.). 1976. 6.95 o.p. (ISBN 0-395-24392-0). HM.

Messenger of Love. Wildorf E. Goodison-Orr. 1972. 6.50 o.p. (ISBN 0-682-47377-4). Exposition-Phoenix.

Messer Rondo & Other Stories by Gay Men. Stephen Airey et al. 157p. (Orig.). 1983. pap. 6.50 o.p. (ISBN 0-907040-21-7, Pub. by GMP England). Alyson Pubns.

Messerschmitt 262 A-1. J. Richard Smith & Eddie J. Creek. LC 83-61695. (Monogram Close-up 17 Ser.). (Illus.). 32p. 1984. 6.95 o.s.i. (ISBN 0-914144-17-0). Monogram Aviation.

Messiah, a Study in Interpretation. Percy M. Young. (Student's Music Library Ser.). 1961. 15.95 o.p. (ISBN 0-234-77215-8). Dufour.

Messiah & the Mandarins. Dennis Bloodworth. LC 82-45182. 384p. 1982. 15.95 o.p. (ISBN 0-689-11297-1, Atheneum). Macmillan.

Messiah in Context: Israel's History & Destiny in Formative Judaism. Jacob Neusner. LC 83-20542. (Foundations of Judaism Ser.). 304p. 1984. 26.95 o.p. (ISBN 0-8006-0716-3, 1-716, Fortress). Augsburg Fortress.

Messiahship of Christ. Franz Delitzsch & P. J. Gloag. 628p. lib. bdg. 23.95 o.p. (ISBN 0-8254-5120-5). Kregel.

Messianic Expectation in the Old Testament. Joachim Becker. Tr. by David E. Green from Ger. LC 79-8891. 96p. 1980. 8.95 o.p. (ISBN 0-8006-0545-4, 1-545, Fortress). Augsburg Fortress.

Messianic Secret. Ed. by Christopher Tuckett. LC 83-5499. (Issues in Religion & Theology Ser.). 176p. 1983. pap. 2.50 o.p. (ISBN 0-8006-1767-3, Fortress). Augsburg Fortress.

Messieurs les Ronds-de-cuirt. Georges Courteline & Francis Pruner. 192p. 1966. 8.95 o.p. (ISBN 0-686-54634-2). French & Eur.

Metabolic Activation of Polynuclear Aromatic Hydrocarbons. Wing-Sum Tsang & Gary W. Griffin. (Illus.). 1979. 50.00 o.p. (ISBN 0-08-023835-1). Pergamon.

Metabolic & Pediatric Eye Disease: Proceedings of the International Society on Metabolic Eye Disease Symposium, 3rd. International Society on Metabolic Eye Disease Staff. Ed. by Heskel M. Haddad. (Illus.). 240p. 1980. pap. 55.00 o.p. (ISBN 0-08-024950-7). Pergamon.

Metabolic Aspects of Food Safety. Ed. by Francis J. Roe. LC 72-142181. 1971. 84.50 o.p. (ISBN 0-12-592550-6). Acad Pr.

Metabolic Bone Disease. Ed. by Louis V. Avioli & Stephen M. Krane. LC 76-27431. 1977-78. Vol. 1. 89.00 o.p. (ISBN 0-12-068701-1); Vol. 2. 98.00 o.p. (ISBN 0-12-068702-X). Acad Pr.

Metabolic Bone Disease in Total Parenteral Nutrition. Ed. by Jack W. Coburn & Gordon L. Klein. (Illus.). 158p. 1984. pap. text ed. 29.00 o.p. (ISBN 0-8067-0351-2). Urban & S.

Metabolic Care. D. E. F. Tweedle. LC 81-70268. (Illus.). 320p. 1983. pap. text ed. 37.00 o.p. (ISBN 0-443-01867-7). Churchill.

Metabolic Changes Induced by Alcohol. Ed. by G. A. Martini & Ch. Bode. LC 77-142386. (Illus.). 1972. 28.40 o.p. (ISBN 0-387-05296-8). Springer-Verlag.

Metabolic Disease: A Guide to Early Recognition. Robert M. Cohn & Karl Roth. (Illus.). 464p. 1983. (ISBN 0-7216-2652-1). Saunders.

Metabolic Interconversion of Enzymes: Proceedings of the Konferenz der Gesellschaft Deutscher Naturforscher und Aerzte, 2nd, Rottach-Egern, 1971. Konferenz der Gesellschaft Deutscher Naturforscher und Aerzte Staff. Ed. by O. Wieland et al. LC 72-85775. (Illus.). xi, 448p. 1972. pap. 43.00 o.p. (ISBN 0-387-05919-9). Springer-Verlag.

Metabolic Interconversion of Enzymes 1975: Fourth International Symposium Held in Arab, April 27th-May 2nd, 1975. Ed. by S. Shaltiel. (Proceedings in Life Sciences). (Illus.). 1976. 43.00 o.p. (ISBN 0-387-07888-6). Springer-Verlag.

Metabolic Regulation. R. M. Denton & C. I. Pogson. 1976. pap. 8.50 o.p. (ISBN 0-412-13150-1, NO. 6085, Pub. by Chapman & Hall England). Routledge Chapman & Hall.

Metabolic Roles of Citrate: Proceedings. Biochemical Society Symposium, 27th. Ed. by T. W. Goodwin. LC 68-17671. (Illus.). 1968. 29.00 o.p. (ISBN 0-12-289878-8). Acad Pr.

Metachromatic Reaction. J. W. Kelly. (Protoplasmatologia: Vol. 2, Pt. D2). (Illus.). 1956. pap. 32.50 o.p. (ISBN 0-387-80422-6). Springer-Verlag.

Metafisica Della Architettura. Alberto Sartoris. (Pamphlet Architecture Ser.: no.10). (Illus.). 35p. (Orig.). 1984. pap. 7.00 o.p. (ISBN 0-910413-30-4). Princeton Arch.

Metal Age, Vol. II. (Illus.). 120p. (YA) (gr. 8-12). 1986. pap. 12.95 o.p. (ISBN 0-317-42981-7, HL00182841, Pub. by Shinko Music Pub Co Ltd). H Leonard Pub Corp.

Metal-Ammonia Solutions. Ed. by William Jolly. LC 72-80134. (Benchmark Papers in Inorganic Chemistry: Vol. 1). 440p. 1982. 62.95 o.p. (ISBN 0-87933-008-2). Van Nos Reinhold.

Metal-Ammonia Solutions: Proceedings of the International Conference on the Nature of Metal-Ammonia Solution, Ithaca, N.Y., 1969. Ed. by J. J. Lagowski & M. J. Sienko. 522p. 1976. 130.00 o.p. (ISBN 0-08-020794-4). Pergamon.

Metal & Inorganic Waste Reclaiming Encyclopedia. Marshall Sittig. LC 80-21669. (Pollution Tech. Rev. 70; Chem. Tech. Rev. 175). (Illus.). 591p. (Orig.). 1981. 54.00 o.p. (ISBN 0-8155-0823-9). Noyes.

Metal-Arc Gas Shielded Welding. Ed. by N. C. Balchin et al. (Engineering Craftsmen: No. F23). (Illus.). 1977. spiral bdg. 39.95x o.p. (ISBN 0-85083-385-X). Trans-Atl Phila.

Metal Bridges. Compiled by American Society of Civil Engineers Staff. 444p. 1974. pap. 49.00x o.p. (ISBN 0-87262-101-4). Am Soc Civil Eng.

Metal Casting of Sculpture & Ornament. 2nd ed. Carl D. Clarke. (Illus.). 250p. 1985. 30.00 o.p. (ISBN 0-685-50214-7). Standard Arts.

Metal Complexes of Chelating Olefin-Group V Ligands see Coordinative Interactions.

Metal Deformation Processes: Friction & Lubrication. John A. Schey. (Illus.). 824p. 1980. 195.00 o.p. (ISBN 0-08-024658-3); pap. 195.00 o.p. (ISBN 0-08-024657-5). Pergamon.

Metal Ion Activation of Dioxygen, Vol. 2. Ed. by Thomas G. Spiro. LC 79-13808. (Metal Ions in Biology Ser.). 247p. 1980. 67.95 o.p. (ISBN 0-471-04398-2, Pub. by Wiley-Interscience). Wiley.

Metal Ions in Biological Systems: High Molecular Complexes, Vol. 3. Ed. by Helmut Sigel. 304p. 1974. 85.00 o.p. (ISBN 0-8247-6030-1). Dekker.

Metal Ions in Biological Systems: Nucleotides & Derivatives--Their Ligating Ambivalency, Vol. 8. Sigel. 256p. 1979. 85.00 o.p. (ISBN 0-8247-6843-4). Dekker.

Metal Manufacturing Technology. Jack W. Chaplin. (gr. 10 up). 1976. text ed. 19.96 o.p. (ISBN 0-87345-132-5). Glencoe.

Metal Monster. Abraham Merritt. (Orig.). 1976. pap. 1.50 o.p. (ISBN 0-380-00862-9, 31294). Avon.

Metal Pi Complexes, 2 Pts, Vol. 2. M. Herberhold. LC 65-13231. 1972-74. Pt. 1: General Survey. 166.00 o.p. (ISBN 0-444-40899-1); Vol. 2: Specific Aspects. 127.75 o.p. (ISBN 0-444-41061-9). Elsevier.

Metal Science of Stainless Steels: Proceedings of the AIME Annual Meeting, Denver, CO, 1987. (Illus.). 206p. 32.00 o.p. (ISBN 0-89520-148-8); members 20.00 o.p. (ISBN 0-317-34886-8); student members 11.00 o.p. (ISBN 0-317-34887-6). ASM.

Metal Sculptures of Eastern India. Bimal Bandyopadhyay. (Illus.). 178p. 1981. text ed. 38.50x o.p. (ISBN 0-391-02658-5). Humanities.

Metal Shots. (Illus.). 32p. 1985. pap. 3.95 o.p. (ISBN 0-88188-372-7). H Leonard Pub Corp.

Metal Toxicity in Mammals. B. Venugopal & T. D. Luckey. Incl. Vol. 1, Physiologic & Chemical Basis for Metal Toxicity. 248p. 1977. 55.00x (ISBN 0-306-37176-6); Vol. 2, Chemical Toxicity of Metals & Metalloids. LC 76-44859. 420p. 1978. 75.00x (ISBN 0-306-37177-4). (Illus.). 1977 (Plenum Pr). Plenum Pub.

Metalcube Pkg 1S-6A. Date not set. (ISBN 0-07-521127-0). McGraw.

Metalcutting: Today's Techniques for Engineers & Shop Personnel. American Machinist Magazine Staff. 1979. text ed. 36.00 o.p. (ISBN 0-07-001545-7). McGraw.

Metalforming: Modern Machines, Methods & Tooling for Engineers & Operating Personnel. American Machinist Magazine Staff. 288p. 1982. text ed. 39.50 o.p. (ISBN 0-07-001546-5). McGraw.

Metallic Bellows & Expansion Joints. Ed. by R. I. Jetter et al. (PVP Ser.: Vol. 51). 154p. 1981. 30.00 o.p. (ISBN 0-686-34510-X, H00187). ASME.

Metallic Cartridge Reloading. Robert S. Anderson. LC 81-70996. (Illus.). 320p. (Orig.). 1982. pap. 13.95 o.p. (ISBN 0-910676-39-9). DBI.

Metallic Contaminants & Human Health: Fogarty International Center Proceedings, Ed. by Douglas H. Lee. (Environmental Science Ser.: No. 2). 1972. 47.00 o.p. (ISBN 0-12-440660-2). Acad Pr.

Metallogeny & Global Tectonics. Ed. by Wilfred Walker. LC 76-3605. (Benchmark Papers in Geology Ser.: Vol. 29). 425p. 1976. 80.00 o.p. (ISBN 0-12-787720-7). Acad Pr.

Metallography As a Quality Control Tool. Ed. by J. L. McCall & P. M. French. LC 78-7224. 308p. 1980. 55.00x o.p. (ISBN 0-306-40423-0, Plenum Pr). Plenum Pub.

Metallurgical Engineering Practice Problem Manual. David S. Goldstein & Rhonda A. Jones. (Engineering Review Manual Ser.). 58p. 1987. pap. text ed. 14.50 o.p. (ISBN 0-932276-67-9). Prof Pubns CA.

Metallurgical Furnaces. V. Krivandin & B. Markov. 1980. 11.50 o.p. (ISBN 0-8285-1830-0, Pub. by Mir Pubs USSR). Imported Pubns.

Metallurgical Plant Design: A Bibliographical Overview. Coppa & Avery Consultants Staff. (Architecture Ser.: Bibliography A 1321). 1985. pap. 2.00 o.p. (ISBN 0-89028-271-4). Vance Biblios.

Metallurgical Progress. McLeod et al. 88p. 1957. (ISBN 0-8022-1022-8). Philos Lib.

Metallurgical Reminiscences & Dialogue. Albert Sauveur. 1981. 20.00 o.p. (ISBN 0-87170-132-4). ASM.

Metallurgical Slags, Pt. 2. C. R. Masson. 1982. pap. 67.00 flexi-cover o.p. (ISBN 0-08-028684-4). Pergamon.

Metallurgical Thermodynamics. 2nd ed. David R. Gaskell. (Materials Engineering Ser.). 560p. 1981. text ed. 55.95 o.p. (ISBN 0-07-022946-5). McGraw.

Metallurgical Treatises. Ed. by John K. Tien & John F. Elliot. LC 81-83754. (Technology of Metallurgy Ser.). 643p. 1983. Repr. of 1981 ed. 60.00 o.p. (ISBN 0-89520-381-2). Minerals Metals.

Metallurgy in Antiquity see Studies in Ancient Technology.

Metallurgy of Continuous Annealed Sheet Steel. Ed. by B. L. Bramfitt & P. L. Magonon. 488p. cancelled o.s.i. Minerals Metals.

Metallurgy of Continuous-Annealed Sheet Steel: Proceedings. AIME Annual Meeting, Dallas, 1982. Ed. by P. L. Mangonon, Jr. & B. L. Bramfitt. (Illus.). 395p. 40.00 o.p.; members 25.00 o.p. (ISBN 0-317-36247-X); student members 15.00 o.p. (ISBN 0-317-36248-8). ASM.

Metallurgy of Nuclear Fuels. V. S. Yemel'yanov & A. I. Yevstyukin. 1969. 145.00 o.p. (ISBN 0-08-012073-3). Pergamon.

Metallurgy: Weldability of Metals. Resource Systems International Staff. 1982. pap. text ed. 15.00 o.p. (ISBN 0-8359-4336-4, Reston). P-H.

Metallurgy: Welding. Resource Systems International Staff. 1982. pap. text ed. 15.00 o.p. (ISBN 0-8359-4335-6, Reston). P-H.

Metals & Micronutrients: Uptake & Utilization by Plants. D. A. Robb & S. Pierpoint. 1983. 79.50 o.s.i. (ISBN 0-12-589580-1). Acad Pr.

Metals for Space Travel: Lectures held at the Fifth Plansee Seminar. Plansee Seminar De Re Metallica-5th-Reutte-1964. Ed. by F. Benesovsky. (Illus.). viii, 879p. 1965. pap. 51.40 o.p. (ISBN 0-387-80730-6). Springer Verlag.

Metals for the Space Age: Papers Presented at the Fifth Plansee Seminar. Plansee Seminar De Re Metallica-5th-Reutte-1964. Ed. by F. Benesovsky. (Illus.). 1965. 51.40 o.p. (ISBN 0-387-80729-2). Springer-Verlag.

Metals Handbook Comprehensive Index. 1985. 98.00 o.p. (ISBN 0-87170-216-9). ASM.

Metals in Biochemistry. P. M. Harrison & R. J. Hoare. LC 79-41813. 80p. 1980. pap. 8.50x o.p. (ISBN 0-412-13160-9, NO. 6361, Pub. by Chapman & Hall England). Routledge Chapman & Hall.

Metals: Thermal & Mechanical Data. S. Allard. 1969. 115.00 o.p. (ISBN 0-08-006588-0). Pergamon.

Metalwork & Enamelling: A Practical Treatise on Gold & Silversmiths' Work & Their Allied Crafts. 5th & rev. ed. Herbert Maryon. (Illus.). 14.00 o.p. (ISBN 0-8446-0198-5). Peter Smith.

Metamassage: How to Massage Your Way to a Beautiful Complexion - All Over. Pyrrha Malouf. (Illus.). 192p. (Orig.). 1983. 5.95 o.p. (ISBN 0-87795-472-0, Arbor Hse). Morrow.

Metamathematical Investigations of Intuitionistic Arithmetic & Analysis. A. S. Troelstra. (Lecture Notes in Mathematics Ser.: Vol. 344). 1973. pap. 23.00 o.p. (ISBN 0-387-06491-5). Springer-Verlag.

Metamorphic Complexes of Asia. Ed. by V. S. Sobolev et al. (Illus.). 350p. 1984. 80.00 o.p. (ISBN 0-08-022854-2). Pergamon.

Metamorphic Map of Asia. V. S. Sobolev. 1979. 150.00x o.p. (ISBN 0-08-022936-0). Pergamon.

Metamorphic Petrology. 2nd ed. Francis J. Turner. LC 79-27496. (International Earth & Planetary Sciences Ser.). (Illus.). 512p. 1980. text ed. 57.95 o.p. (ISBN 0-07-065501-4). McGraw.

Metamorphoseon. Ovid. Ed. by Jacobus Pontanus. LC 75-27868. (Renaissance & the Gods Ser.: Vol. 24). (Illus.). 1977. Repr. of 1618 ed. lib. bdg. 88.00 o.p. (ISBN 0-8240-2073-1). Garland Pub.

Metamorphoses. Ovid. Tr. by Garth et al. LC 75-27884. (Renaissance & the Gods Ser.: Vol. 39). (Illus.). 1976. Repr. of 1732 ed. lib. bdg. 88.00 o.p. (ISBN 0-8240-2088-X). Garland Pub.

Metamorphosis. Alvin Silverstein & Virginia Silverstein. (Illus.). (gr. 3-7). 1971. 6.25 o.p. (ISBN 0-689-20645-3, Atheneum). Macmillan.

Metaphor. H. W. Fowler et al. Ed. by Steele Commager. Incl. English Idioms; English Influence on the French Vocabulary; Briton, British, Britisher; Split Infinitive; Logic & Grammar; Four Words; Subjunctives; Medium Aevum & the Middle Age; Index to Tracts I-XIX. (Society for Pure English Ser.: Vol. 2). 1979. lib. bdg. 46.00 o.p. (ISBN 0-8240-3666-2). Garland Pub.

Metaphor in the Nondramatic Works of Jean Giraudoux. Laurence Le Sage. 1952. pap. 1.00 o.p. (ISBN 0-87114-004-7). U of Oreg Bks.

Metaphors We Live by. George Lakoff & Mark Johnson. LC 80-10783. xiv, 242p. 1980. lib. bdg. 20.00x o.s.i. (ISBN 0-226-46800-3). U of Chicago Pr.

Metaphysical Healing: Principles & Practice. Henry F. Nowell. 1979. 6.00 o.p. (ISBN 0-682-49239-6). Exposition-Phoenix.

Metaphysical Society: Victorian Minds in Crisis, 1869-1880. Alan W. Brown. LC 73-8422. xiv, 372p. 1973. Repr. of 1947 ed. lib. bdg. 27.50x o.p. (ISBN 0-374-91008-1, Octagon). Hippocrene Bks.

Metaphysical Theory of State: A Criticism. Leonard T. Hobhouse. LC 83-22706. 156p. 1984. Repr. of 1918 ed. lib. bdg. 35.00x o.p. (ISBN 0-313-24391-3, HMTS). Greenwood.

Metaphysics. William H. Walsh. LC 66-26470. (Orig.). 1966. pap. 2.25 o.p. (ISBN 0-15-659305-X, Harv). HarBraceJ.

Metaphysics, a Bridge to ECKANKAR. Thomas Flamma. LC 81-80177. 232p. 1981. pap. 4.95 o.p. (ISBN 0-914766-65-1, 0193). Illum Way Pub.

Metaphysics of Wall Street. Justin F. Stone. 143p. 1983. 10.00 o.p. (ISBN 0-89540-134-7, SB-134). Sun Pub.

Metastable Liquids. B. P. Skripov. 284p. 1974. text ed. 57.00x o.p. (ISBN 0-7065-1370-3, Pub. by Keter Pub Jerusalem). Coronet Bks.

Metastatic Tumors of the Central Nervous System. Kintomo Takakura & Keiji Sano. LC 81-18635. (Illus.). 356p. 1982. 58.00 o.p. (ISBN 0-89640-067-0). Igaku-Shoin.

Meteorites. C. B. Moore. (Earth Science Curriculum Project Pamphlet Ser). 1971. pap. 5.76 o.p. (ISBN 0-395-02624-5). HM.

Meteorology. 2nd ed. Joseph S. Weisberg. (Illus.). 432p. 1981. text ed. 34.95 o.p. (ISBN 0-395-29516-5). HM.

Meteorology for Seamen. 4th ed. C. R. Burgess. 251p. 1982. text ed. 25.00x o.p. Sheridan.

Meteorology: The Earth & Its Weather. Joseph S. Weisberg. LC 75-26094. (Illus.). 320p. 1976. text ed. 20.30 o.p. (ISBN 0-395-20673-1). HM.

Meteorology Today. 2nd ed. C. Donald Ahrens. (Illus.). 523p. 1985. pap. text ed. 38.75 o.p. (ISBN 0-314-85212-3). West Pub.

Meter: A Handbook of Activities to Motivate the Teaching of the Metric System. (The Spice Ser.). 1975. 8.95 o.s.i. (ISBN 0-89273-118-4). Educ Serv.

Metering Apparatus & Tariffs for Electricity Supply. Institution of Electrical Engineers (UK) Staff & Peter Peregrims, Ltd. (Conference Publications: No. 217). 229p. 1982. pap. 82.00 o.s.i. (ISBN 0-85296-265-7, IC217). Inst Elect Eng.

Meterology Manual & Lecture Guide. Richard E. Carlson. 112p. 1986. pap. text ed. 8.95 o.p. (ISBN 0-8403-2992-X). Kendall-Hunt.

Methane. Ed. by H. L. Clever & C. L. Young. (Solubility Data Ser.). (Illus.). 801p. 1987. 130.01 o.s.i. (ISBN 0-08-029201-1). Pergamon.

Methane: Fuel for the Future. Ed. by Enoch Durbin & Patrick L. McGeer. LC 82-13120. 350p. 1982. 59.50x o.p. (ISBN 0-306-41122-9, Plenum Pr). Plenum Pub.

Method & Imagination in Coleridge's Criticism. James R. Jackson. LC 77-400918. 1969. 16.00x o.p. (ISBN 0-674-57135-5). Harvard U Pr.

Method for Easy Comprehension of History. Jean Bodin. Tr. by Beatrice Reynolds. (Columbia University Records of Civilization Ser). 1969. pap. 5.95x o.p. (ISBN 0-393-09863-X, NortonC). Norton.

Method Modeling. Valerie Cragin. LC 80-81778. (Illus.). 160p. (Orig.). 1980. pap. 13.95 o.p. (ISBN 0-8227-4045-1). Petersen Pub.

Method of Founding Stereotype As Practised by Charles Brightly. Charles Brightly. Ed. by John Bidwell. (Nineteenth Century Book Arts & Printing History Ser.). 1982. lib. bdg. 36.00 o.p. (ISBN 0-8240-3883-5). Garland Pub.

Method of Fractional Steps: The Solution of Problems of Mathematical Physics in Several Variables. N. N. Yanenko. Ed. by M. Holt. LC 78-139953. (Illus.). 1971. 36.00 o.p. (ISBN 0-387-05272-0). Springer-Verlag.

Method of Zen. Eugen Herrigel. 112p. 1988. (Pub. by Eyre Methuen England). Routledge Chapman & Hall.

Method, Process & Austrian Economics: Essays in Honor of Ludvig von Mises. Ed. by Israel M. Kirzner. LC 82-47573. 272p. 1982. 33.00x o.p. (ISBN 0-669-05545-X). Lexington Bks.

Method Study & the Furniture Industry. R. H. Glossop. LC 75-112711. 1970. 34.00 o.p. (ISBN 0-08-015653-3). Pergamon.

Method to Their Madness: A History of the Actors Studio. Foster Hirsch. LC 83-25515. (Illus.). 1984. 18.45 o.p. (ISBN 0-393-01783-4). Norton.

Methode et Philosophie en Physique Fondamentale Aujourd'Hui. Ed. by C. Chevalley. 104p. 1984. pap. 19.75 o.p. (ISBN 0-08-031846-0). Pergamon.

Methode Orange 2. Reboullet et al. (Methode Orange Ser.). (Illus.). 143p. (gr. 7-12). 1979. pap. text ed. 4.50 o.p. (ISBN 0-88345-415-7, 18933). Prentice ESL.

Methodical Bible Study. Robert A. Traina. 1985. 15.95 o.p. (ISBN 0-310-31230-2, 17031). Zondervan.

Methodological Approaches to Social Science: Integrating Divergent Concepts & Theories. Ian I. Mitroff & Ralph H. Kilmann. LC 78-62565. (Social & Behavioral Science Ser.). (Illus.). 1978. text ed. 27.95x o.p. (ISBN 0-87589-386-4). Jossey-Bass.

Methodologies for Classification of Low-Level Radioactive Wastes from Nuclear Power Plants: AIF-NESP-027. Nuclear Safety Associates Staff & Impell Corporation Staff. (National Environmental Studies Project: NESP Reports). 1983. 50.00 o.p. (ISBN 0-318-02235-4). US Coun Energy Awareness.

Methodologies of Pattern Recognition. Ed. by S. Watanabe. 1969. 82.00 o.p. (ISBN 0-12-737150-8). Acad Pr.

Methodology of Mass Production in Career Education: A System for Successful Teaching. Jack B. De Vore, Jr. & John A. Rolloff. LC 74-76023. 1974. text ed. 5.00 o.p. (ISBN 0-682-47929-2, University). Exposition-Phoenix.

Methodology of Social Impact Assessment. 2nd ed. Ed. by Kurt Finsterbusch & Charles P. Wolf. LC 81-2400. (Community Development Ser.: Vol. 32). 386p. 1982. 39.95 o.p. (ISBN 0-87933-401-0). Van Nos Reinhold.

Methods & Evaluation in Clinical & Counseling Psychology. T. C. Kahn et al. 375p. 1975. 31.00 o.p. (ISBN 0-08-017862-6); pap. 21.00 o.p. (ISBN 0-08-017863-4). Pergamon.

Methods & Issues in Occupational & Environmental Epidemiology. Ed. by Leonard Chiazze, Jr. & Frank E. Lundin. LC 82-72346. (Illus.). 225p. 1983. 49.95 o.p. (ISBN 0-250-40576-8). Butterworth.

Methods & Materials for Secondary School Physical Education. 6th ed. Charles A. Bucher & Constance R. Koenig. LC 82-2243. (Illus.). 454p. 1982. 26.95 o.p. (ISBN 0-8016-0874-0). Mosby.

Methods & Models for Assessing Energy Resources: First IIASA Conference on Energy Resources, 20-21 May, 1975, Laxenburg, Austria. Ed. by M. Grenon. (IIASA Proceedings: Vol. 5). (Illus.). 1979. 140.00 o.p. (ISBN 0-08-024443-2). Pergamon.

Methods & Results of Quantitative Ecosystem Research in the Czechoslovakian IBP Project: Methods & Results of Quantitative Ecosystem Research in the Czechoslovakian IBP Project Ser. Ed. by D. Dykyjova & J. Kvet. (Ecological Studies: Vol. 28). (Illus.). 1978. 58.00 o.p. (ISBN 0-387-08569-6). Springer-Verlag.

Methods & Techniques of Business Forecasting. William Butler et al. 1976. pap. text ed. 39.33 o.p. (ISBN 0-13-578930-3). P-H.

Methods & Techniques of Teaching Adults. National Center for Research in Vocational Education Staff. 60p. 1984. 4.95 o.p. (ISBN 0-318-22151-9, BB74). Natl Ctr Res Voc Ed.

Methods for Analysis of Musts & Wines. M. A. Amerine & C. S. Ough. LC 79-17791. 341p. 1980. 65.00x o.p. (ISBN 0-471-05077-6). Wiley.

Methods for the Estimation of Production of Aquatic Animals. G. G. Winberg. 1971. 39.50 o.p. (ISBN 0-12-758350-5). Acad Pr.

Methods in Adaptive Control: Proceedings. Ed. by H. Unbehauen. (Lecture Notes in Control & Information Sciences Ser.: Vol. 24). (Illus.). 309p. 1980. pap. 26.00 o.p. (ISBN 0-387-10226-4). Springer-Verlag.

Methods in Behavioral Research. 3rd. ed. Paul C. Cozby. 398p. 1985. pap. text ed. 16.95 o.p. (ISBN 0-87484-683-8). Mayfield Pub.

Methods in Bremsstrahlung Research. O. V. Bogdankevich & F. A. Nikolayev. 1966. 51.50 o.p. (ISBN 0-12-110850-3). Acad Pr.

Methods in Carbohydrate Chemistry, Vol. 9: Lipopolysaccharide Methods, General Methods. Ed. by Roy L. Whistler et al. 331p. cancelled o.s.i. (ISBN 0-12-746209-0). Acad Pr.

Methods in Complement for Clinical Immunologists. Ed. by Keith Whaley. LC 84-21418. (Illus.). 330p. 1985. text ed. 32.00 o.p. (ISBN 0-443-02453-7). Churchill.

Methods in Experimental Psychology. David G. Elmes et al. 1981. text ed. 26.50 o.p. (ISBN 0-395-30798-8). HM.

Methods in Microbiology, Vol. 9. Ed. by J. R. Norris & D. W. Ribbons. 1977. 52.50 o.p. (ISBN 0-12-521509-6). Acad Pr.

Methods in Microbiology, Vol. 17. J. R. Norris & D. W. Ribbons. 1984. 90.00 o.p. (ISBN 0-12-521517-7). Acad Pr.

Methods in Narcotics Research. Ed. by S. Ehrenpreis & A Neidel. (Modern Pharmacology-Toxicology Ser.: Vol.5). 424p. 1975. 85.00 o.p. (ISBN 0-8247-6308-4). Dekker.

Methods in Olfactory Research. Ed. by D. G. Moulton. 1975. 112.00 o.p. (ISBN 0-12-508950-3). Acad Pr.

Methods in Pharmacology, Vol. 3: Smooth Muscle. Edwin E. Daniel & David M. Paton. LC 74-34441. (Illus.). 746p. 1975. 95.00x o.p. (ISBN 0-306-35263-X, Plenum Pr). Plenum Pub.

Methods in Pharmacology, Vol. 4A: Renal Pharmacology. Ed. by Manuel Martinez-Maldonado. LC 74-3441. 398p. 1976. 69.50x o.p. (ISBN 0-306-35264-8, Plenum Pr). Plenum Pub.

Methods in Pharmacology, Vol. 4B: Renal Pharmacology. Ed. by Manuel Martinez-Maldonado. LC 74-34441. 414p. 1978. 69.50x o.p. (ISBN 0-306-35265-6, Plenum Pr). Plenum Pub.

Methods in Prenatal Toxicology. Ed. by D. Neubert et al. LC 77-91114. (Illus.). 486p. 1977. 28.00 o.p. (ISBN 0-88416-239-7). Year Bk Med.

Methods in Receptor Research, Pt. 1. Ed. by Melvin Blecher. (Methods in Molecular Biology Ser.: Vol. 9). 1976. 85.00 o.p. (ISBN 0-8247-6414-5). Dekker.

Methods in Teaching Developmental Reading. 2nd ed. Eddie C. Kennedy. LC 80-52445. 354p. 1981. pap. text ed. 16.95 o.p. (ISBN 0-87581-258-9). Peacock Pubs.

Methods In Vitamin B-6 Nutrition: Analysis & Status Assessment. Ed. by James E. Leklem & Robert D. Reynolds. LC 80-29553. 412p. 1981. 75.00x o.p. (ISBN 0-306-40640-3, Plenum Pr). Plenum Pub.

Methods in X-Ray Crystallography. J. W. Jeffrey. 1972. 92.00 o.p. (ISBN 0-12-382250-5). Acad Pr.

Methods of Accelerated Convergence in Nonlinear Mechanics. A. M. Samoilenko et al. Tr. by V. Kumar from Rus. 320p. 1976. 30.70 o.p. (ISBN 0-387-07106-7). Springer-Verlag.

Methods of Analysis for Quick-Frozen Fruits & Vegetables: 1st Series. 6p. 1977. pap. 7.50 o.p. (ISBN 92-5-101747-6, F1980, FAO). UNIPUB.

Methods of Applied Mathematics. 2nd, reference ed. Francis B. Hildebrand. 1965. text ed. 56.67 o.p. (ISBN 0-13-579201-0). P-H.

Methods of Applied Mathematics. N. Queen. 1982. 33.00 o.p. (ISBN 0-442-30750-0). Van Nos Reinhold.

Methods of Biochemical Analysis: Analysis of Biogenic Amines & Their Related Enzymes. Ed. by David Glick. LC 54-7232. 358p. (Orig.). 1971. Supplemental Ed. 38.00 o.p. (ISBN 0-471-30420-4, Pub. by John Wiley). Krieger.

Methods of Construction of Celtic Art. George Bain. (Illus.). 15.50 o.p. (ISBN 0-8446-4706-3). Peter Smith.

Methods of Cultivating Parasites in Vitro. Ed. by Angela Taylor & John Baker. 1978. 82.00 o.p. (ISBN 0-12-685550-1). Acad Pr.

Methods of Electronic Structure Theory. Ed. by Henry F. Schaefer. LC 76-46965. (Modern Theoretical Chemistry Ser.: Vol. 3). (Illus.). 462p. 1977. 75.00x o.p. (ISBN 0-306-33503-4, Plenum Pr). Plenum Pub.

Methods of Knowledge & Values. Robert E. Shiller. LC 66-22005. 1967. (ISBN 0-8022-1554-8). Philos Lib.

Methods of Learning Communication Skills. Peter R. Day. 324p. 1977. 46.00 o.p. (ISBN 0-08-018954-7); pap. text ed. 25.00 o.p. (ISBN 0-08-018953-9). Pergamon.

Methods of Local & Global Differential Geometry in General Relativity: Proceedings. Regional Conference on Relativity, Univ. of Pittsburgh, July 13-17, 1970. Ed. by D. Farnsworth et al. LC 72-75728. (Lecture Notes in Physics: Vol. 14). 194p. 1972. pap. 10.70 o.p. (ISBN 0-387-05793-5). Springer-Verlag.

Methods of Metallurgical Experiment. B. Linchevsky. 296p. 1982. 7.00 o.p. (ISBN 0-8285-2283-9, Pub. by Mir Pubs USSR). Imported Pubns.

Methods of Molecular Quantum Mechanics. R. McWeeny & B. T. Sutcliffe. (Theoretical Chemistry Ser). 1970. 94.00 o.p. (ISBN 0-12-486550-X). Acad Pr.

Methods of Operations Research. Billy E. Gillett. (Illus.). 1976. text ed. 45.00 o.p. (ISBN 0-07-023245-8). McGraw.

Methods of Organ Playing. 6th ed. Harole Gleason. 1979. pap. text ed. 35.00 o.p. (ISBN 0-13-579466-8). P-H.

Methods of Physical Examination in Archaeology. M. S. Tite. LC 76-183476. (International Series of Monographs on Science in Archaeology). 250p. 1973. 102.00 o.p. (ISBN 0-12-785830-X). Acad Pr.

Methods of Protein Separation, Vol. 1. Ed. by Nicholas Catsimpoolas. LC 75-17684. (Biological Separations Ser.). (Illus.). 288p. 1975. 55.00x o.p. (ISBN 0-306-34601-X, Plenum Pr). Plenum Pub.

Methods of Protein Separation, Vol. 2. Ed. by Nicholas Catsimpoolas. LC 75-17684. (Biological Separations Ser.). (Illus.). 344p. 1976. 55.00x o.p. (ISBN 0-306-34602-8, Plenum Pr). Plenum Pub.

Methods of Radioimmunoassay. Ed. by Bernard Jaffe & Harold Behrman. 1974. 48.00 o.p. (ISBN 0-12-379250-9). Acad Pr.

Methods of Research in Communication. Philip Emmert & William D. Brooks. 517p. 1970. text ed. 14.95 o.p. (ISBN 0-395-04396-4). HM.

Methods of Sampling & Analysis of Contaminants in Food: Report of a Joint FAO-WHO Expert Consultation. 19p. 1978. pap. 7.50 o.p. (ISBN 92-5-100572-9, F1472, FAO). UNIPUB.

Methods of Surface Analysis. Ed. by A. W. Czanderna. (Methods & Phenomena Ser.: Vol. 1). 482p. 1975. 108.00 o.p. (ISBN 0-444-41344-8). Elsevier.

Methods of Teaching Reading. Ed. by Florence Shankman. (Illus.). 192p. 1970. 12.95x o.p. (ISBN 0-8290-1652-X); pap. text ed. 6.00 o.p. (ISBN 0-8290-1651-1). Irvington.

Methods of the Allocation of Limited Resources. K. M. Mjelde. 100p. 1983. 37.00x o.p. (ISBN 0-471-10439-6, Pub. by Wiley-Interscience). Wiley.

Methods Toward a Science of Behavior & Experience. 2nd ed. Ray & Ravizza. 1984. text ed. (ISBN 0-534-04041-1). Wadsworth Pub.

Methods Work...If You Do. Keyes, Ken, Center Residents. 1983. pap. 6.00 o.p. (ISBN 0-915972-10-7). Love Line Bks.

Methodus Plantarum Nova. J. Ray. (Illus.). 1962. Repr. of 1682 ed. 24.00x o.p. (ISBN 3-7682-0119-8). Lubrecht & Cramer.

Methuen Handbook of Colour. 3rd ed. A. Kornup & J. H. Wanscher. (Illus.). 1978. 33.00x o.p. (ISBN 0-413-33400-7, NO. 2278). Heinemann Ed.

Methusaleh Enzyme. Fred M. Stewart. LC 76-122333. 1970. 5.95 o.p. (ISBN 0-87795-002-4, Arbor Hse). Morrow.

Metipranolol: Pharmacology of Beta-blocking Agents & Use of Metipranolol in Opthalmology, Contributions to the First Metipranolol Symposium, Berlin 1983. Ed. by H. J. Merte. (Illus.). 180p. 1984. pap. 34.00 o.p. (ISBN 0-387-81824-3). Springer-Verlag.

Metis in the Canadian West, 2 vols. Marcel Giraud. Tr. by George Woodcock. LC 86-6912. (Illus.). 1986. Vol. 1, xxi, 631 pgs. 50.00x o.p. (ISBN 0-8032-2125-8). Vol. 2, vi, 738 pgs. U of Nebr Pr.

Metodo Directo de Conversacion en Espanol, 2 Bks. Juvenal L. Angel & Robert J. Dixson. (gr. 9 up). 1969. Bk. 1. pap. text ed. 3.75 o.p. (ISBN 0-88345-102-6, 17761); Bk. 2. pap. text ed. 3.25 o.p. (ISBN 0-88345-103-4, 17762). Prentice ESL.

Metre, Rhyme, & Free Verse. G. S. Fraser. (Critical Idiom Ser.). 1970. pap. 5.50x o.p. (ISBN 0-416-17300-4, NO. 2203). Routledge Chapman & Hall.

Metric Architectural Construction Drafting & Design. William J. Hornung. (Illus.). 240p. 1981. text ed. 29.67 o.p. (ISBN 0-13-579367-X). P-H.

Metric Debate. Ed. by David F. Bartlett. LC 79-53270. 22.50 o.p. (ISBN 0-87081-083-9). Univ Pr Colo.

Metric Drafting. Paul Wallach. 1979. text ed. 23.76 o.p. (ISBN 0-02-829690-7). Glencoe.

Metric Engineering Drawing Examples. E. McPherson & D. L. Ashton. LC 78-67439. 69p. (Orig.). 1979. pap. 12.00x o.p. (ISBN 0-87201-539-4). Gulf Pub.

Metric Handbook for Teachers. Ed. by Jon L. Higgins. LC 74-13468. 144p. 1974. pap. 6.00 o.p. (ISBN 0-87353-077-2). NCTM.

Metric Module Involute Splines. Part III: Inspection (Replaces Part II of ANSI B92.2M-1980) 50p. 1984. 16.00 o.p. (ANSI B92.2MA-1984). Soc Auto Engineers.

Metric Multibase Mathematics. Verda Holmberg et al. (Illus., Orig.). (gr. 1-9). 1974. pap. 7.95 o.p. (ISBN 0-918932-33-5). Activity Resources.

Metric Pattern Cutting: For Menswear Including Unisex Casual Clothes. Winifred Aldrich. (Illus.). 128p. 1980. text ed. 22.50x o.p. (ISBN 0-246-11219-0, Granada England). Gower Pub Co.

Metric System. Joan E. Rahn. LC 75-29445. (Illus.). (gr. 6-9). 1976. 6.95 o.p. (ISBN 0-689-30510-9, Atheneum). Macmillan.

Metric System of Measurement. Verda Holmberg. (Illus., Orig.). (gr. 4-9). 1973. pap. 7.95 o.p. (ISBN 0-918932-34-3). Activity Resources.

Metric: The Modern Way to Measure. Miriam Schlein. LC 74-22169. (gr. 6 up). 1975. 6.75 o.p. (ISBN 0-15-253187-4, HJ). HarBraceJ.

Metric: The Modern Way to Measure. Miriam Schlein. LC 76-29665. (Illus.). (gr. 3-7). 1977. pap. 1.95 o.p. (ISBN 0-15-659310-6, VoyB). HarBraceJ.

Metrics for Architects, Designers & Builders. Martin Van Buren. 192p. 1982. 25.95 o.p. (ISBN 0-442-28889-1). Van Nos Reinhold.

Metrics for Elementary & Middle Schools. V. Ray Kurtz. 120p. 1978. pap. 5.95 o.p. (ISBN 0-8106-1714-5). NEA.

Metrology. Center for Occupational Research & Development Staff. (High Technology Ser.). (Illus.). 474p. 1984. pap. text ed. 33.00 o.p. (ISBN 1-55502-116-6). Ctr Res & Dev.

Metrology Needs in the Measurement of Environmental Radioactivity: Seminar Sponsored by the International Committee for Radionuclide Metrology. Ed. by J. M. Hutchinson & W. B. Mann. (Illus.). 1980. pap. 43.00 o.p. (ISBN 0-08-022943-3). Pergamon.

Metropol: A Literary Almanac. Ed. by Vasily Aksyonov et al. 1983. 24.95 o.p. (ISBN 0-393-01438-X). Norton.

Metropolis in Transition. Ed. by Ervin Y. Galantay. LC 86-12167. (Illus.). 288p. 1986. 35.95 o.s.i. (ISBN 0-89226-044-0, Pub. by ICUS). Paragon Hse.

Metropolis: New York As Myth, Marketplace, & Magical Land. Jerome Charyn. 1986. 18.95 o.p. (ISBN 0-399-13133-7). Putnam Pub Group.

Metropolitan Kano, 2 vols. B. A. Trevallion. 1967. Set. 120.00 o.p. (ISBN 0-08-012635-9). Pergamon.

Metropolitan Libraries on Their Way into the 80's. Ed. by Marion Beaujean. 1982. 27.00 o.p. (ISBN 3-598-10429-4). K G Saur.

Metropolitan Museum Journal, 1988, Vol. 23. (Illus.). 280p. 1989. 60.00 o.p. Metro Mus Art.

Metropolitan Museum of Art Guide. rev., 3rd ed. Ed. by Kathleen Howard. LC 83-13097. 448p. (Orig.). 1983. 18.50 o.p. (ISBN 0-87099-348-8); pap. 9.95 o.p. (ISBN 0-87099-346-1). Metro Mus Art.

Metropolitan Museum of Art: Notable Acquisitions, 1965-1975. Metropolitan Museum of Art, Curatorial Staff. LC 75-31761. (Illus.). 304p. 1975. pap. 4.95 o.p. (ISBN 0-87099-141-8). Metro Mus Art.

Metropolitan Opera, 1883-1966: A Candid History. Irving Kolodin. 762p. Repr. of 1966 ed. lib. bdg. 89.00 o.p. (Pub. by Am Repr Serv). Reprint Servs.

Metropolitan Tabernacle Pulpit, Vol. 30. C. H. Spurgeon. 700p. 1988. write for info. o.p. (ISBN 0-85151-052-3). Banner of Truth.

Metropolitan Transportation Planning. 2nd ed. John W. Dickey. Ed. by Kiran Verma. (Illus.). 624p. 1983. text ed. 42.95 o.p. (ISBN 0-07-016816-4). McGraw.

Metropolitanism: Its Challenge to Education. Ed. by Robert J. Havighurst. (National Society for the Study of Education Yearbooks Ser: No. 67, Pt. 1). 1968. lib. bdg. 7.50x o.s.i. (ISBN 0-226-60090-4). U of Chicago Pr.

Mets from Mobile: Cleon Jones & Tommie Agee. A. S. Young. LC 70-103832. (Curriculum Related Bks.). (gr. 5 up). 1970. 4.95 o.p. (ISBN 0-15-253190-4, HJ). HarBraceJ.

Mettlach Book: Illustrated Catalog, Current Prices, & Collector's Information. Gary Kirsner. Ed. by Jim Gruhl. LC 82-62880. (Illus.). 332p. (Orig.). 1983. pap. 25.00 o.p. (ISBN 0-911403-18-3). Seven Hills Bk Dists.

Mexican American: His Life Across Four Centuries. Gilbert T. Martinez & Jane Edwards. LC 72-2751. 184p. (gr. 7-12). 1973. pap. 13.24 o.p. (ISBN 0-395-14261-X). HM.

Mexican Americans. 2nd ed. Joan W. Moore. (Ethnic Groups in American Life Ser.). 208p. 1976. pap. text ed. 21.00 o.p. (ISBN 0-13-579508-7). P-H.

Mexican Americans. 2nd ed. Manuel P. Servin. LC 73-8357. Orig. Title: Awakened Minority. 320p. 1974. pap. text ed. write for info. o.p. (ISBN 0-02-477940-7, 47794). Macmillan.

Mexican Caribbean: Twenty Years of Underwater Exploration. Earl J. Wilson. (Illus.). 176p. 1982. 10.00 o.p. (ISBN 0-682-49829-7). Exposition-Phoenix.

Mexican Collection, 1978. 163p. 1978. pap. 10.00 o.p. (ISBN 0-940764-23-7). U of Utah Pr.

Mexican Cookbook. Erna Fergusson. LC 46-214. (Illus.). 126p. 1967. pap. 7.95 o.s.i. (ISBN 0-8263-0035-9). U of NM Pr.

Mexican Cookbook. Barbara Grunes. 64p. (Orig.). 1981. pap. 3.95 o.p. (ISBN 0-8249-3000-2). Ideals.

Mexican Cookery. Barbara Hansen. 1981. pap. 2.95 o.p. (ISBN 0-440-15644-0). Dell.

Mexican Cooking Class Cookbook. Consumer Guide Staff. 1984. pap. 4.98 o.p. (ISBN 0-517-43544-6). Crown.

Mexican Folk Ceramics. Carlos Espejel. (Illus.). 220p. 1982. 35.00 o.p. (ISBN 84-7031-222-7, Pub. by Editorial Blume Spain). Intl Spec Bk.

Mexican Jewelry. Mary L. Davis & Greta Pack. (Illus.). 278p. 1963. pap. 17.95 o.p. (ISBN 0-292-73305-4). U of Tex Pr.

Mexican Masks. Donald Cordry. LC 73-92100. (Illus.). 36p. 1973. pap. 3.00 o.p. (ISBN 0-88360-004-8, Dist. by Univ. of Texas Pr). Amon Carter.

Mexican Mural: The Story of Mexico, Past & Present. Lois Hobart. LC 63-15399. (Illus.). 1963. 5.95 o.p. (ISBN 0-15-253201-3, HJ). HarBraceJ.

Mexican Parish Registers, 1981. 288p. 1981. pap. 15.00 o.p. (ISBN 0-940764-22-9). U of Utah Pr.

Mexican Pet: More "New" Urban Legends & Some Old Favorites. Jan H. Brunvand. 1986. 13.45 o.p. (ISBN 0-393-02324-9). Norton.

Mexican Political System. 2nd ed. Vincent L. Padgett. LC 75-27497. (Illus.). 352p. 1976. pap. 11.50 o.p. (ISBN 0-395-20364-3). HM.

Mexican Revolution, Nineteen Fourteen to Nineteen Fifteen: The Convention of Aguascalientes. Robert E. Quirk. LC 80-28130. 325p. 1981. Repr. of 1960 ed. lib. bdg. 35.00x o.p. (ISBN 0-313-22894-9, QUMR). Greenwood.

Mexican Revolution, 1914-1915. Robert E. Quirk. 1970. pap. 2.45 o.p. (ISBN 0-393-00507-0, Norton Lib). Norton.

Mexican Supplement, 1979. 28p. 1979. pap. 5.00 o.p. (ISBN 0-940764-24-5). U of Utah Pr.

Mexican Tamale Mystery. George E. Stanley. 112p. (YA) (gr. 8-12). 1988. pap. 2.50 o.p. (ISBN 0-380-75458-4, Camelot). Avon.

Mexican War: Changing Interpretations. Ed. by Odie B. Faulk & Joseph A. Stout, Jr. LC 72-94389. 243p. 1973. 12.95x o.p. (ISBN 0-8040-0642-3); pap. 5.95 o.p. (ISBN 0-8040-0643-1). Ohio U Pr.

Mexican Wilderness & Wildlife. Ben Tinker. LC 77-14030. (Illus.). 143p. 1978. 9.95 o.p. (ISBN 0-292-75037-4). U of Tex Pr.

Mexican Women Poets: An Anthology of Poetry. Tr. by Thomas Hocksema. 1987. Lat Am Lit Rev Pr.

Mexicano Resistance in the Southwest: "The Sacred Right of Self-Preservation" Robert J. Rosenbaum. (Illus.). 253p. 1981. pap. 20.00 o.p. (ISBN 0-292-77562-8). U of Tex Pr.

Mexico. Mona King. (Rand McNally Pocket Guides Ser.). (Illus.). 128p. 1986. pap. 5.95 o.p. (ISBN 0-528-84847-X). Rand McNally.

Mexico. rev. ed. Patricia F. Ross. LC 73-90742. (American Neighbors Ser.). (Illus.). 208p. (gr. 5 up). 1975. text ed. 9.95, 5 or more copies 7.96 o.p. (ISBN 0-88296-096-2); tchrs'. guide 6.96 o.p. (ISBN 0-686-67148-1). Gateway Pr MI.

Mexico. Time-Life Books Editors. (Library of Nations). (Illus.). 160p. (YA) (gr. 7 up). 1985. lib. bdg. 23.93 o.p. Time-Life.

Mexico-A Travel Survival Kit. 2nd ed. Doug Richmond. (Illus.). 256p. (Orig.). 1985. pap. 7.95 o.p. (ISBN 0-908086-76-8). Lonely Planet.

Mexico & Its Heritage. Ernest H. Gruening. LC 68-9542. (Illus.). 1969. Repr. of 1940 ed. lib. bdg. 43.75x o.p. (ISBN 0-8371-0457-2, GRMH). Greenwood.

Mexico & the United States in the Oil Controversy, 1917-1942. Lorenzo Meyer. Tr. by Muriel Vasconcellos from Span. LC 76-18690. 389p. 1977. text ed. 23.50x o.p. (ISBN 0-292-75032-3). U of Tex Pr.

Mexico City Blues. Jack Kerouac. 1959. pap. 4.95 o.p. (ISBN 0-394-17287-6, E552, Ever). Grove.

Mexico, Nineteen Eighty. rev. ed. Steve Birnbaum. (Get 'Em & Go Travel Guides Ser.). 1979. 15.00 o.p. (ISBN 0-395-28417-1); pap. 9.95 o.p. (ISBN 0-395-28415-5). HM.

Mexico Nineteen Eighty-Seven. Steve Birnbaum. (Illus.). 528p. 1986. pap. 12.70 o.s.i. (ISBN 0-395-42336-8). HM.

Mexico, Nineteen Eighty-Two. Steve Birnbaum. (Get 'em & Go Travel Guide Ser.). 704p. 1981. pap. 10.95 o.p. (ISBN 0-395-31536-0). HM.

Mexico on Twenty Dollars a Day. Tom Brosnahan. 484p. 1985. pap. 9.95 o.p. (ISBN 0-671-52474-7). Prentice Hall Pr.

Mexico on Twenty-Five Dollars a Day: 1983-84. 512p. 1983. pap. 8.95 o.p. (ISBN 0-671-45297-5). Prentice Hall Pr.

Mexico: Travel Guide. Sunset Magazine & Books Editors. LC 82-83215. (Illus.). 160p. 1983. pap. 9.95 o.p. (ISBN 0-376-06458-7, Sunset Bks). Sunset-Lane.

Mexico: Winter Vacation Guide, 1989. (Illus.). cancelled o.s.i. Wrld Travel.

Mexico, 1981. Steve Birnbaum. (Get 'em & Go Travel Guides). 1980. pap. 9.95 o.p. (ISBN 0-395-29747-8). HM.

Mexico 1983. Steve Birnbaum. (Get 'em & Go Travel Guide Ser.). 1982. pap. 11.45 o.p. (ISBN 0-395-32873-X). HM.

Mexico 1984. Steve Birnbaum. (Get'em & Go Travel Guide Ser.). 1983. pap. 11.45 o.p. (ISBN 0-395-34628-2). HM.

Mexico, 1985. Steve Birnbaum. (Get 'em & Go Travel Guides Ser.). 1984. pap. 11.70 o.p. (ISBN 0-395-36520-1). HM.

Mexico's Miguel Caldera: The Taming of America's First Frontier, 1548-1597. Philip W. Powell. LC 76-62551. 322p. 1977. 14.95x o.p. (ISBN 0-8165-0638-8); pap. 12.50 o.p. (ISBN 0-8165-0569-1). U of Ariz Pr.

Meyerhold: The Art of Conscious Theater. Marjorie L. Hoover. Date not set. price not set o.p. U of Mass Pr.

Mezhdu Sobakoi I Volkom. Sasha Sokolov. 1980. 25.00 o.p. (ISBN 0-88233-339-9); pap. 10.00 o.p. (ISBN 0-88233-340-2). Ardis Pubs.

MG Midget & Sprite. (A205). Clymer Pub.

MG: Past & Present. Rivers Fletcher. 18.95 o.p. (ISBN 0-85614-074-0, F402). Haynes Pubns.

MG: Sports Car Supreme. Joseph H. Wherry. LC 81-3633. (Illus.). 240p. 1982. 25.00 o.p. (ISBN 0-498-02565-9). A S Barnes.

MGA-MGB All Models: 1956-1980 Service, Repair Handbook. Alan Ahlstrand. Ed. by Jeff Robinson. (Illus.). pap. 13.95 o.p. (ISBN 0-89287-279-9, A165). Clymer Pub.

MGMA Digest of Medical Group Employment Contracts & Income Distribution Plans. 2nd ed. (Illus.). 179p. 1978. 30.00 o.p. (ISBN 0-933948-06-9). Med Group Mgmt.

MHD & Fusion Magnets: Field & Force Design Concepts. Richard J. Thome & John M. Tarrh. LC 81-19666. 347p. 1982. 47.50x o.p. (ISBN 0-471-09317-3, Pub. by Wiley-Interscience). Wiley.

MHD Power Generation: Selected Problems of Combustion MHD Generation. R. Buende et al. Ed. by J. Raeder. (Illus.). 320p. 1975. pap. 64.90 o.p. (ISBN 0-387-07296-9). Springer-Verlag.

MHPG (3-Methoxy 4-Hydroxyphenethyle Neglycol) Basic Mechanisms & Psychopathology. Ed. by James W. Maas. LC 82-11640. (Behavioral Biology Ser.). 1983. 39.50 o.p. (ISBN 0-12-462920-2). Acad Pr.

Mi Ani? (Who Am I?) Rochelle S. Sobel. (Illus.). 40p. (Hebrew.). (gr. 2-4). 1982. 3.95 o.p. (ISBN 0-686-83445-3). Kar Ben.

Mi Daguestan. R. Gamzatov. 445p. 1974. 8.95 o.p. (ISBN 0-8285-1720-7, Pub. by Progress Pubs USSR). Imported Pubns.

Mi Maquina Maravillosa. William L. Coleman. 144p. 1982. 3.25 o.p. (ISBN 0-88113-309-4). Edit Betania.

Mi primer diccionario ilustrado de ingles. Dixson. (Illus., Eng.). (gr. 1-6). 1975. pap. 2.75 o.p. (ISBN 0-88345-246-4, 18481). Prentice ESL.

Miami Dolphins. Julian May. LC 74-4139. (Superbowl Champions Ser). 48p. 1974. PLB 10.45 o.p. (ISBN 0-87191-328-3); pap. 3.95 o.p. (ISBN 0-89812-088-8). Creative Ed.

Miami Dolphins. Julian May. (NFL Today Ser.). (gr. 4-8). 1980. lib. bdg. 10.45 o.p. (ISBN 0-87191-725-4); pap. 4.25 o.p. (ISBN 0-89812-228-7). Creative Ed.

Miami Golden Boy. Herbert Kastle. 1976. pap. 1.75 o.p. (ISBN 0-380-00673-1, 29397). Avon.

Miami, Orlando & the Gold Coast. Andy Vladimir & Ute Vladimir. cancelled o.s.i. (ISBN 1-55707-119-5). Wrld Travel.

Micah the Prophet. Hans W. Wolff. Tr. by Ralph D. Gehrke from Ger. LC 80-2380. 240p. 1981. 19.95 o.p. (ISBN 0-8006-0652-3, 1-652, Fortress). Augsburg Fortress.

Mice & the Flying Basket. Rodney Peppe. LC 84-14360. (Illus.). 32p. (ps-3). 1985. 11.75 o.p. (ISBN 0-688-04252-X). Lothrop.

Mice Are Rather Nice. Vardine Moore. LC 80-23121. (Illus.). 112p. (gr. 3 up). 1981. PLB 7.95 o.p. (ISBN 0-689-30819-1, Atheneum). Macmillan.

Mice, Men & Elephants. Herbert S. Zim. LC 42-36123. (Illus.). 215p. (gr. 7 up). 1942. 5.95 o.p. (ISBN 0-15-253305-2, HJ). HarBraceJ.

Mice on My Mind. Bernard Waber. LC 77-9050. (Illus.). (gr. k-5). 1977. PLB 5.95 o.p. (ISBN 0-395-25935-5). HM.

Micelles. Ed. by F. L. Boschke. (Topics in Current Chemistry Ser.: Vol. 87). (Illus.). 1979. 56.00 o.p. (ISBN 0-387-09639-6). Springer-Verlag.

Michael Bloomfield: The Rise & Fall of an American Guitar Hero. Ed Ward. (Illus.). 1983. pap. text ed. 8.95 o.p. (ISBN 0-89524-157-9, 8605). Cherry Lane.

Michael Broadbent's Complete Guide to Wine Tasting & Wine Cellars. Michael Broadbent. 272p. 1984. pap. 12.95 o.s.i. (ISBN 0-671-50889-X). S&S.

Michael Broadbent's Pocket Guide to Wine Tasting. Michael Broadbent. (Illus.). 1982. pap. 6.95 o.p. (ISBN 0-671-45235-5). S&S.

Michael Cardew. Garth Clark. LC 76-9358. (Illus.). 228p. 1976. 27.95 o.p. (ISBN 0-87011-277-5). Kodansha.

Michael Faraday: A List of His Lectures & Published Writings. Alan E. Jeffreys. 1961. 43.00 o.p. (ISBN 0-12-383050-8). Acad Pr.

Michael Field Egg Cookbook. 9.95 o.s.i. (ISBN 0-03-048221-6, Owl Bks.). H Holt & Co.

Michael Field's Cooking School. rev. ed. Michael Field. LC 77-1943. 1977. 18.50 o.s.i. (ISBN 0-03-018476-2). H Holt & Co.

Michael Grows a Wish. Fen H. Lasell. (Illus.). (gr. k-3). 1962. Dolphin bdg. 3.07 o.p. (ISBN 0-395-06880-0). HM.

Michael J. Fox Scrapbook. Mimi Kasbah. 80p. (Orig.). 1987. pap. 7.95 o.p. (ISBN 0-345-34389-1). Ballantine.

Michael Jackson Catalog: A Comprehensive Guide to Records, Videos, Clothing, Posters, Toys & Millions of Collectible Souvenirs. Milt Machlin. (Illus.). 1984. pap. 7.95 o.p. (ISBN 0-87795-664-2, Arbor Hse). Morrow.

Michael Jackson Scrapbook: The Early Days of the Jackson 5. Weldon A. McDougal, III. (Illus.). 128p. 1985. pap. 9.95 o.p. (ISBN 0-380-89588-9). Avon.

Michael Landon. Marsha Daly. 1988. pap. 3.95 o.p. (ISBN 0-7701-1018-5). PaperJacks US.

Michael Sheriff: Arabian Assault. Preston MacAdam. (Shield Ser.: No. 2). 192p. 1985. pap. 2.95 o.p. (ISBN 0-380-89688-5). Avon.

Michael Sheriff, the Shield: African Assignment, No. I. Preston MacAdam. 192p. 1985. pap. 2.95 o.p. (ISBN 0-380-89687-7). Avon.

Michael Whelan's Works of Wonder. Michael Whelan. 1987. pap. 25.00 o.p. (ISBN 0-345-32679-2, Del Rey). Ballantine.

Michael Wurmbrand: The Man & His Work. Kurt R. Grossman. 128p. 1956. (ISBN 0-8022-0638-7). Philos Lib.

Michaelangelo - A Study in the Nature of Art. Adrian Stokes. (Illus.). 160p. 1956. (ISBN 0-8022-1653-6). Philos Lib.

Michel de Klerk, 1884-1923: An Architect of the Amsterdam School. Suzanne S. Frank. Ed. by Stephen Foster. LC 84-132. (Architecture & Urban Design: No. 4). 314p. 1984. 44.95 o.p. (ISBN 0-8357-1546-9). UMI Res Pr.

Michel Guerard's Cuisine Minceur. Michel Guerard. Tr. by Narcisse Chamberlain & Fanny Brennan. LC 76-49719. (Illus.). 1977. 12.95 o.p. (ISBN 0-688-03142-0). Morrow.

Michel-Richard Delalande's "De Profundis" Grand Motet for Soloists, Chorus, Woodwinds, Strings, & Continuo. James R. Anthony. LC 79-29740. (Early Musical Masterworks Ser.). viii, 173p. 1981. 25.00x o.p. (ISBN 0-8078-1439-3). U of NC Pr.

Michelangelo: The Last Judgment. Deoclecio R. De Campos. 1979. 100.00 o.p. (ISBN 0-385-12299-3). Doubleday.

Michelangelo's David: A Search for Identity. Charles Seymour, Jr. (Illus.). 224p. 1974. pap. 3.95 o.p. (ISBN 0-393-00735-9). Norton.

Michelin Green Guide: Allemagne. 8th ed. (Green Guide Ser.). (Fr.). 1984. pap. 7.95 o.p. (ISBN 2-06-005001-4). Michelin.

Michelin Green Guide Belgique et Grand Duche du Luxembourg. 3rd ed. Michelin Guides & Maps Dept. 1981. pap. 9.95 o.p. (ISBN 2-06-005102-9). Michelin.

Michelin Green Guide: Chateaux de la Loire. 28th ed. (Green Guide Ser.). (Fr.). 1984. pap. 7.95 o.p. (ISBN 2-06-003182-6). Michelin.

Michelin Green Guide: Elsass Vogesen. (Green Guide Ser.). (Ger.). 1979. pap. 7.95 o.p. (ISBN 2-06-023741-6). Michelin.

Michelin Green Guide: Espagne. (Green Guide Ser.). (Fr.). 1982. pap. 8.95 o.p. (ISBN 2-06-005182-7). Michelin.

Michelin Green Guide: Espana. (Green Guide Ser.). (Span.). 1982. pap. 9.95 o.p. (ISBN 2-06-045271-6). Michelin.

Michelin Green Guide: Portugal. (Green Guide Ser.). (Fr.). 1982. pap. 8.95 o.p. (ISBN 2-06-005542-3). Michelin.

Michelin Green Guide: Pyrenees. 3rd ed. (Green Guide Ser.). (Fr.). 1982. pap. 7.95 o.p. (ISBN 2-06-003662-3). Michelin.

Michelin Green Guide: Pyrenees-Roussillon. 1987. pap. 9.95 o.p. Michelin.

Michelin Green Guide Rome. 3rd ed. Michelin Guides & Maps Department Staff. (Fr.). 1982. pap. 9.95 o.p. (ISBN 2-06-005582-2). Michelin.

Michelin Green Guide: Spanien. (Green Guide Ser.). (Ger.). 1982. pap. 8.95 o.p. (ISBN 2-06-025240-7). Michelin.

Michelin Green Guide: Suisse. (Green Guide Ser.). (Fr.). 1982. pap. 8.95 o.p. (ISBN 2-06-005601-2). Michelin.

Michelin Green Guide to Alpes. 3rd ed. Michelin Guides & Maps Department Staff. (Fr.). 1984. pap. 9.95 o.p. (ISBN 2-06-003002-1). Michelin.

Michelin Green Guide to Alsace et Lorraine (Vosges) 1986. pap. 9.95 o.p. (ISBN 2-06-003722-0). Michelin.

Michelin Green Guide to Autriche. 10th ed. Michelin Guides & Maps Dept. (Green Guide Ser.). 1984. pap. 8.95 o.p. (ISBN 2-06-005091-X). Michelin.

Michelin Green Guide to Auvergne. 5th ed. (Fr.). 1987. pap. 9.95 o.p. (ISBN 2-06-003033-1). Michelin.

Michelin Green Guide to Auvergne. 4th ed. Michelin Guides & Maps Department Staff. (Green Guide Ser.). (Fr.). 1982. pap. 7.95 o.p. (ISBN 2-06-003032-3). Michelin.

Michelin Green Guide to Belgique-Luxembourg. 4th ed. 1985. pap. 10.95 o.p. (ISBN 2-06-005103-7). Michelin.

Michelin Green Guide to Bourgogne. 18th ed. Michelin Guides & Maps Department Staff. (Fr.). 1982. pap. 7.95 o.p. (ISBN 2-0600-3062-5). Michelin.

Michelin Green Guide to Bretagne. 2nd ed. (Fr.). 1986. pap. 10.95 o.p. (ISBN 2-06-003093-5). Michelin.

Michelin Green Guide to Canada. 2nd ed. Michelin Guides & Maps Department Staff. (Fr.). pap. cancelled o.p. (ISBN 2-06-005161-4). Michelin.

Michelin Green Guide to Causses-Cevennes. 5th ed. Michelin Guides & Maps Department Staff. (Fr.). 1985. pap. 7.95 o.p. (ISBN 2-06-003153-2). Michelin.

Michelin Green Guide to Corse. 6th ed. Michelin Guides & Maps Department Staff. (Fr.). 1985. pap. 9.95 o.p. (ISBN 2-06-003254-7). Michelin.

Michelin Green Guide to Cote D'Azur. 2nd ed. Michelin Guides & Maps Department Staff. (Green Guide Ser.). 1983. pap. 7.95 o.p. (ISBN 2-06-003272-5). Michelin.

Michelin Green Guide to Cote De L'Atlantique. 11th ed. Michelin Guides & Maps Department Staff. (Green Guide Ser.). (Fr.). 1984. pap. 8.95 o.p. (ISBN 2-06-003332-2). Michelin.

Michelin Green Guide to Dordogne. 4th ed. Michelin Guides & Maps Department Staff. (Avail. in Fr.). 1987. pap. 9.95 o.p. (ISBN 2-06-013231-2). Michelin.

Michelin Green Guide to England, the West Country. Michelin Travel Publications Staff. 1985. pap. 10.95 o.p. (ISBN 2-06-015621-1). Michelin.

Michelin Green Guide to Environs De Paris. 22nd ed. Michelin Guides & Maps Department Staff. (Fr.). pap. cancelled o.p. (ISBN 2-06-003363-2). Michelin.

Michelin Green Guide to Flandres-Artois-Picardie. (Fr.). 1985. pap. 9.95 o.p. (ISBN 2-06-003381-0). Michelin.

Michelin Green Guide to French Riviera. 8th ed. Michelin Guides & Maps Dept. (Green Guide Ser.). (Avail. in Fr.). 1982. pap. 9.95 o.p. (ISBN 2-06-013301-7). Michelin.

Michelin Green Guide to Hollande. 3rd ed. Michelin Guides & Maps Department Staff. 1982. pap. 9.95 o.p. (ISBN 2-06-005532-6). Michelin.

Michelin Green Guide to Italy. 10th ed. 1983. pap. 10.95 o.p. (ISBN 2-060-15331-X). Michelin.

Michelin Green Guide to London. 4th ed. Michelin Guides & Maps Department Staff. 1985. pap. 10.95 o.p. (ISBN 2-06-015433-2). Michelin.

Michelin Green Guide to Londres. 2nd ed. Michelin Guides & Maps Dept. (Green Guide Ser.). (Fr.). pap. cancelled o.s.i. (ISBN 2-06-005420-6). Michelin.

Michelin Green Guide to New England. 1987. pap. 10.95 o.p. (ISBN 2-06-015693-9, 569). Michelin.

Michelin Green Guide to New York. 7th ed. (Fr.). 1987. pap. 10.95 o.p. (ISBN 2-06-005483-4). Michelin.

Michelin Green Guide to New York City. 8th ed. (Avail. in Fr.). 1988. pap. 10.95 o.p. (ISBN 2-06-015513-4). Michelin.

Michelin Green Guide to Normandie. 3rd ed. (Fr.). 1984. pap. 9.95 o.p. (ISBN 2-06-003452-3). Michelin.

Michelin Green Guide to Normandy. 6th ed. Michelin Guides & Maps Department Staff. (Avail. in Fr.). pap. cancelled o.p. (ISBN 2-06-013481-1). Michelin.

Michelin Green Guide to Nouvelle Angleterre. 2nd ed. pap. 10.95 o.p. (568). Michelin.

Michelin Green Guide to Nouvelle Angleterre. 2nd ed. Michelin Guides & Maps Department Staff. (Orig., Fr.). 1984. pap. 10.95 o.p. (ISBN 2-06-005681-0). Michelin.

Michelin Green Guide to Provence. 4th ed. (Fr. & Eng.). 1986. pap. 9.95 o.p. (ISBN 2-06-003633-X). Michelin.

Michelin Green Guide to Provence. 1989. pap. 10.95 o.p. (ISBN 2-06-013642-3). Michelin.

Michelin Green Guide to Provence Eng. 2nd ed. Michelin Guides & Maps Dept. (Avail. Fr. & Ger.). 1983. pap. 9.95 o.p. (ISBN 2-06-013641-5). Michelin.

Michelin Green Guide to Switzerland. 8th ed. Michelin Guides & Maps Department Staff. (Green Guide Ser.). (Avail. in Fr.). 1982. pap. 10.95 o.p. (ISBN 2-06-015631-9). Michelin.

Michelin Green Guide to the French Riviera. 9th ed. 1986. pap. 9.95 o.p. (ISBN 2-06-013302-5). Michelin.

Michelin Green Guide to Vosges. 3rd ed. Michelin Guides & Maps Dept. (Green Guide Ser.). 1982. pap. 7.95 o.p. (ISBN 2-06-003721-2). Michelin.

Michelin Red Guide to Benelux, 1986: Michelin Guides & Maps. (Red Guide Ser.). 1985. 13.95 o.p. (ISBN 2-06-006055-9). Michelin.

Michelin Red Guide to Deutschland, 1986: Annual. Michelin Guides & Maps Dept. (Red Guide Ser.). 1985. 15.95 o.p. (ISBN 3-92-107805-9). Michelin.

Michelin Red Guide to France, 1985. (Red Guide Ser.). 1985. pap. 15.95 o.p. (ISBN 2-06-006455-4). Michelin.

Michelin Red Guide to Great Britain & Ireland, 1985: Annual. Michelin Guides & Maps Dept. (Red Guide Ser.). 1985. 14.95 o.p. (ISBN 2-06-006555-0). Michelin.

Michelin Red Guide to Italia, 1985: Annual. Michelin Guides & Maps Dept. (Red Guide Ser.). 1985. 15.95 o.p. (ISBN 2-06-006755-3). Michelin.

Michelin Red Guide to London: Annual. Michelin Guides & Maps Dept. (Red Guide Ser.). 1985. pap. 3.95 o.p. (ISBN 2-06-006655-7). Michelin.

Michelin Red Guide to "Main Cities in Europe" Annual. Michelin Guides & Maps Dept. (Red Guide Ser.). 1985. 13.95 o.p. (ISBN 2-06-007055-4). Michelin.

Michelin Red Guide to Paris Annual: Paris Hotels & Restaurants. Michelin Guides & Maps. (Red Guide Ser.). 1981. Avail. In Fr. & Eng. pap. 3.95 o.p. (ISBN 2-06-006844-4). Michelin.

Michelin Red Guide to Spain & Portugal. Michelin Guides & Maps Dept. (Red Guide Ser.). 1985. 14.95 o.p. (ISBN 2-06-006355-8). Michelin.

Michelle, la Chienne Francais. Joanne Ridley. (gr. k-4). 1979. 4.00 o.p. (ISBN 0-682-49208-6). Exposition-Phoenix.

Michener Miscellany, 1950-1970. James A. Michener. 384p. 1975. pap. 1.95 o.s.i. (ISBN 0-449-22526-7, C2526, Crest). Fawcett.

Michie's Texas Tort Reporter. Michie Company Editorial Staff. 1985. Twelve issues per year. 130.00 o.p. (ISBN 0-87215-728-8). Michie Co.

Michigan. Bruce Catton. (Illus.). 1977. pap. 1.95 o.p. (ISBN 0-393-05645-7). Norton.

Michigan: Agency. 1983. 8.50 o.p. (ISBN 0-686-90809-0). Am Law Inst.

Michigan Business Corporations: 1979. Stanley Siegel & Stephen Schulman. LC 79-15852. 85.00 o.p. (ISBN 0-317-12079-4). Callaghan.

Michigan: Conflict of Laws. 1983. 8.50 o.p. Am Law Inst.

Michigan Criminal Justice Law Manual. George T. Felkenes. (Criminal Justice Ser.). 300p. 1981. pap. text ed. 18.95 o.p. (ISBN 0-8299-0369-0). West Pub.

Michigan Cross Country Skiing Atlas. 3rd ed. Dennis R Hansen. (Illus.). 247p. 1981. pap. 6.95 o.p. (ISBN 0-930098-03-X). Hansen Pub MI.

Michigan Distributors Directory: 1987. 478p. 1987. 123.00 o.p. (ISBN 0-318-23575-7). Manufacturers.

Michigan Hiking & Skiing Trails. Michigan United Conservation Clubs Staff. 1979. 1.75 o.s.i. (ISBN 0-933112-08-4). Mich United Conserv.

Michigan Hiking Opportunities. Ed. by Russell Mckee. 64p. 1982. pap. 6.95 o.p. (ISBN 0-941912-20-5). Mich Nat Res.

Michigan Manufacturers Directory, 1988. 994p. 1988. 127.00 o.p. (ISBN 0-318-02889-1). Manufacturers.

Michigan Probate Code. 200p. pap. 11.50 looseleaf o.p. (ISBN 0-87526-306-2). Gould.

Michigan: Restitution. 1983. 8.50 o.p. (ISBN 0-686-90525-3). Am Law Inst.

Michigan Statutes Annotated: Containing the Text of All General Laws of a Permanent Character in Force in Michigan. James M. Henderson. Ed. by Callaghan & Company Staff. LC 36-18036. 1986. 995.00 o.p. Callaghan.

Michigan's Masterpieces: Art from Public Collections. Commentary by Mary Riordan et al. (Illus.). 96p. 1985. pap. 9.95 o.p. (ISBN 0-89558-112-4). Detroit Inst Arts.

Michigan's Snow Trails. Ed. by Russell McKee. 96p. 1979. pap. 6.95 o.p. (ISBN 0-941912-22-1). Mich Nat Res.

Mick. Mickey Mantle & Herb Gluck. LC 85-2000. (Illus.). 264p. 1985. 15.95 o.p. (ISBN 0-385-19456-0); write for info. ltd. ed. o.p. Doubleday.

Mickey Mouse. Intro. by Floyd Gottfredson. LC 78-15264. (Walt Disney Best Comics Ser.). (Illus.). 204p. (YA) (gr. 7 up). 1978. 15.95 o.p. (ISBN 0-89659-005-4). Abbeville Pr.

Mickey Mouse Says I Can, Can You? Disney Studios & Walt Disney. Ed. by Kate Klimo. (Illus.). 6p. 1983. pap. 9.95 o.s.i. (ISBN 0-671-45821-3, Little Simon). S&S.

Mickey Takes a Bow. Doug Cushman. (Ringling Bros. & Barnum & Bailey Circus Bks.). (Illus.). 32p. (gr. k-3). 1986. 7.95 o.p. (ISBN 0-316-16558-1). Little.

Mickey Visits the Dentist. Ronnie Krauss. (Illus.). 48p. (gr. k-4). 1980. PLB 4.19 o.p. (ISBN 0-448-13640-6, G&D); text ed. 4.95 o.p. (ISBN 0-448-16582-1). Putnam Pub Group.

Mickey's Addition & Subtraction, 24 Bks. (Illus.). 64p. (ps-1). Set. pap. 30.00 o.p. (ISBN 0-448-81735-7). Putnam Pub Group.

Mickey's Advanced Reading Comprehension. (Illus.). 64p. (ps-1). Set. pap. 30.00 o.p. (ISBN 0-448-81736-5). Putnam Pub Group.

Mickey's Begining to Read, 24 bks. (Illus.). 64p. (ps-1). pap. 30.00 o.p. (ISBN 0-448-81734-9). Putnam Pub Group.

Mickey's Christmas Carol. Charles Dickens. Ed. by Disney Studio Staff. LC 84-9491. (Illus.). (gr. k up). 1984. pap. 5.95 o.p. (ISBN 0-517-55525-5). Crown.

Mickey's Dictionary & Word Skills, 24 bks. (Illus.). 64p. (ps-1). Set. pap. 30.00 o.p. (ISBN 0-448-81738-1). Putnam Pub Group.

Mickey's Divison & Fractions, 24 Bks. (Illus.). 64p. (ps-1). Set. pap. 30.00 o.p. (ISBN 0-448-81739-X). Putnam Pub Group.

Mickey's Listening, 24 bks. (Illus.). 64p. (ps-1). Set. pap. 30.00 o.p. (ISBN 0-448-81741-1). Putnam Pub Group.

Mickey's Looking, 24 bks. (Illus.). 64p. (ps-1). Set. pap. 30.00 o.p. (ISBN 0-448-81742-X). Putnam Pub Group.

Mickey's Math Puzzles & Games, 24 bks. (Illus.). 64p. (ps-1). Set. pap. 30.00 o.p. (ISBN 0-448-81743-8). Putnam Pub Group.

Mickey's Multiplcation, 24 bks. (Illus.). 64p. (ps-1). Set. pap. 30.00 o.p. (ISBN 0-448-81744-6). Putnam Pub Group.

Mickey's Neighborhood Friends, 24 bks. (Illus.). 64p. (ps-1). Set. pap. 30.00 o.p. (ISBN 0-317-31371-1). Putnam Pub Group.

Mickey's Numbers Fun, 24 bks. (Illus.). 64p. (ps-1). Set. pap. 30.00 o.p. (ISBN 0-448-81745-4). Putnam Pub Group.

Mickey's Phonics, 24 bks. (Illus.). 64p. (ps-1). Set. pap. 30.00 o.p. (ISBN 0-448-81746-2). Putnam Pub Group.

Mickey's Pop-Up Book of Colors. Disney, Walt, Productions Staff. (Illus.). 14p. (ps-1). 1985. 6.95 o.p. (ISBN 0-394-87344-0, BYR). Random.

Mickey's Pop-Up Book of Numbers. Disney, Walt, Productions Staff. (Illus.). 14p. (gr. 3-6). 1985. 6.95 o.p. (ISBN 0-394-87346-7, BYR). Random.

Mickey's Pop-Up Book of Shapes. Disney, Walt, Productions Staff. (Illus.). 14p. (gr. 1-5). 1985. 6.95 o.p. (ISBN 0-394-87345-9, BYR). Random.

Mickey's Practice Workbook: Division & Fractions, No. 12. Margery A. Steinberg. (Mickey's Practice Workbook Ser.). (Illus.). (gr. 3-5). 1980. pap. 1.25 o.p. (ISBN 0-448-16131-1, G&D). Putnam Pub Group.

Mickey's Practice Workbook: Math Puzzles & Games, No. 11. Margery A. Steinberg. (Mickey's Practice Workbook Ser.). (Illus.). (gr. 3-5). 1980. pap. 1.25 o.p. (ISBN 0-448-16130-3, G&D). Putnam Pub Group.

Mickey's Practice Writing, 24 bks. (Illus.). 64p. (ps-1). Set. pap. 30.00 o.p. (ISBN 0-448-81737-3). Putnam Pub Group.

Mickey's Question & Answer Book. Ronnie Krauss. LC 79-50667. (Illus.). (ps-1). 1979. 5.95 o.p. (ISBN 0-448-16565-1, G&D). Putnam Pub Group.

Mickey's Reading Comprehension, 24 bks. (Illus.). 64p. (ps-1). Set. pap. 30.00 o.p. (ISBN 0-448-81747-0). Putnam Pub Group.

Mickey's Science Fun, 24 bks. (Illus.). 64p. (ps-1). Set. pap. 30.00 o.p. (ISBN 0-448-81729-2). Putnam Pub Group.

Mickey's Words to Know, 24 bks. (Illus.). 64p. (ps-1). Set. pap. 30.00 o.p. (ISBN 0-448-81749-7). Putnam Pub Group.

MICOS: A Microprogrammable Computer Simulator. Lubomir Bic. LC 82-23627. (Digital Systems Design Ser.). 123p. 1984. pap. 18.95 o.p. (ISBN 0-914894-76-5, Computer Sci Pr); IBM diskette 20.00 o.p. (ISBN 0-88175-018-2); Apple diskette 20.00 o.p. (ISBN 0-88175-029-8). W H Freeman.

Micro-Analysis of Computer System Performance. Boris Beizer. (Illus.). 340p. 1978. 26.95 o.p. (ISBN 0-442-20663-1). Van Nos Reinhold.

Micro & Macro Mechanics of Crack Growth: Proceedings. TMS-AIME Fall Meeting, Louisville, 1981. Ed. by K. Sadananda & B. B. Rath. (Illus.). 255p. 30.00 o.p. (ISBN 0-89520-388-X); members 20.00 o.p. (ISBN 0-317-36249-6); student members 10.00 o.p. (ISBN 0-317-36250-X). ASM.

Micro Aspects of Development. Ed. by Eliezer B. Ayal. LC 72-89641. (Special Studies in International Economics & Development). 1973. 59.50x o.p. (ISBN 0-275-28685-1); pap. text ed. 24.50x o.p. (ISBN 0-89197-846-1). Irvington.

Micro Computers in Education II: Papers. 59p. 1981. pap. 28.60x o.p. (ISBN 0-686-97776-9, Pub. by Online Conference England). Gower Pub Co.

Micro Cookbook, Machine Language Programming, Vol. 2. Don Lancaster. 456p. 1983. pap. 15.95 o.p. (21829). Sams.

Micro-Economics: Selected Readings. 2nd ed. Ed. by Edwin Mansfield. (Illus.). 550p. 1975. pap. text ed. 8.95x o.p. (ISBN 0-393-09253-4). Norton.

Micro-Mainframe Connection. Thomas W. Madron. 272p. pap. 29.95 o.s.i. Sams.

Micro-Mainframe Link: The Corporate Guide to Productive Use of the Microcomputer. William E. Perry. LC 84-19563. 269p. 1985. 29.95 o.p. (ISBN 0-471-88212-7). Wiley.

Micro-Model Railways. Robert Kelly. (Illus.). 96p. 1982. 16.95 o.p. (ISBN 0-7153-8326-4). David & Charles.

Micro-Politics of the School Towards a Theory of School Organization. Stephen J. Ball. 256p. 1987. lib. bdg. 57.50x o.p. (ISBN 0-416-00102-5, Pub. by Croom Helm UK). Routledge Chapman & Hall.

Micro Systems in Business. A. Osborne et al. (Micro Monograph: No. 1). 122p. 1980. pap. text ed. 29.00x o.p. (ISBN 0-903796-63-5, Pub. by Online Conferences England). Gower Pub Co.

Micro TSP Cappl II V. 1983. 295.00 o.p. (ISBN 0-07-079126-0). McGraw.

Micro TSP Demo Dis. 1983. 12.00 o.p. (ISBN 0-07-025605-5). McGraw.

Micro TSP 5.0 Demo. 1986. 30.00 o.p. (ISBN 0-07-852207-2). McGraw.

Micro 4.1 Version. McGraw.

Microanalysis by the Ring Oven Technique. 2nd ed. H. Weisz. 1970. 38.00 o.p. (ISBN 0-08-015702-5). Pergamon.

Microanalysis of Assaults on Police in Austin, Texas. Patton N. Morrison & C. Kenneth Meyer. (Criminal Justice Policy & Administration Research Ser: No. 9). 1974. pap. 1.50 o.p. (ISBN 0-686-20787-4). Univ OK Gov Res.

Microanalytic Simulation Models for Analysis of Public Welfare Policies. Robert Harris. 50p. 1978. pap. text ed. 7.00 o.p. (ISBN 0-87766-223-1). Urban Inst.

Microautoradiography & Electron Probe Analysis: Their Application to Plant Physiology. Ed. by U. Luettge. LC 72-97599. (Illus.). 280p. 1973. pap. 29.00 o.p. (ISBN 0-387-05950-4). Springer-Verlag.

Microbeam Analysis in Biology. Ed. by Claude P. Lechene & Ronald Warner. LC 79-24948. 1980. 65.50 o.p. (ISBN 0-12-440340-9). Acad Pr.

Microbes in Your Life. Leo Schneider. LC 66-13796. (Illus.). (gr. 7 up). 1966. 6.50 o.p. (ISBN 0-15-253574-8, HJ). HarBraceJ.

Microbial & Plant Protoplasts. Ed. by J. F. Peberdy et al. 1976. 63.50 o.p. (ISBN 0-12-549050-X). Acad Pr.

Microbial Disease in Nephrology. A. W. Asscher & W. Brumfitt. 366p. 1986. 36.00 o.p. (ISBN 0-471-90826-6, Dist. by A R Liss). Wiley.

Microbial Ecology of Foods: Vol. 1 Factors Affecting Life & Death of Microorganisms. International Commission on Microbial Specifications for Foods. 1980. 32.50 o.p. (ISBN 0-12-363501-2). Acad Pr.

Microbial Energy Conversion. H. G. Schlegel. LC 76-56894. 1977. pap. 155.00 o.p. (ISBN 0-08-021791-5). Pergamon.

Microbial Genetics. Ed. by Morad Abou-Sabe. LC 73-13002. (Benchmark Papers in Microbiology: Vol. 3). 451p. 1982. 59.95 o.p. (ISBN 0-87933-046-5). Van Nos Reinhold.

Microbial Growth. Ed. by P. S. Dawson. LC 74-26644. (Benchmark Papers in Microbiology: Vol. 8). 400p. 1975. 75.00 o.p. (ISBN 0-12-786330-3). Acad Pr.

Microbial Interaction with the Physical Environment. Ed. by D. W. Thayer. LC 75-20439. (Benchmark Papers in Microbiology Ser: Vol. 9). 431p. 1975. 64.50 o.p. (ISBN 0-12-787536-0). Acad Pr.

Microbial Interactions see Queues: Receptors & Recognition Series B.

Microbial Iron Metabolism: A Comprehensive Treatise. J. B. Neilands. 1974. 99.50 o.p. (ISBN 0-12-515250-7). Acad Pr.

Microbial Metabolism. Ed. by H. W. Doelle. LC 73-16370. (Benchmark Papers in Microbiology: Vol. 5). 424p. 1982. 61.95 o.p. (ISBN 0-87933-063-5). Van Nos Reinhold.

Microbial Permeability. Ed. by John P. Reeves. (Benchmark Papers in Microbiology Ser). 442p. 1982. 61.95 o.p. (ISBN 0-87933-032-5). Van Nos Reinhold.

Microbial Perspective. Eugene Nester & Nancy Pearsall. 1982. text ed. 37.95 o.s.i. (ISBN 0-03-047041-2, CBS C). SCP.

Microbial Physiology. I. W. Dawes & I. W. Sutherland. (Illus.). 192p. 1976. pap. text ed. 15.60x o.p. (ISBN 0-632-00278-6). Blackwell Sci.

Microbial Physiology. Albert G. Moat. LC 79-11323. 600p. 1979. 41.50x o.p. (ISBN 0-471-07258-3, Pub. by Wiley-Interscience). Wiley.

Microbial Polysaccharides & Polysaccharases. Ed. by R. C. Berkeley & D. C. Ellwood. (Society for General Microbiology Ser.). 1979. 105.00 o.p. (ISBN 0-12-091450-6). Acad Pr.

Microbial Processes. Ed. by A. Fiechter. LC 72-152360. (Advances in Biochemical Engineering Ser.: Vol. 9). (Illus.). 1978. 38.00 o.p. (ISBN 0-387-08606-4). Springer-Verlag.

Microbial Respiration. Ed. by W. P. Hempfing. LC 78-22097. (Benchmark Papers in Microbiology: Vol. 13). 337p. 1982. 49.95 o.p. (ISBN 0-87933-344-8). Van Nos Reinhold.

Microbial Ribonucleases. F. Egami & K. Nakamura. LC 68-8784. (Molecular Biology, Bichemistry, & Biophysics Ser.: Vol. 6). 1969. 25.00 o.p. (ISBN 0-387-04657-7). Springer-Verlag.

Microbial Testers: Probing Carcinogenesis. Felkner. (Microbiology Ser.: Vol. 5). 1981. 59.75 o.p. (ISBN 0-8247-1244-7). Dekker.

Microbial World. 4th ed. Roger Stanier & M. Doudoroff. (Illus.). 1976. text ed. 45.67x ref. ed. o.p. (ISBN 0-13-581025-6). P-H.

Microbiological Effects on Metallurgical Processes: Proceedings of the AIME Annual Meeting, 114th, New York, February, 1985. AIME Staff. Ed. by L. A. Haas & J. A. Clum. LC 85-28541. 165p. pap. 59.00 o.p. (ISBN 0-87339-010-5). Minerals Metals.

Microbiological Hazards of Infusion Therapy. Ed. by I. Phillips et al. LC 76-47865. (Illus.). 194p. 1976. 22.00 o.p. (ISBN 0-88416-187-0). Year Bk Med.

Microbiology. Neal D. Buffaloe & Dale V. Ferguson. LC 75-19538. (Illus.). 448p. 1976. text ed. 20.90 o.p. (ISBN 0-395-18712-5). HM.

Microbiology. Ernest A. Gray. 180p. 1955. (ISBN 0-8022-0621-2). Philos Lib.

Microbiology. 4th ed. Michael J. Pelczar, Jr. et al. 1977. text ed. 43.95 o.p. (ISBN 0-07-049229-8). McGraw.

Microbiology: An Introduction. 2nd ed. Gerard J. Tortora et al. 820p. 1986. text ed. 43.95 o.p. (ISBN 0-8053-9315-3); instr's. guide 9.95 o.p. (ISBN 0-8053-9317-X); study guide 13.95 o.p. (ISBN 0-8053-9318-8); instr's. resource manual 150.00 o.p. (ISBN 0-8053-9319-6); lab manual by Case-Johnson 18.95 o.p.; transparencies 150.00 o.p. (ISBN 0-8053-9333-1). Benjamin-Cummings.

Microbiology & Pathology. 12th ed. Alice L Smith. LC 79-27338. (Illus.). 856p. 1980. text ed. 36.95 o.p. (ISBN 0-8016-4673-1). Mosby.

Microbiology Experiments. Eugene Nester & Marie Gilstrap. 1982. 19.95 o.s.i. (ISBN 0-03-057008-5, CBS C). SCP.

Microbiology for Environment Science Engineers. Anthony Gaudy & Elizabeth Gaudy. (Water Resources & Environmental Engineering Ser.). (Illus.). 704p. 1980. text ed. 49.95 o.p. (ISBN 0-07-023035-8). McGraw.

Microbiology for Medical Technologists: PreTest Self-Assessment & Review. Ed. by Sheila R. Berg. LC 78-51703. (Illus.). 203p. 1979. pap. 12.95 o.p. (ISBN 0-07-051572-7). McGraw-Pretest.

Microbiology for Sanitary Engineers. R. E. McKinney. (Sanitary & Water Resources Engineering Ser.). 1962. text ed. 46.95 o.p. (ISBN 0-07-045180-X). McGraw.

Microbiology for the Allied Health Professions. 3rd ed. Adrian N. Delaat. LC 83-24833. (Illus.). 1984. 24.50 o.p. (ISBN 0-8121-0910-4). Lea & Febiger.

Microbiology: Fundamentals & Applications. Ronald M. Atlas. 1984. write for info. o.p. (ISBN 0-02-304550-7); write for info. study guide, 400p o.p. (ISBN 0-02-304570-1). Macmillan.

Microbiology in Clinical Dentistry. Frank J. Orland. (Illus.). 288p. 1982. 38.00 o.p. (ISBN 0-88416-171-4). Year Bk Med.

Microbiology of Aerial Plant Surfaces. Ed. by C. Dickinson. 1976. 104.00 o.p. (ISBN 0-12-215050-3). Acad Pr.

Microbiology: PreTest Self-Assesment & Review. 3rd ed. Pre Test Services, Inc. & Richard C. Tilton. (Basic Science Ser.). (Illus.). 200p. 1983. text ed. 12.95 review book o.p. (ISBN 0-07-051933-1). McGraw.

Microbiology: PreTest Self-Assessment & Review. 4th ed. PreTest Service, Inc. Staff. (Illus.). 200p. 1985. 14.95 o.p. (ISBN 0-07-051943-9). McGraw-Pretest.

Microbiology 1986. Ed. by Loretta Leive et al. (Illus.). 378p. 1986. pap. text ed. 38.00 o.p. (ISBN 0-914826-84-0). Am Soc Microbio.

Microchemical Analysis of Nervous Tissue. Neville N. Osborne. 1974. 60.00 o.p. (ISBN 0-08-018100-7). Pergamon.

Microcirculation & Tubular Urine Flow in the Mammalian Kidney Cortex: In Vivo Microscopy. M. Steinhausen & G. A. Tanner. (Illus.). 1976. pap. 28.40 o.p. (ISBN 0-387-07819-3). Springer-Verlag.

Microcirculation As Related to Shock. David Shepro & George P. Fulton. 1968. 60.50 o.p. (ISBN 0-12-639650-7). Acad Pr.

Microcirculation: Current Concepts. Ed. by Richard Effros et al. 1981. 72.50 o.p. (ISBN 0-12-232560-5). Acad Pr.

Microcirculation in Medicine. Ed. by Roe Wells. 1973. 81.00 o.p. (ISBN 0-12-743750-9). Acad Pr.

Microcirculation, Perfusion & Transplantation of Organs. Ed. by T. I. Malinin et al. 1970. 68.00 o.p. (ISBN 0-12-466550-0). Acad Pr.

Microcomputer Applications for Calculus. Gary Bitter. 256p. 1982. pap. text ed. write for info o.p. (ISBN 0-87150-378-6, 8010, Prindle). PWS-Kent Pub.

Microcomputer Art. Ross Edwards. (Illus.). 240p. 1985. pap. text ed. 23.00 o.p. (ISBN 0-13-580218-0). P-H.

Microcomputer Assembly Language Programming. Gary C. Elfring. (Illus.). 224p. 1984. 35.95 o.p. (ISBN 0-442-22261-0). Van Nos Reinhold.

Microcomputer BASIC: Structures, Concepts, & Techniques. Edward J. Coburn. 416p. 1986. pap. 25.95 o.p. (ISBN 0-8273-2480-4); instr's. guide 10.60 o.p. Delmar.

Microcomputer Builder's Bible. Chris Johnston. (Illus.). 320p. (Orig.). 1983. 19.95 o.p. (ISBN 0-8306-2473-2); pap. 14.15 o.p. (ISBN 0-8306-1473-7, 1473). TAB Bks.

Microcomputer Buyer's Guide. 2nd ed. Tony Webster. (Illus.). 400p. 1983. pap. text ed. 19.95 o.p. (ISBN 0-07-068959-8, BYTE Bks). McGraw.

Microcomputer Buyer's Guide. 3rd ed. Tony Webster. (Illus.). 384p. 1984. pap. text ed. 19.95 o.p. (ISBN 0-07-068963-6, BYTE Bks). McGraw.

Microcomputer Communications in Business. Howard Falk. LC 84-45161. 320p. (Orig.). 1984. pap. 18.95 o.p. (ISBN 0-8019-7512-3). Chilton.

Microcomputer-Controlled Toys & Games & How They Work. Van Waterford. (Illus.). 240p. (Orig.). 1983. 17.95 o.p. (ISBN 0-8306-0407-3); pap. 9.95 o.p. (ISBN 0-8306-1407-9, 1407). TAB Bks.

Microcomputer Courseware for Technical Mathematics (Apple II & TRS-80) User's Manual. Ronald S. Burke & Arthur D. Kramer. 1982. pap. text ed. 16.95 o.p. (ISBN 0-07-009050-5). McGraw.

Microcomputer Design. Carol A. Ogdin. (Illus.). 1978. text ed. 35.00 ref. ed. o.p. (ISBN 0-13-580977-0); pap. text ed. 29.00 o.p. (ISBN 0-13-580985-1). P-H.

Microcomputer Markets in Europe. (Reports Ser.: No. 522). 231p. 1982. 1450.00x o.p. (ISBN 0-88694-522-4). Intl Res Dev.

Microcomputer Models for Management Science: Text. Terry L. Dennis & Laurie B. Dennis. (Illus.). 313p. 1985. pap. text ed. 22.50 o.p. (ISBN 0-314-93171-6); Microcomputer Models for Management Decision Making. software 23.75 o.p. (ISBN 0-314-97406-7). West Pub.

Microcomputer Operating System Strategies. International Resource Development, Inc. Staff. 237p. 1983. 1650.00x o.p. (ISBN 0-88694-571-2). Intl Res Dev.

Microcomputer Programming & Interfacing, 6801, 68701 & 6803. Andrew C. Staugaard, Jr. LC 80-51716. 352p. 1980. pap. 14.95 o.p. (ISBN 0-672-21726-0, 21726). Sams.

Microcomputer Publications Survey. International Resource Development, Inc. Staff. 115p. 1983. 895.00x o.p. (ISBN 0-88694-584-4). Intl Res Dev.

Microcomputer System Design & Techniques. Carol A. Ogdin. LC 80-80772. (Tutorial Texts Ser.). 374p. 1980. 24.00 o.p. (ISBN 0-8186-0259-7, Q259). IEEE Comp Soc.

Microcomputer Systems. 1987. 110.00 o.p. DATA Busn Pub.

Microcomputer Tools for Communication Engineering. S. T. Li et al. LC 83-71834. 269p. 1984. disks avail. 54.00 o.p. (ISBN 0-89006-132-7). Artech Hse.

Microcomputers & Laboratory Instrumentation. David J. Malcolme-Lawes. 256p. 1984. 35.00x o.p. (ISBN 0-306-41668-9, Plenum Pr). Plenum Pub.

Microcomputers at a Glance. Donald D. Spencer. LC 77-11920. (gr. 9-12). pap. 3.50x o.s.i. Camelot Pub.

Microcomputers for Business. Claire Summer & Walter A. Levy. 1980. pap. 7.95 o.p. (ISBN 0-8144-7539-6). AMACOM.

Microcomputers for Engineers & Scientists. Glenn A. Gibson & Yu-Cheng Liu. (Illus.). 1980. text ed. 50.67 o.p. (ISBN 0-13-580886-3). P-H.

Microcomputers for Financial Planning. Rodney Drew. 116p. 1983. pap. 38.50x o.p. (ISBN 0-566-03443-3). Gower Pub Co.

Microcomputers in a Law Office. 2nd ed. Gary L. Bakke. LC 86-206956. 106p. 1985. 25.00 o.p. (ISBN 0-941161-06-4). PES Inc WI.

Microcomputers in Amateur Radio. Joe Kasser. 15.95 o.p. (ISBN 0-8306-0024-8, 1305); pap. 10.95 o.p. (ISBN 0-8306-1305-6). TAB Bks.

Microcomputers in Art Education. Ed. by Virginia M. Brouch. 48p. 1988. pap. 7.00 o.p. (ISBN 0-937652-39-3). Natl Art Ed.

Microcomputers in Business: Wordstar, Lotus, Base II & II. Spence & Windsor. 240p. 1987. pap. 17.95 o.p. (ISBN 0-8016-5030-5). Mosby.

Microcomputers in Clinical Practice. D. E. Norris et al. LC 84-13020. 159p. 1985. pap. 14.95 o.p. (ISBN 0-471-90373-6, Dist. by A R Liss). Wiley.

Microcomputers in Education. Lee M. Joiner et al. LC 81-84658. 320p. 1982. 24.95 o.s.i. (ISBN 0-918452-31-7); pap. text ed. 14.95 o.p. (ISBN 0-918452-46-5). Learning Pubns.

Microcomputers in Education: Commodore in the Classroom. Ed. by E. Ramsden & R. N. Green. LC 84-22565. (Computers & Their Applications Ser.). 206p. 1985. 29.95 o.p. (ISBN 0-470-20121-5). Halsted Pr.

Microcomputers in Education: Micro Monograph, No. 2. (Online Conference, 1980). 55p. (Orig.). 1980. pap. text ed. 28.60x o.p. (ISBN 0-903796-64-3, Pub. by Online Conferences England). Gower Pub Co.

Microcomputers in Education: Papers of the Online Conference, Mersey Micro Shoe, 1980. 55p. 1980. pap. 23.00x o.p. (ISBN 0-903796-64-3). Taylor & Francis.

Microcomputers in Financial Institutions. M. Arthur Gillis. LC 84-73254. 1985. 25.00 o.p. (ISBN 0-87094-580-7). Dow Jones-Irwin.

Microcomputers in K-Twelve Education, First Annual Conference Proceedings. Ed. by Pierre Barrette. LC 82-2522. 123p. 1982. pap. text ed. 30.00 o.p. (ISBN 0-914894-32-3, Computer Sci Pr). W H Freeman.

Microcomputers in K-Twelve Education: Second Annual Conference Proceedings. Pierre Barrette. LC 83-2101. 141p. 1983. 30.00 o.p. (ISBN 0-914894-87-0, Computer Sci Pr). W H Freeman.

Microcomputers in Secondary Education: Proceedings. Conference of the British Educational Research Association 1980. Ed. by Jim Howe & Peter Ross. 162p. 1981. pap. 23.50 o.p. (ISBN 0-89397-108-1). Nichols Pub.

Microcomputers in Special Education: Special Issue of Exceptional Children, October 1982. Ed. by M. Angele Thomas. 96p. 1982. pap. 5.00 o.p. (ISBN 0-86586-139-0). Coun Exc Child.

Microcomputers in the Home. (Reports Ser.: No. 537). 166p. 1983. 985.00x o.p. (ISBN 0-88694-537-2). Intl Res Dev.

Microcomputers-Microprocessors: Hardware, Software & Applications. John L. Hilburn & Paul M. Julich. 1976. text ed. 48.00 o.p. (ISBN 0-13-580969-X). P-H.

Microcomputing Systems in Business. Ed. by Derek Pedder. 64p. (Orig.). 1980. pap. text ed. 78.00x o.p. (ISBN 0-566-03010-1). Gower Pub Co.

Microcosm: College & the World. Ann W. Connor & Gerald Kohs. 371p. 1972. pap. text ed. 8.95 o.p. (ISBN 0-15-558600-9, HC). HarBraceJ.

Microcosmic Tales: One Hundred Wondrous Science Fiction Short-Short Stories. Ed. by Isaac Asimov et al. LC 79-66641. 1980. 12.95 o.p. (ISBN 0-8008-5238-9). Taplinger.

Microeconomic Analysis. Hal R. Varian. (Illus.). 1978. pap. text ed. 22.95x o.p. (ISBN 0-393-09036-1). Norton.

Microeconomic Analysis: Essays in Microeconomics & Economic Development. Ed. by D. Currie et al. 495p. 1981. 44.00 o.p. (ISBN 0-7099-0709-5, Pub. by Croom Helm Ltd). Routledge Chapman & Hall.

Microeconomic Analysis of Issues in Business, Government & Society. Roger Beck. (Illus.). 1978. text ed. 34.95 o.p. (ISBN 0-07-004253-5). McGraw.

Microeconomic Decisions. Robert A. Meyer, Jr. LC 75-30259. (Illus.). 384p. 1976. text ed. 25.95 o.p. (ISBN 0-395-19855-0). HM.

Microeconomic Models. K. C. Kogiku. LC 78-11695. 320p. 1982. Repr. of 1971 ed. lib. bdg. 22.50 o.p. (ISBN 0-88275-781-4). Krieger.

Microeconomic Problems. 3rd ed. Edwin Mansfield. 1979. pap. text ed. 5.95x o.p. (ISBN 0-393-95004-2). Norton.

Microeconomic Problems. Ed. by Edwin Mansfield. 1971. pap. text ed. 4.25x o.p. (ISBN 0-393-09390-5). Norton.

Microeconomic Problems: Case Studies and Exercises for Review. 4th ed. Edwin Mansfield. 1982. pap. text ed. 8.95x o.p. (ISBN 0-393-95212-6). Norton.

Microeconomic Theory. DeSerpa. 1985. 29.25 o.p. (ISBN 0-205-08339-0, 098339). Allyn.

Microeconomic Theory. 3rd ed. M. L. Jhingan. 744p. 1984. pap. text ed. 22.50x o.p. (ISBN 0-7069-2628-5, Pub. by Vikas India); text ed. 40.00 o.p. Advent NY.

Microeconomic Theory & Applications. 2nd ed. Edgar K. Browning & Jacqueline M. Browning. 1986. text ed. write for info. o.p. (ISBN 0-673-39117-5); write for info. o.p. (ISBN 0-673-39118-3). Scott F.

Microeconomics. 3rd ed. William J. Baumol & Alan S. Blinder. 560p. 1986. pap. text ed. 20.00 o.p. (ISBN 0-15-518850-X, Pub. by HC). HarBraceJ.

Microeconomics. 3rd ed. Ralph T. Byrns & Gerald W. Stone, Jr. 1987. pap. write for info. o.p. (ISBN 0-673-16685-6). Scott F.

Microeconomics. 2nd ed. Steven T. Call & William L. Holahan. 499p. 1983. text ed. (ISBN 0-534-01314-7). Wadsworth Pub.

Microeconomics. 4th ed. Edwin G. Dolan. 576p. 1986. pap. text ed. 19.95 o.s.i. (ISBN 0-03-005472-9); wkbk. 8.95 o.s.i. (ISBN 0-03-005467-2). Dryden Pr.

Microeconomics. Robert B. Ekelund & Robert D. Tollison. 1986. pap. text ed. write for info. o.p. (ISBN 0-673-39123-X). Scott F.

Microeconomics. Truett. 608p. 1987. pap. text ed. 24.95 o.p. (ISBN 0-8016-5149-2). Mosby.

Microeconomics. Lila F. Truett & Dale B. Truett. (Illus.). 549p. 1982. pap. text ed. 23.00 o.p. (ISBN 0-314-63304-9); study guide 9.25 o.p. (ISBN 0-314-63305-7). West Pub.

Microeconomics: A Contemporary Approach. Charles L Cole. 1973. text ed. 15.95 o.p. (ISBN 0-15-558620-3, HC). HarBraceJ.

Microeconomics: Analysis & Applications. 2nd ed. C. Bach. 1980. pap. text ed. (ISBN 0-13-581298-4). P-H.

Microeconomics of Peasant Economy: China 1920-1940. Thomas B. Wiens. Ed. by Ramon H. Myers. LC 80-8837. (China During the Interregnum 1911-1949, The Economy & Society Ser.). 536p. 1982. lib. bdg. 67.00 o.p. (ISBN 0-8240-4692-7). Garland Pub.

Microeconomics: Resource Allocation & Price Theory. John C. Redman & Barbara J. Redman. (Illus.). 1981. pap. 19.95 o.p. (ISBN 0-87055-367-4). AVI.

Microeconomics: Selected Readings. Ed. by Edwin Mansfield. 1971. pap. text ed. 6.95x o.p. (ISBN 0-393-09989-X). Norton.

Microeconomics: Selected Readings. 3rd ed. Ed. by Edwin Mansfield. (Illus.). 1979. 10.95x o.p. (ISBN 0-393-95015-8). Norton.

Microeconomics: Theory & Applications. Robert Y. Awh. LC 75-38643. 492p. 1976. text ed. 39.45x o o.p. (ISBN 0-471-03849-0); pap. text ed. 17.95x wkbk. o.p. (ISBN 0-471-03853-9); tchrs. manual avail. o.p. (ISBN 0-471-03854-7). Wiley.

Microeconomics: Theory & Applications. Fred R. Glahe & Dwight R. Lee. 558p. 1981. text ed. 30.00 net o.p. (ISBN 0-15-558623-8, HC). HarBraceJ.

Microeconomics: Theory & Applications. 2nd ed. Edwin Mansfield. 500p. 1975. text ed. 12.95x o.p. (ISBN 0-393-09244-5); microeconomic problems wkbk. 4.25x o.p. (ISBN 0-393-09248-8). Norton.

Microeconomics: Theory & Applications. shorter 2nd ed. Edwin Mansfield. (Illus.). 400p. 1975. text ed. 12.50x o.p. (ISBN 0-393-09190-2). Norton.

Microeconomics: Theory & Applications. Edwin Mansfield. 1970. text ed. 10.95x o.p. (ISBN 0-393-09928-8, NortonC). Norton.

Microeconomics: Theory Applications Innovations. Gerald Garb. 342p. 1981. text ed. write for info. o.p. (ISBN 0-02-340400-0). Macmillan.

Microelectronic Circuits. Adele S. Sedra & Kenneth C. Smith. 927p. 1982. text ed. 49.95 o.s.i. (ISBN 0-03-056729-7). HR&W.

Microelectronics: A Standard Manual & Guide. John D. Young. 277p. 1983. 24.95 o.p. (ISBN 0-13-581108-2, Busn). P-H.

Microelectronics Education Programme Policy & Guidelines. R. Fothergill & J. S. Anderson. (Orig.). 1983. pap. text ed. 42.50x o.p. (ISBN 0-318-21731-7). Trans Atl Phila.

Microelectronics Interconnection & Packaging. Electronics Magazine Editors. (Electronics Book Ser.). (Illus.). 1980. text ed. 39.50 o.p. (ISBN 0-07-019184-0). McGraw.

Microelectronics, International Competiton & Development Strategies: The Unavoidable Issues. Ed. by K. Hoffman. 200p. 1985. pap. 26.00 o.p. (ISBN 0-08-032687-0, Pub by PPL). Pergamon.

Microenvironments & Metabolic Compartmentation. Ed. by Paul A. Srere & Ronald W. Estabrook. 1978. 60.50 o.p. (ISBN 0-12-660550-5). Acad Pr.

Microfilaments. Vivianne T. Nachmias. Ed. by J. J. Head. LC 82-73999. (Carolina Biology Readers Ser.: No. 130). (Illus.). 16p. (gr. 10 up). 1984. pap. 1.80 o.p. (ISBN 0-89278-330-3, 45-9730). Carolina Biological.

Microforms of United States Government Publications. Helen McReynolds. (Occasional Papers: No. 69). 13p. 1963. pap. 1.00 o.p. (ISBN 0-317-58850-8). U of Ill Lib Info Sci.

Microgravity Sciences & Processes. L. G. Napolitano. 1983. pap. 37.00 o.p. (ISBN 0-08-029985-7). Pergamon.

Microlight Flying Manual. R. D. Campbell & J. Jones. 240p. (Orig.). 1982. pap. text ed. 21.95x o.p. (ISBN 0-246-11914-4, Pub. by Granada England). Gower Pub Co.

Micromanagement: How to Solve the Problems of Growing Companies. William A. Delaney. 176p. 1981. 14.95 o.p. (ISBN 0-8144-5642-1). AMACOM.

Micromanipulators & Micromanipulation. Hamed M. El-Badry. (Illus.). 1963. 34.90 o.p. (ISBN 0-387-80648-2). Springer-Verlag.

Micromethods in Molecular Biology. V. Neuhoff. (Molecular Biology, Biochemistry & Biophysics Ser.: Vol. 14). (Illus.). xv, 428p. 1973. 66.00 o.p. (ISBN 0-387-06319-6). Springer-Verlag.

Micromorphology of Soils. E. A. FitzPatrick. (Illus.). 330p. 1984. 69.95 o.p. (ISBN 0-412-24200-1, 5067, Pub. by Chapman & Hall England). Routledge Chapman & Hall.

Micronesia under American Rule: An Evaluation of the Strategic Trusteeship 1947-77. Harold F. Nufer. 1978. 15.00 o.p. (ISBN 0-682-49021-0, University). Exposition-Phoenix.

Microorganisms & Nitrogen Sources: Transport & Utilization of Amino Acods, Peptides, Proteins & Related Substrates. J. W. Payne. LC 79-42900. 870p. 1980. 220.00x o.p. (ISBN 0-471-27697-9). Wiley.

Micropolar Elasticity: Proceedings of CISM, Department of Mechanics of Solids, 1972. CISM (International Center for Mechanical Sciences, Department of Mechanics of Solids Staff. Ed. by W. Olszak & W. Nowacki. (CISM International Centre for Mechanical Sciences Ser.: No. 151). (Illus.). vii, 168p. 1974. pap. 15.70 o.p. (ISBN 0-387-81262-8). Springer-Verlag.

Microprobe Analysis As Applied to Cells & Tissues. Ed. by Theodore Hall et al. 1974. 70.50 o.p. (ISBN 0-12-319050-9). Acad Pr.

Microprocessing Programming 6801, 68701, & 6803. Date not set. Sams.

Microprocessor & Microcomputer Basics. Jefferson C. Boyce. (Illus.). 1979. text ed. 46.00 o.p. (ISBN 0-13-581249-6). P-H.

Microprocessor Control Systems, the Concept - The Reality: Proceedings of the Wilmington Section Symposium. Wilmington Section Symposium Staff. LC 82-164810. 84p. 1982. pap. text ed. 20.00x o.p. (ISBN 0-87664-688-7). Instru Soc.

Microprocessor Development & Development Systems. Vincent Tseng. 224p. 1982. text ed. 34.95 o.p. (ISBN 0-07-065380-1). McGraw.

Microprocessor for Managers: A Decision Maker's Guide. R. L. Krutz. 150p. 1983. 29.95 o.p. (ISBN 0-8436-1610-5). Van Nos Reinhold.

Microprocessor-Microcomputer Technology. Frederick F. Driscoll. 520p. 1983. 31.95 o.p. (ISBN 0-442-21827-3). Van Nos Reinhold.

Microprocessor Programming & Software Development. F. Duncan. 1979. text ed. 44.00 o.p. (ISBN 0-13-581405-7). P-H.

Microprocessors. Electronics Magazine Editors. (Illus.). 1975. text ed. 39.50 o.p. (ISBN 0-07-019171-9). McGraw.

Microprocessors & Digital Systems. Douglas V. Hall. 1980. text ed. 33.00 o.p. (ISBN 0-07-025571-7). McGraw.

Microprocessors & Microcomputer Systems. rev. 2nd ed. Guthikonda V. Rao. (Illus.). 592p. 1982. 45.95 o.p. (ISBN 0-442-25626-4). Van Nos Reinhold.

Microprocessors & Microcomputers: Hardware & Software. 2nd ed. Ronald J. Tocci & Lester P. Laskowski. (Illus.). 416p. 1982. pap. text ed. 37.33 o.p. (ISBN 0-13-581322-0); solutions manual avail o.p. P-H.

Microprocessors & Programmed Logic. K. Short. 1981. text ed. 50.67 o.p. (ISBN 0-13-581173-2). P-H.

Microprocessors & Small Digital Computer Systems: For Engineers & Scientists. Granino A. Korn. LC 77-492. 1977. text ed. 51.50 o.p. (ISBN 0-07-035367-0). McGraw.

Microprocessors for Measurement & Control. David Auslander & Paul Sagues. 310p. (Orig.). 1981. pap. text ed. 16.95 o.p. (ISBN 0-07-931057-5). Osborne-McGraw.

Microprocessors in Analytical Chemistry, Vol. 27, No. 7b. R. A. Chalmers. 64p. 1982. pap. 28.00 o.p. (ISBN 0-08-026284-8). Pergamon.

Microprocessors in Industry. Ed. by National Computing Centre, Ltd. Staff. 280p. (Orig.). 1981. pap. 27.50x o.s.i. (ISBN 0-85012-322-4). Intl Pubns Serv.

Microprogrammed APL Implementation. Rodnay Zaks. LC 78-58355. (Illus.). 347p. 1978. pap. 29.95 o.p. (ISBN 0-89588-005-9, Z-10). SYBEX.

Micropublishers' Trade List Annual, 1976. rev. ed. Microform Review, Inc. Staff. 1976. 80.00x o.p. (ISBN 0-913672-06-8). Meckler Corp.

Microreconstruction of Nerve Injuries. Julia K. Terzis. (Illus.). 702p. 1987. 89.00 o.p. Saunders.

Micros: A Pervasive Force. Michael Orme. LC 79-23839. 214p. 1980. 47.95x o.p. (ISBN 0-470-26891-3). Halsted Pr.

Micros in DP: Micro Monograph, Proceeding of the Online Conference, Interface, London, 1980. Online Conference Staff. (Micro Monograph: No. 4). 52p. (Orig.). 1980. pap. text ed. 28.60x o.p. (ISBN 0-903796-65-1, Pub. by Online Conferences England). Online.

Microscope. S. Bradbury. 1968. 70.00 o.p. (ISBN 0-08-012848-3). Pergamon.

Microscope Past & Present. S. Bradbury. 1968. pap. 70.00 o.p. (ISBN 0-08-013249-9). Pergamon.

Microscopic & Endoscopic Surgery with the Carbon Dioxide Laser. Albert H. Andrews, Jr. & Thomas Polanyi. LC 81-15989. (Illus.). 386p. 1982. 50.00 o.p. (ISBN 0-7236-7009-9). Butterworth.

Microscopic Optical Potentials: Proceedings of the Hamburg Topical Workshop on Nuclear Physics, Univ. of Hamburg, Germany, Sept. 25-27, 1978. Ed. by H. von Geramb. (Lecture Notes in Physics Ser.: Vol. 89). 1979. pap. 26.00 o.p. (ISBN 0-387-09106-8). Springer-Verlag.

Microsoft BASIC for the Macintosh. Coan & Coan. 1985. 18.95 o.p. (ISBN 0-8104-6558-2). Sams.

Microsoft BASIC for the Macintosh. Larry J. Goldstein & David Schneider. (Illus.). 576p. 1984. pap. 21.95 o.p. (ISBN 0-89303-662-5). Brady Bks.

Microsoft BASIC Programming for the Mac. Sharon Z. Aker. (Illus.). 336p. 1985. pap. 17.95 o.p. (ISBN 0-673-18167-7). Scott F.

Microsoft BASIC Using Modular Structure. Julia C. Bradley. 464p. 1986. pap. text ed. write for info. o.p. (ISBN 0-697-00455-4). Wm C Brown.

Microsoft BASIC 2.0 for the Apple Macintosh. Merl Miller & Ken Knecht. 329p. (Orig.). 1986. pap. 19.95 o.s.i. (ISBN 0-317-55831-5). Weber Systems.

Microsoft C Programming for the PC. Waite Group. 640p. 1987. pap. 24.95 o.p. (ISBN 0-672-22515-8). Sams.

Microsoft File: Organizing Your Business on the Apple Macintosh. Nancy Andrews. LC 85-29804. 472p. (Orig.). 1986. pap. 18.95 o.p. (ISBN 0-914845-65-9). Microsoft.

Microsoft Macinations: An Introduction to Microsoft BASIC for the Apple Macintosh. Waite Group Staff & Mitchell Waite. (Illus.). 528p. 1985. pap. 19.95 o.p. (ISBN 0-914845-34-9). Microsoft.

Microsoft QuickBASIC. Douglas Hergert. 384p. (Orig.). 1987. pap. 18.95 o.p. (ISBN 0-914845-99-3). Microsoft.

Microsoft Word for the IBM PC. Lieberman & Gloe. 1985. 29.95 o.p. (ISBN 0-672-22348-1, 22348-1). Sams.

Microsoft Word for the MAC. Lambert. 450p. 1987. pap. 19.95 o.p. (ISBN 0-88022-333-2, 803). Que Corp.

Microsoft Word Made Easy. Paul Hoffman. 250p. (Orig.). 1984. pap. text ed. 15.95 o.p. (ISBN 0-07-881144-9). Osborne-McGraw.

Microsoft Word Made Easy: Macintosh Edition. Paul Hoffman. LC 84-22750. 200p. 1984. pap. text ed. 15.95 o.p. (ISBN 0-07-881152-X). Osborne-McGraw.

Microsoft Works Short BASIC Combo 88-89. Robert H. Blissmer et al. 1988. pap. 38.95 o.p. (ISBN 0-471-62340-7). Wiley.

Microsoftware: Operations Research IBM. Ed. by Gary Whitehouse. 1986. 175.00 o.p. (ISBN 0-89806-080-X). Inst Indus Eng.

Microsoftware: Statistical Analysis. rev ed. Ed. by Gary Whitehous. 1984. 175.00 o.p. (ISBN 0-89806-084-2). Inst Indus Eng.

Microstrip Antenna Theory & Design. J. R. James et al. (IEE Electromagnetic Waves Ser.: No. 12). 336p. 1981. casebound 84.00 o.p. (ISBN 0-906048-57-5, EW 012). Inst Elect Eng.

Microstrip Antennas. I. J. Bahl & P. Bhartia. (Illus.). 355p. 1980. 70.00 o.p. (ISBN 0-89006-098-3). Artech Hse.

Microsurgery for Stroke. Ed. by P. Schmeidek. LC 77-21011. 1978. 36.00 o.p. (ISBN 0-387-90250-3). Springer-Verlag.

Microsurgery in Glaucoma: Proceedings of the Ophthalmic Microsurgery Study Group Symposium, 2nd, Buergenstock, 1968. Ophthalmic Microsurgery Study Group Symposium Staff. Ed. by G. Mackensen. (Bibliotheca Ophthalmologica: No. 81). (Illus.). 1970. 78.75 o.p. (ISBN 3-8055-0216-8). S Karger.

Microsurgery Practice Manual. Robert D. Acland. LC 79-17533. (Illus.). 64p. 1979. pap. text ed. 21.95 o.p. (ISBN 0-8016-0076-6). Mosby.

Microteaching. C. Turney et al. 198p. 1974. 9.50x o.p. (ISBN 0-424-06740-4, Pub. by Sydney U Pr); pap. 14.00x o.p. (ISBN 0-424-06750-1, Pub. by Sydney U Pr). Intl Spec Bk.

Microteaching in Higher Education. Elizabeth Perrot. 107p. 1977. pap. 15.00 o.p. (ISBN 0-900868-59-7, Open Univ Pr). Taylor & Francis.

MicroTSP Version 5.0 (Software Package) Ed. by Quantitative Micro Software Staff. 1986. 595.00 o.p. (ISBN 0-07-852205-6). McGraw.

Microwave. 1987. 100.00 o.p. DATA Busn Pub.

Microwave Attenuation Measurement, No. 19. F. L. Warner. (IEE Monograph Ser.). 358p. 1977. casebound 56.00 o.p. (ISBN 0-901223-79-4, MO 019, Pub. by Pereginus London). Inst Elect Eng.

Microwave Cookbook: The Complete Guide. Pat Jester. (Illus.). 534p. 1982. ringbound 22.50 o.p. (ISBN 0-89586-169-0); pap. 14.95 o.p. (ISBN 0-89586-270-0). Price Stern.

Microwave Cooking: Meals in Minutes. Thelma Pressman. Ed. by Betsy Lawrence. LC 83-71038. (Great American Cooking Schools Ser.). (Illus.). 84p. (Orig.). 1983. pap. 5.95 o.p. (ISBN 0-941034-16-X). I Chalmers.

Microwave Discontinued Devices. 1987. 70.00 o.p. DATA Busn Pub.

Microwave Fish Cookbook. Val Collins. (Illus.). 120p. 1983. 16.95 o.p. (ISBN 0-7153-8393-0). David & Charles.

Microwave Fruit & Vegetable Cookbook. Val Collins. LC 81-65958. (Illus.). 120p. 1981. 16.95 o.p. (ISBN 0-7153-8199-7). David & Charles.

Microwave Heating. 2nd ed. David A. Copson. (Illus.). 1975. 50.95 o.p. (ISBN 0-87055-182-5). AVI.

Microwave Integrated Circuits. 2nd ed. Ed. by Jeffrey Frey & Kul Bhasin. 446p. 1985. pap. text ed. 45.00 o.p. (ISBN 0-89006-160-2). Artech Hse.

Microwave Magic. Ed. by Annette Gohlke. 88p. 1977. pap. 3.95 o.s.i. (ISBN 0-89821-020-8). Reiman Assocs.

Microwave Magic II. Ed. by Annette Gohlke. LC 82-62678. 64p. 1982. pap. 3.95 o.s.i. Reiman Assocs.

Microwave Materials & Fabrication Techniques. Thomas S. Laverghetta. 218p. 1984. text ed. 60.00 o.p. (ISBN 0-89006-143-2). Artech Hse.

Microwave Measurements. Ed. by A. E. Bailey. (Electrical Measurement Ser.: No. 3). 472p. 1985. 78.00 o.p. (ISBN 0-86341-048-0, EL003). Inst Elect Eng.

Microwave Solid State Devices & Applications. Ed. by M. J. Howes & D. V. Morgan. (Illus.). 256p. 1980. pap. 52.00 o.p. (ISBN 0-906048-39-7, EM099, Pub. by Peregrinus England). Inst Elect Eng.

Microwave Spectroscopy of Free Radicals. Alan Carrington. 1974. 69.00 o.p. (ISBN 0-12-160750-X). Acad Pr.

Microwave System Engineering Principles. S. J. Raff. 1978. 35.00 o.p. (ISBN 0-08-021797-4). Pergamon.

Microwave Tubes in Systems. (Conference Publications: No. 241). 171p. 1984. pap. 70.00 o.s.i. (ISBN 0-85296-302-5, IC241). Inst Elect Eng.

Microworlds: Writings on Science Fiction & Fantasy. Stanislaw Lem. Ed. by Franz Rottensteiner. (Helen & Kurt Wolff Bk.). 256p. 1985. 14.95 o.p. (ISBN 0-15-159480-5). HarBraceJ.

Mid-Atlantic Bed & Breakfast Book. rev. ed. Corinne M. Ross. LC 85-45692. (Illus.). 208p. (Orig.). 1986. pap. 8.95 o.p. (ISBN 0-88742-061-3). Globe Pequot.

Mid-Century. (Our Nations Heritage Ser.). Date not set. (ISBN 0-07-375429-3). McGraw.

Mid-Century Appraisal of Civilization. Willis D. Warren. 1951. (ISBN 0-8022-1811-3). Philos Lib.

Mid-Century Child & Her Books. Caroline M. Hewins. LC 69-16070. 148p. 1969. Repr. of 1926 ed. 35.00x o.p. (ISBN 0-8103-3857-2). Gale.

Mid-Life Change. Ed. by Arthur A. Hitchcock & Wanda L. Nott. 97p. 1981. pap. text ed. 4.75 o.p. (ISBN 0-911547-56-8, 72190W34). Am Assn Coun Dev.

Mid-Tudor Polity, c. Fifteen Forty to Fifteen Sixty. Ed. by Robert Tittler & Jennifer Loach. 227p. 1980. 23.50x o.p. (ISBN 0-8476-6257-8). Rowman.

Midday Meal. Tom Watson & Jenny Watson. LC 82-19908. (What the World Eats Ser.). 64p. (gr. 5 up). 1983. PLB 11.93 o.p. (ISBN 0-516-01857-4). Childrens.

Middle-Aged Sons & the Meaning of Work. Richard L. Ochberg. Ed. by Peter Nathan. LC 86-30709. (Research in Clinical Psychology Ser.: No. 16). 166p. 1987. 39.95 o.p. (ISBN 0-8357-1779-8). Univ Microfilms.

Middle Ages. abr. ed. Morris Bishop. LC 70-95728. 1970. pap. text ed. 7.95 o.p. (ISBN 0-07-005466-5). McGraw.

Middle Atmosphere Sciences: A Selection of Papers from the Symposium Organised by the IAMAP & IAGA on the Occasion of the XVIII General Assembly of the IUGG, Hamburg, Federal Republic of Germany, August 1983. Ed. by A. Ebel & P. C. Simon. 120p. 1985. pap. 36.00 o.p. (ISBN 0-08-032592-0). Pergamon.

Middle Caraquet: The Lean Years. Albert Gionet. LC 87-91030. (Illus.). 176p. 1987. 16.95 o.p. (ISBN 0-682-40353-9). Exposition-Phoenix.

Middle Colonies. Thomas J. Wertenbaker. LC 63-17541. (Founding of American Civilization Ser). (Illus.). Repr. of 1938 ed. 25.00x o.p. (ISBN 0-8154-0254-6). Cooper Sq.

Middle-Earth Quest: Treason in Helm's Deep. 160p. 1986. pap. 3.50 o.s.i. (ISBN 0-425-08690-9). Berkley Pub.

Middle-Earth Quiz Book. Suzanne Buchholz. 1979. pap. 3.95 o.p. (ISBN 0-395-28428-7). HM.

Middle East. (Traveller's Guides). (Illus.). 190p. (Orig.). 1988. pap. 12.95 o.p. (ISBN 1-55650-036-X). Hunter Pub NY.

Middle East. Jay Walz. LC 65-27595. (New York Times Byline Books). (Orig.). 1965. 3.95 o.p. (ISBN 0-689-10279-8, Atheneum); pap. 1.95 o.p. (ISBN 0-689-10280-1, Atheneum). Macmillan.

Middle East & North Africa: A Bibliography for Undergraduate Libraries. University of the State of New York, Foreign Area Materials Center Staff. Ed. by Harry N. Howard. LC 72-151801. (Occasional Publications Ser: No. 14). 80p. 1971. 8.95 o.s.i. (ISBN 0-87272-018-7). Brodart.

Middle East & North Africa, Nineteen Eighty-Eight. 34th ed. 90p. 1987. 150.00x o.s.i. (ISBN 0-946653-35-6, Pub. by Europa England). Gale.

Middle East & North Africa on Film: An Annotated Filmography. Marsha H. McClintock. LC 82-12114. (Garland Reference Library of the Humanities). 562p. 1982. lib. bdg. 61.00 o.p. (ISBN 0-8240-9260-0). Garland Pub.

Middle East & North Africa 1985-86. 32nd ed. 700p. 120.00x o.p. (ISBN 0-946653-09-7). Intl Pubns Serv.

Middle East & North Africa 1987. 33rd ed. 820p. 1986. 135.00x o.p. (ISBN 0-317-58279-8, Pub. by Europa England). Gale.

Middle East & North Africa 1987. 3rd ed. Taylor & Francis Inc. Staff. 900p. 1987. 135.00x o.p. (ISBN 0-946653-22-4, Pub. by Europa England). Intl Pubns Serv.

Middle East & the Trilateral Countries. Garret Fitzgerald et al. (Triangle Papers: No. 22). 1981. Trilateral Comm.

Middle East & the Western Alliance. Ed. by Center for International & Strategic Affairs, Univ. of California, Los Angeles Staff & Steven Spiegel. 256p. 1982. text ed. 37.95x o.p. (ISBN 0-04-327067-0). Unwin Hyman.

Middle East Annual: Issues & Events 1985, Vol. V. Ed. by David H. Partington. (Reference Bks). 220p. 1986. lib. bdg. 45.00 o.s.i. (ISBN 0-8161-8907-2). G K Hall.

Middle East Business Information Guide. Middle East Economic Digest Staff. (Illus.). 823p. (Orig.). 1987. pap. 150.00 o.p. (ISBN 0-946510-13-X). Lynne Rienner.

Middle East Economic Handbook. (Economic Handbook Ser.). 350p. 1986. 80.00x o.s.i. (ISBN 0-86338-126-X, Pub. by Euromonitor Pubns). Gale.

Middle East Government Directory & Guide to Purchasing Agencies. Ed. by Middle East Executive Reports, High-Level Staff. 150p. 1983. looseleaf binder 175.00 o.s.i. (ISBN 0-915797-00-3). Mid East Exec Reports Ltd.

Middle East in the World Economy, 1800-1914. Roger Owen. 1981. 49.50x o.p. (ISBN 0-416-14270-2, NO. 2235). Routledge Chapman & Hall.

Middle East Mission: The Story of a Major Bid for Peace in the Time of Nasser & Ben-Gurion. Elmore Jackson. 1983. 12.45x o.p. (ISBN 0-393-01785-0). Norton.

Middle East Opportunities. Moshe Arens et al. Trilateral Comm.

Middle East Perspectives: The Next Twenty Years. Ed. by George S. Wise & Charles Issawi. LC 81-2562. 246p. 1981. 19.95 o.p. (ISBN 0-87850-037-5). Darwin Pr.

Middle East Political Dictionary. Lawrence Ziring. LC 82-22673. (Clio Dictionaries in Political Science Ser.: No. 5). 452p. 1984. lib. bdg. 41.00 o.p. (ISBN 0-87436-044-7); pap. 17.00 o.p. (ISBN 0-87436-045-5). ABC-Clio.

Middle East Record, 1969-70, 2 vols in one, Vol. 5-6. Ed. by Daniel Dishon. 1414p. text ed. 89.95 o.p. (ISBN 0-87855-218-9). Transaction Pubs.

Middle East Studies & Libraries: A Felicitation Volume for J. D. Pearson. Ed. by B. C. Bloomfield. 244p. 1980. text ed. 51.00x o.p. (ISBN 0-7201-1512-4). Mansell.

Middle Eastern Cookery. Eva Zane. LC 74-18088. (Illus.). 144p. 1974. pap. 5.95 o.s.i. (ISBN 0-912238-50-X, One Hund One Prods). Ortho.

Middle English Literature. Charles W. Dunn & Edward T. Byrnes. 1973. text ed. 14.95 o.p. (ISBN 0-15-558762-5, HC). HarBraceJ.

Middle English Prose: Essays on Bibliographical Problems. Ed. by A. S. Edwards & Derek Pearsall. LC 80-8595. 150p. 1981. lib. bdg. 31.00 o.p. (ISBN 0-8240-9453-0). Garland Pub.

Middle Game in Chess. Ludek Pachman. Tr. by John Littlewood. (Illus.). 192p. 1983. pap. 7.95 o.p. (ISBN 0-7100-9071-4). Routledge Chapman & Hall.

Middle Level Social Studies: From Theory to Practice. Michael G. Allen & Kenneth McEwin. 58p. 1983. 4.95 o.p. (ISBN 0-318-16920-7, NMSA 012). Natl Middle Schl.

Titles

Titles

Middle Mist. Mary Renault. 288p. 1976. Repr. of 1945 ed. lib. bdg. 21.95x o.p. (ISBN 0-89244-080-5). Queens Hse-Focus Serv.
Middle Moffat. Eleanor Estes. LC 42-36272. (Illus.). (gr. 3-7). 1943. 12.95 o.p. (ISBN 0-15-253663-9, HJ). HarBraceJ.
Middle Moffat. Eleanor Estes. LC 79-11970. (Illus.). (gr. 4-7). 1979. pap. 2.95 o.p. (ISBN 0-15-659536-2, VoyB). HarBraceJ.
Middle of the Journey. Lionel Trilling. 1976. pap. 4.95 o.p. (ISBN 0-380-00520-4, 32904). Avon.
Middle Parts of Fortune. Frederic Manning. (Echoes of War Ser.). 1987. pap. 10.95 o.p. (ISBN 0-907675-55-7, Pub. by Buchan & Enright England). Seven Hills Bk Dists.
Middle Passage: Comparative Studies in the Atlantic Slave Trade. Herbert Klein. LC 77-85544. 1978. 36.00 o.p. (ISBN 0-691-03119-3); pap. 9.75x o.p. LPE (ISBN 0-691-10064-0). Princeton U Pr.
Middle School Research Studies, 1983. Thomas Erb. 110p. 1983. 8.00 o.p. (ISBN 0-318-18600-4). Natl Middle Schl.
Middle School Research Studies, 1984. Hershel Thornburg & Stefinee Pinnegar. 95p. 1984. 8.00 o.p. (ISBN 0-318-17732-3). Natl Middle Schl.
Middle School Research Studies, 1985. David Strahan. 140p. 1985. 8.00 o.p. (ISBN 0-318-18601-2). Natl Middle Schl.
Middle Sea Autumn. Carol McConnell & Malcolm McConnell. (Illus.). 1985. 16.45 o.p. (ISBN 0-393-03304-X). Norton.
Middle Years. Paul E. Johnson. LC 70-154489. (Pocket Counsel Bks). (Orig.). 1971. pap. 1.75x o.p. (ISBN 0-8006-1105-5, 1-1105, Fortress). Augsburg Fortress.
Middleman. David Chandler. LC 80-66504. 1981. 12.95 o.p. (ISBN 0-87795-279-5, Arbor Hse). Morrow.
Middletown in Transition. Lynd. 1937. 6.00 o.p. (ISBN 0-15-159549-6). HarbraceJ.
Midland & Great Northern Joint Railway. A. J. Wrottesley. LC 80-85502. (Illus.). 320p. 1981. 22.95 o.p. (ISBN 0-7153-8173-3). David & Charles.
Midland, Texas. (Panel Advisory Service Report Ser.). 75p. 1980. pap. 10.00 o.p. (ISBN 0-317-06743-5, M-16). Urban Land.
Midnight. Mao Dun. (Illus.). 1980. 15.95 o.p. (ISBN 0-8351-0614-4). China Bks.
Midnight Deception. Lindsey Hanks. (Avon Romance Ser.). 368p. 1987. pap. 3.95 o.p. (ISBN 0-380-75273-5). Avon.
Midnight Fox. Betsy Byars. (gr. 3-7). 1975. pap. 1.25 o.p. (ISBN 0-380-00197-7, 46987, Camelot). Avon.
Midnight Gold. Sylvia Grieg. 272p. (Orig.). 1987. pap. 3.95 o.p. (ISBN 0-380-75073-2). Avon.
Midnight Haul. Max A. Collins. LC 86-16626. 252p. 1986. 14.95 o.s.i. (ISBN 0-88150-077-1, Foul Play). Countryman.
Midnight in the Century. Maurice English. LC 64-20847. 69p. 1964. 5.00 o.p. (ISBN 0-8040-0204-5, Pub. by Swallow). Ohio U Pr.
Midnight Man. Loren D. Estleman. 230p. 1982. 12.45 o.p. (ISBN 0-395-32204-9). HM.
Midnight Raymond Chandler. Raymond Chandler. 1971. 10.00 o.p. (ISBN 0-395-13152-9). HM.
Midnight Specials. Ed. by Bill Pronzini. 1978. pap. 1.75 o.p. (ISBN 0-380-01941-8, 37903). Avon.
Midnight Suppers. Susan Monsky. 233p. 1983. 13.45 o.p. (ISBN 0-395-32558-7). HM.
Midnight Water. Geoffrey Norman. 272p. 1985. pap. 3.95 o.p. (ISBN 0-380-69583-9). Avon.
Midnight's Lady. Sandra Langford. (Avon Romance Ser.). 1986. pap. 3.50 o.p. (ISBN 0-380-75018-X). Avon.
Midrash As Literature: The Primacy of Documentary Discourse. Jacob Neusner. LC 87-6272. (Studies in Judaism). 254p. 1987. lib. bdg. 26.50 o.p. (ISBN 0-8191-6307-4, Pub. by Studies in Judaism); pap. text ed. 14.75 o.p. (ISBN 0-8191-6308-2, Pub. by Studies in Judaism). U Pr of Amer.
Midrash in Context. Jacob Neusner. LC 83-5705. 240p. 1983. 23.95 o.p. (ISBN 0-8006-0708-2, 1-708, Fortress). Augsburg Fortress.
Midsummer Ball. Fay Marden. LC 86-22340. (Flower Fairy Story-Bks.). (Illus.). 24p. (gr. k-3). 1987. 7.95 o.p. (ISBN 0-87226-141-7). P Bedrick Bks.
Midsummer Banquet. (Tales From Fern Hollow Ser.). (Illus.). 22p. (ps-1). 1985. 1.98 o.p. (ISBN 0-517-45799-7). Outlet Bk Co.
Midsummer Nights' Dream. William Shakespeare. LC 77-512. (Illus.). 1977. 32.50 o.p. (ISBN 0-913870-41-2). Abaris Bks.
Midsummer Night's Dream. William Shakespeare. Ed. by J. H. Walter. (Players' Shakespeare Ser). (YA) (gr. 9 up). 1964. 3.50 o.p. (ISBN 0-8238-0108-X). Plays.
Midsummer Night's Dream. William Shakespeare. 48p. (Orig.). 1989. pap. 9.95 o.p. (ISBN 1-55651-585-5); audiocassette tape incl. o.p. (ISBN 1-55651-586-3). Cram Cassettes.
Midsummer's Eve. Philippa Carr. 1986. 17.95 o.p. (ISBN 0-399-13148-5). Putnam Pub Group.
Midwest & Great Plains. rev. ed. Ed. by Walter Havighurst. LC 78-54255. (United States Ser.). (Illus.). (gr. 5 up). 1979. text ed. 9.93 1-4 copies o.p. (ISBN 0-88296-070-9); 5 or more 7.94 o.p. (ISBN 0-88296-070-9); tchrs'. annotated ed. 13.68 o.p. (ISBN 0-88296-347-3). Gateway Pr MI.
Midwest at Noon. Graham Hutton. (Midway Reprint Ser). 368p. 1975. pap. text ed. 10.50x o.s.i. (ISBN 0-226-36343-0). U of Chicago Pr.
Midwest Gem Trails Field Guide. June C. Zeitner. 80p. 1964. pap. 2.50 o.p. (ISBN 0-910652-00-7). Gembooks.
Midwest Meets Mideast. Marjorie H. Barnes. 1979. 4.50 o.p. (ISBN 0-682-49319-8). Exposition-Phoenix.
Midwinter Madness. Anthony Stuart. LC 79-52254. 1979. 8.95 o.p. (ISBN 0-87795-237-X, Arbor Hse). Morrow.
Midwinter Tale. Fay Marden. LC 86-20656. (Flower Fairy Story-Bks.). (Illus.). 24p. (gr. k-3). 1987. 7.95 o.p. (ISBN 0-87226-142-5). P Bedrick Bks.
Miernick Dossier. Charles McCarry. 320p. 1985. pap. 3.95 o.p. (ISBN 0-451-13652-7, Sig). NAL.
Mightier Than the Sword: Cartoon, Caricature, Social Comment. W. G. Rogers. LC 71-82637. (Illus.). 1969. 7.50 o.p. (ISBN 0-15-253860-7, HJ). HarBraceJ.
Mighty & Their Fall. I. Compton-Burnett. 1961. 19.95 o.p. (ISBN 0-575-02704-5, Pub. by Gollancz England). David & Charles.
Mighty Eighth. 2nd ed. Roger A. Freeman. (Illus.). 508p. 1986. 24.95 o.p. (ISBN 0-7106-0355-X). Janes Info Group.
Mighty Eighth War Diary. Roger A. Freeman. (Illus.). 240p. 1981. 29.95 o.p. (ISBN 0-7106-0038-0). Janes Info Group.
Mighty Eighth War Manual. Roger A. Freeman. (Illus.). 320p. 1984. 29.95 o.p. (ISBN 0-7106-0325-8). Janes Info Group.
Mighty Ferment: Britain in the Age of Revolution, 1750-1850. David Snodin. LC 77-16482. (Illus.). 128p. (gr. 6 up). 1979. 8.95 o.p. (ISBN 0-395-28925-4, Clarion). HM.
Mighty God Viracocha: El Dios Poderoso Viracocha. Adapted by Harriet Rohermer. LC 76-17492. (Illus.). 20p. (gr. k-6). 1976. pap. 5.95 spanish bilingual ed. o.p. (ISBN 0-89239-005-0, Imprenta de Libros Infantiles). Childrens Book Pr.
Mighty Lobo. Max Brand. (Lythway Ser.). 319p. 1988. lib. bdg. 20.95x o.s.i. (ISBN 0-7451-0711-7, Pub. by Chivers Pr UK). G K Hall.
Mighty MG's: The Twin-Cam. MGC & MGB GT V8 Stories. Graham Robson. (Illus.). 224p. 1982. 32.95 o.p. (ISBN 0-7153-8226-8, Pub by Gollancz England). David & Charles.
Mighty Mississippi. Bern Keating. Ed. by Donald J. Crump. LC 70-151944. (Special Publications Series 5: No. 4). (Illus.). 1971. 7.95, avail. only from natl. geog. o.p. (ISBN 0-87044-096-9). Natl Geog.
Mighty Mississippi: Biography of a River. Marquis Childs. LC 82-3299. (Illus.). 224p. 1982. 12.45 o.p. (ISBN 0-89919-088-X). Ticknor & Fields.
Mighty Mizzling Mouse & the Red Cabbage House. Friso Henstra. (Illus.). (ps-3). 1984. 12.95 o.p. (ISBN 0-316-35778-2); pap. 4.95 o.p. (ISBN 0-316-35779-0). Little.
Migraine & Its Variants. George Selby. (ADIS Health Science Ser.). (Illus.). 153p. 1983. 24.00 o.p. (ISBN 0-86792-015-7). Year Bk Med.
Migraine: Psychological, Psychiatric & Physiological Aspects. Harold Geist. LC 82-26855. 1983. text ed. 11.50 o.p. (ISBN 0-89874-601-9). Krieger.
Migrant Crime in Australia. Ronald D. Francis. (Illus.). 217p. 1981. text ed. 24.50x o.p. (ISBN 0-7022-1561-9). U of Queensland Pr.
Migrant Labour in Europe, Sixteen Hundred to Nineteen Hundred: The Drift to the North Sea. Jan Lucassen. 288p. 1986. 52.50 o.p. (ISBN 0-7099-4117-X, Pub. by Croom Helm UK). Routledge Chapman & Hall.
Migrant Workers. International Labour Office, Geneva Staff. 196p. (Orig.). 1980. pap. 14.25 o.p. (ISBN 92-2-102093-2). Intl Labour Office.
Migrant Workers in Western Europe & the United States. Jonathan Power et al. LC 78-41199. 1979. 44.00 o.p. (ISBN 0-08-023385-6); pap. 17.00 o.p. (ISBN 0-08-023384-8). Pergamon.
Migration & Unemployment in Hawaii. Robert D. Retherford. LC 81-22204. (Papers of the East-West Population Institute: No. 79). v, 18p. (Orig.). 1982. pap. text ed. 1.00 o.p. (ISBN 0-86638-012-4). EW Ctr HI.
Migration & Uneven Rural Development in Africa: The Case of Zambia. Alifeyo Chilivumbo. (Illus.). 138p. (Orig.). 1986. lib. bdg. 22.75 o.p. (ISBN 0-8191-4929-2); pap. text ed. 10.00 o.p. (ISBN 0-8191-4930-6). U Pr of Amer.
Migration, Kinship & Community: Tradition & Transition in a Spanish Village. Stanley H. Brandes. 1975. 24.95 o.p. (ISBN 0-12-125750-9). Acad Pr.
Migration of Symbols & Their Relations to Beliefs & Customs. Donald A. Mackenzie. LC 68-18029. 238p. 1968. Repr. of 1926 ed. 34.00x o.p. (ISBN 0-8103-3074-1). Gale.
Miguel De Cervantes-Saavedra: Two Cervantes Short Novels: El Curioso Impertinente & El Celoso Extremeno. Miguel De Cervantes-Saavedra. Ed. by F. F. Pierce. 1970. pap. 4.30 o.p. (ISBN 0-08-015781-5). Pergamon.
Mike: A Mother's Prayers. Bette Lawrence. LC 84-21247. 64p. 1985. pap. 2.95 o.p. (ISBN 0-8006-1857-2, 1-1857, Fortress). Augsburg Fortress.
Mike Dime. Barry Fantoni. 208p. 1981. 9.95 o.p. (ISBN 0-531-09948-2). Watts.
Mike Grenby's Money Book: How to Survive Canada's Inflation. 2nd ed. Mike Grenby. 169p. 1979. 5.50 o.p. (ISBN 0-88908-051-8). ISC Pr.
Mike Schmidt: The Human Vacuum Cleaner. Mike Herbert. LC 83-7621. (Sports Stars Ser.). (Illus.). 48p. (gr. 2-8). 1983. lib. bdg. 10.33 o.p. (ISBN 0-516-04332-3); pap. 2.95 o.p. (ISBN 0-516-44332-1). Childrens.
Mikhail Bulgakov: Selected Works. Ed. by Avril Pyman. 259p. 1972. pap. 17.00 o.p. (ISBN 0-08-015506-5). Pergamon.
Mikhail Lermontov. John Garrard. (World Authors Ser.). 1982. lib. bdg. 18.95 o.p. (ISBN 0-8057-6514-X, Twayne). G K Hall.
Mikhail Sholokhov, Collected Works, Vol. 2. Mikhail Sholokhov. 487p. 1985. 9.95 o.p. (ISBN 0-8285-2987-6, Pub. by Raduga Pubs USSR). Imported Pubns.
Mikhail Sholokhov, Collected Works, Vol. 3. Mikhail Sholokhov. 456p. 1985. 9.95 o.p. (ISBN 0-8285-2988-4, Pub. by Raduga Pubs USSR). Imported Pubns.
Mikhail Sholokhov, Collected Works, Vol. 4. Mikhail Sholokhov. 482p. 1985. 9.95 o.p. (ISBN 0-8285-2989-2, Pub. by Raduga Pubs USSR). Imported Pubns.
Mikhail Sholokhov, Collected Works, Vol. 5. Mikhail Sholokhov. 542p. 1985. 9.95 o.p. (ISBN 0-8285-2990-6, Pub. by Raduga Pubs USSR). Imported Pubns.
Mikhail Sholokhov, Collected Works, Vol. 6. Mikhail Sholokhov. 398p. 1985. 9.95 o.p. (ISBN 0-8285-3010-6, Pub. by Raduga Pubs USSR). Imported Pubns.
Mikhail Sholokhov, Collected Works, Vol. 7. Mikhail Sholokhov. 438p. 1985. 9.95 o.p. (ISBN 0-8285-3011-4, Pub. by Raduga Pubs USSR). Imported Pubns.
Mikhail Sholokhov, Collected Works, Vol. 8. Mikhail Sholokhov. 294p. 1985. 9.95 o.p. (ISBN 0-8285-3005-X, Pub. by Raduga Pubs USSR). Imported Pubns.
Mikron Euchologion: An Orthodox Prayer Book. Ed. by Nomikos M. Vaporis. Tr. & pref. by Michael Gelsinger. LC 77-77642. 288p. 1977. 18.95 o.s.i. (ISBN 0-916586-09-X). Holy Cross Orthodox.
Milady in Love. Marion Chesney. 160p. (Orig.). 1987. pap. 2.50 o.s.i. (ISBN 0-449-20932-6, Crest). Fawcett.
Mile Above the Rim. Charles Rosen. LC 76-8640. 1976. 8.95 o.p. (ISBN 0-87795-137-3, Arbor Hse). Morrow.
Mile High Cabin. Ruth G. Plowhead. LC 46-815. (Illus.). 299p. (gr. 6-8). 1945. 2.50 o.p. (ISBN 0-87004-121-5). Caxton.
Milepost. Alaska Northwest Publishing Staff. (Illus.). 530p. 1988. pap. 14.95 o.p. (ISBN 0-88240-212-9). Alaska Northwest.
Milepost. (Illus.). 500p. 1984. 11.95 o.p. (ISBN 0-88240-208-0). Alaska Northwest.
Milepost: All-the-North Travel Guide Annual, 1985. 37th ed. The Milepost Staff. (Illus.). 500p. (Orig.). 1985. pap. 12.95 o.p. (ISBN 0-88240-209-9). Alaska Northwest.
Milepost: All-the-North Travel Guide, 1986. Milepost Staff. (38th). (Illus.). 500p. (Orig.). 1986. pap. 12.95 o.p. (ISBN 0-88240-210-2). Alaska Northwest.
Miles Davis: A Biography. Ian Carr. LC 84-60477. (Illus.). 336p. 1984. pap. 9.70 o.p. (ISBN 0-688-02198-0, Quill). Morrow.
Miles Davis: A Critical Biography. Ian Carr. LC 82-6469. (Illus.). 324p. 1982. 14.95 o.p. (ISBN 0-688-01321-X). Morrow.
Miles from Nowhere: Round-the-World Bicycle Adventure. Barbara Savage. (Illus.). 324p. 1983. 14.95 o.p. (ISBN 0-89886-084-9). Mountaineers.
Milestones of Flight. David Mondey & Michael J. Taylor. (Illus.). 320p. 1983. 17.95 o.p. (ISBN 0-86720-656-X); pap. 10.95 o.p. (ISBN 0-86720-666-7). Janes Info Group.
Milford Malvoisin; or, Pews & Pew-Holders, 1842 see St. Antholin's; or, Old Churches & New: A Tale for the Times, 1841.
Militant. Michael Crick. 200p. (Orig.). 1984. pap. 9.95 o.p. (ISBN 0-571-13256-1). Faber & Faber.
Militant South, Eighteen Hundred to Eighteen Sixty-One. John H. Franklin. LC 56-10160. 1970. Repr. 24.50x o.s.i. (ISBN 0-674-57450-8, Belknap Pr). Harvard U Pr.
Militarism. Guglielmo Ferrero. LC 76-147469. (Library of War & Peace; the Character & Causes of War). 1972. lib. bdg. 46.00 o.p. (ISBN 0-8240-0260-1). Garland Pub.
Militarism in Peking's Policies. G. Apalin & U. Mityayev. 1980. pap. 6.95 o.p. (ISBN 0-8285-1937-4, Pub. by Progress Pubs USSR). Imported Pubns.
Militarism, Politics, & Working Class Attitudes in Late Nineteenth Century Europe. Incl. Army & the Democracy; Militarism in Politics. Jean De Bloch; Armee, Est-Elle, Doit-Elle Etre la Nation? Jules Bourelly; Working Men & War. Thomas Burt; Der Militarismus. F. Wiede. LC 75-147561. (Library of War & Peace; Control & Limitation of Arms). lib. bdg. 46.00 o.p. (ISBN 0-8240-0335-7). Garland Pub.
Militarization of the Middle East. Max Holland. 1981. pap. 1.50 o.p. (ISBN 0-686-95356-8). Am Fr Serv Comm.
Military Aerospace Standard Drawings, 14 vols. Ed. by Jerome H. Lieblich. 6000p. loose-leaf 650.00 o.p. (ISBN 0-912702-15-X). Global Eng.
Military Aircraft in Colour. Hiroshi Seo. 80p. 14.95 o.p. (ISBN 0-7106-0345-2). Janes Info Group.
Military Aircraft of the World. Hiroshi Seo. (Illus.). 96p. 1982. 12.95 o.p. (ISBN 0-86720-559-8). Janes Info Group.
Military & American Society. Ed. by Adam Yarmolinsky & Richard D. Lambert. LC 72-93251. (Annals of the American Academy of Political & Social Science: No. 406). 300p. 1973. 17.00 o.p. (ISBN 0-87761-161-0). Am Acad Pol Soc Sci.
Military Bachelor Chef: A Guide for Getting Started in the Kitchen. Henry Lippincott. (Illus.). 64p. 1974. 8.00 o.p. (ISBN 0-910584-40-0); pap. 2.00 o.p. (ISBN 0-910584-79-6). Filter.
Military Balance, 1980-1981. International Institute for Strategic Studies Staff. 119p. 1980. lib. bdg. 19.50x o.p. (ISBN 0-86079-040-1). Westview.
Military Balance, 1981 to 1982. International Institute for Strategic Studies Staff. 128p. 1982. 17.95x o.p. (ISBN 0-87196-449-X). Facts on File.
Military Balance 1986-87. 232p. 1986. pap. 24.95x o.p. (ISBN 0-86079-098-3). Janes Info Group.
Military Balance, 1987-1988. International Institute for Strategic Studies Staff. (Illus.). 232p. 1987. pap. 27.00x o.p. Janes Info Group.
Military Balance, 1988-89. International Institute for Strategic Studies Staff. (Illus.). 1989. pap. 29.50x o.p. Janes Info Group.
Military Border in Croatia, Seventeen Forty-Eighteen Eighty One: A Study of an Imperial Institution. Gunther Rothenberg. LC 66-13887. 1966. lib. bdg. 15.00x o.s.i. (ISBN 0-226-72944-3). U of Chicago Pr.
Military Communications System Control Symposium. Mitre Corp. Staff. 1980. 60.00 o.s.i. (ISBN 0-686-38472-5). Info Gatekeepers.
Military Eitzen. K. Eitzen. (Ger. & Eng.). 1957. pap. 15.95 o.p. (ISBN 3-87599-035-8, M-7563, Pub. by Vlg. Offene Worte). French & Eur.
Military Electro-Optics Market. International Resource Development, Inc. Staff. 204p. 1983. 1850.00x o.p. (ISBN 0-88694-572-0). Intl Res Dev.
Military Electro-Optics Markets. Int'l. Resource Development, Inc. Staff. 206p. 1986. 2100.00x o.p. (ISBN 0-88694-711-1). Intl Res Dev.
Military Electronic Devices Guide-Microcircuits & Semiconductors. 1987. 195.00 o.p. DATA Busn Pub.
Military Experience in the Age of Reason. Christopher Duffy. 320p. 1987. lib. bdg. 39.95 o.p. (ISBN 0-7102-1024-8, Pub. by Routledge UK). Routledge Chapman & Hall.
Military Fastener Standard Drawings, 5 vols. Ed. by Jerome H. Lieblich. 3000p. loose-leaf 450.00 o.p. (ISBN 0-912702-16-8). Global Eng.
Military Forces in the Persian Gulf. Alvin J. Cottrell & Frank Bray. (Washington Papers: Vol. VI, No. 60). 72p. (Orig.). 1978. pap. text ed. 7.95 o.p. (ISBN 0-8191-6009-1, Pub. by CSIS). U Pr of Amer.
Military Handbook. Intel Staff. 832p. 1986. pap. 18.00 o.p. (ISBN 1-55512-008-3, 210461). Intel Corp.
Military Handbook Nineteen Eighty-Seven. Intel Staff. 700p. 1987. pap. 18.00 o.p. (ISBN 1-55512-059-8, 210461). Intel Corp.
Military Helicopters. (Warbirds Illustrated Ser.: No. 13). 1982. 9.95 o.p. (ISBN 0-85368-572-X, Pub. by Arms & Armour Pr). Sterling.
Military History Calendar, 1989. Raymond R. Lyman. (Illus.). 24p. 1988. pap. 8.95 o.s.i. (ISBN 0-87364-456-5). Paladin Pr.

Military History of Germany: From the 18th Century to the Present Day. Martin Kitchen. 1976. pap. 4.95 o.p. (ISBN 0-8065-0524-9, Pub. by Citadel Pr). Carol Pub Group.
Military Illustration. M. Tamiya. (Illus.). 88p. (Orig.). 1986. pap. 24.95 o.p. (ISBN 4-766-10404-8, Pub. by Graphic Sha Japan). Bks Nippan.
Military in the Third World. Gavin Kennedy. LC 74-7512. 1975. 17.50 o.s.i. (ISBN 0-684-14050-0, ScribT). Scribner.
Military Manners & Customs. James A. Farrer. LC 68-21771. 300p. 1968. Repr. of 1885 ed. 30.00x o.p. (ISBN 0-8103-3510-7). Gale.
Military Memoir of Colonel John Birch. Roe. Ed. by Webb. Repr. of 1873 ed. 27.00 o.p. (ISBN 0-384-51615-7). Johnson Repr.
Military Modelling Guide to Wargaming. Stuart Asquith. (Illus.). 128p. 1987. pap. 16.95 o.s.i. (ISBN 0-85242-903-7, Pub. by Argus Pubs UK). Motorbooks Intl.
Military Music of the American Revolution. Raoul F. Camus. LC 75-38947. (Illus.). xii, 210p. 1976. 25.00x o.p. (ISBN 0-8078-1263-3). U of NC Pr.
Military Obligation in Medieval England. Michael Powicke. LC 75-10217. 263p. 1975. Repr. of 1962 ed. lib. bdg. 22.50x o.p. (ISBN 0-8371-8171-2, POMO). Greenwood.
Military Organization & Society. Stanislav Andreski. LC 68-27161. 1968. pap. 11.95x o.p. (ISBN 0-520-00026-9). U of Cal Pr.
Military Politics in Finland: The Development of Governmental Control Over the Armed Forces. William J. Stover. LC 81-40343. 220p. (Orig.). 1982. lib. bdg. 28.25 o.p. (ISBN 0-8191-2009-X); pap. text ed. 12.50 o.p. (ISBN 0-8191-2010-3). U Pr of Amer.
Military Roads in Scotland. William Taylor. LC 76-9239. (Illus.). 1976. 19.95 o.p. (ISBN 0-7153-7067-7). David & Charles.
Military Small Arms of the Twentieth Century. 4th ed. Ian Hogg & John Weeks. LC 73-83466. (Illus.). 288p. (Orig.). 1981. 12.95 o.p. (ISBN 0-910676-28-3, 9146). DBI.
Military Sociology 1963-1969: A Trend Report & Bibliography. Kurt Lang. (Current Sociology Ser.). 1971. pap. 4.80x o.p. (ISBN 90-2796-578-1). Mouton.
Military Utility of the U. S. Facilities in the Philippines. Alvin J. Cottrell & Robert J. Hanks. (Significant Issues Ser.: Vol. II, No. 11). 44p. (Orig.). 1980. pap. text ed. 6.95 o.p. (ISBN 0-8191-5916-6, Pub. by CSIS). U Pr of Amer.
Militia Christi: The Christian Religion & the Military in the First Three Centuries. Adolf Harnack. Tr. by David M. Gracie from Ger. LC 81-43089. 112p. 1981. 3.00 o.p. (ISBN 0-8006-0673-6, 1-673, Fortress). Augsburg Fortress.
Milk Free & Milk & Egg Free Cookbook. Isobel S. Sainsbury. LC 78-18364. 1979. lib. bdg. 6.95 o.p. (ISBN 0-668-04693-7); pap. 4.95 o.p. (ISBN 0-668-04701-1). Arco.
Milk Proteins, Vols. 1-2. Ed. by Hugh A. McKenzie. 1971. Vol. 1. 104.50 o.p. (ISBN 0-12-485201-7); Vol. 2. 104.50 o.p. (ISBN 0-12-485202-5). Acad Pr.
Mill. James F. Murphy, Jr. 320p. 1981. pap. 2.95 o.p. (ISBN 0-380-77198-5, 77198-5). Avon.
Mill Girls. George Larkin. 304p. 1981. pap. 2.50 o.p. (ISBN 0-505-51618-7, Pub. by Tower Bks). Dorchester Pub Co.
Mill on Liberty: A Defence. John N. Gray. LC 82-16151. (International Library of Philosophy). 143p. 1983. 19.95x o.p. (ISBN 0-7100-9270-9). Routledge Chapman & Hall.
Mill Song. William H. Harding. LC 84-4527. 336p. 1985. 16.95 o.p. (ISBN 0-03-070547-9). H Holt & Co.
Mille Miglia: The Fabulous Story of the Great Road Race. G. Lurani. (Illus.). 1982. 37.50 o.p. (ISBN 2-8800-1113-2). Norton.
Millenium & Charisma among Pathans: A Critical Essay in Social Anthropology. A. S. Ahmed. (International Library of Anthropology). 1980. pap. 10.95x o.p. (ISBN 0-7100-0547-4). Routledge Chapman & Hall.
Millennium Management: Last Chance for America. William Lareau. LC 86-18247. 256p. 1986. 14.95 o.p. (ISBN 0-8329-0431-7). New Century.
Millennium Postponed: Socialism from Sir Thomas More to Mao Tse-Tung. Edward Hyams. LC 74-171. 278p. 1974. 10.95 o.s.i. (ISBN 0-8008-5247-8). Taplinger.
Miller Analogies Test. William Bader & Daniel S. Burt. LC 81-152. 160p. 1982. lib. bdg. 10.00 o.p. (ISBN 0-668-04989-8); pap. 6.95 o.p. (ISBN 0-668-04990-1). Arco.
Miller Freeman, Man of Action. Elizabeth Wright. LC 76-29566. (Illus.). 1977. pap. 10.00 o.p. (ISBN 0-87930-060-4). Miller Freeman.
Miller: The Playwright. 2nd ed. Dennis Welland. (Illus.). 158p. 1983. pap. 10.95 o.p. (ISBN 0-413-52110-9, NO. 3826). Heinemann Ed.
Miller's Comprehensive GAAP Guide. annual Martin A. Miller. 524p. 1982. pap. 15.00 o.p. (ISBN 0-15-003957-3, HC). HarBraceJ.
Miller's Comprehensive GAAP Guide, 1985. Martin A. Miller. 1984. pap. 35.00 o.p. (ISBN 0-15-601761-X, BFP). HarBraceJ.
Miller's Comprehensive GAAS Guide, 1983. Martin A. Miller. (Miller Accounting Series). 1983. pap. 25.00 o.p. (ISBN 0-15-601757-1, BFP). HarBraceJ.
Miller's Comprehensive GAAS Guide, 1985. Martin A. Miller. 1984. pap. 27.50 o.p. (ISBN 0-15-601764-4, BFP). HarBraceJ.
Miller's Comprehensive GAAS Guide 1985. Martin A. Miller & Andrew D. Bailey. 1984. pap. 40.00 o.p. (ISBN 0-15-601763-6, BFP). HarBraceJ.
Miller's Comprehensive Nineteen Eighty-Seven Governmental GAAP Guide. Miller Accounting Staff. 1987. pap. 45.00 o.p. (ISBN 0-15-601739-3, BFP); pap. 35.00 o.p. (ISBN 0-15-601740-7). HarBraceJ.
Miller's Court. Arthur R. Miller. 288p. 1982. 12.95 o.p. (ISBN 0-395-31323-6). HM.
Miller's CPA Exam Solutions: May 1978 Through November 1982, 10 Vols. Millers Editors. (Miller Accounting Series). 1983. pap. 49.75 o.p. (ISBN 0-15-601871-3, BFP). HarBraceJ.
Miller's Personal Income Tax Guide: 1984 Edition. Martin A. Miller et al. 384p. 1983. pap. 7.95 o.p. (ISBN 0-15-659690-3, Harv). HarBraceJ.
Miller's Personal Income Tax Guide, 1985 Edition. Martin A. Miller et al. 1984. pap. 8.95 o.p. (ISBN 0-15-659692-X, Harv). HarBraceJ.
Miller's Solutions to the Uniform CPA Exam, November 1982. Millers Editors. (BFP). 1983. pap. 9.95 o.p. (ISBN 0-15-601723-7). HarBraceJ.
Millicent Maybe. Ellen Weiss. (Illus.). (gr. 3-7). 1980. pap. 1.50 o.p. (ISBN 0-380-49197-4, 49197-4, Camelot). Avon.
Millie Willenheimer & the Chestnut Corporation. Dean Hughes. LC 82-13758. 144p. (gr. 3-7). 1983. 10.95 o.s.i. (ISBN 0-689-30958-9, Atheneum Childrens Bks). Macmillan.
Milling, Vol. 1. 2nd ed. Ed. by C. Plaster et al. (Engineering Craftsmen: No. H4). (Illus.). 1977. spiral bdg. 38.50x o.p. (ISBN 0-85083-404-X). Trans-Atl Phila.
Milling, Vol. 2. Ed. by A. G. Spencer. (Engineering Craftsmen: No. H29). (Illus.). 1969. spiral bdg. 37.50x o.p. Trans-Atl Phila.
Milling Machine Operations. Richard R. Kibbe. LC 84-11798. 192p. 1985. 17.95 o.p. (ISBN 0-471-89020-0). Wiley.
Million & One Nights: A History of the Motion Picture through 1925. Terry Ramsaye. (Illus.). 1986. pap. 15.95 o.p. (ISBN 0-671-62404-0). S&S.
Million Dollar Burn. Trevor Loring. LC 85-90118. 58p. 1985. 7.95 o.p. (ISBN 0-533-06622-0). Vantage.
Million Dollar Contest Cookbook. Jean Sanderson. (Mary Ellen Family Bks.). 224p. 1984. pap. 6.95 o.p. (ISBN 0-385-19145-6); prepack of 12 bks. 83.40 o.p. (ISBN 0-385-19149-9). Doubleday.
Million-Dollar Foxhole: The Story of the Richey Family. Leonard E. Bennett. 1977. 8.00 o.p. (ISBN 0-682-48873-9). Exposition-Phoenix.
Million Memories of You. Henry J. 1977. 5.50 o.p. (ISBN 0-682-48969-7). Exposition-Phoenix.
Million Villages, a Million Decades. 1983. 6.00 o.p. (ISBN 0-905347-41-2). C I D E.
Millionaires. Herbert Kastle. 400p. 1984. pap. 3.95 o.p. (ISBN 0-440-15630-0). Dell.
Millionaires & Managers. S. Menshikov. 288p. 1973. 4.95 o.p. (ISBN 0-8285-0367-2, Pub. by Progress Pubs USSR). Imported Pubns.
Mills Bomb. Clive Egleton. LC 78-55207. 1978. 8.95 o.p. (ISBN 0-689-10910-5, Atheneum). Macmillan.
Mills of the Kavanaughs. Robert Lowell. 1951. 9.95 o.p. (ISBN 0-15-159825-8). HarBraceJ.
Mill's Pharmacy State Board Review. 29th ed. Joseph A. Romano & Matthew B. Wiener. LC 76-14721. 1977. 23.75 o.p. (ISBN 0-87488-430-6). Med Exam.
Milly: A Tribute to Amelia E. Collins. A. Q. Faizi. 52p. pap. 3.75 o.s.i. (ISBN 0-85398-074-8). G Ronald Pub.
Milos Forman Stories. Antonin J. Liehm. LC 73-92806. 191p. 1975. 35.00 o.p. (ISBN 0-87332-051-4). M E Sharpe.
Milton. David Daiches. (Orig.). 1966. pap. 4.95x o.p. (ISBN 0-393-00347-7, Norton Lib). Norton.
Milton. John Milton. (Plain Texts of the Poets Ser). 1968. pap. 2.50x o.p. (ISBN 0-7022-0631-8). U of Queensland Pr.
Milton: A Poem. William Blake. LC 78-58177. (Illus.). 178p. 1978. pap. 17.95 o.p. (ISBN 0-87773-129-2). Shambhala Pubns.
Milton: A Structural Reading. Donald F. Bouchard. 224p. 1974. 15.00x o.p. (ISBN 0-7735-0229-7, McGill Canada). U of Toronto Pr.
Milton: An Introduction. Brijraj Singh. 1977. 5.50x o.p. (ISBN 0-333-90213-0). South Asia Bks.
Milton & Melville. Henry F. Pommer. LC 70-122752. (Illus.). 1970. Repr. of 1950 ed. lib. bdg. 23.50x o.p. (ISBN 0-8154-0338-0). Cooper Sq.
Milton & Others. 2nd ed. George Williamson. LC 74-134913. 1970. lib. bdg. 15.00x o.s.i. (ISBN 0-226-89937-3). U of Chicago Pr.
Milton & the Book of Revelation: The Heavenly Cycle. Austin C. Dobbins. LC 73-22715. (Studies in the Humanities: No. 7). 176p. 1975. 12.50 o.p. (ISBN 0-8173-7320-9); pap. 6.95 o.p. (ISBN 0-8173-7321-7). U of Ala Pr.
Milton & the Miltonic Dryden. Anne D. Ferry. LC 68-25608. 1968. 17.50x o.s.i. (ISBN 0-674-57576-8). Harvard U Pr.
Milton & the Pauline Tradition: A Study of Theme & Symbolism. Timothy J. O'Keeffe. LC 80-5842. 356p. (Orig.). 1982. PLB 34.00 o.p. (ISBN 0-8191-2453-2); pap. text ed. 16.75 o.p. (ISBN 0-8191-2454-0). U Pr of Amer.
Milton in the Puritan Revolution. Don M. Wolfe. 1963. text ed. 22.50x o.p. (ISBN 0-391-00477-8). Humanities.
Milton the Puritan: Portrait of a Mind. A. L. Rowse. 298p. 1985. pap. text ed. 13.25 o.p. (ISBN 0-8191-4778-8). U Pr of Amer.
Milton's Paradise Lost. M. Wilding. (Sydney Studies in Literature Ser.). 1969. 15.00x o.p. (ISBN 0-424-05850-2, Pub. by Sydney U Pr). Intl Spec Bk.
Milwaukee & More. Pam Nonken et al. Ed. by Sue W. McCoy. LC 85-7316. (Illus.). 168p. (Orig.). 1985. pap. 9.95 o.s.i. (ISBN 0-942802-09-8). Northword.
Milwaukee Brewers. rev. ed. Martin. LC 82-16182. (Baseball Today Ser.). 48p. (gr. 4 up). 1982. PLB 11.45 o.p. (ISBN 0-87191-864-1). Creative Ed.
Milwaukee Bucks. Jim Moore. (NBA Today Ser.). (Illus.). 48p. (gr. 4 up). 1984. PLB 10.45 o.p. (ISBN 0-87191-982-6). Creative Ed.
Milwaukee Transport Era: The Trackless Trolley Years. Russell E. Schultz. Ed. by Mac Sebree. (Interurbans Special Ser.: 74). (Illus.). 160p. (Orig.). 1980. pap. 13.95 o.p. (ISBN 0-916374-43-2). Interurban.
Mime: The Theory & Practice of Expressive Gesture. Joan Lawson. LC 72-88968. (Illus.). 167p. pap. 14.95 o.s.i. (ISBN 0-87127-042-0, Pub. by Dance Horiz). Princeton Bk Co.
Mime Themes & Motifs. Pat Keysell. (Illus.). 80p. 80. Repr. of 1975 ed. bds. 9.95 o.p. (ISBN 0-8238-0245-0). Plays.
Mime Time: Forty-Five Complete Routines for Everyone. Happy Jack Feder. (Illus.). 160p. 1985. 12.95 o.p. (ISBN 0-668-06002-6). Arco.
Mimekor Yisrael: Classical Jewish Folktales, 3 vols. Ed. by Micha J. bin Gorion & Emanuel bin Gorion. Tr. by I. M. Lask from Hebrew. LC 74-15713. 1666p. 1976. 100.00 o.p. (ISBN 0-253-15330-1). Ind U Pr.
Mimi Pond's Secrets of the Powder Room: What Every Man Should Know about Women. Mimi Pond. 80p. 1983. pap. 4.95 o.p. (ISBN 0-03-063253-6). H Holt & Co.
Mimicry in Plants & Animals. Wolfgang Wickler. (Illus., Orig.). 1968. pap. text ed. 3.95 o.p. (ISBN 0-07-070100-8). McGraw.
Minature Book of Hours. 480p. 250.00 o.p. (ISBN 0-8115-0905-2). Kraus Repr.
Mind & Art of Giovanni Battista Piranesi. John Wilton-Ely. (Illus.). 1978. 50.00f o.p. (ISBN 0-500-09122-6). Thames Hudson.
Mind & Body Shop. Frank Parkin. LC 86-25953. 224p. 1987. 14.95 o.p. (ISBN 0-689-11895-3, Atheneum). Macmillan.
Mind & Body: The Psychology of Physical Illness. Stephen A. Green. LC 85-13496. 224p. 1985. text ed. 22.50x o.p. (ISBN 0-88048-043-2, 48-043-2). Am Psychiatric.
Mind & Deity. Laird. (ISBN 0-8022-0903-3). Philos Lib.
Mind & Memory Training. Wood. 10.50 o.p. (ISBN 0-8356-5115-0). Theos Pub Hse.
Mind & Soul. Olga E. Muller. LC 72-85034. 72p. 1972. (ISBN 0-8022-2100-9). Philos Lib.
Mind & Spirit of Early America: Sources in American History, 1607-1789. Ed. by Richard Walsh. LC 80-5704. 442p. 1980. lib. bdg. 33.75 o.p. (ISBN 0-8191-1239-9); pap. text ed. 15.00 o.p. (ISBN 0-8191-1240-2). U Pr of Amer.
Mind & Supermind. Ed. by Al Rosenfeld. LC 76-29912. 1977. 9.95 o.s.i. (ISBN 0-03-018961-6). H Holt & Co.
Mind Angel & Other Stories. Michael Orgill et al. Ed. by Roger Elwood. LC 73-21480. 48p. (gr. 4-8). 1974. PLB 3.95g o.p. (ISBN 0-8225-0958-X). Lerner Pubns.
Mind Bandits. Stephen Mooser. (Which Way Bks.: No. 20). (Illus.). (gr. 3-6). pap. 2.25 o.p. (ISBN 0-671-55829-3). Archway.
Mind Benders. Shirley Schwarzrock & C. Gilbert Wrenn. (Coping with Ser.). (gr. 10 up). 1971. pap. text ed. 3.00 o.p. (ISBN 0-913476-16-1). Am Guidance.
Mind Beyond Mind: Perceptive Meditation, Form & Function. Yuvacharya Shri Mahaprajna. 186p. 1980. 9.00 o.p. (ISBN 0-88065-214-4, Pub. by Messers Today & Tomorrow Printers & Publishers). Scholarly Pubns.
Mind-Body Effect. Herbert Benson. 1979. 8.95 o.p. (ISBN 0-671-24143-5). S&S.
Mind Breakers. Dan Streib. 208p. (Orig.). 1984. pap. 2.50 o.s.i. (ISBN 0-449-12682-X, GM). Fawcett.
Mind: Cumulative Index 1967-1976 (Volumes 76-85) 1983. 25.00 o.p. (ISBN 0-317-01051-4). Learned Info.
Mind Drugs. 4th ed. Margaret O. Hyde. (gr. 7-9). 1981. text ed. 9.95 o.p. (ISBN 0-07-031649-X). McGraw.
Mind Forg'd Manacles: Evil in the Poetry of Blake & Shelley. Melanie Bandy. LC 80-18779. (Illus.). 210p. 1981. text ed. 19.95 o.s.i. (ISBN 0-8173-0046-5). U of Ala Pr.
Mind Games. M. Arthur Bogen. (Burchardt & Decker Mystery Ser.). 128p. (Orig.). (gr. 3-7). 1984. pap. 2.25 o.p. (ISBN 0-380-86512-2, 86512, Flare). Avon.
Mind in Nature: Essays on the Interface of Science & Philosophy. Ed. by David R. Griffin & John B. Cobb, Jr. 1977. pap. text ed. 11.25 o.p. (ISBN 0-8191-0157-5). U Pr of Amer.
Mind in the Waters: A Book to Celebrate the Consciousness of Whales & Dolphins. Joan McIntyre. LC 74-13000. (Illus.). 224p. 1984. pap. 16.95 o.p. (ISBN 0-684-14443-3, ScribT). Scribner.
Mind-Influencing Drugs: Effective Management of Patients with Emotional Illness. M. Goldberg & G. Egelston. LC 76-19659. (Illus.). 406p. 1978. 24.50 o.p. (ISBN 0-88416-179-X). Year Bk Med.
Mind Magic: The Science of Microcosmology see Mind Magic: With Mind Experiments.
Mind Magic: With Mind Experiments. 3rd ed. Bill Harvey. LC 80-7457. Orig. Title: Mind Magic: The Science of Microcosmology. (Illus.). 470p. 1980. pap. 14.95 o.p. (ISBN 0-8290-0231-6). Irvington.
Mind, Matter & Purpose: Proceedings, Supplementary Vol. 8. Aristotelian Society for the Systematic Study of Philosophy Staff. 11.00 o.p. (ISBN 0-384-39030-7); pap. 7.00 o.p. (ISBN 0-384-39031-5). Johnson Repr.
Mind Models: New Forms of Musical Experience. Roger Reynolds. (Music Ser.). 238p. 1987. Repr. of 1975 ed. 25.00 o.p. Da Capo.
Mind, Mood & Medicine: A Guide to the New Biopsychiatry. Paul H. Wender & Donald F. Klein. 372p. 1981. 16.95 o.p. (ISBN 0-374-20895-6). FS&G.
Mind-Murders. Janwillem Van de Wetering. 1981. 9.95 o.p. (ISBN 0-395-30544-6). HM.
Mind of an Ape. David Premack & Ann J. Premack. (Illus.). 1983. 14.45 o.p. (ISBN 0-393-01581-5). Norton.
Mind of China. Edwin D. Harvey. LC 73-874. (China Studies: from Confucius to Mao Ser). x, 321p. 1973. Repr. of 1933 ed. 25.50 o.s.i. (ISBN 0-88355-069-5). Hyperion Conn.
Mind of Her Own. Veronica Boyle. LC 84-90132. 180p. 1985. 12.95 o.p. (ISBN 0-533-06205-5). Vantage.
Mind of Matthew. R. E. White. LC 79-23682. 1980. pap. 6.95 o.s.i. (ISBN 0-664-24310-X, Westminster). Westminster John Knox.
Mind of Norman Bethune. Roderick Stewart. LC 77-89097. (Illus.). 160p. 1978. 15.95 o.p. (ISBN 0-88208-091-1, L Hill Bks). Chicago Review.
Mind of the Accused: A Psychiatrist in the Courtroom. David Abrahamsen. 252p. 1983. 15.50 o.p. (ISBN 0-671-47053-1). S&S.
Mind of the Maker. Dorothy L. Sayers. LC 78-19503. 1979. pap. 6.68i o.p. (ISBN 0-06-067071-1, RD 295). HarpR.
Mind of the Murderer. W. L. Neustatter. 232p. 1957. (ISBN 0-8022-1199-2). Philos Lib.
Mind of the Negro As Reflected in Letters Written During the Crisis 1800-1860. Ed. by Carter G. Woodson. 1969. Repr. of 1926 ed. lib. bdg. 22.50 o.p. (ISBN 0-8371-1179-X, WOM&). Greenwood.
Mind of the Oxford Movement. Ed. by Owen Chadwick. 1961. 18.50x o.p. (ISBN 0-8047-0342-6); pap. 3.95 o.p. (ISBN 0-8047-0343-4, SP41). Stanford U Pr.
Mind of the Scientist: Imaginary Conversations with Galileo, Newton, Herschel, Darwin, & Pasteur. Michael Hoskin. LC 72-164020. (Illus.). 1972. 7.95 o.s.i. (ISBN 0-8008-5248-6). Taplinger.
Mind of the Strategist: Business Planning for a Corporate Advantage. Ohmae Kenichi. 304p. 1983. pap. 7.95 o.p. (ISBN 0-14-006722-1). Penguin.

Mind of Watergate: A Study of the Compromise of Integrity. Leo Rangell. 1980. 14.95 o.p. (ISBN 0-393-01308-1). Norton.

Mind or Body: Distinguishing Psychological from Organic Disorders. Robert L. Taylor. (Illus.). 256p. 1982. text ed. 22.95 o.p. (ISBN 0-07-062963-3). McGraw.

Mind over Matter: The Case for Psychokinesis. D. Scott Rogo. 160p. (Orig.). 1986. pap. 7.99 o.p. (ISBN 0-85030-485-7, Pub. by Aquarian Pr England). Sterling.

Mind Palace: A Novel. Steve R. Pieczenick. 1985. 16.45 o.p. (ISBN 0-671-52433-X). S&S.

Mind-Reader. Richard Wilbur. LC 75-42312. 67p. 1977. pap. 3.95 o.p. (ISBN 0-15-659805-1, Harv). HarBraceJ.

Mind Teaches the Brain, 3 vols. Caleb Gattegno. 1975. pap. 5.00 ea. o.p.; Vol. 1. pap. (ISBN 0-87825-067-0); Vol. 2. pap. (ISBN 0-685-64852-4); Vol. 3. pap. (ISBN 0-87825-069-7). Ed Solutions.

Mind Tools: The Five Levels of Mathematical Reality. Rudy Rucker. (Illus.). 320p. 1987. 17.45 o.p. (ISBN 0-395-38315-3). HM.

Mind Your Own Travel Business: A Manual of Retail Travel Practice, 2 vols. Allan Beaver. (Illus.). 1086p. 1980. Set. text ed. 65.00x o.p. (ISBN 0-9504395-1-7, Pub. by Beaver Travel, England); Set. pap. text ed. 50.00x o.p. (ISBN 0-9504395-2-5). Travel & Tourism.

Mindbend. Robin Cook. 1985. lib. bdg. 17.95 o.p. (ISBN 0-8161-3804-4, Large Print Bks). G K Hall.

Mindblock. Jerry Names. 224p. (Orig.). 1981. pap. 2.25 o.p. (ISBN 0-8439-0988-9, Pub. by Leisure Bks CT). Dorchester Pub Co.

Minden Curse. Willo D. Roberts. LC 77-24433. (Illus.). 216p. (gr. 3-7). 1978. 8.95 o.s.i. (ISBN 0-689-30603-2, Atheneum Childrens Bks). Macmillan.

Minder: The Story of the Courtship, Call & Conflicts of John Ledger, Minder & Minister, 1900. Frederick R. Smith. Ed. by Robert L. Wolff. Bd. with Coming of the Preachers: A Tale of the Rise of Methodism, 1901. (Victorian Fiction Ser). 1976. lib. bdg. 73.00 o.p. (ISBN 0-8240-1590-8). Garland Pub.

Minding America's Business: The Decline & Rise of the American Economy. Ira C. Magaziner & Robert C. Reich. LC 81-47901. 350p. 1982. 25.00 o.p. (ISBN 0-15-159954-8, 42779). HarBraceJ.

Minding the Store. Stanley Marcus. LC 74-10833. (Illus.). 1974. 19.95 o.p. (ISBN 0-316-54598-8). Little.

Mindkiller. Spider Robinson. LC 81-20132. 256p. 1982. 14.50 o.p. (ISBN 0-03-059018-3). H Holt & Co.

Minds. David Black. 1985. 6.95 o.p. (ISBN 0-87795-703-7, Arbor Hse). Morrow.

Minds Made Feeble: The Myth & Legacy of the Kallikaks. J. David Smith. LC 84-28416. 244p. 1985. 21.95 o.p. (ISBN 0-87189-093-3). Aspen Pub.

Mindscapes: Poems by Dale Zieroth, Paulette Jiles, Susan Musgrave, Tom Wayman. Ed. by Ann Wall. (HAP 21). 136p. 1971. pap. 5.95 o.p. (ISBN 0-88784-021-3, Pub. by Hse Anansi Pr Canada). U of Toronto Pr.

Mindsong. Joan Cox. 1979. pap. 2.25 o.p. (ISBN 0-380-43638-8, 43638-8). Avon.

Mindstretchers. Incl. Level 1, 3 vols. Wordwright. (gr. 1-3) (ISBN 0-8224-4501-8). Trick or Treat. Ship Ahoy (ISBN 0-8224-4503-4). Grin & Bear It (ISBN 0-8224-4504-2). pap. 5.95 ea. o.p. D S Lake Pubs.

Mindstretchers: Level 2, 4 vols. Pat Carr & Steve Tracey. Incl. Star Gazing. pap. 5.95 (ISBN 0-8224-4505-0); Who Done It? pap. 4.95 o.p. (ISBN 0-8224-4506-9); Great Explorations. pap. 5.95 (ISBN 0-8224-4507-7); Enchantments. pap. 5.95 (ISBN 0-8224-4508-5). (gr. 4-6). 1983. pap. D S Lake Pubs.

Mindy. Dorothy Hamilton. LC 72-5098. (Illus.). 112p. (gr. 7-12). 1973. pap. 3.95 o.p. (ISBN 0-8361-1692-5). Herald Pr.

Mindy's Mysterious Miniature. Jane L. Curry. LC 72-124842. (Illus.). (gr. 4-6). 1970. 5.95 o.p. (ISBN 0-15-254290-6, HJ). HarBraceJ.

Mine! David L. Porter. (Illus.). (gr. k-3). 1981. PLB 7.95 o.p. (ISBN 0-395-31607-3). HM.

Mine Drainage: Proceedings of the International Mine Drainage Symposium, 1st, Denver, Colorado, May, 1979. International Mine Drainage Symposium Staff. Ed. by George O. Argall, Jr. & C. O. Brawner. LC 79-89681. (A World Mining Bk.). (Illus.). 1979. 55.00 o.p. (ISBN 0-87930-122-8). Miller Freeman.

Mine Enemy Grows Older. Alexander King. 1958. 4.50 o.p. S&S.

Mine for a Year. Susan Kuklin. (Illus.). 96p. (gr. 3-7). 1984. 10.95 o.p. (ISBN 0-698-20603-7, Coward). Putnam Pub Group.

Mine for Keeps. Jean Little. (Illus.). (gr. 4-6). 1974. pap. 1.95 o.p. (ISBN 0-671-42455-6). Archway.

Mine Plant. Benjamin F. Tillson. (Illus.). 1976. text ed. 30.00x o.p. (ISBN 0-89520-042-2). SMM&E Inc.

Mine Safety & Health Reporter. looseleaf 760.00 o.p. BNA.

Mine to Kill. David St. Clair. 352p. 1987. pap. 3.95 o.p. (ISBN 1-55547-165-X). Critics Choice Paper.

Mineral Deposits of the Deep-Ocean Floor. K. O. Emery & Brian J. Skinner. LC 78-59181. 72p. 1978. pap. 4.95x o.p. (ISBN 0-8448-1363-X, Pub. by Crane Russak & Co). Taylor & Francis.

Mineral Industry Trends & Economic Opportunities. (Mineral Policy Ser.). 1978. pap. 5.00 o.p. (SSC100, SSC). UNIPUB.

Mineral Names: What Do They Mean? Richard S. Mitchell. 1979. 17.95 o.p. (ISBN 0-442-24593-9). Van Nos Reinhold.

Mineral Processing in Developing Countries. 60p. 1984. pap. 18.00 o.p. (ISBN 0-86010-500-8). Graham & Trotman.

Mineral Processing Plant Design. Ed. by R. B. Bhappu & A. L. Mular. (Illus.). 1978. text ed. 27.00x o.p. (ISBN 0-89520-251-4). SMM&E Inc.

Mineral Processing Plant Design. 2nd ed. Ed. by Andrew L. Mular & Roshan B. Bhappu. LC 79-57345. (Illus.). 958p. 1980. text ed. 10.00x o.p. (ISBN 0-89520-269-7). SMM&E Inc.

Mineral Processing: Proceedings of the Sixth International Conference. Ed. by P. Gy. 1965. 185.00 o.p. (ISBN 0-08-010277-8). Pergamon.

Mineral Processing Technology: An Introduction to the Practical Aspects of Ore Treatment & Mineral Recovery. 2nd ed. B. A. Wills. LC 80-41698. (International Series on Materials Science & Technology: Vol. 29). (Illus.). 450p. 1985. pap. text ed. 21.00 o.p. (ISBN 0-08-031159-8); pap. text ed. 20.00 o.p. (ISBN 0-08-027323-8). Pergamon.

Mineral Resource Development Law. 386p. 1984. 30.00 o.p. (ISBN 0-318-03927-3, 276). PA Bar Inst.

Mineral Resources. Glenn A. Cheney. LC 84-21022. (Natural Resoures Ser.: No. 1). (Illus.). 62p. (gr. 5-8). 1985. lib. bdg. 9.90 o.p. (ISBN 0-531-04915-9). Watts.

Mineralogy & Petrography. A. Milovsky. 437p. 1982. 10.95 o.p. (ISBN 0-8285-2310-X, Pub. by Mir Pubs USSR). Imported Pubns.

Mineralogy of Arizona. John W. Anthony et al. LC 75-44670. 1977. pap. text ed. 9.75x o.p. (ISBN 0-8165-0471-7). U of Ariz Pr.

Minerals & Gemstones: An Identification Guide. G. Brocardo. (Illus.). 220p. (gr. 6 up). 1983. 12.95 o.p. (ISBN 0-88254-756-9). Hippocrene Bks.

Minerals Handbook: 1982-83. Phillip Crowson. 144p. 1983. 36.95 o.p. (ISBN 0-442-21504-5). Van Nos Reinhold.

Minerals Handbook 1986-87. Philip Crowson. LC 86-645605. 331p. 1986. 90.00x o.p. (ISBN 0-935859-00-4, Stockton Pr). Groves Dict Music.

Minerals of Brazil, 3 vols. R. R. Franco & A. Leprevost. (Illus.). 1972. Set. 160.00 o.s.i. (ISBN 0-685-47310-4). E J Brill USA.

Minerals Transportation: Proceedings of the International Symposium, 3rd, Vancouver, British Columbia, Canada, Oct., 1979, Vol. 3. International Symposium on the Transportation & Handling of Minerals Staff. Ed. by George O. Argall, Jr. LC 76-189985. (World Mining Bk.). 1980. pap. 50.00 o.p. (ISBN 0-87930-080-9). Miller Freeman.

Minerals Yearbook, 1983, Area Reports: Domestic, Vol. 2. 624p. 1985. 18.00 o.p. (ISBN 0-318-18788-4, S/N 024-004-02145-4). USGPO.

Minerals Yearbook, 1984: Area Reports, Domestic, Vol. 2. (Illus.). 667p. 1986. 24.00 o.p. (S/N 024-004-02163-2). USGPO.

Miner's Life. David Douglass & Joel Krieger. 116p. (Orig.). 1983. pap. 9.95x o.p. (ISBN 0-7100-9473-6). Routledge Chapman & Hall.

Miners of the Red Mountain: Indian Labor in Potosi, 1545-1650. Peter Bakewell. LC 84-7582. (Illus.). 229p. 1984. 19.95x o.p. (ISBN 0-8263-0769-8). U of NM Pr.

Minerva. Marion Chesney. (Nightingale Large Print Ser.). 1985. pap. text ed. 10.95 o.p. (ISBN 0-8161-3745-5, Large Print Bks). G K Hall.

Mines & Mining Equipment & Service Companies Worldwide, 1986. Compiled by Don Nelson. 700p. 1986. text ed. 99.00 o.p. (ISBN 0-419-13860-9, Pub. by E & FN Spon England). Routledge Chapman & Hall.

Mines & Mining Equipment & Service Companies Worldwide, 1984-85. Don Nelson. 500p. 1985. 79.95 o.p. (ISBN 0-419-13260-0, NO. 6900, Pub. by E & FN Spon England). Routledge Chapman & Hall.

Mines of Churchill Country. William Vanderburg. (Illus.). 144p. 1988. pap. 14.95 o.p. (ISBN 0-913814-73-3). Nevada Pubns.

Ming Dynasty: Its Origins & Evolving Institutions. Charles O. Hucker. LC 78-17354. (Michigan Monographs in Chinese Studies: No. 34). 1978. pap. 6.00 o.s.i. (ISBN 0-89264-034-0). U of Mich Ctr Chinese.

Ming Lo Moves the Mountain. Arnold Lobel. (Illus.). 32p. (ps-3). 1983. pap. 2.95 o.p. (ISBN 0-590-33273-2). Scholastic Inc.

Mingled Yarn: The Life of R. P. Blackmur. Russell A. Fraser. LC 81-47554. (Illus.). 320p. 1982. 19.95 o.p. (ISBN 0-15-160138-0). HarBraceJ.

Mingles: A Home Buying Guide for Unmarried Couples. Robert Irwin. 1984. pap. text ed. 16.95 o.p. (ISBN 0-07-032037-3). McGraw.

Mini-Center Stuff. Imogene Forte & Mary A. Pangle. LC 76-29532. (Learning Center Set). (Illus.). 164p. (gr. 2-6). 1976. pap. 8.95 o.p. (ISBN 0-913916-25-0, IP 25-0). Incentive Pubns.

Mini Page Kids' Cookbook. Betty Debnam. LC 78-59687. (gr. 3 up). 1978. spiral bd. 5.95 o.p. (ISBN 0-8362-4202-5). Andrews & McMeel.

Mini-Truck Repair Manual. Kalton C. Lahue. LC 78-51841. (Illus.). 384p. 1978. pap. 5.95 o.p. (ISBN 0-8227-5016-3). Petersen Pub.

Mini-Wood Community. Paul G. Howes. LC 74-84425. (Illus.). 1975. 20.00 o.p. (ISBN 0-682-48069-X). Exposition-Phoenix.

Miniature Desserts. Pam Dotter. LC 86-11000. (Illus.). 160p. 1986. 14.95 o.p. (ISBN 1-55584-013-2). Weidenfeld.

Miniature Faith. Carrie C. Hayes. LC 84-91276. 81p. 1985. 7.95 o.p. (ISBN 0-533-06357-4). Vantage.

Miniature Mysteries: One Hundred Malicious Little Mystery Stories. Ed. by Isaac Asimov & Martin H. Greenberg. LC 80-28667. 1983. pap. 9.95 o.p. (ISBN 0-8008-5252-4). Taplinger.

Miniature Orchids to Grow & Show. Jack Kramer & Roy L. Crafton. (Illus.). 1982. 15.95 o.p. (ISBN 0-393-01632-3). Norton.

Miniature Paintings. Moreen. Date not set. 35.00 o.p. Ktav.

Miniature Paintings & Painters of Persia, India & Turkey from the 8th to the 18th Century. F. R. Martin. (Illus.). 1972. 125.00x o.p. (ISBN 0-87556-425-9). Saifer.

Miniature Publications of Dawson's Book Shop. Mary Helen & Glen Dawson. Ed. by E. H. Mundell. 36p. 1981. leatherette 15.00 o.p. (ISBN 0-317-11640-1). Dawsons.

Miniatures & Silhouettes of Early American Jews. Hannah R. London. LC 78-87797. (Illus.). 1969. Repr. 16.50 o.p. (ISBN 0-8048-0657-8). C E Tuttle.

Miniatures Frame. Kenneth Royce. 1973. pap. 0.95 o.p. (ISBN 0-380-01415-7, 17459). Avon.

Miniatures: How to Make Them, Use Them & Sell Them. Phyllis Meras. LC 76-16493. 1976. 12.95 o.p. (ISBN 0-395-24344-0); pap. 8.95 o.p. (ISBN 0-395-24586-9). HM.

Miniatures of the Paris Psalter: A Study in Middle Byzantine Painting. Hugo Buchtal. (Warburg Institute Studies: Vol. 2). Repr. of 1938 ed. 88.00 o.p. (ISBN 0-8115-1379-3). Kraus Repr.

Miniatures of the Sacra Parallela: Parsinius Graecus 923. Kurt Weitzmann. LC 78-70320. (Studies in Manuscript Illumination: No. 8). (Illus.). 1979. 86.50 o.p. (ISBN 0-691-03940-2). Princeton U Pr.

Miniaturization of High-Energy Physics Detectors. Ed. by A. Stefanini. LC 82-16495. (Ettore Majorana International Science Series, Physical Sciences: Vol. 14). 260p. 1983. 55.00x o.p. (ISBN 0-306-41133-4, Plenum Pr). Plenum Pub.

Minibibliophilia. Francis J. Weber. 30p. 1979. marbled boards 12.50 o.p. (ISBN 0-317-11686-X). Dawsons.

Minicomputer Systems. Boeing Computer Service Co. Staff & M. Vardell Lines. 217p. 1980. text ed. 25.95 o.p. (ISBN 0-316-52679-7). Little.

Minicomputers: Low-Cost Computer Power for Management. rev. ed. Donald P. Kennedy. (Illus.). 1979. 15.95 o.p. (ISBN 0-8144-5484-4). AMACOM.

Minicomputers: Low-Cost Computer Power for Management. rev. ed. Donald P. Kenney. LC 78-14413. 288p. 1981. pap. 7.95 o.p. (ISBN 0-8144-7560-4). AMACOM.

Minimizing Deicing Chemical Use. (National Cooperative Highway Research Program Synthesis of Highway Practice). 58p. 1974. 4.00 o.p. (ISBN 0-309-02300-9). Transport Res Bd.

Mining. Ed. by Financial Times Staff. 1987. 95.00 o.p. (ISBN 0-912289-66-X); Standing Order. 85.00 o.p. St James Pr.

Mining & Australia. Ed. by W. H. Richmond & P. C. Sharma. LC 82-13357. (Illus.). 320p. 1983. text ed. 34.50x o.p. (ISBN 0-7022-1742-5); pap. text ed. 16.50x o.p. (ISBN 0-7022-1752-2). U of Queensland Pr.

Mining & Concentrating of Lead & Zinc, 2, Vol. I. Ed. by D. O. Rausch & B. C. Mariacher. LC 78-132404. 1017p. 1970. 10.00 o.p. (ISBN 0-89520-038-4, 040-6). SMM&E Inc.

Mining & Social Change: Durham County in the Twentieth Century. Ed. by Martin Bulmer. 320p. 1978. 30.00 o.p. (ISBN 0-85664-509-5, Pub. by Croom Helm Ltd). Routledge Chapman & Hall.

Mining for Development in the Third World: Multinationals, State Enterprises & the International Economy. Ed. by S. Sideri & S. Johns. LC 80-20930. (Pergamon Policy Studies on International Development). 376p. 1981. 95.00 o.p. (ISBN 0-08-026308-9). Pergamon.

Mining in the Outer Continental Shelf & in the Deep Ocean. Marine Board, Asembly of Engineering Staff & National Research Council Staff. 152p. 1975. pap. 7.75 o.p. (ISBN 0-309-02405-6). Natl Acad Pr.

Mining Technology for Energy Resources Advances for the Eighties. Ed. by A. H. Jones. 1978. 8.00 o.p. (ISBN 0-685-66805-3, G00140). ASME.

Minister & the Care of Souls. Daniel D. Williams. LC 76-62929. (Orig.). 1977. pap. 5.95i o.p. (ISBN 0-06-318071-5, RD 213). HarpR.

Ministering Couple. Carl Nelson & Martha Nelson. LC 82-71440. (Orig.). 1983. pap. 4.95 o.p. (ISBN 0-8054-3706-1); wkbk. 2.25 o.p. (ISBN 0-8054-9406-5). Broadman.

Ministering to Single Adults. Gene Van Note. 109p. 1978. pap. 2.95 o.p. (ISBN 0-8341-0556-X). Beacon Hill.

Ministering to the Aging. Bartholomew J. Laurello. LC 79-90992. (Paths of Life Ser.). 96p. (Orig.). 1979. pap. 2.95 o.p. (ISBN 0-8091-2268-5). Paulist Pr.

Minister's Filing System. Paul Gericke. 1978. pap. 2.95 o.p. (ISBN 0-8010-3721-2). Baker Bk.

Minister's Manual for Nineteen Eighty-Five. Ed. by James W. Cox. LC 25-21658. (Doran's Ser.). 288p. 1984. 11.49i o.p. (ISBN 0-06-061599-0). HarpR.

Ministers Manual for Nineteen Eighty-Four. Ed. by James W. Cox. LC 25-21658. 288p. 1983. 10.53i o.p. (ISBN 0-06-061598-2). HarpR.

Ministers Manual for Nineteen Eighty-Six. Ed. by James W. Cox. LC 25-21658. 352p. 1985. 14.45 o.p. (ISBN 0-06-061595-8). HarpR.

Minister's Manual for 1981. 56th annual ed. Charles L. Wallis. LC 25-21658. 288p. 1980. 8.95i o.p. (ISBN 0-06-069026-7). HarpR.

Ministers Manual, 1983. Ed. by Charles L. Wallis. LC 25-21658. 288p. 1982. write for info. o.p. (ISBN 0-06-069027-5). HarpR.

Minister's Wooing. (Illus.). 578p. 1978. pap. 7.95 o.p. (ISBN 0-317-35969-X). Stowe-Day.

Ministry & Ordination. pap. 0.75 o.p. (ISBN 0-8192-1174-5). Morehouse Pub.

Ministry Gifts Study Guide. Kenneth E. Hagin. 1981. pap. 10.00 spiral bdg. o.p. (ISBN 0-89276-092-3). Hagin Ministries.

Ministry of Greed: The Inside Story of the Televangelists & Their Holy Wars. Larry Martz. (Illus.). 272p. 1988. 18.95 o.p. (ISBN 1-55584-216-X). Weidenfeld.

Ministry of Intercession: A Plea for More Prayer. Andrew Murray. 159p. 1987. pap. 3.95 o.p. (ISBN 0-310-55082-3, 19008P). Zondervan.

Ministry of Prayer. Womens Anglow Staff. (Cornerstone Ser.). 32p. 1983. pap. 2.00 o.p. (ISBN 0-930756-77-0, 533008). Aglow Pubns.

Ministry of Sovereign Authority. Dennis Hart. 1978. 4.50 o.p. (ISBN 0-682-49119-5). Exposition-Phoenix.

Ministry of the Glory Cloud. R. E. Hough. 160p. 1956. (ISBN 0-8022-0747-2). Philos Lib.

Ministry of the Word. Robert E. Browne. LC 76-1310. 128p. 1976. pap. 3.50 o.p. (ISBN 0-8006-1229-9, 1-1229, Fortress). Augsburg Fortress.

Ministry of Visitation. John T. Sisemore. LC 54-2969. 1954. 1.25 o.p. (ISBN 0-88243-550-7, 02-0550). Gospel Pub.

Ministry to Word & Sacraments: History & Theology. Bernard Cooke. LC 75-36459. 688p. 1980. pap. 16.95 o.p. (ISBN 0-8006-1440-2, 1-1440, Fortress). Augsburg Fortress.

Minneapolis - St. Paul Bar Guide. 136p. 1986. pap. 4.95 o.p. (ISBN 0-89716-162-9). Peanut Butter.

Minneapolis-St. Paul Epicure. Alexandra Jacobs. Ed. by Isabel Keating & Gretchen Weidenbach. (American Epicure Ser.). 160p. 1986. pap. 7.95 o.p. (ISBN 0-89716-159-9). Peanut Butter.

Minnesota Business Directory, 1987-88. rev. ed. American Directory Publishing Co., Inc. Staff. 1384p. 1987. pap. 85.00 o.p. (ISBN 0-944316-05-0). Amer Directory.

Minnesota: Conflict of Laws. 1983. 8.50 o.p. (ISBN 0-686-90814-7). Am Law Inst.

Minnesota: Contracts. 1983. 9.50 o.p. (ISBN 0-686-90528-8). Am Law Inst.

Minnesota Data Book: 1985-1986. Victor M. Spadaccini. 384p. (Orig.). 1983. pap. 10.00 o.p. (ISBN 0-911493-03-4). Blue Sky.

Minnesota II. Photos by Richard H. Smith. LC 84-80124. (Illus.). 128p. (Text by Richard A. Coffey). 1984. text ed. 32.50 o.s.i. (ISBN 0-912856-87-4). Gr Arts Ctr Pub.

Minnesota Legal Forms, 9 vols. 1981. looseleaf 252.00 o.p. Butterworth MN.

Minnesota Manufacturers Register, 1988. 466p. 1987. 75.00 o.p. (ISBN 0-318-02890-5). Manufacturers.

Minnesota Medical & Healthcare Resources Guide: The 1986 Medical Alley Directory. Minnesota Trade Office Staff. Ed. by Urgil Bolton. (Illus.). 170p. (Orig.). 1986. pap. text ed. 45.00 o.p. (ISBN 0-931833-00-0). Minn Med Alley.

Minnesota No-Fault Automobile Insurance. Michael K. Steenson. 1982. 70.00 o.p. Butterworth MN.

Minnesota: Property, Vols. 1-2. 1983. 8.50 o.p. (ISBN 0-686-90817-1). Am Law Inst.

Minnesota Public Sector Labor Law. Stephen D. Gordon et al. 1983. Looseleaf 55.00 o.p. (ISBN 0-86678-115-3). Butterworth MN.

Minnesota: Restitution. 1983. 8.50 o.p. (ISBN 0-686-90819-8). Am Law Inst.

Minnesota Supplement for Modern Real Estate Practice. 4th ed. Edward J Driscoll & Thomas A. Musil. LC 85-1956. (Illus.). 248p. 1985. pap. 10.95 o.p. (ISBN 0-88462-491-9, 1510-22, Real Estate Ed). Longman Finan.

Minnesota Twins. rev. ed. Hinz. LC 82-239828. (Baseball Today Ser.). 48p. (gr. 4 up). 1982. PLB 11.45 o.p. (ISBN 0-87191-865-X). Creative Ed.

Minolta Camera Handbook. (Your Automatic Camera Ser.). (Illus.). 176p. 1981. pap. 10.95 o.s.i. (ISBN 0-930764-31-5). Curtin & London.

Minolta Maxxum 7000. Herbert Kaspar. (Illus.). 192p. (Orig.). 1986. pap. 12.95 o.p. (ISBN 0-86343-078-3, Pub. by Hove-Fountain UK). Seven Hills Bk Dists.

Minolta XG's. Rick Sammon. (Amphoto Pocket Companion Ser.). (Illus.). 1980. pap. 4.95 o.p. (ISBN 0-8174-4583-8, Amphoto). Watson-Guptill.

Minor American Novelists. Ed. by Charles A. Hoyt. LC 70-86184. (Crosscurrents-Modern Critiques Ser.). 160p. 1970. 8.95x o.p. (ISBN 0-8093-0447-3). S Ill U Pr.

Minor Cemetery at Giza. Clarence S. Fisher. (Eckley B. Coxe Foundation Ser.: Vol. 1). (Illus.). xxiii, 170p. 1924. 25.00X o.p. (ISBN 0-686-11902-9). Univ Mus of U PA.

Minor Characters. Joyce Johnson. 262p. 1983. 13.45 o.p. (ISBN 0-395-32513-7). HM.

Minor Oral Surgery. 2nd ed. Howe. 348p. 1971. pap. 24.00 o.p. (ISBN 0-7236-0433-9, Pub. by John Wright UK). Butterworth.

Minor Poets of the Seventeenth Century. Ed. by R. G. Howarth. 1969. 14.95x o.p. (ISBN 0-460-00873-0, Evman); pap. 4.95x o.p. (ISBN 0-460-01873-6). Biblio Dist.

Minor Prophets: An Expositional Commentary (Hosea-Jonah, Vol. 1. James M. Boice. 272p. 1983. 17.95 o.p. (ISBN 0-310-21550-1, 10423). Zondervan.

Minor Prophets: An Expositional Commentary (Micah-Malachi, Vol. 2. James M. Boice. 1986. 17.95 o.p. (ISBN 0-310-21580-3, 10424). Zondervan.

Minor Royalty. Caroline Light. LC 87-20197. (Starlight Romance Ser.). 192p. 1988. pap. 12.95 o.p. (ISBN 0-385-24338-3). Doubleday.

Minor Surgery. Humphrey Rolleston. (ISBN 0-8022-1370-7). Philos Lib.

Minor White: A Living Remembrance. LC 83-30845. 80p. 1985. 12.50 o.p. Aperture.

Minorities under Communism: Nationalities As a Source of Tension Among Balkan Communist States. Robert R. King. LC 72-95184. 336p. 1973. 25.00x o.p. (ISBN 0-674-57632-2). Harvard U Pr.

Minority Administrator: Blacks & Women in Public Sector Management. Brenda J. Rowe. (Public Administration Ser.: P 1719). 6p. 1985. 2.00 o.p. (ISBN 0-89028-489-X). Vance Biblios.

Minority Group Adolescents in the United States. Eugene B. Brody. LC 78-20769. 256p. 1979. Repr. of 1968 ed. lib. bdg. 16.50 o.p. (ISBN 0-88275-849-7). Krieger.

Minority Participation in Kalamazoo's Apprenticeship Training Programs: Assessments & Recommendations. 62p. 1970. pap. 0.75 o.p. (ISBN 0-911558-50-0). W E Upjohn.

Minority Religions in America. William J. Whalen. LC 79-38979. 312p. (Orig.). 1972. pap. 7.95 o.p. (ISBN 0-8189-0239-6). Alba.

Minority Shareholders. Pennsylvania Bar Institute Staff. 164p. 1985. 50.00 o.p. (ISBN 0-318-19061-3, 318). PA Bar Inst.

Minsky's Burlesque. Morton Minsky & Milt Machlin. (Illus.). 256p. 1985. 15.95 o.p. (ISBN 0-87795-743-6, Arbor Hse). Morrow.

Minstrelsy Ancient & Modern. William Motherwell. LC 68-24477. 532p. 1968. Repr. of 1873 ed. 37.00x o.p. (ISBN 0-8103-3415-1). Gale.

Minstrelsy of Maine. Fanny Eckstorm. LC 79-152248. 408p. 1971. Repr. of 1927 ed. 43.00x o.p. (ISBN 0-8103-3707-X). Gale.

Mint. T. E. Lawrence. 1963. pap. 4.95 o.p. (ISBN 0-393-00196-2, Norton Lib). Norton.

Minting of Antoniniani A. D. 238-249 & the Smyrna Hoard. Samuel K. Eddy. (Numismatic Notes & Monographs: 156). (Illus.). 140p. 1967. pap. 12.00 o.p. (ISBN 0-89722-056-0). Am Numismatic.

Minton Pottery & Porcelain of the First Period, 1793-1850. Geoffrey A. Godden. (Illus.). 168p. 1968. 50.00 o.p. (ISBN 0-257-66717-2, Pub. by Barrie & Jenkins England). Seven Hills Bk Dists.

Minus One Hundred Forty Eight Degrees: The Winter Ascent of Mt McKinley. Art Davidson. LC 69-14695. (Illus.). 1969. 10.95 o.p. (ISBN 0-393-07447-1). Norton.

Minute to Live! Lajos Draviczki. 1977. 6.50 o.p. (ISBN 0-682-48863-1). Exposition-Phoenix.

Minutes No One Owns. Brendan Galvin. LC 77-73464. (Pitt Poetry Ser.). 1977. 15.95x o.p. (ISBN 0-8229-3359-4); ltd. ed 20.00x o.p. (ISBN 0-8229-3364-0); pap. 6.95 o.p. (ISBN 0-8229-5286-6). U of Pittsburgh Pr.

Mira. Daoma Winston. LC 80-68544. 288p. 1981. 11.95 o.p. (ISBN 0-87795-300-7, Arbor Hse). Morrow.

Mirabell: Books of Number. James Merrill. LC 78-4350. 1979. 10.95 o.p. (ISBN 0-689-10901-6, Atheneum); pap. 6.95 o.p. (ISBN 0-689-11167-3, Atheneum). Macmillan.

Miracle at James Towne. Lois M. Parker. Ed. by Gerald Wheeler. LC 83-13740. (Banner Bks.). (Illus.). 96p. (Orig.). (gr. 1 up). 1984. pap. 6.50 o.p. (ISBN 0-8280-0219-3). Review & Herald.

Miracle Babies & Other Happy Endings for Couples with Fertility Problems. Mark Perloe & Linda Gail Christie. LC 85-43088. 288p. 1986. 17.95 o.p. (ISBN 0-89256-301-X). Rawson Assocs.

Miracle Chip: The Microelectronic Revolution. Stanley L. Englebardt. LC 79-2422. (Illus.). (gr. 5 up). 1979. 11.25 o.p. (ISBN 0-688-41908-9); PLB 11.88 o.p. (ISBN 0-688-51908-3). Lothrop.

Miracle Doctor. A. Kuprin. 24p. 1980. pap. 1.99 o.p. (ISBN 0-8285-1820-3, Pub. by Malysh Pubs USSR). Imported Pubns.

Miracle in the Making. Betsy Lee. LC 82-72647. 128p. (Orig.). 1983. pap. 5.50 o.p. (ISBN 0-8066-1954-6, 10-4451, Augsburg). Augsburg Fortress.

Miracle of Dialogue. Reuel L. Howe. 1963. pap. 6.95 o.p. (ISBN 0-86683-886-4, SP9). HarpR.

Miracle of Fasting: For Physical, Mental & Spiritual Prjuvenation. 35th, rev. ed. Paul C. Bragg & Patricia Bragg. LC 84-62771. (Illus.). pap. 6.95 o.p. (ISBN 0-87790-035-3). Health Sci.

Miracle of Flight. Dalton. 1977. text ed. 16.95 o.p. (ISBN 0-07-015207-1). McGraw.

Miracle of Love: Mother Teresa of Calcutta, Her Missionaries of Charity, & Her Co-Workers. Kathryn Spink. LC 81-47717. (Illus.). 256p. 1982. 15.00 o.p. (ISBN 0-06-067497-0). HarpR.

Miracle of Mark. Roy A. Harrisville. LC 67-11725. (Orig.). 1967. pap. 1.75 o.p. (ISBN 0-8066-9354-1, 10-4456, Augsburg). Augsburg Fortress.

Miracle of Mind Power. Dan Custer. 288p. 1983. pap. 6.95 o.p. (ISBN 0-13-585414-8, Reward). P-H.

Miracle of Mindfulness! A Manual on Meditation. Thich N. Hanh. LC 76-7747. (Illus.). 1976. pap. 7.95 o.p. (ISBN 0-8070-1119-3, BP546). Beacon Pr.

Miracle of the Rose. Jean Genet. Tr. by Bernard Frechtman from Fr. 1971. pap. 7.95 o.p. (ISBN 0-394-17470-4, B322, BC). Grove.

Miracle of Universal Psychic Power: How to Build Your Way to Prosperity. Al G. Manning. 1976. pap. 14.95 o.p. (ISBN 0-13-585794-5, Parker). P-H.

Miracle on Thirty-Fourth Street. Valentine Davies. LC 47-4221. 1967. pap. 2.50 o.p. (ISBN 0-15-660453-1, Harv). HarBraceJ.

Miracle Power for Infinite Riches. Joseph Murphy. 1972. 8.95 o.p. (ISBN 0-13-585638-8, Parker); pap. 5.95 o.p. (ISBN 0-13-585612-4). P-H.

Miracle Stories in Christian Antiquity. Susan M. Praeder. LC 86-45909. 288p. 1987. pap. 22.95 o.p. (ISBN 0-8006-2115-8, 1-2115, Fortress). Augsburg Fortress.

Miracle Stories of the Early Christian Tradition. Gerd Theissen. Ed. by John Riches. Tr. by Francis McDonagh. LC 82-48546. 416p. 1983. 9.95 o.p. (ISBN 0-8006-0700-7, 1-700, Fortress); pap. (1-2115). Augsburg Fortress.

Miracle to Proclaim: First-Hand Experience of Healing. Ralph A. DiOrio. LC 83-18218. 224p. 1984. pap. 4.50 o.s.i. (ISBN 0-385-19241-X, Im). Doubleday.

Miracle Worker see Dinny & the Witches: Two Plays.

Miracles: A Parascientific Inquiry into Wonderous Phenomena. D. Scott Rogo. LC 81-17329. (Illus.). 320p. 1982. 17.95 o.p. (ISBN 0-385-27202-2, Dial). Doubleday.

Miracles & Mysteries in the Bible. Bruce Kaye & John Rogerson. 1978. pap. 3.95 o.s.i. (ISBN 0-664-24179-4, Westminster). Westminster John Knox.

Miracles & the Sumrall Family. Leona S. Murphy. 205p. (Orig.). 1984. pap. 6.95 o.p. (ISBN 0-89274-325-5). Harrison Hse.

Miracles In Dispute: A Continuing Debate. Ernst Keller & Marie-Luise Keller. 256p. pap. 8.95 o.p. (ISBN 0-317-31482-3, 30-1012-259, Fortress). Augsburg Fortress.

Miracles in El Paso. Rene Laurentin. (Illus.). 135p. 1982. pap. 6.95 o.p. (ISBN 0-89283-150-2). Servant.

Miracles in Pinafores & Bluejeans. Ardeth G. Kapp. LC 77-4268. 81p. pap. 1.50 o.p. (ISBN 0-87747-741-8). Deseret Bk.

Miracles of Jesus. David Wenham & Craig Blomberg. (Gospel Perspectives Ser.: No. 6). pap. text ed. 14.95x o.s.i. (Pub. by JSOT Pr England). Eisenbrauns.

Miracles of Rare Device: The Poet's Sense of Self in Nineteenth-Century Poetry. Fred Kaplan. LC 73-88818. 188p. 1972. 19.95x o.p. (ISBN 0-8143-1476-7). Wayne St U Pr.

Miracles of Survival: Canada & French Canada. Waris Shere. 160p. 1981. 7.50 o.p. (ISBN 0-682-49730-4, University). Exposition-Phoenix.

Miracles of Urine Therapy: A Practical Guide to Auto-Urine Therapy for Every Man, Woman & Child. 2nd ed. C. P. Mithal. (Modern Approach to Nature Cure Ser.). (Illus.). 82p. 1978. pap. 11.95 o.s.i. (ISBN 0-9609802-9-6). Life Science.

Miracles on Maple Hill. Virginia Sorensen. LC 56-8358. (Illus.). (gr. 4-6). 1956. 7.95 o.p. (ISBN 0-15-254558-1, HJ). HarBraceJ.

Miracles or Law: Lessons by & Experiences with the Masters of Mystery. Volume I-The Yellow Robe. Gijsbert Van der Zeeuw. Tr. by L. W. C. Zonneveld. (Illus.). 1977. 15.00 o.p. (ISBN 0-682-48889-5). Exposition-Phoenix.

Miracles: Poems by Children of the English-Speaking World. Ed. by Richard Lewis. 216p. 1984. 14.50 o.p. (ISBN 0-671-50419-3). S&S.

Miracles: Proof of God's Power. T. L. Osborn. 96p. (Orig.). 1981. pap. 1.50 o.p. (ISBN 0-89274-185-6, HH-185). Harrison Hse.

Miraculous Birth of Language. R. A. Wilson. (ISBN 0-8022-1893-8). Philos Lib.

Miraculous Pigtail. Feng Jicai. 1987. 4.95 o.p. (ISBN 0-8351-2050-3). China Bks.

Mirage. Jean-Pierre Decock. (Warbirs Illustrated Ser.: No. 32). (Illus.). 72p. (Orig.). 1985. pap. 9.95 o.p. (ISBN 0-85368-705-6, Pub. by Arms & Armour). Sterling.

Mirage in the West: A History of the French Image of American Society to 1815. Durand Echeverria. LC 56-8379. 1957. pap. 11.50 o.p. (ISBN 0-691-00560-5). Princeton U Pr.

Mirage of the Ages: A Critique of Christianity. Andrew Tomas. 152p. 1983. 9.00 o.p. (ISBN 0-682-49999-4). Exposition-Phoenix.

Miranda: Crime, Law & Politics. Liva Baker. LC 81-69127. 480p. 1985. pap. 10.95 o.p. (ISBN 0-689-70692-8, 328, Atheneum). Macmillan.

Miranda: The Crime, the Law, the Politics. Liva Baker. LC 81-69127. 320p. 1983. 22.95 o.p. (ISBN 0-689-11240-8, Atheneum). Macmillan.

Miranda the Great. Eleanor Estes. LC 66-10422. (Illus.). 80p. (gr. 4-6). 1967. 4.95 o.s.i. (ISBN 0-15-254600-6, HJ). HarBraceJ.

Miriam: A Novel. Lois T. Henderson. LC 82-48929. 256p. 1983. 10.45 o.p. (ISBN 0-06-063867-2). HarpR.

Miriam's Schooling, Eighteen Ninety see Revolution in Tanner's Lane, 1887.

Miro & Mallorca. Pere A. Serra. LC 85-14329. (Illus.). 294p. 1986. 50.00 o.p. (ISBN 0-8478-0661-8). Rizzoli Intl.

Mirror & the Garden: Realism & Reality in the Writings of Anais Nin. Evelyn J. Hinz. LC 73-4979. 127p. 1973. pap. 2.45 o.p. (ISBN 0-15-660500-7, HB259, Harv). HarBraceJ.

Mirror for Autumn. Tr. by Abdullah Al-Udhari. 1974. saddlestitched in wrappers 1.25 o.p. (ISBN 0-685-78972-1, Pub. by Menard Pr). Small Pr Dist.

Mirror for Gotham: New York As Seen by Contemporaries from Dutch Days to the Present. Bayrd Still. LC 80-16246. (Illus.). xix, 417p. 1980. Repr. of 1956 ed. lib. bdg. 45.50x o.p. (ISBN 0-313-22439-0, STMG). Greenwood.

Mirror Image. Ed. by Nancy Hunt. LC 78-4690. 1978. 8.95 o.s.i. (ISBN 0-03-040646-3). H Holt & Co.

Mirror Man. Paul Virdell. LC 78-57317. 1978. 9.95 o.p. (ISBN 0-87795-190-X). Morrow.

Mirror, Mirror. Alice Gray & Marilyn McAuley. 144p. (Orig.). 1985. pap. 6.95 o.p. (ISBN 0-310-42951-X, 11344P). Zondervan.

Mirror, Mirror on the Wall: An Invitation to Beauty. Gayelord Hauser. (Illus.). 364p. 1961. 5.95 o.p. (ISBN 0-374-21009-8). FS&G.

Mirror of Conrad. E. H. Visiak. 256p. 1956. (ISBN 0-8022-1777-X). Philos Lib.

Mirror of Conscience. Basilea Schlink. (Orig.). 1973. pap. 0.95 o.p. (ISBN 0-87123-371-1, 260371). Bethany Hse.

Mirror of Danger. Pamela Sykes. (gr. 5-7). 1976. pap. 1.95 o.p. (ISBN 0-671-42892-6). Archway.

Mirror of Light. Rodney Collin. LC 84-22141. 89p. 1985. pap. 6.95 o.p. (ISBN 0-87773-314-7, 72996-X). Shambhala Pubns.

Mirror of Love: A Reinterpretation of the "Romance of the Rose" Alan M. Gunn. 592p. 1952. 24.00 o.p. (ISBN 0-89672-005-5). Tex Tech Univ Pr.

Mirror of Myth: T. S. Eliot Memorial Lecture 1984. Jasper Griffin. 1986. 35.00 o.p. (ISBN 0-571-13805-5). Faber & Faber.

Mirror of Nature. Robertson Davies. (Alexander Lectures Ser.). 144p. 1983. pap. 6.95 o.p. (ISBN 0-8020-6536-8). U of Toronto Pr.

Mirror of the Heart. Sara Teasdale. Ed. by William Drake. 192p. 1984. 15.95 o.p. (ISBN 0-02-616870-7). Macmillan.

Mirror of the Invisible World: Tales from the Khamseh of Nizami. Peter J. Chelkowski. LC 75-28305. (Illus.). 128p. 1975. 15.00 o.p. (ISBN 0-87099-142-6). Metro Mus Art.

Mirrors & Windows: American Photography Since 1960. John Szarkowski. 1978. 22.50 o.p. Museum Mod Art.

Mirrors-Messages-Manifestations. Minor White. (Illus.). 242p. 1982. 60.00 o.s.i. (ISBN 0-89381-102-5); original print limited edition 900.00 o.p. (ISBN 0-89381-105-X); 125.00 o.p. Aperture.

Mirrors of Love. Jo Calloway. 224p. 1983. pap. 2.75 o.p. (ISBN 0-380-84434-6, 84434-6). Avon.

Mirrors of the Soul. Kahlil Gibran. Ed. by Joseph Sheban. LC 65-10658. 112p. 1965. Philos Lib.

MIS Design Variables & Decision Making Performance: A Simulation Experiment. A. Milton Jenkins. Ed. by Gary Dickson. LC 82-21858. (Management Information Systems Ser.: No. 3). 269p. 1983. 44.95 o.p. (ISBN 0-8357-1399-7). UMI Res Pr.

Misadventure of the New Satan. A. Tammsaare. 311p. 1978. 6.95 o.p. (ISBN 0-8285-1051-2, Pub. by Progress Pubs USSR). Imported Pubns.

Misadventures of a Fly Fisherman: My Life With & Without Papa. Jack Hemingway. LC 86-1876. (Illus.). 368p. 1986. 17.95 o.p. (ISBN 0-87833-379-7). Taylor Pub.

Misanthrope. Moliere. Tr. by Bernard D. Grebanier from Fr. 1959. pap. text ed. 3.95 o.p. (ISBN 0-8120-0137-0). Barron.

Miscarriages of Justice. Bob Woffinden. 352p. 1988. 34.95 o.p. (ISBN 0-340-37420-9, Pub. by Hodder & Stoughton UK). David & Charles.

Miscellaneous Works. Charles Blount. LC 75-11197. (British Philosophers & Theologians of the 17th & 18th Centuries: Vol. 4). 1979. Repr. of 1695 ed. lib. bdg. 51.00 o.p. (ISBN 0-8240-1753-6). Garland Pub.

Miscellany of American Poetry, 1920. Ed. by Louis Untermeyer. LC 78-57866. (Granger Poetry Library). 1978. Repr. of 1920 ed. 21.50x o.p. (ISBN 0-89609-103-1). Roth Pub Inc.

Mischief-Maker. Molly Katz. (Candlelight Ecstasy Ser.: No. 506). (Orig.). 1987. pap. 2.25 o.p. (ISBN 0-440-15572-X). Dell.

Misdemeanors with Punishments Not Exceeding a Fine of Fifty Dollars or Imprisonment of Thirty Days. Joan G. Brannon. 55p. 1983. 4.75 o.p. (ISBN 0-686-39453-4). Institute Government.

Miser of Mayfair. Marion Chesney. (Large Print Bks., Nightingale Ser.). 298p. 1987. pap. 10.95x o.p. (ISBN 0-8161-4256-4, Large Print Bks). G K Hall.

Miserables see also Les Miserables.

Misery Loves Company. Suzanne Heller. LC 67-17279. (Illus.). 1967. 2.50 o.s.i. (ISBN 0-8397-5816-2). Eriksson.

Misfortunes of Mr. Teal. Leslie Charteris. (Saint Ser.). (Illus.). 336p. 1982. pap. 2.50 o.p. (ISBN 0-441-53476-7). Ace Bks.

Misfortunes of Ogier the Dane. Tr. by Robert Linker. Ed. by M. Butts. LC 64-8377. (Illus.). (gr. 5-7). 1964. PLB 2.98 o.p. (ISBN 0-910244-38-3). Blair.

Misguided Expenditures: An Analysis of the Proposed MX Missile System. David Gold et al. 220p. 1985. pap. 19.95 o.p. (ISBN 0-87871-014-0, Dist. by St Martin). CEP.

Mishmash & the Substitute Teacher. Molly Cone. (Illus.). (gr. 3-5). 1979. pap. 2.25 o.p. (ISBN 0-671-54315-6). Archway.

Mishmash & The Venus Flytrap. Molly Cone. LC 75-44380. (Illus.). 128p. (gr. 2-5). 1976. 6.95 o.p. (ISBN 0-395-24376-9). HM.

Misho School. Koho Hihara. (Ikebana Card Bks.). (Illus.). 84p. (Eng. & Japanese.). 1970. pap. 5.95 ea o.p. (Pub. by Shufunomoto Co Ltd Japan). Kakubana Style 1, 42pgs (ISBN 4-07-973270-8). C E Tuttle.

Mishpokhe: A Study of New York City Jewish Family Clubs. William E. Mitchell. 1978. pap. text ed. 18.95x o.p. (ISBN 0-202-01166-6). Aldine de Gruyter.

Misia: The Life of Misia Sert. Arthur Gold & Robert Fizdale. LC 80-27340. (Illus.). 340p. 1981. Repr. 12.95 o.p. (ISBN 0-688-00391-5, Quill NY). Morrow.

Misnomers: One Hundred Fifty Misnamed Words & Their Twisted Definitions. Mark Dittrick & Diane K. Dittrick. (Illus.). 96p. 1986. pap. 5.95 o.p. (ISBN 0-02-013670-6, Collier). Macmillan.

Misplaced Animals, Plants & Other Living Creatures. Alice L. Hopf. LC 75-10952. 160p. (Orig.). (gr. 7-12). 1975. text ed. 7.95 o.p. (ISBN 0-07-030318-5). McGraw.

Misrule. Tam Dalyell. 152p. 1988. 29.95 o.p. (ISBN 0-241-12170-1, Pub. by Hamish Hamilton). David & Charles.

Miss Dr. Lucy. Carol H. Behrman. Ed. by Gerald Wheeler. LC 83-23008. (Banner Bks.). 96p. (gr. 1 up). 1984. pap. 6.95 o.p. (ISBN 0-8280-0231-2). Review & Herald.

Miss Dog's Christmas Treat. James Marshall. (Illus.). 24p. (gr. k-3). 1973. 2.50 o.p. (ISBN 0-395-18154-2). HM.

Miss Ghost. Ruth M. Arthur. LC 79-63117. (gr. 5-9). 1979. 7.95 o.p. (ISBN 0-689-30702-0, Atheneum). Macmillan.

Miss Herbert: The Suburban Wife. Christina Stead. LC 80-24614. 320p. 1981. pap. 5.95 o.p. (ISBN 0-15-660762-X, Harv). Harbracej.

Miss Josephine's Secret Walk. Yuji Kobayashi. Date not set. 11.95 o.p. (ISBN 0-310-57080-8, 16108). Zondervan.

Miss Julie. August Strindberg. 1976. pap. 1.75 o.p. (ISBN 0-380-01416-5, 77412, Bard). Avon.

Miss Kitty, the New Baby, & Me. Michael J. Pellowski. (Illus.). 112p. (gr. 3-6). 1986. 2.25 o.p. (ISBN 0-87406-063-X). Willowisp Pr.

Miss Liberty Meet Crazyhorse. Don Jones. LC 74-18916. 62p. 1972. 5.00 o.p. (ISBN 0-8040-0584-2, Pub. by Swallow); pap. 3.25 o.p. (ISBN 0-8040-0585-0, Pub. by Swallow). Ohio U Pr.

Miss Macintosh, My Darling, Vols. 1 & 2. Marquerite Young. LC 79-12048. 1979. pap. 12.95 o.p. (ISBN 0-15-660793-X, Harv). HarBraceJ.

Miss Manners' Guide to Rearing Perfect Children. Judith Martin. LC 84-45041. (Illus.). 416p. 1984. 19.95 o.p. (ISBN 0-689-11489-3, Atheneum). Macmillan.

Miss Margarida's Way. Roberto Athayde. 1979. pap. 1.95 o.p. (ISBN 0-380-40568-7, Bard). Avon.

Miss Marks & Miss Wooley. Anna M. Wells. 1978. 10.95 o.p. (ISBN 0-395-25724-7). HM.

Miss Mason Remembers. Harriett S. Mason. LC 85-50946. 140p. 1985. 15.00 o.p. (ISBN 0-317-38094-X). Tradd St Pr.

Miss Mouse Takes a Holiday. (Oak Tree Tales Ser.). (Illus.). (ps-1). 1.98 o.p. (ISBN 0-517-45739-3). Outlet Bk Co.

Miss Patch's Learn to Sew Book. Carolyn Meyer. LC 69-11597. (Illus.). (gr. 4-7). 1969. 4.75 o.p. (ISBN 0-15-254933-1, HJ). HarBraceJ.

Miss Pickerell & the Supertanker. Ellen MacGregor & Dora Pantell. (Miss Pickerell Ser.: No. 6). (Illus.). (gr. 4-6). 1980. pap. 1.75 o.p. (ISBN 0-671-56026-3). Archway.

Miss Pickerell on the Trail. Ellen MacGregor & Dora Pantell. (Illus.). 160p. (gr. 4-6). 1982. text ed. 8.95 o.p. (ISBN 0-07-044591-5). McGraw.

Miss Pickerell Tackles the Energy Crisis. Ellen MacGregor & Dora Pantell. LC 79-24149. (Illus.). (gr. 4-6). 1980. text ed. 10.95 o.p. (ISBN 0-07-044589-3). McGraw.

Miss Pickerell to the Earthquake Rescue. Ellen MacGregor & Dora Pantell. (Illus.). 160p. (gr. 4-6). 1977. text ed. 9.95 o.p. (ISBN 0-07-044586-9). McGraw.

Miss Piggy's Guide to Life. Henson Association & Miss Piggy. LC 80-2708. (Illus.). 192p. 1981. 12.95 o.p. (ISBN 0-394-51912-4); pap. 7.95 o.p. (ISBN 0-394-71521-7). Knopf.

Miss Piggy's Treasury of Art Masterpieces: From the Kermitage Collection. Ed. by Henry Beard. (Illus.). 1984. pap. 12.95 o.p. (ISBN 0-03-000743-7). H Holt & Co.

Miss Plunkett to the Rescue. Jane Flory. LC 82-15797. (Illus.). 84p. (gr. 3-6). 1983. 7.70 o.s.i. (ISBN 0-395-33072-6). HM.

Miss Raggedy Taggedy. Bobbi Balin. LC 85-60793. (Illus.). 36p. (Orig.). (gr. 2-5). 1985. pap. 6.95 o.p. (ISBN 0-932967-02-7). Pacific Shoreline.

Miss Switch to the Rescue. Barbara B. Wallace. (Illus.). (gr. 3-5). 1982. pap. 1.95 o.p. (ISBN 0-671-43848-4). Archway.

Miss Universe Beauty Book. Susan Duff. (Illus.). 240p. 1983. 15.95 o.p. (ISBN 0-698-11195-8, Coward). Putnam Pub Group.

Missabe Road: The Duluth, Missabe & Iron Range Railway. Frank A. King. LC 74-190177. (Illus.). 224p. 1972. 23.95 o.p. (ISBN 0-87095-040-1). Gldn West Bks.

Missiles of the World. 3rd, rev. ed. Michael J. Taylor. 1980. 5.95 o.p. (ISBN 0-684-16593-7, ScribT); 5.95 o.p. (ISBN 0-684-17729-3). Scribner.

Missing. Thomas Hauser. 272p. 1980. pap. 2.75 o.p. (ISBN 0-380-49098-6, 58834-X). Avon.

Missing Chums. rev. ed. Franklin W. Dixon. (Hardy Boys Ser: Vol. 4). (gr. 5-9). 1930. 4.50 o.p. (ISBN 0-448-08904-1, G&D); PLB 3.29 o.p. (ISBN 0-448-18904-6). Putnam Pub Group.

Missing from Home. Dorothy Clewes. LC 78-52826. (gr. 7 up). 1978. 6.95 o.p. (ISBN 0-15-254882-3, HJ). HarBraceJ.

Missing Half: Woman 1975. (Illus.). 47p. 1975. pap. 5.75 o.p. (ISBN 92-5-101646-1, F276, FAO). UNIPUB.

Missing Hazelnuts. Fay Marden. LC 86-25894. (Flower Fairy Story-Bks.). (Illus.). 24p. (gr. k-3). 1987. 7.95 o.p. (ISBN 0-87226-143-3). P Bedrick Bks.

Missing in Action. Bill Linn. 224p. 1981. pap. 2.95 o.p. (ISBN 0-380-77370-8, 83626-2). Avon.

Missing Link: Connecting Adult Learners to Learning Resources. K. Patricia Cross. 80p. 1978. pap. 4.50 o.p. (ISBN 0-87447-062-5, 237402). College Bd.

Missing Links: Golf & the Mind. David Morley. 1976. 8.95 o.p. (ISBN 0-689-10689-0, Atheneum). Macmillan.

Missing Persons. Heinrich Boll. Tr. by Leila Vennewitz from German. LC 77-9351. 1977. text ed. 9.95 o.p. (ISBN 0-07-006424-5). McGraw.

Missing Persons. C. Terry Cline, Jr. LC 80-70215. 320p. 1981. 12.95 o.p. (ISBN 0-87795-304-X, Arbor Hse). Morrow.

Missing Persons. Jack Olsen. LC 80-69375. 1981. 12.95 o.p. (ISBN 0-689-11133-9, Atheneum). Macmillan.

Missing: Stories of Strange Disappearances. Daniel Cohen. (Illus.). (gr. 4 up). 1980. pap. 1.95 o.p. (ISBN 0-671-56052-2). Archway.

Mission. Jean Giono. (Illus.). 1971. 12.50 o.p. (ISBN 0-686-53973-7). French & Eur.

Mission Accomplished: What Today's Christian Must Know About God & Salvation. Michael S. Horton. LC 85-29772. 192p. 1985. pap. 6.95 o.p. (ISBN 0-8407-5947-9). Nelson.

Mission at Rangorwich. Alfred V. Swanberg. 1979. 9.50 o.p. (ISBN 0-682-49367-8). Exposition-Phoenix.

Mission in a New World. Edgar R. Trexler. LC 76-62613. 96p. (Orig.). 1977. pap. 0.50 o.p. (ISBN 0-8006-1257-4, Fortress). Augsburg Fortress.

Mission in Ferment. Russell A. Cervin. 1977. pap. 3.50 o.p. (ISBN 0-910452-33-4). Covenant.

Mission of Jesus. Howard Belben. 96p. 1985. pap. 4.95 o.p. (ISBN 0-89109-529-2). NavPress.

Mission of Man. Katz. LC 74-130843. 1976. (ISBN 0-8022-2039-8). Philos Lib.

Mission of the Nile. James Dempsey. (Illus.). 250p. 1956. (ISBN 0-8022-0377-9). Philos Lib.

Mission of the Teacher. Richard C. Cushing. 1977. 3.00 o.s.i. (ISBN 0-8198-0542-4); pap. 2.00 o.s.i. (ISBN 0-8198-0543-2). Dghtrs St Paul.

Mission of the University. Jose Ortega Y Gasset. 1966. pap. 1.95 o.p. (ISBN 0-393-00127-X, Norton Lib). Norton.

Mission Possible. Robert Schindler & Marian Schindler. 168p. 1984. pap. 6.95 o.p. (ISBN 0-88207-618-3). Victor Bks.

Mission Tales: Stories of the Historic California Missions: Missions San Gabriel, San Fernando Rey, San Buenaventura, Vol. 2. Helen M. Roberts. LC 62-11254. (Illus.). 92p. (gr. 3-6). 1962. 5.95x o.s.i. (ISBN 0-87015-245-9). Pacific Bks.

Mission Tales: Stories of the Historic California Missions: Missions Santa Barbara, Santa Ines, Purisima, Vol. 3. Helen M. Roberts. LC 62-11254. (Illus.). 95p. (gr. 3-6). 1962. 5.95x o.s.i. (ISBN 0-87015-246-7). Pacific Bks.

Mission to Civilize: The French Way. Mort Rosenblum. 432p. 1986. 19.95 o.p. (ISBN 0-15-160580-7). HarBraceJ.

Mission Trends: Faith Meets Faith, No. 5. Ed. by Gerald Anderson & Thomas Stransky. LC 81-80983. 320p. (Orig.). 1981. pap. 4.95 o.p. (ISBN 0-8091-2356-8). Paulist Pr.

Missionary Impact on Modern Nigeria, 1842-1914. Emmanuel A. Ayandele. (Ibadan History Ser.). 1967. pap. text ed. 17.50x o.p. (ISBN 0-582-64512-3). Humanities.

Missionary Kid, MK. rev. ed. Edward E. Danielson. LC 84-12655. (Mission Candidate Aids Ser.). (Illus.). 91p. 1985. pap. 5.95 o.p. (ISBN 0-87808-745-1). William Carey Lib.

Missionary Spirit in the Augustana Church. George F. Hall. LC 84-72945. (Publications Ser.: No. 32). 166p. 1985. 7.50 o.p. (ISBN 0-910184-32-1). Augustana.

Missionary Stew. Ross Thomas. 1983. 15.50 o.p. (ISBN 0-671-49363-9). S&S.

Missionary Stew. Ross Thomas. 1986. 13.95 o.p. (ISBN 0-317-53132-8, Large Print Bks). G K Hall.

Missions of New Mexico Since 1776. John L. Kessell. LC 79-4934. (Illus.). 288p. 1980. 45.00x o.p. (ISBN 0-8263-0514-8). U of NM Pr.

Mississippi: Agency. 1983. 8.50 o.p. (ISBN 0-686-90532-6). Am Law Inst.

Mississippi Manufacturers Directory, 1988. 328p. 1988. pap. 63.00 o.p. (ISBN 0-318-02891-3). Manufacturers.

Mississippi: Property, Vols. 1-2. 1983. 8.50 o.p. (ISBN 0-686-90824-4). Am Law Inst.

Mississippi River: Before & after Mark Twain. Gerald M. Capers. 1977. 8.50 o.p. (ISBN 0-682-48845-3, Lochinvar). Exposition-Phoenix.

Mississippi: Trusts. 8.50 o.p. (ISBN 0-686-90826-0). Am Law Inst.

Missouri. Dana F. Ross. 1985. lib. bdg. 14.95 o.s.i. (ISBN 0-8161-3891-5, Large Print Bks). G K Hall.

Missouri. Stanley Vestal. LC 44-5196. (Illus.). viii, 368p. 1964. pap. 9.95 o.p. (ISBN 0-8032-5207-2, BB 186, Bison). U of Nebr Pr.

Missouri Business Directory, 1988. rev. ed. American Directory Publishing Co., Inc. Staff. 1577p. 1987. pap. 95.00 o.s.i. (ISBN 0-944316-15-8). Amer Directory.

Missouri: Conflict of Laws. 8.50 o.p. (ISBN 0-686-90828-7). Am Law Inst.

Missouri: Contracts. 9.50 o.p. (ISBN 0-686-90829-5). Am Law Inst.

Missouri Criminal Law Handbook. Dee Wampler. (Illus.). 1978. 12.50 o.p. (ISBN 0-686-67703-X). Exposition-Phoenix.

Missouri in the Federal System. Stephen Chen. LC 80-54752. (Illus.). 234p. (Orig.). 1981. lib. bdg. 30.00 o.p. (ISBN 0-8191-1720-X); pap. text ed. 13.00 o.p. (ISBN 0-8191-1721-8). U Pr of Amer.

Missouri Leasing Guide for Nonlawyers. Theodore H. Hellmuth. 204p. 1985. binder 34.50 o.p. (ISBN 0-934055-25-4). Statelaw Guides.

Missouri Manufacturers Register, 1988. 360p. 1987. 75.00 o.p. (ISBN 0-318-22808-4). Manufacturers.

Missouri: Restitution. 8.50 o.p. (ISBN 0-686-90831-7). Am Law Inst.

Missouri: Torts, Vols. 3-4. 8.50 o.p. (ISBN 0-686-90833-3). Am Law Inst.

Missouri: Trusts. 9.00 o.p. (ISBN 0-686-90835-X). Am Law Inst.

Missouri under Radical Rule, 1865-1870. William E. Parrish. LC 65-21794. 397p. 1965. 39.00x o.p. (ISBN 0-8262-0043-5). U of Mo Pr.

Missy & the Duke: Missy y el Duque. Fred Crump, Jr. Tr. by Horst Woyde. (Eng. & Span.). (gr. 3-7). 1977. 7.50 o.p. (ISBN 0-87917-058-1). Ethridge.

Mistakable French: A Dictionary of Words & Phrases Easily Confused. Philip Thody & Howard Evans. 256p. 1985. 19.95 o.s.i. (ISBN 0-684-18324-2, ScribT). Scribner.

Mistaken Identity: Arab Stereotypes In Popular Writing. Janice J. Terry. LC 85-72494. 135p. 1985. pap. 9.95 o.p. (ISBN 0-943182-02-6). Am Arab Affairs.

Mr. American. George M. Fraser. 1981. 16.95 o.p. (ISBN 0-671-42571-4). S&S.

Mr. Billiwicket's Burro: Ten Stories. Margaret S. Decker. (Illus.). (gr. 1-3). 1980. 5.00 o.p. (ISBN 0-682-49565-4). Exposition-Phoenix.

Mr. Bliss. J. R. R. Tolkien. 1983. 11.45 o.p. (ISBN 0-395-32936-1). HM.

Mr. Bumba & the Orange Grove. Pearl A. Harwood. LC 64-19773. (Mr. Bumba Bks.). (Illus.). (gr. k-3). 1964. PLB 3.95 o.p. (ISBN 0-8225-0104-X). Lerner Pubns.

Mr. Charley Cruising Telegraph Avenue. (ISBN 0-87905-261-9). Gibbs Smith Pub.

Mr. Chill. Barbara Dillon. LC 85-3107. (Illus.). 96p. (gr. 2-5). 1985. 10.25 o.p. (ISBN 0-688-04980-X, Morrow Junior Books); lib. bdg. 10.88 o.p. (ISBN 0-688-04981-8). Morrow.

Mr. Computer. Ronda Rasmussen & Richard M. Rasmussen. (Illus.). 12p. (ps-2). pap. 1.75 o.p. (ISBN 0-932967-08-6). Pacific Shoreline.

Mr. Daydream. Roger Hargreaves. (Mr. Bks.). 32p. (ps up). 1982. PLB 6.95 o.p. (ISBN 0-87191-905-2). Creative Ed.

Mr. Daydream. Roger Hargreaves. (Mr. Bks.). (Illus.). 32p. Date not set. PLB 7.95 o.p. Creative Ed.

Mr. Ferdinand Fisk, Cat Detective. Tony Linsell. LC 79-12422. (Illus.). (gr. k-3). 1979. text ed. 6.95 o.p. (ISBN 0-07-037950-5). McGraw.

Mister God, This Is Anna. Fynn. 192p. 1985. pap. 3.50 o.p. (ISBN 0-345-32722-5). Ballantine.

Mr. H in America: Anonymus Redivivus. Wallace Nethery. i, 21p. 1981. leatherette 12.50 o.p. (ISBN 0-317-11692-4). Dawsons.

Mr. Halley's Comet. Sky & Telescope Editors. LC 84-52261. (Illus.). 32p. (Orig.). 1984. saddle stitch 2.00 o.p. (ISBN 0-933346-41-7). Sky Pub.

Mr. Humanity. Albert D. Stave. 256p. 1983. 12.00 o.p. (ISBN 0-682-49993-5). Exposition-Phoenix.

Mr. Jack & Big Ed. Jack D'Ambrosio. 1977. 8.95 o.p. (ISBN 0-682-48729-5). Exposition-Phoenix.

Mr. Jack & the Greenstalks. Gene Horowitz. 1970. 5.95 o.p. (ISBN 0-393-08593-7). Norton.

Mr. Jackson's Mushrooms. H. A. Jackson. Intro. by Mimi Cazort. (Illus.). 1979. 35.00 o.s.i. (ISBN 0-88884-364-X, 56430-4, Pub. by Natl Gallery Canada). U of Chicago Pr.

Mr. Jacobson's War. Richard Hammer. LC 80-8750. 1981. 10.95 o.p. (ISBN 0-15-162828-9). HarBraceJ.

Mister Jensen & Cat. Lenore Blegvad & Erik Blegvad. LC 65-17987. (Illus.). (gr. 1-3). 1965. 4.50 o.p. (ISBN 0-15-256214-1, HJ). HarBraceJ.

Mr. Kipling's Army. Byron Farwell. (Illus.). 1981. 13.95 o.p. (ISBN 0-393-01386-3). Norton.

Mr. Law's Unlawfulness of the Stage Entertainment Examin'd. S. Philomusus. Bd. with Entertainment of the Stage; Some Few Hints in Defence of Dramatical Entertainments. Allan Ramsay. (English Stage Ser.: Vol. 50). lib. bdg. 55.00 o.p. (ISBN 0-8240-0633-X). Garland Pub.

Mr. Lincoln's Camera Man: Matthew B. Brady. 2nd, rev. ed. Roy Meredith. (Illus.). 18.00 o.p. (ISBN 0-8446-5224-5). Peter Smith.

Mr. Lincoln's Military Railroads: A Pictorial History of the United States Civil War Railroads. Roy Meredith & Arthur Meredith. (Illus.). 1979. 18.95 o.p. (ISBN 0-393-05703-8). Norton.

Mr. Magus Is Waiting for You. Gene Kemp. (Illus.). 144p. (gr. 5-8). 1987. 12.95 o.p. (ISBN 0-571-14686-4); pap. 4.95 o.p. (ISBN 0-571-14687-2). Faber & Faber.

Mr. Marley's Main Street Confectionery. John J. Loeper. LC 79-10549. (Illus.). (gr. 4-6). 1979. 6.95 o.p. (ISBN 0-689-30716-0, Atheneum). Macmillan.

Mr. Menu. Luis Garcia. (Illus.). 60p. 1968. 5.00 o.p. Kayak.

Mr. Merlin: Episode No. 2. William Rotsler. 160p. (gr. 3-7). 1981. pap. 2.95 o.s.i. (ISBN 0-671-44480-8). Wanderer Bks.

Mr. Miller the Dog. Helme Heine. LC 80-81298. (Illus.). 64p. (gr. 1 up). 1980. 8.95 o.p. (ISBN 0-689-50174-9, Atheneum). Macmillan.

Mr. Moto Is So Sorry. John P. Marquand. LC 85-7070. 1986. pap. 3.95 o.p. (ISBN 0-316-54702-6). Little.

Mr. Noisy. Roger Hargreaves. (Mr. Bks.). 32p. (ps up). 1980. PLB 6.95 o.p. (ISBN 0-87191-762-9). Creative Ed.

Mr. Noisy. Roger Hargreaves. (Mr. Bks.). (Illus.). 32p. Date not set. PLB 7.95 o.p. Creative Ed.

Mr. O'Malley & the Haunted House. Crockett Johnson. 224p. 1985. pap. 2.95 o.s.i. (ISBN 0-345-32674-1, Del Rey). Ballantine.

Mr. O'Malley Goes for the Gold. Crockett Johnson. (Barnaby Ser.: No. 4). 224p. 1986. pap. 2.95 o.s.i. (ISBN 0-345-32880-9, Del Rey). Ballantine.

Mr. O'Malley, Wizard of Wall Street. Crockett Johnson. 1986. pap. 2.95 o.s.i. (ISBN 0-345-32881-7, Del Rey). Ballantine.

Mister Roberts. Thomas Heggen. 7.95 o.p. (ISBN 0-395-07788-5). HM.

Mister Rogers: Good Neighbor to America's Children. Anthony DiFranco & JoAnn DiFranco. LC 82-14986. (Taking Part Ser.). (Illus.). 48p. (gr. 3 up). 1983. PLB 9.95 o.p. Dillon.

Mr. Romance's Book of Love: Passionate Secrets of America's Greatest Lovers. Langdon Hill. LC 86-82239. 160p. 1987. 12.95 o.p. (ISBN 0-89586-494-0). Price Stern.

Mr. Rumpletop's Gift. Peg Roberts. LC 82-71439. (ps-2). 1984. 5.95 o.p. (ISBN 0-8054-4161-1, 4241-61). Broadman.

Mr. Rusty's New House. (Tales from Fern Hollow Ser.). (Illus.). 22p. (ps-1). 1985. 1.98 o.p. (ISBN 0-517-42787-7). Outlet Bk Co.

Mr. Single Shot's Gunsmithing-Idea Book. Frank De Haas. (Illus.). 176p. (Orig.). 1983. 18.95 o.p. (ISBN 0-8306-0111-2); pap. 13.50 o.p. (ISBN 0-8306-1511-3, 1511). TAB Bks.

Mr. Skinner's Skinny House. Ann McGovern. LC 79-18360. (Illus.). 48p. (gr. k-3). 1980. 8.95 o.s.i. (ISBN 0-02-765730-2, Four Winds). Macmillan.

Mr. Sponge's Sporting Tour. R. S. Surtees. Ed. by Virginia Blain. (Victorian Texts Ser.: No. VI). (Illus.). 483p. 1982. text ed. 27.95x o.p. (ISBN 0-7022-1419-1); pap. text ed. 15.95x o.p. (ISBN 0-7022-1514-7). U of Queensland Pr.

Mr. Squint. Jenny Partridge. LC 81-7065. (Oakapple Wood Stories Ser.). (Illus.). 32p. (gr. k-2). 1982. 4.95 o.p. (ISBN 0-03-061509-7). H Holt & Co.

Mr. Stubbs: Horsepainter. Constance-Anne Parker. (Illus.). 24.50 o.p. (ISBN 0-85131-123-7, Pub. by J A Allen U K). S R Smith Sporting Bks.

Mr. Terwillger's Secret. Dave Wilson & Jeanne Wilson. LC 80-21835. (Easy-Read Story Bks.). (gr. k-3). 1979. 10.40 o.p. (ISBN 0-531-04191-3). Watts.

Mr. Twigg's Mistake. Robert Lawson. (Illus.). 144p. (gr. 3-6). 1985. pap. 4.95 o.p. (ISBN 0-316-51752-6). Little.

Mr. Typewriter. Arthur T. Foulke. 1975. 6.95 o.p. (ISBN 0-8158-0094-0). Chris Mass.

Mr. Wheatfield's Loft. Isabel L. Cusack. LC 79-984. (Illus.). 96p. (gr. 4-8). 1981. 9.95 o.s.i. (ISBN 0-03-049581-4). H Holt & Co.

Mister White Eyes. Herbert Gold. 241p. 1984. 16.95 o.p. (ISBN 0-87795-636-7, Arbor Hse). Morrow.

Mr. Wigley Cums. Philip L. Sherrod. 26p. (Orig.). 1983. pap. 7.95 o.s.i. (ISBN 0-939826-00-3). Carrousel Pubns.

Mr. William Prynn-His Defence of Stage-Plays: Retraction of a Former Book of His Called 'Histrio-Mastix' Bd. with Vindication of William Prynne. William Prynne; Theatrum Redivivum: In Answer to Mr. Pryn's Histrio-Mastix. Sir Richard Baker. (English Stage Ser.: Vol. 15). lib. bdg. 55.00 o.p. (ISBN 0-8240-0598-8). Garland Pub.

Mr. Yesterday. Elliott Chaze. 184p. 1984. 12.95 o.s.i. (ISBN 0-684-18115-0, ScribT). Scribner.

Mr. Yowder & the Windwagon. Glen Rounds. LC 83-6183. 48p. (gr. 3-6). 1983. 8.95 o.p. (ISBN 0-8234-0499-4). Holiday.

Misterioso Viaje a la Eternidad. Albert Pavlic. 1978. 4.50 o.p. (ISBN 0-682-49059-8). Exposition-Phoenix.

Mistress. Photos by Jean-Francois Jonvelle. 1984. 22.95 o.p. (ISBN 0-394-53687-8, GP 910). Grove.

Mistress Devon. Virginia Coffman. LC 72-82177. 1972. 5.95 o.p. (ISBN 0-87795-044-X, Arbor Hse). Morrow.

Mistress Nancy. Barbara Bentley. LC 80-14264. 384p. 1980. text ed. 12.95 o.p. (ISBN 0-07-016722-2). McGraw.

Mistress Nancy. Barbara Bentley. 368p. 1982. pap. 3.50 o.p. (ISBN 0-380-56895-0, 56895-0). Avon.

Mistress of the Sun King. Sandra DuBay. (Orig.). 1980. pap. 2.25 o.p. (ISBN 0-505-51495-8, Pub. by Tower Bks). Dorchester Pub Co.

Mists of Avalon. Marion Zimmer Bradley. Date not set. price not set o.p. Dell.

Mists of Manittoo. Lois Swann. 464p. 1977. pap. 2.95 o.p. (ISBN 0-380-01690-7). Avon.

Misty Isles-Here, There, Nowhere Land. Elizabeth Allen. (Illus.). 1981. 4.50 o.p. (ISBN 0-682-48953-0). Exposition-Phoenix.

Misty Meadows. Marjorie K. Lawrence. 96p. 1981. 6.00 o.p. (ISBN 0-682-49742-8). Exposition-Phoenix.

Misunderstandings of the Self: Cognitive Psychotherapy & the Misconception Hypothesis. Victor Raimy. LC 74-28917. (Social & Behavioral Science Ser.). 1975. 28.95x o.p. (ISBN 0-87589-251-5). Jossey-Bass.

Misunderstood Child: A Guide for Parents of Learning-Disabled Children. Larry B. Silver. 214p. 1984. text ed. 14.95 o.p. (ISBN 0-07-057301-8). McGraw.

Misunderstood Male. Walter Rickell. (Illus.). 64p. 4.00 o.p. (ISBN 0-318-12502-1). Am Donkey.

Misuse of Drugs - Supplement 1. P. Bucknell & H. Ghodse. (Criminal Law Library). 128p. 1986. pap. 8.25 o.p. (ISBN 0-08-033081-9, Pub. by Waterlow). Pergamon.

Misuse of Drugs & the Law. P. Bucknell. (Library of Criminal Law Ser.). 352p. 1986. 49.00 o.s.i. (ISBN 0-08-039203-2). Pergamon.

Mitchell (The All-Around Good Guy) Brian Jim. 32p. 1988. 6.95 o.p. (ISBN 0-8062-3029-0). Carlton.

Mitochandria. Bernard Tandler & Charles L. Hoppel. (Monographs on the Ultrastructure of Cells & Organisms). 1972. 32.00 o.p. (ISBN 0-12-454143-7). Acad Pr.

Mitochondria, Structure & Function. Ed. by L. Ernster & L. Ernster. 1970. 75.00 o.p. (ISBN 0-12-241250-8). Acad Pr.

Mitosis & Meiosis. 2nd ed. Gary E. Parker et al. (EMI Programmed Biology Ser.). (Illus.). (gr. 9 up). 1979. pap. 6.95 o.s.i. (ISBN 0-88462-010-7, 3304-09, Ed Methods). Longman Finan.

Mitral Valve: A Pluridisciplinary Approach. Ed. by Daniel Kalmanson. LC 75-17444. (Illus.). 598p. 1976. 30.00 o.p. (ISBN 0-88416-116-1). Year Bk Med.

Mitteilungen Ueber Die Besiedelung Des Kilimandscharo. Johannes Schanz. Repr. of 1913 ed. 15.00 o.p. (ISBN 0-384-53540-2). Johnson Repr.

Mittelhochdeutsche Vovelle Vom Studentenabrnteuer. Wilhelm Stehmann. (Ger). 27.00 o.p. (ISBN 0-685-02171-8); pap. 22.00 o.p. (ISBN 0-384-57780-6). Johnson Repr.

Mittelkettige Triglyzeride in der Parenteralen Ernaehrung. Ed. by W. Creutzfeldt & P. Schauder. (Beitraege zu Infusionstherapie und Klinische Ernaehrung Ser.: Vol. 20). (Illus.). viii, 198p. 1988. 39.50 o.p. (ISBN 3-8055-4741-2). S Karger.

Mitternachzeitung Fuer Gebildete Stand, Vol 11, Nos 1-212. Ed. by Edward Brinckmeyer. 1973. Repr. of 1836 ed. 155.00 o.p. (ISBN 0-384-39224-5). Johnson Repr.

Mix Design for Asphalt Concrete & Other Hot-Mix Types. (Illus.). 112p. 1984. 9.00 o.p. (ISBN 0-318-13394-6, MS-2). Asphalt Inst.

Mix Me a Person. Carol Weiser et al. LC 74-80418. (Center Enrichment Bks). (Illus.). 72p. 1975. pap. 0.50 o.p. (ISBN 0-8006-5078-6, Fortress). Augsburg Fortress.

Mix 'n Match. Eugenie B. Smith. LC 85-91012. 160p. 1985. 10.00 o.p. (ISBN 0-682-40274-5). Exposition-Phoenix.

Mixed Boundary Value Problems of Plane Anisotropic Bodies. CISM (International Center for Mechanical Sciences), Dept. for Mechanics of Deformable Bodies, 1969. (CISM International Center for Mechanical Sciences Ser.: No. 16). 45p. 1975. pap. 7.20 o.p. (ISBN 0-387-81306-3). Springer-Verlag.

Mixed Company: Women in the Modern Army. Helen Rogan. LC 82-70570. 334p. 1982. pap. 9.95 o.p. (ISBN 0-8070-6707-5, BP642). Beacon Pr.

Mixed Cranial Nerves. Marshall B. Craigmyle. LC 84-29097. 103p. 1985. pap. 13.00 o.p. (ISBN 0-471-90699-9, Dist. by A R Liss). Wiley.

Mixed Gas Blowing in Steelmaking. 133p. 1982. pap. text ed. 28.00 o.p. (ISBN 0-89520-152-6). Iron & Steel.

Mixed-Longitudinal, Interdisciplinary Study of Growth & Development. Ed. by B. Prahl-Andersen & Charles J. Kowalski. LC 78-3346. 1979. 72.50 o.p. (ISBN 0-12-563350-5). Acad Pr.

Mixed-Use Development Projects in North America: Project Profiles. J. Thomas Black et al. LC 82-84338. 70p. (Orig.). 1982. pap. 40.00 o.p. (ISBN 0-87420-618-9, M19). Urban Land.

Mixing of Particulate Solids. Institution of Chemical Engineers Staff. 1982. 58.00 o.s.i. (ISBN 0-08-028763-8). Pergamon.

Miz Lucretia of Falconhurst. Ashley Carter. 320p. (Orig.). 1986. pap. 3.95 o.s.i. (ISBN 0-449-12767-2, GM). Fawcett.

MLA Directory of Periodicals: A Guide to Journals & Series in Languages & Literature; 1984-85 Edition. 720p. 1984. 90.00 o.p. (ISBN 0-87352-442-X). Modern Lang.

MLA Directory of Periodicals: A Guide to Journals & Series in Languages & Literatures, 1986-1987. 750p. 1986. 100.00 o.p. (ISBN 0-87352-453-5). Modern Lang.

MLA Directory of Periodicals: A Guide to Journals & Series in Languages & Literatures - Periodicals Published in the United States & Canada, 1986-87. 300p. 1986. pap. 30.00x o.p. (ISBN 0-87352-454-3). Modern Lang.

MLA Handbook for Writers of Research Papers. 2nd ed. Joseph Gibaldi & Walter S. Achtert. LC 84-10819. 222p. 1984. pap. text ed. 8.75x o.p. (ISBN 0-87352-132-3). Modern Lang.

MLA Handbook for Writers of Research Papers, Theses & Dissertations. Joseph Gibaldi & Walter S. Achtert. LC 77-76954. 163p. (Orig.). 1977. 9.50 o.p. (ISBN 0-87352-450-0); pap. 6.75x o.p. (ISBN 0-87352-000-9). Modern Lang.

MMPI Codebook for Counselors. Lewis E. Drake & Eugene R. Oetting. LC 59-10187. 1959. 10.95 o.p. (ISBN 0-8166-0187-9). U of Minn Pr.

Mnemosyne: The Parallel Between Literature & the Visual Arts. Mario Praz. LC 68-20876. (Bollingen Ser.: Vol. 35). (Illus., A. w. mellon lecture no. 16). 1970. 33.50x o.p. (ISBN 0-691-09857-3); pap. 13.95 o.p. (ISBN 0-691-01803-0). Princeton U Pr.

Mnl Micro TSP UPG Pk. (ISBN 0-07-852210-2). McGraw.

Mobil Major Cities Guide 1988. 1988. 8.95 o.p. (ISBN 0-317-69781-1). Prentice Hall Pr.

Mobil Travel Guide Lodgings for Less: South. (Mobil Travel Guide Lodgings for Less). (Illus.). 1988. pap. 5.95 o.p. (ISBN 0-13-586520-4). Prentice Hall Pr.

Mobil Travel Guide Lodgings for Less: West. (Mobil Travel Guide Lodgings for Less). (Illus.). 250p. 1988. pap. 5.95 o.p. (ISBN 0-13-586538-7). Prentice Hall Pr.

Mobil Travel Guide Lodgings for Less (Northeast & Midwest) (Mobile Travel Guide Lodgings for Less). (Illus.). 1988. pap. 5.95 o.p. (ISBN 0-13-586512-3). Prentice Hall Pr.

Mobil Travel Guide, 1988: California & the West. (Mobil Travel Guide). (Illus.). 1988. pap. 8.95 o.p. (ISBN 0-13-586553-0). Prentice Hall Pr.

Mobil Travel Guide, 1988: Great Lakes Area. (Mobil Travel Guide). (Illus.). 1988. pap. 8.95 o.p. (ISBN 0-13-586561-1). Prentice Hall Pr.

Mobil Travel Guide, 1988: Major Cities. (Mobil Travel Guide). (Illus.). 1988. pap. 8.95 o.p. (ISBN 0-13-586579-4). Prentice Hall Pr.

Mobil Travel Guide, 1988: Middle Atlantic States. (Mobil Travel Guide). (Illus.). 1988. pap. 8.95 o.p. (ISBN 0-13-586587-5). Prentice Hall Pr.

Mobil Travel Guide, 1988: Northeastern States. (Mobil Travel Guide). (Illus.). 1988. pap. 8.95 o.p. (ISBN 0-13-586595-6). Prentice Hall Pr.

Mobil Travel Guide, 1988: Northwest & Great Plains States. (Mobil Travel Guide). (Illus.). 1988. pap. 8.95 o.p. (ISBN 0-13-586603-0). Prentice Hall Pr.

Mobil Travel Guide, 1988: Southeastern States. (Mobil Travel Guide). (Illus.). 1988. pap. 8.95 o.p. (ISBN 0-13-586611-1). Prentice Hall Pr.

Mobil Travel Guide, 1988: Southwest & South Central Area. (Mobil Travel Guide). (Illus.). 1988. pap. 8.95 o.p. (ISBN 0-13-586629-4). Prentice Hall Pr.

Mobile. Michel Butor. 16.50 o.p. (ISBN 0-685-37254-5). Schoenhof.

Mobile Carnival: Mardi Gras History 1947, Vol. 1 No. 1. Alfred Staples. Ed. by Cameron Plummer. (Illus.). (YA) (gr. 7 up). 1947. pap. o.p. (ISBN 0-940882-04-3). HB Pubns.

Mobile Communications. 2nd ed. William G. Duff. (Illus.). 296p. 1980. text ed. 43.00 o.p. (ISBN 0-932263-09-7). White Consult.

Mobile Home Parks: Part Two, An Analysis of Communities. Robinson Newcomb & Max S. Wherly. (Technical Bulletin Ser.: 68). 136p. 1972. 10.50 o.p. (ISBN 0-317-14551-7, M10); 8.00 o.p. (ISBN 0-317-14552-5). Urban Land.

Mobile Homes, 2 pts. Max Wehrly. LC 72-79132. (Illus.). 80p. 1972. Set. pap. 5.00, Pt. II (Pt. I out of print) o.p. (ISBN 0-87420-068-7). An Analysis Of Characteristics. An Analysis Of Communities. Urban Land.

Mobile Manager. Eugene E. Jennings. LC 67-65498. 1971. pap. text ed. 5.95 o.p. (ISBN 0-07-032450-6). McGraw.

Mobile Radio Systems & Techniques. (IEE Conference Publications Ser.: No. 238). 229p. 1984. pap. 80.00 o.s.i. (ISBN 0-85296-297-5, IC238). Inst Elect Eng.

Mobile Retirement Handbook: A Complete Guide to Living & Traveling in an RV. Jurgen Hesse. (Illus.). 240p. (Orig.). 1987. pap. 9.95 o.p. (ISBN 0-88908-663-X, 9557P). ISC Pr.

Mobile Suit Gundam T.V. Storybook, Vols. 3&4. (Illus.). 1984. 8.95 ea. o.p. Bks Nippan.

Mobile: West Florida to Alabama. Marion T. Gaines. (Illus.). 64p. 1952. o.p. (ISBN 0-940882-07-8). HB Pubns.

Mobility & Diffusion of Ions in Gases. Earl W. McDaniel. LC 72-13414. 372p. 1973. 37.50 o.p. (ISBN 0-471-58387-1, Pub. by Wiley). Krieger.

Mobility & Sedentism: The Navajo of Black Mesa Arizona. Belinda Blomberg. LC 82-72265. (Research Paper: No. 32). (Illus.). vii, 66p. 1983. softcover 12.40 o.p. (ISBN 0-88104-002-9). Center Archaeo.

Mobilization & Reassembly of Genetic Information: Vol. 17 of the Miami Winter Symposia. Ed. by Walter A. Scott et al. LC 80-18845. 1980. 65.50 o.p. (ISBN 0-12-633360-2). Acad Pr.

Mobilizing & Managing Economic Resources for Local Institutional Development. Rebecca M. Doan et al. (Special Series on Local Institutional Development: No. 8). 59p. (Orig.). 1985. pap. text ed. 6.25 o.p. (ISBN 0-86731-115-0). Cornell CIS RDC.

Mobilizing Renewable Energy Technology in Developing Countries: Strengthening Local Capabilities & Research. 52p. 1981. 5.00 o.p. (ISBN 0-686-36154-7, BK9431). World Bank.

Moby Dick & Calvinism: A World Dismantled. T. Walter Herbert, Jr. 1977. 27.00x o.p. (ISBN 0-8135-0829-0). Rutgers U Pr.

Moby Dick by Herman Melville. 48p. (Orig.). 1988. pap. 9.95 o.p. (ISBN 1-55651-577-4); cassette o.p. (ISBN 1-55651-578-2). Cram Cassettes.

Moby Dick Centennial Essays. Ed. by Tyrus Hillway & Luther S. Mansfield. LC 53-12917. 1965. 13.95x o.p. (ISBN 0-87074-078-4, X1953). SMU Press.

Moby Dick, or the Whale. new ed. Herman Melville. Ed. by Harrison Hayford & Hershel Parker. (Illus.). 1976. 14.95 o.p. (ISBN 0-393-04402-5). Norton.

Moby's Textbook for Nursing Assistants. Sorrentino. 1984. 23.95 o.p. (ISBN 0-8016-4717-7); incl. wkbk 23.95 o.p. (ISBN 0-8016-4759-2). Mosby.

Moccasin Bend, Chattanooga, Tennessee. (Panel Advisory Service Report Ser.). 70p. 1982. pap. 10.00 o.p. (ISBN 0-317-06738-9, C-23). Urban Land.

Moccasin Tracks & Other Imprints. William Dodrill. 1974. Repr. of 1915 ed. 16.00 o.p. (ISBN 0-87012-157-X). McClain.

Mod-4. Jack Klein. 218p. (Orig.). 1984. pap. text ed. 9.95 o.p. (ISBN 0-930615-00-X). Crest Sftware.

Mode Illustration. Ed. by Graphic-Sha Staff. (Illus.). 171p. 1986. pap. 25.00 o.p. (ISBN 0-8161-8815-7, Pub. by Graphic-Sha Pub Co Ltd Japan). G K Hall.

Model A Ford: Care & Maintenance of Automobiles & Trucks. Victor W. Page. (Illus.). 1948. pap. 4.00 o.p. (ISBN 0-89287-264-0, H524). Clymer Pub.

Model A Ford Restoration Handbook. Gordon E. Hopper. Ed. by Clymer Publications. (Illus.). pap. 6.00 o.p. (ISBN 0-89287-263-2, H523). Clymer Pub.

Model Analysis of Plane Structures. T. M. Charlton. 1966. 9.90 o.p. (ISBN 0-08-011304-4); pap. text ed. 6.00 o.p. (ISBN 0-08-011303-6). Pergamon.

Model Code of Safe Practice, Pt. 12: Pressure Vessel Inspection Safety Code, Pt. 12. Institute of Petroleum Staff. 32p. 1976. 48.95x o.p. (ISBN 0-471-25785-0, Wiley Heyden). Wiley.

Model Code of Safe Practices for the Petroleum Industry: The Petroleum Pipeline, Pt. 6. Institute of Petroleum Staff. LC 82-20211. (Proceedings of the Institute of Petroleum(IP) Series). 1982. 59.95 o.p. (ISBN 0-471-26139-4, Pub. by Wiley Interscience). Wiley.

Model Code of Safety Regulations (Ionising Radiations) see Manual of Industrial Radiation Protection.

Model Company Town: Urban Design Through Private Enterprise in Nineteenth-Century New England. John S. Garner. LC 84-8636. (Illus.). 304p. 1985. lib. bdg. 27.50x o.p. (ISBN 0-87023-442-0). U of Mass Pr.

Model Correctional Rules & Regulations. rev. ed. American Correctional Association Staff. 50p. 1979. pap. 4.50 o.p. (ISBN 0-942974-13-1). Am Correctional.

Model Curriculum for Group Practice Administration. 237p. 1979. 10.00 o.p. (ISBN 0-317-34842-6, 50-0000-913). Med Group Mgmt.

Model Fighter Planes. Ed Radlauer. LC 82-17805. (Model Bks.). (Illus.). 48p. (gr. 3 up). 1983. PLB 11.93 o.p. (ISBN 0-516-08010-5); pap. 2.95 o.p. (ISBN 0-516-48010-3). Childrens.

Model for Christian Wholeness. Dan Ivins. LC 84-9436. 1985. pap. 4.25 o.p. (ISBN 0-8054-2252-8). Broadman.

Model for Planning & Managing National Parks. Lawrence Prosser. 456p. 1977. 3 ring bdr. 15.00 o.p. (ISBN 0-943272-12-2). Inst Recreation Res.

Model for Theses & Research Papers. Stephen V. Ballou. LC 72-125125. (Illus., Orig.). 1970. pap. 8.95 o.p. (ISBN 0-395-10806-3, 3-02700). HM.

Model of Simple Competition. Joel E. Cohen. LC 66-23470. (Annals of the Computation Laboratory). (Illus.). 138p. 1966. 12.00x o.s.i. (ISBN 0-674-57800-7). Harvard U Pr.

Model State Policy, Legislation & State Plan Toward the Education of Gifted & Talented Students: A Handbook for State & Local Districts. John A. Grossi. 224p. (Orig.). 1980. pap. 14.95 o.p. (ISBN 0-86586-101-3). Coun Exc Child.

Model Subdivision Regulations: Text & Commentary. Robert H. Freilich & Peter S. Levi. 190p. 1975. pap. 10.95 o.p. (ISBN 0-318-13031-9); pap. 9.95 members o.p. (ISBN 0-318-13032-7). Am Plan Assn.

Model T Days: Florida or Bust. Carl King. 1983. 12.95 o.s.i. (ISBN 0-932298-37-0). Tri-State Pr Corp.

Model T Ford Restoration Handbook. Leslie R. Henry. Ed. by Clymer Publications. pap. 6.00 o.p. (ISBN 0-89287-256-X, H506). Clymer Pub.

Model T Memories. Les Henry. Ed. by Clymer Publications. (Illus.). pap. 5.00 o.p. (ISBN 0-89287-257-8, H507). Clymer Pub.

Model Theoretic Algebra Selected Topics. G. Cherlin. LC 76-15388. (Lecture Notes in Mathematics Ser.: Vol. 521). 1976. pap. 16.00 o.p. (ISBN 0-387-07696-4). Springer-Verlag.

Model Theory & Topoi. Ed. by C. Maurer & G. C. Wraith. (Lecture Notes in Mathematics Ser). 354p. 1975. pap. 20.00 o.p. (ISBN 0-387-07164-4). Springer-Verlag.

Model Theory of Algebra & Arithmetics. Ed. by L. Pacholski et al. (Lecture Notes in Mathematics Ser.: Vol. 834). 410p. 1980. pap. 28.00 o.p. (ISBN 0-387-10269-8). Springer-Verlag.

Model Trucks. Ed Radlauer. LC 82-17852. (Model Bks.). (Illus.). 48p. (gr. 3 up). 1983. PLB 11.93 o.p. (ISBN 0-516-08011-3); pap. 2.95 o.p. (ISBN 0-516-48011-1). Childrens.

Model Warships. Ed Radlauer. LC 83-21035. (Model Bks.). (Illus.). 48p. (gr. 3 up). 1984. lib. bdg. 11.93 o.p. (ISBN 0-516-08013-X). Childrens.

Model 100 Book: A Guide to Portable Computing. Jonathan Erickson & Robert Sayre. 380p. (Orig.). 1984. pap. text ed. 17.95 o.p. (ISBN 0-07-881124-4). Osborne-McGraw.

Titles

Model 100 Companion: Business & Entertainment Programs for Portable Computing. Ed. by Osborne-McGraw-Hill Editors. 150p. (Orig.). 1984. pap. text ed. 16.95 o.p. (ISBN 0-07-881122-8). Osborne-McGraw.

Modeling an Ocean Pond. H. P. Wang. 58p. 1975. 10.00 o.p. (P454). Sea Grant Pubns.

Modeling & Control of Electric Power Plants: Proceedings of the IFAC Workshop, Como, Italy, 22-23 September 1983. Ed. by C. Maffezzoni. (IFAC Publication Ser.). 176p. 1984. 56.00 o.p. (ISBN 0-08-031163-6). Pergamon.

Modeling & Stimulation: Proceedings of the Annual Pittsburgh Conference, Vol. 15. Instrument Society of America Staff & University of Pittsburgh Staff. 2090p. 1984. pap. 275.00 o.p. (ISBN 0-317-17617-X); pap. 220.00 member o.p. (ISBN 0-317-17618-8). Instru Soc.

Modeling Cajon. Peter Youngblood. Ed. by Mac Sebree. (Trans Anglo Bks.). (Illus.). 72p. 1985. pap. 9.95 o.p. (ISBN 0-87046-073-0). Interurban.

Modeling Crop Responses to Irrigation in Relation to Soils, Climate & Salinity. R. J. Hanks & R. W. Hill. (IIIC Publication: No. 4). 71p. 1981. text ed. 26.00 o.p. (ISBN 0-08-025513-2); pap. text ed. 21.00 o.p. (ISBN 0-08-030762-0). Pergamon.

Modeling of Casting & Welding Processes: Proceedings, Rindge, New Hampshire, 1980. Ed. by D. Apelian & H. Brody. (Illus.). 540p. 40.00 o.p. (ISBN 0-89520-380-4); members 25.00 o.p. (ISBN 0-317-36252-6); student members 14.00 o.p. (ISBN 0-317-36253-4). ASM.

Modeling of Large-scale Energy Systems: Proceedings of the IIASA-IFAC Symposium, Laxenburg, Austria, Feb. 25-29, 1980, Vol. 11. Ed. by W. Hafele & L. K. Kirchmayer. LC 80-41554. (IIASA Proceedings Ser.: Vol 11). 350p. 1981. 120.00 o.p. (ISBN 0-08-025696-1). Pergamon.

Modeling State Growth: New Jersey Nineteen Eighty. Franklin J. James & James W. Hughes. 300p. 1974. (ISBN 0-87855-125-5). Transaction Pubs.

Modeling Wastewater Renovation: Land Treatment. Ed. by I. K. Iskandar. LC 80-39879. (Environmental Science & Technology: a Wiley-Interscience Series of Texts & Monographs). 802p. 1981. 110.00x o.p. (ISBN 0-471-08128-0, Pub. by Wiley-Interscience). Wiley.

Modelling. J. N. Jeffers. (Outline Studies in Ecology). 1982. pap. 8.50 o.p. (ISBN 0-412-24360-1, NO. 6736, Pub. by Chapman & Hall). Routledge Chapman & Hall.

Modelling & Control of Biotechnical Processes: Proceedings of the Symposium, 1st, Helsink, Finland, Aug., 1982. IFAC Symposium Staff & A. Halme. (IFAC Proceedings Ser.). 296p. 1983. 83.00 o.p. (ISBN 0-08-029978-4). Pergamon.

Modelling & Control of Biotechnological Processes: Proceedings of the 1st IFAC Symposium, Noorwijkerhout, The Netherlands, 11-13 December 1985. A. Johnson. (Illus.). 286p. 1986. 80.00 o.p. (ISBN 0-08-032565-3, PBL). Pergamon.

Modelling & Identification of Distributed Parameter Systems: IFIP Working Conference, Rome Italy, June 21-24,1976. Ed. by A. Ruberti. (Lecture Notes in Control & Information Sciences: Vol. 1). 1978. pap. text ed. 25.00 o.p. (ISBN 0-387-08405-3). Springer-Verlag.

Modelling & Optimization of Complex Systems: Proceedings of the IFIP-TC Working Conference, 7th, Novosibirsk, U.S.S.R., July 3-9, 1978. IFIP-TC Working Conference Staff. Ed. by G. I. Marchuk. (Lecture Notes in Control & Information Science: Vol. 18). 1979. pap. 19.00 o.p. (ISBN 0-387-09612-4). Springer-Verlag.

Modelling, Estimation & Control of the Soaking Pit: An Example of the Development & Application of Some Modern Control Techniques to Industrial Processes. Yong-Zai Lu & Theodore J. Williams. LC 83-101. 460p. 1983. text ed. 29.95x o.p. (ISBN 0-87664-740-9, 1740-9). Instru Soc.

Modelling Large Systems: Limits to Growth Revisited. Peter C. Roberts. LC 78-13339. (Orasa Text). 120p. 1978. pap. 29.95x o.p. (ISBN 0-470-26528-0). Halsted Pr.

Modelling Storage Systems. Mahadev Satyanarayanan. Ed. by Harold Stone. LC 86-1312. (Computer Science Ser.: Computer Architecture & Design: No. 5). 290p. 1986. 49.95 o.p. (ISBN 0-8357-1742-9). UMI Res Pr.

Models & Measurements of the Cardiac Electric Field. Ed. by E. Schubert. LC 82-5334. 242p. 1982. 55.00x o.p. (ISBN 0-306-41011-7, Plenum Pr). Plenum Pub.

Models & Metaphors: Studies in Language & Philosophy. Max Black. 278p. 1962. 27.50x o.p. (ISBN 0-8014-0041-4). Cornell U Pr.

Models for Composition. Allan A. Glatthorn & Harold Fleming. (Orig.). 1967. pap. text ed. 8.95 o.p. (ISBN 0-15-558875-3, HC). HarBraceJ.

Models for Optimal Investment & Maintenance Decisions. Birger Rapp. LC 74-25084. 461p. 1975. 62.95x o.p. (ISBN 0-470-70911-1). Halsted Pr.

Models in Geography. Ed. by Richard J. Chorley & Peter Haggett. 1967. 82.00x o.p. (ISBN 0-416-29020-5, NO. 2136). Routledge Chapman & Hall.

Models of America's Past & How to Make Them. C. J. Maginley. LC 69-17116. (Illus.). (gr. 4-7). 1969. 6.25 o.p. (ISBN 0-15-255051-8, HJ). HarBraceJ.

Models of Development: A Comparative Study of Economic Growth in South Korea & Taiwan. Ed. by Lawrence J. Lau. 217p. 1986. 29.95 o.p. (ISBN 0-917616-84-7); pap. 10.95 o.p. ICS Pr.

Models of Employment & Residence Location. Ed. by Franklin J. James. 352p. 1974. 8.95 o.p. (ISBN 0-87855-107-7). Transaction Pubs.

Models of Society: Class, Stratification & Gender in Australia & New Zealand. Frank Jones & Peter Davis. 208p. 1986. 29.00 o.p. (ISBN 0-949614-22-X, Pub. by Croom Helm UK). Routledge Chapman & Hall.

Models of the Atmosphere & Ionosphere: Proceedings of Workshops VIII & X of the COSPAR 25th Plenary Meeting held in Graz, Austria, 25 June-7 July 1984. Ed. by K. Rawer et al. (Illus.). 242p. 1985. pap. 54.00 o.p. (ISBN 0-08-033196-3, Pub. by PPL). Pergamon.

Models of the Nervous System. Deutsch. LC 67-26923. (Illus.). 266p. 1967. text ed. 18.50 o.p. (ISBN 0-471-21137-0, Pub. by Wiley). Krieger.

Models, Planning & Basic Needs: Conference on the Applicability of Global Modelling to Integrated Planning & Developing Countries. Ed. by Sam Cole. (Illus.). 1979. 44.00 o.p. (ISBN 0-08-023732-0). Pergamon.

Modern Abnormal Psychology. Miksell. (ISBN 0-8022-1115-1). Philos Lib.

Modern Accident Investigation & Analysis: An Executive Guide to Accident Investigation. Ted S. Ferry. LC 80-21046. 273p. 1981. 41.95x o.p. (ISBN 0-471-07776-3, Pub. by Wiley-Interscience). Wiley.

Modern Advanced Accounting. 2nd ed. Walter B. Meigs et al. 1979. text ed. 39.95x o.p. (ISBN 0-07-041201-4). McGraw.

Modern Algebra & Trigonometry. 2nd ed. J. Vincent Robison. (Illus.). 448p. 1972. text ed. 38.95 o.p. (ISBN 0-07-053330-X). McGraw.

Modern American & Modern British Poetry. Ed. by Louis Untermeyer. (Revised, shorter ed). 1955. text ed. 14.95 o.p. (ISBN 0-15-558970-9, HC). HarBraceJ.

Modern American English, 6 bks. Robert J. Dixson. Incl. Bk. 1 (ISBN 0-88345-111-5, 17980). wkbk. o.p. (ISBN 0-88345-105-0, 18001); Bk. 2 (ISBN 0-88345-112-3, 17981). wkbk. o.p. (ISBN 0-88345-106-9, 18002); Bk. 3 (ISBN 0-88345-113-1, 17982). wkbk. o.p. (ISBN 0-88345-107-7, 18003); Bk. 4. o.p. (ISBN 0-88345-114-X, 17983); Bk. 5 (ISBN 0-88345-115-8, 17984). wkbk. o.p. (ISBN 0-88345-109-3, 18005); Bk. 6 (ISBN 0-88345-116-6, 17985). wkbk. o.p. (ISBN 0-88345-110-7, 18006). (gr. 7 up). 1971. pap. text ed. 2.25 ea. o.p.; wkbks. 1.25 ea. o.p.; tapes 75.00 ea. o.p.; ea cassettes 75.00 o.p.; posters for bk.1 30.00 o.p. (ISBN 0-685-48103-4). Prentice ESL.

Modern American Graphic Designers: Thirty Years of Design Imagery. R. Siegel. 144p. 1985. pap. text ed. 26.50 o.p. (ISBN 0-07-057314-X). McGraw.

Modern American Poetry. enl. ed. Ed. by Louis Untermeyer. 1962. text ed. 11.95 o.p. (ISBN 0-15-559855-4, HC). HarBraceJ.

Modern American Soldier. Arnold Meisner & Lee Russell. (Uniforms Illustrated Ser.: No. 16). (Illus.). 72p. (Orig.). 1986. pap. 9.95 o.p. (ISBN 0-85368-762-5, Pub. by Arms & Armour). Sterling.

Modern & Modernism: The Sovereignty of the Artist 1885-1925. Frederick Karl. LC 84-45710. (Illus.). 320p. 1985. 30.00 o.p. (ISBN 0-689-11564-4, Atheneum). Macmillan.

Modern Applied Photography. G. A. Jones. (Illus.). 162p. 1957. (ISBN 0-8022-0813-4). Philos Lib.

Modern Archives & Manuscripts: A Select Bibliography. Compiled by Frank B. Evans. LC 75-23058. 209p. 1975. pap. 12.00 o.p. (ISBN 0-931828-03-1). Soc Am Archivists.

Modern Art from Post Impressionisms to the Present. 2nd ed. Sam Hunter & John Jacobus. LC 76-14611. (Illus.). 1985. 40.00 o.p. (ISBN 0-8109-1349-6). Abrams.

Modern Art-19th & 20th Century: Selected Papers, Vol. III. Meyer Schapiro. LC 78-6831. 1978. 20.00 o.p. (ISBN 0-8076-0899-8). Braziller.

Modern Asia Explained. W. R. MacAuliffe. (Illus.). 174p. 1953. (ISBN 0-8022-1008-2). Philos Lib.

Modern Aspects of Graphite Technology. L. C. Blackman. 1970. 52.50 o.p. (ISBN 0-12-103350-3). Acad Pr.

Modern Aspects of Manufacturing Management: Selected Readings, Vol. 3. Ed. by Ivan R. Vernon. LC 70-118841. (Manufacturing Management Ser). (Illus.). 1970. text ed. 11.75 o.p. (ISBN 0-87263-024-2). SME.

Modern Aspects of Medicine, Vol. 3, No. 5. Baum & I. Roman. (Illus.). 133p. 1980. pap. 14.50 o.p. (ISBN 0-08-027378-5). Pergamon.

Modern Atomic Physics: Quantum Theory & Its Application, Vol. 2. B. Cagnac & J. C. Pebay-Peyroula. LC 74-26875. 253p. 1975. 21.00 o.p. (ISBN 0-470-12921-2). Krieger.

Modern Austrian Literature: Special Issue. Ed. by Karl Kraus. (Journal of the International Arthur Schnitzler Research Association). 1977. pap. 7.50x o.p. (ISBN 0-685-55947-5). M S Rosenberg.

Modern Banking: A Practical Guide to Managing Deregulated Financial Institutions. Douglas V. Austin et al. LC 84-21754. (Bankers Management Ser.). 406p. 1985. 49.00 o.p. (ISBN 0-87267-053-8). Bank Admin Inst.

Modern Blood Banking & Transfusion Practices. D. Harmening Pittiglio. LC 82-17989. 580p. 1983. 34.95x o.p. (ISBN 0-8036-6948-8). Davis Co.

Modern Book of Whittling & Woodcarving. E. J. Tangerman. LC 73-9994. (Illus.). 192p. 1973. spiral bdg. 10.95 o.p. (ISBN 0-07-062669-3). McGraw.

Modern Breeds of Livestock. 4th ed. Hilton M. Briggs & Dinus M. Briggs. (Illus.). 1980. text ed. write for info. o.p. (ISBN 0-02-314730-X). Macmillan.

Modern Britain, Eighteen Eighty Five to Nineteen Fifty Five. Henry Pelling. (Illus.). 1966. pap. 6.95 o.p. (ISBN 0-393-00368-X, Norton Lib). Norton.

Modern British Poetry. new & enl. ed. Ed. by Louis Untermeyer. 1962. text ed. 11.95 o.p. (ISBN 0-15-560150-4, HC). HarBraceJ.

Modern British Soldier, No. 2. Simon Dunstan. (Uniforms Illustrated Ser.: No. 2). (Illus.). 72p. 1984. pap. 9.95 o.p. (ISBN 0-85368-630-0, Pub. by Arms & Armour Pr). Sterling.

Modern Building Encyclopedia. N. W. Kay. (Illus.). 768p. 1955. (ISBN 0-8022-0831-2). Philos Lib.

Modern Business: A Systems Approach. 2nd ed. S. Bernard Rosenblatt et al. LC 76-13803. (Illus.). 1977. text ed. 31.50 o.p. (ISBN 0-395-21381-9). HM.

Modern Business Correspondence. 4th ed. Marjorie Hunsinger & Donna C. McComas. (Illus.). 1979. text ed. 23.85 o.p. (ISBN 0-07-031275-3). McGraw.

Modern Business Report Writing. Salvatore J. Iacone. 440p. 1985. text ed. write for info. o.p. (ISBN 0-02-359410-1). Macmillan.

Modern Business Statistics. Ya-Lun Chou & Bertrand Bauer. 576p. 1983. text ed. 25.00 o.p. (ISBN 0-394-32802-7, RanB). Random.

Modern Capitalism: Its Growth & Transformation. John Cornwall. LC 82-5490. 226p. 1982. Repr. of 1977 ed. deluxe ed. 14.95 o.p. (ISBN 0-87332-222-3). M E Sharpe.

Modern Cardiovascular Physiology. Carl R. Honig. 1981. text ed. 18.50 o.p.; pap. text ed. 19.50 o.p. (ISBN 0-316-37215-3). Little.

Modern Carpentry. Willis H. Wagner. LC 79-11956. 1979. text ed. 18.60 o.p. (ISBN 0-87006-274-3); wkbk. 4.00 o.p. (ISBN 0-87006-282-4). Goodheart.

Modern China. John Robottom. (Modern Times Ser.). (Illus.). 172p. (Orig.). (gr. 9-12). 1978. pap. text ed. 4.95 o.p. (ISBN 0-582-20433-X). Longman.

Modern China, 1840-1972: An Introduction to Sources & Research Aids. Andrew J. Nathan. (Michigan Monographs in Chinese Studies: No. 14). 95p. 1973. pap. 6.00 o.p. (ISBN 0-89264-014-6). U of Mich Ctr Chinese.

Modern Chlor-Alkali Technology. M. O. Coulter. LC 80-41236. 289p. 1980. 129.95 o.p. (ISBN 0-470-27005-5). Halsted Pr.

Modern Coating Technology: Radiation Curing, Electrostatic, Plasma, & Laser Methods. Ed. by J. C. Colbert. LC 81-18900. (Chemical Technology Review: No. 201). (Illus.). 317p. 1982. 48.00 o.p. (ISBN 0-8155-0882-4). Noyes.

Modern College Accounting. Vernon F. Linnaus. (Illus.). 1977. text ed. 16.95 o.p. (ISBN 0-15-560390-6, HC). HarBraceJ.

Modern College Algebra. Robinson H. Parson. 1981. 17.95 o.p. (ISBN 0-533-04868-0). Vantage.

Modern College Algebra & Trigonometry: With Applications. Ronald D. Jamison. 1976. text ed. 19.95 o.p. (ISBN 0-15-560430-9, HC). HarBraceJ.

Modern College Algebra: With Applications. Ronald D. Jamison. 1976. text ed. 18.95 o.p. (ISBN 0-15-560415-5, HC). HarBraceJ.

Modern College Typewriting: A Basic Course. Leonard J. West. (Illus.). 1977. text ed. 12.00 o.p. (ISBN 0-15-560550-X, HC). HarBraceJ.

Modern College Typewriting: An Advanced Course. Leonard J. West. 1978. pap. text ed. 10.50 o.p. (ISBN 0-15-560562-3, HC). HarBraceJ.

Modern Comedy. John Galsworthy. 1928. 12.50 o.s.i. (ISBN 0-684-10197-1, ScribT). Scribner.

Modern Communications Switching Systems. 2nd ed. Marivin Hobbs. 1983. 16.95 o.p. (ISBN 0-8306-9635-0); pap. 9.95 o.p. (ISBN 0-8306-1278-5, 1278). TAB Bks.

Modern Comparative Politics. 2nd ed. Peter H. Merkl. LC 76-42162. 1977. pap. text ed. 17.95 o.p. (ISBN 0-03-088361-X). HR&W.

Modern Computing Methods. (Illus.). 128p. (ISBN 0-8022-1128-3). Philos Lib.

Modern Concepts of Gynecological Oncology. Ed. by John R. Van Nagell, Jr. & Hugh R. Barber. (Illus.). 702p. 1982. text ed. 63.00 o.p. (ISBN 0-88416-268-0). Year Bk Med.

Modern Concepts of Oceanography. Ed. by G. E. Deacon & Margaret B. Deacon. LC 81-6239. (Benchmark Papers in Geology Ser.: Vol. 61). 386p. 1982. 51.95 o.p. (ISBN 0-87933-390-1). Van Nos Reinhold.

Modern Constitutional Law, Cases & Notes: 1986 Supplement. 2nd ed. Ronald D. Rotunda. (American Casebook Ser.). 177p. 1986. 5.95 o.p. (ISBN 0-314-28597-0). West Pub.

Modern Construction Management. Frank Harris & Ronald McCaffer. 363p. 1977. pap. text ed. 22.75x o.p. (ISBN 0-258-97164-9, Pub. by Granada England). Gower Pub Co.

Modern Construction Management. 2nd ed. Frank Harris & Ronald McCaffer. 462p. 1983. pap. text ed. 24.50x o.p. (ISBN 0-246-11818-0, Pub. by Granada England). Gower Pub Co.

Modern Copyright Fundamentals. Ben H. Weil & Barbara F. Polansky. 448p. 1985. 34.95 o.p. (ISBN 0-442-29329-1). Van Nos Reinhold.

Modern Corporation & Private Property. rev. ed. Adolf A. Berle & Gardiner C. Means. LC 68-28813. 1969. pap. 5.25 o.p. (ISBN 0-15-661176-7, Harv). HarBraceJ.

Modern Cost Engineering Methods & Data. Chemical Engineering Magazine Editors. 1979. text ed. 51.50 o.p. (ISBN 0-07-010733-5). McGraw.

Modern Course in English Syntax. Herman Wekker & Liliane Haegeman. LC 85-13994. 176p. 1985. 31.00 o.p. (ISBN 0-7099-3646-X, Pub. by Croom Helm Ltd); pap. 15.95 o.p. (ISBN 0-7099-3649-4). Routledge Chapman & Hall.

Modern Cowboy. John R. Erickson. LC 80-28751. (Illus.). xii, 247p. 1981. pap. 6.95 o.p. (ISBN 0-8032-6707-X, BB 864, Bison). U of Nebr Pr.

Modern Criminal Justice. Jack Wright & Peter Lewis. 1978. text ed. 33.95 o.p. (ISBN 0-07-072075-4). McGraw.

Modern Criminal Law: Cases, Comments & Questions. Wayne R. LaFave. (American Casebook Ser.). 739p. 1985. Repr. of 1977 ed. text ed. 27.95 o.p. (ISBN 0-314-33930-2). West Pub.

Modern Dance. John Martin. LC 65-24217. 123p. pap. 10.95 o.s.i. (ISBN 0-87127-001-3, Pub. by Dance Horiz). Princeton Bk Co.

Modern Deep Sea Trawling Gear. 2nd ed. John Garner. (Illus.). 84p. 1977. 22.00 o.p. (ISBN 0-85238-085-2, FN65, FNB). UNIPUB.

Modern Development in Audiology. 2nd ed. Ed. by James Jerger. 1973. 23.25 o.p. (ISBN 0-12-385156-4). Acad Pr.

Modern Developments in Animal Breeding. I. M. Lerner & H. P. Donald. 1966. 82.00 o.p. (ISBN 0-12-444350-8). Acad Pr.

Modern Developments in Composite Materials & Structures, Bk. No. G00154. Ed. by J. R. Vinson. LC 79-54428. 380p. 1979. 40.00 o.p. (ISBN 0-686-62959-0). ASME.

Modern Developments in Heat Transfer. Ed. by Warren E. Ibele. 1963. 63.50 o.p. (ISBN 0-12-369550-3). Acad Pr.

Modern Developments in Investment Management. 2nd ed. James Lorie & Richard Brealy. 758p. 1978. pap. 24.95x o.p. (ISBN 0-03-040716-8). Dryden Pr.

Modern Developments in Powder Metallurgy. rev. ed. Ed. by E. N. Aqua & C. I. Whitman. Incl. Vol. 15. Principles & Processes. LC 66-5483. 864p (ISBN 0-918404-64-9); Vol. 16. Ferrous & Nonferrous Materials. LC 66-5483. 784p (ISBN 0-918404-65-7); Vol. 17. Special Materials. LC 66-5483. 944p (ISBN 0-918404-66-5). LC 66-5483. 2592p. 1985. 3 vol. set 200.00 o.p. (ISBN 0-918404-67-3); 80.00 ea. o.p. Am Powder Metal.

Modern Diplomacy: A Bibliography. Amos Lakos. LC 85-233322. (Public Administration Bibliography Ser.). 1985. 4.50 o.p. (ISBN 0-89028-531-4). Vance Biblios.
Modern Drama. Martin Lamm. 1953. (ISBN 0-8022-0906-8). Philos Lib.
Modern East Asia: Essays in Interpretation. Ed. by James B. Crowley. 1970. pap. text ed. 9.95 o.p. (ISBN 0-15-561000-7, HC). HarBraceJ.
Modern Economic History. 3rd ed. Edmund Seddon. (Illus.). 384p. 1979. pap. text ed. 14.95x o.p. (ISBN 0-7121-1286-3, Pub. by Macdonald & Evans England). Trans-Atl Phila.
Modern Economics: Principles & Policy. 2nd ed. Kevin Lancaster & Ronald A. DeLaney. 1980. text ed. 29.50 o.p. (ISBN 0-395-30650-7). HM.
Modern Electrical Components. G. W. Dummer. (Illus.). 462p. 1959. (ISBN 0-8022-0423-6). Philos Lib.
Modern Electronic Maintenance Principles. D. J. Garland & F. W. Stainer. 1970. pap. text ed. 4.95 o.p. (ISBN 0-08-014188-9). Pergamon.
Modern Elementary Mathematics. 2nd ed. Malcolm Graham. 464p. 1975. text ed. 16.95 o.p. (ISBN 0-15-561039-2, HC). HarBraceJ.
Modern Elementary Mathematics. 3rd ed. Malcolm Graham. 470p. 1979. text ed. 24.95 o.p. (ISBN 0-15-561041-4, HC). HarBraceJ.
Modern Encyclopedia for Children. (Illus.). 640p. 1956. (ISBN 0-8022-1129-1). Philos Lib.
Modern Encyclopedia Religions in Russia & Soviet Union, Vol. 1. Ed. by Paul D. Steeves. 1987. 36.00 o.p. (ISBN 0-317-57760-3). Academic Intl.
Modern Encyclopedia Russia & Soviet History, Vol. 49. Ed. by J. L. Wieczynski. 1988. 38.50 o.p. Academic Intl.
Modern English Short Stories. Ed. by Derek Hudson. Repr. of 1956 ed. 27.00 o.p. (ISBN 0-403-04179-1). Somerset Pub.
Modern English-Yiddish, Yiddish-English Dictionary. Uriel Weinreich. (Eng. & Yiddish.). 1968. text ed. 57.50 o.p. (ISBN 0-07-069038-3). McGraw.
Modern Ethiopia: From the Accession of Menilek II to the Present, Proceedings of the International Conference of the Ethiopian Studies, Nice, 5th, 19-22 December 1977. Ed. by J. Tubiana. 574p. 1980. text ed. 85.00 o.p. (ISBN 90-6191-086-2, Pub. by A A Balkema). Gower Pub Co.
Modern European Verse. Ed. by Dannie Abse. (Pocket Poet Ser.). 1964. pap. 3.50 o.p. (ISBN 0-8023-9037-4). Dufour.
Modern Experiments in Telepathy. Samuel G. Soal & F. Bateman. LC 75-18403. 425p. 1975. Repr. of 1954 ed. lib. bdg. 27.50x o.p. (ISBN 0-8371-8336-7, SOME). Greenwood.
Modern Far Eastern Stories. Ed. by Chong-Wha Chung. (Writing in Asia Ser.). 1978. pap. text ed. 7.50x o.p. (ISBN 0-686-60446-6, 00205). Heinemann Ed.
Modern Federalism: An Analytical Dimension. Peter A. House & Wilber A. Steger. LC 81-47972. 320p. 1982. 33.00x o.p. (ISBN 0-669-05208-6). Lexington Bks.
Modern Ferreting. D. Brian Plummer. (Illus.). 128p. 1981. 18.00 o.p. (ISBN 0-85115-083-7, Pub. by Boydell & Brewer). Longwood Pub Group.
Modern Fictional Theorists. K. K. Sharma. 194p. 1981. text ed. 15.00x o.p. (ISBN 0-391-02253-9). Humanities.
Modern Fighters & Attack Aircraft. Barry C. Wheeler. (Illus.). 1985. 9.95 o.p. (ISBN 0-668-04964-2). Arco.
Modern Filter Theory & Design. Ed. by Gabor C. Temes & Sanjit K. Mitra. 566p. 1973. 58.50x o.p. (ISBN 0-471-85130-2, Pub. by Wiley-Interscience). Wiley.
Modern Financial Accounting. Lee. 1984. pap. 27.95 o.p. (ISBN 0-442-30573-7). Van Nos Reinhold.
Modern Financial Accounting. 3rd. ed. G. Lee. 1982. pap. 27.50 o.p. (ISBN 0-442-30732-2). Van Nos Reinhold.
Modern Florida Government. Ann E. Kelley. LC 83-16725. (Illus.). 416p. 1984. lib. bdg. 43.00 o.p. (ISBN 0-8191-3564-X); pap. text ed. 23.50 o.p. (ISBN 0-8191-3565-8). U Pr of Amer.
Modern Fluid Mechanics. Science Press Staff. 590p. 1981. 48.95 o.p. (ISBN 0-442-20075-7). Van Nos Reinhold.
Modern Fly Dressings for the Practical Angler. Poul Jorgensen. LC 76-2060. 1976. 24.95 o.p. (ISBN 0-8329-2242-0, Pub. by Winchester Pr). New Century.
Modern Food Analysis. F. L. Hart & H. J. Fisher. LC 72-83661. (Illus.). 1971. 90.00 o.p. (ISBN 0-387-05126-0). Springer-Verlag.
Modern Food Preservation. Margaret McWilliams & Harriett Paine. LC 77-76339. (Illus.). 1977. text ed. 13.95x o.p. (ISBN 0-916434-25-7). Plycon Pr.
Modern Food Processing. J. Lamb. 350p. 1987. lib. bdg. 56.00 o.p. (ISBN 0-89573-400-1). VCH Pubs.
Modern Formulas for Statics & Dynamics: A Stress & Strain Approach. Walter D. Pilkey & Pin Yu Chang. LC 77-15093. (Illus.). 1978. text ed. 44.50 o.p. (ISBN 0-07-049998-5). McGraw.
Modern Foundry Practice. E. D. Howard. 1959. (ISBN 0-8022-0749-9). Philos Lib.
Modern France. Angelo Codevilla. LC 74-56. 272p. 1974. 7.95 o.p. (ISBN 0-87548-150-7). Open Court.
Modern French. Dan Desberg & Lucette R. Kenan. 1964. text ed. 15.95 o.p. (ISBN 0-15-561150-X, HC). HarBraceJ.
Modern Gear Production. H. J. Watson. 1970. 90.00 o.p. (ISBN 0-08-015835-8). Pergamon.
Modern Geometry. 2nd ed. Claire F. Adler. 1967. text ed. 27.95 o.p. (ISBN 0-07-000421-8). McGraw.
Modern German. Van Horn Vail & Kimberly Sparks. (Illus., Ger.). 1971. text ed. 16.95 o.p. (ISBN 0-15-561208-5, HC, HC, HC). HarBraceJ.
Modern German Drama. Edgar Lohner & H. G. Hannum. LC 66-3026. 1966. text ed. 25.95 o.p. (ISBN 0-395-04808-7, 3-33585). HM.
Modern Germany. 2nd ed. Koppel S. Pinson. 1966. text ed. write for info. o.p. (ISBN 0-02-395420-5). Macmillan.
Modern Germany & Her Historians. Antoine Guilland. 1970. Repr. of 1915 ed. lib. bdg. 35.00x o.p. (ISBN 0-8371-4506-6, GUMG). Greenwood.
Modern Grammar. Paul Roberts. LC 68-22216. 1968. text ed. 11.50 o.p. (ISBN 0-15-561315-4, HC). HarBraceJ.
Modern Greek Evidence for the Ancient Greek Vocabulary. G. P. Shipp. LC 80-670068. (Gr.). 1980. 43.00x o.p. (ISBN 0-424-00076-8, Pub. by Sydney U Pr). Intl Spec Bk.
Modern Growth of the Totem Pole on the Northwest Coast. facs. ed. Marius Barbeau. (Shorey Indian Ser.). 16p. pap. 0.95 o.s.i. (ISBN 0-8466-0098-6, S98). Shorey.
Modern Gun Values. 4th ed. Jack Lewis. (Illus.). 384p. (Orig.). 1983. pap. 12.95 o.p. (ISBN 0-910676-52-6, 5836). DBI.
Modern Guns. rev., 6th ed. Russell Quertermous & Steve Quertermous. (Illus.). 448p. 1987. pap. 12.95 o.p. (ISBN 0-89145-343-1). Collector Bks.
Modern Gunsmithing. Clyde Baker. LC 81-39911. (Illus.). 608p. 1981. 24.95 o.p. (ISBN 0-8117-0983-3). Stackpole.
Modern Gym Fitness: The Complete Course. Peter Scully & Muriel Scully. (Illus.). 128p. (Orig.). 1987. pap. 10.95 o.p. (ISBN 0-85112-495-X, Pub. by Guinness Superlatives). Sterling.
Modern Gymnastics: Skills & Techniques. Peter Aykroyd. LC 84-2474. (Illus.). 153p. (YA) (gr. 7 up). 1985. 12.95 o.p. (ISBN 0-668-06458-7). Arco.
Modern Handbook of Humor. Ralph L. Wood. 1967. text ed. 54.95 o.p. (ISBN 0-07-071737-0). McGraw.
Modern Hebrew. Eliezer Rieger. 1953. (ISBN 0-8022-1341-3). Philos Lib.
Modern Hebrew for Biblical Scholars: An Annotated Chrestomathy with an Outline Grammar & Glossary. T. Muraoka. (Journal for the Study of the Old Testament Ser.: Manuals 2). 220p. pap. text ed. 14.50 o.s.i. (Pub. by JSOT Pr England). Eisenbrauns.
Modern History of China & Japan. Ed. by Thomas B. Lee. LC 72-86191. 146p. 1972. pap. text ed. 6.95x o.p. (ISBN 0-8422-0212-9). Irvington.
Modern Household Equipment. Ruth E. Brasher & Carolyn L. Garrison. 512p. 1982. text ed. write for info. o.p. (ISBN 0-02-340500-7). Macmillan.
Modern Human Relations at Work. 2nd ed. Richard M. Hodgetts. 528p. 1984. text ed. 32.95x o.p. (ISBN 0-03-062482-7); instr's. manual w/transparency masters 19.95 o.p. (ISBN 0-03-062483-5). Dryden Pr.
Modern Human Sexuality. Peter Kellman & Burt Saxon. LC 76-6829. (Modern Health Investigations). (gr. 7-8). 1976. pap. 7.00 o.p. (ISBN 0-395-21830-6). HM.
Modern Igneous Petrology. Mohan K. Sood. LC 81-820. 244p. 1981. 39.95x o.p. (ISBN 0-471-08915-X, Pub. by Wiley-Interscience). Wiley.
Modern Indian Short Stories. Ed. by Suresh Kohli. (Indian Short Stories Ser.). 164p. 1975. 5.00 o.p. (ISBN 0-88253-737-7). Ind-US Inc.
Modern Indian Stories. Ed. by Pritish Nandy. (Vikas Library for Young Adults). 112p. 1985. pap. text ed. 5.95x o.p. (ISBN 0-7069-2678-1, Pub. by Vikas India). Advent NY.
Modern Intermediate Algebra for College Students. 3rd ed. Susanne Shelley. 1980. text ed. 29.95 o.p. (ISBN 0-03-042581-6, CBS C). SCP.
Modern Introduction to Astrology. Henry Weingarten. LC 74-15939. 1974. pap. 1.95 o.s.i. (ISBN 0-88231-014-3). ASI Pubs Inc.
Modern Introduction to Classical Mechanics & Control. David N. Burghes & A. M. Downs. LC 75-16463. (Mathematics & It's Applications Ser.). 320p. 1980. 48.95 o.p. (ISBN 0-470-12362-1); pap. 52.95x o.p. (ISBN 0-470-26949-9). Halsted Pr.
Modern Italian Stories. W. J. Strachan. 320p. 1956. (ISBN 0-8022-1663-3). Philos Lib.
Modern Japanese Literature in Translation: A Bibliography. Ed. by Yukio Fujino. LC 78-66395. 311p. 1979. 16.95x o.p. (ISBN 0-87011-339-9). Kodansha.
Modern Japanese Poetry. Ed. by A. R. Davis. Tr. by James Kirkup from Japanese. (Asian & Pacific Writing Ser.). 1979. 16.50x o.p. (ISBN 0-7022-1148-6). U of Queensland Pr.
Modern Jazz Dance. P-H.
Modern Jazz Dance. Fred Traguth. (Illus.). 220p. 1983. 18.95 o.p. (ISBN 0-13-595009-0); pap. 9.95 o.p. (ISBN 0-13-594994-7). P-H.
Modern Judicial Remedies: Cases & Materials. Kellis E. Parker. 870p. 1975. 29.95 o.p. (ISBN 0-316-69082-1). Little.
Modern Kongo Prophets: Religion in a Plural Society. Wyatt MacGaffey. LC 82-48554. (African Systems of Thought: Midland Bks: No. 307). (Illus.). 304p. 1983. 22.50x o.p. (ISBN 0-253-33865-4); pap. 15.00X o.p. (ISBN 0-253-20307-4, MB 307). Ind U Pr.
Modern Ku Klux Klan. Henry P. Fry. LC 74-88411. 1970. Repr. of 1922 ed. lib. bdg. 22.50x o.p. (ISBN 0-8371-1929-4, FRM&, Pub. by Negro U Pr). Greenwood.
Modern Labor Economics. 2nd ed. Ronald G. Ehrenberg & Robert S. Smith. 1985. text ed. write for info. o.p. (ISBN 0-673-18105-7). Scott F.
Modern Language Classroom Techniques: A Handbook. Edward D. Allen & Rebecca M. Valette. 320p. 1972. pap. text ed. 8.95 o.p. (ISBN 0-15-561820-2, HC). HarBraceJ.
Modern Language Performance Objectives & Individualization: A Handbook. Rebecca M. Valette & Renee S. Disick. 260p. 1972. pap. text ed. 7.95 o.p. (ISBN 0-15-561893-8, HC). HarBraceJ.
Modern Law Enforcement & Police Science. E. W. Williams. (Illus.). 408p. 1967. 50.00 o.p. (ISBN 0-398-02071-X). C C Thomas.
Modern Literary Criticism: Nineteen Hundred to Nineteen Seventy. Ed. by Walton A. Litz, Jr. & Lawrence I. Lipking. LC 71-152045. 1972. pap. text ed. 12.95 o.p. (ISBN 0-689-10419-7, Atheneum). Macmillan.
Modern Literary Perspectivism. Charles I. Glicksberg. LC 79-125979. 202p. 1970. 14.95x o.p. (ISBN 0-87074-061-X). SMU Press.
Modern Livestock & Poultry Production. 2nd ed. James Gillespie. LC 79-50918. (Illus.). 662p. 1983. text ed. 33.85 o.p. (ISBN 0-8273-2200-3). Delmar.
Modern Loafer. Illus. by Futzie Nutzle. (Illus., Orig.). 1981. pap. 4.95 o.p. (ISBN 0-500-27231-X). Thames Hudson.
Modern Logic: An Introduction. Norman L. Thomas. 254p. 1985. pap. text ed. 13.00 o.p. (ISBN 0-8191-4350-2). U Pr of Amer.
Modern Love. Karen Fredericks. (Illus.). 1984. pap. 6.95 o.p. (ISBN 0-87795-635-9, Arbor Hse). Morrow.
Modern Lurcher. Michael Shaw. (Illus.). 160p. 1985. 20.00 o.p. (ISBN 0-85115-408-5, Pub. by Boydell & Brewer). Longwood Pub Group.
Modern Machinery Magazine. 1986. pap. 5.95 o.p. (ISBN 0-917914-48-1). Lindsay Pubns.
Modern Madness. Douglas LaBier. 1986. 16.95 o.p. (ISBN 0-201-11775-4). Addison-Wesley.
Modern Makonde Sculpture Exhibit Catalog. (Foreign & Comparative Studies Program, African Special Publications: No.5). 103p. 1968. pap. 4.50x o.p. (ISBN 0-686-70991-8). Syracuse U Foreign Comp.
Modern Man & An Old-Fashioned God. David Kingsberg. 1985. 7.95 o.p. (ISBN 0-533-06659-X). Vantage.
Modern Man & Religion. Tomas G. Masaryk. Tr. by H. E. Kennedy et al. LC 78-109783. viii, 320p. 1971. Repr. of 1938 ed. lib. bdg. 35.00x o.p. (ISBN 0-8371-4273-3, MAMR). Greenwood.
Modern Management & Information Systems. Joel E. Ross. (Illus.). 288p. 1976. 24.33 o.p. (ISBN 0-87909-499-0, Reston). P-H.
Modern Management of Wastewater Utilities. William E. Korbitz. LC 81-2162. (STPM Press Ser.). 264p. 1981. lib. bdg. 40.00 o.p. (ISBN 0-8240-7069-0). Garland Pub.
Modern Man's Conflicts. Dane Rudhyar. (ISBN 0-8022-1406-1). Philos Lib.
Modern Marine Engineering. D. W. Rudorff. (Illus.). 160p. 1956. (ISBN 0-8022-1407-X). Philos Lib.
Modern Market Research. Max K. Adler. (Illus.). 160p. 1957. (ISBN 0-8022-0009-5). Philos Lib.
Modern Masonry. Clois E. Kicklighter. LC 80-17966. (Illus.). 256p. 1980. text ed. 16.00 o.p. (ISBN 0-87006-296-4). Goodheart.
Modern Masonry Panel Construction Systems. J. J. Svec & P. E. Jeffers. LC 72-83307. (Illus.). 144p. 1983. 22.95 o.p. (ISBN 0-8436-0114-0). Van Nos Reinhold.
Modern Materials: Advances in Development & Applications. Ed. by Henry Hausner. Incl. Vol. 1. 1958. o.p. (ISBN 0-12-462201-1); Vol. 2. 1960. 77.00 (ISBN 0-12-462202-X); Vol. 3. 1963. 77.00 (ISBN 0-12-462203-8); Vol. 4. Ed. by B. W. Gonser & Henry H. Hausner. 1964. 77.00 (ISBN 0-12-462204-6); Vol. 5. Ed. by B. W. Gonser. 1965. o.p. (ISBN 0-12-462205-4); Vol. 6. 1968. 56.50 o.p. (ISBN 0-12-462206-2); Vol. 7. 1970. 77.00 (ISBN 0-12-462207-0). Acad Pr.
Modern Mauritius: The Politics of Decolonization. Adele S. Simmons. LC 81-47015. (Illus.). 256p. 1982. 22.50x o.p. (ISBN 0-253-38658-6). Ind U Pr.
Modern Metallography. R. E. Smallman & K. H. Ashbee. 1966. text ed. 14.75 o.p. (ISBN 0-08-011571-3); pap. text ed. 6.25 o.p. (ISBN 0-08-011570-5). Pergamon.
Modern Metalworking. John R. Walker. LC 81-6736. (Illus.). 520p. 1981. 22.00 o.p. (ISBN 0-87006-334-0); wkbk. 4.00 o.p. (ISBN 0-87006-335-9). Goodheart.
Modern Methods for the Separation of Rarer Metal Ions. J. Korkisch. 1969. 65.00 o.p. (ISBN 0-08-012921-8). Pergamon.
Modern Methods in Forest Genetics. Ed. by J. P. Miksche. LC 76-8828. (Illus.). 1976. 36.00 o.p. (ISBN 0-387-07708-1). Springer-Verlag.
Modern Methods in Topological Vector Spaces. Albert Wilansky. 1978. text ed. 48.95 o.p. (ISBN 0-07-070180-6). McGraw.
Modern Methods of Amputation. E. Vasconelos. (ISBN 0-8022-1768-0). Philos Lib.
Modern Methods of Pharmaceutical Analysis, Vol. III. Roger E. Schirmer. 256p. 1982. 81.50 o.p. (ISBN 0-8493-5246-0). CRC Pr.
Modern Methods of Steroid Analysis. Ed. by Erich Heftmann. 1973. 109.00 o.p. (ISBN 0-12-336640-2). Acad Pr.
Modern Microeconomics. 2nd ed. Hyman. (Illus.). 640p. 1988. 41.95 o.p. (ISBN 0-8016-2844-X); International ed. 24.95 o.p. (ISBN 0-8016-5502-1). Mosby.
Modern Microeconomics: Analysis & Applications. Hyman. 1985. 41.95 o.p. (ISBN 0-8016-2367-7); study guide 12.95 o.p. (ISBN 0-8016-2329-4). Mosby.
Modern Military Dictionary: Ten Thousand Technical & Slang Terms of Military Usage. 2nd ed. Max B. Garber & P. S. Bond. LC 74-31354. 276p. 1975. Repr. of 1942 ed. 42.00x o.p. (ISBN 0-8103-4208-1). Gale.
Modern Ms. 2nd ed. Helen Whitcomb & L. Cochran. 1975. text ed. 15.24 o.p. (ISBN 0-07-069663-2). McGraw.
Modern Music. Max Graf. (ISBN 0-8022-0615-8). Philos Lib.
Modern Music-Makers: Contemporary American Composers. Madeleine Goss. LC 73-97345. Repr. of 1952 ed. lib. bdg. 35.00x o.p. (ISBN 0-8371-2957-5, GOMM). Greenwood.
Modern Music Notation. Laszlo Boehm. 1961. pap. 8.95 o.p. (ISBN 0-02-870490-8). Schirmer Bks.
Modern Music: The Avant Garde Since 1945. Paul Griffiths. (Illus.). 332p. 1981. 35.00x o.p. (ISBN 0-460-04365-X, Pub. by J. M. Dent England). Biblio Dist.
Modern Nationalities. Florian Znaniecki. LC 72-7875. 196p. 1973. Repr. of 1952 ed. lib. bdg. 22.50x o.p. (ISBN 0-8371-6549-0, ZNMN). Greenwood.
Modern Naval Architecture. W. Muckle. (Illus.). 160p. 1956. (ISBN 0-8022-1162-3). Philos Lib.
Modern Network Theory: An Introduction. R. K. Brayton et al. Ed. by G. S. Moschytz & J. Neirynck. 1978. text ed. 42.00 o.p. (ISBN 2-604-00034-2). Gower Pub Co.
Modern Novel Writing, or the Elegant Enthusiast: And Interesting Emotions of Arabella Bloomville, a Rhapsodical Romance, Interspersed with Poetry, by the Right Hon. Lady Harriet Marlow, 2 vols. William Beckford. (Feminist Controversy in England, 1788-1810 Ser.). 1974. Set. lib. bdg. 121.00 o.p. (ISBN 0-8240-0851-0). Garland Pub.
Modern Oil-Hydraulic Engineering. Jean Thomas. 350p. 1982. 40.00x o.p. (ISBN 0-85461-043-X, Pub. by Trade & Tech England). Gower Pub Co.
Modern Organizational Theory: Contextual, Environment & Socio-Cultural Variables. Ed. by Anant R. Negandhi. LC 72-619605. 404p. 1973. 15.00x o.p. (ISBN 0-87338-133-5). Kent St U Pr.
Modern Orthodox Saints: Vol. 6-St. Arsenios of Paros. Constantine Cavarnos. LC 78-54384. (Illus.). 123p. 1978. 8.00 o.p. (ISBN 0-914744-39-9); pap. 4.50 o.p. (ISBN 0-914744-40-2). Inst Byzantine.
Modern Orthodox Saints: Vol. 7-St. Nectarios of Aegina. Constantine Cavarnos. LC 81-82963. (Illus.). 222p. 1981. 10.00 o.p. (ISBN 0-914744-53-4); pap. 7.00 o.p. (ISBN 0-914744-54-2). Inst Byzantine.

Modern Oxide Materials: Preparation, Properties & Device Applications. Ed. by B. Cockayne & D. W. Jones. 1972. 82.50 o.p. (ISBN 0-12-177750-2). Acad Pr.

Modern Parliamentary Procedure. Ray E. Keesey. 208p. 1974. 5.95 o.p. (ISBN 0-395-19397-4). HM.

Modern Partnership Law. David Milman & Terrence Flanagan. 178p. 1983. pap. 13.50 o.p. (ISBN 0-7099-1015-0, Pub. by Croom Helm Ltd); 31.00 o.p. (ISBN 0-7099-1014-2). Routledge Chapman & Hall.

Modern Personnel Management. Sexton Adams & Adelaide Griffin. LC 80-24173. 350p. (Orig.). 1979. pap. 19.00x o.p. (ISBN 0-87201-662-5). Gulf Pub.

Modern Perspectives in Child Development. Ed. by Albert J. Solnit & Sally A. Provence. LC 63-17671. 666p. 1963. text ed. 50.00x o.s.i. (ISBN 0-8236-3420-5). Intl Univs Pr.

Modern Philosophy of Science: Selected Essays. Hans Reichenbach. Ed. by Maria Reichenbach. LC 81-13344. ix, 214p. 1982. Repr. of 1959 ed. lib. bdg. 35.00x o.p. (ISBN 0-313-23274-1, REMD). Greenwood.

Modern Physics for Engineers. Otto Oldenberg & N. Rasmussen. 1966. text ed. 52.95 o.p. (ISBN 0-07-047653-5). McGraw.

Modern Pilgrimage in New Testament Christology. Norman Perrin. LC 73-88352. 160p. 1974. 6.25 o.p. (ISBN 0-8006-0267-6, Fortress). Augsburg Fortress.

Modern Plumbing. rev. ed. E. Keith Blankenbaker. LC 81-4114. (Illus.). 300p. 1981. text ed. 18.00 o.p. (ISBN 0-87006-325-1). Goodheart.

Modern Poetry in Translation 1983. Ed. by Daniel Weissbort & Ted Hughes. (Persea Series of Poetry in Translation). 214p. (Orig.). 1983. pap. 9.95 o.p. (ISBN 0-89255-075-9). Persea Bks.

Modern Polarographic Methods. Helmut Schmidt & Mark Von Stackelberg. Tr. by R. E. Maddison. 1963. 39.50 o.p. (ISBN 0-12-626950-5). Acad Pr.

Modern Police Administration. Ed. by Donald O. Schultz. LC 78-67436. 172p. 1979. 19.00x o.p. (ISBN 0-87201-720-6). Gulf Pub.

Modern Policing. Ed. by David W. Pope & Norman L. Weiner. 271p. 1981. pap. 14.75 o.p. (ISBN 0-7099-2008-3, Pub. by Croom Helm Ltd). Routledge Chapman & Hall.

Modern Political Parties: Approaches to Comparative Politics. Sigmund Neumann. LC 55-10249. (Midway Reprint Ser). xii, 460p. 1975. pap. text ed. 17.50x o.s.i. (ISBN 0-226-57447-4). U of Chicago Pr.

Modern Portfolio Theory. Robert Hagin. 1980. pap. 19.95x o.p. (ISBN 0-256-02379-4). Irwin.

Modern Postcards: Postcard Reproductions from the Permanent Collection of the San Francisco Museum of Modern Art. (Illus.). 1984. pap. 5.95 o.p. (ISBN 0-87701-337-3). Chronicle Bks.

Modern Practice in Servo Design. D. R. Wilson. (International Series of Monographs in Electrical Engineering: Vol. 2). (Illus.). 328p. 1970. 87.00 o.p. (ISBN 0-08-015812-9). Pergamon.

Modern Prevention: The New Medicine. Isadore Rosenfeld. 448p. 1986. 18.45 o.s.i. (ISBN 0-671-50735-4, Linden Pr). S&S.

Modern Principles of Athletic Training. 6th ed. Daniel D. Arnheim. 1984. 37.95 o.p. (ISBN 0-8016-2683-8). Mosby.

Modern Private Enterprise: Is It Successful. Roland W. Bartlett. LC 72-93331. 1973. pap. 3.95 o.p. (ISBN 0-8134-1540-3, 1540); text ed. 2.95x o.p. Inter Print Pubs.

Modern Problems of Surface Physics: Proceedings-Condensed Matter & Statistical Mechanics. I. J. Lalov. 1982. 46.00 o.p. (ISBN 0-318-23618-4). World Scientific Pub.

Modern Property Law, Cases & Materials. Jon W. Bruce et al. LC 84-2317. (American Casebook Ser.). 1004p. 1984. text ed. 34.95 o.p. (ISBN 0-314-80459-5); tchr's manual 29.95 o.p. (ISBN 0-314-83524-5). West Pub.

Modern Public Finance. 5th ed. Bernard P. Herber. 1983. 37.50 o.p. (ISBN 0-256-02808-7). Irwin.

Modern Public Relations. John E. Marston. (Illus.). 1979. text ed. 29.95 o.p. (ISBN 0-07-040619-7). McGraw.

Modern Quantum Chemistry, 3 Vols. Ed. by Oktay Sinanoglu. (Istanbul Lectures). 1965. Vol. 1. 69.50 o.p. (ISBN 0-12-645001-3); Vol. 2, 1966. 69.50 o.p. (ISBN 0-12-645002-1); Vol. 3, 1966. 69.50 o.p. (ISBN 0-12-645003-X). Acad Pr.

Modern Quarterly: A Journal of Radical Opinion, Vols. 1-11, No. 7. Incl. Vol. 1. lib. bdg. 31.00 (ISBN 0-313-21753-X, M101); Vol. 2. lib. bdg. 31.00 (ISBN 0-313-21754-8, M102); Vol. 3. lib. bdg. 31.00 (ISBN 0-313-21755-6, M103); Vol. 4. lib. bdg. 31.00 (ISBN 0-313-21756-4, M104); Vol. 5. lib. bdg. 31.00 (ISBN 0-313-21757-2, M105); Vol. 6. lib. bdg. 31.00 (ISBN 0-313-21758-0, M106); Vol. 7. lib. bdg. 31.00 (ISBN 0-313-21759-9, M107); Vol. 8. lib. bdg. 31.00 (ISBN 0-313-21760-2, M108); Vol. 9. lib. bdg. 31.00 (ISBN 0-313-21761-0, M109); Vol. 10. lib. bdg. 31.00 (ISBN 0-313-21762-9, M110); Vol. 11. lib. bdg. 31.00 (ISBN 0-313-21763-7, M111). 1968. Repr. of 1940 ed. Set. lib. bdg. 270.00x o.p. (ISBN 0-8371-9202-1, M100). Greenwood.

Modern Railways: Their Engineering, Equipment & Operation. Cecil J. Allen. LC 72-9045. (Illus.). 307p. 1973. Repr. of 1959 ed. lib. bdg. 35.00x o.p. (ISBN 0-8371-6565-2, ALMR). Greenwood.

Modern Real Estate. Frank J. Parker & Norman Schoenfeld. 1979. text ed. 22.50 o.p. (ISBN 0-669-01326-9). Heath.

Modern Real Estate Management. William M. Shenkel. (Illus.). 1980. text ed. 39.95x o.p. (ISBN 0-07-056546-5). McGraw.

Modern Real Estate Practice. 10th ed. Fillmore W. Galaty et al. LC 84-22254. (Illus.). 480p. (Orig.). 1985. pap. 31.95 o.p. (ISBN 0-88462-517-6, 1510-01, Real Estate Ed); study guide, 240p 9.95 o.p. (ISBN 0-88462-519-2, 1510-02). Longman Finan.

Modern Real Estate Principles. rev. ed. William M Shenkel. 1980. 17.95x o.p. (ISBN 0-256-02291-7); study guide 5.50x o.p. (ISBN 0-256-02292-5). Irwin.

Modern Recording Techniques. Robert E. Runstein. LC 73-90292. (Illus.). 1974. 14.95 o.p. (ISBN 0-672-21037-1). Sams.

Modern Refrigeration & Air Conditioning. Andrew Althouse & C. H. Turnquist. LC 81-20002. (Illus.). 1012p. 1982. text ed. 26.00x o.p. (ISBN 0-87006-340-5); lab manual 5.28x o.p. (ISBN 0-87006-422-3). Goodheart.

Modern Researcher. 3rd ed. Jacques Barzun & Henry F. Graff. LC 76-27411. 378p. 1977. pap. text ed. 12.00 net o.p. (ISBN 0-15-562511-X, HC). HarBraceJ.

Modern Retailing Management. 10th ed. Delbert J. Duncan et al. 1983. 33.95x o.p. (ISBN 0-256-02532-0). Irwin.

Modern Retailing: Theory & Practice. rev. ed. J. Barry Mason & Morris L. Mayer. 1981. 21.95x o.p. (ISBN 0-256-02433-2). Irwin.

Modern Retailing: Theory & Practice. 4th ed. J. Barry Mason & Morris L. Mayer. 1987. 38.95 o.p. (ISBN 0-317-61149-6). Irwin.

Modern Rhetoric. 3rd ed. Cleanth Brooks & Robert Penn Warren. 1970. text ed. 10.50 o.p. (ISBN 0-15-562807-0, HC). HarBraceJ.

Modern Russia. John Long. 180p. 1958. (ISBN 0-8022-0995-5). Philos Lib.

Modern Russia. John Robottom. (Moddern Times Ser.). (Illus.). 172p. (Orig.). (gr. 9-12). 1980. pap. text ed. 4.95 o.p. (ISBN 0-582-20440-2). Longman.

Modern Russian I. Clayton L. Dawson et al. 1964. text ed. 7.75 o.p. (ISBN 0-15-562860-7, HC). HarBraceJ.

Modern Russian Stress. R. I. Avanesov. (Pergamon Oxford Russian Ser.). 1965. pap. 4.40 o.p. (ISBN 0-08-010300-6). Pergamon.

Modern Russian Usage. D. E. Rozental. Ed. by C. V. James. 1963. text ed. 11.75 o.p. (ISBN 0-08-009811-8). Pergamon.

Modern Satire. Ed. by Alvin B. Kernan. 234p. (Orig.). 1962. pap. text ed. 12.95 o.p. (ISBN 0-15-563099-7, HC). HarBraceJ.

Modern Sawmill Techniques Vol. 5: Proceedings of the Sawmill Clinic, 5th, Portland, Oregon, March, 1975. Sawmill Clinic Staff. Ed. by Vernon S. White. LC 73-88045. (Sawmill Clinic Library: A Forest Industries Bk.). (Illus.). 400p. 1975. 19.25 o.p. (ISBN 0-87930-047-7). Miller Freeman.

Modern School Superintendent: His Principles & Practices. Robert E. Wilson. LC 77-2905. (Illus.). 1977. Repr. of 1960 ed. lib. bdg. 35.00 o.p. (ISBN 0-8371-9575-6, WIMO). Greenwood.

Modern Science & God. McLaughlin. 96p. 1954. (ISBN 0-8022-1020-1). Philos Lib.

Modern Scribes & Lettering Artists. LC 80-50362. (Illus.). 160p. 1984. pap. 10.95 o.s.i. (ISBN 0-8008-5298-2, Pentalic). Taplinger.

Modern Ships: Elements of Their Design, Construction, & Operation. 2nd ed. John H. La Dage. LC 65-21747. (Illus.). 389p. 1965. 11.50x o.p. (ISBN 0-87033-065-9). Cornell Maritime.

Modern Short Stories. 3rd ed. Ed. by Arthur Mizener. 1971. text ed. 6.95x o.p. (ISBN 0-393-09972-5, NortonC). Norton.

Modern Short Stories in English. rev. ed. Robert J. Dixson. (Illus., Orig., Sequel to Easy Reading Selections in English). (gr. 9-11). 1971. pap. text ed. 3.75 o.p. (ISBN 0-88345-117-4, 17986); 35.00 o.p. tapes (ISBN 0-685-19799-5, 158213); cassettes 40.00 o.p. (ISBN 0-685-19800-6). Prentice ESL.

Modern Singapore. Ed. by Jin-Bee Ooi & Hai D. Chiang. 306p. 1969. 15.00x o.p. (ISBN 0-8214-0478-4, Pub. by Singapore U Pr). Ohio U Pr.

Modern Social Work Management. Ed. by Paul R. Keys & Leon H. Ginsberg. 1988. write for info. o.p. Natl Assn Soc Wkrs.

Modern Socialism, Nos. 1-4. 1968. Repr. of 1941 ed. lib. bdg. 12.25 o.p. (ISBN 0-8371-9204-8, MS00). Greenwood.

Modern Sociological Issues. 2nd ed. Barry J. Wishart & Louis C. Reichman. 1979. pap. text ed. write for info. o.p. (ISBN 0-02-428760-1). Macmillan.

Modern Sociology. Peter Morsley. (Education Ser.). 680p. 1985. pap. 7.95 o.p. (ISBN 0-14-080221-5). Penguin.

Modern Spanish-English & English-Spanish Technical & Engineering Dictionary. R. L. Guinle. (Span. & Eng.). 1969. Repr. of 1938 ed. 27.95 o.p. (ISBN 0-7100-1478-3). Routledge Chapman & Hall.

Modern Sri Lanka: A Society in Transition. Ed. by Tissa Fernando & Robert N. Kearney. LC 79-13077. (Foreign & Comparative Studies Program, South Asian Ser.: No. 4). (Illus.). 297p. 1979. pap. text ed. 9.00x o.p. (ISBN 0-915984-80-6). Syracuse U Foreign Comp.

Modern Statistics for Behavioral Sciences. Daniel S. Lordahl. LC 67-14485. 366p. (Orig.). 1967. 19.50 o.p. (ISBN 0-471-06918-3). Krieger.

Modern Street Ballads. John Ashton. LC 67-23926. (Illus.). 428p. 1968. Repr. of 1888 ed. 34.00x o.p. (ISBN 0-8103-3407-0). Gale.

Modern Surveying. Harold F. Birchal. (Illus.). 528p. 1956. (ISBN 0-8022-0130-X). Philos Lib.

Modern Swedish Grammar. 9th, rev. ed. I. Bjorkhagen. 1966. 12.50 o.p. (ISBN 0-685-47300-7). E J Brill USA.

Modern Syllabus Algebra. D. G. Lloyd. 1971. 60.00 o.p. (ISBN 0-08-015965-6); pap. 60.00 o.p. (ISBN 0-08-015964-8). Pergamon.

Modern Systems Research for the Behavioral Scientist: A Sourcebook. Ed. by Walter Buckley. LC 66-19888. (Illus.). 1968. 45.00 o.p. (ISBN 0-202-30011-0). Aldine de Gruyter.

Modern Technical Communication. D. Godfrey. 300p. 1983. text ed. 12.95 o.p. (ISBN 0-07-548071-9). McGraw.

Modern Technical Mathematics with Calculus. Robert A. Carman & Hal M. Saunders. 1326p. 1985. text ed. (ISBN 0-534-04305-4). Wadsworth Pub.

Modern Technique of Rock Blasting. 3rd ed. U. Langefors & B. Kihlstrom. LC 77-23895. 438p. 1978. 58.95x o.p. (ISBN 0-470-99282-4). Halsted Pr.

Modern Techniques in Physiological Sciences. Ed. by J. F. Gross et al. 1974. 109.00 o.p. (ISBN 0-12-304450-2). Acad Pr.

Modern Tennis Doubles. Stan Smith et al. Ed. by Larry Sheehan. LC 75-13514. (Illus.). 1977. o p 9.95 o.p. (ISBN 0-689-10687-4, Atheneum); pap. 4.95 o.p. (ISBN 0-689-70556-5). Macmillan.

Modern TheoJolites & Levels. 2nd ed. M. A. Cooper. 288p. 1982. 45.00x o.p. (ISBN 0-246-11502-5, NO. 6721). Routledge Chapman & Hall.

Modern Theory of Architechture. Bruce Allsopp. 1978. 16.50 o.p. (ISBN 0-7100-8611-3). Routledge Chapman & Hall.

Modern Theory of Architecture. Bruce Allsopp. (Illus.). 112p. (Orig.). 1981. pap. 8.95 o.p. (ISBN 0-7100-0950-X). Routledge Chapman & Hall.

Modern Therapies. V. Binder et al. 1976. 11.95 o.p. (ISBN 0-13-599001-7, Spec); 6.95 o.p. (ISBN 0-13-598995-7). P-H.

Modern Tongues Movement. Robert G. Gromacki. pap. 5.95 o.p. (ISBN 0-8010-3708-5). Baker Bk.

Modern Trade Unionism. John J. Flagler. LC 79-84424. (Real World of Economics Ser.). (Illus.). (gr. 5-11). 1970. PLB 4.95 o.p. (ISBN 0-8225-0621-1). Lerner Pubns.

Modern Transportation: Selected Readings. 2nd ed. Martin T. Farris & Paul T. McElhiney. LC 72-6891. 1973. pap. 10.95 o.p. (ISBN 0-395-14034-X). HM.

Modern Trends in Housing in Developing Countries. Ed. by A. G. Madhava Rao. (Illus.). 400p. 1984. 58.00 o.p. (ISBN 0-419-13290-2, 6883, Pub. by E & FN Spon England). Routledge Chapman & Hall.

Modern Trends in Human Leukemia IV: Latest Results. Ed. by R. Neth. (Haematology & Blood Transfusion Supplement Ser.: No. 26). (Illus.). 650p. 1981. pap. 78.20 o.p. (ISBN 0-387-10622-7). Springer-Verlag.

Modern Trends in Human Leukemia V: New Results in Clinical & Biological Research Including Pediatric Oncology; Proceedings, Wilsede, FRG, June 1982. Ed. by R. Neth et al. (Haematology & Blood Transfusion Ser.: Vol. 28). 560p. 1983. pap. 84.50 o.p. (ISBN 0-387-11858-6). Springer-Verlag.

Modern Upholstering Methods. William F. Tierney. (gr. 9 up). 1965. text ed. 18.64 o.p. (ISBN 0-87345-482-0). Glencoe.

Modern Verse from Taiwan. Tr. by Angela J. Palandri. LC 79-161994. 1972. 35.00x o.p. (ISBN 0-520-02061-8). U of Cal Pr.

Modern View of Conveyancing. G. H. Glasgow. 1969. 29.00 o.p. (ISBN 0-08-013063-1); pap. 35.00 o.p. (ISBN 0-08-013062-3). Pergamon.

Modern View of the Law for Builders & Surveyors. V. Powell-Smith. 1967. text ed. 25.00 o.p. (ISBN 0-08-012297-3). Pergamon.

Modern Weed Science. O. P. Gupta & P. S. Lamba. (Illus.). 325p. 1977. 25.00 o.p. (ISBN 0-88065-095-8, Pub. by Messers Today & Tomorrow Printers & Publishers). Scholarly Pubns.

Modern Women Poets of Spanish America: The Precursors, Delmira Agustine, Gabriela Mistral, Alfonsina Storni, Juana de Ibarbourou. Sidonia C. Rosenbaum. LC 78-776. 1978. Repr. of 1945 ed. lib. bdg. 37.50x o.p. (ISBN 0-313-20289-3, ROMO). Greenwood.

Modern Working Terrier. Michael Shaw. 1986. 20.00 o.p. (ISBN 0-85115-425-5, Pub. by Boydell & Brewer). Longwood Pub Group.

Moderne Deutsche Erzaehler. 3rd ed. Ed. by Robert Roseler & Audrey Duckert. 1960. 7.95x o.p. (ISBN 0-393-09536-3, NortonC). Norton.

Modernisation & Revolution. Bill Brugger & Kate Hannan. 64p. 1983. pap. 11.50 o.p. (ISBN 0-7099-0695-1, Pub. by Croom Helm Ltd). Routledge Chapman & Hall.

Modernisers in Africa see Tarikh.

Modernism in Quebec Art, Nineteen Sixteen to Nineteen Forty-Six. Jean-Rene Ostiguy. (Illus.). 256p. 1982. 19.95 o.p. (ISBN 0-686-97832-3, 56435-5, Pub. by Natl Mus Canada). U of Chicago Pr.

Modernist Survivors: The Contemporary Novel in England, France, the United States, & Latin America. Morton P. Levitt. LC 87-5616. 304p. 1987. 27.50x o.p. (ISBN 0-8142-0420-1). Ohio St U Pr.

Modernization & Diversity in Soviet Education: With Special Reference to Nationality Groups. Jaan Pennar et al. LC 70-105285. (Special Studies in International Economics & Development). 1971. 59.50x o.p. (ISBN 0-89197-854-2); pap. text ed. 18.50x o.p. (ISBN 0-89197-855-0). Irvington.

Modernization & Its Impact upon Korean Law. Pyong-ho Pak et al. LC 80-84987. (Korea Research Monographs: No. 3). 156p. 1981. pap. 12.50x o.p. (ISBN 0-912966-31-9). IEAS.

Modernization & the Structure of Societies: A Setting for International Affairs, 2 vols. Marion J. Levy. 1966. boxed 69.00 o.p. (ISBN 0-691-09320-2); pap. 7.50 o.p. (ISBN 0-691-02808-7). Princeton U Pr.

Modernization, Dislocation, & Aprismo: Origins of the Peruvian Aprista Party, 1870-1932. Peter F. Klaren. LC 73-4915. (Latin American Monographs, No. 32). 213p. 1973. 12.50x o.p. (ISBN 0-292-76001-9). U of Tex Pr.

Modernizers: Overseas Students, Foreign Employees, & Meiji Japan. Ardath Burks. (Replica Edition Ser.). 525p. 1985. softcover 29.85x o.p. (ISBN 0-86531-826-3). Westview.

Modernizing State Policies: Community Colleges & Lifelong Education. Ed. by Jamison Gilder. (Orig.). 1981. pap. 7.50 o.p. (ISBN 0-87117-107-4). Am Assn Comm Jr Coll.

Moderns & Contemporaries: Novelists, Poets, Critics. John Lucas. LC 84-20349. 230p. 1985. 28.50x o.p. (ISBN 0-389-20530-3, BNB-08092). B&N Imports.

Moderns & Their World. J. Rothenstein. (Illus.). 128p. (ISBN 0-8022-1385-5). Philos Lib.

Modes of Analogy in Ancient Medieval Verse. Phillip Damon. (California Library Reprint Ser.: No. 33). 1973. 13.00x o.p. (ISBN 0-520-02366-8). U of Cal Pr.

Modes of Constitutional Interpretation. Craig R. Ducat. LC 78-8496. 299p. 1978. pap. text ed. 23.75 o.p. (ISBN 0-8299-2009-9). West Pub.

Modes of Literature. J. Bard McNulty. LC 76-10896. (Illus.). 1977. text ed. 17.95 o.p. (ISBN 0-395-24249-5). HM.

Modest Mussorgsky. Michel D. Calvocoressi. 322p. Repr. of 1956 ed. lib. bdg. 49.00 o.p. (Pub. by Am Repr Serv). Reprint Servs.

Modified Cellulosics. R. M. Rowell & R. Youngs. 1978. 59.00 o.p. (ISBN 0-12-599750-7). Acad Pr.

Modifying Retarded Behavior. John T. Neisworth & Robert M. Smith. (Illus.). 200p. 1973. text ed. 27.95 o.p. (ISBN 0-395-14049-8). HM.

Modifying Section Eight: Implications from Experiments with Housing Allowances. James P. Zais et al. 61p. 1979. pap. 6.00x o.p. (ISBN 0-87766-240-1, 24100). Urban Inst.

Modigliani. William Fifield. LC 75-41362. (Illus.). 1976. 11.95 o.p. (ISBN 0-688-03039-4). Morrow.

Modigliani Scandal. Ken Follett. Ed. by Pat Golbitz. LC 84-27278. 224p. 1985. Repr. of 1977 ed. 15.95 o.p. (ISBN 0-688-05119-7). Morrow.

Modigliani Scandal. Ken Follett. 385p. 1986. lib. bdg. 17.95 o.p. (ISBN 0-8161-4016-2, Large Print Bks); pap. 9.95 o.p. (ISBN 0-8161-4017-0). G K Hall.

Modula-2: Seafarer's Manual & Shipyard Guide. Edward J. Joyce. LC 84-28347. 1985. (ISBN 0-201-11587-5). Addison-Wesley.

Modular Computer Lesson Design. 2nd ed. Paul M. Roper & David V. Loertscher. 1985. pap. 15.00x o.p. (ISBN 0-931510-12-0). Hi Willow.

Modular Functions & Dirichlet Series in Number Theory. T. M. Apostol. Ed. by F. W. Gehring & C. C. Moore. LC 76-10236. (Graduate Texts in Mathematics Ser.: Vol. 41). 1976. 28.00 o.p. (ISBN 0-387-90185-X). Springer-Verlag.

Modular Functions of One Complex Variables. H. Maass. (Tata Institute Lectures on Mathematics Ser.). vii, 266p. 1984. pap. 7.10 o.p. (ISBN 0-387-12874-3). Springer-Verlag.

Modular Functions of One Variable Four: Proceedings of the International Summer School for Theoretical Physics, University of Antwerp, RUCA, July-Aug., 1972. International Summer School for Theoretical Physics Staff. Ed. by B. J. Birch & W. Kuyk. (Lecture Notes in Mathematics: Vol. 476). v, 151p. (Orig.). 1975. pap. text ed. 14.00 o.p. (ISBN 0-387-07392-2). Springer-Verlag.

Modular Functions of One Variable: Proceedings of the International Conference, Sonderforsch-ungsbereich Theoretische Mathmatik, University of Bonn, July, 1976, No. 6. Ed. by J. P. Serre & D. B. Zagier. (Lecture Note in Mathematics: Vol. 627). 1977. pap. 22.00 o.p. (ISBN 0-387-08530-0). Springer-Verlag.

Modular Functions of One Variable 5: Proceedings. Ed. by J. P. Serre & D. B. Zagier. LC 77-22148. (Lecture Notes in Mathematics: Vol. 601). 1977. pap. text ed. 18.00 o.p. (ISBN 0-387-08348-0). Springer-Verlag.

Modular Learning Approach to Accompany Educational Aspects of Behavioral Problems in Children & Youth. Lyndal M. Bullock & Gary M. Blackburn. 144p. 1974. pap. 4.75x o.p. (ISBN 0-8422-0390-7). Irvington.

Modular Model Railroading. Jeff W. Griffin. (Illus.). 144p. 1986. pap. 11.60 o.p. (ISBN 0-8306-1783-3, 1783P). Tab Bks.

Modular Study Guide to Fundamentals of Nursing. Watson et al. 1985. 13.95 o.p. (ISBN 0-8016-3963-8). Mosby.

Modular Study Guide to Maternity Care. Irene M. Bobak & Margaret D. Jensen. LC 82-7911. (Illus.). 229p. 1982. pap. text ed. 17.95 o.p. (ISBN 0-8016-0738-8). Mosby.

Module IA: Practical Mathematics (Decimals, Ratios, Proportions, & Per Cent) L. J. Ablon et al. 1975. pap. 7.95 o.p. (ISBN 0-8465-6713-X). Benjamin-Cummings.

Module, Proportion, Symmetry, Rhythm. Ed. by Gyorgy Keppes. LC 66-13044. (Vision & Value Ser). (Illus.). 1966. 12.50 o.p. (ISBN 0-8076-0363-5). Braziller.

Modules for Basic Nursing Skills, 2 vols. 2nd ed. Janice R. Ellis et al. LC 79-89521. (Illus.). 1980. Vol. 1. pap. 14.50 o.p. (ISBN 0-395-28654-9); Vol. 2. pap. 14.50 o.p. (ISBN 0-395-28655-7). HM.

Modules-Hybrids. 1987. 105.00 o.p. DATA Busn Pub.

Modumath: Arithmetic. Miriam Hecht & Caroline Hecht. LC 77-75447. 1978. pap. 20.95 o.p. (ISBN 0-395-24424-2). HM.

Mog at the Zoo. Helen Nicoll & Jan Pienkowski. (Meg & Mog Ser.). (Illus.). 32p. (ps-1). 1983. 12.95 o.s.i. (ISBN 0-434-95429-2, Pub. by W Heinemann Ltd). David & Charles.

Mohammad Mossadegh: A Political Biography. Farhad Diba. 240p. 1986. 43.00 o.p. (ISBN 0-7099-4517-5, Pub. by Croom Helm Ltd). Routledge Chapman & Hall.

Mohammed Wong Spouts: Being an Eyewitness Account of the Antediluvian Sex Life of Atlantis & Other Things. Robin Sanborn. 1978. 4.00 o.p. (ISBN 0-682-49148-9). Exposition-Phoenix.

Mohonk Conference on the Negro Question: Proceedings of the First & Second Conferences, 1890-1891. Mohonk Conference on the Negro Question Staff. 1969. Repr. of 1891 ed. 19.75 o.p. (ISBN 0-8371-2001-2, MOC&, Pub. by Negro U Pr). Greenwood.

Moire Fringes in Strain Analysis. P. S. Theocaris. 1969. 110.00 o.p. (ISBN 0-08-012974-9); pap. text ed. 110.00 o.p. (ISBN 0-08-012973-0). Pergamon.

Moisei Nappelbaum Our Age: Photographs. Ed. by Il'ia Rudiak. 144p. 1983. 35.00 o.p. (ISBN 0-88233-814-5); pap. 15.00 o.p. (ISBN 0-88233-815-3). Ardis Pubs.

Moki. Grace J. Penney. (Illus.). (gr. 3). 1985. pap. 0.95 o.p. (ISBN 0-380-00850-5, 24091, Camelot). Avon.

Moldavia: A Guide. M. Shukhat. 154p. 1985. 7.95 o.p. (ISBN 0-8285-3456-X, Pub. by Raduga Pubs USSR). Imported Pubns.

Molded & Slip Cast Pottery & Ceramics. David Cowley. (Encore Edition Ser.). (Illus.). 1978. encore ed. 3.95 o.p. (ISBN 0-684-17558-4, ScribT). Scribner.

Molding & Casting: Its Technique & Application. 3rd ed. Carl D. Clarke. (Illus.). 380p. 1972. 30.00 o.p. (ISBN 0-685-25470-4). Standard Arts.

Molding Forces. Sam Shankman. 1955. (ISBN 0-8022-1541-6). Philos Lib.

Mole. Dan Sherman. LC 76-50339. 1977. 7.95 o.p. (ISBN 0-87795-162-4, Arbor Hse). Morrow.

Mole Cricket Called Servol: An Account of Experiences in Education & Community Development in Trinidad & Tobago, West Indies. Gerard Pantin. (Illus.). 1979. text ed. 22.00 o.p. (ISBN 0-08-024278-2). Pergamon.

Mole Cricket Called Servol: The Early Years of an Education & Community Development Project in the West Indies. Gerard Pantin. LC 83-8575. (Bernard van Leer International Ser.). 169p. 1983. pap. 8.95 o.p. (ISBN 0-931114-17-9). High-Scope.

Molecular & Cellular Mechanisms of Mutagenesis. Ed. by J. F. Lemontt & W. M. Generoso. LC 82-5300. (Basic Life Sciences Ser.: Vol. 20). 404p. 1982. 69.50x o.p. (ISBN 0-306-41006-0, Plenum Pr.). Plenum Pub.

Molecular & Hormonal Basis of Plant Growth Regulation. Y. Leshem. LC 73-6802. 168p. 1973. 21.00 o.p. (ISBN 0-08-017649-6). Pergamon.

Molecular Approaches to Ecology. Marcel Florkin & Ernest Schoffeniels. 1969. 58.50 o.p. (ISBN 0-12-261046-6). Acad Pr.

Molecular Approaches to Gene Expression & Protein Structure. Ed. by M. A. Siddiqui et al. LC 81-7945. 1981. 43.50 o.p. (ISBN 0-12-641820-9). Acad Pr.

Molecular Approaches to Immunology. Ed. by E. E. Smith & D. W. Ribbons. (Miami Winter Symposia Ser.). 1975. 54.50 o.p. (ISBN 0-12-651050-4). Acad Pr.

Molecular Aspects of Idiopathic Urolithiasis. R. Nath et al. (Illus.). 176p. 1984. pap. 59.00 o.p. (ISBN 0-08-031697-2). Pergamon.

Molecular Aspects of Medicine, Vol. 2. Ed. by H. Baum & J. Gergely. LC 80-40473. (Illus.). 453p. 1980. 85.00 o.p. (ISBN 0-08-026355-0). Pergamon.

Molecular Aspects of Medicine, Vol. 3, No. 6. 1981. pap. 14.50 o.p. (ISBN 0-08-027978-3). Pergamon.

Molecular Aspects of Medicine, Vol. 4. Ed. by H. Baum & J. Gergely. (Illus.). 452p. 1982. 180.00 o.p. (ISBN 0-08-030007-3). Pergamon.

Molecular Aspects of Medicine, Vol. 5. Ed. by H. Baum & J. Gergely. (Illus.). 470p. 1983. 180.00 o.p. (ISBN 0-08-030429-X). Pergamon.

Molecular Aspects of Medicine, Vol. 6. Ed. by H. Baum et al. (Illus.). 584p. 1984. 180.00 o.p. (ISBN 0-08-031724-3). Pergamon.

Molecular Aspects of Medicine, Vol. 7. Ed. by H. Baum et al. (Illus.). 554p. 1985. 205.00 o.p. (ISBN 0-08-033239-0, H210, H125, Pub. by PPL). Pergamon.

Molecular Aspects of Medicine: Vol. 1, Complete. Ed. by H. Baum & J. Gergely. 600p. 1978. 85.00 o.p. (ISBN 0-08-020277-2). Pergamon.

Molecular Aspects of Membrane Phenomena. International Symposium Held at the Battelle Seattle Research Center Seattle, WA, Nov. 4-6, 1974 et al. Ed. by H. R. Kabak & H. Neurath. LC 75-25772. (Illus.). 400p. 1975. 38.00 o.p. (ISBN 0-387-07448-1). Springer-Verlag.

Molecular Aspects of Primary Billiary Cirrhosis. Ed. by O. Epstein. (Illus.). 112p. 1986. pap. 31.00 o.p. (ISBN 0-08-034275-2, Pub. by PPL). Pergamon.

Molecular Associations in Biology. Ed. by Bernard Pullman. LC 68-18679. 1968. 99.00 o.p. (ISBN 0-12-566954-2). Acad Pr.

Molecular Asymmetry in Biology, Vols. 1 & 2. R. Bentley. (Molecular Biology Ser). 1969-70. Vol. 1. 77.00 o.p. (ISBN 0-12-089201-4); Vol. 2. 98.00 o.p. (ISBN 0-12-089202-2). Acad Pr.

Molecular Basis of Biological Degradative Processes. Ed. by Richard Berlin et al. 1978. 52.50 o.p. (ISBN 0-12-092150-2). Acad Pr.

Molecular Basis of Biological Transport. Miami Winter Symposium Staff. Ed. by J. F. Woessner, Jr. & F. Huijing. 1972. 54.50 o.p. (ISBN 0-12-761250-5). Acad Pr.

Molecular Basis of Cancer. Peter B. Farmeer & John M. Walker. 349p. 1985. pap. 39.95 o.p. (ISBN 0-471-82755-X). Wiley.

Molecular Basis of Electron Transport. Miami Winter Symposium Staff. Ed. by Julius Schultz & Bruce F. Cameron. 1972. 54.50 o.p. (ISBN 0-12-632650-9). Acad Pr.

Molecular Basis of Lysosomal Storage Disorders. Ed. by John A. Barranger & Roscoe O. Brady. 1984. 53.50 o.p. (ISBN 0-12-079280-X). Acad Pr.

Molecular Basis of Motility: Proceedings of the Colloquium of the Gesellschaft fuer Biologische Chemie, 26th, Mosbach, Baden, Germany, April 10-12, 1975. Colloquium of the Gesellschaft Fuer Biologische Chemie Staff. Ed. by L. Heilmeyer. (Illus.). 260p. 1976. 40.00 o.p. (ISBN 0-387-07576-3). Springer-Verlag.

Molecular Basis of Odor. John E. Amoore. (Illus.). 216p. 1970. 25.75x o.p. (ISBN 0-398-00039-5). C C Thomas.

Molecular Beam Epitaxy. Brian R. Pamplin. (Illus.). 178p. 1980. 48.00 o.p. (ISBN 0-08-025050-5). Pergamon.

Molecular Beams & Reaction Kinetics. Ed. by C. Schlier. (Italian Physical Society: Course No. 44). 1970. 88.00 o.p. (ISBN 0-12-368844-2). Acad Pr.

Molecular Behavior & the Development of Polymer Materials. Ed. by A. Ledwith & A. M. North. 1975. 65.00x o.p. (ISBN 0-412-12400-9, NO. 6175, Pub. by Chapman & Hall). Routledge Chapman & Hall.

Molecular Biology & Protein Synthesis. Ed. by Robert A. Niederman. LC 76-13388. (Benchmark Papers in Microbiology Ser.: Vol. 10). 1976. 72.50 o.p. (ISBN 0-12-787130-6). Acad Pr.

Molecular Biology of Animal Virus, Vol. 1. Ed. by Debi Nayak. 1977. 85.00 o.p. (ISBN 0-8247-6533-8). Dekker.

Molecular Biology of Animal Viruses, Vol. 2. Ed. by Debi Nayak. 1977. 85.00 o.p. (ISBN 0-8247-6534-6). Dekker.

Molecular Biology of Cancer. Harris Busch. 1974. 95.00 o.p. (ISBN 0-12-147660-X). Acad Pr.

Molecular Biology of Rifomycin. Henry Erlich et al. 182p. 1973. text ed. 28.50x o.p. (ISBN 0-8422-7089-2). Irvington.

Molecular Biology of RNA Tumor Viruses. Ed. by John R. Stephenson. LC 79-29668. (Molecular Biology Ser.). 1980. 77.00 o.p. (ISBN 0-12-666050-6). Acad Pr.

Molecular Biology of the Gene. 3rd ed. J. D. Watson. LC 75-14791. 1976. 39.95 o.p. (ISBN 0-8053-9609-8). Benjamin-Cummings.

Molecular Biology of Viruses. John S. Colter & William Paranchych. 1967. 99.00 o.p. (ISBN 0-12-182250-8). Acad Pr.

Molecular Biology, Pathogenicity, & Ecology of Bacterial Plasmids. Ed. by Stuart B. Levy et al. LC 81-8692. 720p. 1981. 95.00x o.p. (ISBN 0-306-40753-1, Plenum Pr). Plenum Pub.

Molecular Biophysics. Ed. by Bernard Pullman & Mitchel Weissbluth. 1965. 74.50 o.p. (ISBN 0-12-566956-9). Acad Pr.

Molecular Cloning of Recombinant DNA. Ed. by W. A. Scott & R. Werner. 1977. 24.95 o.p. (ISBN 0-12-634250-4). Acad Pr.

Molecular Control of Cell Differentiation & Morphogenesis: A Systematic Theory. G. D. Wassermann. (Quantitative Approach to Life Science Ser.: Vol. 2). 1972. 99.75 o.p. (ISBN 0-8247-1766-X). Dekker.

Molecular Control of Proliferation & Differentiation: Thirty-fifth Symposium on the Society for Developmental Biology. Ed. by John Papaconstantinou & William J. Rutter. 1978. 45.50 o.p. (ISBN 0-12-612981-9). Acad Pr.

Molecular Diffusion & Spectra. William Coffey et al. LC 83-16681. 378p. 1984. 62.50x o.p. (ISBN 0-471-87539-2). Krieger.

Molecular Dynamics & Protein Structure: Proceedings of a Workshop held 13-18 May 1984 at the University of North Carolina. Ed. by Jan Hermans. 194p. 1985. pap. 10.00x o.s.i. (ISBN 0-317-43256-7). Polycrystal Bk Serv.

Molecular Dynamics in Biosystems. Kenneth H. Norwick. 1977. 105.00 o.p. (ISBN 0-08-020420-1). Pergamon.

Molecular Electro-Optics: Electro-Optic Properties of Macromolecules & Colloids in Solution. Ed. by Sonja Krause. LC 81-1314. (NATO ASI Series B, Physics: Vol. 64). 528p. 1981. 85.00x o.p. (ISBN 0-306-40659-4, Plenum Pr). Plenum Pub.

Molecular Electronics: Beyond the Silicon Chip. 2nd, rev. ed. Ed. by M. Todd Jarvis. LC 85-51500. (Emerging Technologies Ser.: No. 9). (Illus.). 148p. 1985. report 390.00 o.p. (ISBN 0-914993-21-6, ME-2RV). Tech Insights.

Molecular Evolution & the Origins of Life. 2nd expanded ed. Sidney W. Fox & Klaus Dose. LC 77-21434. (Biology-a Series of Textbooks: Vol. 2). 1977. 49.75 o.p. (ISBN 0-8247-6619-9). Dekker.

Molecular Genetic Mechanisms in Aging & Development. Ed. by Morris Rockstein & George T. Baker. 1972. 42.50 o.p. (ISBN 0-12-591550-0). Acad Pr.

Molecular Genetic Modification of Eucaryotes. Ed. by Rubenstein et al. 1977. 26.00 o.p. (ISBN 0-12-601150-8). Acad Pr.

Molecular Genetics: An Advanced Treatise, 2 pts. Ed. by J. H. Taylor. (Molecular Biology Ser). Pt. 1, 1962. 82.50 ea. o.p. (ISBN 0-12-684401-1). Pt. 1. Pt. 2, 1967. 82.50 o.p. (ISBN 0-12-684402-X). Acad Pr.

Molecular Genetics: Proceedings. Wissenschaftliche Konferenz der Gesellschaft Deutscher Naturforscher und Aerzte, 4th, Berlin, 1967. Ed. by H. G. Wittmann & H. Schuster. LC 68-28526. 1968. pap. 44.90 o.p. (ISBN 0-387-04276-8). Springer-Verlag.

Molecular Graphics on the Apple Microcomputer. Ed. by Frank H. Clarke & James G. Henkel. 1985. 129.50 o.p. (ISBN 0-12-175780-3). Acad Pr.

Molecular Graphics on the IBM PC Microcomputer. Ed. by James G. Henkel & Frank H. Clarke. 1985. 129.50 o.p. (ISBN 0-12-340820-2). Acad Pr.

Molecular Hydrodynamics. Jean P. Boon & Sidney Yip. (Illus.). 440p. 1980. text ed. 86.95 o.p. (ISBN 0-07-006560-8). McGraw.

Molecular Interactions, Vol. 3. Ed. by H. Ratajczak & W. J. Orville-Thomas. LC 79-40825. (Molecular Interactions Ser.). 561p. 1982. 220.00 o.p. (ISBN 0-471-10033-1, Pub. by Wiley-Interscience). Wiley.

Molecular Ions: Geometric & Electronic Structures. Ed. by Joseph Berkowitz & Karl-Ontjes Groeneveld. (NATO ASI Series B, Physics: Vol. 90). 606p. 1983. 95.00x o.p. (ISBN 0-306-41264-0, Plenum Pr). Plenum Pub.

Molecular Mechanics: A Symposium. Ed. by Delos F. DeTar. LC 77-14614. 1978. pap. 40.00 o.p. (ISBN 0-08-022070-3). Pergamon.

Molecular Mechanisms in the Control of Gene Expression, Vol. 5. Ed. by Donald P. Nierlich et al. 1976. 77.00 o.p. (ISBN 0-12-518550-2). Acad Pr.

Molecular Mechanisms of Complement. Ed. by M. Loos et al. (Complement Ser: Vol. 2). 1976. text ed. 35.50x o.p. (ISBN 0-685-70939-6). Irvington.

Molecular Metals. Ed. by William E. Hatfield. LC 79-4284. (NATO Conference Series VI, Materials Science: Vol. 1). 568p. 1979. 79.50x o.p. (ISBN 0-306-40159-2, Plenum Pr). Plenum Pub.

Molecular Models of Photoresponsiveness. Ed. by G. Montagnoli & B. F. Erlanger. LC 83-13861. (NATO ASI Series A, Life Sciences: Vol. 68). 400p. 1983. 75.00x o.p. (ISBN 0-306-41472-4, Plenum Pr). Plenum Pub.

Molecular Neurobiology. Guroff. LC 79-22812. 1980. 89.00 o.p. (ISBN 0-8247-6862-0). Dekker.

Molecular Orbital Studies in Chemical Pharmacology: Proceedings of the Batelle Seattle Research Center Symposium, 1969. Battelle Seattle Research Center Symposium Staff. Ed. by Lemont B. Kier. LC 77-120374. 1970. 36.00 o.p. (ISBN 0-387-04972-X). Springer-Verlag.

Molecular Orbitals. Ed. by F. Boschke. LC 51-5497. (Topics in Current Chemistry: Vol. 23). 1971. pap. 29.10 o.p. (ISBN 0-387-05504-5). Springer-Verlag.

Molecular Photobiology: Inactivation & Recovery. Kendric C. Smith & Philip C. Hanawalt. (Molecular Biology Ser, Vol. 6). 1969. 54.00 o.p. (ISBN 0-12-651450-X). Acad Pr.

Molecular Processes in Vision. Ed. by Edwin Abrahamson & Sanford E. Ostroy. LC 80-29543. (Benchmark Papers in Biochemistry: Vol. 3). 448p. 1982. 61.95 o.p. (ISBN 0-87933-372-3). Van Nos Reinhold.

Molecular Processes on Solid Surfaces. E. Drauglis et al. (Materials Science & Engineering Ser.). 1969. text ed. 77.50 o.p. (ISBN 0-07-017827-5). McGraw.

Molecular Properties. E. Tsuchida et al. LC 61-642. (Advances in Polymer Science: Vol. 24). (Illus.). 1977. 53.00 o.p. (ISBN 0-387-08124-0). Springer-Verlag.

Molecular Radiation Biology. Action of Ionizing Radiation on Elementary Biological Objects. H. Dertinger & H. Jung. Tr. by R. P. Hueber & P. A. Gresham. LC 73-112314. (Heidelberg Science Library: Vol. 12). (Illus.). 1970. pap. 17.00 o.p. (ISBN 0-387-90013-6). Springer-Verlag.

Molecular Relaxation Processes: Proceedings. Symposium On Relaxation Methods In Relation To Molecular Structure - Aberystwyth - 1965. Ed. by R. C. Cross. 1966. 33.50 o.p. (ISBN 0-12-150450-6). Acad Pr.

Titles

Titles

Molecular Spectra & Molecular Structure, 3 vols. Gerhard Herzberg. Incl. Vol.1. Spectra of Diatomic Molecules. 2nd ed. 1950. 34.95 o.p. (ISBN 0-442-03385-0); Vol. 2. Infrared & Raman Spectra of Polyatomic Molecules. 1945. 34.95 o.p. (ISBN 0-442-03386-9); Vol. 3. Electronic Spectra & Electronic Structure of Polyatomic Molecules. 1966. 34.95 o.p. (ISBN 0-442-03387-7). Pub. by Van Nostrand). Krieger.
Molecular Studies on Halogenated Deoxynucleosides. C. C. Huang et al. 256p. 1972. text ed. 36.50x o.p. (ISBN 0-8422-7013-2). Irvington.
Molecular Thermodynamics. R. E. Dickerson. 1969. pap. text ed. 21.95 o.p. (ISBN 0-8053-2363-5). Benjamin-Cummings.
Molecular Vibrations in Crystals. J. C. Decius & R. M. Hexter. 1977. text ed. 65.95 o.p. (ISBN 0-07-016227-1). McGraw.
Molecular Virology. T. H. Pennington & D. A. Ritchie. (Outline Studies in Biology). 1976. pap. 8.50 o.p. (ISBN 0-412-12590-0, NO. 6216, Pub. by Chapman & Hall). Routledge Chapman & Hall.
Molecules, Cells & Parasites in Immunology. Ed. by Carlos Larralde et al. 1980. 38.00 o.p. (ISBN 0-12-436840-9). Acad Pr.
Molecules R2CXCR2 Including Azomethine, Carbonyl & Thiocarbonyl Ylides: Their Syntheses, Properties & Reactions. Richard M. Kellogg. 1977. pap. 14.00 o.p. (ISBN 0-08-021582-3). Pergamon.
Moliere: Four Comedies. Tr. by Richard Wilbur. LC 82-47657. (Illus.). 640p. 1982. 19.95 o.p. (ISBN 0-15-161781-3). HarBraceJ.
Moll Flanders see also Amorous Adventures of Moll Flanders.
Moll Flanders see also Fortunes & Misfortunes of the Famous Moll FLANDERS.
Moll Flanders. Daniel Defoe. 1982. pap. 2.50x o.p. (ISBN 0-460-01837-X, DEL-04243, Evman); 9.95x o.p. (ISBN 0-460-00837-4). Biblio Dist.
Molloy. Samuel Beckett. Tr. by Samuel Beckett & Patrick Bowles. LC 55-5113. 1955. pap. 6.95 o.p. (ISBN 0-394-17027-X, E18, Ever). Grove.
Mollusca of the Chalk, 4 Pts. D. Sharpe. Repr. of 1909 ed. Set. 23.00 o.p. (ISBN 0-384-55070-3). Johnson Repr.
Molluscicides in Schistosomiasis Control. Ed. by Thomas C. Cheng. 1974. 49.50 o.p. (ISBN 0-12-170740-7). Acad Pr.
Molly Companion. Maura Stanton. 1979. pap. 1.95 o.p. (ISBN 0-380-40436-2, 40436). Avon.
Molly Gallagher. Betty L. Receveur. (Orig.). 1982. pap. 3.50 o.s.i. (ISBN 0-345-29512-9). Ballantine.
Molly Stark: Woman of the Revolution. Olive Tardiff. LC 75-12182. (Illus.). 96p. (gr. 4-6). 1976. pap. 4.95 o.p. (ISBN 0-914016-26-1). Phoenix Pub.
Molly's Lies. Kay Chorao. LC 78-12383. (Illus.). 32p. (ps-3). 1979. 7.50 o.p. (ISBN 0-395-28951-3, Clarion). HM.
Molly's Moe. Kay Chorao. LC 76-3526. (Illus.). 32p. (ps-3). 1979. 7.50 o.p. (ISBN 0-395-28784-7, Clarion). HM.
Molt Brother. Jacqueline Lichtenberg. 256p. 1985. pap. 2.75 o.s.i. (ISBN 0-425-07452-8). Berkley Pub.
Molybdenum in the Environment, Vol. 1: The Biology of Molybdenum. Williard R. Chappell & Kathy K. Paterson. 1976. 89.75 o.p. (ISBN 0-8247-6405-6). Dekker.
Molybdenum in the Environment, Vol. 2: The Geochemistry, Cycling, & Industrial Uses of Molybdenum. Willard Chappell & Kathy Peterson. 1977. 95.00 o.p. (ISBN 0-8247-6495-1). Dekker.
Molybdenum Nutrition in Rice. D. K. Das Gupta. (International Bioscience Monographs: No. 4). 74p. 1978. 8.00 o.p. (ISBN 0-88065-046-X, Pub. by Messers Today & Tomorrow Printers & Publishers). Scholarly Pubns.
Mom Has a Second Job: Prayer Thoughts for Working Mothers. Judith Mattison. LC 80-65548. 96p. (Orig.). 1980. pap. 4.50 o.p. (ISBN 0-8066-1793-4, 10-4534, Augsburg). Augsburg Fortress.
Mom, How Come I'm Not Thin? Bill Bluestein & Enid Bluestein. (Illus.). (gr. 2-5). 1981. 8.95 o.p. (ISBN 0-89638-044-0). CompCare.
Mom LeTourneau. Norman B. Rohrer. Ed. by Isabel A. Throop. 144p. 1985. 6.95 o.p. (ISBN 0-8423-4502-7). Tyndale.
Mom, the Wolf Man & Me. Norma Klein. 160p. (gr. 5-9). 1977. pap. 1.95 o.p. (ISBN 0-380-01725-3, 60458-2, Camelot). Avon.
MOMA-Access. Richard S. Wurman. (Guidebooks). (Illus.). 120p. (Orig.). 1988. pap. 9.95 o.p. (ISBN 0-915461-14-5). Access Pr.
Moment in the Sun. Ann Pinchot. 202p. 1984. 15.95 o.p. (ISBN 0-87795-582-4, Arbor Hse). Morrow.
Moment of Freedom. Jens Bjorneboe. 217p. 1975. 9.95 o.p. (ISBN 0-393-08719-0). Norton.
Moment of Silence. Pierre Janssen. Tr. by William R. Tyler. LC 76-115085. (Illus.). 64p. (gr. 5 up). 1970. PLB 4.25 o.s.i. (ISBN 0-689-20603-8, Atheneum Childrens Bks). Macmillan.
Moment of True Feeling. Peter Handke. Tr. by Ralph Manheim from Ger. 144p. 1977. 7.95 o.p. (ISBN 0-374-17291-9). FS&G.
Momentos Felices Con Dios. Margaret Anderson. 192p. 1977. 3.95 o.p. (ISBN 0-88113-312-4). Edit Betania.
Moments Bright & Shining: Three Hundred & Sixty-Five Thoughts to Enjoy Day by Day. Compiled by Peter Seymour. (Illus.). 1979. 7.95 o.s.i. (ISBN 0-8378-1706-4). Gibson.
Moments of Being: Unpublished Autobiographical Writings. Virginia Woolf. Ed. by J. Ferrone. LC 76-27410. 1977. 8.95 o.p. (ISBN 0-15-162034-2). HarBraceJ.
Moments of Being: Unpublished Autobiographical Writings. Virginia Woolf. Ed. & intro. by Jeanne Schulkind. LC 78-6666. 1978. pap. 3.95 o.p. (ISBN 0-15-661917-2, Harv). HarBraceJ.
Moments: Poems about the Seasons. Ed. by Lee B. Hopkins. LC 80-7983. (Illus.). 64p. (gr. 4-6). 1980. 8.95 o.p. (ISBN 0-15-255291-X, HJ). HarBraceJ.
Moments Without Self. 4th ed. Benito F. Reyes. LC 61-21760. 198p. Date not set. Repr. of 1970 ed. 10.00 o.p. (ISBN 0-939375-36-2). World Univ Amer.
Momentum. Wallace Alcorn. (Living Studies Ser.). 128p. (Orig.). 1986. pap. 5.95 o.p. (ISBN 0-8423-4538-8). Tyndale.
Momentum: A Theory of Social Action. Peter Adler. LC 81-2718. (Sociological Observations Ser.: Vol. 11). (Illus.). 191p. 1981. 29.95 o.p. (ISBN 0-8039-1307-9); pap. 14.95 o.p. (ISBN 0-8039-1581-0). Sage.
Momentum & Heat Transfer Processes in Recirculating Flows: HTD, Vol.13. Ed. by B Launder & J. A. Humphrey. 116p. 1980. 18.00 o.p. (ISBN 0-317-33568-5, G00186); members 9.00 o.p. (ISBN 0-317-33569-3). ASME.
Momentum Transfer in Boundary Layers. Cebeci. 391p. 1977. 32.00 o.p. (ISBN 0-89116-475-8). Hemisphere Pub.
Mommy, Daddy, Look What I'm Saying. Myra Levick & Diana S. Wheeler. (What Your Children Are Telling You Through Their Art Ser.). 192p. 1985. 17.95 o.p. (ISBN 0-87131-462-2). M Evans.
Momoyama: Japanese Art in the Age of Grandeur. (Illus.). 136p. 1975. pap. 5.50 o.p. (ISBN 0-87099-125-6). Metro Mus Art.
Mon Faust. Paul Valery. (Coll. Soleil). 9.95 o.p. (ISBN 0-685-36620-0). Schoenhof.
Mona que le Pisaron la Cola. Rosario Ferre. LC 81-69847. (Illus.). 48p. (gr. 7). 1981. pap. 5.50 o.p. (ISBN 0-940238-61-6). Ediciones Hura.
Monarch Notes in Kant's Philosophy. (gr. 7-12). pap. 2.95 o.p. (ISBN 0-671-00530-8). Monarch Pr.
Monarch Notes: Introduction to American Minority Literature. Ann Semel. 1975. pap. 1.50 o.p. (ISBN 0-671-00962-1). Monarch Pr.
Monarch Notes on a Survey of Pre-Twentieth Century American Poets. Ray Rudnik. (Orig.). pap. 1.50 o.p. (ISBN 0-671-00735-1). Monarch Pr.
Monarch Notes on Austen's Pride & Prejudice. (Orig.). pap. 2.50 o.p. (ISBN 0-671-52852-1). Monarch Pr.
Monarch Notes on Blake's Poetry. Eugenie Harris. (Orig.). pap. 2.95 o.s.i. (ISBN 0-671-00775-0). Monarch Pr.
Monarch Notes on Buck's the Good Earth. Donald Roden. (Orig.). pap. 2.95 o.p. (ISBN 0-671-52868-8). Monarch Pr.
Monarch Notes on Dickens' a Tale of Two Cities. (Orig.). pap. 2.95 o.p. (ISBN 0-671-52853-X). Monarch Pr.
Monarch Notes on Fitzgerald's Great Gatsby. (Orig.). pap. 3.25 o.p. (ISBN 0-671-52876-9). Monarch Pr.
Monarch Notes on Hardy's Jude, the Obscure. Ralph Ranald. (Orig.). pap. 3.50 o.p. (ISBN 0-671-00713-0). Monarch Pr.
Monarch Notes on Hemingway's Farewell to Arms. Lawrence Klibbe. (Orig.). pap. 2.75 o.p. (ISBN 0-671-52865-3). Monarch Pr.
Monarch Notes on Homer's Odyssey. (Orig.). pap. 3.50 o.p. (ISBN 0-671-52862-9). Monarch Pr.
Monarch Notes on Lee's to Kill a Mockingbird. (Orig.). pap. 2.95 o.p. (ISBN 0-671-52875-0). Monarch Pr.
Monarch Notes on London's Call of the Wind. (gr. 7-12). pap. 2.95 o.p. (ISBN 0-671-52867-X). Monarch Pr.
Monarch Notes on Melville's Moby Dick. (Orig.). pap. 2.75 o.p. (ISBN 0-671-52854-8). Monarch Pr.
Monarch Notes on Mitchell's Gone with the Wind. Leila Gemme. 1975. pap. 2.50 o.p. (ISBN 0-671-00946-X). Monarch Pr.
Monarch Notes on Shakespeare's Richard Third. Elizabeth Nugent. (Orig.). pap. 3.50 o.p. (ISBN 0-671-52877-7). Monarch Pr.
Monarch Notes on Shakespeare's Romeo & Juliet. (Orig.). pap. 2.95 o.p. (ISBN 0-671-52880-7). Monarch Pr.
Monarch Notes on Shakespeare's Winter's Tale. Margaret L. Ranald. (Orig.). pap. 3.50 o.p. (ISBN 0-671-00656-8). Monarch Pr.
Monarch Notes on Steinbeck's Of Mice & Men. (Orig.). pap. 2.50 o.p. (ISBN 0-671-52869-6). Monarch Pr.
Monarch Notes on Twain's Huckleberry Finn & Other Works. (Orig.). pap. 2.50 o.p. (ISBN 0-671-52849-1). Monarch Pr.
Monarchia. Dante Alighieri. LC 74-147412. (Library of War & Peace; Proposals for Peace: a History). lib. bdg. 46.00 o.p. (ISBN 0-8240-0210-5). Garland Pub.
Monarch's Complete Guide to Getting into Graduate Business School. Bruce S. Sheiman. (Illus.). 160p. (Orig.). 1981. pap. 6.95 o.p. (ISBN 0-671-09255-3). Monarch Pr.
Monarch's Complete Guide to Law Schools. Arline Glotzer. (Illus.). 192p. (Orig.). 1981. pap. 6.95 o.p. (ISBN 0-671-09192-1). Monarch Pr.
Monarch's Dictionary of Investment Terms. Edith L. Beer. 192p. (Orig.). 1983. pap. 7.95 o.p. (ISBN 0-671-45497-8). Monarch Pr.
Monarch's Dictionary of Legal Terms. Shirley R. Bysiewicz. 192p. (Orig.). 1983. pap. 7.95 o.p. (ISBN 0-671-09232-4). Monarch Pr.
Monarch's Preparation for the Police Officer Exam. Rocky Pomerance & James L. LeGrande. 384p. 1983. 7.95 o.p. (ISBN 0-671-47102-3). Monarch Pr.
Monarchy in the Emperor's Eyes: Image & Reality in the Ch'ien-Lung Reign. Harold L. Kahn. LC 75-135546. (East Asian Ser.: No. 59). 1971. 22.50x o.s.i. (ISBN 0-674-58230-6). Harvard U Pr.
Monastery: Prayer, Work, & the Common Life. M. Basil Pennington. LC 83-47732. (Illus.). 128p. 1983. 21.63 o.p. (ISBN 0-06-066495-9). HarpR.
Monastic Achievement. George Zarnecki. (Illus.). 144p. 1972. pap. text ed. 3.95 o.p. (ISBN 0-07-072735-X). McGraw.
Monastic Breviary. 1976. 17.50x o.p. (ISBN 0-8192-1220-2). Morehouse Pub.
Monastic Realm. Reginald Gregoire et al. LC 85-43046. (Illus.). 288p. 1985. 75.00 o.p. (ISBN 0-8478-0664-2). Rizzoli Intl.
Mondamine Oxidase & Disease. Ed. by Keith Tipton & P. Dostert. 1984. 49.00 o.p. (ISBN 0-12-691660-8). Acad Pr.
Monday Morning Christianity. Harry E. Olson, Jr. LC 75-2833. 128p. (Orig.). 1975. pap. 3.95 o.p. (ISBN 0-8066-1478-1, 10-4535, Augsburg). Augsburg Fortress.
Monday Morning Quarterback. Jim Benagh et al. 1983. pap. 8.95 o.p. (ISBN 0-03-063776-7). H Holt & Co.
Monday Night Football Cookbook & Restaurant Guide. Andy Armentani & Gary Donatelli. LC 82-71965. (Illus.). 160p. 1982. pap. 9.95 o.p. (ISBN 0-8019-7270-1). Chilton.
Monday, Tuesday, Wednesday. Robert Houston. 1978. pap. 1.50 o.p. (ISBN 0-380-01876-4, 37036-0). Avon.
Monday Voices. Joanne Greenberg. 1979. pap. 1.50 o.p. (ISBN 0-380-01417-3, 35212-5). Avon.
Monde de l'Art n'est pas le Morde du Pardon. Rene Char. (Illus.). 132p. 1974. 300.00 o.p. (ISBN 0-686-54161-8). French & Eur.
Mondrian Studies. Kermit S. Champa. LC 85-980. (Illus.). xviii, 150p. 1985. 35.00 o.s.i. (ISBN 0-226-10078-2). U of Chicago Pr.
Monet. Compiled by Anna Barskaya. (Illus.). 50p. 1982. pap. 14.95 o.p. (ISBN 0-8109-2265-7, 2219-3). Abrams.
Monet: The Masterworks. Jean-Paul Crespelle. LC 86-892. (Illus.). 138p. (Orig.). 1986. pap. 17.95 o.p. (ISBN 0-87663-894-9). Universe.
Monetary & Financial Policy in Nineteenth Century Britain. F. W. Fetter & D. Gregory. (Government & Society in 19th Century Britain Ser.). 106p. 1973. 30.00x o.p. (ISBN 0-7165-2217-9, 02038, Pub. by Irish Academic Pr Ireland); pap. 6.00x o. p. o.p. (ISBN 0-7165-2218-7). Biblio Dist.
Monetary Control. Elmer Wood. 238p. 1963. 24.00 o.p. (ISBN 0-8262-0021-4). U of Mo Pr.
Monetary Incentives & Work Standards in Five Cities: Impacts & Implications for Management & Labor. John M. Greiner et al. 94p. 1977. pap. text ed. 7.85 o.p. (ISBN 0-87766-187-1). Urban Inst.
Monetary Policy & Modern Money Markets: Fixed vs. Market-Determined Deposit Rates. Michael G. Hadjimachalakis. LC 82-47638. 272p. 1982. 37.00x o.p. (ISBN 0-669-05550-6). Lexington Bks.
Monetary Policy & Practice: A View from the Federal Reserve Board. Henry C. Wallich. LC 81-47648. 416p. 1981. 23.50x o.p. (ISBN 0-669-04712-0). Lexington Bks.
Monet's Series. Grace Seiberling. LC 79-57497. (Outstanding Dissertations in the Fine Arts Ser.: No. 5). 470p. 1982. lib. bdg. 61.00 o.p. (ISBN 0-8240-3941-6). Garland Pub.
Money, Vol. 4, (incl. 1987 Supplement) Ed. by Eleanor C. Goldstein. 1988. 15.00 o.p. (ISBN 0-89777-131-1). Soc Issues.
Money---Guilt or Excitement? Wilfred Bockelman. 80p. (Orig.). 1986. pap. 3.95 o.p. (ISBN 0-8066-2258-X, 23-1696, Augsburg). Augsburg Fortress.
Money & Banking. G. Krishnan-Kutty. 1979. text ed. 9.95x o.p. (ISBN 0-391-01815-9). Humanities.
Money & Banking. Kenneth H. Smith. LC 72-84417. (Real World of Economics Ser.). Orig. Title: Banking. (Illus.). (gr. 5-11). 1970. PLB 4.95 o.p. (ISBN 0-8225-0614-9). Lerner Pubns.
Money & Banking: A Market Oriented Approach. 2nd ed. Ivan C. Johnson & William Roberts. 672p. 1985. text ed. 32.95x o.p. (ISBN 0-03-001222-8); study guide 10.95x o.p. (ISBN 0-03-001224-4). Dryden Pr.
Money & Banking: Contemporary Policies, Practices & Issues. 2nd ed. Tyrone Black & Donnie L. Daniel. 1985. 33.95x o.p. (ISBN 0-256-03253-X). Irwin.
Money & Capital Markets. Rose. 1983. text ed. 31.95 o.p. (ISBN 0-256-02708-0). Irwin.
Money & Capital Markets. 2nd ed. Peter R. Rose. 1986. 38.95 o.p. (ISBN 0-256-03434-6). Irwin.
Money & Capital Markets in an Asian Setting. Sixto K. Roxas. 1977. pap. 3.50x o.p. (ISBN 0-89955-347-8, Pub. by Japan Sci Soc Pr Japan). Intl Spec Bk.
Money & Class in America: Notes & Observations on the American Character. Lewis Lapham. 320p. 1988. 18.95 o.p. (ISBN 0-317-66208-2). Weidenfeld.
Money & Kids: How to Earn It, Save It, & Spend It. Mary P. Lee. LC 73-7864. (Illus.). 144p. (gr. 4-8). 1973. 4.75 o.s.i. (ISBN 0-664-32536-X, Westminster); pap. 2.75 o.s.i. (ISBN 0-664-34006-7, Westminster). Westminster John Knox.
Money & the Economy. 5th ed. John J. Klein. 538p. 1982. text ed. 20.75 o.p. (ISBN 0-15-564006-2, HC). HarBraceJ.
Money & the Woman: The Embezzler. James M. Cain. (Nightingale Ser.). 256p. (Orig.). 1985. pap. 9.95 o.p. (ISBN 0-8161-3926-1, Large Print Bks). G K Hall.
Money Angles. Andrew Tobias. 192p. 1984. 12.70 o.p. (ISBN 0-671-50804-0, Linden Pr). S&S.
Money Banking & International Trade. 2nd rev. ed. M. C. Vaish. 1980. text ed. 37.50x o.p. (ISBN 0-7069-0559-8, Pub. by Vikas India). Advent NY.
Money, Banking & the Economy, 2nd ed. Thomas Mayer et al. (Illus.). 1984. text ed. 31.95x o.p. (ISBN 0-393-95313-0). Norton.
Money, Banking, & the Nation's Income. Lapkin. Irwin.
Money Burn. Tony Foster. 284p. 1986. pap. 3.95 o.p. (ISBN 1-55547-116-1). Critics Choice Paper.
Money, Credit & Economic Activity. Charles D. Cathcart. 1982. 33.95x o.p. (ISBN 0-256-02491-X). Irwin.
Money Diet: Biblical Prescriptions for Financial Success. Richard T. Case et al. (Life Enrichment Ser.). 1985. pap. 5.95 o.p. (ISBN 0-8010-2512-5). Baker Bk.
Money for a Motorbike see Heinemann Guided Readers.
Money for Sale see Heinemann Guided Readers.
Money-Grubbing: A Student's Guide to Part-time Jobs & Self-Run Businesses. Patrick H. Crowe & Gregory D. Crowe. 150p. 1983. pap. 5.95 o.p. (ISBN 0-914091-29-8). Chicago Review.
Money Guide: Your Taxes an Ongoing Guide for Tax Planning under the New Tax Law. Money Magazine Editors. (Money Guides: No. 3). 144p. (Orig.). 1988. pap. 6.95 o.p. (ISBN 0-8362-2200-8). Andrews & McMeel.
Money Hat & Other Hungarian Folk Tales. Peggy Hoffman & Gyuri Biro. 1969. 4.50 o.s.i. (ISBN 0-664-32458-4, Westminster). Westminster John Knox.
Money: How to Get It, Keep It, & Make It Grow. Michael Hayes. (Illus.). 1979. 15.95 o.p. (ISBN 0-8144-5503-4). AMACOM.
Money: How to Save It, Spend It, & Make It. B. D. Coleman. 1968. text ed. 24.00 o.p. (ISBN 0-08-012936-6); pap. text ed. 10.75 o.p. (ISBN 0-08-012935-8). Pergamon.
Money in the Computer Age. F. P. Thomson. 1968. text ed. 25.00 o.p. (ISBN 0-08-012856-4); pap. text ed. 11.25 o.p. (ISBN 0-08-012855-6). Pergamon.
Money in the Pocket see Getting along Series of Skills.
Money Income of Households, Families & Persons in the United States, 1984. (Current Population Reports, P-60; Consumer Income: No. 151). 204p. 1986. looseleaf 10.00 o.p. (S/N 003-001-91657-6). USGPO.
Money Income of Households, Families, & Persons in the United States, 1985: Consumer Income, P-60. (Current Population Ser.: No. 156). (Illus.). 219p. 1987. pap. 10.00 o.p. (ISBN 0-318-23517-X, S/N 803-005-30002-1). USGPO.

Money is What Money Does: A Mini Book on the Macroeconomy. Glen Peterson. 1978. 7.00 o.p. (ISBN 0-682-49199-3). Exposition-Phoenix.
Money Labyrinth. Shirley E. Woods. LC 84-12103. 192p. 1985. 16.95 o.p. (ISBN 0-385-19651-2). Doubleday.
Money-Making Photography. Bill Hurter. LC 80-81784. (Petersen's Photographic Libray: Vol. 2). (Illus.). 160p. (Orig.). (gr. 8-12). 1980. pap. 8.95 o.p. (ISBN 0-8227-4040-0). Petersen Pub.
Money Making Plans of the New Era, 2 vols. Set. pap. 8.00 o.s.i. (ISBN 0-937514-17-9). Vol. 1 (ISBN 0-937514-18-7). Vol. 2 (ISBN 0-937514-19-5). Prime Pubs.
Money Management Forms. (Easy-to-Make Photocopier Bks.). (Orig.). 1983. pap. 14.95 o.p. (ISBN 0-87280-043-1, Asher-Gallant). Caddylak Systs.
Money Management Teacher's Guide. 64p. 1980. 2.00 o.p. (ISBN 0-317-36398-0). New Readers.
Money Market Calculations. Marcia Stigum. LC 80-66022. 1981. 42.50 o.p. (ISBN 0-87094-192-5). Dow Jones-Irwin.
Money Marriage: A Novel. Elaine Suss. LC 79-23995. 240p. 1980. 9.95 o.s.i. (ISBN 0-8008-5319-9). Taplinger.
Money Matters: The Hassle-Free-Month-by-Month Guide to Money Management. Paul N. Strassels & William B. Mead. LC 86-10733. 288p. 1986. (ISBN 0-201-07222-X). Addison-Wesley.
Money Men & One Shot Deal. Gerald Petievich. LC 79-8756. 1981. 12.95 o.p. (ISBN 0-15-169892-9). HarBraceJ.
Money on the Move: The Modern International Capital Market. M. Stefan Mendelsohn. (Illus.). 1979. text ed. 34.95 o.p. (ISBN 0-07-041474-2). McGraw.
Money Phases. Judith Briles. 1985. pap. 7.95 o.p. (ISBN 0-671-55451-4, Fireside). S&S.
Money Phases: The Six Financial Stages of a Woman's Life. Judith Briles. 224p. 1984. 14.50 o.p. (ISBN 0-671-45609-1). S&S.
Money, Prices, & Foreign Exchange in Fourteenth Century France. Harry A. Miskimin. LC 63-7942. Repr. of 1963 ed. 15.00 o.s.i. (ISBN 0-08-022307-9). Pergamon.
Money Problems & Pastoral Care. Paul G. Schurman. LC 81-70662. (Creative Pastoral Care & Counseling Ser.). 96p. 1982. pap. 4.50 o.p. (ISBN 0-8006-0568-3, 1-568, Fortress). Augsburg Fortress.
Money Question During Reconstruction. Walter T. Nugent. (Orig.). 1967. pap. 1.95 o.p. (ISBN 0-393-09759-5, NortonC). Norton.
Money: Royal Shakespeare Company. Edward G. Bulwer-Lytton. (PIT Playtext Ser.). 56p. 1982. pap. 4.95 o.p. (ISBN 0-413-51240-1, NO. 3761). Heinemann Ed.
Money Saving Recipes Through Sprouting & Gardening. Bruford S. Reynolds. pap. 4.95 o.p. (ISBN 0-89036-134-7). Hawkes Pub Inc.
Money Should Be Fun. William Hamilton. 1980. 9.95 o.p. (ISBN 0-395-28218-7); pap. 5.95 o.p. HM.
Money Stones. Ian St. James. LC 80-65984. 1980. 9.95 o.p. (ISBN 0-689-11104-5, Atheneum). Macmillan.
Money: Study of the Theory of the Medium of Exchange. David Kinley. LC 68-28638. 1968. Repr. of 1904 ed. lib. bdg. 35.00x o.p. (ISBN 0-8371-0515-3, KIMS). Greenwood.
Money Supply, Money Demand, & Macroeconomic Models. 2nd ed. Thomas M. Havrilesky & John T. Boorman. LC 81-174230. (Illus.). 544p. 1982. pap. text ed. 21.95x o.s.i. (ISBN 0-88295-408-3). Harlan Davidson.
Money Talk: The Last Taboo. Carole Phillips. LC 84-12281. 221p. 1984. 16.95 o.p. (ISBN 0-87795-529-8, Arbor Hse). Morrow.
Money Talks: An Irreverent Guide for the Curious, Penurious, Pennywise & Pound Foolish. Richard Skolnik. (Illus.). 224p. 1986. pap. 9.95 o.p. (ISBN 0-684-18623-3). Scribner.
Money Talks: Bob Rosefsky's Complete Program for Financial Success. 2nd ed. Bob Rosefsky. 687p. 1985. pap. 14.95 o.p. (ISBN 0-471-81346-X). Wiley.
Money Talks: The Complete Guide to Creating a Profitable Workshop or Seminar in Any Field. Jeffrey Lant. (Enterprise Ser.: Vol. III). 302p. (Orig.). 1985. pap. 30.00 o.p. (ISBN 0-940374-08-0). JLA Pubns.
Money, the Financial System & the Economy. 3rd ed. George G. Kaufman. 1981. text ed. 40.76 o.p. (ISBN 0-395-30817-8); instr's. manual 1.56 o.p. (ISBN 0-395-30818-6). HM.
Money: The Root of All Evil. Edith C. Taylor. 1978. 5.50 o.p. (ISBN 0-682-49156-X). Exposition-Phoenix.
Money Theory Policy & Institutions. 2nd ed. A. Crockett. 1979. 36.95 o.p. (ISBN 0-442-30735-7). Van Nos Reinhold.
Money Trust Investigation of Financial & Monetary Conditions in the United States. U. S. Congress, House Committee on Banking & Currency. 1970. Repr. of 1913 ed. lib. bdg. 86.50x o.p. (ISBN 0-8371-3181-2, MTIN). Greenwood.
Money War. Terrence L. Smith. LC 78-55022. 1978. 9.95 o.p. (ISBN 0-689-10900-8, Atheneum). Macmillan.
Money: Whence It Came, Where It Went. John Kenneth Galbraith. LC 75-14116. 1975. 10.00 o.p. (ISBN 0-395-19843-7). HM.
Money-Wise Guide to Sports Cars. Peter Bohr. LC 82-47678. (Illus.). 228p. 1983. 19.95 o.p. (ISBN 0-15-162052-0); pap. 9.95 o.p. (ISBN 0-15-661956-3, Harv). HarBraceJ.
Money Workbook for Women: A Step-by-Step Guide to Managing Your Personal Finances. Carole Phillips. LC 81-71673. (Illus.). 1982. 13.00 o.p. (ISBN 0-87795-379-1, Arbor Hse); pap. 9.95 o.p. (ISBN 0-87795-402-X). Morrow.
Money 1987. Money Magazine Editors. (Illus.). 190p. 1987. 19.95 o.p. (ISBN 0-8487-0705-2). Oxmoor Hse.
Moneyman. Judith Liederman. 1979. 10.95 o.p. (ISBN 0-395-27099-5). HM.
Moneypower: How to Make Inflation Make You Rich. Ben Stein & Herbert Stein. 224p. 1981. pap. 2.95 o.p. (ISBN 0-380-54809-7, 54809-7). Avon.
Moneywise! Financial Survival on the Road to Riches. David M. Brownstone. 224p. 1985. 15.95 o.p. (ISBN 0-531-09593-2). Watts.
Mongo Homecoming. Mary Elting & Robin McKown. LC 73-88695. (Two Worlds Bks.). (Illus.). 64p. (gr. 4-6). 1969. 3.95 o.p. (ISBN 0-87131-099-6). M Evans.
Mongolian Epigraphical Dictionary in Reverse Listing. John G. Hangin. LC 67-63757. (Uralic & Altaic Ser.: Vol. 88). 70p. (Mongolian). 1967. pap. text ed. 6.00x o.p. (ISBN 0-87750-078-9). Res Ctr Lang Semiotic.
Monica the Computer Mouse. Donna Bearden. LC 84-51602. (Illus.). 64p. (gr. k-3). 1984. 6.95 o.p. (ISBN 0-89588-214-0). SYBEX.
Monimbo. Robert Moss & Arnaud De Borchgrave. 1983. 16.50 o.p. (ISBN 0-671-43541-8). S&S.
Monitoring Behavior & Supervisory Control. Ed. by T. B. Sheridan & G. Johannsen. LC 76-41687. (NATO Conference Series III, Human Factors: Volume 1). 538p. 1976. 80.00x o.p. (ISBN 0-306-32881-X, Plenum Pr). Plenum Pub.
Monitoring Birth Defects & Environment: The Problem of Surveillance. Ed. by Ernest Hook et al. 1971. 60.50 o.p. (ISBN 0-12-355450-0). Acad Pr.
Monitoring Drug Therapy in the Long-Term Care Facility. LC 77-93746. 1978. 36.00 o.p. (ISBN 0-917330-19-6). Am Pharm Assn.
Monitoring in Anesthesia & Critical Care Medicine. Ed. by Casey D. Blitt. (Illus.). 750p. 1985. text ed. 82.00 o.p. (ISBN 0-443-08277-4). Churchill.
Monitoring of Fish Stock Abundance: The Use of Catch & Effort Data: A Report of the ACMRR Working Party on Fishing Effort & Monitoring of Fish Abundance, Rome, Italy, Dec. 16-20, 1975. (Fisheries Technical Papers: No. 155). (Illus.). 105p. (2nd Printing). 1976. pap. 7.50 o.p. (ISBN 92-5-100050-6, F888, FAO). UNIPUB.
Monitoring Systems for Agricultural & Rural Development Projects. (Economic & Social Development Paper: No. 12, Rev. 1). 81p. 1984. pap. text ed. 7.50 o.p. (ISBN 92-5-101367-5, F2541, FAO). UNIPUB.
Monitoring the Impacts of Prison & Parole Services: An Initial Examination. Louis H. Blair et al. 88p. 1977. pap. 6.00 o.p. (ISBN 0-87766-201-0, 16900). Urban Inst.
Monitoring the Outcome of Social Services, 2 vols. Annie Millar et al. Incl. Vol. 1. Preliminary Suggestions (ISBN 0-87766-194-4); Vol. 2. Review of Past Research & Test Activities. 88p (ISBN 0-87766-200-2). 1977. pap. text ed. 6.50x ea. o.p. Urban Inst.
Monitoring Toxic Gases in the Atmosphere. William Thain. 1980. 45.00 o.p. (ISBN 0-08-023810-6). Pergamon.
Monk. William H. Hallahan. 272p. 1983. pap. 3.95 o.p. (ISBN 0-380-64956-X, 64956-X). Avon.
Monk. Matthew Lewis. 1975. pap. 1.95 o.p. (ISBN 0-380-00468-2, 25411). Avon.
Monk Dawson. Piers P. Read. 192p. 1980. pap. 2.25 o.p. (ISBN 0-380-50617-3, 50617). Avon.
Monkey. Wu Ch'Eng-En. Tr. & pref. by Arthur Waley. 1958. pap. 8.95 o.p. (ISBN 0-394-17211-6, E112, Ever). Grove.
Monkey Crosses the Equator. Paul White. (Jungle Doctor Picture Fable Ser.). 21p. (gr. 1-7). 1986. Set of 8. pap. 26.50 o.p. (ISBN 0-85364-375-X, Pub. by Paternoster UK). Attic Pr.
Monkey Grammarian. Paz. (ISBN 0-8050-0181-6). Seaver Bks.
Monkey in a Lion's Skin. Paul White. (Jungle Doctor Picture Fable Ser.). 21p. (gr. 1-7). 1986. Set of 8. pap. 26.50 o.p. (ISBN 0-85364-371-7, Pub. by Paternoster UK). Attic Pr.
Monkey in the Middle. Eve Bunting. LC 83-18339. (Illus.). 32p. (ps-2). 1984. 10.95 o.p. (ISBN 0-15-255316-9, HJ). HarBraceJ.
Monkey Mountain. Craig Hiler. 1979. pap. 2.25 o.p. (ISBN 0-505-51403-6, Pub. by Tower Bks). Dorchester Pub Co.
Monkeys. Nina Leen. LC 78-4284. (Illus.). (gr. 4-9). 1978. 7.95 o.p. (ISBN 0-03-044001-7). H Holt & Co.
Monkeys & Apes. P-H.
Monkeys & the Eggs. Paul White. (Jungle Doctor Picture Fable Ser.). 21p. (gr. 1-7). 1986. Set of 8. pap. 26.50 o.p. (ISBN 0-85364-374-1, Pub. by Paternoster UK). Attic Pr.
Monkey's Clue & The Stolen Sapphire. Edward D. Hoch. Ed. by Doris Duenewald. LC 78-58882. (Inkpot Mini-Mysteries Ser.). (Illus.). (gr. 3-7). 1978. pap. 0.95 o.p. (ISBN 0-448-16367-5, G&D). Putnam Pub Group.
Monkeys Never Say Please. Alice J. Davidson. (Good Little Books for Good Little Children). 32p. (ps-3). 1986. 6.95 o.s.i. (ISBN 0-8378-5085-1). Gibson.
Monkey's Raincoat. Robert Crais. 208p. (Orig.). 1987. pap. 2.95 o.p. (ISBN 0-553-26336-6). Bantam.
Monk's Retreat. Susannah Curtis. (Orig.). 1976. pap. 1.25 o.p. (ISBN 0-380-00857-2, 31245). Avon.
Mono-Olefins: Chemistry & Technology. H. Asinger. 1969. 290.00 o.p. (ISBN 0-08-011547-0). Pergamon.
Monoamine Oxidase: Structure, Function & Altered Functions. Ed. by Thomas P. Singer et al. LC 79-24107. 1980. 66.00 o.p. (ISBN 0-12-646880-X). Acad Pr.
Monochrome Darkroom Practice. Jack H. Coote. (Illus.). 320p. 1983. 39.95 o.p. (ISBN 0-240-51061-5); pap. 16.95 o.p. (ISBN 0-240-51700-8). Focal Pr.
Monoclonal Antibodies. James W. Goding. 1984. 30.00 o.p. (ISBN 0-12-287020-4). Acad Pr.
Monoclonal Antibodies: Technical Opportunities. Technical Insights, Inc. Staff. LC 83-51745. (Emerging Technology Ser.: No. 10). 243p. 1984. 678.00 o.p. (ISBN 0-914993-02-X). Tech Insights.
Monograph of Cimicidae see Thomas Say Foundation Publications.
Monograph of the Orthoptera of North America (North of Mexico, Vol. 1. James A. Rehn & Harold J. Grant, Jr. (Monograph: No. 12). (Illus.). 257p. (Orig.). 1961. pap. 18.00 o.s.i. (ISBN 0-910006-18-0). Acad Nat Sci Phila.
Monograph of the Sub-Class Cirripedia: 1851-54, 2 vols. in 1. Charles Darwin. (Illus.). 1964. 48.00 o.p. (ISBN 3-7682-0114-7). Lubrecht & Cramer.
Monographs of the Shallow-Water Indo-West Pacific Echinoderms. Ailsa M. Clark & Francis W. Rowe. (Illus.). ix, 238p. 1971. 52.50x o.p. (ISBN 0-565-00690-8, Pub. by Brit Mus Nat Hist England). Sabbot-Natural Hist Bks.
Monographs on Fragrance Raw Materials. Ed. by D. L. Opdyke. (Illus.). 1979. 185.00 o.p. (ISBN 0-08-023775-4). Pergamon.
Mononuclear Phagocytes in the Central Nervous System: Origin, Mode of Distribution, & Function of Progressive Microglia, Perivascular Cells of Intracerebral Vessels, Free Subarachnoidal Cells, & Epiplexus Cells. M. Oehmichen. (Neurology Ser.: Vol. 21). (Illus.). 1978. 49.00 o.p. (ISBN 0-387-08958-6). Springer-Verlag.
Monopoly & Competition in the English Coal Trade: 1550-1850. Paul M. Sweezy. LC 79-139152. 186p. 1972. Repr. of 1938 ed. lib. bdg. 22.50x o.p. (ISBN 0-8371-5768-4, SWEC). Greenwood.
Monopoly Capitalism. Keith Cowling. LC 81-7215. 192p. 1982. 29.95x o.p. (ISBN 0-470-27288-0). Halsted Pr.
Monopoly Power & Economic Performance. 3rd ed. Ed. by Edwin Mansfield. LC 73-18027. (Problems of the Modern Economy Ser). (Illus.). 228p. 1974. 7.95 o.p. (ISBN 0-393-05448-9); pap. 3.25x o.p. (ISBN 0-393-09990-3). Norton.
Monorail. Jacques Audiberti. 344p. 1964. 9.95 o.p. (ISBN 0-686-54496-X). French & Eur.
Monsenor Romero: Martis de la Iglesia Popular see Archbishop Romero: Martyr of Salvador.
Monsieur Bergeret a Paris see Romans et Contes.
Monsieur Monde Vanishes. Georges Simenon. Tr. by Jean Stewart. LC 76-39800. (Helen & Kurt Wolff Bk.). 1977. 6.95 o.p. (ISBN 0-15-162098-9). HarBraceJ.
Monsoon Meteorology. C. S. Ramage. (International Geophysics Ser: Vol. 15). 1971. 46.00 o.p. (ISBN 0-12-576650-5). Acad Pr.
Monster: A Tale of Loch Ness. Jeffrey Konvitz. 388p. (Orig.). 1982. pap. 3.50 o.s.i. (ISBN 0-345-29447-5). Ballantine.
Monster Alphabet Book. Yvonne Ashby. (Illus.). 32p. (ps-k). 1988. 4.95 o.p. (ISBN 0-8249-8205-3). Ideals.
Monster Fun. Stephen Mooser. LC 79-16000. (Illus.). 96p. (gr. 4-6). 1979. PLB 7.29 o.p. (ISBN 0-671-33016-0). Messner.
Monster Island. Van DeMeer. 1981. 9.95 o.p. (ISBN 0-03-059348-4). H Holt & Co.
Monster Knock Knocks. William Cole & Mike Thaler. (Illus., Orig.). (gr. 3-5). 1982. pap. 1.75 o.p. (ISBN 0-671-44254-6). Archway.
Monster Madness Outrageous Jokes about Weird Folks. Jack Stokes. LC 80-2068. (Illus.). 64p. (gr. 6). 1981. 8.95a o.p.; PLB 8.95 o.p. (ISBN 0-385-15691-X). Doubleday.
Monster Mary, Mischief Maker. Kazuko Taniguchi. (Illus.). (ps-3). 1976. 6.95 o.p. (ISBN 0-07-062868-8); text ed. 7.95 o.p. (ISBN 0-07-062869-6). McGraw.
Monster or Messiah? The Computer's Impact on Society. Ed. by Walter M. Mathews. LC 79-16737. 1980. text ed. 9.95x o.p. (ISBN 0-87805-108-2). U Pr of Miss.
Monster Trucks: Car Crushers & Crowd Pleasers. Michael Bargo. LC 86-12775. (Illus.). 128p. 1986. 12.98 o.p. (ISBN 0-87938-221-X). Motorbooks Intl.
Monsters: A Guide to Information on Unaccounted for Creatures, Including Bigfoot, Many Water Monsters, & Other Irregular Animals. George M. Eberhart. LC 82-49029. (Supernatural Studies). 358p. 1983. lib. bdg. 28.00 o.p. (ISBN 0-8240-9213-9). Garland Pub.
Monsters Among Us. Brad Steiger. 1982. pap. 9.95 o.s.i. (ISBN 0-914918-38-9). Whitford Pr.
Monsters & Dinosaurs. Illus. by Louise Nevett. (Make-It-Yourself Ser.). (Illus.). 32p. (gr. k-3). 1984. lib. bdg. 11.90 o.p. (ISBN 0-531-04770-9). Watts.
Monsters in the Sky. Paolo Maffei. 352p. 1981. pap. 8.95 o.p. (ISBN 0-380-55517-4, 55517-4). Avon.
Monstres Sacres see Theatre.
Monstrous American Car Spotter's Guide 1920-1980. Tad Burness. LC 86-12754. (Illus.). 1080p. (gr. 5-12). 1986. 18.98 o.p. (ISBN 0-87938-223-6). Motorbooks Intl.
Mont-Saint-Michel. Germain Bazin. LC 75-24825. (Fr.). 1978. Repr. of 1933 ed. lib. bdg. 100.00 o.p. (ISBN 0-87817-190-8). Hacker.
Montagnards of South Vietnam: A Study of Nine Tribes. Robert L. Mole. LC 70-104198. (Illus.). 1970. pap. 3.25 o.p. (ISBN 0-8048-0724-8). C E Tuttle.
Montaigne: A Biography. Donald M. Frame. LC 65-19055. (Illus.). 1965. 10.00 o.p. (ISBN 0-15-162099-7). HarBraceJ.
Montaigne in France, 1812-1852. Donald M. Frame. 1972. lib. bdg. 20.50x o.p. (ISBN 0-374-92845-2, Octagon). Hippocrene Bks.
Montana: Contracts. 9.50 o.p. (ISBN 0-686-90837-6). Am Law Inst.
Montana Gothic. Dirck Van Sickle. LC 78-14658. 1979. 8.95 o.p. (ISBN 0-15-162101-2). HarBraceJ.
Montana: Images of the Past. William Farr & K. Ross Toole. LC 78-7408. (Illus.). 1978. 35.00 o.p. (ISBN 0-87108-514-3); pap. 19.95 o.p. Pruett.
Montana Industrial Minerals. 1975. 15.20 o.p. (ISBN 0-942218-05-1). Minobras.
Montana Passage. Lawrence F. Small & Harley Henderson. LC 83-82103. 126p. 1983. pap. 6.95 o.s.i. (ISBN 0-934318-25-5). Falcon Pr Mt.
Montana: Trusts. 8.50 o.p. Am Law Inst.
Montana's Genealogical Records. Ed. by Dennis L. Richards. (Genealogy & Local History Ser.: Vol. 11). 384p. 1981. 68.00x o.p. (ISBN 0-8103-1487-8). Gale.
Montauk. Max Frisch. Tr. by Geoffrey Skelton. LC 76-70. (Helen & Kurt Wolff Bks.). 143p. 1976. 7.95 o.p. (ISBN 0-15-162100-4). HarBraceJ.
Montauk Fault. Herbert Mitgang. LC 80-70744. 320p. 1981. 12.95 o.p. (ISBN 0-87795-320-1, Arbor Hse). Morrow.
Montauk Fault. Herbert Mitgang. 224p. 1982. pap. 2.95 o.s.i. (ISBN 0-345-30378-4). Ballantine.
Montcalm & Wolfe. Francis Parkman. LC 84-16850. (Illus.). 640p. 1984. 19.95 o.p. (ISBN 0-689-11527-X, Atheneum). Macmillan.
Monte & the Coons. Ethel B. Johnson. (gr. k-3). 1978. 4.00 o.p. (ISBN 0-682-48978-6). Exposition-Phoenix.
Monte Carlo. Stephen Sheppard. 416p. 1983. 14.50 o.s.i. (ISBN 0-671-44789-0). Summit Bks.
Monte Carlo Method. 2nd ed. I. M. Sobol. Tr. by Peter Fortini et al from Rus. LC 73-98791. (Popular Lectures in Mathematics Ser). (Illus.). 76p. 1975. pap. text ed. 4.50x o.s.i. (ISBN 0-226-76749-3). U of Chicago Pr.
Monte Carlo Method. I. M. Sobol. 72p. 1984. pap. 1.95 o.p. (ISBN 0-8285-2961-2, Pub. by Mir Pubs USSR). Imported Pubns.

Monte Cassino. David Hapgood & David Richardson. 320p. 1984. 17.95 o.p. (ISBN 0-312-92537-9). Congdon & Weed.

Montecito & Santa Barbara. David F. Myrick. Ed. by Jim Walker. (Illus.). 224p. 1988. 42.95 o.p. (ISBN 0-87046-083-8, Pub. by Trans Anglo). Interurban.

Montenegro. M. Spadijer. (Illus.). 1980. text ed. 45.00 o.p. (ISBN 0-686-46540-7). E J Brill USA.

Monterey County Street Atlas 1985. Thomas Bros. Maps Staff. (Illus.). 74p. pap. 7.95 o.p. (ISBN 0-88130-119-1). Thomas Bros Maps.

Monterey County Street Guide & Directory, 1987. Thomas Brothers Maps Staff. (Illus.). 84p. 1987. pap. 10.95 o.p. (ISBN 0-88130-203-1). Thomas Bros Maps.

Montesa Service-Repair Handbook: 123-360cc Singles, 1965-1975. Clymer Publications. (Illus.). 1975. pap. text ed. 8.50 o.p. (ISBN 0-89287-020-6, M356). Clymer Pub.

Montesquieu & Social Theory. Alan Baum. 1979. 44.00 o.p. (ISBN 0-08-024317-7). Pergamon.

Montesquieu Ses Idees et Ses Oeuvres d'apres les Papiers de La Brede. Barckhausen. 49.90 o.p. (ISBN 0-685-34049-X). French & Eur.

Monteverdi Companion. Ed. by Denis Arnold & Nigel Fortune. (Illus.). 1972. pap. 5.95 o.p. (ISBN 0-393-00636-0, Norton Lib). Norton.

Montezuma's Ball. Eugene Wildman. LC 74-112037. 183p. 1970. 10.95x o.p. (ISBN 0-8040-0211-8, Pub. by Swallow); pap. 5.95 o.p. (ISBN 0-8040-0212-6, Pub. by Swallow). Ohio U Pr.

Montgomery Bus Story. Ida S. Meltzer. Ed. by Nestina Thomas. (American Destiny Ser.: Black Americans). (Illus.). 32p. (gr. 4-12). 1972. pap. text ed. 12.95 set of 10 o.p. (ISBN 0-87594-169-9). Book-Lab.

Montgomery Clift. Bosworth. 1978. 12.95 o.p. (ISBN 0-15-162123-3). HarBraceJ.

Montgomery in Europe Nineteen Forty-Three to Nineteen Forty-Five: Success or Failure. Richard Lamb. 1987. 21.95 o.p. (ISBN 0-907675-04-2, Pub. by Buchan & Enright England). Seven Hills Bk Dists.

Montgomery of Alamein. Alun Chalfont. LC 76-12519. 1976. 12.95 o.p. (ISBN 0-689-10744-7, Atheneum). Macmillan.

Montgomery's Children. Richard Perry. LC 83-8447. 288p. 1984. 12.95 o.p. (ISBN 0-15-162124-1). HarBraceJ.

Month in the Country. April Fitzlyon. (Orig.). pap. 6.95 o.p. (ISBN 0-905209-44-3, Pub. by Victoria & Albert Mus UK). Faber & Faber.

Month with St. Paul. James Alberione. 1988. 3.50 o.p. (ISBN 0-317-67462-5, SP0445); pap. 2.50 o.p. (ISBN 0-8198-4721-6). Dghtrs St Paul.

Monthly Mortgage Loan Payment Table. Financial Publishing Co. Staff. 224p. 1981. pap. 7.50 o.p. (ISBN 0-87600-553-9). Finan Pub.

Monthly Review, Nos. 1-5. 1969. Repr. of 1934 ed. lib. bdg. 22.00x o.p. (ISBN 0-8371-9205-6, M200). Greenwood.

Monthly Review: An Independent Socialist Magazine, Vols. 1-12. Incl. Vol. 1. lib. bdg. 26.00 (ISBN 0-313-21764-5, M301); Vol. 2. lib. bdg. 26.00 o.s.i. (ISBN 0-313-21765-3, M302); Vol. 3. lib. bdg. 26.00 (ISBN 0-313-21766-1, M303); Vol. 4. lib. bdg. 26.00 (ISBN 0-313-21767-X, M304); Vol. 5. lib. bdg. 26.00 (ISBN 0-313-21768-8, M305); Vol. 6. lib. bdg. 26.00 (ISBN 0-313-22710-6, M306); Vol. 7. lib. bdg. 26.00 (ISBN 0-313-21770-X, M307); Vol. 8. lib. bdg. 26.00 (ISBN 0-313-21771-8, M308); Vol. 9. lib. bdg. 26.00 (ISBN 0-313-21772-6, M309); Vol. 10. lib. bdg. 26.00 (ISBN 0-313-21773-4, M310); Vol. 11. lib. bdg. 26.00 (ISBN 0-313-21774-2, M311); Vol. 12. lib. bdg. 26.00 (ISBN 0-313-21775-0, M312). Repr. of 1949 ed. Set. lib. bdg. 255.00x o.p. (ISBN 0-8371-9206-4, M300). Greenwood.

Months of the Year in Verse. Evelyn F. Olson. (Illus.). 32p. (gr. k up). 1983. 5.50 o.p. (ISBN 0-682-40152-8). Exposition-Phoenix.

Montmorillon: Portrait of a Provincial Town. I. C. Thimann. 1970. 2.75 o.p. (ISBN 0-08-016005-0); pap. 1.80 o.p. (ISBN 0-08-015821-8). Pergamon.

Montreal Diocesan Theological College. Oswald Howard. 150p. 1963. 5.00 o.p. (ISBN 0-7735-9055-2, McGill Canada). U of Toronto Pr.

Montreal Expos. rev. ed. Shaw. (Baseball Today Ser.). 48p. (gr. 4 up). 1982. PLB 11.45 o.p. (ISBN 0-87191-866-8). Creative Ed.

Monty. Robert LaGuardia. 1978. pap. 2.25 o.p. (ISBN 0-380-01887-X, 49577-7). Avon.

Monty: A Biography of Montgomery Clift. Robert Laguardia. LC 77-78968. 1977. 12.95 o.p. (ISBN 0-87795-155-1, Arbor Hse). Morrow.

Monty Python: Complete & Utter Theory of the Grotesque. Ed. by John O. Thompson. (British Film Institute Bks.). (Illus.). 58p. 1982. pap. 6.95 o.p. (ISBN 0-85170-119-1, Pub. by British Film Inst England). U of Ill Pr.

Monty: The Making of a General 1887-1942. Nigel Hamilton. (Illus.). 864p. 1981. text ed. 22.95 o.p. (ISBN 0-07-025805-8). McGraw.

Monument. Erich Loest. 224p. 1988. 19.95 o.p. (ISBN 0-436-25673-8, Pub. by Secker & Warburg UK). David & Charles.

Monument Maker: A Biography of Frederick Ernst Triebel. Adelaide N. Cooley. (Illus.). 1978. 5.00 o.p. (ISBN 0-682-49051-2). Exposition-Phoenix.

Monumental Brasses in Somerset. A. B. Connor. (Illus.). 1970. 17.50 o.p. (ISBN 0-87556-057-1). Saifer.

Monumental Era: European Architecture & Design 1929-1939. Franco Borsi. Tr. by Pamela Marwood. LC 87-45386. 1987. 40.00 o.p. (ISBN 0-8478-0805-X). Rizzoli Intl.

Monumental Washington: The Planning & Development of the Capital Center. John W. Reps. 1967. 47.50 o.p. (ISBN 0-691-04527-5). Princeton U Pr.

Mood Control. Gene Bylinsky. LC 78-929. 1978. 8.95 o.p. (ISBN 0-684-15586-9, ScribT). Scribner.

Mood Food: A Galaxy of Feasts to Calm You down; Cheer You up; Warm Your Cockles, Excite Your Palate, Comfort, Soothe, & Delight You. Glenn Andrews. LC 74-81234. 256p. 1974. 8.95 o.p. (ISBN 0-689-10639-4, Atheneum). Macmillan.

Moods & Emotions. Ruth Odor. Ed. by Jane Buerger. LC 80-17567. 112p. (gr. k-4). 1980. 5.95 o.p. (ISBN 0-89565-177-7, 4934). Standard Pub.

Moods & Emotions: A Handbook About Feelings. Ruth Odor. LC 80-17567. (Living the Good Life Ser.). (Illus.). 112p. (Orig.). (gr. 1-6). 1980. pap. 5.95 o.p. (ISBN 0-89565-177-7). Childs World.

Moods, Thinks, & Thoughts. Andre Everett. 1977. 4.50 o.p. (ISBN 0-682-48704-X). Exposition-Phoenix.

Moody Moose Buttons. Richard Hefter. LC 77-7255. (Sweet Pickles Ser.). (Illus.). (gr. k-2). 1977. 2.95 o.p. (ISBN 0-03-021446-7). H Holt & Co.

Moominstroll, 7 vols. Tove Jansson. Incl. Comet in Moominland. 1976. Vol. 1. pap. 1.95 o.p. (ISBN 0-380-00436-4, 39784); Finn Family Moomintroll. 1976. Vol. 2. pap. 1.95 o.p. (ISBN 0-380-00350-3, 39776); Moominland Midwinter. 1976. Vol. 3. pap. 1.95 o.p. (ISBN 0-380-00748-7, 30205); Moominpappa at Sea. 1977. Vol. 4. pap. 1.95 o.p. (ISBN 0-380-01726-1, 34157); Moomin's Summer Madness. 1976. Vol. 5. pap. 1.25 o.p. (ISBN 0-380-00633-2, 39768); Moominvalley in November. 1976. Vol. 6. pap. 1.25 o.p. (ISBN 0-380-00765-7, 30544); Tales from Moominvalley. Vol. 8. pap. 1.25 (31773-7). (gr. 6 up). 1978. pap. 8.75 o.p. (ISBN 0-380-34926-4, 34926, Camelot). Avon.

Moon & a Star: And Other Poems. Myra C. Livingston. LC 65-14115. (Illus.). 48p. (gr. 1-4). 1965. 2.75 o.p. (ISBN 0-15-255330-4, HJ). HarBraceJ.

Moon & the Ghetto. Richard R. Nelson. 1977. 7.95x o.p. (ISBN 0-393-05611-2); pap. 4.95x o.p. (ISBN 0-393-09173-2). Norton.

Moon Deluxe. Frederick Barthelme. LC 83-4735. 240p. 1983. 15.50 o.p. (ISBN 0-671-47268-2). S&S.

Moon Dragon. Fran Manushkin. LC 81-20771. (Illus.). 32p. (gr. k-3). 1982. 8.95 o.s.i. (ISBN 0-02-762210-X). Macmillan.

Moon Eyes. Jean Chapman. Tr. by Astra Lacis. LC 79-22088. (Illus.). (gr. k-3). 1980. text ed. 8.95 o.p. (ISBN 0-07-010648-7). McGraw.

Moon Is a Harsh Mistress. Robert A. Heinlein. 304p. 1986. pap. 3.50 o.s.i. (ISBN 0-425-08899-5). Berkley Pub.

Moon is Full. Aileen Adair. 200p. 1957. (ISBN 0-8022-0005-2). Philos Lib.

Moon Is Mine & Other Tales. Jack Neilson. 1978. 8.00 o.p. (ISBN 0-682-49176-4). Exposition-Phoenix.

Moon of Gomrath. Alan Garner. 1981. pap. 1.95 o.s.i. (ISBN 0-345-29041-0). Ballantine.

Moon on a String. Tricia Springstubb. (YA) (gr. 7 up). 1982. 12.45 o.p. (ISBN 0-317-60248-9). Little.

Moon on the One Hand: Poetry in Song. William Crofut. LC 74-18179. (Illus.). 64p. (gr. 1-9). 1975. 9.95 o.p. (ISBN 0-689-50018-1, Atheneum). Macmillan.

Moon Pinnace. Thomas Williams. LC 85-29255. 360p. 1986. 17.95 o.s.i. (ISBN 0-385-23321-3). Doubleday.

Moon Rocks & Minerals. A. A. Levinson & Ross Taylor. 240p. 1972. 44.00 o.p. (ISBN 0-08-016669-5). Pergamon.

Moon-Watch Summer. Lenore Blegvad. LC 74-187855. (Illus.). 63p. (gr. 2-5). 1972. 4.75 o.p. (ISBN 0-15-255350-9, HJ). HarBraceJ.

Moonbird. Grania Davis. LC 85-16077. (Science Fiction Ser.). 192p. 1986. 12.95 o.p. (ISBN 0-385-19555-9). Doubleday.

Moonblood. Kenn S. Roe. 1984. pap. 2.25 o.s.i. (ISBN 0-345-31461-1). Ballantine.

Mooncake. Frank Asch. (Illus.). 28p. (ps-3). 1983. 11.95 o.s.i. (ISBN 0-13-601013-X). P-H.

Mooncake. Frank Asch. (Illus.). 32p. 1986. pap. 4.95 o.s.i. (ISBN 0-13-601048-2). P-H.

Moonchild. Kenneth McKenney. 256p. 1979. pap. 2.50 o.p. (ISBN 0-380-41483-X, 41483-X). Avon.

Moongame. Frank Asch. LC 84-8405. (Illus.). 32p. (gr. k-3). 1984. 11.95 o.s.i. (ISBN 0-13-600503-9). P-H.

Moongame. Frank Asch. 1987. pap. 4.95 o.s.i. (ISBN 0-13-601055-5). P-H.

Moonglow. Judy Baer. 224p. (Orig.). 1984. pap. 5.95 o.p. (ISBN 0-310-47681-X). Zondervan.

Moonheart. Charles De Lint. 496p. 1986. pap. 3.95 o.s.i. (ISBN 0-441-53721-9, Pub. by Charter Bks). Ace Bks.

Moonies in America: Cult, Church, & Crusade. David G. Bromley & Anson D. Shupe, Jr. LC 79-16456. (Sage Library of Social Research: Vol. 92). 269p. 1979. 29.95 o.p. (ISBN 0-8039-1060-6); pap. 12.50 o.p. (ISBN 0-8039-1061-4). Sage.

Moonpath & Other Tales of the Bizarre. Robert E. Swindells. LC 83-7450. (Good Time Library). (Illus.). 80p. (gr. 3-7). 1983. PLB 8.95 o.p. (ISBN 0-87614-251-X). Carolrhoda Bks.

Moonset. Marylu T. Jeans. 1971. 4.00 o.p. (ISBN 0-8233-0047-1). Golden Quill.

Moonshadow. Angela Carter. (Illus.). 32p. (ps-1). 1983. 14.95 o.p. (ISBN 0-575-03026-7, Pub. by Gollancz England). David & Charles.

Moonslasher. Douglas D. Hawk. 388p. (Orig.). 1987. pap. 3.95 o.p. (ISBN 1-55547-170-6). Critics Choice Paper.

Moonstalker. Fred Wrixon. LC 76-58203. 1977. 10.00 o.p. (ISBN 0-682-48811-9, Banner). Exposition-Phoenix.

Moonstone Castle Mystery. Carolyn Keene. (Nancy Drew Ser.: Vol. 40). (gr. 4-7). 1963. 4.50 o.p. (ISBN 0-448-09540-8, G&D); PLB 3.29 o.p. (ISBN 0-448-19540-2). Putnam Pub Group.

Moore's Historical, Biographical, & Miscellaneous Gatherings. John W. Moore. LC 68-17977. 604p. 1968. Repr. of 1886 ed. 60.00x o.p. (ISBN 0-8103-3312-0). Gale.

Moorhaven. Daoma Winston. 408p. 1976. pap. 3.50 o.p. (ISBN 0-380-00244-2, 63925-4). Avon.

Moorings - Past & Present. Isabelle R. Algee. (Illus.). 557p. 1980. lib. bdg. 35.00 o.p. (ISBN 0-918518-18-0, St Luke TN); pap. 20.00 o.p. (ISBN 0-918518-17-2). Peachtree Pubs.

Moose, Goose & Little Nobody. Ellen Raskin. LC 80-15287. (Illus.). 32p. (ps-3). 1980. Repr. of 1974 ed. 8.95 o.s.i. (ISBN 0-02-775750-1, Four Winds). Macmillan.

Moot Court Book. John Gaubatz. 211p. (Orig.). 1980. pap. text ed. 14.00x o.p. (ISBN 0-672-83854-0). Michie Co.

Moped: The Wonder Vehicle. Jerry Murray. (Illus.). (gr. 7-9). 1978. pap. 2.50 o.p. Archway.

Mopeds: A Guide to Models, Maintenance, & Safety. Lawrence Reeves. LC 82-14218. (Illus.). 96p. (gr. 8-11). 1983. lib. bdg. 8.79 o.s.i. (ISBN 0-671-46100-1). Messner.

Moral Alphabet of Vice & Folly. Stan Washburn. (Illus.). 1986. 8.95 o.p. (ISBN 0-87795-872-6). Morrow.

Moral Choices: Memory, Desire, & Imagination in Nineteenth-Century American Abolition. Peter Walker. LC 78-5922. xxiv, 388p. 1978. 37.50 o.p. (ISBN 0-8071-0262-8). La State U Pr.

Moral Development & Moral Education. R. S. Peters. 192p. 1981. pap. text ed. 8.95x o.p. Unwin Hyman.

Moral Dilemmas in Medicine. 3rd ed. Alastair V. Campbell. (Illus.). 210p. 1983. pap. text ed. 13.00 o.p. (ISBN 0-443-02948-2). Churchill.

Moral Education. William Kay. (Unwin Education Books). 1974. pap. text ed. 9.95x o.p. (ISBN 0-04-370053-5). Unwin Hyman.

Moral Education & the Curriculum. J. Wilson. 1969. 35.00 o.p. (ISBN 0-08-013897-7); pap. 35.00 o.p. (ISBN 0-08-013898-5). Pergamon.

Moral Education for the Emotionally Disturbed Early Adolescent: An Application of Kohlbergian Techniques & Spiritual Principles. Eileen M. Gardner. LC 82-49250. (Illus.). 208p. 1983. 25.00x o.p. (ISBN 0-669-06448-3). Lexington Bks.

Moral Fiber: Character & Belief in Recent American Fiction. Wesley A. Kort. LC 81-71389. 160p. 1982. pap. 1.00 o.p. (ISBN 0-8006-1624-3, 1-1624, Fortress). Augsburg Fortress.

Moral Idealists, Bureaucracy, & Catherine the Great. Walter J. Gleason. 261p. 1981. 30.00x o.p. (ISBN 0-8135-0917-3). Rutgers U Pr.

Moral Impulse: Modern Drama from Ibsen to the Present. Morris Freedman. LC 67-10025. (Crosscurrents-Modern Critiques Ser.). 148p. 1967. 7.95x o.p. (ISBN 0-8093-0235-7). S Ill U Pr.

Moral Issues & Christian Responses. 3rd ed. Paul T. Jersild & Dale A. Johnson. 1983. pap. text ed. 25.95 o.p. (ISBN 0-03-062464-9). HR&W.

Moral Issues in Business. 3rd ed. Vincent Barry. 502p. 1986. text ed. (ISBN 0-534-05484-6). Wadsworth Pub.

Moral Judgment. David D. Raphael. LC 77-28440. 1978. Repr. of 1955 ed. lib. bdg. 35.00x o.p. (ISBN 0-313-20246-X, RAMJ). Greenwood.

Moral Judgment of the Child. Jean Piaget. Tr. by Marjorie Gabain. 416p. 1932. 15.95 o.p. (ISBN 0-02-925230-X); pap. text ed. 15.95 o.p. (ISBN 0-02-925240-7). Free Pr.

Moral Life. Rodger Beehler. 226p. 1978. 19.50x o.s.i. (ISBN 0-8476-6107-5). Rowman.

Moral Life of Man. Jacob Kohn. 1957. (ISBN 0-8022-0879-7). Philos Lib.

Moral Perspective in La Princesse de Cleves. Helen K. Kaps. LC 79-4661. 1968. 5.00 o.p. (ISBN 0-87114-021-7). U of Oreg Bks.

Moral Philosophy: Text & Readings. 2nd ed. Andrew Oldenquist. LC 77-77978. (Illus.). 1978. pap. 18.50 o.p. (ISBN 0-395-25433-7). HM.

Moral Principles in Education. John Dewey. 64p. 1958. (ISBN 0-8022-0388-4). Philos Lib.

Moral Principles in the Bible. Ben F. Kimpel. 192p. 1956. (ISBN 0-8022-0858-4). Philos Lib.

Moral Responsibility: Situation Ethics at Work. Joseph Fletcher. LC 67-14515. 256p. (Orig.). 1967. pap. 4.95 o.s.i. (ISBN 0-664-24770-9, Westminster). Westminster John Knox.

Moral Values & Political Behavior in Ancient Greece. A. W. Adkins. (Ancient Culture & Society Ser.). (Illus.). 1973. 5.95x o.p. (ISBN 0-393-04367-3). Norton.

Moral Values & Political Behaviour in Ancient Greece. A. W. Adkins. (Illus.). 176p. 1976. pap. 2.95 o.p. (ISBN 0-393-00826-6). Norton.

Moral Values & the Superego Concept in Psychoanalysis. Ed. by Seymour C. Post. LC 71-160289. 402p. 1972. text ed. 40.00x o.s.i. (ISBN 0-8236-3470-1). Intl Univs Pr.

Morale. John W. Gardner. 1978. 7.95 o.p. (ISBN 0-393-08823-5). Norton.

Morale in the Civil Service: A Study of the Desk Worker. Nigel Walker. LC 76-49867. (Illus.). 1977. Repr. of 1962 ed. lib. bdg. 35.00x o.p. (ISBN 0-8371-9397-4, WAMCS). Greenwood.

Morality & Youth: A Guide for Christian Parents. F. Philip Rice. LC 80-11433. 252p. 1980. pap. 10.95 o.s.i. (ISBN 0-664-24315-0, Westminster). Westminster John Knox.

Morality in the Making: Thought, Action & the Social Context. Helen Weinreich-Haste & Don Locke. (Developmental Psychology & Its Application Ser.). 300p. 1983. 73.95 o.p. (ISBN 0-471-10423-X, Pub. by Wiley Interscience). Wiley.

Morality of Terrorism: Religious Origins & Ethical Implications. Ed. by David C. Rapoport & Yonah Alexander. (Pergamon Policy Studies on International Politics). 280p. 1982. 43.00 o.s.i. (ISBN 0-08-026347-X). Pergamon.

Morarji Papers: Fall of the Janata Government. A. Gandhi. 314p. 1984. text ed. 18.50x o.p. (ISBN 0-391-03099-X). Humanities.

More about BASIC: Supplement. Donald H. Sanders. 352p. 1983. text ed. 8.95 o.p. (ISBN 0-07-054664-9). McGraw.

More about Leemo. Stanley E. Brock. (Illus.). 1968. 7.95 o.s.i. (ISBN 0-8008-5350-4). Taplinger.

More about Names. Leopold Wagner. LC 68-17937. 288p. 1968. Repr. of 1893 ed. 37.00x o.p. (ISBN 0-8103-3099-7). Gale.

More about the Japanese. rev. ed. Jack Seward. LC 74-184528. 250p. (Orig.). 1983. pap. 9.50 o.p. (ISBN 4-89788-001-7, Pub. by Lotus Pr Japan). C E Tuttle.

More about This Business of Music. 3rd., rev. & enl. ed. Sidney Shemel & M. William Krislovsky. Ed. by Lee Zhito. 204p. (Orig.). 1982. Repr. 14.95 o.p. (ISBN 0-8230-7567-2, Billboard Bks). Watson-Guptill.

More About What Plants Do. Joan E. Rahn. LC 74-19280. (Illus.). 80p. (gr. 3-5). 1975. PLB 6.95 o.p. (ISBN 0-689-30454-4, Atheneum). Macmillan.

More African Adventures. Lloyd Fezler. LC 84-62232. 1985. pap. 3.95 o.p. (ISBN 0-89051-105-5). Master Bks.

More All-Jewish Cartoons, Yet: And Just As Kosher As the others. Mort Greberg. (Illus.). 80p. 1987. pap. text ed. 5.95 o.p. (ISBN 0-399-51395-7, Perigee Bks). Putnam Pub Group.

More Andrew Lang Fairy Tale Books in Many Colors, 4 vols. Andrew Lang. (Illus.). 1437p. 1985. pap. 23.80 boxed set o.p. (ISBN 0-486-24236-6). Dover.

More Answers. Dorothy Martin. (Peggy Ser.: No. 3). (gr. 7). 1985. pap. 3.50 o.p. (ISBN 0-8024-8303-8). Moody.

More BASIC: A Guide to Intermediate Level Computer Programming. Shelley Lipson. (Illus.). (gr. 4-6). 1984. 9.95 o.p. (ISBN 0-03-070722-6). H Holt & Co.

More Bible Study Puzzles. Thomas J. Marks. (Orig.). (YA) (gr. 9 up). 1983. pap. 2.95 o.p. (ISBN 0-8054-9108-2). Broadman.

More Cajun Humor. Justin Wilson & Howard Jacobs. 96p. (Orig.). 1984. pap. 5.95 o.s.i. (ISBN 0-88289-454-4). Pelican.

More Calculated Cooking: Practical Recipes for Diabetics & Dieters. Jeanne Jones. LC 80-25179. (Illus.). 192p. (Orig.). 1981. (One Hund One Prods); pap. 6.95 o.p. (ISBN 0-89286-184-3). Ortho.

More Chess & Computers: The Microcomputer Revolution, the Challenge Match. David Levy & Monroe Newborn. LC 80-16057. (Illus.). 1980. pap. 12.95x o.p. (ISBN 0-914894-07-2, Computer Sci Pr). W H Freeman.

More Cricket Songs: Japanese Haiku. Tr. by Harry Behn. LC 77-137755. (Illus., Photos). (gr. 4 up). 1971. 4.50 o.p. (ISBN 0-15-255440-8, HJ). HarBraceJ.

More Cute & Crazy Cats. Ed. by Jill Wolf. (Illus.). 24p. (gr. 2-6). 1985. pap. 1.95 o.p. (ISBN 0-89954-292-1). Antioch Pub Co.

More Dark Than Shark. Brian Eno & Russell Mills. (Illus.). 1986. limited cased ed. 125.00 o.p. (ISBN 0-571-13810-1); pap. 25.00 o.p. (ISBN 0-571-13883-7). Faber & Faber.

More Deadly Than the Male: First Lady of Bridge. Rixi Markus. 144p. 1984. 19.95 o.p. (ISBN 0-571-13339-8); pap. 9.95 o.p. (ISBN 0-571-13340-1). Faber & Faber.

More Deadly Than the Male (The Secrets of Women Exposed) J. E. Vessels. (Illus.). 1979. 7.50 o.p. (ISBN 0-682-49333-3). Exposition-Phoenix.

More Developed Realm: A Population Geography. Ed. by G. T. Trewartha. 1978. 39.00 o.p. (ISBN 0-08-020631-X); pap. 22.00 o.p. (ISBN 0-08-020630-1). Pergamon.

More Dress Pattern Designing. 3rd ed. Natalie Bray. (Illus.). 184p. 1982. pap. text ed. 17.00 o.p. (ISBN 0-246-11848-2). Gower Pub Co.

More Easy Answers. Platt & Munk Editors. (Platt & Munk Cricket Bks.). (Illus.). 24p. (ps-3). 1978. 2.50 o.p. (ISBN 0-448-46516-7, G&D); PLB 3.59 o.p. (ISBN 0-448-13054-8). Putnam Pub Group.

More Favorite Brand Name Recipes Cookbook. Consumer Guide Staff. 1984. pap. 3.98 o.p. (ISBN 0-517-41445-7). Crown.

More Favorite Stories from Borneo. Irene-Anne Monteiro. (Illus.). viii, 52p. (Orig.). (gr. 7-12). 1981. pap. text ed. 2.50 o.p. (ISBN 0-317-17351-0). Heinemann Ed.

More Favorite Stories from Indonesia. Marguerite Siek. (Favorite Stories Ser.). (Illus.). vi, 68p. (Orig.). (gr. 7-12). 1982. pap. text ed. 2.50x o.p. (ISBN 9971-64-038-4). Heinemann Ed.

More Favorite Stories from Sri Lanka. Indi Rani. (Favorite Stories Ser.). (Illus.). vi, 48p. (Orig.). (gr. 7-12). 1983. pap. text ed. 2.50x o.p. (ISBN 9971-64-040-6). Heinemann Ed.

More Favourite Chinese Stories. bilingual ed. Leon Comber. (Favourite Stories Ser.). (Orig.). (gr. 7-12). 1981. pap. 2.50x o.p. (ISBN 0-686-73757-1). Heinemann Ed.

More Favourite Chinese Stories. Retold by Ho Man Yee. (Favourite Stories Ser.). (gr. 7-12). 1969. pap. text ed. 2.50x o.p. (ISBN 0-686-60448-2). Heinemann Ed.

More Favourite Stories from Asia. bilingual ed. Leon Comber. (Favourite Stories Ser.). (Orig.). (gr. 7-12). 1981. pap. text ed. 2.50x o.p. (ISBN 0-686-73758-X). Heinemann Ed.

More Festivals in Asia. Compiled by Asian Cultural Centre for Unesco. LC 75-34740. (Illus.). 68p. (gr. 9-12). 1975. 8.25 o.p. (ISBN 0-87011-273-2). Kodansha.

More Fingerstyle Guitar. Ken Perlman. (Illus.). 256p. 1985. 22.95 o.p. (ISBN 0-13-600842-9); pap. 14.95 o.p. (ISBN 0-13-600834-8). P H.

More Food from Soil Science: The Natural Chemistry of Lime in Agriculture. V. A. Tiedjens. 1965. 15.00 o.p. (ISBN 0-682-43057-9, University). Exposition-Phoenix.

More for Your Money: How to Increase Your Spending Power up to Twenty Percent Without Increasing Your Income. Mary B. Hall. 187p. 1981. 10.95 o.p. (ISBN 0-395-31293-0). HM.

More from Hound & Bear. Dick Gackenbach. LC 79-4310. (Illus.). 48p. (ps-3). 1979. 7.95 o.s.i. (ISBN 0-395-28973-4, Clarion). HM.

More from Your Micro. Charles Platt. 192p. 1985. pap. 2.50 o.p. (ISBN 0-380-89529-3). Avon.

More FYI: Further Tips for Healthful Living. Alton Blakeslee et al. Ed. by Nat Brandt. LC 83-14171. 288p. (Orig.). 1983. 12.95 o.p. (ISBN 0-87131-424-X, 01258-370); pap. 7.95 o.p. (ISBN 0-87131-420-7, 0772-230). M Evans.

More Games for the SuperIntelligent. James F. Fixx. LC 76-7695. 1976. 8.95 o.p. (ISBN 0-385-11039-1). Doubleday.

More Great American Mansions: And Their Stories. Merrill Folsom. (Illus.). 1979. pap. 16.95 o.s.i. (ISBN 0-8038-4723-8). Hastings.

More Great New England Recipes: And the Cooks Who Made Them Famous. Ed. by Neysa Hebbard. LC 85-50085. 288p. 1985. 14.95 o.p. (ISBN 0-89909-081-8). Yankee Bks.

More Gross. Sam Gross. 128p. 1984. pap. 5.95 o.p. (ISBN 0-380-68197-8, 68197-8). Avon.

More Home Cooking in a Hurry. Sarah Howell. LC 86-9716. 1986. 7.95 o.p. (ISBN 0-8054-7003-4). Broadman.

More Horse Stories. Ed. by A. L. Furman. (gr. 5-7). 1966. pap. 1.95 o.p. (ISBN 0-671-43951-0). Archway.

More Houses Architects Design for Themselves. Architectural Record Magazine Editors. (Illus.). 1982. text ed. 47.50 o.p. (ISBN 0-07-002365-4). McGraw.

More Houses for Good Living. Royal Barry Wills Associates. LC 68-31686. (Illus.). 1968. 13.95 o.s.i. (ISBN 0-8038-0162-9). Architectural.

More How Do They Make It? George Sullivan. LC 79-79958. (Illus.). 142p. (gr. 5-8). 1969. 4.95 o.s.i. (ISBN 0-664-32454-1, Westminster). Westminster John Knox.

More Innocent Time. Eugenie Hill. LC 79-5128. 1979. 8.95 o.p. (ISBN 0-8008-5355-5). Taplinger.

More Items from Our Catalog. Alfred Gingold. 80p. 1983. pap. 5.95 o.p. (ISBN 0-380-84657-8, 84657). Avon.

More Joy of Watercolors. David L. Millard. (Illus.). 144p. 1984. 24.95 o.p. (ISBN 0-8230-3126-8). Watson-Guptill.

More Killing Defense at Bridge. H. W. Kelsey. 192p. 1981. pap. 7.95 o.p. (ISBN 0-571-11760-0). Faber & Faber.

More Kindergarten Resources. Josephine Newbury. LC 73-5349. 264p. (Orig.). 1974. pap. 3.99 o.p. (ISBN 0-8042-1360-7, John Knox). Westminster John Knox.

More Kitchen Wisdom. Frieda Arkin. LC 81-7188. (Illus.). 176p. 1982. pap. 5.95 o.p. (ISBN 0-03-071056-1). H Holt & Co.

More Learning in Less Time: A Guide to Effective Study. 2nd, rev. ed. Norma Kahn. 96p. (gr. 9-12). 1984. pap. text ed. 6.50x o.p. (ISBN 0-86709-037-5). Boynton Cook Pubs.

More Lives Than a Cat. Michael C. Doroski. LC 86-91240. (Illus.). 1986. 12.50 o.p. (ISBN 0-682-40304-0). Exposition-Phoenix.

More Make-A-Mix Cookery. Karine Eliason et al. LC 80-82533. (Orig.). 1980. pap. 7.95 o.p. (ISBN 0-89586-055-4). Price Stern.

More Misery. Suzanne Heller. LC 65-15779. (Illus.). 1965. 2.50 o.s.i. (ISBN 0-8397-6001-9). Eriksson.

More Mysterious Wales. Chris Barber. (Illus.). 256p. 1986. 25.95 o.s.i. (ISBN 0-7153-8736-7). David & Charles.

More Needlework Blocking & Finishing. Dorothy Burchette. (Illus.). 1979. encore ed. 2.95 o.p. (ISBN 0-684-16892-8, ScribT). Scribner.

More Oddities & Enigmas. Rupert R. Gould. 128p. 1974. 5.95 o.p. (ISBN 0-8216-0210-1, Pub. by Univ Bks). Carol Pub Group.

More of the Best of Bon Apetit. Jan Steubing. (Illus.). 1984. 24.95 o.p. (ISBN 0-517-55465-8, Knapp Pr Potter Bks). Crown.

More of the Best of Bon Appetit. LC 84-14368. (Illus.). 240p. 1984. 19.95 o.p. (ISBN 0-89535-136-6). Knapp Pr.

More Perfect Union. Betsy Moestro. LC 87-4083. (Illus.). 48p. (YA) (gr. 1-5). 1987. 13.95 o.p.; lib. bdg. 13.88 o.p. Lothrop.

More Pricks Than Kicks. Samuel Beckett. 1972. pap. 4.95 o.p. (ISBN 0-394-17789-4, E588, Ever). Grove.

More Profits, Less Risk: Your New Financial Strategy. Charles A. Cerami. LC 82-7775. 240p. 1982. text ed. 14.95 o.p. (ISBN 0-07-010324-0). McGraw.

More Recipes with a Jug of Wine. Morrison Wood. 416p. 1956. 8.95 o.p. (ISBN 0-374-21260-0). FS&G.

More Sail Trim: An Anthology from Sail Magazine. Ed. by Sail Magazine. (Illus.). 1979. 11.95 o.p. (ISBN 0-393-03237-X). Norton.

More Saints for Our Time. 2nd ed. David Q. Liptak. LC 83-72371. 201p. 1986. pap. 2.95 o.p. (ISBN 0-87973-498-1). Our Sunday Visitor.

More Sixty-Minute Gourmet. Pierre Franey. 304p. 1983. pap. 6.95 o.s.i. (ISBN 0-449-90038-X, Columbine). Fawcett.

More Street Jewellery. Baglee & Morlee. (Illus.). 96p. 1984. 15.00 o.s.i. (ISBN 0-904568-39-3, Pub. by New Cavendish England). Schiffer.

More Synonyms: Shout & Yell & Other Words That Mean the Same Thing but Look & Sound As Different as Loud & Noisy. Joan Hanson. LC 73-11974. (Joan Hanson Word Bks.). (Illus.). 32p. (gr. k-3). 1973. PLB 4.95 o.p. (ISBN 0-8225-0289-5). Lerner Pubns.

More Tales of Pirx the Pilot. Stanislaw Lem. Tr. by Louis Iribarne. LC 80-8753. (Helen & Kurt Wolff Bk.). 216p. 1982. 11.95 o.p. (ISBN 0-15-162138-1). HarBraceJ.

More Than a Century of Investment Banking: The Didder, Peabody & Co. Story. Vincent P. Carosso. (Illus.). 1979. text ed. 23.95 o.p. (ISBN 0-07-010136-1). McGraw.

More Than a Man Can Take: A Study of Job. Wesley C. Baker. (Orig.). 1966. pap. 2.65 o.p. (ISBN 0-664-24702-4, Westminster). Westminster John Knox.

More Than a Summer's Love. Jeannette Eyerly. 176p. (gr. 12 up). 1983. pap. 2.25 o.p. (ISBN 0-671-45660-1). Archway.

More Than Chicken Cookbook. Sara Pitzer. LC 83-48975. (Illus.). 160p. (Orig.). 1984. pap. 6.95 o.p. (ISBN 0-88266-368-2, Garden Way Pub). Storey Comm Inc.

More Than Courage. Michel-Aime Baudouy. Tr. by Marie Ponsot. LC 61-13241. (gr. 7 up). 1966. pap. 1.65 o.s.i. (ISBN 0-15-662145-2, VoyB). HarBraceJ.

More Than Dispensing. Cyrelle K. Gerson. LC 80-65958. 120p. 1980. 24.00 o.p. (ISBN 0-917330-31-5). Am Pharm Assn.

More Than Forever. Susanne Savoy. 320p. 1987. pap. 3.95 o.p. (ISBN 0-380-75142-9). Avon.

More Than Friends. Betty Henrichs. 1983. pap. 2.75 o.p. (ISBN 0-380-84996-8, 84996). Avon.

More Than Friends. William R. Jordan, Sr. Ed. by Sherrian Wilson. 1978. 4.00 o.p. (ISBN 0-682-49194-2). Exposition-Phoenix.

More Than Herbs & Acupuncture. E. Grey Dimond. 224p. 1975. 7.95 o.p. (ISBN 0-393-06400-X). Norton.

More Than Just a Pretty Face: How Cosmetic Surgery Can Improve Your Looks & Your Life. Thomas Rees & Sylvia Simmons. LC 86-27617. 1987. 19.95 o.p. (ISBN 0-316-73707-0). Little.

More Than Just a Smart Girl. Lurlene McDaniel. 128p. (Orig.). (gr. 6-8). 1987. pap. 2.50 o.s.i. (ISBN 0-87406-265-9). Willowisp Pr.

More Than Love. Denise Robins. 1975. pap. 1.25 o.p. (ISBN 0-380-00236-1, 22392). Avon.

More Than Meets the Eye. Carl Mydans. LC 74-19785. 310p. 1975. Repr. of 1959 ed. lib. bdg. 24.75x o.p. (ISBN 0-8371-7808-8, MYME). Greenwood.

More Than Meets the Eye: New Look at Flower Arranging. Sue Phillips. (Illus.). 128p. 1986. 14.95 o.p. (ISBN 0-09-162551-3, Pub. by Century Hutchinson). David & Charles.

More Than Sympathy: The Everyday Needs of Sick & Handicapped Children & Their Families. Richard Lansdown. 1980. write for info. o.p. (ISBN 0-413-47530-1, NO. 2017, Pub. by Tavistock); pap. 12.95x o.p. (ISBN 0-422-76640-2, NO. 2016). Heinemann Ed.

More Than Truth. David Kohn. 180p. 1956. (ISBN 0-8022-0877-0). Philos Lib.

More Than Two Aspirin: Hope for Your Headache Problem. Seymour Diamond & William B. Furlong. 1977. pap. 1.95 o.p. (ISBN 0-380-01772-5, 35055). Avon.

More Than You Dare Ask: The First Year of Living with Cancer. Mac N. Turnage & Anne S. Turnage. LC 75-32940. 1976. 3.99 o.p. (ISBN 0-8042-1129-9, John Knox). Westminster John Knox.

More to Learn, Bk. III. Margaret Dee. 1954. 1.75 o.p. (ISBN 0-913650-34-X). CPP Belwin.

More Twentieth Century Dolls, Vol. 2. Johana G. Anderton. (Illus.). 364p. 19.95 o.s.i. (ISBN 0-87069-292-5). Wallace-Homestead.

More Twentieth Century Dolls: A-H, Vol. 1. Johana G. Anderton. (Illus.). 364p. 1979. 19.95 o.s.i. (ISBN 0-87069-273-9). Wallace-Homestead.

More Wandering Thoughts. Thomas Smyth. 1980. 5.00 o.p. (ISBN 0-682-49613-8). Exposition-Phoenix.

More Washingtoons. Mark A. Stamaty. (Illus.). 96p. 1986. pap. 8.95 o.p. (ISBN 0-13-601154-3). P-H.

More Wife Savers. Ed. by Catherine Schneider. 64p. 1978. pap. 3.95 o.s.i. (ISBN 0-89821-022-4). Reiman Assocs.

More Wisconsin Bike Trips. Phil Van Valkenberg. LC 78-23654. (Illus., Orig.). 1980. pap. 5.95 o.p. (ISBN 0-915024-21-7). WI Trails.

More Words of Science. Isaac Asimov. LC 79-187422. (Illus.). 288p. (gr. 7 up). 1972. 6.95 o.p. (ISBN 0-395-13722-5). HM.

Moreabouts for Brownie Girl Scout Leaders. Girl Scouts of the U. S. A. Staff. (Illus.). 96p. 1980. pap. text ed. 3.75 o.p. (ISBN 0-88441-328-4, 20-703). Girl Scouts USA.

Morenita: Evangelizadora de las Americas. Virgilio P. Elizondo. 96p. (Span.). 1981. pap. 2.50 o.p. (ISBN 0-89243-145-8). Liguori Pubns.

More...Try This One. Ed. by Thom Schultz. LC 80-80947. (Illus.). 80p. (Orig.). 1980. pap. 5.95 o.p. (ISBN 0-936664-00-2). Group Pub.

Morgan. Leo P. Kelley. LC 85-31101. (Double D Western Ser.). 192p. 1986. 12.95 o.p. (ISBN 0-385-19294-0). Doubleday.

Morgan. Leo P. Kelley. LC 87-571. (Double D Western Ser.). 1987. 16.95 o.s.i. (ISBN 0-385-23987-4, GC Large Print). Doubleday.

Morgan & Morgan Darkroom Book. rev. ed. Algis Balsys & Liliane De Cock-Morgan. 232p. (Orig.). 1984. pap. 19.95 o.p. (ISBN 0-87100-196-9, 2196). Morgan.

Morgan Horse Handbook. Jeanne Mellin. LC 72-91799. (Illus.). 1973. 15.00 o.p. (ISBN 0-8289-0181-3). Greene.

Morgan Triumphs. Marden Clark. 123p. 1984. pap. 5.95 o.p. (Orion). Signature Bks.

Morgette in the Yukon. large print ed. G. G. Boyer. LC 84-8747. 269p. 1984. Repr. of 1983 ed. 12.95 o.p. (ISBN 0-89621-562-8). Thorndike Pr.

Morgette on the Barbary Coast. G. G. Boyer. LC 85-20972. 280p. 1985. Repr. of 1984 ed. 14.95 o.p. (ISBN 0-89621-674-8). Thorndike Pr.

Morisco. Hilary Mason. LC 78-73071. 1979. 9.95 o.p. (ISBN 0-689-10960-1, Atheneum). Macmillan.

Mormon Conflict, 1850-1859. Norman F. Furniss. LC 77-5424. (Illus.). 1977. Repr. of 1960 ed. lib. bdg. 35.00x o.p. (ISBN 0-8371-9636-1, FUMC). Greenwood.

Mormon Documents Behind the Zion Curtain. Wallace Tope. 288p. (Orig.). Date not set. pap. 7.95 o.p. (ISBN 0-87123-869-1). Bethany Hse.

Mormonism & the American Experience. Klaus J. Hansen. LC 80-19312. (History of American Religion Ser.). 224p. 1981. lib. bdg. 15.00x o.s.i. (ISBN 0-226-31552-5). U of Chicago Pr.

Mormonism: Challenge & Defense. Rodger S. Gunn. 1979. pap. 8.95 o.p. (ISBN 0-89036-126-6). Hawkes Pub Inc.

Mormons & Women. Ann Terry et al. 150p. (Orig.). 1980. pap. 2.95 o.p. (ISBN 0-942241-17-7, 8599). Pubs Bk Sales.

Mormons, Indians & the Ghost Dance Religion of 1890. Garold D. Barney. LC 85-29509. (Illus.). 258p. (Orig.). 1986. lib. bdg. 29.50 o.p. (ISBN 0-8191-5227-7); pap. text ed. 14.25 o.p. (ISBN 0-8191-5228-5). U Pr of Amer.

Morning Answer. John Fandel. 1984. pap. 3.35 o.p. (ISBN 0-88028-041-7). Forward Movement.

Morning Chores & Other Times Remembered: Poems. Hadley Read. LC 77-22772. (Illus.). 195p. 1977. 14.95 o.p. (ISBN 0-252-00661-5). U of Ill Pr.

Morning Has Broken: A Biography of Eleanore Farjeon. Annabel Farjeon. (Illus.). 320p. 1986. 19.95 o.p. (ISBN 0-531-15020-8). Watts.

Morning Is a Long Time Coming. Bette Greene. (gr. 7-9). 1979. pap. 1.95 o.p. (ISBN 0-671-42456-4). Archway.

Morning News. Cynthia Trembly. 1977. pap. 2.00 o.p. (ISBN 0-89924-005-4). Lynx Hse.

Morning Noon & Night. James G. Cozzens. LC 68-20064. 1968. 5.95 o.p. (ISBN 0-15-162160-8). HarBraceJ.

Morning, Noon & Night: A Teacher's Diary. Ruth M. Twiss. 80p. 1982. 5.50 o.p. (ISBN 0-682-49820-3). Exposition-Phoenix.

Morning of America: 1603-1789. Darrett B. Rutman. LC 77-131289. (Illus., Orig.). 1971. pap. 15.95 o.p. (ISBN 0-395-04333-6). HM.

Morning of the Gods. Edward Fenton. LC 86-16831. 240p. (gr. 7 up). 1987. pap. 14.95 o.p. (ISBN 0-385-29550-2). Delacorte.

Morning of the Gods. Date not set. (ISBN 0-385-29550-2). Delacorte.

Morning of the Magicians. Louis Pauwels & Jacques Bergier. 1980. pap. 1.50 o.p. (ISBN 0-380-00818-1, 30890). Avon.

Morning Ran Red. Stephen Bowman. 304p. 1988. pap. 3.95 o.p. (ISBN 1-55547-225-7). Critics Choice Paper.

Morning Rendezvous. V. Belov. 383p. 1985. pap. 4.00 o.p. (ISBN 0-8285-3006-8, Pub. by Raduga Pubs USSR). Imported Pubns.

Mornings on Horseback. David W. McCullough. (General Ser.). 1981. lib. bdg. 19.95 o.p. (ISBN 0-8161-3332-8, Large Print Bks). G K Hall.

Mornings on Horseback: The Story of an Extraordinary Family, a Vanquished Way of Life, & the Unique Child Who Became Theodore Roosevelt. David McCullough. 1981. 19.95 o.s.i. (ISBN 0-671-22711-4). S&S.

Moro per Amore. Alessandro Stradella. Ed. by Howard M. Brown. LC 76-20990. (Italian Opera Ser.: No. 10). 1978. lib. bdg. 77.00 o.p. (ISBN 0-8240-2609-8). Garland Pub.

Moroccan Islam: Tradition & Society in a Pilgrimage Center. Dale F. Eickelman. (Modern Middle East Ser.: No. 1). 323p. 1976. pap. text ed. 12.95x o.p. (ISBN 0-292-75062-5). U of Tex Pr.

Moroccan Mystery. Thomas McKean. 160p. 1986. pap. 2.50 o.p. (ISBN 0-380-89809-8, Camelot). Avon.

Morpeth: A Victorian Public Career. Diana D. Olien. LC 82-23820. 538p. (Orig.). 1983. lib. bdg. 39.50 o.p. (ISBN 0-8191-2989-5); pap. text ed. 22.00 o.p. (ISBN 0-8191-2990-9). U Pr of Amer.

Morphogenesis: An Essay on Development. John T. Bonner. LC 52-5847. (Illus.). 1963. pap. 1.65 o.p. (ISBN 0-689-70021-0, 28, Atheneum). Macmillan.

Titles

Morphological Astronomy. Fritz Zwicky. (Illus.). 1957. 52.00 o.p. (ISBN 0-387-02233-3). Springer-Verlag.
Morphology & Evolution of the Insect Abdomen. R. Matsuda. Ed. by Kerkut. 568p. 1976. 97.00 o.p. (ISBN 0-08-018753-6). Pergamon.
Morphology & Physiology of Plant Tumors. A. C. Braun & T. Stonier. (Protoplasmatologia: Vol. 10, Pt. 5a). (Illus.). 1958. 24.80 o.p. (ISBN 0-387-80492-7). Springer-Verlag.
Morphology of the Liver. H. Elias & Joseph C. Sherrick. 1969. 59.00 o.p. (ISBN 0-12-237950-0). Acad Pr.
Morphometry of the Placental Exchange Area. R. Baur. LC 77-3148. (Advances in Anatomy, Embryology & Cell Biology: Vol. 53, No. 1). 1977. pap. 22.00 o.p. (ISBN 0-387-08159-3). Springer-Verlag.
Morrow Book of New Words: 8500 Terms Not Yet in Standard Dictionaries. Nathan H. Mager & Sylvia K. Mager. LC 81-14205. 256p. 1982. 13.50 o.p. (ISBN 0-688-00685-X); pap. 6.25 o.p. (ISBN 0-688-00927-1). Morrow.
Morrow Travel Guide to the People's Republic of China see Fielding's People's Republic of China, 1987.
Mort dans l'ame. Jean-Paul Sartre. 296p. 1949. 10.95 o.p. (ISBN 0-686-54985-6). Schoenhof.
Mort dans l'Ame see Chemins de la liberte.
Mort Qui Fait le Trottoir. Henry de Montherlant. (Folio 35). 1972. 3.95 o.p. (ISBN 0-686-55526-0). Schoenhof.
Mort Safety Assurance Systems Book. william G. Johnson. LC 79-27759. 512p. 44.00 o.p. (199021). Natl Safety Coun.
Mort Tres Douce. Simone De Beauvoir. (Coll. Soleil). 1964. 10.50 o.p. (ISBN 0-685-11609-3). Schoenhof.
Mortadella. Justin Wintle. 144p. 1986. 14.95 o.p. (ISBN 0-531-15012-7). Watts.
Mortal Belladaywic. Mark Christensen. LC 86-29264. 264p. 1987. pap. 16.95 o.p. (ISBN 0-385-23763-4, Dolp). Doubleday.
Mortal Condition: Eight Stories of Survival, Hope & Loss. Martha Fay. 352p. 1983. 16.95 o.p. (ISBN 0-698-11251-2, Coward). Putnam Pub Group.
Mortal Engines. Stanislaw Lem. Tr. by Michael Kandel. 272p. 1979. pap. 2.95 o.p. (ISBN 0-380-57406-3, 57406-3, Bard). Avon.
Mortal Fire. Peter Dale. LC 74-29409. x, 181p. 1976. 12.00x o.p. (ISBN 0-8214-0185-8); pap. 7.00 o.p. (ISBN 0-8214-0187-4). Ohio U Pr.
Mortal Flower. Han Suyin. 363p. 1985. pap. 6.95 o.p. (ISBN 0-586-03738-1, Pub. by Granada England). Academy Chi Pubs.
Mortal Lessons, Notes in the Art of Surgery. Richard Selzer. LC 76-25481. 1977. 9.95 o.p. (ISBN 0-671-22356-9). S&S.
Mortal Lessons: Notes on the Art of Surgery. Richard Selzer. 1978. pap. 7.95 o.s.i. (ISBN 0-671-24074-9, Touchstone Bks). S&S.
Mortal Matters. Penelope Gilliatt. LC 83-2090. 176p. 1983. 13.95 o.p. (ISBN 0-698-11245-8, Coward). Putnam Pub Group.
Mortal Spring. Francisco Umbral. Tr. by Helen R. Lane from Span. LC 80-7946. 180p. 1980. Repr. of 1975 ed. 9.95 o.p. (ISBN 0-15-162338-4). HarBraceJ.
Mortal Stakes. Robert Parker. LC 75-20273. 192p. 1975. 6.95 o.p. (ISBN 0-395-21969-8). HM.
Mortal Term. John Penn. 192p. 1985. 12.95 o.s.i. (ISBN 0-684-18317-X, ScribT). Scribner.
Morte D'Arthur, Vol. 1. Thomas Malory. 1972. 14.95x o.p. (ISBN 0-460-00045-4, Evman); pap. 3.95x o.p. (ISBN 0-460-01045-X, Evman). Biblio Dist.
Morte D'Arthur, Vol. 2. Thomas Malory. 1976. 13.95x o.p. (ISBN 0-460-00046-2, Evman); pap. 3.95x o.p. (ISBN 0-460-01046-8, Evman). Biblio Dist.
Mortgage-Backed Securities: Mortgage Pass-Throughs, CMOs, & Builder Bonds, Vol. 250. Practising Law Institute Staff. 740p. 1984. pap. 40.00 o.p. (ISBN 0-317-27676-X, #N4-4430). PLI.
Mortgage Lending: Fundamentals & Practices. 2nd ed. Willis R. Bryant. 1962. text ed. 40.95 o.p. (ISBN 0-07-008609-5). McGraw.
Mortgage Loan Administration. William I. DeHuszar. (Illus.). 480p. 1972. text ed. 38.95 o.p. (ISBN 0-07-016257-3). McGraw.
Mortgage Market: Theory & Practice of Housing Finance. Mark Boleat & Adrian Coles. (Studies in Financial Institutions & Markets: No. 3). 192p. 1987. text ed. 39.95 o.p. (ISBN 0-04-334011-3). Unwin Hyman.
Mortgages (N.Y.) Louis A. Kass. 1964. pap. 1.75x o.p. (ISBN 0-87526-046-2). Gould.
MOS Devices: Design & Manufacture. A. D. Milne. LC 83-110. 186p. 1983. 25.95x o.p. (ISBN 0-470-27421-2). Halsted Pr.
MOS-LSI Design & Application. William N. Carr & Jack P. Mize. LC 72-7407. (Texas Instruments Electronics Ser.). (Illus.). 320p. 1973. text ed. 69.95 o.p. (ISBN 0-07-010081-0). McGraw.
MOS Memory Data Book, Nineteen Eighty-Six. Texas Instruments, Inc., Engineering Staff. (Illus.). 804p. 1986. pap. 8.35 o.p. (ISBN 0-89512-196-4). Tex Instr Inc.
Mosaic. Jo Bannister. LC 86-16551. 192p. 1987. 12.95 o.p. (ISBN 0-385-23797-9). Doubleday.
Mosaic: Russian for Children. V. O. Tolmacheva et al. 108p. 1986. pap. 7.95 incl. cass. o.p. (ISBN 0-8285-3192-7, Pub. by Rus Lang Pubs USSR). Imported Pubns.
Mosaics & Home, Where Love & Contentment Abide. Elizabeth B. Joseph. 64p. 1981. 10.00 o.p. (ISBN 0-682-49674-X). Exposition-Phoenix.
Mosaics from Memories. Lea V. Bludau. 1979. 5.00 o.p. (ISBN 0-682-49301-5). Exposition-Phoenix.
Mosaics in Needlepoint. Xenia L. Parker. LC 77-5045. (Encore Edition Ser.). (Illus.). 1977. 5.95 o.p. (ISBN 0-684-16201-6, ScribT); pap. 2.95 o.s.i. (ISBN 0-684-15036-0, ScribT). Scribner.
Mosaics of Norman Sicily. Otto Demus. 1950. (ISBN 0-8022-0378-7). Philos Lib.
Mosby's Assesstest: A Practice Exam for RN Licensure (Secured Version) 80p. 1987. 25.95 o.p. (ISBN 0-8016-4390-2). Mosby.
Mosby's Assesstest: A Practice Exam for RN Licensure (Unsecured Version. Dolores F. Saxton et al. 80p. 1986. 24.95 o.p. (ISBN 0-8016-4331-7). Mosby.
Mosby's Assesstest: Basic Science. Mosby. 1985. pap. 4.95 o.p. (ISBN 0-8016-4393-7). Mosby.
Mosby's Assesstest: Drugs & Solutions. Mosby. 1985. pap. 4.95 o.p. (ISBN 0-8016-4394-5). Mosby.
Mosby's Assesstest: Fundamentals - Application. Mosby. 1985. pap. 4.95 o.p. (ISBN 0-8016-4398-8). Mosby.
Mosby's Assesstest: Fundamentals - Basic Concepts. Mosby. 1985. pap. 4.95 o.p. (ISBN 0-8016-4397-X). Mosby.
Mosby's Assesstest: Maternity Nursing. Mosby. 1985. pap. 4.95 o.p. (ISBN 0-8016-4391-0). Mosby.
Mosby's Assesstest: Medical - Surgical Nursing. Mosby. 1985. pap. 4.95 o.p. (ISBN 0-8016-4399-6). Mosby.
Mosby's Assesstest: Nutrition. Mosby. 1985. pap. 4.95 o.p. (ISBN 0-8016-4396-1). Mosby.
Mosby's Assesstest: Pediatric Nursing. Mosby. 1985. pap. 4.95 o.p. (ISBN 0-8016-4400-3). Mosby.
Mosby's Assesstest: Pharmacology. Mosby. 1985. pap. 4.95 o.p. (ISBN 0-8016-4395-3). Mosby.
Mosby's Assesstest: Psychiatric Nursing. Mosby. 1985. pap. 4.95 o.p. (ISBN 0-8016-4392-9). Mosby.
Mosby's Assesstest (Secured), 86: A Practice Exam for RN Licensure. Saxton. 1986. 25.95 o.p. (ISBN 0-8016-4388-0). Mosby.
Mosby's Assesstest 86: A Practice Exam for RN Licensure. Saxton. 1985. 23.95 o.p. (ISBN 0-8016-4389-9). Mosby.
Mosby's Atlas of Functional Human Anatomy. Ernest W. Beck & Harry Monsen. LC 81-14110. (Illus.). 310p. 1982. pap. 18.95 o.p. (ISBN 0-8016-0554-7). Mosby.
Mosby's Comprehensive Review of Critical Care. 3rd ed. Zschoche. 816p. 1985. 38.95 o.p. (ISBN 0-8016-5699-0). Mosby.
Mosby's Comprehensive Review of Nursing. 11th ed. Dolores F. Saxton et al. (Illus.). 797p. 1984. pap. text ed. 19.95 o.p. (ISBN 0-8016-3551-9). Mosby.
Mosby's Comprehensive Review of Nursing. 10th ed. Ed. by Dolores F. Saxton et al. LC 80-26510. (Illus.). 690p. 1981. text ed. 17.95 o.p. (ISBN 0-8016-3530-6). Mosby.
Mosby's Handbook of Pharmacology in Nursing. 3rd ed. Bruce D. Clayton. 698p. 1984. pap. text ed. 18.95 o.p. (ISBN 0-8016-4243-4). Mosby.
Mosby's Manual of Clinical Nursing Procedures. University of California, Department of Nursing Service Staff. LC 81-1379. (Illus.). 394p. 1981. pap. text ed. 25.95 o.p. (ISBN 0-8016-3592-6). Mosby.
Mosby's Manual of Critical Care: Practices & Procedures, 1979. Linda F. Abels. LC 78-24358. (Illus.). 440p. 1979. pap. text ed. 28.95 o.p. (ISBN 0-8016-0055-3). Mosby.
Mosby's Manual of Urologic Nursing. Judith Lerner & Zafar Khan. LC 81-18948. (Illus.). 721p. 1982. pap. text ed. 36.95 o.p. (ISBN 0-8016-2947-0). Mosby.
Mosby's Med-Tech Assess Test. Shoemaker. 1986. 21.95 o.p. (ISBN 0-8016-4621-9). Mosby.
Mosby's Rad-Tech Assesstest. Leonard. 1984. pap. 24.95 o.p. (ISBN 0-8016-2950-0). Mosby.
Mosby's Respiratory Therapy Assess Test. Youtsey. 1983. pap. 19.95 o.p. (ISBN 0-8016-5669-9). Mosby.
Mosby's Workbook for Nursing Assistants. Kelly. 1984. pap. 7.95 o.p. (ISBN 0-8016-2641-2). Mosby.
Moscow Abandons Israel for the Arabs: Ten Crucial Years in the Middle East. Alden H. Voth. LC 80-5478. 275p. 1980. lib. bdg. 27.25 o.p. (ISBN 0-8191-1111-2); pap. text ed. 13.50 o.p. (ISBN 0-8191-1112-0). U Pr of Amer.
Moscow & the Vatican. Alexis Floridi. 365p. 1986. 23.50 o.p. (ISBN 0-88233-647-9). Ardis Pubs.
Moscow, Capital of the Soviet Union. G. Lappo. 189p. 1976. 7.95 o.p. (ISBN 0-8285-0519-5, Pub. by Progress Pubns USSR). Imported Pubns.
Moscow Circus School. Leon Harris. LC 72-98611. (Illus.). (gr. 3-7). 1970. PLB 5.50 o.p. (ISBN 0-689-30005-0, Atheneum). Macmillan.
Moscow Kremlin & Red Square. 183p. 1976. 3.95 o.p. (ISBN 0-8285-0538-1, Pub. by Progress Pubs USSR). Imported Pubns.
Moscow-Leningrad-Kiev: A Guide. L. Dubinskaya. 215p. 1981. 7.45 o.p. (ISBN 0-8285-2356-8, Pub. by Progress Pubs USSR). Imported Pubns.
Moscow Rules. Robert Moss. 1985. 19.95 o.p. (ISBN 0-8161-3935-0). G K Hall.
Moscow Symposium on the Chemistry of Transuranium Elements: Proceedings. Ed. by V. I. Spitsyn & J. J. Katz. 1976. 95.00 o.p. (ISBN 0-08-020638-7). Pergamon.
Moscow to Main Street: Among the Russian Emigres. Victor Ripp. 252p. 1984. 16.45i o.p. (ISBN 0-316-74709-2). Little.
Moscow to the End of the Line. Venedikt Erofeev. Tr. by William Tjalsma from Rus. LC 79-5169. 1980. 8.95 o.s.i. (ISBN 0-8008-5374-1). Taplinger.
Moscow Travel Guide. Berlitz Staff. (Berlitz Travel Guides). (Illus.). 1982. pap. 4.95 o.p. (ISBN 0-02-969380-2, Berlitz). Macmillan.
Moscow Women: Thirteen Interviews. Carola Hansson et al. Tr. by Gerry Bothmer. Intro. by Gail W. Lapidus. LC 82-18841. 200p. 1983. 16.45 o.p. (ISBN 0-394-52332-6); pap. 7.95 o.p. (ISBN 0-394-71491-1). Pantheon.
Moscow's Muslim Challenge: Soviet Central Asia. Michael Rywkin. LC 81-14414. (Illus.). 232p. 1982. 25.00 o.p. (ISBN 0-87332-196-0); pap. 13.95 o.p. (ISBN 0-87332-262-2). M E Sharpe.
Mose in Egitto, 2 vols. Gioachino Rossini. Ed. by Phillip Gossett & Charles Rosen. LC 76-49183. (Early Romantic Opera Ser.: No. 9). 1979. lib. bdg. 180.00 o.p. (ISBN 0-8240-2908-9). Garland Pub.
Moses. Elias Auerbach. Tr. by Israel O. Lehman & Robert A. Barclay. LC 72-6589. 255p. 1975. text ed. 25.00x o.p. (ISBN 0-8143-1491-0). Wayne St U Pr.
Moses - Born to Be a Slave, but God... Richard O. Gilpin. 1977. 5.50 o.p. (ISBN 0-682-48843-7). Exposition-Phoenix.
Moses in the Promised Land. R. Howard Bloch. 224p. 1988. pap. 10.95 o.p. (ISBN 0-87905-216-3). Gibbs Smith Pub.
Moses: Leader & Lawgiver. Jean H. Berg. (Bible in Story & Song Ser.). (Illus.). 40p. (gr. k-4). 1982. pap. 4.95 o.p. (ISBN 0-87510-161-5). Chr Science.
Moses Malone. Libman. (Sports Superstars Ser.). (Illus.). 32p. (gr. 4 up). 1985. PLB 8.95 o.p. Creative Ed.
Moses of Rovno: The Stirring Story of Fritz Graeve, a German Christian Who Risked His Life to Lead Hundreds of Jews to Safety During the Holocaust. Douglas K. Huneke. (Holocaust Studies). (Illus.). 236p. 1985. 17.95 o.p. (ISBN 0-396-08714-0). Dodd.
Moses, Who First Saw the Pyramid of Life. Adolph A. Williamson. 1953. (ISBN 0-8022-1889-X). Philos Lib.
Moshe Safdie, Canadian Architect: A Bibliography. Mary E. Huls. (Architecture Ser.: A 1470). 6p. 1985. 2.00 o.p. (ISBN 0-89028-600-0). Vance Biblios.
Mosley's Men: The British Union of Fascists in the West Midlands. John D. Brewer. LC 84-1549. 159p. 1984. text ed. 30.95x o.p. (ISBN 0-566-00696-0). Gower Pub Co.
Mosquito. Philip Birtles. (Illus.). 192p. 1981. 19.95 o.p. (ISBN 0-86720-585-7). Janes Info Group.
Mosquitoes. William Faulkner. 1955. pap. 6.95 o.p. Norton.
Mosquitoes. William Faulkner. 352p. 1984. pap. 6.70 o.p. (ISBN 0-87140-133-9). Liveright.
Mosquitoes of Victoria. N. V. Dobrotworsky. 1965. 25.00x o.p. (ISBN 0-522-83584-8, Pub. by Melbourne U Pr). Intl Spec Bk.
Mossbauer Spectroscopy. Ed. by U. Gonser. (Topics in Applied Physics Ser.: Vol. 5). (Illus.). 240p. 1975. 44.00 o.p. (ISBN 0-387-07120-2). Springer-Verlag.
Mosses of Southern Australia. George Scott & Llma Stone. 1976. 99.00 o.p. (ISBN 0-12-633850-7). Acad Pr.
Most Ancient Egypt. William C. Hayes. Ed. by Keith C. Seele. LC 65-17294. (Midway Reprint Ser.). (Illus.). 1977. pap. text ed. 7.50x o.s.i. (ISBN 0-226-32102-9). U of Chicago Pr.
Most Beautiful Girl in the World. Gene Olson. LC 68-16857. (gr. 8 up). 1968. 3.95 o.s.i. (ISBN 0-664-32421-5, Westminster). Westminster John Knox.
Most Beautiful World. Rodney Hall. 60p. 1982. text ed. 13.50 o.p. (ISBN 0-7022-1587-2); pap. 7.50 o.p. (ISBN 0-7022-1588-0). U of Queensland Pr.
Most Dangerous Women: Feminist Peace Campaigners of the Great War. Anne Wiltsher. (Illus.). 288p. (Orig.). 1985. pap. 11.50 o.p. (ISBN 0-86358-010-6, Pandora Pr). Routledge Chapman & Hall.
Most Instructive Games of Chess Ever Played. Irving Chernev. 1973. pap. 9.95 o.s.i. (ISBN 0-671-21536-1, Fireside). S&S.
Most of the World: The Peoples of Africa, Latin America & the East Today. Ed. by Ralph Linton. 1970. Repr. of 1949 ed. lib. bdg. (ISBN 0-8371-3806-X, LIMW). Greenwood.
Most Popular Subroutines in BASIC. Ken Tracton. (Illus.). 1980. 13.95 o.p. (ISBN 0-8306-9740-3); pap. 7.95 o.p. (ISBN 0-8306-1050-2, 1050). TAB Bks.
Most Secret Place: Boscombe Down 1939-45. Brian Johnson & Terry Hefferman. (Illus.). 288p. 1983. 19.95 o.p. (ISBN 0-86720-641-1). Janes Info Group.
Most Valuable Player. William L. Heath. LC 72-88168. (Illus., Orig.). (gr. 5 up). 1973. 5.25 o.p. (ISBN 0-15-255720-2, HJ). HarBraceJ.
Mostly Mary. Gwynedd Rae. (Orig.). (gr. 1-3). 1972. pap. 0.95 o.p. (ISBN 0-380-01349-5, 08110, Camelot). Avon.
Mostly Motor Racing: A Pictorial Autobiography. A. F. Fletcher. (Illus.). 300p. 1986. 25.95 o.p. (ISBN 0-85429-461-9, Pub. by Haynes Pubns). Haynes Pubns.
Mostly on Martha's Vineyard: A Personal Record. Henry B. Hough. LC 74-22494. 298p. 1975. 7.95 o.p. (ISBN 0-15-106800-3). HarBraceJ.
Mostly Sitting Haiku. 2nd rev., exp. ed. Allen Ginsberg. (Xtras Ser.: No. 6). 36p. (Orig.). 1983. pap. 2.50 o.s.i. (ISBN 0-89120-014-2). From Here.
Mostly True Confessions: Looking for Love in the Eighties. Jean Gonick. LC 85-19364. 224p. 1986. 14.45 o.p. (ISBN 0-394-55131-1). Random.
Mote in God's Eye. Larry Niven & Jerry Pournelle. 576p. 1974. 10.95 o.s.i. (ISBN 0-671-21833-6). S&S.
Mote in Heaven's Eye. Donald Finkel. LC 74-196700. 1975. 7.95 o.p. (ISBN 0-689-10648-3, Atheneum). Macmillan.
Moth. Catherine Cookson. LC 85-26266. 1986. 17.45 o.s.i. (ISBN 0-671-44076-4). Summit Bks.
Moth Hunters: Aboriginal Prehistory of the Australian Alps. J. Flood. (AIAS New Ser.). (Illus.). 1980. text ed. 29.95x o.p. (ISBN 0-391-00993-1); pap. text ed. 18.00x o.p. (ISBN 0-391-00994-X). Humanities.
Mother. Bertolt Brecht. LC 78-10764. 1978. pap. 7.95 o.p. (ISBN 0-394-17065-2, B414, BC). Grove.
Mother. V. I. Pudovkin. (Film Scripts-Classic Ser.). 1970. pap. 1.95 o.p. (ISBN 0-671-20790-3). S&S.
Mother Cee. Nola P. Crist. LC 85-90066. 105p. 1985. 8.95 o.p. (ISBN 0-533-06588-7). Vantage.
Mother Courage & Her Children. Bertolt Brecht. Tr. by Eric Bentley from Ger. (Orig.). 1963. pap. 3.95 o.p. (ISBN 0-394-17106-3, B108, BC). Grove.
Mother Earth Bulletin. Incl. Series 1, Vol. 1. lib. bdg. 27.00 (ISBN 0-313-21733-5, ME11); Series 1, Vol. 2. lib. bdg. 27.00 (ISBN 0-313-21734-3, ME12); Series 1, Vol. 3. lib. bdg. 21.00 (ISBN 0-313-21735-1, ME13); Series 1, Vol. 4. lib. bdg. 21.00 (ISBN 0-313-21736-X, ME14); Series 1, Vol. 5. lib. bdg. 21.00 (ISBN 0-313-21737-8, ME15); Series 1, Vol. 6. lib. bdg. 21.00 (ISBN 0-313-21738-6, ME16); Series 1, Vol. 7. lib. bdg. 21.00 (ISBN 0-313-21739-4, ME17); Series 1, Vol. 8. lib. bdg. 21.00 (ISBN 0-313-21740-8, ME18); Series 1, Vol. 9. lib. bdg. 21.00 (ISBN 0-313-21741-6, ME19); Series 1, Vol. 10. lib. bdg. 21.00 (ISBN 0-313-21742-4, ME30); Series 1, Vol. 11. lib. bdg. 21.00 (ISBN 0-313-21743-2, ME31); Series 1, Vol. 12 & Series 2, Nos. 1-7. lib. bdg. 22.00 (ISBN 0-313-21744-0, ME32). (Series 1: Vols. 1-12, No. 6; Series 2: Nos. 1-7). 1969. Repr. of 1918 ed. Set. lib. bdg. 240.00x o.p. (ISBN 0-8371-9207-2, ME00). Greenwood.
Mother Earth's Hassle-Free Vegetable Cookbook. J. Rapp. (Illus.). 1981. pap. 5.95 o.p. (ISBN 0-380-76851-8, 76851-8). Avon.
Mother Florence: A Biographical History. Angeline Murphy, Sr. (Illus.). 258p. 1980. 15.00 o.p. (ISBN 0-682-49625-1, Testament). Exposition-Phoenix.
Mother Goose. Selected by & illus. by Michael Hague. LC 83-22559. (Illus.). 72p. (gr. k-3). 1984. 12.95 o.p. (ISBN 0-03-070723-4). H Holt & Co.

Mother Goose. Illus. by William Joyce. LC 84-1955. (Knee-High Bks.). (Illus.). (ps-1). 1984. 3.95 o.p. (ISBN 0-394-86534-0, Pub. by BYR); lib. bdg. 4.99 o.p. (ISBN 0-394-96534-5). Random.

Mother Goose. (Illus.). 48p. (gr. 1-7). 1978. 5.95 o.p. (ISBN 0-448-47230-9, G&D). Putnam Pub Group.

Mother Goose. (gr. k-3). 0.79 o.p. (ISBN 0-8431-4180-8). Wonder.

Mother Goose. (Chubby Panoramas Ser.). (Illus.). 1983. 2.85 o.s.i. (ISBN 0-671-47664-5, Little Simon). S&S.

Mother Goose. Dorothy Rose. (Chubby Banana Split Board Bks.). (ps). 1984. 2.95 o.s.i. (ISBN 0-671-50955-1, Little Simon). S&S.

Mother Goose, a Treasury of Best Loved Rhymes. Ed. by Watty Piper. LC 72-185969. (Illus.). 64p. (ps-1). 1971. PLB 5.99 o.p. (ISBN 0-448-13027-0, G&D). Putnam Pub Group.

Mother Goose Book. Illus. by Daniel San Souci. (Illus.). 48p. 1986. pap. 9.95 o.s.i. (ISBN 0-671-62913-1, Little Simon). S&S.

Mother Goose for the Animals' Children. Marjorie Kahl Lawrence. (gr. k-3). 1974. 5.00 o.p. (ISBN 0-682-47885-7). Exposition-Phoenix.

Mother Goose Your Computer: A Grownup's Garden of Silicon Satire. Paul Panish & Anna B. Panish. LC 84-51239. (Illus.). 96p. 1984. 8.95 o.p. (ISBN 0-89588-198-5). SYBEX.

Mother Goose's Picture Puzzles. (Illus.). 48p. (Orig.). (gr. k-4). 1982. pap. 2.95 o.p. (ISBN 0-8431-4081-X). Troubador Pr.

Mother India's Children. Edward Rice. (Illus.). 1972. pap. 2.95 o.p. (ISBN 0-377-12111-8). Friendship Pr.

Mother Ireland. Edna O'Brien. 1976. 12.95 o.p. (ISBN 0-15-162587-5). HarBraceJ.

Mother Less Child. Jacquelyn Mitchard. LC 84-14812. 379p. 1985. 15.45x o.p. (ISBN 0-393-01902-0). Norton.

Mother Load. Cindy Packard. LC 85-47636. 288p. 1986. 15.95 o.p. (ISBN 0-689-11577-6, Atheneum). Macmillan.

Mother Nature's Michigan. Oscar Warbach. (Illus., Orig.). 1976. pap. 6.95 o.p. (ISBN 0-910726-70-1). Hillsdale Educ.

Mother of Carmel: A Portrait of St. Teresa of Jesus. E. A. Peers. 1979. pap. 4.95 o.p. (ISBN 0-8192-1261-X). Morehouse Pub.

Mother of God. Ed. by Lawrence Cunningham. LC 82-47741. 132p. 1982. 4.50 o.p. (ISBN 0-686-97232-5). HarpR.

Mother of the Blues: A Study of Ma Rainey. Sandra R. Lieb. LC 81-1168. (Illus.). 256p. 1981. 20.00x o.p. U of Mass Pr.

Mother Russia. Robert Littel. LC 77-92554. 192p. 1978. 12.95 o.p. (ISBN 0-15-162638-3). HarBraceJ.

Mother Shares: Meditations on Parenting. Susan Nethery. 128p. 1981. 5.95 o.p. (ISBN 0-8010-6736-7). Baker Bk.

Mother Teresa: Caring for All God's Children. Betsy Lee. LC 80-20286. (Taking Part Ser.). (Illus.). 48p. (gr. 3 up). 1981. PLB 8.95 o.p. (ISBN 0-87518-205-4). Dillon.

Mother Teresa of Calcutta. Roy Gasnick. 1.25 o.p. (NCR472). Paulist Pr.

Mother Was a Lovely Beast. Philip Jose Farmer. 1976. pap. 1.25 o.s.i. (ISBN 0-515-04071-1). Jove Pubns.

Motherhood in Bondage: Motherhood in Bondage see Works.

Motherhood: The Second Oldest Profession. Erma Bombeck. (General Ser.). 1984. lib. bdg. 13.95 o.p. (ISBN 0-8161-3602-5, Large Print Bks). G K Hall.

Mothers. abr. ed. Robert Briffault. Ed. & intro. by Gordon R. Taylor. LC 76-28642. (Illus.). 1977. pap. text ed. 5.95x o.p. (ISBN 0-689-70541-7, 232, Atheneum). Macmillan.

Mothers. Mary C. Smith. 1985. 6.95 o.p. (ISBN 0-533-06061-3). Vantage.

Mothers & Children Facing Divorce. Tracy B. Grossman. Ed. by Peter Nathan. LC 86-11336. (Research in Clinical Psychology Ser.: No. 15). 220p. 1986. 39.95 o.p. (ISBN 0-8357-1767-4). UMI Res Pr.

Mothers & Lovers. Elizabeth Wood. 1987. 17.95 o.p. (ISBN 0-531-15062-3). Watts.

Mothers & Sons. Carole Klein. (Non-Fiction Ser.). 272p. 1985. pap. 7.95 o.p. (ISBN 0-8398-2880-2, Gregg). G K Hall.

Mothers Are Special. John W. Drakeford & Robina Drakeford. LC 78-73137. 1979. 8.95 o.p. (ISBN 0-8054-5636-8). Broadman.

Mothers: At the Heart of Life. Sheree Phillips. 140p. (Orig.). 1985. pap. 6.95 o.p. (ISBN 0-89283-274-6, Pub. by Vine Books). Servant.

Mothers, Fathers, & Children: Practical Advice to Parents. A. Furutan. 280p. pap. (ISBN 0-85398-095-0). G Ronald Pub.

Mothers, Grandmothers & Daughters: Personality & Child-Care in Three Generation Families. Bertram J. Cohler & Henry U. Grunebaum. LC 80-17979. (Wiley Personality Processes Ser.). 456p. 1981. 37.95x o.p. (ISBN 0-471-05900-5, Pub. by Wiley-Interscience). Wiley.

Mothers in Prison. Phyllis J. Baunach. 172p. 1985. 19.95 o.p. (ISBN 0-88738-027-1). Transaction Pubs.

Mother's Journal. (Illus.). 96p. 1988. 6.98 o.p. (ISBN 0-89471-608-5, Pub. by Courage Bks.). Running Pr.

Mother's Love. Leon R. Hartshorn. LC 80-81506. 76p. 1980. 5.95 o.p. (ISBN 0-88290-143-5). Horizon Utah.

Mother's Love. Ed. by Susan P. Schutz. (Illus.). 64p. (Orig.). 1980. pap. 4.95 o.p. (ISBN 0-88396-122-9). Blue Mtn Pr CO.

Mothers of the Novel. Dale Spender. 320p. 1988. pap. 13.95 o.p. (ISBN 0-86358-251-6, Pandora Pr). Routledge Chapman & Hall.

Mothers of the Novel: One Hundred Good Women Writers Before Jane Austen. Dale Spender. 320p. 1986. 25.00 o.p. (ISBN 0-86358-081-5, Pandora Pr). Routledge Chapman & Hall.

Mothers on Trial: The Battle for Children & Custody. Phyllis Chesler. LC 86-31573. 558p. 1987. pap. 11.95 o.p. (ISBN 0-931188-46-6). Seal Pr Feminist.

Mother's Problem Solver. Verna Birkey & Jeanette Turnquist. 128p. 1979. pap. 5.95 o.p. (ISBN 0-8007-5050-0, Power Bks). Revell.

Mother's Work. Deborah Fallows. 250p. 1985. 16.45 o.p. (ISBN 0-395-36218-0). HM.

Moths & Mothers, Feathers & Fathers: A Story About a Tiny Owl Named Squib. Larry Shles. 1984. 10.45 o.p. (ISBN 0-395-36695-X); pap. 4.80 o.p. (ISBN 0-395-36555-4). HM.

Motility in Cell Function: Proceedings of the First John M. Marshall Symposium on Cell Biology. Ed. by Frank Pepe et al. LC 78-11880. 1979. 48.50 o.p. (ISBN 0-12-551750-5). Acad Pr.

Motility of Living Cells. P. Cappuccinelli. 80p. 1980. pap. 8.50x o.p. (ISBN 0-412-15770-5, NO. 2887, Pub. by Chapman & Hall England). Routledge Chapman & Hall.

Motion, Motion: Kinetic Art. Jim Jenkins & Dave Quick. (Illus.). 64p. 1989. pap. 14.95 o.p. (ISBN 0-87905-185-X, Peregrine Smith). Gibbs Smith Pub.

Motion of Mercury's Perihelion. Harold S. Slusher & Francisco Ramirez. LC 83-80180. 1984. pap. 6.95 o.p. (ISBN 0-932766-17-X, Inst Creation). Master Bks.

Motion Picture Continuities. Frances Patterson. Ed. by Bruce S. Kupelnick. LC 76-52120. (Classics of Film Literature Ser.). 1977. lib. bdg. 22.00 o.p. (ISBN 0-8240-2888-0). Garland Pub.

Motion Picture Film Maintenance Manual, 16MM. University Film Centers Consortium Staff. 120p. 1983. pap. text ed. 23.95 o.p. (ISBN 0-8403-3030-8). Kendall-Hunt.

Motion Picture Projection & Theatre Presentation Manual. Ed. by Don V. Kloepfel. (Illus.). 190p. pap. text ed. 7.50 o.s.i. (ISBN 0-318-16589-9). Soc Motion Pic & TV Engrs.

Motion Pictures from the Library of Congress Paper Print Collection, 1894-1912. Kemp R. Niver. 1967. 75.00x o.p. (ISBN 0-520-00947-9). U of Cal Pr.

Motion Practice in Georgia. 197p. 1984. 11.00 o.p. (ISBN 0-318-02481-0). ICLE Georgia.

Motions, Discovery, & Negotiated Agreements. Massachusetts Continuing Legal Education-New England Law Institute, Inc. Staff. LC 83-63418. write for info. o.p. Mass CLE.

Motions to Supress in Deportation Cases. 35.00 o.p. Natl Lawyers Guild.

Motivating Classroom Discipline. William J. Gnagey. 148p. 1981. pap. text ed. write for info. o.p. (ISBN 0-02-344140-2). Macmillan.

Motivating People to Work. Ed. by Warren C. Hauk. 1984. pap. text ed. 24.95 o.p. (ISBN 0-89806-057-5). Inst Indus Eng.

Motivating Today's Students. Walter F. Drew et al. LC 74-16805. (Learning Handbooks Ser.). 1974. pap. 5.95 o.p. (ISBN 0-8224-1908-4). D S Lake Pubs.

Motivation. Phil Evans. (Essential Psychology Ser.). 1975. pap. 4.50x o.p. (ISBN 0-416-83160-5, NO. 2777). Routledge Chapman & Hall.

Motivation & Work Behavior. 2nd ed. Richard M. Steers & Lyman W. Porter. (Management Ser.). (Illus.). 1979. text ed. 30.95 o.p. (ISBN 0-07-060941-1, C). McGraw.

Motivation at Work. Hywel Murrell. (Essential Psychology Ser.). 1976. pap. 4.50x o.p. (ISBN 0-416-84090-6, NO. 2332). Routledge Chapman & Hall.

Motivation: Key to Good Management. (AMACOM Reprint Collections). 1974. pap. 8.00 o.p. (ISBN 0-8144-6938-8). AMACOM.

Motivation to Last a Lifetime. Ted W. Engstrom. 96p. 1983. 9.95 o.p. (ISBN 0-310-24250-9, 9570Z); pap. 4.95 o.p. (ISBN 0-310-24251-7, 9570P). Zondervan.

Motivation Training Manual. George L. Wenzel. (Illus.). 272p. 1970. text ed. 42.50 o.p. Radio City.

Motivation Training Manual. William J. Wenzel. 272p. 1983. 28.95 o.p. (ISBN 0-8436-0599-5). Van Nos Reinhold.

Motivational Approach to Selling. James F. Evered. 224p. 1982. 15.95 o.p. (ISBN 0-8144-5738-X). AMACOM.

Motivational Control Systems Analysis. Ed. by D. J. McFarland. 1975. 94.50 o.p. (ISBN 0-12-483860-X). Acad Pr.

Motivational Gifts. Marilyn Hickey. 104p. (Orig.). 1983. pap. text ed. 3.50 o.p. (ISBN 0-914307-06-1). R Tilton Ministries.

Motive for Murder. Edson T. Hamill. (Ryker Ser). 1975. pap. 1.25 o.p. (ISBN 0-685-61047-0, LB315, Pub. by Leisure Bks CT). Dorchester Pub Co.

Motobecane Mopeds '66 - '76: '65 Thru '76. Mansur Darlington. (Haynes Owners Workshop Manuals: No. 258). 1976. 11.50 o.p. (ISBN 0-85696-258-9). Haynes Pubns.

Motocourse 1984-1985. P. Clifford. (Motorcycle Annual Ser.). (Illus.). 192p. 1985. 36.95 o.p. (ISBN 0-905138-33-3, Pub. by Hazelton England). Motorbooks Intl.

Motor Application & Maintenance Handbook. R. W. Smeaton. 1969. text ed. 63.00 o.p. (ISBN 0-07-058438-9). McGraw.

Motor Auto Engines & Electrical Systems. 8th ed. Motor Auto Engines & Electrical Staff. (Illus.). 656p. 1984. 28.50 o.p. (ISBN 0-87851-577-1, Hearst Motor Bk). Morrow.

Motor Auto Repair Manual. 47th ed. Motor Auto Repair Manual Staff. (Illus.). 1400p. 1983. 21.50 o.p. (ISBN 0-87851-570-4). Morrow.

Motor Auto Repair Manual. 8th ed. Motor Auto Repair Manual Staff. (Illus.). 1440p. 1984. 21.50 o.p. (ISBN 0-87851-592-5, Hearst Motor Bk). Morrow.

Motor Auto Repair Manual, 1985. 48th ed. Motor Auto Repair Manual Staff. (Illus.). 1450p. 1984. 21.50 o.p. (ISBN 0-87851-590-9, Hearst Motor Bk). Morrow.

Motor Boat & Yachting Manual. 18th ed. T. Cox. (Illus.). 1973. 17.50 o.p. (ISBN 0-540-00966-0). E J Brill USA.

Motor City Blue. Loren D. Estleman. 1980. 9.95 o.p. (ISBN 0-395-29447-9). HM.

Motor Cruising Manual. John Mellor. (Illus.). 224p. 1987. 29.95 o.p. (ISBN 0-7153-8851-7). David & Charles.

Motor Fitness Testing Manual for the Moderately Mentally Retarded. 80p. 1975. 6.80 o.p. (ISBN 0-88314-135-3, 242-25778). AAHPERD.

Motor Imported Auto Repair Manual. 5th ed. 1200p. 25.50 o.p. (ISBN 0-87851-564-X). Morrow.

Motor Innervation of Muscle. Ed. by S. Thesleff. 1977. 82.00 o.p. (ISBN 0-12-685950-7). Acad Pr.

Motor Learning & Human Performance: An Application to Motor & Movement Behaviors. 3rd ed. Robert N. Singer. (Illus.). 1980. text ed. (ISBN 0-02-410780-8). Macmillan.

Motor Museums of Europe. William Stobbs. (Illus.). 208p. 1983. 22.50x o.p. (ISBN 0-213-16843-X, GWN 04887, Pub. by Weidenfeld & Nicolson England). Biblio Dist.

Motor Vehicle Inspection. William H. Crouse & Donald L. Anglin. (Illus.). 1978. text ed. 38.55 o.p. (ISBN 0-07-014813-9). McGraw.

Motor Vehicle Law. Annotations by Ben F. Loeb, Jr. 155p. 1984. pap. 6.50 o.p. (ISBN 0-686-17564-6). Institute Government.

Motor Vehicle No-Fault Law: Florida. Alpert. 1985. 39.95 o.p. Lawyers Co-Op.

Motor Vehicle Program Manager I. Jack Rudman. (Career Examination Ser.: C-312). (Cloth bdg. avail. on request). pap. 12.00 o.p. (ISBN 0-8373-0312-5). Natl Learning.

Motor Vehicle Program Manager II. Jack Rudman. (Career Examination Ser.: C-313). (Cloth bdg. avail. on request). pap. 14.00 o.p. (ISBN 0-8373-0313-3). Natl Learning.

Motor Vehicle Science, 2 pts. P. W. Kett. (Illus.). 1981. Pt. I. 22.00x o.p. (ISBN 0-412-22359-7, NO. 6623, Pub. by Chapman & Hall England); Pt. II. 22.00x o.p. (ISBN 0-412-23600-1, NO. 6605). Routledge Chapman & Hall.

Motorcycle & Small Engine: Dictionary-Terminology. William H. Kosbab. Ed. by Dianne Greenslade-Moore & Daveta Lamont. LC 82-71155. 350p. 1983. pap. text ed. 14.95x o.p. (ISBN 0-89262-044-7). Career Pub.

Motorcycle Racing. Nicole Puleo. LC 72-5421. (Superwheels & Thrill Sports Bks.). (Illus.). 48p. (gr. 3-6). 1973. PLB 9.95 o.p. (ISBN 0-8225-0401-4). Lerner Pubns.

Motorcycle Repair Encyclopedia. 2nd ed. Tim Lockwood. Ed. by Jeff Robinson. (Illus.). 472p. 1976. pap. text ed. 10.00 o.p. (ISBN 0-89287-021-4, M430). Clymer Pub.

Motorcycles: Fundamentals, Service Repair. Bruce Johns & David Edmundson. 1984. 21.28 o.p. (ISBN 0-87006-438-X). Goodheart.

Motoring Mascots of the World. William Carlos Williams. LC 79-4529. (Illus.). 1979. 34.95 o.p. (ISBN 0-87938-036-5). Motorbooks Intl.

Motorist Information Systems & Services. (Transportation Research Record Ser.). 67p. 1976. 3.00 o.p. (ISBN 0-309-02569-9). Transport Res Bd.

Motorists' Needs & Services on Interstate Highways. (National Cooperative Highway Research Program Report). 88p. 1969. 3.60 o.p. (ISBN 0-317-36094-9, 1718). Transport Res Bd.

Motorsports: A Guide to Information Sources. Ed. by Susan Ebershoff-Coles & Charla Leibenguth. LC 79-13736. (Sports, Games, & Pastimes Information Guide Ser.: Vol. 5). 208p. 1979. 68.00x o.p. (ISBN 0-8103-1446-0). Gale.

Motown Story. Don Waller. (Illus.). 192p. 1985. 24.95 o.p. (ISBN 0-684-18293-9, ScribT); pap. 12.95 o.p. (ISBN 0-684-18347-1). Scribner.

Mots. Jean-Paul Sartre. (Coll. Soleil). 1964. 10.95 o.p. (ISBN 0-685-11407-4). Schoenhof.

Mottoes & Badges of Families, Regiments, Schools, Colleges, States, Towns, Livery Companies, Societies, Etc. W. S. Anson. LC 74-14502. 192p. 1975. Repr. of 1904 ed. 43.00x o.p. (ISBN 0-8103-4055-0). Gale.

Mouche Bleue. Marcel Ayme. 1978. pap. 9.95 o.p. (ISBN 0-686-51917-5). French & Eur.

Mould & Core Material for the Steel Industry. A. D. Sarkar. 1967. text ed. 24.00 o.p. (ISBN 0-08-012486-0); pap. text ed. 10.75 o.p. (ISBN 0-08-012487-9). Pergamon.

Moulded Slip Cast Pottery. encore ed. David Cowley. (ISBN 0-684-17558-4). Scribner.

Moulded Slip Cast Pottery. David Cowley. pap. (ISBN 0-684-15752-7). Scribner.

Moulds: Their Isolation, Cultivation, & Identification. David Malloch. 88p. 1981. 14.95 o.p. (ISBN 0-8020-2418-1). U of Toronto Pr.

Moulds, Toxins & Food. Claude Moreau. LC 78-8715. 477p. 1979. 127.00 o.p. (ISBN 0-471-99681-5, Pub. by Wiley-Interscience). Wiley.

Mounce's Legal Forms Workbook. 6th ed. Townes L. Dawson. 272p. 1979. net 12.00 o.s.i. (ISBN 0-205-11507-1, H1507-6). Allyn.

Mount Lowe: Railway in the Clouds. Charles Seims. LC 76-45760. (Illus.). 232p. 1976. 27.95 o.p. (ISBN 0-87095-063-0). Gldn West Bks.

Mount Pleasant & the Early Quakers of Ohio. J. L. Burke & D. E. Bensch. (Illus.). 45p. 1975. 2.50 o.s.i. (ISBN 0-318-03174-4). Ohio Hist Soc.

Mount St. Helens: A Changing Landscape. LC 80-83472. (Illus.). 128p. (Text by Chuck Williams). 29.50 o.s.i. (ISBN 0-912856-63-7). Gr Arts Ctr Pub.

Mount Washington in Winter 1870-1871. 363p. 1986. pap. 20.00 o.p. (ISBN 1-55613-015-5). Heritage Bk.

Mountain & Water: Essays on the Cultural Ecology of South Coastal China. Eugene Anderson & Marja L. Anderson. (Asian Folklore & Social Life Monograph: No. 54). 194p. 1973. photo copy 25.00x o.p. (ISBN 0-89986-051-6). Oriental Bk Store.

Mountain Bike Book: Choosing, Riding, & Maintaining the Off-Road Bicycle. Rob Van der Plas. LC 83-51788. (Illus.). 144p. (Orig.). 1985. pap. 7.95 o.p. (ISBN 0-933201-10-9). Bicycle Books.

Mountain Bike Book: Choosing, Riding & Maintaining the Off-Road Bicycle. 3nd. rev. ed. Rob Van der Plas. Ed. by Paddy Monk. (Illus.). 208p. 1988. pap. 8.95 o.p. (ISBN 0-933201-18-4). Bicycle Books.

Mountain Blows Its Top. Glen Wright. Ed. by Carol Murphy. (Illus.). (gr. 3-6). 1981. PLB 6.95 o.p. (ISBN 0-89868-111-1, Read Res); pap. text ed. 4.95 o.p. (ISBN 0-89868-118-9, Read Res). ARO Pub.

Mountain Boy. Lee Templeton. 115p. (gr. 4-7). 1983. 6.95 o.p. (ISBN 0-89015-370-1). Eakin Pr.

Mountain Eagles. Jack Bannatyne. 192p. 1986. pap. 2.95 o.p. (ISBN 0-931773-34-2). Critics Choice Paper.

Mountain, Field, & Family: The Economy & Human Ecology of an Andean Valley. Stephen B. Brush. LC 77-24364. 1977. 13.95x o.p. (ISBN 0-8122-7728-7). U of Pa Pr.

Mountain Flying. Sparky Imeson. (Illus.). 246p. 1982. pap. 7.50 o.p. (ISBN 0-911721-22-3, Pub. by Airguide). Aviation.

Mountain Geography: A Critique & Field Study. Roderick Peattie. Repr. of 1936 ed. lib. bdg. 35.00x o.p. (ISBN 0-8371-2243-0, PEMG). Greenwood.

Mountain Gloom & Mountain Glory. Marjorie H. Nicolson. 1963. pap. 2.95 o.p. (ISBN 0-393-00204-7, Norton Lib). Norton.

Mountain Gorilla: Ecology & Behavior. George B. Schaller. LC 63-11401. (Illus.). 1976. pap. text ed. 9.00x o.s.i. (ISBN 0-226-73636-9). U of Chicago Pr.

Mountain in the Clouds: A Search for the Wild Salmon. Bruce Brown. 1982. 12.50 o.p. (ISBN 0-671-43583-3). S&S.

Mountain in the Clouds: A Search for the Wild Salmon. Bruce Brown. 249p. 1983. pap. 6.75 o.p. (ISBN 0-671-49264-0, Touchstone). S&S.

Titles

Mountain in Tibet: The Search for Mount Kailas & the Sources of the Great Rivers of Asia. Charles Allen. (Illus.). 256p. 1982. 30.95 o.s.i. (ISBN 0-233-97281-1, Pub. by A Deutsch England). David & Charles.

Mountain Men of Wyoming. Richard Fetter. (Wyoming Frontier Ser.). 64p. 1982. pap. 3.95 o.p. (ISBN 0-686-97819-6). Johnson Bks.

Mountain of Gems: Fairy Tales of the Peoples of the Soviet Land. 238p. 1984. 8.95 o.p. (ISBN 0-8285-2836-5, Pub. by Raduga Pub USSR). Imported Pubns.

Mountain of Names: A History of the Human Family. Alex Shoumatoff. 1986. pap. 8.95 o.p. (ISBN 0-671-62259-5, Touchstone Bks). S&S.

Mountain of Names: An Informal History of Kinship. Alex Shoumatoff. 320p. 1985. 17.45 o.s.i. (ISBN 0-671-49440-6). S&S.

Mountain of Winter. Shirley Schoonover. 192p. 1980. pap. 2.25 o.p. (ISBN 0-380-76513-6, 76513). Avon.

Mountain Relics. Frances Thompson. LC 75-20605. (Illus.). 188p. 1977. 15.00 o.p. (ISBN 0-498-01774-5). A S Barnes.

Mountain Skiing. Vic Bein. 1983. 15.25 o.p. (ISBN 0-8446-6044-2). Peter Smith.

Mountain Splendour. R. O. Pearse. (Illus.). 239p. 1981. 37.50x o.p. (ISBN 0-86978-156-1, Pub. by Timmins Africa). Intl Spec Bk.

Mountain Standard Time. Paul Horgan. 595p. 1962. 7.95 o.p. (ISBN 0-374-21568-5). FS&G.

Mountain Time. Date not set. (ISBN 0-8052-3932-4). Random.

Mountain Time. Paul Schullery. LC 84-5586. 256p. 1984. 17.95 o.s.i. (ISBN 0-8052-3932-4). Schocken.

Mountain Trailways for Youth: Devotions for Young People. Mrs. Charles E. Cowman. 1979. pap. 7.95 o.p. (ISBN 0-310-37641-6, 6880P). Zondervan.

Mountain Wild Flowers of the Pacific Northwest. Taylor & Douglas. LC 73-89237. (Illus.). 1975. 12.50 o.p. (ISBN 0-8323-0230-9); pap. 8.95 o.p. (ISBN 0-8323-0231-7). Binford-Metropolitan.

Mountaineering Essays. John Muir. Ed. by Richard F. Fleck. (Literature of the American Wilderness Ser.). (Illus.). 208p. 1984. pap. 4.95 o.p. (ISBN 0-87905-169-8, Peregrine Smith). Gibbs Smith Pub.

Mountaineering First Aid: A Guide to Accident Response & First Aid Care. 2nd ed. Dick Mitchell. LC 75-25341. (Illus.). 104p. 1975. pap. 3.95 o.p. (ISBN 0-916890-33-3). Mountaineers.

Mountains at the Bottom of the World. Ian Cameron. (YA) (gr. 7 up). 1980. pap. 1.25 o.p. (ISBN 0-380-00184-5, 21402). Avon.

Mountain's Hostage. J. Wayne Erickson. 290p. 1980. 12.50 o.p. (ISBN 0-682-49654-5, Banner). Exposition-Phoenix.

Mountains of Canada. Randy Morse. LC 78-71667. (Illus.). 1979. 27.50 o.p. (ISBN 0-916890-74-0). Mountaineers.

Mountains of North America. Fred Beckey. LC 82-3315. (Illus.). 288p. 1982. 35.00 o.s.i. (ISBN 0-87156-320-7). Sierra.

Mountains of the Gods. Ian Cameron. (Illus.). 248p. 1985. 24.95 o.p. (ISBN 0-8160-1242-3). Facts on File.

Mountains to Climb. Helen DeLuca. (Illus.). 128p. (Orig.). 1983. pap. 6.95 o.s.i. (ISBN 0-918342-18-X). Cambric.

Mounted Games & Gymkhanas. British Horse Society & Pony Club Staff. LC 76-56448. 1977. 8.95 o.p. (ISBN 0-8120-5124-6). Barron.

Mourners Below. James Purdy. LC 79-57080. 1980. 9.95 o.p. (ISBN 0-87795-263-9, Arbor Hse). Morrow.

Mourning Trees. Velda Johnston. (Nightingale Ser.). 304p. 1988. pap. 12.95x o.p. (ISBN 0-8161-4404-4). G K Hall.

Mourt's Relation. William Bradford & Edward Winslow. LC 72-78652. 1865. Repr. 25.00 o.p. (ISBN 0-686-01725-0). Somerset Pub.

Mouse. Sara B. Stein. LC 84-15872. (Illus.). 32p. (ps-3). 1985. 6.95 o.p. (ISBN 0-15-256021-1, HJ). HarBraceJ.

Mouse about the House. Richard Fowler. (Slot Bks.). 24p. (ps-1). 1984. 8.95 o.s.i. (ISBN 0-88110-154-0). EDC.

Mouse & His Child. Russell Hoban. (Illus.). 192p. (gr. k up). 1977. pap. 2.25 o.p. (ISBN 0-380-00910-2, Camelot). Avon.

Mouse Book: The Story of Apodemus, a Longtailed Field Mouse. David Bellamy. (Illus.). 96p. 1984. 11.95 o.p. (ISBN 0-85362-200-0, Oriel). Routledge Chapman & Hall.

Mouse in House. Judith Schermer. (ps-2). 1979. PLB 6.95 o.p. (ISBN 0-395-27801-5). HM.

Mouse Named Mus. Irene Brady. LC 74-161651. (Illus.). 96p. (gr. 2-5). 1972. 4.95 o.p. (ISBN 0-395-13151-0). HM.

Mouse Numbers & Letters. Jim Arnosky. LC 81-13305. (Illus.). 48p. (ps-3). 1982. 10.95 o.p. (ISBN 0-15-256022-X, HJ). HarBraceJ.

Mouse Sarcoma Virus. new ed. H. Yoshikura et al. (Illus.). 220p. 1972. text ed. 28.50x o.p. (ISBN 0-8422-7086-8). Irvington.

Mouse to Be Free. Joyce W. Warren. (Illus.). (gr. 1-4). 1975. pap. 1.25 o.p. (ISBN 0-380-00349-X, 25700-9, Camelot). Avon.

Mouse Will Play. David N. Bruskin. (Story Bus Subseries: Camp Bus). (Illus.). 10p. (ps-2). 1988. bds. 14.95 o.p. (ISBN 1-55929-010-2). Bound Fun Inc.

Mouse Woman & the Vanished Princesses. Christie Harris. LC 75-23147. (Illus.). 192p. (gr. 4-6). 1976. 7.95 o.p. (ISBN 0-689-30502-8, Atheneum). Macmillan.

Mouse Writing. Jim Arnosky. LC 83-4298. (Illus.). 48p. (ps-3). 1983. 10.95 o.p. (ISBN 0-15-256028-9, HJ). HarBraceJ.

Mousekin's ABC's. Edna Miller. (Illus.). (ps-1). 1974. pap. 5.95 o.s.i. (ISBN 0-13-604371-2, Pub. by Treehouse). P-H.

Mousekin's Easter Basket. Edna Miller. (Illus.). 32p. (ps-3). 1987. 11.95 o.s.i. (ISBN 0-13-604141-8). P-H.

Mouvement. Marie Galanti. 288p. 1984. 14.00 o.p. (ISBN 0-669-06367-3). Heath.

Movable Feasts: The Backpacker Magazine Cookbook. Hasse R. Bunnelle. Ed. by Backpacker Magazine Staff. 1981. 12.95 o.p. (ISBN 0-671-25032-9, Fireside); pap. 9.50 o.p. (ISBN 0-671-25033-7). S&S.

Move Ahead with Possibility Thinking. Robert H. Schuller. 224p. 1973. pap. 2.95 o.p. (ISBN 0-8007-8105-8, Spire Bks). Revell.

Move to Learn: Lessons Plans for Elementary Physical Education. Margaret C. Seagraves. LC 79-63067. (Illus.). 238p. (Orig.). 1981. pap. text ed. 12.95x o.p. (ISBN 0-89459-048-0). Hunter Textbks.

Move with Me from A to Z. Charlene Schade. (Illus.). 72p. (gr. k-1). 1982. pap. 6.95 o.p. (ISBN 0-940156-01-6). Wright Group.

Moved-Outers. Florence C. Means. (gr. 7-9). 1945. 5.95 o.p. (ISBN 0-395-06933-5). HM.

Movement: Anti Persecution Gazette & Register of Progress, Vols. 1-2. 1970. Repr. of 1843 ed. lib. bdg. 31.00x o.p. (ISBN 0-8371-9208-0, MO00). Greenwood.

Movement Control in the Fabric of Buildings. Philip Rainger. (Illus.). 288p. 1983. 48.50 o.s.i. (ISBN 0-89397-168-5). Nichols Pub.

Movement Education. Robert E. Gensemer. 80p. 1979. pap. 6.95 o.p. (ISBN 0-8106-1823-0). NEA.

Movement: English Poetry & Fiction of the 1950's. Blake Morrison. 336p. 1986. pap. text ed. 14.95 o.p. (ISBN 0-416-30250-5, 9897). Routledge Chapman & Hall.

Movements in Animation, 2 vols. Brian G. Salt. LC 76-276. 1976. Set. 275.00 o.p. (ISBN 0-08-020904-1). Pergamon.

Movements in Art since 1945. eev. ed. Edward Lucie-Smith. 16.75 o.p. (ISBN 0-8446-6129-5). Peter Smith.

Movements of the Eyes. R. H. Carpenter. 580p. 1988. text ed. 55.00 o.p. (ISBN 0-85086-109-8, Pub. by Pion England). Routledge Chapman & Hall.

Movements of Thought in Modern Education. George F. Kneller. LC 83-14696. 279p. 1984. text ed. write for info. o.p. (ISBN 0-02-365170-9) (ISBN 0-02-365180-6). Macmillan.

Movie Buff's Book. Ed. by Ted Sennett. (Orig.). 1975. pap. 4.95 o.p. (ISBN 0-515-03649-8, 3649, Harv). HarBraceJ.

Movie Guide for VCR's, Nineteen Eighty-Nine. The Philadelphia Inquirer Staff. 608p. (Orig.). 1989. pap. 5.95 o.p. (ISBN 1-55785-085-2). Bart Books.

Movie Guide for VCRs 1988. The Philadelphia Inquirer Staff. 574p. (Orig.). 1988. pap. 5.95 o.p. (ISBN 1-55785-002-X). Bart Books.

Movie Horses: The Fascinating Techniques of Training. Anthony Amaral. pap. 2.00 o.p. (ISBN 0-87980-274-X). Wilshire.

Movie Makers: Artists in an Industry. Gene D. Phillips. LC 73-75524. (Illus.). 254p. 1973. 26.95x o.s.i. (ISBN 0-911012-43-5). Nelson-Hall.

Movie Mastermind. McGraw.

Movie Stars of the Forties: A Complete Reference Guide for the Film Historian or Trivia Buff. David Ragan. 228p. 1985. 15.95 o.p. (ISBN 0-13-604992-3); pap. 6.95 o.p. (ISBN 0-13-604984-2). P-H.

Movie Stunts & the People Who Do Them. Gloria D. Miklowitz. LC 80-7984. (Illus.). 64p. 1980. 6.95 o.p. (ISBN 0-15-256038-6, HJ). HarBraceJ.

Movie Stunts & the People Who Do Them. Gloria D. Miklowitz. LC 80-7984. (Illus.). 64p. (gr. 4-6). 1980. pap. 3.95 o.p. (ISBN 0-15-256039-4, VoyB). HarBraceJ.

Moviegoer. Walker Percy. (Southern Winter Ser.). 1980. pap. 3.95 o.p. (ISBN 0-380-47076-4). Avon.

Movies. rev. ed. Richard Griffith & Arthur Mayer. (Illus.). 576p. 1983. pap. 16.50 o.p. (ISBN 0-671-45622-9, Fireside). S&S.

Movies. rev. ed. Richard Griffith et al. (Illus.). 1981. 24.95 o.p. (ISBN 0-671-42765-2). S&S.

Movies: A Psychological Study. Martha Wolfenstein & Nathan Leites. LC 50-7374. (Illus.). 1970. pap. text ed. 3.45x o.p. (ISBN 0-689-70252-3, 165, Atheneum). Macmillan.

Movies As Medium. Lewis Jacobs. 1973. lib. bdg. 24.00x o.p. (ISBN 0-374-94139-4, Octagon). Hippocrene Bks.

Movies Made for Television. Alvin H. Marill. LC 81-9752. (Quality Paperbacks Ser.). (Illus.). 400p. 1981. pap. 14.95 o.p. (ISBN 0-306-80156-6). Da Capo.

Movies of Woody Allen: A Short, Neurotic Quiz Book. David Wild. (Illus.). 128p. 1987. pap. 8.95 o.p. (ISBN 0-399-51307-8, Perigee). Putnam Pub Group.

Movimiento Obrero en America Latina: 1917-1959. B. Koval. 184p. 1985. pap. 3.95 o.p. (ISBN 0-8285-3052-1, Pub. by Progress Pubs USSR). Imported Pubns.

Moving Ahead: Black Managers in American Business. R. America & B. Anderson. LC 78-3642. 1978. text ed. 28.50 o.p. (ISBN 0-07-001355-1). McGraw.

Moving & Knowing: Sport, Dance, Physical Education. Elenor Metheny. 1975. pap. text ed. 8.95 o.p. (ISBN 0-917962-26-5). T H Peek.

Moving Coffins: Ghosts & Hauntings Around the World. David C. Knight. LC 83-9447. (Illus.). 150p. (gr. 5-9). 1983. 10.95 o.s.i. (ISBN 0-13-604645-2). P-H.

Moving from the Primary Classroom. Ed. by Maurice Galton & John Willcocks. 260p. (Orig.). 1983. pap. 14.95x o.p. (ISBN 0-7100-9343-8). Routledge Chapman & Hall.

Moving Home. Clare Ungerson. 99p. 1971. pap. text ed. 5.00x o.p. (ISBN 0-686-70851-2, Pub. by Bedford England). Gower Pub Co.

Moving Inward: A Study of Robert Bly's Poetry. Ingegerd Friberg. (Acta Universitatis Gothoburgensis Ser.). 1976. pap. text ed. 22.50x o.p. (ISBN 91-7346-033-8). Humanities.

Moving Out of Education: The Educator's Guide To Career Management & Change. Ronald L. Krannich & William J. Bants. 264p. 1981. 14.95 o.p. (ISBN 0-940010-00-3). Impact VA.

Moving Out of Government: A Guide to Surviving & Prospering in the 1980's. Ronald L. Krannich. LC 82-80730. 152p. (Orig.). 1982. pap. 14.95 o.p. (ISBN 0-942710-00-2). Impact VA.

Moving People: An Introduction to Public Transportation. (Department of Transportation Ser.: No. I-81-8). (Illus.). 46p. (Orig.). 1981. pap. 4.75 o.p. (ISBN 0-318-21873-9, S/N 050-000-00193-8). USGPO.

Moving Shadow Problem. Peter Murphy. LC 85-22726. 170p. 1987. 17.50 o.p. (ISBN 0-7022-1977-0). U of Queensland Pr.

Moving to Los Angeles: The Inside Scoop on Starting out, Settling in & Making It in the Big City. Annie Patton & Pamela Campbell. LC 83-23672. (Moving to...Books). (Illus.). 1984. pap. 8.95 o.p. (ISBN 0-399-50996-8, Perigee). Putnam Pub Group.

Moving to Metrics in Home Economics. J. Oppert. LC 77-81325. 1977. 2.50 o.p. (ISBN 0-686-20043-8, 26108430). Home Econ Educ.

Moving Up: Digging In, Taking Charge, Playing the Power Game & Learning to Like It. George Mazzei. 256p. 1984. 15.45 o.s.i. (ISBN 0-671-50266-2, Pub. by Poseidon). S&S.

Moving Up: Intermediate Functional English. J. E. Lackstrom & R. V. White. 1983. text ed. 15.00 o.p. (ISBN 0-8384-1202-5); instructor's manual avail. 0.00 o.p. (ISBN 0-8384-1203-3); cassette net 12.00 o.p. (ISBN 0-8384-1206-8). Heinle & Heinle.

Moving Up: Proven Strategies for Career Success. Edward F. Mrkvicka, Jr. LC 84-27272. 192p. 1985. 12.95 o.p. (ISBN 0-688-02427-0). Morrow.

Moving Up to Twin-Engine Airplanes. Jeffrey L. Ethell. (Illus.). 1979. 8.95 o.p. (ISBN 0-8306-9790-X); pap. 4.95 o.p. (ISBN 0-8306-2270-5, 2270). TAB Bks.

Moving UpCountry: A Yankee Way of Knowledge. Don Mitchell. LC 83-5111. (Illus.). 224p. 1984. 12.95 o.p. (ISBN 0-89909-035-4); pap. 8.95 o.p. (ISBN 0-89909-031-1). Yankee Bks.

Moving with Change: A Women's Reintegration of the I Ching. Rowena Pattee. 256p. 1986. pap. 9.95 o.p. (ISBN 1-85063-036-4, 30364). Routledge Chapman & Hall.

Mowgli's Brothers. Rudyard Kipling. (Illus.). 48p. (gr. k-6). 1985. 5.95 o.p. (ISBN 0-8249-8094-8). Ideals.

Mowry's Basic Nutrition & Diet Therapy. 7th ed. Sue R. Williams. (Illus.). 240p. 1983. pap. text ed. 18.95 o.p. (ISBN 0-8016-5580-3). Mosby.

Moxie: The American Challenge. Philip S. Weld. 1982. 16.95 o.p. (ISBN 0-316-92929-8, Pub. by Atlantic Monthly Pr). Little.

Moya Zhizn (My Life) Noah Zhordania. LC 68-14736. (Foreign Language Ser: No. 3). (Rus). 1968. 12.00x o.p. (ISBN 0-8179-4031-6). Hoover Inst Pr.

Mozambique & Tanzania: Asking the Big Questions. Frances M. Lappe & Adele Beccar-Varela. LC 81-23769. (Illus.). 126p. 1980. pap. 4.75 o.p. (ISBN 0-935028-05-6). Inst Food & Develop.

Mozambique in the Twentieth Century: From Colonialism to Independence. Luis B. Serapiao & Mohamed A. El-Khawas. LC 79-64964. 1979. pap. text ed. 15.25 o.p. (ISBN 0-8191-0502-3). U Pr of Amer.

Mozart. Sacheverell Sitwell. 1970. Repr. of 1932 ed. lib. bdg. 35.00x o.p. (ISBN 0-8371-4022-6, SIMO). Greenwood.

Mozart & His Times. Erich Schenk. 452p. Repr. of 1960 ed. lib. bdg. 59.00 o.p. (Pub. by Am Repr Serv). Reprint Servs.

Mozart & Masonry. Paul Nettl. 150p. 1957. (ISBN 0-8022-1195-X). Philos Lib.

Mozart: the Man - the Musician. Arthur Hutchings. LC 75-13790. 1976. 45.00 o.p. (ISBN 0-02-871140-8). Schirmer Bks.

Mrcchakatika, the Little Clay Cart. Kind Sudraka. Tr. by Revilo Oliver from Sanskrit. LC 74-14116. (Illinois Studies in Language & Literature: Vol. 23, Nos. 1-2). 250p. 1975. Repr. of 1938 ed. lib. bdg. 35.00x o.p. (ISBN 0-8371-7789-8, SULC). Greenwood.

Mrs. Appleyard's Kitchen Omnibus. Louise A. Kent & Polly Campion. 1977. 12.95 o.p. (ISBN 0-395-25771-9). HM.

Mrs. Browning: The Story of Elizabeth Barrett. Rosalie Mander. (Illus.). 184p. 1980. 13.50x o.s.i. (ISBN 0-297-77802-1). Wedgestone Pr.

Mrs. Cat Hides Something. Eleanor W. Arbeit. (Illus.). 56p. (ps up). 1985. 10.95 o.p. (ISBN 0-87905-205-8). Gibbs Smith Pub.

Mrs. Dalloway. Virginia Woolf. LC 81-47578. (Centenary Ed.). 208p. 1981. 17.95 o.p. (ISBN 0-15-162860-2). HarBraceJ.

Mrs. Dalloway. Virginia Woolf. LC 25-9749. 304p. 1949. 11.95 o.s.i. (ISBN 0-15-162862-9). HarBraceJ.

Mrs. Fish, Ape, & Me, the Dump Queen. Norma F. Mazer. 140p. (gr. 4-7). 1981. pap. 2.25 o.p. (ISBN 0-380-57042-4, Camelot). Avon.

Mrs. Frisby & the Rats of Nimh. Robert C. O'Brien. 1975. pap. 3.95 o.s.i. (ISBN 0-689-70413-5, Aladdin). Macmillan.

Mrs. Gandhi's Second Reign. Arun Shourie. 1984. text ed. 35.00x o.p. (ISBN 0-7069-2554-8, Pub. by Vikas India); pap. 18.95x o.p. Advent NY.

Mrs. Gerald's Niece: A Novel, 1869. Georgiana Fullerton. Ed. by Robert L. Wolff. (Victorian Fiction Ser.). 1976. lib. bdg. 16.50 o.p. (ISBN 0-8240-1534-7). Garland Pub.

Mrs. McDillydally's Candy Store. Holly L. Marks. (Illus.). (ps-3). 1979. 4.00 o.p. (ISBN 0-682-49342-2). Exposition-Phoenix.

Mrs. Merry Weather's Letter. (Tales from Fern Hollow Ser.). (Illus.). 22p. (ps-1). 1985. 1.98 o.p. (ISBN 0-517-45796-2). Outlet Bk Co.

Mrs. Miniver. Jan Struther. LC 40-27553. 1966. pap. 0.50 o.p. (ISBN 0-15-663138-5, Harv). HarBraceJ.

Mrs. Patrick Campbell. Alan Dent. LC 72-9046. (Illus.). 333p. 1973. Repr. of 1961 ed. lib. bdg. 22.50x o.p. (ISBN 0-8371-6560-1, DECA). Greenwood.

Mrs. Pollifax on Safari. Dorothy Gilman. 1985. pap. 3.50 o.p. (ISBN 0-449-21011-1, Crest). Fawcett.

Mrs. Pollifax on the China Station. Dorothy Gilman. LC 82-45972. (Illus.). 192p. 1983. 12.95 o.p. (ISBN 0-385-14525-X). Doubleday.

Mrs. Randall. Christopher T. Leland. 1987. 16.45 o.s.i. (ISBN 0-395-42729-0). HM.

Mrs. Spratt's Buffet Cookbook. Genevieve S. McDaniel. 1977. 10.00 o.p. (ISBN 0-682-48542-X, Banner). Exposition-Phoenix.

Mrs. Tortino's Return to the Sun. Pat Murphy & Shirley Murphy. LC 79-20694. (Illus.). (gr. k-3). 1980. 11.25 o.p. (ISBN 0-688-41921-6); PLB 11.88 o.p. (ISBN 0-688-51921-0). Lothrop.

MS & Us. Barbara Beach. 1976. 7.50 o.p. (ISBN 0-682-48572-1). Exposition-Phoenix.

MS-DOS Bible. Steven Simrin. 400p. 1985. pap. 19.95 o.p. (ISBN 0-672-22408-9, 22408). Sams.

MS-DOS Command Summary, Specialized Systems Consultants, Inc. Staff. 10p. (Orig.). 1985. pap. 3.00 cancelled o.s.i. (ISBN 0-317-40890-9). Specialized Sys.

MS-DOS Handbook. Richard A. King. LC 84-50354. 320p. 1984. pap. 17.95 o.p. (ISBN 0-89588-185-3). Sybex.

MS-DOS Handbook. rev. ed. Richard A. King. LC 86-61063. 339p. (Orig.). 1986. pap. 19.95 o.p. (ISBN 0-89588-352-X). Sybex.

MS-DOS Power User's Guide, Vol. I. Jonathan Kamin. LC 86-61240. 397p. 1986. pap. 19.95 o.p. (ISBN 0-89588-345-7). Sybex.

MS-DOS User's Guide. Chris DeVoney. 330p. 1984. pap. 19.95 o.p. (ISBN 0-88022-061-9, 20). Que Corp.

MS-DOS User's Guide. 2nd ed. Chris DeVoney. LC 86-60356. 500p. (Orig.). 1987. pap. 21.95 o.p. (ISBN 0-88022-293-X, 96). Que Corp.

Ms Isabelle Cornell, Herself. Carol Farley. LC 79-22667. (gr. 5-7). 1980. 7.95 o.p. (ISBN 0-689-30740-3, Atheneum). Macmillan.
Ms. M. D. D. X. Fenten. LC 72-11999. (Illus.). (gr. 7 up). 1973. 5.25 o.s.i. (ISBN 0-664-32524-6, Westminster). Westminster John Knox.
MS: Something Can Be Done & You Can Do It. Robert W. Soll & Penelope B. Grenoble. 272p. 1984. 14.95 o.p. (ISBN 0-8092-5469-7). Contemp Bks.
MSDS Reference for Crop Protection Chemicals: Update One. MSDS Staff. 1988. pap. (ISBN 0-471-61988-4). Wiley.
MSH Peptides. Ed. by A. J. Thody. 1981. 77.00 o.p. (ISBN 0-12-687850-1). Acad Pr.
MSX Book. Paul Hoffman. 224p. (Orig.). 1985. pap. text ed. 15.95 o.p. (ISBN 0-07-881172-4). Osborne McGraw.
MSX Standard - The New Computers. Robert C. Wood. (Illus.). 192p. (Orig.). 1985. 21.95 o.p. (ISBN 0-8306-0907-5, 1907); pap. 14.60 o.p. (ISBN 0-8306-1907-0). TAB Bks.
MTI Radar. Ed. by D. C. Schleher. (Artech Radar Library). (Illus.). 499p. 1978. 40.00x o.p. (ISBN 0-89006-060-6). Artech Hse.
Much Ado about Nothing. William Shakespeare. Ed. by Louis B. Wright & Virginia A. LaMar. (Folger Library). (Illus.). 256p. (gr. 11 up). 1964. pap. text ed. 3.95 o.s.i. (ISBN 0-671-50814-8). WSP.
Much Entertainment: A Visual & Culinary Record of Johnson & Boswell's Tour of Scotland in 1773. Virginia Maclean. 1973. 10.00 o.p. (ISBN 0-87140-568-7). Liveright.
Much Loved Books. James O. Bennett. (Black & Gold Lib). 1927. 7.95 o.p. (ISBN 0-87140-979-8). Liveright.
Muckle Annie. Jan Webster. 224p. 1987. pap. 3.50 o.p. (ISBN 1-55547-171-4). Critics Choice Paper.
Mucus In Health & Disease II. Ed. by Eric N. Chantler & James B. Elder. LC 82-424. (Advances In Experimental Medicine & Biology Ser.: Vol. 144). 458p. 1982. 75.00x o.p. (ISBN 0-306-40906-2, Plenum Pr). Plenum Pub.
Mud Actor. Cyrus Cassells. LC 81-13450. (National Poetry Ser.). 104p. (Orig.). 1982. 14.50 o.p. (ISBN 0-03-061371-X); pap. 7.95 o.p. (ISBN 0-03-061369-8, Owl Bks). H Holt & Co.
Mud Puddles, Rainbows & Asparagus Tips: Learning's Best Language Arts Ideas. Ed. by Bruce Raskin. LC 78-74910. (Learning Ideabooks Ser.). 1979. pap. 15.95 o.p. (ISBN 0-8224-1911-4). D S Lake Pubs.
Mud Show: A Circus Season. Fred Powledge. LC 75-12691. (Illus.). 384p. 1975. 12.95 o.p. (ISBN 0-15-163212-X). HarBraceJ.
Muddling Through: The Art of Properly Unbusinesslike Management. Roger A. Golde. LC 76-888. 1976. 13.95 o.p. (ISBN 0-8144-5411-9). AMACOM.
Muddling Through: The Art of Properly Unbusinesslike Management. Roger A. Golde. LC 76-888. 185p. 1979. pap. 5.95 o.p. (ISBN 0-8144-7523-X). AMACOM.
Muddy Fork. James Crumley. 30p. 1984. Limited signed ed. 50.00 o.p. (ISBN 0-935716-26-2). Lord John.
Muddy Road to Glory. Stephen W. Meader. LC 63-17005. (Illus.). (gr. 7 up). 1963. 4.95 o.p. (ISBN 0-15-256260-5, HJ). HarBraceJ.
Mudhead. Josephine R. Stone. LC 80-11982. 156p. (gr. 5-9). 1980. 8.95 o.p. (ISBN 0-689-30787-X, Atheneum). Macmillan.
Mudhole Smith: Alaska Flier. Lone Janson. LC 81-4529. (Illus.). 160p. 1981. pap. 6.95 o.p. (ISBN 0-88240-139-4). Alaska Northwest.
Muffie Mouse & the Busy Birthday. Joan L. Nixon. LC 77-28866. (Illus.). 48p. (ps-3). 1979. 6.95 o.p. (ISBN 0-395-28868-1, Clarion). HM.
Muffled Drums: The News Media in Africa. facsimile ed. William A. Hachten. (Illus.). 1971. pap. 12.50x o.p. (ISBN 0-8138-2475-3). Iowa St U Pr.
Muhammad: Seal of the Prophets. Muhammad Z. Khan. 400p. 1980. pap. 10.50 o.p. (ISBN 0-7100-0610-1). Routledge Chapman & Hall.
Muhammed: Man of Allah. Seyyed H. Nasr. 61p. (Orig.). 1986. pap. text ed. 9.95 o.p. (ISBN 0-7103-0154-5). Routledge Chapman & Hall.
Mujeres: Conversations from a Hispanic Community. Nan Elsasser et al. (Women's Lives - Women's Work Ser.). (Illus.). 192p. (gr. 11 up). 1981. 9.95 o.p. (ISBN 0-912670-84-3); pap. 9.95 o.p. (ISBN 0-912670-70-3); tchr's. guide 5.00 o.p. (ISBN 0-912670-80-0). Feminist Pr.
Mujeres Sovieticas. E. Z. Danilova et al. 198p. (Span.). 1977. 3.45 o.p. (ISBN 0-8285-1483-6, Pub. by Progress Pubs USSR). Imported Pubns.
Mujeres y Agonias. 2nd ed. Rima Vallbona. 104p. (Span.). 1986. pap. 7.00 o.p. (ISBN 0-317-59984-4). Arte Publico.
Mulata. Miguel A. Asturias. 352p. 1982. pap. 3.50 o.p. (ISBN 0-380-58552-9, 58552-9, Bard). Avon.
Muldoon. Don Bredes. 1982. 15.50 o.p. (ISBN 0-03-058281-4). H Holt & Co.
Mulligan Stew. Gilbert Sorrentino. LC 78-67419. 1979. 14.95 o.s.i. (ISBN 0-394-50717-7, GP823). Grove.
Mulligan Stew. Gilbert Sorrentino. LC 78-67419. 1979. pap. 7.95 o.s.i. (ISBN 0-394-17086-5, E727, Ever). Grove.
Multi-Level & Hillside Home Plans. 2nd ed. Ed. by Garlinghouse, L. F., Co., Staff. LC 84-81890. (Illus.). 112p. 1985. pap. 2.95 o.p. (ISBN 0-938708-12-0). L F Garlinghouse Co.
Multi-Level, Hillside & Solar Home Plans. Ed. by L. F. Garlinghouse, Co., Staff. LC 80-84640. (Illus.). 116p. (Orig.). 1981. pap. 2.95 o.s.i. (ISBN 0-938708-00-7). L F Garlinghouse Co.
Multi-Media Compliance Inspection Manual. 2nd ed. U. S. Environmental Protection Agency Staff. (Illus.). 184p. 1986. pap. 43.00 o.s.i. (ISBN 0-86587-145-0). Gov Insts.
Multi-Media in the Church: A Beginner's Guide for Putting It All Together. W. A. Engstrom. LC 72-11165. (Illus.). 128p. (Orig.). 1973. pap. 3.95 o.p. (ISBN 0-8042-1730-0, John Knox). Westminster John Knox.
Multi-Media Indexes, Lists, & Review Sources: A Bibliographic Guide. T. L. Hart et al. (Books in Library & Information Sciences: Vol. 13). 288p. 1975. 55.00 o.p. (ISBN 0-8247-6340-8). Dekker.
Multi-Vendor Data Communications Networks. QED Information Sciences, Inc. Staff. 480p. 1982. 3-ring binder 95.00 o.p. (ISBN 0-89435-057-9). QED Info Sci.
Multibus Design Guidebook. J. Johnson & S. Kassel. 1984. text ed. 49.95 o.p. (ISBN 0-07-032599-5). McGraw.
Multicompartment Models for Biological Systems. G. L. Atkins. 1974. pap. 9.95x o.p. (ISBN 0-412-21180-7, NO. 6014, Pub. by Chapman & Hall). Routledge Chapman & Hall.
Multicultural Classrooms: Perspectives for Teachers. Louis Cohen & Lawrence Manion. 240p. 1982. 27.25 o.p. (ISBN 0-7099-0719-2, Pub. by Croom Helm Ltd); pap. 13.95 o.p. (ISBN 0-7099-0747-8). Routledge Chapman & Hall.
Multicultural Counseling: Bibliography. 7.50 o.p. (ISBN 0-317-59910-0, 72508C). Am Assn Coun Dev.
Multicultural Nonsexist Education: A Human Relations Approach. Nicholas Colangelo et al. 1979. pap. text ed. 16.95 o.p. (ISBN 0-8403-2052-3). Kendall-Hunt.
Multicultural Teacher Education: Case Studies of Thirteen Programs, Vol. II. Gollnick et al. 1980. 9.50 o.p. (ISBN 0-317-53446-7). AACTE.
Multicultural Teaching: A Guide for the Classroom. M. Saunders. 192p. 1982. text ed. 10.50 o.p. (ISBN 0-07-084133-0). McGraw.
Multidimensionale Optimierung bei der Standortwahl von Grosstechnischen Anlagen. Gunter Halbritter. (Interdisciplinary Systems Research: No. 62). (Illus.). 178p. (Ger.). 1979. pap. 26.95 o.p. (ISBN 0-8176-1055-3). Birkhauser.
Multidisciplinary Readings in Educational Leadership. Harold W. Boles et al. LC 75-44465. 442p. 1976. pap. text ed. 12.95x o.p. (ISBN 0-8422-0461-X). Irvington.
Multiethnic Education: Theory & Practice. 2nd ed. James Banks. 320p. 1988. pap. text ed. 27.00 o.p. (ISBN 0-205-11169-6). Allyn.
Multihandicapped Hearing Impaired: Identification & Instruction. Ed. by David Tweedie & Edgar H. Shroyer. LC 81-84511. (Illus.). xiv, 274p. 1982. 19.95 o.p. (ISBN 0-913580-74-0). Gallaudet Univ Pr.
Multilingual Dictionary of Technical Terms in Cartography. E. Meynen. 572p. (Eng. & Ger.). 1973. pap. 88.00 o.p. (ISBN 3-515-00127-1, M-7564, Pub. by F. Steiner). French & Eur.
MultiMate Tips & Techniques. Dick Anderson & Janet McBean. 275p. (Orig.). 1986. pap. 19.95 o.p. (ISBN 0-912677-88-0). Tate Pub.
MultiMate User's Guide. Barbara Spear. (Illus.). 192p. (Orig.). 1986. 21.95 o.p. (ISBN 0-8306-0423-5, 2623); pap. 14.95 o.p. (ISBN 0-8306-0323-9). Tab Bks.
Multimedia Library: Materials Selection & Use. James Cabeceiras. 275p. 1978. tchrs' ed. 17.50 o.p. (ISBN 0-12-153950-4). Acad Pr.
Multimind. Robert E. Ornstein. LC 85-27296. (Illus.). 1986. 16.45 o.p. (ISBN 0-395-41107-6). HM.
Multinational Banks & Underdevelopment. Maurice A. Odle. (Pergamon Policy Studies on International Development). 216p. 1981. 55.00 o.p. (ISBN 0-08-028043-9). Pergamon.
Multinational Banks: Their Identities & Determinants. Kang Rae Cho. Ed. by Fred Bateman. LC 85-1123. (Research in Business Economics & Public Policy Ser.: No. 8). 190p. 1985. 42.95 o.p. (ISBN 0-8357-1668-6). UMI Res Pr.
Multinational Business Marketing Guide. (Multinational Business Guides). 1980. pap. 80.00 o.p. (ISBN 0-931000-10-6). Suburban Pub CT.
Multinational Business Strategy. W. Dymsza. 1971. pap. text ed. 15.95 o.p. (ISBN 0-07-018570-0, C). McGraw.
Multinational Computer Nets: The Case of International Banking. Richard H. Veith. LC 80-8386. 160p. 1981. 24.50x o.p. (ISBN 0-669-04092-4). Lexington Bks.
Multinational Cooperation for Development in West Africa. John P. Renninger. LC 78-15217. 176p. 1979. 45.00 o.p. (ISBN 0-08-022490-3). Pergamon.
Multinational Corporation, the Nation State & the Trade Unions: A European Perspective. Gunnar Hedlund & Lars Otterbeck. LC 76-42447. (Illus.). 168p. 1977. 17.50x o.p. (ISBN 0-87338-198-X, Pub. by Comparative Adm. Research Institute). Kent St U Pr.
Multinational Corporations & the Control of Culture: The Ideological Apparatuses of Imperialism. Armand Mattelart. Tr. by Michael Chanan. LC 79-221. (Marxist Theory & Contemporary Capitalism: No. 26). 1982. text ed. 33.00x o.p. (ISBN 0-391-00978-8); pap. 19.95x o.p. (ISBN 0-391-02553-8). Humanities.
Multinational Enterprises. Ed. by J. S. Wilson. 1974. 45.00 o.p. (ISBN 9-0286-0124-4). E J Brill USA.
Multinational Enterprises & Social Policy. (Studies & Reports, New Ser.: No. 79). (Eng., Fr. & Span., Second Impression). 1973. pap. 10.00 o.p. (ISBN 92-2-101003-1, ILO1, ILO). UNIPUB.
Multinational Management. David Rutenberg. 1982. text ed. write for info. o.p. (ISBN 0-673-39036-5). Scott F.
Multinational Strategic Planning. Derek F. Channon & Michael Jalland. 1979. 35.00 o.p. (ISBN 0-8144-5575-1). AMACOM.
Multinational Union Organizations in the Manufacturing Industries. Richard L. Rowan et al. LC 80-53989. (Multinational Industrial Relations Ser.: No.7a). 213p. (Orig.). 1980. pap. 15.00 o.p. (ISBN 0-89546-021-1). Indus Res Unit-Wharton.
Multiobjective Analysis with Engineering & Business Applications. Ambrose Goicocchea et al. LC 81-23058. 519p. 1982. text ed. (ISBN 0-471-06401-7). Wiley.
Multiplan: Home & Office Companion. Elna Tymes & Peter Antoniak. 180p. (Orig.). 1984. pap. text ed. 16.95 o.p. (ISBN 0-07-881133-3). Osborne-McGraw.
Multiplan Models. Gilbert Held. LC 85-722. 250p. (Orig.). 1985. pap. 17.95 o.p. (ISBN 0-938862-30-8). Weber Systems.
Multiplan on the Commodore 64. Richard A. King & Stanley R. Trost. LC 84-51980. 225p. 1985. pap. 17.95 o.p. (ISBN 0-89588-231-0). SYBEX.
Multiplan on the Macintosh: Including Word, File & Chart. Stan Schatt. 256p. 1986. pap. 17.95 o.p. (ISBN 0-89303-678-1). Brady Bks.
Multiple Aspects of Soil Mechanics. (Transportation Research Record Ser.). 58p. 1977. 4.00 o.p. (ISBN 0-309-02669-5). Transport Res Bd.
Multiple Choice Questions in Medicine for the MRCP Examination, Part I. P. Bell. 176p. pap. 15.00 o.p. (ISBN 0-7236-0646-3). Butterworth.
Multiple Criteria Decision Making, Kyoto, 1975. Ed. by M. Zeleny. (Lecture Notes in Mathematical Systems Ser.: Vol. 123). 1976. pap. 16.80 o.p. (ISBN 0-387-07684-0). Springer-Verlag.
Multiple Criteria Decision Making: Theory & Application. Proceedings. Ed. by G. Fandel & T. Gal. (Lecture Notes in Economics & Mathematical Systems: Vol. 177). (Illus.). 570p. 1980. 48.00 o.p. (ISBN 0-387-09963-8). Springer-Verlag.
Multiple Criteria Optimization: Theory, Computation & Application. Ralph E. Steuer. LC 85-9564. (Probability & Mathematical Statistics Ser.). 546p. 1986. 61.50 o.p. (ISBN 0-471-88846-X). Wiley.
Multiple Cropping in the Humid Tropics of Asia. A. A. Gomez & K. A. Gomez. 248p. 1983. pap. text ed. 15.00 o.p. (ISBN 0-88936-304-8, IDRC176, IDRC). UNIPUB.
Multiple Decision Procedures: Theory & Methodology of Selecting & Ranking Populations. Shanti S. Gupta & S. Panchapakesan. LC 79-13119. 602p. 1979. 61.95 o.p. (Pub. by John Wiley). Krieger.
Multiple Deformation in Ductile & Brittle Rocks: A Selection of Papers Presented at the International Conference on Multiple Deformation & Foliation Development, Bemagui, NSW, Australia, 4-10 Feb. 1984. Ed. by P. L. Hancock. 242p. 1985. pap. 54.00 o.p. (ISBN 0-08-031419-8, Pub by PPL). Pergamon.
Multiple Equilibria in Proteins. J. Steinhardt & J. A. Reynolds. 1970. 82.50 o.p. (ISBN 0-12-665450-6). Acad Pr.
Multiple Exposure: An American Ambassador's Unique Perspective on East-West Issues. Jacob D. Beam. 1978. 10.95 o.p. (ISBN 0-393-07519-2). Norton.
Multiple Factors in the Causation of Environmentally Induced Disease. Ed. by Douglas H. Lee & Paul Kotin. (Fogarty International Center Proceedings,: No. 12). 1972. 47.00 o.p. (ISBN 0-12-440665-3). Acad Pr.
Multiple Gaussian Hypergeometric Series. H. M. Srivastava & P. W. Karlsson. (Mathematics & Its Applications Ser.). 425p. 1985. 74.95 o.p. (ISBN 0-470-20100-2). Halsted Pr.
Multiple Hypergeometric Functions & Applications. Harold Exton. LC 76-20720. (Mathematics & It's Applications Ser.). 312p. 1977. 61.95x o.p. (ISBN 0-470-15190-0). Halsted Pr.
Multiple Laboratory Screening. Ed. by E. S. Benson & P. E. Strandjord. 1969. 60.50 o.p. (ISBN 0-12-089050-X). Acad Pr.
Multiple Meanings: The Written Word in Japan, Past, Present & Future. Ed. by Thomas J. Rimer. LC 85-600365. 117p. 1986. 10.00 o.p. (ISBN 0-8444-0523-X, S/N 030-000-00180-0). USGPO.
Multiple Objective Decision Making-Methods & Applications: A State-of-the-Art Survey. C. L. Hwang & A. S. Masud. (Lecture Notes in Economics & Mathematical Systems: Vol. 164). (Illus.). 1981. pap. 22.00 o.p. (ISBN 0-387-09111-4). Springer-Verlag.
Multiple Personality: Theory, Diagnosis & Treatment. R. Douglas Smith et al. 93p. 1982. text ed. 18.95x o.s.i. (ISBN 0-8290-0539-0). Irvington.
Multiple Primary Cancers in Connecticut & Denmark. John D. Boice. (National Cancer Institute Monograph: No. 68). 445p. 1985. 23.00 o.p. (ISBN 0-318-19575-5, S/N 017-042-00186-2). USGPO.
Multiple Primary Malignant Neoplasms: Their Incidence & Significance. C. G. Moertel. (Recent Results in Cancer Research: Vol. 7). (Illus.). 1966. 17.70 o.p. (ISBN 0-387-03646-6). Springer-Verlag.
Multiple Residence & Cyclical Migration in Western Societies: A Bibliography. Curtis C. Roseman. (Public Administration Ser.: P 1712). 13p. 1985. 2.00 o.p. (ISBN 0-89028-462-8). Vance Biblios.
Multiple Sclerosis. Ed. by Frederick Wolfgram. (Illus.). 1972. 32.50 o.p. (ISBN 0-12-761950-X). Acad Pr.
Multiple Use of Lands Within Highway Rights-of-Way. (National Cooperative Highway Research Program Report). 68p. 1968. 3.20 o.p. (ISBN 0-317-36095-7, 1587). Transport Res Bd.
Multiples: The First Decade. John L. Tancock. LC 74-156314. (Illus.). 148p. (Orig.). 1971. pap. 3.95 o.p. (ISBN 0-87633-021-9). Phila Mus Art.
Multiplication & Division. R. Hunt. LC 78-730962. 1978. pap. text ed. 159.00 o.s.i. (ISBN 0-89290-093-8, A509-SATC). Soc for Visual.
Multiplication & Division in Mammalian Cells. Ed. by Renato Baserga. (Biochemistry of Disease Ser.: Vol.6). 256p. 1976. 55.00 o.p. (ISBN 0-8247-6353-X). Dekker.
Multiplication of Viruses. S. E. Luria. Bd. with Virus Inclusions in Plant Cells. K. M. Smith; Virus Inclusions in Insect Cells. K. M. Smith; Antibiotika Erzeugende Virus-Ahnliche Faktoren in Bakterien. P. Fredericq. (Protoplasmatologica: Vol. 4, Pts. 3, 4a, 4b, 5). (Illus.). iv, 118p. (Eng. & Ger.). 1958. 32.50 o.p. (ISBN 0-387-80488-9). Springer-Verlag.
Multipliers on Locally Compact Groups. K. R. Parthasarathy. LC 71-84142. (Lecture Notes in Mathematics: Vol. 93). (Orig.). 1969. pap. 10.70 o.p. (ISBN 0-387-04612-7). Springer-Verlag.
Multiply Injured Patient with Complex Fractures. Ed. by Marvin H. Meyers. LC 83-9333. (Illus.). 423p. 1984. text ed. 45.00 o.p. (ISBN 0-8121-0882-5). Lea & Febiger.
Multipurpose Tools for Bible Study. rev. ed. Frederick W. Danker. 1970. pap. 12.95 o.p. (ISBN 0-570-03734-4, 12-2638). Concordia.
Multiscale 2: Four Programs for Multidimensional Scaling by the Method of Maximum Likelihood. James O. Ramsay. pap. 14.00 o.p. (ISBN 0-89498-002-5). Sci Ware.
Multistate Corporate Tax Almanac. 1986 ed. Panel Publishers, Inc. Staff. 1986. pap. 95.00 o.p. (ISBN 0-317-18590-X). Panel Pubs.
Multitude of Men. William D. Smith. 1984. pap. 4.80 o.p. (ISBN 0-671-49650-6). S&S.
Multivariable System Theory & Design. Patel. (International Series on Systems & Control: Vol. 3). 385p. 1981. text ed. 69.00 o.p. (ISBN 0-08-027297-5); pap. text ed. 26.00 o.p. (ISBN 0-08-027298-3). Pergamon.

Multivariate Analysis. Ed. by P. Krishnaiah. 1967. 103.00 o.p. (ISBN 0-12-426650-9). Acad Pr.

Multivariate Analysis & Psychological Theory. Ed. by Joseph R. Royce. 1973. 93.00 o.p. (ISBN 0-12-600750-0). Acad Pr.

Multivariate Analysis: Proceedings of Third International Symposium. Krishnaiah. 1973. 103.00 o.p. (ISBN 0-12-426653-3). Acad Pr.

Multivariate Morphometrics. R. E. Blackith & R. A. Reyment. 1972. 65.00 o.p. (ISBN 0-12-103150-0). Acad Pr.

Mumbo Jumbo. Ishmael Reed. 1978. pap. 3.95 o.p. (ISBN 0-380-01860-8, 65110-6, Bard). Avon.

Mumby's Publishing & Bookselling in the 20th Century. 6th ed. Ed. by Ian Norrie. 1982. 35.00 o.p. (ISBN 0-7135-1341-1, Pub. by Bell & Hyman). Bowker.

Mumkin. Stephen Cosgrove. (Serendipity Bks.). (Illus.). 32p. (gr. 5-9). 1986. pap. 2.50 o.s.i. (ISBN 0-8431-1431-2). Price Stern.

Mummy. Daniel Curley. 256p. 1987. 16.45 o.s.i. (ISBN 0-395-42507-7). HM.

Mummy! A Chrestomathy of Crypt-ology. Bill Pronzini. LC 80-66496. 1980. 10.95 o.p. (ISBN 0-87795-271-X, Arbor Hse). Morrow.

Mummy Case. Elizabeth Peters. (Large Print Books (General Ser.)). 450p. 1985. lib. bdg. 17.95 o.p. (ISBN 0-8161-3934-2). G K Hall.

MUMPS Primer. rev. ed. Ed. by Richard F. Walters et al. J. Bowie & J. C. Wilcox. 1983. pap. 15.00 o.p. (ISBN 0-918118-24-7). MUMPS.

Mundane Data Nineteen Eighty-Four. AFA Staff. 40p. 5.00 o.p. (ISBN 0-318-01885-3). Am Fed Astrologers.

Mundo de Santiago. Anna Mayer. 22p. (Span.). (gr. 3-4). 1980. pap. text ed. 5.95 o.p. (ISBN 0-933982-18-6). Bradt Ent.

Mundo del mas alla. Ed. by Gloria Duran & Manuel Duran. (Illus., Orig., Span.). 1976. pap. text ed. 9.95 o.p. (ISBN 0-15-520970-1, HC). HarBraceJ.

Mundos a Explorar. Girl Scouts of the U. S. A. Staff. 104p. (Span.). (gr. 1-6). 1981. pap. 2.75 o.p. (ISBN 0-88441-332-2, 20-709). Girl Scouts USA.

Mundos a Explorar: Manual para las Brownie y las Junior Girl Scouts. Girl Scouts of the U. S. A. Staff. 293p. (Orig., Span.). (gr. 1-6). 1981. pap. 4.00 o.p. (ISBN 0-88441-331-4, 20-708). Girl Scouts USA.

Muneca Menor. Rosario Ferre. (De Orilla a Orilla Ser.). (Illus.). 16p. 1979. pap. 3.75 o.p. (ISBN 0-940238-29-2). Ediciones Huracan.

Mungobus. Raymond Mungo. 1979. pap. 3.95 o.p. (ISBN 0-380-42929-2, 42929-2, Discus). Avon.

Munich Ten. Lewis Orde. LC 82-72076. 1982. 14.50 o.p. (ISBN 0-87795-423-2, Arbor Hse). Morrow.

Munich: The Price of Peace. Telford Taylor. 1100p. pap. 17.95 o.s.i. (ISBN 0-88184-447-0). Carroll & Graf.

Municipal Accounting for Developing Countries. David C. Jones. 904p. 1984. 30.00 o.p. (ISBN 0-8213-0350-3, BK 0350). World Bank.

Municipal & Local Documents. 156p. 1979. 3.75 o.p. (ISBN 0-931658-14-4). NY Lib Assn.

Municipal Bonding & Taxation. Anthony G. White. LC 78-68296. (Reference Library of Social Sciences Ser.). 1979. lib. bdg. 24.00 o.p. (ISBN 0-8240-9761-0). Garland Pub.

Municipal Bonds. Jerry Oster. 288p. 1981. 10.95 o.p. (ISBN 0-395-30538-1). HM.

Municipal Bonds: The Comprehensive Review of Tax-Exempt Securities & Municipal Finance. Robert Lamb & Stephen P. Rappaport. (Illus.). 384p. 1980. text ed. 28.95 o.p. (ISBN 0-07-036082-0). McGraw.

Municipal Budget & Accounting Systems: A Review of the Periodical Literature, 1980 - 1984. Dale E. Casper. (Public Administration Series: Bibliography P 1771). 8p. 1985. pap. 2.00 o.p. (ISBN 0-89028-571-3). Vance Biblios.

Municipal Disaster Preparedness: A List of Periodical Literature, 1980-1984. Dale E. Casper. (Public Administration Ser.: P 1802). 6p. 1985. 2.00 o.p. (ISBN 0-89028-632-9). Vance Biblios.

Municipal Financial Disclosure: An Empirical Investigation. Julia H. Magann. Ed. by Richard N. Farmer. LC 83-1106. (Research for Business Decisions: No. 58). 110p. 1983. 37.95 o.p. (ISBN 0-8357-1394-6). UMI Res Pr.

Municipal Management & Budget Methods: An Evaluation of Policy Related Research. Wayne A. Kimmel et al. 150p. 1974. pap. 7.95x o.p. (ISBN 0-87766-135-9, 96000). Urban Inst.

Municipal Needs, Services & Financing: Readings on Municipal Expenditures. Ed. by Patrick W. Beaton. 360p. 1974. 15.00 o.p. (ISBN 0-87855-104-2). Transaction Pubs.

Municipal Renewal - Central Business Districts: A Checklist, 1974-1984. Dale E. Casper. (Public Administration Series: Bibliography P 1768). 1985. pap. 2.00 o.p. (ISBN 0-89028-568-3). Vance Biblios.

Municipal Year Book 1980. International City Management Association Staff. LC 34-27121. 1980. 36.00 o.p. (ISBN 0-87326-955-1). Intl City Mgt.

Municipal Year Book 1981. International City Management Association Staff. LC 34-237121. (Illus.). 416p. 1981. text ed. 42.00 o.p. (ISBN 0-87326-956-X). Intl City Mgt.

Municipal Year Book, 1988: International City Management Association. 480p. 1988. 69.50 o.p. (ISBN 0-87326-963-2). Intl City Mgt.

Municipal Yearbook, 1987. Ed. by J. B. Yowell. LC 34-27121. (Illus.). 1987. text ed. 68.00 o.p. (ISBN 0-87326-962-4). Intl City Mgt.

Munster Village. Mary Hamilton. pap. 8.95 o.p. (ISBN 0-317-65249-4, Pandora Pr). Routledge Chapman & Hall.

Muntu: An Outline of the New African Culture. Janheinz Jahn. Tr. by Marjorie Green. (Illus.). (YA) (gr. 9 up). 1961. pap. 5.95 o.p. (ISBN 0-394-17238-8, E332, Ever). Grove.

Muny: St. Louis' Outdoor Theater. Mary Kimbrough. LC 78-6847. 1978. 10.95 o.p. (ISBN 0-8272-2315-3); pap. 6.95 o.p. (ISBN 0-8272-2314-5). CBP.

Muon Physics. Ed. by Vernon Hughes & C. S. Wu. Incl. Vol. 1. 67.50 (ISBN 0-12-360601-2); Vol. 2. Weak Interactions. 111.00 (ISBN 0-12-360602-0); Vol. 3. Chemistry & Solids. 80.00 (ISBN 0-12-360603-9). 1975. Set. 320.00 o.p. Acad Pr.

Muppet Babies' Mother Goose. Illus. by Diane Dawson Hearn. LC 85-60527. (Illus.). 14p. (gr. 2-6). 1985. bds. 3.95 o.p. (ISBN 0-394-87496-X, BYR). Random.

Muppet Babies Playtime Book. LC 84-61137. (Baby Fingers Ser.). (Illus.). 14p. (ps). 1985. bds. 2.95 o.s.i. (ISBN 0-394-87039-5, BYR). Random.

Muppet Babies Take a Bath. Illus. by Manhar Chauhan. (Bath & Beach Play Sets Ser.). (Illus.). 10p. (ps). 1986. 3.95 o.s.i. (ISBN 0-394-88135-4). Random.

Muppet Movie. 7.95 o.s.i. (ISBN 0-89524-061-0). Cherry Lane.

Mur. Jean-Paul Sartre. (Coll. Soleil). 10.95 o.p. (ISBN 0-685-36563-8). Schoenhof.

Murals & Sculpture of Josef Albers. Neal D. Benezra. Ed. by S. J. Freedberg. (Outstanding Dissertations in Fine Arts Ser.). (Illus.). 325p. 1985. Repr. of 1983 ed. 40.00 o.p. (ISBN 0-8240-6873-4). Garland Pub.

Murder America. Jay R. Nash. 1980. 16.95 o.p. (ISBN 0-671-24270-9). S&S.

Murder & Madness. Donald T. Lunde. 1979. pap. 3.95 o.p. (ISBN 0-393-00954-8). Norton.

Murder & the First Lady. Elliott Roosevelt. (Hall Large Print Bk.). 1985. lib. bdg. 14.95 o.p. (ISBN 0-8161-3785-4, Large Print Bks). G K Hall.

Murder at the FBI. Margaret Truman. 1985. 15.95 o.p. (ISBN 0-87795-680-4, Arbor Hse). Morrow.

Murder at the Met. David Black. LC 84-7079. 312p. 1984. 15.95 o.p. (ISBN 0-385-27852-7, Dial). Doubleday.

Murder at the Met. David Black. 1986. pap. 3.50 o.p. (ISBN 0-380-69990-7). Avon.

Murder at the Super Bowl: A Memory of Love. Fran Tarkenton & Herb Resnicow. LC 86-62214. 1986. 15.95 o.p. (ISBN 0-688-06716-6). Morrow.

Murder by Microphone. John Reeves. 224p. 1980. pap. 2.25 o.p. (ISBN 0-380-43729-5, 43729). Avon.

Murder-by-the-Sea. Layne Littlepage. LC 86-19716. (Crime Club Ser.). 192p. 1987. 12.95 o.s.i. (ISBN 0-385-23800-2). Doubleday.

Murder Cure. Ann Ross. 1978. pap. 1.50 o.p. (ISBN 0-380-40915-1, 40915). Avon.

Murder for Lunch. Haughton Murphy. 240p. 1986. 14.70 o.s.i. (ISBN 0-671-60628-X). S&S.

Murder Gets a Degree. Theodora Wender. 160p. (Orig.). 1986. pap. 2.95 o.p. (ISBN 0-380-75014-7). Avon.

Murder Gone Mad. Philip MacDonald. 1984. pap. 3.95 o.p. (ISBN 0-394-72437-2, Vin). Random.

Murder in Advent. David Williams. 192p. 1987. pap. 2.95 o.p. (ISBN 0-380-70257-6). Avon.

Murder in E Minor: A Nero Wolfe Mystery. Robert Goldsborough. 224p. 1986. 13.95 o.p. (ISBN 0-553-05123-7). Bantam.

Murder in Paradise. Jocelyn Davey. 240p. 1983. pap. 2.95 o.p. (ISBN 0-380-64659-5, 64659). Avon.

Murder in the Central Committee. Manuel V. Montalban. 203p. 1985. 13.95 o.p. (ISBN 0-89733-125-7). Academy Chi Pubs.

Murder in the Family. Marc Brandel. 160p. 1985. pap. 2.95 o.p. (ISBN 0-380-89869-1). Avon.

Murder in the First Reel. Bill Pronzini et al. 352p. 1985. pap. 3.25 o.p. (ISBN 0-380-89646-X). Avon.

Murder in the Smithsonian. Margaret Truman. 304p. 1983. 14.95 o.p. (ISBN 0-87795-475-5, Arbor Hse). Morrow.

Murder in the Supreme Court. Margaret Truman. LC 81-71678. 1982. 12.95 o.p. (ISBN 0-87795-384-8, Arbor Hse). Morrow.

Murder in the Title: A Charles Paris Mystery. Simon Brett. 192p. 1983. 11.95 o.s.i. (ISBN 0-684-17898-2, ScribT). Scribner.

Murder in the White House. Margaret Truman. LC 79-54004. 1980. 9.95 o.p. (ISBN 0-87795-245-0, Arbor Hse). Morrow.

Murder in White. Hugh Zachary. 1981. pap. 1.95 o.p. (ISBN 0-8439-0876-9, Pub. by Leisure Bks CT). Dorchester Pub Co.

Murder Ink: Revived, Revised, Still Unrepentant. Dilys Winn. LC 84-40321. (Illus.). 416p. 1984. pap. 9.95 o.p. (ISBN 0-89480-777-3, 777). Workman Pub.

Murder Is Pathological. P. M. Carlson. 192p. 1986. pap. 2.95 o.p. (ISBN 0-380-75071-6). Avon.

Murder Must Advertise. Dorothy L. Sayers. 1985. pap. 2.25 o.p. (ISBN 0-380-00916-1, 60913-4). Avon.

Murder of Chile. Samuel Chavkin. (Illus.). 288p. 1982. 13.95 o.p. (ISBN 0-89696-137-0, Everest House Book). Dodd.

Murder of Herodes & Other Trials from the Athenian Law Courts. Kathleen Freeman. 1963. pap. 2.95 o.p. (ISBN 0-393-00201-2, Norton Lib). Norton.

Murder of My Aunt. Richard Hull. (Seagull Library of Mystery & Suspense Ser). 1968. 4.95 o.p. (ISBN 0-393-08404-3). Norton.

Murder of Sherlock Holmes. James Anderson. (Murder she Wrote Ser.: No. 1). 208p. 1985. pap. 2.95 o.p. (ISBN 0-380-89702-4). Avon.

Murder of the Glass. Michael J. Katz. 224p. pap. 3.50 o.p. (ISBN 0-671-64667-2). Archway.

Murder on a Mystery Tour. Marian Babson. (Nightingale Paperbacks Ser.). 299p. 1987. pap. 11.95 o.p. (ISBN 0-8161-4215-7, Large Print Bks). G K Hall.

Murder on Capitol Hill. Margaret Truman. LC 80-70223. 256p. 1981. 11.95 o.p. (ISBN 0-87795-312-0, Arbor Hse). Morrow.

Murder on Embassy Row. Margaret Truman. 297p. 1984. 15.95 o.p. (ISBN 0-87795-594-8, Arbor Hse). Morrow.

Murder on Embassy Row. Margaret Truman. (General Ser.). 1984. lib. bdg. 16.95 o.p. (ISBN 0-8161-3727-7, Large Print Bks); pap. 9.95 o.p. (ISBN 0-8161-3765-X). G K Hall.

Murder on High. George Kennedy. 208p. (Orig.). 1984. pap. 3.25 o.p. (ISBN 0-380-88062-8, 88062-8). Avon.

Murder on Location. George Kennedy. 208p. 1983. pap. 2.95 o.p. (ISBN 0-380-83857-5, 83857-5). Avon.

Murder on My Street. Edwin M. Lanham. LC 58-5472. 1958. 3.50 o.p. (ISBN 0-15-163551-X). HarBraceJ.

Murder on the Menu. Ed. by Carol-Lynn R. Waugh et al. 320p. 1984. pap. 3.50 o.p. (ISBN 0-380-86918-7, 86918). Avon.

Murder on Usher's Planet. Atanielle A. Noel. 192p. 1987. pap. 2.95 o.p. (ISBN 0-380-75012-0). Avon.

Murder Post-Dated. Anne Morice. (Nightingale Large Print Ser.). 1985. pap. text ed. 11.95 o.p. (ISBN 0-8161-3769-2, Large Print Bks). G K Hall.

Murder under Two Flags: The U. S., Puerto Rico & Cerro Maravilla Cover-Up. Anne Nelson. (Illus.). 272p. 1986. 17.45 o.p. (ISBN 0-89919-371-4). Ticknor & Fields.

Murder Unprompted: A Charles Paris Mystery. Simon Brett. 160p. 1982. 10.95 o.s.i. (ISBN 0-684-17659-9, ScribT). Scribner.

Murdered Heiress, Living Witness. Petti Wagner. LC 84-80413. 211p. (Orig.). 1984. pap. 6.95 o.p. (ISBN 0-910311-09-9). Huntington Hse Inc.

Murders Most Macabre. Henry Slesar. 336p. 1986. pap. 3.50 o.p. (ISBN 0-380-89975-2). Avon.

Murders on Fraternity Row. Harold A. Seward. 96p. 1988. 8.95 o.p. (ISBN 0-8062-3040-1). Carlton.

Murdock. Geoffrey Simmons. LC 82-72056. 224p. 1982. 14.25 o.p. (ISBN 0-87795-429-1, Arbor Hse). Morrow.

Murphy. Samuel Beckett. 1969. pap. 8.95 o.p. (ISBN 0-394-17210-8, E104, Ever). Grove.

Muscle. David S. Smith. (Ultrastructure of Cells & Organisms Monographs). 1972. 32.50 o.p. (ISBN 0-12-454145-3). Acad Pr.

Muscle Shoals Canal...Life with the Canalers. new ed. Joshua N. Winn, III. (Strode History Ser.). (gr. 9-12). 1978. 9.95 o.p. (ISBN 0-87397-140-X). Strode.

Muscles! R. R. Knudson. (Illus.). 96p. (gr. 3-7). 1983. pap. 1.95 o.p. (ISBN 0-380-82172-9, 82172-9, Camelot). Avon.

Muscles & Movement. Gwynne Vevers. LC 83-18757. (Your Body Ser.: No. 4). (Illus.). 24p. (gr. 1-4). 1984. 8.25 o.p. (ISBN 0-688-02825-X); PLB 7.63 o.p. (ISBN 0-688-02826-8). Lothrop.

Muscles & Their Neural Control. Graham Hoyle. LC 82-11045. 689p. 1983. 77.50 o.p. (ISBN 0-471-87709-3). Wiley.

Muscloskeletal Injuries in the Workplace: Proceeding of International Conference Second Copenhagen, Denmark May 27-29 1986. Ed. by Peter L. Ferrara & Margareta C. Nordin. (Special Issue of Ergonomics Ser.: Vol. 30 No.2). 344p. 1987. pap. 37.00x o.p. (ISBN 0-85066-927-8). Taylor & Francis.

Musculo-Skeletal System. C. Fleetcroft. (Penguin Library of Nursing). (Illus.). 1983. pap. text ed. 10.00 o.p. (ISBN 0-443-01611-9). Churchill.

Musculoskeletal Manual. Jacob S. Birnbaum. LC 82-3878. 1982. 34.00 o.p. (ISBN 0-12-788075-5); pap. 44.00 o.p. (ISBN 0-12-788074-7). Acad Pr.

Musculoskeletal Pain: Principles of Physical Diagnosis & Physical Treatment. David A. Zohn & John M. Mennell. 1976. 35.00 o.p. (ISBN 0-316-98893-6). Little.

Musee Guimet, Paris. Madeleine Paul-David et al. LC 80-82645. (Oriental Ceramics Ser.: Vol. 7). (Illus.). 175p. 1981. 65.00 o.p. (ISBN 0-87011-446-8). Kodansha.

Musee Guimet, Paris see Oriental Ceramics: The World's Great Collections.

Musee Imaginaire. Andre Malraux. (Illus.). 256p. 1965. 3.95 o.p. (ISBN 0-686-56332-8). Schoenhof.

Museum Architecture: A Guide to Design, Conservation & Museum Architecture in the United States. Coppa & Avery Consultants Staff. (Architecture Ser.: A 1366). 10p. 1985. 2.00 o.p. (ISBN 0-89028-356-7). Vance Biblios.

Museum Guide to Washington D. C. Betty Ross. (Illus.). 252p. (Orig.). 1986. pap. 12.95 o.p. (ISBN 0-9616144-0-4). Americana Pr.

Museum Masterpieces in Needlepoint. Brande Ormond & Marion Muller. (Illus.). 1978. 14.95 o.p. (ISBN 0-395-27093-6). HM.

Museum of Far Eastern Antiquities, Stockholm. Bo Gyllensvard. LC 80-82645. (Oriental Ceramics Ser.: Vol. 8). (Illus.). 166p. 1982. 68.00 o.p. (ISBN 0-87011-447-6). Kodansha.

Museum of Far Eastern Antiquities, Stockholm see Oriental Ceramics: The World's Great Collections.

Museum of Fine Arts, Boston. Fontein Jan. LC 80-82645. (Oriental Ceramics Ser.: Vol. 10). (Illus.). 180p. 1981. 65.00 o.p. (ISBN 0-87011-449-2). Kodansha.

Museum of the Fine Arts, Boston see Oriental Ceramics: The World's Great Collections.

Museum Pusat, Jakarta. Abu Ridho. LC 80-82645. (Oriental Ceramics Ser.: Vol. 3). (Illus.). 175p. 1982. 68.00 o.p. (ISBN 0-87011-442-5). Kodansha.

Museum Pusat, Jakarta see Oriental Ceramics: The World's Great Collections.

Museum: Vols. 1-23 & General Index 1-25, Paris, 1948-1971. 1986. pap. 2323.00 o.p. (ISBN 0-317-44423-9). Kraus Repr.

Museums & Galleries in Great Britain & Ireland 1987. (Illus.). 160p. (Orig.). 1987. pap. 9.95 o.p. (ISBN 0-935161-99-6). Hunter Pub NY.

Museums & Galleries in Great Britain & Ireland, 1988. (Illus.). 184p. (Orig.). 1988. pap. 10.95 o.p. (ISBN 1-55650-014-9). Hunter Pub NY.

Museums & Sites of Historical Interest in Oregon. LC 74-647323. 206p. 1980. pap. 5.95 o.p. (ISBN 0-87595-075-2). Oregon Hist.

Museums: Architecture, Technics. R. Aloi. (Illus.). 1962. 50.00 o.p. E J Brill USA.

Museums in & Around Moscow. I. Baikova. 197p. 1985. 8.95 o.p. (ISBN 0-8285-2920-5, Pub. by Raduga Pubs USSR). Imported Pubns.

Mushroom Center Disaster. N. M. Bodecker. LC 73-85317. (Illus.). 48p. (ps-3). 1974. 6.95 o.p. (ISBN 0-689-30424-2, Atheneum). Macmillan.

Mushroom Handbook. L. C. Krieger. (Illus.). 14.00 o.p. (ISBN 0-8446-2404-7). Peter Smith.

Mushroom Trail Guide. Phyllis Glick. LC 78-18424. (Illus.). 1979. 9.95 o.s.i. (ISBN 0-03-018306-5); pap. 5.95 o.s.i. (ISBN 0-03-018301-4). H Holt & Co.

Mushrooms & Toadstools: A Colour Field Guide. U. Nonis. (Illus.). 230p. (gr. 6 up). 1983. 12.95 o.p. (ISBN 0-88254-755-0). Hippocrene Bks.

Music. 4th ed. 104p. 1979. pap. 4.95 o.s.i. (ISBN 0-900217-04-9, Pub. by Sufi Pub Co England). Hunter Hse.

Music. Helen Wolfert. (Orig.). 1965. pap. 1.95x o.p. (ISBN 0-393-04169-7). Norton.

Music: A Design for Listening. 3rd ed. Homer Ulrich. 1970. text ed. 12.95 o.p. (ISBN 0-15-564877-2, HC, HC). HarBraceJ.

Music: An Appreciation. 2nd ed. R. Kamien. 1979. text ed. 29.95 o.p. (ISBN 0-07-033279-7). McGraw.

Music: An Appreciation. Roger Kamien. 1976. text ed. 29.95 o.p. (ISBN 0-07-033266-5, C). McGraw.

Music & Art in Society. Francois Lesure. 59p. Repr. of 1968 ed. lib. bdg. 39.00 o.p. (Pub. by Am Repr Serv). Reprint Servs.

Music & Its Instruments. Robert Donington. LC 82-8012. 225p. 1982. 27.00x o.p. (ISBN 0-416-72270-9, NO. 3732); pap. 15.95 o.p. (ISBN 0-416-72280-6, NO. 3733). Routledge Chapman & Hall.

Music & Moonlight. Arthur O'Shaughnessy. Ed. by Ian Fletcher & John Stokes. LC 76-20153. (Decadent Consciousness Ser.: Vol. 31). 1977. Repr. of 1874 ed. lib. bdg. 46.00 o.p. (ISBN 0-8240-2781-7). Garland Pub.

Music & Music Education: Data & Information. Compiled by Daniel V. Steinel. 84p. 1984. pap. 14.50 o.p. (5670). Am Council Arts.

Music & Musical Life in Soviet Russia: 1917-1970. Boris Schwarz. 560p. 1973. pap. 5.95x o.p. (ISBN 0-393-00699-9). Norton.

Music & Society: England & the European Tradition. Winfrid H. Meller. 230p. Repr. of 1950 ed. lib. bdg. 39.00 o.p. (Pub. by Am Repr Serv). Reprint Servs.

Music & Speech Programs for the IBM PC. Robert J. Traister. (Illus.). 192p. 1983. 16.95 o.p. (ISBN 0-8306-0196-1); pap. 11.15 o.p. (ISBN 0-8306-0596-7, 1596). TAB Bks.

Music & the Dance. Elwood R. Priesing. 1978. 10.00 o.p. (ISBN 0-682-48957-3, Banner). Exposition-Phoenix.

Music & Western Man. Peter Garvie. 1958. (ISBN 0-8022-0566-6). Philos Lib.

Music & Your Emotions. new ed. Emil Gutheil. LC 75-131283. 1970. pap. 5.95 o.p. (ISBN 0-87140-232-7). Liveright.

Music at Court: Four Eighteenth Century Studies. Alan Yorke-Long. LC 78-66928. (Encore Music Editions Ser.). (Illus.). 1979. Repr. of 1954 ed. 20.35 o.s.i. (ISBN 0-88355-770-3). Hyperion Conn.

Music Before the Classic Era: An Introductory Guide. Robert Stevenson. LC 73-9131. 215p. 1974. Repr. of 1958 ed. lib. bdg. 35.00x o.p. (ISBN 0-8371-6986-0, STCE). Greenwood.

Music Education: A Guide to Information Sources. Ed. by Ernest E. Harris. LC 74-11560. (Education Information Guide Ser.: Vol. 1). 584p. 1978. 68.00x o.p. (ISBN 0-8103-1309-X). Gale.

Music Festivals in America. Rev. ed. Carol P. Rabin. LC 78-73844. (Illus.). 286p. 1983. pap. 6.95 o.p. (ISBN 0-912944-74-9). Berkshire Traveller.

Music for Analysis: Examples from the Common Practice Period & the Twentieth Century. Thomas E. Benjamin et al. LC 77-78237. 1978. pap. 18.95 o.p. (ISBN 0-395-25507-4). HM.

Music for Conducting Class. James McKelvy. LC 77-76862. 1977. wire bound 15.50 o.p. (ISBN 0-916656-10-1); pap. 14.50 o.p. (ISBN 0-916656-05-5). Mark Foster Mus.

Music for Elementary Teachers. 2nd ed. Parks Grant. LC 60-6665. (Illus.). 1960. 39.50x o.p. (ISBN 0-89197-311-7); pap. text ed. 19.95x o.p. (ISBN 0-89197-861-5). Irvington.

Music for God. Theresa Weiser. 1951. (ISBN 0-8022-1844-X). Philos Lib.

Music for Mohini. Bhabani Bhattacharya. pap. 5.50 o.s.i. (ISBN 0-89253-071-5). Ind-US Inc.

Music for the Piano: A Handbook of Concert & Teaching Material from 1580 to 1952. James Friskin & Irwin Freundlich. 15.50 o.p. (ISBN 0-8446-5109-5). Peter Smith.

Music for Tiny Tots: A Teacher's Manual for Group Teaching of Four-&-Five-Year-Olds. Eileen L. Mabus. 1977. 8.00 o.p. (ISBN 0-682-48719-8). Exposition-Phoenix.

Music from Another Room. James Kelly. 1980. pap. 2.25 o.p. (ISBN 0-8439-0779-7, Pub. by Leisure Bks CT). Dorchester Pub Co.

Music in America: An Anthology from the Landing of the Pilgrims to the Close of the Civil War 1620-1865. W. Thomas Marrocco & Harold Gleason. (Illus.). 384p. 1974. pap. 12.95x o.p. (ISBN 0-393-09296-8). Norton.

Music in American Life. Jacques Barzun. 126p. Repr. of 1960 ed. lib. bdg. 39.00 o.p. (Pub. by Am Repr Serv). Reprint Servs.

Music in Ancient Israel. Alfred Sendry. LC 66-20218. 678p. 1969. (ISBN 0-8022-2300-1). Philos Lib.

Music in Elizabethan England. Dorothy E. Mason. 38p. Repr. of 1958 ed. lib. bdg. 39.00 o.p. (Pub. by Am Repr Serv). Reprint Servs.

Music in Every Room: Around the World in a Bad Mood. John Krich. LC 83-18755. 320p. 1984. text ed. 14.95 o.p. (ISBN 0-07-035302-6). McGraw.

Music in My Heart, Borscht in My Blood. Henry Tobias. (Illus.). 256p. 1987. 18.95 o.p. (ISBN 0-87052-457-7). Hippocrene Bks.

Music in Poland (1975) Ludwik Erhardt. (Illus.). 1977. pap. 5.50 o.s.i. (ISBN 0-685-81371-1). E J Brill USA.

Music in Stone: Great Sculpture Gardens of the World. Sidney Lawrence & George Foy. Ed. by P. Tompkins. LC 84-50549. 204p. 1984. 35.00 o.p. (ISBN 0-935748-61-X). Scala Books.

Music in the Education of Children. 4th ed. Bessie R. Swanson. 408p. 1981. text ed. (ISBN 0-534-00880-1). Wadsworth Pub.

Music in the French Secular Theater 1400-1550. Howard M. Brown. 338p. Repr. of 1963 ed. lib. bdg. 49.00 o.p. (Pub. by Am Repr Serv). Reprint Servs.

Music in Today's Classroom: Creating, Listening, Performing. Lois R. Land & Mary A. Vaughan. 1973. 11.95 o.p. (ISBN 0-15-564893-4, HC). HarBraceJ.

Music in Transition: A Study of Tonal Expansion & Atonality, 1900-1920. Jim Samson. 1977. 12.95x o.p. (ISBN 0-393-02193-9). Norton.

Music: Invent Your Own. Martha Faulhaber & Janet Underhill. LC 74-13315. (Music Involvement Ser). (Illus.). 48p. (gr. 3 up). 1974. PLB 10.25 o.p. (ISBN 0-8075-5355-7). A Whitman.

Music Is for Children. Connie Fortunato. LC 78-50962. 1978. pap. 1.50 o.p. (ISBN 0-89191-128-6). Cook.

Music Locator. Ed. by W. Patrick Cunningham. (Illus.). 1976. pap. 21.95 o.p. (ISBN 0-89390-001-X). Resource Pubns.

Music Locator. 2nd ed. William P. Cunningham. 400p. 1980. 49.95 o.p. (ISBN 0-89390-020-6); pap. 39.95 o.p. (ISBN 0-89390-012-5). Resource Pubns.

Music Locator 1984. 584p. 1984. pap. 89.95 o.p. (ISBN 0-89390-048-6). Resource Pubns.

Music Lover's Europe: A Guidebook & Companion. Kenneth Bernstein. (Illus.). 192p. 1983. 4.95 o.s.i. (ISBN 0-684-17770-6, ScribT). Scribner.

Music Making. George Seltzer. LC 83-42897. 187p. (Orig.). 1983. pap. 15.95x o.p. (ISBN 0-89950-081-1). McFarland & Co.

Music Man of the West. Wellman E. Gerke. 1977. 6.50 o.p. (ISBN 0-682-47824-5). Exposition-Phoenix.

Music Monographs in Series: A Bibliography of Numbered Monograph Series in the Field of Music Current Since 1945. Fred Blum. 197p. Repr. of 1964 ed. lib. bdg. 39.00 o.p. (Pub. by Am Repr Serv). Reprint Servs.

Music, Movement, & the Young Child. rev. ed. Heather Gell. (Illus.). 1973. 10.50 o.p. (ISBN 0-900882-06-9). CPP Belwin.

Music Movement Therapy. Claire-Lise Dutoit. 1971. pap. 4.50 o.p. (ISBN 0-913650-07-2). CPP Belwin.

Music, Mysticism & Magic: A Source Book. Joscelyn Godwin. 384p. 1986. text ed. 50.00 o.p. (ISBN 0-7102-0904-5, 0905W, Pub. by Routledge UK). Routledge Chapman & Hall.

Music, Mysticism & Magic: A Source Book. Joscelyn Godwin. 385p. 1987. pap. 14.95 o.p. (ISBN 0-317-62024-X, Pub. by Routledge UK). Routledge Chapman & Hall.

Music Notation: A Manual of Modern Practice. Gardner Read. LC 68-54213. 1972. 13.95 o.s.i. (ISBN 0-8008-5459-4, Crescendo). Taplinger.

Music Observed. Bernard H. Haggin. 297p. Repr. of 1964 ed. lib. bdg. 39.00 o.p. (Pub. by Am Repr Serv). Reprint Servs.

Music of Black Americans: A History. Eileen Southern. (Illus.). 1971. text ed. 19.95x o.p. (ISBN 0-393-02156-4); pap. text ed. 9.95x o.p. (ISBN 0-393-09899-0). Norton.

Music of Brazil. David P. Appleby. (Illus.). 223p. 1983. text ed. 25.00x o.p. (ISBN 0-292-75068-4). U of Tex Pr.

Music of Central Africa: An Ethnomusicological Study. R. Brandel. (Illus.). 1973. pap. 35.00 o.s.i. (ISBN 9-0247-0634-3). E J Brill USA.

Music of Franz Schmidt, Vol. 1: The Orchestral Music. Harold Truscott. (Illus.). 190p. 22.95 o.s.i. (ISBN 0-907689-11-6, Pub. by Toccata Pr UK); pap. 13.95 o.s.i. (ISBN 0-907689-12-4, Pub. by Toccata Pr UK). David & Charles.

Music of Human Flesh. Mahmoud Darwish. Tr. by Denys Johnson-Davies from Arabic. (Modern Arab Writers Ser.). 96p. (Orig.). 1980. pap. 6.00 o.p. (ISBN 0-89410-203-6). Three Continents.

Music of India. Reginald Massey et al. (Illus.). 189p. 1986. pap. 7.95 o.s.i. (ISBN 0-8008-5451-9). Taplinger.

Music of Our Time. Nick Rossi & Robert Choate. LC 69-16933. 1970. 12.50 o.s.i. (ISBN 0-8008-5456-X, Crescendo). Taplinger.

Music of Schubert. Gerald E. Abraham. 342p. Repr. of 1969 ed. lib. bdg. 49.00 o.p. (Pub. by Am Repr Serv). Reprint Servs.

Music of Szymanowski. Jim Samson. LC 80-51747. 220p. 1981. 11.95 o.s.i. (ISBN 0-8008-7539-7, Crescendo). Taplinger.

Music of the Laws. Daniel Kornstein. (Illus.). 192p. 1982. 14.95 o.p. (ISBN 0-89696-185-0, An Everest House Book). Dodd.

Music of the Whole Earth. David Reck. LC 76-12493. 1977. 19.95 o.s.i. (ISBN 0-684-14631-2, ScribT); pap. 15.95 o.s.i. (ISBN 0-684-14633-9, ScribT). Scribner.

Music Play Past Midnight. Marilyn C. Donahue. (Pennypinchers Ser.). 132p. (gr. 4-7). 1983. 2.25 o.p. (ISBN 0-89191-756-X, 57562). Cook.

Music Publishing in Chicago Before 1871: The Firm of Root & Cady, 1858-1871. Dena J. Epstein. (Detroit Studies in Music Bibliography Ser.: No. 14). 1969. pap. 6.00 o.p. (ISBN 0-911772-36-7). Harmonie Pk Pr.

Music Since 1900. 4th ed. Nicolas Slonimsky. LC 70-114929. 1971. 75.00 o.s.i. (ISBN 0-684-10550-0, ScribT). Scribner.

Music Skills for Classroom Teacher. 6th ed. Robert W. Winslow & Leon Dallin. 336p. 1983. write for info. wire coil o.p. (ISBN 0-697-03566-2). Wm C Brown.

Music Subject Headings, Vol. 1. 2nd enlarged ed. New York Public Library, Research Libraries Staff. 1970. lib. bdg. 70.00 o.p. (ISBN 0-8161-0739-4, Hall Library). G K Hall.

Music Survey: New Series, 1949-1952. Ed. by Donald Mitchell & Hans Keller. (Illus.). 817p. 1983. 59.95 o.p. (ISBN 0-571-10040-6). Faber & Faber.

Music Synthesizers: A Manual of Design & Construction. Delton T. Horn. (Illus.). 336p. (Orig.). 1984. 16.95 o.p. (ISBN 0-8306-0565-7, 1565); pap. 16.60 o.p. (ISBN 0-8306-1565-2). TAB Bks.

Music: The Art of Listening. Jean Ferris. 408p. 1985. pap. text ed. write for info. incl. cassettes o.p. (ISBN 0-697-08278-4); instr's. manual avail. o.p. (ISBN 0-697-00525-9). Wm C Brown.

Music: The Listener's Art. 3rd ed. Leonard G. Ratner. 1977. text ed. 35.95 o.p. (ISBN 0-07-051221-3). McGraw.

Music Therapy. Edward Podolsky. 1954. (ISBN 0-8022-1994-2). Philos Lib.

Music Therapy for the Developmentally Disabled. Edith H. Boxill. LC 84-15752. 269p. 1984. 38.00 o.p. (ISBN 0-89443-555-8). Aspen Pub.

Music Through the Looking Glass. Fritz Spiegl. (Illus., Orig.). 1985. pap. 12.95 o.p. (ISBN 0-7102-0401-9). Routledge Chapman & Hall.

Music Titles in Translation: A Checklist of Musical Compositions. Julian Hodgson. LC 75-42015. viii, 370p. 1976. 34.00 o.p. (ISBN 0-208-01520-5, Linnet). Shoe String.

Music to Murder by. Vernon Hinkle. 1978. pap. 1.75 o.p. (ISBN 0-505-51262-9, Pub. by Tower Bks). Dorchester Pub Co.

Music Video Trivia. Matthew Abeshouse & Tevin Abeshouse. 1985. pap. 2.95 o.p. (ISBN 0-380-89836-5). Avon.

Music Within You. Shelley Katsh & Carole Merle-Fishman. 1985. pap. 8.95 o.s.i. (ISBN 0-671-55554-5). S&S.

Musical Acoustics: Violin Family Functions, 2 pts. Ed. by Carleen M. Hutchins. (Benchmark Papers in Acoustics Ser.: No. 5). 1975-76. Pt. 1. 87.00 o.p. (ISBN 0-12-786691-4); Pt. 2. 87.00 o.p. (ISBN 0-12-786692-2). Acad Pr.

Musical Applications of Microprocessors. Hal Chamberlin. 672p. 1983. pap. 21.95 o.p. (ISBN 0-317-00362-3). Sams.

Musical Autographs from Monteverdi to Hindemith, 2 vols. Emanuel Winternitz. Repr. of 1965 ed. lib. bdg. 108.00 o.p. (Pub. by Am Repr Serv). Reprint Servs.

Musical Companion. Ed. by A. L. Bachrach & J. R. Pearce. LC 78-53917. 1978. 14.95 o.p. (ISBN 0-15-163628-1). HarBraceJ.

Musical Composition. Charles V. Stanford. LC 78-13865. (Encore Music Editions Ser.). 1979. Repr. of 1911 ed. 20.25 o.s.i. (ISBN 0-88355-820-3). Hyperion Conn.

Musical Form: Studies in Analysis & Synthesis. Ellis B. Kohs. 1976. text ed. 30.95 o.p. (ISBN 0-395-18613-7). HM.

Musical Houses: Homes & Secret Retreats of Music Stars. Environmental Communications Staff. LC 80-22152. (Illus., Orig.). 1980. lib. bdg. 19.80 o.p. (ISBN 0-89471-112-1); pap. 7.95 o.p. (ISBN 0-89471-138-5). Running Pr.

Musical Iconography: A Manual for Cataloguing Musical Subjects in Western Art Before 1800. Howard M. Brown & Joan Lascelle. LC 76-180151. (Illus.). 224p. 1972. 18.95x o.s.i. (ISBN 0-674-59220-4). Harvard U Pr.

Musical Instruments: A Comprehensive Dictionary. Sibyl Marcuse. (Illus.). 656p. 1975. pap. 7.95x o.p. (ISBN 0-393-00758-8, Norton Lib). Norton.

Musical Instruments & Their Decoration. Christoph Rueger. (Illus.). 167p. 1986. 24.95 o.p. (ISBN 0-911403-17-5). Seven Hills Bk Dists.

Musical Instruments in Art & History. Roger Bragard. 281p. Repr. of 1968 ed. lib. bdg. 39.00 o.p. (Pub. by Am Repr Serv). Reprint Servs.

Musical Instruments of India. S. Krishnaswamy. LC 74-125041. 1970. pap. 2.95 o.s.i. (ISBN 0-8008-5461-6, Crescendo). Taplinger.

Musical Landscapes. John Burke. 192p. 1983. 23.95 o.p. (ISBN 0-03-063262-5). H Holt & Co.

Musical Laughs: Jokes, Tittle-Tattle, & Anecdotes, Mostly Humorous, About Musical Celebrities. Henry T. Finck. LC 79-159955. 352p. 1971. Repr. of 1924 ed. 40.00x o.p. (ISBN 0-8103-3397-X). Gale.

Musical Life. Irving Kolodin. 266p. Repr. of 1959 ed. lib. bdg. 39.00 o.p. (Pub. by Am Repr Serv). Reprint Servs.

Musical Settings of Early & Mid-Victorian Literature: A Catalogue. Bryan N. Gooch & David S. Thatcher. LC 78-68274. (Reference Library of Humanities Ser.). 1979. lib. bdg. 109.00 o.p. (ISBN 0-8240-9793-9). Garland Pub.

Musical Theatre. 1986. text ed. 24.95 o.p. (ISBN 0-07-037232-2). McGraw.

Musical Thoughts & Afterthoughts. Alfred Brendel. LC 76-3267. (Princeton Essays on the Arts: No. 4). (Illus.). 1977. 20.00x o.p. (ISBN 0-691-09122-6); pap. 9.50 o.p. (ISBN 0-691-02705-6). Princeton U Pr.

Musical Variations on Jewish Thought. Olivier R. D'Allonnes. Tr. by Judith Greenberg. LC 83-15640. 169p. 1984. 10.95 o.s.i. (ISBN 0-8076-1080-1). Braziller.

Musical World of Robert Schumann: A Selection from His Own Writings. Robert A. Schumann. 205p. Repr. of 1965 ed. lib. bdg. 39.00 o.p. (Pub. by Am Repr Serv). Reprint Servs.

Musical Worlds: Ethnomusicology & Folk Music Studies in Multicultural Education. (Ethnic Studies Bulletins: No. 10). 1982. 1.50 o.p. (ISBN 0-686-32674-1). I N Thut World Educ Ctr.

Musicalia: Sources of Information in Music. J. H. Davies. 184p. Repr. of 1969 ed. lib. bdg. 39.00 o.p. (Pub. by Am Repr Serv). Reprint Servs.

MusiCatalog. Resource Publications, Inc. Staff. Ed. by W. P. Cunningham. 1978. pap. 54.90x o.p. (ISBN 0-89390-013-3). Resource Pubns.

Musicians & the Servants. 2nd ed. Carolyn North. 192p. 1985. pap. 7.95 o.p. (ISBN 0-930588-21-5). Heyday Bks.

Musician's Guide to Copyright. rev. ed. J. Gunnar Erickson & Edward R. Hearn. 160p. 14.95 o.s.i. (ISBN 0-684-17900-8, ScribT). Scribner.

Musician's World: Great Composers in their Letters. Hans Gal. 464p. Repr. of 1966 ed. lib. bdg. 59.00 o.p. (Pub. by Am Repr Serv). Reprint Servs.

Music's Connecticut Yankee: An Introduction to the Life & Music of Charles Ives. Helen Sive. LC 76-25000. (Illus.). (gr. 6-9). 1977. 6.95 o.p. (ISBN 0-689-30561-3, Atheneum). Macmillan.

Musings & Reminiscences of A Pseudo-Scientist. John E. Howard. 1985. 6.00 o.p. (ISBN 0-682-40260-5). Exposition-Phoenix.

Musings of a Mild Manic-Depressive. Albert H. Saperstein. 1979. pap. 5.00 o.p. (ISBN 0-682-49432-1). Exposition-Phoenix.

Muskegon County, Harbor of Promise: An Illustrated History. Jonathan Eyler. LC 86-9142. (Illus.). 200p. 1986. 22.95 o.p. (ISBN 0-89781-174-7). Windsor Pubns Inc.

Muskie Murders. Ted Vogel. 1982. pap. 5.95 o.p. (ISBN 0-89803-101-X, Dist. by Kampmann). Green Hill.

Muskies & Muskie Fishing: How to Catch the King of Freshwater Game Fish. C. H. Shook. (Illus.). 144p. (Orig.). 1985. pap. 9.95 o.p. (ISBN 0-8117-2223-6). Stackpole.

Muslim Family Law: A Sourcebook. Keith Hodkinson. 401p. (Orig.). 1984. pap. 25.00 o.p. (ISBN 0-7099-1256-0, Pub. by Croom Helm Ltd). Routledge Chapman & Hall.

Muslim Neoplatonists. I. R. Netton. 160p. 1982. text ed. 19.95x o.p. (ISBN 0-04-297043-1). Unwin Hyman.

Muslim Saints & Mystics: Episodes from the Tadhkirat Al-Auliya (Memorial of the Saints) Farid Attar. Tr. by A. J. Arberry from Persian. (Persian Heritage Ser.). 1979. pap. 8.95 o.p. (ISBN 0-7100-0169-X). Routledge Chapman & Hall.

Muslim Spain. Duncan Townson. LC 78-56805. (Cambridge Topic Bks.). (Illus.). (gr. 5-10). 1978. PLB 8.95 o.p. (ISBN 0-8225-1216-5). Lerner Pubns.

Musorgsky's Days & Works: A Biography in Documents. Alexandra Orlova. Ed. by Malcolm Brown. Tr. by Roy Guenther. LC 82-4826. (Studies in Russian Music: No. 4). 720p. 1983. 74.95 o.p. (ISBN 0-8357-1324-5). UMI Res Pr.

Mussolini. Laura Fermi. LC 61-17075. 1966. pap. 12.95 o.s.i. (ISBN 0-226-24375-3, P216, Phoen). U of Chicago Pr.

Mussolini. Anthony J. Joes. (Illus.). 384p. 1982. 18.95 o.p. (ISBN 0-531-09865-6). Watts.

Mussolini, Twilight & Fall. Roman Dabrowski. LC 78-20460. 1980. Repr. of 1956 ed. 21.00 o.s.i. (ISBN 0-88355-839-4). Hyperion Conn.

Mussorgsky. rev. ed. M. D. Calvocoressi. Ed. by Gerald Abraham. (Master Musicians Ser.: No. M141). (Illus.). 216p. 1974. pap. 7.95 o.p. (ISBN 0-8226-0718-2). Littlefield.

Mussorgsky. rev. ed. M. D. Calvocoressi. (Master Musicians Ser.). (Illus.). 224p. 1974. 17.95x o.p. (ISBN 0-460-03152-X, Pub. by J. M. Dent England). Biblio Dist.

Must Words: The Six Thousand Most Important Words for a Successful & Profitable Vocabulary. Craig T. Norback & Peter Norback. 1979. text ed. 12.95 o.p. (ISBN 0-07-047136-3). McGraw.

Mustang: A Documentary History. Jeffrey Ethell. (Illus.). 160p. 1981. 18.95 o.p. (ISBN 0-86720-561-X). Janes Info Group.

Mustang 1979-1982 Includes Turbo Shop Manual. Ed. by Eric Jorgensen. (Illus., Orig.). pap. text ed. 12.95 o.p. (ISBN 0-89287-335-3, A291). Clymer Pub.

Mustangers. Gary McCarthy. LC 86-23993. (Double D Western Ser.). 192p. 1987. 12.95 o.s.i. (ISBN 0-385-23855-X). Doubleday.

Mustangs, Six-Shooters & Barbed Wire: How the West Was Really Won. Grant Lyons. LC 80-26715. (Illus.). 96p. (gr. 3-5). 1981. lib. bdg. 9.29 o.s.i. (ISBN 0-671-32996-0). Messner.

Mustard Seed: Discourses on the Sayings of Jesus from the Gospel According to Thomas. Bhagwan S. Rajneesh. LC 77-20461. 1978. pap. 9.57i o.p. (ISBN 0-06-066785-0, RD-255). HarpR.

Mustard Seed of Magic. Norma Johnston. LC 77-1214. 1977. 8.95 o.p. (ISBN 0-689-30587-7, Atheneum). Macmillan.

Mustard Seeds & Wineskins: Dramas & Meditations on Seven Parables. LC 79-176471. 1972. pap. 5.50 o.p. (ISBN 0-8066-1201-0, 10-4565, Augsburg); drama bklet 2.50 o.p. (ISBN 0-8066-1202-9, 10-4566). Augsburg Fortress.

Mutagenic Effects of Environmental Contaminants. H. Eldon Sutton. (Environmental Science Ser.). 1972. 48.50 o.p. (ISBN 0-12-677950-3). Acad Pr.

Mutagens & Carcinogens. Ed. by Randall Murray. 147p. 1977. 18.50x o.p. (ISBN 0-8290-2402-6). Irvington.

Mutant. Henry Kuttner. Ed. by Lester Del Ray. (Library of Science Fiction). 1975. lib. bdg. 21.00 o.p. (ISBN 0-8240-1420-0). Garland Pub.

Mutation. Robin Cook. 1988. 18.95 o.p. Presidio Pr.

Mutation Research: Problems, Results & Perspectives. Charlotte Auerbach. 1976. 59.95 o.p. (ISBN 0-412-11280-9, NO. 6017, Pub. by Chapman & Hall). Routledge Chapman & Hall.

Mutiny in Force X. Bill Glenton. (Illus.). 239p. 1987. 30.95 o.p. (ISBN 0-340-38015-2, Pub. by Hodder & Stoughton UK). David & Charles.

Mutiny: In the British & Commonwealth Forces, 1797-1956. Lawrence James. (Illus.). 288p. 1987. 26.95 o.p. (ISBN 0-907675-70-0, Pub. by Buchan & Enright UK). Seven Hills Bk Dists.

Mutiny of the Bounty. Sir John Barrow. Ed. by Gavin Kennedy. LC 80-66459. (Illus.). 216p. 1980. 17.95 o.p. (ISBN 0-87923-343-5). Godine.

Mutiny on the Enterprise. Robert E. Vanderman. (Gregg Fiction Star Trek Ser.). 1985. lib. bdg. 11.95 o.p. (ISBN 0-8398-2887-X, Gregg). G K Hall.

Mutt. Bianca Bradbury. (YA) (gr. 7 up). Dolphin bdg. 3.07 o.p. (ISBN 0-395-06658-1). HM.

Mutt. Bianca Bradbury. (Illus.). 32p. (gr. k-3). 1974. pap. 0.95 o.p. (ISBN 0-395-18560-2, Sandpiper). HM.

Mutual Images: Essays in American-Japanese Relations. Ed. by Akira Iriye. (Harvard Studies in American-East Asian Relations: No. 7). 336p. 1975. 24.50x o.s.i. (ISBN 0-674-59550-5). Harvard U Pr.

MVS JCL for Sequential Data Management, Bk. 2. Joe Leben & Jim Arnold. LC 84-15385. (Data Processing Training Ser.). 256p. 1985. 59.95x o.p. (ISBN 0-471-80138-0). Wiley.

MVS JCL Library. Joe Leben & Jim Arnold. 1987. 94.50 o.p. (ISBN 0-471-62449-7). Wiley.

My ABC Book. Illus. by Art Seiden. (Illus.). (gr. k-3). 1953. 0.79 o.p. (ISBN 0-8431-4105-0). Wonder.

My America. Oscar De Mejo. LC 82-22794. (Contemporary Artists Ser.). (Illus.). 120p. 1983. 40.00 o.p. (ISBN 0-8109-1804-8). Abrams.

My Analysis with Freud: Reminiscences. A. Kardiner. 1977. 6.95 o.p. (ISBN 0-393-01135-6). Norton.

My Antonia. Willa Cather. LC 86-5830. 381p. 1986. Repr. of 1977 ed. 15.95 o.p. (ISBN 0-89621-725-6). Thorndike Pr.

My Appetite Control. large print 16pt. ed. Pearl Brians. 1985. pap. 6.00 o.p. (ISBN 0-914009-40-0). VHI Library.

My Apprenticeship. Colette. Tr. by Helen Beauclerk from Fr. 144p. 1978. 10.00 o.p. (ISBN 0-374-21660-6); pap. 4.95 o.p. (ISBN 0-374-51458-5). FS&G.

My Aunt Otilia's Spirits: Los Espiritus De Mi Tia Otilia. Richard Garcia & Robin Cherin. LC 78-59159. (Fifth World Tales Ser.). (Illus.). (gr. k-6). 1978. pap. text ed. 4.95 spanish bilingual ed. o.p. (ISBN 0-89239-016-6, Imprenta de Libros Infantiles). Children's Book Pr.

My Bar Mitzvah. Richard Rosenblum. LC 84-16685. (Illus.). 32p. (ps-3). 1985. 10.25 o.p. (ISBN 0-688-04143-4); PLB 10.88 o.p. (ISBN 0-688-04144-2). Morrow.

My Barber. Anne Rockwell & Harlow Rockwell. LC 80-24496. (Illus.). 24p. (ps-1). 1981. PLB 8.95 o.s.i. (ISBN 0-02-777630-1). Macmillan.

My Battle with Low Blood Sugar. G. M. Thienell. 1971. 4.00 o.p. (ISBN 0-682-47198-4, Banner). Exposition-Phoenix.

My Best Games of Chess 1929-75. Arnold S. Denker. 190p. 1981. pap. 5.95 o.p. (ISBN 0-486-24035-5). Dover.

My Bible Book. Marian Bennett. (Wipe-Clean Bks.). (Illus.). 12p. (ps). 1985. pap. 1.39 o.p. (ISBN 0-87239-956-7, 3516). Standard Pub.

My Bible Says. Marilyn McAuley. (Peek & Find Bks.). (Illus.). 28p. (ps). 1984. bds. 3.95 o.p. (ISBN 0-89191-877-9, 58776). Cook.

My Birthday Praise Book. Alton Ward. (Little Tuffie Ser.). (Illus.). (ps). 1987. bds. 1.95 o.p. (ISBN 0-570-09064-4). Concordia.

My Body. Sue Porter. (Baby Book Ser.). (Illus.). 12p. (ps). 1985. bds. 3.95 o.p. (ISBN 0-911745-96-3, Bedrick Blackie). P Bedrick Bks.

My Body, My Life. David R. Ellingson & Darcy D. Jensen. LC 79-54122. 160p. (Orig.). 1981. pap. 5.95 o.p. (ISBN 0-8066-1761-6, 10-4590, Augsburg). Augsburg Fortress.

My Book of Prayers. Frances Matranga. (Happy Day Bks.). (Illus.). 24p. (ps-2). 1985. 1.59 o.p. (ISBN 0-87239-877-3, 3677). Standard Pub.

My Book of Prayers: A Personal Prayer Book. Compiled by Melvin A. Hammarberg & Clifford A. Nelson. LC 56-10134. 192p. 1956. pap. 3.95 o.p. (ISBN 0-8006-0454-7, 1-454, Fortress). Augsburg Fortress.

My Brother Tries to Make Me Laugh. Andrew Glass. LC 83-14989. (Illus.). 32p. (ps-1). 1984. 11.75 o.p. (ISBN 0-688-02257-X); PLB 11.88 o.p. (ISBN 0-688-02259-6). Lothrop.

My Brother's Image. Mark Hamilton. 160p. 1983. pap. 2.50 o.p. (ISBN 0-380-82230-X, 82230-X). Avon.

My Brother's Silly. Mike Dickinson. (Illus.). 32p. (ps-1). 1983. 9.95 o.p. (ISBN 0-233-97531-4). Andre Deutsch.

My Browning Family Album. Vivienne Browning. Ed. by Betty A. Coley. (Illus.). 128p. 1979. 10.50x o.s.i. (ISBN 0-905947-22-3). Wedgestone Pr.

My Cash Register Book. Illus. by Amye Rosenberg. (Softies Ser.). (Illus.). 12p. (ps-2). 1981. vinyl 5.95 o.p. (ISBN 0-671-42527-7, Little Simon). S&S.

My Chains Fell Off: William Wells Brown, Fugitive Abolitionist. L. H. Whelchel, Jr. LC 84-21027. 132p. (Orig.). 1985. lib. bdg. 22.75 o.p. (ISBN 0-8191-4367-7); pap. text ed. 9.25 o.p. (ISBN 0-8191-4368-5). U Pr of Amer.

My Children, My Children. Robert Reid. LC 76-54586. 1977. 8.95 o.p. (ISBN 0-15-163651-6). HarBraceJ.

My China Years: A Memoir. Helen F. Snow. LC 83-13477. (Illus.). 335p. 1984. 17.95 o.p. (ISBN 0-688-00786-4). Morrow.

My Christmas ABC Book. Ron Klug & Lyn Klug. LC 81-65643. (Illus., Orig.). (ps-1). 1981. pap. 3.95 o.p. (ISBN 0-8066-1879-5, 10-4623, Augsburg). Augsburg Fortress.

My Christmas Praise Book. Dorothy Oslin. (Little Tuffie Ser.). (Illus.). (ps). 1987. bds. 1.95 o.p. (ISBN 0-570-09066-0, 56-1573). Concordia.

My Church Covenant & I. Robert King & Estelle King. 1979. 5.00 o.p. (ISBN 0-682-49429-1). Exposition-Phoenix.

My Clock Book. Illus. by Amye Rosenberg. (Little Simon Playboards Ser.). (Illus.). 12p. (ps-2). 1981. bds. 3.95 o.p. (ISBN 0-671-42528-5, Little Simon). S&S.

My Clothes. Sue Porter. (Baby Book Ser.). (Illus.). 12p. (ps). 1985. bds. 3.95 o.p. (ISBN 0-911745-97-1, Bedrick Blackie). P Bedrick Bks.

My Color Book. Illus. by Sharon Leyland-DiBlasi. (Little Simon Playboards Ser.). (Illus.). 12p. (ps-2). 1981. bds. 3.95 board o.p. (ISBN 0-671-42529-3, Little Simon). S&S.

My Computer Guide: An Introduction to the IBM-PC. DLW Corporation Staff. 1984. 59.95 o.p. (ISBN 0-07-031740-2). McGraw.

My Conscience Speaks. Ed. by Constance McKenna et al. (Illus.). 48p. 1981. pap. 1.00 o.p. (ISBN 0-915365-05-7). Cath Free Choice.

My Country Is the Whole World: An Anthology of Women's Work on Peace & War. Ed. by Cambridge Women's Peace Collective Staff. (Illus.). 306p. (Orig.). 1984. pap. 8.95 o.p. (ISBN 0-86358-004-1, Pandora Pr). Routledge Chapman & Hall.

My Country Right or Left: Nineteen Forty to Nineteen Forty-Three see Collected Essays, Journalism, & Letters of George Orwell.

My Cousin the King. Edward Frascino. (Illus.). 32p. (gr. k-3). 1985. 12.95 o.s.i. (ISBN 0-13-608423-0). P-H.

My Creator, My Friend. Bruce Larson. 192p. 1986. 10.95 o.p. (ISBN 0-8499-0458-7). Word Bks.

My Dad Lives in a Downtown Hotel. Peggy Mann. 1976. pap. 1.75 o.p. (ISBN 0-380-00096-2, 55038-5, Camelot). Avon.

My Daddy. Mathew Price. LC 85-7573. (Surprise Board Bks.). (Illus.). 12p. (ps). 1986. bds. 3.95 o.s.i. (ISBN 0-394-87537-0). Knopf.

My Daily Partner. Becky Tirabassi. 128p. 1986. 14.95 o.p. (ISBN 0-8423-4637-6). Tyndale.

My Darling. Anne B. Harris. 32p. cancelled o.s.i. (ISBN 0-8062-3142-4). Carlton.

My Darling Darling Doctors. Fay Baker. LC 74-25292. 224p. 1975. 6.95 o.s.i. (ISBN 0-8076-0774-6). Braziller.

My Day. Chris Winn. LC 85-82080. (Busy Day Board Bks.). (Illus.). 14p. (ps-k). 1986. bds. 3.95 o.p. (ISBN 0-8050-0066-6). H Holt & Co.

My Dear Cousin. Peggy Hoffmann. LC 74-78878. 1970. 6.95 o.p. (ISBN 0-15-163671-0). HarBraceJ.

My Dear Parents: The Civil War Seen by an English Union Soldier. James Horrocks. Ed. by A. S. Lewis. LC 83-10717. 192p. 1983. 13.95 o.p. (ISBN 0-15-163674-5). HarBraceJ.

My Dear Runemeister: A Voyage Through the Alphabet. Lloyd J. Reynolds. LC 81-51920. (Illus.). 72p. (Orig.). 1982. pap. 6.95 o.s.i. (ISBN 0-8008-5452-7, Pentalic). Taplinger.

My Dearest Daughter--I Want You to Know. Ginny Hallock. 190p. 1982. 9.50 o.p. (ISBN 0-682-49886-6). Exposition-Phoenix.

My Dinner with Andre. Wallace Shawn & Andre Gregory. LC 81-47639. (Illus.). 240p. (Orig.). 1981. pap. 6.95 o.s.i. (ISBN 0-394-17948-X, E763, Ever). Grove.

My Doctrine Book. George Douma. pap. 2.25 o.p. (ISBN 0-686-23469-3). Rose Pub MI.

My Enemy's Enemy. Kingsley Amis. LC 63-11907. 1963. 4.50 o.p. (ISBN 0-15-163681-8). HarBraceJ.

My Eyes Are My Ears. Ed. by Daniel H. Pokorny. LC 74-14683. 373p. 1974. 32.50x o.p. (ISBN 0-8422-5205-3); pap. text ed. 16.50x o.p. (ISBN 0-8422-0464-4). Irvington.

My Father, My Son. Elmo Zumwalt et al. (Illus.). 320p. 1986. 18.95 o.p. (ISBN 0-02-633630-8). Macmillan.

My Father, the Coach. Alfred Slote. (gr. 3-7). 1977. pap. 1.75 o.p. (ISBN 0-380-01724-5, 54080, Camelot). Avon.

My Father's Glory & My Mother's Castle. Marcel Pagnol. Tr. by Rita Barisse. 352p. 1987. 20.00 o.s.i. (ISBN 0-86547-256-4); pap. 9.95 o.s.i. (ISBN 0-86547-257-2). N Point Pr.

My Father's House. Yigal Allon. Tr. by Reuven Ben-Yosef from Hebrew. (Illus.). 1976. 7.95 o.p. (ISBN 0-393-07498-6). Norton.

My Father's Reply. Anna C. Laing. LC 84-90152. 63p. 1985. 7.95 o.p. (ISBN 0-533-06215-2). Vantage.

My Father's Son. Frank O'Connor. (Non-Fiction Ser.). 256p. 1985. pap. 7.95 o.p. (ISBN 0-8398-2883-7, Gregg). G K Hall.

My Favorite Place. Kathryn H. Sasse. 32p. 1987. 6.50 o.p. (ISBN 0-8062-2832-6). Carlton.

My Favorite Verse. Ann K. Anderson. LC 85-70000. (My Favorite Verse Ser.). 24p. 1986. pap. 3.95 o.p. (ISBN 0-89636-209-4). Accent Bks.

My Favorite Verse. Cynthia Clawson. LC 86-73189. (My Favorite Verse Ser.). 24p. 1987. pap. 3.95 o.p. (ISBN 0-89636-222-1). Accent Bks.

My Favorite Verse. Jerry Falwell. LC 86-72750. (My Favorite Verse Ser.). 24p. 1987. pap. 3.95 o.p. (ISBN 0-89636-235-3). Accent Bks.

My Favorite Verse. John MacArthur. LC 85-73590. 24p. 1986. pap. 3.95 o.p. (ISBN 0-89636-205-1). Accent Bks.

My Favorite Verse. J. Vernon McGee. LC 86-71652. (My Favorite Verse Ser.). 24p. 1987. pap. 3.95 o.p. (ISBN 0-89636-223-X). Accent Bks.

My Favorite Verse. Janette Oke. LC 86-72125. 24p. 1987. pap. 3.95 o.p. (ISBN 0-89636-226-4). Accent Bks.

My Favorite Verse. Harold Sala. LC 86-72986. (My Favorite Verse Ser.). 24p. 1987. pap. 3.95 o.p. (ISBN 0-89636-228-0). Accent Bks.

My Favorite Verse. Luci Swindoll. LC 85-73591. (My Favorite Verse Ser.). 24p. 1986. pap. 3.95 o.p. (ISBN 0-89636-204-3). Accent Bks.

My Favorite Verse. Warren Wiersbe. LC 86-71653. 24p. 1987. pap. 3.95 o.p. (ISBN 0-89636-220-5). Accent Bks.

My Fifty Thousand Dollar Year at the Races. Andrew Beyer. LC 78-53918. 1978. 8.95 o.p. (ISBN 0-15-163693-1). HarBraceJ.

My Fifty Thousand Dollar Year at the Races. Andrew Beyer. LC 79-24212. 163p. 1980. pap. 3.95 o.p. (ISBN 0-15-662327-7, Harv). HarBraceJ.

My First Bible Word Book. Yvonne Russell. (Illus.). 64p. (ps-2). 1984. 8.95 o.p. (ISBN 0-528-82421-X, Checkerboard Pr). Macmillan.

My First Book see My Toys, My First Book, Baby Animals, the Farm.

My First Book About BASIC. Luca Novelli. Tr. by Laura Parma-Veigel from Ital. LC 86-16321. (Microsoft Juvenile Ser.). 64p. (gr. 1-6). 1986. 9.95 o.s.i. (ISBN 0-914845-86-1). Microsoft.

My First Book about Computers. Luca Novelli. Tr. by Laura Parma-Veigel from Ital. LC 86-12831. (Microsoft Juvenile Ser.). 64p. (Orig.). (gr. 5-7). 1986. 9.95 o.s.i. (ISBN 0-914845-85-3). Microsoft.

My First Book about Jesus. Walter Wangerin, Jr. (Illus.). 24p. (gr. 2 up). Date not set. incl. cassette 9.95 o.p. (ISBN 0-02-899505-8, Checkerboard Pr). Macmillan.

My First Book of Nursery Tales: Five Favorite Bedtime Tales. Illus. by William Joyce. LC 82-20452. (Illus.). 48p. (ps-1). 1983. 5.95 o.s.i. (ISBN 0-394-85396-2); lib. bdg. 6.99 o.s.i. (ISBN 0-394-95396-7). Random.

My First Computer Dictionary. Luca Novelli. Tr. by Laura Parma-Veigel from Ital. LC 86-12846. (Microsoft Juvenile Ser.). 64p. (gr. 1-6). 1986. 9.95 o.s.i. (ISBN 0-914845-87-X). Microsoft.

My First Days of School. Jane Hamilton-McRritt. (New Feeling Bks.). (Illus.). 32p. (ps-k). 1982. 4.80 o.s.i. (ISBN 0-671-44417-4, Little Simon). S&S.

My First Dictionary. Ed. by Houghton Mifflin Company Staff. LC 80-10899. (Illus.). 312p. (gr. 1-3). 1980. 10.45 o.p. (ISBN 0-395-29210-7). HM.

My First English-Japanese Picture Dictionary. Dixson et al. (Illus., Eng. & Japanese.). (gr. 1-6). 1978. pap. text ed. 4.50 o.p. (ISBN 0-88345-260-X). Prentice ESL.

My First Forty Years. Placido Domingo. LC 83-48100. (Illus.). 1983. 15.45 o.s.i. (ISBN 0-394-52329-6). Knopf.

My First Sixty Years. Lena B. Morton. LC 65-11951. 187p. 1965. (ISBN 0-8022-1157-7). Philos Lib.

My First Step. Wim Heesakkers. (First Step Ser.). 24p. (ps-1). 1985. 3.95 o.p. (ISBN 0-8120-5642-6). Barron.

My Friend Bear. Carol-Lynn R. Waugh. LC 81-15600. (Illus.). 32p. (ps-1). 1982. 10.45i o.p. (ISBN 0-316-92636-1, Pub. by Atlantic-Little, Brown). Little.

My Friend Charlie. James Flora. LC 64-16265. (Illus.). (gr. 1-4). 1972. pap. 1.25 o.p. (ISBN 0-15-662330-7, VoyB). HarBraceJ.

My Friend Is Moving. Christine Kohler. (Growing up Christian Ser.). 24p. (Orig.). (ps-4). 1985. pap. 3.95 o.p. (ISBN 0-570-04116-3, 56-1527). Concordia.

My Friend Jesus. Marian Bennett. (Wipe-Clean Bks.). (Illus.). 12p. (ps). 1985. pap. 1.39 o.p. (ISBN 0-87239-957-5, 3517). Standard Pub.

My Friend Mac: The Story of Little BAptiste & the Moose. May McNeer. (Illus.). (gr. k-3). 1960. PLB 5.95 o.p. (ISBN 0-395-24371-8). HM.

My Friend, My Love. Hila Colman. (gr. 12 up). 1983. o.p. Archway.

My Friend Next Door. Leone C. Anderson. LC 83-7440. (Illus.). 32p. (gr. 1-3). 1983. PLB 4.95 o.p. (ISBN 0-89693-212-5). Dandelion Hse.

My Friend Wants to Run Away. Margaret O. Hyde. LC 79-14517. (gr. 7-9). 1979. text ed. 9.95 o.p. (ISBN 0-07-031642-2). McGraw.

My Friends Live in Many Places. Dorka Raynor. Ed. by Kathleen Tucker. LC 79-27655. (Albert Whitman Concept Bks.: Level 1). (Illus.). (ps up). 1980. PLB 11.25 o.p. (ISBN 0-8075-5353-0). A Whitman.

My Garden. Zokeisha. (Puffies Ser.). (Illus.). 8p. (ps). 1982. pap. 3.40 o.s.i. (ISBN 0-671-44848-X, Little Simon). S&S.

My God Is Real. David Watson. LC 81-71343. 95p. 1982. pap. 4.95 o.p. (ISBN 0-89107-248-9). Good News.

My Godmother: Theodate Pope Riddle & Reminiscences of Creativity. Phyllis F. Cunningham. LC 83-12202. (Illus.). 96p. 1983. 10.95 o.p. (ISBN 0-914016-97-0). Phoenix Pub.

My Great-Grandfather, the Heroes & I. James Kruss. LC 73-76321. (Illus.). 256p. (gr. 4-6). 1973. 6.95 o.p. (ISBN 0-689-30113-8, Atheneum). Macmillan.

My Green Age: A Memoir. Edwards Weeks. (Illus.). 1974. 14.45 o.p. (ISBN 0-316-92790-2, Pub. by Atlantic Monthly Pr). Little.

My Hands, My World. Catherine Brighton. LC 84-9670. (Illus.). 32p. (gr. k-3). 1984. 11.95 o.s.i. (ISBN 0-02-712900-4). Macmillan.

My Heart, My Temple. Emilia C. Mariani. LC 84-90223. 58p. 1985. 6.95 o.p. (ISBN 0-533-06276-4). Vantage.

My Heart Soars. Chief Dan George & Helmut Hirnschall. (Illus.). 95p. pap. 14.95 o.p. (ISBN 0-919654-15-0). Hancock House.

My House. Zokeisha. (Puffies Ser.). (Illus.). 8p. (ps). 1982. pap. 3.40 o.s.i. (ISBN 0-671-45078-6, Little Simon). S&S.

My House Has Two Doors. Han Suyin. 524p. 1985. pap. 6.95 o.p. (ISBN 0-586-05413-8, Pub. by Granada England). Academy Chi Pubs.

My House of Fairy Tales II Pink. (Illus., Consisting of: Alice in Wonderland, Cinderella, Little Vain Mouse, The Golden Egg, Treasure Island, Ali Baba). (ps-1). 1985. 2.98 o.s.i. (ISBN 0-517-48294-0). Outlet Bk Co.

My Husband, My Friend. Neile M. Toffel. LC 85-47606. 320p. 1986. 17.95 o.p. (ISBN 0-689-11637-3, Atheneum). Macmillan.

My Inventions: Moji Pronalasci. Nikola Tesla. (Illus.). 112p. 1977. 35.00x o.s.i. (ISBN 0-686-63529-9). E J Brill USA.

My Iron Journey: An Autobiography. Otto Kuhler. LC 67-8268. 1967. 9.95 o.p. (ISBN 0-933472-40-4). Johnson Bks.

My Jewish Roots: A Practical Guide to Tracing & Recording Your Genealogy & Family History. David Kranzler. (Illus.). 1979. pap. 8.95 o.s.i. Hermon.

My Journey into God's Realm of Light. Agnes M. Fenwick. 1974. 3.50 o.p. (ISBN 0-682-47865-2). Exposition-Phoenix.

My Kids are My Best Teachers. Bill Butterworth. 168p. 1986. 6.95 o.p. (ISBN 0-8007-5210-4). Revell.

My Lady Ludlow. Gaskell. 198p. 1987. pap. 5.95 o.s.i. (ISBN 0-86299-248-6, Pub. by A Sutton Pub England). Academy Chi Pubs.

My Life a Loaded Gun: Female Creativity & Feminist Poetics. Paula Bennett. LC 85-73366. 288p. 1986. 21.95 o.p. (ISBN 0-8070-6308-8). Beacon Pr.

My Life & Music & Reflections on Music. Artur Schnabel. 248p. Repr. of 1972 ed. lib. bdg. 39.00 o.p. (Pub. by Am Repr Serv). Reprint Servs.

My Life & My Dressage Horses. E. Petushkova. 136p. 1983. pap. 2.95 o.p. (ISBN 0-8285-2575-7, Pub. by Raduga Pubs USSR). Imported Pubns.

My Life & My Films. Jean Renoir. Tr. by Norman Denny from Fr. LC 74-77850. (Illus.). 320p. 1974. pap. 5.95 o.p. (ISBN 0-689-10629-7, 219, Atheneum). Macmillan.

My Life & Times, Vol 1. V. V. Giri. LC 76-904158. 1976. 14.00x o.p. (ISBN 0-333-90133-9). South Asia Bks.

My Life As a Restaurant. Alice M. Brock. LC 75-4378. (Illus.). 144p. 1976. 7.95 o.p. (ISBN 0-87951-032-3). Overlook Pr.

My Life in the Bush of Ghosts. Amos Tutuola. 1962. pap. 6.95 o.p. (ISBN 0-394-17324-4, E559, Ever). Grove.

My Life in the Silver Screen. Gerald Kaufman. LC 85-12927. 1985. 19.95 o.p. (ISBN 0-571-13493-9). Faber & Faber.

My Life in the Southwest. Adah Hadlock. LC 75-97793. 1969. 5.00 o.p. (ISBN 0-87404-017-5). Tex Western.

My Life in the Wild. Ivan Tors. 1979. 10.95 o.p. (ISBN 0-395-27766-3). HM.

My Life Is a Poem. Tony Karlic. 144p. 1985. 6.50 o.p. (ISBN 0-682-40236-2). Exposition-Phoenix.

My Life Is Love. Sue E. Huckins. 1980. pap. 5.00 o.p. (ISBN 0-682-49469-0). Exposition-Phoenix.

My Life on a Diet: Confessions of a Hollywood Diet Junkie. Renee Taylor. 192p. 1986. 15.95 o.p. (ISBN 0-399-13205-8, Perigee). Putnam Pub Group.

My Life on the Plains. George A. Custer. 1976. pap. 1.25 o.p. (ISBN 0-685-69509-3, LB377ZK, Pub. by Leisure Bks CT). Dorchester Pub Co.

My Life with Goya. Andrew Potok. 1986. 17.95 o.p. (ISBN 0-87795-789-4). Morrow.

My Life Without God. William J. Murray. LC 83-14269. 252p. 1984. pap. 5.95 o.p. (ISBN 0-8407-5884-7). Nelson.

My Little Bear. Patricia Crampton. (Illus.). 24p. (ps-2). 1986. 2.95 o.p. (ISBN 0-02-724920-4). Bradbury Pr.

My Little Brother. Wim Heesakkers. (First Step Ser.). 24p. (ps-1). 1985. 3.95 o.p. (ISBN 0-8120-5643-4). Barron.

My Little Bunny. Patricia Crampton. (Illus.). 24p. (ps-2). 1986. 2.95 o.p. (ISBN 0-02-724940-9). Bradbury Pr.

My Little Cat. Patricia Crampton. (Illus.). 24p. (ps-2). 1986. 2.95 o.p. (ISBN 0-02-724950-6). Bradbury Pr.

My Little Cat Woodbook. Wim Heesakkers. (ps). 1985. 7.95 o.p. (ISBN 0-8120-5615-9). Barron.

My Little Church Around the Corner. J. H. Randolph Ray. 1957. 5.00 o.p. S&S.

My Little Duck. Patricia Crampton. (Illus.). 24p. (ps-2). 1986. 2.95 o.p. (ISBN 0-02-724930-1). Bradbury Pr.

My Little Goose Woodbook. Wim Heesakkers. (ps). 1985. 12.95 o.p. (ISBN 0-8120-5626-4). Barron.

My Little Lamb. Patricia Crampton. (Illus.). 24p. (ps-1). 1987. 2.95 o.p. (ISBN 0-02-724980-8). Bradbury Pr.

My Little Panda. Patricia Crampton. (Illus.). 24p. (ps-1). 1987. 2.95 o.p. (ISBN 0-02-724990-5). Bradbury PR.

My Little Pig. Patricia Crampton. 24p. (ps-1). 1987. 2.95 o.p. (ISBN 0-02-724970-0). Bradbury Pr.

My Little Pony: A Book of Favorite Things to Touch & Feel. Carey Timm. LC 85-60497. (Illus.). 14p. (gr. 1-4). 1985. 4.95 o.s.i. (ISBN 0-394-87384-X, BYR). Random.

My Little Pony & The New Friends. Edith Adams. LC 84-60331. (My Little Pony Mini-Storybooks Ser.). (Illus.). 32p. (ps-3). 1984. pap. 1.25 o.s.i. (ISBN 0-394-86810-2, Pub. by BYR). Random.

My Little Pony Sea Ponies Water Fun. Illus. by Mia Woods. (Bath & Beach Play Sets Ser.). (Illus.). 10p. (ps). 1986. 3.95 o.s.i. (ISBN 0-394-88012-9). Random.

My Little Puppy. Patricia Crampton. (Illus.). 24p. (ps-1). 1987. 2.95 o.p. (ISBN 0-02-725000-8). Bradbury Pr.

My Lord & My God. Charles Allen. 48p. 1985. 6.95 o.p. (ISBN 0-8378-5083-5). Gibson.

My Lord Guardian. Elizabeth Kidd. 192p. 1983. pap. 2.50 o.p. (ISBN 0-380-64139-9, 64139-9). Avon.

My Lord Monleigh. Jan C. Speas. 1978. pap. 1.95 o.p. (ISBN 0-380-01847-0, 36442-5). Avon.

My Mane Catches the Wind: Poems About Horses. Ed. by Lee B. Hopkins. LC 79-87518. (Illus.). (gr. 4 up). 1979. 8.95 o.p. (ISBN 0-15-256343-1, HJ). HarBraceJ.

My Marks & Scars I Carry: The Story of Ernst Kisch. Thoburn T. Brumbaugh. (Bold Believers Ser.). 1969. pap. 0.95 o.p. (ISBN 0-377-84151-X). Friendship Pr.

My Masterpiece. Max Wilk. LC 77-116121. 1970. 5.95 o.p. (ISBN 0-393-08610-0). Norton.

My Mind on Trial. Eugen Loebl. LC 76-14482. (Helen & Kurt Wolff Bks.). 1976. 8.95 o.p. (ISBN 0-15-163700-8). HarBraceJ.

My Mind on Trial. Eugen Loebl. 235p. 1978. pap. 3.95 o.p. (ISBN 0-15-663800-2). HarBraceJ.

My Mom Got a Job. Lucia B. Smith. LC 79-1494. (Illus.). (gr. k-3). 1979. 6.95 o.p. (ISBN 0-03-048321-2). H Holt & Co.

My Mom, the Money Nut. Betty Bates. LC 78-24213. 160p. (gr. 4-6). 1979. 12.95 o.p. (ISBN 0-8234-0347-5). Holiday.

My Mommy. Mathew Price. LC 85-23175. (Surprise Board Bks.). (Illus.). 12p. (ps). 1986. bds. 3.95 o.s.i. (ISBN 0-394-88180-X). Knopf.

My Mommy Makes Money. Joyce S. Mitchell. LC 83-17507. (Illus.). 31p. (ps-3). 1984. 12.95 o.p. (ISBN 0-316-57501-1). Little.

My Morning Glory. M. Havill Patterson. 1977. 7.00 o.p. (ISBN 0-682-48669-8). Exposition-Phoenix.

My Most Marvelous Memory Book. Judith King. (Illus.). 64p. 1983. pap. 6.95 plastic comb bdg o.p. (ISBN 0-932620-22-1). Betterway Pubns.

My Mother Golda Meir: A Son's Evocation of Life with Golda Meir. Menahem Meir. LC 82-72053. (Illus.). 304p. 1983. 15.95 o.p. (ISBN 0-87795-415-1, Arbor Hse). Morrow.

My Mother, My Self: Tenth Anniversary Edition. Nancy Friday. 448p. 1987. pap. 19.95 o.p. (ISBN 0-385-29570-7). Delacorte.

My Mother, Myself. 10th ed. Date not set. (ISBN 0-385-29570-7). Delacorte.

My Mother the Witch. Rose Blue. LC 79-23950. (Illus.). (gr. 6-8). 1980. text ed. 8.95 o.p. (ISBN 0-07-006169-6). McGraw.

My Mother Who Fathered Me: A Study of the Family in the Selected Communities in Jamaica. Edith Clark. 1976. pap. text ed. 14.95X o.p. (ISBN 0-04-573010-5). Unwin Hyman.

My Mother's Keeper. B. D. Hyman. 510p. 1986. lib. bdg. 18.95 o.p. (ISBN 0-8161-4024-3, Large Print Bks). G K Hall.

My Mother's Keeper: A Daughter's Candid Portrait of Her Famous Mother. B. D. Hyman. Ed. by Pat Golbitz. LC 85-250. (Illus.). 256p. 1985. 17.95 o.p. (ISBN 0-688-04798-X). Morrow.

My Name Is Christian Woman. Mary H. Wallace. LC 85-31575. (Illus., Orig.). 1982. pap. 6.95 o.p. (ISBN 0-912315-20-2). Word Aflame.

My Neighbors, the Billy Grahams. Betty Frist. LC 83-70368. 1983. 8.95 o.p. (ISBN 0-8054-7229-0). Broadman.

My New Order. Adolph Hitler. Ed. by Raoul De Roussy De Sales. LC 73-3444. 1008p. 1973. Repr. of 1941 ed. lib. bdg. 57.50x o.p. (ISBN 0-374-93918-7, Octagon). Hippocrene Bks.

My Oh My Country Pies. Ed. by Annette Gohlke. LC 83-60923. 64p. 1983. pap. 3.95 o.s.i. (ISBN 0-89821-051-8). Reiman Assocs.

My Old Kentucky Home, Good-night. Mary Ann Kelly. (Illus.). 1978. 15.00 o.p. (ISBN 0-682-49143-8). Exposition-Phoenix.

My Old Sweetheart. Susanna Moore. 211p. 1982. 12.45 o.p. (ISBN 0-395-32516-1). HM.

My One, Two, Three Peter the Pixie. (Illus.). (ps-k). 1.98 o.s.i. (ISBN 0-517-47119-1). Outlet Bk Co.

My Other-Mother, My Other-Father. Harriet L. Sobol. LC 78-24165. (Illus.). 48p. (gr. 3-7). 1979. 9.95 o.s.i. (ISBN 0-02-785960-6). Macmillan.

My Own Book of Secrets. Edith L. Dahlby. 1977. 4.50 o.p. (ISBN 0-682-48776-7). Exposition-Phoenix.

My Own Ground. Hugh Nissenson. 182p. 1976. 7.95 o.p. (ISBN 0-374-21747-5). FS&G.

My Own Reading Book, Vol. 2. Cecelia Pollack. (Intersensory Reading Program). (Illus.). 64p. (Orig.). (gr. 2-5). pap. 2.95 o.p. (ISBN 0-87594-044-7). Book-Lab.

My Own Trumpet: The Memoirs of Sir Adrian Boult. Adrian C. Boult. (Sir). (Illus.). 213p. 1979. 19.95 o.p. (ISBN 0-241-02445-5, Pub. by Hamish Hamilton England). David & Charles.

My Own Writing Book. Cecelia Pollack. (Intersensory Reading Program). (gr. 1-3). pap. 2.95 o.p. (ISBN 0-87594-010-2). Book-Lab.

My Oxford, My Cambridge. Ed. by Ann Thwaite. Ronald Hayman. LC 79-14003. (Illus.). 1979. 12.50 o.s.i. (ISBN 0-8008-5468-3). Taplinger.

My People in Wood. Helen Bullard. (Illus.). 88p. 1984. pap. 9.95 o.p. (ISBN 0-87588-208-0, 2641). Hobby Hse.

My Personal History Workbook. Jeanne W. Pittman. 1979. pap. 3.95 o.p. (ISBN 0-89036-132-0). Hawkes Pub Inc.

My Pets. Eric Hill. LC 82-60625. (Eric Hill's Baby Bear Bks.). (Illus.). 14p. (ps). 1983. pap. 2.50 o.s.i. (ISBN 0-394-85637-6). Random.

My Place in God's World. Ryan Narka. 1974. pap. text ed. 2.35 tchrs' ed o.p. (ISBN 0-8042-1451-4, John Knox); pap. text ed. 1.15 students' ed o.p. (ISBN 0-8042-1450-6); resource packet 5.95 o.p. (ISBN 0-8042-1452-2). Westminster John Knox.

My Pony, Johnny. Marion Hulsizer & Allan Hulsizer. (Illus.). 64p. 1981. 5.00 o.p. (ISBN 0-682-49779-7). Exposition-Phoenix.

My Prayer Journal. Ronald Klug. LC 12-2964. 1982. pap. 3.95 o.p. (ISBN 0-570-03871-5). Concordia.

My Prayerbook. Daughters of St. Paul. (Illus.). (ps). 1988. plastic bdg. 2.00 o.p. (ISBN 0-317-67479-X, CH0390); pap. 1.25 o.p. (ISBN 0-317-67480-3). Dghtrs St Paul.

My Pretty Girl. Bianca Bradbury. LC 73-22061. (Illus.). 176p. (gr. 4-9). 1974. 5.95 o.p. (ISBN 0-395-18518-1). HM.

My Psychic Experience. Georgia Ramsey. 32p. 1987. 5.75 o.p. (ISBN 0-8062-2835-0). Carlton.

My Red Umbrella. Robert Bright. (Illus.). (ps-1). 1959. PLB 10.88 o.p. (ISBN 0-688-31619-0). Morrow.

My Redeemer Lives: Messages from the Book of Job for Lent & Easter. Vernon R. Schreibner. LC 74-14170. 80p. 1974. pap. 2.50 o.p. (ISBN 0-8066-1453-6, 10-4600, Augsburg). Augsburg Fortress.

My Response. Luis Palau. 1985. pap. 3.95 o.p. (ISBN 0-8024-8782-3). Moody.

My Road to Opera: The Recollections of Boris Goldsovsky As Told to Curtis Cate. Boris Goldovsky & Curtis Cate. 1979. 15.00 o.p. (ISBN 0-395-27760-4). HM.

My Robot Buddy. Alfred Slote. (Illus.). 92p. (gr. 2-7). 1978. pap. 1.95 o.p. (ISBN 0-380-40329-3, 64063-5, Camelot). Avon.

My Russia. Peter Ustinov. (Illus.). 224p. 1983. 19.95 o.p. (ISBN 0-316-89052-9, Pub. by Atlantic Monthly Pr.). Little.

My Search for Absolutes: A Credo Perspective. Paul Tillich. Ed. by Ruth N. Anshen. (Illus.). 1984. pap. 6.70 o.p. (ISBN 0-671-50585-8, Touchstone Bks). S&S.

My Search for B. Traven. Jonah Raskin. 252p. 1980. 12.95 o.p. (ISBN 0-416-00741-4, NO. 0199). Routledge Chapman & Hall.

My Servant Job: A Devotional Guide to the Book of Job. Vernon Schreibner. LC 74-14169. 144p. 1974. pap. 0.95 o.p. (ISBN 0-8066-1454-4, 10-4602, Augsburg). Augsburg Fortress.

My Servants the Prophets. Edward J. Young. 1952. pap. 9.95 o.p. (ISBN 0-8028-1697-5). Eerdmans.

My Silent Obligato. Sylvia McCracken. LC 61-15244. 64p. 1962. (ISBN 0-8022-1010-4). Philos Lib.

My Sister Eileen. Ruth McKenney. LC 38-17844. 1968. pap. 0.60 o.p. (ISBN 0-15-663890-8, Harv). HarBraceJ.

My Sister, Life. Boris Pasternak. Tr. by Olga A. Carlisle. (Helen & Kurt Wolff Bk.). 1976. 14.95 o.p. (ISBN 0-15-163964-7). HarBraceJ.

My Sister, My Antigone. Grete Weil. Tr. by Krishna Winston. 208p. 1984. pap. 3.95 o.p. (ISBN 0-380-85522-4, 85522, Bard). Avon.

My Sister, My Spouse: A Biography of Lou Andreas - Salome. H. F. Peters. (Illus.). 328p. 1974. pap. 6.95 o.p. (ISBN 0-393-00748-0, Norton Lib.). Norton.

My Sister's Picture. Cathy Arden. 1986. 17.45 o.p. (ISBN 0-671-50467-3). S&S.

My Soul & I: The Inner Life of Walt Whitman. David Cavitch. LC 85-47525. (Illus.). 224p. 1985. 19.95 o.p. (ISBN 0-8070-7000-9). Beacon Pr.

My Soul Doth Magnify the Lord! Mark Prophet & Elizabeth Prophet. LC 73-83759. (Illus.). 350p. 1974. 9.95 o.s.i. (ISBN 0-916766-06-3). Summit Univ.

My Special Play Group. Pamela Dowling. (Way We Live Ser.). (Illus.). 32p. (gr. 1-3). 1986. 9.95 o.p. (ISBN 0-241-11645-7, Pub. by Hamish Hamilton England). David & Charles.

My Spirit Soars. Dan George & Helmut Hirnschall. (Illus.). 96p. 14.95 o.p. (ISBN 0-88839-154-4). Hancock House.

My Story. Kamala Das. 231p. 1977. 10.00 o.p. (ISBN 0-86578-198-2); pap. 3.00 o.p. (ISBN 0-86578-199-0). Ind-US Inc.

My String of Pearls. Eve Jacques. 64p. 1986. 8.95 o.p. (ISBN 0-8062-2997-7). Carlton.

My Sunday Praise Book. Alton Ward. (Little Tuffie Ser.). (Illus.). (ps). 1987. bds. 1.95 o.p. (ISBN 0-570-09063-6, 56-1570). Concordia.

My Sweet Audrina. V. C. Andrews. 368p. 1982. 14.50 o.s.i. (ISBN 0-671-44327-5, Poseidon). PB.

My Sweet Lord: Hare Krishna Movement. pap. 8.95 o.p. (ISBN 0-85030-432-6, Pub. by Aquarian Pr England). Sterling.

My Sweet Lord: The Hare Krishna Movement. Kim Knott. 112p. 1986. pap. 11.95 o.p. Newcastle Pub.

My Teacher Sleeps in School. Leatie Weiss. LC 83-10427. (Illus.). 32p. (gr. k-3). 1984. 10.95 o.p. (ISBN 0-7232-6253-5). Warne.

My Telephone Book. Illus. by Amye Rosenberg. (Softies Ser.). (Illus.). 12p. (ps-2). 1981. vinyl 5.95 o.p. (ISBN 0-671-42526-9, Little Simon). S&S.

My Thanksgiving Praise Book. Alton Ward. (Little Tuffie Ser.). (Illus.). (ps). 1987. bds. 1.95 o.p. (ISBN 0-570-09065-2, 56-1572). Concordia.

My Theatre Life. August Bournonville. Tr. by Patricia McAndrew. LC 78-27349. (Illus.). 1979. 40.00x o.p. (ISBN 0-8195-5035-3). Wesleyan U Pr.

My Theodosia. Anya Seton. 9.95 o.p. (ISBN 0-395-08174-2). HM.

My Time & What I've Done with It: An Autobiography, Compiled from the Diary, Notes & Personal Recollections of Cecil Colvin, 1874. Francis C. Burnard. (Victorian Fiction Ser.). 1976. lib. bdg. 73.00 o.p. (ISBN 0-8240-1535-5). Garland Pub.

My Times with Dogs. Date not set. (ISBN 0-87605-664-8). Howell Bk.

My Toys see My Toys, My First Book, Baby Animals, the Farm.

My Toys, My First Book, Baby Animals, the Farm, 20 bk. set. Lawrence DiFiori. Incl. My Toys, 5 bks. 26p. pap. 2.95 (ISBN 0-02-730600-3); My First Book, 5 bks. (ps). 2.95 (ISBN 0-02-730610-0); Baby Animals, 5 bks. (ps). 2.95 (ISBN 0-02-730620-8); Farm, 5 bks. (ps). 2.95 (ISBN 0-02-730630-5). (Block Bks.). (Illus.). (ps-6). 1983. of 20, 5 of ea. 59.00 set o.s.i. (ISBN 0-02-730640-2). Macmillan.

My Trip Book. (Affordable Travel Ser.). 68p. 1984. pap. 3.95 o.p. Mar Lor Pr.

My Trip to Alpha I. Alfred Slote. (Illus.). 96p. (gr. 2-5). 1980. pap. 2.25 o.p. (ISBN 0-380-51128-2, Camelot). Avon.

My True Love. Denise Robins. (Large Print Bks. (Nightingale Ser.)). 330p. 1986. pap. 11.95x o.p. (ISBN 0-8161-4081-2). G K Hall.

My Turn. Roz Avrett. 288p. 1983. 14.50 o.p. (ISBN 0-87795-476-3, Arbor Hse). Morrow.

My Two Feet. Alice Schertle. LC 84-12192. (Illus.). 32p. (ps-2). 1985. 11.75 o.p. (ISBN 0-688-02676-1); PLB 11.88 o.p. (ISBN 0-688-02677-X). Lothrop.

My Uncle. Jerry Thorne. LC 81-22786. (Illus.). 32p. (ps-3). 1982. 9.95 o.s.i. (ISBN 0-689-50233-8, M K McElderry). Macmillan.

My Uncle Atahualpa. Paulo De Carvalho-Neto. Tr. by Victor Valle from Span. Ed. by Yvette E. Miller. 253p. 1987. pap. text ed. (ISBN 0-935480-31-5). Lat Am Lit Rev Pr.

My Uncle Oswald. Roald Dahl. 208p. 1981. pap. 2.95 o.s.i. (ISBN 0-345-29410-6). Ballantine.

My Uncle Silas. H. E. Bates. 1986. 13.50 o.p. (ISBN 0-317-53135-2, Large Print Bks). G K Hall.

My Very Own Chanukah Book. Judyth R. Saypol & Madeline Wikler. LC 77-23682. (Illus.). 32p. (ps-5). 1977. pap. 2.95 o.p. (ISBN 0-930494-03-2). Kar-Ben.

My Very Own Dictionary. Charlie Daniel & Becky Daniel. (gr. 1-4). 1978. 6.95 o.p. (ISBN 0-916456-17-X, GA81). Good Apple.

My Violin. Maurice Cellard. 80p. 1987. 6.95 o.p. (ISBN 0-8062-2529-7). Carlton.

My Way: The Way of the White Clouds. rev. ed. Bhagwan Shree Rajneesh. Ed. by Swami Ananda Teertha. LC 79-2303. (Questions & Answers Ser.). (Illus.). 640p. 1975. 10.95 o.p. (ISBN 0-88050-096-4). Chidvilas Inc.

My Wife, the Condesa. Felix Abelard. 1978. 9.50 o.p. (ISBN 0-682-49054-7). Exposition-Phoenix.

My Wisdom. Jean Thompson. 384p. 1982. 15.95 o.p. (ISBN 0-531-09870-2). Watts.

My Work in Films. Eugene Lourie. LC 84-9130. (Illus.). 384p. 1985. 29.95 o.p. (ISBN 0-15-164019-X). HarBraceJ.

My Works & Days: A Personal Chronicle, 1895-1975. Lewis Mumford. LC 78-14077. 1979. 13.95 o.s.i. (ISBN 0-15-164087-4). HarBraceJ.

My World of Birds: Memoirs of an Ornithologist. George J. Wallace. 345p. 1979. 12.50 o.p. (ISBN 0-8059-2586-4). Dorrance.

My "Y" Shaped Travels in China. T. Y. Wong. (Illus.). 1980. 5.00 o.p. (ISBN 0-682-49603-0). Exposition-Phoenix.

My Younger Son. Glenn P. Holman. 304p. 1986. 14.95 o.p. (ISBN 0-8062-2912-8). Carlton.

Myalgic Encephalomyelitis: Post-Viral Fatigue Syndrome & How to Cope with It. Celia Wookey. 144p. (Orig.). 1986. pap. 13.50 o.p. (ISBN 0-7099-3672-9, Pub. by Croom Helm Ltd). Routledge Chapman & Hall.

Myasthenia Gravis. Ed. by E. X. Albuquerque & A. T. Eldefrawi. (Illus.). 512p. 1983. 75.00 o.p. (ISBN 0-412-16310-1, NO. 6779, Pub. by Chapman & Hall). Routledge Chapman & Hall.

Mycanean Greece. J. T. Hooker. (States & Cities of Ancient Greece Ser.). 330p. 1977. 30.00x o.p. (ISBN 0-7100-8379-3). Routledge Chapman & Hall.

Mycardial Imaging. (Landmark Ser.). 1979. 22.50x o.p. (ISBN 0-8422-4107-8). Irvington.

Mycenae. Michael Sargent. Ed. by Kenneth McLeish & Valerie McLeish. (Aspects of Greek Life Ser.). (Illus.). 64p. (Orig.). (gr. 7-12). 1972. pap. text ed. 4.75 o.p. (ISBN 0-582-34401-8). Longman.

Mycetozoans. Lindsay S. Olive. 1975. 66.50 o.p. (ISBN 0-12-526250-7). Acad Pr.

Mycotoxins in Foodstuffs, No. 3. Ed. by M. Jemmali. 1978. 25.00 o.p. (ISBN 0-08-021194-1). Pergamon.

Myeloproliferative Disorders of Animals & Man: Proceedings. Ed. by W. J. Clarke et al. LC 70-605836. (AEC Symposium Ser.). 765p. 1970. pap. 27.25 o.p. (ISBN 0-87079-280-6, CONF-680529); microfiche 4.50 o.p. (ISBN 0-87079-281-4, CONF-680259). DOE.

Myocardial Infarction. 3rd ed. Ary L. Goldberger. (Illus.). 336p. 1984. cloth 46.50 o.p. (ISBN 0-8016-1870-3). Mosby.

Myocardial Infraction. Ed. by Eugene I. Chazov. LC 77-99143. (Illus.). 314p. 1979. 27.50 o.p. (ISBN 0-88416-119-6). Year Bk Med.

Myocardial Injury. Ed. by John J. Spitzer. LC 82-24624. (Advances in Experimental Medicine & Biology Ser.: Vol. 161). 622p. 1983. 95.00x o.p. (ISBN 0-306-41253-5, Plenum Pr). Plenum Pub.

Myocardial Revascularization by Arterial-Ventricular Implants. Arthur M. Vineberg. LC 80-10654. (Illus.). 490p. 1982. text ed. 58.00 o.p. (ISBN 0-88416-191-9). Year Bk Med.

Myra. Barbara Bottner. LC 78-10417. (Illus.). (gr. k-3). 1979. 9.95 o.s.i. (ISBN 0-02-711740-5). Macmillan.

Myra Waldo's Chinese Cooking. Myra Waldo. LC 68-17205. 1985. pap. 3.95 o.p. (ISBN 0-02-010720-X, Collier). Macmillan.

Myriapod Biology. Ed. by Marina Camatini. LC 79-41559. 1980. 139.00 o.p. (ISBN 0-12-155750-2). Acad Pr.

Myron Goldsmith: Concepts & Buildings. Ed. by Werner Blaser. LC 86-29697. (Illus.). 192p. (Orig.). 1987. 25.00 o.p. (ISBN 0-8478-0790-8). Rizzoli Intl.

Mysaskovsky, His Life & Work. A. Ikonnikov. (ISBN 0-8022-0773-1). Philos Lib.

Myself & I. Norma Johnston. LC 80-21855. 216p. (gr. 6 up). 1981. PLB 10.95 o.p. (ISBN 0-689-30814-0, Atheneum). Macmillan.

Mystere des Saints Innocents. Charles Peguy. (Coll. Soleil). 9.95 o.p. (ISBN 0-685-37029-1). Schoenhof.

Mysteries. John Allan. (Book of Beliefs). 1981. 9.95 o.p. (ISBN 0-89191-477-3, 54775). Cook.

Mysteries & Fantasies. Ed. by World Book, Inc. Staff. LC 65-25105. (The How & Why Library-1986 Annual Supplement to Childcraft). (Illus.). 304p. (gr. 3-4). 1986. write for info. o.p. (ISBN 0-7166-0686-0). World Bk.

Mysteries & Marvels of Nature. Barbara Cork & R. Morris. (Mysteries & Marvels Ser.). (Illus.). 96p. (gr. 3-6). 1983. 12.95 o.p. (ISBN 0-86020-757-9). EDC.

Mysteries & Secrets of Magic. C. J. Thompson. LC 78-174119. (Tower Bks). (Illus.). 344p. 1971. Repr. of 1928 ed. 48.00x o.p. (ISBN 0-8103-3213-2). Gale.

Mysteries of Easter Island. Jean-Michael Schwartz. 1975. pap. 1.95 o.p. (ISBN 0-380-00419-4, 38455). Avon.

Mysteries of History, with Accounts of Some Remarkable Characters & Charlatans. C. J. Thompson. LC 76-164056. (Tower Bks). 334p. 1971. Repr. of 1928 ed. 40.00x o.p. (ISBN 0-8103-3908-0). Gale.

Mysteries of Machu Picchu. Simone Waisbard. 1979. pap. 2.75 o.p. (ISBN 0-380-43687-6, 43687). Avon.

Mysteries of Nature: Explained & Unexplained. Roger Caras. (Illus.). (gr. 5 up). 1979. 5.95 o.p. (ISBN 0-15-256346-6, HJ). HarBraceJ.

Mysteries of Stonehenge. Fennand Niel. 1975. pap. 1.95 o.p. (ISBN 0-380-00473-9, 38620). Avon.

Mysteries of the Andes. Robert Charroux. (YA) 1977. pap. 2.25 o.p. (ISBN 0-380-01702-4, 33779). Avon.

Mysteries of the Great Pyramids. Andre Pochan. 1978. pap. 2.25 o.p. (ISBN 0-380-00881-5, 31492). Avon.

Mysteries of the Red Sea. Lev Fishelson. (Illus.). 144p. 1984. 29.95 o.p. (ISBN 0-911378-53-7, Pub. by Massada). Sheridan.

Mysterious Ambassador. Lee Falk. (Phantom Ser.: No. 6). 1973. pap. 0.75 o.p. (ISBN 0-380-01421-1, 15545). Avon.

Mysterious Britain. Janet Bord & Colin Bord. (Illus.). 287p. 1981. pap. 7.95 o.p. (ISBN 0-586-08157-7, Pub. by Granada England). Academy Chi Pubs.

Mysterious Man. Lyubomir Levchev. Tr. by Vladimir Phillipov. LC 80-83426. (International Poetry: Vol. 4). 30p. 1981. 11.95x o.p. (ISBN 0-8214-0594-2); pap. 6.95 o.p. (ISBN 0-8214-0595-0). Ohio U Pr.

Mysterious Prowler. Joan L. Nixon. LC 75-29314. (Let Me Read Ser.). (Illus.). 64p. (gr. 1-5). 1976. 4.95 o.p. (ISBN 0-15-256355-5, HJ). HarBraceJ.

Mysterious Prowler. Joan L. Nixon. LC 75-29314. (Let-Me-Read Ser.). (Illus.). 64p. (ps-3). 1976. pap. 1.95 o.p. (ISBN 0-15-256356-3, VoyB). HarBraceJ.

Mysterious Radio Code. Thomas F. Pursell. LC 77-74009. (Carolrhoda Mini-Mysteries Ser.). (Illus.). (gr. k-4). 1977. PLB 5.95 o.p. (ISBN 0-87614-088-6). Carolrhoda Bks.

Mysterious Schoolmaster. Karin Anckarsvard. Tr. by Annabelle MacMillan. LC 59-10170. (Illus.). (gr. 3-7). 1959. 6.50 o.p. (ISBN 0-15-256527-2, HJ). HarBraceJ.

Mysterious Schoolmaster. Karin Anckarsvard. Tr. by Annabelle MacMillan. LC 59-10170. (Illus.). (gr. 3-7). 1965. pap. 2.95 o.p. (ISBN 0-15-663971-8, VoyB). HarBraceJ.

Mysterious Science of the Law. Daniel J. Boorstin. 11.25 o.p. (ISBN 0-8446-1702-4). Peter Smith.

Mysterious Sea Monsters of California's Central Coast. Randall A. Reinstedt. LC 80-114610. (Illus.). 68p. (Orig.). 1979. pap. 5.50 o.p. (ISBN 0-933818-06-8). Ghost Town.

Mysterious Shroud. Ian Wilson. LC 83-45570. (Illus.). 176p. 1986. 19.95 o.s.i. (ISBN 0-385-19074-3). Doubleday.

Mysterious Signs in the Sky. Israel Norkin. (Illus.). 112p. 1983. 8.00 o.p. (ISBN 0-682-40161-7). Exposition-Phoenix.

Mysterious Toyshop. Cyril W. Beaumont. (Illus.). 32p. 1985. 14.00 o.s.i. (ISBN 0-03-005852-X). H Holt & Co.

Mysterious World: An Atlas of the Unexplained. Francis Hitching. LC 78-14162. (Illus.). 1979. 18.95 o.p. (ISBN 0-03-044036-X); pap. 11.95 o.p. (ISBN 0-03-044031-9). H Holt & Co.

Mysterious Zetabet. Scott Corbett. LC 78-23243. (Illus.). (gr. 1-3). 1979. 9.95 o.p. (ISBN 0-316-15730-9, Joy St Bks). Little.

Mystery & Art of the Apothecary. C. J. Thompson. LC 78-89294. (Illus.). 304p. 1971. Repr. of 1929 ed. 43.00x o.p. (ISBN 0-8103-3210-8). Gale.

Mystery & Lore of Apparitions, with Some Account of Ghosts, Spectres, Phantoms & Boggarts in Early Times. C. J. Thompson. LC 70-167225. (Illus.). 360p. 1975. Repr. of 1930 ed. 40.00x o.p. (ISBN 0-8103-3981-1). Gale.

Mystery & Lure of Perfume. C. J. Thompson. LC 74-75789. 1969. Repr. of 1927 ed. 30.00x o.p. (ISBN 0-8103-3842-4). Gale.

Mystery & Magic of the Occult. John S. Kerr. LC 79-154486. (Orig.). 1971. pap. 0.50 o.p. (ISBN 0-8006-0157-2, Fortress). Augsburg Fortress.

Mystery & Meaning: Personal Logic & the Language of Religion. Douglas A. Fox. LC 75-15738. 1975. pap. 4.95 o.s.i. (ISBN 0-664-24768-7, Westminster). Westminster John Knox.

Mystery & Philosophy. Michael B. Foster. LC 79-8721. (Library of Philosophy & Theology). 96p. 1980. Repr. of 1957 ed. lib. bdg. 35.00x o.p. (ISBN 0-313-20792-5, FOMP). Greenwood.

Mystery at Devil's Paw. Franklin W. Dixon. (Hardy Boys Ser.: Vol. 38). (Illus.). 192p. (gr. 5-9). 1959. Repr. 4.50 o.p. (ISBN 0-448-08938-6, G&D); PLB 3.29 o.p. (ISBN 0-448-18938-0). Putnam Pub Group.

Mystery at Long Crescent Marsh. Remus F. Caroselli. LC 84-15716. 160p. (gr. 4-7). 1985. 11.95 o.s.i. (ISBN 0-03-001414-X). H Holt & Co.

Mystery at October House. Marjory Hall. LC 76-46565. (gr. 6 up). 1977. 7.95 o.s.i. (ISBN 0-664-32606-4, Westminster). Westminster John Knox.

Mystery at Poor Boy's Folly. Bernard Palmer. LC 80-65058. (Powell Family Ser.). 160p. (Orig.). (gr. 7-10). 1981. pap. 2.95 o.p. (ISBN 0-89636-049-0). Accent Bks.

Mystery at Raider Stadium. Jerry B. Jenkins. (Bradford Family Adventures Ser.). (Illus.). 128p. (gr. 3-6). 1986. 2.95 o.p. (ISBN 0-87403-092-7, 2922). Standard Pub.

Mystery at Sans Souci. James Hausman. LC 77-18520. (Illus.). (gr. 4-6). 1978. 7.95 o.p. (ISBN 0-689-30644-X, Atheneum). Macmillan.

Mystery at the Edge of Two Worlds. Christie Harris. LC 78-5326. (Illus.). (gr. 4-6). 1978. 7.95 o.p. (ISBN 0-689-30631-8, Atheneum). Macmillan.

Mystery Babylon - Revelation 17-5: Is It America? Lee Dawkins. 103p. 1983. 7.00 o.p. (ISBN 0-682-49965-X). Exposition-Phoenix.

Mystery Book Mystery. Wylly F. St. John. (gr. 5 up). 1978. pap. 1.50 o.p. (ISBN 0-380-39800-1, 47910-9). Avon.

Mystery in the Mainstream: Suspense Stories by Classic Writers. Ed. by Bill Pronzini et al. LC 86-12410. 416p. 1986. 18.95 o.p. (ISBN 0-688-04965-6). Morrow.

Mystery in the Ravine. Carol Farley. (Illus.). 132p. (gr. 3-7). 1976. pap. 1.95 o.p. (ISBN 0-380-00745-2, 60558-9, Camelot). Avon.

Mystery of Aloha House. Lee Roddy. (Chime Gothic 202 Ser.). 1981. pap. 2.50 o.p. (ISBN 0-89191-293-2, 52936). Cook.

Mystery of Atlantis. Charles Berlitz. (Illus.). 1976. pap. 2.75 o.p. (ISBN 0-380-00546-8, 56747-4). Avon.

Mystery of Christian Hope. Jean Galot. LC 77-1222. 1977. 4.95 o.p. (ISBN 0-8189-0346-5). Alba.

Mystery of Cottage Cove. Aleda Renken. (Haley Adventure Bks). (Illus.). 96p. (gr. 3-7). 1975. pap. 1.00 o.p. (ISBN 0-570-07232-8, 39-1030). Concordia.

Mystery of Golf. Arnold Haultain. 1986. pap. 9.95 o.p. Morrow.

Mystery of Green Hill. Ivan Kusan. Tr. by Michael B. Petrovich. LC 62-8743. (Illus.). (gr. 4-6). 1966. pap. 3.95 o.p. (ISBN 0-15-663972-6, VoyB). HarBraceJ.

Mystery of Hilliard's Castle. Kathy L. Emerson. (gr. 6-9). 1985. pap. 7.95 o.p. (ISBN 0-89272-213-4). Down East.

Mystery of Lost Beach. Thomas F. Pursell. LC 77-74007. (Carolrhoda Mini-Mysteries Ser.). (Illus.). (gr. k-4). 1977. PLB 5.95 o.p. (ISBN 0-87614-086-X). Carolrhoda Bks.

Mystery of Marriage: A Challenge to Forced Divorce. Jan Doctor. 1980. 8.95 o.p. (ISBN 0-682-49302-3, Testament). Exposition-Phoenix.

Mystery of Missions. Henrietta T. Wilkinson. (Illus., Orig.). (gr. 5-7). 1965. pap. 2.95 o.p. (ISBN 0-8042-9412-7, John Knox). Westminster John Knox.

Mystery of Pain. Paul J. Lindell. LC 74-77676. 80p. (Orig.). 1974. pap. 1.75 o.p. (ISBN 0-8066-1424-2, 10-4639, Augsburg). Augsburg Fortress.

Mystery of Prayer. Mac N. Turnage & Anne S. Turnage. (Orig.). (gr. 9-10). 1964. pap. 1.25 o.p. (ISBN 0-8042-9314-7, John Knox). Westminster John Knox.

Mystery of Salvation. Paul De Surgy. Tr. by Rosemary Sheed. 1966. pap. 6.95 o.p. (ISBN 0-268-00185-5). U of Notre Dame Pr.

Mystery of Steamboat Rock. Dorothy Y. Croman. (Outlands Adventure Ser.). 208p. (gr. 4-7). 1984. pap. 2.95 o.p. (ISBN 0-8423-4671-6). Tyndale.

Mystery of Telepathy. Joe Cooper. 1982. 19.95x o.p. (ISBN 0-09-464170-6, Pub. byConstable Pubs UK). Trans-Atl Phila.

Mystery of the Aztec Warrior. Franklin W. Dixon. (Hardy Boys Ser: Vol. 43). (gr. 5-9). 1964. 4.50 o.p. (ISBN 0-448-08943-2, G&D); PLB 3.29 o.p. (ISBN 0-448-18943-7). Putnam Pub Group.

Mystery of the Bewitched Bookmobile. Florence P. Heide & Roxanne Heide. LC 75-6763. (Pilot Bks). (Illus.). (gr. 3-8). 1975. PLB 8.95 o.p. (ISBN 0-8075-5375-1). A Whitman.

Mystery of the Blue Champ. Larry Sutton. LC 80-69289. (Carolrhoda Mini-Mysteries Ser.). (Illus.). 32p. (gr. 1-4). 1981. PLB 5.95 o.p. (ISBN 0-87614-137-8). Carolrhoda Bks.

Mystery of the Brass Bound Trunk. Carolyn Keene. (Nancy Drew Mystery Stories: Vol. 17). (gr. 3-9). 4.50 o.p. (ISBN 0-448-09517-3, G&D). Putnam Pub Group.

Mystery of the Buried Gold. Eda Stertz. (Windrider Ser.). 192p. (gr. 4-7). 1985. pap. 3.50 o.p. (ISBN 0-8423-4649-X). Tyndale.

Mystery of the Crimson Ghost. Phyllis A. Whitney. LC 69-14202. (gr. 5-9). 1969. 5.50 o.s.i. (ISBN 0-664-32440-1, Westminster). Westminster John Knox.

Mystery of the Eagle's Claw. Frances Wosmek. LC 78-12221. 132p. 1979. 7.95 o.s.i. (ISBN 0-664-32640-4, Westminster). Westminster John Knox.

Mystery of the Fiery Message. Carol Farley. (Illus.). 108p. (gr. 3-7). 1983. pap. 1.95 o.p. (ISBN 0-380-81927-9, 81927-9, Camelot). Avon.

Mystery of the Flying Express. Franklin W. Dixon. LC 73-106327. (Hardy Boys Ser.: Vol. 20). (Illus.). (gr. 5-9). 1941. 4.50 o.p. (ISBN 0-448-08920-3, G&D); PLB 3.29 o.p. (ISBN 0-448-18920-8). Putnam Pub Group.

Mystery of the Fog Man. Carol Farley. (Illus.). 112p. 1976. pap. 2.50 o.p. (ISBN 0-380-00102-0, Camelot). Avon.

Mystery of the Funny Money. Ray Broekel. LC 79-52408. (Carolrhoda Mini-Mysteries Ser.). (Illus.). (gr. 1-4). 1980. PLB 5.95 o.p. (ISBN 0-87614-114-9). Carolrhoda Bks.

Mystery of the Gingerbread House. Wylly F. St. John. (Illus.). (YA) (gr. 9-12). 1977. pap. 1.50 o.p. (ISBN 0-380-01731-8, 52084-2, Camelot). Avon.

Mystery of the Golden Horn. Phyllis A. Whitney. (Illus.). (gr. 5-9). 1962. 4.95 o.s.i. (ISBN 0-664-32288-3, Westminster). Westminster John Knox.

Mystery of the Golden Ram. Ruth Malone. LC 75-34158. 1976. 6.00 o.s.i. (ISBN 0-664-32585-8, Westminster). Westminster John Knox.

Mystery of the Great Swamp. (ISBN 0-689-20491-4, Atheneum). Macmillan.

Mystery of the Great Zimbabwe: A New Solution. Wilfrid Mallows. (Illus.). 1984. 34.50 o.p. (ISBN 0-393-01789-3). Norton.

Mystery of the Green Cat. Phyllis A. Whitney. LC 57-5435. (A Junior Literary Guild Selection). (Illus.). 208p. 1957. 6.95 o.s.i. (ISBN 0-664-32160-7, Westminster). Westminster John Knox.

Mystery of the Haunted Pool. Phyllis A. Whitney. LC 60-9715. (Illus.). 224p. (gr. 5-9). 1960. 7.50 o.s.i. (ISBN 0-664-32241-7, Westminster). Westminster John Knox.

Mystery of the Hidden Camera. Dan Cohen. LC 79-84362. (Carolrhoda Mini-Mysteries Ser.). (Illus.). (gr. k-4). 1979. PLB 5.95 o.p. (ISBN 0-87614-098-3). Carolrhoda Bks.

Mystery of the Imposter. R. L. Stine. (Wizards, Warriors & You Ser.: No. 11). 1986. pap. 2.50 o.p. (ISBN 0-380-89948-5). Avon.

Mystery of the Locked Door. Dan Cohen. LC 79-50786. (Carolrhoda Mini-Mysteries Ser.). (Illus.). (gr. k-4). 1979. PLB 5.95 o.p. (ISBN 0-87614-099-1). Carolrhoda Bks.

Mystery of the Marmalade Cat. large type ed. Janet R. Howe. LC 69-12908. (Illus.). (gr. 4-9). 1969. 4.25 o.s.i. (ISBN 0-664-32439-8, Westminster). Westminster John Knox.

Mystery of the Mayan Hieroglyphs: The Vision of an Ancient Tradition. Richard Luxton. Ed. by Pablo Balam. LC 81-48211. 247p. (Orig.). 1982. pap. 7.64i o.p. (ISBN 0-06-065315-9, CN 4035). HarpR.

Mystery of the Mellafeller Elephant. Dan Cohen. LC 79-56198. (Carolrhoda Mini-Mysteries Ser.). (Illus.). (gr. 1-4). 1980. PLB 5.95 o.p. (ISBN 0-87614-118-1). Carolrhoda Bks.

Mystery of the Midnight Message, No. 3. Florence P. Heide & Roxanne Heide. (Spotlight Club Mystery Ser.). (Illus.). (gr. 3-6). 1982. pap. 1.95 o.p. (ISBN 0-671-43980-4). Archway.

Mystery of the Missing Ring. Dan Cohen. LC 79-56200. (Carolrhoda Mini-Mysteries Ser.). (Illus.). (gr. 1-4). 1980. PLB 5.95 o.p. (ISBN 0-87614-120-3). Carolrhoda Bks.

Mystery of the Other Girl. Wylly F. St. John. (YA) 1978. pap. 1.25 o.p. (ISBN 0-380-01926-4, 48207, Camelot). Avon.

Mystery of the Roman Ransom. Henry Winterfeld. Tr. by Edith McCormick. LC 71-137759. Orig. Title: Caius Geht Ein Licht Auf. (Illus.). (gr. 5 up). 1971. 5.50 o.p. (ISBN 0-15-256612-0, HJ). HarBraceJ.

Mystery of the Roman Ransom. Henry Winterfeld. Tr. by Edith McCormick from Ger. LC 77-3673. (Illus.). (gr. 5-9). 1977. pap. 1.75 o.p. (ISBN 0-15-662340-4, VoyB). HarBraceJ.

Mystery of the Scowling Boy. Phyllis A. Whitney. LC 72-7272. 192p. (gr. 5-9). 1973. 5.95 o.s.i. (ISBN 0-664-32523-8, Westminster). Westminster John Knox.

Mystery of the Sea Horse. Lee Falk. (Phantom Ser.: No. 1). 1973. pap. 0.75 o.p. (ISBN 0-380-01422-X, 15867). Avon.

Mystery of the Sexes. Francis H. Buzzacott. (Illus.). 183p. 1914. pap. 13.95 o.s.i. (ISBN 0-88697-015-6). Life Science.

Mystery of the Silver Tag. Florence P. Heide & Sylvia Van Clief. LC 75-188429. (Spotlight Club Mysteries Ser.). (Illus.). 128p. (gr. 3-7). 1972. PLB 8.95 o.p. (ISBN 0-8075-5387-5). A Whitman.

Mystery of the Stolen Painting. Ivan Kusan. Tr. by Drenka Willen. LC 74-24324. (Illus.). 256p. (gr. 5 up). 1975. 7.95 o.p. (ISBN 0-15-243353-8, 15-243353, HJ). HarBraceJ.

Mystery of the Tolling Bell. Carolyn Keene. (Nancy Drew Ser.: Vol. 23). (Illus.). 192p. (gr. 4-7). 1973. Repr. 4.50 o.p. (ISBN 0-448-09523-8, G&D); PLB 3.29 o.p. (ISBN 0-448-19523-2). Putnam Pub Group.

Mystery of the Vanishing Visitor. Florence P. Heide & Roxanne Heide. (Spotlight Club Mystery: No. 2). (Illus.). (gr. 3-7). 1982. pap. 1.75 o.p. (ISBN 0-671-43977-4). Archway.

Mystery of the Whispering Voice. Florence P. Heide & Sylvia Van Clief. LC 74-8511. (Spotlight Club Mysteries Ser.). (Illus.). 128p. (gr. 3-7). 1974. PLB 8.95 o.p. (ISBN 0-8075-5389-1). A Whitman.

Mystery of the Woman in the Mirror. Teri Martini. LC 73-7901. (Illus.). 112p. (gr. 4-7). 1973. 4.75 o.s.i. (ISBN 0-664-32534-3, Westminster). Westminster John Knox.

Mystery of the Zebra Butterfly. Thomas F. Pursell. LC 77-74008. (Carolrhoda Mini-Mysteries Ser.). (Illus.). (gr. k-4). 1977. PLB 5.95 o.p. (ISBN 0-87614-090-8). Carolrhoda Bks.

Mystery of Transforming Love. Adrian Van Kaam. 12.95 o.p. (ISBN 0-87193-182-6). Dimension Bks.

Mystery of Wealth: Political Economy, Its Development & Impact on World Events. John Hutton. LC 78-13743. 412p. 1979. 44.95 o.p. (ISBN 0-470-26515-9). Halsted Pr.

Mystery Picture Puzzles. Anthony Tallarico. (Magic Answer Bks.). (Illus.). 64p. (gr. 3-7). 1984. pap. 2.95 o.s.i. (ISBN 0-671-44923-0). Wanderer Bks.

Mystery Religions. Samuel Angus. 1967. 10.00 o.p. (ISBN 0-8216-0123-7, Pub. by Univ Bks). Carol Pub Group.

Mystery Solved. Dorothy Martin. (Peggy Ser.: No. 4). (gr. 7). 1985. pap. 3.50 o.p. (ISBN 0-8024-8304-6). Moody.

Mystery under the Big Top. Bonnie West. LC 81-68852. (Carolrhoda Mini-Mysteries Ser.). (Illus.). 32p. (gr. 1-4). 1982. PLB 5.95 o.p. (ISBN 0-87614-175-0). Carolrhoda Bks.

Mystery Walk. Robert R. McCammon. LC 82-15419. 396p. 1983. 13.95 o.s.i. (ISBN 0-03-061832-0). H Holt & Co.

Mystery Waters of Tonbridge Wells. Teri Martini. LC 74-28313. (Illus.). (gr. 5 up). 1975. 5.75 o.s.i. (ISBN 0-664-32565-3, Westminster). Westminster John Knox.

Mystic Life of Merlin. R. J. Stewart. 256p. 1987. pap. 11.95 o.p. (ISBN 1-85063-042-9, 30429, Ark Paperbks). Routledge Chapman & Hall.

Mystic Mandrake. C. J. Thompson. LC 74-19199. (Illus.). 266p. 1975. Repr. of 1934 ed. 37.00x o.p. (ISBN 0-8103-4138-7). Gale.

Mystic Poet: Biography-Poetry-Lyrics of a Mysterious Man. Donald R. Tate & Leora B. Tate. 1979. 6.00 o.p. (ISBN 0-682-49467-4). Exposition-Phoenix.

Mystic Rose: A Study of Primitive Marriage & of Primitive Thought in Its Bearing on Marriage, 2 Vols. rev. & enl. ed. Ernest Crawley. Ed. by Theodore Besterman. LC 72-164193. 772p. 1971. Repr. of 1927 ed. 47.00x o.p. (ISBN 0-8103-3781-9). Gale.

Mystic Spiral: Journey of the Soul. Jill Purce. (Art & the Cosmos Ser). (Illus.). 1974. pap. 4.95 o.p. (ISBN 0-380-01499-8, 18739). Avon.

Mystic with the Healing Hands: The Life of Olga Worrall. Edwina Cerutti. LC 75-9317. 1977. pap. 6.95i o.p. (ISBN 0-06-061357-2, RD 244). HarpR.

Mystical Poems. Gaye de Windt. 104p. 1985. 8.00 o.p. (ISBN 0-682-40209-5). Exposition-Phoenix.

Mysticism. Sven S. Hartman & C. M. Edsman. (Illus.). 258p. (Orig.). 1970. pap. text ed. 16.95x o.p. (Pub. by Almqvist & Wiksell). Coronet Bks.

Mysticism of Sound. Hazrat Inayat Khan. (Sufi Message of Hazrat Inayat Khan Ser.: Vol. 2). 262p. 1979. 14.95 o.s.i. (ISBN 90-6077-569-4, Pub. by Servire BV Netherlands). Hunter Hse.

Mysticism of William Law. George Clarkson. 1980. 18.75 o.p. (ISBN 0-227-67838-9). Attic Pr.

Mysticism, Psychology & Oedipus. Israel Regardie et al. LC 85-81908. 96p. (Orig.). 1986. pap. 6.95 o.s.i. (ISBN 0-941404-38-2). Falcon Pr AZ.

Myth, Allegory, & Gospel. Ed. by John W. Montgomery. LC 74-1358. Orig. Title: Names & Titles of Christ. 160p. 1974. pap. 5.95 o.p. (ISBN 0-87123-358-4, 210358). Bethany Hse.

Myth & Cult Among Primitive Peoples. Adolf E. Jensen. LC 63-20909. 1963. lib. bdg. 10.00x o.s.i. (ISBN 0-226-39823-4). U of Chicago Pr.

Myth & History in Revelation: The Book of Revelation. John M. Court. LC 79-16586. 1980. 6.49 o.p. (ISBN 0-8042-0346-6, John Knox). Westminster John Knox.

Myth & the American Experience, Vol. 2. 2nd ed. Nicholas Cords & Patrick Gerster. 1978. pap. text ed. (ISBN 0-02-471880-7). Macmillan.

Myth, Faith & Hermeneutics. Mary E. Hansburg. 85p. (Orig.). 1985. pap. 9.95x o.p. (ISBN 0-932269-23-0). Wyndham Hall.

Myth of Evolution. Donald A. McWilliams. LC 73-88018. 1973. 3.95x o.p. (ISBN 0-916434-08-7). Plycon Pr.

Myth of Evolution. Louise Thomas. LC 85-91013. (Illus.). 128p. 1985. 7.50 o.p. (ISBN 0-682-40231-1). Exposition-Phoenix.

Myth of Freedom. Chogyam Trungpa. 1976. pap. 7.95 o.p. (ISBN 0-394-73180-8). Random.

Myth of God Incarnate. Ed. by John Hick. LC 77-9965. 224p. 1978. pap. 7.95 o.s.i. (ISBN 0-664-24178-6, Westminster). Westminster John Knox.

Myth of Senility: The Truth about the Brain & Aging. Robin M. Henig. 330p. 1985. pap. 14.95 o.p. (ISBN 0-673-24831-3). Am Assn Retire.

Myth of Tantalus: A Scaffolding for an Ontological Personality Theory. Shlomo G. Shoham. (Illus.). 1979. 39.50x o.p. (ISBN 0-7022-1208-3). U of Queensland Pr.

Myth of the All-Destructive Fury of the Thirty Years' War. Robert R. Ergang. 1956. stiff, printed wrappers 7.50x o.p. (ISBN 0-686-17408-9). R S Barnes.

Myth of the Great Depression 1873-1896. 2nd ed. S. B. Saul. (Studies in Economic & Social History). (Illus.). 83p. 1985. pap. text ed. 7.95x o.p. (ISBN 0-333-04972-1). Humanities.

Myth of the Great Depression 1873-1896. 2nd, rev. ed. S. B. Saul. (Studies in Economic & Social History). (Illus.). 1985. pap. text ed. 9.95 o.p. (ISBN 0-333-40212-X, 80541, Co-Pub. by Macmillan Pubs UK). Humanities.

Myth of the Middle Class: Notes on Affluence & Equality. Richard Parker. LC 76-167291. (Illus.). 288p. 1972. 7.95 o.p. (ISBN 0-87140-539-3). Liveright.

Myth of the OPEC Cartel: The Role of Saudi Arabia. Ali D. Johany. LC 80-40959. 107p. 1980. 63.95x o.p. (ISBN 0-471-27864-5, Pub. by Wiley-Interscience). Wiley.

Myth of the Twentieth Century. Alfred Rosenberg. Tr. by James B. Whisker from Ger. LC 82-60770. Orig. Title: Der Mythos des 20. Jahrhunderts. 454p. 1982. 15.00 o.p. (ISBN 0-911038-47-7). Noontide.

Myth, Symbol & Culture. Ed. by Clifford Geertz. (Daedalus Ser., 1973). 224p. 1974. 9.95x o.p. (ISBN 0-393-04254-5); pap. 6.95x o.p. (ISBN 0-393-09409-X). Norton.

Myth: Truth of God Incarnate. Ed. by Durstan R. McDonald et al. Dennis Nineham & Roy Sano. LC 79-91091. 122p. (Orig.). 1979. pap. 4.95 o.p. (ISBN 0-8192-1266-0). Morehouse Pub.

Mythago Wood. Robert Holdstock. 256p. 1985. 14.95 o.p. (ISBN 0-87795-761-4, Arbor Hse). Morrow.

Mythic West in Twentieth-Century America. Robert G. Athearn. (History Book Club Ser.). (Illus.). xii, 324p. 1988. pap. 9.95 o.p. (ISBN 0-7006-0377-8). U Pr of Ks.

Mythical Monsters. Charles Gould. LC 74-75474. 416p. 1969. Repr. of 1886 ed. 37.00 o.p. (ISBN 0-8103-3834-3). Gale.

Mythmakers. Mary Barnard. LC 66-20061. 213p. 1979. 16.95 o.p. (ISBN 0-8214-0024-X); pap. 6.50 o.p. (ISBN 0-8214-0562-4). Ohio U Pr.

Mythologiae. Natalis Comes. LC 75-27853. (Renaissance & the Gods Ser.: Vol. 11). (Illus.). 1976. Repr. of 1567 ed. lib. bdg. 88.00 o.p. (ISBN 0-8240-2060-X). Garland Pub.

Mythological Astronomy of the Ancients Demonstrated, Pt. 1. Samson A. Mackey. Bd. with Pt. 2. Key to Urania. LC 73-84043. (Secret Doctrine Reference Ser.). 380p. 1973. Repr. of 1822 ed. 17.00 o.p. (ISBN 0-913510-06-8). Wizards.

Mythologies of the World: A Concise Encyclopedia. Rhoda A. Hendricks. Ed. by Max S. Shapiro. (McGraw-Hill Paperbacks Ser.). 240p. 1981. pap. text ed. 5.95 o.p. (ISBN 0-07-056421-3). McGraw.

Mythology. Jane E. Harrison. LC 25-821. 1963. pap. 1.95 o.p. (ISBN 0-15-663975-0, H024). HarBraceJ.

Mythology & the Renaissance Tradition in English Poetry. rev. ed. Douglas Bush. 1963. pap. 3.45x o.p. (ISBN 0-393-00187-3, Norton Lib). Norton.

Mythology of Middle Earth. Ruth S. Noel. 1978. pap. 3.95 o.p. (ISBN 0-395-27208-4). HM.

Mythology of Middle Earth. Ruth S. Noel. 1977. 7.95 o.p. (ISBN 0-395-25006-4). HM.

Myths & Dreams. Edward Clodd. LC 70-159918. 264p. 1971. Repr. of 1891 ed. 40.00x o.p. (ISBN 0-8103-3776-2). Gale.

Myths & Legends of Ancient Rome. McLeish. (Illus.). 336p. 1987. text ed. 25.95 o.p. (ISBN 0-582-00288-5). Longman.

Myths & Legends of Australia. A. W. Reed. LC 72-779. (Illus.). 1973. 7.50 o.s.i. (ISBN 0-8008-5463-2). Taplinger.

Myths & Legends of China. Repr. of 1987 ed. 14.95 o.p. (MYLECH). China Bks.

Myths & Legends of Our New Possessions & Protectorate. Charles M. Skinner. LC 73-140399. 358p. 1971. Repr. of 1900 ed. 43.00x o.p. (ISBN 0-8103-3634-0). Gale.

Myths & Legends of the Torres Strait. Ed. by Margaret Lawrie. LC 73-163219. (Illus.). 1972. 25.00 o.s.i. (ISBN 0-8008-5464-0). Taplinger.

Myths & Realities of the Energy Shortage: Contrivance by the Companies or Bungling by the Government. Ray E. Storms. 1974. 6.95 o.p. (ISBN 0-682-48024-X, Banner). Exposition-Phoenix.

Myths, Fables, & Legends for the Young & Old. W. Edger Vinacke. 192p. (gr. 4 up). 1985. 10.00 o.p. (ISBN 0-682-40178-1). Exposition-Phoenix.

Myths of Information: Technology & Post-Industrial Culture. Ed. by Kathleen Woodward. LC 80-23653. (Theories of Contemporary Culture Ser.). (Illus.). 282p. 1980. 20.00x o.p. (ISBN 0-930956-12-5); pap. 7.95x o.p. (ISBN 0-930956-13-3). Ind U Pr.

Myths of the Hindus & Buddhists. A. K. Coomaraswamy & M. E. Noble. (Illus.). 15.25 o.p. (ISBN 0-8446-1896-9). Peter Smith.

Myths of the New World: A Treatise on the Symbolism & Mythology of the Red Race in America. Daniel G. Brinton. LC 74-1038. 358p. 1974. Repr. of 1896 ed. 30.00x o.p. (ISBN 0-8103-3959-5). Gale.

MZ 150 & 250 '69 - '79. Stewart Wilkins. (Owners Workshop Manuals Ser.: No. 253). 1979. 11.50 o.p. (ISBN 0-85696-546-4). Haynes Pubns.

M68000 8-, 16-, 32-Bit Microprocessor's Programmer's Reference Manual. 5th ed. Motorola, Inc. Staff. 240p. 1986. pap. 26.95 o.p. (ISBN 0-13-541475-X). P-H.

M6816 32-Bit Microprocessor: Programmer's Reference Manual. 4th ed. Motorola, Inc. Staff. (Illus.). 240p. 1984. pap. 18.95 o.p. (ISBN 0-13-566795-X). P-H.

N

N-Benzoylphenylhydroxylamine & Its Analogues. A. K. Majumdar. 224p. 1972. 70.00 o.p. (ISBN 0-08-016754-3). Pergamon.

N by E. Rockwell Kent. LC 77-13530. (Illus.). 1978. Repr. of 1930 ed. 25.00x o.p. (ISBN 0-8195-5018-3). Wesleyan U Pr.

N. C. Outdoor Drama: Spanish Autumn. C. D. Huneycutt. 100p. 1985. pap. 4.80 o.p. (ISBN 0-915153-18-1). Gold Star Pr.

N. C. Writers & Writing: Essays. Ed. & intro. by C. D. Huneycutt. (Writer's Ser. 1985). 80p. (Orig.). 1987. pap. 4.80x o.p. (ISBN 0-915153-21-1). Gold Star Pr.

N. C. Writers & Writing: Essays. Ed. by C. D. Huneycutt. (Writer's Ser. 1986). 80p. (Orig.). 1987. pap. 4.80x o.p. (ISBN 0-915153-23-8). Gold Star Pr.

N. F. S. Grundtvig: Selected Writings. Ed. by Johannes Knudsen. LC 76-7873. 192p. 1976. pap. 1.50 o.p. (ISBN 0-8006-1238-8, 1-1238, Fortress). Augsburg Fortress.

N M R & Relaxation of Molecules Absorbed on Solids see N M R of Molecules Oriented in Electric Fields.

N M R of Molecules Oriented in Electric Fields. C. W. Hilbers & C. MacLean. Bd. with N M R & Relaxation of Molecules Absorbed on Solids. H. Pfeifer. (N M R Basic Principles & Progress, Vol. 7). (Illus.). 1972. 38.00 o.p. (ISBN 0-387-05687-4). Springer-Verlag.

N M R Spectroscopy of Annulenes. Ed. by F. Boschke. LC 51-5497. (Topics in Current Chemistry: Vol. 16, Pt. 2). (Illus.). 1971. pap. 55.50 o.p. (ISBN 0-387-05299-2). Springer-Verlag.

N. P. D. E. S. Compliance Inspection Manual. Environmental Protection Agency Staff. 170p. 1985. pap. 47.00 o.p. (ISBN 0-86587-048-9). Gov Insts.

N. U. R. S. E. Nursing Undergraduate Review for Self Evaluation. Sandra Kirby. (Illus.). 300p. 1982. text ed. 19.95 o.p. (ISBN 0-86792-002-5, Pub by Adis Pr Australia). Year Bk Med.

N. Y. Gold. (Illus.). 376p. 1987. 45.00 o.s.i. (ISBN 0-9618685-0-3). Am Showcase.

N. Y. Times Natural Foods Cookbook. Jean Hewitt. 1976. pap. 3.95 o.p. (ISBN 0-380-00951-X, 65474-1). Avon.

NA, K-Atpase: Structure & Kinetics. Ed. by J. C. Skou & J. G. Norby. 1979. 99.00 o.p. (ISBN 0-12-647650-0). Acad Pr.

Na-Linked Transport of Organic Solutes: The Coupling Between Electrolyte & Nonelectrolyte Transport in Cells, Proceedings. International Congress of Physiological Sciences, Satellite Symposium, 1971. Ed. by E. Heinz. LC 72-80293. (Illus.). 205p. 1972. pap. 26.00 o.p. (ISBN 0-387-05849-4). Springer-Verlag.

NAACP: Triumphs of a Pressure Group 1909-1980. Warren St. James. (Illus.). 288p. 1980. 14.95 o.p. (ISBN 0-682-49605-7, University). Exposition-Phoenix.

Nabis: Their History & Their Art, 1888-1896. George Mauner. LC 77-94708. (Outstanding Dissertations in the Fine Arts Ser.). 495p. 1978. lib. bdg. 55.00 o.p. (ISBN 0-8240-3240-3). Garland Pub.

Nabokov's Dozen. Vladimir Nabokov. 1983. pap. 1.95 o.p. (ISBN 0-380-01352-5, 58370-4, Bard). Avon.

Nacar, the White Deer. Elizabeth B. De Trevino. LC 63-20019. (Illus.). 160p. (gr. 4 up). 1963. 3.95 o.p. (ISBN 0-374-35478-2). FS&G.

Nacht Uber dem Tal see Darkness over the Valley.

Nadia: A Case of Extraordinary Drawing Ability in an Autistic Child. Lorna Selfe. LC 78-21714. 137p. 1979. pap. 5.95 o.p. (ISBN 0-15-665320-6, Harv). HarBraceJ.

NAFSA Directory of Institutions & Individuals in International Educational Exchange, 1985. rev. ed. National Association for Foreign Students Affairs Staff. 147p. (Orig.). 1987. pap. text ed. 25.50 o.p. (ISBN 0-912207-04-3). NAFSA Washington.

NAFSA Directory 1985. 126p. 25.00 o.p. (ISBN 0-317-36628-9). NAFSA Washington.

NAGWS Softball Guide 1987-89. 1987. 3.95 o.p. (ISBN 0-88314-354-2). AAHPERD.

NAGWS Tennis Guide 86-88. 1986. 4.50 o.p. (ISBN 0-88314-327-5). AAHPERD.

NAGWS Volleyball Guide. 1988. write for info. o.p. (ISBN 0-88314-399-2). AAHPERD.

Nails: The Inside Story of an Amazin Season. Len Dykstra & Marty Nobel. LC 87-5225. 240p. 1987. 15.95 o.p. (ISBN 0-385-24253-0). Doubleday.

Naked Angels: The Lives & Literature of the Beat Generation. John Tytell. LC 75-22206. 274p. 1986. pap. 8.95 o.s.i. (ISBN 0-394-62179-4, Ever). Grove.

Naked-Eye Astronomy. Patrick Moore. (Illus.). 1966. 8.95 o.p. (ISBN 0-393-06303-8). Norton.

Naked Is the Best Disguise: My Life As a Stripper. Lauri Lewin. (Pandora Autobiography Ser.). 208p. 1986. pap. 8.95 o.p. (ISBN 0-86358-077-7, 80777). Routledge Chapman & Hall.

Naked Island. Russell Braddon. LC 82-13375. (Illus.). 288p. 1982. pap. 8.95 o.p. (ISBN 0-689-70629-4, 282, Atheneum). Macmillan.

Naked Lunch. William S. Burroughs. 1969. pap. 6.95 o.p. (ISBN 0-394-17108-X, B115, BC). Grove.

Naked Range. Steven C. Lawrence. Orig. Title: Thruway West. 1976. pap. 0.95 o.p. (ISBN 0-685-69152-7, LB354NK, Pub. by Leisure Bks CT). Dorchester Pub Co.

Naked Soul of Iceberg Slim. Robert Beck. 1988. pap. 2.95 o.p. (ISBN 0-87067-713-6). Holloway.

Naked Sword. F. W. Kenyon. 1975. pap. 1.50 o.p. (ISBN 0-685-59191-3, LB308, Pub. by Leisure Bks CT). Dorchester Pub Co.

Naked Sword. F. W. Kenyon. 1979. pap. 1.95 o.p. (ISBN 0-505-51341-2, Pub. by Tower Bks). Dorchester Pub Co.

Naked to Naked Goes. Robert Flanagan. 200p. 1986. 14.95 o.p. (ISBN 0-684-18671-3). Scribner.

NALCO Water Handbook. NALCO Chemical Company Staff. (Illus.). 1979. text ed. 52.00 o.p. (ISBN 0-07-045868-5). McGraw.

Name Authority Control for Card Catalogs in the General Libraries. (Contributions to Librarianship Ser.: No. 5). 1981. pap. 10.00 o.p. (ISBN 0-930214-07-2). U TX Austin Gen Libs.

Name for Number Nine. Pete Kersten & Rick Kersten. (Kersten Brothers' Critter Tales Picture Bks.). 32p. (gr. k-3). 1986. 7.95 o.p. (ISBN 0-316-49003-2). Little.

Name Index to the Library of Congress Collection of Mormon Diaries. Meirill Library Staff. (Western Text Society Ser.: Vol. 1, No. 2). 391p. (Orig.). 1971. pap. 12.95 o.p. (ISBN 0-87421-045-3). Utah St U Pr.

Name It & Claim It Game. Helen Hadsell. 1972. 2.50 o.p. (ISBN 0-87516-119-7). DeVorss.

Names & Faces of Heroes. Reynolds Price. LC 63-12414. 1973. pap. 2.95 o.p. (ISBN 0-689-70364-3, 201, Atheneum). Macmillan.

Names & Titles of Christ see Myth, Allegory, & Gospel.

Names, Designations, & Appelations see Persian Words in English.

Names of a Hare in English. David P. Young. LC 79-4704. (Pitt Poetry Ser.). 1979. 15.95x o.p. (ISBN 0-8229-3406-X); pap. 6.95 o.p. (ISBN 0-8229-5311-0). U of Pittsburgh Pr.

Names of Countries. 8th rev. ed. (FAO Terminology Bulletin: No. 20). 120p. (Eng., Fr., Span. & Chinese.). 1986. pap. text ed. 9.75 o.p. (ISBN 92-5-002391-X, F2914, FAO). UNIPUB.

Names of Countries & Their Capital Cities Including Adjectives of Nationality & Currency Units. (Terminology Bulletins: No. 20, Rev. 6). 64p. (Eng., Fr. & Span.). 1982. pap. 7.50 o.p. (ISBN 92-5-001242-X, F2357, FAO). UNIPUB.

Names of Places in a Transferred Sense in English: A Sematological Study. Carl J. Efvergren. LC 68-17922. 136p. 1969. Repr. of 1909 ed. 35.00x o.p. (ISBN 0-8103-3233-7). Gale.

Names of the Land: Cape Cod, Nantucket, Martha's Vineyard & the Elizabeth Islands. Eugene Green & William L. Sachse. LC 82-82167. (Illus.). 192p. (Orig.). 1983. pap. 8.95 o.p. (ISBN 0-87106-974-1). Globe Pequot.

Namibia. 1981. 1.50 o.p. (ISBN 0-910082-05-7). Am Fr Serv Comm.

Namibia: Political & Economic Prospects. Ed. by Robert I. Rotberg. LC 81-48672. 144p. 1982. 26.00x o.p. (ISBN 0-669-05531-X). Lexington Bks.

Namibia: Reclaiming the People's Health. Ed. by Tim Lobstein. 1986. Repr. of 1984 ed. 7.00 o.p. (ISBN 0-317-56002-6). Africa Fund.

Namibia: The Facts. 98p. 1980. 4.00 o.p. (ISBN 0-317-36666-1). Africa Fund.

Namibia: The Ravages of War. Barbara Konig. 60p. 1983. 3.00 o.p. (ISBN 0-317-36662-9). Africa Fund.

Namibia: Transforming a Wasted Land. Richard Moorsom. 114p. 1982. 5.00 o.p. (ISBN 0-317-36663-7). Africa Fund.

Namkwa: Life Among the Bushmen. H. J. Heinz & Marshall Lee. 1979. 10.95 o.p. (ISBN 0-395-27611-X). HM.

NAMRC Eight: Nineteen Eighty Proceedings. LC 76-646280. (Illus.). 429p. 1980. 65.00 o.p. (ISBN 0-87263-105-2). SME.

NAMRC Seven: Nineteen Seventy-Nine Proceedings. LC 79-63779. (Illus.). 1979. 65.00 o.p. (ISBN 0-87263-037-4). SME.

NAMRC 1985 XIII: Proceedings. Society of Manufacturing Engineers Staff. 1985. 70.00 o.p. (ISBN 0-87263-186-9). SME.

Nan: The Life of an Irish Travelling Woman. Sharon Gmelch. 239p. 1986. 15.45x o.p. (ISBN 0-393-02331-1). Norton.

Nana. Delcorta, pseud. Tr. by Victoria Reiter from Fr. (Gorodish-Alba Ser.: No. 2). 128p. 1984. 9.50 o.s.i. (ISBN 0-671-49210-1). Summit Bks.

Nancy Astor. Anthony Masters. 256p. 1981. text ed. 10.95 o.p. (ISBN 0-07-040784-3). McGraw.

Nancy Drew & the Hardy Boys Super Sleuths: Seven New Mysteries. Carolyn Keene & Franklin W. Dixon. (Illus.). 192p. (Orig.). (gr. 3-7). 1981. 8.95 o.p. (ISBN 0-671-44429-8); pap. 3.50 o.p. (ISBN 0-671-43375-X). Wanderer Bks.

Nancy Mitford: A Memoir. Harold Acton. 1986. 16.95 o.p. (ISBN 0-317-53137-9, Large Print Bks). G K Hall.

Nanette. Edwards Park. 1977. 9.95 o.p. (ISBN 0-393-05618-X). Norton.

Nannie Mama. Hazel L. Worthington. 144p. 1986. 7.75 o.p. (ISBN 0-8062-2815-6). Carlton.

Nanny Connection: How to Find & Keep a Perfect Nanny. O. Robin Sweet & Mary-Ellen Siegel. LC 86-47701. 224p. (Orig.). 1987. 14.95 o.p. (ISBN 0-689-11820-1, Atheneum); pap. 9.95 o.p. (ISBN 0-689-11865-1, Atheneum). Macmillan.

Nantucket & Other New England Cooking. Nancy Hawkins et al. 371p. 1986. pap. 12.95 o.p. (ISBN 0-8038-5046-8, Dist. by Kampmann & Co.). Hastings.

Nantucket Lightship Baskets. 3rd ed. Katherine Seeler & Edgar Seeler. (Illus.). 127p. 1982. 15.00x o.p. (ISBN 0-9600596-3-6); 5 or more copies 9.00 o.p. (ISBN 0-686-85860-3). Deermouse.

Nanuck the Polar Bear. (Zoo Babies Ser.). 16p. (gr. k-6). 1982. pap. 1.25 o.p. (ISBN 0-8249-8032-8). Ideals.

Naomikong Point Site & the Dimensions of Laurel in the Lake Superior Region. Donald E. Janzen. (Anthropological Papers: No. 36). (Illus.). 1968. pap. 3.00x o.p. (ISBN 0-932206-34-4). U Mich Mus Anthro.

Nap Master. William Kotzwinkle. LC 78-12178. (Illus.). 32p. 1979. 7.95 o.p. (ISBN 0-15-256704-6, HJ). HarBraceJ.

Nap Master. William Kotzwinkle. LC 78-12178. (Illus.). (gr. k-3). 1979. pap. 2.50 o.p. (ISBN 0-15-665325-7, VoyB). HarBraceJ.

Napa Valley Corporate Park Napa, California. (Panel Advisory Service Report). 72p. 1982. pap. 10.00 o.p. (ISBN 0-317-06730-3, N-17). Urban Land.

Napa Wine Country. LC 75-16054. (Illus., Photos & Text by Earl Roberge). 1975. pap. 12.95 o.p. Gr Arts Ctr Pub.

Naplo: 1945-1957. 2nd ed. Sandor Marai. LC 68-21909. 1968. 15.00 o.p. (ISBN 0-911050-37-X). Occidental.

Napoleon. Patricia Kindle & Susan Finney. (Gifted Learning Ser.). (Illus.). 64p. (gr. 4-8). 1985. 6.95 o.p. (ISBN 0-86653-296-X). Good Apple.

Napoleon. Anthony Masters. (Great Leaders Ser.). (Illus.). 69p. 1981. text ed. 7.95 o.p. (ISBN 0-07-040785-1). McGraw.

Napoleon & the French Empire. David Sylvester. Ed. by Marjorie Reeves. (Then & There Ser.). (Illus.). 96p. (Orig.). (gr. 7-12). 1978. pap. text ed. 4.75 o.p. (ISBN 0-582-20546-8). Longman.

Napoleon of Notting Hill. G. K. Chesterton. LC 77-99307. 228p. 1978. pap. 3.45 o.p. (ISBN 0-8091-2096-8). Paulist Pr.

Napoleon Symphony. Anthony Burgess. 384p. 1980. pap. 4.95 o.p. (ISBN 0-393-00964-5). Norton.

Napoleonic Ideas. Louis Napoleon, 3rd. Ed. & intro. by Brison D. Gooch. 1967. lib. bdg. 17.50x o.p. (ISBN 0-88307-218-1). Gannon.

Napoleonic Wars & Their Impact on Factor Returns & Output Growth in England: 1793-1895. Glenn R. Hueckel. LC 84-46003. (British Economic History Ser.). 216p. 1985. lib. bdg. 25.00 o.p. (ISBN 0-8240-6683-9). Garland Pub.

Napoleon's Diplomatic Service. Edward A. Whitcomb. LC 78-74846. (Illus.). xiii, 218p. 1979. 23.75 o.p. (ISBN 0-8223-0421-X). Duke.

Napoleon's Glands & Other Ventures in Biohistory. Arno Karlen. 288p. 1984. 15.95 o.p. (ISBN 0-316-48319-2). Little.

Napoleon's Invasion of Russia in 1812. Eugene Tarle. LC 77-120670. 1970. Repr. lib. bdg. 27.50x o.p. (ISBN 0-374-97758-5, Octagon). Hippocrene Bks.

Napoleon's Peninsular Marshals: A Reassessment. Richard Humble. LC 74-3874. (Illus.). 256p. 1974. 10.95 o.s.i. (ISBN 0-8008-5465-9). Taplinger.

Narcissa. Julie Penny. 1985. 16.95 o.p. (ISBN 0-87795-585-9, Arbor Hse). Morrow.

Narcissa. Julie Penny. 324p. 1985. pap. 3.75 o.p. (ISBN 0-931773-42-3). Critics Choice Paper.

Narcissa Whitman. Opal S. Allen. (Illus.). 1959. 12.95 o.p. (ISBN 0-8323-0049-7). Binford-Metropolitan.

Narcotic Addiction in Britain & America: The Impact of Public Policy. Edwin M. Schur. LC 75-22646. 1977. Repr. of 1962 ed. lib. bdg. 22.50x o.p. (ISBN 0-8371-8360-X, SCNA). Greenwood.

Narcotics & Drug Addiction. Erich Hesse. (ISBN 0-8022-0713-8). Philos Lib.

Nargun & the Stars. Patricia Wrightson. LC 73-85323. (gr. 4-7). 1974. 6.95 o.p. (ISBN 0-689-30432-3, Atheneum). Macmillan.

Narration: Four Lectures. Gertrude Stein. LC 36-27069. (Illus.). 1969. Repr. of 1935 ed. lib. bdg. 24.75 o.p. (ISBN 0-8371-0939-6, STFL). Greenwood.

Narrative & Its Discontents: Problems of Closure in the Traditional Novel. D. A. Miller. LC 80-8565. 320p. 1981. 28.00 o.p. (ISBN 0-691-06459-8). Princeton U Pr.

Narrative Elements & Religious Meaning. Wesley A. Kort. LC 75-15257. 128p. 1975. pap. 0.50 o.p. (ISBN 0-8006-1433-X, Fortress). Augsburg Fortress.

Narrative Endings: Narrative Endings. Nineteenth-Century Fiction Staff. 1978. pap. 7.95x o.p. (ISBN 0-520-03783-9). U of Cal Pr.

Narrative of an Expedition Against the Revolted Negroes of Surinam. John G. Stedman. Ed. by R. A. Van Lier. LC 70-181361. (Illus.). 512p. 1972. 30.00x o.p. (ISBN 0-87023-093-X). U of Mass Pr.

Narrative of Arthur Gordon Pym. Edgar Allan Poe. (American Century Ser.). 198p. 1984. pap. 6.25 o.p. (ISBN 0-8090-0029-6). Hill & Wang.

Narrative of the Life & Adventures of Henry Bibb, an American Slave. Henry Bibb. LC 76-84686. (Illus.). Repr. of 1850 ed. 35.00x o.p. (ISBN 0-8371-1267-2, BIH&, Pub. by Negro U Pr). Greenwood.

Narratives of Early Carolina, Sixteen Fifty to Seventeen Eight. Ed. by Alexander S. Salley, Jr. (Original Narratives). (Illus.). 388p. 1967. Repr. of 1911 ed. 21.50x o.p. (ISBN 0-06-480758-4). B&N Imports.

Narratives of Early Maryland, Sixteen Thirty-Three to Sixteen Eighty-Four. Ed. by Clayton C. Hall. (Original Narratives). 454p. 1967. Repr. of 1910 ed. 21.50x o.p. (ISBN 0-06-480346-5). B&N Imports.

Narrow Boat Painting: A History & Description of the English Narrow Boats' Traditional Paintwork. A. J. Lewery. LC 74-81074. 1975. 24.95 o.p. (ISBN 0-7153-6771-4). David & Charles.

Narrow Gauge into the Eighties. G. T. Heavyside. LC 79-56067. (Illus.). 96p. 1980. 20.95 o.p. (ISBN 0-7153-7979-8). David & Charles.

Narrow Lane. Meher Baba. Ed. by William Le Page. 148p. 1979. pap. 3.95 o.p. (ISBN 0-913078-39-5). Sheriar Pr.

Narrow Lumbar Canal: Radiologic Signs & Surgery. A. Wackenheim & E. Babin. LC 79-13720. (Illus.). 1980. 110.00 o.p. (ISBN 0-387-09443-1). Springer-Verlag.

Narrow Margin. Richard Fleischer. (RKO CLassic Screenplay Ser.). 1985. pap. 8.95 o.p. (ISBN 0-8044-6135-X). Ungar.

Narrow Rooms. James Purdy. LC 77-90667. 1977. 9.95 o.p. (ISBN 0-87795-183-7, Arbor Hse). Morrow.

NARUC Convention Manual. 98p. 1980. 5.00 o.p. (ISBN 0-318-15010-7). NARUC.

NARUC Convention Manual. 98p. 1980. 5.00 o.p. NARUC.

NAS Thinline Bible. 1983. Brown cloth edition. text ed. 17.95 o.p. (ISBN 0-8024-6283-9); Brown. deluxe ed. 29.95 o.p. (ISBN 0-8024-6281-2); Burgundy. deluxe ed. 29.95 o.p. (ISBN 0-8024-6282-0). Moody.

NAS Thinline Bible. 1985. deluxe ed. 39.95 burgundy leather o.p. (ISBN 0-8024-6286-3); deluxe ed. 39.95 brown leather o.p. (ISBN 0-8024-6284-7). Moody.

Nashville Convention: Southern Movement for Unity, 1849 to 1850. Thelma Jennings. LC 80-12917. 1980. 16.95x o.p. (ISBN 0-87870-097-8). Memphis St Univ.

Nashville Memories: Thirty-Two Historic Postcards. Ed. by James A. Hoobler. LC 82-23841. (Illus.). 16p. 1983. pap. 3.95 o.p. (ISBN 0-87049-385-X). U of Tenn Pr.

Nashville: Music City, U. S. A. John Lomax, III. (Illus.). 224p. 1985. 29.95 o.p. (ISBN 0-8109-1345-3). Abrams.

Nasir-I Khusraw: Forty Poems from the Divan. Ed. by Seyyed H. Nasr. Tr. by Peter L. Wilson & Gholam R. Aavani. 1978. write for info. o.p. (ISBN 0-87773-730-4, Great Eastern). Shambhala Pubns.

Nasser: The Rise to Power. Joachim Joesten. LC 74-3752. (Illus.). 224p. 1974. Repr. of 1960 ed. lib. bdg. 22.50x o.p. (ISBN 0-8371-7471-6, JONA). Greenwood.

NASSP Advisory List of National Contests & Activities: Annual 1985-1986. 1985. pap. 2.50 o.p. (ISBN 0-88210-130-7). Natl Assn Principals.

Nat Divided. (Our Nations Heritage Ser.). Date not set. (ISBN 0-07-375422-6). McGraw.

Nat Expands. (Our Nations Heritage Ser.). Date not set. (ISBN 0-07-375421-8). McGraw.

Nat Heri-Dis Mod. (Our Nations Heritage Ser.). Date not set. (ISBN 0-07-375488-9). McGraw.

Nat Heri-Disp Divid. (Our Nations Heritage Ser.). Date not set. (ISBN 0-07-375489-7). McGraw.

Nat Herit 1. (Our Nations Heritage Ser.). Date not set. (ISBN 0-07-375441-2). McGraw.

Nat Herit 2. (Our Nations Heritage Ser.). Date not set. (ISBN 0-07-375442-0). McGraw.

Nat Heritage 1 B-CS. (Our Nations Heritage Ser.). Date not set. (ISBN 0-07-375463-3). McGraw.

Nat Heritage 1 Box. (Our Nations Heritage Ser.). Date not set. (ISBN 0-07-375485-4). McGraw.

Nat Heritage 2 B-CS. (Our Nations Heritage Ser.). Date not set. (ISBN 0-07-375464-1). McGraw.

Nat Heritage 2 Box. (Our Nations Heritage Ser.). Date not set. (ISBN 0-07-375486-2). McGraw.

Nat Hert-Disp Tray. (Our Nations Heritage Ser.). Date not set. McGraw.

Nat Launched Bd. (Our Nations Heritage Ser.). Date not set. (ISBN 0-07-375419-6). McGraw.

Nat Prosp. (Our Nations Heritage Ser.). Date not set. (ISBN 0-07-375427-7). McGraw.

Nat Tested. (Our Nations Heritage Ser.). Date not set. (ISBN 0-07-375420-X). McGraw.

Nat Turner's Slave Rebellion: Together with the Full Text of the So-Called "Confessions" of Nat Turner Made in Prison in 1831. Ed. by Herbert Aptheker. (AIMS Historical Ser: No. 2). 1966. text ed. 9.95x o.p. (ISBN 0-391-00437-9). Humanities.

Natalie: A Memoir by Her Sister. Lana Wood. 1986. 13.95 o.p. (ISBN 0-317-53138-7, Large Print Bks). G K Hall.

Natalie Dunn: World Roller Skating Champion. Gloria D. Miklowitz. LC 79-78524. (Illus.). (gr. 4-7). 1979. 2.95 o.p. (ISBN 0-15-256716-X, HJ). HarBraceJ.

Natalie Wood: A Biography in Photographs. Christopher Nickens. LC 85-31198. (Illus.). 208p. 1986. 15.95 o.s.i. (ISBN 0-385-23307-8, Dolp). Doubleday.

Natchez. Louise MacKendrick. (Orig.). 1977. pap. 1.75 o.p. (ISBN 0-505-51138-X, Pub. by Tower Bks). Dorchester Pub Co.

Nate the Great Stalks Stupidweed. Marjorie W. Sharmat. LC 85-30161. (Nate the Great Bks.). (Illus.). 48p. (gr. 1-4). 1986. 10.95 o.p. (ISBN 0-698-20626-6, Coward). Putnam Pub Group.

Nate's Lady. Bernadette Parkin. 1981. pap. 2.75 o.p. (ISBN 0-380-78204-9, 78204-9). Avon.

Nathanael West: A Comprehensive Bibliography. William White. LC 74-79149. (Serif Ser.: No. 32). (Illus.). 224p. 1975. 12.00x o.p. (ISBN 0-87338-157-2). Kent St U Pr.

Nathaniel. John Saul. 343p. 1985. lib. bdg. 14.95 o.p. (ISBN 0-8398-2891-8, Gregg). G K Hall.

Nathaniel Hawthorne & His Times. James R. Mellow. 672p. 1980. 19.95 o.p. (ISBN 0-395-27602-0). HM.

Nathaniel Hawthorne in His Times. James R. Mellow. 1982. pap. 10.95 o.p. (ISBN 0-395-32135-2). HM.

Nathaniel Lord Crewe, Bishop of Durham, 1674-1712, & His Diocese. Charles E. Whiting. (Church Historical Society London N. S. Ser.: No. 40). Repr. of 1940 ed. 60.00 o.p. (ISBN 0-8115-3163-5). Kraus Repr.

Nation & the Navy. Christopher Lloyd. LC 74-383. (Illus.). 314p. 1974. Repr. of 1961 ed. lib. bdg. 22.50x o.p. (ISBN 0-8371-7379-5, LLNN). Greenwood.

Nation-Building: A Review of Recent Comparative Research & a Select Bibliography of Analytical Studies. Stein Rokkan et al. (Current Sociology Series - La Sociologie Contemporaine: No. 19-3). 1973. pap. 7.20x o.p. (ISBN 90-2797-220-6). Mouton.

Nation Cornerstone. (Our Nations Heritage Ser.). Date not set. (ISBN 0-07-375397-1). McGraw.

Nation Divided. (Our Nations Heritage Ser.). Date not set. (ISBN 0-07-375401-3). McGraw.

Nation Expands. (Our Nations Heritage Ser.). Date not set. (ISBN 0-07-375400-5). McGraw.

Nation Is Launched. (Our Nations Heritage Ser.). Date not set. (ISBN 0-07-375398-X). McGraw.

Nation Is Tested. (Our Nations Heritage Ser.). Date not set. (ISBN 0-07-375399-8). McGraw.

Nation of Nations: The Ethnic Experience & the Racial Crisis. Ed. by Peter I. Rose. LC 81-40797. 366p. 1981. pap. text ed. 15.25 o.p. (ISBN 0-8191-1801-X). U Pr of Amer.

Nation of Pakistan. R. Kureishi. 1969. 29.00 o.p. (ISBN 0-08-013871-3); pap. 29.00 o.p. (ISBN 0-08-013870-5). Pergamon.

Nation of Sheep. William J. Lederer. (gr. 10 up). 1961. 6.95 o.p. (ISBN 0-393-05288-5). Norton.

Nation Prosperity. (Our Nations Heritage Ser.). Date not set. (ISBN 0-07-375406-4). McGraw.

Nation Transformed: The Creation of an Industrial Society. Ed. by Sigmund Diamond. LC 63-17876. (American Epochs Ser.). 1963. 10.00 o.p. (ISBN 0-8076-0247-7); pap. 4.95 o.p. (ISBN 0-8076-0395-3). Braziller.

National: A Library for the People, Nos. 1-26. 1969. Repr. of 1839 ed. lib. bdg. 20.50x o.p. (ISBN 0-8371-9209-9, NP00). Greenwood.

National Account Marketing Handbook. Ed. by Robert S. Rogers & V. B. Chamberlain, 3rd. 304p. 1981. 24.95 o.p. (ISBN 0-8144-5618-9). AMACOM.

National Air & Space Museum. C. D. Bryan. (Illus.). 1979. 60.00 o.p. (ISBN 0-8109-0666-X). Abrams.

National Anti-Slavery Standard Magazine, Vols. 1-30. Incl. Vol. 1-2. 165.00 (ISBN 0-8371-1588-4, NC0&); Vol. 3-4. 165.00 (ISBN 0-8371-1590-6, NC1&); Vol. 5-6. 165.00 (ISBN 0-8371-1592-2, NC2&); Vol. 7-8. 165.00 (ISBN 0-8371-1594-9, NC3&); Vol. 9-10. 165.00 (ISBN 0-8371-1596-5, NC4&); Vol. 11-12. 165.00 (ISBN 0-8371-1598-1, NC5&); Vol. 13-14. 165.00 (ISBN 0-8371-1600-7, NC6&); Vol. 15-16. 165.00 (ISBN 0-8371-1602-3, NC7&); Vol. 17-18. 165.00 (ISBN 0-8371-1604-X, NC8&); Vol. 19-20. 165.00 (ISBN 0-8371-1606-6, NC9&); Vol. 21-22. 165.00 (ISBN 0-8371-1608-2, ND1&); Vol. 23-24. 165.00 (ISBN 0-8371-1610-4, ND2&); Vol. 25-26. 165.00 (ISBN 0-8371-1612-0, ND3&); Vol. 27-28. 165.00 (ISBN 0-8371-1614-7, ND4&); Vol. 29-30. 165.00 (ISBN 0-8371-1616-3, ND5&). 1840-1870. Repr. Set. 2080.00x o.p. (ISBN 0-8371-1617-1, NAR&, Pub. by Negro U Pr). Greenwood.

National Art-Collections Fund Review 1985. Ed. by Normanby. (Illus.). 186p. (Orig.). 1985. pap. 6.95 o.p. (ISBN 0-9503334-2-5, Pub by Trefoil Bks Ltd UK). Seven Hills Bk Dists.

National Art-Collections Fund Review 1984. Ed. by Normanby. (Illus.). 184p. (Orig.). 1984. pap. 6.95 o.p. (ISBN 0-86294-048-6, Pub by Trefoil Bks Ltd UK). Seven Hills Bk Dists.

National Assessment & Social Studies Education. National Council for the Social Studies Staff. 115p. 1975. 1.95 o.p. (ISBN 0-318-13996-0, EWD-111-748, Natl Assessment Ed Progress). Ed Comm States.

National Association of Realtors Membership Profile: 1978. 54p. 5.00 o.p. (ISBN 0-318-15186-3, 111-101). Natl Assoc Realtors.

National Avocational Organizations: 1986. 6th ed. Intro. by Regina Germain. LC 80-70429. 140p. 1986. pap. 30.00 o.p. (ISBN 0-910416-58-3). Columbia Bks.

National Being: Some Thoughts on An Irish Polity. G. W. Russell. (Co-operative Studies). 184p. 1982. Repr. of 1916 ed. pap. text ed. 8.50x o.p. (ISBN 0-7165-0336-0, BBA 04743, Pub. by Irish Academic Pr Ireland). Biblio Dist.

National Bibliography of Indian Literature, 1901-1953, 4 vols. 1962-1974 ed. B. S. Kesavan. Incl. Vol. 1. Assamese-Bengali-English-Gujaratt. Ed. by V. Y. Kulkarni; Vol. 2. Hindi-Jannada-Kashmiri-Malayalam. Ed. by Y. M. Mulay; Vol. 3. Marathi-Oriya-Panjabi-Sanskrit; Vol. 4. Sindhi-Tamil-Teleyu-Urdu. 1978. 150.00 set o.p.; 40.00 ea. o.p. E J Brill USA.

National Book Awards for Fiction: An Index to the First Twenty-Five Years. Joseph F. Trimmer. 1978. lib. bdg. 44.00 o.p. (ISBN 0-8161-7898-4, Hall Reference). G K Hall.

National Central Library: An Experiment in Library Co-Operation. S. P. L. Filon. 1977. 17.50 o.p. (ISBN 0-85365-249-X). Nichols Pub.

National College Databank: The College Book of Lists. 3rd ed. LC 84-14798. 871p. (Orig.). 1984. pap. 11.95 o.p. (ISBN 0-87866-268-5). Petersons Guides.

National Conference on Catholic School Finance III. 84p. 1977. 3.60 o.p. (ISBN 0-686-29258-8). Natl Cath Educ.

National Conference on Catholic School Finance I. 75p. 1974. 3.60 o.p. (ISBN 0-686-29260-X). Natl Cath Educ.

National Conference on Clays & Minerals, 8th: Proceedings. Ed. by A. Swineford. 1968. 75.00 o.p. (ISBN 0-08-009351-5). Pergamon.

National Conference on Clays & Minerals, 9th: Proceedings. Ed. by A. Swineford. (International Ser. on Earth Sciences: Vol. 11). 1962. 150.00 o.p. (ISBN 0-08-009664-6). Pergamon.

National Conference on the Use of Microcomputers in Special Education, Proceedings, Hartford, CT, March 10-12, 1983. Ed. by Michael M. Behrmann & Liz Lahm. 217p. 1984. 20.00 o.p. (ISBN 0-86586-149-8). Coun Exc Child.

National Conventions: Nominations Under the Big Top. rev. ed. James W. Davis. Ed. by Mary E. Dillon. LC 77-189866. (Politics of Government Ser.). 124p. (Orig.). 1973. pap. 5.95 o.p. (ISBN 0-8120-0443-4). Barron.

National Council Licensure Examination for Registered Nurses. 3rd rev. ed. National Council of State Boards of Nursing Staff. LC 85-4681. 145p. 1985. pap. 10.95 o.p. (ISBN 0-914091-65-4). Chicago Review.

National Data Book, 2 vols. 12th ed. The Foundation Center Staff. Ed. by Barbara Buzan. LC 81-71421. (Annual Ser.). 1988. pap. text ed. 65.00 o.p. (ISBN 0-87954-234-9). Vol. 1, 984 pgs. Vol. 2, 192 pgs. Foundation Ctr.

National Dean's List, 1985-86, 2 vols. 9th ed. LC 79-642835. 1986. 2-vol. set 33.50 ea. o.p. (ISBN 0-930315-23-5). Vol. 1 (ISBN 0-930315-24-3). Vol. 2 (ISBN 0-930315-25-1). Educ Comm.

National Dean's List, 1986-87, 2 vols. 10th ed. LC 79-642835. 1987. Set. 33.50 o.p. (ISBN 0-930315-38-3). Vol. 1 (ISBN 0-930315-39-1). Vol. 2 (ISBN 0-930315-40-5). Educ Comm.

National Directory of Addresses & Telephone Numbers. Ed. by Kristin S. Loomis et al. LC 81-52822. 1981. pap. 19.95 o.p. (ISBN 0-940994-26-7). Concord Ref Bks.

National Directory of Bulletin Board Systems, 1986-87. Ed. by Ric Manning. 1986. pap. text ed. 19.95 o.p. (ISBN 0-88736-092-0). Meckler Corp.

National Directory of Minority-Owned Business Firms. Ed. by Pamela G. Osbourne. 1700p. 1988. 195.00 o.s.i. (ISBN 0-933527-11-X). Business Research.

National Directory of Postcard Deck Media. LC 87-1071. 1987. pap. 49.95 o.p. (ISBN 0-87280-156-X, Asher-Gallant). Caddylak Systs.

National Directory of Speakers. 65p. 10.00 o.p. (ISBN 0-318-15187-1). Natl Assoc Realtors.

National Directory of Women-Owned Business Firms. Ed. by Pamela G. Osbourne. 1500p. 1988. 195.00 o.s.i. (ISBN 0-933527-12-8). Business Research.

National Directory of ZIP Codes & Post Offices, 1986. Steven Spaeth. 2200p. 1986. 29.95 o.p. (ISBN 0-940994-24-0). Concord Ref Bks.

National Economic Accounting. C. O'Loughlin. 1971. 50.00 o.p. (ISBN 0-08-016395-5). Pergamon.

National Economic Environment. Vernon G. Lippitt. (Illus.). 576p. 1975. text ed. 31.95 o.p. (ISBN 0-07-037972-6). McGraw.

National Energy Act's Impact on State Regulation of Natural Gas Distribution Utilities: A Current Assessment. 154p. Date not set. 9.25 o.p. NARUC.

National Energy Policy Plan, 1985. (Illus.). 50p. 1985. pap. 3.00 o.p. (ISBN 0-318-20401-0, S/N 061-000-00663-0). USGPO.

National Era Magazine, 14 vols. Incl. Vol. 1. 88.00 (ISBN 0-8371-1357-1, NE1&); Vol. 2. 88.00 (ISBN 0-8371-1358-X, NE2&); Vol. 3. 88.00 (ISBN 0-8371-1359-8, NE3&); Vol. 4. 88.00 (ISBN 0-8371-1360-1, NE4&); Vol. 5. 88.00 (ISBN 0-8371-1361-X, NE5&); Vol. 6. 88.00 (ISBN 0-8371-1362-8, NE6&); Vol. 7. 88.00 (ISBN 0-8371-1363-6, NE7&); Vol. 8. 88.00 (ISBN 0-8371-1364-4, NE8&); Vol. 9. 88.00 (ISBN 0-8371-1365-2, NE9&); Vol. 10. 88.00 (ISBN 0-8371-1366-0, N10&); Vol. 11. 88.00 (ISBN 0-8371-1367-9, N11&); Vol. 12. 88.00 (ISBN 0-8371-1368-7, N12&); Vols. 13 & 14. 180.00 (ISBN 0-8371-1369-5, N13&). 1970. Repr. of 1860 ed. Set. 1090.00x o.p. (ISBN 0-8371-9114-9, NER&, Pub. by Negro U Pr). Greenwood.

National Experience, Pt. 2. 2nd ed. John M. Blum et al. 1968. 8.95 o.p. (ISBN 0-15-565692-9). HarbraceJ.

National Experience: A History of the United States. 4th ed. John M. Blum et al. LC 76-13664. (Illus.). 1977. One-vol. Ed. text ed. 20.95 o.p. (ISBN 0-15-565680-5, HC); Pt. 1. To 1877. pap. text ed. 13.95 o.p. (ISBN 0-15-565681-3, HC); Pt. 2. To 1865. pap. text ed. 13.95 o.p. (ISBN 0-15-565682-1). HarBraceJ.

National Experience: A History of the United States. 6th ed. John M. Blum et al. 983p. 1985. text ed. 28.00 net o.p. (ISBN 0-15-565664-3, HC). HarBraceJ.

National Experience: A History of the United States. 5th ed. John M. Blum et al. 970p. 1981. One-Vol. Ed. text ed. 20.75 o.p. (ISBN 0-15-565672-4, HC); Vol. 1: A History of the U. S. to 1877. text ed. 14.50 o.p. (ISBN 0-15-565673-2); Vol. 2: A History of the U. S. since 1877. text ed. 14.50 o.p. (ISBN 0-15-565674-0). HarBraceJ.

National Faculty Directory, 1988, 4 vols. 4200p. 1987. 500.00x o.p. (ISBN 0-8103-4399-1). Gale.

National Faculty Directory: 1988 Supplement. 496p. 1987. 170.00x o.p. (ISBN 0-8103-4372-X). Gale.

National Faculty Salary Survey by Discipline & Rank in Private Colleges & Universities 1987-88. 50.00 o.p. (ISBN 0-910402-42-6); 25.00 o.p. Coll & U Personnel.

National Flood Insurance Program: Is It Working? Ed. by League of Women Voters Education Fund. 64p. 1982. 0.85 o.p. (ISBN 0-89959-315-1, 640). LWV US.

National Folk Sports in the U. S. S. R. Y. Lukashin. 125p. 1980. 6.45 o.p. (ISBN 0-8285-1884-X, Pub. by Progress Pubs USSR). Imported Pubns.

National Gallery of Art Early American Guest Book. Ed. by Lisa MacDonald. (Illus.). 80p. 1985. 15.00 o.p. (ISBN 0-939456-14-1). Galison.

National Gallery of Art Small French Paintings: A Book of Days. Ed. by Lisa MacDonald. (Illus.). 32p. 10.95 o.p. (ISBN 0-939456-18-4). Galison.

National Gallery of Art: Washington, D.C. John Walker. LC 74-10716. (Illus.). 1976. 65.00 o.p. (ISBN 0-8109-1370-4). Abrams.

National Grain Policies. annual Incl. 1959. pap. 4.25 o.p. (F283). UNIPUB; 1959 Supplement. pap. 1.25 o.p. (F284). UNIPUB; 1960 Supplement. pap. 4.50 o.p. (F285). UNIPUB; 1961 Supplement. pap. 4.50 o.p. (F286). UNIPUB; 1962 Supplement. pap. 4.50 o.p. (F287). UNIPUB; 1963. pap. 3.00 o.p. (ISBN 0-685-48309-6, F288). UNIPUB; 1964. pap. 4.50 o.p. (ISBN 0-685-48310-X, F289). UNIPUB; 1966. pap. 4.75 o.p. (ISBN 0-685-48311-8, F290). UNIPUB; 1967. pap. 7.25 o.p. (ISBN 0-685-48312-6, F291). UNIPUB; 1968. pap. 7.25 o.p. (ISBN 0-685-48313-4, F292). UNIPUB; 1969. pap. 12.25 o.p. (ISBN 0-685-48314-2, F293). UNIPUB; 1970 Supplement. pap. 6.75 o.p. (ISBN 0-685-48315-0, F294). UNIPUB; 1975, 2 Vols. No. 1. pap. 9.25 o.p. (ISBN 0-685-48316-9, F295); No. 2. pap. 28.75 (ISBN 92-5-100001-8, F296). UNIPUB. (Orig., FAO). UNIPUB.

National Guard in Politics. Martha A. Derthick. LC 65-11588. (Political Studies Ser.). 1965. 16.00x o.s.i. (ISBN 0-674-60200-5). Harvard U Pr.

National Hail Research Experiment: Hailstorms of the Central High Plains, 2 vols. National Center for Atmospheric Research Staff. Ed. by C. A. Knight & P. Squires. LC 81-66733. 32.50x ea. o.p. Vol. 1, 1982 (ISBN 0-87081-096-0). Vol. II, 1982 (ISBN 0-87081-097-9). Univ Pr Colo.

National Health. Peter Nichols. LC 74-8611. 112p. 1975. pap. 3.95 o.s.i. (ISBN 0-394-17836-X, E650, Ever). Grove.

National Health Directory, 1986. John T. Grupenhoff. 670p. 1986. 62.50 o.p. (ISBN 0-87189-367-3). Aspen Pub.

National Health Directory 1987. Ed. by John T. Grupenhoff. 670p. 1987. 64.50 o.p. (ISBN 0-87189-852-7). Aspen Pub.

National Health Insurance & Health Resources: The European Experience. Jan Blanpain et al. LC 77-25818. 320p. 1978. 23.50x o.s.i. (ISBN 0-674-26955-1). Harvard U Pr.

National Health Practitioner Program: Profile. 6th ed. 130p. 1983-84. pap. 10.00 o.p. (ISBN 0-318-13476-4). Assn Phys Asst Prog.

National Health Service: Professionals or Militants? Roger Dyson. 180p. 1987. 22.50 o.p. (ISBN 0-7099-0835-0, Pub. by Croom helm Ltd). Routledge Chapman & Hall.

National Hockey League Official Guide & Record Book, 1988-1989. (Illus.). 352p. (Orig.). 1988. pap. 14.95 o.p. (ISBN 0-89471-639-5). Running Pr.

National Home Sewage Disposal Symposium: Proceedings. 248p. 1974. 17.50 o.p. (ISBN 0-317-33217-1, PO175). Am Soc Ag Eng.

National Housing Finance Systems: A Comparative Study. Mark Boleat. 490p. 1984. 50.00 o.p. (ISBN 0-7099-3249-9, Pub. by Croom Helm Ltd). Routledge Chapman & Hall.

National Human Resource Development Policy: The Role of Postsecondary Vocational Education. Dale Parnell. 12p. 1982. 2.25 o.p. (ISBN 0-318-22158-6, OC83). Natl Ctr Res Voc Ed.

National Incomes Policy & Manpower Problems: Proceedings of the Annual Research Conference, 14th, UCLA, 1972. Annual Research Conference Staff. 2.00 o.p. (ISBN 0-89215-032-7). U Cal LA Indus Rel.

National Incomes Policy for Inflation Control. Charles E. Rockwood. LC 68-65365. 1969. 5.00 o.p. (ISBN 0-8130-0433-0). U Presses Fla.

National Institutes of Health Consensus Development Conference on Adjuvant Chemotherapy & Endocrine Therapy for Breast Cancer. Ed. by Marc E. Lippman. (NCI Monographs, 1986: No. 1). (Illus.). 169p. 1986. pap. 8.50 o.p. (S/N 017-042-00190-1). USGPO.

National Institutes of Health Consensus Development Conference on Limb Sparing Treatment of Adult Soft Tissue Sarcomas & Osteosarcomas, Dec. 3-5, 1984. (Cancer Treatment Symposia: Vol. 3). (Illus.). 168p. 1985. pap. 6.50 o.p. (ISBN 0-318-20126-7, S/N 017-042-00185-4). USGPO.

National Inventory of Documentary Sources in the United States: Federal Records. Index 1985. 352p. 1985. lib. bdg. 6250.00 incl. microfiche o.p. (ISBN 0-89887-026-7). Chadwyck-Healey.

National Inventory of Documentary Sources in the United States, Manuscript Division, Library of Congress Index 1983. Ed. by Sandra S. Tinkham & Bruce B. Hardcastle. LC 83-72351. 219p. 1984. lib. bdg. 3250.00 incl. 900 microfiches o.p. (ISBN 0-89887-028-3). Chadwyck-Healey.

National Issues: A Survey of Politics & Legislation, Nos. 1-9. Communist Labor Party of America Staff. 1969. Repr. of 1939 ed. lib. bdg. 28.00x o.p. (ISBN 0-8371-9210-2, NS00). Greenwood.

National Jail & Adult Detention Directory: 1983-85. rev. ed. 350p. 1983. pap. 15.00 o.p. (ISBN 0-942974-49-2). Am Correctional.

National Job Bank: A Comprehensive Guide to Major Employers in the Nation's Key Job Markets. Adams, Robert Lang, & Associates Staff & Fiedler Michael J. (Job Bank Ser.). 1432p. (Orig.). 1983. hdbk 79.95x o.p. (ISBN 0-937860-07-7). Adams Inc MA.

National Land Symposium: Proceedings, Little Rock, AR, 1974. 122p. 1974. 6.00 o.p. (ISBN 0-317-32465-9, L320). Am Congrs Survey.

National League: An Illustrated History. Donald Honig. LC 83-2072. 352p. 1983. 19.95 o.p. (ISBN 0-517-55041-5). Crown.

National Left Movements in India. Ed. by K. N. Panikkar. 320p. 1980. text ed. 30.00x o.p. (ISBN 0-7069-1000-1, Pub by Vikas India). Advent NY.

National Liberation Revolutions Today, 2 vols. K. Brutents. 555p. 1977. Set. 7.95 o.p. (ISBN 0-8285-3218-4, Pub. by Progress Pubs USSR). Imported Pubns.

National Libraries: Their Problems & Prospects, Proceedings of the Symposium, Vienna, 1958. National Libraries Symposium Staff. 1960. pap. 5.00 o.p. (ISBN 92-3-100442-5, U399, UNESCO). UNIPUB.

National Library Buildings. Ed. by Anthony Thompson. (IFLA Publication Ser.: No. 2). 144p. 1975. lib. bdg. 12.00 o.p. (ISBN 3-7940-4422-3). K G Saur.

National Listing of Providers Furnishing Kidney Dialysis & Transplant Services, 1987. (DHHS Publication HCFA Ser.: No. 03243). (Illus.). 196p. 1987. pap. 9.50 o.p. (ISBN 0-318-22921-8, S/N 017-060-00198-4). USGPO.

National Longitudinal Study of the High School Class of 1972: Postsecondary Education Transcript Study, Data File User's Manual, Contractor Report. Calvin Jones et al. (Education Department Publication CS-221). 535p. 1986. text ed. 24.00 o.p. (ISBN 0-318-21623-X, S/N 065-000-00266-3). USGPO.

National Longitudinal Surveys of Labor Market Experience: An Annotated Bibliography of Research. Kezia V. Sproat et al. LC 84-17194. 448p. 1984. 45.00x o.p. (ISBN 0-669-08171-X). Lexington Bks.

National Monetary Policies & the International Financial System. Ed. by Robert Z. Aliber. LC 74-75610. (Studies in Business & Society - Midway Reprint Ser.). vii, 332p. 1982. pap. text ed. 18.00x o.s.i. (ISBN 0-226-01393-6). U of Chicago Pr.

National Museum of Korea, Seoul. Sunu Choi. LC 80-82645. (Oriental Ceramic Ser.: Vol. 2). (Illus.). 180p. 1982. 68.00 o.p. (ISBN 0-87011-441-7). Kodansha.

National Museum of Korea, Seoul see Oriental Ceramics: The World's Great Collections.

National Music of America & Its Sources. Louis C. Elson. LC 70-159950. (Illus.). 348p. 1975. Repr. of 1911 ed. 43.00x o.p. (ISBN 0-8103-4039-9). Gale.

National Oil Companies. L. E. Grayson. 269p. 1981. 73.95 o.p. (ISBN 0-471-27861-0, Wiley-Interscience). Wiley.

National Parks & Forests: The Administration of the National Park Service & Forest Service, 1977-1984. Glenna Dunning. (Public Administration Ser.: P 1695). 30p. 1985. 4.50 o.p. (ISBN 0-89028-425-3). Vance Biblios.

National Parks: Camping Guide 1986-87. (Illus.). 112p. 1986. pap. 3.50 o.p. (ISBN 0-318-20127-5, S/N 024-005-00987-6). USGPO.

National Parks: Index 1985. 111p. 1985. pap. 3.50 o.p. (ISBN 0-318-20128-3, S/N 024-005-00968-0). USGPO.

National Parks: Lesser Known Areas. (Illus.). 49p. (Orig.). 1985. pap. 1.50 o.p. (ISBN 0-318-18793-0, S/N 024-005-00794-6). USGPO.

National Party Conventions 1831-1980. Congressional Quarterly, Inc. Staff. LC 83-14426. 235p. 1983. 10.25 o.p. (ISBN 0-87187-275-7). Congr Quarterly.

National Plan of Integrated Airport Systems, 1984-1993: Report of the Secretary of Transportation to the Congress Pursuant to PL 97-248. (Illus.). 569p. 1985. pap. 21.00 o.p. (ISBN 0-318-19930-0, S/N 050-007-00709-4). USGPO.

National Policy Game: A Simulation of the American Political Process. John L. Foster et al. LC 74-3411. 108p. 1975. text ed. write for info. o.p. (ISBN 0-02-338720-3); write for info. tchr's manual o.p. (ISBN 0-02-338730-0). Macmillan.

National Political Boundary. John E. Willmer. (CISE Learning Package Ser.: No.15). 56p. (Orig.). 1975. pap. text ed. 3.00x o.p. (ISBN 0-936876-28-X). LRIS.

National Prospectus on Vocational Education: Its Impact on Research & Leadership Development. Charles O. Hopkins. 15p. cancelled o.s.i. (ISBN 0-318-22160-8, OC85). Natl Ctr Res Voc Ed.

National Radio Publicity Directory: 1978. 6th ed. Ed. by Brian J. Smith. 1978. ring bdg. 70.00 o.p. (ISBN 0-87314-098-2). Peter Glenn.

National Radio Publicity Directory 1978-79. 7th ed. Ed. by Brian J. Smith. 1978. ring binder 70.00 o.p. (ISBN 0-87314-099-0). Peter Glenn.

National Recreational, Sporting & Hobby Organizations of the United States, 1981. Ed. by Craig Colgate & Laurie A. Evans. LC 80-70429. 130p. 1981. pap. 25.00 o.p. (ISBN 0-910416-36-2). Columbia Bks.

National Recreational, Sporting & Hobby Organizations of the United States, 1982. Ed. by Craig Colgate, Jr. & Laurie A. Evans. LC 80-70429. 145p. 1982. pap. 25.00 o.p. (ISBN 0-910416-41-9). Columbia Bks.

National Recreational Sporting & Hobby Organizations of the United States, 1983. Ed. by Craig Colgate, Jr. & Stephany J. Freedman. 150p. 1983. pap. 25.00 o.p. (ISBN 0-910416-44-3). Columbia Bks.

National Recreational, Sporting & Hobby Organizations of the United States, 1984. Ed. by Craig Colgate, Jr. & Stephany J. Freedman. LC 80-70429. 134p. 1984. pap. 25.00 o.p. (ISBN 0-910416-48-6). Columbia Bks.

National Recreational, Sporting & Hobby Organizations of the U. S., 1985. 5th ed. Ed. by Craig Colgate, Jr. & Regina Germain. LC 80-70429. 140p. 1985. pap. 30.00 o.p. (ISBN 0-910416-53-2). Columbia Bks.

National Reformer & Manx Weekly Review of Home & Foreign Affairs, Nos. 1-35. 1970. Repr. of 1847 ed. lib. bdg. 31.00x o.p. (ISBN 0-8371-9211-0, NB00). Greenwood.

National Security Affairs: A Guide to Information Sources. Ed. by Arthur D. Larson. LC 70-184013. (Management Information Guide Ser.: No. 27). 418p. 1973. 68.00x o.p. (ISBN 0-8103-0827-4). Gale.

National Security Law. John N. Moore et al. Date not set. Carolina Acad pr.

National Security Policy: The Decision-Making Process. Ed. by Robert L. Pfaltzgraff, Jr. & Uri Ra'anan. LC 84-2932. xiii, 311p. 1984. 32.50 o.p. (ISBN 0-208-02003-9, Archon Bks). Shoe String.

National Strategy for Improving Productivity in Building & Construction. Technology Assessment & Utilization Committee. LC 80-81951. xii, 209p. 1980. pap. text ed. 8.25x o.p. (ISBN 0-309-03080-3). Natl Acad Pr.

National Student Register, 1973. 4th ed. Yvonne Boland. 22.50 o.p. (ISBN 0-912150-04-1). Magna Pubns.

National Survey of Crime Severity. Marvin E. Wolfgang et al. 183p. (Orig.). 1985. pap. 7.00 o.p. (ISBN 0-318-18794-9, S/N 027-000-01243-4). USGPO.

National Survey of Professional, Administrative, Technical, & Clerical Pay: March 1986. 27th annual ed. (Labor Statistics Bureau Bulletin 2271 Ser.). (Illus.). 102p. 1986. pap. 4.75 o.p. (ISBN 0-318-21553-5, S/N 029-001-02914-4). USGPO.

National Survey of Ratings of the Attributes of a Successful Land Data System. Part II: Profiles of 75 Operating Systems. (Monograph: No. 84-3). (Illus.). 1984. pap. text ed. 4.00 o.s.i. (ISBN 0-318-04690-3). Lincoln Inst Land.

National Temper: Readings in American History. Ed. by Lawrence W. Levine & Robert Middlekauff. 1972. Pt. 1, To 1877. pap. 7.95 o.p. (ISBN 0-15-565709-7, HC); Pt. 2, To 1865. pap. 7.95 o.p. (ISBN 0-15-565710-0); One-vol. Ed. pap. text ed. 10.95 o.p. (ISBN 0-15-565708-9). HarBraceJ.

National Trade Index of South Africa, 1986. 150.00 o.p. (ISBN 0-8002-3961-X). Intl Pubns Serv.

National Trust Book of English Architecture. J. M. Richards. (Illus.). 288p. 1981. 24.95 o.p. (ISBN 0-393-01421-5). Norton.

National Trust Book of Picnics. Jackie Gurney. LC 80-69355. (Illus.). 96p. 1982. 13.95 o.s.i. (ISBN 0-7153-8099-0). David & Charles.

National Trust for Scotland Guide. Compiled by Robin Prentice. (Illus.). 1977. 19.95 o.p. (ISBN 0-393-08770-0). Norton.

National Trust Guide. 3rd, rev. ed. Ed. & rev. by Rosemary Joekes. (Illus.). 1984. 24.45x o.p. (ISBN 0-393-01876-8). Norton.

National Trust Guide to England, Wales, & Northern Ireland. rev. ed. Ed. by Robin Fedden & Rosemary Joekes. (Illus.). 1978. 24.95 o.p. (ISBN 0-393-08813-8). Norton.

National Trust Handbook. Date not set. (ISBN 0-7078-0097-8). Salem Hse Pubs.

National Trust Yearbook, 1977-78. (ISBN 0-905118-16-2). Intl Pubns Serv.

National Union Catalogue Author Lists, 1942-1962: A Master Cummulation, 152 vols. Gale Research Company Staff. LC 73-82135. 1969. Set. 3250.00x o.p. (ISBN 0-8103-0950-5). Gale.

National Waste Processing Conference 1978: Energy Conservation Through Waste Utilization. 500p. 1978. 90.00 o.p. (ISBN 0-317-33576-6, 100119); members 45.00 o.p. (ISBN 0-317-33577-4). ASME.

National Water Summary, 1983: Hydrologic Events & Issues. 249p. 1983. pap. 9.00 o.p. (ISBN 0-318-11740-1, S/N 024-001-03505-7). USGPO.

National YMCA Camping Standards. Ed. by Charles C. Kujawa. 79p. 1979. pap. text ed. 5.00x o.p. (ISBN 0-88035-026-1, Pub. by YMCA USA). Human Kinetics.

National YMCA Progressive Gymnastics Program for Youth. YMCA of the U. S. A. Staff. 1978. pap. text ed. 4.00x o.p. (ISBN 0-88035-019-9). Human Kinetics.

Nationalism: A Trend Report & Bibliography Prepared for the International Sociological Association Under the Auspices of the International Committee for Social Sciences Documentation. Anthony D. Smith. (Current Sociology-la Sociologie Contemporaine Ser.: Vol. XXI, 3). 1975. pap. 14.00x o.p. (ISBN 0-686-21792-6). Mouton.

Nationalism & Communism in Asia: The American Response. Norman Graebner. (Problems in American Civilization Ser.). 1976. pap. text ed. 7.00 o.p. (ISBN 0-669-00683-1). Heath.

Nationalism & History: Essays on Old & New Judaism. Simon Dubnow. Ed. by Koppel S. Pinson. LC 58-5590. (Temple Bks.). 1970. pap. 4.25 o.p. (ISBN 0-689-70247-7, T21, Atheneum). Macmillan.

Nationalism & Ideology. Barbara Ward. 1966. pap. 2.50x o.p. (ISBN 0-393-09702-1, NortonC). Norton.

Nationalism, War & Society. Edward K. Krehbiel. LC 75-147474. (Library of War & Peace; the Characters & Causes of War). 1973. lib. bdg. 46.00 o.p. (ISBN 0-8240-0266-0). Garland Pub.

Nationalist China During the Sino-Japanese War, 1937-1945. Ed. by Paul K. Sih. (Illus.). 1977. 20.00 o.p. (ISBN 0-682-48840-2, University). Exposition-Phoenix.

Nationalization in Practice: The British Coal Industry. William W. Haynes. Repr. of 1953 ed. 27.50 o.s.i. (ISBN 0-08-022305-2). Pergamon.

Nations & Households in Economic Growth: Essays in Honor of Moses Abramovitz. Ed. by Paul A. David & Melvin W. Reder. 1973. 44.50 o.p. (ISBN 0-12-205050-9). Acad Pr.

Nations & Internationalism. V. Semyonov. 303p. 1979. 7.45 o.p. (ISBN 0-8285-1503-4, Pub. by Progress Pubs USSR). Imported Pubns.

Nation's Choice. John Craven. LC 84-90156. 130p. 1985. 10.95 o.p. (ISBN 0-533-06212-8). Vantage.

Nation's Health: Some Issues. Ed. by S. E. Berki & Alan W. Heston. LC 77-186411. (Annals of the American Academy of Political & Social Science Ser.: No. 399). 1972. pap. 7.95 o.p. (ISBN 0-87761-146-7). Am Acad Pol Soc Sci.

Nations Heritage TG. (Our Nations Heritage Ser.). Date not set. (ISBN 0-07-375435-8). McGraw.

Nations in Prophecy. John F. Walvoord. 1967. pap. 7.95 o.p. (ISBN 0-310-34101-9, 12159P). Zondervan.

Nation's Response to Its Environment at Risk: Historical Perspectives, 1974-1984. Dale E. Casper. (Public Administration Ser.: P 1710). 11p. 1985. 2.00 o.p. (ISBN 0-89028-460-1). Vance Biblios.

Nationwide Audience. David Morley. (Television Monograph: No. 11). 167p. 1980. pap. 10.95 o.p. (ISBN 0-85170-097-7, Pub. by British Film Inst England). U of Ill Pr.

Nationwide Evaluation of M.D.T.A. (Manpower Development & Training Act) Institutional Job Training Programs. Earl D. Main. (Report Ser.: No. 118). 1966. 6.25x o.p. (ISBN 0-932132-10-3). NORC.

Native American Astronomy. Ed. by Anthony F. Aveni. LC 76-53569. (Illus.). 304p. 1977. text ed. 18.95x o.p. (ISBN 0-292-75511-2). U of Tex Pr.

Native American Indian Novelists: An Annotated Critical Bibliography. Tom Colonnese & Louis Owens. LC 84-49135. (Reference Library of the Humanities). 178p. 1983. lib. bdg. 31.00 o.p. (ISBN 0-8240-9199-X). Garland Pub.

Native Clays & Glazes for North American Potters: A Manual for the Utilization of Local Clay & Glaze Materials. Ralph Mason. LC 81-18493. 150p. 1981. cloth o.p. 24.95 o.p. (ISBN 0-917304-02-0); pap. 17.95 o.p. (ISBN 0-917304-66-7). Timber.

Native Egyptians: The Historical Essence of an Outstanding Early Culture. C. O. Barnard. 1979. 10.00 o.p. (ISBN 0-682-49300-7). Exposition-Phoenix.

Native Land: Sagas of the Indian Americas. Jamake Highwater. 1986. 24.95 o.p. (ISBN 0-316-36087-2). Little.

Native Languages of the Americas, Vol. 1. Ed. by Thomas A. Sebeok. 646p. 1976. 80.00x o.p. (ISBN 0-306-37157-X, Plenum Pr). Plenum Pub.

Native Languages of the Americas, Vol. 2. Ed. by Thomas A. Sebeok. 550p. 1977. 80.00x o.p. (ISBN 0-306-37158-8, Plenum Pr). Plenum Pub.

Native Studies: American & Canadian Indians. John A. Price. 1978. text ed. 31.95x o.p. (ISBN 0-07-082695-1). McGraw.

Native to the Grain. George Troy. LC 61-6646. 1961. 3.95 o.p. (ISBN 0-15-164793-3). HarBraceJ.

Natives & Strangers. Louisa Dawkins. 404p. 1985. 18.45 o.p. (ISBN 0-395-36553-8). HM.

Natives of Hemso. August Strindberg. Tr. by Arvid Paulson from Swedish. 1973. pap. 2.95 o.p. (ISBN 0-87140-284-X). Liveright.

Nativism & Interactionism see Psychology of School Learning.

Nativity of Christ. Ed. by Theodore Heckman. (Music Ser.). 158p. 1974. pap. 10.00 o.p. (ISBN 0-913836-16-8). St Vladimirs.

NATO: A Bleak Picture. S. Vladmirov & L. Teplov. 214p. 1977. pap. 1.95 o.p. (ISBN 0-8285-1920-X, Pub. by Progress Pubs USSR). Imported Pubns.

NATO Air Power in the 1980's. (Warbirds Illustrated Ser.: No. 7). 1982. 9.95 o.p. (ISBN 0-85368-545-2, Pub. by Arms & Armour Pr). Sterling.

NATO Air Power Today. Michael J. Gething. (Warbirds Illustrated Ser.: No. 37). (Illus.). 72p. (Orig.). 1986. pap. 9.95 o.p. (ISBN 0-85368-795-1, Pub. by Arms & Armour). Sterling.

NATO Aircraft in Colour. Robbie Shaw. 96p. 10.95 o.p. (ISBN 0-7106-0399-1). Janes Info Group.

NATO: Alliance for Peace. David R. Mets. LC 81-1841. (Illus.). 224p. (gr. 7 up). 1981. lib. bdg. 10.79 o.s.i. (ISBN 0-671-34065-4). Messner.

NATO & the Defense of the West. Laurence Martin. (Illus.). 160p. 1985. 18.95 o.p. (ISBN 0-03-006018-4). H Holt & Co.

NATO & the European Union Movement. M. Margaret Ball. LC 74-9319. (Library of World Affairs, London, Institute of World Affairs Ser.: No. 45). (Illus.). 486p. 1974. Repr. of 1959 ed. lib. bdg. 35.00x o.p. (ISBN 0-8371-7642-5, BANA). Greenwood.

NATO & Warsaw Pact Submarines since 1955. Eugene M. Kolesnik. (Illus.). 128p. (Orig.). 1988. pap. 14.95 o.p. (ISBN 0-7137-1804-8, Pub. by Blandford Pr England). Sterling.

NATO Arms Co-Operation: A Study in Economics & Politics. Keith Hartley. 240p. 1983. text ed. 44.95x o.p. (ISBN 0-04-341022-7). Unwin Hyman.

NATO Navies of the 1980s, Vol. 1. Paul Beaver. (Warships Illustrated Ser.: No. 3). (Illus.). 72p. (Orig.). 1986. pap. 9.95 o.p. (ISBN 0-85368-723-4, Pub. by Arms & Armour). Sterling.

NATO-the Next Thirty Years: The Changing Political, Economic, & Military Setting. Ed. by Kenneth A. Myers. LC 80-10677. 470p. 1980. lib. bdg. 40.00x o.p. (ISBN 0-89158-965-1); pap. 29.00x o.p. (ISBN 0-86531-331-8). Westview.

Natural Acts. Date not set. (ISBN 0-8052-3967-7). Random.

Natural & Artificial Right of Property Contrasted. Thomas Hodgskin. LC 68-55734. iii, 188p. Repr. of 1832 ed. 29.50x o.s.i. (ISBN 0-678-01121-4). Kelley.

Natural & Induced Cell-Mediated Cytotoxicity: Effector & Regulatory Mechanisms. Ed. by Gert Riethmuller et al. LC 79-14162. (Perspectives in Immunology Ser.). 1979. 38.50 o.p. (ISBN 0-12-584650-9). Acad Pr.

Natural & Political History of the State of Vermont. Ira Allen. LC 69-19611. 1969. Repr. 13.95 o.p. (ISBN 0-8048-0419-2). C E Tuttle.

Natural & Synthetic High Polymers: Lectures Presented at the 7th Colloquium on NMR Spectroscopy. Ed. by P. Diehl et al. LC 70-94160. (NMR, Basic Principles & Progress: Vol. 4). (Illus.). 1971. 47.30 o.p. (ISBN 0-387-05221-6). Springer-Verlag.

Natural & the Supernatural Jew: An Historical and Theological Introduction. Arthur A. Cohen. LC 79-13038. 1979. pap. text ed. 6.95x o.p. (ISBN 0-87441-291-9). Behrman.

Natural Anthraquinone Drugs: Proceedings of the Anthraquinone Symposium, Buergenstock-Luzern, September 1978. Anthraquinone Symposium Staff. Ed. by J. W. Fairbairn. (Pharmacology Journal: Vol. 20, Suppl. 1). (Illus.). 140p. 1980. pap. 26.75 o.p. (ISBN 3-8055-0683-X). S Karger.

Natural Architecture: 40 Earth Sheltered House Designs. Rev. ed. Charles G. Woods. LC 82-83906. (Illus.). 128p. 1984. 28.95 o.p. (ISBN 0-442-29256-2); pap. 16.95 o.p. (ISBN 0-442-29257-0). Van Nos Reinhold.

Natural Birth. Toi Derricotte. LC 83-2071. (Feminist Ser.). 62p. (Orig.). 1983. 19.95 o.p. (ISBN 0-89594-102-3); pap. 6.95 o.p. (ISBN 0-89594-101-5). Crossing Pr.

Natural Causes. Jonathan Valin. (Harry Stoner Mystery Ser.). 304p. 1984. pap. 2.95 o.p. (ISBN 0-380-68247-8, 68247). Avon.

Natural Cell-Mediated Immunity Against Tumors. Ronald B. Herberman. 1980. 108.00 o.p. (ISBN 0-12-341350-8). Acad Pr.

Natural Chelating Polymers. Riccardo A. Muzzarelli. 260p. 1974. 65.00 o.p. (ISBN 0-08-017235-0). Pergamon.

Natural Chicago. Phyllis Thomas & Bill Thomas. (Illus.). 224p. 1985. pap. 12.95 o.p. (ISBN 0-03-059681-5). H Holt & Co.

Natural Childbirth & the Christian Family. 4th, rev. ed. Helen Wessel. LC 82-48943. 384p. 1983. 14.37i o.p. HarpR.

Natural Convection in Enclosures: HTD, Vol.8. Ed. by I. Catton & K. E. Torrance. 128p. 1980. 20.00 o.p. (ISBN 0-317-33570-7, G00168); members 10.00 o.p. (ISBN 0-317-33571-5). ASME.

Natural Coumarins: Occurence, Chemistry & Biochemistry. Robert D. Murray et al. LC 81-14776. 702p. 1982. 232.00 o.p. (ISBN 0-471-28057-7, Pub. by Wiley-Interscience). Wiley.

Natural Crop Protection Based on Local Farm Resources in the Tropics & Subtropics. 2nd ed. Gaby Stoll. Tr. by John Coates from Ger. (Illus.). 188p. (Orig.). 1987. pap. text ed. 19.00x o.p. (ISBN 3-924333-43-2). Agribookstore.

Natural Dietetics: A Handbook on Food, Nutrition & Health. 4th ed. R. J. Jussawalla. 1984. pap. 5.95x o.p. (Pub. by Vikas India). Advent NY.

Natural Enemy. Jane Langton. LC 81-16618. (Joan Kahn Bk.). (Illus.). 288p. 1982. 11.95 o.p. (ISBN 0-89919-081-2). Ticknor & Fields.

Natural Foods Storage Bible: Secrets of Storing, Cooking & Enjoying Natural Foods. Sharon Dienstbier & Sybil D. Hendricks. LC 76-29308. (Illus.). 240p. 1976. 13.95 o.p. (ISBN 0-88290-066-8). Horizon Utah.

Natural Forms & Forces: Abstract Images in American Sculpture. Katy Kline & Douglas Dreishpoon. LC 86-60962. (Illus.). 68p. (Orig.). 1986. pap. 6.00 o.p. (ISBN 0-938437-14-3). MIT List Visual Arts.

Natural Healer's Acupressure Handbook. Blate. pap. 6.95 o.p. (ISBN 0-317-64766-0). H Holt & Co.

Natural Healer's Acupressure Handbook: G-Jo Fingertip Technique. Michael Blate. LC 76-45282. (Illus.). 1977. 8.95 o.p. (ISBN 0-03-020631-6); pap. 6.95 o.p. (ISBN 0-03-020626-X). H Holt & Co.

Natural Healing Annual for 1987. Mark Bricklin. 248p. 1987. 17.95 o.p. (ISBN 0-87857-680-0). Rodale Pr Inc.

Natural Healing Cookbook. Mark Bricklin. 1986. 17.95 o.p. (ISBN 0-87857-600-2). Rodale Pr Inc.

Natural Healing in Gynecology: A Manual for Women. Rina Nissim. 192p. 1986. 25.00 o.p. (ISBN 0-86358-063-7, 80637); pap. 9.95 o.p. (ISBN 0-86358-069-6, 80696). Routledge Chapman & Hall.

Natural History Essays. Henry David Thoreau. Ed. by Robert Sattelmeyer. LC 80-11357. (Literature of the American Wilderness Ser.). 288p. 1980. pap. 4.95 o.p. (ISBN 0-87905-071-3, Peregrine Smith). Gibbs Smith Pub.

Natural History in America, 1609-1860: Printed Works in the Collections of the American Philosophical Society, the Historical Society of Pennsylvania, & the Library Company of Philadelphia. Ed. by Andrea J. Tucher. LC 83-49302. (Referance Library of Social Science- Americana to 1860: Vol. 232). 287p. 1985. lib. bdg. 50.00 o.p. (ISBN 0-8240-8965-0). Garland Pub.

Natural History Notebook of North American Animals. National Museum of Natural Sciences, Canada Staff. (Illus.). 176p. 1985. 21.95 o.p. (ISBN 0-13-610114-3); pap. 11.95 o.p. (ISBN 0-13-610106-2). P-H.

Natural History of American Birds of Eastern & Central North America. Edward H. Forbush. Ed. by John R. May. (Illus.). 1973. 15.45 o.p. (ISBN 0-395-07699-4). HM.

Natural History of Flies. Harold Oldroyd. (World Naturalist Ser). (Illus.). 1966. pap. 2.25x o.p. (ISBN 0-393-00375-2). Norton.

Natural History of Game. John Marchington. (Illus.). 256p. 1984. 27.00 o.p. (ISBN 0-85115-196-5, Pub. by Boydell & Brewer). Longwood Pub Group.

Natural History of Giraffes. Dorcas MacClintock & Ugo Mochi. LC 72-9580. (gr. 5-9). 1973. 7.95 o.p. (ISBN 0-684-13239-7, ScribT). Scribner.

Natural History of Marine Mammals. Victor B. Scheffer. LC 76-14820. (Illus.). 170p. (gr. 8 up). 1981. 7.95 o.p. (ISBN 0-686-96884-0, Pub. by Scribner); pap. 5.95 o.s.i. (ISBN 0-684-16952-5, Pub. by Scribner). Macmillan.

Natural History of Raccoons. Dorcas MacClintock. (Illus.). 160p. (gr. 7 up). 1981. 11.95 o.s.i. (ISBN 0-684-16619-4, Pub. by Scribner). Macmillan.

Natural History of Selbourne. Gilbert White. 1974. pap. 2.95x o.p. (ISBN 0-460-01048-4, Evman). Biblio Dist.

Natural History of Sharks. Thomas H. Lineweaver, III & Richard H. Backus. LC 84-5389. (Illus.). 256p. 1984. pap. 9.95 o.p. Schocken.

Natural History of Termites. Frances L. Behnke. LC 77-1424. (gr. 7 up). 1977. encore ed. 1.79 o.p. (ISBN 0-684-17355-7, ScribT). Scribner.

Natural History of Vermont. Zadock Thompson. LC 77-152112. (Illus.). 1971. pap. 9.25 o.p. (ISBN 0-8048-0983-6). C E Tuttle.

Natural History Photography. Ed. by D. M. Turner Ettlinger. 1975. 76.00 o.p. (ISBN 0-12-703950-3). Acad Pr.

Natural Language: Beyond Single Sentence Systems. James F. Allen & Bonnie L. Webber. (Illus.). 100p. 1988. pap. text ed. 12.00 o.p. (ISBN 0-929280-12-1). Amer Artificial.

Natural Language Communication with Computers. Ed. by L. Bolc. (Lecture Notes in Computer Science Ser.: Vol. 63). 1978. pap. 17.00 o.p. (ISBN 0-387-08911-X). Springer-Verlag.

Natural Law & the Ethics of Love: A New Synthesis. William A. Spurrier. LC 74-6211. 1974. 5.95 o.s.i. (ISBN 0-664-20702-2, Westminster). Westminster John Knox.

Natural Light. Joseph Holmes. Date not set. price not set o.p. (Peregrine Smith). Gibbs Smith Pub.

Natural Magic. David Carroll & Barry Saxe. LC 75-31073. 1977. 9.95 o.p. (ISBN 0-87795-143-8, Arbor Hse); pap. 4.95 o.p. (ISBN 0-87795-152-7). Morrow.

Natural Mind: A New Way of Looking at Drugs & the Higher Consciousness. Andrew Weil. 1973. 9.95 o.p. (ISBN 0-395-13936-8); pap. 7.70 o.p. (ISBN 0-395-16612-8). HM.

Natural Motivation in the Pauline Epistles. rev. ed. Robert J. Austgen. 1969. 12.95 o.p. (ISBN 0-268-00374-2). U of Notre Dame Pr.

Natural New York. Bill Thomas & Phyllis Thomas. LC 81-13218. 320p. 1983. 17.95 o.s.i. (ISBN 0-03-057554-0); pap. 10.95 o.s.i. (ISBN 0-03-057553-2). H Holt & Co.

Natural Prey. Edward Mathis. 240p. 1987. 15.95 o.p. (ISBN 0-684-18852-X). Scribner.

Natural Principles of Land Use. Edward H. Graham. 1969. Repr. of 1944 ed. lib. bdg. 22.50x o.p. (ISBN 0-8371-2394-1, GRLU). Greenwood.

Natural Proteinase Inhibitors. Rosemarie Vogel et al. 1969. 42.00 o.p. (ISBN 0-12-722850-0). Acad Pr.

Natural Radiation Environment. Ed. by John A. Adams & Wayne M. Lowder. LC 64-12256. (Illus.). 1069p. 1964. lib. bdg. 35.00x o.s.i. (ISBN 0-226-00596-8). U of Chicago Pr.

Natural Resources: Allocation, Economics & Policy. Judith Rees. 450p. 1986. text ed. 65.00 o.p. (ISBN 0-416-31990-4, 9813); pap. text ed. 23.00 o.p. (ISBN 0-416-32000-7, 9826). Routledge Chapman & Hall.

Natural Resources: Bureaucratic Myths & Environmental Management. Richard L. Stroup & John A. Baden. LC 83-2607. (Illus.). 148p. 1983. 24.95 o.p.; pap. 9.95 o.p. (ISBN 0-88410-385-4). PRIPP.

Natural Resources, Uncertainty, & General Equilibrium System Memory: Essays in Honor of Rafael Lusky. Ed. by Alan S. Blinder & Philip Friedman. (Economic Theory & Mathematical Economics Ser.). 1977. 29.95 o.p. (ISBN 0-12-106150-7). Acad Pr.

Natural Selection. L. R. Ginzburg. 1983. text ed. 29.95 o.p. (ISBN 0-8053-3180-8). Benjamin-Cummings.

Natural Selection. Margaret Mulvihill. 160p. 1986. 16.95 o.p. (ISBN 0-86358-064-5, Pandora Pr); pap. 8.95 o.p. (ISBN 0-86358-058-0). Routledge Chapman & Hall.

Natural Selection & Heredity. P. M. Sheppard. (Illus.). 224p. 1959. (ISBN 0-8022-1551-3). Philos Lib.

Natural Shocks. Richard Stern. 1987. pap. 6.95 o.p. (ISBN 0-87795-869-6). Morrow.

Natural Substances Formed Biologically from Mevalonic Acid: Proceedings. Biochemical Society Symposium, 29th. Ed. by T. W. Goodwin. 1970. 33.00 o.p. (ISBN 0-12-289865-6). Acad Pr.

Natural Sweets & Treats. Ruth Laughlin. LC 75-17275. (Illus.). 176p. (Orig.). 1975. pap. 5.95 o.p. (ISBN 0-912800-17-8). Woodbridge Pr.

Natural Systems for Water Pollution Control. W. Ray Dinges. (Environmental Engineering Ser.). 352p. 1981. 31.95 o.p. (ISBN 0-442-20166-4). Van Nos Reinhold.

Natural Toxicants in Feeds & Poisonous Plants. Peter R. Cheeke & L. R. Shull. (Illus.). 1985. 75.95 o.s.i. (ISBN 0-87055-482-4). AVI.

Natural Toxins: Proceedings of the 6th International Symposium on Animal, Plant & Microbial Toxins, Uppsala, August, 1979. D. Eaker. Ed. by T. Wadstrom. LC 80-40898. (Illus.). 704p. 1980. 185.00 o.p. (ISBN 0-08-024952-3). Pergamon.

Natural Trigonometric Functions. Robert E. Benson. 6.00 o.p. (ISBN 0-685-19493-0). Powner.

Natural Washington. Thomas. pap. 9.95 o.p. (ISBN 0-8050-0626-5). H Holt & Co.

Natural Washington. Bill Thomas & Phyllis Thomas. LC 79-22744. (Illus.). 240p. (Orig.). 1980. 14.95 o.s.i. (ISBN 0-03-044746-1); pap. 6.95 o.s.i. (ISBN 0-03-044741-0). H Holt & Co.

Natural Way to Health, Vigor & Beauty. Shelon Electric Co. Staff. (Illus.). 36p. 1981. pap. 2.00 o.p. (ISBN 0-940208-02-4). Down There Pr.

Natural Way to Reading: A How-to Method for Parents of Slow Learners, Dyslexic, & Learning Disabled Children. Nancy Stevenson. LC 73-175478. 1974. 12.95 o.p. (ISBN 0-316-81422-9). Little.

Natural Way to Reduce. 16th, rev. ed. Paul C. Bragg & Patricia Bragg. LC 84-62770. pap. 4.95 o.p. (ISBN 0-87790-040-X). Health Sci.

Natural Ways to Relieve Pain. Norman D. Ford. 169p. 1980. 4.95 o.p. (ISBN 0-686-64248-1). Allsport Pub.

Natural Wonders of New Zealand. Dawes Trevern & Anna Dawes. 176p. 1986. pap. 29.95 o.p. (ISBN 0-7233-0775-X, Pub. by Whitcoulls Nz). Intl Spec Bk.

Naturalism. Lillian R. Furst & Peter N. Skrine. (Critical Idiom Ser.). 1971. pap. 5.50x o.p. (ISBN 0-416-65670-6, NO. 2208). Routledge Chapman & Hall.

Naturalist Image of German Literature: A Study of the German Naturalists - Appraisal of Their Literary Heritage. Warren R. Maurer. 269p. bds. cancelled o.s.i. (ISBN 3-7705-0726-6). Adlers Foreign Bks.

Naturalist in Palestine. Victor Howells. (Illus.). 180p. 1957. (ISBN 0-8022-0750-2). Philos Lib.

Naturalist in the Sudan. Charles Sweeney. LC 73-17778. (Illus.). 256p. 1974. 8.50 o.s.i. (ISBN 0-8008-5466-7). Taplinger.

Naturalists of the Frontier. rev. & enl. ed. Samuel W. Geiser. LC 48-7357. (Illus.). 302p. 1948. Repr. of 1937 ed. 14.95x o.p. (ISBN 0-87074-059-8). SMU Press.

Naturally. David Kalugin. (Illus.). 1979. pap. 4.95 o.p. (ISBN 0-933586-02-7). Book Promo Pr.

Naturally Occurring Acetylenes. F. Bohlmann et al. 1973. 134.50 o.p. (ISBN 0-12-111150-4). Acad Pr.

Nature: A Facsimile of the First Edition. Ralph Waldo Emerson. LC 85-47940. 124p. 1986. 15.95 o.p. (ISBN 0-8070-1556-3). Beacon Pr.

Nature & Aesthetics of Design. David Pye. 160p. 1982. pap. 13.95 o.p. (ISBN 0-442-27379-7). Van Nos Reinhold.

Nature & Applications of Mathematics. George J. Kertz. LC 78-20979. (Illus.). 1979. pap. write for info. o.p. (ISBN 0-673-16241-9). Scott F.

Nature & Love in the Middle Ages. Aldo D. Scaglione. LC 76-2688. (Illus.). 250p. 1976. Repr. of 1963 ed. lib. bdg. 24.75x o.p. (ISBN 0-8371-8768-0, SCNL). Greenwood.

Nature & Mission of the Church. Donald G. Miller. LC 57-9443. (Orig.). 1957. pap. 5.95 o.s.i. (ISBN 0-8042-3208-3, John Knox). Westminster John Knox.

Nature & Nurture: Child-Rearing in North & Central Arnhem Land. Annette Hamilton. 1980. pap. text ed. 19.95x o.p. (ISBN 0-391-01937-6). Humanities.

Nature & Origin of Carbohydrates in Soils. M. V. Cheshire. LC 79-40898. 1980. 66.50 o.p. (ISBN 0-12-171250-8). Acad Pr.

Nature & Ornament: Nature the Raw Material of Design. Lewis F. Day. LC 74-137355. (Illus.). 146p. 1971. Repr. of 1930 ed. 34.00x o.p. (ISBN 0-8103-3328-7). Gale.

Nature & Religious Imagination: From Edwards to Bushnell. Conrad Cherry. LC 79-7374. 256p. 1980. 3.00 o.p. (ISBN 0-8006-0550-0, 1-550, Fortress). Augsburg Fortress.

Nature & Truth of the Great Religions: Toward a Philosophy of Religion. August K. Reischauer. LC 65-20612. 1966. 19.50 o.p. (ISBN 0-8048-0420-6). C E Tuttle.

Nature & Types of Sociological Theory. Don A. Martindale. LC 60-50843. 1960. text ed. 21.95 o.p. (ISBN 0-395-04843-5, 3-34640). HM.

Nature & Types of Sociological Theory. 2nd ed. Don A. Martindale. LC 80-68142. (Illus.). 640p. 1980. text ed. 31.50 o.p. (ISBN 0-395-29732-X). HM.

Nature & Use of Ritual. Peter R. De Coppens. 1977. pap. text ed. 9.75 o.p. (ISBN 0-8191-0341-1). U Pr of Amer.

Nature, Children & You. Paul E. Goff. LC 74-80677. 1974. 5.00 o.p. (ISBN 0-682-47996-9, Banner). Exposition-Phoenix.

Nature Close Up: A Fantastic Journey into Reality. Andreas Feininger. (Illus.). 18.00 o.p. (ISBN 0-8446-5885-5). Peter Smith.

Nature Encyclopedia. John Paton & Catherine Dell. LC 82-80986. (Encyclopedia Ser.). (Illus.). 144p. (gr. 4-7). 1982. 14.95 o.s.i. (ISBN 0-02-689203-0, Checkerboard Pr). Macmillan.

Nature Gone Wild! Walter Olesky. LC 82-60645. (Illus.). 64p. (gr. 7-9). 1982. lib. bdg. 9.29 o.s.i. (ISBN 0-671-44007-1). Messner.

Nature in Ornament. Lewis F. Day. LC 70-159852. (Illus.). 288p. 1971. Repr. of 1898 ed. 40.00x o.p. (ISBN 0-8103-3207-8). Gale.

Nature in the Balance. H. F. Hartmann et al. LC 75-184411. (Illus.). 96p. 1972. 6.50 o.s.i. (ISBN 0-8008-5469-1). Taplinger.

Nature in the West. Richard Rabkin & Jacob Rabkin. LC 81-791. (Illus.). 256p. (Orig.). 1982. 17.95 o.p. (ISBN 0-03-053671-5); pap. 10.95 o.p. (ISBN 0-03-053666-9, Owl Bks). H Holt & Co.

Nature Meditations. Hazrat I. Khan. LC 80-50829. (Collected Works of Hazrat Inayat Khan Ser.). (Illus.). 128p. (Orig.). 1980. pap. 6.95 o.p. (ISBN 0-930872-12-6). Omega Pr NY.

Nature, Mind & Death. C. J. Ducasse. (Paul Carus Lecture Ser.). 533p. 1951. 19.95 o.p. (ISBN 0-87548-102-7). Open Court.

Nature of a Humane Society. Ed. by H. Ober Hess. LC 76-62616. 1977. 9.50 o.p. (ISBN 0-8006-0502-0, Fortress). Augsburg Fortress.

Nature of Adolescence. John C. Coleman. 1980. 10.95x o.p. (ISBN 0-416-72620-8, NO. 2894). Routledge Chapman & Hall.

Nature of Christian Worship. J. Alan Kay. 115p. 1954. Philos Lib.

Nature of Creative Activity. 2nd ed. Viktor Lowenfeld. LC 65-7654. 272p. 1959. Repr. 49.00x o.p. (ISBN 0-686-01428-6). Somerset Pub.

Nature of Culture. Alfred L. Kroeber. (Illus.). 1952. lib. bdg. 35.00x o.s.i. (ISBN 0-226-45422-3). U of Chicago Pr.

Nature of Faith. Gerhard Ebeling. Tr. by Ronald G. Smith from Ger. LC 62-7194. 192p. 1967. pap. 6.95 o.p. (ISBN 0-8006-1914-5, 1-1914, Fortress). Augsburg Fortress.

Nature of Human Speech see Society's Work.

Nature of Life & Cancer. Benedict F. Favata & Frank Pirone. LC 67-24572. 109p. 1968. (ISBN 0-8022-0477-5). Philos Lib.

Nature of Mathematics. 4th ed. Karl J. Smith. LC 83-14455. (Mathematics Ser.). 630p. 1984. text ed. 25.00 pub net o.p. (ISBN 0-534-02806-3). Brooks-Cole.

Nature of Multiple Sclerosis. Paavo Riekkinen et al. (Illus.). 220p. 1973. text ed. 29.50x o.p. (ISBN 0-8422-7070-1). Irvington.

Nature of Philosophical Inquiry. Ed. by Joseph Bobik. LC 77-85347. 1970. pap. 5.95x o.p. (ISBN 0-268-00482-X). U of Notre Dame Pr.

Nature of Politics. Ed. by Michael Curtis. (Orig.). 1962. pap. 2.65 o.p. (ISBN 0-380-01423-8, 24364, Discus). Avon.

Nature of Price Theory. Liebhafsky. Irwin.

Nature of Psychotherapy: A Critical Appraisal. Karl Jaspers. Tr. by J. Hoenig & Marian W. Hamilton. LC 75-34897. (Midway Reprint Ser). xii, 52p. 1975. pap. text ed. 3.00x o.s.i. U of Chicago Pr.

Nature of Science. Frederick Aicken. viii, 136p. 1984. pap. text ed. 15.00x o.p. (ISBN 0-435-54020-3). Heinemann Ed.

Nature of Science, & Other Lectures. Edwin Hubble. LC 77-14173. 1977. Repr. of 1954 ed. lib. bdg. 35.00x o.p. (ISBN 0-8371-9841-0, HUNS). Greenwood.

Nature of Some of Our Physical Concepts. P. W. Bridgeman. 64p. 1952. (ISBN 0-8022-0173-3). Philos Lib.

Nature of Special Education: People, Places & Change. Ed. by Tony Booth & June Statham. 450p. 1982. pap. 12.00 o.p. (ISBN 0-7099-0657-9, Pub. by Croom Helm Ltd). Routledge Chapman & Hall.

Nature of Structure-Design & Safety. D. I. Blockley. LC 80-40028. 365p. 1980. 105.95x o.p. (ISBN 0-470-27047-0). Halsted Pr.

Nature of Surrey. Drewett. 1987. text ed. 60.00x o.p. (ISBN 0-86023-247-6, Pub. by Barracuda UK). State Mutual Bk.

Nature of the Elementary Particle. M. H. MacGregor. (Lecture Notes in Physics Ser.: Vol. 81). 1978. pap. 28.00 o.p. (ISBN 0-387-08857-1). Springer-Verlag.

Nature of Theoretical Thinking in Nursing. Hesook S. Kim. 208p. 1983. pap. 19.95 o.p. (ISBN 0-8385-6652-9). Appleton & Lange.

Nature of Theory & Research in Social Psychology. Clyde Hendrick & Russell A. Jones. 1972. text ed. 14.50 o.p. (ISBN 0-12-340750-8). Acad Pr.

Nature of Thermodynamics. P. W. Bridgman. 12.50 o.p. (ISBN 0-8446-0512-3). Peter Smith.

Nature of Things. Don Hawley. 178p. 1959. (ISBN 0-8022-0692-1). Philos Lib.

Nature of Thought, 2 Vol. Set. Brand Blanshard. (Muirhead Library of Philosophy). 1964. text ed. 50.00x o.p. (ISBN 0-391-00923-0); Vol. 1. text ed. (ISBN 0-685-92789-X); Vol. 2. text ed. (ISBN 0-685-92790-3). Humanities.

Nature Photography-Its Art & Technique. Heather Angel. (Illus.). 222p. 1987. 17.95 o.p. (ISBN 0-85242-670-4, Pub. by Fountain Pr UK). Seven Hills Bk Dists.

Nature Photography Yearbook, 1986-1987. Ed. by Fritz Polking. 160p. 1987. pap. 26.95 o.p. (ISBN 0-86343-068-6, Pub. by Fountain Pr UK). Seven Hills Bk Dists.

Nature Stored, Nature Studied: Collections, Conservation & Allied Research at the British Museum (Natural History) British Museum (Natural History) (Illus.). 64p. 1981. pap. 6.50x o.p. (ISBN 0-565-00835-8, Pub. by Brit Mus Nat Hist England). Sabbot-Natural Hist Bks.

Nature vs. Nurture: Gettysburg College Senior Scholars' Seminar 1983-1984. Ed. by Robert D. Barnes & James D. Pickering. 264p. (Orig.). 1985. pap. text ed. 15.50 o.p. (ISBN 0-8191-4554-8). U Pr of Amer.

Nature with Children of All Ages: Adventures for Exploring, Learning, & Enjoying the World Around Us. Edith Sisson. 195p. 1982. 19.95 o.p. (ISBN 0-13-610444-4); pap. 10.95 o.p. (ISBN 0-13-610436-3). P-H.

NatureCrafts: Seasonal Projects from Natural Materials. Mary E. Johnson & Katherine Pearson. LC 79-83705. (Illus.). 1980. 19.95 o.p. (ISBN 0-8487-0494-0). Oxmoor Hse.

Nature's Classroom: A Manual for Teaching Outdoor Education. Michael Link. (Illus.). 1978. 4.25 o.p. (ISBN 0-930698-01-0). Natl Audubon.

Nature's Economy: The Roots of Ecology. Donald Worster. LC 77-7579. 416p. 1977. o.s.i 15.00 o.s.i. (ISBN 0-87156-197-2). Sierra.

Nature's Healing System for Better Eyesight. 17th, erv. ed. Patricia Bragg. pap. 4.95 o.p. (ISBN 0-87790-037-X). Health Sci.

Nature's Place: Conservation Sites & Countryside Change. W. M. Adams. 160p. 1986. text ed. 29.95x o.p. (ISBN 0-04-719009-4). Unwin Hyman.

Nature's Secret World. Ed. by James Harrison. LC 84-9169. (Illus.). 192p. 1984. 19.95 o.p. (ISBN 0-668-06213-4, 6213). Arco.

Naude: Prophet to South Africa. G. McLeod Bryan. LC 77-15746. (Orig.). 1978. pap. 5.95 o.p. (ISBN 0-8042-0942-1, John Knox). Westminster John Knox.

Naughty Jokes Rated "R" JoAnn Box. 1977. 4.00 o.p. (ISBN 0-682-48849-6). Exposition-Phoenix.

Naughty Nicky. Tony Ross. LC 82-21265. (Illus.). 24p. (gr. k-3). 1983. 11.95 o.p. (ISBN 0-03-063522-5). H Holt & Co.

Nausee. Jean-Paul Sartre. (Coll. Soleil). 1960. 12.95 o.p. (ISBN 0-685-11414-7). Schoenhof.

Nautical Almanac for the Year 1987. (Illus.). 310p. 1985. 11.00 o.p. (ISBN 0-318-20399-5, S/N 008-054-00113-1). USGPO.

Nautical Emergencies: Seamanship for the Unexpected. Tony Meisel. (Illus.). 1984. 12.45x o.p. (ISBN 0-393-03285-X). Norton.

Nautilus Bodybuilding Book. Ellington Darden. (Illus.). 256p. 1982. 15.50 o.p. (ISBN 0-8092-5816-1); pap. 8.95 o.p. (ISBN 0-8092-5815-3). Contemp Bks.

Nautilus Diet: Ten Weeks to a Brand-New Body. Ellington Darden. (Illus.). 1987. 19.95 o.p. (ISBN 0-316-17283-9). Little.

Nautilus Handbook for Young Athletes. Ellington Darden. Ed. by Wendy Barish. (Illus.). 128p. (Orig.). (gr. 3 up). 1984. 7.75 o.s.i. (ISBN 0-671-49688-3). Wanderer Bks.

Nautilus Woman: For a Slimmer, Stronger, Sexier Body. Ellington Darden. (Illus.). 192p. 1983. pap. 9.95 o.p. (ISBN 0-671-46126-5, Fireside). S&S.

Navaho Symbols of Healing. Donald Sandner. 1979. pap. 8.95 o.p. (ISBN 0-15-665445-8, Harv). HarBraceJ.

Navajo Changes. Stephen Wallace et al. 107p. Date not set. price not set o.s.i. Navajo Curr.

Navajo Changes: A History of the Navajo People. Materials Development Staff & Teresa McCarty. 107p. 1983. text ed. 10.00 o.s.i. (ISBN 0-936998-22-9). Navajo Curr.

Navajo Neverland. Ennis Skillen. 192p. 1987. text ed. 15.00 o.p. (ISBN 0-682-40334-2). Exposition-Phoenix.

Navajo Police. Alfred Yazzie. LC 80-85450. 144p. 1980. pap. 9.00x o.s.i. Navajo Curr.

Navajo Rugs: How to Find, Evaluate, Buy & Care for Them. Don Dedera. LC 74-31617. (Illus.). 114p. 1975. pap. 8.95 o.p. (ISBN 0-87358-138-5). Northland.

Navajo Weaving: Three Centuries of Change. Kate P. Kent. LC 85-10875. (Illus.). 152p. 1985. 30.00x o.p. (ISBN 0-295-96292-5); pap. 17.95 o.p. (ISBN 0-295-96293-3). U of Wash Pr.

Naval Air Power. Michael Taylor. (Arco Military Bk.). (Illus.). 192p. 1986. 19.95 o.p. (ISBN 0-671-61958-6). Arco.

Naval Air War in Vietnam. Peter Mersky & Norman Polmar. LC 81-80703. (Illus.). 224p. 1981. softcover 14.95 o.p. (ISBN 0-933852-13-4). Nautical & Aviation.

Naval Air War in Vietnam. 2nd ed. Peter Mersky & Norman Polmar. (Illus.). 230p. 1986. pap. 12.95 o.p. (ISBN 0-933852-55-X). Nautical & Aviation.

Naval Architecture of Small Craft. D. Phillips-Birt. (Illus.). 360p. 1958. (ISBN 0-8022-1965-9). Philos Lib.

Naval Armament. Doug Richardson. (Illus.). 160p. 1982. 19.95 o.p. (ISBN 0-86720-553-9). Janes Info Group.

Naval Aviation 1911-1986: A Pictorial Study. Ed. by Sandy Russell et al. (Illus.). 96p. (Orig.). 1986. pap. 4.50 o.p. (ISBN 0-318-21609-4, S/N 008-046-00116-2). USGPO.

Naval Hydrodynamics: Proceedings of the Symposium, 12th, Naval Studies Board. Naval Hydrodynamics Symposium Staff. 1979. 19.25x o.p. (ISBN 0-309-02896-5). Natl Acad Pr.

Naval Night Battles of the Solomons. C. W. Kilpatrick. 288p. text ed. 30.00 o.p. (ISBN 0-682-40333-4). Exposition-Phoenix.

Naval Review 1986. Ed. by Paul Stillwell. (Illus.). 352p. 1986. 16.00 o.p. (ISBN 0-87021-452-7). Naval Inst Pr.

Naval Terms Dictionary. 4th ed. John V. Noel, Jr. & Edward L. Beach. LC 78-56086. 352p. 1978. 14.95x o.p. (ISBN 0-87021-482-9); bulk rates avail. o.p. Naval Inst Pr.

Nave's Topical Living Bible. 1321p. 1988. 24.95 o.p. (ISBN 0-8423-4669-4). Tyndale.

Navier-Stokes Solution for Laminar Transonic Flow over a NACA0012 Airflow, Report No. 140. B. Muller. Ed. by Aeronautical Research Institute of Sweden Staff. (Illus.). 102p. 1986. pap. text ed. 26.50 o.p. (ISBN 0-317-62880-1, Pub. by Almqvist & Wiksell). Coronet Bks.

Titles

Navigating the Rapids, Nineteen Eighteen to Nineteen Seventy-One. Beatrice B. Berle & Travis B. Jacobs. LC 72-88805. 1973. 18.50 o.p. (ISBN 0-15-164820-4). HarBraceJ.
Navigation: An RYA Manual. Royal Yatching Association Staff. (Illus.). 164p. 1984. 22.95 o.p. (ISBN 0-7153-8630-1). David & Charles.
Navigation by Pocket Calculator. Conrad Dixon. (Encore Edition Ser.). (Illus.). 1979. 2.95 o.p. (ISBN 0-684-17560-6, ScribT). Scribner.
Navigation Primer for Fishermen. F. S. Howell. (Illus.). 200p. 1978. pap. 21.75 o.p. (ISBN 0-85238-081-X, FN27, FNB). UNIPUB.
Navigator. Robert D. Foster. LC 83-60287. 240p. 1983. pap. 3.95 o.p. (ISBN 0-89109-495-4). NavPress.
Navy & Empire. James L. Stokesbury. LC 83-13230. (Illus.). 430p. 1987. pap. 12.95 o.p. (ISBN 0-688-06969-X, Quill). Morrow.
Naylors. J. I. Stewart. 1985. 13.45 o.p. (ISBN 0-393-01911-X). Norton.
Naylors. J. I. Stewart. 1986. 16.50 o.p. (ISBN 0-317-53139-5, Large Print Bks). G K Hall.
Nazi Gold. Ian Sayer & Douglas Botting. (Illus.). 388p. 1984. 21.95 o.p. (ISBN 0-943940-19-2). Congdon & Weed.
Nazi Gold. Ian Sayer & Douglas Botting. LC 85-45543. 576p. 1986. pap. 3.95 o.s.i. (ISBN 0-394-62132-8, BC). Grove.
Nazi Legacy: Klaus Barbie & the International Fascist Connection. Neal Ascherson et al. 351p. 1984. pap. 17.95 o.p. (ISBN 0-03-069303-9). H Holt & Co.
Nazi-Soviet Relations, 1939-1941: Documents from Archives of German Foreign Office. Ed. by Raymond J. Sontag & James S. Beddie. LC 75-35371. (U. S. Government Documents Program Ser.). 362p. 1976. Repr. of 1948 ed. lib. bdg. 28.75x o.p. (ISBN 0-8371-8612-9, GENS). Greenwood.
Nazi State. William Ebenstein. 1973. lib. bdg. 26.00x o.p. (ISBN 0-374-92463-5, Octagon). Hippocrene Bks.
Nazism Nineteen Eighteen to Nineteen Forty-Five. M. J. Thornton. 1966. 7.00 o.p. (ISBN 0-08-011622-1); pap. 4.60 o.p. (ISBN 0-08-011621-3). Pergamon.
Nazism 1919-1945: A Documentary Reader No. 3: Foreign Policy, War & Racial Extermination. Ed. by G. Pridham & J. Noakes. (Exeter Studies in History: Vol. 13). 400p. 1987. pap. text ed. 19.95 o.p. (ISBN 0-85989-292-1). Humanities.
NBS Metric Practice Guide & Style Manual. U. S. Department of Commerce Staff & R. A. Hopkins. 5.95 o.p. (ISBN 0-917240-04-9). Am Metric.
NBS Standard Reference Materials Catalog, 1986-87. biennial ed. Ed. by R. W. Seward. (National Bureau of Standards Special Publication 260). (Illus.). 160p. pap. 8.00 o.p. (ISBN 0-318-21345-1, S/N 003-003-02740-5). USGPO.
NC-CNC Machining II. Ed. by R. G. Brewer et al. (E.I.T.B. Training Manuals Ser.). (Illus.). 230p. 1982. 42.50x o.p. Trans-Atl Phila.
NCLEX-LPN Examination. Eileen M. Dvorak & Ray Showalter. 100p. 1982. pap. 6.95 o.p. (ISBN 0-914091-10-7). Chicago Review.
NCLEX Review Questions. 4th ed. Sandra F. Smith. 384p. 1987. 17.95 o.p. (ISBN 0-917010-29-9). Natl Nursing.
NCLEX-RN Sample Tests from American Nursing Review. Ed. by Elizabeth J. Mason. 160p. (Orig.). 1986. wkbk. 12.95 o.p. (ISBN 0-938401-01-7). Am Pro Educ.
NCLIS-SLA Task Force: The Role of the Special Library in Networks & Cooperatives - Executive Summary & Recommendations. 32p. 1984. pap. 5.00 o.p. (ISBN 0-87111-310-4). SLA.
NDT: Acoustic Emission: Advances in Acoustic Emission. W. F. Hartman & H. L. Dunegan. 385p. 1981. 77.35 o.p. (ISBN 0-318-17215-1, 758); 71.40, ASNT member o.p. (ISBN 0-318-17216-X). Am Soc Nondestructive.
NDT: Holographic Testing: An Introduction to Acoustical Holography. B. P. Hildebrand & B. B. Brenden. 224p. 1972. 31.65 o.p. (ISBN 0-318-17210-0, 858). Am Soc Nondestructive.
NEA Handbook for Local, State, & National Associations 1985-86. National Education Association Staff. LC 45-8313. 1985. pap. 10.00 o.p. (ISBN 0-8106-1238-0). NEA.
Neal Parent's Maine. Photos by Neal Parent. (Illus.). 21.95 o.s.i. (ISBN 0-89272-258-4). Down East.
Neanderthal Planet. Brian Aldiss. 192p. 1981. pap. 2.25 o.p. (ISBN 0-380-54197-1, 54197-1). Avon.
Near East: 10,000 Years of History. Isaac Asimov. (Illus.). (gr. 7 up). 1968. 4.95 o.p. (ISBN 0-395-06562-3). HM.
Near Eastern Religious Texts Relating to the Old Testament. Ed. by Walter Beyerlin. Tr. by John Bowden. LC 77-28284. (Old Testament Library). (Illus.). 324p. 1978. 22.00 o.s.i. (ISBN 0-664-21363-4, Westminster). Westminster John Knox.
Near Occasion of Sin. Judy Delton. LC 84-4597. 160p. (gr. 7 up). 1984. 12.95 o.p. (ISBN 0-15-256738-0, HJ). HarBraceJ.
Near the Long Tidal River: Readings in the Historical Geography of Central Connecticut. Thomas R. Lewis. LC 80-6181. 156p. 1981. lib. bdg. 26.00 o.p. (ISBN 0-8191-1464-2); pap. text ed. 11.50 o.p. (ISBN 0-8191-1465-0). U Pr of Amer.
Near the Ocean. Robert Lowell. LC 66-20126. (Illus.). 125p. 1967. 6.95 o.p. (ISBN 0-374-21988-5); pap. 1.95 o.p. (ISBN 0-374-50968-9). FS&G.
Near Thing for Captain Najork. Russell Hoban. LC 75-29464. (Illus.). (gr. k-3). 1976. PLB 7.95 o.p. (ISBN 0-689-30503-6, Atheneum). Macmillan.
Nearer by Far. Richard K. Tipping. LC 85-20287. 137p. 1987. 14.95 o.p. (ISBN 0-7022-1905-3). U of Queensland Pr.
Nearest Fire. Cherry Wilder. LC 79-22114. (Illus.). 1980. 9.95 o.p. (ISBN 0-689-30762-4, Atheneum). Macmillan.
Nearing's Grace. Scott Sommer. LC 79-5131. 175p. 1980. pap. 3.95 o.s.i. (ISBN 0-8008-5477-2). Taplinger.
Nebe. Ignatz Sahula-Dycke. 1978. 4.50 o.p. (ISBN 0-682-49069-5). Exposition-Phoenix.
Nebraska. George Whitmore. 144p. 1987. 15.95 o.s.i. (ISBN 0-8021-0026-0). Grove.
Nebraska: A Pictorial History. Bicentennial ed. Compiled by Bruce H. Nicoll & Gilbert M. Savery. LC 75-3570. (Illus.). 240p. 1975. 17.95 o.p. (ISBN 0-8032-0863-4); pap. 8.95 o.p. (ISBN 0-8032-5825-9). U of Nebr Pr.
Nebraska: Agency. 8.50 o.p. (ISBN 0-686-90841-4). Am Law Inst.
Nebraska Centennial Cookbook. (Illus.). 1966. pap. 6.95 o.p. (ISBN 0-8220-1620-6). Centennial.
Nebraska: Conflict of Laws. 8.50 o.p. (ISBN 0-686-90843-0). Am Law Inst.
Nebraska: Contracts. 8.50 o.p. (ISBN 0-686-90845-7). Am Law Inst.
Nebraska Curriculum for English, Grade 8: Units 82-84, the Hero. Nebraska Curriculum Development Center Staff. (Nebraska Curriculum for English Ser.). 1968. pap. 8.95x student's manual,vi,191p o.p. (ISBN 0-8032-7519-6); pap. 4.45x tchr's. manual, xxiv, 131p. o.p. (ISBN 0-8032-7518-8). U of Nebr Pr.
Nebraska Folklore. Louise Pound. LC 75-36101. 243p. 1976. Repr. of 1960 ed. lib. bdg. 22.50x o.p. (ISBN 0-8371-8616-1, PONF). Greenwood.
Nebraska: Judgments. 8.50 o.p. (ISBN 0-686-90847-3). Am Law Inst.
Nebraska Legal Forms, 9 vols. Set. looseleaf 252.00 o.p. Butterworth MN.
Nebraska Manufacturers Directory, 1986-87. 190p. 1986. pap. 30.00 o.p. (ISBN 0-318-02894-8). Manufacturers.
Nebraska: Security. 8.50 o.p. (ISBN 0-686-90849-X). Am Law Inst.
Nebraska Street & Interurban Railways. E. Bryant Phillips. 1975. pap. 3.75 o.p. (ISBN 0-916170-33-0). J-B Pub.
Nebraska: Torts, Vol. 2. 8.50 o.p. (ISBN 0-686-90851-1). Am Law Inst.
Nebraska: Trusts. 8.50 o.p. (ISBN 0-686-90852-X). Am Law Inst.
Nebula Award Stories Seventeen. Ed. by Joe Haldeman. 228p. 1983. 16.95 o.s.i. (ISBN 0-03-063528-4). H Holt & Co.
Nebula Award Stories Sixteen. Ed. by Jerry Pournelle & John F. Carr. LC 66-20974. 259p. 1982. 15.50 o.p. (ISBN 0-03-059787-0). H Holt & Co.
Nebula Awards, No. 18. Ed. by Robert Silverberg. 1983. 16.95 o.p. (ISBN 0-87795-565-4, Arbor Hse). Morrow.
Nebula Awards, No. 19. Ed. by Marta Randall. 304p. 1984. 16.95 o.p. (ISBN 0-87795-662-6, Arbor Hse). Morrow.
Nebular Variables. John S. Glasby. LC 74-3354. 220p. 1974. 60.00 o.p. (ISBN 0-08-017949-5). Pergamon.
Necessary Angel. Wallace Stevens. 1965. pap. 3.95 o.p. (ISBN 0-394-70278-6, Vin). Random.
Necessary Roughness: The Other Game of Football Revealed by Its Most Controversial Agent. Mike Trope & Steve Delsohn. (Illus.). 256p. 1987. 18.95 o.p. (ISBN 0-8092-4816-6). Contemp Bks.
Necessity of Nuclear Power. G. Greenhalgh. 260p. 1980. 28.00x o.p. (ISBN 0-86010-201-7). Graham & Trotman.
Neck of the Giraffe: Where Darwin Went Wrong. Francis Hitching. LC 81-23266. (Illus.). 288p. 1982. 13.95 o.p. (ISBN 0-89919-102-9). Ticknor & Fields.
Ned. Paxton Davis. LC 78-4187. (Illus.). (gr. 5-9). 1978. 7.95 o.p. (ISBN 0-689-30650-4, Atheneum). Macmillan.
Ned Kelly & the City of the Bees. Thomas Keneally. LC 80-66217. (Illus.). 128p. (gr. 2-7). 1981. 11.95 o.p. (ISBN 0-87923-338-9). Godine.
Ned Kelly & the City of the Bees. Thomas Keneally. 128p. (YA) (gr. 3-7). 1985. pap. 2.50 o.p. (ISBN 0-380-69848-X, Camelot). Avon.
Nedobeck's Twelve Days of Christmas. Don Nedobeck. (Illus.). 32p. (gr. k-6). 1982. pap. 2.95 o.p. (ISBN 0-8249-8113-8). Ideals.
Need for Certainty: A Sociological Study of Conventional Religion. Robert Towler. 180p. 1985. 22.50x o.p. (ISBN 0-7100-9973-8). Routledge Chapman & Hall.
Need I Say More. Beverly Duncombe. LC 83-90386. 45p. 1985. 5.95 o.p. (ISBN 0-533-05888-0). Vantage.
Need to Change. Fay Fransella. (Essential Psychology Ser.). 1975. pap. 4.50x o.p. (ISBN 0-416-82180-4, NO. 2782). Routledge Chapman & Hall.
Need to Testify. Iris Origo. LC 83-48453. (Helen & Kurt Wolff Bk.). (Illus.). 272p. 1984. 14.95 o.p. (ISBN 0-15-164989-8). HarBraceJ.
Needed Research in American English. Thomas L. Clark et al. (Publication of the American Dialect Society Ser.: No. 71). iv, 76p. (Orig.). 1984. pap. 5.30 o.s.i. (ISBN 0-8173-0238-7). U of Ala Pr.
Needed Words. Logan P. Smith et al. Ed. by Steele Commager. Incl. B.B.L.'s Recommendations for Pronouncing Doubtful Words; Bull's Bellow; Possibility of a Universal Language; Robert Bridges Recollections; Colloquial Language in Literature; Oxford English; Arabic Words in English; Best English; Index to Tracts XXI-XXIX. (Society for Pure English Ser.: Vol. 4). 1979. lib. bdg. 46.00 o.p. (ISBN 0-8240-3668-9). Garland Pub.
Needle. Hal Clement. 1979. pap. 2.45 o.p. (ISBN 0-380-00635-9, 44263-9). Avon.
Needle-Made Laces: Materials, Designs, Techniques. Pat Earnshaw. 1989. 24.95 o.p. (Pub. by Ward Lock). David & Charles.
Needle Match. H. W. Kelsey. 192p. 1982. 15.95 o.p. (ISBN 0-571-11872-0). Faber & Faber.
Needlepoint. rev. ed. Hope Hanley. LC 74-14016. (Encore Edition Ser.). (Illus.). 176p. 1975. 5.95 o.p. (ISBN 0-684-16685-2, ScribT). Scribner.
Needlepoint & Beyond: Twenty Seven Lessons in Advanced Canvaswork. Edith Feisner. (Illus.). 1980. 17.95 o.s.i. (ISBN 0-684-16086-2, ScribT). Scribner.
Needlepoint & Beyond: Twenty-Seven Lessons in Advanced Canvas Work. Edith A. Feisner. (Illus.). 176p. 1983. pap. 10.95 o.s.i. (ISBN 0-684-17825-7, ScribT). Scribner.
Needlepoint Bargello. Dorothy Kaestner. 1981. pap. 3.95 o.s.i. (ISBN 0-684-16941-X, ScribT). Scribner.
Needlepoint Bargello. Dorothy Kaestner. LC 75-24259. (Illus.). 160p. 1974. 12.95 o.s.i. (ISBN 0-684-13991-X, ScribT). Scribner.
Needlepoint by Design. Maggie Lane. LC 71-123842. 1970. encore ed. 6.95 o.p. (ISBN 0-684-10338-9, ScribT). Scribner.
Needlepoint by Design: Variations on Chinese Themes. Maggie Lane. (Illus.). 128p. 1981. pap. 9.95 o.s.i. (ISBN 0-684-17315-8, ScribT). Scribner.
Needlepoint Designs from Amish Quilts. Barbara Buchholtz & Laura S. Gilberg. (Encore Editions Ser.). (Illus.). 1977. 4.95 o.p. (ISBN 0-684-16536-8, ScribT). Scribner.
Needlepoint Designs from Oriental Rugs. Grethe Sorensen. (Illus.). 112p. 1981. 17.95 o.s.i. (ISBN 0-684-16622-4, ScribT). Scribner.
Needlepoint Designs from Oriental Rugs. Grethe Sorensen. (Illus.). 112p. 1983. pap. 12.95 o.p. (ISBN 0-684-17895-8, ScribT). Scribner.
Needlepoint Designs from the Metropolitan Museum of Art. Erica Wilson. 1988. Metro Mus Art.
Needlepoint on Plastic Canvas. Elisabeth B. De Nitto. LC 78-705. (Illus.). 1978. encore ed. 4.95 o.p. (ISBN 0-684-15534-6, ScribT); pap. 6.95 o.p. (ISBN 0-684-15577-X, SL779, ScribT). Scribner.
Needlepoint Scrapbook. Loretta Swit & Ellen Appel. LC 86-2190. (Illus.). 144p. 1986. 12.95 o.p. (ISBN 0-385-19905-8); pap. 19.95 o.p. (ISBN 0-385-19904-X). Doubleday.
Needlepoint: Stitch by Stitch. Nancy N. Kurten. (Illus.). 1977. pap. 0.75 o.p. (ISBN 0-684-15291-6, ScribT). Scribner.
Needlepoint Styles For Period Furniture. Hope Hanley. LC 78-3496. (Encore Edition Ser.). (Illus.). 1978. 15.95 o.p. (ISBN 0-684-15582-6, ScribT). Scribner.
Needlepoints to Go: Small Projects for Spare Moments. Brande Ormond. LC 75-6852. 1975. 10.95 o.p. (ISBN 0-395-20422-4). HM.
Needlework Blocking & Finishing. Dorothy Burchette. 1981. pap. 2.50 Encore o.p. (ISBN 0-684-16939-8, ScribT). Scribner.
Needlework: Blocking & Finishing. Dorothy Burchette. LC 73-1096. (Illus.). 160p. 1974. 7.95 o.s.i. (ISBN 0-684-13867-0, ScribT). Scribner.
Needlework Book of Bible Stories. Carolyn Meyer. LC 75-10135. (Illus.). 96p. (gr. 5 up). 1975. 6.95 o.p. (ISBN 0-15-256793-3, HJ). HarBraceJ.
Needlework Treasure from the Orient. P-H.
Needlwork Dragons and Mythical Creatures. Dodd.
Needs Assessment Methodologies in the Development of Impact Statements. Rosalind G. Bauchum. (Public Administration Ser.: Bibliography P 1640). 1985. pap. 2.00 o.p. (ISBN 0-89028-330-3). Vance Biblios.
Needs of the Biotechnology Industry: Growth Markets. 173p. 1984. 1500.00 o.p. (ISBN 0-89336-334-0, C-040). BCC.
Negative Income Tax: An Approach to the Co-Ordination of Taxation and Social Welfare Policies. Organization for Economic Cooperation & Development Staff. 56p. 1974. 2.50x o.p. (ISBN 92-64-11220-0). OECD.
Negative Ions. B. M. Smirnov. 1982. text ed. 70.95 o.p. (ISBN 0-07-058447-8). McGraw.
Negative News. Practising Law Institute Staff. 258p. 1984. pap. 15.00 o.p. (ISBN 0-317-27449-X, #B4-6692). PLI.
Negative Scream: A Story of Young People Who Took an Overdose. Sally O'Brien. 160p. 1986. pap. text ed. 12.95 o.p. (ISBN 0-7102-0310-1). Routledge Chapman & Hall.
Negative Strand Viruses & the Host Cell. Ed. by B. W. Mahy & R. D. Barry. 1978. 137.00 o.p. (ISBN 0-12-465350-2). Acad Pr.
Neglected Battered Child Syndrome: Role Reversal in Parents. Helen E Boardman et al. LC 63-21525. 1963. pap. 3.15 o.p. (ISBN 0-87868-074-8, G-17). Child Welfare.
Negligence Litigation Handbook: Federal & State. Mark A. Dombroff et al. LC 86-1602. (Trial Practice Library). 848p. 1986. 95.00 o.p. (ISBN 0-471-83978-7). Wiley.
Negotiability in the Federal Sector. Henry H. Robinson. 232p. 22.50 o.p. (ISBN 0-318-12387-8); pap. 14.95 o.p. (ISBN 0-318-12388-6). Am Arbitration.
Negotiate Your Way to Financial Success. Ronald J. Posluns. 224p. 1987. 18.95 o.p. (ISBN 0-399-13239-2, Putnam). Putnam Pub Group.
Negotiated Grievance Procedures in Public Employment see Issues in the Public Employee Relations Library: Series 3.
Negotiating Settlements: A Guide to Environmental Mediation. American Arbitration Association Staff & Jane E. McCarthy. LC 84-70963. 107p. 1984. pap. 10.00 o.p. (ISBN 0-943001-17-X). Am Arbitration.
Negotiating While Fighting: The Diary of Admiral C. Turner Joy at the Korean Armistice Conference. Ed. by Allen E. Goodman. LC 77-77565. (Publication Ser: No. 175). (Illus.). 1978. 22.50x o.p. (ISBN 0-8179-6751-6). Hoover Inst Pr.
Negotiations: A Novel of Tomorrow. Herman C. Gilbert. 315p. 14.95 o.p. (ISBN 0-910671-00-1). Chicago Review.
Negotiator. Clayton Matthews. 320p. 1987. pap. 3.95 o.p. (ISBN 1-55547-203-6). Critics Choice Paper.
Negro & Southern Politics: A Chapter of Florida History. Hugh D. Price. LC 73-3027. (Illus.). 133p. 1973. Repr. of 1957 ed. lib. bdg. 22.50x o.p. (ISBN 0-8371-6824-4, PRNS). Greenwood.
Negro & the Communist Party. Wilson Record. LC 76-162279. (Studies in American Negro Life). 1971. pap. text ed. 3.45x o.p. (ISBN 0-689-70279-5, NL29, Atheneum). Macmillan.
Negro Anthology. Nancy Cunard. LC 69-16589. (Illus.). 1969. Repr. of 1934 ed. lib. bdg. 110.00x o.p. (ISBN 0-8371-1952-9, CUN&, Pub. by Negro U Pr). Greenwood.
Negro Combat Troops in the World War: The Story of the Three Hundred Seventy-First Infantry. Chester D. Heywood. LC 76-93675. 1970. Repr. of 1928 ed. lib. bdg. 22.50x o.p. (ISBN 0-8371-2349-6, HET&, Pub. by Negro U Pr). Greenwood.
Negro Education: A Study of the Private & Higher Schools for Colored People in the United States, 2 vols. United States Office of Education Staff. LC 72-75558. (Illus.). 1970. Repr. of 1917 ed. 64.00x o.p. (ISBN 0-8371-2513-8, NEE&, Pub. by Negro U Pr); Vol. 1. 32.00 o.p. (ISBN 0-8371-1118-8, NEF&); Vol. 2. 36.00 o.p. (ISBN 0-8371-1119-6, NEG&). Greenwood.
Negro Education in Alabama: A Study in Cotton & Steel. Horace M. Bond. LC 39-18307. (Studies in American Negro Life Ser). 1969. pap. 3.45 o.p. (ISBN 0-689-70019-9, NL17, Atheneum). Macmillan.
Negro Folktales in Michigan. Richard M. Dorson. LC 73-21099. (Illus.). 245p. 1974. Repr. of 1956 ed. lib. bdg. 35.00x o.p. (ISBN 0-8371-5989-X, DONF). Greenwood.
Negro in American History, 3 vols. (Illus.). 1960. Set. 59.00 o.p. (ISBN 0-87827-007-8). Ency Brit Ed.

Negro in American Life. Ed. by Richard C. Wade & Howard R. Anderson. (Life in America Ser.). (gr. 9-12). 1970. text ed. 13.92 o.p. (ISBN 0-395-03148-6); pap. 9.44 o.p. (ISBN 0-395-03147-8). HM.

Negro in Brazilian Society. Florestan Fernandes. Ed. by P. B. Eveleth et al. Tr. by J. D. Skiles. LC 78-76247. (Studies in American Negro Life). 1971. pap. text ed. 4.50x o.p. (ISBN 0-689-70258-2, NL28, Atheneum). Macmillan.

Negro in Colonial New England. Lorenzo J. Greene. LC 68-16413. (Studies in American Negro Life). 1968. pap. text ed. 4.75x o.p. (ISBN 0-689-70081-4, NL1, Atheneum). Macmillan.

Negro in New Jersey. New Jersey Conference of Social Work Staff. LC 74-78772. (Illus.). 1969. Repr. of 1932 ed. 35.00x o.p. (ISBN 0-8371-1411-X, NNJ&, Pub. by Negro U Pr). Greenwood.

Negro in New York. James E. Allen. 1964. 5.00 o.p. (ISBN 0-682-42082-4). Exposition-Phoenix.

Negro in Savannah, Eighteen Sixty-Five to Nineteen Hundred. Robert Perdue. LC 72-90068. 1973. 7.50 o.p. (ISBN 0-682-47606-4, University). Exposition-Phoenix.

Negro in Texas, 1874-1900. Lawrence D. Rice. LC 70-130665. xii, 310p. 1971. 32.50x o.p. (ISBN 0-8071-0637-2). La State U Pr.

Negro in the French West Indies. Shelby T. McCloy. LC 70-162631. 278p. 1974. Repr. of 1966 ed. lib. bdg. 22.50x o.p. (ISBN 0-8371-6193-2, MNI&, Pub. by Negro U Pr). Greenwood.

Negro in the South Since Eighteen Sixty-Five. Ed. by C. E. Wynes. LC 65-19664. (Southern Historical Ser: Vol. 10). 253p. 1965. 16.50 o.p. (ISBN 0-8173-5215-5). U of Ala Pr.

Negro Musicians & Their Music. Maud Hare. 439p. Repr. of 1936 ed. lib. bdg. 59.00 o.p. (Pub. by Am Repr Serv). Reprint Servs.

Negro Myths from the Georgia Coast. Charles C. Jones, Jr. LC 68-21779. 184p. 1969. Repr. of 1888 ed. 40.00x o.p. (ISBN 0-8103-3836-X). Gale.

Negro People in America. Herbert Aptheker. LC 46-8650. 1946. pap. 15.00 o.p. (ISBN 0-527-02770-7). Kraus Repr.

Negro Poetry & Drama & the Negro in American Fiction. Sterling Brown. LC 69-15521. (Studies in American Negro Life Ser). 1969. pap. text ed. 3.45x o.s.i. (ISBN 0-689-70024-5, NL12, Atheneum). Macmillan.

Negro Potential. Eli Ginzberg et al. LC 80-17250. (Illus.). xvi, 144p. 1980. Repr. of 1963 ed. lib. bdg. 35.00x o.p. (ISBN 0-313-22389-0, GINP). Greenwood.

Negro Professional Man & the Community, with Special Emphasis on the Physician & the Lawyer. Carter G. Woodson. LC 74-89025. 1970. Repr. of 1934 ed. lib. bdg. 25.00x o.p. (ISBN 0-8371-1896-4, WNP&, Pub. by Negro U Pr). Greenwood.

Negro Spirituals: From Bible to Folk Song. Christa K. Dixon. LC 75-36444. 128p. 1976. pap. 3.25 o.p. (ISBN 0-8006-1221-3, Fortress). Augsburg Fortress.

Negroes & the New Southern Politics. Donald R. Matthews & James W. Prothro. LC 66-28289. (Illus.). 551p. 1966. 12.50 o.p. (ISBN 0-15-165011-X). HarBraceJ.

Negroes in Cities: Residential Segregation & Neighborhood Change. Karl E. Taeuber & Alma F. Taeuber. LC 65-12459. (Studies in American Negro Life). 1969. pap. text ed. 3.95x o.p. (ISBN 0-689-70193-4, NL21, Atheneum). Macmillan.

Negroes in the United States, 1920-1932. U. S. Bureau of the Census Staff & Charles E. Hall. 1970. Repr. of 1935 ed. lib. bdg. 44.00 o.p. (ISBN 0-8371-2076-4, NUS&). Greenwood.

Negro's God As Reflected in His Literature. Benjamin Mays. LC 68-9471. (Studies in American Negro Life Ser.). 1968. pap. text ed. 2.75x o.p. (ISBN 0-689-70138-1, NL11, Atheneum). Macmillan.

Negro's Progress in Fifty Years. American Academy of Political And Social Science Staff. LC 71-92737. 1969. Repr. of 1913 ed. 35.00 o.p. (ISBN 0-8371-2187-6, NEP&, Pub. by Negro U Pr). Greenwood.

Nehemiah & the Dynamics of Effective Leadership: Study Guide. Cyril J. Barber. (Illus.). 56p. 1980. pap. text ed. 3.25 o.p. (ISBN 0-87213-022-3). Loizeaux.

Nehemiah: Man in Charge. Donald K. Campbell. 1979. pap. 5.50 o.p. (ISBN 0-88207-781-3). Victor Bks.

Nehrus: Motilal & Jawaharlal. B. R. Nanda. 358p. 1974. pap. text ed. 3.95x o.s.i. (ISBN 0-226-56806-7, P582, Phoen). U of Chicago Pr.

Neid see Envy: A Theory of Social Behaviour.

Neighbor. Laird Koenig. 1978. pap. 1.75 o.p. (ISBN 0-380-41285-3, 41285). Avon.

Neighborhood. Jerry Van Amerongen. 96p. 1984. pap. 4.95 o.s.i. (ISBN 0-671-52322-8). S&S.

Neighborhood Associations: A Selected Checklist. Jamie W. Coniglio. (Public Administration Ser.: P 1766). 4p. 1985. 2.00 o.p. (ISBN 0-89028-566-7). Vance Biblios.

Neighborhood Organization & Interest-Group Processes. David J. O'Brien. LC 75-3468. 304p. 1975. 30.50 o.p. (ISBN 0-691-09363-6); pap. 10.50 o.p. (ISBN 0-691-02818-4). Princeton U Pr.

Neighborhood Policy & Planning. Ed. by Phillip L. Clay & Robert M. Hollister. (Politics of Planning Ser.). 240p. 1983. 28.00x o.p. (ISBN 0-669-06302-9); pap. 17.00x o.p. (ISBN 0-669-06936-1). Lexington Bks.

Neighborhood Renewal: Trends & Strategies. Phillip L. Clay. LC 78-14153. 1979. 19.00X o.p. (ISBN 0-669-02681-6). Lexington Bks.

Neighborhood Revitalization & the Postindustrial City: A Multinational Perspective. Dennis E. Gale. LC 83-47523. (Politics of Planning Ser.). 208p. 1984. 27.00x o.p. (ISBN 0-669-06697-4). Lexington Bks.

Neighborhoods That Work: Sources for Viability in the Inner City. Sandra Schoenberg & Patricia Rosenbaum. 195p. 1980. 23.00x o.p. (ISBN 0-8135-0901-7). Rutgers U Pr.

Neighbors to the South. rev. ed. Delia Goetz. LC 56-5874. (Illus.). (gr. 7 up). 1956. 4.95 o.p. (ISBN 0-15-256885-9, HJ). HarBraceJ.

Neil Diamond: Heartlight. Ed. by Milton Okun & Dan Fox. 63p. 1983. pap. 7.95 o.p. (ISBN 0-89524-177-3, 7703). Cherry Lane.

Neil Diamond: On the Way to the Sky. Milton Okun. Ed. by Dan Fox. 68p. 1982. 7.95 o.p. (ISBN 0-89524-151-X, 7702). Cherry Lane.

Neil Leifer's Sports Stars. Neil Leifer. LC 85-6737. (Illus.). 1985. 35.00 o.s.i. (ISBN 0-385-19562-1, Dolp). Doubleday.

Neil Leifers Sports Stars. Neil Leifer. LC 85-6737. (Illus.). 256p. 1986. pap. 16.95 o.p. (ISBN 0-385-23757-X, Dolp). Doubleday.

Neither Athens nor Sparta? The American Service Academies in Transition. John P. Lovell. LC 78-9509. (Illus.). 384p. 1979. 22.50x o.p. (ISBN 0-253-12955-9). Ind U Pr.

Neither Justice nor Reason: A Legal & Anthropological Analysis of Aboriginal Rights. Marc Gumbert. LC 84-3598. (Illus.). 215p. 1985. text ed. 25.00x o.p. (ISBN 0-7022-1746-8). U of Queensland Pr.

Nekkid Cowboy. Katie Breeze. LC 82-73110. 216p. 1982. 11.95 o.p. (ISBN 0-931722-17-9). Corona Pub.

Neknus & Other Poems. J. A. Bosworth. LC 83-90808. 1984. 10.00 o.p. (ISBN 0-533-05817-1). Vantage.

Nelegko byt' Ruskim Shpionom. Aleksei Korotyukov. LC 82-7341. 132p. (Rus.). 1982. pap. 8.00 o.s.i. (ISBN 0-938920-18-9). Hermitage.

Nellie Cameron. Michele Murray. LC 75-133060. 160p. (gr. 3-6). 1979. 6.95 o.p. (ISBN 0-395-28867-3, Clarion). HM.

Nelson. Carola M. Lenanton. LC 77-100166. (Illus.). xiv, 748p. 1970. Repr. of 1946 ed. lib. bdg. 35.00x o.p. (ISBN 0-8371-3976-7, LENE). Greenwood.

Nelson Essential Hero. Bradford. 1977. 12.95 o.p. (ISBN 0-15-112240-7). HarBraceJ.

Nelson Island Story. Karen Southern. Ed. by Diane Brown. 224p. (Orig.). 1987. pap. 12.95 o.s.i. (ISBN 0-88839-196-X). Hancock House.

Nelson's Complete Concordance of the Revised Standard Version. 2nd ed. John W. Ellison. LC 84-27256. 1136p. 1985. 29.95 o.p. (ISBN 0-8407-4954-6). Nelson.

Nematode Parasite Population in Sheep & on Pasture. Ed. by H. D. Crofton. 104p. 1971. pap. 5.75 o.p. CAB Intl.

Nemesis. Phil Davis. 1979. pap. 2.50 o.p. (ISBN 0-380-41913-0, 41913). Avon.

Neo-African Literature: A History of Black Writing. Janheinz Jahn. 1961. pap. 3.95 o.p. (ISBN 0-394-17319-8, E523, Ever). Grove.

Neo-Colonialism: The Last Stage of Imperialism. Kwame Nkrumah. LC 66-18026. (Illus.). 304p. (Orig.). 1966. pap. 4.95 o.p. (ISBN 0-7178-0140-3). Intl Pubs Co.

Neo-Hegelianism. Hiralal Haldar. LC 83-48508. (Philosophy of Hegel Ser.). 501p. 1984. lib. bdg. 60.00 o.p. (ISBN 0-8240-5631-0). Garland Pub.

Neo-Keynesian Theory of Inflation & Economic Growth. S. Fusino. (Lecture Notes in Economics & Mathematical Systems Ser.: Vol. 104). v, 96p. 1974. pap. 9.90 o.p. (ISBN 0-387-06964-X). Springer-Verlag.

Neo-Ricardian Theory: With Applications to Some Current Economic Problems. B. Naeslund & B. Sellstedt. (Lecture Notes in Economics & Mathematical Systems: Vol. 156). 1978. pap. 14.00 o.p. (ISBN 0-387-08763-X). Springer-Verlag.

Neo-Tech & Business. Frank R. Wallace. 1986. 15.50 o.p. (ISBN 0-911752-52-8). I & O Pub.

Neo-Tech I, the Pre-Discovery. Frank R. Wallace. 224p. 1985. 47.50 o.p. (ISBN 0-911752-42-0). I & O Pub.

Neoclassic to Post-Impressionist Painters. John Canaday. 1972. pap. 2.95 o.p. (ISBN 0-393-00666-2, Norton Lib). Norton.

Neoevangelicalism Today. Robert P. Lightner. LC 78-11426. (Illus.). 1979. pap. 3.95 o.p. (ISBN 0-87227-067-X). Reg Baptist.

Neoliberals: Creating the New American Politics. Randall Rothenberg. 288p. 1984. 16.45 o.p. (ISBN 0-671-45881-7). S&S.

Neon Lovers Glow in the Dark. Lili Lakich. (Illus.). 96p. 1986. pap. 15.95 o.p. (ISBN 0-87905-419-0, Peregrine Smith). Gibbs Smith Pub.

Neon Rain. James L. Burke. LC 86-15222. 1987. 16.95 o.s.i. (ISBN 0-8050-0053-4). H Holt & Co.

Neonatal Hormone Treatment & Adult Sexual Behavior in Rodents. R. D. Lisk et al. (Biology of Sex Ser.). 230p. 1974. text ed. 25.50x o.p. (ISBN 0-8422-7125-2). Irvington.

Neonatal Medicine. Malcolm L. Chiswick. (Illus.). 1978. text ed. 10.50x o.p. (ISBN 0-906141-01-X, Pub. by Update Pubns England). Kluwer Academic.

Neonate with Congenital Heart Disease. 2nd ed. Richard D. Rowe et al. (Major Problems in Clinical Pediatrics Ser.: Vol. 5). (Illus.). 450p. 1981. text ed. write for info. o.p. (ISBN 0-7216-7775-4). Saunders.

Neoplasms of the Colon, Rectum & Anus: Mucosal & Epithelial. John S. Spratt. (Illus.). 459p. 1984. write for info. o.p. (ISBN 0-7216-8534-X). Saunders.

Neoplastic Development. L. R. Foulds. Vol. 1. 1969. 106.00 o.p. (ISBN 0-12-262801-2); Vol. 2. 1975. 167.00 o.p. (ISBN 0-12-262802-0). Acad Pr.

Neoplastic Disorders. Ed. by Helen Hamilton & Minnie B. Rose. (Nurses's Clinical Library). (Illus.). 192p. 1985. text ed. 19.95 o.p. (ISBN 0-916730-73-5). Springhouse Pub.

Neoplastic Transformation in Differentiated Epithelial Cell Systems in Vitro. Ed. by L. M. Franks & C. B. Wigley. LC 79-41276. 1980. 74.50 o.p. (ISBN 0-12-266260-1). Acad Pr.

Neostriatum: Proceedings of a Workshop Sponsored by the European Brain & Behaviour Society, Denmark, 17-19 April 1978. Ed. by Ivan Divac et al. (Illus.). 1979. 59.00 o.p. (ISBN 0-08-023174-8). Pergamon.

Neotropical Colubrid Snake Genus Liophis. I. The Generic Concept. James R. Dixon. (Contributions in Biology & Geology Ser.: No. 31). 40p. 1980. 3.25 o.p. (ISBN 0-89326-055-X). Milwaukee Pub Mus.

Neotropical Primates: Field Studies & Conservation. Institute for Laboratory Animal Resources Staff. Ed. by Richard Thorington, Jr. & Paul Heltne. (Illus.). 1976. pap. 11.75x o.p. (ISBN 0-309-02442-0). Natl Acad Pr.

Neotropical Species of Campanella & Aphyllotus with Notes on some Species of Marasmiellus. R. Singer. (Nova Hedwigia Ser.: No. 26). (Illus.). 50p. 1975. pap. text ed. 15.95x o.p. (ISBN 3-7682-1091-X). Lubrecht & Cramer.

NEPA Decision Criteria for Operating License Reviews: AIF-NESP-024. Envirosphere Company Staff. (National Environmental Studies Project: NESP Reports). 1981. 45.00 o.p. (ISBN 0-318-02232-X). US Coun Energy Awareness.

Nephew. James Purdy. 1987. pap. 7.95 o.p. (ISBN 0-317-66527-8). Weidenfeld.

Nephrology. 3rd ed. Ed. by Sanford Warren, Jr. et al. (Self-Assessment Ser.: Vol. 6). 1982. 32.75 o.p. (ISBN 0-87488-280-X). Med Exam.

Neptune's Apprentice: Adventures of a Commercial Fisherwoman. Marie De Santis. (Illus.). 232p. 1984. 15.95 o.p. (ISBN 0-89141-200-X). Presidio Pr.

Nerilka's Story: A Pern Adventure. Anne McCaffrey. LC 85-26864. 1986. 12.95 o.p. (ISBN 0-345-33159-1, Del Rey). Ballantine.

Nero: Reality & Legend. B. H. Warmington. (Ancient Culture & Society Ser). (Illus.). 1970. pap. 3.95 o.p. (ISBN 0-393-00542-9, Norton Lib.). Norton.

Nerve Endings. William Martin. (General Ser.). 1984. lib. bdg. 18.95 o.p. (ISBN 0-8161-3729-3, Large Print Bks). G K Hall.

Nerve Impulse. rev. ed. R. H. Adrian. Ed. by J. J. Head. LC 78-54975. (Carolina Biology Readers Ser.: No. 67). (Illus.). 16p. (YA) (gr. 10 up). 1981. pap. 1.80 o.p. (ISBN 0-89278-267-6, 45-9667). Carolina Biological.

Nerve Membranes: A Study of the Biological & Chemical Aspects of Neuron Glia Relationships. P. Johnston & B. Roots. 279p. 1972. 80.00 o.p. (ISBN 0-08-013222-7). Pergamon.

Nerve-Muscle Interaction. G. Vrbova et al. 1978. 59.95x o.p. (ISBN 0-412-15720-9, NO. 6308, Pub. by Chapman & Hall). Routledge Chapman & Hall.

Nervous System Theory: An Introductory Study. K. N. Leibovic. 1973. 58.00 o.p. (ISBN 0-12-441250-5). Acad Pr.

Nesting Biology & Associates of Melitoma (Hymenoptera, Anthrophoridae) E. G. Linsley & J. W. MacSwain. (U. C. Publications in Entomolgy Ser.: Vol. 90). 1980. pap. 14.95x o.p. (ISBN 0-520-09618-5). U of Cal Pr.

Net Net. Isadore Barmash. 1973. pap. 1.50 o.p. (ISBN 0-380-01354-1, 14621). Avon.

Net Theory & Applications Proceedings. W. Brauer. (Lecture Notes in Computer Science Ser.: Vol. 84). 537p. 1980. pap. 32.00 o.p. (ISBN 0-387-10001-6). Springer-Verlag.

Net to Catch War. Mary Mian. (gr. 4-6). 1975. 6.95 o.p. (ISBN 0-395-20491-7). HM.

Net Yield Table After Forty-Six Percent Capital Gains Tax. Financial Publishing Co. Staff. 384p. 1982. pap. 19.50 o.p. (ISBN 0-87600-144-4). Finan Pub.

Net Yields Table after Twenty Percent Capital Gains Tax. Financial Publishing Co. Staff. 384p. 1982. pap. 19.50 o.p. (ISBN 0-87600-244-0). Finan Pub.

Nether World. George Gissing. 1983. pap. 7.95 o.p. (ISBN 0-7108-0319-2, NO. 3877). Routledge Chapman & Hall.

Netsuke: Masterpieces from the Metropolitan Museum of Art. Barbara T. Okada. Ed. by Kathleen Howard. Tr. by Hozen Seki & Edwin A. Cranston. (Illus.). 204p. 1982. 29.50 o.p. (ISBN 0-87099-273-2). Metro Mus Art.

Nettlewood. Mary Melwood. LC 74-19426. 352p. (gr. 6 up). 1979. 8.95 o.p. (ISBN 0-395-28919-X, Clarion). HM.

Network Analysis for Technology. Curtis Johnson. (Illus.). 1984. text ed. write for info. o.p. (ISBN 0-02-361050-6). Macmillan.

Network Analysis: Theory & Computer Methods. Randall W. Jensen & Bruce O. Watkins. (Illus.). 544p. 1974. ref. ed. 26.95 o.p. (ISBN 0-13-611061-4). P-H.

Network & Switching Theory. Ed. by Giuseppe Biorci. (Electrical Science Ser). 1968. 98.00 o.p. (ISBN 0-12-099550-6). Acad Pr.

Network Flow, Transportation & Scheduling: Theory & Algorithms. M. Iri. (Mathematics in Science & Engineering Ser., Vol. 57). 1969. 54.00 o.p. (ISBN 0-12-373850-4). Acad Pr.

Network Planning Symposium (Networks 83) Institution of Electrical Engineers (UK) Staff & Peter Peregrinus, Ltd. (IEE Conference Publications Ser.). 315p. 1983. 80.00 o.p. (ISBN 0-85296-269-X, IC215). Inst Elect Eng.

Network Synthesis. Charles A. Vergers. 14.95 o.p. (ISBN 0-8306-0085-X, 1402); pap. 7.95 o.p. (ISBN 0-8306-1402-8). TAB Bks.

Network Systems. Roshan L. Sharma et al. (VNR Data Processing Ser.). 392p. 1982. 32.95 o.p. (ISBN 0-442-26104-7). Van Nos Reinhold.

Network Television & the Public Interest: A Preliminary Inquiry. Ed. by Michael Botein & David Rice. LC 79-1751. 320p. 1980. 27.00x o.p. (ISBN 0-669-02927-0). Lexington Bks.

Network Theorem Book. Harry E. Stockman. 300p. 20.00 o.p. (ISBN 0-918332-11-7). Sercolab.

Networking & Other Forms of Cooperation. Clinic on Library Applications of Data Processing Proceedings, 1973. Ed. by F. W. Lancaster. LC 65-1841. 185p. 1973. 7.00x o.p. (ISBN 0-87845-038-6). U of Ill Lib Info Sci.

Networking Book: People Connecting with People. Jessica Lipnack & Jeffrey Stamps. 256p. 1986. pap. 12.95 o.p. (ISBN 0-7102-0976-2, 09762, Pub. by Routledge UK). Routledge Chapman & Hall.

Networking IBM PCs: A Practical Guide. Michael Durr. 320p. 1984. pap. 18.95 o.p. (ISBN 0-88022-106-2, 125). Que Corp.

Networking Practices & Priorities of Special & Academic Librarians: A Comparison. Marcy Murphy. (Occasional Papers: No. 126). 24p. 1976. pap. 2.00 o.p. (ISBN 0-317-58963-6). U of Ill Lib Info Sci.

Networking: The Great New Way for Women to Get Ahead. Mary S. Welch. LC 79-2767. 1980. 9.95 o.p. (ISBN 0-15-165199-X). HarBraceJ.

Networking With The IBM Network & Cluster. Michael Hurwicz. (Illus.). 224p. (Orig.). 1985. 29.95 o.p. (ISBN 0-8306-0929-6, 1929); pap. 19.60 o.p. (ISBN 0-8306-1929-1). TAB Bks.

Networks of World Trade. (Studies in International Trade: No. 7). (Illus.). 1979. pap. 10.50 o.p. (ISBN 0-685-93846-8, G120, GATT). UNIPUB.

Neue Aspekte Der Medikamentosen Behandlung Von Tachyarrhythmien see New Aspects in the Medical Treatment of Tachyarrhythmias: Role of Amiodarone.

Neue Horizonte. David Dollenmayer et al. LC 87-81430. 350p. 1984. text ed. 26.00 o.p. (ISBN 0-669-04534-9). Heath.

Neue Malerei in Deutschland. Ed. by Jurgen Harten et al. (Illus.). 192p. (Ger.). 1983. 41.00 o.p. (ISBN 3-7913-0641-3, Pub. by Prestel). TeNeues.

Neural Assemblies: An Alternative Approach to Artificial Intelligence. G. Palm. (Studies of Brain Function: Vol. 7). (Illus.). 244p. 1982. 65.00 o.p. (ISBN 0-387-11366-5). Springer-Verlag.

Neural Basis of Oral & Facial Function. Ed. by Ronald Dubner et al. LC 78-4048. (Illus.). 494p. 1978. 75.00x o.p. (ISBN 0-306-31094-5, Plenum Pr). Plenum Pub.

Neural Communication & Control: Satellite Symposium of the 28th International Congress of Physiological Sciences, Debrechen, Hungary, 1980. Ed. by Gy. Szekely et al. (Advances in Physiological Sciences: Vol. 30). (Illus.). 350p. 1981. 50.00 o.p. (ISBN 0-08-027351-3). Pergamon.

Neural Control of Behavior. Ed. by Richard E. Whalen et al. 1970. 65.50 o.p. (ISBN 0-12-745050-5). Acad Pr.

Neural Control of Circulation. Ed. by Maysie J. Hughes & Charles D. Barnes. LC 79-6784. (Research Topics in Physiology Ser.). 1980. 49.00 o.p. (ISBN 0-12-360850-3). Acad Pr.

Neural Mechanisms of Learning & Memory. Ed. by Mark R. Rosenzweig & Edward L. Bennett. LC 75-35780. 1000p. 1976. text ed. 70.00x o.p. (ISBN 0-262-18076-6). MIT Pr.

Neural Network Architectures for Artificial Intelligence. Ed. by Geoffrey E. Hinton & David E. Rumelhart. 75p. 1988. pap. text ed. 12.00 o.p. (ISBN 0-929280-15-6). Amer Artificial.

Neural Principles in Vision. Ed. by F. Zettler & R. Weiler. LC 76-21804. (Proceedings in Life Sciences). (Illus.). 1976. 57.00 o.p. (ISBN 0-387-07839-8). Springer-Verlag.

Neuro-Ophthamology Review Manual. 2nd ed. Rev. by Lanning B. Kline. LC 86-42869. 176p. 1987. text ed. 34.95 o.p. (ISBN 0-943432-96-0). Slack Inc.

Neuro-Orthopedic Screening in Infancy: Schedules, Examination & Findings. Rupprecht Bernbeck & Alexander Sinios. LC 78-2505. (Illus.). 120p. 1978. text ed. 16.50 o.p. (ISBN 0-8067-0231-1). Urban & S.

Neuro-Psychopharmacology: Proceedings of the Collegium Internationale Neuro-Psychopharmacologium 11th Congress, Vienna, 1979. Ed. by B. Saletu et al. (Illus.). 1979. 220.00 o.p. (ISBN 0-08-023089-X). Pergamon.

Neuroanatomical Research Technique. Ed. by Richard T. Robertson. (Methods in Physiological Psych. Ser.: Vol. 2). 1978. 74.50 o.p. (ISBN 0-12-590350-2). Acad Pr.

Neurobehavioral Methods in Occupational Health: Proceedings of an International Symposium on Neurobehavioral Methods in Occupational Health (State of Art & Emerging Trends) Como & Milan, Italy June 1982. Ed. by R. Gilioli et al. LC 83-13466. 328p. 1983. 77.00 o.p. (ISBN 0-08-029802-8). Pergamon.

Neurobiology Invertebrates: Proceedings of a Satellite Symposium of the 28th International Congress of Physiological Sciences, Tihany, Hungary, 1980, Vol. 23. Ed. by J. Salanki. LC 80-42252. (Illus.). 400p. 1981. 69.00 o.p. (ISBN 0-08-027344-0). Pergamon.

Neurobiology of Dopamine. Ed. by A. S. Horn et al. LC 78-72547. 1980. 152.00 o.p. (ISBN 0-12-354150-6). Acad Pr.

Neurobiology of Sleep & Memory. R. R. Drucker- Colin & J. L. McGaugh. 1977. 72.50 o.p. (ISBN 0-12-222350-0). Acad Pr.

Neuroblastoma. Carl Pochedly. LC 75-18337. (Illus.). 314p. 1976. 14.50 o.p. (ISBN 0-88416-117-X). Year Bk Med.

Neuroblastomas: Biochemical Studies. Ed. by C. Bohoun. (Recent Results in Cancer Research: Vol. 2). (Illus.). 1966. 15.40 o.p. (ISBN 0-387-03641-5). Springer-Verlag.

Neurochemical Aspects of Hypothalmic Function. Ed. by L. Martini & J. Meites. 1971. 43.00 o.p. (ISBN 0-12-475560-7). Acad Pr.

Neurodevelopmental Problems in Early Childhood: Assessment & Management. Drillien & Drummond. (Illus.). 512p. 1978. 69.50 o.p. (ISBN 0-632-00409-6, B-1475-9). Mosby.

Neurodynamics of Vertebral Subluxation. A. E. Homewood. LC 77-85117. 1977. text ed. 18.00 o.s.i. (ISBN 0-912760-55-9). Valkyrie Pub Hse.

Neuroendocrinology, 2 vols. Ed. by L. Martini & William F. Ganong. 1966-67. 90.00 ea. o.p. Vol. 1 (ISBN 0-12-475351-5). Vol. 2 (ISBN 0-12-475352-3). Acad Pr.

Neuroendocrinology: Biological & Clinical Aspects. Ed. by A. Polleri & R. M. Macleod. 1979. 72.50 o.p. (ISBN 0-12-560850-0). Acad Pr.

Neurogenic Control of the Brain Circulation. Ed. by Christer Owman & Lars Edvinsson. LC 77-30303. 1977. 105.00 o.p. (ISBN 0-08-021553-X). Pergamon.

Neurogenic Heart Lesions. I. S. Zavodskaya et al. LC 80-40436. (Illus.). 150p. 1980. 89.00 o.p. (ISBN 0-08-025482-9). Pergamon.

Neurohistological Studies of the Hypothalamo-Hypophysial System of Zonotrichia Leucophrys Gambelii. A. Oksche & D. S. Farner. LC 73-19102. (Advances in Anatomy, Embryology & Cell Biology: Vol. 48, Pt. 4). (Illus.). 105p. 1974. pap. 30.70 o.p. (ISBN 0-387-06586-5). Springer-Verlag.

Neurohormones & Neurohumors: Proceedings of the International Society for Neurovegetative Research, Amsterdam, 1967. International Society for Neurovegetative Research Staff. (Illus.). 1969. 116.90 o.p. (ISBN 0-387-80914-7). Springer-Verlag.

Neurologic Critical Care. Joan E. Davis & Celestine B. Mason. 1979. 24.95 o.p. (ISBN 0-442-22004-9). Van Nos Reinhold.

Neurologic Infections in Children. 2nd ed. William E. Bell & William F. McCormick. (Major Problems in Clinical Pediatrics Ser.: Vol. 12). (Illus.). 600p. 1981. text ed. (ISBN 0-7216-1676-3). Saunders.

Neurologic Problems, Vol. 3. Diana I. Bubb. (RN Nursing Assessment Ser.). 160p. 1984. pap. 15.95 o.p. (ISBN 0-87489-287-2). Med Economics.

Neurological Control Systems: Studies in Bioengineering. Lawrence Stark. LC 68-14858. 428p. 1968. 59.50x o.p. (ISBN 0-306-30325-6, Plenum Pr). Plenum Pub.

Neurological Problems in Orthopaedics. Galasko. (Illus.). 250p. 1987. 75.75 o.p. (ISBN 0-317-53478-5, B-1722-7). Mosby.

Neurological Rehabilitation. Umphred. 1984. 41.95 o.p. (ISBN 0-8016-2514-9). Mosby.

Neurology. 8th ed. Paul S. Slosberg. (Medical Examination Review Book Ser.: Vol. 8). 1981. 15.75 o.p. (ISBN 0-87488-092-0). Med Exam.

Neurology for Non-Neurologists. Ed. by Wigbert C. Wiederholt. LC 82-3995. 1982. 43.50 o.p. (ISBN 0-12-788925-6). Acad Pr.

Neurology of Hereditary Metabolic Diseases of Children. Raymond D. Adams & G. Lyon. 1982. text ed. 75.00 o.p. (ISBN 0-07-000318-1). McGraw.

Neurology of Mentality. Jay Carlton. 45p. 1984. 5.00 o.p. (ISBN 0-682-40145-5). Exposition-Phoenix.

Neuromuscular Blocking & Stimulating Agents, Vols. 1 & 2. J. Cheymol. 654p. 1972. 235.00 o.p. (ISBN 0-08-016277-0). Pergamon.

Neuronal Information Transfer. Ed. by Arthur Karlin et al. (P & S Biomedical Sciences Symposia Ser.). 1976. 49.95 o.p. (ISBN 0-12-398450-5). Acad Pr.

Neuronal Mechanisms of Hearing. Ed. by Josef Syka & Lindsay Aitkin. LC 81-1626. 456p. 1981. 75.00x o.p. (ISBN 0-306-40656-X, Plenum Pr). Plenum Pub.

Neurons of the First Optic Ganglion on the Bee (Apis Mellifera) W. A. Ribi. (Advances in Anatomy, Embryology & Cell Biology Ser.: Vol. 50, Pt. 4). (Illus.). 49p. 1975. pap. 16.60 o.p. (ISBN 0-387-07096-6). Springer-Verlag.

Neuropharmacology & Behavior. Ed. by Bernard Haber & M. H. Aprison. LC 77-14178. (Illus.). 236p. 1978. 42.50x o.p. (ISBN 0-306-31056-2, Plenum Pr). Plenum Pub.

Neuropharmacology of Cyclic Nucleotides: Role of CAMP in Affective Disorders, Epilepsy & Modified Behavioral States. Ed. by Gene C. Palmer. LC 78-23490. (Illus.). 316p. 1979. text ed. 22.50 o.p. (ISBN 0-8067-1521-9). Urban & S.

Neuropharmacology of Epilepsy. Michael Trimble. LC 84-25817. 184p. 1985. 29.00x o.p. (ISBN 0-471-90672-7, Dist. by A R Liss). Wiley.

Neurophysiological Correlates of Normal Cognition & Psychopathology. Carlo Parris et al. 268p. 1984. pap. 60.00 o.p. (ISBN 3-8055-3737-9). Transaction Pubs.

Neuropolitique. 1st ed. Timothy Leary. LC 88-81431. (Future History Ser.). (Illus.). 180p. 1987. pap. 9.95 o.p. (ISBN 0-941404-61-7). Falcon Pr Az.

Neurosciences: A Study Program. Ed. by G. C. Quarton. (Illus.). 1088p. (Charts, Photos, Micrographs, Tabs). 1967. write for info. o.p. (ISBN 0-87470-005-1); on microfilm avail. o.p. Rockefeller.

Neurosecretion: Molecules, Cells, Systems. Ed. by Donald S. Farner & Karl Lederis. LC 81-21016. 558p. 1982. 89.50x o.p. (ISBN 0-306-40760-4, Plenum Pr). Plenum Pub.

Neurosecretion: Proceedings. International Symposium on Neurosecretion, 4th, Strasbourg, 1966. Ed. by F. Stutinsky. (Illus.). 1967. 74.40 o.p. (ISBN 0-387-03941-4). Springer-Verlag.

Neuroses. Pieter C. Kuiper. LC 74-180732. 261p. 1972. text ed. 30.00x o.s.i. (ISBN 0-8236-3555-4). Intl Univs Pr.

Neuroses & Their Treatment. Edward Podolsky. 576p. 1958. (ISBN 0-8022-1995-0). Philos Lib.

Neuroses of the Nations. Caroline Playne. LC 77-148371. (Library of War & Peace; the Character & Causes of War). 1973. lib. bdg. 46.00 o.p. (ISBN 0-8240-0453-1). Garland Pub.

Neurosurgery, 6th European Congress: Organized by the European Association of Neurosurgical Societies of Paris, July 15-20, 1979. Ed. by J. Brihaye. (Act Neurochirurgica Supplements: Vol. 28). (Illus.). 1979. pap. 115.10 o.p. (ISBN 0-387-81534-1). Springer-Verlag.

Neurosurgical Approach to Intracranial Infections: A Review of Personal Experiences 1940-1960. F. J. Irsigler. (Illus.). 1961. 52.00 o.p. (ISBN 0-387-02700-9). Springer-Verlag.

Neurotic Distortion of the Creative Process. Lawrence S. Kubie. 152p. 1961. pap. 4.95 o.p. (ISBN 0-374-50180-7). FS&G.

Neurotransmitter Amino Acids. Neil Davidson. 1976. 51.00 o.p. (ISBN 0-12-205950-6). Acad Pr.

Neurotransmitter Interaction & Compartmentation. Ed. by H. F. Bradford. (NATO ASI Series A, Life Sciences: Vol. 48). 852p. 1982. 115.00x o.p. (ISBN 0-306-41015-X, Plenum Pr). Plenum Pub.

Neurotransmitter Receptors, Part 1: Amino Acids, Peptides & Benzodiazepines see Queues: Receptors & Recognition Series B.

Neurotransmitter Receptors, Part 2: Biogenic Amines see Queues: Receptors & Recognition Series B.

Neurotransmitter Systems & Their Clinical Disorders. Ed. by N. Legg. 1979. 43.50 o.p. (ISBN 0-12-443050-3). Acad Pr.

Neurotransmitters & Anterior Pituitary. Eugenio E. Muller et al. 1978. 81.50 o.p. (ISBN 0-12-510550-9). Acad Pr.

Neurotransmitters in Cerebral Coma & Stroke: Proceedings of the Workshop, Vienna, July 11, 1978. Ed. by K. Jellinger et al. LC 79-4083. (Journal of Neural Transmission: Supplementum XIV). (Illus.). 1979. 57.90 o.p. (ISBN 0-387-81510-4). Springer-Verlag.

Neurotransmitters in Invertebrates: Proceedings of a Satellite Symposium of the 28th International Congress of Physiological Sciences, Veszprem, Hungary, 1980. Ed. by K. S. Rozsa. LC 80-42251. (Advances in Physiological Sciences: Vol. 22). (Illus.). 400p. 1981. 69.00 o.p. (ISBN 0-08-027343-2). Pergamon.

Neurotransmitters-Receptor Interactions: Proceedings of the Weizman Institute of Science Conference, Rehovot, Israel, Feb. 1980. Weizman Institute of Science Conference Staff & U. Z. Littauer. LC 80-41130. 570p. 1980. 75.00x o.p. (ISBN 0-471-27893-9, Pub. by Wiley-Interscience). Wiley.

Neurotransmitters-Receptors: Proceedings of 8th International Congress of Pharmacology, Tokyo, Japan, July 19-24, 1981. Ed. by H. Yoshida et al. (Advances in Pharmacology & Therapeutics Ser.: No. II, Vol. 2). (Illus.). 340p. 1982. 105.00 o.p. (ISBN 0-08-028022-6, H130). Pergamon.

Neurovegetative Transmission Mechanisms: Proceedings of the International Society for Neurovegetative Research, Tinany, 1972. International Society for Neurovegetative Research Staff. Ed. by B. Csillik & J. A. Kappers. (Journal of Neural Transmission: Suppl. 11). (Illus.). 350p. 1974. 91.50 o.p. (ISBN 0-387-81173-7). Springer Verlag.

Neutral Proteases of Human Polymorphonuclear Leukocytes: Biochemistry, Physiology & Clinical Significance. Ed. by K. Havemann & A. Janoff. LC 78-7037. (Illus.). 480p. 1978. text ed. 44.50 o.p. (ISBN 0-8067-0801-8). Urban & S.

Neutralism & Nonalignment: The New States in World Affairs. Ed. by Laurence W. Martin. LC 75-32460. 1977. Repr. of 1962 ed. lib. bdg. 22.50x o.p. (ISBN 0-8371-8541-6, MANN). Greenwood.

Neutrality for the U. S. William Lage & Edwin M. Borchard. LC 70-147766. (Library of War & Peace; International Law). lib. bdg. 46.00 o.p. (ISBN 0-8240-0488-4). Garland Pub.

Neutrality or Commitment: The Evolution of Dutch Foreign Policy, 1667-1795. Alice C. Carter. (Foundations of Modern History). (Illus.). 120p. 1976. 10.00x o.p. (ISBN 0-393-05577-9). Norton.

Neutralization & World Politics. Cyril E. Black et al. LC 68-29388. (Center of International Studies, Princeton Univ.). 1968. 25.00 o.p. (ISBN 0-691-05639-0); pap. 10.50x o.p. (ISBN 0-691-01056-0). Princeton U Pr.

Neutrino. Isaac Asimov. 1983. pap. 1.50 o.p. (ISBN 0-380-00483-6, 38109-5, Discus). Avon.

Neutrino Physics & Astrophysics. Ed. by Ettore Fiorini. LC 81-11999. (Ettore Majorana International Science Series, Physical Sciences: Vol. 12). 432p. 1982. 75.00x o.p. (ISBN 0-306-40746-9, Plenum Pr). Plenum Pub.

Neutron Activation Tables. Gerhard Erdtmann. (Topical Presentations in Nuclear Chemistry Ser.: Vol. 6). (Illus.). 146p. 1976. 62.00x o.p. (ISBN 3-527-25693-8). VCH Pubs.

Neutron Data of Structural Materials for Fast Reactors: Proceedings of the Specialists Meeting of the Central Bureau for Nuclear Measurements, Geel, Belgium, Dec. 5-8, 1977. Central Bureau for Nuclear Measurements Staff. Ed. by K. H. Bockhoff. (Illus.). 1979. 210.00 o.p. (ISBN 0-08-023424-0). Pergamon.

Neutron Sources: For Applied & Pure Nuclear Research. Ed. by S. Cierjacks. (Neutron Physics & Nuclear Data in Science & Technology Ser.: Vol. 2). 370p. 1982. 93.00 o.p. (ISBN 0-08-029351-4). Pergamon.

Neutron Transmutation Doping in Semiconductors. Ed. by J. M. Meese. LC 79-395. 382p. 1979. 75.00x o.p. (ISBN 0-306-40155-X, Plenum Pr). Plenum Pub.

Neutron Two Is Critical. Lawrence Dunning. 1977. pap. 1.75 o.p. (ISBN 0-380-01775-X, 35089-0). Avon.

Nevada Civil Practice Manual. State Bar of Nevada. 425p. 1986. 50.00x o.p. (ISBN 0-87215-982-5). Michie Co.

Nevada Industrial Minerals. 1973. 15.00 o.p. (ISBN 0-942218-06-X). Minobras.

Nevada Supplement for Modern Real Estate Practice. James A. Gorzelany. (Orig.). 1979. pap. 9.95 o.s.i. (ISBN 0-88462-346-7, 1510-29, Real Estate Ed). Longman Finan.

Nevada the Compleat Industrial Directory, 1987. 272p. 1987. pap. 45.00 o.p. (ISBN 0-318-02895-6). Manufacturers.

Nevada Towns & Tales: South, Vol. 2. Stanley W. Paher. (Illus.). 224p. 1982. 10.95 o.p. (ISBN 0-317-64826-8). Nevada Pubns.

Nevada: Trusts. suppl. 6.00 o.p. Am Law Inst.

Nevada's Public Museums: A Guide. Ed. by Dave Basso. (Nevada Classics Ser.). (Illus.). 88p. (Orig.). 1983. pap. 5.95 o.p. (ISBN 0-936332-08-5). Falcon Hill Pr.

Never a Dull Moment. Date not set. (ISBN 0-8052-3859-X). Random.

Never Alone. Joan W. Brown. 48p. 1985. 6.95 o.s.i. (ISBN 0-8378-5084-3). Gibson.

Never & Always: Micronesian Stories of the Origin of Islands, Landmarks, & Customs. Micronesian Community College Students Staff. Ed. by Gene Ashby. LC 81-86460. (Illus.). 152p. (Orig.). 1983. pap. 7.95 o.p. (ISBN 0-931742-11-0). Rainy Day Oreg.

Never Before Noon. Afdera Fonda. LC 86-13297. (Illus.). 192p. 1986. 16.95 o.p. (ISBN 1-55584-026-4). Weidenfeld.

Never Bring Her Roses. Susan Marie. LC 85-16175. (Starlight Romance Ser.). 192p. 1986. 12.95 o.p. (ISBN 0-385-23081-8). Doubleday.

Never Brought to Mind. Violet Olsen. LC 84-21664. 180p. (gr. 8 up). 1985. 11.95 o.s.i. (ISBN 0-689-31110-9, Atheneum Childrens Bks). Macmillan.

Never Despair. 168p. 1971. pap. 4.00 o.s.i. (ISBN 0-317-06085-6). C C Brown Pub.

Never Give In. JoAnna Brandon. (Candlelight Ecstasy Ser.: No. 488). (Orig.). 1987. pap. 2.25 o.p. (ISBN 0-440-16429-X). Dell.

Never Give Up. Jill P. Walton. 1980. 6.00 o.p. (ISBN 0-682-49580-8). Exposition-Phoenix.

Never in Doubt: Critical Essays on American Books, 1972-1985. Peter S. Prescott. 1986. 19.95 o.p. (ISBN 0-87795-803-3); pap. text ed. 10.95 o.p. Morrow.

Never Look Back. Rose Abernethy & Diana Lynn. LC 84-90298. 43p. 1985. 6.95 o.p. (ISBN 0-533-06345-0). Vantage.

Never Pick up Hitch Hikers. Ellis Peters. Ed. by J. Barzun & W. H. Taylor. LC 81-47343. (Crime Fiction 1950-1975 Ser.). 255p. 1983. lib. bdg. 18.00 o.p. (ISBN 0-8240-4996-9). Garland Pub.

Never Say Can't. Howard Vann. 80p. 1985. 6.50 o.p. (ISBN 0-682-40226-5). Exposition-Phoenix.

Never Say Old. Bartlett Hess & Margaret Hess. 156p. 1984. pap. 6.50 o.p. (ISBN 0-89693-375-X). Victor Bks.

Never Sniff a Gift Fish. Patrick F. McManus. (General Ser.). 1984. lib. bdg. 15.95 o.p. (ISBN 0-8161-3718-8, Large Print Bks). G K Hall.

Never Such Innocence: A New Anthology of Great War Verse. Ed. by Martin Stephen. (Illus.). 320p. 1987. 29.95 o.p. (ISBN 0-907675-67-0, Pub. by Buchan & Enright UK). Seven Hills Bk Dists.

Never Take a Pig to Lunch. Ed. by Stephanie Calmenson. LC 80-2040. (Illus.). 32p. (gr. 3). 1982. 8.95a o.p.; PLB (ISBN 0-385-15593-X). Doubleday.

Never the Same Again. Aleda Renken. LC 75-133253. (gr. 6-9). 1971. 4.50 o.s.i. (ISBN 0-664-32487-8, Westminster). Westminster John Knox.

Never the Twain: A Novel. G. D. Khosla. (Vikas Library of Modern Moian Writing Ser.: No. 6). 177p. 1981. text ed. 15.00x o.p. (ISBN 0-7069-1270-5, Pub. by Vikas India). Advent NY.

Never-to-Be-Forgotten Adventures with God. Theresa K. Curry. 1977. 9.00 o.p. (ISBN 0-682-48929-8). Exposition-Phoenix.

Never Too Old to Teach. Judith Murphy & Carol Florio. LC 78-50074. 115p. (Orig.). 1978. pap. 5.00 o.p. (ISBN 0-89492-001-4). Acad Educ Dev.

Never Underestimate the Power of God's Woman. Daisy Hepburn. LC 84-3337. (Life with Spice Bible Study Ser.). 1984. 2.95 o.s.i. (ISBN 0-8307-0948-7, 6101856). Regal.

Neverending Story: Official Tie-In Edition. Michael Ende. Tr. by Ralph Manheim from Ger. 352p. 1984. pap. 6.95 o.p. (ISBN 0-14-007619-0). Penguin.

Neville Cardus: Autobiography. Neville Cardus. (Illus.). 288p. 1984. pap. 11.95 o.p. (ISBN 0-241-11286-9, Pub. by Hamish Hamilton England). David & Charles.

New Abelard: A Romance. Robert Buchanan. Ed. by Robert L. Wolff. LC 75-483. (Victorian Fiction Ser.). 1976. lib. bdg. 73.00 o.p. (ISBN 0-8240-1603-3). Garland Pub.

New Acronyms, Initialisms & Abbreviations Dictionary, Vol. 2. 12th ed. Ed. by Julie E. Towell & Helen E. Sheppard. 275p. 1987. 165.00x o.p. (ISBN 0-8103-2506-3). Gale.

New Adapted Physical Education: A Developmental Approach. Janet Seaman & Karen Depauw. LC 81-84691. (Illus.). 507p. 1982. text ed. 28.95 o.p. (ISBN 0-87484-524-6); instr's. manual avail. o.p. Mayfield Pub.

New Adoption Maze & How to Get Through It. Fred Powledge. 1985. text ed. 15.95 o.p. (ISBN 0-8016-4021-0). Mosby.

New Adventures of Peter Rabbit. Beatrix Potter. 1986. incl. cassette 7.98 o.p. (ISBN 0-8317-6797-9, Gallery Bks). Smith Pubs.

New Advertising: Twenty-One Successful Campaigns from Avis to Volkswagon. Robert Glatzer. (Illus.). 1970. 10.00 o.p. (ISBN 0-8065-0009-3, Pub. by Citadel Pr). Carol Pub Group.

New African Song. A. Keach. 1960. 14.95x o.p. New Coll U Pr.

New African Yearbook: Forty-Eight African Countries, 1987-88. 7th, rev. ed. 412p. (Orig.). 1987. pap. 29.95 o.p. (ISBN 0-905268-51-2). Hunter Pub NY.

New Age Musicians. Compiled by Keyboard Magazine Editors & Guitar Player Magazine Editors. 128p. (Orig.). 1988. pap. 12.95 o.p. (ISBN 0-88188-909-1, 00183522). H Leonard Pub Corp.

New Age Training for Fitness & Health. Dyveke Spino. LC 78-65254. (Illus.). 288p. 1980. pap. 7.95 o.p. (ISBN 0-394-17738-X, E766, Ever). Grove.

New Air Transport Policy for the North Atlantic. Jessie J. Friedman. LC 76-15035. 1976. 5.95 o.p. (ISBN 0-689-10761-7, Atheneum). Macmillan.

New Alchemists: Silicon Valley & the Microelectronics Revolution. Dirk Hanson. 1982. 17.45i o.p. (ISBN 0-316-34342-0). Little.

New Alchemists: Silicon Valley & the Microelectronics Revolution. Dirk Hanson. 1983. pap. 4.95 o.p. (ISBN 0-380-65854-2, 65854X). Avon.

New Almond Cookery. Almond Growers Exchange Staff & Michelle Schmidt. 208p. 1984. 19.45 o.p. (ISBN 0-671-52490-9). S&S.

New America? Ed. by Stephen R. Graubard. 1979. 12.95 o.p. (ISBN 0-393-01197-6). Norton.

New America: The Child in Contemporary America. Ed. by Nancy M. Theriot. LC 84-11945. (Illus.). 127p. 1984. pap. 7.95 o.p. (ISBN 0-8263-0786-8). U of NM Pr.

New American Computer Dictionary. rev. ed. New American Computer Dictionary Editors. 1986. pap. 4.50 o.p. (ISBN 0-317-47650-5). NAL.

New American Dramatists, 1960-1980. Ruby Cohn. LC 81-84700. (Modern Dramatists Ser.). 192p. (Orig.). 1982. pap. 7.95 o.p. (ISBN 0-394-17962-5, E793, Ever). Grove.

New American Gothic. Irving Malin. LC 62-15005. (Crosscurrents-Modern Critiques Ser.). 190p. 1962. 11.95x o.p. (ISBN 0-8093-0071-0). S Ill U Pr.

New American Graphics 2. (Illus.). 60p. 1982. 6.50 o.p. (ISBN 0-913883-04-2). Madison Art.

New American Photography. Kathleen M. Gauss. LC 85-9633. (Illus.). 128p. 1985. 38.50 o.p. (ISBN 0-87587-126-7). LA Co Art Mus.

New American Plays, Vol. 1. Ed. by Robert W. Corrigan. Incl. Mister Biggs. Anna M. Barlow; The Hundred & First. Kenneth Cameron; A Summer Ghost. Claude Fredericks; Blood Money. Dennis Jasudowicz; Socrates Wounded. Alfred Levinson; Constantinople Smith. Charles L. Mee, Jr; Pigeons. Lawrence Osgood; The Death & Life of Sneaky Fitch. James L. Rosenberg; Ginger Anne. Deric Washburn; The Golden Bull of Boredom. Lorees Yerby. (Mermaid Dramabook Ser.). 284p. (Orig.). 1965. pap. 7.95 o.p. (ISBN 0-8090-0734-7). Hill & Wang.

New American Plays, Vol. 4. Ed. by William M. Hoffman. Incl. Slaughterhouse Play. Susan Yankowitz; At War with the Mongols. Robert Heide; Captain Jack's Revenge. Michael Smith; African Medea. Jim Magnuson; Icarus. Ken Rubenstein; Moby Tick. Emanuel Peluso. LC 65-14530. (Illus.). 288p. 1971. 6.50 o.p. (ISBN 0-8090-7253-X, Mermaid); pap. 2.45 o.p. (ISBN 0-8090-0748-7). Hill & Wang.

New American Pocket Medical Dictionary. Nancy Roper. 1978. pap. 9.95 o.s.i. (ISBN 0-684-15923-6, ScribT). Scribner.

New American Reformation: A Study of Youth Culture & Religion. James F. Drane. (Quality Paperback Ser.: No. 293). 166p. 1974. pap. 2.95 o.p. (ISBN 0-8226-0293-8). Littlefield.

New American State Papers: Science & Technology Subject Set, 14 vols. Ed. by Nathan Reingold. LC 72-95578. 1973. Set. lib. bdg. 800.00 o.p. (ISBN 0-8420-1575-2). Scholarly Res Inc.

New American Stock Purchase Plan. Nancy Chapel O'Neill. 1981. 5.00 o.s.i. (ISBN 0-682-49755-X). Exposition-Phoenix.

New American Webster Handy College Dictionary. New American Webster Handy College Dictionary Editors. 1986. pap. 2.50 o.p. (ISBN 0-317-47646-7). NAL.

New Americans: Cuban Boat People. James Haskins. LC 82-8906. (Illus.). 64p. (gr. 5-11). 1982. PLB 12.95 o.p. (ISBN 0-89490-059-5). Enslow Pubs.

New Amsterdam Days & Ways: The Dutch Settlers of New York. Dorothy N. Hults. LC 63-15400. (Illus.). (gr. 4-6). 1963. 5.95 o.p. (ISBN 0-15-257030-6, HJ). HarBraceJ.

New & Better Uses of Secondary Resources: Proceedings of the Second Recycling World Congress, Philippine International Conventional Center, Manila, March 1979. Ed. by M. Henstock & M. B. Bever. 278p. 1980. pap. 57.00 o.p. (ISBN 0-08-026245-7). Pergamon.

New & Extraordinary Relief in Intellectual Property Cases, Vol. 198. Practising Law Institute Staff. 432p. 1985. pap. 40.00 o.p. (ISBN 0-317-27501-1, #G4-3765). PLI.

New & Selected Essays. Howard Nemerov. 312p. 24.95 o.p. (ISBN 0-8093-1182-8). S Ill U Pr.

New Answer Book. Mary Elting & Rose Wyler. LC 77-71531. (Illus.). (gr. 3-8). 1977. 6.95 o.p. (ISBN 0-448-12899-3, G&D); PLB 6.99 o.p. (ISBN 0-448-13418-7). Putnam Pub Group.

New Anti-Inflammatory & Antirheumatic Drugs: Proceedings of an International Symposium. Ed. by A. Bertelli et al. (Illus.). 1977. 55.00 o.p. E J Brill USA.

New Apartment Book. rev. ed. Ed. by Apartment Life Editors. 27.50 o.p. (ISBN 0-517-55045-8, Harmony). Crown.

New Approach to Latin. E. G. MacNaughton & T. W. McDougall. (Illus.). No. 1, 1973. pap. text ed. 7.95x o.p. (ISBN 0-05-002185-0); No. 2, 1974. pap. text ed. 8.50 o.p. (ISBN 0-05-002365-9). Longman.

New Approach to Self-Diagnosis: Introducing Applied Kinesiology. Yoshiaki Omura. LC 79-89345. (Illus.). 9.95 o.p. (ISBN 0-87040-468-7). Japan Pubns USA.

New Approach to Sight Singing. rev ed. Sol Berkowitz et al. (Illus.). 346p. 1976. pap. text ed. 18.95x o.p. (ISBN 0-393-09194-5). Norton.

New Approaches In Eukaryotic DNA Replication. Ed. by A. M. De Recondo. LC 82-18550. 376p. 1983. 65.00x o.p. (ISBN 0-306-41182-2, Plenum Pr). Plenum Pub.

New Approaches to Family Pastoral Care. Douglas A. Anderson. LC 79-8898. (Creative Pastoral Care & Counseling Ser.). 96p. (Orig.). 1980. pap. 4.50 o.p. (ISBN 0-8006-0564-0, 1-564, Fortress). Augsburg Fortress.

New Approaches to Ruskin: Thirteen Essays. Ed. by Robert Hewison. 240p. 24.95x o.p. (ISBN 0-7100-0915-1). Routledge Chapman & Hall.

New Approaches to the Evaluation of Abnormal Embryonic Development. Ed. by Diether Neubert & Hans J. Merker. LC 76-4619. (Illus.). 844p. 1975. 35.00 o.p. (ISBN 0-88416-140-4). Year Bk Med.

New Approaches to the Measurement of Public Library Use by Individual Patrons. Philip M. Clark. (Occasional Papers: No. 162). 46p. 1983. pap. 3.00 o.p. (ISBN 0-317-59012-X). U of Ill Lib Info Sci.

New Approaches to the Psychology of Childhood & Adolescence. Lester D. Crow. (Illus.). 1978. 12.50 o.p. (ISBN 0-682-49170-5, University). Exposition-Phoenix.

New Approaches to Travel Forecasting: Ten Reports. (Transportation Research Record Ser.). 151p. 1976. 6.00 o.p. (ISBN 0-309-02482-X). Transport Res Bd.

New Arabian Nights. Robert Louis Stevenson. LC 86-12291. 334p. 1986. Repr. of 1905 ed. 6.95 o.s.i. (ISBN 0-87773-382-1). Shambhala Pubns.

New Architecture. Paul Zucker. Philos Lib.

New Art of Flower Design. Deryck Healey. LC 85-40724. (Illus.). 160p. 1986. 24.50 o.p. (ISBN 0-394-54675-X, Pub. by Villard Bks). Random.

New Art on Paper, Acquired with Funds from the Hunt Manufacturing Co. Ellen S. Jacobowitz et al. (Illus.). 70p. 1988. 13.95 o.p. (ISBN 0-87633-075-8). Phila Mus Art.

New Aspects in the Medical Treatment of Tachyarrhythmias: Role of Amiodarone. Ed. by Gunter Breithardt & Franz Loogen. Orig. Title: Neue Aspekte Der Medikamentosen Behandlung Von Tachyarrhythmien. (Illus.). 283p. 1983. text ed. 29.50 o.p. (ISBN 0-8067-1121-3). Urban & S.

New Aspects of Clinical Nutrition. Ed. by G. Kleinberger & E. Deutsch. (Illus.). x, 662p. 1983. pap. 82.75 o.p. (ISBN 3-8055-3683-6). S Karger.

New Audiences for Teacher Education. Diana Demetrulias & Alleen Deutsch. LC 82-60797. (Fastback Ser.: No. 178). 50p. 1982. pap. 0.90 o.p. (ISBN 0-87367-178-3). Phi Delta Kappa.

New Australian Short Stories. Ed. by Craig Munro. 298p. 1981. pap. 9.75 o.p. (ISBN 0-7022-1595-3). U of Queensland Pr.

New Bankruptcy Rules. 219p. 1983. 6.00 o.p. (ISBN 0-318-02376-8). ICLE Georgia.

New Banks & New Bankers, 1984, Vol. 468. Practising Law Institute Staff. 1017p. 1984. pap. 40.00 o.p. (ISBN 0-317-27454-6, B4-6701). PLI.

New Beethoven Letters. Ludwig van Beethoven. 577p. Repr. of 1957 ed. lib. bdg. 69.00 o.p. (Pub. by Am Repr Serv). Reprint Servs.

New Beginning: How You Can Change Your Life Through Cognitive Therapy. Gary Emery. 1984. pap. 6.75 o.s.i. (ISBN 0-671-50771-0, Touchstone Bks). S&S.

New Better Handwriting. George L. Thomson. 1977. pap. 3.95 o.s.i. (ISBN 0-8008-5496-9, Pentalic). Taplinger.

New Biotechnology Marketplace: Japan. Ed. by Joanne Terminello. 1983. 395.00 o.p. (ISBN 0-317-07625-6, EIC Intell). Bowker.

New Biotechnology Marketplace: U. S. & Canada. 2nd ed. Ed. by Joanne Terminello. 1984. 295.00 o.p. (EIC Intell). Bowker.

New Birth of Freedom: A Theology of Bondage & Liberation. Peter C. Hodgson. LC 75-37145. 320p. 1976. 14.95 o.p. (ISBN 0-8006-0437-7, Fortress); pap. 7.95 o.p. (ISBN 0-8006-1437-2). Augsburg Fortress.

New Boatman's Manual. rev. ed. Carl D. Lane. (Illus.). 1962. 9.95 o.p. (ISBN 0-393-03163-2). Norton.

New Body. James Fritzhand. 1976. pap. 1.95 o.p. (ISBN 0-380-00547-6, 27383). Avon.

New Book of Bests: A Guide to the Best Things Life Has to Offer. Best Report Editors. 480p. 1986. pap. 9.95 o.p. (ISBN 0-8362-7933-6). Andrews & McMeel.

New Book of Knowledge, 21 Vols. rev. ed. Ed. by Jean Reynolds. LC 85-9956. (Illus.). 10500p. (gr. 2-8). 1987. Set. write for info. o.p. (ISBN 0-7172-0519-3). Grolier Inc.

New Book of the Road. rev. ed. Automobile Association of England Staff. (Illus.). 1979. 22.95 o.p. (ISBN 0-393-01229-8). Norton.

New Bouquet. Margaret F. Csovanyos. (Illus.). 1977. 7.50 o.p. (ISBN 0-682-48690-6). Exposition-Phoenix.

New Boy. Reginald Wallis. (gr. 3-7). pap. 1.00 o.p. (ISBN 0-87213-910-7). Loizeaux.

New Boy in Kindergarten. Jane B. Moncure. LC 76-15634. (Values to Live By Ser.). (Illus.). (ps-3). 1976. 6.50 o.p. (ISBN 0-913778-51-6). Childs World.

New Breed. W. E. Griffin. (Brotherhood of War Ser.: Bk VII). 416p. 1987. 16.95 o.p. (ISBN 0-399-13305-4, Putnam). Putnam Pub Group.

New Breed: Getting to Know You. Rubye C. Vaughan. 1979. 6.00 o.p. (ISBN 0-682-49306-6). Exposition-Phoenix.

New Bride's Book of Etiquette. rev. ed. Bride's Magazine Editors. Ed. by Conde Nast. LC 80-84126. (Illus.). 1981. pap. 5.95 o.p. (ISBN 0-399-50775-2, Perigee). Putnam Pub Group.

New British Drama: Fourteen Playwrights Since Osborne & Pinter. Oleg Kerensky. LC 78-56986. (Illus.). 1979. 11.95 o.s.i. (ISBN 0-8008-5499-3). Taplinger.

New British Political Dramatists. John Bull. (Modern Dramatists Ser.). 272p. 1984. 22.50 o.p. (ISBN 0-394-54242-8, GP942). Grove.

New British Political Dramatists. John Bull. (Modern Dramatists Ser.). 1984. pap. 7.95 o.p. (ISBN 0-394-62309-6, E-958, Ever). Grove.

New Broadways: Theatre Across America 1950-1980. Gerald M. Berkowitz. LC 81-21162. (Illus.). 208p. 1982. 28.50x o.s.i. (ISBN 0-8476-7031-7). Rowman.

New Budget Landscaping. Carlton B. Lees. LC 78-10546. (Illus.). 1979. 10.95 o.p. (ISBN 0-03-016851-1); pap. 5.95 o.p. (ISBN 0-03-016846-5). H Holt & Co.

New Burlington: The Life & Death of an American Village. John Baskin. (Illus.). 1976. 9.95 o.p. (ISBN 0-393-08366-7). Norton.

New Business Enterprises: Monographs. Mary Vance. (Public Administration Ser.: P 1792). 24p. 1985. 3.75 o.p. (ISBN 0-89028-592-6). Vance Biblios.

New Business Journalism: The People & Corporations Behind America's Business Publications. Donald Gussow. LC 83-18473. 256p. 1984. 14.95 o.p. (ISBN 0-15-165202-3). HarBraceJ.

New Business Ventures & the Entrepreneur. 2nd ed. Howard H. Stevenson et al. 1985. 37.95x o.p. (ISBN 0-256-02166-X). Irwin.

New Businesses Women Can Start & Successfully Operate. David D. Seltz & Mary Leslie. LC 77-608270. 1977. 9.95 o.s.i. (ISBN 0-87863-129-1, Farnsworth Pub Co). Longman Finan.

New Caledonia or Independent Kanaky? John Connell. 160p. 1986. 29.00 o.p. (ISBN 0-949614-20-3, Pub. by Croom Helm UK); pap. 17.00 o.p. (ISBN 0-949614-21-1, Pub. by Croom Helm UK). Routledge Chapman & Hall.

New Canon Law: Perspectives on the Law, Religious Life & the Laity. LC 82-17889. (Orig.). 1983. pap. 11.00 o.p. (ISBN 0-87125-076-4). Cath Health.

New Carbohydrate Gram Counter. Margaret Sullivan. (Orig.). 1980. pap. 2.95 o.p. (ISBN 0-440-16311-0). Dell.

New Career Books Nineteen Eighty-Eight Set, 7 vols. (Illus.). (gr. 7-12). 1988. Set. lib. bdg. 69.79 o.p. (ISBN 0-8239-0837-2, 0837C). Rosen Group.

New Careers in Nursing. Florence Downs & Dorothy Brooten. LC 82-18449. (Illus.). 192p. 1983. lib. bdg. 12.95 o.p. (ISBN 0-668-05255-4); pap. 7.95 o.p. (ISBN 0-668-05260-0). Arco.

New Caribbean Man. P. D. Sharma. LC 80-68909. 72p. 1981. pap. 5.00 o.p. (Pub. by Carib Hse). Three Continents.

New Catalogue of Historical Records: 1898 to 1908-09. 2nd ed. Robert Bauer. LC 48-1665. 494p. 1970. Repr. of 1947 ed. lib. bdg. 22.50x o.p. (ISBN 0-8371-9104-1, BAHR). Greenwood.

New Celibacy. Gabrielle Brown. 224p. 1981. pap. 2.75 o.s.i. (ISBN 0-345-29803-9). Ballantine.

New Celibacy: Why More Men & Women Are Abstaining from Sex & Enjoying It. Gabrielle Brown. 300p. 1980. text ed. 10.95 o.p. (ISBN 0-07-008430-0). McGraw.

New Century Handbook of Leaders of the Classical World. C. Avery. 1972. 8.95 o.p. (ISBN 0-13-612002-4, Spec). P-H.

New Century Instant German Conversation Guide. Gerda Joseph. LC 82-62312. (Illus., Orig.). 1972. 2.95 o.p. (ISBN 0-8329-4197-2). New Century.

New Century Instant Spanish Conversation Guide. Jack Joseph. LC 75-39823. (Illus., Orig.). 1973. 2.95 o.s.i. (ISBN 0-8329-4199-9). New Century.

New Century Velazquez Spanish-English Dictionary. rev. ed. New Century Editors. (Span. & Eng.). 1977. 19.95 o.p. (ISBN 0-8329-0472-4). New Century.

New Century Vest Pocket French Dictionary. rev. ed. Ed. by Richard Switzer & Herbert S. Gochberg. LC 84-61666. (Orig., Fr.). 1977. 2.95 o.s.i. (ISBN 0-8329-1532-7). New Century.

New Century Vest-Pocket Secretary's Handbook. Mary De Vries. LC 82-81063. 352p. 1980. pap. 2.95 o.p. (ISBN 0-8329-1342-1). New Century.

New Century Vest-Pocket: Webster Dictionary. rev. ed. Norman Allen. LC 81-84631. 304p. 1975. pap. 2.95 o.s.i. (ISBN 0-8329-1536-X). New Century.

New Century World Wide German Dictionary. Robert Appert. LC 82-81061. (Ger.). 1966. pap. 5.95 o.s.i. (ISBN 0-8329-9687-4); 9.95 o.s.i. (ISBN 0-8329-0144-X). New Century.

New Century World-Wide Spanish Dictionary. rev. ed. Ed. by Ida N. Hinojosa. LC 81-83572. (Span. & Eng., Eng). 1966. 9.95 o.p. (ISBN 0-8329-9711-0); pap. 5.95 o.p. (ISBN 0-8329-9712-9). New Century.

New Challenge: The Disadvantaged see Issues in the Public Employee Relations Library: Series 2.

New Choices: The Latest Options in Treating Breast Cancer. Mark Rubinstein & Dennis P. Cirillo. (Illus.). 224p. 1985. 15.95 o.p. (ISBN 0-396-08552-0). Dodd.

New Church Debate: Issues Facing American Lutheranism. Ed. by Carl E. Braaten. LC 83-48008. 176p. 1984. pap. 7.95 o.p. (ISBN 0-8006-1715-0, 1-1715, Fortress). Augsburg Fortress.

New Class? Ed. by B. Bruce-Briggs. LC 78-62999. (McGraw-Hill Paperbacks Ser.). 252p. 1981. pap. text ed. 5.95 o.p. (ISBN 0-07-008573-0). McGraw.

New Classic Cuisine. Albert Roux & Michel Roux. (Illus.). 256p. 1984. 24.95 o.p. (ISBN 0-8120-5600-0). Barron.

New Clinical Laboratory Standardization Methods. Robert G. Hoffmann. LC 73-82089. 1974. 17.50 o.p. (ISBN 0-682-47758-3, University). Exposition-Phoenix.

New Clothes for Alex. Mary Dickinson. LC 84-71670. (Illus.). 32p. (ps-2). 1984. 8.95 o.p. (ISBN 0-233-97685-X). Andre Deutsch.

New Coding System for Electrocardiography. Ed. by E. D. Robles de Medina. 1972. pap. 20.75 o.p. (ISBN 90-219-2073-5, Excerpta Medica). Elsevier.

New Collected Short Stories. E. M. Forster. 1986. 13.50 o.p. (ISBN 0-317-53140-9, Large Print Bks). G K Hall.

New College Encyclopedia of Music. rev. ed. J. A. Westrup & F. L. Harrison. (Illus.). 1976. 19.95 o.p. (ISBN 0-393-02191-2). Norton.

New College Encyclopedia of Music. Ed. by J. A. Westrup & F. L. Harrison. 1964. 15.00 o.p. (ISBN 0-393-02109-2); pap. 7.95 o.p. (ISBN 0-393-00273-X, Norton Lib). Norton.

New Color Photography. Sally Eauclaire. LC 80-70940. (Illus.). 1981. 45.00 o.p. (ISBN 0-89659-190-5); pap. 24.95 o.p. (ISBN 0-89659-196-4). Abbeville Pr.

New Communications. Frederick Williams. 376p. 1984. pap. text ed. (ISBN 0-534-02945-0). Wadsworth Pub.

New Community. Elizabeth O'Connor. LC 76-9964. (Illus.). 1976. pap. 5.72i o.p. (ISBN 0-06-066337-5, RD180). HarpR.

New Comnsultants & Consulting Organizations Directory, 1988: New Consultants - Inter-Edition Supplement. 8th ed. Ed. by Janice McLean. 1988. pap. 325.00x o.p. (ISBN 0-8103-2527-6). Gale.

New Companion to Greek Tragedy. Andrew Brown. LC 83-3842. (Illus.). 210p. 1983. text ed. 25.75x o.p. (ISBN 0-389-20389-0, 07267); pap. text ed. 10.50x o.p. (ISBN 0-389-20396-3, 07274). B&N Imports.

New Complete Beagle. Date not set. (ISBN 0-87605-024-0). Howell Bk.

New Complete Book of Collectibles Cars. rev. ed. R. M. Langworth. 1987. 14.98 o.p. (ISBN 0-517-64744-3). Crown.

New Complete Book of Home Remodeling, Improvement, & Repair. Arthur M. Watkins. (Encore Edition). (Illus.). 1979. 4.95 o.p. (ISBN 0-684-16731-X, ScribT). Scribner.

New Complete Fox Terrier. Date not set. (ISBN 0-87605-120-4). Howell Bk.

New Complete Medical & Health Encyclopdeia. Ed. by Richard Wagman. 1366p. 1987. (ISBN 0-89434-079-4). Ferguson.

New Complete Norwegian Elkhound. 2nd ed. Olav Wallo. (Complete Breed Book Ser.). (Illus.). 1982. 17.95 o.p. (ISBN 0-87605-243-X). Howell Bk.

New Complete Pomeranian. Date not set. (ISBN 0-87605-250-2). Howell Bk.

New Complete Snow Camper's Guide. Raymond Bridge. (Illus.). 416p. 1981. encore ed. 7.95 o.p. (ISBN 0-684-16842-1, ScribT). Scribner.

New Concepts in Alzheimer's Disease. Ed. by M. Briley et al. (Pierre Fabre Monograph). (Illus.). 256p. 1986. text ed. 90.00x o.p. (ISBN 0-333-41356-3, Pub. by Macmillan London). Sheridan.

New Concepts in Finite Element Analysis. Ed. by T. J. Hughes et al. (AMD: Vol. 44). 272p. 1981. 40.00 o.p. (ISBN 0-686-34476-6, G00202). ASME.

New Concepts in Lipid Research in Honor of Stina & Einar Stenhagen, Vol. 16. Ed. by Ralph T. Holman. (Progress in the Chemistry of Fats & Other Lipids). 1978. 86.00 o.p. (ISBN 0-08-022663-9). Pergamon.

New Concepts of Life After Death. Martial Celestin. 40p. 1986. 5.75 o.p. (ISBN 0-8062-2670-6). Carlton.

New Concepts One. Ed. by F. Boschke. LC 51-5497. (Topics in Current Chemistry: Vol. 41). (Illus.). 150p. 1973. 31.00 o.p. (ISBN 0-387-06333-1). Springer-Verlag.

New Concepts Three. R. Zahradnik & H. Hartmann. (Topics in Current Chemistry: Vol. 43). (Illus.). 145p. 1973. 33.00 o.p. (ISBN 0-387-06400-1). Springer-Verlag.

New Concepts Two. Ed. by A. Davison et al. (Topics in Current Chemistry: Vol. 42). (Illus.). iv, 158p. 1973. 35.00 o.p. (ISBN 0-387-06399-4). Springer-Verlag.

New Congress. Stephen Goode. LC 80-19111. 224p. (gr. 7 up). 1980. lib. bdg. 9.49 o.s.i. (ISBN 0-671-34031-X). Messner.

New Consultants. 8th ed. Ed. by Janice McLean. 1988. pap. text ed. 325.00x o.p. (ISBN 0-8103-2342-7). Gale.

New Cookbook. Miriam Polunin. (Illus.). 320p. 1985. 19.95 o.p. (ISBN 0-8120-5666-3). Barron.

New Coping Books - Nineteen Eighty-Eight Library, 9 vols. (gr. 7-12). 1988. Set. lib. bdg. 116.55 o.p. (ISBN 0-8239-0843-7, 0843C). Rosen Group.

New Copyright Law: Questions Teachers & Librarians Ask. 76p. 1977. pap. 3.00 o.p. (ISBN 0-8389-3214-2). ALA.

New Covenant. Robert Coleman. 132p. 1985. pap. 4.95 o.p. (ISBN 0-89109-524-1). NavPress.

New Creation: Marxist & Christian? Jose-Maria Gonzalez-Ruiz. Tr. by Mathew J. O'Connell from Span. LC 76-10226. Orig. Title: Marximo y Cristianismo Frente Al Hombre Nuevo. 160p. (Orig.). 1976. 1.74 o.p. (ISBN 0-88344-327-9). Orbis Bks.

New Critical Essays. Roland Barthes. Tr. by Richard Howard from Fr. 121p. 1980. 10.95 o.p. (ISBN 0-8090-7257-2); pap. 6.95 o.p. (ISBN 0-8090-1396-7). Hill & Wang.

New Cruising Cookbook. Russell K. Jones & C. McKim Norton. (Illus.). 1960. 15.95 o.p. (ISBN 0-393-03151-9). Norton.

New Day. rev. ed. R. Galen Hanson. 64p. 1982. 5.00 o.p. (ISBN 0-682-49825-4). Exposition-Phoenix.

New Day for Dragons. Lynn Hall. (Illus.). 1976. pap. 1.25 o.p. (ISBN 0-380-00763-0, 30528, Camelot). Avon.

New Day Still Dawning: A Sequel to Surgery in Personal Experience & a Reaffirmation of the Joy of Living. R. Galen Hanson. 31p. 1983. 5.50 o.p. (ISBN 0-682-49937-4). Exposition-Phoenix.

New Day: The National Socialist Weekly, Vols. 1-4, No. 29. 1971. Repr. of 1920 ed. lib. bdg. 185.00x o.p. (ISBN 0-8371-9213-7, ND00). Greenwood.

New Deal in Tennessee, Nineteen Thirty-Two to Nineteen Thirty-Eight. John D. Minton & Frank Freidel. LC 78-62388. (Modern American History Ser.: Vol. 13). 1979. lib. bdg. 36.00 o.p. (ISBN 0-8240-3636-0). Garland Pub.

New Deal Mosaic: Roosevelt Confers with His National Emergency Council 1933-1936. Ed. by Lester G. Seligman & Elmer E. Cornwell, Jr. LC 65-5158. 1965. 10.00 o.p. (ISBN 0-87114-017-9). U of Oreg Bks.

New Deal Thought. Ed. by Howard Zinn. LC 66-16755. (Orig.). 1966. pap. write for info. o.p. (ISBN 0-02-431700-4). Macmillan.

New Decade (Poems 1958-1967) Pablo Neruda. Tr. by Ben Belitt & Alastair Reid. (Bilingual ed.). 1969. pap. 5.95 o.s.i. (ISBN 0-394-17275-2, E495, Ever). Grove.

New Definitions of School-Library Service: Proceedings of the 24th Annual Conference of the Graduate Library School. Ed. by Sara I. Fenwick. LC 60-2341. (University of Chicago Studies in Library Science). 1960. lib. bdg. 6.00x o.s.i. (ISBN 0-226-24163-7). U of Chicago Pr.

New Delhi & Sri Lanka. P. Ramaswamy. 1987. 26.50 o.p. (ISBN 0-8364-2368-2, Pub. by Allied India). South Asia Bks.

New Departure Classics. Chichester P. Weldon. LC 86-2508. (Illus.). 80p. 1986. 25.00 o.p. (ISBN 0-914659-18-9). Phoenix Pub.

New Description of Blenheim. William Mavor. Ed. by John D. Hunt. LC 79-56976. (English Landscape Garden Ser.). 146p. 1982. lib. bdg. 26.00 o.p. (ISBN 0-8240-0173-7). Garland Pub.

New Development in Soviet Military Strategy. Andrew C. Goldberg. (Significant Issues Ser. Vol. 9, No. 7). 60p. 1987. pap. 7.95 o.p. (ISBN 0-89206-107-3). CSI Studies.

New Developments & Applications in Composites: Proceedings of the TMS-AIME Fall Meeting, St. Louis, 1978. TMS Staff & AIME Staff. Ed. by Doris Kuhlmann-Wilsdorf & W. C. Harrigan. (Illus.). 370p. 38.00 o.p. (ISBN 0-89520-350-2); members 24.00 o.p. (ISBN 0-317-34888-4); student members 14.00 o.p. (ISBN 0-317-34889-2). ASM.

New Developments in Biotechnology, 2: Public Perceptions of Biotechnology, Background Paper. LC 87-619822. 135p. (Orig.). 1987. pap. 5.50 o.p. (ISBN 0-318-22927-7, S/N 052-003-01068-2). USGPO.

New Developments in Diagnostic Virology. Ed. by P. A. Bachmann. (Current Topics in Microbiology Ser.: Vol. 104). (Illus.). 355p. 1983. 58.00 o.p. (ISBN 0-387-12171-4). Springer-Verlag.

New Developments in Differential Equations: Proceedings of the Scheveningen Conference, 2nd, the Netherlands, 1975. W. Eckhaus. (North Holland Mathematics Studies: Vol. 21). 348p. 1976. 63.25 o.p. (ISBN 0-444-11107-7, North-Holland). Elsevier.

New Developments in Office Technology. Ed. by Alan Simpson. LC 84-13696. 180p. 1984. text ed. 35.50x o.p. (ISBN 0-566-02537-X). Gower Pub Co.

New Developments in Productivity Measurement & Analysis. Ed. by John W. Kendrick & Beatrice N. Vaccara. LC 79-20399. (Studies in Income & Wealth: No. 44). 1980. lib. bdg. 73.00x o.s.i. (ISBN 0-226-43080-4). U of Chicago Pr.

New Developments in River Basin Management. Ed. by S. J. Jenkins. (Illus.). 320p. 1981. pap. 85.00 o.p. (ISBN 0-08-028391-8). Pergamon.

New Developments in Stainless Steel Technology: Proceedings of the 1984 Conference. 391p. 76.00 o.p. (6209L). ASM.

New Diabetic Cookbook, Vol. 1. Mabel Cavaiani. 1984. 16.95 o.p. (ISBN 0-8092-5524-3). Contemp Bks.

New Dictionary of American History. Ed. by Michael Martin & Leonard Gelber. LC 65-23770. 1966. 12.95 o.p. (ISBN 0-8022-1071-6). Philos Lib.

New Dictionary of Americanisms. Sylvia Clapin. LC 68-17985. 596p. 1968. Repr. of 1902 ed. 42.00x o.p. (ISBN 0-8103-3244-2). Gale.

New Dictionary of Economics. 2nd ed. Philip A. Taylor. 321p. (Orig.). 1969. pap. 10.50x o.p. (ISBN 0-7100-7812-9). Routledge Chapman & Hall.

New Dictionary of Thoughts. rev. ed. Ed. by Tryon Edwards. 1955. 17.95 o.p. (ISBN 0-385-00127-4). Doubleday.

New Dimensions in European Social Policy. Ed. by Jacques Vandamme. LC 84-29306. 208p. 1985. 29.00 o.p. (ISBN 0-7099-2473-9, Pub. by Croom Helm Ltd). Routledge Chapman & Hall.

New Dimensions in Judaism: A Creative Analysis of Rabbinic Concepts. Phillip Sigal. LC 72-186485. 1972. 10.00 o.p. (ISBN 0-682-47429-0, University). Exposition-Phoenix.

New Dimensions of Political Economy. Walter Heller. 1967. pap. 3.95x o.p. (ISBN 0-393-09755-2). Norton.

New Dimensions of World Politics. G. L. Goodwin. 200p. 1975. 16.50 o.p. (ISBN 0-85664-241-X, Pub. by Croom Helm Ltd). Routledge Chapman & Hall.

New Diplomacy: International Affairs in the Modern Age. Abba Eban. LC 80-6035. 384p. 1983. 19.45 o.p. (ISBN 0-394-50283-3). Random.

New Directions for a Musical Church. Peter Stapleton. LC 75-13462. 120p. 1975. pap. 5.25 o.p. (ISBN 0-8042-1765-3, John Knox). Westminster John Knox.

New Directions for the Thrift Industry. Practising Law Institute Staff & Donald G. Glascoff. LC 83-62449. (Commercial Law & Practice Course Handbook Ser.: No. 310). (Illus.). 880p. 1983. 40.00 o.p. PLI.

New Directions in Chemical Analysis: Proceedings of the Annual Symposia of the Industry University Cooperative Chemistry Program (IUCCP) of the Texas A&M Univ. Chemistry Department, No. 3. Ed. by Bernard L. Shapiro. LC 85-40053. 527p. 1985. lib. bdg. 45.00x o.p. (ISBN 0-89096-255-3). Tex A&M Univ Pr.

New Directions in Dance: Proceedings. Dance in Canada Annual Conference, 7th, Waterloo, Ontario, June 27-July 2, 1979. Ed. by Taplin. (Pergamon International Series on Dance & the Related Arts). (Illus.). 200p. 1979. pap. 43.00 o.p. (ISBN 0-08-024773-3). Pergamon.

New Directions in Fair Isle Knitting. Patty Knox. (Illus.). 119p. 1987. 29.95 o.p. (ISBN 0-7153-8619-0). David & Charles.

New Directions in Helping: Vol. 1: Recipient Reactions to Aid. Ed. by Jeffrey D. Fisher & Arie Nadler. 1983. 56.00 o.p. (ISBN 0-12-257301-3). Acad Pr.

New Directions In International Law: Essays in Honour of Wolfgang Abendroth. Ed. by R. G. Girardot et al. 592p. 1982. 75.00 o.p. (ISBN 0-317-07423-7). Transnatl Pubs.

New Directions in Organizational Behavior. Barry M. Staw & Gerald R. Salancik. LC 82-9953. 314p. 1982. Repr. of 1977 ed. 19.50 o.p. (ISBN 0-89874-528-4). Krieger.

New Directions in Primary Education. Ed. by Colin Richards. 310p. 1982. text ed. 33.00x o.p. (ISBN 0-905273-27-3, Falmer Pr); pap. 19.00x o.p. (ISBN 0-905273-26-5). Taylor & Francis.

New Directions in Psycholegal Research. Ed. by Paul D. Lipsitt & Bruce D. Sales. 352p. 1980. 27.95 o.p. (ISBN 0-442-26267-1). Van Nos Reinhold.

New Directions in Religious Education. Ed. by John Hull. 226p. 1982. text ed. 25.00x o.p. (ISBN 0-905273-31-1, Falmer Pr); pap. 18.00x o.p. (ISBN 0-905273-30-3). Taylor & Francis.

New Directions in Satellite Communications: Challenges for North & South (Conference Proceedings) Ed. by Heather Hudson. 315p. 1985. pap. text ed. 44.00 o.p. (ISBN 0-89006-162-9). Artech Hse.

New Directions in Sex Research. Ed. by E. A. Rubenstein et al. LC 76-14490. (Perspectives In Sexuality Ser.). 172p. 1976. 45.00x o.p. (ISBN 0-306-30956-4, Plenum Pr). Plenum Pub.

New Directions in Social Skill Training. Ed. by Roger Ellis & Dorothy Whittington. 320p. 1983. 29.95 o.p. (ISBN 0-416-00911-5, NO. 5044). Routledge Chapman & Hall.

New Directions in the Psychophysiology of Individual Differences: A Symposium of Papers from the 22nd Annual Meeting of the Society for Psychophysiological Research, Minneapolis, 21-24 October 1982. Ed. by R. M. Stelmack. 76p. 1983. pap. 15.25 o.p. (ISBN 0-08-030844-9). Pergamon.

New Directions in Theology Today, History & Hermeneutics, Vol. 2. Carl E. Braaten. (Orig.). 1966. pap. 2.85 o.s.i. (ISBN 0-664-24731-8, Westminster); 3.95 o.s.i. (ISBN 0-664-20796-0, Westminster). Westminster John Knox.

New Directions in Theology Today: God & Secularity, Vol. 3. John Macquarrie. 1967. pap. 2.85 o.s.i. (ISBN 0-664-24787-3, Westminster). Westminster John Knox.

New Directions in Theology Today: Man: the New Humanism, Vol. 6. Roger L. Shinn. 1968. pap. 2.85 o.s.i. (ISBN 0-664-24812-8, Westminster). Westminster John Knox.

New Directions in Theology Today: The Church, Vol. 4. Colin W. Williams. LC 68-22647. (New Directions in Theology Today). 1968. pap. 3.25 o.s.i. (ISBN 0-664-24834-9, Westminster). Westminster John Knox.

New Doglike Carnivore, Genus Cynarctus, from the Clarendonian, Pliocene, of Texas. E. Raymond Hall & Walter W. Dalquest. (Museum Ser.: Vol. 14, No. 10). 4p. 1962. 1.25 o.p. (ISBN 0-317-04806-6). U of KS Mus Nat Hist.

New Drama 1900-1914. Jan McDonald. LC 85-808890. 188p. 1986. 27.50 o.s.i. (ISBN 0-394-55138-9). Grove.

New Drama 1900-1914. Jan McDonald. LC 85-80889. 188p. 1986. pap. 11.95 o.s.i. (ISBN 0-394-62112-3, Ever). Grove.

New Economy: An Argument for Economic Reform. F. K. Richter. LC 76-20057. 1976. 9.00 o.p. (ISBN 0-682-48590-X). Exposition-Phoenix.

New Eden: James Kilbourne & the Development of Ohio. Goodwin F. Berquist & Paul C. Bowers, Jr. (Illus.). 306p. (Orig.). 1983. lib. bdg. 32.50 o.p. (ISBN 0-8191-3385-X); pap. text ed. 14.75 o.p. (ISBN 0-8191-3386-8). U Pr of Amer.

New Elite: The Death of Democracy. David Lebedoff. 224p. 1981. 11.95 o.p. (ISBN 0-531-09854-0). Watts.

New Encyclopedia of Sports. Ralph Hickok. (Illus.). 1977. text ed. 54.50 o.p. (ISBN 0-07-028705-8). McGraw.

New Energy Conservation Technologies & Their Commercialization: Proceedings, 3 vols. Ed. by J. P. Millhone & E. H. Willis. 1982. Set. 142.30 o.p. (ISBN 0-387-11124-7). Springer-Verlag.

New England Bed & Breakfast Book. rev. ed. Corinne M. Ross. LC 85-45691. (Illus.). 224p. pap. 8.95 o.p. (ISBN 0-88742-060-5). Globe Pequot.

New England Coast. Photos by Clyde H. Smith. LC 75-41843. (Belding Imprint Ser.). (Illus.). 128p. (Text by M. Cronan Minton). 1976. 32.50 o.s.i. (ISBN 0-912856-24-6). Gr Arts Ctr Pub.

New England Furniture at Williamsburg. Barry A. Greenlaw. LC 73-90536. (Decorative Arts Ser.). (Illus.). 195p. (Orig.). 1974. 10.00 o.s.i. (ISBN 0-87935-020-2); pap. 7.95 o.s.i. (ISBN 0-87935-019-9). Williamsburg.

New England in the Republic. J. T. Adams. (Illus.). 1958. 13.25 o.p. (ISBN 0-8446-1010-0). Peter Smith.

New England Inns Christmas Traditions. Jeanne MacDowell & Effie Conley. (Illus.). write for info. o.s.i. Down East.

New England Life in the Eighteenth Century: Representative Biographies from Sibley's Harvard Graduates. Clifford K. Shipton. LC 63-9562. (Illus.). 1963. 37.00x o.s.i. (ISBN 0-674-61250-7, Belknap Pr). Harvard U Pr.

New England Nun. Mary E. Wilkins Freeman. LC 67-29266. (Americans in Fiction Ser.). Repr. of 1891 ed. lib. bdg. 29.00 o.p. (ISBN 0-8398-0567-5). Irvington.

New England Offering: A Magazine of Industry, Vols. 1-3. 1971. Repr. of 1848 ed. lib. bdg. 34.00x o.p. (ISBN 0-8371-9214-5, NEOO). Greenwood.

New England Patriots. James R. Rothaus. (NFL Today Ser.). (Illus.). 48p. (gr. 4-12). 1981. PLB 10.45 o.p. (ISBN 0-87191-807-2); pap. 4.25 o.p. (ISBN 0-89812-253-8). Creative Ed.

New England Patriots: Triumph & Tragedy. Larry Fox. LC 79-1992. (Illus.). 1979. 11.95 o.p. (ISBN 0-689-10992-X, Atheneum). Macmillan.

New England Politics. Ed. by Josephine Milburn & Victoria Schuck. LC 80-14530. 320p. 1981. text ed. 27.00x o.p. (ISBN 0-87073-356-7); pap. text ed. 11.95x o.p. (ISBN 0-87073-357-5). Schenkman Bks Inc.

New England: The Four Seasons. Arthur Griffin. 1980. 35.00 o.p. (ISBN 0-395-29164-X). HM.

New England Town: The First Hundred Years. Kenneth A. Lockridge. (Essays in American History Ser). 1970. pap. text ed. 5.95x o.p. (ISBN 0-393-09884-2, NortonC). Norton.

New England Village. Eva D. Costabel. LC 82-13738. (Illus.). 64p. (gr. 3 up). 1983. 12.95 o.s.i. (ISBN 0-689-30972-4, Atheneum Childrens Bks). Macmillan.

New England Woman's Perspective on Norfolk, Virginia, 1801-1802: Excerpts from the Diary of Ruth Henshaw Bascom. Ed. by A. G. Roeber. 1979. pap. 4.00x o.p. (ISBN 0-912296-41-0, Dist. by U Pr of Va). Am Antiquarian.

New England Year: A Journal of Vermont Farm Life. Muriel Follett. LC 73-145711. (Illus.). 222p. 1971. Repr. of 1939 ed. 35.00x o.p. (ISBN 0-8103-3393-7). Gale.

New England's Rarities Discovered. John Josselyn. 1986. pap. 10.00 o.p. Morrow.

New English Springer Spaniel. Date not set. (ISBN 0-87605-312-6). Howell Bk.

New Enterprises: A Start-up Case Book. Sue Birley. 215p. 1982. pap. 11.95 o.p. (ISBN 0-7099-0680-3, Pub. by Croom Helm Ltd); 30.00 o.p. (ISBN 0-7099-0614-5). Routledge Chapman & Hall.

New Epicurean & Adventures of a Schoolboy. LC 84-81072. (Victorian Library). 224p. 1984. 15.95 o.p. (ISBN 0-394-54267-3, GP-954). Grove.

New Epicurean & Adventures of a Schoolboy. LC 84-81072. (Victorian Library). 224p. 1984. pap. 5.95 o.s.i. (ISBN 0-394-62320-7, E-970, Ever). Grove.

New Era Challenges Old Patterns: A World History, 1945-1960. Franklin D. Parker. LC 80-6296. 880p. (Orig.). 1981. lib. bdg. 53.50 o.p. (ISBN 0-8191-1839-7); pap. text ed. 34.50 o.p. (ISBN 0-8191-1840-0). U Pr of Amer.

New Era in CATV: The Cable Franchise Policy & Communications Act of 1984, Vol. 194. Practising Law Institute Staff. 284p. 1985. pap. 15.00 o.p. (ISBN 0-317-27495-3, #G4-3761). PLI.

New Ethnicity, Perspectives from Ethnology: Proceedings. American Ethnological Society Staff & John W. Bennett. (AES Ser). 1975. pap. text ed. 18.95 o.p. (ISBN 0-8299-0032-2). West Pub.

New Europe: An Introduction to Its Political Geography. Walter Fitzgerald. LC 80-24065. (Illus.). xiii, 298p. 1980. Repr. of 1946 ed. lib. bdg. 35.00x o.p. (ISBN 0-313-21006-3, FINE). Greenwood.

New Every Morning: Three Hundred Sixty-Six Daily Meditations from Your Favorite Christian Writers. Ed. by Al Bryant. 224p. 1985. 8.99 o.p. (ISBN 0-8499-0507-9, 0507-9). Word Bks.

New Examinations System. Walter Roy. 192p. 1986. 31.00 o.p. (ISBN 0-7099-4217-6, Pub. by Croom Helm Ltd). Routledge Chapman & Hall.

New Extended Family: Day Care Programs That Work. Ellen Galinsky & William Hooks. 1977. 11.95 o.p. (ISBN 0-395-25934-7); pap. 6.95 o.p. (ISBN 0-395-25945-2). HM.

New Face of Mars. V. A. Firsoff. 1982. 17.95x o.p. Trans-Atl Phila.

New Faces, New Spaces: Helping Children Cope with Change. Rev. ed. Ardis Kysar & Dianne McLinn. 67p. 1985. pap. 10.50 o.p. (ISBN 0-934140-03-0). Toys N Things.

New Federal Policies for R & D: Impacts on Government, Industry & Academy - Proceedings of the 38th National Conference on the Advancement of Research. Ed. by Nanette S. Levinson. (Illus.). 226p. (Orig.). 1986. lib. bdg. 28.75 o.p. (ISBN 0-8191-5006-1); pap. text ed. 13.50 o.p. (ISBN 0-8191-5007-X). U Pr of Amer.

New Fiction from New England. Ed. by Deb Navas. LC 85-51875. 272p. 1986. 14.95 o.p. (ISBN 0-89909-087-7). Yankee Bks.

New Findings in Obsessive Compulsive Disorders. Thomas R. Insel. LC 84-2968. (Clinical Insights Monograph). 136p. 1984. pap. text ed. 12.00x o.p. (ISBN 0-88048-065-3, 48-065-3). Am Psychiatric.

New Firm Formation & Regional Development. Michael Cross. 354p. 1981. text ed. 44.50x o.p. (ISBN 0-566-00372-4). Gower Pub Co.

New Firms & Regional Development. Ed. by David Keeble & Egbert Wever. LC 85-28372. 304p. 1986. 34.50 o.p. (ISBN 0-7099-1577-2, Pub. by Croom Helm Ltd). Routledge Chapman & Hall.

New Food for All Palates. Sally Berg & Lucian Berg. (Illus.). 160p. 1980. pap. 9.95 o.p. (ISBN 0-575-02543-3, Pub. by Gollancz England). David & Charles.

New Force on the Left: Tom Hayden & the Campaign Against Corporate America. John H. Bunzel. (Publication Ser.: No. 280). 131p. 1983. pap. 6.95 o.p. (ISBN 0-8179-7802-X). Hoover Inst Pr.

New Forests for a Changing World. LC 84-50483. 640p. (Orig.). 1985. pap. 17.00 o.p. (ISBN 0-939970-23-6, SAF 84-03). Soc Am Foresters.

New Forms of Work Organisation, Vol. 1. ix, 174p. 1982. 24.50 o.p. (ISBN 92-2-102005-3); pap. 17.50 o.p. (ISBN 92-2-101991-8). Intl Labour Office.

New Forms of Work Organisation: German Democratic Republic, India, Italy, U. S. S. R., Economic Costs & Benefits, Vol. 2. International Labour Office Staff. (Illus.). 1979. 19.95 o.p. (ISBN 92-2-102109-2); pap. 14.25 o.p. (ISBN 92-2-102110-6). Intl Labour Office.

New French Imperialism, 1880-1910: The Third Republic & Colonial Expansion. James J. Cooke. (Library of Politics & Society Ser.). 223p. 1973. 26.00 o.p. (ISBN 0-208-01320-2, Archon). Shoe String.

New Frontiers in Psychology. Nicholas DeVore. (ISBN 0-8022-0385-X). Philos Lib.

New Frontiers in Rare Earth Science & Applications, Vol. 1. Ed. by Xu Guangxian & Xiao Jimei. 1986. 90.00 o.p. (ISBN 0-12-767661-9). Acad Pr.

New Frontiers in Rare Earth Science & Applications, Vol. 2. Ed. by Xu Guangxian & Xiao Jimei. 1986. 90.00 o.p. (ISBN 0-12-767662-7). Acad Pr.

New Frontiers in Transport Theory: Selected Papers from the 6th Conference at U. of Ariz, Tuscon, April 1979. Ed. by B. D. Ganapol. 122p. 1980. pap. 45.00 o.p. (ISBN 0-08-026698-3). Pergamon.

New Futures: Changing Women's Education. Ed. by Mary Hughes & Mary Kennedy. 192p. 1985. 22.50x o.p. (ISBN 0-7102-0612-7); pap. 12.50x o.p. (ISBN 0-7100-9988-6). Routledge Chapman & Hall.

New Generation of Environmental Essays. Ed. by George A. Watkins. LC 73-9938. 1973. Vol. 1. 21.00x o.p. (ISBN 0-8422-5126-X); pap. text ed. 6.95x o.p. (ISBN 0-8422-0318-4); Vol. 2. 24.00x o.p. (ISBN 0-8422-5127-8); pap. text ed. 8.95x o.p. (ISBN 0-8422-0348-6). Irvington.

New German Cinema. James Franklin. (Filmmakers Ser.). 1983. lib. bdg. 22.95 o.s.i. (ISBN 0-8057-9288-0, Twayne). G K Hall.

New German Dramatists. Denis Calandra. LC 83-48310. (Modern Dramatists Ser.). (Illus.). 224p. 1984. 17.50 o.p. (ISBN 0-394-53499-9, GP-875). Grove.

New German Dramatists. Denis Calandra. LC 83-48310. (Modern Dramatists Ser.). (Illus.). 224p. 1984. pap. 9.95 o.p. (ISBN 0-394-62487-4, E866, Ever). Grove.

New Girl. Janet A. Bloss. 96p. (gr. 5-8). 1984. 2.25 o.s.i. (ISBN 0-87406-048-6). Willowisp Pr.

New Girls. Beth Gutcheon. 336p. 1981. pap. 2.50 o.p. (ISBN 0-380-50831-1, 50831-1). Avon.

New Glenans Sailing Manual. Ed. by James MacGibbon & Stanley Caldwell. (Illus.). 1978. 35.00 o.p. (ISBN 0-393-03225-6). Norton.

New Gnomes: A Multinational Banks in the Third World. Howard Watchel. 61p. 1977. pap. 4.95x o.p. (ISBN 0-87855-671-0). Transaction Pubs.

New Gospel Parallels, Vol. 1. Robert W. Funk. LC 84-48727. (Foundations & Facets Ser.). 512p. 1985. 29.95 o.p. (ISBN 0-8006-2104-2, 1-2104, Fortress). Augsburg Fortress.

New Gospel Parallels, Vol. 2. Robert W. Funk. LC 84-48727. (Foundations & Facets Ser.). 384p. 1986. 24.95 o.p. (ISBN 0-8006-2106-9, 1-2106, Fortress). Augsburg Fortress.

New Group Therapies. Hendrik M. Ruitenbeek. 1970. pap. 1.95 o.p. (ISBN 0-380-01425-4, 27995, Discus). Avon.

New Guide to Building a One Hundred Thousand Dollar Law Practice. Joseph T. Karcher. LC 81-13180. 427p. 1981. 49.50 o.p. (ISBN 0-87624-402-9, Inst Busn Plan). P-H.

New Guide to the Birds of New Zealand. R. A. Falla & R. B. Sibson. (Illus.). 247p. 1983. 17.95 o.p. (ISBN 0-00-216928-2, Pub. by W Collins New Zealand). Intl Spec Bk.

New Guide to the Birds of Taiwan. Sheldon Severinghaus & Kenneth Blackshaw. Tr. by Lucia L. Severinghaus. (Illus.). 1978. 13.95 o.p. (ISBN 0-915180-05-7). Harrowood Bks.

New Guide to the Birds of Taiwan. Sheldon R. Severinghaus et al. 200p. 1976. 11.25 o.p. (ISBN 0-89955-185-8, Pub. by Mei Ya China). Intl Spec Bk.

New Guide to the Moon. Patrick Moore. 1977. 12.95 o.p. (ISBN 0-393-06414-X). Norton.

New Guide to the Planets. 3rd ed. Patrick Moore. (Illus.). 224p. 1972. 12.95 o.p. (ISBN 0-393-06319-4). Norton.

New Guide to the Stars. Patrick Moore. (Illus.). 1976. 12.95 o.p. (ISBN 0-393-06406-9). Norton.

New Guinea Images in Australian Literature. Nigel Krauth. LC 82-2812. (UQP Australian Authors Ser.). 279p. 1982. text ed. 30.00 o.p. (ISBN 0-7022-1960-6, AACR2); pap. 12.95 o.p. (ISBN 0-7022-1970-3). U of Queensland Pr.

New Guinea Tapeworms & Jewish Grandmothers: Tales of Ecology, Parasites, & Progress. Robert S. Desowitz. 1981. 12.95 o.p. (ISBN 0-393-01474-6). Norton.

New Gulliver. Esme Dodderidge. LC 79-65728. 1979. 9.95 o.s.i. (ISBN 0-8008-5506-X). Taplinger.

New Gulliver. Esme Dodderidge. LC 79-65728. 220p. 1980. pap. 3.95 o.s.i. (ISBN 0-8008-5507-8). Taplinger.

New Hampshire: An Illustrated History of the Granite State. Ronald Jager & Grace Jager. LC 83-17117. (Illus.). 248p. 1983. 27.95 o.s.i. (ISBN 0-89781-069-4). Windsor Pubns Inc.

New Hampshire: Contracts. 9.50 o.p. (ISBN 0-686-90855-4). Am Law Inst.

New Hampshire Genealogical Research Guide. 2nd ed. Laird Towle & Ann A. Brown. (Illus.). vi, 95p. (Orig.). 1983. pap. 12.00 o.p. (ISBN 0-917890-25-6). Heritage Bk.

New Hampshire: Trusts. 8.50 o.p. (ISBN 0-686-90856-2). Am Law Inst.

New Handbook of Handgunning. Paul B. Weston. (Illus.). 112p. 1980. 15.75 o.p. (ISBN 0-398-04092-3). C C Thomas.

New Harvest. Lou S. Pappas & Jane Horn. LC 86-1430. (Illus.). 168p. (Orig.). 1986. pap. 9.95 o.p. (ISBN 0-89286-262-9, TX801.P33, One Hund One Prods). Ortho.

New Haven Colony. Isabel M. Calder. LC 71-95002. vi, 301p. 1970. Repr. of 1934 ed. 28.00 o.p. (ISBN 0-208-00836-5, Archon). Shoe String.

New Health Care Economy: Legal Responses to New Economic Forces, Vol. 336. Practising Law Institute Staff. 514p. 1984. pap. 40.00 o.p. (ISBN 0-317-27408-2, #A4-4103). PLI.

New Healthcare Market: A Guide to PPOs for Purchasers, Payors & Providers. Peter Boland. LC 84-71429. 1985. 65.00 o.p. (ISBN 0-87094-534-3). Dow Jones-Irwin.

New Healthy Trail Food Book. rev. ed. Dorcas S. Miller. LC 79-28172. (Illus.). 80p. (Orig.). 1980. pap. 4.95 o.p. (ISBN 0-914788-25-6). Globe Pequot.

New High Ground: Strategies & Weapons of Space-Age War. Thomas Karas. 1984. pap. 6.70 o.p. (ISBN 0-671-50591-2, Touchstone Bks). S&S.

New High Ground: Systems & Weapons of Space Age War. Thomas Karas. 1983. 14.50 o.p. (ISBN 0-671-47025-6). S&S.

New History of Wind Music. David Whitwell. 1980. pap. 9.00 o.p. (ISBN 0-686-15899-7). Instrumental Co.

New History, the 1980s & Beyond: Studies in Interdisciplinary History. Ed. by Theodore K. Rabb & Robert I. Rotberg. LC 82-47634. 335p. 1982. 30.00x o.p. (ISBN 0-691-05370-7); pap. 11.50 o.p. (ISBN 0-691-00794-2). Princeton U Pr.

New Hobby Computers. Lawrence A. Leventhal et al. Ed. by Rich Force. (Illus.). 96p. 1977. pap. 4.95 o.p. (ISBN 0-88006-022-0, BK 7340). Wayne Green Ent.

New Home - Who'll Follow? Glimpses of Western Life. Caroline Kirkland. 1972. lib. bdg. 18.50 o.p. (ISBN 0-8422-8087-1); pap. text ed. 7.50x o.p. (ISBN 0-8290-1854-9). Irvington.

New Home Sales. Dave Stone. LC 82-15084. 400p. 1982. 19.95 o.p. Nat Assn H Build.

New Homes for Nineteen Eighty-Nine. Ed. by Garlinghouse Corp. Staff. LC 87-83320. (Illus.). 160p. 1988. pap. 3.95 o.s.i. (ISBN 0-938708-21-X). L F Garlinghouse Co.

New Hope for Incurable Diseases. E. Cheraskin, Jr. & W. M. Ringsdorf, Jr. LC 79-176384. 1971. 6.50 o.p. (ISBN 0-682-47387-1, University). Exposition-Phoenix.

New Hope for the Hungry? The Challenge of the World Food Crisis. Larry Minear. (Orig.). 1975. pap. 1.95 o.p. (ISBN 0-377-00043-4). Friendship Pr.

New Hope for Your Marriage. Charles P. Carney. LC 73-82082. 1973. 8.00 o.p. (ISBN 0-682-47745-1, University). Exposition-Phoenix.

New Horizons for Academic Libraries. Ed. by Robert Stuart & Richard Johnson. 582p. 1979. lib. bdg. 50.00 o.p. (ISBN 3-598-40002-0). K G Saur.

New Horizons in Carbonyl Chemistry: Reagents for Nucleophilic Acylation. Ed. by O. W. Lever. 29p. 1976. pap. 12.75 o.p. (ISBN 0-08-021334-0). Pergamon.

New Horizons in Educational Computing. Ed. by Masoud Yazdani. (Artificial Intelligence Ser.: No. 1381). 314p. 1984. text ed. 47.95x o.p. (ISBN 0-470-20022-7). Halsted Pr.

New Horizons in Oncology: Screening & Monitoring of Cancer, Vol. 4. Ed. by Basil A. Stoll. 440p. 1985. text ed. 75.00 o.p. (ISBN 0-471-90483-X, Dist. by A R Liss). Wiley.

New Horizons in Public Employee Bargaining see Issues in the Public Employee Relations Library: Series 3.

New Horizons in Travel-Behavior Research. Ed. by Peter R. Stopher et al. LC 78-24830. 784p. 1981. 48.00x o.p. (ISBN 0-669-02850-9). Lexington Bks.

New Hospital Psychiatry: Proceedings of a Conference. Ed. by Gene M. Abroms & Norman S. Greenfield. LC 77-137633. 1971. 64.00 o.p. (ISBN 0-12-042850-4). Acad Pr.

New House. Lorinda B. Cauley. LC 81-611. (Let Me Read Ser.). (Illus.). 48p. (gr. 6 up). 1981. 7.95 o.p. (ISBN 0-15-257040-3, HJ). HarBraceJ.

New House. Lorinda B. Cauley. LC 81-611. (Let Me Read Ser.). (Illus.). 48p. (gr. 1-5). 1981. pap. 3.50 o.p. (ISBN 0-15-257041-1, VoyB). HarBraceJ.

New Hungarian Agriculture. Lewis A. Fischer & Philip E. Uren. (Illus.). 168p. 1974. 10.00x o.p. (ISBN 0-7735-0136-3, Pub. by McGill Canada). U of Toronto Pr.

New Hydroboration Reagent. Clinton F. Lane & George W. Kabalka. 1976. pap. 12.75 o.p. (ISBN 0-08-021330-8). Pergamon.

New Hydrogenating Catalysts: Urushibara Catalysts. Kazuo Hata. LC 72-2652. 247p. 1972. 31.95 o.p. (ISBN 0-470-35890-4). Halsted Pr.

New Ice Age. Robert Edric. 148p. 1987. 18.95 o.p. (ISBN 0-233-97895-X, Pub. by A Deutsch England). David & Charles.

New Immigrants: What Can Unions Do? 1.80 o.p. Natl Lawyers Guild.

New! Improved! Bob & Ray Book. Bob Elliott & Ray Goulding. (Illus.). 224p. 1985. 14.95 o.p. (ISBN 0-399-13085-3). Putnam Pub Group.

New Industrial State. 3rd, rev. ed. John Kenneth Galbraith. (Sentry Ser.). 1979. pap. 6.95 o.p. (ISBN 0-395-28223-3). HM.

New Information Systems & Services. 7th ed. Amy Lucas & Kathleen Y. Marcaccio. 200p. 1987. pap. 260.00x o.p. (ISBN 0-8103-2495-4). Gale.

New Information Systems & Services. 8th ed. Ed. by Amy Lucas & Annette Novallo. 200p. 1988. pap. text ed. 270.00x o.p. (ISBN 0-8103-2533-0). Gale.

New Information Technologies-New Opportunities: Proceedings of the Clinic on Library Applications of Data Processing, 1981. Ed. by Linda C. Smith. LC 82-10947. 119p. 1982. 11.00 o.p. (ISBN 0-87845-066-1). U of Ill Lib Info Sci.

New Information Technology in Education. David G. Hawkridge. 256p. 1983. 27.50x o.p. (ISBN 0-8018-2980-1). Johns Hopkins.

New Information Technology in Social Science Education: Viewpoints from Europe & the U. S. Ed. by Mary A. Hepburn. 227p. (Orig.). 1985. pap. 10.00 o.p. (ISBN 0-89994-301-2). Soc Sci Ed.

New Inquisition? The Case of Edward Schillebeeckx & Hans Kung. Peter Hebblethwaite. LC 80-7290. 160p. (Orig.). 1980. pap. 4.95i o.p. (ISBN 0-06-063795-1, RD 339). HarpR.

New International, Vols. 1-24, No. 3. Socialist Workers Party. Incl. Vols. 1-3. lib. bdg. 42.00 o.s.i. (ISBN 0-313-21794-7, NI01); Vol. 4. lib. bdg. 42.00 o.s.i. (ISBN 0-313-21795-5, NI04); Vol. 5. lib. bdg. 42.00 o.s.i. (ISBN 0-313-21796-3, NI05); Vols. 6 & 7. lib. bdg. 42.00 (ISBN 0-313-21797-1, NI06); Vol. 8. lib. bdg. 42.00 (ISBN 0-313-21798-X, NI08); Vol. 9. lib. bdg. 42.00 (ISBN 0-313-21799-8, NI09); Vol. 10. lib. bdg. 42.00 (ISBN 0-313-21800-5, NI10); Vols. 11 & 12. lib. bdg. 42.00 (ISBN 0-313-21801-3, NI11); Vol. 13. lib. bdg. 37.50 (ISBN 0-313-21802-1, NI13); Vols. 14 & 15. lib. bdg. 42.00 (ISBN 0-313-21803-X, NI14); Vol. 16. lib. bdg. 31.00 (ISBN 0-313-21804-8, NI16); Vol. 17. lib. bdg. 31.00 (ISBN 0-313-21805-6, NI17); Vol. 18. lib. bdg. 31.00 (ISBN 0-313-21806-4, NI18); Vol. 19. lib. bdg. 31.00 (ISBN 0-313-21807-2, NI19); Vols. 20 & 21. lib. bdg. 31.00 (ISBN 0-313-21808-0, NI20); Vols. 22-24. lib. bdg. 31.00 (ISBN 0-313-21809-9, NI22). 1968. Repr. of 1934 ed. Set. lib. bdg. 510.00x o.p. (ISBN 0-8371-9217-X, NI00). Greenwood.

New International Communism: The Foreign & Defense Policies of the Latin European Communist Parties. Lawrence L. Whetten. LC 81-47963. 288p. 1982. 33.00x o.p. (ISBN 0-669-05146-2). Lexington Bks.

New International Development Strategy: A Systems Analysis Approach. United Nations Institute for Training & Research Staff. 32p. 1981. pap. 5.00 o.p. (ISBN 0-686-97558-8, UN81/15RR26, UNITAR). UNIPUB.

New International Dictionary of Refrigeration in English, French, Russian, German, Italian, Spanish, & Norwegian. International Institute of Refrigeration. 550p. (Eng., Fr., Rus., Ger., Ital., Span. & Norwegian.). 1977. 235.00 o.p. (ISBN 0-08-020368-X). Pergamon.

New International Economic Order (NIEO) Library. Ed. by Ervin Laszlo. (Pergamon Policy Studies on International). 1983. 380.00 o.p. (ISBN 0-08-025109-9). Pergamon.

New International Economic Order: Selected Documents, 1977. Ed. by Hideko Makiyama. 466p. 1982. pap. 50.00 o.p. (ISBN 0-89059-025-7, UPB123, UNITAR). UNIPUB.

Titles

New Investment Opportunities for the Mid-1980's. Russ Von Hoelscher & George Sterne. 320p. 1985. 14.95 o.p. (ISBN 0-940398-11-7). Profit Ideas.

New IRA Handbook: Everyone's Guide to Successful Investing after Tax Reform. Frank Sacks et al. (Illus.). 128p. 1987. pap. 6.95 o.p. (ISBN 0-911445-05-6). M C I Pub.

New Irish Setter. Date not set. (ISBN 0-87605-165-4). Howell Bk.

New Islands & Other Stories. Maria L. Bombal. Tr. by Richard Cunningham from Span. 112p. 1982. 12.95 o.p. (ISBN 0-374-22118-9). FS&G.

New Italian Cooking. Margaret Romagnoli & G. Franco Romagnoli. 384p. 1980. 17.95 o.p. (ISBN 0-316-75565-6, Pub. by Atlantic Monthly Pr). Little.

New Jersey. Joseph Monninger. LC 85-48153. 320p. 1986. 17.95 o.p. (ISBN 0-689-11770-1, Atheneum). Macmillan.

New Jersey Business Kit for Starting & Existing Businesses. Lawless J. Barrientos. LC 84-174276. (Illus.). 1983. pap. 14.95 o.p. (ISBN 0-671-49212-8). S&S.

New Jersey: Contracts. 9.50 o.p. (ISBN 0-686-90858-9). Am Law Inst.

New Jersey Directory of Manufacturers, 1987-88. 524p. 1986. pap. 82.50 o.p. (ISBN 0-318-02898-0, Pub. by Commerce Register Inc). Manufacturers.

New Jersey Income Maintenance Experiment. Ed. by Harold W. Watts & Albert Rees. (Institute for Research on Poverty Monograph Ser.: Vols. 2 & 3). 1977. Vol. 2. 32.50 o.p. (ISBN 0-12-738502-9); Vol. 3. 32.50 o.p. (ISBN 0-12-738503-7). Acad Pr.

New Jersey Manufacturers Directory, 1987-88. 701p. 1987. 57.00 o.p. (ISBN 0-318-02899-9, Pub. by Geo D. Hall Co). Manufacturers.

New Jersey Nets. Jim Moore. (NBA Today Ser.). (Illus.). 48p. (gr. 4 up). 1984. PLB 10.45 o.p. (ISBN 0-87191-983-4). Creative Ed.

New Jersey Services Directory: 1986-87. 700p. 1986. 62.00 o.p. (ISBN 0-318-23576-5, Pub. by Geo D. Hall Co). Manufacturers.

New Jersey: Some Dimensions of Local History. Paul Harrison Silfen. 1975. 4.50 o.p. (ISBN 0-682-48374-5). Exposition-Phoenix.

New Jersey: Spotlight on Government. League of Women Voters of New Jersey Staff. 1983. 30.00x o.p. (ISBN 0-8135-0854-1); pap. 12.95x o.p. (ISBN 0-8135-0977-7). Rutgers U Pr.

New Jersey State Industrial Directory, 1988. 880p. 1988. 110.00 o.p. (ISBN 0-318-22821-1, Pub. by Mac Rae's). Manufacturers.

New Jersey Supplement for Modern Real Estate Practice. 3rd ed. Joseph H. Martin & William Jackson. 130p. (Orig.). 1981. pap. 9.95 o.p. (ISBN 0-88462-481-1, 1510-15, Real Estate Ed). Longman Finan.

New Jersey: Trusts. 8.50 o.p. (ISBN 0-686-90860-0). Am Law Inst.

New Jerusalem: The Labour Party & the Economics of Democratic Socialism. Elizabeth Durbin. 320p. 1985. 32.00x o.p. (ISBN 0-7100-9650-X). Routledge Chapman & Hall.

New Jewish Homemaker: A Treasury of Tips, Crafts, Foods & Stories. Shirley Bogart. 256p. 16.95t o.p. (ISBN 0-940646-20-X). Rossel Bks.

New Jewish Identity in America. Stuart E. Rosenberg. LC 84-10938. 384p. 1985. 19.95 o.p. (ISBN 0-88254-997-9). Hippocrene Bks.

New Jewish Theology in the Making. Eugene B. Borowitz. LC 68-25395. 1968. 6.50 o.s.i. (ISBN 0-664-20836-3, Westminster). Westminster John Knox.

New Jewish Wedding. Anita Diamant. LC 84-24102. (Illus.). 1985. 16.45 o.s.i. (ISBN 0-671-49527-5). Summit Bks.

New Justice: A Radical Magazine, Nos. 1-17. 1970. Repr. of 1919 ed. lib. bdg. 26.00x o.p. (ISBN 0-8371-9218-8, NJ00). Greenwood.

New Kid in Town. Charles Robinson. LC 75-8870. (Illus.). 32p. (gr. 1-3). 1975. 6.95 o.p. (ISBN 0-689-30484-6, Atheneum). Macmillan.

New Kingmakers. David Chagall. LC 80-7932. 288p. 1981. 14.95 o.p. (ISBN 0-15-165203-1). HarBraceJ.

New Kosher Cooking. Colette Rossant. (Illus.). 1986. 18.95 o.p. (ISBN 0-87795-802-5). Morrow.

New Larousse Gastronomique: The Encyclopedia of Food, Wine, & Cooking. Prosper Montagne. Ed. by Charlotte Turgeon. (Illus.). 1977. 40.00 o.p. (ISBN 0-517-53137-2). Crown.

New Lease of Death. Ruth Rendell. Ed. by J. Barzun & W. H. Taqylor. LC 81-47387. (Crime Fiction 1950-1975 Ser.). 214p. 1982. lib. bdg. 18.00 o.p. (ISBN 0-8240-4998-5). Garland Pub.

New Letters of David Hume. David Hume. Ed. by Raymond Klibansky & Ernest C. Mossner. LC 82-48349. (Philosophy of David Hume Ser.). 287p. 1983. lib. bdg. 33.00 o.p. (ISBN 0-8240-5408-3). Garland Pub.

New Library Buildings 1973-74. Ed. by Herbert Ward. 1976. 27.50 o.p. (ISBN 0-85365-089-6, Pub by the Library Assn). Nichols Pub.

New Life. Dante Alighieri. (Most Meaningful Classics in World Culture Ser.). (Illus.). 129p. 1983. 147.50 o.p. Found Class Reprints.

New Life. Bernard Malamud. 352p. 1980. pap. 2.75 o.p. (ISBN 0-380-52530-5, 56572-2, Bard). Avon.

New Life. Bernard Malamud. 367p. 1961. 15.00 o.p. (ISBN 0-374-22128-6). FS&G.

New Life. Dorothy Martin. (Peggy Ser: No. 1). (gr. 7). 1985. pap. 3.50 o.p. (ISBN 0-8024-8301-1). Moody.

New Life for Old Buildings. Architectural Record Magazine Editors. 200p. 1982. text ed. 39.95 o.p. (ISBN 0-07-002364-6). McGraw.

New Life Options. Rosalind K. Loring & Herbert A. Otto. 1976. text ed. 26.95 o.p. (ISBN 0-07-038742-7). McGraw.

New Life: Pregnancy, Birth, & Your Child's First Year. Ed. by John T. Queenan. 1979. 26.95 o.p. (ISBN 0-442-23214-4). Van Nos Reinhold.

New Light Breaks Forth. Lyndon W. Cook & Donald Q. Cannon. pap. 7.95 o.p. (ISBN 0-89036-148-7). Hawkes Pub Inc.

New Linear Polymers. Henry L. Lee et al. 1967. text ed. 28.50 o.p. (ISBN 0-07-036990-9). McGraw.

New Lives: What Happened When Twenty-Two Ordinary People Encountered the Extraordinary Love of God. Bob Ovies. 115p. (Orig.). 1980. pap. text ed. 2.95 o.p. (ISBN 0-89283-077-8). Servant.

New Look at Mechanisms in Bioenergetics. Efraim Racker. 1976. 35.00 o.p. (ISBN 0-12-574670-9); pap. 16.50 o.p. (ISBN 0-12-574672-5). Acad Pr.

New Look at Microwave Cooking. Lila Chalpin. LC 76-41144. (Illus.). 1976. 9.95 o.p. (ISBN 0-916752-04-6). Longman Trade.

New Look at the Apostles Creed. Ed. by Gerhard Rein. Tr. by David LeFort. LC 72-75401. 1969. pap. 2.95 o.p. (ISBN 0-8066-0915-X, 10-4646, Augsburg). Augsburg Fortress.

New Look at the Commonwealth. A. M. Walker. 1978. 31.00 o.p. (ISBN 0-08-021823-7); pap. 15.25 o.p. (ISBN 0-08-021824-5). Pergamon.

New Lower-Cost Way to End Gum Trouble Without Surgery. Vincent M. Cali. LC 81-14702. (Illus.). 206p. 1983. pap. 7.95 o.s.i. (ISBN 0-446-38139-X). Warner Bks.

New Magic of Microwave. pap. write for info. o.s.i. Cy De Cosse.

New Maginot Line: A Documented Expose of Our Fatally Flawed Defense System & What We Can Do about It. Jon Connell. 352p. 1986. 18.95 o.p. (ISBN 0-87795-814-9). Morrow.

New Manual for Vestrymen. Henry B. Luffberry. LC 72-75651. 96p. (Orig.). 1972. pap. 1.00 o.p. (ISBN 0-8006-0122-X, 1-122, Fortress). Augsburg Fortress.

New Maps of Hell. Kingsley Amis. 1960. 4.50 o.p. (ISBN 0-15-165207-4). HarBraceJ.

New Men-New Roles. Perry Yoder & Elizabeth Yoder. 1977. pap. 2.00 o.s.i. (ISBN 0-87303-001-X). Faith & Life.

New Menus from Simca's Cuisine. Simone Beck & Michael James. LC 79-1810. (Illus.). 1979. 12.95 o.p. (ISBN 0-15-165262-7). HarBraceJ.

New Menus from Simca's Cuisine. Simone Beck & Michael James. LC 79-1810. 256p. 1982. pap. 6.95 o.p. (ISBN 0-15-665494-6, Harv). HarBraceJ.

New Merger Game: The Plan & the Players. Don Gussow. 1978. 12.50 o.p. (ISBN 0-8144-5463-1). AMACOM.

New Merger Guidelines. Practising Law Institute Staff & John H. Shenfield. LC 82-61808. (Corporate Law & Practice Course Handbook Ser.: No. 397). 147p. 1982. 45.00 o.p. (B4-6627). PLI.

New Method Supplementary Readers: Bestseller Pack, 40 bks. Ed. by D. K. Swan. Incl. Alice in Wonderland; Black Beauty; Dracula; Frankenstein; King Arthur & the Knights of the Round Table; Secret Garden; Oliver Twist; Robin Hood; Seven Detective Stories; Three Adventures of Sherlock Holmes. (English As a Second Language Bk.). 1981. Set. pap. 115.00 o.p. (ISBN 0-582-52797-X). Longman.

New Methodologies in Studies of Protein Configuration. Tai T. Wu. (Illus.). 224p. 1985. 49.95 o.p. (ISBN 0-442-29212-0). Van Nos Reinhold.

New Methods for Degrading - Detoxifying Chemical Wastes. LC 85-51133. (Emerging Techmologies: No. 18). (Illus.). 350p. 1986. Report 715.00, o.p. (ISBN 0-914993-16-X, DCW). Tech Insights.

New Methods in Chemistry. Ed. by F. Boschke. LC 51-5497. (Topics in Current Chemistry Ser.: Vol. 36). (Illus.). 127p. 1972. pap. 24.30 o.p. (ISBN 0-387-06098-7). Springer-Verlag.

New Methods of Automated Sequence Analysis of Proteins. J. Daniel Lynn et al. (Illus.). 220p. 1973. text ed. 39.50x o.p. (ISBN 0-8422-7099-X). Irvington.

New Mexico Divorce Manual. David Kelsey et al. 404p. 1985. Repr. of 1978 ed. looseleaf 100.00 o.s.i. (ISBN 0-409-25137-2). Butterworth TX.

New Mexico Grasses: A Vegetative Key. Carolyn Barnard & Loren D. Potter. LC 83-21901. (Illus.). 167p. 1984. pap. 8.95 o.p. (ISBN 0-8263-0744-2). U of NM Pr.

New Mexico Populism: A Study of Radical Protest in a Western Territory. Robert W. Larson. LC 73-89256. 1974. 17.50x o.p. (ISBN 0-87081-054-5). Univ Pr Colo.

New Mexico Revisited. Berenard Plossu. LC 83-1079. (Illus.). 103p. 1983. 22.50 o.p. (ISBN 0-8263-0702-7). U of NM Pr.

New Mexico Triptych. Angelico Chavez. LC 75-31416. 84p. 1976. lib. bdg. 9.50x o.p. (ISBN 0-88307-520-2). Gannon.

New Mexico: Trusts. 8.50 o.p. (ISBN 0-686-90862-7). Am Law Inst.

New Militant, Vols. 1-2, No. 22. Worker's Party of Marxist Unification, U.S.A. Staff. 1969. Repr. of 1934 ed. lib. bdg. 96.00x o.p. (ISBN 0-8371-9219-6, NM00). Greenwood.

New Mission for a New People: Voices from the Caribbean. Ed. by David I. Mitchell. (Orig.). 1977. pap. 2.75 o.p. (ISBN 0-377-00062-0). Friendship Pr.

New Missionary Era. Ed. by Padraig Flanagan. LC 81-9595. 192p. (Orig.). 1982. pap. 2.49 o.p. (ISBN 0-88344-331-7). Orbis Bks.

New Mixer's Guide to Low-Alcohol & Non Alcoholic Drinks. Judi Olstein & Sheila Buff. LC 85-82369. (Illus.). 160p. 1986. pap. 9.95 o.p. (ISBN 0-89586-247-6). Price Stern.

New Model Economy: Economic Inventions for the Rest of the Century. Peter G. Elkan. 142p. 1982. 26.00 o.p. (ISBN 0-08-028112-5, L115). Pergamon.

New Moral World, Vols. 1-13. Robert Owen. Incl. Vol. 1. lib. bdg. 39.00 (ISBN 0-313-21779-3, NE01); Vol. 2. lib. bdg. 39.00 (ISBN 0-313-21780-7, NE02); Vol. 3. lib. bdg. 39.00 (ISBN 0-313-21781-5, NE03); Vol. 4. lib. bdg. 39.00 (ISBN 0-313-21782-3, NE04); Vol. 5. lib. bdg. 39.00 (ISBN 0-313-21783-1, NE05); Vol. 6. lib. bdg. 39.00 (ISBN 0-313-21784-X, NE06); Vol. 7. lib. bdg. 39.00 (ISBN 0-313-21785-8, NE07); Vol. 8. lib. bdg. 39.00 (ISBN 0-313-21786-6, NE08); Vol. 9. lib. bdg. 39.00 (ISBN 0-313-21787-4, NE09); Vol. 10. lib. bdg. 39.00 (ISBN 0-313-21788-2, NE10); Vol. 11. lib. bdg. 39.00 (ISBN 0-313-21789-0, NE11); Vol. 12. lib. bdg. 39.00 (ISBN 0-313-21790-4, NE12); Vol. 13. lib. bdg. 39.00 (ISBN 0-313-21791-2, NE13). 1968. Repr. of 1834 ed. Set. lib. bdg. 435.00x o.p. (ISBN 0-8371-9267-6, NE00). Greenwood.

New Mortgage Game. Robert Irwin. LC 81-18665. (Illus.). 240p. 1982. text ed. 22.95 o.p. (ISBN 0-07-032053-5); pap. text ed. 5.95 o.p. (ISBN 0-07-032113-2). McGraw.

New Mother Goose. (Puppet Storybooks Ser.). (ps-2). 1980. pap. 2.95 o.p. (ISBN 0-448-09750-8, G&D). Putnam Pub Group.

New Mother Syndrome. Carol Dix. 320p. pap. 4.50 o.p. (ISBN 0-671-64485-8). Archway.

New Mother's Book of Baby Care. rev. ed. Marjorie Palmer & Ethel Bowman. (Living Books). 144p. 1985. pap. 2.95 o.p. (ISBN 0-8423-4695-3). Tyndale.

New Multinationals: The Spread of Third World Enterprises. Sanjaya Lall. LC 83-6595. (Wiley IRM Series on Multinationals: 1-659). 268p. 1984. 38.95x o.p. (ISBN 0-471-90241-1, Pub. by Wiley-Interscience). Wiley.

New Mythos: The Novel of the Artist As Heroine, 1877-1977. G. B. Stewart. LC 78-74840. 1979. 17.95 o.p. (ISBN 0-88831-030-7). Eden Pr.

New Mythos: The Novel of the Artist As Heroine 1877-1977. 2nd ed. Grace Stewart. 208p. 1981. pap. 8.95 o.p. (ISBN 0-920792-11-1). Eden Pr.

New Nation. Thomas B. Adams. LC 81-82607. (Illus.). 320p. (Orig.). 1982. casebound 16.95 o.p. (ISBN 0-87106-959-8). Globe Pequot.

New Nation: A History of the United States During the Confederation 1781-1789. Merrill Jensen. 1965. pap. 3.95 o.s.i. (ISBN 0-394-70527-0, Vin). Random.

New Nationalism: Implications for Transatlantic Relations. new ed. Ed. by Werner Link & Werner J. Feld. LC 78-17144. (Pergamon Policy Studies). 1979. 45.00 o.p. (ISBN 0-08-023370-8); pap. 45.00 o.p. (ISBN 0-08-023369-4). Pergamon.

New Natural Products & Plant Drugs with Pharmacological, Biological or Therapeutical Activity: Proceedings of the International Congress on Medicinal Plant Research, Section A, University of Munich, Germany, Sept. 6-10, 1976. International Congress on Medicinal Plant Research, Section A Staff. Ed. by H. K. Wagner & P. M. Wolff. (Proceeding in Life Sciences Ser.). (Illus.). 1977. 45.00 o.p. (ISBN 0-387-08292-1). Springer-Verlag.

New Negro of the South. Wilmoth A. Carter. 1967. 4.00 o.p. (ISBN 0-682-45756-6, University). Exposition-Phoenix.

New Office Etiquette: A Guide to Getting along in the Corporate Age. George Mazzei. LC 82-18951. 256p. 1983. 13.50 o.s.i. (ISBN 0-671-45407-2, Poseidon). PB.

New Orlean Saints. James R. Rothaus. (NFL Today Ser.). (Illus.). 48p. (gr. 4-12). PLB 10.45 o.p. (ISBN 0-87191-810-2); pap. 4.25 o.p. (ISBN 0-89812-256-2). Creative Ed.

New Orleans-Access. Richard S. Wurman. (Access Guidebooks). (Illus.). 28p. 1984. pap. 2.95 o.p. (ISBN 0-915461-19-6). Access Pr.

New Orleans Legacy. Alexandra Ripley. 448p. 1987. 14.95 o.p. (ISBN 0-02-603520-0). Macmillan.

New Orleans Restaurant Cookbook. rev. ed. Deirdre Stanforth. LC 75-33266. 320p. 1976. 14.95 o.p. (ISBN 0-385-05032-1). Doubleday.

New Orleans Scrapbook. Ross Yockey. (Illus.). 160p. 0.00 o.s.i. (ISBN 0-938530-43-7); pap. 9.95 o.s.i. (ISBN 0-938530-42-9). Lexikos.

New Orleans 1987-1988. (Frommer's City Guides). 224p. 5.95 o.p. (ISBN 0-671-62358-3). Prentice Hall Pr.

New Outlooks in Psychology. Ed. by Wade Baskin & G. Pat Powers. LC 67-20466. 512p. 1968. 15.95 o.p. (ISBN 0-8022-0080-X). Philos Lib.

New Pacifism. Ed. by Gerald K. Hibbert. LC 74-147447. (Library of War & Peace; Problems of the Organized Peace Movement: Selected Documents). lib. bdg. 38.00 o.p. (ISBN 0-8240-0237-7). Garland Pub.

New Pathways to Piano Technique. Bonpensiere. 1953. (ISBN 0-8022-0153-9). Philos Lib.

New Penguin Book of Scottish Short Stories. Ian Murray. 334p. 1984. pap. 5.95 o.p. (ISBN 0-14-006411-7). Penguin.

New Pension Legislation: ALI-ABA Video Law Review Study Materials. ALI-ABA Committee on Continuing Professional Education & American Bar Association Committee on Continuing Professional Education. LC 83-108222. Date not set. price not set o.p. Am LAw Inst.

New Pentecost? Leon J. Suenens. 1975. pap. 2.95 o.s.i. (ISBN 0-89283-040-9). Servant.

New Peoples: Being & Becoming Metis in North America. Ed. by Jacqueline Peterson & Jennifer S. Brown. LC 85-20859. (Illus.). xxiv, 266p. 1985. 22.50x o.p. (ISBN 0-8032-3673-5). U of Nebr Pr.

New Periodical Title Abbreviations. 5th ed. Ed. by Leland G. Alkire, Jr. 400p. 1986. pap. 125.00x o.p. (ISBN 0-8103-0339-6). Gale.

New Perspective on Cohesion in Expository Paragraphs. Robin B. Markels. 110p. 1984. 10.95 o.p. (ISBN 0-317-37082-0). NCTE.

New Perspectives & Conceptions of International Law: An Afro-American Dialogue. Ed. by K. Ginther & W. Benedek. (Oesterreichische Zeitschrift fuer Oeffentliches Recht und Voeikerrecht: Supp. 6). 280p. 1984. pap. 24.50 o.p. (ISBN 0-387-81780-8). Springer-Verlag.

New Perspectives for Bank Directors. Ed. by Richard B. Johnson. LC 77-12973. 254p. 1977. 15.00x o.p. (ISBN 0-87074-168-3). SMU Press.

New Perspectives in Behavior: A Book of Readings. W. Bugsby. 1970. pap. text ed. 4.75x o.p. (ISBN 0-8290-1168-4). Irvington.

New Perspectives in Public Administration. Ed. by Jae T. Kim. 1973. 34.50x o.p. (ISBN 0-8422-5129-4). Irvington.

New Perspectives on Latin America: Political Conflict & Social Change. Ed. by Karen L. Remmer & Gilbert W. Merkx. 298p. 1976. pap. text ed. 17.50x o.p. (ISBN 0-8422-0533-0). Irvington.

New Perspectives on Older Workers. Harold Sheppard. 90p. 1971. pap. 1.25 o.p. (ISBN 0-911558-10-1). W E Upjohn.

New Perspectives on School Integration. Ed. by Murray Friedman et al. LC 78-21715. 192p. 1979. pap. 6.50 o.p. (ISBN 0-8006-1359-7, 1-1359, Fortress). Augsburg Fortress.

New Perspectives on the American Community. 3rd ed. Roland L. Warren. 1977. pap. 13.95 o.p. (ISBN 0-395-30763-5). HM.

New Perspectives on the Education of Adults in the United States: International Perspectives on Adult & Continuing Education. Huey Long & Peter Jarvis. 288p. 1986. 32.50 o.p. (ISBN 0-7099-1693-0, Pub. by Croom Helm UK). Routledge Chapman & Hall.

New Perspectives on the House of Representatives. 3rd ed. Robert L. Peabody & Nelson W. Polsby. 1977. pap. 11.75 o.p. (ISBN 0-395-30829-1). HM.

New Perspectives on the Presidency. Curtis A. Amlund. LC 77-86502. 121p. 1969. (ISBN 0-8022-2288-9). Philos Lib.

New Physical Education for Elementary School Children. Elsie C. Burton. LC 76-11981. (Illus.). 1977. text ed. 26.95 o.p. (ISBN 0-395-20658-8). HM.

New Physical Trends in Experimental Mechanics, Vol. 264. Ed. by J. T. Pindera. (International Centre for Mechanical Sciences, Courses & Lectures Ser.). (Illus.). 367p. 1982. pap. 31.70 o.p. (ISBN 0-387-81630-5). Springer-Verlag.

New Pioneers Handbook. Date not set. pap. (ISBN 0-8052-0581-0). Random.

New Poems (1968-1970) Pablo Neruda. Ed. & intro. by Ben Belitt. (Eng. & Span., Bilingual ed.). 1972. pap. 3.95 o.s.i. (ISBN 0-394-17793-2, E601, Ever). Grove.

New Poodle. Date not set. (ISBN 0-87605-255-3). Howell Bk.

New Power for the Church. Harvey Seifert. LC 75-40063. 1976. pap. 3.95 o.s.i. (ISBN 0-664-24791-1, Westminster). Westminster John Knox.

New Procedures in Nondestructive Testing: Proceedings, Saarbruecken, FRG, 1982. Ed. by P. Hoeller. (Illus.). 604p. 1983. 51.00 o.p. (ISBN 0-387-12187-0). Springer-Verlag.

New Product Decisions. Edgar A. Pessemier. 1966. pap. text ed. 19.95 o.p. (ISBN 0-07-049517-3). McGraw.

New Product Development Strategies. Frederick D. Buggie. 192p. 1981. 17.95 o.p. (ISBN 0-8144-5626-X). AMACOM.

New Product Planning. Ed. by Sarojini Balachandran. LC 79-24046. (Management Information Guide Ser.: No. 38). 250p. 1980. 68.00x o.p. (ISBN 0-8103-0838-X). Gale.

New Product Trends in Electronics Number One, No. 1. Electronics Magazine Editors. (Electronic Book Ser.). 1978. text ed. 39.50 o.p. (ISBN 0-07-019152-2). McGraw.

New Products. Noreen Heimbold & Jim Betts. 192p. 12.95 o.s.i. (ISBN 0-318-16908-8). Mindsight Pub.

New Products & Diversifications-New Edition. P. Kraushar. 1977. 25.00 o.p. (ISBN 0-8464-0672-1). Beekman Pubs.

New Profits: Business Interruption Insurance. 4th ed. Edward C. Bardwell. 1982. 16.00 o.p. (ISBN 0-942326-20-2, 26621). Rough Notes.

New Program Opportunities in the Electronic Media. Practising Law Institute Staff & George R. Shapiro. LC 83-61576. (Patents, Copyrights, Trademarks, & Literary Property Course Handbook Ser.: No. 164). (Illus.). 616p. 1983. 40.00 o.p. PLI.

New Psychiatry. Nathan Masor. 1959. (ISBN 0-8022-1078-3). Philos Lib.

New Psychiatry: How Modern Psychiatrists Think about Their Patients, Theories, Diagnoses, Drugs, Psychotherapies, Power, Training, Families & Private Lives. Jerrold S. Maxmen. LC 84-22798. (Illus.). 320p. 1985. 17.95 o.p. (ISBN 0-688-04242-2). Morrow.

New Public Policy for Neighborhood Preservation. Roger S. Ahlbrandt. 304p. 1979. 39.95 o.p. (ISBN 0-03-051321-9). H Holt & Co.

New Publications for Architecture Libraries: (April, 1985) Mary Vance. (Architecture Ser.: A 1357). 62p. 1985. 9.00 o.p. (ISBN 0-89028-347-8). Vance Biblios.

New Publications for Architecture Libraries: (August 1985) Mary Vance. (Architecture Ser.: A 1437). 69p. 1985. 10.50 o.p. (ISBN 0-89028-507-1). Vance Biblios.

New Publications for Architecture Libraries: (December, 1985) Mary Vance. (Architecture Ser.: A 1497). 48p. 1985. 7.50 o.p. (ISBN 0-89028-647-7). Vance Biblios.

New Publications for Architecture Libraries (February 1985) Mary Vance. (Architecture Ser.: Bibliography A 1317). 1985. pap. 10.50 o.p. (ISBN 0-89028-267-6). Vance Biblios.

New Publications for Architecture Libraries: (July, 1985) Mary Vance. (Architecture Ser.: A 1418). 65p. 1985. 9.75 o.p. (ISBN 0-89028-468-7). Vance Biblios.

New Publications for Architecture Libraries: (June, 1985) Mary Vance. (Architecture Ser.: A 1397). 70p. 1985. 10.50 o.p. (ISBN 0-89028-427-X). Vance Biblios.

New Publications for Architecture Libraries: (January, 1985) Mary Vance. (Architecture Ser.: A 1298). 68p. 1985. 10.50 o.p. (ISBN 0-89028-228-5). Vance Biblios.

New Publications for Architecture Libraries (March 1985) Mary Vance. (Architecture Ser.: Bibliography A 1337). 1985. pap. 12.75 o.p. (ISBN 0-89028-307-9). Vance Biblios.

New Publications for Architecture Libraries: (May, 1985) Mary Vance. (Architecture Ser.: A 1377). 61p. 1985. 9.00 o.p. (ISBN 0-89028-387-7). Vance Biblios.

New Publications for Architecture Libraries: (November, 1985) Mary Vance. (Architecture Ser.: A 1477). 57p. 1985. 8.25 o.p. (ISBN 0-89028-607-8). Vance Biblios.

New Publications for Architecture Libraries: (October 1985) Mary Vance. (Architecture Ser.: A 1467). 56p. 1985. 8.25 o.p. (ISBN 0-89028-597-7). Vance Biblios.

New Publications for Architecture Libraries: (September 1985) Mary Vance. (Architecture Ser.: A 1457). 71p. 1985. 10.50 o.p. (ISBN 0-89028-547-0). Vance Biblios.

New Pulps for the Paper Industry: Proceedings of the Symposium, Brussels, Belgium, May 1979. New Pulps for the Paper Industry Symposium Staff. Ed. by Leonard E. Haas. LC 79-53919. (PPI Bk.). (Illus.). 160p. 1979. pap. 40.00 o.p. (ISBN 0-87930-121-X). Miller Freeman.

New Puppy. Nicoletta Costa. LC 85-7139. (Macmillan Little Bks.). (Illus.). 16p. (ps-k). 1985. bds. 3.95 o.s.i. (ISBN 0-02-724650-7). Macmillan.

New Puppy. Judith Tabler. LC 85-62016. (Great Big Board Bks.). 14p. (ps). 1986. 3.95 o.s.i. (ISBN 0-394-88038-2, BYR). Random.

New Quest of the Historical Jesus & Other Essays. James M. Robinson. LC 82-48586. 224p. 1983. pap. 12.95 o.p. (ISBN 0-8006-1698-7, Fortress). Augsburg Fortress.

New Rand McNally College World Atlas. rev. ed. Ed. by Jon Leverenz. (Illus.). 528p. 1985. 17.95 o.p. (ISBN 0-528-83187-9). Rand McNally.

New Rand McNally College World Atlas. 528p. 1983. 15.95 o.p. (ISBN 0-528-83133-X). Rand McNally.

New Realities & the Struggle of Ideas. V. Granov. 1980. pap. 4.95 o.p. (ISBN 0-8285-1774-6, Pub. by Progress Pubs USSR). Imported Pubns.

New Recreations with Magic Squares. William H. Benson & Oswald Jacoby. LC 74-28909. 192p. (Orig.). 1976. pap. 4.95 o.p. (ISBN 0-486-23236-0). Dover.

New Reformation. John A. Robinson. 1965. pap. 1.65 o.s.i. (ISBN 0-664-24650-8, Westminster). Westminster John Knox.

New Regime for the Oceans. Michael Hardy et al. 1976. 15.00 o.s.i. (ISBN 0-318-02782-8); pap. 4.95 o.s.i. (ISBN 0-318-02783-6). Trilateral Comm.

New Regime for the Oceans see Trilateral Commission Task Force Reports.

New Renaissance of the Spirit. V. A. McCrossen. (ISBN 0-8022-1012-0). Philos Lib.

New Research Centers. 12th ed. Ed. by Peter Dresser. 150p. 1987. pap. text ed. 240.00x o.p. (ISBN 0-8103-0679-4). Gale.

New Resource for Welfare Reform: The Poor Themselves. Hope H. Pressman. LC 75-2399. 122p. 1975. pap. 4.50x o.p. (ISBN 0-87772-202-1). UCB IGS.

New Results in Boron Chemistry. Ed. by F. Boschke. LC 51-5497. (Topics in Current Chemistry: Vol. 15, Pt. 2). 1970. pap. 48.40 o.p. (ISBN 0-387-04821-9). Springer-Verlag.

New, Revised & Updated McCall's Cookbook. McCall's Food Staff. 1984. 17.45 o.p. (ISBN 0-394-53720-3). Random.

New Right, Nineteen Sixty to Nineteen Sixty-Eight: With Epilogue, 1969-1980. Jonathan M. Kolkey. LC 82-23821. 416p. (Orig.). 1983. lib. bdg. 35.50 o.p. (ISBN 0-8191-2993-3); pap. text ed. 18.75 o.p. (ISBN 0-8191-2994-1). U Pr of Amer.

New Rochelle: Portrait of a City. Robert Merrill et al. LC 80-70248. (Illus.). 224p. 1981. 25.00 o.p. (ISBN 0-89659-186-7). Abbeville Pr.

New Rock Record. Terry Hounsome. 17.95 o.p. (ISBN 0-87196-774-X); pap. 9.95 o.p. (ISBN 0-87196-770-7). Facts on File.

New Roget's Thesaurus in Dictionary Form. rev. ed. Norman Lewis. LC 77-24457. 552p. 10.95 o.p. (ISBN 0-399-12678-3); Thumb-indexed ed. 11.95 o.p. (ISBN 0-399-12679-1). Putnam Pub Group.

New Roles for Public Officials in Labor Relations see Issues in the Public Employee Relations Library: Series 3.

New Rules of Golf: The 1988-1991 Edition. Tom Watson & Frank Hannigan. LC 87-42672. (Illus.). 192p. 1988. 14.95 o.p. (ISBN 0-394-56271-2); pap. 9.95 o.p. (ISBN 0-394-75632-0, Vin). Random.

New Rules of Practice Before the Public Utility Commission. 284p. 1984. 35.00 o.p. (ISBN 0-318-03930-3, 278). PA Bar Inst.

New Russian Tragedy. Anatole Shub. 1970. pap. text ed. 2.95x o.p. (ISBN 0-393-09910-5, NortonC). Norton.

New San Juan Current Guide. rev. ed. Island Canoe Co. Staff. (Illus., Orig.). 1985. pap. 8.95 o.p. (ISBN 0-918439-04-3). Island Canoe.

New Science of Health. 8th ed. Paul C. Bragg & Patricia Bragg. pap. 1.75 o.p. (ISBN 0-87790-021-3). Health Sci.

New Science of Skin & Scuba Diving Workbook. 6th ed. 1.95 o.p. (ISBN 0-8329-0450-3). New Century.

New Scientific Aspect. Ed. by H. J. Canton et al. LC 61-642. (Advances in Polymer Science: Vol. 20). (Illus.). 200p. 1976. 43.00 o.p. (ISBN 0-387-07631-X). Springer-Verlag.

New Scientific Spirit. Gaston Bachelard. Tr. by Arthur Goldhammer from Fr. LC 84-14609. 214p. 1985. 22.95 o.p. (ISBN 0-8070-1500-8). Beacon Pr.

New Season: A Spectator's Guide to the 1988 Election. George F. Will. 320p. 1987. 17.45 o.p. (ISBN 0-671-64837-3). S&S.

New Secondary Education: A Phi Delta Kappa Task Force Report. Maurice Gibbons. LC 75-26386. (Orig.). 1976. 6.50 o.p. (ISBN 0-87367-763-3); pap. 5.00 o.p. (ISBN 0-87367-762-5). Phi Delta Kappa.

New Serial Titles, 1950-1970. 1978. avail. microfilm 100.00 o.p. (ISBN 0-8352-1105-3). Bowker.

New Sex Ethics & Marriage Structure. Marion Bassett. LC 60-53155. 342p. 1961. (ISBN 0-8022-0081-8). Philos Lib.

New Shoe. Jeff MacNelly. 128p. (Orig.). 1981. pap. 6.95 o.p. (ISBN 0-380-78030-5, 78030-5). Avon.

New Short-Term Therapies for Children: A Guide for Parents & the Helping Professions. Lawrence E. Shapiro. (Illus.). 192p. 1984. 16.95 o.p. (ISBN 0-13-615724-6); pap. 7.95 o.p. (ISBN 0-13-615716-5). P-H.

New-Skipper's Bowditch: Piloting from Here to There-& Home Again-with Maximun Pleasure & Minimun Trauma. James R. Louttit. (Illus.). 1984. 24.45 o.p. (ISBN 0-393-03292-2). Norton.

New Song. Leland B. Sateren. (Orig.). 1958. pap. 1.50 o.p. (ISBN 0-8066-0187-6, 11-9299, Augsburg). Augsburg Fortress.

New Songs from a Jade Terrace: An Anthology of Early Chinese Love Poetry. Tr. by Anne Birrell. 374p. 1982. 35.00 o.p. (ISBN 0-04-895026-2). Unwin Hyman.

New Sources of Oil & Gas: Gases from Coal, Liquid Fuels from Coal, Shale, Tar Sands, & Heavy Oil Sources. S. S. Penner. (Illus.). 120p. 1982. 40.00 o.p. (ISBN 0-08-029335-2). Pergamon.

New Sources of Self. T. R. Young. 124p. 1972. 17.50 o.p. (ISBN 0-08-016672-5). Pergamon.

New Southern Photography: Aperture 115. (Illus.). 80p. 1989. pap. 14.50 o.p. (ISBN 0-89381-378-8). Aperture.

New Soviet Legislation to Combat Crime. M. Yevteyev & V. A. Kirin. 75p. 1973. pap. 0.95 o.p. (ISBN 0-8285-0340-0, 130712, Pub. by Progress Pubs USSR). Imported Pubns.

New Spring in China. Leslie T. Lyall. pap. 3.95 o.p. (ISBN 0-340-24549-2). OMF Bks.

New Standard Encyclopedia, 17 vols. Standard Educational Corporation Staff. Ed. by Douglas W. Downey et al. LC 83-429. (gr. 9-12). 1984. Set. 595.50 o.p. (ISBN 0-87392-189-5). Standard Ed.

New Standard Encyclopedia, 17 vols. Standard Educational Corporation Staff. Ed. by Douglas W. Downey et al. LC 86-3742. (gr. 9-12). 1987. Set. 669.50 o.p. (ISBN 0-87392-192-5). Standard Ed.

New State of the World Atlas. Michael Kidron & Ronald Segal. 176p. 1984. 19.95 o.s.i. (ISBN 0-671-50663-3); pap. 12.95 o.s.i. (ISBN 0-671-50664-1). S&S.

New Steinerbooks Dictionary of the Paranormal. George Riland. 368p. (Orig.). 1982. pap. 7.95 o.s.i. (ISBN 0-446-97010-7). Warner Bks.

New Strategy in Indian Agriculture. C. Subramaniam. text ed. 12.50x o.p. (ISBN 0-7069-0921-6, Pub. by Vikas India). Advent NY.

New Student, Vols. 1-8, No. 9. National Student Forum of the Paris Pact Staff. 1970. Repr. of 1922 ed. lib. bdg. 325.00x o.p. (ISBN 0-8371-9222-6, NO00). Greenwood.

New System for Public Housing: Salvaging a National Resource. Raymond J. Struyk. LC 80-53321. 263p. 1980. 21.00 o.p. (ISBN 0-87766-279-7). Urban Inst.

New System of Chemical Philosophy. John Dalton. LC 64-13307. (Illus.). 180p. 1964. (ISBN 0-8022-0336-1). Philos Lib.

New Tax Consequences of Separation & Divorce. 92p. 1984. 30.00 o.p. (ISBN 0-318-03921-4, 269). PA Bar Inst.

New Techniques of Architectural Rendering. 2nd ed. Compiled by Helmut Jacoby. 1981. 24.95 o.p. (ISBN 0-442-21210-0); pap. 19.95 o.p. (ISBN 0-442-21211-9). Van Nos Reinhold.

New Technologies for the Exploration & Exploitation of Oil & Gas Resources. Ed. by Commission of the European Communities et al. 1400p. 1985. Vol. 1. 63.00 o.p. (ISBN 0-86010-675-6); Vol. 2. 63.00 o.p. (ISBN 0-86010-676-4). Graham & Trotman.

New Technology. T. Potter et al. (New Technology Ser.). (Illus.). 144p. (gr. 6up). 1983. 12.95 o.p. (ISBN 0-86020-728-5). EDC.

New Technology & Military Power: General Purpose Military Forces for the Nineteen Eighties & Beyond. Seymour J. Deitchman. (Special Studies in Military Affairs). 315p. 1981. lib. bdg. 32.00x o.p. (ISBN 0-89158-358-0); pap. 13.50x o.p. (ISBN 0-86531-307-5). Westview.

New Technology & Regional Development. Ed. by G. A. Van der Knapp & E. Wever. 208p. 1986. 43.95 o.p. (ISBN 0-7099-3106-9, Pub. by Croom Helm Ltd). Routledge Chapman & Hall.

New Technology & Rural Development see Technology & the Rural Community: The Social Impact.

New Telecommunications Era After the AT&T Divestiture: The Transition to Full Competition. 838p. 1985. 15.00 o.p. (G4-3780). PLI.

New Testament. 48p. (Orig.). 1989. pap. 9.95 o.s.i. (ISBN 1-55651-629-0); audiocassette tape incl. o.s.i. (ISBN 1-55651-630-4). Cram Cassettes.

New Testament: A Guide to Its Writings. Gunther Bornkamm. Tr. by Reginald H. Fuller & Ilse Fuller. LC 73-79009. 176p. (Orig.). 1973. pap. 5.95 o.p. (ISBN 0-8006-0168-8, 1-168, Fortress). Augsburg Fortress.

New Testament: A New Translation. William Barclay. 576p. 1980. pap. 2.95 o.s.i. (ISBN 0-664-24358-4, Westminster). Westminster John Knox.

New Testament & the Literary Imagination. David Jasper. LC 86-18519. 132p. 1987. text ed. 25.00 o.p. (ISBN 0-391-03482-0). Humanities.

New Testament & the Mishnah. Charles R. Gianotti. 1983. pap. 3.50 o.p. (ISBN 0-8010-3791-3). Baker Bk.

New Testament as the Church's Book. Willi Marxsen. Tr. by James E. Mignard from Ger. LC 70-164554. 160p. (Orig.). 1972. pap. 3.95 o.p. (ISBN 0-8006-0102-5, 1-102, Fortress). Augsburg Fortress.

New Testament Commentary: A General Introduction to & a Commentary on the Books of the New Testament. rev. ed. Ed. by Herbert C. Alleman. LC 44-47049. 1944. 8.95 o.p. (ISBN 0-8006-0364-8, Fortress). Augsburg Fortress.

New Testament Express. Terry Hall. 160p. 1986. pap. 4.50 o.p. (ISBN 0-88207-598-5). Victor Bks.

New Testament for English Readers, 4 vols. Henry Alford. 1983. Repr. of 1976 ed. 54.95 o.p. (ISBN 0-8010-0195-1). Baker Bk.

New Testament for Today. A. M. Hunter. LC 75-13463. (Bible Speaks to Us Today Ser.). 88p. 1975. pap. 3.95 o.p. (ISBN 0-8042-0351-2, John Knox). Westminster John Knox.

New Testament Manuscripts in the Freer Collection. Henry A. Sanders. Repr. of 1918 ed. 37.00 o.p. (ISBN 0-384-38809-4). Johnson Repr.

New Testament Men of Faith. F. B. Meyer. LC 79-66338. 1979. pap. 4.95 o.p. (ISBN 0-89107-171-7). Good News.

New Testament Prophecy. David Hill. LC 79-16707. (New Foundations Theological Library). 260p. (Peter Toon & Ralph Martin series editors). 1980. 12.95 o.s.i. (ISBN 0-8042-3702-6). Westminster John Knox.

New Testament Questions of Today. Ernst Kasemann. Tr. by W. J. Montague from Ger. LC 70-81531. 320p. 1979. pap. 7.95 o.p. (ISBN 0-8006-1351-1, 1-1351, Fortress). Augsburg Fortress.

New Testament Studies: Essays in Honor of Ray Summers in His Sixty-Fifth Year. Ed. by Huber L. Drumwright & Curtis Vaughan. LC 75-29815. 195p. 1975. 7.95 o.s.i. (ISBN 0-918954-15-0). Baylor Univ Pr.

New Testament Survey. Robert G. Gromacki. LC 74-83793. 1974. 9.95 o.p. (ISBN 0-87227-018-1). Reg Baptist.

New Testament Understanding of Jesus. Megan McKenna & Darryl Ducote. LC 78-71529. (Followers of the Way Ser.: Vol. 2). (gr. 9-12). 1979. 22.50 o.p. (ISBN 0-8091-9543-7). Paulist Pr.

New Testament Word Lists. Clinton D. Morrison & David H. Barnes. 1964. pap. 4.95 o.p. (ISBN 0-8028-1141-8). Eerdmans.

New Testaments. (Illus.). 348p. 3000.00 o.p. (ISBN 0-8115-0900-1). Kraus Repr.

New Theatre & Film 1934 to 1937: An Anthology. Ed. by Herbert Kline. LC 85-815. (Illus.). 352p. 1985. 24.95 o.p. (ISBN 0-15-165457-3). HarBraceJ.

New Theatre & Film 1934 to 1937: An Anthology. Ed. by Herbert Kline. LC 85-815. (Illus.). 416p. 1985. pap. 13.95 o.s.i. (ISBN 0-15-665507-1, Harv). HarBraceJ.

New Theatres for Old. Mordecai Gorelik. LC 75-14002. 553p. 1975. Repr. of 1940 ed. lib. bdg. 37.50x o.p. (ISBN 0-374-93213-1, Octagon). Hippocrene Bks.

New Theory of Gravitation. Jacob Mandelker. 1951. (ISBN 0-8022-1041-4). Philos Lib.

New Theory of Human Evolution. Arthur Keith. Philos Lib.

New Thinking Man's Guide to Pro Football. Paul Zimmerman. 416p. 1984. 17.45 o.p. (ISBN 0-671-45394-7). S&S.

New Times Network: Groups & Centres for Personal Growth. Ed. by Robert Adams. 192p. 1983. pap. 8.95 o.p. (ISBN 0-7100-9355-1). Routledge Chapman & Hall.

New Tolkien Companion. J. E. Taylor. 672p. 1980. pap. 5.95 o.p. (ISBN 0-380-46904-9, 63743-X). Avon.

New Towns: Monographs Published 1970-1984. Mary Vance. (Architecture Ser.: A 1468). 30p. 1985. 4.50 o.p. (ISBN 0-89028-598-5). Vance Biblios.

New Toxicology for Old, A Critique of Accepted Requirements & Methodology: Proceedings. Ed. by P. L. Chambers & C. M. Chambers. (Archives of Toxicology Supplements: Vol. 5). (Illus.). 394p. 1982. pap. 41.80 o.p. (ISBN 0-387-11406-8). Springer-Verlag.

New Trade Names. 5th ed. Ed. by Donna Wood. (Trade Names Dictionary- Supplement). 300p. 1986. pap. text ed. 220.00x o.p. (ISBN 0-8103-0693-X). Gale.

New Trails in Mexico: Travels among the Papago, Pima & Cocopa Indians. Carl Lumholtz. LC 70-176225. (Beautiful Rio Grande Classics Ser.). (Illus.). 576p. 1983. Repr. of 1912 ed. lib. bdg. 25.00 o.p. (ISBN 0-87380-059-1). Rio Grande.

New Training Organizations. 3rd ed. Ed. by Janice McLean. 250p. 1987. pap. text ed. 105.00x o.p. (ISBN 0-8103-0447-3). Gale.

New Transportation Systems: Seven Reports. (Transportation Research Record Ser.). 76p. 1974. 3.40 o.p. (ISBN 0-309-02367-X). Transport Res Bd.

New Treasury of Judaism. Ed. by Philip Birnbaum. 1977. 15.00 o.p. (ISBN 0-88482-410-1, Sanhedrin Pr); pap. 9.95 o.p. (ISBN 0-88482-411-X, Sanhedrin Pr). Hebrew Pub.

New Trends, Nos. 1-10. 1968. Repr. of 1945 ed. lib. bdg. 13.75 o.p. (ISBN 0-8371-9223-4, NT00). Greenwood.

New Trends in Bio-Inorganic Chemistry. Ed. by R. J. Williams & J. R. Da Silva. 1979. 69.00 o.p. (ISBN 0-12-755050-X). Acad Pr.

New Trends in Development Theory. P. W. Preston. (International Library of Sociology). 256p. 1985. 29.95x o.p. (ISBN 0-7102-0377-2). Routledge Chapman & Hall.

New Trends in Mathematical Anthropology. Gisele De Meur. (International Library of Anthropology). 320p. 1986. text ed. 29.95 o.p. (ISBN 0-7102-0076-5). Routledge Chapman & Hall.

New Trends in Physics Teaching, 3 vols. Incl. Vol. 1. 1965-66. W. Knecht. 271p. 1968. pap. 9.50 o.p. (ISBN 92-3-000707-2, U425). UNIPUB; Vol. 2. 1970. Ed. by E. Nagy. 517p. 1972. pap. 8.50 (ISBN 92-3-000950-4, U426). UNIPUB; Vol. 3. 1976. 282p. pap. 8.00 (ISBN 92-3-101410-2, U427). UNIPUB. (Teaching of Basic Sciences Ser.). (Orig., UNESCO). UNIPUB.

New Trends in Soviet Economics. Ed. by Martin Cave et al. Tr. by Martin Cave from Rus. LC 82-835. 425p. 1982. 45.00 o.p. (ISBN 0-87332-206-1). M E Sharpe.

New Trends in Systems Analysis: International Symposium, Versailles, France, Dec. 13-17, 1976. Ed. by A. Bensoussan & J. L. Lions. (Lecture Notes in Control & Information Sciences Ser.: Vol. 2). 1977. pap. text ed. 34.00 o.p. (ISBN 0-387-08406-1). Springer-Verlag.

New Trends in Urban Planning: Studies in Housing, Urban Design & Planning--Papers Presented at the Symposium Held in Tel Aviv, Israel, December 1977. Ed. by D. Soen. LC 78-41197. (Illus.). 355p. 1979. 65.00 o.p. (ISBN 0-08-024266-9). Pergamon.

New Trip. T. Pfalzer. 1984. 6.95 o.p. (ISBN 0-533-06002-8). Vantage.

New Universities Overseas. Sir Alexander M. Carr-Saunders. LC 77-7518. (Illus.). 1977. Repr. of 1961 ed. lib. bdg. 35.00x o.p. (ISBN 0-8371-9665-5, CSNU). Greenwood.

New Urban Economics, & Alternatives. H. W. Richardson. (Research in Planning & Design Ser.). 266p. 1977. 24.95x o.p. (ISBN 0-85086-058-X, NO. 2926, Pub. by Pion England). Routledge Chapman & Hall.

New Urban Studies Literature: A Review with Special Reference to Australia. M. Huxley & J. B. McLoughlin. 86p. 1985. pap. 22.00 o.p. (ISBN 0-08-033668-X, K120, Pub. by PPL). Pergamon.

New Uses of Ion Accelerators. Ed. by James F. Ziegler. LC 75-16315. 482p. 1975. 75.00x o.p. (ISBN 0-306-30853-3, Plenum Pr). Plenum Pub.

New Venture Analysis: Research, Planning & Finance. Dennis Costello. LC 84-73197. 1985. 45.00 o.p. (ISBN 0-87094-505-X). Dow Jones-Irwin.

New Victor Book of the Opera. Henry W. Simon. 1968. 24.45 o.p. (ISBN 0-671-20054-2). S&S.

New Viewpoints in Georgia History. Albert B. Saye. LC 44-3340. 264p. 1943. 14.00x o.p. (ISBN 0-8203-0132-9). U of Ga Pr.

New Vision: Forty Years of Photography at the Institute of Design. Ed. by Charles Traub. LC 80-68713. (Illus.). 80p. 1982. 20.00 o.p. (ISBN 0-89381-067-3). Aperture.

New Vision: The Ford Motor Company Collection of Photographs in the Metropolitan Museum of Art. (Illus.). 1988. Metro Mus Art.

New Vocal Repertory: An Introduction. Jane Manning. (Illus.). 284p. 1987. pap. 12.95 o.s.i. (ISBN 0-8008-5557-4, Crescendo). Taplinger.

New Voices on the Right: Impact on Schools. (Communication Alert Ser.). 64p. 12.50 o.p. (ISBN 0-87545-024-5, 411-13307). Natl Sch Pr.

New Voices on the Right: Impact on Schools see Communication Alert Series.

New Warfare. C. N. Barclay. 1954. (ISBN 0-8022-0058-3). Philos Lib.

New Ways in Discipline. Dorothy W. Baruch. 1949. text ed. 12.95 o.p. (ISBN 0-07-004040-0). McGraw.

New Ways of Working Metals. David Fishlock. (Illus.). 132p. 1965. (ISBN 0-8022-0509-7). Philos Lib.

New Ways to Enjoy Chicken. Stanley Wolf. (Illus.). 216p. 1983. pap. 6.95 o.p. (ISBN 0-911954-76-7). Bristol Pub Ent CA.

New Weather Satellite Handbook. Ralph E. Taggart. 131p. 1981. pap. 8.95 o.p. (ISBN 0-88006-015-8, BK 7383). Wayne Green Ent.

New Western Garden Book. 4th ed. Sunset Magazine & Books Editors. LC 78-70266. (Illus.). 512p. 1979. pap. 14.95 o.p. (ISBN 0-376-03890-X). Sunset-Lane.

New Wine in Old Bottles? Royston Lambert. 171p. 1968. pap. text ed. 5.00x o.p. (ISBN 0-686-70852-0, Pub. by Bedford England). Gower Pub Co.

New Woman. Janine Boissard. 1982. 15.95 o.p. (ISBN 0-316-10099-4). Little.

New Woman Driver: All a Woman Needs to Know about Cars to Buy One, Drive It, Have It Maintained. Don Sharpe. (Illus.). 410p. 1984. 16.45 o.p. (ISBN 0-395-33971-5); pap. 9.70 o.p. (ISBN 0-395-33972-3). HM.

New Women in Art & Dance. Kathleen Bowman. LC 76-5457. (New Women Ser.). (Illus.). 48p. (gr. 4 up). 1976. PLB 8.95 o.p. (ISBN 0-87191-512-X). Creative Ed.

New Work Schedules in Practice. Stanley D. Nollen et al. (Work in America Institue Ser.). 1981. 21.95 o.p. (ISBN 0-442-26899-8). Van Nos Reinhold.

New World. Alan T. Dale. (Illus.). 429p. (Orig.). 1973. pap. 9.95 o.p. (ISBN 0-8192-1149-4). Morehouse Pub.

New World Book. (Our Nations Heritage Ser.). Date not set. (ISBN 0-07-375391-2). McGraw.

New World Book. (Our Nations Heritage Ser.). Date not set. (ISBN 0-07-375412-9). McGraw.

New World, New Ways, New Management. Philip R. Harris. 320p. 1983. 22.95 o.p. (ISBN 0-8144-5755-X). AMACOM.

New World of Economics: Explorations into the Human Experience. 4th ed. Gordon Tullock & Richard B. McKenzie. 1985. pap. 17.95x o.p. (ISBN 0-256-03095-2). Irwin.

New World of Travel. Arthur Frommer. (Illus.). 1988. pap. 12.95 o.p. (ISBN 0-13-048886-0). Prentice Hall Pr.

New World Review, Vols. 1-28. Incl. Vol. 1. lib. bdg. 53.00 (ISBN 0-313-21816-1, NW01); Vol. 2. lib. bdg. 53.00 (ISBN 0-313-21817-X, NW02); Vol. 3. lib. bdg. 53.00 (ISBN 0-313-21818-8, NW03); Vol. 4. lib. bdg. 53.00 (ISBN 0-313-21819-6, NW04); Vol. 5. lib. bdg. 47.00 (ISBN 0-313-21820-X, NW05); Vol. 6. lib. bdg. 47.00 (ISBN 0-313-21821-8, NW06); Vol. 7. lib. bdg. 47.00 (ISBN 0-313-21822-6, NW07); Vol. 8. lib. bdg. 47.00 (ISBN 0-313-21823-4, NW08); Vol. 9. lib. bdg. 47.00 (ISBN 0-313-21824-2, NW09); Vol. 10. lib. bdg. 47.00 (ISBN 0-313-21825-0, NW10); Vol. 11. lib. bdg. 47.00 (ISBN 0-313-21826-9, NW11); Vol. 12. lib. bdg. 47.00 (ISBN 0-313-21827-7, NW12); Vol. 13. lib. bdg. 47.00 (ISBN 0-313-21828-5, NW13); Vol. 14. lib. bdg. 47.00 (ISBN 0-313-21829-3, NW14); Vol. 15. lib. bdg. 47.00 (ISBN 0-313-21830-7, NW15); Vol. 16. lib. bdg. 47.00 (ISBN 0-313-21831-5, NW16); Vol. 17. lib. bdg. 47.00 (ISBN 0-313-21832-3, NW17); Vol. 18. lib. bdg. 42.50 (ISBN 0-313-21833-1, NW18); Vol. 19. lib. bdg. 47.00 (ISBN 0-313-21834-X, NW19); Vol. 20. lib. bdg. 42.00 (ISBN 0-313-21835-8, NW20); Vol. 21. lib. bdg. 42.00 (ISBN 0-313-21836-6, NW21); Vol. 22. lib. bdg. 42.00 (ISBN 0-313-21837-4, NW22); Vol. 23. lib. bdg. 42.00 (ISBN 0-313-21838-2, NW23); Vol. 24. lib. bdg. 42.00 (ISBN 0-313-21839-0, NW 24); Vol. 25. lib. bdg. 42.00 (ISBN 0-313-21840-4, NW25); Vol. 26. lib. bdg. 42.00 (ISBN 0-313-21841-2, NW26); Vol. 27. lib. bdg. 42.00 (ISBN 0-313-21842-0, NW27); Vol. 28. lib. bdg. 42.00 (ISBN 0-313-21843-9, NW28). 1978. Repr. of 1932 ed. Set. lib. bdg. 1090.00 o.p. (ISBN 0-8371-9224-2, NW00). Greenwood.

New Y-Indian Guide Program, 7 Bks. YMCA of the U. S. A. Staff. (Illus.). 148p. 1982. pap. text ed. 6.00x o.s.i. (ISBN 0-88035-005-9, YMCA USA). Human Kinetics.

New Yacht Racing Rules, 1973-1976. Robert N. Bavier, Jr. (Illus.). 176p. 1974. 7.95 o.p. (ISBN 0-393-03177-2). Norton.

New Yacht, Rules-Racing. Robert N. Bavier, Jr. 1969. 5.95 o.p. (ISBN 0-393-03135-7). Norton.

New York. Carole Chester. 1977. 29.95 o.p. (ISBN 0-7134-0183-4, Pub. by Batsford England). David & Charles.

New York. Juan Fresan. (Illus.). 96p. (Orig.). 1983. pap. 7.95 o.p. (ISBN 0-87663-592-3). Universe.

New York. Arthur S. Harris. LC 72-96127. (This Beautiful World Ser.: Vol. 42). (Illus.). 142p. 1982. pap. 5.25 o.p. (ISBN 0-87011-197-3). Kodansha.

New York. Date not set. (ISBN 0-905522-54-0). Salem Hse Pubs.

New York. Reinhart Wolf. (Illus.). 38p. 1987. pap. 16.95 o.p. (ISBN 3-8228-0043-0). Parkwest Pubns.

New York Academy of Medicine, Illustration Catalog. 3rd. enlarged ed. New York Academy of Medicine Editors. 1976. lib. bdg. 35.00 o.p. (ISBN 0-8161-0038-1, Hall Library). G K Hall.

New York: An Anthology. Ed. by Mike Marqusee & Bill Harris. LC 85-80124. 362p. 1985. 17.95 o.p. (ISBN 0-316-54709-3). Little.

New York Business Kit for Starting & Existing Business. Lawless J. Barrientos. LC 83-113851. (Illus.). 1983. pap. 14.95 o.p. (ISBN 0-671-46522-8). S&S.

New York City. (Pocket Guides). (Illus., Orig.). 1987. pap. 5.95 o.p. (ISBN 0-528-84406-7). Rand McNally.

New York City Architecture & the Empire State Building: A Selected Bibliography. Bibliographic Research Library Staff. (Architecture Ser.: A 1386). 5p. 1985. 2.00 o.p. (ISBN 0-89028-396-6). Vance Biblios.

New York City Electrical Code. 17.50 o.p. Gould.

New York City Folklore: Legends, Tall Tales, Anecdotes, Stories, Sagas, Heroes & Characters, Customs, Traditions & Sayings. Benjamin A. Botkin. LC 76-43977. (Illus.). 1976. Repr. of 1956 ed. lib. bdg. 28.75x o.p. (ISBN 0-8371-9310-9, BONC). Greenwood.

New York City Health Code. 600p. 1988. 25.00 o.p. (ISBN 0-87526-336-4). Gould.

New York City Street Smarts. Saul Miller. (Illus.). 320p. 1983. 17.95 o.p. (ISBN 0-03-060379-X); pap. 9.95 o.p. (ISBN 0-03-060378-1). H Holt & Co.

New York Collection, 1980. Arlene H. Eakle et al. 249p. 1980. pap. 15.00 o.p. (ISBN 0-940764-27-X). U of Utah Pr.

New York Communist, Nos. 1-10. Socialist Workers Party Staff. 1970. Repr. of 1919 ed. lib. bdg. 35.00x o.p. (ISBN 0-8371-9225-0, NY00). Greenwood.

New York Corporations. Eugene R. Canudo. 112p. 1969. pap. text ed. 5.50x o.p. (ISBN 0-87526-215-5). Gould.

New York Court of Appeals Case Names Citator. Shepard's Citation, Inc. Staff. 1400p. 1986. incl. quarterly supplements 95.00 o.p. (ISBN 0-318-20346-4). Shepards McGraw.

New York Criminal Law Appendix. 100p. pap. 5.00 looseleaf o.p. (ISBN 0-317-15581-4). Gould.

New York Cuisine. E. Sieveling. (Illus.). 264p. 1985. text ed. 19.95 o.p. (ISBN 0-07-057295-X). McGraw.

New York d'Arrabal. Fernando Arrabal. 1973. 14.95 o.p. (ISBN 0-686-54458-7). French & Eur.

New York Days, New York Nights. Stephen Brook. LC 84-14575. 304p. 1985. 14.95 o.p. (ISBN 0-689-11511-3, Atheneum). Macmillan.

New York Dictionary Catalog of the Missionary Research Library, 17 vols. Missionary Research Library Staff. 1970. Set. 1680.00 o.p. (ISBN 0-8161-0778-5, Hall Library). G K Hall.

New York Etchings: Nineteen Five to Nineteen Forty-Nine. John Sloan. 1978. pap. 5.00 o.p. (ISBN 0-486-23651-X). Dover.

New York Ethnic Food Market Guide & Cookbook. Vilma L. Chantiles. (Illus.). 416p. 1984. pap. 14.95 o.p. (ISBN 0-396-08282-3). Dodd.

New York Family Court Act. Gould Editorial Staff. 450p. (Supplemented annually). looseleaf 15.00 o.p. (ISBN 0-87526-143-4); abridged ed. 6.95 o.p. (ISBN 0-87526-277-5). Gould.

New York Giants. Julian May. (NFL Today Ser.). (Illus.). (gr. 3-6). 1977. PLB 10.45 o.p. (ISBN 0-87191-598-7); pap. 4.25 o.p. (ISBN 0-686-67476-6). Creative Ed.

New York Gold. 1987. 45.00 o.p. (ISBN 0-8230-3180-2). Watson-Guptill.

New York in the Thirties. Berenice Abbott. Orig. Title: Changing New York. 15.00 o.p. (ISBN 0-8446-5000-5). Peter Smith.

New York Insurance Law. Gould Editorial Staff. 600p. 1985. looseleaf 14.95 o.p. (ISBN 0-87526-316-X). Gould.

New York Insurance Law. 1974 ed. 238p. 5.50 o.p. (ISBN 0-87526-077-2). Gould.

New York Knicks. Molly Martin. (NBA Today Ser.). (Illus.). 48p. (gr. 4 up). 1984. PLB 10.45 o.p. (ISBN 0-87191-984-2). Creative Ed.

New York Landlord-Tenant. Louis A. Kass. 1964. pap. 4.00x o.p. (ISBN 0-87526-043-8). Gould.

New York Magistrate's Association Handbook. 200p. pap. 25.00 looseleaf o.p. (ISBN 0-87526-310-0). Gould.

New York Manufacturers Directory, 1986-87. 860p. 1986. pap. 57.00 o.p. (ISBN 0-318-02901-4, Pub. by George D. Hall Co.). Manufacturers.

New York Mets. rev. ed. Martin. LC 82-239938. (Baseball Today Ser.). 48p. (gr. 4 up). 1982. PLB 11.45 o.p. (ISBN 0-87191-867-6). Creative Ed.

New York Mets - World Series Edition. Lang. 25.00 o.p. (ISBN 0-8050-0467-X). H Holt & Co.

New York Mets World Series Edition. pap. 13.95 o.p. (ISBN 0-8050-0466-1). H Holt & Co.

New York Mets: 25 Years of Baseball Magic. Peter Simon & Jack Lang. LC 86-353. (Illus.). 256p. 1986. pap. 18.95 o.p. (ISBN 0-8050-0054-2). H Holt & Co.

New York-New York: Masterworks of a Street Peddler. David D. Duncan & George Forss. (Illus.). 1984. text ed. 19.95 o.p. (ISBN 0-07-018208-6). McGraw.

New York on Thirty-Five Dollars a Day. Joan Hamburg & Norma Ketay. 336p. 1986. pap. 9.95 o.p. (ISBN 0-671-55619-3). S&S.

New York on Thirty-Five Dollars a Day, 1984-85. (Dollar a Day Guides). 304p. 1983. 8.95 o.p. (ISBN 0-671-47597-5). Prentice Hall Pr.

New York Penal Law. (Span.). 1985. looseleaf 10.00 o.p. Gould.

New York: Poems. Ed. by Howard Moss. 320p. 1980. pap. 5.95 o.p. (ISBN 0-380-76067-3, 76067-3). Avon.

New York State Fair: An Empire Showcase. Henry W. Schramm. (Illus.). 192p. (Orig.). 1985. pap. 9.95 o.p. (ISBN 0-932052-39-8). North Country.

New York State in Story, Pt. 1. rev. ed. Schwarz & Goldberg. 1962. pap. 5.25x o.p. (ISBN 0-88323-096-8, 281). Pendergrass Pub.

New York State Industrial Directory, 1988. 1140p. 1988. 110.00 o.p. (ISBN 0-318-22822-X, Pub. by Mac Rae's). Manufacturers.

New York Supreme Court Appellate Division Case Names Citator, 3 vols. Shepard's Citation, Inc. Staff. 2800p. 1986. incl. quarterly supplements 165.00 o.p. (ISBN 0-318-20343-X). Shepards McGraw.

New York Theatre Annual: 1976-77. Ed. by Catharine R. Hughes. LC 78-50757. (Illus.). 160p. 1978. 66.00x o.p. (ISBN 0-8103-0416-3). Gale.

New York Theatre Annual: 1977-78. Ed. by Catharine R. Hughes. LC 78-50757. (Illus.). 192p. 1978. 66.00x o.p. (ISBN 0-8103-0417-1). Gale.

New York Theatrical Sourcebook 1988. rev ed. Association of Theatrical Artists & Craftspeople Staff. 600p. 1987. pap. 25.50 o.p. (ISBN 0-911747-07-9). Broadway Pr.

New York Times Atlas of the World. Rev, 2nd ed. 1983. 49.45 o.s.i. (ISBN 0-8129-1090-7). Times Bks.

New York Times Everyday Dictionary. The New York Times Staff. Ed. by Thomas M. Paikeday. LC 81-84903. 832p. (Orig.). 1982. 12.45 o.p. (ISBN 0-8129-0910-0); pap. 7.95 o.p. (ISBN 0-8129-6318-0). Times Bks.

New York Times Gourmet Shopper: A Guide to the Best Foods. Moira Hodgson. 384p. 1984. pap. 7.95 o.p. (ISBN 0-380-68114-5, 68114). Avon.

New York Times Guide to Dining Out in N. Y. rev. ed. John Canady. LC 75-13626. 1975. pap. 3.95 o.p. (ISBN 0-689-70528-X, 61, Atheneum). Macmillan.

New York Times Guide to the New Tax Law. Gary L. Klott & New York Times Staff. LC 86-14441. 1986. pap. 6.95 o.s.i. (ISBN 0-8129-1638-7). Times Bks.

New York Times Large Type Cookbook. Jean Hewitt. 453p. 1984. lib. bdg. 14.95 o.p. (ISBN 0-8161-3682-3, Large Print Bks); pap. 11.95 o.p. (ISBN 0-8161-3655-6, Large Print Bks). G K Hall.

New York Times of New York: An Uncommon Guide to the City of Fantasies. Ed. by A. M. Rosenthal & Arthur Gelb. LC 85-40263. 400p. 1986. 17.45 o.s.i. (ISBN 0-8129-1262-4, Dist. by Random House). Times Bks.

New York Times Report from Red China. Tillman Durdin et al. pap. 1.95 o.p. (ISBN 0-380-01363-0, 12435). Avon.

New York Times Sixty-Minute Gourmet. Large-Type ed. Pierre Franey. LC 84-40113. 288p. 1984. 18.95 o.p. (ISBN 0-8129-1126-1). Times Bks.

New York: Trusts. 9.00 o.p. (ISBN 0-686-90864-3). Am Law Inst.

New York Yankees. rev. ed. Ward. LC 82-12652. (Baseball Today Ser.). 48p. (gr. 4 up). 1982. PLB 11.45 o.p. (ISBN 0-87191-868-4). Creative Ed.

New Yorker in Egypt. Hans Koning. LC 76-20535. (Helen &Kurt Wolff Bk). 1976. 10.95 o.p. (ISBN 0-15-165520-0). HarBraceJ.

New York's Chinese Restaurants: A Guide. Stanley Miller et al. LC 76-53403. 1977. pap. 4.95 o.p. (ISBN 0-689-70550-6, Atheneum). Macmillan.

New York's Master Chefs. Bon Appetit Magazine Editors. Ed. by Richard Sax. LC 84-26153. (Illus.). 1985. 9.95 o.p. (ISBN 0-89535-090-4). Knapp Pr.

New York's Other Theatre: A Guide to Off Off Broadway. Off Off Broadway Alliance Staff & Mindy N. Levine. 256p. 1981. pap. 4.50 o.p. (ISBN 0-380-77909-9, 77909-9, Discus). Avon.

New You. Harold Myra. (gr. 9-12). 1980. pap. 4.50 o.p. (ISBN 0-88207-581-0). Victor Bks.

New You. Dede Robertson. 1984. 12.95 o.p. (ISBN 0-8407-5408-6). Nelson.

New Zealand. Sunset Editors. LC 77-90726. (Illus.). 128p. 1978. pap. 7.95 o.p. (ISBN 0-376-06535-4, Sunset Bks). Sunset-Lane.

New Zealand-A Travel Survival Kit. 4th ed. Tony Wheeler. (Illus.). 248p. (Orig.). 1985. pap. 7.95 o.p. (ISBN 0-908086-64-4). Lonely Planet.

New Zealand ABC Frieze. Gwenda Turner. (Illus.). (ps up). 1986. 12.95 o.p. (ISBN 0-7233-0765-2, Pub. by Whitcoulls NZ); pap. (ISBN 0-7233-0798-9). Intl Spec Bk.

New Zealand Architecture: A Selected Bibliography. Anthony G. White. (Architecture Ser.: A 1440). 5p. 1985. 2.00 o.p. (ISBN 0-89028-510-1). Vance Biblios.

New Zealand Business Who's Who. 26th ed. 1985. 144.00x o.p. (ISBN 0-8002-3913-X, FEP Pub). Intl Pubns Serv.

New Zealand Butterflies. George W. Gibbs. (Illus.). 208p. 1983. 45.00 o.p. (ISBN 0-00-216955-X, Pub. by W Collins New Zealand). Intl Spec Bk.

New Zealand Fiction. Joseph Jones & Johanna Jones. LC 83-12662. (World Authors Ser.: No. 643). 114p. 1983. lib. bdg. 22.95 o.s.i. (ISBN 0-8057-6368-6, Twayne). G K Hall.

New Zealand Fish & Shellfish Cookbook. Heather Currie et al. 132p. 1986. pap. 12.95 spiral o.p. (ISBN 0-7233-0776-8, Pub. by Whitcoulls NZ). Intl Spec Bk.

New Zealand Freshwater Fishes: A Guide & Natural History. Robert M. McDowall. (Illus.). 230p. 1983. 25.95 o.p. (ISBN 0-86863-130-2, Pub. by Heinemann Pub New Zealand). Intl Spec Bk.

New Zealand Kiwi. Ken Francis. 20p. 1985. pap. 3.95 o.p. (ISBN 0-7233-0758-X, Pub. by Whitcoulls NZ). Intl Spec Bk.

New Zealand on Twenty-Five Dollars a Day, 1984-85. (Dollar a Day Guides). 272p. 1984. 9.95 o.p. (ISBN 0-671-46797-2). Prentice Hall Pr.

New Zealand on Twenty-Five Dollars a Day. Susan Poole. 240p. 1986. pap. 10.95 o.p. (ISBN 0-671-55628-2). S&S.

New Zealand Whiskey Book. Stuart Perry. (Illus.). 144p. 1982. 15.95x o.p. (ISBN 0-00-216973-8, Pub. by W Collins New Zealand). Intl Spec Bk.

New Zealander's Garden. Julian Matthews & Gordon Collier. (Illus.). 135p. 1987. 37.95 o.p. (ISBN 0-86481-130-6, Pub. by Whitcoulls NZ). Intl Spec Bk.

New Zoning Landmarks in Planned Unit Developments. Lenard L. Wolffe. LC 68-59421. (Technical Bulletin Ser: No. 62). 31p. (Orig.). 1968. pap. 10.50 o.p. (ISBN 0-87420-062-8, N07). Urban Land.

Newberry Library Catalog of Early American Printed Sheet Music. Compiled by Bernard E. Wilson. 1983. lib. bdg. 345.00 o.p. (ISBN 0-8161-0389-5, Hall Library). G K Hall.

Newbery & Caldecott Medal Books, 1976-1987. Ed. by Lee Kingman. (Illus.). 1987. 24.95 o.p. (ISBN 0-317-65532-9). Horn Bk.

Newborn Mother: Stages of Her Growth. Andrea B. Eagen. 192p. 1985. 15.95 o.p. (ISBN 0-316-20056-5). Little.

Newcomers: Negroes & Puerto Ricans in a Changing Metropolis. Oscar Handlin. LC 59-14737. (New York Metropolitan Region Study). 1959. 13.50x o.s.i. (ISBN 0-674-62101-8). Harvard U Pr.

Newell Commentaries, 3 vols. William R. Newell. 1514p. 1987. Set. 49.95 o.p. (ISBN 0-8010-6778-2). Baker Bk.

Newer Methods of Preparative Organic Chemistry, 3 vols. W. Foerst. LC 48-6233. 1968. Vol. IV. 43.60x o.p. (ISBN 3-527-25087-5); Vol. V. 43.60x o.p. (ISBN 3-527-25088-3); Vol. VI. 53.00x o.p. (ISBN 3-527-25338-6). VCH Pubs.

Newly-Free Countries in the Seventies. K. Brutents. 280p. 1984. 6.95 o.p. (ISBN 0-8285-2655-9, Pub. by Progress Pubs USSR). Imported Pubns.

Newly Industrialized Countries in the World Economy. Bela Balassa. LC 80-20787. 450p. 1981. 115.00 o.p. (ISBN 0-08-026336-4); pap. 115.00 o.p. (ISBN 0-08-026335-6). Pergamon.

Newlywed Nonsense a Cartoonist's View of the First Year of Marriage. Val. C. Bagley. (Illus.). 96p. (Orig.). 1980. pap. 3.95 o.p. (ISBN 0-88290-145-1, 2039). Horizon Utah.

Newman & Gladstone: The Vatican Decrees. Ed. by Alvan Ryan. 1962. 17.95 o.p. (ISBN 0-268-00190-1); pap. 4.95x o.p. (ISBN 0-268-00372-6). U of Notre Dame Pr.

Newman's Apologia: A Classic Reconsidered. Ed. by Vincent Blehl & Francis X. Connolly. LC 64-18283. 1964. 4.50 o.p. (ISBN 0-15-165204-X). HarBraceJ.

Newman's Own Cookbook. Compiled by Ursula Hotchner et al. (Illus.). 144p. 1986. pap. 7.95 o.p. (ISBN 0-8092-5155-8). Contemp Bks.

News at Any Cost: How Journalists Compromise Their Ethics to Shape the News. Tom Goldstein. 252p. 1985. 18.45 o.p. (ISBN 0-671-49960-2). S&S.

News Editing. 2nd ed. Bruce H. Westley. LC 79-170163. (Illus.). 1972. text ed. 16.95 o.p. (ISBN 0-395-05529-6, 3-59706). HM.

News Editing & Display. Charles H. Brown. LC 74-109285. (Illus.). 457p. 1971. Repr. of 1952 ed. lib. bdg. 24.75x o.p. (ISBN 0-8371-3828-0, BRNE). Greenwood.

News Writing. George A. Hough. 1975. text ed. 13.50 o.p. (ISBN 0-395-18593-9). HM.

News Writing. 2nd ed. George A. Hough. LC 79-91631. (Illus.). 1980. text ed. 19.95 o.p. (ISBN 0-395-28636-0). HM.

Newsdeath. Ray Connolly. LC 77-15840. 1978. 8.95 o.p. (ISBN 0-689-10872-9, Atheneum). Macmillan.

Newsletters Directory. 3rd ed. Ed. by Brigitte T. Darnay & John Nimchuk. 1162p. 1986. 160.00x o.p. (ISBN 0-8103-2134-3). Gale.

Newsletters Directory: Supplement. 3rd ed. 1987. 80.00x o.p. (ISBN 0-8103-2146-7). Gale.

Newspaper Genealogical Column Directory. 2nd ed. Anita C. Milner. viii, 51p. (Orig.). 1985. pap. 7.50 o.p. (ISBN 0-917890-59-0). Heritage Bk.

Newspaper Know-How. Cherrie Farnette. (Choose-a-Card Ser.). (Illus.). 64p. (gr. 2-6). 1981. pap. text ed. 6.95 o.p. (ISBN 0-86530-011-9, IP-119). Incentive Pubns.

Newspaper Layout & Design. Daryl R. Moen. (Illus.). 276p. 1984. text ed. 21.95x o.p. (ISBN 0-8138-1226-7). Iowa St U Pr.

Newspaper Murders. Joe Gash. LC 85-5423. 192p. 1985. 13.95 o.p. (ISBN 0-03-070544-4). H Holt & Co.

Newspaper Murders. Joe Gash. (Nightingales Ser.). 283p. 1987. pap. 11.95x o.p. (ISBN 0-8161-4219-X, Large Print Bks.). G K Hall.

Newspaper Press in New South Wales 1803-1920. R. B. Walker. (Illus.). 1976. 23.00x o.p. (ISBN 0-424-00023-7, Pub. by Sydney U Pr). Intl Spec Bk.

Newspaper Press in the French Revolution. Hugh Gough. 264p. 1988. text ed. (ISBN 0-534-11263-3); pap. text ed. (ISBN 0-534-11264-1). Wadsworth Pub.

Newspaperman: S. I. Newhouse & the Business of News. Richard H. Meeker. LC 83-5008. (Illus.). 320p. 1983. 17.45 o.p. (ISBN 0-89919-200-9). Ticknor & Fields.

Newspapers & Periodicals by & about Black People: Southeastern Library Holdings. Compiled by African-American Materials Project Staff. 190p. 1978. 24.00 o.p. (ISBN 0-8161-8264-7). G K Hall.

Newspapers & the Antitrust Laws. S. Chesterfield Oppenheim & Carrington Shields. 531p. 1982. 45.00x o.p. (ISBN 0-87215-476-9). Michie Co.

Newspapers Career Directory: 1987. Ed. by Ron Fry. (Career Directory Ser.). 300p. (Orig.). 1987. text ed. 34.95 o.p. (ISBN 0-934829-21-7); pap. text ed. 26.95 o.p. (ISBN 0-934829-15-2); Special Bookstore Edition Distributed by Williamson Publishing Co. pap. 17.95 o.p. (ISBN 0-934829-09-8). Career Pr Inc.

Newsreel. Irvin Faust. LC 79-3349. 312p. 1980. 10.95 o.p. (ISBN 0-15-165421-2). HarBraceJ.

Newswatch: How TV Decides the News. Av Westin. 276p. 1983. pap. 6.75 o.p. (ISBN 0-671-42180-8, Touchstone). S&S.

Newswriting & Reporting. James M. Neal & Suzanne S. Brown. 298p. 1976. text ed. 17.95x o.p. (ISBN 0-8138-1320-4). Iowa St U Pr.

Newton at the Bat: The Science in Sport. Allen L. Hammond. (Illus.). 176p. 1984. 14.95 o.p. (ScribT). Scribner.

Newtonian Classicism & Darwinian Institutionalism. David Hamilton. LC 73-8558. (University of New Mexico Publications in Economics: No. 1). 138p. 1975. Repr. of 1953 ed. lib. bdg. 41.50x o.p. (ISBN 0-8371-6969-0, HANC). Greenwood.

Newtonian Studies. Alexander Koyre. 1968. pap. text ed. 8.50x o.s.i. (ISBN 0-226-45176-3). U of Chicago Pr.

Newtonians & the English Revolution, 1689-1720. Margaret C. Jacob. LC 75-36995. 288p. 1976. 32.50x o.p. (ISBN 0-8014-0981-0). Cornell U Pr.

Nexon on Commercial Real Estate Financing & Developments. Phillip J. Nexon & Massachusetts Continuing Legal Education, Inc. Staff. LC 84-62949. (Illus.). write for info. o.p. Mass CLE.

Next America: The Decline & Rise of the United States. Michael Harrington. (Illus.). 160p. 1981. 18.95 o.p. (ISBN 0-03-057468-4); pap. 10.95 o.p. (ISBN 0-03-057467-6). H Holt & Co.

Next Best Thing. John R. Saul. LC 86-2169. 264p. 1986. 16.95 o.p. (ISBN 0-385-23277-2). Doubleday.

Next Canadian Economy. Dian Cohen & Kristin Shannon. 224p. 1984. pap. 9.95 o.p. (ISBN 0-920792-44-8). Eden Pr.

Next Economy. Paul Hawken. (Illus.). 252p. 1983. 14.50 o.s.i. (ISBN 0-03-062631-5). H Holt & Co.

Next Fifty Years in Space. Patrick Moore. LC 75-26326. (Illus.). 1978. pap. 7.50 o.s.i. (ISBN 0-8008-5529-9). Taplinger.

Next Five Hundred Years. Burnham P. Beckwith. 1968. text ed. 10.00 o.p. (ISBN 0-682-45791-4, University). Exposition-Phoenix.

Next of Kin in Jail. Tom McDonald. 1978. pap. 4.95 o.p. (ISBN 0-87397-143-4). Strode.

Next-to-Last Things: New Poems & Essays. Stanley Kunitz. Ed. by Peter Davison. LC 85-47995. 130p. 1985. 17.95 o.p. (ISBN 0-87113-036-X). Atlantic Monthly.

Next to Nothing: Collected Poems 1926-1977. Paul Bowles. 77p. (Orig.). 1981. 14.00 o.p. (ISBN 0-87685-505-2); pap. o.p. (ISBN 0-87685-504-4). Black Sparrow.

Next Whole Earth Catalog. 2nd ed. Ed. by Stewart Brand. (Illus.). 608p. (Orig., Pub. by Point Fdn., dist. by Random House). 1981. Repr. of 1980 ed. pap. 16.00 o.s.i. (ISBN 0-394-70776-1). Point Calif.

Next-Year Country: A Study of Rural Social Organization in Alberta. Jean Burnet. LC 52-1704. xii, 188p. 1978. pap. 7.50 o.p. (ISBN 0-8020-6340-3). U of Toronto Pr.

Nexus. Henry Miller. (Rosy Crucifixion Ser.: Bk. 3). 640p. 1987. pap. 7.95 o.s.i. (ISBN 0-394-62369-X, BC). Grove.

Ngari the Hunter. Ronald Rose. LC 68-31981. (Children of Other Lands Ser.). (Illus.). (gr. 4-6). 1968. 5.95 o.p. (ISBN 0-15-257295-3, HJ). HarBraceJ.

NGCSA Annual Narrative Report 1985-86. 1986. 7.00 o.p. (ISBN 0-318-21707-4). NGCSA.

NGCSA Membership Directory 1987. 1987. 10.00 o.p. (ISBN 0-318-21706-6). NGCSA.

NGCSA Membership Handbook. 1986. 5.00 o.p. (ISBN 0-318-21708-2). NGCSA.

Niagara Falls & the Glacier. Glenn C. Forrester. LC 76-20135. 1976. 7.50 o.p. (ISBN 0-682-48381-8); pap. 4.50 o.p. (ISBN 0-686-67229-1). Exposition-Phoenix.

Niagara Falls: One Hundred Years of Souvenirs. Virginia Vidler. (Illus.). 140p. (Orig.). 1985. pap. 14.95 o.p. (ISBN 0-932052-40-1). North Country.

Nicaragua Reader: Documents of a Revolution under Fire. John Vandermeer & Peter Rosset. LC 83-48294. (Latin American Ser.). 378p. 1983. 22.50 o.p. (ISBN 0-394-53506-5, GP-884). Grove.

Nicaragua Reader: Documents of a Revolution under Fire. John Vandermeer & Peter Rosset. LC 83-48294. (Latin American Ser.). 378p. 1983. pap. 8.95 o.p. (ISBN 0-394-62498-X, E877, Ever). Grove.

Nicaragua: Unfinished Revolution. Ed. by Peter Rosset & John Vandermeer. LC 86-372. 416p. 1986. pap. 12.95 o.p. (ISBN 0-394-62143-3, Ever). Grove.

Niccolo Machiavelli. Silvia Ruffo-Fiore. (World Authors Ser.). 1982. lib. bdg. 17.95 o.s.i. (ISBN 0-8057-6499-2, Twayne). G K Hall.

Nice Class of Corpse. Simon Brett. 196p. 1987. 14.95 o.p. (ISBN 0-684-18685-3). Scribner.

Nice Fire & Some Moonpennies. Dorris Heffron. LC 70-179721. (gr. 6-9). 1972. 4.50 o.p. (ISBN 0-689-30029-8, Atheneum). Macmillan.

Nice Girl Like You. Norma Johnston. LC 79-22586. (gr. 8 up). 1980. 9.95 o.p. (ISBN 0-689-30765-9, Atheneum). Macmillan.

Nice Girls Do. Irene Kassorla. 1982. pap. 3.50 o.p. (ISBN 0-87216-946-4). Playboy Pbks.

Nice Jewish Girls: A Lesbian Anthology. Ed. by Evelyn T. Beck. (Feminist Ser.). 288p. 1984. 23.95 o.p. (ISBN 0-89594-138-4); pap. 10.95 o.p. (ISBN 0-89594-137-6). Crossing Pr.

Nice Knight for Murder. Philip Daniels. 208p. 1986. pap. 2.95 o.p. (ISBN 0-931773-60-1). Critics Choice Paper.

Nice Rum An' Coca-Cola & Welcome Home Jacko. Mustapha Matura. 1981. pap. 4.95 o.p. (ISBN 0-413-47720-7, NO. 2573). Heinemann Ed.

Nice to See You, Andy Capp! Reginald Smythe. 1981. pap. 1.75 o.s.i. (ISBN 0-449-13848-8, GM). Fawcett.

Nicene Creed: Our Common Faith. Metropolitan Emilianos Timiadis Staff. LC 82-71826. 128p. (Orig.). 1983. pap. 7.95 o.p. (ISBN 0-8006-1653-7, 1-1653, Fortress). Augsburg Fortress.

Niche: Theory & Application. Ed. by Robert H. Whittaker & Simon A. Levin. LC 74-23328. (Benchmark Papers in Ecology Ser.: No. 3). 1975. 71.00 o.p. (ISBN 0-12-787757-6). Acad Pr.

Nicholas. Ginny Cowles. LC 74-11432. (Illus.). 40p. (ps-3). 1979. 6.95 o.p. (ISBN 0-395-28785-5, Clarion). HM.

Nicholas Bacon: The Making of a Tudor Statesman. Robert Tittler. LC 75-36976. (Illus.). 255p. 1976. 15.00x o.p. (ISBN 0-8214-0225-0). Ohio U Pr.

Nicholas Crabbe: Or, The One & the Many, a Romance. Frederick C. Rolfe. LC 77-11680. 1977. Repr. of 1958 ed. lib. bdg. 35.00x o.p. (ISBN 0-8371-9816-X, RONC). Greenwood.

Nicholas Guide to Dog Judging. Date not set. (ISBN 0-87605-665-6). Howell Bk.

Nicholas Knock. Dennis Lee. LC 76-27324. (Illus.). (gr. 3-7). 1977. 7.95 o.p. (ISBN 0-395-24910-4). HM.

Nicholas Nickleby. Charles Dickens. 1977. Repr. of 1907 ed. 10.95x o.p. (ISBN 0-460-00238-4, Evman); pap. 3.95x o.p. (ISBN 0-460-01238-X, Evman). Biblio Dist.

Nicholas of Cusa. Henry Bett. LC 76-1131. (Great Medieval Churchmen Ser). x, 210p. 1976. Repr. of 1932 ed. lib. bdg. 17.50x o.p. (ISBN 0-915172-05-4). Richwood Pub.

Nicholson's Complete London Guide. Nicholson, Robert, Publications Staff. (Illus.). 158p. (Orig.). 1984. pap. 9.95 o.p. (ISBN 0-900568-96-8, Pub. by Automobile Assn Brit). Salem Hse Pubs.

Nicholson's Guide to England & Wales. Nicholson Publications Staff. pap. (ISBN 0-684-16977-0). Scribner.

Nicholson's London Guide. rev. ed. Nicholson Publications Staff. (Illus.). 1978. pap. 4.95 o.p. (ISBN 0-684-15751-9, SL800, ScribT). Scribner.

Nicholson's Visitors London. Nicholson. pap. write for info. o.p. (ISBN 0-684-16976-2). Scribner.

Nick Bollettieri's Junior Tennis. Nick Bollettieri & Barry McDermott. LC 84-10618. (Illus.). 256p. 1984. 17.45 o.p. (ISBN 0-671-50840-7). S&S.

Nickel an Inch: A Memoir. Ed Fitzgerald. LC 85-47777. 320p. 1985. 17.95 o.p. (ISBN 0-689-11590-3, Atheneum). Macmillan.

Nickels & Dimes: The Story of F. W. Woolworth. Nina B. Baker. LC 54-9621. (gr. 4-7). 1966. pap. 0.50 o.p. (ISBN 0-15-665590-X, AVB17, VoyB). HarBraceJ.

Nickerson's No-Risk Way to Real Estate Fortunes. William Nickerson. 224p. 1986. 17.45 o.s.i. (ISBN 0-671-55143-4). S&S.

Nicknames in Sports: A Quiz Book. Bud Christian. 72p. 1986. 6.75 o.p. (ISBN 0-8062-2807-5). Carlton.

Nicknames: Their Origins & Social Consequences. Jane Morgan et al. (Social Worlds of Childhood Ser.). 1979. 19.95x o.p. (ISBN 0-7100-0139-8). Routledge Chapman & Hall.

Nicolai Case: A Biography. Wolf Zuelzer. LC 82-1990. (Illus.). 476p. 1982. 35.00x o.p. (ISBN 0-8143-1701-4). Wayne St U Pr.

Nicolai Fechin. 2nd ed. Mary Balcomb. LC 75-11161. (Illus.). 192p. 1985. Repr. of 1975 ed. 40.00 o.p. (ISBN 0-87358-374-4). Northland.

Nicolette. Herbert M. Katz. LC 76-8636. 1976. 7.95 o.p. (ISBN 0-87795-144-6, Arbor Hse). Morrow.

Nicolo Paganini: His Life & Work. Stephen S. Stratton. LC 75-109856. 1971. Repr. of 1907 ed. lib. bdg. 22.50x o.p. (ISBN 0-8371-4347-0, STNP). Greenwood.

NICSEM Mini-index to Special Education Materials: Functional Communication Skills. National Information Center for Special Education Materials (NICSEM) Staff. LC 80-82540. 1980. pap. 8.00 o.p. (ISBN 0-89320-045-X). Natl Info Ctr NM.

NICSEM Mini-Index to Special Education Materials: Family Life & Sex Education. National Information Center for Special Education Materials (NICSEM) Staff. LC 80-82538. 1980. pap. 8.00 o.p. (ISBN 0-89320-043-3). Natl Info Ctr NM.

NICSEM Mini-index to Special Education Materials: High Interest, Controlled Vocabulary Supplementary Reading Materials for Adolescents & Young Adults. National Information Center for Special Education Materials (NICSEM) Staff. LC 80-82901. 1980. pap. 8.00 o.p. (ISBN 0-89320-047-6). Natl Info Ctr NM.

NICSEM Mini-index to Special Education Materials: Independent Living Skills for Moderately & Severely Handicapped Students. National Information Center for Special Education Materials (NICSEM) Staff. LC 80-82530. 1980. pap. 8.00 o.p. (ISBN 0-89320-044-1). Natl Info Ctr NM.

NICSEM Mini-index to Special Education Materials: Personal & Social Development for Moderately & Severely Handicapped Students. National Information Center for Special Education Materials (NICSEM) Staff. LC 80-82541. 1980. pap. 8.00 o.p. (ISBN 0-89320-046-8). Natl Info Ctr NM.

NICSEM Source Directory. 1st ed. National Information Center for Special Education Materials (NICSEM) Staff. LC 80-83757. 1980. pap. 6.25 o.p. (ISBN 0-89320-050-6). Natl Info Ctr NM.

Niels Bohr: The Man, His Science, & the World They Changed. Ruth Moore. 476p. (Orig.). 1985. pap. 9.95 o.p. (ISBN 0-262-63101-6). MIT Pr.

Nieman Marcus. (ISBN 0-07-017838-0). McGraw.

Nietzsche & Christian Ethics. R. Motson Thompson. 1952. (ISBN 0-8022-1714-1). Philos Lib.

Nietzsche As Educator. Timothy F. Murphy. LC 84-2264. 118p. (Orig.). 1984. lib. bdg. 22.00 o.p. (ISBN 0-8191-3839-8); pap. text ed. 10.00 o.p. (ISBN 0-8191-3840-1). U Pr of Amer.

Nietzsche's View of Socrates. Werner J. Dannhauser. LC 73-20797. 283p. 1974. 29.95x o.p. (ISBN 0-8014-0827-X). Cornell U Pr.

Niger Cereals Project: An Experience in Technical Assistance. Ed. by William E. Hall & Grover E. Murray. 107p. 1983. 9.50 o.s.i. (ISBN 0-318-17669-6, 83-1). Intl Ctr Arid & Semi-Arid.

Nigeria: Absorbing the Oil Wealth. Henry Bienen. 153p. 1982. 150.00 o.p. (ISBN 0-8002-3412-X). Intl Pubns Serv.

Nigerian Children: Developmental Perspectives. Valerie Curran. 224p. 1984. pap. 25.95X o.p. (ISBN 0-7100-9515-5). Routledge Chapman & Hall.

Nigerian Literature: A Bibliography of Criticism, 1952-1976. Claudia Baldwin. 1980. lib. bdg. 24.00 o.s.i. (ISBN 0-8161-8418-6, Hall Reference). G K Hall.

Nigger, Go Home! Bill Lawrence. 1978. 5.00 o.p. (ISBN 0-682-49136-5). Exposition-Phoenix.

Nigger of "Narcissus", Typhoon, Falk, & Other Stories. Joseph Conrad. Ed. by Norman Sherry. 1978. Repr. of 1974 ed. 12.95x o.p. (ISBN 0-460-00980-X, Evman); pap. 3.50x o.p. (ISBN 0-460-01980-5, Evman). Biblio Dist.

Night. Elie Wiesel. 128p. 1981. pap. 1.50 o.p. (ISBN 0-380-00995-1, 46797, Discus). Avon.

Night & Low-light Photography: A Complete Guide. Bob Gibbons & Peter Wilson. (Illus.). 192p. 1987. 29.95 o.p. (ISBN 0-7137-1777-7, Pub. by Blandford Pr England). Sterling.

Night Before Christmas Coloring Book. Clement C. Moore. (Illus.). pap. 3.00 o.p. (ISBN 0-486-22083-4). Dover.

Night Before Xmas. Date not set. bds. 8.95 incl. cassette o.p. Ideals.

Night-Blooming Cactus. Robert Watson. LC 80-65999. 1980. 10.00 o.p. (ISBN 0-689-11090-1, Atheneum); pap. 5.95 o.p. (ISBN 0-689-11091-X, Atheneum). Macmillan.

Night Chills. Dean R. Koontz. LC 75-33122. 352p. 1976. 8.95 o.p. (ISBN 0-689-10660-2, Atheneum). Macmillan.

Night Chills. Kirby E. McCauley. (Orig.). 1986. pap. 1.50 o.p. (ISBN 0-380-00397-X, 26856). Avon.

Night Church. Whitley Strieber. 320p. 1983. 15.50 o.p. (ISBN 0-671-46955-X). S&S.

Night Country. Loren Eiseley. LC 78-162747. (Illus.). 1971. pap. 7.95 o.s.i. (ISBN 0-684-13224-9, ScribT). Scribner.

Night Dancers see There's a Skunk in My Trunk.

Night Drop: The American Airborne Invasion of Normandy. Samuel L. Marshall. (Airborne Ser.: No. 16). (Illus.). 425p. 1982. Repr. of 1962 ed. 18.95 o.p. (ISBN 0-89839-062-1). Battery Pr.

Night Face & Other Stories. Poul Anderson. (Science Fiction, Worlds of Poul Anderson Ser.). 1978. lib. bdg. 10.50 o.p. (ISBN 0-8398-2412-2, Gregg). G K Hall.

Night Fighter. C. F. Rawnsley & Robert Wright. (War Library). 320p. 1983. pap. 2.95 o.s.i. (ISBN 0-345-31025-X). Ballantine.

Night Has a Thousand Eyes. Cornell Woolrich. 304p. 1983. pap. 2.50 o.s.i. (ISBN 0-345-30667-8). Ballantine.

Night Herding Song. Gerald Hausman. (Illus.). 1979. 12.00 o.p. (ISBN 0-914742-39-6); pap. 5.00 o.p. Copper Canyon.

Night in Lisbon. Erich M. Remarque. Tr. by Ralph Manheim. LC 64-11538. 1964. 4.95 o.p. (ISBN 0-15-165595-2). HarBraceJ.

Night Line. Ambrose Clancy & Peter M. Donahoe. (Illus.). 192p. 1989. 25.00 o.p. (ISBN 0-941533-45-X). New Amsterdam Bks.

Night Manhattan Burned. Basil Jackson. 1979. 9.95 o.p. (ISBN 0-393-01248-4). Norton.

Night of Kadar. Garry Kilworth. 208p. 1980. pap. 1.95 o.p. (ISBN 0-380-50070-1, 50070-1). Avon.

Night of Light. Philip Jose Farmer. Ed. by Lester Del Rey. LC 75-404. (Library of Science Fiction). 1975. lib. bdg. 21.00 o.p. (ISBN 0-8240-1409-X). Garland Pub.

Night of Stones. George MacBeth. LC 69-15506. 1968. pap. 2.45 o.p. (ISBN 0-689-10173-2, Atheneum). Macmillan.

Night of the Hammer. Ned O'Gorman. LC 59-6419. 1959. 4.50 o.p. (ISBN 0-15-165621-5). HarBraceJ.

Night of the Ninja. Max Abelard. 216p. 1986. pap. text ed. 10.00 o.p. (ISBN 0-87364-368-2). Paladin Pr.

Night of the Sphinx & Other Stories. Ed. by Roger Elwood. LC 73-21482. Orig. Title: When the Cold Came & Other Stories. (Illus.). (gr. 4-8). 1974. PLB 3.95g o.p. (ISBN 0-8225-0954-7). Lerner Pubns.

Night of the Tribades: A Play from 1889. Per Olov Enquist. Tr. by Ross Shideler from Swedish. 81p. 1977. 9.95 o.p. (ISBN 0-8090-7365-X); pap. 3.95 o.p. (ISBN 0-8090-1237-5). Hill & Wang.

Night of the Unicorn. Diana Blayne. (Candlelight Supreme Ser.: No. 110). (Orig.). 1986. pap. (ISBN 0-440-16382-X). Dell.

Night of the Whale. Jerry Spinelli. 160p. (gr. 6 up). 1985. 12.95 o.p. (ISBN 0-316-80718-4). Little.

Night of the Wolf. James Conway. 1979. pap. 1.75 o.p. (ISBN 0-8439-0700-2, Pub. by Leisure Bks CT). Dorchester Pub Co.

Night Out. Edward Peple. (Illus.). 52p. 1960. 1.00 o.p. (ISBN 0-910244-23-5). Blair.

Night Out, Night School, Revue Sketches: Early Plays. Harold Pinter. 1968. pap. 1.95 o.p. (ISBN 0-394-17310-4, E480, Ever). Grove.

Night Raider & Other Stories. Walter D. Edmonds. 96p. (gr. 7 up). 1980. 10.45i o.p. (ISBN 0-316-21141-9). Little.

Night Sanctuary. Monique Van Vooren. 502p. 1981. 14.95 o.s.i. (ISBN 0-671-40093-2). Summit Bks.

Night She Died. Dorothy Simpson. 192p. 1981. 9.95 o.s.i. (ISBN 0-684-16869-3, ScribT). Scribner.

Night-Side of Nature: Of Ghosts & Ghost-Seers. Catherine Crowe. (Illus.). 452p. (Orig.). 1988. pap. 14.95 o.p. (ISBN 0-85030-519-5, Pub. by Aquarian Pr England). Sterling.

Night Sky. Mary T. Bruck. (Illus.). (gr. 5 up). cancelled o.s.i. (ISBN 0-7214-0104-X). Merry Thoughts.

Night Sky of Lord. Date not set. (ISBN 0-8052-3810-7). Random.

Night Spell. Robert Newman. LC 76-25207. (Illus.). (gr. 5-8). 1977. 8.95 o.p. (ISBN 0-689-30559-1, Atheneum). Macmillan.

Night Stick. Joseph C. Hess. LC 82-61732. (Ser. 419). (Illus.). 1982. pap. 7.50 o.p. (ISBN 0-89750-082-2). Ohara Pubns.

Night Talks. Patricia L. Gauch. 176p. (gr. 7-9). 1984. pap. 2.25 o.p. (ISBN 0-671-49635-2). Archway.

Night Thoughts of an Aging Orphan. Howard A. Wiley. LC 64-13330. 91p. 1964. (ISBN 0-8022-1882-2). Philos Lib.

Night to Remember. Walter Lord. (Illus.). (gr. 9 up). 1955. 7.95 o.s.i. (ISBN 0-03-027615-2). H Holt & Co.

Night Visitor. Laura Wylie. 256p. 1987. pap. 3.50 o.p. (ISBN 1-55547-174-9). Critics Choice Paper.

Night Watch. Paul D. Boles. LC 80-8778. (Illus.). 32p. 1980. 0.95 o.p. (ISBN 0-931948-15-0). Peachtree Pubs.

Night Watch. David A. Phillips. 1977. 9.95 o.p. (ISBN 0-689-10754-4, Atheneum). Macmillan.

Night We Slept Outside. Anne Rockwell & Harlow Rockwell. LC 82-17963. (Ready-to-Read Ser.). (Illus.). 48p. (gr. 1-4). 1983. 8.95 o.s.i. (ISBN 0-02-777450-3). Macmillan.

Night Wind. Mabel E. Allan. LC 73-84819. (Illus.). 224p. (gr. 4-6). 1974. 6.95 o.p. (ISBN 0-689-30127-8, Atheneum). Macmillan.

Night World. Gretchen L. Miller. (Illus.). 1980. 6.00 o.p. (ISBN 0-682-49535-2). Exposition-Phoenix.

Nightbloom. Herbert Lieberman. 432p. 1985. pap. 3.95 o.p. (ISBN 0-380-69819-6). Avon.

Nightbook. William Kotzwinkle. 1986. pap. 2.95 o.p. (ISBN 0-380-01501-3, 49106-0, Bard). Avon.

Nightclerk. Stephen Schneck. LC 83-81373. (Outrider Bk.). 208p. 1983. pap. 4.50 o.s.i. (ISBN 0-394-17975-7, B471, BC). Grove.

Nightclub. Georges Simenon. Tr. by Jean Stewart. LC 79-1845. (Helen & Kurt Wolff Bk.). 1979. 7.95 o.p. (ISBN 0-15-165589-8). HarBraceJ.

Nightfall at Nauvoo. Samuel W. Taylor. 1986. pap. 1.95 o.p. (ISBN 0-380-00247-7, 52696-4). Avon.

Nightingale. Hans Christian Andersen. LC 85-2765. (Illus.). 32p. (ps-3). 1985. 13.95 o.p. (ISBN 0-15-257427-1, Pub. by HJ). HarBraceJ.

Nightingales. M. Dudin. 263p. 1981. 5.00 o.p. (ISBN 0-8285-2045-3, Pub. by Progress Pubs USSR). Imported Pubns.

Nightmare Nina. George Shea. (Challenge Bks.). (Illus.). 56p. (gr. 4 up). 1979. PLB 8.95 o.p. (ISBN 0-87191-682-7). Creative Ed.

Nightmare of the Innocents. Otto Larsen. (Illus.). 240p. 1957. (ISBN 0-8022-0929-7). Philos Lib.

Nightmare Realm of Baba Yaga. Roger E. Moore. LC 86-50358. (Advanced Dungeons & Dragons Adventure Gamebooks: No. 8). 1986. 2.95 o.p. (ISBN 0-88038-286-4). TSR Inc.

Nightmare Universe. Gene DeWeese & Robert Coulson. LC 85-51933. (Amazing Stories Ser.: Bk. 4). 223p. (Orig.). 1985. pap. 2.95 o.p. (ISBN 0-88038-259-7). TSR Inc.

Nightmares of Dream Topping. Merrily Harpur. (Illus.). 78p. 1985. 5.95 o.p. (ISBN 0-88186-275-4). Parkwest Pubns.

Nightmares of Geranium Street. Susan Shreve. (YA) 1979. pap. 1.50 o.p. (ISBN 0-380-42887-3, 42887). Avon.

Night's Black Agents: Witchcraft & Magic in Seventeenth-Century English Drama. Anthony Harris. (Illus.). 210p. 1980. 19.50x o.p. (ISBN 0-8476-6226-8). Rowman.

Nightscape. Thomas Chastain. LC 81-14900. 1982. 10.95 o.p. (ISBN 0-689-11236-X, Atheneum). Macmillan.

Nightstar. Fern Michaels. (Silhouette Romances Ser.). 1984. lib. bdg. 8.95 o.p. (ISBN 0-8398-2811-X, Gregg). G K Hall.

Nightwalker. Thomas Tessier. LC 79-55595. 1980. 9.95 o.p. (ISBN 0-689-11058-8, Atheneum). Macmillan.

Nightwebs: A Collection of Stories by Cornell Woolrich. Ed. by Francis M. Nevins, Jr. 1974. pap. 4.45 o.p. (ISBN 0-380-00025-3, 19539). Avon.

Nightwing: A Novel. Martin C. Smith. 1977. 10.95 o.p. (ISBN 0-393-08783-2). Norton.

Nightwings. Robert Silverberg. 192p. 1976. pap. 2.50 o.p. (ISBN 0-380-41467-8). Avon.

Nihilism & Culture. Johan Goudsblom. 213p. 1980. 27.50x o.p. (ISBN 0-8476-6766-9). Rowman.

Nihilism & Technology: A Heideggerian Investigation. Phillip R. Fandozzi. LC 82-17337. 158p. (Orig.). 1983. lib. bdg. 25.75 o.p. (ISBN 0-8191-2825-2); pap. text ed. 9.75 o. p. o.p. (ISBN 0-8191-2826-0). U Pr of Amer.

Nihilism of John Dewey. Paul Crosser. 256p. 1955. (ISBN 0-8022-0321-3). Philos Lib.

Nijhoff, Van Ostaijen, "De Stijl" Modernism in the Netherlands & Belgium in the First Quarter of the 20th Century.- Six Essays (1976) Ed. by Francis Bulhof. (Illus., Orig.). 1976. pap. 27.50 o.s.i. (ISBN 90-247-1857-0). E J Brill USA.

Nijinsky. Vera Krasovskaya. Tr. by John E. Bowlt from Rus. LC 79-7368. (Illus.). 1979. 17.95 o.s.i. (ISBN 0-02-871870-4). Schirmer Bks.

Nike. Date not set. (ISBN 0-8052-3895-6). Random.

Nikita's Childhood. A. Tolstoy. 197p. 1977. 6.45 o.p. (ISBN 0-8285-1213-2, Pub. by Progress Pubs USSR). Imported Pubns.

Nikola Tesla: Colorado Spring Notes 1899-1900. Tesla Museum Staff. (Illus.). 1978. 85.00x o.p. (ISBN 0-89918-782-X, Y-782). Vanous.

Nikola Tesla: Tribute. Tesla Museaum Staff. (Illus.). 1961. 60.00x o.p. (ISBN 0-89918-691-2, Y-691). Vanous.

Nikola Tesla (1856-1943) Lectures, Patents, Articles. Ed. by Popovic. 1977. 75.00x o.p. (ISBN 0-89918-639-4, Y-639). Vanous.

Nikolai Bukharin: The Last Years. Roy A. Medvedev. Tr. by A. D. Briggs. 1980. 10.95 o.p. (ISBN 0-393-01357-X). Norton.

Nikolai Gogol: A Selection. N. Gogol. (Vol. 2). 397p. 1981. 11.00 o.p. (ISBN 0-8285-2383-5, Pub. by Progress Pubs USSR). Imported Pubns.

Nikolai Gogol & Ivan Turgenev. Nick Worrall. (Grove Press Modern Dramatists Ser.). (Illus.). 196p. 1982. pap. 9.95 o.s.i. (ISBN 0-394-62431-9, Ever). Grove.

Nikolai I. Bukharin: A Bibliography. Ed. by Sidney Heitman. LC 68-28101. (Bibliographical Ser.: No. 37). (Rus.). 1969. 13.95x o.p. (ISBN 0-8179-2371-3). Hoover Inst Pr.

Nikolai Leskov: The Man & His Art. Hugh McLean. 1977. 44.50x o.s.i. (ISBN 0-674-62471-8). Harvard U Pr.

Nikon F-Three: Amphoto Pocket Companion. Milton Heiberg. (Illus.). 112p. 1981. pap. 4.95 o.p. (ISBN 0-8174-5532-9, Amphoto). Watson-Guptill.

Nikon F-Two. Mark Iocolano. (Amphoto Pocket Companion Ser.). (Illus.). 128p. 1980. pap. 4.95 o.p. (ISBN 0-8174-2182-3, Amphoto). Watson-Guptill.

Nikon FM & FE. Mark Iocolano. (Amphoto Pocket Companion Ser.). (Illus.). 128p. 1980. pap. 4.95 o.p. (ISBN 0-8174-2181-5, Amphoto). Watson-Guptill.

Nile. Laurie Devine. LC 82-16960. 476p. 1983. 16.50 o.p. (ISBN 0-671-45170-7). S&S.

Nile--Notes for Travellers in Egypt & the Egyptian Sudan: Notes for Travellers in Egypt & the Egyptian Sudan. 12th ed. Ernest A. Budge. LC 74-106772. (Illus.). 1971. Repr. of 1912 ed. lib. bdg. 47.00x o.p. (ISBN 0-8371-3550-8, BUN&, Pub. by Negro U Pr). Greenwood.

Nile & Its Environment. Ed. by M. Kassas & I. Ghabbour. 136p. 1980. pap. 24.00 o.p. (ISBN 0-08-026081-0). Pergamon.

Nile Shadows. Edward Whittemore. LC 82-2915. 448p. 1983. 17.95 o.s.i. (ISBN 0-03-018531-9). H Holt & Co.

Nile Tributaries of Abyssinia, & the Sword Hunters of the Hamran Arabs. 4th ed. Samuel W. Baker. Bd. with Sword Hunters of the Hamran Arabs. (Landmarks in Anthropology Ser). Repr. of 1867 ed. 58.00 o.p. (ISBN 0-384-03110-2). Johnson Repr.

Niles Cars Catalog. 44p. 1982. pap. 9.95 o.s.i. (ISBN 0-87004-292-0). Caxton.

Nilpotent Groups. R. B. Warfield, Jr. (Lecture Notes in Mathematics Ser.: Vol. 513). 1976. pap. 13.00 o.p. (ISBN 0-387-07683-2). Springer-Verlag.

Nilpotent Lie Groups: Structure & Applications to Analysis. R. W. Goodman. (Lecture Notes on Mathematics Ser.: Vol. 562). 1977. soft cover 17.00 o.p. (ISBN 0-387-08055-4). Springer-Verlag.

Nimby. Jasper Tomkins. Date not set. pap. 6.95 o.p. (ISBN 0-310-57091-3, 16109P). Zondervan.

Nimrod of the Sea. William M. Davis. LC 72-78905. (Illus.). 416p. 1972. 8.95 o.p. (ISBN 0-8158-0283-8). Chris Mass.

Nimzowitsch Defence. Tim Harding. (Illus.). 144p. 1981. pap. 18.95 o.p. (ISBN 0-7134-3596-8, Pub. by Batsford England). David & Charles.

Nine Australian Progressives: Vitalism in Bourgeois Social Thought. Michael Roe. LC 83-23352. (Scholars' Library). 328p. 1985. text ed. 37.50x o.p. (ISBN 0-7022-1974-6). U of Queensland Pr.

Nine Billion Names of God. Arthur C. Clarke. LC 67-16086. 1967. 7.95 o.p. (ISBN 0-15-165890-0). HarBraceJ.

Nine Contemporary Poets: A Critical Introduction. P. R. King. x, 280p. 1979. pap. 10.95x o.p. (ISBN 0-416-71860-4, NO. 3673). Routledge Chapman & Hall.

Nine Critics - Nine Photographs. Ed. by James Alinder. LC 80-68803. (Untitled Ser.: No. 23). (Illus.). 56p. (Orig.). 1980. pap. 8.95 o.p. (ISBN 0-933286-21-X). Friends Photography.

Nine Day Wonder Diet. Seymour Eisenberg & L. Melvin Elting. 1979. pap. 2.25_o.p. (ISBN 0-440-16395-1). Dell.

Nine Days' Queen: A Portrait of Lady Jane Grey. Mary Luke. LC 85-32040. (Illus.). 432p. 1986. 18.95 o.p. (ISBN 0-688-05771-3). Morrow.

Nine Gates to the Chassidic Mysteries. new ed. Jiri Langer. Ed. by Seymour Rossel. Tr. by Stephen Jolly from Czech. & Fr. LC 76-5859. (Jewish Legacy Ser.). 266p. 1976. pap. text ed. 5.95x o.p. (ISBN 0-87441-241-2). Behrman.

Nine Hundred Days: The Siege of Leningrad. Harrison Salisbury. 1983. pap. 1.95 o.p. (ISBN 0-380-01634-6, 35899). Avon.

Nine Hundred Fifty-Nine Plan. Peter Lord. pap. 7.95 o.p. (ISBN 0-8010-5600-4). Baker Bk.

Nine Hundred Thousand Plus Jobs Annually: Published Sources of Employment Listings. S. Norman Feingold & Glenda A. Hansard-Winkler. LC 81-85931. (Illus.). 196p. (Orig.). 1982. pap. 9.95 o.p. (ISBN 0-912048-25-5). Garrett Pk.

Nine Innings. Daniel Okrent. 312p. 1985. 16.45 o.p. (ISBN 0-89919-334-X). Ticknor & Fields.

Nine Little Popples. Virginia Holt. LC 85-63347. (Cuddle Bks.). (Illus.). 14p. (ps). 1986. 1.95 o.s.i. (ISBN 0-394-88254-7, BYR). Random.

Nine Lives of Sterling W. Sill: An Autobiography. Sterling W. Sill. LC 79-89354. 286p. 1979. 8.95 o.p. (ISBN 0-88290-118-4). Horizon Utah.

Nine Modern Soviet Plays. M. Shatrov et al. 464p. 1977. 8.95 o.p. (ISBN 0-8285-1036-9, Pub. by Progress Pubs USSR). Imported Pubns.

Nine Monks. Tr. by Paul Hansen. 1988. 20.00 o.p. (ISBN 0-918116-45-7); pap. 10.00 o.p. (ISBN 0-918116-46-5). Brooding Heron Pr.

Nine Months, Nine Lessons. Gail S. Brewer. (Orig.). 1983. pap. 9.50 o.p. (ISBN 0-671-45788-8, Fireside). S&S.

Nine Nations of North America. Joel Garreau. LC 80-28556. (Illus.). 423p. 1981. 14.95 o.p. (ISBN 0-395-29124-0). HM.

Nine One Act Plays from the Yiddish. Tr. by Bessie F. White. 25.00 o.p. (ISBN 0-8283-1421-7). Branden Pub Co.

Nine Questions People Ask About Judaism. Dennis Prager & Joseph Telushkin. 1981. 16.45 o.s.i. (ISBN 0-671-42593-5). S&S.

Nine Sonatinas for Piano. H. Lichner. (Illus.). 60p. 1909. pap. 9.00 o.p. (ISBN 0-8258-0249-0, L-880). Fischer Inc NY.

Nine-Thirty-Fifty-Five. John Minahan. 1977. pap. 1.75 o.p. (ISBN 0-380-00970-6, 32474). Avon.

Nine Thousand Miles to Freedom. Mehrdad Pourkhesali. 128p. 1987. 9.95 o.p. (ISBN 0-8062-3042-8). Carlton.

Nine White Swans. S. Vorohin. 12p. 1973. pap. 1.49 o.p. (ISBN 0-8285-1214-0, Pub. by Progress Pubs USSR). Imported Pubns.

Nineteen. Aleksandr A. Fadieev. Tr. by R. D. Charques from Rus. LC 72-90293. (Soviet Literature in English Translation Ser). 293p. 1973. Repr. of 1929 ed. 21.25 o.s.i. (ISBN 0-88355-003-2). Hyperion Conn.

Nineteen Artists: Emergent Americans-1981 National Exhibition. Peter Frank. LC 80-54018. (Illus.). 92p. 1981. cover museum catalogue 8.50soft o.p. (ISBN 0-89207-026-9). S R Guggenheim.

Nineteen Eighties, Decade of Shock. John Weldon. LC 78-52320. 1978. pap. 3.95 o.p. (ISBN 0-89051-063-6). Master Bks.

Nineteen Eighty Businessman's Guide to the Arab World & Iran: 1980. Arab World Business Guides Staff. 1980. pap. 30.00 o.p. (ISBN 0-931000-13-0). Suburban Pub CT.

Nineteen Eighty Edition Folio: Annual. Folio Magazine. (Folio Annual Ser.). (Orig.). 1981. pap. 20.00 o.p. (ISBN 0-918110-05-X). Hanson Pub Grp.

Nineteen Eighty-Eight Baseball Card Engagement Book. Michael Gershman. (Illus.). 112p. 1987. pap. 8.95 o.s.i. (ISBN 0-395-44113-7). HM.

Nineteen Eighty-Eight Candidate Profiles: A Look at the Leading Presidential Contenders. Ed. by James Skillen. 96p. 1988. pap. 2.95 o.p. (ISBN 0-310-20862-9, 6328P). Zondervan.

Nineteen Eighty-Eight Coping Library, 8 vols. (gr. 7-12). 1988. Set. lib. bdg. 87.95 o.p. (ISBN 0-8239-0823-2). Rosen Group.

Nineteen Eighty-Eight Summer Theater Guide, from an Actor's Viewpoint. John Allen. 150p. 1988. pap. 10.95 o.p. (ISBN 0-9614419-5-X). Allen Theatr Pubns.

Nineteen Eighty-Eight Supplement to the Directory of Medical Specialists. 23rd ed. 800p. 1988. 60.00 o.s.i. (ISBN 0-8379-0525-7). Marquis.

Nineteen Eighty-Five. Anthony Burgess. LC 78-9583. 1978. 11.45 o.p. (ISBN 0-316-11651-3). Little.

Nineteen Eighty-Five Health Care Cost Containment Legislation. Michelle L. Polchow. 90p. 1986. pap. text ed. 10.00 o.s.i. (ISBN 1-55516-669-5). Natl Conf State Legis.

Nineteen Eighty-Five Supplement to An Estate Planner's Handbook. James F. Farr & Jackson W. Wright, Jr. 1985. pap. 25.00 o.p. (ISBN 0-316-27477-1). Little.

Nineteen Eighty-Five Supplement to Closely Held Corporations in Business and Estate Planning: 1985 Supplement. Edwin T. Hood et al. 1985. pap. text ed. 32.00 o.p. (ISBN 0-316-37225-0). Little.

Nineteen Eighty-Five Supplement to Life Insurance in Estate Planning. James C. Munch, Jr. 1985. pap. 30.00 o.p. (ISBN 0-317-52259-0). Little.

Nineteen Eighty-Five Supplement to Regulation of Money Managers. Tamar Frankel. 1985. pap. 50.00 o.p. (ISBN 0-316-29189-7). Little.

Nineteen Eighty Folio Annual: Supplement to the Handbook of Magazine Publishing. 1980. 20.00 o.p. (ISBN 0-918110-05-X). Hanson Pub Grp.

Nineteen Eighty-Four. George Orwell. 1949. 12.95 o.p. (ISBN 0-15-166035-2). HarBraceJ.

Nineteen Eighty-Four & Animal Farm. George Orwell. 48p. (Orig.). 1988. pap. 9.95 o.p. (ISBN 1-55651-627-4); audiocassette tape incl. o.p. (ISBN 1-55651-628-2). Cram Cassettes.

Nineteen-Eighty-Four in 1984: Autonomy, Control & Communication. Ed. by Paul Aubrey & Crispin Chiltern. (Comedia Social Issues Ser.). 160p. 1984. pap. 7.95 o.p. (ISBN 0-906890-43-8, Dist. by Scribner); 15.00 o.p. (ISBN 0-906890-42-X). M Boyars Pubs.

Nineteen Eighty-Four Olympic Handbook. Norman Giller. (Illus.). 206p. 1984. pap. 7.95 o.p. (ISBN 0-317-06147-X). H Holt & Co.

Nineteen Eighty-Four Supplement to Law of Restitution. George E. Palmer. LC 77-71510. 375p. 1984. pap. 50.00 o.p. (ISBN 0-316-69008-2). Little.

Nineteen Eighty-One Advances in Aerospace Structures & Materials (AD-01) Ed. by S. S. Wang & W. J. Renton. (No. H00194). 311p. 1981. 40.00 o.p. (ISBN 0-686-34472-3). ASME.

Nineteen Eighty-One Advances in Bioengineering. Ed. by D. C. Viano. 232p. 1981. 40.00 o.p. (ISBN 0-686-34502-9, H00199). ASME.

Nineteen Eighty-One Multinational Executive Travel Companion. rev. ed. Multinational Executive, Inc. Staff. 1981. pap. 30.00 o.p. (ISBN 0-931000-14-9). Suburban Pub CT.

Nineteen Eighty-Seven Florida Statistical Abstract. Ed. by Anne Shoemyen. 1987. 28.95 o.p. (ISBN 0-8130-0875-1); pap. 19.95 o.p. (ISBN 0-8130-0876-X). U Presses FLa.

Nineteen Eighty-Seven Pesticule Directors. Lori Harvey & W. T. Thomas. 110p. pap. text ed. 75.00 o.p. (ISBN 0-913702-45-5). Thomson Pubns.

Nineteen Eighty-Six-Eighty-Eight National Jail & Adult Detention Directory. 364p. 1988. 35.00 o.p. Am Correctional.

Nineteen Eighty-Six Family Circle Cookbook. 2nd ed. Family Circle Editors. Ed. by JoAnn Brett-Billowitz. LC 86-4465. 320p. 1986. 19.95 o.p. (ISBN 0-933585-01-2). Family Circle Bks.

Nineteen Eighty-Six San Francisco County Street Atlas & Directory. rev. ed. Thomas Bros. Maps Staff. (Illus.). 90p. pap. 10.95 o.p. (ISBN 0-88130-199-X). Thomas Bros Maps.

Nineteen Eighty-Six Supplement to Corporate Tax Aspects of Closely Held Corporations. William H. Painter. 1986. 35.00 o.p. (ISBN 0-316-68875-4). Little.

Nineteen Eighty-Six Supplement to Discovery Practice. Roger S. Haydock & David F. Herr. 1986. pap. 30.00 o.p. (ISBN 0-316-35177-6). Little.

Nineteen Eighty-Six Supplement to Motion Practice. David F. Herr et al. 688p. 1986. lawyers bk. 67.50 o.p. (ISBN 0-316-35179-2). Little.

Nineteen Eighty-Three Annual Educational Conference Proceeding: Design for the Future, Vol. 25. Ed. by Becky A. Wright. 330p. 1984. text ed. 35.00 o.p. (ISBN 0-89154-222-1). Intl Found Employ.

Nineteen Eighty-Three P. E. Examination for Industrial Engineers. 1987. supl. 9.95 o.p. (ISBN 0-89806-092-3). Inst Indus Eng.

Nineteen Eighty-Two Amendments to the Voting Rights Act. Caroline Bakewell et al. LC 83-622202. (Local Government Law Bulletin Ser.: No. 24). 1983. 3.00 o.p. Institute Government.

Nineteen Fifty-Six. Stephen Marlowe. LC 80-70218. 352p. 1981. 12.95 o.p. (ISBN 0-87795-307-4, Arbor Hse). Morrow.

Nineteen Forty-Five: The World We Fought For. Robert Kee. 384p. 1985. 19.45 o.p. (ISBN 0-316-48509-8). Little.

Nineteen Forty-Three: The Victory That Never Was. John Grigg. (Illus.). 254p. 1980. 12.50 o.p. (ISBN 0-8090-7377-3). Hill & Wang.

Nineteen Forty-Two to Nineteen Forty-Six. F. C. Jones et al. 60.00 o.p. (ISBN 0-384-27745-4); pap. 54.00 o.p. (ISBN 0-384-27744-6). Johnson Repr.

Nineteen Hundred & Eighty Advances in Bioengineering. Ed. by V. C. Mow. 344p. 1980. 40.00 o.p. (ISBN 0-317-33574-X, G00176); members 20.00 o.p. (ISBN 0-317-33575-8). ASME.

Nineteen Hundred and Sixty-Six & All That: Design & the Consumer in Britain, 1960-1969. Jennifer Harris et al. (Illus.). 160p. (Orig.). 1988. pap. 14.95 o.p. (ISBN 0-86294-087-7, Pub. by Trefoil Bks Ltd UK). Seven Hills Bk Dists.

Nineteen Hundred Six: Surviving the Great Earthquake & Fire. Gerstle Mack. LC 81-1660. (Illus.). 128p. (Orig.). 1981. pap. 5.95 o.p. (ISBN 0-87701-176-1). Chronicle Bks.

Nineteen-Hundred to Now: Art from Rhode Island Collections. Commentary by Daniel Rosenfeld. LC 87-63297. (Illus.). 131p. (Orig.). 1988. pap. 18.00 o.p. (ISBN 0-911517-50-2). Mus of Art RI.

Nineteen New American Poets of the Golden Gate. Ed. by Philip Dow. LC 83-6124. 496p. 1984. 26.95 o.p. (ISBN 0-15-136418-4). HarBraceJ.

Nineteen New American Poets of the Golden Gate. Ed. by Philip Dow. LC 83-6124. 496p. 1984. pap. 14.95 o.p. (ISBN 0-15-636101-9, Harv). HarBraceJ.

Nineteen Purchase Street. Gerald A. Browne. LC 82-72051. 1982. 14.95 o.p. (ISBN 0-87795-413-5, Arbor Hse). Morrow.

Nineteen Seventy-Nine Multinational Executive Travel Companion. rev. ed. Multinational Executive Inc. 1978. pap. 20.00 o.p. (ISBN 0-931000-09-2). Suburban Pub CT.

Nineteen Sixties Supercars: A Repair & Restoration Guide. Tony Hossain. LC 82-19389. (Illus.). 214p. 1983. pap. 13.15 o.p. (ISBN 0-8306-2077-X, 2077). TAB Bks.

Nineteen Thirty-Eight: A World Vanishing. Brian Cleeve. 1987. 21.95 o.p. (ISBN 0-907675-08-5, Pub. by Buchan & Enright England). Seven Hills Bk Dists.

Nineteen Thirty-Nine: In the Shadow of War. Robert Kee. (Illus.). 304p. 1984. 19.45i o.p. (ISBN 0-316-48507-1). Little.

Nineteenth & Twentieth Century Architecture. LC 76-14074. (Garland Library of the History of Art). 1976. lib. bdg. 61.00 o.p. (ISBN 0-8240-2421-4). Garland Pub.

Nineteenth Century Aether Theories. Kenneth F. Schaffner. 288p. 1972. 70.00 o.p. (ISBN 0-08-015674-6). Pergamon.

Nineteenth-Century Art. Ariane Ruskin. (Discovering Art Ser.). (Illus.). (gr. 5 up). 1969. text ed. 11.95 o.p. (ISBN 0-07-054292-9); pap. (ISBN 0-07-054293-7). McGraw.

Nineteenth-Century British Drama: An Anthology of Representative Plays. Ed. by Leonard R. Ashley. 714p. 1989. pap. text ed. 17.50 o.p. (ISBN 0-8191-7107-7). U Pr of Amer.

Nineteenth Century Evangelical Theology. Fisher Humphreys. LC 83-71439. (Orig.). 1984. pap. 11.95 o.p. (ISBN 0-8054-6579-0). Broadman.

Nineteenth Century Government Publications: An Historical Guide. Cheryl A. Price. 200p. lib. bdg. (ISBN 0-87287-551-2). Libs Unl.

Nineteenth Century Historians of New Haven. Richard Hegel. LC 70-181318. (Illus.). 105p. 1972. 17.50 o.p. (ISBN 0-208-01262-1, Archon). Shoe String.

Nineteenth Century Home Architecture of Iowa City. Margaret N. Keyes. 126p. 1966. 5.95 o.s.i. (ISBN 0-87745-012-9); pap. 6.00 o.p. (ISBN 0-87745-013-7). U of Iowa Pr.

Nineteenth Century Hungarian Painting. 4th, rev. ed. G. O. Pogany. (Illus.). 1972. 20.00 o.s.i. (ISBN 0-685-47295-7). E J Brill USA.

Nineteenth-Century New York in Rare Photographic Views. Ed. by Frederick S. Lightfoot. 16.50 o.p. (ISBN 0-8446-5901-0). Peter Smith.

Nineteenth Century Opinion: An Anthology of Extracts from the First 50 Volumes of the Nineteenth Century, 1877-1901. Ed. by Michael Goodwin. LC 79-9966. 1979. Repr. of 1951 ed. lib. bdg. 27.50x o.p. (ISBN 0-313-21276-7, TCNC). Greenwood.

Nineteenth-Century Sydney: Studies in Urban History. Ed. by Max Kelly. 1979. pap. 17.00x o.p. (ISBN 0-424-00051-2, Pub. by Sydney U Pr). Intl Spec Bk.

Ninety & Counting. Arthur Pollock. LC 84-91305. 159p. 1985. 10.00 o.p. (ISBN 0-533-06396-5). Vantage.

Ninety Dollar Circle Tour: The Value of Traveling. Bergljot Abrahamson. (Illus.). 1979. 5.00 o.p. (ISBN 0-682-48523-3). Exposition-Phoenix.

Ninety Eight Point Six Meditations to Maintain Spiritual Well-Being. 2nd ed. Francis P. LeBuffe. LC 84-71932. 99p. 1986. pap. 2.95 o.p. (ISBN 0-87973-499-X). Our Sunday Visitor.

Ninety-Five Hikes in the Canadian Rockies: Banff, Kootenay, & Assiniboine Parks. Vicky Spring & Gordon King. (Illus.). 224p. (Orig.). 1982. pap. 9.95o.p. (ISBN 0-89886-019-9). Mountaineers.

Ninety-Five Poems. e. e. Cummings. LC 58-10909. 1958. 8.50 o.s.i. (ISBN 0-15-166450-1). HarBraceJ.

Ninety-Five Questions People Ask Most about the Holy Spirit. Don Stewart. 192p. 1987. pap. 5.95 o.p. (ISBN 0-8423-5108-6). Tyndale.

Ninety-Four Hikes in the Canadian Rockies: Yoho, Jasper, Mt. Robson & Willmore Wilderness Parks. Vicky Spring & Dee Urbick. (Illus.). 224p. (Orig.). 1983. pap. 9.95 o.p. (ISBN 0-89886-056-3). Mountaineers.

Ninety Highest Paying Careers for the 80's. Anita Gates. 176p. 1984. pap. 8.95 o.p. (ISBN 0-671-49869-X, Pub. by Monarch Pr). S&S.

Ninety Most Promising Careers for the 80s. Anita Gates. 192p. (Orig.). 1982. pap. 7.95 o.p. (ISBN 0-671-45272-X). Monarch Pr.

Ninety-Nine Novels: The Best in English since 1939. Anthony Burgess. 1985. pap. 4.95 o.s.i. (ISBN 0-671-55485-9). Summit Bks.

Ninety-Nine Plus One. Gerard A. Pottebaum. LC 72-135225. (Illus.). (ps-2). 1971. 4.95 o.p. (ISBN 0-8066-1108-1, 10-4648, Augsburg). Augsburg Fortress.

Ninety-Nine Pockets. Myrick. (gr. 1-4). PLB 6.19 o.p. (ISBN 0-8313-0079-5). Lantern.

Ninety-Nine Questions People Ask Most about the Bible. Don Stewart. 160p. (Orig.). 1987. pap. 5.95 o.p. (ISBN 0-8423-5107-8). Tyndale.

Ninety-Ninth Congress Children's Directory. 25.00 o.p. (ISBN 0-317-55863-3). Child Welfare.

Ninety-One Prints by Childe Hassam. Childe Hassam. Ed. by Joseph S. Czestochowski. (Illus., Orig.). 1980. 6.95 o.p. (ISBN 0-486-23981-0). Dover.

Ninety Plus & Swinging: One Man's Love Affair with Life. Jack Ruderman. LC 87-90756. 150p. 1987. text ed. 12.95 o.p. (ISBN 0-682-40338-5). Exposition-Phoenix.

Ninevah & the Old Testament. Andre Parrott. 1956. (ISBN 0-8022-1272-7). Philos Lib.

Ninos, Children of Mexico. Bob Schalkwijk & Nina Lincoln. (Illus.). 1980. portfolio 395.00 o.p. (ISBN 0-915998-08-4). Lime Rock Pr.

Ninotchka. Ed. by Richard J. Anobile. (Illus.). 1975. pap. 6.45 o.p. (ISBN 0-380-00290-6, Flare). Avon.

Ninth Amendment: History, Interpretation & Meaning. Mark N. Goodman. 74p. 1981. 5.00 o.p. (ISBN 0-682-49630-8, University). Exposition-Phoenix.

Ninth Century Political Tract: The De Institutione Regia of Jonas of Orleans. R. W. Dyson. 112p. 1983. 7.00 o.p. (ISBN 0-682-40116-1, University). Exposition-Phoenix.

Ninth Decade: Secret Plans for the Coming Communist Takeovers. Jean-Jacques Sensoir. 1977. 7.50 o.p. (ISBN 0-682-48801-1). Exposition-Phoenix.

Ninth International Congress of Carboniferous Stratigraphy & Geology: Compte Rendu, Vol. 1. LC 83-19147. 159p. 1984. pap. 25.00x o.p. (ISBN 0-8093-1168-2). S Ill U Pr.

Ninth Reading Helper. Gloria Orlick. (Classroom Reading Ser). 48p. (Orig., Prog. Bk.). (gr. 4 up). 1973. pap. 3.45 o.p. (ISBN 0-87594-047-1). Book-Lab.

Ninth Vertical Poetry, Tenth Vertical Poetry. Roberto Juarroz. Tr. by Pamela Carmell. 1987. Lat Am Lit Rev Pr.

NIOSH Certified Equipment List, As of Oct. 1, 1986. 490p. 1986. pap. 19.00 o.p. (ISBN 0-318-22601-4, S/N 017-033-00427-7). USGPO.

Nippon: A Charted Survey of Japan, 1985-86. 30th ed. 1985. 66.00 o.p. (ISBN 0-8002-3989-X). Intl Pubns Serv.

Nirgendwo ist Poenichen see Flight of Cranes.

Nirvana Blues. John Nichols. LC 80-22376. 540p. 1981. 14.95 o.s.i. (ISBN 0-03-059256-9). H Holt & Co.

Nirvana Blues. John T. Nichols. 608p. 1988. pap. 4.95 o.p. (ISBN 0-345-30465-9). Ballantine.

Nirvanasara. Da Free John. 280p. (Orig.). 1982. pap. 14.95 o.s.i. (ISBN 0-913922-65-X). Dawn Horse Pr.

Nissan-Datsun: A History of Nissan Motor Corporation in the U. S. A. 1960-1980. John B. Rae. (Illus.). 1981. text ed. 27.50 o.p. (ISBN 0-07-051112-8). McGraw.

Nissan Pick-ups 1970-84. Chilton Automotives Editorial Staff. LC 84-45483. 224p. (Orig.). 1985. pap. 13.50 o.p. (ISBN 0-8019-7567-0). Chilton.

Nitrendipine. Alexander Scriabine et al. 566p. 1984. pap. 34.50 o.p. (ISBN 0-8067-1781-5). Urban & S.

Nitrile Oxides, Versatile Tools of Theoretical & Preparative Chemistry. C. Grundmann & P. Gruenanger. (Organische Chemie in Einzeldarstellungen: Vol. 13). 1971. 52.90 o.p. (ISBN 0-387-05226-7). Springer-Verlag.

Nitrogen & Air: Gas Solubilities. Batino. LC 82-15046. (Solubility Data Ser.: Vol. 10). 1982. 110.00 o.p. (ISBN 0-08-023922-6). Pergamon.

Nitrogen As a Water Pollutant. S. H. Jenkins. 1978. pap. 110.00 flexi-cover o.p. (ISBN 0-08-020900-9). Pergamon.

Nitrogen Fixation: The Chemical-Biochemical-Genetic Interface. Ed. by Achim Muller & William E. Newton. LC 82-24587. 388p. 1983. 72.50x o.p. (ISBN 0-306-41258-6, Plenum Pr). Plenum Pub.

Nitrogen in Desert Ecosystems. Ed. by N. E. West & J. Skujins. LC 78-17672. (US-IBP Synthesis Ser.: Vol. 9). 307p. 1982. 39.95 o.p. (ISBN 0-87933-333-2). Van Nos Reinhold.

Nitrogen Metabolism & the Environment. American Physiological Society & American Society of Zoologists, Joint Symposium. Ed. by J. W. Campbell & L. Goldstein. 1972. 49.50 o.p. (ISBN 0-12-157850-X). Acad Pr.

Nitrogen NMR. Ed. by M. Witanowski & G. A. Webb. LC 72-95065. 404p. 1973. 69.50x o.p. (ISBN 0-306-30734-0, Plenum Pr). Plenum Pub.

Nitroimidazoles: Chemistry, Pharmacology & Clinical Application. Ed. by A. Breccia & B. Cavalleri. (NATO ASI Series A, Life Science: Vol. 42). 224p. 1982. 49.50x o.p. (ISBN 0-306-40916-X, Plenum Pr). Plenum Pub.

Nitrosourea: Current Status & New Development. Ed. by A. W. Prestayko et al. 1981. 53.50 o.p. (ISBN 0-12-565060-4). Acad Pr.

Nittany Lions: A Story of Penn State Football. Ken Rappoport. LC 73-86999. (College Sports Ser.). 1980. 10.95 o.p. (ISBN 0-87397-044-6). Strode.

Nitter Pitter. Stephen Cosgrove. Ed. by Mary H. Manoni. (Serendipity Book Cassettes). (Illus.). (gr. 1-3). 1979. pap. text ed. 24.95 o.p. (ISBN 0-89290-070-9). Soc for Visual.

Nixon Chronicles. Mike Peters. 1976. pap. 6.95 o.p. (ISBN 0-89328-001-1). Lorenz Corp.

Nixon Nobody Knows. Henry D. Spalding. LC 70-188240. (Illus.). 456p. 1972. 8.95 o.p. (ISBN 0-8246-0142-4). Jonathan David.

Njegos: Poet, Prince, Bishop. Milovan Djilas. Tr. by Michael B. Petrovich. LC 66-12915. (Illus.). 1966. 10.00 o.p. (ISBN 0-15-166480-3). HarBraceJ.

Nkrumah & the Ghana Revolution. C. L. James. LC 77-73128. 228p. 1977. 12.95 o.p. (ISBN 0-88208-077-6). Chicago Review.

NLRB Representation Elections: Law, Practice & Procedure. John D. Feerick et al. 1058p. 1980. Supplements avail. press binder 55.00 o.p. (ISBN 0-15-100042-5, H39786, Pub. by Law & Business); Suppl., 1983. 25.00 o.p. (ISBN 0-686-89123-6). HarBraceJ.

NLRB, the First Fifty Years: The Story of the National Labor Relations Board, 1935-1985. (Illus.). 96p. (Orig.). 1986. pap. 6.50 o.p. (ISBN 0-318-22933-1, S/N 031-000-00270-2). USGPO.

NMR Analyses of Molecular Conformations & Conformational Equilibria with the Lanthanide Probe Method, Vol. 14, No. 2. Emsley & T. Miyazawa. (Illus.). 45p. 1981. pap. 28.00 o.p. (ISBN 0-08-027104-9). Pergamon.

NMR & Biochemistry. S. J. Opella & P. Lu. 1979. 79.75 o.p. (ISBN 0-8247-6882-5). Dekker.

NMR & the Periodic Table. Ed. by Robin Harris & Brian Mann. 1979. 141.00 o.p. (ISBN 0-12-327650-0). Acad Pr.

NMR in Medicine. Ed. by R. Danadian. (NMR--Basic Principles & Progress Ser.: Vol. 19). (Illus.). 230p. 1981. 57.90 o.p. (ISBN 0-387-10460-7). Springer-Verlag.

NMR Spectroscopy Using Liquid Crystal Solvents. J. W. Emsley & J. C. Lindon. 367p. 1975. 90.00 o.p. (ISBN 0-08-019919-4). Pergamon.

No-Action Alternative: Research Report. (National Cooperative Highway Research Program Report). 72p. 1979. 6.80 o.p. (ISBN 0-309-03011-0). Transport Res Bd.

No Baths for Tabitha. Sharon K. Thomas & Marjorie Siegal. Ed. by Margaret Holland. LC 84-52561. (Predictable Reading Books Ser.). (Illus.). 24p. (gr. k-3). 1985. 7.95 o.s.i. (ISBN 0-87406-002-8). Willowisp Pr.

No Baths for Tabitha. Sharon K. Thomas & Marjorie Siegel. (Illus.). 24p. (gr. k-2). 1984. 1.95 o.p. (ISBN 0-87406-075-3). Willowisp Pr.

No Beasts! No Children! Beverly Keller. LC 82-14011. 128p. (gr. 3-6). 1983. 10.25 o.p. (ISBN 0-688-01678-2). Lothrop.

No Blade of Grass. John Christopher. 1986. pap. 2.25 o.p. (ISBN 0-380-00319-8, 48009-3). Avon.

No Body: A Jenny Cain Mystery. Nancy Pickard. 224p. 1986. 13.95 o.p. (ISBN 0-684-18593-8). Scribner.

No Book. Drew Babb & Jann Alexander. (Illus.). 112p. 1983. pap. 5.75 o.p. (ISBN 0-671-49196-2). S&S.

No Book: No Buddha, No Teaching, No Discipline. Bhagwan Shree Rajneesh. Ed. by Ma Prem Maneesha. (Initation Talks Ser.). (Illus.). 354p. (Orig.). 1981. 26.95 o.p. (ISBN 0-88050-102-2). Chidvilas Inc.

No Bosses Here: A Manual on Working Collectively & Cooperatively. Vocations for Social Change Staff & Karen Brandow. LC 81-68797. 120p. (Orig.). 1981. pap. 4.95 o.p. (ISBN 0-932870-15-5). Alyson Pubns.

No Bosses Here: A Manual on Working Collectively & Cooperatively. Vocations for Social Change Staff et al. 115p. 1981. 5.75 o.p. (ISBN 0-318-17039-6). NASCO.

No Bugles, No Drums. Charles Durden. 1978. pap. 1.95 o.p. (ISBN 0-441-58320-2). Ace Bks.

No Bugles, No Drums. Charles Durden. (Vietnam Ser.). 240p. 1984. pap. 3.50 o.p. (ISBN 0-380-69260-0, 69260). Avon.

No Cease Fires: The War on Poverty in Roanoke Valley. Edwin L. Cobb. LC 84-5515. 192p. 1984. 13.95 o.p. (ISBN 0-932020-28-3); pap. 8.95 o.p. (ISBN 0-932020-29-1). Seven Locks Pr.

No Certain Harbor. Hilda B. Powicke. (gr. 9 up). 1962. pap. 0.75 o.p. (ISBN 0-377-80231-X). Friendship Pr.

No Child Is Ineducable. 2nd ed. S. S. Segal. LC 73-21571. 412p. 1974. 26.00 o.p. (ISBN 0-08-017815-4). Pergamon.

No Church Is an Island. David S. King. LC 79-27113. (Orig.). 1980. pap. 5.95 o.p. (ISBN 0-8298-0385-8). Pilgrim NY.

No Church Is an Island: Study Guide. King. 1980. pap. 1.00 o.p. (ISBN 0-8298-0389-0). Pilgrim NY.

No Deals Mr. Bond. John Gardner. 320p. 1987. 13.95 o.p. (ISBN 0-399-13254-6, Putnam). Putnam Pub Group.

No Democratic Opening: Human Rights Violations in Guatemala. 4.50 o.p. Natl Lawyers Guild.

No Doubt Mad Idea. Steve Minkin. Ed. by Stella Nathan. 260p. 1978. pap. 4.95 o.p. (ISBN 0-89496-019-9). Ross Bks.

No-Drug Approach to Lowering Your Blood Pressure. George Berkley. 208p. (Orig.). 1984. pap. 3.95 o.s.i. (ISBN 0-915962-32-2). Comm Channels.

No Earthly Shore. Francine Mezo. 256p. 1981. pap. 2.50 o.p. (ISBN 0-380-77347-3, 77347-3). Avon.

No Easy Choice: Political Participation in Developing Countries. Samuel P. Huntington & Joan M. Nelson. (Center for International Affairs Ser.). 224p. 1976. 24.50x o.p. (ISBN 0-674-62530-7). Harvard U Pr.

No Easy Circle. Phyliss R. Naylor. 1973. pap. 0.75 o.p. (ISBN 0-380-01431-9, 14548). Avon.

No End to Yesterday. Shelagh Macdonald. LC 78-74755. (Illus.). (gr. 7 up). 1979. 9.95 o.p. (ISBN 0-233-96865-2). Andre Deutsch.

No Excuse to Lose: Winning Yacht Races. Dennis Conner. (Illus.). 1978. 9.95 o.p. (ISBN 0-393-03212-4). Norton.

No-Fault Divorce, an Expose. Isabelle Andrews. 96p. 1988. 8.75 o.p. (ISBN 0-8062-3054-1). Carlton.

No-Fault Marriage. Marcia Lasswell & Norman M. Lobsenz. 1984. pap. 2.95 o.s.i. (ISBN 0-345-32420-X). Ballantine.

No Flowers by Request. June Thompson. LC 86-29161. (Crime Club Ser.). 192p. 1987. 12.95 o.p. (ISBN 0-385-24175-5). Doubleday.

No Fond Return of Love. Barbara Pym. (General Ser.). 362p. 1986. lib. bdg. 18.95x o.p. (ISBN 0-8161-3860-5, Large Print Bks). G K Hall.

No Fury. Margaret Yorke. 200p. 1988. lib. bdg. 19.95x o.s.i. (ISBN 0-7451-0789-3, Pub. by Chivers Pr UK). G K Hall.

No Go on Jackson Street: A Mystery Introducing Ben Henry. Mike Weiss. LC 86-29635. 1987. 14.95 o.p. (ISBN 0-684-18810-4). Scribner.

No Greater Love: Maximilian Kolbe. Boniface Hanley. LC 82-72656. (Illus.). 80p. (Orig.). (gr. 9-12). 1982. pap. 3.95 o.p. (ISBN 0-87793-257-3). Ave Maria.

No Higher Calling. J. N. Hunt. (Horizon Ser.). 96p. 1981. pap. 5.95 o.p. (ISBN 0-8280-0064-6). Review & Herald.

No Hill Too Fast. Phil Mahre & Steve Mahre. 1985. 17.45 o.p. (ISBN 0-671-55706-8). S&S.

No Holly for Miss Quinn. Miss Read. 1976. 6.95 o.p. (ISBN 0-395-24768-3). HM.

No House Calls: Irreverent Notes on the Practice of Medicine. Peter Gott. 224p. 1986. 17.45 o.s.i. (ISBN 0-671-60433-3, Poseidon). PB.

No Idle Words, & Having the Last Word. Ivor Brown. LC 77-11610. 1977. Repr. of 1951 ed. lib. bdg. 35.00x o.p. (ISBN 0-8371-9800-3, BRNO). Greenwood.

No Job for a Lady. M. Phyllis Lose & Daniel Mannix. 224p. 1982. pap. 2.25 o.s.i. (ISBN 0-345-29016-X). Ballantine.

No Job for a Lady. Martha Thomas. Ed. by Judith Schnell. (Illus.). 256p. (ISBN 0-8117-1020-3). Stackpole.

No Known Survivors: David Levine's Political Plank. David Levine. LC 77-118213. (Illus.). 1970. 10.95 o.p. (ISBN 0-87645-030-3, Pub. by Gambit); signed limited ed. 25.00 o.p. (ISBN 0-87645-106-7). Harvard Common Pr.

No Laughing Matter: A Collection of Political Jokes. Steven Lukes & Itzhak Galnoor. (Illus.). 171p. 1986. 14.95 o.p. (ISBN 0-7100-9965-7). Routledge Chapman & Hall.

No Little Plans: Fairfax County's PLUS Program for Managing Growth. Gene Dawson. 168p. 1977. pap. text ed. 9.00 o.p. (ISBN 0-87766-185-5). Urban Inst.

No Longer Strangers. Larson. 145p. 1985. pap. 5.95 o.p. (ISBN 0-8499-3020-0, 3020-0). Word Bks.

No Love Lost. Large Print ed. Helen Van Slyke. LC 81-18405. 767p. 1982. Repr. 16.95 o.p. (ISBN 0-89621-336-6). Thorndike Pr.

No Man's Brother. Charles Ewert. 320p. (Orig.). 1984. pap. 4.50 o.p. (ISBN 0-380-86215-8, 86215). Avon.

No Man's Land. Harold Pinter. LC 75-13555. 1975. 6.95 o.p. (ISBN 0-394-49931-X, GP769). Grove.

No Man's Land: The Last of White Africa. John Heminway. 300p. 1984. pap. 8.95 o.p. (ISBN 0-15-665967-0, Harv). HarBraceJ.

No Marks for Trying. Stella Allan. 208p. (Orig.). 1982. pap. 2.25 o.p. (ISBN 0-380-57836-0, 57836-0). Avon.

No Message & No Song. Kenneth Parsons. 66p. 1985. 6.95 o.p. (ISBN 0-533-06110-5). Vantage.

No More Alphabet Soup. Nancy B. Irland. Ed. by Bobbie J. Van Dolson. LC 83-3303. (Banner Bks.). 128p. (Orig.). (gr. 1 up). 1984. pap. 6.95 o.p. (ISBN 0-8280-0165-0). Review & Herald.

No More Butts: A Psychologist's Approach to Quitting Cigarettes. Richard W. Olshavsky. LC 76-26421. (Illus.). 192p. 1977. 12.95x o.p. (ISBN 0-253-15832-X). Ind U Pr.

No More Dead Horses. Charlotte Bolton. 160p. 1986. 9.95 o.p. (ISBN 0-8062-2908-X). Carlton.

No More Fat. Ellington Darden. 1986. pap. 5.75 o.p. (ISBN 0-671-49245-4, Fireside). S&S.

No More for the Road: One Man's Journey from Chemical Dependency to Freedom. Duane Mehl. LC 75-22721. 144p. 1976. pap. 7.95 o.p. (ISBN 0-8066-1515-X, 10-4665, Augsburg). Augsburg Fortress.

No More Headaches! Alan C. Turin. 288p. 1981. 12.95 o.p. (ISBN 0-395-30516-0). HM.

No More Loving. Patricia Robbins. (Lythway Ser.). 224p. 1988. lib. bdg. 18.50 o.s.i. (ISBN 0-7451-0669-2, Pub. by Chivers Pr UK). G K Hall.

No More Masks: An Anthology of Poems by Women. Ed. by Florence Howe & Ellen Bass. LC 72-89675. 432p. 1973. pap. 5.95 o.p. (ISBN 0-385-02553-X, Anch). Doubleday.

No More! Piggety Pig. Harriet Ziefert. (Piggety Pig Bks.). (Illus.). 16p. (ps-k). 2.95 o.p. (ISBN 0-316-98763-8). Little.

No More Shacks: The Daring Vision of Habitat for Humanity. Millard Fuller. 1986. 11.95 o.p. (ISBN 0-8499-0604-0); pap. 5.95 o.p. (ISBN 0-8499-3050-2). Word Bks.

No More the Round Mud Hut: Voices of Young Africa. Willard E. Roth. (Orig.). 1971. pap. 1.50 o.p. (ISBN 0-377-11211-9). Friendship Pr.

No More Tomorrow. Reginald Ottley. LC 78-137758. (Illus.). 107p. (gr. 7 up). 1971. 5.25 o.p. (ISBN 0-15-257495-6, HJ). HarBraceJ.

No More Vietnams. Richard Nixon. 224p. 1985. 14.95 o.p. (ISBN 0-87795-668-5, Arbor Hse). Morrow.

No More Vietnams. Richard Nixon. deluxe ed. 50.00 o.p. (ISBN 0-87795-726-6). Morrow.

No Name for Season. Karla M. Hammond. LC 85-82963. 64p. 1985. lib. bdg. 7.95 o.s.i. (ISBN 0-943512-05-0, 1053J). Linwood Pub.

No-Name Man of the Mountain. William O. Steele. LC 64-22272. (Illus.). (gr. 1-5). 1964. 4.50 o.p. (ISBN 0-15-257501-4, HJ); 3.33 o.p. (ISBN 0-15-257502-2). HarBraceJ.

No Nation Alone. Linus Fike. (ISBN 0-8022-0498-8). Philos Lib.

No Need to Count. Leon B. Dubey, Jr. LC 79-23884. (Illus.). 176p. 1981. pap. 9.95 o.s.i. (ISBN 0-498-02465-2). A S Barnes.

No-Nonsense Delegation. Dale D. McConkey. LC 73-93670. (Illus.). 240p. 1974. 14.95 o.p. (ISBN 0-8144-5361-9). AMACOM.

No-Nonsense Delegation. Dale D. McConkey. (Illus.). 1979. pap. 4.95 o.p. (ISBN 0-8144-7517-5). AMACOM.

No-Nonsense Guide to Get You into Medical School. Kent Bransford. LC 78-11160. 1979. pap. 3.95 o.p. (ISBN 0-671-18353-2). Monarch Pr.

No-Nonsense Guide to Starting Your Own Business. Starmark Publishing. 64p. 1980. write for info. spiral bound hard pressboard cover 14.95 o.s.i. (ISBN 0-936572-01-9). Starmark.

No-Nonsense Management. Richard S. Sloma. 176p. 1981. pap. 4.50 o.p. (ISBN 0-553-23382-3). Bantam.

No-Nonsense Nutrition from Toddlers to Pre-Teen. Annette B. Natow & Jo-Ann Heslin. 304p. 1984. text ed. 15.95 o.p. (ISBN 0-07-028413-X). McGraw.

No One Has to Die. Roy Masters. LC 76-20023. 1977. pap. 9.95 o.p. (ISBN 0-933900-03-1). Foun Human Under.

No One Is to Blame: Getting a Loving Divorce from Mom & Dad. Bob Hoffman. LC 79-63271. 1979. pap. 8.95 o.p. (ISBN 0-8314-0057-9). Sci & Behavior.

No One Knows My Name. Joyce Harrington. 240p. 1981. pap. 2.25 o.p. (ISBN 0-380-57349-0, 57349-0). Avon.

No One Rides for Free. Larry Beinhart. LC 85-15386. 256p. 1986. 16.95 o.p. (ISBN 0-688-06057-9). Morrow.

No One Writes to the Colonel & Other Short Stories. Gabriel Garcia Marquez. 1978. pap. 1.75 o.p. (ISBN 0-380-00994-3, 36749, Bard). Avon.

No Ordinary Crime. James R. Wilson. (Illus.). 240p. 1981. softcover 5.95 o.p. (ISBN 0-933586-07-8). Book Promo Pr.

No Part in Your Death. Nicolas Freeling. 1985. 13.95 o.p. (Large Print Bks). G K Hall.

No Past, No Present, No Future. Yulisa A. Maddy. (African Writers Ser.). 1973. pap. text ed. 7.00 o.p. (ISBN 0-435-90137-0). Heinemann Ed.

No Pat Answers. Eugenia Price. 144p. 1983. pap. 6.95 o.p. (ISBN 0-310-31331-7, 16244P). Zondervan.

No Picnic. Julian Thompson. 202p. 1986. pap. 4.95 rack size o.p. (Pub. by Fontana). Parkwest Pubns.

No Promises in the Wind. Irene Hunt. 224p. (gr. 5 up). 1981. pap. 2.25 o.s.i. (ISBN 0-441-58864-6, Pub. by Tempo). Ace Bks.

No Reservations. Molly Katz. (Candlelight Ecstasy Ser.: No. 341). 1985. pap. 2.25 o.p. (ISBN 0-440-16080-4). Dell.

No Respecter of Persons. Lois G. Dickie. LC 85-80195. 272p. 1985. 11.50 o.p. (ISBN 0-682-40253-2). Exposition-Phoenix.

No Retirement: Devotions on Christian Discipleship for Older People. Lillian R. Reynolds. LC 83-48916. 96p. 1984. pap. 0.95 o.p. (ISBN 0-8006-1779-7, 1-1779, Fortress). Augsburg Fortress.

No-Return Trail. Sonia Levitin. LC 77-88964. (gr. 7 up). 1978. 6.95 o.p. (ISBN 0-15-257545-6, HJ). HarBraceJ.

No Risk: Gordon Williams' Step-by-Step Program to Safeguard Your Financial Future. Gordon Williams. 304p. 1984. 15.50 o.p. (ISBN 0-671-45171-5). S&S.

No Scarlet Ribbons. Susan Terris. 160p. 1983. pap. 2.25 o.p. (ISBN 0-380-62844-9, 62844-9, Flare). Avon.

No Schools. Ignacio L. Gotz. 198p. 1971. pap. text ed. 10.95x o.p. (ISBN 0-8422-0163-7). Irvington.

No Second Wind. A. B. Guthrie, Jr. 1980. 9.95 o.p. (ISBN 0-395-29069-4). HM.

No Secrets: Gold Quill Winners Tell All. International Association of Business Communicators Staff. Ed. by Elizabeth Allan. 480p. (Orig.). 1985. pap. text ed. 35.00 o.p. (ISBN 0-943372-04-6). Intl Assn Busn Comm.

No Slipper for Cinderella. Mildred Lawrence. LC 65-17990. (gr. 7 up). 1965. 5.25 o.p. (ISBN 0-15-257575-8, HJ). HarBraceJ.

No Souvenirs: Journal, 1957-1969. Mircea Eliade. LC 76-9969. 1976. 15.00 o.p. (ISBN 0-06-062141-9). HarpR.

No Sugar Cooking. Karen Taggart. (Illus.). 80p. (Orig.). 1985. pap. 4.95 o.p. (ISBN 0-8249-3047-9). Ideals.

No Thank You, Mr. President. John Herbers. 256p. 1976. 7.95 o.p. (ISBN 0-393-05570-1). Norton.

No Through Road. Roy Brown. LC 74-3484. 160p. (gr. 6 up). 1979. 5.95 o.p. (ISBN 0-395-28896-7, Clarion). HM.

No Time for Tears. Cynthia Freeman. LC 80-70542. 448p. 1981. 14.95 o.p. (ISBN 0-87795-317-1, Arbor Hse). Morrow.

No Time for Women: Exploring Women's Health: 1930's vs. 1980's. Charmain Kenner. (Illus.). 128p. (Orig.). 1984. pap. 9.95 o.p. (ISBN 0-86358-032-7, Pandora Pr). Routledge Chapman & Hall.

No Time Lost. Walter S. Mack & Peter Buckley. LC 82-71061. 224p. 1982. 12.95 o.p. (ISBN 0-689-11326-9, Atheneum). Macmillan.

No Time on Our Side. Roger Chapman. (Illus.). 168p. 1975. 7.95 o.p. (ISBN 0-393-03186-1). Norton.

No Violations of Policy: An Informal History of the Independent Insurance Agents of America. 20.00 o.p. (ISBN 0-686-31038-1, 26540). Rough Notes.

No Way. Natalia Ginzburg. 1976. pap. 1.75 o.p. (ISBN 0-380-00838-6, 31054-6, Bard). Avon.

No Way. Natalia Ginzburg. Tr. by Sheila Cudahy. LC 74-7069. (Helen & Kurt Wolff Bks.). 168p. 1974. 5.95 o.p. (ISBN 0-15-167674-7). HarBraceJ.

No Way Back. Tova Sadka. 208p. 1984. 12.00 o.p. (ISBN 0-682-40202-8). Exposition-Phoenix.

No Way of Telling. Emma Smith. LC 74-190560. (gr. 5-9). 1972. 5.50 o.p. (ISBN 0-689-30311-4, Atheneum). Macmillan.

No Way to Treat a Lady. William Goldman. 1968. 4.50 o.p. (ISBN 0-15-167675-5). HarBraceJ.

No Woman's Country. Michael Langley. 1951. (ISBN 0-8022-0917-3). Philos Lib.

Noa Noa. Paul Gauguin. 148p. (Orig.). 1957. pap. 5.95 o.p. (ISBN 0-374-50040-1). FS&G.

NOAA Diving Manual: Diving Science & Technology. 2nd ed. Ed. by James W. Miller. 545p. 1979. pap. 17.00 o.p. (ISBN 0-318-11742-8, S/N 003-017-00468-6). USGPO.

Noah & the Ark. (MacDonald Educational Ser.). (Illus., Arabic.). (gr. 4-6). 3.50x o.p. (ISBN 0-86685-212-3). Intl Bk Ctr.

Noah's Ark. LC 76-11269. (Sunshine Bks.). (Illus.). 20p. 1976. pap. 1.00 o.p. (ISBN 0-8006-1576-X, 1-1576, Fortress). Augsburg Fortress.

Noah's Ark: A Novel. Barbara Trapido. 264p. 1985. 16.95 o.p. (ISBN 0-531-09704-8). Watts.

Noah's Ark Diorama Book. Carol Ferntheil. (gr. k-3). 1977. 3.95 o.p. (ISBN 0-87239-167-1, 3606). Standard Pub.

Noah's Ark in Paper & Card. Charlotte Gerlings & Suzy Ives. (Illus.). 112p. (gr. k-3). 7.95 o.s.i. (ISBN 0-8008-5578-7). Taplinger.

Noah's Ark, Pitched & Parked. Nathan M. Meyer. pap. 4.00 o.p. (ISBN 0-88469-039-3). BMH Bks.

Noah's Arkitecture: A Study of Dicken's Mythology. Bert G. Hornback. LC 70-181681. x, 183p. 1972. 12.00x o.p. (ISBN 0-8214-0100-9). Ohio U Pr.

Nobby Clark's Auckland. K. S. Clark. (Illus.). 84p. 1987. 19.95 o.p. (ISBN 0-86481-100-4, Pub. by Whitcoulls NZ). Intl Spec Bk.

Nobel Lecture: Bilingual Edition. Joseph Brodsky. Tr. by Barry Rubin. cancelled o.s.i. (ISBN 0-374-22304-1, Noonday); pap. cancelled o.s.i. (ISBN 0-374-52117-4). FS&G.

Nobel Prize Lectures in Chemistry, 1901-1970, 4 vols. Nobel Foundation. Incl. Vol. 1. 1901-1921. 1967. 44.00 o.p. (ISBN 0-444-40413-9); Vol. 2. 1922-1941. 1966. 84.25 o.p. (ISBN 0-444-40414-7); Vol. 3. 1942-1962. 1964. 94.75 o.p. (ISBN 0-444-40415-5); Vol. 4. 1963-1970. 1973. 100.00 o.p. (ISBN 0-444-40987-4). Elsevier.

Nobility in Russia & Eastern Europe. Ed. by Ivo Banac & Paul Bushkovitch. LC 83-60391. (Yale Russian & East European Publications: No. 3). xi, 221p. 1983. 18.50 o.p. Yale Russian.

Nobility in Russia & Eastern Europe. Ed. by Ivo Banac & Paul Bushkovitch. (Yale Russian & East European Publications Ser.: No. 3). 221p. 1983. 18.50 o.p. (ISBN 0-936586-02-8). Yale Russian.

Noble Savage. Robert C. Smith. (Illus.). 26p. 1958. pap. 1.00 o.p. (ISBN 0-318-01001-1). Univ Mus of U PA.

Noble Task: The Elder. rev. ed. Andrew A. Jumper. LC 65-14420. 1965. pap. 3.50 o.p. (ISBN 0-8042-3992-4, John Knox). Westminster John Knox.

Nobody Does It Better. Bob Simmins. (Illus.). 144p. 1987. pap. 5.95 o.p. (ISBN 0-7137-1907-9, Pub. by Javelin). Sterling.

Nobody Else Is Just Like Me. Florence Schulz. (Illus.). (ps-1). 1967. pap. 1.50 o.p. (ISBN 0-8042-9712-6, John Knox). Westminster John Knox.

Nobody Ever Died of Old Age. Sharon R. Curtin. LC 72-6157. 1973. 8.95 o.p.; pap. 7.70i o.p. (ISBN 0-316-16547-6, An Atlantic Little, Brown Book). Little.

Nobody Ever Sees You Eat Tuna Fish. David Brenner. (Illus.). 1986. 15.95 o.p. (ISBN 0-87795-730-4). Morrow.

Nobody Here But Us Chickens. Marvin Mudrick. LC 81-4408. 320p. 1981. 16.95 o.p. (ISBN 0-89919-042-1). Ticknor & Fields.

Nobody Here by That Name. Donald McKenzie. LC 86-2126. (Crime Club Ser.). 192p. 1986. 12.95 o.p. (ISBN 0-385-23547-X). Doubleday.

Nobody Is Perfick. Bernard Waber. (Illus.). (gr. k-3). 1971. PLB 8.95 o.p. (ISBN 0-395-15991-1). HM.

Nobody Lives Forever. John Gardner. 1986. 12.95 o.p. (ISBN 0-399-13151-5). Putnam Pub Group.

Nobody Stole the Pie. Sonia Levitin. LC 79-90032. (Illus.). (gr. k-4). 1980. 9.95 o.p. (ISBN 0-15-257469-7, HJ); pap. 3.50 o.p. (ISBN 0-15-665959-X, VoyB). HarBraceJ.

Nobody's Fault? Patricia Hermes. LC 81-47532. 107p. 1981. 8.95 o.p. (ISBN 0-15-257466-2, HJ). HarBraceJ.

Nobody's Orphan. Anne Lindbergh. LC 83-8494. 160p. (gr. 3-7). 1983. 12.95 o.p. (ISBN 0-15-257468-9, HJ). HarBraceJ.

Nobody's Perfect. Terry Powell. LC 78-65556. 116p. 1979. pap. 4.50 o.p. (ISBN 0-88207-577-2). Victor Bks.

Noche Oscura del Nino Aviles. Edgardo Rodriquez-Julia. LC 83-80313. (Coleccion Sur.). 334p. (Span.). 1984. pap. 12.95 o.p. (ISBN 0-940238-10-1). Ediciones Huracan.

Nocturne: A Life of Chopin. Ruth Jordan. LC 78-53797. 1978. 12.50 o.s.i. (ISBN 0-8008-5593-0, Crescendo). Taplinger.

Nocturnes. L. S. Senghor. (African Writers Ser.). 1969. pap. text ed. 6.50x o.p. (ISBN 0-435-90071-4). Heinemann Ed.

Noel Coward Diaries. Ed. by Graham Payn & Sheridan Morley. 704p. 1982. pap. 14.50i o.p. (ISBN 0-316-69551-3). Little.

Noel de Sam et Violet. Nicole Rubel. (Illus.). 32p. (Fr.). (gr. k-3). 1983. pap. 2.25 o.p. (ISBN 0-380-85092-3, 85092-3, Camelot). Avon.

Noel the Coward. Kraus et al. (Illus.). 32p. (ps-3). 1979. 5.95 o.s.i. (ISBN 0-671-96280-9). Windmill Bks.

Noise Control for Engineers. Harold W. Lord et al. (Illus.). 448p. 1980. text ed. 42.00x o.p. (ISBN 0-07-038738-9). McGraw.

Noise Control in Internal Combustion Engines. Donald E. Baxa & Darrell E. Petska. LC 81-147356. 526p. 1982. 71.95 o.p. (ISBN 0-471-05870-X, Pub. by John Wiley). Krieger.

Noise in Physical Systems: Proceedings of the Fifth International Conference on Noise, Bad Nauheim, March 13-16, 1978. Ed. by D. Wolf. (Springer Ser, in Electrophysics: Vol. 2). (Illus.). 1978. 44.00 o.p. (ISBN 0-387-09040-1). Springer-Verlag.

Noise, Noise, Noise. Jerry Grey. (Franklin Institute Bk). (Illus.). (gr. 7-10). 1975. 6.50 o.p. (ISBN 0-664-32575-0, Westminster); pap. 4.50 o.s.i. (ISBN 0-664-34010-5, Westminster). Westminster John Knox.

Noise: Notes from a Rock 'n' Roll Era. Robert Duncan. LC 84-8558. 288p. 1984. 16.45 o.p. (ISBN 0-89919-168-1); pap. 8.70 o.p. (ISBN 0-89919-326-9). Ticknor & Fields.

Noise Pollution: A Guide to Information Sources. Ed. by Clifford R. Bragdon. LC 73-17535. (Man & the Environment Information Guide Ser.: Vol. 5). 544p. 1979. 68.00x o.p. (ISBN 0-8103-1345-6). Gale.

Noise Reduction Techniques in Electronic Systems. Henry W. Ott. LC 75-33165. 294p. 1976. 41.95x o.p. (ISBN 0-471-65726-3). Wiley.

Noise Regulation Reporter. 412.00 o.p. BNA.

Noises Off. pap. 6.95 o.p. Routledge Chapman & Hall.

Noisy Nancy Norris. Louann Gaeddert. LC 65-10180. (ps-1). 1971. PLB 8.95 o.p. (ISBN 0-385-04749-5). Doubleday.

Nomad Queen. James G. White. 320p. (Orig.). 1989. pap. 4.95 o.p. (ISBN 0-8439-2700-3). Dorchester Pub Co.

Nomads of the World. Ed. by Donald J. Crump. LC 78-151946. (Special Publications Series 6: No. 3). (Illus.). 1971. avail. only from Natl. Geog. 7.95 o.p. (ISBN 0-87044-098-5). Natl Geog.

Nomad's Progress: A Biography of Dr. J. E. Zimmerman. Eugene L. Gross. 1977. 6.50 o.p. (ISBN 0-682-48822-4). Exposition-Phoenix.

Nomenclature of Organic Chemistry, Sect. E: Sterochemistry. Ed. by L. C. Cross & W. Klyne. 1976. pap. 35.00 o.p. (ISBN 0-08-021019-8). Pergamon.

Nomenclature of Regular Single-Strand Organic Polymers. Ed. by K. L. Loening. 1977. pap. 10.75 o.p. (ISBN 0-08-021579-3). Pergamon.

Nomenclature, Symbols, Units & Their Usage in Spectrochemical Analysis 11, Data Interpretation, 111 Analytical Flame Spectroscopy & Associated Non-Flame Procedures. International Union of Pure & Applied Chemistry. 1976. pap. 35.00 o.p. (ISBN 0-08-021227-1). Pergamon.

Nomina Anatomica. 4th ed. Ed. by R. Warwick. 1977. 78.50 o.p. (ISBN 0-444-15259-8, Excerpta Medica). Elsevier.

Non-Admitted Insurance in the United States. Samuel H. Weese. (S. S. Huebner Foundation for Insurance Education). 1971. 11.95x o.p. (ISBN 0-256-00683-0). Irwin.

Non-Alcoholic Food Service Beverage Handbook. 2nd ed. Marvin E. Thorner & R. J. Herzberg. (Illus.). 1979. 35.95 o.p. (ISBN 0-87055-279-1). AVI.

Non-Alignment: Perspective & Prospects. Ed. by U. S. Bajpai. 350p. 1983. text ed. 37.50x o.p. (ISBN 0-391-02923-1). Humanities.

Non-Aqueous Electrolytes Handbook, 2 vols. George J. Janz & R. P. T. Tompkins. Vol. 1, 1972. 154.00 o.p. (ISBN 0-12-380401-9); Vol. 2, 1974. 180.00 o.p. (ISBN 0-12-380402-7). Acad Pr.

Non-Commutative Harmonic Analysis. Ed. by J. Carmona et al. 231p. 1975. pap. 16.00 o.p. (ISBN 0-387-07183-0). Springer-Verlag.

Non-Equilibrium Relativistic Kinetic Theory. J. M. Stewart. LC 70-179436. (Lecture Notes in Physics: Vol. 10). iii, 113p. 1971. pap. 10.70 o.p. (ISBN 0-387-05652-1). Springer-Verlag.

Non-Ferrous Metal Works of the World. 4th ed. 1986. 128.00 o.p. (ISBN 0-8002-3990-3). Intl Pubns Serv.

Non-Formal Education in Asia & the Pacific: An Overview. (APEID Occasional Papers). 71p. 1983. pap. 5.00 o.p. (ISBN 0-686-44030-7, UB127, UB). UNIPUB.

Non-Glycolytic Pathways of Metabolism of Glucose. Siegfried Hollmann. Tr. by Oscar Touster. 1964. 53.50 o.p. (ISBN 0-12-352650-7). Acad Pr.

Non-Homogeneous Boundary Value Problems & Applications, Vol. 1. J. L. Lions & E. Magenes. Tr. by P. Kenneth. LC 71-151407. (Grundlehren der Mathematischen Wissenschaften: Vol. 181). 355p. 1972. 38.00 o.p. (ISBN 0-387-05363-8). Springer-Verlag.

Non-Homogeneous Media & Vibration Theory. E. Sanchez-Palencia. (Lecture Notes in Physics Ser.: Vol. 127). 398p. 1980. pap. 28.00 o.p. (ISBN 0-387-10000-8). Springer-Verlag.

Non-Human Primates & Medical Research. Ed. by Geoffrey H. Bourne. 1973. 77.00 o.p. (ISBN 0-12-119150-8). Acad Pr.

Non-Impact Printers in the U. S. International Resource Development, Inc. Staff. 200p. 1983. 985.00x o.p. (ISBN 0-88694-570-4). Intl Res Dev.

Non-Intervention: The Law & Its Import in the Americas. Ann V. Thomas & A. J. Thomas, Jr. LC 56-9845. 496p. 1956. 19.50x o.p. (ISBN 0-87074-112-8). SMU Press.

Non-Invasive Cardiovascular Monitoring by Electrical Impedance Technique. Surya N. Mohapatra. LC 87-3137. 298p. 1989. Repr. of 1981 ed. lib. bdg. write for info. o.p. (ISBN 0-89464-227-8). Krieger.

Non-Isothermal Reaction Analysis. Ed. by E. Koch. 1978. 128.00 o.p. (ISBN 0-12-417350-0). Acad Pr.

Non-Keyboard Data Entry. International Resource Development, Inc. Staff. 201p. 1984. 1650.00x o.p. (ISBN 0-88694-598-4). Intl Res Dev.

Non-Linear Waves in Dispersive Media. V. I. Karpman. Tr. by Ferdinand Cap. 1975. 50.00 o.p. (ISBN 0-08-017720-4). Pergamon.

Non-Negative Matrices in the Mathematical Sciences. Abraham Berman & Robert J. Plemmons. (Computer Sciences & Applied Mathematics Ser.). 1979. 59.00 o.p. (ISBN 0-12-092250-9). Acad Pr.

Non-Parents & Schools: Creating a New Team see Communication Alert Series.

Non-Profit Cultural Organizations. Harvey Horowitz. LC 79-88855. (Patents, Copyrights, Trademards, & Literary Property Course Habndbook Ser.: 1978-1979). 1979. pap. 45.00 o.p. (ISBN 0-686-59555-6, G4-3662). PLI.

Non-Proliferation & Safeguards: Proceedings, American Nuclear Society International Executive Conference. 288p. softcover 40.00 o.p. (ISBN 0-317-33060-8, 650012). Am Nuclear Soc.

Non-Renewable Resource Taxation in the Western States. Ed. by Albert M. Church. (Monograph: No. 77-2). 1977. pap. text ed. 10.00 o.s.i. (ISBN 0-686-20037-3). Lincoln Inst Land.

Non-Sexist Childraising. Carrie Carmichael. LC 76-48497. 1977. 9.95 o.p. (ISBN 0-8070-2738-3); pap. 6.95 o.p. (ISBN 0-8070-2739-1, BP579). Beacon Pr.

Non-Sexual Hormonal Influences on the Electrophysiology of the Brain. James A. Clemens et al. LC 74-6074. (Biology of Sex Ser.). 188p. 1974. text ed. 24.50x o.p. (ISBN 0-8422-7223-2). Irvington.

Non-Sighted & Sighted Adults' Volumetric Perceptions of Functional Objects. T. M. Nelson et al. 21p. 1978. 1.80 o.p. (ISBN 0-89128-965-8, PPR965). Am Foun Blind.

Non-Steroidal Antioestrogens: Molecular Pharmacology & Antitumor Activity. Ed. by R. L. Sutherland & V. C. Jordan. LC 81-67869. (Ludwig Symposia Ser.: No. 1). 1982. 82.50 o.p. (ISBN 0-12-677880-9). Acad Pr.

Non-Stoichiometric Compounds: Tungsten Bronzes; Vanadium Bronzes; & Related Compounds. D. Bevan & P. Hagenmuller. (Pergamon Texts in Inorganic Chemistry: Vol. 1). 154p. 1975. text ed. 29.00 o.p. (ISBN 0-08-018776-5); pap. text ed. 14.00 o.p. (ISBN 0-08-018775-7). Pergamon.

Non-Stop Connolly Show, Nos. 1 & 2. Margaretta D'Arcy & John Arden. (The Non-Stop Connolly Show Ser.). 64p. (Orig., O). 1981. Part 1: Boyhood 1868-1889. pap. 5.95 o.p. (ISBN 0-904383-80-6, NO. 4123). Part 2: Apprenticeship 1889-1896. Routledge Chapman & Hall.

Non-Stop Connolly Show, No. 4. Margaretta D'Arcy & John Arden. (Non-Stop Connolly Show Ser.). 87p. (Orig.). 1981. pap. 5.95 o.p. (ISBN 0-904383-82-2). Routledge Chapman & Hall.

Non-Stop Connolly Show: Professional 1986-1903, No. 3. Margaretta D'Arcy & John Arden. (Non-Stop Connolly Show Ser.). 77p. (Orig.). 1981. pap. 5.95 o.p. (ISBN 0-904383-81-4, NO. 4141). Routledge Chapman & Hall.

Non-Stop Connolly Show: The Great Lockout, 1910-1914, No. 5. Margaretta D'Arcy & John Arden. 112p. (Orig.). 1981. pap. 5.95 o.p. (ISBN 0-904383-83-0). Routledge Chapman & Hall.

Non-Stop Connolly Show: World War & the Rising, No. 6. Margaretta D'Arcy & John Arden. (Non-Stop Connolly Show Ser.). 128p. (Orig.). 1981. pap. 5.95 o.p. (ISBN 0-904383-84-9, NO. 4144). Routledge Chapman & Hall.

Non-Stop Discussion Workbook! Problems for Intermediate & Advanced Students of English. George Rooks. 152p. (Orig.). 1981. pap. text ed. 10.50 o.p. (ISBN 0-88377-171-3). Newbury Hse.

Non-Vocal Communication Techniques & Aids for the Severely Physically Handicapped. Gregg C. Venderheiden & Kate Grilley. LC 76-21835. (Illus.). 246p. 1976. 19.00x o.p. (ISBN 0-936104-57-0, 1108). Pro Ed.

Non-Waste Technology & Production: Proceedings of an International Seminar Held in Paris, Nov.-Dec. 1976. United Nations Economic Commission for Europe. 1978. pap. 180.00 o.p. (ISBN 0-08-022028-2). Pergamon.

Nonaligned Movement in World Politics. Ed. by A. W. Singham. LC 78-51457. 324p. 1978. pap. 7.95 o.p. (ISBN 0-88208-086-5). Chicago Review.

Nonalignment in Contemporary International Relations. Ed. by K. R. Narayanan & K. P. Misra. 275p. 1981. text ed. 27.50x o.p. (ISBN 0-7069-1286-1, Pub by Vikas India). Advent NY.

Nonaqueous Solution Chemistry. Orest Popovych & Reginald P. Tomkins. LC 80-21693. 500p. 1981. 87.00 o.p. (ISBN 0-471-02673-5). Wiley.

Nonbenzenoid Aromatics, Vols. 1-2. Ed. by James P. Snyder. (Organic Chemistry Ser: Vol. 16). 1971. Vol. 2. 77.00 o.p.; Vol. 1. 45.00 o.p. (ISBN 0-12-654002-0); 45.00 o.p. (ISBN 0-685-05139-0). Acad Pr.

Nonbook Cataloguing Sampler. David V. Laertacher. 100p. 1975. pap. 5.00 o.p. (ISBN 0-912556-04-8). Hi Willow.

Nonbroadcast Television Writer's Handbook. William Van Nostran. LC 83-89. (Illus.). 240p. 1983. professional 32.95 o.p. (ISBN 0-914236-82-2). Knowledge Indus.

Noncapitalist Way. I. Andreyev. 195p. 1977. 3.95 o.p. (ISBN 0-8285-0247-1, Pub. by Progress Pubs USSR). Imported Pubns.

Nonclassical Ion Problem. Ed. by H. C. Brown. LC 76-45175. (Illus.). 302p. 1977. 49.50x o.p. (ISBN 0-306-30950-5, Plenum Pr). Plenum Pub.

Noncoherent Optical Processing. G. L. Rogers. LC 77-5453. 192p. 1977. text ed. 33.95 o.p. (ISBN 0-471-73055-6, JW). Krieger.

Nonconformity in the Nineteenth Century. Ed. by David M. Thompson. (Birth of Modern Britain Ser.). 1972. 15.00 o.p. (ISBN 0-7100-7274-0); pap. 9.95x o.p. (ISBN 0-7100-7275-9). Routledge Chapman & Hall.

Nonconscious Social Information Processing. Paul Lewicki. LC 85-15618. 1986. 39.50 o.p. (ISBN 0-12-446120-4); pap. 25.00 o.p. (ISBN 0-12-446121-2). Acad Pr.

Nonconventional Energy Resources. Philip R. Pryde. LC 82-21827. (Environmental Science & Technology Series of Texts & Monographs). 270p. 1983. 40.00 o.p. (ISBN 0-471-86807-8, Pub. by Wiley-Interscience). Wiley.

Nondecision-Making & Community Power: Residential Development Control in Rural Areas. H. Buller & K. Hoggart. (Progress in Planning Ser.: Vol. 25). (Illus.). 74p. 1986. pap. 22.00 o.p. (ISBN 0-08-034277-9, Pub. by PPL). Pergamon.

Nondestructive Evaluation in the Nuclear Industry: Proceedings, American Nuclear Society International Conference, Salt Lake City, February 13-15, 1978. 524p. 44.00 o.p. (ISBN 0-87170-029-8, 700041). Am Nuclear Soc.

Nondestructive Evaluation in the Nuclear Industry. 536p. 1978. 58.00 o.p. (ISBN 0-318-17192-9, 115). Am Soc Nondestructive.

Nondestructive Evaluation: Microstructural Characterization & Reliability Strategies Proceedings. Fall Meeting, Pittsburgh, 1980. Ed. by Otto Buck & Stanley M. Wolf. (Illus.). 410p. 32.00 o.p. (ISBN 0-89520-375-8); members 20.00 o.p. (ISBN 0-317-36255-0); student members 12.00 o.p. (ISBN 0-317-36256-9). ASM.

Nondestructive Examination. (Boiler & Pressure Vessel Code Ser.: Sec. 5). 1980. 65.00 o.p. (ISBN 0-685-76818-X, P00050); pap. 90.00 loose-leaf o.p. (ISBN 0-685-76819-8, V00050). ASME.

Nondestructive Testing in Electronics: Key to Quality-Reliability. LC 86-50205. (Emerging Technologies Ser.: No. 20). (Illus.). 269p. 1986. spiral bound 720.00 o.p. (ISBN 0-914993-28-3). Tech Insights.

None Dare Call it Conspiracy. Gary Allen. 197p. Date not set. 15.00 o.p. (ISBN 0-317-53202-2); pap. 5.00 o.p. Noontide.

None Need Suffer from Asthma: Nor in All Probability Develop Emphysema. Jacob J. Robbins. LC 85-91010. (Illus.). 1985. 25.00 o.p. (ISBN 0-682-40224-9). Exposition-Phoenix.

None of the Above. Rosemary Wells. (gr. 7 up). 1984. pap. 1.25 o.p. (ISBN 0-380-00554-9, 52613). Avon.

None of the Above: Behind the Myth of Scholastic Aptitude. David Owen. 1985. 16.45 o.s.i. (ISBN 0-395-35540-0). HM.

None of These Diseases. S. I. McMillen. 160p. 1963. pap. 2.95 o.p. (ISBN 0-8007-8030-2, Spire Bks). Revell.

None Shall Know. Martha Albrand. 192p. 1973. pap. 0.75 o.p. (ISBN 0-380-01359-2, 14274). Avon.

None to Give Away. Elsie D. Townsend. LC 83-81345. 222p. 1983. pap. 3.95 o.s.i. (ISBN 0-934318-22-0). Falcon Pr Mt.

Nonemissive Electro-Optic Displays. Ed. by A. R. Kmetz & F. K. Von Willisen. LC 76-17060. (Brown Boveri Symposia Ser.). 360p. 1976. 65.00x o.p. (ISBN 0-306-30957-2, Plenum Pr). Plenum Pub.

Nonequilibrium Interfacial Transport Processes. Ed. by J. C. Chen & S. G. Bankoff. 1979. 18.00 o.p. (ISBN 0-686-59664-1, I00124). ASME.

Nonequilibrium Superconductivity. Ed. by V. L. Ginzburg. (Proceedings of the Lebedev Physics Institute of the Academy of Sciences of the U. S. S. R. Ser.: Vol. 174). 282p. 1987. text ed. 89.00 o.p. (ISBN 0-941743-09-8). Nova Sci Pubs.

Nonfamilial Roles of Women & Fertility: Pakistan & the Philippines Compared. Nasra M. Shah & Peter C. Smith. LC 81-12601. (Papers of the East-West Population Institute: No. 73). iv, 47p. (Orig.). 1981. pap. text ed. 1.50 o.p. (ISBN 0-86638-018-3). EW Ctr HI.

Nonfiction Novel. Robert A. Smart. LC 84-22028. 154p. (Orig.). 1985. lib. bdg. 23.00 o.p. (ISBN 0-8191-4200-X); pap. text ed. 9.25 o.p. (ISBN 0-8191-4201-8). U Pr of Amer.

Nongraded Elementary School. rev ed. John I. Goodlad & Robert H. Anderson. (Orig.). 1963. pap. text ed. 7.95 o.p. (ISBN 0-15-566053-5, HC). HarBraceJ.

Noninvasive Assessment of the Cardiovascular System. Ed. by Edward B. Diethrich. LC 82-4785. (Illus.). 432p. 1982. text ed. 50.00 o.p. (ISBN 0-7236-7019-6). Butterworth.

Titles

Noninvasive Brain Imaging: Computed Tomography & Radionuclides. H. J. DeBlanc & J. A. Sorenson. LC 74-27242. (Illus.). 232p. 1975. 23.00 o.p. (ISBN 0-88416-137-4). Year Bk Med.

Noninvasive Cardiac Diagnosis. (Landmark Ser.). 1979. 22.50x o.p. (ISBN 0-8422-4108-6). Irvington.

Noninvasive Cardiovascular Diagnosis. 2nd ed. Ed. by Edward B. Diethrich. LC 80-11233. (Illus.). 630p. 1981. text ed. 59.50 o.p. (ISBN 0-88416-288-5). Year Bk Med.

Nonlinear Analysis: A Collection of Papers in Honor or Eric Rothe. Ed. by Lamberto Cesari & Rangacesari Kannan. 1978. 60.50 o.p. (ISBN 0-12-165550-4). Acad Pr.

Nonlinear & Dynamic Fracture Mechanics, Bk. No. G00152. Ed. by N. Perrone & S. N. Atluri. LC 79-54425. (Applied Mechanics Division Ser.: Vol. 35). 220p. 1979. 30.00 o.p. (ISBN 0-686-62962-0). ASME.

Nonlinear & Random Vibrations. F. Dinca & C. Teodosiu. (Eng.). 1974. 94.50 o.p. (ISBN 0-12-216750-3). Acad Pr.

Nonlinear Differential Equations of Chemically Reacting Systems. George R. Gavalas. LC 68-31619. (Springer Tracts in Natural Philosophy: Vol. 17). 1968. 24.10 o.p. (ISBN 0-387-04345-4). Springer-Verlag.

Nonlinear Equations in Abstract Spaces. Ed. by V. Lakshmikantham. 1978. 60.50 o.p. (ISBN 0-12-434160-8). Acad Pr.

Nonlinear Finite Element Analysis & Adina: Proceedings of the 3rd Adina Conference, Massachussetts, U. S. A., 10-12 June 1981. Ed. by K. J. Bathe. 206p. 1981. 125.00 o.p. (ISBN 0-08-027594-X). Pergamon.

Nonlinear Maxium Entropy Spectral Analysis Methods for Signal Recognition. C. H. Chen. LC 82-8630. (Pattern Recognition & Image Processing Research Studies). 170p. 1982. 52.95 o.p. (ISBN 0-471-10497-3, Pub by Res Stud Pr). Wiley.

Nonlinear Methods of Spectral Analysis. Ed. by S. Haykin. (Topics in Applied Physics: Vol. 34). (Illus.). 1979. 56.00 o.p. (ISBN 0-387-09351-6). Springer-Verlag.

Nonlinear Networks: Theory & Analysis. Ed. by Alan N. Willson, Jr. LC 74-19558. 408p. 1975. 27.65 o.p. (ISBN 0-87942-046-4, PP00414). Inst Electrical.

Nonlinear Operators & the Calculus & Variations: Summer School Held in Bruxelles, 8-19 Sept. 1975. Ed. by J. P. Gossez et al. (Lecture Notes in Mathematics: Vol. 543). 1976. soft cover 17.00 o.p. (ISBN 0-387-07867-3). Springer-Verlag.

Nonlinear Optimatization, 1981. Ed. by M. J. Powell. LC 81-71583. (NATO Conference Ser.). 1982. 82.00 o.p. (ISBN 0-12-563860-4). Acad Pr.

Nonlinear Partial Differential Equations: A Symposium on Methods of Solution. Ed. by W. F. Ames. 1967. 72.00 o.p. (ISBN 0-12-056754-7). Acad Pr.

Nonlinear Partial Differential Equations in Engineering, 2 vols. Ed. by W. F. Ames. (Mathematics in Science & Engineering Ser). Vol. 1, 1965. 49.50 o.p. (ISBN 0-12-056756-3); Vol. 2, 1972. 49.50 o.p. (ISBN 0-12-056755-5). Acad Pr.

Nonlinear Problems in the Physical Sciences & Biology: Proceedings. Battelle Summer Institute, Seattle, Jul. 3-28, 1972. Ed. by I. Stakgold et al. LC 73-78428. (Lecture Notes in Mathematics: Vol. 322). (Illus.). 357p. 1973. pap. 12.90 o.p. (ISBN 0-387-06251-3). Springer-Verlag.

Nonlinear Programming Codes. K. Schittkowski. (Lecture Notes in Economics & Mathematical Systems Ser.: Vol. 183). 242p. 1980. pap. 21.00 o.p. (ISBN 0-387-10247-7). Springer-Verlag.

Nonlinear Programming Three. Ed. by O. L. Mangasarian et al. 1978. 77.00 o.p. (ISBN 0-12-468660-5). Acad Pr.

Nonlinear System Analysis. Austin Blaquiere. (Electrical Science Ser.). 1966. 75.00 o.p. (ISBN 0-12-104350-9). Acad Pr.

Nonlinear Systems: Processing of Random Signals-Classical Analysis. Ed. by Abraham H. Haddad. LC 75-1014. (Benchmark Papers in Electrical Engineering & Computer Science Ser: No. 10). 1975. 74.00 o.p. (ISBN 0-12-786612-4). Acad Pr.

Nonlinear Thermoelasticity. CISM (International Center for Mechanical Sciences Staff. Ed. by R. Stojanovic. (CISM Publications: No. 120). 85p. 1974. pap. 12.40 o.p. (ISBN 0-387-81200-8). Springer-Verlag.

Nonlinear Vibrations in Mechanical & Electrical Systems Pure & Aplied Mechanics, Vol. 2. J. J. Stoker. (Pure & Applied Mathematics Ser.). 294p. 1950. 51.95 o.p. (ISBN 0-470-82830-7). Wiley.

Nonmetropolitan Industrialization. Ed. by Richard E. Lonsdale & H. L. Seyler. LC 78-20887. (Scripta Series in Geography). 196p. 1979. 16.95x o.p. (ISBN 0-470-26631-7). Halsted Pr.

Nonparametric Detection: Theory & Applications. Ed. by S. A. Kassam & J. B. Thomas. LC 79-22557. (Benchmark Papers in Electrical Engineering & Computer Science Ser.: Vol. 23). 349p. 1982. 59.95 o.p. (ISBN 0-87933-359-6). Van Nos Reinhold.

Nonparametric Probability Density Estimation. Richard A. Tapia & James R. Thompson. LC 77-17249. (Illus.). 1978. text ed. 24.50x o.p. (ISBN 0-8018-2031-6). Johns Hopkins.

Nonparametric Trend Analysis. George A. Ferguson. 61p. 1965. pap. 3.95x o.p. (ISBN 0-7735-0161-4, McGill Canada). U of Toronto Pr.

Nonprint in the Elementary Curriculum: Readings for Reference. Ed. by James L. Thomas. LC 81-15672. 155p. 1982. text ed. 17.50 o.p. (ISBN 0-87287-273-4). Libs Unl.

Nonprint Media in Academic Libraries. Ed. by Pearce S. Grove. LC 74-23972. (ACRL Publications in Librarianship: No. 34). 239p. 1975. pap. 11.00x o.p. (ISBN 0-8389-0153-0). ALA.

Nonprofit Firms in a Three-Sector Economy. Ed. by Michelle J. White. LC 81-52791. (Coupe Ser.: No. 6). (Illus.). 181p. (Orig.). 1981. pap. text ed. 12.75 o.p. (ISBN 0-87766-312-2). Urban Inst.

Nonprofit Organization Handbook. Tracy D. Connors. LC 78-26691. (Illus.). 1980. text ed. 62.50 o.p. (ISBN 0-07-012422-1). McGraw.

Nonreactive Measures in the Social Science. 2nd ed. Eugene J. Webb & Donald T. Campbell. 1981. pap. 17.95 o.p. (ISBN 0-395-30767-8). HM.

Nonsalary Compensation for Employees of Independent Schools. Ned A. Miller. 1984. pap. text ed. 10.00 o.p. NAIS.

Nonsense Anthology. facsimile ed. Ed. by Carolyn Wells. LC 76-128160. (Granger Index Reprint Ser.). 289p. 1982. Repr. of 1902 ed. text ed. 18.00 o.p. (ISBN 0-8290-0509-9). Irvington.

Nonsense Mutations & RNA Suppressors. Ed. by J. E. Celis & J. D. Smith. 1979. 82.50 o.p. (ISBN 0-12-164550-9). Acad Pr.

Nonstandard Analysis: A Practical Guide with Applications. R. Lutz & M. Goze. (Lecture Notes in Mathematics Ser.: Vol. 881). 261p. 1981. pap. 16.80 o.p. (ISBN 0-387-10879-3). Springer-Verlag.

Nonstoichiometry, Diffusion, & Electrical Conductivity in Binary Metal Oxides. Per Kofstad. LC 74-177885. 382p. 1972. 31.50 o.p. (ISBN 0-471-49776-2, Pub. by Wiley). Krieger.

Nontraditional Therapy & Counseling with the Aging. S. Stansfeld Sargent. LC 80-11303. (Adulthood & Aging Ser.). 256p. 1980. text ed. 19.95 o.p. (ISBN 0-8261-2800-9); pap. 15.95 o.p. (ISBN 0-8261-2801-7). Springer Pub.

Nonvascular Plants: An Evolutionary Survey. R. F. Scagel et al. 570p. 1982. text ed. (ISBN 0-534-01029-6). Wadsworth Pub.

Nonverbal Behavior: Applications & Cultural Implications. Ed. by Aaron Wolfgang. 1979. 19.95 o.p. (ISBN 0-12-761350-1). Acad Pr.

Nonverbal Communication. Albert Mehrabian. LC 72-172859. 1972. 29.95 o.p. (ISBN 0-202-25091-1). Aldine de Gruyter.

Nonviolence in Peace & War, 1942, 2 vols. Mohandas K. Gandhi. Incl. Nonviolence in Peace & War, 1949. Mohandas K. Ghandi. LC 72-147618. (Library of War & Peace; Non-Resis. & Non-Vio.). Set. lib. bdg. 76.00 o.p. (ISBN 0-8240-0375-6); lib. bdg. 38.00 ea. o.p. Garland Pub.

Nonviolence in Peace & War, 1949 see Nonviolence in Peace & War, 1942.

Nonviolence: Not First for Export. James Bristol. 1972. pap. 0.30 o.p. (ISBN 0-686-95383-5). Am Fr Serv Comm.

Nonviolent Struggle in the Middle East. Scott Kennedy & Mubarak Awad. 40p. 1985. 2.95 o.p. (ISBN 0-86571-062-7). New Soc Pubs.

Noodles du Jour. Wally Armbruster. LC 75-42818. (Illus.). 192p. 1976. pap. 2.25 o.p. (ISBN 0-570-03729-8, 12-2631). Concordia.

Nooks & Crannies of the New England Coast. Samuel A. Drake. LC 69-19883. 464p. 1969. Repr. of 1875 ed. 43.00x o.p. (ISBN 0-8103-3827-0). Gale.

Noonblaze. Milan Chiba. 288p. (Orig.). 1981. pap. 2.95 o.p. (ISBN 0-8439-1013-5, Pub. by Leisure Bks CT). Dorchester Pub Co.

Noonday Devil. Ralph McInerny. LC 84-45042. 288p. 1985. 15.95 o.p. (ISBN 0-689-11488-5, Atheneum). Macmillan.

Nop's Trials. Donald McCaig. 1984. lib. bdg. 16.95 o.p. (ISBN 0-8161-3734-X, Large Print Bks). G K Hall.

Nor Live So Long. Sara Woods. (Large Print Bks., Nightingale Ser.). 331p. 1987. pap. 15.95x o.p. (ISBN 0-8161-4225-4, Large Print Bks). G K Hall.

Norah & the Whale. Robert Swindells. (Illus.). (gr. 4-8). 1981. text ed. 8.50 o.s.i. (ISBN 0-08-024980-9). Pergamon.

Norah's Ark. Ann Cartwright & Reg Cartwright. 1984. 9.50 o.s.i. (ISBN 0-671-50763-X, Little Simon). S&S.

Nordamerika im Kartenbild. Karl Lenz & W. Patzer. (Kartographische Miniaturen Ser.: Nr. 6). (Illus.). pap. 9.85 o.p. (ISBN 3-920597-28-1). M S Rosenberg.

Nordic Area Studies in North America: A Survey & Directory of the Human & Material Resources. Donald E. Askey et al. LC 75-21996. 153p. 1975. pap. text ed. 7.95x o.p. (ISBN 0-89067-056-0). Am Scandinavian.

Nordic Skier's Guide to Montana. Elaine Sedlack. LC 80-71026. 176p. (Orig.). 1981. pap. text ed. 6.95 o.p. (ISBN 0-934318-04-2). Falcon Pr MT.

Nordic Sound. John Yoell. LC 74-773034. 1974. 9.50 o.s.i. (ISBN 0-8008-5603-1, Crescendo). Taplinger.

Norfolk Churches. H. Munro Cautley. (Illus.). 1979. 27.00 o.p. (ISBN 0-85115-022-5, Pub. by Boydell & Brewer). Longwood Pub Group.

Norfolk Island: An Outline of Its History, 1774-1981. 3rd ed. Merval Hoare. LC 82-4719. (Illus.). 188p. 1983. pap. 12.95 o.p. U of Queensland Pr.

Norm & Form: Studies in the Art of the Renaissance, No. I. E. H. Gombrich. LC 84-28113. (Illus.). xii, 164p. 1985. pap. 14.95 o.s.i. (ISBN 0-226-30216-4). U of Chicago Pr.

Normal Adolescence: Its Dynamics & Impact. Group for the Advancement of Psychiatry. LC 68-12511. 1968. pap. 3.45 o.p. (ISBN 0-684-71781-6, SL 143, ScribT). Scribner.

Normal & Malignant Cell Growth. Ed. by R. J. Fry et al. (Recent Results in Cancer Research: Vol. 17). (Illus.). 1969. 47.00 o.p. (ISBN 0-387-04680-1). Springer-Verlag.

Normal & Pathological Development of Energy Metabolism. Ed. by E. A. Hommes & C. J. Van Den Berg. 1976. 48.50 o.p. (ISBN 0-12-354560-9). Acad Pr.

Normal Lung: Its Diseases. Michael E. Whitcomb. LC 81-16816. (Illus.). 360p. 1982. pap. text ed. 24.95 o.p. (ISBN 0-8016-5421-1). Mosby.

Normal Radiologic Patterns & Variances of the Human Skeleton: An X-Ray Atlas of Adults & Children. Rudolf Birkner. LC 78-692. (Illus.). 574p. 1978. text ed. 88.00 o.s.i. (ISBN 0-8067-0211-7). Urban & S.

Norman Conquest of the North: The Region & Its Transformation, 1000-1135. William E. Kapelle. LC 79-10200. 329p. 1980. 27.50x o.p. (ISBN 0-8078-1371-0). U of NC Pr.

Norman Conquests: Table Manners, Living Together, Round & Round the Garden. Alan Ayckbourn. LC 78-73051. 1979. pap. 6.95 o.p. (ISBN 0-394-17082-2, B422, BC). Grove.

Norman England. Peter Lane. (Visual Sources Ser.). (Illus.). 96p. (gr. 7 up). 1980. text ed. 17.95 o.p. (ISBN 0-7134-3356-6, Pub. by Batsford England). David & Charles.

Norman Foster: RIBA Gold Medallist, 1983. Valerie J. Nurcombe. (Architecture Ser.: A 1396). 26p. 1985. 3.75 o.p. (ISBN 0-89028-406-7). Vance Biblios.

Norman Foster, Richard Rogers, James Stirling: New Directions in British Architecture. Deyan Sudjic. LC 86-71618. (Illus.). 208p. 1987. 35.00 o.p. (ISBN 0-500-34101-X). Thames Hudson.

Norman Heritage Ten Sixty-Six to Twelve Hundred. Trevor Rowley. (Making of Britain Ser.). (Illus.). 224p. 1983. 21.95x o.p. (ISBN 0-7100-9413-2). Routledge Chapman & Hall.

Norman Mark's Chicago. Norman Mark. 240p. (Orig.). 1987. pap. 8.95 o.p. (ISBN 1-55652-003-4). Chicago Review.

Norman Monasteries & Their English Possessions. Donald Matthew. LC 78-26293. (Oxford Historical Ser.). 1979. Repr. of 1962 ed. lib. bdg. 35.00x o.p. (ISBN 0-313-20847-6, MANM). Greenwood.

Norman Rockwell Bicycle Tour of Stockbridge. Ed. by SnO Publications Staff. (Illus., Orig.). 1980. pap. 5.00 o.p. (ISBN 0-937814-00-8). SnO Pubns.

Norman Rockwell: Special Days Come to Life. Norman Rockwell. (Abbeville Pop-Up Bks.). (Illus.). 12p. (gr. k-4). 1987. 12.95 o.p. (ISBN 0-89659-505-6). Abbeville Pr.

Norman Rockwell Treasury. Thomas S. Baechner. 1987. 16.98 o.p. (ISBN 0-8317-6412-0, Gallery Bks). Smith Pubs.

Norman Rockwell's America. Christopher Finch. LC 75-15703. (Illus.). 314p. 1975. 45.00 o.p. (ISBN 0-8109-0454-3). Abrams.

Norman Rockwell's America. Christopher Finch. (Illus.). 256p. 1985. 19.95 o.p. (ISBN 0-8109-8071-1). Abrams.

Norman Rockwell's Christmas Book. Ed. by Molly Rockwell. LC 77-7087. (Illus.). 1977. 19.95 o.p. (ISBN 0-8109-1583-9). Abrams.

Norman Table: The Traditional Cooking of Normandy. Claude Guermont & Paul Frumkin. (Illus.). 288p. 1985. 19.95 o.p. (ISBN 0-684-18319-6, ScribT). Scribner.

Norman Thomas. rev. ed. Harry Fleischman. (Illus.). 1969. 6.95 o.p. (ISBN 0-393-07452-8). Norton.

Normandie: Her Life & Times. Harvey Ardman. 432p. 1985. 22.95 o.p. (ISBN 0-531-09784-6). Watts.

Normandie Triangle. Justin Scott. LC 81-67220. 480p. 1981. 13.95 o.p. (ISBN 0-87795-346-5, Arbor Hse). Morrow.

Normandy & Channel Islands Pilot: Calais to St. Malo. 6th ed. Mark Brackenbury. (Adlard Coles Pilotage Ser.). (Illus.). 186p. 1986. 42.50 o.p. (ISBN 0-229-11781-3, Pub. by Adlard Coles). Sheridan.

Norms of Word Association. Ed. by Leo Postman & Geoffrey Keppel. 1970. 60.00 o.p. (ISBN 0-12-563050-6). Acad Pr.

Norris & Campbell's Anaesthetics, Resuscitation, & Intensive Care. 6th ed. Donald Campbell & Alastair A. Spence. (Illus.). 254p. 1985. pap. text ed. 14.75 o.p. (ISBN 0-443-03005-7). Churchill.

Norris Case & Benefit Planning. (Tax Law & Estate Planning Course Handbook Ser.: Vol. 193). 153p. 1983. 45.00 o.p. (ISBN 0-317-11439-5, J4-3535). PLI.

Norse Discoveries & Explorations in America: 982-1362. H. R. Holand. (Illus.). 16.25 o.p. (ISBN 0-8446-0703-7). Peter Smith.

North. Ward Abbott. (Illus.). 1975. lib. bdg. 10.00 o.p. (ISBN 0-916908-38-0); pap. 2.00 o.p. (ISBN 0-916908-01-1). Place Herons.

North America & the Great Ice Age. new ed. Charles L. Matsch. (Earth Science Paperback Ser.). (Illus.). 1976. text ed. 16.95 o.p. (ISBN 0-07-040935-8). McGraw.

North American Dye Plants. Anne Bliss. (Illus.). 1980. pap. 5.95 o.p. (ISBN 0-684-16393-4). Scribner.

North American Game Birds & Mammals. A. Starker Leopold et al. (Illus.). 224p. 1981. 19.95 o.s.i. (ISBN 0-684-17270-4, ScribT). Scribner.

North American Game Birds & Mammals. A. Starker Leopold et al. (Illus.). 208p. 1984. pap. 14.95 o.p. (ISBN 0-684-17923-7, ScribT). Scribner.

North American Geology: Early Writings. Ed. by R. M. Hazen. LC 79-708. (Benchmark Papers in Geology: Vol. 51). 356p. 1983. 46.50 o.p. (ISBN 0-87933-345-6). Van Nos Reinhold.

North American Horticulture. American Horticultural Society Staff. 448p. 1982. 50.00 o.s.i. (ISBN 0-684-17604-1, ScribT). Scribner.

North American Hudsons: The 4-6-4 Steam Locomotive. Lloyd E. Stagner & James J. Reisdorff. (Illus.). 108p. 1987. pap. 20.00 o.p. (ISBN 0-9609568-8-3). South Platte.

North American Indian Artifacts: A Collector's Identification & Value Guide. 2nd ed. Lar Hothem. (Illus.). 440p. 1980. pap. 9.95 o.p. (ISBN 0-89689-015-5). Bks Americana.

North American Indian Captivity. W-llcomb E. Washburn & John Aubrey. LC 76-7664. (Reference Library of the Humanities Ser.: Vol. 70). (Illus.). 1977. lib. bdg. 24.00 o.p. (ISBN 0-8240-1736-6). Garland Pub.

North American Indian Wars. Richard Dillon. (Illus.). 256p. 29.95 o.p. (ISBN 0-87196-641-7). Facts on File.

North American Indians: An Account of the American Indians North of Mexico. Rose A. Palmer. LC 74-11848. (Illus.). 309p. 1975. Repr. of 1929 ed. lib. bdg. 25.00x o.p. (ISBN 0-8154-0494-8). Cooper Sq.

North American Radio-TV Station Guide. 15th ed. Vane A. Jones. LC 63-23371. 232p. 1984. pap. 9.95 o.p. (ISBN 0-672-22296-5). Sams.

North & South. Elizabeth Gaskell. 1968. Repr. of 1914 ed. 9.95x o.p. (ISBN 0-460-00680-0, Evman). Biblio Dist.

North & South. John Jakes. 1985. 29.95 o.p. (ISBN 0-8161-3952-0, Large Print Bks); pap. 14.95 o.p. (ISBN 0-8161-3953-9). G K Hall.

North & South: After Cancun - Where to? Takeshi Watanabe et al. Trilateral Comm.

North Atlantic Civilization. Michael Kraus. 7.75 o.p. (ISBN 0-8446-2403-9). Peter Smith.

North Beach: The Italian Heart of San Francisco. Richard Dillon. Ed. by Lynn L. Davis. (Illus.). 272p. 1985. 35.00 o.p. (ISBN 0-89141-187-9). Presidio Pr.

North Carolina Almanac: And Book of Facts. Ed. by James Crutchfield. LC 86-29752. 1986. 14.95 o.p. (ISBN 0-934395-35-7); pap. 9.95 o.p. (ISBN 0-934395-36-5). Rutledge Hill Pr.

North Carolina Almanac & Book of Facts. James A. Crutchfield. 1988. 16.95 o.p. (ISBN 0-934395-60-8). Rutledge Hill Pr.

North Carolina Artists Exhibition 1984. Ed. by Huston Paschal. (Illus.). 72p. 1984. pap. 5.00 o.p. (ISBN 0-88259-099-5). NCMA.

North Carolina Artists Exhibition, 1987. Ed. by Huston Paschal & Jenny Monbouquette. LC 84-650670. (Illus.). 71p. 1987. pap. 5.00 o.p. (ISBN 0-88259-954-2). NCMA.

North Carolina Collection & Enforcement of Judgments. Wake Forest University School of Law Staff. 55.00cancelled o.s.i. (ISBN 0-318-19518-6). Wake Forest Law.

North Carolina Constitutional & Statutory Provisions with Respect to Higher Education. rev. ed. Ed. by Robert E. Phay. 1984. pap. 7.50 o.p. (ISBN 0-686-17563-8). Institute Government.

North Carolina Crimes: A Guidebook for Law Enforcement Officers. Stevens H. Clarke et al. 360p. 1980. 6.50 o.p. (ISBN 0-686-39462-3). Institute Government.

North Carolina Criminal Law & Procedure. Michie Company Editorial Staff. (State Practice Publications Ser.). 1092p. 1985. pap. 25.00x o.p. (ISBN 0-87215-977-9). Michie Co.

North Carolina Dog Law Manual. Patrice Solberg. 55p. 1978. 3.00 o.p. (ISBN 0-686-39477-1). Institute Government.

North Carolina Dog Law Manual: 1979 Supplement. Compiled by Patricia Solberg. 2.00 o.p. (ISBN 0-686-39478-X). Institute Government.

North Carolina Fifth Annual Review. Wake Forest University School of Law Staff. 80.00cancelled o.s.i. (ISBN 0-318-18445-1). Wake Forest Law.

North Carolina Guidebook for Registers of Deeds. 4th ed. William A. Campbell. 109p. 1982. 7.00 o.p. (ISBN 0-686-39431-3). Institute Government.

North Carolina Hiking Trails. Allen DeHart. (Illus.). 346p. (Orig.). 1982. pap. 12.95 o.p. (ISBN 0-910146-37-3). AMC Books.

North Carolina Land Grants in Tennessee, 1778 to 1791. Goldene F. Burgner. 214p. 1981. 25.00 o.s.i. (ISBN 0-89308-205-8). Southern Hist Pr.

North Carolina Law & the Health Department. Patrice Solberg. 218p. 1978. 8.00 o.p. (ISBN 0-686-39464-X). Institute Government.

North Carolina Legislation, 1981: A Summary of Legislation in the 1981 General Assembly of Interest to North Carolina Public Officials. Ed. by Ann L. Sawyer. 384p. 1981. 10.00 o.p. (ISBN 0-686-39451-8). Institute Government.

North Carolina Legislation, 1982: A Summary of Legislation in the 1982 General Assembly of Interest to North Carolina Public Officials. Ed. by Robert L. Farb. 63p. 1982. 5.00 o.p. (ISBN 0-686-39452-6). Institute Government.

North Carolina Manual for Magistrates. 3rd. ed. Joan G. Brannon. 1988. write for info. o.p. Institute Government.

North Carolina Manufacturers Directory, 1987-88. 682p. 1987. pap. 79.00 o.p. (ISBN 0-318-02904-9). Manufacturers.

North Carolina Modern Erotica. Ed. by David Hunter. (Carolina Blue Series: Vol. 1). (Illus.). 100p. 1987. pap. 5.98x o.p. (ISBN 0-915153-22-X). Gold Star Pr.

North Carolina Modern Erotica. Ed. by David Hunter. (Carolina Blue Ser.: Vol. 3). (Illus.). 100p. (Orig.). 1988. pap. 5.98x o.p. (ISBN 0-915153-30-0). Gold Star Pr.

North Carolina Modern Erotica, Vol. 2. Ed. by David Hunter. (Carolina Blue Ser.). (Illus.). 100p. (Orig.). 1987. pap. 5.98x o.p. (ISBN 0-915153-25-4). Gold Star Pr.

North Carolina: New Directions for an Old Lane: An Illustrated History of Tar Heel Enterprise. David E. Brown. LC 85-22766. 240p. 1985. 24.95 o.p. (ISBN 0-89781-157-7). Windsor Pubns Inc.

North Carolina-North Carolina State Joke Book. S. C. Lee. LC 81-50801. 1981. pap. 2.95 o.p. (ISBN 0-87397-190-6). Strode.

North Carolina: Our People, Places & Past. James D. Charlet et al. (Illus.). 320p. (gr. 4 up). 1988. lib. bdg. 22.95 o.p. (ISBN 0-89089-319-5). Carolina Acad Pr.

North Carolina Professional Malpractice. Wake Forest University School of Law Staff. 55.00cancelled o.s.i. (ISBN 0-318-18432-X). Wake Forest Law.

North Carolina Rules of Court. 908p. 1985. pap. 18.00 o.p. (ISBN 0-314-25091-3). West Pub.

North Carolina, South Carolina, Virginia State Industrial Directory, 1986. 724p. 1986. 100.00 o.p. (ISBN 0-318-22823-8). Manufacturers.

North Carolina Supreme Court Cases on Zoning, Subdivision Regulation & Urban Renewal: Supplements. Philip P. Green. 274p. 1984. pap. 13.00 o.p. Institute Government.

North Carolina: The History of a Southern State. 3rd rev. ed. Hugh T. Lefler & Albert R. Newsome. LC 72-81330. (Illus.). xiv, 808p. 1973. 16.95 o.p. (ISBN 0-8078-1207-2); text ed. 19.95x o.p. (ISBN 0-8078-1202-1). U of NC Pr.

North Carolina Trial Book Criminal: Master Case. Wake Forest University, Continuing Legal Education Staff. LC 82-235375. 1982. 70.00 o.p. Wake Forest Law.

North Carolina Wills & Probate Handbook. Wake Forest University School of Law Staff. 55.00cancelled o.s.i. (ISBN 0-318-18436-2). Wake Forest Law.

North Carolina's Extinct Prehistoric Mammals. C. D. Huneycutt. (Illus.). 100p. (Orig.). 1987. pap. 5.80 o.p. (ISBN 0-915153-24-6). Gold Star Pr.

North Carolina's Fair Sentencing Act: Explanation, Text, & Felony Classification Table. Rev. ed. Stevens H. Clarke & Elizabeth W. Rubinsky. 66p. 1981. 5.00 o.p. (ISBN 0-686-39463-1). Institute Government.

North Central California Counties Public Schools, 1986, Vol. 6. Lillian S. Clancy. (California Public Schools Ser.: How Are They Doing?). 400p. (Orig.). 1985. pap. 24.95 o.p. (ISBN 0-939580-33-0). CA Schl Surveys.

North Central California Counties Public Schools, 1987, Vol. 6. Lillian S. Clancy. (California Public Schools: How Are They Doing? Ser.). 400p. (Orig.). 1987. pap. 24.95 o.p. (ISBN 0-939580-42-X). CA Schl Surveys.

North Central California Counties Public Schools, 1988, Vol. 6. Lillian S. Clancy. (California Public Schools: How Are They Doing? Ser.). 400p. (Orig.). 1988. pap. 25.95 o.p. (ISBN 0-939580-50-0). CA Schl Surveys.

North Dakota Court Rules. 912p. 1986. pap. 43.50 o.p. (ISBN 0-314-23509-4). West Pub.

North Dakota Directory of Manufactures 1987-88. 146p. 1986. pap. 15.00 o.p. (ISBN 0-318-02905-7). Manufacturers.

North Light. Erik Riss-Carstensen. LC 61-17970. 360p. 1962. (ISBN 0-8022-1347-2). Philos Lib.

North of the Circle. Frank Illingworth. 1952. (ISBN 0-8022-0775-8). Philos Lib.

North of the Narrows: Men & Women of the Upper Priest Lake Country Idaho. Claude C. Simpson & Catherine Simpson. LC 80-51781. (Illus.). 332p. (Orig.). 1981. pap. 11.95 o.p. (ISBN 0-89301-069-3). U of Idaho Pr.

North Pacific Cretaceous Trigoniid Genus Yaadia. Lou E. Saul. (UC Publications in Geological Science: Vol. 119). 1978. pap. 20.00x o.p. (ISBN 0-520-09582-0). U of Cal Pr.

North Platte Canteen. James J. Reisdorff. (Illus.). 36p. 1986. pap. 6.50 o.p. (ISBN 0-9609568-5-9). South Platte.

North Runner. R. D. Lawrence. LC 78-23576. (Illus.). 1979. 8.95 o.s.i. (ISBN 0-03-041551-9). H Holt & Co.

North Sea. Heinrich Heine. Tr. by Howard M. Jones. LC 73-83869. 137p. 1916. 14.95 o.p. (ISBN 0-87548-266-X); pap. 4.95 o.p. (ISBN 0-87548-272-4). Open Court.

North Sea Harbours & Pilotage: Calais to Den Helder. 6th ed. Jack Coote. (Adlard Coles Pilotage Ser.). (Illus.). 128p. 1983. 42.50 o.p. (ISBN 0-229-11810-0, Pub. by Adlard Coles). Sheridan.

North Sea Oil & Scotland's Economic Prospects. T. M. Lewis & I. H. McNicoll. 147p. 1978. 25.00 o.p. (ISBN 0-85664-578-8, Pub. by Croom Helm Ltd). Routledge Chapman & Hall.

North Sea Oil: Resource Requirements for U. K. Development. J. Kenneth Klitz. (Illus.). 1981. 51.00 o.p. (ISBN 0-08-024442-4). Pergamon.

North Sea Platform Guide. 1000p. 1985. 280.00 o.s.i. (P1950). PennWell Bks.

North Sea Science: Papers Presented at the NATO Science Committee Conference, November 1971. Ed. by Edward D. Goldberg. (Illus.). 420p. 1973. 45.00x o.p. (ISBN 0-262-07056-1). MIT Pr.

North Sea Subsea Construction Guide. 8th ed. 1000p. 1986. 320.00 o.s.i. (P1952). PennWell Bks.

North South Debate. L. K. Jha. 153p. 1982. text ed. 15.00x o.p. (ISBN 0-391-02769-7, 41257). Humanities.

North to Freedom. Anne S. Holm. Tr. by L. W. Kingsland. LC 65-12612. (gr. 7 up). 1965. 5.95 o.p. (ISBN 0-15-257550-2, HJ). HarBraceJ.

North to Montana. Steven C. Lawrence. 160p. 1981. pap. 1.95 o.p. (ISBN 0-8439-0985-4, Pub. by Leisure Bks CT). Dorchester Pub Co.

North to Rabaul. Christopher Wood. LC 79-52253. 1979. 9.95 o.p. (ISBN 0-87795-233-7, Arbor Hse). Morrow.

Northeast. rev. ed. Ed. by Jerry Jennings. LC 78-54254. (United States Ser.). (Illus.). (gr. 5 up). 1979. text ed. 9.93 ea. 1-4 copies o.p. (ISBN 0-88296-057-1); text ed. 7.94 ea. 5 or more copies o.p.; tchrs.' annotated ed. 13.68 o.p. (ISBN 0-88296-347-3). Gateway Pr MI.

Northeast & Great Lake Wind Atlas. De Harpporte. 1983. 24.95 o.p. (ISBN 0-442-21821-4). Van Nos Reinhold.

Northeast Asia in Prehistory. Chester S. Chard. LC 73-2040. (Illus.). 232p. 1974. 21.50x o.p. (ISBN 0-299-06430-1). U of Wis Pr.

Northeast Asian Security: A Korean Perspective. Young K. Cha. (Significant Issues Ser.). 50p. (Orig.). pap. 6.95 o.p. (ISBN 0-89206-111-1). CSI Studies.

Northern Adirondack Ski Tours: Thirty Selected Tours for the Novice to Expert Skier. Tony Goodwin. LC 81-22785. (Illus.). 1982. pap. 7.95 o.s.i. (ISBN 0-935272-19-4). ADK Mtn Club.

Northern California Job Bank: A Comprehensive Guide to Major Local Employers. Adams, Robert Lang, & Associates Staff. (Job Bank Ser.). 249p. (Orig.). 1982. pap. 9.95 o.p. (ISBN 0-937860-12-3). Adams Inc MA.

Northern California Public Schools: How Are They Doing? (1984) Lillian S. Clancy. (How Are They Doing Ser.). 1200p. (Orig.). 1984. pap. 40.00 o.p. (ISBN 0-939580-07-1). CA Schl Surveys.

Northern Central California Counties Public Schools: How Are They Doing? 1985, Vol. 6. Lillian S. Clancy. (California Public Schools Ser.). 307p. (Orig.). 1984. pap. 23.95 o.p. (ISBN 0-939580-24-1). CA Schl Surveys.

Northern England. Cuchlaine A. King. (Geomorphology of the British Isles Ser.). 216p. 1976. pap. 10.95x o.p. (ISBN 0-416-84460-X, 6527). Routledge Chapman & Hall.

Northern Frontier Problems. Ed. by W. Tietze. 100p. 1975. pap. 23.00 o.p. (ISBN 0-08-019675-6). Pergamon.

Northern Ireland, Nineteen Twenty-One to Nineteen Seventy-Four: A Select Bibliography. Richard R. Deutsch. LC 75-5516. (Reference Library of Social Science: No. 2). 160p. 1974. lib. bdg. 25.00 o.p. (ISBN 0-8240-1060-4). Garland Pub.

Northern Ireland: Report of the National Lawyers Guild. 10.00 o.p. Natl Lawyers Guild.

Northern Ireland Scrapbook. John Chartres et al. (Illus.). 160p. (Orig.). 1987. pap. 14.95 o.p. (ISBN 0-85368-896-6, Pub. by Arms & Armour). Sterling.

Northern Italian Cooking. Biba Caggiano. LC 81-82276. 1981. 12.95 o.p. (ISBN 0-89586-127-5); pap. 9.95 o.p. (ISBN 0-89586-119-4). Price Stern.

Northern Italy: From the Alps to Rome. Alta Macadam. (Blue Guide Ser.). (Illus.). 1982. 24.95 o.p. (ISBN 0-393-01546-7); pap. 15.95 o.p. (ISBN 0-393-00099-0). Norton.

Northern Lights. Howard Norman. 224p. 1987. 17.45 o.s.i. (ISBN 0-671-53231-6). Summit Bks.

Northern Lights. I. Zheleznova. 1976. 6.45 o.p. (ISBN 0-8285-1807-6, Pub. by Progress Pubs USSR). Imported Pubns.

Northern Magic. Janet Dailey. (Nightingales Ser.). 218p. 1987. pap. 10.95x o.s.i. (ISBN 0-8161-4192-4, Large Print Bks.). G K Hall.

Northern Marianas Covenant & American Territorial Relations. Paul M. Leary. LC 80-10945. (IGS Research Report: No. 80-1). 55p. (Orig.). 1980. pap. 3.50x o.p. (ISBN 0-87772-269-2). UCB IGS.

Northern Plainsmen: Adaptive Strategy & Agrarian Life. John W. Bennett. LC 76-75043. (Worlds of Man Ser.). (Illus.). 1970. text ed. 23.95x o.s.i. (ISBN 0-88295-602-7); pap. text ed. 13.95x o.s.i. (ISBN 0-88295-603-5). Harlan Davidson.

Northern Seas, Hardy Sailors. George Whiteley. (Illus.). 320p. 1982. 18.95 o.p. (ISBN 0-393-03270-1). Norton.

Northern Shoshoni. Brigham D. Madsen. LC 78-53138. (Illus.). 262p. (Orig.). 1980. 17.95 o.s.i. (ISBN 0-87004-289-0); pap. 12.95 o.s.i. (ISBN 0-87004-266-1). Caxton.

Northern Sphinx: Iceland & the Icelanders from the Settlement to the Present Day. Sigurdur A. Magnusson. 1977. lib. bdg. 13.00x o.p. (ISBN 0-7735-0277-7, McGill Canada). U of Toronto Pr.

Northern Tribune: A Periodical for the People, Vols. 1-2, No. 9. 1970. Repr. of 1855 ed. lib. bdg. 30.00x o.p. (ISBN 0-8371-9226-9, NU00). Greenwood.

Northern Words in Modern English see Persian Words in English.

Northmen, Columbus & Cabot, Nine Eighty-Five to Fifteen Three. Ed. by Julius E. Olson & Edward G. Bourne. (Original Narratives Ser.). 443p. 1967. Repr. of 1906 ed. 21.50x o.p. (ISBN 0-06-480095-4). B&N Imports.

Northrop Frye on Culture & Literature: A Collection of Review Essays. Northrop Frye. Intro. by Robert D. Denham. LC 77-12917. 1980. pap. text ed. 5.50x o.s.i. (ISBN 0-226-26648-6, P867, Phoen). U of Chicago Pr.

Northrop Frye on Culture & Literature: A Collection of Review Essays. Northrop Frye. Ed. by Robert D. Denham. LC 77-12917. (Illus.). 1978. lib. bdg. 10.00x o.s.i. (ISBN 0-226-26647-8). U of Chicago Pr.

Northstar One. David W. Howell. 1989. price not set o.p. (ISBN 0-538-70021-1, JC40AB). SW Pub.

Northwest Best Places. 6th ed. David Brewster. (Best Places Ser.). Orig. Title: Best Places. (Illus.). 500p. (Orig.). 1985. pap. 12.95 o.p. (ISBN 0-912365-06-4). Sasquatch Bks.

Northwest Coast Photographs of Edward Dossetter. Pamela Haas. 1981. Ayer Co Pubs.

Northwest Mileposts. 1988. 18.00 o.p. (ISBN 0-317-67713-6). Alaska Northwest.

Northwest Mileposts, 1986. Ed. by Alaska Northwest Publishing Staff. (Illus.). 500p. (Orig.). 1986. pap. 12.95 premier ed. o.p. (ISBN 0-88240-275-7). Alaska Northwest.

Northwest North Central & Alaska Wind Atlas. 1983. 24.95 o.p. (ISBN 0-442-21824-9). Van Nos Reinhold.

Northwest Passage. Kenneth Roberts. 1983. pap. 2.95 o.p. (ISBN 0-449-20451-0, Crest). Fawcett.

Northwest Passage. Time-Life Books Editors & Brendan Lehane. (Seafarers Ser.). (Illus.). 192p. 1981. 13.95 o.p. (ISBN 0-8094-2730-3). Time-Life.

Northwest Shore Dives. Steve Fischnaller. LC 86-71709. (Illus.). 240p. (Orig.). 1986. pap. 12.95 o.p. (ISBN 0-9617106-0-8). Bio Marine.

Norton Anthology of American Literature: Shorter Edition. Ed. by Ronald Gottesman et al. 1980. pap. text ed. 16.95x o.p. (ISBN 0-393-95112-X). Norton.

Norton Anthology of English Literature, 2 vols. 3rd ed. Ed. by M. H. Abrams et al. 5000p. 1974. Vol. 1. 12.95 o.p. (ISBN 0-393-09301-8); Vol. 1. pap. 9.95 o.p. (ISBN 0-393-09304-2); Vol. 2. pap. 9.95 o.p. (ISBN 0-393-09306-9). Norton.

Norton Anthology of English Literature, 2 vols. 4th ed. Ed. by M. H. Abrams et al. (Illus.). 1979. Vol. I. text ed. 23.95x o.p. (ISBN 0-393-95039-5); Vol. II. text ed. 23.95x o.p. (ISBN 0-393-95043-3); Vol. I. pap. text ed. 21.95x o.p. (ISBN 0-393-95048-4); Vol II. pap. text ed. 21.95x o.p. (ISBN 0-393-95051-4). Norton.

Norton Anthology of Poetry. Ed. by Arthur M. Eastman et al. 1970. 11.95x o.p. (ISBN 0-393-09916-4, NortonC); pap. text ed. 9.45x o.p. (ISBN 0-393-09922-9). Norton.

Norton Anthology of Poetry. rev. ed. Ed. by Arthur M. Eastman et al. 1975. text ed. 19.95x o.p. (ISBN 0-393-09240-2); pap. text ed. 16.95x complete ed. o.p. (ISBN 0-393-09245-3); pap. text ed. 12.95x shorter ed. o.p. (ISBN 0-393-09251-8). Norton.

Norton Anthology of Poetry, Shorter Edition. Ed. by Arthur M. Eastman et al. 1970. pap. 5.25x o.p. (ISBN 0-393-09935-0, NortonC). Norton.

Norton Anthology of Short Fiction. 2nd. ed. Ed. by R. V. Cassill. 1981. Shorter ed. 13.95x o.p. (ISBN 0-393-95182-0); text ed. 14.95x o.p. (ISBN 0-393-95178-2). Norton.

Norton Anthology of Short Fiction. Ed. by R. V. Cassill. 1472p. 1977. pap. text ed. 10.95x complete edition o.p. (ISBN 0-393-09072-8); pap. text ed. 8.95x shorter edition o.p. (ISBN 0-393-09075-2). Norton.

Norton History of Modern Europe. Ed. by Felix Gilbert. (Illus.). 1971. text ed. 14.95x o.p. (ISBN 0-393-09938-5, NortonC). Norton.

Norton Introduction to Literature. 3rd ed. Ed. by Carl E. Bain et al. 1536p. 1981. pap. text ed. 16.95x o.p. (ISBN 0-393-95146-4). Norton.

Norton Introduction to Literature. 2nd ed. Ed. by Carl E. Bain et al. 1977. pap. 11.95x o.p. (ISBN 0-393-09119-8). Norton.

Norton Introduction to Literature. 3rd ed. 1982. shorter ed. 14.95x o.p. (ISBN 0-393-95244-4). Norton.

Norton Introduction to Literature: Combined Shorter Ed. Carl Bain et al. 1248p. 1973. pap. 7.95x o.p. (ISBN 0-393-09334-4). Norton.

Norton Introduction to Literature: Fiction. Ed. by Jerome Beaty. 600p. 1973. pap. text ed. 8.95x o.p. (ISBN 0-393-09359-X). Norton.

Norton Introduction to Literature: Poetry. Ed. by J. Paul Hunter. 600p. 1973. pap. text ed. 10.95x o.p. (ISBN 0-393-09380-8). Norton.

Norton Introduction to Poetry. 2nd. ed. Ed. by J. Paul Hunter. (gr. 12). 1981. pap. text ed. 12.95x o.p. (ISBN 0-393-95157-X). Norton.

Norton Reader. 5th ed. Ed. by Arthur Eastman et al. 1980. pap. 12.95x o.p. (ISBN 0-393-95109-X); pap. text ed. 10.95x shorter ed. o. p. o.p. (ISBN 0-393-95113-8). Norton.

Norton Reader. 4th ed. Ed. by Arthur M. Eastman et al. LC 76-48128. 1280p. 1977. pap. text ed. 10.95x complete ed. o.p. (ISBN 0-393-09145-7); pap. text ed. 8.95x shorter ed. o.p. (ISBN 0-393-09133-3). Norton.

Norton Sampler: Short Essays for Composition. 2nd ed. Ed. by Thomas Cooley. (gr. 12). 1981. pap. text ed. 8.95x o.p. (ISBN 0-393-95179-0). Norton.

Norton Sampler: Short Essays for Composition. Ed. by Thomas Cooley. 1978. pap. text ed. 6.95x o.p. (ISBN 0-393-09007-8). Norton.

Norton Scores. 3rd ed. Ed. by Roger Kamien. 1000p. (Orig.). 1977. pap. text ed. 17.95x standard ed. o.p. (ISBN 0-393-09111-2). Norton.

Norton Scores: An Anthology for Listening, 2 Vols. Roger Kamien. LC 78-95537. 1970. Vol. 1. pap. 5.95x o.p. (ISBN 0-393-09909-1); Vol. 2. pap. 6.95x o.p. (ISBN 0-393-09920-2). Norton.

Norton Scores: An Anthology for Listening, 2 vols. 3rd ed. Ed. by Roger Kamien. LC 76-52467. (Expanded ed.). 1977. Vol. 2. 12.95x o.p. (ISBN 0-393-09123-6); Vol. 1. pap. 12.95x o.p. (ISBN 0-393-09116-3). Norton.

Norton Scores: Standard Edition. rev. ed. Ed. by Roger Kamien. 1972. 20.00x o.p. (ISBN 0-393-02167-X); pap. 7.50x o.p. (ISBN 0-393-09386-7). Norton.

Titles

Norton Service Repair Handbook: 750 & 850 Commandos, All Years. (Illus.). pap. 13.95 o.p. (ISBN 0-89287-158-X, M361). Clymer Pub.

Norway: Facts About. 20th ed. Ed. by A. Aftenposten. 1986. 11.00x o.p. (ISBN 82-516-1060-5, N451). Vanous.

Norway Motoring. new ed. Welle-Strand. (Illus.). 1983. pap. 20.00x o.p. (ISBN 82-90103-26-3, N411). Vanous.

Norway: Native Art. Hauglid & Asker. 1977. deluxe ed. 48.50x o.p. (ISBN 82-09-01381-5, N-387). Vanous.

Norway: Tourist in. 6th ed. Welle-Strand. Ed. by E. Lundevall. (Illus.). 1980. pap. 20.00x o.p. (ISBN 8-2516-0269-6, N410). Vanous.

Norway, Tourist In. 6th ed. Ed. by E. Welle-Strand. (Illus.). 140p. 1980. pap. 20.00x o.p. (ISBN 82-516-0269-6, N-410). Vanous.

Norwegian Dictionary: English-Norwegian. Ed. by L. Bjerke & H. Soraas. 1963. 35.00x o.p. (N434). Vanous.

Norwegian Music: A Survey. 2nd rev. ed. K. Lange. (Tanum of Norway Tokens Ser). pap. 12.50x o.p. (ISBN 8-2518-1654-8, N507). Vanous.

Norwegian Painting: A Survey. J. Askeland. (Tanum of Norway Tokens Ser). (Illus.). pap. 14.00x o.p. (ISBN 82-518-1122-8, N505). Vanous.

Norwegian Technical Dictionary: English-Norwegian Oil Supplement, Vol. 1. 3rd. ed. J. Ansteinsson. 1983. 65.00x o.p. (ISBN 82-702-8469-6, N433). Vanous.

Norwegian Technical Dictionary: Norwegian-English, Vol. 2. rev. 4th ed. Ed. by J. Ansteinsson. (Norwegian & Eng.). 1985. 65.00x o.p. (ISBN 82-702-8474-2, N432). Vanous.

NOS: Book of Resurrection. Miguel Serrano. (Illus.). 192p. (Orig.). 1984. pap. 7.95 o.p. (ISBN 0-7100-9828-6). Routledge Chapman & Hall.

Nose Knows. E. W. Hildick. 1979. pap. 2.50 o.s.i. (ISBN 0-441-58869-7, Pub. by Tempo). Ace Bks.

Nosferatu: Vampyre. P. Monette. 1979. pap. 2.25 o.p. (ISBN 0-380-44107-1). Avon.

Nostalgia. Heller McAlpin. 272p. 1982. 12.95 o.s.i. (ISBN 0-684-17768-4, ScribT). Scribner.

Nostalgia of the Fortuneteller. Stephen Kessler. 66p. 1976. pap. 2.00 o.p. (ISBN 0-87711-061-1). Story Line.

Nostalgic Almanac. Edna Hong. LC 80-65545. 176p. (Orig.). 1980. pap. 7.95 o.p. (ISBN 0-8066-1790-X, 10-4670, Augsburg). Augsburg Fortress.

Nostradamus: Countdown to Apocalypse. Jean-Charles de Fontbrune. 512p. 1985. 18.95 o.p. (ISBN 0-03-064177-2); pap. 12.95 o.p. (ISBN 0-8050-1048-3). H Holt & Co.

Nostromo. Joseph Conrad. 1979. 16.95x o.p. (ISBN 0-460-00038-1, Evman); pap. 2.95x o.p. (ISBN 0-460-01038-7, Evman). Biblio Dist.

Nostromo. Joseph Conrad. 449p. 35.00 o.p. (ISBN 0-913720-27-5, Sandstone); leather bound o.p. 65.00 o.p. (ISBN 0-913720-26-7). Beil.

Not a Through Street. Ernest Larsen. 240p. 1986. pap. 3.95 o.s.i. (ISBN 0-394-62248-0, BC). Grove.

Not an Average Guy. James Barrett. LC 85-91060. 160p. 1986. 12.50 o.p. (ISBN 0-682-40284-2). Exposition-Phoenix.

Not by Politics Alone: The Other Lenin. Ed. by Tamara Deutscher. LC 75-35301. 256p. 1976. pap. 4.95 o.p. (ISBN 0-88208-063-6, L Hill Bks). Chicago Review.

Not Dead, Only Resting. Simon Brett. (Nightingale-Lythway Ser.). 1985. pap. 10.95 o.p. (ISBN 0-8161-3831-1, Large Print Bks). G K Hall.

Not Dead, Only Resting: A Charles Paris Mystery. Simon Brett. 176p. 1984. 11.95 o.s.i. (ISBN 0-684-18193-2, ScribT). Scribner.

Not for Doctors Only: Breakthrough Reports from the Medical Front. James E. Wasco. 12.95 o.p. (ISBN 0-201-08297-7); pap. 7.95 o.p. (ISBN 0-201-08298-5). Addison-Wesley.

Not for Glory: A Personal History of the 1914-18 War. R. H. Haigh & P. W. Turner. 1969. 35.00 o.p. (ISBN 0-08-007101-5). Pergamon.

Not I, But Christ. Corrie Ten Boom. LC 84-1965. 144p. 1984. 16.95 o.p. (ISBN 0-8407-4112-X). Nelson.

Not in Front of the Servants: A True Portrait of English Upstairs-Downstairs Life. Frank Dawes. LC 73-16961. 1974. 8.95 o.s.i. (ISBN 0-8008-5605-8). Taplinger.

Not in Our Stars. Oliver G. Howard. 208p. 1981. 9.00 o.p. (ISBN 0-682-49778-9). Exposition-Phoenix.

Not in Precious Metals Alone: A Manuscript History of Montana. Montana Historical Society Staff. LC 76-18976. 1976. 15.95 o.s.i. (ISBN 0-917298-01-2). MT Hist Soc.

Not Just a Job: Serving Christ in Your Work. Judith A. Shelly. LC 84-29676. 140p. (Orig.). 1985. pap. 5.95 o.p. (ISBN 0-87784-332-5). Inter-Varsity.

Not Just Yes & Amen: Christians with a Cause. Dorothee Soelle & Fulbert Steffensky. LC 84-48708. 96p. 1985. pap. 1.75 o.p. (ISBN 0-8006-1828-9, 1-1828, Fortress). Augsburg Fortress.

Not Like That, Armadillo. Ida Luttrell. LC 81-20107. (Let-Me-Read Ser.). (Illus.). 64p. (ps-3). 1982. pap. 2.95 o.p. (ISBN 0-15-257585-5, VoyB). HarBraceJ.

Not Like That, Armadillo. Ida Luttrell. LC 81-20107. (Illus.). 64p. (ps-3). 1982. 8.95 o.p. (ISBN 0-15-257584-7, HJ). HarBraceJ.

Not Made for Quitting. Dick Hillis. 144p. 1973. pap. 3.95 o.p. (ISBN 0-87123-396-7, 200396, Dimension Bks). Bethany Hse.

Not Man Apart: Photographs of the Big Sur Coast. Robinson Jeffers. Ed. by David Brower. LC 65-23375. (Exhibit Format Ser.). (Illus.). 160p. 1965. 32.50 o.s.i. (ISBN 0-87156-007-0). Sierra.

Not My Kid: A Parent's Guide to Kids & Drugs. Beth Polson & Miller Newton. LC 84-11069. 256p. 1984. 15.95 o.p. (ISBN 0-87795-633-2, Arbor Hse). Morrow.

Not My Will. Andrew Murray. Tr. by Marian Schoolland. 1977. pap. 3.95 o.p. (ISBN 0-310-29722-2, 10381P). Zondervan.

Not on Our Street: Community Attitudes to Mental Health Care. Michael J. Dear & S. Martin Taylor. 200p. 1982. 19.95 o.p. (ISBN 0-85086-096-2, NO. 8010, Pub. by Pion England). Routledge Chapman & Hall.

Not Quite Human! Batteries Not Included. Seth McCoy. (Illus., Orig.). (gr. 5 up). 1985. pap. 2.25 o.p. (ISBN 0-671-60081-8). Archway.

Not So Wild a Dream. Eric Sevareid. LC 76-11538. 1978. 15.00 o.p. (ISBN 0-689-10741-2, Atheneum); pap. 8.95 o.s.i. (ISBN 0-689-70578-6, 235, Atheneum). Macmillan.

Not-Strictly Vegetarian Cookbook. 4th ed. Lois Fishkin & Susan Dimarco. LC 82-73064. (Illus.). 256p. (Orig.). 1982. pap. 9.95 o.p. (ISBN 0-916870-49-9). Creative Arts Bk.

Not Such a Bad Place to Be. William Kloefkorn. 100p. (Orig.). 1980. pap. 7.00 o.p. (ISBN 0-914742-48-5). Copper Canyon.

Not the Law's Business. Date not set. (ISBN 0-8052-0621-3). Random.

Not Too Dusty. George H. Mizher. 1978. 7.50 o.p. (ISBN 0-682-49066-0). Exposition-Phoenix.

Notable Names in American History. 3rd ed. 1979. 135.00x o.p. (ISBN 0-8103-0409-0). Gale.

Note-Book. Thomas Lechford. Repr. of 1885 ed. 35.00 o.p. (ISBN 0-384-31988-2). Johnson Repr.

Note-Books of Captain Coignet. 232p. 1987. 25.00 o.p. (ISBN 0-947898-49-2). Kraus Repr.

Note for the DRCOG. 2nd ed. Kaye. 1987. write for info. o.p. (ISBN 0-443-03785-X). Churchill.

Notebook of Gismondo Cavalletti. R. M. Lamming. LC 84-45043. 256p. 1985. 11.95 o.p. (ISBN 0-689-11487-7, Atheneum). Macmillan.

Notebook of Medical Physiology: Endocrinology with Aspects of Maternal, Fetal & Neonatal Monitoring. 2nd ed. Ross W. Hawker. (Illus.). 288p. 1986. pap. text ed. 18.00 o.p. (ISBN 0-443-03188-6). Churchill.

Notebook of Medical Physiology: Gastroenterology. Ross W. Hawker. (Illus.). 1981. pap. text ed. 18.00 o.p. (ISBN 0-443-02144-9). Churchill.

Notebooks, 2 vols. Simone Weil. Tr. by Simone Wills from Fr. (Routledge Academic Research Editions Ser.). 648p. 1984. Vol. 1. pap. 20.00x o.p. (ISBN 0-7100-8522-2); Vol. 2. pap. 20.00x o.p. (ISBN 0-7100-8523-0). Routledge Chapman & Hall.

Notebooks for "Crime & Punishment" Fyodor Dostoyevsky. Ed. & tr. by Edward Wasiolek. LC 66-23702. viii, 246p. 1974. pap. text ed. 3.95x o.s.i. (ISBN 0-226-15960-4, P600, Phoen). U of Chicago Pr.

Notebooks, Memoirs, Archives: Reading & Rereading Doris Lessing. Ed. by Jenny Taylor. 240p. 1983. pap. 8.95 o.p. (ISBN 0-7100-9034-X). Routledge Chapman & Hall.

Notebooks-Memoirs-Archives: Readings & Re-readings Doris Lessing. Jenny Taylor. 230p. 1982. 16.95x o.p. (ISBN 0-7100-9033-1). Routledge Chapman & Hall.

Notebooks: Nineteen Forty-Two to Nineteen Fifty-One. Albert Camus. LC 77-16233. 288p. 1978. pap. 3.95 o.s.i. (ISBN 0-15-667401-7, Harv). HarBraceJ.

Notebooks, Nineteen Sixty to Nineteen Seventy-Seven. Athol Fugard. LC 83-49025. 1984. 14.45 o.s.i. (ISBN 0-394-53755-6). Knopf.

Notebooks of F. Scott Fitzgerald. F. Scott Fitzgerald. Ed. by Matthew J. Bruccoli. LC 78-7094. 1978. 14.95 o.s.i. (ISBN 0-15-167260-1). HarBraceJ.

Notebooks of F. Scott Fitzgerald. F. Scott Fitzgerald. Ed. by Matthew J. Bruccoli. LC 79-18490. 1980. pap. 5.95 o.p. (ISBN 0-15-667362-2, Harv). HarBraceJ.

Notebooks of Joseph Joubert: A Selection. Joseph Joubert. Ed. & tr. by Paul Auster. LC 82-73711. 192p. 1983. pap. 12.50 o.p. (ISBN 0-86547-108-8). N Point Pr.

Notebooks of Major Thompson. Pierre Daninos. LC 81-70065. 1982. pap. 7.95 o.p. (ISBN 0-689-70619-7, 273, Atheneum). Macmillan.

Notebooks of Martha Graham. Martha Graham. LC 72-75416. (Illus.). 480p. 1973. 27.50 o.p. (ISBN 0-15-167265-2). HarBraceJ.

Notebooks of Sologdin. Dimitri Panin. LC 75-29051. 352p. 1976. 12.95 o.p. (ISBN 0-15-166995-3). HarBraceJ.

Notebooks: 1935-1942. Albert Camus. 1965. 3.95 o.s.i. (ISBN 0-394-60349-4). Modern Lib.

Notes, Criticism, Translations, & Miscellaneous Writings: A Facsimile of Manuscripts & Typescripts, Vol. 1. James Joyce. 1978. lib. bdg. 89.00 o.p. (ISBN 0-8240-2801-5). Garland Pub.

Notes, Criticism, Translations, & Miscellaneous Writings: A Facsimile of Manuscripts & Typescripts, Vol. 2. James Joyce. 1978. lib. bdg. 89.00 o.p. (ISBN 0-8240-2802-3). Garland Pub.

Notes for a Young Painter: Revised & Expanded Edition of a Classic Handbook for Beginning Artists. Hiram Williams. (Illus.). 224p. 1984. 21.95 o.p. (ISBN 0-13-624123-9); pap. 9.95 o.p. (ISBN 0-13-624115-8). P-H.

Notes for Introductory Courses in Genetics. rev. ed. Charlotte Auerbach. 1965. pap. 2.25 o.p. (ISBN 0-910824-02-9). Kallman.

Notes from a Distant Flute: The Extant Literature of Pre-Mughal Indian Sufism. Bruce B. Lawrence. LC 78-62007. 1979. write for info. o.p. (ISBN 0-87773-735-5). Shambhala Pubns.

Notes from a Naturalist's Sketchbook. Clare W. Leslie. (Illus.). 112p. 1981. pap. 7.95 o.p. (ISBN 0-395-31298-1). HM.

Notes from a School Teacher. James Herndon. 160p. 1985. 15.45 o.p. (ISBN 0-671-54371-7). S&S.

Notes from Marie's Kitchen. Marie W. Newton. Ed. by Elizabeth Speir. LC 84-61095. (Illus.). 140p. pap. cancelled o.s.i. (ISBN 0-939944-42-1). Marmac Pub.

Notes from the Caroline Underground: Alexander Leighton, the Puritan Triumvirate, & the Laudian Reaction to Nonconformity. Stephen Foster. LC 78-9595. (Conference on British Studies: Vol. VI). xviii, 126p. 1978. 16.50 o.p. (ISBN 0-208-01758-5, Archon). Shoe String.

Notes from the City of the Sun: Poems by Bei Dao. Ed. & tr. by Bonnie S. McDougall. LC 83-214673. (East Asia Papers: No. 34). 118p. 1983. 6.00 o.p. (ISBN 0-939657-34-1). Cornell East Asia Pgm.

Notes of a Madman. Adam Powell. 44p. 1987. 5.95 o.p. (ISBN 1-55523-054-7). Winston-Derek.

Notes of a Native Son. James Baldwin. (Modern Classic Ser). 1971. pap. 2.95 o.s.i. (ISBN 0-553-24075-7). Bantam.

Notes of a Processed Brother. Donald Reeves. 148p. 1981. pap. 1.95 o.p. (ISBN 0-380-01360-6, 14175, Discus). Avon.

Notes of an Apprenticeship. Pierre Boulez. 398p. Repr. of 1968 ed. lib. bdg. 49.00 o.p. (Pub. by Am Repr Serv). Reprint Servs.

Notes of Debates in the Federal Convention of 1787 Reported by James Madison. James Madison. Ed. by Adrienne Koch. 1969. pap. 8.95 o.p. (ISBN 0-393-00485-6, Norton Lib). Norton.

Notes of the Debates in the House of Lords in 1624. Great Britain, House of Lords Staff. Ed. by Samuel R. Gardiner. 1879. 27.00 o.p. (ISBN 0-384-19800-7). Johnson Repr.

Notes on Academic Disciplines. A. A. Saxe. 1972. pap. text ed. 5.95x o.p. (ISBN 0-8422-0270-6). Irvington.

Notes on an Emergency. Elizabeth L. Simpson. 160p. 1982. 12.95 o.p. (ISBN 0-393-01514-9). Norton.

Notes on Art & Education. R. Henkes. 1973. pap. text ed. 7.95x o.p. (ISBN 0-8290-1169-2). Irvington.

Notes on Broadway: Conservations with the Great Songwriters. Al Kasha & Joel Hirschhorn. (Illus.). 320p. 1985. 22.95 o.p. (ISBN 0-8092-5162-0). Contemp Bks.

Notes on Chopin. Andre Gide. (ISBN 0-8022-0587-9). Philos Lib.

Notes on Dental Materials. 5th ed. E. C. Combe. LC 86-20754. (Dental Ser.). (Illus.). 395p. (Orig.). 1986. pap. text ed. 19.95 o.p. (ISBN 0-443-03112-6). Churchill.

Notes on Elementary Particle Physics. H. Muirhead. 264p. 1972. 41.00 o.p. (ISBN 0-08-016550-8). Pergamon.

Notes on Epistles of Saint Paul. J. B. Lightfoot. Ed. by J. R. Harmer. (Thornapple Commentaries Ser.). 345p. 1980. pap. 8.95 o.p. (ISBN 0-8010-5602-0). Baker Bk.

Notes on Labor Problems in Nationalist China. Israel Epstein. LC 78-74341. (Modern Chinese Economy Ser.). 159p. 1980. lib. bdg. 20.00 o.p. (ISBN 0-8240-4281-6). Garland Pub.

Notes on Leviticus. George Bush. 282p. lib. bdg. 12.95 o.p. (ISBN 0-8254-5052-7). Kregel.

Notes on Literary Stucture. Daniel Burke. LC 81-40645. 280p. (Orig.). 1982. lib. bdg. 30.25 o.p. (ISBN 0-8191-2119-3); pap. text ed. 14.00 o.p. (ISBN 0-8191-2120-7). U Pr of Amer.

Notes on Medical Nursing. 4th ed. William C. Fream. LC 84-29226. 242p. 1985. pap. text ed. 13.00 o.p. (ISBN 0-443-03381-1). Churchill.

Notes on Medicine for Occupational Health Nurses. Stok. 1986. write for info. o.p. Year Bk Med.

Notes on Prayer. Elisabeth Elliot. 1982. pap. 0.95 o.p. (ISBN 0-89107-254-3). Good News.

Notes on Psychiatry. 6th ed. I. M. Ingram et al. 173p. 1985. pap. text ed. 13.00 o.p. (ISBN 0-443-03218-1). Churchill.

Notes on Relative Clauses see Society's Work.

Notes on Romans. Arthur Pridham. 461p. 1983. 14.95 o.p. (ISBN 0-8254-3519-6). Kregel.

Notes on Rubik's Magic Cube. David Singmaster. LC 80-27751. (Illus.). 73p. 1981. text ed. 13.95x o.p. (ISBN 0-89490-057-9); pap. 5.95 o.p. (ISBN 0-89490-043-9). Enslow Pubs.

Notes on Stagflation. Howard S. Ellis. 1978. pap. 5.00 o.p. (ISBN 0-8447-3323-7). Am Enterprise.

Notes on the Cathedral Libraries of England. Beriah Botfield. LC 68-23138. 544p. 1969. Repr. of 1849 ed. 65.00x o.p. (ISBN 0-8103-3174-8). Gale.

Notes on the Ethnology of the Indians of Puget Sound. T. T. Waterman. LC 72-88406. (Illus., Orig.). 1973. pap. 3.50 o.p. (ISBN 0-934490-31-7). Mus Am Ind.

Notes on the Hauter Experiment: A Journey Through the Inner World of Evelyn B. Chestnut. Bernice Grohskopf. LC 75-6749. (gr. 4-7). 1975. 6.95 o.p. (ISBN 0-689-30477-3, Atheneum). Macmillan.

Notes on the Hebrew Text of Samuel. S. R. Driver. 1986. 24.95 o.p. (ISBN 0-88469-163-2). BMH Bks.

Notes on the Islands of the Unalashka District. Ivan Veniaminov. Ed. by Richard A. Pierce. Tr. by Richard Geoghegan. (Alaska History Ser.: No. 27). 1984. 30.00 o.p. (ISBN 0-919642-03-9). Limestone Pr.

Notes on the Methodology of Scientific Research. Ed. by Walter B. Weimer. LC 78-31093. 257p. 1979. 24.95x o.p. (ISBN 0-470-26650-3). Halsted Pr.

Notes on the Technique of Painting. Hilaire Hiler. 10.00 o.p. (ISBN 0-686-67685-8, Banner). Exposition-Phoenix.

Notes on the Witt Classification of Hermitian Innerproduct Spaces over a Ring of Algebraic Integers. P. E. Conner. 157p. 1979. text ed. 20.00x o.p. (ISBN 0-292-75516-3). U of Tex Pr.

Notes on Thermodynamics & Statistics. Enrico Fermi. LC 66-20581. (Orig.). 1966. pap. text ed. 5.00x o.s.i. (ISBN 0-226-24364-8, P529, Phoen). U of Chicago Pr.

Notes on Visitations: Poems 1936-1975. George Woodcock. (House of Anansi Poetry Ser.: No. 33). 115p. 1975. 2.00 o.p. (ISBN 0-88784-134-1, Pub. by Hse Anansi Pr Canada). U of Toronto Pr.

Notes, Recent Developments in Lining Techniques: July 18-22, 1983. 3.50 o.p. (ISBN 0-318-18696-9). Am Inst Conser Hist.

Notes sur Andre Gide. Roger Martin du Gard. 156p. 1951. 3.95 o.p. (ISBN 0-686-55504-X). Schoenhof.

Notes to a Science Fiction Writer. Ben Bova. 1981. pap. 5.95 o.p. (ISBN 0-395-30521-7). HM.

Notes to My Children: A Simplified Metaphysics. Ken Carey. 170p. 1987. pap. 8.95 o.p. (ISBN 0-913299-36-7, Dist. by NAL). Stillpoint.

Notes Towards the Definition of Culture. T. S. Eliot. 1949. 8.95 o.s.i. (ISBN 0-15-167277-6). HarBraceJ.

Nothing but the Best. Diane Balson. LC 77-92528. 1978. 7.95 o.p. (ISBN 0-15-167327-6). HarBraceJ.

Nothing but the Best for Baby. Barbara Blitzer. 72p. 1986. 14.95 o.p. (ISBN 0-8378-5098-3). Gibson.

Nothing Could Be Finer. Junior League of Wilmington, Inc. Staff. Tr. by Suzanne Nash. (Illus.). 304p. 1982. pap. 10.95 o.p. (ISBN 0-939114-52-6). Wimmer Bks.

Nothing Could Be Finer Than a Crisis That Is Minor in the Morning. Charles Osgood. LC 79-14377. 204p. 1979. 9.95 o.p. (ISBN 0-03-047646-1); pap. 3.95 o.p. (ISBN 0-03-057646-6). H Holt & Co.

Nothing Down. Robert G. Allen. 1980. 16.45 o.p. (ISBN 0-671-24748-4). S&S.

Nothing Ever Happens on My Block. Ellen Raskin. (Illus.). (gr. 1-4). 1977. pap. 3.95 o.s.i. (ISBN 0-689-70436-4, Aladdin). Macmillan.

Nothing Hurts but My Heart. Linda Barr. (Lifelines Ser.). 112p. (Orig.). (gr. 6-8). 1987. pap. 2.25 o.s.i. (ISBN 0-87406-273-X). Willowisp Pr.

Nothing Is Impossible: The Story of Beatrix Potter. Dorothy Aldis. LC 69-13528. (Illus.). (gr. 3-7). 1969. PLB 7.95 o.p. (ISBN 0-689-20618-6, Atheneum). Macmillan.

Nothing Lasts Forever. Roderick Thorp. 1979. 9.95 o.p. (ISBN 0-393-01249-2). Norton.

Nothing Natural. Jenny Diski. 256p. 1987. 16.45 o.s.i. (ISBN 0-671-63459-3). S&S.

Nothing Rhymes with April. Naomi J. Karp. LC 73-17938. (Illus.). (gr. 3-7). 1974. 5.95 o.p. (ISBN 0-15-257579-0, HJ). HarBraceJ.

Nothing Said. Lucy M. Boston. LC 70-137756. (Illus.). (gr. 2-5). 1971. 4.95 o.p. (ISBN 0-15-257580-4, HJ). HarBraceJ.

Nothing Seemed Impossible: Women's Education & Social Change in South Australia 1875-1915. Helen Jones. (Scholars' Library). 272p. 1985. text ed. 37.50x o.p. (ISBN 0-318-04294-0). U of Queensland Pr.

Nothing Stands Still: Essays by Arthur M. Schlesinger Jr. Arthur M. Schlesinger, Jr. LC 69-18045. 1969. 15.00x o.s.i. (ISBN 0-674-62760-1, Belknap Pr). Harvard U Pr.

Nothing to Be Afraid Of. Jan Mark. 1985. 11.95 o.p. (ISBN 0-317-53143-3, Large Print Bks). G K Hall.

Nothing to Cheer About. Marcie Anderson. 96p. (gr. 5-8). 1985. 2.25 o.s.i. (ISBN 0-87406-016-8). Willowisp Pr.

Nothing's Changed: Diary of a Mastectomy. Dorothy Abbott. LC 81-65746. 224p. 1981. 11.95 o.p. (ISBN 0-8119-0423-7). Fell.

Nothing's Wrong with Me! Juanita Duncan. Ed. by Mary Penoi. LC 85-60543. 180p. (Orig.). 1985. pap. 4.75 o.p. (ISBN 0-942316-09-6). Pueblo Pub Pr.

Notices of Florida & the Campaigns. M. M. Cohen. Ed. by O. Z. Tyler, Jr. LC 64-19153. (Floridiana Facsimile & Reprint Ser.). 1964. Repr. of 1836 ed. 10.75 o.p. (ISBN 0-8130-0048-3). U Presses Fla.

Noticiario: Primer Nivel. William F. Smith. 168p. (Orig.). 1981. pap. text ed. 9.00 o.p. (ISBN 0-88377-161-6). Newbury Hse.

Noticiario: Segundo Nivel. Wm. Flint Smith & Frank Medley. (Noticiario Ser.). 184p. 1982. pap. text ed. 9.00 o.p. (ISBN 0-88377-219-1). Newbury Hse.

Noticiario: Tercer Nivel. Wm. Flint Smith & Linda Nieman. (Noticiario Ser.). 186p. 1982. pap. text ed. 9.00 o.p. (ISBN 0-88377-277-9). Newbury Hse.

Notion of Tao in Lao Tzu & Chuang Tsu. Giancarlo Finazzo. 240p. 1980. 11.95 o.p. (ISBN 0-89955-146-7, Pub. by Mei Ya China). Intl Spec Bk.

Notre-Dame-des-Fleurs. Jean Genet. 1966. pap. 8.50 o.p. (ISBN 0-685-11426-0). Schoenhof.

Notre Dame Football: The Golden Tradition. Dave Condon et al. (Illus.). 208p. 1982. 24.95 o.s.i. (ISBN 0-89651-510-9). B L Pub.

Notre Dame: One Hundred Years. Arthur J. Hope. LC 78-23391. 532p. 1979. 15.95 o.s.i. (ISBN 0-89651-500-1); pap. 9.95 o.s.i. (ISBN 0-89651-501-X). B L Pub.

Notre Patrie. Charles Peguy. 12p. 1915. 2.95 o.p. (ISBN 0-686-54861-2). Schoenhof.

Notre Seigneur. Charles Peguy. pap. 2.50 o.p. (ISBN 0-685-37032-1). Schoenhof.

Notre Vin et Notre Patois. Roel Puijk & Jorid Vaagland. (Bergen Studies in Social Anthropology Ser.: No. 23). (Illus.). 272p. (Orig.). 1985. pap. text ed. 10.50x o.p. (ISBN 0-936589-65-5, Pub by Dept Soc Anthropology Norway). Barber Pr.

Nottingham, Nobles, & the North: Aspects of the Revolution of 1688. David H. Hosford. LC 75-19458. (Studies in British History & Culture: Vol. 4). (Illus.). xvi, 182p. 1976. 22.00 o.p. (ISBN 0-208-01565-5, Archon). Shoe String.

Noun-Class Systems of Proto-Benue-Congo. Paul P. De Wolf. 1971. pap. text ed. 30.00 o.p. (ISBN 0-686-22527-9). Mouton.

Nous Tous, Bk. 2. Gilbert A. Jarvis et al. (Fr.). 1983. text ed. 12.96 o.p. (ISBN 0-03-057539-7, Holte). HR&W.

Nouveau Visage Du Monde Francais. 2nd ed. Louis L. Curcio & Marie E. Galanti. 203p. 1981. pap. 25.96 o.p. (ISBN 0-395-30978-6). HM.

Nouvelle Biographie Generale, 23 vols. Ed. by J. C. Hoefer. 22000p. (Fr.). 1981. Repr. of 1866 ed. Set. 1500.00 o.p. (ISBN 0-915346-75-3). A Wofsy Fine Arts.

Nouvelle Cuisine of Jean & Pierre Troisgros. Jean Troisgros & Pierre Troisgros. Tr. by Roberta W. Smoler from Fr. LC 85-19163. (Three-Star Chefs of France Ser.). (Illus.). 254p. 1985. pap. 9.95 o.p. (ISBN 0-688-06151-6, Quill). Morrow.

Novalis Spiritual Saturnalia: Fragments of Existence by Friedrich von Hardenberg. Tr. by John N. Ritter. 1971. 5.95 o.p. (ISBN 0-682-47246-8, University). Exposition-Phoenix.

Novel. Elizabeth A. Drew. 1964. 8.95x o.p. (ISBN 0-393-04213-8). Norton.

Novel Approaches to Cancer Chemotherapy. Ed. by Prasad Sunkara. (Cell Biology Ser.). 1984. 71.50 o.p. (ISBN 0-12-676980-X). Acad Pr.

Novel As Structure & Praxis: From Cervantes to Malraux. Everett Knight. 1981. text ed. 8.50x o.p. (ISBN 0-391-00938-9). Humanities.

Novel Aspects. Ed. by J. D. Dunitz et al. LC 67-11280. (Structure & Bonding: Vol. 34). 1978. 48.00 o.p. (ISBN 0-387-08676-5). Springer-Verlag.

Novel Before the Novel: Essays & Discussions About the Beginnings of Prose Fiction in the West. Arthur Heiserman. LC 76-8102. 1980. pap. text ed. 8.00x o.s.i. (ISBN 0-226-32573-3). U of Chicago Pr.

Novel Drilling Techniques. W. C. Maurer. 1968. 42.00 o.p. (ISBN 0-08-012734-7). Pergamon.

Novel Materials. Ed. by Time-Life Books Staff. LC 74-16950. (Art of Sewing Ser.). (Illus.). (gr. 6 up). 1974. PLB 11.97 o.p. (ISBN 0-8094-1723-5, Pub. by Time-Life). Silver.

Novel of Violence in America. rev ed. Wilbur M. Frohock. LC 57-14767. 254p. 1971. 14.95x o.p. (ISBN 0-87074-054-7). SMU Press.

Novel Techniques in Metal Deformation Testing: Proceedings. TMS-AIME Fall Meeting, St. Louis, 1982. Ed. by R. H. Wagoner. (Illus.). 430p. 45.00 o.p. (ISBN 0-89520-149-6). ASM.

Novel to Nineteen Hundred, 1 of 7 vols. Intro. by A. O. Cockshut. (Great Writers Library). 313p. pap. 9.95 o.p. (ISBN 0-312-34707-3). Academy Chi Pubs.

Novel to Nineteen Hundred. Ed. by James Vinson. (Great Writer's Library). 313p. (Orig.). 1980. pap. 9.95 o.p. (ISBN 0-312-34707-3). St Martin.

Novelist in the Making: A Collection of Student Themes & the Novels Blix & Vandover & the Brute. Frank Norris. Ed. by James D. Hart. LC 72-129124. (John Harvard Library). (Illus.). xiv, 596p. 1970. 37.50x o.s.i. (ISBN 0-674-62820-9). Harvard U Pr.

Novelistas Espanoles de Hoy. Ed. by Rodolfo Cardona. 1959. 6.95x o.p. (ISBN 0-393-09525-8, NortonC). Norton.

Novelists & Political Consciousness: Literary Expression of Indian Nationalism 1919-1947. S. Bald. 175p. 1982. text ed. 17.50x o.p. (ISBN 0-391-02713-1). Humanities.

Novelists on Novelists. Ed. by David Dowling. LC 83-28. 283p. 1983. text ed. 29.95x o.p. (ISBN 0-391-02485-X). Humanities.

Novels & Novelists. Katherine Mansfield. Repr. of 1930 ed. 49.00x o.p. (ISBN 0-403-02290-8). Somerset Pub.

Novels of Flaubert: A Study of Themes & Techniques. Victor Brombert. 1967. 32.00x o.p. (ISBN 0-691-06085-1); pap. 12.95x o.p. (ISBN 0-691-01290-3). Princeton U Pr.

Novels of Hermann Hesse: A Study in Theme & Structure. Theodore Ziolkowski. 1965. 25.00x o.p. (ISBN 0-691-06084-3); pap. 9.50x o.p. (ISBN 0-691-01272-5). Princeton U Pr.

Novels of R. K. Narayan. Lakshmi Holmstrom. (Writers Workshop Greybird Ser.). 130p. 1975. 15.00 o.s.i. (ISBN 0-88253-584-6); pap. text ed. 8.00 o.s.i. (ISBN 0-88253-583-8). Ind-US Inc.

Novels of Thomas Hardy: Illusion & Reality. Penelope Vigar. 236p. 1974. text ed. 17.50x o.p. (ISBN 0-391-00932-X). Humanities.

November. Georges Simenon. Tr. by Jean Stewart from Fr. LC 72-124826. (Helen & Kurt Wolff Bks.). 1970. 9.95 o.p. (ISBN 0-15-167560-0). HarBraceJ.

Novena for Murder. Carol A. O'Marie. 224p. 1984. 12.95 o.s.i. (ISBN 0-684-18087-1, ScribT). Scribner.

Novena of Confidence & Thanksgiving to the Sorrowful & Immaculate Heart of Mary. Tr. by Mary E. Hickey from Fr. (Illus.). 20p. 1962. pap. 0.25 o.p. (ISBN 0-913382-21-3, 107-2). Prow Bks-Franciscan.

Novgorod: A Guide. M. Dunaev. 183p. 1985. 8.95 o.p. (ISBN 0-8285-2958-2, Pub. by Raduga Pubs USSR). Imported Pubns.

Novice License Study Guide. Ed. by Timothy M. Daniel. 98p. 1981. pap. 4.95 o.p. (ISBN 0-88006-018-2, SG7357). Wayne Green Ent.

Now, Ameriky. Betty S. Cummings. LC 79-11750. (gr. 7 up). 9.95 o.p. (ISBN 0-689-30705-5, Atheneum). Macmillan.

Now & Again. Joan Cassity. 480p. 1984. pap. 2.95 o.p. (ISBN 0-380-87353-2, 87353-2). Avon.

Now & at the Hour. Robert Cormier. 144p. 1980. pap. 1.95 o.p. (ISBN 0-380-50195-3, 50195-3). Avon.

Now & Forever. Danielle Steel. (General Ser.). 1982. lib. bdg. 16.95 o.p. (Large Print Bks). G K Hall.

Now & Forever see Danielle Steel.

Now & Future Church. Eugene C. Kennedy. LC 83-20574. 216p. 1985. pap. 7.95 o.p. (ISBN 0-385-23236-5, Im). Doubleday.

Now & Future Church: The Psychology of Being an American Catholic. Eugene C. Kennedy. LC 83-20574. 216p. 1984. 13.95 o.p. (ISBN 0-385-19040-9). Doubleday.

Now Come the Spring. Andrea Edwards. 240p. 1983. pap. 2.95 o.p. (ISBN 0-380-83329-8, 83329-8). Avon.

Now, God Be Thanked, Vol. 1. John Masters. LC 78-27829. 1979. text ed. 12.95 o.p. (ISBN 0-07-040781-9). McGraw.

Now Hear This! Roy P. Adelberg. (Illus., Orig.). (YA) (gr. 9-12). 1965. pap. 1.25 o.p. (ISBN 0-8042-9348-1, John Knox). Westminster John Knox.

Now I Have a Step-Parent, & It's Kind of Confusing. Janet S. Stenson. 1979. pap. 2.95 o.p. (ISBN 0-380-46516-7, 46516-7). Avon.

Now in Mexico. Hudson Strode. LC 47-11420. (Illus.). 1947. 5.00 o.p. (ISBN 0-15-167691-7). HarBraceJ.

Now Is Always the Miraculous Time. Robert Sargent. (Ser. Two). (Illus.). 1977. pap. 2.00 o.p. (ISBN 0-931846-02-1). Wash Writers Pub.

Now Is the Accepted Time. Stephen Bayne. Ed. by Wilbur Woodhams. 80p. (Orig.). 1983. pap. 2.00 o.p. (ISBN 0-88028-022-0). Forward Movement.

Now Is the Time to Prevent a Third World War. Kirby Page. LC 79-147483. (Library of War & Peace; the Character & Causes of War). 1972. lib. bdg. 46.00 o.p. (ISBN 0-8240-0275-X). Garland Pub.

Now Is Your Time to Win. Dave Dean & Marti Hefley. 1983. 8.95 o.p. (ISBN 0-8423-4724-0). Tyndale.

Now It Can Be Told. James Gleeson & Tom Waldron. 188p. 1952. (ISBN 0-8022-0598-4). Philos Lib.

Now Let's Talk About Music. Gordon Merrick. 432p. 1981. pap. 4.95 o.p. (ISBN 0-380-77867-X, 60055-2). Avon.

Now Listen Good! A Collection of Authentic West Indian Recipes. Estella F. Schulman. LC 79-19954. 1979. 8.95 o.p. (ISBN 0-88427-037-8). North River.

Now Molly Knows. Merrill J. Gerber. LC 73-89567. 1974. 7.50 o.p. (ISBN 0-87795-074-1, Arbor Hse). Morrow.

Now That I'm a Christian, Vol. 1. Chuck Miller. 64p. (Orig.). 1974. pap. 5.95 o.s.i. (ISBN 0-8307-0425-6, 5201918). Regal.

Now That You Are a Catholic. rev. & enl. ed. John Kenny. LC 73-80417. 108p. (Orig.). 1986. pap. 2.95 o.p. (ISBN 0-8091-1743-6). Paulist Pr.

Now That You Are Single Again. Gary Chapman. 80p. 1985. wkbk. 3.95 o.p. (ISBN 0-89840-087-2). Heres Life.

Now That You Have Believed: An Exploration of the Life & Walk of Faith. Douglas Vickers. 1981. 10.00 o.p. (ISBN 0-682-49830-0). Exposition-Phoenix.

Now That You Know: What Every Parent Should Know About Homosexuality. Betty Fairchild & Nancy Hayward. 1979. 8.95 o.p. (ISBN 0-15-167707-7). HarBraceJ.

Now What Do I Do? Ronald Rehrer. 1982. pap. 1.75 o.p. (ISBN 0-570-03854-5, 12-2809). Concordia.

Now You Know About: Animals, 5 bks. Barbara Donner et al. Incl. Animal Coverings. 32p; Animal Homes. 32p; How Animals Stay Alive. 32p; Many Animals. 32p (ISBN 0-87827-091-4); Where Animals Live. 32p (ISBN 0-87827-003-5); Where Animals Live. Five vols. with records. avail.. (Illus.). (gr. k-3). 1972. incl. cassettes 99.00 o.p. (ISBN 0-87827-090-6). Ency Brit Ed.

Nowhere. Thomas Berger. 192p. 1984. 14.95 o.p. (ISBN 0-385-29401-8, Sey Lawr). Delacorte.

Nowhere. Thomas Berger. 192p. 1986. pap. 8.95 o.p. (ISBN 0-385-29464-6, Delta). Dell.

Nowhere. Date not set. pap. (ISBN 0-385-29464-6). Delacorte.

NRCSA Directory of Special Interest Programs, 1982-1983: Britain-Ireland. Mibar, Ltd. Staff. 452p. pap. 6.95 o.p. (ISBN 0-937816-21-3). Tech Data.

NRCSA Program Directory Europe, 1982-83. Mibar, Ltd. Staff. 115p. (Orig.). 1982. pap. 6.95 o.p. (ISBN 0-937816-19-1). Tech Data.

NRJD on Three Eighty-Seven Glizzits a Day. Lawrence Casler. (Illus.). 64p. 1986. 5.95 o.p. (ISBN 0-87795-732-0, Arbor Hse). Morrow.

NRL Yearbook Eighty-Six. Minnie Rose & Kellen Hamilton. 256p. 1986. 19.95 o.p. (ISBN 0-317-65342-3). Springhouse Pub.

NRL Yearbook 86. Ed. by Helen Hamilton & Minnie B. Rose. 256p. 1986. 19.95 o.p. (ISBN 0-87434-031-4). Springhouse Pub.

NSC800 Microprocessor Cookbook. Roger C. Alford. (Illus.). 280p. 1983. 18.95 o.p. (ISBN 0-8306-0502-9, 1502); pap. 12.95 o.p. (ISBN 0-8306-1502-4). TAB Bks.

Nu Dang & His Kite. Jacqueline Ayer. LC 59-6561. (Illus.). (gr. 1-4). 1972. pap. 1.25 o.p. (ISBN 0-15-667800-4, AVB62, VoyB). HarBraceJ.

Nubber Bear. William Lipkind & Roger Duvoisin. LC 66-10077. (Illus.). (gr. k-3). 1966. 5.50 o.p. (ISBN 0-15-257590-1, HJ). HarBraceJ.

Nuclear Almanac: Confronting the Atom in War & Peace. Ed. by MIT Faculty Staff. LC 82-20596. (Illus.). 512p. (Orig.). 1984. 34.00 o.p. (ISBN 0-201-05331-4); pap. write for info. o.p. (ISBN 0-201-05332-2). Addison-Wesley.

Nuclear America: A Historical Bibliography. LC 83-12227. (ABC-Clio Research Guides Ser.: No. 3). 183p. 1984. lib. bdg. 28.00 o.p. (ISBN 0-87436-360-8). ABC-Clio.

Nuclear Analogue States. Ed. by D. Robson & J. D. Fox. LC 76-17849. (Benchmark Papers in Nuclear Physics: Vol. 1). 1976. 80.50 o.p. (ISBN 0-12-787356-2). Acad Pr.

Nuclear Apple & the Solar Orange: Alternatives in World Energy. M. Grenon. LC 80-40836. (Illus.). 200p. 1981. 50.00 o.p. (ISBN 0-08-026157-4); pap. 21.00 o.p. (ISBN 0-08-026156-6). Pergamon.

Nuclear Arms Control: With Effective International Agreements. Julie Dahlitz. 256p. 1984. text ed. 37.95x o.p. (ISBN 0-04-341023-5); pap. text ed. 14.95x o.p. (ISBN 0-04-341024-3). Unwin Hyman.

Nuclear Arms: 1984 Annual. Ed. by Bruno Leone. (Opposing Viewpoints SOURCES Ser.). 120p. pap. text ed. 9.95 o.p. (ISBN 0-89908-518-0). Greenhaven.

Nuclear Arms: 1985 Annual. Ed. by Bruno Leone et al. (Opposing Viewpoints Sources Ser.). 100p. 1985. pap. text ed. 9.95 o.p. (ISBN 0-89908-509-1). Greenhaven.

Nuclear Arms, 1986 Annual. Ed. by Bruno Leone et al. (Opposing Viewpoints SOURCES Ser.). 100p. 1986. pap. text ed. 9.95 o.p. (ISBN 0-89908-519-9). Greenhaven.

Nuclear Cardiology: Principles & Methods. Ed. by Aldo Serafini. LC 76-39783. (Topics In Cardiovascular Disease Ser.). (Illus.). 264p. 1977. 49.50x o.p. (ISBN 0-306-30952-1, Plenum Med Bk.). Plenum Pub.

Nuclear Challenge III: Safe Transport of Radioactive Materials. 1979. pap. 5.00 o.p. (ISBN 0-918734-06-1). Reymont.

Nuclear Chemistry. Ed. by G. T. Seaborg & W. Loveland. LC 81-23522. (Benchmark Papers in Physical Chemistry & Chemical Physics: Vol. 5). 489p. 1982. 87.95 o.p. (ISBN 0-87933-422-3). Van Nos Reinhold.

Nuclear Chemistry, 2 Vols. Ed. by L. Yaffe. 1968. 67.50 o.p. Vol. 1 (ISBN 0-12-767901-4). Vol. 2 (ISBN 0-12-767902-2). Acad Pr.

Nuclear Chemistry: Theory & Applications. Ed. by G. Choppin & J. Ryberg. (Illus.). 1980. 125.00 o.p. (ISBN 0-08-023826-2); pap. text ed. 39.00 o.p. (ISBN 0-08-023823-8). Pergamon.

Nuclear Deal. P-H.

Nuclear Destruction of Britain. Magnus Clarke. (Illus.). 290p. 1982. 25.00 o.p. (ISBN 0-7099-0458-4, Pub. by Croom Helm Ltd). Routledge Chapman & Hall.

Nuclear Division in the Fungi. Ed. by I. B. Heath. 1978. 52.00 o.p. (ISBN 0-12-335950-3). Acad Pr.

Nuclear-Electric Power in the Asia-Pacific Region: Proceedings of the Workshop Held in Honolulu, Hawaii, 23-28 January 1983. Ed. by D. J. Rose. 265p. 1985. pap. 61.00 o.p. (ISBN 0-08-031654-9). Pergamon.

Nuclear Electronic Industriments in Tropical Contries. (Technical Reports: No. 13). (Fr. & Eng.). 1963. pap. 6.25 o.p. (IDC13, IAEA). UNIPUB.

Nuclear Electronics. E. Kowalski. LC 72-98149. (Illus.). 1970. 52.10 o.p. (ISBN 0-387-04895-2). Springer-Verlag.

Nuclear Energy & the Environment. Ed. by Essam E. El-Hinnawi. LC 80-40365. (Illus.). 310p. 1980. 90.00 o.p. (ISBN 0-08-024472-6). Pergamon.

Nuclear Energy: In SI Metric Units. 2nd ed. R. L. Murray. 1980. text ed. 52.00 o.p. (ISBN 0-08-024751-2); pap. text ed. 22.00 o.p. (ISBN 0-08-024750-4). Pergamon.

Nuclear Energy Technology. Ronald A. Knief. (Illus.). 624p. 1981. text ed. 47.95 o.p. (ISBN 0-07-035086-8). McGraw.

Nuclear Envelope in Freeze-Etching. J. Kartenbeck et al. (Advances in Anatomy, Embryology & Cell Biology: Vol. 45, Pt. 1). (Illus.). 64p. 1971. pap. 22.50 o.p. (ISBN 0-387-05538-X). Springer-Verlag.

Nuclear Environment Information-Resources & Action Plans: AIF-NESP-001. Arthur D. Little, Inc. (National Environmental Studies Project: NESP Reports). 1974. 10.00 o.p. (ISBN 0-318-02230-3). US Coun Energy Awareness.

Nuclear Ethics. Joseph S. Nye, Jr. 1988. pap. 8.95 o.p. (ISBN 0-317-67528-1). Free Pr.

Nuclear Evolution: A Guide to Cosmic Enlightenment. Christopher Hills. (Illus.). 152p. 1968. 4.00 o.p. (ISBN 0-916438-00-7). Univ of Trees.

Nuclear Explosions & Their Effects. Massey. (ISBN 0-8022-1081-3). Philos Lib.

Nuclear First Use. Neville Brown et al. 1987. pap. 10.95 o.p. (ISBN 0-907675-26-3, Pub. by Buchan & Enright England). Seven Hills Bk Dists.

Titles

Nuclear Fission & Neutron-Induced Fission Cross-Sections. Ed. by A. Michaudon et al. LC 80-41822. (Neutron Physics & Nuclear Data in Science & Technology Ser.: Vol. 1). (Illus.). 270p. 1981. 81.00 o.p. (ISBN 0-08-026125-6). Pergamon.

Nuclear-Free Defence. Ed. by L. McKay & D Fernbach. 223p. 1983. pap. 7.50 o.p. (ISBN 0-946097-04-6, Pub. by GMP England). Alyson Pubns.

Nuclear Fuel Management. Harvey W. Graves. LC 78-19119. 327p. 1979. text ed. 54.95x o.p. (ISBN 0-471-03136-4). Wiley.

Nuclear Holocaust or World Peace. N. Ranganathan. 72p. 1984. Apt Bks.

Nuclear Hostages. Bernard J. O'Keefe. 1983. 14.45 o.p. (ISBN 0-395-34072-1). HM.

Nuclear Isospin. Ed. by J. D. Anderson et al. 1969. 91.00 o.p. (ISBN 0-12-058150-7). Acad Pr.

Nuclear Letters. Graham Lancaster. LC 78-10658. 1979. 8.95 o.p. (ISBN 0-689-10940-7, Atheneum). Macmillan.

Nuclear Litigation Nineteen Eighty-Four. Practising Law Institute Staff. 500p. 1984. pap. 15.00 o.p. (ISBN 0-317-27567-4, H4-4962). PLI.

Nuclear Love. Eugene Wildman. LC 70-189193. 85p. 1972. 7.95 o.p. (ISBN 0-8040-0568-0, Pub. by Swallow); pap. 4.95 o.p. (ISBN 0-8040-0569-9, Pub. by Swallow). Ohio U Pr.

Nuclear Magnetic Resonance & Electron Spin Resonance: Index For 1958-1963. Herbert M. Hershenson. 1965. 54.50 o.p. (ISBN 0-12-343260-X). Acad Pr.

Nuclear Magnetic Resonance Imaging Technology: A Clinical, Industrial, & Policy Analysis. Carl P. Steinberg & Alan B. Cohen. LC 84-601123. (Office of Technology Assessment Case Study Ser.: No. 27). 166p. (Orig.). 1984. pap. 5.50 o.p. (ISBN 0-318-11807-6, S/N 052-003-00964-1). USGPO.

Nuclear Magnetic Resonance in Chemistry: Proceedings. Ed. by Biagio Pesce. 1965. 88.00 o.p. (ISBN 0-12-552350-5). Acad Pr.

Nuclear Magnetic Resonance Shift Reagents. Robert E. Sievers. 1973. 48.50 o.p. (ISBN 0-12-643050-0). Acad Pr.

Nuclear Magnetic Resonance Spectra & Chemical Structure. Werner Brugel. 1968. 58.50 o.p. (ISBN 0-12-137450-5). Acad Pr.

Nuclear Magnetic Resonance Spectroscopy. Frank A. Bovey. LC 68-23485. 1969. 20.95 o.p. (ISBN 0-12-119750-6). Acad Pr.

Nuclear Materials: Accountability Management Safeguards. James E. Lovett. LC 74-78611. (ANS Monographs). 310p. 1974. 32.00 o.p. (ISBN 0-89448-001-4, 300007). Am Nuclear Soc.

Nuclear Medicine & Biology Advances: Proceedings of the Third World Congress on Nuclear Medicine & Biology, August 29 - September 2, 1982, Paris, France, 7 Vols. Ed. by C. Raynaud. 3685p. 1983. Set. 665.00 o.p. (ISBN 0-08-026405-0). Pergamon.

Nuclear Medicine for the General Physician. Thomas A. Verdon, Jr. LC 78-26954. (Illus.). 244p. 1980. 29.00 o.p. (ISBN 0-88416-206-0). Year Bk Med.

Nuclear Medicine in Clinical Pediatrics. Ed. by Hirsch Handmaker & Jerold M. Lowenstein. LC 74-25383. (Illus.). 310p. 1975. lib. bdg. 22.50 o.p. (ISBN 0-88416-036-X). Year Bk Med.

Nuclear Medicine in Japan. M. Iio. 310p. 1975. 60.00x o.p. (ISBN 0-89955-341-9, Pub. by Japan Sci Soc Japan). Intl Spec Bk.

Nuclear Medicine: Technology & Techniques. Donald R. Bernier et al. LC 80-17455. (Illus.). 551p. 1981. text ed. 46.95 o.p. (ISBN 0-8016-0662-4). Mosby.

Nuclear Medicine Technology Continuing Education Review. 2nd ed. E. V. Dubovsky et al. 1981. 21.50 o.p. (ISBN 0-87488-331-8). Med Exam.

Nuclear Medicine Technology Examination Review. Deborah L. Gryniewicz et al. LC 79-17328. (Orig.). 1980. pap. 18.95 o.p. (ISBN 0-668-04724-0). Appleton & Lange.

Nuclear Membrane & Nucleocytoplastic Interchange. C. M. Feldherr et al. (Protoplasmatologia: Vol. 5, Pt. 2). (Illus.). 1964. pap. 16.60 o.p. (ISBN 0-387-80690-3). Springer-Verlag.

Nuclear Methods in Environmental Research: Proceedings, American Nuclear Society Conference, Columbia, August 23-24, 1971. 245p. softcover 6.00 o.p. (ISBN 0-317-33010-1, 700005). Am Nuclear Soc.

Nuclear Navy, Nineteen Forty-Six to Nineteen Sixty-Two. Richard G. Hewlett & Francis Duncan. LC 74-5726. (Illus.). 544p. 1974. lib. bdg. 30.00x o.s.i. (ISBN 0-226-33219-5). U of Chicago Pr.

Nuclear News: Buyers Guide, 1985. American Nuclear Society Staff. 485p. 1985. 64.00 o.p. (130612). Am Nuclear Soc.

Nuclear News: Buyers Guide, 1986. American Nuclear Society Staff. 428p. 1986. 64.00 o.p. Am Nuclear Soc.

Nuclear Nonproliferation: The Spent Fuel Problem. Ed. by Frederick C. Williams & David A. Deese. (Pergamon Policy Studies). 1980. 60.00 o.p. (ISBN 0-08-023887-4). Pergamon.

Nuclear Optical Model Potential. Ed. by S. Boffi & G. Passatore. (Lecture Notes in Physics Ser.: Vol. 55). 1976. pap. 17.00 o.p. (ISBN 0-387-07864-9). Springer-Verlag.

Nuclear Overhauser Effect: Chemical Applications. Joseph H. Noggle & Richard E. Schirmer. 1971. 73.50 o.p. (ISBN 0-12-520650-X). Acad Pr.

Nuclear, Particle & Many Body Physics, 2 vols. Philip M. Morse et al. 1972. Vol. 1. 86.00 o.p. (ISBN 0-12-508201-0); Vol. 2. 70.00 o.p. (ISBN 0-12-508202-9). Acad Pr.

Nuclear Physics. M. G. Bowler. 444p. 1973. 105.00 o.p. (ISBN 0-08-016983-X); pap. text ed. 105.00 o.p. (ISBN 0-08-018990-3). Pergamon.

Nuclear Physics. Werner Heisenberg. 1953. (ISBN 0-8022-0706-5). Philos Lib.

Nuclear Physics. Ed. by Victor F. Weisskopf. (Italian Physical Society: Course 23). 1963. 82.50 o.p. (ISBN 0-12-368823-X). Acad Pr.

Nuclear Physics with Electromagnetic Interactions: Proceedings, International Conference, Mainz, Germany, June 1979. Ed. by H. Arenhovel & D. Drechsel. (Lecture Notes in Physics: Vol. 108). 1979. pap. 28.00 o.p. (ISBN 0-387-09539-X). Springer-Verlag.

Nuclear Plant Owner Certification: Proceedings, American Nuclear Society Executive Conference. 204p. pap. 32.00 o.p. (ISBN 0-89448-308-0, 650011). Am Nuclear Soc.

Nuclear Politics: America, France, & Britain. Wynfred Joshua & Walter F. Hahn. (Washington Papers: Vol. I, No. 9). 90p. (Orig.). 1973. pap. text ed. 7.95 o.p. (ISBN 0-8191-5964-6, Pub. by CSIS). U Pr of Amer.

Nuclear Power. 3rd. ed. Robert W. Deutsch. (Illus.). 42p. 1979. pap. 4.25 o.p. (ISBN 0-87683-299-0). GP Pub.

Nuclear Power. Resource Systems International Staff. 1982. pap. text ed. 15.00 o.p. (ISBN 0-8359-4976-1, Reston). P-H.

Nuclear Power & Its Regulation in the United States, Vol. 7, Pt. 2. Ed. by L. Manning Muntzing. (Illus.). 125p. 1981. pap. 36.00 o.p. (ISBN 0-08-027139-1). Pergamon.

Nuclear Power & Political Surveillance. Jay Peterzell. 110p. 1981. pap. 3.50 o.p. (ISBN 0-86566-015-8). Ctr Natl Security.

Nuclear Power & the Public Safety: A Study in Regulation. Elizabeth S. Rolph. LC 78-24795. (Illus.). 240p. 1979. 21.50x o.p. (ISBN 0-669-02822-3). Lexington Bks.

Nuclear Power, Both Sides: The Best Arguments for & Against the Most Controversial Technology. Ed. by Michio Kaku & Jennifer Trainer. (Illus.). 384p. 1982. 16.95 o.p. (ISBN 0-393-01631-5). Norton.

Nuclear Power Debate: A Guide to the Literature. Jerry W. Mansfield. LC 83-48255. 100p. 1984. lib. bdg. 20.00 o.p. (ISBN 0-8240-9102-7). Garland Pub.

Nuclear Power Decisions: British Policies, 1953-1978. Roger Williams. 365p. 1980. 35.00 o.p. (ISBN 0-7099-0265-4, Pub. by Croom Helm Ltd). Routledge Chapman & Hall.

Nuclear Power Development & the Fuel Cycle: Proceedings, American Nuclear Society 1st Pacific Basin Conference, Honolulu, October 11-14, 1976. 600p. 48.00 o.p. (ISBN 0-317-33026-8, 700018). Am Nuclear Soc.

Nuclear Power Hazard Control Policy. J. C. Chicken. LC 80-40992. (Illus.). 300p. 1981. 57.00 o.p. (ISBN 0-08-023254-X); pap. 21.00 o.p. (ISBN 0-08-023255-8). Pergamon.

Nuclear Power in an Age of Uncertainty. LC 84-601006. (Illus.). 305p. (Orig.). 1984. pap. 10.00 o.p. (S/N 052-003-00941-2). USGPO.

Nuclear Power in Perspective. Eric Addinall & Henry Ellington. 200p. 1982. 32.50 o.p. (ISBN 0-89397-110-3). Nichols Pub.

Nuclear Power Plant. E. Openshaw Taylor. 192p. 1960. (ISBN 0-8022-1695-1). Philos Lib.

Nuclear Power Plant Demographic Siting Criteria. NUS Corporation Staff. (National Environmental Studies Project: NESP Reports). 85p. 1981. 45.00 o.p. (ISBN 0-318-13584-1, AIF-NESP-019); NESP sponsors 15.00 o.p. (ISBN 0-318-13585-X). US Coun Energy Awareness.

Nuclear Power Plant Maintenance International Marketing, Salt Lake City, UT March 23-27, 1986, 2 vols. 1212p. 1986. pap. 96.00 o.p. (ISBN 0-89448-129-0, 700116). Am Nuclear Soc.

Nuclear Power Plant Steam & Mechanical Fundamentals, Vol. 5. 2nd ed. (Illus.). 98p. 1981. pap. text ed. 10.00x o.p. (ISBN 0-87683-305-9). GP Pub.

Nuclear Power Plant Steam & Mechanical Fundamentals, Vol. 7. 2nd ed. (Illus.). 124p. 1981. pap. text ed. 10.00x o.p. (ISBN 0-87683-307-5). GP Pub.

Nuclear Power Plants. softcover 10.00 o.p. (ISBN 0-686-14598-4, NP-1-75). P-PCI.

Nuclear Power, Pollution, & Politics. W. R. Burton & C. J. Hasslam. 240p. 1989. 59.50 o.p. (ISBN 0-415-03065-X). Routledge Chapman & Hall.

Nuclear Power Primer: Issues for Citizens. League of Women Voters Education Fund Staff. 80p. 1981. pap. 4.00 o.p. (ISBN 0-89959-290-2, 575). LWV US.

Nuclear Power Reactor Safety. E. E. Lewis. LC 77-21360. 630p. 1977. 59.95x o.p. (ISBN 0-471-53335-1, Pub. by Wiley-Interscience). Wiley.

Nuclear Power Reactor Safety: Proceedings, European & American Nuclear Societies International Meeting, Pt. I. 2312p. 1979. 30.00 o.p. (ISBN 0-317-33064-0, 120024). Am Nuclear Soc.

Nuclear Power Reactor Safety: Proceedings, European & American Nuclear Societies International Meeting, Pt. II. 256p. 1979. 30.00 o.p. (ISBN 0-317-33065-9, 120025). Am Nuclear Soc.

Nuclear Power Stations. R. Margulova. 432p. 1978. 10.00 o.p. (ISBN 0-8285-0691-4, Pub. by Mir Pubs USSR). Imported Pubns.

Nuclear Power: Status & Trends. 76p. (Orig.). 1987. pap. text ed. 18.50 o.p. (ISBN 92-0-159187-X, ISP680 4, IAEA). UNIPUB.

Nuclear Power Struggles: Industrial Competition & Proliferation Control. William Walker & Mans Lonnroth. (Illus.). 192p. 1983. text ed. 34.95x o.p. (ISBN 0-04-338104-9). Unwin Hyman.

Nuclear Power Waste Technology. Ed. by A. A. Moghissl et al. (Bk. No. G00132). 1978. 40.00 o.p. (ISBN 0-685-37571-4). ASME.

Nuclear Process Heat Applications: Proceedings, American Nuclear Society Conference, Los Alamos, October 1-3, 1974. 286p. 35.00 o.p. (ISBN 0-317-33011-X, 700010). Am Nuclear Soc.

Nuclear Quadrupole Coupling Constants. E. A. Lucken. 1969. 63.50 o.p. (ISBN 0-12-458450-0). Acad Pr.

Nuclear Quadrupole Resonance. Ed. by F. Boschke et al. F. Boschke. (Topics in Current Chemistry Ser.: Vol. 30). (Illus.). 180p. (Eng. & Ger.). 1972. pap. 30.30 o.p. (ISBN 0-387-05781-1). Springer-Verlag.

Nuclear Question. Ann E. Weiss. LC 80-8806. (Illus.). 192p. (gr. 7 up). 1981. 10.95 o.p. (ISBN 0-15-257596-0, HJ). HarBraceJ.

Nuclear Radiation in Geophysics. Ed. by H. Israel & A. Krebs. (Illus., Eng. & Ger.). 1962. 58.50 o.p. (ISBN 0-387-02860-9). Springer-Verlag.

Nuclear Reactions. I. E. McCarthy. 1970. 85.00 o.p. (ISBN 0-08-006630-5); pap. 85.00 o.p. (ISBN 0-08-006629-1). Pergamon.

Nuclear Reactions in Heavy Elements: A Data Handbook. V. M. Gorbachev & A. A. Zamyatnin. LC 79-40928. 460p. 1980. 180.00 o.p. (ISBN 0-08-023595-6). Pergamon.

Nuclear Reactor Instrumentation (In-Core) James F. Boland. LC 76-101310. 230p. 1970. 14.00 o.p. (ISBN 0-677-02420-7, 450015). Am Nuclear Soc.

Nuclear Reactor Kinetics. 2nd ed. Milton S. Ash. (Illus.). 1979. text ed. 75.00 o.p. (ISBN 0-07-002380-8). McGraw.

Nuclear Reactor Kinetics & Control. J. Lewins. LC 77-8107. 1978. 70.00 o.p. (ISBN 0-08-021682-X); pap. 70.00 o.p. (ISBN 0-08-021681-1). Pergamon.

Nuclear Reactors for Power Generation. O. Taylor. (Illus.). 140p. Philos Lib.

Nuclear Research with Low Energy Nuclear Accelerators. Ed. by Jerry B. Marion & Douglas M. Van Patter. 1967. 91.50 o.p. (ISBN 0-12-472259-8). Acad Pr.

Nuclear Safety. M. M. Williams. (Illus.). 1979. pap. 22.00 o.p. (ISBN 0-08-024752-0). Pergamon.

Nuclear Safety: Proceedings, American Nuclear Society Topical Meeting, Tucson, October 1975. 350p. softcover 18.00 o.p. (ISBN 0-317-33037-3, 700013). Am Nuclear Soc.

Nuclear Science & Engineering-Improved Methods for Analysis of Nuclear Systems: Proceedings, American Nuclear Society Topical Meeting, Pt. I. Mathematics & Computation Division Staff. 277p. 1977. 25.60 o.p. (ISBN 0-317-33067-5, 110001). Am Nuclear Soc.

Nuclear Science & Engineering-Improved Methods for Analysis of Nuclear Systems: Proceedings, American Nuclear Society Topical Meeting, Pt. II. Mathematics & Computation Division Staff. 434p. 1977. 39.60 o.p. (ISBN 0-317-33068-3, 110002). Am Nuclear Soc.

Nuclear Solutions to World Energy Problems: Proceedings, American Nuclear Society International Conference, Washington DC, November 13-17, 1972. 788p. 37.00 o.p. (ISBN 0-317-33018-7, 700007). Am Nuclear Soc.

Nuclear Spectroscopy. Ed. by G. Racah. (Italian Physical Society: Course 15). 1962. 82.50 o.p. (ISBN 0-12-368815-9). Acad Pr.

Nuclear Spectroscopy & Reactions, 4 pts. Ed. by Joseph Cerney. Set. 359.00 o.p.; Pt. A 1974. 112.50 o.p. (ISBN 0-12-165201-7); Pt. B 1974. 123.00 o.p. (ISBN 0-12-165202-5); Pt. C 1974. 123.00 o.p. (ISBN 0-12-165203-3); Pt. D 1975. 85.00 o.p. (ISBN 0-12-165204-1). Acad Pr.

Nuclear Stakes: Race to the Finish. Dervla Murphy. LC 81-23277. 272p. 1982. 13.95 o.p. (ISBN 0-89919-105-3). Ticknor & Fields.

Nuclear Structure. Ed. by K. Abrahams et al. LC 81-7291. (NATO ASI Series B, Physics: Vol. 67). 442p. 1981. 79.50x o.p. (ISBN 0-306-40728-0, Plenum Pr). Plenum Pub.

Nuclear Structure. William F. Hornyak. 1975. 111.50 o.p. (ISBN 0-12-356050-0). Acad Pr.

Nuclear Structure & Nuclear Reactions. Ed. by M. Jean. (Italian Physical Society: Course 40). 1969. 99.00 o.p. (ISBN 0-12-368840-X). Acad Pr.

Nuclear Structure Theory. J. M. Irvine. 492p. 1972. 110.00 o.p. (ISBN 0-08-016401-3); pap. 110.00 o.p. (ISBN 0-08-018991-1). Pergamon.

Nuclear Structures of Protocaryotic Organisms. G. W. Fuhs. (Protoplasmatologia: Vol. 5, Pt. 4). (Illus.). 1969. 54.30 o.p. (ISBN 0-387-80917-1). Springer-Verlag.

Nuclear Techniques in Analytical Chemistry. A. J. Moses. LC 64-15736. (International Series on Analytical Chemistry: Vol. 20). 1964. 35.00 o.p. (ISBN 0-08-010695-1). Pergamon.

Nuclear Terrorism Threat: A Bibliography. Amos Lakos. (Public Administration Ser.: P 1779). 20p. 1985. 3.00 o.p. (ISBN 0-89028-579-9). Vance Biblios.

Nuclear Theory, Vol. 1: Nuclear Models. 2nd ed. J. M. Eisenberg & W. Greiner. 486p. 1976. pap. 58.00 o.p. (ISBN 0-444-10790-8, North-Holland). Elsevier.

Nuclear Track Registration: Proceedings of the Pacific Northwest Conference, 5th, Hanford Engineering Development Laboratory, Westinghouse Hanford Company, Richland, WA, July 28-29, 1982. Ed. by E. V. Benton et al. 96p. 1983. pap. 61.00 o.p. (ISBN 0-08-030274-2). Pergamon.

Nuclear War Fun Book. Victor Langer & Walter Thomas. LC 82-12893. (Illus.). 128p. 1983. pap. 5.95 o.p. (ISBN 0-03-063396-6, Owl Bks). H Holt & Co.

Nuclear War, Nuclear Peace. Leon Wieseltier. 128p. 1983. 7.95 o.p. (ISBN 0-03-064082-2); pap. 2.95 o.p. (ISBN 0-03-064029-6). H Holt & Co.

Nuclear Waste Primer. Date not set. (ISBN 0-8052-6007-2); pap. (ISBN 0-8052-6006-4). Random.

Nuclear Waste Reprocessing. Ed. by G. R. Plumb. (Illus.). 72p. 1984. pap. 44.00 o.p. (ISBN 0-08-031509-7). Pergamon.

Nuclear Weapons, Policies & the Test Ban Issue. S. T. Cohen & William R. Van Cleave. 1987. text ed. write for info. o.p. (ISBN 0-8179-8431-3, Co-Pub. by Praeger); pap. text ed. write for info. o.p. (ISBN 0-8179-8432-1). Hoover Inst Pr.

Nuclei & Cerebral Connections of the Human Thalamus see Variations & Connections of the Human Thalamus.

Nucleic Acid Hybridization in the Study of Cell Differentiation. Ed. by H. Ursprung. LC 70-188705. (Results & Problems in Cell Differentiation: Vol. 3). (Illus.). 120p. 1972. 24.00 o.p. (ISBN 0-387-05742-0). Springer-Verlag.

Nucleic Acid Metabolism, Cell Differentiation & Cancer Growth. E. V. Cowdry & S. Seno. 1969. 130.00 o.p. (ISBN 0-08-013252-9). Pergamon.

Nucleic Acid-Protein Recognition. Ed. by H. J. Vogel. 1977. 82.50 o.p. (ISBN 0-12-722560-9). Acad Pr.

Nucleic Acid Structure: An Introduction. W. Guschlbauer. LC 75-11796. (Heidelberg Science Library: Vol. 21). (Illus.). 180p. 1976. pap. 17.60 o.p. (ISBN 0-387-90141-8). Springer-Verlag.

Nucleic Acids & Nucleoproteins: Proceedings, Vol. 12. Cold Spring Harbor Symposia on Quantitative Biology Staff. Repr. of 1947 ed. 27.00 o.p. (ISBN 0-384-42250-0). Johnson Repr.

Nucleic Acids & Proteins: The Proceedings of China-West Germany Symposium on Nucleic Acids & Proteins. Science Press Staff. 662p. 1981. 54.95 o.p. (ISBN 0-442-20072-2). Van Nos Reinhold.

Nucleic Acids in Immunology: Proceedings. Symposium of the Institute of Microbiology, Rutgers University, 1967. Ed. by O. J. Plescia & W. Braun. (Illus.). 1968. 62.10 o.p. (ISBN 0-387-04290-3). Springer-Verlag.

Nucleolus. Ed. by Harris Busch & Karel Smetana. 1970. 104.00 o.p. (ISBN 0-12-147652-9). Acad Pr.

Nucleosides As Biological Probes. Robert J. Suhadolnik. LC 79-10719. 364p. 1979. 101.50 o.p. (ISBN 0-471-05317-1, Pub. by Wiley-Interscience). Krieger.

Nucleosides in Cancer Treatment: Rational Approaches to Antimetabolite Selectivity & Modulation. Ed. by M. H. Tattersall & R. M. Fox. LC 80-70775. (Ludwig Symposia Ser.: Vol. 1). 1981. 54.50 o.p. (ISBN 0-12-683820-8). Acad Pr.

Nucleotide Metabolism. J. Frank Henderson & A. R. Paterson. 1973. 72.50 o.p. (ISBN 0-12-340550-5). Acad Pr.

Nucleus of a Library. 106p. Date not set. pap. 5.45 o.p. (ISBN 0-87506-034-X). Campus.

Nude & the Portrait: How to Pose & Paint Them. John Wynne-Morgan. (Illus.). 12.95 o.p. (ISBN 0-87523-147-0). Emerson.

Nude Before God: A Novel. Shiv K. Kumar. 187p. 1986. text ed. 20.00x o.p. (ISBN 81-207-0009-0, Pub. by Sterling Pubs India). Apt Bks.

Nude Nineteen Hundred. Ed. by J. P. Bourgeron. 64p. 1980. pap. 8.95 o.p. (ISBN 0-87100-169-1, 2169). Morgan.

Nude Nineteen Twenty-Five. J. P. Bourgeron & P. J. Balbo. LC 78-70678. (Illus.). 64p. 1978. pap. 8.95 o.s.i. (ISBN 0-87100-154-3, 2154). Morgan.

Nudge-Nudge Wink-Wink: A Quotebook of Love & Sex. Nigel Rees. (Illus.). 128p. (Orig.). 1987. pap. 3.95 o.p. (ISBN 0-7137-1916-8, Pub. by Javelin England). Sterling.

Nudges: IBM Logo Projects for Children. Steve Tipps et al. 228p. (gr. 4-8). 1984. pap. 16.95 o.p. (ISBN 0-03-000224-9). HR&W.

Nudity As Therapy. Aileen Goodson. Ed. by Art Kunkin. 300p. Date not set. text ed. 24.95 o.p. (ISBN 1-55599-026-6). Elysium.

Nuestra idea de Dios see Our Idea of God.

Nueva Epanortosis al Diccionario de Anonimos Seudonimos de J. T. Medina. Ricardo Victorica. LC 73-78357. 207p. (Span.). 1973. Repr. of 1929 ed. 16.00x o.p. (ISBN 0-87917-028-X). Ethridge.

Nueva Vida. Andrew Murray. 144p. 1979. 2.95 o.p. (ISBN 0-88113-220-9). Edit Betania.

Nuffield Maths Four: Math Five-Eleven. rev. ed. Nuffield Foundation Staff. Ed. by Eric A. Albany. 96p. 1981. tchrs.' ed 15.95 o.p. (ISBN 0-582-19178-5). Longman.

Nuffield Maths Three: Maths Five to Eleven. rev. ed. Nuffield Foundation Staff. Ed. by Eric A. Albany. 112p. 1980. tchrs.' manual 15.95 o.p. (ISBN 0-582-19177-7). Longman.

Nuggets From Numbers. W. G. Heslop. LC 75-13660. (W. G. Heslop Bible Study Aids). 192p. 1975. pap. 4.50 o.p. (ISBN 0-8254-2828-9). Kregel.

Nuggets of Knowledge. George W. Stimpson. LC 75-109182. 1970. Repr. of 1928 ed. 46.00x o.p. (ISBN 0-8103-3860-2). Gale.

Nuits de la Colere: Avec: Poof. Armand Salacrou. (Folio 93). 1972. 3.95 o.p. (ISBN 0-686-55437-X). Schoenhof.

Number Four. Molly Cone. LC 72-2758. (Illus.). 160p. (gr. 5-9). 1972. 6.95 o.p. (ISBN 0-395-13889-2). HM.

Number Puzzles, No. 3. The Diagram Group Staff. 96p. (Orig.). 1983. pap. 1.75 o.s.i. (ISBN 0-345-30479-9). Ballantine.

Number Theory. Z. I. Borevich & I. R. Shafarevich. (Pure and Applied Mathematics: Vol. 20). 1966. text ed. 25.00 o.p. (ISBN 0-12-117850-1). Acad Pr.

Number Theory & Algebra: Collected Papers Dedicated to Henry B. Mann, Arnold E. Ross & Olga Taussky-Todd. Hans Zassenhaus. 1977. 85.00 o.p. (ISBN 0-12-776350-3). Acad Pr.

Number Two: A Look at the Vice Presidency. Robert I. Alotta. LC 81-2109. (Illus.). 256p. (gr. 7 up). 1981. PLB 10.79 o.p. (ISBN 0-671-41628-6). Messner.

Numbers. Leo Lionni. LC 84-10091. (To Talk About Ser.). (Illus.). 12p. (ps). 1985. 3.95 o.s.i. (ISBN 0-394-87002-6, Pant Bks Young). Pantheon.

Numbers. Jan Pienkowski. (Concept Bks.). (Illus.). 32p. (ps-k). 1981. 3.95 o.s.i. (ISBN 0-671-44456-5, Little Simon). S&S.

Numbers. John Rechy. 1967. pap. 3.95 o.p. (ISBN 0-394-17130-6, B171, BC). Grove.

Numbers. Dorothy Rose. (Chubby Banana Split Board Bks.). (ps). 1984. 2.95 o.s.i. (ISBN 0-671-50956-X, Little Simon). S&S.

Numbers. Peter Seymour. (Turn & Learn Bks.). (Illus.). 8p. (ps-1). 1984. 5.95 o.s.i. (ISBN 0-02-782090-4). Macmillan.

Numbers. Gillian Youldon. (Picture Play Ser.). (Illus.). 32p. (ps-2). 1986. PLB 9.40 o.p. (ISBN 0-531-00440-6). Watts.

Numbers: A Commentary. Martin Noth. Tr. by James D. Martin. LC 69-12129. (Old Testament Library). 268p. 1969. 13.95 o.s.i. (ISBN 0-664-20841-X, Westminster). Westminster John Knox.

Numbers & Counting. National Education Association Staff. 1983. pap. 1.95 o.p. (ISBN 0-380-82727-1, 82727). Avon.

Numbers & Mathematics. 2nd ed. Clayton W. Dodge. LC 74-31133. 1975. text ed. write for info. o.p. (ISBN 0-87150-180-5, PWS 1481, Prindle). PWS-Kent Pub.

Numbers & Numerals. Reusable ed. Kitty Wehrli. (Michigan Arithmetic Program Ser.). (ps-2). 1976. 1.00 o.p. (ISBN 0-89039-199-8); wkbk. 7.00 o.p. (ISBN 0-89039-102-5). Ann Arbor Pubs.

Numbers & Units for Science. Frank E. Harris. (gr. 10-12). 1972. pap. text ed. 6.00 o.p. (ISBN 0-8449-0301-9). Carroll CA.

Numbers Game. Margaret Willerding. 1977. pap. text ed. write for info. o.p. (ISBN 0-87150-232-1, PWS 1862, Prindle). PWS-Kent Pub.

Numbers in Theory & Practice. Ed. by Blaise W. Liffick. (Orig.). 1979. pap. text ed. 16.95 o.p. (ISBN 0-07-037827-4, BYTE Bks). McGraw.

Numbers: Their History & Meaning. Date not set. (ISBN 0-8052-3847-6). Random.

Numerical Analysis. 3rd ed. Richard J. Burden et al. 1985. pap. text ed. write for info. o.p. (ISBN 0-87150-243-7, Prindle). PWS-Kent Pub.

Numerical Analysis. I. M. Khabaza. 1965. 33.00 o.p. (ISBN 0-08-010776-1); pap. 17.00 o.p. (ISBN 0-08-010775-3). Pergamon.

Numerical Analysis. Ed. by G. A. Watson. LC 75-45241. (Lecture Notes in Mathematics Ser.: Vol. 506). 1976. pap. 16.00 o.p. (ISBN 0-387-07610-7). Springer-Verlag.

Numerical Analysis for Semiconductor Devices. Mamoru Kurata. LC 80-8374. 288p. 1982. 35.00x o.p. (ISBN 0-669-04043-6). Lexington Bks.

Numerical Analysis of Singular Perturbation Problems. Ed. by P. W. Hemker & J. J. Miller. 1979. 91.00 o.p. (ISBN 0-12-340250-6). Acad Pr.

Numerical & Aphabetical Progressions & Abstract Reasoning. Jack Rudman. (Career Examination Ser.: CS-30). (Cloth bdg. avail. on request). pap. 12.00 o.p. (ISBN 0-8373-3730-5). Natl Learning.

Numerical & Asymptotic Techniques in Electromagnetics. Ed. by R. Mittra. LC 74-30146. (Topics in Applied Physics Ser.: Vol. 3). (Illus.). 290p. 1975. 43.00 o.p. (ISBN 0-387-07072-9). Springer-Verlag.

Numerical & Matrix Methods in Structural Mechanics, with Applications to Computers. Ping-Chun Wang. LC 66-11529. 426p. 1966. 62.95x o.p. (ISBN 0-471-91950-0). Wiley.

Numerical Computing: An Introduction. Lawrence F. Shampine & Richard C. Allen. LC 72-93122. 258p. 1973. text ed. 20.95 o.p. (ISBN 0-7216-8150-6). HR&W.

Numerical Control for Machine Tools. C. H. Barron. 1971. text ed. 44.95 o.p. (ISBN 0-07-003824-4). McGraw.

Numerical Heat Transfer & Fluid Flow. Suhas V. Patankar. LC 79-28286. (Hemisphere Series on Computational Methods in Mechanics & Thermal Sciences). (Illus.). 208p. 1980. text ed. 48.95 o.p. (ISBN 0-07-048740-5). McGraw.

Numerical Methods for Engineers & Scientists. A. C. Bajpai et al. (Series of Programmes on Mathematics for Scientists & Technologists). 380p. 1977. 37.00x o.p. (ISBN 0-471-99542-8, Pub. by Wiley-Interscience). Wiley.

Numerical Methods for Grid Equations. A. A. Samarskii & E. S. Nikolaev. 300p. 1988. 89.00 o.p. (ISBN 0-8176-3099-6). Birkhauser.

Numerical Methods for Non-Linear Variational Problems. R. Olowinski. (Tata Institute Lectures on Mathematics Ser.). 240p. 1981. pap. 10.00 o.p. (ISBN 0-387-08774-5). Springer-Verlag.

Numerical Methods in Geotechnic Engineering. Desai & Christian. 1977. text ed. 59.95 o.p. (ISBN 0-07-016542-4). McGraw.

Numerical Methods in Markov Chains & Bulk Queues. T. P. Bagchi & J. G. Templeton. LC 72-88380. (Lecture Notes in Economics & Mathematical Systems: Vol. 72). xi, 89p. 1972. pap. 7.00 o.p. (ISBN 0-387-05996-2). Springer-Verlag.

Numerical Methods in Weather Prediction. rev. ed. G. I. Marchuk. 1974. 64.00 o.p. (ISBN 0-12-470650-9). Acad Pr.

Numerical Modeling of Manufacturing Processes, PVP-PB-025. Ed. by R. F. Jones, Jr. et al. 188p. 1977. pap. text ed. 20.00 o.p. (ISBN 0-685-86872-9, G00131). ASME.

Numerical Models for Tidal Rivers, Estuaries & Coastal Waters: Bibliography. R. Gordon & M. L. Spaulding. (Technical Report Ser.: No. 32). 55p. 1974. 2.00 o.p. (ISBN 0-938412-31-0, P376). Sea Grant Pubns.

Numerical Optimization of Computer Models. Hans-Paul Schwefel. LC 81-173223. 389p. 1981. 54.95 o.p. (ISBN 0-471-09988-0, Pub. by Wiley-Interscience). Wiley.

Numerical Prediction of Flow, Heat Transfer Turbulence, & Combustion: Selected Works of Professor D. Brian Spalding. Ed. by S. V. Patankar et al. LC 83-12172. 444p. 1983. 130.00 o.p. (ISBN 0-08-030937-2, 11). Pergamon.

Numerical Quadrature & Solution of Ordinary Differential Equations: A Textbook for a Beginning Course in Numerical Analysis. A. H. Stroud. (Applied Mathematical Sciences Ser.: Vol. 10). (Illus.). 350p. 1974. pap. 18.50 o.p. (ISBN 0-387-90100-0). Springer-Verlag.

Numerical Record of University Attendance in Germany in the Last Fifty Years. C. Quetsch. (Illus.). 1961. pap. 7.10 o.p. (ISBN 0-387-02741-6). Springer-Verlag.

Numerical Simulation. (SPE Reprint Ser.). 465p. 1973. 24.00x o.p. (ISBN 0-317-32927-8, 30511). Soc Petrol Engineers.

Numerical Solution of Differential Equations. Isaac Fried. (Computer Science & Applied Math Ser.). 1979. 52.50 o.p. (ISBN 0-12-267780-3). Acad Pr.

Numerical Solution of Ordinary Differential Equations. Leon Lapidus & John H. Seinfeld. (Mathematics in Science & Engineering Ser.: Vol. 74). 1971. 77.00 o.p. (ISBN 0-12-436650-3). Acad Pr.

Numerical Treatment of Differential Equations. 3rd ed. L. Collatz. (Grundlehren der Mathematischen Wissenschaften Ser.: Vol. 60). (Illus.). 1976. 69.70 o.p. (ISBN 0-387-03519-2). Springer-Verlag.

Numerically Controlled or Special Purpose Machining I. Ed. by L. Butlin et al. (E.I.T.B. Training Manuals Ser.). (Illus.). 271p. 1984. pap. 49.95x cancelled o.p. (ISBN 0-85083-542-9). Trans-Atl Phila.

Numerous Numerals. James M. Henle. LC 75-19347. 48p. 1975. pap. 3.00 o.p. (ISBN 0-87353-079-9). NCTM.

Numismatic Art in America: Aesthetics & the United States Coinage. Cornelius Vermeule. LC 76-135549. (Illus.). 1971. 24.00x o.s.i. (ISBN 0-674-62840-3, Belknap Pr). Harvard U Pr.

Numismatic Fine Arts Auction VIII Catalogue (With Prices Realized) Ancient Greek Coins Featuring a Selection from the Museum of Fine Arts, Boston & Other Owners. 1980. 15.00 o.p. (ISBN 0-686-81262-X). Numismatic Fine Arts.

Numismatic Fine Arts Auction XIV Catalogue (With Prices Realized) Ancient Greek & Roman Coins. 1984. pap. 15.00x o.p. (ISBN 0-318-04767-5). Numismatic Fine Arts.

Numismatic Fine Arts Auction XVI Catalogue (With Prices Realized) Ancient Greek & Roman Coins. 1985. 15.00 o.p. (ISBN 0-318-18562-8). Numismatic Fine Arts.

Nun: A Memoir. Mary G. Wong. LC 82-47656. 416p. 1983. 15.95 o.p. (ISBN 0-15-167739-5). HarBraceJ.

Nun in the Concentration Camp. C. M. Target. 1974. pap. text ed. 1.60 o.s.i. (ISBN 0-08-017611-9). Pergamon.

Nunamuit Ethnoarchaeology. Lewis R. Binford. (Studies in Archaeology). 1978. 50.00 o.p. (ISBN 0-12-100040-0). Acad Pr.

Nunchaku & Sai: Ancient Okinawan Martial Arts. Ryusho Sakagami & Setsumei Sakagami. (Okinawan Combat Arts Ser.). (Illus.). 180p. 1974. pap. 11.50 o.p. (ISBN 0-87040-333-8). Japan Pubns USA.

Nungu & the Hippopotamus. Babette Cole. LC 78-12382. (Illus.). (gr. k-2). 1979. text ed. 7.95 o.p. (ISBN 0-07-011695-4). McGraw.

Nuns in Jeopardy. Martin Boyd. LC 74-17476. 217p. 1975. pap. 2.95 o.p. (ISBN 0-15-667820-9, Harv). HarBraceJ.

Nuovissimo Dizionario Tecnico. Giuseppe Ragazzini. 1278p. (Eng. & Ital.). 1983. 75.00 o.p. (ISBN 0-8288-0637-3, M 8305). French & Eur.

Nuremberg: German Views of the War Trials. Ed. by Wilbourn E. Benton & Georg Grimm. LC 55-5739. 1955. 14.95x o.p. (ISBN 0-87074-006-7). SMU Press.

Nurse - Midwifery. Varney. 1980. 37.50 o.p. (ISBN 0-8016-5234-0, B-5234-0). Mosby.

Nurse & the Mental Patient: A Study in Interpersonal Relations. Morris S. Schwartz & Emmy L. Shockley. 284p. 1965. pap. 18.95 o.p. (ISBN 0-471-76610-0). Wiley.

Nurse Assistant. Lucy Brooks. 1978. 14.95 o.p. (ISBN 0-442-20943-6). Van Nos Reinhold.

Nurse Assistant in Long Term Care: A New Era. Betty J. Walston & Keith E. Walston. LC 80-12308. (Illus.). 204p. 1980. pap. text ed. 19.95 o.p. (ISBN 0-8016-5355-X). Mosby.

Nurse-Client Interaction: Implementing the Nursing Process. 3rd ed. Sandra Sundeen et al. LC 80-27585. (Illus.). 264p. 1985. pap. text ed. 14.95 o.p. (ISBN 0-8016-4910-2). Mosby.

Nurse Faculty: Socioeconomic Trends 1985. (Illus.). 88p. (Orig.). 1986. pap. 18.95 o.p. (ISBN 0-88737-102-7, 19-1969). Natl League Nurse.

Nurse Faculty: Socioeconomic Trends 1986. 2nd ed. (Illus.). 82p. 1987. pap. 18.95 o.p. (ISBN 0-88737-355-0, 19-2174). Natl League Nurse.

Nurse-Manager in the Emergency Department. Margaret Miller. LC 82-2264. (Illus.). 338p. 1982. 27.95 o.p. (ISBN 0-8016-3512-8). Mosby.

Nurse Practitioner: Current Practice Issues. Joellen B. Hawkins & Janice A. Thibodeau. LC 82-62154. 160p. (Orig.). 1983. pap. text ed. 7.95 o.p. (ISBN 0-913292-34-6). Tiresias Pr.

Nurse Staffing Based on Patient Classification: An Examination of Case Studies. American Hospital Association Clearinghouse for Hospital Management Engineering Staff. LC 83-2561. 188p. 1983. pap. 20.00 o.p. (ISBN 0-87258-384-8, AHA-154150). Am Hospital.

Nursery Alice. Lewis Carroll. (Illus.). (gr. 5 up). 9.00 o.p. (ISBN 0-8446-1815-2). Peter Smith.

Nursery Babies. Georgeanne Irvine. (Zoo Babies Ser.). (Illus.). 16p. (Orig.). (gr. k-3). 1983. pap. 1.25 o.p. (ISBN 0-8249-8057-3). Ideals.

Nursery Crimes. B. M. Gill. 1987. 15.95 o.p. (ISBN 0-684-18800-7). Scribner.

Nursery Rhymes. Illus. by Douglas Gorsline. LC 76-24168. (Picturebacks Ser). (Illus.). (ps-2). 1977. pap. 1.95 o.s.i. (ISBN 0-394-83550-6, BYR). Random.

Nursery Songs. Joseph Moorat. LC 80-16025. (Illus.). 42p. (ps). 1980. 9.95 o.p. (ISBN 0-87099-242-2). Metro Mus Art.

Nursery Songs. Joseph Moorat & Paul Woodroffe. (Illus.). 1980. 12.95 o.p. (ISBN 0-500-01242-3). Thames Hudson.

Nursery Tales, Traditions, & Histories of the Zulus: In their Own Words, with a Translation. Henry Callaway. LC 72-132641. 1970. Repr. of 1868 ed. lib. bdg. 22.50x o.p. (ISBN 0-8371-2493-X, CNT&, Pub. by Negro U Pr). Greenwood.

Nurses. Richard Frede. 480p. 1985. 17.45 o.p. (ISBN 0-395-38169-X). HM.

Nurse's Aide Handbook. Carmen C. Sanchez. LC 83-19730. 304p. 1984. pap. 10.00 o.p. (ISBN 0-668-05858-7, 5858). Arco.

Nurse's Drug Reference. Stewart M. Brooks. 1978. text ed. 22.50 o.p. (ISBN 0-316-10973-8); pap. text ed. 16.95 o.p. (ISBN 0-316-10975-4). Little.

Nurse's Guide to Diagnostic Procedures. 4th ed. Ruth M. French. (Illus.). 384p. 1975. text ed. 13.95 o.p. (ISBN 0-07-022141-3); pap. text ed. 9.95 o.p. (ISBN 0-07-022140-5). McGraw.

Nurse's Story. Carol Gino. 352p. 1982. 15.50 o.p. (ISBN 0-671-45390-4, Linden Pr). S&S.

Nursing: A Human Needs Approach. Janice R. Ellis & Elizabeth A. Nowlis. LC 76-12023. (Illus.). 416p. 1977. text ed. 17.95 o.p. (ISBN 0-395-24067-0). HM.

Nursing: A Human Needs Approach. 2nd ed. Janice R. Ellis & Elizabeth A. Nowlis. LC 80-82841. (Illus.). 528p. 1981. text ed. 29.95 o.p.; 2.00 o.p. HM.

Nursing Administration: A Selected Annotated Bibliography of Current Periodical Literature in Nursing Administration. rev. ed. 88p. 1984. pap. text ed. 12.95 o.p. (ISBN 0-88737-129-9, 20-1965). Natl League Nurse.

Nursing & Cancer. Nancy Burns. (Illus.). 400p. 1982. pap. (ISBN 0-7216-2184-8). Saunders.

Nursing & Nursing Education: Public Policies & Private Actions. Institute of Medicine Staff & National Research Council Staff. 336p. 1983. pap. text ed. 18.75x o.p. (ISBN 0-309-03346-2). Natl Acad Pr.

Nursing & the American Health Care Delivery System. 2nd ed. Joellen B. Hawkins & Loretta P. Higgins. LC 84-52528. (Illus.). 192p. 1985. pap. 9.00 o.p. (ISBN 0-913292-35-4). Tiresias Pr.

Nursing & the American Health Care Delivery System. Joellen W. Hawkins & Loretta P. Higgins. LC 81-50580. (Illus.). 192p. (Orig.). 1982. flexible bdg. 8.95 o.p. (ISBN 0-913292-33-8). Tiresias Pr.

Nursing & the Law. 2nd ed. Sue D. Calloway. LC 86-230444. 250p. 1987. pap. 30.00 o.p. (ISBN 0-941161-23-4). PES Inc WI.

Nursing Care of Infants & Children. 2nd ed. Lucille F. Whaley & Donna L. Wong. LC 82-8111. (Illus.). 1722p. 1983. text ed. 49.95 o.p. (ISBN 0-8016-5419-X). Mosby.

Nursing Care of the Cancer Patient. 4th ed. Rosemary Bouchard & Norma F. Owens. LC 80-21708. (Illus.). 503p. 1981. pap. text ed. 31.95 o.p. (ISBN 0-8016-0720-5). Mosby.

Nursing Care of the Labor Patient. 2nd ed. Janet S. Malinowski. LC 82-22081. (Illus.). 302p. 1983. pap. text ed. 13.95x o.p. (ISBN 0-8036-5802-8). Davis Co.

Nursing Care of the Patient with Burns. Florence G. Jacoby. 1972. 8.25 o.p. (ISBN 0-318-03563-4). Phoenix Soc.

Nursing Care Planning Guides from Nurseco, 5 sets. 2nd ed. Neal & Cohen. 1980. Set. 59.95 o.p. (ISBN 0-87489-330-5). Med Economics.

Nursing Care Plans for the Pediatric Patient. Children's Hospital & Medical Center Staff, Seattle, Washington. 500p. 1987. 22.95 o.p. (ISBN 0-8016-0988-7). Mosby.

Nursing Care Plans: Nursing Diagnoses in Planning Patient Care. E. Marilynn Doenges et al. LC 83-25211. 696p. 1984. pap. text ed. 27.95 o.p. (ISBN 0-8036-2660-6). Davis Co.

Titles

Nursing Critically Ill Patients Confidently. 2nd ed. Ed. by Susan Williams & Barbara McVan. LC 84-5635. (New Nursing Skillbook Ser.). (Illus.). 192p. 1984. text ed. 14.95 o.p. (ISBN 0-916730-67-0). Springhouse Pub.
Nursing Data Review 1985-1986. (Illus.). 192p. (Orig.). 1986. pap. 24.95 o.p. (ISBN 0-88737-217-1, 19-1994). Natl League Nurse.
Nursing Data Review, 1986. 2nd ed. 200p. 1987. pap. 24.95 o.p. (ISBN 0-88737-357-7). Natl League Nurse.
Nursing Data Review, 1987. 3rd ed. 200p. 1988. pap. 24.95 o.p. (ISBN 0-317-65351-2). Natl League Nurse.
Nursing Eighty-Seven Drug Handbook. 1987. 19.95 o.p. (ISBN 0-317-65343-1). Springhouse Pub.
Nursing Ethics. Ian E. Thompson & Kath M. Melia. LC 82-17696. 143p. 1983. pap. text ed. 12.00 o.p. (ISBN 0-443-02430-8). Churchill.
Nursing Implications of Laboratory Tests. Mary B. McFarland & Moeller M. Grant. LC 82-7077. 407p. 1982. pap. 16.50 o.p. (ISBN 0-471-04692-2). Wiley.
Nursing in the Community. Ed. by Victoria Schoolcraft. LC 83-21592. 572p. 1984. 25.00 o.p. (ISBN 0-471-86409-9, Pub. by Wiley Medic). Wiley.
Nursing Issues & Research in Terminal Care, Vol. 6. Ed. by Jennifer Wilson-Barnett & Jennifer Raiman. (Developments in Nursing Research Ser.). 1988. pap. (ISBN 0-471-91795-8). Wiley.
Nursing Leadership: Concepts & Practice. Ruth M. Tappen. LC 82-22144. (Illus.). 458p. 1983. pap. text ed. 16.95 o.p. (ISBN 0-8036-8334-0). Davis Co.
Nursing Management & Education: A Conceptual Approach. Michael P. Bowman. 320p. (Orig.). 1986. pap. 19.00 o.p. (ISBN 0-7099-3234-0, Pub. by Croom Helm UK). Routledge Chapman & Hall.
Nursing Management of Diabetes Mellitus. 2nd ed. Diana W. Guthrie & Richard A. Guthrie. LC 81-14062. (Illus.). 399p. 1982. pap. text ed. 21.95 o.p. (ISBN 0-8016-1996-3). Mosby.
Nursing Pediatric Patients. Ed. by Jean Robinson & Barbara McVan. LC 82-6273. (Nursing Photobook Ser.). (Illus.). 160p. 1982. 17.95 o.p. (ISBN 0-916730-47-6). Springhouse Pub.
Nursing: Perspectives & Issues. 2nd ed. Gloria M. Grippando. LC 82-71087. 512p. 1983. pap. text ed. 17.50 o.p. (ISBN 0-8273-2078-7). Delmar.
Nursing Photobook Annual, Nineteen Eighty-Seven. Jean Robinson. 160p. 1987. text ed. 16.95 o.p. (ISBN 0-87434-122-1). Springhouse Pub.
Nursing Process in Psychiatric Nursing. Felicity Stockwell. LC 85-9673. 82p. (Orig.). 1985. pap. 8.50 o.p. (ISBN 0-7099-3311-8, Pub. by Croom Helm Ltd). Routledge Chapman & Hall.
Nursing Research: Critical Appraisal & Utilization. Lobiondo et al. 1986. pap. 23.95 o.p. (ISBN 0-8016-3030-4). Mosby.
Nursing Research I. Ed. by Phyllis J. Verhonick. 1975. 15.50 o.p. (ISBN 0-316-90010-9). Little.
Nursing School Entrance Examinations. Marion F. Gooding & Bernice Hughes. LC 81-15003. 368p. (Orig.). 1982. pap. 8.95 o.p. (ISBN 0-668-05217-1, 5217). Arco.
Nursing Student Census with Policy Implications 1985. 1986. pap. 18.95 o.p. (19-2156). Natl League Nurse.
Nursing Student Census with Policy Implications 1986. 3rd ed. (Illus.). 85p. 1987. pap. 18.95 o.p. (ISBN 0-88737-356-9, 19-2175). Natl League Nurse.
Nursing Student Census with Policy Implications, 1987. 4th ed. (Illus.). 96p. 1987. pap. 18.95 o.p. (ISBN 0-88737-388-7). Natl League Nurse.
Nursing Student's Guide to Surgery. Janet Brand & Stephen Tolins. 1979. write for info. o.p. (ISBN 0-673-39371-2). Scott F.
Nursing System: Issues, Ethics & Politics. G. F. Donnelly et al. LC 80-12402. 224p. 1980. pap. 16.00 o.p. (ISBN 0-471-04441-5). Wiley.
Nursing the Elderly. M. A. Hodkinson. 1966. 45.00 o.p. (ISBN 0-08-011987-5). Pergamon.
Nursing Theorists & Their Work. Marriner. 1986. pap. 23.95 o.p. (ISBN 0-8016-3162-9). Mosby.
Nursing Yearbook, 1987. Barbara McVan & Helen Hamilton. (Illus.). 256p. 1987. 21.95 o.p. (ISBN 0-87434-085-3). Springhouse Pub.
Nursing 88 Nursing Diagnosis Cards. Cynthia M. Loxley-Taylor & Sheila S. Cress. 1988. 15.95 o.p. (ISBN 0-87434-125-6). Springhouse Pub.
Nurtured by Love: The Classic Approach to Talent Education. 2nd ed. Shinichi Suzuki. Tr. by Waltraud Suzuki. LC 79-82726. (Illus.). 1982. 9.95 o.s.i. (ISBN 0-682-49930-7, Banner); pap. 6.95 o.s.i. (ISBN 0-682-49910-2). Exposition-Phoenix.
Nutcracker. Rachel Isadora. LC 81-6042. (Illus.). 32p. (gr. k-3). 1981. 11.95 o.s.i. (ISBN 0-02-747470-4). Macmillan.
Nutcracker. Barbara Newman. (Stories of the Ballets Ser.). (Illus.). 48p. 1985. 8.95 o.p. (ISBN 0-8120-5672-8). Barron.
Nutcracker: Based on the Alexandre Dumas pere Version of the Story by E. T. A. Hoffmann. Ed. by Warren Chappell. LC 80-15576. (Illus.). 40p. (gr. k-6). 1987. 5.95 o.s.i. (ISBN 0-8052-0660-4). Schocken.
Nutcracker: Money, Madness, Murder-A Family Album. Shana Alexander. LC 85-7042. 456p. 1985. 17.95 o.p. (ISBN 0-385-19268-1). Doubleday.
Nutcracker: Money, Madness, Murder, A Family Album. Shana Alexander. (General Ser.). 697p. 1986. lib. bdg. 19.95 o.p. (ISBN 0-8161-4051-0, Large Print Bks). G K Hall.
Nutraerobics. Jeffrey Bland. LC 83-47716. 384p. 1985. pap. 16.30 o.p. (ISBN 0-06-250054-6). HarpR.
Nutraerobics: The Complete Individualized Nutrition & Fitness Program for Life after 30. Jeffrey Bland. LC 83-47716. 320p. 1983. 16.30 o.p. (ISBN 0-06-250053-8). HarpR.
Nutrient Requirements of Dairy Cattle, 1978. 5th ed. National Research Council. (Nutrient Requirements of Domestic Animals Ser). 76p. 1978. pap. text ed. 9.50x o.p. (ISBN 0-309-02749-7). Natl Acad Pr.
Nutrient Requirements of Horses. 1978. 6.50x o.p. (ISBN 0-309-02760-8). Natl Acad Pr.
Nutrient Requirements of Swine. 8th rev. ed. National Research Council Board on Agriculture & Renewable Resources. (Nutrient Requirements of Domestic Animals Ser.). (Illus.). 52p. 1979. pap. 7.95x o.p. (ISBN 0-309-02870-1). Natl Acad Pr.
Nutrients & Toxic Substances in Water for Livestock & Poultry. National Research Council Committee on Animal Nutrition. LC 74-2836. (Illus.). v, 93p. 1974. pap. 6.25x o.p. (ISBN 0-309-02312-2). Natl Acad Pr.
Nutrition. 8th ed. Margaret S. Chaney & Margaret L. Ross. LC 76-151636. (Illus.). 1972. text ed. 15.95 o.p. (ISBN 0-395-12425-5, 3-09829). HM.
Nutrition. 9th ed. Margaret S. Chaney et al. LC 78-69546. (Illus.). 1979. text ed. 40.76 o.p. (ISBN 0-395-25448-5). HM.
Nutrition. Cheryl Corbin. LC 80-11138. (Illus.). 208p. 1981. pap. 8.95 o.p. (ISBN 0-03-048276-3, Owl Bks.). H Holt & Co.
Nutrition Additive & Flavor Standards. rev. ed. Lewis J. Minor. (L. J. Minor Foodservice Standards Ser.: Vol. 1). (Illus.). 1983. 25.95 o.s.i. (ISBN 0-87055-520-0). AVI.
Nutrition: An Applied Science. Pat B. Reed. (Illus.). 747p. 1980. text ed. 39.75 o.p. (ISBN 0-8299-0311-9). West Pub.
Nutrition & Behavior in Dogs & Cats: Proceedings of the First Nordic Symposium on Small Animal Veterinary Medicine, Oslo, Norway, September 15-18, 1982. Ed. by R. S. Anderson. LC 83-17281. 246p. 1983. 40.00 o.p. (ISBN 0-08-029778-1). Pergamon.
Nutrition & Diet Therapy. Williams. (Illus.). 1024p. 1984. text ed. 42.95 o.p. (ISBN 0-8016-5566-8). Mosby.
Nutrition & Feeding Strategies in Protozoa. Brenda Nisbet. (Illus.). 280p. 1984. 38.00 o.p. (ISBN 0-7099-1800-3, Pub. by Croom Helm Ltd). Routledge Chapman & Hall.
Nutrition & Food Needs in Developing Countries. Odin K. Knudsen & Pasquale L. Scandizzo. (Working Paper: No. 328). 73p. 1979. 5.00 o.p. (ISBN 0-686-36199-7, WP-0328). World Bank.
Nutrition & Food Processing. Muller. 1980. 30.95 o.p. (ISBN 0-85664-540-0). Van Nos Reinhold.
Nutrition & Good Health. Brooke Beebe et al. LC 78-731300. (Illus.). 1978. pap. text ed. 159.00 o.s.i. (ISBN 0-89290-099-7, A576-SATC). Soc for Visual.
Nutrition & Its Disorders. 3rd ed. Ed. by Donald S. McLaren. (Livingston Medical Text Ser.). (Illus.). 1981. pap. text ed. 18.00 o.p. (ISBN 0-443-02158-9). Churchill.
Nutrition & Medical Practice. Ed. by Lewis A. Barness et al. (Illus.). 1981. 35.95 o.s.i. (ISBN 0-87055-365-8). AVI.
Nutrition & Mental Functions. Ed. by George Serban. LC 74-28371. (Advances in Behavioral Biology Ser.: Vol. 14). (Illus.). 294p. 1975. 39.50x o.p. (ISBN 0-306-37914-7, Plenum Pr). Plenum Pub.
Nutrition & Performance, Vol 7/1-2. C. F. Consolazio. (Illus.). 200p. 1983. pap. 92.00 o.p. (ISBN 0-08-031013-3, 38). Pergamon.
Nutrition & Preventative Health Care. Mary A. Caliendo. (Illus.). 1981. text ed. write for info. o.p. (ISBN 0-02-318330-6). Macmillan.
Nutrition & the Elderly: A Selected Annotated Bibliography for Nutrition & Health Professionals. Ed. by Evelyn Cox & Janet Sandberg. (Bibliographies of Literature & Agriculture Ser.: No. 34). (Illus.). 157p. 1985. pap. 6.00 o.p. (ISBN 0-318-18804-X, S/N 001-024-00218-6). USGPO.
Nutrition & the Surgical Patient. Graham L. Hill. (Clinical Surgery International Ser.: Vol. 2). (Illus.). 323p. 1981. 48.00 o.p. (ISBN 0-443-02249-6). Churchill.
Nutrition & the World Food Problem. Ed. by M. Rechigl, Jr. (Illus.). 1978. 8.50 o.p. (ISBN 3-8055-2779-9). S Karger.
Nutrition & Vitamin Therapy. Michael Lesser. LC 79-52100. 1980. pap. 7.95 o.p. (ISBN 0-394-17600-6, E748, Ever). Grove.
Nutrition Care in Family Planning: A Guide for Administrators. Janet Schwartz et al. 68p. (Orig.). 1981. pap. text ed. 3.00 o.p. (ISBN 0-940050-00-5). Sun Rose.
Nutrition: Codata Directory of Data Sources for Science & Technology, Chapter Twelve. Ed. by CODATA Staff. (Codata Bulletin Ser.). 93p. 1985. pap. 11.00 o.p. (ISBN 0-08-032489-4, Pub. by PPL). Pergamon.
Nutrition Cookbook: 123 Gourmet Recipes Computer Analyzed for Your Specific Daily Requirements. Stephen Kreitzman & Susan Kreitzman. LC 76-54565. 1977. 12.95 o.p. (ISBN 0-15-167750-6). HarBraceJ.
Nutrition Counseling Skills: Assessment, Treatment & Evaluation. Linda G. Snetselaar. LC 83-9932. 304p. 1983. 33.95 o.p. (ISBN 0-89443-880-8). Aspen Pub.
Nutrition-Digestion-Metabolism: Proceedings of the 28th International Congress of Physiological Sciences, Budapest, 1980. Ed. by T. Gati et al. LC 80-42185. (Advances in Physiological Sciences Ser.: Vol. 12). (Illus.). 400p. 1981. 71.00 o.p. (ISBN 0-08-026825-0). Pergamon.
Nutrition, Food & Drug Interactions in Man. Ed. by G. Debry. (World Review of Nutrition & Dietetics: Vol. 43). (Illus.). x, 210p. 1984. 110.75 o.p. (ISBN 3-8055-3800-6). S Karger.
Nutrition for Children. Francis. 1986. 9.50 o.p. (ISBN 0-8016-1645-X). Mosby.
Nutrition for Fitness & Sport. Melvin H. Williams. 416p. 1983. pap. write for info. o.p. (ISBN 0-697-07198-7). Wm C Brown.
Nutrition for the Prime of Your Life. Annette B. Natow & Jo-Ann Heslin. 352p. 1983. text ed. 17.95 o.p. (ISBN 0-07-028414-8). McGraw.
Nutrition for the Working Woman. Audrey T. Cross. 288p. 1986. 16.45 o.p. (ISBN 0-671-61707-9). S&S.
Nutrition for the Working Woman. Audrey T. Cross. 288p. 1986. pap. 7.95 o.p. (ISBN 0-671-54069-6, Fireside). S&S.
Nutrition for Your Child's Most Important Years: Birth to Age Three. Sue Castle. Ed. by Kathi Paton. (Illus.). 192p. (Orig.). 1984. pap. 8.70 o.p. (ISBN 0-671-49403-1, Fireside). S&S.
Nutrition in Early Childhood & Its Effects in Later Years. J. C. Somogyi & H. Haenel. 152p. 1982. pap. 63.50x o.p. Transaction Pubs.
Nutrition in Infancy & Childhood. 3rd ed. Pipes. (Illus.). 352p. 1984. 17.95 o.p. (ISBN 0-8016-3938-7). Mosby.
Nutrition in Medical Practice. Robert E. Hodges. LC 77-11337. (Illus.). 363p. 1980. text ed. write for info. o.p. (ISBN 0-7216-4706-5). Saunders.
Nutrition in Pregnancy & Lactation. 3rd ed. Bonnie S. Worthington-Roberts et al. LC 80-39509. (Illus.). 310p. 1984. pap. text ed. 18.95 o.p. (ISBN 0-8016-5647-8). Mosby.
Nutrition in Preventive Dentistry: Science & Practice. 2nd ed. Abraham E. Nizel. (Illus.). 704p. 1980. text ed. 38.95 o.p. (ISBN 0-7216-6810-0). Saunders.
Nutrition in the Lower Metazoa: Proceedings. Ed. by D. C. Smith & Y. Tiffon. (Illus.). 192p. 1980. 55.00 o.p. (ISBN 0-08-025904-9). Pergamon.
Nutrition, Neurotransmitter Function & Behavior. Ed. by J. Mauron. 88p. 1985. pap. text ed. 15.40 o.p. (ISBN 0-920887-05-8, Pub. by Hans Huber). CJ Hogrefe Pubs.
Nutrition: Principles & Clinical Practice. Sara M. Hunt et al. LC 79-25899. 1980. (ISBN 0-02-358650-8). Macmillan.
Nutrition Requirements of Man: A Conspectus of Research. Journal of Nutrition Staff. 592p. 15.00 o.p. Nutrition Found.
Nutrition Services for Older Americans: Foodservice Systems & Technologies: Administrative Guidelines. Audrey C. McCool & Barbara M. Posner. (Illus.). 52p. 1982. pap. 15.55 o.p. (ISBN 0-88091-003-8). Am Dietetic Assn.
Nutrition Services for Older Americans: Foodservice Systems & Technologies: Program Management Strategies. Audrey C. McCool & Barbara M. Posner. (Illus.). 144p. 1982. pap. 15.55 o.p. (ISBN 0-88091-002-X). Am Dietetic Assn.
Nutrition, Weight Control, & Exercise. Frank I. Katch & William D. McArdle. LC 76-14695. (Illus.). 1977. pap. 16.95 o.p. (ISBN 0-395-24453-6). HM.
Nutritional Ages of Women: A Lifetime Guide to Eating Right for Health, Beauty, & Well-Being. Patricia Long. 1986. 18.95 o.p. (ISBN 0-02-574760-6). Macmillan.
Nutritional Biochemistry & Metabolism, with Clinical Applications. Ed. by Maria C. Linder. 1985. 62.25 o.p. (ISBN 0-444-00910-8). Elsevier.
Nutritional Consequences of Agricultural Projects: Conceptual Relationships & Assessment Approaches. Per Pinstrup-Andersen. (Working Paper: No. 456). 93p. 1981. 5.00 o.p. (ISBN 0-8213-9315-4, WP-0456). World Bank.
Nutritional Considerations in a Changing World. Ed. by Geoffrey H. Bourne. 218p. 1985. 99.00 o.p. (ISBN 0-317-37818-X). Transaction Pubs.
Nutritional Deficiencies in Industrialized Countries. Ed. by J. C. Somogyi & G. Varela. 172p. 1981. pap. 76.95x o.p. Transaction Pubs.
Nutritional Guide to Fast Food. Robert Haas. (Illus.). 160p. 1982. pap. 6.95 o.p. (ISBN 0-682-49909-9, Banner). Exposition-Phoenix.
Nutritional Limits to Animal Production from Pastures. Ed. by J. B. Hacker. 536p. 1982. text ed. 35.30 o.p. (ISBN 0-85198-492-4). CAB Intl.
Nutritional Methods of Blood Regeneration, Pt. 1. Raymond Bernard. 53p. 1960. pap. 13.95 o.s.i. (ISBN 0-88697-037-7). Life Science.
Nutritional Prevention of Cardiovascular Disease. Ed. by Walter Lovenberg & Yukio Yamori. 1984. 42.00 o.p. (ISBN 0-12-456010-5). Acad Pr.
Nutritional Quality Index of Foods. R. Gaurth Hansen & Bonita W. Wyse. (Illus.). 1979. 39.95 o.p. (ISBN 0-87055-320-8). AVI.
Nutritional Research: An International Approach. Ed. by Brita Rolander-Chilo. (Illus.). 1979. 45.00 o.p. (ISBN 0-08-024399-1). Pergamon.
Nutritional Sex Control & Rejuvenation. Raymond Bernard. 51p. 1960. pap. 7.95 o.s.i. (ISBN 0-88697-038-5). Life Science.
Nutritive Value of American Foods in Common Units. Catherine F. Adams. (Agriculture Handbook Ser.). (Illus.). 291p. 1981. pap. 8.50 o.p. (ISBN 0-318-04553-2, S/N 001-000-03184-8). USGPO.
Nuts & Bolts: A Manual for Effective Professional Communication. William W. Neher & David H. Waite. 1978. pap. 11.95 o.p. (ISBN 0-89917-000-5). TIS Inc.
Nuts to Nightingale. Jacquelyn Reinach. Ed. by Ruth L. Perle. LC 77-16325. (gr. k-2). 1978. 2.95 o.p. (ISBN 0-03-042041-5). H Holt & Co.
Nuttier Knock Knocks. Karen Markoe & Louis Phillips. (Funnybones Ser.). 64p. (gr. 3-7). 1981. pap. 1.50 o.s.i. (ISBN 0-671-42248-0). Wanderer Bks.
Nutty Knock Knocks. Karen Markoe & Louis Phillips. (Funnybones Ser.). (Illus.). 64p. (gr. 3-7). 1981. pap. 1.50 o.s.i. (ISBN 0-671-42249-9). Wanderer Bks.
Nutty's Christmas. Claire Schumacher. LC 83-26558. (Illus.). 32p. (ps-1). 1984. 11.75 o.p. (ISBN 0-688-03851-4, Morrow Junior Books); lib. bdg. 11.88 o.p. Morrow.
NVT BSA Easy Rider Mopeds Seventy-Six to Seventy-Nine. Pete Shoemark. pap. 11.50 o.p. (457). Haynes Pubns.
NWWA - API Conference on Petroleum Hydrocarbons & Organic Proceedings. LC 86-713. 1986. 43.75 o.p. (ISBN 0-318-23000-3). Natl Water Well.
NWWA - API Conference on Petroleum Hydrocarbons - 1984: Proceedings. 1984. 43.75 o.p. (ISBN 0-318-22999-4). Natl Water Well.
NWWA Conference on Characterization & Monitoring. 1984. 43.75 o.p. (ISBN 0-318-23018-6). Natl Water Well.
NWWA Conference on Ground Water Management, 1984: Proceedings. 1985. 43.75 o.p. (ISBN 0-318-23027-5). Natl Water Well.
NWWA Western Regional Ground Water Management Conference, 1985: Proceedings. 1984. 43.75 o.p. Natl Water Well.
NYC Access. 2nd ed. Richard S. Wurman. (Access Guidebooks). (Illus.). 248p. 1984. pap. 11.95 o.p. (ISBN 0-915461-07-2, 60341-8, Dist. by S&S). Access Pr.
NYC Access. Ed. by Richard S. Wurman. (Access Guidebook Ser.). (Illus.). 248p. 1982. pap. 11.95 o.p. (ISBN 0-9604858-5-6). Access Pr.
Nye County Brothel Wars: A Tale of the New West. Jeannie Kasindorf. 1985. 16.45 o.p. (ISBN 0-671-41591-3, Linden Pr). S&S.
Nyingma School of Tibetan Buddhism. Dudjom Rinpoche. Ed. by Gyurme Dorje & Matthew Kapstein. (Wisdom Advanced Book - Blue Ser.). (Illus.). 1800p. 1988. 95.00 o.p. (ISBN 0-86171-047-9). Wisdom MA.
Nymph Fishing for Larger Trout. Charles E. Brooks. LC 83-5832. (Illus.). 224p. 1983. pap. 14.95 o.p. (ISBN 0-8329-0330-2). Lyons & Burford.
NYO&W Employee Timetable. LC 72-80428. (Carstens Hobby Bks.: C-10). 1963. pap. 3.00 o.p. (ISBN 0-911868-10-0). Carstens Pubns.
NYSML-ARML Contests 1973-1985. Ed. by Harry D. Ruderman. (Illus.). 176p. (Orig.). 1987. pap. 9.00 o.p. (ISBN 0-87353-247-3, Co-Pub by Mu Alpha Theta). NCTM.

O

O & M in Local Government. T. D. Sherman. 1969. text ed. 24.00 o.p. (ISBN 0-08-013317-7); pap. text ed. 10.75 o.p. (ISBN 0-08-013309-6). Pergamon.

O Beloved Kids: Rudyard Kipling's Letters to His Children. Rudyard Kipling. LC 85-26455. (Illus.). 240p. 1984. 16.95 o.p. (ISBN 0-15-167770-0). HarBraceJ.

O Christian! O Jew! Paul R. Carlson. LC 74-78937. 256p. (Orig.). 1974. pap. 1.95 o.p. (ISBN 0-912692-39-1). Cook.

O, Desert Dream! K Willis Putnam. 1987. 9.95 o.p. (ISBN 0-8062-2957-8). Carlton.

O Enviado do Pai see Sent from the Father: Meditations on the Fourth Gospel.

O. Henry & the Theory of the Short Story. B. M. Ejxenbaum. Tr. by I. R. Titunik. (Michigan Slavic Contributions: No. 1). pap. cancelled o.s.i. (ISBN 0-930042-09-3). Mich Slavic Pubns.

O, How the Wheel Becomes It! Anthony Powell. 1983. 13.95 o.p. (ISBN 0-03-063999-9). H Holt & Co.

O Lord, from You: Prayers & Devotions of Petition in Large Print. 1.00 o.p. (ISBN 0-685-62050-6, Augsburg). Augsburg Fortress.

O My America. Thomas S. Matthews. 1962. 3.95 o.p. S&S.

O S H A Compliance Manual. rev. ed. Daniel C. Petersen. (Illus.). 1979. text ed. 55.00 o.p. (ISBN 0-07-049598-X). McGraw.

O Zebron Falls. Charles Ferry. LC 77-9986. (gr. 7 up). 1977. 7.95 o.p. (ISBN 0-395-25839-1). HM.

O-Zone. Paul Theroux. 528p. 1986. 19.95 o.p. (ISBN 0-399-13186-8, Perigee). Putnam Pub Group.

Oahu: Traveler's Guide. Bill Gleasner & Diana Gleasner. (Illus.). 65p. (Orig.). 1978. pap. 4.00 o.p. (ISBN 0-932596-04-5, Pub. by Oriental). Intl Spec Bk.

Oak Furniture, Styles & Prices. Rev. ed. Wallace-Homestead Co. Staff. 132p. pap. 7.95 o.p. (ISBN 0-87069-368-9). Wallace-Homestead.

Oak Ridge Boys: Our Story. Ellis Widner & Walter Carter. (Illus.). 192p. 1987. 17.95 o.p. (ISBN 0-8092-4842-5). Contemp Bks.

Oak-Tree Fairy Book. Ed. by Clifton Johnson. (Illus.). (gr. 4-12). 9.00 o.p. (ISBN 0-8446-2334-2). Peter Smith.

Oakfield; Or, Fellowship in the East, 1854. 2nd ed. William D. Arnold. Ed. by Robert L. Wolff. LC 75-1522. (Victorian Fiction Ser.). 1976. lib. bdg. 73.00 o.p. (ISBN 0-8240-1594-0). Garland Pub.

Oakland A'S. rev. ed. Martin. LC 82-12701. (Baseball Today Ser.). 48p. (gr. 4 up). 1982. PLB 11.45 o.p. (ISBN 0-87191-869-2). Creative Ed.

Oakland Raiders. Julian May. (NFL Today Ser.). (Illus.). (gr. 3-6). 1977. PLB 10.45 o.p. (ISBN 0-87191-595-2); pap. 4.25 o.p. (ISBN 0-686-67475-8). Creative Ed.

Oakville: A Place of Some Importance. Clare McKeon & Joseph P. McKeon. LC 85-29458. (Illus.). 136p. 1986. 24.95 o.p. (ISBN 0-89781-170-4). Windsor Pubns Inc.

OAS & the Evolution of the Interamerican System. OAS, General Secretariat, Department of Public Information Staff. 46p. 1982. pap. 5.00 o.p. (ISBN 0-8270-1458-9). OAS.

OAS Offical Documents Final Report: Twelfth Meeting of the Inter-American Nuclear Energy Commission, August 31 - September 4, 1981, La Paz, Bolivia. OAS, General Secretariat, Inter-American Nuclear Energy Staff. (Ser. C: No. VIII.12). 52p. 1981. pap. 3.00 o.p. (ISBN 0-8270-1414-7). OAS.

Oasis. Mary McCarthy. 96p. 1981. pap. 2.25 o.p. (ISBN 0-380-54577-2, 54577-2, Bard). Avon.

Oasis in Space: Earth History from the Beginning. Preston Cloud. (Illus.). 1987. 29.45 o.p. (ISBN 0-393-01952-7). Norton.

Oatmeal Is Not for Mustaches. Thomas Rockwell. LC 84-9081. (Illus.). (gr. k-2). 1984. 9.95 o.s.i. (ISBN 0-03-063653-1). H Holt & Co.

Obbligati: Essays in Criticism. Anthony Hecht. LC 84-45707. 1986. 18.95 o.p. (ISBN 0-689-11570-9, Atheneum). Macmillan.

Obeah: Witchcraft in the West Indies. Henry H. Bell. LC 78-106879. 1970. Repr. of 1889 ed. lib. bdg. 22.50x o.p. (ISBN 0-8371-3275-4, BEO&, Pub. by Negro U Pr). Greenwood.

Obedience in Church & State: Three Political Tracts. Stephen Gardiner. Ed. by Pierre Janelle. LC 68-19272. 1968. Repr. of 1930 ed. lib. bdg. 22.50x o.p. (ISBN 0-8371-0081-X, GABW). Greenwood.

Obedience to Authority. Doris Seger. (Illus.). 8p. (gr. k-4). pap. text ed. cancelled o.s.i. CEF Press.

Oberammergau: The Passion-Play-Village & Its Text in German-English-French. Otto Siegner. (Illus.). 1978. 15.00x o.s.i. (ISBN 0-686-63526-4). E J Brill USA.

OBERS BEA Regional Projections 1985: State Projections to 2035, Vol. 1. 132p. (Orig.). 1985. pap. 4.75 o.p. (ISBN 0-318-22420-8, S/N 003-010-00157-7). USGPO.

Obesity. Albert J. Stunkard. LC 79-92616. (Illus.). 470p. 1980. text ed. (ISBN 0-7216-8635-4). Saunders.

Obesity & Leanness: Basic Aspects. Michael Stock & Nancy Rothwell. 100p. 1982. pap. 9.95 o.p. (ISBN 0-317-55162-0). Krieger.

Obesity in Childhood. Ed. by E. Cacciari et al. 1978. 61.00 o.p. (ISBN 0-12-154150-9). Acad Pr.

Obesity: Its Pathogenesis & Management. Trevor Silverstone. LC 75-18338. (Illus.). 250p. 1975. 20.00 o.p. (ISBN 0-88416-038-6). Year Bk Med.

Obeying. Marian Bennett. (Wipe-Clean Bks.). (Illus.). 12p. (ps). 1985. pap. 1.39 o.p. (ISBN 0-87239-958-3, 3518). Standard Pub.

Object of Morality. G. J. Warnock. 1971. pap. 10.95x o.p. (ISBN 0-416-29900-8, NO. 2575). Routledge Chapman & Hall.

Object of My Affection. Stephen McCauley. 336p. 1987. 17.45 o.s.i. (ISBN 0-671-61840-7). S&S.

Objections to Nuclear Defence: Philosophers on Deterrence. Ed. by Nigel Blake & Kay Pole. 208p. (Orig.). 1984. pap. 11.95x o.p. (ISBN 0-7102-0249-0). Routledge Chapman & Hall.

Objective Tests for Nurses, Book 2. Janet T. Riddle & Joan Dinner. (Objective Tests for Nurses Ser.). (Illus.). 112p. 1981. pap. text ed. 7.50 o.p. (ISBN 0-443-01740-9). Churchill.

Objective Tests for Nurses, Bk. 5. Janet T. Riddle. LC 82-9689. 124p. 1983. pap. text ed. 8.00 o.p. (ISBN 0-443-01743-3). Churchill.

Objective Tests for Nurses: The Digestive System & the Urinary System, Bk. 4. Janet T. Riddle. LC 80-40910. 115p. 1982. pap. text ed. 7.50 o.p. (ISBN 0-443-01742-5). Churchill.

Objectives & Multi-Objective Decision Making Under Uncertainty. J. Wilhelm. (Lecture Notes in Economics & Mathematical Systems: Vol. 112). iv, 111p. 1975. pap. 13.00 o.p. (ISBN 0-387-07412-0). Springer-Verlag.

Objectives of the New International Economic Order. Ervin Laszlo et al. LC 78-14766. (Pergamon Policy Studies). 288p. 1978. 29.00 o.p. (ISBN 0-08-023697-9). Pergamon.

Oboe. 3rd ed. Philip Bate. (Instruments of the Orchestra Ser). (Illus.). 1975. 13.95x o.p. (ISBN 0-393-02166-1). Norton.

Oboe. Philip Bate. (ISBN 0-8022-0083-4). Philos Lib.

Obrazovanie Osnovnoi Gosudarstvennoi Territorii Velikorusskoi Narodnosti. M. K. Liubavskii. (Russian Ser.: No. 27). 1969. Repr. of 1929 ed. 30.00 o.p. (ISBN 0-87569-006-8). Academic Intl.

Obscenity Law Today. 1970 ed. William E. Ringel. 1969. pap. text ed. 6.00x o.p. (ISBN 0-87526-048-9). Gould.

Observations. Lennart Bruce. (Illus.). 68p. 1968. 5.00 o.p. Kayak.

Observations. Arthur E. Morgan. LC 68-22796. 1968p. 8.50 o.p. (ISBN 0-317-20771-7). Comm Serv OH.

Observations. Igor D. Radovic. LC 66-26970. 84p. 1967. (ISBN 0-8022-1304-9). Philos Lib.

Observations of a Madman. Johnnie B. Pierce, Jr. 64p. 1984. 5.50 o.p. (ISBN 0-682-40171-4). Exposition-Phoenix.

Observations on Liberal Learning: Careers. 12p. 1982. pap. text ed. 2.00 o.s.i. (ISBN 0-911696-38-5). Assn Am Coll.

Observations on Modern Gardening. Thomas Whatley. Ed. by John D. Hunt. LC 79-56984. (English Landscape Garden Ser.). 263p. 1980. lib. bdg. 40.00 o.p. (ISBN 0-8240-0167-2). Garland Pub.

Observations on the Geology of the United States of America. W. Maclure. Repr. of 1966 ed. text ed. 44.00 o.p. (ISBN 0-934454-67-1). Lubrecht & Cramer.

Observations on the Nature & Tendency of the Doctrine of Mr. Hume Concerning the Relation of Cause & Effect. Thomas Brown. LC 82-48341. (Philosophy of David Hume Ser.). 221p. 1983. lib. bdg. 33.00 o.p. (ISBN 0-8240-5401-6). Garland Pub.

Observations on the Popular Antiquities of Great Britain: Chiefly Illustrating the Origin of Our Vulgar & Provincial Customs, Ceremonies & Superstitions, 3 vols. John Brand. LC 67-23896. 1606p. 1969. Repr. of 1849 ed. Set. 68.00x o.p. (ISBN 0-8103-3256-6). Gale.

Observations on the Theory & Practice of Landscape Gardening. Humphry Repton. (Illus.). 312p. 1985. 325.00 o.s.i. Godine.

Observatories of the Canaries: On the Occasion of Their Inauguration, June 28-29, 1985. Ed. by P. Beers & P. Murdin. (Illus.). 168p. 1985. pap. 44.00 o.p. (ISBN 0-08-033676-0, C150, Pub. by PPL). Pergamon.

Observatory. Carl Jonas. 1966. 4.95 o.p. (ISBN 0-393-08482-5). Norton.

Observing National Holidays & Church Festivals: A Weekday Church School Unit in Christian Citizenship Series for Grades Three & Four. Florence Martin. LC 76-174077. 280p. 1971. Repr. of 1940 ed. 48.00x o.p. (ISBN 0-8103-3804-1). Gale.

Obsession of Emmet Booth. Martha Albrand. 1974. pap. 0.95 o.p. (ISBN 0-380-01433-5, 18010). Avon.

Obstacles to Existential Freedom. James Park. (Existential Freedom Ser.: No. 10). 1976. pap. 5.00x o.p. (ISBN 0-89231-010-3). Existential Bks.

Obstacles to Mineral Development: A Pragmatic View. John S. Carman. Ed. by Benison Varon. LC 78-26807. (Illus.). 1979. 50.00 o.p. (ISBN 0-08-023904-8). Pergamon.

Obstacles to the New International Economic Order. Ervin Laszlo et al. LC 79-28723. (Pergamon Policy Studies on the New International Economic Order). 170p. 1980. 29.00 o.p. (ISBN 0-08-025110-2); pap. 11.00 o.p. (ISBN 0-08-025970-7). Pergamon.

Obstetrical Decision Making. Beth Israel Hospital Staff & Emanuel A. Friedman. LC 82-70759. 222p. 1982. pap. text ed. 38.00 o.p. (ISBN 0-941158-01-2, D1680-8). Mosby.

Obstetrical Diagnosis by Radiographic, Ultrasonic & Nuclear Methods. John A. Campbell. LC 77-6448. 220p. 1977. 25.00 o.p. (ISBN 0-683-01416-1). Krieger.

Obstetrical Procedure Manual: Delivery Suite, Nursery, Post Partum. St. Joseph Medical Center Staff. LC 75-18054. (Illus.). 1975. pap. 5.00 o.p. (ISBN 0-87125-027-6). Cath Health.

Obstetrical Ultrasound. P. Jeanty & R. Romero. (Illus.). 304p. 1984. text ed. 50.00 o.p. (ISBN 0-07-032319-4). McGraw.

Obstetrics & Gynecology. 7th ed. J. Robert Willson & Elsie R. Carrington. LC 82-14177. (Illus.). 746p. 1983. text ed. 44.95 o.p. (ISBN 0-8016-5597-8). Mosby.

Obstetrics & Gynecology: PreTest Self-Assessment & Review. 3rd ed. Pretest Services Inc. & M. I. Evans. (Clinical Science Ser.). 272p. 1985. text ed. 13.95 o.p. (ISBN 0-07-051001-6). McGraw.

Obstetrics for the Nurse. Barbara Anderson & Pamela J Shapiro. 272p. 1981. 19.95 o.p. (ISBN 0-442-21840-0). Van Nos Reinhold.

Obstetrics in Outline. Michael D. Read & Stuart Mellor. LC 85-9367. 256p. 1985. pap. 15.00 o.p. (ISBN 0-471-90799-5, Dist. by A R Liss). Wiley.

Obstruction Theory on the Homotopy Classification of Maps. H. J. Baues. (Lecture Notes in Mathematics Ser: Vol. 628). 1977. pap. 22.00 o.p. (ISBN 0-387-08534-3). Springer-Verlag.

Occasion of Sin. Rachel Billington. 320p. 1983. 14.50 o.s.i. (ISBN 0-671-45938-4). Summit Bks.

Occasion of Sin. Rachel Billington. 1984. pap. 3.50 o.s.i. (ISBN 0-345-31515-4). Ballantine.

Occasional Horseman. George Canning. (Illus.). 4.50 o.p. (ISBN 0-85131-188-1, BL212, Pub. by J A Allen U K). S R Smith Sporting Bks.

Occlusion. Thomson. 288p. 1975. 29.00 o.p. (ISBN 0-7236-0401-0, Pub. by John Wright UK). Butterworth.

Occulation of Imam: A Historical Background. Jassim M. Hussain. 221p. 1986. lib. bdg. 30.00 o.p. (ISBN 0-7103-0158-8). Routledge Chapman & Hall.

Occult Properties of Herbs & Plants. W. B. Crow. (Paths to Inner Power Ser). 1971. pap. 3.95 o.p. (ISBN 0-85030-196-3, Pub. by Thorsons UK). Weiser.

Occult Science & Occult Development: Christ at the Time of the Mystery of Golgotha & Christ in the Twentieth Century. Rudolf Steiner. Tr. by D. S. Osmond. 36p. 1978. pap. 5.00 o.p. (ISBN 0-85440-335-3, Pub. by Steiner Book Centre Canada). Anthroposophic.

Occult Science in India & Among the Ancients. Louis Jacolliot. 1970. 5.95 o.p. (ISBN 0-8216-0130-X, Pub. by Univ Bks). Carol Pub Group.

Occult Sciences. Arthur E. Waite. 7.95 o.p. (ISBN 0-8216-0214-4, Pub. by Univ Bks). Carol Pub Group.

Occult Symbolism in France: Josephin Peladan & the Salons De la Rose-Croix. Robert Pincus-Witten. LC 75-23809. (Outstanding Dissertations in the Fine Arts-20th Century). (Illus.). 300p. 1976. lib. bdg. 50.00 o.p. (ISBN 0-8240-2003-0). Garland Pub.

Occupation: English Teacher. Floyd Bergman. 138p. 1969. looseleaf 10.95 o.p. (ISBN 0-87506-040-4). Campus.

Occupation Writer. Robert Graves. 1977. Repr. of 1950 ed. lib. bdg. 26.00x o.p. (ISBN 0-374-93237-9, Octagon). Hippocrene Bks.

Occupational & Environmental Cancers of the Respiratory System. W. C. Hueper. (Recent Results in Cancer Research: Vol. 3). (Illus.). 1966. 31.90 o.p. (ISBN 0-387-03642-3). Springer-Verlag.

Occupational Asthma. Claude A. Frazier. 384p. 1980. 39.95 o.p. (ISBN 0-442-21687-4). Van Nos Reinhold.

Occupational Attainment: Minorities & Women in Selected Industries, 1969-1979. Robert B. Hill. 150p. 1983. pap. 6.95 o.p. (ISBN 0-87855-606-0). Transaction Pubs.

Occupational Cancer & Carcinogenesis. Ed. by Harri Vainio et al. LC 80-21703. (Illus.). 422p. 1980. 95.50 o.p. (ISBN 0-89116-193-7). Hemisphere Pub.

Occupational Health Hazards. G. Walker Daubenspeck. LC 74-80676. 1974. 4.00 o.p. (ISBN 0-682-48002-9). Exposition-Phoenix.

Occupational Health Nursing. Ed. by Brenda Slaney. 177p. 1979. pap. 11.50 o.p. (ISBN 0-7099-2322-8, Pub. by Croom Helm Ltd). Routledge Chapman & Hall.

Occupational Health of Migrant & Seasonal Farmworkers in the United States. Farmworker Justice Fund Staff & Valerie A. Wilk. Ed. by Ann-Therese Carlozzo. (Illus.). 125p. (Orig.). 1986. pap. text ed. 15.00 o.s.i. (ISBN 0-9616508-1-8). Farmworker Justice.

Occupational Health: Recognizing & Preventing Work-Related Diseases. Ed. by Barry S. Levy & David H. Wegman. 1982. pap. text ed. 31.50 o.p. (ISBN 0-316-52234-1). Little.

Occupational Hearing Loss. Ed. by D. W. Robinson. (British Acoustical Society Special Ser.: Vol. 1). 1971. 60.50 o.p. (ISBN 0-12-590150-X). Acad Pr.

Occupational Hygiene: An Introductory Guide. Alan L. Jones et al. (Illus.). 182p. 1981. 24.50 o.p. (ISBN 0-7099-1404-0, Pub. by Croom Helm Ltd). Routledge Chapman & Hall.

Occupational Information. 4th ed. Robert Hoppock. 1976. text ed. 40.95 o.p. (ISBN 0-07-030330-4). McGraw.

Occupational Injuries & Illnesses in the United States by Industry, 1985. (Labor Statistics Bureau Bulletin Ser.: No. 2278). 87p. 1987. pap. 4.25 o.p. (ISBN 0-317-62876-3, S-N 029-001-02925-0). USGPO.

Occupational Mobility in the United States, 1930-1960. A. Jaffe & R. O. Carleton. LC 73-16947. (Illus.). 105p. 1974. Repr. of 1954 ed. lib. bdg. 35.00x o.p. (ISBN 0-8371-7248-9, JAOM). Greenwood.

Occupational Monopoly & Modern Medicine. Gerald Larkin. LC 82-19553. 220p. 1983. text ed. 29.95 o.p. (ISBN 0-422-78300-5, NO. 3886, Pub. by Tavistock). Routledge Chapman & Hall.

Occupational Outlook Handbook, 1986-87. 17th ed. (Bureau of Labor Statistics Bulletin: No. 2250). (Illus.). 484p. 1986. text ed. 23.00 o.p. (ISBN 0-318-20131-3, S/N 029-001-02864-4); pap. text ed. 20.00 o.p. (ISBN 0-318-20132-1, S/N 029-001-02863-6). USGPO.

Occupational Outlook Handbook, 1986-87. 1987. pap. 17.76 o.p. (ISBN 0-942784-04-9). Rosen Group.

Occupational Profiles. rev. ed. Chronicle Guidance Publications Staff. LC 75-6566. 183p. 1981. pap. 16.25 o.p. (ISBN 0-912578-22-X). Chron Guide.

Occupational Safety & Health: A Guide to Information Sources. Ed. by Theodore P. Peck. LC 74-7199. (Management Information Guide Ser.: No. 28). 268p. 1974. 68.00x o.p. (ISBN 0-8103-0828-2). Gale.

Occupational Safety & Health: An Administrative Overview. Coppa & Avery Consultants Staff. (Public Administration Ser.: P 1789). 10p. 1985. 2.00 o.p. (ISBN 0-89028-589-6). Vance Biblios.

Occupational Safety & Health Law, Nineteen Eighty-Five Pocket Part. Mark A. Rothstein. (Handbook Ser.). 1985. write for info o.p. (ISBN 0-314-90281-3). West Pub.

Occupational Therapy for Children. Clark & Allen. 1984. cloth 45.95 o.p. (ISBN 0-8016-1162-8). Mosby.

Occupational Therapy in Long-Term Psychiatry. Moya Willson. LC 82-9704. 174p. 1983. pap. text ed. 15.25 o.p. (ISBN 0-443-02444-8). Churchill.

Occupational Therapy in the Treatment of Adult Hemiplegia. O. Eggers. (Illus.). 1983. pap. 17.50 o.p. (ISBN 0-433-08170-8). E J Brill USA.

Occupational Therapy Manual. Monte J. Meldman et al. 88p. 1969. 15.75 o.p. (ISBN 0-398-01283-0). C C Thomas.

Occupations & Society: Toward a Sociology of the Labor Market. Paul D. Montagna. LC 76-40121. 456p. 1977. write for info. o.p. (ISBN 0-02-382430-1). Macmillan.

Occupations in Virginia. (Demographics & Labor Force Ser.). 1983. photocopy 1.05 o.p. U VA Ctr Pub Serv.

Occupations One. Caroline Blakely. 64p. 1975. 2.25 o.p. (ISBN 0-317-35476-0). New Readers.

Occupied Haiti: Being the Report of a Committee of Six Disinterested Americans Representing Organizations Exclusively American. Ed. by Emily G. Balch. LC 79-147491. (Library of War & Peace; the Political Economy of War). 1972. lib. bdg. 46.00 o.p. (ISBN 0-8240-0284-9). Garland Pub.
Occupiers' Law. Raja Shehadeh. Ed. by International Commission of Jurists (Geneva, Switzerland) Staff. LC 85-20941. 212p. 1985. 17.95 o.p. (ISBN 0-88728-149-4); pap. 8.95 o.p. (ISBN 0-88728-150-8). Inst Palestine.
Occupy Till I Come see Spiritual Survival in the Last Days.
Occurrence Diagnoses & Sources of Hospital-Associated Diseases. Ed. by W. J. Fahlberg & D. Groschal. (Hospital Associated Disease Ser.: Vol. 1). 1978. 39.75 o.p. (ISBN 0-8247-6724-1). Dekker.
Ocean Alphabet Book. Jerry Pallotta. (Illus.). 30p. Date not set. 10.95 o.p. (ISBN 0-933341-96-2); pap. 4.95 o.p. (ISBN 0-933341-56-3). Quinlan Pr.
Ocean & Its Resources. P. C. Bunich & K. Kharchev. 149p. 1977. pap. 4.95 o.p. (ISBN 0-8285-1513-1, Pub. by Mir Pubs USSR). Imported Pubns.
Ocean Carriage. Edward F. Stevens. 1956. (ISBN 0-8022-1641-2). Philos Lib.
Ocean Disposal Systems for Sewage Sludge & Effluent. National Research Council Ocean Waste Transportation Committee. 126p. 1984. pap. 13.95x o.p. (ISBN 0-309-03490-6). Natl Acad Pr.
Ocean Engineering for OTEC. Ed. by O. M. Griffin & J. G. Gianotti. (OED: Vol. 9). 96p. 1980. 14.00 o.p. (ISBN 0-317-33589-8, 100129); members 7.00 o.p. (ISBN 0-317-33590-1). ASME.
Ocean Freights & Chartering. rev. ed. C. F. Cufley. (Illus.). 1980. 55.00 o.p. (ISBN 0-686-77963-0). E J Brill USA.
Ocean-Going Giants. Ross R. Olney. LC 84-21698. (Illus.). 48p. (gr. 3-6). 1985. 11.95 o.s.i. (ISBN 0-689-31082-X, Atheneum Childrens Bks). Macmillan.
Ocean Racing. Eric Tabarly. LC 71-163378. (Illus.). 1972. 10.00 o.p. (ISBN 0-393-03174-8). Norton.
Ocean Thermal Energy Conversion. A. Lavi. 80p. 1981. pap. 36.00 o.p. (ISBN 0-08-026705-X). Pergamon.
Ocean Tides: Mathematical Models & Numerical Experiments. G. I. Marchuk & B. A. Kagan. Tr. by D. E. Cartwright. LC 82-18898. (Illus.). 240p. 1984. 87.00 o.p. (ISBN 0-08-026236-8). Pergamon.
Ocean Uses & Their Regulation. Luc Cuyvers. LC 84-3587. 179p. 1984. 31.50x o.p. (ISBN 0-471-88676-9); pap. text ed. 21.95x o.p. (ISBN 0-471-88675-0). Wiley.
Ocean Wave Climate. Ed. by M. D. Earle & A. Malahoff. LC 78-24469. (Marine Sciences Ser.: Vol. 8). 380p. 1979. 69.50x o.p. (ISBN 0-306-40079-0, Plenum Pr). Plenum Pub.
Ocean World Encyclopedia. Donald G. Groves & Lee M. Hunt. LC 79-21093. (Illus.). 1980. text ed. 54.50 o.p. (ISBN 0-07-025010-3). McGraw.
Oceania: A Regional Study. Ed. by Frederica M. Bunge & Melinda W. Cooke. LC 85-6043. (DA PAM 550-94. Area Handbook Ser.). (Illus.). 588p. 1985. 16.00 o.p. (ISBN 0-318-18806-6, S/N 008-020-01026-0). USGPO.
Oceanic Fronts in Coastal Processes: Proceedings of a Workshop Held at the Marine Science Research Center, May 25-27, 1977. Ed. by M. J. Bowman & W. E. Esaias. (Illus.). 1978. pap. 15.00 o.p. (ISBN 0-387-08823-7). Springer-Verlag.
Oceanic Music & Dance: An Annotated Bibliography. Mervyn McLean. 252p. 1977. pap. text ed. 15.00x o.p. (ISBN 0-8248-0589-5). UH Pr.
Oceanographic Atlas of the Pacific Ocean. Richard A. Barkley. (Illus.). 1969. text ed. 50.00x o.p. (ISBN 0-87022-050-0). UH Pr.
Oceanographic Data Reduction Manual. Ed. by Pierre G. Dallemagne. 296p. 1974. pap. text ed. 16.50x o.p. (ISBN 0-8422-0467-9). Irvington.
Oceanographic Index: Author Cumulation, 1946-1970: Woods Hole Oceanographic Institution, Mass, 3 vols. Compiled by Mary Sears. 1972. Set. 298.00 o.p. (ISBN 0-8161-0931-1, Hall Library). G K Hall.
Oceanography: An Introduction. 3rd ed. Dale E. Ingmanson & William J. Wallace. 530p. 1985. text ed. (ISBN 0-534-03849-2). Wadsworth Pub.
Oceanography: Concepts & History. Margaret B. Deacon. LC 76-27682. (Benchmark Papers in Geology Ser.: Vol. 35). 1982. 49.95 o.p. (ISBN 0-87933-202-6). Van Nos Reinhold.
Oceanography from Space. Ed. by J. F. Gower. LC 81-12060. (Marine Science Ser.: Vol. 13). 998p. 1981. 135.00x o.p. (ISBN 0-306-40808-2, Plenum Pr). Plenum Pub.
Oceola Kid. Clay Randall. 144p. 1981. pap. 1.75 o.p. (ISBN 0-8439-0984-6, Pub. by Leisure Bks CT). Dorchester Pub Co.
Ocho Mundos: A Cultural Reader. 2nd ed. Brenda Wegmann. (Span.). 1982. pap. text ed. 15.95 o.p. (ISBN 0-03-059746-3). HR&W.
Ochre Robe: An Autobiography. 2nd ed. Agahananda Bharati. 300p. 1980. 14.95 o.p. (ISBN 0-915520-40-0); pap. 7.95 o.p. (ISBN 0-915520-28-1). Ross-Erikson.
Ockham, the Conciliar Theory, & the Canonists. Brian Tierney. Ed. by Heiko A. Oberman. LC 74-157547. (Facet Bks). (Orig.). 1971. pap. 1.00 o.p. (ISBN 0-8006-3064-5, 1-3064, Fortress). Augsburg Fortress.
OCLC in Retrospect. Joseph Z. Nitecki. (Occasional Papers: No. 123). 35p. 1976. pap. 2.00 o.p. (ISBN 0-317-58956-3). U of Ill Lib Info Sci.
Ocran's Acronyms: A Dictionary of Abbreviations & Acronyms Used in Scientific & Technical Writing. Emanuel B. Ocran. 1978. 25.00 o.p. (ISBN 0-7100-8869-8). Routledge Chapman & Hall.
Octavia's Hill. Margaret Dickson. LC 82-15830. 384p. 1983. 14.45 o.p. (ISBN 0-395-33159-5). HM.
October Blood. Francine Du Plessix Gray. 256p. 1985. 16.45 o.p. (ISBN 0-671-55511-1). S&S.
October Circle. Robert Littell. 1977. pap. 1.75 o.p. (ISBN 0-380-00872-6, 31393). Avon.
October Fort. Brom Hoban. LC 80-25995. (Illus.). 32p. (gr. 1-4). 1981. 9.95 o.s.i. (ISBN 0-03-059017-5). H Holt & Co.
October Nineteen Seventeen. Marc Ferro. (Illus.). 1980. 35.00 o.p. (ISBN 0-7100-0534-2). Routledge Chapman & Hall.
Octopus Protests. Jacquelyn Reinach. Ed. by Ruth L. Perle. LC 78-54981. (Sweet Pickles Ser.). (Illus.). (gr. k-2). 1978. 2.95 o.p. (ISBN 0-03-042046-6). H Holt & Co.
Ocular & Cerebrospinal Fluids: Experimental Eye Research Supplement. Ed. by L. Bito & H. Davson. 1978. 76.50 o.p. (ISBN 0-12-102550-0). Acad Pr.
Ocular & Extraocular Processing of Visual Information: Journal: Ophthalmic Research. Ed. by E. Zrenner & H. Meissl. (Vol. 16, Nos. 1-2). (Illus.). 128p. 1984. pap. 53.50 o.p. (ISBN 3-8055-3869-3). S Karger.
Ocular Assessment. Ed. by Barry J. Baressi. 384p. 1983. text ed. 54.95 o.p. (ISBN 0-409-95034-3). Butterworth.
Ocular Needs in Africa. F. M. Mburu. 147p. 1984. pap. 25.00 o.p. (ISBN 0-08-031299-3). Pergamon.
Od Infinitum. Daniel E. Schneider. 176p. 1987. 9.50 o.p. (ISBN 0-8062-2826-1). Carlton.
Odd One Out. Rodney Peppe. (Illus.). 32p. (gr. k-3). 1974. PLB 10.95 o.p. Penguin USA.
Odd Order Group Actions & Witt Classification of Innerproducts. J. P. Alexander et al. (Lecture Notes in Mathematics Ser: Vol. 625). 1977. pap. 18.00 o.p. (ISBN 0-387-08528-9). Springer-Verlag.
Oddities: A Book of Unexplained Facts. Rupert T. Gould. (Illus.). 1965. 5.00 o.p. (ISBN 0-8216-0131-8, Pub. by Univ Bks). Carol Pub Group.
Odds Against Them. Lyn Doudna. LC 85-90046. 189p. 1985. 11.95 o.p. (ISBN 0-533-06574-7). Vantage.
Odds & Ends. Lionel A. Canaan. 1983. 8.95 o.p. (ISBN 0-533-05334-X). Vantage.
Odds Were Against Me. Katherine L. Weems. LC 84-90241. (Illus.). 162p. 1985. 14.50 o.p. (ISBN 0-533-06296-9). Vantage.
Ode. John D. Jump. (Critical Idiom Ser.). 1974. pap. 5.50x o.p. (ISBN 0-416-78820-3, NO. 2260). Routledge Chapman & Hall.
Ode, Inscribed to John Howard, Repr. Of 1780. William Hayley. Ed. by Donald H. Reiman. Bd. with Essay on Painting: in Two Epistles to Mr. Romney...Third Edition Corrected & Enlarged. Repr. of 1781 ed; Triumphs of Temper; a Poem. In Six Cantos. Repr. of 1781 ed; Essay on Epic Poetry: in Five Epistles to the Rev. Mr. Mason. With Notes... Repr. of 1782 ed. LC 75-31207. (Romantic Context Ser.: Poetry 1789-1830: Vol. 58). 1979. lib. bdg. 57.00 o.p. (ISBN 0-8240-2157-6). Garland Pub.
Ode to the Sea & Other Poems. Howard Baker. 77p. 1966. 5.95 o.p. (ISBN 0-8040-0228-2). Ohio U Pr.
Odes of Feeling. Gertrude Libby Ducharme. 1977. 4.00 o.p. (ISBN 0-682-48966-2). Exposition-Phoenix.
Odessa: A Guide. G. Kononova. 191p. 1985. 7.95 o.p. (ISBN 0-8285-2959-0, Pub. by Raduga Pubs USSR). Imported Pubns.
Odometer Law: Nineteen Eighty-Two & 1987 Supplement. LC 82-60509. 63p. 1982. pap. 41.00 o.p. (ISBN 0-943116-05-8). Nat Consumer Law.
Odor Control for Wastewater Facilities. Water Pollution Control Federation Staff. (Manual of Practice Ser.: M0028). 80p. 1985. pap. 11.00 o.p. Water Pollution.
Odors from Stationary & Mobile Sources. National Research Council, Board on Toxicology & Environmental Health Hazards. 1979. pap. 21.95x o.p. (ISBN 0-309-02877-9). Natl Acad Pr.
Odour of White Bread. (Agricultural Research Reports: No. 198). 1973. pap. 5.00 o.p. (ISBN 90-220-0456-2, PDC191, PUDOC). UNIPUB.
Odysseus: Archaeology of the European Image of Man. Bernard Andreae. Tr. by Shapur Shabhazi from Ger. (Centers of Civilization Ser.). (Illus.). 272p. 1989. lib. bdg. (ISBN 0-89089-306-3). Carolina Acad Pr.
Odysseus Elytis: A Poem in Two Voices. Maria Nephele. Tr. by Athan Anagnostopoulos from Gr. 64p. 1981. 10.00 o.p. (ISBN 0-395-29465-7). HM.
Odyssey. John Bierman. 288p. 1984. 16.45 o.p. (ISBN 0-671-50156-9). S&S.
Odyssey of a Film-Maker: Robert Flaherty's Story. Frances H. Flaherty. (Illus.). 80p. 1984. ltd. ed. 15.00 o.p. (ISBN 0-939660-15-6); pap. 8.00 o.p. (ISBN 0-939660-14-8). Threshold VT.
Odyssey of a Santo Domingan Creole. Ed. by Edward L. Tinker. 18p. 1957. pap. 3.00x o.p. (ISBN 0-912296-28-3, Dist. by U Pr of Va). Am Antiquarian.
Odyssey of an American Composer. Otto Luening. (Illus.). 1980. 7.95 o.p. (ISBN 0-684-16496-5, ScribT); encore ed. 7.95 o.p. (ISBN 0-684-17737-4). Scribner.
Odyssey of C. H. Lightoller. Patrick Stenson. (Illus.). 1984. 16.45 o.p. (ISBN 0-393-01924-1). Norton.
Odyssey of Homer. 48p. (Orig.). 1988. pap. 9.95 o.p. (ISBN 1-55651-681-9); cassette o.p. (ISBN 1-55651-682-7). Cram Cassettes.
Odyssey to Omega. Merlin L. Reittinger. 1978. 5.50 o.p. (ISBN 0-682-49120-9). Exposition-Phoenix.
Oecumenica 1966 Yearbook for Ecumenical Studies. Ed. by Vilmos Vatja & Friedrich W. Kantzenback. 1966. 8.50 o.p. (ISBN 0-8066-9330-4, 10-4720, Augsburg). Augsburg Fortress.
Oecumenica 1967 Yearbook for Ecumenical Studies. Ed. by Vilmos Vatja & Friedrich W. Kantzenback. 1967. 8.50 o.p. (ISBN 0-8066-9331-2, 10-4721, Augsburg). Augsburg Fortress.
Oecumenica 1968 Yearbook for Ecumenical Studies. Ed. by Vilmos Vatja & Friedrich W. Kantzenback. 1968. 8.50 o.p. (ISBN 0-8066-9332-0, 10-4722, Fortress). Augsburg Fortress.
Oecumenica 1969 Yearbook for Ecumenical Studies. Ed. by Vilmos Vatja & Friedrich W. Kantzenback. 1969. 8.50 o.p. (ISBN 0-8066-9333-9, 10-4723, Augsburg). Augsburg Fortress.
Oecumenica 1970 Yearbook for Ecumenical Studies. Ed. by Gunther Gassmann & Vilmos Vatja. 1970. 8.50 o.p. (ISBN 0-8066-9334-7, 10-4724, Augsburg). Augsburg Fortress.
Oecumenica 1971 & 72 Yearbook for Ecumenical Studies. Ed. by Vilmos Vatja & Friedrich W. Kantzenback. 1972. 8.50 o.p. (ISBN 0-8066-9335-5, 10-4725, Augsburg). Augsburg Fortress.
Oedipus at Thebes: Sophocles Tragic Hero & His Time. Bernard Knox. 1971. pap. 1.95 o.p. (ISBN 0-393-00563-1, Norton Lib). Norton.
Oedipus Rex see also King Oedipus.
Oedipus Trilogy of Sophocles. 48p. (Orig.). 1988. pap. 9.95 o.p. (ISBN 1-55651-679-7); cassette o.p. (ISBN 1-55651-680-0). Cram Cassettes.
Oeil Ces Sangasses. Michel Butor. 1972. 75.00 o.p. (ISBN 0-686-50136-5). French & Eur.
OEM Systems Handbook. rev. ed. Intel Staff. 1136p. 1986. pap. 18.00 o.p. (ISBN 1-55512-003-2, 210941). Intel Corp.
Oeuvre Poetique, 2 tomes, Tome I. Saint John-Perse. Incl. Eloges; Gloire des Rois; Anabase; Exil. (Coll. Soleil). 1960. 11.95 o.p. (ISBN 0-685-35910-7). Schoenhof.
Oeuvre Poetique, 2 tomes, Tome II. Saint John-Perse. Incl. Vents; Amers; Chronique. (Coll. Soleil). 1960. 16.95 o.p. (ISBN 0-685-35911-5). Schoenhof.
Oeuvres, 4 tomes. Louis-Ferdinand D. Celine. Set. 691.25 o.p. (ISBN 0-685-37273-1). French & Eur.
Oeuvres, 2 tomes, Tome II. Charles-Agustin De Sainte-Beuve. Incl. Portraits Litteraires (Fin; Portraits de Femmes. (Bibl. de Pleiade). 1950. 24.95 o.p. (ISBN 0-685-36019-9). Schoenhof.
Oeuvres, 2 tomes, Tome I. Charles-Agustin De Sainte-Beuve. Incl. Premiers Lundis; Portraits Litteraires. (Bibl. de la Pleiade). 1950. 22.50 o.p. (ISBN 0-685-36018-0). Schoenhof.
Oeuvres. Antoine De Saint-Exupery. (Bibl. de la Pleiade). 1953. 33.95 o.p. (ISBN 0-685-11436-8). Schoenhof.
Oeuvres, 5 vols. Marcel Proust. Incl. Vols. 1-3. A la Recherche du Temps Perdu. Ed. by Ferre & Clarac. Vols. 1. 35.95 (ISBN 0-685-37059-3); Vol. 2. 37.50 (ISBN 0-685-37060-7); Vol. 3. 37.50 (ISBN 0-685-37061-5); Vol. 4. Jean Santeuil et Les Plaisirs et les Jours. Ed. by Sandre & Clarac. 35.95 (ISBN 0-685-37062-3); Vol. 5. Contre Sainte-Beuve & Pastiches et Melanges. Ed. by Sandre & Clarac. 37.95 (ISBN 0-685-37063-1). (Pleiade Ser.). Schoenhof.
Oeuvres Completes, 8 vols. Guillaume Apollinaire. Ed. by Decaudin. Set. deluxe ed. 550.00 o.p. (ISBN 0-685-37179-4). French & Eur.
Oeuvres Completes. Charles Baudelaire. 1931-1952. 75.00 o.p. (ISBN 0-685-11439-2); pap. 115.00 13 vol. ed o.p. (ISBN 0-685-11440-6). French & Eur.
Oeuvres Completes: Avec: Le Momo, Cigit, La Culture Indienne, Lettre a Peter Watson, Vol. 12. Antonin Artaud. 352p. 1974. 19.95 o.p. (ISBN 0-686-53830-7). Schoenhof.
Oeuvres Completes: Avec: Van Gogh, Pour en Finir avec le Jugement de Dieu, Le Theatre de la Cruante, Vol. 13. Antonin Artaud. 400p. 1974. 22.50 o.p. (ISBN 0-686-53831-5). Schoenhof.
Oeuvres Completes Illustrees, 25 tomes. Honore De Balzac. Ed. by Ducourneau. Set. 950.00 o.p. (ISBN 0-685-34068-6). French & Eur.
Oeuvres Completes: Paris, 1826-1831, 27 vols. facsimile ed. Rene de Chateaubriand. 50.00 ea. o.p. French & Eur.
Oeuvres Completes: Supplement Au Tome 1. Antonin Artaud. 248p. 1970. 14.95 o.p. (ISBN 0-686-53826-9). Schoenhof.
Oeuvres Completes: Suppots et Supplications, Vol. 14, Pt. 1. Antonin Artaud. 321p. 1978. 25.00 o.p. (ISBN 0-686-53832-3). Schoenhof.
Oeuvres Completes: Suppots et Supplications, Vol. 14, Pt. 2. Antonin Artaud. 310p. 1978. 25.00 o.p. (ISBN 0-686-53833-1). Schoenhof.
Oeuvres Poetiques, 3 Vols. Christine De Pisan. Ed. by M. Roy. 1965. 109.00 o.p. (ISBN 0-384-46593-5); pap. 91.00 o.p. (ISBN 0-384-46594-3). Johnson Repr.
Oeuvres: Recits (1887-1892, Vol. 2. Anton Chekhov. 1032p. 33.95 o.p. (ISBN 0-686-56580-0). French & Eur.
Oeuvres: Recits (1892-1903, Vol. 3. Anton Chekhov. 1048p. 33.95 o.p. (ISBN 0-686-56581-9). French & Eur.
Oeuvres Romanesques Completes. Jean Giono et al. 1733p. 1977. 49.95 o.p. (ISBN 0-686-53980-X). French & Eur.
Of a Fire on the Moon. Norman Mailer. LC 84-73187. 480p. 1985. pap. 3.95 o.s.i. (ISBN 0-394-62019-4, BC). Grove.
Of Acceptable Risk: Science & the Determination of Safety. William W. Lowrance. LC 76-834. (Illus.). 191p. 1976. 11.95 o.p. (ISBN 0-913232-30-0); pap. 7.95 o.p. (ISBN 0-913232-31-9). W Kaufmann.
Of All Things! A Nibley Quote Book. Compiled by Gary P. Gillum. 178p. 1981. 10.95 o.p. (ISBN 0-941214-03-6). Signature Bks.
Of Battles Long Ago: Memoirs of an American Ambulance Driver in World War I. G. Ripley Cutler. Ed. & intro. by Charles H. Knickerbocker. LC 79-50656. (Illus.). 280p. 1979. 15.00 o.p. (ISBN 0-682-49396-1). Exposition-Phoenix.
Of Blood & Hope. Samuel Pisar. 1980. 12.95 o.p. (ISBN 0-316-70901-8). Little.
Of Blood & Hope. Samuel Pisar. (Illus.). 1982. pap. 9.95 o.p. (ISBN 0-02-006310-5, Collier). Macmillan.
Of Books & Men. Louis B. Wright. LC 76-26493. xx, 180p. 1976. 15.95 o.p. (ISBN 0-87249-344-X). U of SC Pr.
Of Cabbages & Kings. Tillie H. Gandy. 1983. 6.50 o.p. (ISBN 0-8062-2138-0). Carlton.
Of Caesar's Household. Mollie Thompson. Ed. by Charles Clanton. 232p. (Orig.). 1978. pap. 4.95 o.p. (ISBN 0-912315-29-6). Word Aflame.
Of Children: An Introduction to Child Development. 5th ed. Guy R. Lefrancois. 606p. 1986. text ed. (ISBN 0-534-05502-8). Wadsworth Pub.
Of Course I Love You, but... Ann Miller & Charles Miller. LC 73-89084. (Center Enrichment Ser.). (Illus.). 72p. 1974. pap. 0.50x o.p. (ISBN 0-8006-5077-8, Fortress). Augsburg Fortress.
Of Crimes & Rights. Macklin Fleming. 1978. 11.95x o.p. (ISBN 0-393-05650-3). Norton.
Of Everlasting Value, Vol. 1. Ed. by Howard H. Barron. (Orig.). 1978. pap. 5.95 o.p. (ISBN 0-89036-129-0). Hawkes Pub Inc.
Of Everlasting Value, Vol. 2. Ed. by Howard H. Barron. (Orig.). pap. 5.95 o.p. (ISBN 0-89036-130-4). Hawkes Pub Inc.
Of Garry Owen in Glory: The History of the Seventh U. S. Cavalry Regiment. Melbourne C. Chandler. (Illus.). 1960. 50.00 o.p. (ISBN 0-682-40021-1). Exposition-Phoenix.

Of God & Man. Martin C. D'Arcy. 1967. pap. 2.95x o.p. (ISBN 0-268-00197-9). U of Notre Dame Pr.
Of Graves, Worms & Epitaphs. Tobias Wells. LC 87-33967. (Crime Club Ser.). 192p. 1988. 12.95 o.p. (ISBN 0-385-19772-1). Doubleday.
Of Guilt & Hope. Martin Niemoeller. 1947. (ISBN 0-8022-1219-0). Philos Lib.
Of Human Freedom. Jean-Paul Sartre. LC 66-18816. 176p. 1967. (ISBN 0-8022-1488-6). Philos Lib.
Of Human Values. Bernardino Dell'Osso. 1986. 12.95 o.p. (ISBN 0-533-06264-0). Vantage.
Of Ivory Accents. Stevan Treleaven Eldred-Grigg. 1977. 4.00 o.p. (ISBN 0-682-48650-7). Exposition-Phoenix.
Of Jewish Law & Lore. Louis Ginzberg. LC 55-6707. (Temple Bks). 1970. pap. 5.95 o.s.i. (ISBN 0-689-70231-0, T12, Atheneum). Macmillan.
Of Kennedys & Kings: Making Sense of the Sixties. Harris Wofford. 496p. 1980. 17.50 o.p. (ISBN 0-374-22432-3). FS&G.
Of Life & Hope: Toward Effective Witness in Human Rights. Mia Adjali. (Orig.). 1979. pap. 2.95 o.p. (ISBN 0-377-00084-1). Friendship Pr.
Of Life & Love. Emil Ludwig. Philos Lib.
Of Life & Love: Contemporary Poems. William Lowenkamp. 64p. 1982. 5.00 o.p. (ISBN 0-682-49881-5). Exposition-Phoenix.
Of Light. Frank Samperi. 1965. saddlestitched in wrappers 5.00 o.p. (ISBN 0-685-79040-1). Small Pr Dist.
Of Lost Loves & Other People. Eileen C. Rasmussen. 1979. 5.00 o.p. (ISBN 0-682-49473-9). Exposition-Phoenix.
Of Making Many Books. Roger Burlingame. 1971. 10.00 o.s.i. (ISBN 0-684-10047-9, ScribT). Scribner.
Of Man & God. Alfred Pomerantz. LC 65-10996. 192p. 1965. (ISBN 0-8022-2002-9). Philos Lib.
Of Mice & Men by John Steinbeck. 48p. (Orig.). 1988. pap. 9.95 o.p. (ISBN 1-55651-677-0); cassette o.p. (ISBN 1-55651-678-9). Cram Cassettes.
Of Music & Music-Making. Bruno Walter. 1964. pap. 3.95 o.p. (ISBN 0-393-00242-X, Norton Lib). Norton.
Of Nightingales That Weep. Katherine Paterson. (Illus.). 172p. (gr. 5 up). 1980. pap. 2.50 o.p. (ISBN 0-380-51110-X, Camelot). Avon.
Of Other Realms: A Journey of the Soul. Patricia A. Lewis. LC 82-60760. (Illus.). 112p. (Orig.). 1982. pap. 5.50 o.p. (ISBN 0-935834-08-7). Rainbow Books.
Of Our Soup, Of Our People. Donna D. De La Torriente. LC 85-72693. (Illus.). 168p. 1985. 19.95 o.p. (ISBN 0-931494-78-8). Brunswick Pub.
Of Outer & Inner Space. Harry H. Sisler. 80p. 1981. 7.95 o.p. (ISBN 0-89116-229-1). Hemisphere Pub.
Of Oxygen, Fuels & Living Matter, Vol. 2, Pt. 2. G. Semenza. LC 80-41420. (Evolving Life Sciences Ser.). 508p. 1982. 97.95x o.p. (ISBN 0-471-27924-2, Pub. by Wiley-Interscience). Wiley.
Of Presidents, Prime Ministers & Princes: A Decade in Fleet Street. Anthony Holden. LC 83-45074. 325p. 1984. 12.95 o.p. (ISBN 0-689-11400-1, Atheneum). Macmillan.
Of Prisons & Ideas. Milovan Djilas. Tr. by Michael B. Petrovich from Serbo-Croatian. 144p. 1986. 17.95 o.p. (ISBN 0-15-167979-7). HarBraceJ.
Of Roses & Other Poems. Frank J. Fitzgerald. 36p. 1981. 4.00 o.p. (ISBN 0-682-49747-9). Exposition-Phoenix.
Of Shadow, Song, & Soul. Sharon L. Housen. 40p. 1985. 4.95 o.p. (ISBN 0-317-18031-2). Dorrance.
Of Solitude & Silence: Writings on Robert Bly. Ed. by Richard Jones & Kate Daniels. LC 81-68357. (Illus.). 192p. 1982. 14.50x o.p. (ISBN 0-8070-6360-6); pap. 8.25x o.p. (ISBN 0-8070-6361-4, BP 630). Beacon Pr.
Of Space-Time & the River. Gregory Benford. (Illus.). 72p. (Orig.). 1985. casebound, numbered, signed, Collector's ed. 80.00 o.p. (ISBN 0-941826-14-7). Cheap St.
Of Suchness: Glimpses of the Anatomy & Pathology of God. John J. Robinson. (Illus.). 1980. 10.50 o.p. (ISBN 0-682-49465-8, Banner). Exposition-Phoenix.
Of the Press, by the Press, for the Press (& Others, Too) 2nd ed. Washington Post Writers Group. 1976. pap. 11.95 o.p. (ISBN 0-395-24016-6). HM.
Of Thee I Sing. Donald Kipfer. 299p. 1987. 18.00 o.p. (ISBN 0-682-40350-4). Exposition-Phoenix.
Of This Man: The Biography of William A. Hillenbrand. Garven Dalglish. LC 82-310. (Illus.). 304p. 1982. 15.00 o.p. (ISBN 0-914016-86-5). Phoenix Pub.
Of Time & of Seasons. Norma Johnston. LC 75-9748. 320p. (gr. 7 up). 1975. 7.95 o.p. (ISBN 0-689-30479-X, Atheneum). Macmillan.
Of Time & People. E. Yekovlev. 397p. 1979. 7.95 o.p. (ISBN 0-8285-1074-1, Pub. by Progress Pubs USSR). Imported Pubns.
Of Time, Space, & Other Things. Isaac Asimov. 1977. pap. 1.50 o.p. (ISBN 0-380-00325-2, 35584, Discus). Avon.
Of Time, Work & Leisure (20th Cent. Fund) Sebastian De Grazia. LC 73-12379. 572p. 1973. lib. bdg. (ISBN 0-527-22100-7); pap. 20.00 o.p. Kraus Repr.
Of Times & People from Ohio: Distant Cousins, Vol. I. Alberta M. Detering. LC 85-90998. (Illus.). 304p. 1985. 15.00 o.p. (ISBN 0-682-40248-6). Exposition-Phoenix.
Of Virtue Rare: Margaret Beaufort, Matriarch of the House of Tudor. Linda Simon. (Illus.). 192p. 1982. 12.95 o.p. (ISBN 0-395-31563-8). HM.
Of Woman Born: Motherhood As Experience & Institution. Adrienne Rich. 1976. 12.95 o.p. (ISBN 0-393-08750-6). Norton.
Of Woman Born: Motherhood As Experience & Institution. Adrienne Rich. 320p. 1985. pap. 6.70 o.p. (ISBN 0-393-30292-X). Norton.
Off Balance: The Real World of Ballet. Suzanne Gordon. LC 82-18806. (Illus.). 256p. 1983. 15.45 o.p. (ISBN 0-394-51985-X). Pantheon.
Off-Broadway Theater. Julia S. Price. LC 73-8256. (Illus.). 279p. 1974. Repr. of 1962 ed. lib. bdg. 24.75x o.p. (ISBN 0-8371-6972-0, PROB). Greenwood.
Off Duty. Andrew Coburn. 1980. 10.95 o.p. (ISBN 0-393-01369-3). Norton.
Off for the Sweet Hereafter. T. R. Pearson. 283p. 1986. 17.45 o.s.i. (ISBN 0-671-61437-1, Linden Pr). S&S.
Off-Key Angel. H. R. Schneider. 1977. 4.00 o.p. (ISBN 0-682-48672-8). Exposition-Phoenix.
Off-Road Transportation & Soil-Working: Means to Promote Development & Operations. Ed. by S. Areskoug et al. 120p. 1985. pap. 33.00 o.p. (ISBN 0-08-031652-2). Pergamon.
Off Season Angler. Gary Saindon. 94p. (Orig.). 1985. pap. 9.95 o.s.i. (ISBN 0-934318-53-0). Falcon Pr MT.
Off-Site Costs of Soil Erosion. Ed. by Thomas E. Waddell. 284p. (Orig.). 1986. pap. 25.00 o.p. (ISBN 0-89164-097-5). Conservation Foun.
Off Stage & On: An Introduction to Youth Drama. Alison Taylor. 1969. pap. 35.00 o.p. (ISBN 0-08-012968-4). Pergamon.
Off the Cuff. D. J. Trombley. 1987. 8.95 o.p. (ISBN 0-533-06955-6). Vantage.
Off the Record. Buzzie Bavasi & John Strege. (Illus.). 256p. 1987. 16.95 o.p. (ISBN 0-8092-4885-9). Contemp Bks.
Off the Record with F. D. R., Nineteen Forty-Two to Forty-Five. William D. Hassett. LC 80-16200. (Illus.). 366p. 1908. Repr. of 1958 ed. lib. bdg. 35.00x o.p. (ISBN 0-313-22585-0, HAOR). Greenwood.
Off to a Great Start: How to Relax & Enjoy Your Baby. Loraine Stern & Kathleen McKay. LC 85-18863. 1986. 15.45 o.p. (ISBN 0-393-02269-2). Norton.
Off to College: The Survival Manual for High School Students & Their Parents. Melody Martin. 144p. (Orig.). 1984. pap. 7.95 o.p. (ISBN 0-671-52781-9). Monarch Pr.
Off to Mt. Hood: An Autobiography of the Old Road. Ivan Woolley. (Illus.). 109p. 1959. pap. 4.95 o.p. (ISBN 0-87595-015-9). Oregon Hist.
Off with His Head. Ngaio Marsh. (Portway Ser.). 400p. 1988. lib. bdg. 18.50x o.s.i. (ISBN 0-7451-7092-7, Pub. by Chivers Pr UK). G K Hall.
Offbeat Oregon: A Connoisseur's Collection of Travel Discovery in Oregon. Mimi Bell. LC 83-5229. (Illus.). 144p. (Orig.). 1983. pap. 6.95 o.p. (ISBN 0-87701-274-1). Chronicle Bks.
Offender Assessment: A Casebook in Corrections. Robert B. Mills. 200p. 1980. pap. 14.95 o.p. (ISBN 0-87084-568-3). Anderson Pub Co.
Offensive Football. Gayle Sayers & Bob Griese. Ed. by Bill Bonderunt. LC 72-78293. (Illus.). 1972. 6.95 o.p. (ISBN 0-689-10529-0, Atheneum). Macmillan.
Offering. 1986. pap. 7.95 o.p. (ISBN 0-918222-70-2). Morrow.
Offering of Swans. Oliver Gogarty. 40p. 1971. Repr. of 1923 ed. 15.00x o.p. (ISBN 0-7165-1360-9, BBA 02054, Pub. by Cuala Press Ireland). Biblio Dist.
Offical Liars' Handbook. David Dale. (Illus.). 64p. 1987. pap. 4.95 o.p. (ISBN 0-399-51398-1, Perigee Bks). Putnam Pub Group.
Office. Fredric Brown. 1987. signed, ltd. ed. 30.00x o.p. (ISBN 0-939767-01-5). D McMillan.
Office Administration. C. Deverell. 1980. pap. 19.95 o.p. (ISBN 0-85258-187-4). Van Nos Reinhold.
Office Administration Handbook. B. H. Walley. 470p. 1975. text ed. 25.75x o.p. (ISBN 0-220-66281-9, Pub. by Busn Bks England). Gower Pub Co.
Office at Home. Robert Scott. 320p. 1985. 15.95 o.p. (ISBN 0-684-18212-2); write for info. o.p. (ISBN 0-684-18218-1). Scribner.
Office at Home: Everything You Need to Know to Work Efficiently & Happily from Home. Robert Scott. 320p. 1986. pap. 9.95 o.p. (ISBN 0-684-18650-0). Scribner.
Office Automation. Ed. by Nancy M. Edwards. 1983. pap. 37.95 o.p. (ISBN 0-442-22202-5). Van Nos Reinhold.
Office Automation: A Manager's Guide. Harry Katzan, Jr. 224p. 1982. 32.50 o.p. (ISBN 0-8144-5752-5). AMACOM.
Office Automation & Word Processing Buyer's Guide. Tony Webster. LC 83-18694. (Illus.). 328p. 1984. pap. text ed. 19.95 o.p. (ISBN 0-07-068962-8, BYTE Bks). Mcgraw.
Office Automation: Concepts & Application. 3rd ed. Paula B. Cecil. 1984. 31.95 o.p. (ISBN 0-8053-1763-5); instr's guide 5.95 o.p. (ISBN 0-8053-1764-3); study guide 7.95 o.p. (ISBN 0-8053-1765-1). Benjamin-Cummings.
Office Bulletins & Announcements. (Easy-to-Make Photocopier Bks.). (Orig.). 1983. pap. 14.95 o.p. (ISBN 0-87280-027-X, Asher-Gallant). Caddylak Systs.
Office Design & Decoration: A Bibliography. Mary Vance. (Architecture Ser.: Bibliography A 1333). 22p. 1985. pap. 3.00 o.p. (ISBN 0-89028-283-8). Vance Biblios.
Office Diagnosis & Management of Chronic Obstructive Pulmonary Disease. Geoffrey M. Davies. LC 81-8386. (Illus.). 135p. 1981. text ed. 8.95 o.p. (ISBN 0-8121-0823-X). Lea & Febiger.
Office Dynamics Company: An Office Services & Temporary Help Agency Practice Set. Olive Church. 250p. 1981. pap. text ed. 16.00 o.s.i. (ISBN 0-205-07136-8, EDP 087136); tchr's. ed. avail. o.s.i. (ISBN 0-205-07361-1). Allyn.
Office Furniture: A Bibliography. Mary Vance. (Architecture Ser.: Bibliography A 1336). 21p. 1985. pap. 3.00 o.p. (ISBN 0-89028-286-2). Vance Biblios.
Office Layout: A Bibliography. Mary Vance. (Architecture Ser.: Bibliography A 1334). 24p. 1985. pap. 3.75 o.p. (ISBN 0-89028-284-6). Vance Biblios.
Office Lighting: A Bibliography. Mary Vance. (Architecture Ser.: Bibliography A 1335). 16p. 1985. pap. 2.25 o.p. (ISBN 0-89028-285-4). Vance Biblios.
Office Machines: A Practical Approach. 2nd ed. Jimmy C. McKenzie & Robert J. Hughes. 352p. 1983. 22.00 o.p. (ISBN 0-205-11509-8, H1509-2); instr's. manual avail. o.p. (ISBN 0-205-11513-6, H1513-4); practice set 13.00 o.p. (ISBN 0-205-11510-1, H1510-0). Allyn.
Office Management. Burton S. Kaliski. 452p. 1983. text ed. 22.00 o.p. (ISBN 0-15-567391-2, HC). HarBraceJ.
Office Management Problem Solver. Joseph L. Kish. LC 80-70349. 224p. 1983. 27.50 o.p. (ISBN 0-8019-7011-3); pap. 17.95 o.p. (ISBN 0-8019-7370-8). Chilton.
Office of the Madonna. 226p. 250.00 o.p. (ISBN 0-8115-0907-9). Kraus Repr.
Office Procedure Forms for the Professional Psychologist. Ohio Psychology Publishing Co. Staff. 44p. (Orig.). 1981. pap. text ed. 6.00x o.p. (ISBN 0-910707-04-9). Ohio Psych Pub.
Office Signs. (Easy-to-Make Photocopier Bks.). 78p. (Orig.). 1983. pap. 14.95 o.p. (ISBN 0-87280-028-8, Asher-Gallant). Caddylak Systs.
Office Supply Industry. Ed. by Peter Allen. 300p. 1988. pap. 995.00 o.p. (ISBN 0-941285-27-8). Find SVP.
Office Systems Management. 9th ed. John J. Stallard & George R. Terry. 1984. 34.95x o.p. (ISBN 0-256-03085-5). Irwin.
Office Work Measurement. rev. ed. Harold Nance. LC 82-20887. 164p. 1983. 19.50 o.p. (ISBN 0-89874-314-1). Krieger.
Officer & a Gentleman. Stephen P. Smith. 1982. pap. 2.95 o.p. (ISBN 0-380-80853-6, 88294-9). Avon.
Officer Candidate Tests. Solomon Wiener. 592p. Date not set. pap. 12.95 o.p. (ISBN 0-668-05665-7). Arco.
Officer Pay Plan. Fred C. Ballman. 125p. 1986. 8.50 o.p. (ISBN 0-8062-2898-9). Carlton.
Officers' & Directors' Liability: A Review of the Business Judgment Rule. 733p. 1985. pap. 15.00 o.p. (ISBN 0-317-27492-9, #B4-6718). PLI.
Officers' & Directors' Liability: A Review of the Business Judgement Rule. 733p. 1985. 40.00 o.p. (B4-6718). PLI.
Official Arrow Street Map Atlas of Metro Boston, MA. 1973. 9.95 o.p. (ISBN 0-913450-96-0). Arrow Pub.
Official Arrow Street Map Atlas of Metro Hartford, CT. 1984. 7.95 o.p. (ISBN 0-913450-89-8). Arrow Pub.
Official Arrow Street Map Atlas of Western MA. 1986. 9.95 o.p. (ISBN 0-913450-88-X). Arrow Pub.
Official Catalogue of the Uffizi. Intro. by Luciano Berti. 1980. 550.00x o.p. (ISBN 0-8103-4355-X, Centro Di). Gale.
Official Catholic Directory. National Register Publishing Co. Staff. LC 81-30961. 1987. 115.00 o.p. (ISBN 0-317-65762-3). Natl Register.
Official Commentary for Sharing the Light of Faith. Berard L. Marthaler. 119p. 1981. pap. 7.50 o.p. (ISBN 1-55586-694-8). US Catholic.
Official Directory of Industrial & Commercial Traffic Executives, 1986. Ed. by Khin S. Hla. LC 72-626342. (Illus.). 614p. 1985. 75.00 o.p. (ISBN 0-87408-034-7). Intl Thom Trans Pr.
Official Directory of Industrial & Commercial Traffic Executives: 1981 Edition. Ed. by Callie Possinger. LC 72-626342. (Illus.). 490p. 1980. 45.00 o.p. (ISBN 0-87408-021-5). Intl Thom Trans Pr.
Official Directory of Industrial & Commercial Traffic Executives, 1983. Ed. by Callie Possinger. LC 72-626342. (Illus.). 566p. 1982. 50.00 o.p. (ISBN 0-87408-023-1). Intl Thom Trans Pr.
Official Directory of Industrial & Commercial Traffic Executives, 1984. Ed. by Callie Possinger. LC 72-626342. (Illus.). 578p. 1983. 60.00 o.p. (ISBN 0-87408-025-8). Intl Thom Trans Pr.
Official Fantasy Football League Manual: How to Own Your Own Pro Football Team, Coach Your Players, Outsmart Your Friends, & Win Big. Jim Donaldson. (Illus.). 160p. (Orig.). 1984. pap. 6.95 o.p. (ISBN 0-8092-5388-7). Contemp Bks.
Official Foodie Handbook. Ann Barr & Paul Levy. (Illus.). 1985. 17.95 o.p. (ISBN 0-87795-770-3, Arbor Hse); pap. 12.95 o.p. (ISBN 0-87795-727-4). Morrow.
Official Guide to Food Service & Hospitality Management. Alexander C. Morton. (Illus.). 128p. 1983. pap. 8.95 o.p. (ISBN 0-668-05750-5, 5750-5). Arco.
Official Guide to the Small Country Hotels & Inns of France, 1985. French Government Tourist Office Staff. 250p. (Orig.). 1985. pap. 7.95 o.p. (ISBN 2-904394-07-9). Faber & Faber.
Official Guidebook to China. rev. & 4th ed. Ed. by China International Travel Service Staff. (Illus.). 372p. 1986. pap. 11.95 o.p. (ISBN 0-87052-249-3). Hippocrene Bks.
Official Handbook of the American Quarter Horse Association. 36th ed. (Illus.). 160p. 1988. write for info. o.p. Am Qtr Horse.
Official History of Colonial Development, 5 vols. D. J. Morgan. Incl. Vol. 1. The Origins of British Aid Policy 1924-1945. 253p (ISBN 0-391-01684-9); Vol. 2. Developing British Colonial Resources 1945-1951. 398p (ISBN 0-391-01685-7); Vol. 3. Reassessment of British Aid Policy 1951-1965. 334p (ISBN 0-391-01686-5); Vol. 4. Changes in British Aid Policy 1951-1970. 275p (ISBN 0-391-01687-3); Vol. 5. Guidance Towards Self-Government on British Colonies 1941-1971. 382p (ISBN 0-391-01688-1). 1980. text ed. 38.50x ea. o.p. Humanities.
Official I Hate Cats Book. Skip Morrow. LC 80-81251. 64p. (Orig.). 1980. pap. 3.95 o.p. (ISBN 0-03-057708-X). H Holt & Co.
Official I Hate Love Book. Skip Morrow. (Illus.). 1982. pap. 3.95 o.p. (ISBN 0-03-060417-6, Owl Bks). H Holt & Co.
Official Kerryman Joke Book. Des MacHale. 48p. 1983. pap. 3.95 o.p. (ISBN 0-85342-609-0, Pub. by Mercier Pr Ireland). Irish Bks Media.
Official Little League Guide to Fitness. Frank W. Jobe & Diane R. Moynes. LC 84-1268. (Illus.). 96p. 1984. pap. 5.95 o.p. (ISBN 0-671-50719-2). S&S.
Official MBA Handbook of Great Business Quotations. Jim Fisk & Robert Barron. (Orig.). 1984. pap. 5.70 o.p. (ISBN 0-671-50318-9, Fireside). S&S.
Official Monogram Painting Guide to German Aircraft: 1935-1945. LC 80-80846. 1980. 39.95 o.s.i. (ISBN 0-914144-29-4). Monogram Aviation.
Official National Football League Record & Fact Book,1985. Compiled by National Football League Staff. 320p. (Orig.). 1985. pap. 11.95 o.p. (ISBN 0-89480-841-9, 841). Workman Pub.
Official National Football League Record & Fact Book, 1986. Compiled by National Football League Staff. 320p. (Orig.). 1986. pap. 12.95 o.p. (ISBN 0-89480-012-4). Workman Pub.
Official NFL Record & Fact Book 1984. Ed. by NFL. (Illus.). 320p. (Orig.). 1984. pap. 9.95 o.s.i. (ISBN 0-89480-730-7, 730). Workman Pub.
Official Nineteen Eighty-Seven NFL Record & Fact Book. Compiled by N. F. L. Staff. (Illus.). 320p. (Orig.). 1987. pap. 12.95 o.p. (ISBN 0-89480-467-7). Workman Pub.
Official Price Guide to Football Cards, 1988. 7th ed. Ed. by James Beckett. (Illus.). 1987. pap. 4.95 o.p. (ISBN 0-87637-359-7, Hse of Collectibles). Ballantine.

Official Price Guide to Football Cards, 1987. 6th ed. Ed. by James Beckett. (Illus.). 1986. pap. 4.95 o.p. (ISBN 0-87637-520-4, Hse of Collectibles). Ballantine.

Official Professional Rodeo Guide 1987. Ed. by Steve Fleming. (Illus.). 264p. 1987. pap. 10.95 o.p. (ISBN 1-55566-015-0). Johnson Bks.

Official Professional Rodeo Guide, 1989. Professional Rodeo Cowboys Association Staff. (Illus.). 264p. pap. cancelled o.s.i. Johnson Bks.

Official Publishing, an Overview: An International Survey & Review of the Role, Organization & Principles of Official Publishing. J. J. Cherns. LC 78-41157. (Guides to Official Publication Ser.: Vol. 3). 1979. 132.00 o.p. (ISBN 0-08-023340-6). Pergamon.

Official Transcript of the Perfect Pitch Workshop. David L. Burge. (Illus.). 1984. pap. 10.00 o.p. (ISBN 0-942542-98-3). Am Ed Mus Pubns.

Official Transcript of the Perfect Pitch Master Class. David L. Burge. (Orig.). 1984. pap. 10.00 o.p. (ISBN 0-942542-99-1). Am Ed Mus Pubns.

Official Workers' Compensation Practice Mannual. 1984. looseleaf 12.00 o.p. (ISBN 0-318-02492-6); looseleaf without binder 7.00 o.p. ICLE Georgia.

Official World Series Records Nineteen Three to Nineteen Eighty. 13.00 o.p. (ISBN 0-89204-065-3). Sporting News.

Official 1986 Price Guide to Dolls. 1983. pap. 2.95 o.p. (ISBN 0-87637-316-3). Hse of Collectibles.

Officina Bodoni. John Barr. (Illus.). 96p. 1981. pap. 20.00 o.p. (ISBN 0-913720-33-X, Sandstone). Beil.

Officium of the Urban Prefecture During the Later Roman Empire. W. G. Sinnigen. 126p. 1957. 22.00x o.p. (ISBN 0-271-00466-5). Pa St U Pr.

Offshore Ecology Investigation. Ed. by C. H. Ward et al. (Rice University Studies: Vol. 65, Nos. 4 & 5). (Illus.). 600p. (Orig.). 1980. pap. 20.00x o.p. (ISBN 0-89263-243-7). Rice Univ.

Offshore Medicine: Medical Care of Employees in the Offshore Oil Industry. Ed. by R. A. Cox. (Illus.). 208p. 1982. 35.60 o.p. (ISBN 0-387-11111-5). Springer-Verlag.

Offshore Operation: Proceedings. Seminar on Petroleum Legislation Staff. (Mineral Resources Development Ser.: No. 40). pap. 5.00 o.p. (E.73.11.F.13). UN.

Offshore Structures Engineering, Vol. 1. F. L. Lobo et al. LC 78-74102. (Offshore Structures Engineering Ser.). 424p. 1979. 48.00x o.p. (ISBN 0-87201-608-0). Gulf Pub.

Ogden's Revised California Real Property Law, 2 Vols. Melvin B. Ogden & Arthur G. Bowman. LC 73-620258. 1975. 65.00 o.p. (ISBN 0-88124-032-X); 65.00 o.p. (ISBN 0-88124-034-6). Cal Cont Ed Bar.

Oggi in Italia: A First Course in Italian. Ferdinando Merlonghi et al. LC 77-83330. 1978. text ed. 34.76 o.p. (ISBN 0-395-26244-5); tchr's. ed. 35.96 o.p. (ISBN 0-395-26243-7); wkbk. 13.56 o.p. (ISBN 0-395-26242-9); tapes 298.76 o.p. (ISBN 0-395-26245-3). HM.

Oggi in Italia: A First Course in Italian. 2nd ed. Ferninando Merlonghi et al. LC 81-85378. 1982. text ed. 34.76 o.p. (ISBN 0-395-31872-6); instr's. annot. ed. 35.96 o.p. (ISBN 0-395-31873-4); wkbk. 13.56 o.p. (ISBN 0-395-31874-2); tapes 298.76 o.p. (ISBN 0-395-31876-9); Pt. 1. cassette 23.96 o.p. (ISBN 0-395-32946-9); Pt. 2. cassettes 23.96 o.p. (ISBN 0-395-32947-7); tapescript 7.56 o.p. (ISBN 0-395-32948-5); reel-to-reel tapes 270.00 o.p. HM.

Oglethorpe in America. Phinizy Spalding. LC 76-8092. 1977. lib. bdg. 15.00x o.s.i. (ISBN 0-226-76846-5). U of Chicago Pr.

Oh, Boy! Joy Roy! Mary C. Carmichael. (Illus.). 23p. (gr. 1-5). 1985. 4.95 o.p. (ISBN 0-533-05795-7). Vantage.

Oh, for the Life of a Guide. Don De Hart. (Illus.). 120p. 1968. pap. 3.95 o.p. (ISBN 0-933472-42-0). Johnson Bks.

Oh Lucky Country. Rose Cappiello. Tr. by Gaetano Rando from Ital. 236p. 1985. 12.95 o.p. (ISBN 0-7022-1789-1). U of Queensland Pr.

Oh Mountains Be My Refuge. Arlene F. Sande. (Illus.). 208p. (Orig.). pap. 5.95 o.s.i. (ISBN 0-934318-85-9). Falcon Pr MT.

Oh, My Son, Forgive Me. Yoshiko C. Sturgis. 1985. 7.95 o.p. (ISBN 0-533-06076-1). Vantage.

Oh, My Word! Becky Daniel & Charlie Daniel. (gr. 2-6). 1980. 7.95 o.p. (ISBN 0-916456-74-9, GA 189). Good Apple.

Oh! Pascal! Doug Cooper & Michael Clancy. 1982. pap. 20.95x o.p. (ISBN 0-393-95205-3). Norton.

Oh Promise Me But Put It in Writing: Living Together Agreements Without, Before, During & After Marriage. Paul P. Ashley. 1980. pap. text ed. 3.95 o.p. (ISBN 0-07-002414-6). McGraw.

Oh, Susannah! Kate Wilhelm. 256p. 1982. 12.45 o.p. (ISBN 0-395-32054-2). HM.

Oh That Kaola. Gina Ruck-Pauquet. (gr. k-3). 1979. text ed. 7.95 o.p. (ISBN 0-07-054192-2). McGraw.

Oh, the Anguish of English. John Plank. LC 84-90266. 58p. 1985. 7.95 o.p. (ISBN 0-533-06300-0). Vantage.

Oh, to Be Fifty Again: On Being Too Old for a Mid-Life Crisis. Eda J. LeShan. LC 86-5829. 320p. 1986. 16.45 o.s.i. (ISBN 0-8129-1238-1). Times Bks.

"Oh, What a Wonderful Wedding" Book: How to Be a Beautiful Bride on a Budget. Diane M. Reed. (Illus.). 252p. 1984. 15.95 o.p. (ISBN 0-13-633421-0); pap. 6.95 o.p. (ISBN 0-13-633413-X). P-H.

Ohau see Exploring Hawaii.

Ohio Bank Law & Regulation Manual. 3rd ed. Susan B. Collins. 825p. 1978. annual 78.00 o.p. (ISBN 0-8322-0001-8); pap. text ed. 10.00 o.p. Banks-Baldwin.

Ohio Cemeteries. Ohio Genealogical Society Staff. LC 78-67919. 1978. 29.50 o.p. (ISBN 0-935057-04-8). OH Genealogical.

Ohio Criminal Code: Handbook for Law Enforcement Officers 1987. 6th, rev. ed. Anderson Publishers Staff. 220p. 1987. pap. text ed. 6.95 o.p. (ISBN 0-87084-630-2). Anderson Pub Co.

Ohio Criminal Justice, 1987. The Center for Criminal Justice Case Western Reserve University. 900p. 1987. pap. text ed. 29.50 o.p. (ISBN 0-8322-0214-2). Banks Baldwin.

Ohio Criminal Law Handbook, Seventh Annual Edition. revised ed. 1000p. 1987. pap. 26.95 o.p. (ISBN 0-87084-647-7). Anderson Pub Co.

Ohio Gang: The World of Warren G. Harding. Charles L. Mee, Jr. (Illus.). 256p. 1981. 14.95 o.p. (ISBN 0-87131-340-5). M Evans.

Ohio Impromptu, Catastrophe, & What Where: Three Plays. Samuel Beckett. LC 83-49372. 64p. (Orig.). 1984. pap. 4.95 o.p. (ISBN 0-394-62061-5, E905, Ever). Grove.

Ohio in the American Revolution. Ed. by Thomas H. Smith. (Illus.). 34p. 1976. pap. 2.00 o.s.i. (ISBN 0-318-00837-8). Ohio Hist Soc.

Ohio Jury Instructions 1968-1985, 4 vols. Ohio Judicial Conference Staff. 1809p. 1984. Set. 235.00 o.p.; Suppl. 1985. 57.50 o.p.; Vols. 1-3. 205.00 o.p.; Vol. 4. 68.50 o.p. Anderson Pub Co.

Ohio Manufacturers Directory, 1988. 1104p. 1987. 104.00 o.p. (ISBN 0-318-02906-5). Manufacturers.

Ohio Monthly Record. Administrative Agencies Staff. 1977. ann. subscr. 1987-88 245.00 o.p. (ISBN 0-8322-0188-X). Banks-Baldwin.

Ohio Municipal Code 1962-1981, 3 vols. 11th ed. James W. Farrell. 2368p. 162.50 o.p.; Suppl. 1988. 39.50 o.p. Anderson Pub Co.

Ohio: Off the Beaten Path. George Zimmermann. LC 82-48994. (Illus.). 160p. 1983. pap. 5.95 o.p. (ISBN 0-914788-67-1). Globe Pequot.

Ohio Probate Code: Including the Fiduciary Laws, Ohio Estate Tax Law, & Veterans' Guardianship Annotated, 1988. pap. 23.00 o.p. (ISBN 0-8322-0084-0). Banks-Baldwin.

Ohio Probate Practice 1973-1985, 3 vols. 6th ed. Chase M. Davies. 3000p. 1983. Set. 225.00 o.p. (Pub by Addams & Hosford); Suppl. 1986. 72.50 o.p. Anderson Pub Co.

Ohio Public Health Manual. 31.50 o.p. (ISBN 0-8322-0052-2). service 1983 35.00 o.p. Banks-Baldwin.

Ohio Real Estate Law. 3rd ed. Carol K. Irvin & James D. Irvin. (Illus.). 442p. 1985. pap. text ed. 25.00x o.p. (ISBN 0-89787-908-2). Gorsuch Scarisbrick.

Ohio: Restitution. 8.50 o.p. (ISBN 0-686-90866-X). Am Law Inst.

Ohio Savings & Loan Laws. 1974. 40.00 o.p.; Suppl. 1987. 21.50 o.p. Anderson Pub Co.

Ohio Supplement for Modern Real Estate Practice. 6th ed. J. Terence Burke et al. LC 84-2139. 128p. 1984. pap. text ed. 10.95 o.p. (ISBN 0-88462-489-7, 1510-04, Real Estate Ed). Longman Finan.

Ohio Symposium on Stress Management: Proceedings of the First & Second Symposia. Ohio Psychology Publishing Co. Staff. 43p. (Orig.). 1980. pap. text ed. 4.00x o.p. (ISBN 0-910707-03-0). Ohio Psych Pub.

Ohio: Trusts. 8.50 o.p. (ISBN 0-686-90868-6). Am Law Inst.

Ohio Water Law Conference: Proceedings. 1984. 18.75 o.p. (ISBN 0-318-22993-5). Natl Water Well.

Ohn - Shipper. (Our Nations Heritage Ser.). Date not set. (ISBN 0-07-375490-0). McGraw.

Oikos: A Practical Approach to Family Evangelism. Joseph W. Hinkle et al. LC 81-69328. 1982. pap. 4.95 o.p. (ISBN 0-8054-6234-1). Broadman.

Oil & Development in the Arab Gulf States: A Selected Annotated Bibliography. Walid I. Sharif. LC 84-23086. 450p. 1985. 50.00 o.p. (ISBN 0-7099-3368-1, Pub. by Croom Helm Ltd). Routledge Chapman & Hall.

Oil & Gas. Ed. by Financial Times Staff. 1987. 95.00 o.p. (ISBN 0-912289-67-8); Standing Order. 85.50 o.p. St James Pr.

Oil & Gas. Ed. by Financial Times Staff. 1989. 125.00 o.p. (ISBN 1-55862-008-7); Standing Order. 112.50 o.p. St James Pr.

Oil & Gas Financings: Current Practice & Anticipated Developments. Practising Law Institute Staff & Lawrence C. Tondel. (Corporate Law & Practice Course Handbook Ser.: No. 417). 553p. 1983. 45.00 o.p. (B4-6649). PLI.

Oil & Gas: From Fossils to Fuel. Hershell H. Nixon & Joan Lowery. LC 77-1671. (Let Me Read Ser.). (Illus.). 64p. (gr. 1-4). 1977. 5.95 o.p. (ISBN 0-15-257700-9, HJ). HarBraceJ.

Oil & Gas in a Nutshell. John S. Lowe. LC 83-6811. (Nutshell Ser.). 443p. 1983. pap. text ed. 10.95 o.p. (ISBN 0-314-73469-4). West Pub.

Oil & Gas Industry & the Bankruptcy Laws: A Course Handbook. Alan Grover. 555p. 1985. pap. 15.00 o.p. (A4-4128). PLI.

Oil & Gas Industry & the Bankruptcy Laws. Alan Gover. LC 85-209570. (Commercial Law & Practice Course & Handbook Ser.: No. 361). 1985. 15.00 o.p. (A44128). PLI.

Oil & Gas Journal DataBook, 1987. Ed. by Barbara Rock. 325p. 1987. 26.95 o.p. (ISBN 0-87814-314-9). Pennwell Bks.

Oil & Gas Journal Datebook, 1988. 1988. 34.95 o.p. (D4460). Pennwell Bks.

Oil & Gas Journal Energy Statistics Sourcebook, 1987. 445p. 1987. 95.00 o.p. (P1187). PennWell Bks.

Oil & Gas Supplies in the Lower Forty-Eight States. Y. Y. Kim & R. G. Thompson. LC 78-53816. 110p. 1978. 21.00x o.p. (ISBN 0-87201-816-4). Gulf Pub.

Oil & Gas Taxation Nineteen Eighty-Six. John P. Klingstedt & Horace R. Brock. 300p. (Orig.). 1985. pap. text ed. 29.95x o.p. (ISBN 0-940966-09-3). UNTX Pro Dev Inst.

Oil & Honor: The Texaco-Pennzoil Wars. Thomas Petzinger, Jr. (Illus.). 416p. 1987. 19.95 o.p. (ISBN 0-399-13276-7, Putnam). Putnam Pub Group.

Oil & Its Impact: A Case Study of Community Change. John J. Pfuhl. LC 80-5090. 164p. 1980. text ed. 19.50 o.p. (ISBN 0-8191-1043-4); pap. text ed. 12.00 o.p. (ISBN 0-8191-1044-2). U Pr of Amer.

Oil & Natural Gas. rev. ed. Betsy H. Kraft. (First Bks). (Illus.). (gr. 4 up). 1978. PLB 10.40 o.p. (ISBN 0-531-01411-8). Watts.

Oil & Natural Gas Resources of Canada 1976: Oil Sands & Heavy Oils - the Prospects, 2 pts. 1978. pap. 5.50 set o.p. (ISBN 0-685-89403-7, SSC97, SSC); Vol. 1. pap. (ISBN 0-660-00859-9); Vol. 2. pap. (ISBN 0-685-89404-5). UNIPUB.

Oil & Oilfield Equipment & Service Companies Worldwide Nineteen Eighty-Five. Don Nelson. 600p. 1985. 99.00 o.p. (ISBN 0-419-13330-5, NO. 9167). Routledge Chapman & Hall.

Oil & Turmoil: America Faces OPEC & the Middle East. Dankwart A. Rustow. 320p. 1982. 14.95x o.p. (ISBN 0-393-01597-1). Norton.

Oil & Water. Glen Swanson. (Illus.). (gr. 3-7). 1981. 7.95 o.s.i. (ISBN 0-13-633677-9). P-H.

Oil & Water: The Struggle for Georges Bank. William H. MacLeish. Ed. by Peter Davison. LC 84-72093. (Illus.). 304p. 1986. pap. 8.95 o.p. (ISBN 0-87113-068-8). Atlantic Monthly.

Oil & Wine. Bob Yandian. 58p. (Orig.). 1987. pap. 2.95 o.p. (ISBN 0-89274-435-9). Harrison Hse.

Oil & World Power: Background to the Oil Crisis. 3rd rev. ed. Peter R. Odell. LC 75-148830. (Illus.). 256p. 1975. 9.95 o.s.i. (ISBN 0-685-51711-X). Taplinger.

Oil Crisis. Ed. by Raymond Vernon. 1976. pap. 6.95x o.p. (ISBN 0-393-09186-4). Norton.

Oil Debt & Development: OPEC in the Third World. C. Paul Hallwood & Stuart W. Sinclair. 208p. 1981. pap. text ed. 10.95x o.p. (ISBN 0-04-382027-1); pap. 15.95 o.p. Unwin Hyman.

Oil in Freshwater: Chemistry, Biology, Countermeasure: Proceedings of the Symposium on Oil Pollution in Freshwater, Edmonton, Alberta, Canada, 15-19 October 1984. Ed. by J. H. Vandermeulen & S. E. Hrudey. 550p. 1987. 75.00 o.s.i. (ISBN 0-08-031861-4, E140, G135, A125, Pub. by PPC). Pergamon.

Oil in the People's Republic of China: Industry Structure, Production, Exports. Wolfgang Bartke. (Illus.). 1977. lib. bdg. 11.95x o.p. (ISBN 0-7735-0309-9, McGill Canada). U of Toronto Pr.

Oil, Industrialization & Development in the Arab Gulf States. Atif A. Kubursi. LC 84-19988. 144p. 1984. 28.00 o.p. (ISBN 0-7099-1566-7, Pub. by Croom Helm Ltd). Routledge Chapman & Hall.

Oil Painter's Guide to Painting Skies. S. Allyn Schaeffer. (Illus.). 144p. 1985. 27.50 o.p. (ISBN 0-8230-3266-3). Watson-Guptill.

Oil Painter's Guide to Painting Trees. S. Allyn Schaeffer. (Illus.). 144p. 1985. 24.95 o.p. (ISBN 0-8230-3267-1). Watson-Guptill.

Oil Painting for the Beginner. Frederic Taubes. (Illus.). 168p. 1986. pap. 14.95 o.p. (ISBN 0-8230-3276-0). Watson-Guptill.

Oil Painting: From Van Eyck to Rothko. Jean-Luc Daval. LC 85-42920. (Illus.). 140p. 1985. 37.50 o.p. (ISBN 0-8478-0628-6). Rizzoli Intl.

Oil Painting Pure & Simple. Ron Ranson & Trevor Chamberlain. (Illus.). 128p. 1987. 24.95 o.p. (ISBN 0-7137-1744-0, Pub. by Blandford Pr England). Sterling.

Oil: Piper. (gr. 4-6). 1980. PLB 9.40 o.p. (ISBN 0-531-04175-1). Watts.

Oil, Politics, & Seapower: The Indian Ocean Vortex. Ian W. Adie. LC 74-29073. (Strategy Paper Ser.: No. 24). 98p. 1975. 6.95x o.p. (ISBN 0-8448-0617-X, Pub. by Crane Russak & Co); pap. o.p. (ISBN 0-8448-0618-8). Taylor & Francis.

Oil Prices & the Future of OPEC: The Political Economy of Tension & Stability in the Organization of Petroleum Exporting Countries. Theodore H. Moran. 102p. 1978. 10.00 o.p. (ISBN 0-317-60218-7). Resources Future.

Oil Prices Effects & OPEC's Pricing Policy: An Optimal Control Approach. Jaime R. Marquez. LC 83-49503. (Wharton Econometric Studies). 224p. 1984. 42.00x o.p. (ISBN 0-669-08200-7). Lexington Bks.

Oil Pricing, the Oil Weapon & the Arms Race in the Middle East. Arab World & Iran Business Guides. 1978. pap. 10.00 o.p. (ISBN 0-931000-07-6). Suburban Pub CT.

Oil Refining & Petroleum Chemistry Multi-Lingual Dictionary: English-French-German-Russian. Ed. by Walter Leipnitz et al. 35.00 o.s.i. (ISBN 0-685-86402-2). E J Brill USA.

Oil Sand & Oil Shale Chemistry. Ed. by Otto P. Strausz & Elizabeth M. Lown. LC 78-19168. (Illus.). 384p. 1978. pap. 37.80x o.p. (ISBN 0-89573-102-9). VCH Pubs.

Oil Spills. Ed. by A. A. Moghissi. 80p. 1980. pap. 15.50 o.p. (ISBN 0-08-026237-6). Pergamon.

Oils & Gases from Coal: A Review of the State-of-the-Art in Europe & North America Based on the Work of the Symposium on the Gasification & Liquefaction of Coal Held Under the Auspices of the UNECE, Katowice, Poland. 23-27 April 1979. United Nations Economic Commission for Europe, Geneva, Switzerland. (ECE Seminars & Symposia Ser.). (Illus.). 316p. 1980. 89.00 o.p. (ISBN 0-08-025678-3). Pergamon.

Oilseed & Vegetable Oil Processing Technology, 1976: Proceedings, World Conference. 330p. 15.00 o.p. (ISBN 0-318-12904-3). Am Oil Chemists.

Oiseaux de Lune. Marcel Ayme. 1956. pap. 9.95 o.p. (ISBN 0-686-51921-3). French & Eur.

Ojibwa Indian Legends. Wah-Be-Gwo-Nese, pseud. (Illus.). (gr. 3 up). 1972. 6.95 o.p. (ISBN 0-918616-05-0). Northern Mich.

Ojibwa Woman. Ruth Landes. 1971. pap. 4.95 o.p. (ISBN 0-393-00574-7, Norton Lib.). Norton.

Okagami: A Japanese Historical Tale. Tr. by Joseph K. Yamagiwa. LC 77-83045. 1977. pap. 5.25 o.p. (ISBN 0-8048-1247-0). C E Tuttle.

Okara Mask. Rex Wiseman. 1979. pap. 1.95 o.p. (ISBN 0-505-51434-6, Pub. by Tower Bks). Dorchester Pub Co.

Okavango Adventure. Jeremy Mallinson. (Illus.). 208p. 1974. 6.95 o.p. (ISBN 0-393-08687-9). Norton.

Okeechobee Hurricane. Lawrence E. Will. (Illus.). 1978. pap. 4.00 o.p. (ISBN 0-8200-1001-4). Great Outdoors.

Okinawa: The History of an Island People. George H. Kerr. LC 58-12283. (Illus.). 1975. Repr. of 1958 ed. 27.50 o.p. (ISBN 0-8048-0437-0). C E Tuttle.

Oklahoma. Photos by David Fitzgerald. LC 79-92730. (Belding Imprint Ser.). (Illus.). 128p. (Text by Bill Burchardt). 1980. 29.50 o.p. (ISBN 0-912856-57-2). Gr Arts Ctr Pub.

Oklahoma. Marcia Keegan. LC 79-5087. (Illus.). 112p. 1979. pap. 14.95 o.p. (ISBN 0-89659-063-1). Abbeville Pr.

Oklahoma: Agency. 8.50 o.p. (ISBN 0-686-90870-8). Am Law Inst.

Oklahoma Business Directory, 1987-88. American Directory Publishing Co., Inc. Staff. 1350p. (Orig.). 1987. pap. 95.00 o.s.i. (ISBN 0-944316-14-X). Amer Directory.

Oklahoma: Conflict of Laws. 8.50 o.p. (ISBN 0-686-90872-4). Am Law Inst.

Oklahoma: Contracts. 9.50 o.p. (ISBN 0-686-90874-0). Am Law Inst.

Oklahoma: Land of the Fair God. Odie B. Faulk. LC 86-1573. (Illus.). 344p. 1986. 29.95 o.p. (ISBN 0-89781-173-9). Windsor Pubns Inc.

Oklahoma Legislative Voting: A Roll Call Analysis for 1970-1974. F. Ted Hebert. (Legislative Research Ser.: No. 12). 29p. 1978. 2.00 o.p. (ISBN 0-686-04909-8). Univ OK Gov Res.

Oklahoma Score. Tom Cutter. (Tracker Ser.: No. 5). 144p. 1985. pap. 2.25 o.p. (ISBN 0-380-89531-5). Avon.

Oklahoma State University Supplement to Governing the Nation: American National Government. Robert L. Spurrier, Jr. et al. 64p. 1981. pap. text ed. 2.95 o.p. (ISBN 0-8403-2406-5). Kendall-Hunt.

Ol' Jake's Lucky Day. Anatoly Ivanov. LC 83-25645. (Illus.). 24p. (ps-2). 1984. 12.00 o.p. (ISBN 0-688-02866-7); lib. bdg. 11.04 o.p. (ISBN 0-688-02867-5). Lothrop.

Old Age among the Ancient Greeks: The Greek Portrayal of Old Age in Literature, Art & Inscriptions. Bessie E. Richardson. Repr. of 1933 ed. lib. bdg. 35.00x o.p. (ISBN 0-8371-0637-0, RIOA). Greenwood.

Old Age in Modern Society. Christina R. Victor. 352p. 1987. 38.95 o.p. (ISBN 0-7099-2628-6, Pub. by Croom Helm UK); pap. 18.95 o.p. (ISBN 0-7099-2630-8, Pub. by Croom Helm UK). Routledge Chapman & Hall.

Old & New Problems in Elementary Particles. Ed. by G. Puppi. 1968. 79.50 o.p. (ISBN 0-12-567250-0). Acad Pr.

Old Bores Almanack, Nineteen Eighty-Six AD. Ken Bromfield. (Illus.). 64p. (Orig.). 1986. pap. 2.50 o.p. (ISBN 0-903852-70-5, Pub. by Milestone Pubns UK). Seven Hills Bk Dists.

Old Boston Taverns & Tavern Clubs. Samuel A. Drake. LC 78-162511. 130p. 1971. Repr. of 1917 ed. 40.00x o.p. (ISBN 0-8103-3293-0). Gale.

Old Boy Networks: Who We Know & How We Use Them. Tim Heald. LC 83-24286. 288p. 1984. 16.45 o.p. (ISBN 0-89919-284-X). Ticknor & Fields.

Old Calabria. Norman Douglas. (Century Classic Ser.). 352p. 1988. pap. 13.95 o.p. (ISBN 0-7126-0113-9, Pub. by Century Hutchinson). David & Charles.

Old Chicago Houses. John Drury. (Illus.). xviii, 518p. 1975. pap. 6.95 o.s.i. (ISBN 0-226-16555-8). U of Chicago Pr.

Old Christmas. Washington Irving. LC 77-8465. (Illus.). 208p. 1977. Repr. of 1875 ed. 10.00 o.s.i. (ISBN 0-912882-30-1). Sleepy Hollow.

Old Christmas-Bracebridge Hall. Washington Irving. (Illus.). 528p. 1980. boxed set 22.00 o.s.i. (ISBN 0-912882-43-3). Sleepy Hollow.

Old Civilizations of Inca Land. Charles W. Mead. LC 72-85431. (Illus.). 140p. 1972. Repr. of 1935 ed. lib. bdg. 18.50x o.p. (ISBN 0-8154-0430-1). Cooper Sq.

Old Colonial System, 2 vols. George L. Beer. 14.50 ea. o.p. (ISBN 0-8446-1066-6). Peter Smith.

Old Cookery Books & Ancient Cuisine. William C. Hazlitt. LC 68-30612. 280p. 1968. Repr. of 1886 ed. 30.00x o.p. (ISBN 0-8103-3306-6). Gale.

Old Country School: The Story of Rural Education in the Middle West. Wayne E. Fuller. LC 85-8454. (Illus.). x, 302p. 1985. lib. bdg. 30.00 o.s.i. (ISBN 0-226-28215-5). U of Chicago Pr.

Old Creed for a New Day. Dana P. Smith. LC 74-26331. 144p. 1975. pap. 0.50x o.p. (ISBN 0-8006-1093-8, Fortress). Augsburg Fortress.

Old Curiosity Shop. Charles Dickens. LC 87-62830. (Illus.). 528p. 1988. 13.95 o.p. (ISBN 0-89577-292-2). RD Assn.

Old Curiousity Shop: T. V. Tie-In. Charles Dickens. Ed. by Angus Easson. 1979. pap. 3.95 o.p. (ISBN 0-14-005436-7). Penguin.

Old El Paso Sun Mexican Cookbook II. Old El Paso Staff. (Illus.). 127p. spiral binding 6.95 o.p. (ISBN 0-914091-32-8). Chicago Review.

Old England & the Destruction of Its Prehistoric Remains. Frederick Roe. (Illus.). 149p. 1982. Repr. of 1910 ed. 127.75 o.p. Found Class Reprints.

Old English & Medieval Literature. Ed. by Gordon H. Gerould. LC 78-95100. Repr. of 1929 ed. lib. bdg. 35.00x o.p. (ISBN 0-8371-2703-3, GEOE). Greenwood.

Old English Customs Extant at the Present Time. P. H. Ditchfield. LC 68-21765. 360p. 1968. Repr. of 1896 ed. 40.00x o.p. (ISBN 0-8103-3427-5). Gale.

Old English Grammar. 2nd ed. Randolph Quirk & C. L. Wrenn. 166p. 1958. pap. 12.95x o.p. (ISBN 0-416-77240-4, NO. 2396). Routledge Chapman & Hall.

Old English Home & Its Dependencies. Sabine Baring-Gould. LC 74-77085. 344p. 1969. Repr. of 1898 ed. 40.00x o.p. (ISBN 0-8103-3847-5). Gale.

Old English Language & Literature. James L. Rosier & Albert Marckwardt. 1972. text ed. 10.95x o.p. (ISBN 0-393-09991-1). Norton.

Old English Libraries. Ernest A. Savage. LC 68-26177. (Illus.). 314p. 1968. Repr. of 1912 ed. 40.00x o.p. (ISBN 0-8103-3179-9). Gale.

Old English Literature. Ed. by Michael Alexander. LC 83-3018. (History of Literature Ser.). (Illus.). 328p. 1987. 28.00 o.s.i. (ISBN 0-8052-3862-X). Schocken.

Old English Metrical Psalter: An Annotated Set of Collation Lists with the Psalter Glosses. Sarah L. Keefer. LC 79-7920. (Garland Reference Library of the Humanities). 200p. 1979. lib. bdg. 36.00 o.p. (ISBN 0-8240-9538-3). Garland Pub.

Old English Riddles. A. J. Wyatt. 1982. 42.50 o.p. (ISBN 0-686-81939-X). Bern Porter.

Old English Rune Poem: A Critical Edition. Maureen Halsall. (McMaster Old English Studies and Texts). 224p. 1981. 25.00x o.p. (ISBN 0-8020-5477-3). U of Toronto Pr.

Old English Sheepdogs. Sylvia Woods & Ray Owen. LC 81-670122. (Illus.). 224p. 1981. 17.95 o.p. (ISBN 0-571-11620-5). Faber & Faber.

Old Estonian Folk Religion. Ivar Paulson. LC 76-63029. (Uralic & Altaic Ser: Vol. 108). (Orig.). 1971. pap. text ed. 19.95x o.p. (ISBN 0-87750-154-8). Res Ctr Lang Semiotic.

Old Farm Buildings. Nigel Harvey. (Shire Album Ser.: No. 10). (Illus.). 32p. (Orig.). 1979. pap. 2.95 o.p. (ISBN 0-85263-351-3, 3382089, Pub. by Shire Pubns England). Seven Hills Bk Dists.

Old Farmer's Almanac Book of Old-Fashioned Puzzles. Ed. by Clarissa M. Silitch. LC 76-46762. (Illus.). 64p. (Orig.). 1976. pap. 5.95 o.p. (ISBN 0-911658-72-6). Yankee Bks.

Old Farmer's Almanac Colonial Cookbook. Rev. ed. Ed. by Clarissa Silitch. LC 82-50962. (Illus.). 64p. 1982. pap. 5.95 o.p. (ISBN 0-89909-008-7). Yankee Bks.

Old Farmer's Almanac Heritage Cookbook. Ed. by Clarissa Silitch. LC 82-70482. (Illus.). 64p. (Orig.). 1982. pap. 4.95 o.p. (ISBN 0-911658-39-4). Yankee Bks.

Old Farmer's Almanac, Nineteen Eighty-Eight. 1987. pap. 2.50 o.p. (ISBN 0-89909-130-X). Yankee Bks.

Old Farmer's Almanac 1983: 191st Anniversary Edition. Ed. by Judson Hale & Rob Trowbridge. (Illus.). 192p. 1982. pap. 1.50 o.p. (ISBN 0-89909-006-0). Yankee Bks.

Old Farmer's Almanac, 1984. Ed. by Rob Trowbridge & Judson Hale. LC 56-29681. (Illus.). 224p. 1983. pap. 1.75 o.p. (ISBN 0-89909-018-4). Yankee Bks.

Old Farmer's Almanac, 1985. Ed. by Rob Trowbridge & Judson D. Hale. LC 56-29681. (Illus.). 224p. 1984. pap. 1.75 o.p. (ISBN 0-89909-040-0). Yankee Bks.

Old Farmer's Almanac, 1986. Robert B. Thomas. 1985. pap. 1.95 o.p. (ISBN 0-89909-067-2). Yankee Bks.

Old Farmer's Almanac 1987. Ed. by Judson Hale. 1986. pap. 2.25 o.p. (ISBN 0-89909-108-3). Yankee Bks.

Old Fashioned Country Christmas. Susan Wheeler. (Illus.). 14p. 1986. 6.95 o.p. (ISBN 0-02-792740-7). Bradbury Pr.

Old-Fashioned Desserts. Richard Sax. Ed. by Jean Atcheson. LC 83-71445. (Great American Cooking Schools Ser.). (Illus.). 84p. (Orig.). 1983. pap. 5.95 o.p. (ISBN 0-941034-18-6). I Chalmers.

Old-Fashioned Garden: Four Delightful Pop-Up Plans. Nancy Lynch. LC 87-4759. (Illus.). 12p. 1987. 16.95 o.p. (ISBN 0-8478-0833-5). Rizzoli Intl.

Old-Fashioned Girl. Louisa May Alcott. (Louisa May Alcott Library). (gr. 5-9). 1971. Repr. 5.95 o.p. (ISBN 0-448-02365-2, G&D). Putnam Pub Group.

Old-Fashioned Mystery. Runa Fairleigh. Ed. by L. A. Morse. 256p. 1984. pap. 2.95 o.p. (ISBN 0-380-69286-4, 69286-4). Avon.

Old Fashioned Nursery Rhymes & Tales. Illus. by John Hassall. (Illus.). 62p. (gr. k up). Date not set. 7.95 o.p. (ISBN 1-85170-109-5, Pub. by Key Porter Canada). U of Toronto Pr.

Old Fasnacht. Barbara Mitchell. LC 82-23619. (Carolrhoda on My Own Bks.). (Illus.). 64p. (gr. k-4). 1984. PLB 8.95 o.p. (ISBN 0-87614-221-8). Carolrhoda Bks.

Old Favorite Honey Recipes. Ed. by American Honey Institute Staff. (Illus.). 1977. pap. 3.95 o.p. (ISBN 0-916638-03-0). Meyerbooks.

Old Fears. John Wooley & Ron Wolfe. 288p. 1982. 13.95 o.p. (ISBN 0-531-09866-4). Watts.

Old Fishing Lures & Tackle: Identification & Value Guide. Carl F. Luckey. (Illus.). 312p. 1980. pap. 14.95 o.p. (ISBN 0-89689-018-X). Bks Americana.

Old Forest & Other Stories. Peter Taylor. LC 83-40133. 360p. 1985. 16.95 o.p. (ISBN 0-385-27983-3). Doubleday.

Old Furniture: Understanding the Craftsman's Art. Nancy A. Smith. (Illus.). 1976. pap. 12.95 o.p. (ISBN 0-316-79932-7). Little.

Old Garden Tools. Kay N. Sanecki. (Shire Album Ser.: No. 41). (Illus.). 32p. pap. 2.95 o.p. (ISBN 0-85263-470-6, 3380659, Pub. by Shire Pubns England). Seven Hills Bk Dists.

Old Girl. Joshua Gidding. LC 79-26850. 264p. 1980. 12.95 o.p. (ISBN 0-03-052196-3); pap. 5.95 o.p. (ISBN 0-03-057998-8). H Holt & Co.

Old Glass: Its Manufacture Styles Uses. O. N. Wilkinson. (Illus.). 200p. 1968. (ISBN 0-8022-1883-0). Philos Lib.

Old Goriot. Honore De Balzac. Tr. by Ellen Marriage. 1970. Repr. of 1948 ed. 12.95x o.p. (ISBN 0-460-00170-1, Evman). Biblio Dist.

Old Hippo's Easter Egg. Jan Wahl. LC 79-9199. (Illus.). (gr. k-3). 1980. 9.95 o.p. (ISBN 0-15-257835-8, HJ). HarBraceJ.

Old Hippo's Easter Egg. Jan Wahl. LC 79-9199. (Illus.). 32p. (gr. k-3). 1980. pap. 3.50 o.p. (ISBN 0-15-668452-7, VoyB). HarBraceJ.

Old House & Other Tales. Fedor Teternikov. LC 74-11995. 294p. 1974. Repr. of 1915 ed. lib. bdg. 35.00x o.p. (ISBN 0-8371-7715-4, TEOH). Greenwood.

Old-House Journal Catalog, 1988 Edition: A Buyers Guide for the Pre-1939 House. The Old-House Journal Staff. 248p. 1987. pap. 14.95 o.p. (ISBN 0-317-61726-5). Old Hse Journ Corp.

Old-House Journal Nineteen Seventy-Eight Yearbook: A One-Volume Compilation of All the Editorial Pages Printed in the Old-House Journal in 1978. The Old-House Journal Staff. Ed. by Patricia Poore & Clem Labine. (Old-House Journal Yearbook). (Illus.). 152p. (Orig.). 1981. pap. 16.00 o.p. (ISBN 0-942202-02-3). Old Hse Journ Corp.

Old-House Journal Nineteen Seventy-Nine Yearbook: A One-Volume Compilation of All the Editorial Pages Printed in the Old-House Journal in 1979. The Old-House Journal Staff. Ed. by Patricia Poore & Clem Labine. (Old-House Journal Yearbooks). (Illus.). 152p. (Orig.). 1981. pap. 16.00 o.p. (ISBN 0-942202-03-1). Old Hse Journ Corp.

Old-House Journal Nineteen Seventy-Six Yearbook: A One-Volume Compilation of All the Editorial Pages Printed in the Old-House Journal in 1976. The Old-House Journal Staff. Ed. by Patricia Poore & Clem Labine. (Old-House Journal Yearbook). (Illus.). 152p. (Orig.). 1981. pap. 16.00 o.p. (ISBN 0-942202-00-7). Old Hse Journ Corp.

Old-House Journal Nineteen Seventy-Seven Yearbook: A One-Volume Compilation of All the Editorial Pages Printed in the Old-House Journal in 1977. The Old-House Journal Staff. Ed. by Patricia Poore & Clem Labine. (Old-House Journal Yearbook). (Illus.). 152p. (Orig.). 1981. pap. 16.00 o.p. (ISBN 0-942202-01-5). Old Hse Journ Corp.

Old House Journal, 1985 Catalog: A Buyer's Guide for the Pre-1939 House. The Old-House Journal Staff. (Old House Journal Catalog Ser.). 212p. 1984. pap. 12.95 o.p. (ISBN 0-942202-10-4). Old Hse Journ Corp.

Old-House Journal, 1986 Catalog: A Buyer's Guide for the Pre-1939 House. Old-House Journal Staff. 216p. 1985. pap. 12.95 o.p. (ISBN 0-942202-11-2). Old Hse Journ Corp.

Old Illinois Houses. John Drury. (Illus.). 1977. pap. 3.95 o.s.i. (ISBN 0-226-16552-3). U of Chicago Pr.

Old Indian Temples, Idols & Worship. Eduard F. Herrick. (Illus.). 154p. 1985. Repr. of 1882 ed. 127.75 o.p. Found Class Reprints.

Old Jules Country. Mari Sandoz. (Illus.). 424p. 1955. 12.95 o.p. (ISBN 0-8038-5345-9). Hastings.

Old Korea. Elizabeth Keith. (ISBN 0-8022-0839-8). Philos Lib.

Old Lady in Dubuque. Albert Kwasky. 1979. 7.95 o.p. (ISBN 0-533-03615-1). Vantage.

Old Landmarks & Historic Personages of Boston. Samuel A. Drake. LC 76-99068. (Illus.). 506p. 1970. Repr. of 1900 ed. 43.00x o.p. (ISBN 0-8103-3582-4). Gale.

Old Law & the New Law. William Barclay. LC 72-1412. (Illus.). 128p. 1972. pap. 3.95 o.s.i. (ISBN 0-664-24958-2, Westminster). Westminster John Knox.

Old London. Ed. by John Cadfryn-Roberts. LC 79-81859. (Golden Ariels Ser). (Illus.). 1969. 3.95 o.s.i. (ISBN 0-8008-5690-2). Taplinger.

Old Long Island. Compiled by Skip Whitson. (Sun Historical Ser). (Illus., Orig.). 1976. pap. 3.50 o.p. (ISBN 0-89540-020-0, SB-020). Sun Pub.

Old MacDonald Had a Farm. Rowan Barnes-Murphy. (ps). 1985. 8.95 o.p. (ISBN 0-8120-5693-0); bk. & cassette 12.95 o.p. (ISBN 0-8120-7380-0). Barron.

Old Magic. Ruth M. Arthur. LC 77-8335. (Illus.). (gr. 5-9). 1977. 7.95 o.p. (ISBN 0-689-30577-X, Atheneum). Macmillan.

Old Maids: A Selection of Short Stories by Nineteenth-Century Women Writers. Compiled by Susan Koppelman. 208p. (Orig.). 1985. pap. 8.95 o.p. (ISBN 0-86358-014-9, Pandora Pr). Routledge Chapman & Hall.

Old Man. Yuri Trifonov. Tr. by Jacqueline Edwards & Mitchell Schneider. 288p. (Rus.). 1984. 16.45 o.s.i. (ISBN 0-671-25283-6). S&S.

Old Man & the Boy. Robert Ruark. LC 57-10425. 1957. 15.95 o.s.i. (ISBN 0-03-027910-0). H Holt & Co.

Old Man & the Sea by Ernest Hemingway. 48p. (Orig.). 1988. pap. 9.95 o.p. (ISBN 1-55651-675-4); cassette o.p. (ISBN 1-55651-676-2). Cram Cassettes.

Old Manor House. Charlotte Smith. pap. 9.95 o.p. (ISBN 0-317-65250-8, Pandora Pr). Routledge Chapman & Hall.

Old Manors in the Colony of Maryland. Annie L. Sioussat. (Illus.). 64p. 1913. 7.50 o.p. (ISBN 0-686-36503-8). Md Hist.

Old Man's Diary. A. J. Taylor. 145p. 1984. 19.95 o.p. (ISBN 0-241-11247-8, Pub. by Hamish Hamilton England). David & Charles.

Old Man's Gold & Other Stories. Ovid Pierce. LC 75-19101. x, 70p. 1976. 10.95 o.p. (ISBN 0-8078-1257-9). U of NC Pr.

Old Merchants of New York City, 5 vols. Joseph A. Scoville. LC 68-28645. 1971. Repr. of 1870 ed. Set. lib. bdg. 105.00x o.p. (ISBN 0-8371-0214-6, SCOM). Greenwood.

Old Mother West Wind. Thornton W. Burgess. (Mother West Wind Ser.: Vol. 1). (Illus.). (gr. k-3). 1976. 3.09 o.p. (ISBN 0-448-13728-3, G&D). Putnam Pub Group.

Old Norse Poems. L. M. Hollander. LC 36-10020. Repr. of 1936 ed. 30.00 o.p. (ISBN 0-527-41890-0). Kraus Repr.

Old Norse Sagas. H. Koht. (Lowell Institute Lectures Ser). Repr. of 1931 ed. 30.00 o.p. (ISBN 0-527-52400-X). Kraus Repr.

Old North Country Bridges: Upstate New York. Richard S. Allen. (Illus.). 112p. 1983. 16.95 o.p. (ISBN 0-932052-28-2). North Country.

Old Nyack: The Finest Written Historical Sketch of Old Nyack Village. Compiled by George H. Budke & J. Elmer Christie. (Illus.). 1984. pap. 5.00 o.p. (ISBN 0-911183-25-6). Rockland County Hist.

Old One-Toe. Michel-Aime Baudouy. Tr. by Marie Ponsot. LC 59-10944. (Illus.). (gr. 4 up). 1959. 6.50 o.p. (ISBN 0-15-257780-7, HJ). HarBraceJ.

Old Ones of New Mexico. Robert Coles. LC 84-6736. (Illus.). 96p. 1984. pap. 12.95 o.p. (ISBN 0-15-668508-6, Harv). HarBraceJ.

Old Patagonian Express: By Train Through the Americas. Paul Theroux. 1979. 11.95 o.s.i. (ISBN 0-395-27788-4). HM.

Old Patchwork Quilts. Ruth E. Finley. (Illus.). 1971. 10.75 o.s.i. (ISBN 0-8231-5025-9). Branford.

Old Paths & Legends of New England: Saunterings over Historic Roads with Glimpses of Picturesque Fields & Old Homesteads in Massachusetts, Rhode Island & New Hampshire. Katherine M. Abbott. LC 76-75228. 518p. Repr. of 1903 ed. 40.00x o.p. (ISBN 0-8103-3564-6). Gale.

Old Paths & Legends of the New England Border: Connecticut, Deerfield, Berkshire. Katherine M. Abbott. LC 72-75227. 424p. 1970. Repr. of 1907 ed. 40.00x o.p. (ISBN 0-8103-3562-X). Gale.

Old People. Theodore Handelman. 1985. 12.50 o.p. (ISBN 0-682-40258-3). Exposition-Phoenix.

Old People & London Government. Kathleen M. Slack. 82p. 1970. pap. text ed. 5.00 o.p. (ISBN 0-7135-1620-8, Pub. by Bedford England). Gower Pub Co.

Old Poor Law 1795-1834. 2nd ed. J. D. Marshall. (Studies in Economic & Social History). 49p. 1968. pap. text ed. 9.95 o.p. (ISBN 0-333-09365-8). Humanities.

Old Priest Remembers, Eighteen Ninety-Two to Nineteen Seventy-Eight. 2nd ed. John K. Sharp. 1978. 10.00 o.p. (ISBN 0-682-49183-7). Exposition-Phoenix.

Old Priory. Norah Lofts. 304p. 1983. pap. 3.50 o.p. (ISBN 0-380-62380-3, 62380-3). Avon.

Old Quantum Theory. D. Ter Haar. 1967. 55.00 o.p. (ISBN 0-08-012102-0); pap. 55.00 o.p. (ISBN 0-08-012101-2). Pergamon.

Old Ramon. Jack Schaefer. (Illus.). (gr. 6-10). 1975. 7.95 o.p. (ISBN 0-395-07087-2). HM.

Old Ramon. Jack Schaefer. LC 60-5211. (Sandpiper Ser.). (Illus.). 102p. (gr. 6 up). 1973. pap. 2.95 o.p. (ISBN 0-395-15056-6, Sandpiper). HM.

Old Religion in the Brave New World: Reflections on the Relation Between Christendom & the Republic. Sidney Mead. LC 76-24588. (Jefferson Memorial Lectures Ser.: No. 4). 1977. 20.00x o.p. (ISBN 0-520-03322-1). U of Cal Pr.

Old Rhinebeck Aerodrome. E. Gordon Bainbridge. 1977. 12.50 o.p. (ISBN 0-682-48883-6, Banner). Exposition-Phoenix.

Old Shanghai: Gansters in Paradise. Pan Ling. (Illus.). viii, 239p. (Orig.). 1984. pap. 16.50 o.p. (ISBN 962-225-164-1, 00163). Heinemann Ed.

Titles

Old Ship: A Prospect of Brighton. Raymond Flower. (Illus.). 192p. 1986. 24.00 o.p. (ISBN 0-7099-1077-0, Pub. by Croom Helm Ltd). Routledge Chapman & Hall.

Old Stone Age. Francois Bordes. (Illus., Orig.). 1968. pap. text ed. 3.95 o.p. (ISBN 0-07-006500-4). McGraw.

Old Stone Age. rev. ed. Miles Burkitt. LC 56-10678. (Illus.). 1963. pap. 1.45 o.p. (ISBN 0-689-70028-8, 26, Atheneum). Macmillan.

Old Stone Age. Geoffrey Grigson. (Illus.). 96p. 1957. Philos Lib.

Old Stories for a New Time. James Limburg. LC 82-49019. 127p. 1983. pap. 8.95 o.s.i. (ISBN 0-8042-0148-X, John Knox). Westminster John Knox.

Old Tales of San Francisco. Arthur B. Chandler. LC 77-78491. (History Ser.). (Illus.). 1977. pap. text ed. 11.95 o.p. (ISBN 0-8403-1746-8). Kendall-Hunt.

Old Tavern Signs: An Excursion into the History of Hospitality. Fritz A. Endell. LC 68-26572. (Illus.). 320p. 1968. Repr. of 1916 ed. 40.00x o.p. (ISBN 0-8103-3505-0). Gale.

Old Testament. 48p. (Orig.). 1989. pap. 9.95 o.p. (ISBN 1-55651-687-8); audiocassette tape incl. o.p. (ISBN 1-55651-688-6). Cram Cassettes.

Old Testament: A Guide to Its Writings. Hans W. Wolff. Tr. by Keith R. Crim from Gr. LC 73-79010. 160p. (Orig.). 1973. pap. 1.95 o.p. (ISBN 0-8006-0169-6, 1-169, Fortress). Augsburg Fortress.

Old Testament & Jesus Christ. Claus Westerman. Tr. by Omar Kaste. LC 71-101108. 1970. pap. 4.50 o.p. (ISBN 0-8066-1005-0, 10-4736, Augsburg). Augsburg Fortress.

Old Testament & the Literary Critic. David Robertson. Ed. by Gene M. Tucker. LC 76-62620. (Guides to Biblical Scholarship Ser). 96p. (Orig.). 1977. pap. 4.50 o.p. (ISBN 0-8006-0463-6, 1-463, Fortress). Augsburg Fortress.

Old Testament & the Proclamation of the Gospel. Elizabeth Achtemeier. LC 73-7863. 224p. 1973. 7.50 o.p. (ISBN 0-664-20974-2, Westminster). Westminster John Knox.

Old Testament & the Proclamation of the Gospel. Elizabeth Achtemeier. LC 73-7863. 224p. 1980. pap. 5.95 o.s.i. (ISBN 0-664-24287-1, Westminster). Westminster John Knox.

Old Testament & the World. Walther Zimmerli. Tr. by John J. Scullion from Ger. LC 75-32946. 1976. 8.50 o.p. (ISBN 0-8042-0139-0, John Knox). Westminster John Knox.

Old Testament As the Book of Christ: An Appraisal of Bonhoeffer's Interpretation. Martin Kuske. Ed. by S. T. Kimbrough, Jr. LC 76-25495. 1976. 12.95 o.s.i. (ISBN 0-664-20772-3, Westminster). Westminster John Knox.

Old Testament Books for Pastor and Teacher. Brevard S. Childs. LC 76-52457. 120p. 1977. pap. 4.95 o.s.i. (ISBN 0-664-24120-4, Westminster). Westminster John Knox.

Old Testament Commentary Survey. 2nd ed. John Goldingay. Ed. by Robert Hubbard & Mark L. Branson. 66p. 1981. pap. 6.95 o.p. (ISBN 0-8308-5499-1). Inter-Varsity.

Old Testament Covenant: A Survey of Current Opinions. Dennis J. McCarthy. LC 71-37117. (Growing Points in Theology Ser). (Orig.). 1972. pap. 5.75 o.p. (ISBN 0-8042-0020-3, John Knox). Westminster John Knox.

Old Testament Criticism in the Nineteenth Century. John W. Rogerson. LC 84-47933. 448p. 1985. 3.95 o.p. (ISBN 0-8006-0737-6, 1-737, Fortress). Augsburg Fortress.

Old Testament Express. Terry Hall. 160p. 1985. pap. 4.50 o.p. (ISBN 0-88207-599-3). Victor Bks.

Old Testament for Modern Readers. D. B. Campbell. LC 73-16913. 144p. 1974. 5.95 o.p. (ISBN 0-8042-0197-8, John Knox). Westminster John Knox.

Old Testament: God's People-Our Story. DeVere Ramsay. LC 84-51829. (Illus.). 1985. 6.50 o.p. (ISBN 0-8358-0500-X). Upper Room.

Old Testament Journeys in Faith. Megan McKenna & Darryl Ducote. LC 78-71528. (Followers of the Way Ser.: Vol. 1). (gr. 9-12). 1979. 22.50 o.p. (ISBN 0-8091-9542-9). Paulist Pr.

Old Testament Made Easy. Julie C. Tatham. LC 85-90957. (Illus.). 720p. 1985. 25.00 o.p. (ISBN 0-682-40263-X). Exposition-Phoenix.

Old Testament Men of Faith. F. B. Meyer. 1979. pap. 5.95 o.p. (ISBN 0-89107-170-9). Good News.

Old Testament of the Early Church: A Study of Canon. A. C. Sundberg, Jr. (Harvard Theological Studies). 1964. 26.00 o.p. (ISBN 0-527-01020-0). Kraus Repr.

Old Testament Prophets. rev. ed. E. W. Heaton. LC 77-79589. 1977. pap. 4.95 o.p. (ISBN 0-8042-0140-4, John Knox). WEstminster John Knox.

Old Testament Roots of Our Faith. Paul J. Achtemeier & Elizabeth Achtemeier. LC 78-14659. 160p. 1979. pap. 5.95 o.p. (ISBN 0-8006-1348-1, 1-1348, Fortress). Augsburg Fortress.

Old Testament Theology. Ronald E. Clements. LC 79-16704. (New Foundations Theological Library). (Peter Toon & Ralph Martin series editors). 1980. 12.95 o.p. (ISBN 0-8042-3701-8, John Knox). Westminster John Knox.

Old Testament Theology in Outline. Walther Zimmerli. Tr. by David E. Green. LC 76-44969. 1977. 12.50 o.p. (ISBN 0-8042-0141-2, John Knox). Westminster John Knox.

Old Thad Stevens: A Story of Ambition. Richard N. Current. LC 80-15189. (Illus.). v, 344p. 1980. Repr. of 1942 ed. lib. bdg. 35.00x o.p. (ISBN 0-313-22569-9, CUOT). Greenwood.

Old Timbers. Chilton Thomson. (Illus.). 64p. 1981. 5.00 o.p. (ISBN 0-682-49757-6). Exposition-Phoenix.

Old Times. John Ashton. LC 67-23944. (Illus.). 366p. 1969. Repr. of 1885 ed. 35.00x o.p. (ISBN 0-8103-3252-3). Gale.

Old Times. Walter C. Meller. LC 68-26592. (Illus.). 266p. 1968. Repr. of 1925 ed. 35.00x o.p. (ISBN 0-8103-3453-4). Gale.

Old Times in the Adirondacks. 2nd ed. Seneca R. Stoddard. Ed. by Maitland C. De Sormo. LC 77-182699. (Illus.). 1972. 15.00 o.s.i. (ISBN 0-9601158-0-3). North Country.

Old Times in the Faulkner Country. John B. Cullen & Floyd C. Watkins. LC 61-1874. xvi, 132p. 1975. 16.95 o.p. (ISBN 0-8071-0099-4). La State U Pr.

Old Traditions-New Traditions. Rebecca A. Stevens. LC 81-51494. (Illus.). 32p. 1981. pap. 6.00 o.p. (ISBN 0-87405-017-0). Textile Mus.

Old Washington, D. C. in Early Photographs Eighteen Forty-Six to Nineteen Thirty-Two. Robert Reed. (Illus.). 19.00 o.p. (ISBN 0-8446-5804-9). Peter Smith.

Old Wilderness Road: An American Journey. William O. Steele. LC 68-25197. (Illus.). (gr. 7 up). 1968. 5.95 o.p. (ISBN 0-15-257847-1, HJ). HarBraceJ.

Old Wives' Lore for Gardeners. Bridget Boland & Maureen Boland. (Illus.). 64p. 1977. pap. 3.95 o.p. (ISBN 0-374-51639-1). FS&G.

Old World, New Horizons: Britain, Europe, & the Atlantic Alliance. Edward M. Heath. LC 71-106959. (Godkin Lecture Ser: 1967). 1970. 7.95x o.s.i. (ISBN 0-674-63260-5). Harvard U Pr.

Older Americans: An Untapped Resource. National Committee on Careers for Older Americans. LC 79-51560. 63p. (Orig.). 1979. pap. 8.50 o.p. (ISBN 0-89492-006-5). Acad Educ Dev.

Older Employees: New Roles for Valued Resources. Benson Rosen & Thomas H. Jerdee. LC 83-73720. 200p. 1984. 19.95 o.p. (ISBN 0-87094-439-8). Dow Jones-Irwin.

Older Kind of Magic. Patricia Wrightson. LC 70-167839. (Illus.). 192p. (gr. 3-7). 1972. 5.50 o.p. (ISBN 0-15-203600-8, HJ). HarBraceJ.

Older Patient & the Role of the Physiologist. 2nd ed. Margot Hawker et al. Intro. by Donald Dick. (Illus.). 160p. 1985. pap. 8.95 o.p. (ISBN 0-571-13427-0). Faber & Faber.

Older People Have Choices: Information for Decisions about Health, Home, & Money. Nancy Manser. 32p. (Orig.). 1984. pap. 3.95 o.p. (ISBN 0-8066-2098-6, 10-4741, Augsburg). Augsburg Fortress.

Older Soldier. Jack M. Lambert. 1959. 3.50 o.p. S&S.

Older Woman's Health Guide. Mary Egginton et al. 272p. 1985. text ed. 16.95 o.p. (ISBN 0-07-042424-1). McGraw.

Older Women in Twentieth Century America: A Selected Annotated Bibliography. Audrey Borenstein. LC 82-6082. (Women Studies, Facts & Issues: Vol. 3). 351p. 1982. 48.00 o.p. (ISBN 0-8240-9396-8). Garland Pub.

Oldest Library Motto & Other Library Essays. Cora E. Lutz. LC 79-16757. 176p. 1979. 19.50 o.p. (ISBN 0-208-01816-6, Archon). Shoe String.

Oldsmobile. (Popular Mechanics-Motor Car Care Guide Ser.). (Illus.). 192p. pap. 6.95 o.p. (ISBN 0-87851-946-7). Hearst Bks.

Oldsmobile Omega, 1980. 12.95 o.p. (ISBN 0-89287-350-7, A286). Clymer Pub.

Ole Bull Returns to Pennsylvania: The Biography of a Norwegian Violin Virtuoso & Pioneer in the Keystone State. Inez Bull. (Illus.). 1961. 5.00 o.p. (ISBN 0-686-67700-5). Exposition-Phoenix.

Ole Bull's Activities in the United States Between 1843 & 1880. Inez Bull. (Illus.). 144p. 1982. pap. 12.95 o.p. (ISBN 0-682-49801-7). Exposition-Phoenix.

Ole Nell, Mama, & Me. Spurgeon Q. Bryant, Sr. LC 78-55926. 1978. 4.95 o.p. (ISBN 0-87397-137-X). Strode.

Olefins, Diolefins & Acetylene see Petrochemical Manufacturing & Marketing Guide.

Olfaction & Odours: An Osphresiological Essay. W. McCartney. 1968. 34.30 o.p. (ISBN 0-387-04262-8). Springer-Verlag.

Olfaction & Taste, Vol. 1. Ed. by Yngve Zotterman. 1963. 100.00 o.p. (ISBN 0-08-009814-2). Pergamon.

Olga Worrall: Mystic with the Healing Hands. Edwina Cerutti. LC 75-9317. 192p. 1975. 7.95i o.p. (ISBN 0-06-061358-0). HarpR.

Oligarchy in Fraternal Organizations: A Study in Organizational Leadership. Alvin J. Schmidt. LC 73-15732. 104p. 1973. 35.00x o.p. (ISBN 0-8103-0345-0). Gale.

Oligosaccharides. Jaroslav Stanek et al. Tr. by Karel Mayer. 1965. 88.00 o.p. (ISBN 0-12-663756-3). Acad Pr.

Olimpiade. Antonio Caldara. Ed. by Howard M. Brown. LC 76-20980. (Italian Opera 1640-1770 Ser.). 1978. lib. bdg. 77.00 o.p. (ISBN 0-8240-2631-4). Garland Pub.

Olimpiade. Baldassare Galuppi. Ed. by Howard M. Brown. LC 76-20965. (Italian Opera 1640-1770 Ser.). 1978. lib. bdg. 77.00 o.p. (ISBN 0-8240-2639-X). Garland Pub.

Olive Schreiner: Feminism on the Frontier. Joyce Berkman. LC 78-74842. 1979. 11.95 o.p. (ISBN 0-88831-031-5). Eden Pr.

Olive Schreiner Reader: Writings on Women & South Africa. Carol Barsh. 200p. 1987. 32.00 o.p. (ISBN 0-86358-180-3, 81803, Pub by Pandora Pr); pap. 12.95 o.p. (ISBN 0-86358-118-8, 81188). Routledge Chapman & Hall.

Oliver Goldsmith. William Freeman. 1952. (ISBN 0-8022-0535-6). Philos Lib.

Oliver Messel. Roger Pinkham. (Illus.). 200p. (Orig.). 1984. pap. 13.95 o.p. (ISBN 0-905209-50-8, Pub. by Victoria & Albert Mus UK). Faber & Faber.

Oliver Twist. Charles Dickens. 1978. 12.95x o.p. (ISBN 0-460-10233-8, DEL-04273, Evman); pap. 2.95 o.p. (ISBN 0-460-11233-3). Biblio Dist.

Oliver Twist. Charles Dickens. (Enriched Classics Ser.). 1981. pap. 3.50 o.s.i. (ISBN 0-671-44242-2). PB.

Oliver Twist. Charles Dickens. LC 86-63584. (Illus.). 416p. (gr. 5-12). 1987. 12.95 o.p. (ISBN 0-89577-258-2). RD Assn.

Oliver Twist see New Method Supplementary Readers: Bestseller Pack.

Oliver Wants a Pony. Artis Johnson. (gr. 2-4). 1978. 4.00 o.p. (ISBN 0-682-49028-8). Exposition-Phoenix.

Oliver Wendell Holmes. Miriam R. Small. (Twayne's United States Authors Ser). 1962. pap. 10.95 o.p. (ISBN 0-8084-0237-4, T29, Twayne). New Coll U Pr.

Oliver's ADF Directory. 2nd ed. Robert Oliver. 96p. 1981. pap. 6.50 o.p. (ISBN 0-911721-50-9). Aviation.

Oliver's Story. Erich Segal. (YA) (gr. 9-12). 1978. pap. 2.25 o.p. (ISBN 0-380-01844-6). Avon.

Olivier: The Complete Career. Robert Tanitch. LC 85-7455. 192p. 1985. 29.95 o.p. (ISBN 0-89659-590-0). Abbeville Pr.

Olivos: California Crossroad. Jim Norris. (Illus.). 84p. (Orig.). 1987. pap. 5.00 o.p. (ISBN 0-933380-01-1). Olive Pr Pubns.

Olivos y Abedules. Julio Mateu. 167p. (Span.). 1977. pap. 2.95 o.p. (ISBN 0-8285-1325-2, Pub. by Progress Pubs USSR). Imported Pubns.

Olode the Hunter & Other Tales from Nigeria. Harold Courlander & Ezekiel A. Eshugbayi. LC 68-13370. (Illus.). (gr. 3 up). 1968. 4.50 o.p. (ISBN 0-15-257826-9, HJ). HarBraceJ.

Olrik. Alfred Konner. Date not set. 6.95 o.p. (ISBN 0-317-63442-9). Acropolis.

Olson's Encyclopedia of Small Arms. John Olson. LC 84-29587. (Illus.). 336p. 1985. 22.95 o.p. (ISBN 0-8329-0374-4, Pub. by Winchester Pr). New Century.

Olson's Push: Origin, Black Mountain, & Recent American Poetry. Sherman Paul. LC 78-6694. xxvi, 296p. 1978. 32.50 o.p. (ISBN 0-8071-0461-2). La State U Pr.

Olvida los Tambores. Ana Diosdado. Ed. by Angel R. Maroto. 112p. (Orig.). (gr. 11-12). 1974. pap. text ed. 4.75x o.p. (ISBN 0-88334-063-1). Ind Sch Pr.

Olvidados. Peter McCurtin. (Sundance Ser.: No. 30). 1980. 1.75 o.p. (ISBN 0-686-71012-6, Pub. by Leisure Bks CT). Dorchester Pub Co.

Olympia. Elgin Groseclose. 1981. 8.95 o.p. (ISBN 0-89191-290-8). Cook.

Olympian. Peter L. Dixon. 265p. 1987. pap. 3.95 o.p. (ISBN 1-55547-157-9). Critics Choice Paper.

Olympian. Brian Glanville. 1980. pap. 4.95 o.p. (ISBN 0-395-29086-4). HM.

Olympian & Pthyian Odes. Pindar. Ed. by B. L. Gildersleeve. 395p. Repr. of 1890 ed. lib. bdg. 62.50x o.p. (Pub. by A M Hakkert). Coronet Bks.

Olympian Games in Athens: The First Modern Olympics, 1896. Burton Holmes. LC 83-49389. (Illus.). 112p. (Orig.). 1984. pap. 6.95 o.p. (ISBN 0-394-62115-8, E913, Ever). Grove.

Olympian Nights. 224p. 1986. 15.00 o.p. (ISBN 0-947898-38-7). Kraus Repr.

Olympic Games. David Chester. LC 75-18816. (Encore Edition). 1975. 3.50 o.p. (ISBN 0-684-15688-1, ScribT). Scribner.

Olympic Games see Heinemann Guided Readers.

Olympic Games of 1932 & 1984: The Planning & Administration of the Los Angeles Games. Glenna Dunning. (Public Administration Ser.: P 1661). 23p. 1985. 3.75 o.p. (ISBN 0-89028-371-0). Vance Biblios.

Olympic Gold: A Runner's Life & Times. Frank Shorter & Marc Bloom. 320p. 1984. 15.45 o.p. (ISBN 0-395-35403-X). HM.

Olympic Stamps. V. Foorman. 195p. 1981. 5.95 o.p. (ISBN 0-8285-2514-5, Pub. by Progress Pubs USSR). Imported Pubns.

Olympics Handbook, 1984. Norman Giller. LC 83-17168. (Illus.). 208p. 1984. pap. 7.95 o.s.i. H Holt & Co.

Olympiques. Henry De Montherlant. 13.25 o.p. (ISBN 0-685-23905-5). Schoenhof.

Olympiques. Henry de Montherlant. (Folio 323). 1973. 3.95 o.p. (ISBN 0-686-55527-9). Schoenhof.

Olympus OM-2 Spot-Program. Michael Huber. (Illus.). 192p. (Orig.). 1987. pap. 12.95 o.p. (ISBN 0-317-52843-2, Pub. by Hove-Fountain UK). Seven Hills Bk Dists.

Oman. 2nd ed. Middle East Economic Digest Staff. Ed. by John Whelan. (MEED Practical Guides Ser.). (Illus.). 248p. (Orig.). 1985. pap. 16.95x o.p. (ISBN 0-946510-02-4). Lynne Rienner.

Oman: A Middle East Economic Digest Guide. Ed. by John Whelan. (MEED Practical Guide Ser.). (Illus.). 198p. (Orig.). 1982. pap. 15.00 o.p. (ISBN 0-7103-0013-1, Kegan Paul). Routledge CHapman & Hall.

Oman Before Nineteen Seventy: The End of an Era. rev. ed. Ian Skeet. 224p. 1985. pap. 8.95 o.p. (ISBN 0-571-13580-3). Faber & Faber.

Oman in the Twentieth Century: Political Foundations of an Emerging State. John E. Peterson. LC 78-761. (Illus.). 286p. 1978. text ed. 29.50x o.p. (ISBN 0-06-495522-2). B&N Imports.

Omar Sharif's Life in Bridge. Omar Sharif. Tr. by Terence Reese from Fr. 144p. 1983. pap. 7.95 o.p. (ISBN 0-571-13098-4). Faber & Faber.

Ombudsman or Citizen's Defender: A Modern Institution. Ed. by Roy V. Peel & Thorsten Sellin. LC 68-21996. (Annals of the American Academy of Political & Social Science: No. 377). (Orig.). 1968. pap. 15.00 o.p. (ISBN 0-87761-107-6). Am Acad Pol Soc Sci.

Omega. D. Brian Plummer. (Illus.). 234p. 1984. 20.00 o.p. (ISBN 0-85115-189-2, Pub. by Boydell & Brewer). Longwood Pub Group.

Omega-Three Phenomenon. Donald O. Rudin et al. 304p. 1988. pap. 4.50 o.p. (ISBN 0-380-70595-8). Avon.

Omega-3 Breakthrough: The Revolutionary, Medically-Proven Fish Oil Diet. Julius Fast. 1987. 15.95 o.p. (ISBN 0-89586-625-0). Price Stern.

Omelette Book. Narcissa Chamberlain. LC 55-10130. (Illus.). 192p. 1976. pap. text ed. 3.95 o.p. (ISBN 0-07-010450-6). McGraw.

Omelettes & Souffles. Anne Byrd. Ed. by Irene Rich. LC 81-68839. (Great American Cooking Schools Ser.). (Illus.). 84p. 1982. pap. 5.95 o.p. (ISBN 0-941034-08-9). I Chalmers.

Omits for Obits: Memoirs. Anna Marie Fisher. 1978. 7.00 o.p. (ISBN 0-682-49168-3). Exposition-Phoenix.

Omni-Horizon 1978-1984: Repair & Tune-up Guide. Chilton Automotives Editorial Staff. LC 83-45319. 248p. 1984. pap. 13.50 o.p. (ISBN 0-8019-7485-2). Chilton.

Omni Interviews. Ed. by Pamela Weintraub. LC 83-26501. 336p. 1984. 17.45 o.p. (ISBN 0-89919-215-7); pap. 9.70 o.p. (ISBN 0-89919-269-6). Ticknor & Fields.

Omnibook Three. Ed. by RotoVision Staff. 250p. 1987. 59.50 o.p. (ISBN 0-8230-5790-9). Watson-Guptill.

Omni's Catalog of the Bizarre. Omni Magazine Editors. Ed. by Pamela Weintraub. LC 84-26043. (Illus.). 256p. 1985. pap. 9.95 o.p. (ISBN 0-385-19261-4, Dolp). Doubleday.

Omni's Screen Flights-Screen Fantasies: The Future According to Science Fiction Cinema. Ed. by Danny Peary. Omni Editors. LC 84-4022. (Illus.). 288p. 1984. 35.00 o.p. (ISBN 0-385-19199-5, Dolp); pap. 17.95 o.p. (ISBN 0-385-19202-9, Dolp). Doubleday.

On a Field Azure. Aleksei Remizov. Tr. by Beatrice Scott from Rus. LC 75-25267. (Illus.). 125p. 1976. Repr. of 1946 ed. lib. bdg. 24.75x o.p. (ISBN 0-8371-8387-1, REFAZ). Greenwood.

On a General Economic Theory of Motion. M. J. Magill. LC 74-135961. (Lecture Notes in Operations Research & Mathematical Systems: Vol. 36). 1970. pap. 10.70 o.p. (ISBN 0-387-04959-2). Springer-Verlag.

On a Pale Horse. Piers Anthony. (Incarnations of Immortality Ser.: Bk. 1). 288p. 12.95 o.p. (ISBN 0-345-30924-3, Del Rey). Ballantine.

On a Sacred Hill. Anita P. Pileggi. 48p. 1983. 5.50 o.p. (ISBN 0-682-40118-8). Exposition-Phoenix.

On a White Bud. Alexis Rotella. 1984. pap. 4.95 o.p. (ISBN 0-934536-20-1). Merging Media.

On Account of Murder. Elizabeth Powers. 272p. (Orig.). 1984. pap. 2.95 o.p. (ISBN 0-380-89250-2). Avon.

On Aggression. Konrad Lorenz. Tr. by Marjorie K. Wilson. LC 66-12369. (Helen & Kurt Wolff Bk). (Illus.). 1966. 9.50 o.p. (ISBN 0-15-168960-1). HarBraceJ.

On All Hallows' Eve. Grace Chetwin. LC 84-4391. 160p. (gr. 6 up). 1984. 10.25 o.p. (ISBN 0-688-03012-2). Lothrop.

On & off the Record: A Memoir of Walter Legge. Elisabeth Schwarzkopf. (Illus.). 320p. 1982. 17.95 o.p. (ISBN 0-684-17451-0, ScribT). Scribner.

On Art & Artists. Aldous Huxley. Ed. by Morris Philipson. Repr. of 1960 ed. 21.00 o.p. (ISBN 0-527-43800-6). Kraus Repr.

On Art & the Mind. Richard Wollheim. LC 73-94137. 1974. text ed. 27.00x o.s.i. (ISBN 0-674-88757-3). Harvard U Pr.

On Arts & Artists. Auguste Rodin. 1957. (ISBN 0-8022-1363-4). Philos Lib.

On Bear's Head. Philip Whalen. LC 68-24399. 1969. pap. 3.95 o.p. (ISBN 0-15-668742-9, Harv). HarBraceJ.

On Bear's Head: Poems 1950-1967. Philip Whalen. LC 68-24399. 1969. 17.50 o.p. (ISBN 0-15-168966-0). HarBraceJ.

On Becoming a Leader: Leadership Training for Women in Higher Education. Barnetta M. White. 1985. text ed. 39.50x o.s.i. (ISBN 0-8290-1357-1). Irvington.

On Becoming a Social Scientist: From Survey Research & Participant Observation to Experiential Analysis. Shulamit Reinharz. LC 79-83577. (Social & Behavioral Science Ser.). 1979. 32.95x o.p. (ISBN 0-87589-416-X). Jossey-Bass.

On Becoming American. Ted Morgan. 1978. 10.95 o.p. (ISBN 0-395-26283-6). HM.

On Being a Caring Father. Ed. by Ted Miller. LC 82-48421. 128p. (Orig.). 1983. pap. 5.72i o.p. (ISBN 0-06-061384-X, RD 437). HarpR.

On Being a Jewish Feminist. Date not set. (ISBN 0-8052-3837-9). Random.

On Being a Mother. Mary G. Boulton. LC 83-9150. 240p. 1984. 33.00x o.p. (ISBN 0-422-78540-7, NO. 4005); pap. 15.95x o.p. (ISBN 0-422-78550-4, NO. 4006). Routledge Chapman & Hall.

On Being a Poet. Judson Jerome. LC 84-15286. 313p. 1984. 14.95 o.p. (ISBN 0-89879-148-0). Writers Digest.

On Being a Woman. Fay Fransella. (Tavistock Women's Studies). 1977. pap. 10.95 o.p. (ISBN 0-422-76080-3, NO. 2783, Pub. by Tavistock England). Routledge Chapman & Hall.

On Being a Woman in 1976: Selected Issues & Research. National Association for Women Deans, Administrators & Counselors Staff. 1976. pap. 6.00 o.p. (ISBN 0-686-17544-1). Natl Assn Women.

On Being Blue. William Gass. LC 75-43013. 96p. 1976. 10.00 o.s.i. (ISBN 0-87923-183-1). Godine.

On Being Free. Frithjof Bergmann. LC 77-89760. 1977. text ed. 22.95 o.s.i. (ISBN 0-268-01492-2). U of Notre Dame Pr.

On Being Freer. Caleb Gattegno. 1975. pap. 10.00 o.p. (ISBN 0-87825-070-0). Ed Solutions.

On Being Grandmotherly: The Evolution of IMF Conditionality. Sidney Dell. LC 81-6888. (Essays in International Finance Ser.: No. 144). 1981. pap. text ed. 4.50x o.p. (ISBN 0-88165-051-X). Princeton U Int Finan Econ.

On Being Human: A Systematic View. G. Marian Kinget. 272p. (Orig.). 1975. pap. text ed. 12.95 o.p. (ISBN 0-15-567491-9, HC). HarBraceJ.

On Being Human: Essays in Theological Anthropology. Ray S. Anderson. 234p. (Orig.). 1982. pap. 10.95 o.p. (ISBN 0-8028-1926-5). Eerdmans.

On Being Responsible: Issues in Personal Ethics. Ed. by James M. Gustafson & James T. Laney. LC 68-17602. (Forum Bks.). 1968. pap. 6.95xi o.p. (ISBN 0-06-063531-2, RD 5). HarpR.

On Bended Knees: The Night Rider Story. Bill Cunningham. LC 83-60651. (Illus.). 256p. (gr. 7-12). 1983. 15.95 o.p. (ISBN 0-913383-00-7). McClanahan Pub.

On Beyond A-I-S. Ed. by Vangie Piper & Phyllis Tickle. LC 81-21343. (Tennessee Arts Commission Bks). 196p. 1982. pap. 4.95 o.p. (ISBN 0-686-79842-2, St Luke TN). Peachtree Pubs.

On Beyond Koch. Phyllis A. Tickle. LC 80-28172. (Brooks Memorial Gallery Bks.). (Illus.). 194p. 1981. pap. 4.95 o.p. (ISBN 0-918518-20-2, St Luke TN). Peachtree Pubs.

On Call. Lois Rowe. 1984. 8.95 o.p. (ISBN 0-8010-7724-9). Baker Bk.

On Camera: My Ten Thousand Hours on Television. Hugh Downs. (Illus.). 256p. 1986. 17.95 o.p. (ISBN 0-399-13203-1, Putnam). Putnam Pub Group.

On Christian Truth. Harry Blamires. 168p. (Orig.). pap. 5.95 o.p. (ISBN 0-89283-130-8). Servant.

On Christmas Day in the Morning. Ed. by John M. Langstaff & Antony Groves-Raines. (Illus.). (gr. k-3). 1959. 5.95 o.p. (ISBN 0-15-257959-1, HJ). HarBraceJ.

On Christmas Morning. Jane B. Moncure. LC 83-10104. (Illus.). 32p. (ps-k). 1983. PLB 6.95 o.p. (ISBN 0-89693-210-9). Dandelion Hse.

On Civilized Stars: The Search for Intelligent Life in Outer Space. Joseph F. Baugher. (Illus.). 288p. 1985. 21.95 o.p. (ISBN 0-13-634429-1); pap. 9.95 o.p. (ISBN 0-13-634411-9). P-H.

On Codevelopmental Markers: Biologic Diagnostic & Monitoring Aspects, Vol. 1. Ed. by William H. Fishman. 1983. 91.50 o.p. (ISBN 0-12-257701-9). Acad Pr.

On Colonialism: Selections. Karl Marx & Friedrich Engels. LC 72-80130. 382p. 1972. 7.50 o.p. (ISBN 0-7178-0258-2); pap. 2.65 o.p. (ISBN 0-7178-0259-0). Intl Pubs Co.

On Communications: A Fundamental Approach to Reading, Writing, Speaking & Listening. Richard W. Swanson & Charles E. Marquardt. LC 73-7370. (Illus.). 192p. 1974. pap. text ed. write for info. o.p. (ISBN 0-02-478750-7). Macmillan.

On Complementation in Icelandic. Hoskuldur Thrainsson. LC 78-67736. (Outstanding Dissertations in Linguistics Ser.). 523p. 1985. lib. bdg. 64.00 o.p. (ISBN 0-8240-9671-1). Garland Pub.

On Composition & Computers. Deborah H. Holdstein. LC 87-22917. (Technology & the Humanities 3). 137p. 1988. 30.00 o.p. (ISBN 0-317-67437-4, S803C/S803P); pap. 16.50 o.p. (ISBN 0-317-67438-2). Modern Lang.

On Deadline: Managing Media Relations. Carole Howard & Wilma Mathews. (Public Communication Ser.). (Illus.). 352p. 1985. 34.95x o.p. (ISBN 0-582-28436-8). Longman.

On Dearborn Street. Miles Franklin. LC 81-11570. 224p. (YA) 1982. 16.95 o.p. (ISBN 0-7022-1636-4). U of Queensland Pr.

On Dirichlet's Boundary Value Problem. C. G. Simader. LC 72-85089. (Lecture Notes in Mathematics: Vol. 268). iv, 238p. 1972. pap. 11.00 o.p. (ISBN 0-387-05903-2). Springer-Verlag.

On Earth As It Is... Gladys S. Lewis. LC 83-70006. (Orig.). 1983. pap. 6.50 o.p. (ISBN 0-8054-6332-1). Broadman.

On Edgar Bergen's Lap: An Ironic History of the Human Condition. Bill Leverette. 184p. 1987. 12.95 o.p. (ISBN 0-934601-16-X). Peachtree Pubs.

On English Homophones see Preliminary Announcement.

On Equal Terms: Jews in America, 1881-1981. Lucy S. Dawidowicz. 200p. 1982. 12.95 o.s.i. (ISBN 0-03-061658-1). H Holt & Co.

On Equal Terms: Jews in America 1881-1981. Lucy S. Dawidowicz. 1984. pap. 6.95 o.s.i. (ISBN 0-03-071058-8). H Holt & Co.

On Extended Wings. Diane Ackerman. LC 84-45606. 288p. 1985. 16.95 o.p. (ISBN 0-689-11540-7, Atheneum). Macmillan.

On Foot in the Grand Canyon. Sharon Spangler. LC 86-4909. (Illus.). 322p. 1986. pap. 11.95 o.p. (ISBN 0-87108-708-1). Pruett.

On Gender & Writing. Ed. by Michelene Wandor. 232p. (Orig.). 1983. pap. 5.95 o.p. (ISBN 0-86358-021-1, Pandora Pr). Routledge Chapman & Hall.

On Gide's Promethee: Private Myth & Public Mystification. Kurt Weinberg. LC 70-173760. (Princeton Essays in Literature Ser.). 144p. 1972. 22.50x o.p. (ISBN 0-691-06222-6). Princeton U Pr.

On Going to Bed. Anthony Burgess. LC 81-22757. (Illus.). 96p. 1982. 12.95 o.p. (ISBN 0-89659-280-4). Abbeville Pr.

On Grammatical Inversion see Preliminary Announcement.

On Having No Head: Zen & the Rediscovery of the Obvious. rev. ed. D. E. Harding. (Illus.). 96p. 1986. pap. 4.95 o.p. (ISBN 0-317-40544-6). Routledge Chapman & Hall.

On Hegel's Logic: Fragments of a Commentary. J. W. Burbidge. 280p. 1981. text ed. 17.50x o.p. (ISBN 0-391-02387-X). Humanities.

On Higher Than Commercial Grounds: The Factory Controversy, 1830-1853. Ann P. Robson. LC 84-46010. (British Economic History Ser.). 450p. 1985. 50.00 o.p.; lib. bdg. 45.00 o.p. (ISBN 0-8240-6690-1). Garland Pub.

On His Majesty's Service: The Origins of Uganda's African Civil Service, 1912-1940. Nizar Motani. (Foreign & Comparative Studies Program, African Ser.: No. 29). 72p. 1978. pap. text ed. 6.00x o.p. (ISBN 0-915984-51-2). Syracuse U Foreign Comp.

On Historians. J. H. Hexter. LC 78-16635. 1979. 24.50x o.p. (ISBN 0-674-63426-8). Harvard U Pr.

On Historical Materialism. Karl Marx & Frederick Engels. LC 73-87991. 751p. 1975. 11.00 o.p. (ISBN 0-7178-0402-X); pap. 4.25 o.p. (ISBN 0-7178-0411-9). Intl Pubs Co.

On Holy Ground. Kirkie Morrissey. 144p. (Orig.). 1983. pap. 5.95 o.p. (ISBN 0-89109-051-7). NavPress.

On Human Dignity: Political Theology & Ethics. Jurgen Moltmann. Tr. by M. Douglas Meeks from Ger. LC 83-48913. 240p. 1984. 3.95 o.p. (ISBN 0-8006-0715-5, 1-715, Fortress). Augsburg Fortress.

On Hyphens & Shall & Will, Should & Would see Preliminary Announcement.

On Iowa: A University & Its People. Louise Roalson. LC 83-62320. (Illus.). 88p. 1983. pap. 4.95 o.p. (ISBN 0-941016-13-7). Penfield.

On Justifying Democracy. William Nelson. (International Library of Philosophy). 208p. 1980. 21.95x o.p. (ISBN 0-7100-0653-5). Routledge Chapman & Hall.

On Keeping Women. Hortense Calisher. LC 77-79531. 1977. 9.95 o.p. (ISBN 0-87795-169-1, Arbor Hse). Morrow.

On Language. William Safire. (Illus.). 348p. 1981. pap. 6.95 o.p. (ISBN 0-380-56457-2, 63446). Avon.

On Language. George Bernard Shaw. Ed. by A. Tauber. LC 63-13483. 1963. 4.75 o.p. (ISBN 0-8022-1544-0). Philos Lib.

On Learning to Plan & Planning to Learn: The Social Psychology of Changing Toward Future-Responsive Societal Learning. Donald N. Michael. LC 73-7153. (Social & Behavioral Science Ser.). 1973. 29.95x o.p. (ISBN 0-87589-187-X). Jossey-Bass.

On Leaving Paradise. Frank Hercules. LC 79-3354. 324p. 1980. 10.95 o.p. (ISBN 0-15-169921-6). HarBraceJ.

On Life's Expanses. Y. Kolas. 232p. 1982. 5.45 o.p. (ISBN 0-8285-2488-2, Pub. by Progress Pubs USSR). Imported Pubns.

On-Line Cataloging. O.C.L.C. Staff. LC 73-620155. 1973. 2.00 o.p. (ISBN 0-88215-037-5). Friends Ohio St U Lib.

On Line Revolution in Libraries. Kent & Galvin. (Library Science Ser.: Vol. 23). 1978. 75.00 o.p. (ISBN 0-8247-6754-3). Dekker.

On Literary Farces see Popeiana.

On Literature. Maxim Gorky. 347p. 1979. 9.45 o.p. (ISBN 0-8285-1713-4, Pub. by Progress Pubs USSR). Imported Pubns.

On Love & Life. Linda Bircheat. 1978. 4.00 o.p. (ISBN 0-682-49024-5). Exposition-Phoenix.

On Maiden Lane. Bruce Nicolaysen. (Novel of New York Ser.: Vol. 2). 560p. 1981. pap. 2.95 o.p. (ISBN 0-380-77800-9, 77800-9). Avon.

On Man & Nature. Henry David Thoreau. 1960. 5.95 o.s.i. (ISBN 0-88088-513-0). Peter Pauper.

On Manpower Forecasting. J. E. Morton. 51p. 1968. pap. 1.95 o.p. (ISBN 0-911558-44-6). W E Upjohn.

On Meeting Life's Challenges. Ed. by Ted Miller. LC 82-4824. (Christian Reader Ser.). 128p. (Orig.). 1983. pap. 5.72i o.p. (ISBN 0-06-061388-2, RD 440). HarpR.

On Mountains. Jerome. 1978. 8.95 o.p. (ISBN 0-15-169948-8). HarBraceJ.

On Mountains: Thinking About Terrain. John Jerome. LC 78-24273. 1979. pap. text ed. 4.95 o.p. (ISBN 0-07-032535-9). McGraw.

On My Back, Looking Up! Evelyn Orser. Ed. by Richard W. Coffen. LC 83-13882. (Banner Bk.). (Illus.). 94p. (Orig.). 1984. pap. 6.95 o.p. (ISBN 0-8280-0218-5). Review & Herald.

On Native Grounds. Alfred Kazin. LC 42-24811. 541p. 1972. pap. 5.95 o.p. (ISBN 0-15-668750-X, Harv). HarBraceJ.

On Nature Lucretuis. Russel M. Geer. 1965. pap. text ed. write for info. o.p. (ISBN 0-02-341210-0). Macmillan.

On Neoclassicism. Mario Praz. Tr. by Angus Davidson from Ital. (Illus.). 400p. 1988. pap. 24.95 o.p. (ISBN 0-8101-0774-0). Northwestern U Pr.

On Not Being Able to Paint. 2nd, rev. ed. Marion Milner. (Illus.). 184p. (Orig.). 1967. text ed. 27.50x o.s.i. (ISBN 0-8236-3820-0); pap. text ed. 6.95 o.s.i. (ISBN 0-8236-8202-1, 023820). Intl Univs Pr.

On Organizing Macro-Analysis Seminars: Study & Action for a New Society. Philadelphia Macro-Analysis Collective of Movement for a New Society Staff. 76p. (Orig.). 1980. pap. 3.95 o.p. (ISBN 0-86571-009-0); reading unit 1.75 o.p. (ISBN 0-86571-010-4). New Soc Pubs.

On Our Father's Knee: Devotions for Times of Illness. Fredrik Wisloff. LC 72-90264. 144p. 1973. pap. 5.95 o.p. (ISBN 0-8066-1309-2, 10-4765, Augsburg). Augsburg Fortress.

On Our Way Rejoicing. Ingrid Trobisch. 240p. (Orig.). 1986. pap. 6.95 o.p. (ISBN 0-8423-4745-3). Tyndale.

On Our Way to Christmas: A Family Activity Book for Advent. Mary P. Warren. 32p. (Orig.). (gr. k-3). 1980. pap. 4.95 o.p. (ISBN 0-8066-1784-5, 10-4768, Augsburg). Augsburg Fortress.

On Photography. Susan Sontag. LC 77-11916. 207p. 1977. 7.95 o.p. (ISBN 0-374-22626-1). FS&G.

On Photography. Ed. by Susan Sontag. 1978. pap. 9.95 o.p. (ISBN 0-385-28757-7, Delta). Dell.

On Playing with Lions. Virginia McKenna & Bill Travers. LC 66-25625. (Helen & Kurt Wolff Bks.). (Illus.). 1967. 3.95 o.p. (ISBN 0-15-169954-2). HarBraceJ.

On Poetry & Style Aristotle. G. M. Grube. 1958. pap. text ed. (ISBN 0-02-348500-0). Macmillan.

On Polar Trails. John W. Goodsell. 214p. 1984. 12.95 o.p. (ISBN 0-89015-431-7). Eakin Pr.

On Political Economy & Econometrics. Oskar Lange. 1966. 85.00 o.p. (ISBN 0-08-011588-8). Pergamon.

On Prayer: The Lord's Prayer in Today's World. Gerhard Ebeling. Tr. by James W. Leitch from Ger. LC 78-5079. 112p. 1978. pap. 2.95 o.p. (ISBN 0-8006-1336-8, 1-1336, Fortress). Augsburg Fortress.

On Protectionism in the Netherlands. K. A. Koekkoek et al. (Working Paper: No. 493). ii, 68p. 1981. pap. 5.00 o.p. (ISBN 0-686-39773-8, WP-0493). World Bank.

On Reagan: The Man & His Presidency. Ronnie Dugger. LC 83-9833. 1983. text ed. 19.95 o.p. (ISBN 0-07-017974-3). McGraw.

On Regenerative Processes in Queueing Theory. J. W. Cohen. (Lecture Notes in Economics & Mathematical Systems Ser.: Vol. 121). 1976. pap. 11.00 o.p. (ISBN 0-387-07627-1). Springer-Verlag.

On Round-off Errors in Linear Programming. H. Mueller-Merbach. LC 76-137141. (Lecture Notes in Operations Research & Mathematical Systems: Vol. 37). 1970. pap. 10.90 o.p. (ISBN 0-387-04960-6). Springer-Verlag.

On St. Basil the Great. LC 79-20045. (Word & Spirit Ser.: Vol. I). 1979. pap. 4.95 o.p. (ISBN 0-932506-07-0). St Bedes Pubns.

On St. Benedict. LC 80-25958. (Word & Spirit Ser.: Vol. II). 1980. pap. 6.00 o.p. (ISBN 0-932506-09-7). St Bedes Pubns.

On Scotland & the Scotch Intellect. Henry T. Buckle. Ed. by H. J. Hanham & John Clive. LC 78-114958. (Classics of British Historical Literature Ser). 1970. lib. bdg. 22.50x o.s.i. (ISBN 0-226-07976-7). U of Chicago Pr.

On Seashore Far, a Green Oak Tower. Aleksandr Pushkin et al. 126p. 1983. 6.95 o.p. (ISBN 0-8285-2718-0, Pub. by Raduga Pubs USSR). Imported Pubns.

On Seeing Things. Bill Nelson. (Illus., Orig.). 1983. pap. 20.00 Ltd. signed ed. o.p. (ISBN 0-937596-07-8). Pentagram.

On Shame & the Search for Identity. Helen M. Lynd. LC 58-5921. 1970. pap. 2.95 o.p. (ISBN 0-15-681680-6, HB171, Harv). HarBraceJ.

On Shares: Ed Brown's Story. Jane Maguire. 224p. 1976. 9.95 o.p. (ISBN 0-393-07495-1). Norton.

On Sledge & Horseback to Outcast Siberian Lepers. Kate Marsden. (Century Travellers Ser.). 432p. 1986. pap. 11.95 o.p. (ISBN 0-7126-9461-7, Pub. by Century Hutchinson). David & Charles.

On Some Disputed Points in English Grammar see Society's Work.

On Stage for Christmas. Ed. by Sylvia E. Kamerman. LC 78-15517. (gr. 4-12). 1978. 13.95 o.p. (ISBN 0-8238-0226-4). Plays.

On Stage with Flip Wilson. Thomas Braun. (gr. 6-12). 1975. PLB 5.95 o.p. (ISBN 0-87191-489-1); pap. 3.95 o.p. (ISBN 0-89812-149-3). Creative Ed.

On Stage with John Denver. Meagon McGreane. (gr. 6-12). 1975. pap. 3.25 o.p. (ISBN 0-87191-104-3); pap. 3.95 o.p. (ISBN 0-89812-143-4). Creative Ed.

On Stories & Other Essays on Literature. C. S. Lewis. LC 81-48014. 144p. 1982. 9.95 o.p. (ISBN 0-15-169964-X). HarBraceJ.

On Tangled Paths. George MacDonald. Ed. by Dan Hamilton. 288p. 1987. pap. 5.95 o.p. (ISBN 0-89693-791-7). Victor Bks.

On Taste, Seventeen Thirty-Two to Seventeen Thirty-Five see Popeiana.

On Television: A Survival Guide for Media Interviews. Jack Hilton & Mary Knoblauch. (Illus.). 176p. 1980. 13.95 o.p. (ISBN 0-8144-5627-8). AMACOM.

On Testing the Freshness of Frozen Fish. pap. 10.00 o.p. (FN18, FNB). UNIPUB.

On the Banks of the Blanco. Bevon Varnon. 172p. 1984. 9.95 o.p. (ISBN 0-89015-436-8). Eakin Pr.

On the Banks of the Ganga: The Sojourn of Jews in Calcutta. Ezekiel N. Musleah. (Illus.). 555p. 1975. 12.95 o.p. (ISBN 0-8158-0313-3). Chris Mass.

On the Banks of the Wabash: A Photograph Album of Greater Terre Haute, 1900-1950. Ed. by Dorothy W. Jerse & Judith Calvert. LC 82-47955. (Midland Bks: No. 309). (Illus.). 128p. (Orig.). 1983. 20.00x o.p. (ISBN 0-253-19035-5); pap. 12.95 o.p. (ISBN 0-253-20309-0). Ind U Pr.
On the Beat: Policemen at Work. Barry Robinson & Martin J. Dain. LC 68-13816. (Curriculum Related Bks.). (Illus.). (gr. 2-4). 1968. 5.95 o.p. (ISBN 0-15-257892-7, HJ). HarBraceJ.
On the Causes of War, & the Means of Reducing Their Number see Paix et Liberte, ou le Budget Republicain.
On the Choice of a Mistress. Benjamin Franklin. 1976. 5.95 o.p. (ISBN 0-88088-187-9). Peter Pauper.
On the Classification of Frogs. William E. Duellman. (Occasional Papers: No. 42). 14p. 1975. 1.25 o.p. (ISBN 0-317-04852-X). U of KS Mus Nat Hist.
On the Composition of Paradise Lost. Allan H. Gilbert. 1966. lib. bdg. 17.00x o.p. (ISBN 0-374-93059-7, Octagon). Hippocrene Bks.
On the Crest of the Wave: Leader's Guide. Janet Hermansen. LC 83-8616. 64p. 1985. pap. 3.95 o.s.i. (ISBN 0-8307-1010-8, 6101974). Regal.
On the Cutting Edge: Reflections of a Minister in Suburbia. Raymond J. Pontier. 1978. 8.00 o.p. (ISBN 0-682-49166-7). Exposition-Phoenix.
On the Defense of the Comedy of Dante: Introduction & Summary. Giacopo Mazzoni. Tr. by Robert L. Montgomery from Ital. LC 83-3579. Orig. Title: Della Difesa della Comedia di Dante. 149p. 1983. 15.00 o.p. (ISBN 0-8130-0749-6). U Presses Fla.
On the Economic Theory of Socialism. Oskar Lange & Fred M. Taylor. 1956. pap. text ed. 3.95 o.p. (ISBN 0-07-036259-9). McGraw.
On the Edge of the Organization: The Role of the Outside Director. Anne Spencer. LC 82-11135. 137p. 1983. 39.95 o.p. (ISBN 0-471-90018-4, Pub. by Wiley-Interscience). Wiley.
On the Evolution of Manpower Statistics. J. Morton. 113p. 1969. pap. 0.50 o.p. (ISBN 0-911558-11-X). W E Upjohn.
On the Field of Honor: A History of the Knight's Cross Bearers, Vol. 2. John R. Angolia. (Illus.). 368p. 1981. 17.95 o.p. (ISBN 0-912138-21-1). Bender Pub CA.
On the Fringe of the Getto. Nathaniel Hudson. LC 86-81967. 150p. 1986. pap. 5.95 o.p. Authors Unltd.
On the Frontiers of Science: Strange Machines You Can Build. G. Harry Stine. LC 84-45632. (Illus.). 256p. 1985. pap. 8.95 o.p. (ISBN 0-689-11562-8, Atheneum). Macmillan.
On the Influence of Germanic Languages on Finnish & Lapp. Vilhelm Thomsen. LC 67-63427. (Uralic & Altaic Ser: Vol. 87). (Ger.). 1967. Repr. of 1870 ed. pap. text ed. 15.00x o.p. (ISBN 0-87750-035-5). Res Ctr Lang Semiotic.
On the Interpretation of Plato's Timaeus. John C. Wilson. Ed. by Leonardo Taran. Bd. with On the Platonist Doctrine of the Classical Review XVIII. LC 78-66577. (Ancient Philosophy Ser.). 160p. 1982. lib. bdg. 20.00 o.p. (ISBN 0-8240-9571-5). Garland Pub.
On the Island. Iain C. Smith. 1979. 16.95 o.p. (ISBN 0-575-02689-8, Pub. by Gollancz England). David & Charles.
On the Job. Ann A. Weaver & Margaret W. Hudson. 1965. pap. 2.50x o.p. (ISBN 0-88323-059-3, 157). Pendergrass Pub.
On the Knowledge of Good & Evil. Philip B. Rice. LC 75-8968. 299p. 1975. Repr. of 1955 ed. lib. bdg. 22.50x o.p. (ISBN 0-8371-8124-0, RIGE). Greenwood.
On the Lesson Tee: Basic Golf Fundamentals. Jack Grout. LC 81-86517. (Athletic Institute Bk.). (Illus.). 131p. (Orig.). 1982. pap. 6.95 o.p. (ISBN 0-8069-7622-5). Sterling.
On the Meaning & Future of the European Monetary System. Tom De Vries. LC 80-20510. (Essays in International Finance Ser.: No. 138). 1980. pap. text ed. 4.50x o.p. (ISBN 0-88165-045-5). Princeton U Int Finan Econ.
On the Meaning of Victory: Essays on Strategy. Edward N. Luttwak. LC 85-26145. 335p. 1986. 18.45 o.p. (ISBN 0-671-61089-9). S&S.
On the Meaning of Victory: Essays on Strategy. Edward N. Luttwak. 320p. 1987. pap. 9.95 o.s.i. (ISBN 0-671-63317-1, Touchstone Bks). S&S.
On the Mesa. John Nichols. LC 85-26190. (Illus.). 208p. 1986. 7.00 o.p. (ISBN 0-87905-220-1). Gibbs Smith Pub.
On the Music of the North American Indians (1976) bilingual ed. Theodore Baker. Ed. by Frank Harrison. (Source Materials & Studies in Ethnomusicology: Vol. 9). (Illus., Eng. & Ger.). pap. 40.00 o.p. (ISBN 0-685-85950-9). E J Brill USA.
On the Other Side of Anger. Drew Davis. LC 74-7618. 1978. pap. 2.95 o.p. (ISBN 0-8042-1047-0, John Knox). Westminster John Knox.
On the Other Side of the Gate. Yuri Suhl. 1976. pap. 1.25 o.p. (ISBN 0-380-00854-8, 31237). Avon.
On the Periphery. Veronica Forrest-Thompson. (Illus.). 1976. pap. 4.00 o.p. (ISBN 0-685-83036-5, Pub. by St Edns). Small Pr Dist.
On the Place of the Progressive Palatalization of Velars in the Relative Chronology of Slavic. Robert Channon. 57p. 1972. 4.95 o.p. (ISBN 90-279-3450-9). Mouton.
On the Platonist Doctrine of the Classical Review XVIII see On the Interpretation of Plato's Timaeus.
On the Point of My Pen: The Best of Cummings. Michael Cummings. (Illus.). 240p. 1986. 19.95 o.p. (ISBN 0-903852-69-1, Pub. by Milestone Pubns UK). Seven Hills Bk Dists.
On the Pointwise Convergence of Fourier Series. C. J. Mozzochi. LC 79-162399. (Lecture Notes in Mathematics: Vol. 199). 1971. pap. 9.00 o.p. (ISBN 0-387-05475-8). Springer-Verlag.
On the Potter's Wheel: The Diaries of Heber C. Kimball. Heber C. Kimball. Intro. by Stanley B. Kimball. LC 87-23421. (Illus.). 224p. 1988. 50.00 o.p. (ISBN 0-941214-60-5). Signature Bks.
On the Prehistory of Marriage. Josef Kohler. Ed. by R. H. Barnes. LC 74-11626. (Classics in Anthropology Ser). x, 298p. 1979. pap. text ed. 12.50x o.s.i. (ISBN 0-226-45025-2, Midway Reprint). U of Chicago Pr.
On the Probable Fall in the Value of Gold. Michel Chevalier. Ed. by Richard Cobden. LC 68-28619. Repr. of 1859 ed. lib. bdg. 35.00x o.p. (ISBN 0-8371-0045-3, CHPF). Greenwood.
On the Problem of Plateau-Subharmonic Functions. T. Rado. LC 71-160175. (Illus.). 1971. pap. 22.50 o.p. (ISBN 0-387-05479-0). Springer-Verlag.
On the Range: Cooking Western Style. Marian Pfommer. LC 80-18380. (Illus.). 112p. (gr. 3-7). 1981. PLB 8.95 o.p. (ISBN 0-689-30826-4, Atheneum). Macmillan.
On the Rise. Karl S. McDaniel. 40p. 1986. 6.75 o.p. (ISBN 0-8062-3013-4). Carlton.
On the Royal Road: A Decade of Photographing the Royal Family. Tim Graham. (Illus.). 160p. 1984. 19.45 o.p. (ISBN 0-316-32300-4). Little.
On the Run. Eric Dickerson & Steve Delsohn. (Illus.). 160p. (Orig.). 1986. pap. 7.95 o.p. (ISBN 0-8092-4973-1). Contemp Bks.
On the Shores of the Mediterranean. Eric Newby. (Illus.). 320p. 1985. 19.95 o.p. (ISBN 0-316-60422-4). Little.
On the Side of Truth: An Evaluation with Readings. new ed. George Shuster. Ed. by Vincent P. Lannie. LC 73-11564. 352p. 1974. text ed. 24.95 o.p. (ISBN 0-268-00520-6). U of Notre Dame Pr.
On the Social Contract & Discourse on the Origin of Inequality & Discourse on Political Economy & Rousseau's Notes to Discourse on the Origin of Inequality. Jean-Jacques Rousseau. Tr. by Donald A. Cress from Fr. LC 83-4301. (HPC Philosophical Classics Ser.). 208p. 1983. lib. bdg. 15.00 o.p. (ISBN 0-915145-57-X); pap. text ed. 5.95 o.p. (ISBN 0-915145-56-1). Hackett Pub.
On the Socio-Political Fault Line. Bernard M. Bane. 56p. 1986. pap. 5.00 o.s.i. (ISBN 0-930924-23-1). BMB Pub Co.
On the Study & Difficulties of Mathematics. 2nd ed. Augustus De Morgan. 295p. 19.95 o.p. (ISBN 0-87548-187-6). Open Court.
On the Subject of Tongues: From the New Testament. Don Welborn. 56p. pap. 0.50 o.p. (ISBN 0-937396-48-6). Walterick Pubs.
On the Take. William Riordan. (Orig.). 1976. pap. 1.25 o.p. (ISBN 0-685-64015-9, LB342ZK, Pub. by Leisure Bks CT). Dorchester Pub Co.
On the Theory & Practice of Voice Identification. National Research Council. 1979. pap. text ed. 7.50x o.p. (ISBN 0-309-02873-6). Natl Acad Pr.
On the Thermodynamics of Elastic Materials & of Reacting Fluid Mixtures. M. E. Gurtin. (CISM - International Centre for Mechanical Sciences, Courses & Lectures: Vol. 75). (Illus.). 47p. 1975. pap. 7.10 o.p. (ISBN 0-387-81178-8). Springer-Verlag.
On the Viability of 1300 Operation in the MX-C3 Program. Robert L. Gallawa. 1980. 50.00 o.p. (ISBN 0-686-39231-0). Info Gatekeepers.
On the Volterra & Other Nonlinear Models of Interacting Populations. N. S. Goel et al. (Reviews of Modern Physics Monographs). 1971. 43.00 o.p. (ISBN 0-12-287450-1). Acad Pr.
On the Wasteland. Ruth M. Arthur. (Illus.). 176p. (gr. 4-8). 1975. 5.95 o.p. (ISBN 0-689-30473-0, Atheneum). Macmillan.
On the Way! David R. Currie. LC 81-69403. 1982. pap. 3.95 o.p. (ISBN 0-8054-5336-9, 4253-36). Broadman.
On the Way Home. Sandol S. Warburg. LC 73-6578. (Illus.). 144p. (gr. 5 up). 1973. 4.95 o.p. (ISBN 0-395-17510-0). HM.
On the Way to the Future: A Christian View of Eschatology in the Light of Current Trends in Religion, Philosophy & Science. Hans Schwarz. LC 78-176479. 1972. 6.95 o.p. (ISBN 0-8066-1208-8, 10-4760, Augsburg). Augsburg Fortress.
On the Way to the Future: A Christian View of Eschatology in the Light of Current Trends in Religion, Philosophy, & Science. rev. ed. Hans Schwarz. LC 78-176479. 294p. 1979. pap. 11.95 o.p. (ISBN 0-8066-1731-4, 10-4761, Augsburg). Augsburg Fortress.
On the Winds of Love. Lori Leigh. 384p. 1986. pap. 3.95 o.p. (ISBN 0-380-75072-4). Avon.
On Third Thought. Deda R. Gamble. LC 86-71786. 120p. (Orig.). 1987. pap. 6.95 o.p. (ISBN 1-55666-003-0). Authors Unltd.
On This Rock. Lloyd Palmer. LC 66-20217. 328p. 1967. (ISBN 0-8022-1259-X). Philos Lib.
On Tobacco Road: Basketball in North Carolina. Smith Barrier. LC 83-80743. (Illus.). 208p. (Orig.). 1983. pap. 10.95 o.p. (ISBN 0-88011-175-5). Scribner.
On Tour. Mel Arrighi. LC 79-7315. 352p. 1979. 10.95 o.p. (ISBN 0-689-10984-9, Atheneum). Macmillan.
On Trial: Being a Summary of Eyewitness Reports Concerning the Early Church. Luke the Physician. LC 82-60668. (Illus.). 120p. (gr. 4-8). 1982. pap. 1.65 o.p. (ISBN 0-87973-648-8, 648). Our Sunday Visitor.
On Trial: The Soviet State vs. "Abram Tertz" & "Nikolai Arzhak" Andrei D. Siniavskii. Ed. by Max Hayward. LC 80-16756. vi, 310p. 1980. Repr. of 1967 ed. lib. bdg. 35.00x o.p. (ISBN 0-313-22457-9, HAOT). Greenwood.
On We Go, Bk. II. Margaret Dee. 1953. 1.75 o.p. (ISBN 0-913650-33-1). CPP Belwin.
On Wings of Eagles. Ken Follett. 664p. 1984. lib. bdg. 16.95 o.p. (ISBN 0-8161-3642-4, Large Print Bks). G K Hall.
On with the Shoe. Jeff MacNelly. LC 85-81673. (Illus.). 1982. pap. 5.95 o.p. (ISBN 0-03-061656-5, Owl Bks). H Holt & Co.
On Writing, Editing, & Publishing: Essays Explicative & Hortatory. Jacques Barzun. LC 71-161602. 1971. pap. 1.50 o.s.i. (ISBN 0-226-03848-3, P430, Phoen). U of Chicago Pr.
On Your Own. Pearson et al. (Gregg McGraw-Hill Series for Independent Living). (Illus.). 1977. text ed. 12.00 o.p. (ISBN 0-07-049051-1). McGraw.
Onawa Bestiary: An Opinionated Survey with Digressions. Henry D. Sherrerd, Jr. (Illus.). 176p. (Orig.). 1987. pap. 9.90 o.p. (ISBN 0-916153-04-5). Ten-Thirty Pr.
Once a Month. Katharina Dalton. LC 79-88572. 1979. pap. 8.45 o.p. (ISBN 0-89793-005-3). Hunter Hse.
Once a Month. 2nd ed. Katharina Dalton. LC 83-81699. (Illus.). 256p. 1983. pap. 8.45 o.p. (ISBN 0-89793-030-4). Hunter Hse.
Once a Warrior King: Memories of an Officer in Vietnam. D. Donovan. 384p. 1985. text ed. 15.95 o.p. (ISBN 0-07-017592-6). McGraw.
Once a Week. A. A. Milne. LC 77-91380. (Short Story Index in Reprint Ser.). 1978. Repr. of 1925 ed. 18.75x o.p. (ISBN 0-8486-5002-6). Roth Pub Inc.
Once & Future Film: British Cinema in the 70's & 80's. Alexander Walker. (Orig.). 1985. 25.00x o.p. (ISBN 0-413-53540-1, 9416); pap. 9.95x o.p. (ISBN 0-413-53550-9, 9462). Heinemann Ed.
Once at the Weary Why. Mildred Lawrence. LC 76-84773. (gr. 5-8). 1969. 5.25 o.p. (ISBN 0-15-257880-3, HJ). HarBraceJ.
Once in a Lifetime, You Can't Take It With You, The Man Who Came to Dinner: Three Plays. George S. Kaufman & Moss Hart. 1988. pap. 8.95 o.p. (ISBN 0-394-17744-4, B443, BC); pap. 10.95 o.p. (ISBN 0-8021-5064-0). Grove.
Once in Golconda: A True Dream of Wall Street, 1920-1938. John Brooks. 1981. 15.95 o.p. (ISBN 0-393-01375-8). Norton.
Once More from the Middle: A Philosophical Anthropology. James F. Sheridan, Jr. LC 72-85543. ix, 157p. 1973. 10.00x o.p. (ISBN 0-8214-0108-4). Ohio U Pr.
Once More the Hawks. Max Hennessy. LC 83-45492. 256p. 1984. 11.95 o.p. (ISBN 0-689-11452-4, Atheneum). Macmillan.
Once There Were Dragons. John Mole. LC 79-64262. (Illus.). (gr. 3-7). 1979. 5.95 o.p. (ISBN 0-233-97112-2). Andre Deutsch.
Once to Every Man. William S. Coffin. LC 77-76547. 1977. 12.95 o.p. (ISBN 0-689-10811-7, Atheneum). Macmillan.
Once upon a Christmas. Oxtoby & Sandison. (ps up). 1986. 14.95 o.p. (ISBN 0-8120-5755-4). Barron.
Once upon a Christmas Time. Thyra F. Bjorn. 1964. 5.95 o.p. (ISBN 0-03-047195-8). H Holt & Co.
Once upon a Friendship. Jane Sorenson. (Jennifer Bks.). 144p. (gr. 5-8). 1985. 2.95 o.p. (ISBN 0-87239-932-X, 2982). Standard Pub.
Once upon a Test: Three Light Tales of Love. Vivian Vande Velde. Ed. by Ann Fay. LC 84-17283. (Illus.). 32p. (gr. 4up). 1984. PLB 8.25 o.p. (ISBN 0-8075-6070-7). A Whitman.
Once upon an Earth. Denton Cantwell. LC 85-73041. 144p. (Orig.). 1986. pap. 6.95 o.p. (ISBN 0-86666-243-X): Authors Unltd.
Once upon the Future: A Woman's Guide to Tomorrow's Technology. Jan Zimmerman. 224p. 1986. pap. 7.95 o.p. (ISBN 0-86358-009-2, 80092, Pandora Pr). Routledge Chapman & Hall.
Once We Were Men. Gordon Nimse. 224p. 1985. pap. 2.95 o.p. (ISBN 0-931773-23-7). Critics Choice Paper.
Onchocerciasis in Zaire. Ed. by Frederick C. Rodger. 1977. 81.00 o.p. (ISBN 0-08-020619-0). Pergamon.
Onco-Developmental Gene Expression. Ed. by William H. Fishman & Stewart Sell. 1976. 98.00 o.p. (ISBN 0-12-257660-8). Acad Pr.
Oncogenesis & Other Pathological Results of Herpesvirus Infection II. Jay A. Levy et al. LC 74-3205. 206p. 1974. text ed. 22.50x o.p. (ISBN 0-8422-7156-2). Irvington.
Oncogenesis & Other Pathological Results of Herpesvirus Infection I. Daniel Miller et al. LC 74-3205. 229p. 1974. text ed. 24.50x o.p. (ISBN 0-8422-7155-4). Irvington.
Oncogenic Viruses & Host Cell Genes. Ed. by Yoji Ikawa & Tadeshi Odaka. LC 78-31253. 1979. 55.00 o.p. (ISBN 0-12-370650-5). Acad Pr.
Oncology. Ed. by Jerome B. Block. LC 81-318. 364p. 1982. 42.95 o.p. (ISBN 0-471-09511-7). Krieger.
One-Act Plays by Modern Authors. Ed. by Helen L. Cohen. LC 34-8319. 1934. 8.95 o.p. (ISBN 0-15-169347-1). HarBraceJ.
One-Act Plays of Today: Second Series. Ed. by James W. Marriott. LC 79-50028. (One-Act Plays in Reprint Ser.). 1980. Repr. of 1925 ed. 24.75x o.p. (ISBN 0-8486-2051-8). Roth Pub Inc.
One America: The History, Contributions, & Present Problems of Our Racial & National Minorities. Francis J. Brown. LC 72-111566. 1971. Repr. of 1952 ed. lib. bdg. 34.00x o.p. (ISBN 0-8371-4587-2, BMR&). Greenwood.
One American Must Die: A Hostage's Personal Account of the Hijacking of Flight 847. Kurt Carlson. (Illus.). 224p. 1986. 13.95 o.p. (ISBN 0-86553-161-7). Congdon & Weed.
One & Other Poems. Thomas Kinsella. 1979. pap. 8.95 o.p. (ISBN 0-85105-341-6, Pub. by Colin Smythe Ltd Britain). Dufour.
One April Vacation. Ruth Wallace-Brodeur. LC 81-3482. 96p. (gr. 3-7). 1981. 9.95 o.s.i. (ISBN 0-689-50211-7, M K McElderry). Macmillan.
One Arrow, One Life: Zen, Archery & Daily Life. Kenneth Kushner. (Illus.). 160p. 1988. pap. 10.95 o.p. (ISBN 1-85063-080-1). Routledge Chapman & Hall.
One Bad Thing about Birthdays. David R. Collin. LC 80-23104. (Let Me Read Ser.). (Illus.). 32p. (ps-3). 1981. 6.95 o.p. (ISBN 0-15-258288-6, HJ). HarBraceJ.
One Bad Thing about Birthdays. David R. Collin. LC 80-23104. (Let Me Read Ser.). (Illus.). 32p. (ps-3). 1981. pap. 2.95 o.p. (ISBN 0-15-258289-4, VoyB). HarBraceJ.
One Better. William Francis McElroy, Jr. 1977. 5.00 o.p. (ISBN 0-682-48686-8). Exposition-Phoenix.
One Big Bed. John Krich. 368p. 1986. text ed. 16.95 o.p. (ISBN 0-07-035408-1). McGraw.
One Billion. Jay Mathews & Linda Mathews. 448p. 1985. pap. 4.95 o.s.i. (ISBN 0-345-29895-0). Ballantine.
One-Burner Cookbook. Mary B. Jung. 256p. 1986. 12.95 o.p. (ISBN 0-02-009850-2, Collier). Macmillan.
One Country or Two? Ed. by R. M. Burns. 1971. 8.25 o.p. (ISBN 0-7735-0104-5, McGill Canada); pap. 4.00 o.p. (ISBN 0-7735-0176-2, McGill Canada). U of Toronto Pr.
One Culture. W. H. Davenport. LC 70-106054. 1971. 20.00 o.p. (ISBN 0-08-016322-X). Pergamon.
One Day at a Time. Lauri J. Shewell. 1977. pap. 2.95 o.p. (ISBN 0-89036-097-9). Hawkes Pub Inc.
One Day at School. Ida Luttrell. LC 83-18341. (Let Me Read Ser.). (Illus.). 32p. (ps-3). 1984. pap. 4.95 o.p. (ISBN 0-15-258314-9, VoyB). HarBraceJ.
One Day at School. Ida Luttrell. LC 83-18341. (Let-Me-Read Ser.). (Illus.). 32p. (ps-3). 1984. 9.95 o.p. (ISBN 0-15-258313-0, HJ). HarBraceJ.
One Day in Aztec Mexico. G. B. Kirtland. LC 63-7897. (Illus.). (gr. 4-6). 1963. 4.50 o.p. (ISBN 0-15-258381-5, HJ). HarBraceJ.
One Day in Our World. Associated Press Editors. 224p. 1986. pap. 14.95 o.p. (ISBN 0-380-89940-X). Avon.
One Day U. S. A. A Self Portrait of America's Cities. Ed. by Richard Carver & Judith Carver. (Illus.). 256p. 1986. 35.00 o.p. (ISBN 0-8109-0837-9). Abrams.

One Day You'll Go. Sheila Schwartz. 160p. (Orig.). (YA) (gr. 7 up). 1981. pap. 1.95 o.p. (Wildfire). Scholastic Inc.

One Deadly Summer. Sebastien Japrisot. Tr. by Alan Sheridan. LC 79-3356. (Helen & Kurt Wolff Bk.). 288p. 1980. 9.95 o.p. (ISBN 0-15-169381-1). HarBraceJ.

One-Dimensional Cohen-Macaulay Rings. E. Matlis. (Lecture Notes in Mathematics Ser.: Vol. 327). xii, 157p. 1973. pap. 14.00 o.p. (ISBN 0-387-06327-7). Springer-Verlag.

One-Dimensional Compressible Flow. M. Danenshyar. 1977. 45.00 o.p. (ISBN 0-08-020414-7); pap. 45.00 o.p. (ISBN 0-08-020413-9). Pergamon.

One-Dimensional Conductors: Proceedings. GPS Summer School, Saarbruecken, F. R. Germany, Jul 10-12, 1974. Ed. by H. G. Schuster. LC 74-30060. (Lecture Notes in Physics Ser: Vol. 34). x, 371p. 1975. pap. 19.00 o.p. (ISBN 0-387-07024-9). Springer-Verlag.

One-Dish Meals. Bon Appetit Magazine Editors. LC 85-24004. (Cooking with Bon Appetit). (Illus.). 144p. 12.95 o.p. (ISBN 0-89535-171-4). Knapp Pr.

One Dollar League. Jim Byrne. 288p. 1987. 17.95 o.p. (ISBN 0-13-331760-9). P-H.

One Doubles Enough. Eric Bowles. 176p. 1986. 9.95 o.p. (ISBN 0-8062-3028-2). Carlton.

One Dragon to Another. Ned Delaney. LC 75-33250. (Illus.). 48p. (gr. k-3). 1976. reinforced bdg. 6.95 o.p. (ISBN 0-395-24209-6). HM.

One Eyed Merchants. Kathleen Timms. 236p. 1987. pap. 2.95 o.p. (ISBN 1-55547-173-0). Critics Choice Paper.

One Fairy Story Too Many: The Brothers Grimm & Their Tales. John M. Ellis. LC 83-1193. 219p. 1983. lib. bdg. 17.50x o.s.i. (ISBN 0-226-20546-0). U of Chicago Pr.

One Family under God. Ed. by Daughters of St. Paul. (Divine Master Ser.). (Orig.). 1968. 3.00 o.s.i. (ISBN 0-8198-0109-7); pap. 2.00 o.s.i. (ISBN 0-8198-0110-0). Dghtrs St Paul.

One Fat Englishman. Kingsley Amis. LC 64-11532. 1964. 4.50 o.p. (ISBN 0-15-169400-1). HarBraceJ.

One Fearful Yellow Eye. John D. MacDonald. (Travis McGee Ser.). 1985. pap. 3.50 o.p. (ISBN 0-449-12933-0, GM). Fawcett.

One Fine Day. Leon Arden. 1981. 10.95 o.p. (ISBN 0-393-01423-1). Norton.

One Flew Over the Cuckoo's Nest. Ken Kesey. 48p. (Orig.). 1988. pap. 9.95 o.p. (ISBN 1-55651-685-1); audiocassette tape incl. o.p. (ISBN 1-55651-686-X). Cram Cassettes.

One for the Gods. Gordon Merrick. 1976. pap. 4.95 o.p. (ISBN 0-380-01366-5). Avon.

One for the Money. Dick Belsky. 191p. 1985. 14.95 o.s.i. (ISBN 0-89733-148-6). Academy Chi Pubs.

One for the Road: A Play. Harold Pinter. (Illus.). 80p. 1986. 15.00 o.s.i. (ISBN 0-394-54575-3). Grove.

One Good Death Deserves Another. Ritchie Perry. LC 76-54326. 1977. 6.95 o.p. (ISBN 0-395-25295-4). HM.

One Great Fellowship Travels of a Global Minister. Allan W. Lee. 1974. pap. 2.50 o.p. (ISBN 0-682-48095-9, Banner). Exposition-Phoenix.

One Hand Shaking: A California Campaign Diary. Lowell Darling. LC 79-3345. 224p. 1980. 10.95 o.p. (ISBN 0-15-169516-4). HarBraceJ.

One Hand Shaking: A California Campaign Diary. Lowell Darling. LC 79-3345. 224p. 1980. pap. 5.95 o.p. (ISBN 0-15-668747-X, Harv). HarBraceJ.

One Holy Passion: The Consuming Thirst to Know God. R. C. Sproul. LC 87-1617. 192p. 1987. 13.95 o.p. (ISBN 0-8407-5528-7). Oliver-Nelson.

One Hundred & Fifty Years of Modern Britain. S. Hopewell. 1965. 3.15 o.p. (ISBN 0-08-011254-4). Pergamon.

One Hundred & One Great Golf Jokes' & Stories. McDougal. 1.95 o.p. (ISBN 0-8065-0326-2, Pub. by Citadel Pr). Carol Pub Group.

One Hundred & One Ideas to Help You Sell More Typesetting. Wade Dowdle. (Illus.). 147p. 28.50 o.p. (ISBN 0-318-03249-X). Print Indus Am.

One Hundred & One Parsi Recipes. Jeroo Mehta. (Illus.). 146p. 1975. comb. bound 4.95 o.s.i. (ISBN 0-88253-438-6). Ind-US Inc.

One Hundred & One Practical Activities for Use in Classes of Pupils Who Are Retarded. Alpha Brown. 1970. pap. 3.25x o.p. (ISBN 0-88323-058-5, 156). Pendergrass Pub.

One Hundred & One Ranch. Ellsworth Collings & Alma England. LC 73-167774. (Illus.). 255p. 1937. 5.95 o.p. (ISBN 0-8061-0986-6); pap. 5.95 o.p. U of Okla Pr.

One Hundred & One Select Dream Houses. Andy Lang. LC 82-2964. (Illus.). 224p. 1982. pap. 9.95 o.p. (ISBN 0-8437-3243-1). Hammond Inc.

One Hundred & One Tips & Hints for Your Boat. Jacques Damour. Tr. by Jeremy Howard-Williams from Fr. (Illus.). 1981. 13.95 o.p. (ISBN 0-393-03262-0). Norton.

One Hundred & One Uses of a Condom. Russell Jones. (Illus.). 96p. 1988. pap. 4.95 o.p. (ISBN 0-8069-6832-X). Sterling.

One Hundred & One Ways to Protect Your Job. G. Demare & Joanne Summerfield. 1984. text ed. 15.95 o.p. (ISBN 0-07-016289-1). McGraw.

One Hundred & Twenty Year Diet: How to Double Your Vital Years. Roy Walford. 400p. 1987. 18.45 o.s.i. (ISBN 0-671-46677-1). S&S.

One-hundred Best IBM Utilities. Mark R. Sawusch. 230p. 1988. 24.95 o.p. (ISBN 0-8306-9606-7, 3006); pap. 16.95 o.p. (ISBN 0-8306-9306-8). TAB Bks.

One Hundred Billion Dollar Market: How to Do Business with the U. S. Government. Herman R. Holtz. 1982. 10.95 o.p. (ISBN 0-8144-7570-1). AMACOM.

One Hundred Dollar Misunderstanding. Robert Gover. LC 62-20506. 256p. 1981. pap. 2.95 o.p. (ISBN 0-394-17764-9, B448, BC). Grove.

One Hundred Eleven & Garden Projects-from Boxes & Bins to Tables & Tools. Percy W. Blandford. (Illus.). 416p. 1986. 25.95 o.p. (ISBN 0-8306-0344-1, 2644); pap. 16.60 o.p. (ISBN 0-8306-0444-8). Tab Bks.

One Hundred Eleven Proven Techniques & Strategies for Getting the Job Interview. Burdette Bostwick. LC 80-26454. 285p. 1981. 16.95 o.p. (ISBN 0-471-07762-3, Pub. by Wiley-Interscience). Wiley.

One Hundred Fabulicious Drinks. Tyronne Oliver. 5.95 o.p. (ISBN 0-918544-44-0). Wimmer Bks.

One Hundred Fifty Progressive Exercises for Melodic Dictation. Maurice Whitney. (For use with Backgrounds in Music Theory). 1954. pap. 2.95 o.p. (ISBN 0-02-872880-7). Schirmer Bks.

One Hundred Fifty-Two House Plans. Home Planners, Inc. Staff. 128p. 1984. pap. 3.95 o.p. (ISBN 0-918894-42-5). Home Planners.

One Hundred Forty-Four Home Designs for All Americans. Home Planners Staff. 128p. 1985. pap. 2.95 o.p. (ISBN 0-918894-48-4). Home Planners.

One Hundred Great Kings, Queens & Rulers of the World. Ed. by John Canning. LC 68-23429. 1978. pap. 7.95 o.s.i. (ISBN 0-8008-5776-3). Taplinger.

One Hundred Great Science Fiction Short Short Stories. Ed. by Isaac Asimov et al. LC 77-76221. 1978. 8.95 o.s.i. (ISBN 0-385-13044-9). Doubleday.

One Hundred Greatest Golf Courses--& Then Some. Ed. by Golf Digest Editors. William H. Davis. LC 82-81714. 280p. 1982. 30.95 o.p. (ISBN 0-914178-57-1). Golf Digest.

One Hundred Hikes in the North Cascades. Ira Spring & Harvey Manning. (One Hundred Hikes Ser.). (Illus.). 240p. (Orig.). 1985. pap. 9.95 o.p. (ISBN 0-89886-102-0). Mountaineers.

One Hundred Libraries Statistical Survey, 1984. Academic Library Statistics Task Force Staff. 92p. 1985. pap. text ed. 12.00 o.p. (ISBN 0-8389-6951-8). Assn Coll & Res Libs.

One Hundred Luscious Diet Drinks. Millicent Brower & Naomi Koshkin. 112p. 1983. pap. 6.75 o.p. (ISBN 0-671-46019-6, Fireside). S&S.

One Hundred One Best Jazz Albums: A History of Jazz on Records. Len Lyons. 1980. 17.95 o.p. (ISBN 0-688-03720-8). Morrow.

One-Hundred One Experiments for the Young Scientist. Dave Prochnow. (Illus.). 240p. 1988. 19.95 o.p. (ISBN 0-8306-0252-6); pap. 12.60 o.p. (ISBN 0-8306-2952-1). TAB Bks.

One Hundred One Language Arts Activities. Trudy Aarons & Francine Koelsch. (Illus.). 134p. 1979. pap. text ed. 11.95 o.p. (ISBN 0-88450-795-5, 3053-B). Communication Skill.

One Hundred One Math Activities. Trudy Aarons & Francine Koelsch. 118p. 1981. pap. text ed. 11.95 o.p. (ISBN 0-88450-740-8, 2065-B). Communication Skill.

One Hundred One Microprocessor Software & Hardware Projects. Frank P. Tedeschi & Gary Kueck. (Illus.). 294p. 16.95 o.p. (ISBN 0-8306-0030-2); pap. 9.95 o.p. (ISBN 0-8306-1333-1, 1333). TAB Bks.

One Hundred One Model Railroad Layouts. Paul Garrison. (Illus.). 160p. (Orig.). 1983. 17.95 o.p. (ISBN 0-8306-0514-2, 1514); pap. 11.15 o.p. (ISBN 0-8306-1514-8). TAB Bks.

One Hundred One Patriotic Poems. 186p. 1986. leatherette 7.95 o.p. (ISBN 0-8092-4930-8). Contemp Bks.

One-Hundred One Practical Uses for Propane Torches. Robert Brightman. (Illus.). 1978. 6.95 o.p. (ISBN 0-8306-9976-7); pap. 5.95 o.p. (ISBN 0-8306-1030-8, 1030). TAB Bks.

One Hundred One Programming Surprises & Tricks for Your Commodore 64 Computer. David L. Heiserman. (Illus.). 208p. (Orig.). 1985. 18.95 o.p. (ISBN 0-8306-0951-2, 1951); pap. 11.60 o.p. (ISBN 0-8306-1951-8). TAB Bks.

One Hundred One Projects, Plans & Ideas for the High-Tech Household. Julie Knott & Dave Prochnow. (Illus.). 352p. 1986. 24.95 o.p. (ISBN 0-8306-0342-5, 2642); pap. 16.60 o.p. (ISBN 0-8306-0442-1). Tab Bks.

One Hundred One Reading Activities. Trudy Aarons & Francine Koelsch. 125p. (ps-4). 1982. pap. text ed. 11.95 o.p. (ISBN 0-88450-833-1, 2079-B). Communication Skill.

One Hundred One Saving Secrets Your Phone Company Won't Tell You. Harry Newton. 96p. (Orig.). 1983. pap. text ed. 7.95 o.p. (ISBN 0-936648-15-5). Telecom Lib.

One Hundred One Science Activities. Trudy Aarons & Francine Koelsch. 156p. (Orig.). 1981. pap. text ed. 11.95 o.p. (ISBN 0-88450-879-X, 7018-B). Communication Skill.

One Hundred One Secrets of Gourmet Chefs. Jacqueline Killeen. LC 75-10394. (Illus., Orig.). 1969. pap. 4.95 o.s.i. (ISBN 0-912238-01-1, One Hund One Prods). Ortho.

One Hundred One Uses for an Unused Home Computer. Frank Saidis. (Illus.). 112p. 1986. pap. 4.95 o.p. (ISBN 0-934601-09-7). Peachtree Pubs.

One Hundred One Ways to Answer the Request: Would You Please Put Out That Cigar! Warren Leight et al. (Illus.). 128p. 1987. pap. 5.95 o.s.i. (ISBN 0-671-63500-X, Fireside). S&S.

One Hundred One Ways to Market Your Books: For Publishers & Authors. John Kremer. LC 86-7995. (Illus.). 304p. (Orig.). 1986. 19.95 o.p. (ISBN 0-912411-08-2); pap. 14.95 o.p. (ISBN 0-912411-09-0). Ad-Lib.

One Hundred Percent Natural, Purely Organic, Cholesterol-Free, Megavitamin, Low Carbohydrate Nutrition Hoax. Elizabeth M. Whelan & Fredrick J. Stare. LC 82-71260. 320p. 1984. pap. 7.95 o.p. (ISBN 0-689-70680-4, 320, Atheneum). Macmillan.

One Hundred Plays for Children. Ed. by A. S. Burack. (gr. 1-6). 1970. 15.95 o.p. (ISBN 0-8238-0002-4). Plays.

One Hundred Questions in Auditing with Suggested Answers for Accountancy Examinees. D. Kirkby. 1968. text ed. 18.00 o.p. (ISBN 0-08-012901-3); pap. text ed. 9.25 o.p. (ISBN 0-08-012900-5). Pergamon.

One Hundred Selected Poems. e. e. Cummings. (Orig.). (YA) (gr. 9 up). 1959. pap. 5.95 o.p. (ISBN 0-394-17219-1, E190, Ever). Grove.

One Hundred Seventeen Practical IC Projects You Can Build. R. H. Warring & Delton T. Horn. (Illus.). 196p. 1986. 16.95 o.p. (ISBN 0-8306-0445-6); pap. 10.60 o.p. (ISBN 0-8306-2645-X, NO. 2645). TAB Bks.

One Hundred Seventy-Two Most Popular Homes. Home Planners, Inc. Staff. 128p. 1985. pap. 2.95 o.p. (ISBN 0-918894-47-6). Home Planners.

One Hundred Short Cases for the MRCP. K. Gupta. LC 82-23477. 144p. 1983. pap. 12.95 o.p. (ISBN 0-412-25230-9, NO. 6797, Pub. by Chapman & Hall). Routledge Chapman & Hall.

One Hundred Sixty-Six Most Popular Homes. Home Planners, Inc. Staff. 112p. 1984. 2.95 o.p. (ISBN 0-918894-37-9). Home Planners.

One Hundred Ten Super Songs of the Super Stars: All Organ Edition. 1977. pap. 8.95 o.p. (ISBN 0-89328-018-6). Lorenz Corp.

One Hundred Terrific Ideas of QC People That Made Management Hundred Percent Happy. 1988. 12.85 o.p. Media Intl Promo.

One Hundred Thirty Distinctive Home Designs. 112p. 1984. pap. 2.75 o.p. (ISBN 0-918894-39-5). Home Planners.

One Hundred Thirty Feet Down: Handbook for Hydronauts. Hank Frey & Shaney Frey. LC 61-7687. (Illus.). 1961. 6.95 o.p. (ISBN 0-15-169623-3). HarBraceJ.

One Hundred Thousand Dollars a Year Selling Real Estate! The 5000 System. Jess Mason. 160p. 1981. 12.50 o.p. (ISBN 0-682-49728-2, Banner). Exposition-Phoenix.

One Hundred Three Hikes in Southwestern British Columbia. 2nd ed. Mary Macaree & David Macaree. LC 80-17573. (Illus.). 224p. (Orig.). 1980. pap. 9.95 o.p. (ISBN 0-916890-96-1). Mountaineers.

One Hundred Twelve Traditional & Contemporary Family Homes. Home Planners, Inc. Staff. 96p. 1983. 2.95 o.p. (ISBN 0-918894-35-2). Home Planners.

One Hundred Twenty-Eight Home Plans for Varying Building Budgets. (Illus.). 128p. 1986. pap. 2.95 o.p. (ISBN 0-918894-57-3). Home Planners.

One Hundred Twenty-Five Masterpieces from the Collection of the Albright-Knox Art Gallery. LC 86-14092. (Illus.). 264p. 1987. 40.00 o.p. (ISBN 0-8478-0786-X). Rizzoli Intl.

One Hundred Twenty-Five Ways to Cut Your Business Health Costs. Judy Haberek. Ed. by Robert Varela. LC 85-54175. 285p. pap. cancelled o.s.i. (ISBN 0-914176-28-5); pap. cancelled o.s.i. Wash Busn Info.

One Hundred Twenty-Three Questions & Answers: From the Edgar Cayce Readings. rev. ed. Gladys D. Turner & Mae G. St. Clair. 58p. 1974. pap. 3.95 o.p. (ISBN 0-87604-073-3). ARE Pr.

One Hundred Two Home Plans. 96p. 1984. pap. 2.95 o.p. (ISBN 0-317-65101-3). Home Planners.

One Hundred White Horses. Mildred Lawrence. LC 53-7866. (Illus.). (gr. 4-6). 1953. 5.25 o.p. (ISBN 0-15-258675-X, HJ). HarBraceJ.

One Hundred Years of Dance Posters. Jack Rennert & Walter Terry. 1975. pap. 8.45 o.p. (ISBN 0-380-00485-2, 25874, Flare). Avon.

One Hundred Years of Geosciences in Romania. Ed. by V. Mihailescu. 1975. pap. 30.00 o.p. (ISBN 0-08-019969-0). Pergamon.

One Hundred Years of Health Progress in Japan: Progress in Japan. F. Ontani. 130p. 1971. pap. 16.00x o.p. (ISBN 0-89955-342-7, Pub. by Japan Sci Soc Japan). Intl Spec Bk.

One Hundred Years of Psychiatry. Emil Kraepelin. Tr. by Wade Baskin. LC 61-15241. 163p. 1962. (ISBN 0-8022-0887-8). Philos Lib.

One Hundred Years of Science Fiction Illustration. Anthony Freus'N. 1975. pap. 4.95 o.p. (ISBN 0-515-03863-6, Harv). HarBraceJ.

One Hundred Years of the American Two-Move Chess Problem. Kenneth S. Howard. 1962. pap. 2.95 o.p. (ISBN 0-486-20997-0). Dover.

One Hundred Years of Thomism: Aeterni Patris & Afterwards - A Symposium. Ed. by Victor B. Brezik. LC 85-14986. 210p. 1983. pap. text ed. 9.95 o.s.i. (ISBN 0-9605456-0-3). U of Notre Dame Pr.

One in Five: The Assessment & Incidence of Special Educational Needs. Paul Croll & Diana Moses. (Special Needs in Education Ser.). 192p. 1985. 24.95x o.p. (ISBN 0-7102-0322-5). Routledge Chapman & Hall.

One in the Gospel. Friedemann Hebart. 1981. pap. 4.25 o.p. (ISBN 0-570-03830-8, 12-2796). Concordia.

One-Inch Helical Video Recording. 136p. 5.00 o.p. (ISBN 0-318-16590-2). Soc Motion Pic & TV Engrs.

One Is a Wanderer: Selected Stories. Francis King. LC 85-19705. 336p. 1986. 16.95 o.p. (ISBN 0-316-49350-3). Little.

One Is for the Sun. Lenore Blegvad & Erik Blegvad. LC 67-17151. (Illus.). (gr. k-3). 1968. 5.50 o.p. (ISBN 0-15-258685-7, HJ). HarBraceJ.

One Is Not a Woman, One Becomes: The African Woman in a Transitional Society. Ed. by Daphne W. Ntiri. (Illus.). 137p. (Orig.). 1982. pap. text ed. 8.95 o.p. (ISBN 0-911557-00-8). Bedford Publishers.

One Is Unique. Marnie Luce. LC 68-56701. (Math Concept Bks.). (Illus.). (gr. 3-6). 1969. PLB 3.95 o.p. (ISBN 0-8225-0572-X). Lerner Pubns.

One Kick. Michael Hardcastle. 144p. (gr. 5-6). 1986. 14.95 o.p. (ISBN 0-571-13775-X). Faber & Faber.

One Life at a Time, Please. Edward Abbey. LC 87-8812. (Owl Bks.). 1988. 17.95 o.p. (ISBN 0-317-66822-6); pap. 9.95 o.p. (ISBN 0-317-66823-4). H Holt & Co.

One Life Is Not Enough. Barbara Barondess-MacLean. (Illus.). 320p. 1986. 19.95 o.p. (ISBN 0-87052-338-4). Hippocrene Bks.

One Little Room, an Everywhere. Ed. by Myra C. Livingston. LC 75-8859. (Illus.). 152p. (gr. 7 up). 1975. 5.95 o.p. (ISBN 0-689-50032-7, Atheneum). Macmillan.

One Man, One Matchet. T. M. Aluko. (African Writers Ser.). 1965. pap. text ed. 6.00x o.p. (ISBN 0-435-90011-0). Heinemann Ed.

One Man's Freedom. Edward B. Williams. LC 62-11689. 1977. pap. 4.95 o.p. (ISBN 0-689-70544-1, 227, Atheneum). Macmillan.

One Man's Story. Fredrik A. Schiotz. LC 80-67790. 192p. (Orig.). 1980. pap. 7.95 o.p. (ISBN 0-8066-1851-5, 10-4780, Augsburg). Augsburg Fortress.

One Man's Wilderness: An Alaskan Odyssey. Sam Keith & Richard Proenneke. LC 72-92089. (Illus.). 116p. 1973. 14.95x o.p. (ISBN 0-88240-092-4); pap. 9.95 o.s.i. (ISBN 0-88240-013-4). Alaska Northwest.

One Master for Another: Populism As Patriarchal Rhetoric in Dominican Novels. Doris Sommer. LC 83-19688. 296p. (Orig.). 1984. lib. bdg. 29.25 o.p. (ISBN 0-8191-3605-0); pap. text ed. 14.00 o.p. (ISBN 0-8191-3606-9). U Pr of Amer.

One Million Poor: The Challenge of Irish Inequality. Stanislaus Kennedy. (Turoe Press Ser.). 272p. text ed. 17.95 o.p. (ISBN 0-905223-30-6, Dist. by Scribner). M Boyars Pubs.

Titles

One-Minute Scolding. Gerald E. Nelson. LC 83-18410. (Illus.). 150p. 1984. 13.95 o.p. (ISBN 0-87773-260-4); pap. 6.95 o.p. (ISBN 0-87773-272-8). Shambhala Pubns.

One-Minute Scolding see Who's the Boss? Love, Authority & Parenting.

One Miracle at a Time: How to Get Help for Your Disabled Child from the Experience of Other Parents. Irving R. Dickman & Sol Gordon. 256p. 1986. 17.45 o.p. (ISBN 0-671-50292-1). S&S.

One Miracle at a Time: Understanding Your Disabled Child. Irving R. Dickman & Sol Gordon. 352p. 1987. pap. 8.95 o.s.i. (ISBN 0-671-63458-5, Fireside). S&S.

One Misty Moisty Morning: Rhymes from Mother Goose. Ed. & illus. by Mitchell Miller. LC 70-149215. (Illus.). 48p. (ps up). 1971. 5.95 o.p. (ISBN 0-374-35647-5). FS&G.

One Month Lighter: The Lean Line Way to 30 Day Slimness. Toni Marotta et al. 1985. 15.95 o.p. (ISBN 0-87795-671-5, Arbor Hse). Morrow.

One More Day's Journey: The Story of a Family & a People. A. B. Ballard. 320p. 1984. text ed. 17.95 o.p. (ISBN 0-07-003486-9). McGraw.

One More Popple. Virginia Holt. LC 85-63429. (Gatefold Bks.). (Illus.). (ps-1). 1986. 3.95 o.s.i. (ISBN 0-394-88258-X, BYR). Random.

One More Time. Elizabeth Hunter. (Silhouette Romances Ser.). 1984. lib. bdg. 8.95 o.p. (ISBN 0-8398-2816-0, Gregg). G K Hall.

One More Time for Rhyme. Eugenie Smith. 1976. 4.50 o.s.i. (ISBN 0-682-48571-3). Exposition-Phoenix.

One Nation under God. Rus Walton. LC 86-28585. 240p. 1987. pap. 9.95 o.p. (ISBN 0-8407-3093-4). Nelson.

One of Benny's Faces: A Study of Benjamin Bufano (1886-1970) the Man Behind the Artist. Virginia B. Lewin. (Illus.). 1980. 10.50 o.p. (ISBN 0-682-49484-4). Exposition-Phoenix.

One of Our Bombers Is Missing. Dan Brennan. 1977. pap. 1.50 o.s.i. (ISBN 0-505-51140-1, Pub. by Tower Bks). Dorchester Pub Co.

One of the Crowd. Paul Gillette. LC 77-90669. 1980. 12.95 o.p. (ISBN 0-87795-184-5, Arbor Hse). Morrow.

One Old Oxford Ox. Illus. by Nicola Bayley. LC 77-77866. (ps-3). 1977. 6.95 o.p. (ISBN 0-689-30608-3, Atheneum). Macmillan.

One on One: Exercising Together, the Sensual Way to Superbly Conditioned Bodies. Jeff Aquilon & Nancy D. Aquilon. (Illus.). 160p. 1984. 16.45 o.p. (ISBN 0-671-50399-5). S&S.

One on One: Wrestling's Most Loved vs. Most Hated. (Illus.). 32p. (gr. 4-12). 1985. pap. 4.95 o.p. (ISBN 0-88188-392-1, 00183540, Robus Bks). H Leonard Pub Corp.

One Order to Go. Mel Glenn. LC 84-5018. 192p. (gr. 7 up). 1984. 11.45 o.p. (ISBN 0-89919-257-2, Clarion). HM.

One People. John R. Stott. LC 84-72468. 127p. pap. 4.95 o.p. (ISBN 0-87509-324-8); leader's guide 2.95 o.p. Chr Pubns.

One Piece of Paper. Michael Grater. LC 75-165523. (Illus.). (gr. 4-6). 7.50 o.s.i. (ISBN 0-8008-5825-5). Taplinger.

One Pinch of Sunshine, One-Half Cup of Rain. Ruth Cavin. LC 72-86928. Orig. Title: Cooking What Comes Naturally. (Illus.). 96p. (gr. 4-7). 1973. 7.95 o.p. (ISBN 0-689-30099-9, Atheneum). Macmillan.

One-Point Embroidery & Applique. Ondori Publishing Company Staff. (Ondori Young Handicraft Ser.). (Illus.). 1977. pap. 3.95 o.p. (ISBN 0-87040-397-4). Japan Pubns USA.

One-Pot Meals. Maggie Gin. LC 76-41173. (Illus.). 192p. 1986. pap. 7.95 o.p. (ISBN 0-89286-269-6, One Hund One Prods). Ortho.

One-Pot Meals. Margaret Gin. LC 76-41173. (Illus.). 1976. pap. 6.95 o.p. (ISBN 0-89286-100-2, One Hund One Prods). Ortho.

One Potato, Two Potato: The Secret Education of American Children. Mary Knapp & Herbert Knapp. (Illus.). 1976. 9.95 o.p. (ISBN 0-393-08745-X). Norton.

One Red Wagon: A Wrinkles Book of Numbers. Photos by Anita Shevett & Steve Shevett. LC 86-60365. 12p. (ps). 1986. 2.95 o.s.i. (ISBN 0-394-88432-9, BYR). Random.

One Ring to Bind Them All: Tolkien's Mythology. Anne C. Petty. LC 78-19148. 122p. 1979. o. p. 10.75 o.p. (ISBN 0-8173-7328-4); pap. 7.95 o.p. (ISBN 0-8173-0215-8). U of Ala Pr.

One-Room Rural Schools: The Building Blocks for Today's Schools. Harold R. Bare. (Illus.). 64p. 1984. pap. 7.50 o.p. (ISBN 0-682-40134-X). Exposition-Phoenix.

One Shoe Fits All. Jeff MacNelly. (Illus.). 128p. 1987. pap. 7.95 o.p. (ISBN 0-8050-0102-6). H Holt & Co.

One Show Nine. 450p. 1988. 55.00 o.p. (ISBN 0-8230-5809-3). Watson-Guptill.

One Show, Vol. 6: Radio, T. V. & Print's Best Ads. The One Club for Art & Copy Staff. (Illus.). 400p. 1985. 45.00 o.p. (ISBN 2-88046-048-4). R Silver.

One Sister Too Many. Sherry Shahan. (Treetop Tales Ser.). (Illus.). 112p. (Orig.). (gr. 3-5). 1987. pap. 2.25 o.s.i. (ISBN 0-87406-254-3). Willowisp Pr.

One Small Candle: The Pilgrims' First Year in America. Thomas Fleming. 1976. 8.95 o.p. (ISBN 0-393-05540-X). Norton.

One Small Flame: Twenty Five Year Documentary. 1978. pap. 2.50 o.p. (ISBN 0-85363-122-0). OMF Bks.

One-Step Sparring. Shin Duk Kung. LC 78-60159. (Ser. 132). (Illus.). 1978. pap. 8.95 o.p. (ISBN 0-89750-057-1). Ohara Pubns.

One Summer in Montana. Dayton O. Hyde. LC 85-7961. 180p. (YA) (gr. 9-12). 1985. 11.95 o.s.i. (ISBN 0-689-31144-3, Atheneum Childrens Bks). Macmillan.

One Thousand & One Questions Answered about Earthquakes, Avalanches, Floods, & Other Natural Disasters. Barbara Tufty. LC 78-51736. 1978. lib. bdg. 12.50x o.p. (ISBN 0-88307-612-8). Gannon.

One Thousand & One Things to Do with Your Commodore 64. Mark R. Sawusch & Tan A. Summers. (Illus.). 256p. (Orig.). 1984. 15.95 o.p. (ISBN 0-8306-0836-2, 1836); pap. 10.60 o.p. (ISBN 0-8306-1836-8). TAB Bks.

One Thousand Monsters. Alan Benjamin. LC 79-10682. (Illus.). 10p. (ps-2). 1979. spiral 4.95 o.s.i. (ISBN 0-02-708870-7, Four Winds). Macmillan.

One Thousand One Great Housekeeping Hints. Jane Keely. 128p. 1980. 11.95 o.p. (ISBN 0-87851-032-X); pap. 6.95 o.p. (ISBN 0-87851-033-8). Hearst Bks.

One Thousand One Health Tips. Lawrence Galton. 1984. 17.45 o.p. (ISBN 0-671-47689-0); pap. 8.95 o.p. (ISBN 0-671-50935-7). S&S.

One Thousand One Temple Avenue. Rosetta T. Albanese. 1985. 7.95 o.p. (ISBN 0-533-06541-0). Vantage.

One Thousand One Things to Do with Your Personal Computer. Mark Sawusch. (Illus.). 336p. (Orig.). 1980. 15.95 o.p. (ISBN 0-8306-9963-5); pap. 10.60 o.p. (ISBN 0-8306-1160-6, 1160). TAB Bks.

One Thousand Quaint Cuts from Books of Other Days. Andrew W. Tuer. LC 68-31097. 184p. 1968. Repr. of 1886 ed. 40.00x o.p. (ISBN 0-8103-3494-1). Gale.

One Thousand Sayings of History, Presented as Pictures in Prose. Walter Fogg. LC 79-143634. 928p. 1971. Repr. of 1929 ed. 53.00x o.p. (ISBN 0-8103-3779-7). Gale.

One Thousand Souls. Aleksei F. Pisemskii. Tr. by Ivy Litvinov. Repr. of 1959 ed. lib. bdg. 38.50x o.p. (ISBN 0-8371-2239-2, PIOS). Greenwood.

One Thousand Space Monsters--(Have Landed) Alan Benjamin. LC 79-55339. (Illus.). 10p. (ps-2). 1980. spiral 4.95 o.s.i. (ISBN 0-02-708880-4, Four Winds). Macmillan.

One Thousand Two Hundred Russian Proverbs. Isaac A. Langnas. pap. 0.95 o.p. (ISBN 0-685-19410-8, 60, Pub. by Citadel Pr). Carol Pub Group.

One Thousand Years: Western Europe in the Middle Ages. Richard L. Demolen et al. 325p. 1974. pap. 12.50 o.p. (ISBN 0-395-14032-3). HM.

One Times One. e. e. Cummings. LC 54-10935. 72p. 1972. pap. 2.95 o.p. (ISBN 0-15-668800-X, Harv). HarBraceJ.

One to Ten, Count Again. Elaine Livermore. LC 73-5744. (Illus.). 48p. (gr. k-3). 1973. PLB 7.95 o.p. (ISBN 0-395-17514-3). HM.

One Track Mind. Ernest A. Obeng. (Illus.). 64p. 1985. pap. 5.50 o.p. (ISBN 0-682-40201-X). Exposition-Phoenix.

One Tree. Stephen R. Donaldson. (Second Chronicles of Thomas Covenant: Bk. 2). 1982. 14.50 o.p. (ISBN 0-345-29898-5, Del Rey). Ballantine.

One Twenty Year Diet: How to Double Your Vital Years. Roy L. Walford. 432p. pap. 4.95 o.p. (ISBN 0-671-64904-3). Archway.

One, Two, Three---Ah-Choo! Marjorie N. Allen. (Illus.). 64p. (gr. 3-5). 1980. PLB 6.99 o.p. (ISBN 0-698-30718-6, Coward). Putnam Pub Group.

One-Two-Three Business Formula Handbook. Ron Person. 219p. 1986. pap. 19.95 o.p. (ISBN 0-88022-198-4, 196); IBM PC format. disk 39.95 o.p. (ISBN 0-88022-234-4). Que Corp.

One-Two-Three for Business. Douglas Cobb et al. 338p. 1984. pap. 18.95 o.p. (ISBN 0-88022-038-4, 34); IBM-PC format. disk 79.90 o.p. (240). Que Corp.

One, Two, Three for the Library. Mary E. Little. LC 74-75564. (Illus.). 32p. (ps-1). 1974. 5.95 o.p. (ISBN 0-689-30411-0, Atheneums Bk). Macmillan.

One-Two-Three from A to Z: 59 Complete Templates. Elna Tymes & Tony Dowden. 1985. pap. 18.95 o.p. (ISBN 0-8104-6600-7). Sams.

One, Two, Three, Go! Julia Killingback. LC 84-27288. (Illus.). 24p. (ps-k). 1985. 6.25 o.p. (ISBN 0-688-05784-5, Morrow Junior Books). Morrow.

One-Two-Three Macro Library. David P. Ewing. LC 84-62755. (One-Two-Three Ser.). 281p. 1985. pap. 19.95 o.p. (ISBN 0-88022-147-X, 174); IBM Format. disk 79.90 o.p. (245). Que Corp.

One-Two-Three Tips, Tricks, & Traps. Dick Andersen & Douglas Cobb. 257p. 1984. pap. 19.95 o.p. (ISBN 0-88022-110-0, 127). Que Corp.

One, Two, Three to the Zoo. Eric Carle. LC 68-26967. (Illus.). (ps-2). 1982. 13.95 o.p. (ISBN 0-399-61172-X, Philomel); pap. 5.95 o.p. (ISBN 0-399-20847-X). Putnam Pub Group.

One-Way Street. Mary S. English. 339p. 1983. pap. 5.00 o.p. (ISBN 0-682-49998-6). Exposition-Phoenix.

One Way Ticket: Migration & Female Labour. Ed. by Annie Phizacklea. 176p. 1983. pap. 9.95x o.p. (ISBN 0-7100-9489-2). Routledge Chapman & Hall.

One Way to do Research: The A-Z for Those Who Must. J. Calnan. 1976. pap. 15.00 o.p. (ISBN 0-433-05012-8). E J Brill USA.

One Way to Spell Man. Wallace Stegner. LC 81-43428. 192p. 1982. 14.95 o.p. (ISBN 0-385-17720-8). Doubleday.

One Way to Write Your Novel. Dick Perry. LC 81-16415. 138p. 1981. pap. 7.95 o.p. (ISBN 0-89879-069-7). Writers Digest.

One Who Listens. Michael Hollings & Etta Gullick. pap. 2.75 o.p. (ISBN 0-8192-1134-6). Morehouse Pub.

One Winter Night in August & Other Nonsense Jingles. X. J. Kennedy. LC 74-18185. (Illus.). 64p. (gr. 3 up). 1975. 5.95 o.p. (ISBN 0-689-50022-X, Atheneum). Macmillan.

One Woman Lost. Abigail McCarthy & Jane G. Muskie. LC 85-48140. 320p. 1986. 15.95 o.p. (ISBN 0-689-11804-X, Atheneum). Macmillan.

One Word Leads to Another: A Light History of Words. Milton Paisner. LC 82-2505. 1982. 14.95 o.p. (ISBN 0-934878-17-X). Dembner Bks.

One Word to the Other. Octavio Paz. 1989. pap. 7.00 o.p. (ISBN 0-941179-15-X). Latitudes Pr.

One World, One People: A Collection of Photographs & Essays on the Power of the Human Experience. Robert White & Koichi Shimazu. (Illus.). 108p. 1984. 39.95 o.p. (ISBN 4-900422-01-0, Pub. by ARC Inter Ltd). Kampmann.

One World under God. Natalie R. Berez. 1985. 6.75 o.p. (ISBN 0-533-05900-3). Vantage.

One Writer's Beginnings. Eudora Welty. 1985. 13.95 o.p. (ISBN 0-8161-3914-8, Large Print Bks). G K Hall.

One Year Accounting Course, 2 pts. Trevor Gambling. 1969. Pt. 1. 18.00 o.p. (ISBN 0-08-013025-9); Pt. 1. pap. 8.50 o.p. (ISBN 0-08-013024-0); Pt. 2. pap. text ed. 8.50 o.p. (ISBN 0-08-013026-7). Pergamon.

O'Neal's Oppression of Minority Shareholders. 2nd ed. F. Hodge O'Neal. LC 85-7867. 1985. 165.00 o.p. Callaghan.

O'Neill, Son & Playwright. Louis Sheaffer. LC 68-17278. (Illus.). 1968. 17.50 o.p. (ISBN 0-316-78335-8); pap. 8.95 o.p. (ISBN 0-316-78338-2). Little.

Onh Display Modu. (Our Nations Heritage Ser.). Date not set. (ISBN 0-07-375492-7). McGraw.

Onh-Display Shipper. (Our Nations Heritage Ser.). Date not set. (ISBN 0-07-375491-9). McGraw.

Onh Display Tray. (Our Nations Heritage Ser.). Date not set. (ISBN 0-07-375493-5). McGraw.

Online Catalog: Improving Public Access to Library Materials. Emily G. Fayen. LC 83-12009. (Professional Librarian Ser.). 148p. 1983. professional o.s.i. 34.50 o.s.i. (ISBN 0-86729-054-4); pap. 27.50 professional o.s.i. (ISBN 0-86729-053-6). G K Hall.

Online Database Search Services Directory, 2 pts. Ed. by John Schmittroth, Jr. 1983. Set. pap. 130.00x o.p. (ISBN 0-8103-1698-6). Gale.

Online Information: Abstracts of the First National Meeting. 1983. 5.00 o.p. (ISBN 0-317-01055-7). Learned Info.

Online Information Retrieval Bibliography 1964-1979. Donald Hawkins. 175p. 1980. 25.00x o.p. (ISBN 0-938734-00-8). Learned Info.

Online Information Retrieval Bibliography, 1964-1982. Donald T. Hawkins. 311p. 1982. pap. 36.00 o.p. (ISBN 0-317-66388-7). Learned Info.

Online Research & Retrieval with Microcomputers. Nahum Goldmann. LC 85-10047. (Illus.). 192p. 1985. 24.00 o.p. (ISBN 0-8306-1947-X, NO. 1947). Tab Bks.

Online Searching: A Dictionary & Bibliographic Guide. Greg Byerly. LC 83-853. 288p. 1983. lib. bdg. 27.50 o.p. (ISBN 0-87287-381-1). Libs Unl.

Online Searching: A Primer. 2nd ed. Carol H. Fenichel & Thomas H. Hogan. 188p. 1984. text ed. 14.95x o.p. (ISBN 0-938734-01-6). Learned Info.

Only a Free Man: War Memories of Two Dutch Doctors (1940-1945) Peter Voute. LC 81-83223. (Illus.). 188p. 1982. 14.95 o.s.i. (ISBN 0-89016-062-7). Lightning Tree.

Only a Gringo Would Die for an Anteater: The Adventures of a Veterinarian. Michael H. Milts & Carl Larson. (Illus.). 1979. 12.95 o.p. (ISBN 0-393-01251-4). Norton.

Only Child. Frank O'Connor. (Non-Fiction Ser.). 1985. pap. 7.95 o.p. (ISBN 0-8398-2879-9, Gregg). G K Hall.

Only Dance There Is. Ram Dass. LC 74-6963. 200p. 1976. Repr. 17.50x o.s.i. (ISBN 0-87668-237-9). Aronson.

Only Earth We Have. Laurence Pringle. LC 71-78076. (Science for Survival Ser.). (Illus.). 96p. (gr. 5-9). 1969. 9.95 o.s.i. (ISBN 0-02-775210-0). Macmillan.

Only for Peace. A. A. Gromyko. (Illus.). 1979. text ed. 49.00 o.p. (ISBN 0-08-023582-4); pap. text ed. 20.00 o.p. (ISBN 0-08-024513-7). Pergamon.

Only Girl in the Game. John D. MacDonald. 224p. 1982. pap. 2.50 o.p. (ISBN 0-449-12358-8, GM). Fawcett.

Only Great Changes. Meredith S. Willis. 288p. 1985. 15.95 o.s.i. (ISBN 0-684-18240-8, ScribT). Scribner.

Only Investment Guide You'll Ever Need. Andrew Tobias. LC 77-84395. 1978. 5.95 o.p. (ISBN 0-15-169941-0). HarBraceJ.

Only Living Witness. Stephen G. Michaud & Hugh Aynesworth. (Illus.). 464p. 1983. 15.50 o.p. (ISBN 0-671-44961-3, Linden Pr). S&S.

Only My Dreams. Denise Robins. 1976. pap. 1.25 o.p. (ISBN 0-380-00597-2, 28712). Avon.

Only Place To Be. Joan J. Buck. 1982. 14.45 o.s.i. (ISBN 0-394-52300-8). Random.

Only Sin. Julie Ellis. 1985. 17.95 o.p. (ISBN 0-87795-733-9, Arbor Hse). Morrow.

Only the Best: A Love Story. Toby Stein. 1984. 16.95 o.p. (ISBN 0-87795-596-4, Arbor Hse). Morrow.

Only the Best: The Discriminating Software Guide for Preschool-Grade 12, 1986 Edition. Ed. by School Tech News Staff. 128p. 1986. 21.95 o.p. (ISBN 0-936423-00-5). Ed News Serv.

Only the Brave Are Free. Donald R. Richberg & Albert Britt. LC 58-5332. 355p. 1958. 6.00 o.p. (ISBN 0-87004-142-8). Caxton.

Only to the House of Israel? Jesus & the Non-Jews. T. W. Manson. Ed. by John Reumann. LC 64-11860. (Facet Bks). 1964. pap. 1.00 o.p. (ISBN 0-8006-3005-X, 1-3005, Fortress). Augsburg Fortress.

Only Way. Karl Barth. 392p. 1959. (ISBN 0-8022-0075-3). Philos Lib.

Onset of Parenthood: A Comprehensive, Illustrated Guide to Pregnancy, Birth & Infant Care. L. Jed Morrison & M. K. Morrison. LC 75-17105. (Illus.). 238p. 1975. 12.95 o.p. (ISBN 0-88290-056-0). Horizon Utah.

Onslaught: The German Drive to Stalingrad. Intro. by Heinrich Von Einsiedel. (Illus.). 1985. 24.45 o.p. (ISBN 0-393-01939-X). Norton.

ONTAP: Online Training & Practice Manual for ERIC Data Base Searchers. rev. ed. Karen Markey & Pauline A. Cochrane. 176p. 1981. 8.50 o.s.i. (IR-2456). ERIC Clear.

Ontario & the Canadian North. William F. Morley. LC 78-4976. (Canadian Local Histories to 1950: a Bibliography Ser.). 1978. 30.00x o.p. (ISBN 0-8020-2281-2). U of Toronto Pr.

Ontogenesis of Cortical Circuitry: The Spatial Distribution of Synapses in Somesthetic Cortex of Newborn Dog. M. E. Molliver & H. Van Der Loos. LC 64-20582. (Advances in Anatomy Embryology & Cell Biology: Vol. 42, Pt. 4). (Illus.). 1970. pap. 18.90 o.p. (ISBN 0-387-04797-2). Springer-Verlag.

Ontogenesis of the Skeleton & the Intrinsic Muscles of the Human Hand & Foot. R. Cihak. LC 79-183955. (Advances in Anatomy, Embryology & Cell Biology: Vol. 46, Pt. 1). (Illus.). 240p. 1972. pap. 52.00 o.p. (ISBN 0-387-05673-4). Springer-Verlag.

Ontogeny of Vertebrate Behavior. Howard Moltz. 1971. 85.50 o.p. (ISBN 0-12-504350-3). Acad Pr.

Onyx Flame. Jan Moss. (Avon Romance Ser.). 320p. (Orig.). 1984. pap. 2.95 o.p. (ISBN 0-380-87627-2, 87627-2). Avon.

Onze Mille Virges. Guillaume Apollinaire. Tr. by Nina Rootes from Fr. LC 78-24595. 1979. 7.95 o.s.i. (ISBN 0-8008-2384-2). Taplinger.

Oom-Pah. William Crane. LC 80-18404. 204p. (gr. 5-8). 1981. PLB 10.95 o.p. (ISBN 0-689-30804-3, Atheneum). Macmillan.

OPEC & the Petroleum Industry. M. S. Al-Otaiba. 208p. 1976. 25.00 o.p. (ISBN 0-85664-262-2, Pub. by Croom helm Ltd). Routledge Chapman & Hall.

OPEC Behavior & World Oil Prices. Ed. by James M. Griffin & David J. Teece. 256p. 1982. text ed. 34.95x o.p. (ISBN 0-04-338102-2); pap. text ed. 14.95X o.p. (ISBN 0-04-338103-0). Unwin Hyman.

OPEC, the Trilateral World, & the Developing Countries-New Arrangements for Cooperation, 1976-1980. Richard N. Gardner et al. (Triangle Papers: No. 7). 1975. pap. 6.00 o.p. Trilateral Comm.

Opel Service Repair Handbook: All Models, 1966-1975. Ray Hoy. (Illus.). pap. 13.95 o.p. (ISBN 0-89287-171-7, A175). Clymer Pub.

Open & Closed Systems: The Nonequilibrium Statistical Mechanics of Nonlinear Processes. Katja Lindenburg & Bruce J. West. 430p. 1987. lib. bdg. 49.95x o.p. (ISBN 0-89573-347-1). VCH Pubs.

Open Boat - Across the Pacific. Webb Chiles. (Illus.). 224p. 1982. 16.95 o.p. (ISBN 0-393-03268-X). Norton.

Open Book. James Matlock. 1980. 4.00 o.p. (ISBN 0-682-49211-6). Exposition-Phoenix.

Open Door to Spanish, 2 bks. Margarita Madrigal. (gr. 7 up). 1972. Bk. 1. pap. text ed. 3.50 o.p. (ISBN 0-88345-186-7, 18098); Bk. 2. pap. text ed. 2.75 o.p. (ISBN 0-88345-187-5, 17704); records 20.00 ea. o.p.; tapes o.p. 30.00 ea. o.p.; cassettes 40.00 ea. o.p. Prentice ESL.

Open Doors. Dorothy Martin. (Peggy Ser.: No. 2). (gr. 7). 1985. pap. 3.50 o.p. (ISBN 0-8024-8302-X). Moody.

Open Doorways. Philip Appleman. 1976. 7.95 o.p. (ISBN 0-393-04443-2); pap. 2.95 o.p. (ISBN 0-393-04451-3). Norton.

Open Education Goes to Church. Mary Duckert. LC 75-45195. 1976. pap. 3.45 o.s.i. (ISBN 0-664-24796-2, Westminster). Westminster John Knox.

Open Education: Promise & Problems. Vito Perrone. LC 72-190068. (Fastback Ser.: No. 3). (Illus.). 1972. pap. 0.90 o.p. (ISBN 0-87367-003-5). Phi Delta Kappa.

Open Form: Essays for Our Time. 3rd ed. Alfred Kazin. 1970. pap. text ed. 2.50 o.p. (ISBN 0-15-567533-8, HC). HarBraceJ.

Open Gate. Jean McVayne. 1977. 4.50 o.p. (ISBN 0-682-48922-0). Exposition-Phoenix.

Open Goal of My Life. Susanne Cook. LC 84-90269. 74p. 1985. 7.95 o.p. (ISBN 0-533-06303-5). Vantage.

Open Heart. Frederick Buechner. LC 76-190401. 1972. 5.95 o.p. (ISBN 0-689-10498-7, Atheneum). Macmillan.

Open Heaven: The Study of Apocalyptic in Judaism & Early Christianity. Christopher Rowland. LC 82-7409. 540p. 1982. 29.50x o.p. (ISBN 0-8245-0455-0). Crossroad NY.

Open-Hole Fishing. 2nd, rev. ed. (Rotary Drilling Ser.: Unit III, Lesson 2). (Illus.). 40p. 1975. pap. text ed. 6.95 o.p. (ISBN 0-88698-050-X, 2.30220). PETEX.

Open House. William Katz. 1985. text ed. 14.95 o.p. (ISBN 0-07-033329-7). McGraw.

Open House Cookbook. Sarah L. Chase. (Illus.). 288p. 1987. 19.95 o.p. (ISBN 0-89480-476-6); pap. 11.95 o.p. (ISBN 0-89480-465-0). Workman Pub.

Open Learning in Action. Ed. by Roger Lewis. (Orig.). 1984. pap. text ed. 26.50x o.p. (ISBN 0-86184-123-9). Trans Atl Phila.

Open Marriage: A New Lifestyle for Couples. Nana O'Neill & George O'Neill. 1986. pap. 2.25 o.p. (ISBN 0-380-00271-X). Avon.

Open Meeting & Conflict of Interest Laws. Municipal Law Conference Staff. LC 84-60194. 238p. write for info. o.p. Mass CLE.

Open Messencephalotomy & Thalamotomy for Intractable Pain. B. Zapletal. LC 75-82429. (Illus.). 1969. 33.70 o.p. (ISBN 0-387-80936-8). Springer-Verlag.

Open Net. George Plimpton. (Illus.). 1985. 16.45 o.p. (ISBN 0-393-02255-2). Norton.

Open Pit Mine Planning & Design. Ed. by John T. Crawford, III & William A. Hustrulid. LC 79-52269. (Illus.). 367p. 1979. text ed. 5.00x o.p. (ISBN 0-89520-253-0). SMM&E Inc.

Open Plan Offices. 1978. text ed. 19.95 o.p. (ISBN 0-07-084497-6). McGraw.

Open Prison. J. I. Stewart. 1985. 13.95 o.p. (Large Print Bks). G K Hall.

Open Rapture. Sakae Kubo. (Flame Ser.). 1978. pap. 1.25 o.p. (ISBN 0-8127-0170-4). Review & Herald.

Open Road. Donovan. pap. 3.50 o.p. (ISBN 0-686-09058-6, Pub. by Peer-Southern). CPP Belwin.

Open Road: Truckin' on the Biting Edge. Axel Madsen. LC 82-47666. (Illus.). 224p. 1982. 12.95 o.p. (ISBN 0-15-170029-X). HarBraceJ.

Open Sea: Its Natural History. Alister Hardy. 1971. 20.00 o.p. (ISBN 0-395-07777-X). HM.

Open-Shop Building Construction Cost Data, 1986. 2nd ed. Means, R. S., Company, Inc. Staff. Ed. by Dwayne Lehigh. 458p. 1985. pap. 44.95 o.p. (ISBN 0-87629-026-8). R S Means.

Open Space & Peace. Ed. by Frederick J. Ossenbeck & Patricia C. Kroeck. LC 64-18827. (Publications Ser.: No. 35). 1964. 10.95x o.p. (ISBN 0-8179-1351-3). Hoover Inst Pr.

Open Spaces: Monographs Published since 1970. Mary Vance. (Architecture Ser.: A 1459). 15p. 1985. 2.25 o.p. (ISBN 0-89028-549-7). Vance Biblios.

Open to the Spirit. Ed. by Alan Craston. 172p. 1987. pap. 8.10 o.s.i. (ISBN 0-88028-073-5). Forward Movement.

Open University: History & Evaluation of a Dynamic Innovation in Higher Education. Walter Perry. LC 76-55917. (Higher Education Ser.). 1977. text ed. 27.95x o.p. (ISBN 0-87589-305-8). Jossey-Bass.

Open Windows. Neal Stanford. 80p. 1984. 8.00 o.p. (ISBN 0-682-40172-2). Exposition-Phoenix.

Open Your Eyes to Opportunity. Oliver K. Whiting. 1975. 6.00 o.p. (ISBN 0-682-48182-3, Banner). Exposition-Phoenix.

Open Your Eyes, Your Heart, & Your Soul: A Philosophy of Life for Every Individual. Hugh W. Van Resseh. 1977. 10.00 o.p. (ISBN 0-682-48751-1). Exposition-Phoenix.

Opened Treasures. Frances R. Havergal. LC 62-21063. 1962. 7.95 o.p. (ISBN 0-87213-320-6). Loizeaux.

Opening & Penetration of Foreign Influence in Samoa to 1880. Joseph W. Ellison. (Studies in History: No. 1). 108p. 1938. pap. 4.95x o.p. (ISBN 0-87071-071-0). Oreg St U Pr.

Opening Closed Doors: The Deinstitutionalization of Disabled Individuals. David Braddock. LC 77-72050. 1977. pap. text ed. 3.75 o.p. (ISBN 0-86586-059-9). Coun Exc Child.

Opening Doors to the Job Market. James L. Sheard & Rodney E. Stalley. LC 82-72642. 176p. 1983. pap. 9.95 o.p. (ISBN 0-8066-1948-1, 10-4811, Augsburg). Augsburg Fortress.

Opening Game in Chess. Ludek Pachman. Tr. by John Littlewood. (Illus.). 192p. 1983. pap. 7.95 o.p. (ISBN 0-7100-9222-9). Routledge Chapman & Hall.

Opening of the Mississippi: A Struggle for Supremacy in the American Interior. Frederic A. Ogg. LC 68-57500. Repr. of 1904 ed. 24.00x o.p. (ISBN 0-8154-0283-X). Cooper Sq.

Opening the Door of Faith: The Why, When & Where of Evangelism. John R. Hendrick. LC 76-12404. 1977. pap. 4.75 o.p. (ISBN 0-8042-0675-9, John Knox). Westminster John Knox.

Opening the Door to Good Nutrition. Marion Franz et al. (Illus.). 188p. 1985. pap. 7.95 o.p. (ISBN 0-937721-15-8). DCI Publishing.

Openings. Wendell Berry. LC 68-20061. 67p. 1968. 4.50 o.s.i. (ISBN 0-15-170025-7). HarBraceJ.

Opera, 3 Vols. Saint Ambrosius. Set. 210.00 o.p. (ISBN 0-384-01038-5). Johnson Repr.

Opera. Jean Cocteau. 121p. 1959. 8.95 o.p. (ISBN 0-686-54543-5). French & Eur.

Opera. Saint Hilarius. Ed. by A. Feder. (Corpus Scriptorum Ecclesiasticorum Latinorum Ser: Vol. 65). 1916. 50.00 o.p. (ISBN 0-384-23110-1). Johnson Repr.

Opera, 2 Vols. Quintus S. Tertullianus. (Lat). Repr. of 1890 ed. Set. 100.00 o.p. (ISBN 0-384-59850-1). Johnson Repr.

Opera: Avec: Plain-Chant. Jean Cocteau. 159p. 1967. pap. 8.95 o.p. (ISBN 0-686-54542-7). French & Eur.

Opera Dos Mortos see Voices of the Dead: A Novel.

Opera du Monde. Jacques Audiberti. 360p. 1947. 8.95 o.p. (ISBN 0-686-54497-8). French & Eur.

Opera Gazetteer. Hugh Cannin. LC 86-42738. (Illus.). 240p. 1987. 17.50 o.p. (ISBN 0-8478-0727-4). Rizzoli Intl.

Opera House Album: A Collection of Turn-of-the-Century Postcards. Ed. by Charles Osborne. LC 79-64978. (Illus.). 1980. 9.95 o.s.i. (ISBN 0-8008-5836-0, Crescendo). Taplinger.

Opera House Murders. David Hanna. 256p. (Orig.). 1982. pap. 2.50 o.p. (ISBN 0-8439-1027-5, Pub. by Leisure Bks CT). Dorchester Pub Co.

Opera on Record. Alan Blyth. (Illus.). 672p. 1980. 29.95 o.p. (ISBN 0-09-139980-7, NO. 0215, Pub. by Hutchinson England). Routledge Chapman & Hall.

Opera Pars 1. Orationum Gregorii Nazianzeni Novem Interpretation. Tyrannius Rufinius. Ed. by A. Engelbrecht. Repr. of 1910 ed. 40.00 o.p. (ISBN 0-384-52540-7). Johnson Repr.

Opera Philosophica Quae Latine Scripsit Omnia, 5 Vols. Thomas Hobbes. Ed. by W. Molesworth. Set. cancelled o.s.i. (ISBN 3-511-02230-4). Adlers Foreign Bks.

Opera Psychotherapy. Bartalini. (Illus.). 88p. 1981. 12.50 o.p. (ISBN 0-682-49703-7). Exposition-Phoenix.

Opera Themes & Plots. Rudolph Fellner. 1971. pap. 9.70 o.p. (ISBN 0-671-21215-X, Fireside). S&S.

Operas of Leos Janacek. E. Chisholm. 1971. 100.00 o.p. (ISBN 0-08-012854-8); pap. 100.00 o.p. (ISBN 0-08-012853-X). Pergamon.

Operating Criteria for Credit Departments: Revised Feb., 1987. 49p. 40.00 o.p. (ISBN 0-939050-48-X). Credit Res NYS.

Operating Handbook of Mineral Underground Mining, Vol. III. Engineering & Mining Journal Editors. (Library of Operating Handbooks). 1978. text ed. 33.50 o.p. (ISBN 0-07-019521-8). McGraw.

Operating Manual for Spaceship Earth. R. Buckminster Fuller. 1970. pap. 7.75 o.p. (ISBN 0-671-20783-0, Touchstone Bks). S&S.

Operating the IBM-PC Networks. Paul Berry. LC 85-63777. 363p. (Orig.). 1986. pap. 19.95 o.p. (ISBN 0-89588-307-4). Sybex.

Operation & Effects of the Generalized System of Preferences. UNCTAD, Secretariat. (Trade, Finance & Commerce Reports & Studies). 266p. 1978. First Review. pap. 12.00 o.p. (E.73.11.D.16); Second Review. pap. 11.00 o.p. (E.75.11.D.9); Third Review. pap. 17.00 o.p. (ISBN 0-686-99417-5, E.78.11.D.2); Fourth Review. pap. 11.00 o.p. (ISBN 0-686-68964-X, E.79.11.D.6); Sixth Review. pap. 9.00 o.p. (E.82.11D.10); pap. 9.00 o.p. (ISBN 92-1-112081-0). UN.

Operation & Maintenance of Gas Cleaning Equipment. Air Pollution Control Association Specialty Conference, Pittsburgh, PA, 1980. 190p. 1980. 15.00 o.p. (ISBN 0-318-12263-4, SP-35); members 12.00 o.p. (ISBN 0-318-12264-2). Air & Waste.

Operation Arctic. Leif Hamre. Tr. by Dag Ryen from Norwegian. LC 73-75441. 160p. (YA) (gr. 7 up). 1973. 4.95 o.p. (ISBN 0-689-30418-8, Atheneum). Macmillan.

Operation Avalanche: The Salerno Landings, 1943. Des Hickey & Gus Smith. 379p. 1984. text ed. 17.95 o.p. (ISBN 0-07-028682-5). McGraw.

Operation Barbarossa. Steven J. Zaloga & James Grandsen. (Illus.). 64p. (Orig.). 1985. pap. 9.95 o.p. (ISBN 0-85368-702-1, Pub. by Arms & Armour). Sterling.

Operation Brogue. John M. Feehan. 138p. 1984. pap. 8.95 o.p. (ISBN 0-85342-729-1, Pub. by Mercier Pr Ireland). Irish Bks Media.

Operation Chastise: The True Story of the Famous Dams Raid. John Sweetman. (Illus.). 256p. 1982. 19.95 o.p. (ISBN 0-86720-557-1). Janes Info Group.

Operation Emerald. Dominic McCartan. LC 86-6243. 1986. 14.95 o.p. (ISBN 0-934878-77-3). Dembner Bks.

Operation Garbo: The Personal Story of the Most Successful Double Agent of World War II. Juan Pujol & Nigel West. LC 85-10809. (Illus.). 224p. 1986. 17.45 o.p. (ISBN 0-394-54777-2). Random.

Operation Golden Buddha. Ellis Edwards. 264p. 1985. 16.95 o.p. (ISBN 0-87364-342-9). Paladin Pr.

Operation Gomorrah. Gordon Musgrove. (Illus.). 288p. 1981. 18.95 o.p. (ISBN 0-86720-562-8). Janes Info Group.

Operation Intercept. Lawrence A. Gooberman. 1975. 31.00 o.p. (ISBN 0-08-017837-5); pap. 55.00 o.p. (ISBN 0-08-017836-7). Pergamon.

Operation Lila. Marvin H. Albert. LC 82-72067. 304p. 1983. 14.95 o.p. (ISBN 0-87795-411-9, Arbor Hse). Morrow.

Operation Norfolk. Carl Ramm. (Hawker Ser.: No. 11). (Orig.). 1987. pap. 2.75 o.p. (ISBN 0-440-16624-1). Dell.

Operation Nuke. Martin Caidin. LC 72-97689. 1974. 6.95 o.p. (ISBN 0-87795-041-5, Arbor Hse). Morrow.

Operation of the European Social Fund. Doreen Collins. (Illus.). 144p. 1983. 25.00 o.p. (ISBN 0-7099-0782-6, Pub. by Croom Helm Ltd). Routledge Chapman & Hall.

Operation Time Search. Andre Norton. LC 67-17156. (gr. 8 up). 1967. 5.75 o.p. (ISBN 0-15-258700-4, HJ). HarBraceJ.

Operation Titan. Dilwyn Horvat. LC 84-71417. 128p. (gr. 9-12). 1984. pap. 3.95 o.p. (ISBN 0-89107-322-1, Crossway Bks). Good News.

Operation Tombola. Roy Farran. (Special Forces Library). 256p. 1987. 24.95 o.p. (ISBN 0-85368-749-8, Pub. by Arms & Armour). Sterling.

Operation Willi: The Nazi Plot to Capture the Duke of Windsor. Michael Bloch. LC 86-10975. (Illus.). 288p. 1986. 18.95 o.p. (ISBN 1-55584-020-5). Weidenfeld.

Operational Audits of Production Control. Gary L. Holstrum & William Collins. LC 77-80966. (Research Reports Ser.). 1978. pap. 13.50 o.p. (ISBN 0-89413-056-0). Inst Inter Aud.

Operational Calculus. Gregors Krabbe. LC 75-30722. 350p. 1976. pap. 15.95x o.p. (ISBN 0-306-20017-1, Plenum Pr). Plenum Pub.

Operational Gaming: An International Approach. Ed. by I. Stahl. LC 83-17199. (Frontiers of Operational Research & Applied Systems Analysis: Vol. 3). 340p. 1983. 44.00 o.p. (ISBN 0-08-030836-8); pap. 22.00 o.p. (ISBN 0-08-030870-8). Pergamon.

Operational Organic Chemistry: A Laboratory Course. new ed. John W. Lehman. 640p. 1981. text ed. write for info. o.p. (ISBN 0-205-07146-5, 687146-1); tchr's. ed. avail. o.p. (ISBN 0-205-07147-3). Allyn.

Operational Research 1975: Proceedings of the IFIP International Conference on Operational Research, 7th, Japan, 1975. IFORS International Conference Staff & K. B. Haley. 698p. 1976. 85.00 o.p. (ISBN 0-7204-0384-7, North-Holland). Elsevier.

Operations & Production Management. Michael Peters & Terence Oliva. LC 80-29618. 527p. 1981. text ed. (ISBN 0-87150-312-3, 33L 2491, Prindle). PWS-Kent Pub.

Operations Management in Practice. Ed. by C. D. Lewis. LC 81-6445. 454p. 1981. 59.95x o.p. (ISBN 0-470-27204-X). Halsted Pr.

Operations Management: Planning & Control of Operations & Operating Resources. Richard J. Schonberger. 1981. text ed. 22.50x o.p. (ISBN 0-256-02442-1). Irwin.

Operations Management: Productivity & Quality. 2nd ed. Richard J. Schonberger. 1985. 39.95x o.p. (ISBN 0-256-03074-X); study guide 12.95 o.p. (ISBN 0-256-03541-5). Irwin.

Operations Management: Text & Cases. Paul W. Marshall et al. 1975. 36.95x o.p. (ISBN 0-256-01682-8). Irwin.

Operations Manager. Roy D. Harris & Richard F. Gonzalez. (Illus.). 478p. 1981. text ed. 41.00 o.p. (ISBN 0-8299-0332-1). West Pub.

Operations Manual. 178p. 6.00 o.p. (ISBN 0-318-15188-X, NO. 111-836). Natl Assoc Realtors.

Operations of the National Weather Service, 1985. (Illus.). 245p. 1985. pap. 7.50 o.p. (ISBN 0-318-21879-8, S/N 003-018-00111-0). USGPO.

Operations Research: A Methodological Approach. E. Wentzel. 256p. 1983. 5.95 o.p. (ISBN 0-8285-2569-2, Pub. by Mir Pubs USSR). Imported Pubns.

Operations Research & Economic Theory: Essays in Honor of Martin J. Beckmann. Ed. by H. Hauptmann et al. (Illus.). xi, 378p. 1984. 39.00 o.p. (ISBN 0-387-13652-5). Springer-Verlag.

Operations Research Problem Solver. rev. ed. Research & Education Association Staff. LC 83-62276. (Illus.). 1088p. 1988. pap. text ed. 28.85 o.p. (ISBN 0-87891-548-6). Res & Educ.

Operative Dentistry. 3rd ed. H. William Gilmore et al. LC 76-30465. (Illus.). 1977. text ed. 32.95 o.p. (ISBN 0-8016-1822-3). Mosby.

Operative Dentistry Procedures for Dental Auxiliaries. Eric E. Spohn et al. LC 81-907. (Illus.). 298p. 1981. pap. text ed. 24.95 o.p. (ISBN 0-8016-2580-7). Mosby.

Operative Plastic & Reconstructive Surgery, Vols. 1 & 2. J. Barron & M. N. Saad. 1981. text ed. 222.00 o.p. (ISBN 0-443-02522-3). Churchill.

Operative Plastic & Reconstructive Surgery, Vol. 3. J. Barron. Ed. by M. N. Saad. (Illus.). 352p. 1981. text ed. 79.90 o.p. (ISBN 0-443-02212-7). Churchill.

Operative Surgery & Management. Ed. by Gerald Keen. (Illus.). 880p. 1981. text ed. 65.00 o.p. (ISBN 0-7236-0548-3, Pub. by John Wright UK). Butterworth.

Operative Surgery: Principles & Techniques. 2nd ed. Ed. by Paul F. Nora. LC 79-28112. (Illus.). 1181p. 1980. text ed. 96.00 o.p. (ISBN 0-8121-0670-9). Lea & Febiger.

Operative Ultrasonography. Bernard Sigel. LC 81-18599. (Illus.). 186p. 1982. text ed. 20.00 o.p. (ISBN 0-8121-0837-X). Lea & Febiger.

Operator of Uninspected Towing Vessels (200-Tons-200-Miles) Ed. by Richard A. Block. (Illus.). 68p. (Orig.). 1984. pap. text ed. 10.00 o.p. (ISBN 0-934114-55-2, BK200). Marine Educ.

Opere, 7 vols. Alessandro G. Volta. (Sources of Science Ser.). Repr. of 1929 ed. Set. 315.00 o.p. (ISBN 0-384-64900-9). Johnson Repr.

Ophiolites: Ancient Oceanic Lithosphere. R. G. Coleman. (Minerals & Rocks Ser.: Vol. 12). (Illus.). 1977. 43.00 o.p. (ISBN 0-387-08276-X). Springer-Verlag.

Ophthalmic Assistant: Fundamentals & Clinical Practice. 4th ed. Harold A. Stein & Bernard J. Slatt. LC 75-43808. (Illus.). 632p. 1982. pap. text ed. 39.95 o.p. (ISBN 0-8016-4776-2). Mosby.

Ophthalmic Drug Delivery Systems. Ed. by Joseph R. Robinson. LC 80-66335. 144p. 1980. 18.00 o.p. (ISBN 0-917330-32-3). Am Pharm Assn.

Ophthalmic Lasers: Photocoagulation, Photoradiation & Surgery. 2nd ed. L'Esperance. (Illus.). 512p. 1982. 97.50 o.p. (ISBN 0-8016-2823-7). Mosby.

Ophthalmologic Nursing. Joan F. Smith & Delbert P. Nachazel. 1980. text ed. 20.50 o.p. (ISBN 0-316-80158-5). Little.

Ophthalmology Annual, 1986, Vol. 2. Ed. by Robert Reinecke. (Illus.). 253p. 1985. 59.95 o.p. (ISBN 0-8385-7431-9). Appleton & Lange.
Opinion Letters of Counsel. 1984. pap. 15.00 o.p. (B4-6689). PLI.
Opinions. Melvin Bernasconi. 1980. 5.00 o.p. (ISBN 0-682-49520-4). Exposition-Phoenix.
Opinions of the Attorney General of the Republic of Liberia, September, 1964-August 1968. Liberia, Republic of. Ed. by Milton R. Konvitz. LC 28-17298. (Liberian Code of Law & Supreme Court Reports). 224p. 1969. 40.00x o.p. (ISBN 0-8014-0529-7). Cornell U Pr.
Opium. Tony Cohan. 463p. 1984. 19.45 o.p. (ISBN 0-671-47327-1). S&S.
Opium-Eater: A Life of Thomas De Quincey. Grevel Lindop. LC 81-5662. (Illus.). 433p. 1982. 19.95 o.s.i. (ISBN 0-8008-5841-7). Taplinger.
Opium of the Intellectuals. Raymond Aron. 1962. pap. 3.45 o.p. (ISBN 0-393-00106-7, Norton Lib). Norton.
Opium: The Diary of a Cure. Jean Cocteau. Tr. by Margaret Crosland & Sinclair Road. LC 58-5967. (Illus.). 176p. 1980. pap. 6.95 o.p. (ISBN 0-394-17737-1, E771, Ever). Grove.
Opportunities & Constraints. Institution of Chemical Engineers. 1982. 50.00 o.s.i. (ISBN 0-08-028775-1). Pergamon.
Opportunities & Uses of the Ocean. D. A. Ross. LC 79-12694. (Illus.). 1979. 26.50 o.p. (ISBN 0-387-90448-4). Springer-Verlag.
Opportunities for Adult Education. Ed. by Malcolm Tight. 321p. 1983. pap. 12.00 o.p. (ISBN 0-7099-2454-2, Pub. by Croom Helm Ltd). Routledge Chapman & Hall.
Opportunities in Biology. 568p. 1988. 42.50 o.p. (ISBN 0-309-03927-4); pap. 32.50 o.p. (ISBN 0-309-03893-6). Natl Acad Pr.
Opportunities in Food Science & Technology. Joseph G. Endres. (gr. 8 up). 1969. pap. 1.25 o.p. (ISBN 0-8442-6480-6). Natl Textbk.
Opportunities in Management Careers. 2nd ed. Irene Place & Leonard Robertson. LC 78-60546. (gr. 8 up). 1979. 10.95 o.p. (VGM Career Horzns); pap. 7.95 o.p. (VGM Career Horzns). Natl Textbk.
Opportunities in Mechanical Engineering. 2nd ed. Seichi Konzo & James W. Bayne. LC 77-166404. 1978. 10.95 o.p. (VGM Career Horzns); pap. 7.95 o.p. (VGM Career Horzns). Natl Textbk.
Opposites. Peter Seymour. (Turn & Learn Bks.). (Illus.). (ps-1). 1984. 5.95 o.s.i. (ISBN 0-02-782130-7). Macmillan.
Opposites. Richard Wilbur. LC 72-88175. (Illus., Orig.). (gr. 3-7). 1973. 4.95 o.p. (ISBN 0-15-258720-9, HJ). HarBraceJ.
Opposites Attract. Alicia Meadows. 240p. 1983. pap. 2.75 o.p. (ISBN 0-380-84111-8, 84111). Avon.
Opposites: Poems & Drawings. Richard Wilbur. LC 78-71154. (Illus.). 1979. pap. 1.75 o.p. (ISBN 0-15-670087-5, VoyB). HarBraceJ.
Opposition & Dissent in Contemporary China. Peter R. Moody, Jr. LC 77-72054. (Publication Ser.: No. 177). (Illus.). 360p. 1977. 15.95x o.p. Hoover Inst Pr.
Oppression & Liberty. Simone Weil. 208p. 1988. pap. text ed. 9.95 o.p. (ISBN 0-7448-0090-0, Pub. by Ark Paperbks). Routledge Chapman & Hall.
Oppression, Violence & Repression. J. M. Sanchez-Perez. 1975. 7.00 o.p. (ISBN 0-682-48267-6). Exposition-Phoenix.
Optati Milevitani Libri Septum. Saint Optatus. (Corpus Scriptorum Ecclesiasticorum Latinorum Ser: Vol. 26). (Lat). pap. 50.00 o.p. (ISBN 0-384-43390-1). Johnson Repr.
Optical Anecdotes. D. J. Lovell. 148p. 20.00 o.p. (ISBN 0-317-34704-7); members 17.00 o.p. (ISBN 0-317-34705-5). SPIE.
Optical Aspects of Oceanography. N. G. Jerlov. 1973. 84.00 o.p. (ISBN 0-12-384950-0). Acad Pr.
Optical Bistability One. Ed. by Charles M. Bowden et al. LC 81-2559. 626p. 1981. 95.00x o.p. (ISBN 0-306-40722-1, Plenum Pr). Plenum Pub.
Optical-Electronic Publishing Directory, 1986. Richard A. Bowers. 110p. 1986. pap. 30.00 o.p. (ISBN 0-317-52867-X). Learned Info.
Optical Engineering for Cold Environments, Vol. 414. Ed. by G. W. Aitken. 231p. 42.00 o.p. (ISBN 0-89252-449-9). SPIE.
Optical Fiber Technology II. C. K. Kao. LC 80-25665. 343p. 1981. 32.95x o.p. (ISBN 0-471-09169-3, Pub. by Wiley-Interscience); pap. 21.50x o.p. (ISBN 0-471-09171-5, Pub. by Wiley-Interscience). Wiley.
Optical-Fibre Waveguides. Ed. by P. J. Clarricoats. (IEE Reprint Ser.: No. 1). 335p. 1975. pap. 32.00 o.s.i. (ISBN 0-901223-76-X, RE001). Inst Elect Eng.
Optical Instrumentation: A Problem-Solving Tool in Automotive Safety Engineering & Bio-Mechanics, Proceedings, Vol. 34. Society of Photo-Optical Instrumentation Engineers Staff. 28.00 o.p. (ISBN 0-89252-045-0). SPIE.
Optical Instrumentation: A Tool for Solving Problems in Security, Surveillance & Law Enforcement, Proceedings, Vol. 33. Society of Photo-Optical Instrumentation Engineers Staff. 28.00 o.p. (ISBN 0-89252-044-2). SPIE.
Optical Measurements in the Printing Industry. J. M. Adams. 1965. pap. text ed. 9.75 o.p. (ISBN 0-08-011240-4). Pergamon.
Optical Model of the Atomic Nucleus. Ivan Ulehla et al. Tr. by G. Alter. 1965. 45.50 o.p. (ISBN 0-12-707450-3). Acad Pr.
Optical Physics. Max Garbuny. 1965. 43.50 o.p. (ISBN 0-12-275350-X). Acad Pr.
Optical Properties & Band Structures of Semiconductors. D. L. Greenaway & G. Harbeke. 1968. 45.00 o.p. (ISBN 0-08-012648-0). Pergamon.
Optical Properties of Solids. Ed. by S. Nudelman & S. S. Mitra. LC 68-15008. (Optical Physics & Engineering Ser). (Illus.). 624p. 1969. 95.00x o.p. (ISBN 0-306-30321-3, Plenum Pr). Plenum Pub.
Optical Properties of Solids. Ed. by J. Tauc. (Italian Physical Society: Course 34). 1967. 88.00 o.p. (ISBN 0-12-368834-5). Acad Pr.
Optical Publishing Directory. Richard A. Bowers. 1987. 45.00 o.p. Learned Info.
Optical Specifications: Components & Systems, Vol. 406. Ed. by W. J. Smith et al. 139p. 1983. 46.00 o.p. (ISBN 0-89252-441-3). SPIE.
Optical Systems Engineering: Proceedings of the SPIE Annual Technical Symposium, 23rd, San Diego, 1979. (SPIE Seminar Proceedings: Vol. 193). 302p. 1979. 38.00 o.p. (ISBN 0-89252-221-6); members 30.00 o.p. (ISBN 0-317-34719-5). SPIE.
Opticks, or a Treatise of the Reflections, Refractions, Inflections & Colours of Light. Isaac Newton. 16.00 o.p. (ISBN 0-8446-5799-9). Peter Smith.
Optics, 2 pts. Jean P. Mathieu. Incl. Pt. 1. Electromagnetic Optics; Pt. 2. Quantum Optics. LC 73-10408. 1975. 71.00 o.p. (ISBN 0-08-017157-5). Pergamon.
Optics see Physics Programs.
Optics & Information Theory. Francis T. Yu. LC 83-16273. 240p. 1984. Repr. of 1976 ed. lib. bdg. 31.50 o.p. (ISBN 0-89874-678-7). Krieger.
Optics & Lasers: Including Fibers & Integrated Optics. 2nd, rev. ed. M. Young. (Springer Series on Optical Sciences: Vol. 5). (Illus.). 290p. 1984. pap. 26.70 o.p. (ISBN 0-387-13014-4). Springer Verlag.
Optics Replacement PA. 1970. 32.32 o.p. (ISBN 0-07-521254-4). McGraw.
Optimal Adaptive Control Systems. David D. Sworder. (Mathematics in Science & Engineering Ser.: Vol. 25). 1966. 54.50 o.p. (ISBN 0-12-679550-9). Acad Pr.
Optimal Control & Differential Equation. Ed. by A. B. Schwarzkopf et al. 1978. 45.50 o.p. (ISBN 0-12-632250-3). Acad Pr.
Optimal Control of Discrete Time Stochastic Systems. C. Striebel. (Lecture Notes in Economics & Mathematical Systems Ser.: Vol. 110). 208p. 1975. pap. 14.00 o.p. (ISBN 0-387-07181-4). Springer-Verlag.
Optimal Control of Nuclear Reactors. R. R. Mohler & C. N. Shen. (Nuclear Science & Technology Ser.: Vol. 6). 1970. 84.00 o.p. (ISBN 0-12-504150-0). Acad Pr.
Optimal Control Systems. A. A. Feldbaum. (Mathematics in Science & Engineering Ser.: Vol. 22). 1966. 81.00 o.p. (ISBN 0-12-251950-7). Acad Pr.
Optimal Control Theory. L. D. Berkovitz. LC 74-20837. (Applied Mathematical Sciences Ser.: Vol. 12). (Illus.). 1974. pap. 29.80 o.p. (ISBN 0-387-90106-X). Springer-Verlag.
Optimal Control Theory for the Damping of Vibrations of Simple Elastic Systems. V. Komkov. (Lecture Notes in Mathematics: Vol. 253). 240p. 1972. pap. 7.90 o.p. (ISBN 0-387-05734-X). Springer-Verlag.
Optimal Decisions. Oskar Lange. 304p. 1972. 50.00 o.p. (ISBN 0-08-016053-0). Pergamon.
Optimal Design of Flexural Systems. G. I. Rozvany. 200p. 1976. 51.00 o.p. (ISBN 0-08-020517-8); pap. 29.00 o.p. (ISBN 0-08-020516-X). Pergamon.
Optimal Expansion of a Water Resources System. D. T. O'Laoghaire. 1974. 71.00 o.p. (ISBN 0-12-525450-4). Acad Pr.
Optimal Rate Structures & the Electric Utility Problem. 53p. 1974. 3.75 o.p. (ISBN 0-318-15015-8). NARUC.
Optimal Shutdown Control of Nuclear Reactors. Milton Ash. (Mathematics in Science and Engineering Ser.: Vol. 26). 1966. 54.50 o.p. (ISBN 0-12-065150-5). Acad Pr.
Optimal Subset Selection: Multiple Regression, Interdependence & Optimal Network Algorithms. D. E. Boyce et al. (Lecture Notes in Economics & Mathematical Systems: Vol. 103). xiv, 187p. 1974. pap. 12.00 o.p. (ISBN 0-387-06957-7). Springer-Verlag.
Optimization & Industrial Experimentation. William E. Biles & James J. Swain. LC 79-9516. 382p. 1980. 56.95 o.p. (ISBN 0-471-04244-7, Pub. by Wiley-Interscience). Krieger.
Optimization & Operations Research. Ed. by W. K. Oettli & K. G. Ritter. (Lecture Notes in Economies & Math Systems: Vol. 117). 316p. 1976. pap. 17.00 o.p. (ISBN 0-387-07616-6). Springer-Verlag.
Optimization & Optimal Control: Proceedings. Ed. by A. Auslender et al. (Lecture Notes in Control & Information Sciences Ser.: Vol. 30). 254p. 1981. pap. 18.00 o.p. (ISBN 0-387-10627-8). Springer-Verlag.
Optimization in Economic Analysis. Gordon Mills. (Illus.). 208p. 1984. text ed. 39.95x o.p. (ISBN 0-04-311001-0); pap. text ed. 14.95 o.p. (ISBN 0-04-311002-9). Unwin Hyman.
Optimization in Locational & Transport Analysis. A. G. Wilson et al. LC 80-42068. 283p. 1981. 73.95x o.p. (ISBN 0-471-28005-4, Pub. by Wiley-Interscience). Wiley.
Optimization Models for Planning & Allocation: Text & Cases in Mathematical Programming. Roy D. Shapiro. LC 83-21878. 650p. 1984. (ISBN 0-471-09468-4). Wiley.
Optimization of Density & Moisture Content Measurement by Nuclear Method. (National Cooperative Highway Research Provram Report). 68p. 1971. 4.40 o.p. (ISBN 0-309-02005-0). Transport Res Bd.
Optimization of Stochastic Systems. Masanao Aoki. (Mathematics in Science & Engineering Ser: Vol. 32). 1967. 75.50 o.p. (ISBN 0-12-058850-1). Acad Pr.
Optimization Techniques, Part 2: Proceedings of the 8th IFIP Conference & Optimization Techniques, Wuerzburg, Sept. 5-9, 1977. Ed. by J. Stoer. (Lecture Notes in Control & Information Sciences: Vol. 7). (Illus.). 1978. pap. 29.00 o.p. (ISBN 0-387-08708-7). Springer-Verlag.
Optimization Techniques: Proceedings, Pt. 2. Ed. by K. Iracki et al. (Lecture Notes in Control & Information Sciences Ser.: Vol. 23). 621p. 1980. pap. 40.00 o.p. (ISBN 0-387-10081-4). Springer-Verlag.
Optimization Techniques: Proceedings of the 8th IFIP Conference on Optimization Techniques, Wuerzburg, Sept 5-9, 1977, Pt. 1. Ed. by J. Stoer. (Lecture Notes in Control & Information Sciences Ser.: Vol. 6). (Illus.). 1978. pap. 29.00 o.p. (ISBN 0-387-08707-9). Springer-Verlag.
Optimization Techniques: Proceedings the IFIP Technical Conference, Novosibirsk, 1974. IFIP Technical Conference Staff. Ed. by G. I. Marchuk. (Lecture Notes in Computer Science Ser.: Vol. 27). 515p. 1975. pap. 25.00 o.p. (ISBN 0-387-07165-2). Springer-Verlag.
Optimization Theory: The Finite Dimensional Case. Magnus R. Hestenes. LC 80-11516. 464p. 1981. Repr. of 1975 ed. lib. bdg. 38.50 o.p. (ISBN 0-89874-143-2). Krieger.
Optimizing Development Profits in Large Scale Real Estate Projects. Michael D. Wilburn & Robert M. Gladstone. LC 72-79135. (Technical Bulletin Ser.: No. 67). (Illus.). 64p. 1972. pap. 14.00 o.p. (ISBN 0-87420-067-9, N11). Urban Land.
Optimizing Flow on Existing Street Networks. (National Cooperative Highway Research Project Report). 414p. 1971. 15.60 o.p. (ISBN 0-309-01903-6). Transport Res Bd.
Optimizing Methods in Statistics: Proceedings of an International Conference. Ed. by Jagdish S. Rustagi. LC 79-10487. 1979. 71.50 o.p. (ISBN 0-12-604580-1). Acad Pr.
Optimum Design of Digital Control Systems Via Dynamic Programming. Ed. by Julius Tou. (Mathematics in Science & Engineering: Vol. 10). 1963. 60.50 o.p. (ISBN 0-12-696250-2). Acad Pr.
Option Football: Concepts & Techniques for Winning. Stan Scarborough & William E. Warren. (Illus.). 300p. 26.95x o.p. (ISBN 0-205-07749-8, EDP 627749, Pub. by Longwood Div). Wm C Brown.
Option Pricing. Robert Jarrow & Andrew Rudd. LC 83-70860. 225p. 1983. 40.00 o.p. (ISBN 0-87094-378-2). Dow Jones-Irwin.
Option Pricing: Theory & Applications. Menachem Brenner. (Salomon Brothers Center Bks.). 256p. 1983. 37.00x o.p. (ISBN 0-669-05714-2). Lexington Bks.
Option Writing & Hedging Strategies: With Special Chapters on the Chicago Board Options Exchange, Convertible Strategies, Warrant Strategies. Rolf Auster. LC 74-21435. 1975. 12.50 o.p. (ISBN 0-682-48162-9, Banner). Exposition-Phoenix.
Options As a Strategic Investment. Lawrence G. McMillan. (Illus.). 1980. text ed. 35.00 o.p. (ISBN 0-13-638387-4). P-H.
Options Handbook. Standard's & Poor's Staff. 1982. pap. text ed. 29.95 o.p. (ISBN 0-07-051884-X). McGraw.
Optoacoustic Spectroscopy & Detection. Ed. by Y. H. Pao. 1977. 53.50 o.p. (ISBN 0-12-544150-9). Acad Pr.
Optoelectronic Data Book. Texas Instruments Engineering Staff. LC 83-70442. 480p. 1983. pap. 11.50 o.p. (ISBN 0-89512-115-8, SOYDOO1E). Tex Instr Inc.
Optoelectronics Discontinued Devices. 1987. 70.00 o.p. DATA Busn Pub.
Optometric Instrumentation. David B. Henson. 256p. 1983. 54.95 o.p. (ISBN 0-407-00241-3). Butterworth.
Opulence: The Kimonos & Robes of Itchiku Kubota. Itchiku Kubota. Ed. by Tomoyuki Yamanobe. LC 83-48290. (Illus.). 128p. 1984. pap. 39.95 o.p. (ISBN 0-87011-636-3). Kodansha.
Opus Est: Six Composers from Northern Europe. Paul Rapport. (Illus.). 200p. 1985. pap. 7.95 o.s.i. (ISBN 0-8008-5845-X). Taplinger.
Opus Pistorum. Henry Miller. LC 83-80498. 272p. 1983. 12.95 o.s.i. (ISBN 0-394-53374-7, GP-872). Grove.
Opus Pistorum see Under the Roofs of Paris.
Opus Two Hundred. Isaac Asimov. 1979. 10.95 o.p. (ISBN 0-395-27625-X). HM.
Opvuscula. Lucifer of Cagliari. (Corpus Scriptorum Ecclesiasticorum Latinorum Ser: Vol. 14). (Lat). pap. 40.00 o.p. (ISBN 0-384-34090-3). Johnson Repr.
Oral & Maxillofacial Surgery Abstracts. 1986. 12.95 o.p. (ISBN 0-8016-0039-1). Mosby.
Oral & the Written Gospel: The Hermeneutics of Speaking & Writing in the Synoptic Tradition, Mark, Paul, & Q. Werner H. Kelber. LC 82-7450. 272p. 1983. 9.95 o.p. (ISBN 0-8006-0689-2, 1-689, Fortress). Augsburg Fortress.
Oral Communication of the Scripture: Insights from African Oral Art. Herbert V. Klem. LC 81-10052. (Applied Cultural Anthropology Ser.). (Illus.). 256p. (Orig.). 1982. pap. text ed. 9.95x o.p. (ISBN 0-87808-332-4). William Carey Lib.
Oral Communication: The Essential Skill. Michael Minchew & Norma Minchew. 102p. 1980. pap. 8.95x o.p. (ISBN 0-89459-198-3). Hunter Textbks.
Oral Diagnosis. 6th ed. Donald A. Kerr et al. LC 82-6291. (Illus.). 383p. 1982. 37.95 o.p. (ISBN 0-8016-2656-0). Mosby.
Oral Diagnosis. 2nd ed. W. R. Tyldesley. 172p. 1978. text ed. 55.00 o.p. (ISBN 0-08-021543-2). Pergamon.
Oral Diagnosis, Oral Medicine & Treatment Planning. Robert P. Langlais et al. (Illus.). 400p. 1984. 40.95 o.p. (ISBN 0-7216-5618-8). Saunders.
Oral Health Care Systems. Ed. by Harald A. Arnljot et al. 218p. (Orig.). 1985. pap. text ed. 34.00x o.p. (ISBN 1-85097-001-7). Quint Pub Co.
Oral Histology: Development, Structure, & Function. 3rd ed. (Illus.). 480p. 1989. 51.95 o.p. (ISBN 0-8016-4902-1). Mosby.
Oral Histology: Development, Structure & Function. 2nd ed. A. Richard Ten Cate. (Illus.). 472p. 1985. text ed. 49.95 o.p. (ISBN 0-8016-4908-0). Mosby.
Oral History of an American High School. Michael Arkush. 215p. 1988. 24.50 o.p. (ISBN 0-8419-1094-4). Holmes & Meier.
Oral Hypoglycaemic Agents. G. D. Campbell. (Medicinal Chemistry Ser.: Vol. 9). 1969. 99.00 o.p. (ISBN 0-12-157350-8). Acad Pr.
Oral Interpretations. 6th ed. Charlotte I. Lee & Timothy Gura. LC 76-13095. (Illus.). 1981. text ed. 29.95 o.p. (ISBN 0-395-31705-3). HM.
Oral Microbiology: With Basic Microbiology & Immunology. 4th ed. William A. Nolte. LC 81-14102. (Illus.). 806p. 1982. 39.95 o.p. (ISBN 0-8016-3697-3). Mosby.
Oral Physiology. N. Emmelin & Yngve Zotterman. 311p. 1972. 115.00 o.p. (ISBN 0-08-016972-4). Pergamon.
Oral Physiology & Occlusion: An International Symposium. Ed. by James H. Perryman. LC 78-17812. 268p. 1979. 48.00 o.p. (ISBN 0-08-023183-7). Pergamon.
Oral Radiology: Principles & Interpretations. Paul W. Goaz & Stuart C. White. LC 81-18802. (Illus.). 672p. 1982. cloth 39.95 o.p. (ISBN 0-8016-1886-X). Mosby.
Oral Reading of the Scriptures. Charlotte I. Lee. 1974. text ed. 16.50 o.p. (ISBN 0-395-18940-3). HM.
Orange County Public Schools: How Are They Doing? (1984) Lillian S. Clancy. (How Are They Doing Ser.). 120p. (Orig.). 1984. pap. 13.95 o.p. (ISBN 0-939580-13-6). CA Schl Surveys.
Orange County Street Atlas 1984. Thomas Brothers Maps Staff. (Illus.). 144p. 1983. pap. 9.50 o.p. (ISBN 0-88130-049-7). Thomas Bros Maps.
Orange County Street Atlas, 1985. Thomas Bros. Maps. (Illus.). 144p. 1985. pap. 9.95 o.p. (ISBN 0-88130-099-3). Thomas Bros Maps.
Orange County Street Atlas, 1986. Thomas Bros. Maps Staff. (Illus.). 144p. 1986. pap. 10.95 o.p. (ISBN 0-88130-168-X). Thomas Bros Maps.

Orange County Street Atlas 1987. Thomas Bros Maps, Staff. (Illus.). 144p. 1987. pap. 12.95 o.p. (ISBN 0-88130-220-1). Thomas Bros Maps.

Orange County Zip Code Street Atlas, 1986. Thomas Bros. Maps Staff. (Illus.). 146p. 1986. pap. 14.95 o.p. (ISBN 0-88130-182-5). Thomas Bros Maps.

Orange County Zip Code Street Atlas 1987. (Illus.). 146p. pap. 15.95 o.p. (ISBN 0-88130-234-1). Thomas Bros Maps.

Orange Grove Boyhood: Growing up in Southern California 1910-1928. Lawrence C. Powell. (Illus.). 74p. 12.95 o.p. (ISBN 0-88496-275-X). Capra Pr.

Orange Illustrated, Nineteen Hundred Four: A Pictorial of a Massachusetts Town. Pref. by Allen Young. (Illus.). 56p. 1988. pap. 7.00 o.p. (ISBN 0-912395-14-1). Millers River Pub Co.

Orange-Los Angeles Counties Street Atlas, 1986. Thomas Bros. Maps Staff. (Illus.). 432p. 1986. pap. 19.95 o.p. (ISBN 0-88130-163-9). Thomas Bros Maps.

Orange-Los Angeles Counties Street Atlas 1987. Thomas Bros Maps, Staff. (Illus.). 432p. 1987. pap. 21.95 o.p. (ISBN 0-88130-215-5). Thomas Bros Maps.

Orangutan: Endangered Ape. Aline Amon. LC 76-41354. (Illus.). 160p. (gr. 4-6). 1977. 7.95 o.p. (ISBN 0-689-30563-X, Athenuem). Macmillan.

Orbit. Thomas H. Block. 320p. 1983. pap. 3.50 o.s.i. (ISBN 0-425-05740-2). Berkley Pub.

Orchard. Benjamin Tammuz. Tr. by Richard Flantz from Hebrew. LC 84-15571. 88p. (Orig.). 1985. pap. 6.00 o.p. (ISBN 0-914278-43-6). Copper Beech.

Orchard Children. Rachel Maddux. 1978. pap. 1.95 o.p. (ISBN 0-380-01933-7, 37820). Avon.

Orchestral Composer's Point of View: Essays on Twentieth-Century Music by Those Who Wrote It. Robert S. Hines. 254p. Repr. of 1970 ed. lib. bdg. 39.00 o.p. (Pub. by Am Repr Serv). Reprint Servs.

Orchestral Percussion Technique. James Blades. 85p. Repr. of 1961 ed. lib. bdg. 39.00 o.p. (Pub. by Am Repr Serv). Reprint Servs.

Orchestrating Symphony. Waite Group Staff. Ed. by Dan Schafer. 288p. 1985. pap. 18.95 o.p. (ISBN 0-553-34200-2). Bantam.

Orchid Hunting in the Lost World (& Elsewhere in Venezuela) G. C. Dunsterville & E. Dunsterville. (Illus.). 300p. 1988. write for info. o.p. Amer Orchid Soc Inc.

Orchid Tree. Virginia Coffman. 1984. 15.95 o.p. (ISBN 0-87795-532-8, Arbor Hse). Morrow.

Orchids. Lee Chew Kang. (Illus.). 1979. 15.00 o.p. (ISBN 0-89860-032-4). Eastview.

Orchids. Thomas H. Cook. 252p. 1982. 12.45 o.p. (ISBN 0-395-32503-X). HM.

Orchids: A Guide to All Species Found in Maine. P. E. Keenan. (Maine Geographic Ser.). (Illus.). 48p. 1983. pap. 2.95 o.p. (ISBN 0-89933-068-1). Delorme Map.

Orchids of America. J. Stewart & E. F. Hennessey. LC 81-6589. 159p. 1981. 50.00 o.s.i. (ISBN 0-395-31771-1). HM.

Orchids of the Western Himalaya. J. F. Duthie. (Illus.). 1967. Repr. of 1906 ed. 180.00x o.p. (ISBN 3-7682-0465-0). Lubrecht & Cramer.

ORD & CD in Chemistry & Biochemistry: An Introduction. Pierre Crabbe. 1972. 54.50 o.p. (ISBN 0-12-194650-9). Acad Pr.

Ordained to Service: A Theology of the Permanent Diaconate. Norbert Brockman. 1976. 7.50 o.p. (ISBN 0-682-48561-6, University). Exposition-Phoenix.

Ordeal, 3 vols. A. Tolstoi. 1150p. 1976. Set. 16.50 o.p. (ISBN 0-8285-1053-9, Pub. by Progress Pubs USSR). Imported Pubns.

Ordeal by Slander. Owen Lattimore. LC 72-138156. 1971. Repr. of 1950 ed. lib. bdg. 22.50x o.p. (ISBN 0-8371-5613-0, LAOS). Greenwood.

Ordeal of a Latter Day Oedipus. T. W. Familia. 1979. 8.00 o.p. (ISBN 0-682-49371-6). Exposition-Phoenix.

Ordeal of Civility: Freud, Marx, Levi-Strauss, & the Jewish Struggle with Modernity. John M. Cuddihy. LC 86-47757. 272p. 1987. pap. 9.95 o.p. (ISBN 0-8070-3609-9, BP-738). Beacon Pr.

Ordeal of Faith. F. P. Weisenburger. 392p. 1959. (ISBN 0-8022-1843-1). Philos Lib.

Ordeal of Power: A Political Memoir of the Eisenhower Years. Emmet J. Hughes. LC 63-12783. 1975. pap. text ed. 5.95x o.s.i. (ISBN 0-689-70523-9, 213, Athenuem). Macmillan.

Ordeal of the Union, 8 vols. Allan Nevins. Incl. Vol. 1. Ordeal of the Union: Fruits of Manifest Destiny, 1847-1852. 1947 (ISBN 0-684-10423-7); Vol. 2. Ordeal of the Union: A House Dividing, 1852-1857. 1947 (ISBN 0-684-10424-5); Vol. 3. Emergence of Lincoln: Douglas, Buchanan, & Party Chaos, 1857-1859. 1950 (ISBN 0-684-10415-6); Vol. 4. Emergence of Lincoln: Prologue to Civil War, 1859-1861. 1950 (ISBN 0-684-10416-4); Vol. 5. War for the Union: The Improvised War, 1861-1862. LC 47-11072. 1959 (ISBN 0-684-10426-1); Vol. 6. War for the Union: War Becomes Revolution, 1862-1863. LC 59-3690. 1960 (ISBN 0-684-10427-X); Vol. 7. War for the Union: The Organized War, 1863-1864. LC 47-11072. 1971 (ISBN 0-684-10428-8); Vol. 8. War for the Union: The Organized War to Victory, 1864-1865. LC 47-11072. 1971 (ISBN 0-684-10429-6). (Illus.). 29.50 ea o.s.i. Scribner.

Ordeal of the Union: A House Dividing, 1852-1857 see Ordeal of the Union.

Ordeal of the Union: Fruits of Manifest Destiny, 1847-1852 see Ordeal of the Union.

Ordeal of Twentieth-Century America: Interpretive Readings. Jordan A. Schwarz. 464p. 1974. pap. 9.95 o.p. (ISBN 0-395-14519-8). HM.

Ordeal: One Family's Experience with Stroke. Fern Starr. 1984. 10.95 o.p. (ISBN 0-533-05936-4). Vantage.

Order in Court: The Organization of Verbal Interaction in Judicial Settings. J. Maxwell Atkinson. (Oxford Sociolegal Studies). 1979. text ed. 32.50x o.p. (ISBN 0-391-01025-5). Humanities.

Order of Battle at Trafalgar & Other Essays. John Bayley. LC 86-29013. 224p. 1987. 15.95 o.s.i. (ISBN 1-55584-137-6). Weidenfeld.

Order of Liberalization of the Balance of Payments: Should the Current Account Be Opened Up First? Sebastian Edwards. (Working Paper: No. 710). 114p. 1985. 5.00 o.p. (ISBN 0-8213-0469-0, WP 0170). World Bank.

Order of Poetry: An Introduction. Ed. by Edward A. Bloom et al. 192p. 1961. pap. text ed. write for info. o.p. (ISBN 0-02-311080-5). Macmillan.

Orderly Career Opportunities. Richard O. Carlson. LC 79-54079. 1979. 4.95 o.p. (ISBN 0-936276-09-6). Ctr Educ Policy Mgmt.

Orders of Knighthood, Awards & the Holy See: A Historical Juridical & Practical Compendium. 3rd, rev., enl. ed. H. E. Cardinale. 1985. text ed. 55.00x o.p. (ISBN 0-905715-26-8). Humanities.

Ordinary & Delay Differential Equations. R. Driver. LC 76-58452. (Applied Mathematical Sciences Ser.: Vol. 20). 1977. pap. 27.50 o.p. (ISBN 0-387-90231-7). Springer-Verlag.

Ordinary & Partial Differential Equations: Proceedings of Conference, 4th, Dundee, Scotland, March 30 - April 2, 1976. Ed. by W. N. Everitt & B. D. Sleeman. (Lecture Notes in Mathematics Ser.: Vol. 564). 1977. soft cover 29.00 o.p. (ISBN 0-387-08058-9). Springer-Verlag.

Ordinary Differential Equations. M. Krasnov. 151p. 1987. pap. 4.95 o.s.i. (ISBN 0-8285-3444-6, Pub. by Mir Pubs USSR). Imported Pubns.

Ordinary Differential Equations. E. R. Lapwood. LC 68-21278. 1968. 38.00 o.p. (ISBN 0-08-012551-4). Pergamon.

Ordinary Differential Equations in Banach Spaces. K. Deimling. (Lecture Notes in Mathematics: Vol. 596). 1977. 13.00 o.p. (ISBN 0-387-08260-3). Springer-Verlag.

Ordinary Life of a Temporary Pantyhose Salesman. Aldo Busi. Tr. by Raymond Rosenthal. 400p. 19.95 o.p. (ISBN 0-317-60291-8). FS&G.

Ordinary Marriage. Harriet Robey. 228p. 1984. 14.45i o.p. (ISBN 0-316-75127-8, Pub. by Atlantic Monthly Pr). Little.

Ordinary Princess. M. M. Kaye. LC 82-46036. (Illus.). 128p. (gr. 4-8). 1984. pap. 11.95 o.p. (ISBN 0-385-17855-7). Doubleday.

Ordination of Women. Raymond Tiemeyer. 1970. 1.00 o.p. (ISBN 0-8066-1013-1, 10-4815, Augsburg). Augsburg Fortress.

Ordination of Women: Pro & Con. Michael P. Hamilton & Nancy S. Montgomery. (Orig.). 1975. pap. 4.95 o.p. (ISBN 0-8192-1203-2). Morehouse Pub.

Ore Fields & Continental Weathering. Jean-Claude Samama. (Evolution of Ore Fields Ser.). (Illus.). 352p. 1986. 44.95 o.p. (ISBN 0-442-28025-4). Van Nos Reinhold.

Oregon! Dana F. Ross. (Reader's Request Ser.). 1982. lib. bdg. 16.95 o.p. (ISBN 0-8161-3317-4, Large Print Bks). G K Hall.

Oregon Coast. Photos by Ray Atkeson. LC 75-188295. (Belding Imprint Ser.). (Illus.). 128p. (Text by Archie Satterfield). 1972. 29.50 o.s.i. (ISBN 0-912856-06-8). Gr Arts Ctr Pub.

Oregon II. Photos by Ray Atkeson. LC 74-75124. (Belding Imprint Ser.). (Illus.). 192p. (Text by Archie Satterfield). 1974. 29.50 o.s.i. (ISBN 0-912856-15-7). Gr Arts Ctr Pub.

Oregon Imprints 1845-1870. George N. Belknap. LC 78-1013. (Illus.). 1968. 10.00 o.p. (ISBN 0-87114-019-5). U of Oreg Bks.

Oregon Indians: Culture, History & Current Affairs; an Atlas & Introduction. Jeff Zucker & Bob Hogfoss. (Illus.). 192p. (Orig.). 1983. pap. 15.95 o.p. (ISBN 0-87595-094-9, Western Imprints). Oregon Hist.

Oregon Manufacturers Directory, 1987-88. 345p. 1987. pap. 82.00 o.p. (ISBN 0-318-02865-4). Manufacturers.

Oregon Question: Essays in Anglo-American Diplomacy & Politics. Frederick Merk. LC 67-14345. 1967. 29.50x o.s.i. (ISBN 0-674-64200-7, Belknap Pr). Harvard U Pr.

Oregon Uniform Commercial Code, Vol. 2. Henry J. Bailey, III. LC 82-73190. 575p. 1984. incl. suppl. 1986 thru. 1988 65.00 o.p. (ISBN 0-409-20043-3). Butterworth WA.

Oregon Uniform Commercial Code, Vol. 3. Henry J. Bailey, III. LC 82-73190. 550p. 1986. 75.00 o.p. Butterworth WA.

Oresteia: Iconography & Narrative. A. J. Prag. (Illus.). 300p. 1985. 59.00 o.p. (ISBN 0-86516-121-6). Bolchazy-Carducci.

Oresteia, Pt. 1 see Agamemnon.

Oresteia, Pt. 2 see Libation-Bearers.

Oresteia, Pt. 3 see Eumenides.

Orfeo ed Euridice. Johann J. Fux. Ed. by Howard M. Brown. LC 76-21040. (Italian Opera 1640-1770 Ser.). 1978. lib. bdg. 77.00 o.p. (ISBN 0-8240-2618-7). Garland Pub.

Organ & Species Specificity in Chemical Carcinogenesis. Ed. by Robert Langenbach & Stephen Nesnow. (Basic Life Sciences Ser.: Vol. 24). 704p. 1983. 95.00x o.p. (ISBN 0-306-41184-9, Plenum Pr). Plenum Pub.

Organ & Tissue Regeneration in Mammals II. new ed. R. F. Kempczinski et al. LC 72-13503. 157p. 1973. text ed. 25.50x o.p. (ISBN 0-8422-7059-0). Irvington.

Organ & Tissue Regeneration in Mammals I. P. Nettesheim et al. LC 72-13503. 167p. 1972. text ed. 27.50x o.p. (ISBN 0-8422-7048-5). Irvington.

Organ Culture. Ed. by J. Andre Thomas. (Fr). 1970. 95.00 o.p. (ISBN 0-12-688150-2). Acad Pr.

Organ: Its Evolution, Principles, Construction & Use. William L. Sumner. (Illus.). 468p. 1955. (ISBN 0-8022-1670-6). Philos Lib.

Organic Chemical Drugs & Their Synonyms, 3 vols. 5th ed. Martin Negwer. 1863p. 1978. Set. 125.00x o.p. (ISBN 0-89573-100-2). VCH Pubs.

Organic Chemistry. Ed. by F. L. Boschke. LC 77-14137. (Topics in Current Chemistry: Vol. 73). 1978. 63.00 o.p. (ISBN 0-387-08480-0). Springer-Verlag.

Organic Chemistry. K. N. Houk & L. A. Paquette. (Topics in Current Chemistry: Vol. 79). (Illus.). 1979. 51.00 o.p. (ISBN 0-387-09301-X). Springer-Verlag.

Organic Chemistry. John McMurry. LC 83-7744. 1051p. 1983. text ed. 36.00 pub net o.p. (ISBN 0-534-01204-3); pub net study guide 17.50 o.p. (ISBN 0-534-02675-3). Brooks-Cole.

Organic Chemistry. V. Potapov & S. Tatarindrick. 517p. 1979. 10.00 o.p. (ISBN 0-8285-1529-8, Pub. by Mir Pubs USSR). Imported Pubns.

Organic Chemistry: A Brief Survey of Concepts & Applications. 3rd ed. Philip S. Bailey & Christina A. Bailey. 1985. text ed. 45.00 o.p. (ISBN 0-205-08195-9, 688195); study guide avail. o.p. (ISBN 0-205-08197-5, 688197). Allyn.

Organic Chemistry: A Short Course. 5th ed. Harold Hart & Robert D. Schuetz. LC 77-75880. (Illus.). 1978. text ed. 22.95 o.p. (ISBN 0-395-25161-3). HM.

Organic Chemistry in Colour. P. F. Gordon & P. Gregory. (Illus.). 300p. 1983. 74.20 o.p. (ISBN 0-387-11748-2). Springer-Verlag.

Organic Chemistry Laboratory Survival Manual: A Student's Guide to Techniques. 2nd ed. James W. Zubrick. LC 83-21808. 244p. 1984. pap. text ed. 14.95 o.p. (ISBN 0-471-87131-1). Wiley.

Organic Chemistry of Boron. W. Gerrard. 1961. 86.00 o.p. (ISBN 0-12-281250-6). Acad Pr.

Organic Chemistry of Iron, Vol. 2. Ed. by Ernest A. Von Gustorf. (Organometallic Chemistry Ser.). 1981. 65.50 o.p. (ISBN 0-12-417102-8). Acad Pr.

Organic Chemistry of Nucleic Acids, Pts. A & B. Ed. by N. K. Kochetkov & E. I. Budovsky. LC 77-178777. 280p. 1972. Pt. A. 240pp. 59.50x o.p. (ISBN 0-306-37531-1, Plenum Pr); Pt. B. 330pp. 65.00 o.p. (ISBN 0-306-37532-X). Plenum Pub.

Organic Chemistry of Sulfur. Ed. by S. Oae. LC 72-95072. 714p. 1977. 95.00x o.p. (ISBN 0-306-30740-5, Plenum Pr). Plenum Pub.

Organic Chemistry: Syntheses & Reactivity. L. Birkofer. (Topics in Current Chemistry Ser.: Vol. 88). (Illus.). 200p. 1980. 61.00 o.p. (ISBN 0-387-09817-8). Springer-Verlag.

Organic Compounds in Soils: Sorption, Degradation & Persistence. L. G. Morrill et al. 1982. text ed. 45.00 o.p. (ISBN 0-250-40514-8). Butterworth.

Organic Compounds: Syntheses, Stereochemistry, Reactivity. (Topics in Current Chemistry: Vol. 74). (Illus.). 1978. 37.00 o.p. (ISBN 0-387-08633-1). Springer-Verlag.

Organic Electrochemistry. L. Eberson. LC 70-31906. (Topics in Current Chemistry: Vol. 21). (Illus.). 1971. pap. 48.40 o.p. (ISBN 0-387-05463-4). Springer-Verlag.

Organic Electrochemistry. A. J. Frey & G. Dryhurst. LC 51-5497. (Topics in Current Chemistry: Vol. 34). (Illus.). iii, 85p. 1972. pap. 23.10 o.p. (ISBN 0-387-06074-X). Springer-Verlag.

Organic Electron Spectral Data, Vol.13. Ed. by John P. Phillips et al. LC 60-16428. 1190p. 1977. 69.50 o.p. (ISBN 0-471-03563-7). Krieger.

Organic Electronic Spectral Data, Vol. XVIII. John P. Phillips et al. LC 60-16428. 1053p. 1982. text ed. 126.00 o.p. (ISBN 0-471-87178-8, Pub. by John Wiley). Krieger.

Organic Electronic Spectral Data, Vol. XIX, 1977. John P. Phillips & B. S. Thyagarajan. LC 60-16428. (Organic Electronic Spectral Data Ser.). 1068p. 1983. 137.00 o.p. (ISBN 0-471-88637-8, 2197). Krieger.

Organic Electronic Spectral Data, Vol. 14. Ed. by J. P. Phillips et al. LC 60-16428. 1178p. 1978. 108.50 o.p. (ISBN 0-471-05076-8). Krieger.

Organic Electronic Spectral Data: 1975, Vol. 17. John P. Phillips et al. LC 60-16428. 1076p. 1981. 137.00 o.p. (ISBN 0-471-08614-2, Pub. by Wiley-Interscience). Krieger.

Organic Electronic Spectral Data 1978, Vol. XX. Ed. by J. P. Phillips et al. (Organic Electronic Spectral Data Ser.: No. 2-197). 1040p. 1984. 120.00 o.p. (ISBN 0-471-81808-9, Pub. by John Wiley). Krieger.

Organic Electronics Spectral Data, Vol. 18. Phillips. LC 60-16428. 1070p. 1982. lib. bdg. 126.00 o.p. (ISBN 0-317-57932-0). Krieger.

Organic Electronics Spectral Data, Vol. 20. Phillips. LC 60-16408. 1056p. 1984. lib. bdg. 125.00 o.p. (ISBN 0-317-57923-1). Krieger.

Organic Functional Group Analysis, Theory & Development. G. H. Schenk. LC 67-28668. 1968. 75.00 o.p. (ISBN 0-08-012626-X); pap. 75.00 o.p. (ISBN 0-08-012625-1). Pergamon.

Organic Functional Group Preparations, 3 vols. Stanley R. Sandler & Wolf Karo. (Organic Chemistry Ser.: Vol. 12). Vol.1. 1969. 77.00 o.p.; Vol.2. 1971. 98.00 o.p. (ISBN 0-12-618552-2); Vol. 3. 1972. 89.00 o.p. Acad Pr.

Organic Gardener. Catharine O. Foster. 1972. 10.95 o.p. (ISBN 0-394-47210-1); pap. 8.95 o.p. (ISBN 0-394-71785-6). Knopf.

Organic Gardeners Complete Guide to Vegetables & Fruits. Rodale Press, Inc. Editors. Ed. by Anne Halpin. (Illus.). 528p. 1982. 21.95 o.p. (ISBN 0-87857-386-0, 01-025-0). Rodale Pr Inc.

Organic Gardening in the West: Raising Vegetables in a Short, Dry Growing Season. Robert F. Smith, Jr. (Illus.). 1976. pap. 4.95 o.p. (ISBN 0-913270-60-1). Sunstone Pr.

Organic Geochemistry Two: A Selection of Papers from the Second Australian Geochemistry Conference, University of Melbourne, 28-29 May 1984. Ed. by E. W. Baker. 98p. 1985. pap. 40.00 o.p. (ISBN 0-08-032640-4, Pub by PPL). Pergamon.

Organic Liquids: Structure, Dynamics & Chemical Properties. Ed. by A. D. Buckingham et al. LC 78-8462. 352p. 1979. 110.00 o.p. (ISBN 0-471-99673-4, Pub. by Wiley-Interscience). Wiley.

Organic Materials & Soil Productivity. W. Flaig et al. (Soils Bulletins: No. 35). 127p. (2nd Printing). 1977. pap. 13.50 o.p. (ISBN 92-5-100510-9, F1404, FAO). UNIPUB.

Organic Phosphorous Compounds, Vol. 3. G. M. Kosolapoff & L. Maier. 508p. 1972. 44.50 o.p. (ISBN 0-471-50442-4, John Wiley). Krieger.

Organic Photochemistry of Benzene-I. D. Bryce-Smith & A. Gilbert. 18p. 1976. pap. 15.50 o.p. (ISBN 0-08-020464-3). Pergamon.

Organic Polymer Chemistry. K. J. Saunders. 1973. 32.00x o.p. (ISBN 0-412-10580-2, NO. 6245, Pub. by Chapman & Hall England). Routledge Chapman & Hall.

Organic Reactions, Vol. 29. William G. Dauben. LC 79-642486. 468p. 1989. Repr. of 1983 ed. 53.50 o.p. (ISBN 0-471-87490-6). Krieger.

Organic Reactions, Vol. 31. Ed. by William G. Dauben. LC 42-20265. (Organic Reactions Ser.: 2-201). 376p. 1984. 55.00 o.p. (ISBN 0-471-88671-8, Pub by Wiley Interscience). Wiley.

Organic Reagents in Metal Analysis. K. Burger. 270p. 1973. 70.00 o.p. (ISBN 0-08-016929-5). Pergamon.

Organic Recycling in Asia: Papers Presented at the FAO-SIDA Workshop on the use of Organic Materials as Fertilizers in Asia, Bangkok, Oct. 26-Nov 5, 1976. (Soils Bulletins: No. 36). 423p. 1978. pap. 24.50 o.p. (ISBN 92-5-100655-5, F1550, FAO). UNIPUB.

Organic Scintillators & Liquid Scintillation Counting. Ed. by Donald L. Horrocks & Chin-Tzu Peng. LC 77-137625. 1971. 96.50 o.p. (ISBN 0-12-356250-3). Acad Pr.

Organic Semiconductors: Dark & Photoconductivity of Organic Solids. H. Meier. LC 74-76846. (Monographs in Modern Chemistry: Vol. 2). (Illus.). 661p. 1974. 88.00 o.p. (ISBN 3-527-25438-2). VCH Pubs.

Organic Solid-State Chemistry-2: Proceedings of An International Symposium, Rehovot, Israel, 1970. Ed. by M. D. Cohen. 230p. 1976. 60.00 o.p. (ISBN 0-08-020803-7). Pergamon.

Organic Structural Analysis. Joseph B. Lambert et al. (Illus.). 640p. 1976. text ed. (ISBN 0-02-367290-0). Macmillan.

Organic Syntheses, Vol. 59. Ed. by Robert M. Coates. LC 21-17747. (Series on Organic Synthesis). 1980. 26.95 o.p. (ISBN 0-471-05963-3, Pub. by Wiley-Interscience). Wiley.

Organic Syntheses, Vol. 60. Ed. by Orville L. Chapman. LC 21-17747. (Organic Syntheses Ser.). 156p. 1981. 26.50 o.p. (ISBN 0-471-09359-9, Pub. by Wiley-Interscience). Wiley.

Organic Syntheses: Collective Volumes, 1-49, 6 Vols. R. L. Shriner. 1983. 295.00 set o.p. (ISBN 0-471-80555-6). Wiley.

Organic Synthesis--Today & Tomorrow: Third IUPAC Symposium on Organic Synthesis, Madison, Wisconsin, U. S. A., 15-20 June 1980. Ed. by Barry M. Trost & C. R. Hutchinson. (IUAC Symposium Ser.). (Illus.). 360p. 1981. 100.00 o.p. (ISBN 0-08-025268-0). Pergamon.

Organic Vegetable Gardening. Bob Percival. (Illus.). 544p. (Orig.). 1984. 25.95 o.p. (ISBN 0-8306-0660-2, 1660H); pap. 16.50 o.p. (ISBN 0-8306-1660-8, 1660P). TAB Bks.

Organicum: A Practical Handbook of Organic Chemistry. B. J. Hazzard et al. 1973. 190.00 o.p. (ISBN 0-08-012789-4); pap. text ed. 24.00 o.p. (ISBN 0-08-018964-4). Pergamon.

Organisation of Nematodes. Ed. by N. A. Croll. 1977. 95.50 o.p. (ISBN 0-12-196850-2). Acad Pr.

Organisational Aspects of Police Behaviour. J. Mervyn Jones. 188p. 1980. 35.25x o.p. (ISBN 0-566-00402-X). Gower Pub Co.

Organised Work: A Female Perspective. Ulla Ressner & Evy Gunnarson. 1986. text ed. write for info. o.p. (Pub. by Gower Pub England). Gower Pub Co.

Organising Social Services Departments. David Billis et al. 1981. text ed. 28.50x o.p. (ISBN 0-435-82085-0). Gower Pub Co.

Organisms & Biological Communities As Indicators of Environmemtal Quality: A Symposium, the Ohio State University, March 25,1974. Charles C. King & Lynn E. Elfner. 1975. 3.00 o.p. (ISBN 0-86727-078-0). Ohio Bio Survey.

Organization & Administration of the Union Army 1861-1865, 2 vols. Fred A. Shannon. Set. 25.00 o.p. Peter Smith.

Organization & Collective Bargaining in Public Employment: Proceedings of the Institute of Industrial Relations Conference on Employee Relations in Public Agencies. Institute of Industrial Relations Staff. 50p. 1968. 2.00 o.p. (ISBN 0-89215-035-1). U Cal LA Indus Rel.

Organization & Expression of Chromosomes. Ed. by V. G. Allfrey et al. (Dahlem Workshop Reports Ser.: L.S.R.R. No. 4). 349p. 1976. pap. 36.50x o.p. (ISBN 0-89573-088-X). VCH Pubs.

Organization & Expression of the Eukaryotic Genome. Ed. by E. M. Bradbury & K. Javaherian. 1977. 107.50 o.p. (ISBN 0-12-123550-5). Acad Pr.

Organization & Management: A Systems & Contingency Approach. 3rd rev. ed. Fremont Kast & James Rosenzweig. (Management Ser.). (Illus.). 1979. text ed. 39.95x o.p. (ISBN 0-07-033346-7). McGraw.

Organization & Structure of FAO Including Titles of Staff. Incl. (No. 15, Rev. 1). 54p. 1971. pap. 8.25 o.p. (F1201, F). UNIPUB; (No. 15, Rev. 2). 88p. 1974. pap. 7.50 (F1202, F). UNIPUB. (Terminology Bulletin Ser., FAO). UNIPUB.

Organization & Technical Problems of Transfusion; Clinical Problems of Transfusion see Proceedings of the International Society of Blood Transfusion, 12th Congress, Moscow, 1969.

Organization Design: Theoretical Perspectives & Empirical Findings. Ed. by Elmer H. Burack & Anant Negandhi. LC 77-24228. 400p. 1977. 17.50x o.p. (ISBN 0-87338-206-4, Pub. by Comparative Adm. Research Institute). Kent St U Pr.

Organization Development: A Total Systems Approach to Positive Change in Any Business Organization. Karl Albrecht. 254p. 1983. 18.45 o.p. (ISBN 0-13-641696-9). P-H.

Organization Development & Management. Ed. by Jim Hammons. LC 81-48473. (Community College Ser.: No. 37). 1982. 12.95x o.p. (ISBN 0-87589-883-1). Jossey-Bass.

Organization Development in Transition: Evidence of an Evolving Profession. A. J. McLean et al. 140p. 1982. 38.95x o.p. (ISBN 0-471-10142-7, Pub. by Wiley-Interscience). Wiley.

Organization for Manufacturing, Vol. 2. Ed. by Ivan R. Vernon. LC 79-110568. (Manufacturing Management Ser.). (Illus.). 252p. 1970. text ed. 11.25 o.p. (ISBN 0-87263-018-8). SME.

Organization, Functioning & Activities of National Documentary Information Systems in the Scientific, Technical & Economic Fields. V. Taraboi. LC 67-1784. 88p. 1973. pap. 38.00 o.p. (ISBN 0-08-017725-5). Pergamon.

Organization Guerrilla: Playing the Game to Win. Allen Weiss. 1975. 8.95 o.p. (ISBN 0-689-10685-8, Atheneum). Macmillan.

Organization in Plants. 3rd ed. W. M. Baron. LC 78-12085. 264p. 1979. pap. 31.95x o.p. (ISBN 0-470-26558-2). Halsted Pr.

Organization of American States. Ann Van Wynen Thomas & A. J. Thomas, Jr. LC 63-9754. 544p. 1965. Repr. of 1963 ed. 22.50x o.p. (ISBN 0-87074-113-6). SMU Press.

Organization of Interests: Incentives & the Internal Dynamics of Political Interest Groups. Terry M. Moe. LC 79-13238. (Illus.). x, 282p. 1982. pap. text ed. 10.00x o.s.i. (ISBN 0-226-53352-2). U of Chicago Pr.

Organization of Medical Record Departments in Hospitals. Margaret F. Skurka. Ed. by Mary E. Converse. LC 83-21535. 124p. 1984. pap. 19.95 o.p. (ISBN 0-939450-52-6, 148151). AHPI.

Organization of Phonology. Stephen R. Anderson. 1974. 24.95 o.p. (ISBN 0-12-785031-7). Acad Pr.

Organization of Prose & Its Effects on Memory. B. J. Meyer. (N-H Studies in Theoretical Poetics: Vol. 1). 249p. 1975. pap. 66.00 o.p. (ISBN 0-444-10946-3, North-Holland). Elsevier.

Organization of Space in Developing Countries. E. A. Johnson. LC 74-122216. 1970. 29.50x o.p. (ISBN 0-674-64338-0). Harvard U Pr.

Organization of the Library Profession. 2nd ed. Ed. by H. Chaplin. (IFLA Publication Ser.: No. 6). 132p. 1976. lib. bdg. 12.00 o.p. (ISBN 3-7940-4309-X). K G Saur.

Organization Strategy: A Marketing Approach. E. Raymond Corey & Steven H. Star. LC 79-132151. 1971. 27.95x o.p. (ISBN 0-87584-088-4, Dist. by Harper & Row Pubs., Inc.). Harvard Busn.

Organization: The Effect on Large Corporations. Barry C. Harris. Ed. by Fred Bateman. LC 83-3589. (Research in Business Economics & Public Policy Ser.: No. 2). 138p. 1983. 37.95 o.p. (ISBN 0-8357-1435-7). UMI Res Pr.

Organization Theory: An Integrated Approach. Richard N. Osborn et al. LC 83-27537. 632p. 1984. Repr. of 1980 ed. lib. bdg. 37.50 o.p. (ISBN 0-89874-738-4). Krieger.

Organizational America. William G. Scott & David K. Hart. 1979. 13.95 o.p. (ISBN 0-395-27599-7). HM.

Organizational America. William G. Scott & David K. Hart. 1980. pap. 8.70 o.p. (ISBN 0-395-29698-6). HM.

Organizational Barriers & Their Impact on Women in Higher Education. Myra J. Stokes. 1984. 8.00 o.p. (ISBN 0-317-42937-X). Natl Assn Women.

Organizational Behavior. 2nd ed. W. Jack Duncan. LC 80-82460. (Illus.). 464p. 1981. text ed. 41.16 o.p. (ISBN 0-395-29640-4); 1.25 o.p. HM.

Organizational Behavior. W. Jack Duncan. LC 77-76344. (Illus.). 1978. text ed. 17.95 o.p. (ISBN 0-395-25744-1). HM.

Organizational Behavior. George Strauss et al. 1976. pap. text ed. (ISBN 0-534-00466-0). PWS-Kent Pub.

Organizational Behavior, Vol. 8. Compiled by James W. Dean & Richard Schwindt. 207p. 1985. 14.00 o.p. (ISBN 0-88024-108-X). Eno River Pr.

Organizational Behavior: A Management Approach. Harry R. Knudson & C. Patrick Fleenor. (Orig.). 1978. pap. text ed. 14.95 o.p. (ISBN 0-316-50000-3). Little.

Organizational Behavior: A Managerial Viewpoint. Robert Albanse & David D. Van Fleet. 640p. 1983. 33.95x o.p. (ISBN 0-03-050736-7); instr's. manual 19.95 o.p. (ISBN 0-03-050741-3). Dryden Pr.

Organizational Behavior: An Applied Psychological Approach. 2nd ed. Dennis W. Organ & Clay Hamner. 1982. 31.95x o.p. (ISBN 0-256-02431-6). Irwin.

Organizational Behavior & Management: A Contingency Approach. 3rd ed. Ed. by Henry L. Tosi & W. Clay Hamner. LC 81-16443. (St. Clair Series in Management & Organizational Behavior). 581p. 1982. 29.50 o.p. (ISBN 0-471-08504-9). Wiley.

Organizational Behavior & Management. John M. Ivancevich & Michael T. Matteson. 1987. 40.95 o.p. (ISBN 0-256-05608-0). Irwin.

Organizational Behavior & Management. Laurie G. Larwood. LC 83-22241. 576p. 1984. text ed. 32.00 o.p. (ISBN 0-534-03135-8). PWS-Kent Pub.

Organizational Behavior & Management. 4th ed. Henry L. Tosi & W. Clay Hamner. LC 84-19768. 569p. 1985. pap. 26.95 o.p. (ISBN 0-88244-277-5); pap. text ed. 22.95 o.p. Pub Horizons.

Organizational Behavior: Contemporary Viewpoints. Ed. by Kerry M. Andrade & Suzanne R. Ontiveros. LC 86-1220. (Human Resources Management Ser.). 250p. 1986. lib. bdg. 39.00 o.p. (ISBN 0-87436-465-5). ABC-Clio.

Organizational Behavior: Foundation for Organizational Effectiveness. J. C. Wofford. LC 81-50040. 480p. 1982. 21.75 o.p. (ISBN 0-534-01106-3). PWS-Kent Pub.

Organizational Behavior Reading & Cases. 2nd ed. Ed. by Theodore T. Herbert. 403p. 1981. pap. text ed. write for info. o.p. (ISBN 0-02-353610-1). Macmillan.

Organizational Behavior: Understanding Life at Work. Gary Johns. 1983. text ed. write for info. o.p. (ISBN 0-673-15366-5). Scott F.

Organizational Biosynthesis. Ed. by Henry J. Vogel et al. 1967. 82.50 o.p. (ISBN 0-12-722556-0). Acad Pr.

Organizational Change by Choice. D. C. Dunphy & B. Dick. 312p. 1983. text ed. 21.00 o.p. (ISBN 0-07-072947-6). McGraw.

Organizational Climates & Careers: The Work Lives of Priests. Douglas T. Hall & Benjamin Schneider. LC 78-187261. (Quantitative Studies in Social Relation). 280p. 1973. 52.50 o.p. (ISBN 0-12-785300-6). Acad Pr.

Organizational Communication Nineteen Seventy-Seven: Abstracts, Analysis, & Overview. new ed. Howard H. Greenbaum & Raymond L. Falcione. 1979. pap. 9.00 o.p. (ISBN 0-931874-08-4). Assn Busn Comm.

Organizational Concept for Information Management Programs. 91p. 1980. 16.00 o.p. (ISBN 0-933887-04-3). Assn Recs Mgrs & Admin.

Organizational Development: Theory, Practice, Research. 2nd ed. Wendell L. French, Jr. et al. 1983. pap. 28.95 o.p. (ISBN 0-256-02689-0). Irwin.

Organizational Environments: Ritual & Rationality. John W. Meyer et al. LC 83-13698. 302p. 1985. 29.95 o.s.i. (ISBN 0-8039-2081-4); pap. 14.95 o.p. (ISBN 0-8039-2469-0). Sage.

Organizational Functioning in Cross-Cultural Perspective. George W. England et al. LC 78-31169. 325p. 1979. 17.50x o.p. (ISBN 0-87338-225-0). Kent St U Pr.

Organizational Policy & Strategic Management: Text & Cases. 2nd ed. James M. Higgins. 816p. 1983. 33.95x o.p. (ISBN 0-03-061961-0); instr's. manual 19.95 o.p. (ISBN 0-03-061962-9). Dryden Pr.

Organizational Renewal in a School District: Self-Help Through a Cadre of Organizational Specialists. Philip J. Runkel et al. LC 79-57252. 168p. (Orig.). 1980. pap. 7.50 o.p. (ISBN 0-936276-12-6). Ctr Educ Policy Mgmt.

Organizational Shock. W. Clay Hamner. LC 80-11910. (St. Clair Series in Management & Organizational Behavior). 430p. 1980. pap. text ed. 27.50 o.p. (ISBN 0-471-06251-0). Wiley.

Organizational Strategy & Policy: Text & Cases. 3rd ed. Frank T. Paine & William Naumes. 618p. 1982. 32.95x o.p. (ISBN 0-03-060067-7); instr's. manual 20.00 o.p. (ISBN 0-03-060068-5). Dryden Pr.

Organizational Surveys: An Internal Assessment of Organizational Health. Frank J. Smith & Randall Dunham. 1979. pap. text ed. write for info. o.p. (ISBN 0-673-15143-3). Scott F.

Organizational Training for a School Faculty. Richard A. Schmuck & Philip J. Runkel. LC 73-629555. 1970. 2.50 o.p. (ISBN 0-936276-07-X). Ctr Educ Policy Mgmt.

Organizational Transitions: Managing Complex Change. R. Beckhard & R. T. Harris. 1977. 11.95 o.p. (ISBN 0-201-00335-X). Addison-Wesley.

Organizational World. Harold J. Leavitt et al. 335p. 1973. pap. text ed. 11.00 o.p. (ISBN 0-15-567562-1, HC). HarBraceJ.

Organizational Writing. Larry Bielawski & A. Franklin Parks. 535p. 1987. pap. (ISBN 0-534-06534-1). Wadsworth Pub.

Organizations Alike & Unlike. Ed. by Cornelius J. Lammers & David J. Hickson. (International Studies in the Sociology of Organizations). 1979. pap. 22.95x o.p. (ISBN 0-7100-0385-4). Routledge Chapman & Hall.

Organizations: An Information Systems Perspective. Kenneth Knight & Reuben McDaniel. 1979. pap. (ISBN 0-534-00583-7). PWS-Kent Pub.

Organizations: An Information Systems Perspective. Kenneth E. Knight & Reuben R. McDaniel, Jr. LC 78-8929. 191p. 1979. pap. text ed. 9.95x o.p. (ISBN 0-534-00583-7). PWS-Kent Pub.

Organizations: Behavior, Structure, Processes. 5th ed. James L. Gibson et al. 1985. 38.95x o.p. (ISBN 0-256-03265-3). Irwin.

Organizations by Design. Mariann Jelinek et al. 1981. pap. 21.95x o.p. (ISBN 0-256-02561-4). Irwin.

Organizations Closeup: A Book of Readings. 5th ed. James L. Gibson et al. 1985. pap. 18.95 o.p. (ISBN 0-256-03266-1). Irwin.

Organizations in the Computer Age. David A. Buchanan & David Boddy. 279p. 1983. text ed. 45.00 o.p. (ISBN 0-566-00488-7). Gower Pub Co.

Organized Crime in America. Jay S. Albanese. LC 85-70121. (Criminal Justice Studies). v, 142p. 1985. 13.95 o.p. (ISBN 0-87084-024-X). Anderson Pub Co.

Organized Executive: New Ways to Manage Time, Paper, & People. Stephanie Winston. (Illus.). 265p. 1983. 14.50 o.p. (ISBN 0-393-01813-X). Norton.

Organized Religion. Hiram Elfenbein. LC 67-26264. 246p. 1968. Philos Lib.

Organizing Course Materials for Industrial Education see Planning & Organizing Instruction.

Organizing Space Activities for World Needs. Ed. by Ernst A. Steinhoff. 1971. 120.00 o.p. (ISBN 0-08-006851-0). Pergamon.

Organizing Staff Development: Programs That Work. Terry O'Banion. 1978. 5.00 o.p. (ISBN 0-87117-074-4, 1028). Am Assn Comm Jr Coll.

Organizing the Library's Support: Donors, Volunteers, Friends. Ed. by Donald W. Krummel. LC 80-14772. (Allerton Park Institute Ser.: No. 25). 119p. 1980. 10.00 o.p. (ISBN 0-87845-054-8). U of Ill Lib Info Sci.

Organizing the Presidency. Stephen Hess. LC 76-28668. 228p. 1976. 26.95 o.p. (ISBN 0-8157-3588-X); pap. 9.95 o.p. (ISBN 0-8157-3587-1). Brookings.

Organo-Transition Metal Compounds & Related Aspects of Homogenous Catalysis. B. L. Shaw & N. I. Tucker. (Pergamon Texts in Inorganic Chemistry: Vol. 23). 214p. 1975. text ed. 34.00 o.p. (ISBN 0-08-018872-9); pap. text ed. 17.50 o.p. (ISBN 0-08-018871-0). Pergamon.

Organoborane Chemistry. Thomas Onak. (Organoborane Chemistry Ser.). 1975. 93.50 o.p. (ISBN 0-12-526550-6). Acad Pr.

Organochlorine Insecticides: Persistent Organic Pollutants. Ed. by F. Moriarty. 1975. 81.00 o.p. (ISBN 0-12-506750-X). Acad Pr.

Organochromium Compounds. R. P. Sneeden. (Organometalic Chemistry Ser.). 1975. 88.00 o.p. (ISBN 0-12-653850-6). Acad Pr.

Organometallic Compounds-Models of Synthesis, Physical Constants & Chemical Reactions, Vol. 1: Compounds of Transition Metals. 2nd ed. K. Bauer & G. Haller. Ed. by M. Dub. LC 66-28249. xxvi, 1171p. 1975. 91.30 o.p. (ISBN 0-387-07196-2). Springer-Verlag.

Organometallic Compounds-Synthesis, Stucture, & Theory: Proceedings of the Annual Symposia of the Industry-University Cooperative Chemistry Program (IUCCP) of the Texas A&M University Department of Chemistry, No. 1. Ed. by B. L. Shapiro. LC 83-45137. 512p. 1983. 40.00x o.p. (ISBN 0-89096-170-0). Tex A&M Univ Pr.

Organometallic Compounds, Vol 1, Pt. 2: Groups IV & V. 4th ed. B. J. Aylett. 1979. 89.95 o.p. (ISBN 0-412-13020-3, NO. 6018, Pub. by Chapman & Hall). Routledge Chapman & Hall.

Organometallic Polymers. Ed. by Charles E. Carraher & John Sheats. 1978. 59.00 o.p. (ISBN 0-12-160850-6). Acad Pr.

Organometallics in Organic Synthesis: General Discussions & Organometallics of Main Group Metals in Organic Synthesis, Vol. 1. Ei-Ichi Negishi. LC 79-16818. 532p. 1980. 45.00 o.p. (ISBN 0-471-03193-3, Pub. by Wiley-Interscience). Wiley.

Organophosphorous Stereochemistry, 2 pts. Ed. by W. E. McEwen & K. D. Berlin. Incl. Pt. 1. Origins of P(3&4) Compounds. 387p. 1975. 77.00 (ISBN 0-12-787031-8); Pt. 2. P(5) Compounds. 1975. 70.00 (ISBN 0-12-787032-6). (Benchmark Papers on Organic Chemistry: Vols. 3 & 4). 1975. Acad Pr.

Organophosphorus Monomers & Polymers. Y. Gefter. 1962. 50.00 o.p. (ISBN 0-08-009655-7). Pergamon.

Organosilicon Chemistry--1: Proceedings of an International Symposium, Prague, 1965. International Union of Pure & Applied Chemistry. 336p. 1976. 85.00 o.p. (ISBN 0-08-020807-X). Pergamon.

Organs of Our Time. Ed. by Homer D. Blanchard. (Illus.). 1975. pap. 17.50 o.p. (ISBN 0-930112-01-6). Organ Lit.

Orgone Energy: The Answer to Atomic Suicide. Jerome Eden. LC 72-75477. 1972. 8.95 o.p. (ISBN 0-682-47477-0). Exposition-Phoenix.

Orgone, Reich & Eros. W. Edward Mann. 1974. pap. 6.95 o.p. (ISBN 0-671-21726-7, Touchstone Bks). S&S.

Orient Travel Guide. Sunset Magazine & Books Editors. LC 82-83216. (Illus.). 160p. 1983. pap. 9.95 o.p. (ISBN 0-376-06633-4, Sunset Bks). Sunset-Lane.

Oriental Art: A Quarterly Journal Devoted to All Forms of Oriental Art. Incl. Vols. 1-3, London, 1948-49-1950-51. 177.00 (ISBN 0-317-44424-7); pap. text ed. 168.00 (ISBN 0-317-44425-5); Vols. 1-17, London, 1955-1971. 1284.00 (ISBN 0-317-44426-3); pap. text ed. 1221.00 (ISBN 0-317-44427-1); Vols. 18-28, London, 1972-1982. pap. 1100.00 (ISBN 0-317-44428-X). 1986. Kraus Repr.

Oriental Ceramics: The World's Great Collections, 8 vols. Incl. Vol. 1. Tokyo National Museum. 68.00 (ISBN 0-317-55050-0); Vol. 2. National Museum of Korea, Seoul. 68.00 (ISBN 0-317-55051-9); Vol. 3. Museum Pusat, Jakarta. 68.00 (ISBN 0-317-55052-7); Vol. 4. Iran Bastan Museum, Teheran. 65.00 (ISBN 0-317-55053-5); Vol. 5. British Museum, London. 68.00 (ISBN 0-317-55054-3); Vol. 6. Percival David Foundation of Chinese Art, London. Date not set. 68.00 (ISBN 0-317-55055-1); Vol. 7. Musee Guimet, Paris. 65.00 (ISBN 0-317-55056-X); Vol.8. Museum of Far Eastern Antiquities, Stockholm. 68.00 (ISBN 0-317-55057-8); Vol. 9. Freer Gallery of Art, Washington DC. 65.00 (ISBN 0-317-55058-6); Vol. 10. Museum of the Fine Arts, Boston. Date not set. 65.00 (ISBN 0-317-55059-4). Eight-volume set. 500.00 o.p. (ISBN 0-317-55049-7). Apollo.

Oriental Coins & Their Values: The Ancient & Classical World, Vol. 2. Michael Mitchiner. 760p. 1978. lib. bdg. 125.00 o.p. (ISBN 0-904173-16-X, Pub. by Seaby UK). Numismatic Fine Arts.

Oriental Cooking the Fast Wok Way. Jacqueline Heriteau. 1984. pap. 3.50 o.p. (AE2052, Sig). NAL.

Oriental Favorites. Bon Appetit Magazine Editors. LC 85-31230. (Cooking with Bon Appetit Ser.). 1986. 12.95 o.p. (ISBN 0-89535-177-3). Knapp Pr.

Oriental Magic. Sayed I. Shah. 206p. 1957. (ISBN 0-8022-1539-4). Philos Lib.

Oriental Rugs & Carpets Today: How to Choose & Enjoy Them. Georges Izmidlian. (Illus.). 128p. 1983. 19.95 o.p. (ISBN 0-88254-800-X); pap. 11.95 o.p. (ISBN 0-88254-801-8). Hippocrene Bks.

Oriental Rugs in the Metropolitan Museum of Art. M. S. Dimand & Jean Mailey. LC 73-2846. (Illus.). 356p. 1973. 45.00 o.p. (ISBN 0-87099-124-8). Metro Mus Art.

Oriental Sex Manners. Howard S. Levy. 1978. text ed. 15.00x o.p. (ISBN 0-685-67212-3). Oriental Bk Store.

Oriental Tales. Marguerite Yourcenar. Tr. by Alberto Manguel. 147p. 1986. pap. 7.95 o.p. (ISBN 0-374-51997-8). FS&G.

Orientalisierende Glaser, Vol. 1: J. & L. Lobmeyr. Waltraud Neuwirth. (Illus.). 423p. (Ger.). 1986. pap. 30.00 o.p. (ISBN 3-900282-16-1, Pub. by Waltraud Neuwirth). Seven Hills Bk Dists.

Orientalistes, Peintres Voyageurs 1828-1908. Lynne Thornton. (Illus.). 272p. sewn bdg. 95.00 o.p. (ISBN 0-317-54956-1). Apollo.

Orientalists, Painter-Travellers 1828-1908. Lynne Thornton. (Illus.). 272p. 1983. 75.00 o.p. (ISBN 0-911403-00-0, Pub. by ACR Edn Fr). Seven Hills Bk Dists.

Orientation & Form. Irvin Rock. 1974. 31.50 o.p. (ISBN 0-12-591250-1). Acad Pr.

Orientation to Total Fitness. 3rd ed. Vincent J. Melograno & James E. Klinzing. 1984. pap. text ed. 12.95 o.p. (ISBN 0-8403-3179-7). Kendall-Hunt.

Oriented Nuclei: Polarized Targets & Beams. James M. Daniels. (Pure & Applied Physics Ser.: Vol. 20). 1965. 65.50 o.p. (ISBN 0-12-202950-X). Acad Pr.

Origami & Paper Craft. Paul Jackson. (Illus.). 1989. 9.98 o.p. (ISBN 0-517-66804-1). Crown.

Origial Roadkill Cookbook. B. R. Peterson. 64p. 1987. pap. 4.95 o.p. (ISBN 0-317-60855-X). Ten Speed Pr.

Origin & Chemistry of Petroleum: Proceedings of the Third Annual Karcher Symposium, Oklahoma, 1979. G. Atkinson. Ed. by J. J. Zuckerman. (Illus.). 120p. 1981. 35.00 o.p. (ISBN 0-08-026179-5). Pergamon.

Origin & Conclusion of the Paris Pact. Denys P. Myers. Bd. with Renunciation of War. Kirby Page. LC 75-147608. (Library of War & Peace; Kellogg Pact & the Outlawry of War). lib. bdg. 46.00 o.p. (ISBN 0-8240-0368-3). Garland Pub.

Origin & Continuity of Cell Organelles. Ed. by J. Reinert & H. Ursprung. LC 75-132272. (Results & Problems in Cell Differentiation: Vol. 2). (Illus.). 1971. 44.00 o.p. (ISBN 0-387-05239-9). Springer-Verlag.

Origin & Destiny of the Earth's Magnetic Field. Thomas Barnes. LC 73-79065. (ICR Technical Monograph: No. 4). (Illus.). 132p. 1973. pap. 7.95 o.p. (ISBN 0-89051-013-X). Master Bks.

Origin & Development of Early Christian Church Architecture. J. Gordon Davies. (Illus.). 147p. 1953. (ISBN 0-8022-0350-7). Philos Lib.

Origin & Development of Living Systems. J. Brooks & G. Shaw. 1973. 67.50 o.p. (ISBN 0-12-135740-6). Acad Pr.

Origin & Development of the Army Security Agency, 1917-1947. U. S. Army, Security Agency, Historical Section Staff. (Cryptographic Ser.). 1978. 8.80 o.p. (ISBN 0-89412-114-6); lib. bdg. 16.80 o.p. (ISBN 0-89412-025-5). Aegean Park Pr.

Origin & Distribution of the Elements: First & Second Symposium. L. H. Ahrens. 1979. 230.00 o.p. (ISBN 0-08-022947-6). Pergamon.

Origin & Early Form of Greek Tragedy. Gerald F. Else. 144p. 1972. pap. 2.45 o.p. (ISBN 0-393-00656-5, Norton Lib). Norton.

Origin & Evolution of the Priesthood. James A. Mohler. 137p. 1976. pap. 3.95 o.p. (ISBN 0-8189-0342-2). Alba.

Origin & Significance of Hegel's Logic. James B. Baillie. LC 83-48502. (Philosophy of Hegel Ser.). 398p. 1984. lib. bdg. 50.00 o.p. (ISBN 0-8240-5625-6). Garland Pub.

Origin & Significance of the Frankfurt School, a Marxist Perspective. Phil Slater. (International Library of Sociology). 1980. pap. 9.95x o.p. (ISBN 0-7100-0490-7). Routledge Chapman & Hall.

Origin, Nature & Evolution of Protoplasmic Individuals & their Associations: Protoplasmic Action & Experience. Faustino Cordon. (Illus.). 650p. 1982. 145.00 o.p. (ISBN 0-08-027990-2). Pergamon.

Origin of Cerebral Field Potentials. E. J. Speckman & H. Caspers. LC 78-24682. (Illus.). 230p. 1979. text ed. 28.00 o.p. (ISBN 0-88416-281-8). Year Bk Med.

Origin of Consciousness in the Breakdown of the Bicameral Mind. Julian Jaynes. 1977. 19.95 o.p. (ISBN 0-395-20729-0). HM.

Origin of Continents & Ocean Basins. M. Muratov. 191p. 1977. 6.45 o.p. (ISBN 0-8285-0797-X, Pub. by Mir Pubs USSR). Imported Pubns.

Origin of English Place-Names. P. H. Reaney. 277p. 1985. pap. 9.95 o.p. (ISBN 0-7102-0728-X). Routledge Chapman & Hall.

Origin of History as Metaphysics. Marjorie Burke. Philos Lib.

Origin of Life. A. I. Oparin. Tr. & annotations by Sergius Morgulis. LC 53-10161. lib. bdg. 12.50x o.p. (ISBN 0-88307-223-8). Gannon.

Origin of Local Government in New South Wales 1831-58. new ed. F. A. Larcombe. (Illus.). 352p. 1974. 36.00x o.p. (ISBN 0-424-06610-6, Pub. by Sydney U Pr). Intl Spec Bk.

Origin of Major Invertebrate Groups. M. R. House. (Systematics Association Ser.: No. 12). 1979. 130.50 o.p. (ISBN 0-12-357450-1). Acad Pr.

Origin of Species. Charles Darwin. 1982. pap. 8.00x o.p. (ISBN 0-318-04039-5, DEL-05136, Evman). Biblio Dist.

Origin of Terrestrial Vertebrates. Ivan I. Schmalhausen. Tr. by Leon Kelso. 1968. 72.50 o.p. (ISBN 0-12-625750-7). Acad Pr.

Origin of the Icelandic Family Sagas. Knut Liestol. LC 73-17630. 261p. 1975. Repr. of 1930 ed. lib. bdg. 24.75x o.p. (ISBN 0-8371-7253-5, LIIF). Greenwood.

Origin of the Land Tenure System in the United States. Marshall D. Harris. 1970. Repr. of 1953 ed. lib. bdg. 22.50x o.p. (ISBN 0-8371-3731-4, HATS). Greenwood.

Origin of the Solar System. John C. Whitcomb. (Biblical & Theological Studies). pap. 2.50 o.p. (ISBN 0-8010-9590-5). Baker Bk.

Origin of the Solar System: Proceedings. Ed. by R. Jastrow & A. G. Cameron. 1963. 54.00 o.p. (ISBN 0-12-381150-3). Acad Pr.

Origin of the Species. Charles Darwin. (ISBN 0-8022-0342-6). Philos Lib.

Origin of the Universe. Harold S. Slusher. LC 78-70532. (ICR Technical Monograph). 1978. pap. 6.95 o.p. (ISBN 0-932766-00-5, Inst Creation). Master Bks.

Origin of the West German Republic. Peter H. Merkl. LC 82-6267. xviii, 269p. 1982. Repr. of 1963 ed. lib. bdg. 38.50x o.p. (ISBN 0-313-23591-0, MEOR). Greenwood.

Origin, Prevention & Treatment of Affective Disorders. Ed. by M. Schou & E. Stromgren. 1979. 52.00 o.p. (ISBN 0-12-628950-6). Acad Pr.

Original Colored House of David. Martin Quigley. (gr. 7 up). 1981. 8.95 o.p. (ISBN 0-395-31608-1). HM.

Original Face: An Anthology of Rinzai Zen. Ed. by Thomas Cleary. LC 77-91354. 1978. pap. 4.95 o.p. (ISBN 0-394-17038-5, E707, Ever). Grove.

Original Record Collectors Price Guide: Blues-Rhythm & Blues-Soul. Jerry Osborne. LC 80-16711. 192p. 1980. pap. 9.95 o.p. (ISBN 0-89019-071-2). Norwalk Pr.

Original Record Collectors Price Guide: Record Album Price Guide. 3rd ed. Jerry Osborne & Bruce Hamilton. 208p. 1980. pap. 9.95 o.p. (ISBN 0-89019-074-7). Norwalk Pr.

Original Sin: Two Major Trends in Contemporary Roman Catholic Reinterpretation. G. Vandervelde. LC 81-40000. 364p. 1982. lib. bdg. 34.25 o.p. (ISBN 0-8191-1849-4); pap. text ed. 15.75 o.p. (ISBN 0-8191-1850-8). U Pr of Amer.

Original Teachings of Ch'an Buddhism. Ed. by Chang Chung-Yuan. LC 82-48003. (Grove Press Eastern Philosophy & Religion Ser.). 320p. 1982. pap. 9.95 o.p. (E813, Ever). Grove.

Original Thai Cookbook. Jennifer Brennan. (Illus.). 276p. 1981. 14.95 o.p. (ISBN 0-399-90110-8, Perigee); pap. 9.95 o.p. (ISBN 0-399-51033-8). Putnam Pub Group.

Originality & Competition in Science: A Study of the British High Energy Physics Community. Jerry Gaston. LC 73-81313. 1973. lib. bdg. 16.00x o.s.i. (ISBN 0-226-28429-8). U of Chicago Pr.

Origins. 4th ed. Morton Marcus. (Illus.). 80p. pap. 2.95 o.p. Brown Bear.

Origins: A Short Etymological Dictionary of Modern English. Eric Partridge. 972p. 1977. 45.00 o.p. (ISBN 0-02-594840-7). Macmillan.

Origins: A Skeptic's Guide to the Genesis of Life on Earth. Robert Shapiro. 320p. 1986. 17.45 o.s.i. (ISBN 0-671-45939-2). Summit Bks.

Origins & Course of Psychopathology: Methods of Longitudinal Research. Ed. by John S. Strauss et al. LC 77-2874. (Illus.). 468p. 1977. 59.50x o.p. (ISBN 0-306-31028-7, Plenum Pr). Plenum Pub.

Origins & Development of Labor Economics. Paul J. McNulty. 320p. 1980. text ed. 30.00x o.p. (ISBN 0-262-13162-5). MIT Pr.

Origins & Developments of the English Language. 2nd ed. Thomas Pyles & John Algeo. 1971. 14.50 o.p. (ISBN 0-15-567603-2). HarbraceJ.

Origins & History of Religions. John Murphy. 1952. (ISBN 0-8022-1175-5). Philos Lib.

Origins & Prehistory of Language. G. Revesz. 250p. 1956. (ISBN 0-8022-1328-6). Philos Lib.

Origins of Agriculture: An Evolutionary Perspective (Monograph) David Rindos. 1984. 29.50 o.p. (ISBN 0-12-589280-2). Acad Pr.

Origins of American Politics. Bernard Bailyn. 1983. 13.50 o.p. (ISBN 0-8446-6034-5). Peter Smith.

Origins of Britain. Lloyd Laing & Jennifer Laing. (Britain Before the Conquest Ser.). 256p. 1983. pap. 9.95 o.p. (ISBN 0-586-08370-7, Pub. by Granada England). Academy Chi Pubs.

Origins of British Sociology: Eighteen Thirty-Four to Nineteen Fourteen: An Essay with Selected Papers. Philip Abrams. LC 68-54221. (Heritage of Sociology Ser). 304p. 1972. 15.00x o.s.i. (ISBN 0-226-00170-9); pap. text ed. 3.25x o.s.i. (ISBN 0-226-00171-7). U of Chicago Pr.

Origins of Calvin's Theology of Music: 1536-1543. Charles Garside, Jr. LC 78-73171. (Transactions Ser.: Vol. 69, Pt. 4). 1979. 10.00 o.p. (ISBN 0-87169-694-0). Am Philos.

Origins of Cast Iron Architecture in America. D. D. Badger & James Bogardus. LC 68-25760. (Architecture & Decorative Art Ser.: Vol. 13). (Illus.). 1970. Repr. of 1856 ed. lib. bdg. 55.00 o.p. (ISBN 0-306-71039-0). Da Capo.

Origins of Central Banking in the United States. Richard H. Timberlake, Jr. LC 78-4622. 1978. 21.00x o.s.i. (ISBN 0-674-64480-8). Harvard U Pr.

Origins of Chemistry. Robert P. Multhauf. 1967. lib. bdg. 15.00 o.p. (ISBN 0-685-52442-6). Watson Pub Intl.

Origins of Church Wealth in Mexico: Ecclesiastical Revenues & Church Finances, 1523-1600. John F. Schwaller. LC 85-1122. (Illus.). 251p. 1985. 22.50x o.p. (ISBN 0-8263-0813-9). U of NM Pr.

Origins of Communism in Turkey. George S. Harris. LC 67-26980. (Publications Ser.: No. 63). 1967. 9.95x o.p. (ISBN 0-8179-1631-8). Hoover Inst Pr.

Origins of Culture. Edward Tylor. (Primitive Culture Ser.: Pt. 1). 1988. 18.00 o.p. Peter Smith.

Origins of Day Care: Selections from the Conferences on Day Nurseries, 1893-1925, 2 vols. Ed. by Sheila M. Rothman & David J. Rothman. (Women & Children First Ser.). 1000p. 1986. lib. bdg. 125.00 o.p. (ISBN 0-8240-7691-5). Garland Pub.

Origins of Entrepreneurship in Meiji Japan. Johannes Hirschmeier. LC 64-20973. (East Asian Ser: No. 17). 1964. 24.50x o.s.i. (ISBN 0-674-64475-1). Harvard U Pr.

Origins of General Nursing. Christopher J. Maggs. 183p. 1983. 25.25 o.p. (ISBN 0-7099-1734-1, Pub. by Croom Helm Ltd). Routledge Chapman & Hall.

Origins of General Nursing. Christopher J. Maggs. LC 85-16663. 224p. 1985. pap. 17.00 o.p. (ISBN 0-7099-4614-7, Pub. by Croom Helm Ltd). Routledge Chapman & Hall.

Origins of Human Competence: The Final Report of the Harvard Preschool Project. Burton L. White et al. LC 77-81793. 464p. 1979. 24.50x o.p. (ISBN 0-669-01943-7). Lexington Bks.

Origins of Human Social Relations: Proceedings. Centre for Advanced Study in the Developmental Sciences Study Group Staff. Ed. by H. R. Schaffer. 1971. 69.00 o.p. (ISBN 0-12-622550-8). Acad Pr.

Origins of Life: Evolution As Creation. Hoimar Ditfurth. Tr. by Peter Heinegg from Ger. LC 82-47757. (Illus.). 220p. 1982. 14.45 o.p. (ISBN 0-06-250909-8). HarpR.

Origins of Madness: The Psychopathology of Animal Life. J. D. Keehn. (Illus.). 1979. 83.00 o.p. (ISBN 0-08-023725-8). Pergamon.

Origins of Man & the Universe: The Myth That Came to Life. Barry Long. 256p. (Orig.). 1984. pap. 12.95 o.p. (ISBN 0-7102-0337-3). Routledge Chapman & Hall.

Origins of Molecular Biology: A Tribute to Jacques Monod. Ed. by Andre Lwoff & Agnes Ullman. 1979. 24.95 o.p. (ISBN 0-12-460480-3). Acad Pr.

Origins of Papal Infallibility 1150-1350. B. Tierney. 1972. 45.00 o.p. (ISBN 90-04-03440-4). E J Brill USA.

Origins of Physiological Regulations. E. F. Adolph. 1968. 42.00 o.p. (ISBN 0-12-044360-0). Acad Pr.

Origins of Printing & Engraving. Andre Blum. Tr. by H. M. Lydenberg from Fr. LC 74-78543. Repr. of 1940 ed. 50.00 o.p. (ISBN 0-87817-154-1). Hacker.

Origins of Rhodesia. Stanlake Samkange. 1969. pap. text ed. 17.50x o.p. (ISBN 0-435-94488-6). Heinemann Ed.

Origins of Russia. George Vernadsky. LC 75-11804. (Illus.). 354p. 1975. Repr. of 1959 ed. lib. bdg. 37.50x o.p. (ISBN 0-8371-8052-X, VEOR). Greenwood.

Origins of Soviet-American Diplomacy. Robert P. Browder. LC 84-19123. xi, 256p. 1984. Repr. of 1953 ed. lib. bdg. 38.50x o.p. (ISBN 0-313-24616-5, BROS). Greenwood.

Origins of the American Indians: European Concepts, 1492-1729. Lee E. Huddleston. (Latin American Monographs: No. 11). 189p. 1967. 10.00x o.p. (ISBN 0-292-73693-2). U of Tex Pr.

Origins of the Christian Doctrine of Sacrifice. Robert J. Daly. LC 77-78628. 168p. (Orig.). 1978. pap. 5.50 o.p. (ISBN 0-8006-1267-1, 1-1267, Fortress). Augsburg Fortress.

Origins of the Cold War & Contemporary Europe. Ed. by Charles S. Maier. LC 78-17915. (Modern Scholarship on European History Ser.). 249p. 1978. pap. text ed. 8.95 o.p. (ISBN 0-531-05607-4). Wiener Pub Inc.

Origins of the Gospel Traditions. Birger Gerhardsson. Tr. by Gene J. Lund from Swedish. LC 78-19634. 96p. 1979. 7.95 o.p. (ISBN 0-8006-0543-8, 1-543, Fortress). Augsburg Fortress.

Origins of the Infant's Social Responsiveness, Vol. 1. Ed. by Evelyn B. Thoman. LC 79-16625. (The Johnson & Johnson Baby Products Pediatric Round Table). 470p. 1979. 31.95x o.p. (ISBN 0-470-26813-1). Halsted Pr.

Origins of the Novel. Marthe Robert. Tr. by Sacha Rabinovitch. LC 80-7970. 244p. 1981. 19.95x o.p. (ISBN 0-253-18824-5). Ind U Pr.

Origins of the Sacred. Anne Bancroft. 240p. 1987. pap. 12.95 o.p. (ISBN 1-85063-028-3, 30283, Ark Paperbks). Routledge Chapman & Hall.

Origins of the Second World War. Joachim Remak. 1976. pap. write for info. o.p. (ISBN 0-13-642751-0, S-384, Spec); pap. 4.95 o.p. (ISBN 0-13-642744-8). P-H.

Origins of the Second World War. A. J. Taylor. LC 62-7543. (Illus.). 1962. 6.95 o.p. (ISBN 0-689-10268-2, Atheneum). Macmillan.

Origins of the Social Democratic Party. Noel Tracy. (Illus.). 69p. 1983. pap. 11.50 o.p. (ISBN 0-7099-2426-7, Pub. by Croom Helm Ltd). Routledge Chapman & Hall.

Origins of the State & Civilization: The Process of Cultural Evolution. Elman R. Service. 1975. pap. text ed. 13.95x o.p. (ISBN 0-393-09224-0). Norton.

Origins of the Theology of Hope. M. Douglas Meeks. LC 73-88351. 192p. 1974. 8.50 o.p. (ISBN 0-8006-0265-X, 1-265, Fortress). Augsburg Fortress.
Origins of Theoretical Population Genetics. William Provine. LC 73-153711. (History of Science & Medicine Ser.). 1971. lib. bdg. 18.00x o.s.i. (ISBN 0-226-68465-2). U of Chicago Pr.
Origins of Totalitarian Democracy. J. L. Talmon. 1970. pap. 5.95x o.p. (ISBN 0-393-00510-0, Norton Lib). Norton.
Origins of Totalitarianism. rev. ed. Hannah Arendt. LC 66-22273. 1966. 11.00 o.p. (ISBN 0-15-170154-7). HarBraceJ.
Origins of Trotskyism in Ceylon. George J. Lerski. LC 68-9405. (Publications Ser.: No. 74). 1968. 12.95x o.p.; pap. 7.95x o.p. (ISBN 0-8179-1742-X). Hoover Inst Pr.
Origins of Western Art. Ann Powell. LC 74-183245. (Illus.). 1973. 7.95 o.p. (ISBN 0-15-170157-1). HarBraceJ.
Origins: Two Models. rev ed. Richard Bliss. Ed. by Duane T. Gish & John N. Moore. LC 76-20178. (Illus.). 1978. 3.95 o.p. (ISBN 0-89051-027-X); avail. tchr's. guide 6.95 o.p. Master Bks.
Orion Blue Book Audio 1988. Orion Research Corporation Staff. 640p. 1988. text ed. 125.00 o.p. (ISBN 0-932089-22-4). Orion Res.
Orion Line. Nicholas Luard. LC 76-12456. 1977. 8.95 o.p. (ISBN 0-15-170158-X). HarBraceJ.
Orisha: The Gods of Yorubaland. Judith Gleason. LC 74-19493. (Illus.). (gr. 6 up). 1971. 5.25 o.p. (ISBN 0-689-20639-9, Atheneum). Macmillan.
Orlando, Disney World & EPCOT 1987-1988. (Frommer's City Guides). 224p. 5.95 o.p. (ISBN 0-671-62359-1). Prentice Hall Pr.
Orlando Gibbons. Ed. by P. C. Buck. (Tudor Church Music Ser.: Vol. 4). 1963. Repr. of 1925 ed. 85.00x o.p. Broude.
Orme du Mail see Romans et Contes.
Ormerod's Landing. Leslie Thomas. LC 78-21412. 1979. 8.95 o.p. St Martin.
Ornament & Its Application. Lewis F. Day. LC 71-136735. (Illus.). 360p. 1971. Repr. of 1904 ed. 40.00x o.p. (ISBN 0-8103-3324-4). Gale.
Ornithological Gazetteer of Paraguay. Raymond A. Paynter, Jr. & Alastair M. Caperton. (Illus.). iv, 43p. 1977. 2.25 o.p. (ISBN 0-686-35829-5). Mus Comp Zoo.
Oro-Facial Pain & Neuromuscular Dysfunction: Mechanisms & Clinical Correlates. Ed. by I. Klineberg & B. Sessle. (Illus.). 216p. 1985. 105.00 o.p. (ISBN 0-08-032001-5, Pub. by PPL). Pergamon.
Orofacial Pain: Aetiology, Diagnosis & Treatment. 3rd ed. J. M. Mumford. LC 81-69055. 406p. 1982. text ed. 67.00 o.p. (ISBN 0-443-02631-9). Churchill.
Orogeny. Ed. by J. G. Dennis. LC 81-6436. (Benchmark Papers in Geology: Vol. 62). 380p. 1982. 51.95 o.p. (ISBN 0-87933-394-4). Van Nos Reinhold.
Orphan Drugs: Your Complete Guide to Effective, Proven Medications Available Outside the U. S. - & How to Get Them. Kenneth Anderson. 288p. 1983. 17.25 o.p. (ISBN 0-671-47172-4, Linden Pr); pap. 7.75 o.p. (ISBN 0-671-49521-6). S&S.
Orphan for Nebraska. Charlene J. Talbot. LC 78-12179. (Illus.). 216p. (gr. 3-7). 1979. 10.95 o.s.i. (ISBN 0-689-30698-9, Atheneum Childrens Bks). Macmillan.
Orphans. Lyle Kessler. 96p. 1987. 17.95 o.s.i. (ISBN 0-8021-0005-8); pap. 6.95 o.s.i. (ISBN 0-8021-3005-4, Ever). Grove.
Orphans' Court Litigation. 204p. 1988. 65.00 o.p. (ISBN 0-318-03913-3, 436). PA Bar Inst.
Orphans of the Wind. Erik C. Haugaard. (Illus.). (gr. 7 up). 1966. 7.95 o.p. (ISBN 0-395-06805-3). HM.
Orphans: Real & Imaginary. Eileen Simpson. LC 86-28921. 272p. 1987. 16.95 o.p. (ISBN 1-55584-077-9). Weidenfeld.
Orpheus in the New World. Philip Hart. (Illus.). 544p. 1973. 20.00x o.p. (ISBN 0-393-02169-6). Norton.
Orrery. Richard Kenney. LC 85-47604. 128p. (Orig.). 1985. 17.50 o.p. (ISBN 0-689-11631-4, Atheneum); pap. 10.95 o.p. (ISBN 0-689-11640-3, Atheneum). Macmillan.
Orson Hyde: Missionary, Apostle, Colonizer. Howard H. Barron. LC 77-74490. (Illus.). 336p. 1977. 10.95 o.p. (ISBN 0-88290-076-5). Horizon Utah.
Orson Squire Fowler & the Octagon House: A Selected Bibliography. Bibliographic Research Library Staff. (Architecture Ser.: A 1390). 6p. 1985. 2.00 o.p. (ISBN 0-89028-400-8). Vance Biblios.
Orson Welles: A Celebration. John R. Taylor. (Illus.). 1986. 22.50 o.p. (ISBN 0-316-83309-6). Little.
Ortega, Pt. I: Veronica. Lois M. Parker. 192p. 1987. 11.95 o.p. (ISBN 0-8062-2921-7). Carlton.
Orthodontic Theory & Technique. 3rd ed. P. R. Begg & Peter C. Kesling. LC 76-14673. (Illus.). 1977. text ed. write for info. o.p. (ISBN 0-7216-1670-4). Saunders.
Orthodontics in Daily Practice. Rudolf Hotz. 415p. 1974. 40.25 o.p. (Pub. by W & W). Krieger.
Orthodox Hymns of Christmas, Easter, & Holy Week. Alexander Bogolepov. LC 65-16177. 78p. 1965. pap. 1.95 o.p. (ISBN 0-913836-02-8). St Vladimirs.
Orthodox Veneration of the Mother of God. John Maximovitch. Tr. by Seraphim Rose. (Orthodox Theological Texts Ser.: No. 1). (Illus.). 56p. 1987. pap. 5.00 o.p. (ISBN 0-317-64376-2). St Herman AK.
Orthodoxy. G. K. Chesterton. (Thomas More Books to Live Ser.). 1985. Repr. of 1908 ed. 10.95 o.p. (ISBN 0-88347-184-1). Thomas More.
Orthodoxy & Heresy in Earliest Christianity. Walter Bauer. Ed. by Robert A. Kraft & Gerhard Krodel. LC 71-141252. 360p. 1979. pap. 2.50 o.p. (ISBN 0-8006-1363-5, 1-1363, Fortress). Augsburg Fortress.
Orthogonal Transforms for Digital Signal Processing. N. Ahmed & K. R. Rao. LC 73-18912. (Illus.). 280p. 1975. text ed. 30.70 o.p. (ISBN 0-387-06556-3). Springer-Verlag.
Orthogonale Polynome. G. Freud. (Mathematische Eihe Ser.: No. 33). (Illus.). 294p. (Ger.). 1969. 49.95x o.p. (ISBN 0-8176-0127-9). Birkhauser.
Orthopaedic Surgery of the Limbs in Paraplegia. L. S. Michaelis. (Illus.). 1964. pap. 17.70 o.p. (ISBN 0-387-03182-0). Springer-Verlag.
Orthopedic Diseases: Physiology, Pathology, Radiology. 4th ed. Ernest E. Aegerter & John A. Kilpatrick, Jr. LC 74-4551. (Illus.). 791p. 1975. text ed. write for info. o.p. (ISBN 0-7216-1062-5). Saunders.
Orthopedic Nursing: A Programmed Approach. 4th ed. Nancy A. Brunner. LC 78-32020. (Illus.). 264p. 1983. pap. text ed. 19.95 o.p. (ISBN 0-8016-0839-2). Mosby.
Orvis Fly-Fishing Guide. Tom Rosenbauer. LC 83-25898. (Nick Lyons Bks.). (Illus.). 1984. 17.95 o.p. (ISBN 0-8329-0350-7); pap. 14.95 o.p. (ISBN 0-8329-0304-3). Lyons & Burford.
Orwell: The Transformation. Peter Stansky & William Abrahams. (Illus.). 253p. 1981. pap. 6.95 o.s.i. (ISBN 0-586-08375-8, Pub. by Granada Enland). Academy Chi Pubs.
Orwell's Fiction. Robert A. Lee. LC 74-75151. 205p. 1972. 8.50 o.p. (ISBN 0-268-00310-6); pap. 7.95x o.p. (ISBN 0-268-00458-7). U of Notre Dame Pr.
OS Debugging for the COBOL Programmer. Wayne Clary. LC 80-84122. (Illus.). 312p. (Orig.). 1981. pap. 20.00 o.p. (ISBN 0-911625-10-0). M Murach & Assoc.
Osage Indians, Vol. Five: Findings of Fact, & Opinion. Indian Claims Commission. (American Indian Ethnohistory Ser.: Plains Indians). (Illus.). 1975. lib. bdg. 51.00 o.p. (ISBN 0-8240-0751-4). Garland Pub.
Osage Indians, Vol. One: Osage Research Project. Fred W. Voget. (American Indian Ethnohistory Ser.: Plains Indians). (Illus.). 1974. lib. bdg. 51.00 o.p. (ISBN 0-8240-0747-6). Garland Pub.
Osage Indians, Vol. Two: Osage Research Report, & Bibliography of Basic Research References. Alice Marriott. (American Indian Ethnohistory Ser.: Plains Indians). (Illus.). 1974. lib. bdg. 51.00 o.p. (ISBN 0-8240-0748-4). Garland Pub.
Osborn on Osborn. Robert Osborn. LC 81-18492. (Illus.). 192p. 1982. 34.00 o.p. (ISBN 0-89919-051-0). Ticknor & Fields.
Osborne-McGraw-Hill Business System Buyer's Guide. 2nd ed. Adam Osborne et al. 200p. (Orig.). 1984. pap. text ed. 10.95 o.p. (ISBN 0-07-881125-2). Osborne-McGraw.
Osborne-McGraw Hill CP-M-86 User's Guide. Jonathan Sachs. 350p. (Orig.). 1984. pap. text ed. 19.95 o.p. (ISBN 0-07-881143-0). Osborne-McGraw.
Osborne, McGraw-Hill Guide to Using Lotus 1-2-3. Edward Baras. 250p. (Orig.). 1984. pap. text ed. 17.95 o.p. (ISBN 0-07-881123-6). Osborne-McGraw.
Osborne-McGraw-Hill Home Computer Guide. Steve Ditlea. 1984. pap. text ed. 11.95 o.p. (ISBN 0-07-881107-4). Mcgraw.
Oscar, Laddie, Came Home. Martha H. Graupner. LC 84-90199. (Illus.). 65p. 1985. 7.95 o.p. (ISBN 0-533-06250-0). Vantage.
Oscar Lincoln Busby Stokes. Frances C. Sayers. LC 69-13778. (Illus.). (gr. 1-4). 1970. 4.50 o.p. (ISBN 0-15-258814-0, HJ). HarBraceJ.
Oscar Lobster's Fair Exchange. George Selden. (Illus.). 172p. (gr. 3-7). 1976. pap. 1.25 o.p. (ISBN 0-380-00703-7, 61085X, Camelot). Avon.
Oscar the Otter. Alice L. Mason. (Illus.). 16p. (gr. k-6). 1984. pap. 1.50 o.p. (ISBN 0-8249-8065-4). Ideals.
Oscar Wilde. Martin Fido. LC 85-9028. (Illustrated Biographies Ser.). (Illus.). 144p. 1985. pap. 9.95 o.p. (ISBN 0-87226-032-1). P Bedrick Bks.
Oscar Wilde. Katharine Worth. LC 83-49387. (Modern Dramatists Ser.). 224p. 1984. 19.50 o.s.i. (ISBN 0-394-53843-9, GP907). Grove.
Oscar Wilde. Katharine Worth. LC 83-49387. (Modern Dramatists Ser.). 224p. 1984. pap. 9.95 o.s.i. (ISBN 0-394-62031-3, E927, Ever). Grove.
Oscar Wilde & His World. Vyvyan Holland. (Illus.). 1978. 3.95 o.p. (ISBN 0-684-15305-X, ScribT); encore ed. 3.95 o.p. (ISBN 0-684-17233-X). Scribner.
Osceola. Matthew G. Grant. LC 73-12407. (We the People Ser.). 1974. PLB 7.95 o.p. (ISBN 0-87191-266-X). Creative Ed.
Oscillation Theorem for Algebraic Eigenvalue Problems & Its Applications. F. W. Sinden. (Mittelungen des Institutes fur AngewandteMathematik: No. 4). (Illus.). 57p. 1967. pap. 15.95x o.p. (ISBN 0-8176-0340-9). Birkhauser.
Oscilloscope at Work. A. Haas & R. W. Hallows. (Illus.). 176p. 1956. (ISBN 0-8022-0652-2). Philos Lib.
Oscilloscope Measuring Technique: Principles & Applications of Modern Cathode Ray Oscilloscopes. Josef Czech. (Illus.). 1966. 24.00 o.p. (ISBN 0-387-91003-4). Springer-Verlag.
Oscilloscopes: Functional Operation & Measuring Examples. Rien Van Erk. 1978. text ed. 49.95 o.p. (ISBN 0-07-067050-1). McGraw.
OSGLAS: General Ledger Accounting System for Osborne Computers. Sheldon W. Philips & Brian L. King. (Key-By-Key Ser.). (Illus.). 240p. (Orig.). 1983. pap. write for info. o.p. (ISBN 0-534-02872-1); write for info. templates on disk o.p. PWS-Kent Pub.
OSGLAS: Payroll for Osborne Computers. Sheldon W. Philips & Brian L. King. (Key-By-Key Ser.). (Illus.). 150p. 1983. pap. write for info. o.p. (ISBN 0-534-02874-8); write for info. o.p. Brooks-Cole.
OSHA Field Operations Manual. U. S. Department of Labor. (OSHA Inspection Manual Ser.). 452p. 1986. pap. 59.00 o.p. (ISBN 0-86587-147-7). Gov Insts.
OSHA Handbook. Robert D. Moran. 270p. 1987. pap. text ed. 65.00 o.p. (ISBN 0-86587-734-3). Gov Insts.
OSHA, Toxic Substances in the Workplace. Practising Law Institute Staff & Richard D. Hinds. LC 83-61042. (Litigation & Administrative Practice Ser.: No. 223). 440p. 1983. 40.00 o.p. PLI.
Osip Mandelstam: Fifty Poems. Osip Mandelstam. Tr. by Bernard Meares. LC 76-52274. (Poetry in Translation Ser.). 1977. o. p. 7.95 o.s.i. (ISBN 0-89255-005-8); pap. 8.95 o.s.i. (ISBN 0-89255-006-6). Persea Bks.
Oskar Kokoschka - Drawings 1906-1965. Compiled by Ernest G. Rathenau. LC 76-129665. (Illus.). 1970. 19.95 o.p. (ISBN 0-87024-176-1). U of Miami Pr.
Oskar Kokoschka: A Life. Frank Whitford. (Illus.). 288p. 1986. 21.95 o.p. (ISBN 0-689-11794-9, Atheneum). Macmillan.
Oskar Kokoschka: The Painter As Playwright. Henry I. Schvey. LC 82-2871. (Illus.). 168p. 1982. 29.95X o.p. (ISBN 0-8143-1702-2). Wayne St U Pr.
Oslo Travel Guide. Berlitz Editors. (Travel Guides Ser.). 1980. pap. 4.95 o.p. (ISBN 0-317-12113-8, Berlitz). Macmillan.
Osmonds: The Official Story of the Osmond Family. Paul H. Dunn. 1977. pap. 1.75 o.p. (ISBN 0-380-01717-2, 34066). Avon.
Osmosis & Tensile Solvent. H. T. Hammel & P. F. Scholander. LC 76-3684. 1976. pap. 15.00 o.p. (ISBN 0-387-07663-8). Springer-Verlag.
Osmotic Investigations. Wilhelm Pfeffer. (Illus.). 304p. 1985. 39.95 o.p. (ISBN 0-442-27583-8). Van Nos Reinhold.
Osprey Island. Ann L. Feydy. LC 74-9379. (Illus.). 192p. (gr. 3-7). 1974. 5.95 o.p. (ISBN 0-395-19498-9). HM.
OSS Sabotage & Demolition Manual. Office of Strategic Services Staff. (Illus.). 139p. 1971. pap. 15.95 o.p. (ISBN 0-87364-005-5). Paladin Pr.
Ossa Service - Repair Handbook: 125-250cc Singles, 1971-1978. 2nd ed. Ed. by Jeff Robinson. (Illus.). 160p. 1976. pap. text ed. 10.95 o.p. (ISBN 0-89287-092-3, M362). Clymer Pub.
Ossining New York: An Informal Bicentennial History. Carl Oechsner. LC 75-11853. (Illus.). 144p. 1975. 12.00 o.s.i. (ISBN 0-88427-016-5). North River.
Osten und Westen. Stefan Grunwald. (Ger). 1970. pap. text ed. 3.95 o.p. (ISBN 0-15-567644-X, HC). HarBraceJ.
Osteoarthromechanics. D. N. Ghista. 1982. text ed. 58.00 o.p. (ISBN 0-07-023168-0). McGraw.
Osteology of the Reptiles. Alfred S. Romer. 1976. pap. text ed. 15.00x o.s.i. (ISBN 0-226-72491-3, Phoen). U of Chicago Pr.
Osteoporosis. Michael MacAdams. 250p. write for info. o.s.i. (ISBN 0-942028-30-9). R D Anderson.
Osteoporosis: How to Prevent the Brittle-Bone Disease. Wendy Smith & Stanton H. Cohn. (Illus.). 128p. 1985. pap. 5.95 o.p. (ISBN 0-671-55252-X, Pub. by Fireside). S&S.
Osteoporosis: Proceedings of an International Symposium Held at the Jerusalem Osteoporosis Center in June, 1981. Ed. by J. Menczel et al. LC 81-19822. 440p. 1983. 58.00x o.p. (ISBN 0-471-10156-7). Wiley.
Ot Legal 'nostik Podpol'-Iu (From Legality to the Underground) Boris Dvinov. LC 67-19592. (Foreign Language Ser.: No. 2). (Rus). 1968. 12.95x o.p. (ISBN 0-8179-4021-9). Hoover Inst Pr.
Otage: Theatre. Paul Claudel. (Coll. Soleil). 1962. 13.95 o.p. (ISBN 0-685-11472-4). Schoenhof.
Otasukeman. (Big Little Bks.: No. 72). (Illus.). 350p. 1984. 6.95 o.p. (ISBN 0-318-02710-0). Bks Nippan.
OTC Handbook. Standard's & Poor's Staff. 1982. pap. text ed. 39.50 o.p. (ISBN 0-07-051885-8). McGraw.
Othello see also Tragedy of Othello.
Othello. William Shakespeare. Ed. by J. H. Walter. LC 76-25235. 1977. 3.50 o.p. (ISBN 0-8238-0208-6). Plays.
Othello. William Shakespeare. 48p. (Orig.). 1988. pap. 9.95 o.p. (ISBN 1-55651-683-5); audiocassette tape incl. o.p. (ISBN 1-55651-684-3). Cram Cassettes.
Othello of Shakespeare's Audience. John W. Draper. 1967. lib. bdg. 19.00x o.p. (ISBN 0-374-92338-8, Octagon). Hippocrene Bks.
Other. Thomas Tryon. 1986. pap. 3.95 o.p. (ISBN 0-449-21066-9, Crest). Fawcett.
Other Britain: A New Society Collection. Ed. by Paul Barker. 276p. 1983. 24.95x o.p. (ISBN 0-7100-9308-X); pap. 11.95x o.p. (ISBN 0-7100-9340-3). Routledge Chapman & Hall.
Other Casanova. Paul Nettl. 1954. (ISBN 0-8022-1196-8). Philos Lib.
Other Child. Michael Hale. 304p. 1986. pap. 3.95 o.p. (ISBN 0-380-89950-7). Avon.
Other David. Carolyn Coker. 224p. 1984. 13.95 o.p. (ISBN 0-396-08390-0). Dodd.
Other Devil's Name. E. X. Ferrars. LC 86-16489. (Crime Club Ser.). 192p. 1987. 12.95 o.s.i. (ISBN 0-385-23553-4). Doubleday.
Other Door: Poetic Exhortations, Vol. I. Dennis L. Siluk. (Illus.). 64p. 1981. 5.00 o.p. (ISBN 0-682-49716-9). Exposition-Phoenix.
Other Echos. Adele Geras. LC 81-8080. 144p. (gr. 6 up). 1982. PLB 9.95 o.p. (ISBN 0-689-30877-9, Atheneum). Macmillan.
Other Foot. D. Knight. 1966. pap. 7.50 o.p. (ISBN 0-08-007043-4). Pergamon.
Other Girl. Marjory Hall. LC 73-18334. 184p. (gr. 5-8). 1974. 5.25 o.s.i. (ISBN 0-664-32542-4, Westminster). Westminster John Knox.
Other Guy Blinked: How Pepsi Won the Cola Wars. Roger Enrico & Jesse Kornbluth. 288p. 1986. 17.95 o.p. (ISBN 0-553-05177-6). Bantam.
Other Lips & Other Hearts. Joan Sanders. 1982. 13.45 o.p. (ISBN 0-395-32523-4). HM.
Other Mafia. Joseph Goldbach. 1977. 5.00 o.p. (ISBN 0-682-48307-9). Exposition-Phoenix.
Other Man: Conversations with Graham Greene. Marie-Francoise Allain. Tr. by Guido Waldman. 1983. 13.50 o.p. (ISBN 0-671-44767-X). S&S.
Other Marilyn: A Biography of Marilyn Miller. Warren Harris. LC 84-18515. (Illus.). 1985. 16.95 o.p. (ISBN 0-87795-584-0, Arbor Hse). Morrow.
Other Men's Daughters. Richard Stern. 1986. pap. 5.95 o.p. (ISBN 0-87795-792-4). Morrow.
Other Nine. Colleen L. Reece. (Orig.). 1981. pap. 7.50 o.p. (ISBN 0-8309-0288-0). Herald Hse.
Other Paris. Mavis Gallant. (Hall Fiction Ser.). 256p. 1986. pap. 5.95 o.p. (ISBN 0-8398-2895-0). G K Hall.
Other Paths to Glory. Anthony Price. 256p. 1987. pap. 3.95 o.p. (ISBN 0-445-40666-6). Mysterious Pr.
Other People. Sol Stein. LC 78-14082. 1979. 10.00 o.p. (ISBN 0-15-170447-3). HarBraceJ.
Other People's Letters: A Memoir. Mina Curtiss. 1978. 9.95 o.p. (ISBN 0-395-26291-7). HM.
Other Places: A Kind of Alaska; Victoria Station: Family Voices. Harold Pinter. 96p. 1983. 15.00 o.p. (ISBN 0-394-53131-0, GP866). Grove.
Other Poe: Comedies & Satires. Edgar Allan Poe. Ed. by David Galloway. (Penguin American Library). 256p. 1983. pap. 4.95 o.p. (ISBN 0-14-039035-9). Penguin.
Other Racquet Sports. Dick Squires. (Illus.). 1980. pap. text ed. 7.95 o.p. (ISBN 0-07-060531-9). McGraw.
Other Shoe Book. Jeff MacNelly. 128p. 1980. pap. 5.95 o.p. (ISBN 0-380-75341-3, 75341-3). Avon.

Other Shore. Lucinda Mays. LC 79-10448. (gr. 5-10). 1979. 8.95 o.p. (ISBN 0-689-30717-9, Atheneum). Macmillan.

Other Side: How Soviets & Americans Perceive Each Other. Robert D. English & Jonathan J. Halperin. (Illus.). 1987. pap. 9.95 o.p. Comm Natl Security.

Other Side of Darkness. Gidada Solon. Ed. by Marion Fairman. (Orig.). 1972. pap. 2.50 o.p. (ISBN 0-377-12001-4). Friendship Pr.

Other Side of Death. Raymond Bayless. 1972. 5.95 o.p. (ISBN 0-8216-0134-2, Pub. by Univ Bks). Carol Pub Group.

Other Side of Medicine see Health Care: Its Psychosocial Dimensions.

Other Side of Midnight. Sidney Sheldon. 1975. pap. 3.95 o.p. (ISBN 0-440-16067-7). Dell.

Other Side of Paradise: Foreign Control in the Caribbean. Tom Barry et al. LC 83-49377. 1985. pap. 9.95 o.p. (ISBN 0-394-62056-9, E-904, Ever). Grove.

Other Side of Power. Claude M. Steiner. LC 80-8921. 256p. 1981. 16.50 o.s.i. (ISBN 0-394-51950-7, GP 842). Grove.

Other Side of Rape. Paul R. Wilson. 1978. 19.95x o.p. (ISBN 0-7022-1188-5); pap. 9.95x o.p. (ISBN 0-7022-1167-2). U of Queensland Pr.

Other Side of Silence. Margaret Perko. 1979. pap. 3.25 o.p. (ISBN 0-8439-0698-7, Pub. by Leisure Bks CT). Dorchester Pub Co.

Other Side of Sorrow. Sandy Derksen & Connie Nash. LC 81-52281. 128p. (Orig.). 1982. pap. 5.95 o.p. (ISBN 0-8066-1913-9, 10-4840, Augsburg). Augsburg Fortress.

Other Side of the Coin. Edward C. Rochette. LC 85-24442. (Illus.). 200p. (Orig.). 1985. pap. 9.95 o.p. (ISBN 0-939650-24-X). R H Pub.

Other Side of the Couch: What Therapists Believe. Ed. by E. Mark Stern. LC 81-12017. 196p. 1981. 12.95 o.p. (ISBN 0-8298-0462-5). Pilgrim NY.

Other Side of the Fence. Molly Cone. (gr. 5-8). 1967. 6.95 o.p. (ISBN 0-395-06713-8). HM.

Other Side of the River: A Novel. Douglass Wallop. 295p. 1984. 14.45 o.p. (ISBN 0-393-01864-4). Norton.

Other Side of the Sky. Arthur C. Clarke. LC 58-5477. 1958. 8.95 o.s.i. (ISBN 0-15-170451-1). HarBraceJ.

Other Side of the Story. Jody Powell. LC 84-60200. 322p. 1984. 15.95 o.p. (ISBN 0-688-03646-5). Morrow.

Other Side of the Universe. Kurt Dreifuss. 1961. 15.95 o.p. New Coll U Pr.

Other Side of Western Civilization-Readings in Everyday Life: The Ancient World to the Reformation, Vol. 1. 2nd ed. Stanley Chodorow. 363p. 1979. pap. text ed. 12.95 o.p. (ISBN 0-15-567648-2, HC). HarBraceJ.

Other Side of Western Civilization-Readings in Everyday Life: The Sixteenth Century to the Present, Vol. 2. Ed. by Peter N. Stearns. 370p. 1979. pap. text ed. 12.95 o.p. (ISBN 0-15-567649-0, HC). HarBraceJ.

Other Six Hundred Thirty-Seven Best Things Anybody Ever Said. Robert Byrne. LC 84-45057. (Illus.). 192p. 1984. 10.95 o.p. (ISBN 0-689-11472-9, Atheneum). Macmillan.

Other Spaces: New Theatre & the Royal Shakespeare Company. Colin Chambers. 80p. 1981. pap. 7.95 o.p. (ISBN 0-413-46880-1, NO. 2121). Heinemann Ed.

Other Than That I Have No Opinion. Chuck Snyder. 240p. (Orig.). 1985. pap. 5.95 o.p. (ISBN 0-8423-4763-1). Tyndale.

Other Woman & Other Stories. Dina Mehta. (Vikas Library of Modern Indian Writing: No. 11). 175p. 1981. text ed. 15.95x o.p. (ISBN 0-7069-1290-X, Pub. by Vikas India). Advent NY.

Other Worlds: Space, Superspace & the Quantum Universe. Paul Davies. 1981. 11.95 o.p. (ISBN 0-671-42227-8). S&S.

Other You: Develop Your Psychic Potential. Andrew Laurance. 192p. (Orig.). 1987. pap. 7.95 o.p. (ISBN 0-7137-1719-X, Pub. by Javelin England). Sterling.

Otis Family in Provincial & Revolutionary Massachusetts. John J. Waters, Jr. 256p. 1975. pap. 3.45x o.p. (ISBN 0-393-00757-X, Norton Lib). Norton.

Ou Est Os? Laura Palmer. (Illus.). 32p. (Fr.). 1982. pap. 1.95 o.p. (ISBN 0-380-81299-1, 81299, Camelot). Avon.

Ouch! All about Cuts & Other Hurts. Rita G. Gelman & Susan K. Buxbaum. LC 76-46310. (Illus.). (gr. 1-4). 1977. 6.95 o.p. (ISBN 0-15-258839-6, HJ). HarBraceJ.

Ouch! My Back Is Killing Me! Joanne P. Levy. 1978. 6.50 o.p. (ISBN 0-682-48952-2). Exposition-Phoenix.

Ounce of Prevention: A Parent's Guide to Moral & Spiritual Growth in Children. S. Bruce Narramore. 160p. 1973. pap. 5.95 o.p. (ISBN 0-310-30301-X, 11035P). Zondervan.

Ounce of Prevention Plus a Pound of Cure: Tests & Techniques for Aiding Individual Readers. Ronald W. Bruton. LC 76-20600. (Illus.). 1977. 11.95 o.p. (ISBN 0-673-16412-8); pap. 10.95 o.p. (ISBN 0-685-93396-2). Scott F.

Our African Safari. Ilene Hogancamp. 48p. 1987. 6.95 o.p. (ISBN 0-8062-3008-8). Carlton.

Our American Artists: With Portraits, Studios & Engravings of Paintings, Repr. Of 1879 Ed. S. G. Benjamin. Bd. with Second Series. Painters, Sculptors, Illustrators, Engravers & Architects. Repr. of 1881 ed. LC 75-28870. (Art Experience in Late 19th Century America Ser.: Vol. 6). (Illus.). 1977. lib. bdg. 70.00 o.p. (ISBN 0-8240-2230-0). Garland Pub.

Our American Heritage in Song. Compiled by Geoffrey Reiff. (Illus.). 1978. pap. 5.95 o.p. (ISBN 0-89328-019-4). Lorenz Corp.

Our Baby: A Gift from God. (Illus.). 48p. 1982. padded cover boxed 12.95 o.p. (ISBN 0-8007-1290-0). Revell.

Our Best Recipes, Vol. 3. Jean Wickstrom. LC 78-55774. (Illus.). 416p. 1978. 17.95 o.p. (ISBN 0-8487-0489-4). Oxmoor Hse.

Our Best Recipes: Vol. 1. Ed. by Lena Sturges. LC 70-140493. (Illus.). 404p. 1970. 17.95 o.p. (ISBN 0-8487-0185-2). Oxmoor Hse.

Our Blue Planet: The Story of the Earth's Evolution. Heinz Haber. LC 77-85276. 1969. 6.95 o.s.i. (ISBN 0-684-31048-1, ScribT); pap. 1.95 o.p. (ISBN 0-684-12735-0, ScribT). Scribner.

Our Burro & Other Animal Friends. Allan Hulsizer. (Illus.). 64p. (gr. 5 up). 1982. pap. 5.00 o.p. (ISBN 0-682-49870-X). Exposition-Phoenix.

Our Challenging World: Food for Christians, Food for Thinkers. Jacy Of Chickdedee Land. (Illus.). 112p. 1981. 6.50 o.p. (ISBN 0-686-72346-5). Exposition-Phoenix.

Our Changing Climate. James D. Hays. LC 77-5055. (Illus.). (gr. 5 up). 1977. 6.95 o.p. (ISBN 0-689-30586-9, Atheneum). Macmillan.

Our Changing Geopolitical Premises. Thomas P.. Rona. LC 81-16192. (Illus.). 360p. 1982. pap. text ed. 9.95 o.p. (ISBN 0-87855-897-7). Transaction Pubs.

Our Child: Preparation for Parenting. Carol A. Hallenbeck. 231p. Date not set. 18.95 o.p. (ISBN 0-317-62063-0). Our Child Pr.

Our Christian Heritage: Revised & Expanded. 4th ed. Powel M. Dawley. LC 78-62062. 1978. pap. 5.95 o.p. (ISBN 0-8192-1243-1); leader's guide 3.95x o.p. (ISBN 0-8192-4086-9). Morehouse Pub.

Our Christian Wedding. (Illus.). 48p. 1982. padded cover boxed 12.95 o.p. (ISBN 0-8007-1309-5). Revell.

Our Christian Wedding Guest Book. (Illus.). 48p. 1983. padded cover 8.50 o.p. (ISBN 0-8007-1345-1). Revell.

Our Church at Work in the World. Lucy Pennell & Jackie M. Smith. (Illus., Orig.). (gr. 3-5). 1967. pap. 2.25 o.p. (ISBN 0-8042-9452-6, John Knox). Westminster John Knox.

Our Claim on the Future: A Controversial Collection from Latin America. Ed. by Jorge Lara-Braud. (Illus., Orig.). 1970. pap. 1.95 o.p. (ISBN 0-377-10071-4). Friendship Pr.

Our Common History. Paul Thompson. 334p. 1982. text ed. 19.95x o.p. (ISBN 0-391-02606-2). Humanities.

Our Constitution & What It Means. 5th ed. William A. Kottmeyer. 1975. text ed. 7.48 o.p. (ISBN 0-07-033640-7). McGraw.

Our Cosmic Journey: Christian Anthropology in the Light of Current Trends in the Sciences, Philosophy, & Theology. Hans Schwarz. LC 77-72460. 1977. 16.95 o.p. (ISBN 0-8066-1551-6, 10-4861, Augsburg); pap. 12.95 o.p. (ISBN 0-8066-1592-3, 10-4860). Augsburg Fortress.

Our Cup Is Broken. Florence C. Means. LC 69-19935. (Illus.). (gr. 7 up). 1969. 6.95 o.p. (ISBN 0-395-06937-8). HM.

Our Deaf Children: Into the 80's. Rev. ed. Freddy Bloom. 160p. 1978. 15.00x o.p. (ISBN 0-905418-21-2, Pub. by Gresham England). State Mutual Bk.

Our Earth. rev. ed. Marion H. Smith & Carol S. Prescott. LC 76-17685. (Fideler Social Studies Ser.). (Illus.). 160p. (gr. 3-4). 1978. text ed. 7.45 ea., 1-4 copies o.p. (ISBN 0-88296-019-9); text ed. 5.96 ea., 5 or more copies o.p.; tchrs. ed. 5.96 o.p. (ISBN 0-88296-334-1). Gateway Pr MI.

Our Endangered Children: Growing up in a Changing World. Vance Packard. 384p. 1983. 18.45i o.p. (ISBN 0-316-68751-0). Little.

Our Energy-Regaining Control. Marc H. Ross & Robert H. Williams. (Illus.). 320p. 1981. text ed. 28.95 o.p. (ISBN 0-07-053894-8). McGraw.

Our Faces, Our Words. Lillian Smith. (Illus.). 1964. pap. 1.95 o.p. (ISBN 0-393-00251-9, 4, Norton Lib). Norton.

Our Faith: Basic Christian Belief. Max Thurian. Tr. by Emily Chisholm from Fr. LC 82-72008. 192p. 1982. 12.95 o.p. (ISBN 0-8245-0547-6). Crossroad NY.

Our Family Got a Divorce. Carolyn E. Phillips. LC 78-74006. (gr. 1-6). 1987. pap. 5.95 o.p. (ISBN 0-8307-1228-3, 5419212). Regal.

Our Farm Years. Essye Price Flaten. 1981. 5.00 o.p. (ISBN 0-682-49737-1). Exposition-Phoenix.

Our Father Who Art in Heaven. Kurt Rommel. Tr. by Edward A. Cooperrider from Ger. LC 80-2373. 96p. 1981. pap. 4.95 o.p. (ISBN 0-8006-1448-8, 1-1448, Fortress). Augsburg Fortress.

Our Favorite Verse. Stuart Briscoe & Jill Briscoe. LC 86-71753. (My Favorite Verse Ser.). 24p. 1987. pap. 3.95 o.p. (ISBN 0-89636-224-8). Accent Bks.

Our Favorite Verse. Tim LaHaye & Beverly LaHaye. LC 86-70647. 24p. 1986. pap. 3.95 o.p. (ISBN 0-89636-215-9). Accent Bks.

Our Favorite Verse. David Mains & Karen Mains. LC 86-73188. (My Favorite Verse Ser.). 24p. 1987. pap. 3.95 o.p. (ISBN 0-89636-232-9). Accent Bks.

Our Federal Union: The United States from 1816-1865. Isaac Asimov. LC 74-32378. (Illus.). 304p. (gr. 7 up). 1975. 8.95 o.s.i. (ISBN 0-395-20283-3). HM.

Our Finite Resources. S. E. Kesler. 1975. text ed. 19.95 o.p. (ISBN 0-07-034245-8). McGraw.

Our Forgotten Past: Seven Centuries of Life on the Land. Jerome Blum. LC 81-85070. (Illus.). 1982. 29.95 o.s.i. (ISBN 0-500-25080-4). Thames Hudson.

Our Gift: Sunshine. 5.00 o.p. (ISBN 0-8198-6830-2); 4.00 o.p. (ISBN 0-8198-6831-0). Dghtrs St Paul.

Our Government. (Federal Textbook on Citizenship, Becoming a Citizen Ser.: No. M-163). (Illus.). 149p. 1981. pap. 7.00 o.p. (ISBN 0-318-21880-1, S/N 027-002-00136-2). USGPO.

Our Grandmothers' Cures & Remedies. Pete Amato. LC 84-91323. 38p. 1985. 6.95 o.p. (ISBN 0-533-06410-4). Vantage.

Our Green & Living World: The Wisdom to Save It. Edward S. Ayensu et al. Ed. by Joseph Goodwin. LC 84-600181. (Illus.). 256p. 1984. 25.00 o.p. (ISBN 0-89599-016-4, Dist. by Cambridge). Smithsonian Bks.

Our Harvard: Reflections on College Life by Twenty-Two Distinguished Graduates. Ed. by Jeffrey L. Lant. LC 81-18471. 394p. 1982. 19.95 o.s.i. (ISBN 0-8008-6139-6). Taplinger.

Our Hearts Were Young & Gay. Cornelia Otis Skinner & Emily Kimbrough. LC 42-36388. (Illus.). 1942. 6.95 o.p. (ISBN 0-396-02401-7). Dodd.

Our Home Memory & Maintenance Album. (Illus.). 127p. 1982. 6.95 o.p. (ISBN 0-86718-257-1). Nat Assn H Build.

Our Idea of God. Juan L. Segundo. Tr. by John Drury from Span. LC 73-77358. (Theology for Artisans of a New Humanity Ser.: Vol. 3). Orig. Title: Nuestra idea de Dios. 212p. (Orig.). 1974. 7.95x o.p. (ISBN 0-88344-483-6); pap. 4.95 o.p. (ISBN 0-88344-489-5). Orbis Bks.

Our Invaded Universities: Form, Reform & New Starts. Ronnie Dugger. LC 73-18366. (Illus.). 457p. 1974. 14.95x o.p. (ISBN 0-393-05511-6). Norton.

Our Kind of People: The Ethical Dimensions of Church Growth in America. C. Peter Wagner. LC 77-1574. pap. 9.95 o.p. (ISBN 0-8042-0838-7, John Knox). Westminster John Knox.

Our Lady & Vatican II. William J. Gilligan. 33p. (Orig.). 1971. pap. 0.35 o.p. (ISBN 0-913382-08-6, 105-5). Prow Bks-Franciscan.

Our Lady: Eight Hundred & Sixty-Eight Pronouncements from Benedict Fourteenth to John Twenty-Third. Ed. by Monks of Solesmes Staff. 5.50 o.s.i. (ISBN 0-8198-0111-9). Dghtrs St Paul.

Our Lady of the Flowers. Jean Genet. Tr. by Bernard Frechtman from Fr. LC 61-6715. 1976. pap. 3.95 o.p. (ISBN 0-394-17903-X, B389, BC). Grove.

Our Lady of the Flowers. Jean Genet. Tr. by Bernard Frechtman from Fr. 320p. 1987. pap. 8.95 o.p. (ISBN 0-8021-3013-5, Ever). Grove.

Our Lady's Knight. Lawrence Lovasik. 3.50 o.p. (ISBN 0-8198-0112-7). Dghtrs St Paul.

Our Legacy from Ma & Pa. Chester Butler. LC 84-91308. 70p. 1985. 7.95 o.p. (ISBN 0-533-06392-2). Vantage.

Our Life in God's Light: Essays by Hugh T. Kerr. Hugh T. Kerr, Jr. LC 78-24089. 1979. o.s.i 12.50 o.s.i. (ISBN 0-664-21372-3, Westminster); softcover 7.95 o.s.i. (ISBN 0-664-24235-9, Westminster). Westminster John Knox.

Our Life's Aim. Naftali Hofner. 1978. 7.95 o.s.i. (ISBN 0-87306-125-X); pap. 5.95 o.s.i. (ISBN 0-87306-190-X). Feldheim.

Our Like Will Not Be There Again: Notes from the West of Ireland. Lawrence Millman. 1977. 12.95 o.p. (ISBN 0-316-57386-8). Little.

Our Lord & Our Lady. Alexander P. Schorsch & M. Delores Schorsch. 1958. (ISBN 0-8022-1514-9). Philos Lib.

Our Love Reachin' Out to Earth. Martin R. Jones. LC 85-51405. 104p. 1986. 6.95 o.p. (ISBN 0-938232-93-2, Dist. by Baker & Taylor Co.). Winston-Derek.

Our Man in Mongoa. Alex Alben. 240p. 1987. 17.95 o.p. (ISBN 0-684-18827-9). Scribner.

Our Market System of Capitalism Close-Up. W. Richard. 1971. pap. text ed. 3.50x o.p. (ISBN 0-8422-0121-1). Irvington.

Our Modern Stone Age. Robert L. Bates & Julie Jackson. LC 81-17219. (Illus.). 150p. (Orig.). 1981. 18.95 o.p. (ISBN 0-86576-027-6). W Kaufmann.

Our Money & Our Misery: A Diagnosis & Prescription. Ardron B. Lewis. (Illus.). 240p. 1983. 11.00 o.p. (ISBN 0-682-40115-3). Exposition-Phoenix.

Our Nation Heritage. (Our Nations Heritage Ser.). Date not set. (ISBN 0-07-375410-2). McGraw.

Our National Parks: America's Spectacular Wilderness Heritage. Reader's Digest Editors. LC 84-15085. (Illus.). 352p. 1985. 26.95 o.p. (ISBN 0-89577-197-7, Pub. by RD Assn). Random.

Our Needs. rev. ed. Carol S. Prescott & Marion H. Smith. LC 76-17684. (Fideler Social Studies Ser.). (Illus.). 112p. (gr. 2-3). 1978. text ed. 6.20, 5 or more copies 4.96 o.p. (ISBN 0-88296-013-X); tchr's guide 4.96 o.p. (ISBN 0-88296-328-7). Gateway Pr MI.

Our Neighbor World. V. A. Firsoff. (Illus.). 336p. 1953. (ISBN 0-8022-0505-4). Philos Lib.

Our New Baby. Jan Grant. LC 79-22048. (Social Values Ser.). (Illus.). 32p. (gr. k-3). 1980. PLB 11.27 o.p. (ISBN 0-516-01480-3); pap. 3.95 o.p. (ISBN 0-516-41480-1). Childrens.

Our Overloaded Economy: Inflation, Unemployment & the Crisis in American Capitalism. Wallace C. Peterson. LC 81-51288. 288p. 1982. 29.95 o.p. (ISBN 0-87332-187-1). M E Sharpe.

Our Own Worst Enemy: The Unmaking of American Foreign Policy. I. M. Destler et al. 294p. 1984. 17.45 o.p. (ISBN 0-671-44278-3). S&S.

Our Precious Heritage. Sarah J. McDonnall. 112p. 1988. 9.50 o.p. (ISBN 0-8062-3076-2). Carlton.

Our Reader. Jack Tancer. (Illus.). 1964. pap. 3.00x o.p. (ISBN 0-88323-060-7, 158). Pendergrass Pub.

Our Reasonable Faith: A Survey of Christian Doctrine. Herman Bavinck. Tr. by Henry Zylstra. (Twin Brooks Ser). 1977. pap. 13.95 o.p. (ISBN 0-8010-0513-2). Baker Bk.

Our Region: The Pacific Northwest. Ruth Pelz. LC 81-2579. (Illus.). 275p. (gr. 4). 1981. text ed. 17.25x o.p. (ISBN 0-87905-107-8, Peregrine Smith). Gibbs Smith Pub.

Our Road to Prayer. Francis Line & Helen Line. 1974. pap. 1.25x o.p. (ISBN 0-8358-0305-8). Upper Room.

Our Roots Are Still Alive: The Story of the Palestinian People. People's Press Palestine Book Project Staff et al. LC 77-10952. (Illus.). 182p. pap. 5.45 o.p. (ISBN 0-917654-12-9). IISJ.

Our Search for Identity: Humanity in the Image of God. Marianne H. Micks. LC 81-70592. 176p. 1982. pap. 1.00 o.p. (ISBN 0-8006-1627-8, Fortress). Augsburg Fortress.

Our Search for Wilderness: The Story of a Sixty-Year Marriage. Edward C. Graves. 224p. 1975. 8.00 o.p. (ISBN 0-682-48321-4, Lochinvar). Exposition-Phoenix.

Our Second Revolution. James T. Hunter. LC 68-9126. (Orig.). 1968. pap. 2.00 o.p. (ISBN 0-87004-068-5). Caxton.

Our Secular Cathedrals: Change & Continuity in the University. Alan Richardson et al. Ed. by Taylor Littleton. LC 75-181495. (Franklin Lectures in the Sciences & Humanities: No. 3). 1973. 12.95 o.p. (ISBN 0-8173-6643-1). U of Ala Pr.

Our Share of Time. Yves Navarre. Tr. by Dominic DiBernardi & Noelle Domke. LC 86-72136. Orig. Title: Temps Uoulu. 240p. 1987. 20.00 o.p. (ISBN 0-916583-17-1). Dalkey Arch.

Our Sisters in the Bible. Jerrie W. Hurd. LC 83-50986. 168p. 1983. 8.95 o.p. (ISBN 0-87747-981-X). Deseret Bk.

Our Sixth Sense: An Organic Theory of the Unknown. J. M. Sanchez-Perez. 1979. 5.50 o.p. (ISBN 0-682-49072-5). Exposition-Phoenix.

Our Social Bees. Andrew Wynter. LC 67-23950. (Social History Reference Ser.). (Illus.). 544p. 1969. Repr. of 1861 ed. 35.00x o.p. (ISBN 0-8103-3265-5). Gale.

Our Spiritual Resources. Joel S. Goldsmith. LC 62-7965. 1978. 8.95i o.p. (ISBN 0-06-063211-9). HarpR.

Our Teachers Are Crying: A Positive Approach to Solving Classroom Problems. Ann G. Ruben. 132p. 1975. pap. 4.75 o.p. (ISBN 0-8422-0525-X). Irvington.

Titles

Our Tempestuous Day. Carolly Erickson. LC 85-15389. (Illus.). 320p. 1986. 18.95 o.p. (ISBN 0-688-06086-2). Morrow.

Our Town. Thornton Wilder. 1976. pap. 2.25 o.p. (ISBN 0-380-00557-3, 69013-6, Bard). Avon.

Our Tragic Inflation Orgy & What to Do About It: An Introduction to the Fascinating Economics of Tomorrow. Clyde G. Chenoweth. 1978. 8.00 o.p. (ISBN 0-682-49097-0, University). Exposition-Phoenix.

Our Trails to Triumphant Living. Rev. Roy E. Dickert. 1976. 6.00 o.p. (ISBN 0-682-48445-8). Exposition-Phoenix.

Our Urban Planet. Ellen A. Switzer. LC 80-12225. (Illus.). 288p. (gr. 7 up). 1980. 12.95 o.s.i. (ISBN 0-689-30788-8, Atheneum Childrens Bks). Macmillan.

Our Useless Fears. Joseph Wolpe & David Wolpe. 185p. 1981. 10.95 o.p. (ISBN 0-395-31334-1). HM.

Our Way-Their Way. Ed. by A. K. Islam. 200p. 1974. 24.50x o.p. (ISBN 0-8422-5185-5); pap. text ed. 5.00x o.p. (ISBN 0-8422-0436-9). Irvington.

Our World of Things. Patricia A. Reuse. LC 84-12705. 1985. pap. 3.95 o.p. (ISBN 0-8054-5246-X). Broadman.

Our Yes to God. Chiara Lubich. Tr. by Hugh J. Moran from Ital. LC 81-82064. 112p. (Orig.). 1981. pap. cancelled o.s.i. (ISBN 0-911782-38-9). New City.

Our Youngest Parents: A Study of the Use of Support Services by Adolescent Mothers. Rosalind Zitner & Shelby M. Miller. 96p. (Orig.). 1980. pap. text ed. 9.95 o.p. (ISBN 0-87868-144-2, 1442). Child Welfare.

Out from the Heart. James Allen. 1975. soft bdg. 1.25 o.p. (ISBN 0-87707-144-6). CSA Pr.

Out of Africa. Isak Dinesen. 416p. 1972. pap. 4.95 o.s.i. (ISBN 0-394-71740-6, V740, Vin). Random.

Out of Africa. Isak Dinesen. (Illus.). 288p. 1987. 24.95 o.p. Crown.

Out of Africa & Shadows on the Grass. Isak Dinesen. (Large Print Bks (General Ser.)). 597p. 1986. lib. bdg. 19.95x o.p. (ISBN 0-8161-4181-9); pap. 12.95x o.p. (ISBN 0-8161-4182-7). G K Hall.

Out of Canaan. Keith A. Rice. 192p. 1983. 12.95 o.s.i. (ISBN 0-684-17857-5, ScribT). Scribner.

Out of Chaos. Louis J. Halle. 1977. 20.00 o.p. (ISBN 0-395-25357-8). HM.

Out of Control. Sam Bittman. (Going for It Ser: No. 4). 144p. 1985. pap. 2.50 o.p. (ISBN 0-380-89902-7, Flare). Avon.

Out of Court. 1983. 37.50 o.p. (ISBN 0-317-43440-3, LEG-SIM 595). Dushkin Pub.

Out of Crisis: A Project for European Recovery. Ed. by Stuart Holland. (European Socialist Thought Ser.: No. 11). (Illus.). 204p. 1983. text ed. 29.95 o.p. (ISBN 0-317-52165-9, Pub. by Spokesman UK). Humanities.

Out of Danger. Suzanne Lipsett. LC 87-14409. 256p. 1987. 18.95 o.p. (ISBN 0-689-11825-2, Atheneum). Macmillan.

Out of Forever into Forever. Ronald L. Pelton. 1978. 5.50 o.p. (ISBN 0-682-49131-4). Exposition-Phoenix.

Out of Heartland Hell. Earl D. Hunter. 1985. 13.95 o.p. (ISBN 0-317-38085-0). Vantage.

Out of India: Selected Stories. Ruth P. Jhabvala. 384p. 1986. 16.95 o.p. (ISBN 0-688-06382-9). Morrow.

Out of My Head. Robert Bloch. Ed. by Jim Mann. LC 85-63158. (Illus.). 193p. 1986. 15.00 o.p. (ISBN 0-915368-30-7). New Eng SF Assoc.

Out of My Later Years. Albert Einstein. 256p. (ISBN 0-8022-0439-2). Philos Lib.

Out of Order. Roger Sycamore. LC 84-91347. 91p. 1985. 7.95 o.p. (ISBN 0-533-06176-8). Vantage.

Out of Our Depth. Mike Peyton. (Illus.). 96p. (Orig.). 1985. 13.95 o.p. (ISBN 0-85177-353-2, Pub. by Conway Maritime Press England). Sheridan.

Out of Phaze. Piers Anthony. (Apprentice Adept Ser.: Bk. 4). 288p. 1987. 17.95 o.p. (ISBN 0-399-13272-4). Putnam Pub Group.

Out of School: Modern Perspectives in Truancy & School Refusal. Ed. by Lionel Hersov & Ian Berg. LC 79-41725. (Studies in Child Psychiatry). 377p. 1980. 79.95 o.p. (ISBN 0-471-27743-6, Pub. by Wiley-Interscience). Wiley.

Out of Step. Joseph Trenaman. 224p. 1953. (ISBN 0-8022-1735-4). Philos Lib.

Out of the Blackout. Robert Barnard. 270p. 1986. pap. 10.95x o.p. (ISBN 0-8161-3920-2, Large Print Bks). G K Hall.

Out of the Bleachers: Writings on Women & Sport. Ed. by Stephanie L. Twin. (Women's Lives-Women's Work Ser). (Illus.). 272p. 1979. pap. 5.00 o.p. (ISBN 0-912670-59-2); teaching guide, 96p. o.p. 5.00 o.p. (ISBN 0-912670-64-9). Feminist Pr.

Out of the Blue: Role of Luck in Air Warfare. Ed. by Laddie Lucas. (Illus.). 317p. 1986. 24.95 o.p. (ISBN 0-09-162410-X, Pub. by Century Hutchinson). David & Charles.

Out of the Desert. Michael A. Keen. LC 63-11482. 64p. 1963. (ISBN 0-8022-0836-3). Philos Lib.

Out of the Forties. Nicholas Lemann. 1985. pap. 12.95 o.p. (ISBN 0-671-55419-0). S&S.

Out of the Night, Into the Wind. Johnson Levering. LC 84-91348. 192p. 1985. 12.95 o.p. (ISBN 0-533-06444-9). Vantage.

Out of the Night: The Spiritual Journey of Vietnam Vets. William P. Mahedy. 1986. 15.45 o.p. (ISBN 0-345-32911-2). Ballantine.

Out of the Rolling Ocean & Other Love Poems. Robert Bly. LC 84-6442. 1984. Handcased & Signed o.p. 30.00x o.s.i. (ISBN 0-915408-29-5); pap. 4.00 o.s.i. (ISBN 0-915408-28-7). Ally Pr.

Out of the Whirlwind. Albert Friedlander. 1968. 10.95 o.p. (ISBN 0-8074-0043-2, 959065). UAHC.

Out of This Century. Peggy Guggenheim. 1987. pap. 14.95 o.p. (ISBN 0-233-97601-9). Basil Blackwell.

Out of Work. Stephen Ludwig. 56p. 1975. 2.00 o.p. (ISBN 0-317-35481-7). New Readers.

Out of Yesterday & Into Tomorrow: Selected Poems 1935-1970. H. Silverman. 1970. pap. text ed. 3.50 o.p. (ISBN 0-8290-1170-6). Irvington.

Out, Out, Brief Candle! R. W. Myres. 1978. 4.00 o.p. (ISBN 0-682-49220-5). Exposition-Phoenix.

Out West. Mike Flanagan. (Illus.). 208p. 1987. 27.50 o.p. (ISBN 0-8109-1409-3). Abrams.

Out with the In Crowd. Jane Sorenson. (Jennifer Bks.). 144p. (gr. 5-8). 1986. 2.95 o.p. (ISBN 0-87403-087-0, 2987). Standard Pub.

Outback. Aaron Fletcher. 448p. (Orig.). 1982. pap. 3.25 o.p. (ISBN 0-8439-1028-3, Pub. by Leisure Bks CT). Dorchester Pub Co.

Outback. Aaron Fletcher. 1978. pap. 2.25 o.s.i. (ISBN 0-8439-0533-6, Pub. by Leisure Bks CT). Dorchester Pub Co.

Outback. Aaron Fletcher. 448p. 1983. pap. 3.50 o.s.i. (ISBN 0-8439-2013-0, Pub. by Leisure Bks CT). Dorchester Pub Co.

Outboard Book. Nigel Warren. (Illus.). 200p. 1978. 8.95 o.p. (ISBN 0-910990-43-3). Hearst Bks.

Outboard Motor Maintenance & Tune-up Manual, Vol. 1. Intertec Publishing Corp. Staff. (Illus.). 400p. 1986. pap. 12.95 o.p. (ISBN 0-87288-224-1, OMM1-1). Intertec Pub.

Outboard Motor Maintenance Tune-up Manual, Vol. 2. Intertec Publishing Corp. Staff. (Illus.). 364p. 1986. pap. 12.95 o.p. (ISBN 0-87288-225-X, OMM2-1). Intertec Pub.

Outbreak. Robin Cook. 368p. 1986. 17.95 o.p. (ISBN 0-399-13187-6, Perigee). Putnam Pub Group.

Outbreak. Robin Cook. 1987. 17.95 o.p. (ISBN 0-317-56209-6). Putnam Pub Group.

Outcast Gun. Giles A. Lutz. 1984. pap. 1.95 o.p. (ISBN 0-449-12718-4, GM). Fawcett.

Outcome of Severe Damage to the Central Nervous System. Ciba Foundation Staff. (CIBA Foundation Symposium Ser.: No. 34). 340p. 1976. 44.75 o.p. (ISBN 0-444-15182-6, Excerpta Medica). Elsevier.

Outcome Uncertain: Science & the Political Process. Mary E. Ames. 1982. pap. 3.50 o.p. (ISBN 0-380-59535-4, 59535-4, Discus). Avon.

Outdoor Design: A Handbook for the Architect & Planner. Olwen C. Marlowe. 301p. 1977. text ed. 76.00x o.p. (ISBN 0-258-97017-0, Pub. by Granada England). Gower Pub Co.

Outdoor Guide to the San Francisco Bay Area. 4th ed. Dorothy L. Whitnah. LC 82-62812. (Illus.). 416p. (Orig.). 1984. pap. 11.95 o.p. (ISBN 0-89997-026-5). Wilderness Pr.

Outdoor Leadership Handbook. Paul Green. 42p. 1982. pap. 3.50 o.p. (ISBN 0-913724-32-7). Emerg Response Inst.

Outdoor Recreation & Camping Guide to Michigan's U. P. (Illus.). 1982. pap. 3.25 o.p. (ISBN 0-686-92000-7). Avery Color.

Outdoor Safety & Survival. Paul H. Risk. LC 82-23810. 340p. 1983. pap. (ISBN 0-02-401800-7). Macmillan.

Outdoor Survival Handbook. David Platten. (Illus.). 160p. 1986. 20.95 o.p. (ISBN 0-7153-8879-7); pap. 15.95 o.p. (ISBN 0-7153-8880-0). David & Charles.

Outdoors Canada. Reader's Digest Association, Canada. (Illus.). 1980. 24.95 o.p. (ISBN 0-393-01366-9). Norton.

Outer City: Geographical Consequences of the Urbanization of the Suburbs. Peter O. Muller. Ed. by Salvatore J. Natoli. LC 76-29264. (Resource Papers for College Geography Ser.). (Illus.). 1976. pap. text ed. 5.00 o.p. (ISBN 0-89291-114-X). Assn Am Geographers.

Outer Continental Shelf Frontier Technology. Marine Board, Assembly of Engineering Staff & National Research Council Staff. LC 80-82152. 1980. pap. text ed. 9.95x o.p. (ISBN 0-309-03084-6). Natl Acad Pr.

Outer Space: Battlefield of the Future? 180p. 1978. 18.00x o.p. (ISBN 0-85066-130-7). Taylor & Francis.

Outfit. Richard Stark. 1981. lib. bdg. 11.50 o.p. (ISBN 0-8398-2710-5, Gregg). G K Hall.

Outlaw: The Saga of Claude Dallas. Jeff Long. LC 84-1178. 1985. 12.95 o.p. (ISBN 0-688-04165-5). Morrow.

Outlaw Valley. Thomas Thompson. LC 87-13689. (Double D Western Ser.). 192p. 1987. 12.95 o.s.i. (ISBN 0-385-23959-9). Doubleday.

Outlaw Years: The History of the Land Pirates of the Natchez Trace. Robert M. Coates. LC 74-1087. (Illus.). 348p. 1974. Repr. of 1930 ed. 48.00x o.p. (ISBN 0-8103-3961-7). Gale.

Outlawry of War see Outlawry of War: A Constructive Policy for World Peace.

Outlawry of War: A Constructive Policy for World Peace. Charles C. Morrison. Bd. with Outlawry of War. Salmon O. Levinson. LC 71-147607. (Library of War & Peace; Kellogg Pact & the Outlawry of War). 1972. lib. bdg. 46.00 o.p. (ISBN 0-8240-0367-5). Garland Pub.

Outlaw's Empire. Ray Hogan. LC 85-13082. (Double D Western Ser.). 192p. 1986. 12.95 o.p. (ISBN 0-385-23254-3). Doubleday.

Outlaws in the Promised Land: Mexican Immigrant Workers & America's Future. James D. Cockcroft. LC 84-73206. (Latin America Ser.). 288p. (Orig.). 1986. pap. 10.95 o.p. (ISBN 0-394-62365-7, Ever). Grove.

Outlaws of Medieval Legend. Maurice Keen. (Studies in Social History). 235p. 1977. 26.95x o.p. (ISBN 0-7100-8682-2). Routledge Chapman & Hall.

Outlaws of the Marsh, 2 vols. Nai'an Shi & Luo Guanzhong. Tr. by Sidney Shapiro. LC 80-8665. (Illus.). 1638p. 1981. 37.50x o.p. (ISBN 0-253-12574-X). Ind U Pr.

Outlaws of the Ocean: The Complete Book of Crime on the High Seas. Gerhard Mueller & Freda Adler. LC 84-19255. (Illus.). 360p. 1985. 17.95 o.p. (ISBN 0-688-04170-1, Pub. by Hearst Marine Bks). Morrow.

Outline Course of Pure Mathematics. A. F. Horadam. 1969. text ed. 23.00 o.p. (ISBN 0-08-012593-X). Pergamon.

Outline Life of Christ. Frank E. Wilson & Clifford P. Morehouse. (Orig.). 1947. pap. 1.95 o.p. (ISBN 0-8192-1090-0). Morehouse Pub.

Outline of a Plan for Scientific Research & Training in Africa: Proceedings of the Lagos Conference, 1964. Lagos Conference Staff. 1964. pap. 2.25 o.p. (ISBN 92-3-100557-X, U444, UNESCO). UNIPUB.

Outline of Balanced Cross-Sections. 2nd ed. N. B. Woodward et al. (University of Tennessee Studies in Geology). (Illus.). 170p. (Orig.). 1985. pap. 11.00 o.p. (ISBN 0-910249-10-5). U of Tenn Geo.

Outline of Bible Study. G. Dallas Smith. pap. 2.95 o.p. (ISBN 0-89225-192-1); pap. 2.95 o.p. (ISBN 0-686-96726-7). Gospel Advocate.

Outline of China's Physical Geography. Ed. by Ren Mei'E et al. Tr. by Zhang Tingquan & Hu Genkang. (China Knowledge Ser.). (Illus.). 471p. 1985. pap. 9.95 o.p. (ISBN 0-8351-1192-X). China Bks.

Outline of Chinese Acupuncture. Academy of Traditional Chinese Medicine, Shanghai Staff. 1978. 36.00 o.p. (ISBN 0-08-021545-9). Pergamon.

Outline of Christian Symbolism. Frank E. Wilson. (Orig.). 1938. pap. 1.50 o.p. (ISBN 0-8192-1068-4). Morehouse Pub.

Outline of Christian Theology. W. N. Clarke. 498p. 1898. text ed. 10.95x o.p. (ISBN 0-567-02069-X). Attic Pr.

Outline of Clinical Diagnosis. B. J. Prout. (Illus.). 276p. 1983. pap. 23.00 o.p. (ISBN 0-7236-0678-1). Butterworth.

Outline of Developmental Physiology. 3rd ed. C. P. Raven. 1966. 23.00 o.p. (ISBN 0-08-011343-5). Pergamon.

Outline of English Painting. R. H. Wilensky. (ISBN 0-8022-1881-4). Philos Lib.

Outline of Fractures. 8th ed. John C. Adams. LC 77-30525. (Illus.). 1984. pap. text ed. 18.50 o.p. (ISBN 0-443-02897-4). Churchill.

Outline of History, 4 vols. H. G. Wells. 1920. Repr. 250.00x o.p. (ISBN 0-403-03082-X). Somerset Pub.

Outline of History of Science. Walter Shepherd. LC 68-18734. 142p. 1968. (ISBN 0-8022-1550-5). Philos Lib.

Outline of Metaphysics. Franklin J. Matchette. 1952. (ISBN 0-8022-1083-X). Philos Lib.

Outline of Modern Russian Literature: 1880-1940. Ernest J. Simmons. LC 75-138599. 1971. Repr. of 1943 ed. lib. bdg. 22.50x o.p. (ISBN 0-8371-5801-X, SIMR). Greenwood.

Outline of Oral Surgery, Pt. 1. H. Killey & G. Seward. (Illus.). 196p. 1975. 16.00 o.p. (ISBN 0-7236-0406-1, Pub. by John Wright UK). Butterworth.

Outline of Organic Chemistry. 3rd ed. J. Ernest Simpson et al. (Illus.). 448p. 1975. text ed. 25.95 o.p. (ISBN 0-07-057436-7). McGraw.

Outline of Philosophy. Bertrand Russell. 1927. text ed. 17.95x o.p. (ISBN 0-04-192017-1). Unwin Hyman.

Outline of Piaget's Developmental Psychology. Ruth M. Beard. (Student's Library of Education). 144p. 1983. pap. 7.95 o.p. (ISBN 0-7100-6344-X). Routledge Chapman & Hall.

Outline of Piano Pedagogy. Beryl Rubinstein. 70p. 1967. pap. 5.00 o.p. (ISBN 0-8258-0171-0, 01836). Fischer Inc NY.

Outline of Plant Classification. S. B. Holmes. 192p. 1983. 17.95 o.p. (ISBN 0-470-20394-3, Co-Pub. with Longman). Wiley.

Outline of Psychology As Applied to Medicine. J. Weinman. 288p. 1981. pap. text ed. 13.00 o.p. (ISBN 0-7236-0591-2). Butterworth.

Outline of Scientific Criminology. Nigel Morland. (ISBN 0-8022-1150-X). Philos Lib.

Outline of Structural Geology. B. E. Hobbs et al. LC 75-20393. 571p. 1976. (ISBN 0-471-40156-0). Wiley.

Outline of the Old Testament & Apocrypha. Frank E. Wilson. (Orig.). 1935. pap. 1.75 o.p. (ISBN 0-8192-1091-9). Morehouse Pub.

Outline of Theatre Law. Milton C. Jacobs. LC 72-5454. xii, 148p. 1972. Repr. of 1949 ed. lib. bdg. 35.00x o.p. (ISBN 0-8371-6436-2, JATL). Greenwood.

Outline of Weather Control. Anthony G. Vieira. 64p. 1984. 5.50 o.p. (ISBN 0-682-40196-X). Exposition-Phoenix.

Outline Research Programme for the African Regional Aquaculture Centre: Report of a Task Force Sponsored by the FAO-UNDP Aquaculture Development & Coordination Programme, Port Harcourt, Rivers State, Nigeria, Feb. 3-19, 1980. 21p. 1980. pap. 7.50 o.p. (ISBN 92-5-101019-6, F2142, FAO). UNIPUB.

Outlines & Readings in Educational Tests & Measurements. Ed. by William J. Beausay. 194p. 1972. pap. text ed. 8.95x o.p. (ISBN 0-8422-0199-8). Irvington.

Outlines for Christian Youth. R. P. Daniel. pap. 6.95 o.p. (ISBN 0-88172-019-4). Believers Bkshelf.

Outlines of a Philosophy of Art. Robin G. Collingwood. LC 25-26891. 104p. 1925. Repr. 39.00x o.p. (ISBN 0-403-07231-X). Somerset Pub.

Outlines of Bible Study: An Easy-to-Follow Guide to Greater Bible Knowledge. Ed. by G. Dallas Smith. 120p. 1986. pap. text ed. 3.95 o.p. (ISBN 0-89225-287-1). Gospel Advocate.

Outlines of General & Systemic Pathology. 1st ed. Herbert Braunstein. LC 81-14145. (Illus.). 616p. 1981. pap. text ed. 27.95 o.p. (ISBN 0-8016-0869-4). Mosby.

Outlines of Modern Legal Logic. Ilmar Tammelo. 182p. (Orig.). 1969. pap. 42.50x o.p. (ISBN 3-515-00185-9, Pub by Franz Steiner). Coronet Bks.

Outlines of the Moral Philosophy. Dugald Stewart. LC 75-11255. (British Philosophers & Theologians of the 17th & 18th Centuries: Vol. 54). 322p. 1976. Repr. of 1793 ed. lib. bdg. 51.00 o.p. (ISBN 0-8240-1805-2). Garland Pub.

Outlines of Tudor & Stuart Plays, Fourteen Ninety-Seven to Sixteen Forty-Two. Karl J. Holznecht. Repr. of 1947 ed. 69.00 o.p. (ISBN 0-403-04196-1). Somerset Pub.

Outpatient Surgery. 2nd ed. George J. Hill, II. LC 77-27749. (Illus.). 1457p. 1980. text ed. write for info. o.p. (ISBN 0-7216-4676-X). Saunders.

Outperforming Wall Street: Stock Market Profits Through Patience. Daniel A. Seiver. (Illus.). 192p. 1987. 19.95 o.p. (ISBN 0-13-645235-3). P-H.

Outplacement Techniques: A Positive Approach to Terminating Employees. William J. Morin & Lyle Yorks. 208p. 1982. 16.95 o.p. (ISBN 0-8144-5579-4). AMACOM.

Outposts of Monopoly Capitalism: Southern Africa in the Changing Global Economy. Ann Seidman & Neva S. Makgetla. LC 80-80525. 384p. (Orig.). 1980. 16.95 o.p. (ISBN 0-88208-114-4); pap. 8.95 osi o.p. (ISBN 0-88208-115-2). Chicago Review.

Outrage. Henry Denker. 320p. 1983. pap. 3.95 o.p. (ISBN 0-380-62802-3, 62802). Avon.

Outrageous Acts & Everyday Rebellions. Gloria Steinem. LC 84-6875. 288p. 1983. 14.95 o.p. (ISBN 0-03-063236-6). H Holt & Co.

Outrageous Fortune: The Tragedy of Leopold III of the Belgians, 1901-1941. Roger Keyes. (Illus.). 544p. 1984. 39.95 o.p. (ISBN 0-436-23320-7, Pub. by Secker & Warburg UK). David & Charles.

Outrageous Fortunes: The Story of the Medici, the Rothschilds, & J. Pierpont Morgan. Cass Canfield. LC 80-24299. (Illus.). 120p. 1981. 10.95 o.p. (ISBN 0-15-170513-5). HarBraceJ.

Outrageous Good Fortune. Michael Burke. 480p. 1984. 19.45i o.p. (ISBN 0-316-11679-3). Little.

Outrageous Herb Lady: How to Make a Mint in Selling & Multi-Level Marketing. Venus C. Andrecht. Ed. by Margaret L. McWhorter. LC 82-60388. 144p. (Orig.). 1982. pap. 6.95 o.p. (ISBN 0-9604342-2-4). Ransom Hill.

Outrageously Yours: The Explosive West Letters. Bruce West. 1987. pap. 7.95 o.p. (ISBN 0-399-51410-4, Perigee Bks). Putnam Pub Group.

Outreach Preaching: The Role of Preaching in Evangelism. Elton P. Richards, Jr. 56p. (Orig.). 1986. pap. 4.95 o.p. (ISBN 0-8066-2232-6, 10-4859, Augsburg). Augsburg Fortress.

Outside. Marguerite Duras. Tr. by Arthur Goldhammer from Fr. LC 86-47507. 272p. 1986. 19.95 o.p. (ISBN 0-8070-6310-X). Beacon Pr.

Outside. Andre Norton. (gr. 4-7). 1976. pap. 1.50 o.p. (ISBN 0-380-00435-6, 52720-0, Camelot). Avon.

Outside Looking in. Richard Montrois. 1979. 5.00 o.p. (ISBN 0-682-49536-0). Exposition-Phoenix.

Outside the Dream: Lacan & French Styles of Psychoanalysis. Martin Stanton. 108p. 1983. pap. 9.95 o.p. (ISBN 0-7100-9273-3). Routledge Chapman & Hall.

Outside the State: Voluntary Organisations in Three English Towns. Stephen Hatch. 154p. 1980. 20.00x o.p. (ISBN 0-7099-0234-4, Pub. by Croom Helm Ltd). Routledge Chapman & Hall.

Outsider. Howard Fast. 1984. lib. bdg. 17.95 o.p. (ISBN 0-8161-3760-9, Large Print Bks). G K Hall.

Outsider. Furan Illustrators Staff & Collen L. Reece. Ed. by Howard Schroeder. LC 81-3298. (Roundup Ser.). (Illus.). 48p. (Orig.). (gr. 3 up). 1981. PLB 4.95 o.p. (ISBN 0-89686-150-3); pap. text ed. 3.95 o.s.i. (ISBN 0-89686-158-9). Crestwood Hse.

Outsider in Amsterdam. Janwillem Van de Wetering. LC 75-12579. 256p. 1975. 6.95 o.p. (ISBN 0-395-20705-3). HM.

Outstanding American Illustrators Today. Ed. by Satoru Fujii. 344p. 1985. 54.95 o.p. (ISBN 0-8161-8749-5). G K Hall.

Outstanding Books for the College Bound. Mary Ann Paulin & Susan T. Berlin. LC 83-25714. vi, 92p. 1984. pap. 5.95x o.p. (ISBN 0-8389-3302-5). ALA.

Outstretched Arm: The History of the Jewish Colonization Association. Theodore Norman. 352p. 1984. 32.00x o.p. (ISBN 0-7102-0253-9). Routledge Chapman & Hall.

Outstretched Hand: Advances in Modern Medicine. Moira S. Reynolds. (Illus.). 147p. (gr. 7-12). 1980. lib. bdg. 10.97 o.p. (ISBN 0-8239-0502-0). Rosen Group.

Outstretched Hand: Poems, Prayers, & Meditations. Rod McKuen. LC 78-20589. 160p. 1980. 9.57i o.p. (ISBN 0-06-250568-8). HarpR.

Outta Sight, Luther. Brumsic Brandon, Jr. LC 77-170318. (Illus.). 1972. pap. 1.95 o.p. (ISBN 0-8397-6481-2). Eriksson.

Ouvrage Collectif Sous la Direction de Denise Escarpit. (Publications de la Maison des Sciences de l'homme d'Aquitaine Ser.: No. 12). (Illus.). 1978. pap. 16.50x o.p. (ISBN 90-279-7804-2). Mouton.

Ouvre-Boite: Colloque Abhumaniste. Jacques Audiberti. 9.95 o.p. (ISBN 0-686-54498-6). French & Eur.

Ovarian Malignancies: The Clinical Care of Adults & Adolescents. M. Steven Piver. LC 82-4364. (Current Reviews in Obstetrics & Gynecology Ser.: No. 4). (Illus.). 204p. 1983. pap. text ed. 21.50 o.p. (ISBN 0-443-02553-3). Churchill.

Ovarian Tumors. L. W. Brady et al. (Oncologic Ser.: Vol. 20). (Illus.). 232p. 1984. pap. 120.00 o.p. (ISBN 0-08-027472-2). Pergamon.

Ovary, 2 vols. 2nd ed. Ed. by Solly Zuckerman. Incl. Vol. 1. General Aspects. 1977. 73.50 (ISBN 0-12-782601-7); Vol. 2. Physiology. 1977. 78.00 (ISBN 0-12-782602-5); Vol. 3. Regulation of Oogenesis & Sleriodogenesis. 1978. 67.50 (ISBN 0-12-782603-3). 1977. Acad Pr.

Ove Arup; Ove Arup & Partners, Architects; & Arup Associates: A Bibliography of Articles. Carole A. Cable. (Architecture Ser.: Bibliography A 1343). 1985. pap. 2.00 o.p. (ISBN 0-89028-313-3). Vance Biblios.

Over & Under. John Misterly, Jr. 448p. 1987. 14.50 o.p. (ISBN 0-8062-2845-8). Carlton.

Over Cape Cod & the Islands. Steven Proehl. 1979. o.s. 20.00 o.p. (ISBN 0-395-27064-2); pap. 11.95 o.p. (ISBN 0-395-27937-2). HM.

Over Fifty-Five Is Not Illegal. Frances Tenenbaum. 1979. 14.95 o.p. (ISBN 0-395-27595-4); pap. 7.95 o.p. (ISBN 0-395-27936-4). HM.

Over Forty Wellness Diet. R. A. Gegan & Ray C. Wunderlick. (Illus.). 40p. 1985. pap. 2.95 o.p. (ISBN 0-318-11693-6). Consumer Info Pubns.

Over in the Meadow. Paul Galdone. (Illus.). 32p. (ps-1). 1986. 12.95 o.s.i. (ISBN 0-13-646654-0). P-H.

Over in the Meadow. Olive A. Wadsworth. (gr. k-3). 1971. pap. 1.95 o.p. (ISBN 0-590-09195-6). Scholastic Inc.

Over New York: An Aerial View. Stephen Proehl. 1980. 24.95 o.p. (ISBN 0-395-29096-1); pap. 12.95 o.p. (ISBN 0-395-29097-X). HM.

Over Sea, under Stone. Susan Cooper. LC 79-10489. (Illus.). (gr. 4-7). 1979. pap. 5.95 o.p. (ISBN 0-15-670542-7, VoyB). HarBraceJ.

Over-Sexed, Over-Paid & Over Here: Americans in Australia 1941-1945. John H. Moore. (Illus.). 303p. 1982. text ed. 27.50x o.p. (ISBN 0-7022-1575-9). U of Queensland Pr.

Over the Hills & Far Away. Lavinia Russ. LC 68-13371. (gr. 5 up). 1968. 5.50 o.p. (ISBN 0-15-258946-5, HJ). HarBraceJ.

Over the Moon: A Book of Sayings. Ed. by Shirley Hughes. (Illus.). 48p. (gr. k-4). 1980. 6.95 o.p. (ISBN 0-571-11594-2). Faber & Faber.

Over the Sea's Edge. Jane L. Curry. LC 70-152693. (Illus.). 182p. (gr. 4-6). 1971. 5.25 o.p. (ISBN 0-15-259010-2, HJ). HarBraceJ.

Overboard. Hank Searls. 1977. 8.95 o.p. (ISBN 0-393-08364-0). Norton.

Overcoming. Rick Yohn. 96p. 1985. pap. 4.95 o.p. (ISBN 0-89109-055-X). NavPress.

Overcoming Breast Cancer. Genell J. Subak-Sharpe. LC 86-24099. (Illus.). 1987. pap. 16.95 o.p. (ISBN 0-385-18770-X). Doubleday.

Overcoming Childlessness: Its Causes & What to Do About Them. Elliot Philipp. LC 75-8201. (Illus.). 192p. 1975. 8.50 o.s.i. (ISBN 0-8008-6161-2). Taplinger.

Overcoming Clumsiness: Physical Dexterity for People Who Thought It Was Impossible. David L. Chandler & Johnathan Eisen. LC 85-31730. (Illus.). 128p. 1986. 12.95 o.p. (ISBN 0-8069-6348-4); pap. 6.95 o.p. (ISBN 0-8069-6350-6). Sterling.

Overcoming Dyslexia: A Straightforward Guide for Families & Teachers. Beve Hornsby. (Illus.). 112p. 1985. 12.95 o.p. (ISBN 0-668-05689-4); pap. 7.95 o.p. (ISBN 0-668-05692-4). Arco.

Overcoming Loneliness. David Jeremiah. LC 83-48411. 143p. 1983. pap. 5.95 o.p. (ISBN 0-89840-049-X). Heres Life.

Overcoming Murphy's Law. William C. Waddell. 618p. 1981. 14.95 o.p. (ISBN 0-8144-5628-6); pap. 5.95 o.p. (ISBN 0-8144-7561-2). AMACOM.

Overcoming Procrastination. Albert Ellis & William J. Knaus. LC 76-26333. 1977. pap. 3.95 o.p. (ISBN 0-917476-04-2). Inst Rational-Emotive.

Overdeveloped Nations. Date not set. (ISBN 0-8052-3683-X). Random.

Overdrive: A Personal Documentary. William F. Buckley, Jr. (Illus.). 272p. 1984. pap. 8.95 o.p. (ISBN 0-316-11449-9). Little.

Overexposed Society see Media Power: Who Is Shaping Your Picture of the World?.

Overheard by God: Fiction & Prayer in Herbert, Milton, Dante & St. John. A. D. Nuttall. 160p. 1980. 25.00x o.p. (ISBN 0-416-73980-6, NO. 6349); pap. 9.95 o.p. (ISBN 0-416-35230-8, NO. 4162). Routledge Chapman & Hall.

Overland & Beyond. 5th ed. Theresa Hewat & Joanathan Hewat. 160p. 1980. 9.95 o.p. (ISBN 0-903909-13-8). Bradt Ent.

Overland on the California Trail, 1846-1859. Marlin L. Heckman. LC 83-51609. (American Trails Ser.: Vol. XIII). 159p. 1984. 65.00 o.p. (ISBN 0-87062-155-6). A H Clark.

Overland Route. Krause & Grenard. (Carstens Hobby Bks.). 1979. pap. 10.00 o.p. (ISBN 0-911868-36-4, C36). Carstens Pubns.

Overlook Guide to Smallscale Goatkeeping. Billie Luisi. LC 85-8910. (Orig.). 1985. pap. 8.95 o.p. (ISBN 0-87951-230-X). Overlook Pr.

Overlook Treasury of Federal Antiques. George Michael. 1986. 22.95 o.p. (ISBN 0-87951-254-7). Overlook Pr.

Overlord: D-Day & The Invasion of Europe. Albert Marrin. LC 82-1745. (Illus.). 224p. (gr. 5 up). 1982. 12.95 o.s.i. (ISBN 0-689-30931-7, Atheneum Childrens Bks). Macmillan.

Overlord: D-Day, June 6, 1944. Max Hastings. (Illus.). 384p. 1984. 17.45 o.s.i. (ISBN 0-671-46029-3). S&S.

Overseas Economic Survey, Turkey, April 1950. T. G. Muntz. 1951. (ISBN 0-8022-1172-0). Philos Lib.

Overseas List: Opportunities for Living & Working in Developing Countries. David M. Beckmann & Elizabeth A. Donnelly. LC 79-50095. 192p. 1979. pap. 11.95 o.p. (ISBN 0-8066-1719-5, 10-4865, Augsburg). Augsburg Fortress.

Oversoul Seven & the Museum of Time. Jane Roberts. 134p. 1984. 14.95 o.p. (ISBN 0-13-647453-5); pap. 7.95 o.p. (ISBN 0-13-647446-2). P-H.

Overview & Analysis of School Mathematics. National Advisory Committee on Mathematical Education. LC 75-34807. 157p. (gr. k-12). 1975. pap. 5.00 o.p. (ISBN 0-87353-146-9). NCTM.

Overview of All Programs. Kitty Wehrli. (Michigan Arithmetic Program). 48p. 1974. tchrs. manual 3.00 o.p. (ISBN 0-89039-117-3). Ann Arbor Pubs.

Overview of Body Mechanics. Luella J. Lilly. 1976. pap. text ed. 3.95 o.p. (ISBN 0-917962-05-2). T H Peek.

Overview of Decommissioning Nuclear Power Plants. Atomic Industrial Forum Staff. (Technical & Economic Reports: Decommissioning). 1983. 30.00 o.p. (ISBN 0-318-02246-X). US Coun Energy Awareness.

Overview of International Studies. Ed. by John R. Howard. LC 72-86185. 232p. 1972. 29.50x o.p. (ISBN 0-8422-5030-1); pap. text ed. 9.95x o.p. (ISBN 0-8422-0229-3). Irvington.

Overview of Simulation in Highway Transportation, 2 vols, Pts. 1 & 2. Ed. by James E. Bernard. (SCS Simulation Ser.: Vol. 7, Nos. 1 & 2). 36.00 ea. o.p. (ISBN 0-686-36672-7). Soc Computer Sim.

Overwash Processes. Ed. by Stephen P. Leatherman. LC 80-28753. (Benchmark Papers in Geology Ser.: Vol. 58). 400p. 1982. 51.95 o.p. (ISBN 0-87933-375-8). Van Nos Reinhold.

Overweight Ladies. large type ed. Pearl Brians. 37p. 1984. pap. 6.00x o.p. (ISBN 0-914009-23-0). VHI Library.

Ovid-The Roman World: Selections from the Poems. Ed. by Jon Hazel. (Illus.). 122p. 1971. pap. text ed. 4.50x o.p. (ISBN 0-04-871001-6). Bolchazy-Carducci.

Ovulation in the Human. Ed. by P. G. Crosignani & D. Mishell. (Serono Symposium: No. 8). 1977. 65.50 o.p. (ISBN 0-12-198340-4). Acad Pr.

Ovulation Method of Birth Regulation. Mercedes Wilson. 202p. 1981. pap. 11.95 o.p. (ISBN 0-442-29432-8). Van Nos Reinhold.

Ovulation Method of Birth Regulation: The Latest Advances for Achieving or Postponing Pregnancy--Naturally. Mercedes A. Wilson. 240p. 1980. 24.95 o.p. (ISBN 0-442-29515-4). Van Nos Reinhold.

Owen Morrel Works: Nineteen Seventy-Six to Nineteen Eighty-Four. Trent Myers. (Illus.). 48p. (Orig.). 1984. pap. 11.95 art catalog o.p. Madison Art.

Owl & the Pussy Cat. Edward Lear. LC 77-77869. (gr. k-4). 1977. 6.95 o.p. (ISBN 0-689-30609-1, Atheneum). Macmillan.

Owl Hoots Twice at Catfish Bend. Ben L. Burman. 132p. (gr. 3-5). 1981. pap. 1.95 o.p. (ISBN 0-380-53496-7, 53496-7, Camelot). Avon.

Owl Hoots Twice at Catfish Bend see Three from Catfish Bend.

Owl in the Garden. Bernice Freschet. LC 84-5724. (Illus.). 32p. (ps-3). 1985. 11.75 o.p. (ISBN 0-688-04047-0); PLB 11.88 o.p. (ISBN 0-688-04048-9). Lothrop.

Owl Mystique. P-H.

Owl Service. Alan Garner. 192p. 1981. pap. 1.95 o.s.i. (ISBN 0-345-29044-5, Del Rey). Ballantine.

Owl That Could Not Fly. Joseph Chappelle. 40p. 1986. 5.75 o.p. (ISBN 0-8062-2622-6). Carlton.

Owlet the Great Horned Owl. Irene Brady. LC 74-5483. (Illus.). (gr. 4-6). 1974. reinforced bdg. 9.95 o.p. (ISBN 0-395-18519-X). HM.

Owliver. Robert Kraus. LC 80-13664. (Illus.). 32p. (gr. 4 up). 1987. 10.95 o.s.i. (ISBN 0-13-647538-8). Prentice Hall Pr.

Owls. Clive Catchpole. LC 77-8371. (New Biology Ser.). (Illus.). (gr. 4-9). 1978. text ed. 7.95 o.p. (ISBN 0-07-010232-5). McGraw.

Owls: Their Natural & Unnatural History. John Sparks & Tony Soper. LC 76-126994. (Illus.). 1970. 14.95 o.s.i. (ISBN 0-8008-6170-1). Taplinger.

Owls: Their Natural & Unnatural History. John Sparks & Tony Soper. LC 76-126994. (Illus.). 1979. pap. 8.50 o.s.i. (ISBN 0-8008-6171-X). Taplinger.

Owner-Built Adobe House. Duane Newcomb. (Illus.). 224p. 1980. pap. 8.95 o.s.i. (ISBN 0-684-17459-6). Scribner.

Owner-Built Home. Ken Kern. LC 75-5653. 1975. pap. 8.95 o.s.i. (ISBN 0-684-14223-6, ScribT). Scribner.

Owner Built Homestead. Barbara Kern & Ken Kern. LC 77-4032. (Illus.). 1977. pap. 7.95 o.s.i. (ISBN 0-684-14926-5, ScribT). Scribner.

Owner Occupation in Britain. Stephen Merrett & Fred Gray. 480p. 1983. 35.00x o.p. (ISBN 0-7100-9280-6). Routledge Chapman & Hall.

Ownership of the Image. Bernard Edelman. Tr. by Elizabeth Kingdom from Fr. 1979. 22.95x o.p. (ISBN 0-7100-0103-7). Routledge Chapman & Hall.

Oxford & Cambridge. Richard Gloucester & Hermione Hobhouse. (Illus.). 184p. 1980. 8.98 o.s.i. (ISBN 0-500-34081-1). Thames Hudson.

Oxford & Cambridge. Mercia Mason. (Blue Guides Ser.). (Illus.). 1982. 18.95 o.p. (ISBN 0-393-01547-5); pap. 11.95 o.p. (ISBN 0-393-00100-8). Norton.

Oxford & Stratford Travel Guide. Berlitz Editors. (Travel Guides Ser.). 1981. pap. 4.95 o.p. (ISBN 0-317-12116-2, Berlitz). Macmillan.

Oxford & the Idea of Commonwealth. Ed. by Frederick Madden & David K. Fieldhouse. 256p. 1982. 26.00 o.p. (ISBN 0-7099-1021-5, Pub. by Croom Helm Ltd). Routledge Chapman & Hall.

Oxford Blood: A Jemima Shore Mystery. Fraser Antonia. 1985. 13.45 o.p. (ISBN 0-393-02229-3). Norton.

Oxford Book of American Essays. Ed. by Brander Matthews. LC 77-92511. (Essay Index in Reprint Ser.). 1978. Repr. 38.50x o.p. (ISBN 0-8486-3008-4). Roth Pub Inc.

Oxford Book of Ballads, 2 vols in one. Ed. by Arthur Quiller-Couch. 800p. Repr. of 1955 ed. 55.00x o.p. (ISBN 0-403-08625-6). Somerset Pub.

Oxford Book of Pseuds. Private Eye "Pseud Corner" Column Staff. (Illus.). 1984. pap. 7.95 o.p. (ISBN 0-233-97586-1, Pub. by Private Eye UK). David & Charles.

Oxford English see Needed Words.

Oxford Travel Guide. Oxford Travel Guide Editors. (Berlitz Travel Guides). (Illus.). 1982. pap. 4.95 o.p. (ISBN 0-02-969500-7, Berlitz). Macmillan.

Oxidases & Related Redox Systems: Proceedings of a Conference Held in New York, 3-7 July 1979, 2 vols. Ed. by T. E. King et al. (Advances in the Biosciences Ser.: Vol. 33 & 34). 1250p. 1982. 415.00 o.p. (ISBN 0-08-024421-1). Pergamon.

Oxidation Numbers & Oxidation States. C. K. Jorgensen. LC 68-56944. 1969. 42.00 o.p. (ISBN 0-387-04658-5). Springer-Verlag.

Oxidation of Organic Compounds by Permanganate Ion & Hexavalent Chromium. Donald G. Lee. 174p. 1980. 14.95 o.p. (ISBN 0-87548-351-8). Open Court.

Oxidation of Organic Compounds: Solvent Effects in Radical Reactions. N. M. Emanuel et al. 350p. 1984. 155.00 o.p. (ISBN 0-08-022067-3). Pergamon.

Oxidation of Petrochemicals: Chemistry & Technology. T. Dumas & W. Bulani. LC 74-11232. 186p. 1974. 37.95x o.p. (ISBN 0-470-22480-0). Halsted Pr.

Oxide Minerals. Ed. by Rumble, III. (Reviews in Mineralogy: Vol. 3). 502p. 1976. 18.00 o.p. (ISBN 0-939950-03-0). Mineralogical Soc.

Oxide Semiconductors. Z. M. Jarzebski. LC 73-6971. 304p. 1974. 65.00 o.p. (ISBN 0-08-016968-6). Pergamon.

Oxides of Nitrogen, Sulfur & Chlorine: Gas Solubilities. Young. (IUPAC Solubility Data Ser.: Vol. 8). 1981. 110.00 o.p. (ISBN 0-08-023924-2). Pergamon.

Oxocarbons. Robert West. LC 80-515. (Organic Chemistry Ser.). 1980. 47.50 o.p. (ISBN 0-12-744580-3). Acad Pr.

Oxtail Cocktail: A Modern Western. Shirley Hicks. LC 86-60442. 352p. 1986. 16.95 o.s.i. (ISBN 0-934318-97-2). Falcon Pr MT.

Oxter English Dictionary: Uncommon Words Used by Uncommonly Good Writers. George S. Saussy. LC 84-13789. 272p. 1984. 19.95 o.p. (ISBN 0-87196-962-9). Facts on File.

Oxy-Acetylene Welding. Ed. by N. C. Balchin et al. (Engineering Craftsmen: No. F25). (Illus.). 1977. spiral bdg. 39.95x o.p. (ISBN 0-85083-396-5). Trans-Atl Phila.

Oxygen & Oxy-Radicals in Chemistry & Biology. Ed. by M. A. Rodgers & E. L. Powers. LC 81-19096. 1981. 83.00 o.p. (ISBN 0-12-592050-4). Acad Pr.

Oxygen & Ozone: Gas Solubilities. Battino. (Solubility Data Ser.). 1981. 110.00 o.p. (ISBN 0-08-023915-3). Pergamon.

Oxygen Transport to Tissue IV. Ed. by Haim I. Bicher & Duane F. Bruley. LC 82-19010. (Advances In Experimental Medicine & Biology: Vol. 159). 646p. 1983. 95.00x o.p. (ISBN 0-306-41192-X, Plenum Pr). Plenum Pub.

Oxygenases. Ed. by Osamu Hayaishi. 1962. 93.50 o.p. (ISBN 0-12-333650-3). Acad Pr.

Oxytocin: Current Research, 5 vols, Vol. 1. P. Richard et al. LC 73-21688. (Hormones Ser.). (Illus.). 169p. 1974. text ed. 23.50x o.p. (ISBN 0-8422-7181-3). Irvington.

Oxytocin: Current Research, 5 vols, Vol. 2. Per Melin et al. LC 73-21688. (Hormones Ser.). (Illus.). 212p. 1974. text ed. 23.50x o.p. (ISBN 0-8422-7182-1). Irvington.

Oxytocin: Current Research, 5 vols, Vol. 3. W. Y. Chan et al. LC 73-21688. (Hormones Ser.). (Illus.). 213p. 1974. text ed. 23.50x o.p. (ISBN 0-8422-7183-X). Irvington.

Oxytocin: Current Research, 5 vols, Vol. 4. D. G. Smyth et al. LC 73-21688. (Hormones Ser.). (Illus.). 162p. 1974. text ed. 23.50x o.p. (ISBN 0-8422-7184-8). Irvington.

Oxytocin: Current Research, 5 vols, Vol. 5. M. J. Webb et al. LC 73-21688. (Hormones Ser.). (Illus.). 185p. 1974. 23.50x o.p. (ISBN 0-8422-7185-6). Irvington.

Oysters: A Culinary Celebration. Jean Reardon & Ruth Ebling. (Illus.). 256p. 1984. 25.00 o.p. (ISBN 0-940160-26-9). Parnassus Imprints.

Ozark Log Cabin Folks: The Way They Were. Paul Faris. LC 82-82816. (Illus.). 143p. 1983. pap. 14.95 o.s.i. (ISBN 0-914546-43-0). Rose Pub.

Ozark Magic & Folklore. Vance Randolph. Orig. Title: Ozark Superstitions. (YA) (gr. 5 up). 15.50 o.p. (ISBN 0-8446-0866-1). Peter Smith.

Ozark, Ozark: A Hillside Reader. Ed. by Miller Williams. LC 80-26242. 200p. 1981. 19.95 o.p. (ISBN 0-8262-0331-0). U of Mo Pr.

Ozark, Ozark: A Hillside Reader. Ed. by Miller Williams. LC 80-26242. 208p. (Orig.). 1984. pap. 12.95 o.p. (ISBN 0-8262-0472-4). U of Mo Pr.

Ozark Superstitions see Ozark Magic & Folklore.

Ozone & Other Photochemical Oxidants. Ed. by National Research Council, Division of Medical Sciences Medical & Biologic Effects of Environmental Pollutants. LC 77-1293. 719p. 1977. 19.50x o.p. (ISBN 0-309-02531-1). Natl Acad Pr.

Ozone Layer: Synthesis of Papers Based on the UNEP Meeting on the Ozone Layer, Washington DC, March 1977. Ed. by Asit K. Biswas. LC 79-42879. (Environmental Sciences & Applications Ser.: Vol. 4). 1980. 89.00 o.p. (ISBN 0-08-022429-6). Pergamon.

Ozone Oxidants: Interactions with the Total Environment II. Air Pollution Control Association Specialty Conference, Houston, 1979. 542p. 1980. 25.00 o.p. (ISBN 0-318-12265-0, SP-32); members 20.00 o.p. (ISBN 0-318-12266-9). Air & Waste.

Ozzy Osbourne: Diary of a Madman. Garry Bushell et al. (Illus.). 208p. 1986. pap. 8.95 o.s.i. (ISBN 0-946391-46-7, Pub. by Zomba Bks England). H Leonard Pub Corp.

Ozzy Osbourne: The Authorized Biography. 128p. 1986. 9.95 o.p. (ISBN 0-946391-46-7). Cherry Lane.

P

P. A. Stolypin & the Third Duma: An Appraisal of the Three Major Issues. George Tokmakoff. LC 81-40349. (Illus.). 258p. (Orig.). 1982. lib. bdg. 30.50 o.p. (ISBN 0-8191-2058-8); pap. text ed. 14.00 o.p. (ISBN 0-8191-2059-6). U Pr of Amer.

P. B. The Paul Brown Story. Paul Brown & Jack Clary. LC 79-7314. (Illus.). 1979. 12.95 o.p. (ISBN 0-689-10985-7, Atheneum). Macmillan.

P. E. P.-The Productivity Effectiveness Program. Robert Gedaliah. 1984. pap. 2.95 o.p. (ISBN 0-03-069866-9). H Holt & Co.

P. G. Wodehouse: A Portrait of a Master. rev. ed. David A. Jasen. (Illus.). 352p. 1981. pap. 8.95 o.p. (ISBN 0-8264-0033-7). Continuum.

P. H. Emerson: The Fight for Photography As a Fine Art. Nancy Newhall. LC 74-76911. (Aperture Monograph). (Illus.). 266p. 50.00 o.p. (ISBN 0-89381-383-4); pap. 19.95 o.p. (ISBN 0-912334-59-2). Aperture.

P. J. Andrea Balis & Robert Reiser. 160p. (gr. 3-6). 1984. 10.45 o.p. (ISBN 0-395-36006-4, 5-81180). HM.

P. J. Clover, Private Eye: The Case of the Stolen Laundry. Susan Meyers. (Illus.). 128p. (Orig.). (gr. 3-7). 1981. pap. 2.50 o.s.i. (ISBN 0-671-43360-1). Wanderer Bks.

Pablo Picasso. Paul Eluard. 1965. (ISBN 0-8022-0452-X). Philos Lib.

Pablo Picasso, Twentieth Century Genius. Patricia D. Frevert. Ed. by Ann Redpath. (People to Remember Ser.). (Illus.). 32p. (gr. 4 up). 1981. PLB 8.95 o.p. (ISBN 0-87191-800-5). Creative Ed.

PABX Peripherals Market. International Resource Development, Inc. Staff. 163p. 1983. 1850.00x o.p. (ISBN 0-88694-575-5). Intl Res Dev.

Pacific Atoll Populations. Ed. by Vern Carroll. LC 75-1264. (Asao Monograph Ser.: No. 3). (Illus.). 547p. 1975. text ed. 22.50x o.p. (ISBN 0-8248-0354-X, Eastwest Ctr). UH Pr.

Pacific Business Guide, 1987. World of Information Editorial Staff. (Illus.). 210p. 1987. pap. 9.95 o.p. (ISBN 0-317-55332-1, Pub. by World Info England). Hippocrene Bks.

Pacific Cavalcade. Virginia Coffman. LC 80-66502. 1981. 12.95 o.p. (ISBN 0-87795-277-9, Arbor Hse). Morrow.

Pacific Challenge in International Business. Ed. by W. Chan Kim & Philip K. Y. Young. LC 87-5008. (Research for Business Decisions Ser.: No. 72). 350p. 1987. 54.95 o.p. (ISBN 0-8357-1620-1). UMI Res Pr.

Pacific Coast Nudibranchs. David W. Behrens. LC 80-51439. (Illus.). 112p. 1980. pap. 14.95 o.p. (ISBN 0-930118-05-7). Western Marine Ent.

Pacific Coast Nudibranchs: A Guide to the Opisthobranchs of the Northeastern Pacific. David W. Behrens. LC 80-51439. (Illus.). 112p. 1980. 24.95 o.p. (ISBN 0-930118-04-9); pap. 14.95 o.s.i. (ISBN 0-930118-05-7). Sea Chall.

Pacific Coast Shay. Dan Ranger. LC 64-8046. 112p. 16.95 o.p. (ISBN 0-87095-022-3). Gldn West Bks.

Pacific Coast Studies in Shakespeare. Ed. by Waldo F. McNeir & Thelma N. Greenfield. LC 66-9575. 1966. 7.50 o.p. (ISBN 0-87114-014-4). U of Oreg Bks.

Pacific Crest Trail: Vol. 1, California. 4th ed. Jeffery P. Schaffer et al. LC 81-70345. (Illus.). 470p. (Orig.). 1982. pap. 19.95 o.p. (ISBN 0-89997-015-X). Wilderness Pr.

Pacific Destiny: The Story of America in the Western Sea in the Early 1800's to the 1980's. Edwin P. Hoyt. 1981. 16.95 o.p. (ISBN 0-393-01472-X). Norton.

Pacific Electric Railway. Donald Duke. LC 56-12943. (Illus.). 64p. pap. 7.95 o.p. (ISBN 0-87095-030-4). Gldn West Bks.

Pacific Fresh: A Seafood Cookbook. Maryana Vollstedt. (Illus.). 128p. (Orig.). 1984. pap. 5.95 o.p. (ISBN 0-910983-15-1). Cookbook Fact.

Pacific Interlude. Sloan Wilson. LC 81-67221. 256p. 1982. 14.95 o.p. (ISBN 0-87795-333-3, Arbor Hse). Morrow.

Pacific Islands under Japanese Mandate. Tadao Yanaihara. LC 76-18921. (Institute of Pacific Relations: International Research Ser.). (Illus.). 312p. 1976. Repr. of 1940 ed. lib. bdg. 22.50x o.p. (ISBN 0-8371-8667-6, YAPI). Greenwood.

Pacific Northwest, 1542-1846. Cecil K. Byrd. (Lilly Library Publications: No. 42). (Illus., Orig.). 1988. pap. 12.50x o.p. IN Univ Lilly Library.

Pacific Research Centres. 1986. 230.00x o.p. (ISBN 0-582-90028-X, Pub. by Longman). Gale.

Pacific Rim: Area of Change, Area of Opportunity. David Aikman. 1986. pap. 8.95 o.p. (ISBN 0-316-02039-7). Little.

Pacific Rim Computer Law Institute. 1984. 45.00 o.p. (ISBN 0-88129-116-1). Wash Bar CLE.

Pacific Theater of Operations see Combat World War II.

Pacifism & the Just War: A Study in Applied Philosophy. Jenny Teichman. 19.95 o.p. (ISBN 0-317-58502-9). Basil Blackwell.

Package Design: An Introduction to the Art of Packaging. Lazlo Roth. (Illus.). 224p. 1981. 24.95 o.p. (ISBN 0-13-647842-5, Spec); 13.95 o.p. (ISBN 0-13-647834-4). P-H.

Package Production Management. 2nd ed. Harold J. Raphael & David L. Olsson. (Illus.). 1976. 29.95 o.p. (ISBN 0-87055-217-1); pap. text ed. 21.50 o.p. (ISBN 0-87055-307-0). AVI.

Package X, Nineteen Eighty-Six: Informational Copies of Federal Tax Forms, Vol. 1-2. annually ed. (Illus.). 500p. (Orig.). 1986. Set. pap. 17.00 o.p. (ISBN 0-318-21372-9, S/N 648-004-00001-0). USGPO.

Packaging Design Two. Industrial Design Magazine Editors & Paul Schmitt. LC 84-25554. (Illus.). 256p. 1985. 55.00 o.p. (ISBN 0-86636-005-0). PBC Intl Inc.

Packaging Information Sources. Ed. by Gwendolyn Jones. LC 67-18370. (Management Information Guide Ser.: No. 10). 288p. 1967. 68.00x o.p. (ISBN 0-8103-0811-8). Gale.

Packaging Regulations. Stanley Sacharow. (Illus.). 1979. 35.95 o.p. (ISBN 0-87055-274-0). AVI.

Packaging: The Sixth Sense. Ernest Dichter. LC 73-76439. 160p. 1983. 27.95 o.p. (ISBN 0-8436-1103-0). Van Nos Reinhold.

Packet of Pictures. Joan W. Anglund & Joan Walsh. (Illus.). (gr. 1 up). 1970. 2.95 o.p. (ISBN 0-15-259190-7, HJ). HarBraceJ.

Packing & Outfitting Field Manual. University of Wyoming Staff. 78p. pap. 4.00 o.p. (ISBN 0-318-12508-0). Am Donkey.

Paddington & the Knickerbocker Rainbow. Michael Bond. LC 84-11564. (Paddington Bks.). (Illus.). 32p. (ps-1). 1985. 5.95 o.p. (ISBN 0-399-21202-7, Putnam). Putnam Pub Group.

Paddle Steamers: An Illustrated History of Steamboats on the Mississippi & Its Tributaries. Ken Watson. (Illus.). 192p. 1985. 18.45 o.p. (ISBN 0-393-01865-2). Norton.

Paddy: A Naturalist's Story of an Orphaned Beaver. R. D. Lawrence. 1978. pap. 2.25 o.p. (ISBN 0-380-42580-7). Avon.

Paddy Finds a Job: A Pop-up Story. John S. Goodall. LC 81-43103. (Illus.). 12p. 1981. 6.95 o.p. (ISBN 0-689-50213-3, Atheneum). Macmillan.

Paddy's New Hat. John S. Goodall. LC 80-80129. (Illus.). 64p. (ps up). 1980. 6.95 o.p. (ISBN 0-689-50172-2, Atheneum). Macmillan.

Pade & Rational Approximation: Theory & Applications. Ed. by E. B. Saff & R. S. Varga. 1977. 56.50 o.p. (ISBN 0-12-614150-9). Acad Pr.

Pade Approximant in Theoretical Physics. Ed. by George A. Baker, Jr. & John L. Gammel. (Mathematics in Science & Engineering Ser.: Vol. 71). 1970. 95.00 o.p. (ISBN 0-12-074850-9). Acad Pr.

Pade Approximants & Their Applications. P. R. Graves-Morris. 1973. 86.00 o.p. (ISBN 0-12-295950-7). Acad Pr.

Pade Approximants Methods & Its Applications to Mechanics. Ed. by H. Cabannes. (Lecture Notes in Physics: Vol. 47). 285p. 1976. pap. 17.00 o.p. (ISBN 0-387-07614-X). Springer-Verlag.

Paderewski. Adam Zamoyski. LC 81-69136. (Illus.). 1982. 19.95 o.p. (ISBN 0-689-11248-3, Atheneum). Macmillan.

Paediatric Cardiology Vol. 1, 1977. Ed. by Robert H. Anderson & Elliot A. Shinebourne. (Illus.). 1978. text ed. 63.50 o.p. (ISBN 0-443-01623-2). Churchill.

Paediatric Dianostic Imaging. Catherine Gyll & Noel S. Blake. 232p. 1986. 50.00 o.p. (ISBN 0-471-84479-9). Wiley.

Paediatric Emergencies. C. Bacon. 1982. pap. 17.50 o.p. (ISBN 0-433-01051-7). E J Brill USA.

Paediatric Haematology. Michael L. Willoughby. (Illus.). 1977. 66.75 o.p. (ISBN 0-443-01442-6). Churchill.

Paediatric Immunology. Soothill et al. (Illus.). 496p. 1983. text ed. 69.95 o.p. (ISBN 0-632-00724-9, B4632-4). Mosby.

Paediatric Neuroradiology. Kurt Decker & Herbert Backmund. LC 75-18339. (Illus.). 192p. 1975. 36.50 o.p. (ISBN 0-88416-132-3). Year Bk Med.

Paediatric Operative Dentistry. 2nd ed. D. B. Kennedy. (Illus.). 288p. 1979. pap. 26.00 o.p. (ISBN 0-7236-0525-4, Pub. by John Wright UK); 31.00 o.p. Butterworth.

Paediatric Otolaryngology. J. F. Birrell. (Illus.). 216p. 1978. pap. text ed. 31.00 o.p. (ISBN 0-7236-0479-7, Pub. by John Wright UK). Butterworth.

Paediatric Perspectives on Epilepsy: A Symposium Held at the Grand Hotel, Eastbourne, December 1984. Ed. by Euan Ross. LC 85-12009. 163p. 1985. 35.00 o.p. (ISBN 0-471-90817-7, Dist. by A R Liss). Wiley.

Paediatrics. H. M. Coles. 1976. 30.00x o.p. (ISBN 0-272-00102-3). State Mutual Bk.

Pagan & Christian Anxiety: A Response to E. R. Dodds. Ed. by Robert C. Smith & John Lounibos. LC 83-27345. 248p. 1984. lib. bdg. 26.75 o.p. (ISBN 0-8191-3823-1); pap. text ed. 13.00 o.p. (ISBN 0-8191-3824-X). U Pr of Amer.

Pagan Place: A Play. Edna O'Brien. 64p. 1973. 8.50 o.p. (ISBN 0-571-10336-7); pap. 4.95 o.p. (ISBN 0-571-10316-2). Faber & Faber.

Paganini. Renee De Saussine. Tr. by Marjorie Laurie. 1982. Repr. of 1954 ed. lib. bdg. 90.50x o.p. (ISBN 0-8371-4013-7, AESAPA). Greenwood.

Page a Day Advent & the Christmas Season, 1988. Stephanie Collins. 48p. 1988. pap. 1.95 o.p. (ISBN 0-8091-2987-6). Paulist Pr.

Page a Day for Lent 1987. Barbara Sullivan. 56p. (Orig.). 1987. pap. 2.95 o.p. (ISBN 0-8091-2852-7). Paulist Pr.

Page a Day for the Advent & the Christmas Season, 1987. Stephanie Collins. 48p. 1987. pap. 1.95 o.p. (ISBN 0-8091-2901-9). Paulist Pr.

Pageant of Medieval Art & Life. Richard McLanathan. (Illus.). (gr. 7 up). 1966. 6.95 o.s.i. (ISBN 0-664-32379-0, Westminster). Westminster John Knox.

Pages & Pictures from Forgotten Children's Books. Andrew W. Tuer. LC 68-31096. (Illus.). 512p. 1969. Repr. of 1899 ed. 40.00x o.p. (ISBN 0-8103-3488-7). Gale.

Pages Francaises. Ed. by Georges Lannois. 1969. text ed. 14.50 o.p. (ISBN 0-08-006379-9). Pergamon.

Pages from the Life of Dmitri Shostakovich. Dmitri Sollertinsky & Ludmilla Sollertinsky. Tr. by Graham Hobbs & Charles Midgely. LC 79-3364. 1980. 12.95 o.p. (ISBN 0-15-170730-8). HarBraceJ.

Pages: The World of Books, Writers & Writing, Vol. 1. Ed. by C. E. Clark, Jr. & Matthew J. Bruccoli. LC 76-20369. (Illus.). 304p. 1976. 38.00x o.p. (ISBN 0-8103-0925-4). Gale.

Paget's Disease of Bone. Ed. by Frederick Singer. LC 77-1303. (Topics In Bone & Mineral Disorders Ser.). (Illus.). 172p. 1977. 39.50x o.p. (ISBN 0-306-30996-3, Plenum Med Bk). Plenum Pub.

Pagoda Ridge & Other Stories. Gu Hua. Tr. by Gladys Yang from Chinese. 260p. 1985. pap. 5.95 o.p. (ISBN 0-8351-1335-3). China Bks.

Pai-Pai Pig. Joy Anderson. LC 67-17150. (Illus.). (gr. 4-6). 1967. 4.50 o.p. (ISBN 0-15-259415-9, HJ); 4.50 o.p. (ISBN 0-15-259416-7). HarBraceJ.

Pain. Ed. by Katherine W. Carey & Barbara McVan. (Nursing Now Ser.). (Illus.). 128p. 1985. text ed. 13.95 o.p. (ISBN 0-916730-81-6). Springhouse Pub.

Pain & Society. Ed. by H. W. Kosterlitz & L. Y. Terenius. (Dahlem Workshop Reports, Life Sciences Research Report Ser.: No. 17). (Illus.). 523p. (Orig.). 1980. pap. 46.30x o.p. (ISBN 0-89573-099-5). VCH Pubs.

Pain Dur: Theatre. Paul Claudel. (Coll. Soleil). 1918. 11.50 o.p. (ISBN 0-685-11474-0). Schoenhof.

Pain Erasure: The Bonnie Prudden Way. Bonnie Prudden. LC 80-20688. (Illus.). 288p. 1980. 14.95 o.p. (ISBN 0-87131-328-6). M Evans.

Pain Erasure the Bonnie Prudden Way. Bonnie Prudden. 1982. pap. 7.95 o.p. (ISBN 0-345-29489-0). M Evans.

Pain-Its Nature, Analysis, & Treatment. 2nd ed. Michael R. Bond. (Churchill-Livingstone Medical Text Ser.). (Illus.). 1984. pap. text ed. 13.50 o.p. (ISBN 0-443-03000-6). Churchill.

Pain: New Perspectives In Therapy & Research. Ed. by M. Weisenberg & B. Tursky. LC 76-40023. 240p. 1976. 49.50x o.p. (ISBN 0-306-30983-1, Plenum Pr). Plenum Pub.

Pain, Penance & Peace: A Selection of Poems. Marion Hyde-Pritchard. 1979. 5.00 o.p. (ISBN 0-682-49515-8). Exposition-Phoenix.

Pain: Research & Treatment. Ed. by Benjamin L. Crue, Jr. (City of Hope Symposium Ser.). 1975. 91.50 o.p. (ISBN 0-12-198950-X). Acad Pr.

Pain: The Essence of a Mental Illness. Anna E. Anderson. 64p. 1979. 5.00 o.p. (ISBN 0-682-49527-1). Exposition-Phoenix.

Paine Webber Handbook to Stock & Bond Analysis. new ed. Kiril Sokoloff. (Illus.). 1979. text ed. 62.50 o.p. (ISBN 0-07-059576-3). McGraw.

Painless Public Speaking. Sharon A. Bower. (Illus.). 272p. 1981. 12.95 o.p. (ISBN 0-13-647933-2, Spec); 6.95 o.p. (ISBN 0-13-647925-1). P-H.

Paint! John F. Mills. (Illus.). 64p. 1986. pap. 4.95 o.p. (ISBN 0-563-16458-1, Pub. by BBC). Parkwest Pubns.

Paint Magic. Jocasta Innes. LC 86-42519. (Illus.). 240p. 1986. pap. 19.95 o.p. (ISBN 0-394-74654-6). Pantheon.

Paintbox Summer. Betty Cavanna. (Illus.). (gr. 6-9). 1949. 5.50 o.p. (ISBN 0-664-32052-X, Westminster). Westminster John Knox.

Painted Bird. 2nd ed. Jerzy Kosinski. 1976. 7.95 o.p. (ISBN 0-395-24291-6). HM.

Painted Dresses. Shelby Hearon. LC 80-69644. 1981. 12.95 o.p. (ISBN 0-689-11155-X, Atheneum). Macmillan.

Painted Men. T. C. Lethbridge. (Illus.). 202p. 1954. (ISBN 0-8022-0961-0). Philos Lib.

Painted Sky. Jeanine C. D'Hyon. 200p. 11.95 o.p. (ISBN 0-8062-2846-6). Carlton.

Painting & Decorating: An Information Manual. 2nd ed. A. Fulcher et al. (Illus.). 226p. 1981. pap. text ed. 17.25x o.p. (ISBN 0-246-11613-7, Pub. by Granada England). Gower Pub Co.

Painting & Decorating: An Information Manual. A. Fulcher et al. 229p. 1975. pap. text ed. 17.25x o.p. (ISBN 0-258-97020-0, Pub. by Granada England). Gower Pub Co.

Painting & Drawing Animals: Practical & Colorful Lessons on Painting Mammals, Fish, Birds, & Insects. Graeme Sims. (Illus.). 144p. 1983. 27.50 o.p. (ISBN 0-8230-3556-5). Watson-Guptill.

Painting & Sculpture in the Museum of Modern Art: Catalog of the Collection, 1987. rev. ed. Ed. by Alicia Legg & Mary B. Smalley. 136p. 1988. pap. 8.95 o.p. (ISBN 0-87070-572-5). Museum Mod Art.

Painting & Sculpture in the Museum of Modern Art with Selected Works on Paper: A Catalog. Ed. by Alicia Legg. LC 77-81324. 1977. pap. 6.95 o.p. (ISBN 0-87070-544-X). Museum Mod Art.

Painting Animals in Watercolor. Sally Michel. (Illus.). 128p. 1985. 19.95 o.p. (ISBN 0-8230-3559-X). Watson-Guptill.

Painting Children. Benedict Rubbra. LC 79-63839. (Start to Paint Ser.). (Illus.). 1979. pap. 3.95 o.s.i. (ISBN 0-8008-6203-1, Pentalic). Taplinger.

Painting Classes. Carol Jones. 189p. 1987. 18.95 o.p. (ISBN 0-340-38599-5, Pub. by Hodder & Stoughton UK). David & Charles.

Painting Figures in Light. Jane Corsellis. (Illus.). 144p. 1982. 23.95 o.p. (ISBN 0-8230-3631-6). Watson-Guptill.

Painting in Eighteenth-Century France. Philip Conisbee. LC 81-66151. 224p. 1981. 60.00x o.p. (ISBN 0-8014-1424-5). Cornell U Pr.

Painting in France Eighteen Ninety-Five to Nineteen Forty-Nine. G. Di San Lazzaro. 1954. (ISBN 0-8022-0943-2). Philos Lib.

Painting in Islam. Thomas W. Arnold. (Illus.). 16.25 o.p. (ISBN 0-8446-1553-6). Peter Smith.

Painting in Naples: From Caravaggio to Giordano. Ed. by Clovis Whitfield & Jane Martineau. (Illus.). 302p. 1983. 37.50 o.p. (ISBN 0-8390-0316-1). Abner Schram Ltd.

Painting in Towns & Cities. Hans Schwarz. LC 79-56606. (Start to Paint Ser.). (Illus.). 1980. pap. 3.95 o.s.i. (ISBN 0-8008-6204-X, Pentalic). Taplinger.

Painting in Watercolors. Ed. by Yvonne Deutsch. (Illus.). 128p. 1984. 18.95 o.p. (ISBN 0-89134-092-0, North Light). Writers Digest.

Painting in Watercolors. Leslie Worth et al. LC 81-85922. (Illus.). 128p. 1982. pap. 8.95 o.s.i. (ISBN 0-8008-6201-5, Pentalic). Taplinger.

Painting Nature. Franklin Jones. (Illus.). 176p. 1985. pap. 17.95 o.p. (ISBN 0-89134-119-6). North Light Bks.

Painting Nature's Quiet Places. Thomas A. Daly. (Illus.). 144p. 1984. 27.50 o.p. (ISBN 0-8230-3724-X). Watson-Guptill.

Painting of the Passions in Theory, Practice & Criticsm in Later Eighteen Century France. John M. Wilson. LC 79-57493. (Outstanding Dissertations in tne Fine Arts Ser.: No. 5). 355p. 1982. lib. bdg. 46.00 o.p. (ISBN 0-8240-3945-9). Garland Pub.

Painting on Fabric. Serene Miller. LC 84-2078. (Illus.). 168p. (Orig.). 1984. pap. 14.95 o.p. (ISBN 0-8329-0356-6). New Century.

Painting on Silence: An Orchestra of Poems. Joseph Gallagher. 1973. 6.00 o.p. (ISBN 0-682-47699-4). Exposition-Phoenix.

Painting Seascapes. John Raynes. LC 79-56607. (Start to Paint Ser.). (Illus.). 104p. 1980. pap. 3.95 o.s.i. (ISBN 0-8008-6205-8, Pentalic). Taplinger.

Painting the Day: Thomas Chruchyard of Hoodbridge. Wallace Morfey. (Illus.). 192p. 1986. 45.00 o.p. (ISBN 0-85115-426-3, Pub. by Boydell & Brewer). Longwood Pub Group.

Painting the Head in Oil. John H. Sanden. (Illus.). 152p. 1976. 27.50 o.p. (ISBN 0-8230-3640-5). Watson-Guptill.

Painting the Landscape. Elizabeth Leonard. (Illus.). 144p. 1984. 27.50 o.p. (ISBN 0-8230-3655-3). Watson-Guptill.

Painting the Still Life. Olga Zaferatos. (Illus.). 144p. 1985. 27.50 o.p. (ISBN 0-8230-3860-2). Watson-Guptill.

Painting Weathered Textures in Watercolor. Richard Bolton. (Illus.). 144p. 1982. 27.50 o.p. (ISBN 0-8230-3876-9). Watson-Guptill.

Painting with Oils. Barclay Sheaks. Ed. by George F. Horn & Sarita R. Rainey. LC 77-78827. (Illus.). 1977. 14.95 o.p. (ISBN 0-87192-093-X, Dist. by Sterling). Davis Mass.

Painting with Pastel. Ed. by Peter D. Johnson. (Illus.). 160p. 1984. 16.95 o.p. (ISBN 0-89134-081-5, North Light). Writers Digest.

Paintings from Collection of Palace Museum: No. 2, Song Dynasty, Part 1. (Paintings of Palace Museum Ser.). (Illus.). 146p. 1981. 250.00 o.p. (ISBN 0-8351-1138-5). China Bks.

Paintings in the Kunsthistorisches Museum, Vienna, Guide. (Illus.). 68p. (Orig.). 1984. pap. text ed. 750.00 incl. microfiche o.p. (ISBN 0-85964-158-9). Chadwyck-Healey.

Paintings in the Studiolo of Isabella d'Este at Mantua. Egon Verheyen. LC 76-164021. (College Art Association Monograph Ser.: Vol. 23). (Illus.). 122p. 1985. Repr. of 1971 ed. 30.00x o.s.i. (ISBN 0-271-00409-6). Pa St U Pr.

Paintings of Cornelis Engebrechtsz. Walter S. Gibson. LC 76-23620. (Outstanding Dissertations in the Fine Arts - 16th Century). (Illus.). 1977. Repr. of 1969 ed. lib. bdg. 68.00 o.p. (ISBN 0-8240-2691-8). Garland Pub.

Paintings of Franz A. Bischoff (1864-1929) Jean Stern. Ed. by Carol E. Stern. LC 80-80157. (Illus.). 56p. 1980. lib. bdg. 25.00 o.p. (ISBN 0-8227-8028-3, Dist. by DeRu's Fine Art). Petersen Pub.

Paintings of J. M. W. Turner, 2 vols. rev. ed. Martin Butlin & Evelyn Joll. (Illus.). 1987. Set. pap. 60.00 o.p. (ISBN 0-318-23664-8). Yale-U-Pr.

Paintings of Sam Hyde Harris (1889-1977) Jean Stern & Ruth Westphal. LC 80-83993. (Illus.). 64p. 1980. lib. bdg. 25.00 o.p. (ISBN 0-8227-8036-4, Dist. by DeRu's Fine Art). Petersen Pub.

Paintings of the Casa Vasari. Liana Cheney. Ed. by S. J. Freedberg. (Outstanding Dissertations in Fine Arts Ser.). (Illus.). 675p. 1985. Repr. of 1978 ed. 65.00 o.p. (ISBN 0-8240-6852-1). Garland Pub.

Paintings, Pastels, Drawings, Prints & Copper Plates by & Attributed to American & European Artists. rev. ed. Compiled by Burns A. Stubbs. (Occasional Papers Ser: Vol. 1, No. 2). 1967. pap. 3.50 o.p. (ISBN 0-934686-00-9). Freer.

Paints & Coating Handbook. 2nd ed. A. Banov. 1981. text ed. 36.50 o.p. (ISBN 0-07-003664-0). McGraw.

Paints & Protective Coatings for Wastewater Treatment Facilities ('69) (Manual of Practice No. 17). 86p. pap. 10.00 o.p. Water Pollution.

Paisius Velichkovsky. Monk Metrophan. (Illus.). 300p. Date not set. 25.00 o.p. St Herman AK.

Paix et Liberte, ou le Budget Republicain. Frederic Bastiat. Bd. with On the Causes of War, & the Means of Reducing Their Number. Emile L. Laveleye. LC 72-147492. (Library of War & Peace; the Political Economy of War). lib. bdg. 46.00 o.p. (ISBN 0-8240-0286-5). Garland Pub.

Pajama Walking. Vicki K. Artis. (Illus.). (gr. k-3). 1981. 6.95 o.p. (ISBN 0-395-30343-5). HM.

Pakistan. B. L. Johnson. LC 79-10749. 1980. text ed. 22.50x o.p. (ISBN 0-435-35484-1). Heinemann Ed.

Pakistan: A Travel Survival Kit. 2nd ed. Jose R. Santiago. (Illus.). 214p. (Orig.). 1984. pap. 7.95 o.p. (ISBN 0-908086-53-9). Lonely Planet.

Pakistan: Energy Planning in a Strategic Vortex. Charles K. Ebinger. LC 80-8767. (Illus.). 176p. 1981. 25.00x o.p. (ISBN 0-253-37645-9). Ind U Pr.

Palace: My Life in the Royal Family of Monaco. Christian De Massy & Charles Higham. LC 86-47674. 1986. 17.95 o.p. (ISBN 0-689-11636-5, Atheneum). Macmillan.

Palace of Mirrors. 3rd ed. Hazrat Inayat Khan. 66p. 1979. pap. 4.95 o.s.i. (ISBN 0-900217-07-3, Pub. by Sufi Pub Co England). Hunter Hse.

Palace Politics: An Inside Account of the Ford Years. R. T. Hartmann. 1980. text ed. 15.95 o.p. (ISBN 0-07-026951-3). McGraw.

Palace Without Chairs. Brigid Brophy. LC 77-18387. 1978. 9.95 o.p. (ISBN 0-689-10883-4, Atheneum). Macmillan.

Palaces. Neal Travis. 384p. 1983. pap. 4.75 o.p. (ISBN 0-380-84517-2, 84517-2). Avon.

Palaces & Progresses of Elizabeth First. Ian Dunlop. LC 72-107009. 1970. 10.00 o.s.i. (ISBN 0-8008-6209-0). Taplinger.

Palaces of Leningrad. Audrey Kennett. LC 84-50030. (Illus.). 1984. 35.00f o.s.i. (ISBN 0-500-24087-6). Thames Hudson.

Palaces of the People: A Social History of Commercial Hospitality. Arthur White. LC 70-107011. 1970. 5.50 o.s.i. (ISBN 0-8008-6207-4). Taplinger.

Paladin. George Shipway. LC 73-9887. 1973. 7.95 o.p. (ISBN 0-15-170740-5). HarBraceJ.

Palaeography Collection, 2 Vols. University of London Library Staff. 1968. Set. 170.00 o.p. (ISBN 0-8161-0789-0, Hall Library). G K Hall.

Palaeontology: An Introduction. James Scott. 1978. 9.95 o.s.i. (ISBN 0-8008-6213-9). Taplinger.

Palate Pleasing Pork. Ed. by Annette Gohlke. LC 83-63080. 64p. 1983. pap. 3.95 o.s.i. (ISBN 0-89821-056-9). Reiman Assocs.

Palazzo Incantato overo la Guerriera Amante. Luigi Rossi. Ed. by Howard M. Brown. LC 76-21077. (Italian Opera 1640-1770 Ser.). 1977. lib. bdg. 77.00 o.p. (ISBN 0-8240-2601-2). Garland Pub.

Palazzo Medici & a Ledger for the Church of San Lorenzo. Isabelle Hyman. LC 76-23631. (Outstanding Dissertations in the Fine Arts-Fifteenth Century). (Illus.). 583p. 1977. Repr. of 1968 ed. lib. bdg. 83.00 o.p. (ISBN 0-8240-2700-0). Garland Pub.

Pale Betrayer. Dorothy S. Davis. 224p. 1987. pap. 2.95 o.p. (ISBN 0-380-70132-4). Avon.

Pale Gray for the Guilt. John D. MacDonald. (Large Print Books). 357p. 1986. lib. bdg. 15.95x o.p. (ISBN 0-8161-4006-5, Large Print Bks). G K Hall.

Pale Grey for Guilt. John D. MacDonald. 1985. pap. 3.95 o.p. (ISBN 0-449-12897-0, GM). Fawcett.

Pale Invaders. G. R. Kesteven. LC 75-305052. 192p. (gr. 6-9). 1976. 6.95 o.p. (ISBN 0-689-30505-2, Atheneum). Macmillan.

Paleoanthropology. G. E. Kennedy. 1980. text ed. 39.95 o.p. (ISBN 0-07-034046-3). McGraw.

Paleobiogeography. Ed. by C. A. Ross. LC 76-12969. (Benchmark Papers in Geology Ser.: Vol. 31). 1976. 81.00 o.p. (ISBN 0-12-787365-1). Acad Pr.

Paleobiology of the Invertebrates: Data Retrieval from the Fossil Record. 2nd ed. Paul Tasch. LC 79-14929. 975p. 1980. text ed. (ISBN 0-471-05272-8). Wiley.

Paleohistoria: Acta et Communicationes Instituti Bio-Archaeologici Universitatis Groninganae. 200p. 1951. text ed. 79.00 o.p. (ISBN 0-317-64954-X, Pub. by A A Balkema). Gower Pub Co.

Paleoneurology Eighteen-Four to Nineteen Sixty-Six: An Annotated Bibliography. T. Edinger. (Advances in Anatomy, Embryology, & Cell Biology Ser.: Vol. 49). 275p. 1975. pap. 47.20 o.p. (ISBN 0-387-07060-5). Springer-Verlag.

Paleontology & Paleoenvironments. Ed. by Brian J. Skinner. (Earth & Its Inhabitants: Selected Readings from American Scientist Ser.). (Illus.). 210p. (Orig.). 1981. pap. 10.95x o.p. (ISBN 0-913232-93-9). W Kaufmann.

Paler Shade of White: The History of White People in America, Vol. II. Martin Mull & Allen Rucker. 1986. pap. 5.95 o.p. (ISBN 0-399-51300-0, Perigee). Putnam Pub Group.

Palestine: Concordance of United Nations Resolutions 1967-71. Fayez Sayegh & Sohair Soukkary. LC 77-181998. 93p. (Orig.). 1971. pap. text ed. 4.00 o.p. (ISBN 0-911026-07-X). New World Press NY.

Palestine under the Mandate, 1920-1948. Albert M. Hyamson. LC 72-5399. 210p. 1976. Repr. of 1950 ed. lib. bdg. 35.00x o.p. (ISBN 0-8371-5996-2, HYPU). Greenwood.

Palestinian Arab Politics. Moshe Ma'oz. 147p. 1975. (ISBN 0-87855-234-0). Transaction Pubs.

Palestinian Catastrophe: The 1984 Expulsion of a People from Their Homeland. Michael Palumbo. 250p. 1987. 19.95 o.p. (ISBN 0-571-14864-6). Faber & Faber.

Palestinian Resistance: Organization of a Nationalist Movement. John W. Amos, II. LC 80-16134. (Pergamon Policy Studies on International Politics). 496p. 1981. 75.00 o.p. (ISBN 0-08-025094-7); pap. 52.00 (Reproduction on Demand) o.p. Pergamon.

Pali Metre: A Contribution to the History of Indian Literature. A. K. Warder. 252p. 1967. 18.50x o.p. (ISBN 0-7102-0139-7). Routledge Chapman & Hall.

Palio: History Rites & Images of Siena's Festival. Alessandro Falassi & Guiliano Catoni. Tr. by Christopher Evans & Elizabeth Borgese. (Illus.). 369p. 1983. 65.00x o.p. (ISBN 0-8103-1643-9, Pub. by Electra Editrice). Gale.

Palladio in America. Electa-Rizzoli Staff & Walter M. Whitehill. LC 77-95342. (Illus.). 120p. 1976. pap. 9.95 o.p. (ISBN 0-8478-0169-1). Rizzoli Intl.

Palm-Aire Spa's Seven-Day Plan to Change Your Life: A Diet, Fitness & Beauty Program. Eleanor Berman. (Illus.). 224p. 1987. 19.45 o.p. (ISBN 0-13-648361-5). P-H.

Palm Beach County: An Illustrated History. Donald W. Curl. LC 86-9133. (Illus.). 224p. 1986. 24.95 o.p. (ISBN 0-89781-167-4). Windsor Pubns Inc.

Palm Beach Long-Life Diet. E. Joan Barice & Kathleen Jonah. 224p. 1985. 14.70 o.p. (ISBN 0-671-50363-4). S&S.

Palm Reading in Winter. Ira Sadoff. LC 77-17147. 1978. 6.95 o.p. (ISBN 0-395-25766-2); pap. 4.50 o.p. (ISBN 0-395-26285-2). HM.

Palm-Wine Drinkard. Amos Tutuola. LC 83-49449. 144p. 1984. pap. 4.50 o.p. (ISBN 0-394-62168-9, B507, BC). Grove.

Paloma. Theresa Conway. 672p. (Orig.). 1984. pap. 3.95 o.s.i. (ISBN 0-345-31566-9). Ballantine.

Paloverde. Jacqueline Briskin. 1978. text ed. 10.95 o.p. (ISBN 0-07-007915-3). McGraw.

Palpable God. Reynolds Price. LC 77-10613. 1978. 8.95 o.p. (ISBN 0-689-10837-0, Atheneum). Macmillan.

Paludes. Andre Gide. pap. 6.95 o.p. (ISBN 0-685-23909-8). Schoenhof.

Palynology, Pt. 1& 2. M. Muir. 1983. 99.95 o.p. (ISBN 0-87933-096-1). Van Nos Reinhold.

Pamela, 2 Vols. Samuel Richardson. (Paper Pub. 1978, repr. from 1914). 1974. Repr. of 1914 ed. Vol. 1. 9.50x o.p. (ISBN 0-460-00683-5, Evman); Vol. 2. 9.95x o.p. (ISBN 0-460-00684-3); Vol. 1. pap. 5.50x o.p. (ISBN 0-460-01683-0, Evman); Vol. 2. pap. 4.95x o.p. (ISBN 0-460-01684-9). Biblio Dist.

Pamela Deck. Rudolph L. Williams. 112p. 1987. 6.95 o.p. (ISBN 0-8062-2895-4). Carlton.

Pamela Harlech's Practical Guide to Cooking, Entertaining & Household Management. Pamela Harlech. LC 80-65991. (Illus.). 1981. 16.95 o.p. (ISBN 0-689-11108-8, Atheneum). Macmillan.

Pamella Asquith's Ultimate Chocolate Cake Book. Pamella Z. Asquith. (Illus.). 256p. 1985. pap. 8.95 o.p. (ISBN 0-345-31929-X). Ballantine.

Pamella Z. Asquith's Ultimate Chocolate Cake Book. Pamella Asquith. LC 83-41. (Illus.). 240p. 1983. 16.95 o.p. (ISBN 0-03-062196-8). H Holt & Co.

Pamphlets of the American Revolution, 1750-1776: Vol. 1, 1750-1765. Ed. by Bernard Bailyn & Jane N. Garrett. (John Harvard Library). 1965. 35.00x o.s.i. (ISBN 0-674-65250-9). Harvard U Pr.

Pamphlets on the First World War: An Annotated Bibliography. Donald Hendricks. (Occasional Papers: No. 79). 57p. 1966. pap. 1.00 o.p. (ISBN 0-317-58861-3). U of Ill Lib Info Sci.

Pan-Africanism & East African Integration. Joseph S. Nye, Jr. LC 65-22063. (Center for International Affairs Ser). (Illus.). 1965. 21.00x o.s.i. (ISBN 0-674-65300-9). Harvard U Pr.

Pan-Africanism: New Directions in Strategy. Ed. by W. Ofuatey-Kodjoe. LC 86-20191. 472p. (Orig.). 1986. lib. bdg. 30.25 o.p. (ISBN 0-8191-5363-X); pap. text ed. 19.75 o.p. (ISBN 0-8191-5364-8). U Pr of Amer.

Pan American Nuclear Technology Exchange: PRoceedings of the American Nuclear Society, Executive Conference. American Nuclear Society Staff Executive Conference. 448p. pap. 44.00 o.p. (ISBN 0-317-33003-9, 650008). Am Nuclear Soc.

Pan Am's U. S. A. Guide. 4th ed. Ed. by Pan Am World Airways, Inc. Staff. 1982. pap. text ed. 8.95 o.p. (ISBN 0-07-048434-1). McGraw.

Pan-Turkism & Islam in Russia. Serge A. Zenkovsky. LC 60-5399. (Russian Research Center Studies: No. 36). 1960. 27.00x o.s.i. (ISBN 0-674-65350-5). Harvard U Pr.

Panada & the Bushfire. Michael Foreman. (Illus.). 32p. (gr. k-4). 1986. 12.95 o.s.i. (ISBN 0-13-648395-X). P-H.

Panama Paradox. Michael Wolfe. 250p. 1986. pap. 3.50 o.p. (ISBN 1-55547-117-X). Critics Choice Paper.

Panama Red. Stephen Diamond. 1979. pap. 2.75 o.p. (ISBN 0-380-45237-5, 45237-5). Avon.

Panama Story. Jean Niemeier. LC 68-19528. 1968. pap. 5.95 o.p. (ISBN 0-8323-0195-7). Binford-Metropolitan.

Pancakes at Four. Frank A. Sherman, III. 1979. 5.00 o.p. (ISBN 0-682-49427-5). Exposition-Phoenix.

Pancakes, Crepes & Waffles. Martha Lomask. (Illus.). 96p. 1984. 8.95 o.p. (ISBN 0-86188-200-8). Salem Hse Pubs.

Panchatantra. Tr. by Arthur W. Ryder. 1925. lib. bdg. 20.00x o.s.i. (ISBN 0-226-73248-7). U of Chicago Pr.

Pancreas: Principles of Medical & Surgical Practice. Ed. by Luis H. Toledo-Pereyra. LC 84-13165. 496p. 1985. 59.95 o.p. (ISBN 0-471-09265-7). Wiley.

Pancreatic Function Diagnostant. Ed. by Masasuke Masuda. LC 80-80942. (Illus.). 145p. 1980. 22.50 o.p. (ISBN 0-89640-044-1). Igaku-Shoin.

Pandemic. Geoffrey Simmons. LC 79-56017. 1980. 9.95 o.p. (ISBN 0-87795-258-2, Arbor Hse). Morrow.

Pandora. Pamela Kaufman. (Orig.). 1977. pap. 1.75 o.p. (ISBN 0-380-01104-2, 32896). Avon.

Pandora Plague. Lee A. Matthias. 1981. pap. 2.25 o.s.i. (ISBN 0-8439-0917-X, Pub. by Leisure Bks CT). Dorchester Pub Co.

Pandora Secret: A Captain Justice Story. Anthony Forrest. 303p. 1982. 15.50 o.p. (ISBN 0-8090-7504-0). Hill & Wang.

Pandora's Box. Parker Abell. 64p. 1987. 6.50 o.p. (ISBN 0-8062-2808-3). Carlton.

Pandora's Box: The Changing Aspects of a Mythical Symbol. 2nd ed. Erwin Panofsky & D. Panofsky. (Bollingen Ser.: Vol. 52). (Illus.). 1962. 20.00x o.p. (ISBN 0-691-09809-3); pap. 8.50x o.p. (ISBN 0-691-01824-3). Princeton U Pr.

Pandora's Galley. MacDonald Harris. LC 78-22254. 1979. 10.95 o.p. (ISBN 0-15-170802-9). HarBraceJ.

Pandora's Last Voyage. Geoffrey Rawson. LC 64-18291. (Illus.). 1964. 3.95 o.p. (ISBN 0-15-170826-6). HarBraceJ.

Panel Reviews & Relevant Papers. Fisheries Advisory Commission, Major Communicable Fish Diseases in Europe & Their Control Symposium Staff. (European Inland Fisheries Advisory Commission (EIFAC): Technical Papers: No. 17, Suppl. 2). 255p. (Eng. & Fr.). 1973. pap. 18.50 o.p. (ISBN 92-5-002069-4, F759, FAO). UNIPUB.

Paneling with Solid Lumber, Including Projects. Dan Ramsey. (Illus.). 192p. (Orig.). 1985. 18.95 o.p. (ISBN 0-8306-0868-0, 1868); pap. 12.60 o.p. (ISBN 0-8306-1868-6). TAB Bks.

Panfish. Dick Sternberg & Bill Ignizio. (Hunting & Fishing Library). 1985. 16.95 o.p. (ISBN 0-13-648379-8). P-H.

Panhandle Personalities. Claude Simpson. LC 84-50761. (Illus.). 352p. (Orig.). 1984. pap. 14.95 o.p. (ISBN 0-89301-100-2). U of Idaho Pr.

Panic in Box C. John Dickson Carr. 273p. 1987. pap. 3.50 o.p. (ISBN 1-55547-149-8). Critics Choice Paper.

Panic in the Pantry. Elizabeth Whelan & Fredrick J. Stare. LC 75-7952. 1975. pap. 3.95 o.s.i. (ISBN 0-689-70553-0, 236, Atheneum). Macmillan.

Panique: Inedit. Fernando Arrabal. 320p. 1973. 9.95 o.p. (ISBN 0-686-54459-5). French & Eur.

Panky & William. Nancy Saxon. LC 83-2633. (Illus.). 104p. (gr. 3-7). 1983. 10.95 o.s.i. (ISBN 0-689-30997-X, Atheneum Childrens Bks). Macmillan.

Panky in the Saddle. Nancy Saxon. LC 83-15910. (Illus.). 160p. (gr. 3-7). 1984. 11.95 o.s.i. (ISBN 0-689-31038-2, Atheneum Childrens Bks). Macmillan.

Panna Maria: Which in English Means "Virgin Mary" Jerome Charyn. LC 81-66960. 320p. 1982. 17.50 o.p. (ISBN 0-87795-328-7, Arbor Hse); pap. 9.50 o.p. (ISBN 0-87795-408-9). Morrow.

Panorama de las Americas. 5th ed. John A. Crow & G. D. Crow. (Span.). 1980. pap. text ed. 16.50 o.p. (ISBN 0-03-050561-5). HR&W.

Panorama du Zoe Siecle: Encyclopedie du Monde Contemporain, 9 vols. 2988p. (Fr.). 1976. Set. 495.00 o.p. (ISBN 0-686-57267-X, M-464). French & Eur.

Panorama of British India. Martin R. Montgomery. 192p. 1984. Repr. of 1853 ed. text ed. 75.00 o.p. (ISBN 0-86590-288-7, Pub. by Inter India Pubns N. Delhi). Apt Bks.

Panorama of the Soviet Union. N. Mikhailov. Tr. by Glanys A. Lipatov. (Illus.). 264p. 1984. 11.95 o.p. (ISBN 0-8285-2917-5, Pub by Progress Pubs USSR). Imported Pubns.

Pantheisticon. John Toland. Ed. by Rene Wellek. LC 75-11260. (British Philosophers & Theologians of the 17th & 18th Centuries: Vol. 59). 1977. Repr. of 1751 ed. lib. bdg. 51.00 o.p. (ISBN 0-8240-1810-9). Garland Pub.

Pantheon. Andrew Tooke. LC 75-27880. (Renaissance & the Gods Ser.: Vol. 35). (Illus.). 1976. Repr. of 1713 ed. lib. bdg. 88.00 o.p. (ISBN 0-8240-2084-7). Garland Pub.

Pantographia: Containing Accurate Copies of All the Known Alphabets in the World, Together with an English Explanation of the Peculiar Force or Power of Each Letter. Edmund Fry. LC 79-104956. 320p. 1983. lib. bdg. 49.95x o.p. (ISBN 0-89370-778-3). Borgo Pr.

Pantyhose Craft Book: Making Things from Run Pantyhose & Nylons. Jean R. Laury & Joyce Aiken. LC 76-53871. (Illus.). 1977. 12.95 o.s.i. (ISBN 0-8008-6235-X); pap. 5.95 o.s.i. (ISBN 0-8008-6234-1). Taplinger.

Panza Collection. Panza Di Biumo. LC 87-43270. (Illus.). 248p. 1988. 60.00 o.p. (ISBN 0-8478-0916-1). Rizzoli Intl.

Papa: A Personal Memoir. Gregory H. Hemingway. 1976. 7.95 o.p. (ISBN 0-395-24348-3). HM.

Papa Albert. Lilian Moore. (Illus.). (gr. k-4). 1964. 3.95 o.p. (ISBN 0-689-20294-6, Atheneum); PLB 3.79 o.p. (ISBN 0-689-20295-4). Macmillan.

Papa & Mama Biederbeck. Gerda B. Mantinband. LC 82-15619. (Illus.). 48p. (gr. 2-5). 1983. 7.70 o.s.i. (ISBN 0-395-33228-1). HM.

Papa Babe's Stamp Collection. Gladys T. Turner. (Illus.). 39p. (gr. 1-8). 1983. 5.50 o.p. (ISBN 0-682-49944-7). Exposition-Phoenix.

Papa Hemingway: The Ecstasy & Sorrow. A. E. Hotchner. LC 82-22852. (Illus.). 352p. 1983. Repr. 16.95 o.p. (ISBN 0-688-02041-0). Morrow.

Papa Hemingway: The Ecstasy & Sorrow. A. E. Hotchner. LC 82-22852. (Illus.). 352p. 1982. pap. 8.95 o.p. (ISBN 0-688-02042-9, Quill NY). Morrow.

Papa Was a Preacher. Alyene Porter. 192p. 1979. 3.50 o.p. (ISBN 0-8007-8359-X, Spire Bks). Revell.

Papago Indians, Vol. 2: Papago Population Studies. William S. King & Delmos J. Jones. (American Indian Ethnohistory Ser: Indians of the Southwest). (Illus.). lib. bdg. 51.00 o.p. (ISBN 0-8240-0701-8). Garland Pub.

Papal Crusading Policy, Twelve Hundred Forty-Four to Twelve Hundred Ninety-One. M. Purcell. 1975. 40.00 o.p. (ISBN 90-04-04317-9). E J Brill USA.

Papal Ideology of Social Reform: A Study in Historical Development, 1878-1967. R. L. Camp. 1969. 30.00 o.p. E J Brill USA.

Papal Infallibility: An Application of Lonergan's Theological Method. Ed. by Terry J. Tekippe. LC 82-23837. 416p. (Orig.). 1983. lib. bdg. 36.25 o.p. (ISBN 0-8191-2995-X); pap. text ed. 17.75 o. p. o.p. (ISBN 0-8191-2996-8). U Pr of Amer.

Papal Power. Henry T. Hudson. 1981. pap. 9.95 o.p. (ISBN 0-87552-919-4, Evangel Pr UK). Presby & Reformed.

Papa's Razor Strop. Lela G. Garrett. (Illus.). 128p. 1981. 8.00 o.p. (ISBN 0-682-49775-4). Exposition-Phoenix.

Papel de la Educacion Ambiental en America Latina. (Span.). 1979. pap. 5.00 o.p. (ISBN 92-3-301574-2, U858, UNESCO). UNIPUB.

Papel del Sector Publico en los Paises en Desarrollo: Costa Rica. (ICPE Country Studies). 174p. 1984. pap. 9.00x o.p. (ISBN 92-9038-803-X). Kumarian Pr.

Paper Americana: A Collector's Guide. Lou W. McCulloch. LC 78-75317. (Illus.). 1980. 25.00 o.s.i. (ISBN 0-498-02392-3). A S Barnes.

Paper Circus: How to Create Your Own Circus. Robin West. LC 83-23580. (Illus.). 72p. (gr. k-4). 1983. PLB 10.95 o.p. (ISBN 0-87614-212-9). Carolrhoda Bks.

Paper Daughter: Paper Daughter. Jill Johnston. Ed. by Robert Gottlieb. Martha Kaplan. LC 84-25028. (Autobiography in Search of a Father Ser.: Vol. II). (Illus.). 287p. 1985. 16.45 o.s.i. (ISBN 0-394-53939-7). Knopf.

Paper Dolls of China. Museum of Science & Industry Staff. (Illus.). 16p. (Orig.). (gr. 4 up). 1983. pap. 6.95 o.p. (ISBN 0-914091-34-4). Chicago Review.

Paper Flower Sculpture. Jeanette Westcott. (Illus.). 128p. 1986. 24.95 o.p. (ISBN 0-7137-1673-8, Pub. by Blandford Pr England). Sterling.

Paper Folding Magic. Richard Chen. 32p. 1987. 7.50 o.p. (ISBN 0-8062-2896-2). Carlton.

Paper Jungle. Satoshi Kitamura. (Illus.). 32p. (gr. k up). 1986. pap. 4.50 o.p. (ISBN 0-03-007453-3). H Holt & Co.

Paper Making in Pioneer America. Dard Hunter. LC 78-74388. (Nineteenth Century Book Arts & Printing History Ser.: Vol. 3). 1980. lib. bdg. 26.00 o.p. (ISBN 0-8240-3877-0). Garland Pub.

Paper of Pins. Illus. by Margaret Gordon. LC 74-8767. (Illus.). 32p. (ps-3). 1979. 6.95 o.p. (ISBN 0-395-28814-2, Clarion). HM.

Paper Sword of Bill Rentschler. Ed. by Bill Rentschler. LC 86-26827. 250p. 1986. 17.95 o.p. (ISBN 0-914091-98-0). Chicago Review.

Paper Two to Accompany Financial Accounting. Eugene J. Laughlin. 40p. 1984. pap. 13.95 o.p. (ISBN 0-471-88120-1). Wiley.

Paper UFO's. Yoong Bae. (Illus.). 32p. (gr. 1-12). 1981. pap. 3.95 o.p. (ISBN 0-89844-080-7). Troubador Pr.

Paperback Writers: The History of the Beatles in Print. Bill Harry. 192p. 1985. pap. 9.95 o.p. (ISBN 0-380-89558-7). Avon.

Paperbound Books in Print-Spring, 1988, 3 vols. Ed. by Bowker, R. R., Staff. 6842p. 1988. Set. 129.95 o.p. (ISBN 0-8352-2451-1). Vol. 1 (ISBN 0-8352-2453-8). Vol. 2 (ISBN 0-8352-2454-6). Vol. 3 (ISBN 0-8352-2455-4). Bowker.

Paperless Consumer Information Services. International Resource Development, Inc. Staff. 195p. 1983. 1450.00x o.p. (ISBN 0-88694-565-8). Intl Res Dev.

Papermaking Machine. R. H. Clapperton. 1968. 195.00 o.p. (ISBN 0-08-010896-2). Pergamon.

Papers Concerning the Palaeontology of the Pleistocene of California & the Tertiary of Oregon. Carnegie Institution of Washington Staff. Repr. of 1925 ed. 22.00 o.p. (ISBN 0-685-02123-8). Johnson Repr.

Papers in Language Variation: Samla-Ads Collection. Ed. by David L. Shores & Carole P. Hines. LC 76-23162. 1977. 25.00 o.p. (ISBN 0-8173-0504-1). U of Ala Pr.

Papers in Political Science. John S. Ambler et al. (Rice University Studies: Vol. 54, No. 3). 88p. 1968. pap. 10.00x o.p. (ISBN 0-89263-197-X). Rice Univ.

Papers in Urban & Regional Analysis. Alan G. Wilson. 261p. 1972. pap. text ed. 14.95x o.p. (ISBN 0-85086-033-4, NO. 2904, Pub. by Pion England). Routledge Chapman & Hall.

Papers of Adlai E. Stevenson, Vol. 1: Beginnings of Education, 1900-1941. Ed. by Walter Johnson & Carol Evans. (Illus.). 576p. 1972. 24.50 o.p. (ISBN 0-316-46750-2). Little.

Papers of Adlai E. Stevenson, Vol. 2: Washington to Springfield 1941-1948. Ed. by Walter Johnson & Carol Evans. (Illus.). 1973. 24.50 o.p. (ISBN 0-316-46751-0). Little.

Papers of Adlai E. Stevenson, Vol. 3: Governor of Illinois 1949-1953. Ed. by Walter Johnson & Carol Evans. 1973. 24.50 o.p. (ISBN 0-316-46752-9). Little.

Papers of Adlai E. Stevenson, Vol. 6: Toward a New America, 1955-1957. Ed. by Walter Johnson et al. (Illus.). 1976. 22.50 o.p. (ISBN 0-316-46731-6). Little.

Papers of Adlai E. Stevenson, Vol. 7: Continuing Education & the Unfinished Business of American Society 1957-1961. Ed. by Walter Johnson & Carol Evans. (Illus.). 1977. 24.50 o.p. (ISBN 0-316-46724-3). Little.

Papers of Adlai E. Stevenson, Vol. 8: Ambassador to the United Nations 1961-1965. Ed. by Walter Johnson et al. LC 73-175478. 1979. 25.00 o.p. (ISBN 0-316-46944-0). Little.

Papers of George Wyatt. Ed. by Royal Historical Society Staff. (Camden Fourth Ser.: No. 5). 200p. 1979. 27.00 o.p. (ISBN 0-901050-01-6, Pub. by Boydell & Brewer). Longwood Pub Group.

Papers of Henry Laurens, Vol. XI. Ed. by David R. Chesnutt. 786p. 1988. text ed. 39.95x o.p. (ISBN 0-87249-516-7). U of SC Pr.

Papers of Jefferson Davis, 1853-1855, Vol. 5. Lynda L. Crist. LC 76-15270. 592p. 1985. text ed. 37.50 o.p. (ISBN 0-317-59943-7). La State U Pr.

Papers on Inter-Racial Problems. Universal Races Congress Staff. LC 78-90139. 1969. Repr. of 1911 ed. 24.75 o.p. (ISBN 0-8371-2002-0, IRP&, Pub. by Negro U Pr). Greenwood.

Papers on Methodolgy: Theory & Methods of Social Research, Vol. 2. Johan Galtung. 1979. pap. 22.50x o.p. (ISBN 0-391-01133-2). Humanities.

Papers on the Science of Administration. Ed. by Luther H. Gulick & Lydall Urwick. LC 68-55727. (Illus.). 195p. 1969. Repr. of 1937 ed. 27.50x o.p. (ISBN 0-678-00512-5). Kelley.

Papiamentu Textbook. 4th ed. E. R. Goilo. pap. 12.50 o.p. E J Brill USA.

Papier Mache: An Introduction to the Art of Modeling in Paper. Peter Rush. (Illus.). 1980. pap. 8.95 o.p. (ISBN 0-374-51611-1). FS&G.

Papillon. Henri Charriere. 1983. pap. 3.95 o.s.i. (ISBN 0-671-47345-X). PB.

Papillon Butterfly Dog. Clarice Waud & Mark Hutchings. (Illus.). 300p. 1985. 60.00 o.p. (ISBN 0-947647-01-5, Pub. by Nimrod Bk Serv England). Kathleen Rais.

Papo Impala Esta Quitao. Juan A. Ramos. LC 83-82117. 96p. (Span.). 1983. pap. 4.95 o.p. (ISBN 0-940238-68-3). Ediciones Huracan.

Papua New Guinea. Ernst Loffler. (Illus.). 206p. 1979. 29.00 o.p. (ISBN 0-09-135430-7, NO. 0220, Pub. by Hutchinson England). Routledge Chapman & Hall.

Papua New Guinea: A Travel Survival Kit. 3rd ed. Tony Wheeler. (Illus.). 256p. (Orig.). 1985. pap. 8.95 o.p. (ISBN 0-908086-59-8). Lonely Planet.

Papua New Guinea: Guide to Sources in Education. John F. Cleverly & Christabel Wescombe. LC 79-670399. 1979. pap. 22.00x o.p. (ISBN 0-424-00043-1, Pub. by Sydney U Pr). Intl Spec Bk.

Papua New Guinea: Initiation & Independence. Don Woolford. 1977. 25.00x o.p. (ISBN 0-7022-1313-6); pap. 12.95x o.p. (ISBN 0-7022-1334-9). U of Queensland Pr.

Paquin's Master Guide to a Successful Will Practice. Claude Paquin. LC 79-15962. 214p. 1979. 59.50 o.p. (ISBN 0-87624-423-1, Inst Busn Plan). P-H.

Parable of a Siamese Cat That Kept Purring among Thorns. Kasimir B. Slania. LC 84-90148. 44p. 1985. 6.95 o.p. (ISBN 0-533-06219-5). Vantage.

Parable of Jesus. Jamie Buckingham. 176p. 7.95 o.p. (ISBN 1-55725-004-9). Paraclete Pr.

Parable of the Father's Heart. G. Campbell Morgan. (Morgan Library). 96p. 1981. pap. 2.95 o.p. (ISBN 0-8010-6118-0). Baker Bk.

Parables & Presence. Robert W. Funk. LC 82-71827. 224p. 1982. 3.00 o.p. (ISBN 0-8006-0688-4, 1-688, Fortress). Augsburg Fortress.

Parables in Matthew's Gospel: Matthew 13. R. K. Campbell. tchr's lesson outline 3.95 o.p. (ISBN 0-88172-011-9). Believers Bkshelf.

Parables of Jesus. Norman Bull. (Bible Story & Its Background Ser.: Vol. 6). (gr. 2-7). 10.95 o.p. (ISBN 0-7175-0452-2). Dufour.

Parables of Jesus, Vol. 1. Neil Lightfoot. 1986. pap. 3.95 o.p. Abilene Christ U.

Parables of Our Lord. William Arnot. LC 80-8065. 532p. 1981. 14.95 o.p. (ISBN 0-8254-2119-5). Kregel.

Parables of Peanuts. Robert L. Short. LC 68-29566. (Illus.). 1968. pap. 6.95i o.p. (ISBN 0-06-067379-6, RD-27). HarpR.

Parables of the Triple Tradition. Charles E. Carlston. LC 74-26347. 272p. 1975. pap. 14.95 o.p. (ISBN 0-8006-0402-4, 1-402, Fortress). Augsburg Fortress.

Parables: Their Literary & Existential Dimension. Dan O. Via, Jr. LC 67-11910. 232p. 1974. pap. 6.95 o.p. (ISBN 0-8006-1392-9, 1-1392, Fortress). Augsburg Fortress.

Parachute Rigger Question Book. (FAA-T-8080-9). (Illus.). 37p. (Orig.). 1986. pap. 1.75 o.p. (ISBN 0-318-20392-8, S/N 050-007-00735-3). USGPO.

Parachuting Manual for Square-Tandem Equipment. 3rd, rev. ed. Dan Poynter. LC 84-27374. (Illus.). 24p. (Orig.). 1986. pap. 2.00 o.p. (ISBN 0-915516-41-1). Para Pub.

Parachuting: The Skydivers' Handbook. 4th ed. Dan Poynter. LC 77-83469. (Illus.). 180p. 1983. pap. 7.95 o.p. (ISBN 0-915516-16-0); pap. 11.95 span. ed. o.p. (ISBN 84-283-1386-5). Para Pub.

Parade: Cubism As Theater. Richard H. Axsom. LC 78-74361. (Outstanding Dissertations in the Fine Arts, Fourth Ser.). (Illus.). 1979. lib. bdg. 46.00 o.p. (ISBN 0-8240-3950-5). Garland Pub.

Parade Pony. Illus. by Ellen Blonder. (Fast Rolling Bks.). (Illus.). (ps up). 1986. 6.95 o.p. (ISBN 0-448-09882-2, G&D). Putnam Pub Group.

Paradiddle. Gus Weill. LC 73-90946. 256p. 1974. 6.95 o.p. (ISBN 0-8065-0402-1, Pub. by Citadel Pr). Carol Pub Group.

Paradise. Donald Barthelme. 208p. 1986. 16.95 o.p. (ISBN 0-399-12921-9). Putnam Pub Group.

Paradise. Patrick Dennis. LC 79-142085. 1971. 6.95 o.p. (ISBN 0-15-170965-3). HarBraceJ.

Paradise Found & Lost. O. H. Spate. (Illus.). 410p. 1988. 46.00 o.s.i. (ISBN 0-08-034400-3). Pergamon.

Paradise Loot. Don Blanding. (Illus.). 1978. Repr. of 1925 ed. pap. 2.95 o.p. (ISBN 0-912180-35-8). Petroglyph.

Paradise Lost. G K. Hunter. (Unwin Critical Library). 213p. 1982. pap. 11.95 o.p. (ISBN 0-04-800007-8). Unwin Hyman.

Paradise Lost. John Milton. 48p. (Orig.). 1988. pap. 9.95 o.p. (ISBN 1-55651-727-0); audiocassette tape incl. o.p. (ISBN 1-55651-728-9). Cram Cassettes.

Paradise Lost: A Humanist Approach. K. G. Hamilton. (Scholars' Library). 122p. 1982. text ed. 34.50x o.p. U of Queensland Pr.

Paradise Rehearsal Club. Margaret C. Fisk & Alan Fisk. 480p. 1982. 14.95 o.s.i. (ISBN 0-671-40023-1). Summit Bks.

Paradise Reviewed: An Interpretation of Gauguin's Polynesian Symbolism. Jehanne Teilhet-Fisk. Ed. by Stephen C. Foster. LC 82-4904. (Studies in the Fine Arts: The Avant-Garde: No. 31). 315p. 1983. 49.95 o.p. (ISBN 0-8357-1334-2). Univ Microfilms.

Paradox Companion. Douglas Cobb et al. Ed. by Marjorie Phifer & Linda Baughman. LC 86-70871. (Illus.). 618p. (Orig.). 1986. pap. 24.95 o.p. (ISBN 0-936767-02-2). Cobb Group.

Paradox in the Religious Poetry of Zinaida Gippius. Olga Matich. bds. cancelled o.s.i. (ISBN 3-7705-0653-7). Adlers Foreign Bks.

Paradox of Cause & Other Essays. John W. Miller. 192p. 1981. pap. 5.95 o.p. (ISBN 0-393-00032-X). Norton.

Paradox of Helping: Introduction to the Philosophy of Scientific Practice. Martin Bloom. LC 74-13524. 283p. 1975. text ed. write for info. o.p. (ISBN 0-02-310890-8). Macmillan.

Paradox of Pleasure & Relativity. Dominick Garan. LC 63-15602. 499p. 1964. (ISBN 0-8022-0561-5). Philos Lib.

Paradoxes of Freedom. Sidney Hook. LC 83-22539. ix, 152p. 1984. Repr. of 1970 ed. lib. bdg. 35.00x o.p. (ISBN 0-313-24289-5, H0PA). Greenwood.

Paragraph & Essay Book. Lee A. Jacobus. 161p. (Orig.). 1977. pap. text ed. 8.00 o.p. (ISBN 0-15-567980-5, HC). HarBraceJ.

Paragraph Book. C. Jeriel Howard & Richard F. Tracz. (Orig.). 1982. pap. text ed. write for info. o.p. (ISBN 0-673-39270-8). Scott F.

Paragraph of Life: Killer-Your Friend? Dino Manuel. 64p. (YA) (gr. 7 up). 1981. 5.00 o.p. (ISBN 0-682-49724-X). Exposition-Phoenix.

Paragraph Practice: Writing the Paragraph & the Short Composition. 4th ed. Kathleen E. Sullivan. (Illus.). 1980. pap. text ed. write for info. o.p. (ISBN 0-02-418280-X). Macmillan.

Paragraph Sense: A Basic Rhetoric. Enno Klammer. 197p. 1978. 8.75 o.p. (ISBN 0-15-567985-6, HC). HarbraceJ.

Paraguay under Stroessner. Paul H. Lewis. LC 79-28554. xi, 256p. 1980. 26.00x o.p. (ISBN 0-8078-1437-7). U of NC Pr.

Paralegals. (Career Blazers Guides Ser.). 192p. (Orig.). 1983. pap. 7.95 o.p. (ISBN 0-671-45870-1). Monarch Pr.

Paralegals & Successful Law Practice. Robert G. Kurzman & Rita K. Gilbert. LC 81-13157. 401p. 1981. 49.50 o.p. (ISBN 0-87624-426-6, Inst Busn Plan). P-H.

Parallax View. Loren Singer. LC 80-54848. 192p. 1981. Repr. of 1970 ed. 15.95 o.p. (ISBN 0-933256-20-5). Second Chance.

Parallel Developments: A Comparative History of Ideas. Hajime Nakamura. LC 75-24947. 567p. 1975. 36.00x o.p. (ISBN 0-87011-272-4). Kodansha.

Parallel Models of Intelligence. Ed. by Danny Hillis. 105p. 1988. pap. text ed. 20.00x o.p. (ISBN 0-929280-02-4). Amer Artificial.

Parallel Pipeline Computer Architecture for Speech Processing. Vassilios J. Georgiou. Ed. by Harold Stone. LC 83-18133. (Computer Science: Computer Architecture & Design Ser.: No. 2). 122p. 1984. 37.95 o.p. (ISBN 0-8357-1524-8). UMI Res Pr.

Parallel Processing: Proceedings. Sagamore Computer Conference, Aug. 20-23, 1974. Ed. by Tse-Yun Feng. (Lecture Notes in Computer Science Ser.: Vol. 24). vi, 433p. 1975. pap. 21.00 o.p. (ISBN 0-387-07135-0). Springer-Verlag.

Paralysis of International Institutions & the Remedies: A Study of Self-Determination, Concord among the Major Powers & Political Arbitration. Istvan Bibo. LC 75-17182. 152p. 1976. 39.95x o.p. (ISBN 0-470-07208-3). Halsted Pr.

Paramagnetic Resonance, 2 Vols. Ed. by William Low. 1963. Set. 130.50 o.s.i. (ISBN 0-12-456266-3); Vol. 1. 97.00 o.p. (ISBN 0-12-456201-9); Vol. 2. 97.00 o.p. (ISBN 0-12-456202-7). Acad Pr.

Paramartha Katha Prasang: Spiritual Conversations with Swami Muktananda. Swami Muktananda. 356p. 7.50 o.s.i. (ISBN 0-914602-90-X). SYDA Found.

Paramedic Review Manual. Ed. by Jonathan Politis et al. 1985. 14.95 o.p. (ISBN 0-917010-19-1). Natl Nursing.

Parameters of Personality. R. Roth. 1970. pap. text ed. 9.95x o.p. (ISBN 0-8290-1171-4). Irvington.

Paraprofessionals in Counseling, Guidance & Personnel Services. David G. Zimpfer. (APGA Reprint Ser.: No. 5). 280p. 1974. pap. 9.75 o.p. (ISBN 0-911547-58-4, 72097W34). Am Assn Coun Dev.

Paraprofessionals in Mental Health. Benjamin Pope & James P. McGee. 275p. 1985. text ed. 29.50x o.s.i. (ISBN 0-8290-0532-3). Irvington.

Paraprofessions: Careers of the Future & the Present. Sarah Splaver. LC 72-1417. (Messner Career Bks.). 192p. (gr. 9 up). 1972. lib. bdg. 8.29 o.s.i. (ISBN 0-671-32546-9). Messner.

Paraproteins in Disease: Investigation of Plasma Cell Dyscrasia. W. Pruzanski & E. C. Keystone. LC 84-11415. (Practical Method in Clinical Immunology Ser.). (Illus.). 195p. 1985. text ed. 74.00 o.p. (ISBN 0-443-02060-4). Churchill.

Parapsychology Today. Rhine & Brier. 6.00 o.p. (ISBN 0-8065-0344-0, Pub. by Citadel Pr). Carol Pub Group.

Paras: The British Parachute Regiment. James G. Shortt. (Illus.). 72p. (Orig.). 1985. pap. 9.95 o.p. (ISBN 0-85368-699-8, Pub. by Arms & Armour). Sterling.

Paraside Then, & Again. Mildred Richards. 154p. (Orig.). 1985. pap. 12.95x o.p. (ISBN 0-317-39414-2). Wyndham Hall.

Parasite. Michel Serres. Tr. by Lawrence R. Schehr from Fr. LC 81-19277. 272p. 1982. text ed. 29.50x o.p. (ISBN 0-8018-2456-7). Johns Hopkins.

Parasitic Diseases: Their Biology, Clinical Diagnosis & Therapy. Crewe. 218p. 1985. 25.00 o.p. (ISBN 0-471-01063-4). Wiley.

Parasitology: The Biology of Animal Parasites. 5th ed. Elmer R. Noble & Glenn A. Noble. LC 81-20686. (Illus.). 522p. 1982. text ed. 34.50 o.p. (ISBN 0-8121-0819-1). Lea & Febiger.

Paratransit Services. (Transportation Research Record Ser.). 69p. 1977. 4.80 o.p. (ISBN 0-309-02679-2). Transport Res Bd.

Parco Advertisement Art. (Illus.). 96p. 1986. pap. 34.95 o.s.i. (ISBN 4-8-9194133-2, Parco Pub Japan). Bks Nippan.

Pardes Rimonim. Moshe Tendler. 96p. 1982. 4.95 o.p. (ISBN 0-910818-09-6). Judaica Pr.

Pardon Me While I Be Myself. Doris C. Travis. 1985. 7.95 o.p. (ISBN 0-533-06648-4). Vantage.

Pardon My Convicts: Memoirs of a Prison Warden. J. Jerry Sylvia. 265p. 1983. 15.50 o.p. (ISBN 0-682-49962-5). Exposition-Phoenix.

Parent & Child in the Christian Kitchen. Louann Bernthal. 128p. 1987. pap. 12.95 o.p. (ISBN 0-570-09062-8, 12-3029). Concordia.

Parent & Family Issues Related to Health Care for Children: An Annotated Bibliography. 67p. 1982. 10.50 o.p. (ISBN 0-318-17763-3); members 7.00 o.p. (ISBN 0-318-17764-1). Assn Care Child.

Parent Child Fun Kit. Robert Stafford & Carolyn Stafford. (Illus.). 318p. 1980. pap. 10.00 o.p. (ISBN 0-933586-00-0). Book Promo Pr.

Parent-Child Interaction & Youth Rebellion. Marianne Marschak. 1980. text ed. 24.95 o.p. (ISBN 0-89876-049-6). Gardner Pr.

Parent-Child Relations: A Reader. Ed. by Norman Poppel. 221p. 1971. pap. text ed. 9.50x o.p. (ISBN 0-8422-0156-4). Irvington.

Parent-Child Relationship in the Law: Recent Actions & Cases, 1980-1985. Dale E. Casper. (Public Administration Ser.: P 1832). 12p. 1985. 2.00 o.p. (ISBN 0-89028-682-5). Vance Biblios.

Parent in the Shadows. Phyllis J. McAdams. 1972. pap. 19.95 pkg.of 25 o.p. (ISBN 0-87868-103-5, FP-1). Child Welfare.

Parent-Infant Communication: A Program of Clinical & Home Training for Parents & Hearing Impaired Infants, 2 vols. V. Schuyler et al. LC 84-62996. 201p. 1985. 37.50 o.p. (ISBN 0-318-23144-1). Infant Hearing Resc.

Parent Power: A Common Sense Approach to Raising Your Children in the Eighties. John Rosemond. LC 81-9716. 240p. 1981. 12.95 o.p. (ISBN 0-914788-42-6). Globe Pequot.

Parent Teacher Conferencing. Joseph C. Rotter & Edward H. Robinson. (What Research Says to the Teacher Ser.). 32p. 1982. 2.50 o.p. (ISBN 0-8106-1057-4). NEA.

Parent-Teacher Interaction: A Special Educational Perspective. Edward Kelly. LC 73-82979. 151p. 1974. pap. 5.50x o.p. (ISBN 0-87562-048-5). Spec Child.

Parental Behavior in Birds. Ed. by Rae Silver. (Benchmark Papers in Animal Behavior: Vol. 11). 1982. 51.95 o.p. (ISBN 0-87933-289-1). Van Nos Reinhold.

Parental Child-Support Obligation: Research, Practice, & Social Policy. Ed. by Judith Cassetty. LC 81-48464. 320p. 1982. 36.00x o.p. (ISBN 0-669-05376-7). Lexington Bks.

Parental Death & Psychological Development. Ellen B. Berlinsky & Henry B. Biller. LC 82-48015. 176p. 1982. 25.00x o.p. (ISBN 0-669-05875-0). Lexington Bks.

Parental Leave: Judicial & Legislative Trends: Current Practices in the Workplace. Mary E. Radford. 1988. 9.00 o.p. (ISBN 0-89154-340-6). Intl Found Employ.

Parenteral Nutrition in Acute Metabolic Illness. Ed. by H. A. Lee. 1974. 101.00 o.p. (ISBN 0-12-441750-7). Acad Pr.

Parenting Education at Medford & Churchill High Schools. M. C. Jensen. 1986. 4.00 o.p. U of Oreg Bks.

Parenting with Love & Limits. Bruce Narramore. 312p. 1987. pap. 8.95 o.p. (ISBN 0-310-30541-1, 11246P). Zondervan.

Parents & Children in the Hospital: The Family's Role in Pediatrics. Carol B. Hardgrove & Rosemary B. Dawson. 276p. 1972. 12.95 o.p. (ISBN 0-316-34600-4). Little.

Parents & Teenagers. Frank S. Caprio & Frank B. Caprio. LC 68-19127. 1969. 5.00 o.p. (ISBN 0-685-08134-6, Pub. by Citadel Pr); pap. 2.00 o.p. (ISBN 0-8065-0082-4). Carol Pub Group.

Parents' Book of Physical Fitness for Children. Martin I. Lorin. LC 78-3151. (Illus.). 290p. 1981. pap. 5.95 o.p. (ISBN 0-689-70604-9, 264, Atheneum); 9.95 o.p. (ISBN 0-689-10922-9). Macmillan.

Parent's Emergency Guide: An Action Handbook for Childhood Illness & Accidents. The Diagram Group. (Illus.). 128p. 1984. pap. 6.95 o.p. (ISBN 0-87196-821-5). Facts on File.

Parents' Financial Survival Guide. Theodore E. Hughes & David Klein. 228p. 1987. 19.95 o.p. (ISBN 0-89586-644-7); pap. 13.95 o.p. (ISBN 0-89586-583-1). Price Stern.

Parents' Guide to Austin, 1986. rev. ed. Lynda Crowell & Maryanne Mariotti. (Illus.). 202p. 1986. pap. 7.95 o.p. (ISBN 0-938934-12-0). C&M Pubns.

Parents Guide to Cleft Palate Habilitation: The Team Approach. Aaron H. Bleiberg & Harry Leubling. 1971. 10.00 o.p. (ISBN 0-682-47183-6, University). Exposition-Phoenix.

Parent's Guide to Computers in Education. David Moursund. 80p. 1983. 3.50 o.p. (ISBN 0-924667-14-1). Intl Council Comp.

Parent's Guide to Learning Disabilities. Johanna Fisher. LC 78-9950. 1979. 2.95 o.s.i. (ISBN 0-684-15899-X, ScribT); pap. 2.95 o.s.i. (ISBN 0-684-17180-5). Scribner.

Parent's Guide to Personal Computers & Software. Consumer Guide Editors & Danny Goodman. 80p. 1983. pap. 6.75 o.p. (ISBN 0-671-49173-3, 22083, Touchstone). S&S.

Parents' Guide to Sex Education. Mary A. Mayo. 208p. pap. 7.95 o.p. (ISBN 0-310-44581-7, 11357P). Zondervan.

Parents Guide to Successful Child Rearing: How to Say No Without Guilt. Esther Laden Cava. 1977. pap. 4.00 o.p. (ISBN 0-682-48777-5, Banner). Exposition-Phoenix.

Parents' Guide to "Teacherese" A Glossary of Special Education Terms. Nancy O. Wilson. 96p. (Orig.). 1981. pap. text ed. 7.50x o.p. (ISBN 0-87562-069-8, 069-8). Spec Child.

Parents in Contemporary America: A Sympathetic View. 4th ed. E. E. LeMasters & John Defrain. 304p. 1983. pap. text ed. (ISBN 0-534-10669-2). Wadsworth Pub.

Parents in Reading: Parents' Booklet Spanish-English Version. Northwest Regional Educational Laboratory Staff. (Illus., Orig.). 3.95 o.p. (ISBN 0-89354-402-7). Northwest Regional.

Parents in the Workplace: A Management Resource for Employers. Ed. by Tom Copeland. (Illus.). 30p. folder 10.00 o.p. (ISBN 0-934140-17-0). Toys N Things.

Parent's Journey into Magic Moments in the Kingdom of Kids. Marlee Alex & Ben Alex. 64p. 1986. 10.95 o.p. (ISBN 0-8407-6699-8). Nelson.

Parents, Kids & the Commodore 64. Lynne Alper & Meg Holmberg. LC 84-51796. 110p. 1984. pap. 9.95 o.p. (ISBN 0-89588-234-5). SYBEX.

Parents Not Guilty of Their Children's Neuroses. Edmund Bergler. LC 71-131274. 1964. 6.95x o.p. (ISBN 0-87140-977-1). Liveright.

Parents of Newborns. Susan B. Borstein. LC 80-5950. 153p. 1980. 14.95 o.s.i. (ISBN 0-86618-000-1). Family Serv.

Parent's Pediatric Companion. Gil Simon & Marcia Cohen. LC 84-27302. (Illus.). 416p. 1985. 17.95 o.p. (ISBN 0-688-03791-7). Morrow.

Parents' Solution Book. Lea Bramnick & Anita Simon. 320p. 1983. 14.95 o.p. (ISBN 0-531-09881-8). Watts.

Parents' Solution Book: Your Child from Five to Twelve. Lea Bramnick & Anita Simon. 1984. pap. 9.95 o.p. (ISBN 0-399-51076-1, Perigee). Putnam Pub Group.

Parents, Take Charge! Perry L. Draper. 1982. pap. 5.95 o.p. (ISBN 0-8423-4822-0). Tyndale.

Parents, Teachers, Kids. William R. Van Osdol. 292p. 1974. 24.00x o.p. (ISBN 0-8422-5167-7); pap. text ed. 9.50x o.p. (ISBN 0-8422-0395-8). Irvington.

Parents Terribles see Theatre.

Parents Terribles: Avec: La Machine a Ecrire. Jean Cocteau. 282p. 1971. 16.95 o.p. (ISBN 0-686-54547-8). French & Eur.

Pargiters: The Novel Essay Portion of the Years. Virginia Woolf. 167p. 1978. pap. 4.95 o.s.i. (ISBN 0-15-671380-2). HarBraceJ.

Pariah & Other Stories. Joan Williams. (Southern Writers Ser.). 1985. pap. 3.50 o.p. (ISBN 0-380-69979-6). Avon.

Paris. Anne Corbierre. LC 80-50996. (Rand McNally Pocket Guide Ser.). (Illus.). 1983. pap. 5.95 o.p. (ISBN 0-528-84294-3). Rand McNally.

Paris. (Berlitz Deluxe Guides). (Illus.). 336p. 1988. 10.95 o.p. (ISBN 0-02-968210-X, Berlitz). Macmillan.

Paris: A Picture Book to Remember Her By. (Illus.). 1970. 3.98 o.p. (ISBN 0-517-28828-1). Crown.

Paris & Environs. 5th ed. Ian Robertson. (Blue Guides Ser.). (Illus.). 1983. 24.95 o.p. (ISBN 0-393-01561-0); pap. 14.95 o.p. (ISBN 0-393-30013-7). Norton.

Paris & Environs. 6th ed. Ian Robertson. (Blue Guides Ser.). (Illus., Orig.). 1985. pap. 16.95 o.p. (ISBN 0-393-30073-0). Norton.

Paris & the American Avant-Garde, 1900-1925. Detroit Institute of Arts Staff & Museum Practice Program Students. (Illus.). 98p. 1980. 3.50 o.p. (ISBN 0-318-18404-4). Michigan Mus.

Paris & the American Avant-Garde, 1900-1925. 1980. pap. 3.50 o.p. (ISBN 0-912303-22-0). Michigan Mus.

Paris Atlas, No. 011. 10th ed. 1986. pap. 8.95 o.p. (ISBN 2-06-000118-8). Michelin.

Paris Cumulative Index to English Translations, 1948-1968, 2 vols. UNESCO Staff. 1973. lib. bdg. 429.00 o.p. (ISBN 0-8161-1042-5, Hall Library). G K Hall.

Paris de ma Fenetre. Colette. 160p. 1976. pap. 8.95 o.p. (ISBN 0-686-54602-4). French & Eur.

Paris Dining Guide. Waverley Root. LC 69-15514. 1969. pap. 2.95 o.p. (ISBN 0-689-30001-8, Atheneum). Macmillan.

Paris in the Age of Absolutism. Orest Ranum. LC 79-2603. (Midland Bks.: No. 238). (Illus.). 336p. 1980. 20.00x o.p. (ISBN 0-253-19677-9); pap. 6.95x o.p. (ISBN 0-253-20238-8). Ind U Pr.

Paris in the Terror. Stanley Loomis. 1973. pap. 1.50 o.p. (ISBN 0-380-01369-X, 14977). Avon.

Paris in the Third Reich: A History of the German Occupation, 1940-1944. David Pryce-Jones. LC 80-21256. (Illus.). 304p. 1981. 25.00 o.s.i. (ISBN 0-03-045621-5). H Holt & Co.

Paris in Your Pocket. Loomis. 208p. 1985. pap. 2.95 o.p. (ISBN 0-8120-2696-9). Barron.

Paris Index & Map, No. 12. 4th ed. Michelin Guides & Maps. 1980. pap. 4.95 o.p. (ISBN 2-06-000123-4). Michelin.

Paris Index Plan, No. 14. 4th ed. Michelin. 1984. pap. 5.95 o.p. (ISBN 2-06-000144-7). Michelin.

Paris Journal: Vol. II, 1965-1971. Janet Flanner. Ed. by William Shawn. LC 76-45462. 444p. 1977. pap. 9.95 o.p. (ISBN 0-15-670951-1, Harv). HarBraceJ.

Paris! Paris! Irwin Shaw & Ronald Searle. LC 76-27415. (Illus.). 1977. 10.95 o.p. (ISBN 0-15-170968-8). HarBraceJ.

Paris Phaidon Cultural Guide. (Phaidon Cultural Guide Ser.). (Illus.). 1987. 17.95 o.p. (ISBN 0-13-650136-2). P-H.

Paris Puzzle. Vincent McConnor. 1984. pap. 2.50 o.s.i. (ISBN 0-345-30811-5). Ballantine.

Paris 1987-1988. (Frommer's City Guides). 224p. 5.95 o.p. (ISBN 0-671-62340-0). Prentice Hall Pr.

Parish As Learning Community. Thomas Downs. LC 78-70816. 128p. 1979. pap. 3.95 o.p. (ISBN 0-8091-2172-7). Paulist Pr.

Parish Life in the United States, Final Report to the Bishops of the United States by the Parish Project, November, 1982. 90p. 1983. pap. 7.50 o.p. (ISBN 1-55586-876-2). US Catholic.

Parish Life: Manual for Spiritual Leadership Formation. Nancy Westmeyer. 1983. pap. 8.95 o.p. (ISBN 0-8091-2489-0). Paulist Pr.

Parish of Rich Women. James Buchan. LC 84-45611. 256p. 1985. 14.95 o.p. (ISBN 0-689-11534-2, Atheneum). Macmillan.

Parish Secretary's Handbook. Wayne Paulson. 180p. (Orig.). 1982. pap. 14.95 o.p. (ISBN 0-8066-1898-1, 10-4868, Augsburg). Augsburg Fortress.

Parishes & Families: A Model for Christian Formation Through Liturgy. Ed. by Gabe Huck & Virginia Sloyan. 1973. pap. 5.00 o.p. (ISBN 0-918208-11-4). Liturgical Conf.

Parisian Frolics. LC 83-83189. (Classics of the Victorian Imagination Ser.). 144p. 1984. 12.50 o.p. (ISBN 0-394-53881-1, GP 916). Grove.

Parisian Girl. John Hohenberg. 304p. 1986. pap. 3.50 o.p. (ISBN 0-380-89615-X). Avon.

Pariswalks. Alison Landes & Sonia Landes. LC 81-47475. (Illus.). 256p. (Orig.). 1982. 15.95 o.s.i. (ISBN 0-03-059747-1, Owl Bks.); pap. 9.95 o.s.i. (ISBN 0-03-060076-6). H Holt & Co.

Park. Eric Hill. LC 82-60615. (Eric Hill's Baby Bear Bks.). (Illus.). 14p. (ps). 1983. pap. 2.50 o.s.i. (ISBN 0-394-85636-8). Random.

Park & Recreation Management. Robert E. Sternloff & Roger Warren. 326p. 1984. text ed. (ISBN 0-02-417210-3). Macmillan.

Parker, America's Finest Shotgun. Peter H. Johnson. (Classic Gun Book Ser.). (Illus.). 272p. 1985. 17.95 o.p. (ISBN 0-8117-1240-0). Stackpole.

Parker on Writing. Robert B. Parker. 50p. 1985. deluxe signed ed. 50.00 o.p. (ISBN 0-935716-34-3). Lord John.

Parking Discounts & Carpool Formation in Seattle. Marie Olsson & Gerald Miller. 115p. (Orig.). 1978. pap. text ed. 6.00x o.p. (ISBN 0-87766-226-6). Urban Inst.

Parkinson: The Law 1980. C. Northcote Parkinson. (Illus.). 1980. 8.95 o.p. (ISBN 0-395-29131-3). HM.

Parkinson's Disease: A New Approach to Treatment. Ed. by G. F. Birdwood et al. 1971. 27.50 o.p. (ISBN 0-12-100150-4). Acad Pr.

Parks of the Pacific Coast: The Complete Guide to the National & Historic Parks, California, Oregon, Washington. Doug Tatreau & Bobbe Tatreau. LC 84-48892. (Illus.). 160p. (Orig.). 1985. pap. 10.95 o.p. (ISBN 0-88742-050-8). Globe Pequot.

Parlement of Foulys. new ed. Geoffrey Chaucer. Ed. by D. S. Brewer. (Old & Middle English Texts). 168p. 1976. pap. 11.25x o.p. (ISBN 0-06-491190-X). B&N Imports.

Parliament & the Ombudsman in New Zealand. Larry B. Hill. (Legislative Research Ser.: No. 8). 1973. pap. 3.50 o.p. (ISBN 0-686-18649-4). Univ OK Gov Res.

Parliament of Great Britain: A Bibliography. Robert Goehlert & Fenton Martin. LC 82-47920. (Special Series in Libraries & Librarianship). 240p. 1983. 30.00x o.p. (ISBN 0-669-05700-2). Lexington Bks.

Parliamentary Debates in Sixteen Ten. Great Britain, House of Commons Staff. 1862. 24.00 o.p. (ISBN 0-384-19780-9). Johnson Repr.

Parliamentary Democracy & Socialist Politics. Barry Hindess. 200p. 1983. pap. 10.95x o.p. (ISBN 0-7100-9319-5). Routledge Chapman & Hall.

Parliamentary Government in the Commonwealth. Ed. by S. D. Bailey. 1953. (ISBN 0-8022-0052-4). Philos Lib.

Parliamentary Law Textbook. Narcissa T. Shawhan. pap. 2.95 o.p. (ISBN 0-8042-1776-9, John Knox). Westminster John Knox.

Parliamentary Procedure: How to Conduct a Meeting: A Pictorial Presentation Based on the Parliamentary Writings of General Henry M. Roberts. rev. ed. (Illus.). 8p. 1981. pap. 1.95 o.p. (ISBN 0-8040-0390-4, Swallow). Ohio U Pr.

Parliaments & Estates in Europe: To 1789. A. R. Myers. (History of European Civilization Library). 180p. 1975. pap. text ed. 9.95 o.p. (ISBN 0-15-568123-0, HC). HarBraceJ.

Parliaments of the World. Ed. by V. Herman & F. Mendel. 1976. 105.00 o.s.i. (ISBN 3-11-006975-X). De Gruyter.

Parlour Four & Other Stories. J. I. Stewart. 1986. 14.45 o.p. (ISBN 0-393-02292-7). Norton.

Parma Legacy. Dorothy Backer. 1978. 10.95 o.p. (ISBN 0-393-08817-0). Norton.

Parmer County History. Palmer County Historical Society Staff. (Illus.). 414p. 1974. 25.00 o.p. (ISBN 0-89015-073-7). Eakin Pr.

Parnassus on Wheels. Christopher Morley. 160p. 1983. pap. 4.95 o.p. (ISBN 0-380-62703-5, 62703-5). Avon.

Parody Anthology. Carolyn Wells. LC 67-14060. 432p. 1968. Repr. of 1904 ed. 30.00x o.p. (ISBN 0-8103-3224-8). Gale.

Parole Board Votes, County Houses of Correction, 1982. Massachusetts Parole Board Staff & Ellen M. Gilmore. LC 83-622994. 1983. write for info. o.p. Mass CLE.

Paroles. Jacques Prevert. 296p. 1949. 25.00 o.p. (ISBN 0-686-54915-5). Schoenhof.

Parousia. J. Stuart Russel. pap. 12.95 o.p. (ISBN 0-8010-7725-7). Baker Bk.

Parramore Sketches. Dock D. Parramore. LC 75-8096. 1975. 10.00 o.p. (ISBN 0-87404-054-X). Tex Western.

Parrot Guide. 2nd ed. Cyril H. Rogers. (Illus.). 256p. 14.95 o.p. (ISBN 0-87666-546-6, PL-2984). TFH Pubns.

Parrot in the Garret & Other Rhymes about Dwellings. Ed. by Lenore Blegvad. LC 81-10859. (Illus.). 32p. (ps-3). 1982. 8.95 o.s.i. (ISBN 0-689-50217-6, M K McElderry). Macmillan.

Parsifal Mosaic. Robert Ludlum. (General Ser.). 1984. lib. bdg. 19.95 o.p. (ISBN 0-8161-3719-6, Large Print Bks). G K Hall.

Titles

Parsley, Sage, Rosemary & Time. Jane L. Curry. LC 74-18181. (Illus.). 112p. (gr. 3-7). 1975. 5.95 o.p. (ISBN 0-689-50019-X, Atheneum). Macmillan.

Parson Weems of the Cherry-Tree. Harold Kellock. LC 75-107137. 224p. 1971. Repr. of 1928 ed. 35.00x o.p. (ISBN 0-8103-3785-1). Gale.

Part of Fortune. Laurel Goldman. LC 86-11079. 288p. 1987. 15.95 o.s.i. (ISBN 1-55584-004-3). Weidenfeld.

Part of My Life: The Memoirs of a Philosopher. A. J. Ayer. LC 77-73110. 1977. 14.95 o.p. (ISBN 0-15-170973-4). HarBraceJ.

Part of the Main. Edward M. Holmes. 1976. pap. 4.95 o.s.i. (ISBN 0-89101-031-9). U Maine Pr.

Part of the Story. Richard Jackson. Ed. by Robert Pack. (Grove Press Poetry Ser.). 96p. 1983. 12.50 o.s.i. (ISBN 0-394-53133-7, GP863). Grove.

Part of the Story. Richard Jackson. Ed. by Robert Pack. (Grove Press Poetry Ser.). 96p. 1983. pap. 5.95 o.p. (ISBN 0-394-62451-3, Ever). Grove.

Part-Time Career for Full-Time You. JoAnne Alter. (Illus.). 320p. 1982. 15.95 o.p. (ISBN 0-395-31284-1); pap. 8.95 o.p. (ISBN 0-395-31868-8). HM.

Part Time Job Book. Arthur R. Pell. 128p. 1984. pap. 7.95 o.p. (ISBN 0-671-46270-9). Monarch Pr.

Parthenon. Ed. by Vincent J. Bruno. (Critical Studies in Art History Ser). (Illus.). 334p. 1974. 12.50 o.p. (ISBN 0-393-04373-8); pap. 6.95x o.p. (ISBN 0-393-09354-9). Norton.

Partial Dentures. 5th ed. Lammie. 1986. 32.95 o.p. (ISBN 0-8016-2825-3). Mosby.

Partial Differential Equations. 2nd ed. George F. Carrier. 340p. 1988. 39.95 o.p. (ISBN 0-12-160451-9). Acad Pr.

Partial Figure in Modern Sculpture, from Rodin to 1969. Albert E. Elsen. LC 73-106903. (Illus.). 1969. pap. 10.00 o.p. (ISBN 0-912298-03-0); pap. 8.00 o.p. (ISBN 0-912298-04-9). Baltimore Mus.

Partial Recall. John Verdery. LC 81-66007. 1981. 12.95 o.p. (ISBN 0-689-11158-4, Atheneum). Macmillan.

Participants in the Information Marketplace see Understanding U. S. Information Policy.

Participating Life Insurance Sold by Stock Companies. Joseph M. Belth. 1965. 10.00x o.p. (ISBN 0-256-00639-3). Irwin.

Participation. Ann Richardson. (Concepts in Social Policy Ser.). 160p. 1983. pap. text ed. 8.95x o.p. (ISBN 0-7100-9469-8). Routledge Chapman & Hall.

Participation by Employers & Workers Organisations in Economic & Social Planning: A General Introduction. viii, 247p. 1971. 11.20 o.p. (ISBN 92-2-100129-6). Intl Labour Office.

Participation in American Presidential Nominations-1976. Austin Ranney. 1977. pap. 5.00 o.p. (ISBN 0-8447-3246-X). Am Enterprise.

Participation in Urban Planning. John Ferris. 95p. 1972. pap. text ed. 6.25 o.p. (ISBN 0-7135-1714-X, Pub. by Bedford England). Gower Pub Co.

Participation Training for Adult Education. Paul Bergevin & John McKinley. LC 65-18205. (Orig.). 1965. pap. 3.95 o.p. (ISBN 0-8272-2900-3). CBP.

Participatory & Self-Managed Firms: Evaluating Economic Performance. Ed. by Derek C. Jones & Jan Svejnar. LC 80-8612. (Illus.). 416p. 1982. 45.00x o.p. (ISBN 0-669-04328-1). Lexington Bks.

Participatory Management for Public Administrators: A Selective Bibliography. Lorna Peterson. (Public Administration Ser.: P 1834). 6p. 1985. 2.00 o.p. (ISBN 0-89028-684-1). Vance Biblios.

Particle Acceleration Processes, Shockwaves, Nucleosynthesis & Cosmic Rays: Proceedings of Symposia 6 & 8 & the Joint Sessions 6-8 of the COSPAR Twenty-fifth Plenary Meeting Held in Graz, Austria, 25 June to 7 July 1984. Ed. by L. Koch-Miramond & M. A. Lee. (Illus.). 542p. 1985. pap. 110.00 o.p. (ISBN 0-08-032711-7). Pergamon.

Particle Connection: The Most Exciting Scientific Chase since DNA & the Double Helix. Christine Sutton. LC 84-10595. 352p. 1984. 16.45 o.p. (ISBN 0-671-49659-X). S&S.

Particle Physics: Proceedings. International University Courses on Nuclear Physics, 8th, Schladming, Austria, 1969. Ed. by P. Urban. (Acta Physica Austriaca: Suppl. 6). (Illus.). 1969. 67.90 o.p. (ISBN 0-387-80915-5). Springer-Verlag.

Particle Size Analysis in Industrial Hygiene. Leslie Silverman. (Atomic Energy Commission Monographs). 315p. 1971. 40.00 o.p. (ISBN 0-12-643750-5). Acad Pr.

Particle Technology. Institution of Chemical Engineers Staff. 1982. 79.00 o.s.i. (ISBN 0-08-028761-1). Pergamon.

Particles & Fields 1. Ed. by D. H. Boal & A. N. Kamal. LC 78-2509. 470p. 1978. 69.50x o.p. (ISBN 0-306-31147-X, Plenum Pr). Plenum Pub.

Particles & Fields 2. Ed. by Anton Z. Capri & Abdul N. Kamal. 696p. 1983. 110.00x o.p. (ISBN 0-306-41162-8, Plenum Pr). Plenum Pub.

Particles, Currents, Symmetries: Proceedings. International University Courses on Nuclear Physics, 7th, Schladming, Austria, 1968. Ed. by P. Urban. (Acta Physica Austriaca: Suppl. 5). (Illus.). 1968. 63.80 o.p. (ISBN 0-387-80878-7). Springer-Verlag.

Particular Account of the Emperor of China's Gardens Near Peking with Unconnected Thoughts on Gardening & Other Items: An Essay on Design in Gardening. Jean D. Attiret & William Shenstone. Ed. by John D. Hunt. LC 79-56989. (English Landscape Garden Ser.). 194p. 1982. lib. bdg. 26.00 o.p. (ISBN 0-8240-0165-6). Garland Pub.

Particular Friendships. Martin Allen. 80p. (Orig.). 1986. pap. 7.95 o.p. (ISBN 0-571-14537-X). Faber & Faber.

Particularly Cats. Doris Lessing. (Illus.). 1979. pap. 3.95 o.p. (ISBN 0-671-24414-0, Fireside). S&S.

Particulate Carbon: Atmospheric Life Cycle. Ed. by George T. Wolff & Richard L. Klimisch. LC 81-21017. (General Motors Symposia Ser.). 422p. 1982. 75.00x o.p. (ISBN 0-306-40918-6, Plenum Pr); Set of 2 vols. 115.00 o.p. Plenum Pub.

Particulate Carbon: Formation During Combustion. Ed. by Donald C. Siegla & George W. Smith. LC 81-15363. (General Motors Research Symposia Ser.). 516p. 1981. 79.50x o.p. (ISBN 0-306-40881-3, Plenum Pr); Set of 2 vols. 115.00 o.p. Plenum Pub.

Particulates & Fine Dust Removal: Processes & Equipment. M. Sittig. LC 77-77018. (Pollution Technology Review Ser.: No. 34). (Illus.). 1977. 48.00 o.p. (ISBN 0-8155-0664-3). Noyes.

Parties in Crisis: Party Politics in America. 2nd ed. Ruth K. Scott & Ronald J. Hrebenar. LC 83-17089. 394p. 1983. text ed. write for info. o.p. (ISBN 0-02-408420-4). Macmillan.

Parties, Parties. Fran Chiles. LC 83-18572. (Illus.). 120p. 1984. 17.95x o.p. (ISBN 0-87201-656-0). Gulf Pub.

Parting. Dorothy Dobson. 1980. 7.00 o.p. (ISBN 0-682-49502-6). Exposition-Phoenix.

Parting Company: How to Survive the Loss of a Job & Find Another Successfully. William J. Morin & James C. Cabrera. LC 82-48045. 264p. 1982. 12.95 o.p. (ISBN 0-15-170966-1). HarbraceJ.

Parting Shots. Dan Issel & Buddy Martin. (Illus.). 224p. 1986. pap. 6.95 o.p. (ISBN 0-8092-5070-5). Contemp Bks.

Partisan Guide to the Jewish Problem. Milton Steinberg. LC 86-1509. (Brown Classics in Judaica). 312p. 1986. pap. text ed. 14.25 o.p. (ISBN 0-8191-4493-2). U Pr of Amer.

Partition of Africa. J. M. McKenzie. (Lancaster Pamphlet Ser.). 60p. 1983. pap. 3.95 o.p. (ISBN 0-416-35050-X, NO. 3850). Routledge Chapman & Hall.

Partly Right. Anthony Campolo. 192p. 1985. pap. 9.99 o.p. (ISBN 0-8499-0368-8, 0368-8). Word Bks.

Partners. Louis Auchincloss. 1974. 6.95 o.p. (ISBN 0-395-18279-4). HM.

Partners. Susan Washburn. LC 80-65985. 1981. 11.95 o.p. (ISBN 0-689-11103-7, Atheneum). Macmillan.

Partners Against Hunger: The Consultative Group on International Agricultural Research. Warren C. Baum. 352p. 1986. 29.95 o.p. (ISBN 0-8213-0827-0, BK 0827); pap. 10.95 o.p. (ISBN 0-8213-0829-7, BK 0829). World Bank.

Partners in Crime. Agatha Christie. 240p. 1984. pap. 3.50 o.s.i. (ISBN 0-425-10352-8). Berkley Pub.

Partners in Love. 3rd rev. ed. Eleanor Hamilton. LC 79-51018. 1981. Repr. 9.95 o.s.i. (ISBN 0-498-02431-8). A S Barnes.

Partners in Process. Truman Esau & Beverly Burch. 156p. 1986. pap. 6.50 o.p. (ISBN 0-89693-372-5). Victor Bks.

Partners in Prosperity: Strategic Industries in the United States & Japan. Julian Gresser. LC 83-24925. 432p. 1984. text ed. 15.95 o.p. (ISBN 0-07-024671-8). McGraw.

Partners in Public Service: Government & the Nonprofit Sector in Rhode Island. Diane M. Disney et al. 164p. (Orig.). 1984. pap. text ed. 14.95x o.p. (ISBN 0-87766-344-0). Urban Inst.

Partners: Inside America's Most Powerful Law Firms. James A. Stewart. 384p. 1983. 17.25 o.p. (ISBN 0-671-42023-2). S&S.

Partnership Book. 2nd ed. Denis Clifford & Ralph Warner. (Illus.). 221p. 1984. pap. 17.95 o.p. (ISBN 0-917316-91-6). Nolo Pr.

Partnership Desk Book. Burton J. Defren. LC 76-27990. 1978. 39.50 o.p. (ISBN 0-87624-427-4, Inst Busn Plan). P-H.

Partnership of Hearts. Vicki Page. (Lythway Ser.). 1987. lib. bdg. 16.50x o.p. (ISBN 0-7451-0583-1, Pub. by Chivers Pr UK). G K Hall.

Partnership Taxation: An Advanced Tax Program, 1985. Herschel M. Bloom & David W. Mills. LC 86-107597. (Tax Law & Estate Planning Ser.). 560p. 1984. 3.40 o.p. PLI.

Partnership Taxation: An Advanced Tax Program, 1984. Practising Law Institute Staff & David W. Mills. LC 84-213352. (Tax Law & Estate Planning Ser.). 1984. 40.00 o.p. PLI.

Partnerships, UPA, ULPA, Taxation, Securities, & Bankruptcy. 8th ed. Frwd. by Paul A. Wolkin. 897p. Date not set. pap. text ed. 50.00 o.p. (ISBN 0-8318-0166-2). Am Law Inst.

Partridges. G. E. Robbins. (Illus.). 144p. 1985. 22.00 o.p. (ISBN 0-85115-191-4, Pub. by Boydell & Brewer). Longwood Pub Group.

Parts of a Lifetime. Milovan Djilas. LC 75-1307. 442p. 1975. 15.00 o.s.i. (ISBN 0-15-170969-6). HarBraceJ.

Parts Unknown. Frances P. Keyes. 1976. pap. 1.50 o.p. (ISBN 0-380-00152-7, 20768). Avon.

Parturient Hypocalcemia. Ed. by J. J. Anderson. 1970. 66.00 o.p. (ISBN 0-12-058350-X). Acad Pr.

Party & Factional Division in Texas. James R. Soukup et al. 239p. 1964. 14.95x o.p. (ISBN 0-292-73323-2). U of Tex Pr.

Party & Political Opposition in Revolutionary America. Ed. by Patricia U. Bonomi. LC 80-13480. 176p. 1980. text ed. 17.50 o.s.i. (ISBN 0-912882-39-5). Sleepy Hollow.

Party at the Old Farm: A Halloween Story. Nancy W. Parker. LC 75-6754. (Illus.). 40p. (gr. 1-5). 1975. 5.95 o.p. (ISBN 0-689-50034-3, Atheneum). Macmillan.

Party Builder, Nos. 1-88. Socialist Workers Party Staff. 1970. Repr. of 1912 ed. lib. bdg. 130.00x o.p. (ISBN 0-8371-9243-9, PB00). Greenwood.

Party Politics in America. 5th ed. Frank J. Sorauf. 1984. text ed. write for info. o.p. (ISBN 0-673-39482-4). Scott F.

Party Time. Caroline Pitcher. (Make-It-Yourself Ser.). (Illus.). 32p. 1984. lib. bdg. 11.90 o.p. (ISBN 0-531-04814-4). Watts.

Pas a pas. Ed. by Jean Sareil & Jacqueline Sareil. (Illus.). 175p. (Orig., Fr.). 1975. pap. text ed. 7.95 o.p. (ISBN 0-15-568225-3, HC). HarBraceJ.

Pasadena: Crown of the Valley. Ann Scheid. LC 86-4023. (Illus.). 288p. 1986. 24.95 o.p. (ISBN 0-89781-163-1). Windsor Pubns Inc.

Pascal. James Richards. 1982. 24.30 o.p. (ISBN 0-12-587520-7); instr's. manual 13.50i o.p. (ISBN 0-12-587521-5). Acad Pr.

Pascal: A Considerate Approach. David Price. 198p. 1982. 17.95 o.p. (ISBN 0-13-652818-X); pap. 9.95 o.p. (ISBN 0-13-652800-7). P-H.

Pascal: An Introduction to the Art & Science of Programming. W. J. Savitch. 1984. 26.95 o.p. (ISBN 0-8053-8370-0). Benjamin-Cummings.

Pascal & the Mystical Tradition. Fletcher. 1954. (ISBN 0-8022-0513-5). Philos Lib.

Pascal for Beginners. Christopher Lampton. (Computer Literacy Skills Ser.). (Illus.). 96p. (gr. 7 up). 1984. lib. bdg. 11.90 o.p. (ISBN 0-531-04748-2). Watts.

Pascal for Electrical Engineers. Attikioyzel. 1984. pap. 20.95 o.p. (ISBN 0-442-30597-4). Van Nos Reinhold.

Pascal for Electronic Engineers. J. Attikiouzel. 160p. 1984. 24.95 o.p. (ISBN 0-442-30596-6). Van Nos Reinhold.

Pascal for Engineers. David T. Barnard & David B. Skillcorn. 1988. pap. text ed. write for info. o.p. (ISBN 0-697-06755-6). Instr's manual (ISBN 0-697-06988-5). Wm C Brown.

Pascal for FORTRAN Programmers. Robert Weiss & Charles Seiter. 1630p. 1984. 16.30 o.p. (ISBN 0-201-08296-9). Addison-Wesley.

Pascal for the IBM-PC: Turbo Pascal, PC-DOS Pascal, & UCSD p-System Pascal. rev. & expanded ed. Kevin W. Bowyer & Sherryl J. Tomboulian. (Illus.). 438p. 1984. pap. 19.95 o.p. (ISBN 0-89303-766-4). Brady Bks.

Pascal Handbook. Jacques Tiberghien. LC 80-53283. (Illus.). 485p. 1981. pap. 19.95 o.p. (ISBN 0-89588-053-9, P320). SYBEX.

Pascal: His Life & His Works. Jean Mesnard. 1953. (ISBN 0-8022-1105-4). Philos Lib.

Pascal Plus Data Structures, Algorithms, & Advanced Programming. Nell Dale & Susan C. Lilly. LC 84-82073. 490p. 1985. pap. text ed. 26.00 o.p. (ISBN 0-669-07239-7). Heath.

Pascal Primer. David Fox & Mitchell Waite. LC 80-53275. 208p. 1981. pap. 17.95 o.p. (ISBN 0-672-21793-7, 21793). Sams.

Pascal Programming Business, Management Science, & Social Science Applications. Irvine H. Forkner. 250p. 1984. pap. text ed. Brooks-Cole.

Pascal Programs for Business. Swan. 1983. 18.95 o.p. (ISBN 0-317-02343-8, 6270); disks & documentation 59.95 o.p. (7270). Sams.

Pascal Programs for Scientists & Engineers. Alan R. Miller. LC 81-51128. (Scientists & Engineers Ser.: No. 1). (Illus.). 374p. 1981. pap. 17.95 o.p. (ISBN 0-89588-058-X, P340). SYBEX.

Pascal with Style: Programming Proverbs. Henry F. Ledgard et al. 1979. pap. text ed. 10.50 o.p. (ISBN 0-8104-5124-7). Sams.

PASCAL 86 User's Guide for DOS Systems. Intel Staff. 382p. 1985. pap. 25.00 o.p. (ISBN 0-917017-71-4, 122426). Intel Corp.

Paschal Cycle. Paul Bosch. 1979. pap. 6.75 o.p. (ISBN 0-570-03796-4, 12-2778). Concordia.

Pasmore. David Storey. 1978. pap. 1.50 o.p. (ISBN 0-380-00276-0, 38547-3). Avon.

PASRO Pascal for Robots. C. Blume & W. Jakob. (Illus.). 145p. 1985. 31.00 o.p. (ISBN 0-387-15120-6). Springer-Verlag.

Pass It on. Larry Richards. LC 77-87260. (Bible Alive Ser.). (Illus.). 1978. pap. text ed. 2.95 o.p. (ISBN 0-89191-089-1); tchr's ed. 3.95 o.p. (ISBN 0-89191-090-5). Cook.

Pass Thy Hand for the Finishing Touch: The Homemaker's Guide to Refinishing & Restoring Antiques. Julia Spurlock. (Illus.). 1965. 6.00 o.p. (ISBN 0-682-43054-4, Banner). Exposition-Phoenix.

Passage Between Rivers: A Portfolio of Photographs with a History of the Delaware & Raritan Canal. Elizabeth G. Menzies. (Illus.). 1976. 12.50 o.p. (ISBN 0-8135-0831-2); pap. 9.95 o.p. (ISBN 0-8135-0832-0). Rutgers U Pr.

Passage East. Carleton Mitchell. (Illus.). 1977. 10.95 o.p. (ISBN 0-393-03208-6). Norton.

Passage fo Peshawar: Pakistan: Between the Hindu Kush & the Arabian Sea. Richard Reeves. 1985. pap. 7.95 o.p. (ISBN 0-671-60539-9, Touchstone Bks.). S&S.

Passage from Russia: A Personal History. Robert N. Maupin. 432p. 13.95 o.p. (ISBN 0-8062-2799-0). Carlton.

Passage Through Armageddon: The Russians in War & Revolution 1914-1918. W. Bruce Lincoln. 640p. 1986. 22.45 o.s.i. (ISBN 0-671-55709-2). S&S.

Passage Through El Dorado. Jonathan Kandell. 320p. (gr. 7 up). 1985. pap. 5.95 o.p. (ISBN 0-380-69959-1, Discus). Avon.

Passage Through the Red Sea. Zofia Romanowicz. Tr. by Virgilia Peterson. LC 62-19588. (Helen & Kurt Wolff Bks.). 1962. 3.75 o.p. (ISBN 0-15-170995-5). HarBraceJ.

Passage to Peshawar: Pakistan: Between the Hindu Kush & the Arabian Sea. Richard Reeves. (Illus.). 210p. 1984. 15.45 o.p. (ISBN 0-671-50842-3). S&S.

Passage West. Dallas Miller. 1980. pap. 2.75 o.p. (ISBN 0-380-50278-X, 50278-X). Avon.

Passages from Finnegans Wake: A Free Adaptation for the Theater. James Joyce. Ed. by Mary Manning. (Poets' Theatre Ser: No. 3). 1957. 9.95x o.s.i. (ISBN 0-674-65650-4). Harvard U Pr.

Passages from the Letter of John Butler Yeats. John B. Yeats. Ed. by Ezra Pound. 76p. 1971. Repr. of 1917 ed. 15.00x o.p. (ISBN 0-7165-1351-X, BBA 02087, Pub. by Cuala Press Ireland). Biblio Dist.

Passe-Muraille. Marcel Ayme. (Illus.). deluxe ed. 61.25 o.p. (ISBN 0-685-37183-2). SChoenhof.

Passenger. Thomas Keneally. LC 78-22258. 1979. 8.95 o.p. (ISBN 0-15-171282-4). HarBraceJ.

Passenger & Immigration Lists Bibliography, 1538-1900: Supplement. Ed. by P. William Filby. 125p. 1984. pap. 66.00x o.p. (ISBN 0-8103-1644-7). Gale.

Passenger Train Annual, 1987. Mike Schafer & Kevin McKinney. (PTJ Annuals). (Illus.). 80p. 1987. pap. 15.95 o.p. (ISBN 0-937658-12-X). Interurban.

Passenger Travel Demand Forecasting. (Transportation Research Record Ser.). 52p. 1976. 2.80 o.p. (ISBN 0-309-02585-0). Transport Res Bd.

Passenger Travel Forecasting. (Transportation Research Record Ser.). 89p. 1979. 5.00 o.p. (ISBN 0-309-02981-3). Transport Res Bd.

Passin' Through. Louis L'Amour. (General Ser.). 357p. 1986. lib. bdg. 14.95 o.p. (ISBN 0-8161-4067-7, Large Print Bks); pap. 10.95 o.p. (ISBN 0-8161-4068-5, Large Print Bks.). G K Hall.

Passing Age. A. Kukarkin. 1979. 10.00 o.p. (ISBN 0-8285-1860-2, Pub. by Progress Pubs USSR). Imported Pubns.

Passing the Love of Women: A Study of Gide's Saul & Its Biblical Roots. Anne L. Lerner. LC 80-5477. 148p. 1980. lib. bdg. 20.50 o.p. (ISBN 0-8191-1109-0); pap. text ed. 10.00 o.p. (ISBN 0-8191-1110-4). U Pr of Amer.

Passion. Peter Nichols. 106p. 1983. pap. 6.95 o.p. (NO. 3927). Routledge Chapman & Hall.

Passion According to Luke: The Special Material of Luke 22. Marion L. Soards. (JSOT Supplement Ser.: No. 14). 150p. pap. text ed. 11.95x o.s.i. (Pub. by JSOT Pr England). Eisenbrauns.

Passion & Affect. Laurie Colwin. 1976. pap. 1.50 o.p. (ISBN 0-380-00454-2, 27235). Avon.

Passion & Perfection. Norman W. Pittenger. 1985. pap. 2.00 o.p. (ISBN 0-88028-044-1). Forward Movement.

Passion & Rebellion: The Expressionist Heritage. Ed. by Stephen Bronner & Douglas Kellner. LC 81-40492. (Illus.). 468p. 1983. text ed. 35.00x o.p. Universe.

Passion & the Passion: Sex & Religion in Modern Literature. Francis L. Kunkel. LC 75-20085. 1975. softcover 4.95 o.s.i. (ISBN 0-664-24778-4, Westminster). Westminster John Knox.

Passion As Story: The Plot of Mark. John Blackwell. LC 85-16209. (Fortress Resources for Preaching Ser.). 96p. 1986. pap. 5.95 o.p. (ISBN 0-8006-1144-6, 1-1144, Fortress). Augsburg Fortress.

Passion for Friends: Toward a Philosophy of Female Affection. Janice G. Raymond. LC 85-47942. 320p. 1986. 22.95 o.p. (ISBN 0-8070-6724-5). Beacon Pr.

Passion for Identity: An Introduction to Canadian Studies. Eli Mandel & David Taras. 460p. 1987. pap. 15.95 o.p. (Pub. by Routledge UK). Routledge Chapman & Hall.

Passion for Jesus: A Passion for Justice. Esther B. Bruland & Stephen C. Mott. 176p. 1983. pap. 9.95 o.p. (ISBN 0-8170-0994-9). Judson.

Passion for Life: A Messianic Lifestyle. Jurgen Moltmann. Tr. & intro. by M. Douglas Meeks. LC 77-78636. 130p. 1978. 3.00 o.p. (ISBN 0-8006-0508-X, 1-508, Fortress). Augsburg Fortress.

Passion Fruit. Ed. by Jeannette Winterspoon. 232p. 1986. pap. 6.95 o.p. (ISBN 0-86358-070-X, 8070X). Routledge Chapman & Hall.

Passion Game. Nancy Geyer. 464p. 1987. pap. 3.95 o.p. (ISBN 0-380-70290-8). Avon.

Passion in China. Morris B. Blumberg. LC 85-91081. 1986. 15.00 o.p. (ISBN 0-682-40290-7). Exposition-Phoenix.

Passion in Mark: Studies on Mark 14-16. Ed. by Werner H. Kelber. LC 75-36453. 224p. 1976. 5.50 o.p. (ISBN 0-8006-0439-3, 1-439, Fortress). Augsburg Fortress.

Passion: New Poems, Nineteen Seventy-Seven to Nineteen Eighty. June Jordan. LC 80-66073. 120p. 1980. 13.95x o.p. (ISBN 0-8070-3218-2); pap. 8.95x o.p. (ISBN 0-8070-3219-0, BPA5, Pub. by Adriadne Bks). Beacon Pr.

Passion of Ayn Rand. Barbara Branden. LC 85-20704. (Illus.). 456p. 1986. 19.95 o.p. (ISBN 0-385-19171-5). Doubleday.

Passion of Loreen Bright Weasel. James Polk. 192p. 1981. 9.95 o.p. (ISBN 0-395-30351-6). HM.

Passion of New Eve. Angela Carter. LC 76-54629. 1977. 7.95 o.p. (ISBN 0-15-171285-9). HarBraceJ.

Passion Rose. Mallory Burgess. 400p. (Orig.). 1987. pap. 3.95 o.p. (ISBN 0-380-75169-0). Avon.

Passion Star. Rita Gallagher. (Orig.). 1987. pap. 3.95 o.p. (ISBN 0-440-18105-4). Dell.

Passion Stone. Harriette DeJarnette. 1980. pap. 2.75 o.p. (ISBN 0-8439-0840-8, Pub. by Leisure Bks CT). Dorchester Pub Co.

Passion to Know: Twenty Profiles in Science. Ed. by Allen L. Hammond. (Illus.). 240p. 1984. 15.95 o.p. (ISBN 0-684-18209-2, ScribT). Scribner.

Passionate Crusader: The Life of Marie Stopes. Ruth Hall. LC 77-73054. (Illus.). 1977. 14.95 o.p. (ISBN 0-15-171288-3). HarBraceJ.

Passionate Flower. Betsy McCarty. 352p. 1983. pap. 2.95 o.p. (ISBN 0-380-85167-9, 85167-9). Avon.

Passionate Stranger. Flora Kidd. 1986. pap. 10.95 o.p. (ISBN 0-8161-3999-7, Large Print Bks). G K Hall.

Passionate War: A Narrative History of the Spanish Civil War, 1936-1939. Peter Wyden. (Illus.). 500p. 1983. 19.25 o.p. (ISBN 0-671-25330-1). S&S.

Passions. Ellen White. 1985. pap. 6.00 o.p. (ISBN 0-914009-55-9). VHI Library.

Passions & Prejudices. Leo Rosten. LC 77-16562. 1978. text ed. 9.95 o.p. (ISBN 0-07-053984-7). McGraw.

Passion's Gold. Susan Sackett. 352p. (Orig.). 1987. pap. 3.95 o.p. (ISBN 0-380-75318-9). Avon.

Passion's Honor. (Avon Romance Ser.). 352p. 1987. pap. 3.95 o.p. (ISBN 0-380-75097-X). Avon.

Passions of Medora Graeme. Elsie Lee. LC 72-82172. 1972. 6.95 o.p. (ISBN 0-87795-047-4, Arbor Hse). Morrow.

Passions of the Heart. Donna DeLorean. 1985. 10.95 o.p. (ISBN 0-533-06642-5). Vantage.

Passion's Price. Donna K. Vitek. (Candlelight Ecstacy Ser.: No. 110). (Orig.). 1983. pap. 1.95 o.s.i. (ISBN 0-440-17036-2). Dell.

Passion's Promise see Danielle Steel.

Passions, Realms & Visions. Natari Shirani Kali. 1979. 4.00 o.p. (ISBN 0-682-49406-2). Exposition-Phoenix.

Passion's Torment. Victoria Pade. (Avon Romance Ser.). 432p. 1985. pap. 2.95 o.p. (ISBN 0-380-89681-8). Avon.

Passive & Low Energy Alternatives I: The First International PLEA Conference, Bermuda, September 13-15, 1982. Ed. by A. Bowen & R. Vagner. (Illus.). 475p. 1982. 120.00 o.p. (ISBN 0-08-029405-7). Pergamon.

Passive Smoking: A Bibliography. Susan M. Neumeister. (Public Administration Ser.: Bibliography P 1651). 32p. 1985. pap. 4.50 o.p. (ISBN 0-89028-341-9). Vance Biblios.

Passive Solar Architecture: 35 Outstanding Houses Across the United States. Wright & Andrejko. 1982. 32.95 o.p. (ISBN 0-442-23860-6). Van Nos Reinhold.

Passive Solar Construction Handbook. Emanuel Levy. 584p. 1981. pap. 18.00 o.p. (ISBN 0-318-11812-2, S/N 061-000-00525-1). USGPO.

Passive Solar Design Handbook. Compiled by Bruce Anderson. (Illus.). 752p. 1984. 62.95 o.s.i. (ISBN 0-442-20810-3). Van Nos Reinhold.

Passive Solar Design in Australia. Jack Greenland & Steve Szokolay. 101p. 1986. pap. 15.95 o.p. (ISBN 0-909724-64-4, Pub. by RAIA Australia). Intl Spec Bk.

Passive Solar Heating. J. Richard Williams. LC 82-72857. (Illus.). 304p. 1983. 39.95 o.p. (ISBN 0-250-40601-2). Butterworth.

Passive Solar Heating Design. Ralph M. Lebens. LC 80-40255. 234p. 1980. 64.95x o.p. (ISBN 0-470-26977-4). Halsted Pr.

Passive Solar Homes. (ISBN 0-396-08531-8). Dodd.

Passivity & Its Breakdown on Iron & Iron Base Alloys. LC 76-5317. (Illus.). 191p. 1976. 45.00 o.p. (ISBN 0-915567-73-3). Natl Corrosion Eng.

Passkey for Life Insurance Licensing. 1985. pap. 11.10 o.p. (ISBN 0-317-42417-3, 5306-02, Longman Fin Serv Pub). Longman Finan.

Passkey: Health Insurance. 100p. 1986. pap. text ed. 11.95 o.p. (ISBN 0-317-57620-8). Longman Finan.

Passkey: Life Insurance. rev. ed. 100p. 1986. pap. text ed. 11.95 o.p. (ISBN 0-88462-648-2). Longman Finan.

Passkey: Property-Casualty Insurance Licensing. rev. ed. 614p. 1986. pap. text ed. 27.95 o.p. (ISBN 0-317-57621-6, 5311-07). Longman Finan.

Passover. Howard Greenfeld. LC 77-13910. (Illus.). 32p. (gr. 7-9). 1978. 6.95 o.s.i. (ISBN 0-03-039921-1). H Holt & Co.

Passport South America. Arleta Richardson. (Illus.). 60p. (Orig.). (gr. 4-6). 1988. pap. 4.50 o.p. (ISBN 0-89367-130-4). Light & Life.

Passport to Europe's Small Hotels & Inns. Beverly Beyer. LC 82-24704. 253p. 1983. pap. 4.95 o.p. (ISBN 0-471-88960-1, Pub by Wiley Pr). Wiley.

Passport to Paradise. Bernard Finch. 192p. 1960. (ISBN 0-8022-0500-3). Philos Lib.

Passport to World Band Radio. Ed. by Lawrence Magne & Tony Jones. LC 87-22739. (Illus.). 400p. (Orig.). 1988. pap. 14.95 o.p. (ISBN 0-914941-15-1). IBS PA.

Passport's European Atlas for Travelers. (Illus.). 252p. vinyl binding 17.95 o.p. (ISBN 0-8442-9494-2, Passport Bks). Natl Textbk.

Password to Larkspur Lane. Carolyn Keene. (Nancy Drew Ser.: Vol. 10). (gr. 4-7). 1960. 4.50 o.p. (ISBN 0-448-09510-6, G&D); PLB 3.29 o.p. (ISBN 0-448-19510-0). Putnam Pub Group.

Password 'Victory' The 1941-1945 Great Patriotic War, 2 vols. V. Sevruk. 906p. 1985. 13.95 o.p. (ISBN 0-8285-3046-7, Pub. by Raduga Pubs USSR). Imported Pubns.

Past. Hugh Fleetwood. 199p. 1988. 19.95 o.p. (ISBN 0-241-11984-7, Pub. by Hamish Hamilton). David & Charles.

Past All Dishonour. James M. Cain. LC 84-71471. (Arbor House Library of Contemporary Americana). 128p. 1984. pap. 6.95 o.p. (ISBN 0-87795-651-0, Arbor Hse). Morrow.

Past & the Present. Lawrence Stone. 288p. 1981. 21.95x o.p. (ISBN 0-7100-0628-4). Routledge Chapman & Hall.

Past As Prologue: Present Perspectives. League of Women Voters Education Fund Staff. (Federalist Papers Reexamined: No. 1). 1976. pap. 1.00 o.p. (ISBN 0-89959-037-3, 622). LWV US.

Past Due: How to Collect Money. Norman King. 174p. 19.95x o.p. (ISBN 0-87196-140-7). Facts on File.

Past Has Another Pattern: Memoirs. George W. Ball. LC 81-18924. (Illus.). 510p. 1982. 19.95 o.p. (ISBN 0-393-01481-9). Norton.

Past Imperfect: An Autobiography. Joan Collins. LC 84-1263. 336p. 1984. 16.45 o.p. (ISBN 0-671-47360-3). S&S.

Past in Perspective. J. Burke et al. 1971. pap. text ed. 3.50x o.p. (ISBN 0-8290-1172-2). Irvington.

Past Is Human: Ancient Mysteries Explained. Peter White. LC 75-21680. (Illus.). 165p. 1976. 9.95 o.s.i. (ISBN 0-8008-6265-1); pap. 4.95 o.s.i. (ISBN 0-8008-6266-X). Taplinger.

Past Tense. Isobel Lambot. (Lythway Ser.). 216p. 1988. lib. bdg. 18.50 o.s.i. (ISBN 0-7451-0649-8, Pub. by Chivers Pr UK). G K Hall.

Past Through Tomorrow. Robert A. Heinlein. 832p. 1986. pap. 4.95 o.p. (ISBN 0-425-09350-6). Berkley Pub.

Past Years: Characteristics of the Population below the Poverty Level see Poverty in the United States 1985: 1985.

Pasta & Pizza. Bon Appetit Magazine Editors. LC 85-9829. (Cooking with Bon Appetit Ser.). (Illus.). 144p. 1985. 12.95 o.p. (ISBN 0-89535-167-6). Knapp Pr.

Pasta & Rice Italian Style. Efrem F. Calingaert & Jacquelyn D. Serwer. (Illus.). 256p. 1983. 16.95 o.p. (ISBN 0-684-17878-8, ScribT). Scribner.

Pasta Cookbook. San Giorgio Staff & Skinner Hersey Staff. (Illus.). 64p. (Orig.). 1983. pap. 3.95 o.p. (ISBN 0-8249-3019-3). Ideals.

Pasta! Cooking It, Loving It. Carlo Middione. Ed. by Richard Atcheson. LC 81-70442. (Great American Cooking Schools Ser.). (Illus.). 84p. 1982. pap. 5.95 o.p. (ISBN 0-941034-12-7). I Chalmers.

Pasta International. Gertrude Harris. LC 78-11295. (Illus.). 1978. pap. 7.95 o.p. (ISBN 0-89286-143-6, One Hund One Prods). Ortho.

Pasta, Please. Ed. by Annette Gohlke. LC 82-50005. 68p. 1982. pap. 3.95 o.s.i. (ISBN 0-89821-042-9). Reiman Assocs.

Pastel City. M. John Harrison. 1976. pap. 0.95 o.p. (ISBN 0-380-00057-1, 29637). Avon.

Pastels for Beginners. Ernest Savage. LC 79-56680. (Start to Paint Ser.). (Illus.). 1980. pap. 3.95 o.s.i. (ISBN 0-8008-6238-4, Pentalic). Taplinger.

Pasternak. Ed. by Donald Davie & Angela Livingstone. LC 75-127562. (Modern Judgement Ser). 1970. pap. text ed. 2.50 o.p. (ISBN 0-87695-096-9). Aurora Pubs.

Pastor & Parish: A Systems Approach. E. Mansell Pattison. Ed. by Howard J. Clinebell & Howard W. Stone. LC 76-62619. (Creative Pastoral Care & Counseling Ser.). 96p. 1977. pap. 0.50 o.p. (ISBN 0-8006-0559-4, 1-559, Fortress). Augsburg Fortress.

Pastor As Worship Leader: A Manual for Corporate Worship. Frank C. Senn. LC 77-72452. 1977. 4.95 o.p. (ISBN 0-8066-1593-1, 10-4871, Augsburg). Augsburg Fortress.

Pastor Goode & His Marvelous Micro. rev. ed. 1986. pap. 6.95 o.s.i. (ISBN 0-9615086-4-7). Church Bytes.

Pastor of the Range. R. J. Sherman. (Illus.). 224p. 1985. 13.00 o.p. (ISBN 0-682-40225-7). Exposition-Phoenix.

Pastor to the Outports: The Story of William & Emma McKirdy. Margaret M. Sherman. 1978. 9.00 o.p. (ISBN 0-682-49057-1). Exposition-Phoenix.

Pastora. Joanna Barnes. LC 77-79533. 1980. 12.95 o.p. (ISBN 0-87795-170-5, Arbor Hse). Morrow.

Pastora. Joanna Barnes. 768p. 1981. pap. 4.50 o.p. (ISBN 0-380-56184-0). Avon.

Pastoral Care: A Thematic Approach. Donald Capps. LC 78-15093. (Illus.). 162p. 1979. softcover 8.95 o.s.i. (ISBN 0-664-24222-7, Westminster). Westminster John Knox.

Pastoral Care & Hermeneutics. Donald Capps. LC 84-47909. (Theology & Pastoral Care Ser.). 128p. 1984. pap. 2.95 o.p. (ISBN 0-8006-1732-0, 1-1732, Fortress). Augsburg Fortress.

Pastoral Care & the Jewish Tradition: Empathic Process & Religious Counseling. Robert L. Katz. LC 84-47925. (Theology & Pastoral Care Ser.). 128p. 1984. pap. 2.95 o.p. (ISBN 0-8006-1731-2, 1-1731, Fortress). Augsburg Fortress.

Pastoral Care: Its Roots & Renewal. Herbert T. Mayer. LC 78-52444. 1978. 7.25 o.p. (ISBN 0-8042-1130-2, John Knox). Westminster John Knox.

Pastoral Care with Handicapped Persons. Lowell G. Colston. Ed. by Howard J. Clinebell & Howard W. Stone. LC 77-15229. (Creative Pastoral Care & Counseling Ser). 96p. (Orig.). 1978. pap. 4.50 o.p. (ISBN 0-8006-0560-8, 1-560, Fortress). Augsburg Fortress.

Pastoral Counseling. Wayne E. Oates. LC 73-19719. 1974. 8.50 o.s.i. (ISBN 0-664-20992-0, Westminster). Westminster John Knox.

Pastoral Counseling with People in Distress. Harold I. Haas. LC 77-99316. 1969. pap. 6.95 o.p. (ISBN 0-570-03794-8, 12-2776). Concordia.

Pastoral Counselor in Social Action. Speed Leas & Paul Kittlaus. Ed. by Howard J. Clinebell & Howard W. Stone. LC 80-8059. (Creative Pastoral Care & Counseling Ser.). 96p. (Orig.). 1981. pap. 4.50 o.p. (ISBN 0-8006-0565-9, 1-565, Fortress). Augsburg Fortress.

Pastoral Dreams. Anita Schorsch. LC 77-91892. pap. 5.95 o.p. (ISBN 0-87663-975-9, Pica Spec Stud). Universe.

Pastoral Epistles see Word Studies in the Greek New Testament, for the English Reader.

Pastoral Evangelism. Samuel Southard. LC 80-82196. 192p. 1981. pap. 4.50 o.s.i. (ISBN 0-8042-2037-9, John Knox). Westminster John Knox.

Pastoral Ministry of Church Officers. Charlie W. Shedd. LC 65-11504. 1965. pap. 4.95 o.p. (ISBN 0-8042-1788-2, John Knox). Westminster John Knox.

Pastoral Presence & the Diocesan Priest. Paul T. Keyes. LC 78-22009. 142p. 1978. pap. 4.95 o.p. (ISBN 0-89571-004-8). Affirmation.

Pastoral Psychology & the Gospel. W. H. Peacey. 1985. 10.00x o.p. (ISBN 0-317-62217-X, Guild of Pastoral Psych). State Mutual Bk.

Pastors & Masters. I. Compton-Burnett. 1952. 16.95 o.p. (ISBN 0-575-02705-3, Pub. by Gollancz England). David & Charles.

Pastors' Barracks. Robert Wise. 192p. 1986. pap. 11.95 o.p. (ISBN 0-89693-157-9). Victor Bks.

Pastor's Counseling Manual for Ministry to Those Who Must Sustain a Loved One in Crisis. Theodore W. Schroeder. 1981. pap. 2.75 o.p. (ISBN 0-570-08250-1, 12YY2922). Concordia.

Pastor's Handbook. C & MA Home Department Board Staff. 102p. 4.45 o.p. (ISBN 0-87509-118-0). Chr Pubns.

Pasture & Politics: Economics, Conflict & Ritual among Shahsevan Nomads of Northwestern Iran. Richard Tapper. (Studies in Anthropology). 1979. 68.00 o.p. (ISBN 0-12-683660-4). Acad Pr.

Pat Benatar: Get Nervous. Ed. by Milton Okun & Dan Fox. (Illus.). 79p. 1983. pap. 7.95 o.p. (ISBN 0-89524-179-X, 27610). Cherry Lane.

Pat Nixon: The Untold Story. Julie N. Eisenhower. 480p. 1986. 19.45 o.s.i. (ISBN 0-671-24424-8). S&S.

Pat Widmer's Cat Book: Straight Talk for City & Suburban Cat Owners. Patricia P. Widmer. (Illus.). 256p. 1983. 5.95 o.s.i. (ISBN 0-684-17297-6, ScribT); pap. 7.95 o.p. (ISBN 0-684-18041-3). Scribner.

Patagonia Revisited. Bruce Chatwin & Paul Theroux. 1986. 9.45 o.p. (ISBN 0-395-38401-X). HM.

Patch. C. H. Frick. LC 57-6559. (gr. 7 up). 1957. 5.25 o.p. (ISBN 0-15-259570-8, HJ). HarBraceJ.

Patch of Blue. Grace L. Hill. (Large Print Bks., Nightingale Ser.). 237p. 1987. pap. 10.95x o.p. (ISBN 0-8161-4261-0, Large Print Bks). G K Hall.

Patch of Earth. Lani Van Ryzin. LC 80-25969. (Illus.). 64p. (gr. 3-5). 1981. lib. bdg. 8.29 o.s.i. (ISBN 0-671-33092-6). Messner.

Patch of the Odin Soldier. Geoffrey Marsh. LC 86-24032. (Science Fiction Ser.). 192p. 1987. 12.95 o.s.i. (ISBN 0-385-15938-2). Doubleday.

Patch Testing. S. Fregert et al. LC 75-2387. (Illus.). 100p. 1976. pap. 18.00 o.p. (TAB ISBN 0-387-07229-2). Springer-Verlag.

Patch Unit. George G. Bailey. (Orig.). 1981. pap. 1.95 o.p. (ISBN 0-505-51624-1, Pub. by Tower Bks). Dorchester Pub Co.

Patchwork. Carolyn Banks. 272p. 1987. pap. 3.95 o.p. (ISBN 0-380-70306-8). Avon.

Patchwork Fish Tale. Stewart Moskowitz. LC 82-7959. (Illus.). 48p. (gr. k-3). 1982. lib. bdg. 8.29 o.s.i. (ISBN 0-671-45890-6). Messner.

Patchwork for Your Home. Ondori Publishing Company Staff. 126p. (Orig.). 1984. pap. 9.95 o.p. (ISBN 0-87040-585-3). Japan Pubns USA.

Patchwork from Mosaics. P-H.

Patchwork Quilt Design & Coloring Book. Judith L. Larsen & Carol W. Gull. Ed. by Evelyn Brannon. LC 76-52138. (Illus.). 1983. pap. 12.95 o.p. (ISBN 0-8329-0186-5). New Century.

Patchworking: A Quilt Design & Coloring Book. Judith LaBelle & Carol Waugh. LC 82-14470. (Illus.). 256p. (Orig.). 1983. pap. 13.95 o.p. (ISBN 0-8329-0250-0). New Century.

Patent Antitrust, 1984. (Patents, Copyrights, Trademarks & Literary Property Course Handbook Ser.: Vol. 177). 340p. 1984. 15.00 o.p. (ISBN 0-317-11432-8, G4-3743). PLI.

Patent Information & Documentation in Western Europe. 2nd, rev. & enl. ed. Ed. by H. Bank et al. 268p. 1981. lib. bdg. 34.00 o.p. (ISBN 3-598-10158-9). K G Saur.

Patent Interference: Law & Practice. Maurice H. Klitzman. 300p. 1984. 45.00 o.p. (ISBN 0-317-04076-6). PLI.

Patent It: A Do It Yourself Handbook. Hrand M. Muncheryan. (Illus.). 180p. (Orig.). 1982. 14.95 o.p. (ISBN 0-8306-2429-5, 1429); pap. 9.70 o.p. (ISBN 0-8306-1429-X). TAB Bks.

Patent It Yourself. David Pressman. Ed. by Stephen Elias. LC 85-63111. (Illus.). 421p. (Orig.). 1985. pap. 29.95 o.p. (ISBN 0-917316-94-0). Nolo Pr.

Patent Law, Cases & Materials Also Including Trade Secrets - Copyrights - Trademaks. 2nd ed. Robert A. Choate & William H. Francis. LC 80-27863. (American Casebook Ser.). 1110p. 1981. text ed. 32.95 o.p. (ISBN 0-8299-2124-9). West Pub.

Titles

Patent Law Handbook, 1986-87. Helene J. Pines. (Intellectual Property Library). 1986. 47.50 o.p. (ISBN 0-87632-525-8). Clark Boardman.

Patent Profiles: Robots. U. S. Department of Commerce, National Technical Information Service Staff. 157p. (Orig.). 1985. pap. 17.95 o.p. (ISBN 0-317-39384-7). Robot Inst Am.

Patents, Trademarks, Copyrights & Trade Secrets: Pennsylvania Legal Practice Course Materials. Pennsylvania Bar Institute Staff. 86p. 1985. 25.00 o.p. (ISBN 0-318-02157-9, PLP-85). PA Bar Inst.

Pater Sato-Portfolio. P. Sato. (Illus.). 104p. 1986. pap. 29.95 o.p. (ISBN 0-318-23207-3, Pub. by Genko Sha). Bks Nippan.

Pater Sato Portfolio. P. Sato. 104p. 29.95 o.p. (ISBN 4-7683-0002-2). Bks Nippan.

Paternity. Charlie Peters. 1981. pap. 2.25 o.p. (ISBN 0-380-78527-7, 78527-7). Avon.

Path Breaking. Date not set. (ISBN 0-8052-0322-2). Random.

Path of Love. Bhagwan Shree Rajneesh. Ed. by Ma Yoga Sudha. LC 83-181255. (Kabir Ser.). (Illus.). 350p. (Orig.). 1978. 9.95 o.p. (ISBN 0-88050-112-X); pap. 12.95 358p o.p. (ISBN 0-88050-612-1). Chidvilas Inc.

Path of Pregnancy. rev. ed. Bob Flaws. 113p. pap. 10.95 o.p. (ISBN 0-912111-01-1). Paradigm Pubns.

Path of the Righteous Gentile, Chain Clorfine: A Philosophical & Historical Presentation of the Doctrine of the Seven Laws of Noah. 142p. 1987. 10.95 o.p. (ISBN 0-87306-433-X). Feldheim.

Path of Transcendence. Bennett Penn. 144p. 1987. pap. text ed. 10.00 o.p. (ISBN 0-682-40332-6). Exposition-Phoenix.

Path to Pain Control. Meg Bogin. 288p. 1982. 12.95 o.p. (ISBN 0-395-31287-6). HM.

Path to Parnassus. Eduard C. Hargrave. 1979. 7.50 o.p. (ISBN 0-682-49381-3). Exposition-Phoenix.

Path to Wing Chun. rev. ed. Samuel Kwok. (Illus.). 96p. 1986. pap. text ed. 12.00 o.p. (ISBN 0-87364-367-4). Paladin Pr.

Pathfinders Guide to Understanding Computers. Ernie Philipp & Donald L. Day. 176p. 1984. pap. text ed. 14.95 o.p. (ISBN 0-8403-3297-1). Kendall Hunt.

Pathobiology of Cell Membranes, 2 vols, Vol. 1. Ed. by Benjamin F. Trump & A. U. Arstila. 1975. 82.50 o.p. (ISBN 0-12-701501-9). Acad Pr.

Pathobiology of Cell Membranes, Vol. 2. Ed. by Benjamin F. Trump & Antti U. Arstila. LC 74-27793. 1980. 71.50 o.p. (ISBN 0-12-701502-7). Acad Pr.

Pathobiology of Cell Membranes, Vol. 3. Ed. by Benjamin F. Trump & A. U. Arstila. 1983. 54.50 o.p. (ISBN 0-12-701503-5). Acad Pr.

Pathobiology of Development. E. V. Perrin & M. J. Feingold. LC 72-13417. 163p. 1974. 25.00 o.p. (Pub by Williams & Wilkins). Krieger.

Pathogenesis of Arteriosclerosis. Ed. by Robert W. Wissler & J. C. Geer. LC 78-187919. 315p. 1972. 25.00 o.p. (ISBN 0-683-09195-6, Pub. by W & W). Krieger.

Pathogenesis of Colorectal Cancer. Bosil C. Morson. LC 78-1792. (Major Problems in Pathology: Vol. 10). 1978. text ed. write for info. o.p. (ISBN 0-7216-6558-6). Saunders.

Pathogenesis of Cyathostome (Trichonema) Infections of the Horse: A Review. Ed. by C. P. Ogbourne. 25p. 1978. 11.45 o.p. (ISBN 0-85198-434-7). CAB Intl.

Pathogenesis of Hypertensive Encephalography. L. Auer. (Acta Neurochirurgica: Supplementum 27). (Illus.). 1979. pap. 44.90 o.p. (ISBN 0-387-81490-6). Springer-Verlag.

Pathogenesis of Infectious Disease. 2nd ed. Cedric A. Mims. 1982. 31.50 o.p. (ISBN 0-12-498254-9); pap. 15.50 o.p. (ISBN 0-12-498255-7). Acad Pr.

Pathologic Mechanisms & Human Disease. Roderick A. Cawson & Alexander W. McCracken. LC 81-16834. (Illus.). 594p. 1982. pap. text ed. 37.95 o.p. (ISBN 0-8016-0939-9). Mosby.

Pathology. C. H. Bloor. (Illus.). pap. text ed. write for info. o.p. (ISBN 0-443-08073-9). Churchill.

Pathology & Surgery of the Veins of the Lower Limb. Harold Dodd & Frank B. Cockett. LC 75-599. (Illus.). 1976. text ed. 74.00 o.p. (ISBN 0-443-01292-X). Churchill.

Pathology Annual, 1982, Vol. 17, Pt. 2. Sheldon C. Sommers & Paul P. Rosen. 416p. 1983. 45.00 o.p. (ISBN 0-8385-7767-9). Appleton & Lange.

Pathology Annual, 1982, Vol. 17, Pt. 1. Shedlon C. Sommers & Paul Peter Rosen. 432p. 1982. text ed. 42.50x o.p. (ISBN 0-8385-7765-2). Appleton & Lange.

Pathology Annual, 1985, Vol. 20, Pt. 2. Ed. by Sheldon C. Sommers et al. (Pathology Ser.). 544p. 1985. 61.50 o.p. (ISBN 0-8385-7771-7). Appleton & Lange.

Pathology of Cerebral Microcirculation: Proceedings. International Symposium, Berlin, Sep, 1973. Ed. by J. Cervos-Navarro et al. LC 73-90619. 1974. pap. 88.00 o.p. (ISBN 3-11-004472-2). De Gruyter.

Pathology of Domestic Animals, 2 Vols. 2nd ed. K. V. Jubb & P. C. Kennedy. Vol. 1 1970. 59.50 o.p. (ISBN 0-12-391501-5); Vol. 2 1971. 59.50 o.p. (ISBN 0-12-391502-3). Acad Pr.

Pathology of Laboratory Animals, 2 vols. Ed. by K. Benirschke et al. (Illus.). 1978. Set. 450.00 o.p. (ISBN 0-387-90292-9). Springer-Verlag.

Pathology of Soft Tissue Tumors. Steven I. Hajdu. LC 79-21735. (Illus.). 599p. 1979. text ed. 65.00 o.p. (ISBN 0-8121-0693-8). Lea & Febiger.

Pathology of the Colon, Small Intestine, & Anus. Ed. by H. Thomas Norris. (Contemporary Issues in Surgical Pathology Ser.: Vol. 2). (Illus.). 338p. 1983. text ed. 55.00 o.p. (ISBN 0-443-08235-9). Churchill.

Pathology of the Placenta. Harold Fox. (Major Problems in Pathology Ser.: Vol. 7). (Illus.). 491p. 1978. (ISBN 0-7216-3831-7). Saunders.

Pathology of Transcription & Translation. Ed. by E. Farber. (Biochemistry of Disease Ser: Vol. 2). 192p. 1972. 49.75 o.p. (ISBN 0-8247-1180-7). Dekker.

Pathology: PreTest Self-Assessment & Review. 4th ed. Ed. by Paul H. Duray. (Illus.). 216p. 1986. 14.95 o.p. (ISBN 0-07-051944-7). McGraw-Pretest.

Pathology: PreTest Self-Assessment & Review. 3rd ed. Pretest Service Inc. Ed. by Paul Duray. (Basic Science Ser.). (Illus.). 216p. 1982. text ed. 12.95x o.p. (ISBN 0-07-051934-X). McGraw.

Pathology Specialty Board Review. 4th ed. Ed. by Myron E. Tracht & Majid Ali. 1976. spiral bdg. 34.25 o.p. (ISBN 0-87488-305-9). Med Exam.

Pathophysiology: Adaptations & Alterations in Function. Ed. by Barbara Bullock et al. 1984. text ed. write for info. o.p. (ISBN 0-673-39386-0). Scott F.

Pathophysiology: An Introduction to Mechanisms of Disease. Bernice L. Muir. LC 79-27791. 612p. 1980. 28.95 o.p. (ISBN 0-471-03202-6). Wiley.

Pathophysiology in Small Animal Surgery. Ed. by M. Joseph Bojrab. LC 80-25780. (Illus.). 906p. 1981. text ed. 75.00 o.p. (ISBN 0-8121-0696-2). Lea & Febiger.

Pathophysiology of Blood. Ed. by Archie A. Mackinney, Jr. LC 83-26040. (Series in Pathophysiology: Nos. 1-411). 363p. (Orig.). 1984. pap. 25.00 o.p. (ISBN 0-471-08245-7, Pub by Wiley Med). Wiley.

Pathophysiology of Human Immunologic Disorders. Jeremiah J. Twomey. LC 82-8675. (Illus.). 281p. 1982. 42.50 o.p. (ISBN 0-8067-1921-4). Urban & S.

Pathophysiology of Muscle Tone. M. Wiesendanger. LC 72-189294. (Neurology Series: Vol. 9). (Illus.). 52p. 1972. 20.10 o.p. (ISBN 0-387-05761-7). Springer-Verlag.

Pathophysiology of Renal. Avery R. Harrington & Stephen W. Zimmerman. LC 81-7454. (Pathophysiology Ser.). 258p. 1982. 19.50 o.p. (ISBN 0-471-07815-8). Wiley.

Pathophysiology of Renal Disease. Burton D. Rose. (Illus.). 1981. text ed. 34.00 o.p. (ISBN 0-07-053616-3); pap. text ed. 24.95 o.p. (ISBN 0-07-053615-5). McGraw.

Pathophysiology of Respiration. Meir H. Kryger. LC 81-2113. (Pathophysiology Ser.). 352p. 1981. pap. text ed. 19.95 o.p. (ISBN 0-471-05923-4). Wiley.

Paths in Dreams: Selected Prose of Ho Chi-Fang. Ho Chi-Fang. Tr. by Bonnie McDougall from Chinese. (Asian & Pacific Writing). 1977. 22.50x o.p. (ISBN 0-7022-1260-1); pap. 8.95x o.p. (ISBN 0-7022-1261-X). U of Queensland Pr.

Paths into American Culture: Psychology, Medicine, & Morals. John C. Burnham. 384p. 1988. 37.95 o.p. (ISBN 0-87722-505-2). Temple U Pr.

Paths of Development in Capitalist Agriculture. Ed. by A. Hussain & K. Tribe. 240p. 1984. text ed. 38.50x o.p. (ISBN 0-333-26839-3, Pub. by Macmillan UK). Humanities.

Paths to Power: Elite Mobility in Contemporary China. David M. Lampton. (Michigan Monographs in Chinese Studies Ser.: No. 55). (Illus.). 379p. (Orig.). 1986. text ed. 17.50 o.s.i. (ISBN 0-89264-063-4); pap. text ed. 10.00 o.s.i. (ISBN 0-89264-064-2). U of Mich Ctr Chinese.

Paths to the Present. 2nd ed. Fred R. Mabbutt. 1987. write for info. o.p. (ISBN 0-89874-886-0). Krieger.

Paths to the Present: Thoughts on the Contemporary Relevance of America's Past. Thomas J. Osborne & Fred R. Mabbutt. LC 84-29748. 182p. 1985. Repr. of 1974 ed. lib. bdg. 13.50 o.p. (ISBN 0-89874-842-9). Krieger.

Paths to Writing: Developing Prose Power. Don A. Edwards. 1976. text ed. 12.50 o.p. (ISBN 0-682-48343-5, University). Exposition-Phoenix.

Pathway to the Bible. Samuel Umen & Mark Strickland. LC 63-19258. 284p. 1963. (ISBN 0-8022-1751-6). Philos Lib.

Pathways. Compiled by Jo Petty. 1983. 7.95 o.s.i. (ISBN 0-8378-1709-9). Gibson.

Pathways of Life: Poems by Phyllis Morton. Phyllis Morton. (Illus.). 64p. 1984. 5.50 o.p. (ISBN 0-682-40173-0). Exposition-Phoenix.

Pathways of the Pulp. 3rd ed. Stephen Cohen & Richard C. Burns. (Illus.). 896p. 1983. text ed. 57.95 cloth o.p. (ISBN 0-8016-1128-8). Mosby.

Pathways to the Gods: The Mystery of the Andes Lines. Tony Morrison. (Illus.). 256p. 1983. pap. 7.95 o.p. (Pub. by Granada England). Academy Chi Pubs.

Patience & Fortitude: Fiorello la Guardia. William Manners. (Illus.). 320p. 1976. 12.95 o.p. (ISBN 0-15-171290-5). HarBraceJ.

Patient & Family Education: Tools, Techniques & Theory. Rose-Marie McCormick & Tamar J. Parkavich. LC 79-10014. 372p. 1979. pap. 27.50 o.p. (ISBN 0-471-04269-2). Wiley.

Patient Assessment in Psychiatric Nursing. Philip J. Barker. 368p. 1985. pap. 18.95 o.p. (ISBN 0-7099-3254-5, Pub. by Croom Helm Ltd). Routledge Chapman & Hall.

Patient Care Audit Criteria: Standards for Hospital Quality Assurance. Jean G. Carroll. LC 82-73622. 250p. 1983. 55.00 o.p. (ISBN 0-87094-392-8). Dow Jones-Irwin.

Patient Care Flow Chart Manual. 3rd ed. Patient Care Magazine Editors. 608p. 1982. casebound 49.95 o.p. (ISBN 0-87489-295-3). Med Economics.

Patient Care in Cardiac Surgery. 3rd ed. Douglas M. Behrendt & W. Gerald Austen. (Little, Brown SPIRAL TM Manual Ser.). 1980. pap. 16.95 o.p. (ISBN 0-316-08756-4). Little.

Patient Care in Radiography. 2nd ed. Ruth A. Ehrlich & Ellen M. Givens. (Illus.). 190p. 1984. pap. text ed. 26.95 o.p. (ISBN 0-8016-1561-5). Mosby.

Patient Care Services Policy Manual for the Nursing Department. Leone Douville. LC 73-88318. (Illus.). 1974. pap. 8.00 o.p. (ISBN 0-87125-011-X). Cath Health.

Patient Care Standards. 3rd ed. Susan M. Tucker et al. (Illus.). 736p. 1983. pap. text ed. 28.95 o.p. (ISBN 0-8016-5143-3). Mosby.

Patient-Centered Care Manual for the Nursing Department. St. Joseph Hospital Staff. LC 77-71736. 1977. pap. 13.00 o.p. (ISBN 0-87125-041-1). Cath Health.

Patient Contact & Public Relations see Doctors' Administrative Program.

Patient Lifting Devices in Hospitals. Frank Bell. 236p. 1984. 25.00 o.p. (ISBN 0-7099-3229-4, Pub. by Croom Helm Ltd). Routledge Chapman & Hall.

Patient Patients: Women & Their Doctors. Helen Roberts. 200p. (Orig.). 1985. pap. 8.95 o.p. (ISBN 0-86358-019-X). Routledge Chapman & Hall.

Patient Records Control, Vol 6. A. Ziegler. (Illus.). 1979. pap. 21.95 o.p. (ISBN 0-87489-155-8). Med Economics.

Patients. Toynbee. 1977. 8.95 o.p. (ISBN 0-15-171295-6). HarBraceJ.

Patient's Guide to Surgery. Laurence Galton. 1977. pap. 2.50 o.p. (ISBN 0-380-00683-9, 32987). Avon.

Patient's Revenge. Ed. by Steven Heller & Seymour Chwast. (Illus.). 64p. 1983. pap. 4.80 o.p. (ISBN 0-671-49402-3, Fireside). S&S.

Patient's Rights & Professional Practice. James T. Ziegenfuss, Jr. 256p. 1983. 26.95 o.p. (ISBN 0-442-29434-4). Van Nos Reinhold.

Patient's Rights: Ethical & Legal Issues in Health Case & Nursing. J. Storch. 288p. 1982. text ed. 14.95 o.p. (ISBN 0-07-548477-3). McGraw.

Patients: The Experience of Illness. Mark L. Rosenberg. LC 79-67115. (Illus.). 208p. (Orig.). 1980. 14.95 o.s.i. (ISBN 0-03-056743-2); pap. 8.95 o.s.i. (ISBN 0-03-056742-4). H Holt & Co.

Patio Roofs: How to Build. 3rd ed. Sunset Magazine & Books Editors. LC 73-89579. (Illus.). 80p. 1974. pap. 4.95 o.p. (ISBN 0-376-01455-5, Sunset Bks.). Sunset-Lane.

Patriarcha & Other Political Works of Sir Robert Filmer. Robert Filmer. LC 83-48568. (Philosophy of John Locke Ser.). 326p. 1985. lib. bdg. 40.00 o.p. (ISBN 0-8240-5604-3). Garland Pub.

Patriarchs & Politics. Marilyn Warenski. (Illus.). 1978. text ed. 10.95 o.p. (ISBN 0-07-068270-4). McGraw.

Patriarchs & Prophets. Stanley B. Frost. 232p. 1963. 20.00 o.p. (ISBN 0-7735-0010-3, Pub. by McGill Canada). U of Toronto Pr.

Patriarch's Wife: Literary Evidence & the History of the Family. Margaret J. Ezell. 284p. Date not set. 24.95 o.p. U of NC Pr.

Patricide in the House Divided: A Psychological Interpretation of Lincoln & His Age. George B. Forgie. 1979. 14.95x o.p. (ISBN 0-393-05695-3). Norton.

Patrick. Keith Hetherington. 1980. pap. 1.95 o.p. (ISBN 0-380-48363-7, 48363). Avon.

Patrick & the Fairy Thief. Margaret K. Wetterer. LC 79-22576. (Illus.). 32p. (gr. 1-4). 1980. 7.95 o.p. (ISBN 0-689-50160-9, Atheneum). Macmillan.

Patrick Campbell's Travels. Patrick Campbell. LC 78-50738. (Illus.). 96p. 1978. 12.50x o.p. (ISBN 0-8139-0858-2). U Pr of Va.

Patrick Caulfield. Tate Gallery, London Staff & Walker Art Gallery Staff. (Illus.). 88p. 1982. pap. 35.99 o.p. (ISBN 0-8120-2579-2). Barron.

Patrick Duncan. C. J. Driver. text ed. 25.00x o.p. (ISBN 0-435-96200-0). Heinemann Ed.

Patrick Henry, Patriot. Teri Martini. LC 78-148106. (Illus.). (gr. 3-6). 1972. 4.95 o.s.i. (ISBN 0-664-32507-6, Westminster). Westminster John Knox.

Patrick Kavanagh: Complete Poems. Ed. by Peter Kavanagh. 1972. 34.50x o.p. (ISBN 0-904984-79-6); pap. 18.00 o.p. Natl Poet Foun.

Patrick Pearse: The Triumph of Failure. Ruth D. Edwards. LC 78-58294. (Illus.). 1978. 14.95 o.s.i. (ISBN 0-8008-6267-8). Taplinger.

Patrick: Sixteen Centuries with Ireland's Patron Saint. Ed. by Alice B. Proudfoot. (Illus.). 160p. 1983. 19.95 o.p. (ISBN 0-02-599280-5). Macmillan.

Patrick White. John Colmer. (Contemporary Writers Ser.). 96p. 1984. pap. 5.95 o.p. (ISBN 0-416-36790-9, NO. 4066). Routledge Chapman & Hall.

Patrick's Problem. Kees Moerbeek. (Did It Happen? Bks.). Date not set. 4.95 o.p. (ISBN 0-317-62068-1). Price Stern.

Patrimony. Elsie L. Hartung. 160p. 1987. 9.95 o.p. (ISBN 0-8062-2878-4). Carlton.

Patriot Games. Tom Clancy. (Large Print Bks.). 800p. 1988. lib. bdg. 21.95x o.s.i. (ISBN 0-8161-4382-X, Large Print Bks); pap. 13.95x o.s.i. (ISBN 0-8161-4383-8, Large Print Bks). G K Hall.

Patriot or Traitor: The Case of General Mihailovich. Intro. by David Martin. (Serbian Special Project Ser.: No. 29). 507p. (Serbian.). 1981. pap. 12.50x o.p. (ISBN 0-8179-4292-0). Hoover Inst Pr.

Patriotic Announcements & Letterheads. (Easy-to-Make Photocopier Bks.). (Orig.). 1984. pap. 14.95 o.p. (ISBN 0-87280-025-3, Asher-Gallant). Caddylak Systs.

Patriots: The American Revolution, Generation of Genius. Ed. by Virginius Dabney. 1975. 14.95 o.p. (ISBN 0-689-10690-4, Atheneum). Macmillan.

Patron & the Panca. Bengt-Erik Borgstrom. 184p. 1980. text ed. 17.50x o.p. (ISBN 0-7069-0997-6, Pub. by Vikas India). Advent NY.

Patronage. Maria Edgeworth. (Mothers of the Novel Reprints Ser.). 592p. 1986. pap. 8.95 o.p. (ISBN 0-86358-106-4, 81064). Routledge Chapman & Hall.

Patrons & Patriotism: The Encouragement of the Fine Arts in the United States, 1790-1860. Lillian B. Miller. LC 66-13880. (Illus.). 352p. 1974. pap. text ed. 5.75x o.s.i. (ISBN 0-226-52773-5, P611, Phoen). U of Chicago Pr.

Pat's Pointers: The Needlepoint Handbook. Pat Trexler. 200p. 1983. 15.00 o.p. (ISBN 0-8362-2500-7); pap. 8.95 o.p. (ISBN 0-8362-2502-3). Andrews & McMeel.

Patsy Cline. Ellis Nassour. (Orig.). 1981. pap. 2.95 o.p. (ISBN 0-505-51679-9, Pub. by Tower Bks). Dorchester Pub Co.

Patten's Elements of Embryology. Clark E. Corliss. (Illus.). 1976. text ed. 30.00 o.p. (ISBN 0-07-013150-3). McGraw.

Pattern & Operators: The Foundation of Data Representation. J. Simon. 256p. 1986. text ed. 39.95 o.p. (ISBN 0-07-057533-9). McGraw.

Pattern Crimes. William Bayer. 1987. 17.45 o.s.i. (ISBN 0-394-55876-6, Pub. by Villard Bks). Random.

Pattern Design. Lewis F. Day. LC 78-21373. (Illus.). 1979. 14.95 o.s.i. (ISBN 0-8008-6268-6, Pentalic); pap. 9.95 o.s.i. (ISBN 0-8008-6270-8, Pentalic). Taplinger.

Pattern Designing & Adaptation for Beginners. Pamela Lee & Rozanne Hawksley. (Illus.). 240p. 1981. text ed. 21.95 o.p. (ISBN 0-246-11235-2, Granada England). Gower Pub Co.

Pattern Drills for Introductory Russian. Robert D. Sholiton & Joseph A. Van Campen. 1968. pap. 3.95x o.p. (ISBN 0-393-09772-2, NortonC). Norton.

Pattern for Failure: Socialist Economies in Crisis. Sven Rydenfelt. LC 84-12909. 352p. 1985. 22.95 o.p. (ISBN 0-15-171333-2). HarBraceJ.

Pattern for Profit in Southern Africa. Ian Mackler. LC 74-17614. 1975. pap. text ed. 2.95x o.p. (ISBN 0-689-70525-5, 215, Atheneum). Macmillan.

Pattern Formation by Dynamic Systems & Pattern Recognition. Ed. by H. Haken. (Springer Series in Synergetics). (Illus.). 305p. 1979. 42.00 o.p. (ISBN 0-387-09770-8). Springer-Verlag.

Pattern in Islamic Art. David Wade. LC 75-33464. (Illus.). 144p. 1976. 27.95 o.s.i. (ISBN 0-87951-042-0). Overlook Pr.

Pattern Models. Narendra Ahuja & Bruce J. Schachter. LC 82-11070. 309p. 1983. 45.95 o.p. (ISBN 0-471-86194-4, Pub. by Wiley-Interscience). Wiley.

Pattern of a Dependent Economy: The National Income of British Honduras. N. S. Carey Jones. LC 77-157955. (Illus.). 162p. Repr. of 1953 ed. lib. bdg. 35.00x o.p. (ISBN 0-8371-6178-9, CADE). Greenwood.

Pattern of Animal Communities. C. S. Elton. 1966. pap. 19.95 o.p. (ISBN 0-412-21880-1, NO. 6579, Pub. by Chapman & Hall). Routledge Chapman & Hall.

Pattern of Sound in Lucretius. Rosamund E. Deutsch. Ed. by Steele Commager. LC 77-70763. (Latin Poetry Ser.). 1979. Repr. of 1939 ed. lib. bdg. 25.00 o.p. (ISBN 0-8240-2967-4). Garland Pub.

Pattern of Tragicomedy in Bernard Shaw. C. D. Sidhu. (English Language & Literature Ser.: No. 5). 239p. 1979. text ed. 15.00x o.p. (ISBN 0-391-02544-9). Humanities.

Pattern Recognition & Artificial Intelligence: Proceedings of a Joint Workshop held at Hyannis, Mass., June 1976. Ed. by C. H. Chen. 1976. 79.50 o.p. (ISBN 0-12-170950-7). Acad Pr.

Pattern Recognition in Biological & Technical Systems: Proceedings-Deutsche Gesellschaft Fuer Kybernetik, 4th Congress, Berlin, 1970. Ed. by O. J. Gruesser & R. Klinke. LC 78-152359. (Illus.). 1971. 58.50 o.p. (ISBN 0-387-05385-9). Springer-Verlag.

Pattern Recognition in Chemistry. K. Varmuza. (Lecture Notes in Chemistry Ser.: Vol. 21). (Illus.). 217p. 1980. pap. 25.00 o.p. (ISBN 0-387-10273-6). Springer-Verlag.

Patternmaking & Founding. Robert E. Smith. (gr. 9 up). 1959. pap. 6.36 o.p. (ISBN 0-87345-020-5). Glencoe.

Patternmaster. Octavia E. Butler. 1979. pap. 1.75 o.p. (ISBN 0-380-41806-1, 41806-1). Avon.

Patterns & Systems of Elementary Mathematics. Jonathan Knaupp et al. LC 76-13087. (Illus.). 1977. text ed. 21.95 o.p. (ISBN 0-395-20638-3). HM.

Patterns for Better Living, Vol. 6. U-Bild Enterprises Staff. 112p. 1985. pap. 2.95 o.p. (ISBN 0-910495-03-3). U-Bild.

Patterns for Canvas Embroidery. Diana Jones. (Illus.). 96p. 1985. pap. 12.95 o.s.i. (ISBN 0-7134-4014-7, Pub. by Batsford England). David & Charles.

Patterns for Educational Growth. Theodore M. Hesburgh. 1958. 8.95x o.p. (ISBN 0-268-00202-9). U of Notre Dame Pr.

Patterns for Power. D. Stuart Briscoe. LC 78-68850. (Bible Commentary for Laymen Ser.). 160p. 1979. pap. 3.95 o.s.i. (ISBN 0-8307-0701-8, S331101). Regal.

Patterns for Practical Communications: Combined Sentence & Composition Packages. Doris C. Weddington. 1976. 40 wkbks., 20 cassettes, 2 scripts, 2 tchrs' manuals 450.00 o.p. (ISBN 0-13-653899-1). P-H.

Patterns in Action. Robert Schwegler. 1985. pap. text ed. (ISBN 0-673-39237-6). Scott F.

Patterns in Clause, Sentence & Discourse in Selected Languages in India & Nepal, 4 vols. Ed. by Ronald Trail. (Publications in Linguistics: No. 41). Set. pap. 35.00, microfiche (16) 32.00x 0-88312-447-5 o.p. (ISBN 0-88312-047-X); Pt. 1. pap. 9.00x o.p. (ISBN 0-88312-048-8); Pt. 2. pap. 10.00x o.p. (ISBN 0-88312-049-6); Pt. 3. pap. 9.50x o.p. (ISBN 0-88312-050-X); Pt. 4. pap. 4.73 Pt. 1 microfiche (4) 0-88312-448-3, 5.72 Pt. 2 microfiche (5) 0-88312-449-1, 4.73 Pt. 3 microfiche (4) 0-88312-450-5 3.80 Pt. 4 microfiche (3) 0-88312-487-4 o.p. (ISBN 0-88312-051-8). Summer Inst Ling.

Patterns in Mathematics. Ellery B. Golos. LC 80-25883. 456p. 1981. text ed. write for info. o.p. (ISBN 0-87150-301-8, Prindle). PWS-Kent Pub.

Patterns in Nature. Peter S. Stevens. LC 73-19720. (Illus.). 256p. 1974. 19.45 o.p. (ISBN 0-316-81328-1, Pub. by Atlantic Monthly Pr); pap. 12.45 o.p. (ISBN 0-316-81331-1). Little.

Patterns of Acute Head Injury. R. Hooper. 175p. 1969. 15.00 o.p. (ISBN 0-683-04134-7, Pub. by Williams & Wilkins). Krieger.

Patterns of Care for the Mentally Subnormal. M. Craft & L. Miles. 1967. 29.00 o.p. (ISBN 0-08-012265-5); pap. 35.00 o.p. (ISBN 0-08-012264-7). Pergamon.

Patterns of Change in Earth Evolution: Report of the Dahlem Workshop on Patterns of Change in Earth Evolution, Berlin, 1983, May 1-6. Ed. by S. Bernhard. (Dahlem Workshop Reports, Physical, Chemical, & Earth Sciences Research Report: Vol. 5). (Illus.). 450p. 1984. 26.00 o.p. (ISBN 0-387-12749-6). Springer-Verlag.

Patterns of Control in Post-Industrial Society: Magnificent Myth. A. Wiener. 1978. 58.00 o.p. (ISBN 0-08-021474-6); pap. 22.00 o.p. (ISBN 0-08-023100-4). Pergamon.

Patterns of Discovery in the Social Sciences. Paul R. Diesing. LC 72-106978. 360p. 1971. 36.95x o.p. (ISBN 0-202-30101-X). Aldine de Gruyter.

Patterns of Evolution: As Illustrated by the Fossil Record. Ed. by A. Hallam. (Developments in Paleontology & Stratigraphy Ser.: Vol. 5). 592p. 1977. 129.00 o.p. (ISBN 0-444-41495-9). Elsevier.

Patterns of Faith: A Study in the Relationship Between the New Testament & Christian Doctrine. J. L. Houlden. LC 76-55829. (Orig.). 1977. pap. 3.25 o.p. (ISBN 0-8006-0493-8, Fortress). Augsburg Fortress.

Patterns of Financing Local Government Services. (Legislative Finance Papers Ser.). 23p. 1984. 6.25 o.s.i. (ISBN 1-55516-044-1). Natl Conf State Legis.

Patterns of French. 3rd ed. Rodney K. Ketcham. (Illus.). 340p. (Orig., Fr.). 1975. pap. text ed. 10.95 o.p. (ISBN 0-15-568714-X, HC); tapes, 7 reels 75.00 o.p. (ISBN 0-685-53407-3). HarBraceJ.

Patterns of Grace: Human Experience As Word of God. Tom F. Driver. 214p. 1985. pap. text ed. 10.25 o.p. (ISBN 0-8191-4637-4). U Pr of Amer.

Patterns of Kingship & Authority in Traditional Asia. Ed. by Ian W. Mabbett. LC 84-45701. 202p. 1985. 26.00 o.p. (ISBN 0-7099-3509-9, Pub. by Croom Helm Ltd). Routledge Chapman & Hall.

Patterns of Local Community Leadership. Linton C. Freeman. LC 68-23259. 1968. pap. text ed. 3.95x o.p. (ISBN 0-672-60838-3). Irvington.

Patterns of Metropolitan Area & County Population Growth: 1980-1984. Donald E. Starsinic. (Current Population Reports Series P-25, Population Estimates & Projections: No. 976). (Illus.). 69p. (Orig.). 1985. pap. 2.75 o.p. (ISBN 0-318-20391-X, S/N 003-001-91473-5). USGPO.

Patterns of Personality Judgement. Rudolf Cohen. Tr. by Dirk L. Schaeffer. 1973. 69.50 o.p. (ISBN 0-12-178950-0). Acad Pr.

Patterns of Primary Production in the Biosphere. Ed. by Helmut F. Lieth. LC 78-18691. (Benchmark Papers in Ecology: Vol. 8). 342p. 1982. 51.95 o.p. (ISBN 0-87933-327-8). Van Nos Reinhold.

Patterns of Race in the Americas. Marvin Harris. 144p. 1974. pap. 4.95 o.p. (ISBN 0-393-00727-8, Norton Lib). Norton.

Patterns of Reproduction of Four Species of Vespertiliohia Bats in Paraguay. Philip Myers. (UC Publications in Zoology: Vol. 107). 1977. pap. 19.00x o.p. (ISBN 0-520-09554-5). U of Cal Pr.

Patterns of Spoken English: An Introduction to English Phonetics. G. Knowles. (Illus.). 262p. 1987. pap. text ed. 13.95 o.p. (ISBN 0-582-29132-1). Longman.

Patterns on the Earth. 4th ed. Rhoads Murphey. 1981. text ed. 31.50 o.p. (ISBN 0-395-30827-5). HM.

Patton's Tanks. Steven J. Zaloga. (Tanks Illustrated Ser.: Vol. 11). (Illus.). 1984. pap. 9.95 o.p. (ISBN 0-85368-671-8, Arms & Armour Pr). Sterling.

Patty Cannon Administers Justice. R. W. Messenger. LC 60-15801. 320p. 1960. pap. 5.00 o.p. (ISBN 0-87033-079-9). Tidewater.

Paul. Martin Dibelius. Ed. by W. G. Kuemmel. 1953. 4.95 o.s.i. (ISBN 0-664-20093-1, Westminster). Westminster John Knox.

Paul: A Son's Torment, a Mother's Anguish. Bertha Plitt. (Illus.). 136p. 1985. 10.00 o.p. (ISBN 0-682-40230-3). Exposition-Phoenix.

Paul & His Letters. Leander E. Keck. Ed. by Gerhard Krodel. LC 78-54554. (Proclamation Commentaries, The New Testament Witnesses for Preaching). 144p. 1979. pap. 4.95 o.p. (ISBN 0-8006-0587-X, 1-587, Fortress). Augsburg Fortress.

Paul & Power: The Structure of Authority in the Primitive Church Reflected in the Pauline Epistles. Bengt Holmberg. LC 79-8905. 240p. 1980. 3.00 o.p. (ISBN 0-8006-0634-5, 1-634, Fortress). Augsburg Fortress.

Paul & Rabbinic Judaism: Some Rabbinic Elements in Pauline Theology. W. D. Davies. LC 80-8049. 448p. 1980. pap. 14.95 o.p. (ISBN 0-8006-1438-0, 1-1438, Fortress). Augsburg Fortress.

Paul & the Law. Heikki Raisanen. 330p. 1983. lib. bdg. 67.50x o.p. (ISBN 3-16-144629-1, Pub. by J C B Mohr BRD). Coronet Bks.

Paul & the Salvation of Mankind. Johannes Munck. LC 60-5412. 1977. pap. 8.95 o.s.i. (ISBN 0-8042-0373-3, John Knox). Westminster John Knox.

Paul & Thomas Sandby. Luke Herrmann. (British Watercolour Ser.). (Illus.). 200p. 1986. 35.95 o.p. (ISBN 0-7134-4788-5); pap. 20.95 o.p. (ISBN 0-7134-4789-3). David & Charles.

Paul, Apostle of Jesus Christ. Lillian R. Reynolds. (Illus., Orig.). (gr. 7-10). 1965. pap. 1.25 o.p. (ISBN 0-8042-9340-6, John Knox). Westminster John Knox.

Paul, Apostle to the Gentiles: Studies in Chronology. Gerd Luedemann. Tr. by Stanley F. Jones from Ger. LC 83-48919. 320p. 1984. 9.95 o.p. (ISBN 0-8006-0714-7, 1-714, Fortress). Augsburg Fortress.

Paul Celan: Poems. Paul Celan. Tr. by Michael Hamburger from Ger. LC 79-9117. (Poetry in Translation Ser.). 286p. (Orig.). 1981. 20.00 o.p. (ISBN 0-89255-043-0); pap. 7.95 o.s.i. (ISBN 0-89255-060-0). Persea Bks.

Paul Claudel: The Man & the Mystic. Louis Chaigne. LC 78-5951. 1978. Repr. of 1961 ed. lib. bdg. 35.00x o.p. (ISBN 0-313-20465-9, CHCL). Greenwood.

Paul De Lamerie, Citizen & Goldsmith of London 1688-1751. Philip A. Phillips. 75.00x o.p. (ISBN 0-87556-510-7). Saifer.

Paul Delaroche: A Study in 19th Century French History Painting. Norman D. Ziff. LC 76-23663. (Outstanding Dissertations in the Fine Arts-19th Century). (Illus.). 1977. Repr. of 1974 ed. lib. bdg. 68.00 o.p. (ISBN 0-8240-2741-8). Garland Pub.

Paul Delvaux: Graphic Work. Mira Jacob. (Illus.). 166p. 1984. 125.00 o.p. (ISBN 0-915346-92-3). A Wofsy Fine Arts.

Paul Gauguin in the Context of Symbolism. Vojtech Jirat-Wasiutynski. LC 77-25773. (Outstanding Dissertations in the Fine Arts Ser.). 560p. 1982. lib. bdg. 67.00 o.p. (ISBN 0-8240-3219-5). Garland Pub.

Paul Hindemith: The Man Behind the Music. Geoffrey Skelton. (Illus.). 1977. 10.00 o.s.i. (ISBN 0-87597-107-5, Crescendo). Taplinger.

Paul Jenkins. Albert E. Elsen. LC 75-101622. (Contemporary Artists Ser.). (Illus.). 288p. 1973. 65.00 o.p. (ISBN 0-8109-0215-X). Abrams.

Paul Klee & Primitive Art. James S. Pierce. LC 75-23807. (Outstanding Dissertations in the Fine Arts - 20th Century). 1976. lib. bdg. 37.00 o.p. (ISBN 0-8240-2001-4). Garland Pub.

Paul Klee: The Formative Years. Charles W. Haxthausen. LC 79-57507. 724p. 1982. lib. bdg. 94.00 o.p. (ISBN 0-8240-3932-7). Garland Pub.

Paul McCartney. Gelfand. (Rock 'n Pop Stars Ser.). (Illus.). 32p. (gr. 4 up). PLB 8.95 o.p. (ISBN 0-317-31142-5). Creative Ed.

Paul McCartney: In His Own Words. Paul Gambaccini. LC 76-8068. 1983. pap. 6.95 o.p. (ISBN 0-399-41008-2, Perigee). Putnam Pub Group.

Paul McLean. Malcolm McGregor. LC 85-1082. (Illus.). 217p. 1986. text ed. 25.00x o.p. (ISBN 0-7022-1885-5). U of Queensland Pr.

Paul: Mystic & Missionary. Bernard T. Smyth. LC 80-14041. 191p. (Orig.). 1980. pap. 3.98 o.p. (ISBN 0-88344-380-5). Orbis Bks.

Paul Newman: An Illustrated Biography. J. Landry. (Illus.). 144p. 1983. pap. text ed. 8.95 o.p. (ISBN 0-07-036189-4). McGraw.

Paul Robeson: The Man & His Mission. Ron Ramdin. LC 88-60469. 223p. 1988. 35.00 o.p. (ISBN 0-7206-0684-5, Pub. by P Owen Ltd). Dufour.

Paul Scott. K. Bhaskara Rao. (English Authors Ser.). 1980. 15.95 o.p. (ISBN 0-8057-6773-8, Twayne). G K Hall.

Paul Strassels' Quick & Easy Guide to Tax Management for 1985-1986. Paul N. Strassels. 300p. 1985. pap. 14.95 o.p. (ISBN 0-87094-707-9). Dow Jones-Irwin.

Paul the Leader. J. O. Sanders. LC 83-62737. 192p. 1984. pap. 5.95 o.p. (ISBN 0-89109-515-2). NavPress.

Paul the Teacher: A Resource for Teachers in the Church. Kent L. Johnson. LC 86-17384. 128p. (Orig.). 1986. pap. 6.95 o.p. (ISBN 0-8066-2226-1, 10-4905, Augsburg). Augsburg Fortress.

Paul: The Theology of the Apostle in the Light of Jewish Religious History. Hans J. Schoeps. Tr. by Harold Knight. LC 61-10284. 304p. 1979. Repr. of 1961 ed. softcover 7.95 o.s.i. (ISBN 0-664-24273-1, Westminster). Westminster John Knox.

Paul Tillich. John P. Newport. 320p. 1984. 12.95 o.p. (ISBN 0-8499-2952-0). Word Bks.

Paul Tillich. J. Heywood Thomas. Ed. by D. E. Nineham & E. H. Robertson. LC 66-11072. (Makers of Contemporary Theology Ser). 1966. pap. 1.99 o.p. (ISBN 0-8042-0678-3, John Knox). Westminster John Knox.

Paul Tillich's Radical Social Thought. Ronald H. Stone. LC 79-87740. 180p. 1980. pap. 3.99 o.p. (ISBN 0-8042-0679-1, John Knox). Westminster John Knox.

Paul Valery & the Civilized Mind. Norman Suckling. LC 77-25965. (University of Durham Publications). 1978. Repr. of 1954 ed. lib. bdg. 35.00x o.p. (ISBN 0-313-20095-5, SUPV). Greenwood.

Paul Wallach's Guide to Restaurants of Los Angeles & Southern California. Paul Wallach. 592p. 1985. pap. 11.95 o.p. (ISBN 0-87905-214-7). Gibbs Smith Pub.

Paul Wallach's Guide to the Restaurants of Northern California. Paul Wallach. (Illus.). 600p. 1984. pap. 9.95 o.p. (ISBN 0-87905-408-5, Peregrine Smith). Gibbs Smith Pub.

Paul Young. Philip Kamin. (Illus.). 32p. (gr. 3-12). 1985. pap. 4.95 o.p. (ISBN 0-88188-411-1, 00183876, Robus Bks). H Leonard Pub Corp.

Paula Modersohn-Becker: The Letters & Journals, 1876-1907. Paula Modersohn-Becker. Ed. by Gunter Busch & Liselotte Von Reinken. Tr. by Arthur S. Wensinger & Carole C. Hoey. LC 82-19232. (Illus.). 608p. 1984. 29.95 o.s.i. (ISBN 0-8008-6264-3). Taplinger.

Paulician Heresy: A Study of the Origin & Development of Paulicianism in Armenia & the Eastern Provinces of the Byzantine Empire. N. G. Garsoian. (Publications in Near & Middle East Ser.: No. 6). 1967. text ed. 32.80x o.p. (ISBN 90-2790-096-5). Mouton.

Pauline Parallels. Ed. by Fred O. Francis & J. Paul Sampley. LC 74-26346. 400p. 1975. pap. 10.95x spiral bdg. o.p. (ISBN 0-8006-1206-X, 1-1206, Fortress). Augsburg Fortress.

Pauline Partnership in Christ: Christian Community & Commitment in Light of Roman Law. J. Paul Sampley. LC 79-8895. 144p. 1980. 2.00 o.p. (ISBN 0-8006-0631-0, 1-631, Fortress). Augsburg Fortress.

Paulji: A Memoir. Patti Simpson. LC 85-81716. (Illus.). 306p. (Orig.). 1985. pap. 4.95 o.p. (ISBN 0-88155-036-1, 0190). Illum Way Pub.

Paul's Ethic of Freedom. Peter Richardson. LC 78-27440. 182p. 1979. pap. 6.95 o.s.i. (ISBN 0-664-24261-8, Westminster). Westminster John Knox.

Paul's Faith & the Power of the Gospel: A Structural Introduction to the Pauline Letters. Daniel Patte. LC 82-7416. 432p. (Orig.). 1983. 21.95 o.p. (ISBN 0-8006-1682-0, 1-1682, Fortress). Augsburg Fortress.

Paul's Gospel & Mission: The Outlook from His Letter to the Romans. Arland J. Hultgren. LC 85-4430. 176p. 1985. pap. 9.95 o.p. (ISBN 0-8006-1871-8, 1-1871, Fortress). Augsburg Fortress.

Paul's Thorn in the Flesh. Charles Capps. 60p. (Orig.). 1983. pap. text ed. 4.95 o.s.i. (ISBN 0-914307-09-6, Dist. by Harrison Hse). R Tilton Ministries.

Pavement & Soil Characteristics: Seven Reports. (Transportation Research Record Ser.). 81p. 1975. 3.80 o.p. (ISBN 0-309-02388-2). Transport Res Bd.

Pavement Design & Management Systems: Eight Reports. (Transportation Research Record Ser.). 73p. 1974. 3.40 o.p. (ISBN 0-309-02356-4). Transport Res Bd.

Pavement Distress, Evaluation, & Performance. (Transportation Research Record Ser.). 76p. 1979. 3.00 o.p. (ISBN 0-309-02962-7). Transport Res Bd.

Pavement Evaluation & Overlay Design: A Symposium & Related Papers. (Transportation Research Record Ser.). 114p. 1979. 6.20 o.p. (ISBN 0-309-02848-5). Transport Res Bd.

Pavement Surface Properties & Performance. (Transportation Research Record Ser.). 50p. 1977. 2.80 o.p. (ISBN 0-309-02659-8). Transport Res Bd.

Pavement Surface Properties & Vehicle Interaction: Five Reports. (Transportation Research Record Ser.). 64p. 1976. 2.80 o.p. (ISBN 0-309-02498-6). Transport Res Bd.

Pavement Surface Properties, Evaluation & Shoulders. (Transportation Research Record Ser.). 60p. 1978. 4.00 o.p. (ISBN 0-317-36097-3). Transport Res Bd.

Pavement Systems: Assessment of Load Effects, Design, & Bases. (Transportation Research Record Ser.). 88p. 1979. 5.00 o.p. (ISBN 0-309-02975-9). Transport Res Bd.

Pavilion of Passion. Jocelyn Carew. 320p. 1983. pap. 2.95 o.p. (ISBN 0-380-84681-0, 84681-0). Avon.

Pavillons of the Eighteenth Century. Jerome Zerbe & Cyril Connolly. (Illus.). 1982. pap. 9.95 o.p. (ISBN 0-393-00070-2). Norton.

Pavillons of the Eighteenth Century. Jerome Zerbe & Cyril Connolly. (Illus.). 1980. 14.98 o.p. (ISBN 0-393-01279-4). Norton.

Pavlova: Repertoire of a Legend. John Lazzarini & Roberta Lazzarini. LC 80-5560. (Illus.). 1980. 35.00 o.s.i. (ISBN 0-02-871970-0). Schirmer Bks.

Pavlovian Approach to Psychopathology. W. H. Gantt et al. 1970. 90.00 o.p. (ISBN 0-08-013016-X). Pergamon.

Pawcatuck River Estuary & Little Narragansett Bay. R. Ehinger et al. 56p. 1978. free o.p. (P728). Sea Grant Pubns.

Pawns of War: The Loss of the U. S. S. Langley & the U. S. S. Pecos. Dwight R. Messimer. LC 82-14415. (Illus.). 228p. 1983. 19.95 o.p. (ISBN 0-87021-515-9). Naval Inst Pr.

Pax Britannica: The Climax of an Empire. James Morris. LC 68-24395. (Helen & Kurt Wolff Bks.). (Illus.). 1968. 11.95 o.p. (ISBN 0-15-171425-8). HarBraceJ.

Pay Rates in the Public Service. (International Personnel Management Association). 25.00 o.p. (ISBN 0-686-81155-0); members 10.00 o.p. Intl Personnel Mgmt.

Pay: The Experiences of a Junior Supply Officer During World War II. John W. Hempstead. 65p. 1985. 7.95 o.p. (ISBN 0-533-06283-7). Vantage.

Pay Yourself First: The High Beta No-Load Way to Stock Market Profits. Michael Hayes. LC 78-27414. 224p. 1980. pap. 6.95 o.p. AMACOM.

Paying for Performance & Position: Dilemmas in Salary Compression & Merit Pay. James W. Steele. 1982. 13.50 o.p. (ISBN 0-8144-3145-3). AMACOM.

Paying Your Way. J. A. Marts. 1975. 28.00 o.p. (ISBN 0-07-086495-0). McGraw.

Payment for Milk on Quality: Report. (Agricultural Planning Studies: No. 89). 90p. (Orig.). 1973. pap. 5.75 o.p. (ISBN 0-685-39006-3, F308, FAO). UNIPUB.

Payment for Physician Services: Strategies for Medicare. LC 85-606641. (OTA-H-294 Ser.). (Illus.). 287p. (Orig.). 1986. pap. 9.00 o.p. (ISBN 0-318-19927-0, S/N 052-003-01020-8). USGPO.

Payment Systems in Britain. Michael White. 160p. 1981. text ed. 39.75x o.p. (ISBN 0-566-02294-X). Gower Pub Co.

Payroll. McGraw.

Paysan Parvenu: Or, the Fortunate Peasant. Pierre C. De Chamblain De Marivaux. LC 78-60836. (Novel 1720-1805 Ser.: Vol. 2). 1979. lib. bdg. 37.00 o.p. (ISBN 0-8240-3651-4). Garland Pub.

PBX Switchboard Workbook. Elizabeth L. Stockton. 1970. 15.00x o.p. (ISBN 0-89262-040-4). Career Pub.

PC-Bilog. Robert Mislevy & R. Darrell Bock. looseleaf binder 20.00 o.p. (ISBN 0-89498-013-0). Sci Ware.

PC Board Connectors. Ed. by Steven D'Adolf. 1100p. 1987. 95.00 o.p. (ISBN 0-317-57580-5). DATA Busn Pub.

PC CAD-CAM-CAE Software & Systems Directory. 2nd., rev ed. Ed. by Lawrence Rosenbaum & Jonathan Linden. 90p. 1986. 49.00 o.p. (ISBN 0-932007-10-4, B49). Mgmt Roundtable.

PC COBOL. Kahn. 400p. 1987. pap. text ed. 39.00 net o.p. (ISBN 0-205-11165-3). Wm C Brown.

PC-DOS Companion. Murtha & Petrie. LC 83-50996. 168p. 1983. pap. 15.95 o.p. (ISBN 0-672-22039-3, 22039). Sams.

PCBs & the Environment: Differences Between Yusho & Other Kinds of Poisoning Involving Only PCBs. Ed. by John S. Waid. 304p. 1987. 3 volume set 415.00 o.p. (ISBN 0-317-61078-3). CRC Pr.

PCBs & the Environment: Polychlorinated Biphenyls: Accumulation & Effects upon Plants, Vol. II. Ed. by John S. Waid. 200p. 1987. 3 volume set 415.00 o.p. (ISBN 0-317-61073-2). CRC Pr.

PCC-From Coast to Coast. Fred W. Schneider & Stephen P. Carlson. (Special Ser.: No. 86). (Illus.). 288p. 1983. 36.95 o.p. (ISBN 0-916374-57-2). Interurban.

PCI Architectural Precast Concrete Drafting Handbook. 224p. 25.00 o.p. (ISBN 0-13-044602-5, MNL-119-75). P-PCI.

PCs vs. CWPs in the Clerical Workstation of the Future. International Resource Development, Inc. Staff. 257p. 1983. 1650.00x o.p. (ISBN 0-88694-566-6). Intl Res Dev.

Peace: A Dream Unfolding. Ed. by Patrick Crean & Penney Kome. LC 86-42633. (Illus.). 256p. (Orig.). 1986. 35.00 o.s.i. (ISBN 0-87156-770-9); pap. 18.95 o.s.i. (ISBN 0-87156-700-8). Sierra.

Peace & Social Structure. J. Galtung. (Essays in Peace Research Ser.: Vol. 3). 1978. pap. text ed. 33.00x o.p. (ISBN 87-7241-370-0). Humanities.

Peace & World Order Studies: A Curriculum Guide. Ed. by Barbara J. Wien. 742p. 1975. pap. 14.95 o.p. Transaction Pubs.

Peace & World Order Studies: A Curriculum Guide. 4th ed. Ed. by Barbara J. Wien. 742p. 1985. pap. 14.95 o.p. (ISBN 0-317-56948-1). Transaction Pubs.

Peace & World Structure. J. Galtung. (Essays in Peace Research Ser.: Vol. 4). 1980. pap. text ed. 85.00x o.p. (ISBN 0-391-01159-6). Humanities.

Peace as It Can Be. Irving Rikon. LC 76-97938. 188p. 1970. 6.95 o.p. (ISBN 0-8022-2325-7). Philos Lib.

Peace Breaks Out. John Knowles. LC 80-19678. 192p. 1981. 10.95 o.p. (ISBN 0-03-056908-7). H Holt & Co.

Peace Corps: Ambassadors of Good Will. Henry B. Lent. (Illus.). (YA) (gr. 9 up). 1966. 4.50 o.s.i. (ISBN 0-664-32383-9, Westminster). Westminster John Knox.

Peace, Detente, & Soviet-American Relations: A Collection of Public Statements by Leonid Brezhnev. Leonid I. Brezhnev. LC 78-22244. 1979. 12.95 o.p. (ISBN 0-15-185921-3). HarBraceJ.

Peace in the Valley. Willias Young. 64p. 1987. 7.75 o.p. (ISBN 0-8062-2959-4). Carlton.

Peace of Jesus: Reflections on the Gospel for the A-Cycle. Joseph G. Donders. LC 83-4240. 312p. (Orig.). 1983. pap. 9.95 o.p. (ISBN 0-88344-379-1). Orbis Bks.

Peace on Earth Handbook. Loren Halvorson. LC 75-22718. 128p. 1976. pap. 4.50 o.p. (ISBN 0-8066-1516-8, 10-4873, Augsburg). Augsburg Fortress.

Peace, Politics, & the People of God. Ed. by Paul Peachey. LC 85-45490. 208p. 1986. pap. 4.95 o.p. (ISBN 0-8006-1898-X, 1-1898, Fortress). Augsburg Fortress.

Peace Porridge, No. 2: Russia, to Begin With. Teddy Milne. LC 86-64052. (Illus.). 195p. (Orig.). (gr. 3 up). 1987. pap. 9.95 o.s.i. (ISBN 0-938875-06-X). Pittenbruach Pr.

Peace, Print & Protestantism: 1450 to 1558. C. S. Davies. (Paladin History of England Ser.). 365p. 1983. pap. 7.95 o.p. (ISBN 0-586-08266-2, Pub. by Granada England). Academy Chi Pubs.

Peace Where Is It? Annie Gagiati. LC 73-91996. 1974. pap. 1.95 o.p. (ISBN 0-8198-0507-6). Dghtrs St Paul.

Peaceable Kingdom. Jan De Hartog. LC 76-168256. 1972. 10.00 o.p. (ISBN 0-689-10482-0, Atheneum). Macmillan.

Peaceable Kingdoms: An Anthology of Utopian Writings. Robert L. Chianese. 1971. pap. text ed. 5.95 o.p. (ISBN 0-15-569053-1, HC). HarBraceJ.

Peaceable Kingdoms: New England Towns in the Eighteenth Century. Michael Zuckerman. 1978. pap. 5.95x o.p. (ISBN 0-393-00895-9, N895, Norton Lib). Norton.

Peaceable Nature: An Optimistic View of Life on Earth. Stephen Lackner. LC 83-48985. 192p. 1984. 13.45 o.p. (ISBN 0-06-250489-4). HarpR.

Peaceful Change in Modern Society. Ed. by E. Berkeley Tompkins. LC 74-152429. (Publications Ser.: No. 101). 158p. 1971. pap. 8.95x o.p. (ISBN 0-8179-6011-2). Hoover Inst Pr.

Peacemaking from Vergennes to Napoleon. Thomas M. Iiams. LC 79-14922. 240p. 1980. lib. bdg. 14.00 o.p. (ISBN 0-88275-997-3). Krieger.

Peacemaking in the Middle East. Lester Sobel. (Checkmark Bk.). 304p. 1980. lib. bdg. 24.95x o.p. (ISBN 0-87196-267-5). Facts on File.

Peacemongers. Robert D. Culver. Ed. by Mark Carpenter. 160p. 1985. pap. 5.95 o.p. (ISBN 0-8423-4789-5). Tyndale.

Peaceways: Sixteen Christian Perspectives on Security in a Nuclear Age. Charles P. Lutz & Jerry L. Folk. LC 83-70500. 224p. (Orig.). 1983. pap. 10.95 o.p. (ISBN 0-8066-2006-4, 10-4904, Augsburg). Augsburg Fortress.

Peaches, Cream & Sour Apples. Jean Downing. 80p. 1986. 7.75 o.p. (ISBN 0-8062-2844-X). Carlton.

Peachtree Island. Mildred Lawrence. LC 48-9018. (Illus.). (gr. 3-6). 1966. pap. 2.95 o.p. (ISBN 0-15-671560-0, VoyB). HarBraceJ.

Peacock & the Lions. Sheilagh Murray. (Illus.). 240p. 1983. 25.00 o.p. (ISBN 0-85362-197-7, Oriel). Routledge Chapman & Hall.

Peacock Ate My Lunch. Craig B. McKee & Margaret Holland. LC 85-51101. (Predictable Reading Bks.). (Illus.). 24p. (gr. k-4). 1985. 7.95g o.s.i. (ISBN 0-87406-036-2). Willowisp Pr.

Peaking Power Generation. E. S. Miliaras. 56p. 1980. 16.00 o.p. (ISBN 0-317-33591-X, G00195); members 8.00 o.p. (ISBN 0-317-33592-8). ASME.

Peaks & People of the Adirondacks. rev. ed. Russell M. Carson. LC 85-31796. (Illus.). 350p. 1986. pap. 9.95 o.s.i. (ISBN 0-935272-32-1). ADK Mtn Club.

Peanut Butter Favorites. Ed. by Annette Gohlke. LC 83-61904. 64p. 1983. pap. 3.95 o.s.i. (ISBN 0-89821-053-4). Reiman Assocs.

Peanut Butter for Dinner Again? Lurlene McDaniel. (Illus.). 112p. (gr. 3-5). 1985. 2.25 o.p. (ISBN 0-87406-028-1). Willowisp Pr.

Peanuts Double, Vol. I. Charles M. Schulz. 256p. 1976. pap. 1.50 o.s.i. (ISBN 0-449-22782-0, Q2782, Crest). Fawcett.

Peanuts Double, Vol. II. Charles M. Schulz. (YA) 1981. pap. 2.25 o.s.i. (ISBN 0-449-23027-9, Crest). Fawcett.

Peanuts Jubilee. Charles M. Schulz. LC 74-15471. 224p. 1975. 29.95 o.p. (ISBN 0-03-015081-7). H Holt & Co.

Peanuts Treasury. Charles M. Schulz. (gr. 5 up). 8.95 o.s.i. (ISBN 0-03-072585-2). H Holt & Co.

Pearl. Nancy Flynn. (La Mer Press Ser.). 24p. (Orig.). 1985. pap. 5.00 o.p. (ISBN 0-917573-02-1). CAO TIMES.

Pearl. Anne Leaton. LC 84-48538. 256p. 1985. 14.45 o.s.i. (ISBN 0-394-53923-0). Knopf.

Pearl Harbor: The Verdict of History. Gordon W. Prange & Donald M. Goldstein. 752p. 1985. text ed. 19.95 o.p. (ISBN 0-07-050668-X). McGraw.

Pearlkillers: Four Novellas. Rachel Ingalls. 1987. 15.45 o.s.i. (ISBN 0-671-63340-6). S&S.

Pearls Before Swine. Ann Drysdale. 160p. 1985. 16.95 o.p. (ISBN 0-7102-0466-3). Routledge Chapman & Hall.

Pearls of Wisdom, Nineteen Eighty-Two: Kuan Yin Opens the Door to the Golden Age, Vol. 25, Bks. I & II. LC 83-50756. (Illus.). Bk. 1, 322 pgs. 25.00 o.s.i. (ISBN 0-916766-58-6); Bk. 2, 476 pgs. 25.00 o.s.i. (ISBN 0-916766-59-4). Summit Univ.

Pearl's Place. Bob Graham. LC 85-47503. (Illus.). 32p. (gr. 1-5). 1985. 10.95 o.p. (ISBN 0-87226-019-4). P Bedrick Bks.

Pearls, Points, & Poems for My Lady. Joseph Di Napoli. 1977. 5.00 o.p. (ISBN 0-682-48757-0). Exposition-Phoenix.

Peasant & the Fly. Osmond Molarsky. LC 80-11609. (Illus.). (gr. k-3). 1980. 7.95 o.p. (ISBN 0-15-260152-X, HJ). HarBraceJ.

Peasant & the Fly. Osmond Molarsky. LC 80-11609. (Illus.). 48p. (gr. k-3). 1980. pap. 3.95 o.p. (ISBN 0-15-260153-8, VoyB). HarBraceJ.

Peasant Life in China: A Field Study of Country Life in the Yangtze Valley. Hsiao-Tung Fei. (International Library of Sociology). (Illus.). 1980. 25.00x o.p. (ISBN 0-7100-0590-3). Routledge Chapman & Hall.

Peasant Renaissance in Yugoslavia, 1900-1950. Ruth Trouton. LC 72-11339. 344p. 1973. Repr. of 1952 ed. lib. bdg. 35.00x o.p. (ISBN 0-8371-6662-4, TRPR). Greenwood.

Peasant Revolts in China 1840-1949. Jean Chesneaux. Ed. by Geoffrey Barraclaugh. Tr. by C. A. Curwen from Fr. LC 72-13015. (Library of the World Civilization). (Illus.). 180p. 1973. 7.95 o.p. (ISBN 0-393-05485-3); pap. 5.95x o.p. (ISBN 0-393-09344-1). Norton.

Peasant Society & Culture see Little Community.

Peasant Society in the Late Byzantine Empire: A Social & Demographic Study. A. E. Laiou-Thomadakis. 1977. 38.50x o.p. (ISBN 0-691-05252-2). Princeton U Pr.

Peasant Urbanites: A Study of Rural-Urban Mobility in Serbia. Andrei Simic. (Studies in Anthropology). 150p. 1972. 40.50 o.p. (ISBN 0-12-785790-7). Acad Pr.

Peasantry in the Old Regime: Conditions & Protests. Isser Woloch. 12.00 o.p. (ISBN 0-8446-0970-6). Peter Smith.

Peasantry of Eastern Europe: Roots of Rural Transformation, Vol. I. Ed. by Ivan Volgyes. LC 78-18483. 200p. 1979. 50.00 o.p. (ISBN 0-08-023124-1). Pergamon.

Peasants in the Hills. Violeta Lopez-Gonzaga. 258p. 1984. text ed. 15.50x o.p. (ISBN 0-8248-0901-7, Pub. by U of Philippines Pr); pap. text ed. 10.50x o.p. (ISBN 0-8248-0902-5). UH Pr.

Peat Deposits of Florida, Their Occurrence, Development, & Uses. John H. Davis, Jr. (Illus.). 250p. 1946. 1.00 o.p. (ISBN 0-318-17292-5, B 30). FL Bureau Geology.

Peat Moss & Ivy & the Birthday Present. Michael Berenstain. LC 86-611. (Picturebacks Ser.). (Illus.). 32p. (ps-2). 1986. lib. bdg. 5.99 o.s.i. (ISBN 0-394-97605-3, BYR); pap. 1.95 o.s.i. (ISBN 0-394-87605-9, BYR). Random.

Peatlands. P. D. Moore & D. J. Bellamy. LC 73-76673. (Illus.). 224p. 1974. 17.90 o.p. (ISBN 0-387-91112-X). Springer-Verlag.

Peau de Chagrin. Honore De Balzac. 1973. 125.00 o.p. (ISBN 0-686-53922-2). French & Eur.

Peckham's Marbles. Peter DeVries. 256p. 1986. 17.95 o.p. (ISBN 0-399-13188-4, Putnam). Putnam Pub Group.

Peckinpah: A Portrait in Montage. Garner Simmons. (Illus.). 308p. 1982. pap. 17.95 o.p. (ISBN 0-292-77570-9). U of Tex Pr.

Pecos Bill & Lightning. Leigh Peck. (Illus.). (gr. 4-8). 1940. reinforced bdg. 6.95 o.p. (ISBN 0-395-13933-3). HM.

Peculiar Architecture of Turrets & Towers in Europe. Thomas Parmenter. (Illus.). 146p. 1988. 137.75 o.p. (ISBN 0-86650-249-1). Gloucester Art.

Peculiar Truth. Duvie Clark. LC 78-55206. 1978. 9.95 o.p. (ISBN 0-689-10909-1, Atheneum). Macmillan.

Peculiarities of Behavior, 2 Vols. Wilhelm Stekel. 1943. 14.95x o.p. (ISBN 0-87140-839-2). Liveright.

Pedaling the Ends of the Earth. David Duncan. LC 85-10824. 312p. 1985. 17.45 o.s.i. (ISBN 0-671-49289-6). S&S.

Pedestrian Accidents. Ed. by Antony J. Chapman et al. 250p. 1982. 91.95 o.p. (ISBN 0-471-10057-9, Pub. by Wiley-Interscience). Wiley.

Pediatric & Adolescent Gynecology. Ed. by V. Bruni et al. 1983. 82.50 o.p. (ISBN 0-12-137880-2). Acad Pr.

Pediatric Anesthesia, 2 vols. George A. Gregory. (Illus.). 1051p. 1983. Set. text ed. 98.00 o.p. (ISBN 0-443-08177-8). Churchill.

Pediatric Anesthesia: Current Practice, Vol. 1. M. Ramez Salem. 1981. 37.00 o.p. (ISBN 0-12-615201-2). Acad Pr.

Pediatric Anesthesia Handbook. 3rd ed. Richard M. Levin & Babette J. Horn. (Medical Handbook Ser.: Vol. 3). 1984. pap. text ed. 35.50 o.p. (ISBN 0-87488-413-6). Med Exam.

Pediatric Cardiac Anesthesia. Carol L. Lake. 464p. 1987. 65.00 o.p. (ISBN 0-8385-7783-0). Appleton & Lange.

Pediatric Clinical Chemistry. Jocelyn M. Hicks & Roger L. Boeckx. (Illus.). 752p. 1984. write for info. o.p. (ISBN 0-7216-4661-1). Saunders.

Pediatric Critical Care Nursing. Katherine W. Vestal. LC 80-22913. 450p. 1981. 28.95 o.p. (ISBN 0-471-05674-X, Pub. by Wiley Med). Wiley.

Pediatric Dental Medicine. Ed. by Donald J. Forrester et al. LC 80-10694. (Illus.). 692p. 1981. text ed. 48.50 o.p. (ISBN 0-8121-0663-6). Lea & Febiger.

Pediatric Developmental Diagnosis. Ed. by William K. Frankeburg & Susan M. Thornton. (Illus.). 244p. 1981. pap. 19.95 o.p. (ISBN 0-86577-019-0). Thieme Med Pubs.

Pediatric Hematology-Oncology: A Treatise for the Clinician. Philip Lanzkowsky. (Illus.). 1980. text ed. 55.00 o.p. (ISBN 0-07-036340-4). McGraw.

Pediatric Liver Disease. Ed. by M. M. Fisher & C. C. Roy. LC 82-18046. (Hepatology: Vol. 5). 306p. 1983. 59.50x o.p. (ISBN 0-306-41164-4, Plenum Pr). Plenum Pub.

Pediatric Neurology Case Studies. 2nd ed. Kenneth F. Swaiman & Stephen Ashwal. LC 84-493. (Case Study Ser.: Vol. 29). 1984. pap. text ed. 47.50 o.p. (ISBN 0-87488-071-8). Med Exam.

Pediatric Neurosonography: Clinical Tomographic & Neuropathologic Correlates. Asma Q. Fischer et al. LC 85-3219. 267p. 1985. 45.00x o.p. (ISBN 0-471-89252-1). Wiley.

Pediatric Nursing. Patricia A Lesner. LC 81-82910. (Illus.). 544p. (Orig.). 1982. pap. text ed. 25.95 o.p. (ISBN 0-8273-1932-0). Delmar.

Pediatric Nursing Policies, Procedures, & Personnel. Eileen M. Sporing et al. 264p. 1984. pap. 26.95 o.p. (ISBN 0-87489-339-9). Med Economics.

Pediatric Oncology. Philip Lanzkowsky. (Illus.). 576p. 1983. text ed. 55.00 o.p. (ISBN 0-07-036341-2). McGraw.

Pediatric Optometry. Jerome Rosner. (Illus.). 458p. 1982. text ed. 47.95 o.p. (ISBN 0-409-95014-9). Butterworth.

Pediatric Orthopedic Radiology. M. B. Ozonoff. LC 76-54040. (Monographs in Clinical Radiology: Vol. 15). (Illus.). 1979. text ed. write for info. o.p. (ISBN 0-7216-7034-2). Saunders.

Pediatric Policy & Procedure Manual. Linda Black. LC 79-19681. 1980. pap. 9.50 o.p. (ISBN 0-87125-060-8). Cath Health.

Pediatric Procedures. 2nd ed. Walter T. Hughes & E. Stephen Buescher. (Illus.). 400p. 1980. text ed. write for info. o.p. (ISBN 0-7216-4826-6). Saunders.

Pediatric Radiographic Interpretation. Charles Dixter et al. LC 79-67303. (Exercises in Dental Radiology Ser.: Vol. 3). (Illus.). 271p. 1980. pap. write for info. o.p. (ISBN 0-7216-3095-2). Saunders.

Pediatric Radiology. 2nd ed. Alan E. Oestreich. (Medical Outline Ser.). 1981. 44.50 o.p. (ISBN 0-87488-658-9). Med Exam.

Pediatric Surgery. Thomas M. Holder & Keith W. Ashcraft. LC 78-54513. (Illus.). 1200p. 1980. text ed. write for info. o.p. (ISBN 0-7216-4737-5). Saunders.

Pediatric Surgery in Tropical Countries. Ed. by P. P. Rickham. LC 81-24085. (Progress in Pediatric Surgery Ser.: Vol. 15). (Illus.). 311p. 1982. text ed. 32.00 o.p. (ISBN 0-8067-1515-4). Urban & S.

Pediatricks. Medical Economics Company. (Illus.). 1974. pap. 9.95 o.p. (ISBN 0-87489-052-7). Med Economics.

Pediatrics. Richard M. Heller & Lucy F. Squire. (Exercises in Diagnostic Radiology: Vol. 5). (Illus.). 162p. 1973. pap. write for info. o.p. (ISBN 0-7216-4630-1). Saunders.

Pediatrics: An Approach to Independent Learning. Ed. by C. William Daeschner. LC 82-8438. 646p. 1983. pap. 27.50x o.p. (ISBN 0-471-05992-7). Wiley.

Pediatrics for the Practical Nurse. Catherine M. Brigley. LC 72-9384. (Illus.). 224p. 1973. pap. 15.95 o.p. (ISBN 0-8273-0332-7); instr's. guide o.s.i. 5.00 o.p. (ISBN 0-8273-0333-5). Delmar.

Pediatrics: PreTest, Self-Assessment & Review. 3rd ed. PreTest Service, Inc. Staff. (Clinical Science Ser.). 272p. 1985. text ed. 13.95 o.p. (ISBN 0-07-051006-7). McGraw.

Pedigree & Progress: Essays in the Genealogical Interpretation of History. Anthony Wagner. 333p. 1975. 37.50x o.p. (ISBN 0-87471-782-5). Rowman.

Pedigree Unknown. Dorothy Lyons. LC 73-5242. (gr. 7 up). 1973. 5.95 o.p. (ISBN 0-15-260170-8, HJ). HarBraceJ.

Pedlar of Swaffham. Kevin C. Crossley-Holland. LC 70-129208. (Illus.). 48p. (gr. 1-4). 1979. 6.95 o.p. (ISBN 0-395-28786-3, Clarion). HM.

Pedlar's Pack of Ballads & Songs. William H. Logan. LC 67-23929. 496p. 1968. Repr. of 1869 ed. 44.00x o.p. (ISBN 0-8103-3534-4). Gale.

Pedlock & Sons. Stephen Longstreet. 1976. pap. 1.75 o.p. (ISBN 0-380-00500-X, 27730). Avon.

Pedrin, el Conejo Travieso: Peter Rabbit. Beatrix Potter. (Illus., Span.). (gr. 3-7). 1931. 5.00 o.p. (ISBN 0-7232-1797-1). Warne.

Pedrini Supplementary Aid to the Administration of the Stanford-Binet Intelligence Scale (Form L-M) A Handbook. Duilio T. Pedrini & Lura N. Pedrini. LC 74-95256. (Professional Handbook). 50p. 1970. pap. 14.10x o.p. (ISBN 0-87424-114-6). Western Psych.

Pedro Calderon de la Barca: Los Cabellos de Absalon. Ed. by R. A. Edwards & G. Edwards. LC 73-4292. 168p. 1973. 25.00 o.p. (ISBN 0-08-017161-3); pap. 8.50 o.p. (ISBN 0-08-017162-1). Pergamon.

Pedro Paramo: A Novel of Mexico. Juan Rulfo. Tr. by Lysander Kemp from Span. 1959. pap. 3.95 o.p. (ISBN 0-394-17446-1, B207, BC). Grove.

Pedro Vial & the Roads to Santa Fe. Noel M. Loomis & Abraham P. Nasatir. (American Exploration & Travel Ser.: Vol. 49). (Illus.). 1967. 27.50 o.p. (ISBN 0-8061-0730-8); pap. 16.95 o.p. (ISBN 0-8061-1110-0). U of Okla Pr.

Peek-A-Boo. Carla Dijs & Kees Moerbeek. LC 86-80651. (Illus.). 10p. (ps-k). 1986. 4.95 o.p. (Revolving Board Bks.). H Holt & Co.

Peel & Put Complete Program for Speech & Language Development. rev. ed. V. D. Blockcolsky et al. 1986. pap. 69.00 o.p. (ISBN 0-88450-173-6, 2040-B); games incl. o.p. Communication Skill.

Peep into the Twentieth Century. Christopher Davis. 1985. 5.95 o.p. (ISBN 0-87795-711-8, Arbor Hse). Morrow.

Peeping Tom. Howard Jacobson. 312p. 1985. 15.45 o.p. (ISBN 0-89919-347-1). Ticknor & Fields.

Peer Gynt. Henrik Ibsen. Tr. by Michael Meyer. 192p. 1981. pap. 6.95 o.p. (ISBN 0-413-29460-9). Heinemann Ed.

Peer Gynt. Henrik Ibsen. Tr. by Horace M. Finney. 208p. 1955. Philos Lib.

Peer Pressure. Rich Wilkerson. 26p. (Orig.). 1985. pap. text ed. 1.95 o.s.i. (ISBN 0-914307-46-0). R Tilton Ministries.

Peer Program for Youth. Ardyth Hebeisen. LC 73-78257. 1973. 6.50 o.p. (ISBN 0-8066-1322-X, 10-4875, Augsburg). Augsburg Fortress.

Peer Review: A Legal Update. 42p. 1981. pap. 8.00 o.p. (ISBN 0-89970-257-0, OP-202). AMA.

Peerless Eye: The Art of Bruno Lilefors. Bruno Liljefors. LC 87-20176. (Illus.). 180p. 1987. 60.00 o.s.i. (ISBN 0-385-24361-8). Doubleday.

Peers, Tents, & Owls: Some Solutions to Problems of the Clergy Today. James L. Lowery, Jr. 160p. (Orig.). 1973. pap. 3.95 o.p. (ISBN 0-8192-1155-9). Morehouse Pub.

Pegasus Bridge: June 6, 1944. Stephen E. Ambrose. 208p. 1985. 14.70 o.p. (ISBN 0-671-52374-0). S&S.

Peggy. Roy J. Campbell. 187p. 1983. 10.00 o.p. (ISBN 0-682-49952-8). Exposition-Phoenix.

Peggy & Her Boyfriend: A True Love Story. Louisa C. Culver. (Illus.). 61p. 1979. pap. 2.50 o.p. (ISBN 0-682-49251-5). Exposition-Phoenix.

Peggy & Pete: A Story of Lasting Love & Success. Louisa C. Culver. (Illus.). 224p. 1979. 7.50 o.p. (ISBN 0-682-49252-3). Exposition-Phoenix.

Peintre-Graveur Illustre, 32 vols, Vols. 17-32. Ed. by Loys Delteil. Incl. Vol. 17. Camille Pissaro, Alfred Sisley, Auguste Renoir. 75.00 o.s.i. (ISBN 0-306-78517-X); Vol. 18. Theodore Gericault. 35.00 o.s.i. (ISBN 0-306-78518-8); Vol. 19. Henri Leys, Henri de Braekeleer, James Ensor. 65.00 (ISBN 0-306-78519-6); Vols. 20-29. Honore Daumier. Set. 650.00 (ISBN 0-306-78520-X); Vol. 30. Albert Besnard. 55.00 (ISBN 0-306-78530-7); Vol. 31. Jean Frelaut. lib. bdg. 55.00 (ISBN 0-306-78531-5); Vol. 32. Appendix. Herman J. Wechsler. 30.00 o.s.i. (ISBN 0-306-78532-3). LC 68-27720. (Graphic Art Ser). Da Capo.

Peinture Sur Porcelaine see Art of Painting on Porcelain.

Peiping Municipality & the Diplomatic Quarter. Robert Duncan. LC 78-74355. (Modern Chinese Economy Ser.). 146p. 1980. lib. bdg. 20.00 o.p. (ISBN 0-8240-4271-9). Garland Pub.

Peirce's Cosmology. Peter T. Turley. LC 77-79173. 126p. 1977. 8.95 o.p. (ISBN 0-8022-2208-0). Philos Lib.

Peking Opera. Rewi Alley. (Illus.). 103p. (Orig.). 1984. pap. 19.95 o.p. (ISBN 0-8351-1617-4). China Bks.

Pele. Don Kowet. LC 75-38344. (YA) (gr. 9 up). 1976. 6.95 o.p. (ISBN 0-689-10713-7, Atheneum). Macmillan.

Pele & Hiiaka: A Myth from Hawaii. Nathaniel B. Emerson. LC 77-83040. (Illus.). 1978. 15.00 o.p. (ISBN 0-8048-1251-9). C E Tuttle.

Pele, Volcano Goddess of Hawaii. L. R. McBride. (Illus.). 1968. pap. 3.95 o.s.i. (ISBN 0-912180-11-0). Petroglyph.

Pele's New World. Peter Bodo & David Hishey. (Illus.). 1977. 8.95 o.p. (ISBN 0-393-08758-1). Norton.

Pelican Guide to New Orleans. 6th ed. Thomas K. Griffin. LC 74-182889. (Pelican Guide Ser.). (Illus.). 160p. 1980. pap. 4.95 o.p. (ISBN 0-88289-010-7). Pelican.

Pelican Guide to Plantation Homes of Louisiana. 5th ed. Ed. by Nancy Calhoun & James Calhoun. LC 75-162347. (Pelican Guide Ser.). (Illus.). 128p. 1980. pap. 4.95 o.p. (ISBN 0-911116-50-8). Pelican.

Pelican Guide to the Bahamas. James E. Moore. 320p. 1983. pap. 9.95 o.p. (ISBN 0-88289-380-7). Pelican.

Pellagra. Ed. by Kenneth Carpenter. LC 81-6514. (Benchmark Papers in Biochemistry Ser.: Vol. 2). 416p. 1982. 56.95 o.p. (ISBN 0-87933-364-2). Van Nos Reinhold.

Peloubet's Sunday School Notes 1988-1989 September - August. Ralph Earle. 372p. (Orig.). 1988. pap. 7.95 o.p. (ISBN 0-8010-3446-9). Baker Bk.

Peltries or Plantations: The Economic Policies of the Dutch West India Company in New Netherland, 1623-1639. Van Cleaf Bachman. LC 74-91336. (Studies in Historical & Political Science: Eighty-Seventh Series). 292p. 1970. 30.00x o.p. (ISBN 0-8018-1064-7). Johns Hopkins.

Pen Calligraphy. John Cataldo. LC 78-72583. (Illus.). 1979. pap. 12.95 o.p. (ISBN 0-87192-108-1). Davis Mass.

Pen Renderings of Elmer Rising: New England in Black & White. Gwenn E. Wells. (Illus.). 112p. 1986. text ed. 75.00 o.p. Globe Pequot.

Penal Code of Michigan. Gould Editorial Staff. 450p. loose leaf 13.00 o.p. Gould.

Penal Colony. Date not set. (ISBN 0-8052-3198-6); pap. (ISBN 0-8052-0418-0). Random.

Penal Law of New York Question & Answers. Gould Editorial Staff. (Supplemented annually). looseleaf 6.95 o.p. (ISBN 0-87526-225-2). Gould.

Penal Law of New York: Spanish Edition. Gould Editiorial Staff. (Supplemented annually). looseleaf 10.00 o.p. Gould.

Penalty-Finite Elements Methods in Mechanics. Ed. by J. N. Reddy. (AMD Ser.: Vol. 51). 1982. 40.00 o.p. (H00235). ASME.

Penance: God's Gift for Forgiveness. Blanche Twigg. (Illus.). 64p. 1974. pap. 2.50 o.p. (ISBN 0-912228-15-6). St Anthony Mess Pr.

Pendleton District & Anderson County, S. C. Wills, Estates & Legal Records, 1793 to 1857. Virginia Alexander & Colleen M. Elliott. 350p. 1979. 38.50 o.s.i. (ISBN 0-89308-143-4). Southern Hist Pr.

Pendragon. Douglas Carmichael. (Illus.). 1977. 9.00 o.p. (ISBN 0-682-48905-0). Exposition-Phoenix.

Pendragon Castle. Peter Seymour. Designed by Keith Moseley. LC 82-80753. (Illus.). (gr. 1-4). 1982. 7.75 o.p. (ISBN 0-03-062076-7). H Holt & Co.

Pendulum. Robert Eastman. LC 78-22250. 1979. 8.95 o.p. (ISBN 0-15-171652-8). HarBraceJ.

Pendulum Power. Greg Nielsen & Joseph Polansky. 190p. pap. 4.95 o.p. (ISBN 0-89281-157-9). Inner Tradit.

Pendulums. 2nd ed. Elementary Science Study Staff. 1975. tchr's guide 15.64 o.p. (ISBN 0-07-018585-9). McGraw.

Penelope Devereux. Sheila Bishop. 1978. pap. 1.75 o.p. (ISBN 0-8439-0551-4, Pub. by Leisure Bks CT). Dorchester Pub Co.

Penelope Hall's Social Services of England & Wales. 10th ed. Penelope Hall. Ed. by J. B. Mays & Anthony Forder. (International Library of Sociology). 384p. (Orig.). 1983. pap. 15.95x o.p. (ISBN 0-7100-0837-6). Routledge Chapman & Hall.

Penetrating Beam: Reflections on Light. Edith Levin. 115p. (gr. 7-12). 1978. PLB 10.97 o.p. (ISBN 0-8239-0416-4). Rosen Group.

Penet's Square. Thomas Powell. 206p. 1976. 8.95 o.p. (ISBN 0-932052-10-X). North Country.

Penguin Atlas of Recent History: Europe Since 1815. Colin McEvedy. 1982. pap. 6.95 o.p. (ISBN 0-14-070834-0). Penguin.

Penguin Book of American Folk Songs. Alan Lomax. 159p. Repr. of 1966 ed. lib. bdg. 39.00 o.p. (Pub. by Am Repr Serv). Reprint Servs.

Penguin Guide to London. F. R. Banks. (Handbooks Ser.). 608p. 1984. pap. 6.95 o.p. (ISBN 0-14-070419-1). Penguin.

Penguins. Tony Soper & John Sparks. LC 67-25577. 1967. 12.50 o.s.i. (ISBN 0-8008-6275-9). Taplinger.

Penguins. Bernard Stonehouse. LC 79-13661. (New Biology Ser.). (Illus.). (gr. 4 up). 1980. text ed. 9.95 o.p. (ISBN 0-07-061740-6). McGraw.

Peninsula Trails. Jean Rusmore & Frances Spangle. LC 81-70343. (Illus.). 216p. (Orig.). 1982. pap. 9.95 o.p. (ISBN 0-89997-014-1). Wilderness Pr.

Penitent. Isaac Bashevis Singer. (General Ser.). 1984. lib. bdg. 13.95 o.p. (ISBN 0-8161-3641-6, Large Print Bks). G K Hall.

Penkovskiy Papers. Oleg Penkovskiy. 1982. pap. 3.50 o.s.i. (ISBN 0-345-30093-9). Ballantine.

Penmarric. Susan Howatch. 704p. 1981. pap. 3.95 o.p. (ISBN 0-449-24090-8, Crest). Fawcett.

Penn. Sara Berkeley. 48p. 1986. pap. 7.95 o.p. (Pub. by Raven Arts Pr). Dufour.

Penn's Woods: A Love Story. Bernard C. Barnick. 145p. 1980. 8.95 o.p. (ISBN 0-682-49660-X, Banner). Exposition-Phoenix.

Pennsylvania - Architecture & Culture: A Bibliography. E. Willard Miller & Ruby M. Miller. (Architecture Ser.: A 1508). 55p. 1985. 8.25 o.p. (ISBN 0-89028-658-2). Vance Biblios.

Pennsylvania - Natural Resources & Economic Development: A Bibliography. E. Willard Miller & Ruby M. Miller. (Public Administration Ser.: P 1819). 66p. 1985. 9.75 o.p. (ISBN 0-89028-669-8). Vance Biblios.

Pennsylvania - Transportation: A Bibliography. E. Willard Miller & Ruby M. Miller. (Public Administration Ser.: P 1818). 25p. 1985. 3.75 o.p. (ISBN 0-89028-668-X). Vance Biblios.

Pennsylvania: Agency. suppl. 6.00 o.p. Am Law Inst.

Pennsylvania Agriculture & Country Life: 1640-1840. Stevenson W. Fletcher. LC 50-9470. 605p. 1971. 9.50 o.p. (ISBN 0-911124-33-0). Pa Hist & Mus.

Pennsylvania Appellate Practice. Pennsylvania Bar Institute Staff. 146p. 1983, 15.00 o.p. (ISBN 0-318-02166-8, 235). PA Bar Inst.

Pennsylvania Civil Practice & Procedure. Pennsylvania Bar Institute Staff. 254p. 1984. 25.00 o.p. (ISBN 0-318-02202-8, 258). PA Bar Inst.

Pennsylvania Civil Procedure Law & Rules, 2 vols. Gould Editorial Staff. 600p. 1983. text ed. 14.00 looseleaf o.p. (ISBN 0-87526-295-3). Gould.

Pennsylvania Corporate Taxes. 187p. 1984. 25.00 o.p. (ISBN 0-318-03917-6, 264). PA Bar Inst.

Pennsylvania Dutch Cookbook. J. George Frederick. 12.75 o.p. (ISBN 0-8446-0099-7). Peter Smith.

Pennsylvania Dutch Farm: To Cut Out & Assemble. Edmund V. Gillon, Jr. (Encore Edition). (Illus., Orig.). 1979. pap. 2.49 o.p. (ISBN 0-684-17368-9). Scribner.

Pennsylvania Evidence. 280p. 1984. 35.00 o.p. (ISBN 0-318-03931-1, 280). PA Bar Inst.

Pennsylvania Job Bank: A Comprehensive Guide to Major Local Employers. Adams, Robert L., & Associates Staff. (Job Bank Ser.). 258p. (Orig.). 1982. pap. 9.95 o.p. (ISBN 0-937860-09-3). Adams Inc MA.

Pennsylvania: Judgments. 26.00 o.p. (ISBN 0-686-90877-5). Am Law Inst.

Pennsylvania Legal Practice Manuals, 18 vols. Pennsylvania Bar Institute Staff. 1985. 125.00 o.p. (ISBN 0-318-02163-3). PA Bar Inst.

Pennsylvania Manufacturers Register, 1988. 840p. 1987. 99.00 o.p. (ISBN 0-318-02866-2). Manufacturers.

Pennsylvania Old Assyrian Texts. Gwaltney. Date not set. 18.75 o.p. Ktav.

Pennsylvania Place Names. Abraham H. Espenshade. LC 68-30591. 380p. 1969. Repr. of 1925 ed. 34.00x o.p. (ISBN 0-8103-3234-5). Gale.

Pennsylvania: Property, Vols. 3-5. 8.50 o.p. (ISBN 0-686-90878-3). Am Law Inst.

Pennsylvania: Security. 8.50 o.p. (ISBN 0-686-90880-5). Am Law Inst.

Pennsylvania: Trusts. 2nd ed. 11.50 o.p. (ISBN 0-686-90881-3). Am Law Inst.

Pennsylvania Workers' Compensation Practice & Procedure. Pennsylvania Bar Institute Staff. 293p. 1985. 55.00 o.p. (ISBN 0-318-19064-8, 299). PA Bar Inst.

Penny & a Periwinkle. Josephine H. Aldridge. LC 60-15036. (Illus.). (gr. k-3). 1961. PLB 5.95 o.p. (ISBN 0-395-27691-8, Pub. by Parnassus). HM.

Penny Crossword Puzzles No. 39. Ed. by Ned Webster. (Orig.). 1976. pap. 0.95 o.s.i. (ISBN 0-671-80812-5). PB.

Penny Dreadfuls & Comics: English Periodicals for Children from Victorian Times to the Present Day. Kevin Carpenter. (Illus.). 128p. (Orig.). pap. 17.95 o.p. (ISBN 0-905209-47-8, Pub. by Victoria & Albert Mus UK). Faber & Faber.

Penny Ferry. Rick Boyer. 1984. 13.45 o.p. (ISBN 0-395-35288-6). HM.

Penny for a Song: A Comedy. John Whiting. 1964. text ed. 5.50x o.p. (ISBN 0-435-22941-9). Heinemann Ed.

Penny Links: A Novel. Ursula Golden. 156p. 1981. pap. 8.95 o.p. (ISBN 0-416-00891-7, NO. 0213). Routledge Chapman & Hall.

Penny Murders. Lionel Black. 1980. pap. 1.95 o.p. (ISBN 0-380-48090-5, 48090-5). Avon.

Penny Pincher's Wine Guide. Lucy Waverman. 224p. 1983. pap. 5.95 o.p. (ISBN 0-380-85027-3, 85027). Avon.

Penny Puzzles No. 44. Ed. by Ned Webster. 1977. pap. 0.95 o.s.i. (ISBN 0-671-81068-5). PB.

Penny the Medicine Maker: The Story of Penicillin. Sherrie S. Epstein. LC 60-14006. (Medical Books for Children). (Illus.). (gr. k-5). 1960. PLB 4.95 o.p. (ISBN 0-8225-0006-X). Lerner Pubns.

Penobscot Expedition. John E. Cayrord. LC 76-21153. (Illus.). 1976. 9.95 o.p. (ISBN 0-318-23480-7); pap. 6.95 o.p. (ISBN 0-318-23481-5). Cay Bel.

Penross Manor. Joan W. Brown. 192p. 1986. 11.95 o.p. (ISBN 0-8499-0517-6). Word Bks.

Pensees. Charles Peguy. pap. 1.95 o.p. (ISBN 0-685-37035-6). Schoenhof.

Pension & Profit Sharing: Sample Plans & Workbook. Panel Publishers, Inc. Staff. (Orig.). 1985. pap. 75.00 o.p. (ISBN 0-916592-58-8). Panel Pubs.

Pension & Retirement Plans: Issues & Strategies. Panel Publishers, Inc. Staff. (Orig.). 1985. pap. 45.00 o.p. (ISBN 0-317-20147-6). Panel Pubs.

Pension Answer Book. 3rd ed. Stephen J. Krass & Richard L. Keschner. LC 84-25510. 1984. 45.00 o.p. (ISBN 0-916592-52-9). Panel Pubs.

Pension Crisis. Robert J. Lynn. LC 82-48795. 192p. 1983. 25.00x o.p. (ISBN 0-669-06374-6). Lexington Bks.

Pension Funds & the Bottom Line: Managing the Corporate Pension Fund as a Financial Business. Keith P. Ambachtsheer. 200p. 1986. 35.00 o.p. (ISBN 0-87094-708-7). Dow Jones-Irwin.

Pension Integration: Concepts, Issues & Proposals. James H. Schulz & Thomas D. Leavitt. Ed. by Patricia G. Moore & Lynn Ann Johnson. LC 83-1527. 103p. (Orig.). 1983. pap. 15.00 o.p. (ISBN 0-86643-032-6). Employee Benefit.

Pension Mathematics: With Numerical Illustrations. Howard E. Winklevoss. 1977. 16.95x o.p. (ISBN 0-256-01886-3). Irwin.

Pension Planning: Readings. Ed. by Life Office Management Association Staff. (FLMI Insurance Education Program Ser.). 177p. 1982. pap. text ed. 10.00 o.p. (ISBN 0-915322-49-8). LOMA.

Pension Planning Within a Major Company. Ronald J. Lucas. 1979. 55.00 o.p. (ISBN 0-08-024045-3). Pergamon.

Pension Plans: Answers to the Questions on Subject Matter, CEBS Course, No.2. 7th ed. (Orig.). 1985. pap. text ed. 15.00 o.p. Intl Found Employ.

Pension Plans: Learning Guide CEBS Course 2. 6th ed. (Orig.). 1984. Spiral bdg. 18.00 o.p. Intl Found Employ.

Pension Plans: Learning Guide, CEBS Course, No. 2. 7th ed. (Orig.). 1985. 18.00 o.p. Intl Found Employ.

Pensions: An ERISA Accounting & Management Guide. 2nd ed. Richard M. Steinberg & Harold Danker. LC 82-13396. 381p. 1983. 68.95x o.p. (ISBN 0-471-09798-5). Wiley.

Pensions & Industrial Relations: A Practical Guide for All Involved in Pensions. Harry Lucas. 1977. 34.00 o.p. (ISBN 0-08-021947-0); pap. 15.25 o.p. (ISBN 0-08-021946-2). Pergamon.

Pensions & New York City's Fiscal Crisis. Damodar Gujarati. 1978. pap. 7.00 o.p. (ISBN 0-8447-3314-8). Am Enterprise.

Titles

Pensions in Perspective: A Guide to Qualified Retirement Plans. Ed. by Judith T. Boyers. LC 85-62947. 240p. (Orig.). 1986. pap. 20.00 o.p. (ISBN 0-87218-439-0). Natl Underwriter.

Pensions' Policy in Britain: Socialist Analysis. Eric Shragge. (Radical Social Policy Ser.). 256p. (Orig.). 1984. pap. 25.00x o.p. (ISBN 0-7100-9842-1). Routledge Chapman & Hall.

Pentagon & the Art of War: The Question of Military Reform. Edward N. Luttwak. 352p. 1985. 18.45 o.p. (ISBN 0-671-52432-1). S&S.

Pentagon & the Making of U. S. Foreign Policy: A Case Study of Vietnam 1960-1968. Jaya K. Baral. LC 77-13333. 1978. text ed. 17.50x o.p. (ISBN 0-391-00549-9). Humanities.

Pentagon Papers Case Collection: Annotated Procedural Guide & Index. Meiklejohn Civil Liberties Institute Staff & Ann F. Ginger. LC 75-14531. 200p. 1975. pap. 10.00x o.p. (ISBN 0-913876-07-0). Meiklejohn Civ Lib.

Pentagon Tidbits. Nita Scoggan. (Illus.). 28p. (Orig.). 1984. pap. 1.95 o.p. (ISBN 0-910487-01-4). Royalty Pub.

Pentamerone. Giovanni Basile. 1943. 6.95 o.p. (ISBN 0-87140-982-8). Liveright.

Pentateuch in Its Cultural Environment. 2nd ed. G. Herbert Livingston. 1974. 13.95 o.p. (ISBN 0-8010-5540-7). Baker Bk.

Pentax SLR Cameras. Carl Shipman. LC 76-51908. (Illus.). 1977. pap. 12.95 o.p. (ISBN 0-912656-57-3). Price Stern.

Pentecost & the Chosen One. W. J. Corbett. LC 86-19738. 240p. (ps up). 1987. pap. 14.95 o.p. (ISBN 0-385-29549-9). Delacorte.

Pentecost & the Chosen One. Date not set. (ISBN 0-385-29549-9). Delacorte.

Pentecost Cycle. R. W. Kemper. LC 12-2965. 1982. pap. 7.95 o.p. (ISBN 0-570-03872-3). Concordia.

Pentecost One. Frederick H. Borsch. LC 84-18756. (Proclamation Three C Ser.). 64p. 1986. pap. 3.75 o.p. (ISBN 0-8006-4130-2, 1-4130, Fortress). Augsburg Fortress.

Pentecost One. Leander E. Keck & Francis W. Hobbie. LC 79-7377. (Proclamation 2: Aids for Interpreting the Lessons of the Church Year, Series B). 64p. 1982. pap. 3.75 o.p. (ISBN 0-8006-4089-6, 1-4089, Fortress). Augsburg Fortress.

Pentecost One. Howard C. Kee & Peter J. Gomes. Ed. by Elizabeth Achtemeier et al. LC 79-7377. (Proclamation 2: Aids for Interpreting the Lessons of the Church Year, Ser. C). 64p. 1980. pap. 3.75 o.p. (ISBN 0-8006-4081-0, 1-4081, Fortress). Augsburg Fortress.

Pentecost One: Proclamation 3B. David A. Hubbard. LC 84-18756. (Proclamation Ser.). 64p. 1985. pap. 3.75 o.p. (ISBN 0-8006-4106-X, 1-4106, Fortress). Augsburg Fortress.

Pentecost Three. Paul J. Achtemeier. LC 84-18756. (Proclamation Three C Ser.). 64p. 1986. pap. 3.75 o.p. (1-4132, Fortress). Augsburg Fortress.

Pentecost Three. Schuyler Brown & Don E. Saliers. Ed. by Elizabeth Actemeier et al. LC 79-7377. (Proclamation Ser.: No. 2). 64p. 1982. pap. 3.75 o.p. (ISBN 0-8006-4099-3, 1-4099, Fortress). Augsburg Fortress.

Pentecost Three: Proclamation 3B. John B. Rogers, Jr. LC 84-18756. (Proclamation Ser.). 64p. 1985. pap. 3.75 o.p. (ISBN 0-8006-4108-6, 1-4108, Fortress). Augsburg Fortress.

Pentecost Two. Adela Y. Collins & Charles Rice. LC 79-7377. (Proclamation 2: Aids for Interpreting the Lessons of the Church Year, Series B). 64p. 1982. pap. 3.75 o.p. (ISBN 0-8006-4090-X, 1-4090, Fortress). Augsburg Fortress.

Pentecost Two. R. Alan Culpepper. LC 84-18756. (Proclamation Three C Ser.). 64p. 1986. pap. 3.75 o.p. (ISBN 0-8006-4131-0, 1-4131, Fortress). Augsburg Fortress.

Pentecost Two: Proclamation 3B. Daniel J. Harrington. LC 84-18756. (Proclamation Ser.). 64p. 1985. pap. 3.75 o.p. (ISBN 0-8006-4107-8, 1-4107, Fortress). Augsburg Fortress.

Pentecost 1. Virgil P. Howard. LC 84-18756. (Proclamation 3 A). 64p. 1987. pap. 3.75 o.p. (ISBN 0-8006-4122-1, 1-4122). Augsburg Fortress.

Pentecost 1. Morris Niedenthal & Andre Lacocque. LC 74-76929. (Proclamation 1: Aids for Interpreting the Lessons of the Church Year, Ser. A). 64p. 1975. pap. 2.95 o.p. (ISBN 0-8006-4066-7, 1-4066, Fortress). Augsburg Fortress.

Pentecost 1. David Randolph & Jack D. Kingsbury. LC 75-24959. (Proclamation 1: Aids for Interpreting the Lessons of the Church Year, Ser. B). 64p. 1975. pap. 2.95 o.p. (ISBN 0-8006-4076-4, 1-4076, Fortress). Augsburg Fortress.

Pentecost 1. Ronald E. Sleeth & John R. Donahue. LC 73-88347. (Proclamation 1: Aids for Interpreting the Lessons of the Church Year, Ser. C). 64p. 1974. pap. 2.95 o.p. (ISBN 0-8006-4056-X, 1-4056, Fortress). Augsburg Fortress.

Pentecost 1. David L. Tiede & Aidan Kavanagh. Ed. by Elizabeth Achtemeier et al. LC 79-7377. (Proclamation 2: Aids for Interpreting the Lessons of the Church Year, Ser. A). 64p. (Orig.). 1981. pap. 3.75 o.p. (ISBN 0-8006-4096-9, 1-4096, Fortress). Augsburg Fortress.

Pentecost 2. George W. Hoyer & Wolfgang Roth. LC 73-88347. (Proclamation 1: Aids for Interpreting the Lessons of the Church Year, Ser. C). 64p. 1974. pap. 2.95 o.p. (ISBN 0-8006-4057-8, 1-4057, Fortress). Augsburg Fortress.

Pentecost 2. Donald H. Juel & David Buttrick. Ed. by Elizabeth Achtemeier et al. LC 79-7377. (Proclamation 2: Aids for Interpreting the Lessons of the Church Year, Ser. C). 64p. 1980. pap. 3.75 o.p. (ISBN 0-8006-4083-7, 1-4083, Fortress). Augsburg Fortress.

Pentecost 2. Donald Macleod & J. T. Forestell. LC 74-76929. (Proclamation 1: Aids for Interpreting the Lessons of the Church Year, Ser. C). 64p. 1975. pap. 2.95 o.p. (ISBN 0-8006-4067-5, 1-4067, Fortress). Augsburg Fortress.

Pentecost 2. Patrick D. Miller, Jr. LC 84-18756. (Proclamation 3 A). 64p. 1987. pap. 3.75 o.p. (ISBN 0-8006-4123-X). Augsburg Fortress.

Pentecost 2. Paul S. Minear & Harry B. Adams. Ed. by Elizabeth Achtemeier et al. LC 79-7377. (Proclamation 2: Aids for Interpreting the Lessons of the Church Year, Ser. A). 64p. (Orig.). 1981. pap. 3.75 o.p. (ISBN 0-8006-4097-7, 1-4097, Fortress). Augsburg Fortress.

Pentecost 2. Eduard Riegert & Richard H. Hiers. LC 75-24960. (Proclamation 1: Aids for Interpreting the Lessons of the Church Year, Ser. B). 64p. 1965. pap. 2.95 o.p. (ISBN 0-8006-4077-2, 1-4077, Fortress). Augsburg Fortress.

Pentecost 3. Fred Craddock & Leander Keck. LC 75-24971. (Proclamation 1: Aids for Interpreting the Lessons of the Church Year, Ser. B). 64p. 1975. pap. 2.95 o.p. (ISBN 0-8006-4078-0, 1-4078, Fortress). Augsburg Fortress.

Pentecost 3. O. C. Edwards, Jr. & Gardner C. Taylor. Ed. by Elizabeth Achtemeier et al. LC 79-7377. (Proclamation 2: Aids for Interpreting the Lessons of the Church Year, Ser. C). 64p. (Orig.). 1980. pap. 3.75 o.p. (ISBN 0-8006-4084-5, 1-4084, Fortress). Augsburg Fortress.

Pentecost 3. Victor P. Furnish & Richard L. Thulin. Ed. by Elizabeth Achtemeier et al. LC 79-7377. (Proclamation 2: Aids for Interpreting the Lessons of the Church Year, Ser. A). 64p. (Orig.). 1981. pap. 3.75 o.p. (ISBN 0-8006-4098-5, 1-4098, Fortress). Augsburg Fortress.

Pentecost 3. George Peck. LC 84-18756. (Proclamation 3 A). 64p. 1987. pap. 3.75 o.p. (ISBN 0-8006-4124-8, 1-4124). Augsburg Fortress.

Pentecost 3. Gerard S. Sloyan & Howard C. Kee. LC 73-88347. (Proclamation 1: Aids for Interpreting the Lessons of the Church Year, Ser. C). 64p. 1974. pap. 2.95 o.p. (ISBN 0-8006-4058-6, 1-4058, Fortress). Augsburg Fortress.

Pentecost 3. Bruce Vawter & John H. Elliott. LC 74-76929. (Proclamation 1: Aids for Interpreting the Lessons of the Church Year, Ser. A). 64p. 1975. pap. 2.95 o.p. (ISBN 0-8006-4068-3, 1-4068, Fortress). Augsburg Fortress.

Pentecostals. Walter J. Hollenwager. Tr. by R. A. Wilson from Ger. LC 70-176103. 1977. pap. 10.95 o.p. (ISBN 0-8066-1632-6, 10-4901, Augsburg). Augsburg Fortress.

Peonies, Outdoors & in. Arno Nehrling & Irene Nehrling. (Illus.). 14.75 o.p. (ISBN 0-8446-5230-X). Peter Smith.

People Above: Politics & Administration in Mid-18th Century Scotland. Alexander Murdoch. (Illus.). 210p. 1980. text ed. 32.50x o.p. (ISBN 0-85976-053-7). Humanities.

People among Peoples: Quaker Benevolence in Eighteenth Century America. Sydney V. James. LC 62-20248. (Center for the Study of the History of Liberty in America Ser). 1963. 27.50x o.s.i. (ISBN 0-674-66050-1). Harvard U Pr.

People: An International Choice, the Multilateral Approach to Population. Rafael M. Salas. 1976. 31.00 o.p. (ISBN 0-08-021030-9); pap. 40.00 o.p. (ISBN 0-08-021029-5). Pergamon.

People & Ideas: A Rhetoric Reader. J. Baylor & James Moore. (Illus.). 1980. text ed. 18.95 o.p. (ISBN 0-07-004162-8). McGraw.

People & Information. Harold B. Pepinsky. 1970. 90.00 o.p. (ISBN 0-08-015624-X). Pergamon.

People & Organizations: Cases in Management & Organizational Behavior. 2nd ed. John E. Dittrich & Robert A. Zawacki. 1985. pap. 21.95x o.p. (ISBN 0-256-03257-2). Irwin.

People & Places of Constantinople. Charles Newton. (Illus.). 112p. (Orig.). 1985. pap. 7.95 o.p. (ISBN 0-948107-03-0, Pub. by Victoria & Albert Mus UK). Faber & Faber.

People & Plants in Australia. Ed. by D. J. Carr & S. G. Carr. 450p. 1981. 55.00 o.p. (ISBN 0-12-160720-8); pap. 30.50 o.p. (ISBN 0-12-160722-4). Acad Pr.

People & Productivity: The New York Stock Exchange Guide to Financial Incentives & the Quality of Work Life. Eugene Epstein & William C. Freund. LC 84-71126. 132p. 1984. 19.95 o.p. (ISBN 0-87094-510-6). Dow Jones-Irwin.

People & Progress in West Africa. R. Hallett. 1966. 6.05 o.p. (ISBN 0-08-011326-5); pap. text ed. 5.25 o.p. (ISBN 0-08-011325-7). Pergamon.

People & Races. Alice M. Brues. 1977. write for info. o.p. (ISBN 0-02-315670-8, 31567). Macmillan.

People & the Countryside. H. E. Bracey. 1970. 24.00x o.p. (ISBN 0-7100-6686-4). Routledge Chapman & Hall.

People & the Sea, 2 vols. P. H. Nixon. 1977. Vol. 1. 2.00 o.p. (ISBN 0-686-36988-2); Vol. II. 2.00 o.p.; Vol. III. 2.00 o.p. Sea Grant Pubns.

People & Weather. P. J. Kavanagh. 176p. (Orig.). 1986. pap. 5.95 o.s.i. (ISBN 0-7145-3666-0). Riverrun NY.

People Are Legends. Kevin Gilbert. (Paperback Poets Ser.). 1979. 12.95x o.p. (ISBN 0-7022-1238-5); pap. 8.95x o.p. (ISBN 0-7022-1239-3). U of Queensland Pr.

People at Work see Unblocking Your Organization.

People at Work: Nineteen Thirty to the Nineteen Eighty's. Cherry Gilchrist. (Illus.). 72p. (gr. 7-12). 1983. 19.95 o.p. (ISBN 0-7134-1366-2, Pub. by Batsford England). David & Charles.

People, Evaluation & Achievement. George Nixon. LC 72-94066. (Building Blocks of Human Potential Ser.). 1973. 13.95x o.p. (ISBN 0-87201-663-3). Gulf Pub.

People, Families & God. Mac Turnage & Anne Turnage. pap. 4.25 o.p. (ISBN 0-8042-9077-6, John Knox). Westminster John Knox.

People Ideology-People Theology: New Perspectives on Religious Dogma. Dario Lisiero. 226p. 1980. 10.95 o.p. (ISBN 0-682-49664-2, Banner). Exposition-Phoenix.

People in My Camera. Michael Gnade. (Illus.). 200p. 15.50 o.p. (ISBN 0-85242-632-1, Pub. by Fountain Pr UK). Seven Hills Bk Dists.

People in the Web of Life. Gwendolyn L. Baines. 1978. 5.00 o.p. (ISBN 0-682-48832-1). Exposition-Phoenix.

People, Law & the Futures Perspective. Betty B. Franks & Mary K. Howard. 56p. 1979. pap. 5.95 o.p. (ISBN 0-8106-1676-9). NEA.

People Need Each Other. Cherrie Farnette et al. LC 78-70902. (Kids & Careers Ser.). (Illus.). 104p. (gr. 2-6). 1979. pap. text ed. 6.95 o.p. (ISBN 0-913916-63-3, IP633). Incentive Pubns.

People of Chaco: A Canyon & Its Culture. Kendrick Frazier. 1986. 19.45 o.p. (ISBN 0-393-02313-3). Norton.

People of Darkness. Tony Hillerman. 192p. 1983. pap. 2.95 o.p. (ISBN 0-380-57778-X). Avon.

People of God. Markus Barth. (Journal for the Study of the New Testament, Supplement Ser.: No. 5). 100p. pap. text ed. 7.95x o.s.i. (ISBN 0-905774-55-8, Pub. by JSOT Pr England). Eisenbrauns.

People of Hope: The Story Behind the Modern Church. Anthony E. Gilles. 1988. pap. 6.95 o.p. (ISBN 0-317-68169-9). St Anthony Mess Pr.

People of Rimrock: A Study of Values in Five Cultures. Ed. by Evon Z. Vogt & Ethel M. Albert. LC 66-23469. (Illus.). 1970. pap. text ed. 4.95x o.p. (ISBN 0-689-70222-1, 155, Atheneum). Macmillan.

People of the Bible. Cecil Northcott. (gr. 5-7). 1967. 4.95 o.s.i. (ISBN 0-664-20764-2, Westminster). Westminster John Knox.

People of the Church. L. C. Rudolph. (Illus., Orig.). (gr. 1-3). 1967. pap. 1.95 o.p. (ISBN 0-8042-9462-3). Westminster John Knox.

People of the City. Cyprian Ekwensi. (African Writers Ser.). 1963. pap. text ed. 6.00 o.p. (ISBN 0-435-90005-6). Heinemann Ed.

People of the Dawn. Richard B. Lyttle. LC 79-22766. (Illus.). (gr. 6 up). 1980. 10.95 o.p. (ISBN 0-689-30750-0, Atheneum). Macmillan.

People of the Earth. 5th ed. Brian M. Fagan. 1986. write for info. o.p. (ISBN 0-673-39004-7). Scott F.

People of the Ice Whale: Eskimos, White Men & the Whale. David Boeri. (Illus.). 300p. 1985. pap. 6.95 o.p. (ISBN 0-15-671660-7, Harv). HarBraceJ.

People of the Lie: The Hope for Healing Human Evil. M. Scott Peck. LC 83-13631. 269p. 1983. 15.45 o.s.i. (ISBN 0-671-45492-7). S&S.

People of the Polar North. Knud Rasmussen. LC 75-167126. 586p. 1975. Repr. of 1908 ed. 34.00x o.p. Gale.

People of the Short Blue Corn: Tales & Legends of the Hopi Indians. Harold Courlander. LC 75-115756. (Illus.). (gr. 4-6). 1970. 6.95 o.p. (ISBN 0-15-260525-8, HJ). HarBraceJ.

People of Uganda in the 19th Century see Tarikh.

People Pat Cos CS. Webster. Date not set. (ISBN 0-07-102850-1). McGraw.

People, Power & Politics: An Introduction to Political Science. John C. Donovan et al. (Illus.). 384p. 1985. pap. text ed. 15.00 o.p. (ISBN 0-394-34928-8, RanC). Random.

People, Power, Change. Luther P. Gherlach & Virginia H. Hine. 1970. pap. text ed. write for info. o.p. (ISBN 0-02-341620-3). Macmillan.

People Pray. Ellwyn Nichols. 120p. 1985. pap. 1.60 o.p. (ISBN 0-88028-043-3). Forward Movement.

People Shall Continue. Simon J. Ortiz & Sharol Graves. LC 77-83856. (Fifth World Tales Ser.). (Illus.). 24p. (gr. 2-9). 1977. pap. 5.95 o.p. (ISBN 0-89239-015-8). Childrens Book Pr.

People Shapers. Vance Packard. 1977. 12.50 o.p. (ISBN 0-316-68750-2). Little.

People Skills: How to Assert Yourself, Listen to Others & Resolve Conflicts. Robert H. Bolton. (Illus.). 1979. 13.95 o.p. (ISBN 0-13-655779-1, Spec); pap. 6.95 o.p. (ISBN 0-13-655761-9). P-H.

People Speak. Anna L. Arnott. 64p. (Orig.). 1982. pap. 4.50 o.p. (ISBN 0-682-49857-2). Exposition-Phoenix.

People, States, & World Order. Louis R. Beres. LC 80-83099. 237p. 1981. pap. text ed. 14.95 o.p. (ISBN 0-87581-267-8). Peacock Pubs.

People Therein. Mildred Lee. 320p. (gr. 7 up). 1980. 10.95 o.s.i. (ISBN 0-395-29434-7, Clarion). HM.

People Who Make Things: How American Craftsmen Live & Work. Carolyn Meyer. LC 74-18189. (Illus.). 208p. (gr. 7 up). 1975. 6.50 o.p. (ISBN 0-689-50012-2, Atheneum). Macmillan.

People Will Always Be Kind. Wilfrid Sheed. LC 72-97000. 374p. 1973. 7.95 o.p. (ISBN 0-374-23071-4). FS&G.

People Without Government: An Anthropology of Anarchism. Harold Barclay. 150p. (Orig.). 1982. pap. 11.00 o.s.i. (ISBN 0-904564-47-9). Left Bank.

People Without Names. Ray W. Rosevear. 96p. 1985. 6.50 o.p. (ISBN 0-682-40179-X). Exposition-Phoenix.

Peoplemaking. Virginia M. Satir. LC 73-188143. 1972. pap. 9.95 o.p. (ISBN 0-8314-0031-5). Sci & Behavior.

Peoples & Cultures of Cambodia, Laos & Vietnam. Language & Orientation Resource Center Staff. (Illus.). 81p. (Orig.). 1981. pap. 9.95x o.p. (ISBN 0-15-599114-0). Ctr Appl Ling.

People's College: Little Rock Junior College & Little Rock University, 1927-1969. Jim Lester. (Illus.). 239p. 1987. 19.95 o.p. (ISBN 0-87483-052-4). August Hse.

People's Guide to Camping in Mexico. Carl Franz. (Illus.). 416p. (Orig.). 1982. pap. 10.00 o.s.i. (ISBN 0-912528-24-9). John Muir.

People's Guide to Mexico. rev. ed. Carl Franz. (Illus.). 576p. (Orig.). 1986. pap. 13.95 o.p. (ISBN 0-912528-56-7). John Muir.

People's Guide to Mexico. Carl Franz. 1975. pap. 10.95 o.p. (ISBN 0-912528-15-X). John Muir.

People's History of England. A. L. Morton. (Illus.). 562p. 1980. pap. 2.95 o.p. (ISBN 0-7178-0150-0). Intl Pubs Co.

People's History of Live Oak County, Texas. Ervin L. Sparkman. Ed. by Mary S. Roberts. LC 81-2937. (Illus.). 305p. 1981. 27.50 o.p. (ISBN 0-86663-402-9). Ide Hse.

People's Hospital Book. Gots & Kaufman. 1981. pap. 3.95 o.p. (ISBN 0-380-53058-9, 53058-9). Avon.

Peoples of Asiatic Russia. Vladimir I. Jochelson. 1928. 27.00 o.p. (ISBN 0-384-27560-5). Johnson Repr.

Peoples of Kenya. Joy Adamson. 1975. 19.50 o.p. (ISBN 0-15-171681-1). HarBraceJ.

Peoples of the Arctic. Kirk Reynolds. (Peoples of North America Ser.). (Illus.). 112p. 1988. lib. bdg. 15.95x o.p. (ISBN 0-87754-894-3). Chelsea Hse.

People's Pharmacy. Joe Graedon. 1977. pap. 5.95 o.p. (ISBN 0-380-00902-1, 76299-4). Avon.

Peoples' Pottage. Garet Garrett. 174p. Date not set. 10.00 o.p. (ISBN 0-317-53238-3). Noontide.

People's Republic of China: A Documentary History of Revolutionary Change. Ed. by Mark Selden. LC 78-13916. 718p. 1979. 20.00 o.p. (ISBN 0-85345-466-3). Monthly Rev.

People's Republic of China Year-Book 1983. Xinhua News Agency, Beijing, China, Staff. 1046p. 1984. 125.00 o.p. (ISBN 0-13-656612-X, Busn). P-H.

People's Republic of China Year Book: 1986. 673p. 1986. 120.00 o.p. (ISBN 962-7167-03-7, Pub. by NCN). Taylor & Francis.

Peoples: The Ethnic Dimension in Human Relations. Jerry D. Rose. 1976. pap. 18.50 o.p. (ISBN 0-395-30716-3). HM.

People's Verdict: DCM Computer-Based Study. G. G. Mirchandani. (Illus.). 194p. 1980. text ed. 22.50x o.p. (ISBN 0-7069-1060-5, Pub. by Vikas India). Advent NY.

Pepper & All the Legs. Dick Gackenbach. LC 78-5084. (Illus.). 32p. (ps-3). 1979. 7.95 o.s.i. (ISBN 0-395-28797-9, Clarion). HM.

Peppermint Gang & the Impossible Houseboat. Laurie B. Clifford. (Peppermint Gang Ser.). 192p. (Orig.). (gr. 1-3). 1985. pap. 3.50 o.p. (ISBN 0-8423-1594-2). Tyndale.

Peptide & Protein Reviews, Vol. 1. (Illus.). 256p. 1983. 65.00 o.p. (ISBN 0-8247-7053-6). Dekker.

Peptide & Protein Reviews, Vol. 2. Hearn. 336p. 1983. 65.00 o.p. (ISBN 0-8247-7135-4). Dekker.

Peptide & Protein Reviews, Vol. 3. (Illus.). 240p. 1984. 65.00 o.p. (ISBN 0-8247-7241-5). Dekker.

Peptide & Protein Reviews, Vol. 4. Ed. by Milton W. Hearn. (Illus.). 256p. 1984. 65.00 o.p. (ISBN 0-8247-7292-X). Dekker.

Peptides, 2 vols. Ed. by Eberhard Schroder & Kraus Lubke. Incl. Vol. 1. Methods of Peptide Synthesis. 1965. 92.00 (ISBN 0-12-629801-7); Vol. 2. Synthesis, Occurrence & Action of Biologically Active Polypeptides. 1966. 93.00 o.p. (ISBN 0-12-629802-5). Acad Pr.

Peptides 1984: Proceedings of the Eighteenth European Peptide Symposium. Ed. by Ulf Ragnarsson. 668p. 1984. pap. 115.00x o.p. (ISBN 91-22-00715-6, Pub. by Almqvist & Wiksell). Coronet Bks.

Pepys. Richard Ollard. LC 84-45029. 384p. 1984. pap. 6.95 o.p. (ISBN 0-689-70679-0, 319, Atheneum). Macmillan.

Pequena Enciclopedia de la Gran Cibernetica. V. Pekelis. 423p. (Span.). 1977. 8.95 o.p. (ISBN 0-8285-1467-4, Pub. by Mir Pubs USSR). Imported Pubns.

Pequeno Diccionario Tecnologico: Farmacia, Quimica, Fisica, Medicina y Ciencias Naturales. M. Busto. 226p. (Span.). 1964. 13.50 o.p. (ISBN 0-686-57357-9, S-50248). French & Eur.

Perceiving Time: A Psychological Investigation with Men & Women. Thomas J. Cottle. LC 76-18768. 267p. 1976. 19.50 o.p. (ISBN 0-471-17530-7, JW). Krieger.

Perceiving Women. Ed. by Shirley Ardener. 192p. 1982. pap. text ed. 9.95x o.p. (ISBN 0-460-12536-2, BKA 04659, Pub. by J M Dent England). Biblio Dist.

Perception. Margaret Matlin. 500p. 1983. write for info. o.p. (ISBN 0-205-07849-4, 797849). Allyn.

Perception: An Adaptive Process. Ed. by Thomas L. Bennett. LC 73-9612. 1973. 24.50x o.p. (ISBN 0-8422-5133-2); pap. text ed. 8.95x o.p. (ISBN 0-8422-0325-7). Irvington.

Perception: An Annotated Bibliography of Philosophical & Related Writings. Kathleen Emmett & Peter Machamer. LC 75-24086. (Reference Library of the Humanities: Vol. 39). 400p. 1975. lib. bdg. 26.00 o.p. (ISBN 0-8240-9966-4). Garland Pub.

Perception: An Applied Approach. William Schiff. LC 79-88717. 1980. text ed. 29.95 o.p. (ISBN 0-395-27054-5). HM.

Perception & Aesthetic Value. Harold N. Lee. Repr. of 1938 ed. 24.00 o.p. (ISBN 0-384-32040-6). Johnson Repr.

Perception & Design in Tennyson's "Idylls of the King" John R. Reed. LC 77-122100. 270p. 1969. 15.00x o.p. (ISBN 0-8214-0078-9). Ohio U Pr.

Perception & Evocation of Literature. Leland H. Roloff. 1973. text ed. write for info. o.p. (ISBN 0-673-07550-8). Scott F.

Perception & Information. Paul J. Barber & David Legge. (Essential Psychology Ser.). 1976. pap. 4.50x o.p. (ISBN 0-416-82040-9, NO. 2615). Routledge Chapman & Hall.

Perception & Lighting as Formgivers for Architecture. W. Lam. 1977. text ed. 67.50 o.p. (ISBN 0-07-036094-4). McGraw.

Perception & Performance Underwater. John A. Adolfson & Thomas E. Berghage. LC 73-23009. 380p. 1974. 26.50 o.p. (ISBN 0-471-00900-8, Pub. by Wiley). Krieger.

Perception & the Physical World. David M. Armstrong. (International Library of Philosophy & Scientific Method). 1961. text ed. 29.95x o.p. (ISBN 0-7100-3603-5). Humanities.

Perception & Values in Travel Demand. (Transportation Research Record Ser.). 49p. 1976. 2.80 o.p. (ISBN 0-309-02561-3). Transport Res Bd.

Perception, Decision Making & Conflict. Robert Mandel. LC 78-65350. 1978. pap. text ed. 11.50 o.p. (ISBN 0-8191-0652-6). U Pr of Amer.

Perception of Asian Personality. A. Mehta. 264p. 1978. 16.95 o.p. Asia Bk Corp.

Perception of Poetry. Eugene R. Kintgen. LC 82-48387. 288p. 1983. 22.50x o.p. (ISBN 0-253-34345-3). Ind U Pr.

Perception of Stimulus Relations: Discrimination Learning & Transposition. Hayne W. Reese. (Child Psychology Ser.). 1968. 82.50 o.p. (ISBN 0-12-585550-8). Acad Pr.

Perception, Theory & Commitment: The New Philosophy of Science. Harold I. Brown. LC 76-22991. (Illus.). 1977. 19.95 o.s.i. (ISBN 0-913750-13-1). Precedent Pub.

Perceptions in Literature. Philip J. McFarland et al. (Literature Ser.). (Illus.). (gr. 10). 1972. text ed. 27.48 o.p. (ISBN 0-395-11200-1). HM.

Perceptions of the Police Organization: A Sociometric Analysis. Patton N. Morrison & Charles D. Hale. (Criminal Justice Policy & Administration Research Ser: No. 8). 26p. 1974. pap. 1.50 o.p. (ISBN 0-686-20789-0). Univ OK Gov Res.

Perceptual - Motor Learning: Theory & Practice. Lerch et al. 1974. pap. text ed. 8.95 o.p. (ISBN 0-917962-36-2). T H Peek.

Perceptual - Motor Training for Handicapped Children. Ed. by John P. Glavin. 246p. 1975. 29.50x o.p. (ISBN 0-8422-5234-7); pap. text ed. 14.95x o.p. (ISBN 0-8422-0518-7). Irvington.

Perceptual & Cognitive Aspects of Body Experience. F. C. Shontz. 1969. 64.00 o.p. (ISBN 0-12-640650-2). Acad Pr.

Perceptual Development. Richard D. Walk. LC 81-2516. 180p. (Orig.). 1981. pap. text ed. 10.25 pub net o.p. (ISBN 0-8185-0447-1). Brooks-Cole.

Perceptual World. Kai Von Fieandt & I. K. Mousgaard. 1978. 134.00 o.p. (ISBN 0-12-725050-6). Acad Pr.

Perceptualistic Theory of Knowledge. Peter Fireman. 1954. (ISBN 0-8022-0504-6). Philos Lib.

Perceval: The Story of the Grail. Chretien De Troyes. Tr. by Nigel Bryant. LC 82-3696. (Arthurian Studies: No. V). 318p. 1982. text ed. 47.50x o.p. (ISBN 0-8476-7201-8). Rowman.

Percival David Foundation of Chinese Art, London. Margaret Medley. LC 80-82645. (Oriental Ceramics Ser.: Vol. 6). (Illus.). 180p. 1982. 68.00 o.p. (ISBN 0-87011-445-X). Kodansha.

Percival David Foundation of Chinese Art, London see Oriental Ceramics: The World's Great Collections.

Percutaneous Absorption of Steroids. Ed. by P. Mauvais-Jarvis et al. LC 80-40243. 1980. 66.00 o.p. (ISBN 0-12-480680-5). Acad Pr.

Percutaneous Vascular Recanalization: Technique - Application - Clinical Results. Ed. by E. Zeitler. (Illus.). 1979. pap. 33.50 o.p. (ISBN 0-387-08875-X). Springer-Verlag.

Percy Grainger: The Pictorial Biography. Robert Simon. LC 83-62148. (Illus.). 150p. 1983. 27.50x o.p. (ISBN 0-87875-281-1). Whitston Pub.

Perdita. Isabelle Holland. 252p. (gr. 7 up). 1983. 13.95 o.p. (ISBN 0-316-37001-0). Little.

Perdition Express. Brad Lang. (Orig.). 1976. pap. 1.25 o.p. (ISBN 0-685-62587-7, LB328, Pub. by Leisure Bks CT). Dorchester Pub Co.

Pere Goriot see also Old Goriot.

Peregrine Falcon. Robert Murphy. 1981. pap. 4.95 o.p. (ISBN 0-395-30860-7). HM.

Perennial Rebel. Bernard B. Parun. 1979. 10.00 o.p. (ISBN 0-682-49292-2). Exposition-Phoenix.

Perennial Scope of Philosophy. Karl Jaspers. (ISBN 0-8022-0792-8). Philos Lib.

Perenning Apprentice. George F. Bennett. (Illus.). 240p. 25.00 o.p. (ISBN 0-317-66671-1). Mid Atlantic.

Perfect End. William Marshall. LC 82-15502. 204p. 1983. 13.50 o.s.i. (ISBN 0-03-047481-7). H Holt & Co.

Perfect End. William Marshall. 1984. pap. 3.95 o.p. (ISBN 0-03-071062-6). H Holt & Co.

Perfect Fiction. Gilbert Sorrentino. (Orig.). 1968. 4.95 o.p. (ISBN 0-393-04298-7). Norton.

Perfect Freedom. Gordon Merrick. 432p. 1982. pap. 4.50 o.p. (ISBN 0-380-80127-2, Flare). Avon.

Perfect Gas. J. S. Rowlinson. (International Encyclopedia of Physical Chemistry & Chemical Physics, Topic 10: The Fluid State: Vol. 5). 1963. 8.80 o.p. (ISBN 0-08-010188-7). Pergamon.

Perfect Hostess Cookbook. Mildred Knopf. LC 85-47640. 560p. 1985. pap. 14.95 o.p. (ISBN 0-689-70696-0, 333, Atheneum). Macmillan.

Perfect Martini Book. Robert Herzbrum. LC 79-1858. (Illus.). 1979. pap. 5.95 o.p. (ISBN 0-15-644642-1, Harv). HarBraceJ.

Perfect Mouse. Retold by & illus. by Dick Gackenbach. LC 84-877. (Illus.). 32p. (ps-3). 1984. 10.95 o.s.i. (ISBN 0-02-736760-6). Macmillan.

Perfect Name for Your Pet. Texe Marrs & Wanda Marrs. (Illus.). 128p. (Orig.). 1983. pap. 5.95 o.p. (ISBN 0-89346-221-7). Heian Intl.

Perfect Nude Photography. Michael Gnade. (Illus.). 198p. 19.95 o.p. (ISBN 0-86343-036-8, Pub. by Fountain Pr UK). Seven Hills Bk Dists.

Perfect Pal. Jack Gantos. (Illus.). (gr. k-3). 1979. PLB 7.95 o.p. (ISBN 0-395-28380-9). HM.

Perfect Symmetry: The Search for the Beginning of Time. Heinz Pagels. 1985. 18.45 o.p. (ISBN 0-671-46548-1). S&S.

Perfect Vacuum. Stanislaw Lem. Tr. by Michael Kandel. LC 78-14076. (Helen & Kurt Wolff Bk.). 1979. 8.95 o.p. (ISBN 0-15-171697-8). HarBraceJ.

Perfect Windsurfing. Ernstfried Prade. 120p. 1986. 10.95 o.p. (ISBN 0-8120-3683-2). Barron.

Perfect Writer Made Perfectly Clear. Elyse Sommer. LC 83-45394. 192p. (Orig.). 1984. pap. 12.95 o.p. (ISBN 0-8019-7427-5). Chilton.

Perfected American Watch: Waltham. 1976. Repr. pap. 4.00 o.p. (ISBN 0-913902-19-5). Heart Am Pr.

Perfected Millenial Kingdom. Robert Millet. 1974. pap. 2.00 o.p. (ISBN 0-89036-034-0). Hawkes Pub Inc.

Perfection of Wisdom: The Career of the Predestined Buddhas. Tr. by E. J. Thomas from Sanskrit. LC 78-12005. 1979. Repr. of 1952 ed. lib. bdg. 35.00x o.p. (ISBN 0-313-20646-5, MAPWI). Greenwood.

Perfidious P. Bd. with Glorious Life & Actions of St. Whigg; Life & Adventures of Captain John Avery, the Famous English Pirate ... Now in Possession of Madagascar. (Novel in England, 1700-1775 Ser). lib. bdg. 61.00 o.p. (ISBN 0-8240-0518-X). Garland Pub.

Perforating Veins. Robert May et al. (Illus.). 262p. 1981. 32.50 o.p. (ISBN 0-8067-1261-9). Urban & S.

Performance Activities in Mathematics, 6 bks. Terry Shoemaker. Incl. Bk. 1 (ISBN 0-913688-10-X); Bk. 2 (ISBN 0-913688-11-8); Bk. 3 (ISBN 0-913688-12-6); Bk. 4 (ISBN 0-913688-13-4); Bk. 5 (ISBN 0-913688-14-2); Bk. 6 (ISBN 0-913688-15-0). pap. cancelled o.s.i. Pawnee Pub.

Performance Advances in Small Boat Racing. Stuart H. Walker. LC 68-54959. (Illus.). 1969. 15.00 o.p. (ISBN 0-393-03124-1). Norton.

Performance & Progress in Working Life. W. L. T. Isbister. 1968. text ed. 34.00 o.p. (ISBN 0-08-013031-3). Pergamon.

Performance Budgeting System for Highway Maintenance Management. (National Cooperative Highway Research Program Report). 213p. 1972. 8.40 o.p. Transport Res Bd.

Performance Evaluation Systems. Wilbert Steffy & Daniel R. Darby. (Illus.). 99p. 1980. 12.00 o.p. (ISBN 0-938654-10-1, PERF E.). Indus Dev Inst Sci.

Performance Guide to Word Processing Software. W. Hession & M. Rubel. 1985. pap. text ed. 23.95 o.p. (ISBN 0-07-028451-2). McGraw.

Performance Measurement & Municipalities: A Selected Bibliography. Jamie W. Coniglio. (Public Administration Ser.: P 1772). 5p. 1985. 2.00 o.p. (ISBN 0-89028-572-1). Vance Biblios.

Performance Measurements of Scintillation Cameras. 1983. 11.50 o.p. (ISBN 0-318-18018-9, NU 1-1980). Natl Elec Mfrs.

Performance Measures for Oklahoma Public Libraries. 115p. 1982. 10.00x o.p.; members 9.00x o.p. ALA.

Performance Monitoring for Transportation Programs. Theodore H. Poister. LC 81-47574. 256p. 1982. 33.50x o.p. (ISBN 0-669-04683-3). Lexington Bks.

Performance of Off-Road Vehicles & Machines: Proceedings of the 8th International ISTVS Conference, Cambridge, August 1984. Ed. by M. J. Dwyer. 120p. 1984. pap. 33.00 o.p. (ISBN 0-08-031655-7). Pergamon.

Performance of Pavements Designed with Low-Cost Materials. (Transportation Research Record Ser.). 49p. 1980. 4.20 o.p. (ISBN 0-309-02999-6). Transport Res Bd.

Performance of Pressure Vessels with Clad & Overlayed Stainless Steel Linings. Ed. by L. I. Sluzalis & P. E. Dempsey. (MPC Ser.: Vol. 16). 72p. 1981. 20.00 o.p. (ISBN 0-686-34501-0, H00205). ASME.

Performance of Textiles. Dorothy S. Lyle. LC 76-54110. 592p. 1977. write for info. o.p. (ISBN 0-02-372860-4). Macmillan.

Performance of the U. S. Railroads since World War II. Kent T. Healy. (Illus.). 368p. 1984. 18.00 o.s.i. (ISBN 0-682-40170-6). Exposition-Phoenix.

Performance of the U. S. Railroads since World War II. Kent T. Healy. LC 83-90465. 296p. 1985. 17.95 o.p. (ISBN 0-533-06561-5). Vantage.

Performance Prediction of Centifugal Pumps & Compressors. Ed. by S. Gopalakrishnan & P. Cooper. 296p. 1980. 38.00 o.p. (ISBN 0-317-33593-6, 100127); members 19.00 o.p. (ISBN 0-317-33594-4). ASME.

Performance Programming Under MS-DOS. Michael J. Young. 436p. (Orig.). 1987. pap. 19.95 o.p. (ISBN 0-89588-420-8). Sybex.

Performance Recording in Sheep. Ed. by J. B. Owen. 132p. 1971. 10.00 o.p. (ISBN 0-85198-020-1). CAB Intl.

Performance Testing: Issues Facing Vocational Education. Janet E. Spirer. 193p. 1980. 11.00 o.p. (ISBN 0-318-15529-X, RD 190). Natl Ctr Res Voc Ed.

Performance Zoning. Lane H. Kendig & Susan Connor. 350p. 1980. 39.95 o.p. (ISBN 0-318-13042-4); members 37.95 o.p. (ISBN 0-318-13043-2). Am Plan Assn.

Performers & Their Plays. Ed. by Shirley S. Kenny & P. R. Backscheider. LC 78-66655. (Eighteenth Century English Drama Ser.). lib. bdg. 73.00 o.p. (ISBN 0-8240-3577-1). Garland Pub.

Performer's Guide to Baroque Music. Robert Donington. LC 72-3659. (Illus.). 320p. 1974. 30.00 o.s.i. (ISBN 0-684-13155-2, ScribT). Scribner.

Performing Artist's Handbook. Janice Papolos. LC 84-3671. (Illus.). 224p. 1984. 15.95 o.p. Writers Digest.

Performing Arts in Contemporary China. Colin Mackerras. (Illus.). 220p. 1981. 30.00x o.p. (ISBN 0-7100-0778-7). Routledge Chapman & Hall.

Performing Arts: The Economic Dilemma. William G. Baumol & William G. Bowen. 1968. pap. 14.50x o.p. (ISBN 0-262-52011-7). MIT Pr.

Performing G. I. Procedures. Ed. by Jean Robinson & Barbara McVan. LC 81-965. (Nursing Photobook Ser.). (Illus.). 1981. text ed. 17.95 o.p. (ISBN 0-916730-31-X). Springhouse Pub.

Peridineen der Plankton-Expedition der Humboldt-Stiftung I: Allgemeiner Teil. F. Schuett. (Illus.). 1978. Repr. of 1895 ed. 60.00x o.p. (ISBN 3-7682-0806-0). Lubrecht & Cramer.

Periglacial Environment: Past & Present. Ed. by Troy L. Pewe. 1969. 25.00x o.p. (ISBN 0-7735-0042-1, McGill Canada). U of Toronto Pr.

Periglacial Processes. Ed. by C. A. King. LC 75-33696. (Benchmark Papers in Geology Ser.: Vol. 27). 1976. 81.00 o.p. (ISBN 0-12-786846-1). Acad Pr.

Perilous Presidency. Bernard Hirschhorn. (Social Studies Student Ser.). 212p. (gr. 7-12). 1979. PLB 10.97 o.p. (ISBN 0-8239-0418-0). Rosen Group.

Perilous Road. William O. Steele. LC 58-6820. (gr. 3-7). 1958. 9.95 o.p. (ISBN 0-15-260644-0, HJ). HarBraceJ.

Perilous Road. William O. Steele. LC 58-6820. (Illus.). (gr. 3-7). 1965. pap. 3.95 o.p. (ISBN 0-15-671696-8, VoyB). HarBraceJ.

Perils of Cultism. J. C. Da Nobrega. 1980. 6.00 o.p. (ISBN 0-682-49453-4). Exposition-Phoenix.

Perils of Putney. Stephen Krensky. LC 78-5324. (Illus.). (gr. 4-6). 1978. 7.95 o.p. (ISBN 0-689-30657-1, Atheneum). Macmillan.

Perimeter of Social Repair. Ed. by W. H. Armytage & John Peel. 1978. 76.00 o.p. (ISBN 0-12-062750-7). Acad Pr.

Perimeters. Helena Worthen. LC 79-3372. 288p. 1980. 11.95 o.p. (ISBN 0-15-162729-0). HarBraceJ.

Perinatal Brain Damage. Pape & Wigglesworth. 1986. 35.00 o.p. (ISBN 0-8016-3787-2). Mosby.

Perinatal Health Services in Europe: Searching for Better Childbirth. Ed. by J. M. Phaff. 224p. 1986. 34.50 o.p. (ISBN 0-7099-3666-4, Pub. by Croom Helm Ltd). Routledge Chapman & Hall.

Perinatal Medicine. Ed. by Peter J. Huntingford et al. 1970. 32.00 o.p. (ISBN 0-12-362550-5). Acad Pr.

Perinatal Medicine: Clinical & Biochemical Aspects of the Evaluation, Diagnosis & Management of the Fetus & Newborn. Ed. by S. Kumar & M. Rathi. LC 78-40219. 1978. 69.00 o.p. (ISBN 0-08-021517-3). Pergamon.

Perinatal Medicine: Fourth European Congress. Ed. by Z. K. Stembera et al. LC 75-46148. (Illus.). 556p. 1975. 28.00 o.p. (ISBN 0-88416-080-7). Year Bk Med.

Perinatal Medicine: Proceedings. European Congress on Perinatal Medicine, Sixth, Vienna, 1978. Ed. by O. Thalhammer et al. (Illus.). 324p. 1979. pap. text ed. 35.00 o.p. (ISBN 0-88416-289-3). Year Bk Med.

Perinatal Pathology. Ed. by E. Grundmann & W. H. Kirsten. LC 79-450. (Current Topics in Pathology: Vol. 66). (Illus.). 1979. 62.00 o.p. (ISBN 0-387-09207-2). Springer-Verlag.

Perinatal Physiology. Ed. by Uwe Stave. LC 77-12596. (Illus.). 874p. 1978. 95.00x o.p. (ISBN 0-306-30999-8, Plenum Pr). Plenum Pub.

Period. JoAnn G. Loulan et al. 6.00 o.p. (ISBN 0-317-43160-9, Pub. by Volcano Pr). Down There Pr.

Period Piece. Gwen Raverat. (Illus.). 288p. 1976. pap. 3.95 o.p. (ISBN 0-393-00822-3). Norton.

Titles

Periodate Oxidation of Diol & Other Functional Groups. G. Dryhurst. LC 72-101490. 1970. 50.00 o.p. (ISBN 0-08-006877-4). Pergamon.

Periodical Scholarship on Islamic Architecture Published 1973-1983: A Bibliography. Carole Cable. (Architecture Ser. Bibliography A-1307). 7p. 1985. pap. 2.00 o.p. (ISBN 0-89028-237-4). Vance Biblios.

Periodical Title Abbreviations: By Abbreviation, Vol. I. 5th ed. Ed. by Leland G. Alkire, Jr. 1100p. 1986. 155.00x o.p. (ISBN 0-8103-0531-3). Gale.

Periodical Title Abbreviations: By Title, Vol. II. 5th ed. Ed. by Leland G. Alkire, Jr. 1100p. 1986. 155.00x o.p. (ISBN 0-8103-0532-1). Gale.

Periodicals for South-East Asian Studies: A Union Catalogue of Holdings in British & Selected European Libraries. Compiled by Brenda E. Moon. 630p. 1979. 85.00 o.p. (ISBN 0-7201-0730-X). Mansell.

Periodicals from Africa: A Bibliography & Union List of Periodicals Published in Africa. Standing Conference on Library Materials on Africa Staff. Ed. by Carole Travis. 1977. lib. bdg. 68.00 o.p. (ISBN 0-8161-7946-8, Hall Reference). G K Hall.

Periodontic Syllabus. Ed. by Peter Fedi, Jr. LC 84-27787. (Illus.). 190p. 1985. pap. 23.50 o.p. (ISBN 0-8121-0982-1). Lea & Febiger.

Periodontics in the Tradition of Orban & Gottlieb. 5th ed. Daniel A. Grant et al. LC 79-10615. (Illus.). 974p. 1979. text ed. 54.95 cloth o.p. (ISBN 0-8016-1961-0). Mosby.

Perioperative Management in Cardiothoracic Surgery. Benson B. Roe. 247p. 1980. text ed. 30.00 o.p. (ISBN 0-316-75376-9). Little.

Perioperative Patient Care: The Nursing Perspective. Kneedler & Dodge. 1983. 38.95 o.p. (ISBN 0-8016-2711-7). Mosby.

Peripatos Uber das Greisenalter. Adolf Dyroff. 1939. pap. 12.00 o.p. (ISBN 0-384-13655-9). Johnson Repr.

Peripheral Arterial Disease. 3rd ed. Max R. Gaspar & Wiley F. Barker. (Major Problems in Clinical Surgery Ser.: Vol. 4). (Illus.). 528p. 1981. text ed. write for info. o.p. (ISBN 0-7216-4054-0). Saunders.

Peripheral Nerve. Ed. by D. H. Landon. 1976. 86.00x o.p. (ISBN 0-412-11740-1, NO. 6173, Pub. by Chapman & Hall). Routledge Chapman & Hall.

Peripheral Nerve Surgery. Julia K. Terzis. 1986. (ISBN 0-7216-1268-7). Saunders.

Peritonial Dialysis. Ed. by Robert C. Atkins. (Illus.). 426p. 1981. 74.00 o.p. (ISBN 0-443-02394-8). Churchill.

Perks & Parachutes: How to Get the Ideal Employment Package. John Tarrant. 320p. 1986. pap. 8.95 o.p. (ISBN 0-671-62807-0, Fireside). S&S.

Permafrost Fourth International Conference: Final Proceedings. National Academy of Sciences Staff. 413p. 1985. text ed. 32.50x o.p. (ISBN 0-309-03533-3). Natl Acad Pr.

Permanency Planning: Past, Present, & Future. Elizabeth Cole. (ISBN 0-87868-226-0, F-66, 2260). Child Welfare.

Permanent Campaign. Sidney Blumenthal. 1983. pap. 6.75 o.p. (ISBN 0-671-45341-6, Touchstone Bks). S&S.

Permanent Campaign: Inside the World of Elite Political Operatives. Sidney Blumenthal. LC 79-53755. 1980. 19.95x o.p. (ISBN 0-8070-3208-5). Beacon Pr.

Permanent Court of International Justice, 1920-1942: A Treatise. Manley O. Hudson. LC 74-147605. (Library of War & Peace; Kellogg Pact & the Outlawry of War). lib. bdg. 46.00 o.p. (ISBN 0-8240-0366-7). Garland Pub.

Permanent Errors. Reynolds Price. LC 70-124974. 1970. 6.50 o.p. (ISBN 0-689-10357-3, Atheneum). Macmillan.

Permanent War Economy. Seymour Melman. 1976. pap. 8.95 o.s.i. (ISBN 0-671-22261-9, Touchstone Bks). S&S.

Permissible Dose for Internal Radiation. International Commission on Radiological Protection. (ICRP Publication Ser.: No. 2). 1960. pap. 10.45 o.p. (ISBN 0-08-009254-3). Pergamon.

Permissive Universe. Kirtley F. Mather. LC 85-24618. 231p. 1986. 14.95 o.p. (ISBN 0-8263-0856-2). U of NM Pr.

Permissiveness & Control: The Fate of the Sixties Legislation. Ed. by National Deviancy Conference Staff. LC 79-55914. 199p. 1980. text ed. 27.50x o.p. (ISBN 0-06-495090-5). B&N Imports.

Permit Explosion: Coordination of the Proliferation. Fred Bosselman et al. LC 76-55844. (Management & Control of Growth Ser.). 86p. 1976. pap. 16.00 o.p. (ISBN 0-87420-570-0, P04). Urban Land.

Permits, Licenses, & Registrations: New England Edition. Frank Kirkpatrick. Ed. by Roger Griffith. LC 84-51488. 82p. 1984. 6.95 o.p. (ISBN 0-88266-374-7, Storey Pub); pap. 4.95 o.p. (ISBN 0-317-13949-5). Storey Comm Inc.

Peron & the Enigmas of Argentina. Robert Crassweller. 1987. 22.45 o.p. (ISBN 0-393-02381-8). Norton.

Peron Tapes. Julian Rathbone. (ISBN 0-394-54344-0). Pantheon.

Perpectives on Adult Career Development & Guidance. Ed. by Robert E. Campbell & Paul Shaltry. 197p. 1980. 10.50 o.p. (ISBN 0-318-15530-3, RD181). Natl Ctr Res Voc Ed.

Perplexing History of the European Empires, 2 vols. Charles H. Andrews. (Illus.). 455p. 1988. Set. 187.75 o.p. (ISBN 0-89266-633-1). Am Classical Coll Pr.

Perplexities & Paradoxes. Miguel Unamuno. (ISBN 0-8022-1754-0). Philos Lib.

Persatuan Islam: Islamic Reform in Twentieth Century Indonesia. Howard Federspiel. (Monograph Ser.). (Orig.). 1970. pap. 7.50 o.p. (ISBN 0-87763-013-5). Cornell Mod Indo.

Persecution & Martyrdom: From Experience to Theology in Paul. John S. Pobee. (JSNT Supplement Ser.: No. 6). 150p. pap. text ed. 14.95x o.s.i. (Pub. by JSOT Pr. England). Eisenbrauns.

Persecution & the Art of Writing. Leo Strauss. LC 73-1407. 204p. 1973. Repr. of 1952 ed. lib. bdg. 19.75 o.p. (ISBN 0-8371-6801-5, STPA). Greenwood.

Persepolis - The Archaeology of Persa, Seat of the Persian Kings. rev. ed. Donald N. Wilber. LC 87-27438. (Illus.). 144p. 1989. 24.95 o.p. (ISBN 0-87850-062-6). Darwin Pr.

Persian Carpets. Michael C. Hillmann. (Illus.). 112p. 1984. 24.95 o.p. (ISBN 0-292-76490-1). U of Tex Pr.

Persian Corridor: The Little-Known Story of the Signal Corps in the Middle East During World War II. Douglas S. Sherwen. 1979. 9.50 o.p. (ISBN 0-682-49337-6). Exposition-Phoenix.

Persian-English, English-Persian Shorter Dictionary, 2 vols. rev., enl. ed. S. Haim. (Persian, Modern & Eng.). Set. 50.00 o.s.i. (ISBN 0-686-77974-6). E J Brill USA.

Persian Gulf. Ed. by B. H. Purser. LC 72-97023. (Illus.). viii, 471p. 1978. 55.00 o.p. (ISBN 0-387-06156-8). Springer-Verlag.

Persian Gulf & United States Policy: A Guide to Issues & References. Bruce R. Kuniholm. LC 84-9853. (Guides to Contemporary Issues Ser.: No. 3). 228p. 1984. 21.95x o.p. (ISBN 0-941690-12-1); pap. 13.95x o.p. (ISBN 0-941690-11-3); pap. text ed. 8.75x o.p. Regina Bks.

Persian Language. Reuben Levy. 1952. (ISBN 0-8022-0967-X). Philos Lib.

Persian Letters, Pt. 2. Charles D. Montesquieu. LC 73-170550. (Novel in England, 1700-1775 Ser). lib. bdg. 61.00 o.p. (ISBN 0-8240-0550-3). Garland Pub.

Persian Notes. Robin Magowan. 1972. pap. 3.00 o.p. (ISBN 0-685-37095-X). Small Pr Dist.

Persian Paintings. B. W. Robinson. (Orig.). pap. 3.95 o.p. (ISBN 0-317-02537-6, Pub. by Victoria & Albert Mus UK). Faber & Faber.

Persian Words in English. A. A. Daryusl et al. Ed. by Steele Commager. Incl. German Influence on the English Vocabulary; H.W. Fowler; Dutch Influence on English Vocabulary; American Variations; Fine Writing; Names, Designations, & Appelations; Linguistic Self-Criticism; Formation & Use of Compound Epithets in English Poetry; Northern Words in Modern English. (Society for Pure English Ser.: Vol. 5). 1979. lib. bdg. 46.00 o.p. (ISBN 0-8240-3669-7). Garland Pub.

Persistent Dominion in History of the Theory of Masters & Slaves & Its Significance for the Human Race. Charles J. Lowell. (Illus.). 133p. 1984. 87.45x o.p. (ISBN 0-86722-060-0). Inst Econ Pol.

Persistent Virus Infections. Ed. by Morris Pollard. (Perspectives in Virology: Vol. 8). 1973. 54.50 o.p. (ISBN 0-12-560560-9). Acad Pr.

Persistent Viruses. Ed. by Jack G. Stevens et al. (ICN-UCLA Symposia on Molecular & Cellular Biology, 1978 Ser.: Vol. 11). 1978. 66.00 o.p. (ISBN 0-12-668350-6). Acad Pr.

Person & Community: A Philosophical Exploration. Ed. by Robert J. Roth. LC 73-93143. xii, 175p. 1975. 25.00 o.p. (ISBN 0-8232-0975-X). Fordham.

Person & God in a Spanish Valley. William A. Christian, Jr. LC 72-7697. (Studies in Social Discontinuity). 210p. 1972. 30.50 o.p. (ISBN 0-12-785119-4). Acad Pr.

Person & Work of the Holy Spirit in the Life of the Believer. George B. Duncan. LC 74-21900. 87p. 1975. pap. 1.99 o.p. (ISBN 0-8042-0681-3, John Knox). Westminster John Knox.

Person Circle: A First Book on Group Psychotherapy & the Small Group Field. Sidney Jacob Fields. LC 76-667. 1976. 8.50 o.p. (ISBN 0-682-48509-8, University). Exposition-Phoenix.

Person from England. F. Maclean et al. 384p. 1988. pap. 11.95 o.p. (ISBN 0-317-61230-1, Pub. by Century Hutchinson). David & Charles.

Person Identification by Means of the Teeth: A Practical Guide. S. Keiser-Nielsen. (Illus.). 124p. 1980. pap. text ed. 26.00 o.p. (ISBN 0-7236-0557-2, Pub. by John Wright UK). Butterworth.

Personal Aircraft. McGraw.

Personal Aircraft Business at Airports. L. L. Bollinger & J. R. Tully. 1948. Repr. of 1946 ed. 85.00 o.p. (ISBN 0-08-018742-0). Pergamon.

Personal Aircraft Maintenance. Kas Thomas. (Aviation Ser.). (Illus.). 256p. 1981. text ed. 39.50 o.p. (ISBN 0-07-064241-9). McGraw.

Personal & Community Health. Olive Keywood. (Illus.). 272p. 1982. pap. text ed. 9.95 o.p. (ISBN 0-632-00807-5, B 2675-7). Mosby.

Personal & Family Safety. Nancy Z. Olson. LC 80-11549. (Strang Ser.). 128p. 1981. 11.95 o.p. (ISBN 0-03-048271-2); pap. 5.95 o.p. (ISBN 0-03-048266-6). H Holt & Co.

Personal & Public Speaking. Donald W. Klopf & Ronald E. Cambra. 256p. 1983. pap. text ed. 12.95x o.p. (ISBN 0-89582-085-4). Morton Pub.

Personal & Social Education in the Curriculum. Richard Pring. (Studies in Teaching & Learning). 184p. (Orig.). 1984. pap. text ed. 16.95 o.s.i. (ISBN 0-340-33422-3). Princeton Bk Co.

Personal Anthology. Jorge L. Borges. Ed. & frwd. by Anthony Kerrigan. 1967. pap. 6.95 o.p. (ISBN 0-394-17270-1, E472, Ever). Grove.

Personal Awareness: A Psychology of Adjustment. 2nd ed. Richard G. Warga. LC 78-69531. (Illus.). 1979. pap. 16.95 o.p. (ISBN 0-395-26795-1). HM.

Personal Bible Study Journal, 1989. 1988. pap. 6.95 spiral o.p. (ISBN 0-89066-105-7). World Wide Pubs.

Personal Characteristics of Assaulted & Non-Assaulted Officers. Charles D. Hale & Wesley R. Wilson. (Criminal Justice Policy & Administration Research Ser.: No. 4). 1974. pap. 4.50 o.p. (ISBN 0-686-18641-9). Univ OK Gov Res.

Personal Choice: A Celebration of Twentith Century Photographs. Mark Haworth-Booth. (Illus.). 136p. (Orig.). 1984. pap. 18.95 o.p. (ISBN 0-905209-38-9, Pub. by Victoria & Albert Mus UK). Faber & Faber.

Personal Computer in Business Book. Peter A. McWilliams. LC 84-10352. (Illus.). 384p. 1984. pap. 9.95 o.p. (ISBN 0-385-19686-5, Quantum Pr). Doubleday.

Personal Computers. Hoo-min D. Toong & Amar Gupta. LC 83-7290. (Illus.). 130p. 1983. pap. 9.95 o.s.i. (ISBN 0-89708-127-7). And Bks.

Personal Computers & Data Communications. Dimitris N. Chorafas. LC 84-19972. (Personal Computing Ser.). 341p. 1986. pap. text ed. 25.95 o.p. (ISBN 0-88175-052-2, Computer Sci Pr). W H Freeman.

Personal Computers & Special Needs. Frank G. Bowe. LC 84-51240. 175p. 1984. pap. 9.95 o.p. (ISBN 0-89588-193-4). SYBEX.

Personal Computers & the Disabled. Peter A. McWilliams. LC 84-10309. (Illus.). 416p. 1984. pap. 9.95 o.p. (ISBN 0-385-19685-7, Quantum Pr). Doubleday.

Personal Computers in Business. Donald P. Kenny. LC 84-45204. 224p. 1984. pap. 15.95 o.p. (ISBN 0-8144-7627-9). AMACOM.

Personal Computers in Business. Ed. by Online Conferences Ltd. 1978. pap. text ed. 42.00x o.p. (ISBN 0-903796-33-3, Pub. by Online Conferences England). Gower Pub Co.

Personal Computing & C. J. A. Gainsborough. 1985. pap. text ed. 19.95 o.p. (ISBN 0-07-912645-6). McGraw.

Personal Computing & C. John A. Gainsborough. 200p. 1985. pap. 19.95 o.p. (ISBN 0-912677-45-7). Tate Pub.

Personal Computing for Professionals in Government & Business. P. Carr. pap. write for info. o.s.i. Meghan-Kiffer.

Personal Computing: Hardware & Software Basics. Electronics Magazine Editors. 1979. text ed. 38.50 o.p. (ISBN 0-07-019151-4). McGraw.

Personal Effects: A Novel of Hollywood. Rex Reed. 1986. 17.95 o.p. (ISBN 0-87795-685-5). Morrow.

Personal Equation. American Society of Association Executives Staff. 1989. text ed. write for info. o.p. (ISBN 0-88034-021-5). Am Soc Assn Execs.

Personal Evangelism among Roman Catholics. Aniceto Sparagna. (Orig.). 1978. pap. 3.95 o.p. (ISBN 0-89900-122-X). College Pr Pub.

Personal Experience of Time. Ed. by B. S. Gorman & A. E. Wessman. LC 77-21964. (Emotions, Personality, & Psychotherapy Ser.). (Illus.). 310p. 1977. 42.50x o.p. (ISBN 0-306-31039-2, Plenum Pr). Plenum Pub.

Personal Finance. 6th ed. Jerome B. Cohen. 1979. 33.95x o.p. (ISBN 0-256-02154-6). Irwin.

Personal Finance. 3rd ed. Jerome B. Cohen. (Plaid Ser.). 1981. 10.95 o.p. (ISBN 0-256-02126-0). Dow Jones-Irwin.

Personal Finance. Tom Garman et al. LC 84-80173. 704p. 1985. text ed. 41.96 o.p. (ISBN 0-395-35663-6). HM.

Personal Finance. 3rd ed. Lawrence J. Gitman. 750p. 1984. text ed. 30.95x o.s.i. (ISBN 0-03-068911-2); instr's. manual 20.00 o.s.i. (ISBN 0-03-068912-0). Dryden Pr.

Personal Finance. 7th ed. Harold A. Wolf. 1984. text ed. 38.00 o.p. (ISBN 0-205-08060-X, 108060); write for info instrs' manual o.p. (ISBN 0-205-08061-8). Allyn.

Personal Finance Four Cassette Pak. Dolan. 1987. pap. 35.95 o.p. (ISBN 0-471-60860-2). Wiley.

Personal Finance: Getting Along & Getting Ahead. J. Norman Swaton. LC 79-67018. 453p. 1981. pap. text ed. 16.95x o.p. PWS-Kent Pub.

Personal Finances for Ministers. rev. ed. John C. Banker. LC 73-4838. 128p. 1973. pap. 1.95 o.s.i. (ISBN 0-664-24972-8, Westminster). Westminster John Knox.

Personal Financial Management. David West & Glenn Wood. LC 75-172124. 80p. (Orig.). 1972. text ed. 23.50 o.p. (ISBN 0-395-12428-X). HM.

Personal Financial Management with dBASE III. George Geis. 250p. 1985. pap. 29.95 incl. disk o.p. (ISBN 0-912677-47-3). Tate Pub.

Personal Financial Planner. 1988 ed. Financial Publishing Co. Staff. 128p. 1988. pap. 6.25 o.p. (ISBN 0-87600-503-2). Finan PUb.

Personal Financial Planning. 3rd ed. G. Victor Hallman & Jerry S. Rosenbloom. 448p. 1985. text ed. 31.50 o.p. (ISBN 0-07-025648-9). McGraw.

Personal Financial Planning for Executives, updated ed. Randle & Swensen. 1981. 21.95 o.p. (ISBN 0-534-97964-5). Van Nos Reinhold.

Personal Financial Planning for Physicians & Dentists. Paul A. Randle & Philip R. Swenson. (Fin. Ser.). (Illus.). 268p. 1982. 32.95 o.p. (ISBN 0-534-97944-0, Lifetime Learn). Van Nos Reinhold.

Personal Growth & Behavior 1988-89. 8th, rev. ed. Ed. by Karen G. Duffy. LC 75-20757. (Annual Editions Ser.). (Illus.). 256p. 1988. pap. text ed. 9.95x o.p. (ISBN 0-87967-726-0). Dushkin Pub.

Personal History of Douglas F. Roby. Joseph F. Clayton. 529p. 1986. After Thoughts Inc.

Personal Income Tax Practice Set. R. Armstrong. 1987. pap. text ed. 12.75 o.p. (ISBN 0-07-002529-0). McGraw.

Personal Income Tax Practice Set: 1983 Edition. R. Armstrong. 1983. 7.60 o.p. (ISBN 0-07-002525-8). McGraw.

Personal Injury National Verdict Survey. Jury Verdict Research, Inc. Staff. LC 84-245660. 1986. 600.00 o.p. Jury Verdict.

Personal Inspirations & Reflections. Gertrude T. Reisberg. LC 83-90251. 76p. 1984. 8.95 o.p. (ISBN 0-533-05757-4). Vantage.

Personal Integrity. Ed. by William M. Schutte & Erwin R. Steinberg. (Illus., Orig.). 1961. pap. 3.95x o.p. (ISBN 0-393-09571-1, NortonC). Norton.

Personal Investing. 4th ed. Wilbur W. Widicus & Thomas E. Stitzel. 1985. 31.95x o.p. (ISBN 0-256-03006-5). Irwin.

Personal Involvement in Current Psychological Issues. Richard J. Hammersma et al. LC 72-13800. (Illus.). 250p. 1973. 29.00x o.p. (ISBN 0-8422-5084-0); pap. text ed. 12.50x o.p. (ISBN 0-8422-0290-0). Irvington.

Personal Justice. Ann Hilborn. 272p. 1982. pap. 2.95 o.p. (ISBN 0-380-81109-X, 81109-X). Avon.

Personal Justice Denied: Report of the Commission on Wartime Relocation & Interment of Civilians. 479p. (Orig.). 1982. pap. 8.50 o.p. (ISBN 0-318-11745-2, S/N 052-003-00897-1). USGPO.

Personal Learning Aid for Introductory Sociology. 3rd ed. Paul B. Horton & Robert L. Horton. 1983. pap. text ed. (ISBN 0-534-10585-8). Wadsworth Pub.

Personal Matter. Kenzaburo Oe. Tr. by John Nathan from Japanese. 1968. pap. 6.95 o.p. (ISBN 0-394-17141-1, B199, BC). Grove.

Personal Money Management with Your Micro. Wendy L. Milner. (Illus.). 384p. (Orig.). 1984. 18.95 o.p. (ISBN 0-8306-0709-9, 1709); pap. 13.15 o.p. (ISBN 0-8306-1709-4). TAB Bks.

Personal Name Index to Orton's Records of California Men in the War of the Rebellion, 1861 to 1867. Compiled by J. Carlyle Parker. LC 78-15674. (Genealogy & Local History Ser.: Vol. 5). 168p. 1978. 68.00x o.p. (ISBN 0-8103-1402-9). Gale.

Personal Name Index to the Eighteen Fifty-Six City Directories of California. Ed. by Nathan C. Parker. LC 79-24246. (Genealogy & Local History Ser.: Vol. 10). 280p. 68.00x o.p. (ISBN 0-8103-1414-2). Gale.

Personal Name Index to the Eighteen Fifty-Six City Directories of Iowa. LaVerne Sopp. (Genealogy & Local History Ser.: Vol. 13). 168p. 1980. 68.00x o.p. (ISBN 0-8103-1486-X). Gale.

Personal Name Index to the New York Times Index, 1975-1979 Supplement: Vol. 25, N-Z. Byron A. Falk & Valerie R. Falk. 434p. 1985. lib. bdg. 51.00 o.p. (ISBN 0-89902-125-5). Roxbury Data.

Personal Names: A Bibliography. Elsdon C. Smith. LC 66-31855. 226p. 1965. Repr. of 1952 ed. 35.00x o.p. (ISBN 0-8103-3134-9). Gale.

Personal Pension Plan Strategies for Physicians. C. Colburn Hardy & Howard J. Wiener. 144p. 1984. casebound 28.95 o.p. (ISBN 0-87489-345-3). Med Economics.

Personal Perspectives: A Guide to Decision Making. Beatrice Paolucci et al. LC 72-8842. (Illus.). 480p. (gr. 11-12). 1973. text ed. 22.28 o.p. (ISBN 0-07-048437-6). McGraw.

Personal Philosophy: The Art of Living. Thomas O. Buford. 1984. text ed. 25.95 o.p. (ISBN 0-03-059341-7). HR&W.

Personal Pocket Promise Book. David Wilkerson. 1987. gift ed. 16.95 o.s.i. (ISBN 0-8307-1236-4, 5111745). Regal.

Personal Prayer Journal, 1989. 1988. pap. 6.95 spiral o.p. (ISBN 0-89066-104-9). World Wide Pubs.

Personal-Professional Computers: How Can They Help You? North Texas State University Faculty of Computer Science Staff. LC 83-50902. 264p. 1983. pap. 12.95 o.p. (ISBN 0-89512-098-4). Tex Instr Inc.

Personal Psychology for Life & Work. R. K. Baltus. 1976. text ed. 17.25 o.p. (ISBN 0-07-003592-X, G). McGraw.

Personal Psychopathology: Early Formulations. Harry S. Sullivan. 416p. 1972. 12.50x o.p. (ISBN 0-393-01088-0). Norton.

Personal Publishing with the Macintosh. Terry Ulick. 207p. 1986. pap. 24.95 o.p. (ISBN 0-8104-6572-8). Sams.

Personal Recollections of Joan of Arc by the Sieur Louis De Conte. Samuel L. Clemens. LC 80-23663. (Illus.). xiv, 461p. 1980. Repr. of 1906 ed. lib. bdg. 60.50x o.p. (ISBN 0-313-22373-4, CLPR). Greenwood.

Personal Record. Joseph Conrad. LC 82-73728. xvii, 220p. 1982. pap. 6.95 o.p. (ISBN 0-910395-05-5). Marlboro Pr.

Personal Relationships: An Approach to Marriage & Family. Ernest J. Green. (Illus.). 1978. text ed. 36.95 o.p. (ISBN 0-07-024270-4). McGraw.

Personal Relationships, Vol. 2: Developing Personal Relationships. Ed. by S. Duck & R. Gilmour. LC 80-41360. 1981. 68.00 o.p. (ISBN 0-12-222802-2). Acad Pr.

Personal Robot Book. Texe Marrs. (Illus.). 192p. 1985. 21.95 o.p. (ISBN 0-8306-0896-6, 1896); pap. 12.60 o.p. (ISBN 0-8306-1896-1, 1896P). TAB Bks.

Personal Selling: Foundations, Process, & Management. Ben Enis. LC 78-12171. (Illus.). 1979. text ed. write for info. o.p. (ISBN 0-673-16132-3). Scott F.

Personal Selling: Function, Theory, & Practice. 2nd ed. James R. Young & Robert W. Mondy. LC 81-67246. 536p. 1981. text ed. 32.95x o.p. (ISBN 0-03-060291-2); instr's manual 20.00 o.p. (ISBN 0-03-060296-3). Dryden Pr.

Personal Shorthand Master Dictionary. Joanne Piper. 1978. 12.85 o.p. (ISBN 0-89420-043-7, 212000). Natl Book.

Personal Skill Building for the Emerging Manager. Dick Pinkstaff & Marlene A. Pinkstaff. LC 79-16920. 193p. 1983. pap. 16.95 o.p. (ISBN 0-8436-0785-8). Van Nos Reinhold.

Personal Skills for the Manager. Leonard Nadler. LC 82-72869. 275p. 1982. ringed binder 29.95x o.p. (ISBN 0-87094-349-9). Dow Jones-Irwin.

Personal Soulwinning. Jimmy Hester. 40p. (Orig.). 1986. wkbk. 4.95 o.s.i. (ISBN 0-914307-56-8). R Tilton Ministries.

Personal Style. James Wagenvoord. LC 85-14075. (Illus.). 222p. 1985. 16.95 o.p. (ISBN 0-03-004068-X). H Holt & Co.

Personal Styles in Neurosis: Implications for Small Group Psychotherapy & Behavior Therapy. Tom Caine et al. (International Library of Group Psychotherapy & Group Process). 224p. 27.95x o.p. (ISBN 0-7100-0617-9). Routledge Chapman & Hall.

Personal Subsidiary Farming under Socialism. G. Shmelev. 110p. 1986. pap. 1.95 o.p. (ISBN 0-8285-3242-7, Pub. by Progress Pubs USSR). Imported Pubns.

Personal Travel Budgets. Ed. by Howard R. Kirby. 124p. 1981. pap. 32.00 o.p. (ISBN 0-08-027420-X). Pergamon.

Personal Values in Public Policy. John Haughey. LC 79-84401. (Woodstock Studies: No. 3). 288p. (Orig.). 1979. pap. 6.95 o.p. (ISBN 0-8091-2201-4). Paulist Pr.

Personal View: Photography in the Collection of Paul F. Walter. John Pultz. pap. 40.00 o.p. (ISBN 0-87070-628-4). Museum Mod Art.

Personalities of the West & Midwest. 8th. ed. Ed. by J. M. Evans. LC 68-56857. 366p. 1985. 55.00x o.p. (ISBN 0-934544-26-3). Am Biog Inst.

Personality. Fay Fransella. (Psychology in Progress Ser.). 1981. 26.50x o.p. (ISBN 0-416-72770-0, NO. 2226); pap. 11.95x o.p. (ISBN 0-416-72780-8, NO. 2236). Routledge Chapman & Hall.

Personality: An Introduction. John Lamberth et al. 1978. text ed. 21.00 o.p. (ISBN 0-394-31190-6, RanC). Random.

Personality & Adjustment. Lu Hsien. 97p. 1972. pap. text ed. 5.95x o.p. (ISBN 0-8290-1089-0). Irvington.

Personality & Adjustment in the Aged. R. D. Savage et al. 1978. 52.00 o.p. (ISBN 0-12-619550-1). Acad Pr.

Personality & Hypnosis: A Study of Imaginative Involvement. 2nd ed. Josephine R. Hilgard. LC 79-13387. 1979. lib. bdg. 19.50x o.s.i. (ISBN 0-226-33443-0); pap. text ed. 5.95 o.s.i. (ISBN 0-226-33442-2, P852). U of Chicago Pr.

Personality & Ideology. Peter Leonard. (Critical Texts in Social Work & the Welfare State). 224p. 1984. text ed. 35.00x o.p. (ISBN 0-391-03056-6). Humanities.

Personality & National Character. R. Lynn. 1971. text ed. 27.00 o.p. (ISBN 0-08-016516-8). Pergamon.

Personality & Politics: Problems of Evidence, Inference, & Conceptualization. Fred I. Greenstein. 352p. 1975. pap. 4.95 o.p. (ISBN 0-393-00767-7, Norton Lib). Norton.

Personality & Salesmanship, Speedways to Success. O. William Bill Hayes. 1978. 6.00 o.p. (ISBN 0-682-49158-6, Banner). Exposition-Phoenix.

Personality & Social Encounter: Selected Essays. Gordon W. Allport. LC 80-39538. x, 388p. 1981. pap. text ed. 17.00x o.s.i. (ISBN 0-226-01494-0). U of Chicago Pr.

Personality Assessment. Philip E. Vernon. (Methuen's Manuals of Psychology Ser.). 1979. pap. 11.95x o.p. (ISBN 0-422-72560-9, NO. 2565, Pub. by Tavistock England). Routledge Chapman & Hall.

Personality Decorating. Lynda G. Barbaer & Elizabeth V. Warren. 288p. (Orig.). 1986. pap. 14.95 o.s.i. (ISBN 0-449-90111-4, Columbine). Fawcett.

Personality Development. Jerome Kagan. (Illus.). 181p. 1971. pap. text ed. 9.00 net o.p. (ISBN 0-15-569750-1, HC). HarBraceJ.

Personality Development & Psychopathology: A Dynamic Approach. Norman Cameron. LC 63-6438. 1963. text ed. 29.95 o.p. (ISBN 0-395-04251-8). HM.

Personality Development in Preschool Years, Latency, & Adolescence see Teaching Program in Psychiatry.

Personality Differences & Biological Variations: A Study of Twins. Gordon S. Claridge et al. LC 72-10132. 1973. 50.00 o.p. (ISBN 0-08-017124-9). Pergamon.

Personality: Dynamics, Development & Assessment. Irving L. Janis et al. 1969. text ed. 18.95 o.p. (ISBN 0-15-569585-1, HC). HarBraceJ.

Personality in Politics. Alan C. Elms. (Illus.). 200p. 1976. pap. text ed. 9.50 o.p. (ISBN 0-15-569762-5, HC). HarBraceJ.

Personality Language: Power Pack. Stefan Neilson & Shay Thoelke. (Illus.). 44p. 1985. Repr. of 1981 ed. coil bdg. 7.95 o.p. (ISBN 0-9606110-4-5). AEON-Hierophant.

Personality Language: Youth's Road to Excellence. Stefan Neilson & Shay Thoelke. (Illus.). 138p. 1987. pap. text ed. 20.00 coil o.p. (ISBN 0-317-55247-3); tchr's. ed 30.00 o.p. (ISBN 0-317-55248-1); participant's manual 10.00 o.p. (ISBN 0-317-55249-X). Aeon-Hierophant.

Personality Psychology in Europe: Current Trends & Controversies. Ed. by A. Angleitner et al. 266p. (Orig.). 1986. pap. 33.50 o.p. (ISBN 9-02650-597-3). CJ Hogrefe Pubs.

Personality: Research & Theory. Nathan Brody. 1972. 46.00 o.p. (ISBN 0-12-134850-4). Acad Pr.

Personality: The Human Potential. M. L. Weiner. 200p. 1973. 28.00 o.p. (ISBN 0-08-016946-5). Pergamon.

Personality Theories: An Introduction. Barbara O. Engler. LC 78-69596. (Illus.). 1979. text ed. 26.95 o.p. (ISBN 0-395-26772-2). HM.

Personality Theories, Research & Assessment. Raymond J. Corsini & Anthony J. Marsella. LC 82-61261. 703p. 1983. text ed. 32.50 o.p. (ISBN 0-87581-288-0). Peacock Pubs.

Personalized Guide to Computers & Your Dental Practice, Vol. 6. Ed. by Thomas L. Snyder & Charles J. Felmeister. (Mosby's Dental Practice Management Ser.). (Illus.). 150p. 1983. pap. text ed. 19.95 o.p. (ISBN 0-8016-4721-5). Mosby.

Personalized Guide to Establishing Associateships & Partnerships, Vol. 3. Thomas L. Snyder & Jeffrey C. Bauer. LC 82-14347. (Dental Practice Management Ser.). (Illus.). 152p. 1982. pap. text ed. 17.95 o.p. (ISBN 0-8016-4714-2). Mosby.

Personalized Guide to Financial Planning, Vol. 5. Ed. by Thomas L. Snyder et al. LC 82-14356. (Dental Practice Management Ser.). 122p. 1982. pap. text ed. 17.95 o.p. (ISBN 0-8016-4713-4). Mosby.

Personalized Guide to Legal Issues, Vol. 7. Thomas L. Snyder & Randall K. Berning. LC 84-8259. (Mosby's Dental Practice Management Ser.: Vol. 7). 140p. 1984. pap. text ed. 17.95 o.p. (ISBN 0-8016-4751-7). Mosby.

Personalized Guide to Marketing Strategy, Vol. 4. Ed. by Thomas L. Snyder & Charles J. Felmeister. LC 82-14158. (Dental Practice Management Ser.). (Illus.). 120p. 1983. pap. text ed. 17.95 o.p. (ISBN 0-8016-4725-8). Mosby.

Personalized Guide to Practice Evaluation, Vol. 1. Thomas L. Snyder & Larry R. Domer. LC 82-14306. (Dental Practice Management Ser.). 208p. 1982. pap. text ed. 17.95 o.p. (ISBN 0-8016-4715-0). Mosby.

Personalized Guide to Stress Evaluation, Vol. 2. Ed. by Thomas L. Snyder & Charles J. Felimeister. (Dental Practice Management Ser.). (Illus.). 103p. 1982. pap. text ed. 17.95 o.p. (ISBN 0-8016-4724-X). Mosby.

Personalizing Reading Instruction in Middle Junior & Senior High Schools. 2nd ed. Martha H. Dillner & Joanne P. Olson. 544p. 1982. pap. text ed. write for info. o.p. (ISBN 0-02-329780-8). Macmillan.

Personnel. Andrew J. Dubrin. 1981. 22.50 o.p. (ISBN 0-534-25407-1). PWS-Kent Pub.

Personnel: A Book of Readings. Ed. by William F. Glueck. 1979. pap. 16.95x o.p. (ISBN 0-256-02078-7). Irwin.

Personnel & Human Resource Management (International Edition) 2nd ed. Randall S. Schuler. (Illus.). 700p. 1984. 17.00 o.p. (ISBN 0-314-77789-X). West Pub.

Personnel & Human Resources Administration. 5th ed. Leon C. Megginson. 1985. 35.95x o.p. (ISBN 0-256-03229-7). Irwin.

Personnel Classification Schemes. (SPEC Kit & Flyer Ser.: No. 85). 98p. 1982. (10.00 for ARL members) 20.00 o.p. (ISBN 0-318-03469-7); members 10.00 o.p. OMS.

Personnel Forms. (Easy-to-Make Photocopier Bks.). (Orig.). 1983. pap. 14.95 o.s.i. (ISBN 0-87280-037-7, Asher-Gallant). Caddylak Systs.

Personnel-Human Resource Management. 3rd ed. Herbert G. Heneman, Jr. et al. 1986. 36.95 o.p. (ISBN 0-256-03360-9). Irwin.

Personnel: Human Resource Management. 4th ed. Robert L. Mathis & John H. Jackson. (Illus.). 659p. 1985. text ed. 39.75 o.p. (ISBN 0-314-85276-X). West Pub.

Personnel-Human Resources Management: A Diagnostic Approach. 4th. ed. George T. Milkovich & William F. Glueck. 1985. 38.95x o.p. (ISBN 0-256-03267-X). Irwin.

Personnel Interviewing: The Working Woman's Resource Book. 2nd ed. Felix M. Lopez. (Illus.). 384p. 1975. text ed. 43.95 o.p. (ISBN 0-07-038726-5). McGraw.

Personnel Job of Government Managers. O. Glenn Stahl. 185p. 1971. 12.00 o.p. (ISBN 0-87373-058-5). Intl Personnel Mgmt.

Personnel Law Handbook. Wake Forest University School of Law Staff. 125.00cancelled o.s.i. (ISBN 0-318-18442-7). Wake Forest Law.

Personnel Management: A Situational Approach. Donald P. Crane. 1974. (ISBN 0-534-00356-7). PWS-Kent Pub.

Personnel Management & Organization Development: Fields in Transition. Ed. by Wendell L. French & Don Hellriegel. LC 73-144320. 1972. pap. 12.95 o.p. (ISBN 0-395-12035-7). HM.

Personnel Management for the Smaller Company: A Hands-on Manual. Linda A. Roxe. (Illus.). 1979. 14.95 o.p. (ISBN 0-8144-5509-3). AMACOM.

Personnel Management in Merchant Ships. D. H. Moreby. 1968. text ed. 29.00 o.p. (ISBN 0-08-012993-5); pap. 14.00 o.p. (ISBN 0-08-012992-7). Pergamon.

Personnel: Management of Human Resources. 3rd ed. Mondy & Noe. 736p. 1986. 41.00 o.s.i. (ISBN 0-205-08946-1). Allyn.

Personnel Management Process. 4th ed. Wendell L. French. LC 77-73992. (Illus.). 1978. text ed. 22.95 o.p. (ISBN 0-395-25529-5). HM.

Personnel Management Process: Cases in Human Resources Administration. 5th ed. Wendell French. LC 81-86540. 1982. text ed. 37.95 o.p. (ISBN 0-395-31713-4). HM.

Personnel Management Process: Cases on Human Resources Administration. Wendell L. French et al. LC 77-74422. (Illus.). 1978. pap. 11.50 o.p. (ISBN 0-395-25531-7). HM.

Personnel Manual: An Outline for Libraries. LC 77-5539. 46p. 1977. pap. 5.00x o.p. (ISBN 0-8389-0239-1). ALA.

Personnel of Fairyland: A Short Account of the Fairy People of Great Britain for Those Who Tell Stories to Children. Katherine M. Briggs. LC 70-147084. (Illus.). 234p. 1971. Repr. of 1953 ed. 35.00x o.p. (ISBN 0-8103-3372-4). Gale.

Personnel Practices of the Retail Industry. National Retail Merchants Association Staff. pap. 5.00 o.p. (ISBN 0-87102-033-5, 55-7596). Natl Ret Merch.

Personnel Program Appraisal Workbook. Gloria W. White. 10.00 o.p. (ISBN 0-910402-66-3); 6.00 o.p. Coll & U Personnel.

Personnel Services in Education. Ed. by Melvene D. Hardee. LC 59-3793. (National Society for the Study of Education Yearbooks Ser: No. 58, Pt. 2). 1959. pap. text ed. 4.50x o.s.i. (ISBN 0-226-60051-3). U of Chicago Pr.

Personnel: The Management of Human Resources. 2nd ed. R. Wayne Mondy & Robert M. Noe. 1983. text ed. write for info. o.p. (ISBN 0-205-08058-8, 088058); instr's. manual 11.43 o.p. (ISBN 0-205-08256-4, 088256). Allyn.

Persons & Persuasions. Oren Root. (Illus.). 1974. 7.95 o.p. (ISBN 0-393-07482-X). Norton.

Persons Lowly Born. Jennie Charsky, pseud. (ISBN 0-8022-0233-0). Philos Lib.

Perspectivas: Temas de Hoy y de Siempre. 3rd ed. Mary E. Kiddle & Brenda Wegmann. (Span.). 1983. pap. text ed. 16.95 o.p. (ISBN 0-03-061482-1). HR&W.

Perspective. Charles Rembar. LC 73-90111. 1974. 8.95 o.p. (ISBN 0-87795-105-5, Arbor Hse). Morrow.

Perspective Drawings by Programmable Calculator: A Method with Graphic Arts. David Yue. (Illus.). 220p. 1984. 32.95 o.p. (ISBN 0-442-29035-7). Van Nos Reinhold.

Perspective for Interior Designers. John Pile. (Illus.). 160p. 1985. 24.95 o.p. (ISBN 0-8230-7420-X). Watson-Guptill.

Perspective for the Artist. Sal Amendola. (Illus.). 64p. (Orig.). 1983. pap. 4.95 o.s.i. (Pentalic). Taplinger.

Perspective in Alcohol & Drug Abuse: Similarities & Differences. Joel Solomon & Kim Keeley. 270p. 1982. pap. 28.00 o.p. (ISBN 0-88416-306-7). Year Bk Med.

Perspective in Art. Michael Woods. LC 84-20660. (Illus.). 144p. 1985. 12.95 o.p. (ISBN 0-89134-101-3). North Light Bks.

Perspective on Budgeting (Par Classics, Vol. II. Ed. by Allen Schick. LC 80-81208. 1980. 10.95 o.p. (ISBN 0-936678-01-1). Am Soc Pub Admin.

Perspective on Energy Modeling. Ed. by Bruce A. Smith. 1976. pap. 35.00 o.p. (ISBN 0-08-019985-2). Pergamon.

Perspectives in Consumer Behavior. 3rd ed. Harold Kassarjian & Thomas Robertson. 1981. pap. text ed. write for info. o.p. (ISBN 0-673-15394-0). Scott F.

Perspectives in Creep Fracture. Ed. by M. F. Ashby & L. M. Brown. 180p. 1983. 45.00 o.p. (ISBN 0-08-030541-5). Pergamon.

Perspectives in Educational Psychology: Old Wine in New Bottles. Ed. by Gary L. Sapp. 249p. 1975. 29.00x o.p. (ISBN 0-8422-5230-4); pap. text ed. 12.50x o.p. (ISBN 0-8422-0524-1). Irvington.

Perspectives in Hemostasis: Proceedings of a Symposium Held at Loyola University, Maywood, Ill., U. S. A. 11 May 1979. Ed. by Jawed Fareed. (Illus.). 400p. 1981. 115.00 o.p. (ISBN 0-08-025092-0). Pergamon.

Perspectives in Immigrant & Minority Education. Ed. by Ronald J. Samuda & Sandra L. Woods. 390p. (Orig.). 1983. lib. bdg. 34.00 o.p. (ISBN 0-8191-3062-1); pap. text ed. 16.75 o.p. (ISBN 0-8191-3063-X). U Pr of Amer.

Perspectives in Interactional Psychology. Ed. by Lawrence A. Pervin & Michael Lewis. LC 78-13514. 352p. 1978. 39.50x o.p. (ISBN 0-306-31146-1, Plenum Pr). Plenum Pub.

Perspectives in Musicology. Ed. by Barry S. Brook et al. 400p. 1975. pap. 5.95 o.p. (ISBN 0-393-00784-7, N784, Norton Lib). Norton.

Perspectives in Personal Construct Theory. Ed. by D. Bannister. 1971. 60.00 o.p. (ISBN 0-12-077960-9). Acad Pr.

Perspectives in Perspective. Lawrence Wright. (Illus.). 300p. 1983. 75.00x o.p. (ISBN 0-7100-0791-4). Routledge Chapman & Hall.

Perspectives in Phytochemistry: Proceedings. Phytochemical Society Staff. Ed. by J. B. Harborne & T. Swain. 1969. 61.50 o.p. (ISBN 0-12-324660-1). Acad Pr.

Perspectives in Political Sociology. Ed. by Andrew Effrat. LC 73-4329. pap. text ed. 9.95x o.p. (ISBN 0-8290-1763-1). Irvington.

Perspectives in Reading. N. Hartman. 1971. pap. text ed. 4.75x o.p. (ISBN 0-8422-0158-0). Irvington.

Perspectives In the Sociology of Science. Stuart S. Blume. LC 76-30827. 237p. 1977. 73.95 o.p. (ISBN 0-471-99480-4, Pub. by Wiley-Interscience). Wiley.

Perspectives in Urban Entomology. Ed. by G. W. Frankie & C. S. Koehler. 1978. 65.00 o.p. (ISBN 0-12-265250-9). Acad Pr.

Perspectives in World Agriculture. 532p. 1980. 48.50 o.p. (ISBN 0-85198-458-4). CAB Intl.

Perspectives in Zoology. A. A. Boyden. LC 73-1279. 294p. 1973. 50.00 o.p. (ISBN 0-08-017122-2). Pergamon.

Perspectives of Wages & Prices. Henry P. Brown & Sheila V. Hopkins. 256p. 1981. 30.00x o.p. (ISBN 0-416-31950-5, NO. 3478). Routledge Chapman & Hall.

Perspectives on a Regional Culture: Essays About the Coimbatore Area of South India. Brenda E. Beck. 1979. text ed. 27.50x o.p. (ISBN 0-7069-0723-X, Pub. by Vikas India). Advent NY.

Perspectives on Academic Gaming & Simulations: Games & Simulations - the Real & the Ideal, No. 6. Society for Academic Gaming & Simulation in Education & Training Staff. Ed. by Betty Hollinshead & Mantz Yorke. 220p. 1981. 35.00x o.p. (ISBN 0-85038-422-2). Nichols Pub.

Perspectives on Academic Gaming & Simulation: Human Factors in Games & Simulation, No. 4. Ed. by Jacquetta Megarry. 190p. 1979. 35.00 o.p. (ISBN 0-85038-196-7, Pub. by Kogan Pg.). Nichols Pub.

Perspectives on Academic Gaming & Simulation: Simulation in Management & Business Education, No. 7. Ed. by Lynton Gray & Ian Waitt. 160p. 1982. 35.00 o.p. (ISBN 0-89397-139-1). Nichols Pub.

Perspectives on Adult Career Development & Guidance. (gr. 5 up). cancelled o.s.i. (ISBN 0-318-23262-6, RD 181). Natl Ctr Res Voc Ed.

Perspectives on Aging. Ed. by Gari Lesnoff-Caravaglia. 141p. 1977. pap. text ed. 7.95x o.p. (ISBN 0-8290-1655-4). Irvington.

Perspectives on American Composers. Ed. by Benjamin Boretz & Edward T. Cone. 1971. pap. 5.95 o.p. (ISBN 0-393-00549-6, Norton Lib). Norton.

Perspectives on British Sign Language & Deafness. Ed. by B. Woll et al. (Illus.). 268p. 1981. 29.95 o.p. (ISBN 0-7099-2703-7, Pub. by Croom Helm Ltd). Routledge Chapman & Hall.

Perspectives on Canadian Airline Regulation. G. B. Reschenthaler & B. Roberts. 266p. 1979. pap. text ed. 13.50x o.p. (ISBN 0-409-88604-1, Pub. by Inst Res Pub Canada). Gower Pub Co.

Perspectives on Congress: Performance & Prospects. League of Women Voters Education Fund Staff. (Federalist Papers Reexamined: No. 3). 32p. 1977. pap. 1.00 o.p. (ISBN 0-89959-039-X, 213). LWV US.

Perspectives on Contemporary Music Theory. Ed. by Benjamin Boretz & Edward T. Cone. 304p. (Orig.). 1972. pap. 5.95 o.p. (ISBN 0-393-00548-8, Norton Lib). Norton.

Perspectives on Counseling Adults. Nancy K. Schlossberg et al. LC 77-16292. 152p. 1978. 16.95 o.p. (ISBN 0-8185-0261-4). Krieger.

Perspectives on Environment & Behavior: Theory, Research & Applications. Ed. by Daniel Stokols. LC 76-45326. (Illus.). 374p. 1977. 39.50x o.p. (ISBN 0-306-30954-8, Plenum Pr). Plenum Pub.

Perspectives on Equity. 1982. 30.00 o.p. (ISBN 0-318-23570-6, RD 214). Natl Ctr Res Voc Ed.

Perspectives on Geomorphic Processes. G. H. Drury. LC 78-80970. (CCG Resource Papers Ser.: No. 3). (Illus.). 1969. pap. text ed. 5.00 o.p. (ISBN 0-89291-050-X). Assn Am Geographers.

Perspectives on Health Policy: Australia, New Zealand, United States. Ed. by Marshall Raffel & Norma K. Raffel. LC 87-2168. 292p. 1987. 48.50 o.p. (ISBN 0-471-91510-6, Dist. by A R Liss). Wiley.

Perspectives on Helping Relationships. Arthur W. Combs & Avila. 250p. (Orig.). 1985. pap. text ed. 24.00 o.p. (ISBN 0-205-08325-0, 248325). Allyn.

Perspectives on History. William Dray. 192p. 1980. 23.95x o.p. (ISBN 0-7100-0569-5); pap. 10.00 o.p. (ISBN 0-7100-0570-9). Routledge Chapman & Hall.

Perspectives on Indian Prose in English. M. K. Naik. 277p. 1982. text ed. 17.50x o.p. (ISBN 0-391-02660-7). Humanities.

Perspectives on Landscape. Bill Gaskind. (British Image Ser.: No. 5). 84p. 1980. pap. 10.00 o.p. (ISBN 0-7287-0168-5). Eastview.

Perspectives on Minority Group Mental Health. Ed. by Faye U. Munoz & Russell Endo. LC 81-40848. 192p. (Orig.). 1982. lib. bdg. 29.00 o.p. (ISBN 0-8191-2343-9); pap. text ed. 12.50 o.p. (ISBN 0-8191-2344-7). U Pr of Amer.

Perspectives on Modernization: Toward a General Theory of Third World Development. M. Francis Abraham. LC 79-6811. 262p. 1980. pap. text ed. 14.25 o.p. (ISBN 0-8191-0961-4). U Pr of Amer.

Perspectives on Notation & Performance. Ed. by Benjamin Boretz & Edward T. Cone. (Illus.). 1976. 10.00x o.p. (ISBN 0-393-02190-4, Norton Lib); pap. 3.95 o.p. (ISBN 0-393-00809-6). Norton.

Perspectives on Nursing Leadership: Proceedings of the Conference on Research in Nursing, Sixteenth Conference. Stewart Conference on Research in Nursing Staff. Ed. by Shake Ketefian. LC 80-27464. (Orig.). 1981. pap. text ed. 8.95x o.p. (ISBN 0-8077-2637-0). Tchrs Coll.

Perspectives on Paul. Ernst Kasemann. Tr. by Margaret Kohl from Ger. LC 79-157540. 184p. 1971. 7.25 o.p. (ISBN 0-8006-0030-4, 1-30, Fortress). Augsburg Fortress.

Perspectives on Paul. Ernst Kasemann. LC 79-157540. 184p. 1982. pap. 7.95 o.p. (ISBN 0-8006-1730-4, 1-1730, Fortress). Augsburg Fortress.

Perspectives on R. K. Narayan. Atma Ram. (Indo-English Writers: No. 3). 222p. 1981. text ed. 15.00x o.p. (ISBN 0-391-02514-7). Humanities.

Perspectives on Raja Rao. K. K. Sharma. (Indo-English Writers Ser.: No. 2). 237p. 1980. text ed. 15.00x o.p. (ISBN 0-391-02520-1). Humanities.

Perspectives on Resource Management. T. O'Riordan. (Illus.). 184p. 1971. 10.50x o.p. (ISBN 0-85086-024-5, NO. 2931, Pub by Pion England); pap. 10.50x o.p. (ISBN 0-85086-025-3, NO. 2920). Routledge Chapman & Hall.

Perspectives on Revolution & Evolution. Ed. by Richard A. Preston. LC 78-74448. xii, 294p. 1979. 30.00 o.p. (ISBN 0-8223-0425-2). Duke.

Perspectives on Schoenberg & Stravinsky. Ed. by Benjamin Boretz & Edward T. Cone. 304p. 1972. pap. 4.95 o.p. (ISBN 0-393-00618-2, Norton Lib). Norton.

Perspectives on Social Welfare: An Introductory Anthology. 2nd ed. P. E. Weinberger. 1974. pap. (ISBN 0-02-425160-7). Macmillan.

Perspectives on Strategic Marketing Management. Roger Kerin & Robert M. Peterson. 480p. 1983. text ed. 28.00 o.p. (ISBN 0-205-07922-9, 087922). Allyn.

Perspectives on Teaching: Learning & Development. Andrew Garrod et al. 536p. 1984. pap. text ed. 25.95 o.p. (ISBN 0-8403-3482-6). Kendall Hunt.

Perspectives on the Development of a Comprehensive Labor Market Information System for Michigan. Rodgers Lawson. 74p. 1973. pap. 1.75 o.p. (ISBN 0-911558-42-X). W E Upjohn.

Perspectives on the European Past: Conversations with Historians. Norman F. Cantor. 1971. write for info. combined ed. o.p. (ISBN 0-02-319180-5); pap. 7.50 ea. o.p.; Vol. 1. pap. (ISBN 0-02-319050-7); Vol. 2. pap. (ISBN 0-685-01461-4). Macmillan.

Perspectives on the Group Process: A Foundation for Counseling with Groups. 2nd ed. C. Gratton Kemp. LC 64-346. 1970. text ed. 28.95 o.p. (ISBN 0-395-04723-4). HM.

Perspectives on the Parables: An Approach to Multiple Interpretations. Mary Ann Tolbert. LC 78-54563. 144p. 1978. 4.95 o.p. (ISBN 0-8006-0527-6, 1-527, Fortress). Augsburg Fortress.

Perspectives on the Royal Commission on Corporate Concentration. P. K. Gorecki & W. T. Stanbury. 308p. 1979. pap. text ed. 15.95x o.p. (ISBN 0-409-88606-8, Pub. by Inst Res Pub Canada). Gower Pub Co.

Perspectives: Understanding & Evaluating Today's World Views. Norman L. Geisler & Williams D. Watkins. LC 84-70487. 269p. (Orig.). 1984. pap. 8.95 o.p. (ISBN 0-89840-073-2). Heres Life.

Perspecture, Optics, & Delft Artists Around Sixteen Fifty. Arthur K. Wheelock, Jr. LC 76-23661. (Outstanding Dissertations in the Fine Arts - 17th Century). (Illus.). 1977. Repr. of 1973 ed. lib. bdg. 68.00 o.p. (ISBN 0-8240-2740-X). Garland Pub.

Persuaders: Propaganda in War & Peace. Gladys Thum & Marcella Thum. LC 72-75288. (gr. 6 up). 1972. 7.95 o.p. (ISBN 0-689-30071-9, Atheneum). Macmillan.

Persuasion: How Opinions & Attitudes Are Changed. 2nd ed. Marvin Karlins & Herbert Abelson. LC 78-100098. 179p. 1970. pap. 17.95 o.p. (ISBN 0-8261-0364-2). Springer Pub.

Persuasion: Reception & Responsibility. 4th ed. Charles U. Larson. 349p. 1986. pap. text ed. (ISBN 0-534-06162-1). Wadsworth Pub.

Persuasion: Understanding, Practice & Analysis. Herbert W. Simons. (Illus.). 400p. 1976. text ed. 18.00 o.p. (ISBN 0-394-34983-0, RanC). Random.

Perturbation Expansions in Axiomatic Field Theory. O. Steinmann. LC 72-183483. (Lecture Notes in Physics: Vol. 11). iii, 126p. 1971. pap. 10.70 o.p. (ISBN 0-387-05698-X). Springer-Verlag.

Perturbation Methods in Non-Linear Systems. G. E. Giacaglia. LC 72-87714. (Applied Mathematical Sciences Ser: Vol. 8). 378p. 1972. pap. 13.10 o.p. (ISBN 0-387-90054-3). Springer-Verlag.

Pertussis Toxin. Ed. by Ronald Sekura & Joel Moss. 1985. 39.50 o.p. (ISBN 0-12-635480-4). Acad Pr.

Peru: A Country Study. 3rd ed. Ed. by Richard F. Nyrop. LC 81-3456. (Area Handbook Ser.: DA Pam 550-42). 330p. 1981. 11.00 o.p. (ISBN 0-318-21885-2, S/N 008-020-00869-9). USGPO.

Peru & the United States, 1900-1962. James C. Carey. 1964. 19.95x o.p. (ISBN 0-268-00206-1). U of Notre Dame Pr.

Perverse & Foolish. L. M. Boston. LC 78-71593. 180p. 1979. 8.95 o.p. (ISBN 0-689-50136-6, Atheneum). Macmillan.

Perversity of Politics. E. Beuhrig. 128p. 1985. 27.50 o.p. (ISBN 0-7099-3201-4, Pub. by Croom Helm Ltd). Routledge Chapman & Hall.

Pervert. Jose E. Contreras. 96p. 1986. 8.75 o.p. (ISBN 0-8062-3041-X). Carlton.

Pervigilium Veneris: A Late Latin Poem of Love & Springtime. Ed. by Vincent J. Cleary & Theodore W. Wells. 46p. (Lat.). (gr. 10-12). 1981. pap. text ed. 3.75x o.p. (ISBN 0-88334-151-4). Ind Sch Pr.

Pest Management Programs for Deciduous Tree Fruits & Nuts. Ed. by D. J. Boethal & R. D. Eikenbary. LC 79-12616. 268p. 1979. 52.50x o.p. (ISBN 0-306-40178-9, Plenum Pr). Plenum Pub.

Pest Resistance to Pesticides in Agriculture. 38p. 1970. pap. 7.50 o.p. (ISBN 0-686-70624-2, F1984, FAO). UNIPUB.

Peste. Albert Camus. (Coll. Soleil). 1942. 15.75 o.p. (ISBN 0-685-11487-2). Schoenhof.

Pesticide Application & Safety Training. M. W. Stimmann. LC 80-52766. 1977. pap. text ed. 8.00x o.p. (ISBN 0-931876-17-6, 4070). ANR Pubns CA.

Pesticide Chemistry-Three: Proceedings, Helsinki, 1974. Ed. by P. Varo. 1976. 95.00 o.p. (ISBN 0-08-020973-4). Pergamon.

Pesticide Decision Making. National Research Council. LC 77-94524. (Analytical Studies for the U. S. Environmental Protection Agency Ser.). (Illus.). 1978. pap. text ed. 7.50 o.p. (ISBN 0-309-02734-9). Natl Acad Pr.

Pesticide Residues in Food: Report of the 1974 Joint FAO-WHO Expert Meeting. (Agricultural Planning Studies: No. 97). pap. 6.25 o.p. (F314, FAO). UNIPUB.

Pesticide Terminal Residues (Additional Publication) Proceedings of an International Symposium. Ed. by A. S. Tahori. 374p. 1976. 97.00 o.p. (ISBN 0-08-020809-6). Pergamon.

Pesticides: A Community Action Guide. Ed. by Cynthia McGrath et al. 22p. 1985. pap. text ed. 3.00 o.p. (ISBN 0-937345-02-4). Concern.

Pesticides & the Environment: Monographs. Mary Vance. (Public Administration Ser.: Bibliography P 1638). 1985. pap. 6.75 o.p. (ISBN 0-89028-328-1). Vance Biblios.

Pesticides Guide. Keller, J. J., & Associates, Inc. Staff. LC 79-54216. (22G). 600p. 1985. 95.00 o.p. (ISBN 0-934674-12-4). J J Keller.

Pesticides Residues in Food: Report of the Joint Meeting, Geneva, December 1968. (Agricultural Planning Studies: No. 78). 40p. 1969. pap. 5.75 o.p. (ISBN 92-5-101532-5, F309, FAO). UNIPUB.

Pesto Manifesto. Lovel Nazzaro. 120p. 1987. pap. 6.95 o.p. (ISBN 1-55652-028-X). Chicago Review.

Pests of Grain Legumes: Ecology & Control. Ed. by S. R. Singh et al. 1979. 76.00 o.p. (ISBN 0-12-646350-6). Acad Pr.

Pet Aerobics: How to Solve Your Pets Behavior Problems, Improve Their Health, Lengthen Their Lives & Have Fun Doing It. Warren Eckstein & Fay Eckstein. 1984. 14.95 o.p. (ISBN 0-03-063882-8). H Holt & Co.

PET Fun & Games. J. R. Jeffries & G. Fisher. 1982. pap. text ed. 11.95 o.p. (ISBN 0-07-047859-7). McGraw.

Pet Pers Comp. (ISBN 0-07-931030-3). McGraw.

P.E.T. Pierre Elliott Trudeau & His Unearthly Adventures. Jude Waples. 64p. 1983. pap. 4.95 o.p. (ISBN 0-380-83543-6, 83543-6). Avon.

Pet Sematary. Stephen King. 1984. 18.95 o.p. (ISBN 0-8161-3691-2, Large Print Bks); pap. 9.95 o.p. (ISBN 0-8161-3756-0). G K Hall.

Pet Store. Peter Spier. LC 80-1846. (Balloon Bks.). (Illus.). 14p. (ps-3). 1981. 3.95 o.p. (ISBN 0-385-15730-4). Doubleday.

Peta, Wild Rose of the Mountain. Marjorie Miller. (Illus.). 33p. (gr. 3-7). 1985. 4.95 o.p. (ISBN 0-533-06347-7). Vantage.

Pete Turner Photographs. Owen Edwards. (Illus.). 144p. 1987. 29.95 o.p. (ISBN 0-8109-1691-6). Abrams.

Peter. William Coleman. LC 81-85894. 160p. (Orig.). 1982. pap. 4.95 o.p. (ISBN 0-89081-305-1). Harvest Hse.

Peter & Anthony Shaffer: A Reference Guide. Dennis A. Klein. 1982. lib. bdg. 23.00 o.p. (ISBN 0-8161-8574-3, Hall Reference). G K Hall.

Peter & the Wolf. Date not set. pap. (ISBN 0-8052-0684-1). Random.

Peter & the Wolf. Sergei Prokofiev. (Illus.). 32p. (gr. 1-2). 1979. 4.95 o.p. (ISBN 0-571-18004-3). Faber & Faber.

Peter & the Wolf. Sergei Prokofiev. LC 79-92902. (Illus.). 32p. (gr. 2-5). 1980. 12.95 o.p. (ISBN 0-87923-331-1). Godine.

Peter Blake. Marina Vaizey. (Royal Academy Painters & Sculptors Ser.). (Illus.). 92p. 1986. 16.95 o.p. (ISBN 0-89733-182-6). Academy Chi Pubs.

Peter Finch: A Biography. Trader Faulkner. LC 79-2400. (Illus.). 1980. 12.95 o.s.i. (ISBN 0-8008-6281-3). Taplinger.

Peter Fischli David Weiss. Katy Kline et al. LC 87-62759. (Illus.). 28p. (Orig.). 1987. pap. 4.00 o.p. (ISBN 0-938437-19-4). MIT List Visual Arts.

Peter Gets a Hearing Aid. Nigel Snell. (Illus.). 32p. (ps-1). 1980. 9.95 o.p. (ISBN 0-241-89918-4, Pub. by Hamish Hamilton England). David & Charles.

Peter Gets the Chickenpox. Marguerite R. Lerner. LC 59-15144. (Medical Books for Children). (Illus.). (gr. k-5). 1959. PLB 4.95 o.p. (ISBN 0-8225-0002-7). Lerner Pubns.

Peter Goes to School. (gr. k-3). 1953. 0.79 o.p. (ISBN 0-8431-4106-9). Wonder.

Peter in Blueberry Land. Elsa Beskow. (Illus.). 34p. 1984. bds. 11.95 laminated o.p. (ISBN 0-510-00129-7). Salem Hse Pubs.

Peter in the Land of Musical Instruments. Klara C. Robitzek. 1977. 4.95 o.s.i. (ISBN 0-8008-6283-X, Crescendo). Taplinger.

Peter in the Land of Musical Theory. Klara C. Robitzek. 1977. 4.95 o.s.i. (ISBN 0-8008-6284-8, Crescendo). Taplinger.

Peter in the New Testament. Raymond E. Brown et al. LC 73-83787. 1973. 7.95 o.p. (ISBN 0-8066-1401-3, 10-4930, Augsburg). Augsburg Fortress.

Peter McWilliams Personal Computer Buying Guide. Peter A. McWilliams. LC 85-3636. (Illus.). 448p. 1985. pap. 12.95 o.p. (ISBN 0-385-19688-1, Quantum Pr). Doubleday.

Peter Martins: Prince of the Dance. Steven Caras. (Illus.). 64p. 1986. pap. 14.95 o.p. (ISBN 0-8109-2324-6). Abrams.

Peter Norton Programmer's Guide to the IBM PC: The Ultimate Reference Guide to the Entire Family of IBM Personal Computers. Peter Norton. (Illus.). 448p. (Orig.). 1985. pap. 21.95 o.p. (ISBN 0-914845-46-2). Microsoft.

Peter Pan. James M. Barrie. (Illus.). 224p. (gr. 4 up). 1987. deluxe ed. 13.95 o.p. (ISBN 0-448-06033-7, G&D). Putnam Pub Group.

Peter Pan. (Children's Classics Ser.). 32p. (gr. k-3). 1988. 5.95 o.p. (ISBN 0-8249-8261-4). Ideals.

Peter Pan Bag. Lee Kingman. LC 78-98520. (gr. 9-12). 1973. 5.95 o.p. (ISBN 0-395-06866-5). HM.

Peter Pan: Or the Boy Who Would Not Grow Up. James M. Barrie. 208p. (gr. k up). 1982. pap. 2.95 o.p. (ISBN 0-380-57752-6, Bard). Avon.

Peter Pears: A Tribute on His 75th Birthday. Ed. by Marion Thorpe. LC 85-20435. (Illus.). 145p. 1985. ltd. ed. 35.00 o.p. (ISBN 0-571-10063-5). Faber & Faber.

Peter, Peter, Pumpkin Eater. James Reid. (Big Books for Little People). (Illus.). (ps-3). 1970. pap. 0.50 o.p. (ISBN 0-8006-0424-5, Fortress). Augsburg Fortress.

Peter Pindar's Poems. Selected by P. M. Zall. 1972. 17.95x o.p. (ISBN 0-87249-251-6). U of SC Pr.

Peter Pirate's Hospital Coloring Book. Janet O'Rourke & Lee Wallat. 32p. (Orig.). 1982. pap. 2.95 o.p. (ISBN 0-89716-111-4). Peanut Butter.

Peter Pyramid. Laurence J. Peter. 1987. pap. 3.95 o.p. (ISBN 0-553-26347-1). Bantam.

Peter Rabbit. Beatrix Potter. (Puppet Storybooks). (Illus.). 18p. (gr. k-2). 1981. 3.95 o.p. (ISBN 0-448-09755-9, G&D); PLB 2.29 o.p. (ISBN 0-448-13084-X). Putnam Pub Group.

Peter Rabbit & His Friends. (Beatrix Potter Board Bks.). (Illus.). 14p. (ps-k). 1982. bd. 3.50 o.s.i. (ISBN 0-671-44519-7, Little Simon). S&S.

Peter Rabbit Diary. Beatrix Potter. (Illus.). 90p. 1982. 3.95 o.p. (ISBN 0-7232-2982-1). Warne.

Peter Schulthorpe: His Music & Ideas 1929-1979. Michael Hannan. LC 81-11696. (Illus.). 235p. 1982. text ed. 25.00x o.p. (ISBN 0-7022-1589-9). U of Queensland Pr.
Peter Spier's Little Bible Storybooks. Peter Seymour. (Illus.). (ps-3). 1983. 7.95 o.p. (ISBN 0-385-19061-1). Doubleday.
Peter the Caterpillar. Joanne Keegan. 32p. (ps-3). 1986. 5.95 o.p. (ISBN 0-8062-2866-0). Carlton.
Peter the Great, 2 vols. A. Tolstoy. 838p. 1985. 15.95 o.p. (ISBN 0-8285-3392-X, Pub. by Raduga Pubs USSR). Imported Pubns.
Peter the Great. Kazimierz Waliszewski. Tr. by Mary Loyd. Repr. of 1897 ed. lib. bdg. 38.50x o.p. (ISBN 0-8371-0734-2, WAPG). Greenwood.
Peter Tudebode: Historia De Hierosolymitano Itinere. John H. Hill & Laurita L. Hill. LC 74-78091. (Memoirs Ser.: Vol. 101). 1974. 12.00 o.p. (ISBN 0-87169-101-9). Am Philos.
Peterkin Meets a Star. Emilie Boon. LC 83-9691. (Illus.). 32p. (gr. k-2). 1984. 4.95 o.p. (ISBN 0-394-86284-8, BYR); lib. bdg. 6.99 o.p. (ISBN 0-394-96284-2). Random.
Peterkin Pollensnuff. Jenny Partridge. (Oakapple Wood Stories Ser.). (Illus.). 32p. (gr. k-2). 1982. 4.95 o.p. (ISBN 0-03-061508-9). H Holt & Co.
Peterkin's Very Own Garden. Emilie Boon. LC 86-62244. (Great Big Board Bks.). (Illus.). 14p. (ps). 1987. 3.95 o.s.i. (ISBN 0-394-88666-6, BYR). Random.
Peter's Kingdom: Inside the Papal City. Jerrold M. Packard. (Illus.). 352p. 1985. 17.95 o.p. (ISBN 0-684-18430-3, ScribT). Scribner.
Peter's Pocket. Judith Barrett. LC 74-75555. (Illus.). 32p. (ps-k). 1974. 6.95 o.p. (ISBN 0-689-30403-X, Atheneum). Macmillan.
Petersburg & Paris Period, 2 vols. Mihail Chemiakin. Incl. Vol. II. Transformation: New York Period. 286p. (Illus.). 504p. 1986. pap. 250.00 sold as boxed set only o.p. (ISBN 0-317-56275-4, Pub. by Mosaic Pr Canada). Riverrun NY.
Petersen's Big Book of Auto Repair. 10th ed. 896p. 1985. pap. 14.95 o.p. (ISBN 0-89803-157-5, Dist. by Kampmann). Green Hill.
Petersen's Big Book of Photography. Ed. by Kalton Lahue. LC 77-86527. (Petersen "How-to" Photographic Library). (Illus.). (gr. 9-12). 1977. pap. 12.95 o.p. (ISBN 0-8227-4029-X). Petersen Pub.
Peterson's Annual Guide to Independent Secondary Schools, 1983-84. Ed. by Rebecca A. Shepherd. LC 80-64511. 1046p. 1983. pap. 10.95 o.p. (ISBN 0-87866-212-X). Petersons Guides.
Peterson's Applying to Graduate School in the United States: A Handbook for International Students. 250p. (Orig.). pap. cancelled o.s.i. (ISBN 0-87866-728-8). Petersons Guides.
Peterson's Competitive Colleges. 3rd ed. Ed. by Karen C. Hegener. 344p. 1984. pap. 7.95 o.p. (ISBN 0-87866-267-7). Petersons Guides.
Peterson's Competitive Colleges. 5th ed. 358p. (Orig.). 1986. pap. 9.95 o.p. (ISBN 0-87866-441-6). Petersons Guides.
Peterson's Competitive Colleges. 6th ed. 356p. (Orig.). 1987. pap. 9.95 o.p. (ISBN 0-87866-539-0). Petersons Guides.
Peterson's Guide to College Admissions: Getting into the College of Your Choice. 3rd. ed. R. Fred Zuker & Karen C. Hegener. LC 83-4219. 366p. (Orig.). 1983. pap. 9.95 o.p. (ISBN 0-87866-224-3). Peterson's Guides.
Peterson's Guide to Colleges in New England. Ed. by Kim R. Kaye. (Peterson's Regional Guides Ser.). 114p. 1984. pap. 6.95 o.p. (ISBN 0-87866-274-X). Petersons Guides.
Peterson's Guide to Colleges in New England 1987. 3rd ed. (Peterson's Regional Guides to Colleges Ser.). 132p. (Orig.). 1986. pap. 7.95 o.p. (ISBN 0-87866-365-7). Petersons Guides.
Peterson's Guide to Colleges in New England 1988. 4th ed. (Peterson's Regional Guides to Colleges Ser.). 136p. (Orig.). 1987. pap. 7.95 o.p. (ISBN 0-87866-564-1). Petersons Guides.
Peterson's Guide to Colleges in New York. Ed. by Kim R. Kaye. (Peterson's Regional Guides ser.). 107p. 1984. pap. 6.95 o.p. (ISBN 0-87866-225-1). Petersons Guides.
Peterson's Guide to Colleges in New York 1988. 4th ed. (Peterson's Regional Guides to Colleges Ser.). 131p. (Orig.). 1987. pap. 7.95 o.p. (ISBN 0-87866-565-X). Petersons Guides.
Peterson's Guide to Colleges in the Middle Atlantic States. Ed. by Kim R. Kaye. (Peterson's Regional Guides Ser.). 176p. 1984. pap. 6.95 o.p. (ISBN 0-87866-226-X). Petersons Guides.
Peterson's Guide to Colleges in the Middle Atlantic States 1987. 3rd ed. (Peterson's Regional Guides to Colleges Ser). 206p. (Orig.). 1986. pap. 7.95 o.p. (ISBN 0-87866-369-X). Petersons Guides.
Peterson's Guide to Colleges in the Middle Atlantic States 1988. 4th ed. (Peterson's Regional Guides to Colleges Ser.). 216p. (Orig.). 1987. pap. 7.95 o.p. (ISBN 0-87866-566-8). Petersons Guides.
Peterson's Guide to Colleges in the Midwest. Ed. by Kim R. Kaye. (Peterson's Regional Guides Ser.). 274p. 1984. pap. 7.95 o.p. (ISBN 0-87866-228-6). Petersons Guides.
Peterson's Guide to Colleges in the Midwest 1987. 3rd ed. (Peterson's Regional Guides to Colleges Ser). 304p. (Orig.). 1986. pap. 8.95 o.p. (ISBN 0-87866-366-5). Petersons Guides.
Peterson's Guide to Colleges in the Midwest 1988. 4th ed. (Peterson's Regional Guides to Colleges Ser.). 318p. (Orig.). 1987. pap. 8.95 o.p. (ISBN 0-87866-568-4). Petersons Guides.
Peterson's Guide to Colleges in the Southeast 1987. 2nd ed. (Peterson's Regional Guides to Colleges Ser). 208p. (Orig.). 1986. pap. 7.95 o.p. (ISBN 0-87866-368-1). Petersons Guides.
Peterson's Guide to Colleges in the Southwest 1988. 3rd ed. (Peterson's Regional Guides to Colleges Ser.). 116p. (Orig.). 1987. pap. 7.95 o.p. (ISBN 0-87866-570-6). Petersons Guides.
Peterson's Guide to Colleges in the Southeast 1988. 3rd ed. (Peterson's Regional Guides to Colleges Ser.). 224p. (Orig.). 1987. pap. 7.95 o.p. (ISBN 0-87866-567-6). Petersons Guides.
Peterson's Guide to Colleges in the West 1987. 1st ed. (Peterson's Regional Guides to Colleges Ser.). 175p. (Orig.). 1986. pap. 7.95 o.p. (ISBN 0-87866-447-5). Petersons Guides.
Peterson's Guide to Colleges in the West 1988. 2nd ed. (Peterson's Regional Guides to Colleges Ser.). 185p. (Orig.). 1987. pap. 7.95 o.p. (ISBN 0-87866-569-2). Petersons Guides.
Peterson's Guide to Colleges with Programs for Learning-Disabled Students. LC 85-3497. 322p. (Orig.). 1985. pap. 13.95 o.p. (ISBN 0-87866-327-4). Petersons Guides.
Peterson's Higher Education Directory 1988. 1063p. (Orig.). 1988. pap. 34.95 o.p. (ISBN 0-87866-644-3). Petersons Guides.
Peterson's State & Federal Aid Programs for College Students 1987. 60p. (Orig.). 1986. pap. 3.00 o.p. (ISBN 0-87866-525-0). Petersons Guides.
Petit Fleur Red. 1988. 4.98 o.p. (ISBN 0-517-67084-4). Crown.
Petit Littre. 32.50 o.p. (ISBN 0-685-36077-6). French & Eur.
Petit Mal Epilepsy: A Search for the Precursors of Spike-Wave Activity. M. Myslobodsky. 1976. 55.00 o.p. (ISBN 0-12-511950-X). Acad Pr.
Petit Prince. Antoine De Saint-Exupery. (Illus., Fr.). 1946. pap. 1.50 o.p. (ISBN 0-685-11488-0). Schoenhof.
Petit Prince. Antoine De Saint-Exupery. (Fr.). (gr. 3-8). 10.95 o.p. (ISBN 0-685-28443-3). Schoenhof.
Petits Maitres de la Peinture Valeur de Demain, 1820-1920, Vol. IV. Gerald Schurr. (Illus.). 189p. (Fr.). 1979. 55.00 o.p. (ISBN 2-85917-009-X, 2390069, Pub. by Editions de l'Amateur FR). Seven Hills Bk Dists.
Petits Maitres de la Peinture Valeur de Demain, 1820-1920, Vol. V. Gerald Schurr. (Illus.). 189p. (Fr.). 1981. 65.00 o.p. (ISBN 2-85917-016-2, 2390079, Pub. by Editions de l'Amateur FR). Seven Hills Bk Dists.
Petits Maitres de la Peinture Valeur de Demain, 1820-1920, Vol. II. Gerald Schurr. (Illus.). 150p. (Fr.). 1982. 50.00 o.p. (ISBN 2-85917-022-7, 2390049, Pub. by Editions de l'Amateur FR). Seven Hills Bk Dists.
Petits Maitres de la Peinture Valeur de Demain, 1820-1920, Vol. III. Gerald Schurr. (Illus.). 175p. (Fr.). 1982. 50.00 o.p. (ISBN 2-85917-006-5, 2390059, Pub. by Editions de l'Amateur FR). Seven Hills Bk Dists.
Petits Maitres de la Peinture Valeur de Demain, 1820-1920, Vol. 1. Gerald Schurr. (Illus.). 160p. (Fr.). 1982. 50.00 o.p. (ISBN 2-85917-013-8, 2390039, Pub. by Editions de l'Amateur FR). Seven Hills Bk Dists.
Petits Miroirs. Michel Butor. 1972. pap. 9.95 o.p. (ISBN 0-686-51945-0). French & Eur.
Petits Mots Croises. A. John Gaudet. (gr. 8-10). pap. text ed. 3.25x ans. key avail. o.p. (ISBN 0-88334-160-3). Ind Sch Pr.
Petrarch, Scipio & the "Africa" The Birth of Humanism's Dream. Aldo S. Bernardo. LC 78-19065. 1978. Repr. of 1962 ed. lib. bdg. 35.00x o.p. (ISBN 0-313-20535-3, BEPA). Greenwood.
Petri Riage Biblia Versificato: Petri Rigue Biblia Versificato, a Verse Commentary on the Bible, 2 vols. Paul E. Beichner. (Mediaeval Studies Ser.: No. 19). 1965. 50.00 set o.p. (ISBN 0-268-00016-6). U of Notre Dame Pr.
Petrochemical Manufacturing & Marketing Guide, 2 vols. Robert B. Stobaugh, Jr. Incl. Vol. 1. Aromatics & Derivatives. 1967. (ISBN 0-87201-665-X); Vol. 2. Olefins, Diolefins & Acetylene. 1968. (ISBN 0-87201-666-8). 12.95x ea. o.p. Gulf Pub.
Petrography: An Introduction to the Study of Rocks in Thin Sections. 2nd ed. Howel Williams et al. LC 82-5072. (Illus.). 626p. 1983. text ed. 38.95 o.p. (ISBN 0-7167-1376-4). W H Freeman.
Petroleum. Wilbur Cross. (Science & Technology Ser.). (Illus.). 100p. (gr. 5 up). 1983. PLB 17.27 o.p. (ISBN 0-516-00509-X). Childrens.
Petroleum Accounting Practices. Stanley Porter. 1965. text ed. 57.50 o.p. (ISBN 0-07-050524-1). McGraw.
Petroleum & Hard Minerals from the Sea. Fillmore C. Earney. LC 80-17653. (Scripta Series in Geography). 291p. 1980. 59.95x o.p. (ISBN 0-470-27009-8, Pub. by Halsted Pr). Wiley.
Petroleum & the Continental Shelf of North-West Europe: Environmental Protection, Vol. 2. Ed. by H. A. Cole. LC 75-14329. 126p. 1975. 47.95x o.p. (ISBN 0-470-16483-2). Halsted Pr.
Petroleum & the Economy of the United Arab Emirates. Mana Saeed Al-Otaiba. 304p. 1977. 90.00 o.p. (ISBN 0-85664-519-2, Pub. by Croom Helm Ltd). Routledge Chapman & Hall.
Petroleum Concession Agreements of the United Arab Emirates: Adu Dhabi 1939-1981, 2 vols. Mana S. Al-Otaiba. 578p. 1982. Set. 165.00 o.p. (ISBN 0-7099-1915-8, Pub. by Croom Helm Ltd). Routledge Chapman & Hall.
Petroleum Conservation in Eastern Europe, Pt. I. Victor Merkin. Ed. by Andreas Tamberg. 197p. (Orig.). 1987. pap. text ed. 42.50 o.p. (ISBN 1-55831-080-0). Delphic Associates.
Petroleum Dictionary. David F. Tver & Richard W. Berry. 384p. 1982. pap. 21.95 o.p. (ISBN 0-442-28529-9). Van Nos Reinhold.
Petroleum Encyclopedia. Levin. (ISBN 0-8022-0963-7). Philos Lib.
Petroleum Engineering Practice Problem Manual. David S. Goldstein & Rhonda A. Jones. (Engineering Review Manual Ser.). 138p. 1987. pap. text ed. 19.50 o.p. (ISBN 0-932276-65-2). Prof Pubns CA.
Petroleum Exploration Handbook: A Practical Manual Summarizing the Application of Earth Sciences to Petroleum Exploration. Graham B. Moody. (Illus.). 1961. text ed. 75.00 o.p. (ISBN 0-07-042867-0). McGraw.
Petroleum Industry in Oil-Importing Developing Countries. Fariborz Ghadar & Robert Stobaugh. LC 81-48556. 240p. 1983. 30.00x o.p. (ISBN 0-669-05419-4). Lexington Bks.
Petroleum Industry in Western Europe: A Guide to Information Sources. Lawrence G. Franco et al. LC 75-20065. (Reference Library of Social Science: Vol. 13). 178p. 1975. lib. bdg. 34.00 o.p. (ISBN 0-8240-9990-7). Garland Pub.
Petroleum Industry of the People's Republic of China. Hsien C. Ling. LC 74-22168. (Publications Ser.: No. 142). 264p. 1975. 11.95x o.p. (ISBN 0-8179-6421-5). Hoover Inst Pr.
Petroleum Measurement Manual: Fidelity & Security of Measurement - Data Transmission Systems Section 1, Pt. XIII. Institute of Petroleum Staff. 32p. 1976. 48.95x o.p. (ISBN 0-471-25782-6). Wiley.
Petroleum Measurement Manual: Tank Calibration Section I- Liquid Calibration Methods, Pt. II. Institute of Petroleum Staff. 120p. 1981. 59.95x o.p. (ISBN 0-471-25802-4). Wiley.
Petroleum Politics & the Texas Railroad Commission. David F. Prindle. (Elma Dill Russell Spencer Foundation Ser.: No. 12). 240p. 1981. pap. 14.95 o.p. (ISBN 0-292-76474-X). U of Tex Pr.
Petroleum Processing. V. Sukhanov. 408p. 1982. 8.95 o.p. (ISBN 0-8285-2438-6, Pub. by Mir Pubs USSR). Imported Pubns.
Petroleum Refinery Engineer's Handbook. Strachan. (Illus.). 350p. 1956. (ISBN 0-8022-1662-5). Philos Lib.
Petroleum Training Directory, 1988. Ed. by John J. Connor. 326p. Date not set. pap. 95.00 o.p. (ISBN 0-945820-02-X). Training Resc Catalogs.
Petrology. Walter T. Huang. 1962. text ed. 60.95 o.p. (ISBN 0-07-030750-4). McGraw.
Petrozavodsk & Kizhi: A Guide. A. Frolov. 168p. 1984. 6.95 o.p. (ISBN 0-8285-2801-2, Pub. by Raduga Pubs USSR). Imported Pubns.
Petrushka. Geoffrey Ashton. (Stories of the Ballets Ser.). (Illus.). 48p. 1985. 8.95 o.p. (ISBN 0-8120-5671-X). Barron.
Pets Are Wonderful Family Album. Pets Are Wonderful Council Editors. 1986. pap. 7.95 o.p. (ISBN 0-399-51232-2). Putnam Pub Group.
Pets, Pets, Pets. (Animals & Their Babies Ser.). (Illus.). 32p. (ps-3). 1987. pap. 5.95 o.s.i. (ISBN 0-671-63490-9, Little Simon). S&S.
Petunia, Beware! Roger Duvoisin. (Pinwheel Bks). (Illus.). 32p. (gr. k-3). 1974. pap. 1.45 o.s.i. (ISBN 0-394-82801-1). Pantheon.
Peugeot Moped Owners Service-Repair, 1976-1978. Ed Scott. (Illus.). pap. 6.00 o.p. (ISBN 0-89287-202-0, M436). Clymer Pub.
Peuple Esquimau Aujourd'hui et Demain-The Eskimo People Today & Tomorrow: Quatrieme Congres International De la Fondation Francaise D'etudes Nordiques. Ed. by Jean Malaurie. (Bibliotheque Arctique et Antarctique: No. 4). 1973. pap. 40.40x o.p. (ISBN 90-2797-242-7). Mouton.
Pew for One, Please. William Lyon. LC 76-41976. 1977. 6.95 o.p. (ISBN 0-8164-0374-0). HarpR.
Peyton Place. Grace Metalious. 1956. 7.95 o.p. (ISBN 0-671-56683-0). S&S.
PFS on the IBM PC, Using. Linda L. Rice. (Illus.). 147p. (Orig.). 1984. pap. text ed. 12.95 o.p. (ISBN 0-942728-20-3). Custom Pub Co.
PG: A Parental Guide to Rock. David Scheer. 275p. 1986. pap. 7.95 o.s.i. (ISBN 0-87509-378-7). Chr Pubns.
PGL-2, Over the P-Adics: Its Representations, Spherical Functions, & Fourier Analysis. A. J. Silberger. LC 70-139951. (Lecture Notes in Mathematics: Vol. 166). 1970. pap. 15.10 o.p. (ISBN 0-387-05193-7). Springer-Verlag.
PH Global Employee Guide. (ISBN 0-13-699018-5). P-H.
PH of Animal Cells see PH of Plant Cells.
PH of Plant Cells. J. Small. Bd. with PH of Animal Cells. F. J. Wiercinski. (Protoplasmatologica: Vol. 2B, Pt. 2c). (Illus.). iv, 172p. 1955. pap. 40.20 o.p. (ISBN 0-387-80386-6). Springer-Verlag.
Phaedra. Jean Racine. Tr. by Richard Wilbur. (Illus.). 128p. 1986. 15.95 o.p. (ISBN 0-15-171731-1). HarBraceJ.
Phaidon Guide to Antique Weapons & Armour. (ISBN 0-13-661935-5). P-H.
Phallic Critiques: Masculinity & Twentieth Century Literature. Peter Schwenger. 256p. 1984. 24.95x o.p. (ISBN 0-7102-0164-8). Routledge Chapman & Hall.
Phanomenologische Idealismus Husserls. Theodor Celms. Ed. by Natanson. LC 78-66733. (Phenomenology: Vol. 3). 192p. 1979. lib. bdg. 26.00 o.p. (ISBN 0-8240-9567-7). Garland Pub.
Phantastes. Date not set. (ISBN 0-8052-3815-8). Random.
Phantasy in Childhood. Audrey Davidson & Judith Fay. 188p. 1953. (ISBN 0-8022-0346-9). Philos Lib.
Phantom. Thomas Tessier. LC 82-71058. 256p. 1982. 13.95 o.p. (ISBN 0-689-11328-5, Atheneum). Macmillan.
Phantom Caravan or Abd el Kader, Emir of Algeria (1808-1883) Vista Clayton. LC 75-10617. 1975. 15.00 o.p. (ISBN 0-682-48263-3, University). Exposition-Phoenix.
Phantom Homestead: A Circuit of Our People. Otis Dunbar Richardson. 1975. 10.00 o.p. (ISBN 0-682-48062-2). Exposition-Phoenix.
Phantom Ice Cream Man: More Nonsense Verse. X. J. Kennedy. LC 78-23681. (Illus.). 80p. (gr. 3 up). 1979. 7.95 o.p. (ISBN 0-689-50132-3, Atheneum). Macmillan.
Phantom Lady. Cornell Woolrich. 256p. 1982. pap. 2.50 o.s.i. (ISBN 0-345-30652-X). Ballantine.
Phantom Major. V. Cowles. LC 79-21890. Repr. of 1958 ed. 15.95 o.p. (ISBN 0-89201-088-6). Zenger Pub.
Phantom of Pine Hill. Carolyn Keene. (Nancy Drew Ser.: Vol. 42). (gr. 4-7). 1965. 4.50 o.p. (ISBN 0-448-09542-4, G&D); PLB 3.29 o.p. (ISBN 0-448-19542-9). Putnam Pub Group.
Phantom of the Temple. Robert Van Gulik. (Judge Dee Mystery). 1979. pap. 4.95 rack size o.s.i. (ISBN 0-684-16178-8, ScribT). Scribner.
Phantom Submarine. Richard Brightfield. (Choose Your Own Adventure Ser.: No. 26). (Illus.). 111p. (gr. 3-6). 1983. pap. 2.25 o.p. (ISBN 0-553-25916-4). Bantam.
Phantoms & Fairies. T. Bringsvaard. (Tanum of Norway Tokens Ser). (Illus.). 1979. pap. 18.50x o.s.i. (ISBN 82-518-0853-7, N498). Vanous.
Pharmaceutical Chemistry-2: Proceedings of an International Symposium, Muenster, 1968. International Union of Pure & Applied Chemistry. 272p. 1976. 70.00 o.p. (ISBN 0-08-020810-X). Pergamon.
Pharmaceutical Industry. (UNIDO Guides to Information Sources: No. 20). pap. 4.00 o.p. (ISBN 92-1-106150-4, ID/162). UN.
Pharmaceutical Microbiology. 3rd ed. A. D. Russell. Ed. by W. B. Hugo. (Illus.). 480p. 1983. pap. text ed. 29.00x o.p. (ISBN 0-632-01048-7). Blackwell Sci.
Pharmaceutical Quality Control. William F. Head, Jr. (Illus.). 99p. 1983. 20.00 o.p. (ISBN 0-682-49983-8). Exposition-Phoenix.
Pharmaceuticals for Developing Countries. Institute of Medicine Staff. 1979. pap. 13.95 o.p. (ISBN 0-309-02891-4). Natl Acad Pr.
Pharmaceuticals in Developing Countries. Ed. by S. J. Patel. 100p. 1983. 25.00 o.p. (ISBN 0-08-030210-6). Pergamon.

Pharmacokinetics & Pharmacodynamics of Psychoactive Drugs. Ed. by Gene Barnett & C. Nora Chang. LC 85-70734. (Illus.). 500p. 1985. text ed. 54.00 o.p. (ISBN 0-931890-20-9, Biomed Pubns). Year Bk Med.

Pharmacologic Principles of Cancer Treatment. Bruce A. Chabner. (Illus.). 480p. 1982. write for info. o.p. (ISBN 0-7216-2477-4). Saunders.

Pharmacologic Review for Intensive Cardiopulmonary Therapy. L. J. Fields. 1979. 11.50 o.p. (ISBN 0-8151-3219-0). Year Bk Med.

Pharmacological Experiments on Isolated Preparations. 2nd ed. Edinburgh University Staff. (Illus.). 1971. 17.25 o.p. (ISBN 0-443-00730-6). Churchill.

Pharmacological Facts & Figures. F. Lembeck et al. Tr. by H. Heller & D. R. Ferguson. LC 75-82689. (Heidelberg Science Library: Vol. 9). 1969. pap. 12.00 o.p. (ISBN 0-387-90010-1). Springer-Verlag.

Pharmacological Modifications of Evolked Brain Potentials. A. A. Barbely. 138p. 1973. 60.00 o.p. (ISBN 3-456-00356-0, Pub. by Holdan Bk Ltd UK). State Mutual Bk.

Pharmacology. National Medical Series for Independent Study Staff. (National Medical Series for Independent Study). 281p. 1984. pap. text ed. 19.00 o.p. (ISBN 0-471-09626-1, 1-635). Wiley.

Pharmacology & Pharmaco-Therapeutics. rev. ed. V. Iswaran & M. N. Guruswami. 1979. text ed. 45.00x o.p. (ISBN 0-7069-0803-1, Pub. by Vikas India). Advent NY.

Pharmacology & Therapeutics, Vol. 12, No. 1. Ed. by W. C. Bowman. LC 77-25743. (Illus.). 283p. 1981. pap. 73.00 o.p. (ISBN 0-08-026854-4). Pergamon.

Pharmacology & Therapeutics, Vol. 12, No. 2. Ed. by W. C. Bowman. (Illus.). 190p. 1981. pap. 73.00 o.p. (ISBN 0-08-026855-2). Pergamon.

Pharmacology & Toxicology of Naturally Occurring Toxins, 2 vols. Ed. by H. Raskova. LC 77-130797. 1971. Vol. 1. 100.00 o.p. (ISBN 0-08-016319-X); Vol. 2. 93.00 o.p. (ISBN 0-08-016798-5); Set. 170.00 o.p. (ISBN 0-08-016797-7). Pergamon.

Pharmacology: Drug Actions & Reactions. 3rd ed. Ruth R. Levine. 526p. 1983. pap. text ed. 21.00 o.p. Little.

Pharmacology for Respiratory Therapists. 2nd ed. Hugh S. Mathewson. LC 80-25212. (Illus.). 97p. 1981. pap. text ed. 15.95 o.p. (ISBN 0-8016-3161-0). Mosby.

Pharmacology for the Dental Hygienist. 2nd ed. Ed. by Austin H. Kutscher et al. LC 81-19395. (Illus.). 389p. 1982. text ed. 19.50 o.p. (ISBN 0-8121-0802-7). Lea & Febiger.

Pharmacology of Central Synapses. V. V. Zakusov. (Illus.). 1980. 85.00 o.p. (ISBN 0-08-020549-6). Pergamon.

Pharmacology of Cerebral Circulation. Ed. by Amilcare Carpi. LC 70-182263. 370p. 1972. 180.00 o.p. (ISBN 0-08-016209-6). Pergamon.

Pharmacology of Gastrointestinal Motilation. Ed. by Pamela Holton & N. Emmelin. 700p. 1973. Set. 200.00 o.p. (ISBN 0-08-016552-4). Pergamon.

Pharmacology of Hearing: Experimental & Clinical Bases. R. Don Brown & Ernest A. Daigneault. LC 81-437. 364p. 1981. 64.95 o.p. (ISBN 0-471-05074-1). Krieger.

Pharmacology of Immunoregulation: Present Concepts As a Basis for the Development of Immunopharmacological Agents. Ed. by G. H. Werner & F. Floc'h. 1979. 89.00 o.p. (ISBN 0-12-745650-3). Acad Pr.

Pharmacology of Intestinal Absorption: Gastrointestinal Absorption of Drugs. Ed. by W. Forth & W. Rummel. 1975. 230.00 o.p. (ISBN 0-08-016210-X). Pergamon.

Pharmacology of Lipid Transport & Atherosclerotic Processes. Ed. by E. J. Masoro. 1975. 170.00 o.p. (ISBN 0-08-017762-X). Pergamon.

Pharmacology of Naturally Occurring Polypeptides & Lipid Soluble Acids, Vol. VI. John M. Walker. 320p. 1971. 80.00 o.p. (ISBN 0-08-016347-5). Pergamon.

Pharmacology of Pain: Proceedings - Vol. 9. Ed. by R. K. Lim. 1968. 65.00 o.p. (ISBN 0-08-012374-0). Pergamon.

Pharmacology of Reproduction, Vol. 2. Ed. by E. Diczfalusy. LC 67-19416. 1968. 50.00 o.p. (ISBN 0-08-012368-6). Pergamon.

Pharmacology of Synapses. J. W. Phillis. 376p. 1970. 95.00 o.p. (ISBN 0-08-015558-8). Pergamon.

Pharmacology: Pretest Self-Assessment & Review. 3rd ed. Pre Test Service, Inc. 192p. 1983. text ed. 12.95 o.p. (ISBN 0-07-051935-8). McGraw.

Pharmacology: PreTest Self-Assessment & Review. 4th ed. PreTest Service, Inc. Staff et al. Ed. by Edward J. Barbieri & G. John DiGregorio. 192p. 1985. pap. 14.95 o.p. (ISBN 0-07-051945-5). McGraw-Pretest.

Pharmacy Issues in Long Term Care. National Foundation for Long Term Care Staff. 193p. 10.00 o.p. (ISBN 0-318-17116-3, 00301). Am Health Care Assn.

Pharmacy Museums & Collections in the United States & Canada. rev. ed. George Griffenhagen & Ernst Stieb. 130p. 1988. pap. 6.50 o.p. Am Inst Hist Pharm.

Pharmacy School Admission Requirements. 7th ed. 1986. 6.00 o.p. (ISBN 0-937526-07-X). AACP Alexandria.

Phase & Caste Determination in Insects - Endocrine Aspects: Proceedings of the International Congress of Entomology, 15th, Washington, D.C., 1976. Ed. by Martin Luscher. 1976. 37.00 o.p. (ISBN 0-08-021256-5). Pergamon.

Phase Equilibria. Arnold Reisman. (Physical Chemistry Ser: Vol. 19). 1970. 98.50 o.p. (ISBN 0-12-586350-0). Acad Pr.

Phase Lock & Frequency Feedback Systems: Principles & Techniques. Jacob Klapper & John T. Frankle. (Electrical Science Ser.). 1972. 106.50 o.p. (ISBN 0-12-410850-4). Acad Pr.

Phase Stability During Irradiation: Proceedings. TMS-AIME Fall Meeting, Pittsburgh, 1980. Ed. by J. R. Holland & L. K. Mansur. (Illus.). 612p. 50.00 o.p. (ISBN 0-89520-376-6); members 32.00 o.p. (ISBN 0-317-36257-7); student members 16.00 o.p. (ISBN 0-317-36258-5). ASM.

Phase Stability under Irradiation. K. C. Russell. (Illus.). 206p. 1985. pap. 83.00 o.p. (ISBN 0-08-032722-2, Pub. by Aberdeen Scotland). Pergamon.

Phase Transfer Catalysis in Organic Synthesis. W. P. Weber & G. W. Gokel. LC 77-22798. (Reactivity & Structure: Vol. 4). 1977. 39.50 o.p. (ISBN 0-387-08377-4). Springer-Verlag.

Phase Transition in Solids: An Approach to the Study of Chemistry & Physics of Solids. C. N. Rao & K. J. Rao. (Illus.). 1978. text ed. 61.95x o.p. (ISBN 0-07-051185-3). McGraw.

Phase Transitions & Critical Phenomena: Series Expansion for Lattice Models, Vol. 3. Ed. by C. Domb & M. Green. 1974. 141.00 o.p. (ISBN 0-12-220303-8). Acad Pr.

Phase Transitions & Their Applications in Materials Science. Ed. by H. K. Henisch et al. LC 73-14411. 300p. 1974. 59.00 o.p. (ISBN 0-08-017955-X). Pergamon.

Phase Transitions in Surface Films. Ed. by J. G. Dash & J. Ruvalds. LC 79-28484. (NATO ASI Series B, Physical Sciences: Vol. 51). 380p. 1980. 69.50x o.p. (ISBN 0-306-40348-X, Plenum Pr). Plenum Pub.

Phases & Faces of the Moon: A Critical Evaluation of the Unification Church & Its Principles. Donald A. Tingle & Richard A. Fordyce. 1979. 5.00 o.p. (ISBN 0-682-49264-7). Exposition-Phoenix.

Pheasant Book. Keith Proud & John Foyster. (Illus.). 208p. 1988. 34.95 o.p. (ISBN 0-7153-8981-5). David & Charles.

Phenomena, Atoms & Molecules. Irving Langmuir. (ISBN 0-8022-0922-X). Philos Lib.

Phenomenological Sense of John Dewey: Habit & Meaning. Victor Kestenbaum. 1977. text ed. 15.00x o.p. (ISBN 0-391-00668-1). Humanities.

Phenomenology & Art. Jose Ortega y Gasset. Tr. by Philip W. Silver from Span. 228p. 1975. 8.95x o.p. (ISBN 0-393-08714-X). Norton.

Phenomenology & Literature: An Introduction. Robert R. Magliola. LC 76-21584. 218p. 1977. 10.95 o.p. (ISBN 0-911198-46-6). Purdue U Pr.

Phenomenology of Mind. Georg W. Hegel. Tr. by J. B. Baillie. (Muirhead Library of Philosophy). 1966. text ed. 39.95 o.p. (ISBN 0-391-00690-8). Humanities.

Phenomenon of Architecture in Cultures in Change. D. Oakley. 1970. 100.00 o.p. (ISBN 0-08-016075-1). Pergamon.

Phenomenon of Money. Thomas Crump. (Library of Man). 304p. 1981. 40.00x o.p. (ISBN 0-7100-0856-2). Routledge Chapman & Hall.

Pheochromocytoma. W. M. Manger & R. W. Gifford. 1977. 94.00 o.p. (ISBN 0-387-90217-1). Springer-Verlag.

Phil Collins. Philip Kamin. (Illus.). 32p. 1985. pap. 4.95 o.p. (ISBN 0-318-04248-7, Pub. by Robus Bks). H Leonard Pub Corp.

Phil Collins Story. Johnny Waller. (Illus.). 156p. 1986. pap. 7.95 o.p. (ISBN 0-946391-78-5, Pub. by Zomba Bks England). H Leonard Pub Corp.

Philadelphia Experiment. William Moore & Charles Berlitz. 224p. 1981. pap. 2.95 o.p. (ISBN 0-449-24280-3, Crest). Fawcett.

Philadelphia Houston Exchange. Suzanne Delehanty & James Harithas. (Illus.). 1976. pap. 7.00 o.p. (ISBN 0-88454-020-0). U of Pa Contemp Art.

Philadelphia Phillies. Martin. LC 82-13972. (Baseball Today Ser.). 48p. (gr. 4 up). 1982. PLB 11.45 o.p. (ISBN 0-87191-870-6). Creative Ed.

Philadelphia Seventy-Sixers. Pam Banks. (NBA Today Ser.). (Illus.). 48p. (gr. 4 up). 1984. PLB 10.45 o.p. (ISBN 0-87191-985-0). Creative Ed.

Philadelphia Taxes on Business & Related Activities. Pennsylvania Bar Institute Staff. 92p. 1984. 25.00 o.p. (ISBN 0-318-02182-X, 248). PA Bar Inst.

Philadelphia 1987-1988. (Frommer's City Guides). 224p. 5.95 o.p. (ISBN 0-671-62361-3). Prentice Hall Pr.

Philadelphia's Philosopher Mechanics: A History of the Franklin Institute, 1824-1865. Bruce A. Sinclair. LC 74-6843. (History of Technology Ser). (Illus.). 352p. 1974. 37.50x o.p. (ISBN 0-8018-1636-X). Johns Hopkins.

Philately: The Catalog of the Collectors Club Library. Collectors Club Library Editors, New York. 1974. lib. bdg. 120.00 o.p. (ISBN 0-8161-1047-6, Hall Library). G K Hall.

Philip Freneau, the Poet of the Revolution. Mary S. Austin. Ed. by Helen K. Vreeland. LC 67-23885. 302p. 1968. Repr. of 1901 ed. 35.00x o.p. (ISBN 0-8103-3040-7). Gale.

Philip II: Alexander the Great & the Macedonian Heritage. Ed. by W. Lindsay Adams & Eugene N. Borza. LC 81-43664. (Illus.). 318p. (Orig.). 1982. PLB 33.75 o.p. (ISBN 0-8191-2447-8); pap. text ed. 16.25 o.p. (ISBN 0-8191-2448-6). U Pr of Amer.

Philip K. Dick. Ed. by Joseph D. Olander & Martin H. Greenberg. LC 77-76723. 1983. 12.95 o.s.i. (ISBN 0-8008-6292-9); pap. 5.95 o.s.i. (ISBN 0-8008-6291-0). Taplinger.

Philip K. Dick: In His Own Words. Gregg Rickman. 278p. 1984. softcover 9.95 o.p. (ISBN 0-916063-01-1). Fragments West.

Philip Larkin. Andrew Motion. (Contemporary Writers Ser.). 96p. 1982. pap. 5.95x o.p. (ISBN 0-416-32270-0, NO. 3555). Routledge Chapman & Hall.

Philip Paternoster: A Tractarian Love Story, 1858. Charles M. Davies. Ed. by Robert L. Wolff. LC 75-477. (Victorian Fiction Ser.). 1975. lib. bdg. 66.00 o.p. (ISBN 0-8240-1555-X). Garland Pub.

Philip Pearlstein: The Complete Paintings. Russell Bowman. (Illus.). 364p. sewn bdg. 50.00 o.p. (ISBN 0-317-54904-9). Apollo.

Philip Roth. Hermione Lee. LC 82-8223. (Contemporary Writers Ser.). 96p. 1982. pap. 5.95 o.p. (ISBN 0-416-32980-2, NO. 3750). Routledge Chapman & Hall.

Philip Second of Spain. Martin A. Hume. Ed. by Henry Ketcham. 1970. Repr. of 1903 ed. lib. bdg. 35.00x o.p. (ISBN 0-8371-4091-9, HUPH). Greenwood.

Philip the Second & Macedonian Imperialism. J. R. Ellis. (Illus.). 320p. 1986. pap. text ed. 12.50x o.p. (ISBN 0-691-00602-4). Princeton U Pr.

Philip Wylie: The Man & His Work. Robert H. Barshay. LC 79-63682. 1979. pap. text ed. 10.00 o.p. (ISBN 0-8191-0733-6). U Pr of Amer.

Philippians see Word Studies in the Greek New Testament, for the English Reader.

Philippians: A Good News Commentary. F. F. Bruce. LC 82-48919. 176p. (Orig.). 1983. pap. 7.95 o.p. (ISBN 0-06-061138-3, RD/446). HarpR.

Philippians, Colossians, Philemon, Vol. IX. Beacon Bible Expositions Staff. 300p. 1985. text ed. 6.95 o.p. (ISBN 0-8010-0788-7). Baker Bk.

Philippine Social History: Global Trade & Local Transformations. Ed. by Alfred W. McCoy & Ed. C. De Jesus. 488p. 1982. pap. text ed. 12.95x o.p. (ISBN 0-8248-0803-7). UH Pr.

Philippine Yearbook, 1982-83. Intl Pubns Serv.

Philippines. Richard Z. Chesnoff. LC 77-99197. (Illus.). 288p. 1978. 125.00 o.p. (ISBN 0-8109-1458-1). Abrams.

Philippines. Mitsusada Fukasaku. LC 76-9352. (This Beautiful World Ser.: Vol. 57). (Illus., Orig.). 1976. pap. 5.25 o.p. (ISBN 0-87011-282-1). Kodansha.

Philippines: A Framework for Economic Recovery. World Bank Staff. 1987. 10.00 o.p. (ISBN 0-8213-0615-4, BK0942). World Bank.

Philippines: A Travel Survival Kit. 2nd ed. Jens Peters. (Illus.). 320p. (Orig.). 1983. pap. 8.95 o.p. (ISBN 0-908086-49-0). Lonely Planet.

Philippines: Post Report. rev. ed. (Department of State Publication 9159. Department & Foreign Service Ser.: No. 212). (Illus.). 40p. 1985. pap. 1.75 o.p. (ISBN 0-318-19580-1, S/N 044-000-02090-4). USGPO.

Philip's Girl. Date not set. (ISBN 0-8052-3976-6). Random.

Philip's Little Sister. Ellen Benson. LC 78-12627. (Social Values Ser.). (Illus.). (gr. 3). 1979. PLB 11.27 o.p. (ISBN 0-516-02023-4); pap. 3.95 o.p. (ISBN 0-516-42023-2). Childrens.

Philisophical Study of the Human Mind. Jospeh Barrell. 1954. (ISBN 0-8022-0069-9). Philos Lib.

Phillipines. rev. ed. (Hildebrand Travel Guides). (Illus.). 320p. (Orig.). pap. cancelled o.s.i. (ISBN 3-88989-089-X). Hunter Pub NY.

Phillipps Manuscripts: Catalogus Liberorum Maniscriptorum in Bibliotheca, 1837-71. D. Thomas Phillipps. 300.00 o.p. (ISBN 0-87556-663-4). Saifer.

Phillis. Billie L. Watt & Martin Newman. (Orig.). 1967. pap. 1.50 o.p. (ISBN 0-377-80591-2). Friendship Pr.

Phillis Wheatley: A Bio-Bibliography. William H. Robinson. 1981. 20.00 o.p. (ISBN 0-8161-8318-X, Hall Reference). G K Hall.

Philosophe in the Age of Revolution: Destutt de Tracy & the Origins of "Ideology" Emmet Kennedy. LC 78-56704. (Memoirs Ser.: Vol. 129). (Illus.). 1978. pap. 15.00 o.p. (ISBN 0-87169-129-9). Am Philos.

Philosopher's Annual, 1978, Vol. 1. Ed. by David L. Boyer et al. 223p. 1978. 25.00x o.s.i. (ISBN 0-8476-6105-9); pap. 12.50x o.s.i. (ISBN 0-8476-6106-7). Rowman.

Philosopher's Diet. Richard Watson. LC 84-45818. 153p. 1985. 12.95 o.p. (ISBN 0-87113-016-5). Atlantic Monthly.

Philosopher's Index: A Retrospective Index to U. S. Publications from 1940, 3 vols. Philosophy Documentation Center Staff. Ed. by Richard H. Lineback. 1619p. 1978. 195.00 set o.p. (ISBN 0-912632-09-7). Philos Document.

Philosophers Look at Science. LC 65-15789. 128p. 1965. (ISBN 0-8022-1863-6). Philos Lib.

Philosophers Speak for Themselves: From Aristotle to Plotinus. 2nd ed. Ed. by Thomas V. Smith. LC 56-4949. 1956. pap. text ed. 7.50 o.s.i. (ISBN 0-226-76479-6, P9, Phoen). U of Chicago Pr.

Philosopher's Stone. Jane Little. LC 74-154754. (Illus.). (gr. 3-7). 1971. 4.50 o.p. (ISBN 0-689-20692-5, Atheneum). Macmillan.

Philosophic History of Civilizations. J. C. Wise. (Illus.). 1955. (ISBN 0-8022-1913-6). Philos Lib.

Philosophic Problems. 2nd ed. Ed. by Maurice Mandelbaum et al. 1967. text ed. write for info. o.p. (ISBN 0-02-375360-9). Macmillan.

Philosophical Analysis: A Collection of Essays. Ed. by Max Black. LC 78-152158. (Essay Index Reprint Ser.). 405p. 1984. pap. 14.95 o.p. (ISBN 0-8290-1567-1). Irvington.

Philosophical Analysis & Educational Theory: Contemporary Readings. D. Reitz et al. 1972. pap. text ed. 9.95x o.p. (ISBN 0-8422-0193-9). Irvington.

Philosophical & Political History of the Settlements & Trade of the Europeans in the East & West Indies, 6 vols. 2nd ed. Guillaume T. Raynal. Tr. by J. O. Justamond. LC 69-18996. (Illus.). 1970. Repr. of 1798 ed. lib. bdg. 110.00 o.p. (ISBN 0-8371-9945-X, RAW&); Vol. 1. lib. bdg. 19.25 o.p. (ISBN 0-8371-1551-5, RAT&); Vol. 2. lib. bdg. 19.25 o.p. (ISBN 0-8371-1552-3, RAU&); Vol. 3. lib. bdg. 19.25 o.p. (ISBN 0-8371-1553-1, RAV&); Vol. 4. lib. bdg. 19.25 o.p. (ISBN 0-8371-1554-X, RAX&); Vol. 5. lib. bdg. 19.25 o.p. (ISBN 0-8371-1555-8, RAY&); Vol. 6. lib. bdg. 19.25 o.p. (ISBN 0-8371-1556-6, RAZ&). Greenwood.

Philosophical Aspects of the Mind-Body Problem. Ed. by Chung-ying Cheng. 226p. 1975. text ed. 16.00x o.p. (ISBN 0-8248-0342-6). UH Pr.

Philosophical Diary. Leonardo Da Vinci. 96p. 1959. (ISBN 0-8022-0355-8). Philos Lib.

Philosophical Dictionary. Voltaire. Tr. by Peter Gay. LC 62-9371. 1967. pap. 2.95 o.p. (ISBN 0-15-671750-6, HB122, Harv). HarBraceJ.

Philosophical Essays. Bertrand Russell. 1984. pap. 5.75 o.s.i. (ISBN 0-671-50583-1, Touchstone). S&S.

Philosophical Essays on Dance: With Responses from Choreographers, Critics & Dancers. Ed. by Gordon Fancher & Gerald Myers. LC 81-67061. 178p. (Orig.). 1981. pap. 14.95 o.s.i. (ISBN 0-87127-126-5, Pub. by Dance Horiz). Princeton Bk Co.

Philosophical Foundations of the Three Sociologies. Ted Benton. (International Library of Sociology Ser). 1977. 23.95x o.p. (ISBN 0-7100-8593-1). Routledge Chapman & Hall.

Philosophical Fragments. 2nd ed. Soren Kierkegaard. Ed. by H. V. Hong. Tr. by David Swenson. (American-Scandinavian Foundation Ser.). 1962. pap. 6.95x o.p. (ISBN 0-691-01955-X). Princeton U Pr.

Philosophical Investigations on Space, Time & Continuum. Franz Bretano. Tr. by Barry Smith from Ger. 224p. 1987. PLB 30.00x o.p. (ISBN 0-7099-4476-4, Pub. by Croom Helm UK). Routledge Chapman & Hall.

Philosophical Letters. Rene Descartes. Ed. & tr. by Anthony Kenny. LC 81-3431. 287p. 1981. pap. 11.95 o.p. (ISBN 0-8166-1060-6). U of Minn Pr.

Philosophical Redirection of Educational Research. Ed. by Lawrence G. Thomas. LC 6-16938. (National Society for the Study of Education Yearbooks Ser: No. 71, Pt. 1). 1972. lib. bdg. 8.00x o.s.i. (ISBN 0-226-60109-9). U of Chicago Pr.

Philosophical Studies by Heinrich Gomperz. Heinrich Gomperz. Ed. by Daniel S. Robinson. 1953. 9.50 o.p. (ISBN 0-8158-0100-9). Chris Mass.

Philosophical Themes in Modern Education. Robert S. Brumbaugh & Nathaniel Lawrence. LC 72-4796. 368p. 1973. pap. 9.75 o.p. (ISBN 0-395-04239-9, 3-07152). HM.

Philosophical Theology. James F. Ross. 366p. 1982. pap. text ed. 24.95x o.p. (ISBN 0-8290-1764-X). Irvington.

Philosophical Works: Phenomenology-Background, Foreground & Influences, 3 vols. James F. Ferrier. Ed. by Maurice Natanson. LC 78-66732. 1980. lib. bdg. 200.00 set o.p. (ISBN 0-8240-9566-9). Garland Pub.

Philosophical Writings. Gottlob Frege. (ISBN 0-8022-0537-2). Philos Lib.

Philosophical Writings of Richard Burthogge. Richard Burthogge. Ed. by Margaret W. Landes. 266p. 1921. 19.95 o.p. (ISBN 0-87548-048-9). Open Court.

Philosophies of Education. John S. Brubacher. (National Society for the Study of Education Yearbooks Ser: No. 41, Pt. 1). 1942. 6.00x o.s.i. (ISBN 0-226-59974-4); pap. text ed. 4.50x o.s.i. (ISBN 0-226-59975-2). U of Chicago Pr.

Philosophies of F. R. Tenant & John Dewey. J. Oliver Buswell, Jr. (ISBN 0-8022-0203-9). Philos Lib.

Philosophy: An Outline for the Intending Student. Ed. by R. J. Hirst. (Outlines Ser). 1968. 16.95x o.p. (ISBN 0-7100-2038-4); pap. 6.95 o.p. (ISBN 0-7100-6099-8). Routledge Chapman & Hall.

Philosophy & Archaic Experience, Vol. 38. Ed. by John Sallis. LC 82-5112. (Duquesne Studies: Philosophical). 225p. 1981. text ed. 19.50x o.p. (ISBN 0-8207-0152-1). Duquesne.

Philosophy & Care of the Mentally Retarded: A Worldwide Status Report. J. L. Matson. 120p. 1983. pap. 15.25 o.p. (ISBN 0-08-028093-5). Pergamon.

Philosophy & Foundations of Vocational Education. H. C. Kazanas et al. 188p. 1973. text ed. 29.50x o.p. (ISBN 0-8422-7124-4). Irvington.

Philosophy & Human Movement. David Best. (Unwin Education Bks.). 1979. text ed. 21.95x o.p. (ISBN 0-04-370088-8); pap. text ed. 7.95x o.p. (ISBN 0-04-370089-6). Unwin Hyman.

Philosophy & Law. Ed. by Jules Coleman & Ellen F. Paul. 240p. 1987. pap. text ed. 14.95x o.p. (ISBN 0-631-15257-1). Basil Blackwell.

Philosophy & Personal Relations: An Anglo-French Study. Ed. by Alan Montefiore. 208p. 1973. 12.50x o.p. (ISBN 0-7735-0179-7, McGill Canada). U of Toronto Pr.

Philosophy & Philosophical Authors of the Jews: A Historical Sketch With Explanatory Notes. S. Munk. Tr. by Isidor Kalisch. (Reprints in Philosophy Ser.). 1986. pap. text ed. 6.95x o.p. (ISBN 0-8290-1881-6). Irvington.

Philosophy & Psychology: Classification Schedule, Author & Title Listing, Chronological Listing, 2 vols. Harvard University Library Staff. LC 72-83389. (Widener Library Shelflist Ser: No. 42-43). 1973. 100.00x o.p. (ISBN 0-674-66486-8). Harvard U Pr.

Philosophy & Religion in Colonial America. Claude Newlin. LC 61-15245. 224p. 1962. Philos Lib.

Philosophy & Religion: Six Lectures Delivered at Cambridge. Hastings Rashdall. Repr. of 1910 ed. lib. bdg. 35.00x o.p. (ISBN 0-8371-3025-5, RAPR). Greenwood.

Philosophy & the Civilizing Arts: Essays Presented to Herbert W. Schneider. Ed. by Craig Walton & John P. Anton. LC 73-92907. xxii, 508p. 1974. 18.00x o.p. (ISBN 0-8214-0145-9, 82-81487). Ohio U Pr.

Philosophy & the Modern World. Albert W. Levi. (Midway Reprints). 1977. pap. text ed. 16.00x o.s.i. (ISBN 0-226-47391-0). U of Chicago Pr.

Philosophy Applied to Controversial Issues in a Democratic Society. Bradley G. Moore. LC 79-84650. 1979. pap. text ed. 10.00 o.p. (ISBN 0-8191-0741-7). U Pr of Amer.

Philosophy, Evolution & Human Nature. Florian Von Schilcher & Neil Tennant. 269p. 1984. 29.95X o.p. (ISBN 0-7100-9767-0). Routledge Chapman & Hall.

Philosophy for Pleasure. Hector Hawton. 1950. (ISBN 0-8022-0693-X). Philos Lib.

Philosophy for the Common Man. Heinrich F. Wolf. (ISBN 0-8022-1914-4). Philos Lib.

Philosophy in America from Puritans to James. Paul R. Anderson & Max H. Fisch. 1969. lib. bdg. 31.50x o.p. (ISBN 0-374-90248-8, Octagon). Hippocrene Bks.

Philosophy in the Flesh: A Reader. Ed. by Donald Brady. 149p. 1975. pap. text ed. 6.95x o.p. (ISBN 0-8422-0492-X). Irvington.

Philosophy in Wit. Emil Froeschels. (ISBN 0-8022-0553-4). Philos Lib.

Philosophy Looks to the Future: Confrontation, Commitment & Utopia. 2nd ed. Walter L. Fogg & Peyton E. Richter. 1978. pap. text ed. 28.58 o.s.i. (ISBN 0-205-06030-7, 6060307). Allyn.

Philosophy Now. 3rd ed. Karsten J. Struhl & Paula R. Struhl. 608p. 1980. pap. text ed. 15.00 o.p. (ISBN 0-394-32354-8, RanC). Random.

Philosophy of Andy Warhol: From A to B & Back Again. Andy Warhol. LC 74-31107. 256p. 1975. 7.95 o.p. (ISBN 0-15-189050-1). HarBraceJ.

Philosophy of As If: A System of the Theoretical, Practical & Religious Fictions of Mankind. H. Vaihinger. (Illus.). 428p. 1984. pap. 30.00 o.p. (ISBN 0-7100-3019-3). Routledge Chapman & Hall.

Philosophy of Benedetto Croce. Angelo A. De Gennaro. LC 61-12620. 128p. 1961. (ISBN 0-8022-0371-X). Philos Lib.

Philosophy of Benedetto Croce, an Introduction. Angelo A. De Gennaro. LC 69-10084. Repr. of 1961 ed. lib. bdg. 35.00x o.p. (ISBN 0-8371-0058-5, DEBC). Greenwood.

Philosophy of Brentano. Ed. by Linda McAlister. 200p. 1977. text ed. 28.50x o.p. (ISBN 0-391-00653-3); pap. text ed. 13.00x o.p. (ISBN 0-391-00654-1). Humanities.

Philosophy of Christian Education. Pierre J. Marique. 1970. Repr. of 1939 ed. lib. bdg. 22.50x o.p. (ISBN 0-8371-4271-7, MAED). Greenwood.

Philosophy of Creation. Charles J. Fitti. LC 63-156011. 112p. 1963. Philos Lib.

Philosophy of David Hume. Norman Kemp-Smith. LC 82-48335. (Philosophy of David Hume Ser.). 592p. 1983. lib. bdg. 55.00 o.p. (ISBN 0-8240-5412-1). Garland Pub.

Philosophy of Death & Dying. M. V. Kamath. 350p. pap. 11.95 o.p. (ISBN 0-89389-046-4). Himalayan Pubs.

Philosophy of Education. John Dewey. (Quality Paperback: No. 126). 312p. 1971. pap. 4.95 o.p. (ISBN 0-8226-0126-5). Littlefield.

Philosophy of Education. William K. Frankena. 1965. pap. write for info. o.p. (ISBN 0-02-339490-0, 33949). Macmillan.

Philosophy of Epictetus. John Bonforte. 180p. 1955. (ISBN 0-8022-0151-2). Philos Lib.

Philosophy of Existence. Marcel Cabriel. LC 69-12353. 96p. 1969. 7.95 o.p. (ISBN 0-8022-2286-2). Philos Lib.

Philosophy of Existentialism. Jean-Paul Sartre. LC 65-20329. 448p. 1965. (ISBN 0-8022-1489-4). Philos Lib.

Philosophy of Free Expression & Its Constitutional Applications. Robert F. Ladenson. LC 82-18106. (Philosophy & Society Ser.). 224p. 1983. text ed. 37.50 o.s.i. (ISBN 0-8476-6761-8). Rowman.

Philosophy of Friedrich Nietzsche. H. L. Mencken. 325p. 1982. pap. 7.00 o.p. Noontide.

Philosophy of Geohistory. Claude C. Albritton. LC 74-10559. (Benchmark Papers in Geology Ser: Vol. 13). 400p. 1975. 29.95 o.p. (ISBN 0-12-786049-5). Acad Pr.

Philosophy of God, & Theology. Bernard J. Lonergan. LC 73-22011. 1974. 4.50 o.s.i. (ISBN 0-664-20888-6, Westminster). Westminster John Knox.

Philosophy of Grammar. Otto Jespersen. (Illus.). 1965. pap. 7.95 o.p. (ISBN 0-393-00307-8, Norton Lib.). Norton.

Philosophy of Humanism. Corliss Lamont. LC 58-633. 256p. 1958. (ISBN 0-8022-0909-2). Philos Lib.

Philosophy of John Dewey: A Critical Analysis. William T. Feldman. LC 68-19271. 1968. Repr. of 1934 ed. lib. bdg. 35.00x o.p. (ISBN 0-8371-0414-9, FEPD). Greenwood.

Philosophy of Jonathan Edwards, from His Private Notebooks. Jonathan Edwards. Ed. by Harvey G. Townsend. LC 72-7503. (Studies in Philosophy, No. 2). 270p. 1973. Repr. of 1955 ed. lib. bdg. 35.00x o.p. (ISBN 0-8371-6511-3, EDPH). Greenwood.

Philosophy of Language Primer. Thomas S. Vernon. LC 80-489. 136p. 1980. text ed. 24.25 o.p. (ISBN 0-8191-1023-X); pap. text ed. 9.25 o.p. (ISBN 0-8191-1024-8). U Pr of Amer.

Philosophy of Life. Richard N. Bender. (ISBN 0-8022-0100-8). Philos Lib.

Philosophy of Life. Chen Li-Fu. (ISBN 0-8022-0974-2). Philos Lib.

Philosophy of Literature. Gustave E. Mueller. (ISBN 0-8022-1165-8). Philos Lib.

Philosophy of Literature. Raymond Tschumi. 20.00 o.p. (ISBN 0-87556-338-4). Saifer.

Philosophy of Logical Atomism & Other Essays, 1914-1919. Bertrand Russell. Ed. by John G. Slater. (Collected Papers of Bertrand Russell: Vol. 8). 418p. 1986. lib. bdg. 60.00 o.p. (ISBN 0-04-920074-7). Unwin Hyman.

Philosophy of Magic. Arthur Versluis. (Illus.). 166p. 1985. pap. 7.95 o.p. (ISBN 0-317-40548-9). Routledge Chapman & Hall.

Philosophy of Martin Heidegger. Ed. by Howard A. Slaatte & Henry Sendaydiego. LC 83-16901. 148p. (Orig.). 1984. lib. bdg. 22.75 o.p. (ISBN 0-8191-3597-6); pap. text ed. 9.25 o.p. (ISBN 0-8191-3598-4). U Pr of Amer.

Philosophy of Mathematics & Natural Science. Hermann Weyl. LC 49-9797. 1963. pap. 1.65 o.p. (ISBN 0-689-70207-8, 31, Atheneum). Macmillan.

Philosophy of Medicine: An Introduction. Wulff. 1986. 35.50 o.p. (ISBN 0-8016-5692-3); pap. 15.95 o.p. (ISBN 0-8016-5718-0). Mosby.

Philosophy of Meditation. Haridas Chaudhuri. LC 65-11635. 64p. 1965. Philos Lib.

Philosophy of Natural Magic. Henry C. Agrippa. 1974. 8.95 o.p. (ISBN 0-8216-0218-7, Pub. by Univ Bks). Carol Pub Group.

Philosophy of Nature. Jacques Maritain. 1951. (ISBN 0-8022-1060-0). Philos Lib.

Philosophy of Psychiatry: Psychiatric Prolegonema. Harold Palmer. 1952. (ISBN 0-8022-1256-5). Philos Lib.

Philosophy of Religion: An Annotated Bibliography of Twentieth-Century Writings in English. William J. Wainwright. LC 77-83374. (Library of Humanities Reference Bks.: No. 111). lib. bdg. 83.00 o.p. (ISBN 0-8240-9849-8). Garland Pub.

Philosophy of Religion: Selected Readings. Ed. by William L. Rowe & William J. Wainwright. 489p. 1973. pap. text ed. 14.00 net o.p. (ISBN 0-15-570580-6, HC). HarBraceJ.

Philosophy of Science & Sociology: From the Methodological Doctrine to Research Practice. E. Mokrzycki. (International Library of Sociology). 180p. 1983. 21.95x o.p. (ISBN 0-7100-9444-2). Routledge Chapman & Hall.

Philosophy of Shakespeare. K. H. Spalding. 190p. 1953. (ISBN 0-8022-1614-5). Philos Lib.

Philosophy of the Christian Religion. Edward J. Carnell. (Twin Brooks Ser.). 525p. 1981. pap. 10.95 o.p. (ISBN 0-8010-2464-1). Baker Bk.

Philosophy of the Humanistic Society. Ed. by Alfred E. Koenig et al. LC 80-1425. 290p. (Orig.). 1981. lib. bdg. 27.25 o.p. (ISBN 0-8191-1414-6); pap. text ed. 14.50 o.p. (ISBN 0-8191-1415-4). U Pr of Amer.

Philosophy of the Present. George H. Mead. Ed. by Arthur E. Murphy. (Paul Carus Lecture Ser.). 239p. 1959. 14.95 o.p. (ISBN 0-87548-103-5). Open Court.

Philosophy of the Religions of Ancient Greeks & Israelites. Ben Kimpel. LC 83-6512. 362p. (Orig.). 1983. lib. bdg. 31.50 o.p. (ISBN 0-8191-3225-X); pap. text ed. 16.50 o.p. (ISBN 0-8191-3226-8). U Pr of Amer.

Philosophy of the Second Advent. Howard A. Redmond. 1986. text ed. 12.95 o.p. (ISBN 0-8010-7740-0). Baker Bk.

Philosophy of the State As Educator. Thomas Dubay. LC 78-6256. 1978. Repr. of 1959 ed. lib. bdg. 35.00x o.p. (ISBN 0-313-20416-0, DUPH). Greenwood.

Philosophy of Time. Louis A. Reitmeister. LC 72-10699. 452p. 1974. Repr. of 1962 ed. lib. bdg. 25.00x o.p. (ISBN 0-8371-6618-7, REPT). Greenwood.

Philosophy of Upanishads. B. Singh. 160p. 1983. text ed. 10.50x o.p. (ISBN 0-391-02935-5). Humanities.

Philosophy of W. V. Quine: An Expository Essay. Roger F. Gibson. 1986. pap. 12.00x o.p. (ISBN 0-8130-0855-7); 22.00 o.p. U Presses Fla.

Philosophy: Paradox & Discovery. Arthur J. Minton. 512p. 1976. text ed. 21.95 o.p. (ISBN 0-07-042412-8, C). McGraw.

Philsophical Lectures (1818-19) Samuel Taylor Coleridge. (ISBN 0-8022-0281-0). Philos Lib.

Philsophical Problems of Mathematics. Bruno B. Von Freytag & General Loringhoff. 1951. (ISBN 0-8022-0542-9). Philos Lib.

Phiz!: Illustrator of Dickens' World. John Buchanan-Brown. (Encore Editions). (Illus.). 1978. 4.95 o.p. (ISBN 0-684-16675-5, ScribT). Scribner.

Phlebography of the Lower Limb. M. Lea Thomas. (Illus.). 220p. 1982. 52.00 o.p. (ISBN 0-443-01841-3). Churchill.

Phobias: Their Nature & Control. S. Rachman. (Illus.). 136p. 1968. 18.00 o.p. (ISBN 0-398-01535-X). C C Thomas.

Phoebe. Patricia Dizenzo. (gr. 9 up). 1970. text ed. 7.95 o.p. (ISBN 0-07-017096-7). McGraw.

Phoenix & Other Stories. Swee H. Wong. (Writing in Asia Ser.). 124p. (Orig.). 1985. pap. text ed. 6.00 o.p. (ISBN 9971-64-072-4, 00269). Heinemann Ed.

Phoenix & Vicinity Street Atlas, 1986. Thomas Bros. Maps Staff. (Illus.). 184p. 1986. pap. 11.95 o.p. Thomas Bros Maps.

Phoenix Ascent. Chris Ananyi. LC 83-91408. 70p. 1985. 7.95 o.p. (ISBN 0-533-06031-1). Vantage.

Phoenix Factor: Surviving & Growing Through Personal Crisis. Karl Slaikeu & Steve Lawhead. LC 85-4254. 256p. 1985. 15.45 o.s.i. (ISBN 0-395-35405-6). HM.

Phoenix Harvest. Han Suyin. 1985. pap. 6.95 o.p. (ISBN 0-586-05414-6, Pub. by Granada England). Academy Chi Pubs.

Phoenix House: Studies in a Therapeutic Community (1968-1973) Ed. by George De Leon. 214p. 1974. text ed. 34.75x o.p. (ISBN 0-8422-7238-0). Irvington.

Phoenix Metropolitan Area Street Atlas & Directory, 1986. rev. ed. Thomas Bros. Maps Staff. (Illus.). 192p. 1986. pap. 11.95 o.p. (ISBN 0-88130-158-2). Thomas Bros Maps.

Phoenix of His Age: Interpretations of Erasmus, Fifteen Fifty to Seventeen Fifty. Bruce Mansfield. LC 79-14960. (Erasmus Studies). (Illus.). 1979. 30.00x o.p. (ISBN 0-8020-5457-9). U of Toronto Pr.

Phoenix Suns. Jim Moore. (NBA Today Ser.). (Illus.). 48p. (gr. 4 up). 1984. PLB 10.45 o.p. (ISBN 0-87191-986-9). Creative Ed.

Phoenix Syndrome. Lucilla Andrews. 196p. 1988. 19.95 o.p. (ISBN 0-434-02131-8, Pub. by W Heinemann Ltd). David & Charles.

Phoenix Syndrome. Lucilla Andrews. (Lythway Ser.). 280p. 1988. lib. bdg. 19.50x o.p. (ISBN 0-7451-0708-7, Pub. by Chivers Pr UK). G K Hall.

Phone Calls from the Dead. Beth Bentley. LC 76-122096. 78p. 1970. 8.95 o.p. (ISBN 0-8214-0076-2). Ohio U Pr.

Phonetic Rules in Reading. Mary H. Manoni & Robert Cienkus. LC 78-730055. (Illus.). 1978. text ed. 159.00 o.s.i. (ISBN 0-89290-103-9, A329-SATC). Soc for Visual.

Phonic Dictionary. Linda Hayward. (Illus.). 96p. (gr. k-4). 1981. PLB 3.99 o.p. (ISBN 0-448-13923-5, G&D); pap. 4.95 o.p. (ISBN 0-448-47336-4). Putnam Pub Group.

Phonics Combinations. Compiled by Constance McAllister. (Illus., Orig.). (gr. 1-4). 1978. pap. 2.95 o.p. (ISBN 0-87534-173-X). Highlights.

Phonics Crossword Puzzles Series. Kramer. Incl. Early Phonics Crossword Puzzle Book. (gr. k). 1974. pap. text ed. 1.60 o.p. (ISBN 0-8009-0438-9); Bk. A. (gr. 1-2). 1971. pap. text ed. 3.96 (ISBN 0-8009-0441-9); Bk. B. (gr. 3-4). 1971. pap. text ed. 3.96 (ISBN 0-8009-0445-1); Bk. C. (gr. 5-6). 1971. pap. text ed. 3.96 (ISBN 0-8009-0449-4). (gr. k-6). Bks. A-C. pap. text ed. 1.76 ea. o.p.; tchr's. eds. Bks. A-C 3.32 ea. o.p.; Spirit masters Early Phonics-Bk. C. spirit masters Early Phonics- 6.88 ea. o.p. Random Sch Div.

Phonics Fun Crossword Puzzles. Beth Seiler. (Illus.). 48p. (gr. k-3). 1987. pap. 1.95 incl. clipboard o.s.i. (ISBN 0-8431-1920-9). Price Stern.

Phonics Fun for Beginners. Compiled by Constance McAllister. (Illus., Orig.). (gr. 1-3). 1977. pap. 2.95 o.p. (ISBN 0-87534-167-5). Highlights.

Phonics in Learning to Read. Ellen C. Henderson. 1967. pap. text ed. 5.00 o.p. (ISBN 0-682-45712-4, University). Exposition-Phoenix.

Phonological Interpretation of Ancient Greek: A Pandialectal Analysis. Vit Bubenik. (Phoenix Supplementary Ser.: Vol. 19). 352p. 1983. 37.50x o.p. (ISBN 0-8020-5476-5). U of Toronto Pr.

Phonology & Syntax: The Relation Between Sound & Structure. Elisabeth O. Selkirk. 496p. 1986. pap. text ed. 12.50x o.p. (ISBN 0-262-69098-5). MIT Pr.

Phosphate & Other Minerals International Workshop: On Phosphate & Other Minerals, 5th International Workshop Abstracts. International Workshop on Phosphate & Other Minerals Staff. Ed. by S. G. Massry. (Mineral & Electrolyte Metabolism Journal: Vol. 6, No. 4-5, 1981). (Illus.). 52p. 1981. pap. 11.25 o.p. (ISBN 3-8055-3441-8). S Karger.

Phosphates in Agriculture. Vincent Sauchelli. LC 65-27055. 228p. 1965. 17.50 o.p. (ISBN 0-442-15040-7, Pub. by Van Nos Reinhold). Krieger.

Phosphatidylcholine. Ed. by H. Peeters. (Illus.). 1976. 22.50 o.p. (ISBN 0-387-07828-2). Springer-Verlag.

Phosphorimetry: The Application of Phosphoresence to the Analysis of Organic Compounds. Maximilian Zander. Tr. by Thomas H. Goodwin. LC 68-18686. 1968. 61.00 o.p. (ISBN 0-12-775650-7). Acad Pr.

Photo & Thermoelectric Effects in Semiconductors. J. Tauc. 1962. 35.00 o.p. (ISBN 0-08-009611-5); pap. 23.00 o.p. (ISBN 0-08-013636-2). Pergamon.

Photo Crimes, Vol. 3. (Illus.). 64p. 1986. pap. 7.95 o.p. (ISBN 0-671-62756-2, Fireside). S&S.

Photo Crimes, Vol. 1. 64p. 1986. pap. 7.95 o.p. (ISBN 0-671-61762-1, Fireside). S&S.

Photo Crimes, Vol. 2. 64p. 1986. pap. 7.95 o.p. (ISBN 0-671-60568-2, Fireside). S&S.

Photo Dictionary of Football. Melvin Berger. (Illus.). 60p. (gr. 3-7). 1980. 9.95 o.p. (ISBN 0-416-30131-2, NO. 0148). Routledge Chapman & Hall.

Photo-Enolisation. P. G. Sammes. 1976. pap. 15.50 o.p. (ISBN 0-08-020475-9). Pergamon.

Photo Equipment You Can Make, Vol. 2. Parry Yob. LC 73-82539. (Photography How-to Ser.). 1977. 3.95 o.p. (ISBN 0-8227-4013-3). Petersen Pub.

Photo Filters & Lens Attachments. Kalton C. Lahue. (Petersen's Photographic Library: Vol. 5). (Illus.). 160p. 1981. pap. 8.95 o.p. (ISBN 0-8227-4044-3). Petersen Pub.

Photo-Optical Data Reduction: Proceedings of the SPIE Seminar, St. Louis, 1964, Vol. 2. Society of Photo-Optical Instrumentation Engineers Staff. (SPIE Seminar Proceedings). 236p. 1964. 29.00 o.p. (ISBN 0-89252-003-5). SPIE.

Photo-Optical Techniques in Simulators I: Proceedings of the SPIE Seminar, New York, 1969, Vol. 17. Society of Photo-Optical Instrumentation Engineers Staff. (SPIE Seminar Proceedings). 172p. 1969. 29.00 o.p. (ISBN 0-89252-020-5). SPIE.

Photo Retouching & Restoration. Kalton C. Lahue. LC 78-78395. (Photography How-to Ser.). (Illus.). 1979. pap. 4.50 o.p. (ISBN 0-8227-4034-6). Petersen Pub.

Photo School: A Step by Step Course in Photography. Michael Freeman. (Illus.). 224p. 1982. 27.50 o.p. (ISBN 0-8174-5402-0, Amphoto). Watson-Guptill.

Photo Typesetter Comparison Charts: 1988 Edition. Harold Durbin. 1988. pap. 25.00 o.p. (ISBN 0-936786-05-1). Durbin Assoc.

Photoacoustics & Photoacoustic Spectroscopy, Vol. 57. Allan Rosencraig. LC 80-17286. (Chemical Analysis: A Series of Monographs on Analytical Chemistry & Its Applications). 309p. 1980. 79.00 o.p. (ISBN 0-471-04495-4). Krieger.

Photochemical & Transport Processes in the Upper Atmosphere. Ed. by L. Thomas & H. Rishbeth. LC 76-26741. 1977. pap. 33.00 o.p. (ISBN 0-08-021312-X). Pergamon.

Photochemical Conversion & Storage of Solar Energy. John S. Connolly. LC 81-12853. 1981. 79.50 o.p. (ISBN 0-12-185880-4). Acad Pr.

Photochemical Processes in High Polymers: Proceedings of the Second International Symposium on Photochemical Processes in Polymer Chemistry, Leuven, Belgium, 1976. Ed. by G. Smets. 1977. 53.00 o.p. (ISBN 0-08-021205-0). Pergamon.

Photochemical Processes in Polymer Chemistry: Proceedings of the First International Symposium, on Photochemical Processes in Polymer Chemistry, Leuven, Belgium, 1972. Ed. by G. Smets & F. C. De Schryver. 188p. 1976. 48.00 o.p. (ISBN 0-08-020811-8). Pergamon.

Photochemistry. Ed. by F. Boschke. (Topics in Current Chemistry Ser.: Vol. 46). (Illus.). iv, 236p. 1974. 45.00 o.p. (ISBN 0-387-06592-X). Springer-Verlag.

Photochemistry. Ed. by F. Boschke. LC 51-5497. (Topics in Current Chemistry: Vol. 13, Pt. 2). (Illus.). 1969. pap. 42.50 o.p. (ISBN 0-387-04489-2). Springer-Verlag.

Photochemistry & Photobiology of Nucleic Acids, 2 vols. Ed. by Shih Y. Wang. 1976. Vol. 1. 95.00 o.p. (ISBN 0-12-734601-5); Vol. 2. 93.50 o.p. (ISBN 0-12-734602-3). Acad Pr.

Photochemistry of Proteins & Nucleic Acids. A. D. McLaren & D. Shugar. 1964. 115.00 o.p. (ISBN 0-08-010139-9); pap. text ed. 115.00 o.p. (ISBN 0-08-013569-2). Pergamon.

Photoelasticity for Designers. R. B. Heywood. (International Series in Mechanical Engineering: Vol. 2). 1969. 110.00 o.p. (ISBN 0-08-013005-4). Pergamon.

Photoelectron Spectra of Nonmetallic Solids & Consequences for Quantum Chemistry see Photoelectron Spectrometry.

Photoelectron Spectrometry. Incl. Photoelectron Spectra of Nonmetallic Solids & Consequences for Quantum Chemistry. C. K. Jrgensen; Fractional Prentage Methods for Ionisation of Open Shells of D & F Electrons. P. A. Cox; X-Ray Photoelectron Spectroscopy: Application to Metals & Alloys. R. E. Watson & M. L. Perlman; Ultraviolet Photoelectron Spectroscopy of Gases Absorbed on Metal Surfaces. A. M. Bradshaw et al. (Structure & Bonding: Vol. 24). (Illus.). iv, 170p. 1975. 45.00 o.p. (ISBN 0-387-07364-7). Springer-Verlag.

Photoelectron Spectroscopy. J. H. Eland. LC 73-17763. 239p. 1974. 45.95x o.p. (ISBN 0-470-23485-7). Halsted Pr.

Photoelectron Spectroscopy: Chemical & Analytical Aspects. A. D. Baker & D. Betteridge. 190p. 1972. 50.00 o.p. (ISBN 0-08-016910-4). Pergamon.

Photogrammetry, Water Quality, Safety Appurtenances & Shoulder Design. (Transportation Research Record Ser.). 64p. 1976. 2.80 o.p. (ISBN 0-309-02563-X). Transport Res Bd.

Photograms of the Year. Ed. by R. H. Mason. 1957. (ISBN 0-8022-1077-5). Philos Lib.

Photograph Collector's Resource Directory. 2nd ed. Ed. by Peter H. Falk. 1985. pap. 24.95 o.p. (ISBN 0-913069-05-1). Photo Arts Ctr.

Photographed All the Best Scenery: Jack Hillers's Diary of the Powell Expeditions 1871-1875. Ed. by Don D. Fowler. LC 78-189755. (University of Utah Publications in the American West: Vol. 9). (Illus.). 1972. 19.95 o.p. (ISBN 0-87480-066-8). U of Utah Pr.

Photographer's Almanac. Peter Miller & Janet Nelson. (Illus.). 352p. 1983. 24.95 o.p. (ISBN 0-316-57364-7); pap. 15.00 o.p. (ISBN 0-316-57365-5). Little.

Photographer's Build-It-Yourself Book. Tom Branch. (Illus.). 160p. (Orig.). 1982. 24.95 o.p. (ISBN 0-8174-5406-3, Amphoto); pap. text ed. 14.95 o.p. (ISBN 0-8174-5407-1). Watson-Guptill.

Photographer's Complete Guide to Exhibition & Sales Spaces. Ed. by Peter H. Falk. 1985. pap. 19.95 o.p. (ISBN 0-913069-06-X). Photo Arts Ctr.

Photographers Index I. (Illus.). 450p. 1986. 90.00 o.p. (ISBN 0-8161-8814-9, Pub. by Graphic-Sha Pub Co Ltd Japan). G K Hall.

Photographer's Market, 1985. Robert D. Lutz. 576p. 1984. 15.95 o.p. (ISBN 0-89879-153-7). Writers Digest.

Photographer's Market 1986. Ed. by Robin Weinstein. 576p. 1985. 16.95 o.p. (ISBN 0-89879-199-5, 1822). Writers Digest.

Photographer's Market 1987. Ed. by Connie Eidenier. 576p. 1986. 16.95 o.p. (ISBN 0-89879-245-2). Writers Digest.

Photographer's Market 88. Ed. by Connie Eidenier. 624p. 1987. 18.95 o.p. (ISBN 0-89879-274-6). Writers Digest.

Photographic Art of Hoyningen-Huene. William A. Ewing. LC 86-6510. 1986. 60.00 o.p. (ISBN 0-8478-0718-5). Rizzoli Intl.

Photographic Artifacts of Timothy O'Sullivan. Rick Dingus. LC 82-8472. (Illus.). 175p. 1982. 45.00 o.p. (ISBN 0-8263-0607-1). U of NM Pr.

Photographic Atlas. Trilobites Levi-Setti. 1977. pap. text ed. 9.95x o.s.i. (ISBN 0-226-47449-6, P719, Phoen). U of Chicago Pr.

Photographic Atlas of Reconstructive Arterial Surgery. R. J. Van Dongen. (Illus.). xvi, 209p. 1970. 48.00 o.p. (ISBN 0-387-91059-X). Springer-Verlag.

Photographic Composition. Tom Grill & Mark Scanlon. (Illus.). 144p. 23.95 o.p. (ISBN 0-86343-060-0, Pub. by Fountain Pr UK). Seven Hills Bk Dists.

Photographic Composition. Ave Phildas. (Illus.). 160p. (Orig.). pap. 14.95 o.p. (ISBN 0-8227-4053-2). Petersen Pub.

Photographic Gelatin II. Ed. by R. J. Cox. 1976. 91.50 o.p. (ISBN 0-12-194452-2). Acad Pr.

Photographic Gelatin: Proceedings of the Symposium, 2nd, Trinity College, Cambridge, 1970. Photographic Gelatin Symposium Staff. Ed. by R. J. Cox. 1972. 87.50 o.p. (ISBN 0-12-194450-6). Acad Pr.

Photographic Information Recording. Hellmut Frieser. LC 75-20097. 592p. 1975. 113.95 o.p. (ISBN 0-470-28117-0). Halsted Pr.

Photographic Lenses. (Petersen's Photographic Library: Vol. 8). (Illus.). 160p. (Orig.). (gr. 9-12). 1982. pap. text ed. 9.95 o.p. (ISBN 0-8227-4054-0). Petersen Pub.

Photographic Modeling. Valerie Cragin. LC 75-10066. (Photography How-to Ser.). 1977. pap. 4.50 o.p. (ISBN 0-8227-0102-2). Petersen Pub.

Photographic Processing Chemistry. L. F. Mason. (Illus.). 328p. 1979. 54.95 o.p. (ISBN 0-317-54398-9). Focal Pr.

Photographic Recording of High-Speed Processes. A. S. Dubovik. 1968. 93.00 o.p. (ISBN 0-08-012017-2). Pergamon.

Photographic Self-Assignments. Ben Helprin. LC 79-51528. (Photography How-to Ser.). (Illus.). 1979. pap. 4.50 o.p. (ISBN 0-8227-4015-X). Petersen Pub.

Photographic Techniques in Scientific Research, Vol. 2. Ed. by A. A. Newman. 1976. 99.00 o.p. (ISBN 0-12-517960-X). Acad Pr.

Photographic Techniques in Scientific Research, Vol. 3. Ed. by A. A. Newman. 1979. 115.00 o.p. (ISBN 0-12-517963-4). Acad Pr.

Photographic Theory for the Motion Picture Cameraman. Compiled by Russell Campbell. LC 70-130298. (Illus.). 160p. 1981. pap. 7.95 o.s.i. (ISBN 0-498-07776-4). A S Barnes.

Photographs from Welsh Collections. Ed. by Welsh Arts Council Staff. 130p. 1977. pap. 3.95x o.p. (ISBN 0-905171-25-X, Pub. by Welsh Arts Wales). Intl Spec Bk.

Photography. McKnight Staff & Wilbur R. Miller. LC 78-53393. (Basic Industrial Arts Ser.). (Illus.). 1978. 7.28 o.p. (ISBN 0-87345-797-8); softbound 5.28 o.p. (ISBN 0-87345-789-7). Glencoe.

Photography. 3rd ed. Barbara L. Upton & John Upton. 1985. pap. text ed. (ISBN 0-673-39618-5). Scott F.

Photography: A Handbook of History, Materials & Processes. 2nd ed. 24.95 o.s.i. (ISBN 0-03-059236-4). H Holt & Co.

Photography: A Practical & Creative Introduction. A. E. Woolley. (Illus.). 336p. 1974. text ed. 37.95 o.p. (ISBN 0-07-071860-1). McGraw.

Photography: A Sense of Order. Janet Kardon. (Illus.). 60p. 1981. pap. 15.00 o.p. (ISBN 0-88454-027-8). U of Pa Contemp Art.

Photography & the Art of Seeing. Freeman Patterson. (Illus.). 156p. 1987. pap. 16.95 o.p. (ISBN 0-919493-81-5, Pub. by Key Porter Canada). U of Toronto Pr.

Photography: Art & Technique. Alfred A. Blaker. LC 79-23536. (Illus.). 460p. 1980. text ed. 34.95 o.p. (ISBN 0-7167-1115-X); pap. text ed. 19.95 o.s.i. (ISBN 0-7167-1116-8); reference manual incl. o.p. W H Freeman.

Photography: Art & Technique. Alfred A. Blaker. (Illus.). 460p. (Orig.). 1980. 32.95x o.p. (ISBN 0-240-51748-2); pap. 22.95x o.p. (ISBN 0-240-51741-5). Focal Pr.

Photography for the Hiker & Backpacker. Michael Krohn. (Illus.). 78p. 1981. pap. 5.95 o.p. (ISBN 0-913140-46-5, Pub. by Ptarmigan Pr). Signpost Bk Pub.

Photography for the Joy of It. Freeman Patterson. (Illus.). 168p. 1987. pap. 16.95 o.p. (ISBN 0-442-29893-5, Pub. by Key Porter Canada). U of Toronto Pr.

Photography for the Scientist. Ed. by Charles E. Engel. 1968. 53.00 o.p. (ISBN 0-12-238650-7). Acad Pr.

Photography Ser. Close-up. D. J. Herda. LC 76-45947. (Photography). (Illus.). (gr. 4-6). 1977. PLB 13.31 o.p. (ISBN 0-8172-0019-3). Raintree Pubs.

Photography Simplified for Archivists. Ken Lawrence. Ed. by Rowland P. Gill. (Collegiate Guide to Archival Science Ser.: No. 5). 120p. (Orig.). 1988. pap. text ed. 6.65 o.p. (ISBN 0-910653-10-0, 8101-K). Archival Servs.

Photography: Three Generations. Ken Dibert. LC 76-15520. 9.95 o.p. (ISBN 0-912216-11-5). Angel Pr.

Photography Through the Microscope. Ed. by Eastman Kodak Company. LC 79-54858. (Illus.). 96p. 1980. pap. 13.00 o.p. (ISBN 0-87985-248-8, P-2). Eastman Kodak.

Photography Year Book 1985. Ed. by Peter Wilkinson. (Photography Yearbook Ser.). (Illus.). 240p. 1985. 22.95 o.s.i. (ISBN 0-86343-027-9, 3279). Morgan.

Photography Yearbook, 1986-1987. Ed. by Peter Wilkinson. (Illus.). 234p. 29.95 o.p. (ISBN 0-86343-077-5, Pub. by Fountain Pr UK). Seven Hills Bk Dists.

Photohistory of the Twentieth-Century. Jonathan Grimwood. (Illus.). 192p. 1987. 29.95 o.p. (ISBN 0-7137-1802-1, Pub. by Blandford Pr England). Sterling.

Photolab Design. Eastman Kodak Company. 52p. 1977. pap. 2.00 o.p. (ISBN 0-87985-098-1, K-13). Eastman Kodak.

Photon-Hadron Interactions, 1: Proceedings of the International Summer Institute in Theoretical Physics, Desy, 1971. International Summer Institute in Theoretical Physics Staff. Ed. by G. Hoehler. LC 25-9130. (Springer Tracts in Modern Physics: Vol. 62). (Illus.). 152p. 1972. 37.80 o.p. (ISBN 0-387-05757-9). Springer-Verlag.

Photonuclear Reactions. Ed. by E. G. Fuller & E. Hayward. (Benchmark Papers in Nuclear Physics: Vol. 2). 1976. 80.50 o.p. (ISBN 0-12-786495-4). Acad Pr.

Photopion Nuclear Physics. Ed. by P. Stoler. LC 78-31569. 448p. 1979. 75.00x o.p. (ISBN 0-306-40148-7, Plenum Pr). Plenum Pub.

Photoprocesses, Photoreceptors, & Evolution. Jerome J. Wolken. 1975. 53.00 o.p. (ISBN 0-12-762050-8). Acad Pr.

Photoreceptor Optics. Ed. by A. W. Snyder & R. Menzel. LC 75-6700. (Illus.). 550p. 1975. 59.00 o.p. (ISBN 0-387-07216-0). Springer-Verlag.

Photosynthesis. rev. ed. C. P. Whittingham. Ed. by J. J. Head. LC 76-50840. (Carolina Biology Readers Ser.). (Illus.). 16p. (gr. 10 up). 1977. pap. 1.65 o.p. (ISBN 0-89278-209-9, 45-9609). Carolina Biological.

Photosynthetic Oxygen Evolution. Ed. by H. Metzner. 1978. 77.00 o.p. (ISBN 0-12-491750-X). Acad Pr.

Phototypesetter Comparison Charts: 1985 Edition. Harold C. Durbin. 1985. pap. 25.00 o.s.i. (ISBN 0-936786-05-1). Durbin Assoc.

Phototypesetting: A Design Manual. James Craig. Ed. by Margit Malmstrom. (Illus.). 224p. 1978. 27.95 o.p. (ISBN 0-8230-4011-9). Watson-Guptill.

Photovoltaics & Materials see Sharing the Sun.

Phrase & Paraphrase: Some Innovative Uses of Language. Lila Gleitman & Henry Gleitman. (Illus.). 1971. 14.95x o.p. (ISBN 0-393-04333-9). Norton.

Phthor. Piers Anthony. 208p. 1984. pap. 2.95 o.s.i. (ISBN 0-425-09135-X). Berkley Pub.

Phylogenetic Development of Vertebrate Immunity, No. 2. new ed. Joel M. Goodman et al. (Illus.). 220p. 1972. text ed. 28.50x o.p. (ISBN 0-8422-7057-4). Irvington.

Phylogenetic Development of Vertebrate Immunity, No. 1. William Neidermeier et al. (Illus.). 206p. 1973. text ed. 28.50x o.p. (ISBN 0-8422-7056-6). Irvington.

Phylogeny & Biogeography of Fossil & Recent Gars (Actincopterygii: Lepisosteidae) E. O. Wiley. (Miscellaneous Publications: No. 64). 111p. 1976. pap. 5.75 o.p. (ISBN 0-686-79832-5). U of KS Mus Nat Hist.

Physical Acoustics. R. Bruce Lindsay. LC 73-12619. (Benchmark Papers in Acoustics Ser.: Vol. 4). 480p. 1982. 59.95 o.p. (ISBN 0-87933-040-6). Van Nos Reinhold.

Physical Activities for Fitness & Fun. 2nd ed. Ed. by Richard A. Lauffer & Robert B. Gantt. LC 77-89262. (Illus.). 241p. 1980. text ed. 8.95x o.s.i. (ISBN 0-89459-109-6). Hunter Textbks.

Physical Agents for Physical Therapists. James Griffin. 1982. C C Thomas.

Physical & Biological Approaches to Computational Vision. Ed. by J. Martin Tenenbaum & Andrew Witken. (Illus.). 137p. 1988. pap. text ed. 20.00x o.p. (ISBN 0-929280-06-7). Amer Artificial.

Physical & Geotechnical Properties of Soils. Joseph E. Bowles. (Illus.). 560p. 1979. text ed. 38.95 o.p. (ISBN 0-07-006760-0). McGraw.

Physical & Sexual Abuse of Children: Causes & Treatment. David R. Walters. LC 75-1940. 196p. 1976. 15.00x o.p. (ISBN 0-253-34490-5); pap. 6.95x o.p. (ISBN 0-253-34491-3). Ind U Pr.

Physical & Transcendental Analysis of the Soul. School of Philosophy Editorial Committee. 74p. 1986. 117.50 o.p. (ISBN 0-89266-565-3). Am Classical Coll Pr.

Physical Aspects of Soil, Water & Salts in Ecosystems. Ed. by A. Hadas et al. LC 72-95753. (Ecological Studies: Vol. 4). (Illus.). xvi, 460p. 1973. 52.30 o.p. (ISBN 0-387-06109-6). Springer-Verlag.

Physical Assessment Skills for Nursing Practice. 2nd ed. Josephine M. Sana & Richard P. Judge. 1982. text ed. 26.95 o.p. (ISBN 0-316-76997-5). Little.

Physical Basis of Electronics. rev. ed. D. J. Harris & P. D. Robson. LC 74-996. 1974. 70.00 o.p. (ISBN 0-08-017900-2); pap. text ed. 11.25 o.p. (ISBN 0-08-017901-0). Pergamon.

Physical Behavior of Macromolecules with Biological Functions. S. P. Spragg. LC 80-40280. (Molecular Biophysics & Biochemistry Monographs). 202p. 1980. 67.95 o.p. (ISBN 0-471-27784-3, Pub. by Wiley-Interscience). Wiley.

Physical Behavior of PCBs in the Great Lakes. Ed. by S. Eisenreich. LC 82-72347. (Illus.). 442p. 1983. 52.95 o.p. (ISBN 0-250-40584-9). Butterworth.

Physical Change & Aging: A Guide for the Helping Professions. 2nd ed. Sue V. Saxon & Mary J. Etten. 1987. pap. (ISBN 0-913292-11-7). Tiresias Pr.

Physical Chemistry. 6th ed. Robert A. Alberty. LC 82-11058. 824p. 1983. text ed. 46.95 o.p. (ISBN 0-471-09284-3). Wiley.

Physical Chemistry, 2 vols. Ed. by Ya. Gerasimov. 1233p. 1974. Set. 12.40 o.p. (ISBN 0-8285-0657-4, Pub. by Mir Pubs USSR). Imported Pubns.

Physical Chemistry. Frank T. Gucker & Ralph T. Seifert. (Illus.). 1966. 16.95x o.p. (ISBN 0-393-09691-2, NortonC). Norton.

Physical Chemistry. Joseph H. Noggle. 1984. text ed. write for info. o.p. (ISBN 0-673-39550-2). Scott F.

Physical Chemistry of Extractive Metallurgy. Ed. by V. Kudryk & Y. K. Rao. LC 84-29561. (Illus.). 497p. 1985. 70.00 o.p. (ISBN 0-89520-486-X). Minerals Metals.

Physical Chemistry of Fast Reactions, Vol. 1: Gas Phase Reactions of Small Molecules. Ed. by B. P. Levitt. LC 74-161304. 332p. 1974. 55.00x o.p. (ISBN 0-306-35091-2, Plenum Pr). Plenum Pub.

Physical Chemistry of Organic Solvent Systems. Ed. by A. K. Covington & T. Dickinson. LC 72-77042. 824p. 1973. 125.00x o.p. (ISBN 0-306-30569-0, Plenum Pr). Plenum Pub.

Physical Chemistry of Polymers. A. Tager. 653p. 1979. 9.95 o.p. (ISBN 0-8285-0661-2, Pub. by Mir Pubs USSR). Imported Pubns.

Physical Constants of Linear Homopolymers. O. Lewis. (Chemie, Physik und Technologie der Kunstoffe in Einzeldarstellungen: Vol. 12). 1968. 38.50 o.p. (ISBN 0-387-04064-1). Springer-Verlag.

Physical Cosmology. P. J. Peebles. LC 74-181520. (Princeton Series in Physics). 296p. 1972. 34.00x o.p. (ISBN 0-691-08137-9); pap. 13.50x o.p. (ISBN 0-691-08108-5). Princeton U Pr.

Physical Data Base Record Design. Jon Clark & Jeffrey A. Hoffer. (Data Base Monograph Ser.: No. 7). (Illus.). 1979. pap. 15.00x o.s.i. (ISBN 0-89435-008-0). QED Info Sci.

Physical Diagnosis in Medicine. A. E. Davis & T. D. Bolin. 122p. 1974. pap. text ed. 12.00 o.p. (ISBN 0-08-017376-4). Pergamon.

Physical Disability & Human Behavior. 2nd ed. James W. McDaniel. 232p. 1976. 60.00 o.p. (ISBN 0-08-019722-1); pap. 60.00 o.p. (ISBN 0-08-019721-3). Pergamon.

Physical Education. Ed. by Celeste Ulrich. (Education in the Eighties Ser.). 104p. 1982. 12.95 o.p. (ISBN 0-8106-3160-1, 3160-1-06); pap. 8.95 o.p. (ISBN 0-8106-3159-8, 3159-8-06). NEA.

Physical Education Activities: For Lifetime Sports Participation. 2nd ed. Virden Evans et al. 153p. (Orig.). 1981. pap. text ed. 8.95x o.p. (ISBN 0-89459-094-4). Hunter Textbks.

Physical Education: An Overview. 2nd ed. Beverly L. Seidel & Matthew C. Resnick. LC 77-79453. (Physical Education Ser.). (Illus.). 214p. 1978. text ed. 15.00 o.p. (ISBN 0-394-34897-4, RanC). Random.

Physical Education & Recreation for the Visually Impaired. 80p. 1982. 4.95 o.p. (ISBN 0-88314-139-6). AAHPERD.

Physical Education for Children. D. Cyril Joynson. (Illus.). 215p. 1955. (ISBN 0-8022-0818-5). Philos Lib.

Physical Education for Children: Movement Foundations & Experiences. Ed. by Charles A. Bucher & Nolan A. Thaxton. 1979. write for info. o.p. (ISBN 0-02-316300-3). Macmillan.

Physical Education in a Changing Society. William Freeman. LC 76-10898. (Illus.). 1977. text ed. 18.50 o.p. (ISBN 0-395-24408-0). HM.

Physical Education: NCATE Guidelines. 1987. 15.00 o.p. (ISBN 0-88314-393-3). AAHPERD.

Physical Education Programming for Exceptional Learners. M. Rhonda Folio. 234p. 1985. 36.00 o.p. (ISBN 0-87189-243-X). Aspen Pub.

Physical Education Student Teaching Guide. Clyde G. Knapp & Ann E. Jewett. 1962. pap. 5.60x o.p. (ISBN 0-87563-012-X). Stipes.

Physical Education: The Behavior Modification Approach. Robert J. Presbie & Paul L. Brown. 128p. 1977. pap. 5.95 o.p. (ISBN 0-8106-1702-1). NEA.

Physical Education: The Profession. Janet B. Parks. LC 79-24507. (Illus.). 162p. 1980. pap. text ed. 12.95 o.p. (ISBN 0-8016-3759-7). Mosby.

Physical Evaluation of the Dental Patient. Charles L. Halstead et al. LC 81-18676. (Illus.). 422p. 1982. text ed. 38.95 cloth o.p. (ISBN 0-8016-0887-2). Mosby.

Physical Fitness. Marilyn S. Halper & Ira Neiger. LC 80-10847. (Strang Clinic Ser.). (Illus.). 160p. 1981. 12.95 o.s.i. (ISBN 0-03-048291-7); pap. 6.95 o.p. (ISBN 0-03-048286-0). H Holt & Co.

Physical Fitness & Mental Health Before & After Retirement. Helen Hall Peters. 1977. 6.50 o.p. (ISBN 0-682-48837-2, Banner). Exposition-Phoenix.

Physical Fitness & the Child's Reading Problem. Pearl M. Rosborough. 1963. 5.00 o.p. (ISBN 0-682-41062-4, University). Exposition-Phoenix.

Physical Fitness: The Pathway to Healthful Living. 5th ed. Robert V. Hockey. (Illus.). 1985. pap. text ed. 15.95 o.p. (ISBN 0-8016-2231-X). Mosby.

Physical Fitness Through Water Exercise. YMCA of the U. S. A. Staff. 1982. 3 ring notebook 18.00x o.p. (ISBN 0-88035-051-2, Pub. by YMCA USA). Human Kinetics.

Physical Fitness Workbook for Adults. T. K. Cureton. 1970. 10.00x o.p. (ISBN 0-87563-039-1). Stipes.

Physical Fluid Dynamics. D. J. Tritton. 1977. pap. 19.95 o.p. (ISBN 0-442-30132-4). Van Nos Reinhold.

Physical Geography. William E. Powers. LC 66-10964. (Illus.). 1966. 39.50x o.p. (ISBN 0-89197-344-3); pap. text ed. 14.95x o.p. (ISBN 0-89197-886-0). Irvington.

Physical Geology. 3rd ed. Charles C. Plummer & David McGeary. 528p. 1985. text ed. write for info. o.p. (ISBN 0-697-00794-4); pap. write for info. o.p. (ISBN 0-697-05046-7); instr's. manual avail. o.p. (ISBN 0-697-00566-6); student study guide avail. o.p. (ISBN 0-697-00564-X); lab manual avail. o.p. (ISBN 0-697-00351-5); transparencies avail. o.p. (ISBN 0-697-00565-8); slides avail. o.p. (ISBN 0-697-00596-8); instr's. lab manual avail. o.p. (ISBN 0-697-00595-X). Wm C Brown.

Physical Geology Laboratory Text & Manual: A Guide for the Study of Earth. 2nd ed. R. David Dallmeyer. 1980. wire coil bdg. 15.95 o.p. (ISBN 0-8403-1231-8). Kendall-Hunt.

Physical Growth & Development: From Conception to Maturity. Isabelle Valadian & Douglas Porter. LC 75-41572. 1977. text ed. 18.50 o.p. (ISBN 0-316-89525-3). Little.

Physical Health see Individualized Health Incentive Program Modules For Physically Disabled Students.

Physical Hydrogeology. Ed. by R. A. Freeze & W. Back. LC 82-2976. (Benchmark Papers in Geology: Vol. 72). 431p. 1983. 57.95 o.p. (ISBN 0-87933-431-2). Van Nos Reinhold.

Physical Metallurgy, 2 vols. A. P. Gulyaev. 650p. 1980. 11.00 set o.p. (ISBN 0-8285-2031-3, Pub. by Mir Pubs USSR). Imported Pubns.

Physical Metallurgy of Metal Joining: Proceedings of the TMS-AIME Fall Meeting, St. Louis, MO, 1978. (Illus.). 271p. 36.00 o.p. (ISBN 0-89520-365-0); members 20.00 o.p. (ISBN 0-317-34890-6); student members 12.00 o.p. (ISBN 0-317-34891-4). ASM.

Physical Metallurgy of Steels. Leslie. 396p. 1981. 51.00 o.p. (ISBN 0-89116-497-9). Hemisphere Pub.

Physical Metallurgy of Steels. William C. Leslie. (M-H Materials Science & Engineering Ser.). 368p. 1981. text ed. 45.00 o.p. (ISBN 0-07-037780-4). McGraw.

Physical Methods in Determinative Mineralogy. 2nd ed. Ed. by J. Zussman. 1978. 90.00 o.p. (ISBN 0-12-782960-1). Acad Pr.

Physical Methods in Physiology. W. T. Catton. (Illus.). 376p. 1958. (ISBN 0-8022-0222-5). Philos Lib.

Physical Modalities in Dermatologic Therapy: Radiotherapy, Electrosurgery, Phototherapy, Cryosurgery. Ed. by H. Goldschmidt. 1978. 84.00 o.p. (ISBN 0-387-90267-8). Springer-Verlag.

Physical Organic Chemistry-Three. Ed. by A. Fruchier. 1977. 31.00 o.p. (ISBN 0-08-021197-6). Pergamon.

Physical Principles & Techniques of Protein Chemistry. Ed. by Sidney J. Leach. (Molecular Biology Ser.). Pt. A, 1969. 103.00 o.p. (ISBN 0-12-440101-5); Pt. B, 1971. 96.50 o.p. (ISBN 0-12-440102-3); Pt. C, 1973. 113.00 o.p. (ISBN 0-12-440103-1). Acad Pr.

Physical Principles of Chemical Engineering. Peter Grassman. 928p. 1971. 225.00 o.p. (ISBN 0-08-012817-3). Pergamon.

Physical Properties. Chemical Engineering Magazine Editors. 1979. text ed. 54.50 o.p. (ISBN 0-07-010715-7). McGraw.

Physical Properties of Foods. Ed. by Micha Peleg & Edward B. Bagley. (IFT Ser.). 1983. 64.95 o.s.i. (ISBN 0-87055-418-2). AVI.

Physical Properties of Magnetically Ordered Crystals. E. A. Turov. Tr. by Scripta Technica. 1965. 64.00 o.p. (ISBN 0-12-704950-9). Acad Pr.

Physical Properties of Rocks & Minerals, Vol. II. Y. S. Touloukian & C. Y. Ho. (M-H-CINDAS Data Series on Material Properties). (Illus.). 576p. 1981. text ed. 59.95 o.p. (ISBN 0-07-065032-2). McGraw.

Physical Properties of Steroid Conjugates. Seymour Bernstein et al. LC 68-9218. 1968. 42.00 o.p. (ISBN 0-387-04060-9). Springer-Verlag.

Physical Rehabilitation: Evaluation & Treatment Procedures. Susan B. O'Sullivan et al. LC 80-10890. (Illus.). 521p. 1980. pap. text ed. 26.95x o.p. (ISBN 0-8036-6697-7). Davis Co.

Physical Research. Johnson. 180p. 1956. Philos Lib.

Physical Science: A Study of Matter & Energy. 3rd ed. Verne H. Booth & Mortimer Bloom. (Illus.). 800p. 1972. text ed. write for info. o.p. (ISBN 0-02-312280-3, 31228). Macmillan.

Physical Science & Physical Reality. L. O. Kattsoff. 1957. 17.50 o.s.i. (ISBN 0-685-12038-4). E J Brill USA.

Physical Science in the Modern World. Jerry B. Marion. 1974. 33.75 o.p. (ISBN 0-12-472260-1). Acad Pr.

Physical Science: Introductory Experiments. Jannie B. Huffman. 128p. 1986. pap. text ed. 12.95 o.p. (ISBN 0-8403-4134-2). Kendall Hunt.

Physical Science with Environmental Applications. Arthur W. Wiggins. 384p. 1974. text ed. 27.50 o.p. (ISBN 0-395-17072-9). HM.

Physical Science, with Modern Applications. 3rd ed. Mel Merken. 576p. 1985. text ed. 42.75 o.s.i. (ISBN 0-03-070448-0, CBS C). SCP.

Physical Structure in Modelling: Proceedings of the Bond Graph Workshop Held at the Twente University of Technology, Enschede, The Netherlands, 1983. Ed. by J. Van Dixhoorn & D. Karnopp. 150p. 1985. pap. 48.00 o.p. (ISBN 0-08-032593-9). Pergamon.

Physical Structure in Systems Theory: Network Approaches Engineering & Economics. Ed. by J. J. Van Dixhoorn & F. J. Evans. 1975. 65.00 o.p. (ISBN 0-12-712450-0). Acad Pr.

Physical Surfaces. J. J. Bikerman. (Physical Chemistry Ser.: Vol. 20). 1970. 110.00 o.p. (ISBN 0-12-097851-2). Acad Pr.

Physical Techniques in Biological Research. Ed. by Gerald Oster et al. Incl. Vol. 1A. Optical Techniques. 2nd ed. Ed. by Gerald Oster. 1971. 74.50 o.p. (ISBN 0-12-529601-0); Vols. 2A-2B. Physical Chemical Techniques. 2nd ed. Ed. by Dan H. Moore. 1968-69. Vol. 2A. 74.50 (ISBN 0-12-505552-8); Vol. 2B. 74.50 (ISBN 0-12-505554-4); Vol. 3. Cells & Tissues, 3 Pts. 2nd ed. Ed. by Arthur W. Pollister. 1966-69. Pt. A. 74.50 (ISBN 0-12-560903-5); Pt. B. 74.50 (ISBN 0-12-560943-4); Pt. C. 74.50 (ISBN 0-12-560953-1); Vol. 4. Special Methods. Ed. by William L. Nastuk. 1962. 55.00 o.p. (ISBN 0-12-514104-1); Vol. 5. Electrophysiological Methods, Pt. A. Ed. by William L. Nastuk. 1964. 74.50 (ISBN 0-12-514105-X); Vol. 6. Electrophysiological Methods, Pt. B. 1963. 74.50 (ISBN 0-12-514106-8). Acad Pr.

Physical Therapy Licensure Examination Review. Jane E. Hogencamp & Patricia R. Evans. Date not set. Appleton & Lange.

Physical Therapy Procedures: Selected Techniques. 3rd ed. Ann H. Downer. (Illus.). 320p. 1981. 21.75x o.p. (ISBN 0-398-03840-6). C C Thomas.

Physically Handicapped Child: An Interdisciplinary Approach to Management. Gillian T. McCarthy. (Illus.). 384p. 1984. 29.95 o.p. (ISBN 0-571-13263-4); pap. 15.95 o.p. (ISBN 0-571-13204-9). Faber & Faber.

Physican & the Mental Health of the Child, 2 Vols. Incl. Vol. 1. Assessing Development & Treating Disorders Within a Family (ISBN 0-89970-120-5, OP-006); Vol. 2. Psychological Concomitants of Illnes. 155p (ISBN 0-89970-008-X, OP-079); Vol. 3. Issues & Skills in Relating Primary Medical Care to the Other Human Services (ISBN 0-89970-108-6, OP-118). pap. 8.00 ea. o.p. AMA.

Physician. Noah Gordon. 624p. 1986. 18.45 o.s.i. (ISBN 0-671-47748-X). S&S.

Physician & Sexuality in Victorian America. John S. Haller & Robin M. Haller. (Illus.). 1977. pap. 7.95x o.p. (ISBN 0-393-00845-2, Norton Lib). Norton.

Physician Characteristics & Distribution in the U. S. American Medical Association Staff. (Orig.). 1987. pap. 45.00 o.p. (ISBN 0-89970-302-X, OP-180/7). AMA.

Physician Characteristics & Distribution in the U. S., 1986. 300p. 1986. pap. 42.00 o.p. (ISBN 0-89970-227-9, OP-180-6). AMA.

Physician in Literature. Ed. by Norman Cousins. LC 81-50841. 500p. 1981. 16.95 o.p. (ISBN 0-03-059653-X, HoltC). H Holt & Co.

Physician or Magician: The Myths & Realities of Patient Care. Benjamin J. Fuller & B. Frank Fuller. (Illus.). 1978. pap. text ed. 14.95 o.p. (ISBN 0-07-022617-2). McGraw.

Physician-Oriented Review: Criteria Development & Analysis of Patient Care: QRB Special Edition. 64p. 1981. pap. 20.00 o.s.i. (ISBN 0-86688-049-6). Joint Comm Hlthcare.

Physician Reimbursement under DRG's: Problems & Prospects. LC 85-110322. 23p. pap. 2.50 o.p. (ISBN 0-89970-260-0, OP-232). AMA.

Physicians' & Pharmacists' Guide to Your Medicines. United States Pharmacopoeial Convention Staff. 500p. (Orig.). 1981. 20.00 o.s.i. (ISBN 0-345-29724-5); pap. 9.95 o.s.i. (ISBN 0-345-29635-4). Ballantine.

Physicians & Sportsmedicine Guide to Raquetball & Squash. Robert S. Scott. (Physician & Sportsmedicine Guides). (Illus.). 1980. text ed. 7.95 o.p. (ISBN 0-07-055586-9). McGraw.

Physicians' Desk Reference, 1988. 42nd ed. Ed. by Ed Barnhart. 1988. 38.95 o.p. (ISBN 0-87489-844-7). Med Economics.

Physicians Guide to Preferred Provider Organization. 91p. 1984. pap. 5.25 o.p. (ISBN 0-89970-242-2, OP 166). AMA.

Physician's Guide to Professional Corporations. 23p. 1984. pap. 9.75 o.p. (ISBN 0-89970-258-9, OP-168). AMA.

Physician's Handbook on Orthomolecular Medicine. Ed. by Roger J. Williams & Dwight K. Kalita. LC 77-8304. 1977. text ed. 49.00 o.p. (ISBN 0-08-021533-5). Pergamon.

Physicians Observed. David R. Slavitt. LC 86-33109. 336p. 1987. 17.95 o.p. (ISBN 0-385-18884-6). Doubleday.

Physician's Resource Guide to Health Delivery Systems. 122p. 1987. pap. 15.00 o.p. (ISBN 0-89970-238-4, OP-157). AMA.

Physician's Responsibility As a Leader. Lewis A. Alesen. LC 53-10247. 1953. pap. 1.00 o.p. (ISBN 0-87004-001-4). Caxton.

Physicists. C. P. Snow. LC 81-80861. (Illus.). 103p. 1981. 15.95 o.p. (ISBN 0-316-80221-2). Little.

Physicist's ABC on Plasma. L. Artsimovich. 1978. pap. 3.95 o.p. (ISBN 0-8285-5196-0, Pub. by Mir Pubs USSR). Imported Pubns.

Physico-Chemical & Theoretical Studies see Biomolecular Structure, Conformation, Function & Evolution.

Physicochemical Measurements: Catalogue of Reference Materials from National Laboratories. Ed. by J. P. Cali. 1977. pap. 35.00 o.p. (ISBN 0-08-021578-5). Pergamon.

Physicochemical Methods of Mineral Analysis. Ed. by A. W. Nicol. LC 72-95070. 508p. 1975. 85.00x o.p. (ISBN 0-306-30739-1, Plenum Pr). Plenum Pub.

Physics. Nigel Henbest & Heather Couper. (Science World Ser.). 40p. (gr. 4-6). 1983. PLB 10.90 o.p. (ISBN 0-531-04652-4). Watts.

Physics. 2nd ed. Joseph W. Kane & Morton M. Sternheim. LC 82-10955. 716p. 1982. text ed. (ISBN 0-471-08323-2). Wiley.

Physics & Astronomy of the Moon. 2nd ed. Ed. by Zdenek Kopal. 1971. 63.50 o.p. (ISBN 0-12-419340-4). Acad Pr.

Physics & Chemistry of the Earth, Vol. 10. L. H. Ahrens. (Illus.). 270p. 1980. 115.00 o.p. (ISBN 0-08-020287-X). Pergamon.

Physics & Computers: Problems, Simulations, & Data Analysis. Robert Ehrlich. LC 72-5640. 125p. (Orig.). 1973. pap. 12.25 o.p. (ISBN 0-395-18010-4). HM.

Physics & Contemporary Needs, Vol. 5. Ed. by Riazuddin & Asghar Qadir. 638p. 1982. 95.00x o.p. (ISBN 0-306-40905-4, Plenum Pr). Plenum Pub.

Physics & Geology. 2nd ed. John A. Jacobs et al. (International Series in the Earth & Planetary Sciences). (Illus.). 448p. 1974. text ed. 31.00 o.p. (ISBN 0-07-032148-5, C). McGraw.

Physics & Mathematics of the Nervous Systems. Ed. by M. Conrad et al. (Lecture Notes in Biomathematics Ser.: Vol. 4). (Illus.). xii, 584p. 1975. pap. 22.40 o.p. (ISBN 0-387-07014-1). Springer-Verlag.

Physics & Music. Harvey E. White & Donald H. White. 422p. 1980. text ed. 37.95x o.p. (ISBN 0-03-045246-5). SCP.

Physics: Answers to Problems. Hans C. Ohanian. (Orig.). 1986. pap. text ed. 2.95x o.p. (ISBN 0-393-95587-7). Norton.

Physics As a Liberal Art. James S. Trefil. LC 77-6729. 1978. text ed. 125.00 o.p. (ISBN 0-08-019863-5). Pergamon.

Physics: Elementary. 3rd, rev. ed. Weidner & Sells. 1988. Physics Part II. pap. text ed. 60.00 o.s.i. (ISBN 0-205-10455-X). Allyn.

Physics: Extended Version. Richard Wolfson & Jay M. Pasachoff. Date not set. text ed. price not set o.p. (ISBN 0-673-39836-6). Scott F.

Physics for Everyone: Electrons. A. I. Kitaigorodsky. 1981. 6.60 o.p. (ISBN 0-8285-1904-8, Pub. by Mir Pubs USSR). Imported Pubns.

Physics for Everyone: Molecules. L. Landau & A. I. Kitaigorodsky. 224p. 1980. 6.60 o.p. (ISBN 0-8285-1725-8, Pub. by Mir Pubs USSR). Imported Pubns.

Physics for Everyone: Photons & Nuclei. A. I. Kitaigorodsky. 235p. 1981. 6.60 o.p. (ISBN 0-8285-1996-X, Pub. by Mir Pubs USSR). Imported Pubns.

Physics for Everyone: Physical Bodies. L. Landau & A. I. Kitaigorodsky. 248p. 1980. 6.60 o.p. (ISBN 0-8285-1716-9, Pub. by Mir Pubs USSR). Imported Pubns.

Physics for O.N.C. Courses. R. A. Edwards. LC 71-82381. 1970. text ed. 25.00 o.p. (ISBN 0-08-013432-7); pap. text ed. 9.75 o.p. (ISBN 0-08-013431-9). Pergamon.

Physics for Scientists & Engineers. Raymond Serway. 920p. 1982. 45.00 o.p. (ISBN 0-03-057903-1, CBS C); instr's manual o.s.i. 20.00 o.p. (ISBN 0-03-058561-9); overhead transparencies o.s.i. 400.00 o.p. (ISBN 0-03-062079-1); study guide 21.50 o.p. (ISBN 0-03-058458-2); solutions manual o.s.i. 16.95 o.p. (ISBN 0-03-062463-0). SCP.

Physics for Scientists & Engineers: Combined Volume. Jerry B. Marion & William F. Hornyak. 1982. text ed. 51.00 o.s.i. (ISBN 0-03-062831-8, CBS C). SCP.

Physics for the Health Professions. 3rd ed. J. Trygve Jensen. LC 82-70068. 329p. 1982. pap. 19.95 o.p. (ISBN 0-471-08696-7, Pub. by Wiley Med). Wiley.

Physics: Foundations & Applications, Combined Vol. Robert M. Eisberg & Lawrence S. Lerner. (Illus.). 1552p. 1981. text ed. 52.95 o.p. (ISBN 0-07-019110-7). McGraw.

Physics Handbook: Elementary Constants & Units, Tables, Formulae & Diagrams & Mathematical Formulae. Carl Nording & Jonny Osterman. 431p. 1982. text ed. 23.95x o.p. (ISBN 0-86238-000-6, Pub. by Chartwell-Bratt England). Gower Pub Co.

Physics in Collision: High-Energy ee-ep-pp Interactions, Vol. 1. Ed. by W. Peter Trower & Gianpaolo Bellini. LC 82-620. 526p. 1982. 85.00x o.p. (ISBN 0-306-40996-8, Plenum Pr). Plenum Pub.

Physics in Collision: High-Energy ee-ep-pp Interactions, Vol. 2. Ed. by Per Carlson & W. Peter Trower. 430p. 1983. 79.50x o.p. (ISBN 0-306-41249-7, Plenum Pr). Plenum Pub.

Physics in Collision: Proceedings of the Seventh International Conference. Ed. by K. Takahashi & T. Kondo. 600p. 1988. 90.00 o.p. (ISBN 9971-50-471-5). World Scientific Pub.

Physics in High Magnetic Fields: Proceedings. Ed. by N. Miura & S. Chikazumi. (Springer Ser. in Solid-State Sciences: Vol. 24). (Illus.). 358p. 1981. 47.00 o.p. (ISBN 0-387-10587-5). Springer-Verlag.

Physics in Industry: Proceedings of an International Conference, Dublin, 1976. Ed. by Eon O'Mongain & C. P. O'Toole. LC 76-17504. 1976. 150.00 o.p. (ISBN 0-08-020922-X). Pergamon.

Physics in One Dimension: Proceedings. Ed. by J. Bernasconi & Toni Schneider. (Springer Ser. in Solid-State Sciences: Vol. 23). (Illus.). 368p. 1981. 39.00 o.p. (ISBN 0-387-10586-7). Springer-Verlag.

Physics in the Twentieth Century. Pascual Jordan. (ISBN 0-8022-0816-9). Philos Lib.

Physics in Your World. 2nd ed. Karl F. Kuhn & Jerry S. Faughn. 1980. pap. text ed. 30.95 o.p. (ISBN 0-03-056791-2, CBS C); instr's manual 6.95 o.p. (ISBN 0-03-056792-0). SCP.

Physics Modeling Using Lotus 1-2-3 Release 2. David Stetser. Ed. by Kim Thomas. 400p. (Orig.). 1988. pap. 39.95 with disk o.p. (ISBN 0-317-58958-X). MIS Press.

Physics of Amorphous Materials. S. R. Elliott. 432p. 1984. 61.95 o.p. (ISBN 0-470-20472-9, Co-Pub. with Longman). Wiley.

Physics of Computer Memory Devices. S. Middelhoek et al. 1976. 76.00 o.p. (ISBN 0-12-495050-7). Acad Pr.

Physics of Deformation & Flow. E. W. Billington & A. Tate. (Illus.). 720p. 1981. text ed. 82.95 o.p. (ISBN 0-07-005285-9). McGraw.

Physics of Electrolytes, 2 vols. Ed. by J. Hladik. Incl. Vol. 1. Transport Processes in Solid Electrolytes. 89.50 (ISBN 0-12-349801-5); Vol. 2. Thermodynamics & Electrode Processes in Solid State Electronics. 97.00 o.p. (ISBN 0-12-349802-3). 1972. Acad Pr.

Physics of High Temperature Reactors. L. Massimo. 1975. 57.00 o.p. (ISBN 0-08-019616-0). Pergamon.

Physics of Large Deformation of Crystalline Solids. James F. Bell. (Springer Tracts in Natural Philosophy: Vol. 14). (Illus.). 1968. 35.00 o.p. (ISBN 0-387-04343-8). Springer-Verlag.

Physics of Materials. Ed. by D. W. Borland et al. LC 79-67059. 1980. 42.00x o.p. (ISBN 0-643-02449-2, Pub by CSIRO). Intl Spec Bk.

Physics of MOS Insulators. Lucovsky et al. 400p. 1980. 90.00 o.p. (ISBN 0-08-025969-3). Pergamon.

Physics of Music. 7th ed. Ed. by Alexander Wood. 1975. pap. 15.95x o.p. (ISBN 0-412-21140-8, NO. 6326, Pub. by Chapman & Hall). Routledge Chapman & Hall.

Physics of Planetary Ionospheres. S. J. Bauer. LC 72-15455. (Physics & Chemistry in Space Ser.: Vol. 6). (Illus.). 230p. 1973. 55.00 o.p. (ISBN 0-387-06173-8). Springer-Verlag.

Physics of Planetary Magnetospheres. Ed. by K. Knott. (Advances in Space Research Ser.: Vol. 1, Pt. 1). (Illus.). 390p. 1981. pap. 56.00 o.p. (ISBN 0-08-027151-0). Pergamon.

Physics of Plasma Close to Thermonuclear Conditions, 2 vols. Ed. by B. Coppi et al. (Commission of the European Communities). 750p. 1981. pap. 115.00 o.p. (ISBN 0-08-024475-0). Pergamon.

Physics of Selenium & Tellurium. W. C. Cooper. 1969. 100.00 o.p. (ISBN 0-08-013895-0). Pergamon.

Physics of Semiconductors: Proceedings. International Conference on Physics of Semiconductors Staff. Ed. by Michel Hulin. (Vol. 1). 1965. 114.00 o.p. (ISBN 0-12-532301-8). Acad Pr.

Physics of Semimetals & Narrow-Gap Semiconductors. D. L. Carter & R. T. Bate. 1971. 170.00 o.p. (ISBN 0-08-016661-X). Pergamon.

Physics of Solids at High Pressures. Ed. by Carl Tomizuka & Roy Emrick. 1965. 91.00 o.p. (ISBN 0-12-693850-4). Acad Pr.

Physics of Solids: Radiation Damage in Solids. Ed. by Douglas S. Billington. (Italian Physical Society Ser.: Course 18). 1963. 99.00 o.p. (ISBN 0-12-368818-3). Acad Pr.

Physics of the Expanding Universe. Ed. by M. Demianski. (Lecture Notes in Physics: Vol. 109). 1979. pap. 17.00 o.p. (ISBN 0-387-09562-4). Springer-Verlag.

Physics of the Future. Thomas G. Barnes. LC 83-81788. (ICR Technical Monograph). 1983. pap. 12.95 o.p. (ISBN 0-932766-09-9, Inst Creation). Master Bks.

Physics of the Interstellar Medium. J. E. Dyson & D. A. Williams. LC 80-13713. 194p. 1980. 31.95x o.p. (ISBN 0-470-26983-9). Halsted Pr.

Physics of Time Asymmetry. 2nd ed. P. C. Davies. 1985. pap. 9.95 o.p. U of Cal Pr.

Physics of Transmission Lines at High & Very High Frequencies, Vol. 1. P. Grivet. (Fr). 1970. 73.50 o.p. (ISBN 0-12-303601-1). Acad Pr.

Physics of Transmission Lines at High & Very High Frequencies: Microwave Circuits & Amplifiers, Vol. 2. Ed. by P. Grivet. 1976. 99.50 o.p. (ISBN 0-12-303602-X). Acad Pr.

Physics of Welding. Ed. by International Institute of Welding Staff. 1984. text ed. 61.00 o.p. (ISBN 0-08-030554-7); pap. text ed. 28.00 o.p. (ISBN 0-08-030555-5). Pergamon.

Physics: Principles & Applications. Michels et al. LC 76-14119. (Illus.). 1977. text ed. 34.95 o.p. (ISBN 0-395-24789-6). HM.

Physics Programs. A. D. Boardman. Incl. Applied Physics. LC 80-40121. 126p. 1980. 36.95 (ISBN 0-471-27740-1); Magnetism. LC 80-40124. 219p. pap. text ed. 36.95 (ISBN 0-471-27733-9); Optics. LC 80-40123. 123p. 0.00 o.p. (ISBN 0-471-27729-0); Solid State Physics. LC 80-40125. 353p. 31.95 o.p. (ISBN 0-471-27734-7). 1980. 24.95x ea. o.p. Wiley.

Physics Review for the MCAT. Robert C. Reno. (Illus.). 82p. (Orig.). 1984. pap. 6.95 o.p. (ISBN 0-916615-00-6). Bks of Sci.

Physics with Applications in Life Sciences. G. K. Strother & Robert L. Weber. (Illus.). 1977. text ed. 34.95 o.p. (ISBN 0-395-21718-0). HM.

Physics with Intersecting Storage Rings. Ed. by B. Touschek. (Italian Physical Society: Course 46). 1971. 101.50 o.p. (ISBN 0-12-368846-9). Acad Pr.

Physiochemical Mechanisms of Carcinogenesis: Proceedings. Ed. by E. D. Bergmann & B. Pullman. 1969. 70.00 o.p. (ISBN 0-12-091050-0). Acad Pr.

Physiochemical Methods for Water & Wastewater Treatment. L. Pawlowski. 1980. 89.00 o.p. (ISBN 0-08-024013-5). Pergamon.

Physiological Acoustics. Ed. by Juergen Tonndorf. LC 81-6488. (Benchmark Papers in Acoustics: Vol. 15). 416p. 1982. 56.95 o.p. (ISBN 0-87933-404-5). Van Nos Reinhold.

Physiological Adaptations: Proceedings of the Symposium Held in Honor of David B. Dill, April 1971. Symposium Held in Honor of David B. Dill Staff. Ed. by Mohamed K. Yousef et al. (Environmental Science: An Interdisciplinary Monograph Ser). 1972. 60.50 o.p. (ISBN 0-12-774650-1). Acad Pr.

Physiological Aspects of Anaesthetics & Inert Gases. A. G. Macdonald & K. T. Wann. 1978. 60.50 o.p. (ISBN 0-12-464150-4). Acad Pr.

Physiological Basis of Memory. Ed. by J. A. Deutsch. 1973. 55.00 o.p. (ISBN 0-12-213450-8). Acad Pr.

Physiological Clock: Circadian Rhythms & Biological Chronometry. 3rd ed. Erwin Buenning. LC 73-77343. (Heidelberg Science Library: Vol. 1). (Illus.). xiii, 258p. 1973. pap. 11.70 o.p. (ISBN 0-387-90067-5). Springer-Verlag.

Physiological Correlates of Emotion: Based Upon a Symposium. Ed. by Perry Black. 1970. 60.50 o.p. (ISBN 0-12-102850-X). Acad Pr.

Physiological Correlates of Human Behaviour, Vol. 1. Ed. by Anthony Gale. John A. Edwards. 1983. Vol. 1. 59.00 o.p. (ISBN 0-12-273901-9); Vol. 2. 59.00 o.p. (ISBN 0-12-273902-7); Vol. 3, 1984. 59.00 o.p. (ISBN 0-12-273903-5). Acad Pr.

Physiological Ecology: An Evolutionary Approach to Resource Use. Ed. by Colin R. Townsend & Peter Calow. LC 81-13559. (Illus.). 480p. text ed. 29.95x cancelled o.s.i. (ISBN 0-87893-827-3); pap. text ed. 29.95x o.s.i. (ISBN 0-87893-828-1). Sinauer Assocs.

Physiological Ecology of North American Plant Communities. Ed. by Brain F. Chabot & Hal. A Mooney. 400p. 1985. 39.95 o.p. (ISBN 0-412-23240-5, NO. 6536, Pub. by Chapman & Hall England). Routledge Chapman & Hall.

Physiological Effects of Air Pollution. Murray B. Gardner et al. 222p. 1973. text ed. 29.75x o.p. (ISBN 0-8422-7137-6). Irvington.

Physiological Measures of the Audiovestibular System. Ed. by Larry J. Bradford. 1975. 49.95 o.p. (ISBN 0-12-123650-1). Acad Pr.

Physiological Pharmacology: A Comprehensive Treatise, 4 vols. Ed. by W. S. Root & F. G. Hoffman. Incl. Vol. 1. The Nervous System, Part A. 1963. 98.50 o.p. (ISBN 0-12-595701-7); Vol. 2. The Nervous System, Part B. 1965. 77.50 o.p. (ISBN 0-12-595702-5); Vol. 3. The Nervous System, Part C. 1967. 80.50 o.p. (ISBN 0-12-595703-3); Vol. 4. The Nervous System, Part D. 1967. 80.50 o.p. (ISBN 0-12-595704-1); Vol. 5. The Nervous System, Part E. 1974. 98.50 o.p. (ISBN 0-12-595705-X). Acad Pr.

Physiological Psychology. John Blundell. (Essential Psychology Ser.). 1975. pap. 4.95x o.p. (ISBN 0-416-81950-8, NO. 2610). Routledge Chapman & Hall.

Physiological Psychology. Thomas S. Brown & Patricia Wallace. 1980. tchrs' ed. 25.00i o.p. (ISBN 0-12-136660-X); study guide 8.00i o.p. (ISBN 0-12-136663-4). Acad Pr.

Physiological Psychology. Mark R. Rosenzweig & Arnold L. Leiman. (Illus.). 736p. 1982. text ed. 28.00 o.p. (ISBN 0-669-02901-7). Heath.

Physiological Psychology: An Introduction. William C. Watson. LC 80-82838. (Illus.). 592p. 1981. text ed. 42.36 o.p. (ISBN 0-395-30221-8). HM.

Physiology. 2nd ed. Berne & Levy. 1987. International Standard ed. 30.00 o.p. Mosby.

Physiology. Ed. by Robert M. Berne & Matthew N. Levy. LC 82-22943. (Illus.). 1184p. 1983. 49.95 o.p. (ISBN 0-8016-0644-6). Mosby.

Physiology: A Clinical Approach. 3rd ed. G. R. Kelman. (Livingstone Medical Text). (Illus.). 1981. pap. text ed. 12.00 o.p. (ISBN 0-443-01820-0). Churchill.

Physiology & Behaviour of Marine Organisms: Proceedings. European Symposium on Marine Biology, 12th. Ed. by D. S. McLusky & A. J. Berry. LC 77-30559. 1978. 105.00 o.p. (ISBN 0-08-021548-3). Pergamon.

Physiology & Biochemistry of Algae. Ed. by Ralph A. Lewin. 1962. 112.00 o.p. (ISBN 0-12-446150-6). Acad Pr.

Physiology & Biochemistry of Drought Resistance in Plants. Ed. by L. G. Paleg & D. Aspinall. LC 80-70894. 1982. 83.00 o.p. (ISBN 0-12-544380-3). Acad Pr.

Physiology & Biochemistry of Exercise. Roy J. Shephard. LC 81-1833. 682p. 1985. pap. 35.00 o.p. (ISBN 0-275-91664-2, B1664). Praeger.

Physiology & Biochemistry of Haemocyanins. Ed. by F. Ghiretti. LC 68-17675. (Illus.). 1968. 26.00 o.p. (ISBN 0-12-281550-5). Acad Pr.

Physiology & Biochemistry of Seed Dormancy & Germination. Ed. by A. A. Khan. 548p. 1983. 170.00 o.p. (ISBN 0-444-80423-4, I-439-82, Biomedical Pr). Elsevier.

Physiology & Biophysics. 20th ed. Ed. by Theodore C. Ruch & Harry D. Patton. Incl. Vol. 1. The Brain & Neural Function. text ed. write for info. (ISBN 0-7216-7821-1); Vol. 2. Circulation, Respiration & Fluid Balance. 495p. text ed. write for info. (ISBN 0-7216-7818-1); Vol. 3. Digestion, Metabolism, Endocrine Function & Reproduction. text ed. write for info. (ISBN 0-7216-7819-X); Vol. 4. Excitable Tissues & Reflex Control of Muscle. write for info. (ISBN 0-7216-7817-3). LC 73-180188. (Illus.). 1973-82. Saunders.

Physiology & Pathology in the Perinatal Period: Proceedings. Boerhaave Course, Univ of Leiden, Netherlands, 1969. Ed. by R. H. Gevers & J. H. Ruys. (Illus.). 1971. 18.00 o.p. (ISBN 0-387-91081-6). Springer-Verlag.

Physiology & Pathology of Adaptation Mechanisms: Neural-Neuroendocrine-Hormonal. Ed. by E. Bajusz. 598p. 1969. 145.00 o.p. (ISBN 0-08-012023-7). Pergamon.

Physiology & Pathophysiology of Plasma Protein Metabolism. Ed. by G. Birke et al. 1969. 65.00 o.p. (ISBN 0-08-012965-X). Pergamon.

Physiology of Echinoderms. J. Binyon. 212p. 1972. 55.00 o.p. (ISBN 0-08-016991-0). Pergamon.

Physiology of Excitable Membranes: Proceedings of the 28th International Congress of Physiological Sciences, Budapest, 1980. Ed. by J. Salanki et al. LC 80-41853. (Advances in Physiological Sciences: Vol. 4). (Illus.). 350p. 1981. 57.00 o.p. (ISBN 0-08-026816-1). Pergamon.

Physiology of Faith: A Theory of Theological Relativity. John W. Dixon, Jr. LC 79-1782. 1979. 15.00i o.p. (ISBN 0-06-061926-0). HarpR.

Physiology of Host Pathogen Interaction, 1977. Ed. by A. Mahadevan. (Current Trends in Life Sciences Ser.: Vol. 6). viii, 496p. 1979. 40.00 o.p. (ISBN 0-88065-152-0, Pub. by Messers Today & Tomorrow Printers & Publishers). Scholarly Pubns.

Physiology of Insect Reproduction. F. Engelmann. LC 70-114850. 1970. 85.00 o.p. (ISBN 0-08-015559-6). Pergamon.

Physiology of Man in Space: Proceedings. Ed. by Jack H. Brown. 1963. 78.50 o.p. (ISBN 0-12-136350-3). Acad Pr.

Physiology of Marriage. Honore De Balzac. (Black & Gold Lib). 1943. 6.95 o.p. (ISBN 0-87140-983-6, Co-Pub with Tudor). Liveright.

Physiology of Non-Excitable Cells: Proceedings of the 28th International Congress of Physiological Sciences, Budapest, 1980. Ed. by J. Salanki et al. LC 80-41874. (Advances in Physiological Sciences: Vol. 3). (Illus.). 350p. 1981. 57.00 o.p. (ISBN 0-08-026815-3). Pergamon.

Physiology of Peripheral Nerve Disease. Austin J. Sumner. (Illus.). 544p. 1980. text ed. write for info. o.p. (ISBN 0-7216-8639-7). Saunders.

Physiology of Taste. Jean Brillat-Savarin. Tr. by M. F. Fisher. LC 78-7199. 1978. pap. 9.95 o.p. (ISBN 0-15-671770-0, Harv). HarBraceJ.

Physiology of Taste: Meditations on Transcendental Gastronomy. new ed. Jean A. Brillat-Savarin. LC 75-131275. 1948. 7.95 o.p. (ISBN 0-87140-972-0). Liveright.

Physiology of the Garden Pea. Ed. by J. F. Sutcliffe & J. S. Pate. 1978. 99.00 o.p. (ISBN 0-12-677550-8). Acad Pr.

Physiology of the Gastrointestinal Tract, 2 vols. Ed. by Leonard Johnson et al. 1526p. 1979. 195.00 o.p. (ISBN 0-89004-440-6). Raven.

Physiology of the Insecta. 2nd ed. Rockstein. 1974. Vol. 1, 1973. 99.00 o.p. (ISBN 0-12-591601-9); Vol. 2, 1974. 99.00 o.p. (ISBN 0-12-591602-7); Vol. 3, 1974. 99.00 o.p. (ISBN 0-12-591603-5); Vol. 4, 1974. 92.00 o.p. (ISBN 0-12-591604-3); Vol. 5, 1974. 106.00 o.p. (ISBN 0-12-591605-1); Vol. 6, 1974. 103.50 o.p. (ISBN 0-12-591606-X). Acad Pr.

Physiology of the Kidney. 2nd ed. Lawrence P. Sullivan & Jared J. Grantham. LC 81-18569. (Illus.). 236p. 1982. pap. 14.50 o.p. (ISBN 0-8121-0839-6). Lea & Febiger.

Physiology of the Kidney & Body Fluids. 3rd ed. Robert F. Pitts. (Illus.). 307p. 1974. pap. 20.00 o.p. (ISBN 0-8151-6703-2). Year Bk Med.

Physiology of the Kidney & of Water Balance. P. Deetjen et al. LC 72-85949. (Illus.). 145p. 1975. pap. 26.50 o.p. (ISBN 0-387-90048-9). Springer-Verlag.

Physiology of Trees. Paul J. Kramer & T. T. Kozlowski. (Botanical Sciences Ser.). 1960. text ed. 54.95 o.p. (ISBN 0-07-035351-4). McGraw.

Physiology: PreTest Self-Assessment & Review. 3rd ed. PreTest Service, Inc. Staff. Ed. by Craig A. Dise. (Basic Science Ser.). 196p. 1982. text ed. 12.95 review book o.p. (ISBN 0-07-051936-6). McGraw.

Physiopathology & Therapy of Human Blood Diseases. E. Kelemen. LC 68-18525. 1969. 150.00 o.p. (ISBN 0-08-012786-X). Pergamon.

Physiotherapy & the Asthmatic Child. Myra Kendall. 176p. 1988. text ed. 85.00 o.p. (ISBN 0-8385-7866-7). Appleton & Lange.

Physiotherapy in Paediatrics. 2nd, rev., enl. ed. R. B. Shepherd. (Illus.). 1980. 40.00 o.s.i. (ISBN 0-433-30131-7). E J Brill USA.

Phytochemical Methods. J. B. Harborne. 1973. pap. 16.95x o.p. (ISBN 0-412-23050-X, NO. 2001, Pub. by Chapman & Hall). Routledge Chapman & Hall.

Phytochemical Phylogeny: Proceedings. Phytochemical Society Staff. Ed. by J. B. Harborne. 1970. 85.00 o.p. (ISBN 0-12-324666-0). Acad Pr.

Phytohormones. R. W. Went et al. (Landmark Reprint in Plant Science Ser.). 1978. Repr. of 1937 ed. text ed. 22.50x o.s.i. (ISBN 0-86598-004-7, Pub. by Allanheld). Rowman.

Phytoplankton Ecology: Structure, Function & Fluctuation. Graham P. Harris. 370p. 1986. text ed. 45.00 o.p. (ISBN 0-412-24330-X, 6706, Pub. by Chapman & Hall England). Routledge Chapman & Hall.

PI-Algebras: An Introduction. N. Jacobson. LC 75-6644. (Lecture Notes in Mathematics Ser: Vol. 441). v, 115p. 1975. pap. 13.00 o.p. (ISBN 0-387-07143-1). Springer-Verlag.

PI Complexes of Transition Metals. G. Boschke et al. (Topics in Current Chemistry: Vol. 28). (Illus.). 205p. 1972. pap. 27.90 o.p. (ISBN 0-387-05728-5). Springer-Verlag.

Piaf. Lange. (ISBN 0-8050-0182-4). Seaver Bks.

Piaf. Monique Lange. Tr. by Richard S. Woodward from Fr. LC 81-4792. Orig. Title: Histoire De Piaf. (Illus.). 252p. 1981. 22.50 o.p. Seaver Bks.

Piaget: A Practical Consideration. G. A. Helmore. LC 75-94933. 1969. text ed. 6.05 o.p. (ISBN 0-08-006893-6). Pergamon.

Piaget & His School: A Reader in Developmental Psychology. Ed. by B. Inhelder et al. LC 75-8903. (Illus.). 320p. 1976. pap. 26.40 o.p. (ISBN 0-387-07248-9). Springer-Verlag.

Piaget: Dictionary of Terms. Ed. by E. R. Hermann et al. 1973. text ed. 28.00 o.p. (ISBN 0-08-017039-0). Pergamon.

Piaget, Philosophy & the Human Sciences. Hugh Silverman. 1980. text ed. 17.50x o.p. (ISBN 0-391-00958-3). Humanities.

Piagetian Psychology. Pierre Dasen. 1977. 33.95 o.p. (ISBN 0-89876-080-1). Gardner Pr.

Piaget's Theory of Cognitive & Affective Development. 3rd ed. Barry J. Wadsworth. LC 83-13637. 190p. 1984. pap. text ed. 13.95 o.p. (ISBN 0-582-28425-2). Longman.

Pianist's Talent. Harold Taylor. LC 78-68764. (Illus.). 96p. 1982. pap. 4.95 o.s.i. (ISBN 0-8008-6295-3, Crescendo). Taplinger.

Piano Beneath the Skin. George Hitchcock. 1979. pap. 5.00 o.p. (ISBN 0-914742-38-8). Copper Canyon.

Piano Breakthrough: How to Revolutionize Your Playing Through Chords & Broken Chords. Duane Shinn. 1978. pap. 19.95 o.p. (ISBN 0-912732-44-X). Duane Shinn.

Piano Makers. David Anderson. (Illus.). 56p. (gr. 8-12). 1982. 10.95 o.p. (ISBN 0-394-85353-9); lib. bdg. 10.99 o.p. (ISBN 0-394-95353-3). Pantheon.

Piano Peek-a-Boo: Opus-One Note Learner. Mike Gallatin. 40p. (ps-5). 1988. plastic spiral 5.95 o.s.i. (ISBN 0-943851-10-6). QED Pr Ann Arbor.

Pirates of the Vistula. William H. Keith, Jr. (Twilight: 2000 Ser.). (Illus.). 49p. (Orig.). 1985. pap. 7.00 o.s.i. (ISBN 0-943580-52-8). Game Designers.

Pirke Aboth. Isaac Unterman. LC 63-9782. 1979. pap. 8.95x o.s.i. (ISBN 0-8197-0472-5). Bloch.

Pishtosh, Bullwash & Wimple. James Flora. LC 71-190554. (Illus.). 32p. (ps-4). 1972. 4.50 o.p. (ISBN 0-689-30304-1, Atheneum). Macmillan.

Pissarro. John Rewald. (Library of Great Painters Ser.). (Illus.). 160p. 45.00 o.p. (ISBN 0-8109-0413-6). Abrams.

Pissing in the Snow & Other Ozark Folktales. Vance Randolph. 1977. pap. 3.95 o.p. (ISBN 0-380-01797-0, 60091-9, Bard). Avon.

Pistol & Revolver Shooting. A. Himmelwright. (Library Classics Ser.). (Illus.). 496p. Repr. of 1928 ed. deluxe ed. cancelled o.s.i. (ISBN 0-935632-59-X). Wolfe Pub Co.

Pistons & Powderpuffs. Gene Olson. LC 67-10613. 186p. (gr. 7-10). 1967. 3.75 o.s.i. (ISBN 0-664-32393-6, Westminster). Westminster John Knox.

Pit Bull. Scott Ely. Ed. by John Herman. LC 87-37161. 192p. 1988. 15.95 o.s.i. (ISBN 1-55584-046-9). Weidenfeld.

Pit Stop. Illus. by Mones. (Fast Rolling Race Cars Ser.). (Illus.). (ps-2). 1987. 3.95 o.p. (ISBN 0-448-09888-1, G&D). Putnam Pub Group.

Pitcher Mountain Inn Cookbook. Bill Matthews & Dawn Matthews. LC 84-51153. (Illus.). 160p. (Orig.). 1985. pap. 8.95 o.p. (ISBN 0-89909-047-8). Yankee Bks.

Pitching. Jim Palmer. Ed. by Joel Cohan. LC 74-77855. 1975. 6.95 o.p. (ISBN 0-689-10627-0, Atheneum). Macmillan.

Pitfalls & Planning in Student Teaching. John Heywood. 192p. 1982. 25.00 o.p. (ISBN 0-89397-133-2). Nichols Pub.

Pitfalls in Human Research: Ten Pivotal Points. Theodore X. Barber. LC 76-13488. 128p. 1977. text ed. 15.25 o.p. (ISBN 0-08-020935-1). Pergamon.

Pittori Viterbesi Di Cinque Secoli. Italo Faldi. LC 77-106770. (Illus., Ital.). 1970. 87.50x o.s.i. (ISBN 0-271-00119-4). Pa St U Pr.

Pittsburgh: Fulfilling Its Destiny. Vince Gagetta. LC 86-22382. (Illus.). 624p. 1986. 34.95 o.p. (ISBN 0-89781-189-5). Windsor Pubns Inc.

Pittsburgh Gazette Abstracts, 1797-1803. Clara E. Duer. 430p. 1986. 24.95 o.s.i. (ISBN 0-933227-51-5). Closson Pr.

Pittsburgh Glass, 1797-1891: A History & Guide for Collectors. Lowell Innes. 1976. 30.00 o.p. (ISBN 0-395-20733-9). HM.

Pittsburgh Moments. Lynn Johnson et al. LC 84-40827. (Illus.). 124p. 1984. 19.95 o.p. (ISBN 0-8229-3501-5). U of Pittsburgh Pr.

Pittsburgh Pirates. rev. ed. Martin. LC 82-13027. (Baseball Today Ser.). 48p. (gr. 4 up). 1982. PLB 11.45 o.p. (ISBN 0-87191-871-4). Creative Ed.

Pittsburgh Steelers. James R. Rothaus. (NFL Today Ser.). (gr. 4 up). 1986. PLB 10.45s.p. o.p. (ISBN 0-88682-045-6). Creative Ed.

Pittsburgh: The Story of an American City. Stefan Lorant. LC 75-24970. (Illus.). 1986. Repr. of 1980 ed. 24.95 o.p. (ISBN 0-317-56929-5). Authors Edn MA.

Pittsylvania County Inventory: Circuit Court Clerk. Compiled by B. Kirke White. 50p. (Orig.). 1977. pap. 2.00 o.p. (ISBN 0-686-98188-X). VA State Lib.

Pituitary-A Current Review: Proceedings of the Symposium, Medical College of Georgia, Augusta, Georgia, May 20-22, 1976. Pituitary Symposium Staff. Ed. by Marshall B. Allen, Jr. & Vivenda B. Mahesh. LC 76-53006. 1977. 71.50 o.p. (ISBN 0-12-051850-3). Acad Pr.

Pituitary Adenomas. Glenn E. Sheline et al. (Oncologic Multidisciplinary Decisions in Onology Ser.). (Illus.). 248p. 1981. pap. 135.00 o.p. (ISBN 0-08-027463-3). Pergamon.

Pituitary Microadenomas. G. Faglia et al. LC 79-41478. (Serono Symposia: No. 29). 1980. 109.00 o.p. (ISBN 0-12-248150-X). Acad Pr.

Pius XII & the Third Reich. Saul Friedlander. LC 80-12830. 238p. 1980. Repr. of 1966 ed. lib. bdg. 21.50x o.p. (ISBN 0-374-92930-0, Octagon). Hippocrene Bks.

Pivot of Civilization see Works.

Pixel Pixie's Birthday Party. Barbara Belle. (Pixel Ser.: No. 1). (Illus.). 24p. (Orig.). (gr. 1-5). 1985. pap. 2.95 o.p. (ISBN 0-935163-00-X). Pixel Prods Pubns.

Pizarro & the Incas. Nicholas Tate. Ed. by Marjorie Reeves. (Then & There Ser.). (Illus.). 79p. (gr. 7-12). 1981. pap. text ed. 4.95 o.p. (ISBN 0-582-20547-6). Longman.

Pizza. Vincenzo Buonassissi. (Illus.). 183p. 1984. 14.95 o.s.i. (ISBN 0-316-11515-0). Little.

Pizza Cookery. C. Dyer. 224p. 1983. text ed. 12.95 o.p. (ISBN 0-07-018542-5); pap. text ed. 6.95 o.p. (ISBN 0-07-018543-3). McGraw.

Pizzas, Hamburgers & Relishes. Martha Lomask. (Illus.). 96p. 1984. bds. 8.95 laminated o.p. (ISBN 0-86188-402-7). Salem Hse Pubs.

Pizzazz for Pennies: Designer Clothes for Children. Barb Forman. LC 86-47610. (Creative Machine Arts Ser.). 1986. pap. 12.95 o.p. (ISBN 0-8019-7729-0). Chilton.

PL-C Essentials. L. J. Mazlack. 1977. text ed. 28.95 o.p. (ISBN 0-07-041170-0). McGraw.

PL-M 286 User's Guide for DOS. Intel Staff. 350p. 1985. pap. 22.00 o.p. (ISBN 0-917017-81-1, 122466). Intel Corp.

PL-One Programming with PL-C. Melvin G. Davidson. LC 72-7635. 224p. (Orig.). 1973. pap. 19.95 o.p. (ISBN 0-395-14518-X). HM.

PL 94 - 142: An Act of Congress. Erwin L. Levine & Elizabeth Wexler. 128p. 1981. pap. text ed. write for info. o.p. (ISBN 0-02-370270-2). Macmillan.

PLA Forces. Conmilit Press Staff. (Illus.). 200p. 1987. 34.95 o.p. (ISBN 0-7106-0483-1). Janes Info Group.

Place & Placelessness. E. Relph. (Research in Planning & Design Ser.). 156p. 1976. 15.50x o.p. (ISBN 0-85086-055-5, NO. 2929, Pub. by Pion England). Routledge Chapman & Hall.

Place & Placelessness. E. Relph. (Pion Research in Planning & Design Ser.). (Illus.). 156p. 1984. pap. 7.50x o.p. (ISBN 0-85086-111-X, NO. 5074). Routledge Chapman & Hall.

Place Apart: Canaveral National Seashore. David Whitman et al. (Illus.). 48p. 1987. pap. 5.95 o.p. (ISBN 0-915992-34-5). Eastern Acorn.

Place at the Table. Steve Orlen. LC 81-47470. 64p. 1982. 12.95 o.p. (ISBN 0-03-059714-5); pap. 6.95 o.p. (ISBN 0-03-059713-7). H Holt & Co.

Place Called Princeton. Samuel A. Schreiner, Jr. (Illus.). 225p. 1984. 16.95 o.p. (ISBN 0-87795-573-5, Arbor Hse). Morrow.

Place For Murder. Emma Lathen. 1985. 9.95 o.p. (ISBN 0-317-53041-0, Large Print Bks). G K Hall.

Place in the Country. John Brookes. LC 83-51677. (Illus.). 240p. 1984. 24.95f o.p. (ISBN 0-500-01327-6). Thames Hudson.

Place in the Country. Sarah Gainham. 1976. pap. 1.75 o.p. (ISBN 0-380-00642-1, 27524). Avon.

Place in the Country: A Narrative on the Imperfect Art of Homesteading & the Value of Ignorance. Peter H. Matson. LC 78-6074. (Illus.). 1978. pap. 3.95 o.p. (ISBN 0-15-672008-6, Harv). HarBraceJ.

Place in the Sun. Nina Lambert. (Lythway). 288p. 1988. lib. bdg. 19.50 o.s.i. (ISBN 0-7451-0648-X, Pub. by Chivers Pr UK). G K HAll.

Place Made Fast. Mark Halperin. 80p. (Orig.). 1982. pap. 6.00 o.p. (ISBN 0-914742-62-0). Copper Canyon.

Place Names in the Writings of William Butler Yeats. James McGarry. Ed. by E. Malins. (Illus.). 1976. text ed. 9.95x o.p. (ISBN 0-7705-1468-5). Humanities.

Place-Names of the Northern Neck of Virginia. Mary R. Miller. xiv, 189p. 1983. pap. 10.00 o.p. (ISBN 0-88490-099-1). VA State Lib.

Place Names of the White Mountains. Hixson. 446p. 1980. pap. 8.95 o.p. (ISBN 0-89272-069-7). Down East.

Place of Birth. David Kherdian. LC 83-7082. 70p. 1983. 13.00 o.s.i. (ISBN 0-932576-17-6); pap. 7.00 o.s.i. (ISBN 0-932576-24-9). Breitenbush Bks.

Place of Dead Roads. William S. Burroughs. 320p. 1983. 100.00 o.p. (ISBN 0-03-070416-2, Owl Bks); pap. 17.95 o.p. H Holt & Co.

Place of Houses. Charles Moore & Gerald Allen. LC 70-182776. (Illus.). 356p. 1979. 9.70 o.p.; pap. 16.95 o.p. (ISBN 0-8050-1044-0). H Holt & Co.

Place of Ideology in Political Life. D. J. Manning & T. J. Robinson. LC 84-45822. 128p. 1985. 31.00 o.p. (ISBN 0-7099-1796-1, Pub. by Croom Helm Ltd). Routledge Chapman & Hall.

Place of Light & Learning: The University of Queensland's First Seventy-Five Years. Malcolm I. Thomis. (Illus.). 429p. 1986. text ed. 44.50x o.p. (ISBN 0-7022-1797-2). U of Queensland Pr.

Place of Power: The American Episode in Human Evolution. Walter Anderson. LC 76-12809. 1976. text ed. 15.95 o.p. (ISBN 0-87620-080-3); pap. text ed. write for info. o.p. (ISBN 0-673-16268-0). Scott F.

Place of Shine & Shadow. Helen C. Rhodes. 85p. (Orig.). 1985. pap. 6.95x o.p. (ISBN 0-932269-32-X). Wyndham Hall.

Place of the Dawn. Gordon Taylor. 1977. pap. 1.50 o.p. (ISBN 0-380-01765-2, 34983). Avon.

Place of the Swan. Lola Irish. 448p. 1986. 16.95 o.p. (ISBN 0-531-15029-1). Watts.

Place of Trust: Martin Luther. Ed. by Martin E. Marty. LC 83-47727. 128p. 1983. 9.57 o.p. (ISBN 0-06-065449-X). HarpR.

Place to Hide. Evelyn Anthony. 256p. 1987. 17.95 o.p. (ISBN 0-399-13207-4, Putnam). Putnam Pub Group.

Place to Live in Later Years. Paul B. Maves. LC 82-72650. 112p. 1982. pap. 5.95 o.p. (ISBN 0-8066-1957-0, 10-4987, Augsburg). Augsburg Fortress.

Place to Place Indexes of the Price of Housing: Some New Estimates & a Comparative Analysis. James Follain et al. 98p. 1979. pap. text ed. 6.00x o.p. (ISBN 0-87766-265-7). Urban Inst.

Placebo Play. E. A. Davis. 1980. 5.50 o.p. (ISBN 0-682-49646-4). Exposition-Phoenix.

Placenta - a Neglected Experimental Animal. P. Beaconsfield. 1979. 105.00 o.p. (ISBN 0-08-024430-0); pap. 40.00 o.p. (ISBN 0-08-024435-1). Pergamon.

Placenta in Twin Pregnancy. S. J. Strong & G. Corney. 1966. 75.00 o.p. (ISBN 0-08-012223-X). Pergamon.

Placenta: The Largest Human Biopsy. Ed. by R. Beaconsfield & G. Birdwood. (Illus.). 174p. 1982. 57.00 o.p. (ISBN 0-08-028028-5). Pergamon.

Places. James Morris. LC 72-88806. 1973. 6.95 o.p. (ISBN 0-15-172023-1). HarBraceJ.

Places for People: Hotel, Restaurants, Bars, Clubs, Community Recreation Facilities Camps, Parks, Plazas, Playgrounds. Architectural Record Magazine Editors. 1976. text ed. 47.50 o.p. (ISBN 0-07-002201-1). McGraw.

Places Rated Almanac: Your Guide to Finding the Best Places to Live in America. 2nd ed. Richard Boyer & David Savageau. (Illus.). 450p. 1985. 24.95 o.p. (ISBN 0-528-81091-X); pap. 14.95 o.p. (ISBN 0-528-88008-X). Rand McNally.

Places to Go with Children in Northern California: More Than 350 Attractions Throughout Northern California to Delight Children & Parents. Elizabeth Pomada. LC 85-3804. (Illus.). 168p. 1985. pap. 7.95 o.p. (ISBN 0-87701-328-4). Chronicle Bks.

Places to Go with Children in Northern California. rev. ed. Elizabeth Pomada. LC 73-77335. (Illus.). 192p. 1980. pap. 5.95 o.p. (ISBN 0-87701-210-5). Chronicle Bks.

Places to Go with Children in Southern California: More Than 350 Attractions Throughout Southern California to Delight Children & Parents. rev. ed. Stephanie Kegan. LC 85-23281. (Illus.). 160p. 1986. pap. 7.95 o.p. (ISBN 0-87701-375-6). Chronicle Bks.

Places to Go with Children in Southern California. Stephanie Kegan. LC 81-18052. (Illus.). 160p. (Orig.). 1982. pap. 6.95 o.p. (ISBN 0-87701-194-X). Chronicle Bks.

Places Where Children Succeed: A Profile of Outstanding Public Elementary Schools. Bruce L. Wilson & Thomas B. Corcoran. (Education Department Publication Ser.: No. 88-827). 71p. (Orig.). 1987. pap. 3.50 o.p. (S/N 065-000-00323-6). USGPO.

Plague: The Greatest Threat to the Civilized World. John L. Poulsen. 48p. 1987. 6.50 o.p. (ISBN 0-8062-2810-5). Carlton.

Plague Years: A Chronicle of Aids, Epidemic of Our Times. David Black. 200p. 1986. 16.45 o.p. (ISBN 0-671-61224-7). S&S.

Plain & Easy Introduction to Practical Music. Thomas Morley. Ed. by R. Alec Harmon. (Illus.). 352p. 1973. pap. 6.95 o.p. (ISBN 0-393-00682-4). Norton.

Plain Bread. Ben Kinchlow & Bob Slosser. 224p. 1985. 7.99 o.p. (ISBN 0-8499-3064-2, 0461-7). Word Bks.

Plain Brown Wrapper Book of Computers. Anna M. Burke. 184p. (Orig.). 1983. pap. 9.95 o.p. (ISBN 0-936602-59-7). Kampmann.

Plain Girl. Virginia Sorensen. LC 55-8681. (gr. 4-6). 1955. 6.50 o.p. (ISBN 0-15-262434-1, HJ). HarBraceJ.

Plain Jane. Marion Chesney. (Nightingale Paperbacks Ser.). 280p. 1987. pap. 11.95 o.p. (ISBN 0-8161-4319-6, Large Print Bks). G K Hall.

Plain People of the Confederacy. B. I. Wiley. 11.25 o.p. (ISBN 0-8446-0294-9). Peter Smith.

Plain Song. Jim Harrison. 1965. 4.50 o.p. (ISBN 0-393-04240-5). Norton.

Plain Tales from the Raj. Charles Allen. (Illus.). 240p. 1985. pap. 13.95 o.s.i. (ISBN 0-03-005862-7). H Holt & Co.

Plain Talk. Ed. by Carol Burke. LC 82-81678. (Illus.). 152p. 1983. pap. 3.50 o.s.i. (ISBN 0-911198-67-9). Purdue U Pr.

Plain Talk about Grants: A Basic Handbook. Robert E. Geller. 76p. 1982. write for info. o.p. CA State Library Fndtn.

Plain Talk, Guidelines for Speaking Out to Your Community About Health Care Costs. 58p. 1984. 15.00 o.p. (ISBN 0-317-36952-0, C-166556). Am Hospital.

Plain Truth about Seventh Day Adventists. Hoehn. 36p. 1988. pap. 6.00 o.p. (ISBN 0-914009-87-7). VHI Library.

Plains. Gerald Murnane. 126p. 1985. 12.95 o.p. (ISBN 0-8076-1123-9). Braziller.

Plains Indian Autobiographies. Lynne W. O'Brien. LC 73-8339. (Western Writers Ser: No. 10). 1973. pap. 2.95x o.p. (ISBN 0-88430-009-9). Boise St Univ.

Plaintiff's Master Exhibit on Conditions in Haiti. Haitian Refugee Center Staff. 85.00 o.p. Natl Lawyers Guild.

Plan for Restoration & Adaptive Use of the Frank Lloyd Wright Home & Studio. Frank Lloyd Wright. LC 78-67224. (Illus.). 1979. 25.00 o.s.i. (ISBN 0-226-90832-1). U of Chicago Pr.

Plan for the Dictionary of Old English. Ed. by Roberta Frank & Angus Cameron. LC 72-97152. (Toronto Old English Ser.). 1973. 35.00x o.p. (ISBN 0-8020-3303-2). U of Toronto Pr.

Plan Paris, No. 12. 5th ed. 1986. pap. 5.95 o.p. (ISBN 2-060-00124-2). Michelin.

Plan Termination: Asset or Liability? (Tax Law & Estate Planning Course Handbook Ser.: Vol. 205). 673p. 1984. 45.00 o.p. (ISBN 0-317-11449-2, J4-3546). PLI.

Plan to Win. Bill Glass & James E. McEachern. 160p. 1984. 8.95 o.p. (ISBN 0-8499-0431-5, 0431-5). Word Bks.

Plan Your Estate, Wills, Probate, Avoidance, Trusts & Taxes: California Edition. 6th, rev. ed. Denis Clifford. 230p. 1987. pap. 15.95 o.p. (ISBN 0-87337-057-0). Nolo Pr.

Planar & Linear Fabrics of Deformed Rocks: A Selection of Papers Delivered at an International Conference held at ETH Zurich 30 August to 2 September 1982. Ed. by P. L. Hancock et al. 218p. 1984. pap. 48.00 o.p. (ISBN 0-08-031428-7). Pergamon.

Plane Crazy: A Celebration of Flying. Burton Bernstein. LC 85-8155. (Illus.). 165p. 1985. 16.45 o.s.i. (ISBN 0-89919-390-0). Ticknor & Fields.

Plane Elastic Systems. 2nd ed. L. M. Milne-Thomson. LC 68-56947. (Ergebnisse der Angewandten Mathematik: Vol. 6). 1965. pap. 19.00 o.p. Springer-Verlag.

Plane Figures & Sections: How to Construct Them Given Specific Conditions. P. V. Pritulenko. 1980. 8.45 o.p. (ISBN 0-8285-1778-9, Pub. by Mir Pubs USSR). Imported Pubns.

Plane Ride. Florance W. Taylor. LC 71-165321. (Felipe Adventure Stories Ser.). (Illus.). (gr. 2-4). 1971. PLB 3.95g o.p. (ISBN 0-8225-0147-3). Lerner Pubns.

Plane Talk: Aviators' & Astronauts' Own Stories. Carl Oliver. (gr. 7 up). 1980. 7.95 o.s.i. (ISBN 0-395-29743-5). HM.

Plane Trigonometry. 3rd ed. Nathan O. Niles. LC 75-28337. 394p. 1976. text ed. 34.00 o.p. (ISBN 0-471-64025-5). Wiley.

Plane Trigonometry with Tables. 4th ed. Gordon Fuller. (Illus.). 1971. text ed. 29.95 o.p. (ISBN 0-07-022608-3, C). McGraw.

Plane Vector Fields. M. A. Krasnoselskiy et al. 1966. 55.00 o.p. (ISBN 0-12-425950-2). Acad Pr.

Planemakers: Boeing. Ed. by Michael J. Taylor. (Planemakers Ser.). (Illus.). 160p. 1982. 17.95 o.p. (ISBN 0-86720-554-7). Janes Info Group.

Planemakers: DeHavilland. Philip Birtles. (Planemakers Ser.). (Illus.). 160p. 1984. 17.95 o.p. (ISBN 0-7106-0303-7). Janes Info Group.

Planemakers Four: Shorts. Michael J. Taylor. (Planemakers Ser.). (Illus.). 160p. 1984. 17.95 o.p. (ISBN 0-7106-0237-5). Janes Info Group.

Planemakers: 2 Westland. David Mondey. (Planemakers Ser.). (Illus.). 160p. 1982. 15.95 o.p. (ISBN 0-86720-555-5). Janes Info Group.

Planes & Airports. Chris McAllister. (Illus.). 64p. 1981. pap. 7.95 o.p. (ISBN 0-7134-3911-4, Pub. by Batsford England). David & Charles.

Planet. Arthur Vogelsang. 96p. 1983. pap. 6.95 o.p. (ISBN 0-03-062107-0, Owl Bks). H Holt & Co.

Planet Earth. D. York. 1975. text ed. 20.95 o.p. (ISBN 0-07-072290-0). McGraw.

Planet-Girded Suns. Sylvia L. Engdahl. LC 73-84825. (Illus.). 208p. (gr. 8 up). 1974. 7.50 o.p. (ISBN 0-689-30135-9, Atheneum). Macmillan.

Planet in Trouble: The UFO Assault on Earth. Jerome Eden. 1973. 8.50 o.p. (ISBN 0-682-47822-9). Exposition-Phoenix.

Planet of Reason: A Sociological Study of the Interrelation of Society & Nature. I. Laptev. (Current Problems Ser.). 1977. 4.95 o.p. (ISBN 0-8285-3327-X, Pub. by Progress Pubs USSR). Imported Pubns.

Planet Savers. Marion Zimmer Bradley. 1980. lib. bdg. 11.95 o.p. (ISBN 0-8398-2514-5, Gregg). G K Hall.

Planet Savers. Marion Zimmer Bradley. Bd. with Sword of Aldones. 1985. pap. 3.50 o.s.i. (ISBN 0-441-67026-1, Pub. by Ace Science Fiction). Ace Bks.

Planet Venus. Garry Hunt & Patrick Moore. LC 82-5045. (Illus.). 240p. 1983. 22.00 o.p. (ISBN 0-571-09050-8). Faber & Faber.

Planetarium. Nathalie Sarraute. 1965. pap. 8.50 o.p. (ISBN 0-685-23937-3, 1452). Schoenhof.

Planetariums: A Bibliography on Their Architecture, Construction & Development. Glenna Dunning. (Architecture Ser.: A 1489). 23p. 1985. 3.75 o.p. (ISBN 0-89028-619-1). Vance Biblios.

Planetary Aeronomy & Astronomy. Ed. by S. K. Atreya & J. J. Caldwell. (Advances in Space Research Ser.: Vol. 1, No.9). (Illus.). 216p. 1981. pap. 34.00 o.p. (ISBN 0-08-028385-3). Pergamon.

Planetary Astronomy: Proceedings. Conference on Origins of Life, 3rd, California, 1970. Ed. by L. Margulis. LC 72-91514. (Illus.). 268p. 1973. 33.00 o.p. (ISBN 0-387-06065-0). Springer-Verlag.

Planetary Exploration Through Year 2000: An Augmented Program, Pt. 2. (Illus.). 239p. (Orig.). 1986. pap. 12.00 o.p. (ISBN 0-318-21305-2, S/N 033-000-00987-9). USGPO.

Planetary Interiors. Ed. by H. Stiller & R. Z. Sagdeev. (Advances in Space Research Ser.: Vol. 1, No. 7). (Illus.). 265p. 1981. pap. 41.00 o.p. (ISBN 0-08-028382-9). Pergamon.

Planetary, Lunar & Solar Positions Six Hundred-One B. C to A. D One at Five-Day & Ten-Day Intervals. Bryant Tuckerman. (Memoirs Ser.: Vol. 56). 333p. 1979. Repr. of 1962 ed. 20.00 o.p. (ISBN 0-87169-056-X). Am Philos.

Planetoid One Hundred Twenty Seven. 144p. 1987. 15.00 o.p. (ISBN 0-947898-47-6). Kraus Repr.

Planets. Heather Couper. LC 84-52571. (Space Scientist Ser.). (Illus.). 32p. (gr. 4-9). 1985. PLB 11.90 o.p. (ISBN 0-531-10001-4). Watts.

Planets in Synthesis: Interpreting the Whole Horoscope. Robert Hand. (Planets Ser.). 1980. 20.00 o.s.i. (ISBN 0-914918-13-3). Whitford Pr.

Planets in Youth: Patterns of Early Development. Robert Hand. (Planets Ser.). 384p. 1977. 16.00 o.p. (ISBN 0-914918-06-0). Whitford Pr.

Planets of Rock & Ice: From Mercury to the Moons of Saturn. Clark R. Chapman. (Illus.). 256p. 1982. 13.95 o.p. (ISBN 0-684-17484-7, ScribT). Scribner.

Planets, Stars & Galaxies: Descriptive Astronomy for Beginners. Anthony E. Fanning. (Illus.). 13.00 o.p. (ISBN 0-8446-2042-4). Peter Smith.

Plank on Frame: The Who, What & Where of 150 Boatbuilders. Paul Lipke. LC 80-80779. (Illus.). 416p. 1980. pap. 1.95 o.p. (ISBN 0-87742-121-8). Intl Marine.

Planned Organizational Change & Its Evaluation: A Checklist. Lorna Peterson. (Public Administration Ser.: P 1720). 7p. 1985. 2.00 o.p. (ISBN 0-89028-490-3). Vance Biblios.

Planned Parenthood in Europe: A Human Rights Perspective. Ed. by Philip Meredith & Lyn Thomas. LC 85-26888. 300p. 1986. 40.00 o.p. (ISBN 0-7099-1331-1, Pub. by Croom Helm Ltd). Routledge Chapman & Hall.

Planned Speaking & Your Career. Vera Gough & B. R. Grier. 1967. 13.25 o.p. (ISBN 0-08-012589-1); pap. 5.50 o.p. (ISBN 0-08-012588-3). Pergamon.

Planned Unit Development: New Communities American Style. Robert Burchell. 300p. 1972. (ISBN 0-87855-058-5). Transaction Pubs.

Planner's Guide to Land Use Law. Ed. by Stuart Meck & Edith M. Netter. LC 83-60683. (Illus.). 369p. 1983. pap. text ed. 36.95 o.s.i. (ISBN 0-918286-29-8). Planners Pr.

Planners, Politics & Health Services. Gregory Parston. 196p. 1980. 25.50 o.p. (ISBN 0-85664-909-0, Pub by Croom Helm Ltd). Routledge Chapman & Hall.

Planner's Use of Information: Techniques for Collection, Organization & Communication. Ed. by Hemalata C. Dandekar. LC 82-3119. (Environmental Design Ser.: Vol. 2). 224p. 1982. 34.95 o.p. (ISBN 0-87933-429-0). Van Nos Reinhold.

Planning a Christian Funeral: A Minister's Guide. Ed. by W. A. Poovey. LC 78-52198. 1978. pap. 8.95 o.p. (ISBN 0-8066-1668-7, 10-4990, Augsburg). Augsburg Fortress.

Planning a Socialist Economy, 2 vols. Ed. by L. Y. Berri. 572p. 9.45 o.p. (ISBN 0-8285-0371-0, Pub. by Progress Pubs USSR). Imported Pubns.

Planning a Tragedy: The Americanization of the War in Vietnam. Larry Berman. 192p. 1982. 14.95 o.p. (ISBN 0-393-01602-1). Norton.

Planning Adult Learning: Issues, Practices & Directions. William M. Rivera. 208p. 1987. lib. bdg. 30.00x o.p. (ISBN 0-317-64377-0, Pub. by Croom Helm UK). Routledge Chapman & Hall.

Planning & Administration of a Large Estate 1985, Vol. 159. Practising Law Institute Staff. 899p. 1985. pap. 15.00 o.p. (ISBN 0-317-27549-6, #D4-5178). PLI.

Planning & Building Fences & Gates. American Association of Vocational Instructional Materials Staff. (Illus.). 192p. 1986. 22.95 o.p. (ISBN 0-8306-0443-X, 2643); pap. 14.60 o.p. (ISBN 0-8306-2643-3). TAB Bks.

Planning & Controlling Manufacturing Resources. Michael Donovan & Harrison Appleby. 1979. pap. 10.00 o.p. (ISBN 0-8144-2235-7). AMACOM.

Planning & Design of Rapid Transit Facilities. (Transportation Research Record Ser.). 49p. 1978. 3.40 o.p. (ISBN 0-309-02691-1). Transport Res Bd.

Planning & Design of Townhouses & Condominiums. Robert E. Engstrom & Marc Putman. LC 79-64813. (Illus.). 246p. 1979. pap. 38.00 o.p. (ISBN 0-87420-587-5, P20). Urban Land.

Planning & Designing the Office Environment. David Harris. 1981. 39.95 o.p. (ISBN 0-442-28418-7). Van Nos Reinhold.

Planning & Development in Modern Libya. Mukhtar Buru et al. 234p. 1985. lib. bdg. 27.50x o.p. (ISBN 0-906559-19-7). Lynne Rienner.

Planning & Development of Quality Services in the Schools. Sandra R. Wright. 117p. 1984. write for info. manual o.p. (ISBN 0-910329-13-3); manual avail. o.p. Am Speech Lang Hearing.

Planning & Ecology. Ed. by R. D. Roberts & T. M. Roberts. (Illus.). 400p. 1984. 55.00x o.p. (ISBN 0-412-23560-9, NO. 6896). Routledge Chapman & Hall.

Planning & Equipping Educational Music Facilities. Harold P. Geerdes. LC 75-15271. (Illus.). 96p. (Orig.). 1975. pap. 8.75 o.p. (ISBN 0-940796-13-9, 1036). Music Ed Natl.

Planning & Financing Your Business. W. Osgood. 1984. pap. 32.95 o.p. (ISBN 0-442-27073-9). Van Nos Reinhold.

Planning & Financing Your Business: A Complete Working Guide. William R. Osgood. 280p. 1983. pap. 27.95 o.p. (ISBN 0-8436-0883-8). Van Nos Reinhold.

Planning & Management of Zoological Parks: A Selected Annotated Bibliography. Jerry E. Green. (Architecture Ser.: A 1430). 18p. 1985. 3.00 o.p. (ISBN 0-89028-480-6). Vance Biblios.

Planning & Organisation of National Research Programs in Information Science. Ed. by V. Slamecka & H. Borka. (Illus.). 83p. 1982. pap. 73.00 o.p. (ISBN 0-08-026472-7). Pergamon.

Planning & Organizing Instruction. rev. ed. G. Harold Silvius & Ralph C. Bohn. Orig. Title: Organizing Course Materials for Industrial Education. 1976. text ed. 19.35 o.p. (ISBN 0-87345-720-X). Glencoe.

Planning & Producing Handmade Slides & Filmstrips for the Classroom. Arthur Ring. LC 73-80403. 1974. pap. 5.95 o.p. (ISBN 0-8224-5430-0). D S Lake Pubs.

Planning & Profit in Socialist Economies. Jean-Charles Asselain. (International Library of Economics). 256p. 1984. 35.00x o.p. (ISBN 0-7102-0257-1). Routledge Chapman & Hall.

Planning & Programming for Transportation: Five Reports. (Transportation Research Record Ser.). 58p. 1976. 2.60 o.p. (ISBN 0-309-02488-9). Transport Res Bd.

Planning & Reasoning about Time. Thomas Dean & Yoav Shoham. (Illus.). 75p. 1988. pap. text ed. 12.00 o.p. (ISBN 0-929280-13-X). Amer Artificial.

Planning & the Growth of the Firm. John Bridge & J. C. Dodds. 211p. 1978. 28.00 o.p. (ISBN 0-85664-362-9, Pub. by Croom Helm Ltd). Routledge Chapman & Hall.

Planning & Vocational Education. G. Copa & J. Moss. 208p. 1983. text ed. 25.95 o.p. (ISBN 0-07-013049-3). McGraw.

Planning Basics for Managers. D. Ellis & P. Pekar. 1983. pap. 6.95 o.p. (ISBN 0-317-31398-3). AMACOM.

Planning Cogeneration Systems. Dilip R. Limaye. LC 84-48107. 250p. 1985. text ed. 39.00 o.p. (ISBN 0-915586-95-9). Fairmont Pr.

Planning Continuing Professional Development. Frankie Todd. Ed. by P. J. Hills. (New Patterns in Learning Ser). 260p. 1987. 34.50 o.p. (ISBN 0-7099-4326-1, Pub. by Croom Helm UK). Routledge Chapman & Hall.

Planning Development Projects. Dennis A. Rodinelli. LC 77-23072. (Community Development Ser.: Vol. 35). 1982. 38.95 o.p. (ISBN 0-87933-280-8). Van Nos Reinhold.

Planning Education in Relation to Rural Development. G. M. Coverdale. (Fundamentals of Educational Planning: No. 21). 37p. (Orig.). 1974. pap. 5.00 o.p. (ISBN 92-803-1062-3, U450, UNESCO). UNIPUB.

Planning Employee Share Schemes. Ed. by G. R. Cyriax. 54p. (Orig.). 1981. pap. text ed. 47.50x o.p. (ISBN 0-566-03024-1). Gower Pub Co.

Planning, Engineering & Construction of Electric Power Generation Facilities. Jack H. Willenbrock & H. Randoph Thomas. LC 79-21427. 896p. 1980. 78.50 o.p. Krieger.

Planning Flexible Learning Places. S. Leggett et al. 1977. text ed. 29.50 o.p. (ISBN 0-07-037060-5). McGraw.

Planning for a Successful Retirement: A Home Study Course. Berthold Sheffield. (Home Study Ser.). 28.00 o.p. (ISBN 0-939926-26-1); tape incl. o.p. (ISBN 0-939926-25-3). Fruition Pubns.

Planning for Creative Learning. 2nd ed. Bruce M. Mitchell et al. 200p. 1983. pap. text ed. 12.95 o.p. (ISBN 0-8403-2969-5, 40296901). Kendall-Hunt.

Planning for Data Base Systems. Robert M. Curtice. (Data Base Monograph: No. 2). 1976. pap. 15.00x o.s.i. (ISBN 0-89435-018-8). QED Info Sci.

Planning for Information Handling. Ed. by Alan Simpson. (The Office of the Future Ser.: Vol. 6). 154p. (Orig.). 1982. pap. text ed. 23.50x o.p. (ISBN 0-566-03417-4). Gower Pub Co.

Planning for Innovation Through Dissemination & Utilization of Knowledge. Ronald G. Havelock et al. LC 78-634679. 538p. 1969. 24.00x o.p. (ISBN 0-87944-075-9). Inst Soc Res.

Planning for Man & Motor. Paul Ritter. 1964. text ed. (ISBN 0-08-010417-7). Pergamon.

Planning for Non-Planners. Darryl J. Ellis & Peter P. Pekar. 1981. 12.95 o.p. (ISBN 0-8144-5593-X). AMACOM.

Planning for Office Microcomputers. Ed. by Alan Simpson. (Office of the Future Ser.: Vol. 5). 110p. (Orig.). 1982. pap. text ed. 21.00x o.p. (ISBN 0-566-03416-6). Gower Pub Co.

Planning for People. Maurice Broady. 119p. 1968. pap. text ed. 7.25x o.p. (ISBN 0-7199-0765-9, Pub. by Bedford England). Gower Pub Co.

Planning for Platted Lands: Land Use Remedies for Lot Sale Subdivisions. Frank Schnidman & R. Lisle Baker. (Lincoln Institute Monograph: No. 85-2). 92p. 1985. pap. text ed. 6.00 o.s.i. (ISBN 0-318-04691-1). Lincoln Inst Land.

Planning for Social Recreation. Israel C. Heaton & Clark T. Thorstenson. LC 77-85148. (Illus.). 1978. pap. 19.50 o.p. (ISBN 0-395-25052-8). HM.

Planning for Telecommunications. Ed. by Alan Simpson. (Office of the Future Ser.: Vol. 4). 164p. (Orig.). 1982. pap. text ed. 23.50x o.p. (ISBN 0-566-03415-8). Gower Pub Co.

Planning for the Elderly: Alternative Community Analysis Techniques. Victor Regnier. LC 79-90975. 152p. 1980. pap. 8.00x o.p. (ISBN 0-88474-093-5, 05748-7). Lexington Bks.

Planning for the Electronic Mail. Ed. by Alan Simpson. (Office of the Future Ser.: Vol. 2). 144p. 1981. pap. text ed. 23.50x o.p. (ISBN 0-566-03406-9). Gower Pub Co.

Planning for the Future: Long-Range Planning for Associations. Stephen P. Gibert. 80p. 1988. pap. text ed. 30.00 o.p. (ISBN 0-88034-030-4). Am Soc Assn Execs.

Planning for the Mobilization of the Nation's Medical Resources. John R. Beatty. (Illus.). 208p. 1985. pap. 7.50 o.p. (ISBN 0-318-22424-0, S/N 008-020-01058-8). USGPO.

Planning for the Office of the Future. Ed. by Alan Simpson. (Office of the Future Ser.: Vol 1). 152p. 1981. pap. text ed. 23.50x o.p. (ISBN 0-566-03404-2). Gower Pub Co.

Planning for the Second Marriage. Massachusetts Continuing Legal Education-New England Law Institute, Inc. Staff. LC 84-61781. write for info. o.p. Mass CLE.

Planning for the Word Processing. Ed. by Alan Simpson. (Office of the Future Ser.: Vol. 3). 160p. 1982. pap. text ed. 23.50x o.p. (ISBN 0-566-03414-X). Gower Pub Co.

Planning for Water Reuse. Ed. by Duane D. Baumann & Daniel M. Dworkin. 1980. 25.00x o.p. (ISBN 0-416-60121-9, NO. 2864). Routledge Chapman & Hall.

Planning for Wellness: A Guidebook for Achieving Optimal Health. 2nd ed. Donald Ardell & Mark J. Tager. 208p. 1982. pap. text ed. 13.50 o.p. (ISBN 0-8403-2717-X). Kendall-Hunt.

Planning for Wildlife in Cities & Suburbs. Urban Wildlife Research Center, Inc. Staff et al. (PAS Reports: No. 331). 64p. 1978. 10.00 o.p. (ISBN 0-318-13051-3). Am Plan Assn.

Planning Games: Case Study Simulations in Land Management & Development. Martin Wynn. (Illus.). 200p. 1985. 35.00 o.p. (ISBN 0-419-12810-7, NO. 9153). Routledge Chapman & Hall.

Planning Grain-Feed Handling for Livestock & Cash-Grain Farms. 1st ed. Midwest Plan Service Engineers Staff. (Illus.). 70p. 1974. pap. 5.00 o.p. (ISBN 0-89373-007-6, MWPS-13). Midwest Plan Serv.

Planning Guide for Information System Evaluation Studies. William A. Smith, Jr. & Ben L. Wechsler. 1983. 13.00 o.p. (ISBN 0-89806-016-8, 108). Inst Indus Eng.

Planning, Implementing & Evaluating Career Preparation Programs. Dwight Davis & Joe Borgen. 1974. 50.00 o.p. (ISBN 0-87345-590-8). Glencoe.

Planning in America: Learning from Turbulence. Ed. by David R. Godschalk. 240p. 1974. pap. 10.00 o.p. (ISBN 0-318-13052-1); pap. 8.00 members o.p. (ISBN 0-318-13053-X). Am Plan Assn.

Planning in Brazil: Monographs Published since 1950. Mary Vance. (Architecture Ser.: A 1419). 25p. 1985. 3.75 o.p. (ISBN 0-89028-469-5). Vance Biblios.

Planning in Chess. Janos Flesch. (Illus.). 96p. 1983. pap. 19.95 o.p. (ISBN 0-7134-1597-5, Pub. by Batsford England). David & Charles.

Planning in Developing Countries: Theory & Methodology. 358p. 1980. pap. 18.50 o.p. (UN80/15/ST17, UNITAR). UNIPUB.

Planning in France: Monographs Published since 1950. Mary Vance. (Architecture Ser.: A 1420). 32p. 1985. 4.50 o.p. (ISBN 0-89028-470-9). Vance Biblios.

Planning in Germany: Monographs Published since 1950. Mary Vance. (Architecture Ser.: A 1421). 45p. 1985. 6.75 o.p. (ISBN 0-89028-471-7). Vance Biblios.

Planning in India: Monographs Published since 1950. Mary Vance. (Architecture Ser.: A 1422). 20p. 1985. 3.00 o.p. (ISBN 0-89028-472-5). Vance Biblios.

Planning in Italy: Monographs Published since 1950. Mary Vance. (Architecture Series Bibliography: A 1423). 51p. 1985. pap. 7.50 o.p. (ISBN 0-89028-473-3). Vance Biblios.

Planning in Residential Conservation Areas. A. D. Thomas. (Illus.). 88p. 1983. pap. 22.00 o.p. (ISBN 0-08-031039-7). Pergamon.

Planning in the Netherlands: Monographs. Mary Vance. (Architecture Ser.: Bibliography A-1302). 42p. 1985. pap. 6.00 o.p. (ISBN 0-89028-232-3). Vance Biblios.

Planning in the United States & the United Kingdom 1970-1985: An Annotated Bibliography. Richard Cline et al. 294p. 1987. 56.00x o.p. (ISBN 0-7201-1666-X). Mansell.

Planning Individual Speech & Language Intervention Programs. Nickola W. Nelson. 240p. 1979. pap. 16.95 o.p. (ISBN 0-88450-790-4, 3099-B). Communication Skill.

Planning Industrial Development. Ed. by David F. Walker. LC 79-40519. 350p. 1980. 97.95x o.p. (ISBN 0-471-27621-9, Pub. by Wiley-Interscience). Wiley.

Planning Learning Resource Centres in Schools & Colleges. Rosemary Raddon. 256p. 1984. text ed. 33.95x o.p. (ISBN 0-566-03435-2). Gower Pub Co.

Planning Legislation in North Carolina. Compiled by Philip Green. 274p. 1986. 19.00 o.p. (ISBN 0-686-39446-1). Institute Government.

Planning Legislation in North Carolina. 11th ed. Philip P. Green, Jr. 1978. looseleaf 8.50 o.p. (ISBN 0-686-17570-0). Institute Government.

Planning Legislation in North Carolina: 1982 Replacement Pages. Compiled by Philip Green. 43p. 1982. 5.00 o.p. (ISBN 0-686-39445-3). Institute Government.

Planning Manual for Colleges. rev. ed. National Association of College & University Business Officers Staff et al. Ed. by Jeanne Nevin. LC 80-12096. 73p. 1980. pap. text ed. 20.00 o.p. (ISBN 0-915164-09-4); pap. text ed. 17.50 ea. 2-4 copies o.p.; pap. text ed. 12.50 ea. 5 or more copies o.p. NACUBO.

Planning Manual for Utility Application of Large Wind Energy Conversion Systems. Gerald L. Park et al. 243p. (Orig.). 1983. pap. 49.50 o.p. (ISBN 0-88016-005-5). Windbks.

Planning Nineteen Eighty-One. 326p. 1982. pap. 16.95 o.p. (ISBN 0-318-17103-1). Am Plan Assn.

Planning Nineteen Eighty-One. Intro. by Frank So. LC 81-71929. 326p. (Orig.). 1982. pap. 16.95 o.s.i. (ISBN 0-918286-26-3). Planners Pr.

Planning of London: Monographs & Journal Articles Published since 1950. Mary Vance. (Architecture Series Bibliography: A 1424). 71p. 1985. pap. 10.50 o.p. (ISBN 0-89028-474-1). Vance Biblios.

Planning Profitable New Product Strategies. James W. Taylor. (Alexander Hamilton Institute Bk.). 240p. 1984. 35.00 o.p. (ISBN 0-8019-7551-4); pap. 19.95 o.p. (ISBN 0-8019-7522-0). Chilton.

Planning Profits in the Food & Lodging Industry. Peter Dukas. 192p. 1983. 18.95 o.p. (ISBN 0-8436-2080-3). Van Nos Reinhold.

Planning, Programming, Budgeting Systems in Academic Libraries: An Exploratory Study of PPBS in University Libraries Having Membership in the Association of Research Libraries. Harold C. Young. LC 76-10667. 246p. 1976. 64.00x o.p. (ISBN 0-8103-0264-0). Gale.

Planning Techniques in Divorce Transactions under the Tax Reform Act of 1984: Video Law Review Study Materials. ALI-ABA Committee on Continuing Professional Education. 159p. Date not set. price not set o.p. Am Law Inst.

Planning the Electronic Office. Aaron Cohen & Elaine Cohen. (Illus.). 256p. 1983. text ed. 48.00 o.p. (ISBN 0-07-011583-4). McGraw.

Planning the Electronic Office. John Whitehead. LC 85-21275. (Information Technology Ser.). 192p. 1985. 29.00 o.p. (ISBN 0-7099-3621-4, Pub. by Croom Helm Ltd). Routledge Chapman & Hall.

Planning the Fourth Migration: The Neglected Vision of the Regional Planning Association of America. Ed. by Carl Sussman. 1976. 27.50x o.p. (ISBN 0-262-19148-2). MIT Pr.

Planning the New Corporate Headquarters. Byrant P. Gould. LC 82-23897. 196p. 1983. 42.95x o.p. (ISBN 0-471-09025-5). Wiley.

Planning the New Office. M. Saphier. (Illus.). 1978. text ed. 38.50 o.p. (ISBN 0-07-054721-1). McGraw.

Planning Theory-Prospects for the Nineteen Eighties: Selected Papers from a Conference Held in Oxford, U. K., 2-4 April 1981. Ed. by P. Healey & G. McDougall. (Urban & Regional Planning Ser.). 330p. 1983. 53.00 o.p. (ISBN 0-08-027449-8); pap. 17.25 o.p. (ISBN 0-08-030824-4). Pergamon.

Planning Trips with Girl Scouts: A Guide for Leaders. rev. ed. Girl Scouts of the U. S. A. Staff. 24p. (gr. 1-8). 1982. pap. 2.50 o.p. (ISBN 0-88441-142-7, 19-998). Girl Scouts USA.

Planning Your Career Pathways: Employee's Career Development Workbook. rev. ed. Ed. by Carol Nalbandian & Colleen Ryan. 50p. 1981. wkbk. 8.00 o.p. (ISBN 0-936352-11-6). U of KS Cont Ed.

Planning Your Career Pathways: Supervisor's Manual. rev. ed. Ed. by Colleen Ryan & Carol Nalbandian. 85p. (Orig.). 1981. pap. 14.00 spiral bdg. o.p. (ISBN 0-936352-12-4). U of KS Cont Ed.

Planning Your First Vacation to Australia. Brian Lewis. (Illus.). 50p. 1987. pap. 2.95 o.p. (ISBN 0-940749-01-7). A A Pub.

Planning Your Future: A Workbook for Personal Goal Setting. George A. Ford & Gordon L. Lippitt. LC 76-11357. Orig. Title: Life Planning Workbook for Guidance in Planning & Personal Goal Setting. 49p. 1976. pap. 8.50 o.p. (ISBN 0-88390-120-X). Univ Assocs.

Plans for City Police Jails & Village Lockups. Hastings H. Hart. (Russell Sage Foundation Reprint Ser.). (Illus.). 1986. pap. text ed. 7.95x o.p. (ISBN 0-8290-1883-2). Irvington.

Plans for Departure. Nayantara Sahgal. LC 85-3037. 1985. 14.45 o.p. (ISBN 0-393-02221-8). Norton.

Plant & Animal Products in the U. S. Food System. National Research Council. 254p. 1978. pap. 12.25x o.p. (ISBN 0-309-02769-1). Natl Acad Pr.

Plant & Insect Mycoplasma Techniques. M. J. Daniels & P. G. Markham. LC 81-13142. 369p. 1982. 59.95x o.p. (ISBN 0-470-27262-7). Halsted Pr.

Plant & Insect Mycoplasma Techniques. Ed. by M. J. Daniels & P. G. Markham. 368p. 1982. 37.00 o.p. (ISBN 0-7099-0272-7, Pub. by Croom Helm Ltd). Routledge Chapman & Hall.

Plant & Production Forms. (Easy-to-Make Photocopier Bks.). (Orig.). 1982. pap. 14.95 o.p. (ISBN 0-87280-033-4, Asher-Gallant). Caddylak Systs.

Plant Bacterial Diseases: A Diagnostic Guide. Ed. by Garrielle J. Persley & Peter C. Fahy. 1983. 61.50 o.p. (ISBN 0-12-247660-3). Acad Pr.

Plant Between Sun & Earth. George Adams & Olive Whicher. LC 82-50276. (Illus.). 224p. (Orig.). 1982. 12.95 o.p. (ISBN 0-87773-232-9, 71231-5). Shambhala Pubns.

Plant Biochemistry. 3rd ed. Ed. by James Bonner & Joseph Varner. 1976. text ed. 47.00 o.p. (ISBN 0-12-114860-2). Acad Pr.

Plant Biology Laboratory Manual. 2nd ed. Curt M. Peterson. 1975. pap. text ed. 14.95 o.p. (ISBN 0-8403-1405-1). Kendall-Hunt.

Plant Book. Maria Vermiglio & Bill Henkin. LC 77-73862. (Illus.). 1977. 11.95 o.s.i. (ISBN 0-03-022096-3). H Holt & Co.

Plant Cell Cultures, Vol. 2. Ed. by A. Fiechter. (Advances in Biochemical Engineering: Vol. 18). (Illus.). 250p. 1980. 50.00 o.p. (ISBN 0-387-09936-0). Springer-Verlag.

Plant Closing Legislation in the United States: A Bibliogrphy. Edward Duensing. LC 85-184586. (Public Administration Ser.: P 1691). 1985. 2.00 o.p. (ISBN 0-89028-421-0). Vance Biblios.

Plant Cytogenetics. D. M. Moore. 1976. pap. 8.50 o.p. (ISBN 0-412-13440-3, NO. 6202, Pub. by Chapman & Hall England). Routledge Chapman & Hall.

Plant Doctor: Growing & Healing Indoor Plants. Richard E. Nicholls. LC 74-31542. (Illus.). 110p. (Orig.). 1975. lib. bdg. 12.90 o.p. (ISBN 0-914294-13-X); pap. 4.95 o.p. (ISBN 0-914294-14-8). Running Pr.

Plant Dreaming Deep. May Sarton. LC 68-10885. (Illus.). 1968. 10.95 o.p. (ISBN 0-393-07403-X). Norton.

Plant Energy System: Energy Systems Engineering. Power Editors. 1967. text ed. 69.95 o.p. (ISBN 0-07-050588-8). McGraw.

Plant Galls of the California Region. Ronald A. Russo. (Illus.). 1979. pap. 8.95 o.p. (ISBN 0-910286-71-X). Boxwood.

Plant Geography. Martin C. Kellman. 1980. pap. 12.50x o.p. (ISBN 0-416-73860-5, NO. 2971). Routledge Chapman & Hall.

Plant Growth & Development. rev. ed. A. Leopold et al. 1975. text ed. 48.00 o.p. (ISBN 0-07-037200-4). McGraw.

Plant Growth Regulation: Proceedings. Conference on Plant Growth Substances, 9th. (Proceedings in Life Sciences). 1977. 39.00 o.p. (ISBN 0-387-08113-5). Springer-Verlag.

Plant Growth Regulators & Herbicide Antagonists: Recent Advances. Ed. by J. C. Johnson. LC 82-7966. (Chemical Technology Rev. 212). (Illus.). 303p. 1983. 45.00 o.p. (ISBN 0-8155-0915-4). Noyes.

Plant Growth Substances, 1970: Proceedings of the International Conference, 7th, Canberra. International Conference on Plant Growth Substances Staff. Ed. by D. J. Carr. LC 72-80291. (Illus.). 849p. 1972. pap. 31.00 o.p. (ISBN 0-387-05850-8). Springer-Verlag.

Plant Health Handbook. Louis L. Pyenson. (Illus.). 1981. 21.95 o.s.i. (ISBN 0-87055-377-1). AVI.

Plant Health: The Scientific Basis for Administrative Control of Plant Diseases & Pests, Vol. 2. Ed. by D. L. Ebbels & J. E. King. (Organized by the Federation of British Plant Pathologists). 322p. 1980. 74.95x o.p. (ISBN 0-470-26954-5). Halsted Pr.

Plant Kingdom. George W. Burns. (Illus.). 640p. 1974. text ed. write for info. o.p. (ISBN 0-02-317200-2, 31720). Macmillan.

Plant Life. Mark Lambert. (Illus.). 96p. (gr. 4-6). 1983. PLB 8.90 o.p. (ISBN 0-531-09216-X). Watts.

Plant Life of the Great Barrier Reef & Adjacent Shores. A. B. Cribb & J. W. Cribb. LC 84-3704. (Illus.). 294p. 1985. text ed. 25.00x o.p. (ISBN 0-7022-1984-3). U of Queensland Pr.

Plant Membranes: Endo- & Plasma Membranes. David G. Robinson. LC 84-7539. (Cell Biology: A Series of Monographs: Vol. 3). 1075p. 1985. 83.95x o.p. (ISBN 0-471-86210-X). Wiley.

Plant Metabolism. 2nd ed. H. E. Street & W. Cockburn. LC 76-174629. 332p. 1972. 85.00 o.p. (ISBN 0-08-016752-7); pap. 85.00 o.p. (ISBN 0-08-016753-5). Pergamon.

Plant Microtechnique. Donald A. Johansen. (Botanical Sciences Ser.). 1940. text ed. 69.95 o.p. (ISBN 0-07-032540-5). McGraw.

Plant Names. Thomas Lindsay. LC 75-16423. viii, 100p. 1976. Repr. of 1923 ed. 40.00x o.p. (ISBN 0-8103-4160-3). Gale.

Plant Nurseries: Training Element & Technical Guide for SPWP Workers. (Special Labour-Intensive Public Works Programme Ser.: No. 6). (Illus.). 61p. (Orig.). 1985. pap. 7.00 o.p. (ISBN 92-2-105236-2). Intl Labour Office.

Plant Nutrition, 1982, 2 vols. Ed. by A. Scaife. 750p. 1982. Set. pap. 44.00 o.p. (ISBN 0-85198-505-X). CAB Intl.

Plant Observer's Guidebook: A Field Botany Manual for the Amateur Naturalist. Charles E. Roth. (Illus.). 240p. 1984. 17.95 o.p. (ISBN 0-13-680752-6); pap. 9.95 o.p. (ISBN 0-13-680745-3). P-H.

Plant Pathology. George N. Agrios. 1969. text ed. 21.00 o.p. (ISBN 0-12-044550-6). Acad Pr.

Plant Pathology. 2nd ed. George N. Agrios. 1978. 47.95 o.p. (ISBN 0-12-044560-3). Acad Pr.

Plant Pathology. 3rd ed. John C. Walker. (Agricultural Sciences Ser.). (Illus.). 1968. text ed. 66.95 o.p. (ISBN 0-07-067860-X). McGraw.

Plant Physiology. D. Hess. LC 73-22278. (Springer Study Edition). (Illus.). 320p. 1975. 35.10 o.p. (ISBN 0-387-06643-8). Springer Verlag.

Plant Physiology. M. Thomas. (Illus.). 700p. 1956. (ISBN 0-8022-1712-5). Philos Lib.

Plant Propagation & Cultivation. William A. Hutchinson. (Illus.). 1980. pap. 21.95 o.s.i. (ISBN 0-87055-340-2). AVI.

Plant Propagation: Principles & Practices. 4th ed. Hudson T. Hartmann & Dale E. Kester. (Illus.). 704p. 1983. text ed. 43.00 o.p. (ISBN 0-13-681007-1). P-H.

Plant Regulation & World Agriculture. Ed. by Tom Scott. LC 79-14597. (NATO ASI Series A, Life Sciences: Vol. 22). 586p. 1979. 95.00x o.p. (ISBN 0-306-40180-0, Plenum Pr). Plenum Pub.

Plant Science Catalog: Botany Subject Index, 15 vols. U. S. Department of Agriculture Staff. 1958. Set. lib. bdg. 1485.00 o.p. (ISBN 0-8161-0506-5, Hall Library). G K Hall.

Plant Seed: Development, Preservation & Germination. Ed. by Irwin Rubenstein et al. 1979. 29.95 o.p. (ISBN 0-12-602050-7). Acad Pr.

Plant, Technology, & Safety Management Handbook. 144p. 1985. pap. 50.00 o.p. (ISBN 0-86688-081-X). Joint Comm Hlthcare.

Plant Tissue Culture & Its Agricultural Applications. Lyndsey A. Withers & P. G. Alderson. (Nottingham Easter Schools in Agricultural Science Ser.). (Illus.). 448p. 1986. 140.00 o.p. (ISBN 0-407-00921-3). Butterworth.

Plant Tissue Culture & Its Bio-Technical Application: Proceedings. Ed. by W. Barz et al. LC 77-7216. (Life Sciences Ser.). 1977. 53.00 o.p. (ISBN 0-387-08227-1). Springer-Verlag.

Plantain Season. Harriet Hahn. 207p. 1976. 6.95 o.p. (ISBN 0-393-08729-8). Norton.

Plantation: An International Bibliography. Edgar T. Thompson. 215p. (gr. 10-12). 1983. lib. bdg. 39.00 o.s.i. (ISBN 0-8161-8593-X, Hall Reference). G K Hall.

Plantations: Forty-Four of Louisiana's Most Beautiful Antebellum Plantation Houses. Joseph A. Arrigo & Cara M. Batt. (Illus.). 96p. (Orig.). 1983. pap. 7.95 o.p. (ISBN 0-938530-19-4, 19-4). Lexikos.

Plantcraft: A Guide to the Everyday Use of Wild Plants. Richard Mabey. LC 77-82824. (Illus.). 1978. 10.00x o.p. (ISBN 0-87663-303-3). Universe.

Planter; or, Thirteen Years in the South. David Brown. LC 71-100281. Repr. of 1902 ed. lib. bdg. 12.75x o.p. (ISBN 0-8371-2910-9, BTP&). Greenwood.

Plantes: Guerisseuses Magiques. Paul Twitchell. Tr. by Denis R. Lasnier et al. 240p. (Orig., Fr.). 1980. pap. 3.95 o.p. (ISBN 0-914766-59-7, 0308). Illum Way Pub.

Planting Design. Brian Hackett. (Illus.). 1979. text ed. 29.95 o.p. (ISBN 0-07-025402-8). McGraw.

Plants: A Guide to Plant Hobbies. Herbert S. Zim. LC 47-11866. (Illus.). 1948. 8.50 o.p. (ISBN 0-15-262613-1, HJ). HarBraceJ.

Plants & Ancient Man - Studies in Palaeoethnobotany: Proceedings of the 6th Symposium of the International Work Group for Palaeoethnobotany, Groningen, 30 May - 3 June 1983. Ed. by W. Van Zeist & W. A. Casarie. 374p. 1984. text ed. 48.50 o.p. (ISBN 90-6191-528-7, Pub. by A A Balkema). Gower Pub Co.

Plants & Man in Australia. Ed. by D. J. Carr & S. G. Carr. 350p. 1981. 55.00 o.p. (ISBN 0-12-160723-2); pap. 30.50 o.p. (ISBN 0-12-160724-0). Acad Pr.

Plants Consumed by Man. B. Brouk. 1975. 112.00 o.p. (ISBN 0-12-136450-X). Acad Pr.

Plants Humanity & the Environment: Discussion Guide. 2nd ed. Lawrence Kapustka. 148p. 1984. pap. text ed. 10.95 o.p. (ISBN 0-89917-407-8, Pub. by College Town Pr). Tichenor Pub.

Plants in Saline Environments. Ed. by A. Poljakoff-Mayber & J. Gale. LC 75-1272. (Ecological Studies: Vol. 15). (Illus.). 215p. 1975. 40.70 o.p. (ISBN 0-387-07193-8). Springer-Verlag.

Plants, Man & Life. rev. ed. Edgar Anderson. LC 52-5870. (YA) (gr. 9 up). 1967. pap. 6.95x o.p. (ISBN 0-520-00021-8). U of Cal Pr.

Plants of Rocky Mountain National Park. rev. ed. Ruth A. Nelson. LC 80-522. 1981. pap. 6.95 o.s.i. (ISBN 0-87081-092-8). Univ Pr Colo.

Plants of the Bible. A. W. Anderson. (Illus.). 72p. 1957. (ISBN 0-8022-0032-X). Philos Lib.

Plants, People, & Environment. Ed. by Peter B. Kaufman & Don La Croix. 1979. text ed. write for info. o.p. (ISBN 0-02-362120-6). Macmillan.

Plants That Grow on Air. Jack Kramer. LC 74-23414. (Illus.). 96p. 1975. 6.95 o.p. (ISBN 0-671-21955-3). S&S.

Plants Without Flowers. Harold Bastin. (Illus.). 140p. 1955. (ISBN 0-8022-0082-6). Philos Lib.

Plasma & Current Instabilities in Semiconductors. J. Pozhela. Tr. by O. A. Germogenova. (International Series in the Science of the Solid State: Vol. 18). (Illus.). 314p. 1981. 89.00 o.p. (ISBN 0-08-025048-3). Pergamon.

Plasma Astrophysics. S. A. Kaplan & V. N. Tsytovich. LC 73-5785. 316p. 1973. 110.00 o.p. (ISBN 0-08-017190-7). Pergamon.

Plasma Astrophysics. Ed. by P. A. Sturrock. (Italian Physical Society: Course 39). 1967. 77.00 o.p. (ISBN 0-12-368839-6). Acad Pr.

Plasma Chemistry: Font Romeu & Rome, 1975. Ed. by A. T. Bell & C. Bonet. 1977. 45.00 o.p. (ISBN 0-08-020999-8). Pergamon.

Plasma Chemistry: Proceedings of an International Symposium, Kiel, Germany, 1973. Ed. by Jensen. 138p. 1976. 50.00 o.p. (ISBN 0-08-020815-0). Pergamon.

Plasma Diagnostic Techniques. Ed. by Richard Huddlestone & Stanley L. Leonard. (Pure & Applied Physics Ser.: Vol. 21). 1965. 92.50 o.p. (ISBN 0-12-359150-3). Acad Pr.

Plasma Diagnostics with Microwaves. M. A. Heald & C. B. Wharton. LC 77-13781. 470p. 1978. Repr. of 1965 ed. 32.50 o.p. (ISBN 0-88275-626-5). Krieger.

Plasma Instabilities & Nonlinear Effects. A. Hasegawa. LC 74-18072. (Physics & Chemistry in Space Ser.: Vol. 8). (Illus.). xi, 217p. 1975. 49.00 o.p. (ISBN 0-387-06947-X). Springer-Verlag.

Plasma Membrane: Dynamic Perspectives, Genetics & Pathology. D. F. Wallach. LC 72-85948. (Heidelberg Science Library: Vol. 18). (Illus.). 179p. 1973. pap. 19.00 o.p. (ISBN 0-387-90047-0). Springer-Verlag.

Plasma Membrane: Models for Its Structure & Function. B. D. Gomperts. 1977. 61.50 o.p. (ISBN 0-12-289450-2). Acad Pr.

Plasma Membranes & Diseases. Donald Wallach. LC 79-50529. 1980. 79.50 o.p. (ISBN 0-12-733150-6). Acad Pr.

Plasma Physics. Setsuo Ichimaru. (Frontiers in Physics Ser: No. 41). (Illus.). 352p. 1973. text ed. 29.50 o.p. (ISBN 0-8053-8752-8, Adv Bk Prog MSP); pap. text ed. write for info. o.p. (ISBN 0-8053-8753-6, Adv Bk Prog MSP). Addison-Wesley.

Plasma Physics: Proceedings of the EUR-CNEN Association Meeting, 1969. Ed. by J. F. Linhart. 1975. pap. 16.25 o.p. (ISBN 0-08-020450-3). Pergamon.

Plasma Processing & Synthesis of Materials: Proceedings of Symposium, 1983, Boston, MA, Materials Research Society. Ed. by J. Szekely & D. Apelian. (Materials Research Society Symposia Ser.: Vol. 30). 306p. 1984. 82.25 o.p. (ISBN 0-444-00895-0, North Holland). Elsevier.

Plasma Protein Metabolism: Regulation of Synthesis, Distribution & Degradation. Ed. by Marcus A. Rothschild & Thomas Waldmann. 1970. 79.50 o.p. (ISBN 0-12-598750-1). Acad Pr.

Plasma Protein Pathology: A Workshop on Plasma Proteins, Their Availability, Assay & Therapeutic Uses--Proceedings of a Round Table Meeting, Seville, Spain, October-November 1977. H. Peeters & P. H. Wright. LC 78-40994. (Illus.). 72p. 1979. 46.00 o.p. (ISBN 0-08-023766-5). Pergamon.

Plasma Spectrochemistry: Proceeding of the 1984 Winter Conference on Plasma Spectrochemistry, San Diego, Jan. 2-6, 1984, No. 2. R. M. Barnes. 412p. 1985. 72.00 o.p. (ISBN 0-08-030246-7, Pub. by P P L). Pergamon.

Plasma Spectrochemistry: Proceedings of the Winter Conference, Orlando, Florida, January 4-9, 1982. Ed. by R. M. Barnes. 436p. 1983. pap. 55.00 o.p. (ISBN 0-08-028745-X). Pergamon.

Plasma Spectrochemistry 3: Proceedings of the 1985 European Winter Conference on Plasma Spectrochemistry, 7-11 January 1985, Leysin, Switzerland. Ed. by P. W. Boumans. 1986. pap. 64.00 o.p. (ISBN 0-08-033925-5, Pub. by PPL). Pergamon.

Plasma State. J. L. Shohet. 1971. 26.00 o.p. (ISBN 0-12-640550-6). Acad Pr.

Plasma Transport Heat & MHD Theory: Proceedings of a Workshop at Varenna, Italy, 12-16 Sept. 1977. T. Stringer. Ed. by R. Rozzoli. LC 78-40822. 1979. pap. 110.00 o.p. (ISBN 0-08-023426-7). Pergamon.

Plasma Wall Interaction: Proceedings of the International Symposium EUR 5782e, Kernsfoschungsanlage Julich, 1976. Commission of the European Communities. LC 77-75794. 1977. pap. 190.00 o.p. (ISBN 0-08-021989-6). Pergamon.

Plasmids & Transposons: Environmental Efforts & Maintenance Mechanisms. Ed. by Colins Stuttard & K. R. Rozee. LC 80-338. 1980. 46.00 o.p. (ISBN 0-12-675550-7). Acad Pr.

Plasmids: Medical & Theoretical Aspects. Ed. by S. Mitsuhashi et al. (Illus.). 1977. 63.00 o.p. (ISBN 0-387-07946-7). Springer-Verlag.

Plasminogen: Function Assay & Clinical Significance. Ed. by E. Wenzel & Leipnitz. (Journal: Haemostasis: Vol. 18, Supplement 1, 1988). iv, 196p. 1989. pap. 46.75 o.p. (ISBN 3-8055-4765-X). S Karger.

Plastering: A Craftsman's Encyclopedia. Brian F. Pegg & William D. Stagg. 276p. 1976. text ed. 14.75 o.p. (ISBN 0-258-97007-3, Pub. by Granada England). Gower Pub Co.

Plastic Analysis of Structures. rev. ed. Philip G. Hodge. LC 80-26340. 444p. 1981. 36.50 o.p. (ISBN 0-89874-161-0). Krieger.

Plastic & Reconstructive Surgery of the Face & Neck. American Academy of Facial Plastic & Reconstructive Surgery Staff. 1984. 175.00 o.p. (ISBN 0-8016-0067-7). Mosby.

Plastic & Reconstructive Surgery of the Genital Area. Ed. by Charles E. Horton. (Illus.). 1973. 82.00 o.p. (ISBN 0-316-37381-8). Little.

Plastic Deformation of Simple Ionic Crystals. M. T. Sprackling. 1977. 66.00 o.p. (ISBN 0-12-657850-8). Acad Pr.

Plastic Flow & Fracture in Solids. Tracy Y. Thomas. (Mathematics in Science & Engineering Ser: Vol. 2). 1961. 66.00 o.p. (ISBN 0-12-688450-1). Acad Pr.

Plastic Repair of Benito Urinary Defects. George Bankoff. (Illus.). 350p. 1956. (ISBN 0-8022-0057-5). Philos Lib.

Plastic Surgery. 4th ed. Barclay & Kernahan. (Rob & Smith's Operative Surgery Ser.). 1986. 112.00 o.p. (ISBN 0-8016-4416-X, C-4416-X). Mosby.

Plastic Surgery in Infancy & Childhood. 2nd ed. Ed. by John C. Mustarde. (Illus.). 1979. text ed. 120.00 o.p. (ISBN 0-443-01629-1). Churchill.

Plastic Theory of Structures: In SI-Metric Units. 2nd ed. M. R. Horne. 1979. 50.00 o.p. (ISBN 0-08-022737-6); pap. 50.00 o.p. (ISBN 0-08-022738-4). Pergamon.

Plastic Tooling: Techniques & Applications. William P. Benjamin. LC 75-39845. (Illus.). 256p. 1972. text ed. 57.00 o.p. (ISBN 0-07-004554-2). McGraw.

Plastic Tubing 3-4 ID. Date not set. (ISBN 0-07-521271-4). McGraw.

Plasticity & Recovery of Function in the Central Nervous System. Ed. by Donald G. Stein et al. 1974. 29.95 o.p. (ISBN 0-12-664350-4). Acad Pr.

Plasticity: Proceedings, Symposium on Naval Structural Mechanics, 2nd, Brown University, 1960. Ed. by E. H. Lee & P. S. Symonds. 1961. 165.00 o.p. (ISBN 0-08-009459-7). Pergamon.

Plasticity Theory & Its Application in Metal Forming. V. Gopinathan. 211p. 1982. 29.95 o.p. (ISBN 0-470-27529-4). Halsted Pr.

Plasticity Today: New Solutions & Trends in Plasticity: Special Memorial Issue in Honor of Prof. Waclaw Olszak. Proceedings of the Plasticity Today Symposium, Udine, Italy, 27-30 June 1983. A. Sawczuk. (Illus.). 466p. 1985. pap. 61.00 o.p. (ISBN 0-08-031657-3, Pub. by PPL). Pergamon.

Plastics - Projects & Techniques. Alvin R. Lappin. (gr. 9 up). 1965. text ed. 14.64 o.p. (ISBN 0-87345-159-7). Glencoe.

Plastics & Building. Mactaggart & Chambers. (Illus.). 190p. 1955. (ISBN 0-8022-1035-X). Philos Lib.

Plastics Chemistry & Technology. Walter E. Driver. LC 78-24011. 1979. 36.95 o.p. (ISBN 0-442-22156-8). Van Nos Reinhold.

Plastics Common Object. Date not set. 37.00 o.p. (ISBN 0-317-57790-5). T-C Pubns CA.

Plastics Engineering. R. J. Crawford. (Illus.). 360p. 1981. text ed. 91.00 o.p. (ISBN 0-08-026262-7); pap. text ed. 32.00 o.p. (ISBN 0-08-026263-5). Pergamon.

Plastics History, U. S. A. J. Harry DuBois. LC 79-156480. (Illus.). 464p. 1983. 32.95 o.p. (ISBN 0-8436-1203-7). Van Nos Reinhold.

Plastics Materials & Processes. Seymour Schwartz & Sidney Goodman. 832p. 1982. 94.50 o.p. (ISBN 0-442-22777-9). Van Nos Reinhold.

Plastics Mold Engineering Handbook. 3rd ed. Ed. by J. Harry DuBois & Wayne I. Pribble. (Polymer Technology Ser.). (Illus.). 1978. 42.50 o.p. (ISBN 0-442-22180-0). Van Nos Reinhold.

Plate Collecting: A Guide to a Fascinating Hobby. Eleanor Clark. (Illus.). 1977. 17.95 o.p. (ISBN 0-8065-0478-1, Pub. by Citadel Pr). Carol Pub Group.

Plate of Red Herrings. Richard Lockridge. (Nightingale-Lythway Ser.). 1985. pap. 10.95 o.p. (ISBN 0-8161-3832-X, Large Print Bks). G K Hall.

Platelet Aggregation & Drugs. Ed. by Luciano Caprino. 1975. 76.00 o.p. (ISBN 0-12-158950-1). Acad Pr.

Platelet Aggregation in the Pathogenesis of Cerebrovascular Disorders. Round Table Conference, Rome, Oct. 30-31, 1974. Ed. by A. Agnoli & C. Fazio. 1977. 29.00 o.p. (ISBN 0-387-08165-8). Springer-Verlag.

Platelets & Thrombosis. Ed. by D. C. Mills & F. I. Pareti. (Serono Symposium Ser.: No. 10). 1978. 37.00 o.p. (ISBN 0-12-497550-X). Acad Pr.

Platelets in Biology & Pathology. 2nd ed. J. L. Gordon. (RMC Ser.: Vol. 5). 1987. 127.00 o.p. (ISBN 0-317-65937-5). Elsevier.

Platero & I. Juan R. Jimenez. Tr. by Eloise Roach from Span. (Illus.). 228p. 1957. pap. 12.95x o.p. (ISBN 0-292-73328-3). U of Tex Pr.

Platform Margin & Deep Water Carbonates. Harry E. Cook, III & Albert C. Hine. (Short Course Notes Ser.: No. 12). 573p. 1983. pap. 33.00 o.p. (ISBN 0-918985-22-6). SEPM.

Platforms on the Prairies: A Public Speaker's Odyssey from Southside Gym to St. Louis & Beyond. R. Galen Hanson. 47p. 1984. 5.50 o.p. (ISBN 0-682-40147-1). Exposition-Phoenix.

Plating Waste Treatment. Kenneth F. Cherry. LC 81-68033. 324p. 1982. 59.95 o.p. (ISBN 0-250-40417-6). Butterworth.

Platinum Rainbow: How to Succeed in the Music Business Without Selling Your Soul. Bob Monaco & James Riordan. (Swordsman Press Bk.). 280p. 9.95 o.p. (ISBN 0-940018-00-4). Contemp Bks.

Plato. Robert W. Hall. (Political Thinkers Ser.). 1981. text ed. 24.95x o.p. (ISBN 0-04-320145-8); pap. text ed. 9.95x o.p. (ISBN 0-04-320146-6). Unwin Hyman.

Plato. William S. Sahakian & Mabel L. Sahakian. (World Leaders Ser.). 1977. lib. bdg. 13.50 o.p. (ISBN 0-8057-7690-7, Twayne). G K Hall.

Plato & the Christians. Adam Fox. 206p. 1957. Philos Lib.

Plato on Beauty, Wisdom & the Arts. Ed. by Julius Moravcsik & Phillip Temko. LC 81-23434. (American Philosophical Quarterly Library of Philosophy). 160p. 1982. 33.50x o.s.i. (ISBN 0-8476-7030-9). Rowman.

Plato on Knowledge & Reality see Examination of Plato's Doctrines.

Plato on Man & Society see Examination of Plato's Doctrines.

Plato: The Founder of Philosophy as a Dialectic. Gustav E. Mueller. LC 64-13312. 352p. 1965. (ISBN 0-8022-1166-6). Philos Lib.

Plato: True & Sophistic Rhetoric. Ed. by Keith V. Erickson. (Orig.). 1980. pap. text ed. 70.00x o.p. (ISBN 90-6203-489-6). Humanities.

Platonic Ideas in Spenser. Mohinimohana Bhattacharya. LC 73-98858. Repr. of 1935 ed. lib. bdg. 35.00x o.p. (ISBN 0-8371-3129-4, MOPI). Greenwood.

Platonic Myth & Platonic Writing. Robert Zaslavsky. LC 80-5563. 306p. 1981. lib. bdg. 30.50 o.p. (ISBN 0-8191-1382-4); pap. text ed. 15.00 o.p. (ISBN 0-8191-1381-6). U Pr of Amer.

Platonic Studies. 2nd ed. Gregory Vlastos. LC 80-8732. 520p. 1981. 37.50x o.p. (ISBN 0-691-07162-4); pap. 16.00x o.s.i. (ISBN 0-691-10021-7). Princeton U Pr.

Platonis Sophista: Recentsuit, Prolegomenis et Commentariis Instruxit. Otto Apelt. Ed. by Leonardo Taran. LC 78-66612. (Ancient Philosophy Ser.: Vol. 1). 225p. lib. bdg. 26.00 o.p. (ISBN 0-8240-9611-8). Garland Pub.

Platonism. Paul E. More. LC 69-14004. 1970. Repr. of 1931 ed. lib. bdg. 35.00x o.p. (ISBN 0-8371-1627-9, MOPL). Greenwood.

Platonism of Plutarch & Selected Papers. Roger M. Jones. Ed. by Leonardo Taran. LC 78-66589. (Ancient Philosophy Ser.). 250p. 1980. lib. bdg. 29.00 o.p. (ISBN 0-8240-9593-6). Garland Pub.

Plato's Analytic Method. Kenneth M. Sayre. LC 69-15496. 1969. lib. bdg. 17.50x o.s.i. (ISBN 0-226-73555-9). U of Chicago Pr.

Plato's Mathematical Imagination: The Mathematical Passages in the Dialogues & Their Interpretation. Robert S. Brumbaugh. LC 55-62013. (Illus.). 1954. 26.00 o.p. (ISBN 0-527-12900-3). Kraus Repr.

Plato's Phaedo. R. S. Bluck. 1955. pap. text ed. write for info. o.p. (ISBN 0-02-311090-2). Macmillan.

Plato's Poetics: The Authority of Beauty. Morriss H. Partee. 240p. 1981. 24.95x o.p. (ISBN 0-87480-197-4). U of Utah Pr.

Plato's Trilogy: Theaetetus, the Sophist & the Statesman. Jacob Klein. LC 76-25642. 1977. lib. bdg. 16.00x o.s.i. (ISBN 0-226-43951-8). U of Chicago Pr.

Plato's Trilogy: Theaetetus, the Sophist, & the Statesman. Jacob Klein. LC 76-25642. viii, 200p. 1980. pap. text ed. 7.50x o.s.i o.s.i. (ISBN 0-226-43952-6). U of Chicago Pr.

Plautus - Bacchides. Plautus. 49.00x o.s.i. (ISBN 0-86516-096-1); pap. 16.50 o.s.i. (ISBN 0-86516-071-6). Bolchazy Carducci.

Plautus in Performance: The Theatre of the Mind. Niall W. Slater. LC 84-15958. 208p. 1985. text ed. 26.50 o.p. (ISBN 0-691-06624-8). Princeton U Pr.

Play Ball, McGill! Amelia Walden. LC 72-76437. 192p. (gr. 6 up). 1972. 4.95 o.s.i. (ISBN 0-664-32516-5, Westminster). Westminster John Knox.

Play Begins. Toni Handy. 1979. pap. 1.75 o.p. (ISBN 0-380-45427-0, 45427). Avon.

Play Fair with Love. Patricia Robins. (Nightingale Ser.). 249p. 1988. pap. 12.95x o.s.i. (ISBN 0-8161-4439-7). G K HAll.

Play, Games, & Sports in Cultural Contexts. Ed. by Janet C. Harris & Roberta J. Park. LC 82-83148. 532p. 1983. text ed. 24.95x o.p. (ISBN 0-931250-36-6, BHAR0036). Human Kinetics.

Play It Safe: The Kids' Guide to Personal Safety & Crime Prevention. Kathy S. Kyte. LC 83-6086. (Illus.). 128p. (gr. 5 up). 1983. lib. bdg. 8.99 o.p. (ISBN 0-394-95964-7); pap. 5.95 o.p. (ISBN 0-394-85964-2). Knopf.

Play Kitten. Emanuel Schongut. Ed. by Kate Klimo. (Kitten Board Bks.). (Illus.). 14p. 1983. 3.80 o.s.i. (ISBN 0-671-46387-X, Little Simon). S&S.

Play Me the Song of Death. Dale Pierce. 159p. 1983. pap. 5.95 o.p. (ISBN 0-682-40121-8). Exposition-Phoenix.

Play of Consciousness. Swami Muktananda. LC 78-15841. (Illus.). 1979. pap. 7.64 o.p. (ISBN 0-06-066044-9, RD 223). HarpR.

Play, Plays, Play: Seven One-Act Plays for Stage & Screen. Robert T. Baxter. LC 76-44160. 1977. 6.50 o.p. (ISBN 0-682-48712-0). Exposition-Phoenix.

Play Safe: How to Avoid Getting Sexually Transmitted Diseases. 2nd ed. Bea Mandel & Byron Mandel. LC 85-70063. 98p. 1986. pap. 4.95 o.p. (ISBN 0-932567-01-0). Ctr Health Info.

Play Strindberg. Friedrich Durrenmatt. Tr. by James Kirkup. 1973. pap. 1.95 o.p. (ISBN 0-394-17798-3, E-612, Ever). Grove.

Play with a Purpose: Learning Games for Children Six Weeks to Ten Years. Dorothy Einon. LC 85-6301. (Illus.). 256p. (ps-5). 1986. 15.45 o.p. (ISBN 0-394-54493-5); pap. 9.95 o.p. (ISBN 0-394-74214-1). Pantheon.

Playa Lake Symposium. Ed. by C. C. Reeves, Jr. 334p. 1972. 16.70 o.s.i. (ISBN 0-318-14559-6, 4). Intl Ctr Arid & Semi-Arid.

Playas & Dried Lakes: Occurrence & Development. Ed. by James T. Neal. LC 74-31134. (Benchmark Papers in Geology: No. 20). 411p. 1975. 82.00 o.p. (ISBN 0-12-787110-1). Acad Pr.

Playback: The Story of Recording Devices. rev. ed. Robert K. Krishef. LC 62-18817. (Musical Books for Young People). (Illus.). (gr. 5-11). 1974. PLB 3.95 o.p. (ISBN 0-8225-0056-6). Lerner Pubns.

Playboy Comes Home. C. M. Ward. LC 75-32603. 112p. (Orig.). 1976. pap. 1.25 o.p. (ISBN 0-88243-572-8, 02-0572). Gospel Pub.

Playboy of the Western World. John Millington Synge. Ed. by Henry Popkin. 1967. pap. 0.95 o.p. (ISBN 0-380-01508-0, 22046, Bard). Avon.

Playboy's Guide to Casino Gambling: Craps, Blackjack, Roulette, & Baccarat. Edwin Silberstang. LC 80-7727. (Playboy's Lifestyles Library). (Illus.). 512p. 1980. 15.95 o.p. (ISBN 0-87223-618-8, Perigee); pap. 7.95 o.p. (ISBN 0-399-50947-X). Putnam Pub Group.

Played by Ear. Daniel A. Lord. LC 56-7099. (Illus.). 1956. 11.95 o.p. (ISBN 0-8294-0049-4). Loyola.

Player King. Earl H. Rovit. LC 65-11993. 1965. 5.95 o.p. (ISBN 0-15-172038-X). HarBraceJ.

Player on the Other Side. Ellery Queen. 1983. pap. 2.25 o.s.i. (ISBN 0-345-31551-0). Ballantine.

Player Queens. Richard Findlater. LC 76-53912. (Illus.). 1977. 10.95 o.s.i. (ISBN 0-8008-6324-0). Taplinger.

Players & Pretenders: The Basketball Team That Couldn't Shoot Straight. Charles Rosen. LC 81-180. (Illus.). 320p. 1981. 14.95 o.p. (ISBN 0-03-053786-X). H Holt & Co.

Playes Confuted in Five Actions. Stephen Gosson. LC 74-170407. (English Stage Ser.: Vol. 6). lib. bdg. 61.00 o.p. (ISBN 0-8240-0589-9). Garland Pub.

Playful Gourmet: For Ladies Only. Stephen Cornwell & Debbie Cornwell. (Illus.). 64p. (Orig.). 1987. pap. 4.95 o.p. (ISBN 0-943678-21-8). Wellton Enter.

Playful Gourmet: For Men Only. Stephen Cornwell & Debbie Cornwell. (Illus.). 64p. (Orig.). 1987. pap. 4.95 o.p. (ISBN 0-943678-22-6). Wellton Enter.

Playful Gourmet: Quickies. Stephen Cornwell & Debbie Cornwell. (Illus.). 64p. (Orig.). 1987. pap. 4.95 o.p. (ISBN 0-943678-23-4). Wellton Enter.

Playful Pets. (Moving Eye Board Bks.). (Illus.). (ps). bds. 1.98 o.s.i. (ISBN 0-517-47117-5). Outlet Bk Co.

Playgirl Love & Sex Adviser. Ed. by Playgirl Editors. 1984. pap. 5.95 o.p. (ISBN 0-671-50133-X, Fireside). S&S.

Playgrounds. Alan Gelb. 304p. 1987. 18.95 o.p. (ISBN 0-399-13277-5, Putnam). Putnam Pub Group.

Playing Cards Around the World. Sid Sackson. (Illus.). (gr. 5 up). 1981. 9.95 o.s.i. (ISBN 0-13-683003-X). P-H.

Playing Consequences. Niel Micklem. 1985. 10.00x o.p. (ISBN 0-317-62253-6, Guild of Pastoral Psych). State Mutual Bk.

Playing Favorites. James Knudsen. 128p. 1987. pap. 2.50 o.p. (ISBN 0-380-89736-9, Flare). Avon.

Playing for Change. Bruce Pollock. LC 76-62498. (gr. 7 up). 1977. 6.95 o.p. (ISBN 0-395-25149-4). HM.

Playing for Keeps: Sport, the Media, & Society. John Goldlust. 189p. (Orig.). 1988. pap. text ed. 17.95 o.p. (ISBN 0-582-71143-6). Longman.

Playing for Time. Fania Fenelon. LC 77-5502. 1977. 8.95 o.p. (ISBN 0-689-10796-X, Atheneum). Macmillan.

Playing God in the Nursery. Jeff Lyon. 1985. 18.45 o.p. (ISBN 0-393-01898-9). Norton.

Playing God in Yellowstone: The Destruction of America's First National Park. Alston Chase. Ed. by Upton Brady. LC 86-1087. 446p. 1986. 24.95 o.p. (ISBN 0-87113-025-4). Atlantic Monthly.

Playing Popular Piano. Neil Thomas. (Illus.). 112p. 1982. 15.95 o.p. (ISBN 0-13-683052-8); 7.95 o.p. (ISBN 0-13-683045-5). P-H.

Playing Safe. Eileen Dewhurst. LC 86-19714. (Crime Club Ser.). 192p. 1987. 12.95 o.p. (ISBN 0-385-23557-7). Doubleday.

Playing Tennis. Sue Barker. LC 79-66012. (Illus.). 134p. 1982. pap. 5.95 o.s.i. (ISBN 0-8008-6322-4). Taplinger.

Playing the Jack. Mary Brown. 584p. 1985. 16.45 o.p. (ISBN 0-671-54252-4). S&S.

Playing the Piano for Pleasure. Charles Cooke. 1960. pap. 6.95 o.s.i. (ISBN 0-671-57801-4, Fireside). S&S.

Playmakers. Stuart W. Little & Arthur Cantor. (Illus.). 1970. 7.95 o.p. (ISBN 0-393-04315-0). Norton.

Playmates. Jean Bethell. LC 80-20542. 32p. (gr. k-2). 1981. 7.95 o.p. (ISBN 0-03-053821-1). H Holt & Co.

Playmates. J. N. Williamson. 304p. (Orig.). 1982. pap. 2.95 o.p. (ISBN 0-8439-1072-0, Leisure NY). Dorchester Pub Co.

Plays. John Galsworthy. 1928. 12.50 o.s.i. (ISBN 0-684-10198-X, ScribT). Scribner.

Plays & Players: Thirty Years of British Theatre 1953-1983 Vol. Two 1969-1983. Peter Roberts. (Illus.). 256p. 1987. lib. bdg. 35.00x o.p. (ISBN 0-317-61820-2); pap. 15.95x o.p. (ISBN 0-317-61821-0). Routledge Chapman & Hall.

Plays & Players: Thirty Years of British Theatre 1953-1983, Vol. One-1953-1968. Ed. by Peter Roberts. (Illus.). 256p. 1987. lib. bdg. 35.00x o.p. (ISBN 0-317-61817-2); pap. 15.95x o.p. (ISBN 0-317-61818-0). Routledge Chapman & Hall.

Plays & Puppets et Cetera. Courtaney Brooks. LC 81-68933. (Illus.). 100p. (Orig.). (gr. k up). 1981. pap. 11.95x o.p. (ISBN 0-941274-00-4). Belnice Bks.

Plays by American Women: The Early Years. Ed. by Judith Barlow. 368p. 1981. pap. 3.95 o.p. (ISBN 0-380-76620-5, 76620-5, Bard). Avon.

Plays by Scots 1660-1800. Terence Tobin. LC 73-82159. 255p. 1974. text ed. 25.00 o.p. (ISBN 0-87745-047-1). U of Iowa Pr.

Plays for an Imaginary Theater. Judson Jerome. LC 79-107339. 296p. 1970. 29.95 o.p. (ISBN 0-252-00103-6). U of Ill Pr.

Plays for Clowns in Christ: Four Short Plays for the Fun of Playing!! Richard Urdahl. LC 72-91527. (Open Bks.). (Illus.). 160p. 1973. pap. 2.95 o.p. (ISBN 0-8006-0145-9, 1-145, Fortress). Augsburg Fortress.

Plays: Four. Noel Coward. 512p. (Orig.). 1981. pap. 9.95 o.s.i. (ISBN 0-394-17943-9, B-462, BC). Grove.

Plays in Review: 1956-1980. Ed. by Gareth Evans & Barbara L. Evans. 256p. 1985. 17.95 o.p. (ISBN 0-416-01171-3, 9684). Routledge Chapman & Hall.

Plays Introduction One. 352p. (Orig.). 1984. pap. 9.95 o.p. (ISBN 0-571-13038-0). Faber & Faber.

Plays of Arthur Murphy, 4 vols. Arthur Murphy. Ed. by Paula R. Backscheider. LC 78-66610. (Eighteenth-Century English Drama Ser.: Vol. 30). 1980. Set. lib. bdg. 290.00 o.p. (ISBN 0-8240-3604-2); lib. bdg. 50.00 ea. o.p. Garland Pub.

Plays of Charles Gildon. Charles Gildon. Ed. by Paula R. Backscheider. LC 78-66609. (Eighteenth-Century English Drama Ser.: Vol. 17). 1979. lib. bdg. 73.00 o.p. (ISBN 0-8240-3591-7). Garland Pub.

Plays of Colley Cibber, 2 vols. Colley Cibber. Ed. by Rodney Hayley. LC 78-66634. (Eighteenth Century English Drama Ser.). 1980. Set. lib. bdg. 145.00 o.p. (ISBN 0-8240-3582-8). Garland Pub.

Plays of David Garrick, 4 vols. David Garrick. Ed. by Gerald Berkowitz. (Eighteenth Century English Drama Ser.). 1981. lib. bdg. 290.00 o.p. (ISBN 0-8240-3590-9). Garland Pub.

Plays of Edward Moore. Ed. by J. Paul Hunter. LC 78-66606. (Eighteenth Century English Drama Ser.). 1982. lib. bdg. 73.00 o.p. (ISBN 0-8240-3603-4). Garland Pub.

Plays of Eliza Haywood. Valerie C. Rudolph. LC 78-66619. (Eighteenth Century English Drama Ser.). 1982. lib. bdg. 73.00 o.p. (ISBN 0-8240-3592-5). Garland Pub.

Plays of Elizabeth Inchbald, 2 Vols. Elizabeth Inchbald. Ed. by Paula R. Backscheider. LC 78-66648. (Eighteenth Century English Drama Ser.). lib. bdg. 145.00 o.p. (ISBN 0-8240-3597-6). Garland Pub.

Plays of George Chapman: The Comedies. George Chapman. Ed. by Alan Holaday. LC 69-11044. 594p. 1970. 39.95 o.p. (ISBN 0-252-78423-5). U of Ill Pr.

Plays of George Chapman: The Comedies. Allan Holaday. 1982. 90.00 o.p. (ISBN 0-85991-266-3, Pub. by Boydell & Brewer). Longwood Pub Group.

Plays of George Colman, the Younger. George the Younger Colman. Ed. by Peter A. Tasch. (Eighteenth Century English Drama Ser.). 1981. lib. bdg. 145.00 o.p. (ISBN 0-8240-3585-2). Garland Pub.

Plays of George Lillo, 2 Vols. George Lillo. Ed. by Trudy Drucker. LC 78-66658. (Eighteenth-Century English Drama Ser.: Vol. 27). 1980. lib. bdg. 145.00 o.p. (ISBN 0-8240-3601-8). Garland Pub.

Plays of Grillparzer. G. A. Wells. 1969. 21.00 o.p. (ISBN 0-08-012950-1); pap. 10.25 o.p. (ISBN 0-08-012949-8). Pergamon.

Plays of Hannah Cowley, 2 vols. Hannah Cowley. Ed. by Frederick M. Link. LC 78-66646. (Eighteenth-Century English Drama Ser.: Vol. 12). 1980. Set. lib. bdg. 145.00 o.p. (ISBN 0-8240-3586-0); lib. bdg. 50.00 ea. o.p. Garland Pub.

Plays of Henry Carey. Henry Carey. Ed. by Samuel C. Macey. LC 78-66613. (Eighteenth Century English Drama Ser.). 1980. lib. bdg. 73.00 o.p. (ISBN 0-8240-3580-1). Garland Pub.

Plays of Henry Medwall: A Critical Edition. M. E. Moeslein. LC 79-54353. (Renaissance Drama Ser.). 400p. 1982. lib. bdg. 53.00 o.p. (ISBN 0-8240-4470-3). Garland Pub.

Plays of Hugh Kelly. Hugh Kelly. Ed. by Larry Carver. LC 78-66653. (Eighteenth Century English Drama Ser.). 1980. lib. bdg. 73.00 o.p. (ISBN 0-8240-3600-X). Garland Pub.

Plays of Isaac Bickerstaff, 3 vols. Issac Bickerstaff. Ed. by Peter A. Tasch. (Eighteenth Century English Drama Ser.). 1981. lib. bdg. 218.00 o.p. (ISBN 0-8240-3578-X). Garland Pub.

Plays of J. M. Barrie. James M. Barrie. 1928. 8.95 o.s.i. (ISBN 0-684-10017-7, ScribT). Scribner.

Plays of James Boaden. James Boaden. Ed. by P. R. Backscheider & Steven Cohan. LC 78-66608. (Eighteenth Century English Drama Ser.). lib. bdg. 73.00 o.p. (ISBN 0-8240-3579-8). Garland Pub.

Plays of James Thomson. James Thomson. Ed. by Paula R. Backscheider. LC 78-66637. (Eighteenth-Century English Drama Ser.: Vol. 35). 1980. lib. bdg. 73.00 o.p. (ISBN 0-8240-3609-3). Garland Pub.

Plays of John Dennis. John Dennis. Ed. by Paula R. Backscheider. LC 78-66657. (Eighteenth-Century English Drama Ser.: Vol. 14). 1980. lib. bdg. 73.00 o.p. (ISBN 0-8240-3588-7). Garland Pub.

Plays of John Hoole. John Hoole. Ed. by Donald T. Siebert & Paula R. Backscheider. LC 78-66635. (Eighteenth-Century English Drama Ser.: Vol. 21). 1980. lib. bdg. 73.00 o.p. (ISBN 0-8240-3595-X). Garland Pub.

Plays of John Marston, 3 vols. John Marston. Repr. of 1934 ed. 225.00x o.p. (ISBN 0-403-04206-2). Somerset Pub.

Plays of John O'Keefe, 4 vols. John O'Keefe. Ed. by Frederick M. Link. (Eighteenth Century English Drama Ser.). 1981. lib. bdg. 290.00 o.p. (ISBN 0-8240-3605-0). Garland Pub.

Plays of Mary Pix & Catherine Trotter, 2 Vols. Mary Pix & Catherine Trotter. Ed. by Edna L. Steeves & P. R. Backscheider. LC 78-66620. (Eighteenth Century English Drama Ser.). Set. lib. bdg. 145.00 o.p. (ISBN 0-8240-3606-9). Garland Pub.

Plays of Oscar Wilde. Oscar Wilde. LC 83-42944. 6.95 o.s.i. (ISBN 0-394-60490-3). Modern Lib.

Plays of Richard Cumberland: Eighteenth Century English Drama Ser, 3 Vols. Richard Cumberland. Ed. by Roberta F. Borkat. LC 78-66651. lib. bdg. 436.00 o.p. (ISBN 0-8240-3587-9). Garland Pub.

Plays of Robert Jephson. Robert Jephson. Ed. by Temple Maynard & Paula R. Backscheider. LC 78-66647. (Eighteenth-Century English Drama Ser.: Vol. 24). 1980. lib. bdg. 73.00 o.p. (ISBN 0-8240-3598-4). Garland Pub.

Plays of Samuel Johnson of Cheshire. Samuel Johnson. Ed. by P. R. Backscheider & Valerie C. Rudolph. LC 78-66642. (Eighteenth Century English Drama Ser.). lib. bdg. 73.00 o.p. (ISBN 0-8240-3599-2). Garland Pub.

Plays of Susanna Centlivre, 3 vols. Susanna Centlivre. Ed. by Richard C. Frushell. LC 78-66629. (Eighteenth Century English Drama Ser.). 1437p. 1982. lib. bdg. 218.00 o.p. (ISBN 0-8240-3581-X). Garland Pub.

Plays of Tehophilus & Susanna Cibber. Tehophilus Cibber & Susanna Cibber. Ed. by David Mann. (Eighteen Century English Drama Ser.). 1981. lib. bdg. 73.00 o.p. (ISBN 0-8240-3583-6). Garland Pub.

Plays of Thomas Holcroft, 2 vols. Thomas Holcroft. Ed. by Joseph Rosenblum. LC 78-66630. (Eighteenth Century English Drama Ser.). 1980. Set. lib. bdg. 145.00 o.p. (ISBN 0-8240-3594-1). Garland Pub.

Plays: One. Noel Coward. 384p. (Orig.). 1981. pap. 9.95 o.s.i. (ISBN 0-394-17940-4, B-459, BC). Grove.

Plays: One. Terence Rattigan. LC 81-83895. 288p. (Orig.). 1982. pap. 5.95 o.s.i. (ISBN 0-394-17743-6, B-467, BC). Grove.

Plays, Prose Writings, & Poems. Oscar Wilde. 1980. Repr. of 1975 ed. 9.95x o.p. (ISBN 0-460-00858-7, Evman); pap. 4.50x o.p. (ISBN 0-460-01858-2). Biblio Dist.

Plays: Three. Noel Coward. 432p. (Orig.). 1981. pap. 9.95 o.s.i. (ISBN 0-394-17942-0, B-461, BC). Grove.

Plays: Two. Noel Coward. 384p. (Orig.). 1981. pap. 9.95 o.s.i. (ISBN 0-394-17941-2, B-460, BC). Grove.

Plays, Vol. 4: Everything in the Garden, Malcolm, the Ballad of the Sad Cafe. Edward Albee. LC 81-3616. 512p. 1982. pap. 10.95 o.s.i. (ISBN 0-689-70616-2, Atheneum). Macmillan.

Playtime. Sue Tarsky. (Time to Talk Ser.). (Illus.). 32p. (ps-2). 1983. 1.50 o.s.i. (ISBN 0-671-47109-0, Little Simon). S&S.

Playtime. Zokeisha. (Puffies Ser.). (Illus.). 8p. (ps). 1982. pap. 3.40 o.s.i. (ISBN 0-671-44845-5, Little Simon). S&S.

Playtime! Americans at Leisure. Mark Jury. LC 77-73123. (Illus.). 1977. pap. 5.95 o.p. (ISBN 0-15-672037-X, Harv). HarBraceJ.

Playtime in Africa. Efua Sutherland. (Illus.). (gr. 2-6). 1962. PLB 6.95 o.p. (ISBN 0-689-20589-9, Atheneum). Macmillan.

Playtime Rhymes. Illus. by Blanche F. Wright. (Real Mother Goose Mini Boxed Set Ser.). (Illus.). (ps-1). bds. 5.95 o.p. (ISBN 0-02-689018-6, Checkerboard Pr). Macmillan.

Playtime with Music. rev. ed. Marion Abeson & Charity Bailey. (Illus.). 1952. 4.95 o.p. (ISBN 0-87140-999-2). Liveright.

Playtime, Worktime. Peter Seymour. (Turn & Learn Bks.). (Illus.). 8p. (ps-1). 1984. 5.95 o.s.i. (ISBN 0-02-782140-4). Macmillan.

Playwright As Thinker. Eric Bentley. LC 55-5157. (YA) 1967. pap. 6.95 o.p. (ISBN 0-15-672040-X, Harv). HarBraceJ.

Playwright's Theatre: The English Stage Company of the Royal Court. Jerry Browne. 160p. 1975. 12.95 o.p. (ISBN 0-8464-1330-2). Beekman Pubs.

Plea Bargaining. 1983. 37.50 o.p. (ISBN 0-317-43441-1, LEG-SIM 594). Dushkin Pub.

Pleasant Dreams. Anna B. Francis. LC 83-6171. (Illus.). 32p. (gr. k-2). 1983. 11.95 o.p. (ISBN 0-03-060574-1). H Holt & Co.

Pleasant Memoirs of the Marquis De Bradomin. Ramon Valle-Inclan. Tr. by May Heywood Broun & Thomas Walsh. LC 76-28508. 1983. Repr. of 1924 ed. 35.00x o.p. (ISBN 0-86527-294-8). Fertig.

Pleasant Paths. Vance Havner. (Direction Bks.). 96p. 1983. pap. 2.95 o.p. (ISBN 0-8010-4268-2). Baker Bk.

Pleasant Places. Samuel A. Schreiner, Jr. LC 76-8639. 1977. 8.95 o.p. (ISBN 0-87795-140-3, Arbor Hse). Morrow.

Pleasant River. Dale R. Coman. (Illus.). 1976. pap. 3.95 o.p. (ISBN 0-89272-031-X). Down East.

Please Change Me, God! Donald L. Deffner. 128p. 1987. pap. 6.50 o.p. (ISBN 0-570-03994-0, 12-3022). Concordia.

Please Dr., I'd Rather Do It Myself with Vitamins & Minerals. LaDean Griffin. 1979. pap. 3.95 o.p. (ISBN 0-89036-120-7). Hawkes Pub Inc.

Please Don't Eat the Daisies. Jean Kerr. LC 57-12467. (Illus.). 1959. 4.95 o.p. (ISBN 0-385-04860-2). Doubleday.

Please Explain. Isaac Asimov. LC 73-7908. (Illus.). 224p. (gr. 7 up). 1973. 5.95 o.s.i. (ISBN 0-395-17517-8). HM.

Please, God: Prayers for Young Children. Ron Klug & Lyn Klug. LC 80-67799. 32p. (Orig.). (ps-1). 1981. pap. 4.95 o.p. (ISBN 0-8066-1861-2, 10-4999, Augsburg). Augsburg Fortress.

Please Love Me. Keith Miller. 316p. 1985. pap. 8.95 o.p. (ISBN 0-8499-3021-9, 3021-9). Word Bks.

Please Make Me Cry! Cookie Rodriguez. 1974. pap. 2.95 o.p. (ISBN 0-88368-042-4). Whitaker Hse.

Please Quote Me: Selected Poems. Alice G. Gaydos. 64p. 1980. 5.00 o.p. (ISBN 0-682-49626-X). Exposition-Phoenix.

Please Save My World: Children Speak Out Against Nuclear War. Ed. by Bill Adler. (Illus.). 80p. 1984. 8.95 o.p. (ISBN 0-87795-634-0, Arbor Hse). Morrow.

Please Talk to Me, God! Donald Deffner. (Continued Applied Christianity). 1983. pap. 2.08 o.p. (ISBN 0-570-03899-5, 12-2981). Concordia.

Please Touch. Edwin McMahon & Peter Campbell. 48p. pap. 4.95 o.p. (LL9210). Sheed & Ward MO.

Pleasure & Danger: Exploring Female Sexuality. Ed. by Carole Vance. 350p. 1984. cloth 25.00X o.p. (ISBN 0-7100-9974-6); pap. 11.95 o.p. (ISBN 0-7102-0248-2). Routledge Chapman & Hall.

Pleasure-Dome. Judith Liederman. LC 80-66503. 384p. 1981. 14.50 o.p. (ISBN 0-87795-278-7, Arbor Hse). Morrow.

Pleasure in Words. Eugene Maleska. 1981. 15.95 o.p. (ISBN 0-671-24881-2). S&S.

Pleasure of Being Oneself. C. E. Joad. 1951. (ISBN 0-8022-0804-5). Philos Lib.

Pleasure of Their Company. Alister Kershaw. LC 85-22603. (Illus.). 199p. 1987. 19.50 o.p. (ISBN 0-7022-1987-8). U of Queensland Pr.

Pleasure of Their Company: How to Have More Fun with Your Children. Ed. by William Hooks et al. LC 80-70382. 480p. (Orig.). 1981. pap. 9.95 o.p. (ISBN 0-8019-6882-8). Chilton.

Pleasure of Your Company. Diana Von Welanetz & Paul Von Welanetz. LC 75-41855. (Illus.). 1979. pap. 8.95 o.p. (ISBN 0-689-70593-X, 253, Atheneum). Macmillan.

Pleasure Principle. Snoo Wilson. 1981. pap. 6.95 o.p. (ISBN 0-413-32010-3, NO. 6482). Heinemann Ed.

Pleasure, Reward, Preference: Their Nature, Determinants, & Role in Behavior (Based Upon a Symposium Held at the Klarskovgaard Training Institute, Near Korsor, Denmark, June, 1972) D. E. Berlyne & K. B. Madsen. 1973. 66.00 o.p. (ISBN 0-12-092550-8). Acad Pr.

Pleasures & Palaces: After-School Activities of Russian Children. Miriam Morton. LC 72-76477. (gr. 5-8). 1972. 5.25 o.p. (ISBN 0-689-30057-3, Atheneum). Macmillan.

Pleasures of Chinese Cooking. Grace Z. Chu. (Illus.). 239p. 1975. pap. 6.75 o.p. (ISBN 0-671-22181-7, Fireside). S&S.

Pleasures of Philosophy. Charles Frankel. LC 76-158085. 1972. 8.95 o.p. (ISBN 0-393-01089-9). Norton.

Pleasures: Women Write Erotica. Lonnie G. Barbach. LC 84-5922. 264p. 1984. 14.95 o.p. (ISBN 0-385-18811-0). Doubleday.

Plebeians Rehearse the Uprising. Gunter Grass. Tr. by Ralph Manheim. LC 66-23810. (Orig.). 1966. pap. 2.35 o.p. (ISBN 0-15-672050-7, HB115, Harv). HarBraceJ.

Plecoptera Nymphs of North America see Thomas Say Foundation Publications.

Plecoptera or Stoneflies of America North of Mexico see Thomas Say Foundation Publications.

Pleistocene Mammals of Florida. Ed. by S. David Webb. LC 74-3115. (Illus.). 270p. 1974. 12.00 o.p. (ISBN 0-8130-0361-X). U Presses Fla.

Pleistocene Mustelidae. S. H. Reynolds. Repr. of 1912 ed. 16.00 o.p. (ISBN 0-384-50426-4). Johnson Repr.

Pleneurethic: A World Class Philosophy. Richard B. Collier. (Illus.). 368p. 1981. 20.00 o.p. (ISBN 0-682-49753-3). Exposition-Phoenix.

Pleneurethic: Its Evolution & Scientific Basis. Richard B. Collier. 318p. 1980. 15.00 o.p. (ISBN 0-682-49623-5). Exposition-Phoenix.

Pleneurethic: Way of Life, System of Therapeutics. Richard B. Collier. (Illus.). 1979. 10.00 o.p. (ISBN 0-682-49372-4). Exposition-Phoenix.

Plenty. Dorothy L. Thompson. LC 84-91266. 187p. 1985. 12.95 o.p. (ISBN 0-533-06353-1). Vantage.

Plenty & Want: A Social History of Diet in England from 1815 to the Present Day. John Burnett. 388p. (Orig.). 1985. pap. 10.95 o.p. (ISBN 0-85967-461-4, NO. 9344). Routledge Chapman & Hall.

Pleural Diseases. Richard W. Light. LC 83-760. (Illus.). 269p. 1983. text ed. 33.00 o.p. (ISBN 0-8121-0886-8). Lea & Febiger.

Plexus. Henry Miller. (Orig.). 1965. pap. 6.95 o.s.i. (ISBN 0-394-17431-3, B100, BC). Grove.

Plippen's Palace. Madye L. Chastain. LC 61-6346. (Illus.). (gr. 4-7). 1961. 4.50 o.p. (ISBN 0-15-262792-8, HJ). HarBraceJ.

PLL Synthesizer Cookbook. Harold Kinley. 13.95 o.p. (ISBN 0-8306-9707-1, 1243); pap. 7.95 o.p. (ISBN 0-8306-1243-2). TAB Bks.

Plop! Plop! 1982. 3.95 o.p. (ISBN 0-8351-1245-4). China Bks.

Plot. Elizabeth Dipple. (Critical Idiom Ser.: Vol. 12). 1970. pap. 5.50x o.p. (ISBN 0-416-19780-9, NO. 2165). Routledge Chapman & Hall.

Plot It Yourself Horror Stories, No. 8: Dungeon Demons. Hilary Milton. Ed. by Diane Arico. (Illus.). 128p. (gr. 3-7). 1985. pap. 3.95 o.s.i. (ISBN 0-671-54448-9). Wanderer Bks.

Plot to Kill the Pope. Paul B. Henze. 224p. 1984. 14.95 o.s.i. (ISBN 0-684-18060-X, ScribT). Scribner.

Plot to Kill the Pope. Paul B. Henze. 224p. 1985. pap. 4.50 o.s.i. (ISBN 0-684-18357-9). Scribner.

Plot to Replace the Constitution. Robert L. Preston. 128p. 1972. pap. 2.00 o.p. (ISBN 0-89036-026-X). Hawkes Pub Inc.

Plot to Steal Florida: James Madison's Phony War. Joseph B. Smith. 356p. 1983. 16.95 o.p. (ISBN 0-87795-477-1, Arbor Hse). Morrow.

Plot-Your-Own-Adventure: Distress Call. William Rotsler. Ed. by Wendy Barish. (Star Trek II). (Illus., Orig.). (gr. 3-7). 1982. pap. 2.85 o.s.i. (ISBN 0-671-46389-6). Wanderer Bks.

Plot-Your-Own Horror Stories: Craven House Horrors, No. 1. Hilary Milton. Ed. by Meg Schneider. LC 82-7020. (Illus.). 128p. (Orig.). (gr. 3-7). 1982. pap. 2.85 o.s.i. (ISBN 0-671-45631-8). Wanderer Bks.

Plough in Field Arable: Western Agribusiness in Third World Agriculture. Sarah P. Voll. LC 80-50490. (Illus.). 223p. 1980. 20.00x o.p. (ISBN 0-87451-186-0). U Pr of New Eng.

Plow a New Furrow. Emma Hedman. 176p. (Orig.). 1985. pap. 8.95 o.s.i. (ISBN 0-934318-47-6). Falcon Pr MT.

Plow-Horse Cavalry: The Carey Creek Boys of the Thirty-Fourth Texas. Robert S. Weddle. LC 74-75208. 1974. 12.00 o.p. (ISBN 0-89052-004-6). Madrona Pr.

Plowden: Circus Press Agent. Gene Plowden. 1984. 12.95 o.s.i. (ISBN 0-87004-299-8). Caxton.

Plowing My Own Furrow. Howard W. Moore. LC 84-22610. (Illus.). 1985. 12.45 o.p. (ISBN 0-393-01977-2). Norton.

Pluie et le Beau Temps. Jacques Prevert. (Coll. Folio). 1955. pap. 4.50 o.p. (ISBN 0-685-23897-0, 847). Schoenhof.

Plum Bun: A Novel Without a Moral. Jessie Fauset. 400p. 1985. 15.95 o.p. (ISBN 0-86358-057-2, Pandora Pr); pap. 8.95 o.p. (ISBN 0-86358-044-0, Pandora Pr). Routledge Chapman & Hall.

Plum Cobbler. Bill Elliott. 1977. 4.00 o.p. (ISBN 0-682-48864-X). Exposition-Phoenix.

Plumbing: Cold Water Supplies. Hall. 1981. pap. 15.95 o.p. (ISBN 0-442-30393-9). Van Nos Reinhold.

Plumbing Estimating Handbook. Joseph J. Galeno. LC 76-57182. (Plumbing Ser.). 256p. 1976. pap. text ed. 19.95 o.s.i. (ISBN 0-8273-1764-6). Delmar.

Plumbing Estimating Handbook. Joseph J. Galeno. 160p. 1976. 28.95 o.p. (ISBN 0-442-12157-1). Van Nos Reinhold.

Plumbing: Hot Water Supplies. F. Hall. 1981. pap. 15.95 o.p. (ISBN 0-442-30395-5). Van Nos Reinhold.

Plumes & Visibility. Ed. by Warren White. (Illus.). 230p. 1982. pap. 73.00 o.p. (ISBN 0-08-028733-6); pap. 36.00 suppl. o.p. (ISBN 0-08-028741-7). Pergamon.

Plunderbund & Proletariat: A History of the IWW in B. C. Jack Scott. 169p. 1975. pap. 3.95 o.p. (ISBN 0-919888-04-6). Left Bank.

Pluperfect of Love. Dorothy Crayder. LC 79-154758. (gr. 5-8). 1971. PLB 5.25 o.p. (ISBN 0-689-20677-1, Atheneum). Macmillan.

Plural Societies & New States: A Conceptual Analysis. Robert Jackson. LC 77-620004. (Research Ser.: No. 30). 1977. pap. 2.00x o.s.i. (ISBN 0-87725-130-4). U of Cal Intl St.

Pluralities-Nineteen Eighty-Pluralite. Philip Fry. Ed. by Jessica Bradley. 1980. pap. 19.95 o.s.i. (ISBN 0-226-56478-9, Dist. by National Museum of Canada). U of Chicago Pr.

Plurals. Joan Hanson. LC 78-70463. (Joan Hanson Word Bks.). (Illus.). (gr. k-3). 1979. PLB 4.95 o.p. (ISBN 0-8225-1114-2). Lerner Pubns.

Plutarch's Historical Methods: An Analysis of the Mulierum Virtutes. Philip A. Stadter. LC 65-13850. 1965. 13.50x o.p. (ISBN 0-674-67400-6). Harvard U Pr.

Plutocrats & Socialists: Reports by German Diplomats & Agents on the American Labor Movement, 1878 to 1917. Ed. by Dirk Hoerder. 422p. 1981. lib. bdg. 40.00 o.p. (ISBN 3-598-10347-6). K G Saur.

Plutonium Fuel Cycle: Proceedings, American Nuclear Society Topical Meeting, Bar Harbour, May 2-4. 320p. 14.00 o.p. (ISBN 0-317-33038-1, 700019). Am Nuclear Soc.

Plutonium, Health Implications for Man: Proceedings of the 2nd Los Alamos Life Sciences Symposium. J. W. Healy. 1976. 50.00 o.p. (ISBN 0-08-019751-5). Pergamon.

Plutonium-Oxygen & Uranium-Plutonium-Oxygen Systems: A Thermochemical Assessment. (Technical Reports Ser.: No. 79). (Illus.). 86p. 1967. pap. 9.00 o.p. (ISBN 92-0-145167-9, IAEA). UNIPUB.

Plutonium Recycle: Reports of Three Contract Studies, 3 pts. in. Incl. Pt.i. Legal Aspects of Nuclear Regulatory Commission's Provisional Policy Statement on GESMO. Gerald Charnoff & J. E. Silberg; Part II. A Cost Impact Analysis of Delay in Plutonium Recycle. W. V. Macnabb et al; Part III. (Technical & Economic Reports: Nuclear Fuelcycle). 120p. 1975. 20.00 o.p. (ISBN 0-318-13587-6); members 10.00 o.p. (ISBN 0-318-13588-4). US Coun Energy Awareness.

Plymouth: A New History, 2 vols. Crispin Gill. Incl. Vol. 1. Ice Age of Elizabethans (ISBN 0-7153-4018-2); Vol. 2. Sixteen Hundred & Three to Present Day (ISBN 0-7153-7617-9). LC 66-6718. (Illus.). 1979. 23.50 ea. o.p. David & Charles.

Plymouth & De Soto Story. F. Donald Butler. Ed. by George H. Dammann. LC 77-93182. (Automotive Ser.). (Illus.). 1979. 29.95 o.p. (ISBN 0-912612-14-2). Crestline.

Plymouth Arrow: 1976-1980 Shop Manual. Ed. by Eric Jorgensen. (Illus.). pap. 12.95 o.p. (ISBN 0-89287-275-6, A178). Clymer Pub.

Plymouth Horizon: 1978-1981 Shop Manual. Ed. by Eric Jorgensen. (Illus.). pap. text ed. 11.95 o.p. (ISBN 0-89287-298-5, A177). Clymer Pub.

Plymouth Owner's Handbook, 1946-1955. Clymer Publications. (Illus.). 1956. pap. 7.00 o.p. (ISBN 0-89287-272-1, A281). Clymer Pub.

Plymouth Tune-Up-Maintenance, 1967-1978 Models. Ed. by Jeff Robinson. (Illus.). pap. 8.95 o.p. (ISBN 0-89287-142-3, A-179). Clymer Pub.

Plymouth Volare: 1976-1979 Shop Manual. Ed. by Eric Jorgensen. (Illus.). 328p. (Orig.). pap. text ed. 11.95 o.p. (ISBN 0-89287-312-4, A236). Clymer Pub.

Plywood Projects Illustrated. Kenn Oberrecht. (Illus.). 256p. 1983. 24.95 o.s.i. (ISBN 0-684-17972-5, ScribT); pap. 14.95 o.p. Scribner.

PMR Spectroscopy in Medicinal & Biological Chemistry. Ed. by A. F. Casy. 1972. 74.00 o.p. (ISBN 0-12-164050-7). Acad Pr.

PMS: An Infobook for Teenage Women, Their Friends & Families. Gilda Berger. LC 85-14473. (Illus.). 96p. (gr. 7-12). 1985. pap. 6.95 o.p. (ISBN 0-89793-035-5). Hunter Hse.

Pneumatic & Hydraulic Components & Instruments in Automatic Control: Proceedings of the IFAC Symposium, Warsaw, Poland, May, 1980. IFAC Symposium Staff. Ed. by H. J. Leskiewicz & M. Zaremba. LC 80-41658. (IFAC Proceedings Ser.). (Illus.). 308p. 1981. 85.00 o.p. (ISBN 0-08-027317-3). Pergamon.

Pneumatic Conveying of Bulk Materials. Chemical Engineering Magazine Editors & Milton N. Kraus. (Chemical Engineering Bks.). 352p. 1980. text ed. 48.00 o.p. (ISBN 0-07-010724-6). McGraw.

Pneumatic Data, Vol. 2. Trade & Technical Press Editors. 130p. 1967. 20.00x o.p. (ISBN 0-85461-012-X, Pub by Trade & Tech England). Gower Pub Co.

Pneumatic Handbook. 5th ed. Ed. by Trade & Technical Press Ltd. (Illus.). 1978. 115.00x o.p. Coronet Bks.

Pneumatic Power Glossary. Trade & Technical Press Editors. 80p. 1970. 17.00x o.p. (ISBN 0-686-65529-X, Pub. by Trade & Tech England). Gower Pub Co.

Pnin. Vladimir Nabokov. 1976. pap. 2.95 o.p. (ISBN 0-380-00819-X, 62182-7, Bard). Avon.

Pnume. Jack Vance. 224p. 1983. lib. bdg. 15.95 o.p. (ISBN 0-934438-57-9). Underwood-Miller.

Poacher. H. E. Bates. 1985. 13.95 o.p. (ISBN 0-317-53146-8, Large Print Bks). G K Hall.

Poacher's Companion. E. G. Walsh. (Illus.). 286p. 1983. 22.00 o.p. (ISBN 0-85115-177-9, Pub. by Boydell & Brewer). Longwood Pub Group.

Pocket Beatles. Ed. by Milton Okun. (Pocket Guitar Ser.). 253p. (Orig.). 1980. pap. 4.95 o.s.i. (ISBN 0-89524-126-9, 1323). Cherry Lane.

Pocket Billiards. Jean Balukas. Ed. by Joel H. Cohen. LC 78-3193. (Illus.). 1980. 9.95 o.p. (ISBN 0-689-10926-1, Atheneum). Macmillan.

Pocket Book Crossword, No. 11. Margaret Farrar. 1985. pap. 2.50 o.s.i. (ISBN 0-671-55151-5). PB.

Pocket Book Crossword, No. 12. Margaret Farrar. 1985. pap. 2.50 o.s.i. (ISBN 0-671-55152-3). PB.

Pocket Book of Crossword Puzzles, No. 22. Margaret Farrar. (Orig.). 1980. pap. 1.75 o.s.i. (ISBN 0-671-82919-X). PB.

Pocket Book of Pro Football, 1980. Ed. by Herb Furlow. (Orig.). 1980. pap. 2.75 o.s.i. (ISBN 0-671-41019-9). PB.

Pocket Dictionary. rev. ed. Ed. by Houghton Mifflin Company Staff. LC 78-13455. (Illus.). 256p. 1978. pap. text ed. 21.00 o.p. (ISBN 0-395-27224-6). HM.

Pocket Dictionary: English-Slovak-English. 6th ed. J. Smejkalova et al. 793p. 1979. text ed. 12.50x o.p. (C170). Vanous.

Pocket Encyclopedia of California Wines. Robert Thompson. 1980. pap. 4.95 o.s.i. (ISBN 0-671-41791-6). S&S.

Pocket Encyclopedia of Calories & Nutrition. Arnold Bender & Tony Nash. 1979. pap. 4.95 o.s.i. (ISBN 0-671-24839-1). S&S.

Pocket English-Croatian-English Dictionary: Short Grammar. 40th ed. B. Grujic. 624p. (Serbian, Croatian & Eng.). 1985. text ed. 18.00x o.p. (Y-647). Vanous.

Pocket Gems. Nelson Mink. 128p. 1985. pap. 2.95 o.p. (ISBN 0-8423-4927-8). Tyndale.

Pocket Guide to Cambridge. Date not set. (ISBN 0-86145-671-8, Pub. by Auto Assn England). Salem Hse Pubs.

Pocket Guide to Depression Glass. 5th ed. Gene Florence. (Illus.). 160p. 1987. pap. 9.95 o.p. (ISBN 0-89145-344-X). Collector Bks.

Pocket Guide to Differential Diagnosis. Eastham. 474p. 1980. pap. 17.50 o.p. (ISBN 0-7236-0542-4, Pub. by John Wright UK). Butterworth.

Pocket Guide to Dublin. Date not set. (ISBN 0-86145-672-6, Pub. by Auto Assn England). Salem Hse Pubs.

Pocket Guide to Edinburgh. Date not set. (ISBN 0-86145-673-4, Pub. by Auto Assn England). Salem Hse Pubs.

Pocket Guide to French Food & Wine. Tessa Youell & George Kimball. 1986. pap. 5.95 o.p. (ISBN 0-671-62205-6, Fireside). S&S.

Pocket Guide to Glasgow. Date not set. (ISBN 0-86145-674-2, Pub. by Auto Assn England). Salem Hse Pubs.

Pocket Guide to Indoor Plants. George Seddon. (Illus.). 1980. pap. 4.95 o.p. (ISBN 0-671-25249-6). S&S.

Pocket Guide to Injectable Drugs. 3rd ed. Lawrence A. Trissel. vi, 209p. 1987. pap. text ed. 15.00 o.p. (ISBN 0-930530-72-1). Am Soc Hosp Pharm.

Pocket Guide to Northern & Central Europe. Ed. by Philippe Gloaguen & Pierre Josse. (Collier World Traveler Ser.). (Illus.). 192p. 1985. pap. 6.95 o.p. (ISBN 0-02-097030-7, Collier). Macmillan.

Pocket Guide to Nursing Diagnosis. Kim & McFarland. 1984. pap. 11.95 o.p. (ISBN 0-8016-2672-2). Mosby.

Pocket Guide to York. Date not set. (ISBN 0-86145-675-0, Pub. by Auto Assn England). Salem Hse Pubs.

Pocket History of Free Masonry. Fred L. Pick & G. Norman Knight. 1954. (ISBN 0-8022-1972-1). Philos Lib.

Pocket in a Petticoat: Memoirs. Florence E. Barrett. 1974. 4.00 o.p. (ISBN 0-682-48075-4, Lochinvar). Exposition-Phoenix.

Pocket Income Tax Calculator. 5th ed. Alfred G. Yates, Jr. LC 85-63768. 80p. 1986. pap. 5.65 o.p. (ISBN 0-87218-441-2). Natl Underwriter.

Pocket Interlinear New Testament. Ed. by Jay P. Green. 1981. pap. 5.95 o.p. (ISBN 0-8010-3777-8). Baker Bk.

Pocket Nurse Guide to Nutrition. Williams. 1986. 14.95 o.p. (ISBN 0-8016-4645-6). Mosby.

Pocket Nurse Guide to Physical Assessment. Potter. 1985. pap. 16.95 o.p. (ISBN 0-8016-3962-X). Mosby.

Pocket Obstetrics. 10th ed. Stanley Clayton & John R. Newton. (Illus.). 1983. pap. text ed. 8.50 o.p. (ISBN 0-443-02008-6). Churchill.

Pocket Prayer Book: Large-Type Edition. Compiled by Ralph S. Cushman. 1977. 5.00x o.p. (ISBN 0-8358-0361-9). Upper Room.

Pocket Publisher: A Business Communication & Desktop Publishing Style Guide. Ed. by John Spilker & Karen Strudwick. LC 88-62379. (Illus.). 1989. pap. 7.95 o.p. (ISBN 0-945264-03-8). Resolution Busn Pr.

Pocket Size Teddy Bears. Date not set. pap. 4.98 o.p. (ISBN 0-317-03199-6). Gick.

Pocketful of Proverbs. Joan W. Anglund. LC 64-12373. (Illus.). (gr. k-3). 1964. 2.95 o.p. (ISBN 0-15-262955-6, HJ). HarBraceJ.

Pocketguide to the Art Institute of Chicago. Ed. by Robert Sharp. (Illus.). 64p. (Orig.). 1983. pap. 2.00 o.p. (ISBN 0-86559-054-0). Art Inst Chi.

Poco. Garry Smith & Vesta Smith. LC 75-17874. (Illus.). 40p. (Eng. & Span.). (gr. k-3). 1975. 5.95 o.p. (ISBN 0-88468-006-1). Ethridge.

Pocosin Wetlands: An Integrated Analysis of Coastal Plain Freshwater Bogs in North Carolina. Ed. by Curtis J. Richardson. LC 81-7158. 364p. 1982. 33.95 o.p. (ISBN 0-87933-418-5). Van Nos Reinhold.

Pocumtuck Housewife: A Guide to Domestic Cookery. 1986. pap. 4.95 o.p. Morrow.

Podiatric Sports Medicine of the Lower Extremity. 2nd ed. Steven I. Subotnick. 400p. cancelled o.s.i. (ISBN 0-89116-315-8). Hemisphere Pub.

Podzols: Temperate Regions. Ed. by Peter Buurman. (Benchmark Papers in Soil Science). 464p. 1984. 54.95 o.p. (ISBN 0-442-21129-5). Van Nos Reinhold.

Poe Poe Poe Poe Poe Poe Poe. Daniel Hoffman. 1978. pap. 2.95 o.p. (ISBN 0-380-41459-7, Discus). Avon.

Poem As Process. David J. Swanger. 256p. (Orig.). 1974. pap. text ed. 7.95 o.p. (ISBN 0-15-570747-7, HC). HarBraceJ.

Poem As Utterance. R. A. York. 210p. 1986. text ed. 36.95 o.p. (ISBN 0-416-42250-0, 9795); pap. text ed. 13.95 o.p. (ISBN 0-416-42260-8, 9806). Routledge Chapman & Hall.

Poem of the Cid. Cid Campeador. Tr. by Archer M. Huntington. LC 42-50955. Repr. of 1942 ed. 24.00 o.p. (ISBN 0-527-17420-3). Kraus Repr.

Poemes. Andre Breton. (Coll. Soleil). 12.50 o.p. (ISBN 0-685-37236-7). French & Eur.

Poemes Choisis. Joachim Du Bellay. (Illus.). 56p. 1973. 7.95 o.p. (ISBN 0-686-56040-X). French & Eur.

Poems. Evan T. Cole. 1985. 5.95 o.p. (ISBN 0-533-06090-7). Vantage.

Poems. Alexander Scott. Ed. by James Cranstoon. Repr. of 1896 ed. 24.00 o.p. (ISBN 0-384-54440-1). Johnson Repr.

Poems, 2 Vols. Alfred Tennyson. 1965. 6.00x ea. o.p. (Evman). Vol. 1 (ISBN 0-460-00044-6). Vol. 2 (ISBN 0-460-00626-6). Biblio Dist.

Poems. Boris Vetrov. 1985. 3.95 o.s.i. RWCPH.

Poems & Dramas of Fulke Greville First Lord Brooke, 2 vols. Fulke G. Brooke. Repr. of 1939 ed. 49.00 o.p. (ISBN 0-403-04210-0). Somerset Pub.

Poems & Epigrams. Richard O'Connell. pap. 25.00 o.p. (ISBN 0-87556-227-2). Saifer.

Poems & Essays. Edgar Allan Poe. 1975. Repr. of 1927 ed. 12.95x o.p. (ISBN 0-460-00791-2, Evman); pap. 4.50x o.p. (ISBN 0-460-01791-8, Evman). Biblio Dist.

Poems & Prayers of Inspiration. Oleen T. Hinson. 1978. 5.50 o.p. (ISBN 0-682-49108-X). Exposition-Phoenix.

Poems & Problems. Vladimir Nabokov. (McGraw-Hill Paperback Ser.). 1981. pap. text ed. 5.95 o.p. (ISBN 0-07-045726-3). McGraw.

Poems & Prose: 1949-1977. Harold Pinter. LC 78-56046. 1978. 10.00 o.s.i. (ISBN 0-394-50290-6, GP814). Grove.

Poems & Short Stories. Rudyard Kipling. 458p. 1983. 25.00x o.p. (ISBN 0-317-39521-1, Pub. by Collets UK). State Mutual Bk.

Poems & Translations. Thanasis Makaleris. (Illus.). 88p. 1969. 5.00 o.p. Kayak.

Poems Beyond Reality. Gaye De Windt. (Illus.). 126p. 1983. 8.00 o.p. (ISBN 0-682-49997-8). Exposition-Phoenix.

Poems by James Lyndon Willcox. James L. Willcox. 65p. 1986. 5.95 o.p. (ISBN 1-55523-025-3). Winston-Derek.

Poems by Olive Hunt. G. P. Hunt. 1986. 5.95 o.p. Vantage.

Poems by Richard Thomas. Richard Thomas. 1974. pap. 1.25 o.p. (ISBN 0-380-00539-5, 45286). Avon.

Poems for Children. Illus. by Gyo Fujikawa. (Pandaback Ser.). (Illus.). 24p. (ps-3). 1980. PLB 4.99 o.p. (ISBN 0-448-13143-9, G&D); pap. 1.25 o.p. (ISBN 0-448-49616-X). Putnam Pub Group.

Poems for My Mother & the Women I Have Loved. Kimi Reith. Ed. by A. D. Winans. 1978. pap. 3.00x o.p. (ISBN 0-915016-23-0). Second Coming.

Poems for the Fireside. Joseph Marshall. 32p. 1986. 5.75 o.p. (ISBN 0-317-60688-3). Carlton.

Poems from Angola. Michael Wolfers. (African Writers Ser.). 1980. pap. text ed. 7.00 o.p. (ISBN 0-435-90215-6). Heinemann Ed.

Poems from Oby. George MacBeth. LC 82-73012. 72p. (Orig.). 1983. 12.95 o.p. (ISBN 0-689-11373-0, Atheneum); pap. 5.95 o.p. (ISBN 0-689-11374-9). Macmillan.

Poems from the Eighteen-Thirties by a Poor Son of Ireland. Nicholas Duffy. Ed. by George H. Duffy. 1977. 6.50 o.p. (ISBN 0-682-48834-8). Exposition-Phoenix.

Poems from the Heart. Frances C. Emmons. iv, 50p. 1984. pap. 5.95x o.p. (ISBN 0-932269-08-7). Wyndham Hall.

Poems from the Heart. Lorraine B. Swindler. 64p. 1986. 7.00 o.p. (ISBN 0-8062-2793-1). Carlton.

Poems from the Medical World. Howard Sergeant. 192p. 1980. 19.95 o.p. (ISBN 0-85200-289-0). Year Bk Med.

Poems from Williamsburg. G. Maylon Miller. LC 73-82890. (Illus.). 1973. scrapbook (ribbon tied) 3.00 o.p. (ISBN 0-88265-007-6). North Am Intl.

Poems in Context. Lee A. Jacobus & William T. Moynihan. 416p. (Orig.). 1974. pap. text ed. 10.95 o.p. (ISBN 0-15-570652-7, HC). HarBraceJ.

Poems in English. Samuel Beckett. 1964. pap. 2.95 o.p. (ISBN 0-394-17196-9, E379, Ever). Grove.

Poems in Persons: An Introduction to the Psychoanalysis of Literature. Norman N. Holland. 192p. 1975. pap. 3.95 o.p. (ISBN 0-393-00776-6, Norton Lib). Norton.

Poems: Nineteen Sixty-Five to Nineteen Seventy-Five. Seamus Heaney. LC 80-68753. 228p. 1980. 12.95 o.p. (ISBN 0-374-23496-5); pap. 7.95 o.p. (ISBN 0-374-51652-9). FS&G.

Poems, Nineteen Thirty-Eight to Nineteen Forty-Five. Robert Graves. 58p. 1946. 4.95 o.p. (ISBN 0-374-23472-8). FS&G.

Poems Now. Joseph A. Stepka. (Contemporary Poets of Dorrance Ser.). 32p. 1983. 3.95 o.p. (ISBN 0-8059-2890-1). Dorrance.

Poems of American Life. Merrill Moore. 288p. 1958. (ISBN 0-8022-1142-9). Philos Lib.

Poems of Andrew Marvell. Andrew Marvell. Ed. by Hugh MacDonald. (Muses' Library). 206p. 1969. pap. 5.95 o.p. (ISBN 0-7100-4920-X). Routledge Chapman & Hall.

Poems of Black Africa. Ed. by Wole Soyinka. 384p. 1975. 12.95 o.p. (ISBN 0-8090-7747-7); pap. 4.95 o.p. (ISBN 0-8090-1376-2). Hill & Wang.

Poems of Catullus. Catullus. Ed. & tr. by Horace Gregory. 208p. 1972. pap. 3.95 o.p. (ISBN 0-393-00654-9, NortonC). Norton.

Poems of Charles. Charles L. Dickerson. 1977. 4.00 o.p. (ISBN 0-682-48909-3). Exposition-Phoenix.

Poems of Francois Villon. Tr. by Galway Kinnell. (Eng. & Fr.). 1977. 10.00 o.p. (ISBN 0-395-25717-4); pap. 6.95 o.p. (ISBN 0-395-25952-5). HM.

Poems of Gray, Collins, Goldsmith. Thomas Gray. Ed. by Roger Lonsdale. (Annotated English Poets Ser.). 1972. 9.95x o.p. (ISBN 0-393-04366-5). Norton.

Poems of Laura Riding. Laura R. Jackson. LC 79-91169. 420p. 1980. 20.00 o.p. (ISBN 0-89255-044-9). Persea Bks.

Poems of Sappho. Tr. by P. Maurice Hill. 96p. 1954. (ISBN 0-8022-0720-0). Philos Lib.

Poems of Sidney Lanier. Sidney Lanier. Ed. by Mary Lanier. 262p. 1944. 15.00 o.p. (ISBN 0-8203-0249-X). U of Ga Pr.

Poems of Tennyson. Alfred Tennyson. Ed. by Christopher Ricks. (Annotated English Poets Ser.). 1972. 17.50x o.p. (ISBN 0-393-04356-8). Norton.

Poems of the Holocaust. Date not set. pap. (ISBN 0-8052-5059-X). Random.

Poems of the Holocaust: Painful Echoes. (Illus.). 80p. 1985. 12.95 o.p. Schocken.

Poems of the Soul & the Sprit. Roxanne M. Collyer. 40p. 1986. 5.75 o.p. (ISBN 0-8062-2796-6). Carlton.

Poems of To-Day: First & Second Series. Ed. by English Association Staff. LC 77-88079. (Granger Poetry Library). 1976. Repr. of 1915 ed. 27.50x o.p. (ISBN 0-89609-036-1). Roth Pub Inc.

Poems on a Boy's Paintings. 1981. pap. 5.95 o.p. (ISBN 0-8351-0880-5). China Bks.

Poems Pennyeach. James Joyce. 1986. 42.50 o.p. (ISBN 0-317-55098-5). Bern Porter.

Poems: Selected & New, 1950-1974. Adrienne Rich. 256p. 1975. 12.95 o.p. (ISBN 0-393-04392-4). Norton.

Poems: Selected & New, 1950-1974. Adrienne Rich. 272p. 1975. pap. 5.95 o.p. (ISBN 0-393-04395-9). Norton.

Poems, Short Stories & Plays for Youth. Bessie Frazier. 80p. 1980. 6.00 o.p. (ISBN 0-682-49591-3). Exposition-Phoenix.

Poems: The Touch of Love. Paolo Di Iorio. 1977. 4.00 o.p. (ISBN 0-682-48698-1). Exposition-Phoenix.

Poems to Drink By. Adam Haddem. 1979. 4.50 o.p. (ISBN 0-682-49326-0). Exposition-Phoenix.

Poems to Read Aloud. rev. ed. Ed. by Edward Hodnett. 1967. 12.95 o.p. (ISBN 0-393-04292-8). Norton.

Poems Toward the Twenty-First Century. Holly Chetta. LC 84-90189. 58p. 1985. 6.95 o.p. (ISBN 0-533-06246-2). Vantage.

Poesie Critique, Vol. 1. Jean Cocteau. 352p. 1959. 8.95 o.p. (ISBN 0-686-54550-8). French & Eur.

Poesie Graphique. Jean Cocteau. (Illus.). 1974. 25.00 o.p. (ISBN 0-686-54552-4). French & Eur.

Poesies. Joachim Du Bellay. 96p. 1978. 18.95 o.p. (ISBN 0-686-56041-8). French & Eur.

Poesies. Paul Valery. Bd. with Album de Vers Anciens; Jeune Parque; Charmes; Pieces Diverses; Cantate du Narcisse; Amphion; Semiramis. (Coll. Soleil). 14.50 o.p. (ISBN 0-685-36606-5). Schoenhof.

Poesies Completes. Arthur Rimbaud. 256p. 1960. 3.95 o.p. (ISBN 0-686-54739-X). French & Eur.

Poesies Libres. Guillaume Apollinaire. 1978. 16.95 o.p. (ISBN 0-686-51899-3). French & Eur.

Poet & the Donkey. May Sarton. LC 72-80024. (Illus.). 1969. 4.50 o.p. (ISBN 0-393-08590-2). Norton.

Poet: Anthology Nineteen Seventy to Nineteen Eighty-Five. Dick Sutphen. Ed. by Dawn Abbey. 144p. (Orig.). 1985. pap. 5.95 o.p. (ISBN 0-911842-63-2). Valley Sun.

Poet Auden: A Personal Memoir. A. L. Rowse. Ed. by Bill Strachan. LC 87-33975. 144p. 1988. 14.95 o.p. (ISBN 1-55584-198-8). Weidenfeld.

Poet in New York. Federico Garcia Lorca. 1981. pap. 4.95 o.p. (ISBN 0-394-17205-1, E54, Ever). Grove.

Poet Physicians: An Anthology of Medical Poetry Written by Physicians. Ed. by Mary Lou McDonough. LC 78-74819. (Granger Poetry Library). 1979. Repr. of 1945 ed. 23.75x o.p. (ISBN 0-89609-138-4). Roth Pub Inc.

Poetae Latini Minores, Leipzig, 1879-1883, 5 vols. Aemilius Bae Hrens. Ed. by Steele Commager. LC 77-70775. (Latin Poetry Ser.). 1979. Set. lib. bdg. 206.00 o.p. (ISBN 0-8240-2950-X). Garland Pub.

Poetaster's Scrapbook. Lewis E. Walton. LC 84-90087. 85p. 1985. 6.95 o.p. (ISBN 0-533-06165-2). Vantage.

Poetic Edda. Lee M. Hollander. 1962. pap. write for info. o.p. (ISBN 0-292-73330-5). U of Tex Pr.

Poetic Justice. Fred A. Keagle. LC 86-918080. 176p. 1987. text ed. 15.00 o.p. (ISBN 0-682-40324-5). Exposition-Phoenix.

Poetic Meditations. Roland R. Daneault. 64p. 1982. 4.00 o.p. (ISBN 0-682-49883-1). Exposition-Phoenix.

Poetical Tributes to the Memory of Abraham Lincoln. Ed. by J. N. Plotts. 1986. pap. text ed. 6.95x o.p. (ISBN 0-8290-1937-5). Irvington.

Poetical Works of John Keats, 2 vols. John Keats. (Illus.). 211p. 1986. Set. 187.45 o.p. (ISBN 0-86650-187-8). Gloucester Art.

Poetical Works of Oliver Wendell Holmes. Oliver W. Holmes. Intro. by Eleanor M. Tilton. LC 74-30148. (Cambridge Editions Ser.). 496p. 1975. 12.50 o.s.i. (ISBN 0-395-18497-5). HM.

Poetics of Biblical Narrative. Robert W. Funk. LC 85-47733. (Foundations & Facets Ser.). 288p. 1986. 19.95 o.p. (ISBN 0-8006-2107-7, 1-2107, Fortress). Augsburg Fortress.

Poetics of Murder: Detective Fiction & Literary Theory. Ed. by Glenn W. Most & William W. Stowe. LC 82-23429. 416p. 1983. 22.95 o.p. (ISBN 0-15-172280-3). HarBraceJ.

Poetry: A Modern Guide. Elizabeth A. Drew. 1959. 5.95x o.p. (ISBN 0-393-04212-X). Norton.

Poetry & Children. Helen W. Painter. LC 73-121417. 104p. 1970. 6.50 o.p. (ISBN 0-87207-923-6). Intl Reading.

Poetry & Courtliness in Renaissance England. Daniel Javitch. LC 77-85541. 1978. 24.00x o.p. (ISBN 0-691-06354-0). Princeton U Pr.

Poetry & Drama, Fifteen Seventy to Seventeen Hundred: Essays in Honor of Harold F. Brooks. Ed. by Antony Coleman & Antony Hammond. LC 81-18813. 1982. 36.00x o.p. (ISBN 0-416-74470-2, NO. 3607). Routledge Chapman & Hall.

Poetry & Experience. Archibald MacLeish. 1972. 6.95 o.p. (ISBN 0-395-07955-1). HM.

Poetry & Politics: An Anthology of Essays. Ed. by Richard M. Jones. LC 84-15017. 397p. 1984. 18.95 o.p. (ISBN 0-688-03987-1). Morrow.

Poetry & Politics: An Anthology of Essays. Ed. by Richard M. Jones. LC 84-15017. 397p. 1984. pap. 10.00 o.p. (ISBN 0-688-03988-X, Quill). Morrow.

Poetry & Prose of E. E. Cummings. Robert E. Wegner. LC 64-11544. 1965. 6.95 o.s.i. (ISBN 0-15-172295-1). HarBraceJ.

Poetry & Song in Late Eighteenth Century Germany: A Study in the Musical Sturm und Drang. Margaret M. Stoljar. LC 85-6631. 217p. 1985. 43.00 o.p. (ISBN 0-7099-3358-4, Pub. by Croom Helm Ltd). Routledge Chapman & Hall.

Poetry Anthology Nineteen Twelve to Nineteen Seventy-Seven: 65 Years of America's Most Distinguished Verse Magazine. Ed. by Daryl Hine & Joseph Parisi. 1978. 20.00 o.p. (ISBN 0-395-26548-7); pap. 10.95 o.p. (ISBN 0-395-26874-5). HM.

Poetry As Metaconsciousness: Readings in William Blake. G. Singh. 170p. 1983. text ed. 17.50 o.p. (ISBN 0-391-02950-9). Humanities.

Poetry Collection. Rose Haft. 1980. 4.00 o.p. (ISBN 0-682-48666-3). Exposition-Phoenix.

Poetry Experience: Teaching & Writing Poetry in Secondary Schools. S. Tunnicliffe. (Teaching Secondary English Ser.). 272p. (Orig.). 1984. text ed. 25.00 o.p. (ISBN 0-416-34600-6, 9217); pap. text ed. 10.95 o.p. (ISBN 0-416-34610-3, 9218). Routledge Chapman & Hall.

Poetry for Children. Charles Lamb & Mary Lamb. i, 32p. 1982. leatherette 15.00 o.p. (ISBN 0-317-11689-4). Dawsons.

Poetry for Pleasure: A Choice of Poetry & Verse on a Variety of Themes. Ian Parsons. 1978. 10.95 o.p. (ISBN 0-393-04515-3). Norton.

Poetry from Heaven. Michael Durachko. LC 84-90275. 45p. 1985. 5.95 o.p. (ISBN 0-533-06310-8). Vantage.

Poetry in the Therapeutic Experience. Ed. by Arthur Lerner. LC 77-24999. 1978. 23.00 o.p. (ISBN 0-08-022222-6). Pergamon.

Poetry Introduction, No. 6. Susannah Amoore et al. LC 70-424610. 112p. (Orig.). 1985. pap. 7.95 o.p. (ISBN 0-571-13543-9). Faber & Faber.

Poetry Is. James P. Wood. LC 71-187420. 192p. (gr. 7 up). 1972. 7.95 o.p. (ISBN 0-395-13736-5). HM.

Poetry Is You. Douglas P. Hinkle. LC 77-2207. 1977. 5.95 o.p. (ISBN 0-918518-05-9, St Luke TN). Peachtree Pubs.

Poetry of Civic Virtue: Eliot, Malraux, Auden. Nathan A. Scott, Jr. LC 76-7871. 192p. 1976. 8.50 o.p. (ISBN 0-8006-0483-0, Fortress). Augsburg Fortress.

Poetry of Earth: A Collection of English Nature Writings. Ed. by E. D. Johnson. LC 65-23661. 1974. pap. text ed. 4.25x o.s.i. (ISBN 0-689-70514-X, 205, Atheneum). Macmillan.

Poetry of Erica Jong. Erica Jong. 1976. pap. 11.95 o.s.i. (ISBN 0-03-018321-9). H Holt & Co.

Poetry of Experience: The Dramatic Monologue in Modern Literary Tradition. Robert Langbaum. 1963. pap. 4.95 o.p. (ISBN 0-393-00215-2, Norton Lib). Norton.

Poetry of Ezra Pound. Hugh Kenner. LC 51-12356. 1951. 35.00 o.p. (ISBN 0-527-48500-4). Kraus Repr.

Poetry of Keats: Language & Experience. David Pollard. LC 84-6435. 186p. 1984. 28.50x o.p. (ISBN 0-389-20490-0, 08052). B&N Imports.

Poetry of Li Shang-Yin, Ninth-Century Baroque Chinese Poet. James J. Liu. LC 68-30695. 1969. lib. bdg. 18.00x o.s.i. (ISBN 0-226-48690-7). U of Chicago Pr.

Poetry of Love & Life. Christina Mlinaric. 1985. 9.95 o.p. (ISBN 0-533-06526-7). Vantage.

Poetry of Robert Lowell. Vivian Smith. (Studies in Literature). 144p. 1974. 16.00x o.p. (ISBN 0-424-06510-X, Pub. by Sydney U Pr). Intl Spec Bk.

Poetry of Samuel Taylor Coleridge: An Annotated Bibliography of Criticism, 1935 to 1970. Mary Lee Milton. LC 80-83650. 250p. 1981. lib. bdg. 39.00 o.p. (ISBN 0-8240-9451-4). Garland Pub.

Poetry of Sir Thomas Wyatt: A Selection & Study by E. M. W. Tillyard. Thomas Wyatt. Repr. of 1929 ed. 29.00x o.p. (ISBN 0-403-08614-0). Somerset Pub.

Poetry of Surrealism: An Anthology. Ed. by Michael Benedikt. LC 74-8014. 1975. pap. 10.95 o.s.i. (ISBN 0-316-08898-6). Little.

Poetry of the Codex Vercellensis, with an English Translation. Book Vercelli. Repr. of 1856 ed. 60.00 o.p. (ISBN 0-384-00369-9). Johnson Repr.

Poetry of the Romantic Period. J. R. Jackson. (Routledge History of English Poetry Ser.). 1980. 30.00x o.p. (ISBN 0-7100-0289-0). Routledge Chapman & Hall.

Poetry of Thomas Kinsella. Maurice Harmon. 126p. 1975. text ed. 15.00X o.p. (ISBN 0-391-00386-0); pap. text ed. 7.95x o.p. (ISBN 0-391-00387-9). Humanities.

Poetry of William Cowper. Bill Hutchings. 246p. 1983. 29.95 o.p. (ISBN 0-7099-1249-8, Pub. by Croom Helm Ltd). Routledge Chapman & Hall.

Poetry Pack Rat. Schurr. (Choose-a-Card Ser.). 64p. (gr. 4-6). 1979. pap. text ed. 6.95 o.p. (ISBN 0-913916-86-2, IP86-2). Incentive Pubns.

Poetry: Sight & Insight. James W. Kirkland & F. David Sanders. 456p. 1981. pap. text ed. 12.00 o.p. (ISBN 0-394-32353-X, RanC). Random.

Poets' Grammar: Person, Time, & Mood in Poetry. Francis Berry. LC 73-14192. 190p. 1974. Repr. of 1958 ed. lib. bdg. 22.50x o.p. (ISBN 0-8371-7147-4, BEPG). Greenwood.

Poet's Handbook, One Thousand Two Hundred Ninety-Nine Places to Send Poems. Lincoln B. Young. 188p. 1988. pap. 9.95 o.p. (ISBN 0-911666-33-8). Fine Arts Pr.

Poets Laureate of England. Walter Hamilton. LC 68-30621. 336p. 1968. Repr. of 1879 ed. 40.00x o.p. (ISBN 0-8103-3150-0). Gale.

Poet's Market 1986. Ed. by Judson Jerome. 360p. 1985. 16.95 o.p. (ISBN 0-89879-197-9, 1838). Writers Digest.

Poet's Market 1987. 2nd ed. Ed. by Judson Jerome. 372p. 1986. 16.95 o.p. (ISBN 0-89879-244-4). Writers Digest.

Poet's Market 88. 3rd ed. Judson Jerome. 432p. 1987. 17.95 o.p. (ISBN 0-89879-277-0). Writers Digest.

Poets of Darkness. James B. Goode. LC 80-29653. (Center for the Study of Southern Culture Ser.). 1981. 7.95 o.p. (ISBN 0-87805-133-3). U Pr of Miss.

Poets of Ireland. David J. O'Donoghue. LC 68-30622. 242p. 1968. Repr. of 1912 ed. 47.00x o.p. (ISBN 0-8103-3152-7). Gale.

Poets of Reality: Six Twentieth Century Writers. J. Hillis Miller. LC 65-22055. 1969. pap. text ed. 4.25x o.p. (ISBN 0-689-70144-6, 143, Atheneum). Macmillan.

Poets of the Early Seventeenth Century. Ed. by Bernard Davis & Elizabeth Davis. (Routledge English Texts). 1967. pap. 5.95x o.p. (ISBN 0-7100-4512-3). Routledge Chapman & Hall.

Poets of the River City. Ed. by Marilou B. Thompson. LC 78-15274. 1978. pap. 1.00 o.p. (ISBN 0-918518-08-3, St Luke TN). Peachtree Pubs.

Poet's Work: Twenty-Nine Masters of Twentieth Century Poetry on the Origins & Practice of Their Art. Ed. by Reginald Gibbons. 1979. 12.50 o.p. (ISBN 0-395-27616-0); pap. 6.95 o.p. (ISBN 0-395-28057-5). HM.

Poganuc People. Fords et al. (Illus.). 416p. 1977. pap. 7.95 o.p. (ISBN 0-317-35972-X). Stowe-Day.

Pogo's Body Politic. Walt Kelly. Ed. by Selby Kelly. 1976. pap. 2.95 o.p. (ISBN 0-671-22302-X, Fireside). S&S.

Poids du Ciel. Jean Giono. 319p. 1971. 4.95 o.p. (ISBN 0-686-53981-8). French & Eur.

Poincons de Garantie Internationaux pour L'or, Le Platine et Le Palladium. 10th ed. Tardy. (Illus.). 406p. (Orig., Fr.). 1981. pap. 21.00 o.p. (ISBN 0-317-06099-6, 2390209, Pub. by Tardy FR). Seven Hills Bk Dists.

Poincons d'Etain. Tardy et al. (Illus.). 288p. (Orig., Fr.). pap. 19.00 o.p. (ISBN 0-317-06100-3, 2390159, Pub. by Tardy Fr). Seven Hills Bk Dists.

Point After: Advice from God's Athletes. Elliot Johnson. 128p. 1987. pap. 5.95 o.p. (ISBN 0-310-26171-6, 12416P). Zondervan.

Point Blank. Sonny Grosso & Philip Rosenberg. 1979. pap. 2.75 o.p. (ISBN 0-380-45229-4, 45229-4). Avon.

Point in Time...Readings in Early Childhood Education. Paula W. Smith et al. 1973. 7.95x o.p. (ISBN 0-8422-0337-0). Irvington.

Point Mapping Stability. J. Bernussou. 1977. 35.00 o.p. (ISBN 0-08-021283-2). Pergamon.

Point of Departure. James Cameron. 318p. 1986. 17.95 o.p. (ISBN 0-85362-175-6, Oriel). Routledge Chapman & Hall.

Point of View: Talks on Education. Edward H. Levi. LC 49-11213. 1970. 4.50x o.s.i. (ISBN 0-226-47412-7). U of Chicago Pr.

Point Sets. E. Cech. 1969. 71.50 o.p. (ISBN 0-12-164850-8). Acad Pr.

Point 045 Automatic. (Weaponry Ser.). 1986. lib. bdg. 79.95 o.p. (ISBN 0-8490-3853-7). Gordon Pr.

Pointed Spade Coins of the Chou Dynasty. Arthur B. Coole. LC 72-86806. (Encyclopedia of Chinese Coins Ser: Vol. 4). (Illus.). 464p. 1975. 35.00x o.p. (ISBN 0-88000-012-0). Quarterman.

Pointlike Structures Inside & Outside Hadrons. Ed. by Antonio Zichichi. LC 80-25632. (Subnuclear Ser.: Vol. 17). 748p. 1982. 120.00x o.p. (ISBN 0-306-40568-7, Plenum Pr). Plenum Pub.

Points for Emphasis. William J. Fallis. (Orig.). 1989. pap. 2.95 pocket-size o.p. (ISBN 0-8054-1566-1). Broadman.

Points for Emphasis, Nineteen Eighty-Eight to Nineteen Eighty-Nine. William J. Fallis. (Orig.). 1988. pap. 3.95 large size o.p. (ISBN 0-8054-1565-3). Broadman.

Points of Departure: Aspects of the Tao. James B. Klee. LC 82-72609. 325p. (Orig.). 1982. pap. 8.95 o.s.i. (ISBN 0-89708-105-6). And Bks.

Points of Entry. Ed. by Mildred Schell. (Orig.). 1973. pap. 1.35 o.p. (ISBN 0-377-80301-4). Friendship Pr.

Points of Modern English Syntax. P. A. Erades. Ed. by N. J. Robat. (Contributions to English Studies). 260p. 1975. pap. text ed. 22.00 o.p. (ISBN 90-265-0184-6, Pub. by Swets Pub Serv Holland). Swets North Am.

Points of View. George W. Pifer & Nancy W. Mutoh. LC 77-972. 152p. 1977. pap. text ed. 8.25 o.p. (ISBN 0-88377-072-5). Newbury Hse.

Poison on the Land. J. Wentworth Day. 256p. 1957. (ISBN 0-8022-0365-5). Philos Lib.

Poison Oracle. Peter Dickenson Book. (International Crime Ser.). 1982. pap. 3.95 o.p. (ISBN 0-394-71023-1). Pantheon.

Poison Tree: A True Story of Family Violence & Revenge. Alan Prendergast. 352p. 1986. 18.95 o.p. (ISBN 0-399-13138-8). Putnam Pub Group.

Poisoning of Michigan. Joyce Egginton. (Illus.). 1980. 13.95 o.p. (ISBN 0-393-01347-2). Norton.

Poisonous Snakes of North America. Leonard Stejneger. (Shorey Lost Arts Ser.). (Illus.). 190p. pap. 5.95 o.p. (ISBN 0-8466-6016-4, U16). Shorey.

Poker Game. Fletcher Knebel. LC 82-45613. 264p. 1983. 14.95 o.p. (ISBN 0-385-18429-8). Doubleday.

Poland. Frank Bren. (World Cinema Ser.: No. 1). (Illus.). 1988. 24.95 o.p. (ISBN 0-948911-46-8, Pub. by Flicks Books England). U of Ill Pr.

Poland. T. Gronowski & R. Gronoswska. (Illus.). 1977. 40.00 o.p. E J Brill USA.

Poland. Marc Heine. (Illus.). 160p. 1980. 14.95 o.p. (ISBN 0-88254-503-5). Hippocrene Bks.

Poland. James A. Michener. (General Ser.). 1984. lib. bdg. 18.95 o.p. (ISBN 0-8161-3689-0, Large Print Bks). G K Hall.

Poland: A Historical Atlas. 2nd, rev. ed. Iwo C. Pogonowski. (Illus.). 320p. 1988. 27.50 o.p. (ISBN 0-87052-282-5); deluxe ed. 60.00 ltd. ed. leather bnd. & signed o.p. (ISBN 0-87052-504-2). Hippocrene Bks.

Poland: A Tourist Guide. A. Bajcar. (Illus.). 1977. pap. 10.00 o.s.i. (ISBN 0-686-77959-2). E J Brill USA.

Poland: Communism Adrift. Jan B. De Weydenthal. (Washington Papers: Vol. VII, No. 72). 88p. (Orig.). 1979. pap. text ed. 7.95 o.p. (ISBN 0-8191-6019-9, Pub. by CSIS). U Pr of Amer.

Poland Nineteen Eighty to Nineteen Eighty-Two: The Making of the Revolution. Jan B. De Weydenthal et al. LC 82-48527. 368p. 1983. 30.00x o.p. (ISBN 0-669-06214-6). Lexington Bks.

Poland-Solidarity-Walesa. Michael Dobbs et al. 1981. pap. text ed. 9.95 o.p. (ISBN 0-07-006681-7). McGraw.

Poland Statistical Data, 1979. (ISBN 0-8002-2328-4). Intl Pubns Serv.

Poland Under Jaruzelski: A Comprehensive Sourcebook on Poland During & after Martial Law. Ed. by Survey Magazine Staff & Leopold Labedz. 432p. 1984. 19.95 o.s.i. (ISBN 0-684-18116-9, ScribT). Scribner.

Poland's Postwar Recovery: Economic Reconstruction, Nationalization & Agrarian Reform in Poland after World War II. Joseph V. Yakowicz. 1979. 12.50 o.p. (ISBN 0-682-49257-4, University). Exposition-Phoenix.

Polanski. Barbara Leaming. 1983. pap. 6.75 o.p. (ISBN 0-671-24986-X, Touchstone Bks). S&S.

Polar Fleet. Warren C. Norwood. 1985. pap. 2.95 o.p. (ISBN 0-553-24877-4). Bantam.

Polar Geomorphology. Ed. by R. J. Price & D. E. Sugen. (Institute of British Geographers Special Publication Ser.: No. 4). 1980. 25.00 o.p. (ISBN 0-12-564550-3). Acad Pr.

Polaris Snowmobile Service-Repair: 1973-1977. Ed. by Eric Jorgensen. (Illus.). pap. 8.95 o.p. (ISBN 0-89287-177-6, X952). Clymer Pub.

Polaris! The Concept & Creation of a New & Mighty Weapon. James Baar & William E. Howard. LC 60-12731. (Illus.). 1960. 4.95 o.p. (ISBN 0-15-172659-0). HarBraceJ.

Polarities of Man's Existence in Biblical Perspective. Frank Stagg. LC 73-8812. 1973. 8.95 o.s.i. (ISBN 0-664-20976-9, Westminster). Westminster John Knox.

Polarity Sensitivity As Inherent Scope Relations. William A. Ladusaw & Jorge Hankamer. LC 79-6614. (Outstanding Dissertations in Linguistics Ser.). 236p. 1985. lib. bdg. 35.00 o.p. (ISBN 0-8240-4555-6). Garland Pub.

Polarization Gradient in Elastic Dielectric. CISM (International Center for Mechanical Sciences) Staff. Ed. by R. D. Mindlin. (CISM Publications: No. 24). (Illus.). 55p. 1973. pap. 10.40 o.p. (ISBN 0-387-81087-0). Springer-Verlag.

Polarization Microscopy of Dental Tissues. W. J. Schmidt & A. Keil. Tr. by P. Middle. 604p. 1971. 150.00 o.p. (ISBN 0-08-010787-7). Pergamon.

Polarized Light. Ed. by William Swindell. LC 74-26881. (Benchmark Papers in Optics Ser: No. 1). 418p. 1975. 78.00 o.p. (ISBN 0-12-787498-4). Acad Pr.

Polarized Light & Optical Measurements. D. Clarke & J. F. Grainger. 1971. 50.00 o.p. (ISBN 0-08-016320-3). Pergamon.

Polarography of Molecules of Biological Significance. Ed. by W. Franklin Smyth. 1979. 86.00 o.p. (ISBN 0-12-653050-5). Acad Pr.

Pole Apart: The Emerging Issues of Antarctica. P. W. Quigg. (New Press Ser.). 288p. 1982. text ed. 19.95 o.p. (ISBN 0-07-051053-9). McGraw.

Poles. Julie Ellis. (Orig.). 1984. pap. 3.95 o.p. (ISBN 0-440-06989-0). Dell.

Police. Jaydie Putterman & Rosalynde Lesur. (Illus.). 192p. 1983. 19.95 o.p. (ISBN 0-03-062429-0); pap. 11.95 o.p. (ISBN 0-03-059597-5). H Holt & Co.

Police! A Precinct at Work. Sara A. Friedman & David Jacobs. LC 75-10137. (Illus.). 192p. (gr. 7 up). 1975. 6.95 o.p. (ISBN 0-15-263027-9, HJ). HarBraceJ.

Police Administration. rev. ed. John P. Kenney. (Illus.). 376p. 1975. 32.25x o.p. (ISBN 0-398-03398-6). C C Thomas.

Police & People in London. David J. Smith & Jeremy Gray. 280p. (Orig.). 1985. text ed. 48.50 o.p. (ISBN 0-566-00850-5). Gower Pub Co.

Police & Pretrial Release. Floyd Feeney, Jr. LC 79-9629. 240p. 1982. 26.50x o.p. (ISBN 0-669-03597-1). Lexington Bks.

Police at Work: Policy Issues & Analysis. Ed. by Richard R. Bennett. (Perspectives in Criminal Justice Ser.: Vol. 5). 174p. 1983. 25.00 o.p. (ISBN 0-8039-1956-5); pap. 12.95 o.p. (ISBN 0-8039-1957-3). Sage.

Police Careers for Women. Diane P. Muro. LC 78-26708. (Messner Career Bks.). (Illus.). 192p. (YA) (gr. 7 up). 1979. lib. bdg. 9.29 o.s.i. (ISBN 0-671-32931-6). Messner.

Police Collective Bargaining see Issues in the Public Employee Relations Library: Series 2.

Police-Community Action: A Program for Change in Police-Community Behavior Patterns. Terry. Eisenberg et al. LC 72-86839. (Special Studies in U. S. Economic, Social & Political Issues). 1973. 46.00x o.p. (ISBN 0-275-28831-5). Irvington.

Police-Community Problems: Essays on Malice in Blunderland. S. H. Cohen. 1975. text ed. 26.50x o.p. (ISBN 0-8422-5216-9); pap. text ed. 7.25x o.p. (ISBN 0-8422-0487-3). Irvington.

Police Community Relations. Hale. LC 73-11827. 208p. 1974. pap. 18.95 o.p. (ISBN 0-8273-1423-X); instr's. guide 5.00 o.p. (ISBN 0-8273-1424-8). Delmar.

Police, Crimes & Offenses & Motor Vehicle Laws of Virginia, 3 vols. Michie Company Editorial Staff. 1985. Set. 60.00 o.p. (ISBN 0-87215-853-5); 1985 supplement 15.00 o.p. (ISBN 0-87215-978-7). Michie Co.

Police, Crimes & Offenses & Motor Vehicle Laws of Virginia, 3 vols. Michie Company Editorial Staff. 1986. Set. 65.00x o.p. (ISBN 0-87215-990-6). Michie Co.

Police Divers. Paul C. Scotti. LC 82-8295. (Illus.). 64p. (gr. 4-6). 1982. lib. bdg. 8.79 o.s.i. (ISBN 0-671-44247-3). Messner.

Police Drugs. Jean Rolin. 200p. 1956. (ISBN 0-8022-1368-5). Philos Lib.

Police Handgun Ammunition: Incapacitation Effects. U. S. Department of Justice Staff. (Illus.). 52p. 1985. pap. 6.00 o.p. (ISBN 0-87364-334-8). Paladin Pr.

Police Ju Jitsu. J. McCauslin Moynahan, Jr. (Illus.). 132p. 1962. 10.75 o.p. (ISBN 0-398-01366-7). C C Thomas.

Police of the World. Roy D. Ingleton. (Illus.). 1979. 4.95 o.p. (ISBN 0-684-16258-X, ScribT); pap. 4.95 o.p. (ISBN 0-684-17259-3, ScribT). Scribner.

Police Operational Intelligence. rev. ed. D. O. Schultz & L. A. Norton. (Illus.). 244p. 1973. 29.75 o.p. (ISBN 0-398-02832-X). C C Thomas.

Police Organization & Administration. Sam S. Souryal. (Criminal Justice Ser.). 150p. 1981. pap. text ed. 10.95 o.p. (ISBN 0-15-570701-9, HC). HarBraceJ.

Police Powers & Accountability. J. L. Lambert. LC 85-21282. 1985. 29.00 o.p. (ISBN 0-7099-1660-4, Pub. by Croom Helm Ltd). Routledge Chapman & Hall.

Police Procedures & Defense Tactics Training Manual. Harry Aziz. Ed. by Sydney S. Halet. (Illus.). 1979. 20.95 o.p. (ISBN 0-87040-451-2). Japan Pubns USA.

Police Pursuit Driving Handbook. Donald O. Schultz. LC 79-50244. 96p. (Orig.). 1979. pap. 9.00x o.p. (ISBN 0-87201-771-0). Gulf Pub.

Police Report Writing. Robert A. Johnson & Ralph W. Pease. (HBJ Criminal Justice Ser.). 160p. 1982. pap. text ed. 9.95 o.p. (ISBN 0-15-570708-6, HC). HarBraceJ.

Police Selection & Training: The Role of Psychology. NATO Advanced Study Institute Staff & Greece Skiathos. (Pub. by Martinus Nijhoff). E J Brill USA.

Police Team. rev. ed. Educational Research Council of America Staff. Ed. by Theodore N. Ferris & John P. Marchak. (Real People at Work Ser.: B). (Illus.). 36p. 1976. pap. text ed. 2.70 o.p. (ISBN 0-89247-018-6, 9218). Changing Times.

Police Work: Strategies & Outcomes in Law Enforcement. Ed. by David M. Petersen. LC 79-9530. (Sage Research Progress Ser. in Criminology: Vol. 12). (Illus.). 128p. 1979. 20.00 o.p. (ISBN 0-8039-1325-7); pap. 9.95 o.p. (ISBN 0-8039-1326-5). Sage.

Police Work with Juveniles & the Administration of Juvenile Justice. 6th ed. John P. Kenney et al. (Illus.). 378p. 1982. 24.00x o.p. (ISBN 0-398-04670-0). C C Thomas.

Policies & Politics in Western Europe: The Impact of Recession. Ed. by F. F. Ridley. LC 84-45284. 224p. 1984. 25.00 o.p. (ISBN 0-7099-2280-9, Pub. by Croom Helm Ltd). Routledge Chapman & Hall.

Policies for Lifelong Education. Ed. by Jamison Gilder. 1979. pap. 5.00 o.p. (ISBN 0-87117-091-4). Am Assn Comm Jr Coll.

Policing & Its Context. Date not set. (ISBN 0-8052-3891-3). Random.

Policing the City: Boston, Eighteen Eighty-Two to Eighteen Eighty-Five. Roger Lane. LC 67-17313. 1971. pap. text ed. 4.95x o.p. (ISBN 0-689-70261-2, 169, Atheneum). Macmillan.

Policing the Victorian Community: The Formation of English Provincial Police Forces, 1856-1880. Carolyn Steedman. 300p. (Orig.). 1984. pap. 17.95x o.p. (ISBN 0-7100-9575-9). Routledge Chapman & Hall.

Policy Alternatives for Mobile Homes. Constance B. Gibson. 59p. 1972. pap. (ISBN 0-87855-552-8). Transaction Pubs.

Policy Alternatives for Nonindustrial Private Forests. Roger A. Sedjo & David M. Ostermeier. LC 78-53432. 71p. (Orig.). 1978. pap. 4.00 o.p. (ISBN 0-939970-10-4). Soc Am Foresters.

Policy & Action: Essays on the Implementation of Public Policy. Ed. by Susan Barrett & Colin Fudge. 1981. 33.00x o.p. (ISBN 0-416-30670-5, NO. 3526); pap. 18.95x o.p. (ISBN 0-416-30680-2, NO. 3525). Routledge Chapman & Hall.

Policy & Politics in American Governments. Ira Sharkansky & Donald Van Meter. (Illus.). 360p. 1975. text ed. 28.95 o.p. (ISBN 0-07-056428-0). McGraw.

Policy Approach to Political Representation: Lessons from the Four Corners States. Helen M. Ingram et al. 270p. 1980. 23.00 o.p. (ISBN 0-317-60219-5). Resources Future.

Policy Choices: Critical Issues in American Foreign Policy. John Stack. LC 83-70927. (Contemporary Focus Paperback Ser.). 240p. 1983. pap. 7.95 o.p. (ISBN 0-87967-442-3). Dushkin Pub.

Policy Cycle. Ed. by Judith V. May & Aaron B. Wildavsky. LC 78-15351. (Sage Yearbooks in Politics & Public Policy: Vol. 5). 332p. 1979. 25.00 o.p. (ISBN 0-8039-0825-3); pap. 12.50 o.p. (ISBN 0-8039-0826-1). Sage.

Policy Formulation. William L. Dejon. LC 79-10329. 643p. 1980. text ed. 23.95x o.p. (ISBN 0-8436-0781-5); keys to the cases 8.95x o.p. (ISBN 0-8436-0787-4). PWS-Kent Pub.

Policy in Urban Planning: Structure Plans, Local Plans, & Urban Development. William Solesbury. 1974. text ed. 23.00 o.p. (ISBN 0-08-017758-1). Pergamon.

Policy Interventions for Technological Innovation in Developing Countries. Charles Cooper. (Working Paper: No. 441). 59p. 1980. 5.00 o.p. (ISBN 0-686-36148-2, WP-0441). World Bank.

Policy Issues in Personal Health Services: Current Perspectives. Ed. by Sagar C. Jain. LC 82-22702. 468p. 1983. 38.50 o.p. (ISBN 0-89443-672-4). Aspen Pub.

Policy-Making & Planning in the Health Sector. Kenneth Lee & Anne Mills. (Illus.). 208p. 1982. 30.00 o.p. (ISBN 0-85664-965-1, Pub. by Croom Helm). Routledge Chapman & Hall.

Policy-Making in a New State: Papua New Guinea 1972-77. Ed. by J. A. Ballard. (Illus.). 331p. 1981. text ed. 37.50x o.p. (ISBN 0-7022-1529-5). U of Queensland Pr.

Policy Making in Communist Party States. Gary K. Bertsch. (CISE Learning Package Ser.: No. 10). (Illus.). 114p. (Orig.). 1975. pap. text ed. 4.00x o.p. (ISBN 0-936876-25-5). LRIS.

Policy-Making in the European Community. 2nd ed. Helen Wallace et al. 451p. 1983. 75.00x o.p. (ISBN 0-471-90149-0, Pub. by Wiley-Interscience). Wiley.

Policy Planning & Local Government. Robin Hambleton. LC 78-73593. (Landmark Study). (Illus.). 384p. 1979. Repr. of 1978 ed. text ed. 22.00x o.s.i. (ISBN 0-916672-92-1, Pub. by Allanheld). Rowman.

Policy Science: Methodologies & Cases. Ed. by Arie Y. Lewin & Melvin F. Shakum. 450p. 1976. 65.00 o.p. (ISBN 0-08-019601-2); pap. 32.00 o.p. (ISBN 0-08-019600-4). Pergamon.

Policy Systems in An Australian Metropolitan Region: Political & Economic Determinants of Change in Victoria, Vols. 22 & 23. N. P. Low & J. M. Power. (Illus.). 70p. 1984. pap. 22.00 o.p. (ISBN 0-08-032329-4). Pergamon.

Policymaking for the Mentally Handicapped. Gregory S. Donges. 144p. 1982. text ed. 32.00x o.p. (ISBN 0-566-00514-X). Gower Pub Co.

Polish Amber. J. Grabowska. (Illus.). 1985. 45.00x o.p. (ISBN 83-223-1985-1). E J Brill USA.

Polish-English, English-Polish Dictionary. T. Grzebieniowski. 22.50 o.s.i. (ISBN 0-685-39853-6). E J Brill USA.

Polish-English, English-Polish Dictionary (The Great) 1975, 4 vols. J. Stanislawski. (Pol. & Eng.). 1978. Set. 110.00 o.p.; Polish-English, 8th Ed. 55.00 o.p.; English-Polish, 4th Ed. 55.00 o.p. E J Brill USA.

Polish-English, English-Polish Pocket Dictionary. (Pol. & Eng.). pap. 6.50 o.p. (ISBN 0-88431-387-5). E J Brill USA.

Polish-English, English-Polish Practical Dictionary, 2 vols. J. Stanislawski. (Pol. & Eng.). Set. 43.00 o.p.; Polish-English, 6th Ed. 21.50 o.p.; English-Poslish, 7th Ed. 21.50 o.p. E J Brill USA.

Polish Profiles: The Land, the People & Their History. Antoni Gronowicz. LC 75-23929. (Illus.). 256p. 1976. 10.00 o.p. (ISBN 0-88208-060-1). Chicago Review.

Polish Romantic Drama: Three Plays in English Translation. Ed. by Harold B. Segel. LC 76-50264. (Illus.). 304p. 1977. 32.50x o.p. (ISBN 0-8014-0871-7). Cornell U Pr.

Polish Scholarly Prose: A Humanities & Social Sciences Reader. Robert Rothstein & Halina Rothstein. xii, 226p. (Orig.). 1981. pap. text ed. 14.95 o.p. (ISBN 0-89357-075-3). Slavica.

Polishing & Waxing Compositions: Recent Developments. Ed. by M. G. Halpern. LC 82-7691. (Chemical Technology Rev. 213). (Illus.). 301p. 1983. 36.00 o.p. (ISBN 0-8155-0916-2). Noyes.

Politica & Moral. Benedetto Croce. (ISBN 0-8022-0316-7). Philos Lib.

Political Adaptation in Sa'udi Arabia: A Study of the Council of Ministers. Summer S. Huyette. (Westview Special Studies on the Middle East). 175p. 1985. softcover 26.50x o.p. (ISBN 0-8133-0203-X). Westview.

Political Allocation of Benefits & Burdens. Norman Wengert. LC 76-20702. 1976. pap. 2.50x o.p. (ISBN 0-87772-214-5). UCB IGS.

Political Analysis: Shifting Trends & Questionable Assumptions. John Pulparampil. LC 76-904610. 1976. 8.50x o.p. (ISBN 0-88386-804-0). South Asia Bks.

Political Anatomy of Ireland. W. Petty. 260p. 1970. Repr. of 1691 ed. 32.50x o.p. (ISBN 0-7165-0093-0, BBA 03502, Pub. by Irish Academic Pr Ireland). Biblio Dist.

Political & Administrative Development. Ed. by Ralph J. Braibanti. LC 75-79965. (Commonwealth Studies Center: No. 36). xii, 700p. 1969. 40.95 o.p. (ISBN 0-8223-0022-2). Duke.

Political & Civil Rights in the United States: 1981 Supplement to Vol. II. suppl. ed. Norman Dorsen et al. LC 78-69780. 337p. 1981. text ed. 10.95 o.p. (ISBN 0-316-23628-4). Little.

Political & Economic Structures. Bela Hubbard. LC 56-7403. 1964. 4.00 o.p. (ISBN 0-87004-067-7). Caxton.

Political & Social Advertising: A Selected Bibliography. Robert Goehlert. (Public Administration Ser.: Bibliography P 1654). 1985. pap. 2.00 o.p. (ISBN 0-89028-344-3). Vance Biblios.

Political & Social Thought of Charles A. Beard. Bernard C. Borning. LC 84-703. xxv, 315p. 1984. Repr. of 1962 ed. lib. bdg. 48.50x o.p. (ISBN 0-313-24462-6, BOPS). Greenwood.

Political Animal: Studies in Political Philosophy from Machiavelli to Marx. Leo Rauch. LC 81-3070. 264p. 1981. lib. bdg. 22.50x o.p. (ISBN 0-87023-338-6). U of Mass Pr.

Political Animal: Studies in Political Philosophy from Machiavelli to Marx. Leo Rauch. LC 81-3070. 264p. 1985. pap. text ed. 9.95x o.p. (ISBN 0-87023-489-7). U of Mass Pr.

Political Behavior in the United States: Readings in American Government. Ed. by Fred W. Grupp, Jr. & Marvin Maurer. LC 71-182885. (Illus.). 1972. pap. text ed. 14.95x o.p. (ISBN 0-89197-348-6). Irvington.

Political Bestiary. Eugene J. McCarthy & James J. Kilpatrick. (Illus.). 1978. text ed. 7.95 o.p. (ISBN 0-07-044395-5). McGraw.

Political Campaign Debates: Images, Strategies, & Tactics. Myles Martel. LC 82-20862. (Professional Studies in Political Communication & Policy). (Illus.). 256p. 1983. 25.00x o.p. (ISBN 0-582-28366-3); pap. text ed. 15.95x o.p. (ISBN 0-582-28367-1). Longman.

Political Change & Development: A Selected Bibliography. Robert Goehlert. (Public Administration Ser.: P 1689). 27p. 1985. 3.75 o.p. (ISBN 0-89028-419-9). Vance Biblios.

Political Change in a West African State: A Study of the Modernization Process in Sierra Leone. Martin Kilson. LC 66-23468. (Illus.). 1969. pap. text ed. 3.25x o.p. (ISBN 0-689-70117-9, 148, Atheneum). Macmillan.

Political Change in the Metropolis. 3rd ed. John J. Harrigan. 1984. pap. text ed. write for info. o.p. (ISBN 0-673-39444-1); tchr's. ed. avail. o.p. Scott F.

Political Christians: A Guide for Christians in Public Service. John W. Johnson. LC 78-66950. 1979. pap. 3.95 o.p. (ISBN 0-8066-1689-X, 10-5005, Augsburg). Augsburg Fortress.

Political Communication & Information: A Selected Bibliography. Robert Goehlert. (Public Administration Ser.: P 1688). 18p. 1985. 3.00 o.p. (ISBN 0-89028-418-0). Vance Biblios.

Political Conflict & Ethnic Strategies: A Case Study of Burundi. Warren Weinstein & Robert Schrire. LC 76-22649. (Foreign & Comparative Studies Program, Eastern African Ser.: No. 23). 68p. 1976. pap. text ed. 5.50x o.p. (ISBN 0-915984-20-2). Syracuse U Foreign Comp.

Political Control: A Selected Bibliography. Robert Goehlert. (Public Administration Ser.: P 1814). 19p. 1985. 3.00 o.p. (ISBN 0-89028-644-2). Vance Biblios.

Political Control of Czechoslovakia. Ivan Gadourek. LC 74-2841. 285p. 1974. Repr. of 1953 ed. lib. bdg. 35.00x o.p. (ISBN 0-8371-7437-6, GACZ). Greenwood.

Political Corruption: A Selected Bibliography. Robert Goehlert. (Public Administration Ser.: P 1816). 19p. 1985. 3.00 o.p. (ISBN 0-89028-646-9). Vance Biblios.

Political Corruption: The Ghana Case. Victor T. Le Vine. LC 74-13629. (Publications Ser.: No. 138). 169p. 1975. 8.95x o.p. (ISBN 0-8179-1381-5). Hoover Inst Pr.

Political Culture & Leadership in Soviet Russia: From Lenin to Gorbachev. Robert C. Tucker. LC 87-11025. 1987. 22.00 o.p. (ISBN 0-393-02489-X). Norton.

Political Culture of the American Whigs. Daniel W. Howe. LC 79-12576. 1980. lib. bdg. 25.00x o.p. (ISBN 0-226-35478-4). U of Chicago Pr.

Political Disintegration of Europe & the Cultural Collapse of the Human Race. Robert W. Bransonnard. (Illus.). 139p. 1986. 175.50 o.p. (ISBN 0-86722-127-5). Inst Econ Pol.

Political Dissent: An International Guide to Dissident, Extra-Parliamentary, Guerrila & Illegal Political Movements. Ed. by Henry W. Degenhardt & Alan J. Degenhardt. 600p. 1983. 90.00x o.p. (ISBN 0-8103-2050-9, Pub. by Longman). Gale.

Political Doctrine of Montesquieu's Esprit Des Lois: Its Classical Background. Lawrence M. Levin. 359p. 1973. Repr. of 1936 ed. lib. bdg. 22.50x o.p. (ISBN 0-8371-6569-5, LEME). Greenwood.

Political Economy. Ed. by Richard G. Fox. (American Ethnologist Ser.: Vol. 5, No. 3). 1978. 12.50 o.s.i. (ISBN 0-317-66314-3). Am Anthro Assn.

Political Economy, 2 vols. Oskar Lange. LC 65-367. 1972. Vol. 1, 1963. 90.00 o.p. (ISBN 0-08-013561-7); Vol. 2, 1972. 65.00 o.p. (ISBN 0-08-016572-9). Pergamon.

Political Economy. A. M. Rumyantsev. 678p. 1983. 11.95 o.p. (ISBN 0-8285-2595-1, Pub. by Progress Pubs USSR). Imported Pubns.

Political Economy: A Condensed Course. L. Leontyev. LC 75-10971. 282p. 1975. pap. 2.25 o.p. (ISBN 0-7178-0412-7). Intl Pubs Co.

Political Economy of Australian Urbanization, Vol. 22. M. Berry. (Illus.). 84p. 1984. pap. 22.00 o.p. (ISBN 0-08-031741-3). Pergamon.

Political Economy of British Capitalism: A Marxist Analysis. S. Aaronovitch & R. Smith. 416p. 1981. text ed. 17.00 o.p. (ISBN 0-07-084121-7). McGraw.

Political Economy of British Regional Policy. D. W. Parsons. LC 85-24261. 320p. 1985. 34.50 o.p. (ISBN 0-7099-4013-0, Pub. by Croom Helm Ltd). Routledge Chapman & Hall.

Political Economy of Coal. Ferdinand E. Banks. LC 82-48522. 288p. 1984. 29.00x o.p. (ISBN 0-669-06169-7). Lexington Bks.

Political Economy of Development: Theoretical & Empirical Contributions. Ed. by Norman T. Uphoff & Warren F. Ilchman. LC 77-161999. 1972. 24.50 o.p. (ISBN 0-520-02062-6); pap. 11.95x o.p. (ISBN 0-520-02314-5). U of Cal Pr.

Political Economy of East-West-South Cooperation. G. Alder-Karlsson. (Studien Uber Wirtschaftsund Systemvergleiche: Vol. 7). 1977. pap. 31.00 o.p. (ISBN 0-387-81385-3). Springer-Verlag.

Political Economy of EEC Relations with African, Caribbean & Pacific States: Contributions to the Understanding of the Lome Convention on North-South Relations. Ed. by Frank Long. 192p. 1980. 37.00 o.p. (ISBN 0-08-024077-1). Pergamon.

Political Economy of Income Distribution in Sri Lanka. Masihur Rahman. 120p. 1988. text ed. 25.00x o.p. (ISBN 81-207-0807-5, Pub. by Sterling Pubs India). Apt Bks.

Political Economy of Indirect Rule: Mysore 1881-1947. Bjorn Hettne. (Scandanavian Institute of Asian Studies Monograph: No. 32). (Illus., Orig.). 1978. pap. text ed. 15.00x o.p. (ISBN 0-7007-0106-0). Humanities.

Political Economy of International Commodity Trade. Karen Mingst. (CISE Learning Package Ser.: No. 22). (Illus.). 94p. (Orig.). 1976. pap. text ed. 3.50x o.p. (ISBN 0-936876-34-4). LRIS.

Political Economy of Manufacturing Protection. Ed. by Ross Garnaut & Christopher Findlay. 320p. (Orig.). 1987. pap. text ed. 24.95x o.p. (ISBN 0-04-330378-1). Unwin Hyman.

Political Economy of Oil. Ferdinand E. Banks. LC 79-3340. 256p. 1980. 32.00x o.p. (ISBN 0-669-03402-9). Lexington Bks.

Political Economy of Prosperity. Arthur Okun. 1970. pap. text ed. 3.95x o.p. (ISBN 0-393-09912-1, NortonC). Norton.

Political Economy of Reaganomics: A Critique. Stephen Rousseas. LC 82-10659. 160p. 1982. 20.00 o.p. (ISBN 0-87332-227-4); pap. 14.95 o.p. (ISBN 0-87332-239-8). M E Sharpe.

Political Economy of Revolution. K. Zarodov. 232p. 1981. 6.50 o.p. (ISBN 0-8285-1900-5, Pub. by Progress Pubs USSR). Imported Pubns.

Political Economy of Tolerable Survival. Ed. by Maxwell Gaskin. (Illus.). 220p. 1981. 30.00 o.p. (ISBN 0-7099-0266-2, Pub. by Croom Helm Ltd). Routledge Chapman & Hall.

Political Economy of Underdevelopment. S. B. De Silva. (International Library of Sociology). 640p. 1982. 50.00x o.p. (ISBN 0-7100-0469-9). Routledge Chapman & Hall.

Political Economy of Underdevelopment. S. B. DeSilva. (International Library of Sociology). 645p. 1984. pap. 23.95x o.p. (ISBN 0-7102-0273-3). Routledge Chapman & Hall.

Political Economy of Urban Poverty. Charles Sackrey. 172p. 1972. pap. 4.95x o.p. (ISBN 0-393-09410-3, NortonC). Norton.

Political Economy of Urban Schools. Martin C. Katzman. LC 70-139723. (Joint Center for Urban Studies Publications). 1971. 18.50x o.s.i. (ISBN 0-674-68576-8). Harvard U Pr.

Political Economy of War & Peace. Richard K. Ashley. 320p. 1980. 35.00 o.p. (ISBN 0-89397-087-5). Nichols Pub.

Political Education. Robert Brownhill & Patricia Smart. 224p. 1988. lib. bdg. 33.00x o.p. (ISBN 0-7099-3972-8, Pub. by Croom Helm UK). Routledge Chapman & Hall.

Political Education of Arnold Brecht: An Autobiography: 1884-1970. Arnold Brecht. LC 77-100994. 1970. 50.00x o.p. (ISBN 0-691-07527-1). Princeton U Pr.

Political Effectiveness. James R. Hatfield. (Illus.). 1977. pap. text ed. 4.95 o.p. (ISBN 0-917962-40-0). T H Peek.

Political Elites: A Bibliography. Robert Goehlert. (Public Administration Ser.: P 1784). 22p. 1985. 3.00 o.p. (ISBN 0-89028-584-5). Vance Biblios.

Political Elites & Political Development in the Middle East. Ed. by Frank Tachau. LC 74-20507. 1975. text ed. 21.95x o.p. (ISBN 0-470-84314-4). Halsted Pr.

Political Fictions. Michael Wilding. 1980. 26.95x o.p. (ISBN 0-7100-0457-5). Routledge Chapman & Hall.

Political Forecasting: A Selected Bibliography. Robert Goehlert. (Public Administration Ser.: P 1813). 12p. 1985. 2.00 o.p. (ISBN 0-89028-643-4). Vance Biblios.

Political Geography. 2nd ed. Norman J. Pounds. (Geography Ser.). (Illus.). 448p. 1972. text ed. 51.95 o.p. (ISBN 0-07-050566-7). McGraw.

Political Handbook of the World: 1981. Ed. by Arthur S. Banks. 407p. 1981. text ed. 49.95 o.p. (ISBN 0-07-003629-2). McGraw.

Political History of Finland: 1809-1966. L. A. Puntila. 248p. 1976. 24.00x o.p. (ISBN 0-8448-0913-6, Pub. by Crane Russak & Co). Taylor & Francis.

Political History of National Liberation Movement in Asia & Africa, 1914-1985. Andras Balogh & Zafar Imam. 300p. 1988. text ed. 32.50x o.p. (Pub. by ABC Pub Hse). Advent NY.

Political History of Slavery in the United States. James Z. George. LC 72-181080. 1970. Repr. of 1915 ed. 35.00x o.p. (ISBN 0-8371-1991-X, GEP&). Greenwood.

Political History of the Special Impact Program. Lawrence F. Parachini. 1980. 8.95 o.p. (ISBN 0-87855-828-4). Transaction Pubs.

Political Ideas in Modern Britain. Rodney Barker. 1978. 24.00x o.p. (ISBN 0-416-76250-6, NO. 2033); pap. 15.95x o.p. (ISBN 0-416-76260-3, NO. 2079). Routledge Chapman & Hall.

Political Identity: A Case Study from Uganda. Marshall H. Segall et al. LC 76-21273. (Foreign & Comparative Studies Program, Eastern Africa Ser.: No. 24). 179p. 1976. pap. text ed. 6.50x o.p. (ISBN 0-915984-21-0). Syracuse U Foreign Comp.

Political Institutions in Britain. Lynton Robins. (Contemporary Politics Ser.). 256p. 1987. pap. text ed. 12.95 o.p. (ISBN 0-582-35495-1). Longman.

Political Institutions of the German Revolution, 1918-1919. Ed. by Charles B. Burdick & Ralph H. Lutz. LC 66-13464. (Publications Ser.: No. 40). 305p. 1966. 10.95x o.p. (ISBN 0-8179-1401-3). Hoover Inst Pr.

Political Integration of the Philippine Chinese. Gerald A. McBeath. (Research Monograph: No. 8). (Illus.). 280p. 1983. pap. text ed. 13.50 o.p. (ISBN 0-8191-3124-5). U Pr of Amer.

Political Issues in Nursing: Past, Present & Future, Vol. 3. Ed. by Rosemary White. 1988. pap. (ISBN 0-471-91256-5). Wiley.

Political Justice: The Use of Legal Procedure for Political Ends. Otto Kirchheimer. LC 80-14279. xiv, 452p. 1980. Repr. of 1961 ed. lib. bdg. 41.50x o.p. (ISBN 0-313-22509-5, KIPJ). Greenwood.

Political Kidnapping. William L. Cassidy. 70p. 1978. pap. 6.00 o.p. (ISBN 0-87364-141-8). Paladin Pr.

Political Language & Oratory in Traditional Society. Ed. by Maurice Bloch. 1975. 55.50 o.p. (ISBN 0-12-106850-1). Acad Pr.

Political Languages: Words That Succeed & Policies That Fail. M. Edelman. (Institute for Research on Poverty Monograph). 1977. 17.95 o.p. (ISBN 0-12-230660-0); pap. 14.95 o.p. (ISBN 0-12-230662-7). Acad Pr.

Political Leadership in Africa. Victor T. Le Vine. LC 67-25788. (Studies Ser.: No. 18). 114p. 1967. pap. 5.95x o.p. (ISBN 0-8179-3182-1). Hoover Inst Pr.

Political Legacy of Malcolm X. Obu T'Shaka. pap. 11.95 o.p. Third World.

Political Legitimacy: A Bibliography. Robert Goehlert. (Public Administration Ser.: P 1783). 13p. 1985. 2.00 o.p. (ISBN 0-89028-583-7). Vance Biblios.

Political Letters & Pamphlets by William Carpenter, 34 vols. William Carpenter. 1971. Repr. of 1830 ed. Set. lib. bdg. 53.00x o.p. (ISBN 0-8371-9136-X, BC00). Greenwood.

Political Life & Letters of Cavour, 1848-1861. Arthur J. Whyte. LC 74-30983. (Illus.). 478p. 1975. Repr. of 1930 ed. lib. bdg. 35.00x o.p. (ISBN 0-8371-7939-4, WHPL). Greenwood.

Political Manipulation & Administrative Power: A Comparative Study. Eva Etzioni-Halevy. (International Library of Sociology). 1980. 26.95x o.p. (ISBN 0-7100-0352-8). Routledge Chapman & Hall.

Political Memoir, 1880-1892. Joseph Chamberlain. Ed. by C. H. Howard. LC 75-7235. (Illus.). 340p. 1975. Repr. of 1953 ed. lib. bdg. 22.50x o.p. (ISBN 0-8371-8101-1, CHPOM). Greenwood.

Political Mobilization & Economic Extraction: Chinese Communist Agrarian Policies During the Kiangi Period. Hsu King-Yi. LC 78-74335. (Modern Chinese Economy Ser.). 400p. 1980. lib. bdg. 53.00 o.p. (ISBN 0-8240-4275-1). Garland Pub.

Political Modernization: A Selected Bibliography. Robert Goehlert. (Public Administration Ser.: P 1815). 23p. 1985. 3.75 o.p. (ISBN 0-89028-645-0). Vance Biblios.

Political Nature of a Ruling Class Capital & Ideology in South Africa, 1890-1933. Belinda Bozzoli. (International Library of Sociology). 356p. 1981. 40.00x o.p. (ISBN 0-7100-0722-1). Routledge Chapman & Hall.

Political Novels of Joseph Conrad. Eloise K. Hay. LC 80-29356. 1981. pap. text ed. 16.00x o.s.i. (ISBN 0-226-32042-1). U of Chicago Pr.

Political Obligation. Richard E. Flathman. LC 75-181460. 1972. pap. text ed. 4.95x o.p. (ISBN 0-689-70330-9, 188, Atheneum). Macmillan.

Political Odyssey: Alone & Together. Alfred B. Lewis. 1979. 8.00 o.p. (ISBN 0-682-49343-0). Exposition-Phoenix.

Political Operas 1: Satire & Allegory. Ed. by Walter H. Rubsamen. (Ballad Opera Ser.). 1974. lib. bdg. 61.00 o.p. (ISBN 0-8240-0919-3). Garland Pub.

Political Operas 2: Attack upon Excise. Ed. by Walter H. Rubsamen. (Ballad Opera Ser.). 1974. lib. bdg. 61.00 o.p. (ISBN 0-8240-0920-7). Garland Pub.

Political Organization of Attica. John S. Traill. LC 74-17324. (Hesperia Ser.: Supplement 14). 1975. pap. 12.50x o.p. (ISBN 0-87661-514-0). Am Sch Athens.

Political Organization of Space. E. W. Soja. LC 70-135471. (CCG Resource Papers Ser.: No. 8). (Illus.). 1971. pap. text ed. 5.00 o.p. (ISBN 0-89291-055-0). Assn Am Geographers.

Political Participation in the U. S. C. Q. Press Staff & M. Margaret Conway. LC 85-15186. 170p. 1985. pap. 18.95 o.p. (ISBN 0-87187-331-1). Congr Quarterly.

Political Parties. 2nd ed. David W. Abbot & Edward T. Rogowsky. 1978. pap. 19.95 o.p. (ISBN 0-395-30780-5). HM.

Political Parties in Western Democracies. Leon D. Epstein. LC 79-64858. 401p. 1980. pap. text ed. 9.95x o.p. (ISBN 0-87855-716-4). Transaction Pubs.

Political Parties: Their Organization & Activity in the Modern State. 3rd rev. ed. Maurice Duverger. Tr. by Barbara North & Robert North. 1964. pap. 13.95x o.p. (ISBN 0-416-68320-7, NO. 2173). Routledge Chapman & Hall.

Political Party Organizations: A Bibliography. Robert Goehlert. (Public Administration Ser.: P 1785). 21p. 1985. 3.00 o.p. (ISBN 0-89028-585-3). Vance Biblios.

Political Philosophy. Alan Gewirth. 1965. write for info. o.p. (ISBN 0-02-341670-X, 34167). Macmillan.

Political Philosophy of Plato & Hegel. Michael B. Foster. LC 83-48506. (Philosophy of Hegel Ser.). 220p. 1984. lib. bdg. 30.00 o.p. (ISBN 0-8240-5629-9). Garland Pub.

Political Power. Gilbert M. Cuthbertson. LC 68-5794. (Rice University Studies: Vol. 54, No. 1). 72p. 1968. pap. 10.00x o.p. (ISBN 0-89263-195-3). Rice Univ.

Political Power & the Press. William J. Small. 424p. 1972. 8.95 o.p. (ISBN 0-393-05339-3). Norton.

Political Power in the Soviet Union: A Study of Decision Making in Stalingrad. Philip D. Stewart. 1968. pap. text ed. 5.45x o.p. (ISBN 0-8290-1766-6). Irvington.

Political Process in Modern Organization. Rolf E. Rogers. LC 79-171712. (Illus.). 158p. 1971. 6.50 o.p. (ISBN 0-682-47350-2, University). Exposition-Phoenix.

Political Pulpit. Roderick P. Hart. LC 76-12290. 160p. 1977. 7.95 o.p. (ISBN 0-911198-44-X); pap. 3.50 o.p. (ISBN 0-911198-45-8). Purdue U Pr.

Political Reform in California: Evaluation & Perspective. Ed. by Phil Mullins et al. LC 77-26850. (Research Report 78-3). 1978. pap. 6.50x o.p. (ISBN 0-87772-252-8). UCB IGS.

Political Research & Knowledge: A Bibliography. Robert Goehlert. (Public Administration Ser.: P 1782). 15p. 1985. 2.25 o.p. (ISBN 0-89028-582-9). Vance Biblios.

Political Research Methods: Foundations & Techniques. Barbara L. Smith et al. (Illus.). 352p. 1976. text ed. 27.95 o.p. (ISBN 0-395-20363-5). HM.

Political Resource Directory: National Edition 1988-1989. Ed. by Carol Hess. 480p. pap. text ed. 95.00 o.p. (ISBN 0-944320-00-7). Politic Rescs.

Political Risk in Thirty-Five Countries. 1984. 150.00x o.p. (ISBN 0-8002-3172-4). Intl Pubns Serv.

Political Risk in Thirty-Five Countries: Nineteen Eighty-Three Edition. 160p. 1983. 185.00x o.p. (ISBN 0-8002-3409-X). Intl Pubns Serv.

Political Science Abstracts: 1983 Annual Supplement. Compiled by IFI-Plenum Data Company, Staff. 2548p. 1985. 450.00x o.p. (ISBN 0-306-69033-0, Plenum Pr). Plenum Pub.

Political Science Abstracts: 1984 Annual Supplement. Compiled by IFI-Plenum Data Company, Staff. 3260p. 1986. 475.00x o.p. (ISBN 0-306-69034-9, Plenum Pr). Plenum Pub.

Political Science: An Introduction to Politics. Neal Riemer. 468p. 1983. pap. text ed. 13.00 o.p. (ISBN 0-15-570715-9, HC). HarBraceJ.

Political Science in Indonesia. Alfian. (Illus.). x, 58p. 1979. pap. 4.95x o.p. (ISBN 0-8214-0775-9). Ohio U Pr.

Political Science of Criminal Justice. Stuart Nagel et al. (Illus.). 304p. 1983. 36.25 o.p. (ISBN 0-398-04731-6). C C Thomas.

Political Socialization of Children & Adolescents: A Bibliography. Joseph J. Galin. (Public Administration Ser.: Bibliography P 1653). 1985. pap. 3.00 o.p. (ISBN 0-89028-343-5). Vance Biblios.

Political Society. Ted G. Goertzel. 1976. pap. 17.50 o.p. (ISBN 0-395-30608-6). HM.

Political Status of the Negro in the Age of F. D. R. Ralph J. Bunche. Ed. by Dewey W. Grantham. LC 72-96327. (Illus.). xxxiv, 682p. 1975. pap. text ed. 10.00x o.s.i. (ISBN 0-226-08029-3). U of Chicago Pr.

Political Studies from Spatial Perspectives: Anglo-American Essays on Political Geography. Ed. by Alan D. Burnett & Peter J. Taylor. LC 80-41384. 519p. 1982. 91.95x o.p. (ISBN 0-471-27909-9); pap. 63.95 o.p. (ISBN 0-471-27910-2). Wiley.

Political Suicide. Robert Barnard. (Nightingale Paperbacks Ser.). 304p. 1987. pap. 12.95 o.p. (ISBN 0-8161-4221-1, Large Print Bks). G K Hall.

Political Syncretism in Italy: Historical Coalition Strategies & the Present Crisis. Giuseppe Di Palma. LC 78-620042. (Policy Papers in International Affairs Ser.: No. 7). 1978. pap. 3.95x o.s.i. (ISBN 0-87725-507-5). U of Cal Intl St.

Political System of Napoleon 3rd. Theodore Zeldin. (Illus.). 1971. pap. 4.95x o.p. (ISBN 0-393-00580-1, Norton Lib). Norton.

Political System of the United States. John D. Lees. 1969. text ed. 9.95x o.p. (ISBN 0-571-08498-2). Humanities.

Political Terrorism: A New Guide to Actors & Authors, Databases, & Literature. rev. & updated ed. Alex P. Schmid & A. J. Jongman. 625p. 1987. 59.95 o.p. (ISBN 0-317-64530-7). Transaction Pubs.

Political Terrorism: A Research Guide To Concepts, Theories, Data Bases, & Literature. Alex P. Schmid. 597p. 1984. 34.95 o.p. Transaction Pubs.

Political Theatre: A History 1914-1929. Erwin Piscator. 1978. pap. 5.95 o.p. (ISBN 0-380-40188-6). Avon.

Political Theology. Dorothee Soelle. Tr. by John Shelley from Ger. LC 73-88349. 128p. 1974. pap. 3.50 o.p. (ISBN 0-8006-1065-2, 1-0165, Fortress). Augsburg Fortress.

Political Theology & the Life of the Church. Andre Dumas. Tr. by John Bowden. LC 78-16813. 158p. 1979. softcover 5.95 o.s.i. (ISBN 0-664-24226-X, Westminster). Westminster John Knox.

Political Theory & Praxis: New Perspectives. Ed. by Terence Ball. LC 77-73320. 1977. 16.75x o.p. (ISBN 0-8166-0816-4). U of Minn Pr.

Political Theory & Public Policy. Robert E. Goodin. LC 81-23120. 1982. lib. bdg. 27.50x o.s.i. (ISBN 0-226-30296-2). U of Chicago Pr.

Political Theory As Public Confession. Peter D. Bathory. LC 80-15667. 180p. 1981. 24.95 o.p. (ISBN 0-87855-405-X); text ed. 24.95 o.p. Transaction Pubs.

Political Theory of John Wyclif. Lowrie J. Daly. LC 62-20515. (Jesuit Studies). 1962. 4.95 o.p. (ISBN 0-8294-0020-6). Loyola.

Political Thought of Hannah Arendt. Margaret Canovan. LC 74-3037. 144p. 1974. 6.50 o.p. (ISBN 0-15-172815-1). HarBraceJ.

Political Thought of the American Revolution. rev. ed. Clinton Rossiter. LC 63-24720. 1963. pap. 2.95 o.p. (ISBN 0-15-672680-7, Harv). HarBraceJ.

Political Tolerance in America: Freedom & Equality in Political Attitudes. Michael Corbett. LC 81-11799. (Illus.). 240p. 1982. pap. text ed. 16.45 o.p. (ISBN 0-582-28262-4). Longman.

Political Unification: A Comparitive Study of Leaders & Forces. Amitai Etzioni. LC 74-12176. 366p. 1974. Repr. of 1965 ed. 18.50 o.p. (ISBN 0-88275-196-4). Krieger.

Political Uses of Symbols. Charles D. Elder & Roger W. Cobb. Ed. by Irving Rockwood. LC 82-12722. (Professional Studies in Political Communication). (Illus.). 192p. 1983. text ed. 22.50x o.p. (ISBN 0-582-28392-2); pap. text ed. 14.95 o.p. (ISBN 0-582-28393-0). Longman.

Political Verse & Song from Britain & Ireland. Mary Asbraf. 1976. 9.95x o.p. (ISBN 0-8464-0731-0). Beekman Pubs.

Political Violence in the United States, 1875-1974: A Bibliography. Jarol B. Manheim & Melanie Wallace. LC 74-34143. (Reference Library of Social Science: No. 8). 118p. 1974. lib. bdg. 25.00 o.p. (ISBN 0-8240-1093-0). Garland Pub.

Political Works of Concealed Authorship: Relating to the United States 1789-1810. 3rd ed. Pierce W. Gaines. LC 76-178861. xx, 226p. 1972. 25.00 o.p. (ISBN 0-208-01241-9, Archon). Shoe String.

Political Writings. George W. Hegel. LC 83-48510. (Philosophy of Hegel Ser.). 342p. 1984. lib. bdg. 40.00 o.p. (ISBN 0-8240-5633-7). Garland Pub.

Political Writings: Psychopathology & Politics; Politics: Who Gets What, When, How; Democratic Character. Harold D. Lasswell. LC 78-11498. vii, 525p. 1979. Repr. of 1951 ed. lib. bdg. 32.50x o.p. (ISBN 0-313-20761-5, LAPW). Greenwood.

Politicos. Matthew Josephson. LC 38-27301. 760p. 1963. pap. 5.95 o.p. (ISBN 0-15-672799-4, Harv). HarBraceJ.

Politics. Edward I. Koch & William Rauch. (Illus.). 256p. 1986. 17.45 o.p. (ISBN 0-671-53296-0). S&S.

Politics & Development. Ed. by Brian Head. 280p. 1987. text ed. 34.95x o.p. (ISBN 0-86861-811-X). Unwin Hyman.

Politics & Economics Policy; From Hoover to Reagan. William Withers. 1986. 10.95 o.p. (ISBN 0-8062-2722-2). Carlton.

Politics & Government: How People Decide Their Fate. 2nd ed. Karl W. Deutsch. 650p. 1974. text ed. 16.50 o.p. (ISBN 0-395-17840-1). HM.

Politics & Government in Japan. 2nd ed. Theodore McNelly. LC 74-186377. (Contemporary Government Ser.). (Illus.). 256p. (Orig.). 1972. pap. 15.50 o.p. (ISBN 0-395-12649-5). HM.

Politics & Jurisprudence. Paul Woelfl. LC 65-26035. (Orig.). 1966. pap. 2.95 o.p. (ISBN 0-8294-0083-4). Loyola.

Politics & Policy in States & Communities. 2nd ed. John J. Harrigan. 1984. text ed. write for info. o.p. (ISBN 0-673-39443-3). Scott F.

Politics & Policy Making in Britain. Lynton Robins. LC 86-10351. (Contemporary Politics Ser.). 224p. 1987. pap. text ed. 12.95 o.p. (ISBN 0-582-35494-3). Longman.

Politics & Political Systems. J. W. Ellsworth & A. A. Stahnke. 1976. text ed. 27.95x o.p. (ISBN 0-07-019250-2). McGraw.

Politics & Religion in Seventeenth-Century France. W. J. Stankiewicz. LC 76-2075. 269p. 1976. Repr. of 1960 ed. lib. bdg. 22.50x o.p. (ISBN 0-8371-8770-2, STPR). Greenwood.

Politics & Society in Rural India: A Case Study of Darauli Gram Panchayat, Siwan District, Bihar. S. N. Mishra. 184p. 1980. text ed. 11.75x o.p. (ISBN 0-391-02123-0). Humanities.

Politics & Society in the Third World. Jean-Yves Calvez. Tr. by Matthew J. OConnell from Fr. LC 72-85792. 256p. (Orig.). 1973. pap. 3.48 o.p. (ISBN 0-88344-389-9). Orbis Bks.

Politics & the Athenian Constitution. Aristotle. Tr. by John Warrington. 1961. Repr. of 1959 ed. 8.95x o.p. (ISBN 0-460-00605-3, Evman). Biblio Dist.

Politics & the Media: Film & Television for the Political Scientist & Historian. M. J. Clark. (Audio-Visual Media Education & Research: Vol. 1). 1979. 36.00 o.p. (ISBN 0-08-022483-0); pap. 18.75 o.p. (ISBN 0-08-022484-9). Pergamon.

Politics & the Media in Canada. A. Siegel. 192p. 1983. text ed. 10.95 o.p. (ISBN 0-07-077866-3). McGraw.

Politics As Symbolic Action: Mass Arousal & Quiescence. Murray Edelman. (Institute for Research on Poverty Monograph). 1971. 20.00 o.p. (ISBN 0-12-230650-3); pap. 14.95 o.p. (ISBN 0-12-230652-X). Acad Pr.

Politics at God's Funeral: The Spiritual Western Civilization. Michael Harrington. LC 83-73. 283p. 1984. 16.45 o.s.i. (ISBN 0-03-062152-6). H Holt & Co.

Politics, Geography & Social Stratification. Ed. by Keith Hoggart & Eleonore Kofman. 304p. 1986. 50.00 o.p. (ISBN 0-7099-3784-9, Pub. by Croom Helm Ltd). Routledge Chapman & Hall.

Politics: How to Get Involved. Levenson. (gr. 7 up). 1980. PLB 9.90 o.p. (ISBN 0-531-04166-2, G09). Watts.

Politics, Ideology & the State: Papers from the Communist University of London. Ed. by Sally Hibbin. 1978. pap. text ed. 8.50x o.p. (ISBN 0-85315-462-7, Pub. by Lawrence & Wishare UK). Humanities.

Politics in Africa: The Former British Territories. J. F. Maitland-Jones. (Comparative Modern Government Ser.). (Illus.). 236p. 1974. pap. 3.25x o.p. (ISBN 0-393-09305-0). Norton.

Politics in America: Members of Congress in Washington & at Home, 1984. Alan Ehrenhalt & Michael Glennon. LC 81-9848. 1734p. 1983. 29.95 o.p. (ISBN 0-87187-259-5). Congr Quarterly.

Politics in America: Readings & Documents. Ed. by Philip J. Briggs. LC 72-86017. 266p. 1972. 29.00x o.p. (ISBN 0-8422-5037-9); pap. text ed. 14.50x o.p. (ISBN 0-8290-0664-8). Irvington.

Politics in America: Studies in Policy Analysis. Smith, Michael P., & Associates Staff. LC 81-40768. 188p. 1981. pap. text ed. 10.00 o.p. (ISBN 0-8191-1828-1). U Pr of Amer.

Politics in Art. Joan A. Mondale. LC 72-266. (Fine Art Bks.). (Illus.). 72p. (gr. 5-12). 1972. PLB 5.95 o.p. (ISBN 0-8225-0170-8); pap. 3.95 o.p. (ISBN 0-8225-9950-3). Lerner Pubns.

Politics in Central America: Guatemala, El Salvador, Honduras, & Nicaragua. Thomas P. Anderson. Ed. by Robert Wesson. LC 81-15787. (Politics in Latin America, A Hoover Institution Ser.). 240p. 1982. lib. bdg. 31.95 o.s.i. (ISBN 0-275-90755-4, C0755). Praeger.

Politics in England. 4th ed. Richard Rose. (Comparative Politics Ser.). 1986. pap. text ed. write for info. o.p. (ISBN 0-673-39473-5). Scott F.

Politics in High Latitudes: The Svalbard Archipelago. Willy Olstreng. 1978. 18.95x o.p. (ISBN 0-7735-0312-9, McGill Canada). U of Toronto Pr.

Politics in Liberia: The Conservative Road to Development. Martin Lowenkopf. LC 75-27010. (Publications Ser.: No. 151). 260p. 1976. 11.95x o.p. (ISBN 0-8179-6511-4). Hoover Inst Pr.

Politics in Mexico. Ed. by George Philip. LC 85-3791. 223p. 1985. 34.50 o.p. (ISBN 0-7099-2085-7, Pub. by Croom Helm Ltd). Routledge Chapman & Hall.

Politics in Mexico: An Introduction & Overview. Wayne A. Cornelius & Ann L. Craig. (Reprint Ser.: No. 1). (Illus.). 57p. (Orig.). 1984. pap. 6.00 o.p. (ISBN 0-935391-54-1, RS-01). Ctr Mex Studies.

Politics in New Caledonia. Myriam Dornoy. (Illus.). 302p. 1984. text ed. 52.00x o.p. (ISBN 0-424-00101-2, Pub. by Sydney U Pr Australia). Intl Spec Bk.

Politics in the Twentieth Century. abr. ed. Hans W. Morgenthau. LC 70-148581. 1971. pap. text ed. 4.95x o.s.i. (ISBN 0-226-53825-7, P425, Phoen). U of Chicago Pr.

Politics Is a Funny Business. Joel Rothman. (Illus.). 78p. 1985. pap. 2.95 o.p. (ISBN 0-86051-233-9). Parkwest Pubns.

Politics, Language & Time: Essays on Political Thought & History. J. G. Pocock. LC 73-139322. 1971. pap. text ed. 3.25x o.p. (ISBN 0-689-70342-2, 198, Atheneum). Macmillan.

Politics, Medicine & Christian Ethics: A Dialogue with Paul Ramsey. Charles E. Curran. LC 72-91521. 240p. (Orig.). 1973. 1.50 o.p. (ISBN 0-8006-0500-4, 1-500, Fortress). Augsburg Fortress.

Politics of African & Middle Eastern States: An Annotated Bibliography. Anne G. Drabek & Wilfred Knapp. LC 76-26649. 1977. 34.00 o.p. (ISBN 0-08-020584-4); pap. 16.25 o.p. (ISBN 0-08-020583-6). Pergamon.

Politics of Agrarian Change in Asia & Latin America. Ed. by Howard Handelman. LC 81-47565. (Illus.). 148p. 1981. 22.50x o.p. (ISBN 0-253-34548-0). Ind U Pr.

Politics of Alternative Technology. David Dickson. LC 75-7919. 224p. 1975. pap. 8.00x o.p. (ISBN 0-87663-224-X). Universe.

Politics of American Cities: Private Power & Public Policy. 2nd ed. Dennis R. Judd. 1984. pap. text ed. 17.50 o.p. (ISBN 0-673-39453-0). Scott F.

Politics of Antipolitics: The Military in Latin America. Ed. by Brian Loveman & Thomas M. Davies, Jr. LC 77-25256. x, 309p. 1978. 21.95x o.p. (ISBN 0-8032-0954-1); pap. 7.50x o.p. (ISBN 0-8032-7900-0, BB 672, Bison). U of Nebr Pr.

Politics of Anxiety: Sellafield's Cancer-Link Controversy. Sally MacGill. 209p. 1987. text ed. 28.95x o.p. (ISBN 0-85086-127-6, Pub. by Pion England). Routledge Chapman & Hall.

Politics of Authenticity: Radical Individualism & the Emergence of Modern Society. Marshall Berman. LC 77-124968. 1970. pap. 5.95x o.s.i. (ISBN 0-689-70288-4, 170, Atheneum). Macmillan.

Politics of Autonomy: A Kantian Reading of Rousseau's "Social Contract" Andrew Levine. LC 76-8757. 224p. 1976. 15.00x o.p. (ISBN 0-87023-215-0). U of Mass Pr.

Politics of Bhutan. Leo E. Rose. LC 77-4792. 304p. 1977. 35.00x o.p. (ISBN 0-8014-0909-8). Cornell U Pr.

Politics of Bureaucracy: A Comparative Analysis. B. Guy Peters. LC 77-24584. (Comparative Studies of Political Life). (Illus.). 1983. text ed. 33.95 o.p. (ISBN 0-582-28317-5); pap. text ed. 17.95 o.p. (ISBN 0-582-28316-7). Longman.

Politics of California Coastal Legislation: The Crucial Year, 1976. Peverill Squire & Stanley Scott. LC 84-715. 104p. 1984. pap. 3.95 o.p. (ISBN 0-87772-298-6). UCB IGS.

Politics of Cancer. Samuel S. Epstein. LC 78-985. 600p. 1978. 12.50 o.s.i. (ISBN 0-87156-193-X). Sierra.

Politics of Compromise: Coalition Government in Colombia. Ed. by R. Albert Berry et al. LC 78-64478. 488p. 1980. 29.95 o.p. (ISBN 0-87855-301-0); pap. text ed. 7.95x o.p. (ISBN 0-87855-723-7). Transaction Pubs.

Politics of Congressional Elections 1983. Gary C. Jacobson. 1982. 12.00 o.p. (ISBN 0-316-45563-6). Little.

Politics of Consumer Protection. Mark V. Nadel. 1971. pap. text ed. write for info. o.p. (ISBN 0-02-385870-2). Macmillan.

Politics of Contraception, Nineteen Eighty. Carl Djerassi. (Illus.). 1980. 12.95 o.p. (ISBN 0-393-01264-6). Norton.

Politics of Cotton Textiles in Kuomintang China, 1927-1937: China During the Interregnum 1911-1949, the Economy & Society. Richard C. Bush. Ed. by Ramon H. Myers. LC 80-8836. 360p. 1982. lib. bdg. 36.00 o.p. (ISBN 0-8240-4691-9). Garland Pub.

Politics of Crime & Criminal Justice. Erika Fairchild & Vincent J. Webb. LC 84-27590. 1985. 25.00 o.p. (ISBN 0-8039-2423-2); pap. 12.95 o.p. (ISBN 0-8039-2424-0). Sage.

Politics of Crude Oil Pricing in the Middle East, 1970 to 1975: A Study in International Bargaining. Richard C. Weisberg. LC 77-620041. (Research Ser.: No. 31). (Illus.). 1977. pap. 4.95x o.s.i. (ISBN 0-87725-131-2). U of Cal Intl St.

Politics of De-Industrialisation: The Contraction of the West European Shipbuilding Industry. Bo Strath. 320p. 1987. lib. bdg. 57.50x o.p. (ISBN 0-7099-5401-8, Pub. by Croom Helm UK). Routledge Chapman & Hall.

Politics of Defense Contracting: The Iron Triangle. Gordon Adams. 465p. 1981. 39.95 o.p. (ISBN 0-87855-457-2); pap. 15.00 o.s.i. (ISBN 0-87871-012-4). CEP.

Politics of Education: 76th Yearbook, Part 2. Ed. by Jay Scribner. LC 74-44918. (National Society for the Study of Education Ser.). 1980. pap. text ed. 7.50x o.s.i. (ISBN 0-226-60104-8). U of Chicago Pr.

Politics of Educational Reform 1920-1940. Brian Simon. (Studies History of Education: No. 3). 400p. 1974. 29.95 o.p. (ISBN 0-8464-0732-9); pap. 16.95 o.p. (ISBN 0-8464-0733-7). Beekman Pubs.

Politics of Fantasy: C. S. Lewis & J. R. R. Tolkien. Lee D. Rossi. Ed. by Robert Scholes. LC 84-16116. (Studies in Speculative Fiction: No. 10). 154p. 1984. 37.95 o.p. (ISBN 0-8357-1597-3). UMI Res Pr.

Politics of Federal Grants. Marian L & George E. Hale. LC 81-960. 191p. (Orig.). 1981. pap. 8.75 o.p. (ISBN 0-87187-161-0). Congr Quarterly.

Politics of Federal Judicial Administration. Peter G. Fish. LC 76-39785. 488p. 1973. 54.00x o.p. (ISBN 0-691-09226-5); pap. 19.50x o.p. (ISBN 0-691-10013-6). Princeton U Pr.

Politics of Friendship: Pompey & Cicero. Beryl Rawson. (Sources in Ancient History Ser.). 1978. pap. 17.00x o.p. (ISBN 0-424-06800-1, Pub. by Sydney U Pr). Intl Spec Bk.

Politics of Health. Ed. by DouglasS Cater & Philip R. Lee. LC 77-28732. 248p. 1979. Repr. of 1972 ed. lib. bdg. 16.50 o.p. (ISBN 0-88275-640-0). Krieger.

Politics of Homosexuality. Toby Marotta. 384p. 1981. 16.95 o.p. (ISBN 0-395-29477-0); pap. 9.95 o.p. (ISBN 0-395-31338-4). HM.

Politics of Human Rights. Andrei Sakharov et al. (ISBN 0-318-03636-3). Trilateral Comm.

Politics of Inflation: A Comparative Analysis. Ed. by Richard Medley. (Pergamon Policy Studies on International Politics). 264p. 1982. 65.00 o.p. (ISBN 0-08-024625-7). Pergamon.

Politics of International Investment. Earl H. Fry. 224p. 1983. text ed. 29.95 o.p. (ISBN 0-07-022610-5). McGraw.

Politics of Irish Literature: From Thomas Davis to W. B. Yeats. Malcolm Brown. LC 72-152328. (Washington Paperback Ser.: No. 67). 443p. 1972. 20.00x o.p. (ISBN 0-295-95170-2); pap. 7.95x o.p. (ISBN 0-295-95280-6). U of Wash Pr.

Politics of Israel: The First Decade of Statehood. Marver H. Bernstein. LC 69-13825. 1969. Repr. of 1957 ed. lib. bdg. 22.50 o.p. (ISBN 0-8371-2036-5, BEPI). Greenwood.

Politics of Law: A Progressive Critique. Kairys David. 1982. pap. 7.00 o.p. Natl Lawyers Guild.

Politics of Linguistics. Frederick J. Newmeyer. LC 86-11225. 192p. 1987. 23.95x o.s.i. (ISBN 0-226-57720-1). U of Chicago Pr.

Politics of Local Socialism. John Gyford. (Local Government Briefings Ser.). 170p. 1985. text ed. 29.95x o.p. (ISBN 0-04-352213-0); pap. text ed. 11.95x o.p. (ISBN 0-04-352214-9). Unwin Hyman.

Politics of Massacre: Political Processes in South Vietnam. Charles A. Joiner. LC 72-95882. 362p. 1974. 19.95 o.p. (ISBN 0-87722-060-3). Temple U Pr.

Politics of Massive Resistance. Francis M. Wilhoit. 1973. 8.95 o.p. (ISBN 0-8076-0700-2); pap. 3.95 o.p. (ISBN 0-8076-0701-0). Braziller.

Politics of Modernization. David Apter. LC 65-24421. 1967. pap. text ed. 2.95 o.s.i. (ISBN 0-226-02347-8, P281, Phoen). U of Chicago Pr.

Politics of Moralism: The New Christian Right in American Life. Erling Jorstad. LC 81-65641. 128p. (Orig.). 1981. pap. 6.95 o.p. (ISBN 0-8066-1877-9, 10-5011, Augsburg). Augsburg Fortress.

Politics of National Despair: French Royalism in the Post-Reformation Era. George D. Balsama. 1977. pap. text ed. 10.00 o.p. (ISBN 0-8191-0142-7). U Pr of Amer.

Politics of New Town Planning: The Newfields, Ohio, Story. Frederick Steiner. LC 80-12783. (Illus.). xiv, 266p. 1981. 17.95x o.p. (ISBN 0-8214-0414-8). Ohio U Pr.

Politics of Normalcy: Governmental Theory & Practice in the Harding-Coolidge Era. Robert K. Murray. (Norton Essays in American History Ser.). 160p. 1973. pap. text ed. 3.95x o.p. (ISBN 0-393-09422-7). Norton.

Politics of Pollution. 2nd ed. Barbara S. Davies & J. Clarence Davies, 3rd. LC 74-20996. (Studies in Contemporary America). 256p. 1975. pap. write for info. o.p. (ISBN 0-02-327900-1). Macmillan.

Politics of Positive Discrimination: An Evaluation of the Urban Programme, 1967-1977. John Edwards & Richard Batley. 1978. 27.00x o.p. (ISBN 0-422-76660-7, NO. 2176, Pub. by Tavistock). Routledge Chapman & Hall.

Politics of Power: A Critical Introduction to American Government. Ira Katznelson & Mark Kesselman. 513p. (Orig.). 1975. pap. text ed. 11.95 o.p. (ISBN 0-15-570744-2, HC). HarBraceJ.

Politics of Power: A Critical Introduction to American Government. 2nd ed. Ira Katznelson & Mark Kesselman. 435p. 1979. pap. text ed. 16.00 o.p. (ISBN 0-15-570746-9, HC). HarBraceJ.

Politics of Provincialism: The Democratic Party in Transition, 1918-1932. David Burner. 320p. 1975. pap. 3.95 o.p. (ISBN 0-393-00792-8, N792, Norton Lib). Norton.

Politics of Public-Facility Planning. John E. Seley. LC 82-47802. (Politics of Planning Ser.). (Illus.). 256p. 1983. 32.00x o.p. (ISBN 0-669-05642-1). Lexington Bks.

Politics of Repeal. Kevin B. Nowlan. LC 75-35339. 248p. 1976. Repr. of 1965 ed. lib. bdg. 17.00x o.p. (ISBN 0-8371-8562-9, NOPR). Greenwood.

Politics of Reproduction. Mary O'Brien. 1983. pap. 10.95 o.p. (ISBN 0-7100-9498-1). Routledge Chapman & Hall.

Politics of Riot Behavior. L. Alex Swan. LC 79-5510. 1980. pap. text ed. 13.50 o.p. (ISBN 0-8191-0905-3). U Pr of Amer.

Politics of School Management. Eric Hoyle. (Studies in Teaching & Learning). 188p. (Orig.). 1986. pap. text ed. 20.95 o.s.i. (ISBN 0-340-38993-1). Princeton Bk Co.

Politics of Teacher Unionism: International Perspectives. Ed. by Martin Lawn. LC 85-4176. 302p. 1985. 31.00 o.p. (ISBN 0-7099-1696-5, Pub. by Croom Helm Ltd). Routledge Chapman & Hall.

Politics of Territorial Identity: Studies in European Regionalism. European Consortium for Political Research Staff & Stein Rokkan. LC 82-80204. (Illus.). 438p. 1982. 27.50 o.p. (ISBN 0-8039-9788-4). Sage.

Politics of the Eighth Central Committee of the Communist Party of China. Peter R. Moody, Jr. LC 73-4308. (Foreign Area Studies). xi, 346p. 1973. 35.00 o.p. (ISBN 0-208-01328-8, ARCHON). Shoe String.

Politics of the Labour Party. Ed. by Denis Kavanagh. 240p. 1982. text ed. 39.95x o.p. (ISBN 0-04-329037-X); pap. text ed. 9.95x o.p. (ISBN 0-04-329038-8). Unwin Hyman.

Politics of the Pacific Nations. Ed. by F. Q. Quo. (Replica Edition Ser.). 275p. cancelled o.s.i. (ISBN 0-86531-951-0). Westview.

Politics of the Second Electorate: Women & Public Participation: Britain, U. S. A., Canada, Australia, France, Spain, West Germany, Italy, Sweden, Finland, Eastern Europe, U. S. S. R., & Japan. Ed. by Joni Lovenduski & Jill Hills. 280p. (Orig.). 1981. pap. 16.95x o.p. (ISBN 0-7100-0806-6). Routledge Chapman & Hall.

Politics of the Tanzania-Zambia Railproject. Kasuka S. Mutuwka. 1977. pap. text ed. 13.50 o.p. (ISBN 0-8191-0301-2). U Pr of Amer.

Politics of the Yorkshire Miners. Andrew Taylor. 256p. 1984. 34.50 o.p. (ISBN 0-7099-2447-X, Pub. by Croom Helm Ltd). Routledge Chapman & Hall.

Politics of Uncertainty: Regulating Recombinant DNA Research in Britain. David Bennett et al. 256p. 1986. text ed. 24.95 o.p. (ISBN 0-7102-0503-1). Routledge Chapman & Hall.

Politics of Upheaval (The Age of Roosevelt, Vol. 3. Arthur M. Schlesinger, Jr. pap. 7.95 o.p. (ISBN 0-395-08396-6). HM.

Politics of Urban Change. David McKay & Andrew W. Cox. 297p. 1979. 32.00x o.p. (ISBN 0-85664-436-6, Pub. by Croom Helm Ltd); pap. 10.75 o.p. (ISBN 0-85664-847-7). Routledge Chapman & Hall.

Politics of Violence: The New Urban Blacks & the Watts Riot. David O. Sears & John B. McConahay. 1973. pap. 8.50 o.p. (ISBN 0-395-11927-8). HM.

Politics of Western Europe. Ed. by Gerald Dorfman & Peter Duignan. (Publications Ser.: No. P-360). (Orig.). 1987. pap. text ed. 16.95 o.p. Hoover Inst Pr.

Politics, Oil & the Western Mediterranean. R. M. Burrell & Alvin J. Cottrell. (Washington Papers: Vol. I, No. 7). 88p. (Orig.). 1973. pap. text ed. 7.95 o.p. (ISBN 0-8191-5963-8, Pub. by CSIS). U Pr of Amer.

Politics, Philosophy, Culture: Interviews & Other Writings, 1977-1984. Michel Foucault. Ed. by Lawrence D. Kritzman. Tr. by Alan Sheridan. 280p. 1988. text ed. 30.00x o.p. (ISBN 0-416-01951-X); pap. text ed. 11.95x o.p. Routledge Chapman & Hall.

Politics, Principle & Prejudice 1865-1866: Dilemma of Reconstruction in America. John H. Cox & Lawanda Cox. LC 63-10647. (Studies in American Negro Life). 1969. pap. 4.95 o.p. (ISBN 0-689-70053-9, NL18, Atheneum). Macmillan.

Politics, the Constitution & the Warren Court. Philip B. Kurland. LC 74-124734. 1973. pap. text ed. 4.50x o.s.i. (ISBN 0-226-46407-5, P554, Phoen). U of Chicago Pr.

Politics Thro' the Looking Glass. Stan Windass. (Illus.). 188p. (Orig.). 1981. pap. 3.75x o.p. (ISBN 0-907650-00-7). LRIS.

Politisch motivierte Kriminalitaet-Echte Kriminalitaet. Ed. by Institut fuer Konfliktforschung Staff. (Schriftenreihe des Instituts fuer Konfliktforschung: Heft 4). 1978. 9.50 o.p. (ISBN 3-8055-2846-9). S Karger.

Polk County Folks, Vol. 1. Don Hendrix. LC 84-80314. 167p. (Orig.). 1984. pap. 15.95 o.p. (ISBN 0-911317-30-9). Ericson Bks.

Pollen: Biology, Biochemistry, & Management. R. G. Stanley & H. F. Linskens. (Illus.). x, 307p. 1975. 36.00 o.p. (ISBN 0-387-06827-9). Springer-Verlag.

Pollination of Flowers by Insects. Ed. by A. J. Richard. (Linnean Society Symposium Ser.). 1979. 49.50 o.p. (ISBN 0-12-587460-X). Acad Pr.

Polling on the Issues. Ed. by Albert H. Cantril et al. Jack Germond & Irving Grespi. LC 80-23439. 224p. 1980. 11.95 o.p. (ISBN 0-932020-02-X); pap. 7.95 o.p. (ISBN 0-932020-03-8). Seven Locks Pr.

Pollock Personal Shorthand: A Primer. John Pollock. 1972. 3.50 o.p. (ISBN 0-682-47360-X). Exposition-Phoenix.

Polluted Homes. Peter Gregory. 64p. 1965. pap. text ed. 3.75x o.p. (ISBN 0-686-70853-9, Pub. by Bedford England). Gower Pub Co.

Polluted Nursery Rhymes. Jerry B. German. 1974. pap. 2.50 o.p. (ISBN 0-682-47864-4). Exposition-Phoenix.

Polluted Pond: The Myth about Aging. Kata Lekich. 104p. 1986. 8.95 o.p. (ISBN 0-8062-2863-6). Carlton.

Pollution Control Problems & Related Federal Legislation. Ed. by T. J. Morrisey. 290p. 1974. text ed. 29.50x o.p. (ISBN 0-8422-5175-8); pap. text ed. 12.50x o.p. (ISBN 0-8422-0418-0). Irvington.

Pollution Engineering Practice Handbook. Paul N. Cheremisinoff & Richard A. Young. LC 74-14427. 1975. 59.95 o.p. (ISBN 0-250-40075-8). Butterworth.

Pollution Japan: Historical Chronology. Nobuku Iijima. 401p. 1980. 93.00 o.p. (ISBN 0-08-026242-2). Pergamon.

Pollution Research Index: A Guide to World Research in Environmental Pollution. 2nd ed. Ed. by Andrew I. Sors & David Coleman. 555p. 220.00x o.p. (ISBN 0-582-90006-9, Pub. by Longman). Gale.

Pollution, Resources & the Environment. new ed. Ed. by Alain C. Enthoven & A. Myrick Freeman, 3rd. (Problems of Modern Economy Ser.). (Illus.). 1973. pap. 7.95x o.p. (ISBN 0-393-09933-4). Norton.

Pollution: The Neglected Dimensions. Denis Hayes. LC 79-63578. (Worldwatch Papers). 1979. pap. 4.00 o.p. (ISBN 0-916468-26-7). Worldwatch Inst.

Pollution, Vol. 4 (incl. 1985-1987 Supplement) Ed. by Eleanor C. Goldstein. (Social Issues Resources Ser.). 1987. 45.00 o.p. (ISBN 0-89777-118-4). Soc Issues.

Polly. Betty Neels. 262p. 1986. pap. 10.95x o.p. (ISBN 0-8161-4107-X, Large Print Bks). G K Hall.

Polnoe Sobranie Sochinenii, Vol. I. Aleksandr Vvedenskii. Ed. by M. Meilakh. (Rus.). 1980. 25.00 o.p. (ISBN 0-88233-321-6); pap. 7.50 o.p. (ISBN 0-88233-322-4). Ardis Pubs.

Polonaise. Piers P. Read. 1977. pap. 1.95 o.p. (ISBN 0-380-01714-8, 33894-7). Avon.

Poltergeists. Alan Gauld & A. D. Cornell. (Illus.). 1979. 26.95 o.p. (ISBN 0-7100-0185-1). Routledge Chapman & Hall.

Polyacetal Resins. Marshall Sittig. LC 63-1271. 152p. 1963. 6.95x o.p. (ISBN 0-87201-722-2). Gulf Pub.

Polyamines in Biomedical Research. Ed. by Joseph M. Gaugas. LC 79-40651. 474p. 1980. 140.00 o.p. (ISBN 0-471-27629-4). Wiley.

Polyandry in Ancient India. Sarva D. Singh. 1980. text ed. 30.00x o.p. (ISBN 0-7069-0729-9, Pub. by Vikas India). Advent NY.

Polychaeta of Southern Africa, 2 pts. J. H. Day. (Illus.). 1967. text ed. 60.00x o.p. (ISBN 0-565-00656-8, Pub. by Brit Mus Nat Hist England). Sabbot-Natural Hist Bks.

Polychlorinated Biphenyls. National Research Council Staff. 1979. pap. 8.75x o.p. (ISBN 0-309-02885-X). Natl Acad Pr.

Polycyclic Hydrocarbons, 2 Vols. E. Clar. 1964. Vol. 1. 87.50 o.p. (ISBN 0-12-174701-8); Vol. 2. 110.00 o.p. (ISBN 0-12-174702-6). Acad Pr.

Polyelectrolyte Solutions: A Theoretical Introduction. Stuart A. Rice. (Molecular Biology Ser.). 1961. 92.00 o.p. (ISBN 0-12-587350-6). Acad Pr.

Polyelectrolytes. Kurt C. Frisch et al. LC 76-177446. (Illus.). 1976. 35.00 o.p. (ISBN 0-87762-076-8). Technomic.

Polyglot of Foreign Proverbs - with English Translations. Ed. by Henry G. Bohn. LC 67-23915. (Polyglot Ser.). 590p. 1968. Repr. of 1857 ed. 40.00x o.p. (ISBN 0-8103-3197-7). Gale.

Polymer Applications of Renewable-Resource Materials. Ed. by Charles E. Carraher, Jr. & L. H. Sperling. LC 82-10127. (Polymer Science & Technology Ser.: Vol. 17). 484p. 1983. 79.50x o.p. (ISBN 0-306-41033-8, Plenum Pr). Plenum Pub.

Polymer Chemistry. B. Vollmert. Tr. by E. H. Immergut. LC 72-175905. (Illus.). 736p. 1973. 24.80 o.p. (ISBN 0-387-05631-9). Springer-Verlag.

Polymer Colloids I. Ed. by Robert M. Fitch. LC 70-153721. 188p. 1971. 49.50x o.p. (ISBN 0-306-30536-4, Plenum Pr). Plenum Pub.

Polymer Colloids II. Ed. by Robert M. Fitch. LC 80-112. 696p. 1980. 110.00x o.p. (ISBN 0-306-40350-1, Plenum Pr). Plenum Pub.

Polymer Concrete: Seven Reports. (Transportation Research Record Ser.). 67p. 1975. 3.20 o.p. (ISBN 0-309-02395-5). Transport Res Bd.

Polymer Conformation & Configuration. Frank A. Bovey. (Current Chemical Concepts Monographs). 1969. 59.00 o.p. (ISBN 0-12-119760-3). Acad Pr.

Polymer Fractionation. Ed. by M. J. Cantow. 1967. 102.00 o.p. (ISBN 0-12-158850-5). Acad Pr.

Polymer Materials. C. Hall. (Illus.). 198p. 1985. pap. 25.00 o.p. (ISBN 0-333-28908-0, 0805). T-C Pubns CA.

Polymer Membranes. (Advances in Polymer Science Ser.: Vol. 64). (Illus.). 150p. 1985. 32.00 o.p. (ISBN 0-387-13483-2). Springer-Verlag.

Polymer Mixing Technology. G. A. Matthews. (Illus.). 280p. 1982. 66.75 o.p. (ISBN 0-85334-133-8, Pub. by Elsevier Applied Sci England). Elsevier.

Polymer Solution Properties: Part I, Statistics & Thermodynamics. Ed. by J. J. Hermans. LC 87-820. (Benchmark Papers in Polymer Chemistry: Vol. 1). 234p. 1983. 48.95 o.p. (ISBN 0-87933-322-7); Set. 96.95 o.p. (ISBN 0-87933-094-5). Van Nos Reinhold.

Polymer Spectroscopy. Dieter O. Hummel. LC 73-90783. (Monographs in Modern Chemistry: Vol. 6). (Illus.). 401p. 1974. 96.90x o.p. (ISBN 3-527-25411-0). VCH Pubs.

Polymerization of Heterocycles (Ring-Opening) Ed. by S. Penczek. LC 76-44623. 1977. 40.00 o.p. (ISBN 0-08-021367-7). Pergamon.

Polymerization Reactions. Incl. Stable Organic Cation Salts: Ion Pair Equilibria & Use in Cationic Polymerization. A. Ledwith & D. C. Sherrington; Cationic Isomerization: Polymerization of Three-Methyl-One-Butene & Four-Methyl-One-Penene. J. P. Kennedy & J. E. Johnston; Grafting on Polyamides. E. B. Mano & F. M. Coutinho; Rigid Rods & the Characterization of Polyisozyanides. F. Millich. (Advances in Polymer Science: Vol. 19). (Illus.). 150p. 1976. 42.00 o.p. (ISBN 0-387-07460-0). Springer-Verlag.

Polymers at Surfaces & Colloid Stability. E. Eisenreighler & P. Pincus. (Advanced Series in Surface Science: Vol. 2). 220p. 1989. 37.00 o.p. (ISBN 9971-50-234-8). World Scientific Pub.

Polymers in Medicine & Surgery. Ed. by Richard L. Kronenthal et al. LC 75-33684. (Polymer Science & Technology Ser.: Vol. 8). 346p. 1975. 65.00x o.p. (ISBN 0-306-36408-5, Plenum Pr). Plenum Pub.

Polymetis. Joseph Spence. LC 75-27886. (Renaissance & the Gods Ser.: Vol. 41). (Illus.). 1976. Repr. of 1747 ed. lib. bdg. 88.00 o.p. (ISBN 0-8240-2090-1). Garland Pub.

Polynesian Languages: A Guide, Vol. 5. Viktor Krupa. (Languages of Asia & Africa Ser.). 200p. (Orig., Pol.). 1982. pap. 17.95x o.p. (ISBN 0-7100-9075-7). Routledge Chapman & Hall.

Polynomial Response Maps. E. D. Sontag. (Lecture Notes in Control & Information Sciences: Vol. 13). 1979. pap. 14.00 o.p. (ISBN 0-387-09393-1). Springer-Verlag.

Polyoma Virus: Current Research, Vol. 1. James B. Hudson et al. LC 73-8643. (Oncogenic Viruses Ser.). 172p. 1973. text ed. 27.50x o.p. (ISBN 0-8422-7117-1). Irvington.

Polyoma Virus: Current Research, Vol. 2. P. E. Branton et al. LC 73-8643. (Oncogenic Viruses Ser.). 160p. 1973. text ed. 27.50x o.p. (ISBN 0-8422-7118-X). Irvington.

Polypeptide Hormones: Molecular & Cellular Aspects. Ciba Foundation Staff. (CIBA Foundation Symposium Ser.: No. 41). 1976. 54.25 o.p. (ISBN 0-444-15207-5, Excerpta Medica). Elsevier.

Polyphase Flow & Transport Technology. Ed. by R. A. Bajura. 270p. 1980. 40.00 o.p. (ISBN 0-686-69858-4, H00158). ASME.

Polyphemus. Michael Shea. (Illus.). 256p. 1987. 16.95 o.p. (ISBN 0-87054-155-2). Arkham.

Polyploidy. Ed. by R. C. Jackson & Donald P. Hauber. LC 82-21388. (Benchmark Papers in Genetics: Vol. 12). 400p. 1983. 44.95 o.p. (ISBN 0-87933-088-0). Van Nos Reinhold.

Polysaccharide-Protein Complexes in Invertebrates. S. Hunt. 1970. 55.00 o.p. (ISBN 0-12-362050-3). Acad Pr.

Polyunsaturated Fatty Acids in Nutrition: Proceedings of a Round Table in Polyunsaturated Fatty Acids in Nutrition, Milan, Italy, April 1979. Ed. by C. Galli & P. Avogaro. (Progress in Food & Nutrition Sciences Ser.: Vol. 4, No. 5). (Illus.). 80p. 1980. pap. 32.00 o.p. (ISBN 0-08-027362-9). Pergamon.

Polyurethanes World Congress 1987: Fifty Years of Polyurethanes-Proceedings of the FSK/SPI. LC 87-51022. 974p. 1987. pap. 95.00 o.p. (ISBN 0-87762-561-1). Technomic.

Polyvinyl Chloride. Harold A. Sarvetnick. LC 77-689. (Plastics Applications Ser.). (Illus.). 268p. 1977. Repr. of 1969 ed. 21.50 o.p. (ISBN 0-88275-532-3). Krieger.

Pom Pon U. S. A. Lynda Haller. 109p. 1986. spiral bdg. 8.00 o.p. (ISBN 0-9614174-1-2). Cheertime USA.

Pomeroy. Gordon Williams. LC 81-71680. 1982. 12.95 o.p. (ISBN 0-87795-389-9, Arbor Hse). Morrow.

Pomp & Pestilence. Ronald Hare. 224p. 1955. (ISBN 0-8022-0677-8). Philos Lib.

Pompeii. Ian Andrews. LC 80-7447. (Cambridge Topic Bks.). (Illus.). (gr. 5-10). 1980. PLB 8.95 o.p. (ISBN 0-8225-1220-3). Lerner Pubns.

Pompeii: The Casa dei Dioscuri & Its Painters. L. Richardson, Jr. 165p. 1955. 45.00x o.s.i. (ISBN 0-271-00462-2). Pa St U Pr.

Pompey: The History of Portsmouth Football Club. Mike Neasom et al. (Illus.). 256p. 1987. 19.95 o.p. (ISBN 0-903852-50-0, Pub. by Milestone Pubns UK). Seven Hills Bk Dists.

Ponca Chiefs: An Account of the Trial of Standing Bear. Thomas H. Tibbles. Ed. by Kay Graber. LC 73-181595. xiv, 143p. 1972. 14.95x o.p. (ISBN 0-8032-0814-6); pap. 5.95 o.p. (ISBN 0-8032-5763-5, BB 547, Bison). U of Nebr Pr.

Pond & Brook: A Guide to Nature Study in Freshwater Environments. Michael J. Caduto. (Illus.). 256p. 1985. 21.95 o.p. (ISBN 0-13-685108-8); pap. 12.95 o.p. (ISBN 0-13-685090-1). P-H.

Ponder Heart. Eudora Welty. LC 54-5248. (Illus.). 1954. 6.95 o.p. (ISBN 0-15-173073-3). HarBraceJ.

Ponderings. Kenneth Grant. 48p. 1986. 6.95 o.s.i. (ISBN 0-8378-5087-8). Gibson.

Ponies for Hire. Margaret M. MacPherson. LC 67-10208. (Illus.). (gr. 6-7). 1967. 4.50 o.p. (ISBN 0-15-263165-8, HJ). HarBraceJ.

Pontiac. Matthew G. Grant. LC 73-12193. (We the People Ser.). 1974. PLB 6.95 o.p. (ISBN 0-87191-268-6). Creative Ed.

Pontiac. (Popular Mechanics-Motor Car Care Guide Ser.). (Illus.). 192p. pap. 6.95 o.p. (ISBN 0-87851-945-9). Hearst Bks.

Pontiac: Phoenix 1980 Shop Manual. Ron Wright. Ed. by Sydnie A. Wauson. (Illus.). 1982. pap. 10.95 o.p. (ISBN 0-89287-347-7, A237). Clymer Pub.

Pony Engine. (gr. k-3). 0.79 o.p. (ISBN 0-8431-4152-2). Wonder.

Poodles from Hell. Mick Stevens & Charles Monagram. 160p. 1984. pap. 5.95 o.p. (ISBN 0-380-86769-9, 86769). Avon.

Poof: Avec: L'Achipel Lenoir. Armand Salacrou. 264p. 1950. 4.50 o.p. (ISBN 0-686-55438-8). Schoenhof.

Pooh's Birthday Book. A. A. Milne. (Illus.). 160p. (gr. 1-3). 1975. pap. 1.25 o.s.i. (ISBN 0-440-46934-1, YB). Dell.

Poole Potteries. Jennifer Hawkins. (Illus.). 224p. 1989. 55.00 o.s.i. (ISBN 0-09-142410-0, Pub. by Century Hutchinson). David & Charles.

Poor & the Poorest. Brian Abel-Smith. 78p. 1965. pap. text ed. 5.00x o.p. (ISBN 0-686-70854-7, Pub. by Bedford England). Gower Pub Co.

Poor Boy & a Long Way from Home. James Sherburne. 1984. 14.45 o.p. (ISBN 0-395-35400-5). HM.

Poor Boy Is the Name. Oliver McGee, Jr. 1978. 5.00 o.p. (ISBN 0-682-49036-9). Exposition-Phoenix.

Poor Britain. Joanna Mack & Stewart Lansley. 280p. 1985. text ed. 34.95x o.p. (ISBN 0-04-336082-3); pap. text ed. 13.95 o.p. (ISBN 0-04-336083-1). Unwin Hyman.

Poor-Country Borrowing in Private Financial Markets & the Repudiation Issue. Jonathan Eaton & Mark Gersovitz. LC 81-2925. (Princeton Studies in International Finance Ser.: No. 47). 1981. pap. text ed. 6.50x o.p. (ISBN 0-88165-218-0). Princeton U Int Finan Econ.

Poor Esme. Victoria Chess. LC 82-2924. (Illus.). 32p. (ps-3). 1982. Reinforced bdg. 12.95 o.p. (ISBN 0-8234-0455-2). Holiday.

Poor Labouring Men: Rural Radicalism in Norfolk, 1870-1923. Alun Howkins. (History Workshop Ser.). (Illus.). 224p. (Orig.). 1985. pap. 14.95x o.p. (ISBN 0-7102-0295-4). Routledge Chapman & Hall.

Poor Little Star. Cynthia L. Ohrt. 32p. 1987. 6.95 o.p. (ISBN 0-8062-3053-3). Carlton.

Poor Man's Advocate & Workman's Guide, Nos. 1-50. 1969. Repr. of 1833 ed. lib. bdg. 22.00x o.p. (ISBN 0-8371-9230-7, PW00). Greenwood.

Poor Mouth. O'Brein. (ISBN 0-8050-0183-2). Seaver Bks.

Poor Mouth: A Bad Story about the Hard Life. Flann O'Brien. Tr. by Patrick Power from Gaelic. LC 80-54558. (Illus.). 128p. 1981. pap. 4.95 o.p. Seaver Bks.

Poor Old Ernie. Marian R. Bartch & Jerry J. Mallett. (Bartch & Mallett's Ernie Ser.: Bk. 2). 1983. 7.95 o.p. (ISBN 0-8062-2108-9). Carlton.

Poor People's Lawyers. Marjorie Girth. LC 76-673. 1976. 7.50 o.p. (ISBN 0-682-48506-3, University). Exposition-Phoenix.

Poor Policies: Australian Income Security Nineteen Seventy-Two to Nineteen Seventy-Seven. Patricia Tulloch. 188p. 1979. 24.00 o.p. (ISBN 0-85664-901-5, Pub. by Croom Helm). Routledge Chapman & Hall.

Pop Annual, Nineteen Fifty-Five to Nineteen Seventy-Seven. new ed. Joel Whitburn. LC 78-60195. (Record Research Ser.). 623p. (Orig.). 1978. text ed. 50.00 o.p. (ISBN 0-89820-001-6); pap. text ed. 40.00 o.p. (ISBN 0-89820-002-4). Record Research.

Pop Annual 1955-1982. rev. ed. Joel Whitburn. 679p. 1983. text ed. 40.00 o.p. (ISBN 0-89820-049-0). Record Research.

Pop Sixties: A Personal & Irreverent Guide. Andrew J. Edelstein. (Illus.). 256p. (Orig.). 1985. pap. 8.95 o.p. (ISBN 0-345-32623-7). Pharos Bks NY.

Popcorn Book. Tomie DePaola. LC 77-21456. (Illus.). 32p. (gr. k-3). 1984. pap. 5.95 o.p. (ISBN 0-8234-0533-8). Holiday.

Pope & the Neo-Classicists. Alexander Pope. (Plain Texts of the Poets Ser.). 1968. pap. 2.50x o.p. (ISBN 0-7022-0646-6). U of Queensland Pr.

Pope in Space. Barbara Ann Blatner. 36p. (Orig.). 1986. pap. 20.00 limited ed. o.p. (ISBN 0-912767-05-7). Intertxt Ak.

Pope John Paul II. Mary Craig. (Profiles Ser.). (Illus.). 64p. (gr. 3-6). 1982. 9.95 o.p. (ISBN 0-241-10711-3, Pub. by Hamish Hamilton England). David & Charles.

Pope John Twenty-Third: A Clever, Pastoral Leader. Bernard R. Bonnot. LC 79-1770. 1980. 9.95 o.p. (ISBN 0-8189-0388-0). Alba.

Pope John XXIII: Shepherd of the Modern World. Peter Hebblethwaite. LC 82-45484. (Illus.). 576p. 1985. 19.95 o.s.i. (ISBN 0-385-17298-2). Doubleday.

Pope Marcellus Mass. new ed. Giovani Pierluigi da Palestrina. Ed. by Lewis Lockwood. (Critical Scores Ser.). 1975. 8.95x o.p. (ISBN 0-393-02185-8); pap. 3.95x o.p. (ISBN 0-393-09242-9). Norton.

Pope on Classic Ground. G. F. C. Plowden. LC 82-14413. x, 174p. 1983. text ed. 20.95x o.p. (ISBN 0-8214-0664-7). Ohio U Pr.

Pope Pius XII. Kees Van Hoek. (ISBN 0-8022-1767-2). Philos Lib.

Popeiana, 25 vols. Incl. Vol. 1. Early Criticism, Seventeen Eleven to Seventeen Sixteen (ISBN 0-8240-1239-9); Vol. 2. Pope's Homer, One (ISBN 0-8240-1240-2); Vol. 3. Pope's Homer, Two. o.s.i. (ISBN 0-8240-1241-0); Vol. 4. On Literary Farces (ISBN 0-8240-1242-9); Vol. 5. Pope's Shakespeare. O.s.i. (ISBN 0-8240-1243-7); Vol. 6. Dunciad, One. Repr. of 1728 ed (ISBN 0-8240-1244-5); Vol. 7. Dunciad, Two. Repr. of 1728 ed (ISBN 0-8240-1245-3); Vol. 8. Dunciad, Three. Repr. of 1729 ed (ISBN 0-8240-1246-1); Vol. 9. Attack of Thomas Cooke (ISBN 0-8240-1247-X); Vol. 10. Dunciad & Other Matters. Repr. of 1730 ed (ISBN 0-8240-1248-8); Vol. 11. On Taste, Seventeen Thirty-Two to Seventeen Thirty-Five (ISBN 0-8240-1249-6); Vol. 12. Essay on Man, Crousaz (ISBN 0-8240-1250-X); Vol. 13. Essay on Man, Crousaz Two (ISBN 0-8240-1251-8); Vol. 14. Essay on Man, Warburton, Etc (ISBN 0-8240-1252-6); Vol. 15. Cibber & the Dunciad (ISBN 0-8240-1253-4); Vol. 16. Dunciad. Repr. of 1742 ed (ISBN 0-8240-1254-2); Vol. 17. Pope's Death & the Critical Aftermath. O.s.i. (ISBN 0-8240-1255-0); Vols. 18-19. Warton on Pope, 2 vols (ISBN 0-8240-1256-9); Vols. 20-21. Biography (ISBN 0-8240-1257-7); Vol. 22. Biography (ISBN 0-8240-1258-5); Vol. 23. Biography (ISBN 0-8240-1259-3); Vol. 24. Biography (ISBN 0-8240-1260-7); Vol. 25. Folio Verse: Attacks, Defences, & Imitations (ISBN 0-8240-1261-5). (Life & Times of Seven Major British Writers Ser). 1974. lib. bdg. 61.00 ea. o.p. Garland Pub.

Pope's Death & the Critical Aftermath see Popeiana.

Pope's Homer, One see Popeiana.

Pope's Homer, Two see Popeiana.

Pope's Jews. Sam Waagenaar. (Illus.). 500p. 1974. 9.95 o.p. (ISBN 0-912050-49-7, Library Pr). Open Court.

Pope's Shakespeare see Popeiana.

Pope's Wedding. Edward Bond. 111p. 1971. pap. 6.95 o.p. (ISBN 0-416-09210-1, NO. 2983). Routledge Chapman & Hall.

Popeye & the Haunted House. (gr. k-3). 1980. 0.79 o.p. (ISBN 0-8431-4132-8). Wonder.

Popeye Climbs a Mountain. (gr. k-3). 1980. 0.79 o.p. (ISBN 0-8431-4129-8). Wonder.

Popeye Goes Fishing. (gr. k-3). 1980. 0.79 o.p. (ISBN 0-8431-4130-1). Wonder.

Popeye Goes on a Picnic. (gr. k-3). 0.79 o.p. (ISBN 0-8431-4131-X). Wonder.

Popeye's Big Surprise. (gr. k-3). 0.79 o.p. (ISBN 0-8431-4128-X). Wonder.

POPism: The Warhol Sixties. Andy Warhol & Pat Hackett. LC 79-1851. 1980. 12.95 o.p. (ISBN 0-15-173095-4). HarBraceJ.

Popol Vuh: The Great Mythological Book of the Ancient Maya. Tr. by Ralph Nelson. 1977. 5.95 o.p. (ISBN 0-395-24302-5); pap. 4.95 o.p. (ISBN 0-395-25168-0). HM.

Titles

Popper & After: Four Modern Irrationalists. David Stove. 192p. 1982. 35.00 o.p. (ISBN 0-08-026792-0); pap. 35.00 o.p. (ISBN 0-08-026791-2). Pergamon.

Poppies in the Wind. Louise O'Flaherty. 448p. (Orig.). 1981. pap. 2.95 o.s.i. (ISBN 0-345-29201-4). Ballantine.

Poppy. True Summers. 1978. pap. 2.25 o.p. (ISBN 0-380-39446-4, 39446-4). Avon.

Poppy Visits Holiday Lane. Sonia Moon. (ps-2). 1978. 5.00 o.p. (ISBN 0-682-49096-2). Exposition-Phoenix.

Pops Foster: The Autobiography of a New Orleans Jazzman As Told to Tom Stoddard. Pops Foster. 208p. Repr. of 1971 ed. lib. bdg. 39.00 o.p. (Pub. by Am Repr Serv). Reprint Servs.

Popular American Novel, 1865-1920. Herbert F. Smith. (United States Authors Ser.). 1980. lib. bdg. 15.95 o.p. (ISBN 0-8057-7310-X, Twayne). G K Hall.

Popular Antiques Yearbook. Ed. by Huon Mallalieu. (Illus.). 240p. 1986. pap. 14.95 o.p. (ISBN 0-317-55013-6). Apollo.

Popular Arts in America: A Reader. William M. Hammel. 436p. 1972. pap. text ed. 8.95 o.p. (ISBN 0-15-570743-4, HC). HarBraceJ.

Popular Beliefs & Superstitions: A Compendium of American Folklore, 3 vols. Compiled by Newbell N. Puckett. 1903p. 1981. Set. lib. bdg. 125.50 o.p. (ISBN 0-8161-8585-9, Hall Reference). G K Hall.

Popular Christianity & the Early Theologians. H. J. Carpenter. Ed. by Clarence L. Lee. LC 66-12387. (Orig.). 1966. pap. 0.50 o.p. (ISBN 0-8006-3025-4, 1-3025, Fortress). Augsburg Fortress.

Popular Crowd. Anne Emery. (gr. 7-10). 1961. 5.50 o.s.i. (ISBN 0-664-32254-9, Westminster). Westminster John Knox.

Popular Culture in Late Imperial China. Ed. by David Johnson et al. (Asian Studies). 466p. 1987. pap. 12.95 o.p. (ISBN 0-520-06172-1). U of Cal Pr.

Popular Culture, Leisure & Social Order. Susan Easton et al. 220p. 1986. text ed. 33.00 o.p. (ISBN 0-566-05123-0). Gower Pub Co.

Popular Culture Reader. Jack Nachbar. LC 78-61077. 1978. 14.95 o.p. (ISBN 0-87972-095-6); pap. 7.95 o.p. (ISBN 0-87972-094-8). Bowling Green Univ.

Popular Dictionary of Buddhism. C. Humphreys. 1984. pap. 12.50 o.p. (ISBN 0-7007-0184-2). E J Brill USA.

Popular Fly Patterns. Terry Hellekson. LC 76-49452. (Illus.). 250p. 1975. pap. 14.95 o.p. (ISBN 0-87905-065-9, Peregrine Smith). Gibbs Smith Pub.

Popular Guide to New Testament Criticism. H. P. Hamann. 1977. pap. 4.75 o.p. (ISBN 0-570-03760-3, 12-2671). Concordia.

Popular Lectures on Mathematical Logic. Hao Wang. 286p. 1980. 34.95 o.p. (ISBN 0-442-23109-1). Van Nos Reinhold.

Popular Mechanics Complete Car Repair. Popular Mechanics Editors. 336p. 1978. pap. 5.95 o.p. (ISBN 0-380-01902-7, 49726-3). Avon.

Popular Mechanics Complete Manual of Home Repair & Improvement. Richard E. Nunn. (Illus.). 1978. pap. 5.95 o.p. (ISBN 0-380-00431-3, 46607-4). Avon.

Popular Music: A Teacher's Guide. Graham Vulliamy & Edward Lee. (Routledge Popular Music Ser.). (Orig.). 1982. pap. 12.95x o.p. (ISBN 0-7100-0895-3). Routledge Chapman & Hall.

Popular Participation as a Strategy for Promoting Community-Level Action & National Development. 26p. 1981. pap. 5.00 o.p. (ISBN 92-1-130061-4, E.81.IV.2). UN.

Popular Pottery. Shirley Bates. (Illus.). 128p. 1982. 16.95 o.p. (ISBN 0-7134-4168-2, Pub. by Batsford England). David & Charles.

Popular Rhymes & Nursery Tales. James O. Halliwell-Phillipps. LC 68-23470. 288p. 1968. Repr. of 1849 ed. 34.00x o.p. (ISBN 0-8103-3484-4). Gale.

Popular Rhymes of Scotland. Robert Chambers. LC 68-58902. 404p. 1969. Repr. of 1870 ed. 40.00x o.p. (ISBN 0-8103-3828-9). Gale.

Popular Science Do-It-Yourself Yearbook 1985. Mike McClintock. (Illus.). 248p. 1985. 19.95 o.p. (ISBN 0-943822-38-6). Rodale Pr Inc.

Popular Science Woodworking Projects Yearbook, Vol. I. Mike McClintock. (Illus.). 192p. 18.95 o.p. (ISBN 0-943822-28-9). Rodale Pr Inc.

Popular Sporting Rifle Cartridges. Clay Harvey. LC 84-70735. 320p. 1984. pap. 13.95 o.p. (ISBN 0-910676-74-7). DBI.

Popular Superstitions. Charles Platt. LC 70-167114. 246p. 1973. Repr. of 1925 ed. 46.00x o.p. (ISBN 0-8103-3170-5). Gale.

Popular Tales from the Norse: With an Introductory Essay on the Origin & Diffusion of Popular Tales. 3rd ed. George W. Dasent. LC 74-136733. clii, 598p. 1971. Repr. of 1888 ed. 43.00x o.p. (ISBN 0-8103-3796-7). Gale.

Popular Tales of the West Highlands, 4 Vols. John F. Campbell. LC 67-23921. 1892p. 1969. Repr. of 1890 ed. 150.00x o.p. (ISBN 0-8103-3458-5). Gale.

Popular Tropical Fish for Your Aquarium. Cliff Harrison. (Illus.). 104p. (Orig.). 1984. pap. 11.15 o.p. (ISBN 0-8306-1631-4, 1631P). TAB Bks.

Population: An Introduction to Concepts & Issues. 3rd ed. John R. Weeks. 525p. 1986. text ed. (ISBN 0-534-06138-9). Wadsworth Pub.

Population & Economic Change in Developing Countries. Ed. by Richard A. Easterlin. LC 79-12569. (National Bureau of Economic Research Ser.). 581p. 1979. lib. bdg. 56.00x o.s.i. (ISBN 0-226-18026-3). U of Chicago Pr.

Population & Family Planning in Bangladesh: A Study of the Research. Mohammad Alauddin & Rashid Faruqee. (Working Paper: No. 557). 176p. 1983. 8.00 o.p. (ISBN 0-8213-0150-0, WP 0557). World Bank.

Population & History. E. A. Wrigley. (Illus., Orig.). 1969. pap. text ed. 3.95 o.p. (ISBN 0-07-072115-7). McGraw.

Population & Land in World Agriculture. Joginder Kumar. LC 76-4571. (Population Monograph Ser.: No. 12). 1976. Repr. of 1973 ed. lib. bdg. 37.50x o.p. (ISBN 0-8371-8833-4, KUPL). Greenwood.

Population Biology. John M. Emlen. 1984. text ed. write for info. o.p. (ISBN 0-02-333660-9). Macmillan.

Population, Capital & Growth. Simon Kuznets. 1974. 14.95x o.p. (ISBN 0-393-05497-7). Norton.

Population Dispersal: A National Imperative. John Oosterbaan. LC 79-9672. 160p. 1980. 23.00x o.p. (ISBN 0-669-03615-3). Lexington Bks.

Population Distribution Policies in Asia & the Pacific: Current Status & Future Prospects. Roland J. Fuchs. LC 83-1608. (Papers of the East-West Population Institute: No. 83). vii, 40p. (Orig.). 1983. pap. text ed. 1.50 o.p. (ISBN 0-86638-008-6). EW Ctr HI.

Population Dynamics & Educational Development. pap. 11.95 o.p. (UB48, UB). UNIPUB.

Population: Dynamics, Ethics & Policy. Ed. by Priscilla Reining & Irene Tinker. 1975. 32.50 o.p. (ISBN 0-12-586750-6); pap. 19.00 o.p. (ISBN 0-12-586751-4). Acad Pr.

Population Dynamics of Nepal. Judith Banister & Shyam Thapa. LC 81-19444. (Papers of the East-West Population Institute: No. 78). vii, 119p. (Orig.). 1981. pap. text ed. 2.50 o.p. (ISBN 0-86638-013-2). EW Ctr HI.

Population Ecology: A Unified Study of Animals & Plants. 2nd, rev. ed. Michael Begon & Martin Mortimer. LC 85-27712. (Illus.). 216p. (Orig.). 1986. pap. text ed. 19.95 o.s.i. (ISBN 0-87893-065-5). Sinauer Assocs.

Population Education: A Knowledge Base. Willard J. Jacobson. LC 78-13398. 1979. text ed. 18.95x o.p. (ISBN 0-8077-2533-1). Tchrs Coll.

Population Education in Non-Formal Education & Development Programmes: A Manual for Field Workers. UNESCO, Regional Office for Education in Asia & the Pacific Staff. (Population Education Programme Service Ser.). 260p. 1981. pap. 12.25 o.p. (ISBN 0-686-82543-8, UB107, UB). UNIPUB.

Population Education Sourcebook for Sub-Saharan Africa. Ed. by Reuben K. Udo. 1980. pap. text ed. 25.00x o.p. (ISBN 0-435-95917-4). Heinemann Ed.

Population Forecasting & Uncertainty at the National & Local Scale. R. Baxter & I. Williams. 1978. pap. 13.25 o.p. (ISBN 0-08-023112-8). Pergamon.

Population Genetics: Outline Studies in Biology. L. M. Cook. 1976. pap. 8.50 o.p. (ISBN 0-412-13930-8, NO. 6064, Pub. by Chapman & Hall). Routledge Chapman & Hall.

Population Growth & Economic Development in Africa. Ed. by S. H. Ominde & C. N. Ejiogu. 1972. 38.95x o.p. (ISBN 0-435-97470-X). Heinemann Ed.

Population Index Bibliography: Cumulated 1969 to 1981. Princeton University, Office of Population Research Staff. 1700p. 1984. lib. bdg. 335.00 o.p. (ISBN 0-8161-0906-0, Hall Library). G K Hall.

Population Index Bibliography Cumulated 1935-1968 by Authors & Geographical Areas, 9 vols. Princeton University Office of Population Research Staff. 1971. Set. lib. bdg. 890.00 o.p. (ISBN 0-8161-0880-3, Hall Library); lib. bdg. 435.00 By Author o.p. (ISBN 0-8161-0231-7); lib. bdg. 515.00 By Geographical Area o.p. (ISBN 0-8161-0116-7). G K Hall.

Population Mobility & Wealth Transfers in Indonesia & Other 3rd World Societies. Graeme J. Hugo. LC 83-14008. (Papers of the East-West Population Institute: No. 87). v, 50p. (Orig.). 1983. pap. text ed. 1.75 o.p. (ISBN 0-86638-045-0). EW Ctr HI.

Population Mobility in the People's Republic of China. Sidney Goldstein & Alice Goldstein. (Papers of the East-West Population Institute: No. 95). 52p. (Orig.). 1985. pap. 3.00 o.p. (ISBN 0-86638-069-8). EW Ctr Hi.

Population of Kalamazoo County, Michigan: Estimates As of July 1, 1973 & Projections to 2000. Rodger S. Lawson. 63p. 1975. pap. 2.95 o.p. (ISBN 0-911558-47-0). W E Upjohn.

Population of Thailand: Its Growth & Welfare. Susan Hill Cochran. (Working Paper: No. 337). iv, 73p. 1979. 5.00 o.p. (ISBN 0-686-36201-2, WP-0337). World Bank.

Population of Vietnam. Judith Banister. (International Population Reports Series P-95: No. 77). (Illus.). 47p. (Orig.). 1985. pap. 2.00 o.p. (ISBN 0-318-19926-2, S/N 003-024-06360-3). USGPO.

Population Perils. Ed. by George W. Forell & William H. Lazareth. LC 78-54548. (Justice Bks.). 64p. 1978. pap. 0.95 o.p. (ISBN 0-8006-1554-9, 1-1554, Fortress). Augsburg Fortress.

Population Policy Compendium. United Nations Fund for Population Activities Staff. 1980. write for info. o.p. (UNFPA). UNIPUB.

Population Primer. Francis Frech. o.p. (ISBN 0-913631-00-0). Anastasia VA.

Population Regulation. Ed. by R. H. Tamarin. LC 77-16178. (Benchmark Papers in Ecology: Vol. 7). 389p. 1982. 49.95 o.p. (ISBN 0-87933-324-3). Van Nos Reinhold.

Population: The Dynamics of Demographic Change. Charles B. Nam & Susan O. Gustavus. LC 75-31031. (Illus.). 352p. 1976. text ed. 19.50 o.p. (ISBN 0-395-20627-8). HM.

Population: un choix international: Approche multilaterale au probleme demographique. Rafael M. Salas. LC 71-11610. 1977. 28.00 o.p. (ISBN 0-08-021818-0); pap. 16.50 o.p. (ISBN 0-08-021819-9). Pergamon.

Population, Vol. 4 (incl. 1985-1987 Supplement) Ed. by Eleanor C. Goldstein. (Social Issues Resources Ser.). 1988. 45.00 o.p. (ISBN 0-89777-119-2). Soc Issues.

Populism. Margaret Canovan. LC 80-22245. 360p. 1981. 17.95 o.p. (ISBN 0-15-173078-4). Harbracej.

Populist Nationalism in Pre-War Japan: A Biography of Nakano Seigo. Leslie Oates. 135p. 1985. text ed. 29.95x o.p. (ISBN 0-86861-111-5). Unwin Hyman.

Por la Salud de Nuestros Ninos. M. Studenikin. 255p. (Span.). 1976. 5.45 o.p. (ISBN 0-8285-1697-9, Pub. by Mir Pubs USSR). Imported Pubns.

Porcelaines Francaises. Tardy. (Illus.). 836p. (Fr.). 1981. pap. 37.50 o.s.i. (ISBN 0-911403-08-6, Pub. by Tardy FR). Seven Hills Bk Dists.

Porche du Mystere de la Deuxieme Vertu. Charles Peguy. (Coll. Soleil). 9.95 o.p. (ISBN 0-685-37036-4). Schoenhof.

Porcupine Dilemma. Leopold Bellak. 1970. 5.95 o.p. (ISBN 0-8065-0223-1, Pub. by Citadel Pr). Carol Pub Group.

Porcupine Stew. Beverly Major. LC 82-2268. (Illus.). 40p. (gr. k-3). 1982. 11.75 o.p. (ISBN 0-688-01272-8). Morrow.

Porfirio Diaz, Dictator of Mexico. Carleton Beals. LC 72-135241. (Illus.). 463p. 1971. Repr. of 1932 ed. lib. bdg. 0.90 o.p. (ISBN 0-8371-5159-7, BEPD). Greenwood.

Porius. John C. Powys. 1952. (ISBN 0-8022-2009-6). Philos Lib.

Pork Butcher. Date not set. (ISBN 0-8052-3984-7). Random.

Pork Chop War. Gary Provost. LC 82-9589. 192p. (gr. 6-8). 1982. 9.95 o.s.i. (ISBN 0-02-775180-5). Bradbury Pr.

Porn Row: An Inside Look at the Sex-for-Sale District of a Major American City. Jack M. Weatherford. LC 86-1187. 1986. 16.95 o.p. (ISBN 0-87795-798-3). Morrow.

Pornada. Mary F. Shura. LC 68-18459. (Illus.). (gr. 2-6). 1968. PLB 4.50 o.p. (ISBN 0-689-20617-8, Atheneum). Macmillan.

Pornography: A Human Tragedy. Ed. by Tom Minnery. 350p. 1986. pap. 14.95 o.p. (ISBN 0-8423-4947-2). Tyndale.

Pornography: The Conflict over Sexually Explicit Materials in the United States. An Annotated Bibliography. Greg Byerly & Rick Rubin. LC 80-1436. (Garland Reference Library of Social Science). 162p. 1980. 24.00 o.p. (ISBN 0-8240-9514-6). Garland Pub.

Porous Carbon Solids. Ed. by R. L. Bond. (Atomic Energy Commission Monographs). 1968. 72.00 o.p. (ISBN 0-12-113560-8). Acad Pr.

Porphyrins & Related Compounds: Proceedings. Biochemical Society Symposium, 28th. Ed. by T. W. Goodwin. 1969. 33.00 o.p. (ISBN 0-12-289879-6). Acad Pr.

Porphyrios Kommentar zur Harmonienlehre des Ptolemaios see Harmonienlehre des Klaudios Ptolemaios.

Porsche Owners Handbook & Service Manual: Covers All Porsche Models up to 356c. Clymer Publications Ser. (Illus.). pap. 7.95 o.p. (ISBN 0-89287-251-9, A181). Clymer Pub.

Porsche: 914 Series, 1970-1976-Service, Repair Handbook. 3rd ed. Ed. by Jeff Robinson. (Illus.). pap. 12.95 o.p. (ISBN 0-89287-203-9, A184). Clymer Pub.

Porsche: 924 Series, 1976-1980. Service Repair Handbook. Ed. by Eric Jorgensen. (Illus.). pap. 12.95 o.p. (ISBN 0-89287-204-7, A182). Clymer Pub.

Porsches for the Road. Henry Rasmussen. LC 81-11314. (Survivor's Ser.). (Illus.). 128p. 1984. 12.98 o.p. (ISBN 0-87938-152-3). Motorbooks Intl.

Port. George Robertson. (Faber Wine Bk.). 192p. 1982. pap. 7.95 o.p. (ISBN 0-571-11766-X). Faber & Faber.

Port: An Introduction to Its Histroy & Delights. Wyndham Fletcher. (Illus.). 128p. 22.50 o.p. (ISBN 0-85667-044-8). Sotheby Pubns.

Port & Harbor Planning & Management: A Selected Bibliography. Jerry E. Green. (Architecture Ser.: A 1446). 11p. 1985. 2.00 o.p. (ISBN 0-89028-516-0). Vance Biblios.

Port & Ocean Engineering under Arctic Conditions: Selected Papers from the 3rd International Conference. Ed. by Michael E. McCormick. 1977. pap. 29.00 o.p. (ISBN 0-08-021421-5). Pergamon.

Port Development in the United States. Maritime Transportation Research Board Staff & National Research Council Staff. LC 76-5180. xv, 244p. 1976. pap. 7.95 o.p. (ISBN 0-309-02448-X). Natl Acad Pr.

Port Dues, Charges & Accommodation Throughout the World. 37th ed. Ed. by M. C. Andrews. 1978-79. 80.00 o.s.i. (ISBN 0-540-07386-5). E J Brill USA.

Port of Bellingham: 1919-1979. Hitchman. (Occasional Papers: No. 1). WWU CPNS.

Port of Dover: Two Centuries of Shipping on the Cochecho. Robert A. Whitehouse & Cathleen C. Beaudoin. (Portsmouth Marine Society Ser.: No. 11). (Illus.). 1987. 24.95 o.p. (ISBN 0-915819-10-4). Portsmouth Marine Soc.

Port of Los Angeles: From Wilderness to World Port. Charles F. Queenan. x, 206p. 1983. 35.00 o.p. (ISBN 0-317-11660-6). Dawsons.

Port-Royal. Henry De Montherlant. (Fr.). 1960. 13.25 o.p. (ISBN 0-685-11501-1). Schoenhof.

Port Royal, 3 vols. Saint-Beuve. Vol. 1. 37.50 o.p. (ISBN 0-686-56564-9); Vol. 2. 37.50 o.p. (ISBN 0-686-56565-7); Vol. 3. 35.95 o.p. (ISBN 0-686-56566-5). Schoenhof.

Portable Back School. Ray C. Mulry & Arthur H. White. LC 81-3960. (Illus.). 53p. 1981. pap. text ed. 13.95 o.p. (ISBN 0-8016-3597-7). Mosby.

Portable Computer Buyer's Guide. Tony Webster. (Illus.). 151p. 1985. pap. text ed. 11.95 o.p. (ISBN 0-07-068969-5). McGraw.

Portable Computers. International Resource Development, Inc. Staff. 215p. 1983. 1650.00x o.p. (ISBN 0-88694-568-2). Intl Res Dev.

Portable Feast: A Cookbook for Food on the Move. Diane D. Macmillan. LC 72-94896. (Illus.). 192p. 1973. pap. 4.95 o.p. (ISBN 0-912238-35-6, One Hund One Prods). Ortho.

Portable Needlepoint Boutique. Joyce Aiken. LC 76-53870. (Illus.). 1977. 10.95 o.s.i. (ISBN 0-8008-6416-6). Taplinger.

Portage to San Cristobel of A.H. George Steiner. 1982. 13.50 o.p. (ISBN 0-671-44572-3). S&S.

Porte Etroite. Andre Gide. 1960. 11.50 o.p. (ISBN 0-685-11503-8). Schoenhof.

Portents of Rebellion: Rhetoric & Revolution in Philadelphia, 1765-1776. Stephen E. Lucas. LC 75-30281. 355p. 1976. 22.95 o.p. (ISBN 0-87722-087-5). Temple U Pr.

Portes du Tonnere. Dennis Adair & Janet Rosenstock. (Fr.). 1984. pap. 3.50 o.p. (ISBN 0-380-86181-X, 86181). Avon.

Portfolio of Dramatic & Romantic Illustrations in Full Colours of the Great Railroads of the Past. Gloucester Art Press Editors. (Illus.). 87p. 1985. 165.50 o.p. (ISBN 0-86650-166-5). Gloucester Art.

Portfolio of New Zealand Birds. Bruce Harvey. LC 71-138066. (Illus.). 1971. 25.00 o.p. (ISBN 0-8048-0666-7). C E Tuttle.

Portland & Vicinity Street Atlas & Directory, 1987. rev. ed. Thomas Bros. Maps Staff. (Illus.). 168p. 1986. pap. 13.95 o.p. Thomas Bros Maps.

Portland Cement Concrete: Six Reports. (Transportation Research Record Ser.). 71p. 1974. 3.40 o.p. (ISBN 0-309-02295-9). Transport Res Bd.

Portland City Directory, 1987. Ed. by Tower Publishing Company Staff. 1075p. 1987. 175.00 o.p. (ISBN 0-89442-072-0). Tower Pub Co.

Portland: Gateway to the Northwest. Carl Abbott. LC 85-9520. 272p. 1985. 24.95 o.p. (ISBN 0-89781-155-0). Windsor Pubns Inc.

Portland Metropolitan Street Atlas 1989. Thomas Bros. Maps Staff. (Illus.). 168p. 1988. pap. 13.95 o.p. (ISBN 0-88130-296-1). Thomas Bros Maps.

Portland Murders. Charles R. Larson. (Nightingale Paperbacks). 1985. pap. 10.95 o.p. (ISBN 0-8161-3867-2, Large Print Bks). G K Hall.

Portland Suburban Directory 1986. 700p. 150.00 o.p. (ISBN 0-89442-063-1). Tower Pub Co.

Portland Trailblazers. Molly Martin. (NBA Today Ser.). (Illus.). 48p. (gr. 4 up). 1984. PLB 10.45 o.p. (ISBN 0-87191-987-7). Creative Ed.

Portly McSwine. James Marshall. (gr. k-3). 1979. reinforced bdg. 5.95 o.p. (ISBN 0-395-28003-6). HM.

Portrait Bust, Renaissance to Enlightenment. Brown University, Department of Art Staff. (Illus.). 1969. 1.00 o.p. (ISBN 0-911517-30-8). Mus of Art RI.

Portrait Catalog, 5 vols. New York Academy of Medicine Staff. 1960. Set. 340.00 o.p. (ISBN 0-8161-0233-3, Hall Library); First Suppl. 1959-65. 110.00 o.p. (ISBN 0-8161-0733-5); Second Suppl. 1965-71. 110.00 o.p. (ISBN 0-8161-0900-1). G K Hall.

Portrait Catalog: Third Supplement, 1971-1975. New York Academy of Medicine Staff. 1976. lib. bdg. 110.00 o.p. (ISBN 0-8161-0034-9, Hall Library). G K Hall.

Portrait Drawing: A Practical Guide for Today's Artists. Lois McArdle. (Illus.). 224p. 1984. 24.95 o.p. (ISBN 0-13-687509-2); pap. 14.95 o.p. (ISBN 0-13-687491-6). P-H.

Portrait d'un Inconnu. Nathalie Sarraute. 1957. 14.95 o.p. (ISBN 0-686-54968-6). Schoenhof.

Portrait in Black. Joan V. Frost. 256p. (Orig.). 1985. pap. 2.95 o.s.i. (ISBN 0-449-12795-8, GM). Fawcett.

Portrait in Blood. Mary Kirchoff. LC 85-50142. (Amazing Bks.). 220p. (Orig.). 1985. pap. 2.95 o.p. (ISBN 0-88038-258-9). TSR Inc.

Portrait of a Country Artist: Charles Tunnicliffe R. A. 1901-1979. Ian Niall. 1980. 29.95 o.s.i. (ISBN 0-575-02868-8, Pub. by Gollancz England). David & Charles.

Portrait of a Port: Boston, 1852-1914. William H. Bunting. LC 77-145893. (Illus.). 1971. 27.50 o.p. (ISBN 0-674-69075-3, Belknap Pr). Harvard U Pr.

Portrait of a Statesman. Dennis Bardens. (Illus.). 326p. 1956. (ISBN 0-8022-0060-5). Philos Lib.

Portrait of a Tortoise. Gilbert White. 64p. 1982. pap. 2.50 o.p. (ISBN 0-380-58123-X, 58123-X, Discus). Avon.

Portrait of a Woman Down East: Selected Writings of Mary Bolte. Ed. by Charles Bolte. 1981. 7.95 o.p. (ISBN 0-89272-129-4). Down East.

Portrait of America, Vol. 1 & 2. 3rd ed. Stephen B. Oates. LC 82-81984. 480p. 1983. Vol. 1. pap. 14.95 o.p. (ISBN 0-395-32778-4); Vol. 2. pap. 14.95 o.p. (ISBN 0-395-32779-2); write for info. instr's manual o.p. (ISBN 0-395-32780-6). HM.

Portrait of America: Vol. 1, from the Cliff Dwellers to the End of Reconstruction. 2nd ed. Stephen B. Oates. LC 77-77432. (Illus.). 1978. pap. 12.50 o.p. (ISBN 0-395-25372-1). HM.

Portrait of America: Vol. 2, from Reconstruction to the Present. 2nd ed. Stephen B. Oates. LC 77-77432. (Illus.). 1978. pap. 12.50 o.p. (ISBN 0-395-25373-X). HM.

Portrait of Andre Gide. Justin O'Brien. 390p. 1976. Repr. of 1953 ed. lib. bdg. 29.00x o.p. (ISBN 0-374-96139-5, Octagon). Hippocrene Bks.

Portrait of California. Photos by Ray Atkeson. LC 79-55978. (Portrait of America Ser.). (Illus.). 80p. (Orig., Text by Lee Foster). 1980. pap. 5.95 o.s.i. (ISBN 0-912856-54-8). Gr Arts Ctr Pub.

Portrait of Chicago. Photos by Bob Glaze. LC 81-81322. (Portrait of America Ser.). (Illus.). 80p. (Orig., Text by Les Krantz). 1981. pap. 6.95 o.s.i. (ISBN 0-912856-70-X). Gr Arts Ctr Pub.

Portrait of Elie Halevy. Michele B. Bramsen. 1978. pap. text ed. 28.50x o.p. (ISBN 90-6032-100-6). Humanities.

Portrait of Essex. Marie Moore. LC 69-12343. (Illus.). 112p. 1979. pap. 5.95 o.p. (ISBN 0-87106-022-1). Globe Pequot.

Portrait of Margarita. Ruth M. Arthur. LC 68-12230. (Illus.). (gr. 5 up). 1968. 6.95 o.p. (ISBN 0-689-30013-1, Atheneum). Macmillan.

Portrait of My Father: The Wonder of Knowing God. Peter Law. LC 85-15458. (Living Theology Ser.). 1985. pap. 7.95 o.p. (ISBN 0-88070-107-2). Multnomah.

Portrait of Myself: Margaret Bourke-White. Margaret B. White. (Nonfiction Ser.). (Illus.). 384p. 1985. pap. 9.95 o.p. (ISBN 0-8398-2858-6, Gregg). G K Hall.

Portrait of Nationalised Banks. H. N. Agrawal. 334p. 1980. text ed. 19.95x o.p. (ISBN 0-391-02130-3). Humanities.

Portrait of Seattle. Photos by Ed Cooper. LC 79-55980. (Portrait of America Ser.). (Illus.). 80p. (Orig., Text by Archie Satterfield). 1980. pap. 7.50 o.s.i. (ISBN 0-912856-56-4). Gr Arts Ctr Pub.

Portrait of the Artist As a Young Man: A Facsimile of the Manuscript Fragments of Stephen Hero, 3 vols. James Joyce. Ed. by Michael Groden. LC 78-12105. (James Joyce Archive Ser.: Vol. 7-10). 1979. lib. bdg. 375.00 o.p. (ISBN 0-8240-2807-4). Garland Pub.

Portrait of the Artist As a Young Man. James Joyce. 48p. (Orig.). 1989. pap. 9.95 o.p. (ISBN 1-55651-729-7); audiocassette tape incl. o.p. (ISBN 1-55651-730-0). Cram Cassettes.

Portrait of the Enemy. David Chanoff & Doan Van Toai. LC 85-25701. 288p. 1986. 17.45 o.s.i. (ISBN 0-394-53671-1). Random.

Portrait of the Irish in America. William D. Griffin. (Illus.). 272p. 1982. pap. 14.95 o.s.i. (ISBN 0-684-17856-7, ScribT). Scribner.

Portrait of Wagner: An Illustrated Biography. Hans Mayer. 175p. Repr. of 1972 ed. lib. bdg. 39.00 o.p. (Pub. by Am Repr Serv). Reprint Servs.

Portrait of Washington. Photos by Ray Atkeson. LC 79-55977. (Portrait of America Ser.). (Illus.). 80p. (Orig., Text by Tom Barr). 1980. pap. 8.50 o.s.i. (ISBN 0-912856-53-X). Gr Arts Ctr Pub.

Portrait Painting in Watercolor. Charles Reid. (Illus.). 160p. 1973. 27.50 o.p. (ISBN 0-8230-4192-1). Watson-Guptill.

Portraits. Cynthia Freeman. LC 78-73865. 1979. 11.95 o.p. (ISBN 0-87795-219-1, Arbor Hse). Morrow.

Portraits de Femmes see Oeuvres.

Portraits de L'artiste en Jeune Singe. Michel Butor. pap. 9.95 o.p. (ISBN 0-685-37256-1). French & Eur.

Portraits from Life. Ford Madox Ford. 256p. 1980. pap. 4.95 o.p. (ISBN 0-395-29911-X). HM.

Portraits in Roses: One Hundred Nine Years of Kentucky Derby Winners. Beverley Bryant & Jean Williams. LC 83-23872. (Illus.). 160p. 1984. text ed. 49.95 o.p. (ISBN 0-07-008602-8). McGraw.

Portraits in the Wild: Behavior Studies of East Africa Mammals. Cynthia Moss. LC 75-20284. (Illus.). 368p. 1975. 12.50 o.p. (ISBN 0-395-20722-3). HM.

Portraits Litteraires see Oeuvres.

Portraits Litteraires (Fin; see Oeuvres.

Portraits of Chinese Women in Revolution. Agnes Smedley. Ed. by Jan MacKinnon & Steve MacKinnon. (Illus.). 208p. 1976. pap. 10.95 o.s.i. (ISBN 0-912670-44-4). Feminist Pr.

Portraits of Poverty. Edythe A. Shewbridge. 112p. 1972. pap. 1.25x o.p. (ISBN 0-393-01096-1). Norton.

Ports, Inland Waterways & Civil Aviation. R. E. Baxter & C. Phillips. Ed. by W. F. Maunder. 1979. 85.00 o.p. (ISBN 0-08-022460-1). Pergamon.

Portugal. Reginald A. Dixon. LC 83-62036. (Pocket Guide Ser.). (Illus.). 1984. pap. 5.95 o.p. (ISBN 0-528-84890-9). Rand McNally.

Portugal. Ian Robertson. (Blue Guides Ser.). (Illus.). 1982. 29.95 o.p. (ISBN 0-393-01549-1); pap. 16.95 o.p. (ISBN 0-393-30001-3). Norton.

Portugal. 2nd, rev. ed. Ian Robertson. (Blue Guides Ser.). (Illus.). 1985. 16.95 o.p. (ISBN 0-393-30068-4). Norton.

Portugese-English (Only) Dictionary of Economy, Finance, Sociology, Commerce & Related Fields. J. Knox. (Port. & Eng.). 1968. pap. 10.00 o.s.i. (ISBN 0-685-47314-7). E J Brill USA.

Portuguese-American Cookbook. E. Donald Asselin. LC 66-20571. 1966. pap. 3.95 o.p. (ISBN 0-8048-0480-X). C E Tuttle.

Portuguese Armed Forces & the Revolution. Douglas Porch. (Publications Ser.: No. 188). (Illus.). 12.50x o.p. Hoover Inst Pr.

Portuguese-English, English-Portuguese Dictionary. J. A. Ferreira. (Port. & Eng.). 30.00 o.p. (ISBN 0-685-12039-2). E J Brill USA.

Portuguese-English, English-Portuguese Dictionary. Michaelis. 50.00 o.p. (ISBN 0-317-40184-X). E J Brill USA.

Portuguese in America, 590 BC-1974: A Chronology & Fact Book. Manoel D. Cardozo. LC 75-45203. (Ethnic Chronology Ser.: No. 22). 154p. 1976. lib. bdg. 8.50 o.p. (ISBN 0-379-00520-4). Oceana.

Pose & Jealousy. Philip M. Kalavros. LC 62-9768. 176p. 1963. (ISBN 0-8022-0822-3). Philos Lib.

Position of Trust. Roy Hart. 208p. 1987. pap. 3.95 o.p. (ISBN 0-380-70278-9). Avon.

Position of Woman in Early China. Albert O'Hara. 563p. 1980. 6.95x o.p. (ISBN 0-89955-174-2, Pub. by Mei Ya China). Intl Spec Bk.

Positioning in Anesthesia & Surgery. John T. Martin. LC 77-16972. 1978. text ed. write for info. o.p. (ISBN 0-7216-6133-5). Saunders.

Positioning: The Battle for Your Mind. Al Ries & Jack Trout. 224p. 1981. text ed. 19.95 o.p. (ISBN 0-07-065263-5). McGraw.

Positive Accounting: Problems & Solutions. Trevor Gambling. 200p. 1984. 33.00x o.p. (ISBN 0-8448-1470-9, Pub. by Crane Russak & Co). Taylor & Francis.

Positive Approach to Head Injury: Guidelines for Professionals & Families. Beverly Slater. LC 86-42635. 200p. 1987. 24.95 o.p. (ISBN 0-943432-85-5). Slack Inc.

Positive Experiences in Constructing & Operating Nuclear Power Plants Worldwide. Atomic Industrial Forum Staff. (Technical & Economic Reports: Construction). 76p. 1984. 100.00 o.p. (ISBN 0-318-02250-8). US Coun Energy Awareness.

Positive Obedience: The Christian's Response to the Ten Commandments. John Bisagno. 80p. (Orig.). 1987. pap. 4.95 o.p. (ISBN 0-310-38141-X, 9249P). Zondervan.

Positive Power of Christian Partnership. Richard Andersen. 1982. pap. 1.00 o.p. (ISBN 0-570-03844-8, 12-2947). Concordia.

Positive Staining for Electron Microscopy. M. Arif Hayat. 1975. 31.95 o.p. (ISBN 0-442-25684-1). Van Nos Reinhold.

Positive Use of Commercial Television with Children. Rosemary L. Potter. 126p. 1981. 7.95 o.p. (ISBN 0-8106-1686-6). NEA.

Positivism & Sociology. Ed. by Anthony Giddens. 1974. pap. text ed. 11.95x o.p. (ISBN 0-435-82341-8). Gower Pub Co.

Positron Emission Tomography of the Brain. Ed. by W. D. Heiss & M. F. Phelps. (Illus.). 244p. 1983. 54.00 o.p. (ISBN 0-387-12130-7). Springer-Verlag.

Positronium Chemistry. James Green & John Lee. 1964. 35.00 o.p. (ISBN 0-12-298650-4). Acad Pr.

Poslednyaya lyubov' Maykovskogo. Semen Chertok. LC 83-173. (Illus., Orig., Rus.). 1983. pap. 7.00 o.s.i. (ISBN 0-938920-31-6). Hermitage.

Possedees: Theatre. Albert Camus. 1959. pap. 3.95 o.p. (ISBN 0-685-11508-9). Schoenhof.

Possessed see also Devils.

Possessed. Fyodor Dostoyevsky. Tr. by Constance Garnett. Ed. by Avrham Yarmolinsky. LC 36-3324. 736p. 1936. 7.95 o.s.i. (ISBN 0-394-60441-5). Modern Lib.

Possession. Nicholas Delbanco. LC 81-20994. (Sherbrookes Trilogy Ser.). 216p. 1982. pap. 7.25 o.p. (ISBN 0-688-00980-8, Quill NY). Morrow.

Possession: A Novel. Ann Rule. 1983. 15.00 o.p. (ISBN 0-393-01641-2). Norton.

Possession of Amber. Nicholas Jose. 285p. 1981. text ed. 17.50 o.p. (ISBN 0-7022-1537-6); pap. 7.25 o.p. (ISBN 0-7022-1538-4). U of Queensland Pr.

Possessions. Judith Michael. 416p. 1984. 16.45 o.s.i. (ISBN 0-671-50421-5, Pub. by Poseidon). S&S.

Possessors & the Possessed. Samuel A. Schreiner, Jr. LC 79-54009. 1980. 12.95 o.p. (ISBN 0-87795-229-9, Arbor Hse). Morrow.

Possibility of a Universal Language see Needed Words.

Possibility Thinkers Bible: The New King James Version. Robert H. Schuller. 1984. 22.95 o.p. (ISBN 0-8407-0043-1); bonded leather 39.95 o.p. (ISBN 0-8407-0048-2). Nelson.

Possible Dream: Toward Understanding the Black Experience. Peter A. Angeles. (Orig.). 1971. pap. 1.95 o.p. (ISBN 0-377-01211-4). Friendship Pr.

Possible Impact of the European Economic Community, in Particular the Common Market, Upon World Trade. pap. 5.00 o.p. (G50, GATT). UNIPUB.

Possible Impossibilities: A Look at Parapsychology. Elizabeth Hall. (gr. 5 up). 1976. 6.95 o.p. (ISBN 0-395-25299-7). HM.

Post-Harvest Food Crop Conservation: Association of Consulting Scientists Symposium on Post-Harvest Food Crop Conservation, Harrogate, 13-15 November, 1979. (Progress in Food & Nutrition Ser.: Vol. 4). (Illus.). 138p. 1980. pap. 48.00 o.p. (ISBN 0-08-025907-3). Pergamon.

Post-Impressionist Group Exhibitions. Ed. by Theodore Reff. (Modern Art in Paris Ser.). 302p. 1981. lib. bdg. 48.00 o.p. (ISBN 0-8240-4728-1). Garland Pub.

Post-Liberation Works of Mao Zedong: A Bibliography & Index. John B. Starr & Nancy A. Dyer. LC 67-65707. (China Research Monographs: Special). 1976. pap. 3.75x o.p. (ISBN 0-912966-16-5). IEAS.

Post-Marital Dissolution Proceedings. 166p. 1984. 25.00 o.p. (ISBN 0-88129-134-X). Wash Bar CLE.

Post-Miocene Stratigraphy Central & Southern Atlantic Coastal Plain. Ed. by Robert Q. Oaks, Jr. & Jules R. DuBar. 275p. 1974. 13.00 o.p. (ISBN 0-87421-065-8). Utah St U Pr.

Post-Mortem Estate Planning. Massachusetts Continuing Legal Education, Inc. Staff. LC 83-63424. (Illus.). 1985. 50.00 o.p. Mass CLE.

Post-Mortem Estate Planning. Pennsylvania Bar Institute Staff. 159p. 1985. 50.00 o.p. (313). PA Bar Inst.

Post Mortem Estate Planning 1985. (Tax Law & Estate Planning Ser.). 1985. 15.00 o.p. (D4-5182). PLI.

Post O-Level Studies in Modern Languages. C. V. Russell. 1970. 70.00 o.p. (ISBN 0-08-016194-4). Pergamon.

Post Office Cat. Gail E. Haley. LC 76-8377. (Macmillan Encore Editions). (Illus.). 32p. (gr. 1-5). 1976. 1.79 o.s.i. (ISBN 0-684-17373-5, Pub. by Scribner). Macmillan.

Post Office Clerk-Carrier. 13th ed. Arco Editorial Board. LC 78-23985. 1979. pap. 6.00 o.p. (ISBN 0-668-04846-8, 4846-8). Arco.

Post Office Clerk-Carrier. 14th ed. Eve P. Steinberg. LC 82-1666. 160p. 1982. pap. 7.95 o.p. (ISBN 0-668-05388-7, 5388). Arco.

Post-Partum Document. Mary Kelly. (Illus.). 172p. (Orig.). 1983. cloth 29.95 o.p. (ISBN 0-7100-9495-7). Routledge Chapman & Hall.

Post-Resurrection Ministry of Christ. Alexander Maclaren & H. B. Swete. 480p. lib. bdg. 17.95 o.p. (ISBN 0-8254-5173-6). Kregel.

Post-School Education: Educational Values in America & England in the Nineteenth Century. G. W. Roderick & M. D. Stephens. LC 84-9549. 272p. 1984. 28.00 o.p. (ISBN 0-7099-2386-4, Pub. by Croom Helm Ltd). Routledge Chapman & Hall.

Post-Traditional Societies. Ed. by S. N. Eisenstadt. 257p. 1974. pap. text ed. 5.95x o.p. (ISBN 0-393-09303-4). Norton.

Post-Traumatic Stress Disorder: Psychological & Biological Sequelae. Bessel A. Van Der Kolk. LC 84-6375. (Clinical Insights Monograph). 160p. 1984. pap. text ed. 12.00x o.p. (ISBN 0-88048-053-X, 48-053-X). Am Psychiatric.

Post-Victorian Britain: 1902-1951. L. C. Seaman. 531p. 1968. 15.95x o.p. (ISBN 0-416-69760-7, NO. 2433). Routledge Chapman & Hall.

Post-War British Theatre. rev. ed. John Elsom. (Illus.). 1979. pap. 9.50 o.p. (ISBN 0-7100-0168-1). Routledge Chapman & Hall.

Postage Stamps of Mexico, 1856-1868. Samuel Chapman. LC 75-40501. (Illus.). 1976. Repr. 40.00x o.p. (ISBN 0-88000-079-1). Quarterman.

Postal Applications of Operations Research. J. N. D. Gupta. 1978. pap. 42.00 o.p. (ISBN 0-08-023011-3). Pergamon.

Postal History of Nebraska. William F. Rapp. (Pt. 2). (Illus.). 150p. 1985. 18.00 o.p. (ISBN 0-916170-27-6). J-B Pub.

Postal History of the United States Forces in British Solomon Islands Protectorate During World War 2. Stanley C. Jersey. LC 79-50817. (Illus.). 1968. 10.00 o.p. (ISBN 0-686-09668-1). Am Philatelic Society.

Postbuckling Behavior of Structures. M. Esslinger & B. Geier. (International Centre for Mechanical Sciences: No. 236). (Illus.). 1976. soft cover 27.00 o.p. (ISBN 0-387-81369-1). Springer-Verlag.

Postcards from Old Kansas City. Mrs. Sam Ray. LC 80-84468. 48p. 1980. pap. 9.50 o.p. Lowell Pr.

Postcards of Alphonse Mucha. Q. David Bowers & Mary L. Martin. (Illus.). 120p. 1980. 9.95 o.p. (ISBN 0-911572-18-X, A-239). Vestal.

Postdoctoral Appointments & Disappointments. National Research Council. 1981. pap. text ed. 15.75x o.p. (ISBN 0-309-03132-X). Natl Acad Pr.

Poster Book of Antique Auto Ads. Ed. by Howard Garrett. 96p. 1975. pap. 7.95 o.p. (ISBN 0-8065-0467-6, Pub. by Citadel Pr). Carol Pub Group.

Posterior & Predictive Densities for Simultaneous Equation Models. J. F. Richard. (Lecture Notes in Economics & Mathematics Systems: Vol. 90). 226p. 1973. pap. 12.00 o.p. (ISBN 0-387-06525-3). Springer-Verlag.

Posters of Jules Cheret. Jules Cheret & Lucy Broido. (Illus.). 19.00 o.p. (ISBN 0-8446-5742-5). Peter Smith.

Postgraduate Obstetrical & Gynaecological Pathology. H. Fox & F. A. Langley. 596p. 1973. 150.00 o.p. (ISBN 0-08-016992-9). Pergamon.

Postharvest Biology & Handling of Fruits & Vegetables. Norman F. Haard & D. K. Salunkhe. (Illus.). 1975. 40.95 o.p. (ISBN 0-87055-187-6). AVI.

Posthumous Poems of Shelley: Mary Shelley's Fair Copy Book. Irving Massey. 328p. (Bodleian MS Shelley adds. d. 9). 1969. 22.00x o.p. (ISBN 0-7735-0018-9, McGill Canada). U of Toronto Pr.

Posthumous Works. Robert Hooke. (Sources of Science Ser., No. 73). 1969. Repr. of 1705 ed. 40.00 o.p. (ISBN 0-384-24165-4). Johnson Repr.

Titles

Posthumous Writings. Gottlob Frege. Ed. by Hans Hermes et al. Tr. by Roger White & Peter Long. LC 79-10986. 1979. Repr. lib. bdg. 35.00x o.s.i. (ISBN 0-226-26199-9). U of Chicago Pr.

Postmodernism: A Bibliography. Mary E. Huls. (Architecture Ser.: A 1515). 6p. 1985. 2.00 o.p. (ISBN 0-89028-665-5). Vance Biblios.

Postmodernism-Jameson-Critique. Ed. by Douglas Kellner. (Post Modern Positions Ser.: Vol. 4). 1988. lib. bdg. 26.00 o.p.; pap. 15.00 o.p. Maisonneuve Pr.

Postmoderns: New American Poetry Revised. Donald Allen & George F. Butterick. 1984. 17.50 o.p. (ISBN 0-8446-6082-5). Peter Smith.

Postmoderns: The New American Poetry Revised. Ed. by Donald M. Allen & George F. Butterick. LC 79-52054. 480p. (Orig.). 1982. pap. 12.95 o.p. (ISBN 0-394-17458-5, E732, Ever). Grove.

Postnatal Growth & Restoration of Internal Organs in Vertebrates. Vera F. Sidorova. Ed. & intro. by Bruce M. Carlson. LC 77-88071. (Illus.). 210p. 1978. 20.00 o.p. (ISBN 0-88416-212-5). Year Bk Med.

Postponed Generation: Why America's Grown-Up Kids Are Growing Up Later. Susan Littwin. Ed. by Pat Golbitz. LC 85-18831. 256p. 1986. 16.95 o.p. (ISBN 0-688-04890-0). Morrow.

Postranslational Covalent Modification of Proteins: MS Repro Symposium. Ed. by B. Connor Johnson. 1983. 47.50 o.p. (ISBN 0-12-387560-9). Acad Pr.

Postscript to the Name of the Rose. Umberto Eco. Tr. by William Weaver from Ital. LC 84-15652. (Helen & Kurt Wolff Bk.). (Illus.). 96p. 1984. 8.95 o.p. (ISBN 0-15-173156-X). HarBraceJ.

Postsecondary Business & Industry Needs Assessment Model. Leonard Nasman. 59p. 1981. 5.10 o.p. (ISBN 0-318-22169-1, RD223). Natl Ctr Res Voc Ed.

Postsecondary Program Evaluation. Compiled by Catharine P. Warmbrod & Jon J. Persavich. 272p. 1982. 14.25 o.p. (ISBN 0-318-22170-5, RD222). Natl Ctr Res Voc Ed.

Postsecondary Student Personnel Services: Bibliography. 7.50 o.p. (ISBN 0-317-59911-9, 72507C). Am Assn Coun Dev.

Postsecondary Vocational Education. ERIC Clearinghouse on Adult, Career, & Vocational Education Staff. 56p. 1983. 4.95 o.p. (ISBN 0-318-22171-3, BB65). Natl Ctr Res Voc Ed.

Postulates & Implications. Ray H. Dotterer. 516p. 1956. (ISBN 0-8022-0412-0). Philos Lib.

Posture. Robert Roaf. 1978. 26.50 o.p. (ISBN 0-12-589350-7). Acad Pr.

Postwar America: The Search for Identity. Donald G. Baker & Charles H. Sheldon. (Insight Series: Studies in Contemporary Issues). 1969. pap. (ISBN 0-02-473840-9, 47384). Macmillan.

Postwar Fertility Trends & Differentials in the United States. Ed. by R. R. Rindfuss & James Sweet. (Studies in Population Ser.). 1977. 30.00 o.p. (ISBN 0-12-589250-0). Acad Pr.

Postwar Italy: A Study in Economic Contrasts. George H. Hildebrand. 1957. 1.00 o.p. (ISBN 0-89215-047-5). U Cal LA Indus Rel.

Postwar Paintings from Brandeis University. Text by Carl Betz. 46p. 1989. pap. 15.95 o.p. Moyer Bell Limited.

Pot of Gold. Julia N. Grandle. LC 84-90490. 115p. 1985. 8.95 o.p. (ISBN 0-533-06370-1). Vantage.

Potash Mining Processing Transportation: Proceedings of the International Potash Technology Conference, Saskatoon, Saskatchewan, Canada, October 3-5, 1983. Ed. by R. M. McKercher. (Illus.). 887p. 1983. 230.00 o.p. (ISBN 0-08-025401-2). Pergamon.

Potassium Argon Dating. Ed. by O. A. Schaeffer & J. Zaehringer. (Illus.). 1966. 37.80 o.p. (ISBN 0-387-03637-7). Springer-Verlag.

Potato Crop: The Scientific Basis for Improvement. Ed. by P. M. Harris. 1978. 88.00x o.p. (ISBN 0-412-12830-6, NO. 6143, Pub. by Chapman & Hall). Routledge Chapman & Hall.

Potato Famine & the Irish Emigrants. P. F. Speed. Ed. by Marjorie Reeves. (Then & There Ser.). (Illus.). 96p. (Orig.). (gr. 7-12). 1976. pap. text ed. 4.75 o.p. (ISBN 0-582-21721-0). Longman.

Potbellied Possums. Elizabeth Winthrop. LC 76-17829. (Illus.). 32p. (ps-3). 1977. reinforced bdg. 4.95 o.p. (ISBN 0-8234-0289-4). Holiday.

Potential Benefits of Reducing Occupational Radiation Exposure (AIF-NESP-010R) rev. ed. NES Division of Science Applications, Inc. (National Environment Studies Project: NESP Reports). 60p. 1979. 45.00 o.p. (ISBN 0-318-13589-2); to NESP sponsors 15.00 o.p. (ISBN 0-318-13590-6). US Coun Energy Awareness.

Potential Carcinogenic Hazards from Drugs: Evaluation of Risks. Ed. by R. Truhaut. (UICC Monograph: Vol. 7). (Illus.). 1967. 57.90 o.p. (ISBN 0-387-04009-9). Springer-Verlag.

Potential Effects of Income Redistribution on Selected Growth Constraints: A Case Study of Kenya. Osman S. Ahmed. LC 80-6093. (Illus.). 368p. (Orig.). 1982. lib. bdg. 34.00 o.p. (ISBN 0-8191-2112-6); pap. text ed. 16.75 o.p. (ISBN 0-8191-2113-4). U Pr of Amer.

Potential Energy Surfaces & Dynamics Calculations for Chemical Reactions & Molecular Energy Transfer. Ed. by D. G. Truhlar. LC 81-8666. 878p. 1981. 125.00x o.p. (ISBN 0-306-40755-8, Plenum Pr). Plenum Pub.

Potential for Appropriate Water Resource Technology in Guinea, West Africa. David Eaton. (Working Paper Ser.: No. 19). 52p. 1981. pap. 3.00 o.p. (ISBN 0-318-00171-3). LBJ Sch Pub Aff.

Potential for Field Beans-Phaseolus Vulgaris L.- In West & North Africa. Centro Internacional de Agricultura Tropical Staff. 143p. (Orig.). 1985. pap. text ed. 14.95x o.s.i. (ISBN 84-89206-45-7, Pub. by CIAT Colombia). Agribookstore.

Potential for Spiritual Direction in the New Rite of Penance. Frederick Schroeder & Craig Meyers. 1.85 o.p. (ISBN 0-89942-530-5, 530/04). Catholic Bk Pub.

Potential of Earth-Shelter & Underground Space: Today's Resource for Tomorrow's Space & Energy Viability: Proceedings of the Underground Space Conference & Exposition, Kansas City, MO, June 8-10, 1981. Ed. by T. Lance Holthusen. (Illus.). 501p. 1981. 92.00 o.p. (ISBN 0-08-028050-1). Pergamon.

Potential Scattering in Atomic Physics. P. G. Burke. LC 76-28965. (Illus.). 138p. 1977. 32.50x o.p. (ISBN 0-306-30933-5, Plenum Pr). Plenum Pub.

Potential Theory. 2nd ed. J. Wermer. (Lecture Notes in Mathematics Ser.: Vol. 408). 166p. 1981. pap. 11.80 o.p. (ISBN 0-387-10276-0). Springer-Verlag.

Potential Theory. J. Wermer. LC 74-14663. (Lecture Notes in Mathematics Ser.: Vol. 408). vii, 146p. 1974. pap. 9.40 o.p. (ISBN 0-387-06857-0). Springer-Verlag.

Potentially Violent Patient & the Tarasoff Decision in Psychiatric Practice. James C. Beck. LC 84-28241. (Clinical Insights Monograph Ser.). 160p. 1985. pap. text ed. 12.00x o.p. (ISBN 0-88048-075-0, 48-075-0). Am Psychiatric.

Poteries-Faiences Porcelaines, Europeennes: Characteristiques Marques, Vol. 1. Tardy. 606p. (Fr.). 1983. pap. 37.50 o.p. (ISBN 2-901622-09-7, Pub. by Tardy FR). Seven Hills Bk Dists.

Poteries-Faiences Porcelaines, Europeennes: Characteristiques Marques, Vol. 2. Tardy. (Illus.). 518p. (Fr.). 1983. pap. 37.50 o.p. (ISBN 2-901622-10-0, Pub. by Tardy FR). Seven Hills Bk Dists.

Potlatch Family. Evelyn S. Lampman. LC 75-28328. 144p. (gr. 5-9). 1976. 6.95 o.p. (ISBN 0-689-50039-4, Atheneum). Macmillan.

Potomac Fever. Fred R. Harris. 1977. 8.95 o.p. (ISBN 0-393-05610-4). Norton.

Potomac Squire. Elswyth Thane. 432p. 4.00 o.p. (ISBN 0-931917-04-2). Mt Vernon Ladies.

Potomak. Jean Cocteau. 352p. 1951. 8.95 o.p. (ISBN 0-686-54554-0). French & Eur.

Potpourri: Clipbook Number Two of Line Artwork. Norman Ludlow, Jr. (Illus.). 1982. pap. 12.50x o.p. (ISBN 0-916706-28-1). N H Ludlow.

Potpourri of Ideas for Student Development Specialists. National Association for Women Deans, Administrators & Counselors. 1976. pap. 3.00 o.p. (ISBN 0-686-16256-0). Natl Assn Women.

Potpourri...Easy As One, Two, Three. Dody Lyness. 1987. 6.00 o.p. (ISBN 0-933863-01-2). Berry Hill Pr.

Potted Plant Book. Sue Tarsky. (Illus.). 48p. (gr. 5 up). 1981. 6.95 o.p. (ISBN 0-316-83206-5). Little.

Potter's Book of Glaze Recipes. Emanuel Cooper. 1980. encore ed. 3.95 o.p. (ISBN 0-684-16670-4, ScribT). Scribner.

Potter's Complete Book of Clay & Glazes. James Chappel. 448p. 1977. 29.95 o.p. (ISBN 0-8230-4202-2). Watson-Guptill.

Potter's Guide to Raw Glazing & Oil Firing. Dennis Parks. (Encore Edition Ser.). (Illus.). 1980. 3.79 o.p. (ISBN 0-684-17563-0). Scribner.

Pottery & Early Commerce: Characterization & Trade in Roman & Later Ceramics. Ed. by D. P. Peacock. 1977. 82.50 o.p. (ISBN 0-12-547850-X). Acad Pr.

Pottery in Ancient Times. Rivka Gonen. LC 72-10796. (Lerner Archaeology Ser.). (Illus.). 96p. (gr. 5 up). 1974. PLB 8.95 o.p. (ISBN 0-8225-0829-X). Lerner Pubns.

Pottery of Pecos: The Dull Paint Wares, Vol. 1. Alfred V. Kidder. LC 78-66502. (Classics of Anthropology Ser.). 176p. 1985. lib. bdg. 31.00 o.p. (ISBN 0-8240-9629-0). Garland Pub.

Poultry. Bon Appetit Magazine Editors. LC 83-24867. (Cooking with Bon Appetit Ser.). (Illus.). 1984. 12.95 o.p. (ISBN 0-89535-134-X). Knapp Pr.

Poultry & Egg Statistics, 1960-85. Allen Baker & Eunice Armstrong. (Statistical Bulletin Ser.: No. 747). 1986. pap. 4.25 o.p. (ISBN 0-318-22425-9, S/N 001-019-00495-9). USGPO.

Poultry & Game Birds. Ed. by Georgia Orcutt & Sandra Taylor. LC 81-51690. (Flavor of New England Ser.). (Illus.). 144p. (Orig.). 1982. pap. 8.95 o.p. (ISBN 0-911658-29-7). Yankee Bks.

Poultry: Feeds & Nutrition. 2nd ed. Homer Patrick & P. J. Schaible. (Illus.). 1980. 35.95 o.p. (ISBN 0-87055-353-4). AVI.

Poultry Health & Management. David Sainsbury. 168p. 1980. text ed. 22.00x o.p. (ISBN 0-246-11173-9, Pub. by Granada England); pap. text ed. 17.00x o.p. (ISBN 0-246-11350-2). Gower Pub Co.

Poultry on the Farm. Cliff Moon. LC 83-71631. (Down on the Farm Bks.). (Illus.). 33p. (ps-2). 1983. PLB 9.40 o.p. (ISBN 0-531-04697-4). Watts.

Pound Conference: Perspectives on Justice in the Future. Ed. by Leo A. Levin & Russell R. Wheeler. LC 80-14618. 368p. 1980. text ed. 25.00 o.p. (ISBN 0-8299-2096-X). West Pub.

Pound Revised. Paul Smith. (Illus.). 192p. 1983. 29.25 o.p. (ISBN 0-7099-2346-5, Pub. by Croom Helm Ltd). Routledge Chapman & Hall.

Pour Dante. Saint-John Perse, pseud. pap. 4.50 o.p. (ISBN 0-685-36546-8). Schoenhof.

Pour la Patrie see For My Country.

Pourboire Sixteen: Peter Kaplan's Book. Peter Kaplan et al. (Pourboire Ser.). 1979. pap. 5.00 o.p. (ISBN 0-930900-59-6). Burning Deck.

Poverty, Achievement, & the Distribution of Compensatory Education Services. Mary M. Kennedy & Richard K. Jung. (Education Department Publication OR 86-001). (Illus.). 321p. 1986. pap. 16.00 o.p. (ISBN 0-318-21348-6, S/N 065-000-00255-8). USGPO.

Poverty Amid Affluence. Oscar Ornati. Ed. by J. S. Sweet. LC 66-18565. (Twentieth Century Fund Ser.). 1976. pap. 22.00 o.p. (ISBN 0-527-02833-9). Kraus Repr.

Poverty & Charity in Aix-en-Provence, 1640-1789. Cissie C. Fairchilds. LC 75-36930. (Studies in Historical & Political Science Ninety-Fourth Ser.: No. 1 (1976)). (Illus.). 216p. 1976. 25.00x o.p. (ISBN 0-8018-1677-7). Johns Hopkins.

Poverty & Policy in Tudor Stuart England. Slack. (Themes in British Social History Ser.). (Illus.). 288p. 1988. pap. text ed. 15.95 o.p. (ISBN 0-582-48965-2). Longman.

Poverty & Progress: Social Mobility in a Nineteenth Century City. Stephan Thernstrom. LC 64-21793. 1969. pap. text ed. 3.95x o.p. (ISBN 0-689-70195-0, 144, Atheneum). Macmillan.

Poverty & the Development of Human Resources: Regional Perspective. Willem Bussink & David Davies. (Working Paper: No. 406). iii, 193p. 1980. 10.00 o.p. (ISBN 0-8213-9268-9, WP-0406). World Bank.

Poverty in Affluence: The Social, Political & Economic Dimensions of Poverty in the United States. 2nd ed. Ed. by Robert E. Will & Harold G. Vatter. (Orig.). 1970. pap. text ed. 8.95 o.p. (ISBN 0-15-570751-5, HC). HarBraceJ.

Poverty in Rural Asia. ILO Asian Employment Programme Staff. Ed. by Azizur Rahman Khan & Eddy Lee. 276p. 1985. pap. 12.00 o.p. (ISBN 92-2-103286-8, ILO391, ILO). UNIPUB.

Poverty in the United States 1985: 1985. (Current Population Reports Series P-60, Consumer Income: No. 158). Orig. Title: Past Years: Characteristics of the Population below the Poverty Level. 188p. (Orig.). 1987. pap. 9.00 o.p. (ISBN 0-318-23840-3, 803-005-30004-8). USGPO.

Poverty, Participating, Protest, & Black Americans: A Selected Bibliography for Use in Social Work Education. Compiled by Charlotte Dunmore. Date not set. 3.00 o.s.i. (70-382-02). Coun Soc WK Ed.

Poverty: Wealth of Mankind. Albert Tevoedjre. 1979. 39.00 o.p. (ISBN 0-08-023367-8); pap. 18.75 o.p. (ISBN 0-08-023366-X). Pergamon.

Povest' OB Ugolovnom Rozyske. Nagornyi et al. 512p. 1984. 59.00x o.p. (ISBN 0-317-42704-0, Pub. by Collets (UK)). State Mutual Bk.

P.O.W. J. G. Hubbell. 1976. text ed. 15.00 o.p. (ISBN 0-07-030831-4). McGraw.

Powder Burn. William L. Montalbano & Carl Hiaasen. LC 81-65997. 1981. 12.95 o.p. (ISBN 0-689-11174-6, Atheneum). Macmillan.

Powder Metallurgy in Defense Technology, 3 Vols. Incl. Vol. 3. 1977. 37.50 (ISBN 0-918404-42-8); Vol. 4. 1978. 26.00 (ISBN 0-918404-46-0); Vol. 5. Yuma Arizona. 1979 (ISBN 0-918404-50-9). (Defense Technology Seminar). Metal Powder.

Powder Metallurgy in the Nuclear Age: Papers Presented at the Fourth Plansee Seminar. Plansee Seminar De Re Metallica, Reutte, 4th, 1961. Ed. by F. Benesovsky. (Illus., Eng. & Fr.). 1962. 46.10 o.p. (ISBN 0-387-80609-1). Springer-Verlag.

Powder Metallurgy in the Nuclear Atomic Energy. Plansec Seminar De Re Metallica, Reutte, 4th, 1961. Ed. by F. Benesovsky. (De Re Metallica). (Illus.). viii, 829p. 1962. pap. 46.10 o.p. (ISBN 0-387-80610-5). Springer Verlag.

Powder Metallurgy of Titanium Alloys: Proceedings of the AIME Annual Meeting , Las Vegas, NV, 1980. (Illus.). 313p. 36.00 o.p. (ISBN 0-89520-367-7); members 22.00 o.p. (ISBN 0-317-34892-2); student members 14.00 o.p. (ISBN 0-317-34893-0). ASM.

Powder River. Gary McCarthy. 384p. (Orig.). 1985. pap. 3.50 o.s.i. (ISBN 0-345-30435-7). Ballantine.

Powdersmoke Lawyer. Lee Floren. (Gunsmoke Western Ser.). 176p. 1988. text ed. 12.95x o.p. (ISBN 0-85997-856-7, Pub. by Firecrest Pub Ltd). Prescott Pr NH.

Powell, Pressburger & Others. Ed. by Ian Christie. 124p. 1978. pap. 5.95 o.p. (ISBN 0-85170-086-1, Pub. by British Film Inst England). U of Ill Pr.

Power. Adolf A. Berle. LC 69-12026. 1969. 14.50 o.p. (ISBN 0-15-173081-4). HarBraceJ.

Power. Bertrand Russell. 1969. pap. 6.95 o.p. (ISBN 0-393-00479-1, Norton Lib). Norton.

Power, Action & Belief: A New Sociology of Knowledge? Ed. by John Law. (Sociological Review Monograph: No. 32). 300p. (Orig.). 1986. pap. text ed. 18.95 o.p. (ISBN 0-7102-0802-2). Routledge Chapman & Hall.

Power & Authority in British Universities. Graeme C. Moodie & Rowland Eustace. 256p. 1974. 10.50x o.p. (ISBN 0-7735-0223-8, McGill Canada). U of Toronto Pr.

Power & Balance: An Introduction to American Constitutional Government. Ira H. Carmen. (Illus.). 582p. 1978. pap. text ed. 16.95 o.p. (ISBN 0-15-570753-1, HC). HarBraceJ.

Power & Crisis in the City. Date not set. (ISBN 0-8052-3838-7). Random.

Power & History: The Political Thought of James Burnham. Samuel T. Francis. 154p. (Orig.). 1984. lib. bdg. 23.75 o.p. (ISBN 0-8191-3752-9); pap. text ed. 9.75 o.p. (ISBN 0-8191-3753-7). U Pr of Amer.

Power & Immortality. Ramon R. Lopez-Reyes. LC 70-146911. 1971. 10.00 o.p. (ISBN 0-682-47247-6, University). Exposition-Phoenix.

Power & Innocence. Rollo May. 1976. pap. 7.95 o.p. (ISBN 0-385-28795-X, Delta). Dell.

Power & Interdependence: World Politics in Transition. Robert O. Keohane & Joseph S. Nye. 1977. text ed. 11.95 o.p. (ISBN 0-316-48935-2); pap. text ed. write for info. o.p. (ISBN 0-673-39454-9). Scott F.

Power & International Relations. Inis L. Claude, Jr. 1962. text ed. 15.00 o.p. (ISBN 0-394-30133-1, RanC). Random.

Power & Peace in Prayer. R. A. Torrey. (One Evening Christmas Classic Ser.). 1976. pap. 2.50 o.p. (ISBN 0-89107-019-2). Good News.

Power & Responsibility: Case Studies in American Leadership. David M. Kenny & Michael E. Parrish. 257p. 1986. pap. text ed. 12.00 net o.p. (ISBN 0-15-570755-8). HarBraceJ.

Power & Shared Values in the Corporate Culture. Cathy A. Enz. Ed. by Richard Farmer. LC 86-4298. (Research for Business Decisions Ser.: No. 90). 190p. 1986. 39.95 o.p. (ISBN 0-8357-1738-0). UMI Res Pr.

Power & Society: An Introduction to the Social Sciences. 3rd ed. Thomas R. Dye. LC 82-14579. (Political Science Ser.). 400p. 1982. pap. text ed. 17.00 pub net o.p. (ISBN 0-534-01237-X). Brooks-Cole.

Power & the Corporate Mind. Abraham Zaleznik & Manfred E. Kets De Vries. LC 75-17784. 304p. 1975. 11.95 o.p. (ISBN 0-395-20426-7). HM.

Power & the Prize. Chet Cunningham. 1977. pap. 1.95 o.p. (ISBN 0-8439-0483-6, Pub. by Leisure Bks CT). Dorchester Pub Co.

Power at Sea: A Portrait of U. S. Naval Aviation. International Defense Images Staff. Ed. by Mi Seitelman. LC 86-50843. 96p. 1986. pap. 15.95 o.p. (ISBN 0-9616878-1-9). Howell Pr VA.

Power at the Top: A Critical Survey of the Nationalized Industries. Clive Jenkins. LC 75-45383. 292p. 1976. Repr. of 1959 ed. lib. bdg. 35.00x o.p. (ISBN 0-8371-8661-7, JEPT). Greenwood.

Power Base Attribution & the Perceived Legitimacy of Managerial Accounting. Roger W. Bartlett. Ed. by Richard N. Farmer. LC 82-23697. (Research for Business Decisions Ser.: No. 57). 145p. 1983. 42.95 o.p. (ISBN 0-8357-1393-8). Univ Microfilms.

Power Condenser Heat Transfer Technology: Computer Modeling-Design-Fouling. P. J. Marto & R. H. Nunn. 496p. 1981. text ed. 57.50 o.p. (ISBN 0-07-040662-6). McGraw.

Power Crazy: How the Long Island Lighting Company Became America's Biggest Utilities Scandal. Karl Grossman. 224p. 1986. 17.95 o.p. (ISBN 0-394-55461-2); pap. 7.95 o.p. Grove.

Power Development in India. K. Venkataraman. LC 72-10341. 178p. 1973. 23.95x o.p. (ISBN 0-470-90578-6). Halsted Pr.

Power Economy: Building an Economy That Works. John O. Wilson. 320p. 1985. 19.95 o.p. (ISBN 0-316-94502-1). Little.

Power Electronics & Variable Speed Drives. (Conference Publications: No. 234). 431p. 1984. pap. 116.00 o.p. (ISBN 0-85296-291-6). Inst Elect Eng.

Power Electronics: Thyristor Controlled Power For Electric Motors. R. S. Ramshaw. (Modern Electrical Studies). 1975. pap. 19.95 o.p. (ISBN 0-412-14160-4, NO. 6230, Pub. by Chapman & Hall). Routledge Chapman & Hall.

Power, Empire Building, & Mergers. Stephen A. Rhoades. LC 82-49255. 176p. 1983. 27.00x o.p. (ISBN 0-669-06439-4). Lexington Bks.

Power Fngineering & Technology: Energy Efficient Use of Working Fluids, Alternative Processes, Heat Pumps& Organic Rankine Cycle. Ed. by H. D. Baehr et al. 1984. 179.50 o.p. (ISBN 0-89116-436-7). Hemisphere Pub.

Power Food: Exciting New Recipes for Vigorous Good Health, Energy & Strength. James McNair. LC 85-29938. (Illus.). 120p. (Orig.). 1986. pap. 9.95 o.p. (ISBN 0-87701-369-1). Chronicle Bks.

Power for Abundant Living. Victor P. Wierwille. LC 72-164674. 380p. 6.95 o.p. (ISBN 0-910068-01-1). Am Christian.

Power Forward. Walter Kaylin. LC 78-20438. 1979. 9.95 o.p. (ISBN 0-689-10972-5, Atheneum). Macmillan.

Power from the Earth: Geothermal Energy. Dorothy C. Tompkins. LC 72-8628. (Public Policy Bibliographies: No. 3). (Orig.). 1972. pap. 2.50x o.p. (ISBN 0-87772-165-3). UCB IGS.

Power, Greed & Stupidity in the Mental Health Racket. Walter Fisher et al. 1973. 5.95 o.s.i. (ISBN 0-664-20958-0, Westminster). Westminster John Knox.

Power Hockey. Ken Hodge et al. LC 74-77845. (Illus.). (gr. 3-7). 1975. 6.95 o.p. (ISBN 0-689-10618-1, Atheneum). Macmillan.

Power Ideas for a Happy Family. Robert H. Schuller. 1987. 8.95 o.p. (ISBN 0-8007-1528-4). Revell.

Power in Management. John P. Kotter. 1979. 11.95 o.p. (ISBN 0-8144-5507-7). AMACOM.

Power in the Land: An Inquiry into Unemployment, the Profits Crisis & Land Speculation. Fred Harrison. LC 83-10576. (Illus.). 316p. 1983. text ed. 17.50x o.p. (ISBN 0-87663-424-2). Universe.

Power in the Pacific: The Origins of Naval Arms Limitation, 1914-1922. Roger Dingman. LC 75-36402. 1976. lib. bdg. 22.50x o.s.i. (ISBN 0-226-15331-2). U of Chicago Pr.

Power Look. Egon Von Furstenberg & Camille Duhe. LC 78-1995. (Illus.). 1978. 10.00 o.s.i. (ISBN 0-03-020456-9). H Holt & Co.

Power: Mechanics of Energy Control. Angus J. MacDonald. (gr. 9-12). 1970. text ed. 15.96 o.p. (ISBN 0-87345-486-3); mechanical control man. 7.32 o.p. (ISBN 0-87345-484-7); fluid control man. 7.32 o.p. (ISBN 0-87345-488-X); electric control man. 7.32 o.p. (ISBN 0-87345-487-1); optional experiments 7.32 o.p. (ISBN 0-87345-489-8); wkbk. & tests 4.67 o.p. (ISBN 0-87345-498-7); tchr's guide 46.67 o.p. (ISBN 0-87345-497-9); lab manual set 28.00 o.p. (ISBN 0-685-04238-3). Glencoe.

Power of Affirmations: You Can Heal Your Life with Words & Thoughts. Alexis Rotella. 140p. (Orig.). Date not set. pap. (ISBN 0-917951-04-2). Jade Mtn.

Power of Attorney Book. Denis Clifford. LC 85-61925. (Illus.). 248p. (Orig.). 1985. 15.95 o.p. (ISBN 0-917316-95-9). Nolo Pr.

Power of Attorney: The Rise of the Big Ten Law Firms. Mark Stevens. LC 86-10494. 208p. 1987. text ed. 17.95 o.p. (ISBN 0-07-061290-0). McGraw.

Power of Babel: A Study of Logophilia. Michel Pierssens. Tr. by Carl R. Lovitt from Fr. Orig. Title: Tour De Babil. 144p. 1980. Repr. of 1976 ed. 21.95x o.p. (ISBN 0-7100-0373-0). Routledge Chapman & Hall.

Power of Commitment. Jerry White. (Christian Character Library). 176p. 1985. 8.95 o.p. (ISBN 0-89109-532-2). NavPress.

Power of God Within You. W. W. VauDell. 1980. 5.50 o.p. (ISBN 0-682-49157-8). Exposition-Phoenix.

Power of Light: Daguerreotypes from the Robert Harshorn Shimshak Collection. Robert F. Johnson & Robert H. Shimshak. LC 86-81908. (Illus.). 48p. (Orig.). 1986. pap. 9.95 o.p. (ISBN 0-317-52336-8). Fine Arts Mus.

Power of Money Dynamics. Venita VanCaspel. 1983. 22.00 o.p. (ISBN 0-8359-5570-2, Reston). P-H.

Power of Music. Music Educators National Conference Staff. LC 72-88397. (Illus.). 94p. 1972. pap. 7.50 o.p. (ISBN 0-940796-14-7, 1037). Music Ed Natl.

Power of Negative Thinking. Woodie Hall. Ed. by Arlene A. Wright. 104p. (Orig.). 1985. pap. 5.95 o.p. (ISBN 0-940156-49-0). Wright Group.

Power of Non-Violence. rev. ed. Richard B. Gregg. 192p. 1960. pap. 4.95 o.p. (ISBN 0-227-67567-3). Attic Pr.

Power of Nothingness. Alexandra David-Neel & Lama Yongden. Tr. by Janwillem Van de Wetering. LC 81-23737. 160p. 1982. 10.95 o.p. (ISBN 0-395-31557-3). HM.

Power of Oil: Economic, Social, Political. Richard J. Walton. LC 76-43985. 192p. (gr. 6 up). 1979. 7.95 o.p. (ISBN 0-395-28929-7, Clarion). HM.

Power of Poetry. Sterling W. Sill. LC 83-83267. 141p. 1984. 7.95 o.p. (ISBN 0-88290-238-5). Horizon Utah.

Power of Positive Nonsense. Leo Rosten. 1977. text ed. 9.95 o.p. (ISBN 0-07-053985-5). McGraw.

Power of Positive Persuasion: A Professional's Guide to Communications. Francis A. Acquaviva & Robert A. Malone. 96p. pap. 9.95 o.p. (RAMSCO 00200). Ramsco Pub.

Power of Positive Self Image. Baird. 1983. 6.50 o.p. (ISBN 0-88207-316-8). Victor Bks.

Power of Positive Thinking. Norman Vincent Peale. 1954. pap. 9.95 o.p. (ISBN 0-13-686402-3). P-H.

Power of Prevention: Reduce Your Risk of Cancer Through Diet & Nutrition. Oliver Alabaster. 432p. 1986. pap. 8.95 o.p. (ISBN 0-671-62798-8, Fireside). S&S.

Power of Professional Management. George S. Dively. LC 77-151052. 1971. 12.95 o.p. (ISBN 0-8144-5188-8). AMACOM.

Power of Propaganda: Imagination & Idealism. Ronald Jackson. (Illus.). 224p. 1983. 4.00 o.p. (ISBN 0-682-49942-0). Exposition-Phoenix.

Power of Sex. Frank S. Caprio. 1962. pap. 1.50 o.p. (ISBN 0-8065-0074-3, 86, Pub. by Citadel Pr). Carol Pub Group.

Power of Sound. Edmund Gurney. 559p. Repr. of 1966 ed. lib. bdg. 69.00 o.p. (Pub. by Am Repr Serv). Reprint Servs.

Power of Steam: An Illustrated History of the World's Steam Age. Asa Briggs. LC 82-40321. (Illus.). 208p. 1983. 22.50x o.s.i. (ISBN 0-226-07495-1); pap. 10.00 o.s.i. (ISBN 0-226-07497-8). U of Chicago Pr.

Power Of: Step-by-Step Through LOGO Turtle Graphics. Ann Rose. (Illus.). 47p. 1983. pap. 6.95 o.s.i. (ISBN 0-943518-11-3). MIS Press.

Power of the Pendulum. T. C. Lethbridge. (Illus.). 160p. 1984. pap. 5.95 o.p. (ISBN 1-85063-003-8, Ark Paperbks). Routledge Chapman & Hall.

Power of the Plus Factor. Norman Vincent Peale. 1987. 14.95 o.p. (ISBN 0-8007-1526-8). Revell.

Power of the Purse: A History of American Public Finance. E. James Ferguson. LC 61-325. (Institute of Early American History & Culture Ser.). xvii, 358p. Repr. of 1961 ed. 32.50x o.p. (ISBN 0-8078-0804-0). U of NC Pr.

Power of the TRS-80 Color Computer. Tom Seluca. 1983. pap. 14.95 o.p. (ISBN 0-916752-62-3). Longman Trade.

Power of VisiCalc, Vol. 2. Robert E. Williams & Brian King. 97p. 1982. pap. 14.95 o.p. (ISBN 0-13-687426-6). P-H.

Power of Words. Stuart Chase & Marian T Chase. LC 54-5980. 308p. 1954. 9.95 o.p. (ISBN 0-15-173487-9). HarBraceJ.

Power of 3: A New Model for Hospital and Nursing Home Care. Mary D. Scheller. 284p. 1988. pap. 7.95 o.p. (ISBN 0-933071-22-1). Saybrook Pub Co.

Power Persuasion: A Surefire System to Get Ahead in Business. William D. Coplin et al. LC 85-11159. 224p. 1985. (ISBN 0-201-11201-9). Addison-Wesley.

Power Picture. Estelle McCarthy & Charles McCarthy. (Orig.). 1973. pap. 1.95 o.p. (ISBN 0-377-03031-7). Friendship Pr.

Power-Places of Central Tibet: A Pilgrim's Guide. Keith Dowman. 320p. 1988. pap. text ed. 15.95 o.p. (ISBN 0-7102-1370-0, Pub. by Routledge UK). Routledge Chapman & HAll.

Power Plant Cost Escalation: Nuclear & Coal Capital Costs, Regulation, & Economics. Charles Komanoff. 336p. 1982. 34.95 o.p. (ISBN 0-442-24903-9). Van Nos Reinhold.

Power Plant Entrainment: A Biological Assessment. Ed. by Jerry R. Schubel & Barton C. Marcy, Jr. 1978. 43.50 o.p. (ISBN 0-12-631050-5). Acad Pr.

Power Plant Fitting & Testing, 2 vols. W. Atherton et al. (Illus.). 492p. 1981. Repr. of 1981 ed. spiral 89.95x o.p. Trans-Atl Phila.

Power Plant Siting. John V. Winter & David A. Conner. 1978. 29.95 o.p. (ISBN 0-442-29554-5). Van Nos Reinhold.

Power Plants: Effects on Fish & Shellfish Behavior. Charles H. Hocutt et al. 1980. 51.00 o.p. (ISBN 0-12-350950-5). Acad Pr.

Power Play. Matt Christopher. (Illus.). (gr. 1-3). 1976. 10.45i o.p. (ISBN 0-316-14015-5). Little.

Power Play. Andrea Edwards. 368p. 1984. pap. 2.95 o.p. (ISBN 0-380-87692-2, 87692-2). Avon.

Power Politics. Martin Wight. Ed. by Hedley Bull. LC 77-11020. 317p. 1978. 35.00x o.s.i. (ISBN 0-8419-0344-1). Holmes & Meier.

Power: Prime Mover of Technology. rev. ed. Joseph Duffy. (gr. 11-12). 1972. text ed. 21.97 o.p. (ISBN 0-87345-420-0). Glencoe.

Power Real Estate Listing. William H. Pivar. LC 82-24108. 187p. 1983. 12.95 o.p. (ISBN 0-88462-480-3, 1907-01, Real Estate Ed). Longman Finan.

Power Real Estate Selling. William H. Pivar. LC 82-24107. 212p. 1983. 14.95 o.p. (ISBN 0-88462-479-X, 1907-02, Real Estate Ed). Longman Finan.

Power Seekers. Clayton Matthews. 438p. 1987. pap. 3.95 o.p. (ISBN 1-55547-154-4). Critics Choice Paper.

Power Selling. James Brewer et al. 200p. 1985. 16.95 o.p. (ISBN 0-13-688425-3); pap. 8.95 o.p. (ISBN 0-13-688417-2). P H.

Power Sits at Another Table & Other Observations on the Business of Power. Earl Shorris. 1986. pap. 9.95 o.s.i. (ISBN 0-671-62293-5, Fireside). S&S.

Power Skills. Kahn. McGraw.

Power Skills in Mathematics. Martine R. Wiznitzer. 1979. pap. text ed. 4.95 o.p. (ISBN 0-07-055225-8). McGraw.

Power Skills in Mathematics II. Frank Cerreto. (Illus.). 1979. pap. text ed. 4.95 o.p. (ISBN 0-07-010338-0). McGraw.

Power Skills in Reading, Bk. 1. Aliyah Abdul-Karim. 1979. pap. text ed. 4.95 o.p. (ISBN 0-07-000041-7). McGraw.

Power Skills in Reading II. Roger B. Goodman & William Ince. (Illus.). 1978. pap. text ed. 4.95 o.p. (ISBN 0-07-023732-8). McGraw.

Power Skills in Science II. Robert Kahn & Herbert Nestler. 1978. pap. text ed. 4.95 o.p. (ISBN 0-07-033194-4). McGraw.

Power Skills in Writing I. Roger B. Goodman & William Ince. 1979. pap. text ed. 4.95 o.p. (ISBN 0-07-023744-1). McGraw.

Power Skills in Writing II. Roger B. Goodman & William Ince. (Illus.). 1979. pap. text ed. 4.95 o.p. (ISBN 0-07-023731-X). McGraw.

Power Sources Five: Research & Development in Non-Mechanical Electrical Power Sources. Ed. by D. H. Collins. 1975. 134.50 o.p. (ISBN 0-12-181450-5). Acad Pr.

Power Sources Six. Ed. by D. H. Collins. (Power Sources Ser.). 1978. 134.00 o.p. (ISBN 0-12-181452-1). Acad Pr.

Power Sources Two: Proceedings, International Symposium on Batteries, 6th. Ed. by D. H. Collins. LC 62-22327. 1970. 150.00 o.p. (ISBN 0-08-013435-1). Pergamon.

Power Spots. Jose A. Rosa & Nathaniel Altman. 96p. (Orig.). 1987. pap. 6.99 o.p. (ISBN 0-85030-474-1, Pub. by Aquarian Pr England). Sterling.

Power Station Engineering & Economy. 2nd ed. Bernhardt G. Skrotzki & W. A. Vopat. 1960. text ed. 49.95 o.p. (ISBN 0-07-057940-7). McGraw.

Power Supplies. 1987. 100.00 o.p. DATA Busn Pub.

Power System & Electric Machines. Syed A. Nasar. 425p. 1985. text ed. write for info. o.p. (ISBN 0-02-385960-1). Macmillan.

Power System Monitoring & Control. (IEE Conference Publication Ser.: No. 187). (Illus.). 234p. 1980. pap. 56.50 o.p. (ISBN 0-85296-219-3). Inst Elect Eng.

Power System Monitoring & Control. (IEE Conference Publication). 404p. 1986. 78.00 o.p. (ISBN 0-85296-331-9, 1C266). Inst Elect Eng.

Power System Protection: Static Relays. T. S. Rao. 1981. text ed. 39.00 o.p. (ISBN 0-07-096574-9). McGraw.

Power Systems Engineering & Mathematics. U. G. Knight. 304p. 1975. pap. 70.00 o.p. (ISBN 0-08-018294-1). Pergamon.

Power Systems for Space Flight, PAAS11. Ed. by M A. Zipkin & R. N. Edwards. LC 63-13306. (Illus.). 943p. 89.50 o.p. (ISBN 0-317-36826-5). AIAA.

Power Thyristor & Its Applications. David Finney. (Illus.). 320p. 1980. text ed. 34.95 o.p. (ISBN 0-07-084533-6). McGraw.

Power to Change: Issues for the Innovative Educator. Carmen M. Culver & Gary J. Hoban. Ed. by John I. Goodlad. (IDEA Reports on Schooling). (Illus.). 380p. 1974. text ed. 21.95 o.p. (ISBN 0-07-014890-2). McGraw.

Power to Lead: The Crisis of the American Presidency. James M. Burns. 273p. 1984. 16.45 o.p. (ISBN 0-671-42731-8). S&S.

Power Tool Safety & Operation. Thomas Hoerner & Mervin Bettis. (Illus.). 94p. 1973. pap. 5.50x o.p. (ISBN 0-913163-06-6). Hobar Pubns.

Power Transmission & Automation for Ships & Submersibles. I. Mortimer Datz. (Illus.). 190p. 45.00 o.p. (ISBN 0-85238-074-7, FN23, FNB). UNIPUB.

Power Up! Kids' Guide to the Apple IIe-IIc. Marty DeJonghe & Caroline Earhart. LC 84-51647. (Illus.). 180p. (gr. 3-6). 1984. pap. 10.95 o.p. (ISBN 0-89588-212-4). SYBEX.

Power Up! Kids' Guide to the Commodore 64. Marty DeJonghe & Caroline Earhart. LC 84-50363. (Illus.). 192p. (gr. 3-6). 1984. pap. 10.95 o.p. (ISBN 0-89588-188-8). SYBEX.

Power User's Guide to Hard Disk Management. Jonathan Kamin. 315p. (Orig.). 1987. pap. 21.95 o.p. (ISBN 0-89588-401-1). Sybex.

Power User's Guide to 1-2-3. Pete Antoniak. 368p. (Orig.). 1987. pap. 19.95 o.p. (ISBN 0-89588-421-6). Sybex.

Power Volleyball for Girls & Women. 2nd ed. Janet Thigpen. 158p. 1974. pap. text ed. write for info. o.p. (ISBN 0-697-07317-3). Wm C Brown.

Power Within You. Pat Williams & Jerry Jenkins. LC 82-24825. 180p. 1983. 12.95 o.s.i. (ISBN 0-664-27008-5, Westminster). Westminster John Knox.

Power Without Property: A New Development in American Political Economy. Adolf A. Berle. LC 59-11771. 1962. pap. 1.65 o.p. (ISBN 0-15-673349-8, Harv). HarBraceJ.

Powerboat Maintenance. Ed. by Jeff Robinson. (Illus.). 288p. pap. text ed. 10.00 o.p. (ISBN 0-89287-069-9, B620). Clymer Pub.

Powercise: The Elaine Powers Total Body Workout. (Illus.). 128p. 1983. pap. 9.50 o.p. (ISBN 0-671-49428-7, Fireside). S&S.

Powerholders. David Kipnis. LC 75-43230. (Illus.). 1976. lib. bdg. 15.00x o.s.i. (ISBN 0-226-43731-0). U of Chicago Pr.

Powerplay: What Really Happened at Bendix. Mary Cunningham & Fran Schumer. 320p. 1984. 15.45 o.p. (ISBN 0-671-47563-0, Linden Pr). S&S.

Powers & Dominations. Robert Early. LC 74-20575. 192p. 1975. 6.95 o.p. (ISBN 0-395-20285-X). HM.

Powers of Attorney. Louis Auchincloss. 1980. pap. 3.95 o.p. (ISBN 0-395-29846-6). HM.

Powers of Psychiatry. Jonas Robitscher. 1980. 17.95 o.p. (ISBN 0-395-28222-5). HM.

Powers of Tamil Women. Ed. by Susan S. Wadley. LC 80-25410. (Foreign & Comparative Studies Program, South Asian Ser.: No. 6). xix, 170p. (Orig.). 1980. pap. 9.00x o.p. (ISBN 0-915984-82-2). Syracuse U Foreign Comp.

Powers of Ten: About the Relative Size of Things in the Universe. Eames, Charles & Ray, Staff et al. LC 82-5504. (Scientific American Library). (Illus.). 164p. 1982. 29.95 o.p. (ISBN 0-7167-1409-4); pap. 19.95 o.p. W H Freeman.

Powtech: 1983. Institution of Chemical Engineers Staff. 1983. 115.00 o.s.i. (ISBN 0-08-028785-9). Pergamon.

Practica Musica: A Music Fundamentals Textbook & Software fo the Macintosh. Jeffrey Evans. LC 88-71355. 200p. 1988. pap. text ed. 125.00 o.p. (ISBN 0-929444-00-0). Ars Nova SW.

Practical Absorption Spectrometry. Ed. by A. Knowles & C. Burgess. (Techniques in Ultraviolet Spectrometry Ser.: Vol. 3). 300p. 1984. 42.00x o.p. (ISBN 0-412-24390-3, NO. 6850). Routledge Chapman & Hall.

Practical Accounting. 3rd ed. John G. Black & Delmar S. Stanley. LC 75-40983. 1980. pap. text ed. write for info. o.p. (ISBN 0-673-16133-1). Scott F.

Practical Accounting for Small Businesses. 2nd ed. Laura T. Kirsner & Lyn Taetzsch. (Illus.). 272p. 1983. 26.95 o.p. (ISBN 0-442-28420-9). Van Nos Reinhold.

Practical Alcoholism Programming: An Honorable Approach to Man's Alcoholism Problem. J. G. Strachan. 1971. 17.50 o.s.i. (ISBN 0-685-25493-3). E J Brill USA.

Practical Analytical Electron Microscopy in Materials Science. David B. Williams. 153p. 1984. text ed. 38.00x o.p. (ISBN 0-89573-307-2). VCH Pubs.

Practical Answers to Common Questions about Sex in Marriage. Tim LaHaye & Beverly LaHaye. 72p. (Orig.). 1984. pap. 1.95 o.p. (ISBN 0-310-27042-1, 18340P). Zondervan.

Practical Answers to Everyday Zoning Problems. Massachusetts Continuing Legal Education-New England Law Institute, Inc. Staff & Massachusetts Continuing Legal Education-New England Law Institute Staff. LC 83-171877. (Illus.). 1983. write for info. o.p. Mass CLE.

Practical Applework Uses. David K. Simerly. LC 85-71777. 313p. 1985. pap. 19.95 o.p. (ISBN 0-89588-274-4). SYBEX.

Practical Approach to COBOL Programming. Sharad Kant. LC 82-23247. 506p. 1985. 21.95x o.p. (ISBN 0-470-27392-5). Halsted Pr.

Practical Approach to Industrial Relations for Line Supervisors. R. M. Bielstein. 109p. 1965. 9.00x o.p. (ISBN 0-87201-381-2). Gulf Pub.

Practical Approach to Quality Control. 3rd ed. R. H. Caplen. 310p. 1978. pap. text ed. 14.75x o.p. (ISBN 0-220-66368-8, Pub. by Busn Bks England). Gower Pub Co.

Practical Approach to Teaching Reading. Dorothy Rubin. 1982. text ed. 29.95 o.p. (ISBN 0-03-059103-1). HR&W.

Practical Art of Diagnostic Interviewing. Gerald R. Pascal. (Professional Bks.). 132p. 1983. (ISBN 0-534-10452-5). Wadsworth Pub.

Practical Aspects of Memory. Ed. by M. M. Gruneberg et al. 1979. 59.50 o.p. (ISBN 0-12-305050-2). Acad Pr.

Practical Astral Projection. Yram. LC 75-16548. (Orig.). 1974. pap. 5.95 o.p. (ISBN 0-87728-267-6). Weiser.

Practical Astrologer. Nicholas Campion. (Illus.). 240p. 1987. 24.95 o.p. (ISBN 0-8109-1492-1); pap. 14.95 o.p. (ISBN 0-8109-2354-8). Abrams.

Practical Astrologer. Nicholas Campion. 1989. 12.98 o.p. (ISBN 0-517-67969-8). Crown.

Practical Astronomy. W. Schroeder. (Illus.). 206p. 1957. (ISBN 0-8022-1515-7). Philos Lib.

Practical Baking Manual. William J. Sultan. (Illus.). 1976. 13.95 o.p. (ISBN 0-87055-213-9). AVI.

Practical Bar Management. H. L. Grossman. 23.50x o.p. (ISBN 0-911202-26-9). Radio City.

Practical Beginning Theory. 5th ed. Bruce Benward & Barbara G. Jackson. 464p. 1982. write for info. plastic comb o.p. (ISBN 0-697-03545-X). Wm C Brown.

Practical Biomechanics for the Orthopedic Surgeon. Eric L. Radin et al. LC 78-11671. 168p. 1979. 37.50x o.p. (ISBN 0-471-02703-0). Wiley.

Practical Blood Transfusion. 3rd ed. Douglas W. Huestis et al. (Series in Laboratory Medicine). 1981. text ed. 33.50 o.p. (ISBN 0-316-37952-2). Little.

Practical Bonsai for Beginners. Kenji Murata. LC 64-7611. (Illus.). 1977. pap. 7.95 o.p. (ISBN 0-87040-230-7). Japan Pubns USA.

Practical Bronchoscopy. Doty et al. 1986. 27.75 o.p. (ISBN 0-8016-1366-3). Mosby.

Practical Business & Tax Guide for the Craftsperson. rev. ed. James E. Norris & Fred Bair. (Illus.). 100p. 1986. pap. 16.00x o.p. (ISBN 0-942280-23-7). Pub Horizons.

Practical Business Communications. Robert Nixon. 594p. 1984. text ed. 24.00 net o.p. (ISBN 0-15-570875-9, HC). HarBraceJ.

Practical Business Law. Frances E. Zollers & Gail H. Foreman. 1978. 15.95 o.p. (ISBN 0-442-29580-4). Van Nos Reinhold.

Practical Business Research Methods. Steven Blank. (Illus.). 1984. 30.95 o.s.i. (ISBN 0-87055-455-7). AVI.

Practical Cardiology. William J. French & J. Michael Criley. LC 82-2641. 320p. 1983. 19.95 o.p. (ISBN 0-317-54507-8, Pub. by John Wiley). Krieger.

Practical Chess Playing. Raymond Edwards. (Routledge Chess Handbooks Ser.). 128p. (Orig.). 1984. pap. 7.95 o.p. (ISBN 0-7100-9653-4). Routledge Chapman & Hall.

Practical Christian Living. Ken Stewart. 32p. (Orig.). 1983. wkbk 3.00 o.s.i. (ISBN 0-914307-07-X). R Tilton Ministries.

Practical Clinical Chemistry. Gelson Toro & Philip G. Ackermann. LC 74-4945. 1975. text ed. 29.95 o.p. (ISBN 0-316-85057-8). Little.

Practical Clinical Neurology. John K. Wolf. LC 79-91846. 1980. pap. 20.50 o.p. (ISBN 0-87488-728-3). Med Exam.

Practical Cogitator. 3rd ed. Charles P. Curtis, Jr. & Ferris Greenslet. 1963. 10.95 o.p. (ISBN 0-395-07590-4). HM.

Practical Considerations in Piping Analysis. Ed. by E. Van Stijgeren & L. Krawzya. (PVP Ser.: Vol. 69). 181p. 1982. 34.00 o.p. (H00226). ASME.

Practical Contraception. Saroja Ramaswamy & Tony Smith. (Illus.). 149p. 1977. text ed. 9.00x o.p. (ISBN 0-89313-004-4). G F Stickley Co.

Practical Conversation in English. Eugene J. Hall. Incl. For Beginning Students. 1972 (ISBN 0-88345-129-8, 18010); For Intermediate Students. 1965 (ISBN 0-88345-130-1, 17412); For Advanced Students. 1967 (ISBN 0-88345-128-X, 17411). (gr. 7 up). pap. 2.75 ea. o.p.; cassettes 60.00 ea. o.p.; tapes o.p. 60.00 ea. o.p. Prentice ESL.

Practical Cost Reduction. Trevor J. Bentley. 176p. 1981. text ed. 27.95 o.p. (ISBN 0-07-084537-9). McGraw.

Practical Curriculum Study. Douglas Barnes. (Rutledge Education Bks.). 160p. 1983. pap. 19.95x o.p. (ISBN 0-7100-0979-8). Routledge Chapman & Hall.

Practical Designs for Wood Turning. Roland Seale. LC 79-65084. (Home Craftsman Bk.). (Illus.). 152p. 1979. pap. 7.95 o.p. (ISBN 0-8069-8874-6). Sterling.

Practical Dissector & Textbook of Human Anatomy: Emphasizing the Musculoskeletal System. Donald J. Hobart. (Allied Health Bks.: Vol. I). 1984. pap. text ed. 30.00 o.p. (ISBN 0-87488-425-X). Med Exam.

Practical Education, 2 vols. Maria Edgeworth & Richard L. Edgeworth. Ed. by Gina Luria. (Feminist Controversy in England, 1788-1810 Ser.). 1974. Set. lib. bdg. 121.00 o.p. (ISBN 0-8240-0857-X). Garland Pub.

Practical Electrical Wiring. 12th ed. Herbert P. Richter & W. Creighton Schwan. (Illus.). 672p. 1982. text ed. 29.95 o.p. (ISBN 0-07-052389-4). McGraw.

Practical Electrical Wiring: Residential, Farm & Industrial. 13th ed. Herbert P. Richter & W. Creighton Schwan. (Illus.). 685p. 1984. text ed. 32.95 o.p. (ISBN 0-07-052390-8). McGraw.

Practical Electricity. Joseph F. McPartland & W. J. Novak. 1964. text ed. 35.95 o.p. (ISBN 0-07-045694-1). McGraw.

Practical Encyclopedia of Natural Healing. Mark Bricklin. LC 76-26864. 1976. 19.95 o.p. (ISBN 0-87857-136-1). Rodale Pr Inc.

Practical Endocrine Diagnosis. 3rd ed. Nelson B. Watts & Joseph H. Keffer. LC 81-15607. (Illus.). 166p. 1982. pap. 18.75 o.p. (ISBN 0-8121-0818-3). Lea & Febiger.

Practical English Handbook. 5th ed. Floyd C. Watkins & William B. Dillingham. LC 77-75888. (Illus.). 1980. pap. 8.95 o.p. (ISBN 0-395-25825-1). HM.

Practical English Handbook. 6th ed. Floyd C. Watkins & William B. Dillingham. 1982. pap. 12.95 o.p. (ISBN 0-395-31734-7). HM.

Practical English Workbook. 2nd ed. Floyd C. Watkins et al. 1982. pap. 11.95 o.p. (ISBN 0-395-31736-3). HM.

Practical English Workbook. Floyd C. Watkins et al. LC 77-75888. 1978. pap. 8.50 o.p. (ISBN 0-395-25830-8). HM.

Practical English Workbook Form B. 2nd ed. Floyd C. Watkins et al. 312p. 1982. pap. 13.56 o.p. (ISBN 0-395-33187-0); instr's. manual 2.36 o.p. (ISBN 0-395-33186-2). HM.

Practical Entertaining. Irma Rhode. LC 78-53801. 1978. 9.95 o.p. (ISBN 0-689-10915-6, Atheneum). Macmillan.

Practical Financial Management for Dental Practice Administration, 4 vols. Eldon L. Schafer et al. Ed. by Center for Research in Ambulatory Health Care Administration Staff. 1982. Set. slipcase 65.00 o.p. (ISBN 0-933948-73-5). Ctr Res Ambulatory.

Practical Fishing Knots. Lefty Kreh & Mark Sosin. LC 83-61444. (Illus.). 160p. 1983. pap. 9.95 o.p. (ISBN 0-8329-0246-2). Lyons & Burford.

Practical Football Coaching Techniques. Bernie Taylor. 228p. (Orig.). 1981. pap. 10.00 spiral bdg. o.p. (ISBN 0-936352-06-X). U of KS Cont Ed.

Practical Formwork & Mould Construction. 2nd ed. Ed. by J. G. Richardson. (Illus.). xv, 294p. 1976. 52.00 o.p. (ISBN 0-85334-629-1, Pub. by Elsevier Applied Sci England). Elsevier.

Practical Geometry & Engineering Graphics. 8th ed. W. Abbot. (Illus.). 1971. pap. text ed. 23.50x o.p. (ISBN 0-216-89450-6). Trans-Atl Phila.

Practical Geriatric Medicine. Ed. by A. Norman Exton-Smith. Marc E. Weksler. LC 84-21439. (Illus.). 475p. 1985. text ed. 50.00 o.p. (ISBN 0-443-02702-1). Churchill.

Practical Goat-Keeping. John Halliday & Jill Halliday. (Illus.). 104p. 1982. 12.95x o.p. (ISBN 0-8464-1290-X). Beekman Pubs.

Practical Goat-Keeping. John Halliday & Jill Halliday. (Illus.). 104p. 1988. pap. 11.95 o.p. (ISBN 0-7063-6486-4, Pub. by Ward Lock). David & Charles.

Practical Guide for Altar Guilds. A. E. Bockelman. LC 62-16936. (Illus., Orig.). 1962. pap. 4.95 o.p. (ISBN 0-8066-0223-6, 10-5050, Augsburg). Augsburg Fortress.

Practical Guide for the Genealogist in English. Rachael Mellen. (Illus.). vi, 84p. (Orig.). 1986. pap. 10.00 o.p. (ISBN 0-917890-85-X). Heritage Bk.

Practical Guide for the Obstetric Team. M. D. Read & D. Wellby. 285p. 1985. pap. 16.00 o.p. (ISBN 0-471-90584-4, Dist. by A R Liss). Wiley.

Practical Guide to Cardiac Pacing. H. Weston Moses & George J. Taylor. 149p. 1983. pap. text ed. 16.00 o.p. (ISBN 0-316-58555-6). Little.

Practical Guide to Computer Programming Management. 1982. pap. 14.95 o.p. (ISBN 0-442-20920-7). Van Nos Reinhold.

Practical Guide to Data Base Management. 1982. pap. 14.95 o.p. (ISBN 0-442-20916-9). Van Nos Reinhold.

Practical Guide to Data Center Operations Management. 1982. pap. 14.95 o.p. (ISBN 0-442-20912-6). Van Nos Reinhold.

Practical Guide to Data Communications Management. 1982. pap. 9.95 o.p. (ISBN 0-442-20918-5). Van Nos Reinhold.

Practical Guide to Data Processing Management. 1982. pap. 14.95 o.p. (ISBN 0-442-20922-3). Van Nos Reinhold.

Practical Guide to Distributed Processing Management. 1982. pap. 14.95 o.p. (ISBN 0-442-20900-2). Van Nos Reinhold.

Practical Guide to EDP Auditing Management. 1982. pap. 14.95 o.p. (ISBN 0-442-20909-6). Van Nos Reinhold.

Practical Guide to Fund Accounting & Auditing. David L. Gittes. LC 81-20907. 270p. 1982. text ed. 89.50 o.p. (ISBN 0-87624-433-9, Inst Busn Plan). P-H.

Practical Guide to Multi-Level Modular ESL. Dorthea Canzano & Phyllis Canzano. 1975. pap. 12.95 o.p. (ISBN 0-87789-130-3); cassettes intermediate 70.00 o.p. (ISBN 0-87789-133-8); cassettes advanced 75.00 o.p. (ISBN 0-87789-136-2). ELS Educ Servs.

Practical Guide to Optimal Nutrition: Nutri-Plan. Virginia Aronson. 240p. (Orig.). 1982. pap. text ed. 17.50 o.p. (ISBN 0-7236-7018-8). Butterworth.

Practical Guide to Portrait Photography. Frank Herramann. (Illus.). 144p. 1988. 29.95 o.p. (ISBN 0-946609-45-4). Haynes Pubns.

Practical Guide to Preaching. George Fitzgerald. LC 79-67742. 160p. (Orig.). 1980. pap. 5.95 o.p. (ISBN 0-8091-2281-2). Paulist Pr.

Practical Guide to Press Photography. Philip Dunn. (Illus.). 128p. 1988. 29.95 o.p. (ISBN 0-946609-54-3). Haynes Pubns.

Practical Guide to Quality Assurance in Medical Imaging. B. M. Moores et al. LC 86-24529. 1987. 29.90 o.p. (ISBN 0-471-91186-0, Dist. by A R Liss). Wiley.

Practical Guide to Small Computers for Business & Professional Use. rev. ed. Robert M. Rinder. 288p. 1983. pap. 11.95 o.p. (ISBN 0-671-47091-4). Monarch Pr.

Practical Guide to Structured Systems Design. Jones Page. 1986. pap. 35.00 o.p. (ISBN 0-13-690694-X). P-H.

Practical Guide to Systems Development Management. 1982. pap. 14.95 o.p. (ISBN 0-442-20915-0). Van Nos Reinhold.

Practical Guide to the Bankruptcy Reform Act, 2 vols. Harvey R. Miller & Michael L. Cook. 1434p. 1979. 110.00 o.p. (ISBN 0-15-100045-X, C00191, Pub. by Law & Business). HarBraceJ.

Practical Guide to the Cable Communications Policy Act of 1984. Practising Law Institute Staff & George R.. Dorsari. LC 85-196289. (Patents, Copyrights, Trademarks, & Literary Property Course Handbooks: No. 200). 1985. 15.00 o.p. (G43771). PLI.

Practical Guide to Word Processing & Office Management Systems. Mary J. Forbes. 200p. pap. 22.00 o.p. (ISBN 0-318-02633-3). Digital Pr.

Practical Handbook for College Teachers. Barbara S. Fuhrmann & Anthony F. Grasha. 315p. 1983. text ed. 30.75 o.p.; pap. text ed. 14.25 o.p. (ISBN 0-673-39151-5). Scott F.

Practical Handbook of Amateur Radio FM & Repeaters. Bill Pasternak. (Illus., Orig.). 1980. 15.95 o.p. (ISBN 0-8306-9959-7); pap. 12.95 o.p. (ISBN 0-8306-1212-2, 1212). TAB Bks.

Practical Handbook of Solid State Troubleshooting. Robert C. Genn. (Illus.). 1984. pap. 12.95 o.p. (ISBN 0-13-691295-8, Busn). P-H.

Practical Handbook of Warehousing. Kenneth B. Ackerman. LC 83-50503. (Illus.). 550p. 1983. 32.50 o.p. (ISBN 0-87408-027-4). Intl Thom Trans Pr.

Practical Horticulture. Robert P. Rice & Laura W. Rice. LC 79-17985. 501p. 1980. text ed. 27.95x o.p. (ISBN 0-03-041455-5, CBS C). SCP.

Practical House Carpentry: Simplified Methods for Building. 3rd ed. J. Douglas Wilson. (Illus.). 1979. pap. text ed. 5.95 o.p. (ISBN 0-07-070889-4). McGraw.

Practical Human Relations. rev ed. Robert M. Fulmer. 1983. 30.95x o.p. (ISBN 0-256-02629-7). Irwin.

Practical Hunter's Dog Book. John R. Falk. LC 84-2419. (Illus.). 1984. pap. 13.95 o.p. (ISBN 0-8329-0317-5, Pub. by Winchester Pr). New Century.

Practical Hydromet 'Eighty-Four: Proceedings of the Seventh Annual Symposium on Uranium & Precious Metals. (Illus.). 126p. 1984. pap. 28.00x o.p. (ISBN 0-89520-423-1). SMM&E Inc.

Practical Ideas for Metalworking Operations, Tooling & Maintenance. American Machinist Magazine Staff. 352p. 1986. text ed. 37.50 o.p. (ISBN 0-07-001551-1). McGraw.

Practical Illustrated Histology. N. A. Ratcliffe & P. J. Llewellyn. 246p. 1982. text ed. write for info. o.p. (ISBN 0-02-398560-7). Macmillan.

Practical Inferences. D. S. Clarke, Jr. (International Library of Philosophy). 192p. 1985. 32.50x o.p. (ISBN 0-7102-0415-9). Routledge Chapman & Hall.

Practical Inorganic Chemistry: Preparations, Reactions & Instrumental Methods. 2nd ed. G. Pass & H. Sutcliffe. 256p. 1979. pap. 12.95x o.p. (ISBN 0-412-16150-8, NO. 6214, Pub. by Chapman & Hall England). Routledge Chapman & Hall.

Practical Interfacing Projects with the Commodore Computers. Robert H. Luetzow. (Illus.). 256p. (Orig.). 1986. 24.95 o.p. (ISBN 0-8306-0983-0, 1983); pap. 16.60 o.p. (ISBN 0-8306-1983-6). Tab Bks.

Practical Introduction to Borehole Geophysics. James A. Labo. Ed. by Samuel H. Mentemeier & Gerald H. Gardner. LC 87-60425. (Geophysical Reference Ser.: No. 2). (Illus.). 336p. 1987. text ed. 56.00 o.p. (ISBN 0-931830-39-7). Soc Expl Geophys.

Practical Introduction to Business. 4th ed. Koontz & Fulmer. 1984. 9.95 o.p. Irwin.

Practical Introduction to Copyright Law. Gavin McFarlane. 256p. 1982. text ed. 38.50 o.p. (ISBN 0-07-084569-7). McGraw.

Practical Introduction to the New Logic Symbols. 2nd ed. Ian Kampel. (Illus.). 176p. 1986. text ed. 21.95 o.p. (ISBN 0-408-03010-0). Butterworth.

Practical Inventor's Handbook. Orville Greene & Frank Durr. LC 78-26666. (Illus.). 1979. text ed. 43.50 o.p. (ISBN 0-07-024320-4). McGraw.

Practical Kinetography Laban. Valerie Preston-Dunlop. 224p. 19.95 o.s.i. (ISBN 0-7121-1609-5). Princeton Bk Co.

Practical Knots & Ropework. Percy W. Blandford. (Illus., Orig.). 1980. 14.95 o.p. (ISBN 0-8306-9956-2); pap. 10.60 o.p. (ISBN 0-8306-1237-8, 1237). TAB Bks.

Practical Law for Correctional Personnel: A Resource Manual & a Training Curriculum (by the National Street Law Institute) Edward L. O'Brien & Margaret E. Fisher. (Illus.). 250p. 1980. pap. text ed. 7.75 o.p. (ISBN 0-8299-1034-4). West Pub.

Practical Liquid Chromatography. S. G. Perry et al. LC 75-179760. 230p. 1972. 39.50x o.p. (ISBN 0-306-30548-8, Plenum Pr); pap. 14.95x o.p. (ISBN 0-306-20002-3). Plenum Pub.

Practical Malaria Control. Carl Gunther. (ISBN 0-8022-0646-8). Philos Lib.

Practical Management for Productivity. John R. Hinrichs. (Work In America Institute Ser.). 160p. 1982. pap. 15.95 o.p. (ISBN 0-442-23210-1). Van Nos Reinhold.

Practical Management of Asthma. T. Clark & J. Rees. (Practical Problems in Medicine Ser.). (Illus.). 174p. 1985. lib. bdg. 45.00 o.p. (ISBN 0-906348-74-9, Pub. by Martin Dunitz Ltd UK). VCH Pubs.

Practical Management of Spinal Injuries for Nurses. 2nd ed. Alan G. Hardy & Reginald Elson. LC 75-29262. (Illus.). 176p. 1976. text ed. 15.00 o.p. (ISBN 0-443-01320-9). Churchill.

Practical Manual of Pediatrics: A Pocket Reference for Those Who Treat Children. 2nd ed. William W. Waring & Louis O. Jeansonne. LC 81-14148. (Illus.). 483p. 1981. pap. text ed. 16.95 o.p. (ISBN 0-8016-5347-9). Mosby.

Practical Map Production. John Loxton. LC 80-40118. 137p. 1980. 19.95 o.p. (ISBN 0-471-27782-7, Pub. by Wiley-Interscience); pap. 31.95x o.p. (ISBN 0-471-27783-5). Wiley.

Practical Math for Business. 2nd ed. Alan R. Curtis. LC 77-73944. (Illus.). 1978. pap. 16.50 o.p. (ISBN 0-395-25431-0). HM.

Practical Math for Business. 3d ed. Alan R. Curtis. LC 82-84521. 368p. 1983. pap. 26.95 o.p. (ISBN 0-395-32698-2). HM.

Practical Mathematics Appraisal of the Learning Disabled. Ed. by John F. Cawley. LC 84-20499. 350p. 1984. 36.50 o.p. (ISBN 0-89443-559-0). Aspen Pub.

Practical Mathematics in Allied Health: A Textbook for the Medical Disciplines. Marian Waterhouse. LC 79-15317. (Illus.). 256p. 1979. spiral bdg. 15.95 o.p. (ISBN 0-8067-2121-9). Urban & S.

Practical Meat Cutting & Merchandising, Vol. 1: Beef. 2nd ed. Thomas Fabbricante & William J. Sultan. (Illus.). 1978. pap. 17.95 o.p. (ISBN 0-87055-273-2). AVI.

Practical Metal Projects. M. J. Ruley. (gr. 9 up). text ed. 15.28 o.p. (ISBN 0-87345-137-6). Glencoe.

Practical Methods of Optimization: Constrained Optimization, Vol. 2. R. Fletcher. 224p. 1981. 51.95x o.p. (ISBN 0-471-27828-9, Pub. by Wiley Interscience). Wiley.

Practical Methods of Optimization: Unconstrained Optimization, Vol. 1. R. Fletcher. LC 79-41486. 120p. 1980. 46.95x o.p. (ISBN 0-471-27711-8, Pub. by Wiley-Interscience). Wiley.

Practical Microwaves. Thomas S. Laverghetta. LC 83-51119. 39.95 o.p. (ISBN 0-672-21945-X, 21945). Sams.

Practical Modern Greek for English Speaking People. S. D. Stouriotis. 1971. pap. 15.00 o.p. E J Brill USA.

Practical Navigation for the Yachtsman. Frederick L. Devereux, Jr. (Illus.). 316p. 1972. 19.95 o.p. (ISBN 0-393-03171-3). Norton.

Practical Nutritional Support. S. J. Karran & K. G. Alberti. LC 79-56645. 364p. 1980. 45.00 o.p. (ISBN 0-471-08024-1, JW). Krieger.

Practical Optimization. Margaret Wright. LC 81-66366. 1982. 32.00 o.p. (ISBN 0-12-283952-8). Acad Pr.

Practical Oscilloscope Handbook. 2nd ed. Bierman et al. 184p. pap. 8.95 o.p. (ISBN 0-8104-0851-1). Sams.

Practical Oscilloscope Handbook. Rufus Turner. (Illus.). (YA) (gr. 10 up). 1964. pap. 5.95 o.p. (ISBN 0-8104-0476-1). Vol. 1. Sams.

Practical Paediatric Haematology: A Laboratory Worker's Guide to Blood Disorders in Children. Ed. by R. F. Hinchliffe & J. S. Lilleyman. LC 86-32497. 1987. (ISBN 0-471-91029-5, Dist. by A R Liss). Wiley.

Practical Paediatrics. Ed. by M. J. Robinson. LC 85-14945. (Illus.). 625p. (Orig.). 1986. text ed. 49.00 o.p. (ISBN 0-443-02817-6). Churchill.

Practical Pascal Programs. Lon Poole & Gregory Davidson. 206p. (Orig.). 1982. pap. text ed. 4.00 o.p. (ISBN 0-07-931074-5). Osborne-McGraw.

Practical Pediatrics, Vol. 1. Ed. by Richard H. Rapkin. 1981. 26.00 o.p. (ISBN 0-88416-342-3, 342). Year Bk Med.

Practical Photography. rev ed. Robert A. McCoy. (Illus.). (gr. 10-12). 1972. text ed. 17.28 o.p. (ISBN 0-87345-431-6). Glencoe.

Practical Physics. Jerry D. Wilson. 560p. 1986. text ed. 41.25 incl. home study experiment pkg. o.s.i. (ISBN 0-03-007508-4). SCP.

Practical Physics: The Production & Conservation of Energy. Joseph F. Mulligan. (Illus.). 1980. text ed. 32.95 o.p. (ISBN 0-07-044032-8). McGraw.

Practical Planning Law: A Handbook for Planners, Architects & Surveyors. J. F. Garner. 246p. 1981. pap. 11.50 o.p. (ISBN 0-7099-1107-6, Pub. by Croom Helm Ltd); 31.50 o.p. (ISBN 0-7099-1106-8). Routledge Chapman & Hall.

Practical Points in Plastic Surgery. Stephen H. Miller et al. LC 79-91201. 1980. pap. 29.50 o.p. (ISBN 0-87488-719-4). Med Exam.

Practical Polish-English Dictionary: Polish-English; English-Polish. Iwo Pogonowski. LC 78-64764. (Pol. & Eng.). 1981. pap. 6.95 o.p. (ISBN 0-88254-494-2). Hippocrene Bks.

Practical Polymerization for Polystyrene. Richard B. Bishop. LC 75-132666. (Illus.). 480p. 1983. 41.95 o.p. (ISBN 0-8436-1200-2). Van Nos Reinhold.

Practical Prescribing. Ed. by Martin J. Brodie & P. Ian Harrison. LC 85-20926. (Illus.). 295p. 1986. pap. text ed. 25.50 o.p. (ISBN 0-443-03304-8). Churchill.

Practical Printing: A Handbook of the Art of Typography. John Southward. LC 78-74412. (Nineteenth Century Book Arts & Printing Ser.). 640p. 1980. lib. bdg. 67.00 o.p. (ISBN 0-8240-3896-7). Garland Pub.

Practical Problem Solving, Level A. Intentional Educations, Inc. Staff. (Problem Solving Ser.). (Illus.). 20p. (gr. 4). 1984. duplicating master cancelled 6.00 o.s.i. (ISBN 0-88049-067-5, 7746). Milton Bradley Co.

Practical Problem Solving, Level B. Intentional Educations, Inc. Staff. (Problem Solving Ser.). (Illus.). 20p. (gr. 5). 1984. duplicating master cancelled 6.00 o.s.i. (ISBN 0-88049-068-3, 7747). Milton Bradley Co.

Practical Problem Solving, Level C. Intentional Educations, Inc. Staff. (Problem Solving Ser.). (Illus.). 20p. (gr. 6). 1984. cancelled 6.00 o.s.i. (ISBN 0-88049-069-1, 7748). Milton Bradley Co.

Practical Problems in Dermatology. R. Marks. (Practical Problems in Medicine Ser.). (Illus.). 255p. 1984. lib. bdg. 45.00 o.p. (Pub. by Martin Dunitz Ltd UK). VCH Pubs.

Practical Problems in Mathematics--Metric System. 2nd ed. Frank R. Schell. LC 78-73133. 1980. pap. text ed. 9.50 o.p. (ISBN 0-8273-1418-3). Delmar.

Practical Problems in Mathematics for Mechanical Drafting. J. Larkin. LC 77-78236. 1979. pap. 9.50 o.p. (ISBN 0-8273-1670-4); instr's. guide o.s.i. 7.00 o.p. (ISBN 0-8273-1671-2). Delmar.

Practical Problems in Mathematics for Carpenters. 3rd ed. H. C. Huth. LC 77-82373. 1979. pap. text ed. 9.50 o.p. (ISBN 0-8273-1275-X). Delmar.

Practical Problems in Mathematics for Consumers. Connie Littman. LC 74-24811. 1975. pap. 9.50 o.p. (ISBN 0-8273-0266-5); 4.50 o.s.i. instr's. guide (ISBN 0-8273-0267-3). Delmar.

Practical Problems in Mathematics for Machinists. 2nd ed. Edward G. Hoffman. LC 78-74432. (Mathematics Ser.). 1980. 9.50 o.p. (ISBN 0-8273-1281-4); instr's. guide 7.00 o.p. (ISBN 0-8273-1282-2). Delmar.

Practical Problems in Mathematics for Welders. 2nd ed. Frank R. Schell & Bill J. Matlock. LC 80-70699. (Practical Problems in Mathematics Ser.). (Illus.). 218p. (Orig.). 1982. pap. text ed. 9.50 o.p. (ISBN 0-8273-2076-0). Delmar.

Practical Problems in Rheumatology. F. D. Hart. (Practical Problems in Medicine Ser.). 255p. 1985. lib. bdg. 45.00 o.p. (ISBN 0-906348-47-1, Pub. by Martin Dunitz Ltd UK). VCH Pubs.

Practical Process Instrumentation & Control. Jay Matley & Chemical Engineering Magazine Editors. (Chemical Engineering Ser.). 512p. 1980. text ed. 46.50 o.p. (ISBN 0-07-010712-2). McGraw.

Practical Programs for the BBC Micro. Owen Bishop & Audrey Bishop. (Illus.). 120p. (Orig.). 1983. pap. 13.95 o.p. (ISBN 0-246-12405-9, Pub. by Granada England). Sheridan.

Practical Protocol: A Guide to International Courtesies. James E. Lott. LC 73-75393. 198p. 1973. 19.95x o.p. (ISBN 0-87201-746-X). Gulf Pub.

Practical Pruning. Ed. by Roger Grounds. LC 77-70395. (Illus.). 1978. pap. 5.95 o.p. (ISBN 0-8120-0797-2). Barron.

Practical Quality Control Manual with Eight Simple Chart Systems. International Technical Information Institute Staff. 60p. 1981. 83.00 o.p. (ISBN 0-318-04393-9). Media Intl Promo.

Practical Rabbit-Keeping. Katie Thear. (Illus.). 96p. 1988. pap. 11.95 o.p. (ISBN 0-7063-6487-2, Pub. by Ward Lock). David & Charles.

Practical Radio Servicing. 2nd ed. William Marcus & Alex Levy. LC 79-26498. 632p. 1980. Repr. of 1963 ed. lib. bdg. 37.50 o.p. (ISBN 0-89874-061-4). Krieger.

Practical Seamanship Illustrated. Robert Das & Harald Schwarzlose. (Illus.). 256p. 1987. 19.95 o.p. (ISBN 0-671-63100-4). S&S.

Practical Security in Commerce & Industry. 4th ed. Eric Oliver & John Wilson. 604p. 1983. text ed. 49.95x o.p. (ISBN 0-566-02429-2). Gower Pub Co.

Practical Soil Science. N. N. Nikol'skil. 248p. 1963. text ed. 54.00x o.p. (ISBN 0-7065-0252-3, Pub. by Keter Pub Jerusalem). Coronet Bks.

Practical Tables, Vol. 3: Six-Figure Trigonometrical Functions of Angles in Degrees & Minutes. 5th ed. Ed. by C. Attwood. 1965. 11.25 o.p. (ISBN 0-08-009894-0); pap. text ed. 4.20 o.p. (ISBN 0-08-009893-2). Pergamon.

Practical Tax Guide for the Horse Owner, 1986 Edition. John Talbott. (Illus.). 97p. 1986. pap. 15.00x o.p. (ISBN 0-317-40030-4). Pub Horizons.

Practical Techniques in MS Word. Alan R. Neibauer. LC 85-63780. 431p. (Orig.). 1986. pap. 18.95 o.p. (ISBN 0-89588-316-3). Sybex.

Practical Techniques of Electronic Circuit Design. Robert L. Bonebreak. LC 81-11394. 306p. 1982. 39.95 o.p. (ISBN 0-471-09612-1, Pub. by Wiley Interscience). Wiley.

Practical Time Management - How to Get More Done in Less Time. Bradley C. McRae. 160p. 1988. pap. 6.95 o.s.i. (ISBN 0-88908-673-7, 9559). TAB Bks.

Practical Transistors & Linear Integrated Circuits, Experiments. Joseph D. Greenfield. 132p. (Orig.). 1988. pap. price not set o.p. (ISBN 0-471-63830-7). Wiley.

Practical Treatise on the Law of Slavery. Jacob D. Wheeler. LC 68-58073. Repr. of 1837 ed. 35.00x o.p. (ISBN 0-8371-0748-2, WHL&, Pub. by Negro U Pr). Greenwood.

Practical Troubleshooting with Modern Electronic Test Instruments. Robert L. Goodman. (Illus.). 1979. pap. 9.95 o.p. (ISBN 0-8306-1177-0, 1177). TAB Bks.

Practical Wood Turner. rev. ed. F. Pain. LC 74-6436. (Home Craftsman Bk.). (Illus.). 1979. pap. 7.95 o.p. (ISBN 0-8069-8580-1). Sterling.

Practical Woodwork for Laboratory Technicians. A. S. Eyers. LC 79-117463. 1970. text ed. 16.00 o.p. (ISBN 0-08-015962-1). Pergamon.

Practical Writer: From Paragraph to Theme. 2nd ed. Edward P. Bailey, Jr. 1983. pap. text ed. 15.95 o.p. (ISBN 0-03-061739-1). HR&W.

Practical Yoga: A Pictorial Approach. Masahiro Oki. LC 76-115846. (Illus.). 1973. pap. 6.95 o.p. (ISBN 0-87040-224-2). Japan Pubns USA.

Practical Yoga: Thoroughly Practical Lessons upon the Philosophy & Practice of Yoga. 6th ed. O. Hashnu Hara. 79p. 1970. pap. 4.95 o.s.i. (ISBN 0-88697-032-6). Life Science.

Practice & Procedure for the Quantity Surveyor. 8th ed. Arthur J. Willis & Christopher J. Willis. 239p. 1980. text ed. 30.75x o.p. (ISBN 0-246-11172-0, Pub. by Granada England); pap. text ed. 19.25x o.p. (ISBN 0-246-11242-5, Pub. by Granada England). Gower Pub Co.

Practice & Theory of Tibetan Buddhism. Geshe L. Sopa & Jeffrey Hopkins. LC 75-42898. 1976. pap. 4.95 o.p. (ISBN 0-394-17905-6, E672, Ever). Grove.

Practice Development for Professional Firms. Aubrey Wilson. 256p. 1984. text ed. 39.50 o.p. (ISBN 0-07-084761-4). McGraw.

Practice for Air Force Placement Tests. 5th ed. E. P. Steinberg. LC 82-4068. 272p. 1982. pap. 8.00 o.p. (ISBN 0-668-05355-0). Arco.

Practice for Army Placement Tests. E. P. Steinberg. LC 82-8914. 288p. 1982. pap. 8.00 o.p. (ISBN 0-668-05452-2). Arco.

Practice for Officer Candidate Tests. 4th ed. LC 74-20760. (Military Examination Ser.). 1974. lib. bdg. 12.00 o.p. (ISBN 0-668-01507-1); pap. 12.00 o.p. (ISBN 0-668-01304-4). Arco.

Practice for Operational Procedures: Inspection & Quality Control of First-Generation Silver-Gelatin Microfilm of Documents (ANSI-AIIM MS23-1983) rev. ed. Association for Information & Image Management. 1979. pap. text ed. 12.00 o.p. (ISBN 0-89258-067-4). Assn Inform & Image Mgmt.

Practice for the SAT (Scholastic Aptitude Test) Martin McDonough & Alvin H. Hansen. 352p. 1982. pap. 3.50 o.p. (ISBN 0-668-05425-5, 5425). Arco.

Practice for Understanding & Using English: Eighty Exercises Workbook. 2nd ed. Newman P. Birk & Genevieve B. Birk. 168p. 1972. pap. text ed. (ISBN 0-02-310090-7). Macmillan.

Practice for Uniform Product Disclosure for Unitized Microform Readers (Microfiche, Jackets & Image Cards) ANSI/AIIM MS22-1979. Association for Information & Image Management. (Standards & Recommended Practices). 1979. 30.00 o.p. (ISBN 0-89258-057-7, MS21). Assn Inform & Image Mgmt.

Practice Makes Perfect. Edward Vernon. (Lythway Ser.). 1987. lib. bdg. 17.50x o.p. (ISBN 0-7451-0596-3, Pub. by Chivers Pr UK). G K Hall.

Practice Manual for Social Security Claims: Plus 1983 Supplement. Dennis M. Sweeney & James J. Lyko. 441p. 1980. text ed. 45.00 o.p. (C6-1178). PLI.

Practice Manual for Social Security Claims: 1983 Supplement. Dennis M. Sweeney & James J. Lyko. 89p. 1983. pap. 15.00 o.p. (ISBN 0-686-82489-X, C5-1175). PLI.

Practice of Astrology. Dane Rudhyar. LC 77-90881. 1978. pap. 6.95 o.p. (ISBN 0-87773-125-X). Shambhala Pubns.

Practice of Collective Bargaining. 7th ed. Jame P. Begin & Edwin F. Beal. 1985. 34.95 o.p. (ISBN 0-256-03214-9). Irwin.

Practice of Comparative Politics: A Reader. 2nd ed. Ed. by Paul G. Lewis & David C. Potter. (Open University Set Bk.). 1979. pap. text ed. 15.95 o.p. (ISBN 0-582-49033-2). Longman.

Practice of Continuing Education in the Human Services. Armand Lauffer. (Illus.). 1977. text ed. 21.95 o.p. (ISBN 0-07-036625-X). McGraw.

Practice of Coronary Artery Bypass Surgery. D. W. Miller. LC 77-10975. (Topics in Cardiovascular Disease Ser.). (Illus.). 254p. 1977. 45.00x o.p. (ISBN 0-306-31065-1, Plenum Med. Bk.). Plenum Pub.

Practice of Decision Making. Ed. by S. R. Watson. 100p. 1983. pap. 17.00 o.p. (ISBN 0-08-028162-1). Pergamon.

Practice of Entrepreneurship, 1982. 196p. 19.95x o.p. (ISBN 92-2-102839-9). Intl Pubns Serv.

Practice of Godliness. Jerry Bridges. (Christian Character Library). 272p. 1985. hdbk. 8.95 o.p. (ISBN 0-89109-466-0). NavPress.

Practice of Hospitality Management I. Abraham Pizam et al. (Illus.). 1982. 32.95 o.p. (ISBN 0-87055-401-8). AVI.

Practice of Literary Criticism. Lars O. Sauerberg et al. (Odense University Studies in English: Vol. 5). 223p. 1983. pap. text ed. 17.50x o.p. (ISBN 87-7492-414-1). Humanities.

Practice of Management for Health Care Professionals. Rita E. Numerof. 608p. 1982. 29.95 o.p. (ISBN 0-8144-5735-5). AMACOM.

Practice of Managerial Psychology. Andrew J. DuBrin. 1975. 31.00 o.p. (ISBN 0-08-016764-0); pap. 19.25 o.p. (ISBN 0-08-018126-0). Pergamon.

Practice of Marketing Research. James E. Nelson. LC 81-20742. 672p. 1982. text ed. write for info. o.p. (ISBN 0-534-01068-7). PWS-Kent Pub.

Practice of Modern Internal Auditing. 2nd rev. & enl. ed. Larry B. Sawyer. Ed. by Ceel Pasternak. LC 81-810325. 912p. 1981. text ed. 63.00 o.p. (ISBN 0-89413-092-7). Inst Inter Aud.

Practice of NMR Spectroscopy: With Spectra-Structure Correlations for Hydrogen-One. Nugent F. Chamberlain. LC 74-11479. (Illus.). 424p. 1974. 65.00x o.p. (ISBN 0-306-30766-9, Plenum Pr). Plenum Pub.

Practice of Piety: Puritan Devotional Disciplines in Seventeenth-Century New England. Charles E. Hambrick-Stowe. LC 81-19806. (Institute of Early American History & Culture Ser.). (Illus.). xvi, 298p. 1982. 30.00x o.p. (ISBN 0-8078-1518-7). U of NC Pr.

Practice of Prayer. G. Campbell Morgan. (Morgan Library). pap. 3.95 o.p. (ISBN 0-8010-5896-1). Baker Bk.

Practice of Psychoanalytic Criticism. Ed. by Leonard Tennenhouse. LC 76-26079. 280p. 1976. 12.50 o.p. (ISBN 0-8143-1562-3); pap. 9.95x o.p. (ISBN 0-8143-1563-1). Wayne St U Pr.

Practice of Rhetorical Criticism. James R. Andrews. 288p. 1983. text ed. write for info. o.p. (ISBN 0-02-303490-4). Macmillan.

Practice of Social Research. 4th ed. Earl Babbie. 577p. 1986. text ed. (ISBN 0-534-05658-X). Wadsworth Pub.

Practice of Social Work. 2nd ed. Charles Zastrow. 545p. 1985. text ed. (ISBN 0-534-11277-3). Wadsworth Pub.

Practice of Supervision: Achieving Results Through People. Andrew J. Dubrin. 1980. 25.95x o.p. (ISBN 0-256-02272-0). Irwin.

Practice Problems in Intermediate I Accounting (Val's Videoland) rev. ed. James J. Benjamin & Stanley H. Kratchman. 1989. 9.95x o.p. (ISBN 0-87393-091-6). Dame Pubns.

Practice Set One to Accompany Financial Accounting. Eugene J. Laughlin. 49p. 1984. pap. 13.95 o.p. (ISBN 0-471-88119-8). Wiley.

Practice Soccer Tactics. 1984. pap. 4.95 o.p. (ISBN 0-02-499390-5). Macmillan.

Practicing Before the International Trade Commission, Vol. 284. Practising Law Institute Staff. 549p. 1985. pap. 15.00 o.p. (ISBN 0-317-27617-4, #H4-4971). PLI.

Practicing Educational Psychology. Margaret M. Clifford. (Illus.). 752p. 1981. text ed. 34.76 o.p. (ISBN 0-395-29921-7); pap. 33.56 o.p. (ISBN 0-395-29922-5); instr's. manual .76 o.p. (ISBN 0-395-29923-3); test bank 1.56 o.p. (ISBN 0-395-29925-X). HM.

Practicing Texas Politics. 5th ed. Eugene W. Jones & Lyle C. Brown. LC 82-81521. 576p. 1982. pap. 18.95 o.p. (ISBN 0-395-32793-8). HM.

Practicing Texas Politics. 4th ed. Eugene W. Jones et al. LC 79-88888. 1980. pap. 12.50 o.p. (ISBN 0-395-28257-8). HM.

Practicing Texas Politics: A Brief Survey. Eugene W. Jones et al. LC 83-81616. 256p. 1984. pap. 18.50 o.p. (ISBN 0-395-34935-4). HM.

Practicioner Perspectives on Residential Child & Youth Care Work: A Special Issue of Child Care. Ed. by Mark A. Krueger & Christopher D. Webster. 96p. 1984. pap. 12.95 o.p. (ISBN 0-89885-225-0). Human Sci Pr.

Practicum in Teacher Education: Research, Practice & Supervision. C. Turney & L. G. Cairns. (Illus.). 208p. 1983. pap. 21.00x o.p. (ISBN 0-424-00096-2, Pub. by Sydney U Pr). Intl Spec Bk.

Practising Before the U. S. Court of Appeals for the Federal Court, Vol. 282. Practising Law Institute Staff. 250p. 1985. pap. 15.00 o.p. (ISBN 0-317-27602-6, #H4-4970). PLI.

Practitioners' Probate Manual. 22nd ed. Ed. by R. F. Yeldham & A. Plumb. (Waterlow Practitioners Library). 320p. 1985. 29.00 o.p. (ISBN 0-08-039242-3, Pub by Waterlow). Pergamon.

Praepostini Tractatus De Officiis. James A. Corbett. (Mediaeval Studies Ser.: Vol. 21). (Lat). 1969. 21.95x o.p. (ISBN 0-268-00326-2). U of Notre Dame Pr.

Praesidium of Archive. Jefferson P. Swycaffer. 197p. 1986. pap. 2.95 o.p. (ISBN 0-380-89663-X). Avon.

Praeventivmassnahmen in der Gynaekologie und ihre oekonomischen Aspekte: Proceedings of the Schweizerische Gesellschaft fuer Gynakologie, Bericht Ueber die Jahresversammlung, Lugano, June 30 - July 2, 1977. Schweizerische Gesellschaft fuer Gynaekologie Staff. Ed. by E. Dreher. (Gynaekologische Rundschau: Vol. 17, Suppl. 1). (Illus., Fr. & Ger.). 1977. 19.50 o.p. (ISBN 3-8055-2867-1). S Karger.

Pragmatic Programming & Sensible Software. Ed. by Online Conferences Ltd. 1978. text ed. 103.50 o.p. (ISBN 0-903796-20-1, Pub by Online Conferences England). Gower Pub Co.

Pragmatic Thought from Its Origins to the Eighteenth Century, Vol. I. Ed. by Herbert Stachowiak. (Pragmatics: Handbook of Pragmatic Thought Ser.). 528p. 1987. 79.95 o.p. (ISBN 3-7873-0643-9). Transaction Pubs.

Pragmatic View of Distributed Processing Systems. Kenneth J. Thurber. LC 80-81350. (Tutorial Texts Ser.). 626p. 1980. 32.00 o.p. (ISBN 0-8186-0299-6, Q299). IEEE Comp Soc.

Prague. Ed. by Vladimir Denkstein et al. LC 78-58354. (Great Centers of Art Ser.). (Illus.). 252p. 1979. 35.00 o.s.i. (ISBN 0-8390-0225-4, Allanheld & Schram). Abner Schram Ltd.

Prairie City, Iowa: Three Seasons at Home. Douglas Bauer. 330p. 1982. pap. 8.95 o.p. (ISBN 0-8138-1329-8). Iowa St U Pr.

Prairie Dancers: A Novel. Jonathan W. Bell. 1987. 17.95 o.p. (ISBN 0-907675-36-0, Pub. by Buchan & Enright England). Seven Hills Bk Dists.

Prairie Grass Dividing. J. Iverne Dowie. LC 60-2575. (Augustana Historical Society Ser.: Vol. 18). xvi, 262p. 1959. pap. 7.50 o.p. (ISBN 0-910184-18-6). Augustana.

Prairie Poet: This Land Called South Dakota & Other Poems. Joyce S. Whitcomb. 1978. 4.00 o.p. (ISBN 0-682-49235-3). Exposition-Phoenix.

Prairie-Town Boy. Carl Sandburg. LC 55-5239. (Illus.). 1955. 6.95 o.s.i. (ISBN 0-15-263329-4, HJ). HarBraceJ.

Prairie Vengeance. M. L. Warren. (Orig.). 1980. pap. 1.75 o.p. (ISBN 0-505-51532-6, Pub. by Tower Bks). Dorchester Pub Co.

Praise All the Moons of Morning. Josephine R. Stone. LC 78-12633. 1979. 7.95 o.p. (ISBN 0-689-30697-0, Atheneum). Macmillan.

Praise Avenue. Don Gossett. 128p. 1976. pap. 2.95 o.p. (ISBN 0-88368-059-9). Whitaker Hse.

Praise God for This New Day: Second Thoughts for Busy Women. Catharine Brandt. LC 75-2831. (Illus.). 128p. (Orig.). 1975. pap. 3.50 o.p. (ISBN 0-8066-1477-3, 10-5053, Augsburg). Augsburg Fortress.

Praise Him! Praise Him! Jennie Davis. LC 82-7238. (Illus.). 32p. (ps-k). 1982. lib. bdg. 4.95 o.p. Dandelion Hse.

Praise of Worthy Women & Other Poems. George Nesbitt. 53p. 1985. 5.95 o.p. (ISBN 0-533-06055-9). Vantage.

Praise Singer. Mary Renault. LC 78-53495. 1978. 12.95 o.p. (ISBN 0-394-50273-6). Pantheon.

Praktische Andrologie. 2nd ed. C. Schirren. (Illus.). 1982. pap. 26.75 o.p. (ISBN 3-8055-3474-4). S Karger.

Prams, Bassinets & Mailcarts. Jack Hampshire. 1981. 69.00x o.p. (ISBN 0-85936-121-7, Pub. by Midas Bks England). State Mutual Bk.

Prater Violet. Christopher Isherwood. 1978. pap. 2.25 o.p. (ISBN 0-380-01836-5, 63016-8, Bard). Avon.

Pratfall. T. A. Schock. (Orig.). 1981. pap. 2.25 o.p. (ISBN 0-8439-0919-6, Pub. by Leisure Bks CT). Dorchester Pub Co.

Pratidwandi. Sunil Gangopadhyay. Tr. by Enakshi Chatterjee from Bengali. LC 74-900546. 1974. lib. bdg. 4.50x o.p. (ISBN 0-8364-0447-5). South Asia Bks.

Pravo na Ostrov. Vasily Aksenov. LC 83-8924. 180p. (Orig.). 1983. pap. 7.00 o.p. (ISBN 0-938920-34-0). Hermitage.

Praxis & Reason: Studies in the Philosophy of Nicholas Rescher. Ed. by Robert Almeder. LC 81-43602. (Nicholas Rescher Ser.). 276p. (Orig.). 1982. lib. bdg. 33.75 o.p. (ISBN 0-8191-2648-9); pap. text ed. 14.50 o.p. (ISBN 0-8191-2649-7). U Pr of Amer.

Pray: How to Be Effective in Prayer. Warren Myers & Ruth Myers. LC 83-61679. 204p. 1984. pap. 5.95 o.p. (ISBN 0-89109-510-1). NavPress.

Pray in This Way. Dorothy F. Richards. LC 83-7342. (Illus.). 32p. (gr. 3-4). 1983. PLB 4.95 o.p. (ISBN 0-89693-215-X). Dandelion Hse.

Prayer. O. Hallesby. Tr. by Clarence J. Carlsen. 1931. 3.50 o.p. (ISBN 0-8066-0059-4, 10-5065, Augsburg). Augsburg Fortress.

Prayer. Abraham Kon. 12.95x o.p. (ISBN 0-900689-05-6). Bloch.

Prayer. Olive Wyon. LC 78-2965. 72p. 1978. pap. 0.50 o.p. (ISBN 0-8006-1335-X, 1-1335, Fortress). Augsburg Fortress.

Prayer & Action. Tom Boone & Edna Boone. 1974. pap. 1.25x o.p. (ISBN 0-8358-0309-0). Upper Room.

Prayer & Life. Piet Penning De Vries. LC 73-91091. 1974. 8.50 o.p. (ISBN 0-682-47985-3). Exposition-Phoenix.

Prayer & Personal Religion. John B. Coburn. LC 57-5397. (Layman's Theological Library). 96p. 1957. pap. 4.95 o.s.i. (ISBN 0-664-24005-4, Westminster). Westminster John Knox.

Prayer & the Common Life. Thomas Langford. LC 83-51396. 96p. (Orig.). 1984. pap. 3.95 o.p. (ISBN 0-8358-0473-9). Upper Room.

Prayer Answered. Dorothy Martin. (Peggy Ser.: No. 10). (gr. 7). 1985. pap. 3.50 o.p. (ISBN 0-8024-8310-0). Moody.

Prayer As a Political Problem. Jean Danielou. Ed. by J. R. Kirwan. 1967. 3.50 o.p. (ISBN 0-8362-0278-3, Pub. by Sheed). Guild Bks.

Prayer Book Epistles & Gospels: Jerusalem Bible Version. pap. 3.50 o.p. (ISBN 0-8192-2101-5). Morehouse Pub.

Prayer for Our Day. E. Lee Phillips. LC 81-82349. 156p. 1982. pap. 7.95 o.s.i. (ISBN 0-8042-2583-4, John Knox). Westminster John Knox.

Prayer He Taught: Seven Dramas & Meditations on the Lord's Prayer. W. A. Poovey. LC 76-27077. 1977. pap. 5.95 o.p. (ISBN 0-8066-1564-8, 10-5077, Augsburg); drama bklet 2.95 o.p. (ISBN 0-8066-1563-X, 10-5078). Augsburg Fortress.

Prayer in Baptist Life. Charles W. Deweese. LC 85-21301. 1986. pap. 4.95 o.p. (ISBN 0-8054-6941-9). Broadman.

Prayer in Life: Life in Prayer. George A. Buttrick. 1976. pap. 0.85x o.p. (ISBN 0-8358-0346-5). Upper Room.

Prayer: Key to Revival. Paul Y. Cho & R. Whitney Manzano. 224p. 1984. 9.95 o.p. (ISBN 0-8499-0453-6, 0453-6). Word Bks.

Prayer Life: A Guide to the Inner Chamber. Andrew Murray. 128p. 1987. pap. 3.95 o.p. (ISBN 0-310-55072-6, 19007P). Zondervan.

Prayer Meeting at Our House. large print ed. Pearl Brians. 25p. 1985. pap. 4.00 o.p. (ISBN 0-914009-33-8). VHI Library.

Prayer: More Than Words. LeRoy Eims. LC 82-61301. 162p. 1983. pap. 3.95 o.p. (ISBN 0-89109-493-8). NavPress.

Prayer-Poems. 3rd ed. Wm. Armstrong. LC 79-100082. (Illus.). 50p. (Orig.). 1968. pap. 1.00 o.s.i. (ISBN 0-913452-00-9). Jesuit Bks.

Prayer Times for Intermediate Grades. Marilyn Brokamp. (Prayer Times Ser.). 56p. (Orig.). 1987. pap. text ed. 4.95 o.p. (ISBN 0-86716-089-6, SBN 896). St Anthony Mess Pr.

Prayerfully. Helen S. Rice. 32p. 1971. 6.95 o.p. (ISBN 0-8007-0475-4). Revell.

Prayers. Michael Quoist. 1980. pap. 4.95 o.p. (ISBN 0-380-00406-2, 60244-X). Avon.

Prayers: Alone, Together. Sarah Klos. LC 71-117977. 1970. 1.00 o.p. (ISBN 0-8006-0044-4, Fortress). Augsburg Fortress.

Prayers at Midpoint: Conversations with God for Those in Life's Second Half. William A. Miller. LC 83-72110. 96p. 1984. pap. 6.50 o.p. (ISBN 0-8066-2054-4, 10-5081, Augsburg). Augsburg Fortress.

Prayers: Disturbance & Transfiguration. Donald H. Stewart. 1978. 4.50 o.p. (ISBN 0-682-49153-5). Exposition-Phoenix.

Prayers for Children & Young People. Ed. by Nancy Martin. LC 75-42383. 1976. 5.95 o.s.i. (ISBN 0-664-20746-4, Westminster). Westminster John Knox.

Prayers for Every Need. William H. Kadel. pap. 5.95 o.s.i. (ISBN 0-8042-2496-X, John Knox). Westminster John Knox.

Prayers for Help & Healing. William Barclay. LC 74-25682. 128p. 1975. pap. 4.95i o.p. (ISBN 0-06-060481-6, RD-89). HarpR.

Prayers for Inner Strength: In Times of Bereavement: A Book-Greeting Card. Ed. by John Beilenson. 1986. 2.50 o.p. (ISBN 0-88088-882-2, 888822). Peter Pauper.

Prayers for Lay Ministry. Carl T. Uehling. LC 73-88341. 96p. (Orig.). 1974. pap. 0.50 o.p. (ISBN 0-8006-1062-8, Fortress). Augsburg Fortress.

Prayers for Little Ones. rev. ed. George L. Conrad. (Orig.). (gr. k-2). 1952. pap. 0.95 o.p. (ISBN 0-8066-0153-1, 10-5080, Augsburg). Augsburg Fortress.

Prayers for Protestants. Ed. by William E. Wegener. LC 66-10158. 1965. fabrikoid 0.50 o.p. (ISBN 0-8006-0006-1, Fortress). Augsburg Fortress.

Prayers for Public Worship. Carl T. Uehling. LC 72-75657. 160p. 1972. 10.95 o.p. (ISBN 0-8006-0234-X, Fortress). Augsburg Fortress.

Prayers for Sunday. Madeleine L'Engle. (Illus.). (ps-3). 1974. pap. 1.95 o.p. (ISBN 0-8192-1153-2). Morehouse Pub.

Prayers for the Dead. Orthodox Eastern Church Staff. pap. 2.95 o.p. (ISBN 0-686-05659-0). Eastern Orthodox.

Prayers for Today's Church. Dick Williams. LC 76-27081. 1977. pap. 7.95 o.p. (ISBN 0-8066-1565-6, 10-5088, Augsburg). Augsburg Fortress.

Prayers for Worship Leaders. Arnold Kenseth & Richard P. Unsworth. LC 77-15249. 132p. (Orig.). 1978. pap. 2.95 o.p. (ISBN 0-8006-1331-7, 1-1331, Fortress). Augsburg Fortress.

Prayers from a Mother's Heart. Judith Mattison. LC 74-14177. (Illus.). 96p. (Orig.). 1975. pap. 5.95 o.p. (ISBN 0-8066-1460-9, 10-5095, Augsburg). Augsburg Fortress.

Prayers from a Troubled Heart. George Appleton. LC 83-48010. 64p. 1983. pap. 0.95 o.p. (ISBN 0-8006-1711-8, 1-1711, Fortress). Augsburg Fortress.

Prayers from a Woman's Heart. Judith Mattison. LC 72-78551. (Illus.). 96p. 1972. 5.95 o.p. (ISBN 0-8066-1219-3, 10-5100, Augsburg). Augsburg Fortress.

Prayers from an Island. Richard W. Wong. LC 68-25014. 1980. pap. 2.49 o.p. (John Knox). Westminster John Knox.

Prayers from an Island. Richard W. Wong. LC 68-25014. 1968. 4.50 o.p. (ISBN 0-8042-2499-4, John Knox). Westminster John Knox.

Prayers from Prison. Dietrich Bonhoeffer. Tr. by Johann C. Hampe from Ger. LC 77-15228. 1978. pap. 4.95 o.p. (ISBN 0-8006-1334-1, 1-1334, Fortress). Augsburg Fortress.

Prayers of Susanna Wesley. W. L. Doughty. 64p. 1956. (ISBN 0-8022-0413-9). Philos Lib.

Prayers We Have in Common. Ed. by Ronald Jasper & Harold Winstone. (Orig.). 1975. pap. 0.50 o.p. (ISBN 0-8006-1207-8, 1-1207, Fortress). Augsburg Fortress.

Prayers Written at Vailima. Robert Louis Stevenson. xi, 61p. 1973. 40.00 o.p. (ISBN 0-317-11648-7). Dawsons.

Prayerways: For Those Who Feel Discouraged or Distraught, Frightened or Frustrated, Angry or Anxious, Powerless or Purposeless, Over-Extended or Under-Appreciated, Burned Out or Just Plain Worn Out. Louis M. Savary & Patricia H. Berne. LC 80-7737. 176p. 1984. pap. 7.95 o.p. (ISBN 0-06-067064-9, RD 526). HarpR.

Praying for Inner Healing. Robert Faricy. LC 79-92857. 94p. (Orig.). 1979. pap. 3.95 o.p. (ISBN 0-8091-2250-2). Paulist Pr.

Praying More Effectively. David Mains. (Chapel Talks Ser.). 64p. 1.75 o.p. (ISBN 0-89191-261-4, 52613). Cook.

Praying the Psalms. Leslie E. Stradling. LC 76-46340. (Orig.). 1977. pap. 3.50 o.p. (ISBN 0-8006-1247-7, Fortress). Augsburg Fortress.

Praying Together. Peter Gilmour. LC 77-91623. (Illus.). 64p. 1978. pap. 1.95 o.p. (ISBN 0-88489-097-X); leader's manual o.p. 1.00 o.p. (ISBN 0-88489-120-8). St Mary's.

Praying Together: Making Marriage Last. Charlie Shedd & Martha Shedd. 128p. 1987. pap. 5.95 o.p. (ISBN 0-310-43291-X, 18361P). Zondervan.

Praying Wrong: New & Selected Poems, 1957-1984. Peter Davison. LC 84-45061. 192p. 1984. 18.95 o.p. (ISBN 0-689-11499-0, Atheneum); pap. 9.95 o.p. (ISBN 0-689-11500-8, Atheneum). Macmillan.

Pre-Calculus Problem Solver. Research & Education Association Staff. LC 84-61812. (Illus.). 960p. 1988. pap. text ed. 22.85 o.p. (ISBN 0-87891-556-7). Res & Educ.

Pre-Capitalist Modes of Production. Barry Hindess & Paul Q. Hirst. 1977. pap. 11.95x o.p. (ISBN 0-7100-8169-3). Routledge Chapman & Hall.

Pre-Clinical Carcinoma of the Cervix Uteri. M. Coppleson & B. Reid. 1967. 80.00 o.p. (ISBN 0-08-012433-X). Pergamon.

Pre-Colombian Civilizations: The World of the Maya, Aztecs & Incas. Henri Stierlin. (Illus.). 1980. 7.98 o.s.i. (ISBN 0-8317-7116-X). Smith Pubs.

Pre-Colonial Africa: An Economic and Social History. Robert W. July. LC 75-6920. 1975. pap. text ed. 6.95x o.p. (ISBN 0-684-14319-4, ScribC). Scribner.

Pre-Columbian America: The Art & Archeology of South, Central & Middle America. Lee A. Parsons. (Illus.). 193p. 1974. 7.50 o.p. (ISBN 0-89326-010-X). Milwaukee Pub Mus.

Pre-Columbian Architecture of Mesoamerica. rev. ed. Doris Heyden & Paul Gendrop. LC 87-43257. (History of World Architecture Ser.). (Illus.). 224p. 1988. pap. 25.00 o.p. (ISBN 0-8478-0917-X). Rizzoli Intl.

Pre-Columbian Mind. F. Guerra. LC 75-183465. 350p. 1972. 65.00 o.p. (ISBN 0-12-785286-7). Acad Pr.

Pre-Conquest Church in England. 2nd ed. Margaret Deanesly. (Ecclesiastical History of England Ser.). 376p. 1963. text ed. 30.00x o.p. (ISBN 0-06-491638-3). B&N Imports.

Pre-Contract Practice for Architects & Quality Surveyors. 6th ed. AQUA Group Staff. 101p. 1980. pap. text ed. 12.50x o.p. (ISBN 0-246-11338-3, Pub. by Granada England). Gower Pub Co.

Pre-Fascist Italy: The Rise & Fall of the Parliamentary Regime. Margot Hentze. LC 70-120628. 1970. Repr. of 1939 ed. lib. bdg. 26.00x o.p. (ISBN 0-374-93809-1, Octagon). Hippocrene Bks.

Pre-Historic Background of Indian Culture. Douglas H. Gordon. Ed. by D. Barrett & Desai Madhuri. LC 75-31825. (Illus.). 199p. 1975. lib. bdg. 35.00x o.p. (ISBN 0-8371-8440-1, GOIC). Greenwood.

Pre-Historic Sequence in the Middle Pecos Valley, New Mexico. Arthur Jelinek. (Anthropological Papers: No. 31). 1967. pap. 3.00x o.p. (ISBN 0-686-86802-1). U Mich Mus Anthro.

Pre-Raphaelite Papers. Taite Gallery Staff. Ed. by Leslie Parris. (Illus.). 256p. 1984. 25.00 o.p. (ISBN 0-7139-1639-7). Allen Lane.

Pre-Raphaelite Writing. Ed. by Derek Stanford. (Illus.). 246p. 1984. pap. 5.95x o.p. (ISBN 0-460-11033-0, DEL-05073, Pub. by Evman England). Biblio Dist.

Pre-Raphaelites. Taite Gallery Staff. Ed. by Leslie Parris. (Illus.). 320p. 1984. 35.00 o.p. (ISBN 0-7139-1638-9). Allen Lane.

Pre-School Education in the Arab World: The Experience of Kuwait. Huda Nashif. 224p. 1985. 29.00 o.p. (ISBN 0-7099-0952-7, Pub. by Croom Helm Ltd). Routledge Chapman & Hall.

Pre-University Chemistry, Vol. 1. 2nd & rev. ed. K. R. Acharya et al. 267p. 1985. pap. text ed. 5.95x o.p. (ISBN 0-7069-2665-X, Pub. by Vikas India). Advent NY.

Preach the Word. Denis Lane. 1986. pap. 5.95 o.p. (ISBN 9971-972-42-5). OMF Bks.

Preacher Had Ten Kids. Frances Bradsher. 1980. pap. 3.50 o.p. (ISBN 0-8423-4886-7). Tyndale.

Preacher's Outline & Sermon Bible, Vol. 9: Galatians, Eph., Phil., Col. J. B. Lyles. 1989. text ed. 19.95 notebk. o.p. (ISBN 0-945863-08-X). Chrstn Pubs & Ministries.

Preaching about Death: Eighteen Sermons Dealing with the Experience of Death from the Christian Perspective. Ed. by Alton M. Motter. LC 74-26336. 94p. 1975. pap. 1.00 o.p. (ISBN 0-8006-1098-9, 1-1098, Fortress). Augsburg Fortress.

Preaching & Pastoral Care. Arthur L. Teikmanis. LC 64-23551. 1968. pap. 0.50x o.p. (ISBN 0-8006-5014-X, Fortress). Augsburg Fortress.

Preaching Christian Doctrine. William J. Carl, II. LC 83-48923. pap. 8.95 o.p. (ISBN 0-8006-1788-6, Fortress). Augsburg Fortress.

Preaching in the Witnessing Community. Ed. by Herman G. Stuempfle, Jr. LC 72-91524. 112p. 1973. pap. 0.50 o.p. (ISBN 0-8006-0135-1, Fortress). Augsburg Fortress.

Preaching in Today's World. Ed. by James C. Barry. LC 83-24021. (Orig.). 1984. pap. 6.95 o.p. (ISBN 0-8054-2113-0). Broadman.

Preaching Law & Gospel. Herman G. Stuempfle, Jr. LC 77-15247. 96p. (Orig.). 1978. pap. 3.50 o.p. (ISBN 0-8006-1329-5, 1-1329, Fortress). Augsburg Fortress.

Preaching on National Holidays. Alton M. Motter. LC 75-36445. 96p. 1976. pap. 0.50x o.p. (ISBN 0-8006-1222-1, Fortress). Augsburg Fortress.

Preaching on Peace. Ed. by Ronald J. Sider & Darrel J. Brubaker. LC 82-10958. 96p. 1982. pap. 0.50 o.p. (ISBN 0-8006-1681-2, Fortress). Augsburg Fortress.

Preaching on Suffering & a God of Love. Ed. by Henry J. Young. LC 77-15250. 96p. (Orig.). 1978. pap. 0.50 o.p. (ISBN 0-8006-1332-5, 1-1332, Fortress). Augsburg Fortress.

Preaching on the Parables. David Granskou. LC 74-165512. 144p. 1972. pap. 3.50 o.p. (ISBN 0-8006-4011-X, 1-4011, Fortress). Augsburg Fortress.

Preaching Paul. Daniel Patte. LC 84-47931. (Fortress Resources for Preaching Ser.). 96p. 1984. pap. 4.95 o.p. (ISBN 0-8006-1140-3, Fortress). Augsburg Fortress.

Preaching the Gospel. Ed. by Henry J. Young. LC 75-36449. 96p. (Orig.). 1976. pap. 0.75 o.p. (ISBN 0-8006-1223-X, 1-1223, Fortress). Augsburg Fortress.

Preaching the Gospel of Jesus Christ. Clarke E. Goodman. LC 84-90077. 101p. 1985. 8.95 o.p. (ISBN 0-533-06156-3). Vantage.

Preaching the Story. Edmund A. Steimle et al. LC 78-14675. 208p. 1980. 9.95 o.p. (ISBN 0-8006-0538-1, 1-538, Fortress). Augsburg Fortress.

Preaching the Theology of the Cross: Sermons & Worship Ideas for Lent & Easter. Peter L. Steinke. LC 82-72638. 128p. (Orig.). 1983. pap. 6.95 o.p. (ISBN 0-8066-1944-9, 10-5144, Augsburg). Augsburg Fortress.

Preaching Through the Bible. 2nd ed. Edwin V. Hayden. LC 81-82987. 557p. 1981. pap. 8.95 cancelled o.p. (ISBN 0-89900-145-9). College Pr Pub.

Preaching Through the Year. David Steel. LC 80-82191. 168p. 1980. pap. 1.79 o.s.i. (ISBN 0-8042-1801-3, John Knox). Westminster John Knox.

Precalculus: A Functional Approach with Applications. Salvatore Barbasso & John Impagliazzo. (Illus.). 1977. text ed. 18.95 o.p. (ISBN 0-15-571050-8, HC). HarBraceJ.

Precalculus & Mathematics: Algebra & Trigonometry. Steven Bryant & Daniel Saltz. (Illus.). 1980. text ed. write for info. o.p. (ISBN 0-673-16242-7). Scott F.

Precalculus: Functions & Graphs. Bernard Kolman & Arnold Shapiro. 1984. 25.00 o.p. (ISBN 0-12-417894-4); instr's manual 5.00 o.p. (ISBN 0-12-417895-2); test bank 50.00 o.p. (ISBN 0-12-417896-0). Acad Pr.

Precalculus Mathematics. David G. Crowdis & Brandon W. Wheeler. 1976. text ed. write for info. o.p. (ISBN 0-02-472030-5). Macmillan.

Precalculus Mathematics: Algebra, Trigonometry & Analytical Geometry. H. Braverman. 533p. 1975. 18.50 o.p. Krieger.

Precalculus Mathematics: New Impressions. Michael Payne. (Illus.). 1978. text ed. 30.95 o.s.i. (ISBN 0-7216-7126-8). HR&W.

Precambrian of the Northern Hemisphere. L. J. Salop. (Developments in Paleontology & Stratigraphy Ser.: Vol. 3). 382p. 1977. 129.00 o.p. (ISBN 0-444-41510-6). Elsevier.

Presidential Power in the United States. Raymond Tatalovich & Byron W. Daynes. LC 83-7490. (Political Science Ser.). 400p. 1983. pap. text ed. 14.75 pub net o.p. (ISBN 0-534-02737-7). Brooks-Cole.

Presidential Rhetoric, Nineteen Sixty-One to the Present. 3rd ed. Theodore Windt. LC 83-81606. x, 368p. 1983. 15.95 o.p. (ISBN 0-8403-3746-9, 40308401). Kendall-Hunt.

Presidential Seizure in Labor Disputes. John L. Blackman. LC 67-20871. (Wertheim Publications in Industrial Relations). 367p. 1967. 25.50x o.s.i. (ISBN 0-674-70201-8). Harvard U Pr.

Presidential Vetoes. U. S. Congress, Senate Staff. LC 68-55111. (Illus.). 1969. Repr. of 1961 ed. lib. bdg. 22.50x o.p. (ISBN 0-8371-0703-2, PRVE). Greenwood.

Presidents & Chancellors. Intro. by Dale Parnell. 132p. (Orig.). 1982. pap. 15.00 o.p. (ISBN 0-87117-113-9). Am Assn Comm Jr Coll.

President's Gold Mine. Albert Harding. 1977. 7.50 o.p. (ISBN 0-682-48938-7). Exposition-Phoenix.

Presidents: Washington to Reagan. Sam J. Patrick. 1984. 9.98 o.p. (ISBN 0-517-43350-8). Crown.

President's Women. June F. Singer. 1944. pap. (ISBN 0-449-14600-6). Fawcett.

Presleyana Price Guide. Jerry Osborne & Bruce Hamilton. (Original Record Collectors Price Guide Ser.). 304p. 1980. pap. 9.95 o.p. (ISBN 0-89019-073-9). Norwalk Pr.

Press & People, Seventeen Ninety to Eighteen Fifty. Donald Read. LC 74-3747. (Illus.). 227p. 1975. Repr. of 1961 ed. lib. bdg. 35.00x o.p. (ISBN 0-8371-7465-1, REPP). Greenwood.

Press & Politics: Monographs. Mary Vance. (Public Administration Ser.: P 1781). 15p. 1985. 2.25 o.p. (ISBN 0-89028-581-0). Vance Biblios.

Press Box: Red Smith's Favorite Sport Stories. Ed. by Red Smith. 192p. 1983. pap. 2.95 o.p. (ISBN 0-380-63685-9, 63685-9, Discus). Avon.

Press Box: Red Smith's Favorite Sports Stories. Ed. by Red Smith. 192p. 1976. 7.95 o.p. (ISBN 0-393-08360-8). Norton.

Press Boycott of Aesthetic Realism: Documentation. Ed. by Martha Baird & Ellen Reiss. LC 77-80498. 1978. pap. 2.50 o.p. (ISBN 0-910492-30-1). Definition.

Press Coverage of the Falklands Conflict. J. Laurence Day. LC 83-198373. (UFSI Reports Ser.: No. 47). U Field Staff Intl.

Press, Party, & Presidency. Richard L. Rubin. (Illus.). 1982. 18.95 o.p. (ISBN 0-393-01497-5). Norton.

Press Point Therapy. G. Bendix. 1978. pap. 3.50 o.p. (ISBN 0-380-39867-2, 64782-6). Avon.

Press Toolmaking. 2nd ed. Ed. by F. Ballard et al. (Engineering Craftsmen: No. H21). (Illus.). 1972. spiral bdg. 39.95x o.p. Trans-Atl Phila.

Pressure! James M. Campbell. (gr. 7-9). 1967. pap. 1.25 o.p. (ISBN 0-8042-9370-8, John Knox). Westminster John Knox.

Pressure Cooker. Don Biggs. (Illus.). 1979. 14.95 o.p. (ISBN 0-393-08815-4). Norton.

Pressure Enthalpy Charts. Byron Short et al. LC 70-11431. (Orig.). 1970. pap. 18.00x o.p. (ISBN 0-87201-105-4). Gulf Pub.

Pressure Vessel & Piping: Design & Analysis - A Decade of Progress: Materials & Fabrication, Vol. 3. Ed. by R. Roberts. 1976. text ed. 50.00 o.p. (ISBN 0-685-68906-9, G00100). ASME.

Pressure Vessels Analysis for Design: Proceedings of the Conference in Honour of Emeritus Professor Sidney Gill, held at UMIST, Manchester, U. K., April 1981. Ed. by W. Johnson. (Illus.). 80p. 1983. pap. 21.00 o.p. (ISBN 0-08-029349-2). Pergamon.

Pressure Vessels & Piping - Computer Program Evaluation & Qualification, Series PVP-PB-024. Ed. by D. E. Dietrich. 1977. pap. text ed. 16.00 o.p. (ISBN 0-685-86875-3, G00124). ASME.

Pressure Vessels: Division 1. (Boiler & Pressure Vessel Code Ser.: Sec. 8). 1980. 150.00 o.p. (ISBN 0-685-76824-4, P00081) (ISBN 0-685-76825-2, V00081). ASME.

Pressure Vessels: Division 2-Alternative Rules. (Boiler & Pressure Vessel Code Ser.: Sec. 8). 1980. 110.00 o.p. (ISBN 0-685-76826-0, P00082); pap. 150.00 loose-leaf o.p. (ISBN 0-685-76827-9, V00082). ASME.

Pressurized Water Reactor Transient Response. (Illus.). 1978. Set. 295.00x o.p. (ISBN 0-87683-069-6); spiral bdg. 40.00x o.p. (ISBN 0-87683-070-X); Videotape 1: Turbine & Plant Startup. 90.00x o.p. (ISBN 0-87683-071-8); Videotape 2: Rapid Load Reduction. 90.00x o.p. (ISBN 0-87683-072-6); Videotape 3: Reactor Coolant System Leakage. 90.00x o.p.; Videotape 4: Malfunction Response. 90.00x o.p. (ISBN 0-87683-074-2). GP Pub.

Presto! Roberta Smoodin. LC 81-69200. (Illus.). 288p. 1982. 13.95 o.s.i. (ISBN 0-689-11273-4, Atheneum). Macmillan.

Presto: Or the Adventures of a Turnspit Dog. Marilynne K. Roach. (gr. 5-9). 1979. 8.95 o.p. (ISBN 0-395-28269-1). HM.

Prestressed Concrete Design & Construction. 2nd rev. ed. F. Leonhardt. (Illus.). 1964. 75.00 o.s.i. (ISBN 0-685-12040-6). E J Brill USA.

Presumed Dead. Ritchie Perry. LC 86-19709. (Crime Club Ser.). 192p. 1987. 12.95 o.p. (ISBN 0-385-23558-5). Doubleday.

Presumption of Innocence. Dave Pedneau. 256p. 1985. pap. 2.95 o.p. (ISBN 0-380-89514-5). Avon.

Presynaptic Receptors: Mechanisms & Functions. J. DeBelleroche. LC 82-3044. 223p. 1982. 79.95 o.p. (ISBN 0-470-27345-3). Halsted Pr.

Presystemic Drug Elimination (BIMR Clinical Pharmacology & Therapeutics, Vol. 1) Charles F. George & Andrew G. Renwick. (International Medical Reviews Ser.). 320p. 1982. 59.95 o.p. (ISBN 0-407-02322-4). Butterworth.

Pretending to Be Asleep. Peter Davison. LC 70-103824. (Orig.). 1970. pap. 2.95 o.p. (ISBN 0-689-10309-3, Atheneum). Macmillan.

Pretentious Young Ladies. Moliere. Tr. by Herma Briffault from Fr. 1977. pap. text ed. 3.95 o.p. (ISBN 0-8120-0150-8). Barron.

PreTest for Physicians Preparing for the American Board of Internal Medicine Certifying Examination. 4th ed. PreTest Editors. (Illus.). 96p. 1982. pap. 34.00 o.p. (ISBN 0-07-079093-0). McGraw-Pretest.

Pretrial Detention: A Bibliography. Mary E. Hulls. LC 85-233397. (Public Administration Bibliography Ser.). 1985. 2.00 o.p. (ISBN 0-89028-533-0). Vance Biblios.

Pretty Babies: An Insider's Look at the World of the Hollywood Child Star. A. Darvi. 288p. 1983. text ed. 14.95 o.p. (ISBN 0-07-015402-3). McGraw.

Pretty Good Club: The Founding Fathers of the U. S. Foreign Services. Martin Weil. (Illus.). 1978. 12.95 o.p. (ISBN 0-393-05658-9). Norton.

Pretty Lace. Yoko Suzuki. (Illus., Orig.). 1985. pap. 9.95 o.p. (ISBN 0-87040-646-9). Japan Pubns USA.

Pretty Maids All in a Row. Anthea Fraser. LC 86-16219. (Crime Club Ser.). 192p. 1987. 12.95 o.s.i. (ISBN 0-385-23798-7). Doubleday.

Pretty Penny. Tilly Amstrong. (Lythway). 200p. 1988. lib. bdg. 17.50x o.p. (ISBN 0-7451-0632-3, Pub. by Chivers Pr UK). G K Hall.

Pretty Penny. John D. Scott. LC 64-22672. 1964. 3.95 o.p. (ISBN 0-15-173951-X). HarBraceJ.

Pretty Redwing. Helen Henslee. LC 82-6052. 192p. 1983. 13.95 o.p. (ISBN 0-03-061372-8). H Holt & Co.

Preventing Burnout in Education: A Self-Help Approach to Managing Stress. Christopher Wilson & Deborah Hall. (Illus.). 154p. (Orig.). 1981. pap. text ed. 9.95 o.p. (ISBN 0-940156-02-4). Wright Group.

Preventing Cancer. Elizabeth M. Whelan. (Illus.). 1978. 12.95 o.p. (ISBN 0-393-06431-X). Norton.

Preventing Cancer. Elizabeth M. Whelan. 1980. pap. 4.95 o.p. (ISBN 0-393-00990-4, N990). Norton.

Preventing Classroom Disruption: Policy, Practice & Evaluation in Urban Schools. David Coulby & Tim Harper. LC 85-11359. 189p. 1985. 28.00 o.p. (ISBN 0-7099-3424-6, Pub. by Croom Helm Ltd); pap. 14.00 o.p. (ISBN 0-7099-3425-4). Routledge Chapman & Hall.

Preventing Hardening of the Arteries: The Bowling Green Study. William E. Feeman, Jr. 1986. 10.00 o.p. (ISBN 0-533-06601-8). Vantage.

Preventing Legal Malpractice. Jeffery M. Smith. LC 80-26759. 142p. 1981. pap. text ed. 11.95 o.p. (ISBN 0-8299-2118-4). West Pub.

Prevention & Cure of Cancer. Mulhim A. Hassan. (Illus.). 232p. 1983. 11.50 o.p. (ISBN 0-682-49957-9). Exposition-Phoenix.

Prevention in Mental Health: Research, Policy, & Practice. Ed. by Richard H. Price et al. LC 80-14676. (Sage Annual Reviews of Community Mental Health Ser.: Vol. 1). (Illus.). 320p. 1981. 35.00 o.p. (ISBN 0-8039-1468-7); pap. 14.95 o.s.i. (ISBN 0-8039-1469-5). Sage.

Prevention of Baldness. 1p. pap. 2.00 o.s.i. (ISBN 0-317-52798-3). Truth Seeker.

Prevention of Coronary Heart Disease: Practical Management of Risk Factors. Norman M. Kaplan & Jeremiah Stamler. (Illus.). 232p. 1983. (ISBN 0-7216-5277-8). Saunders.

Prevention of Cruelty to Children. Leslie Housden. (ISBN 0-8022-0748-0). Philos Lib.

Prevention of Mental Retardation & Other Developlmental Disabilities. Ed. by Michael K. McCormack. (Pediatric Habilitation Ser.: Vol. 1). (Illus.). 680p. 1980. 79.75 o.p. (ISBN 0-8247-6950-3). Dekker.

Prevention of Occupational Cancer, 1982. 680p. 32.00x o.p. (ISBN 92-2-002907-3). Intl Pubns Serv.

Prevention of Respiratory Distress Syndrome: Effect of Antenatal Dexamethasone Administration. (Illus.). 85p. (Orig.). 1985. pap. 3.25 o.p. (ISBN 0-318-18820-1, S/N 017-043-00110-9). USGPO.

Prevention of Sexual Disorders: Issues & Approaches. Ed. by C. Brandon Qualls et al. LC 78-1700. (Perspectives In Sexuality Ser.). 212p. 1978. 32.50x o.p. (ISBN 0-306-31118-6, Plenum Pr). Plenum Pub.

Prevention of Youthful Crime: The Great Stumble Forward. James C. Hackler. 1979. pap. 12.00x o.p. (ISBN 0-416-60001-8, NO. 2825). Routledge Chapman & Hall.

Preventive Dentistry. Ed. by Dominick P. DePaola et al. LC 77-94885. (Illus.). 308p. 1979. 33.00 o.p. (ISBN 0-88416-162-5). Year Bk Med.

Preventive Health Care for Adults: A Study of Medical Practice. Rodney M. Coe & Henry P. Brehm. 1972. 13.95x o.p. (ISBN 0-8084-0040-1); pap. 9.95x o.p. (ISBN 0-8084-0041-X). New Coll U Pr.

Preventive Labor Relations. John G. Kilgour. 1981. 25.95 o.p. (ISBN 0-8144-5637-5). AMACOM.

Price Controls, Physician Fees, & Physician Incomes from Medicare & Medicaid. John Holahan & William Scanlon. 110p. 1978. pap. text ed. 6.50x o.p. (ISBN 0-87766-219-3). Urban Inst.

Price Guide of United States, Canada & United Nations: 1988 Edition, Vol. I. Ed. by Brookman Stamp Co. 240p. 1988. pap. 5.95 o.s.i. (ISBN 0-936937-08-4). Brookman Stamp.

Price Guide of United States Stamps: 1988 Edition. Ed. by Brookman Stamp Co. 132p. 1988. pap. 4.50 o.s.i. (ISBN 0-936937-10-6). Brookman Stamp.

Price Guide Popular & Rock Records 1948-1978: 45 & 78 R P M. 2nd ed. Jerry Osborne. 1978. pap. 7.95 o.p. (ISBN 0-89019-065-8). Norwalk Pr.

Price Guide to Antique & Classic Cameras: 1985-1986. 5th. ed. James M. McKeown & Joan McKeown. (Illus.). 544p. (Orig.). 1985. pap. 19.95 o.p. (ISBN 0-931838-08-8). Centennial Photo Serv.

Price Guide to Antique Furniture. 2nd ed. John Andrews. (Price Guide Ser.). (Illus.). 290p. 1978. 39.50 o.p. (ISBN 0-907462-79-0). Antique Collect.

Price Guide to Antique Silver. 2nd ed. Peter Waldron. (Price Guide Ser.). (Illus.). 365p. 1982. 49.50 o.p. (ISBN 0-907462-08-1). Antique Collect.

Price Guide to Clocks, 1840-1940. Alan Shenton & Rita Shenton. (Price Guide Ser.). (Illus.). 540p. 1978. 29.50 o.p. (ISBN 0-907462-66-9). Antique Collect.

Price Guide to Crested China, 1985. Sandy Andrews & Nicholas Pine. (Illus.). 288p. 1985. 17.95 o.p. (ISBN 0-903852-44-6, Pub. by Milestone Pubns UK). Seven Hills Bk Dists.

Price Guide to Goss China, 1984. Nicholas Pine. (Illus.). 254p. 1985. 17.95 o.p. (ISBN 0-903852-41-1, Pub. by Milestone Pubns UK). Seven Hills Bk Dists.

Price Guide to Metal Toys. G. Gardiner & A. Morris. (Price Guide Ser.). (Illus.). 214p. 1980. 39.50 o.p. (ISBN 1-85149-016-7). Antique Collect.

Price Guide to Miniature Lamps Combining Book I & II. rev. ed. Ruth E. Smith & Hellen A. Feltner. 48p. 1987. pap. 10.00 o.p. (ISBN 0-88740-085-X). Schiffer.

Price Guide to Nineteenth & Twentieth Century British Pottery. David Battie & Michael Turner. (Price Guide Ser.). (Illus.). 244p. 1979. 49.50 o.p. (ISBN 1-85149-009-4). Antique Collect.

Price Guide to Nineteenth Century European Furniture. Christopher Payne. (Illus.). 506p. 1985. 69.50 o.p. Apollo.

Price Guide to Old Sheffield Plate. T. W. Frost. (Price Guide Ser.). (Illus.). 396p. 1977. (ISBN 0-902028-07-3). Antique Collect.

Price Guide to Pot-Lids & Other Underglaze Multicolour Prints on Ware. 2nd ed. A. Ball. (Price Guide Ser.). (Illus.). 320p. 1980. 49.50 o.p. (ISBN 0-902028-56-1). Antique Collect.

Price Guide to Victorian, Edwardian & 1920's Furniture. John Andrews. (Price Guide Ser.). (Illus.). 218p. 1980. 49.50 o.p. (ISBN 1-85149-018-3). Antique Collect.

Price Guide to Victorian Silver. Ian Harris. (Price Guide Ser.). (Illus.). 276p. 1977. (ISBN 0-902028-09-X). Antique Collect.

Price Guide to Wallace Nutting Pictures. 2nd ed. Michael Ivankovich. LC 85-73342. (Illus.). 64p. 1985. pap. 7.95 o.p. (ISBN 0-9615843-2-7). Diamond Pr PA.

Price of a Life: One Woman's Death from Toxic Shock. Tom Riley. LC 85-15063. 293p. 1986. 15.95 o.p. (ISBN 0-917561-06-6). Adler & Adler.

Price of Genius. April Fitzlyon. (Orig.). 1981. pap. 5.95 o.p. (ISBN 0-7145-0488-2). Riverrun NY.

Price of Leisure. John D. Owen. 1970. 10.00x o.p. (ISBN 0-7735-0094-4, McGill Canada). U of Toronto Pr.

Price of Peace: Living with the Nuclear Dilemma. Lawrence Freedman. (New Republic Bks). 304p. 1986. 18.95 o.p. (ISBN 0-8050-0041-0). H Holt & Co.

Price of Power: Kissinger in the Nixon White House. Seymour Hersh. 480p. 1983. 19.25 o.s.i. (ISBN 0-671-44760-2). Summit Bks.

Price System & Resource Allocation. 9th ed. Richard H. Leftwich & Ross D. Eckert. 656p. 1985. text ed. 32.95 o.p. (ISBN 0-03-071477-X). Dryden Pr.

Price Theory & Its Uses. 4th ed. Donald S. Watson & Mary A. Holman. LC 76-14003. (Illus.). 1977. text ed. 19.80 o.p. (ISBN 0-395-24422-6). HM.

Price Theory in Action. 4th ed. Donald S. Watson & Malcolm Getz. LC 81-80260. 448p. 1981. pap. 21.50 o.p. (ISBN 0-395-30058-4). HM.

Price Theory in Action: A Book of Readings. 3rd ed. Ed. by Donald S. Watson. LC 72-85910. 450p. (Orig.). 1973. pap. 12.50 o.p. (ISBN 0-395-15073-6, 3-58884). HM.

Price Was High: The Last Uncollected Stories of F. Scott Fitzgerald. Matthew J. Bruccoli. LC 78-14074. 785p. 1981. 19.95 o.s.i. (ISBN 0-15-174020-8); pap. 12.95 o.s.i. (ISBN 0-15-673872-4). HarBraceJ.

Priceless Possesion of a Few. Eugene T. Fuller. 1974. 10.00 o.p. (ISBN 0-913902-41-1). Heart Am Pr.

Prices & Profits in the Pharmaceutical Industry. M. H. Cooper. 1967. 33.00 o.p. (ISBN 0-08-012178-0); pap. 17.00 o.p. (ISBN 0-08-012177-2). Pergamon.

Prices, Taxes & Subsidies in Pakistan Agriculture, 1960-1976. Carl Gotsch & Gilbert Brown. (Working Paper: No. 387). 108p. 1980. 5.00 o.p. (ISBN 0-686-36073-7, WP-0387). World Bank.

Prices, Wages & Incomes Policies in Industrialised Market Economies. 3rd ed. H. A. Turner & H. Zoeteweij. 172p. 1971. 7.00 o.p. (ISBN 92-2-100130-X). Intl Labour Office.

Pricing Employee Benefits see Issues in the Public Employee Relations Library: Series 2.

Pricing for Higher Profit. Spencer A. Tucker. 1966. text ed. 42.50 o.p. (ISBN 0-07-065419-0). McGraw.

Pricing Petroleum Products: Strategies of Eleven Industrial Nations, Vol. 1. Ed. by Edward N. Krapels. (Illus.). 272p. 1982. text ed. 88.50 o.p. (ISBN 0-07-035374-3). McGraw.

Pricing Strategies. Alfred R. Oxenfeldt. LC 74-78207. (Illus.). 272p. 1975. 18.95 o.p. (ISBN 0-8144-5368-6). AMACOM.

Pricing Strategies. Alfred R. Oxenfelt. 1982. pap. 10.95 o.p. (ISBN 0-8144-7572-8). AMACOM.

Prick of Noon. Peter DeVries. 240p. 1985. 14.95 o.p. (ISBN 0-316-18205-2). Little.

Pride. William Wharton. LC 85-40125. 304p. 1985. 16.45 o.s.i. (ISBN 0-394-53636-3). Knopf.

Pride & Prejudice. Jane Austen. 1978. Repr. of 1965 ed. 10.95x o.p. (ISBN 0-460-00022-5, Evman); pap. 2.95x o.p. (ISBN 0-460-01022-0, DEL-04305, Evman). Biblio Dist.

Pride & Prejudice. Jane Austen. LC 84-60894. (Illus.). 368p. 1984. 12.95 o.p. (ISBN 0-89577-198-5). RD Assn.

Pride & Prejudice by Jane Austen. 48p. (Orig.). 1988. pap. 9.95 o.p. (ISBN 1-55651-725-4); cassette o.p. (ISBN 1-55651-726-2). Cram Cassettes.

Pride of Hannah Wade. Janet Dailey. 1985. 15.95 o.p. (ISBN 0-8161-3885-0, Large Print Bks). G K Hall.

Pride of Lions. Norma Johnston. LC 79-12463. (gr. 7 up). 1979. 7.95 o.p. (ISBN 0-689-30711-X, Atheneum). Macmillan.

Pride of Our Hearts. Wilbert L. Walker. 1978. 10.00 o.p. Exposition-Phoenix.

Pride of Royals. Justin Scott. LC 81-71676. 570p. 1983. 15.95 o.p. (ISBN 0-87795-382-1, Arbor Hse). Morrow.

Pride of the Peacock. Victoria Holt. 304p. 1983. pap. 2.95 o.p. (ISBN 0-449-20493-6, Crest). Fawcett.

Pride's Captive. Mary R. Daheim. 352p. 1986. pap. 3.95 o.p. (ISBN 0-380-89849-7). Avon.

Pride's Passion. Linda P. Sandifer. 400p. 1986. pap. 3.95 o.p. (ISBN 0-380-75171-2). Avon.

Priest. Ralph McInerny. 1976. pap. 1.95 o.p. (ISBN 0-380-00580-8, 27268). Avon.

Priest & Parish in Eighteenth-Century France. T. Tackett. 1977. 38.00 o.p. (ISBN 0-691-05243-3). Princeton U Pr.

Priester und Beamtentum der Altbabylonischen Kontrakte. Ernest Lindl. Repr. of 1913 ed. 37.00 o.p. (ISBN 0-384-32780-X). Johnson Repr.

Priesthood. Spencer W. Kimball et al. LC 81-5394. viii, 359p. 1981. 8.95 o.p. (ISBN 0-87747-859-7). Deseret Bk.

Priestly Celibacy: Recurrent Battle & Lasting Values. Albert J. Hebert. 198p. 1971. 6.00 o.p. (ISBN 0-912414-01-4). Lumen Christi.

Priestly Murders: A Chicago Police Mystery. Joe Gash. 163p. 1984. 11.95 o.p. (ISBN 0-03-070543-6). H Holt & Co.

Priests of Ancient Egypt. Serge Sauneron. LC 59-10792. (Illus.). 192p. 1980. pap. 3.50 o.s.i. (ISBN 0-394-17410-0, B433, BC). Grove.

Priglashenie Na Kazn. Vladimir Nabokov. (Rus.). 1979. 25.00 o.p. (ISBN 0-88233-429-8); pap. 7.95 o.p. (ISBN 0-88233-430-1). Ardis Pubs.

Primacy of Peter. Meyendorff et al. 134p. 1963. 8.95 o.p. (ISBN 0-913836-20-6). St Vladimirs.

Primacy or World Order: American Foreign Policy since the Cold War. Stanley Hoffmann. 1978. text ed. 29.15 o.p. (ISBN 0-07-029205-1). McGraw.

Primacy or World Order: American Foreign Policy Since the Cold War. Stanley Hoffmann. 252p. 1980. pap. text ed. 6.95 o.p. (ISBN 0-07-029207-8). McGraw.

Primal Place. Robert Finch. 256p. 1985. pap. 5.70 o.p. (ISBN 0-393-30228-8). Norton.

Primal Power in Man: The Kundalini Shakti Yoga. Swami Narayananda. 155p. 1971. pap. 11.95 o.s.i. (ISBN 0-88697-027-X). Life Science.

Primal Printing. Ed. by Paul Woodbine. 1978. 7.00 o.p. (ISBN 0-916258-08-4). Woodbine Pr.

Primary & General Election Law & Procedure. rev. ed. H. Rutherford Turnbull, 3rd. 1978. looseleaf 6.00 o.p. (ISBN 0-686-17566-2); replacement pgs. 1978 6.50 o.p. (ISBN 0-686-17567-0); replacement pgs. 1980 6.00 o.p. (ISBN 0-686-28570-0). Institute Government.

Primary Care & the Public Health: Judging Impacts, Goals, & Polices Public's. Nancy Milio. LC 81-47275. 272p. 1983. 35.00x o.p. (ISBN 0-669-04571-3). Lexington Bks.

Primary Care Nursing. Ed. by Lisbeth Hockey. LC 82-4339. (Recent Advances in Nursing Ser.: No. 5). (Illus.). 220p. (Orig.). 1983. pap. text ed. 34.00 o.p. (ISBN 0-443-02367-0, AACR2). Churchill.

Primary Care of Facial Injuries. Ed. by Elvin G. Zook. LC 79-16117. (Illus.). 184p. 1980. text ed. 29.00 o.p. (ISBN 0-88416-205-2). Year Bk Med.

Primary Care of Hand Injuries. William L. Newmeyer. LC 78-31444. (Illus.). 297p. 1979. text ed. 22.50 o.p. (ISBN 0-8121-0669-5). Lea & Febiger.

Primary Care Optometry: A Clinical Manual. Theodore P. Grosvenor. LC 81-84965. 60p. 1982. 60.00 o.p. (ISBN 0-87873-038-9). Prof Pr Bks NYC.

Primary Cinema Resources: An Index of Screen Plays, Interviews & Special Collections at the University of Southern California. Chistopher S. Wheaton. 1975. lib. bdg. 27.50 o.p. (ISBN 0-8161-1198-7, Hall Reference). G K Hall.

Primary Commodity Exports & Economic Development: Theory, Evidence, & a Study of Malaysia. John T. Thoburn. LC 76-26337. 310p. 1977. 67.95x o.p. (ISBN 0-471-99441-3, Pub. by Wiley-Interscience). Wiley.

Primary Crushing Plant Design. Frank W. McQuiston, Jr. & Robert S. Shoemaker. LC 77-94869. (Illus.). 1978. 33.00x o.p. (ISBN 0-89520-252-2). SMM&E Inc.

Primary Elections in the South: A Study in Uniparty Politics. Cortez A. Ewing. LC 80-12616. (Illus.). xii, 112p. 1980. Repr. of 1953 ed. lib. bdg. 35.00x o.p. (ISBN 0-313-22452-8, EWPR). Greenwood.

Primary Generalized Epilepsy with Sporadic Myoclonias of Myoclonic Petit Mal Type: A Clinical, Electroencephlographic, Statistical & Genetic Study of 399 Probands. T. Tsuboi. Ed. by Peter E. Becker et al. LC 75-32668. (Illus.). 122p. 1977. pap. 25.00 o.p. (ISBN 0-88416-078-5). Year Bk Med.

Primary Health Care Buildings. Ruth Cammock. (Illus.). 96p. 1981. 25.00 o.p. (ISBN 0-85139-962-2). Nichols Pub.

Primary Langauge Learning with Microcomputers. G. R. Keith & M. Glover. 165p. 1986. 34.95 o.p. (ISBN 0-7099-1586-1, Pub. by Croom Helm UK). Routledge Chapman & Hall.

Primary Love & Psycho-Analytic Technique. Michael Balint. Ed. by Ernest Jones. (Psychoanalysis: Examined & Re-Examined Ser.). 288p. Date not set. lib. bdg. 27.50 o.p. (ISBN 0-306-76296-X). Da Capo.

Primary Philosophy. Michael Scriven. 1966. text ed. 31.95 o.p. (ISBN 0-07-055860-4). McGraw.

Primary Prevention in Mental Health & Social Work. Date not set. 8.80 o.s.i. Coun Soc Wk Ed.

Primary Processes in Photosynthesis. Martin D. Kamen. (Advanced Biochemistry Ser). (Orig.). 1964. pap. 30.00 o.p. (ISBN 0-12-394856-8). Acad Pr.

Primary School Potpourri. Marcus Ballenger et al. Ed. by Monroe D. Cohen. LC 75-45119. (Illus.). 1980. Repr. of 1976 ed. 3.25 o.p. (ISBN 0-87173-072-3). ACEI.

Primary Source: Tropical Forests & Our Future. Norman Myers. LC 83-13494. (Illus.). 352p. 1984. 17.45 o.p. (ISBN 0-393-01795-8). Norton.

Primate Behavior: Developments in Field & Laboratory Research, 4 vols. Ed. by Leonard A. Rosenblum. Vol. 2, 1971. 60.00 o.p. (ISBN 0-12-534002-8); Vol. 3, 1974. 55.00 o.p. (ISBN 0-12-534003-6); Vol. 4, 1975. 75.00 o.p. (ISBN 0-12-534004-4). Acad Pr.

Primate Ecology: Problem Oriented Field Studies. Robert W. Sussman. LC 78-17828. 596p. 1979. text ed. 27.00 o.p. (ISBN 0-394-34409-X). Random.

Primate Evolution: An Introduction to Man's Place in Nature. Elwyn L. Simons. (Illus.). 352p. 1972. pap. text ed. write for info. o.p. (ISBN 0-02-410680-1). Macmillan.

Primate Locomotion. Ed. by Farish A. Jenkins. 1974. 80.50 o.p. (ISBN 0-12-384050-3). Acad Pr.

Primate Social Relationships. Ed. by Robert A. Hinde. LC 83-12023. (Illus.). 400p. 1983. text ed. 47.50x o.p. (ISBN 0-87893-275-5); pap. text ed. 29.95x o.p. (ISBN 0-87893-276-3). Sinauer Assocs.

Primates: Comparative Anatomy & Taxonomy. W. C. Hill. Incl. Vol. 2. 367p. 1955. 59.95 o.p. (ISBN 0-471-39699-0); Vol. 3. 376p. 1957. o.p. (ISBN 0-471-39732-6); Vol. 4. 523p. 1960. o.p. (ISBN 0-471-39765-2); Vol. 5. 537p. 1962. o.p. (ISBN 0-471-39798-9); Vol. 6. 757p. 1966. o.p. (ISBN 0-471-39831-4); Vol. 7. 1974. 139.95 o.p. (ISBN 0-471-39835-7); Vol. 8. 692p. 1970. o.p. (ISBN 0-471-39836-5). Halsted Pr.

Primavera. Marjorie David. 208p. 1983. 14.50 o.s.i. (ISBN 0-671-45273-8, Poseidon). PB.

Primavera: The Restoration of Botticelli's Masterpiece. Umberto Baldini. (Illus.). 120p. 1986. pap. 9.95 o.p. (ISBN 0-8109-2314-9). Abrams.

Prime Mover. Paul Mariani. Ed. by Robert Pack. LC 85-14838. (Poetry Ser.). 98p. 1985. 22.50 o.p. (ISBN 0-394-55015-3). Grove.

Prime Mover. Paul Mariani. Ed. by Robert Pack. LC 85-14838. (Poetry Ser.). 98p. 1985. pap. 7.95 o.p. (ISBN 0-394-62083-6, Ever). Grove.

Prime of Your Life: The Book That Makes Old Age Obsolete. Arthur S. Freese. LC 77-90662. Orig. Title: End of Senility. 192p. 1981. pap. 5.95 o.p. (ISBN 0-87795-316-3). Morrow.

Prime Rib & Apple. Jill Briscoe. 1976. pap. 6.95 o.p. (ISBN 0-310-21811-X, 9257P). Zondervan.

Prime Target. Martin Russell. (Lythway Ser.). 248p. 1988. lib. bdg. 19.50 o.p. (ISBN 0-7451-0639-0, Pub. by Chivers Pr UK). G K HAll.

Prime Time for Families: Over Fifty Activities for Personal & Family Growth. Michael G. Pappas. (Illus.). 120p. (Orig.). 1980. pap. 6.95 o.p. (ISBN 0-03-056672-X). HarpR.

Prime Time: Sexual Health for Men over Fifty. Leslie R. Schover. (Illus.). 225p. 1984. 15.95 o.p. (ISBN 0-03-064028-8). H Holt & Co.

Prime-Time Soap Opera Trivia. Chris Vautour. LC 86-60596. (Illus.). 167p. (Orig.). 1986. pap. 6.95 o.s.i. (ISBN 0-933341-47-4). Quinlan Pr.

Prime Time Tennis. Vic Seixas, Jr. & Joel Cohen. (Illus.). 256p. 1982. 14.95 o.s.i. (ISBN 0-684-17904-0, ScribT). Scribner.

Prime Time Tennis. Vic Seixas, Jr. & Joel Cohen. (Illus.). 252p. 1984. pap. 7.95 o.s.i. (ISBN 0-684-18201-7). Scribner.

Primer for Christian Meditation. Robert F. Willett. 1976. pap. 4.25 o.p. (ISBN 0-8192-1202-4). Morehouse Pub.

Primer for Pickles & a Reader for Relishes. Ruby C. Guthrie & Jack S. Guthrie. LC 74-18029. (Illus.). 144p. 1974. 4.95 o.s.i. (ISBN 0-912238-53-4, One Hund One Prods); pap. 4.95 o.s.i. (ISBN 0-912238-52-6). Ortho.

Primer of Biostatistics. Stanton A. Glantz. (Illus.). 384p. 1981. text ed. 18.95 o.p. (ISBN 0-07-023370-5). McGraw.

Primer of Chess. Jose R. Capablanca. LC 35-3374. (Illus.). 1935. 7.95 o.p. (ISBN 0-15-174039-9). HarBraceJ.

Primer of Epidemiology. 2nd ed. Gary D. Friedman. (Illus.). 1980. text ed. 19.95 o.p. (ISBN 0-07-022434-X). McGraw.

Primer of Labor Relations. 23rd ed. John J. Kenny. 178p. 1986. pap. 20.00 o.p. (ISBN 0-87179-510-8, 0510). BNA.

Primer of Left-Handed Embroidery. Carole R. Myers. LC 73-1105. (Illus.). 160p. 1974. 8.95 o.p. (ISBN 0-684-13841-7); pap. 5.95 o.s.i. (ISBN 0-684-15143-X, ScribT). Scribner.

Primer of Medical Radiobiology. E. L. Travis. (Illus.). 1975. 35.50 o.p. (ISBN 0-8151-8836-6). Year Bk Med.

Primer of Multivariate Statistics. Richard J. Harris. 1975. text ed. 22.50i o.p. (ISBN 0-12-327250-5). Acad Pr.

Primer on SQL. Ageloff. 208p. 1988. pap. 17.95 o.p. (ISBN 0-8016-0085-5). Mosby.

Primer on the Atonement. John H. Gerstner. LC 84-3467. 32p. 1984. pap. 1.50 o.p. (ISBN 0-87552-278-5). Presby & Reformed.

Primer on the Deity of Christ. John H. Gerstner. LC 84-1706. 40p. 1984. pap. 1.75 o.p. (ISBN 0-87552-277-7). Presby & Reformed.

Primer on the Law of Mergers: A Guide for the Businessman. Earl W. Kintner. (Illus.). 480p. 1973. write for info. o.p. (ISBN 0-02-364420-6). Macmillan.

Primer, Presses, & Composing Sticks: Women Printers of the Colonial Period. Richard L. Demeter. 1979. 7.50 o.p. (ISBN 0-682-49195-0, University). Exposition-Phoenix.

Primitive Architecture: A Selected Bibliography. Anthony G. White. (Architecture Ser.: A 1363). 6p. 1985. 2.00 o.p. (ISBN 0-89028-353-2). Vance Biblios.

Primitive Folk-Moots: Or, Open-Air Assemblies in Britain. George L. Gomme. LC 67-23899. 328p. 1968. Repr. of 1880 ed. 40.00x o.p. (ISBN 0-8103-3433-X). Gale.

Primitive Gospel Sources. B. Stather Hunt. 1951. (ISBN 0-8022-0760-X). Philos Lib.

Primitive Marriage. John F. McLennan. Ed. by Peter Riviere. LC 72-111602. 1970. Repr. lib. bdg. 9.50x o.s.i. (ISBN 0-226-56080-5). U of Chicago Pr.

Primitive Motile Systems in Cell Biology. Ed. by Robert D. Allen & Noburo Kamiya. 1964. 91.50 o.p. (ISBN 0-12-052950-5). Acad Pr.

Primitive Mythology: The Mythic World of the Australian & Papuan Natives. Lucien Levy-Bruel. Tr. by Brian Elliott. LC 82-17332. 332p. 1984. text ed. 32.50 o.p. (ISBN 0-7022-1667-4). U of Queensland Pr.

Primitive Reader: An Anthology of Myths, Tales, Songs, Riddles, & Proverbs of Aboriginal Peoples Around the World. John Greenway. LC 65-21986. viii, 224p. Repr. of 1965 ed. 35.00x o.p. (ISBN 0-8103-5014-9). Gale.

Primitive Religion. John J. Collins. (Quality Paperback Ser.: No. 342). 256p. 1978. pap. 4.95 o.p. (ISBN 0-8226-0342-X). Littlefield.

Primitive Religion. new ed. Robert H. Lowie. LC 75-114373. 1970. pap. 5.95 o.p. (ISBN 0-87140-209-2). Liveright.

Primitive Revolutionaries of China: A Study of Secret Societies in the Late Nineteenth Century. Fei-Ling Davis. LC 76-45585. 261p. 1977. 14.00x o.p. (ISBN 0-8248-0522-4). UH Pr.

Primitive Sensory & Communication Systems, Taxes & Tropisms of Microorganisms & Cells. Ed. by M. Carlile. 1976. 52.50 o.p. (ISBN 0-12-159950-7). Acad Pr.

Primitivism & Related Ideas in Antiquity. Arthur O. Lovejoy & George Boas. 1965. lib. bdg. 34.50x o.p. (ISBN 0-374-95130-6, Octagon). Hippocrene Bks.

Primrose. Joanna Crawford. LC 74-31042. 216p. 1975. 6.95 o.p. (ISBN 0-15-174220-0). HarBraceJ.

Prince. Gordon Matthews. (In the Spotlight Ser.). 64p. (gr. 3-7). 1985. 8.79 o.p.; pap. 3.50 o.p. Messner.

Prince. Mark Rowland & Margy Rochlin. 224p. (Orig.). 1985. pap. 2.95 o.p. (ISBN 0-931773-27-X). Critics Choice Paper.

Prince among Slaves. Terry Alford. Ed. by Daniel Okrent. LC 77-73109. 1977. 12.95 o.p. (ISBN 0-15-174250-2). HarBraceJ.

Prince & the Pauper. (Guild Books Classics Illustrated Ser.). (Illus.). pap. 0.59 o.p. (ISBN 0-685-74088-9, 29). Guild Bks.

Prince & the Pauper. LC 88-60077. 224p. 1988. 13.95 o.p. (ISBN 0-89577-295-7). RD Assn.

Prince & the Pauper. Mark Twain. (Dent's Illustrated Children's Classics Ser.). (Illus.). (gr. 6 up). 11.00x o.p. (ISBN 0-460-05080-X, BKA 01628, Pub. by J. M. Dent, England). Biblio Dist.

Prince & the Pretender: A Study in the Writing of History. A J. Youngson. LC 84-29350. 270p. 1985. 29.00 o.p. (ISBN 0-7099-2912-9, Pub. by Croom Helm Ltd). Routledge Chapman & Hall.

Prince Caspian. C. S. Lewis. (Chronicles of Narnia Ser.: Vol. 2). (Illus.). 249p. (gr. 4-8). 1986. lib. bdg. 13.95x o.p. (ISBN 0-8161-4090-1, Large Print Bks.). G K Hall.

Prince Charles. Anthony Holden. LC 82-52176. (Illus.). 432p. 1983. pap. 10.95 o.p. (ISBN 0-689-70638-3, 287, Atheneum). Macmillan.

Prince Charles: A Biography. Anthony Holden. LC 79-52176. (Illus.). 1979. 15.00 o.p. (ISBN 0-689-10998-9, Atheneum). Macmillan.

Prince Charles: England's Future King. Jean Nugent. LC 81-22183. (Taking Part Ser.). (Illus.). 48p. (gr. 3 up). 1982. PLB 9.95 o.p. (ISBN 0-87518-226-7). Dillon.

Prince Charles: The Making of a Prince. Helen Cathcart. LC 77-73686. (Illus.). 1977. 8.50 o.s.i. (ISBN 0-8008-6555-3). Taplinger.

Prince Harry's First Quiz Book. Sean Hardie & John Lloyd. 96p. (Orig.). 1986. pap. 9.95 o.p. (ISBN 0-571-13558-7). Faber & Faber.

Prince Junior Gorg. Jennifer Taubner. LC 84-81839. (Illus.). 12p. (ps-k). 1985. bds. 2.95 o.s.i. (ISBN 0-03-002558-3). H Holt & Co.

Prince of Abissinia: A Tale, 1759, 2 vols. in 1. Samuel Johnson. Bd. with Candide; or, All for the Best, 1759. Voltaire. LC 74-17303. (Novel in England, 1700-1775 Ser). 1974. lib. bdg. 61.00 o.p. (ISBN 0-8240-1150-3). Garland Pub.

Prince of Berlin. Dan Sherman. 304p. 1983. 15.95 o.p. (ISBN 0-87795-480-1, Arbor Hse). Morrow.

Prince of Evil. Grant Stockbridge. (Spider Ser.: No. 3). 192p. 1985. pap. 2.95 o.p. (ISBN 0-89300-011-6). Blazing Pubns.

Prince of Librarians: The Life & Times of Antonio Panizzi of the British Museum. Edward Miller. LC 67-26123. (Illus.). 356p. 1967. 17.00x o.p. (ISBN 0-8214-0030-4). Ohio U Pr.

Prince of Peace. James Carroll. 512p. 1984. 17.45i o.p. (ISBN 0-316-13014-1). Little.

Prince of the Church: Schleiermacher & the Beginnings of Modern Theology. B. A. Gerrish. LC 83-48924. 80p. 1984. pap. 1.50 o.p. (ISBN 0-8006-1787-8, 1-1787, Fortress). Augsburg Fortress.

Prince of the City: The True Story of the Cop Who Knew Too Much. Robert Daley. 1979. 10.95 o.p. (ISBN 0-395-27096-0). HM.

Prince of the Dolomites. Tomie De Paola. LC 79-18524. (Illus.). (gr. k-3). 1980. 8.95 o.s.i. (ISBN 0-15-263528-9, HJ). HarBraceJ.

Prince of Thieves. Chris Martindale. LC 88-90039. (Advanced Dungeons & Dragons Gamebook Ser.: No. 18). (Illus.). 192p. (Orig.). (gr. 5 up). 1988. pap. 2.95 o.p. (ISBN 0-88038-596-0). TSR Inc.

Prince Philip, Duke of Edinburgh. Denis Judd. LC 80-22691. 1981. 16.95 o.p. (ISBN 0-689-11131-2, Atheneum). Macmillan.

Prince Rupert of the Rhine. Patrick Morrah. 1976. 28.50x o.s.i. (ISBN 0-09-460910-1, Pub. by Constable Pubs UK). Trans-Atl-Phila.

Princes & Peasants: Smallpox in History. Donald R. Hopkins. LC 83-6472. (Illus.). xx, 380p. 1985. pap. 12.95 o.s.i. (ISBN 0-226-35177-7). U of Chicago Pr.

Princes of the Earth: Subcultural Diversity in a Mexican Municipality. Barbara L. Margoli (Special Publication: No. 2). 1975. pap. 7.50 o.s.i. (ISBN 0-686-36567-4). Am Anthro Assn.

Princess & Curdie. George MacDonald. (Illus.). 224p. (gr. 4 up). 1966. pap. 2.50 o.p. (ISBN 0-14-030260-3, Puffin). Penguin.

Princess & the Enchanted Wood & Other Fairy Tales. Marjorie D. Ashe. (Illus.). 80p. (gr. k up). 1982. 5.50 o.p. (ISBN 0-682-49842-4). Exposition-Phoenix.

Princess & the Pea. Retold by & illus. by Dick Gackenbach. LC 82-17954. (Illus.). 32p. (ps-3). 1983. 9.95 o.s.i. (ISBN 0-02-735800-3). Macmillan.

Princess & the Thorn. Paul Fisher. LC 80-12309. 256p. (gr. 4-8). 1980. 9.95 o.p. (ISBN 0-689-30776-4, Atheneum). Macmillan.

Princess & the Unicorn. Lily Arbore. LC 70-171068. (Illus.). (gr. k-4). 1972. PLB 4.95 o.p. (ISBN 0-87614-028-2). Carolrhoda Bks.

Princess Bride. William Goldman. LC 73-6812. 1973. 7.95 o.p. (ISBN 0-15-173085-7). HarBraceJ.

Princess de Cleves. Jean Cocteau. Ed. by Delannoy. 9.95 o.p. (ISBN 0-686-54555-9). French & Eur.

Princess in Berlin. Arthur R. Solmssen. 1981. pap. 2.75 o.s.i. (ISBN 0-345-29807-1). Ballantine.

Princess of Celle. Jean Plaidy. 597p. 1986. lib. bdg. 18.95 o.p. (ISBN 0-8161-3973-3, Large Prints Bks). G K Hall.

Princess of the Iron Palace. Gustavo Sainz. Tr. by Andrew Hurley. 320p. 1987. 17.95 o.s.i. (ISBN 0-394-56066-3). Grove.

Princess Pamela. Ed. by Ray Russell. 1979. 11.95 o.p. (ISBN 0-395-28210-1). HM.

Princess Remembers. Gayatri Devi & Santha R. Rau. LC 85-7442. (Illus.). 320p. 1985. pap. 11.95 o.p. (ISBN 0-385-19937-6, Anchor). Doubleday.

Princess Who Always Ran Away. Marijke Reesink. (Illus.). 32p. (gr. k-4). 1981. text ed. 9.95 o.p. (ISBN 0-07-051714-2). McGraw.

Princess Zettie & the Teeny Weeny People. Vera Steele. 32p. 1987. 5.95 o.p. (ISBN 0-8062-2855-5). Carlton.

Princeton Alumni Collections: Works on Paper. Princeton University Art Museum Staff. LC 81-80640. (Illus.). 264p. 1981. 42.00x o.p. (ISBN 0-691-03977-1). Princeton U Pr.

Princeton Architecture: A Pictorial History of Town & Campus. Constance M. Greiff et al. LC 65-17138. (Illus.). 1967. 37.00 o.p. (ISBN 0-691-04556-9); pap. 11.50 o.p. (ISBN 0-691-00583-4). Princeton U Pr.

Princeton Journal: Thematic Studies in Architecture. Ed. by Raymond Beeler. (Landscape Ser.: Vol. 2). (Illus.). 232p. (Orig.). 1986. pap. text ed. 17.00 o.p. (ISBN 0-910413-08-8). Princeton Arch.

Principal Functions. R. Rodin & L. Sario. (Illus.). xviii, 347p. 1968. 22.00 o.p. (ISBN 0-387-90129-9). Springer-Verlag.

Principal Winners Abroad of 1978. 10.00 o.p. (ISBN 0-936032-06-5). Blood-Horse.
Principal Winners Abroad of 1979. Ed. by Blood-Horse, Inc. Staff. (Annual Supplement, the Blood-Horse). (Orig.). 1980. pap. 10.00 o.p. (ISBN 0-936032-07-3). Blood-Horse.
Principal Winners Abroad of 1980. Ed. by Blood-Horse, Inc. Staff. (Annual Supplement of the Blood-Horse). (Orig.). 1981. pap. 10.00 o.p. (ISBN 0-936032-38-3). Blood-Horse.
Principios of Electricidad. Kurt Schick. 1973. text ed. 26.60 o.p. (ISBN 0-07-091840-6). McGraw.
Principle of Changes: Understanding the I Ching. Jung Y. Lee. 1971. 10.00 o.p. (ISBN 0-8216-0139-3, Pub. by Univ Bks). Carol Pub Group.
Principle of Inertia in the Middle Ages. Allan Franklin. LC 76-10515. 100p. (Orig.). 1976. pap. 8.95x o.p. (ISBN 0-87081-069-3). Univ Pr Colo.
Principle of Non-Resistance As Held by the Mennonite Church. John Horsch. Bd. with Hutterian Brethren, Fifteen Twenty-Eight to Nineteen Thirty-One. John Horsch. LC 74-147672. (Library of War & Peace; Relig. & Ethical Positions on War). lib. bdg. 46.00 o.p. (ISBN 0-8240-0430-2). Garland Pub.
Principles & Applications of Electrochemistry. 2nd ed. D. R. Crow. LC 79-75. (Chemistry Textbook Ser.). 238p. 1979. pap. 14.95x o.p. (ISBN 0-412-16020-X, NO. 6071, Pub. by Chapman & Hall England). Routledge Chapman & Hall.
Principles & Applications of Medicolegal Alcohol Determination. E. M. Widmark. LC 81-66542. Orig. Title: Theoretische Grundlagen und die Praktische Verwendbarkeit der Gerichtlich-Medizinischen Alkoholbestimmung (1932) (Illus.). 200p. 1981. text ed. 41.50 o.p. (ISBN 0-931890-07-1, Biomed Pubns). Year Bk Med.
Principles & Applications of Tribology. D. F. Moore. 1975. 100.00 o.p. (ISBN 0-08-017902-9); pap. 100.00 o.p. (ISBN 0-08-019007-3). Pergamon.
Principles & Management of Human Reproduction. Duncan E. Reid et al. LC 70-118593. (Illus.). 1972. (ISBN 0-7216-7532-8). Saunders.
Principles & Management of Human Reproduction. Duncan E. Reid et al. LC 70-118593. (Illus.). Repr. of 1972 ed. (2016678). Bks Demand UMI.
Principles & Methods for Determining Ecological Criteria on Hydrobiocenoses. Ed. by R. Amavis & Commission of the European Communities. LC 76-14624. 1976. pap. 120.00 o.p. (ISBN 0-08-021233-6). Pergamon.
Principles & Methods of Adapted Physical Education & Recreation. 5th ed. David Auxter & Jean Pyfer. 1985. 29.95 o.p. (ISBN 0-8016-0378-1). Mosby.
Principles & Methods of Musical Criticism. M. D. Calvocoressi. LC 79-9864. (Music Reprint Ser.). 1979. Repr. of 1931 ed. 29.50 o.p. (ISBN 0-306-79557-4). Da Capo.
Principles & Methods of Phylogenetic Systematics: A Cladistics Workbook. Daniel R. Brooks et al. (Special Publication Ser.: No. 12). (Illus.). v, 92p. (Orig.). 1984. pap. 6.50 o.p. (ISBN 0-89338-022-9). U of KS Mus Nat Hist.
Principles & Practice of Clinical Gynecology. Ed. by Nathan G. Kase & Allan B. Weingold. LC 83-1140. 1099p. 1983. 70.00x o.p. (ISBN 0-471-04594-2). Wiley.
Principles & Practice of Clinical Virology. Ed. by A. J. Zuckerman et al. 1986. (ISBN 0-471-90341-8, Dist. by A R Liss). Wiley.
Principles & Practice of Electrical & Electronics Troubleshooting. Daniel R. Tomal & David V. Gedeon. (Illus.). 256p. (Orig.). 1985. 21.95 o.p. (ISBN 0-8306-0842-7, 1842); pap. 14.60 o.p. (ISBN 0-8306-1842-2). TAB Bks.
Principles & Practice of Freedom of Speech. Haig Bosmajian. (Orig.). 1971. pap. 11.95 o.p. (ISBN 0-395-04216-X, 3-05250). HM.
Principles & Practice of Geriatric Medicine. M. S. J. Pathy. 1323p. 1985. 95.00 o.p. (ISBN 0-471-10346-2, Dist. by A R Liss). Wiley.
Principles & Practice of Health Visiting. R. Hale et al. 1968. 18.25 o.p. (ISBN 0-08-012700-2). Pergamon.
Principles & Practice of Infectious Diseases. 2nd ed. Ed. by Gerald Mandell et al. LC 84-13076. 1760p. 1985. Repr. 160.00 o.p. (ISBN 0-471-87643-7). Wiley.
Principles & Practice of Management. S. S. Chaterjee. 301p. 1983. text ed. 27.50 o.p. (ISBN 0-7069-2311-1, Pub. by Vikas India). Advent NY.
Principles & Practice of Medical Genetics, 2 vols. Ed. by Alan E. Emery & David L. Rimoin. (Illus.). 1594p. 1983. text ed. 198.00 o.p. (ISBN 0-443-02129-5). Churchill.
Principles & Practice of Medicine. 21st ed. Ed. by A. M. Harvey et al. (Illus.). 1618p. 1984. 59.95 o.p. (ISBN 0-8385-7928-0). Appleton & Lange.
Principles & Practice of Nurse Education. F. M. Quinn. 336p. 1981. 29.95 o.p. (ISBN 0-85664-891-4, Pub. by Croom Helm Ltd); pap. 15.00 o.p. (ISBN 0-7099-0363-4). Routledge Chapman & Hall.
Principles & Practice of Oral Dynamics. Thomas H. Forde. 1964. 25.00 o.p. (ISBN 0-682-42059-X, University). Exposition-Phoenix.
Principles & Practice of Psychiatric Nursing. 2nd ed. Gail W. Stuart & Sandra J. Sundeen. LC 82-12540. (Illus.). 1024p. 1983. text ed. 37.95 o.p. (ISBN 0-8016-4885-8). Mosby.
Principles & Practice of Supervision. D. A. Peters. 1968. 35.00 o.p. (ISBN 0-08-012684-7); pap. 35.00 o.p. (ISBN 0-08-012683-9). Pergamon.
Principles & Practice of Surgery: A Surgical Supplement to Davidson's Principles & Practice of Medicine. A. P. Forrest et al. LC 84-9619. (Illus.). 672p. 1985. pap. text ed. 34.00 o.p. (ISBN 0-443-01565-1). Churchill.
Principles & Practice of Surgical Pathology. Ed. by Steven G. Silverberg. LC 81-21891. 1711p. 1983. 172.50 o.p. (ISBN 0-471-05221-3). Wiley.
Principles & Practices of Dryland Farming. Kenneth G. Brengle. LC 80-70691. 1982. 15.00x o.p. (ISBN 0-87081-095-2). Univ Pr Colo.
Principles & Practices of Harvesting & Handling Fruits & Nuts. Michael O'Brien & Burton F. Cargill. (Illus.). 1983. 75.95 o.s.i. (ISBN 0-87055-413-1). AVI.
Principles & Practices of Nursing Care. Donna K. Story & Caroline B. Rosdahl. 1976. text ed. 29.20 o.p. (ISBN 0-07-061770-8). McGraw.
Principles & Practices of Teaching Young Children. Patricia L. Fagan. LC 77-14804. 1977. pap. (ISBN 0-918772-05-2). Daye Pr.
Principles & Procedures of Numerical Analysis. Ed. by F. Szidarovszky & S. Yakowitz. LC 78-12070. (Mathematical Concepts & Methods in Science & Engineering Ser.: Vol. 14). 344p. 1978. 39.50x o.p. (ISBN 0-306-40087-1, Plenum Pr). Plenum Pub.
Principles & Techniques of Effective Business Communication: A Text-Workbook. Isabelle A. Krey & Bernadette V. Metzler. (Illus.). 532p. 1976. pap. text ed. 18.95 o.p. (ISBN 0-15-571310-8, HC). HarBraceJ.
Principles & Techniques of Electron Microscopy, Vol. 5: Biological Applications. M. Arif Hayat. 1975. 24.95 o.p. (ISBN 0-442-25681-7). Van Nos Reinhold.
Principles & Techniques of Electron Microscopy, Vol. 8: Biological Applications. M. Arif Hayat. 1978. 31.95 o.p. (ISBN 0-442-25693-0). Van Nos Reinhold.
Principles & Techniques of Electron Microscopy, Vol. 3. M. Arif Hayat. 1973. 19.95x o.p. (ISBN 0-442-25674-4). Van Nos Reinhold.
Principles & Techniques of Electron Microscopy, Vol. 4. M. Arif Hayat. 1974. 24.95 o.p. (ISBN 0-442-25680-9). Van Nos Reinhold.
Principles & Techniques of Electron Microscopy, Vol. 6. M. Arif Hayat. 1976. 31.95 o.p. (ISBN 0-442-25688-4). Van Nos Reinhold.
Principles & Techniques of Electron Microscopy, Vol. 7. M. Arif Hayat. 1977. 31.95 o.p. (ISBN 0-442-25691-4). Van Nos Reinhold.
Principles & Techniques of Electron Microscopy, Vol. 9. M. Arif Hayat. 1978. 31.95 o.p. (ISBN 0-442-25694-9). Van Nos Reinhold.
Principles & Techniques of Engineering Estimating. G. Calder. 180p. 1976. 34.00 o.p. (ISBN 0-08-019704-3); pap. 10.75 o.p. (ISBN 0-08-019703-5). Pergamon.
Principles & Techniques of Histochemistry. Henry Troyer. LC 80-80592. 1980. text ed. 28.00 o.p. (ISBN 0-316-85310-0). Little.
Principles & Techniques of Mental Health Consultation. Ed. by Stanley C. Plog & Paul I. Ahmed. LC 76-42189. (Current Topics In Mental Health Ser.). (Illus.). 248p. 1977. 45.00x o.p. (ISBN 0-306-30963-7, Plenum Med. Bk.). Plenum Pub.
Principles & Techniques of Scanning Electron Microscopy, Vol. 4. M. Arif Hayat. 278p. 1975. 29.95 o.p. (ISBN 0-442-25686-8). Van Nos Reinhold.
Principles & Techniques of Scanning Electron Microscopy, Vol. 5. M. Arif Hayat. 1976. 29.95 o.p. (ISBN 0-442-25692-2). Van Nos Reinhold.
Principles & Techniques of Scanning Electron Microscopy, Vol. 6. M. Arif Hayat. 1978. 31.95 o.p. (ISBN 0-442-25687-6). Van Nos Reinhold.
Principles & Techniques of Scanning Electron Microscopy: Biological Applications, Vol. 1. M. Arif Hayat. 224p. 1974. 24.50x o.p. (ISBN 0-442-25677-9). Van Nos Reinhold.
Principles & Techniques of Scanning Electron Microscopy, Vol. 2: Biological Applications. M. Arif Hayat. 186p. 1974. 29.95 o.p. (ISBN 0-442-25678-7). Van Nos Reinhold.
Principles & Types of Speech Communication. 9th ed. Douglas Ehninger et al. 1982. (ISBN 0-673-15538-2). Scott F.
Principles for Developing Coastal Water Quality Criteria. (GESAMP Reports & Studies: No. 5). (Illus.). 23p. 1976. pap. 7.50 o.p. (ISBN 92-5-100078-6, F1072, FAO). UNIPUB.
Principles of a New Energy Mechanics. Jakob Mandelker. (ISBN 0-8022-1042-2). Philos Lib.
Principles of Accounting. 4th ed. James J. Benjamin et al. LC 83-70550. 1007p. 1988. 38.95x o.p. (ISBN 0-87393-077-0); study guide 12.95x o.p. (ISBN 0-87393-078-9); Vol. I. working papers 9.95x o.p.; Vol. II. working papers 9.95x o.p. Dame Pubns.
Principles of Accounting. Belverd E. Needles et al. LC 80-80503. (Illus.). 1008p. 1981. text ed. 27.95 o.p. (ISBN 0-395-29527-0). HM.
Principles of Accounting. 2nd ed. Belverd E. Needles et al. Incl. Instructor's Handbook. 1984. 5.96 o.p. (ISBN 0-395-34331-3); Study Guide & Selected Readings. 1983. 17.96 o.p. (ISBN 0-395-34332-1); Working Papers. 1984. Pt. 1A. pap. 18.36 o.p. (ISBN 0-395-34333-X); Pt. 1B. pap. 18.36 o.p. (ISBN 0-395-34334-8); Pt. 2A. pap. 18.36 (ISBN 0-395-34335-6); Pt. 2B. pap. 18.36 o.p. (ISBN 0-395-34336-4); Tranparencies. 1984. 315.96 (ISBN 0-395-34341-0); Checklist of Key Figures. 1984. 16.36 o.p. (ISBN 0-395-34342-9); Achievement Tests 1-7A. 1984. 9.96 o.p. (ISBN 0-395-34343-7); Achievement Tests 1-7B. 1984. 9.96 o.p. (ISBN 0-395-34344-5); Achievement Tests 8-14A. 1980. 8.50 o.p. (ISBN 0-395-34345-3); Achievement Tests 8-14B. 1980. 9.96 o.p. (ISBN 0-395-34346-1); Computer Casebook of Accounting Problems. 1984. 14.36 o.p. (ISBN 0-395-34533-2). 1984. text ed. 47.96 o.p. (ISBN 0-395-34329-1). HM.
Principles of Accounting. Loren A. Nikolai et al. LC 81-18619. 1136p. 1982. write for info. o.p. (ISBN 0-534-01049-0); Practice Set 1. write for info. o.p. (ISBN 0-534-01052-0); Practice Set 2. pap. text ed. write for info. o.p. (ISBN 0-534-01053-9); write for info. study guide o.p. (ISBN 0-534-01050-4); write for info. working papers o.p. PWS-Kent Pub.
Principles of Accounting. 3rd ed. Isaac N. Reynolds et al. 1056p. 1984. text ed. 33.95x o.s.i. (ISBN 0-03-063313-3); study guide 10.95x o.s.i. (ISBN 0-03-063321-4); instr'.s manual 19.95 o.s.i. (ISBN 0-03-063314-1); Working papers I 12.95x o.s.i. (ISBN 0-03-063328-1); Working Papers II 12.95x o.s.i. (ISBN 0-03-063329-X); Practice Set A 13.95x o.s.i. (ISBN 0-03-063316-8); Practice Set B 13.95x o.s.i. (ISBN 0-03-063318-4); Practice Set C 13.95x o.s.i. (ISBN 0-03-063319-2); solutions manual 11.95 o.s.i. (ISBN 0-03-063322-2). Dryden Pr.
Principles of Accounting. Jack Topiol. 1976. pap. 8.95 working papers o.p. (ISBN 0-7216-8873-X). HR&W.
Principles of Accounting. 2nd ed. Paul H. Walgenbach et al. 1065p. 1980. text ed. 22.50 o.p. (ISBN 0-15-571336-1, HC); study guide by Imogene Posey 8.95 o.p. (ISBN 0-686-64998-2). HarBraceJ.
Principles of Accounting. Paul H. Walgenbach et al. (Illus.). 1976. text ed. 20.95 o.p. (ISBN 0-15-571320-5, HC). HarBraceJ.
Principles of Accounting. 3rd ed. Paul H. Walgenbach et al. 1065p. 1984. text ed. 25.50 o.p. (ISBN 0-15-571350-7, HC). HarBraceJ.
Principles of Accounting. 3rd ed. Paul H. Walgenbach et al. 1984. write for info. o.p. (HC). HarBraceJ.
Principles of Air Conditioning. 3rd ed. V. Paul Lang. LC 77-78900. (Air Conditioning, Refrigeration Ser.). 1979. pap. text ed. 21.95 o.p. (ISBN 0-8273-1009-9). Delmar.
Principles of American Nuclear Chemistry: A Novel. Thomas McMahon. 1970. 7.95 o.p. (ISBN 0-316-56221-1, Pub. by Atlantic Monthly Pr.). Little.
Principles of American Prosperity. Leighton A. Wilkie & Richard S. Rimanoczy. LC 81-66941. 100p. 1981. pap. 3.95 o.p. (ISBN 0-933028-18-0). Fisher Inst.
Principles of Anesthesiology. 2nd ed. Vincent J. Collins. LC 76-2054. (Illus.). 1671p. 1976. text ed. 60.00 o.p. (ISBN 0-8121-0463-3). Lea & Febiger.
Principles of Animal Environment. Merle L. Esmay. 1978. 30.95 o.s.i. (ISBN 0-87055-263-5). AVI.
Principles of Animal Physiology. 2nd ed. James A. Wilson. 1979. text ed. write for info. o.p. (ISBN 0-02-428360-6). Macmillan.
Principles of Applied Clinical Chemistry: Chemical Background & Medical Applications, 2 vols. Ed. by Samuel Natelson & Ethan A. Natelson. Incl. Vol. 1, Maintenance of Fluid & Electrolyte Balance. 394p. 1975. 55.00x (ISBN 0-306-35231-1); Vol. 2, The Erythrocyte Chemical Composition, Normal & Aberrant Metabolism. 584p. 1978. 79.50x (ISBN 0-306-35232-X). LC 75-4798. (Illus., Plenum Pr). Plenum Pub.
Principles of Applied Geophysics. 3rd ed. D. S. Parasnis. 1979. 32.00 o.p. (ISBN 0-412-15140-5, NO. 6304, Pub. by Chapman & Hall); pap. 15.95x o.p. (ISBN 0-412-15810-8, NO. 6387). Routledge Chapman & Hall.
Principles of Applied Statistics. Myron Melnyk. LC 73-7943. 1974. 36.00 o.p. (ISBN 0-08-017108-7). Pergamon.
Principles of Arable Crop Production. F. Harper. 336p. (Orig.). 1983. pap. text ed. 21.95x o.p. (ISBN 0-246-11741-9, Pub. by Granada England). Gower Pub Co.
Principles of Art Teaching. Ruth Mock. (Illus.). 100p. 1956. (ISBN 0-8022-1127-5). Philos Lib.
Principles of Association Management. 446p. (Orig.). 1975. pap. text ed. 30.00 o.p. (ISBN 0-88034-003-7). Am Soc Assn Execs.
Principles of Auditing. 8th ed. Walter B. Meigs et al. 1985. 41.95x o.p. (ISBN 0-256-03176-2). Irwin.
Principles of Automatic Control. Martin Healey. 333p. 1968. 19.50 o.p. (ISBN 0-442-33279-3, Pub. by Van Nos Reinhold). Krieger.
Principles of Behavioral Analysis. 2nd ed. J. R. Millenson & Julian C. Leslie. 1979. text ed. write for info. o.p. (ISBN 0-02-381280-X). Macmillan.
Principles of Biological Regulation: An Introduction to Feedback Systems. Richard W. Jones. 1973. 39.95 o.p. (ISBN 0-12-389950-8). Acad Pr.
Principles of Biology Laboratory Manual. Lauren D. Howard. (Illus.). 1980. pap. 18.95 o.s.i. (ISBN 0-87055-354-2). AVI.
Principles of Biosystematics. 2nd ed. Thomas R. Mertens & Judy L. Lines. (Programmed Biology Studies). (Illus.). 1978. pap. text ed. 6.95 o.s.i. (ISBN 0-88462-038-7, 3304-34, Ed Methods). Longman Finan.
Principles of Biotechnology. Ed. by Alan Wiseman. 192p. 1983. pap. 23.95 o.p. (ISBN 0-412-00261-2, NO. 5029). Routledge Chapman & Hall.
Principles of Business Communication: Theory Application & Technology. 1984. pap. (ISBN 0-471-82592-1). Wiley.
Principles of Business Law & the Legal Environment: Brief. Joseph L. Frascona et al. 992p. 1987. text ed. write for info. o.p. (ISBN 0-697-03463-1). Instr's Manual (ISBN 0-697-05588-4). Student Study Guide (ISBN 0-697-05590-6). Transparencies (ISBN 0-697-05591-4). Test Item File (ISBN 0-697-05589-2). Wm C Brown.
Principles of California Real Estate. 4th, rev. ed. David L. Rockwell et al. (Illus.). 491p. 1987. pap. 29.95 o.p. (ISBN 0-915799-29-4). Natl Real Estate Inst.
Principles of Chemistry Laboratory: Manual for CH 111A & 112A. H. W. Cain & R. L. Hunt. 1984. pap. text ed. 16.25 o.s.i. (ISBN 0-89917-431-0). Tichenor Pub.
Principles of Color: A Review of Past Traditions & Modern Theories. Faber Birren. 1977. pap. 10.95 o.p. (ISBN 0-442-20774-3). Van Nos Reinhold.
Principles of Color Sensitometry. 3rd ed. Ed. by Roderick T. Ryan. (Illus.). 128p. 1974. 2.00 o.p. (ISBN 0-318-16591-0). Soc Motion Pic & TV Engrs.
Principles of Communciations: Systems Modulation & Noise. Rodger E. Ziemer & William Tranter. LC 75-25015. (Illus.). 736p. 1976. text ed. 41.50 o.p. (ISBN 0-395-20603-0). HM.
Principles of Cost Accounting with Managerial Implications. 3rd ed. L. Gayle Rayburn. 1986. 41.95x o.p. (ISBN 0-256-03324-2); study guide 14.95x o.p. (ISBN 0-256-03457-5). Irwin.
Principles of Criminal Law. Wayne R. LaFave. (Criminal Justice Ser.). 656p. 1978. text ed. 37.00 o.p. (ISBN 0-8299-0215-9); instrs.' manual avail. o.p. (ISBN 0-8299-0595-2). West Pub.
Principles of Criminology. G. Avanesov. 344p. 1982. 7.95 o.p. (ISBN 0-8285-2511-0, 230065, Pub. by Progress Pubs USSR). Imported Pubns.
Principles of Data Processing: Concepts, Cases & Applications. 2nd ed. Ralph M. Stair. 1984. 29.95x o.p. (ISBN 0-256-02991-1); study guide 10.50x o.p. (ISBN 0-256-02992-X). Irwin.
Principles of Digital Audio. Ken C. Pohlmann. (Illus.). 1985. 19.95 o.p. (ISBN 0-672-22388-0, 22388-0). Sams.
Principles of Dispersal in Higher Plants. 2nd ed. L. Van der Pijl. LC 72-83445. (Illus.). 170p. 1972. 17.90 o.p. (ISBN 0-387-05881-8). Springer-Verlag.
Principles of Dynamics. 2nd ed. R. Hill. 1964. 50.00 o.p. (ISBN 0-08-010571-8); pap. text ed. 9.75 o.p. (ISBN 0-08-013540-4). Pergamon.
Principles of Economic Science. B. N. Ghosh. 1983. text ed. 15.95x o.p. (ISBN 0-686-45575-4, Pub. by Vikas India). Advent NY.

Principles of Economic Sociology: The Economics of Primitive Life as Illustrated from the Bantu Peoples of South & East Africa. David M. Goodfellow. LC 78-106836. 1970. Repr. of 1939 ed. lib. bdg. 22.50x o.p. (ISBN 0-8371-3458-7, GES&). Greenwood.

Principles of Economics, 2 vols. 6th ed. Willis L. Peterson. 1986. pap. 21.95x macro o.p. (ISBN 0-256-03346-3); pap. 21.95x micro o.p. (ISBN 0-256-03348-X); pap. 9.95x study guide, macro o.p. (ISBN 0-256-03347-1); pap. 9.95x study guide, micro o.p. (ISBN 0-256-03349-8). Irwin.

Principles of Economics. 2nd ed. Roy Ruffin & Paul Gregory. 1986. write for info. o.p. (ISBN 0-673-18225-8); instr's. manual avail. o.p. Scott F.

Principles of Economics. Robert H. Scott & Nic Nigro. 1982. text ed. write for info. o.p. (ISBN 0-02-408360-7). Macmillan.

Principles of Economics. Truett. 960p. 1986. text ed. 42.95 o.p. Mosby.

Principles of Education: A Study of Aristotelian Thomism Contrasted with Other Philosophies. Mary M. Spangler. LC 82-24757. 306p. (Orig.). lib. bdg. 31.25 o.p. (ISBN 0-8191-3015-X); pap. text ed. 15.00 o.p. (ISBN 0-8191-3016-8). U Pr of Amer.

Principles of Educational & Psychological Measurement & Evaluation. 2nd ed. Gilbert Sax. 688p. 1980. text ed. (ISBN 0-534-00832-1). Wadsworth Pub.

Principles of Electrical Measurements. H. Buckingham & E. M. Price. 418p. 1957. (ISBN 0-8022-0194-6). Philos Lib.

Principles of Electrical Transmission Lines in Power & Communication. J. H. Grindley. 1967. text ed. 27.00 o.p. (ISBN 0-08-012111-X); pap. 13.25 o.p. (ISBN 0-08-012112-8). Pergamon.

Principles of Electroplating & Electroforming. William Blum & George B. Hogaboom. 455p. 1949. 34.00 o.p. (ISBN 0-318-12556-0). Am Electro Surface.

Principles of Engineering Mechanics. H. R. Harrison & T. Nettleton. (Illus.). 255p. 1984. pap. text ed. 24.00x o.p. (ISBN 0-7131-3378-3). Trans-Atl Phila.

Principles of Engineering Organization. S. H. Wearne. (Illus.). 1973. pap. text ed. 21.50x o.p. (ISBN 0-7131-3290-6). Trans-Atl Phila.

Principles of Extractive Metallurgy. 2nd ed. Terkel Rosenqvist. (Materials Science & Electronics Ser.). 608p. 1983. text ed. 53.95 o.p. (ISBN 0-07-053910-3). McGraw.

Principles of Family Medicine. Robert F. Rakel. LC 76-41541. (Illus.). 1977. text ed. write for info. o.p. (ISBN 0-7216-7449-6). Saunders.

Principles of Field Crop Production. J. E. Prately. 1979. 25.00x o.p. (Pub. by Sydney U Pr); pap. 5.50x o.p. (ISBN 0-424-00058-X, Pub. by Sydney U Pr). Intl Spec Bk.

Principles of Field Ionization & Field Desorption Mass Spectrometry. H. D. Beckey. LC 77-33014. 1971. 83.00 o.p. (ISBN 0-08-017557-0). Pergamon.

Principles of Financial Intermediation. Alex N. McLeod. LC 83-27418. (Illus.). 252p. (Orig.). 1984. lib. bdg. 26.75 o.p. (ISBN 0-8191-3831-2); pap. text ed. 13.25 o.p. (ISBN 0-8191-3832-0). U Pr of Amer.

Principles of Financial Management. Burton Kolb. 1983. text ed. 36.95 o.p. (ISBN 0-256-02879-6); study guide 12.95 o.p. (ISBN 0-256-02880-X). Irwin.

Principles of Food Sanitation. N. G. Marriott. (Food Science & Technology Ser.). (Illus.). 1985. 43.95 o.p. (ISBN 0-87055-485-9). AVI.

Principles of Forest Policy. A. C. Worrell. 1970. text ed. 43.95 o.p. (ISBN 0-07-071891-1). McGraw.

Principles of Forest Yield Study. E. Assmann. 1971. 130.00 o.p. (ISBN 0-08-006658-5). Pergamon.

Principles of Gardening. Hugh Johnson. 1979. 29.95 o.s.i. (ISBN 0-671-24273-3). S&S.

Principles of Genetic Epistemology. Jean Piaget. pap. 7.95 o.p. (ISBN 0-7100-8660-1). Routledge Chapman & Hall.

Principles of Genetic Toxicology. David Brusick. LC 80-16514. 300p. 1980. 32.50x o.p. (ISBN 0-306-40414-1, Plenum Pr). Plenum Pub.

Principles of Geochemistry. 4th ed. Brian Mason & Carleton B. Moore. LC 82-8649. (Intermediate Geology Ser.). 344p. 1982. text ed. (ISBN 0-471-57522-4). Wiley.

Principles of Gestalt Psychology. Kurt Koffka. LC 35-7711. 1967. pap. 6.95 o.s.i. (ISBN 0-15-674460-0, Harv). HarBraceJ.

Principles of Group Solidarity. Michael Hechter. 234p. (Orig.). 1988. pap. text ed. 8.95x o.p. (ISBN 0-520-06462-3). U of Cal Pr.

Principles of Home Inspection: A Guide to Residential Construction, Inspection & Maintenance. Joseph McNeill. 346p. 1979. 25.95 o.p. (ISBN 0-442-23606-9). Van Nos Reinhold.

Principles of Hospital Business Office Management. Beaufort B. Longest, Jr. 1975. 11.75 o.p. (ISBN 0-930228-02-2); instr's manual o.p. 23.50 o.p. (ISBN 0-686-77078-1, 1448). Healthcare Fin Man Assn.

Principles of Industrial Metalworking Processes. G. W. Rowe. 407p. 1977. 69.00x o.p. (ISBN 0-8448-1219-6, Pub. by Crane Russak & Co). Taylor & Francis.

Principles of Industrial Microbiology. A. Rhodes & D. L. Fletcher. 1966. 85.00 o.p. (ISBN 0-08-011906-9); pap. 85.00 o.p. (ISBN 0-08-011905-0). Pergamon.

Principles of Inland Transportation. Stuart Daggett. LC 78-31183. (Illus.). 1979. Repr. of 1955 ed. lib. bdg. 47.50x o.p. (ISBN 0-313-20956-1, DAPI). Greenwood.

Principles of Instructional Design. (Instructor Training Ser.). (Illus.). 330p. 1983. pap. text ed. 49.50 o.p. (ISBN 0-87683-382-2); looseleaf instr's. guide 75.00 o.p. (ISBN 0-87683-045-9). GP Pub.

Principles of Insurance. 8th ed. Robert I. Mehr et al. 1985. 40.95x o.p. (ISBN 0-256-03008-1). Irwin.

Principles of Insurance. 2nd ed. George E. Rejda. 1986. text ed. write for info. o.p. (ISBN 0-673-18209-6). Scott F.

Principles of Interpretation in Echocardiography. Pamela Harrigan. LC 84-13198. 373p. 1985. 65.00 o.p. (ISBN 0-471-87952-5, Pub. by Wiley Med). Wiley.

Principles of Investment. 3rd ed. Frederick Amling. (Plaid Ser.). 198p. 1983. pap. 12.95 o.p. (ISBN 0-87094-336-7). Dow Jones-Irwin.

Principles of Jewish Law. Ed. by Menachem Elon. 866p. 1975. 50.00 o.p. (ISBN 0-87855-188-3). Transaction Pubs.

Principles of Language & Mind: An Evolutionary Theory of Meaning. T. P. Waldron. 224p. 1985. 29.95x o.p. (ISBN 0-7102-0323-3). Routledge Chapman & Hall.

Principles of Lasers. 2nd ed. Orazio Svelto. Tr. by David C. Hanna from Ital. LC 82-484. 392p. 1982. 35.00x o.p. (ISBN 0-306-40862-7, Plenum Pr). Plenum Pub.

Principles of Learning: From Laboratory to Field. Douglas J. Navarick. LC 78-62546. 448p. 1979. text ed. 20.00 o.p. (ISBN 0-394-34774-9, RanC). Random.

Principles of Legislation: The Uses of Political Authority. Michael D. Bayles. LC 78-3220. 280p. 1978. 27.50x o.p. (ISBN 0-8143-1599-2). Wayne St U Pr.

Principles of Leisure Counseling. Larry C. Loesch & Paul T. Wheeler. Ed. by Don L. Sorenson. LC 8-82902. 280p. (Orig.). 1982. pap. text ed. 10.95x o.p. (ISBN 0-932796-10-9). Ed Media Corp.

Principles of Life & Health Insurance. Gene Morton. Ed. by Dani Long. LC 83-83153. (FLMI Insurance Education Program Ser.). 1984. text ed. 15.00 o.p. (ISBN 0-915322-58-7). LOMA.

Principles of Life Insurance, Vol. 1. rev. ed. Janice E. Greider & William T. Beadles. 1973. pap. 13.95x o.p. (ISBN 0-256-01396-9). Irwin.

Principles of Logic. Josiah Royce. LC 61-15247. 1965. (ISBN 0-8022-1402-9). Philos Lib.

Principles of Machining by Cutting, Abrasion & Erosion. J. Kaczmerek. 551p. 1976. casebound 79.00 o.p. (ISBN 0-901223-66-2, NS005). Inst Elect Eng.

Principles of Macroeconomics. Edwin Mansfield. 400p. 1974. pap. text ed. 6.75x o.p. (ISBN 0-393-09275-5). Norton.

Principles of Macroeconomics. 4th ed. Edwin Mansfield. 600p. 1982. text ed. 18.95x o.p. (ISBN 0-393-95266-5). Norton.

Principles of Macroeconomics. 2nd ed. Ed. by Edwin Mansfield. Incl. Reading, Issues, & Cases. 1974. pap. text ed. 3.25x o.p. (ISBN 0-393-09271-2). 1977. pap. text ed. 4.95x o.p. (ISBN 0-393-09108-2). Norton.

Principles of Macroeconomics. 2nd ed. Roy Ruffin & Paul Gregory. 1986. pap. write for info. o.p. (ISBN 0-673-18226-6); instr's. manual avail. o.p. Scott F.

Principles of Macroeconomics. Robert H. Scott & Nic Nigro. 502p. 1982. pap. write for info. o.p. (ISBN 0-02-408380-1). Macmillan.

Principles of Macroeconomics: Theory & Practice. Hyman. (Illus.). 672p. 1989. pap. text ed. 26.95 o.p. (ISBN 0-8016-2422-3). Mosby.

Principles of Magnesium Technology. E. F. Emley. 1966. 165.00 o.p. (ISBN 0-08-010673-0). Pergamon.

Principles of Metal Surface Treatment & Protection. 2nd ed. D. R. Gabe. (International Series on Materials Science & Technology: Vol. 28). (Illus.). 1978. 55.00 o.p. (ISBN 0-08-022703-1); pap. text ed. 55.00 o.p. (ISBN 0-08-022707-4). Pergamon.

Principles of Microeconomics. Edwin Mansfield. 400p. 1974. pap. text ed. 6.75x o.p. (ISBN 0-393-09265-8). Norton.

Principles of Microeconomics. 2nd ed. Edwin Mansfield. (Illus.). 1977. pap. text ed. 9.95x o.p. (ISBN 0-393-09113-9). Norton.

Principles of Microeconomics. 4th ed. Edwin Mansfield. 1982. 18.95x o.p. (ISBN 0-393-95267-3). Norton.

Principles of Microeconomics. 2nd ed. Roy Ruffin & Paul Gregory. 1986. pap. text ed. write for info. o.p. (ISBN 0-673-18227-4); instr's. manual avail. o.p. Scott F.

Principles of Microeconomics: Theory & Practice. Hyman. (Illus.). 720p. 1989. pap. text ed. 26.95 o.p (ISBN 0-8016-2421-5). Mosby.

Principles of Modern Marketing. Stewart W. Husted et al. 752p. 1988. text ed. write for info. o.p. (ISBN 0-697-00538-0). Wm C Brown.

Principles of Modern Soccer. George Beim. LC 76-11986. (Illus.). 1977. text ed. 24.50 o.p. (ISBN 0-395-24415-3). HM.

Principles of Moral & Political Philosophy. William Paley. Ed. by Rene Wellek. LC 75-11246. (British Philosophers & Theologians of the 17th & 18th Centuries Ser.: Vol. 45). 1977. Repr. of 1785 ed. lib. bdg. 51.00 o.p. (ISBN 0-8240-1797-8). Garland Pub.

Principles of Mossbauer Spectroscopy. Terence C. Gibb. 254p. 1976. 43.00x o.p. (ISBN 0-412-13960-X, NO. 6123, Pub. by Chapman & Hall England); pap. 19.95x o.p. (ISBN 0-412-23060-7, NO. 6586, Pub. by Chapman & Hall England). Routledge Chapman & Hall.

Principles of Musik, in Singing & Setting. Charles Butler. LC 68-13273. (Music Ser.). 1970. Repr. of 1636 ed. lib. bdg. 23.50 o.p. (ISBN 0-306-70939-2). Da Capo.

Principles of Neurotransmission: Proceedings of the International Symposium of the Austrian Society for Electron Microscopy, Vienna, Nov. 30, 1973. Austrian Society for Electron Microscopy Staff. Ed. by L. Stockinger. LC 75-2395. (Journal of Neural Transmission Ser.: Suppl. 12). (Illus.). vii, 151p. 1975. 52.60 o.p. (ISBN 0-387-81277-6). Springer-Verlag.

Principles of Nuclear Radiation Detection. G. G. Eichholz & J. W. Poston. LC 85-19720. (Illus.). 379p. 1985. 39.95 o.p. (ISBN 0-87371-062-2). Lewis Pubs Inc.

Principles of Oil Well Production. 2nd ed. T. E. Nind. (Illus.). 384p. 1981. text ed. 54.00 o.p. (ISBN 0-07-046576-2). McGraw.

Principles of Oral Surgery. J. R. Moore. (Pergamon Series on Dentistry: Vol. 3). 1965. 65.00 o.p. (ISBN 0-08-011395-8). Pergamon.

Principles of Orchestration: With Musical Examples Drawn from His Own Works, 2 Vols. in 1. Nikolay Rimsky-Korsakov. Ed. by Maximilian Steinberg. 15.50 o.p. (ISBN 0-8446-2813-1). Peter Smith.

Principles of Organic Chemistry. 4th ed. James English, Jr. et al. 1901. text ed. 37.95 o.p. (ISBN 0-07-019520-X). McGraw.

Principles of Organometallic Chemistry. G. E. Coates et al. 1968. 18.95 o.p. (ISBN 0-412-15350-5, NO. 6062, Pub. by Chapman & Hall). Routledge Chapman & Hall.

Principles of Pathology. 2nd ed. A. Reese. 280p. 1981. pap. 20.00 o.p. (ISBN 0-7236-0603-X). Butterworth.

Principles of Pathology in Surgery. K. A. Myers et al. (Illus.). 466p. 1981. pap. text ed. 34.75 o.p. (ISBN 0-632-00413-4, B-3612-4). Mosby.

Principles of Pediatrics Patient Management Cases Pre-Test Self-Assessment. Robert A. Hoekelman. 234p. 1981. text ed. 35.00 o.p. (ISBN 0-07-051653-7). McGraw.

Principles of Personal Defense. Jeff Cooper. 30p. 1972. pap. 5.00 o.s.i. (ISBN 0-87364-001-2). Paladin Pr.

Principles of Personnel Management. 4th ed. Edwin B. Flippo. 1976. text ed. 34.95 o.p. (ISBN 0-07-021316-X, C). McGraw.

Principles of Pharmaceutical Marketing. 3rd ed. Ed. by Mickey C. Smith. LC 82-6624. (Illus.). 529p. 1983. text ed. 29.75 o.p. (ISBN 0-8121-0858-2). Lea & Febiger.

Principles of Physical & Chemical Metallurgy. Giles F. Carter. 1979. 63.00 o.p. (ISBN 0-87170-080-8). ASM.

Principles of Physical Geography. F. J. Monkhouse. (Illus.). 511p. 1964. (ISBN 0-8022-1140-2). Philos Lib.

Principles of Physical Security. Donald Schultz. LC 77-86192. 168p. 1978. 19.00x o.s.i. (ISBN 0-87201-748-6). Gulf Pub.

Principles of Physics. James P. Hurley & Claude Garrod. LC 77-75475. (Illus.). 1978. text ed. 36.95 o.p. (ISBN 0-395-25036-6). HM.

Principles of Physics. Jerry B. Marion & William F. Hornyak. LC 83-7709. 772p. 1984. text ed. 39.95x o.s.i. (ISBN 0-03-049481-8). SCP.

Principles of Plant & Animal Pest Control, Vol. 1, Plant-Disease Development & Control. National Research Council. 1968. pap. 7.00x o.p. (ISBN 0-309-01596-0). Natl Acad Pr.

Principles of Plant & Animal Pest Control, Vol. 2, Weed Control. National Research Council. 1968. pap. 11.50x o.p. (ISBN 0-309-01597-9). Natl Acad Pr.

Principles of Plant & Animal Pest Control, Vol. 6: Effects of Pesticides on Fruit & Vegetable Physiology. National Research Council. 1968. pap. 5.95x o.p. (ISBN 0-309-01698-3). Natl Acad Pr.

Principles of Political Economy, Applied to the Condition, the Resources, & the Institutions of the American People. Francis Bowen. (Neglected American Economists Ser.). 1974. lib. bdg. 61.00 o.p. (ISBN 0-8240-1011-6). Garland Pub.

Principles of Polymer Systems. 2nd ed. F. Rodriguez. 1982. text ed. 56.95 o.p. (ISBN 0-07-053382-2). McGraw.

Principles of Population Genetics. Daniel L. Hartl. LC 79-28384. (Illus.). 225p. 1980. text ed. 32.95x o.p. (ISBN 0-87893-272-0). Sinauer Assocs.

Principles of Powder Metallurgy. Franz Skaupy. (ISBN 0-8022-1582-3). Philos Lib.

Principles of Power: The Great Political Crises of History. Guglielmo Ferrero. LC 84-12765. ix, 333p. 1984. Repr. of 1942 ed. lib. bdg. 41.50x o.p. (ISBN 0-313-24570-3, FEPP). Greenwood.

Principles of Preaching. Robert F. Morneau. 1983. pap. 6.95 o.p. (ISBN 0-941850-11-0). Liturgical Pubns.

Principles of Programming Languages. Bruce J. MacLennan. 1983. text ed. 38.95 o.p. (ISBN 0-03-061711-1). HR&W.

Principles of Prosecution: A Guide for the Anatomic Pathologist. K. Kendall Pierson. LC 80-12400. 252p. Repr. of 1980 ed. 32.50 o.p. (ISBN 0-471-05811-4, JW). Krieger.

Principles of Psychological Measurement. Elmer Lemke & William Wiersma. LC 80-80803. 380p. 1976. text ed. 34.50 o.p. (ISBN 0-395-30821-6). HM.

Principles of Psychology, Vol. III. William James. LC 81-4194. (Works of William James). 480p. 1981. text ed. 27.50x o.p. (ISBN 0-674-70555-6). Harvard U Pr.

Principles of Psychology. Richard H. Price et al. 1982. text ed. 33.95 o.p. (ISBN 0-03-048411-1). HR&W.

Principles of Quantum Chemistry. D. V. George. 280p. 1973. 70.00 o.p. (ISBN 0-08-016925-2). Pergamon.

Principles of Radionuclide Emission Imaging. Ed. by D. E. Kuhl. 318p. 1983. 34.00 o.p. (ISBN 0-08-027093-X). Pergamon.

Principles of Random Walk. 2nd ed. LC 75-26883. (Graduate Texts in Mathematics Ser.: Vol. 34). 425p. 1976. 30.95 o.p. (ISBN 0-387-90150-7). Springer-Verlag.

Principles of Real Estate. Paul T. O'Donnell & Eugene L. Maleady. LC 75-14863. 610p. 1975. pap. text ed. 28.95 o.p. (ISBN 0-7216-6911-5). HR&W.

Principles of Real Estate Analysis. Michael J. Crean. LC 78-62189. 474p. 1979. text ed. 18.95x o.p. (ISBN 0-442-21249-6). PWS-Kent Pub.

Principles of Real Estate Law. Philip B. Bergfield. (Illus.). 1979. text ed. 38.95 o.p. (ISBN 0-07-004890-8). McGraw.

Principles of Self Damage. Edmund Bergler. 480p. 1959. (ISBN 0-8022-0105-9). Philos Lib.

Principles of Sentencing: The Sentencing Policy of the Court of Appeal, Criminal Division. 2nd ed. David A. Thomas. LC 79-315920. (Cambridge Studies in Criminology). 1979. pap. text ed. 24.00 o.p. (ISBN 0-435-82882-7). Gower Pub Co.

Principles of Shakespearian Production with Special Reference to the Tragedies. George W. Knight. Repr. of 1936 ed. 39.00x o.p. (ISBN 0-403-04222-4). Somerset Pub.

Principles of Social Psychology. 2nd ed. Kelley G. Shaver. 1981. text ed. 21.95 o.p. (ISBN 0-316-78329-3). Little.

Principles of Sociology, 3 vols. Herbert Spencer. LC 74-16259. 1975. Repr. Set. lib. bdg. 90.00x o.p. (ISBN 0-8371-4103-6, SPPS). Greenwood.

Principles of Solar Engineering. Frank Kreith & Jan F. Kreider. LC 77-27861. (McGraw-Hill - Hemisphere Thermal & Fluids Engineering Ser.). (Illus.). 1978. text ed. 50.95 o.p. (ISBN 0-07-035476-6). McGraw.

Principles of Solid State Power Conversion. Ralph E. Tarter. 44.95 o.p. (ISBN 0-672-22018-0, 22018). Sams.

Principles of Spaceflight Propulsion. E. M. Goodger. LC 77-88306. 1970. 50.00 o.p. (ISBN 0-08-013884-5). Pergamon.

Principles of Speech Communication. 9th ed. Douglas Ehninger & Bruce E. Gronbeck. 1984. pap. text ed. write for info. o.p. (ISBN 0-673-15877-2). Scott F.

Principles of Statistics & Econometrics. Thad W. Mirer. 560p. 1983. text ed. write for info. o.p. (ISBN 0-02-381810-7). Macmillan.

Principles of Surgery. 2nd ed. D. J. DuPlessis. 192p. 1976. pap. text ed. 18.00 o.p. (ISBN 0-7236-0445-2, Pub. by John Wright UK). Butterworth.

Principles of Surgery, 2 Vol. Set. 4th ed. Ed. by Seymour I. Schwartz et al. (Illus.). 2256p. 1984. text ed. 110.00 o.p. (ISBN 0-07-079819-2). McGraw.

Principles of Surgery. 4th ed. Ed. by Seymour I. Schwartz et al. (Illus.). 2256p. 1984. text ed. 92.00 o.p. (ISBN 0-07-055795-0). McGraw.

Principles of Surgical Oncology. Ed. by Ronald W. Raven. LC 77-1804. (Illus.). 520p. 1977. 75.00x o.p. (ISBN 0-306-30979-3, Plenum Med. Bk.). Plenum Pub.

Principles of Survey. 4th ed. Olliver. 1978. pap. 26.95 o.p. (ISBN 0-442-30222-3). Van Nos Reinhold.

Principles of Systematic Zoology. Ernst Mayr. LC 68-54937. (Illus.). 1969. text ed. 54.95 o.p. (ISBN 0-07-041143-3). McGraw.

Principles of Teaching. rev. ed. Harold Spears. LC 72-106671. (Illus.). 339p. 1974. Repr. of 1951 ed. lib. bdg. 22.50x o.p. (ISBN 0-8371-3374-2, SPPT). Greenwood.

Principles of the In-Finite Philosophy. Jefferson C. Barnhart. 1955. (ISBN 0-8022-0066-4). Philos Lib.

Principles of the Theory of the Historical Process in Philosophy. T. I. Oizerman & A. S. Bogomolov. 348p. 1986. 9.95 o.p. (ISBN 0-8285-3188-9, Pub. by Progress Pubs USSR). Imported Pubns.

Principles of the Use of Radioisotope Tracers in Clinical & Research Investigations. Ray Oliver. 1971. pap. text ed. 10.75 o.p. (ISBN 0-08-015718-1). Pergamon.

Principles of Training. D. H. Holding. 1965. text ed. 15.50 o.p. (ISBN 0-08-011162-9); pap. text ed. 8.50 o.p. (ISBN 0-08-011161-0). Pergamon.

Principles of Tunnel Diode Circuits. W. F. Chow. LC 64-20080. 387p. 1964. text ed. 26.50 o.p. (ISBN 0-471-15615-9, Pub. by Wiley). Krieger.

Principles of Turbomachinery. R. K. Turton. 200p. (Orig.). 1984. text ed. 39.95 o.p. (ISBN 0-419-12490-X, 9111, Pub. by E & FN Spon England); pap. text ed. 17.95 o.p. (ISBN 0-419-12500-0, 9173, Pub. by E & FN Spon England). Routledge Chapman & Hall.

Principles of Wheel Alignment Service: A Text-Workbook. 2nd ed. E. M. Bacon. LC 76-29363. (Illus.). 1977. text ed. 29.95 o.p. (ISBN 0-07-002855-9). McGraw.

Principles of Zoophysiology, Vol. 1. B. Rybak. 1969. 120.00 o.p. (ISBN 0-08-012158-6). Pergamon.

Print Collector's Handbook. Alfred Whitman. LC 72-177279. (Tower Bks). (Illus.). xii, 164p. 1972. Repr. of 1901 ed. 42.00x o.p. (ISBN 0-8103-3938-2). Gale.

Print Collector's Quarterly: An Anthology of Essays on Eminent Printmakers of the World, 10 vols. Ed. by Lauris Mason & Joan Ludman. LC 77-161. (Illus.). 1977. lib. bdg. 840.00 set o.p. (ISBN 0-527-62205-2). Kraus Intl.

Print in Germany. Frances Carey & Antong Griffiths. 272p. 1985. pap. write for info. o.p. (ISBN 0-8419-1025-1). Holmes & Meier.

Printcrafts for Fun & Profit. Seymour Fleishman. Ed. by Caroline Rubin. LC 76-78907. (Albert Whitman How-to Ser.). (Illus.). (gr. 3-6). 1977. PLB 10.25 o.p. (ISBN 0-8075-6633-0). A Whitman.

Printed Circuit Board Industry: A Strategic Analysis. Business Communications Staff. 117p. 1985. pap. 1750.00 o.p. (ISBN 0-89336-451-7, GO67R). BCC.

Printed Circuits Handbook. Clyde F. Coombs. 1979. text ed. 64.95 o.p. (ISBN 0-07-012608-9). McGraw.

Printed Textiles: A Guide to Creative Design Fundamentals. Terry Gentille. LC 87-26098. 144p. (Orig.). 1988. pap. 14.95 o.p. (ISBN 0-937274-37-2, Dist. by Sterling). Lark Bks.

Printed Textiles: Seventeen Sixty to Eighteen Sixty. Gillian Moss. Ed. by Nancy Aakre. (Collection Handbk Ser.). (Illus.). 32p. (Orig.). 1987. pap. text ed. 3.95 o.p. (ISBN 0-910503-57-5). Cooper-Hewitt Museum.

Printers & Technology. Elizabeth Baker. LC 74-12847. (Illus.). 545p. 1974. Repr. of 1957 ed. lib. bdg. 35.00x o.p. (ISBN 0-8371-7763-4, BAPT). Greenwood.

Printers Arithmetic. F. C. Avis. 150p. 1957. (ISBN 0-8022-0048-6). Philos Lib.

Printer's Guide: Or, an Introduction to the Art of Printing Including an Essay on Punctuation & Remarks on Orthography. Cornelius S. van Winkle. LC 78-74408. (Nineteenth Century Book Arts & Printing Ser.). 290p. 1980. lib. bdg. 33.00 o.p. (ISBN 0-8240-3892-4). Garland Pub.

Printer's Manual, a Practical Guide for Compositors & Pressmen. Thomas Lynch. LC 78-74410. (Nineteenth Century Book Arts & Printing). 270p. 1980. lib. bdg. 33.00 o.p. (ISBN 0-8240-3894-0). Garland Pub.

Printer's Manual, an Abridgement of Stower's Grammar, Comprising All the Plans in That Work for Imposing Forms, Several Tables & Other Useful Articles. Caleb Stower. LC 78-74405. (Nineteenth Century Book Arts & Printing Ser.). 200p. 1980. lib. bdg. 26.00 o.p. (ISBN 0-8240-3891-6). Garland Pub.

Printer's Terms Dictionary. R. Hostettler. (Illus., Eng., Fr., Ger., Ital. & Dutch.). 1983. price not set o.s.i. (ISBN 0-685-12041-4). E J Brill USA.

Printers' Vocabulary. Charles T. Jacobi. LC 68-30613. 176p. 1975. Repr. of 1888 ed. 35.00x o.p. (ISBN 0-8103-3309-0). Gale.

Printing & Embroidery. Mary Newland & Carol Walklin. 1977. 20.95 o.p. (ISBN 0-7134-0136-2, Pub. by Batsford England). David & Charles.

Printing Arts in Texas. Al Lowman. (Illus.). 1975. 150.00 o.p. (ISBN 0-911796-03-7). Beacham.

Printing Calculator: Student Guide. 2nd ed. Charlotte Butsch. 1971. pap. text ed. 3.85 o.p. (ISBN 0-89420-022-4, 126855); cassette recordings 50.20 o.p. (ISBN 0-89420-174-3, 156760). Natl Book.

Printing Color Negatives (E-66) rev. ed. Eastman Kodak Company Staff. (Illus.). 72p. 1982. pap. 8.95 o.p. (ISBN 0-87985-322-0). Eastman Kodak.

Printing Ink Manual. 3rd ed. Ed. by D. E. Bissett et al. R. H. Leach & C. H. Williams. (Illus.). 480p. 1979. 52.95 o.p. (ISBN 0-442-30600-8). Van Nos Reinhold.

Printing Technology. 2nd ed. J. Michael Adams & David D. Faux. LC 81-81070. 611p. 1982. text ed. 30.95 o.p. (ISBN 0-8273-2616-5). 12.00 o.p. (ISBN 0-8273-2617-3). Delmar.

Printing Trades Blue Book: 1986-1987 Northeastern Edition. rev. ed. 700p. pap. 70.00 o.p. (ISBN 0-910880-28-X). Lewis.

Printing Unwins. Philip Unwin. (Illus.). 159p. 1976. 17.00 o.p. (ISBN 0-913720-14-3, Sandstone). Beil.

Prints of Reginald Marsh. Norman Sasowsky. 287p. 1976. 75.00 o.s.i. (ISBN 0-686-87740-3). A Wofsy Fine Arts.

Prints of Rockwell Kent. Dan B. Jones. 219p. 1975. 75.00 o.s.i. (ISBN 0-686-87739-X). A Wofsy Fine Arts.

Prior Betrothal. Elsie Lee. LC 73-82183. 1973. 6.95 o.p. (ISBN 0-87795-066-0, Arbor Hse). Morrow.

Prior Consent & Nuclear Cooperation. Myron B. Kratzer. (Technical & Economic Reports: Proliferation & Safeguards). 1983. 50.00 o.p. (ISBN 0-318-02239-7). US Coun Energy Awareness.

Priorities for Academic Libraries. Ed. by Thomas J. Galvin & Beverly P. Lynch. LC 81-48572. (Higher Education Ser.: No. 39). 1982. 11.95x o.p. (ISBN 0-87589-897-1). Jossey-Bass.

Priority Concerns of Five Groups Involved in Experiential Education Programs. Lester F. Jipp & Richard J. Miguel. 81p. 1980. 5.50 o.p. (ISBN 0-318-15538-9, RD195). Natl Ctr Res Voc Ed.

Priority Queues. N. K. Jaiswal. (Mathematics in Science & Engineering Ser.: Vol. 50). 1968. 77.00 o.p. (ISBN 0-12-380050-1). Acad Pr.

Prise De Cordres et De Sebille. 1896. 38.00 o.p. (ISBN 0-384-47941-3); pap. 32.00 o.p. (ISBN 0-384-47931-6). Johnson Repr.

Prisling. Susan Eastwood. 1977. pap. 1.00 o.p. (ISBN 0-931832-07-1). Fithian Pr.

Prison & a Prisoner. Susan Sheehan. 1978. 10.95 o.p. (ISBN 0-395-26684-X). HM.

Prison & the Prisoner. Dorothy C. Tompkins. LC 73-39480. (Public Policy Bibliographies: No. 1). 156p. (Orig.). 1972. pap. 4.00x o.p. (ISBN 0-87772-140-8). UCB IGS.

Prison Before Trial. A. Keith Bottomley. 117p. 1970. pap. text ed. 5.00 o.p. (ISBN 0-7135-1816-2, Pub. by Bedford England). Gower Pub Co.

Prison-Breakers: A Book of Escapes from Captivity. Alban M. Phillip. LC 76-174093. (Illus.). 296p. 1971. Repr. of 1927 ed. 40.00x o.p. (ISBN 0-8103-3803-3). Gale.

Prison Homosexuality: Myth & Reality. Alice M. Propper. LC 79-48003. 256p. 1981. 27.50x o.p. (ISBN 0-669-03628-5). Lexington Bks.

Prison Letters. Corrie Ten Boom. 1975. 3.95 o.p. (ISBN 0-87508-027-8). Chr Lit.

Prison Life & Reflections. George Thompson. LC 75-75556. 1970. Repr. of 1847 ed. lib. bdg. 25.00 o.p. (ISBN 0-8371-1130-7, THP&). Greenwood.

Prison Reform. Charles R. Henderson. (Russell Sage Foundation Reprint Ser.). (Illus.). 1986. pap. text ed. 6.95x o.p. (ISBN 0-8290-1891-3). Irvington.

Prisoner & Yet. Corrie Ten Boom. (Orig.). 1982. pap. 2.50 o.s.i. (ISBN 0-515-06736-9). Jove Pubns.

Prisoner of Blackwood Castle. Ron Goulart. 176p. 1984. pap. 2.50 o.p. (ISBN 0-380-88005-9, 88005-9). Avon.

Prisoner of Martial Law: Camp Journal-Poland, 1981-1982. Jan Mur. Tr. by Lillian Vallee. (Illus.). 224p. 1984. 19.95 o.p. (ISBN 0-15-173088-1). HarBraceJ.

Prisoner of War Resistance. U. S. Army Staff. (Illus.). 112p. 1985. pap. 12.00 o.p. (ISBN 0-87364-348-8). Paladin Pr.

Prisoner of Zenda. pap. 1.95x o.p. (ISBN 0-460-01637-7, Pub. by Evman England). Biblio Dist.

Prisoners of Culture. George A. Pettitt. LC 68-57070. 1970. 8.50 o.s.i. (ISBN 0-684-31100-3, ScribT). Scribner.

Prisoners of Psychiatry. Bruce Ennis. LC 72-79923. 252p. 1972. 7.95 o.p. (ISBN 0-15-173084-9). HarBraceJ.

Prisoners of Psychiatry. Bruce J. Ennis. 1974. pap. 1.65 o.p. (ISBN 0-380-00021-0, 19299, Discus). Avon.

Prisoner's Plaint. June A. Simpson. LC 82-90657. 1985. 7.95 o.p. (ISBN 0-533-05569-5). Vantage.

Prisoners Rights Nineteen Seventy-Nine, 2 vols. Alvin J. Bronstein & Philip J. Hirschkop. (Litigation & Administrative Practice Course Handbook Ser. 1978-79: Vols. 105 & 106). 1979. pap. 45.00 o.p. (ISBN 0-685-94312-7, C6-4133). PLI.

Prisons. Mary L. Settle. 244p. 1981. pap. 3.50 o.s.i. (ISBN 0-345-29312-6). Ballantine.

Prisons, Education & Work: Towards a National Employment Strategy for Prisoners. John Braithwaite. (Illus.). 240p. 1980. text ed. 12.95 o.p. (ISBN 0-7022-1524-4). U of Queensland Pr.

Prisons for Women: A Practical Guide to Administration Problems. Joy S. Eyman. 200p. 1971. 21.75x o.p. (ISBN 0-398-00537-0). C C Thomas.

Prisons in Transformation: Proceedings. American Academy of Political & Social Science, Philadelphia Staff. Ed. by Thorsten Sellin. LC 79-90462. 227p. 1974. Repr. of 1954 ed. lib. bdg. 35.00x o.p. (ISBN 0-8371-6170-3, PRIT). Greenwood.

Pritikin Promise: Twenty-Eight Days to a Longer, Healthier Life. Nathan Pritikin. 448p. 1983. 20.45 o.p. (ISBN 0-671-49447-3). S&S.

Privacy & Confidentiality of Health Care Information. Jo Anne Czecowski Bruce. LC 84-9231. (Illus.). 168p. (Orig.). 1984. pap. 27.50 o.p. (ISBN 0-939450-06-2, 148171). AHPI.

Privacy Issues: A Bibliographic Update. Anthony G. White. 1987. pap. 3.75 o.p. (ISBN 1-55590-286-3). Vance Biblios.

Privacy: The Right to Be Let Alone. Morris L. Ernst & Alan U. Schwartz. LC 77-10983. (Milestones of Law Ser.). 1977. Repr. of 1962 ed. lib. bdg. 22.50x o.p. (ISBN 0-8371-9805-4, ERPR). Greenwood.

Private Accounts. Ursula Bentley. 256p. 1988. 18.95 o.p. (ISBN 0-436-04021-2, Pub. by Secker & Warburg UK). David & Charles.

Private Affairs. Judith Michael. 520p. 1986. 18.45 o.s.i. (ISBN 0-671-54102-1, Poseidon). S&S.

Private Aviation: A Guide to Information Sources. Ed. by Floyd N. Reister. LC 79-84660. (Sports, Games, & Pastimes Information Guide Ser.: Vol. 3). 160p. 1979. 68.00x o.p. (ISBN 0-8103-1440-1). Gale.

Private Bank Lending to Developing Countries. Richard O'Brien. (Working Paper: No. 482). vi, 54p. 1981. pap. 5.00 o.p. (ISBN 0-686-39746-0, WP-0482). World Bank.

Private Battle. Cornelius Ryan & Kathryn M. Ryan. 1979. 12.95 o.p. (ISBN 0-671-22594-4). S&S.

Private Capital Flows to Developing Countries & Their Determinations: Historical Perspective, Recent Experience, & Future Prospects. Alex Fleming. (Working Paper: No. 484). 484p. 1981. pap. 3.50 o.p. (ISBN 0-686-39747-9, WP-0484). World Bank.

Private Consultants & Municipalities: A Selected Checklist. Jamie W. Coniglio. (Public Administration Ser.: P 1774). 3p. 1985. 2.00 o.p. (ISBN 0-89028-574-8). Vance Biblios.

Private Consulting: How to Turn Experience into Employment Dollars. Barbara Johnson. (Illus.). 147p. 1982. 13.95 o.p. (ISBN 0-13-710889-3); pap. 7.95 o.p. (ISBN 0-13-710871-0). P-H.

Private Cosmos. Philip Jose Farmer. 288p. 1981. pap. 2.50 o.s.i. (ISBN 0-441-67954-4). Ace Bks.

Private Enterprise in Developing Countries. W. M. Clarke. 1969. pap. 5.50 o.p. (ISBN 0-08-012142-X). Pergamon.

Private Eye in Hammett & Chandler. Robert B. Parker. 75p. 1984. Limited signed ed. 50.00 o.p. (ISBN 0-935716-24-6). Lord John.

Private Franklin: The Man & His Family. Claude-Anne Lopez & Eugenia W. Herbert. (Illus.). 361p. 1975. 11.95 o.p. (ISBN 0-393-07496-X). Norton.

Private Independent Schools: The Bunting & Lyon Blue Book, 1988. 41st ed. 1988. 65.00x o.p. (ISBN 0-913094-41-2). Bunting.

Private International Investment: An Exercise in Theory & Policy. rev. ed. Robert R. Miller & John Kilpatrick. (CISE Learning Packages on International Studies). 56p. pap. text ed. 3.00x o.p. (ISBN 0-317-34810-8). LRIS.

Private Investors Index. Matthew Bender Publishers Staff. 1983. write for info. o.p. (#662). Bender.

Private Justice: Towards Integrative Theorising in the Sociology of Law. Stuart Henry. LC 83-10926. 245p. (Orig.). 1984. pap. 14.95x o.p. (ISBN 0-7100-9703-4). Routledge Chapman & Hall.

Private Landlords in England. John Greve. 54p. 1965. pap. text ed. 3.75x o.p. (ISBN 0-686-70855-5, Pub. by Bedford England). Gower Pub Co.

Private Law Library in the High-Tech Era. Jean Strohofer & Marie Wallce. Ed. by Practising Law Institute Staff. LC 83-220469. (Commercial Law & Practice Course Handbook Ser.: No. 308). (Illus.). 288p. 1983. 45.00 o.p. (A4-4068). PLI.

Private Letters from an American in England to His Friends in America, 1769. (Novel in England, 1700-1775 Ser). 1974. lib. bdg. 61.00 o.p. (ISBN 0-8240-1186-4). Garland Pub.

Private Life. Cynthia P. Seton. 192p. 1982. 10.95 o.p. (ISBN 0-393-01515-7). Norton.

Private Life & Public Order. Ed. by Theodore J. Lowi. (Problems of Modern Government Ser.). 1968. pap. 4.95x o.p. (ISBN 0-393-09727-7, NortonC). Norton.

Private Life of Florence Nightingale. Richard Gordon. LC 78-56342. 1979. 9.95 o.p. (ISBN 0-689-10929-6, Atheneum). Macmillan.

Private Life of Henry VIII. Lajos Biro & Arthur Wimperis. Ed. by Bruce S. Kupelnick. LC 76-52090. (Classics of Film Literature Ser.). 1978. lib. bdg. 22.00 o.p. (ISBN 0-8240-2866-X). Garland Pub.

Private Life of the Queen. 256p. 1984. 27.00x o.p. (ISBN 0-905418-66-2, Pub. by Gresham England). State Mutual Bk.

Private Life of the Rabbit. R. M. Lockley. (Illus.). 1975. pap. 3.95 o.p. (ISBN 0-380-00447-X, 38224). Avon.

Private Lives & Public Accounts. Thomas J. Cottle. 1978. pap. 4.95 o.p. (ISBN 0-531-05614-7). Watts.

Private Matter. Kathryn Ewing. LC 74-23673. (gr. 4-8). 1975. 7.95 o.p. (ISBN 0-15-263576-9, HJ). HarBraceJ.

Private Memoirs & Confessions of a Justified Sinner. James Hogg. 1970. pap. 4.95x o.p. (ISBN 0-393-00515-1, Norton Lib). Norton.

Private Mythology. May A. Sarton. (Orig.). 1966. 4.00 o.p. (ISBN 0-393-04175-1). Norton.

Private Parties. Jonathan Penner. 176p. 1985. pap. 3.95 o.p. (ISBN 0-380-69846-3, Bard). Avon.

Private Pilot: Airplane. Dale Crane. (Capstan Guide, Fast-Track Method Ser.). (Illus.). 176p. (Orig.). 1985. pap. text ed. 8.95 o.p. (ISBN 0-914565-06-0). Av Suppl & Acad.

Private Pilot-Airplane Written Test Guide. rev. ed. Federal Aviation Administration Staff. 148p. 1979. pap. text ed. 3.50 o.p. (ISBN 0-939158-08-6). Flightshops.

Private Pilot-Practical Test Standards-ASMEL. rev. ed. Federal Aviation Administration Staff. 92p. 1975. pap. text ed. 3.95 o.p. (ISBN 0-939158-09-4). Flightshops.

Private Pilot Question Book. (FAA-T-8080-1A). (Illus.). 120p. 1986. pap. 7.50 o.p. (ISBN 0-318-20389-8, S/N 050-007-00718-3). USGPO.

Private Pilot's License Program. Ben P. Mellspaugh. (Illus.). 192p. 1985. vinyl 19.95 o.p. (ISBN 0-8306-2371-X, 2371). Tab Bks.

Private Placement of Securities: Cumulative Supplement 1986. Jack H. Halperin. (Business Practice Library). 65p. 1986. pap. 30.00 o.p. (ISBN 0-471-00913-X). Wiley.

Private Placements: National & International Markets, 1984. 120.00 o.p. (ISBN 0-8002-3161-9). Intl Pubns Serv.

Private Practice in Britain. Samuel Mencher. 95p. 1967. pap. text ed. 5.00x o.p. (ISBN 0-686-70856-3, Pub. by Bedford England). Gower Pub Co.

Private Prosecution. Eileen Dewhurst. LC 86-32867. (Crime Club Ser.). 192p. 1987. 12.95 o.p. (ISBN 0-385-24146-1). Doubleday.

Private Screening. Richard N. Patterson. 448p. 1986. pap. 3.95 o.s.i. (ISBN 0-345-31139-6). Ballantine.

Private Sector: Rent-a-Cops, Private Spies, & the Police-Industrial Complex. George O'Toole. 1978. 10.95 o.p. (ISBN 0-393-05647-3). Norton.

Private Side of American History: Readings in Everyday Life, 2 vols. Ed. by Gary B. Nash & Thomas R. Frazier. (Illus.). 1975. Vol. 1, To 1877. 9.95 o.p. (ISBN 0-15-571962-9, HC); Vol. 2, Since 1865. 9.95 o.p. (ISBN 0-15-571963-7). HarBraceJ.

Titles

Private Side of American History: Readings in Everyday Life, 2 vols. 3rd ed. Ed. by Gary B. Nash & Thomas R. Frazier. Incl. Vol. 1. To 1877. 430p. 1983. pap. 10.50 o.p. (ISBN 0-15-571966-1); Vol. 2. Since 1865. 427p. 1983. pap. 10.50 o.p. (ISBN 0-15-571967-X). 1983. pap. text ed. 12.95 ea. o.p. (HC). HarBraceJ.

Private-Stock Cookbook. United Airlines Friendship Guild Staff. 410p. (Orig.). 1982. pap. 11.95 o.s.i. (ISBN 0-89716-109-2). Peanut Butter.

Privatisation & Planning in Declining Areas. Stephen Young. 240p. 1987. lib. bdg. 42.00x o.p. (ISBN 0-317-64368-1, Pub. by Croom Helm UK). Routledge Chapman & Hall.

Privatizing the Public Sector: How to Shrink Government. E. S. Savas. LC 82-4207. (Chatham House Series on Change in American Politics). 192p. 1982. 15.00 o.p. (ISBN 0-934540-15-2); pap. text ed. 11.95x o.p. (ISBN 0-934540-14-4). Chatham Hse Pubs.

Privilege & Creative Destruction: The Charles River Bridge Case. Stanley I. Kutler. 1978. pap. 4.95x o.p. (ISBN 0-393-00885-1, Norton Lib). Norton.

Privileged Class: Senior Year at Beverly Hills High School. Michael Leahy. 1988. 17.95 o.p. Little.

Privileged Generation: Children in the Soviet Union. N. Vishneva-Sarafanova. Tr. by Galina Glasgoleva. 214p. 1984. pap. 3.95 o.p. (ISBN 0-8285-2832-2, Pub. by Progress Pubs USSR). Imported Pubns.

Prize Pig Surprise. Lisa C. Ernst. LC 83-26760. (Illus.). 32p. (ps-2). 1984. 10.25 o.p. (ISBN 0-688-03797-6); lib. bdg. 9.55 o.p. (ISBN 0-688-03798-4). Lothrop.

Prize Stories 1986: The O. Henry Awards. William Abrahams. 288p. 1986. pap. 8.95 o.s.i. (ISBN 0-385-23156-3, Anchor Pr). Doubleday.

Prize Stories 1986: The O. Henry Awards. Ed. by William Abrahams. 288p. 1986. 8.95 o.s.i. (ISBN 0-385-23155-5). Doubleday.

Prize Tomatoes Mystery. Thomas F. Pursell. LC 77-74010. (Carolrhoda Mini-Mysteries Ser.). (Illus.). (gr. k-4). 1977. PLB 5.95 o.p. (ISBN 0-87614-089-4). Carolrhoda Bks.

Prize-Winning Recipes. Selma Glasser. 128p. 1984. 9.95 o.p. (ISBN 0-531-09829-X). Watts.

Prize-Winning Stories from China, 1980-1981. Ke Yunlu et al. Tr. by W. C. Chau et al from Chinese. (Illus.). 437p. (Orig.). 1985. pap. 9.95 o.p. (ISBN 0-8351-1313-2). China Bks.

Prizzi's Family. Richard Condon. 1986. 17.95 o.p. (ISBN 0-399-13210-4, Perigee). Putnam Pub Group.

Pro Football: NFL Facts & Statistics. Herman E. Burke. 1986. 15.00 o.p. (ISBN 0-533-06758-8). Vantage.

Pro Sports Champions. Bill Gutman. LC 80-28131. (Illus.). 192p. (gr. 7 up). 1981. lib. bdg. 9.79 o.s.i. (ISBN 0-671-34028-X). Messner.

Pro Techniques of Making Home Video Movies. Thomas I. Ford. LC 85-80600. 160p. 1986. 12.95 o.p. (ISBN 0-89586-300-6). Price Stern.

Pro Techniques of Photographing Children. Erika Stone. LC 86-80359. 128p. 1986. 9.95 o.p. (ISBN 0-89586-390-1). Price Stern.

Proactive Vocational Habilitation. Eric H. Rudrud et al. LC 83-26302. 200p. (Orig.). 1984. pap. text ed. 16.95 o.p. (ISBN 0-933716-38-9, 389). P H Brookes.

Prob Cards Attribute. Date not set. (ISBN 0-07-018480-1). McGraw.

Probabilistic Algorithms. Andrew Yao. (Progress in Computer Science Ser.: No. 8). 280p. 1988. 35.00 o.p. (ISBN 0-8176-3374-X). Birkhauser.

Probabilistic Methods of Signal & System Analysis. George R. Cooper & Clare D. McGillem. LC 73-136170. 1971. text ed. 41.95 o.p. (ISBN 0-03-084291-3). HR&W.

Probabilistic Modeling & Analysis in Science & Engineering. T. T. Soong. LC 80-39804. 384p. 1981. text ed. 45.00 o.p. (ISBN 0-471-08061-6). Wiley.

Probability Algebras & Stochastic Spaces. Demetrios Kappos. LC 70-84234. (Mathematics in Science & Engineering Ser.: Vol. 7). 1969. 80.50 o.p. (ISBN 0-12-397650-2). Acad Pr.

Probability & Certainty in Seventeenth Century England: A Study of the Relationships Between National Science, Religion, History, Law & Literature. Barbara J. Shapiro. LC 82-61385. 360p. 1985. 37.00x o.p. (ISBN 0-691-05379-0); pap. 12.50x o.p. (ISBN 0-691-00790-X). Princeton U Pr.

Probability & Chi Square. 2nd ed. Thomas R. Mertens & Sandra F. Cooper. LC 77-79901. (Programed Biology Ser.). 1974. pap. text ed. 6.95 o.s.i. (ISBN 0-88462-024-7, 3304-21, Ed Methods). Longman Finan.

Probability & Random Variables. G. P. Beaumont. (Mathematics & its Applications Ser.). 1986. 64.95 o.p. (ISBN 0-470-20307-2). Halsted Pr.

Probability & Statistics for Engineers & Scientists. 3rd ed. Ronald E. Walpole & Raymond H. Myers. 650p. 1985. text ed. write for info. o.p. (ISBN 0-02-424170-9). Macmillan.

Probability & Statistics for Engineering & the Physical Sciences. Jay Devore. LC 81-21744. (Statistics Ser.). (Illus.). 700p. 1982. pap. text ed. 32.50 pub net o.p. (ISBN 0-8185-0514-1). Brooks-Cole.

Probability & Stochastic Processes, with a View Toward Applications. Leo Breiman. LC 78-3566. (Illus.). 1969. text ed. 25.95 o.p. (ISBN 0-395-04231-3, 3-05970). HM.

Probability Based on Radon Measures. Tue Tjur. LC 80-40503. (Probability & Mathematical Statistics Ser.). 232p. 1980. 91.95x o.p. (ISBN 0-471-27824-6). Wiley.

Probability in Banach Spaces: Proceedings of the International Conference, First, Oberwolfach, July 20-26, 1975. International Conference on Probability in Banach Spaces Staff. Ed. by A. Beck. (Lecture Notes in Mathematics Ser.: Vol. 526). 1976. soft cover 19.00 o.p. (ISBN 0-387-07793-6). Springer-Verlag.

Probability, Objectivity & Evidence. F. C. Benenson. (International Library of Philosophy). 224p. 1984. 35.00x o.p. (ISBN 0-7100-9598-8). Routledge Chapman & Hall.

Probability, Statistics & Time: A Collection of Essays. M. S. Bartlett. (Monographs on Applied Probability & Statistics). 1975. 17.95x o.p. (ISBN 0-412-14150-7, NO. 6029, Pub. by Chapman & Hall England); pap. 12.95x o.p. (ISBN 0-412-22260-4, NO. 2964). Routledge Chapman & Hall.

Probability Theory & Mathematical Statistics. Pugachev. Tr. by I. V. Sinitsyna. Ed. by P. Eykhoff. 450p. 1984. 115.00 o.p. (ISBN 0-08-029148-1). Pergamon.

Probability Winter School: Proceedings of the Winter School on Probability, 4th, Karpacz, Poland, Jan., 1975. Winter School on Probability Staff et al. (Lecture Notes in Mathematics: 472). 283p. 1975. 19.00 o.p. (ISBN 0-387-07190-3). Springer-Verlag.

Probate Records of S. C. An Index to Inventories, 1746-1785, Vol. 1. Brent Holcomb. 1978. 15.00 o.s.i. (ISBN 0-89308-052-7). Southern Hist Pr.

Probate Records of S. C. Journal of the Court of Ordinary, 1764-1771, Vol. 3. Brent Holcomb. 1979. 20.00 o.s.i. (ISBN 0-89308-149-3). Southern Hist Pr.

Probation & Parole. Rodney J. Henningsen. (Criminal Justice Ser.). 144p. 1981. pap. text ed. 10.95 o.p. (ISBN 0-15-571980-7, HC). HarBraceJ.

Probation & Parole: Crime Control in the Community. John O. Smykla. LC 83-849. 384p. 1984. (ISBN 0-02-413050-8). Macmillan.

Probation & Parole: Legal & Social Dimensions. Louis P. Carney. (Illus.). 1977. text ed. 44.95 o.p. (ISBN 0-07-010126-4). McGraw.

Probation & Social Adjustment. Jay Rumney & Joseph P. Murphy. LC 68-28593. 285p. 1968. Repr. of 1952 ed. lib. bdg. 35.00x o.p. (ISBN 0-8371-0208-1, RUPS). Greenwood.

Probation & the Community: A Practice & Policy Reader. Ed. by John Harding. 240p. 1987. text ed. 39.95 o.p. (ISBN 0-422-79590-9, 1134, Pub. by Tavistock England). Routledge Chapman & Hall.

Probe Probe. Jane D. Mook. (Illus., Orig.). (gr. 3-10). 1970. pap. 1.75 o.p. (ISBN 0-377-62051-3). Friendship Pr.

Proben Deutscher Prosa. Robert Kauf & Daniel C. McCluney. 1970. pap. text ed. 6.95x o.p. (ISBN 0-393-09911-3, NortonC). Norton.

Probes of Structure & Function of Macromolecules & Membranes, 2 Vols. Ed. by Britton Chance et al. 1971. Vol. 1. 82.50 o.p. (ISBN 0-12-167801-6); Vol. 2. 82.50 o.p. (ISBN 0-12-167802-4). Acad Pr.

Probes: Processes & Resources of the Bering Sea Shelf. Ed. by D. Hood. 300p. 1985. pap. 48.00 o.p. (ISBN 0-08-032630-7, Pub. by PPL). Pergamon.

Probings in Prayer: Why the Closet? Ray Owen. 1975. 4.00 o.p. (ISBN 0-682-48334-6). Exposition-Phoenix.

Probity Chorus. Richard Lemon. LC 85-18880. 1986. 15.45 o.p. (ISBN 0-393-02265-X). Norton.

Problem Behavior & Psychological Development. R. Jessor. 1977. 34.00 o.p. (ISBN 0-12-384750-8). Acad Pr.

Problem Behaviour in the Secondary School: A Systems Approach. Ed. by Bill Gillham. 195p. 1981. 26.00 o.p. (ISBN 0-7099-0129-1, Pub. by Croom Helm Ltd); pap. 9.75 o.p. (ISBN 0-7099-1102-5). Routledge Chapman & Hall.

Problem Clergymen Don't Talk About. Charles L. Rassieur. LC 75-40306. 156p. 1976. pap. 5.95 o.s.i. (ISBN 0-664-24790-3, Westminster). Westminster John Knox.

Problem-Finding in Educational Administration: Trends in Research & Theory. Ed. by Glenn L. Immegart & William L. Boyd. LC 78-19912. 320p. 1979. 29.00x o.p. (ISBN 0-669-02438-4). Lexington Bks.

Problem of Chemical & Biological Warfare: A Study of the Historical, Technical, Military, Legal & Political Aspects of CBW, & Possible Disarmament Measures, Vol. 6, Technical Aspects of Early Warning & Verification 1975. Stockholm International Peace Research Institute Staff. 1975. text ed. 24.00x o.p. (ISBN 0-391-00205-8). Humanities.

Problem of Christian Unity in Early 19th Century America. Lefferts A. Loetscher. Ed. by Richard C. Wolf. LC 69-14622. (Facet Bks.). 1969. pap. 1.00 o.p. (ISBN 0-8006-3053-X, 1-3053, Fortress). Augsburg Fortress.

Problem of Freedom & Determinism. Edward D'Angelo. LC 68-63295. 1968. 13.00x o.p. (ISBN 0-8262-7713-6). U of Mo Pr.

Problem of History in Mark & Other Markan Studies. James M. Robinson. LC 81-70594. 160p. 1982. pap. 8.95 o.p. (ISBN 0-8006-1628-6, 1-1628). Augsburg Fortress.

Problem of International Confrontations see Trilateral Commission Task Force Reports.

Problem of International Consultations. Egidio Ortano et al. (Triangle Papers: No. 12). 1976. 15.00 o.s.i. (ISBN 0-318-02788-7); pap. 6.00 o.s.i. (ISBN 0-318-02789-5). Trilateral Comm.

Problem of Miracle in Primitive Christianity. Anton Fridrichsen. Tr. by Roy A. Harrisville & John S. Hanson. LC 72-176480. 1972. 10.95 o.p. (ISBN 0-8066-1211-8, 10-5170, Augsburg). Augsburg Fortress.

Problem of Religious Knowledge. Margaret L. Furse et al. (Rice University Studies: Vol. 60, No. 1). 129p. 1974. pap. 10.00x o.p. (ISBN 0-89263-219-X). Rice Univ.

Problem of the Hexateuch & Other Essays. Gerhard Von Rad. 352p. pap. 15.95 o.p. (ISBN 0-317-31485-8, 30-1310-259, Fortress). Augsburg Fortress.

Problem of the Historical Jesus. Joachim Jeremias. Ed. by John Reumann. Tr. by Norman Perrin from Ger. LC 64-23064. (Facet Bks.). 48p. 1964. pap. 2.50 o.p. (ISBN 0-8006-3015-7, 1-3015, Fortress). Augsburg Fortress.

Problem of the Picts. Wainwright. (Illus.). 196p. 1956. (ISBN 0-8022-1791-5). Philos Lib.

Problem of the Self. Henry W. Johnstone, Jr. LC 71-84666. 1970. 19.95 o.s.i. (ISBN 0-271-00102-X). Pa St U Pr.

Problem of Unbelief in the Sixteenth Century: The Religion of Rabelais. Lucien Febvre. Tr. by Beatrice Gottlieb from Fr. (Illus.). 528p. 1982. text ed. 42.00x o.p. (ISBN 0-674-70825-3). Harvard U Pr.

Problem-Orientated Medical Record in Clinical Practice. Ed. by J. C. Petrie & Neil McIntyre. 1979. pap. text ed. 22.50 o.p. (ISBN 0-443-01405-1). Churchill.

Problem-Oriented Record: A Self-Learning Module. Jacqueline J. Birmingham. (Illus.). 1978. pap. text ed. 19.95 o.p. (ISBN 0-07-005385-5). McGraw.

Problem Solvers: A History of Arthur D. Little, Inc. E. J. Kahn, Jr. 1986. 19.95 o.p. (ISBN 0-316-48212-9). Little.

Problem Solving & Chemical Calculations. Mildred D. Johnson. 1969. pap. text ed. 10.95 o.p. (ISBN 0-15-571982-3, HC). HarBraceJ.

Problem Solving & Mathematics for Physics. Thomas Nykl. 298p. 1986. pap. text ed. 19.95 o.p. (ISBN 0-8403-4150-4). Kendall Hunt.

Problem Solving Approach for Business. Steven L. Holder & Chris Sherman. LC 84-3674. 252p. 1985. pap. 11.95 o.p. (ISBN 0-471-80652-8). Wiley.

Problem Solving Approach to Mathematics for Elementary School Teachers. R. Billstein et al. 1981. text ed. 28.95 o.p. (ISBN 0-8053-0851-2); instr.'s manual 5.95 o.p. (ISBN 0-8053-0857-1). Addison-Wesley.

Problem Solving in General Chemistry. 2nd ed. Kenneth W. Whitten & Kenneth D. Gailey. 1984. pap. text ed. 19.50 o.s.i. SCP.

Problem-Solving in General Chemistry. Christopher Willis. LC 76-14004. (Illus.). 1977. pap. 16.50 o.p. (ISBN 0-395-24532-X). HM.

Problem Solving in Immunohematology. 3rd ed. Ed. by Herbert Silver et al. (Illus.). 148p. 1988. 22.00 o.p. (ISBN 0-317-62396-6). Am Soc Clinical.

Problem-Solving in the Mathematics Laboratory. Carole E. Greenes et al. 158p. 1972. pap. text ed. write for info. o.p. (ISBN 0-87150-156-2, PWS 1225, Prindle). PWS-Kent Pub.

Problem Solving: Learning & Teaching. Claire C. Hill. (Illus.). 143p. 1979. 28.50x o.p. (ISBN 0-89397-069-7). Nichols Pub.

Problem-Solving Process: A Planner's Handbook for Program Improvement. Carol P. Kowle et al. 119p. cancelled o.s.i. (ISBN 0-318-22181-0, LT63). Natl Ctr Res Voc Ed.

Problem-Solving Strategies for Writing. Linda Flower. 210p. 1981. pap. text ed. 12.95 o.p. (ISBN 0-15-571983-1, HC). HarBraceJ.

Problem-Solving Strategies for Writing. 2nd ed. Linda Flower. 256p. 1985. pap. text ed. 14.00 net o.p. (ISBN 0-15-571976-9, HC). HarBraceJ.

Problem-Solving Therapy: New Strategies for Effective Family Therapy. Jay Haley. LC 76-11889. (Social & Behavioral Science Ser.). 1976. 21.95x o.p. (ISBN 0-87589-300-7). Jossey-Bass.

Problem-Solving Therapy with Socially Anxious Children. J. J. Meijers. 290p. 1978. pap. text ed. 26.50 o.p. (ISBN 90-265-0282-6, Pub. by Swets & Zeitlinger Netherlands). CJ Hogrefe Pubs.

Problem Solving with Ada. Brian H. Mayoh. LC 81-14675. 233p. 1982. 37.00 o.p. (ISBN 0-471-10025-0); Japanese Ed. pap. 17.90 o.p. (ISBN 0-471-88692-0). Wiley.

Problem Solving with Computers. Paul Calter. 1973. text ed. 33.95 o.p. (ISBN 0-07-009648-1). McGraw.

Problem Solving with FORTRAN 77. Richard W. Dillman. 354p. 1985. pap. text ed. 23.95 o.p. (ISBN 0-03-063734-1). HR&W.

Problem with Management: Is It a Science or a Lot of Nonsense Taken Seriously? Anselm Z. Villeneuve. (Illus.). 131p. 1988. 55.85 o.p. (ISBN 0-86654-259-0). Inst Econ Finan.

Problemas Elementales de Maximo y Minimo y Suma de Cantidades Infintamente Pequenas. I. P. Natanson. 107p. (Span.). 1977. pap. 1.95 o.p. (ISBN 0-8285-1690-1, Pub. by Mir Pubs USSR). Imported Pubns.

Problemas y Experimentos Recreativos. Ya Perelman. 423p. (Span.). 1975. 8.95 o.p. (ISBN 0-8285-1698-7, Pub. by Mir Pubs USSR). Imported Pubns.

Problems Among Nations. P. Chen. 1969. pap. text ed. 7.95x o.p. (ISBN 0-8290-1173-0). Irvington.

Problems & Cases in Trial Advocacy: CLE Ed, 2 vols. 4th ed. (Continuing Legal Education Edition). 1986. 45.00 set o.p. (ISBN 1-55681-004-0). Teacher's manual $17.50. Natl Inst Trial Ad.

Problems & Cases in Trial Advocacy: Volume II (Cases) 4th ed. (Continuing Legal Education Edition). 571p. 1986. 25.00 o.p. (ISBN 1-55681-006-7). Natl Inst Trial Ad.

Problems & Cases in Trial Advocacy: Volume I (Problems) 4th ed. (Continuing Legal Education Edition). 1986. 20.00 o.p. (ISBN 1-55681-005-9). Natl Inst Trial Ad.

Problems & Exercises in General Chemistry. N. L. Glinka. 288p. 1981. 7.95 o.p. (ISBN 0-8285-2407-6, Pub. by Mir Pubs USSR). Imported Pubns.

Problems & Exercises in Organic Chemistry. A. Gronomov. 341p. 1974. 7.45 o.p. (ISBN 0-8285-0663-9, Pub. by Mir Pubs USSR). Imported Pubns.

Problems & Failures in Library Automation: Proceedings of the Clinic on Library Applications of Data Processing, 1978. Ed. by F. W. Lancaster. LC 78-31801. 109p. 1979. 9.00 o.p. (ISBN 0-87845-050-5). U of Ill Lib Info Sci.

Problems & Issues in the Education of Exceptional Children. Reginald L. Jones. LC 74-142329. 1971. pap. 15.50 o.p. (ISBN 0-395-11228-1, 3-28340). HM.

Problems & Materials on Decedents' Estates & Trusts. 3rd ed. Eugene F. Scoles & Edward C. Halbach. 850p. 1981. text ed. 31.00 o.p. (ISBN 0-316-77632-7). Little.

Problems & Possibilities for Religious Education. Edwin Cox. (Studies in Teaching & Learning). 152p. (Orig.). 1983. pap. text ed. 16.95 o.s.i. (ISBN 0-340-28433-1). Princeton Bk Co.

Problems & Practices in Advertising Research: Readings & Workbook. Alan D. Fletcher & Donald W. Jugenheimer. 215p. 1984. pap. 21.50 o.p. (ISBN 0-471-84159-5). Wiley.

Problems & Prospects of Presidential Leadership in the Nineteen-Eighties, Vol. I. Ed. by James S. Young. LC 82-19981. (Problems & Prospects of the Presidency). (Illus.). 136p. (Orig.). 1982. lib. bdg. 23.00 o.p. (ISBN 0-8191-2837-6); pap. text ed. 7.75 o.p. (ISBN 0-8191-2838-4). U Pr of Amer.

Problems & Solutions Resulting from Inability to Pay in the Public Sector. Charles C. Mulcahy & Marion C. Smith. (Public Employee Relations Library: No. 57). 53p. 1978. pap. 12.00 o.p. (ISBN 0-686-81159-3); pap. 10.00 members o.p. Intl Personnel Mgmt.

Problems & Theorems in Analysis, Vol. 2: Theory of Functions, Zeros, Polynomials, Determinants, Number Theory, Geometry. rev. ed. G. Polya & G. Szego. Tr. by C. E. Billigheimer from Ger. LC 75-189312. (Grundlehren der Mathematischen Wissenschaften Ser.: Vol. 216). Orig. Title: Aufgaben und Lehrsatze Aus der Analysis. 400p. 1976. 65.00 o.p. (ISBN 0-387-06972-0). Springer-Verlag.

Problems in Class Analysis. Guglielmo Carchedi. 300p. (Orig.). 1983. pap. 14.95x o.p. (ISBN 0-7100-9426-4). Routledge Chapman & Hall.
Problems in Contract Negotiation & Problems & Goals in Manpower Policy: Proceedings. Annual Research Conference, 11th & 12th, UCLA, 1968-1969. Annual Research Conference Staff. 1970. 2.00 o.p. (ISBN 0-89215-030-0). U Cal LA Indus Rel.
Problems in Differential Geometry & Topology. A. S. Mischenko et al. 207p. 1985. 6.95 o.p. (ISBN 0-317-47666-1, Pub. by Mir Pubs USSR). Imported Pubns.
Problems in Electronics with Solutions. 5th ed. F. A. Benson. 1976. pap. 14.95x o.p. (ISBN 0-412-14770-X, NO. 6036, Pub. by Chapman & Hall). Routledge Chapman & Hall.
Problems in Engineering Soils. 3rd ed. P. L. Capper et al. 1980. 14.95x o.p. (ISBN 0-419-11840-3, NO. 2966, Pub. by E & FN Spon). Routledge Chapman & Hall.
Problems in General Physics. I. E. Irodov. 387p. 1981. 10.00 o.s.i. (ISBN 0-8285-1966-8, Pub. by Mir Pubs USSR). Imported Pubns.
Problems in Geometry. A. Kutepov. 208p. 1975. 5.45 o.p. (ISBN 0-8285-0739-2, Pub. by Mir Pubs USSR). Imported Pubns.
Problems in High-School Mathematics. A. I. Prilepko. 279p. 1985. 7.95 o.p. (ISBN 0-8285-3042-4, Pub. by Mir Pubs USSR). Imported Pubns.
Problems in Macroeconomics. Robert A. Meyer, Jr. 352p. 1974. pap. 9.95 o.p. (ISBN 0-395-17824-X). HM.
Problems in Mechanical Drawing. 5th ed. A. S. Levens & S. J. Cooper. 224p. 1980. text ed. 23.16 o.p. (ISBN 0-07-037440-6). McGraw.
Problems in Obstetric Anaesthesia. Ed. by Barbara Morgan. LC 85-26542. 1986. (ISBN 0-471-90957-2, Dist. by A R Liss). Wiley.
Problems in Pediatric Endocrinology. C. La Cuaza & A. W. Root. LC 80-49991. (Serono Symposia: No. 32). 1980. 92.00 o.p. (ISBN 0-12-432450-9). Acad Pr.
Problems in Physical Electronics. Ed. by R. L. Ferrari & A. K. Jonscher. 1973. 32.00x o.p. (ISBN 0-85086-038-5, NO. 2956, Pub. by Pion England). Routledge Chapman & Hall.
Problems in Play: First Book of Bridge Problems. Denis Priest. LC 81-19815. 167p. (Orig.). 1982. 9.95 o.p. (ISBN 0-7022-1675-5). U of Queensland Pr.
Problems in Play: Second Book of Bridge Problems. Denis Priest. LC 83-14740. 197p. (Orig.). 1984. pap. 9.95 o.p. (ISBN 0-7022-1964-9). U of Queensland Pr.
Problems in Price Theory. Robert A. Meyer, Jr. LC 72-7636. (Illus.). 224p. 1973. pap. 9.95 o.p. (ISBN 0-395-14751-4). HM.
Problems in Primary Education. R. F. Dearden. (Students Library of Education Ser.). 1976. 18.95x o.p. (ISBN 0-7100-8363-7); pap. 8.95x o.p. (ISBN 0-7100-8364-5). Routledge Chapman & Hall.
Problems in Pulmonary Medicine for the Primary Physician. Ed. by Robert H. Poe & Robert H. Israel. LC 82-8972. (Illus.). 410p. 1982. text ed. 32.50 o.p. (ISBN 0-8121-0829-9). Lea & Febiger.
Problems in Quantum Mechanics. I. Goldman & V. D. Krivchenkov. 1963. text ed. 26.00 o.p. (ISBN 0-08-009462-7). Pergamon.
Problems in Quantum Mechanics. Ed. by D. Ter Haar. 1975. 32.00x o.p. (ISBN 0-85086-050-4, NO. 2927, Pub. by Pion England). Routledge Chapman & Hall.
Problems in Rock Mechanics. N. G. Cook. (Illus.). cancelled o.s.i. (ISBN 0-412-24110-2, NO. 6750, Pub. by Chapman & Hall). Routledge Chapman & Hall.
Problems in Solid Geometry. I. F. Sharygin. 247p. 1986. pap. 4.95 o.p. (ISBN 0-8285-3299-0, Pub. by Mir Pubs USSR). Imported Pubns.
Problems in Solid State Physics. Ed. by H. J. Goldsmid. 1968. 32.00x o.p. (ISBN 0-85086-000-8, NO. 2940, Pub. by Pion England). Routledge Chapman & Hall.
Problems in the Classification of Antagonistic Actinomycetes. G. F. Gauze. Tr. by F. Danga. 1959. 5.00 o.p. (ISBN 0-934454-69-8). Lubrecht & Cramer.
Problems in the Origins & Development of the English Language. 2nd ed. John Algeo. 1972. 11.95 o.p. (ISBN 0-15-567604-0). HarbraceJ.
Problems in the Strength of Materials. N. M. Belyayev. 1966. 140.00 o.p. (ISBN 0-08-010306-5); pap. 140.00 o.p. (ISBN 0-08-013664-8). Pergamon.
Problems in Thermodynamics & Statistical Physics. Ed. by P. T. Landsberg. 1971. 34.95x o.p. (ISBN 0-85086-023-7, NO. 2938, Pub. by Pion England). Routledge Chapman & Hall.
Problems in Todays Education. Ed. by Alan Gorr. 1974. 29.00x o.p. (ISBN 0-8422-5141-3); pap. text ed. 8.95x o.p. (ISBN 0-8422-0364-8). Irvington.
Problems of a New International Economic Order. Ed. by H. Moller. 1977. pap. 8.90 o.p. (ISBN 0-387-08467-3). Springer-Verlag.
Problems of Accelerating Aircraft Production During World War II. T. Lilley. (Harvard Graduate School of Business Administration: Studies in Aviation Research). 1957. Repr. of 1957 ed. 35.00 o.p. (ISBN 0-08-018743-9). Pergamon.
Problems of Adolescence in the Secondary School. Ed. by Geoff Lindsay. (Illus.). 240p. 1984. 31.00 o.p. (ISBN 0-7099-1621-3, Pub. by Croom Helm Ltd); pap. 15.95 o.p. (ISBN 0-7099-1643-4). Routledge Chapman & Hall.
Problems of Adolescents. Edelston. 192p. (ISBN 0-8022-1956-X). Philos Lib.
Problems of Biblical Theology in the 20th Century. Henning G. Reventlow. LC 86-4722. 1986. pap. 14.95 o.p. (ISBN 0-8006-1935-8, 1-1935, Fortress). Augsburg Fortress.
Problems of British Economic Policy, 1870-1945. Jim Tomlinson. 1981. 22.00x o.p. (ISBN 0-416-30430-3, NO. 3442); pap. 9.95x o.p. (ISBN 0-416-30440-0, NO. 3441). Routledge Chapman & Hall.
Problems of Contemporary French Politics. Dorothy Pickles. LC 81-18804. 190p. 1982. 22.00x o.p. (ISBN 0-416-73230-5, NO. 3612); pap. 9.95x o.p. (ISBN 0-416-73240-2, NO. 3613). Routledge Chapman & Hall.
Problems of Early Childhood: An Annotated Bibliography & Guide. Elisabeth Hirsch. LC 82-49031. 225p. 1983. lib. bdg. 30.00 o.p. (ISBN 0-8240-9216-3). Garland Pub.
Problems of Fluid Mechanics: Proceedings, Vol. 2. International Conference on Numerical Methods in Fluid Mechanics, 3rd. Ed. by H. Cabannes & R. Temam. LC 73-75009. (Lecture Notes in Physics: Vol. 19). (Illus.). vii, 275p. 1973. pap. 14.70 o.p. (ISBN 0-387-06171-1). Springer-Verlag.
Problems of Human Pleasure & Behavior. Michael Balint. 1957. text ed. 8.95x o.p. (ISBN 0-87140-985-2). Liveright.
Problems of Labour & Inflation. Hilde Behrend. LC 84-14263. 256p. 1984. 29.00 o.p. (ISBN 0-7099-3222-7, Pub. by Croom Helm Ltd). Routledge Chapman & Hall.
Problems of Life Research. W. Blasius. (Illus.). 1976. softcover 11.70 o.p. (ISBN 0-387-07731-6). Springer-Verlag.
Problems of Linear Electron Transport Theory in Semiconductors. M. I. Klinger. LC 78-40821. 1979. 240.00 o.p. (ISBN 0-08-018224-0). Pergamon.
Problems of Men. John Dewey. 1946. (ISBN 0-8022-0389-2). Philos Lib.
Problems of Modern Music. Ed. by Paul H. Lang. 1962. pap. 2.95 o.p. (ISBN 0-393-00115-6, Norton Lib). Norton.
Problems of Modern Music. Adolf Weissmann. LC 78-66930. (Encore Music Editions Ser.). (Illus.). 1980. Repr. of 1925 ed. 24.75 o.p. (ISBN 0-88355-768-1). Hyperion Conn.
Problems of Nonstoichiometry. Ed. by A. Rabenau. 1970. 31.75 o.p. (ISBN 0-444-10047-4, North-Holland). Elsevier.
Problems of Pain & Stress: Twenty-Sixth Annual Conference of the Society for Psychosomatic Research. Ed. by A. Steptoe. 96p. 1984. pap. 32.00 o.p. (ISBN 0-08-031301-9). Pergamon.
Problems of Perception. R. J. Hirst. (Muirhead Library of Philosophy). 1978. Repr. of 1959 ed. text ed. 19.95x o.p. (ISBN 0-391-00566-9). Humanities.
Problems of Product Design & Development. C. H. Buck. 1963. text ed. 18.00 o.p. (ISBN 0-08-009794-4); pap. text ed. 6.25 o.p. (ISBN 0-08-009793-6). Pergamon.
Problems of Psychiatry & Neuropathology, 2 vol. 672p. 1961. Set. text ed. 135.00 o.p. (ISBN 0-7065-0128-4, Pub. by Keter Pub Jerusalem). Coronet Bks.
Problems of Reduplication in Biology. Ed. by P. Sitte. (Illus.). viii, 412p. 1966. 49.60 o.p. (ISBN 0-387-03638-5). Springer-Verlag.
Problems of Spelling Reform see Fate of French-E in English: The Plural of Nouns Ending in-th.
Problems of Stability & Progress in International Relations. Quincy Wright. LC 76-3755. 378p. 1976. Repr. of 1954 ed. lib. bdg. 26.25x o.p. (ISBN 0-8371-8788-5, WRPS). Greenwood.
Problems of the Agricultural Development of Less-Favoured Areas. United Nations Economic Commission for Europe. (European Committee for Economic Perspectives). 1979. 77.00 o.p. (ISBN 0-08-024456-4). Pergamon.
Problems of the Communist Movement. S. P. Novoselov. 336p. 1981. pap. 6.00 o.p. (ISBN 0-8285-2276-6, Pub. by Progress Pubs USSR). Imported Pubns.
Problems of the Modern Economy. Ed. by Edmund S. Phelps. (Orig.). 1966. pap. 7.95x o.p. (ISBN 0-393-09690-4, NortonC). Norton.
Problems of the Pleural Space. G. Hugh Lawrence. (Major Problems in Clinical Surgery Ser.: Vol. 28). (Illus.). 144p. 1983. write for info. o.p. (ISBN 0-7216-1093-5). Saunders.
Problems of Wave Optics. S. Frish. 69p. 1976. pap. 1.95 o.p. (ISBN 0-8285-0831-3, Pub. by Mir Pubs USSR). Imported Pubns.
Problems of Weather Forecasting. Ed. by F. Steinhauser. (Ger. & Eng.). 1966. 37.80 o.p. (ISBN 0-387-80778-0). Springer-Verlag.
Problems with Meat As Human Food. John A. Scharffenberg. LC 89-5314. (Illus., Orig.). pap. 5.95 o.p. (ISBN 0-912800-65-8). Woodbridge Pr.
Procedural Justice: A Psychological Analysis. John Thibaut & Laurens Walker. LC 75-15944. 150p. 1975. pap. 7.50 o.p. (ISBN 0-470-85868-0, Pub. by Wiley). Krieger.
Procedure Before Trial. Delmar Karlen. (Nutshell Ser.). 258p. 1972. 7.95 o.p. (ISBN 0-317-00005-5). West Pub.
Procedure Guides for Evaluation of Speech & Language Disorders in Children. 4th ed. Lois J. Sanders. LC 78-71498. 1979. pap. 6.95x o.p. (ISBN 0-8134-2074-1, 2074). Inter Print Pubs.
Procedures & Practices in Activated Sludge Process Control. Robert M. Arthur. 42.95 o.p. (ISBN 0-250-40630-6). Butterworth.
Procedures & Standards for a Multipurpose Cadastre. National Research Council. 1983. pap. text ed. 8.50x o.p. (ISBN 0-309-03343-8). Natl Acad Pr.
Procedures for the Detection & Identification of Certain Fish Pathogens. rev. ed. American Fisheries Society Fish Health Section Staff. Ed. by D. W. McDaniel. 118p. 1979. pap. 12.00 o.p. (ISBN 0-913235-29-6). Am Fisheries Soc.
Proceedings. Algebraic Topology Symposium Staff. Ed. by P. J. Hilton. LC 79-185401. (Lecture Notes in Mathematics: Vol. 249). 111p. 1972. pap. 9.00 o.p. (ISBN 0-387-05715-3). Springer-Verlag.
Proceedings. Boulder Conference on High Energy Physics Staff. Ed. by K. T. Mahanthappa et al. LC 71-115692. (Illus.). 1970. 19.50x o.p. (ISBN 0-87081-002-2). Univ Pr Colo.
Proceedings, 5 vols. Canadian Cancer Conference Staff. Ed. by R. W. Begg. Incl. Vol. 1. 1st Conference, 1954. 1955 (ISBN 0-12-149001-7); Vol. 2. 2nd Conference, 1956. 1957 (ISBN 0-12-149002-5); Vol. 3. 3rd Conference, 1958. 1959 (ISBN 0-12-149003-3); Vol. 4. 4th Conference, 1960. 1961 (ISBN 0-12-149004-1); Vol. 5. 5th Conference, 1962. 1963 (ISBN 0-12-149005-X). 75.00 ea. o.p. Acad Pr.
Proceedings. Colloquium on Automata, Languages & Programming, 2nd, University of Saarbrucken, 1974. Ed. by J. Loeckx. (Lecture Notes in Computer Science Ser.: Vol. 14). viii, 611p. 1974. pap. 29.00 o.p. (ISBN 0-387-06841-4). Springer-Verlag.
Proceedings. Conference on Aerospace Adhesives & Elastomers, NSTC 2, Dallas, Texas, Oct. 6-8, 1970. (National Society for the Advancement of Material & Process Engineering Technical Conference Ser.). 10.00 o.p. (ISBN 0-686-09872-2). SAMPE.
Proceedings. Conference on Applications of Numerical Analysis, Dundee, Scotland, 1971. Ed. by J. L. Morris. (Lecture Notes in Mathematics: Vol. 228). 358p. 1971. pap. 18.00 o.p. (ISBN 0-387-05656-4). Springer-Verlag.
Proceedings. Conference On Categorical Algebra - La Jolla - 1965. Ed. by S. Eilenberg et al. 1966. 41.70 o.p. (ISBN 0-387-03639-3). Springer-Verlag.
Proceedings. Conference on Commutative Algebra. Ed. by J. W. Brewer & E. A. Rutter. LC 72-96859. (Lecture Notes in Mathematics: Vol. 311). 251p. 1973. pap. 14.00 o.p. (ISBN 0-387-06140-1). Springer-Verlag.
Proceedings. Conference on Federal Taxation & Land Use. (Lincoln Institute Monograph: 78-7). (Orig.). 1978. pap. text ed. 5.00 o.s.i. (ISBN 0-686-25526-7). Lincoln Inst Land.
Proceedings. Conference on Local Fields - NUFFIC Summer School - Driebergen - 1966. Ed. by T. A. Springer. (Illus.). 1967. 40.80 o.p. (ISBN 0-387-03953-8). Springer-Verlag.
Proceedings. Conference on Numerical Solution of Ordinary Differential Equations. Ed. by D. G. Bettis. LC 73-20914. (Lecture Notes in Mathematics Ser.: Vol. 362). viii, 490p. 1974. pap. 22.00 o.p. (ISBN 0-387-06602-0). Springer-Verlag.
Proceedings. Conference on Operator Theory, Dalhousie Univ., Halifax, 1973. Ed. by P. A. Fillmore. LC 73-14482. (Lecture Notes in Mathematics: Vol. 345). 1973. pap. 16.00 o.p. (ISBN 0-387-06496-6). Springer-Verlag.
Proceedings. European Symposium on Calcified Tissues, 3rd, Davos, 1965. Ed. by H. J. Fleisch et al. 1966. 46.00 o.p. (ISBN 0-387-03474-9). Springer-Verlag.
Proceedings. Igu Commission on Quantitative Geography, Meeting, 1972. Ed. by Maurice Yeates. 190p. 1974. pap. 7.00 o.p. (ISBN 0-7735-0168-1, McGill Canada). U of Toronto Pr.
Proceedings, 2 Vols. International Astronautical Congress, 12th, Washington, 1961. Ed. by R. M. Baker & M. W. Makemson. (Eng. & Fr.). 1963. Set. 103.90 o.p. (ISBN 0-387-80635-0). Springer-Verlag.
Proceedings, 2 Vols. International Astronautical Congress, 13th, Varna, 1962. Ed. by N. Boneff & I. Hersey. (Fr. & Ger., Vol, 1 Eng, Vol, 2 Eng, & Fr). 1964. Set. 144.60 o.p. (ISBN 0-387-80671-7). Springer-Verlag.
Proceedings, 2 vols. International Astronautical Congress, 11th, Stockholm, 1960. Ed. by C. W. Reuterswaerd & A. Hjertstrand. Incl. Vol. 1. Main Session. Ed. by C. W. Reuterswaerd. (Illus.). xii, 714p; Vol. 2. Small Sounding Rockets Symposium. Ed. by A. Hjertstrand. (Illus.). vi, 102p. (Eng., Fr. & Ger.). 1961. Set. 109.20 o.p. (ISBN 0-387-80571-0). Springer-Verlag.
Proceedings. International Cancer Congress, 9th, Tokyo, 1966. Ed. by R. J. Harris. (UICC Monograph Ser.: Vol. 9). (Illus.). 1967. 25.40 o.p. (ISBN 0-387-04011-0). Springer-Verlag.
Proceedings. International Cancer Congress, 9th, Tokyo, 1966. Ed. by R. J. Harris. LC 67-27724. (UICC Monograph Ser.: Vol. 10). 1967. 57.90 o.p. (ISBN 0-387-04012-9). Springer-Verlag.
Proceedings. International Clean Air Congress, 2nd. Ed. by Harold M. Englund & W. T. Beery. 1971. 125.00 o.p. (ISBN 0-12-239450-X). Acad Pr.
Proceedings. International Conference on Computing Methods in Optimization Problems - 2nd San Remo, Italy - 1968. Ed. by A. V. Balakrishnan. LC 78-94162. (Lecture Notes in Operations Research & Mathematical Economics: Vol. 14). (Orig.). 1969. pap. 10.70 o.p. (ISBN 0-387-04637-2). Springer-Verlag.
Proceedings. International Conference On Nuclidic Masses - 2nd - Vienna - 1963. Ed. by W. H. Johnson, Jr. (Illus.). 1964. 85.00 o.p. (ISBN 0-387-80687-3). Springer-Verlag.
Proceedings. International Congress of Histochemistry & Cytochemistry, 2nd, Frankfurt Am Main, 1964. Ed. by T. H. Schiebler et al. (Illus.). 1964. pap. 20.10 o.p. (ISBN 0-387-03169-3). Springer-Verlag.
Proceedings. International Congress on Suicide Prevention 7th. Ed. by N. Speyer et al. (Illus.). 661p. (Ger. & Fr.). 1975. pap. text ed. 29.50x o.p. Humanities.
Proceedings. International Congress on X-Ray Optics & Microanalysis, 5th, 1968. Ed. by K. H. Gaukler & G. Moellenstedt. LC 74-94153. 1969. 170.00 o.p. (ISBN 0-387-04571-6). Springer-Verlag.
Proceedings. International Summer School on Mathematical Systems Theory & Economics, Varenna, Italy, 1967. Ed. by H. W. Kuhn & G. P. Szegoe. LC 70-81409. (Lecture Notes in Operations Research and Mathematical Economics: Vols. 11 & 12). 1969. pap. 21.90 o.p. (ISBN 0-387-04635-6). Springer-Verlag.
Proceedings. International Symposium On Basic Environmental Problems Of Man In Space - 2nd - Paris - 1965. Ed. by H. Bjurstedt. (Illus., Eng., Fr & Rus.). 1967. 99.20 o.p. (ISBN 0-387-80830-2). Springer-Verlag.
Proceedings. International Symposium On Basic Environmental Problems Of Man In Space - 1st - Paris - 1962. Ed. by H. Bjurstedt. (Illus., Eng., Fr. & Rus.). 1965. 69.70 o.p. (ISBN 0-387-80731-4). Springer-Verlag.
Proceedings. International Symposium On Classification Of Brain Tumors - Cologne - 1961. Ed. by K. J. Zuelch & A. L. Woolf. (Acta Neurochimurgica: Suppl. 10). (Illus.). 1965. pap. 49.60 o.p. (ISBN 0-387-80712-8). Springer-Verlag.
Proceedings. International Symposium on Control Theory, Numerical Methods & Computer Systems Modelling, June, 1974. Ed. by A. Bensoussan & J. L. Lions. LC 74-28484. (Lecture Notes in Economics & Mathematical Systems Ser.: Vol. 107). viii, 757p. 1975. pap. 29.00 o.p. (ISBN 0-387-07020-6). Springer-Verlag.
Proceedings. International Symposium On Echo-Encephalography - Erlangen - 1967. Ed. by E. Kazner et al. Tr. by M. Lewke. (Illus.). 1968. 45.30 o.p. (ISBN 0-387-04300-4). Springer-Verlag.
Proceedings. International Symposium on Electromagnetic Separation of Radioactive Isotopes, Vienna, 1960. Ed. by M. J. Higatsberger & F. P. Viehboeck. (Illus.). 1961. 46.10 o.p. (ISBN 0-387-80575-3). Springer-Verlag.
Proceedings. International Symposium on Feto-Placental Insufficiency, 1st, Italy, 1974. Ed. by B. Salvadori. LC 74-22028. (Illus.). xiii, 354p. 1975. 42.50 o.p. (ISBN 0-387-07032-X). Springer-Verlag.
Proceedings. International Symposium On Hypotensive Peptides - Florence - 1965. Ed. by E. G. Erodes. (Illus.). 1966. 58.00 o.p. (ISBN 0-387-03572-9). Springer-Verlag.

Proceedings. International Symposium on Malignant Lymphomas of the Nervous System. Ed. by K. Jellinger & F. Seitelberger. (Acta Neuropathologica Ser: Suppl. 6). (Illus.). 320p. 1975. pap. 49.60 o.p. (ISBN 0-387-07208-X). Springer-Verlag.

Proceedings. International Symposium on Metabolism, Physiology & Clinical Use of Pentoses & Pentitols, Hakone, Japan, 1967 et al. LC 75-97994. (Illus.). 1970. 66.10 o.p. (ISBN 0-387-04572-4). Springer-Verlag.

Proceedings. International Symposium on Operating Systems, 1974. Ed. by E. Gelenbe & C. Kaiser. (Lecture Notes in Computer Science Ser.: Vol. 16). (Illus.). vii, 310p. 1974. pap. 19.00 o.p. (ISBN 0-387-06849-X). Springer-Verlag.

Proceedings, 3 Vols. Lunar Science Conference, 8th, Houston, 1977. Compiled by Lunar Science Institute, Houston, Texas. (Lunar Science Ser.: No. 8). (Illus.). 1978. 960.00 o.p. (ISBN 0-08-022052-5). Pergamon.

Proceedings. 450p. 1978. pap. 110.00 o.p. (ISBN 0-08-022678-7). Pergamon.

Proceedings. (Illus.). 404p. 8.00 o.p. (ISBN 0-318-13358-X); members 4.00 o.p. (ISBN 0-318-13359-8). ASP & RS.

Proceedings. (Illus.). 224p. 9.00 o.p. (ISBN 0-318-13360-1); members 5.00 o.p. (ISBN 0-318-13361-X). ASP & RS.

Proceedings. 256p. 19.50 o.p. (ISBN 0-318-13364-4); members 15.00 o.p. (ISBN 0-318-13365-2). ASP & RS.

Proceedings, 2 vols. 799p. 7.00 o.p. (ISBN 0-318-13374-1); members 5.00 o.p. (ISBN 0-318-13375-X). ASP & RS.

Proceedings. 552p. 6.00 o.p. (ISBN 0-318-13376-8); members 4.00 o.p. (ISBN 0-318-13377-6). ASP & RS.

Proceedings. Seminar on Differential Equations & Dynamical Systems, 2nd, 1969. Ed. by J. A. Yorke. LC 68-31622. (Lecture Notes in Mathematics: Vol. 144). 1970. pap. 14.70 o.p. (ISBN 0-387-04933-9). Springer-Verlag.

Proceedings. Summer School in Logic, Leeds, 1967. Ed. by M. H. Loeb. LC 68-56951. (Lecture Notes in Mathematics: Vol. 70). 1968. 18.30 o.p. (ISBN 0-387-04240-7). Springer-Verlag.

Proceedings. Summer Workshop on Invariant Imbedding - University of Southern California - Jun-Aug, 1970. LC 79-170660. (Lecture Notes in Operations Research & Mathematical Systems: Vol. 52). (Illus.). 1971. pap. 10.70 o.p. (ISBN 0-387-05549-5). Springer-Verlag.

Proceedings. Symposium on Biophysics & Physiology of Biological Transport, Frascati, 1965. Ed. by L. Bolis et al. (Illus.). 1968. 69.70 o.p. (ISBN 0-387-80837-X). Springer-Verlag.

Proceedings. Symposium on Computer Applications in the Mineral Industry, 10th, South Africa, 1972. 36.00 o.p. (ISBN 0-620-00774-5). SMM&E Inc.

Proceedings. Symposium on Filament Winding, Pasedena, Ca. Mar. 28-30, 1961. (Science of Advanced Materials & Process Engineering Ser., Vol. 1). pap. 3.00 o.p. (ISBN 0-938994-07-7). SAMPE.

Proceedings. Symposium on Germinal Centers in Immune Responses - University Of Bern-Switzerland - 1966. Ed. by H. Cottier et al. (Illus.). 1967. 59.80 o.p. (ISBN 0-387-03807-8). Springer-Verlag.

Proceedings. Symposium on High-Energy Electrons, Montreux, 1964. Ed. by A. Zuppinger & G. Poretti. (Illus., Ger. & Fr.). 1965. 74.40 o.p. (ISBN 0-387-03412-9). Springer-Verlag.

Proceedings. Symposium on Mechanical Behavior of Materials Under Dynamic Loads, San Antonio, 1967. Ed. by U. S. Lindholm. (Illus.). 1968. 43.10 o.p. (ISBN 0-387-04263-6). Springer-Verlag.

Proceedings. Symposium on Neuroglia, 12th Meeting, Berlin, 1966. Ed. by F. Erbsloeh et al. LC 68-21406. (Illus.). 1968. 62.00 o.p. (ISBN 0-387-04355-1). Springer-Verlag.

Proceedings. Symposium on Pathology of Axons & Axonal Flow, Vienna, 1970. Ed. by R. L. Friede & F. Seitelberger. LC 72-167274. (Illus.). 1971. 85.00 o.p. (ISBN 0-387-05433-2). Springer-Verlag.

Proceedings. Symposium on Presenile Spongy Encephalopathies, Vienna, 1965. Ed. by G. L. Guazzi & F. Seitelberger. (Illus.). 1967. 55.50 o.p. (ISBN 0-387-03997-X). Springer-Verlag.

Proceedings. Symposium on the Biochemistry of Sensory Functions, Colloquium Mosbach, Apr. 1974. Ed. by L. Jaenicke. LC 74-23671. (Illus.). xvi, 642p. 1975. 83.00 o.p. (ISBN 0-387-07038-9). Springer-Verlag.

Proceedings. Symposium on the Theory of Scheduling & Its Applications. Ed. by S. E. Elmaghraby. LC 73-14483. (Lecture Notes in Economics & Mathematical Systems: Vol. 86). vi, 436p. 1973. pap. 21.00 o.p. (ISBN 0-387-06437-0). Springer-Verlag.

Proceedings. Symposuim on Bicentennial of Materials Progress, los Angeles, California, April 26-28, 1976. (Science of Advanced Materials & Process Energy Ser: Vol. 21). 40.00 o.p. (ISBN 0-686-17254-X). SAMPE.

Proceedings, Pt. 1. Conference on Optimization Techniques, 5th. Ed. by A. Ruberti. (Lecture Notes in Computer Science: Vol. 3). (Illus.). 565p. 1973. pap. 21.00 o.p. (ISBN 0-387-06583-0). Springer-Verlag.

Proceedings, Pt. 2. Conference on Optimization Techniques, 5th. Ed. by A. Ruberti. (Lecture Notes in Computer Science: Vol. 4). (Illus.). 389p. 1973. pap. 21.00 o.p. (ISBN 0-387-06600-4). Springer-Verlag.

Proceedings, Vols. 2-6. European Society for the Study of Drug Toxicity. (International Congress Ser.: Nos. 73, 75, 81, 90 & 97). 1964-66. Vol. 2: Leyden Symposium, 1963. 14.00 o.p. (ISBN 90-219-0036-X, Excerpta Medica); Vol. 3: Lausanne Symposium, 1964. 16.00 o.p. (ISBN 90-219-0037-8); Vol. 4: Cambridge Meeting, 1964. 13.75 o.p. (ISBN 90-219-0040-8); Vol. 5: Hamburg Meeting, 1965. 13.75 o.p. (ISBN 90-219-0049-1); Vol. 6: Stockholm Meeting, 1965. 20.00 o.p. (ISBN 90-219-0050-5). Elsevier.

Proceedings in Parliament Sixteen Ten, 2 vols. Ed. by Elizabeth R. Foster. Incl. Vol. 1. The House of Lords. (Illus.). lxix, 366p; Vol. 2. The House of Commons. (Illus.). xxi, 422p. (Historical Publications, Manuscripts & Edited Texts Ser.: No. 22 & 23). 1966. Set. 50.00x o.p. (ISBN 0-300-00462-1). Yale U Pr.

Proceedings: International Conference on Photoconductivity, 3rd, Stanford University, Aug. 12, 1969. Ed. by Erik M. Pell. 1971. 125.00 o.p. (ISBN 0-08-016137-5). Pergamon.

Proceedings: Ninth National Passive Solar Conference, Columbus. Ed. by John Hayes & Alex Wilson. 1984. 120.00x o.s.i. (ISBN 0-89553-200-X). Am Solar Energy.

Proceedings of a Forensic Science Symposium on the Analysis of Sexual Assault Evidence, July 6-8, 1983. LC 84-601146. (Illus.). 212p. (Orig.). 1985. pap. 9.50 o.p. (S/N 027-001-00037-8). USGPO.

Proceedings of a Symposium on Radiation Effects in Breeder Reactor Structural Materials, Scottsdale, AZ, 1977. 919p. (Reproduction on Demand - UMI) 55.00 o.p. (ISBN 0-89520-111-9). Minerals Metals.

Proceedings of Conferenceon Hyperfunctions, Katata, 1971. Conference on Hyperfunctions & Pseudo-Differential Equations Staff. Ed. by H. Komatsu. LC 72-88782. (Lecture Notes in Mathematics: Vol. 287). vii, 529p. 1973. pap. 23.00 o.p. (ISBN 0-387-06218-1). Springer-Verlag.

Proceedings of MIT Conference on Advanced Research in VLSI, Cambridge, Massachusetts, Jan. 1982. MIT Conference on Advanced Research in VLSI Staff. Ed. by Paul Penfield, Jr. (Illus.). 209p. 1981. pap. 20.00 o.p. (ISBN 0-89006-116-5). Artech Hse.

Proceedings of the Animal Orientation Symposium, Garmisch, Partenkirchen, 1962. Animal Orientation Symposium Staff. Ed. by H. Autrum et al. (Advances in Biology: Vol. 26). (Illus.). 1963. 34.30 o.p. (ISBN 0-387-02963-X). Springer-Verlag.

Proceedings of the Annual Congress of Correction of the American Correctional Association, 115th. Ed. by Linda Dziobek. 140p. (Orig.). 1986. pap. 10.00 o.p. (ISBN 0-942974-75-1). Am Correctional.

Proceedings of the Automatic Demonstration Symposium, Versaille, 1968. Automatic Demonstrations Symposium Staff. Ed. by M. Laudet et al. LC 79-117526. (Lecture Notes in Mathematics: Vol. 125). (Illus.). 1970. pap. 18.80 o.p. (ISBN 0-387-04914-2). Springer-Verlag.

Proceedings of the Biochemistry & Physiology of Visual Pigments Symposium, Bochum University, Germany, 1972. Biochemistry & Physiology of Visual Pigments Symposium Staff. Ed. by H. Langer. (Illus.). xiv, 366p. 1973. 38.00 o.p. (ISBN 0-387-06204-1). Springer-Verlag.

Proceedings of the Brain Edema Symposium, Vienna, 1965. Brain Edema Symposium Staff. Ed. by I. Klatzo & F. Seitelberger. (Illus.). 1967. 75.00 o.p. (ISBN 0-387-80802-7). Springer-Verlag.

Proceedings of the Cambridge Summer School in Mathematical Logic, 1971. Cambridge Summer School in Mathematical Logic Staff. Ed. by A. R. Mathias & H. Rogers. LC 73-12410. (Lecture Notes in Mathematics Ser: Vol. 337). ix, 660p. 1973. pap. 30.00 o.p. (ISBN 0-387-05569-X). Springer-Verlag.

Proceedings of the Cell in Mitosis Symposium. Cell in Mitosis Symposium Staff. Ed. by Lawrence Levine. 1963. 54.00 o.p. (ISBN 0-12-444950-6). Acad Pr.

Proceedings of the Christmas Foundation Meeting of the General Anthroposophical Society. Rudolf Steiner. Ed. by Sabine Seiler. Tr. by Frances Dawson from Ger. 250p. cancelled o.s.i. (ISBN 0-88010-193-8); pap. cancelled o.s.i. (ISBN 0-88010-194-6). Anthroposophic.

Proceedings of the Classical & Quantum Mechanical Aspects of Heavy Ion Collisions Symposium, Max Planck Institut Fuer, Kernphysik, Heidelberg, Oct. 2-5, 1974. Classical & Quantum Mechanical Aspects of Heavy Ion Collisions Symposium Staff. Ed. by H. L. Harney et al. LC 74-32179. (Lecture Notes in Physics Ser: Vol. 33). viii, 312p. 1975. pap. 19.00 o.p. (ISBN 0-387-07025-7). Springer-Verlag.

Proceedings of the Clean Energy Research Institute, 1st, Miami Beach, 1976. Ed. by T. Nejat Veziroglu. 1977. pap. 355.00 o.p. (ISBN 0-08-021561-0). Pergamon.

Proceedings of the Clinic on Library Data Processing, 1969. Clinic on Library Applications of Data Processing Staff. Ed. by Dewey E. Carroll. LC 65-1841. 149p. 1970. 7.00x o.p. (ISBN 0-87845-018-1). U of Ill Lib Info Sci.

Proceedings of the Combinational Theory Seminar, Eindhoven University of Technology. Combinational Theory Seminar Staff. Ed. by J. H. Van Lint. (Lecture Notes in Mathematics: Vol. 382). vi, 131p. 1974. pap. text ed. 13.00 o.p. (ISBN 0-387-06735-3). Springer-Verlag.

Proceedings of the Conference on Finite Groups. Ed. by William R. Scott & Fletcher Gross. 1976. 78.00 o.p. (ISBN 0-12-633650-4). Acad Pr.

Proceedings of the Conference on Stochastic Differential Equations & Applications. Ed. by J. David Mason. 1977. 32.50 o.p. (ISBN 0-12-478050-4). Acad Pr.

Proceedings of the Conference on the Lunar Highlands Crust: Houston, Texas, U. S. A., 14-16 November 1979. Lunar & Planetary Institute Staff. 550p. 1980. 69.00 o.p. (ISBN 0-08-026304-6). Pergamon.

Proceedings of the Cyclic AMP, Cell Growth, & the Immune Response Symposium, Marco Island, Fla., 1973. Cyclic AMP, Cell Growth, & the Immune Response Symposium Staff. Ed. by W. Braun et al. (Illus.). 432p. 1974. 49.50 o.p. (ISBN 0-387-06654-3). Springer-Verlag.

Proceedings of the Deutsche Gesellschaft fuer Neurochirurgie, 25th Bochum, Germany, Sept. 1974. Deutsche Gesellschaft Fuer Neurochirurgie Staff. Ed. by W. Klug et al. LC 75-8941. (Advances in Neurosurgery Ser.: Vol. 2). (Illus.). 500p. 1975. pap. 50.00 o.p. (ISBN 0-387-07237-3). Springer-Verlag.

Proceedings of the Eighth Northeast Conference. Ed. by Igor Paul. LC 80-81642. 552p. 1980. pap. 125.00 flexi-cover o.p. (ISBN 0-08-026000-4). Pergamon.

Proceedings of the Eleventh International Cryogenic Engineering Conference. Ed. by Gustav Klipping & Ingrid Klipping. 842p. 1986. text ed. 149.95 o.p. (ISBN 0-408-01258-7). Butterworth.

Proceedings of the Eleventh Symposium Neuroradiologicum: Wiesbaden, June 4-10, 1978. Ed. by S. Wende. 1979. 116.90 o.p. (ISBN 0-387-08782-6). Springer-Verlag.

Proceedings of the Eleventh World Conference on Nondestructive Testing, 3 vols. Ed. by Linda Jones et al. (Illus.). 2136p. 1985. 125.00 o.p. (ISBN 0-931403-07-3, 1317). Am Soc Nondestructive.

Proceedings of the European Society for Neurochemistry, Vol. 1. V. Neuhoff. (Illus.). 658p. 1978. 51.80x o.p. (ISBN 0-89573-018-9). VCH Pubs.

Proceedings of the Fifth International Congress of Aesthetics. Ed. by Jan Aler. 1968. pap. 140.00x o.p. (ISBN 90-2791-059-6). Mouton.

Proceedings of the First International Congress on Toxicology: Toxicology As a Predictive Science. Ed. by Gabriel L. Plaa & W. A. Duncan. 1979. 69.50 o.p. (ISBN 0-12-558050-9). Acad Pr.

Proceedings of the First U. S. National Conference on Earthquake Engineering: Held in Ann Arbor, MI, June 18-20,1975. 1975 ed. 660p. 20.00 o.p. Earthquake Eng.

Proceedings of the Fourth Agricultural Symposium. Ed. by Ted J. Davis. 374p. 1984. 23.95 o.p. (ISBN 0-8213-0417-8, BK 0417). World Bank.

Proceedings of the Fourth International Conference on Electron Microscopy, Berlin, 1958, 2 vols. International Conference on Electron Microscopy Staff. Ed. by G. Mollenstedt et al. 1960. Vol. 1. 134.60 o.p. (ISBN 0-387-02562-6); Vol. 2. 115.70 o.p. (ISBN 0-387-02563-4). Springer-Verlag.

Proceedings of the French Colonial Historical Society, 5th Meeting. French Colonial Historical Society Staff. Ed. by James J. Cooke. LC 80-5683. 125p. lib. bdg. 20.50 o.p. (ISBN 0-8191-1146-5); pap. text ed. 10.00 o.p. (ISBN 0-8191-1147-3). U Pr of Amer.

Proceedings of the General Topology & Its General Relations to Modern Analysis & Algebra Symposium, 2nd, Prague, 1967. General Topology & Its Relations to Modern Analysis & Algebra Symposium Staff. Ed. by J. Novak. 1967. 76.00 o.p. (ISBN 0-12-522556-3). Acad Pr.

Proceedings of the IFAC-FIP International Conference on Digital Computer a 75211, 2 pts. IFAC-FIP International Conference Staff. Ed. by M. Mansour & W. Schaufelberger. LC 73-21003. (Lecture Notes in Economics & Mathematical Systems, Vol. 93 & 94). 1974. Pt. 1. pap. 24.00 o.p. (ISBN 0-387-06620-9); Pt. 2. pap. 23.00 o.p. (ISBN 0-387-06621-7). Springer-Verlag.

Proceedings of the International Colloquium on the Law of Outer Space XXIX. 350p. 1987. 59.50 o.p. (ISBN 0-930403-27-4). AIAA.

Proceedings of the International Congress for Hypnosis & Psychosomatic Medicine, Paris, 1965. International Congress for Hypnosis & Psychosomatic Medicine Staff. Ed. by J. Lassner. (Illus., Eng, Fr & Ger.). 1965. 52.20 o.p. (ISBN 0-387-03879-5). Springer-Verlag.

Proceedings of the International Conference on Atherosclerosis, November, 1977. International Conference on Atherosclerosis, Milan Staff. Ed. by Lars A. Carlson et al. LC 78-66345. 796p. 1978. 95.00 o.p. (ISBN 0-89004-267-5). Raven.

Proceedings of the International Conference on Comparative Mammalian Cytogenetics, Dartmouth Medical School, 1968. International Conference on Comparative Mammalian Cytogenetics Staff. Ed. by K. Benirschke. (Illus.). 1969. 79.50 o.p. (ISBN 0-387-04442-6). Springer-Verlag.

Proceedings of the International Conference on Industrial Robot Technology, 1st, University of Nottingham, Eng, March 1973. International Conference on Industrial Robot Technology Staff. 322p. 1977. softbound 30.00x o.p. (ISBN 0-685-89047-3). Scholium Intl.

Proceedings of the International Congress of Microbiological Standardization, 11th, Milan, 1968. International Congress of Microbiological Standardization Staff. Ed. by R. H. Regamey et al. (Progress in Immunobiological Standardization: Vol. 4). 1970. 60.00 o.p. (ISBN 3-8055-0400-4). S Karger.

Proceedings of the International Conference on Pipeline Inspection. Ed. by R. W. Revie et al. 643p. 1984. text ed. 54.00x o.p. (ISBN 0-660-11601-4, Pub. by Canmet). Gower Pub Co.

Proceedings of the International Conference on Raman Spectroscopy, 10th. Ed. by B. Hudson & W. L. Peticolas. 850p. 1986. 45.00x o.p. (ISBN 0-87114-176-0). U of Oreg Bks.

Proceedings of the International Congress of the International Association of Gerontology, 10th. International Association of Gerontology Staff. Ed. by J. Andrews. (Gerontology: Vol. 23, No. 1). (Illus.). 1976. 20.75 o.p. (ISBN 3-8055-2442-0). S Karger.

Proceedings of the International Conference on Water Pollution Research, 8th, Sydney, Australia, 1978. S. H. Jenkins. 1978. 200.00 o.p. (ISBN 0-08-020902-5). Pergamon.

Proceedings of the International Marine & Shipping Conference, 1969. International Marine & Shipping Conference Staff. (Illus.). 832p. 1970. 36.00x o.p. (ISBN 0-900976-93-4, Pub. by Inst Marine Eng). Intl Spec Bk.

Proceedings of the International School of Nuclear Physics, Erice, 2-14 Sept. 1976. Ed. by D. Wilkinson. (Progress in Particle & Nuclear Physics Ser.: Vol. 1). 1978. 98.00 o.p. (ISBN 0-08-020327-2). Pergamon.

Proceedings of the International Seminar on Trends in Mathematical Modelling, Venice, Dec., 1971. International Seminar on Trends in Mathematical Modelling Staff. Ed. by N. Hawkes. LC 72-96971. (Lecture Notes in Economics & Mathematical Systems: Vol. 80). 288p. 1973. pap. 18.00 o.p. (ISBN 0-387-06144-4). Springer-Verlag.

Proceedings of the International Society of Blood Transfusion, 12th Congress, Moscow, 1969, 2 pts. International Society of Blood Transfusion Staff. Ed. by K. Stampfli. Incl. Pt. 1. Immunhematology-Immunology, Transplantation Problems, Leukemia, Coagulation; Pt. 2. Organization & Technical Problems of Transfusion; Clinical Problems of Transfusion. (Bibliotheca Haematologica: Vol. 38). 1972. Set. 426.75 o.p. (ISBN 3-8055-1287-2); Pt. 1. 178.00 o.p. (ISBN 3-8055-1240-6); Pt. 2. 178.00 o.p. (ISBN 3-8055-1241-4). S Karger.

Proceedings of the International Symposium on Atherosclerosis, 3rd, 1973. International Symposium on Atherosclerosis Staff. Ed. by G. Schettler & A. Weizel. LC 74-14636. (Illus.). xxxvii, 1034p. 1975. 54.00 o.p. (ISBN 0-387-06909-7). Springer-Verlag.

Proceedings of the International Symposium on Fosfomycin, Madrid, 1975. International Symposium on Fosfomycin Staff. Ed. by A. Gallego & J. M. Rubio. (Chemotherapy: Vol. 23, Suppl. 1). 1977. 55.00 o.p. (ISBN 3-8055-2368-8). S Karger.

Proceedings of the International Symposium on Industrial Robots, 9th. International Symposium on Industrial Robots Staff & Robots Institute of America Staff. LC 78-75113. (Illus.). 1979. 65.00 o.p. (ISBN 0-87263-048-X). SME.

Proceedings of the International Symposium on Metabolic Interconversion of Enzymes, 3rd, Seattle, 1973. International Symposium on Metabolic Interconversion of Enzymes Staff. Ed. by E. H. Fischer. (Illus.). 400p. 1974. 45.00 o.p. (ISBN 0-387-06650-0). Springer-Verlag.

Proceedings of the International Symposium on Quantum Chemistry, No. 20. Lowdin. 788p. 1986. pap. 99.95 o.p. (ISBN 0-471-85972-9). Wiley.

Proceedings of the International Symposium on the Aerodynamics & Ventilation of Vehicle Tunnels, 1st. International Symposium on the Aerodynamics & Ventilation of Vehicle Tunnels Staff. 1973. text ed. 47.00x o.p. (ISBN 0-900983-28-0, Dist. by Air Science Co.). BHRA Fluid.

Proceedings of the International Symposiums on the Glomerular Basement Membrane, 1st, Vienna, Sept., 1980. International Symposium on the Glomerular Basement Membrane Staff. Ed. by G. Lubec. (Renal Physiology Journal: Vol. 4, No. 2-3). (Illus.). 100p. 1981. pap. 20.75 o.p. (ISBN 3-8055-3491-4). S Karger.

Proceedings of the International Symposium on X-Ray Optics & X-Ray Microanalysis, 3rd, Stanford, California, 1962. International Symposium on X-Ray Optics & X-Ray Microanalysis Staff. Ed. by Howard H. Pattee, Jr. et al. 1964. 97.00 o.p. (ISBN 0-12-547050-9). Acad Pr.

Proceedings of the International Workshop on Ergot Alkaloids, Rome, Dec. 6-7, 1976. International Workshop on Ergot Alkaloids Staff. Ed. by B. B. Brodie et al. (Pharmacology: Vol. 16, Suppl. 1). (Illus.). 1977. 36.00 o.p. (ISBN 3-8055-2769-1). S Karger.

Proceedings of the Interntional Symposium on Mathematical Problems, Kyoto University, Kyoto, Japan, Jan. 23-29, 1975. International Symposium on Mathematical Problems Staff. (Lecture Notes in Physics Ser.). 562p. 1975. pap. 28.00 o.p. (ISBN 0-387-07174-1). Springer-Verlag.

Proceedings of the IUCN General Assembly & Technical Meeting, 14th, Ashkhabad, 1978. IUCN Staff. 1980. pap. 10.00 o.p. (ISBN 0-686-93141-6, IUCN). UNIPUB.

Proceedings of the Jamaica Assembly, 1795-1796: In Regard to the Maroon Negroes. Jamaica Assembly Staff. LC 79-111581. 1971. Repr. of 1796 ed. 22.50x o.s.i. (ISBN 0-8371-4606-2, JMN&). Greenwood.

Proceedings of the Leukocyte Culture Conference, 5th. Leukocyte Culture Conference Staff. Ed. by Jules Harris. 1971. 74.50 o.p. (ISBN 0-12-327050-2). Acad Pr.

Proceedings of the Leukocyte Culture Conference, 6th. Leukocyte Culture Conference Staff. Ed. by M. Roy Schwarz. 1972. 89.00 o.p. (ISBN 0-12-633150-2). Acad Pr.

Proceedings of the Logic Conference, Kiel, 1974. Logic Conference Staff. Ed. by G. H. Muller et al. LC 75-40481. (Lecture Notes in Mathematics: Vol. 499). 1976. pap. 31.00 o.p. (ISBN 0-387-07534-8). Springer-Verlag.

Proceedings of the Machine Tool Design & Research International Conference, 12th. Machine Tool Design & Research International Conference Staff et al. Ed. by S. A. Tobias. LC 72-6276. 582p. 1973. 150.00x o.p. (ISBN 0-470-49745-9). Halsted Pr.

Proceedings of the Manufacturing Productivity Solutions Conference, 2nd, Washington D. C., Oct. 2-3, 1979. Society of Manufacturing Engineers Staff. 239p. 20.00 o.p. (ISBN 0-317-35741-7, 494); members 16.00 o.p. (ISBN 0-317-35742-5). SME.

Proceedings of the National Academy of the Avant Garde. National Academy of the Avant Garde Staff. Ed. by Henry Korn. 1975. pap. 1.50 o.p. (ISBN 0-685-63821-9). Assembling Pr.

Proceedings of the National Conference on Addictions in the Jewish Community. 56p. cancelled o.s.i. Coun Jewish Feds.

Proceedings of the Optimization Symposium, Nice, 1969. Optimization Symposium Staff. Ed. by A. V. Balakrishna et al. LC 70-120380. (Lecture Notes in Mathematics: Vol. 132). (Illus.). 1970. pap. 18.80 o.p. (ISBN 0-387-04921-5). Springer-Verlag.

Proceedings of the Optimiztion & Stability Problems in Continuum Mechanics Symposium, Los Angeles, 1971. Optimization & Stability Problems in continuum Mechanics Symposium Staff. Ed. by P. K. Wang. (Lecture Notes in Physics: Vol. 21). vi, 94p. 1973. pap. 10.70 o.p. (ISBN 0-387-06214-9). Springer-Verlag.

Proceedings of the Probability Methods in Analysis Symposium, Loutraki, Greece, 1966. Probability Methods in Analysis Symposium Staff. (Lecture Notes in Mathematics: Vol. 31). 1967. pap. 18.30 o.p. (ISBN 0-387-03902-3). Springer-Verlag.

Proceedings of the Research Symposium on Complexes of Biologically Active Substances with Nucleic Acids & Their Modes of Action. Research Symposium on Complexes of Biologically Active Substances with Nucleic Acids & Their Modes of Action Staff. Ed. by F. E. Hahn et al. (Progress in Molecular & Subcellular Biology: Vol. 2). (Illus.). 1971. 45.00 o.p. (ISBN 0-387-05321-2). Springer-Verlag.

Proceedings of the Rutherford Jubilee International Conference-Manchester, 1962. Ed. by J. B. Birks & J. B. Birks. 99.00 o.p. (ISBN 0-12-101162-3). Acad Pr.

Proceedings of the Salt Lake City Meeting: Third Regular Meeting of the Division of Particles & Fields of the American Physical Society, Salt Lake City, Utah 14-17 January 1987. Ed. by J. Ball & C. DeTar. 800p. 1987. 78.00 o.p. (ISBN 0-318-23788-1, Z0366P-P); pap. 46.00 o.p. (ISBN 0-318-23789-X). World Scientific Pub.

Proceedings of the San Diego Biomedical Symposium. Ed. by James I. Martin. 1977. 77.00 o.p. (ISBN 0-12-474660-8). Acad Pr.

Proceedings of the Second International Congress for the Study of Child Language, Vol. I. Ed. by Carolyn E. Johnson & Carol L. Thew. LC 82-16145. (Illus.). 614p. (Orig.). 1983. lib. bdg. 45.50 o.p. (ISBN 0-8191-2738-8); pap. text ed. 26.75 o.p. (ISBN 0-8191-2739-6). U Pr of Amer.

Proceedings of the Second National Conference on Business Ethics. Ed. by W. Michael Hoffman. LC 79-64514. 1979. pap. text ed. 21.50 o.p. (ISBN 0-8191-0762-X). U Pr of Amer.

Proceedings of the Seventeenth International Conference on Low Temperature Physics, Pts. I & II. U. Eckern et al. 1400p. 1985. Set. 250.00 o.p. (ISBN 0-444-86910-7). Elsevier.

Proceedings of the Seventeenth International Machine Tool Design & Research Conference. Ed. by S. A. Tobias & T. Koenigsberger. 671p. 1978. 155.00 o.p. (ISBN 0-470-99076-7). Halsted Pr.

Proceedings of the Seventh New England (Northeast) Bioengineering Conference: Held March 22-23, 1979, at Rensselaer Polytechnic Institute, Troy, New York. Lee E. Ostrander. LC 79-83927. (New England Bio-Engineering Conference Ser.: Vol. 7). (Illus.). 1979. pap. 135.00 o.p. (ISBN 0-08-024634-6). Pergamon.

Proceedings of the Seventy-First Annual Meeting: Challenges of Professionalism. 414p. pap. 21.00 o.p. (ISBN 0-317-59283-1). Assn Phys Plant Admin.

Proceedings of the Seventy-Fourth Annual Meeting: Patterns for Progress. 300p. pap. 21.00 o.p. (ISBN 0-317-59292-0). Assn Phys Plant Admin.

Proceedings of the Seventy-Third Annual Meeting: Improving Management Through New Technologies. 304p. pap. 21.00 o.p. (ISBN 0-317-59290-4). Assn Phys Plant Admin.

Proceedings of the Several Complex Variables Symposium, Park City, Utah, 1970. Several Complex Variables Symposium Staff. Ed. by R. M. Brooks. LC 76-153464. (Lecture Notes in Mathematics: Vol. 184). (Illus.). 1971. pap. 13.00 o.p. (ISBN 0-387-05370-0). Springer-Verlag.

Proceedings of the Shambaugh Fifth International Workshop on Middle Ear Microsurgery & Fluctant Hearing Loss. George Shambaugh & John J. Shea. LC 77-79552. 1977. 35.00 o.p. (ISBN 0-87397-125-6). Strode.

Proceedings of the Sixth Lunar Science Conference. R. B. Merrill. 1976. 566.00 o.p. (ISBN 0-08-020566-6). Pergamon.

Proceedings of the Sixth World Congress on the Theory of Machines & Mechanisms: December 15-20, 1983, 2 vols. Ed. by J. S. Rao & K. N. Gupta. 1984. Set. 178.00 o.p. (ISBN 0-470-20037-5); Vol. 1. 79.95 o.p. (ISBN 0-470-20028-6); Vol. 2. 79.95 o.p. (ISBN 0-470-20032-4). Halsted Pr.

Proceedings of the Society of Photo-Optical Instrumentation Engineers, 13th Annual Technical Symposium, Washington D. C. Proceedings. Society of Photo-Optical Instrumentation Engineers Staff. 1968. 8.00 o.p. (ISBN 0-89252-086-8). SPIE.

Proceedings of the Society of Photo-Optical Instrumentation Engineers, 14th Annual Technical Symposium, San Francisco: Proceedings. Society of Photo-Optical Instrumentation Engineers Staff. 1969. 8.00 o.p. (ISBN 0-89252-087-6). SPIE.

Proceedings of the Symposium Trnassonicum, Aachen, 1962. Symposium Transsonicum Staff. Ed. by K. Oswatitisch. (Eng., Ger. & Fr.). 1964. 77.90 o.p. (ISBN 0-387-03223-1). Springer-Verlag.

Proceedings of the Tenth International Conference on Raman Spectroscopy. Ed. by W. L. Peticolas & B. Hudson. 850p. 1986. 45.00x o.p. (ISBN 0-317-58442-1). U of Oreg Bks.

Proceedings of the Third Caltech Conference on VLSI. (Digital Systems Design Ser.). 430p. 1983. 39.95 o.p. (ISBN 0-914894-86-2, Computer Sci Pr). W H Freeman.

Proceedings of the Third General Conference, Vol. 3. I. P. R. A. Staff. 1970. pap. text ed. 59.50x o.p. (ISBN 90-232-0839-0). Humanities.

Proceedings of the Third International Biodegradation Symposium. Ed. by J. Miles Sharpley & Arthur M. Kaplan. (Illus.). xiv, 1138p. 1976. 197.00 o.p. (ISBN 0-85334-679-8, Pub. by Elsevier Applied Sci England). Elsevier.

Proceedings of the Third International Congress on Marine Corrosion & Fouling. Ed. by Robert F. Acker et al. 1974. 36.00x o.s.i. (ISBN 0-8101-0445-8). Northwestern U Pr.

Proceedings of the Third Southeast Asia Wood Industry Conference. Miller Freeman Publications, Inc. Staff. (Illus.). 412p. 1980. pap. 77.00 o.p. (ISBN 0-87930-136-8). Miller Freeman.

Proceedings of the Thirteenth International Machine Tool Design & Research Conference. Ed. by S. A. Tobias & F. Koenigsberger. LC 73-2955. 573p. 1973. 150.00x o.p. (ISBN 0-470-87529-1). Halsted Pr.

Proceedings of the Victoria Conference on Mathematical Problems in Biology. Victoria Conference on Mathematical Problems in Biology Staff. Ed. by P. Van Den Dreissche. (Lecture Notes in Biomathematics Ser.: Vol. 2). vi, 280p. 1974. pap. 14.50 o.p. (ISBN 0-387-06847-3). Springer-Verlag.

Proceedings of the World Congress of Anaesthesiology, 3rd, Sao Paulo, 1964. World Congress of Anaesthesiology, 3rd, Sao Paulo, 1964. Ed. by R. Frey et al. (Anaesthesiology & Resuscitation Ser.: Vol. 8). 1966. pap. 23.10 o.p. (ISBN 0-387-03450-1). Springer-Verlag.

Proceedings of the 1st International Congress of Ecology, The Hague, Netherlands, Sept. 1974. 250p. 1975. pap. 40.00 o.p. (ISBN 9-0220-0525-9, Pub. by PUDOC). UNIPUB.

Proceedings of the 1974 Briefing Conference on the Consumer Product Safety Act. cancelled o.s.i. (ISBN 0-914176-03-X); cancelled o.s.i.; cancelled o.s.i.; cancelled o.s.i. Wash Busn Info.

Proceedings of the 2nd International Conference on Automation in Warehousing, University of Nottingham, England, April 1975. International Conference on Automation in Warehousing Staff. 380p. 1977. pap. 39.00x o.p. (ISBN 0-685-89048-1). Scholium Intl.

Proceedings of the 2nd International Conference on Automation in Warehousing, Keele, England, March 1977. International Conference on Automation in Warehousing Staff. 300p. 1977. softbound 70.00x o.p. (ISBN 0-685-89050-3). Scholium Intl.

Proceedings of the 2nd International Symposium on Nitrite in Meat Proucts, Zeist, The Netherlands 7-10 Sept., 1976. Ed. by B. J. Tinbergen. 1977. pap. 52.00 o.p. (ISBN 90-220-0607-7, Pub. by PUDOC). UNIPUB.

Proceedings of the 2nd International Symposium on Protein Metabolism & Nutrition, The Netherlands, May 2-6, 1977. (European Association for Animal Production (EAAP) Ser.: No. 20). 1977. pap. 28.00 o.p. (ISBN 9-0220-0634-4, Pub. by PUDOC). UNIPUB.

Proceedings of the 3rd International Conference on Plant Pathogenic Bacteria. 1972. 45.00 o.p. (ISBN 9-0220-0357-4, PUDOC). UNIPUB.

Proceedings: Papers on Eskimo & Aleut Linguistics. Ed. by Eric P. Hamp. LC 76-45708. 327p. 1976. pap. 6.00 o.p. (ISBN 0-914203-06-1). Chicago Ling.

Proceedings: Proceedings of the Basic Environmental Problems of Man in Space II, International Symposium, 6th, Bonn, Germany, November 3-6, 1980. Basic Environmental Problems of Man in Space II, International Symposium Staff & K. E. Klein. Ed. by J. R. Hordinsky. 250p. 1982. pap. 77.00 o.p. (ISBN 0-08-028697-6, A140). Pergamon.

Proceedings: Proceedings of the International Seaweed Symposium, 7th, Sappora, Japan, Aug., 1971. International Seaweed Symposium Staff. Ed. by Science Council of Japan Staff. 607p. 1973. 77.95x o.p. (ISBN 0-470-77090-2). Halsted Pr.

Proceedings: Proceedings of the New England Anti-Slavery Convention, 4th, Boston, 1837. New England Anti-Slavery Convention Staff. LC 78-138014. 1973. Repr. of 1837 ed. 10.00 o.p. (ISBN 0-8371-5661-0, NAS&). Greenwood.

Proceedings: Second Technology Exchange Week in Panama. American Society of Photogrammetry Staff. 724p. (Eng. & Span.). 1982. eng. ed. (10.00 member) 14.00 o.p. (ISBN 0-937294-53-5); sp. ed. (10.00 member) 14.00 o.p. (ISBN 0-937294-54-3). ASP & RS.

Proceedings: Tenth National Passive Solar Conference, Raleigh. Ed. by Alex Wilson & W. Glennie. 1985. 135.00x o.s.i. (ISBN 0-89553-201-8). Am Solar Energy.

Process Analysis & Design for Chemical Engineers. W. Resnick. 1981. text ed. 45.95 o.p. (ISBN 0-07-051887-4). McGraw.

Process & Action in Work with Groups: The Preconditions for Treatment & Growth. Ken Heap. 1979. 46.00 o.p. (ISBN 0-08-023023-7); pap. 15.25 o.p. (ISBN 0-08-023022-9). Pergamon.

Process & Divinity: The Hartshorne Festschrift. Ed. by William L. Reese & Eugene Freeman. LC 64-13547. 644p. 1964. 32.95 o.p. (ISBN 0-87548-054-3). Open Court.

Process & Industrial Pipe Estimating. Lloyd K. Burkholder, Sr. LC 82-2448. 240p. (Orig.). 1982. pap. 18.25 o.p. (ISBN 0-910460-94-9). Craftsman.

Process Chemistryar Energy, Vol. 4. C. E. Stevenson et al. 1970. 115.00 o.p. (ISBN 0-08-013401-7). Pergamon.

Process Control in the Construction Industry. (Transportation Research Record Ser.). 63p. 1978. 3.60 o.p. (ISBN 0-309-02837-X). Transport Res Bd.

Process Control Instrumentation Technology. 2nd ed. Curtis D. Johnson. LC 81-10488. (Electronic Technology Ser.). 497p. 1982. (ISBN 0-471-05789-4). Wiley.

Process Control Systems. 2nd ed. F. Gregg Shinskey. 1979. text ed. 49.00 o.p. (ISBN 0-07-056891-X). McGraw.

Process Dynamics & Control. 172p. 1961. pap. 24.00 o.p. (ISBN 0-8169-0302-6, S-36). Am Inst Chem Eng.

Process Energy Conservation: Methods & Technology. Chemical Engineering Magazine Editors. (Illus.). 300p. 1982. text ed. 41.50 o.p. (ISBN 0-07-010697-5). McGraw.

Process Engineering in the Food Industry. R. J. Clarke. 360p. 1958. (ISBN 0-8022-0257-8). Philos Lib.

Process Engineering of Size Reduction: Ball Milling. L. G. Austin et al. LC 83-73512. (Illus.). 561p. 1984. text ed. 15.00x o.p. (ISBN 0-89520-421-5). SMM&E Inc.

Process Ethics. James R. Gray. LC 83-6564. 110p. 1983. lib. bdg. 24.75 o.p. (ISBN 0-8191-3237-3); pap. text ed. 9.25 o.p. (ISBN 0-8191-3238-1). U Pr of Amer.

Process in Neurobiology, Vol. 21. Ed. by G. A. Kerkut & J. W. Phillis. (Illus.). 360p. 1985. 150.00 o.p. (ISBN 0-08-032321-9). Pergamon.

Process Modification for Industrial Pollutants Source Reduction. Ed. by James W. Patterson. LC 84-21257. (Industrial Waste Management Ser.). (Illus.). 160p. 1985. 24.95 o.p. (ISBN 0-87371-003-7). Lewis Pubs Inc.

Process of Change: From a Closed to an Open System in a Mental Hospital. Maxwell Jones. (Therapeutic Communities Section, International Library of Group Psychotherapy & Group Processes). 220p. 1982. 26.95x o.p. (ISBN 0-7100-9255-5). Routledge Chapman & Hall.

Process of Child Therapy. Group for the Advancement of Psychiatry, Committee on Child Psychiatry. LC 82-45469. (Publications Ser.: No. 111). 224p. 1982. 17.50 o.p. (ISBN 0-87630-311-4, Pub. by GAP). Brunner-Mazel.

Process of Communication: An Introduction to Theory & Practice. David K. Berlo. 1960. pap. text ed. 15.95 o.p. (ISBN 0-03-055686-4). HR&W.

Process of Evolution. 2nd ed. Paul R. Ehrlich et al. LC 74-3030. (Population Biology Ser.). (Illus.). 416p. 1974. text ed. 40.95 o.p. (ISBN 0-07-019133-6). McGraw.

Titles

Process of Government. Arthur F. Bentley. LC 82-19509. (Social Science Classics Ser.). 551p. 1983. pap. 19.95 o.p. (ISBN 0-87855-934-5). Transaction Pubs.
Process of Industrial Development & Alternative Development Strategies. Bela Balassa. LC 81-1033. (Essays in International Finance Ser.: No. 141). 1980. pap. text ed. 4.50x o.p. (ISBN 0-88165-048-X). Princeton U Int Finan Econ.
Process of Learning Mathematics. L. R. Chapman. LC 71-178683. 405p. 1972. 100.00 o.p. (ISBN 0-08-016623-7); pap. 100.00 o.p. (ISBN 0-08-017357-8). Pergamon.
Process of Opposition in India: Two Case Studies of How Policy Shapes Politics. Robert W. Stern. LC 78-116029. 1970. lib. bdg. 16.00x o.s.i. (ISBN 0-226-77314-0). U of Chicago Pr.
Process of Patient Teaching in Nursing. 5th ed. Barbara K. Redman. (Illus.). 360p. 1983. pap. text ed. 19.95 o.p. (ISBN 0-8016-4185-3). Mosby.
Process of Planning Nursing Care: A Theoretical Model. 3rd ed. Fay L. Bower. LC 81-14164. (Illus.). 219p. 1982. pap. text ed. 16.95 o.p. (ISBN 0-8016-0721-3). Mosby.
Process Piping Systems. Chemical Engineering Magazine Editors. Ed. by David J. Deutsch. LC 80-13774. (Chemical Engineering Ser.). 484p. 1980. text ed. 54.50 o.p. (ISBN 0-07-010706-8). McGraw.
Process Systems Engineering 1985: Computers in Chemical Engineering. Proceedings of the Symposium, Cambridge, U. K., March 31 - April 4, 1985. Ed. by Institution of Chemical Engineers Staff. (Institution of Chemical Engineers Symposium Ser.: Vol. 92). 708p. 1985. 70.00 o.s.i. (ISBN 0-08-031417-1, Pub by PPL). Pergamon.
Processes of Criminal Justice: Investigation. 2nd ed. H. Richard Uviller. (American Casebook Ser.). 550p. 1979. pap. text ed. 33.95 o.p. (ISBN 0-8299-2065-X). West Pub.
Processes of the Earth's Surface. Susan Vuke. 96p. 1980. pap. 5.00 o.p. (ISBN 0-87842-125-4). Mountain Pr.
Processing & Properties of High School Tool Steels: Proceedings. AIME Annual Meeting, Las Vegas, 1980. Ed. by M. G. H. Wells & L. W. Lherbier. (Illus.). 201p. 24.00 o.p. (ISBN 0-89520-369-3); members 15.00 o.p. (ISBN 0-317-36259-3); student members 10.00 o.p. (ISBN 0-317-36260-7). ASM.
Processing Equipment for Agricultural Products. 2nd ed. Carl W. Hall & Denny C. Davis. (Illus.). 1979. 35.95 o.p. (ISBN 0-87055-270-8). AVI.
Processing of Crystalline Ceramics. Ed. by R. F. Davis et al. LC 78-18441. (Materials Science Research Ser.: Vol. 11). 696p. 1978. 105.00x o.p. (ISBN 0-306-40035-9, Plenum Pr). Plenum Pub.
Processing of Metal & Ceramic Powders: Proceedings. TMS-AIME Fall Meeting, Louisville, 1981. Ed. by R. M. German & K. W. Lay. (Illus.). 337p. 45.00 o.p. (ISBN 0-89520-396-0, 219); members 30.00 o.p. (ISBN 0-317-36310-7); student members 15.00 o.p. (ISBN 0-317-36311-5). ASM.
Processing of Optical Data by Organisms & by Machines. Ed. by W. Reichardt. (Italian Physical Society: Course No. 43). 1970. 104.00 o.p. (ISBN 0-12-368843-4). Acad Pr.
Processing the News: How People Tame the Information Tide. Doris A. Graber. LC 83-19537. (Political Communication & Policy Ser.). (Illus.). 256p. 1984. text ed. 27.50x o.p. (ISBN 0-582-28394-9); pap. 16.95x o.p. (ISBN 0-582-28510-0). Longman.
Procession. Kahlil Gibran. 1958. 5.00 o.p. (ISBN 0-8022-0580-1). Philos Lib.
Prochronisms - Anachronisms. Joslin Deeks. LC 65-28762. 196p. 1967. (ISBN 0-8022-0370-1). Philos Lib.
Proclaiming the Promise: Christian Preaching from the Old Testament. Foster R. McCurley, Jr. LC 74-76921. 176p. (Orig.). 1974. pap. 5.75 o.p. (ISBN 0-8006-1083-0, 1-1083, Fortress). Augsburg Fortress.
Proclaiming the Truth. Donald E. Demaray. 1980. pap. 6.95 o.p. (ISBN 0-8010-2898-1). Baker Bk.
Proclamation from Prophecy & Pattern: Lucan Old Testament Christiology. Darrell L. Bock. (JSOT Supplement Ser.: No. 12). 350p. pap. text ed. 15.95x o.s.i. (Pub. by JSOT Pr England). Eisenbrauns.
Proclamation of the Gospel in a Pluralistic World: Essays on Christianity & Culture. George W. Forell. LC 73-79354. 144p. (Orig.). 1973. pap. 1.00x o.p. (ISBN 0-8006-1035-0, Fortress). Augsburg Fortress.
Proctology. Dr. Dale G. Keighley. 1979. 30.00 o.p. (ISBN 0-682-49191-8, University). Exposition-Phoenix.
Procurement & Inventory Ordering Tables. Jerry Banks & Charles L. Hohenstein, Jr. LC 77-8663. 1978. pap. 19.25 o.p. (ISBN 0-08-021945-4). Pergamon.
Procurement Management: Strategy, Organization & Decision-Making. E. Raymond Corey. LC 78-5826. 320p. 1983. 24.95 o.p. (ISBN 0-8436-0759-9). Van Nos Reinhold.
Prodigal Apprentice. George MacDonald. 288p. 1986. pap. 5.95 o.p. (ISBN 0-89693-151-X). Victor Bks.
Prodigal Century. Henry P. Fairchild. (ISBN 0-8022-0468-6). Philos Lib.
Prodigal Daughter. Jeffrey Archer. 1982. 15.95 o.p. (ISBN 0-671-42229-4, Linden Pr). S&S.
Prodigal Women. Nancy Hale. 736p. 1981. pap. 3.50 o.p. (ISBN 0-380-53553-X, 53553-X). Avon.
Prodigals & Publicans: Dramas. W. A. Poovey. LC 79-54111. 72p. 1980. pap. 2.95 o.p. (10-5248, Augsburg). Augsburg Fortress.
Prodigious Builders. Bernard Rudofsky. LC 78-23534. 383p. 1979. pap. 7.95 o.p. (ISBN 0-15-674625-5, Harv). HarBraceJ.
Prodigious Builders. Bernard Rudofsky. 1977. 14.95 o.p. (ISBN 0-15-193050-3). HarBraceJ.
ProDOS & Beyond: Applesoft File Techniques. Gary Cornell. LC 85-17897. 238p. 1985. pap. 16.95 o.p. (ISBN 0-471-83181-6). Wiley.
ProDOS Quick & Simple: For the Apple II Family. John Burdick & Peter B. Weiser. (Illus.). 256p. 1985. pap. 19.95 o.p. (ISBN 0-673-18077-8). Scott F.
Prodrome d'Une Histoire Naturelle des Agaricinees. V. Fayod. 1968. Repr. of 1889 ed. 17.00x o.p. (ISBN 90-6123-064-0). Lubrecht & Cramer.
Prodromus Lichenographiae Galliae et Algeriae. W. Nylander. 1968. pap. 36.00x o.p. (ISBN 3-7682-0343-3). Lubrecht & Cramer.
Producers & Scroungers Strategics of Exploitation & Parasitism. Ed. by C. J. Barnard. 267p. 1984. 39.95 o.p. (ISBN 0-412-00541-7, NO. 9017, Pub. by Chapman & Hall England). Routledge Chapman & Hall.
Producing Hit Records. Dennis Lambert & Ronald Zalkind. LC 79-91505. (Illus.). 1980. 17.50 o.s.i. (ISBN 0-02-871950-6); pap. 9.95 o.s.i. (ISBN 0-02-871960-3). Schirmer Bks.
Producing Theatre. rev. ed. Donald C. Farber. LC 86-27312. 472p. 1987. text ed. 32.50 o.p. (ISBN 0-87910-074-5); pap. text ed. 19.95 o.p. (ISBN 0-87910-103-2). Limelight Edns.
Product Counterfeiting: Remedies. (Patents, Copyrights, Trademarks & Literary Property Course Handbook: Vol. 180). 332p. 1984. 15.00 o.p. (ISBN 0-317-11486-7, G4-3744). PLI.
Product Defects & Recalls: What Government Wanted & What Industry Did, Vol. 1. Judy Haberek. Ed. by Robert Varela. 45p. pap. cancelled o.s.i. (ISBN 0-914176-27-7); pap. cancelled o.s.i. Wash Busn Info.
Product Life Cycle & International Trade. Ed. by Louis T. Wells, Jr. LC 78-184791. (Illus.). 259p. 1972. pap. 4.95x o.p. (ISBN 0-87584-095-7, Dist. by Harper & Row Pubs., Inc.). Harvard Busn.
Product Management Handbook: A Practical Guide for Bank Product Managers. 84p. 1983. 54.00 o.p. (ISBN 0-318-03430-1, 711). Bank Admin Inst.
Product of Web Impregnation of Saturation. (Bibliographic Ser.: No. S40.). 166p. 1971. 24.00 o.p. (ISBN 0-317-34425-0). Inst Paper Chem.
Product Planning & Management. William S. Sachs & George Benson. 376p. 1981. text ed. write for info. o.p. (ISBN 0-02-308220-8). Macmillan.
Product Rendering with Markers. Mark Arends. (Illus.). 180p. 1985. 36.95x o.s.i. (ISBN 0-442-20952-5). Van Nos Reinhold.
Production & Distribution Theories: The Formative Period. George J. Stigler. LC 68-16356. 1941. 12.00x o.p. (ISBN 0-87586-008-7). Agathon.
Production & Hazards of a Hyperbaric Oxygen Environment: Proceedings. Ed. by G. S. Innes. 1970. 35.00 o.p. (ISBN 0-08-006767-0). Pergamon.
Production & Inventory Control Handbook. J. H. Greene. 1970. text ed. 76.50 o.p. (ISBN 0-07-024332-8). McGraw.
Production & Inventory Management in the Computer Age. Oliver W. Wight. LC 74-7127. 300p. 1983. 29.95 o.p. (ISBN 0-442-29367-4). Van Nos Reinhold.
Production & Operations Management: A Life Cycle Approach. 4th ed. Richard B. Chase & Nicholas J. Aquilano. 1985. 42.00x o.p. (ISBN 0-256-03226-2). Irwin.
Production & Operations Management: A systems Concept. 2nd ed. Richard A. Johnson et al. 500p. 1974. text ed. 26.95 o.p. (ISBN 0-395-18029-5). HM.
Production & Planning Applied to Building. 2nd ed. R. J. Hollins. 1971. 29.95x o.p. (ISBN 0-7121-4606-7). Trans-Atl Phila.
Production Control. 3rd ed. Franklin G. Moore & Ronald Jablonski. LC 68-28418. 1969. text ed. 38.95 o.p. (ISBN 0-07-042921-9). McGraw.
Production Control for the Small & Medium Sized Firms. Wilbert Steffy et al. (Illus.). 104p. 1977. 12.00 o.p. (ISBN 0-938654-11-X, PROD C). Indus Dev Inst Sci.
Production Control in Engineering. 2nd ed. D. K. Corke. (Illus.). 1977. 42.50x o.p. (ISBN 0-7131-3380-5). Trans-Atl Phila.
Production Control Packages. Ed. by National Computing Centre, Ltd. Staff. LC 72-97122. (Factfinder Ser: No. 13). 100p. 1976. pap. 15.00x o.s.i. (ISBN 0-85012-160-4). Intl Pubns Serv.
Production Management Analysis. 2nd ed. Leonard J. Garrett & Milton Silver. LC 73-7831. (Harbrace Business & Economics Ser.). 721p. 1973. text ed. 23.95 o.p. (ISBN 0-15-571991-2, HC). HarBraceJ.
Production of the Boranes & Related Research. Richard I. Holzmann. 1967. 92.00 o.p. (ISBN 0-12-354950-7). Acad Pr.
Production Operations, 2 vols. 2nd ed. T. O. Allen & Alan P. Roberts. 1982. Set. 90.00 o.p. (ISBN 0-317-13016-1); Vol. 1, 290p. 47.50 o.p. (ISBN 0-930972-05-8); Vol. 2, 250p. 47.50 o.p. (ISBN 0-930972-04-X). Oil & Gas.
Production-Operations Management. Richard I. Levin et al. (Management Ser). (Illus.). 416p. 1972. text ed. 36.95 o.p. (ISBN 0-07-037369-8). McGraw.
Production Planning & Control: An Introduction to Quantitative Methods. J. R. King. 1975. 140.00 o.p. (ISBN 0-08-017721-2). Pergamon.
Production Planning & Inventory Control. Dennis W. McLeavey & Seetharama L. Narasimhan. 1985. 45.00 o.s.i. (ISBN 0-205-08147-9, 088147). Allyn.
Production Planning & Repro Mechanicals for Offset Printing. Henry C. Latimer. (Illus.). 1980. text ed. 41.50 o.p. (ISBN 0-07-036621-7). McGraw.
Production Relations, Class & Black Liberation: A Marxist Perspective in Afro-American Studies. Clarence J. Munford. (Philosophical Currents Ser. 24: No. 24). 1978. pap. text ed. 28.50x o.p. (ISBN 90-6032-107-3). Humanities.
Production Systems: Planning, Analysis & Control. 3rd ed. James L. Riggs. LC 80-19186. (Management Ser.). 649p. 1981. (ISBN 0-471-05946-3). Wiley.
Production Theory: Proceedings of the International Seminar, University of Karlsruhe, May-July, 1973. Ed. by W. Eichhorn et al. (Lecture Notes in Economics & Mathematical Systems Ser.: Vol. 99). viii, 386p. 1974. pap. 21.00 o.p. (ISBN 0-387-06890-2). Springer-Verlag.
Productive Conflict Management: Perspectives for Organizations. Dean Tjosvold & David W. Johnson. 224p. 1983. 29.95x o.p. (ISBN 0-8290-1266-4). Irvington.
Productivity Bargaining: A Study in Contract Construction. William F. Maloney. (Illus.). 157p. 1977. 12.00 o.p. (ISBN 0-938654-12-8, BARG). Indus Dev Inst Sci.
Productivity, Bargaining & Industrial Change. N. Stettner. 1969. 21.00 o.p. (ISBN 0-08-006756-5); pap. 10.25 o.p. (ISBN 0-08-006757-3). Pergamon.
Productivity Challenge: How to Make It Work for America & You. Michael LeBoeuf. 256p. 1982. text ed. 12.95 o.p. (ISBN 0-07-036970-4). McGraw.
Productivity Gains Through Worklife Improvement. Edward M. Glaser. LC 76-2044. 1976. 20.85 o.p. (ISBN 0-15-800095-1). HarBraceJ.
Productivity Improvement Manual. National Association of Home Builders Staff. 36p. 1978. pap. 7.50 o.p. (ISBN 0-86718-027-7). Nat Assn H Build.
Productivity Improvements in Emergency Departments: Clearinghouse for Hospital Management Engineering - An Examination of Case Studies. LC 81-7898. 208p. (Orig.). 1981. pap. 15.00 o.p. (ISBN 0-87258-357-0, AHA-052135). Am Hospital.
Productivity Improvements in Operating Rooms: An Examination of Case Studies. LC 80-22838. 236p. (Orig.). 1981. pap. 25.00 o.p. (ISBN 0-87258-335-X, 156121). Am Hospital.
Productivity Improvements in Respiratory Therapy Departments: An Examination of Case Studies. LC 81-14970. 196p. 1981. 15.00 o.p. (ISBN 0-87258-362-7). Am Hospital.
Productivity in Railroads: Proceedings of a Symposium Held at Princeton University, July, 1977. Ed. by Arnold D. Kerr & Alain L. Kornhauser. (Pergamon Policy Studies). 1980. 36.00 o.p. (ISBN 0-08-023871-8). Pergamon.
Productivity in Service Organizations: Organizing for People. Herbert Heaton. (Illus.). 1977. text ed. 34.50 o.p. (ISBN 0-07-027705-2). McGraw.
Productivity Management: Test & Cases. K. C. Chen & Robert E. McGarrah. 564p. 1982. text ed. 33.95x o.p. (ISBN 0-03-048901-6); instr's manual 20.95 o.p. (ISBN 0-03-052231-5). Dryden Pr.
Productivity Measurement in Education. Ed. by Anita A. Sommers. LC 81-48588. (Testing & Measurement Ser.: No. 16). 1982. pap. text ed. 13.95x o.p. Jossey-Bass.
Productivity of World Ecosystems. International Biological Program Staff & National Research Council Staff. 1975. pap. 17.50 o.p. (ISBN 0-309-02317-3). Natl Acad Pr.
Productivity-Performance Measures for Public Services at the Local Level: A Bibliography. Mary E. Huls. (Public Administration Ser.: P 1742). 6p. 1985. 2.00 o.p. (ISBN 0-89028-522-5). Vance Biblios.
Productivity Primer. National Center for Research in Vocational Education Staff. 1982. 25.00 o.p. (ISBN 0-318-22182-9, SN35). Natl Ctr Res Voc Ed.
Productivity: Prospects for Growth. Ed. by Jerome M. Rosow. (Work in America Ser.). 1981. 23.95 o.p. (ISBN 0-442-29326-7). Van Nos Reinhold.
Productivity, Technology, & Capital Economic Analysis, Managerial Strategies, & Government Policies. Bela Gold. LC 79-4749. 352p. 1979. 35.00x o.p. (ISBN 0-669-02957-2). Lexington Bks.
Productivity versus OSHA & EPA Regulations. Wayne B. Gray. Ed. by Richard Farmer. LC 85-28873. (Research for Business Decisions: No. 86). 132p. 1986. 39.95 o.p. (ISBN 0-8357-1721-6). UMI Res Pr.
Products Liability. Pennsylvania Bar Institute Staff. 169p. 1985. 35.00 o.p. (ISBN 0-318-19069-9, 300). PA Bar Inst.
Products Liability. 179p. 1979. 7.50 o.p. (ISBN 0-318-02483-7). ICLE Georgia.
Products Liability. 1984. (ISBN 0-88129-145-5). Wash Bar CLE.
Products Liability in a Nutshell. 2nd ed. Dix W. Noel & Jerry J. Phillips. LC 80-39726. (Nutshell Ser.). 341p. 1981. pap. text ed. 9.95 o.p. (ISBN 0-8299-2121-4). West Pub.
Products Liability: The First 25 Years, 2 vols. Ed. by Jeffrey R. White. LC 83-70668. 1279p. 1983. Set. 45.00 o.p. (ISBN 0-941916-06-5). Vol. 1 (ISBN 0-941916-07-3). Vol. 2 (ISBN 0-941916-08-1). Assn Trial Ed.
Products Liability, 1984. Ed. by Anne R. Grant. (Trial Annuals Ser.). (Illus., Orig.). 1985. pap. 18.00 o.p. (ISBN 0-941916-20-0). Assn Trial Ed.
Products of Binns Road. Peter Randall. (Hornby Companion Ser. II: No. II). (Illus.). 225p. 1984. 35.00 o.s.i. (ISBN 0-904568-06-7, Pub. by New Cavendish England). Schiffer.
Produzentenhaftpflicht in U. S. A. und Deutschland: Product Liability in Germany & the U. S. A. 2nd ed. Martin Peltzer & Walter Treumann. Ed. by German American Chamber of Commerce Staff. Tr. by Annette Fischer-Theurer. 54p. (Ger. & Eng.). 1981. pap. 15.00 o.p. (ISBN 0-86640-002-8). German Am Chamber.
Professing History. Sir Keith Hancock. 1977. 19.00x o.p. (ISBN 0-424-00024-5, Pub. by Sydney U Pr). Intl Spec Bk.
Profession of a Civil Engineer: Studies in Honour of John Roderick. E. H. Davis & D. Campbell-Allen. LC 79-670361. 1979. 29.00x o.p. (ISBN 0-424-00064-4, Pub. by Sydney U Pr). Intl Spec Bk.
Profession of English. G. B. Harrison. LC 73-5607. 183p. 1973. pap. 2.45 o.p. (ISBN 0-15-674650-6, HB257, Harv). HarBraceJ.
Profession '78. Ed. by Richard I. Brod & Jasper P. Neel. 60p. 1978. pap. 7.50x o.p. (ISBN 0-87352-313-X). Modern Lang.
Professional. W. C. Heinz. LC 57-11798. (Library of Contemporary Americana). 346p. 1984. pap. 7.95 o.p. (ISBN 0-87795-646-4, Arbor Hse). Morrow.
Professional. Otto J. Scott. 1976. 15.00 o.p. (ISBN 0-689-10726-9, Atheneum). Macmillan.
Professional & Administrative Career Examination. Gary Gruber. (Exam Prep Ser.). 1975. pap. 6.95 o.p. (ISBN 0-671-18090-8). Monarch Pr.
Professional & Credentialing Issues: Bibliography. 7.50 o.p. (ISBN 0-317-59912-7, 72504C). Am Assn Coun Dev.
Professional & Judicial Conduct Citations. Shepard's Citation, Inc. Staff. (Specialized Citations). 1985. write for info. o.p. Shepards-McGraw.
Professional Apartmenteering. C. D. Ellington. 348p. 1979. pap. 13.00 o.p. (ISBN 0-86718-086-2). Nat Assn H Build.
Professional Bar Service Management. Harris Thayse. 224p. 1983. 34.95 o.p. (ISBN 0-13-725440-7). P-H.
Professional Bowlers Association Guide to Better Bowling: 25th Anniversary Edition. rev. ed. Chuck Pezzano. (Illus.). 240p. 1983. pap. 8.95 o.s.i. (ISBN 0-671-47244-5, Fireside). S&S.
Professional Broadcast Announcing. Lee Dudek. 336p. 1981. text ed. 33.33 o.p. (ISBN 0-205-07660-2, 4876601). Allyn.

Professional Care: Its Meaning & Practice. Alastair W. Campbell. LC 84-4081. 160p. 1984. pap. 7.95 o.p. (ISBN 0-8006-1812-2, Fortress). Augsburg Fortress.

Professional Chef's Art of Garde Manger. 3rd ed. Fritz Sonnenschmidt & Jean Nicholas. 258p. 1983. 31.95 o.p. (ISBN 0-8436-2223-7). Van Nos Reinhold.

Professional Choices: Values at Work. Ann A. Abbott. 128p. 1988. 12.95 o.p. (ISBN 0-87101-159-X). Natl Assn Soc Wkrs.

Professional Cleaning & Building Maintenance: How to Organize a Money Saving Service Business or a Department for Floor & Building Cleaning. Bill Clark. 1960. text ed. 7.50 o.p. (ISBN 0-682-40024-6, Banner). Exposition-Phoenix.

Professional Corporations after TEFRA. Pennsylvania Bar Institute Staff. 118p. 1983. 30.00 o.p. (ISBN 0-318-02185-4, 237). PA Bar Inst.

Professional Corporations & Small Businesses after the Tax Reform Act of 1984. LC 82-61269. (Tax Law & Estate Planning Course Handbook Ser.: Vol. 216). 653p. 1984. pap. 45.00 o.p. (J4-3556). PLI.

Professional Counselor: Competencies, Performance Guidelines & Assessment. Ed. by Joseph Dameton. 102p. 1980. 7.25 o.p. (ISBN 0-911547-63-0, 72141W34); members 6.50 o.p. (ISBN 0-686-37319-7). Am Assn Coun Dev.

Professional Development for College & University Librarians: A Selective Bibliography. Lorna Peterson. (Public Administration Ser.: P 1675). 14p. 1985. 2.25 o.p. (ISBN 0-89028-385-0). Vance Biblios.

Professional Development: The Dynamics of Success. Mary Wilkes & C. Bruce Crosswait. 406p. 1981. text ed. 18.50 o.p. (ISBN 0-15-572001-5, HC). HarBraceJ.

Professional Development: The Dynamics of Success. 2nd ed. Mary Wilkes & C. Bruce Crosswait. 406p. 1984. text ed. 22.00 o.p. (ISBN 0-15-572004-X, HC). HarBraceJ.

Professional Diplomacy in the United States, 1779-1939. Warren F. Ilchman. LC 61-11991. (Midway Reprint Ser.). vii, 254p. 1974. pap. text ed. 10.50x o.s.i. (ISBN 0-226-37052-6). U of Chicago Pr.

Professional Diplomat. John E. Harr. 1969. 39.50x o.p. (ISBN 0-691-07524-7). Princeton U Pr.

Professional Discotheque Management. Daniel A. Emenheiser. LC 80-20910. 248p. 1983. 28.95 o.p. (ISBN 0-8436-0768-8). Van Nos Reinhold.

Professional Dominance: The Social Structure of Medical Care. Eliot Freidson. LC 72-116538. 1970. 29.95x o.p. (ISBN 0-202-30203-2). Aldine de Gruyter.

Professional Engineering Practice: Ethical Aspects. C. Morrison & P. Hughes. 1982. text ed. 15.95 o.p. (ISBN 0-07-548550-8). McGraw.

Professional Engineer's Examination Questions & Answers. 3rd ed. William S. LaLonde & William Stack-Staikidis. 1981. 35.50 o.p. (ISBN 0-07-036093-6); pap. text ed. 19.95 o.p. (ISBN 0-07-036095-2). McGraw.

Professional English. Mark Ellis et al. 104p. (Orig.). 1984. pap. text ed. 12.95 o.p. (ISBN 0-582-74882-8). Longman.

Professional Examination Questions & Answers: A Self-Study Approach to Accompany Horngren, Cost Accounting, 5th Edition. John K. Harris. (Illus.). 304p. 1982. pap. text ed. (ISBN 0-13-179598-8). P-H.

Professional Forecaster: The Forecasting Process Through Data Analysis. James P. Cleary & Hans Levenbach. (Quantitative Methods for Managers Ser.). (Illus.). 402p. 1981. 33.95 o.p. (ISBN 0-534-97960-2, Lifetime Learn). Van Nos Reinhold.

Professional Guide to Drugs. 2nd ed. Ed. by Helen Hamilton & Minnie B. Rose. LC 81-19996. (Illus.). 1320p. 1986. text ed. 24.95 o.p. (ISBN 0-916730-51-4). Springhouse Pub.

Professional Handbook for Patrol & Security Guards. Guy R. Rankin. LC 77-77264. 1977. 5.00 o.p. (ISBN 0-682-48838-0). Exposition-Phoenix.

Professional Housekeeper. 2nd ed. Georgina Tucker & Madelin Schneider. 1983. 37.95 o.p. (ISBN 0-8436-2252-0). Van Nos Reinhold.

Professional Income of Engineers 1985. Engineering Manpower Commission & R. A. Eliis. 125p. (Orig.). 1986. pap. 75.00 o.p. (ISBN 0-87615-137-3). AAES.

Professional Income of Engineers, 1987. R. A. Ellis & Engineering Manpower Commission Staff. 1988. pap. 77.50 o.p. (ISBN 0-87615-139-X). AAES.

Professional Inspection of Construction: Proceedings of a Symposium Sponsored by the Construction Division. 62p. 1984. 14.00x o.p. (ISBN 0-87262-421-8). Am Soc Civil Eng.

Professional Issues for Social Workers in Schools: Proceedings from Second NASW Natl Conference on Social Work. 1982. 10.95x o.p. (ISBN 0-87101-095-X). Natl Assn Soc Wkrs.

Professional Job Search Program: How To Market Yourself. Burton E. Lipman. LC 82-25089. 292p. 1983. 17.95 o.p. (ISBN 0-471-89159-2, Pub. by Wiley-Interscience). Wiley.

Professional Management in General Electric, 4 vols. General Electric Company Staff. Incl. Vol. 1. General Electric's Growth. Repr. of 1953 ed. o.p.; Vol. 2. General Electric's Organization. Repr. of 1955 ed. o.p.; Vol. 3. The Work of a Professional Manager. Repr. of 1954 ed. o.p.; Vol. 4. The Work of a Functional Individual Contributor. Repr. of 1959 ed. (Management History Ser.: No. 76). (Illus.). 1200p. 1975. Set. 87.50 o.s.i. (ISBN 0-87960-113-2). Hive Pub.

Professional Mediation of Civil Disputes. Robert Coulson. LC 84-72418. 62p. pap. 7.50 o.p. (ISBN 0-943001-18-8); pap. 6.50 members o.p. Am Arbitration.

Professional Multihousing Management. Frank Basile. (Illus.). 250p. 1984. 39.00 o.p. (ISBN 0-86718-221-0). Nat Assn H Build.

Professional PAIR, Vol. VIII. Ed. by Dale Yoder & Herbert G. Heneman, Jr. (ASPA Handbook of Personnel & Industrial Relations). 268p. 1979. pap. 12.00 o.p. (ISBN 0-87179-207-9, 0207). BNA.

Professional Photographic Illustration Techniques. LC 77-99272. (Illus.). 136p. 1978. pap. 7.50 o.p. (ISBN 0-87985-190-2, 0-16). Eastman Kodak.

Professional Power & Social Welfare. Paul Wilding. 192p. (Orig.). 1982. pap. 10.95x o.p. (ISBN 0-7100-0885-6). Routledge Chapman & Hall.

Professional Powers: A Study of the Institutionalization of Formal Knowledge. Eliot Freidson. LC 85-20789. xviii, 242p. 1986. 22.50x o.s.i. (ISBN 0-226-26224-3). U of Chicago Pr.

Professional Psychology Review, Vol. II. Ed. by Donald R. Peterson. (Rutgers Professional Psychology Review Ser.). 200p. 1985. text ed. 29.95x o.p. (ISBN 0-88738-011-5). Transaction Pubs.

Professional Responsibility. Ronald D. Rotunda. LC 84-15262. (Black Letter Ser.). 429p. 1984. pap. text ed. 14.95 o.p. (ISBN 0-314-83764-7). West Pub.

Professional Secretary: Skills & Techniques for Recognition & Success. Diane Daniels & Anne D. Barron. 224p. 1982. 15.95 o.p. (ISBN 0-8144-5599-9); pap. 7.95 o.p. (ISBN 0-8144-7576-0). AMACOM.

Professional Selling. 4th. ed. David L. Kurtz et al. 1985. text ed. 34.95x o.p. (ISBN 0-256-03271-8). Irwin.

Professional Selling: A Practical Approach. R. J. Kranz & M. K. Kranz. LC 79-65551. 248p. 1980. text ed. 16.95x o.p. (ISBN 0-442-26242-6). PWS-Kent Pub.

Professional Service Management. William Joseph. (Illus.). 256p. 1983. text ed. 34.95 o.p. (ISBN 0-07-039267-6). McGraw.

Professional Service of Food & Beverage in Britain. Joseph Houston & Neil Glenesk. (Illus.). 144p. 1982. 16.95 o.p. (ISBN 0-7134-3529-1, Pub. by Batsford England). David & Charles.

Professional Smithing. Donald Streeter. (Illus.). 144p. 1980. 19.95 o.s.i. (ISBN 0-684-16530-9, ScribT). Scribner.

Professional Sound Blue Book, 1986. 480p. Date not set. 99.50 o.p. (ISBN 0-932089-08-9). Orion Res.

Professional Sound Blue Book, 1987. Ed. by Orion Research Corporation Staff. 500p. 1986. 99.50 o.p. (ISBN 0-932089-13-5). Orion Res.

Professional Staffs of Congress. 3rd rev. ed. Kenneth Kofmehl. LC 62-63211. 312p. 1977. pap. 6.95 o.p. (ISBN 0-911198-03-2). Purdue U Pr.

Professional Status, Concerns, & Reflections. National Association for Women Deans, Administrators & Counselors Staff. 1971. pap. 6.00 o.p. (ISBN 0-686-09575-8). Natl Assn Women.

Professional Suicide. Donald W. Cole. 256p. 1981. text ed. 23.95 o.p. (ISBN 0-07-011697-0). McGraw.

Professional Suicide. McGraw.

Professional Tax Record Book. B. J. Worth. pap. 9.95 o.p. (ISBN 0-8010-9670-7). Baker Bk.

Professional Teachers Handbook: A Guide for Improving Instruction in Today's Middle & Secondary Schools. 3rd ed. Hoover. 1985. 31.43 o.p. (ISBN 0-205-07724-2, 237724). Allyn.

Professional Thief. Ed. by Edwin H. Sutherland. LC 37-36112. 1956. pap. text ed. 2.95 o.s.i. (ISBN 0-226-78054-6, P10, Phoen). U of Chicago Pr.

Professional Treasure Hunter. George Mroczkowski & Chara Bishop. Ed. by B. J. Nelson. LC 79-65322. (Illus.). 154p. (Orig.). 1981. pap. 7.95 o.p. (ISBN 0-915920-41-7). Ram Pub.

Professional Values. Ann A. Abbott. 1988. write for info. o.p. Natl Assn Soc Wkrs.

Professional Writing Skills for Health Care Managers. Health Care Education Associates Staff. 100p. 1986. 19.95 o.p. (ISBN 0-8016-2123-2). Mosby.

Professionalism & Flexibility in Learning: SRHE Leverhulme VI. Ed. by Donald Bligh. 167p. 1982. 19.00x o.p. (ISBN 0-900868-87-2, Open Univ Pr). Taylor & Francis.

Professionalism & Pastoral Care. Alastair V. Campbell. LC 84-48710. (Theology & Pastoral Care Ser.). 128p. 1985. pap. 3.50 o.p. (ISBN 0-8006-1733-9, Fortress). Augsburg Fortress.

Professionalization of Librarianship. Michael F. Winter. (Occasional Papers: No. 160). 46p. 1983. pap. 3.00 o.p. (ISBN 0-317-59007-3). U of Ill Lib Info Sci.

Professional's Guide to the Estate Tax Audit. Jordan C. Berger & Marvin D. Brody. LC 81-7147. 394p. 1982. 89.50 o.p. (ISBN 0-87624-440-1, Inst Busn Plan). P-H.

Professions in Government. Ed. by Richard Stillman & Frederick C. Mosher. LC 79-93072. 102p. 1981. pap. 9.95 o.s.i. (ISBN 0-87855-863-2). Transaction Pubs.

Professor. Jack Lynn. LC 84-62280. 278p. 1985. 16.95 o.p. (ISBN 0-88186-329-7). Parkwest Pubns.

Professor Branestawm's Crunchy Crockery. Norman Hunter. (Illus.). 48p. 1984. bds. 7.95 Laminated o.p. (ISBN 0-370-30954-5, Pub. by Bodley Head). Salem Hse Pubs.

Professor Branestawm's Hair-Raising Idea. Norman Hunter. (Illus.). 48p. 1984. bds. 7.95 Laminated o.p. (ISBN 0-370-30955-3, Pub. by Bodley Head). Salem Hse Pubs.

Professor Coconut & the Thief. Rita Gelman & Joan Richter. LC 76-27846. (gr. 1-5). 1977. reinforced bdg. 6.95 o.s.i. (ISBN 0-03-016931-3). H Holt & Co.

Professor Diggins' Dragons. Felice Holman. LC 66-16103. (Illus.). 144p. (gr. 4-6). 1974. pap. 0.95 o.s.i. (ISBN 0-02-043680-7, Collier). Macmillan.

Professor Dowell's Head. G. V. Alekseeva. 88p. 1985. pap. 1.95 o.p. (ISBN 0-8285-2872-1, Pub. by Rus Lang Pubs USSR). Imported Pubns.

Professor E. McSquared's Original, Fantastic, & Highly Edifying Calculus Primer. 214p. 1987. pap. 12.50 o.p. (ISBN 0-913232-47-5, GK110). Janson Pubns.

Professor Longfellow of Harvard. Carl L. Johnson. LC 44-42422. 1943. pap. 1.00 o.p. (ISBN 0-87114-003-9). U of Oreg Bks.

Professor's Daughter. Piers P. Read. 1980. pap. 2.25 o.p. (ISBN 0-380-49981-9, 49981). Avon.

Professor's Odyssey: A Portrait of a Profession. John E. Jacobi. LC 76-27821. 1976. 4.00 o.p. (ISBN 0-682-48646-9). Exposition-Phoenix.

Proficiency Plus. Michael McCarthy et al. 256p. 1985. pap. 12.95x o.p. (ISBN 0-631-90320-8) (ISBN 0-631-90016-0). Basil Blackwell.

Profile of a Museum Registrar. Marjorie Hoachlander. 120p. (Orig.). 1980. pap. 3.00 o.p. (ISBN 0-89492-038-3). Acad Educ Dev.

Profile of Current Developments in Atomic Spectroscopy: Dedicated to Kurt Laqua on the Occasion of His 65th Birthday. Ed. by P. W. Boumans et al. 400p. 1985. pap. 91.00 o.p. (ISBN 0-08-031447-3). Pergamon.

Profile of General Meade & the Four Military Installations Named for the Victor at Gettysburg. B. C. Corrigan. (Historic Marker Ahead Ser.). (Illus., Orig.). 1985. pap. 1.95 o.p. (ISBN 0-9612956-1-9). ADS Pr.

Profile of Pacific Schools. 121p. 1987. 9.95 o.p. (ISBN 0-317-66079-9). Northwest Regional.

Profile of Small or Rural Hospitals 1980-1984. 48p. (Orig.). 1986. pap. 15.00 o.p. (ISBN 0-87258-446-1, 184200). Am Hospital.

Profile of the Dixon Family. Mary W. Moss. (Illus.). 1980. pap. 4.50 o.p. (ISBN 0-682-49572-7). Exposition-Phoenix.

Profile Survey 8-B: Arts Programs, Finances & Attendance. Charles L. Shakal. 50p. pap. 13.50 o.p. (ISBN 0-318-13413-6); pap. 8.00 member o.p. (ISBN 0-318-13414-4). Assn Perf Arts Presenters.

Profiles: Educational Institutions. 3rd ed. Compiled by Elizabeth S. Hall & Gweneth G. Whitman. 500p. 1988. 206.00 o.p. (ISBN 0-89964-257-8). Coun Adv & Supp Ed.

Profiles in Exploration. Andrew M. Weber. 272p. 1988. pap. text ed. 18.95 o.p. (ISBN 0-8403-4247-0). Kendall-Hunt.

Profiles in Innocence by Quentin K. Y. Huang: With an Introduction by Himself. J. Gareth Hitchcock. 64p. 1980. 8.00 o.p. (ISBN 0-682-49669-3). Exposition-Phoenix.

Profiles in Liberation: Thirty-Six Portraits of Third World Theologians. Deane W. Ferm. 1988. pap. 7.95 o.p. (ISBN 0-317-67568-0). Twenty-Third.

Profiles of American Colleges. 14th ed. Ed. by Elliot M. Epstein et al. 1984. Vol. I, Descriptions of the Colleges. pap. 12.95 o.p. (ISBN 0-8120-2791-4); Vol. II, Index of College Majors. pap. 10.95 o.p. (ISBN 0-8120-2792-2); (Cloth Vol. I) 28.95 o.p. (ISBN 0-8120-5552-7); (Cloth Vol. II) 19.95 o.p. (ISBN 0-8120-5553-5). Barron.

Profiles of American Colleges, Vol. 1. 15th ed. 1248p. 1986. 28.95 o.p.; pap. 12.95 o.p. (ISBN 0-8120-3656-5). Barron.

Profiles of American Colleges: Index to College Majors, Vol. 2. 15th. rev. ed. 400p. 1986. 19.95 o.p. (ISBN 0-8120-5713-9); pap. 10.95 o.p. (ISBN 0-8120-3657-3). Barron.

Profiles of American Colleges Regional Edition Northeast. 7th ed. 400p. 1986. pap. 8.95 o.p. (ISBN 0-8120-3715-4). Barron.

Profiles of an Era: The Nixon-Ford Years. Eleanora W. Schoenebaum. LC 79-3374. 787p. 1980. pap. 9.95 o.p. (ISBN 0-15-674662-X, Harv). HarBraceJ.

Profiles of International Private Lease, DATEL & Packet Switched Service Markets for the Years 1976 to 1979. National Telecommunications Administration, Office of International Affairs Staff. 1981. 50.00 o.s.i. (ISBN 0-686-37966-7). Info Gatekeepers.

Profiles of Lutherans in the U. S. A. Carl F. Reuss. LC 82-70947. 128p. 1982. pap. 5.95 o.p. (ISBN 0-8066-1922-8, 10-5253, Augsburg). Augsburg Fortress.

Profiles of Selected ESL Programs & Their Staff Employment Conditons: ESOL Programs Outside the U. S, Vol. II. TESOL Professional Standards Committee. 46p. 1984. 2.00 o.s.i. (ISBN 0-939791-05-6). Tchrs Eng Spkrs.

Profiles of Selected ESL Programs & Their Staff Employment Conditions: ESL in Higher Education, Vol. 1. TESOL Professional Standards Committee. 46p. 1983. 2.00 o.s.i. (ISBN 0-939791-04-8). Tchrs Eng Spkrs.

Profiles of Supplies to the Steel Industry in the United States. 89p. 1979. 30.00 o.p. (ISBN 0-317-40463-6). Iron & Steel.

Profiles of the Future: An Inquiry into the Limits of the Possible. rev. ed. Athur C. Clarke. 1984. 15.95 o.p. (ISBN 0-03-069783-2). H Holt & Co.

Profit & Sheen. James Colbert. 1986. 16.45 o.s.i. (ISBN 0-395-39411-2). HM.

Profit from Foodservice: A Q & A Approach. Pat Levings. LC 74-706. 168p. 1983. 19.95 o.p. (ISBN 0-8436-0584-7). Van Nos Reinhold.

Profit from Your Money Making Ideas: How to Build a New Business or Expand an Existing One. Herman R. Holtz. 304p. 1980. 14.95 o.p. (ISBN 0-8144-5590-5). AMACOM.

Profit from Your Moneymaking Ideas: How to Build a New Business or Expand an Existing One. Herman R. Holtz. 1982. pap. 8.95 o.p. (ISBN 0-8144-7553-1). AMACOM.

Profit-Line Management: Managing a Growing Business Successfully. Herman R. Holtz. 200p. 1981. 17.95 o.p. (ISBN 0-8144-5690-1). AMACOM.

Profit Planning Decisions with the Break-Even System. Spencer A. Tucker. 1980. 32.95 o.p. (ISBN 0-442-88014-6). Van Nos Reinhold.

Profitability of Food Processing - 1984 Onwards - the Chemical Engineers' Contribution: Proceedings of the Conference Held at Bath, U. K., 10-12 April 1984. Ed. by Institution of Chemical Engineers. (Institution of Chemical Engineers Symposium Ser.: Vol. 84). 430p. 1984. 67.00 o.s.i. (ISBN 0-08-030279-3). Pergamon.

Profitable Crafts Marketing: A Complete Guide to Successful Selling. Brian T. Jefferson. (Madrona Crafts Business Bks.). (Illus.). 256p. pap. 10.95 o.p. (ISBN 0-88089-013-4). Madrona Pubs.

Profitable People Planning: A Guide to Effective Human Resource Management. Jon D. Council. (Illus.). 159p. 1978. 12.50 o.p. (ISBN 0-682-49104-7). Exposition-Phoenix.

Profitable Public Speaking. Charles Kebbe. LC 82-45167. 128p. 1983. 8.95 o.p. (ISBN 0-689-11309-9, Atheneum). Macmillan.

Profitable Thesis Typing. E. Pokress. 5.50 o.p. (ISBN 0-685-22757-X). Aurea.

Profound Simplicity. Will Schutz. LC 81-84776. 183p. 1982. pap. 13.95 o.p. (ISBN 0-89384-066-1). Univ Assocs.

Progesterone Physiology. J. A. Sundsfjord et al. 1976. 34.50x o.p. (ISBN 0-8422-7256-9). Irvington.

Program Analysis for State & Local Governments. Harry P. Hatry et al. 155p. 1976. pap. 9.95x o.p. (ISBN 0-87766-157-X, 13700). Urban Inst.

Program Design. Ed. by Blaise W. Liffick. LC 78-8649. 1980. pap. text ed. 10.95 o.p. (ISBN 0-07-037825-8, BYTE Bks). McGraw.

Program Design & Development for Gifted & Talented Students. 2nd ed. Frederick B. Tuttle, Jr. & Laurence A. Becker. 128p. 1983. 8.95 o.p. (ISBN 0-8106-0733-6). NEA.

Titles

Program Evaluation in Education: When? How? to What Ends? National Research Council Committee on Program Evaluation in Education. 1981. pap. 8.50x o.p. (ISBN 0-309-03143-5). Natl Acad Pr.
Program Evaluation Kit. rev. ed. Lynn L. Morris et al. LC 78-59613. (Illus.). 1080p. 1978. pap. 59.95 o.p. (ISBN 0-8039-1073-8). Sage.
Program for Change: Affirmative Action in Australia. Ed. by Marian Sawer. 204p. 1986. text ed. 24.95x o.p. (ISBN 0-86861-719-9). Unwin Hyman.
Program Guide for CIM Implementation. 2nd ed. 204p. 1987. 38.00 o.p. (ISBN 0-87263-295-4). SME.
Program Guide for CIM Implementation. Society of Manufacturing Engineers Staff. 110p. 1985. 38.00 o.p. (ISBN 0-87263-206-7). SME.
Program Housing Standards in the Experimental Housing Allowance Program: Analyzing Differences in the Demand & Supply Experiments. Joseph J. Valenza. write for info o.p. Urban Inst.
Program Issues in Developmental Disabilities: A Resource Manual for Surveyors & Reviewers. Ed. by James F. Gardner et al. LC 80-12555. (Illus.). 176p. (Orig.). 1980. pap. text ed. 19.50 o.p. (ISBN 0-933716-05-2, 052). P H Brookes.
Program Management Handbook. 99p. 1976. pap. 5.00 o.p. (ISBN 0-318-14780-7). Lit Vol Am.
Program Materials for Fourth Annual Corporate & Banking Law Institute: October 24-26, 1985, Sea Island. LC 86-620858. Date not set. price not set o.p. ICLE Georgia.
Program Materials for Insurance Law Institute: September 25-27, 1986, St. Simons Island, Georgia. Insurance Law Institute & Institute of Continuing Legal Education in Georgia. LC 86-623179. Date not set. price not set o.p. ICLE Georgia.
Program Materials for Seminar on Construction Litigation, April 4, 1986, Atlanta, Georgia. LC 86-621892. Date not set. price not set o.p. ICLE Georgia.
Program Materials for Seminar on Federal Practice & Procedure: March 7, 1986, Savannah, March 14, 1986, Atlanta, GA. Institute of Continuing Legal Education in Georgia. LC 86-621894. Date not set. price not set o.p. ICLE Georgia.
Program Materials for Seminar on Forensic Evidence for the Civil & Criminal Practitioner: March 21, 1986, Atlanta, Georgia. LC 86-622083. Date not set. price not set o.p. ICLE Georgia.
Program Materials for Seminar on Motion Practice, September 20, 1985, Savannah & September 27, 1985, Atlanta. LC 86-620855. Date not set. price not set o.p. ICLE Georgia.
Program Materials for Seminar on Recent Developments in Georgia Law: November 8, 1985, Amelia Island & November 15, 1985, Atlanta. LC 86-621681. Date not set. price not set o.p. ICLE Georgia.
Program Materials for Seminar on Secured Lending Under the UCC: December 5, 1985, Atlanta, Georgia. LC 86-621679. Date not set. price not set o.p. ICLE Georgia.
Program Materials for Seminar on Will Drafting & Estate Planning, April 18, 1986, Savannah, April, 25, 1986, Atlanta. Institute of Continuing Legal Education in Georgia. LC 86-623186. Date not set. price not set o.p. ICLE Georgia.
Program Materials for Seminar on Workers' Compensation for the General Practitioner: Proceedings of the Seminar, Savannah, April 11, 1986 & Atlanta, April 18, 1986. LC 86-622082. Date not set. price not set o.p. ICLE Georgia.
Program Models for Mainstreaming: Intergrating Students with Moderate to Severe Disabilities. Michael S. Berres & Peter Knoblock. 320p. 1987. 36.00 o.p. (ISBN 0-87189-622-2). Aspen Pub.
Program Planning for Youth Ministry. John E. Forliti. LC 75-143. 60p. 1975. pap. 4.50 o.p. (ISBN 0-88489-061-9). St Marys.
Program Testing Aids. Ed. by National Computing Centre, Ltd. Staff. (Factfinder Ser: No. 8). 60p. (Orig.). 1972. pap. 10.00x o.s.i. (ISBN 0-85012-054-3). Intl Pubns Serv.
Programme-Maker's Handbook or Goodbye Totter TV. Harris Watts. (Illus.). 230p. (Orig.). 1982. text ed. 20.90x o.p. (ISBN 0-9507582-1-3); pap. 7.50x o.s.i. (ISBN 0-9507582-0-5). Kumarian Pr.
Programmed Astronomy: The Night Sky. Sullivan & Sullivan. 1972. pap. text ed. 9.00 o.s.i. (ISBN 0-8449-0504-6); tchrs' manual 4.00 o.s.i.; test 3.00 o.s.i. Carroll CA.
Programmed Business Mathematics, Bk. 1. 4th ed. Harry Huffman. 1980. text ed. 20.20 o.p. (ISBN 0-07-030901-9). McGraw.
Programmed Course in Basic Pulse Circuits. New York Institute of Technology Staff. 1978. text ed. 28.85 o.p. (ISBN 0-07-046375-1). McGraw.
Programmed Gregg Shorthand. Russell J. Hosler et al. (Diamond Jubilee Ser.). (Experimental Ed). 1969. text ed. 35.95 o.p. (ISBN 0-07-030440-8). McGraw.
Programmed Guide to Accompany Fundamentals of Algebra & Trigonometry. Roy A. Dobyns. 1978. pap. text ed. write for info. o.p. (ISBN 0-87150-258-5, PWS 2075, Prindle). PWS-Kent Pub.
Programmed Guide to Tax Research. James E. Parker. (Business Ser.). 260p. 1979. pap. text ed. 10.95x o.p. (ISBN 0-534-00796-1). PWS-Kent Pub.
Programmed Introduction to Critical Path Methods. Cambridge Consultants Training Ltd. 1967. pap. text ed. 6.25 o.p. (ISBN 0-08-014027-0). Pergamon.
Programmed Study Guide for Introduction to Probability & Statistics. 4th ed. Robert J. Beaver & William Mendenhall. 1975. pap. 5.95x o.s.i. (ISBN 0-87872-095-2). PWS-Kent Pub.
Programmed Text in Statistics, 4 bks. J. Hine & G. B. Wetherill. 1975. pap. 10.95x ea. o.p. (NO. 6152, Pub. by Chapman & Hall England); Bk. 1, Summarizing Data. (ISBN 0-412-13590-6, NO. 6152); Bk. 2, Basic Theory. (ISBN 0-412-13730-5, NO. 6431); Bk. 3, The T-text & X-squared Goodness Of Fit. (ISBN 0-412-13740-2, NO. 6153); Bk. 4, Tests On Variance & Regression. (ISBN 0-412-13750-X, NO. 6154). Routledge Chapman & Hall.
Programmer's Book of Rules. George Ledin, Jr. & Victor Ledin. LC 79-13746. 248p. 1981. pap. 19.95 o.p. (ISBN 0-534-97993-9, Lifetime Learn). Van Nos Reinhold.
Programmer's Desk Reference for Commodore 64 BASIC. Mona Rienhardt. (Illus.). 176p. 1985. pap. 15.95 o.p. (ISBN 0-89303-770-2). Brady Bks.
Programmer's Guide to COBOL. William J. Harrison. 240p. 1984. 26.95 o.p. (ISBN 0-442-80040-1); pap. 19.95 o.p. (ISBN 0-442-23224-1). Van Nos Reinhold.
Programmer's Guide to GEM. Phillip Balma & William Fitler. 504p. (Orig.). 1986. pap. 19.95 o.p. (ISBN 0-89588-297-3). Sybex.
Programmer's Guide to MS-DOS. Dennis N. Jump. (Illus.). 1984. pap. 16.95 o.p. (ISBN 0-8359-5655-5, Reston). P-H.
Programmer's Guide to OS-2. Michael J. Young. 625p. (Orig.). 1988. pap. 24.95 o.p. (ISBN 0-89588-464-X). Sybex.
Programmer's Guide to TopView. Alan R. Miller. LC 85-62541. 280p. (Orig.). 1985. pap. 21.95 o.p. (ISBN 0-89588-273-6). Sybex.
Programmer's Guide to Windows. David Durant et al. 645p. (Orig.). 1987. pap. 21.95 o.p. (ISBN 0-89588-362-7). Sybex.
Programmer's Market, 1985. 2nd ed. Brad M. McGehee. 300p. 1984. pap. 16.95 o.p. (ISBN 0-89879-155-3). Writers Digest.
Programmers Reference Guide For the Atari 400-800 Computers. David Heiserman. LC 83-51616. 21.95 o.p. (ISBN 0-672-22277-9). Sams.
Programmer's Reference Guide to TI 99-4A. C. Regena. 312p. 1983. 14.95 o.p. (ISBN 0-942386-12-4). Compute Pubns.
Programmes for Animation Fifty-Seven: Handbook for Animation Technicians. B. Salt. 1978. text ed. 230.00 o.p. (ISBN 0-08-023153-5). Pergamon.
Programmgesteuerte Digitale Rechengerate. H. Rutishauser et al. (MIM Ser.: No. 2). (Illus.). 102p. (Ger.). 1958. pap. 13.95x o.p. (ISBN 0-8176-0321-2). Birkhauser.
Programming ALGOL. D. J. Malcome. 1969. 35.00 o.p. (ISBN 0-08-006385-3); pap. 35.00 o.p. (ISBN 0-08-006384-5). Pergamon.
Programming & Interfacing the Sixty-Five Two, with Experiments. Marvin De Jong. LC 79-67130. 416p. 1980. pap. 17.95 o.p. (ISBN 0-672-21651-5, 21651). Sams.
Programming & Metaprogramming in the Human Biocomputer. John C. Lilly. LC 73-79777. 190p. 1972. 10.95 o.p. (ISBN 0-517-52757-X); pap. 4.95 o.p. (ISBN 0-517-52758-8). Crown.
Programming & Utilization of Research Reactors: Proceedings, 3 vols, Vol. 3. International Atomic Energy Agency Staff. Ed. by Sigvard Eklund. (International Atomic Energy Agency Symposia). 1963. 29.50 o.p. (ISBN 0-12-572503-5). Acad Pr.
Programming Business Applications in FORTRAN IV. Phillip T. May. LC 72-7634. 1973. pap. 32.76 o.p. (ISBN 0-395-14047-1). HM.
Programming Concepts & Problem Solving: An Introduction to Computer Science Using Pascal. Peter Linz. 1983. 34.95 o.p. (ISBN 0-8053-5710-6); Instr's guide with transparency masters. 4.95 o.p. (ISBN 0-8053-5711-4). Benjamin-Cummings.
Programming Digital's Personal Computer: BASIC. Howard Bomze. 1986. text ed. 17.75 o.p. (ISBN 0-03-063729-5). HR&W.
Programming for Real. Harvey G. Lord. LC 84-2990. (Illus.). 224p. 1984. 12.95 o.p. (ISBN 0-689-31064-1, Atheneum). Macmillan.
Programming in BASIC: Structured Programming, Cases, Applications & Modules. 3rd ed. Ralph M. Stair, Jr. Ed. by Robert B. Fetter & Claude McMillan. LC 84-81735. (Irwin Series in Information & Decision Sciences). (Illus.). 454p. 1985. pap. 24.95x o.p. (ISBN 0-256-03213-0). Irwin.
Programming in BASIC, with Applications. Bernard M. Singer. 1973. text ed. 26.90 o.p. (ISBN 0-07-057480-4). McGraw.
Programming in C. Stephen G. Kochan. 384p. pap. 18.95 o.p. (6261). Sams.
Programming in C. Stephen G. Kochan. 1985. 21.95 o.p. (ISBN 0-8104-6261-3). Sams.
Programming in COBOL. G. T. Lancaster. 152p. 1971. pap. text ed. 11.25 o.p. (ISBN 0-08-016384-X). Pergamon.
Programming in Prolog. W. F. Clocksin & C. S. Mellish. 279p. 1982. pap. 16.95 o.p. (ISBN 0-387-11046-1). Springer-Verlag.
Programming in Prolog. 2nd ed. W. F. Clocksin & C. S. Mellish. xv, 297p. 1984. pap. 19.95 o.s.i. (ISBN 0-387-15011-0). Springer-Verlag.
Programming in Structured BASIC. Ronald Brinkman. 416p. 1984. pap. text ed. write for info. o.p. (ISBN 0-02-314870-5). Macmillan.
Programming Language Design. Anthony I. Wasserman. LC 80-83087. (Tutorial Texts Ser.). 527p. 1980. 30.00 o.p. (ISBN 0-8186-0312-7, Q312). IEEE Comp Soc.
Programming Language Standardization. I. D. Hill & B. L. Meek. LC 80-41092. (Computers & Their Applications Ser.). 261p. 1981. pap. 31.95x o.p. (ISBN 0-470-27276-7). Halsted Pr.
Programming Languages. Ed. by F. Genuys. 1969. 68.00 o.p. (ISBN 0-12-279750-7). Acad Pr.
Programming Languages: A Grand Tour. Ed. by Ellis Horowitz. 644p. 1983. 39.95 o.p. (ISBN 0-914894-67-6, Computer Sci Pr). W H Freeman.
Programming Languages: A Grand Tour. 2nd ed. Ed. by Ellis Horowitz. LC 84-14214. 758p. 1985. 43.95 o.p. (ISBN 0-88175-073-5, Computer Sci Pr). W H Freeman.
Programming Languages for Knowledge-Based Systems. John V. Cugini. LC 86-600602. (National Bureau of Standards Special Publication: No. 500-145: Computer Science & Technology). (Illus.). 77p. (Orig.). 1987. pap. 4.00 o.p. (ISBN 0-318-22760-6, S/N 003-003-02783-9). USGPO.
Programming Macintosh BASIC. DiElsie et al. 350p. 1986. pap. text ed. write for info. o.p. (ISBN 0-8087-6404-7). Burgess MN Intl.
Programming Microcomputers with Pascal. Martin Beer. 256p. 1982. pap. 21.95 o.p. (ISBN 0-442-21368-9). Van Nos Reinhold.
Programming Principles: Modula II. John Motil. 1988. pap. text ed. write for info. o.p. (ISBN 0-697-06758-0). Wm C Brown.
Programming Symposium: Proceedings. Colloque Sur la Programmation, Paris, 9-11 April, 1974. Ed. by B. Robinet. LC 74-19256. (Lecture Notes in Computer Science Ser.: Vol. 19). v, 425p. 1974. pap. 22.00 o.p. (ISBN 0-387-06859-7). Springer-Verlag.
Programming the Finite Element Method with Application to Geomechanics. I. M. Smith. LC 82-145525. 351p. 1982. 47.50x o.p. (ISBN 0-471-28003-8, Pub. by Wiley-Interscience); pap. 41.95x o.p. (ISBN 0-471-10098-6, Pub. Bu Wiley-Interscience). Wiley.
Programming the IBM PC & XT: A Guide to Languages. Clarence B. Germain. LC 84-289. (Illus.). 352p. 1984. pap. 19.95 o.p. (ISBN 0-89303-783-4). Brady Bks.
Programming the IBM Personal Computer: Pascal. Neill Graham. 1984. 19.45 o.s.i. (ISBN 0-03-061982-3). HR&W.
Programming the IBM Personal Computer: UCSD Pascal. Seymour V. Pollack. LC 82-21249. 400p. 1983. pap. 40.45 with diskette o.s.i. (ISBN 0-03-063669-8); pap. 23.95 o.s.i. (ISBN 0-03-062637-4). HR&W.
Programming the PL-1 Way. Dan Smedley. (Illus.). 300p. 1982. 15.95 o.p. (ISBN 0-8306-0092-2); pap. 9.95 o.p. (ISBN 0-8306-1414-1, 1414). TAB Bks.
Programming the Sixty-Eight Thousand: An Apple Press Book. Ed Rosenzweig & Harland Harrison. 24.95 o.p. (ISBN 0-8104-6310-5). Sams.
Programming the TI-59 & HP-41 Calculators. Paul Garrison. (Illus.). 300p. (Orig.). 1982. 18.95 o.p. (ISBN 0-8306-2442-2); pap. 13.15 o.p. (ISBN 0-8306-1442-7, 1442). TAB Bks.
Programming the VIC-20. Raeto West. 602p. 1984. pap. 24.95 o.p. (ISBN 0-942386-52-3). Compute Pubns.
Programming the 6502. 3rd ed. Rodnay Zaks. LC 80-51037. (Illus.). 386p. 1980. pap. 13.95 o.p. (ISBN 0-89588-046-6). SYBEX.
Programming the 65816. William Labiak. 370p. (Orig.). 1986. pap. 22.95 o.p. (ISBN 0-89588-324-4). Sybex.
Programming Tools for the IBM PC: Screen Design, Code Generator & High Memory Access. James K. Fugate. (Illus.). 272p. 1985. pap. 19.95 o.p. (ISBN 0-89303-784-2); diskette 30.00 o.p. (ISBN 0-89303-785-0). Brady Bks.
Programming with dBASE MAC. Cary N. Prague & James E. Hammitt. 1988. 26.95 o.p. (ISBN 0-8306-2166-0, 2866); pap. 16.95 o.p. (ISBN 0-8306-2866-5). Tab Bks.
Programming with Pascal. Sanford Leestma & Larry Nyhoff. 384p. 1984. pap. text ed. write for info. o.p. (ISBN 0-02-369460-2). Macmillan.
Programming with the Common Lisp Object System. Daniel Bobrow & Gregor Kiczales. (Illus.). 90p. 1988. pap. text ed. 12.00 o.p. (ISBN 0-929280-25-3). Amer Artificial.
Programming with Windows. Tim Farrell. 600p. 1987. pap. 22.95 o.p. (ISBN 0-88022-299-9, 99). Que Corp.
Programming with Windows Software. Date not set. (ISBN 0-88022-330-8). Que Corp.
Programming Your Apple II Computer. Paul Bryan. (Illus.). 294p. 1982. 15.95 o.p. (ISBN 0-8306-0081-7); pap. 9.95 o.p. (ISBN 0-8306-1394-3, 1394). TAB Bks.
Programs for Electronic Circuit Design. David Leithauser. (Illus.). 128p. (Orig.). 1984. Apple II, II. pap. 24.95 Spiral bound incl. disk o.p. (ISBN 0-88006-079-4, CC7409). Wayne Green Ent.
Programs for Electronic Circuit Design. David Leithauser. (Illus.). 128p. (Orig.). 1984. IBM-PC. pap. 24.95 spiral bound incl. disk o.p. (ISBN 0-88006-080-8, CC7410). Wayne Green Ent.
Programs for Electronic Circuit Design: Package with Software for TRS-80 Model I- Model III Computers. David Leithauser. (Illus.). 128p. (Orig.). 1984. TRS-80 Model I, Model III. pap. 24.95 spiral bound incl. disk o.p. (ISBN 0-88006-081-6, CC7411). Wayne Green Ent.
Programs for Your Timex-Sinclair 1000. Melbourne House Publishers Staff. 108p. 1983. 13.95 o.p. (ISBN 0-13-729798-X); pap. 5.95 o.p. (ISBN 0-13-729780-7). P-H.
Programs in Digital Signal Processing. Institute of Electrical & Electronics Engineers, Inc. Digital Signal Processing Committee. 576p. 1979. 46.95x o.p. (ISBN 0-471-05962-5, Pub. by Wiley-Interscience); pap. 30.50x o.p. (ISBN 0-471-05961-7, Pub. by Wiley-Interscience). Wiley.
Programs of Promise: Art in the Schools. Al Hurwitz. (Illus.). 163p. 1972. pap. text ed. 7.95 o.p. (ISBN 0-15-572150-X, HC). HarBraceJ.
Progres. Louis-Ferdinand D. Celine. 1978. pap. 14.95 o.p. (ISBN 0-686-51955-8). Schoenhof.
Progress & Prospects in Endocrinology. Ed. by Institute of Endocrinology, Gunma Univ. (Gunma Symposia on Endocrinology Ser.: Vol. 20). (Illus.). 152p. 1983. 28.00x o.p. (ISBN 4-905648-03-3, Pub by Sci Soc Japan). Intl Spec Bk.
Progress, Coexistence & Intellectual Freedom. Andrei D. Sakharov. 1968. 7.95 o.p. (ISBN 0-393-05362-8); pap. text ed. 3.95x o.p. (ISBN 0-393-09822-2, Norton C). Norton.
Progress, Coexistence & Intellectual Freedom. rev. ed. Andrei D. Sakharov. 1970. 5.95 o.p. (ISBN 0-393-05428-4). Norton.
Progress in Acetabularia Research. Ed. by C. L. Woodcock. 1977. 49.50 o.p. (ISBN 0-12-763750-8). Acad Pr.
Progress in Aerospace Sciences, Vol. 18, No. 1. Ed. by J. A. Bagley & P. J. Finley. LC 74-618347. 1977. pap. 35.00 o.p. (ISBN 0-08-022133-5). Pergamon.
Progress in Aerospace Sciences, Vol. 19. Ed. by P. J. Finley. (Illus.). 320p. 1982. 145.00 o.p. (ISBN 0-08-029097-3, A140, A999). Pergamon.
Progress in Aerospace Sciences, Vol. 20. Ed. by A. D. Young. (Illus.). 332p. 1985. 145.00 o.p. (ISBN 0-08-032756-7, Pub. by PPL). Pergamon.
Progress in Aerospace Sciences, Vol. 21. Ed. by A. D. Young. (Illus.). 350p. 1986. 132.00 o.p. (ISBN 0-08-033202-1, Pub. by PPL). Pergamon.
Progress in Analytical Atomic Spectroscopy, 2 vols. C. L. Chakrabarti. (Illus.). 282p. 1981. Set. 100.00 o.p. (ISBN 0-08-027126-X). Pergamon.
Progress in Analytical Atomic Spectroscopy, Vol. 1, Pt. 1. Ed. by C. L. Chakrabarti. 1978. 44.00 o.p. (ISBN 0-08-022924-7). Pergamon.
Progress in Analytical Atomic Spectroscopy, Vol. 3. Ed. by C. L. Chakrabarti. 368p. 1981. 92.00 o.p. (ISBN 0-08-029081-7, E130). Pergamon.
Progress in Analytical Atomic Spectroscopy, Vol. 4. Ed. by C. L. Chakrabarti. 440p. 1982. 125.00 o.p. (ISBN 0-08-029659-9). Pergamon.
Progress in Analytical Atomic Spectroscopy, Vol. 5. Ed. by C. L. Chakrabarti. (Illus.). 470p. 1983. 125.00 o.p. (ISBN 0-08-030418-4). Pergamon.

Progress in Analytical Atomic Spectroscopy, Vol. 6. Ed. by C. L. Chakrabarti & R. E. Sturgeon. (Illus.). 444p. 1985. 145.00 o.p. (ISBN 0-08-032307-3). Pergamon.

Progress in Analytical Atomic Spectroscopy, Vol. 7. Ed. by C. L. Chakrabarti. R. E Sturgeon. (Illus.). 426p. 1986. 132.00 o.p. (ISBN 0-08-034141-1, Pub. by PPL). Pergamon.

Progress in Biocybernetics, 3 vols. Norbert Wiener & J. P. Schade. Incl. Vol. 1. 20.75 o.p. (ISBN 0-444-40639-5); Vol. 2. Progress in Biocybernetics. Ed. by N. Wiener & J. Schade. 1965. 23.75 o.p. (ISBN 0-444-40640-9); Vol. 3. 22.00 o.p. (ISBN 0-444-40641-7). 1964-66. Elsevier.

Progress in Biocybernetics see Progress in Biocybernetics.

Progress in Biophysics & Molecular Biology, Vol. 34. D. Noble. 1979. 76.00 o.p. (ISBN 0-08-024858-6). Pergamon.

Progress in Biophysics & Molecular Biology, Vol. 35. Ed. by D. Noble & T. L. Blundell. (Illus.). 206p. 1981. 76.00 o.p. (ISBN 0-08-027122-7). Pergamon.

Progress in Biophysics & Molecular Biology, Vol. 36, Nos. 1-3 Complete. D. Noble & T. L. Blundell. (Illus.). 130p. 1981. 83.00 o.p. (ISBN 0-08-028394-2). Pergamon.

Progress in Biophysics & Molecular Biology, Vol. 37. Ed. by D. Noble & T. L. Blundell. (Illus.). 229p. 1982. 95.00 o.p. (ISBN 0-08-029120-1). Pergamon.

Progress in Biophysics & Molecular Biology, Vol. 38. Ed. by D. Noble & T. L. Blundell. (Illus.). 210p. 1982. 94.00 o.p. (ISBN 0-08-029683-1). Pergamon.

Progress in Biophysics & Molecular Biology, Vol. 39. Ed. by D. Noble & T. L. Blundell. (Illus.). 230p. 1983. 86.00 o.p. (ISBN 0-08-030015-4). Pergamon.

Progress in Biophysics & Molecular Biology, Vol. 41. Ed. by D. Noble & T. L. Blundell. (Illus.). 260p. 1983. 99.00 o.p. (ISBN 0-08-031020-6). Pergamon.

Progress in Biophysics & Molecular Biology, Vol. 42. Ed. by D. Noble & T. L. Blundell. LC 50-11295. (Illus.). 202p. 1984. 99.00 o.p. (ISBN 0-08-031691-3). Pergamon.

Progress in Biophysics & Molecular Biology, Vol. 43. Ed. by D. Noble & T. L. Blundell. (Illus.). 268p. 1985. 110.00 o.p. (ISBN 0-08-032324-3). Pergamon.

Progress in Biophysics & Molecular Biology, Vol. 44. D. Noble & T. L. Blundell. (Illus.). 288p. 1985. 110.00 o.p. (ISBN 0-08-033210-2, Pub. by PPL). Pergamon.

Progress in Biophysics & Molecular Biology, Vol. 45. D. Noble. LC 50-11295. (Illus.). 256p. 1986. 102.00 o.p. (ISBN 0-08-033225-0, Pub. by PPL). Pergamon.

Progress in Boron Chemistry, 3 vols. Ed. by H. Steinberg & A. L. McCloskey. LC 64-13501. 1970. Vol. 1, 1964. 125.00 o.p. (ISBN 0-08-010619-6); Vol. 2, 1970. 75.00 o.p. (ISBN 0-08-013079-8); Vol. 3, 1970. 100.00 o.p. (ISBN 0-08-013080-1). Pergamon.

Progress in Botany, Vol. 36. W. Franke et al. LC 33-15850. (Illus.). xvii, 359p. 1974. 70.80 o.p. (ISBN 0-387-07036-2). Springer-Verlag.

Progress in Botany, Vol. 37. LC 33-15850. (Illus.). 460p. 1976. 75.00 o.p. (ISBN 0-387-07504-6). Springer-Verlag.

Progress in Botany, Vol. 38. Ed. by H. Ellenberg et al. LC 33-15850. 1977. 67.00 o.p. (ISBN 0-387-07966-1). Springer-Verlag.

Progress in Botany, Vol. 39. Ed. by H. Ellenberg et al. LC 33-15850. (Illus.). 1977. 62.00 o.p. (ISBN 0-387-08501-7). Springer-Verlag.

Progress in Botany, Vol. 41. Ed. by H. Ellenberg et al. (Illus.). 1980. 70.30 o.p. (ISBN 0-387-09769-4). Springer-Verlag.

Progress in Botany, Vol. 42. Ed. by H. Ellenberg. 430p. 1981. 61.40 o.p. (ISBN 0-387-10430-5). Springer-Verlag.

Progress in Botany, Vol. 43. Ed. by H. Ellenberg et al. 400p. 1981. 60.00 o.p. (ISBN 0-387-11091-7). Springer-Verlag.

Progress in Botany, Vol. 44. Ed. by H. Ellenberg et al. (Illus.). 450p. 1983. 72.40 o.p. (ISBN 0-387-11840-3). Springer-Verlag.

Progress in Botany, Vol. 45. (Illus.). 440p. 1983. 66.40 o.p. (ISBN 0-387-12997-9). Springer-Verlag.

Progress in Botany, Vol. 46. (Illus.). 410p. 1985. 90.30 o.p. (ISBN 0-387-13731-9). Springer-Verlag.

Progress in Botany: Vol. 40. Ed. by H. Ellenberg et al. (Illus.). 1978. 77.70 o.p. (ISBN 0-387-09074-6). Springer-Verlag.

Progress in Boundary Element Methods. C. A. Brebbia. LC 81-6454. 325p. 1981. 62.95x o.p. (ISBN 0-470-27223-6). Halsted Pr.

Progress in Cardiology, No. 13. Ed. by Paul N. Yu & John F. Goodwin. LC 77-157474. (Illus.). 204p. 1985. text ed. 30.00 o.p. (ISBN 0-8121-0973-2). Lea & Febiger.

Progress in Cardiology, No. 14. Ed. by Paul N. Yu & John F. Goodwin. LC 77-157474. (Illus.). 336p. 1986. text ed. 48.50 o.p. (ISBN 0-8121-1018-8). Lea & Febiger.

Progress in Ceramic Science. J. E. Burke. 1966. Vol. 3. 1964. 85.00 o.p. (ISBN 0-08-010026-0); Vol. 4. 1966. 70.00 o.p. (ISBN 0-08-011842-9). Pergamon.

Progress in Clinical Medicine, Vol. 8. Ed. by A. R. Horler & J. B. Foster. LC 82-19884. (Illus.). 340p. 1983. pap. text ed. 32.00 o.p. (ISBN 0-443-02541-X). Churchill.

Progress in Crystal Growth, Vol. 2, Complete. Ed. by Brian R. Pamplin. (Illus.). 404p. 1981. 140.00 o.p. (ISBN 0-08-026040-3). Pergamon.

Progress in Crystal Growth & Characterization, Vol. 1. Ed. by Brian R. Pamplin. (Illus.). 248p. 1980. 140.00 o.p. (ISBN 0-08-026013-6). Pergamon.

Progress in Crystal Growth & Characterization, Vol. 1. Ed. by Brian R. Pamplin. 1979. Pt. 1, 1977. pap. 35.00 o.p. (ISBN 0-08-021663-3); Pt. 2, 1978. pap. 28.00 o.p. (ISBN 0-08-023050-4); Pt. 3, 1978. pap. 28.00 o.p. (ISBN 0-08-023051-2); Pt. 4. pap. 21.00 o.p. (ISBN 0-08-023083-0). Pergamon.

Progress in Crystal Growth & Characterization, Vol. 3 Complete. Ed. by B. Pamplin. (Illus.). 390p. 1982. 130.00 o.p. (ISBN 0-08-028405-1). Pergamon.

Progress in Crystal Growth & Characterization, Vol. 3, No. 2-3. Ed. by Brian R. Pamplin. (Illus.). 166p. 1981. pap. 72.00 o.p. (ISBN 0-08-027149-9). Pergamon.

Progress in Crystal Growth & Characterization, Vol. 5. Ed. by Brian R. Pamplin. (Illus.). 425p. 1983. 155.00 o.p. (ISBN 0-08-031011-7). Pergamon.

Progress in Crystal Growth & Characterization, Vol. 6. Ed. by B. Pamplin. (Illus.). 424p. 1984. 155.00 o.p. (ISBN 0-08-030997-6). Pergamon.

Progress in Crystal Growth & Characterization, Vol. 8. Ed. by B. Pamplin. (Illus.). 475p. 1985. 180.00 o.p. (ISBN 0-08-032736-2, Pub. by PPL). Pergamon.

Progress in Crystal Growth & Characterization, Vol. 9. Ed. by B. Pamplin. (Illus.). 385p. 1985. 180.00 o.p. (ISBN 0-08-032737-0, Pub. by PPL). Pergamon.

Progress in Crystal Growth & Characterization, Vol. 10: Proceedings of the 6th International Conference on Ternary & Multinary Compounds, Car acas, Venezuela, 15-17 August 1984. Ed. by B. R. Pamplin et al. (Illus.). 430p. 1985. 180.00 o.p. (ISBN 0-08-032344-8). Pergamon.

Progress in Crystal Growth & Characterization, Vol. 4. Ed. by B. Pamplin. (Illus.). 345p. 1982. 160.00 o.p. (ISBN 0-08-029681-5). Pergamon.

Progress in Cybernetics & Systems Research, Vol. 11. Ed. by Robert Trappl. 1982. text ed. 110.00 o.p. (ISBN 0-07-065071-3). McGraw.

Progress in Drug Metabolism, Vol. 5. J. W. Bridges & L. F. Chasseaud. LC 80-40128. (Progress in Drug Metabolism Ser.). 362p. 1980. 135.00 o.p. (ISBN 0-471-27776-2, Pub. by Wiley-Interscience). Wiley.

Progress in Energy & Combustion Science, Vol. 4. N. A. Chigier. 224p. 1980. 140.00 o.p. (ISBN 0-08-024257-X). Pergamon.

Progress in Energy & Combustion Science, Vol. 6. Ed. by N. A. Chigier. (Illus.). 388p. 1981. 145.00 o.p. (ISBN 0-08-027153-7). Pergamon.

Progress in Energy & Combustion Science, Vol. 6, Pt. 2. Ed. by N. A. Chigier. 102p. 1980. pap. 30.00 o.p. (ISBN 0-08-026059-4). Pergamon.

Progress in Energy & Combustion Science, Vol. 7. Ed. by N. A. Chigier. (Illus.). 316p. 1982. 160.00 o.p. (ISBN 0-08-029124-4). Pergamon.

Progress in Energy & Combustion Science, Vol. 8. Ed. by N. A. Chigier. 354p. 1983. 160.00 o.p. (ISBN 0-08-031041-9). Pergamon.

Progress in Energy & Combustion Science, Vol. 9. Ed. by N. A. Chigier. (Illus.). 378p. 1984. 160.00 o.p. (ISBN 0-08-031727-8). Pergamon.

Progress in Energy & Combustion Science, Vol. 10. Ed. by N. A. Chigier. (Illus.). 478p. 1986. 162.00 o.p. (ISBN 0-08-033677-9, B110, Pub. by PPL). Pergamon.

Progress in Engineering Optimization, 1981. Ed. by R. W. Mayne & K. M. Ragsdell. 151p. 1981. 30.00 o.p. (ISBN 0-686-34507-X, I00141). ASME.

Progress in Enzyme & Ion-Selective Electrodes. Ed. by D. W. Luebbers et al. (Illus.). 240p. 1981. pap. 27.70 o.p. (ISBN 0-387-10499-2). Springer-Verlag.

Progress in Fatigue & Fracture, Vol. 8 No. 1. Ed. by H. Liebowitz. 1976. pap. 73.00 o.p. (ISBN 0-08-020866-5). Pergamon.

Progress in Flying Machines. Octave Chanute. 12.50 o.p. (ISBN 0-916494-00-4, Pub. by Lorenz & Herwig). Aviation.

Progress in Food & Nutrition Science. Ed. by R. K. Chandra. (Illus.). 198p. 1984. pap. 92.00 o.p. (ISBN 0-08-030928-3). Pergamon.

Progress in Food & Nutrition Science, Vol. 2, No. 11-12. H. M. Sinclair. LC 75-7734. (Illus.). 70p. 1979. pap. 28.00 o.p. (ISBN 0-08-023758-4). Pergamon.

Progress in Fracture Mechanics: Fracture Mechanics Research & Technological Activities of Nations Around the World. Ed. by G. C. Sih & D. Francois. (International Series on Strength & Fracture of Materials). (Illus.). 96p. 1983. 47.00 o.p. (ISBN 0-08-028691-7). Pergamon.

Progress in Geomorphology: Papers in Honour of David L. Linton. Ed. by E. H. Brown & R. S. Waters. (Special Publication of the Institute of British Geographers: No. 7). 1980. 28.50 o.p. (ISBN 0-12-137780-6). Acad Pr.

Progress in Heat & Mass Transfer, Vol. 19, No. 10: Alan Ede Memorial Issue: Developments in Heat & Mass Transfer. Ed. by Dudley B. Spalding. 1977. pap. 39.00 o.p. (ISBN 0-08-021285-9). Pergamon.

Progress in Immunology. Ed. by Bernard Amos. 1971. 169.00 o.p. (ISBN 0-12-057550-7). Acad Pr.

Progress in Industrial Geography. Ed. by Michael Pacione. LC 85-14938. (Progress in Geography Ser.). 287p. 1985. 43.00 o.p. (ISBN 0-7099-2072-5, Pub. by Croom Helm Ltd). Routledge Chapman & Hall.

Progress in Lipid Research, Vol. 17. Ed. by R. T. Holman. 396p. 1980. 84.00 o.p. (ISBN 0-08-023797-5). Pergamon.

Progress in Lipid Research, Vol. 18. Ed. by R. T. Holman. (Illus.). 180p. 1981. 91.00 o.p. (ISBN 0-08-027129-4). Pergamon.

Progress in Lipid Research, Vol. 22. Ed. by R. T. Holman. (Illus.). 306p. 1984. 150.00 o.p. (ISBN 0-08-031507-0). Pergamon.

Progress in Lipid Research: Golden Jubilee International Conference, Minnesota, May 4-7, 1980, Vol. 20. Ed. by R. J. Holman. (Illus.). 968p. 1982. 240.00 o.p. (ISBN 0-08-028011-0, H115, H125). Pergamon.

Progress in Material Science, Vol. 24. Ed. by J. W. Christian et al. (Illus.). 346p. 1980. 115.00 o.p. (ISBN 0-08-027107-3). Pergamon.

Progress in Materials Analysis, Vol. 1. Ed. by M. Grasserbauer & M. K. Zacherl. (Mikrochimica Acta Ser.: Supplement 10). (Illus.). 350p. 1983. pap. 49.70 o.p. (ISBN 0-387-81759-X). Springer-Verlag.

Progress in Materials Science, Vol. 23. Ed. by B. Chalmers. 280p. 1980. 115.00 o.p. (ISBN 0-08-024846-2). Pergamon.

Progress in Materials Science, Vol. 25. J. W. Christian et al. 1982. 120.00 o.p. (ISBN 0-08-029096-5). Pergamon.

Progress in Materials Science, Vol. 26. Ed. by J. W. Christian & P. Haasen. (Illus.). 420p. 1982. 145.00 o.p. (ISBN 0-08-029122-8). Pergamon.

Progress in Materials Science, Vol. 27. Ed. by J. W. Christian & P. Haasen. (Illus.). 460p. 1983. 145.00 o.p. (ISBN 0-08-030029-4). Pergamon.

Progress in Materials Science, Vol. 28. Ed. by J. W. Christan et al. (Illus.). 450p. 1985. 170.00 o.p. (ISBN 0-08-032741-9, Pub. by PPL). Pergamon.

Progress in Materials Science, Vol. 29. Ed. by J. W. Christian et al. (Illus.). 394p. 1986. 156.00 o.p. (ISBN 0-08-034154-3, Pub. by PPL). Pergamon.

Progress in Metallurgical Technology. Institution of Metallurgists Staff. (Illus.). 1960. 15.00x o.p. (ISBN 0-677-60150-6). Gordon & Breach.

Progress in Molecular & Subcellular Biology, Vol. 1. B. W. Agranoff et al. Ed. by F. E. Hahn et al. (Illus.). 230p. 1970. 42.00 o.p. (ISBN 0-387-04674-7). Springer-Verlag.

Progress in Molecular & Subcellular Biology, Vol. 3. Ed. by F. E. Hahn. LC 75-79748. (Illus.). 400p. 1973. 45.00 o.p. (ISBN 0-387-06227-0). Springer-Verlag.

Progress in Molecular & Subcellular Biology, Vol. 6. Ed. by F. E. Hahn. (Illus.). 1978. 54.00 o.p. (ISBN 0-387-08588-2). Springer-Verlag.

Progress in Molecular & Subcellular Biology, Vol. 7. Ed. by F. E. Hahn et al. (Illus.). 260p. 1980. 56.00 o.p. (ISBN 0-387-10150-0). Springer-Verlag.

Progress in Multiple Sclerosis: Research & Treatment. Ed. by Uri Leibowitz. 1972. 50.50 o.p. (ISBN 0-12-441350-1). Acad Pr.

Progress in Nephrology: Proceedings. Gesellschaft Fuer Nephrologie, 5th Symposium, Switzerland, 1967. Ed. by G. Peters & F. Roch-Ramel. (Illus.). 1969. 77.90 o.p. (ISBN 0-387-04672-0). Springer-Verlag.

Progress in Neurobiology, Vol. 11. Ed. by G. A. Kerkut & J. W. Phillis. 1979. 125.00 o.p. (ISBN 0-08-024857-8). Pergamon.

Progress in Neurobiology, Vol. 12. G. A. Kerkut. (Illus.). 312p. 1980. 125.00 o.p. (ISBN 0-08-024888-8). Pergamon.

Progress in Neurobiology, Vol. 13, Complete. Ed. by G. A. Kerkut. (Illus.). 440p. 1980. 125.00 o.p. (ISBN 0-08-026039-X). Pergamon.

Progress in Neurobiology, Vol. 14 Complete. Ed. by G. A. Kerkut & J. W. Phillis. 344p. 1980. 125.00 o.p. (ISBN 0-08-027114-6). Pergamon.

Progress in Neurobiology, Vol. 15. Ed. by G. A. Kerkut & J. W. Phillis. (Illus.). 344p. 1981. 140.00 o.p. (ISBN 0-08-029084-1, H999). Pergamon.

Progress in Neurobiology, Vol. 15, No.4. 1981. pap. 32.00 o.p. (ISBN 0-08-027148-0). Pergamon.

Progress in Neurobiology, Vol. 17. Ed. by G. A. Kerkut & J. W. Phillus. 289p. 1983. 125.00 o.p. (ISBN 0-08-029697-1). Pergamon.

Progress in Neurobiology, Vol. 18. Ed. by G. A. Kerkut & J. W. Phillis. (Illus.). 338p. 1983. 130.00 o.p. (ISBN 0-08-031046-X). Pergamon.

Progress in Neurobiology, Vol. 19. Ed. by G. A. Kerkut & J. W. Phillis. (Illus.). 370p. 1984. 130.00 o.p. (ISBN 0-08-031508-9). Pergamon.

Progress in Neurobiology, Vol. 20. Ed. by G. A. Kerkut & J. W. Phillis. LC 72-12616. (Illus.). 348p. 1984. 130.00 o.p. (ISBN 0-08-031706-5). Pergamon.

Progress in Neurobiology, Vol. 22. Ed. by G. A. Kerkut & J. W. Phillis. LC 72-12616. (Illus.). 374p. 1985. 150.00 o.p. (ISBN 0-08-032757-5, Pub. by PPL). Pergamon.

Progress in Neurobiology, Vol. 23. Ed. by G. A. Kerkut & J. W. Phillis. LC 72-12616. (Illus.). 358p. 1985. 150.00 o.p. (ISBN 0-08-033211-0, Pub. by PPL). Pergamon.

Progress in Neurobiology, Vol. 24. Ed. by G. A. Kerkut & J. W. Phillis. (Illus.). 350p. 1986. 138.00 o.p. (ISBN 0-08-033679-5, H140, H110, Pub. by PPL). Pergamon.

Progress in Neurobiology, Vol. 16. Ed. by G. A. Kerklit & J. W. Phillis. (Illus.). 320p. 1982. 125.00 o.p. (ISBN 0-08-029105-8). Pergamon.

Progress in Neuropsychopharmacology, Vol. 4, No. 6. Ed. by C. Radouco-Thomas & F. Garcin. (Illus.). 110p. 1981. pap. 31.00 o.p. (ISBN 0-08-027157-X). Pergamon.

Progress in NMR Spectroscopy, Vol. 12. J. W. Emsley. 288p. 1980. 100.00 o.p. (ISBN 0-08-024874-8). Pergamon.

Progress in NMR Spectroscopy: Vol. 11 Complete. Ed. by J. W. Emsley & L. H. Sutcliffe. LC 66-17931. 282p. 1978. 105.00 o.p. (ISBN 0-08-020325-6). Pergamon.

Progress in Nuclear Energy, Vol. 3, No. 2. Ed. by M. M. Williams. (Illus.). 92p. 1979. pap. 47.00 o.p. (ISBN 0-08-024253-7). Pergamon.

Progress in Nuclear Energy, Vol. 3, No. 3. Ed. by M. M. Williams. 96p. 1979. pap. 47.00 o.p. (ISBN 0-08-024844-6). Pergamon.

Progress in Nuclear Energy, Vol. 3. Ed. by M. M. Williams. (Illus.). 252p. 1979. 115.00 o.p. (ISBN 0-08-024875-6). Pergamon.

Progress in Nuclear Energy, Vol. 5 Complete. Ed. by M. M. Williams. (Illus.). 292p. 1980. 115.00 o.p. (ISBN 0-08-027115-4). Pergamon.

Progress in Nuclear Energy, Vol. 7, No. 1. Ed. by M. M. Williams & N. J. McCormick. (Illus.). 71p. 1981. pap. 36.00 o.p. (ISBN 0-08-027146-4). Pergamon.

Progress in Nuclear Energy, Vol. 7. Ed. by M. M. Williams & N. J. McCormick. (Illus.). 228p. 1981. 125.00 o.p. (ISBN 0-08-029090-6, A999, B120). Pergamon.

Progress in Nuclear Energy, Vol. 8. Ed. by M. R. Williams & N. J. McCormick. 318p. 1982. 145.00 o.p. (ISBN 0-08-029684-X). Pergamon.

Progress in Nuclear Energy, Vol. 10. Ed. by M. M. Williams & N. J. McCormick. (Illus.). 408p. 1983. 130.00 o.p. (ISBN 0-08-030420-6). Pergamon.

Progress in Nuclear Energy, Vol. 11. Ed. by M. M. Williams & N. J. McCormick. (Illus.). 310p. 1984. 130.00 o.p. (ISBN 0-08-031029-X). Pergamon.

Progress in Nuclear Energy, Vol. 12. Ed. by M. M. Williams & N. J. McCormick. (Illus.). 300p. 1985. 130.00 o.p. (ISBN 0-08-031695-6). Pergamon.

Progress in Nuclear Energy, Vol. 13. Ed. by M. M. Williams & N. J. McCormick. (Illus.). 300p. 1985. 150.00 o.p. (ISBN 0-08-032322-7). Pergamon.

Progress in Nuclear Energy, Vol. 14. Ed. by M. M. Williams & N. J. McCormick. (Illus.). 260p. 1985. 150.00 o.p. (ISBN 0-08-032323-5, Pub. by PPL). Pergamon.

Progress in Nuclear Energy, Vol. 16. Ed. by M. M. Williams & N. J. McCormick. (Illus.). 322p. 1986. 138.00 o.p. (ISBN 0-08-034139-X, Pub. by PPL). Pergamon.

Progress in Nuclear Energy: New Series. Ed. by M. M. Williams & R. Sher. (Illus.). 1978. Vol. 1, No. 1, 1977. pap. 33.00 o.p. (ISBN 0-08-022118-1); Vol. 2, Nos. 4, 1978. pap. 23.00 o.p. (ISBN 0-08-023260-4); Vol. 2, No. 1, 1978. pap. 32.00 o.p. (ISBN 0-08-022710-4). Pergamon.

Progress in Nuclear Energy New Series, Vol. 1 Complete. Ed. by M. M. Williams & R. Sher. (Illus.). 1979. 205.00 o.p. (ISBN 0-08-023257-4). Pergamon.

Progress in Nuclear Energy: Selected Staff Reports to the President's Commission on the Accident at Three Mile Island, Vol. 6. Ed. by M. M. Williams & N. J. McCormick. (Illus.). 436p. 1981. 115.00 o.p. (ISBN 0-08-027124-3). Pergamon.

Titles

Progress in Nuclear Energy: The Role of the Boltzmann Transport Equation in Radiation Damage Calculations, Vol. 3, No. 1. M. M. Williams. LC 77-25743. (Progress in Nuclear Energy Ser.). (Illus.). 66p. 1979. pap. 47.00 o.p. (ISBN 0-08-024243-X). Pergamon.

Progress in Nuclear Magnetic Resonance Spectroscopy, Vol. 13. 1980. Complete. 105.00x o.p. (ISBN 0-08-026027-6). Pergamon.

Progress in Nuclear Magnetic Resonance Spectroscopy, Vol. 14. Ed. by J. W. Emsley & J. Feeney. 370p. 1982. 140.00 o.p. (ISBN 0-08-029698-X). Pergamon.

Progress in Nuclear Magnetic Resonance Spectroscopy, Vol. 15. Ed. by J. W. Emsley et al. (Illus.). 430p. 1984. 130.00 o.p. (ISBN 0-08-031510-0). Pergamon.

Progress in Nuclear Magnetic Resonanance Spectroscopy, Vol. 16. Ed. by J. W. Emsley et al. 382p. 1985. 150.00 o.p. (ISBN 0-08-033238-2, Pub. by PPL). Pergamon.

Progress in Nuclear Physics, Vol. 13: Rudolf Peierls & Theoretical Physics - Proceedings of the Peierls Symposium. Ed. by Ian J. Aitchison & J. E. Paton. 1977. 89.00 o.p. (ISBN 0-08-020606-9); pap. 18.25 o.p. (ISBN 0-08-021621-8). Pergamon.

Progress in Obstetrics & Gynaecology, Vol. 5. Ed. by John Studd. LC 81-21699. (Illus.). 411p. 1985. pap. text ed. 35.00 o.p. (ISBN 0-443-03268-8). Churchill.

Progress in Oceanography, Vol. 8. M. V. Angel. (Illus.). 296p. 1980. 125.00 o.p. (ISBN 0-08-022963-8). Pergamon.

Progress in Oceanography, Vol. 9, Nos. 1-4. M. V. Angel & J. O'Brien. (Illus.). 246p. 1982. 125.00 o.p. (ISBN 0-08-027116-2). Pergamon.

Progress in Oceanography, Vol. 10. Ed. by M. V. Angel & J. O'Brien. (Illus.). 226p. 1982. 115.00 o.p. (ISBN 0-08-029121-X). Pergamon.

Progress in Oceanography, Vol. 12. Ed. by M. V. Angel & J. J. O'Brien. (Illus.). 470p. 1984. 165.00 o.p. (ISBN 0-08-031504-6). Pergamon.

Progress in Oceanography, Vol. 13. Ed. by M. V. Angel & J. J. O'Brien. (Illus.). 520p. 1985. 175.00 o.p. (ISBN 0-08-032724-9, Pub. by Aberdeen Scotland). Pergamon.

Progress in Oceanography, Vol. 13, Nos. 3-4. H. S. Roe. (Illus.). 276p. 1984. pap. 83.00 o.p. (ISBN 0-08-031735-9). Pergamon.

Progress in Particle & Nuclear Physics: Mesons, Isobars, Quarks & Nuclear Excitations, Vol. 11. Ed. by Denys Wilkinson. (Illus.). 630p. 1984. 110.00 o.p. (ISBN 0-08-031489-9). Pergamon.

Progress in Particle & Nuclear Physics, Vol. 3. Ed. by Denys Wilkinson. 1980. 98.00 o.p. (ISBN 0-08-025020-3). Pergamon.

Progress in Particle & Nuclear Physics, Vol. 4. Ed. by Denys Wilkinson. (Illus.). 600p. 1980. 98.00 o.p. (ISBN 0-08-025039-4). Pergamon.

Progress in Particle & Nuclear Physics, Vol. 5. Ed. by Denys Wilkinson. (Illus.). 280p. 1981. 98.00 o.p. (ISBN 0-08-027109-X). Pergamon.

Progress in Particle & Nuclear Physics, Vol. 6. Ed. by Denys Wilkinson. 350p. 1981. 98.00 o.p. (ISBN 0-08-027117-0). Pergamon.

Progress in Particle & Nuclear Physics, Vol. 7. Ed. by Denys Wilkinson. (Illus.). 270p. 1981. 100.00 o.p. (ISBN 0-08-027152-9). Pergamon.

Progress in Particle & Nuclear Physics, Vol. 12. Ed. by Denys Wilkinson. (Illus.). 470p. 1984. 110.00 o.p. (ISBN 0-08-031500-3). Pergamon.

Progress in Particle & Nuclear Physics, Vol. 14. Ed. by A. Faessler. (Illus.). 300p. 1985. 110.00 o.p. (ISBN 0-08-032300-6, Pub. by PPL). Pergamon.

Progress in Particle & Nuclear Physics, Vol. 16. Ed. by A. Faessler. 268p. 1985. 140.00 o.p. (ISBN 0-08-033667-1, Pub. by PPL). Pergamon.

Progress in Particle & Nuclear Physics, Vol. 13: Nuclear & Subnuclear Degrees of Freedom & Lepton Nucleus Scattering. Ed. by A. Faessler. (Illus.). 540p. 1985. 110.00 o.p. (ISBN 0-08-031743-X). Pergamon.

Progress in Particle & Nuclear Physics, Vol. 15: Nucleus-Nucleus Collisions from the Coulomb Barrier to the Quark-Gluon Plasma. Ed. by A. Faessler. 1985. 140.00 o.p. (ISBN 0-08-034005-9, Pub. by PPL). Pergamon.

Progress in Particle Physics: Proceedings of the International University Courses on Nuclear Physics, 13th, Schladming, Austria, 1974. International University Courses on Nuclear Physics Staff. Ed. by A. Basetto et al. LC 74-13975. (Acta Physica Austriaca Ser.: Supplementum 13). (Illus.). vi, 773p. 1974. 87.40 o.p. (ISBN 0-387-81268-7). Springer-Verlag.

Progress in Perinatology. Harold Kaminetzky & Leslie Iffy. LC 77-838000005. (Illus.). 384p. 1977. text ed. 17.50 o.p. (ISBN 0-89313-006-0). G F Stickley Co.

Progress in Physical Organic Chemistry, Vol. 11. Ed. by A. Streitwieser & R. W. Taft. LC 63-19364. 440p. 1974. 33.00 o.p. (ISBN 0-471-83357-6). Krieger.

Progress in Phytochemistry, 2 vols, Vols. 4-5. Ed. by L. Reinhold et al. LC 68-24347. 1978. Vol. 4. 100.00 o.p. (ISBN 0-08-021004-X); Vol. 5. 105.00 o.p. (ISBN 0-08-022645-0). Pergamon.

Progress in Phytochemistry, Vol. 6. Ed. by L. Reinhold et al. LC 68-24347. (Illus.). 1980. 105.00 o.p. (ISBN 0-08-024946-9). Pergamon.

Progress in Phytochemistry, Vol. 7. L. Reinhold et al. LC 68-24347. (Illus.). 410p. 1981. 105.00 o.p. (ISBN 0-08-026362-3). Pergamon.

Progress in Planetary Exploration. Ed. by R. W. Shorthill. (Advances in Space Research: Vol. 1, No. 8). (Illus.). 224p. 1981. pap. 35.00 o.p. (ISBN 0-08-028384-5). Pergamon.

Progress in Planning, Vol. 9. Ed. by D. R. Diamond & J. B. McLoughlin. 300p. 1979. 61.00 o.p. (ISBN 0-08-025221-4). Pergamon.

Progress in Planning, Vol. 10. Ed. by D. R. Diamond & J. B. McLoughlin. (Illus.). 247p. 1980. 61.00 o.p. (ISBN 0-08-025788-7). Pergamon.

Progress in Planning, Vol. 11. Ed. by D. R. Diamond & J. B. McLoughlin. (Illus.). 280p. 1980. 61.00 o.p. (ISBN 0-08-025802-6). Pergamon.

Progress in Planning, Vol. 12. Ed. by D. R. Diamond & J. B. McLoughlin. 224p. 1980. 61.00 o.p. (ISBN 0-08-026100-0). Pergamon.

Progress in Planning, Vol. 13, (complete) D. R. Diamond & J. B. McLoughlin. (Illus.). 174p. 1981. 68.00 o.p. (ISBN 0-08-028398-5). Pergamon.

Progress in Planning, Vol. 17. Ed. by D. R. Diamond & J. B. McLoughlin. 268p. 1982. 68.00 o.p. (ISBN 0-08-029701-3). Pergamon.

Progress in Planning, Vol. 18. Ed. by D. R. Diamond & J. B. McLoughlin. (Illus.). 384p. 1983. 66.00 o.p. (ISBN 0-08-030415-X). Pergamon.

Progress in Planning, Vol. 19. Ed. by D. R. Diamond & J. B. McLoughlin. (Illus.). 280p. 1983. 66.00 o.p. (ISBN 0-08-031035-4). Pergamon.

Progress in Planning, Vol. 20. Ed. by D. R. Diamond. (Illus.). 260p. 1984. 66.00 o.p. (ISBN 0-08-031490-2). Pergamon.

Progress in Planning, Vol. 21. Ed. by D. R. Diamond & J. B. McLoughlin. (Illus.). 230p. 1985. 66.00 o.p. (ISBN 0-08-032325-1). Pergamon.

Progress in Planning, Vol. 22. Ed. by D. R. Diamond & J. B. McLoughlin. LC 73-66. (Illus.). 266p. 1985. 66.00 o.p. (ISBN 0-08-033206-4, Pub. by PPL). Pergamon.

Progress in Planning, Vol. 23. Ed. by D. R. Diamond. (Illus.). 260p. 1985. 66.00 o.p. (ISBN 0-08-033213-7, Pub. by PPL). Pergamon.

Progress in Planning, Vol. 24. Ed. by D. R. Diamond & J. B. McLoughlin. (Illus.). 250p. 1986. 60.00 o.p. (ISBN 0-08-034144-6, Pub. by PPL). Pergamon.

Progress in Plastics. Philip Morgan. 1958. (ISBN 0-8022-1145-3). Philos Lib.

Progress in Political Geography. Ed. by Michael Pacione. (Progress in Geography Ser.). 275p. 1985. 33.75 o.p. (ISBN 0-7099-2087-3, Pub. by Croom Helm Ltd). Routledge Chapman & Hall.

Progress in Polymer Science, Vol. 6. Ed. by A. D. Jenkins. (Illus.). 266p. 1980. 100.00 o.p. (ISBN 0-08-020335-3). Pergamon.

Progress in Polymer Science, Vol. 8. Ed. by A. D. Jenkins & V. T. Stannett. (Illus.). 490p. 1983. 125.00 o.p. (ISBN 0-08-031007-9). Pergamon.

Progress in Polymer Science, Vol. 9. Ed. by A. D. Jenkins. (Illus.). 380p. 1984. 145.00 o.p. (ISBN 0-08-031734-0). Pergamon.

Progress in Polymer Science, Vol. 10. Ed. by A. D. Jenkins & V. T. Stannett. (Illus.). 364p. 1985. 145.00 o.p. (ISBN 0-08-032721-4, Pub. by Aberdeen Scotland). Pergamon.

Progress in Proctology: Proceedings. International Congress of Hedrologicum Conlegium, 3rd, Erlangen-Nuremberg Germany, 1968. Ed. by J. Hoferichter. LC 77-83795. 1969. 42.50 o.p. (ISBN 0-387-04673-9). Springer-Verlag.

Progress in Quantum Electronics, Vol. 6, Complete. T. S. Moss & S. Stenholm. (Illus.). 292p. 1981. 88.00 o.p. (ISBN 0-08-028387-X). Pergamon.

Progress in Quantum Electronics, Vol. 9. Ed. by T. S. Moss et al. (Illus.). 346p. 1986. 126.00 o.p. (ISBN 0-08-034010-5, Pub. by PPL). Pergamon.

Progress in Radiation Processing: Proceedings of the International Meeting, 5th, San Diego, California, October 24-26, 1984. S. Nablo. 916p. 1985. pap. 205.00 o.p. (ISBN 0-08-032620-X, Pub. by PPL). Pergamon.

Progress in Reaction Kinetics, Vol. 10 Complete. Ed. by K. R. Jennings & R. B. Cundall. 402p. 1981. 100.00 o.p. (ISBN 0-08-027155-3). Pergamon.

Progress in Reaction Kinetics, Vol. 12. Ed. by K. R. Jennings et al. (Illus.). 268p. 1985. 130.00 o.p. (ISBN 0-08-032326-X, Pub. by Aberdeen Scotland). Pergamon.

Progress in Reaction Kinetics, Vol. 13. Ed. by K. R. Jennings et al. (Illus.). 314p. 1986. 120.00 o.p. (ISBN 0-08-033228-5, E120, E115, E125, Pub. by PPL). Pergamon.

Progress in Reaction Kinetics: Vol. 9 Complete. Ed. by K. R. Jennings & R. B. Cundall. 368p. 1980. 92.00 o.p. (ISBN 0-08-020343-4). Pergamon.

Progress in Refrigeration Science & Technology, Munich Conference, 3 vols. International Institute of Refrigeration. 1965. Set. 480.00 o.p. (ISBN 0-08-011439-3). Pergamon.

Progress in Research & Clinical Applications of Corticosteroids. H. Lee & T. J. Fitzgerald. 1982. 85.00 o.p. (ISBN 0-471-26210-2). Wiley.

Progress in Resource Management & Environmental Planning, Vol. 4. Ed. by Timothy O'Riordan & R. Kerry Turner. 304p. 1984. 91.95x o.p. (ISBN 0-471-10534-1, 1469, Pub. by Wiley-Interscience). Wiley.

Progress in Rural Extension & Community Development, Vol. 1: Extension & Relative Advantage in Rural Development. Ed. by Gwyn E. Jones & Maurice J. Rolls. LC 81-13064. (Progress in Rural Extension & Community Development Ser.). 336p. 1982. 71.95x o.p. (ISBN 0-471-10038-2, Pub. by Wiley-Interscience). Wiley.

Progress in Sexology. Ed. by Robert Gemme & C. C. Wheeler. LC 77-13011. (Perspectives In Sexuality Ser.). 634p. 1978. 60.00x o.p. (ISBN 0-306-31104-6, Plenum Pr). Plenum Pub.

Progress in Solid State Chemistry, Vol. 12. Ed. by G. M. Rosenblatt. (Illus.). 332p. 1980. 90.00 o.p. (ISBN 0-08-022846-1). Pergamon.

Progress in Solid State Chemistry, Vol. 13. Ed. by G. M. Rosenblatt & W. L. Worrell. (Illus.). 376p. 1982. 140.00 o.p. (ISBN 0-08-029712-9). Pergamon.

Progress in Solid State Chemistry, Vol. 14. Ed. by G. M. Rosenblatt & W. L. Worrell. (Illus.). 302p. 1983. 130.00 o.p. (ISBN 0-08-030998-4). Pergamon.

Progress in Solid State Chemistry, Vol. 15. Ed. by G. M. Rosenblatt & W. L. Worrell. (Illus.). 374p. 1985. 145.00 o.p. (ISBN 0-08-033664-7, E115, E125, C140, Pub. by PPL). Pergamon.

Progress in Statistics, 2 vols. Ed. by J. Gani et al. (Colloquia Mathematica Societatis Janos Bolyai: No. 9). 912p. 1975. Set. 94.75 o.p. (ISBN 0-444-10702-9, North-Holland). Elsevier.

Progress in Surface Science, Vol. 10, No. 1. Ed. by S. G. Davison. (Illus.). 164p. 1981. pap. 31.00 o.p. (ISBN 0-08-027154-5). Pergamon.

Progress in Surface Science, Vol. 11. Ed. by S. G. Davison. LC 77-141188. 378p. 1983. 115.00 o.p. (ISBN 0-08-030875-9, 17). Pergamon.

Progress in Surface Science, Vol. 12. Ed. by S. G. Davison. 436p. 1984. 120.00 o.p. (ISBN 0-08-030876-7). Pergamon.

Progress in Surface Science, Vol. 13. Ed. by S. G. Davison. LC 77-141188. 355p. 1985. 120.00 o.p. (ISBN 0-08-030886-4). Pergamon.

Progress in Surface Science, Vol. 14. Ed. by S. G. Davison. LC 77-141188. 423p. 1985. 120.00 o.p. (ISBN 0-08-030887-2). Pergamon.

Progress In Surface Science, Vol. 15. Ed. by S. G. Davison. 494p. 1985. 120.00 o.p. (ISBN 0-08-030894-5, Pub. by PPL). Pergamon.

Progress in Surface Science, Vol. 16. Ed. by S. G. Davison. 1985. 120.00 o.p. (ISBN 0-08-030904-6, Pub. by PPL). Pergamon.

Progress in Surface Science, Vol. 17. Ed. by S. G. Davison. LC 77-141188. 328p. 1986. 126.00 o.p. (ISBN 0-08-030905-4, Pub. by PPL). Pergamon.

Progress in Surface Science, Vol. 18. Ed. by S. G. Davison. LC 77-141188. 541p. 1986. 126.00 o.p. (ISBN 0-08-030906-2, Pub. by PPL). Pergamon.

Progress in the Psychology of Personality. Kassakowski & Obudhowski. 71.00 o.p. (ISBN 0-444-86347-8). Elsevier.

Progress in Theoretical Biology, 4 vols. Ed. by Frank M. Snell. Vol. 1. 1967. 52.50 o.p. (ISBN 0-12-543101-5); Vol. 2 1972. 76.50 o.p. (ISBN 0-12-543102-3); Vol. 3. 1974. 76.50 o.p. (ISBN 0-12-543103-1); Vol. 4. 1976. 76.50 o.p. (ISBN 0-12-543104-X). Acad Pr.

Progress in Theoretical Biology, Vol. 5. Ed. by Robert Rosen. 1978. 76.50 o.p. (ISBN 0-12-543105-8). Acad Pr.

Progress in Theoretical Biology, Vol. 6. Ed. by Robert Rosen. 1981. 52.50 o.p. (ISBN 0-12-543106-6). Acad Pr.

Progress in Toxicology, Volume 2: Special Topics. G. Zbinden. (Illus.). v, 117p. 1976. 19.00 o.p. (ISBN 0-387-07566-6). Springer-Verlag.

Progress in Transfusion Medicine, Vol. 1. Ed. by John D. Cash. (Illus.). 190p. 1986. text ed. 55.50 o.p. (ISBN 0-443-03261-0). Churchill.

Progress in Writing: A Learning Program. James A. Gowen. 230p. 1973. text ed. 19.95 o.p. (ISBN 0-07-023859-6). McGraw.

Progress of a Fire. Robert Abel. 1985. 18.45 o.p. (ISBN 0-671-50931-4). S&S.

Progress of God's People. M. J. Evans. (Discovering the Bible Ser.). (gr. 8-10). pap. 8.95 o.p. (ISBN 0-7175-1161-8). Dufour.

Progress of Society in Europe: A Historical Outline from the Subversion of the Roman Empire to the Beginning of the 16th Century. William Robertson. Ed. by Felix Gilbert & Leonard Krieger. LC 75-190283. (Classic European Historians Ser.). xxviii, 186p. 1975. pap. text ed. 2.45 o.s.i. (ISBN 0-226-72134-5, P466, Phoen). U of Chicago Pr.

Progress of Stories. enl. ed. Laura R. Jackson. 1982. 15.95 o.p. (ISBN 0-385-27212-X, Dial). Doubleday.

Progress on Family Problems: A Nationwide Study of Clients' & Counselors' Views on Family Agency Services. Dorothy F. Beck & Mary Ann Jones. LC 73-81256. 1973. pap. 17.00 o.p. (ISBN 0-87304-107-0). Family Serv.

Progress: Social Progress from Mercury to Kennedy. Tertius Chandler. 1976. 10.00 o.p. (ISBN 0-682-48361-3, University). Exposition-Phoenix.

Progression. Vera Blaine & Scott Clark. (Educational Dance Score Registry Ser.: No. 3). (Illus.). 194p. 1981. dance score 10.00 o.s.i. (ISBN 0-932582-36-2). Dance Notation.

Progression of Consciousness. William C. Fry. 208p. 1986. 10.95 o.p. (ISBN 0-8062-2887-3). Carlton.

Progressive Education Movement: An Annotated Bibliography. Mariann P. Winick. LC 76-24764. (Reference Library of Social Science Ser.: Vol. 29). 1976. lib. bdg. 23.00 o.p. (ISBN 0-8240-9913-3). Garland Pub.

Progressive Exercises in Chinese Pronunciation. Charles F. Hockett. 1.95 o.p. (ISBN 0-88710-058-9). Yale Far Eastern Pubns.

Progressive in Particle & Nuclear Physics: Collective Bands in Nuclei, Vol. 9. Ed. by Denys Wilkinson. (Illus.). 563p. 1983. 110.00 o.p. (ISBN 0-08-030036-7). Pergamon.

Progressive Presidents: Theodore Roosevelt, Woodrow Wilson, Franklin D. Roosevelt, Lyndon B. Johnson. John M. Blum. 1980. 11.95 o.p. (ISBN 0-393-01330-8). Norton.

Progressive Years: The Spirit & Achievement of American Reform. Ed. by Otis Pease. LC 62-18227. (American Epochs Ser). 10.00 o.p. (ISBN 0-8076-0203-5); pap. 4.95 o.p. (ISBN 0-8076-0396-1). Braziller.

Progressivity Issue in Taxation: A Bibliography. Robert M. Kozub. (Public Administration Ser.: P 1667). 12p. 1985. 2.00 o.p. (ISBN 0-89028-377-X). Vance Biblios.

Prohibition & the Progressive Movement, 1900-1920. James H. Timberlake. LC 63-9564. 1970. pap. text ed. 2.95x o.p. (ISBN 0-689-70249-3, 162, Atheneum). Macmillan.

Project Analysis. Enabling Technologies Staff. (Decision Maker Series for Frame Work II). (Orig.). 1985. pap. text ed. 69.95 o.p. (ISBN 0-912677-75-9). Tate Pub.

Project & Cost Engineers' Handbook. Ed. by F. C. Jelen. (Illus.). 1979. write for info. o.s.i. (ISBN 0-930284-06-2). Am Assn Cost Engineers.

Project Brochure Fall Meeting 1981 Philadelphia, Pennsylvania. Incl. Project Brochure Fall Meeting 1982 Denver, Colorado. 1982. pap. 13.25 (D-20); Project Brochure Fall Meeting 1983 Miami Beach, Florida. 1983. pap. 13.25 (M-20). 1981. pap. 15.00 o.p. (ISBN 0-317-06719-2, P-34). Urban Land.

Project Brochure Fall Meeting 1982 Denver, Colorado see Project Brochure Fall Meeting 1981 Philadelphia, Pennsylvania.

Project Brochure Fall Meeting 1983 Miami Beach, Florida see Project Brochure Fall Meeting 1981 Philadelphia, Pennsylvania.

Project Brochure Spring Meeting 1981 Portland, Oregon. Incl. Project Brochure Spring Meeting 1982 Houston, Texas. 1982. pap. 13.25 (H-98); Project Brochure Spring Meeting 1983 Seattle, Washington. 1983. pap. 15.00 (S-21); Project Brochure Spring Meeting 1984 San Antonio, Texas. 1984. pap. 15.00 (S-25). 1981. pap. 15.00 o.p. (ISBN 0-317-06714-1, P-30). Urban Land.

Project Brochure Spring Meeting 1982 Houston, Texas see Project Brochure Spring Meeting 1981 Portland, Oregon.

Project Brochure Spring Meeting 1983 Seattle, Washington see Project Brochure Spring Meeting 1981 Portland, Oregon.

Project Brochure Spring Meeting 1984 San Antonio, Texas see Project Brochure Spring Meeting 1981 Portland, Oregon.

Project Cancelled: The Disaster of Britain's Abandoned Aircraft Projects. Derek Wood. 224p. 1987. 27.95 o.p. (ISBN 0-7106-0441-6). Janes Info Group.

Project Control by Critical Pathanalysis: A Basic Guide of CPA. C. W. Lowe. 258p. 1978. text ed. 36.75x o.p. (ISBN 0-220-67012-9, Pub. by Busn Bks England). Gower Pub Co.

Project Finance. 4th ed. Peter Nevitt. 220p. 1983. 120.00 o.p. (ISBN 0-8002-3401-4). Intl Pubns Serv.

Project Finance: The Credit Perspective. Stewart A. Schoder. 48p. 1984. 15.00 o.s.i. (ISBN 0-318-04575-3). Robt Morris Assocs.

Project Financing. 4th ed. 270p. 1984. 120.00 o.p. (ISBN 0-8002-3171-6). Intl Pubns Serv.

Project Financing 1986: Power Generation, Waste Recovery, & Other Industrial Facilities. Robert T. Smith & Practising Law Institute Staff. LC 86-232595. (Real Estate Law & Practise Course Handbook Ser.: No. 284). (Illus.). 998p. 1986. 45.00x o.p. (ISBN 0-317-60057-5). PLI.

Project Management. 2nd ed. D. Lock. 272p. 1977. text ed. 34.95x o.p. (ISBN 0-566-02034-3). Gower Pub Co.

Project Management. 15.00 o.p. (ISBN 0-317-65066-1). Am Consul Eng.

Project Management: A Systems Approach to Planning, Scheduling & Controlling. 2nd ed. Harold Kerzner. 672p. 1984. 44.95 o.p. (ISBN 0-442-24879-2). Van Nos Reinhold.

Project Management for Small & Medium Size Businesses. Kerzner. 1983. 29.95 o.p. (ISBN 0-442-24660-9). Van Nos Reinhold.

Project Management Handbook. Cleland & King. 752p. 1983. 48.95 o.p. (ISBN 0-442-23878-9). Van Nos Reinhold.

Project Management: How to Make It Work. Charles C. Martin. LC 75-37884. (Illus.). 312p. 1976. 16.95 o.p. (ISBN 0-8144-5408-9). AMACOM.

Project Management with the IBM PC. Ira Krukow. 128p. 1985. 11.95 o.p. (ISBN 0-89303-774-5). Brady Bks.

Project Norouz. Rebecca Swift. 512p. (Orig.). 1982. pap. 3.50 o.p. (ISBN 0-505-51834-1, Pub. by Tower Bks). Dorchester Pub Co.

Project Paperclip: German Scientists & the Cold War. Clarence Lasby. LC 75-108824. 1975. pap. text ed. 4.50x o.p. (ISBN 0-689-70524-7, 214, Atheneum). Macmillan.

Project Planning & Management: An Integrated Approach. Ed. by Louis J. Goodman & Ralph N. Love. LC 79-25990. (Pergamon Policy Studies). 312p. 1980. 47.00 o.p. (ISBN 0-08-024667-2); pap. 16.00 o.p. (ISBN 0-08-025962-6). Pergamon.

Project-Readiness: A Guide to Family Emergency Preparedness. Louise E. Nelson. LC 75-307239. (Illus.). 270p. 1975. 13.95 o.p. (ISBN 0-88290-036-6). Horizon Utah.

Project Selection & Economic Appraisal. William E. Souder. 240p. 1983. 34.95 o.p. (ISBN 0-442-21607-6). Van Nos Reinhold.

Project Studies in Fugue. Hugo Norden. 1977. pap. 6.95 o.s.i. (ISBN 0-8008-6553-7, Crescendo). Taplinger.

Project Work in the Geography Curriculum: An Advanced Level Primer. John R. Beaumont & Stephen W. Williams. 332p. 1983. pap. 25.00 o.p. (ISBN 0-7099-3211-1, Pub. by Croom Helm Ltd). Routledge Chapman & Hall.

Project You. Paris & Casey. 1984. pap. 6.00 o.p. (ISBN 0-87980-408-4). Wilshire.

Projecting a Picture of Home Economics: Public Relations in Secondary Programs. E. P. Anderson et al. 4.00 o.p. (ISBN 0-317-52227-2, A261-08452). Home Econ Educ.

Projective Geometry. J. W. Young. (Carus Monograph: No. 4). 185p. 1930. 21.00 o.p. (ISBN 0-88385-004-4). Math Assn.

Projective Varieties & Modular Forms. Martin Eichler. LC 78-166998. (Lecture Notes in Mathematics: Vol. 210). 1971. pap. 11.00 o.p. (ISBN 0-387-05519-3). Springer-Verlag.

Projects & Demonstrations in Astronomy. D. Tattersfield. LC 79-84264. 1979. 42.95x o.p. (ISBN 0-470-26715-1). Halsted Pr.

Projects & Designs in Woodwork. Ian Punter. (Illus.). 96p. 1981. 20.95 o.p. (ISBN 0-7134-3549-6, Pub. by Batsford England). David & Charles.

Projects for Design & Technology in Wood, Metal & Plastics. W. R. Hodder & S. L. Molesworth. (Illus.). 92p. (gr. 11 up). 1983. spiral binding 17.50x o.p. (ISBN 0-7195-3952-8). Coronet Bks.

Projects in Electricity. Merle D. Collings. (gr. 9-12). 1941. pap. text ed. 5.28 o.p. (ISBN 0-685-04240-5). Glencoe.

Projects in Wood. David Field. 224p. 1985. 24.95 o.p. (ISBN 0-399-13089-6). Putnam Pub Group.

Projects: Made in Philadelphia Four. Jeanne Silverthorne et al. LC 80-84522. (Illus.). 1979. pap. 7.00 o.p. (ISBN 0-88454-058-8). U of Pa Contemp Art.

Prol to America Bk. (Our Nations Heritage Ser.). Date not set. (ISBN 0-07-375411-0). McGraw.

Prolactin, Vol. 4. David F. Horrobin. (Annual Research Reviews Ser.). 1976. 24.00 o.p. (ISBN 0-904406-47-4). Eden Pr.

Prolactin Secretion: A Multidisciplinary Approach. Ed. by Flavio Mena & Carlos M. Valverde. 1984. 53.00 o.p. (ISBN 0-12-490620-6). Acad Pr.

Proletarian Hegemony in the Chinese Revolution & the Canton Commune of 1927. S. Bernard Thomas. (Michigan Monographs in Chinese Studies: No. 23). 187p. 1975. pap. 5.00 o.p. (ISBN 0-89264-023-5). U of Mich Ctr Chinese.

Proletarian Revolution & the Renegade Kautsky. Vladimir I. Lenin. 114p. 1970. pap. 0.95 o.p. (ISBN 0-8285-0163-7, Pub. by Progress Pubs USSR). Imported Pubns.

Proletarianisation in the Third World: Studies in the Creation of a Labour Force under Dependent Capitalism. Ed. by Barry Munslow & Henry Finch. LC 84-12739. 320p. 1984. 29.00 o.p. (ISBN 0-7099-1764-3, Pub. by Croom Helm Ltd). Routledge Chapman & Hall.

Proletarians & Parties: Five Essays in Social Class. Leslie Benson. 1978. pap. 10.50x o.p. (ISBN 0-422-76580-5, NO. 2829, Pub. by Tavistock England). Routledge Chapman & Hall.

Proliferation, Plutonium & Policy: Institutional & Technological Impediments to Nuclear Weapons Propogation. Alexander De Volpi. (Pergamon Policy Studies). (Illus.). 1979. 64.00 o.p. (ISBN 0-08-023872-6). Pergamon.

Prologomena to an Anthropological Physiology. F. J. Buytendijk. LC 72-90636. (Psychological Ser.: No. 6). 1974. text ed. 15.00x o.p. (ISBN 0-391-00332-1). Duquesne.

Prologue to America. (Our Nations Heritage Ser.). Date not set. (ISBN 0-07-375390-4). McGraw.

Prologue to Conflict: The Crisis & Compromise of 1850. Holman Hamilton. 1966. pap. 3.95 o.p. (ISBN 0-393-00345-0, Norton Lib). Norton.

Prologue to the Present: A Narrative World History, Vol. I to 1415. Elizabeth Pool. (Illus.). 448p. (Orig.). (gr. 9-12). 1984. pap. 10.95x o.p. (ISBN 0-88334-142-5). Ind Sch Pr.

Prologue to War: England & the United States, 1805-1812. Bradford Perkins. 1961. pap. 11.95x o.p. (ISBN 0-520-00996-7). U of Cal Pr.

Prolongevity II: An Updated Report on the Scientific Prospects for Adding Good Years to Life. Albert Rosenfeld. Ed. by Charles Elliott. LC 84-48662. 335p. 1985. 18.45 o.s.i. (ISBN 0-394-53475-1). Knopf.

Promesas de Jesus. David Wilkerson. 95p. (Span.). 1974. pap. 2.95 o.p. (ISBN 0-89922-027-4). Edit Caribe.

Promesas Personales de la Biblia. 128p. (Span.). 1982. pap. 2.50 o.p. (ISBN 0-87788-692-X). Shaw Pubs.

Prometheus Bound. Robert Lowell. 67p. 1969. 5.95 o.p. (ISBN 0-374-23780-8). FS&G.

Prometheus Design. Sondra Marshak & Myrna Culbreath. (Gregg Press Science Fiction - Star Trek Ser.). 192p. 1986. lib. bdg. 11.95x o.p. (ISBN 0-8398-2936-1, Gregg). G K Hall.

Prometheus Operation. Mark Elder. LC 80-14577. 312p. 1980. text ed. 11.95 o.p. (ISBN 0-07-019191-3). McGraw.

Promise. Evelyn Bence. (Illus.). 48p. 1987. 6.95 o.s.i. (ISBN 0-8378-1823-0). Gibson.

Promise Forever. Dee Austin. (Dawn of Love Ser.). 183p. 1985. pap. 2.50 o.p. (ISBN 0-671-55156-6). Archway.

Promise Is a Promise. Molly Cone. (Illus.). (gr. 7-9). 1964. 8.95 o.p. (ISBN 0-395-06703-0). HM.

Promise Made, A Promise Kept. Joshua F. Edwards. (ISBN 0-682-49419-4). Exposition-Phoenix.

Promise Me Love. Lynn M. Bartlett. 1982. pap. 3.95 o.p. (ISBN 0-380-60418-3, 69815-3). Avon.

Promise Me Tomorrow. Kaye Dobkin. 368p. 1986. pap. 3.95 o.p. (ISBN 0-380-89609-5). Avon.

Promise of a New Spring: The Holocaust & Renewal. Gerda W. Klein. (Illus.). 64p. (gr. 2-5). 1981. 10.95 o.s.i. (ISBN 0-940646-50-1); pap. 5.95 o.s.i. (ISBN 0-940646-51-X). Rossel Bks.

Promise of Bultmann. Norman Perrin. LC 78-19639. 112p. 1979. pap. 3.95 o.p. (ISBN 0-8006-1357-0, 1-1357, Fortress). Augsburg Fortress.

Promise of Eden: The Canadian Expansionist Movement & the Idea of the West, 1856-1900. Doug Owram. 1980. pap. 13.95c o.p. (ISBN 0-8020-6385-3). U of Toronto Pr.

Promise of Eternal Life: Biblical Witness to Christian Hope. Janis Rozentals. LC 86-26456. 112p. (Orig.). 1987. pap. 6.95 o.p. (ISBN 0-8066-2254-7, 10-5257, Augsburg). Augsburg Fortress.

Promise of Narrative Theology: Recovering the Gospel in the Church. George W. Stroup. LC 80-84654. 216p. (Orig.). 1982. pap. 9.95 o.p. (ISBN 0-8042-0683-X, John Knox). Westminster John Knox.

Promise of Spring. Jean Hager. (Candlelight Ecstasy Ser.: No. 258). 192p. (Orig.). 1984. pap. 1.95 o.p. (ISBN 0-440-17312-4). Dell.

Promise of the Rose. Jean Bothwell. LC 58-9744. 1958. 4.50 o.p. (ISBN 0-15-263687-0, HJ). HarBraceJ.

Promise to Keep: A Narrative of the American Encounter with Anti-Semitism. Nathan C. Belth. LC 81-40403. (Illus.). 1987. pap. 7.95 o.s.i. (ISBN 0-8052-0682-5). Schocken.

Promised-Land Living. J. Oswald Sanders. 1984. pap. 5.95 o.p. (ISBN 0-8024-0372-7). Moody.

Promised Land on the Solomon: Black Settlement at Nicodemus, Kansas. (Illus.). 151p. 1986. pap. 7.50 o.p. (ISBN 0-318-21350-8, S/N 024-005-00971-0). USGPO.

Promised Lands 1: Subdivisions in Deserts & Mountains, Vol. 1. Leslie Allan et al. LC 76-46735. (Promised Lands Ser.). (Illus.). 560p. 1976. pap. 20.00x o.p. (ISBN 0-918780-04-7). INFORM.

Promised Lands 3: Subdivisions & the Law, Vol. 3. Patricia A. Simko et al. LC 77-90919. (Promised Lands Ser.). (Illus.). 535p. 1978. pap. 10.00x o.p. (ISBN 0-918780-06-3). INFORM.

Promised Year. Yoshiko Uchida. LC 59-9270. (Illus.). (gr. 4-6). 1959. 6.50 o.p. (ISBN 0-15-263866-0, HJ). HarBraceJ.

Promises. Catherine Gaskin. 1983. pap. 3.95 o.p. (ISBN 0-380-65151-3, 65151). Avon.

Promises, 3 bks. Anita L. Wheatcroft. (Illus.). 80p. (Orig.). (gr. 3-4). 1973. Set. pap. 2.95 o.p. (ISBN 0-8192-4043-5); tchrs'. guide 4.75x o.p. (ISBN 0-8192-4044-3). Morehouse Pub.

Promises: A Guide to Christian Commitment. Frances L. Carroll. 228p. 1985. 14.95 o.p. (ISBN 0-13-731076-5); pap. 7.95 o.p. (ISBN 0-13-731068-4). P H.

Promises of Steel, Covenants of Glass. Conrad Weiser. LC 73-79328. (Illus.). 128p. 1973. pap. 0.50 o.p. (ISBN 0-8006-5075-1, Fortress). Augsburg Fortress.

Promises to Keep. Paige Dixon. LC 74-75560. 176p. (gr. 6 up). 1974. 7.95 o.p. (ISBN 0-689-30408-0, Atheneum). Macmillan.

Promises to Keep. Valerie Ferris. (Candlelight Ecstasy Ser.: No. 30). 192p. (Orig.). 1981. pap. 1.75 o.p. (ISBN 0-440-17159-8). Dell.

Promises to Keep: A Workbook of Experiences for Covenant Living. Dennis C. Benson & Marilyn J. Benson. (Orig.). 1978. pap. 3.95 o.p. (ISBN 0-377-00077-9). Friendship Pr.

Promises to the Fathers: Studies on the Patriarchal Narratives. Claus Westermann. Tr. by David E. Green from Ger. LC 79-7395. 208p. 1980. 13.95 o.p. (ISBN 0-8006-0580-2, 1-580, Fortress). Augsburg Fortress.

Promising Replacements for Conventional Aggregates for Highway Use. (National Cooperative Highway Research Program Report). 53p. 1972. 3.60 o.p. (ISBN 0-317-36100-7). Transport Res Bd.

Promontory's Locomotives. Gerald M. Best. (Illus.). 48p. pap. 2.95 o.s.i. (ISBN 0-87095-082-7). Gldn West Bks.

Promoting & Selling Your Art. Carole Katchen. 192p. 1978. 19.95 o.p. (ISBN 0-8230-4422-X). Watson-Guptill.

Promoting Effectively for Downtown Business: Dynamic New Case Studies. Ed. by Laurence A. Alexander. LC 83-71250. (Illus.). 64p. (Orig.). 1983. pap. 27.50 o.p. (ISBN 0-915910-20-9). Downtown Res.

Promoting Nature in Cities & Towns. Malcolm J. Emery. (Illus.). 320p. 1986. 34.50 o.p. (ISBN 0-7099-0966-7, Pub. by Croom Helm Ltd); pap. 17.00 o.p. (ISBN 0-7099-0970-5, Pub. by Croom Helm Ltd). Routledge Chapman & Hall.

Promoting Psychological Comfort. 3rd ed. Gloria M. Francis & Barbara A. Munjas. (Foundations of Nursing Ser.). 120p. 1979. pap. text ed. write for info. o.p. (ISBN 0-697-05544-2). Wm C Brown.

Promoting Rock Concerts: A Practical Guide. Howard Stein & Ronald Zalkind. LC 79-63032. 1979. 12.95 o.s.i. (ISBN 0-02-872490-9); pap. 6.95 o.s.i. (ISBN 0-02-872470-4). Schirmer Bks.

Promoting the Social Development of Young Children. Charles A. Smith. LC 81-83085. 261p. 1981. pap. 13.95 o.p. (ISBN 0-87484-528-9); instr's. guide avail. o.p. Mayfield Pub.

Promoting Wellness in Nursing Practice: A Step-by-Step Approach in Patient Education. Rita J. DuBrey. LC 81-22321. (Illus.). 387p. 1982. pap. text ed. 18.95 o.p. (ISBN 0-8016-1480-5). Mosby.

Promoting Your Church Library. Marian S. Johnson. LC 68-25805. 1968. pap. 4.50 spiral bdg o.p. (ISBN 0-8066-0831-5, 10-5280, Augsburg). Augsburg Fortress.

Promotion Course. Jack Rudman. (Career Examination Ser.: CS-2). 1987. pap. 14.00 o.p. (ISBN 0-317-62920-4). Natl Learning.

Promotion in Food Service. S. Laine & I. Laine. 1972. text ed. 25.25 o.p. (ISBN 0-07-035843-5). McGraw.

Promotion Management: A Strategic Approach. John J. Burnett. (Illus.). 500p. 1984. text ed. 36.50 o.p. (ISBN 0-314-77851-9); tchrs.' manual avail. o.p. (ISBN 0-314-77855-1). West Pub.

Promotion of Small & Medium-Sized Enterprises: Report VI. International Labour Conference, 72nd Session, 1986. iv, 104p. 1986. pap. 12.25 o.p. (ISBN 92-2-105178-1). Intl Labour Office.

Promotion of the Relationship Between Research & Industry in Mechanical Production. O. Kienzle et al. 1970. pap. 35.00 o.p. (ISBN 0-08-006607-0). Pergamon.

Promotional & Program Artwork. Lauren Reinertsen. 62p. 1988. 11.95 o.p. Galloway.

Pronoia und Paideusis: Studien Uber Origenes und Sein Verhaltnis Zum Platonismus. Hal Koch. LC 78-66597. (Ancient Philosophy Ser.). 347p. 1979. lib. bdg. 41.00 o.p. (ISBN 0-8240-9592-8). Garland Pub.

Pronouncing Dictionary of English-Place Names. Klaus Forster. 308p. 1981. 30.00 o.p. (ISBN 0-7100-0756-6). Routledge Chapman & Hall.

Pronunciation of English: Phonetics & Phonetic Transcriptions. 1985. pap. 20.00 o.p. (ISBN 0-87556-693-6). Saifer.

Pronunciation of English Words see Preliminary Announcement.

Pronunciation of French: Articulation & Intonation. Jeanne V. Pleasants. (Illus.). 1978. pap. text ed. 11.50x o.p. (ISBN 0-940630-00-1, JVP-PFAI). Playette Corp.

Proof. Dick Francis. 1985. 17.95 o.p. (ISBN 0-8161-3927-X, Large Print Bks); pap. 10.95 o.p. (ISBN 0-8161-3944-X). G K Hall.

Propaganda & Myth in Time of War. Charles H. Hamlin. Bd. with War Myth in U. S. History; Educators Present Arms: The Use of the Schools & Colleges As Agents of War Propaganda, 1914-1918. LC 77-147725. (Library of War & Peace; the Character & Causes of War). lib. bdg. 46.00 o.p. (ISBN 0-8240-0261-X). Garland Pub.

Propaganda & the American Revolution. Philip Davidson. (Illus.). 476p. 1973. pap. 3.45x o.p. (ISBN 0-393-00703-0). Norton.

Propaganda of Adolf Hitler. rev. ed. Ed. by Jonathan R. Manning. LC 75-14093. (Illus.). 144p. 1975. pap. 5.95 o.s.i. (ISBN 0-89019-024-0). Norwalk Pr.

Propagation of Electromagnetic Waves in Plasmas. 2nd rev. ed. V. L. Ginzburg. 1971. 135.00 o.p. (ISBN 0-08-015569-3). Pergamon.

Propagation of Gamma Quanta in Matter. O. I. Leipunskii et al. 1965. text ed. 53.00 o.p. (ISBN 0-08-010553-X); pap. 60.00 o.p. (ISBN 0-08-013564-1). Pergamon.

Propagation of Waves. P. David & J. Voge. 1969. text ed. 37.00 o.p. (ISBN 0-08-012114-4). Pergamon.

Propagation Wizard's Handbook. J. H. Nelson. 136p. 1978. pap. 6.95 o.p. (ISBN 0-88006-000-X, BK7302). Wayne Green Ent.

Propane Conversion of Cars, Trucks & RVs. Larry W. Carley. (Illus.). 224p. 1982. 14.95 o.p. (ISBN 0-8306-3103-8); pap. 9.95 o.p. (ISBN 0-8306-2103-2, 2103). TAB Bks.

Propellanes: Structure & Reactions. David Ginsburg. (Monographs in Modern Chemistry: Vol. 7). 272p. 1975. 88.00 o.p. (ISBN 3-527-25602-4). VCH Pubs.

Propellants Manufacture, Hazards, & Testing. Ed. by Carl Boyars & Karl Klager. LC 75-87208. (Advances in Chemistry Ser.: No. 88). 1969. 34.95 o.p. (ISBN 0-8412-0089-0). Am Chemical.

Proper Forcing. S. Shelah. (Lecture Notes in Mathematics Ser.: Vol. 940). 496p. 1982. pap. 27.00 o.p. (ISBN 0-387-11593-5). Springer-Verlag.

Properties & Applications of Transistors. J. P. Vasseur. 1964. 45.00 o.p. (ISBN 0-08-010244-1); pap. text ed. 18.50 o.p. (ISBN 0-08-013647-8). Pergamon.

Properties & Selection of Tool Materials. 1975. 38.00 o.p. (ISBN 0-87170-054-9). ASM.

Properties of Amorphous Silicon. Ed. by N. Parkman et al. (EMIS Datareviews Ser.: No. 1). 262p. 1985. casebound 195.00 o.p. (DA001). Inst Elect Eng.

Properties of Gases & Liquids. 3rd ed. Robert C. Reid & John M. Prausnitz. 1977. text ed. 63.00 o.p. (ISBN 0-07-051790-8). McGraw.

Properties of Infinite Dimensional Hamiltonian Systems. P. R. Chernoff & J. E. Marsden. LC 74-22373. (Lecture Notes in Mathematics Ser.: Vol. 425). iv, 160p. 1975. pap. 14.00 o.p. (ISBN 0-387-07011-7). Springer-Verlag.

Properties of Materials for Electrical Engineers. K. J. Pascoe. LC 72-8612. 324p. 1974. (ISBN 0-471-66910-5, Pub. by Wiley-Interscience); pap. 42.95x o.p. (ISBN 0-471-66911-3, Pub. by Wiley-Interscience). Wiley.

Properties of Matter. (Illus.). 336p. 1959. (ISBN 0-8022-0231-4). Philos Lib.

Titles

Properties of Nonmetallic Fluid Elements, Vol. III. Y. S. Touloukian & C. Y. Ho. (M-H-CINDAS Data Series on Material Properties). 224p. 1981. text ed. 59.95 o.p. (ISBN 0-07-065033-0). McGraw.
Properties of Petroleum Fluids. William D. McCain, Jr. LC 73-78008. 325p. 1974. 54.95 o.p. (ISBN 0-87814-021-2, P-4025). Pennwell Bks.
Properties of Refractory Metals. Walter D. Wilkinson. LC 72-75349. 355p. 1969. 32.00 o.p. (ISBN 0-685-58275-2, 450010). Am Nuclear Soc.
Properties of Steel Weldments for Elevated Temperature Pressure Containment Applications: MPC-9. Ed. by G. V. Smith. 1978. 30.00 o.p. (ISBN 0-685-66811-8, H00133). ASME.
Property & Political Theory. Alan Ryan. 240p. 1984. 45.00x o.p. (ISBN 0-631-13691-6). Basil Blackwell.
Property & Riches in the Early Church: Aspects of a Social History of Early Christianity. Martin Hengel. Tr. by John Bowden from Ger. LC 75-305658. 104p. 1974. pap. 4.50 o.p. (1-1201, Fortress). Augsburg Fortress.
Property Development: Effective Decision Making in Uncertain Times. John W. McMahan. 1976. text ed. 44.95 o.p. (ISBN 0-07-045450-7). McGraw.
Property Management. 2nd ed. Robert C. Kyle. LC 84-3325. 440p. (Orig.). 1984. pap. text ed. 31.95 o.p. (ISBN 0-88462-498-6, 1551-10, Real Estate Ed). Longman Finan.
Property Management. D. Scarrett. (Illus.). 1983. 29.95 o.p. (ISBN 0-419-12380-6, NO. 6828, Pub. by E & FN Spon); pap. 14.95 o.p. (ISBN 0-419-12390-3, NO. 6829). Routledge Chapman & Hall.
Property Rights: Philosophic Foundations. Lawrence C. Becker. 1977. 21.95x o.p. (ISBN 0-7100-8679-2). Routledge Chapman & Hall.
Property Tax in North Carolina: An Introduction. 3rd ed. Henry W. Lewis. 1978. pap. 2.75 o.p. (ISBN 0-686-17569-7). Institute Government.
Property Tax Preferences for Agricultural Land. Ed. by Neal A. Roberts & H. James Brown. LC 79-52473. (Illus.). 140p. 1980. text ed. 19.50x o.s.i. (ISBN 0-916672-32-8, Pub. by Allanheld). Rowman.
Property Tax Reform. Ed. by George Peterson. 188p. 1973. pap. text ed. 10.50 o.p. (ISBN 0-87766-099-9). Urban Inst.
Property Values & Race: Studies in Seven Cities. Luigi Laurenti. LC 76-5437. (Illus.). 256p. 1976. Repr. of 1961 ed. lib. bdg. 35.00x o.p. (ISBN 0-8371-8795-8, LAPV). Greenwood.
Prophecies & Revelations about the Jesuits. Tr. by James S. Terrien. 143p. pap. 3.98 o.p. (ISBN 0-913452-27-0). Jesuit Bks.
Prophecy & Hermeneutics in Early Christianity: New Testament Essays. E. Earle Ellis. 306p. 1978. lib. bdg. 62.50x o.p. Coronet Bks.
Prophecy & History in Luke-Acts. David L. Tiede. LC 79-8897. 180p. 1980. write for info o.p. (ISBN 0-8006-0632-9, 1-632, Fortress). Augsburg Fortress.
Prophecy & Politics: Militant Evangelists on the Road to Nuclear War. Grace Halsell. 256p. 1986. 14.95 o.p. (ISBN 0-88208-210-8). Chicago Review.
Prophecy & the Church. Oswald T. Allis. 1977. pap. 9.95 o.p. (ISBN 0-8010-0110-2). Baker Bk.
Prophecy & Tradition. R. E. Clements. LC 74-3713. 96p. 1975. pap. 2.75 o.p. (ISBN 0-8042-0110-2, John Knox). Westminster John Knox.
Prophecy in Ancient Israel. J. Lindblom. LC 63-907. 480p. 1962. 17.95 o.p. (ISBN 0-8006-0916-6, 1-916, Fortress). Augsburg Fortress.
Prophecy in Early Christianity & the Ancient Mediterranean World. David E. Aune. 400p. 1983. 29.95 o.p. (ISBN 0-8028-3584-8). Eerdmans.
Prophecy Interpreted. John P. Milton. LC 60-6437. 1960. 6.50 o.p. (ISBN 0-8066-0001-2, 10-5261, Augsburg). Augsburg Fortress.
Prophet Eshref & Other Short Stories: A Panorama of Psychic Adventures. Ismail Ersevim. 96p. 1983. 6.50 o.p. (ISBN 0-682-49974-9). Exposition-Phoenix.
Prophet of Community: The Romantic Socialism of Gustav Landauer. Eugene Lunn. LC 70-186105. 1973. 40.00x o.p. (ISBN 0-520-02207-6). U of Cal Pr.
Prophethood of All Believers. James L. Adams. Ed. by George K. Beach. LC 85-73368. 324p. 1987. 25.00 o.p. (ISBN 0-8070-1602-0). Beacon Pr.
Prophetic Faith in Isaiah. Sheldon H. Blank. (Waynebooks Ser: No. 24). 1967. pap. 4.95x o.p. (ISBN 0-8143-1324-8). Wayne St U Pr.
Prophetic Lectures on Daniel & Revelations. F. G. Smith. 260p. pap. 3.50 o.p. (ISBN 0-686-29136-0). Faith Pub Hse.
Prophetic Light in the Present Darkness see **Word Studies in the Greek New Testament, for the English Reader.**
Prophetic Melville: Experience, Transcendence, & Tragedy. Rowland A. Sherrill. LC 78-20436. 292p. 1979. 19.00x o.p. (ISBN 0-8203-0455-7). U of Ga Pr.
Prophetic Persona: The Language of Self-Reference in Jeremiah. Timothy Polk. (JSOT Supplement Ser.: No. 32). 240p. pap. text ed. 14.95x o.s.i. (Pub. by JSOT Pr England). Eisenbrauns.
Prophetic Vision of Merlin: Prediction, Psychic Transformation, & the Foundation of the Grail Legends in an Ancient Set of Visionary Verses. R. J. Stewart. (Illus.). 195p. 1986. pap. 9.95 o.p. (ISBN 1-85063-018-6). Routledge Chapman & Hall.
Prophetic Warnings to Modern America. Duane S. Crowther. LC 77-87431. 415p. 1977. 12.95 o.p. (ISBN 0-88290-016-1). Horizon Utah.
Prophetical, Educational & Playing Cards. Mrs. John K. Van Rensselaer. LC 77-78249. (Illus.). 392p. 1971. Repr. of 1912 ed. 43.00x o.p. (ISBN 0-8103-3867-X). Gale.
Prophets & Prophecies of the Old Testament. 2nd ed. Duane S. Crowther. LC 66-25508. (Comprehensive Bible Ser.). (Illus.). 644p. 1973. Repr. of 1967 ed. 12.95 o.p. (ISBN 0-88290-022-6). Horizon Utah.
Prophets & Prophecy: Seven Key Messengers. Frank H. Seilhamer. LC 76-62603. 96p. (Orig.). 1977. pap. 0.50 o.p. (ISBN 0-8006-1254-X, 1-1254). Augsburg Fortress.
Prophets & the Powerless. James Limburg. LC 76-12397. 1976. pap. 6.95 o.s.i. (ISBN 0-8042-0156-0, John Knox). Westminster John Knox.
Prophets & Their Times. rev ed. John M. Smith. Ed. by William A. Irwin. LC 25-6864. 1941. lib. bdg. 20.00x o.s.i. (ISBN 0-226-76356-0). U of Chicago Pr.
Prophets Denied Honor: An Anthology on the Hispanic Church in the U. S. Ed. by Antonio Stevens-Arroyo. LC 79-26847. 397p. (Orig.). 1982. pap. 12.95 o.p. (ISBN 0-88344-395-3). Orbis Bks.
Prophets of Israel. C. Ross Milley. 160p. 1959. (ISBN 0-8022-1119-4). Philos Lib.
Prophets of Israel. William R. Smith. (Social Science Classics Ser.). 446p. 19.95 o.p. (ISBN 0-87855-318-5); text ed. (ISBN 0-87855-700-8); pap. 7.95 o.p.; pap. text ed. (ISBN 0-686-68060-X). Transaction Pubs.
Prophets of Israel: From Ahijah to Hosea. H. L. Ellison. 176p. 1974. pap. 5.75 o.p. (ISBN 0-8028-1590-1). Attic Pr.
Prophets of Prosperity: America's First Political Economists. Paul K. Conkin. LC 79-3251. 352p. 1980. 25.00x o.p. (ISBN 0-253-30843-7). Ind U Pr.
Prophets on Main Street. rev. ed. J. Elliott Corbett. LC 77-79597. 1977. pap. 7.25 o.p. (ISBN 0-8042-0841-7, John Knox). Westminster John Knox.
Prophets, Poets, Priests, & Kings: The Old Testament Story. F. Washington Jarvis. 288p. 1975. pap. 6.95 o.p. (ISBN 0-8164-2089-0). HarpR.
Prophets Speak Again: A Brief Introduction to Old Testament Prophecy. Barbara Jurgensen. LC 76-27084. 1977. pap. 4.50 o.p. (ISBN 0-8066-1566-4, 10-5265, Augsburg). Augsburg Fortress.
Prophets Speak to Us Anew. David Wanefsky. 1952. (ISBN 0-8022-1805-9). Philos Lib.
Propjet 1988. Harry B. Adams. (Illus.). 170p. 1988. pap. 9.95 o.p. (ISBN 0-941024-08-3). Avcom Intl.
Propjet 1989. Harry Adams & R. W. Simpson. (Illus.). 148p. Date not set. pap. 9.95 o.p. (ISBN 0-317-57095-1, Pub. by AvCom Intl). Aviation.
Proposal Preparation & Management Handbook. Roy J. Loring & Harold Kerzner. 416p. 1982. 28.95 o.p. (ISBN 0-442-25437-7). Van Nos Reinhold.
Proposals for Changes in the United Nations. Francis O. Wilcox & Carl M. Marcy. LC 79-26764. xiv, 537p. 1980. Repr. of 1955 ed. lib. bdg. 42.50x o.p. (ISBN 0-313-22290-8, WIPF). Greenwood.
Proposed Amendments to the Constitution of the United States: During the First Century of Its History. Herman V. Ames. 1896. 26.00 o.p. Ayer Co Pubs.
Proposed Amendments to the Constitution of the United States Introduced in Congress from Dec. 4, 1889 to July 2, 1926. U. S. Library of Congress, Legislative Reference Service Staff. Ed. by Charles C. Tansill. LC 75-35363. (U. S. Government Documents Program Ser.). 148p. 1976. Repr. of 1926 ed. lib. bdg. 35.00x o.p. (ISBN 0-8371-8606-4, USPA). Greenwood.
Proposed SOx & Particulate Standard: Proceedings, Atlanta, Ga. Air Pollution Control Association Specialty Conference. 300p. 1980. 18.00 o.p. (ISBN 0-318-12269-3, SP-38); members 15.00 o.p. (ISBN 0-318-12270-7). Air & Waste.
Proposition Fourteen: A Secessionist Remedy. Richard Cummings. LC 80-8917. 128p. (Orig.). 1981. pap. 3.95 o.s.i. (ISBN 0-394-17890-4, E776, BC). Grove.
Proposition Thirteen: A First Anniversary Assessment. (Lincoln Institute Monograph: No. 80-5). (Illus.). 1980. pap. text ed. 5.00 o.s.i. (ISBN 0-686-29506-4). Lincoln Inst Land.
Proposition Thirteen, Property Transfers, & the Real Estate Markets. Frederick E. Balderston et al. LC 79-10332. (Research Report: No. 79-1). 1979. pap. 3.00x o.p. (ISBN 0-87772-264-1). UCB IGS.
Propositional Logic of Boethius. Karl Durr. LC 80-18931. (Studies in Logic & the Foundations of Mathematics). 79p. 1980. Repr. of 1951 ed. lib. bdg. 35.00x o.p. (ISBN 0-313-21102-7, DUPL). Greenwood.
Proprietor. Ann Schlee. LC 83-6183. (William Abrahams Bk.). 336p. 1983. 15.95 o.p. (ISBN 0-03-063948-4). H Holt & Co.
Prose in Practice: A Rhetorical Reader. James Weldon Johnson. 1971. pap. text ed. 9.95 o.p. (ISBN 0-15-572270-0, HC). HarBraceJ.
Prose in Practice: A Rhetorical Reader. 2nd ed. James Weldon Johnson. (Orig.). 1976. pap. text ed. 10.95 o.p. (ISBN 0-15-572272-7, HC). HarBraceJ.
Prose Models. 5th ed. Gerald Levin. 372p. 1981. pap. text ed. 10.95 o.p. (ISBN 0-15-572280-8, HC). HarBraceJ.
Prose Models. 3rd ed. Gerald Levin. (Orig.). 1975. pap. text ed. 8.95 o.p. (ISBN 0-15-572277-8, HC). HarBraceJ.
Prose Models. 6th ed. Gerald Levin. 534p. 1984. pap. 11.25 o.p. (ISBN 0-15-572282-4, HC). HarBraceJ.
Prose Models. 4th ed. Ed. by Gerald Levin. 1978. pap. text ed. 8.95 o.p. (ISBN 0-15-572278-6, HC). HarBraceJ.
Prose of Sir Thomas Browne. Thomas Browne. Ed. by Norman J. Endicott. 1972. pap. 5.95x o.p. (ISBN 0-393-00619-0, N619, Norton Lib). Norton.
Prose Quotations from Socrates to Macauley. Samuel A. Allibone. LC 68-30642. 764p. 1973. Repr. of 1876 ed. 37.00x o.p. (ISBN 0-8103-3181-0). Gale.
Prose Style. 3rd ed. Wilfred Stone & Jess G. Bell. (Illus.). 1976. text ed. 11.95 o.p. (ISBN 0-07-061732-5). McGraw.
Prose Style of Samuel Johnson. William K. Wimsatt, Jr. LC 78-179568. (Yale Studies in English Ser.: No. 94). xvi, 166p. 1972. Repr. of 1941 ed. 21.00 o.p. (ISBN 0-208-01141-2, Archon). Shoe String.
Prose Writings of Donald Lamont, 1874-1958. Ed. by Thomas M. Murchison. 1958. 15.00x o.p. (ISBN 0-7073-0038-X, Pub. by Scot Acad Pr). Longwood Pub Group.
Prosecutor. Ed. by William F. McDonald. LC 79-14388. (Sage Criminal Justice System Annuals Ser.: Vol. 11). (Illus.). 279p. 1979. 29.95 o.p. (ISBN 0-8039-0815-6); pap. 14.95 o.p. (ISBN 0-8039-0816-4). Sage.
Prosecutor: An Inquiry into the Exercise of Discretion. Brian A. Grosman. LC 76-461526. 1969. pap. 7.50 o.p. (ISBN 0-8020-6341-1). U of Toronto Pr.
Prosecutorial & Judicial Misconduct. Dolores A. Donovan. LC 79-53126. (California Criminal Law Practice Ser.). xi, 148p. 1979. 30.00 o.p. (ISBN 0-88124-062-1). Cal Cont Ed Bar.
Prosecutorial Discretion. Rev. ed. James I. Knapp et al. LC 80-112695. (California Criminal Law Practice Ser.). xvii, 135p. 1979. 30.00 o.p. Cal COnt Ed Bar.
ProSet Eighty-One. Harry Adams. (Illus.). 176p. 1981. pap. 6.95 o.p. (ISBN 0-686-73506-4, Pub. by AvCom Intl). Aviation.
Proskauer, His Life & Times. Louis M. Hacker & Mark D. Hirsch. LC 77-1697. 240p. 1978. 18.00 o.p. (ISBN 0-8173-9361-7). U of Ala Pr.
Prospect for Metaphysics. Ed. by Ian Ramsey. 256p. 1961. (ISBN 0-8022-1310-3). Philos Lib.
Prospect for Presidential-Congressional Government. Ed. by Albert Lepawsky. LC 77-17083. 1978. pap. 6.00x o.p. (ISBN 0-87772-250-1). UCB IGS.
Prospecting to Riches in Real Estate. Albert L. Friedman. 224p. 1986. 10.95 o.p. (ISBN 0-8062-2803-2). Carlton.
Prospective Payments: Health Care Revolution. Ed. by Barbara Dreyfuss. 565p. (Orig.). pap. text ed. cancelled o.s.i. (ISBN 0-914176-25-0). Wash Busn Info.
Prospects for Oil & Gas from Silurian-Niagaran Trend Areas in Michigan. William F. Yellig, Jr. & M. Rasin Tek. (Illus.). 35p. 1976. 12.00 o.p. (ISBN 0-938654-00-4). Indus Dev Inst Sci.
Prospects for Recovery in the British Economy. Ed. by F. V. Meyer. LC 84-29366. 237p. 1985. 34.50 o.p. (ISBN 0-7099-1772-4, Pub. by Croom Helm Ltd). Routledge Chapman & Hall.
Prospects for Synthetic Fuels in the United States. John M. Deutch. 1982. 2.50x o.p. (ISBN 0-317-06611-0). Univ Pr Colo.
Prospects for the World Oil Industry. Ed. by Tim Niblock & Richard Lawless. LC 85-4186. 131p. 1985. 29.00 o.p. (ISBN 0-7099-4104-8, Pub. by Croom Helm Ltd). Routledge Chapman & Hall.
Prospects for Traditional & Non-Conventional Energy Sources in Developing Countries. David P. Hughart. (Working Paper: No. 346). ii, 132p. 1979. 8.00 o.p. (ISBN 0-686-36159-8, WP-0346). World Bank.
Prospects in Mathematics. F. E. Hirzebruch et al. LC 72-155007. (Annals of Mathematics Studies: No. 70). 1971. 24.00 o.p. (ISBN 0-691-08094-1). Princeton U Pr.
Prosperity & Depression: A Theoretical Analysis of Cyclical Movement. Gottfried Haberler. LC 59-6133. 1963. pap. text ed. 1.95x o.s.i. (ISBN 0-689-70083-0, 24, Atheneum). Macmillan.
Prosperity & Poverty: The Compassionate Use of Resources in a World of Sacrity. E. Calvin Beisner. 1988. pap. 9.95 o.p. (ISBN 0-89107-499-6, Crossway Bks). Good News.
Prosperity for Welfare: Proceedings of the International Labour Conference, 58th Session, Geneva, 1973. International Labour Office Staff. 1973. 7.15 o.p. (ISBN 92-2-100964-5). Intl Labour Office.
Prosperity Through Competition. Ludwig Erhard. Tr. by Edith T. Roberts & John B. Wood. LC 75-27681. 260p. 1976. Repr. of 1958 ed. lib. bdg. 22.50x o.p. (ISBN 0-8371-8457-6, ERPC). Greenwood.
Prostaglandin Biosynthesis. (Landmark Ser.). 1979. 27.50x o.p. (ISBN 0-8422-4116-7). Irvington.
Prostaglandin E-1 in Atherosclerosis. Ed. by H. Sinzinger & W. Rogatti. (Illus.). 120p. 1986. pap. 26.40 o.p. (ISBN 0-387-17240-8). Springer-Verlag.
Prostaglandin Research. Ed. by Pierre Crabbe. (Organic Chemistry Ser.). 1977. 85.00 o.p. (ISBN 0-12-194660-6). Acad Pr.
Prostaglandin Synthesis. Jasjit S. Bindra. 1977. 66.00 o.p. (ISBN 0-12-099460-7). Acad Pr.
Prostaglandins. Ed. by Ulf S. Von Euler & Rune Eliasson. 1968. 46.00 o.p. (ISBN 0-12-724950-8). Acad Pr.
Prostaglandins & Cyclic AMP: Biological Actions & Clinical Applications. Ed. by Raymond H. Kahn & William E. M. Lands. 1973. 52.50 o.p. (ISBN 0-12-394450-3). Acad Pr.
Prostaglandins & Reproduction. (Landmark Ser.). 1979. 22.50x o.p. (ISBN 0-8422-4109-4). Irvington.
Prostaglandins & the Alimentary Tract. (Landmark Ser.). 1979. 22.50x o.p. (ISBN 0-8422-4115-9). Irvington.
Prostaglandins & Thromboxins: Proceedings of the Third International Symposium on Prostaglandins & Thromboxanes in the Cardiovascular System, Hale-Salle, GDR, 5-7 May 1980. Werner Forster et al. LC 80-41802. (Illus.). 500p. 1981. 97.00 o.p. (ISBN 0-08-027369-6). Pergamon.
Prostaglandins I: Basic Physiology, Vol. 1. Donald P. Wallach et al. (Illus.). 220p. 1973. text ed. 29.00x o.p. (ISBN 0-8422-7047-7). Irvington.
Prostaglandins II: Clinical Aspects. Elisman M. Coutinho et al. LC 73-510. 1973. 29.00x o.p. (ISBN 0-8422-7109-0). Irvington.
Prostate Cancer. Ed. by W. Duncan. (Recent Results in Cancer Research Ser.: Vol. 78). (Illus.). 192p. 1981. 48.00 o.p. (ISBN 0-387-10676-6). Springer-Verlag.
Prostitution & Drugs. Paul J. Goldstein. LC 78-24766. 208p. 1979. 29.00x o.p. (ISBN 0-669-02833-9). Lexington Bks.
Prostitution & Prejudice. Date not set. (ISBN 0-8052-3866-2). Random.
Protamines: Isolation, Characterization, Structure & Function. T. Ando et al. LC 73-77821. (Molecular Biology, Biochemistry & Biophysics Ser: Vol. 12). (Illus.). 114p. 1973. 34.00 o.p. (ISBN 0-387-06221-1). Springer-Verlag.
Proteas for Pleasure. Sima Eliovson. (Illus.). 228p. 1982. 31.95 o.p. (ISBN 0-86954-006-8, Pub. by Macmillan S Africa). Intl Spec Bk.
Protect Your Child: A Parent's Safeguard Against Child Abduction & Sexual Abuse. Laura M. Huchton. 180p. 1985. 16.95 o.p. (ISBN 0-13-731456-6); pap. 6.95 o.p. (ISBN 0-13-731449-3). P-H.
Protect Yourself in Real Estate: The Complete Beginner's Guide. Robert Irwin. 320p. 1980. pap. text ed. 6.95 o.p. (ISBN 0-07-032059-4). McGraw.
Protecting Engineering Ideas & Inventions. 2nd ed. 1988. 54.00 o.p. Penn Inst.
Protecting Industrial-Business Facilities & Personnel from Terrorist Activities. 1977. pap. 5.00 o.p. (ISBN 0-918734-22-3). Reymont.
Protecting Information on Local Area Networks. James A. Schweitzer. 144p. 1987. text ed. 24.95 o.p. (ISBN 0-409-90138-5). Butterworth.

Protecting Our Children: The Fight Against Molestation, a National Symposium, Oct. 1-4, 1984. LC 85-20124. 259p. 1984. pap. 9.00 o.p. (ISBN 0-318-21665-5, S/N 027-000-01260-4). USGPO.

Protecting the Working Man: The Quest for Safety in Logging & Milling in the State of Oregon. David James. 24.95x o.s.i. (ISBN 0-87595-122-8). Oregon Hist.

Protecting Your Rights As Creditors in Bankruptcy. Diane Sigmund & Erwin Steiner. LC 83-152776. (Illus.). 203p. 1983. write for info. o.p. Natl Busn Inst.

Protection Against Trichothecene Mycotoxins. National Research Council, Toxicology & Environmental Health Hazards Board Staff. 1983. pap. text ed. 17.95x o.p. (ISBN 0-309-03430-2). Natl Acad Pr.

Protection & Industrial Policy in Europe. Joan Pearce & John Sutton. 208p. (Orig.). 1986. text ed. 29.95 o.p. (ISBN 0-7102-0733-6). Routledge Chapman & Hall.

Protection of Educational Buildings Against Earthquakes. A. S. Arya. (Educational Building Report Ser.: No. 13). 67p. (Orig.). 1987. pap. text ed. 7.50 o.p. (ISBN 0-317-66951-6, UB363, UB). UNIPUB.

Protection of Exothermic Reactors & Pressurised Storage Vessels: Proceedings of the Symposium, Chester, U. K., April 25-27, 1984. Ed. by Institution of Chemical Engineers Staff. (Institution of Chemical Engineers Symposium Ser.: Vol. 85). 378p. 1984. 50.00 o.s.i. (ISBN 0-08-030280-7). Pergamon.

Protection of the Patient in X-Ray Diagnosis. International Commission on Radiological Protection. (ICRP Publication Ser.: No. 16). 1971. pap. 11.75 o.p. (ISBN 0-08-016452-8). Pergamon.

Protective Groups in Organic Chemistry. Ed. by J. F. McOmie. LC 72-91038. 418p. 1973. 65.00x o.p. (ISBN 0-306-30717-0, Plenum Pr). Plenum Pub.

Protective Relays: Their Theory & Practice, 2 vols. A. R. Warrington. Incl. Vol. 1, 2nd ed. LC 70-385616. 484p. 1968. text ed. 44.95x (ISBN 0-412-09060-0, NO. 6310); Vol. 2, 3rd ed. 434p. 1978. 44.95x (ISBN 0-412-15380-7, NO. 6311). Pub. by Chapman & Hall England). Routledge Chapman & Hall.

Protein & Nucleic Acids see Submicroscopic Cytochemistry.

Protein & Nucleic Acids Structure. Ed. by Jonathan King. 1985. text ed. 34.95 o.p. (ISBN 0-8053-5403-4). Benjamin-Cummings.

Protein Biosynthesis. Ed. by Robert J. Harris. 1961. 64.50 o.p. (ISBN 0-12-327184-3). Acad Pr.

Protein Biosynthesis. Ed. by Herbert Weissbach & Sidney Pestka. (Molecular Biology Ser.). 1977. 99.00 o.p. (ISBN 0-12-744250-2). Acad Pr.

Protein Biosynthesis In Eukaryotes. Ed. by R. Perez-Bercoff. LC 81-22770. (NATO ASI Series A, Life Sciences: Vol. 41). 520p. 1982. 85.00x o.p. (ISBN 0-306-40893-7, Plenum Pr). Plenum Pub.

Protein-Calorie Malnutrition: Proceedings. Nestle Foundation Symposium Staff. Ed. by A. Von Muralt. (Illus.). 1971. Repr. of 1969 ed. 34.90 o.p. (ISBN 0-387-04677-1). Springer-Verlag.

Protein Conformation As an Immunological Signal. Ed. by Franco Celada et al. LC 83-13999. 520p. 1983. 85.00x o.p. (ISBN 0-306-41463-5, Plenum Pr). Plenum Pub.

Protein Phosphorylation. M. Weller. (Advanced Biochemistry Ser.). 557p. 1979. 70.00x o.p. (ISBN 0-85086-062-8, NO. 2924, Pub. by Pion England). Routledge Chapman & Hall.

Protein Phosphorylation in Control Mechanisms. Ed. by F. Huijing & E. Y. Lee. (Miami Winter Symposia: No. 5). 1973. 54.50 o.p. (ISBN 0-12-360950-X). Acad Pr.

Protein Phosphorylation in the Nervous System. Erie J. Nestler & Paul Greengard. LC 84-2235. (Neuroscience Institute Monograph Ser.: 1-693). 398p. 1984. 75.00 o.p. (ISBN 0-471-80558-0, Pub. by Wiley-Interscience). Wiley.

Protein Quality in Humans: Assessment & in Vitro Estimation. C. E. Bodwell & J. S. Adkins. (Illus.). 1982. 56.95 o.p. (ISBN 0-87055-388-7). AVI.

Protein Structure. Harold A. Scheraga. (Molecular Biology Ser: Vol. 1). 1961. 60.50 o.p. (ISBN 0-12-623850-2). Acad Pr.

Protein: Structure, Function & Industrial Applications. Ed. by E. Hoffman & E. Pfeil. (Federation of European Biochemical Society Ser.: Vol. 52). (Illus.). 1979. 93.00 o.p. (ISBN 0-08-023176-4). Pergamon.

Protein Turnover & Lysosome Function. Ed. by Harold Segal & Darrell J. Doyle. 1978. 85.50 o.p. (ISBN 0-12-636150-9). Acad Pr.

Proteinase Inhibitors: Proceedings. Bayer Symposium, 5th - Proteinase Conference, 2nd, Cologne, Germany, 1973. Ed. by H. Fritz et al. LC 74-6880. (No. 5). (Illus.). xvi, 751p. 1975. 72.00 o.p. (ISBN 0-387-06775-2). Springer-Verlag.

Proteinases & Their Inhibitors: Structure, Function & Applied Aspects. V. Turk & L. J. Vitale. LC 81-319. (Illus.). 500p. 1981. 105.00 o.p. (ISBN 0-08-027377-7). Pergamon.

Proteins & Peptides Hormones. Ed. by John G. Pierce. LC 82-6159. (Benchmark Papers in Biochemistry: Vol. 4). 459p. 1982. 63.95 o.p. (ISBN 0-87933-417-7). Van Nos Reinhold.

Protest & Crime in China: A Bibliography. Ssu-Yu Teng. (History, Political Science & International Affairs Catalog Ser.). 300p. 1981. lib. bdg. 43.00 o.p. (ISBN 0-8240-9354-2). Garland Pub.

Protest & Survive. Ed. by E. P. Thompson & Dan Smith. LC 81-81692. 288p. 1981. pap. 4.95 o.p. (ISBN 0-85345-582-1). Monthly Rev.

Protest, Direct Action, Repression. Dissent in American Society from Colonial Times to the Present. Ed. by Dirk Hoerder. xxvi, 434p. 1977. lib. bdg. 28.00 o.p. (ISBN 3-7940-7009-7). K G Saur.

Protest Movements in America. Michael Useem. 1975. pap. text ed. write for info. o.p. (ISBN 0-02-422150-3). Macmillan.

Protest, Politics & Prosperity: Black Americans & White Institutions. Dorothy K. Newman et al. LC 77-5191. 1978. 15.95 o.s.i. (ISBN 0-394-41202-8); pap. 6.95 o.p. (ISBN 0-394-73448-3). Pantheon.

Protestant Challenge to Corporate America: Issues of Social Responsibility. Roy W. Morano. Ed. by Richard Farmer. LC 84-8514. (Research for Business Decisions Ser.: No. 69). 256p. 1984. 44.95 o.p. (ISBN 0-8357-1592-2). UMI Res Pr.

Protestant Church Music. Friedrich Blume et al. (Illus.). 912p. 1975. 29.95x o.p. (ISBN 0-393-02176-9). Norton.

Protestant Church Music in America: A Short Survey of Men & Movements from 1564 to the Present. Robert Stevenson. (Illus.). 1970. pap. 2.95 o.p. (ISBN 0-393-00535-6, Norton Lib). Norton.

Protestant Dictionary. Vergilius Ferm. 292p. 1951. Philos Lib.

Protestant Dictionary: Containing Articles on the History, Doctrines, & Practices of the Christian Church. Ed. by Charles Wright & Charles Neil. LC 73-155436. 840p. 1971. Repr. of 1933 ed. 65.00x o.p. (ISBN 0-8103-3388-0). Gale.

Protestant in Purgatory: Richard Whately, Archbishop of Dublin. Donald H. Akenson. LC 81-3522. (Conference on British Studies (CBS) Biography: Vol. II). xiii, 276p. 1981. 25.00 o.p. (ISBN 0-208-01917-0, Archon). Shoe String.

Protestant Movement in Bolivia. C. Peter Wagner. LC 76-126079. (Illus.). 240p. (Orig.). 1970. pap. 3.95 o.p. (ISBN 0-87808-402-9). William Carey Lib.

Protestant Quest for a Christian America, 1830-1930. Robert T. Handy. Ed. by Richard C. Wolf. LC 67-22986. (Facet Bks.). 1967. pap. 0.50 o.p. (ISBN 0-8006-3041-6, 1-3041, Fortress). Augsburg Fortress.

Protestantism in Latin America: A Bibliographical Guide. rev. ed. Ed. by John H. Sinclair. LC 73-12837. 414p. 1976. pap. text ed. 8.95x o.p. (ISBN 0-87808-126-7). William Carey Lib.

Protestants & Catholics: A Guide to Understanding the Differences. Peter Toon. 160p. (Orig.). 1984. pap. 5.95 o.p. (ISBN 0-89283-188-X). Servant.

Proteus: His Lies, His Truth. Robert M. Adams. 192p. 1973. 7.95x o.p. (ISBN 0-393-04353-3). Norton.

Proto-Indo-European Syntax. Winfred P. Lehmann. LC 52-2570. 290p. 1974. 20.00x o.p. (ISBN 0-292-76419-7). U of Tex Pr.

Proto-Indo-European Syntax: The Order of Meaningful Elements. Paul Friedrich. (Journal of Indo-European Studies Monograph: No. 1). 78p. 1984. pap. 20.00x o.p. (ISBN 0-941694-25-9). Inst Study Man.

Proto-Oceanic Palatals. Robert A. Blust. 193p. 1979. pap. text ed. 15.00x o.p. (ISBN 0-8248-0684-0, Pub. by Polynesian Soc). UH Pr.

Protocols for Nurse Practitioners in Gynecologic Settings. Joellen Hawkins et al. LC 86-50615. 296p. 1987. spiral bdg. 26.00 o.p. (ISBN 0-913292-15-X). Tiresias Pr.

Protocols of the Meetings of the Learned Elders of Zion. Tr. by Victor E. Marsden from Rus. 1978. pap. 4.00x o.p. (ISBN 0-911038-42-6). Noontide.

Protohistoric Period in the North American Southwest, A. D. 1470-1700. Ed. by D. Wilcox & W. B. Masse. (No. 31). (Illus.). vi, 445p. 1981. 17.50 o.p. (ISBN 9-9933433-4-X). AZ Univ ARP.

Protoplasmic Streaming. N. Kamiya. (Protoplasmatologia: Vol. 8, Pt. 3a). (Illus.). 1959. pap. 57.90 o.p. (ISBN 0-387-80524-9). Springer-Verlag.

Prototype Employee Opinion Survey. 1980. pap. 3.00 o.p. (ISBN 0-918734-09-6). Reymont.

Prototype Locomotives. Robert Tufnell. (Illus.). 96p. 1985. 24.95 o.p. (ISBN 0-7153-8397-3). David & Charles.

Protozoology. 2nd, rev. ed. K. G. Grell. LC 73-77394. (Illus.). vii, 554p. 1977. 33.00 o.p. (ISBN 0-387-06239-4). Springer-Verlag.

Proud Castles. Clayton Matthews. 416p. (Orig.). 1986. pap. 3.95 o.p. (ISBN 1-55547-100-5). Critics Choice Paper.

Proud Glory. Ann F. Barron. 384p. 1987. pap. 3.95 o.p. (ISBN 0-380-89599-4). Avon.

Proud Surrender. Karen Johns. 400p. (Orig.). 1987. pap. 3.95 o.p. (ISBN 0-380-75379-0). Avon.

Proust. Samuel Beckett. (Orig.). 1956. pap. 7.95 o.p. (ISBN 0-394-17414-3, E50, Ever). Grove.

Proust: A Collection of Critical Essays. Ed. by Rene Girard. LC 77-9577. 1977. Repr. of 1962 ed. lib. bdg. 24.75x o.p. (ISBN 0-8371-9710-4, GIPR). Greenwood.

Proust Screenplay. Harold Pinter. 1977. 10.00 o.s.i. (ISBN 0-394-42202-3, GP794). Grove.

Proust's "Recherche" A Psychoanalytic Interpretation. Randolph Splitter. 176p. 1981. 21.95x o.p. (ISBN 0-7100-0664-0). Routledge Chapman & Hall.

Proust's Way. Francois Mauriac. (ISBN 0-8022-1090-2). Philos Lib.

Prout: The Alternative to Capitalism & Marxism. Ravi Batra. LC 80-67184. 221p. 1980. lib. bdg. 23.50 o.p. (ISBN 0-8191-1187-2); pap. text ed. 10.75 o.p. (ISBN 0-8191-1188-0). U Pr of Amer.

Proven Partners: Business, Labor, & Community Colleges. Dale Parnell & Roger Yarrington. (Pocket Reader Ser.: No. 1). 56p. (Orig.). 1982. pap. 5.00 o.p. (ISBN 0-87117-116-3); pap. 25.00 12 copies o.p. Am Assn Comm Jr Coll.

Provenance. Frank McDonald. 512p. 1980. pap. 2.75 o.p. (ISBN 0-380-50120-1, 50120-1). Avon.

Provence. Jean Giono. deluxe ed. 57.75 o.p. (ISBN 0-685-34173-9). French & Eur.

Provence & the Cote D'Azur: Phaidon Cultural Guides. 1986. 14.95 o.p. (ISBN 0-13-731761-1). P-H.

Proverb Lore. F. Edward Hulme. LC 67-23913. 280p. 1968. Repr. of 1902 ed. 34.00x o.p. (ISBN 0-8103-3202-7). Gale.

Proverbs: A Commentary on an Ancient Book of Timeless Advice. Robert L. Alden. 222p. 1984. 12.95 o.p. (ISBN 0-8010-0194-3). Baker Bk.

Proverbs, God's Powerhouse of Wisdom. Chuck Colclasure. 1981. pap. 2.50 o.p. (ISBN 0-8423-4928-6). Tyndale.

Proverbs of Scotland. Alexander Hislop. LC 68-21774. 368p. 1968. Repr. of 1868 ed. 43.00x o.p. (ISBN 0-8103-3201-9). Gale.

Proverbs, Proverbial Expressions, & Popular Rhymes of Scotland. Ed. by Andrew Cheviot. LC 68-23144. 448p. 1969. Repr. of 1896 ed. 40.00x o.p. (ISBN 0-8103-3198-5). Gale.

Providing Early Mobility. Ed. by Jean Robinson & Barbara McVan. LC 80-25062. (Nursing Photobook Ser.). (Illus.). 160p. 1980. text ed. 17.95 o.p. (ISBN 0-916730-27-1). Springhouse Pub.

Providing Respiratory Care. Ed. by Jean Robinson & Barbara McVan. LC 79-21639. (Nursing Photobook Ser.). (Illus.). 1979. text ed. 17.95 o.p. (ISBN 0-916730-17-4). Springhouse Pub.

Province & Court Records of Maine. Maine Historical Society Staff. (Province & Court Records of Maine Ser.). (Earliest known records of Maine). Vol. 4, 1958. 18.00 o.p. (ISBN 0-915592-01-0); Vol. 5, 1964. 18.00 o.p. (ISBN 0-915592-02-9); Vol. 6, 1975. 30.00 o.p. (ISBN 0-915592-03-7). Maine Hist.

Province of Darkness. Patricia Morton. 144p. 1973. pap. 0.75 o.p. (ISBN 0-380-01378-9, 14324). Avon.

Provinces of Early Mexico: Variants of Spanish American Regional Evolution. Ed. by Ida Altman & James Lockhart. LC 76-620055. (Latin American Studies: Vol. 36). (Illus.). 1976. text ed. 12.00 o.p. (ISBN 0-87903-036-4); pap. 11.95 o.p. (ISBN 0-87903-110-7). UCLA Lat Am Ctr.

Provincetown Painters. Dorothy G. Seckler. Ed. by Ronald A. Kuchta. (Illus.). 292p. 1977. pap. 9.95 o.p. (ISBN 0-940160-09-9). Parnassus Imprints.

Provincial Society, Sixteen Ninety to Seventeen Sixty-Three. James T. Adams. LC 84-19128. (Illus.). xvii, 374p. 1984. Repr. of 1927 ed. lib. bdg. 48.50x o.p. (ISBN 0-313-24618-1, ADPS). Greenwood.

Provincial Towns of Georgian England: A Study of the Building Process, 1740-1820. C. W. Chalklin. (Studies in Urban History: No. 3). (Illus.). 416p. 1974. 25.00x o.p. (ISBN 0-7735-0200-9, McGill Canada). U of Toronto Pr.

Provincials. Eli Evans. LC 73-80747. 1976. pap. 7.95 o.s.i. (ISBN 0-689-70532-8, 221, Atheneum). Macmillan.

Proving Operating Systems Correct. Richard A. Karp. Ed. by Harold Stone. LC 82-13378. (Computer Science: System Programming: No. 16). 172p. 1983. 42.95 o.p. (ISBN 0-8357-1365-2). UMI Res Pr.

Prudie Finds Out. Natania Jansz & Litza Jansz. 32p. 1983. pap. 5.95 o.p. (ISBN 0-86358-003-3, Pandora Pr). Routledge Chapman & Hall.

Prune. Ramon R. Ross. LC 84-3018. (Illus.). 192p. (gr. 3 up). 1984. 11.95 o.s.i. (ISBN 0-689-31056-0, Atheneum Childrens Bks). Macmillan.

Pruning of Trees, Shrubs & Conifers. George E. Brown. 1977. pap. 13.95 o.p. (ISBN 0-571-11084-3). Faber & Faber.

P's Three Women. Paulo E. Gomes & Salles Gomes. 144p. 1984. pap. 3.50 o.p. (ISBN 0-380-86256-5, 86256-5, Bard). Avon.

Psalmody & Prophecy. W. H. Bellinger. (JSOT Supplement Ser.: No. 27). 146p. pap. text ed. 11.95x o.s.i. (Pub. by JSOT Pr England). Eisenbrauns.

Psalms: A Form-Critical Introduction. Hermann Gunkel. Ed. by John Reumann. Tr. by Thomas M. Horner from Ger. LC 67-22983. (Facet Bks.). 64p. (Orig.). 1967. pap. 3.95 o.p. (ISBN 0-8006-3043-2, 1-3043, Fortress). Augsburg Fortress.

Psalms in Christian Worship: A Practical Guide. Massey H. Shepherd, Jr. LC 76-3873. 128p. (Orig.). 1976. pap. 3.95 o.p. (ISBN 0-8066-1533-8, 10-5310, Augsburg). Augsburg Fortress.

Psalms, Job. Roland E. Murphy. LC 77-78637. (Proclamation Commentaries: the Old Testament Witnesses for Preaching). (Orig.). 1977. pap. 4.95 o.p. (ISBN 0-8006-0588-8, 1-588, Fortress). Augsburg Fortress.

Psalms That Touch Us Where We Live. David Mains. (Chapel Talks Ser.). 64p. 0.95 o.p. (ISBN 0-89191-265-7, 52654). Cook.

Pseudarthroses & Their Treatment. Ed. by George Chapchal. LC 79-84230. (Illus.). 258p. 1979. text ed. 40.00 o.p. (ISBN 0-88416-286-9). Year Bk Med.

Pseudo Differential Equations. M. Taylor. (Lectures Notes in Mathematics Ser.: Vol. 416). iv, 155p. 1974. pap. text ed. 9.90 o.p. (ISBN 0-387-06961-5). Springer-Verlag.

Pseudo-Philo's Liber Antiquitatum Biblicarum. Ed. by Guido Kisch. (Mediaeval Studies Ser.: No. 10). (Lat). 1949. pap. 16.95 o.p. (ISBN 0-268-00371-8). U of Notre Dame Pr.

Pseudo-Spin Method in Magnetism & Ferroelectricity. L. Novakovic. 200p. 1975. 50.00 o.p. (ISBN 0-08-018060-4). Pergamon.

Pseudoepilepsy: The Clinical Aspects of False Seizures. Ed. by Meir Gross. LC 82-49081. 288p. 1983. 30.00x o.p. (ISBN 0-669-06418-1). Lexington Bks.

Pseudomonas Aeruginosa: Clinical Manifestations of Infection & Current Therapy. Ed. by R. G. Doggett. 1979. 86.00 o.p. (ISBN 0-12-219550-7). Acad Pr.

Pseudonyms of God. Robert M. Brown. LC 77-178813. 1972. 6.50 o.s.i. (Westminster); pap. 3.25 o.s.i. (ISBN 0-664-24948-5, Westminster). Westminster John Knox.

PSI & the Consciousness Explosion. Stuart Holroyd. 1976. 9.95 o.s.i. (ISBN 0-8008-6556-1). Taplinger.

PSI Development Systems. Jeffrey Mishlove. LC 81-23615. 304p. 1983. lib. bdg. 29.95x o.p. (ISBN 0-89950-035-8). McFarland & Co.

PSI Trek. Laile Bartlett. 300p. 1981. text ed. 12.95 o.p. (ISBN 0-07-003915-1). McGraw.

Psionic Medicine: The Study & Treatment of the Causative Factors in Illness. J. H. Reyner et al. 160p. 1982. pap. 8.95 o.p. (ISBN 0-7100-9088-9). Routledge Chapman & Hall.

Psych City. Ed. by Robert Cohen et al. LC 72-11593. 348p. 1974. 28.00 o.p. (ISBN 0-08-017082-X); pap. text ed. 17.25 o.p. (ISBN 0-08-017083-8). Pergamon.

Psych Wards. Russell C. Packard. 288p. 1985. 15.95 o.p. (ISBN 0-8397-6904-0). Eriksson.

Psyche & History. Marvin Goldwert. 85p. (Orig.). 1985. pap. 9.95x o.p. (ISBN 0-932269-41-9). Wyndham Hall.

Psyche, Culture & the New Science: The Role of PN. E. W. Tomlin. 192p. (Orig.). 1985. pap. 12.95 o.p. (ISBN 0-7102-0199-0). Routledge Chapman & Hall.

Psychedelic Prayers. Timothy Leary. 2.95 o.p. (ISBN 0-8216-0002-8, Pub. by Univ Bks). Carol Pub Group.

Psychiatric Diagnosis: A Review of Research. George Frank. LC 74-13884. 1974. 36.00 o.p. (ISBN 0-08-017712-3). Pergamon.

Psychiatric Implications of Acquired Immune Deficiency Syndrome. Stuart Nichols & David G. Ostrow. LC 84-6187. (Clinical Insights Monograph). 160p. 1984. pap. text ed. 12.00x o.p. (ISBN 0-88048-063-7, 48-063-7). Am Psychiatric.

Titles

Psychiatric-Mental Health Assessment. Bonnie K. Hagerty & Karen L. Packard. 320p. 1984. adhesive notchbound 17.95 o.p. (ISBN 0-8016-2012-0). Mosby.

Psychiatric Novels of Oliver Wendell Holmes. abr. ed. 2nd ed. Oliver W. Holmes. LC 72-156193. 1971. Repr. of 1946 ed. lib. bdg. 35.00x o.p. (ISBN 0-8371-6142-8, HOPN). Greenwood.

Psychiatric Nursing. Ed. by Annie T. Altschul. LC 84-12661. (Recent Advances in Nursing Ser.: Vol. 12). (Illus.). 220p. 1985. pap. text ed. 23.00 o.p. (ISBN 0-443-02985-7). Churchill.

Psychiatric Nursing: A Basic Text. Patricia C. Pothier. 1980. pap. text ed. 14.00 o.p. (ISBN 0-316-71484-4). Little.

Psychiatric Nursing Described. Desmond F. Cormack. LC 82-9447. (Studies in Nursing Ser.). (Illus.). 224p. 1983. pap. text ed. 16.00 o.p. (ISBN 0-443-02722-6). Churchill.

Psychiatric Nursing: PreTest Self-Assessment & Review. Nancy Rozendal & Patricia Fallon. LC 78-50596. 193p. 1978. pap. 13.95 o.p. (ISBN 0-07-051569-7). McGraw-Pretest.

Psychiatric Programming of People: Neo-Behavioral Orthomolecular Psychiatry. H. L. Newbold. 170p. 1972. 27.00 o.p. (ISBN 0-08-016791-8). Pergamon.

Psychiatric Services in the Community: Developments & Innovations. Ed. by John Reed & Gillian Lomas. 256p. 1984. 28.50 o.p. (ISBN 0-7099-2264-7, Pub. by Croom Helm Ltd). Routledge Chapman & Hall.

Psychiatric Therapies. Ed. by Toksoz B. Karasu. LC 84-3053. 932p. 1984. text ed. 49.95x o.p. (ISBN 0-89042-102-1, 42-102-1). Am Psychiatric.

Psychiatrist Says Murder. Lucy Freeman. LC 73-82190. 1973. 6.95 o.p. (ISBN 0-87795-045-8, Arbor Hse). Morrow.

Psychiatrist's Casebook (The DSM Case Book) Robert L. Spitzer & Andrew E. Skodol. 384p. 1986. pap. 12.50 o.s.i. (ISBN 0-446-38371-6). Warner Bks.

Psychiatry & Its History: Methodological Problems in Research. George Mora & Jeanne L. Brand. 304p. 1970. 34.00 o.p. (ISBN 0-398-01342-X). C C Thomas.

Psychiatry & Law. Ralph Slovenko. 1973. 38.50 o.p. (ISBN 0-316-79868-1). Little.

Psychiatry & Philosophy. E. W. Straus et al. Ed. by M. Natanson. Tr. by E. Eng & S. C. Kennedy. LC 77-79751. 1969. 24.90 o.p. (ISBN 0-387-04726-3). Springer-Verlag.

Psychiatry: Common Drug Treatments. R. Spector et al. (Practical Problems in Medicine Ser.). (Illus.). 192p. 1984. lib. bdg. 45.00 o.p. (ISBN 0-906348-64-1, Pub. by Martin Dunitz Ltd UK). VCH Pubs.

Psychiatry for Every Man. J. A. Brown. (ISBN 0-8022-0186-5). Philos Lib.

Psychiatry for Social Workers. A. Munro & W. McCullough. LC 75-80842. 1969. text ed. 18.50 o.p. (ISBN 0-08-006366-7); pap. 9.75 o.p. (ISBN 0-08-006365-9). Pergamon.

Psychiatry for Students. 6th ed. Andrew C. Smith & David Stafford-Clark. (Illus.). 368p. 1983. pap. text ed. 16.95x o.p. (ISBN 0-04-132020-4). Unwin Hyman.

Psychiatry for the Primary Care Physician. Ed. by Arthur M. Freeman, III et al. LC 78-18737. 432p. (Orig.). 1979. pap. 24.50 o.p. (ISBN 0-683-00316-X, WW). Krieger.

Psychiatry in Britain: Meaning & Policy. Shulamit Ramon. LC 85-4170. 327p. 1985. 31.00 o.p. (ISBN 0-7099-2279-5, Pub. by Croom Helm Ltd). Routledge Chapman & Hall.

Psychiatry in General Medical Practice. Ed. by Gene Usdin & Jerry M. Lewis. (Illus.). 1979. text ed. 29.00 o.p. (ISBN 0-07-066670-9). McGraw.

Psychiatry in Psychoperception. Nicholas Galagotis. 1985. 7.50 o.p. (ISBN 0-682-40215-X). Exposition-Phoenix.

Psychiatry: Pre-test Self-Assessment & Review. 3rd ed. PreTest Service, Inc. Staff & D. Greenfeld. (Clinical Science Ser.). (Illus.). 272p. 1985. text ed. 13.95 o.p. (ISBN 0-07-051002-4). McGraw.

Psychiatry: PreTest Self-Assessment & Review. 2nd ed. PreTest Service, Inc. Staff. Ed. by J. Craig Nelson. (Illus.). 225p. 1982. 12.95 o.p. (ISBN 0-07-050974-3). McGraw.

Psychic Adventure on Wall Street: Or, You Can Win the Wall Street Game! Mark Ashford. 1979. 6.00 o.p. (ISBN 0-682-49400-3). Exposition-Phoenix.

Psychic Conflict in Spanish America: Six Essays on the Psychohistory of the Region. Marvin Goldwert. LC 82-45059. 86p. (Orig.). 1982. lib. bdg. 21.75 o.p. (ISBN 0-8191-2413-3); pap. text ed. 8.25 o.p. (ISBN 0-8191-2414-1). U Pr of Amer.

Psychic Dependence: Definition, Assessment in Animals & Man, Theoretical and Clinical Implications. Bayer Symposium, 4th. Ed. by F. Hoffmeister & L. Goldberg. LC 73-13497. (Illus.). 244p. 1973. 49.00 o.p. (ISBN 0-387-06478-8). Springer-Verlag.

Psychic Powers. Time-Life Books Editors. (Mystery of the Unknown Ser.). 160p. 1987. 17.27 o.p.; lib. bdg. 21.27 o.p. (ISBN 0-8094-6309-1). Time-Life.

Psychic Reality of Dreams. Iyonne C. Barber. 1978. 6.50 o.p. (ISBN 0-682-49207-8). Exposition-Phoenix.

Psychic Warfare: Threat or Illusion? Martin Ebon. 304p. 1983. text ed. 15.95 o.p. (ISBN 0-07-018860-2). McGraw.

Psyching Out Sex. Ingrid Rimland. LC 74-26537. 1975. 6.00 o.s.i. (ISBN 0-664-20724-3, Westminster); pap. 3.25 o.s.i. (ISBN 0-664-24815-2, Westminster). Westminster John Knox.

Psychism & the Unconscious Mind. Theosophical Research Centre, London Staff. (Orig.). 1968. pap. 2.75 o.p. (ISBN 0-8356-0412-8, Quest). Theos Pub Hse.

Psycho. Ed. by Richard J. Anobile. (Film Classics Library). (Illus.). 256p. 1974. pap. 5.45 o.p. (ISBN 0-380-00085-7, 21063, Flare). Avon.

Psycho-Birds. Robert J. Lifton. LC 78-13463. (Illus.). 1978. pap. 3.95 o.p. (ISBN 0-914378-41-4). Countryman.

Psycho-Educational Battery. Lillie Pope. 1976. incl. specimen set 15.95 o.p. (ISBN 0-87594-155-9). Book-Lab.

Psycho-Social Matrix of Psychiatry. M. Shepherd. LC 83-456. 1983. 27.00 o.p. (ISBN 0-422-78350-1, NO. 3808, Pub. by Tavistock). Routledge Chapman & Hall.

Psychoanalysis. Lawrence J. Friedman. LC 68-8037. 192p. 1977. pap. 4.95 o.p. (ISBN 0-8397-6901-6). Eriksson.

Psychoanalysis & Psychotherapy. Franz Alexander. 1956. 5.50x o.p. (ISBN 0-393-01013-9, NortonC). Norton.

Psychoanalysis & Society: The Social Thought of Sigmund Freud. Arthur K. Berliner. LC 82-21932. 216p. (Orig.). 1983. lib. bdg. 26.00 o.p. (ISBN 0-8191-2893-7); pap. text ed. 12.25 o.p. (ISBN 0-8191-2894-5). U Pr of Amer.

Psychoanalysis & the Family Neurosis. Martin Grotjahn. 1960. 5.95x o.p. (ISBN 0-393-01037-6, NortonC). Norton.

Psychoanalysis of Culture. C. R. Badcock. 272p. 1980. 60.00x o.p. (ISBN 0-631-11701-6); pap. 24.95 o.p. (ISBN 0-631-13033-0). Basil Blackwell.

Psychoanalysis of Culture & History, 7 vols. Ed. by Richard A. Koenigsberg. (Foundations of Social Science). Set. (ISBN 0-915042-11-8). Lib Art Soc Sci.

Psychoanalysis of the Prostitute. Maryse Choisy. LC 60-15951. 1961. (ISBN 0-8022-0243-8). Philos Lib.

Psychoanalytic Forum, Vol. 3. annual Ed. by John A. Lindon. 1972. text ed. 25.00 o.s.i. (ISBN 0-8236-4423-5). Intl Univs Pr.

Psychoanalytic Politics: Freud's French Revolution. Sherry Turkle. 288p. 1981. pap. 9.95x o.p. (ISBN 0-262-70022-0). MIT Pr.

Psychoanalytic Studies of the Sighted & the Blind. Dorothy Burlingham. LC 76-184213. 406p. 1972. text ed. 45.00x o.s.i. (ISBN 0-8236-4510-X). Intl Univs Pr.

Psychobabble. R. D. Rosen. LC 77-76465. 1977. 8.95 o.p. (ISBN 0-689-10775-7, Atheneum). Macmillan.

Psychobabble. R. D. Rosen. 1979. pap. 2.25 o.p. (ISBN 0-380-42291-3, 42291-3). Avon.

Psychobiological Aspects of Cognitive Growth. R. Kohen-Raz. 1977. 19.95 o.p. (ISBN 0-12-418050-7). Acad Pr.

Psychobiology: Behavior from a Biological Perspective. Ed. by James L. McGaugh. 1971. 56.50 o.p. (ISBN 0-12-483750-6). Acad Pr.

Psychobiology of Cancer: Automatization & Boredom in Health & Disease. Augustin De la Pena. 256p. 1983. 34.95x o.s.i. (ISBN 0-03-062872-5). Bergin & Garvey.

Psychobiology of Human Food Selection. Lewis M. Barker. (Illus.). 1982. 35.95 o.s.i. (ISBN 0-87055-409-3). AVI.

Psychobiology of Schizophrenia, In Memory of C. & O. Vogt & M. Hayashi: Proceedings of a Satellite Symposium to the 8th International Congress of Pharmacology, Gifu, Japan, June 27-29, 1981. Ed. by M. Namba & H. Kaiya. (Advances in the Biosciences Ser.: Vol. 39). 342p. 1982. 80.00 o.p. (ISBN 0-08-028007-2). Pergamon.

Psychobiology of Sex Differences & Sex Roles. Tom Farley. Ed. by Jacqueline Parsons. 320p. 1980. text ed. 38.50 o.p. (ISBN 0-07-048540-2). McGraw.

Psychobiology of Stress: A Study of Coping Men. Ed. by Holger Ursin et al. (Behavioral Biology Ser.). 1978. 24.95 o.p. (ISBN 0-12-709250-1). Acad Pr.

Psychochemical Research in Man: Methods, Strategy & Theory. Ed. by A. J. Mandell & M. P. Mandell. 1969. 84.00 o.p. (ISBN 0-12-468050-X). Acad Pr.

Psychodiagnosis: Selected Papers. Paul E. Meehl. 1977. pap. 8.95 o.p. (ISBN 0-393-00855-X, N855, Norton Lib). Norton.

Psychodietetics. Emanuel Cheraskin. 1976. pap. 3.95 o.p. (ISBN 0-553-25607-6). Bantam.

Psychodynamic Approach to Adolescent Psychiatry. D. Heacock. (Experimental & Clinical Psychiatry Ser.: Vol. 2). 384p. 1980. 49.75 o.p. (ISBN 0-8247-6873-6). Dekker.

Psychodynamic Approach to Drug Therapy. Ed. by Mortimer Ostow. 352p. 1980. 17.95 o.p. (ISBN 0-442-20410-8). Van Nos Reinhold.

Psychodynamic Perspectives on Religion, Sect & Cult. D. A. Halperin. 416p. 1983. pap. text ed. 49.00 o.p. (ISBN 0-7236-7029-3). Butterworth.

Psychodynamics of Race: Vicious & Benign Spirals. Rae Sherwood. 608p. 1980. text ed. 55.00x o.p. (ISBN 0-391-01804-3). Humanities.

Psychoeducational Development of Gifted & Talented Learners. Don Sellin & Jack Birch. LC 81-3467. 335p. 1981. text ed. 35.00 o.p. (ISBN 0-89443-362-8). Aspen Pub.

Psychoeducational Diagnosis of Exceptional Children. Milton V. Wisland. (Illus.). 408p. 1977. 48.25 o.p. (ISBN 0-398-02843-5). C C Thomas.

Psychogeriatrics: An Introduction to the Psychiatry of Old Age. 2nd ed. Brice Pitt. (Illus.). 224p. 1982. pap. 11.50 o.p. (ISBN 0-443-01598-8). Churchill.

Psychohistorical Inquiry: A Comprehensive Bibliography. William J. Gilmore. LC 82-49165. (Reference Library of Social Science). 400p. 1983. lib. bdg. 53.00 o.p. (ISBN 0-8240-9167-1). Garland Pub.

Psychohistory & Religion: The Case of Young Man Luther. Ed. by Roger A. Johnson. LC 76-7870. 240p. 1977. 10.95 o.p. (ISBN 0-8006-0459-8, Fortress). Augsburg Fortress.

Psycholinguistics. Alan Garnham. 300p. 1986. text ed. 35.00 o.p. (ISBN 0-416-36610-4, 9622); pap. text ed. 16.95 o.p. (ISBN 0-416-36620-1, 9623). Routledge Chapman & Hall.

Psycholinguistics: Experiments in Spontaneous Speech. F. Goldman-Eisler. 1968. 38.00 o.p. (ISBN 0-12-289250-X). Acad Pr.

Psychologica: Being Notes & Observations on Christian Wolf's Psychologica Empirica. Emanuel Swedenborg. Tr. & pref. by Alfred Acton. 169p. (Lat.). 1923. 7.00 o.p. (ISBN 0-915221-02-0). Swedenborg Sci Assn.

Psychological Analysis of Economic Behavior. George Katona. LC 77-10945. (Illus.). 1977. Repr. of 1951 ed. lib. bdg. 26.75x o.p. (ISBN 0-8371-9814-3, KAPS). Greenwood.

Psychological & Medical Aspects of the Use of Nuclear Energy, Vol. 4. Group for the Advancement of Psychiatry Staff. (Symposium No. 6). 1960. pap. 2.00 o.p. (ISBN 0-87318-059-3, Pub. by GAP). Brunner-Mazel.

Psychological Aspects of Community: Alienation, Identity & Social Breakdown. H. Winthrop. 1971. pap. text ed. 4.50x o.p. (ISBN 0-8290-1174-9). Irvington.

Psychological Aspects of Obesity: A Handbook. Benjamin B. Wolman. 336p. 1981. 28.95 o.p. (ISBN 0-442-22609-8). Van Nos Reinhold.

Psychological Aspects of Physical Illness & Disability. Franklin C. Shontz. (Illus.). 256p. 1975. pap. text ed. write for info. o.p. (ISBN 0-02-410150-8). Macmillan.

Psychological Aspects of the Aging Process: With Sociological Implications. 2nd ed. Harold Geist. LC 80-13233. 208p. 1981. text ed. 13.50 o.p. (ISBN 0-89874-073-8). Krieger.

Psychological Atlas. Katz. Philos Lib.

Psychological Basis of Education. E. A. Peel. 328p. 1968. (ISBN 0-8022-1297-2). Philos Lib.

Psychological Complex: Social Relation & the Psychology of the Individual. Nikolas Rose. 288p. (Orig.). 1985. pap. 18.95x o.p. (ISBN 0-7100-9808-1). Routledge Chapman & Hall.

Psychological Conflict & Defense. George F. Mahl. 1971. pap. text ed. 8.95 o.p. (ISBN 0-15-572411-8). HarBraceJ.

Psychological Deprivation in Childhood. 3rd ed. J. Langmeier & Z. Matejcek. LC 75-16185. 496p. 1975. 29.50 o.p. (ISBN 0-470-51718-2, Pub. by Wiley). Krieger.

Psychological Dimensions of U. S.-Japanese Relations. Hiroshi Kitamura. (Occasional Papers in International Affairs: No. 28). (Illus.). 58p. 1984. pap. text ed. 5.50 o.p. (ISBN 0-8191-4044-9). U Pr of Amer.

Psychological Disorder & Crime. Lindesay Neustatter. 250p. 1957. (ISBN 0-8022-1200-X). Philos Lib.

Psychological Examination & Report Writing. James Mack. 1978. 7.50 o.p. (ISBN 0-682-48964-6). Exposition-Phoenix.

Psychological Experiment: A Practical Accomplishment. Harold B. Pepinsky & Michael J. Patton. LC 75-134829. 208p. 1972. 50.00 o.p. (ISBN 0-08-016515-X). Pergamon.

Psychological Experiments with Autistic Children. B. Hermelin & N. O'Connor. 1970. 40.00 o.p. (ISBN 0-08-016088-3). Pergamon.

Psychological Factors of Peace & War. Ed. by T. H. Pear. 1951. (ISBN 0-8022-1292-1). Philos Lib.

Psychological Fitness: Twenty-One Days to Feeling Good. Richard Corriere & Joseph Hart. LC 78-14073. (Illus.). 1979. 9.95 o.p. (ISBN 0-15-175280-X). HarBraceJ.

Psychological Foundations of Attitudes. Anthony G. Greenwald et al. (Social Psychology Ser.). 1968. text ed. 16.00 o.p. (ISBN 0-12-300750-X). Acad Pr.

Psychological Problems: The Social Context. Ed. by Philip Feldman & Jim Orford. 405p. 1980. 86.00x o.p. (ISBN 0-471-27741-X, Pub. by Wiley-Interscience). Wiley.

Psychological Research in the Classroom: Issues for Educators & Researchers. Ed. by Teresa M Amabile & Margaret L. Stubbs. LC 81-21114. (General Psychology Ser.: No. 108). (Illus.). 280p. 1982. 70.00 o.p. (ISBN 0-08-028042-0, J120); pap. 70.00 o.p. (ISBN 0-08-028041-2). Pergamon.

Psychological Research: Selected Readings for Introductory Psychology. L. Plant. 1969. pap. text ed. 14.95x o.p. (ISBN 0-8422-0022-3). Irvington.

Psychological Stress. Irving Janis. 1974. 23.00 o.p. (ISBN 0-12-380750-6). Acad Pr.

Psychological Testing Workbook. Peter R. Prunkl. 1979. pap. text ed. 6.40 o.p. (ISBN 0-918296-13-7). Inst Personality & Ability.

Psychological Theory of Work Adjustment: An Individual-Differences Model & Its Applications. Rene V. Dawis & Lloyd Lofquist. LC 83-23381. (Illus.). 192p. 1984. 25.00 o.p. (ISBN 0-8166-1316-8). U of Minn Pr.

Psychological Thought from Pythagoras to Freud: An Informal Introduction. Gardner Murphy. LC 68-25371. (Orig.). 1968. pap. 3.65 o.p. (ISBN 0-15-674701-4, Harv). HarBraceJ.

Psychological Twin Research. Torsten Husen. (Illus.). 153p. 1959. pap. text ed. 18.50x o.p. (Pub. by Almqvist & Wiksell). Coronet Bks.

Psychologists on Psychology. David Cohen. 1976. pap. 6.50 o.p. Taplinger.

Psychology. 2nd ed. Andrew B. Crider et al. 1986. text ed. write for info. o.p. (ISBN 0-673-18217-7); instr's. manual avail. o.p. Scott F.

Psychology. 2nd ed. John P. Dworetzky. (Illus.). 708p. 1985. text ed. 38.50 o.p. (ISBN 0-314-85231-X). West Pub.

Psychology. 2nd ed. Spencer A. Rathus. LC 83-10647. 645p. 1984. text ed. 31.95 o.p. (ISBN 0-03-063177-7). HR&W.

Psychology: A Biographical Approach. Malinda Levin. (Illus.). 1978. text ed. 32.95 o.p. (ISBN 0-07-037387-6). McGraw.

Psychology: A Concise Introduction. Terry F. Pettijohn. LC 86-72445. (Illus.). 416p. 1987. pap. text ed. 19.95 o.p. (ISBN 0-87967-421-0). Dushkin Pub.

Psychology: Adapted Readings. Jerome Kagan et al. 1971. pap. text ed. 11.95 o.p. (ISBN 0-15-572560-2, HC). HarBraceJ.

Psychology: Advanced Test for the G. R. E. James W. Morrison. LC 79-11444. 144p. 1980. pap. 6.95 o.p. (ISBN 0-668-04762-3, 4762-3). Arco.

Psychology: An Introduction. Josh R. Gerow. 1986. text ed. write for info. o.p. (ISBN 0-673-18622-9). Scott F.

Psychology: An Introduction. 3rd ed. Jerome Kagan & Ernest Havemann. 1976. text ed. 18.95 o.p. (ISBN 0-15-572617-X, HC). HarBraceJ.

Psychology: An Introduction. 4th ed. Jerome Kagan & Ernest Havemann. 647p. 1980. text ed. 23.95 o.p. (ISBN 0-15-572625-0, HC). HarBraceJ.

Psychology: An Introduction. 5th ed. Jerome Kagan et al. 667p. 1984. 25.00 o.p. (ISBN 0-15-572633-1, HC). HarBraceJ.

Psychology: An Introduction. 2nd ed. Jerome Kagan et al. 1972. 13.95 o.p. (ISBN 0-15-572609-9). HarbraceJ.

Psychology, Ancient & Modern. George Brett. LC 63-10293. (Our Debt to Greece & Rome Ser). Repr. of 1930 ed. 18.50x o.p. (ISBN 0-8154-0031-4). Cooper Sq.

Psychology & Children: Current Research & Practice. Ed. by Sandra Scarr. (Special Issues American Psychologist, Oct., 1979). 16.00 o.p. (ISBN 0-912704-59-4, 4013410). Am Psychol.

Psychology & Deterrence. Robert Jervis et al. LC 85-8060. (Perspectives in Security Ser.). 288p. 1985. text ed. 28.50x o.p. (ISBN 0-8018-3277-2). Johns Hopkins.

Psychology & Education: An Introduction. Jerome Kagan & Cynthia Lang. (Illus.). 626p. 1978. pap. text ed. 16.00 o.p. (ISBN 0-15-572770-2, HC). HarBraceJ.

Psychology & FolkLore. Robert R. Marett. LC 74-10825. 286p. Repr. of 1920 ed. 34.00x o.p. (ISBN 0-8103-4045-3). Gale.

Psychology & Human Living. Walter C. Langer. 1943. 34.50x o.p. (ISBN 0-89197-517-9). Irvington.
Psychology & Industry Today. 3rd ed. Duane P. Schultz. 1982. text ed. write for info. o.p. (ISBN 0-02-408020-9). Macmillan.
Psychology & Its Bearing on Education. C. W. Valentine. 1951. (ISBN 0-8022-1757-5). Philos Lib.
Psychology & Life. 11th ed. Philip G. Zimbardo. 1985. text ed. write for info. o.p. (ISBN 0-673-15418-1). Scott F.
Psychology & Life. 10th ed. Philip G. Zimbardo & Floyd L. Ruch. 1979. text ed. 26.95x o.p. (ISBN 0-673-15183-2). Scott F.
Psychology & Physiology of Stress. Ed. by P. G. Bourne. 1969. 29.95 o.p. (ISBN 0-12-119550-3). Acad Pr.
Psychology & Psychotherapy: Current Trends & Issues. David Pilgrim. 224p. (Orig.). 1984. pap. 13.95x o.p. (ISBN 0-7100-9551-1). Routledge Chapman & Hall.
Psychology & Psychotherapy of Otto Rank. 1953. (ISBN 0-8022-0826-6). Philos Lib.
Psychology & Social Structure. Barrie Stacey. (Essential Psychology Ser.). 1976. pap. 4.50x o.p. (ISBN 0-416-84360-3, NO. 2522). Routledge Chapman & Hall.
Psychology & the Environment. Terence Lee. (Essential Psychology Ser.). 1976. pap. 4.50x o.p. (ISBN 0-416-81920-6, NO. 2290). Routledge Chapman & Hall.
Psychology & the Human Dilemma. Rollo May. 1978. 14.95 o.p. (ISBN 0-393-01195-X). Norton.
Psychology & the Stock Market. new ed. David N. Dreman. LC 76-49986. 1977. 14.95 o.p. (ISBN 0-8144-5429-1). AMACOM.
Psychology & Work. D. R. Davies & V. J. Schackleton. (Essential Psychology Ser.). 1975. pap. 4.50x o.p. (ISBN 0-416-82290-8, NO. 2728). Routledge Chapman & Hall.
Psychology & You. David Dempsey & Philip G. Zimbardo. 1978. text ed. write for info. o.p. (ISBN 0-673-15086-0). Scott F.
Psychology Applied to Teaching. 3rd ed. Robert F. Biehler. LC 77-77665. (Illus.). 1978. pap. 19.95 o.p. (ISBN 0-395-25489-2). HM.
Psychology Applied to Teaching. 4th ed. Robert F. Biehler & Jack Snowran. LC 81-82572. 1982. pap. 26.95 o.p. (ISBN 0-395-31681-2). HM.
Psychology Applied to Teaching: Selected Readings. Ed. by Robert F. Biehler. LC 77-18726. (Illus., Orig.). 1972. pap. 18.95 o.p. (ISBN 0-395-13341-6). HM.
Psychology As Science & Art. James Deese. 120p. 1972. pap. text ed. 9.95 o.p. (ISBN 0-15-572967-5, HC). HarBraceJ.
Psychology East & West. Ed. by Swami Ajaya. 104p. (Orig.). pap. 3.95 o.p. (ISBN 0-89389-019-7). Himalayan Pubs.
Psychology for Management. Thomas V. Bonoma & Gerald Zaltman. 337p. 1981. text ed. 16.95x o.p. (ISBN 0-534-00904-2). PWS-Kent Pub.
Psychology for Our Times. 2nd ed. Philip Zimbardo & Christina Maslach. 1977. pap. 12.35x o.p. (ISBN 0-673-15052-6). Scott F.
Psychology for Preaching. Edgar N. Jackson. LC 81-47430. (Harper's Ministers Paperback Library). 208p. 1981. pap. 5.72i o.p. (ISBN 0-06-064111-8, RD366). HarpR.
Psychology for Psychiatrists. C. G. Costello. 1966. 85.00 o.p. (ISBN 0-08-011729-5); pap. 85.00 o.p. (ISBN 0-08-011728-7). Pergamon.
Psychology for the Paramedical Professions. K. T. Strongman. 290p. 1979. 32.00x o.p. (ISBN 0-85664-652-0, Pub. by Croom Helm Ltd); pap. 13.50 o.p. (ISBN 0-85664-852-3, Pub. by Croom Helm Ltd). Routledge Chapman & Hall.
Psychology: General - Industrial - Social. J. M. Fraser. 320p. 1956. (ISBN 0-8022-0532-1). Philos Lib.
Psychology in Australia. Mary Nixon & Ronald Taft. 1977. 85.00 o.p. (ISBN 0-08-021043-0); pap. 85.00 o.p. (ISBN 0-08-020561-5). Pergamon.
Psychology in Contemporary China. L. B. Brown. 320p. 1981. 55.00 o.p. (ISBN 0-08-026063-2). Pergamon.
Psychology in Foreign Language Teaching. Steven H. McDonough. (Illus.). 176p. 1981. text ed. 24.95x o.p. (ISBN 0-04-418002-0); pap. text ed. 13.95x o.p. (ISBN 0-04-418003-9). Unwin Hyman.
Psychology in Industrial Organizations. 4th ed. Norman R. Maier. LC 74-4797. 750p. 1973. text ed. 20.95 o.p. (ISBN 0-395-14046-3). HM.
Psychology in Social Context. Ed. by Allan R. Buss. 421p. 1979. text ed. 49.50x o.s.i. (ISBN 0-8290-0855-1). Irvington.
Psychology in the Classroom. Ed. by Robert K. Hartman & Nancy Hartman. 142p. 1971. pap. text ed. 5.95x o.p. (ISBN 0-8422-0175-0). Irvington.
Psychology in the Service of School. M. F. Cleugh. 1952. (ISBN 0-8022-0263-2). Philos Lib.
Psychology Is about People. H. J. Eysenck. LC 73-39003. 385p. 1972. 23.95 o.p. (ISBN 0-912050-19-5, Library Pr). Open Court.
Psychology-Judaism Reader. Reuven P. Bulka & Moshe H. Spero. (Illus.). 338p. 1982. pap. 37.25x o.p. (ISBN 0-398-04582-8). C C Thomas.
Psychology, Mon Amour: A Countertext. Klaus F. Riegel. LC 77-89422. (Illus.). 1978. pap. 11.50 o.p. (ISBN 0-395-25748-4). HM.
Psychology of Adjustment: Current Concepts & Applications. 3rd ed. Walter Katkosky & Leon Gorlow. LC 75-17619. (Illus.). 1975. text ed. 29.95 o.p. (ISBN 0-07-033345-9). McGraw.
Psychology of Adolescence. 4th ed. John E. Horrocks. LC 75-26086. (Illus.). 608p. 1976. text ed. 24.95 o.p. (ISBN 0-395-21918-3). HM.
Psychology of Adolescence. 3rd ed. Arthur T. Jersild. (Illus.). 1978. text ed. write for info. o.p. (ISBN 0-02-360610-X, 36061). Macmillan.
Psychology of Anomalous Experience. Graham Reed. 176p. 1974. pap. 2.95 o.p. (ISBN 0-395-19844-5, 81, SenEd). HM.
Psychology of Architectural Design. Akin Omer. (Architecture & Design Ser.). 205p. 1986. 29.95 o.p. (ISBN 0-85086-120-9, 9982, Pub. by Pion England). Routledge Chapman & Hall.
Psychology of Childhood. B. Siegel. 1970. pap. text ed. 12.95x o.p. (ISBN 0-8422-0075-4). Irvington.
Psychology of Computer Programming. Gerald M. Weinberg. (Computer Science Ser.). (Illus.). 304p. 1971. 26.95 o.s.i. (ISBN 0-442-29264-3). Van Nos Reinhold.
Psychology of Death: Dying & Bereavement. Richard Schulz. LC 77-83030. (Illus.). 199p. 1978. text ed. 12.00 o.p. (ISBN 0-394-34813-3, RanC). Random.
Psychology of Deductive Reasoning. Jonathan S. Evans. (International Library of Psychology). 190p. 1982. 29.95x o.p. (ISBN 0-7100-0923-2). Routledge Chapman & Hall.
Psychology of Development & History. Klaus F. Riegel. LC 76-26547. (Illus.). 272p. 1976. 45.00x o.p. (ISBN 0-306-30930-0, Plenum Pr). Plenum Pub.
Psychology of Fate & of Free Will. Socrates & Plato. (Illus.). 121p. 1983. 75.85 o.p. (ISBN 0-89920-067-2). Am Inst Psych.
Psychology of Fear & Stress. Jeffrey Gray. LC 70-104742. (Illus., Orig.). 1971. pap. text ed. 3.95 o.p. (ISBN 0-07-024225-9). McGraw.
Psychology of Fear: The Nightmare Formula of Edgar Allan Poe. David R. Saliba. LC 80-8267. 277p. 1980. lib. bdg. 28.25 o.p. (ISBN 0-8191-1269-0); pap. text ed. 14.00 o.p. (ISBN 0-8191-1270-4). U Pr of Amer.
Psychology of Imagination. Jean-Paul Sartre. 1948. (ISBN 0-8022-1490-8). Philos Lib.
Psychology of Individual & Group Differences. Lee Willerman. LC 78-9865. (Psychology Ser.). (Illus.). 531p. 1978. text ed. 29.95x o.p. (ISBN 0-7167-0292-4). W H Freeman.
Psychology of Industrial Behavior. 3rd ed. Henry C. Smith & John H. Wakeley. 400p. 1972. text ed. 40.95 o.p. (ISBN 0-07-058900-3). McGraw.
Psychology of Laughter. Ralph Piddington. 6.00 o.s.i. (ISBN 0-8008-6558-8); pap. 1.95 o.s.i. (ISBN 0-685-45969-1). Taplinger.
Psychology of Learning. Thomas R. McConnell. (National Society for the Study of Education Yearbooks Ser.: No 41, Pt. 2). 1942. lib. bdg. 7.00x o.s.i. (ISBN 0-226-59976-0). U of Chicago Pr.
Psychology of Learning: An Introduction for Students of Education. Gordon R. Cross. 1974. 37.00 o.p. (ISBN 0-08-018136-8); pap. 23.00 o.p. (ISBN 0-08-018135-X). Pergamon.
Psychology of Learning & Behavior. 2nd ed. Barry Schwartz. 440p. 1984. text ed. 33.95x o.p. (ISBN 0-393-95276-2). Norton.
Psychology of Learning & Technique of Teaching. James M. Thyne. 240p. 1964. (ISBN 0-8022-1723-0). Philos Lib.
Psychology of Learning Disabilities: Applications & Educational Practice. James A. DeRuiter & William L. Wansart. LC 82-4108. 252p. 1982. 33.00 o.p. (ISBN 0-89443-687-2). Aspen Pub.
Psychology of Leisure Travel: Effective Marketing & Selling of Travel Services. Edward J. Mayo & Lance P. Jarvis. 448p. 1983. 25.95 o.p. (ISBN 0-8436-2204-0). Van Nos Reinhold.
Psychology of Life & the Psychology of Death. Paul R. Latimer. (Illus.). 1979. 87.75 o.p. (ISBN 0-89920-000-1). Am Inst Psych.
Psychology of Literature. Ralph J. Hallman. LC 60-13646. 272p. 1961. (ISBN 0-8022-0663-8). Philos Lib.
Psychology of Love. Samuel Kahn. LC 68-22347. 1968. (ISBN 0-8022-0821-5). Philos Lib.
Psychology of Management of Labor Collectives. A. Stolyarenko. 206p. 1983. 6.95 o.p. (ISBN 0-8285-2652-4, Pub. by Progress Pubs USSR). Imported Pubns.
Psychology of Mathematical Abilities in School Children. Kruteskii. U of Chicago Pr.
Psychology of Murder & of Murderers, 2 Vols. Stephen N. Whittington. (Illus.). 1980. deluxe ed. 187.45 o.p. (ISBN 0-89920-004-4). Am Inst Psych.
Psychology of Music. Carl E. Seashore. (Illus.). 14.25 o.p. (ISBN 0-8446-2898-0). Peter Smith.
Psychology of Musical Ability. 2nd ed. Rosamund Shuter-Dyson & Clive Gabriel. 1982. 25.00x o.p. (ISBN 0-416-71300-9, NO. 3498). Routledge Chapman & Hall.
Psychology of Nonviolence. Leroy H. Pelton. LC 74-2156. 310p. 1974. 80.00 o.p. (ISBN 0-08-018099-X). Pergamon.
Psychology of Nothingness. William F. Kraft. LC 73-21809. 160p. 1974. 5.95 o.s.i. (ISBN 0-664-20997-1, Westminster, Westminster). Westminster John Knox.
Psychology of Perception: A Philosophical Examination of Gestalt Theory & Derivative Theories of Perception. D. W. Hamlyn. (Studies in Philosophical Psychology). 1961. pap. text ed. 7.95x o.p. (ISBN 0-391-01104-9). Humanities.
Psychology of Person Identification. Brian Clifford & Ray Bull. 1978. 29.95x o.p. (ISBN 0-7100-8867-1). Routledge Chapman & Hall.
Psychology of Personal Constructs. George A. Kelly. 1974. Repr. of 1955 ed. Vol. 1. text ed. 25.00x o.p. (ISBN 0-393-09484-7); Vol. 2. text ed. 25.00x o.p. (ISBN 0-393-09485-5). Norton.
Psychology of Personality. 3rd ed. William S. Sahakian. 1977. pap. 25.95 o.p. (ISBN 0-395-30833-X). HM.
Psychology of Play. Susanna Millar. LC 74-4394. 288p. 1974. 20.00x o.p. (ISBN 0-87668-140-2). Aronson.
Psychology of Private Events. Alfred Jacobs & Lewis B. Sachs. 1971. 46.50 o.p. (ISBN 0-12-379650-4). Acad Pr.
Psychology of Reading. John Downing & Che Kan Leong. 1982. text ed. write for info. o.p. (ISBN 0-02-330020-5). Macmillan.
Psychology of Reading. Alan Kennedy. 180p. 1984. pap. 9.95 o.p. (ISBN 0-416-35940-X, NO. 3931); 22.00 o.p. (ISBN 0-416-38220-7, 3930). Routledge Chapman & Hall.
Psychology of Schizophrenia. John Cutting. LC 84-15578. (Illus.). 457p. 1985. text ed. 72.00 o.p. (ISBN 0-443-02663-7). Churchill.
Psychology of School Learning, 2 vols. Ed. by William M. Bart & Martin R. Wong. Incl. Vol. 1. Environmentalism. 249p. pap. text ed. 9.95x (ISBN 0-8422-0447-4); Vol. 2. Nativism & Interactionism. 29.50x (ISBN 0-8422-5210-X); pap. text ed. 9.95x (ISBN 0-8422-0466-0). 1974. pap. Irvington.
Psychology of Scientific Thinking. Ernst Friedlander. LC 65-11636. 1965. 5.95 o.p. (ISBN 0-8022-0548-8). Philos Lib.
Psychology of Seeing. Herman F. Brandt. (ISBN 0-8022-0168-7). Philos Lib.
Psychology of Seeing. 3rd ed. Richard L. Gregory. (Illus.). 1978. pap. text ed. 4.95 o.p. (ISBN 0-07-024665-3, SP). McGraw.
Psychology of Sex. Havelock Ellis. 15.95 o.s.i. (ISBN 0-87523-013-X). Emerson.
Psychology of Sex. 2nd ed. Havelock Ellis. LC 78-7414. 377p. 1978. pap. 4.95 o.p. (ISBN 0-15-674702-2, Harv). HarBraceJ.
Psychology of Speech & Language: An Introduction to Psycholinguistics. Joseph DeVito. LC 81-40762. (Illus.). 320p. 1981. pap. text ed. 13.50 o.p. (ISBN 0-8191-1820-6). U Pr of Amer.
Psychology of Successful Living: An Advanced Guide to All Achievement Based on the Laws & Psychology of Right Human Relationship with Oneself, Mankind, & God. Gene H. Lawrence. 1985. pap. 4.95 o.p. (ISBN 0-682-40252-4). Exposition-Phoenix.
Psychology of Superstition. Gustav Jahoda. LC 74-9667. 158p. 1974. Repr. 20.00x o.p. (ISBN 0-87668-185-2). Aronson.
Psychology of the Actor. Yoti Lane. LC 72-6685. 224p. 1973. Repr. of 1960 ed. lib. bdg. 24.75x o.p. (ISBN 0-8371-6496-6, LAPA). Greenwood.
Psychology of Women. 2nd ed. Juanita H. Williams. (Illus.). 1982. pap. text ed. 16.95x o. p. o.p. (ISBN 0-393-95198-7). Norton.
Psychology of Women: Behavior in a Biosocial Context. Juanita H. Williams. LC 76-56740. (Illus.). 1977. 19.95x o.p. (ISBN 0-393-01134-8); pap. 10.95x o.p. (ISBN 0-393-09142-2). Norton.
Psychology of Women: Selected Readings. Ed. by Juanita H. Williams. 1979. pap. text ed. 13.95x o.p. (ISBN 0-393-09068-X). Norton.
Psychology of Written Communication. Ed. by James Hartley. 301p. 1980. 35.00x o.p. (ISBN 0-89397-081-6). Nichols Pub.
Psychology, the Nurse, & the Patient. Doris M. Odlum. 168p. 1954. (ISBN 0-8022-1239-5). Philos Lib.
Psychology: The Personal Science. John C. Ruch. 674p. 1984. text ed. (ISBN 0-534-02672-9). Wadsworth Pub.
Psychology: The Science of Mind & Behavior. John W. Santrock. 712p. 1986. text ed. write for info. o.p. (ISBN 0-697-00310-8); pap. text ed. write for info. o.p. (ISBN 0-697-00576-3); write for info. student study guide o.p. (ISBN 0-697-00577-1); write for info. instr's. manual o.p. (ISBN 0-697-00578-X); write for info. transparencies o.p. (ISBN 0-697-01029-5); write for info. test item file o.p. (ISBN 0-697-00579-8). Wm C Brown.
Psychology: The Study of Human Experience. Robert E. Ornstein. 784p. 1985. text ed. 25.00x o.p. (ISBN 0-15-572670-6, HC). HarBraceJ.
Psychology: Vol. 6, Investigations of Man As Socius, Their Place in Psychology, in the Social Sciences. Ed. by S. Koch. 1963. text ed. 62.95 o.p. (ISBN 0-07-035277-1). McGraw.
Psychology 1988-89. 18th, rev. ed. Ed. by Hiram Fitzgerald & Michael G. Walraven. LC 79-180263. (Annual Editions Ser.). (Illus.). 288p. 1988. pap. text ed. 9.95x o.p. (ISBN 0-87967-715-5). Dushkin Pub.
Psychometrics of Similarity. Robert Gregson. 1975. 44.00 o.p. (ISBN 0-12-301550-2). Acad Pr.
Psychoneurosis, Organic Brain Disease, Psychopharmacology see Teaching Program in Psychiatry.
Psychopathic Disorders. Ed. by M. Craft. 1966. 60.00 o.p. (ISBN 0-08-011618-3); pap. 60.00 o.p. (ISBN 0-08-011617-5). Pergamon.
Psychopathic Personalities. Harold Palmer. 1957. (ISBN 0-8022-1257-3). Philos Lib.
Psychopathology & Pictorial Expression, Vol. III. Ed. by Sandoz, Ltd. Staff. (Series 13-18). 1973. 96.00 o.p. (ISBN 3-8055-1627-4). S Karger.
Psychopathology & Society. Peter E. Nathan & Sandra L. Harris. (Illus.). 576p. 1975. text ed. 33.95 o.p. (ISBN 0-07-046046-9). McGraw.
Psychopathology & Society. 2nd ed. Peter E. Nathan & Sandra L. Harris. LC 79-15683. (Illus.). 1980. text ed. 42.95 o.p. (ISBN 0-07-046053-1). McGraw.
Psychopathology in Animals: Research & Clinical Duplications. Ed. by J. D. Keehn. LC 79-51679. 1979. 46.00 o.p. (ISBN 0-12-403050-5). Acad Pr.
Psychopathology in Childhood: Social, Diagnostic, & Therapeutic Aspects. Mary Engel. 183p. 1972. pap. text ed. 10.00 net o.p. (ISBN 0-15-573028-2, HC). HarBraceJ.
Psychopharmacologic Drugs: A Pocket Reference. R. G. Sample et al. LC 78-56085. (Illus.). 140p. 1978. pap. text ed. 7.95 o.p. (ISBN 0-89313-010-9). G F Stickley Co.
Psychopharmacological Agents, 3 vols. Ed. by Maxwell Gordon. Incl. Vol. 1. 1964. 90.00 (ISBN 0-12-290550-4); Vol. 2. 1967. 80.00 (ISBN 0-12-290556-3); Vol. 3. 1974. 80.00 (ISBN 0-12-290558-X). (Medicinal Chemistry Ser.). Acad Pr.
Psychopharmacological Treatment: Theory & Practice. Ed. by Herman C. Denber. (Modern Pharmacology-Toxicology Ser: Vol. 2). 320p. 1975. 65.00 o.p. (ISBN 0-8247-6229-0). Dekker.
Psychopharmacology: A Behavioral & Biochemical Approach. Lewis S. Seiden & Linda A. Dykstra. 1977. 32.95 o.p. (ISBN 0-442-27481-5). Van Nos Reinhold.
Psychopharmacology: A Biochemical & Behavioral Approach. Lewis S. Seiden & Linda A. Dykstra. 462p. 1980. pap. 24.95 o.p. (ISBN 0-442-21938-5). Van Nos Reinhold.
Psychopharmacology: An Introduction. Rene Spiegel & Hans-J. Aebi. Tr. by Kathleen Kerr from Ger. LC 83-10185. 250p. 1983. text ed. 51.95x o.p. (ISBN 0-471-90173-3, Pub. by Res Stud Pr). Wiley.
Psychopharmacology Case Studies. David S. Janowsky et al. 1978. pap. 22.00 o.p. (ISBN 0-87488-052-1). Med Exam.
Psychopharmacology of Aversively Motivated Behavior. Ed. by H. Anisman & G. Bignami. LC 77-17998. (Illus.). 576p. 1978. 79.50x o.p. (ISBN 0-306-31055-4, Plenum Pr). Plenum Pub.
Psychopharmacology of Hallucinogens. Ed. by R. C. Stillman & R. E. Willette. LC 78-14019. 1979. 66.00 o.p. (ISBN 0-08-021938-1). Pergamon.
Psychophysical Analysis of Visual Space. J. C. Baird. 1970. 80.00 o.p. (ISBN 0-08-013876-4). Pergamon.
Psychophysiological Mechanisms of Hypnosis: Proceedings. International Brain Research Organization. Ed. by L. Chertok. (Illus.). 1969. 29.00 o.p. (ISBN 0-387-04678-X). Springer-Verlag.
Psychophysiological Perspectives: Festchrift for Beatrice & John Lacey. Michael Coles et al. 320p. 1984. 35.95 o.p. (ISBN 0-442-21746-3). Van Nos Reinhold.
Psychophysiology. Ed. by S. W. Porges & G. H. Coles. LC 76-17287. (Benchman Papers in Animal Behavior: Vol. 6). 1976. 65.50 o.p. (ISBN 0-12-787246-9). Acad Pr.

Psychorheumatologie. A. Weintraub. (Illus.). viii, 92p. 1983. 12.75 o.p. (ISBN 3-8055-3628-3). S Karger.

Psychosocial Care of the Dying Patient. Charles A. Garfield. (Illus.). 1978. text ed. 28.00 o.p. (ISBN 0-07-022860-4). McGraw.

Psychosocial Development of Children. 2nd ed. Irene M. Josselyn. LC 78-3112. 1977. pap. 10.95 o.p. (ISBN 0-87304-154-2). Family Serv.

Psychosocial Family Interventions In Chronic Pediatric Illness. Ed. by Adolph E. Christ & Kalman Flomenhaft. LC 82-5309. (Downstate Series of Research In Psychiatry & Psychology: Vol. 4). 224p. 1982. 49.50x o.p. (ISBN 0-306-41013-3, Plenum Pr). Plenum Pub.

Psychosocial Needs of the Aged: A Health Care Perspective. rev. ed. Ed. by Eugene Seymour. LC 78-60818. 1978. pap. 8.00x o.p. (ISBN 0-88474-048-X, 05750-9). Lexington Bks.

Psychosocial Nursing Care of the Aged. 2nd ed. Irene M. Burnside. (Illus.). 1980. text ed. 24.95 o.p. (ISBN 0-07-009210-9). McGraw.

Psychosocial Nursing Care of the Emergency Patient. Sharon G. Fought & Anita N. Throwe. LC 84-12024. 247p. 1984. pap. text ed. 17.95 o.p. (ISBN 0-471-87562-7). Wiley.

Psychosocial Occupational Therapy: Practice in a Pluralistic Arena. R. Barris & G. Kielhofner. LC 83-62206. (Illus.). 352p. 1983. pap. text ed. 22.50 o.p. (ISBN 0-943596-03-3, RAMSCO 00600). Ramsco Pub.

Psychosocial Principles Applied to Classroom Teaching. William F. White. LC 69-13228. (Illus.). 1969. text ed. 29.95 o.p. (ISBN 0-07-069760-4). McGraw.

Psychosocial Therapies. APA Commission on Psychiatric Therapies. Ed. by Toksoz B. Karasu. LC 84-3058. 616p. 1984. pap. text ed. 25.00x o.p. (ISBN 0-89042-103-X, 42-103-X). Am Psychiatric.

Psychosomatic Approach to Prevention of Disease: Proceedings of the 20th Annual Conference for Psychosomatic Research, London, Nov. 15-16, 1976. Annual Conference for Psychosomatic Research Staff. Ed. by M. Carruthers & R. Priest. 1978. pap. 26.00 o.p. (ISBN 0-08-022253-6). Pergamon.

Psychosomatic Medicine. Franz Alexander. 1965. pap. 4.45 o.p. (ISBN 0-393-00300-0, NortonC). Norton.

Psychosomatic Medicine: Theoretical, Clinical & Transcultural Aspects. Ed. by Adam J. Krakowski & Chase P. Kimbell. LC 83-3977. 846p. 1983. 125.00x o.p. (ISBN 0-306-41279-9, Plenum Pr). Plenum Pub.

Psychosomatic Practice & Research: International College of Psychosomatic Medicine, 7th. World Congress, Hamburg, July 1983. Ed. by A. J. Krakowski & C. P. Kimball. (Psychotherapy & Psychosomatics: Vol. 42, Nos. 1-4, 1984). (Illus.). 224p. 1984. pap. 86.75 o.p. (ISBN 3-8055-3975-4). S Karger.

Psychosomatic Research & Practice. Ed. by Adam J. Krakowski & Chase P. Kimball. 248p. 1985. pap. 78.00x o.p. Transaction Pubs.

Psychosomatics & Pleasure: Proceedings of the Twenty-Third Annual Conference of the Society for Psychosomatic Research Held at the Royal College of Physicians, London, 19-20 November 1979. Ed. by C. Aitken. 88p. 1981. pap. 24.00 o.p. (ISBN 0-08-026797-1). Pergamon.

Psychosomatics & Suggestion Therapy in Dentistry. Jacob Stolzenberg. (ISBN 0-8022-1654-4). Philos Lib.

Psychosomatics in War & Peace: Proceedings of the Society for Psychosomatic Research, 22nd, Royal College of Physicians, London, Nov. 27-28, 1978. Society for Psychosomatic Research Staff. Ed. by P. Williams. 112p. 1980. pap. 26.00 o.p. (ISBN 0-08-026064-0). Pergamon.

Psychotherapeutic Attraction. Arnold P. Goldstein. LC 79-119598. 260p. 1971. 25.00 o.p. (ISBN 0-08-016398-X). Pergamon.

Psychotherapy & Counseling. 2nd ed. William S. Sahakian. 1976. pap. 30.36 o.p. (ISBN 0-395-30834-8). HM.

Psychotherapy & Drug Addiction I: Diagnosis & Treatment. Charles P. Cohen et al. LC 73-11097. (Drug Abuse Ser.). 263p. 1974. text ed. 24.00x o.p. (ISBN 0-8422-7143-0). Irvington.

Psychotherapy & Drug Addiction, II. Irving Silverman et al. LC 73-11097. (Drug Abuse Ser.). 1974. text ed. 24.00x o.p. (ISBN 0-8422-7144-9). Irvington.

Psychotherapy & Existentialism. Victor E. Frankl. 1968. pap. 9.95 o.p. (ISBN 0-671-20056-9, Touchstone Bks). S&S.

Psychotherapy & the Modification of Abnormal Behavior. H. Strupp. 1971. pap. text ed. 9.95 o.p. (ISBN 0-07-062231-0). McGraw.

Psychotherapy for Methadone Maintained Opiate Addicts: A Report of Two Studies. (DHHS Publication ADM Ser.: No. 86-1289). 29p. 1986. pap. 1.75 o.p. (ISBN 0-318-21669-8, S/N 017-024-01307-2). USGPO.

Psychotherapy in the Soviet Union. Vsesoiuznaia Konferentsiia Po Voprosam Psikhoterapil Staff. Tr. by Ralph B. Winn. Repr. of 1961 ed. lib. bdg. 35.00x o.p. (ISBN 0-8371-2396-8, PSSV). Greenwood.

Psychotherapy Maze: A Consumer's Guide to Getting In & Out of Therapy. rev. ed. Otto Ehrenberg & Miriam Ehrenberg. 1986. pap. 6.95 o.s.i. (ISBN 0-671-62287-0, Fireside). S&S.

Psychotherapy: Theoretical & Technical Readings. Ed. by Walter E. O'Connell. 350p. 1976. pap. text ed. 12.50x o.p. (ISBN 0-8422-0472-5). Irvington.

Psychotherapy Through the Group Process. Dorothy S. Whitaker & Morton A. Lieberman. LC 64-10206. 1964. 30.95x o.p. (ISBN 0-202-26056-9). Aldine de Gruyter.

Psychotherapy Versus Iatrogeny: A Confrontation for Physicians. Nikola Schipkowensky. LC 76-49515. 508p. 1977. text ed. 35.00x o.p. (ISBN 0-8143-1555-0). Wayne St U Pr.

Psychotherapy: What It's All about. Hendrik Ruitenbeek. 1976. pap. 1.95 o.p. (ISBN 0-380-00811-4, 30858). Avon.

Psychotic States: A Psychoanalytic Approach. Herbert A. Rosenfeld. 264p. 1966. text ed. 30.00x o.s.i. (ISBN 0-8236-5700-0). Intl Univs Pr.

Psychotropic Drugs & Nursing Intervention. Patricia Irons. (Illus.). 1978. text ed. 20.95 o.p. (ISBN 0-07-032052-7). McGraw.

Psychotropic Drugs & Related Compounds. 2nd ed. Earl Usdin & Daniel H. Efron. LC 79-42886. 780p. 1979. 63.00 o.p. (ISBN 0-08-025510-8). Pergamon.

Psychotropic Drugs: Plasma Concentration & Clinical Response. Ed. by Graham D. Burrows & Trevor R. Norman. (Experimental & Clinical Psychiatry Ser.: Vol. 4). (Illus.). 528p. 1981. 85.00 o.p. (ISBN 0-8247-1009-6). Dekker.

PsycINFO Retrospective: Learning & Communication Disorders, 1971-1980. 1982. pap. 31.50 o.p. (ISBN 0-912704-71-3, 3120010). Am Psychol.

Ptolemaios und Porphyrios Uber Die Musik. Ingemar During. LC 78-20290. (Ancient Philosophy Ser.). 293p. 1980. lib. bdg. 34.00 o.p. (ISBN 0-8240-9599-5). Garland Pub.

Ptolia, Bk. 1. Fred Baker. LC 82-81453. 175p. (Orig.). 1982. pap. 4.95 o.p. (ISBN 0-914766-83-X, 0197). Illum Way Pub.

Puberty & Adolescence. Jean C. Lipke. LC 70-104888. (Being Together Bks.). (Illus.). (gr. 5-11). 1971. PLB 5.95 o.p. (ISBN 0-8225-0591-6). Lerner Pubns.

Puberty to Manhood in Italy & America. Harben B. Young & Lucy R. Ferguson. (Development Psychology Ser.). 294p. 1981. 19.95 o.p. (ISBN 0-12-773150-4). Acad Pr.

Public Access Microcomputers: A Handbook for Librarians. Patrick R. Dewey. LC 83-26776. (Professional Librarian Ser.). 151p. 1984. 34.50 o.s.i. (ISBN 0-86729-086-2); pap. 27.50 o.s.i. (ISBN 0-86729-085-4). G K Hall.

Public Access to Government Publications. Peter Hernon & Charles R. McClure. LC 83-25797. (Libraries & Information Science Ser.). 472p. 1984. text ed. 59.50 o.p. (ISBN 0-89391-100-3); pap. text ed. 29.50 o.p. Ablex Pub.

Public Access to Library Automation: Proceedings of the Clinic on Library Applications of Data Processing,1980. LC 81-11685. 128p. 1981. 10.00 o.p. (ISBN 0-87845-065-3). U of Ill Lib Info Sci.

Public Administration. 6th ed. Robert Presthus. 432p. 1975. text ed. write for info. o.p. (ISBN 0-02-396570-3). Macmillan.

Public Administration. 4th ed. Ira Sharkansky. 1978. text ed. 24.50 o.p. (ISBN 0-395-30836-4). HM.

Public Administration & Policy Analysis. R. A. Rhodes. 128p. 1979. text ed. 28.50x o.p. (ISBN 0-566-00239-6). Gower Pub Co.

Public Administration & the Public: Perspectives Toward Government in a Metropolitan Community. Morris Janowitz & D. Wright. LC 76-49866. (Michigan Governmental Studies, University of Michigan: No. 36). 1977. Repr. of 1958 ed. lib. bdg. 22.50x o.p. (ISBN 0-8371-9396-6, JAPU). Greenwood.

Public Administration: Concepts & Cases. Richard J. Stillman. LC 75-31022. (Illus.). 384p. 1976. pap. 9.50 o.p. (ISBN 0-395-20606-5). HM.

Public Administration: Concepts & Cases. 2nd ed. Richard J. Stillman, II. LC 79-89817. (Illus.). 1980. pap. 14.50 o.p. (ISBN 0-395-28634-4). HM.

Public Administration: Readings in Institutions, Processes, Behavior Policy. 3rd ed. Robert T. Golembiewski & Frank Gibson. 1976. pap. 17.50 o.p. (ISBN 0-395-30805-4). HM.

Public & Business Planning in the United States: A Bibliography. Ed. by Martha B. Lightwood. LC 79-165488. (Management Information Guide Ser.: No. 26). 314p. 1972. 68.00x o.p. (ISBN 0-8103-0826-6). Gale.

Public & Private Conformity: Competing Explanations by Improvisation, Cognitive Dissonance & Attribution Theories. Ed. by Barry E. Collins. LC 73-7252. (Illus.). 182p. 1974. pap. text ed. 9.95x o.p. (ISBN 0-8422-9105-9). Irvington.

Public & Private Education: The Australian Dimension. Don Anderson. 238p. 1986. 39.00 o.p. (ISBN 0-949614-26-2, Pub. by Croom Helm UK); pap. 19.00 o.p. (ISBN 0-949614-27-0, Pub. by Croom Helm UK). Routledge Chapman & Hall.

Public Art: New Directions. Louis G. Redstone. 1981. text ed. 52.00 o.p. (ISBN 0-07-051345-7). McGraw.

Public Assistance Data Book. Toby H. Campbell & Marc Bendick, Jr. 344p. 1977. pap. 12.75x o.p. (ISBN 0-87766-207-X, 20300). Urban Inst.

Public Assistance in France. Cindy Stevens. 94p. 1973. pap. text ed. 5.00x o.p. (ISBN 0-7135-1846-4, Pub. by Bedford England). Gower Pub Co.

Public Authorities & the Right to Protection of Trade Union Funds & Property. 1974. 11.40 o.p. (ISBN 92-2-101048-1). Intl Labour Office.

Public Budgeting. 3rd ed. Fremont J. Lyden & Ernest G. Miller. 1978. pap. 14.95 o.p. (ISBN 0-395-30661-2). HM.

Public Buildings: A Bibliography for Architects, Planners & Administrators. Mary Vance. (Architecture Ser.: A 1471). 47p. 1985. 6.75 o.p. (ISBN 0-89028-601-9). Vance Biblios.

Public Communication: Behavioral Perspectives. Jerry W. Koehler et al. (Illus.). 1978. pap. text ed. write for info. o.p. (ISBN 0-02-365610-7). Macmillan.

Public Company Auditor Changes & Big Eight Firms: Disagreements & Other Issues. Donald K. McConnell, Jr. Ed. by Richard Farmer. LC 83-5953. (Research for Business Decisions Ser.: No. 62). 330p. 1983. 49.95 o.p. (ISBN 0-8357-1425-X). UMI Res Pr.

Public Control of the British Bus Industry. Stephen Glaiser & Corinne Mulley. 146p. 1983. text ed. 33.00x o.p. (ISBN 0-566-00560-3). Gower Pub Co.

Public Data Bases for Design Firms. 42p. 1984. 10.00 o.p. (97). Am Consul Eng.

Public Diplomacy & Political Change: Four Case Studies - Okinaws, Peru, Czechoslavakia, Guinea. Gregory Henderson et al. (Special Studies in International Politics & Government). 1988. pap. text ed. 12.95x o.p. (ISBN 0-8290-2140-X). Irvington.

Public Domain. Richard Schechner. 1970. pap. 1.65 o.p. (ISBN 0-380-01379-7, 12104, Bard). Avon.

Public-Domain Software: Untapped Resources for the Business User. Rusel DeMaria & George R. Fontaine. 364p. book & disk 34.95 o.s.i. (ISBN 0-934375-47-X). M&T Pub Inc.

Public Education & the Children of Illegal Aliens. Patrick H. Kellough & Jean L. Kellough. (Public Administration Ser.: P 1733). 6p. 1985. 2.00 o.p. (ISBN 0-89028-503-9). Vance Biblios.

Public Employee Benefit Plans, 1983. Ed. by Mary E. Brennan. 94p. (Orig.). 1983. pap. text ed. 10.00 o.p. (ISBN 0-89154-215-9). Intl Found Employ.

Public Employee Compensation: A Twelve City Comparison. 2nd ed. Elizabeth Dickson & George Peterson. LC 81-53060. 213p. 1981. pap. text ed. 12.00x o.p. (ISBN 0-87766-310-6, URI 32800). Urban Inst.

Public Employees Conference, Dec. 7-10, 1980, Monterey, CA: Proceedings. Ed. by Mary E. Brennan. Incl. Public Employees Conference Proceedings, December 5-8, 1982, Orlando, Florida. Ed. by Mary E. Brennan. 110p. (Orig.). 1983. pap. 10.00 o.p. (ISBN 0-89154-207-8); Public Employees Conference Proceedings, Nov. 11-14, 1981, Williamsburg. Ed. by Mary E. Brennan. 119p. (Orig.). 1982. pap. 10.00 (ISBN 0-89154-173-X). 114p. (Orig.). 1981. pap. 10.00 o.p. (ISBN 0-89154-151-9). Intl Found Employ.

Public Employees Conference Proceedings, December 5-8, 1982, Orlando, Florida see Public Employees Conference, Dec. 7-10, 1980, Monterey, CA: Proceedings.

Public Employees Conference Proceedings, Nov. 11-14, 1981, Williamsburg see Public Employees Conference, Dec. 7-10, 1980, Monterey, CA: Proceedings.

Public Employment in Canada. David K. Foot. (Statistical Ser.). 217p. 1979. pap. text ed. 15.00x o.p. (ISBN 0-409-88603-3, Pub. by Inst Res Pub Canada). Gower Pub Co.

Public Enemies: The Mayor, the Mob, & the Crime That Was. George Walsh. 1980. 14.95 o.p. (ISBN 0-393-01306-5). Norton.

Public Enterprise & the Developing World. Ed. by V. V. Ramanadham. 234p. 1984. 28.00 o.p. (ISBN 0-7099-2275-2, Pub. By Croom Helm Ltd). Routledge Chapman & Hall.

Public Enterprise: Economics & Transport Problems. Tillo E. Kuhn. LC 76-5904. (Illus.). 243p. 1976. Repr. of 1962 ed. lib. bdg. 35.00x o.p. (ISBN 0-8371-8798-2, KUPE). Greenwood.

Public Enterprise in Europe. Henry Parris. 256p. 1986. 43.00 o.p. (ISBN 0-7099-0548-3, Pub. by Croom Helm UK). Routledge Chapman & Hall.

Public Enterprises & Privatization in Africa. African Association of Public Administration & Management Staff. 1987. text ed. 50.00x o.p. (ISBN 0-7069-3341-9, Pub. by Vikas India). Advent NY.

Public Eye: Television & the Politics of Canadian Broadcasting, 1952-68. Frank W. Peers. 1979. 27.50 o.p. (ISBN 0-8020-5436-6). U of Toronto Pr.

Public Finance. 8th ed. H. L. Bhatia. 400p. 1982. text ed. 40.00x o.p. (ISBN 0-7069-2055-4, Pub. by Vikas India); pap. text ed. 22.50x o.p. (ISBN 0-7069-2836-9). Advent NY.

Public Finance. Harvey S. Rosen. LC 84-80446. (Irwin Publications in Economics Ser.). (Illus.). 641p. 1985. 36.95 o.p. (ISBN 0-256-02813-3). Irwin.

Public Finance. Sharp & Sliger. Irwin.

Public Finance: A Contemporary Application of Theory to Policy. David N. Hyman. 689p. 1983. 31.95x o.p. (ISBN 0-03-059349-2). Dryden Pr.

Public Finance: A Normative Theory. Richard W. Tresch. 1981. text ed. 32.95x o.p. (ISBN 0-256-02391-3). Irwin.

Public Finance & Stabilization Policy. Ed. by W. L. Smith & J. M. Culbertson. 368p. 1974. 73.75 o.p. (ISBN 0-444-10682-0, North-Holland). Elsevier.

Public Finance & Welfare: Essays in Honor of C. Ward Macy. Ed. by Paul L. Kleinsorge. LC 66-4750. 1966. 7.50 o.p. (ISBN 0-87114-013-6). U of Oreg Bks.

Public Finance: In Theory & Practice. 6th ed. A. R. Prest & N. A. Barr. (Illus.). 568p. 1979. 37.50x o.p. (ISBN 0-297-77648-7, GWN 03699, Pub. by Weidenfeld & Nicolson England). Biblio Dist.

Public Finance Information Sources. Ed. by Vera H. Knox. LC 64-16503. (Management Information Guide Ser.: No. 3). 150p. 1964. 68.00x o.p. (ISBN 0-8103-0803-7). Gale.

Public Health Administration. S. L. Goel. xiii, 472p. 1984. text ed. 50.00x o.p. (ISBN 0-86590-527-4, Pub. by Sterling Pubs India). Apt Bks.

Public Health Administration: An Instrument for Evaluation. Ray Biggerstaff. 123p. 1983. pap. text ed. 10.95 o.p. (ISBN 0-89917-382-9). Tichenor Pub.

Public Health & Community Optometry. Robert D. Newcomb & Jerry L. Jolley. (Illus.). 534p. 1980. 60.00x o.p. (ISBN 0-398-03918-6). C C Thomas.

Public Health Law Manual. Ed. by Frank Grad. LC 74-120960. 234p. 1981. 6.50x o.p. (ISBN 0-87553-058-3, 060). Am Pub Health.

Public Health Nursing & the Law. Patrice Solberg. 306p. 1979. 17.00 o.p. (ISBN 0-686-39465-8). Institute Government.

Public Health Risks of Exposure to Asbestos. Commission of the European Communities. Ed. by R. L. Zielhuis. LC 76-51964. 1977. pap. 35.00 o.p. (ISBN 0-08-021580-7). Pergamon.

Public Health Risks of the Dioxins: Proceedings of the Life Sciences Symposium, New York, October 19-20, 1983. Life Sciences Symposium Staff. Ed. by William W. Lowrance. (Illus.). 390p. 1984. pap. text ed. 25.00 o.p. (ISBN 0-86576-076-4). W Kaufmann.

Public Hospitals under Private Management: The California Experience. William Shonick & Ruth Roemer. LC 82-25854. 127p. pap. 7.75x o.s.i. (ISBN 0-87772-290-0). UCB IGS.

Public Housing & Private Property. Stephanie Cooper. 200p. text ed. cancelled o.s.i. (ISBN 0-566-05004-8). Gower Pub Co.

Public Housing Policy. Eugene J. Meehan. 200p. 1975. (ISBN 0-87855-118-2). Transaction Pubs.

Public International Air Transportation Law in a New Era: Economic Regulation of International Air Carrier Operations. H. A. Wassenbergh. ix, 165p. 1976. text ed. 25.75x o.p. (ISBN 90-268-0860-7). Rothman.

Public Involvement in Maritime Facility Development. Maritime Transportation Research Board Staff & National Research Council Staff. 1979. pap. text ed. 7.50 o.p. (ISBN 0-309-02868-X). Natl Acad Pr.

Public Landscape: Six Essays on Government & Environmental Design in the San Francisco Bay Area. Garrett Eckbo. LC 77-15997. (Illus.). 1978. pap. 7.75x o.p. (ISBN 0-87772-249-8). UCB IGS.

Public Law Two-Eighty. Carole E. Goldberg. (American Indian Treaties Publications Ser.). 60p. 1975. pap. 5.00 o.p. (ISBN 0-935626-19-0). U Cal AISC.

Public Libraries: Legislation, Administration & Finance. B. J. Phillips et al. 1979. 5.25x o.p. (ISBN 0-85365-750-5, Pub by the Library Assn). Nichols Pub.

Public Library in the Nineteen Eighties: The Problems of Choice. Lawrence J. White. LC 82-48604. (Lexington Books Special Series in Libraries & Librarianship). 244p. 1983. 26.00x o.p. (ISBN 0-669-06342-8). Lexington Bks.

Public Life in Renaissance Florence. Richard C. Trexler. LC 80-979. (Studies in Discontinuity). 1980. 24.95 o.p. (ISBN 0-12-699550-8). Acad Pr.

Public Man: An Interpretation of Latin American & Other Catholic Cultures. Glenn C. Dealy. Date not set. price not set o.p. U of Mass Pr.

Public Ministry of Christ. William G. Blaikie. 356p. lib. bdg. 13.95 o.p. (ISBN 0-8254-5032-2). Kregel.

Public, Municipal & Community Buildings. Architectural Record Magazine Editors. 1980. text ed. 44.95 o.p. (ISBN 0-07-002351-4). McGraw.

Public Opinion & Nuclear Energy. Stanley Nealey et al. LC 78-75319. (Battelle Human Affairs Research Centers Ser.). (Illus.). 224p. 1983. 29.00x o.p. (ISBN 0-669-02843-6). Lexington Bks.

Public Opinion & the Immigrant: Mass Media Coverage, 1880 to 1980. Rita J. Simon. LC 81-48146. (Illus.). 256p. 1984. 27.00x o.p. (ISBN 0-669-05291-4). Lexington Bks.

Public Opinion During the Reagan Administration. John L. Goodman. (Changing Domestic Priorities Ser.). 1983. pap. text ed. 5.95x nfo. o.p. (ISBN 0-87766-330-0). Urban Inst.

Public Opinion of Criminal Justice in California: A Survey Conducted by Field Research Corporation. Field Research Corporation Staff. LC 75-8959. 156p. 1975. pap. 7.00x o.p. (ISBN 0-87772-203-X). UCB IGS.

Public Opinion: The Visible Politics. 2nd ed. Jerry L. Yeric & John R. Todd. LC 82-81415. 243p. 1987. pap. text ed. 14.95 o.p. (ISBN 0-87581-281-3). Peacock Pubs.

Public Parks & Recreation Administration: Behavior & Dynamics. Linn Rockwood. LC 82-1294. (Brighton Recreation & Leisure Ser.). 397p. 1986. 30.00x o.p. (ISBN 0-89832-021-6); text ed. 25.00 o.p. Pub Horizons.

Public Participation in Britain. Anthony Barker. 192p. 1979. pap. text ed. 19.50x o.p. (ISBN 0-7199-1029-3, Pub. by Bedford England). Gower Pub Co.

Public Personnel Administration. 1986. pap. text ed. 45.00x o.p. (ISBN 0-86590-764-1). Apt Bks.

Public Personnel Administration: Critique & Credo see Issues in the Public Employee Relations Library: Series 3.

Public Personnel Management: Contexts & Strategies. Donald E. Klingner. 480p. 1980. non-members 16.95 o.p. (ISBN 0-13-737981-1); members 13.50 o.p. Intl Personnel Mgmt.

Public Personnel Management: Readings, Cases & Contingency Plans. Ed. by Marvin J. Levine. 424p. 1980. 26.95x o.p. (ISBN 0-89832-006-2); pap. text ed. 24.95 o.p. Pub Horizons.

Public Planning & Control of Urban & Land Development Cases & Materials. 2nd ed. Donald G. Hagman. LC 80-36684. (American Casebook Ser.). 1301p. 1980. text ed. 37.95 o.p. (ISBN 0-8299-2100-1). West Pub.

Public Planning & Control of Urban & Land Development-Cases & Materials: 1982 Supplement to Teacher's Manual. 2nd ed. Donald G. Hagman. (American Casebook Ser.). 51p. 1982. pap. text ed. (ISBN 0-314-66383-5). West Pub.

Public Policies for an Aging Population. Ed. by Elizabeth Markson & Gretchen Batra. LC 79-3249. (Boston University Series in Gerontology). 1980. 25.00x o.p. (ISBN 0-669-03398-7). Lexington Bks.

Public Policies Toward Adoption. Barbara Joe. 84p. 1979. pap. text ed. 11.75x o.p. (ISBN 0-87766-253-3). Urban Inst.

Public Policies Toward Business: Readings & Cases. rev ed. Ed. by William G. Shepherd. 1979. pap. 20.95x o.p. (ISBN 0-256-02236-4). Irwin.

Public Policy: A Guide to Information Sources. Ed. by William J. Murin et al. LC 80-25872. (American Government & History Information Guide Ser.: Vol. 13). 296p. 1981. 68.00x o.p. (ISBN 0-8103-1490-8). Gale.

Public Policy & the Corporation. M. A. King. (Cambridge Studies in Applied Econometrics). 1977. 36.00x o.p. (ISBN 0-412-15330-0, NO. 6171, Pub. by Chapman & Hall). Routledge Chapman & Hall.

Public Policy Decision Making & Regulation. Douglas G. Hartle. 218p. 1979. pap. text ed. 12.95x o.p. (ISBN 0-920380-20-4, Pub. by Inst Res Pub Canada). Gower Pub Co.

Public Policy for Local Government. J. A. Chandler. 192p. 1988. lib. bdg. 49.95x o.p. (ISBN 0-317-64369-X, Pub. by Croom Helm UK). Routledge Chapman & Hall.

Public Policy in Britain. Martin Burch & Bruce Wood. 256p. 1983. 55.00x o.p. (ISBN 0-85520-586-5). Basil Blackwell.

Public Policy in Texas. 2nd ed. Wendell M. Bedichek & Neal Tannahill. 1986. pap. text ed. write for info. o.p. (ISBN 0-673-18001-8). Scott F.

Public Policy-Making. 2nd ed. James E. Anderson. LC 73-8174. 188p. 1978. 13.50 o.p. (ISBN 0-88275-737-7, (K)). Krieger.

Public Policy Study Skills Manual. rev. ed. William D. Coplin & Michael K. O'Leary. 253p. (Orig.). 1986. pap. text ed. 14.00x o.p. (ISBN 0-936826-21-5). PS Assocs Croton.

Public Pressures & the Practice of U. S. Foreign Policy: A Checklist, 1979 to 1983. Dale E. Casper. (Public Administration Ser.: Bibliography P 1645). 1985. pap. 2.00 o.p. (ISBN 0-89028-335-4). Vance Biblios.

Public-Private Interplay in Social Protection. Ed. by Martin Rein & Lee Rainwater. 256p. 1986. 35.00 o.p. (ISBN 0-87332-383-1). M E Sharpe.

Public-Private Partnership in American Cities: Seven Case Studies. Scott Fosler & Renee A. Berger. LC 82-48016. 368p. 1982. 33.00x o.p. (ISBN 0-669-05834-3). Lexington Bks.

Public Prosecutor & Other Plays. Fritz Hochwalder. LC 78-8814. 1980. 16.50x o.p. (ISBN 0-8044-2391-1). Ungar.

Public Purchasing & Materials Management. Harry R. Page. LC 79-2039. 528p. 1980. 34.95x o.p. (ISBN 0-669-06575-7); pap. 26.00x o.p. Lexington Bks.

Public Radiation Exposure of the Population from Nuclear Power Generation in the United States. LC 87-24696. (NCRP Report Ser.: No. 92). pap. text ed. NCRP Pubns.

Public Relations & Advertising for Architects. Mary Vance. (Architecture Ser.: Bibliography A-1300). 1985. pap. 2.00 o.p. (ISBN 0-89028-230-7). Vance Biblios.

Public Relations & Fund Development Handbook. 100p. 1976. 4.00 o.p. (ISBN 0-317-35482-5). New Readers.

Public Relations Career Directory 1986: 25 Top PR Professionals. Intro. by Kerryn King. (Career Directory Ser.). 320p. (Orig.). 1986. pap. 24.95 o.p. (ISBN 0-934829-03-9). Career Pr Inc.

Public Relations Career Directory: 1987. 2nd ed. Ed. by Ronald W. Fry. (Career Directory Ser.). 380p. 1987. text ed. 34.95 o.s.i. (ISBN 0-934829-18-7); pap. text ed. 26.95 o.s.i. (ISBN 0-934829-12-8); Special Bookstore Edition Distributed by Williamson Publishing Co. pap. 17.95 o.s.i. (ISBN 0-934829-05-5). Career Pr Inc.

Public Relations for Community & Junior Colleges. Fred A. Woodress. LC 75-13703. 1976. 3.95x o.p. (ISBN 0-8134-1778-3, 1778). Inter Print Pubs.

Public Relations for Management Success. Frank Jefkins. LC 84-17669. 134p. 1984. 29.00 o.p. (ISBN 0-7099-1436-9, Pub. by Croom Helm Ltd). Routledge Chapman & Hall.

Public Relations for Schools. Adolph Unruh & Robert A. Willier. LC 73-91798. 1974. pap. 7.95 o.p. (ISBN 0-8224-5750-4). D S Lake Pubs.

Public Relations Information Sources. Ed. by Alice Norton. LC 77-137574. (Management Information Guide Ser.: No. 22). 160p. 1970. 68.00x o.p. (ISBN 0-8103-0822-3). Gale.

Public Relations: Principles, Cases & Problems. 9th ed. H. Frazier Moore. 1985. 35.95x o.p. (ISBN 0-256-03185-1). Irwin.

Public School & Finances. Mary F. Williams. LC 80-20771. (Education of the Public & the Public School Ser.). 64p. 1980. pap. 3.95 o.p. (ISBN 0-8298-0414-5). Pilgrim NY.

Public School & Moral Education. Henry C. Johnson, Jr. LC 80-20768. (Education of the Public & the Public School Ser.). 96p. (Orig.). 1981. pap. 5.95 o.p. (ISBN 0-8298-0420-X). Pilgrim NY.

Public School & Public Policy. Stanley. 1980. pap. 1.95 o.p. (ISBN 0-8298-0419-6). Pilgrim NY.

Public School & the Challenge of Ethnic Pluralism. Carl A. Grant et al. LC 80-21315. 1981. pap. 2.95 o.p. (ISBN 0-8298-0421-8). Pilgrim NY.

Public School & the Family. Leichter. 1980. pap. 1.95 o.p. (ISBN 0-8298-0416-1). Pilgrim NY.

Public School & the Whole Person. Mary Richards. 1980. pap. 2.95 o.p. (ISBN 0-8298-0417-X). Pilgrim NY.

Public School Monopoly: A Critical Analysis of Education & the State in American Society. Ed. by Robert B. Everhart. LC 81-20635. (Illus.). 583p. 1982. 34.95 o.p.; pap. 14.95 o.p. (ISBN 0-88410-388-9). PRIPP.

Public School Word-Book. John S. Farmer. LC 68-17988. 256p. 1968. Repr. of 1900 ed. 35.00x o.p. (ISBN 0-8103-3280-9). Gale.

Public Sector Accountability: A Selected Bibliography with Emphasis on Canada. Ontario Ministry of Treasury & Economics, Library Services Staff. (Public Administration Ser.: P 1669). 16p. 1985. 2.25 o.p. (ISBN 0-89028-379-6). Vance Biblios.

Public-Sector Bargaining. 2nd ed. Ed. by Benjamin Aaron et al. LC 87-32025. 334p. 1988. write for info. o.p. (207). BNA.

Public Sector Decision-Making. D. Pearce. 1980. pap. 24.00 o.p. (ISBN 0-08-025832-8). Pergamon.

Public Sector Labor Markets. Ed. by P. Mieszkowski & G. Peterson. 216p. 1981. pap. 12.00x o.p. (ISBN 0-87766-285-1, 29100). Urban Inst.

Public Sector Labor Relations: Analysis & Readings. 2nd. ed. David Lewin et al. LC 82-3021. 1981. pap. 18.95x o.p. (ISBN 0-913878-23-5); pap. 18.95x o.p. T Horton & Dghts.

Public Servants & Patronage: The Foundation & Rise of the New South Wales Public Service, 1786-1859. Arthur McMartin. (Illus.). xiii, 345p. 1983. 36.95x o.p. (ISBN 0-424-00097-0, Pub. by Sydney U Pr). Intl Spec Bk.

Public Speaking. Wayne C. Minnick. LC 78-69580. (Illus.). 1979. pap. 12.50 o.p. (ISBN 0-395-26791-9). HM.

Public Speaking. rev. ed. Lois S. Roets. 40p. 1984. 8.00 o.p. (ISBN 0-911943-01-3). Leadership Pubs.

Public Speaking: A Rhetorical Approach. Neher. 196p. 1984. pap. text ed. 15.95 o.p. (ISBN 0-8403-3424-9). Kendall Hunt.

Public Speaking Today. Gordon I. Zimmerman. (Illus.). 1979. pap. text ed. 22.75 o.p. (ISBN 0-8299-0259-7); instr's. manual avail. o.p. (ISBN 0-8299-0586-3). West Pub.

Public Streets for Public Use. Ed. by Anne V. Moudon. (Illus.). 352p. 1987. 44.95 o.s.i. (ISBN 0-442-26404-6). Van Nos Reinhold.

Public Technology: Key to Improved Government Productivity. Ed. by James L. Mercer & Ronald J. Philips. 344p. 1981. 24.95 o.p. (ISBN 0-8144-5643-X). AMACOM.

Public Transportation Planning Issues: Eight Reports. (Transportation Research Record Ser.). 85p. 1974. 3.80 o.p. (ISBN 0-309-02364-5). Transport Res Bd.

Public Transportation Planning: Ten Reports. (Transportation Research Record Ser.). 96p. 1976. 8.00 o.p. (ISBN 0-309-02473-0). Transport Res Bd.

Public Treasury of Colonial South Carolina. Maurice Crouse. LC 76-56125. (Tricentennial Studies Ser.: No. 10). xvi, 142p. 1977. 21.95x o.p. (ISBN 0-87249-255-9). U of SC Pr.

Public Utilities Information Sources. Ed. by Florine E. Hunt. LC 65-24658. (Management Information Guide Ser.: No. 7). 204p. 1965. 68.00x o.p. (ISBN 0-8103-0807-X). Gale.

Public Utilities Law Anthology Index (1987) Ed. by Allison P. Zabriskie. (National Law Anthology Ser.). 120p. 1987. pap. text ed. 29.95x o.s.i. (ISBN 0-914250-32-9). Intl Lib.

Public Utilities: Regulation, Management, & Ownership. Martin T. Farris & Roy J. Sampson. LC 72-85908. 420p. 1973. text ed. 25.95 o.p. (ISBN 0-395-13884-1). HM.

Public Utilities Reports Digest: Supplements A & B, 1983-1986, 10 vols. Lucien E. Smart & Bruce W. Radford. LC 86-192780. (Third Ser., 1953-1982). Date not set. Set & Suppl. 805.00 o.p. (ISBN 0-317-57194-X). Public Util.

Public Utility Regulation of an Exhaustible Resource: The Case of Natural Gas. John C. Gault. LC 78-75016. (Outstanding Dissertations in Economics). 1980. lib. bdg. 37.00 o.p. (ISBN 0-8240-4051-1). Garland Pub.

Public Welfare Directory, 1975. Ed. by Perry Frank & Michele Moore. LC 41-4981. 1975. pap. 25.00x o.p. (ISBN 0-910106-06-1). Am Pub Welfare.

Public Welfare Directory, 1976-1977. Ed. by Perry Frank & Michele Moore. LC 41-4981. 1976. pap. 25.00x o.p. (ISBN 0-910106-07-X). Am Pub Welfare.

Public Welfare Directory, 1977-1978. Ed. by Michele Moore. LC 41-4981. 1977. pap. 25.00x o.p. (ISBN 0-910106-08-8). Am Pub Welfare.

Public Welfare Directory, 1978-1979. Ed. by Michele Moore. LC 41-4981. 1978. pap. 25.00x o.p. (ISBN 0-910106-09-6). Am Pub Welfare.

Public Welfare Directory, 1979-1980. Ed. by Michele Moore. LC 41-4981. 1979. pap. 35.00x o.p. (ISBN 0-910106-10-X). Am Pub Welfare.

Public Welfare Directory, 1980-1981. Ed. by Deborah Cunha. LC 41-4981. 1980. pap. 35.00x o.p. (ISBN 0-910106-11-8). Am Pub Welfare.

Public Welfare Directory, 1981-1982. Ed. by Amy Weinstein. LC 41-4981. 1981. pap. 40.00x o.p. (ISBN 0-910106-12-6). Am Pub Welfare.

Public Welfare Directory, 1982-83. Ed. by Amy Weinstein. LC 41-4981. 448p. (Orig.). 1982. pap. 40.00x o.p. (ISBN 0-910106-13-4). Am Pub Welfare.

Public Welfare Directory, 1983-84. Ed. by Amy Weinstein. LC 41-4981. 456p. 1983. pap. 40.00x o.p. (ISBN 0-910106-14-2). Am Pub Welfare.

Public Welfare Directory, 1984-85. Ed. by Amy Weinstein. LC 41-4981. 464p. 1984. pap. 50.00x o.p. (ISBN 0-910106-15-0). Am Pub Welfare.

Public Welfare Directory, 1985-86. Ed. by Amy Weinstein. LC 41-4981. 464p. 1985. pap. 50.00x o.p. (ISBN 0-910106-16-9). Am Pub Welfare.

Public Welfare Directory 1986-87. Ed. by Amy Weinstein. LC 41-4981. 464p. 1986. pap. 50.00x o.p. (ISBN 0-910106-17-7). Am Pub Welfare.

Public Welfare in the U. S. Monographs. Mary Vance. (Public Administration Series Bibliography: P 1809). 72p. 1985. pap. 10.50 o.p. (ISBN 0-89028-639-6). Vance Biblios.

Publication Design: A Guide to Page Layout, Typography, Format & Style. rev ed. Allen Hurlburt. 134p. 1976. pap. 15.95 o.p. (ISBN 0-442-23592-5). Van Nos Reinhold.

Publication Papers: An Appraisal of the Future of Paper Printing & Publishing at the Start of the Electronic Era, Proceedings of the PPI Publications Papers Conference, Amsterdam, September, 1982. Miller Freeman Publications, Inc. Staff. Ed. by John Kalish. LC 83-61154. (Illus.). 79p. 1983. pap. 65.00 o.p. (ISBN 0-87930-150-3). Miller Freeman.

Publications by Women on American Domestic Architecture. Lamia Doumato. (Architecture Ser.: A 1491). 12p. 1985. 2.00 o.p. (ISBN 0-89028-621-3). Vance Biblios.

Publications in Economics, Vols. 1-15. University of California Staff. 1908-50. pap. 360.00 o.p. (ISBN 0-384-07034-5). Johnson Repr.

Publications in International Relations, 5 Vols. University of California Staff. 1923-57. 155.00 o.p. (ISBN 0-384-07037-X); pap. 125.00 o.p. (ISBN 0-685-13625-6). Johnson Repr.

Publications in Mathematical & Physical Sciences, Vol. 1-3. University of California Staff. (Partly in the original edition). pap. 55.00 o.p. (ISBN 0-384-07038-8). Johnson Repr.

Publications of the Institute of Government: Cumulative Supplement, 1963-1979. Compiled by Rebecca Ballentine. 133p. 1980. Institute Government.

Publications of the International Agricultural Research & Development Centers: 1986 Supplement. 167p. (Orig.). 1986. pap. 9.70x o.p. (ISBN 971-104-145-6, Pub. by Intl Rice Res Philippines). Agribookstore.

Publications of the Venice Biennale 1895-1977 on Microfiche: Bibliography & Subject Index. (Illus.). 60p. (Orig.). 1986. pap. text ed. 4000.00 incl. 1105 microfiche o.p. (ISBN 0-85964-162-7). Chadwyck-Healey.

Publications of William Pain, 1730 to 1790: Architect & Carpenter. Carole Cable. (Architecture Ser.: Bibliography A 1338). 1985. pap. 2.00 o.p. (ISBN 0-89028-308-7). Vance Biblios.

Publicity & Diplomacy with Special Reference to England & Germany (1890-1914) O. J. Hale. 11.75 o.p. (ISBN 0-8446-1215-4). Peter Smith.

Publicity & Public Relations in Libraries: A Selected Bibliography. Dittakavi N. Rao. (Public Administration Ser.: Bibliography P 1636). 1985. pap. 2.25 o.p. (ISBN 0-89028-306-0). Vance Biblios.

Publicity: How to Make the Media Work for You. Ted Klein & Fred Danzig. (Illus.). 304p. 1985. 17.95 o.p. (ISBN 0-684-18244-0). Scribner.

Published in Paris. Hugh Ford. 1980. pap. 14.95 o.p. (ISBN 0-916366-09-X). Pushcart Pr.

Published Radio, Television & Film Scripts: A Bibliography. G. Howard Poteet. LC 74-18201. iii, 245p. 1975. 15.00x o.p. (ISBN 0-87875-063-0). Whitston Pub.

Published Screenplays: A Checklist. Clifford McCarty. LC 73-138656. (Serif Ser.: No. 18). 137p. 1971. 12.00x o.p. (ISBN 0-87338-112-2). Kent St U Pr.

Publisher's Catalogs Annual, 1983-84. Ed. by Nancy Jean Melin. 70p. bk. with microfiche 165.00 o.p. (ISBN 0-930466-91-8). Meckler Corp.

Publishers' Catalogs Annual: 1986-1987. 1985. pap. text ed. 235.00 with microfiche o.p. (ISBN 0-317-46491-4). Chadwyck-Healey.

Publishers Directory, 2 vols. 8th ed. Ed. by Linda S. Hubbard. 2206p. 1987. Set. 275.00x o.p. (ISBN 0-8103-2513-6). Gale.

Publishers Directory, 1988: Supplement. 8th ed. Ed. by Linda S. Hubbard. 250p. 1987. 155.00x o.p. (ISBN 0-8103-2516-0). Gale.

Publisher's International Directory with ISBN Index, 1988, 2 vols. 15th ed. Ed. by Helmut Opitz & Karl H. Strasser. 3444p. 1988. 275.00 o.p. (ISBN 3-598-20537-6). K G Saur.

Titles

Publishers' Trade List Annual 1987, 4 vols. 1987. 165.00 o.p. (ISBN 0-8352-2386-8). Bowker.

Publishing: A Complete Guide for Schools, Small Presses, & Entrepreneurs. Robert L. Holt. LC 82-83565. (Calif. Financial Publications Ser.). 1982. 25.95 o.p. (ISBN 0-930926-08-0); pap. 19.95 o.p. (ISBN 0-930926-09-9). Calif Health.

Publishing for the People: The Firm Posrednik, 1885-1905. Robert C. Otto. Ed. by William H. McNeill & Barbara Jelavich. 260p. 1987. lib. bdg. 40.00 o.p. (ISBN 0-8240-8060-2). Garland Pub.

Publishing in Boston, 1726-1757. Rollo G. Silver. 1956. pap. 3.00 o.p. (ISBN 0-912296-30-5, Dist. by U Pr of Va). Am Antiquarian.

Publishing Job Finder. Mainstream Access, Inc. Staff. 224p. 1981. 15.95 o.p. (ISBN 0-13-739516-7); pap. 7.95 o.p. (ISBN 0-13-739508-6). P-H.

Publishing Newsletters. Howard P. Hudson. (Illus.). 224p. 1982. 19.95 o.p. (ISBN 0-684-17496-0, ScribT). Scribner.

Puch Maxi Mopeds '69 - '80. Jeff Clew & Chris Rogers. (Owners Workshop Manuals Ser.: No. 107). 1979. 13.50 o.p. (ISBN 0-85696-582-0). Haynes Pubns.

Puch Moped Owner Service-Repair: 1976-1977. Ed. by Eric Jorgensen. (Illus.). pap. 6.00 o.p. (ISBN 0-89287-213-6, M437). Clymer Pub.

Puch MS, MV, M2, M3, & VS Mopeds '68-'76. Pete Shoemark. pap. 13.50 o.p. (255). Haynes Pubns.

Puddums: The Cathcarts' Orange Cat. Nancy W. Parker. LC 79-23088. (Illus.). 32p. (ps-4). 1980. 8.95 o.p. (ISBN 0-689-50159-5, Atheneum). Macmillan.

Puebla & Beyond. Ed. by John Eagleson & Philip J. Scharper. LC 79-24098. 370p. (Orig.). 1979. pap. 9.95 o.p. (ISBN 0-88344-399-6). Orbis Bks.

Pueblo Indians, Vol. Two: Archaeologic & Ethnologic Data: Acoma-Laguna Land Claims. Florence H. Ellis. (American Indian Ethnohistory Ser: Indians of the Southwest). (Illus.). lib. bdg. 51.00 o.p. (ISBN 0-8240-0726-3). Garland Pub.

Pueblo No Solo Es Testigo. Margaret Randall. (Illus.). 120p. 1979. pap. 4.25 o.p. (ISBN 0-940238-35-7). Ediciones Huracan.

Puerto Rican Experience: A Sociological Sourcebook. Francesco Cordasco et al. (Quality Paperback: No. 259). 370p. (Orig.). 1975. pap. 5.95 o.p. (ISBN 0-8226-0259-8). Littlefield.

Puerto Rican Task Force Report. Ed. by Emelicia Mizio. LC 78-24582. (Project on Ethnicity Ser.). 51p. (Orig.). 1979. pap. 4.00 o.p. (ISBN 0-87304-170-4). Family Serv.

Puerto Ricans: From Island to Mainland. Arlene H. Kurtis. LC 69-13128. (Illus.). (gr. 4 up). 1969. lib. bdg. 3.64 o.s.i. (ISBN 0-671-32085-8). Messner.

Puerto Ricans in the U. S. Ed. by Catarino Garza. LC 77-81291. 1977. 12.00 o.p. (ISBN 0-87348-552-1); pap. 2.95 o.p. (ISBN 0-87348-553-X). Path Pr NY.

Puerto Rico: A Political & Cultural Odyssey. Arturo M. Carrion et al. (Illus.). 1983. 19.00 o.p. (ISBN 0-393-01740-0). Norton.

Puerto Rico: Identidad Nacional y Clases Sociales. Angel G. Quintero et al. LC 81-65310. 150p. 1981. pap. 5.75 o.p. (ISBN 0-940238-36-5). Ediciones Huracan.

Puerto Rico: Long Ago. Irving Gerber. (American Destiny Ser.: Puerto Rico). (Illus.). (gr. 4-12). 1978. of 10 12.95 set o.p. (ISBN 0-87594-177-X). Book-Lab.

Puff, Wrinkle & Squint. John Koenig. (Orig.). (ps-3). pap. 1.00 o.s.i. (ISBN 0-8198-0129-1). Dghtrs St Paul.

Puffin. Naomi Lewis. LC 83-23864. (Illus.). 32p. (gr. k-3). 1984. 11.00 o.p. (ISBN 0-688-03783-6); PLB 10.08 o.p. (ISBN 0-688-03784-4). Lothrop.

Puget Sound Current Guide. Island Canoe Co. Staff. (Illus., Orig.). 1984. pap. 9.95 o.p. (ISBN 0-918439-02-7). Island Canoe.

Pulitzer Prizes 1987, Vol. 1. Ed. by Kendall Wills & Phyllis Quinn. 1988. 19.45 o.s.i. (ISBN 0-671-65956-1). S&S.

Pull of the Earth. Alfred Alcorn. 299p. 1985. 15.45 o.p. (ISBN 0-395-36804-9). HM.

Pullman. Julian Morel. (Illus.). 192p. (Orig.). 1983. 24.95 o.p. (ISBN 0-7153-8382-5). David & Charles.

Pulmonary & Antiallergic Drugs. Ed. by John P. Delvin. LC 84-11905. (Chemistry & Pharmacology of Drugs Ser. (1-406)). 400p. 1985. text ed. 75.00 o.p. (ISBN 0-471-87395-0, Pub. by Wiley-Interscience). Wiley.

Pulmonary Disease. Paul A Selecky. LC 82-1903. 358p. 1982. 42.95 o.p. (ISBN 0-471-09554-0, JW). Krieger.

Pulmonary Disease Reviews, Vol. 3. Ed. by Roger C. Bone. 758p. 1982. 65.00 o.p. (ISBN 0-471-86595-8). Wiley.

Pulmonary Diseases. N. K. Burki. (Medical Outline Ser.). 1982. pap. text ed. 29.50 o.p. (ISBN 0-87488-583-3). Med Exam.

Pulmonary Diseases & Disorders, 2 vols. Alfred P. Fishman. (Illus.). 1696p. 1980. Set. text ed. 225.00 o.p. (ISBN 0-07-021116-7). McGraw.

Pulmonary Diseases & Disorders: Update 1. Ed. by Alfred P. Fishman. (Illus.). 496p. 1982. text ed. 60.00 o.p. (ISBN 0-07-021119-1). McGraw.

Pulmonary Emphysema & Proteolysis. Ed. by Charles Mittman. (City of Hope Symposium Ser). 1972. 82.50 o.p. (ISBN 0-12-500750-7). Acad Pr.

Pulmonary Pathology & Aging, Vol. 1. Ed. by E. Beregi et al. LC 74-6167. 202p. 1974. text ed. 24.50x o.p. (ISBN 0-8422-7224-0). Irvington.

Pulmonary Pathology & Aging, Vol. 2. Ed. by Albert P. Seltzer et al. 150p. 1974. text ed. 24.50x o.p. (ISBN 0-8422-7225-9). Irvington.

Pulmonary Physiology. M. G. Levitzky. 1982. text ed. 16.95 o.p. (ISBN 0-07-037431-7). McGraw.

Pulmonary Reactions to Coal Dust: A Review of the U. S. Experience. Ed. by Marcus M. Key et al. (Environmental Science Ser.). 1971. 54.50 o.p. (ISBN 0-12-405950-3). Acad Pr.

Pulmonary Rehabilitation: Guidelines to Success. Ed. by John E. Hodgkin et al. 1984. text ed. 44.95 o.p. (ISBN 0-409-95061-0). Butterworth.

Pulp & Paper Industry Division Index to Technical Papers, 1960-1983. 80p. 1984. pap. text ed. 16.00x o.p. (ISBN 0-87664-804-9, 1804-9). Instru Soc.

Pulpit & Press. Mary Baker Eddy. 1984. pap. 6.00 o.p. (ISBN 0-87952-163-5). First Church.

Pulpwood Editor. Harold B. Hersey. LC 74-4841. 301p. 1974. Repr. of 1937 ed. lib. bdg. 35.00x o.p. (ISBN 0-8371-7490-2, HEPE). Greenwood.

Pulse & Switching Circuit Action. H. C. Veatch. 1971. text ed. 44.95 o.p. (ISBN 0-07-067386-1). McGraw.

Pulse Circuits. V. Frolkin. 390p. 1982. 9.45 o.p. (ISBN 0-8285-2467-X, Pub. by Mir Pubs USSR). Imported Pubns.

Pulse of Freedom: American Liberties 1920s-1970s. Alan Reitman. 228p. 1975. 12.50x o.p. (ISBN 0-393-05527-2). Norton.

Pulse Radiolysis. Ed. by M. Ebert. 1965. 54.50 o.p. (ISBN 0-12-228750-9). Acad Pr.

Pulsed Fusion Reactors: Proceedings of a Symposium, Erice-Trapani, Sicily, 1974. Ed. by R. S. Pease. 1975. pap. 190.00 o.p. (ISBN 0-08-019749-3). Pergamon.

Pulsed Neutron Scattering. Colin G. Windsor. LC 81-6363. 432p. 1981. 95.00x o.p. (ISBN 0-470-27131-0). Halsted Pr.

Pump Application Engineering. Tyler G. Hicks & T. Edwards. 1970. text ed. 51.50 o.p. (ISBN 0-07-028741-4). McGraw.

Pump Functional Testing. (Mechanical Inspection Ser.: Module 30-2). (Illus.). 50p. 1979. spiral bdg. 7.00x o.p. (ISBN 0-87683-124-2). GP Pub.

Pump Handbook. Igor J. Karassik & William C. Krutzch. 1000p. 1976. text ed. 66.75 o.p. (ISBN 0-07-033301-7). McGraw.

Pumping Data, Vol. 3. Trade & Technical Press Editors. 84p. 1969. 16.00x o.p. (ISBN 0-85461-033-2, Pub by Trade & Tech England). Gower Pub Co.

Pumping Iron. Charles Gaines & George Butler. (Illus.). 1974. 17.95 o.p. (ISBN 0-671-21898-0); pap. 9.95 o.p. (ISBN 0-671-21922-7). S&S.

Pumping of Liquids. F. A. Holland & F. S. Chapman. LC 66-29034. 414p. 1966. 25.50 o.p. (ISBN 0-442-15118-7). Krieger.

Pumping Plastic: The Jump Rope Fitness Plan. John Cassidy. (Illus.). 96p. (Orig.). 1983. pap. 9.95 incl. jump rope o.p. (ISBN 0-932592-06-6). Klutz Pr.

Punch! R. R. Knudson. (Illus.). 96p. (gr. 3-7). 1983. pap. 1.95 o.p. (ISBN 0-380-82164-8, 82164-8, Camelot). Avon.

Punch Book of Dogs. Ed. by Alan Coren. (Illus.). 160p. (gr. 10 up). 1985. pap. 4.95 o.p. (ISBN 0-88186-828-0). Parkwest Pubns.

Punch Book of Kids. Ed. by Alan Coren. (Illus.). 192p. (Orig.). (gr. 10 up). 1985. pap. 6.95 o.p. (ISBN 0-88186-826-4). Parkwest Pubns.

Punched-Card Data Processing System. 2nd ed. C. A. Clow & R. D. MacDonald. 1975. text ed. 9.00 o.p. (ISBN 0-07-011424-2). McGraw.

Punctuation Power. Imogene Forte. (Skill Stretchers Set). (Illus.). 32p. (gr. 2-5). 1981. pap. 3.95 o.p. (ISBN 0-86530-031-3, IP 31-3). Incentive Pubns.

Punctuation Through Proofreading. Barbara Gregorich & Therese F. Waldowski. LC 78-730056. (Illus.). 1977. pap. text ed. 159.00 o.s.i. (A325). Soc for Visual.

Punctured Poems. Richard Armour. LC 66-12564. (Illus.). 1971. pap. text ed. 1.95 o.p. (ISBN 0-07-002293-3). McGraw.

Punctured Thumb: Cactus & Other Succulents. George Ashley. LC 77-21212. (Illus.). 1977. pap. 4.95 o.s.i. (ISBN 0-89286-124-X, One Hund One Prods). Ortho.

Punished Peoples: The Deportation & Fate of Soviet Minorities at the End of the Second World War. Aleksandr M. Nekrich. 256p. 1981. pap. 5.95 o.p. (ISBN 0-393-00068-0). Norton.

Punishment: A Philosophical & Criminological Inquiry. Philip Bean. 224p. 1982. pap. 15.95x o.p. (ISBN 0-85520-478-8). Basil Blackwell.

Punishment & - or Treatment for Driving under the Influence of Alcohol & Other Drugs: Current Concepts, Experiences, & Prospective. (Illus.). 272p. (Orig.). 1985. pap. text ed. 68.50x o.p. (Pub. by Almqvist & Wiksell). Coronet Bks.

Punjab Painting. Rajeshwar Srivastava. (Illus.). 112p. 1983. text ed. 100.00 o.p. (ISBN 0-391-02560-0). Humanities.

Punjab: The Fatal Miscalculation. Ed. by Patwant Singh & Harji Malik. 252p. 1985. 12.00 o.p. (ISBN 0-318-23241-3, Pub. by Patwant Singh). Nataraj Bks.

Pupil Experience. John F. Schostak & Tom Logan. 258p. 1984. 26.50 o.p. (ISBN 0-7099-2391-0, Pub. by Croom Helm Ltd); pap. 14.50 o.p. (ISBN 0-7099-3332-0). Routledge Chapman & Hall.

Pupil Services: Development, Coordination, Administration. Dean L. Hummel & Charles W. Humes. 1984. text ed. (ISBN 0-02-358460-2). Macmillan.

Pupil Strategies: Explorations in the Sociology of the School. Ed. by Peter Woods. 219p. 1980. 28.00 o.p. (Pub. by Croom Helm Ltd); pap. 11.50 o.p. (ISBN 0-7099-0343-X). Routledge Chapman & Hall.

Puppet for a Corpse: A Luke Thanet Mystery. Dorothy Simpson. 192p. 1983. 11.95 o.s.i. (ISBN 0-684-17909-1, ScribT). Scribner.

Puppet Master. Liz Greene. (Arkana Fiction Ser.). 352p. 1987. pap. 10.95 o.p. (ISBN 0-317-54014-9, 30577, Pub. by Routledge UK). Routledge Chapman & Hall.

Puppeteer. Kathryn Lasky. LC 84-42987. (Illus.). 64p. (gr. 3-7). 1985. 10.95 o.s.i. (ISBN 0-02-751660-1). Macmillan.

Puppetry & Creative Dramatics in Storytelling. Connie Champlin. Ed. by Ann W. Schwalb. (Illus., Orig.). (YA) 1980. 17.95 o.p.; pap. 12.95 o.p. (ISBN 0-931044-03-0). Renfro Studios.

Puppets. Barbara Snook. (Illus.). 96p. 1985. Repr. of 1966 ed. 19.95 o.p. (ISBN 0-85219-618-0, Pub. by Batsford England). David & Charles.

Puppets & Moving Toys. Tony Hart. (Tony Hart Fun Bks.). (Illus.). 32p. (gr. 1-4). 1984. 5.95 o.p. (ISBN 0-7182-2951-7, Pub. by Kaye & Ward). David & Charles.

Puppets, Creative Ideas & Other Neat Things. Frances S. Walker. 64p. 1980. pap. 4.95 o.p. (ISBN 0-87534-216-7). Highlights.

Puppy Gets Around. Dennis Kyte. (Illus.). 1985. 3.95 o.s.i. (ISBN 0-671-54742-9, Little Simon). S&S.

Puppy in the Garden. Dennis Kyte. (Illus.). (gr. 1 up). 1985. 3.95 o.s.i. (ISBN 0-671-54743-7, Little Simon). S&S.

Puppy in Wonderland: And Other Tales. Enid Blyton. (Read for Fun Ser.). (Illus.). 64p. (gr. k-3). 1987. 6.95 o.p. (ISBN 0-09-167180-9, Pub. by Century Hutchinson). David & Charles.

Puppy Plays a Song. Dennis Kyte. (Illus.). (gr. 1 up). 1985. 3.95 o.s.i. (ISBN 0-671-54744-5, Little Simon). S&S.

Puppy Sees. Hargrave Hands. (First Look Nature Ser.). (Illus.). 12p. (ps). 1985. 2.95 o.p. (ISBN 0-448-10580-2, G&D). Putnam Pub Group.

Puppy Tidies Up. Dennis Kyte. (Illus.). (gr. 1 up). 1985. 3.95 o.s.i. (ISBN 0-671-54741-0, Little Simon). S&S.

Puppy's New Adventures: A B C. Illus. by Jean Rudegeair. (Saturday Morning Bks.). (Illus.). 22p. (ps-2). 1983. 2.50 o.p. (ISBN 0-89954-226-3). Antioch Pub Co.

Puppy's New Adventures: Hide & Seek. (Saturday Morning Bks.). (Illus.). 12p. (gr. 2-5). 1983. pap. 2.95 o.p. (ISBN 0-89954-228-X). Antioch Pub Co.

Puppy's New Adventures: The Puppy Who Wanted a Boy. Illus. by Jean Rudegeair. (Saturday Morning Bks.). (Illus.). 24p. (gr. 3-6). 1983. pap. 1.95 o.p. (ISBN 0-89954-227-1). Antioch Pub Co.

Pups, Dogs, Foxes & Wolves. Lee B. Hopkins. Ed. by Kathy Pacini. LC 79-253. (Illus.). (gr. 3-6). 1979. PLB 9.75 o.p. (ISBN 0-8075-6672-1). A Whitman.

Purcell. Jack A. Westrup. (Master Musicians: No. M139). (Illus.). 323p. 1975. pap. 7.95 o.p. (ISBN 0-8226-0720-4). Littlefield.

Purcell. rev. ed. Jack A. Westrup. (Master Musicians Ser.). (Illus.). 325p. 1980. 19.75x o.p. (ISBN 0-460-03177-5, Pub. by J. M. Dent England). Biblio Dist.

Purchase & Sale of Small Businesses: 1987 Cumulative Supplement. Lane. (Business Practice Library). 96p. 1987. pap. (ISBN 0-471-62497-7). Wiley.

Purchasing & Materials Management. 3rd ed. Lamar Lee, Jr. & Donald W. Dobler. 1977. text ed. 40.95 o.p. (ISBN 0-07-037027-3). McGraw.

Purchasing & Materials Management. 8th ed. Michael R. Leenders et al. 1985. 40.95x o.p. (ISBN 0-256-03029-4). Irwin.

Purchasing & Materials Management. N. K. Nair. 400p. 1984. pap. text ed. 18.95x o.p. (ISBN 0-7069-2719-2, Pub. by Vikas India); text ed. 32.50x o.p. (ISBN 0-7069-3006-1). Advent NY.

Purchasing & Supply Management. P. J. Baily. 1978. pap. 18.50x o.p. (ISBN 0-412-15690-3, NO. 6021, Pub. by Chapman & Hall England). Routledge Chapman & Hall.

Purchasing Guide for Banks. 68p. 1978. 24.00 o.p. (ISBN 0-317-33808-0, 652). Bank Admin Inst.

Purdue Thirty-Eighth Industrial Waste Conference: Proceedings. Ed. by John M. Bell. 1000p. 1984. text ed. 90.00 o.p. (ISBN 0-250-40639-X). Butterworth.

Purdue Thirty-Ninth Industrial Waste Conference. Ed. by John B. Bell. 1008p. 1985. text ed. 90.00 o.p. (ISBN 0-250-40640-3). Butterworth.

Pure & Simple. Marian Burros. 1979. pap. 3.50 o.s.i. (ISBN 0-425-04860-8). Berkley Pub.

Pure & the Impure. Colette. Tr. by Herma Briffault from Fr. 175p. 1975. 7.95 o.p. (ISBN 0-374-23920-7); pap. 6.25 o.p. (ISBN 0-374-50692-2). FS&G.

Pure Daughter. Debra Bruce. LC 83-4811. 80p. 1983. 9.95 o.p. (ISBN 0-938626-21-3); pap. 5.95 o.p. (ISBN 0-938626-22-1). U of Ark Pr.

Pure English of the Soil see Fate of French-E in English: The Plural of Nouns Ending in-th.

Pure Magic. Henry Gross. (Illus.). 1979. pap. 7.95 o.p. (SL 751, ScribT); encore ed. 4.95 o.p. (ISBN 0-684-16544-9). Scribner.

Pure Magic see Werefox.

Pure Mischief. Jo A. Algermissen. (Loveswept Ser.: No. 135). 192p. (Orig.). 1986. pap. 2.50 o.p. (ISBN 0-553-21717-8). Bantam.

Pure Nostalgia: Memories of Early Iowa. Ed. by Carl Hamilton. (Illus.). 1979. 11.95 o.p. (ISBN 0-8138-0975-4); pap. 11.95 o.p. (ISBN 0-8138-0976-2). Iowa St U Pr.

Pure Prairie League Songbook. 8.95 o.s.i. (ISBN 0-89524-127-7). Cherry Lane.

Pure Theory of International Trade & Distortions. Bharat R. Hazari. LC 78-9092. 206p. 1978. 42.95x o.p. (ISBN 0-470-26430-6). Halsted Pr.

Pure Thoughts. Eileen C. Wood. 1985. 5.95 o.p. (ISBN 0-533-06662-X). Vantage.

Purge: The Fate of French Collaborators after World War II. Herbert R. Lottman. LC 86-2370. (Illus.). 320p. 1986. 19.95 o.p. (ISBN 0-688-04940-0). Morrow.

Puri Paintings. J. P. Das. 200p. 1982. text ed. 55.00x o.p. (ISBN 0-391-02577-5). Humanities.

Purification of Laboratory Chemicals. 2nd ed. D. D. Perrin et al. LC 79-41708. 580p. 1980. 110.00 o.p. (ISBN 0-08-022961-1). Pergamon.

Purim. Howard Greenfeld. LC 82-3058. (Illus.). 32p. (gr. 2-9). 1983. 9.95 o.p. (ISBN 0-03-061478-3). H Holt & Co.

Purim Anthology. Ed. by Philip Goodman. (Illus.). 525p. 1949. 9.95 o.p. (ISBN 0-8276-0022-4, 248). JPS Phila.

Purinergic Receptors see Queues: Receptors & Recognition Series B.

Purines, Vol. 4. Jerusalem Symposia on Quantum Chemistry & Biochemistry Staff. Ed. by E. D. Bergmann & B. Pullman. 1972. 86.00 o.p. (ISBN 0-12-091060-8). Acad Pr.

Puritan Gentry: The Great Puritan Families of Early Stuart England. J. T. Cliffe. 300p. 1984. 25.00x o.p. (ISBN 0-7102-0007-2). Routledge Chapman & Hall.

Puritan in Voodoo-Land. Edna Taft. LC 73-174115. (Tower Bks). (Illus.). 414p. 1971. Repr. of 1938 ed. 43.00x o.p. (ISBN 0-8103-3919-6). Gale.

Puritan Migration to Connecticut: The Saga of the Seymour Family, 1129-1746. Malcolm Seymour. LC 82-548. (Illus.). 136p. 1982. 29.50 o.p. (ISBN 0-914016-85-7). Phoenix Pub.

Puritanism in America. Everett Emerson. (World Leaders Ser.). 1977. lib. bdg. 13.50 o.s.i. (ISBN 0-8057-7692-3, Twayne). G K Hall.

Puritans & Yankees: The Winthrop Dynasty of New England, 1630-1717. Richard S. Dunn. 1971. pap. 3.25x o.p. (ISBN 0-393-00597-6, Norton Lib). Norton.

Purple Bird. Yu. Kovol. 156p. 1985. pap. 2.99 o.p. (ISBN 0-8285-2797-0, Pub. by Raduga Pubs USSR). Imported Pubns.

Purple Cow. Gelett Burgess. 23p. 1966. leatherette 9.00 o.p. (ISBN 0-317-11646-0). Dawsons.

Purple Land. William H. Hudson. LC 79-50264. (Illus.). 360p. 1979. pap. 5.95 o.p. (ISBN 0-916870-21-9). Creative Arts Bk.

Purple Shit! Onspot - On Location in the Street. Philip L. Sherrod. 1986. write for info. o.s.i. Carrousel Pubns.

Purpose of a Christian School. Ed. by David Cummings. 1979. pap. 4.50 o.p. (ISBN 0-87552-157-6). Presby & Reformed.

Purposes of Higher Education. Huston Smith. LC 76-138130. 218p. 1971. Repr. of 1955 ed. lib. bdg. 22.50x o.p. (ISBN 0-8371-4698-4, SMHE). Greenwood.

Purposes of Pentecost. Derek Prince. (Foundation Ser.: Bk. IV). 1965-66. pap. 3.95 o.p. (ISBN 0-934920-03-6). Derek Prince.

Pursuing Justice in a Sinful World. Stephen V. Monsma. 100p. (Orig.). 1984. pap. 6.95 o.p. (ISBN 0-8028-0023-8). Eerdmans.

Pursuing the Pursuit-the Black Plight in White America: The Black Plight in White America. Jon Eckels. LC 77-77263. 1977. 5.50 o.p. (ISBN 0-682-48815-1, University). Exposition-Phoenix.

Pursuit of Diana. Allen Wold. (Children of the Lion Ser.: Bk. 5). 1985. lib. bdg. 12.95 o.p. (ISBN 0-8398-2868-3, Gregg). G K Hall.

Pursuit of Dignity: New Living Alternatives for the Elderly. Bert K. Smith. LC 76-48536. 1977. 12.50x o.p. (ISBN 0-8070-2736-7); pap. 5.95 o.p. (ISBN 0-8070-2737-5, BP587). Beacon Pr.

Pursuit of Happiness. Mervyn Jones. 1977. pap. 1.75 o.p. (ISBN 0-380-01660-5, 33282). Avon.

Pursuit of Holiness. Jerry Bridges. (Christian Character Library). 158p. 1985. hdbk. 8.95 o.p. (ISBN 0-89109-467-9). NavPress.

Pursuit of Isolationism in the United States Senate from Versailles to Pearl Harbor. Thomas N. Guinsburg. LC 80-8478. (Modern American History Ser.). 339p. 1982. lib. bdg. 44.00 o.p. (ISBN 0-8240-4854-7). Garland Pub.

Pursuit of National Interest Through Neutralism: India's Foreign Policy in the Nehru Era. Sauripad Bhattacharya. 1978. 15.00x o.p. (ISBN 0-8364-0139-5). South Asia Bks.

Pursuit of Perfection: A Life of Maggie Teyte. Garry O'Connor. LC 78-20366. (Illus.). 1979. 15.95 o.p. (ISBN 0-689-10964-4, Atheneum). Macmillan.

Pursuit of Science in Revolutionary America, 1735-1789. Brooke Hindle. (Illus.). 432p. 1974. pap. 3.95 o.p. (ISBN 0-393-00710-3, Norton Lib). Norton.

Pursuit of the Present: Journal of Twenty Years in the Gurdjieff Work. Henri Thomasson. Tr. by Rina Hands. 1980. 12.95 o.p. (ISBN 0-89756-003-5). Two Rivers.

Pursuit of Wisdom. F. Laurier Roderigue. 272p. 1984. 12.50 o.p. (ISBN 0-682-40139-0). Exposition-Phoenix.

Pursuivant of Arms; or, Heraldry Founded upon Facts. James R. Planche. LC 72-10610. (Illus.). 300p. 1973. Repr. of 1874 ed. 35.00x o.p. (ISBN 0-8103-3171-3). Gale.

Pushbutton Butterfly. Kin Platt. 1979. pap. 1.95 o.p. (ISBN 0-441-65215-8). Ace Bks.

Pushcart Prize I: Best of the Small Presses. Ed. by Bill Henderson. 1976. pap. 6.95 o.p. (ISBN 0-380-00752-5, 47407-7). Avon.

Pushcart Prize II: Best of the Small Presses. Ed. by Bill Henderson. 1978. pap. 5.95 o.p. (ISBN 0-380-01895-0, 37275-4). Avon.

Pushcart Prize III: Best of the Small Presses. Ed. by Bill Henderson. 1979. pap. 6.95 o.p. (ISBN 0-380-43059-2). Avon.

Pushcart Prize IV: Best of the Small Presses. Ed. by Bill Henderson. 600p. 1980. pap. 7.95 o.p. (ISBN 0-380-48827-2, 48827-2). Avon.

Pushcart Prize IX: Best of the Small Presses. Ed. by Bill Henderson. 592p. 1985. pap. 9.95 o.p. (ISBN 0-380-69915-X). Avon.

Pushcart Prize V: Best of the Small Presses. Ed. by Bill Henderson. 1981. pap. 8.95 o.p. (ISBN 0-380-53041-4, 53041-4). Avon.

Pushcart Prize VI: Best of the Small Presses. Ed. by Bill Henderson. 544p. 1982. pap. 9.95 o.p. (ISBN 0-380-57646-5, 57646-5). Avon.

Pushcart Prize VII: The Best of the Small Presses. Ed. by Bill Henderson. 576p. 1983. pap. 8.95 o.p. (ISBN 0-380-62851-1, 62851-1). Avon.

Pushcart Prize VIII: The Best of the Small Presses. Ed. by Bill Henderson. 528p. 1984. pap. 9.95 o.p. (ISBN 0-380-67868-3, 67868). Avon.

Pushcart Prize XII: Best of the Small Presses, 1987-88 Edition. Ed. by Bill Henderson. LC 76-58675. 600p. 1987. 26.50 o.p. (ISBN 0-317-64444-0). Pushcart Pr.

Pusher. Ed McBain. (Large Print Bks., Nightingale Ser.). 266p. 1987. pap. 11.95x o.p. (ISBN 0-8161-4258-0, Large Print Bks). G K Hall.

Pussycats Need Love, Too. George Booth. 128p. 1981. pap. 6.95 o.p. (ISBN 0-380-55533-6, 55533-6). Avon.

Put a Little Starch in Your Faith. Otis Bernard. 150p. 1980. pap. 4.95 o.p. (ISBN 0-89221-095-8). New Leaf.

Put Earned Value into Your Management Control System. Quentin W. Fleming. LC 83-3054. (Illus.). 380p. (Orig.). 1983. 35.95x o.p. (ISBN 0-942280-04-0); pap. 22.00x o.p. (ISBN 0-942280-03-2). Pub Horizons.

Put It in Writing. Arthur Daigon et al. 208p. 1978. pap. text ed. 9.00 o.p. (ISBN 0-15-573822-4, HC). HarBraceJ.

Put Ka Ostravenju Demokratije. Slavoljub Stefanovic. 1980. 8.00 o.p. (ISBN 0-682-49549-2). Exposition-Phoenix.

Put the Law on Your Side: Strategies for Winning the Legal Game. Bertram Harnett. LC 84-25196. 384p. 1985. 17.95 o.p. (ISBN 0-15-175352-0). HarBraceJ.

Putnam Division. Daniel Gallo & Frederick Kramer. 1981. pap. 8.95 o.p. (ISBN 0-915276-29-1). Quadrant Pr.

Putting It All Together: A Guide to Strategic Thinking. William E. Rothschild. LC 76-10535. (Illus.). 272p. 1976. 17.95 o.p. (ISBN 0-8144-5405-4). AMACOM.

Putting It All Together: A Guide to Strategic Thinking. William E. Rothschild. LC 76-10535. 272p. 1981. pap. 7.95 o.p. (ISBN 0-8144-7555-8). AMACOM.

Putting Management Theories to Work. Marion S. Kellogg. LC 68-5675. 286p. 1968. 17.00x o.p. (ISBN 0-87201-463-0). Gulf Pub.

Putting up with Sherwood. Ellen Matthews. LC 80-17574. (Illus.). 138p. (gr. 3-5). 1980. 9.95 o.s.i. (ISBN 0-664-32672-2, Westminster). Westminster John Knox.

Putting Your Faith on the Line. Hubert Mitchell. (Orig.). 1981. pap. 5.95 o.p. (ISBN 0-89840-027-9). Heres Life.

Putt's Law & the Successful Technocrat. A. Putt. (Illus.). 175p. 1981. 9.25 o.p. (ISBN 0-682-49702-9, Banner). Exposition-Phoenix.

Puzzle for Fiends. Patrick Quentin. 1979. pap. 2.25 o.p. (ISBN 0-380-45518-8, 45518-8). Avon.

Puzzle King's Baffler. Craig T. Norback. (Orig.). 1982. pap. 6.95 o.p. (ISBN 0-440-57032-8, Dell Trade Pbks). Dell.

Puzzle Master. Time-Life Books Editors. (Understanding Computers Ser.). 128p. (YA) (gr. 7 up). 1988. 19.93 o.p.; lib. bdg. 23.93 o.p. Time-Life.

Puzzle Palace: A Report on America's Most Secret Agency. James Bamford. (Illus.). 436p. 1982. 16.45 o.p. (ISBN 0-395-31286-8). HM.

Puzzlers Gamebook. John Hall. (gr. 4 up). 1974. pap. 2.95 o.p. (ISBN 0-912300-50-7). Troubador Pr.

Puzzles for Geniuses, No. I. David Pritchard. 160p. 1984. 12.95 o.p. (ISBN 0-13-744608-X); pap. 5.95 o.p. (ISBN 0-13-744632-2). P-H.

Puzzles for Geniuses, No. II. David Pritchard. 160p. 1984. 12.95 o.p. (ISBN 0-13-744616-0); pap. 5.95 o.p. (ISBN 0-13-744624-1). P-H.

Pylos Four Hundred Twenty-Five B. C. Thucydides. Ed. by J. Wilson. 49.00 o.s.i. (ISBN 0-86516-111-9); pap. 16.50 o.s.i. (ISBN 0-86516-112-7). Bolchazy Carducci.

Pyongyang Between Peking & Moscow: North Korea's Involvement in the Sino-Soviet Dispute, 1958-1975. Chin O. Chung. LC 76-44261. 240p. 1978. 17.95 o.s.i. (ISBN 0-8173-4728-3). U of Ala Pr.

Pyramids. John Weeks. LC 76-22457. (Cambridge Topic Bks.). (Illus.). (gr. 5-10). 1977. PLB 8.95 o.p. (ISBN 0-8225-1209-2). Lerner Pubns.

Pyramids: Tombs for Eternity. Mildred M. Pace. (Illus.). 192p. (gr. 7-10). 1981. text ed. 10.95 o.p. (ISBN 0-07-048054-0). McGraw.

Pyrazines, Vol. 41. G. B. Barlin. (Chemistry of Heterocyclic Compounds, A Series of Monographs). 712p. 1982. 203.50 o.p. (ISBN 0-471-38119-5, Pub. by Wiley-Interscience). Wiley.

Pyrethrum: The Natural Insecticide. Ed. by John E. Casida. 1973. 49.50 o.p. (ISBN 0-12-162950-3). Acad Pr.

Pyridazines, Vol. 28. Ed. by Raymond N. Castle. LC 72-13270. (Hetercyclic Compounds Ser.). 905p. 1973. 109.00 o.p. (ISBN 0-471-38213-2, JW). Krieger.

Pyridine Nucleotide Coenzymes. Ed. by Johannes Everse et al. 416p. 1982. 78.50 o.p. (ISBN 0-12-244750-6). Acad Pr.

Pythagoras: Lover of Wisdom. Ward Rutherford. 128p. 1984. pap. 13.95 o.p. (ISBN 0-85030-379-6, Pub. by Thorsons UK). Weiser.

Pzyche. Amanda Hemingway. 288p. 1983. 13.95 o.p. (ISBN 0-87795-479-8, Arbor Hse). Morrow.

Q

Q & A. Edwin Torres. 1978. pap. 1.95 o.p. (ISBN 0-380-01862-4, 36590). Avon.

Q Clearance. Peter Benchley. LC 85-28092. 336p. 1986. 16.45 o.s.i. (ISBN 0-394-55360-8). Random.

Q Machines. R. W. Motley. 1975. 51.50 o.p. (ISBN 0-12-508650-4). Acad Pr.

Qabala Trilogy. Carlo Suares. Tr. by Micheline Stuart & Vincent Stuart. LC 85-8179. 565p. 1985. 17.95 o.s.i. (ISBN 0-87773-337-6, 74220-6). Shambhala Pubns.

Qatar. 2nd. ed. Middle East Economic Digest Staff. Ed. by John Whelan. (MEED Practical Guides Ser.). (Illus.). 176p. (Orig.). 1985. pap. 16.95x o.p. (ISBN 0-9505211-9-1). Lynne Rienner.

Qatar: Energy & Development. Ragaei E. Mallakh. LC 84-29317. 184p. 1985. 31.00 o.p. (ISBN 0-7099-0955-1, Pub. by Croom Helm Ltd). Routledge Chapman & Hall.

QB Seven. Leon Uris. LC 70-129894. 14.95 o.s.i. (ISBN 0-385-03452-0). Doubleday.

QE Two Is Missing. Harry Harrison. 1982. pap. 2.95 o.p. (ISBN 0-686-80906-8). Dell.

QF-Three & QF-One Rings. H. Tachikawa. Ed. by C. M. Ringel. (Lecture Notes in Mathematics: Vol. 351). 172p. 1973. pap. 19.00 o.p. (ISBN 0-387-06501-6). Springer-Verlag.

QRB Special Edition - Drug & Antibiotic Review: Effect on Quality & Cost. 90p. 1984. pap. 25.00 o.s.i. (ISBN 0-86688-074-7). Joint Comm Hlthcare.

QRB Tenth Anniversary Publication. 300p. 1984. pap. 25.00 o.s.i. (ISBN 0-86688-087-9, QRB-84-12). Joint Comm Hlthcare.

Q's Legacy. Helene Hanff. 192p. 1985. 14.45i o.p. (ISBN 0-316-34340-4). Little.

QSL Adress Book see KODAK Complete Darkroom DATAGUIDE: Processing & Printing Information for Black-&-White & Color.

Quacks of Old London. C. J. Thompson. LC 75-89296. (Tower Bks). (Illus.). 364p. 1971. Repr. of 1929 ed. 43.00x o.p. (ISBN 0-8103-3212-4). Gale.

Quacky & the Crazy Curve Ball. Walter Oleksy. 1981. text ed. 9.95 o.p. (ISBN 0-07-047752-3). McGraw.

Quacky & the Haunted Amusement Park. Walter Oleksy. (gr. 6-9). 1981. text ed. 8.95 o.p. (ISBN 0-07-047753-1). McGraw.

Quadram Connection. Robert J. Traister. (Illus.). 256p. (Orig.). 1985. 23.95 o.p. (ISBN 0-8306-0956-3, 1956); pap. 15.60 o.p. (ISBN 0-8306-1956-9). TAB Bks.

Quadrangle: The History of Fort Sam Houston. Eldon B. Cagle. (Illus.). 200p. 1985. 14.95 o.p. (ISBN 0-89015-463-5). Eakin Pr.

Quadrant: Twenty-Five Years. Ed. by Peter Coleman & Lee Shrubb. LC 82-19998. 568p. 1983. 27.50 o.p. (ISBN 0-7022-1820-0). U of Queensland Pr.

Quadratic Forms & Matrices: An Introductory Approach. N. V. Yefimov. (Eng.). 1964. pap. 19.50 o.p. (ISBN 0-12-769956-2). Acad Pr.

Quadrifariam. Frank Samperi. 1973. 15.00 o.p. (ISBN 0-685-78988-8, Pub. by Mushinsha Bks). Small Pr Dist.

Quadriphobia. Alan Ryan. LC 85-20451. (Science Fiction Ser.). 192p. 1986. 12.95 o.p. (ISBN 0-385-19839-6). Doubleday.

Quadrus & Goliath. Alvin L. Ben-Moring. LC 75-43633. (Illus.). (gr. 6-9). 1976. 6.95 o.s.i. (ISBN 0-664-32590-4, Westminster). Westminster John Knox.

Quail Can't Decide. Jacquelyn Reinach. LC 77-7249. (Sweet Pickle Ser.). (ps-2). 1977. 2.95 o.p. (ISBN 0-03-021451-3). H Holt & Co.

Quaint Furniture: Stickley Bros. (Illus.). 88p. 1985. pap. 5.95 o.p. (ISBN 0-87905-412-3). Gibbs Smith Pub.

Quaker Struggle for the Rights of Women. pap. 0.75 o.p. (ISBN 0-686-95360-6). Am Fr Serv Comm.

Quakers in Peace & War. Margaret E. Hirst. LC 70-147671. (Library of War & Peace; Relig. & Ethical Positions on War Ser.). lib. bdg. 46.00 o.p. (ISBN 0-8240-0429-9). Garland Pub.

Quaking Lands. Robert E. Vardeman. (Jade Demons Ser. No. 1). 208p. 1985. pap. 2.95 o.p. (ISBN 0-380-89518-8). Avon.

Qualified Plans which Invest in Employer Securities. William N. Kravitz. LC 84-60673. 288p. 45.00 o.p. PLI.

Qualified Products List & Sources, No. 66. Global Engineering Documents Staff. 304p. 1987. perfect binding 59.95 o.s.i. (ISBN 0-912702-33-8). Global Eng.

Qualified Retirement & Other Employee Benefit Plans, 1988. Michael J. Canan. (Handbook Ser.). (Illus.). 983p. 1988. pap. text ed. (ISBN 0-314-77713-X). West Pub.

Qualified Retirement Plans. Michael J. Canan & David R. Baker. (Handbook Ser.). 730p. 1986. write for info. o.p. (ISBN 0-314-28486-9). West Pub.

Qualitative Data Analysis for Educational Research: A Guide to Uses of Systemic Networks. Joan Bliss et al. (Illus.). 224p. 1983. 29.00 o.p. (ISBN 0-7099-0698-6, Pub. by Croom Helm Ltd). Routledge Chapman & Hall.

Qualitative Organic Microanalysis. Frank L. Schneider. 1964. 85.50 o.p. (ISBN 0-12-627750-8). Acad Pr.

Qualitative Organic Microanalysis: Cognition & Recognition of Carbon Compounds. F. Schneider. (Aus Dem Gebiet der Qualitativen Mikroanalyse). (Illus.). 1964. 57.90 o.p. (ISBN 0-387-80686-5). Springer-Verlag.

Qualitative Simulation & Causal Models. Benjamin Kuipers & Brian Williams. (Illus.). 85p. 1988. pap. text ed. 12.00 o.p. (ISBN 0-929280-07-5). Amer Artificial.

Qualitative Theory of Dynamic Systems of Second Order. A. A. Andronow et al. 550p. 1973. text ed. 110.00 o.p. (ISBN 0-7065-1292-8, Pub. by Keter Pub Jerusalem). Coronet Bks.

Qualities & Quantities in the Laboratory. Richard N. McCurdy & Howard M. Greene. 1975. pap. text ed. 6.95 o.p. (ISBN 0-15-574102-0, HC). HarBraceJ.

Qualities & Quantities: Preparation for College Chemistry. Richard M. McCurdy. 448p. 1975. text ed. 17.95 o.p. (ISBN 0-15-574100-4, HC). HarBraceJ.

Qualities of Community Life: Measurement of Environment & Behavior in an American & an English Town. Roger G. Barker & Phil Schoggen. LC 72-13601. (Social & Behavioral Science Ser.). 1973. 54.95x o.p. (ISBN 0-87589-172-1). Jossey-Bass.

Quality & Profit in Building Design. Ed. by Peter S. Brandon & James A Powell. 400p. 1985. 52.00 o.p. (ISBN 0-419-13390-9, NO. 9191, Pub. by E & FN Spon England). Routledge Chapman & Hall.

Quality Assurance-Applications-Components, Vol. IV. Ed. by H. H. Waite. 601p. 1976. 50.00 o.p. (ISBN 0-317-33603-7, G00101); members 25.00 o.p. (ISBN 0-317-33604-5). ASME.

Quality Assurance for Internal Auditing. Urton Anderson & Richard Holman. (Illus.). 176p. 1983. text ed. 60.00 o.p. (ISBN 0-89413-098-6, 510). Inst Inter Aud.

Quality Assurance in Air Pollution Measurement. Air Pollution Control Association Specialty Conference, New Orleans, 1979. 486p. 1979. 24.00 o.p. (ISBN 0-318-12271-5, SP-27); members 18.00 o.p. (ISBN 0-318-12272-3). Air & Waste.

Quality Assurance in Clinical Chemistry. 2nd ed. Whitehead. 1988. (ISBN 0-471-86329-7). Churchill.

Quality Assurance in Health Care. Ed. by Richard H. Egdahl & Paul M. Gertman. LC 76-15770. 372p. 1976. 46.95 o.p. (ISBN 0-912862-23-8). Aspen Pub.

Quality Assurance of Pharmaceuticals Manufactured in the Hospital: Proceedings of the International Symposium on Drug Quality Assurance in the Hospital, Toronto, Ontario, Canada, June 10-14, 1984. Ed. by Ann Warbick-Cerone & Linda G. Johnston. (Illus.). 240p. 1985. pap. 73.00 o.p. (ISBN 0-08-025414-4, Pub. by Aberdeen Scotland). Pergamon.

Quality Assurance: Proceedings, American Nuclear Society Executive Conference, San Diego, 23-26 April 1976. 174p. softcover 14.00 o.p. (ISBN 0-317-33075-6, 650001). Am Nuclear Soc.

Quality Circle Handbook for Financial Institutions. 3rd ed. Donald L. Dewar. (Illus.). 496p. 1982. pap. 69.00 o.p. (ISBN 0-937670-14-6). Quality Circle.

Quality Circle Handbook for Health Care Facilities. 2nd ed. Donald L. Dewar. (Illus.). 496p. (Orig.). 1982. pap. 60.00 o.p. (ISBN 0-937670-07-3). Quality Circle.

Quality Circle Leader Manual & Instructional Guide for Financial Institutions. 3rd ed. Donald L. Dewar. (Illus.). 235p. (Orig.). 1982. 18.50 o.p. (ISBN 0-937670-12-X). Quality Circle.

Quality Circle Leader Manual & Instructional Guide for Health Care Facilities. 2nd ed. (Illus.). 235p. (Orig.). 1982. pap. 18.50 o.p. (ISBN 0-937670-06-5). Quality Circle.

Quality Circle Member Manual for Financial Institutions. 3rd ed. Donald L. Dewar. (Illus.). 268p. 1982. pap. 12.75 o.p. (ISBN 0-937670-13-8). Quality Circle.

Quality Circle Member Manual for Health Care Facilities. 2nd ed. Donald L. Dewar. (Illus.). 268p. (Orig.). 1982. pap. 12.75 o.p. (ISBN 0-937670-05-7). Quality Circle.

Quality Circle: What You Should Know about It - Financial Institutions. 3rd ed. Donald L. Dewar. (Illus.). 29p. 1982. pap. 1.15 o.p. (ISBN 0-937670-17-0). Quality Circle.

Quality Circle: What You Should Know about It - Health Care Facilities. 2nd ed. Donald L. Dewar. (Illus.). 29p. (Orig.). 1982. pap. 1.15 o.p. (ISBN 0-937670-16-2). Quality Circle.

Quality Circles. Philip C. Thompson. 16.95 o.p. (ISBN 0-8144-5731-2). AMACOM.

Quality Circles at Work & Spreading in Utility Systems of Today. Jeffrey D. Dewar. (Illus.). 64p. 1984. pap. 0.95 o.p. (ISBN 0-937670-31-6). Quality Circle.

Quality Circles Guidebook: How to Install Quality Circles in Your Organization. Donald L. Dewar. 81p. (Orig.). 1982. pap. 14.00 o.p. (ISBN 0-937670-28-6). Quality Circle.

Quality Circles: Implications for Training. Carl L. Harshman. 74p. cancelled o.s.i. (ISBN 0-318-22184-5, IN243). Natl Ctr Res Voc Ed.

Quality Control for the Food Industry, Vol. 1: Fundamentals. 3rd ed. Amihud Kramer & Bernard A. Twigg. (Illus.). 1970. 39.95 o.p. (ISBN 0-87055-072-1). AVI.

Quality Control Handbook. rev. 3rd ed. Joseph M. Juran. 1600p. 1974. text ed. 85.00 o.p. (ISBN 0-07-033175-8). McGraw.

Quality Control in Haematology. Ed. by S. M. Lewis & J. Coster. 1976. 51.50 o.p. (ISBN 0-12-446850-0). Acad Pr.

Quality Criteria for Water Reuse. National Research Council Board on Toxicology & Environmental Health Hazards. 1982. pap. text ed. 11.25x o.p. (ISBN 0-309-03326-8). Natl Acad Pr.

Quality in Liberal Learning: Curricular Innovations in Higher Education. Katherine S. Guroff. 272p. (Orig.). 1981. pap. 7.00 o.s.i. (ISBN 0-911696-09-1). Assn Am Coll.

Quality Interviewing. Robert Maddux. 1988. 6.95 o.p. (115). Am Bartenders.

Quality Living in a Complicated Age. Stephen Bly. LC 84-47803. 170p. (Orig.). 1984. 3.95 o.p. (ISBN 0-89840-071-6). Heres Life.

Quality of Irrigation Water. I. Shainberg & J. D. Oster. 1983. 16.25 o.s.i. (ISBN 0-08-023822-X); pap. 16.25 o.s.i. (ISBN 0-08-030768-X). Pergamon.

Quality of Mercy: Cambodia, Holocaust, & Modern Conscience. William Shawcross. (Illus.). 320p. 1984. 19.45 o.p. (ISBN 0-671-44022-5). S&S.

Quality of Mercy: Cambodia, Holocaust & Modern Conscience. rev. & updated ed. William Shawcross. 1985. pap. 9.95 o.s.i. (ISBN 0-671-60640-9, Touchstone Bks). S&S.

Quality of Pig Meat: Progress of Food & Nutrition Science. Mogens Jul & Peter Zeuthen. (Vol. 4, No. 6). 80p. 1981. pap. 24.00 o.p. (ISBN 0-08-026831-5). Pergamon.

Quality of Telephone Service in the U. S. The Role of Regulation. 60.00 o.p. (ISBN 0-686-32968-6). Info Gatekeepers.

Quality of the Informant. Gerald Petievich. 1985. 14.95 o.p. (ISBN 0-87795-619-7, Arbor Hse). Morrow.

Quality of Working Life in the United States: Problems & Prospects. (Center for Quality of Working Life Position Paper Ser.: No. 1). 1976. 3.50 o.p. (ISBN 0-89215-071-8). U Cal LA Indus Rel.

Quality of Worklife Programs & Organizational Structure & Change: The Case of Parkside Hospital. Martin D. Hanlon et al. LC 84-13189. (Wiley Series on Organizational Assessment & Change: 1-430). 256p. 1985. text ed. 39.95X o.p. (ISBN 0-471-88766-8, Pub. by Wiley-Interscience). Wiley.

Quality-Productivity Connection in Service-Sector Management. John C. Shaw. 1978. 21.95 o.p. (ISBN 0-442-27542-0). Van Nos Reinhold.

Quandaries & Virtues: Against Reductivism in Ethics. Edmund L. Pincoffs. LC 86-13352. x, 190p. 1988. pap. 9.95x o.p. (ISBN 0-7006-0363-8). U Pr of KS.

Quantification in American History: Theory & Research. Ed. by Robert P. Swierenga. LC 76-108827. (Orig.). 1970. pap. text ed. 5.95x o.p. (ISBN 0-689-70238-8, 161, Atheneum). Macmillan.

Quantifying the Benefits of Separating Pedestrians & Vehicles. (National Cooperative Highway Research Program Report). 127p. 1978. 7.00 o.p. (ISBN 0-317-36102-3). Transport Res Bd.

Quantitation, Modeling & Control in Aneasthesia. Horst Stoekel. (Illus.). 324p. 1985. text ed. 34.95 o.p. (ISBN 0-86577-209-6). Thieme Med Pubs.

Quantitative Acid-Base Physiology. Poul Kildeberg. LC 80-81619. (Illus.). 142p. 1981. 27.50 o.p. (ISBN 0-89640-048-4). Igaku-Shoin.

Quantitative Analysis. Charles T. Kenner & Kenneth W. Busch. 1979. text ed. write for info. o.p. (ISBN 0-02-362490-6). Macmillan.

Quantitative Analysis by NMR Spectroscopy. F. Kasler. 1973. 43.00 o.p. (ISBN 0-12-400850-X). Acad Pr.

Quantitative Analysis for Management. 2nd ed. Render & Stair. 1985. 30.00 o.p. (ISBN 0-205-08335-8, 108335). Allyn.

Quantitative Analysis of Drugs. Garrett. (Illus.). 672p. 1955. (ISBN 0-8022-0564-X). Philos Lib.

Quantitative & Qualitative Games. A. Blaquiere et al. (Mathematics in Science & Engineering Ser.: Vol. 58). 1969. 49.50 o.p. (ISBN 0-12-104360-6). Acad Pr.

Quantitative & Theoretical Geography. Ed. by A. Kilchenman. 100p. 1975. pap. 23.00 o.p. (ISBN 0-08-019680-2). Pergamon.

Quantitative Aspects of Risk Assessment in Chemical Carcinogenesis. Ed. by J. Clemmensen. (Illus.). 350p. 1980. pap. 39.00 o.p. (ISBN 0-387-09584-5). Springer-Verlag.

Quantitative Biology of Metabolism: Proceedings of the International Symposium on Models of Metabolism, Metabolic Parameters, Damageto Metabolism, Metabolic Control, 3rd, Anstalt Helgoland, 1967. International Symposium Biologische Staff. Ed. by A. Locker. LC 68-55620. (Illus.). 1969. pap. 40.00 o.p. (ISBN 0-387-04301-2). Springer-Verlag.

Quantitative Construction Management: Uses of Linear Optimization. Robert M. Stark & Robert H. Mayer. LC 83-6907. (Construction Management & Engineering Ser.). 162p. 1983. 37.50x o.p. (ISBN 0-471-86959-7, 1-102, Pub. by Wiley-Interscience). Wiley.

Quantitative Cytochemistry & Its Application. Ed. by J. R. Pattison et al. 1979. 54.00 o.p. (ISBN 0-12-546750-8). Acad Pr.

Quantitative Economic Policy & Planning: Theory & Models of Economic Control. new ed. Nicolas Spulber & Ira Horowitz. (Illus.). 550p. 1976. text ed. 18.95x o.p. (ISBN 0-393-09181-3). Norton.

Quantitative Electron Microprobe Analysis. R. Theisen. (Illus.). 1965. 23.00 o.p. (ISBN 0-387-03415-3). Springer-Verlag.

Quantitative Evaluation & Prediction of Donor-Acceptor Interactions see Coordinative Interactions.

Quantitative Geography in Britain: Retrospect & Prospect. Ed. by Neil Wrigley & Robert J. Bennett. 448p. 1981. 65.00x o.p. (ISBN 0-7100-0731-0). Routledge Chapman & Hall.

Quantitative Imagery in the Bio-Medical Sciences, 2: Proceedings, Vol. 40. Society of Photo-Optical Instrumentation Engineers Staff. Ed. by R. E. Herron. 28.00 o.p. (ISBN 0-89252-052-3). SPIE.

Quantitative Industrial Hygiene. Harry J. Beaulieu & Roy M. Buchan. 1981. lib. bdg. 19.00 o.p. (ISBN 0-8240-7180-8). Garland Pub.

Quantitative Laboratory Experiments in General Chemistry. Francis Collier et al. LC 75-26087. (Illus.). 288p. 1976. pap. 18.95 o.p. (ISBN 0-395-18982-9). HM.

Quantitative Methods for Business Decisions. 2nd ed. Lawrence L. Lapin. 774p. 1981. text ed. 28.95 o.p. (ISBN 0-15-574319-8, HC). HarbraceJ.

Quantitative Methods for Business Decisions, with Cases. 3rd ed. Lawrence L. Lapin. 780p. 1985. text ed. 29.00x o.p. (ISBN 0-15-574324-4, HC). HarBraceJ.

Quantitative Methods for Business Decisions: With Cases. 2nd ed. Lawrence L. Lapin. 1976. 22.95 o.p. (ISBN 0-15-574317-1). HarbraceJ.

Quantitative Methods for Decision Making in Business. Richard E. Trueman. LC 80-65810. 736p. 1981. text ed. 38.95x o.p. (ISBN 0-03-051356-1). Dryden Pr.

Quantitative Methods for Management. Ross H. Johnson & Paul R. Winn. LC 75-25239. (Illus.). 448p. 1976. text ed. 31.50 o.p. (ISBN 0-395-20633-2). HM.

Quantitative Methods for Managers. A. I. Godfrey. 1977. pap. text ed. 22.50x o.p. (ISBN 0-7131-3349-X). Trans-Atl Phila.

Quantitative Methods in Accounting. Wayne E. Leininger. LC 79-66015. 353p. 1980. text ed. 23.95x o.p. PWS-Kent Pub.

Quantitative Methods in Business. Curwin & Slater. 1985. pap. 25.95 o.p. (ISBN 0-442-30640-7). Van Nos Reinhold.

Quantitative Methods in Economics. Geoffrey Lewis. (Illus.). 1978. pap. 19.00x o.p. (ISBN 0-424-00038-5, Pub. by Sydney U Pr). Intl Spec Bk.

Quantitative Methods in Geography: An Introduction to Spatial Analysis. Peter J. Taylor. LC 75-26097. (Illus.). 384p. 1977. text ed. 26.50 o.p. (ISBN 0-395-18699-4). HM.

Quantitative Models for Business Decisions. No Kyoon Kwak & Stephen A. DeLurgio. LC 78-27175. (Illus.). 1979. text ed. (ISBN 0-87872-215-7, Duxbury Pr). PWS-Kent Pub.

Quantitative Models for Management. K. Roscoe Davis & Patrick G. McKeown. 735p. 1981. text ed. 28.95x o.p. (ISBN 0-534-00935-2). PWS-Kent Pub.

Quantitative Obstetrical Ultrasonography. Deter L. Russell et al. LC 86-3462. 377p. 1986. 45.00 o.p. (ISBN 0-471-79994-7). Wiley.

Quantitative Organic Analysis Via Functional Groups. 4th ed. Sidney Siggia & J. Gordon Hanna. LC 78-5940. 883p. 1979. 103.00 o.p. (ISBN 0-471-03273-5, Pub. by Wiley-Interscience). Wiley.

Quantitative Organic Microanalysis. 2nd ed. Al Steyermark. 1961. 77.00 o.p. (ISBN 0-12-670450-3). Acad Pr.

Quantitative Planning & Control: In Honor of William W. Cooper. Ed. by Yuji Ijiri & Andrew B. Whinston. LC 78-22529. 1979. 59.00 o.p. (ISBN 0-12-370450-2). Acad Pr.

Quantitative-Qualitative Measure of Information. CISM (International Center for Mechanical Sciences), Department of Automation & Information Staff. Ed. by G. Longo. (CISM Publications: No. 138). (Illus.). 51p. 1973. pap. 8.80 o.p. (ISBN 0-387-81182-6). Springer-Verlag.

Quantitative Research in Public Administration & Policy Analysis: A Methodologically Annotated Bibliography. T. R. Carr et al. 1977. 4.50 o.p. (ISBN 0-686-22970-3). Univ OK Gov Res.

Quantitative Stratigraphic Correlation: Proceedings of the 6th Geochautauqua, Syracuse University, October 1977. Ed. by D. F. Merriam. (Illus.). 112p. 1979. pap. 50.00 o.p. (ISBN 0-08-023979-X). Pergamon.

Quantitative Studies in Life Science. S. J. Poti. 250p. 1983. text ed. 55.00x o.p. (ISBN 0-7069-1247-0, Pub by Vikas India). Advent NY.

Quantitative Techniques for Management Decisions. Frank S. McLaughlin & Robert C. Pickhardt. LC 78-69586. (Illus.). 1979. text ed. 32.95 o.p. (ISBN 0-395-26669-6). HM.

Quantitative Techniques for Managerial Decision Making: Concepts, Illustrations, & Problems. U. K. Srivastava et al. LC 82-21242. 923p. 1983. 39.95x o.p. (ISBN 0-470-27375-5). Halsted Pr.

Quantitative Techniques for the Analysis of Sediments. Ed. by D. F. Merriam. 1976. 50.00 o.p. (ISBN 0-08-020613-1). Pergamon.

Quantities & Units of Measurement: A Dictionary & Handbook. J. V. Drazil. 320p. 1983. 33.00x o.p. (ISBN 0-7201-1665-1). Mansell.

Quantity Food Production, Planning & Management. John B. Knight & Lendal H. Kotschevar. LC 79-12094. 589p. (Orig.). 1985. pap. 24.95 o.s.i. (ISBN 0-442-25745-7). Van Nos Reinhold.

Quantity of Money. H. Visser. LC 75-4762. 294p. 1975. text ed. 26.95x o.p. (ISBN 0-470-90845-9). Halsted Pr.

Quantization. Ed. by Peter F. Swaszek. 352p. 1985. 54.95 o.p. (ISBN 0-442-28124-2). Van Nos Reinhold.

Quantum Aspects of Heterocyclic Compounds in Chemistry & Biochemistry: Proceedings. Ed. by B. Pullman & E. Bergman. 1970. 79.50 o.p. (ISBN 0-12-567050-8). Acad Pr.

Quantum Chemistry: An Introduction. W. Kauzmann. 1957. 70.50 o.p. (ISBN 0-12-402950-7). Acad Pr.

Quantum Chemistry Integrals & Tables. James Miller et al. 1225p. 1959. 45.00x o.p. (ISBN 0-292-73343-7). U of Tex Pr.

Quantum Dynamics of Molecules: The New Experimental Challenge to Theorists. Ed. by R. G. Woolley. LC 80-16321. (NATO ASI Series B, Physics: Vol. 57). 572p. 1980. 95.00x o.p. (ISBN 0-306-40462-1, Plenum Pr). Plenum Pub.

Quantum Effects in Organic Chemistry. Peter Hedvig. 1975. 75.50 o.p. (ISBN 0-12-336450-7). Acad Pr.

Quantum Electrochemistry. J. O. M. Bockris & S. U. Khan. LC 78-11167. 538p. 1978. 79.50x o.p. (ISBN 0-306-31143-7, Plenum Pr). Plenum Pub.

Quantum Electrodynamics. G. Kaellen. Tr. by C. Iddings & M. Mizushima. LC 76-172529. 230p. 1973. 32.00 o.p. (ISBN 0-387-05574-6). Springer-Verlag.

Quantum Electronics & Coherent Light. Ed. by C. H. Townes & P. A. Miles. (Italian Physical Society Ser.: Course 31). 1965. 88.00 o.p. (ISBN 0-12-368831-0). Acad Pr.

Quantum Electronics: Maser Amplifiers & Oscillators, Vols. 1 & 2. V. M. Fain & Ya Khanin. 1969. 80.00 o.p. (ISBN 0-08-012238-8). Pergamon.

Quantum Field Theoretical Methods in Statistical Physics. A. A. Abrikosov et al. (Vol. 4). 1966. 90.00 o.p. (ISBN 0-08-013470-X); pap. 90.00 o.p. (ISBN 0-08-010406-1). Pergamon.

Quantum Field Theory, Vol. 1. A. Visconti. LC 66-18237. 1969. 75.00 o.p. (ISBN 0-08-011821-6). Pergamon.

Quantum Flavordynamics, Quantum Chromodynamics & Unified Theories. Ed. by K. T. Mahanthappa & James Randa. LC 80-12289. (NATO ASI Series B, Physics: Vol. 54). 506p. 1980. 85.00x o.p. (ISBN 0-306-40436-2, Plenum Pr). Plenum Pub.

Quantum Many Particle Physics. John W. Negele & Henri Orland. 1987. 42.95 o.p. (Adv Bk Prog MSP). Addison-Wesley.

Quantum Mechanical Three-Body Problem. E. W. Schmid & H. Ziegelmann. 222p. 1974. 63.00 o.p. (ISBN 0-08-018240-2). Pergamon.

Quantum Mechanics. A. Sokolov. 496p. 1984. 10.95 o.p. (ISBN 0-8285-2967-1, Pub. by Mir Pubs USSR). Imported Pubns.

Quantum Mechanics: A Physical World Picture. Antal Muller. LC 73-18062. 1974. 35.00 o.p. (ISBN 0-08-017936-3). Pergamon.

Quantum Mechanics for Applied Physics & Engineering. A. T. Fromhold. LC 80-19001. 1981. 39.50 o.p. (ISBN 0-12-269150-4). Acad Pr.

Quantum Mechanics in a New Key. Alfred Lande. LC 73-77586. 1973. 6.50 o.p. (ISBN 0-682-47667-6, University). Exposition-Phoenix.

Quantum Mechanics in Mathematics, Chemistry, & Physics. Ed. by Karl E. Gustafson & William P. Reinhardt. LC 81-5846. 512p. 1981. 85.00x o.p. (ISBN 0-306-40737-X, Plenum Pr). Plenum Pub.

Quantum Mechanics of One & Two Electron Atoms. Hans A. Bethe & E. E. Salpeter. (Illus.). 1957. 40.80 o.p. (ISBN 0-387-02118-3). Springer-Verlag.

Quantum Metrology & Fundamental Physical Constants. Ed. by Paul H. Cutler & A. A. Lucas. (NATO ASI Series B, Physics). 670p. 1983. 105.00x o.p. (ISBN 0-306-41372-8, Plenum Pr). Plenum Pub.

Quantum Optics. Ed. by R. J. Glauber. (Italian Physical Society: Course 42). 1970. 110.00 o.p. (ISBN 0-12-368842-6). Acad Pr.

Quantum Radiation of Radioactive Nuclides. new ed. N. G. Gusev & P. P. Dimitriev. 1979. 220.00 o.p. (ISBN 0-08-023058-X). Pergamon.

Quantum-Statistical Theories of Spontaneous Emission & Their Relation to Other Approaches. G. S. Agarwal. LC 25-9130. (Tracts in Modern Physics Ser: Vol. 70). 140p. 1974. 46.70 o.p. (ISBN 0-387-06630-6). Springer-Verlag.

Quantum Theory & Gravitation. A. R. Marlow. LC 79-277837. 1980. 35.50 o.p. (ISBN 0-12-473260-7). Acad Pr.

Quantum Theory of Atoms, Molecules & the Solid State. Ed. by Per-Olov Lowdin. 1966. 59.95 o.p. (ISBN 0-12-456856-4). Acad Pr.

Quantum Theory of Scattering Processes, Vol. 2, Pts. 4 & 5. John E. Farina. LC 72-10162. 164p. 1973. 60.00 o.p. (ISBN 0-08-017047-1); pap. text ed. 35.00 o.p. (ISBN 0-08-018985-7). Pergamon.

Quantum Theory of Scattering Processes, Pt. 1: General Principles & Advanced Topics. John E. Farina. Ed. by R. McWeeny. LC 74-22357. 144p. 1975. 45.00 o.p. (ISBN 0-08-018130-9). Pergamon.

Quarks & Hadronic Structure. Ed. by G. Morpurgo. LC 76-47490. 328p. 1977. 59.50x o.p. (ISBN 0-306-38141-9, Plenum Pr). Plenum Pub.

Quarreling, They Met the Dragon. Sharon Baker. 288p. 1984. pap. 2.95 o.p. (ISBN 0-380-89201-4, 89201-4). Avon.

Quarterdeck & Saddlehorn: The Story of Edward F. Beale, 1822-1893. Carl Briggs & Clyde F. Trudell. (Western Frontiersmen Ser.: Vol. xx). (Illus.). 300p. 1983. 29.50 o.p. (ISBN 0-87062-148-3). A H Clark.

Quarterly Review of Higher Education among Negroes, 28 vols. Incl. Vols. 1 & 2. 36.00 (ISBN 0-8371-1241-9, QU1&); Vols. 3 & 4. 36.00 (ISBN 0-8371-1242-7, QU3&); Vols. 5 & 6. 36.00 (ISBN 0-8371-1243-5, QU5&); Vols. 7 & 8. 36.00 (ISBN 0-8371-1244-3, QU7&); Vols. 9 & 10. 36.00 (ISBN 0-8371-1245-1, QU9&); Vols. 11 & 12. 36.00 (ISBN 0-8371-1246-X, Q11&); Vols. 13 & 14. 36.00 (ISBN 0-8371-1247-8, Q13&); Vols. 15 & 16. 36.00 (ISBN 0-8371-1248-6, Q15&); Vols. 17-19. 36.00 (ISBN 0-8371-1249-4, Q17&); Vols. 20-22. 36.00 (ISBN 0-8371-1250-8, Q20&); Vols. 23 & 24. 36.00 (ISBN 0-8371-1251-6, Q23&); Vols. 25 & 26. 36.00 (ISBN 0-8371-1252-4, Q25&); Vols. 27 & 28. 36.00 (ISBN 0-8371-1253-2, Q27&). 1970. Repr. of 1933 ed. Set. 435.00x o.p. (ISBN 0-8371-9120-3, QUR&). Greenwood.

Quarternary Extinctions: A Prehistoric Revolution. Ed. by Paul S. Martin & Richard G. Klein. LC 83-18033. 892p. 1989. 65.00x o.s.i. (ISBN 0-8165-0812-7). U of Ariz Pr.

Quarternary Stratigraphy of North America: Proceedings of the Symposium, 1975. Quarternary Stratigraphy Symposium Staff. Ed. by W. C. Mahaney. 1976. 78.50 o.p. (ISBN 0-12-787045-8). Acad Pr.

Quartiere de Banchi: Urban Planning in Rome in the First Half of the Cinquecento. Allan Ceen. Ed. by S. J. Freedberg. (Outstanding Dissertations in Fine Arts Ser.). (Illus.). 295p. 1985. Repr. of 1977 ed. 50.00 o.p. (ISBN 0-8240-6884-X). Garland Pub.

Quartzsite Trip. William Hogan. LC 79-55601. 1980. 10.95 o.p. (ISBN 0-689-11043-X, Atheneum). Macmillan.

Quasars, Pulsars, & Black Holes: A Scientific Detective Story. Frederic Golden. LC 75-37646. (Illus.). 128p. 1976. 9.95 o.s.i. (ISBN 0-684-14501-4, ScribT). Scribner.

Quasi One-Dimensional Conductors Two. Ed. by S. Barsic. (Lecture Notes in Physics: Vol. 96). 1979. pap. 26.00 o.p. (ISBN 0-387-09241-2). Springer-Verlag.

Quasilinearization & Invariant Imbedding. E. Stanley Lee. (Mathematics in Science & Engineering Ser.,: Vol. 41). 1968. 83.00 o.p. (ISBN 0-12-440250-X). Acad Pr.

Quaternary in Britain: Essays Reviews & Original Work on the Quarternary Published in Honour of Lewis Penny on His Retirement. Ed. by J. Neale & J. Flenley. (Illus.). 278p. 1981. 45.00 o.p. (ISBN 0-08-026254-6). Pergamon.

Quaternary Plant Ecology: Fourteenth Symposium of the British Ecological Society, University of Cambridge, 28-30 March 1972. Ed. by H. J. Birks & R. G. West. LC 73-10215. (British Ecological Society Symposia Ser.). 326p. 1974. 91.00x o.p. (ISBN 0-470-07534-1). Halsted Pr.

Quaternary Science Reviews, Vol. 1. Ed. by D. Q. Bowen. (Illus.). 340p. 1984. 92.00 o.p. (ISBN 0-08-031491-0). Pergamon.

Quaternary Science Reviews, Vol. 2. Ed. by D. Q. Bowen. (Illus.). 328p. 1984. 105.00 o.p. (ISBN 0-08-031736-7). Pergamon.

Que es el Marxismo-Leninismo? V. Buzuev & V. Gorodnov. 288p. 1987. pap. 1.95 o.p. (ISBN 0-8285-3759-3, Pub. by Progress Pubs USSR). Imported Pubns.

Que Ma Joie Demeure. Jean Giono. (Coll. Soleil). 1959. 18.50 o.p. (ISBN 0-685-11519-4). Schoenhof.

Quebec & Related Silver at the Detroit Institute of Arts. Ross C. Fox. LC 77-4850. (Illus.). 160p. 1978. 15.95x o.p. (ISBN 0-8143-1575-5). Wayne St U Pr.

Quebec & the Constitution: Nineteen Sixty to Nineteen Seventy-Eight. Edward McWhinney. 1979. 15.00x o.p. (ISBN 0-8020-5456-0); pap. 9.50 o.p. (ISBN 0-8020-6364-0). U of Toronto Pr.

Quebec Prehistory. J. V. Wright. (Canadian Prehistory Ser.). (Illus.). 128p. 1985. pap. text ed. 10.00x o.s.i. (ISBN 0-226-56487-8, 56487-8, Pub. by Natl Mus Canada). U of Chicago Pr.

Queen Against Defoe & Other Stories. Stefan Heym. LC 73-20380. (Illus.). 128p. 1974. 6.95 o.p. (ISBN 0-88208-041-5). Chicago Review.

Queen Alexandra's Christmas Gift Book. Queen Alexandra. Intro. by Georgina Battiscombe. (English Heritage Ser.). (Illus.). 160p. 1987. Repr. of 1908 ed. 34.00 o.s.i. (ISBN 0-948285-01-X). Archival Facsimiles.

Queen Anne Churches: A Catalogue of the Papers in Lambeth Palace Library of the Commission for Building Fifty New Churches in London & Westminster, 1711-1759. Compiled by E. G. Bill. 280p. 1979. 53.00x o.p. (ISBN 0-7201-0919-1). Mansell.

Queen Anne's American Kings. Richmond P. Bond. 1972. lib. bdg. 18.00x o.p. (ISBN 0-374-90783-8, Octagon). Hippocrene Bks.

Queen Christina. Pam Gems. 80p. 1983. pap. 4.95 o.p. (ISBN 0-9508443-0-6, NO.3938). Routledge Chapman & Hall.

Queen Dolley: The Life & Times of Dolly Madison. Dorothy C. Wilson. LC 86-8862. 384p. 1987. 17.95 o.s.i. (ISBN 0-385-19762-4). Doubleday.

Queen Elizabeth at War. Chris Konings. (Illus.). 128p. 1985. 17.95 o.p. (ISBN 0-85059-725-0, Pub. by PSL P Stephens England). Sterling.

Queen Juliana: The Story of the Richest Woman in the World. William Hoffman. Ed. by Carol Hill. LC 79-1827. 1979. 11.95 o.p. (ISBN 0-15-146531-2). HarBraceJ.

Queen Lucia. E. F. Benson. (Large Print Bks). 369p. 1987. lib. bdg. 16.95 o.p. (ISBN 0-8161-4163-0, Large Print Bks). G K Hall.

Queen Mary: The Official Pictorial History. Robert O. Maguglin. (Illus.). 120p. 1985. 19.95 o.s.i. (ISBN 0-86679-023-3); pap. 10.95 o.s.i. (ISBN 0-86679-015-2). Oak Tree Pubns.

Queen Mother. Elizabeth Longford. (Illus.). 185p. 1986. pap. 10.95 o.s.i. (ISBN 0-586-05603-3). Academy Chi Pubs.

Queen of Death. John Milne. (Heinemann Guided Readers). 1979. pap. text ed. 3.00x o.p. (ISBN 0-435-27049-4). Heinemann Ed.

Queen of Hearts. Dan McCall. LC 84-25145. 244p. 1985. 15.95 o.p. (ISBN 0-03-001688-6). H Holt & Co.

Queen of Shaba: The Story of an African Leopard. Joy Adamson. LC 80-7931. (Helen & Kurt Wolff Bk.). (Illus.). 256p. 1980. 14.95 o.p. (ISBN 0-15-175651-1). HarBraceJ.

Queen of the What Ifs. Norma Klein. 221p. 1982. pap. 2.50 o.p. (ISBN 0-449-70026-7, Juniper). Fawcett.

Queen Victoria's Highland Journals. Ed. by David Duff. (Illus.). 240p. 1983. pap. 10.95 o.s.i. (ISBN 0-03-063549-7). H Holt & Co.

Queen Victoria's Maharajah: Duleep Singh, 1838-1893. Michael Alexander & Shushila Anand. LC 79-5426. (Illus.). 1980. 14.95 o.s.i. (ISBN 0-8008-6567-7). Taplinger.

Queen Wanda & the Wawel Dragon. Barbara Seidler. Tr. by Jane Kedron. (Kosciuszko Young People's Ser.). (Illus.). (gr. 1-4). 1974. pap. text ed. 1.00x o.s.i. (ISBN 0-917004-06-X). Kosciuszko.

Queen Who Flew. Ford Madox Ford. LC 65-23176. (Illus.). (gr. 4-6). 1965. 4.35 o.p. (ISBN 0-8076-0324-4). Braziller.

Queener: The Man Behind the Preaching. Foster Bell & Darlene Bell. 1976. pap. 2.95 o.p. (ISBN 0-934942-13-7). White Wing Pub.

Queenie. Hortense Calisher. LC 70-141640. 1971. 6.95 o.p. (ISBN 0-87795-010-5, Arbor Hse). Morrow.

Queenie. Michael Korda. 640p. 1985. 17.45 o.p. (ISBN 0-671-46668-2, Linden Pr). S&S.

Queenie. Michael Korda. 1985. 18.95 o.p. (ISBN 0-8161-3970-9, Large Print Bks); pap. 10.95 o.p. (ISBN 0-8161-3971-7). G K Hall.

Queens. George Alpert. LC 74-30498. (Photography Ser). (Illus., Orig.). 1975. pap. 5.95 o.p. (ISBN 0-306-80012-8). Da Capo.

Queen's Gambit Declined: Exchange Variation. Jerzy Konikowski. 58p. (Orig.). pap. 4.00 o.s.i. (ISBN 0-931462-48-7). Chess Ent Inc.

Queen's Gambit: Tartakower System. Jerzy Konikowski. Tr. by Paul Janicki. (Illus.). 107p. (Orig.). 1983. pap. 5.00 o.s.i. (ISBN 0-931462-25-8). Chess Ent Inc.

Queens Health Systems Agency District G: A Profile of Health Status & Health Resources. Susan S. Laudicinda. pap. cancelled o.s.i. (ISBN 0-318-00883-1). Comm Serv Soc NY.

Queen's Heart of Gold: The Complete Story of Our Lady of Beauraing. Sr. Mary Amatora. LC 78-188443. 1972. 7.50 o.p. (ISBN 0-682-47467-3, Banner); pap. 5.00 o.p. (ISBN 0-682-47480-0, Banner). Exposition-Phoenix.

Queen's Indian, 1982. Ed. by David Levy et al. (Illus.). 1982. 19.95 o.s.i. (ISBN 0-907352-13-8, Capablanca). Imprint Edns.

Queen's Portrait: The Story of Guadalupe. Sr. Mary Amatora. LC 74-188442. 1972. 7.50 o.p. (ISBN 0-682-47468-1, Lochinvar); pap. 5.00 o.p. (ISBN 0-682-47479-7, Lochinvar). Exposition-Phoenix.

Queensblade. Susan Shwartz. (Heirs to Byzantium: Bk. 3). 288p. (Orig.). 1988. pap. 3.50 o.s.i. (ISBN 0-445-20360-9, Pub. by Popular Lib). Warner Bks.

Queenscote. Margaret MacWilliams. LC 87-10039. (Starlight Romance Ser.). 192p. 1987. 12.95 o.p. (ISBN 0-385-24336-7). Doubleday.

Queenslanders. Hugh Lunn. LC 84-13134. (Illus.). 224p. 1985. text ed. 22.50x o.p. (ISBN 0-7022-1816-2). U Of Queensland Pr.

Queer, the Quaint, the Quizzical. Francis H. Stauffer. LC 68-22052. 368p. 1968. Repr. of 1882 ed. 35.00x o.p. (ISBN 0-8103-3096-2). Gale.

Queer Things about Japan, to Which Is Added a Life of the Emperor of Japan. 4th ed. Douglas Sladen. LC 68-26607. (Illus.). 518p. 1968. Repr. of 1913 ed. 43.00x o.p. (ISBN 0-8103-3500-X). Gale.

Quellen und Forschungen zur Reformationgeschichte, Vols. 1-23, Lacking Vols. 3 & 7. Set. 895.00 o.p. (ISBN 0-384-49010-7); Set. pap. 775.00 o.p. (ISBN 0-685-02139-4). Johnson Repr.

Quellen zur Geschichte der Taufer in der Schweiz, Vol. 2: Ostschweiz. Heinhold Fast. (Ger.). 1974. 59.00x o.p. (ISBN 0-8361-1197-4). Herald Pr.

Querelle. Jean Genet. Tr. by Anselm Hollo from Fr. LC 74-24898. 1975. pap. 4.95 o.p. (ISBN 0-394-17838-6, B382, BC). Grove.

Querelle: The Film Book. Rainer Werner Fassbinder. LC 83-80816. (Illus.). 180p. 1983. pap. 16.95 o.p. (ISBN 0-394-62477-7, E861, Ever). Grove.

Quest. W. J. Wotten. LC 84-90150. 132p. 1985. 10.95 o.p. (ISBN 0-533-06216-0). Vantage.

Qu'est-ce Que C'est. Ed. by David Fisher & Reginald Bragonier, Jr. Tr. by Alain Fantapie & Marcel Brule. (Illus.). 594p. 1984. 40.00 o.p. (ISBN 0-8437-3328-4). Hammond Inc.

Qu'est-ce Qui Se Passe? Conversation-Revision de Grammaire. Robert S. Balas. 448p. 1980. pap. 22.95 o.p. (ISBN 0-395-30955-7). HM.

Quest for a Black Theology. Ed. by James J. Gardiner & J. Deotis Roberts. LC 76-151250. 128p. 1971. 6.95 o.p. (ISBN 0-8298-0196-0). Pilgrim NY.

Quest for a Sustainable Society. Ed. by James C. Coomer. LC 80-24158. (Pergamon Policy Studies on International Development). 230p. 1981. 65.00 o.p. (ISBN 0-08-027168-5). Pergamon.

Quest for Artificial Intelligence. Dorothy H. Patent. LC 85-27042. (Illus.). 224p. (gr. 7-8). 1986. 13.95 o.s.i. (ISBN 0-15-264550-0, HJ). Harbracej.

Quest for Federal Manpower Partnership. Sar A. Levitan & Joyce K. Zickler. LC 74-16541. 144p. 1974. text ed. 11.00x o.s.i. (ISBN 0-674-74125-0). Harvard U Pr.

Quest for Freedom. Velma B. Clark. LC 86-91155. 1986. 15.00 o.p. (ISBN 0-682-40298-2). Exposition-Phoenix.

Quest for Le Carre. Ed. by Alan Bold. (Critical Studies Ser.). 224p. 1988. 28.50 o.p. (ISBN 0-389-20762-4, N 8321). B&N Imports.

Quest for Merlin. Nikolai Tolstoy. LC 85-52405. (Illus.). 368p. 1985. 19.45i o.p. (ISBN 0-316-85066-7). Little.

Quest for Peace. Bernard Reich. 495p. 1977. 24.95 o.p. (ISBN 0-87855-226-X). Transaction Pubs.

Quest for Peace: U. S. - Israeli Relations & the Arab-Israeli Conflict. Bernard Reich. LC 76-45940. 495p. 1977. text ed. 24.95 o.p. (ISBN 0-87855-226-X). Transaction Pubs.

Quest for Rananim: D.H. Lawrence's Letters to S.S. Koteliansky, 1914-1930. Ed. by George J. Zytaruk. 1970. 14.00 o.p. (ISBN 0-7735-0054-5, McGill Canada). U of Toronto Pr.

Quest for Security, 1715-1740. Penfield Roberts. LC 83-10689. (Rise of Modern Europe Ser.). (Illus.). x, 300p. 1983. Repr. of 1947 ed. lib. bdg. 48.50x o.p. (ISBN 0-313-24086-8, ROQU). Greenwood.

Quest for the Historical Israel. George W. Ramsey. LC 80-82188. 208p. (Orig.). 1981. pap. 13.95 o.p. (ISBN 0-8042-0187-0, John Knox). Westminster John Knox.

Quest for the Killers. June Goodfield. (Illus.). 300p. 1985. 24.95 o.p. (ISBN 0-8176-3313-8). Birkhauser.

Quest of a Hemisphere. Donzella C. Boyle. LC 71-113036. (Illus.). (gr. 7 up). 1970. PLB 18.00 o.p. (ISBN 0-88279-218-0). Western Islands.

Quest of Prince Ferdinand. Jessie Hale. 1985. 4.95 o.p. (ISBN 0-533-06182-2). Vantage.

Quest of the Colonial. Robert Shackleton & Elizabeth Shackleton. LC 72-99075. (Illus.). 440p. 1970. Repr. of 1907 ed. 43.00x o.p. (ISBN 0-8103-3574-3). Gale.

Quest of the Dawnstar. Gordon McBain. 144p. (Orig.). (gr. 7 up). 1984. pap. 2.25 o.p. (ISBN 0-380-86520-3, 86520, Flare). Avon.

Quest: Reflections on Medicine, Science & Mankind. Rene Dubos & Jean-Paul Escande. LC 79-3347. 128p. 1980. Repr. of 1979 ed. 9.95 o.p. (ISBN 0-15-175705-4). HarBraceJ.

Questing Christ. A. O. Steele. LC 64-20427. 208p. 1965. (ISBN 0-8022-1632-3). Philos Lib.

Question of Animal Awareness: Evolutionary Continuity of Mental Experience. Donald R. Griffin. LC 76-18492. 144p. 1976. 7.00x o.p. (ISBN 0-87470-020-5). Rockefeller.

Question of Animal Awareness: Evolutionary Continuity of Mental Experience. 2nd ed. Donald R. Griffin. LC 81-51221. (Illus.). 221p. pap. 9.95 o.p. (ISBN 0-86576-002-0). W Kaufmann.

Question of Guilt: The Curious Case of Dr. Crippen. Richard Gordon. LC 81-66026. 1981. 9.95 o.p. (ISBN 0-689-11192-4, Atheneum). Macmillan.

Question of Harmony. Gretchen A. Sprague. LC 65-13511. (gr. 7 up). 1965. 36.00 o.p. (ISBN 0-396-05111-1). Dodd.

Question of Height Revisited: Assaults on Police. Cheryl Swanson & Charles D. Hale. (Criminal Justice Policy & Administration Research Ser: No. 7). 12p. 1974. pap. 1.00 o.p. (ISBN 0-686-20791-2). Univ OK Gov Res.

Question of Innocence. Lawrence Spiegel. Ed. by William McGuire. 280p. 1987. 16.95 o.p. (ISBN 0-88101-055-3). Unicorn Pub.

Question of Max. Amanda Cross. 1976. 7.95 o.p. (ISBN 0-394-48223-9); pap. 2.50 o.p. (ISBN 0-345-31385-2). Knopf.

Question of Survival: Quakers in Australia in the Nineteenth Century. William N. Oats. LC 84-2351. (Illus.). 409p. 1985. text ed. 35.00x o.p. (ISBN 0-7022-1708-5). U of Queensland Pr.

Questioned Stock Manual: A Guide to Determining the True Worth of Old & Collectible Securities. Albert F. Gargiulo & Rocco Carlucci. (Illus.). 1979. text ed. 24.95 o.p. (ISBN 0-07-022865-5). McGraw.

Questioning & Teaching: A Manual of Practice. J. T. Dillon. (Croom Helm Curriculum Policy & Research Ser.). 208p. 1988. lib. bdg. 45.00 o.p. (ISBN 0-7099-0897-0, Pub. by Croom Helm UK). Routledge Chapman & Hall.

Questionnaire. Jiri Grusa. LC 83-48031. (Library of Contemporary World Literature). 304p. 1983. pap. 7.95 o.s.i. (ISBN 0-394-72212-4, Vin). Random.

Questionnaire: Or, Prayer for a Town & a Friend. Jiri Grusa. Tr. by Peter Kussi from Czech. 282p. 1982. 15.95 o.p. (ISBN 0-374-24010-8). FS&G.

Questions about the Beginning of Life. Ed. by Edward D. Schneider. LC 85-15617. 192p. (Orig.). 1985. pap. 10.95 o.p. (ISBN 0-8066-2167-2, 10-5360, Augsburg). Augsburg Fortress.

Questions & Answers about Acne. John R. Reeves. LC 76-28514. (Illus.). (gr. 7 up). 1977. 9.95 o.s.i. (ISBN 0-13-748434-8). P-H.

Questions & Answers about Love & Sex. Bride's Magazine Editors & Mary Calderone. 144p. 1980. pap. 2.95 o.p. (ISBN 0-380-52977-7, 65615-9). Avon.

Questions & Answers for Electricians Examinations. 7th ed. Roland E. Palmquist. LC 78-50280. 1982. 9.95 o.p. (ISBN 0-672-23363-0). G K Hall.

Questions & Answers for Plumbers Examinations. 2nd ed. Jules Oravetz, Sr. LC 73-85726. (Illus.). 1985. pap. 9.95 o.p. (ISBN 0-8161-1703-9, Pub. by Audel). Macmillan.

Questions & Answers on American Citizenship. new rev. ed. Solomon Wiener. (gr. 9 up). 1970. pap. text ed. 2.95 o.p. (ISBN 0-88345-136-0, 17862). Prentice ESL.

Questions & Answers on the Pension & Profit Sharing Provisions of the New Tax Law: With an Explanation of the Retirement Plan Provisions of TEFRA. Prentice-Hall Editorial Staff. LC 83-126276. 96p. 7.50x o.p. (ISBN 0-13-749002-X, 74900-2). P-H.

Questions & Answers on the Soviet Threat & National Security. 1981. 1.00 o.p. (ISBN 0-910082-06-5). Am Fr Serv Comm.

Questions & Answers: Sermon Outlines & Bible Study Notes. H. Leo Boles. 1985. pap. 8.95 o.p. (ISBN 0-89225-274-X). Gospel Advocate.

Questions Christians Ask about Prayer & Intercession. Barry Wood. 160p. (Orig.). 1984. pap. 5.95 o.p. (ISBN 0-8007-5177-9, Power Bks). Revell.

Questions from the Past. new ed. W. Shepperson et al. LC 72-94356. (Nevada Studies in History & Political Science Ser: No. 11). (Illus.). xii, 216p. 1973. pap. 3.50x o.p. (ISBN 0-87417-036-2). U of Nev Pr.

Quests Beyond the Mirror: A Trio of Tales. Elbert Rynberg. 64p. 1981. 5.00 o.p. (ISBN 0-682-49735-5). Exposition-Phoenix.

Quetzal. Amilcar Lobos & Leland Mellot. Ed. by Rolando Castellon & Carlos Perez. LC 73-74385. 112p. (Orig., Eng. & Span.). 1973. pap. 3.50 o.p. (ISBN 0-912078-29-4). Volcano Pr.

Quetzalcoatl & Guadalupe: The Formation of Mexican National Consciousness, 1531-1813. Jacques Lafaye. Tr. by Benjamin Keen from Fr. LC 75-20889. 1976. lib. bdg. 26.00x o.s.i. (ISBN 0-226-46794-5). U of Chicago Pr.

Queues: Receptors & Recognition Series B. D. R. Cox & W. L. Smith. Incl. Vol. 13. Receptor Regulation. 59.95 (2245); Vol. 12. Purinergic Receptors. 63.00 (2142); Vol. 11. Membrane Receptors. 49.95 (2156); Vol. 10. Neurotransmitter Receptors, Part 2: Biogenic Amines. 49.95 (49.95); Vol. 9. Neurotransmitter Receptors, Part 1: Amino Acids, Peptides & Benzodiazepines. 49.95 (NO.6456); Vol. 8. Virus Receptors, Part 2: Animal Viruses. 43.00 (NO.6413); Vol. 7. Virus Receptors, Part 1: Bacterial Viruses. 43.00 (NO.6416); Vol. 6. Bacterial Adherence. 69.95 (6453); Vol. 5. Taxis & Behavior. 63.00 (NO.6452); Vol. 4. Specificity of Embryological Interactions. 49.95 (NO.6118); Vol. 3. Microbial Interactions. 49.95 (NO.6236); Vol. 2. Intercellular Junctions & Synapses. 53.00 (NO.6107); Vol. 1. Specificity & Action of Animal, Bacterial & Plant Toxins. 63.00 (NO. 6078). Pub. by Chapman & Hall England). Routledge Chapman & Hall.

Quiche & Pate. Peter Kump. Ed. by Gladys Topkis. LC 81-70444. (Great American Cooking Schools Ser.). (Illus.). 84p. 1982. pap. 5.95 o.p. (ISBN 0-941034-10-0). I Chalmers.

Quichean Civilization: The Ethnohistoric, Ethnographic & Archaeological Sources. Robert M. Carmack. LC 70-149948. (Illus.). 1973. 45.00x o.p. (ISBN 0-520-01963-6). U of Cal Pr.

Quick. Leigh Ellis. 208p. 1982. pap. 2.25 o.p. (ISBN 0-380-79640-6, 79640-6). Avon.

Quick & Dirty Guide to War: Briefings on Present & Potential Wars. James F. Dunnigan & Austin Bay. LC 84-22797. (Illus.). 384p. 1985. 17.95 o.p. (ISBN 0-688-04199-X). Morrow.

Quick & Easy Adventures of Huck Finn. P-H.

Quick & Easy Catcher in the Rye. P-H.

Quick & Easy Chinese Cooking. Kenneth H. Lo. 1972. 6.95 o.p. (ISBN 0-395-13523-0). HM.

Quick & Easy Math. Isaac Asimov. (gr. 7 up). 1964. 10.45 o.p. (ISBN 0-395-06573-9). HM.

Quick & Easy Monarch Notes on Bronte's Jane Eyre. (Orig.). pap. 2.50 o.p. (ISBN 0-671-52855-6). Monarch Pr.

Quick & Easy Monarch Notes on Miller's Death of a Salesman. Joan T. Nourse. (Orig.). pap. 1.95 o.p. (ISBN 0-671-52851-3). Monarch Pr.

Quick & Easy Monarch Notes on Salinger's Catcher in the Rye. (Orig.). pap. 2.25 o.p. (ISBN 0-671-52870-X). Monarch Pr.

Quick & Easy Romeo & Juliet: Monarch Quick & Easy Notes. 1985. pap. 2.50 o.p. (ISBN 0-671-52863-7). Monarch Pr.

Quick & Easy Taxes. The J. K. Lasser Tax Institute Staff. 80p. 1987. pap. 3.95 o.p. (ISBN 0-13-509639-1). P-H.

Quick & Easy Wordstar 2000. Janet Crider. LC 85-80116. 192p. pap. 14.95 o.p. (ISBN 0-89586-408-8). Price Stern.

Quick & Friendly: Book One: Working on Pomo Valley Ranch. Moe E. Waltenspiel. 1984. 7.95 o.p. (ISBN 0-533-05779-5). Vantage.

Quick Arithmetic. Robert A. Carman & Marilyn J. Carman. LC 74-2476. (Self-Teaching Guides Ser.). 252p. 1974. pap. text ed. 7.95 o.p. (ISBN 0-471-13496-1, Pub. by Wiley Pr). Wiley.

Quick Cuisine International: Easy French Country Classics. (Illus.). 128p. 1984. 10.00 o.p. (ISBN 0-89535-146-3). Knapp Pr.

Quick Cuisine International: New Recipes for Italian Favorites. LC 84-14402. (Illus.). 128p. 1984. 10.00 o.p. (ISBN 0-89535-147-1). Knapp Pr.

Quick Meals Cookbook. Lorene Froehling. (Illus.). 64p. (Orig.). 1985. pap. 3.95 o.p. (ISBN 0-8249-3056-8). Ideals.

Quick Red Fox. John D. MacDonald. (Travis McGee Ser.). 1981. pap. 2.95 o.p. (ISBN 0-449-14264-7, GM). Fawcett.

Quick Reference Guide to MS-DOS Commands. rev. ed. Date not set. Microsoft.

Quick Reference Guide to MS-DOS Commands. Van Wolverton. (Quick Reference Ser.). 48p. (Orig.). 1987. pap. text ed. 4.95 o.p. (ISBN 1-55615-025-3). Microsoft.

Quick Reference Guide to MS-DOS Commands. rev. ed. Van Wolverton. LC 86-31146. (Quick Reference Ser.). 96p. (Orig.). 1988. pap. 5.95 o.p. (ISBN 1-55615-182-9). Microsoft.

Quick Reference Guide to Polygraph Admissibility, Licensing Laws & Limiting Laws. 10th ed. Norman Ansley. LC 85-108798. 1985. Am Polygraph.

Quick Reference Guide to Polygraphy Admissibility, Licensing Laws & Limiting Laws. 11th ed. Norman Ansley. 1987. 4.95 o.p. Am Polygraph.

Quick Reference Guide to Tax Reform Act of 1986. 44p. 1987. 3.50 o.p. (ISBN 0-88462-593-1, 5606-10, Pub. by Longman Fin Serv Pub). Longman Finan.

Quick Reference Guide to the Tax Reform Act of 1986. H. David Megaw. LC 86-21438. Date not set. (ISBN 0-88462-578-8). Longman Finan.

Quick Reference Guide to the Tax Reform Act, 1988. Ernst & Whinney. 44p. 1987. pap. 27.00 o.p. (ISBN 0-88462-720-9). Longman Finan.

Quick Reference of Common Emergency Drugs. P. Howard Cummings & Stephen R. Porter. LC 83-10386. 421p. 1983. pap. 15.50x o.p. (ISBN 0-471-87703-4, Pub. by Wiley Med). Wiley.

Quick Reference to the Biographical Directory. American Psychiatric Association Staff. 452p. 1984. pap. text ed. 12.95x o.p. (ISBN 0-89042-183-8, 42-183-8). Am Psychiatric.

Quick Reference World Atlas. LC 77-72301. 48p. 1985. pap. 2.95 o.p. (ISBN 0-528-83030-9). Rand McNally.

Quickie Quizzes from the Bible. Charles Vander Meer. (Quiz & Puzzle Bks.: No. 1). 48p. (gr. 7 up). 1976. pap. 2.50 o.p. (ISBN 0-8010-9252-3). Baker Bk.

Quicksand Book. Tomie DePaola. LC 76-28762. (Illus.). (gr. k-3). 1984. pap. 5.95 o.p. (ISBN 0-8234-0532-X). Holiday.

Quicksilver. James Farnsworth. (Gunsmoke Western Ser.). 176p. 1988. text ed. 12.95x o.p. (ISBN 0-85997-853-2, Pub. by Firecrest Pub Ltd). Prescott Pr NH.

Quicksilver. Norman Hartley. LC 78-73070. 1979. 8.95 o.p. (ISBN 0-689-10958-X, Atheneum). Macmillan.

Quicksilver. Norman Hartley. 240p. 1980. pap. 2.50 o.p. (ISBN 0-380-51482-6, 51482-6). Avon.

Quid Pro Quo: Equity & Claims of Money. Michael Kirchberger. 1981. 3.00 o.p. (ISBN 0-682-49779-7). Exposition-Phoenix.

Quien Sabe? A Preliminary List of Chicano Reference Materials. Francisco Garcia-Avyens. (Bibliography & Reference Ser.: No. 11). 116p. (Orig.). 1981. pap. text ed. 6.00 o.p. (ISBN 0-89551-000-6). UCLA Chicano Stud.

Quienes Amenazan a la Paz. URSS, Ministerio de Defensa Staff. (Illus.). 78p. (Span.). pap. 1.95 o.p. (ISBN 0-8285-2207-3, Pub. by Military Pubs USSR). Imported Pubns.

Quiet Crisis. Stewart L. Udall. 1978. pap. 1.75 o.p. (ISBN 0-380-01515-3, 36376). Avon.

Quiet Days in Clichy & The World of Sex. Henry Miller. LC 77-91353. 1978. pap. 2.95 o.s.i. (ISBN 0-394-17037-7, B409, BC). Grove.

Quiet Eye Engagement Calendar 1988. Sylvia S. Judson. (Illus.). 64p. 1987. pap. 9.95 o.p. (ISBN 0-317-62457-1); Eight copy Prepak. 79.60 o.p. (ISBN 0-89526-554-0). Regnery Gateway.

Quiet Heart: Prayers & Meditations for Each Day of the Year. George Appleton. LC 84-6019. 480p. 1984. pap. 7.95 o.p. (ISBN 0-8006-1789-4, Fortress). Augsburg Fortress.

Quiet Imperative: Meditations on Justice & Peace Based on Readings from the New Testament. John Carmody. 176p. (Orig.). 1986. pap. 6.95 o.p. (ISBN 0-8358-0518-2). Upper Room.

Quiet Killers, Vol. 1. J. David Truby. (Illus.). 80p. 1972. pap. 8.00 o.p. (ISBN 0-87364-014-4). Paladin Pr.

Quiet Killers II: Silencer Update. J. David Truby. (Illus.). 92p. (Orig.). 1979. pap. 8.00 o.p. (ISBN 0-87364-163-9). Paladin Pr.

Quiet Money. Robert McDowell. LC 86-25714. 1987. pap. 6.40 o.p. (ISBN 0-8050-0345-2). H Holt & Co.

Quiet Neighborhood. George MacDonald. 240p. 1985. pap. 5.95 o.p. (ISBN 0-89693-328-8). Victor Bks.

Quiet Neighbors: Prosecuting Nazi War Criminals in America. Allan A. Ryan. LC 84-6540. 400p. 1984. 15.95 o.p. (ISBN 0-15-175823-9). HarBraceJ.

Quiet Night of Fear. Charles L. Grant. (Orig.). 1981. pap. 2.25 o.s.i. (ISBN 0-425-04844-6). Berkley Pub.

Quiet Rebel: How to Survive As a Woman & Businessperson. Glynis M. Breakwell. 224p. 1987. Repr. of 1985 ed. 15.95 o.p. (ISBN 0-394-55560-0). Grove.

Quiet Revolution. Peter Ambrose. 1974. 15.00x o.p. (ISBN 0-85621-034-X, Pub. by Scot Acad Pr). Longwood Pub Group.

Quiet Riot. (Metal Mania Ser.). (Illus.). 48p. (gr. 4-12). 1984. 6.95 o.p. (ISBN 0-88188-298-4, Robus Books). H Leonard Pub Corp.

Quiet Road to Death. Sheila Radley. 176p. 1984. 11.95 o.s.i. (ISBN 0-684-18124-X, ScribT). Scribner.

Quiet Way: Selections from the Letters of Gerhart Tersteegen. (ISBN 0-8022-1706-0). Philos Lib.

Quietimes. Becky Tirabassi. 128p. Date not set. notebook 12.95 o.p. (ISBN 0-8423-4636-8). Tyndale.

Quilt for All Seasons. Chris W. Edmonds. (Illus.). 40p. 1982. pap. 6.00 cancelled o.p. (ISBN 0-932946-08-9). Burdett CA.

Quilt Hoops. Date not set. pap. 4.98 o.p. (ISBN 0-317-03195-3). Gick.

Quiltcraft: New Dimensions from Past Traditions. Elaine DeLancy. LC 85-21791. 160p. 1986. 12.95 o.p. (ISBN 0-8329-0391-4). New Century.

Quilter's Precise Yardage Guide. Carol Waugh & Judith LaBelle. LC 82-24622. (Illus.). 144p. 1983. pap. 8.95 o.s.i. (ISBN 0-8329-0275-6). New Century.

Quilting: An Annotated Bibliography. Leinhauser Weiss. 1985. lib. bdg. 18.00 o.p. (ISBN 0-8240-9101-9). Garland Pub.

Quilting in Squares. Katherine Fisher & Elizabeth Kay. LC 77-16137. (Illus.). 1978. pap. 5.95 o.p. (ISBN 0-684-17453-7, ScribT). Scribner.

Quilting, Patchwork, & Applique. Conran Octopus. 1986. pap. 9.95 o.p. (ISBN 0-345-33610-0, Pub. by Ballantine Trade). Ballantine.

Quiltmaker's Big Book of Twelve Inch Patterns. 2nd ed. Anthony Lehman. (Illus.). 1985. 14.95 o.p. (ISBN 0-942786-19-X). Leone Pubns.

Quilts for Babies & Children. P-H.

Quilts to Wear. Virginia Avery. (Illus.). 192p. 1982. 22.95 o.s.i. (ISBN 0-684-17615-7, ScribT). Scribner.

Quimica General. B. V. Nekrasov. 296p. (Span.). 1981. 15.00 o.p. (ISBN 0-8285-1998-6, Pub. by Mir Pubs USSR). Imported Pubns.

Quincannon. Bill Pronzini. LC 85-17292. 263p. 1985. Repr. of 1985 ed. 13.95 o.p. (ISBN 0-89621-671-3). Thorndike Pr.

Quinoline. (American Petroleum Institute Monograph Series). 56p. 1979. 8.00 o.p. (ISBN 0-317-33095-0, 82271100). Am Petroleum.

Quin's Shanghai Circus. Edward Wittemore. 304p. 1982. pap. 3.50 o.p. (ISBN 0-380-61200-3, 61200-3, Bard). Avon.

Quintescence of Irving Langmuir. A. Rosenfeld. 1966. 16.25 o.p. (ISBN 0-08-011049-5); pap. 7.50 o.p. (ISBN 0-08-011048-7). Pergamon.

Quintessence of Ibsenism. George Bernard Shaw. (Drama Bk.). 188p. 1959. pap. 6.25 o.p. (ISBN 0-8090-0509-3). Hill & Wang.

Quintessential Woman. Cory Kenyon. (Candlelight Ecstasy Ser.: No. 496). (Orig.). 1987. pap. 2.25 o.p. (ISBN 0-440-17218-7). Dell.

Quips & Quotes. William E. Darton. 64p. 1986. 6.95 o.p. (ISBN 0-8062-2934-9). Carlton.

Quirigua: A Classic Maya Center & Its Sculptures. Robert J. Sharer. LC 86-71809. (Centers of Civilization Ser.). (Illus.). 144p. 1989. lib. bdg. 29.75 o.p. (ISBN 0-89089-260-1); pap. 12.95 o.p. (ISBN 0-89089-261-X). Carolina Acad Pr.

Quirk. Gordon Merrick. 1978. pap. 3.95 o.p. (ISBN 0-380-38992-4, 84970-4). Avon.

Quit for Life: The Sensational New Program for Smokers. Robert S. Sobel. LC 88-90751. 164p. (Orig.). 1988. pap. 9.50 o.p. (ISBN 0-929517-00-8). MDTA Pr.

Quit Pulling My Leg! A Story of Davy Crockett. Robert Quackenbush. (Illus.). (gr. 2-6). 1987. 11.95 o.s.i. (ISBN 0-13-749755-5). P-H.

Quit Smoking: Forty Major Techniques to Help You Stop Smoking. Curtis Casewit. Intro. by Sidney L. Werkman. LC 83-60346. 160p. 1983. pap. 7.95 o.p. (ISBN 0-914918-44-3). Whitford Pr.

QuitSmart: A Guide to Freedom from Cigarettes. Robert H. Shipley. LC 85-80177. (Illus.). 92p. (Orig.). 1985. pap. 3.95 o.p. (ISBN 0-9614881-0-7); bk. & cassette 12.95 o.p. (ISBN 0-9614881-2-3). J B Pr.

Quiz Book on Black America. Clarence N. Blake & Donald F. Martin. (Illus.). 224p. (gr. 7 up). 1976. 6.95 o.p. (ISBN 0-395-24389-0). HM.

Quizzical Pursuits: Test Yourself & Discover the Real You. Sherry S. Cohen. 128p. (Orig.). 1985. pap. 4.95 o.p. (ISBN 0-671-53070-4, Pub. by Fireside). S&S.

Quizzism & Its Key. Albert P. Southwick. LC 68-22051. 238p. 1970. Repr. of 1884 ed. 35.00x o.p. (ISBN 0-8103-3094-6). Gale.

Qumran & Corinth. Martin H. Scharlemann. 78p. 1962. Concordia Schl Grad Studies.

Qumran & History: The Place of the Teachers in Religion. Olive K. Gilliam. 3.95 o.p. (ISBN 0-533-01167-1). Vantage.

Quonsett. James F. Murphy, Jr. 1979. pap. 1.95 o.p. (ISBN 0-380-45484-X, 45484). Avon.

Quotations from Chairman Mao Tse-Tung. 2nd ed. Mao Tse-Tung. 1967. plastic bdg. 4.95 o.p. (ISBN 0-8351-0284-X). China Bks.

Quotations from Chairman Mao Tse-Tung see Box.

Quotations in History: A Dictionary of Historical Quotations, c800 A. D. to the Present. Compiled by Alan Palmer. LC 76-1801. 354p. 1976. text ed. 26.50x o.p. (ISBN 0-06-495368-8). B&N Imports.

Quote: Because I Must. Gwendolyn Clancy. LC 85-90981. 64p. 1985. 8.00 o.p. (ISBN 0-682-40271-0). Exposition-Phoenix.

Quotemanship: The Use & Abuse of Quotations for Polemical & Other Purposes. Paul F. Boller, Jr. LC 66-29656. 468p. 1968. 17.50x o.p. (ISBN 0-87074-022-9). SMU Press.

Quotes & Notes to Share. Paul J. Molnar. Ed. by Patrice Goebel. (Orig.). 1982. pap. 4.95 o.p. (ISBN 0-938736-06-X). Life Enrich.

Quotienten-Diferenzen-Algorithmus. H. Rutishauser. (MIM Ser.: No. 7). 74p. (Ger.). 1957. pap. 11.95x o.p. (ISBN 0-8176-0323-9). Birkhauser.

Qur'an & Bible: Studies in Interpretation & Dialogue. M. S. Seale. 124p. 1978. 23.50 o.p. (ISBN 0-85664-818-3, Pub. by Croom Helm Ltd). Routledge Chapman & Hall.

Qur'an in Islam: Its Impact & Influence on the Life of Muslims. Allamah S. Tabataba'i. 111p. 1988. pap. text ed. 14.95 o.p. (ISBN 0-7103-0266-5, Kegan Paul). Routledge Chapman & Hall.

Quran, the Ultimate Miracle. A. Deedat. pap. 2.95 o.p. (ISBN 0-686-63913-8). Kazi Pubns.

Quternary Science Reviews, Vol. 3. Ed. by D. Q. Bowen. (Illus.). 328p. 1985. 105.00 o.p. (ISBN 0-08-032760-5, Pub. by PPL). Pergamon.

R

R. A. Fisher: An Appreciation. Ed. by S. E. Fienberg & D. H. Hinkley. (Lecture Notes in Statistics Ser.: Vol. 1). 208p. 1980. pap. 18.00 o.p. (ISBN 0-387-90476-X). Springer-Verlag.

R & D for National Strength. David Williamson, Jr. (Panel Report Ser.). 35p. 1982. 6.00 o.p. (ISBN 0-89206-036-0). CSI Studies.

R & D in FY 1987: R & D & the Budget Crisis. Nina Graybill. 166p. 1986. pap. 10.00 o.p. (ISBN 0-317-59877-5). AAAS.

R: BASE System V: Techniques & Applications. Michael R. Parretta. LC 86-61150. 278p. (Orig.). 1987. pap. 21.95 o.p. (ISBN 0-88022-259-X, 57); disk 39.95 o.p. (ISBN 0-88022-305-7, 267). Que Corp.

R: Base System V User's Guide. 2nd ed. Allen G. Taylor. LC 86-63835. 385p. 1987. pap. 19.95 o.p. (ISBN 0-88022-282-4, 80). Que Corp.

R. Buckminster Fuller on Education. R. Buckminster Fuller et al. Ed. by Peter H. Wagschal & Robert D. Kahn. LC 79-4023. 192p. 1979. 12.50x o.p. (ISBN 0-87023-276-2). U of Mass Pr.

R. D. Laing: His Work & Its Relevance to Sociology. Martin Howarth-Williams. (Direct Editions Ser.). (Orig.). 1977. pap. 14.50 o.p. (ISBN 0-7100-8624-5). Routledge Chapman & Hall.

R. D. Mindlin & Applied Mechanics: A Collection of Studies in the Development of Applied Mechanics Dedicated to Prof. R. D. Mindlin by His Former Students. Ed. by George Herman. LC 73-22346. 1974. 71.00 o.p. (ISBN 0-08-017710-7). Pergamon.

R. E. Lee's Cheat Mountain Campaign. Jack Zinn. 1984. 10.00 o.p. (ISBN 0-87012-151-0). McClain.

R. K. Narayan. P. S. Sundaram. (Indian Writers Ser.). 1973. 8.50 o.s.i. (ISBN 0-89253-510-5). Ind-US Inc.

R. Tait McKenzie: The Sculptor of Athletes. Andrew J. Kozar. LC 74-34421. (Illus.). 140p. 1975. 16.50x o.p. (ISBN 0-87049-168-7). U of Tenn Pr.

R. Taylor's Wrong Bag. Richard Taylor. 1961. 3.95 o.p. (ISBN 0-671-63080-6, 03080-6). S&S.

Rabbinic Mind. 3rd ed. Max Kadushin. LC 75-189016. 1972. 15.00 o.s.i. (ISBN 0-8197-0007-X); pap. 9.75x o.p. (ISBN 0-685-30561-9). Bloch.

Rabbi's Manual. rev. ed. 1961. 7.50 o.p. (ISBN 0-916694-26-7). Central Conf.

Rabbit Express. Michael Gay. LC 84-29608. (Illus.). 40p. (ps-3). 1985. 11.75 o.p. (ISBN 0-688-04647-9, Morrow Junior Books); lib. bdg. 11.88 o.p. (ISBN 0-688-04648-7). Morrow.

Rabbit Feeding for Meat & Fur. 2nd ed. Ed. by F. C. Aitken & W. K. Wilson. 63p. 1962. text ed. 5.75 o.p. CAB Intl.

Rabbit Island. Jorg Steiner. Tr. by Ann C. Lammers. LC 78-1512. (Illus.). (gr. 1 up). 1978. Repr. of 1977 ed. 8.95 o.p. (ISBN 0-15-265034-2, HJ). HarBraceJ.

Rabbit Pie. Gerald Rose. 32p. (ps-5). 1986. pap. 4.95 o.p. (ISBN 0-571-13930-2). Faber & Faber.

Rabbits. Graham Tarrant. LC 83-4633. (Natural Pop-Ups Ser.). (Illus.). 10p. (gr. k-2). 1984. 6.95 o.p. (ISBN 0-399-21005-9, Putnam). Putnam Pub Group.

Rabbits & Rainbows. Margaret Hillert. (Happy Day Bks.). (Illus.). 24p. (ps-2). 1985. 1.59 o.p. (ISBN 0-87239-878-1, 3678). Standard Pub.

Rabbits Are Eating Mrs. Koster's Marigolds. William Troy. (Illus.). 64p. 1986. text ed. 10.00 o.p. (ISBN 0-682-40307-5). Exposition-Phoenix.

Rabbitskin Cap. George Baldry. Ed. by Lilias R. Haggard. (Illus.). 258p. 1979. Repr. of 1939 ed. 20.00 o.p. (ISBN 0-85115-045-4, Pub. by Boydell & Brewer). Longwood Pub Group.

Rabelais. John C. Powys. 1951. (ISBN 0-8022-2010-X). Philos Lib.

Rabelais in English Literature. Huntington Brown. 1967. Repr. lib. bdg. 23.00x o.p. (ISBN 0-374-91027-8, Octagon). Hippocrene Bks.

Rabelasian Reprise. Jayge Carr. LC 87-24648. (Science Fiction Ser.). 192p. 1988. pap. 12.95 o.p. (ISBN 0-385-24436-3). Doubleday.

Raccoons, Coatimundis, & Their Family. Dorothy H. Patent. LC 79-10468. (Illus.). 128p. (gr. 5 up). 1979. 8.95 o.p. (ISBN 0-8234-0360-2). Holiday.

Race & Culture: A Psychological Insight into the Present & Past. Leo Cohen & Ralph J. Erickson. LC 74-21439. 1975. 6.00 o.p. (ISBN 0-682-48183-1, University). Exposition-Phoenix.

Race & Ethnic Relations. 4th ed. Brewton Berry & Henry L. Tischler. LC 77-78901. (Illus.). 1978. text ed. 25.50 o.p. (ISBN 0-395-25508-2). HM.

Race & Kinship in a Midwestern Town: The Black Experience in Monroe Michigan, 1900-1915. James E. DeVries. LC 83-6508. (Blacks in the New World Ser.). (Illus.). 206p. 1984. 19.95 o.p. (ISBN 0-252-01084-1). U of Ill Pr.

Race & Modern Science. Robert E. Kuttner. 1986. 11.00 o.p. (ISBN 0-317-53271-5). Noontide.

Race & Races. 2nd ed. Richard A. Goldsby. 1977. write for info. o.p. (ISBN 0-02-344310-3, 34431). Macmillan.

Race & Residence in American Cities. Ed. by Wade C. Roof & Ralph B. Ginsberg. LC 78-72993. (Annals: No. 441). 1979. 15.00 o.p. (ISBN 0-87761-236-6); pap. 6.00 o.p. (ISBN 0-87761-237-4). Am Acad Pol Soc Sci.

Race & the Renewal of the Church. Will D. Campbell. (Orig.). 1962. pap. 1.25 o.s.i. (ISBN 0-664-24403-3, Westminster). Westminster John Knox.

Race, Class & Education. Ed. by Len Barton & Stephen Walker. 235p. 1983. pap. 13.95 o.p. (ISBN 0-7099-0684-6, Pub. by Croom Helm Ltd). Routledge Chapman & Hall.

Race Distinctions in American Law. Gilbert T. Stephenson. LC 76-84694. xiv, 388p. 1970. Repr. of 1910 ed. 35.00x o.p. (ISBN 0-8371-1669-4, STR&, Pub. by Negro U Pr). Greenwood.

Race, Ethnicity & Power: A Comparative Study. Ed. by Donald G. Baker. 224p. 1983. 24.95x o.p. (ISBN 0-7100-9467-1). Routledge Chapman & Hall.

Race for Electric Power. Jerry Grey. LC 72-1411. (Illus.). 125p. (gr. 6up). 1972. 5.95 o.s.i. (ISBN 0-664-32518-1, Westminster). Westminster John Knox.

Race for Life: The Joel Sonnenberg Story. Janet Sonnenberg. 1983. 9.95x o.p. (ISBN 0-310-25930-4). Phoenix Soc.

Race for Your Life, Charlie Brown. Charles M. Schulz. LC 77-15208. (Illus.). 1978. 12.95 o.s.i. (ISBN 0-03-042646-4). H Holt & Co.

Race, Language & Culture. Franz Boas. LC 81-21998. (Illus.). xx, 648p. 1982. pap. text ed. 18.00x o.s.i. (ISBN 0-226-06241-4). U of Chicago Pr.
Race Problems of the South. Southern Society for the Promotion of the Study of Race Conditions & Problems in the South Staff. LC 73-88451. Repr. of 1900 ed. 19.75 o.p. (ISBN 0-8371-1788-7, RAP&). Greenwood.
Race Relations in Ancient Egypt. S. Davis. 1952. (ISBN 0-8022-0362-0). Philos Lib.
Race Relations in Malaysia. Wan Hashim. xvii, 127p. 1983. pap. text ed. 8.50x o.p. (ISBN 967-925-003-2, 00158). Heinemann Ed.
Race Relations in the United States: Material Published 1980-1984. Mary Vance. (Public Administration Ser.: P 1702). 27p. 1985. 3.75 o.p. (ISBN 0-89028-452-0). Vance Biblios.
Race Relations in World Perspective: Papers. Conference on Race Relations in World Perspective, Honolulu, 1954. Ed. by Andrew W. Lind. LC 73-7074. 488p. 1973. Repr. of 1955 ed. lib. bdg. 35.00x o.p. (ISBN 0-8371-6907-0, RRWP). Greenwood.
Race Riot at East St. Louis, July 2, 1917. Elliot Rudwick. LC 64-13634. (Studies in American Negro Life). 1972. pap. text ed. 3.95x o.s.i. (ISBN 0-689-70336-8, NL31, Atheneum). Macmillan.
Race, Rock & Religion: Profiles from a Southern Journalist. Frye Gaillard. LC 82-11325. (Illus.). 192p. 1982. 12.95 o.p. (ISBN 0-914788-59-0). Globe Pequot.
Race, Science, & Society. UNESCO Staff. 368p. 1975. 39.00x o.p. (ISBN 0-231-03908-5); pap. 19.00x o.p. (ISBN 0-231-03910-7). Columbia U Pr.
Race to Win. Roger Marshall. (Illus.). 1980. 15.95 o.p. (ISBN 0-393-03236-1). Norton.
Racecourse for Andy. Patricia Wrightson. LC 68-11507. (gr. 4-6). 1968. 5.95 o.p. (ISBN 0-15-265080-6, HJ). HarBraceJ.
Races of Mankind. C. I. Kephart. LC 60-1364. 456p. 1960. Philos Lib.
Raceway Charger. Margaret Ogan & George Ogan. LC 74-2280. (Hiway Bks.: A High Interest-Low Reading Level Book). 144p. (gr. 6 up). 1974. 5.50 o.s.i. (ISBN 0-664-32550-5, Westminster). Westminster John Knox.
Rachel. Arthur A. Smith. LC 74-80386. 64p. (Orig.). 1975. pap. 1.95 o.p. (ISBN 0-8192-1175-3). Morehouse Pub.
Rachel of Old Louisiana. Avery O. Craven. LC 74-15921. (Illus.). xiv, 122p. 1975. 16.95 o.p. (ISBN 0-8071-0095-1). La State U Pr.
Rachel's Walk. Jonathan Berman. LC 84-90285. 83p. 1985. 8.95 o.p. (ISBN 0-533-06325-6). Vantage.
Rachz: The True Story of a Fox. Sue Chambers. (Illus.). 160p. Date not set. 16.00 o.p. (ISBN 0-85362-217-5, Oriel). Routledge Chapman & Hall.
Racial & Ethnic Groups. 2nd ed. Richard T. Schaefer. 1984. text ed. write for info. o.p. (ISBN 0-673-39595-2). Scott F.
Racial Equality in America. John H. Franklin. LC 76-26168. 1976. 7.95x o.s.i. (ISBN 0-226-26073-9). U of Chicago Pr.
Racial Hybridity. Philip T. Jones. (Illus.). 241p. (Orig.). 1979. pap. 5.50x o.p. (ISBN 0-911038-77-9, Uriel Pubns). Winning.
Racial Inequality: A Political-Economic Analysis. Michael Reich. LC 80-8573. 345p. 1981. 34.00x o.p. (ISBN 0-691-04227-6); pap. 9.95x o.p. (ISBN 0-691-00365-3). Princeton U Pr.
Racial Problems in Hungary. R. W. Seton-Watson. 540p. 1973. Repr. of 1908 ed. 45.00x o.p. (ISBN 0-86527-163-1). Fertig.
Racial Thinking of Richard Wagner. Leon Stein. (ISBN 0-8022-1638-2). Philos Lib.
Racially Separate or Together. T. F. Pettigrew. 1971. pap. text ed. 19.95 o.p. (ISBN 0-07-049718-4). McGraw.
Racines du Ciel. Romain Gary. 512p. 1972. 3.95 o.p. (ISBN 0-686-55885-5). Schoenhof.
Racine's Mid-Career Tragedies. Jean Racine. Tr. by Lacy Lockert. 1958. 30.50x o.p. (ISBN 0-691-06106-8). Princeton U Pr.
Racing Dragsters. Angelo G. Resciniti. (Winning Streak Ser.). (Illus.). 32p. (gr. 3-8). 1986. 2.95 o.s.i. (ISBN 0-87406-039-7). Willowisp Pr.
Racing Driver's Diary. Y. Klemanov. 150p. 1982. pap. 2.95 o.p. (ISBN 0-8285-2513-7, Pub. by Progress Pubs USSR). Imported Pubns.
Racing Minicycles. Ray Paprocki. (Winning Streak Ser.). (Illus.). 32p. (Orig.). (gr. 3-8). 1987. 2.50 o.s.i. (ISBN 0-87406-217-9). Willowisp Pr.
Racing Sports Car. Anthony Pritchard. (Illus.). 1971. 8.95 o.p. (ISBN 0-393-08627-5). Norton.
Racing to Love. Caroline Cooney. (Follow Your Heart Romance Ser.: No. 7). (Orig.). (gr. 5 up). 1985. pap. 2.25 o.p. Archway.
Racing Toward Judgment. David Wilkerson. 160p. 1976. pap. 2.50 o.p. (ISBN 0-8007-8276-3, Spire Bks). Revell.
Racing Yachts. A. Whipple & Time-Life Books Editors. (Seafarers Ser.). (Illus.). 176p. 1981. 13.95 o.p. (ISBN 0-8094-2693-5). Time-Life.
Racism-a Philosophic Probe. Fr. Chukwudum Barnabas Okolo. LC 73-92851. 1974. 6.00 o.p. (ISBN 0-682-47904-7, University). Exposition-Phoenix.
Racism, a World Issue. Edward D. Soper. LC 75-98731. Repr. of 1947 ed. 35.00x o.p. (ISBN 0-8371-2788-2, SOR&). Greenwood.
Racism, Diversity & Education. Ed. by Jagdish Gundara et al. (Studies in Teaching & Learning). 192p. (Orig.). 1986. pap. text ed. 19.95 o.s.i. (ISBN 0-340-34192-0). Princeton Bk Co.
Racism, Education & the State: The Racialisation of Education Policy. Barry Troyna & Jenny Williams. LC 85-22340. 192p. 1985. 26.00 o.p. (ISBN 0-7099-2498-4, Pub. by Croom Helm Ltd); pap. 12.00 o.p. (ISBN 0-7099-4316-4). Routledge Chapman & Hall.
Racism, the Australian Experience, Volume One: Prejudice & Xenophobia. Ed. by Frank S. Stevens. LC 70-179992. 193p. 1972. 12.50x o.s.i. (ISBN 0-8008-6580-4). Taplinger.
Racism, the Australian Experience, Volume Two: Black Versus White. F. S. Stevens. LC 70-179992. 266p. 1972. 12.50x o.s.i. (ISBN 0-8008-6581-2). Taplinger.
Racism, the Australian Experience, Volume Three: Colonialism. F. S. Stevens. LC 70-179992. 185p. 1973. 12.50x o.s.i. (ISBN 0-8008-6582-0). Taplinger.
Rack & Panel Connectors. Ed. by Steven D'Adolf. 300p. 1987. 95.00 o.p. (ISBN 0-317-57581-3). DATA Busn Pub.
Rack WD Notched Tube. Date not set. (ISBN 0-07-521000-2). McGraw.
Racket & Paddle Games: A Guide to Information Sources. Ed. by David A. Peele. LC 80-23977. (Sports, Games & Pastimes Information Guide Ser.: Vol. 9). 264p. 1980. 68.00x o.p. (ISBN 0-8103-1480-0). Gale.
Racquetball. Philip E. Allsen & Pete Witbeck. 96p. 1987. pap. text ed. write for info. o.p. (ISBN 0-697-07238-X). Wm C Brown.
Racquetball. Gabert. 96p. 1984. pap. text ed. 8.95 o.p. (ISBN 0-8403-3214-9). Kendall-Hunt.
Racquetball Book. Margaret Poynter. LC 79-24534. (Illus.). 128p. (gr. 4 up). 1980. lib. bdg. 8.79 o.s.i. (ISBN 0-671-33014-4). Messner.
Racquetball the Easy Way. Charles Garfinkel. LC 78-53835. (Illus., Orig.). 1978. pap. 6.95 o.p. (ISBN 0-689-70560-3, Atheneum). Macmillan.
Radar Calculations Using Personal Computers. William. A Skillman. 150p. 1984. text ed. 54.00 o.p. (ISBN 0-89006-141-6). Artech Hse.
Radar Calculations Using the TI-59 Programmable Calculator. William Skillman. (Illus.). 405p. 1983. 49.00 o.p. (ISBN 0-89006-112-2). Artech Hse.
Radar Cross Section Handbook. George T. Ruck et al. LC 68-26774. 950p. 1970. 125.00x o.p. (ISBN 0-306-30343-4, Plenum Pr). Plenum Pub.
Radar Principles for the Non-Specialist. John C. Toomay. (Engineering Ser.). 173p. 1982. 26.95 o.p. (ISBN 0-534-97943-2, Lifetime Learn). Van Nos Reinhold.
Radar System Analysis. David K. Barton. LC 76-45811. (Artech Radar Library). 608p. 1977. Repr. of 1964 ed. 55.00x o.p. (ISBN 0-89006-043-6). Artech Hse.
Radars: Radar Clutter, Vol. 5. Ed. by David K. Barton. LC 74-82597. (Artech Radar Library). 420p. 1975. pap. 29.00 o.p. (ISBN 0-89006-034-7). Artech Hse.
Radars: The Radar Equation, Vol. 2. 2nd ed. Ed. by David K. Barton. LC 74-82597. (Artech Radar Library). 232p. 1974. pap. 29.00 o.p. (ISBN 0-89006-031-2). Artech Hse.
Radcliffe. David Storey. 1985. pap. 1.95 o.p. (ISBN 0-380-00426-7, 47241-4). Avon.
RADCURE '84 Conference Proceedings. Society of Manufacturing Engineers Staff. 1984. 54.00 o.p. (ISBN 0-87263-158-3). SME.
Radiant Universe. George W. Hill. 1952. (ISBN 0-8022-0718-9). Philos Lib.
Radiation & Cellular Control Processes. Ed. by J. Kiefer. (Illus.). 1976. 43.00 o.p. (ISBN 0-387-07878-9). Springer-Verlag.
Radiation & Immune Mechanisms. William H. Taliaferro et al. (Atomic Energy Commission Monographs). (Illus.). 1964. 17.00 o.p. (ISBN 0-12-682450-9). Acad Pr.
Radiation & Propagation of Electromagnetic Waves. G. Tyras. (Electrical Science Ser). 1969. 95.00 o.p. (ISBN 0-12-705650-5). Acad Pr.
Radiation & Reentry. S. S. Penner & Daniel B. Olfe. LC 67-22773. (Reentry Physics Ser.). 1968. 95.50 o.p. (ISBN 0-12-550450-0). Acad Pr.
Radiation & Shielding in Space. James W. Haffner. 1967. 55.00 o.p. (ISBN 0-12-313250-9). Acad Pr.
Radiation Biochemistry, 2 vols. Kurt I. Altman. Incl. Vol. 1. Cells. Shigefumi Okada (ISBN 0-12-054501-2); Vol. 2. Tissues & Body Fluids. Kurt I. Altman & Georg B. Gerber (ISBN 0-12-054502-0). 1970. Vol. 1. o.p. 75.00 ea. o.p.; Vol. 2. 98.00 o.p. Acad Pr.
Radiation Chemistry in Nuclear Reactor Technology. Ed. by A. W. Boyd. 70p. 1983. pap. 25.00 o.p. (ISBN 0-08-029156-2). Pergamon.
Radiation Chemistry of Carbohydrates. Ed. by N. K. Kochetkov et al. (Illus.). 1979. 70.00 o.p. (ISBN 0-08-022962-X). Pergamon.
Radiation Chemistry of Macromolecules, 2 vols. Ed. by Malcolm Dole. 1972. Vol. 1. 87.50 o.p. (ISBN 0-12-219801-8). Acad Pr.
Radiation Chimeras. O. Van Bekkum & H. De Vries. 1967. 81.00 o.p. (ISBN 0-12-710350-3). Acad Pr.
Radiation Damage: Proceedings of CISM, Department for Mechanics of Defamable Bodies, Univ. of Vienna, 1970. CISM (International Center for Mechanical Sciences), Department for Mechanics of Defamable Bodies Staff. Ed. by E. Schmid & K. Lintner. Incl. Behavior of Insonated Metals. (CISM Publications: No. 64). (Illus.). 88p. 1973. pap. 10.60 o.p. (ISBN 0-387-81124-9). Springer-Verlag.
Radiation Education Notebook. Atomic Industrial Forum Staff. (Public Affairs & Information Program: General). 1983. 15.00 o.p. (ISBN 0-318-02249-4). US Coun Energy Awareness.
Radiation Exposure of the U. S. Population From Consumer Products & Miscellaneous Sources. LC 87-24724. (NCRP Report Ser.: No. 95). pap. text ed. NCRP Pubns.
Radiation Gas Dynamics. Pai Shih-I. (Illus.). 1966. 31.90 o.p. (ISBN 0-387-80776-4). Springer-Verlag.
Radiation Heat Transfer: Augmented Edition. E. M. Sparrow & R. D. Cess. LC 77-24158. (McGraw-Hill Series in Thermal & Fluids Engineering). (Illus.). 1978. text ed. 49.95 o.p. (ISBN 0-07-059910-6). McGraw.
Radiation Hydrodynamics. G. C. Pomraning. 304p. 1973. 70.00 o.p. (ISBN 0-08-016893-0). Pergamon.
Radiation Injury of Bone: Bone Injuries Following Radiation Therapy of Tumors. K. Shimanovskaya & Alexander Shiman. Tr. by Basil Haigh. (Illus.). 300p. 1983. 61.00 o.p. (ISBN 0-08-028821-9). Pergamon.
Radiation, Isotopes, & Bone. F. C. McLean & A. M. Budy. (Atomic Energy Commission Monographs). 1964. 14.50 o.p. (ISBN 0-12-484950-4). Acad Pr.
Radiation Issues for the Nuclear Industry: Set of Papers from AIF Conference on Radiation. Atomic Industrial Forum Staff. (Technical & Economic Reports: Radiation Protection & Environmental Considerations). 1982. 150.00 o.p. (ISBN 0-318-02244-3). US Coun Energy Awareness.
Radiation Oncology: Rationale, Technique, Results. 5th ed. William T. Moss et al. LC 79-14367. (Illus.). 660p. 1979. 67.95 o.p. (ISBN 0-8016-3556-X). Mosby.
Radiation Physics & Chemistry: Magat Memorial Issue, Vols. 2 & 3. Ed. by F. Kieffer. 300p. 1980. pap. 51.00 o.p. (ISBN 0-08-025069-6). Pergamon.
Radiation Processing for Environmental Conservation. Ed. by S. Machi. 202p. 1985. pap. 30.00 o.p. (ISBN 0-08-031435-X). Pergamon.
Radiation Processing: Fourth International Meeting on Radiation Processing, Dubrovnik, Yugoslavia, October 1982, 2 vols. Ed. by V. Markovic. 980p. 1984. Set. pap. 155.00 o.p. (ISBN 0-08-029162-7). Pergamon.
Radiation Protection: A Systematic Approach to Safety: Proceedings of the 5th Congress of the International Radiation Protection Society, March 1980, Jerusalem, 2 vols. Ed. by Eisenberg. (Illus.). 1055p. 1980. Set. 255.00 o.p. (ISBN 0-08-025912-X). Pergamon.
Radiation Protection in Mining & Milling of Uranium & Thorium. (Occupational Safety & Health Ser.: No. 32). pap. 24.50 o.p. (ISBN 92-2-101504-1, ILO25, ILO). UNIPUB.
Radiation Protection in Schools for Pupils up to the Age of 18 Years. International Commission on Radiological Protection. (ICRP Publication Ser: No. 13). 1970. pap. 8.50 o.p. (ISBN 0-08-016356-4). Pergamon.
Radiation Protection in the Mining & Milling of Radioactive Ores see Manual of Industrial Radiation Protection.
Radiation Protection Measurement. H. Kiefer & R. Maushart. Tr. by Ralf Friese. LC 70-133884. 576p. 1972. 81.00 o.p. (ISBN 0-08-015838-2). Pergamon.
Radiation Protection: Proceedings of the First International Congress. Ed. by W. S. Snyder et al. LC 67-30114. 1968. 415.00 o.p. (ISBN 0-08-012413-5). Pergamon.
Radiation Protection Standards. Lauriston S. Taylor. (Monotopic Reprint Ser.). 112p. 1971. 29.00 o.p. (ISBN 0-8493-0111-4). CRC Pr.
Radiation Sterilization of Plastic Medical Devices: Seminar under the Auspices of the University of Lowell, Mass., March 1979. H. K. Mann. 128p. 1980. pap. 25.00 o.p. (ISBN 0-08-025067-X). Pergamon.
Radiationless Processes. Ed. by Baldassare Di Bartolo. LC 80-21961. (NATO ASI Series B, Physical Sciences: Vol. 62). 566p. 1981. 89.50x o.p. (ISBN 0-306-40577-6, Plenum Pr). Plenum Pub.
Radiationless Transition. Ed. by Sheng H. Lin. LC 79-26781. 1980. 70.50 o.p. (ISBN 0-12-450650-X). Acad Pr.
Radical Approaches to Adult Education. Tom Lovett. 240p. 1988. lib. bdg. 42.00x o.p. (ISBN 0-415-00561-2, Pub. by Croom Helm UK). Routledge Chapman & Hall.
Radical Approaches to Adult Education. Ed. by Tom Lovett. (Radical Forum on Adult Education Ser.). 240p. 1986. 34.50 o.p. (ISBN 0-7099-4141-2, Pub. by Croom Helm UK). Routledge Chapman & Hall.
Radical Approaches to Social Skills Training. Ed. by Peter Trower. 384p. 1984. 33.00 o.p. (ISBN 0-416-00931-X, NO. 5076). Routledge Chapman & Hall.
Radical Attack on Business: A Critical Analysis. Charles Perrow. 288p. 1972. pap. text ed. 9.95 o.p. (ISBN 0-15-575092-5, HC). HarBraceJ.
Radical Christian Living. Richard Booker. LC 84-90103. (Illus.). 124p. (Orig.). pap. cancelled o.s.i. (ISBN 0-932081-03-7). Victory Hse.
Radical Citizenship: The New American Activism. David Bouchier. LC 86-29705. 288p. 1987. 19.95 o.p. (ISBN 0-8052-4031-4). Schocken.
Radical Departures: Desperate Detours to Growing Up. Saul V. Levine. LC 83-26491. 288p. 1984. 15.95 o.p. (ISBN 0-15-175840-9). HarBraceJ.
Radical Earnestness: English Social Theory, 1880-1980. Fred Inglis. 264p. 1982. 24.95x o.s.i. (ISBN 0-85520-328-5); pap. 9.95x o.p. (ISBN 0-85520-401-X). Basil Blackwell.
Radical Education: A Critique of Preschooling & Deschooling. Robin Barrow. 207p. 1979. pap. 23.95 o.p. (ISBN 0-470-26845-X). Halsted Pr.
Radical Imperative: From Theology to Social Ethics. John C. Bennett. LC 75-15538. 208p. 1975. 8.50 o.s.i. (ISBN 0-664-20824-X, Westminster); pap. 7.95 o.s.i. (ISBN 0-664-24769-5, Westminster). Westminster John Knox.
Radical Innocence: The Contemporary American Novel. Ihab Hassan. 1971. 41.00x o.p. (ISBN 0-691-06107-6); pap. 10.50x o.p. (ISBN 0-691-01301-2). Princeton U Pr.
Radical Moves. Lee Daniels. (Surf City Ser.: No. 6). 144p. (Orig.). (YA) (gr. 5-9). 1989. pap. 2.95 o.p. (ISBN 1-55802-070-5). Lynx Bks.
Radical Perspectives in Psychology. Nick Heather. (Essential Psychology Ser.). 1976. pap. 4.50x o.p. (ISBN 0-416-81860-9, NO. 2745). Routledge Chapman & Hall.
Radical Politics in West Bengal. Marcus F. Franda. (Studies in Communism, Revisionism, & Revolution). 1971. 30.00x o.p. (ISBN 0-262-06040-X). MIT Pr.
Radical Probe: The Logic of Student Rebellion. Michael W. Miles. LC 76-139320. Orig. Title: Student Movement. 1971. pap. text ed. 3.25x o.p. (ISBN 0-689-70340-6, 196, Atheneum). Macmillan.
Radical Protest & Social Structure: The Southern Farmer's Alliance & Cotton Tenancy, 1880-1890. Michael Schwartz. (Studies in Social Discontinuity Ser.). 1976. 48.50 o.p. (ISBN 0-12-632850-1). Acad Pr.
Radical Reformation. George H. Williams. LC 62-7066. (Illus.). 960p. 1962. 24.95 o.s.i. (ISBN 0-664-20372-8, Westminster). Westminster John Knox.
Radical Review, Vols. 1-2, No. 3. 1968. Repr. of 1917 ed. Set. lib. bdg. 32.00x o.p. (ISBN 0-8371-9385-0, RR00); Vol. 1. lib. bdg. 18.25 o.p. (ISBN 0-313-21938-9, RR01); Vol. 2. lib. bdg. 18.25 o.p. (ISBN 0-313-21939-7, RR02). Greenwood.
Radical Soap Opera. David Z. Mairowitz. 1976. pap. 2.45 o.p. (ISBN 0-380-00616-2, 28308). Avon.
Radical Socioeducational Analysis. Scott B. Sigmon. 136p. 1985. pap. text ed. 12.95x o.s.i. (ISBN 0-8290-1584-1). Irvington.
Radical Sociology: A Critical Introduction to American Behavioral Science. David J. Sternberg. LC 77-71591. (Illus.). 1977. 15.00 o.p. (ISBN 0-682-48807-0, University); pap. 7.50 o.p. (ISBN 0-682-48808-9). Exposition-Phoenix.
Radical Theater Notebook. Arthur Sainer. 1975. pap. 2.65 o.p. (ISBN 0-380-00287-6, 22442, Discus). Avon.
Radical's America. Harvey Swados. LC 73-5209. 347p. 1973. Repr. of 1962 ed. lib. bdg. 22.50x o.p. (ISBN 0-8371-6869-4, SWRA). Greenwood.
Radicals in Social Work. Daphne Statham. (Radical Social Policy Ser.). 1978. 18.95x o.p. (ISBN 0-7100-8801-9); pap. 8.95x o.p. (ISBN 0-7100-8802-7). Routledge Chapman & Hall.
Radicals in the University. Edward E. Ericson, Jr. LC 75-27011. (Publications Ser.: No. 144). 1975. 12.95x o.p. (ISBN 0-8179-6441-X). Hoover Inst Pr.

Radikalismus Untersuchungen Zur Persoenlichkeitsentwicklung Westdeutscher Studenten in den Jahren-1973. Ed. by W. De Boor & R. Grossarth-Maticek. (Schriftenreihe des Instituts fuer Konfliktforschung: No. 5). (Illus.). 1979. 8.75 o.p. (ISBN 3-8055-3035-8). S Karger.

Radio Amateur's Microwave Communications Handbook. Dave Ingram. (Illus.). 192p. (Orig.). 1985. 18.95 o.p. (ISBN 0-8306-0194-5, 1594); pap. 12.60 o.p. (ISBN 0-8306-0594-0). Tab Bks.

Radio & Line Transmission, Vol. 2. D. Roddy. 1972. text ed. 30.00 o.p. (ISBN 0-08-016289-4); pap. text ed. 12.75 o.p. (ISBN 0-08-016288-6). Pergamon.

Radio & Television Servicing. R. N. Wainwright. (Illus.). 800p. 1986. text ed. 57.50x o.p. (ISBN 0-356-12359-6, Pub. by MacD & Co). Trans-Atl Phila.

Radio & TV Programming. Herbert H. Howard & Michael S. Kievman. LC 82-6079. (Advertising & Journalism Ser.). 372p. 1983. text ed. write for info. o.p. (ISBN 0-02-357240-X, Pub. by Grid). Macmillan.

Radio Astronomy for Amateurs. Frank W. Hyde. (Illus.). 1963. 5.00 o.p. (ISBN 0-393-06331-3). Norton.

Radio City. Fanny Howe. 128p. (YA) (gr. 7 up). 1984. pap. 2.25 o.p. (ISBN 0-380-86025-2, 86025, Flare). Avon.

Radio Control Model Helicopter Handbook. Don Lodge. (Illus.). 192p. (Orig.). 1983. pap. 10.60 o.p. (ISBN 0-8306-1509-1, 1509). TAB Bks.

Radio Database International. Ed. by Lawrence Magne & Tony Jones. (Illus.). 200p. (Orig.). 1983. pap. 9.95 o.p. (ISBN 0-914941-00-3). IBS PA.

Radio Database International. Ed. by Lawrence Magne & Tony Jones. (Illus.). 240p. 1985. pap. 9.95 o.p. (ISBN 0-914941-01-1). IBS PA.

Radio Database International: Tropical Bands Edition, Pt. 2. Ed. by Lawrence Magne & Tony Jones. 1985. pap. 4.95 o.p. (ISBN 0-914941-02-X). IBS PA.

Radio Database International: Worldwide Broadcasting Edition. 1987 ed. Ed. by Lawrence Magne & Tony Jones. 352p. 1986. 14.95 o.p. (ISBN 0-914941-03-8). IBS PA.

Radio Electronic Measurements. G. Mirsky. 503p. 1978. 10.20 o.p. (ISBN 0-8285-0692-2, Pub. by Mir Pubs USSR). Imported Pubns.

Radio Emission of the Sun & Planets. V. V. Zheleznyakov. LC 75-76797. 1970. 180.00 o.p. (ISBN 0-08-013061-5). Pergamon.

Radio Frequency Testers. James Lee et al. Ed. by Sandy Cole & Rich Force. (Seventy-Three Test Equipment Library: Vol. 3). 112p. pap. text ed. 4.95 o.p. (ISBN 0-88006-012-3, LB 7361). Wayne Green Ent.

Radio Galaxies: Radiation Transfer, Dynamics, Stability & Evolution of a Synchroton Plasmon. A. G. Pacholczyk. LC 76-27283. 1977. 75.00 o.p. (ISBN 0-08-021031-7). Pergamon.

Radio Handbook. 22nd ed. William I. Orr. LC 40-33904. (Illus.). 1982. 21.95 o.p. (ISBN 0-672-21874-7). Editors.

Radio Operator's License Q & A Manual. 9th, rev. ed. Milton Kaufman. 1979. 16.80 o.p. (ISBN 0-8104-0651-9); pap. 10.95 o.p. (ISBN 0-8104-0650-0). Sams.

Radio Operator's License Q & A Manual. 10th Rev. ed. Milton Kaufman. 658p. 1986. pap. text ed. 16.95 o.p. (ISBN 0-8104-0666-7). Sams.

Radio Systems for Technicians. D. C. Green. 1985. 12.95 o.p. (ISBN 0-672-22464-X, 22464-X). Sams.

Radioactive Contamination. Virginia Brodine. Ed. by Barry Commoner. (Environmental Issues Ser.). (Illus.). 208p. 1975. pap. text ed. 9.95 o.p. (ISBN 0-15-575121-2, HC). HarBraceJ.

Radioactive Substances: A Translation from the French of the Classical Thesis Presented to the Faculty of Sciences in Paris. Marie Curie. LC 79-139128. (Illus.). 1971. Repr. of 1961 ed. lib. bdg. 22.50x o.p. (ISBN 0-8371-5744-7, CURS). Greenwood.

Radioactive Waste Disposal: A Bibliography. Mary Vance. (Public Administration Ser.: P-1676). 102p. 1985. pap. 15.00 o.p. (ISBN 0-89028-386-9). Vance Biblios.

Radioactively Labeled Iododeoxyuridine in the Study of Experimental Liver Regeneration see Aortic Alterations in Rabbits Following Sheathing with Silastic & Polyethylene Tubes.

Radioactivity Measuring Instruments. M. C. Nokes. (Illus.). 74p. 1959. (ISBN 0-8022-1225-5). Philos Lib.

Radioassay Systems in Clinical Endocrinology. Abraham. (Basic & Clinical Endocrinology Ser.: Vol. 1). 904p. 1981. 110.00 o.p. (ISBN 0-8247-6953-8). Dekker.

Radioastronomical Methods of Antenna Measurements. A. D. Kuzmin & A. E. Salomonovich. (Electrical Science Monographs). 1967. 59.00 o.p. (ISBN 0-12-431150-4). Acad Pr.

Radioecology. V. M. Klechkovskii et al. LC 73-4697. 371p. 1973. 79.95x o.p. (ISBN 0-470-49035-7). Halsted Pr.

Radioecology & Energy Resources: Proceedings of the Ecological Society of America Radioecology Symposium, Oregon State University, May 12-14, 1975. Ecological Society of America Radioecology Symposium Staff. Ed. by C. E. Cushing, Jr. (Ecological Society of America Special Publications Ser.: No. 1). 1976. 64.00 o.p. (ISBN 0-12-786290-0). Acad Pr.

Radiographer's Handbook of Hospital Practice. Chesney. 1986. 21.00 o.p. (ISBN 0-8016-1409-0). Mosby.

Radiographic Index. 6th ed. Goldman & Cope. 104p. 1978. pap. 8.50 o.p. (ISBN 0-7236-0496-7, Pub. by John Wright UK). Butterworth.

Radiographic Index. Myer Goldman & David Cope. (Illus.). 112p. 1982. pap. text ed. 12.00 o.p. (ISBN 0-7236-0660-9). Butterworth.

Radiographic Technique in Veterinary Practice. 2nd ed. James W. Ticer. (Illus.). 528p. 1984. 55.00 o.p. (ISBN 0-7216-8861-6). Saunders.

Radiographic Techniques Related to Pathology. 2nd ed. Margaret A. Clifford & Ann E. Drummond. 88p. 1977. pap. text ed. 10.50 o.p. Butterworth.

Radioimmunoassay. Ed. by Rosalyn S. Yalow. LC 83-8594. (Benchmark Papers in Microbiology: Vol. 20). 416p. 1983. 55.95 o.p. (ISBN 0-87933-109-7). Van Nos Reinhold.

Radioimmunoassay: Methodology & Applications in Physiology & in Clinical Studies. Luft & Yalow. (Illus.). 206p. 1975. lib. bdg. 24.00 o.p. (ISBN 0-88416-059-9). Year Bk Med.

Radioimmunoassay-Renin-Angiotensin: Principles of Radioimmunoassay & Their Application in Measuring Renin & Angiotensin. Ed. by Dieter K. Krause et al. (Illus.). 222p. 1978. 39.50 o.p. (ISBN 0-88416-258-3). Year Bk Med.

Radioisotope & Radiation Physics: An Introduction. M. Mladjenovic. 1973. 66.00 o.p. (ISBN 0-12-502350-2). Acad Pr.

Radioisotopes in Cardiology. Ed. by Marco Salvatore & Ernesto Porta. LC 82-24690. 342p. 1983. 65.00x o.p. (ISBN 0-306-41267-5, Plenum Pr). Plenum Pub.

Radiologic Interpretation of ERCP: A Clinical Atlas. Errol M. Bellon. 1983. pap. text ed. 45.25 o.p. (ISBN 0-87488-707-0). Med Exam.

Radiologic Science for Technologists: Physics, Biology, & Protection. 3rd ed. Stewart C. Bushong. (Illus.). 544p. 1984. cloth 36.95 o.p. (ISBN 0-8016-0933-X). Mosby.

Radiologic Technology: A Future for You. T. J. Jackson. LC 73-83226. (Illus.). 123p. 1974. flexible bdg. 4.95 o.p. (ISBN 0-913292-18-4). Tiresias Pr.

Radiological Atlas of Gastrointestinal Disease. Daniel J. Nolan. 313p. 1983. 75.00 o.p. (ISBN 0-471-25917-9, Dist. by A R Liss). Wiley.

Radiological Exploration of the Ventricles & Subarachnoid Space. G. Ruggiero et al. LC 73-19548. (Illus.). 200p. 1974. 105.00 o.p. (ISBN 0-387-06572-5). Springer-Verlag.

Radiological Investigation: A Guide to the Use of Medical Imaging in Clinical Practice. Hiram Baddeley. LC 82-23777. 411p. 1985. 60.00 o.p. (ISBN 0-471-25589-0, Dist. by A R Liss). Wiley.

Radiology & Imaging for Medical Students. 4th ed. David Sutton. 1982. pap. text ed. 22.50 o.p. (ISBN 0-443-02669-6). Churchill.

Radiology: Focus on Clinical Diagnosis. H. Joachim Burhenne & David K. Li. 1984. text ed. 56.25 o.p. (ISBN 0-87488-406-3). Med Exam.

Radiology for Dental Auxiliaries. 3rd ed. Herbert H. Frommer. (Illus.). 1982. pap. text ed. 23.95 o.p. (ISBN 0-8016-1704-9). Mosby.

Radiology in Disorders of the Liver, Biliary Tract & Pancreas. Joe Ariyama et al. LC 81-82117. (Illus.). 208p. 1981. text ed. 41.00 o.p. (ISBN 0-89640-059-X). Igaku-Shoin.

Radiology of Bone Tumors & Allied Disorders, 4 vols. Daniel Wilner. (Illus.). 4248p. 1982. Set. text ed. write for info. o.p. (ISBN 0-7216-9459-4); Vol. 1, 1180p. write for info. o.p. (ISBN 0-7216-9476-4); Vol. 2, 711p. write for info. o.p. (ISBN 0-7216-9477-2); Vol. 3, 1115p. write for info. o.p. (ISBN 0-7216-9478-0); Vol. 4, 1175p. write for info. o.p. (ISBN 0-7216-9479-9). Saunders.

Radiology of Renal Failures. Harry J. Griffiths. LC 74-17754. (Monographs in Clinical Radiology: Vol. 9). (Illus.). 1976. text ed. write for info. o.p. (ISBN 0-7216-4283-7). Saunders.

Radiology of Skeletal Disorders: Exercises in Diagnosis, 4 vols. 2d ed. Ronald O. Murray & Harold G. Jacobson. LC 76-28430. (Illus.). 1977. text ed. 295.00 o.p. (ISBN 0-443-01267-9). Churchill.

Radiology of the Ear. Phelps & Lloyd. 1983. 68.50 o.p. (ISBN 0-632-01083-5, B-38747). Mosby.

Radiology of the Gallbladder & Bile Ducts: Diagnosis & Intervention. Robert N. Berk et al. (Illus.). 608p. 1983. (ISBN 0-7216-1728-X). Saunders.

Radiology of the Gallbladder & Bile Ducts. Robert N. Berk & Arthur R. Clemett. LC 76-54037. (Saunders Monographs in Clinical Radiology Ser.: Vol. 12). (Illus.). 1977. text ed. write for info. o.p. (ISBN 0-7216-1702-6). Saunders.

Radiology of the Gallbladder & Bile Ducts. Philip M. Hatfield & Robert E. Wise. LC 76-3460. 276p. 1976. 31.00 o.p. (ISBN 0-683-03908-3). Krieger.

Radionuclide Imaging in Drug Research. Ed. by Clive G. Wilson et al. (Illus.). 330p. 1982. 44.00 o.p. (ISBN 0-7099-2716-9, Pub. by Croom Helm Ltd). Routledge Chapman & Hall.

Radionuclide Technology. K. Chackett. 1981. 47.95 o.p. (ISBN 0-442-30170-7); pap. 21.95 o.p. (ISBN 0-442-30171-5). Van Nos Reinhold.

Radionuclides in Nephrology. Ed. by Zum Winkel et al. LC 75-16106. 344p. 1975. lib. bdg. 18.50 o.p. (ISBN 0-88416-062-9). Year Bk Med.

Radionuclides in Pharmacology, 2 vols. Y. Cohen. 1971. Set. 270.00 o.p. (ISBN 0-08-016152-9). Pergamon.

Radiopharmaceuticals. Ed. by Gopal Subramanian. LC 75-16093. 500p. 1975. lib. bdg. 30.00 o.p. (ISBN 0-88416-041-6). Year Bk Med.

Radiopharmaceuticals & Other Compounds Labelled with Short-Lived Radionuclides. Ed. by Michael J. Welch. LC 76-26764. 1977. pap. 48.00 o.p. (ISBN 0-08-021344-8). Pergamon.

Radioprotection: Chemical Compounds - Biological Means. Ed. by Alfred Locker & Kurt Flemming. (Illus.). cancelled o.s.i. (ISBN 3-7643-0871-0). Adlers Foreign Bks.

Radish Day Jubilee. Sheilah Bruce. (Fraggle Rock Bks.). (Illus.). 48p. (gr. 1-4). 1983. 6.95 o.s.i. (ISBN 0-03-068678-4). H Holt & Co.

RAF Colour Album. T. Malcolm English. 96p. 14.95 o.p. (ISBN 0-7106-0204-9). Janes Info Group.

RAF Fighter Squadrons in the Battle of Britain. Anthony Robinson. (Illus.). 224p. 1988. 24.95 o.p. (ISBN 0-85368-846-X, Pub. by Arms & Armour). Sterling.

Rafa's Dog. Helen Griffiths. LC 83-4384. 112p. (gr. 3-6). 1983. 9.95 o.p. (ISBN 0-8234-0492-7). Holiday.

Rag Doll Looks for a House. Lin Songying. (Illus.). 37p. (gr. 1-3). 1983. pap. 2.95 o.p. (ISBN 0-8351-1296-9). China Bks.

Rage for Falcons. Date not set. Random.

Rage of the Vulture. Barry Unsworth. 443p. 1983. 15.45 o.p. (ISBN 0-395-32526-9). HM.

Rage Within: Anger in Modern Life. Willard Gaylin. 320p. 1984. 16.45 o.p. (ISBN 0-671-42130-1). S&S.

Ragged Statue & Other Stories. Ray L. Caley. (Illus.). 75p. 1982. 12.95 o.p. (ISBN 0-910987-01-7); pap. 8.95 o.p. (ISBN 0-910987-00-9). Dragon's Lair.

Raggity & the Cloud. S. Prokofieva. 160p. 1982. 5.45 o.p. (ISBN 0-8285-2530-7, Pub. by Progress Pubs USSR). Imported Pubns.

Raging Hearts. Patricia Hagan. (Trilogy Bk.: No. 2). 480p. 1979. pap. 3.95 o.p. (ISBN 0-380-46201-X, 60028-5). Avon.

Raging Talent. Jack Hoffenberg. 1976. pap. 1.95 o.p. (ISBN 0-380-00836-X, 31021). Avon.

Ragnarok-the Age of Fire & Gravel. I. Donnelly. 1970. 12.50 o.p. (ISBN 0-8216-0142-3, Pub. by Univ Bks). Carol Pub Group.

Ragnar's Tall Tales. Ragnar Benson. 90p. 1983. pap. 6.00 o.p. (ISBN 0-87364-263-5). Paladin Pr.

Rags of Glory. Stuart Cloete. 1973. pap. 1.50 o.p. (ISBN 0-380-01516-1, 15792). Avon.

Ragtime: Its History, Composers, & Music. Ed. by John E. Hasse. 380p. 1985. 29.95 o.s.i. (ISBN 0-02-871650-7). Schirmer Bks.

Ragweed the Pixie & Other Tales. F. F. Foss. (Illus.). 48p. 1983. pap. 4.00 o.p. (ISBN 0-682-49923-4). Exposition-Phoenix.

Rahel Varnhagen: The Life of a Jewish Woman. rev ed. Hannah Arendt. Tr. by Richard Winston & Clara Winston. LC 74-6478. (Illus.). 266p. 1974. 7.95 o.p. (ISBN 0-15-175850-6). HarBraceJ.

Rahne. Susan Coon. 1980. pap. 1.95 o.p. (ISBN 0-380-75044-9, 75044-9). Avon.

Rahner Handbook. Robert Kress. LC 81-85333. 118p. 1982. pap. 10.95 o.p. (ISBN 0-8042-0652-X, John KNox). Westminster John Knox.

Raid see Heinemann Guided Readers.

Raid on the Inarticulate: An Invitation to Adult Religion. Michael G. Lawler. LC 80-1438. 168p. 1980. pap. text ed. 10.00 o.p. (ISBN 0-8191-1186-4). U Pr of Amer.

Raigne of King Edward the Third. Fred Lapides. LC 79-54346. (Renaissance Drama Ser.). 265p. 1982. lib. bdg. 36.00 o.p. (ISBN 0-8240-4463-0). Garland Pub.

Rail & Motor Carrier Reports. (Special Report). 80p. 1979. 4.40 o.p. (ISBN 0-309-02971-6). Transport Res Bd.

Rail Planning. (Transportation Research Record Ser.). 72p. 1977. 4.80 o.p. (ISBN 0-309-02685-7). Transport Res Bd.

Rail Transit Development: Five Reports. (Transportation Research Record Ser.). 57p. 1975. 2.60 o.p. (ISBN 0-309-02458-7). Transport Res Bd.

Rail Transit Planning & Rail Sections. (Transportation Research Record Ser.). 53p. 1980. 5.40 o.p. (ISBN 0-309-03100-1). Transport Res Bd.

Rail Transportation Proceedings 1973. 278p. 1973. 25.00 o.p. (ISBN 0-317-33585-5, G00023); members 12.50 o.p. (ISBN 0-317-33586-3). ASME.

Rail Ventures. Jack Swanson & Jeff Karsh. (Illus.). 240p. 1985. pap. 16.95 o.p. (ISBN 0-9608764-3-X). Wayfinder Pr.

Railfan's Guide to Colorado. Edgar H. Sibert. (Illus.). pap. 7.95 o.p. (ISBN 0-87108-556-9). Pruett.

Railroad Car Builders Pictorial Dictionary. Matthias N. Forney. (Illus.). 13.25 o.p. (ISBN 0-8446-5187-7). Peter Smith.

Railroad Electrification: The Issues. (Special Report). 85p. 1978. 3.80 o.p. (ISBN 0-309-02654-7). Transport Res Bd.

Railroad-Highway Crossings, Visibility & Human Factors. (Transportation Research Record Ser.). 68p. 1976. 3.20 o.p. (ISBN 0-309-02587-7). Transport Res Bd.

Railroad Scene. William D. Middleton. LC 69-20446. (Illus.). 1969. 15.95 o.p. (ISBN 0-87095-000-2). Gldn West Bks.

Railroad to Freedom. Hildegarde H. Swift. LC 32-25841. (Illus.). 1932. 8.50 o.p. (ISBN 0-15-265119-5, HJ). HarBraceJ.

Railroad Track & Electrification Studies. (Transportation Research Record Ser.). 72p. 1978. 4.00 o.p. Transport Res Bd.

Railroad Track & Facilities. (Transportation Research Record Ser.). 66p. 1980. 5.20 o.p. (ISBN 0-309-03052-8). Transport Res Bd.

Railroad Track Briefs for the Plant Engineer. W. L. Anderson. (Illus.). 1979. 10.00 o.p. (ISBN 0-682-49448-8). Exposition-Phoenix.

Railroaded! The Battle for Woodhead Pass. Simon Bain. (Orig.). 1986. pap. 9.95 o.p. (ISBN 0-571-13909-4). Faber & Faber.

Railroading in the Carolina Sandhills: "The Hoffman & Troy Railroad" & "Sandhill Shays, Vol. 3. S. David Carriker. (Illus.). 80p. Date not set. 16.00 o.p. (ISBN 0-936013-03-6); Set. price not set o.p. Herit Pub NC.

Railroads. Leonard E. Fisher. LC 79-1458. (Nineteenth Century America Ser.). (Illus.). 64p. (gr. 5 up). 1979. 9.95 o.p. (ISBN 0-8234-0352-1). Holiday.

Railroads in the Nineteenth Century. Robert L. Frey. (Illus.). 352p. 1988. 75.00 o.p. (ISBN 0-8160-2012-4). Facts on File.

Railroads of Hawaii. Gerald M. Best. LC 78-23666. 194p. 1978. 22.95 o.p. (ISBN 0-87095-049-5). Gldn West Bks.

Railroads of Northern Colorado. Kenneth C. Jessen. LC 82-395. (Illus.). 300p. 1982. 29.95 o.p. (ISBN 0-87108-599-2). Pruett.

Rails Across the Midlands. 2nd ed. Richard J. Cook. LC 64-16409. (Illus.). 1968. 16.95 o.p. (ISBN 0-87095-018-5). Gldn West Bks.

Rails Across the Ranchos. Loren Nicholson. (Illus.). 197p. 1980. 18.95 o.p. (ISBN 0-913548-72-3, Valley Calif). Western Tanager.

Rails I Tote: A Collection of Short Stories. Christopher Manson. (Illus.). 96p. 1987. pap. 7.95 o.p. (ISBN 0-8050-0113-1). H Holt & Co.

Rails in Richmond. Carlton N. McKenney. Ed. by William F. Fulton. (Interurbans Special Ser.: No. 102). 216p. 1986. 32.95 o.p. (ISBN 0-916374-71-8). Interurban.

Rails in the Isle of Wight. P. C. Allen & A. B. MacLeod. (Illus.). 128p. 1987. 24.95 o.p. (ISBN 0-7153-8701-4). David & Charles.

Rails in the Northwest, a Contemporary Glimpse. Ronald C. Hill & Dave Stanley. LC 78-2825. 1978. pap. 9.95 o.p. (ISBN 0-918654-27-0). CO RR Mus.

Rails of the Silver Gate. R. V. Dodge. LC 75-97231. (Illus.). 144p. 1975. 15.95 o.p. (ISBN 0-87095-019-3). Gldn West Bks.

Rails, Sagebrush & Pine. Mallory H. Ferrell. LC 67-28315. (Illus.). 1967. 21.95 o.p. (ISBN 0-87095-007-X). Gldn West Bks.

Railway Barons. David Mountfield. (Illus.). 1980. 14.95 o.p. (ISBN 0-393-01325-1). Norton.

Railway Directory & Yearbook, 1986. 91st ed. 1986. 90.00 o.p. (ISBN 0-617-00443-9). Intl Pubns Serv.

Railway History in Pictures: Chilterns & Cotswolds. R. Davies & M. D. Grant. 1977. 16.95 o.p. (ISBN 0-7153-7299-8). David & Charles.

Railway Modelling: An Introduction. W. A. Corkill. 1979. 14.95 o.p. (ISBN 0-7153-7571-7). David & Charles.

Railway Navvy. D. Brooke. (Illus.). 216p. 1983. 24.95 o.p. (ISBN 0-7153-8449-X). David & Charles.
Railway Paintings of Alan Fearnley. Alan Fearnley. 95p. 1988. 65.00 o.p. (ISBN 0-7153-9088-0). David & Charles.
Railway Paintings of Don Breckon. Don Breckon. LC 81-67015. (Illus.). 200p. 1982. 40.00 o.p. (ISBN 0-7153-8206-3). David & Charles.
Railway Paintings of Don Breckon. Don Breckon. (Illus.). 80p. 1988. 24.95 o.p. (ISBN 0-7153-9078-3). David & Charles.
Railway Walks: Exploring Disused Railways in Britain. Gareth L. Jones. (Illus.). 288p. 1983. 18.95 o.p. (ISBN 0-7153-8543-7). David & Charles.
Railways the World Over. G. Freeman Allen. (Illus.). 128p. 1956. (ISBN 0-8022-0023-0). Philos Lib.
Raiment of Light: A Study of the Human Aura. David Tansley. (Illus.). 224p. (Orig.). 1985. pap. 9.95 o.p. (ISBN 0-7100-9972-X). Routledge Chapman & Hall.
Rain in the Lyle Hollow. Douglas F. Miller. 192p. 1986. 10.95 o.p. (ISBN 0-8062-2916-0). Carlton.
Rain of Darts: The Mexica Aztecs. Burr C. Brundage. LC 72-680. (Texas Pan American Ser.). 372p. 1972. 20.00x o.p. (ISBN 0-292-77002-2). U of Tex Pr.
Rain of Wisdom. Chogyam Trungpa. Tr. by Nalanda Translation Committee. LC 85-2454. 384p. 1985. 18.95 o.s.i. (ISBN 0-87773-345-7, 74199-4). Shambhala Pubns.
Rainbow. Fitzgerald. (Dear God Kids Ser.). 1985. 3.95 o.s.i. (ISBN 0-671-50681-1). S&S.
Rainbow. William H. Harding. LC 79-1245. 1979. 10.95 o.p. (ISBN 0-03-050396-5). H Holt & Co.
Rainbow. D. H. Lawrence. LC 83-42939. 6.95 o.s.i. (ISBN 0-394-60491-1). Modern Lib.
Rainbow Bags: Instructions for Making Six Colorful Bags of Soft Toys. Lois Brokering. 48p. (Orig.). 1986. pap. 5.95 o.p. (ISBN 0-8066-2256-3, 10-5380, Augsburg). Augsburg Fortress.
Rainbow Below. Hugh Atkinson. Ed. by Kent Oswald. 304p. 1987. 17.95 o.p. (ISBN 0-531-15037-2). Watts.
Rainbow Cadenza: A Novel in Logosta Form. Neil J. Schulman. 320p. 1983. 15.50 o.p. (ISBN 0-671-42003-8). S&S.
Rainbow Drive. Roderick Thorp. 320p. 1986. 18.45 o.s.i. (ISBN 0-671-49981-5). Summit Bks.
Rainbow Fairy Book. Date not set. pap. (ISBN 0-8052-0571-3). Random.
Rainbow Flower. V. Katayev. 23p. 1977. pap. 1.49 o.p. (ISBN 0-8285-1221-3, Pub. by Progress Pubs USSR). Imported Pubns.
Rainbow Grocery. William Dickey. LC 78-53381. 80p. 1978. 8.00x o.p. (ISBN 0-87023-252-5); pap. 4.50 o.p. (ISBN 0-87023-253-3). U of Mass Pr.
Rainbow in the Sky. Ed. by Louis Untermeyer. LC 35-27286. (Illus.). (gr. 4-6). 1935. 12.95 o.p. (ISBN 0-15-265477-1, HJ). HarBraceJ.
Rainbow in Your Hands. Albert R. Davis & Walter C. Rawls, Jr. 1976. 8.00 o.p. (ISBN 0-682-48543-8). Exposition-Phoenix.
Rainbow Incentive Collection I, 5 pkgs. Imogene Forte. (Illus.). (gr. 2-6). 1984. Set. 6.00 o.p. (ISBN 0-86530-074-7, IP 74-7). Incentive Pubns.
Rainbow Incentive Collection II. Imogene Forte. (ps-6). 1985. 6.00 o.p. (1P79-6). Incentive Pubns.
Rainbow Incentive Collection III. (gr. 6). 6.00 o.p. (ISBN 0-317-65411-X). Incentive Pubns.
Rainbow People: A Gaudy World of the Very Rich & Those Who Serve Them. Richard Collier. (Illus.). 304p. 1984. 17.95 o.p. (ISBN 0-396-08389-7). Dodd.
Rainbow Quest. Richard Ramella. (Illus.). 120p. (Orig.). (gr. 3-6). 1984. Apple II, II Plus, IIe. pap. 24.95 spiral bound incl. disk o.p. (ISBN 0-88006-082-4, CC7407). Wayne Green Ent.
Rainbow Quest. Richard Ramella. (Illus.). 120p. (Orig.). (gr. 3-6). 1984. IBM-PCjr. spiral bound incl. disk 24.95 o.p. (ISBN 0-88006-083-2, CC7408). Wayne Green Ent.
Rainbow Quest: Color Computer Version. Richard Ramella. (Illus.). 120p. (gr. 3-6). 1984. spiralbound incl. cassette 24.97 o.p. (ISBN 0-88006-064-6, CC7391). Wayne Green Ent.
Rainbow Quest: Commodore 64. Richard Ramella. (Illus.). 120p. (gr. 3-6). 1984. spiralbound incl. cassette 24.95 o.p. (ISBN 0-88006-069-7, CC7401); incl. disk 24.95 o.p. (ISBN 0-88006-076-X, CC7405). Wayne Green Ent.
Rainbow Roun' Mah Shoulder. Linda B. Bragg. 140p. (Orig.). 1984. pap. 7.00 o.p. (ISBN 0-932112-20-X). Carolina Wren.
Rainbow Saga. Chet Cunningham. 1979. pap. 1.95 o.p. (ISBN 0-8439-0622-7, Pub. by Leisure Bks CT). Dorchester Pub Co.
Rainbow Trail. Zane Grey. 1984. pap. 2.95 o.s.i. (ISBN 0-671-50523-8). PB.
Rainbow Walkers. Doris Schwerin. 384p. 1986. pap. 3.95 o.s.i. (ISBN 0-345-30387-3). Ballantine.
Rainbows of Promise. Ivy D. Doherty. Ed. by Gerald Wheeler. (Banner Bks.). (Illus.). 92p. (Orig.). (gr. 2 up). 1984. pap. 6.95 o.p. (ISBN 0-8280-0213-4). Review & Herald.
Raincrow. Jane G. Rushing. 1979. pap. 1.95 o.p. (ISBN 0-380-41749-9, 41749). Avon.
Rainer Maria Rilke: His Life & Work. F. W. Van Heerikhuizen. 1952. (ISBN 0-8022-1766-4). Philos Lib.
Rainer Maria Rilke: Letters to Benvenuta. M. Von Hattingberg. 1951. (ISBN 0-8022-0691-3). Philos Lib.
Rainmaker. Jan Ostergren. Tr. by John Matthais & Goran Printz-Pohlson. LC 82-24554. viii, 52p. 1983. 13.95x o.p. (ISBN 0-8214-0745-7); pap. 7.95 o.p. (ISBN 0-8214-0746-5). Ohio U Pr.
Rains in Meadow Valley. Bryant R. Clark. 1979. 8.50 o.p. (ISBN 0-682-49329-5). Exposition-Phoenix.
Raintree County. Ross Lockridge, Jr. 15.00 o.p. (ISBN 0-395-07919-5). HM.
Raintree County. Ross Lockridge, Jr. 1066p. 1984. pap. 10.95 o.p. (ISBN 0-87795-606-5, Arbor Hse). Morrow.
Rainy Day Activities for the Atari. Nancy K. Mayer. (gr. 3up). 1983. pap. 16.95 o.p. (ISBN 0-8359-6390-X, Reston). P-H.
Rainy Day Man. Rita Garitano. LC 84-16712. 378p. 1985. 14.45 o.p. (ISBN 0-393-01949-7). Norton.
Rainy River Country: A Brief History of the Region Bordering Minnesota & Ontario. Grace L. Nute. LC 71-96385. (Illus.). 143p. 1950. Repr. of 1950 ed. pap. 4.95 o.p. (ISBN 0-87351-008-9). Minn Hist.
Raisin in the Sun. Lorraine Hansberry. Bd. with Sign in Sidney Brustein's Window. pap. 3.50 o.p. (ISBN 0-451-12415-4, Sig). NAL.
Raising a Child Conservatively in a Sexually Permissive World. Sol Gordon & Judith Gordon. 1983. 13.50 o.p. (ISBN 0-671-46748-4). S&S.
Raising a Joyful Family. Ed. by Jeanne Hunt. LC 82-4823. (Christian Reader Ser.). 128p. (Orig.). 1983. pap. 5.72i o.p. (ISBN 0-06-061387-4, RD/439). HarpR.
Raising a Responsible Child: Practical Steps to Successful Family Relationships. Don Dinkmeyer & Gary D. McKay. LC 72-86989. 1973. 11.95 o.p. (ISBN 0-671-21445-4). S&S.
Raising a Son: The Essential Guide to a Healthy Mother-Son Relationship. Joan S. Weiss. 224p. 1985. 16.45 o.s.i. (ISBN 0-671-45269-X). Summit Bks.
Raising & Caring for Animals, a Handbook of Animal Husbandry & Veterinary Care. Guy Lockwood. LC 79-14025. (Encore Edition). 1979. pap. 3.50 o.p. (ISBN 0-684-17742-0). Scribner.
Raising Cash: A Guide to Financing & Controlling Your Business. Sol Postyn & Jo K. Postyn. (Finance Ser.). (Illus.). 309p. 1981. 31.95 o.p. (ISBN 0-534-97966-1, Lifetime Learn). Van Nos Reinhold.
Raising Chickens. Cynthia Haynes. (Illus.). 272p. (Orig.). 1985. 21.95 o.p. (ISBN 0-8306-0963-6, 1963); pap. 13.60 o.p. (ISBN 0-8306-1963-1, 1963P). Tab Bks.
Raising Kids O. K. Dorothy E. Babcock & Terry D. Keepers. 1977. pap. 1.95 o.p. (ISBN 0-380-00937-4, 31989-6). Avon.
Raising Rabbits the Modern Way. Robert Bennett. LC 75-31601. (Illus.). 156p. 1975. pap. 7.95 o.p. (ISBN 0-88266-067-5, Garden Way Pub). Storey Comm Inc.
Raising Sheep the Modern Way. Paula Simmons. Ed. by Roger Griffith. LC 76-44530. (Illus.). 240p. 1976. pap. 8.95 o.p. (ISBN 0-88266-093-4, Garden Way Pub). Storey Comm Inc.
Raising Your Own Meat for Pennies a Day. Will Graves. Ed. by Fred Stetson. LC 83-1595. (Illus.). 160p. (Orig.). 1983. pap. 6.95 o.p. (ISBN 0-88266-330-5, Garden Way Pub). Storey Comm Inc.
Raj Quartet, 4 vols. Paul Scott. 1984. Boxed Set. pap. 18.00 o.p. (ISBN 0-380-46698-8). Avon.
Rajasthan: India's Enchanted Land. Ed. by Raghubir Singh. (Illus.). 1981. 27.50 o.p. (ISBN 0-500-54070-5). Thames Hudson.
Rajpur: Last of the Bengal Tigers. Robert M. McClung. LC 82-3478. (Illus.). 96p. (gr. 4-6). 1982. 10.25 o.p. (ISBN 0-688-01495-X). Morrow.
Rake. Karen Lynn. LC 86-11575. (Starlight Rommance Ser.). 192p. 1986. 12.95 o.p. (ISBN 0-385-23566-6). Doubleday.
Rakhmaninov. Geoffrey Norris. (Master Musicians Ser.: M-175). (Illus.). 1978. pap. 7.95 o.p. (ISBN 0-8226-0701-8). Littlefield.
Ralegh's Lost Colony. David Durant. LC 80-65992. (Illus.). 320p. 1981. 12.95 o.p. (ISBN 0-689-11098-7, Atheneum). Macmillan.
Rally: The Twelve Greatest Notre Dame Football Comebacks. Jeff Jeffers. (Illus.). 176p. 1981. 12.95 o.s.i. (ISBN 0-89651-651-2). B L Pub.
Rallying Idea. Erich Kahler. 1973. pap. 4.00 o.p. (ISBN 0-87775-073-4). Unicorn Pr.
Ralph Fozbek & the Amazing Black Hole Patrol. Steve Senn. 112p. (gr. 3-7). 1986. pap. 2.50 o.p. (ISBN 0-380-89905-1, Camelot). Avon.
Ralph Hodgson: A Bibliography. Wesley D. Sweetser. LC 79-7932. (Garland Reference Library of the Humanities). 185p. 1980. lib. bdg. 31.00 o.p. (ISBN 0-8240-9524-3). Garland Pub.
Ralph Ingersoll: A Biography. Roy Hoopes. LC 84-45624. (Illus.). 562p. 1985. 19.95 o.p. (ISBN 0-689-11554-7, Atheneum). Macmillan.
Ralph Lutz & the Hoover Institution. Charles B. Burdick. LC 72-87287. (Publications Ser.: No. 131). 185p. 1974. 11.95x o.p. Hoover Inst Pr.
Ralph Nader see Investigation of Ralph Nader.
Ralph Richardson: An Actor's Life. Garry O'Connor. LC 82-45178. 320p. 1982. 14.95 o.p. (ISBN 0-689-11313-7, Atheneum). Macmillan.
Ralph Waldo Emerson: Days of Encounter. John McAleer. (Illus.). 704p. 1984. 27.00i o.p. (ISBN 0-316-55341-7). Little.
Rama, the Gypsy Cat. Betsy Byars. (gr. 3-9). 1976. pap. 1.25 o.p. (ISBN 0-380-00630-8, 41608, Camelot). Avon.
Ramage & the Guillotine. Dudley Pope. 256p. 1981. pap. 2.50 o.p. (ISBN 0-380-55491-7, 55491-7). Avon.
Ramage & the Renegades. Dudley Pope. 288p. 1982. pap. 2.75 o.p. (ISBN 0-380-60137-0, 60137-0). Avon.
Raman Spectra of Hydrocarbons: A Data Handbook. K. E. Sterin et al. LC 79-42704. 360p. 1980. 120.00 o.p. (ISBN 0-08-023596-4). Pergamon.
Ramayana. 3rd ed. Valmiki. Ed. & tr. by Chakravarti Rajagopalachari. 320p. (Orig.). 1980. pap. 6.50 o.p. (ISBN 0-934676-17-8). Greenlf Bks.
Ramblings in the Clover-Absorbing Shock. Eileen M. Greco. (Illus.). 48p. 1982. 5.00 o.s.i. (ISBN 0-682-49885-8). Exposition-Phoenix.
Ramesses the Great. Rita Freed. 208p. 1987. 24.95 o.p. (ISBN 0-918518-57-1, St Luke TN); pap. 15.95 o.p. (ISBN 0-918518-56-3). Peachtree Pubs.
Ramon Betances: Father of the Poor. Irving Gerber. (American Destiny Ser.: Puerto Rico: Puerto Rico). (gr. 4-12). 1979. 12.95 set o.p. (ISBN 0-87594-180-X). Book-Lab.
Ramon Makes a Trade. Marilynne K. Ritchie. LC 59-13838. (Illus., Eng. & Span.). (gr. 3-8). 1959. 7.95 o.p. (ISBN 0-395-28055-9, Pub. by Parnassus). HM.
Ramona Quimby Diary. Beverly Cleary. 1970. pap. 7.95 o.p. (ISBN 0-688-06778-6). Greenwillow.
Rampage. Justin Scott. 432p. 1986. 17.45 o.s.i. (ISBN 0-671-53047-X). S&S.
Ramprasad: The Melodius Mystic. Ramprasad. Tr. by Buddhananda. 72p. 1985. pap. 1.95 o.p. (ISBN 0-87481-568-1, Pub. by Ramakrishna Math Madras India). Vedanta Pr.
Ran. Akira Kurosawa et al. LC 86-13016. (Illus.). 110p. (Orig.). 1986. 19.95 o.s.i. (ISBN 0-87773-387-2). Shambhala Pubns.
Ranade & the Roots of Indian Nationalism. Richard P. Tucker. (Midway Reprint Ser.). 1976. pap. text ed. 11.00x o.s.i. (ISBN 0-226-81532-3). U of Chicago Pr.
Ranch Life in the Far West. Theodore Roosevelt. LC 68-56221. (Western Classic Bk.). (Illus.). 96p. 1985. Repr. of 1968 ed. 11.95 o.p. (ISBN 0-87358-376-0). Northland.
Rand McNally Atlas of the United States. 192p. 1983. 29.95 o.p. (ISBN 0-528-83099-6). Rand McNally.
Rand McNally Business Traveler's Road Atlas. 1984. pap. 9.95 o.p. (ISBN 0-528-89607-5). Rand McNally.
Rand McNally Camp California. (Camp U. S. A. Ser.). 128p. (Orig.). 1987. pap. 3.95 o.p. (ISBN 0-528-84699-X). Rand McNally.
Rand McNally Camp Florida. (Camp U. S. A. Ser.). 80p. (Orig.). 1986. pap. 2.95 o.p. (ISBN 0-528-84703-1). Rand McNally.
Rand McNally Camp Texas. (Camp U. S. A. Ser.). 80p. (Orig.). 1987. pap. 2.95 o.p. (ISBN 0-528-84705-8). Rand McNally.
Rand McNally Children's Atlas of the World. Bruce Ogilvie & Douglas Waitley. (Illus.). 96p. (gr. 4 up). 1985. 11.95 o.p. (ISBN 0-528-82418-X). Rand McNally.
Rand McNally Contemporary World Atlas. rev. ed. Jon Leverenz. (Illus.). 224p. 1986. pap. 9.95 o.p. (ISBN 0-528-83146-1). Rand McNally.
Rand McNally Cosmopolitan World Atlas: New Census Edition. 392p. 1984. 55.00 o.p. (ISBN 0-528-83149-6). Rand McNally.
Rand McNally Deluxe Motor Carriers Road Atlas. rev. ed. (Illus.). 208p. (Orig.). 1988. pap. 59.95 o.p. (ISBN 0-528-89826-4). Rand McNally.
Rand McNally Family World Atlas: New Census Edition. LC 73-3377. (Illus.). 320p. 1981. 16.95 o.p. (ISBN 0-528-83122-4); deluxe ed. 16.95 o.p. (ISBN 0-528-83115-1). Rand McNally.
Rand McNally Goode's World Atlas. Ed. by Edward B. Espenshade, Jr. & Joel L. Morrison. (Illus.). 367p. 1986. 22.95 o.p. (ISBN 0-528-83127-5). Rand McNally.
Rand McNally Green Guide: U. S. Places with over 100 People. (Illus.). 298p. 1983. pap. 17.95 o.p. (ISBN 0-528-21066-1). Rand McNally.
Rand McNally Handy Railroad Atlas of the United States. rev. ed. Rand McNally & Company Staff. 1985. pap. 11.95 o.p. (ISBN 0-528-21673-2). Rand McNally.
Rand McNally Interstate Road Atlas: United States, Canada, Mexico. Ed. by John Manning. 1988. pap. 3.95 o.p. (ISBN 0-528-89812-4). Rand McNally.
Rand McNally Mathematics Encyclopedia. Leslie Foster. LC 86-70402. (Encyclopedia Ser.). 144p. (gr. 4 up). 1986. 14.95 o.s.i. (ISBN 0-02-689202-2, Checkerboard Pr). Macmillan.
Rand McNally Motor Carriers' Road Atlas, 1988. 1988. pap. 14.95 o.p. (ISBN 0-528-89810-8). Rand McNally.
Rand McNally New Century World Atlas. Ed. by Jon Leverenz. 504p. 1986. 39.95 o.p. (ISBN 0-528-83213-1). Rand McNally.
Rand McNally Retirement Places Rated. 2nd, rev. ed. Richard Boyer & David Savageau. (Places Rated Ser.). (Illus.). 200p. 1987. pap. 12.95 o.p. (ISBN 0-528-88081-0). Rand McNally.
Rand McNally Road Atlas & City Guide of Europe. 1984. pap. 12.95 o.p. (ISBN 0-528-89517-6). Rand McNally.
Rand McNally Road Atlas & City Guide of Europe, 1988. 1988. pap. 12.95 o.p. (ISBN 0-528-89817-5). Rand McNally.
Rand McNally Road Atlas & Vacation Guide, 1984. 1983. pap. 12.95 o.p. (ISBN 0-528-89512-5). Rand McNally.
Rand McNally Road Atlas & Vacation Guide, 1988. 1988. pap. 13.95 o.p. (ISBN 0-528-89808-6). Rand McNally.
Rand McNally Road Atlas of Britain. 1984. pap. 12.95 o.p. (ISBN 0-528-89518-4). Rand McNally.
Rand McNally Road Atlas of Britain, 1988. 1988. pap. 13.95 o.p. (ISBN 0-528-89818-3). Rand McNally.
Rand McNally Road Atlas of Europe. 1984. pap. 5.95 o.p. (ISBN 0-528-89520-6). Rand McNally.
Rand McNally Road Atlas of Europe, 1988. 1988. pap. 6.95 o.p. (ISBN 0-528-89816-7). Rand McNally.
Rand McNally Road Atlas of France. (Illus.). 128p. (Orig.). 1988. pap. 12.95 o.p. (ISBN 0-528-89837-X). Rand McNally.
Rand McNally Road Atlas: United States, Canada, Mexico. 1984. deluxe ed. 8.95 o.p. (ISBN 0-528-89505-2); pap. 5.95 o.p. (ISBN 0-528-89500-1); gift ed. 7.95 o.p. (ISBN 0-528-89503-6). Rand McNally.
Rand McNally Road Atlas 1986. Rand McNally & Company Staff. pap. 5.95 o.p. (ISBN 0-317-39730-3). Rand McNally.
Rand McNally Road Atlas, 1988: United States, Canada, Mexico. 1988. deluxe ed. 9.95 o.p. (ISBN 0-528-89805-1); pap. 6.95 o.p. (ISBN 0-528-89823-X); gift ed. 8.95 o.p. (ISBN 0-528-89803-5). Rand McNally.
Rand McNally Student's World Atlas. 96p. 1984. 3.95 o.p. (ISBN 0-528-83140-2). Rand McNally.
Rand McNally Vacation & Travel Guide, 1983. 1983. pap. 5.95 ea. o.p. Western (ISBN 0-528-84248-X). Eastern (ISBN 0-528-84247-1). Rand McNally.
Rand McNally Yellow Guide. Rev. ed. 332p. 1984. pap. 17.95 o.p. (ISBN 0-528-21067-X). Rand McNally.
Rand McNally Zip Code Atlas. Rand McNally & Company Staff. 142p. 1984. pap. 17.95 o.p. (ISBN 0-528-21068-8). Rand McNally.
Randall Jarrell. Sr. Bernetta Quinn. (United States Authors Ser.). 1981. lib. bdg. 13.50 o.p. (ISBN 0-8057-7266-9, Twayne). G K Hall.
Randlords: The Exploits & Exploitations of South Africa's Mining Magnates. Geoffrey Wheatcroft. LC 85-18680. (Illus.). 336p. 1986. 17.95 o.p. (ISBN 0-689-11795-7, Atheneum). Macmillan.
Randolph Caldecott. Henry Blackburn. LC 68-21757. 232p. 1969. Repr. of 1886 ed. 35.00x o.p. (ISBN 0-8103-3490-9). Gale.
Random Excitation of Structures by Earthquakes & Atmospheric Turbulence. Ed. by H. Parkus. (CISM-International Center for Mechanical Sciences: Vol. 225). (Illus.). 1978. pap. 33.00 o.p. (ISBN 0-387-81444-2). Springer-Verlag.
Random Fields. C. Preston. (Lecture Notes in Mathematics: Vol. 534). 1976. pap. 16.00 o.p. (ISBN 0-387-07852-5). Springer-Verlag.

Titles

Random Functions & Turbulence. S. Panchev. LC 70-124852. 1971. 87.00 o.p. (ISBN 0-08-015826-9). Pergamon.

Random House Basic Dictionary: German. Ed. by Jenni H. Moulton. (Ger. & Eng.). 1981. pap. 1.50 o.p. (ISBN 0-345-29619-2). Ballantine.

Random Integral Equations with Applications to Life Sciences & Engineering. Chris P. Tsokos & W. J. Padgett. 1974. 77.00 o.p. (ISBN 0-12-702150-7). Acad Pr.

Random Integral Equations with Applications to Stochastic Systems. C. P. Tsokos & W. J. Padgett. (Lecture Notes in Mathematics: Vol. 233). 174p. 1972. pap. 10.00 o.p. (ISBN 0-387-05660-2). Springer-Verlag.

Random Measures. O. Kallenberg. 1984. 54.00 o.p. (ISBN 0-12-394960-2). Acad Pr.

Random Notes on Men, Women & Books at USC. Wallace Nethery. i, 48p. 1980. Repr. of 1966 ed. leatherette 15.00 o.p. (ISBN 0-317-11649-5). Dawsons.

Random Processes: A First Look. Syski. (Statistics; Textbooks & Monographs Ser.: Vol. 29). 352p. 1979. 34.75 o.p. (ISBN 0-8247-6893-0). Dekker.

Random Processes & the Growth of Firms: A Study of the Pareto Law. J. Steindl. 249p. 1965. text ed. 22.00x o.p. (ISBN 0-85264-063-3). Lubrecht & Cramer.

Random Processes in Geology. D. Merriam. LC 75-6848. 1976. 29.00 o.p. (ISBN 0-387-07277-2). Springer Verlag.

Random Processes in Nonlinear Control Systems. A. A. Pervozvanskii. (Mathematics in Science & Engineering Ser.: Vol. 15). 1965. 85.00 o.p. (ISBN 0-12-551650-9). Acad Pr.

Random Processes in Nuclear Reactors. M. M. Williams. LC 74-4066. 1974. 65.00 o.p. (ISBN 0-08-017920-7). Pergamon.

Random Processes: Multiplicity & Canonical Decompositions, Pt. 1. Ed. by A. Ephremides. LC 75-1287. (Benchmark Papers in Electrical Engineering & Computer Science: No. 11). 352p. 1982. 59.95 o.p. (ISBN 0-87933-022-8). Van Nos Reinhold.

Random Theory of Deformation of Structured Media: Thermodynamics of Deformation in Structured Media. CISM (International Center for Mechanical Sciences), Department of Mechanics of Solids Staff. Ed. by D. R. Axelrad & J. W. Provan. (CISM Publications: No. 71). (Illus.). 57p. 1973. pap. 9.50 o.p. (ISBN 0-387-81175-3). Springer-Verlag.

Random Walk down Wall Street. rev. ed. Burton G. Malkiel. (Illus.). 1974. 13.95 o.p. (ISBN 0-393-05500-0); pap. 5.95x o.p. (ISBN 0-393-09246-1). Norton.

Range Development & Improvements. 2nd ed. John F. Vallentine. LC 79-26676. (Illus.). 1980. text ed. 18.95x o.p. (ISBN 0-8425-1708-1). Brigham.

Range Rover Conversions. Nick Dimbleby. (Illus.). 72p. 1988. pap. 15.95 o.p. (ISBN 0-85429-615-8). Haynes Pubns.

Range Science: A Guide to Information Sources. Ed. by John F. Vallentine & Phillip L. Sims. (Natural World Information Guide Ser.: Vol. 2). 248p. 1980. 68.00x o.p. (ISBN 0-8103-1420-7). Gale.

Rangeland Avenger. Max Brand. 340p. 1986. lib. bdg. 14.95x o.p. (ISBN 0-8161-3962-8, Large Print Bks). G K Hall.

Ranger Battalion: American Rangers in World War II. Milton Shapiro. LC 79-9548. (Illus.). 192p. (gr. 7 up). 1979. PLB 8.79 o.p. (ISBN 0-671-32928-6). Messner.

Rangoon. Christine Monson. 464p. 1985. pap. 3.95 o.p. (ISBN 0-380-89611-7). Avon.

Ranibow Cadenza. J. Neil Schulman. 368p. 1986. pap. 3.50 o.p. (ISBN 0-380-75123-2). Avon.

Rank & File Movement in Social Work. Rick Spano. LC 81-40161. 290p. (Orig.). 1982. lib. bdg. 28.50 o.p. (ISBN 0-8191-2539-3); pap. text ed. 13.25 o.p. (ISBN 0-8191-2540-7). U Pr of Amer.

Rank & File: Personal Histories by Working Class Organizers. rev. ed. Ed. by Staughton Lynd & Alice Lynd. LC 81-47284. (Illus.). 296p. 1981. pap. 9.50x o.p. (ISBN 0-691-02825-7). Princeton U Pr.

Ransomed Heart. Sparky Ascani. 208p. 1983. pap. 2.95 o.p. (ISBN 0-380-83287-9). Avon.

Rantin' Pipe & Tremblin' String: A History of Scottish Dance Music. George S. Emmerson. (Illus.). 1971. 14.50 o.p. (ISBN 0-7735-0116-9, McGill Canada). U of Toronto Pr.

Raoul Dufy: Catalogue Raisonne des Aquarelles, Gouaches, et Pastels, 2 Vols, Fr. Fanny L. Guilion. 48p. 1981. 385.00x o.p. (ISBN 2-86574-002-1). Hacker.

Rap. Ernest Brawley. LC 73-91631. 1974. 10.00 o.p. (ISBN 0-689-10563-0, Atheneum). Macmillan.

Rape & Rape Related Issues: An Annotated Bibliography. Elizabeth J. Kemmer. (Reference Library of Social Science: Vol. 39). (LC 76-052701). 1977. lib. bdg. 26.00 o.p. (ISBN 0-8240-9873-0). Garland Pub.

Rape & Woman's Identity. William B. Sanders. LC 80-13346. (Sage Library of Social Research: Vol. 106). (Illus.). 184p. 1980. 24.50 o.p. (ISBN 0-8039-1449-0); pap. 12.50 o.p. (ISBN 0-8039-1450-4). Sage.

Rape of Detroit. Argie W. Post. 50p. 1975. 4.00 o.p. (ISBN 0-682-48133-5). Exposition-Phoenix.

Rape of Manhood: A Plan. Kunle Adedoyin. 1977. 5.50 o.p. (ISBN 0-682-48833-X). Exposition-Phoenix.

Rape of Owens Valley & Mono Lake. George J. Williams, III. (Western Americana History Ser.). (Illus., Orig.). 1985. pap. 7.95 o.p. (ISBN 0-935174-09-5). Tree by River.

Rape of Tamar. Dan Jacobson. 1973. pap. 0.95 o.p. (ISBN 0-380-01517-X, 15180). Avon.

Rape of the American Worker. John J. Parker. LC 76-20051. 1976. 15.00 o.p. (ISBN 0-682-48560-8). Exposition-Phoenix.

Rape: The Power of Consciousness. Susan Griffin. LC 78-20587. 1979. pap. 7.64i o.p. (ISBN 0-685-90558-6, RD 174). HarpR.

Rapeseed. Ed. by L. A. Appelqvist & R. Ohlson. 391p. 1973. 144.75 o.p. (ISBN 0-444-40892-4). Elsevier.

Raphael. Luciano Berti. (Illus.). 1962. 5.95 o.p. (ISBN 0-393-04244-8). Norton.

Rapid Assessement Procedures for Nutrition & Primary Health Care: Anthropological Approaches to Improving Programme Effectiveness, Vol.11. Susan C. Scrimshaw & Elena Hurtado. LC 87-3193. 70p. 1987. pap. 8.95 o.p. (ISBN 0-317-65403-9). UCLA Lat Am Ctr.

Rapid Construction: A Bibliography. Mary Vance. (Architecture Ser.: Bibliography A 1330). 1985. pap. 2.00 o.p. (ISBN 0-89028-280-3). Vance Biblios.

Rapid Electrical Estimating & Pricing: A Handy, Quick Method of Directly Determining the Selling Prices of Electrical Construction Work. 3rd ed. C. Kenneth Kolstad & Gerald V. Kohnert. (Illus.). 1979. text ed. 48.50 o.p. (ISBN 0-07-035129-5). McGraw.

Rapid Electrical Estimating & Pricing. 2nd ed. C. Kenneth Kolstad. (Illus.). 320p. 1974. text ed. 32.50 o.p. (ISBN 0-07-035316-6, P&RB). McGraw.

Rapid Inexpensive Tests for Determining Fracture Toughness. National Materials Advisory Board, National Research Council Staff. LC 76-39632. 1976. pap. 9.75 o.p. (ISBN 0-309-02537-0). Natl Acad Pr.

Rapid Lighting Design & Cost Estimating. Prafulla C. Sorcar. LC 79-4690. (Illus.). 1980. text ed. 46.50 o.p. (ISBN 0-07-059651-4). McGraw.

Rapid Math Without a Calculator. A. Frederick Collins. 120p. 1987. pap. 4.95 o.p. (Pub. by Citadel Pr). Carol Pub Group.

Rapid Mixing & Sampling Techniques in Biochemistry. Ed. by Britton Chance. 1964. 71.50 o.p. (ISBN 0-12-167868-7). Acad Pr.

Rapid Population Growth, Consequences & Policy Implications. National Academy of Sciences Staff. Incl. Vol. I. Summary & Recommendations. 116p. pap. 5.00x o.p. (ISBN 0-8018-1264-X); Vol. II. Research Papers. 700p. pap. 8.50x o.p. (ISBN 0-8018-1427-8). LC 75-148952. (Illus.). 1971p. 1971. pap. Johns Hopkins.

Rapid Practical Designs of Active Filters. D. E. Johnson & J. L. Hilburn. LC 75-14074. 264p. 1975. 39.95x o.p. (ISBN 0-471-44304-2, Pub. by Wiley-Interscience). Wiley.

Rapid Reading: A Home Study Course. 2nd ed. Stephen F. Holbrook. (Home Study Ser.). 67p. Repr. of 1981 ed. 28.00 o.p. (ISBN 0-939926-18-0); audio tape incl. o.p. (ISBN 0-939926-06-7). Fruition Pubns.

Rapid System Development Using Structured Analysis & Relational Technology. Chris Gene. 220p. (Orig.). 1987. pap. 45.00 o.p. (ISBN 0-317-61819-9). Rapid Syst Dev.

Rapidfile Simplified. Neil Dunlop. (Illus.). 272p. 1987. pap. 15.60 o.p. (ISBN 0-8306-2934-3). TAB Bks.

Rapidly Quenched Metals III, 2 vols. (Orig.). 1978. pap. text ed. 60.00x o.p. (ISBN 0-904357-22-8, Pub. by Inst Metals). Gower Pub Co.

Rapidly-Solidified Amorphous Materials. Business Communications Staff. 184p. 1984. pap. 1500.00 o.p. (ISBN 0-89336-396-0, GB-079). BCC.

Rappel a l'Ordre. Jean Cocteau. 1949. 8.95 o.p. (ISBN 0-686-54556-7). French & Eur.

Rappelling. 2nd ed. Tom Martin. LC 86-61694. (Illus.). 304p. 1987. 14.95 o.p. (ISBN 0-930871-01-4). Search.

Rapto. Francisco Ayala. Ed. by Phyllis Z. Boring. (Span). 1971. pap. text ed. 7.95 o.p. (ISBN 0-15-522435-2, HC). HarBraceJ.

Raptors. Ray Hogan. (Large Print Books). 1985. lib. bdg. 12.95 o.p. (ISBN 0-8161-3723-4). G K Hall.

Rapunzel. Jacob Grimm & Wilhelm K. Grimm. Ed. & illus. by Felix Hoffmann. LC 61-2865. (Illus.). (gr. k-3). 1961. 7.95 o.p. (ISBN 0-15-265656-1, HJ). HarBraceJ.

Rapunzel. Jacob Grimm & Wilhelm K. Grimm. LC 81-13284. (Illus.). 32p. (gr. k-4). 1982. 10.95 o.s.i. (ISBN 0-03-061219-5). H Holt & Co.

Rapunzel. Jacob Grimm & Wilhelm K. Grimm. LC 81-6419. (Illus.). 32p. (ps-3). 1987. pap. 5.95 o.p. (ISBN 0-8234-0652-0). Holiday.

Raquel: The Raquel Welch Total Beauty & Fitness Program. Raquel Welch. LC 84-4574. (Illus.). 1984. 19.95 o.p. (ISBN 0-03-069549-X). H Holt & Co.

Rare & Undone Saints. Phyllis Demong. LC 80-16731. (Illus.). 96p. 1981. 4.95 o.p. (ISBN 0-8397-7071-5). Eriksson.

Rare & Undone Saints. Phyllis Demong. 96p. 1983. pap. 3.95 o.p. (ISBN 0-380-63081-8, 63081-8). Avon.

Rare & Unusual Animals. Nina Leen. (Illus.). 80p. (gr. 3-7). 1981. 8.95 o.p. (ISBN 0-03-057478-1). H Holt & Co.

Rare Animals. I. Akimushkin. (Illus.). 16p. 1978. pap. 1.99 o.p. (ISBN 0-8285-8817-1, Pub. by Progress Pubs USSR). Imported Pubns.

Rare Earth Intermetallics. W. E. Wallace. (Materials Science Ser.). 1973. 77.00 o.p. (ISBN 0-12-732850-5). Acad Pr.

Rare Gas Solids, Vol. 1. Ed. by M. L. Klein & J. A. Venables. 1976. 167.00 o.p. (ISBN 0-12-413501-3). Acad Pr.

Rare Gas Solids, Vol. 2. Ed. by M. L. Klein & J. A. Venables. 1977. 123.50 o.p. (ISBN 0-12-413502-1). Acad Pr.

Rarefield Gas Dynamics. Ed. by K. Karamcheti. 1974. 84.50 o.p. (ISBN 0-12-398150-6). Acad Pr.

Ras Shamra & the Bible. Charles F. Pfeiffer. (Baker Studies in Biblical Archaeology). 1976. pap. 2.95 o.p. (ISBN 0-8010-7003-1). Baker Bk.

Rasa Tantra: Blood Marriage, The Sacred Initiation, A Marriage of the Faiths of East & West. Tsampa Yeshe Norbu. (Illus.). 36p. 1980. pap. 6.95 o.s.i. (ISBN 0-9609802-2-9). Life Science.

Rascal. Sterling North. (gr. 5 up). 1976. pap. 2.50 o.p. (ISBN 0-380-01518-8, Flare). Avon.

Rasputin: Prophet, Libertine, Plotter. T. Vogel-Jorgensen. Tr. by William F. Harvey from Danish. 1971. 5.00 o.p. (ISBN 0-8216-0143-1, Pub. by Univ Bks). Carol Pub Group.

Rastafarians: Sounds of Cultural Dissonance. Leonard E. Barrett. LC 76-48491. (Illus.). 1977. pap. 9.95 o.p. (ISBN 0-8070-1115-0, BP559). Beacon Pr.

Rastaman: The Rastafarian Movement in England. Ernest Cashmore. (Illus.). 272p. 1980. pap. text ed. 12.95 o.p. (ISBN 0-04-301116-0). Unwin Hyman.

Rat Brain in Stereotoxic Coordinates. G. Paxinos & C. Watson. 1983. 45.50 o.p. (ISBN 0-12-547620-5). Acad Pr.

Rat-Catcher's Daughter. Laurence Housman. Ed. by Ellin Greene. LC 73-75436. (Illus.). (gr. 4-7). 1974. 6.95 o.p. (ISBN 0-689-30420-X, Atheneum). Macmillan.

Rat Stew. Craig Silvis. (Illus.). (gr. k-3). 1979. 6.95 o.p. (ISBN 0-395-27803-1). HM.

Rate Control in Drug Therapy. Ed. by L. F. Prescott & W. S. Nimmo. LC 84-23894. (Illus.). 315p. 1985. text ed. 74.00 o.p. (ISBN 0-443-02998-9). Churchill.

Ratemaking & Capacity Determination in International Air Transport: A Legal Analysis. Peter P. C. Haanappel. 200p. cancelled o.s.i. (Pub. by Kluwer Law Netherlands). Kluwer Academic.

Rates & Mechanisms of Chemical Reactions. W. C. Gardiner, Jr. 1969. pap. 21.95 o.p. (ISBN 0-8053-3101-8). Benjamin-Cummings.

Rathnam's Cost & Management Accounting: Problems & Solutions. 2nd, rev. ed. P. V. Rathnam. 1984. text ed. 45.00x o.p. (ISBN 0-86590-414-6, Pub. by Sterling Pubs India). Apt Bks.

Rating the Movies. Consumer Guide Staff. 1988. pap. 5.98 o.p. (ISBN 0-517-67559-5). Crown.

Rating the Movies. rev. ed. 1987. pap. 5.98 o.p. (ISBN 0-517-65573-X). Crown.

Ratio Analysis. Morley. 1984. pap. 14.95 o.p. (ISBN 0-85258-233-1). Van Nos Reinhold.

Rational Belief Systems. Brian Ellis. (American Philosophical Quarterly Library of Philosophy). 118p. 1979. 19.50x o.p. (ISBN 0-8476-6108-3). Rowman.

Rational-Emotive Therapy: Fundamentals & Innovations. Windy Dryden. 192p. 1983. 25.00 o.p. (ISBN 0-7099-0848-2, Pub. by Croom Helm Ltd). Routledge Chapman & Hall.

Rational Metric Notation: The Mathematical Basis of Meters, Symbols, a Note-Values. Paul Creston. 1979. 7.50 o.p. (ISBN 0-682-49052-0, University). Exposition-Phoenix.

Rational Politics: Decisions, Games & Strategies. C Q Press Staff & Steven J. Brams. LC 85-17117. 233p. 1985. pap. 18.95 o.p. (ISBN 0-87187-337-0). Congr Quarterly.

Rationalism & Romanticism in Architecture: A Selected Inquiry into the Nature of Both Trends. W. Lesnikowski. 1982. text ed. 34.95 o.p. (ISBN 0-07-037417-1). McGraw.

Rationalist Encyclopaedia: A Book of Reference on Religion, Philosophy, Ethics, & Science. Joseph McCabe. LC 79-164054. 642p. 1971. Repr. of 1948 ed. 51.00x o.p. (ISBN 0-8103-3754-1). Gale.

Rationality & Sciences: A Memorial Volume for Moritz Schlick. Ed. by E. T. Gadol. (Illus.). 228p. 1983. 27.10 o.p. (ISBN 0-387-81721-2). Springer-Verlag.

Rationality & the Social Sciences: Contributions to the Philosophy & Methodology of the Social Sciences. Ed. by S. I. Benn & G. W. Mortimore. 400p. 1976. 36.95x o.p. (ISBN 0-7100-8170-7). Routledge Chapman & Hall.

Rationality in Planning: Critical Essays on the Role of Rationality in Urban & Regional Planning. Ed. by M. Breheny & A. Hooper. 252p. 1985. 25.95x o.p. (ISBN 0-85086-112-8, 9130, Pub. by Pion England). Routledge Chapman & Hall.

Rationality in the Calvinian Tradition. Ed. by Hendrik Hart & Johan Van Der Hoeven. LC 83-19672. (Christian Studies Today). 420p. (Orig.). 1984. lib. bdg. 34.00 o.p. (ISBN 0-8191-3616-6); pap. text ed. 17.75 o.p. (ISBN 0-8191-3617-4). U Pr of Amer.

Rationalization of Russia. George Bernard Shaw. Ed. by Harry M. Geduld. LC 75-3997. 1977. Repr. of 1964 ed. lib. bdg. 35.00x o.p. (ISBN 0-8371-7926-2, SHRR). Greenwood.

Rationing Health Care in America: Perceptions & Principles of Justice. Larry R. Churchill. LC 86-40582. 200p. 1987. text ed. 21.95x o.p. (ISBN 0-268-01630-5). U of Notre Dame Pr.

Ratt. Jay Byrd. (Metal Mania Ser.). (Illus.). 32p. (gr. 4-12). 1985. 4.95 o.p. (ISBN 0-88188-329-8, Robus Books). H Leonard Pub Corp.

Rattle-Rat. Janwillem Van de Wetering. (Large Print Bks (General Ser.)). 427p. 1986. lib. bdg. 17.95x o.p. (ISBN 0-8161-4121-5). G K Hall.

Rattlesnake Cave. Evelyn S. Lampman. LC 72-85918. (Illus.). (gr. 4-7). 1974. 7.95 o.p. (ISBN 0-689-30429-3, Atheneum). Macmillan.

Rattlesnake Karma. Richard Sutphen. LC 85-50289. 128p. 1985. pap. 5.95 o.p. (ISBN 0-911842-39-X). Valley Sun.

Rattlesnakes. Venetia Gleason. 1977. pap. 1.00 o.p. (ISBN 0-931832-08-X). Fithian Pr.

Rattling of Old Bones. Jonathan Ross. 192p. 1982. 10.95 o.s.i. (ISBN 0-684-17335-2, ScribT). Scribner.

Raum, Zeit und Relativitat. R. Nevanlinna. (Science & Civilization Ser.: No. 19). (Illus.). 229p. (Ger.). 1964. 29.95 o.p. (ISBN 0-8176-0277-1). Birkhauser.

Rauschenberg Photographs. Robert Rauschenberg. (Illus.). 1981. 29.50 o.p. (ISBN 0-394-52054-8). Pantheon.

Ravaged Garden: A Critical Study of Shelley's Epipsychidion. Ann Shealy. LC 85-90944. 80p. 1985. 15.00 o.s.i. (ISBN 0-682-40270-2). Exposition-Phoenix.

Ravel. Vladimir Jankelevitch. Tr. by Margaret Crosland. LC 75-28925. (Illus.). 192p. 1976. Repr. of 1959 ed. lib. bdg. 38.50 o.p. (ISBN 0-8371-8473-8, JARA). Greenwood.

Ravel'd Sleave of Care. Dennis K. Murphy. LC 84-90169. 145p. 1985. 10.95 o.p. (ISBN 0-533-06225-X). Vantage.

Raven & the Paperhangers. Donald MacKenzie. 204p. 1980. 9.95 o.p. (ISBN 0-395-29450-9). HM.

Raven Settles a Score. Donald MacKenzie. 1978. 7.95 o.p. (ISBN 0-395-27100-2). HM.

Ravena. Olivier Dunrea. LC 82-23244. (Illus.). 32p. (ps-3). 1984. reinforced bdg. 13.95 o.p. (ISBN 0-8234-0487-0). Holiday.

Raven's Ghosts. Harry D. Renner. 1979. 10.00 o.p. (ISBN 0-682-49240-X). Exposition-Phoenix.

Raven's Revenge. Donald Mackenzie. 192p. 1982. 10.95 o.p. (ISBN 0-395-32050-X). HM.

Ravenswyke. Alan White. 1980. 12.95 o.p. (ISBN 0-395-28589-5). HM.

Ravissement de Lol V. Stein. Marguerite Duras. (Coll. Soleil). 1964. 13.50 o.p. (ISBN 0-685-11522-4). Schoenhof.

Rawhide. Frank Bosworth. (Lythway Ser.). 160p. 1988. lib. bdg. 17.50x o.s.i. (ISBN 0-7451-0661-7, Pub. by Chivers Pr UK). G K HAll.

Rawhide Justice. Max Brand. (General Ser.). 1984. lib. bdg. 14.95 o.p. (ISBN 0-8161-3532-0, Large Print Bks). G K Hall.

Rawhide Redeemer. Jerome Gardner. (Lythway Ser.). 1987. lib. bdg. 16.50x o.p. (ISBN 0-7451-0580-7, Pub. by Chivers Pr UK). G K Hall.

Rawhiders. Ray Hogan. (General Ser.). 255p. 1986. lib. bdg. 14.95x o.p. (ISBN 0-8161-4053-7, Large Print Bks). G K Hall.

Ray Bradbury. Ed. by Joseph D. Olander & Martin H. Greenberg. LC 77-76721. (Writers of the 21st Century Ser.). 1980. 12.95 o.p. (ISBN 0-8008-6638-X); pap. 5.95 o.s.i. (ISBN 0-8008-6639-8). Taplinger.

Ray Bradbury. William F. Touponce. Ed. by Roger C. Schlobin. (Reader's Guides to Contemporary Science Fiction & Fantasy Authors Ser.: Vol. 31). (Orig.). 1988. 17.95x o.p. (ISBN 0-930261-23-2); pap. 9.95x o.p. (ISBN 0-930261-22-4). Starmont Hse.

Raymond Chandler Speaking. Raymond Chandler. Ed. by Dorothy Gardiner & Katherine S. Walker. 1977. pap. 5.95 o.p. (ISBN 0-395-25017-X). HM.

Raymond D'Aguilers: Historia Francorum Qui Ceperunt Iherusalem. John H. Hill & Laurita L. Hill. LC 68-24358. (Memoirs Ser: Vol. 71). (Illus.). 1968. 12.00 o.p. (ISBN 0-87169-071-3). Am Philos.

Raymond IV, Count of Toulouse. John H. Hill & Laurita L. Hill. LC 80-11116. (Illus.). viii, 177p. 1980. Repr. of 1962 ed. lib. bdg. 35.00x o.p. (ISBN 0-313-22362-9, HIRA). Greenwood.

Razor's Edge: Television Edition. W. Somerset Maugham. 320p. 1984. pap. 4.95 o.p. (ISBN 0-14-007313-2). Penguin.

RCIA Team Manual: How to Implement the Rite of Christian Initiation of Adults in Your Parish. Patricia Barbernitz. 88p. 1986. pap. 7.95 o.p. (ISBN 0-8091-2814-4). Paulist Pr.

RCRA Hazardous Wastes Handbook. 6th ed. Ridgway M. Hall, Jr. et al. 552p. 1985. pap. text ed. 89.00 o.p. (ISBN 0-86587-046-2). Gov Insts.

RCT Reading: A Workbook. Marie Lackner & Cynthia Paterno. 165p. 1982. pap. 6.47 o.p. (ISBN 0-937820-25-3). Westsea Pub.

Rd-Sp Cht, Set A. Kottmeyer. (ISBN 0-07-033711-X). McGraw.

Rd-Sp Web, Set A. Kottmeyer. (ISBN 0-07-033712-8). McGraw.

RDF Sourcebook. Frank Frey. (Twilight: 2000 Ser.). (Illus.). 49p. (Orig.). 1986. pap. 7.00 o.s.i. (ISBN 0-943580-14-5). Game Designers.

Re-Discovery of America: An Introduction to the Philosophy of American Life. Waldo D. Frank. LC 81-20286. x, 353p. 1982. Repr. of 1929 ed. lib. bdg. 35.00x o.p. (ISBN 0-313-23451-5, FRRD). Greenwood.

Re-Entry II. John W. White. 1986. pap. 4.95 o.p. (ISBN 0-8010-9680-4). Baker Bk.

Reach a Little Deeper. Mattie H. Pouncy. LC 85-90035. 229p. 1985. 11.95 o.p. (ISBN 0-533-06567-4). Vantage.

Reach for a Different Sky. Linda Grone. 1984. 5.95 o.p. (ISBN 0-8062-2411-8). Carlton.

Reach for a Star. Florence C. Means. (Illus.). (gr. 7 up). 1957. 7.95 o.p. (ISBN 0-395-06934-3). HM.

Reach for It. Ardy Friedberg. (Illus.). 96p. 1983. pap. 7.75 o.p. (ISBN 0-671-45997-X, Fireside). S&S.

Reach for the Sky. Paul Brickhill. 1954. 6.95 o.p. (ISBN 0-393-07376-9). Norton.

Reach for Tomorrow. Arthur C. Clarke. LC 71-95869. 1970. 5.75x o.s.i. (ISBN 0-15-175960-X). HarBraceJ.

Reach of Song. Ed. by Edward D. Vickers. 160p. 1982. pap. 6.95 o.s.i. (ISBN 0-932298-34-6). Tri-State Pr Corp.

Reaching & Teaching Black Young Adults. Walter A. McCray. LC 86-71996. 120p. 1987. pap. 5.95 o.p. (ISBN 0-933176-07-4). Black Light Fellow.

Reaching for the Stars. Moina Ejaz. 176p. 1987. 10.95 o.p. (ISBN 0-8062-3073-8). Carlton.

Reaching Out - How to Love & Be Loved. Georgie Moore. 1980. 5.00 o.p. (ISBN 0-682-49610-3). Exposition-Phoenix.

Reaching Out: Together, Through the Holy Spirit. Vincent Therrien. 1978. 6.00 o.p. (ISBN 0-682-49162-4, Testament). Exposition-Phoenix.

Reaching Teenagers: Learning Centers for the Secondary Classroom. Don M. Beach. LC 76-40778. (Illus.). 1977. 14.95 o.p. (ISBN 0-673-16416-0); pap. 12.95 o.p. (ISBN 0-673-16417-9). Scott F.

Reaching the Aged: Social Services in Forty-Four Countries. Ed. by Morton I. Teicher et al. LC 79-18525. (Social Service Delivery Systems: Vol. 4). 256p. 1979. 29.95 o.p. (ISBN 0-8039-1365-6); pap. 14.95 o.p. (ISBN 0-8039-1366-4). Sage.

Reaching the Morning After. Al Kasha & Joel Hirschhorn. LC 86-805. 224p. 1986. 14.95 o.p. (ISBN 0-8407-5509-0). Nelson.

Reaching the People: A Public Affairs Training Manual for Civil Legal Services Programs. National Legal Aid & Defender Association Staff. 100p. 10.00 o.p. (ISBN 0-318-18222-X); members 5.00 o.p. (ISBN 0-318-18223-8). Natl Legal Aid & Defender.

Reaching the Silent Billion. David Mason. 190p. 1967. 2.50 o.p. (ISBN 0-317-35483-3). New Readers.

Reaching the Unreached: The Old-New Challenge. Ed. by Harvie M. Conn. 192p. 1985. pap. 8.95 o.p. (ISBN 0-8010-2508-7). Baker Bk.

Reaching Young People Through Media. Nancy B. Pillon. 279p. 1983. lib. bdg. 23.50 o.p. (ISBN 0-87287-369-2). Libs Unl.

Reaching Your World. Beth Mainhood. 118p. 1986. pap. 5.95 o.p. (ISBN 0-89109-537-3). NavPress.

Reaction Kinetics, 2 vols. K. J. Laidler. 1963. Vol. 2. 21.00 o.p. (ISBN 0-08-009836-3); Vol. 1. 25.00 o.p. (ISBN 0-08-009834-7); Vol. 2. pap. 8.50 o.p. (ISBN 0-08-009835-5); Vol. 1. pap. 10.50 o.p. (ISBN 0-08-009833-9). Pergamon.

Reaction Kinetics Progress, Vol. 10, No. 4. Jennings. (Illus.). 98p. 1980. pap. 25.00 o.p. (ISBN 0-08-027135-9). Pergamon.

Reaction Mechanisms in Sulphuric Acid & Other Strong Acid Solutions. M. Liler. (Organic Chemistry Ser.). 1971. 75.50 o.p. (ISBN 0-12-450050-1). Acad Pr.

Reaction Time & Attention after Closed Head Injury. A. H. Zomeren. 176p. 1981. pap. text ed. 17.75 o.p. (ISBN 90-265-0369-5, Pub. by Swets & Zeitlinger Netherlands). CJ Hogrefe Pubs.

Reactions of Organosulfur Compounds. Ed. by Eric Block. 1978. 38.50 o.p. (ISBN 0-12-107050-6). Acad Pr.

Reactive Free Radicals. J. M. Hay. 1974. 37.50 o.p. (ISBN 0-12-333550-7). Acad Pr.

Reactive Intermediates. Ed. by F. Boschke. LC 51-5497. (Topics in Current Chemistry: Vol. 16, Pt. 1). (Illus.). 1970. pap. 48.40 o.p. (ISBN 0-387-05103-1). Springer-Verlag.

Reactivite des hypobromites. P. Brun & B. Waegell. 1976. pap. 12.75 o.p. (ISBN 0-08-021014-7). Pergamon.

Reactivities. T. Shimidzu et al. LC 61-642. (Advances in Polymer Science: Vol. 23). (Illus.). 1977. 35.00 o.p. (ISBN 0-387-07943-2). Springer-Verlag.

Reactivity Coefficients in Large Fast Power Reactors. Hummel Okrent. LC 73-119000. (ANS Monographs). 386p. 1970. 21.00 o.p. (ISBN 0-89448-006-5, 300002). Am Nuclear Soc.

Reactor Core Fuel Management. P. Silvennoinen. 250p. 1976. 65.00 o.p. (ISBN 0-08-019853-8); pap. 25.00 o.p. (ISBN 0-08-019852-X). Pergamon.

Reactor Noise - Smorn II: Proceedings of the 2nd Specialists' Meeting on Reactor Noise 1977. Ed. by M. M. Williams. 1978. pap. 220.00 o.p. (ISBN 0-08-022157-2). Pergamon.

Reactor Noise - Smorn III: Proceedings of the Third Specialists Meeting on Reactor Noise at Tokyo, Japan, October 26-30, 1981. Ed. by M. M. Williams. (Illus.). 620p. 1982. 170.00 o.p. (ISBN 0-08-027619-9). Pergamon.

Reactor Noise - Smorn IV. Ed. by M. M. Williams & N. J. McCormick. (Illus.). 1024p. 1985. 150.00 o.p. (ISBN 0-08-031648-4, Pub. by PPL). Pergamon.

Reactor Noise: An International Symposium: Special Multi Issue of Journal of Annals of Nuclear Energy. Ed. by M. M. Williams. 400p. 1975. pap. 67.00 o.p. (ISBN 0-08-019895-3). Pergamon.

Reactor Safeguards. C. R. Russell. 1962. 57.00 o.p. (ISBN 0-08-009706-5); pap. 55.00 o.p. (ISBN 0-08-013610-9). Pergamon.

Read about It Series, 3 vols. Imogene Forte. (Illus.). 1982. Set. 19.95 o.p. (IP 12-7). Incentive Pubns.

Read All About It! The Collected Adventures of a Maverick Reporter. Sidney Zion. 368p. 1982. 15.95 o.s.i. (ISBN 0-671-43458-6). Summit Bks.

Read-Along with "Atariba & Niguayona" Harriet Rohmer & Jesus G. Rea. 1988. Incl. audiocassette. 15.95 o.p. (ISBN 0-89239-039-5). Childrens Book Pr.

Read-Along with "My Aunt Otilia's Spirits" Richard Garcia. 15.95 o.p. Childrens Book Pr.

Read-Along with "The Legend of Food Mountain" Harriet Rohmer. 1988. Incl. Audiocassette. 15.95 o.p. (ISBN 0-89239-035-2). Childrens Book Pr.

Read & Do with Professor Riddle. Jim Maraccini. 1972. 3.00x o.p. (ISBN 0-88323-091-7, 195). Pendergrass Pub.

Read That Label: How to Tell What's Inside a Wine Bottle from What's on the Outside. Bruce M. Fingerhut & Steve Haskin. (Illus.). 128p. (Orig.). 1983. pap. 4.95 o.s.i. (ISBN 0-89651-652-0). B L Pub.

Read to Write. Halsey P. Taylor & Sheila F. Taylor. 1981. pap. text ed. write for info. o.p. (ISBN 0-673-15388-6). Scott F.

Read to Write: Using Children's Literature As a Springboard for Teaching Writing. rev ed. John W. Stewig. LC 80-19047. (Orig.). 1980. pap. 13.95 o.p. (ISBN 0-03-056123-X). HR&W.

Read Your Child's Thoughts: Pre-School Learning Piaget's Way. Mary Sime. (Illus.). 1980. 13.95 o.p. (ISBN 0-500-01217-2). Thames Hudson.

Readable People of George Meredith. Judith Wilt. 284p. 1975. 30.50x o.p. (ISBN 0-691-06275-7). Princeton U Pr.

Reader for Writers. 3rd ed. Jerome W. Archer & A. Schwartz. 1971. text ed. 29.95 o.p. (ISBN 0-07-002193-7). McGraw.

Reader in Contemporary Theology. Ed. by John Bowden & James Richmond. (Orig.). 1967. pap. 1.95 o.s.i. (ISBN 0-664-24777-6, Westminster). Westminster John Knox.

Reader in Cultural Anthropology. Carleton S. Coon. LC 76-78. 634p. 1977. Repr. of 1948 ed. lib. bdg. 28.50 o.p. (ISBN 0-88275-394-0). Krieger.

Reader in Political Theology. Ed. by Alistair Kee. LC 74-19047. 1975. pap. 2.95 o.s.i. (ISBN 0-664-24816-0, Westminster). Westminster John Knox.

Reader of Modern Urdu Poetry. M. A. Barker et al. 334p. 1968. pap. 5.00x o.p. (ISBN 0-7735-9066-8, Pub. by McGill Canada). U of Toronto Pr.

Readers & Library Users: A Study of Reading Habits & Public Library Use. M. L. Ward. 1977. 9.00x o.p. (ISBN 0-85365-479-4, Pub by the Library Assn). Nichols Pub.

Reader's Companion to the Bible. Ralph D. Heim. LC 74-26329. 144p. 1975. pap. 0.50 o.p. (ISBN 0-8006-1090-3, 1-1090, Fortress). Augsburg Fortress.

Reader's Digest Almanac & Yearbook, 1986. Reader's Digest Editors. LC 66-14383. (Illus.). 1024p. 1985. 8.50 o.p. (ISBN 0-89577-216-7, Pub. by RD Assn). Random.

Reader's Digest-Bartholomew Atlas of the World. LC 83-61162. 176p. 1987. 17.95 o.p. (ISBN 0-89577-172-1). RD Assn.

Reader's Digest Bible: Condensed from the Revised Standard Version. LC 81-51531. 816p. 1982. 21.95 o.p. (ISBN 0-89577-106-3); deluxe ed. 24.95 o.p. (ISBN 0-89577-148-9). RD Assn.

Reader's Digest Good Health Cookbooks 1-M Fish & Meat. Reader's Digest Editors. LC 85-62336. (Illus.). 192p. 1986. 14.45 o.p. (ISBN 0-89577-222-1, Pub. by RD Assn). Random.

Reader's Digest Good Health Cookbooks 1-M Vegetables & Desserts. Reader's Digest Editors. LC 85-62573. (Illus.). 192p. 1986. 14.45 o.p. (ISBN 0-89577-226-4, Pub. by RD Assn). Random.

Reader's Digest Great Biographies, Vol. 1. Ed. by Reader's Digest Editors. LC 86-29816. (Open-Ended Ser.). (Illus.). 608p. 1987. 13.95 o.p. (ISBN 0-89577-259-0). RD Assn.

Reader's Digest Great Biographies, Vol. 2. Ed. by Reader's Digest Editors. LC 86-29816. (Open-Ended Ser.). (Illus.). 640p. 1987. 13.95 o.p. (ISBN 0-89577-260-4). RD Assn.

Reader's Digest Great Biographies, Vol. 3. Ed. by Reader's Digest Editors. LC 86-29816. (Open-ended Ser.). (Illus.). 576p. 1987. 13.95 o.p. (ISBN 0-89577-261-2). RD Assn.

Reader's Digest Great Biographies, Vol. 5. Reader's Digest Editors. LC 86-29816. (Open-Ended Ser.). (Illus.). 576p. 1989. 13.95 o.p. (ISBN 0-89577-297-3). RD Assn.

Reader's Digest Great Biographies, Vol. 6. LC 86-29816. (Open-Ended Ser.). (Illus.). 608p. 1989. 13.95 o.p. (ISBN 0-89577-298-1). RD Assn.

Reader's Digest Wide World Atlas. rev. ed. (Illus.). 240p. 1986. 34.95 o.p. (ISBN 0-528-83148-8). Rand McNally.

Reader's Digest 1981 Almanac & Yearbook. 16th ed. Ed. by Reader's Digest Editors. (Illus.). 1981. 6.45 o.p. (ISBN 0-89577-090-3, Pub. by RD Assoc). Random.

Reader's Guide to A. E. van Vogt. Jeffrey M. Elliot. Ed. by Roger C. Schlobin. (Starmont Reader's Guides to Contemporary Science Fiction & Fantasy Authors Ser.: Vol. 17). (Illus., Orig.). Date not set. pap. text ed. 9.95x o.s.i. (ISBN 0-916732-45-2). Starmont Hse.

Reader's Guide to Fantasy. Michael Franklin et al. 224p. 1982. pap. 2.95 o.p. (ISBN 0-380-80333-X, 80333-X). Avon.

Reader's Guide to Fifty British Poets: 1300-1900. Michael Schmidt. (Reader's Guide Ser.). 430p. 1980. 24.50x o.p. (ISBN 0-389-20137-5). B&N Imports.

Reader's Guide to Isaac Asimov. Donald M. Hassler. Ed. by Roger C. Schlobin. (Starmont Reader's Guides to Contemporary Science Fiction & Fantasy Authors Ser.: Vol. 40). (Illus., Orig.). 1988. 17.95x o.p. (ISBN 0-930261-32-1); pap. text ed. 9.95x o.p. (ISBN 0-930261-31-3). Starmont Hse.

Reader's Guide to James Joyce. William Y. Tindall. 304p. 1959. pap. 9.95 o.p. (ISBN 0-374-50112-2). FS&G.

Reader's Guide to Non-Controversial Books for Children, Young People & Discriminating Adults: National Committee for Good Reading. 1986. 5.00 o.p. (ISBN 0-931510-15-5). Hi Willow.

Reader's Guide to Science Fiction. Baird Searles. 1979. pap. 2.95 o.p. (ISBN 0-380-46128-5, 89483). Avon.

Reader's Guide to the Everyman's Library. Ed. by Donald A. Ross. 1976. 14.95x o.p. (ISBN 0-460-00889-7, Evman); pap. 2.50x o.p. (ISBN 0-460-01889-2). Biblio Dist.

Reader's Guide to the Short Stories of Ernest Hemingway. Paul Smith. 1989. 55.00 o.p. (ISBN 0-8161-8794-0). G K Hall.

Reader's Guide to the Silmarillion. Paul H. Kocher. 1980. 9.95 o.p. (ISBN 0-395-28950-5). HM.

Readers Theatre Comes to Church. Gordon C. Bennett. LC 72-1763. (Illus.). 128p. (Orig.). 1972. pap. 4.95 o.p. (ISBN 0-8042-1963-X, John Knox). Westminster John Knox.

Reading About Language. Charlton Laird & Robert M. Gorrell. 1971. pap. text ed. 11.95 o.p. (ISBN 0-15-575535-8, HC). HarBraceJ.

Reading Activities Handbook. Wilma H. Miller. LC 80-17117. (Illus.). 476p. (gr. 1-8). 1980. pap. 22.95 o.p. (ISBN 0-03-051371-5). HR&W.

Reading & Analyzing Medical Records. 232p. 1983. 15.00 o.p. (ISBN 0-318-02486-1). ICLE Georgia.

Reading & Preaching the Bible: A New Approach. Walter Vogels. LC 85-47758. (Background Bks.: Vol. 4). 1986. pap. 8.95 o.p. (ISBN 0-89453-472-6). M Glazier.

Reading & the Adult Learner. Ed. by Laura S. Johnson. 76p. (Orig.). 1980. pap. text ed. 4.00 o.p. (ISBN 0-87207-606-7, 606). Intl Reading.

Reading Architectural Plans for Residential & Commercial Construction. 2nd ed. Ernest R. Weidhaas. 336p. 1980. text ed. 44.00 o.p. (ISBN 0-205-07155-4, 3271552); tchr's. guide avail. o.p. (ISBN 0-205-07167-8). Allyn.

Reading Beyond Words. 2nd ed. W. Royce Adams & Jane Brody. 1983. pap. text ed. 16.95x o.p. (ISBN 0-03-060281-5). HR&W.

Reading Blake's "Songs" Zachery Leader. (Illus.). 256p. 1981. 27.50x o.p. (ISBN 0-7100-0635-7). Routledge Chapman & Hall.

Reading Diagnosis & Direct Instruction: A Guide for the Classroom. 2nd ed. William H. Rupley & Timothy R. Blair. LC 82-84609. 1983. pap. 15.95 o.p. (ISBN 0-395-32787-3). HM.

Reading Diagnosis & Remediation. William H. Rupley & Timothy R. Blair. 1979. text ed. 23.95 o.p. (ISBN 0-395-30720-1). HM.

Reading Diagnosis & Remediation: Classroom & Clinic. 2d ed. William H. Rupley & Timothy R. Blair. LC 82-83365. 496p. 1983. text ed. 34.50 o.p. (ISBN 0-395-32785-7). HM.

Reading Disability: Progress & Research Needs in Dyslexia. Ed. by John Money. 208p. 1962. 19.50x o.p. (ISBN 0-8018-0466-3). Johns Hopkins.

Reading Enhancement & Development. Rhonda H. Atkinson & Debbie Longman. (Illus.). 479p. 1985. pap. text ed. 19.25 o.p. (ISBN 0-314-85215-8). West Pub.

Reading Faces. Leopold Bellak & Samm S. Baker. LC 80-19235. (Illus.). 163p. 1981. 10.95 o.p. (ISBN 0-03-057869-8). H Holt & Co.

Reading for Meaning. Halsey P. Taylor. 317p. (Orig.). 1975. pap. text ed. 9.95 o.p. (ISBN 0-15-575634-6, HC). HarBraceJ.

Reading for Results. Laraine Flemming. LC 77-76422. (Illus.). 1978. pap. 11.95 o.p. (ISBN 0-395-25419-1). HM.

Reading for Results. 2d ed. Laraine Flemming. 468p. 1983. pap. 18.95 o.p. (ISBN 0-395-32605-2). HM.

Reading French in the Arts & Sciences. 3rd ed. E. M. Stack. 1979. pap. 18.50 o.p. (ISBN 0-395-27505-9). HM.

Reading from the Literature. Ed. by Gert H. Brieger. LC 76-165053. 348p. 1972. 35.00x o.p. (ISBN 0-8018-1237-2). Johns Hopkins.

Reading Games & Activities. Mary E. Dorsey. LC 72-80026. 1972. pap. 7.50 o.p. (ISBN 0-8224-5810-1). D S Lake Pubs.

Reading Imaginative Literature. Vernon Thompson. LC 74-24533. 1975. pap. 5.00x o.p. (ISBN 0-912112-06-9). Everett-Edward.

Reading in a Second Language: Hypotheses, Organization & Practice. Ronald Mackay et al. 224p. 1979. pap. text ed. 13.50 o.p. (ISBN 0-88377-134-9). Newbury Hse.

Reading in the Content Areas. Jane Kahn & Gwendolyn Trotter. LC 78-730059. (Illus.). 1978. pap. text ed. 159.00 o.s.i. (ISBN 0-89290-102-0, A328-SATC). Soc for Visual.

Reading in the Content Fields. rev. ed. Compiled by Leo Fay. (Annotated Bibliographies Ser.). 1975. 1.25 o.p. (ISBN 0-87207-302-5). Intl Reading.

Reading in the High School & College. Ed. by William S. Gray. LC 57-6273. (National Society for the Study of Education Yearbooks Ser: No. 47, Pt. 2). 1958. lib. bdg. 6.00x o.s.i. (ISBN 0-226-60002-5); pap. text ed. 4.50x o.s.i. (ISBN 0-226-60003-3). U of Chicago Pr.

Reading in Your School. John R. Newton. 1960. text ed. 26.95 o.p. (ISBN 0-07-046410-3). McGraw.

Reading Instruction. Barbara D. Stoodt. 1981. text ed. 30.50 o.p. (ISBN 0-395-30749-X). HM.
Reading Instruction for Classroom & Clinic. Edward Fry. (Illus.). 448p. 1972. text ed. 29.95 o.p. (ISBN 0-07-022604-0). McGraw.
Reading Instruction in the Content Areas. Walter J. Lamberg & Charles E. Lamb. 1980. text ed. 30.95 o.p. (ISBN 0-395-30648-5). HM.
Reading Instruction in the Secondary School. rev. ed. Betty D. Roe et al. 1978. text ed. 21.95 o.p. (ISBN 0-395-30710-4). HM.
Reading of Shakespeare's "Antony & Cleopatra" A. Riemer. (Sydney Studies in Literature Ser). 1968. 15.00x o.p. (ISBN 0-424-05630-5, Pub by Sydney U Pr). Intl Spec Bk.
Reading Paul Today: A New Introduction to the Man & His Letters. Hubert Richards. LC 79-26287. (Biblical Foundations Ser.). (Illus.). 152p. 1980. pap. 2.49 o.p. (ISBN 0-8042-0392-X, John Knox). Westminster John Knox.
Reading Power. 2nd ed. James I. Brown. 400p. 1982. pap. text ed. 15.00 o.p. (ISBN 0-669-05318-X). Heath.
Reading Power & Study Skills for College Work. Carl A. Lefevre & Helen E. Lefevre. 241p. 1978. pap. text ed. 11.95 o.p. (ISBN 0-15-575757-1, HC). HarBraceJ.
Reading Prescriptions: Phonics Skills, Vol.1 see Diagnostic Prescriptive Reading Program.
Reading Relations - Structures of Literary Production: A Dialectical Text-Book. Bernard Sharratt. 341p. 1982. text ed. 40.00x o.p. (ISBN 0-391-02557-0). Humanities.
Reading Retardation & Multi-Sensory Teaching. Charles Hulme. (International Library of Psychology Ser.). 200p. 1981. 31.95x o.p. (ISBN 0-7100-0761-2). Routledge Chapman & Hall.
Reading Skillbuilder: Comprehension Skills. Harry W. Forgan. 1982. pap. 6.95 o.p. (ISBN 0-673-16549-3). Scott F.
Reading Skillbuilder: Word Recognition Skills. Harry W. Forgan. 1982. pap. 6.95 o.p. (ISBN 0-673-16548-5). Scott F.
Reading Skills for College Study. James F. Shepherd. LC 79-89520. (Illus.). 1983. pap. 13.50 o.p. (ISBN 0-395-28503-8). HM.
Reading Skills Handbook. 2nd ed. Harvey Wiener & Charles Bazerman. 1982. pap. 15.95 o.p. (ISBN 0-395-31710-X). HM.
Reading Skills Handbook. Harvey S. Wiener & Charles Bazerman. LC 77-74097. (Illus.). 1978. pap. 10.95 o.p. (ISBN 0-395-24556-7). HM.
Reading Success for School & Home. Lucy C. LeGros. (Illus.). 212p. (Orig.). (gr. k-4). 1979. pap. 10.95 o.p. (ISBN 0-937306-01-0). Creat Res NC.
Reading the New Testament: An Introduction. Pheme Perkins. LC 78-51892. 352p. 1978. pap. 5.95 o.p. (ISBN 0-8091-9535-6). Paulist Pr.
Reading the New Testament for Today: An Introduction to the Study of the New Testament. Brian E. Beck. LC 78-14420. (Biblical Foundations Ser.). 1978. pap. 4.95 o.p. (ISBN 0-8042-0391-1, John Knox). Westminster John Knox.
Reading the News. Ed. by Robert K. Manoff & Michael Schudson. LC 86-72639. 256p. 1986. 19.45 o.p. (ISBN 0-394-54362-9); pap. 9.95 o.p. (ISBN 0-394-74649-X). Pantheon.
Reading the Old Testament Prophets Today. Harry Mowvley. LC 79-87744. (Biblical Foundations Ser.). 1979. pap. 4.95 o.p. (ISBN 0-8042-0167-6, John Knox). Westminster John Knox.
Reading the Ramayana: A Bibliographic Guide for Students & College Teachers. Indian Variants on the Rama Theme in English Translations. H. Daniel Smith. (Foreign & Comparative Studies Program, South Asian Special Publications: No. 4). (Orig.). 1983. pap. text ed. 6.50x o.p. (ISBN 0-915984-87-3). Syracuse U Foreign Comp.
Reading Through Romans. C. K. Barrett. LC 76-55828. 96p. 1977. pap. 3.95 o.p. (ISBN 0-8006-1250-7, 1-1250, Fortress). Augsburg Fortress.
Reading to Learn. Sheila Harri-Augstein & Michael Smith. LC 82-7864. 120p. 1982. pap. 8.50 o.p. (ISBN 0-416-72660-7, NO. 3747). Routledge Chapman & Hall.
Reading: Who? What? When? Where? Why? How? Floyd Bergman. 314p. 1969. looseleaf 11.55 o.p. (ISBN 0-87506-041-2). Campus.
Reading with Your Child: A Number One Priority. Jane Ervin. 1983. 35.95scp o.p. (ISBN 0-205-07554-1, 237554). Allyn.
Reading, Writing & Newspapers: A Special Issue Devoted Wholly to a Discussion of the Conditions that Affect Newspaper Writing. Ed. by Nieman Reports Staff. pap. 7.00 o.p. (ISBN 0-384-41560-1). Johnson Repr.
Reading, Writing & Speech Problems in Children. Samuel T. Orton. 1973. 5.00x o.p. (ISBN 0-393-01107-0). Norton.
Reading, Writing & the Exceptional Child: A Psycho-socio-linguistic Approach. M. Suzanne Hasenstab & Joan M. Laughton. LC 82-3974. 240p. 1982. text ed. 32.00 o.p. (ISBN 0-89443-654-6). Aspen Pub.
Reading, Writing, Chattering Chimps. Aline Amon. LC 75-9524. (Illus.). 128p. (gr. 3-7). 1975. 7.95 o.p. (ISBN 0-689-30472-2, Atheneum). Macmillan.
Reading 1967-1977: A Decade of Change & Promise. Jeanne Chall. LC 77-89841. (Fastback Ser.: No. 97). 1977. pap. 0.90 o.p. (ISBN 0-87367-097-3). Phi Delta Kappa.
Readings & Applications in School Counseling. Ed. by Vincente N. Noble. 144p. 1976. pap. text ed. 4.75x o.p. (ISBN 0-8422-0523-3). Irvington.
Readings & Cases in Contemporary Labor Relations 1980. Kenneth A. Kovach. LC 80-1429. 359p. 1981. pap. text ed. 15.25 o.p. (ISBN 0-8191-1362-X). U Pr of Amer.
Readings & Cases in Personnel Management. Lloyd L. Byars et al. 1979. 14.95x o.s.i. (ISBN 0-7216-2252-6). Dryden Pr.
Readings & Writing Termcap Entries. John Strang. Ed. by Dale Dougherty. (Nutshell Handbook). 72p. 1985. pap. 7.50 o.p. (ISBN 0-937175-03-X). O'Reilly & Assocs.
Readings for an Introduction to Philosophy. James R. Hamilton et al. 544p. 1976. text ed. write for info. o.p. (ISBN 0-02-349550-2). Macmillan.
Readings for Democrats. Ed. by Edward Reed. LC 60-7433. (Docket Ser.: Vol. 15). 256p. (Orig.). 1960. pap. 2.50 o.p. (ISBN 0-379-11315-5). Oceana.
Readings for Foundations of Education. Ed. by Nevin S. Alwine. 121p. 1969. pap. text ed. 9.95x o.p. (ISBN 0-8290-1310-5). Irvington.
Readings for Resident Assistants. D. Kilbourn. 1969. pap. text ed. 5.95x o.p. (ISBN 0-8290-1179-X). Irvington.
Readings for the Managerial Accounting Specialty. (FLMI Insurance Education Program Ser.). 207p. 1981. pap. text ed. 9.50 o.p. (ISBN 0-915322-45-5). LOMA.
Readings for Writers. 4th ed. Jo R. McCuen & Anthony C. Winkler. 606p. 1983. pap. text ed. 11.25 o.p. (ISBN 0-15-575831-4, HC). HarBraceJ.
Readings for Writers. 3rd ed. Jo Ray McCuen & Anthony C. Winkler. 1980. 10.95 o.p. (ISBN 0-15-575829-2). HarbraceJ.
Readings for Writers. 5th ed. Jo Ray McCuen & Anthony C. Winkler. 741p. 1986. pap. text ed. 14.00 net o.p. (ISBN 0-15-575833-0, Pub. by HC). HarBraceJ.
Readings From Chinese Writers: Nineteen Nineteen to Nineteen Forty-Nine, Bk. 2. Ed. by Beijing Language Institute Staff. (Readings From Chinese Writers Ser.). 360p. (Orig.). 1982. pap. 8.95 o.p. (ISBN 0-8351-1122-9). China Bks.
Readings From Chinese Writers Series: Nineteen Nineteen to Nineteen Forty-Nine, Bk. 1. Ed. by Beijing Language Institute Staff. (Readings From Chinese Writers). 333p. (Orig.). 1982. pap. 8.95 o.p. (ISBN 0-8351-1117-2). China Bks.
Readings from the Frankfurt School. Ed. by Tom Bottomore. (Key Text Ser.). pap. cancelled o.s.i. (ISBN 0-85312-853-7, 9584, Pub. by Tavistock England). Routledge Chapman & Hall.
Readings in Abnormal Behavior: Toward a Sociopsychological Model. Ed. by Richard Dana. 1970. pap. text ed. 9.95x o.p. (ISBN 0-8422-0059-2). Irvington.
Readings in Abnormal Psychology. P. Scott Lawrence et al. LC 73-10220. 1973. 29.50x o.p. (ISBN 0-8422-5112-X); pap. text ed. 12.00x o.p. (ISBN 0-8422-0330-3). Irvington.
Readings in Adult Development & Aging. Warner K. Schaie & James Geiwitz. (Orig.). 1982. pap. text ed. 18.75 o.p. (ISBN 0-316-77272-0). Scott F.
Readings in American History, 2 vols. 4th ed. Robert C. Cotner. LC 75-37038. (Illus.). 1976. Vol. 1. pap. 13.50 o.p. (ISBN 0-395-17810-X); Vol. 2. pap. 17.50 o.p. (ISBN 0-395-17811-8). HM.
Readings in American Politics & Education. Donna E. Shalala et al. LC 73-11237. 1973. 26.00x o.p. (ISBN 0-8422-5124-3); pap. text ed. 8.50x o.p. (ISBN 0-8422-0342-7). Irvington.
Readings in American Social Studies. R. Johnson et al. 1971. pap. text ed. 9.95x o.p. (ISBN 0-8422-0138-6). Irvington.
Readings in Animal Energetics. Robert H. Catlett. LC 73-11003. 237p. 1973. text ed. 29.50x o.p. (ISBN 0-8422-7119-8); pap. text ed. 9.75x o.p. (ISBN 0-8290-0668-0). Irvington.
Readings in Biology & Man. Ed. by Miguel A. Santos. LC 73-12020. 1974. 29.00x o.p. (ISBN 0-8422-5048-4); pap. text ed. 9.75x o.p. (ISBN 0-8422-0334-6). Irvington.
Readings in Black American Music. Ed. by Eileen Southern. LC 70-98892. 1972. pap. 4.95x o.p. (ISBN 0-393-09892-3). Norton.
Readings in Canadian Industrial Relations. Ed. by Gary N. Chaison & Joseph B. Rose. LC 74-11073. 299p. 1974. text ed. 28.50x o.p. (ISBN 0-8422-5191-X); pap. text ed. 8.75x o.p. (ISBN 0-8422-0441-5). Irvington.
Readings in Child Behavior & Development. 3rd ed. Celia S. Lavatelli & Faith Stendler. (Orig.). 1972. pap. text ed. 11.95 o.p. (ISBN 0-15-575805-5, HC). HarBraceJ.
Readings in Child Psychology. W. Coggan. 1969. pap. text ed. 7.95x o.p. (ISBN 0-8422-0033-9). Irvington.
Readings in Child Socialization. Kurt Danziger. 1970. 85.00 o.p. (ISBN 0-08-006882-0); pap. 85.00 o.p. (ISBN 0-08-006881-2). Pergamon.
Readings in Chinese Geography: Vol. 1, Chinese Text, Vol. 2, Vocabulary, Notes & Translations. Jack Williams & Yung Teng Chia-Yee. Set. pap. text ed. 15.00x o.p. (ISBN 0-87022-862-5). UH Pr.
Readings in Christian Humanism. Ed. by Joseph M. Shaw et al. LC 82-70963. (Orig.). 1982. pap. 25.95 o.p. (ISBN 0-8066-1938-4, 10-5400, Augsburg). Augsburg Fortress.
Readings in Classroom Management. R. Karraker et al. 1969. pap. text ed. 9.50x o.p. (ISBN 0-8422-0004-5). Irvington.
Readings in Consumer Behavior: A Student's Choice. Ed. by J. Peter Vernon & Eugene H. Fram. 1974. pap. text ed. 12.95x o.p. (ISBN 0-8422-0369-9). Irvington.
Readings in Consumer Behavior: Individuals, Groups, & Organizations. 2nd ed. Melanie Wallendorf & Gerald Zaltman. LC 83-21608. (Theories in Marketing Ser.: 1-358). 456p. 1984. pap. 27.95 o.p. (ISBN 0-471-09307-6). Wiley.
Readings in Contemporary Physical Distance & Logistics. 4th ed. James C. Johnson. 352p. 1981. pap. text ed. write for info. o.p. (ISBN 0-02-360960-5). Macmillan.
Readings in Contemporary Problems, Issues & Values. J. Nutsch. 1970. pap. text ed. 4.75x o.p. (ISBN 0-8422-0363-X). Irvington.
Readings in Contemporary Transportation. 2nd ed. Donald F. Wood & James C. Johnson. 336p. 1983. pap. text ed. write for info. o.p. (ISBN 0-02-429500-0). Macmillan.
Readings in Cost & Managerial Accounting. Jae K. Shim & Louis Geller. 448p. 1980. 13.95 o.p. (ISBN 0-8403-3047-2, 40304701). Kendall-Hunt.
Readings in Criminal Psychology. Ed. by William L. McCraney. LC 72-8687. 192p. 1972. pap. text ed. 6.95x o.p. (ISBN 0-8422-0246-3). Irvington.
Readings in Deviant Behavior. Ed. by Denzel E. Benson. LC 73-14998. 1973. 29.50x o.p. (ISBN 0-8422-5107-3). Irvington.
Readings in Econometric Theory. Ed. by M. Dowling & F. R. Glahe. LC 79-128867. 1970. pap. 17.50 o.p. (ISBN 0-87081-004-9). Univ Pr Colo.
Readings in Economics. 3rd ed. Ed. by Eileen Applebaum et al. LC 86-71537. 171p. 1986. pap. 13.00 o.p. (ISBN 0-89463-047-4). Am Inst Property.
Readings in Economics for China. C. F. Remer. LC 78-74358. (Modern Chinese Economy Ser.). 685p. 1980. lib. bdg. 94.00 o.p. (ISBN 0-8240-4278-6). Garland Pub.
Readings in Education & Psychology. L. Cohen. 1969. pap. text ed. 5.95x o.p. (ISBN 0-8422-0028-2). Irvington.
Readings in Education & Psychology. Ed. by Paul Grob & Nina W. Brown. 333p. 1969. pap. text ed. 12.95x o.p. (ISBN 0-686-84056-9). Irvington.
Readings in Educational Psychology. L. Njaa. 1975. pap. text ed. 17.00x o.p. (ISBN 0-8422-0462-8). Irvington.
Readings in Educational Psychology. Joseph L. Wolff. 1969. pap. text ed. 14.95x o.p. (ISBN 0-8290-1311-3). Irvington.
Readings in Embryology. R. Grey et al. 1969. pap. text ed. 4.95x o.p. (ISBN 0-8290-1182-X). Irvington.
Readings in Experimental Psychology. David G. Elmes. 1978. pap. 18.50 o.p. (ISBN 0-395-30797-X). HM.
Readings in Family Therapy. H. Goldstein. 1969. pap. text ed. 9.95x o.p. (ISBN 0-8290-1184-6). Irvington.
Readings in Financial Analysis. 5th ed. Institute of C. F. A. Staff. 1981. pap. 12.00x o.p. (ISBN 0-256-02583-5). Irwin.
Readings in Foundations of Education. Ed. by Ronald Haas & Lawrence Hamel. 263p. 1971. pap. text ed. 9.95x o.p. (ISBN 0-8422-0159-9). Irvington.
Readings in General Psychology. O. Desiderato. 1969. pap. text ed. 12.95x o.p. (ISBN 0-8422-0047-9). Irvington.
Readings in Government & Non-Profit Accounting. Richard J. Vargo. 1977. pap. text ed. (ISBN 0-534-00547-0). PWS-Kent Pub.
Readings in Guidance. W. Hitchcock. 1971. pap. text ed. 6.00x o.p. (ISBN 0-8422-0149-1). Irvington.
Readings in Health Science. Benjamin A. Kogan. 1971. pap. text ed. 8.95 o.p. (ISBN 0-15-575841-1, HC). HarBraceJ.
Readings in Human Behavior. John G. Whittle. 143p. 1977. pap. text ed. 6.95x o.p. (ISBN 0-87655-545-8). Irvington.
Readings in Human Development: A Humanist Approach. Ed. by Theron M. Covin. 197p. 1974. pap. text ed. 6.95x o.p. (ISBN 0-8422-0439-3). Irvington.
Readings in Industrial Ancient Prevention. Daniel C. Petersen & Jerry Goodale. (Illus.). 1980. text ed. 20.95 o.p. (ISBN 0-07-049591-2). McGraw.
Readings in Industrial Economics, 2 vols. Charles K. Rowley. LC 73-76642. 288p. 1973. Vol. 1. pap. 11.50x o.p. (ISBN 0-8448-0207-7, Pub. by Crane Russak & Co); Vol. 2. pap. 11.50x o.p. (ISBN 0-8448-0208-5). Taylor & Francis.
Readings in International & Agricultural Economic Development. M. Blase et al. 1970. pap. text ed. 7.25x o.p. (ISBN 0-8422-0107-6). Irvington.
Readings in Introductory Sociology. Hiltz. 1976. pap. write for info. o.p. (ISBN 0-8191-0089-7); pap. 6.75 o.p. U Pr of Amer.
Readings in Investments. Jack C. Francis. 1980. text ed. 23.95 o.p. (ISBN 0-07-019963-9). McGraw.
Readings in Kinship in Urban Society. C. C. Harris. 1970. 100.00 o.p. (ISBN 0-08-016039-5); pap. 100.00 o.p. (ISBN 0-08-016038-7). Pergamon.
Readings in Labor Relations. Ed. by Karl O. Mann. 110p. 1974. pap. text ed. 4.95x o.p. (ISBN 0-87128-850-8). Irvington.
Readings in Land Reform. Ed. by Sein Lin. 374p. 1970. pap. 2.50 o.s.i. (ISBN 0-686-01013-2). Lincoln Inst Land.
Readings in Learning & Memory. Roger Tarpy & Richard Mayer. 1979. pap. text ed. (ISBN 0-673-15110-7). Scott F.
Readings in Management Information Systems. Gordon B. Davis & Gordon Everest. 1976. text ed. 28.95 o.p. (ISBN 0-07-015835-5). McGraw.
Readings in Management: Making Organization Peform. Hugh J. Smith et al. (Illus.). 1980. pap. text ed. write for info. o.p. (ISBN 0-02-412520-2). Macmillan.
Readings in Management Science. Ed. by Efraim Turban & N. Paul Loomba. 1976. pap. 10.95x o.p. (ISBN 0-256-01705-0). Irwin.
Readings in Managerial Economics. 4th ed. Coyne. 1985. 19.95x o.p. (ISBN 0-256-03056-1). Irwin.
Readings in Managerial Economics. 3rd ed. Thomas J. Coyne. 1981. pap. 9.95x o.p. (ISBN 0-256-02422-7). Irwin.
Readings in Managerial Economics. I. Ibrahim et al. LC 75-4618. 1976. 110.00 o.p. (ISBN 0-08-019605-5); pap. 110.00 o.p. (ISBN 0-08-019604-7). Pergamon.
Readings in Marketing Strategy. Joseph P. Guiltinan & P. Gordon. (Marketing Ser.). 624p. 1982. text ed. 19.95 o.p. (ISBN 0-07-048922-X). McGraw.
Readings in Mathematics. Irving Adler. 188p. 1972. pap. 5.60 o.s.i. (ISBN 0-663-24123-5). NCTM.
Readings in Medieval Rhetoric. Ed. by Joseph M. Miller et al. LC 73-77857. 320p. 1973. 9.95X o.p. (ISBN 0-253-34878-1); pap. 9.95x o.p. (ISBN 0-253-34879-X). Ind U Pr.
Readings in Microeconomics. Breit et al. 1985. pap. 16.95 o.p. (ISBN 0-8016-0795-7). Mosby.
Readings in Minnesota Government: Politics & Administration. T. Pahl. 1970. pap. text ed. 6.95x o.p. (ISBN 0-8290-1183-8). Irvington.
Readings in Multiple Regression & Intermediate Educational Statistics. J. Williams et al. 1971. pap. text ed. 4.95x o.p. (ISBN 0-8422-0144-0). Irvington.
Readings in Organizational Behavior. Steven Altman & Richard M. Hodgetts. 1979. pap. text ed. 15.95 o.p. (ISBN 0-7216-1140-0). HR&W.
Readings in Organizational Behavior: Dimensions of Management Actions. Richard C. Huseman & Archie B. Carroll. 1979. text ed. 25.00 o.p. (ISBN 0-205-06515-5, 086515); instr's. manual avail. o.p. (ISBN 0-205-06538-4, 086538). Allyn.
Readings in Political Economy. W. Richard. 1969. pap. text ed. 9.75x o.p. (ISBN 0-8422-0039-8). Irvington.
Readings in Psychology. S. Hochman. 1972. pap. text ed. 6.00x o.p. (ISBN 0-8422-0164-5). Irvington.
Readings in Psychology: Foundations & Applications. David Wrench. 1971. text ed. 9.95 o.p. (ISBN 0-07-071921-7). McGraw.
Readings in "Psychology Today" 4th ed. CRM Books Staff. 1978. pap. text ed. 9.00 o.p. (ISBN 0-394-32244-4, RanC). Random.

Readings in Psychopathology. Ed. by Alfred D. Kornfeld & Leo Schneiderman. LC 72-86189. 146p. 1972. pap. text ed. 5.95x o.p. (ISBN 0-8422-0196-3). Irvington.

Readings in Race & Ethnic Relations. Anthony H. Richmond. 350p. 1972. pap. 85.00 o.p. (ISBN 0-08-016212-6). Pergamon.

Readings in Records Management - from Records Management Quarterly. 175p. 1977-1980. 18.00 o.p. (ISBN 0-933887-02-7, 4517). Assn Recs Mgrs & Admin.

Readings in Rehabilitation Counseling. Timothy F. Field et al. LC 74-11373. 287p. 1975. pap. text ed. 9.50x o.p. (ISBN 0-8422-0427-X). Irvington.

Readings in Russian History: From Ancient Times to the Eighteenth Century, Vol. I. Ed. by Warren B. Walsh. 1963. 10.95x o.p. (ISBN 0-8156-2048-9). Syracuse U Pr.

Readings in Secondary School Mathematics. 2nd ed. Douglas B. Aichele & Robert E. Reys. 1977. pap. text ed. write for info. o.p. (ISBN 0-87150-202-X, PWS 1742, Prindle). PWS-Kent Pub.

Readings in Semantics. Ed. by Farhang Zabeeh et al. LC 73-84699. 853p. 1974. 35.00 o.p. (ISBN 0-252-00196-6); pap. 12.50 o.p. (ISBN 0-252-00421-3). U of Ill Pr.

Readings in Social Evolution & Development. Ed. by S. N. Eisenstadt. LC 78-96463. 1969. 115.00 o.p. (ISBN 0-08-006813-8); pap. 100.00 o.p. (ISBN 0-08-006812-X). Pergamon.

Readings in Social Problems & Deviance. P. Friedman. 1969. pap. text ed. 6.00x o.p. (ISBN 0-8290-1177-3). Irvington.

Readings in Social Studies Education. David Zodikoff. 135p. 1971. pap. text ed. 7.95x o.p. (ISBN 0-8422-0155-6). Irvington.

Readings in Sociology. L. Cross et al. 1969. pap. text ed. 7.25x o.p. (ISBN 0-8290-1181-1). Irvington.

Readings in Soil & Water Conservation. Ed. by Peter E. Black. 275p. 1974. text ed. 38.50x o.p. (ISBN 0-8422-5204-5); pap. text ed. 14.95x o.p. (ISBN 0-8422-0452-0). Irvington.

Readings in Technical Writing. David C. Leonard & Peter J. McGuire. 304p. 1983. pap. text ed. write for info. o.p. (ISBN 0-02-369840-3). Macmillan.

Readings in the Economics of Education. Ed. by John D. Murgo. LC 72-86194. 230p. 1972. text ed. 28.50x o.p. (ISBN 0-8422-5045-X); pap. text ed. 8.95x o.p. (ISBN 0-8422-0217-X). Irvington.

Readings in the Physical, Social & Psychological Dimensions of Education. J. Sullivan. 1971. pap. text ed. 9.75x o.p. (ISBN 0-8422-0161-0). Irvington.

Readings in the Psychology of Early Childhood. Ed. by Theron M. Covin. LC 72-85868. 488p. 1976. text ed. 18.50x o.p. (ISBN 0-8422-5238-X); pap. text ed. 14.50x o.p. (ISBN 0-8422-0491-1). Irvington.

Readings in the Sociology of Migration. C. J. Jansen. LC 72-105954. 1970. 105.00 o.p. (ISBN 0-08-006915-0); pap. 105.00 o.p. (ISBN 0-08-006914-2). Pergamon.

Readings in the Sociology of Religion. Ed. by J. Brothers. 1967. 65.00 o.p. (ISBN 0-08-012186-1); pap. 65.00 o.p. (ISBN 0-08-012187-X). Pergamon.

Readings in the Swedish Class Structure. Ed. by Richard Scase. 1976. 55.00 o.p. (ISBN 0-08-016663-6); pap. 23.00 o.p. (ISBN 0-08-020633-6). Pergamon.

Readings in Urban Economics. Matthew Edel & Jerome Rothenberg. (Illus.). 544p. 1972. pap. text ed. write for info. o.p. (ISBN 0-02-331480-X, 33148). Macmillan.

Readings in Urban Economics & Spatial Patterns. Ed. by Michael R. Greenberg. 336p. 1974. (ISBN 0-87855-106-9). Transaction Pubs.

Readings in Urban Geography. Ed. by Harold M. Mayer & Clyde F. Kohn. LC 59-11973. (Illus.). 1959. lib. bdg. 22.50x o.s.i. (ISBN 0-226-51270-3). U of Chicago Pr.

Readings in Urban Sociology. Ed. by R. E. Pahl. 1968. pap. text ed. 9.25 o.p. (ISBN 0-08-013293-6). Pergamon.

Readings on Fundamental Issues on Learning & Memory. Ed. by Bruce Bridgeman & Dinae Bridgeman. 343p. 1977. pap. text ed. 14.95x o.p. (ISBN 0-8422-0548-9). Irvington.

Readings on National & Regional Foreign Policies. A. Dunlap. 1971. pap. text ed. 7.95x o.p. (ISBN 0-8290-1175-7). Irvington.

Readings on Parties & Elections in the United States. Chester L. Jones. LC 70-129946. Repr. of 1912 ed. 35.00x o.p. (ISBN 0-8371-4994-0, JPE&). Greenwood.

Readings on Police-Community Relations. 2nd ed. Paul F. Cromwell, Jr. & George Keefer. (Criminal Justice Ser.). 1978. pap. 27.25 o.p. (ISBN 0-8299-0156-6). West Pub.

Readings on the Behavior Disorders of Childhood. Ed. by James R. Frazier & Donald K. Routh. LC 72-86267. 320p. 1972. pap. text ed. 12.50x o.p. (ISBN 0-8422-0202-1). Irvington.

Readings on the Management of Working Capital. 2nd ed. Keith V. Smith. (Illus.). 1980. pap. 28.75 o.p. (ISBN 0-8299-0296-1). West Pub.

Ready Foods Systems for Health Care Facilities. Friesen International, Inc. Staff. LC 72-95360. 736p. 1983. 19.95 o.p. (ISBN 0-8436-0562-6). Van Nos Reinhold.

Ready for Sea: Check Your Boat. Basil Mosenthal & Dick Hewitt. 1981. pap. 3.95 encore ed. o.p. (ISBN 0-684-17587-8, ScribT). Scribner.

Ready for the Defense. Martin Garbus. 304p. 1979. pap. 1.50 o.p. (ISBN 0-380-01381-9, 11403). Avon.

Ready, Set...Read! Becky Daniel & Charlie Daniel. (ps-5). 1979. 5.95 o.p. (ISBN 0-916456-45-5, GA114). Good Apple.

Ready to Play, Bk. IV. Margaret Dee. 1954. 1.75 o.p. (ISBN 0-913650-35-8). CPP Belwin.

Ready to Restore. Jay E. Adams. (Orig.). 1981. pap. 4.95 o.p. (ISBN 0-8010-0171-4). Baker Bk.

Reagan Detour: Conservative Revolutionary. Richard Reeves. 139p. 1985. 14.70 o.p. (ISBN 0-671-60652-2); pap. 7.95 o.p. (ISBN 0-671-60702-2). S&S.

Reagan Report. Off the Wall Street Journal, Inc. Staff & Bob Adelman. LC 84-4100. 64p. 1984. pap. 5.95 o.p. (ISBN 0-385-19516-8, Dolp). Doubleday.

Reagan's Ruling Class: Portraits of the President's Top 100 Officials. Ronald Brownstein & Nina Easton. 1983. pap. 9.95 o.s.i. (ISBN 0-394-71495-4). Pantheon.

Reagents for Organic Synthesis, 12 vols. Fieser. (Fieser's Reagents for Organic Synthesis Ser.). 643p. 1986. Set. 575.00 o.p. (ISBN 0-471-83468-8). Wiley.

Real Analytic Theory of Teichmueller Space. W. Abikoff. (Lecture Notes in Mathematics Ser.: Vol. 820). (Illus.). 144p. 1980. pap. 15.00 o.p. (ISBN 0-387-10237-X). Springer-Verlag.

Real & Complex Analysis. 2nd ed. Walter Rudin. (Higher Mathematics Ser.). 416p. 1973. text ed. 49.95 o.p. (ISBN 0-07-054233-3). McGraw.

Real Anti-Semitism in America. Nathan Perlmutter & Ruth A. Perlmutter. LC 81-71672. 1982. 15.50 o.p. (ISBN 0-87795-378-3, Arbor Hse). Morrow.

Real Bernard Shaw. (ISBN 0-8022-0278-0). Philos Lib.

Real Estate. 2nd ed. William R. Beaton et al. 1982. text ed. write for info. o.p. (ISBN 0-673-16003-3). Scott F.

Real Estate Acquisition Handbook: Money-Making Techniques for the Serious Investor. William T. Tappan. 1979. 16.95 o.p. (ISBN 0-13-762633-9, Spec); 7.95 o.p. (ISBN 0-13-762625-8). P-H.

Real Estate Agent's & Investor's Tax Book. Robert Irwin & Richard Brickman. (Illus.). 1981. text ed. 26.95 o.p. (ISBN 0-07-032061-6). McGraw.

Real Estate Appraiser's Kit. Barbara S. Miller. LC 80-22719. (Illus.). 323p. 1980. 59.50 o.p. (ISBN 0-87624-478-9, Inst Busn Plan). P-H.

Real Estate Appraising. M. A. Hines. LC 80-25962. 1982. pap. 8.95 o.p. (ISBN 0-15-600070-9, BFP). HarBraceJ.

Real Estate Brokerage: A Success Guide. John Cyr & Joan Sobeck. 336p. 1982. 29.95 o.p. (ISBN 0-88462-359-9, 1965-01, Real Estate Ed). Longman Finan.

Real Estate Brokerage in the Eighties: Survival among the Giants. Thomas W. Dooley. 1980. 18.95 o.p. (ISBN 0-88462-364-5, 1978-01, Real Estate Ed). Longman Finan.

Real Estate Broker's Guide to Resort Timesharing. Richard Lynge & Keith W. Trowbridge. LC 83-19239. 256p. 1983. 24.95 o.p. (ISBN 0-88462-442-0, 1965-03, Real Estate Ed). Longman Finan.

Real Estate By the Numbers. Wayne E. Brasch. LC 81-6779. 230p. 1981. 24.50 o.p. (ISBN 0-87624-479-7, Inst Busn Plan). P-H.

Real Estate Closings. 2nd ed. Raymond J. Werner. LC 79-89067. 290p. 1979. text ed. 40.00 o.p. (ISBN 0-686-58548-8, N1-1320). PLI.

Real Estate Contracts with 1987 Supplement. Karl B. Holtzschue. 333p. 1987. text ed. 60.00 o.p. (ISBN 0-317-52200-0, N6-1542). PLI.

Real Estate Desk Book. 5th ed. IBP Research & Editorial Staff. LC 76-27989. 1976. 29.95 o.p. (ISBN 0-87624-492-4, Inst Busn Plan). P-H.

Real Estate Desk Book. 6th ed. IBP Research & Editorial Staff. LC 79-17735. 498p. 1979. text ed. 49.50 o.p. (ISBN 0-87624-490-8, Inst Busn Plan). P-H.

Real Estate Development & Construction Financing, 1984. Practising Law Institute Staff & Charles Zalaznick. LC 84-225257. (Real Estate Law & Practice Course Handbook Ser.: No. 248). (Illus.). 1984. 40.00 o.p. PLI.

Real Estate European Style or What You Should Know About Real Estate in 32 Countries. Eugene P. Conser. LC 75-41552. 1976. 30.00 o.p. (ISBN 0-682-48461-X, Banner). Exposition-Phoenix.

Real Estate Exchange Desk Book. James Saylor. LC 78-57270. 1978. 29.95 o.p. (ISBN 0-87624-486-X, Inst Busn Plan). P-H.

Real Estate Exchanges. Mark L. Levine. Ed. by Pat Allen. LC 81-50724. 622p. 1981. 24.95 o.s.i. (ISBN 0-913652-27-X, BK 143); members 19.96 o.s.i. Realtors Natl.

Real Estate Finance. M. A. Hines. LC 80-25965. 1982. pap. 8.95 o.p. (ISBN 0-15-600071-7, BFP). HarBraceJ.

Real Estate Finance. William M. Shenkel. 1988. 38.95 o.p. (ISBN 0-256-02206-2); software 15.95 o.p. (ISBN 0-256-06505-5). Irwin.

Real Estate Financial Feasibility Analysis Handbook & Workbook. James C. Canestano. 280p. 1982. Set. 25.00 o.p. (ISBN 0-318-03322-4); wkbk. o.p. (ISBN 0-936954-04-3); handbk. o.p. (ISBN 0-936954-05-1). Natl Assoc Realtors.

Real Estate Financing. Massachusetts Continuing Legal Education Inc. & American Law Institute-American Bar Association Committee for Continuing Professional Education. LC 87-107439. (ALI-ABA Course of Study Materials Ser.). Date not set. price not set o.p. Am Law Inst.

Real Estate Financing Desk Book. 3rd ed. Joseph R. Bagby. LC 81-170. 454p. 1981. 59.50 o.p. (ISBN 0-87624-493-2, Inst Busn Plan). P-H.

Real Estate Financing Desk Book. 2nd ed. Joseph R. Bagby. LC 77-88878. 1977. 29.95 o.p. (ISBN 0-87624-494-0, Inst Busn Plan). P-H.

Real Estate Forms Desk Book. IBP Research & Editorial Staff. LC 76-27986. 1976. 34.95 o.p. (ISBN 0-87624-498-3, Inst Busn Plan). P-H.

Real Estate Guide to Microcomputers. Christopher B. Reade. (Guides to Microcomputing Ser.). (Illus.). 300p. pap. (ISBN 0-88462-606-7, 1302-02, Pub. by Longman Fin. Serv. Pub.). Longman Finan.

Real Estate Information Sources. Ed. by Janice B. Babb & B. F. Dordick. LC 63-16246. (Management Information Guide Ser.: No. 1). 318p. 1963. 68.00x o.p. (ISBN 0-8103-0801-0). Gale.

Real Estate Investment. M. A. Hines. LC 80-25964. 1982. pap. 8.95 o.p. (ISBN 0-15-600072-5, BFP). HarBraceJ.

Real Estate Investment & Finance. Sherman J. Maisel & Stephen E. Roulac. (Illus.). 1976. text ed. 40.95x o.p. (ISBN 0-07-039730-9). McGraw.

Real Estate Investment by Objective. Judith Creedy & Norbert Wall. LC 79-14085. (Illus.). 416p. 1979. text ed. 31.95 o.p. (ISBN 0-07-013495-2). McGraw.

Real Estate Investment for High Yield & Profit. Harry S. Gillig. LC 77-79831. 1977. 24.95 o.p. (ISBN 0-87624-499-1, Inst Busn Plan). P-H.

Real Estate Investments & How to Make Them: The Only Guide You'll Ever Need. Milt Tanzer. LC 80-15706. (Illus.). 355p. 1980. 34.95 o.p. (ISBN 0-87624-482-7, Inst Busn Plan); pap. 10.95 o.p. (ISBN 0-87624-481-9). P-H.

Real Estate Investments: Tax & Financial Planning. Ed. by Richard M. Horwood & Steven J. Katz. 1985. 125.00 o.p. (ISBN 0-916592-59-6). Panel Pubs.

Real Estate Job Finder. Mainstream Access, Inc. Staff. 216p. 1981. 15.95 o.p. (ISBN 0-13-763193-6); pap. 7.95 o.p. (ISBN 0-13-763185-5). P-H.

Real Estate Law. 3rd ed. William L. Atteberry et al. LC 83-14704. 378p. 1984. (ISBN 0-471-87170-2). Wiley.

Real Estate Law. Frank Gibson et al. LC 82-22998. 620p. 1983. text ed. 34.95 o.p. (ISBN 0-88462-454-4, 1560-01, Real Estate Ed). Longman Finan.

Real Estate License Examinations: Salesperson & Broker. Joseph H. Martin. LC 79-15351. 1979. lib. bdg. 12.00 o.p. (ISBN 0-668-04986-3); pap. 8.00 o.p. (ISBN 0-668-04794-1). Arco.

Real Estate Management Office: Income, Expenses & Profits, No. 859. 49p. 1984. pap. 25.00 o.p. (ISBN 0-317-57158-3). Inst Real Estate.

Real Estate Mathematics Simplified. Susan Shulman. LC 78-15542. 1979. pap. 6.95 o.p. (ISBN 0-668-04713-5). Arco.

Real Estate Office Management: People, Functions, Systems. LC 75-17139. 1975. 15.95 o.p. (ISBN 0-913652-06-7). Realtors Natl.

Real Estate Periodicals Index, 1983, Vol. 3, No. 1. Robert A. Munro. Ed. by Munro, John A., Associates, Inc. Staff. 75p. (Orig.). 1983. pap. text ed. 80.00x o.p. (ISBN 0-911553-02-9). Munro Assocs.

Real Estate Periodicals Index, 1983, Vol. 3, No. 2. Robert A. Munro. Ed. by Munro, John A., Associates, Inc. Staff. 75p. (Orig.). 1983. pap. text ed. 80.00x o.p. (ISBN 0-911553-04-5). Munro Assocs.

Real Estate Portfolio Analysis. M. Chapman Findlay, III et al. (Special Series in Real Estate & Urban Land Economics). 240p. 1983. 28.00x o.p. (ISBN 0-669-02397-3). Lexington Bks.

Real Estate Practice, 2 vols. Pennsylvania Bar Institute Staff. 457p. 1988. 50.00 o.p. (ISBN 0-318-02191-9, 431). PA Bar Inst.

Real Estate Practice: Pennsylvania Legal Practice Course Materials. Pennsylvania Bar Institute Staff. 153p. 1985. 25.00 o.p. (ISBN 0-318-02178-1, PLP-85). PA Bar Inst.

Real Estate Principles. M. A. Hines. LC 80-25963. 1982. pap. 8.95 o.p. (ISBN 0-15-600073-3, BFP). HarBraceJ.

Real Estate: Principles & Practices. 3rd ed. Karl G. Pearson & Michael P. Litka. LC 79-20017. 360p. 1984. text ed. (ISBN 0-471-84191-9). Wiley.

Real Estate Principles & Practices: A Contemporary Approach. Arlyne Geschwender. 280p. (Orig.). 1983. pap. text ed. 19.00x o.p. (ISBN 0-89787-907-4). Gorsuch Scarisbrick.

Real Estate Principles for License Preparation. 3rd ed. Dennis Tosh & Nicholas Ordway. 1984. pap. text ed. 24.00 ETS ed. o.p. (ISBN 0-8359-6570-8, Reston); ACT ed. 23.33 o.p. (ISBN 0-8359-6569-4). P-H.

Real Estate Quick & Easy. 8th, rev. ed. Roy T. Maloney. LC 83-11702. (Illus.). 1987. pap. 14.95 o.p. (ISBN 0-913257-00-1, Dist. by Publishers Group West). Dropzone Pr.

Real Estate Resource Book. 4th ed. Bruce M. Harwood & Jack Ellis. 1985. pap. text ed. 15.00 o.p. (ISBN 0-8359-6555-4, Reston). P-H.

Real Estate Revolution! Who Will Survive. Thomas Ervin. 1980. 12.95 o.s.i. (ISBN 0-88462-387-4, 1983-01, Real Estate Ed). Longman Finan.

Real Estate Sales Handbook. 7th ed. Ed. by Peg Keilholz. LC 73-85748. 1975. 7.90 o.p. (ISBN 0-913652-01-6). Realtors Natl.

Real Estate Syndication: A Selected Bibliography of Articles, Books & Serials. Nathan A. Rosen. (Public Administration Ser.: P 1796). 20p. 1985. 3.00 o.p. (ISBN 0-89028-596-9). Vance Biblios.

Real Estate Syndications. Pennsylvania Bar Institute Staff. 438p. 1985. 40.00 o.p. (ISBN 0-318-19070-2, 293). PA Bar Inst.

Real Estate Syndications - Tax, Securities & Business Aspects: 1986 Cumulative Supplement. Stephen P. Jarchow. (Tax & Business Guides for Professionals Ser.). 351p. 1986. pap. 37.50 o.p. (ISBN 0-471-85004-7). Wiley.

Real Estate Syndications Tax Handbook. Robert J. Haft & Peter M. Fass. 1986-1987. pap. 95.00 o.p. (ISBN 0-87632-506-1). Clark Boardman.

Real Estate Syndications: Tax, Securities & Business Aspects. Stephen P. Jarchow. LC 84-15193. (Tax & Business Guides for Professionals Ser.). 921p. 1985. text ed. 75.00x o.p. (ISBN 0-471-88969-5); Cumulative Supplement, 1985. pap. 32.75x o.p. (ISBN 0-471-83946-9). Wiley.

Real Estate Tax-Shelter Desk Book. 2nd ed. Mark L. Levine. LC 77-90141. 1978. 59.50 o.p. (ISBN 0-87624-502-5, Inst Busn Plan). P-H.

Real Estate Tax Shelter Desk Book. 3rd ed. Mark L. Levine. LC 81-22569. 463p. 1982. text ed. 49.50 o.p. (ISBN 0-87624-489-4, Inst Busn Plan). P-H.

Real Estate Title Matters. 397p. 1984. 17.00 o.p. (ISBN 0-318-02434-9). ICLE Georgia.

Real Estate Transactions Answer Book. 1986. 45.00 o.p. (ISBN 0-916592-63-4). Panel Pubs.

Real Estate Transactions, Tax Planning & Consequences: 1987 Edition. Mark L. Levine. 1227p. 1987. pap. text ed. write for info. o.p. (ISBN 0-314-40359-0). West Pub.

Real Gases. Ali B. Cambel et al. 1963. 48.50 o.p. (ISBN 0-12-155950-5). Acad Pr.

Real Jazz, Old & New. Stephen Longstreet. Repr. of 1956 ed. lib. bdg. 35.00x o.p. (ISBN 0-8371-2524-3, LORJ). Greenwood.

Real Jesus. 128p. (gr. 2-9). pap. 2.95 o.p. (ISBN 0-89191-066-2, 08243). Cook.

Real Lexikon der Musikinstrumente Zugleich ein Polyglossar fur das Gesamte Instrumentengebiet. Curt Sachs. 451p. Repr. of 1964 ed. lib. bdg. 59.00 o.p. (Pub. by Am Repr Serv). Reprint Servs.

Real Life: Louisville in the Twenties. Michael Lesy. LC 76-9977. 1976. pap. 7.95 o.p. (ISBN 0-394-73235-9). Pantheon.

Real Life of Domingos Xavier. Luandino Vieira. (African Writers Ser.). 1978. pap. text ed. 6.50 o.p. (ISBN 0-435-90202-4). Heinemann Ed.

Real Men Do. ken Olson. 224p. 1987. pap. 6.95 o.p. (ISBN 0-8007-5243-0). Revell.

Real Mother Goose. 1987. pap. 2.98 o.p. (ISBN 0-517-65635-3). Crown.

Real Mother Goose Piano Book. Illus. by Blanche F. Wright. 24p. (ps-3). 1987. pap. 9.95 o.p. (ISBN 0-02-899500-7, Checkerboard Pr). Macmillan.

Real Poland: An Anthology of National Self-Perception. Ed. by Alfred Bloch. LC 82-1559. 224p. 1982. 14.95x o.p. (ISBN 0-8264-0060-4). Continuum.

Real Prayer Book, Fifteen Forty-Nine to the Present. William Sydnor. LC 78-61774. 1978. pap. 3.95 o.p. (ISBN 0-8192-1242-3). Morehouse Pub.

Real Presence: The Holy Spirit in the Works of C. S. Lewis. Leanne Payne. LC 78-71945. 183p. 1979. pap. 6.95 o.p. (ISBN 0-89107-164-4, Crossway Bks). Good News.

Real Property Commercial Real Estate. 392p. 1981. 6.00 o.p. (ISBN 0-318-02422-5). ICLE Georgia.

Real Property Law. 350p. 1982. 6.50 o.p. (ISBN 0-318-02428-4). ICLE Georgia.

Real Property Law. 736p. 1984. 27.00 o.p. (ISBN 0-318-02431-4). ICLE Georgia.

Real Property Law Commercial Seminar. 353p. 1983. 16.00 o.p. (ISBN 0-318-02432-2). ICLE Georgia.

Real Property: New York. Louis A. Kass. (Orig.). 1964. pap. 2.50x o.p. (ISBN 0-87526-054-3). Gould.

Real Property Tax Delinquency & Urban Land Policy. John J. Lawlor et al. (Lincoln Institute Monograph: No. 78-2). 1978. pap. 3.00 o.s.i. (ISBN 0-686-12252-6). Lincoln Inst Land.

Real Property Tax: Monographs. Mary Vance. (Public Administration Ser.: P1795). 54p. 1985. pap. 8.25 o.p. (ISBN 0-89028-595-0). Vance Biblios.

Real Reason Why Johnnie Still Can't Read. Stanley L. Sharp. (Illus.). 240p. 1982. 12.95 o.p. (ISBN 0-682-49771-1, University). Exposition-Phoenix.

Real Rewards of Real Estate. Venita VanCaspel. 1981. 1.50 o.p. (ISBN 0-8359-6605-4, Reston). P-H.

Real Satan. James Kallas. LC 74-14184. 112p. (Orig.). 1975. pap. 5.50 o.p. (ISBN 0-8066-1466-8, 10-5410, Augsburg). Augsburg Fortress.

Real Socialism & Ideological Struggle. B. I. Korolyov. 133p. 1985. pap. 1.95 o.p. (ISBN 0-8285-3093-9, Pub. by Progress Pubs USSR). Imported Pubns.

Real Stories from Baltimore County History. Isobel Davidson. LC 70-9245. (Illus.). x, 312p. Repr. of 1917 ed. 35.00x o.p. (ISBN 0-8103-5033-5). Gale.

Real Supply-Side Economics. Anthony P. Carnevale. 15p. 1982. 1.90 o.p. (ISBN 0-318-22185-3, OC80). Natl Ctr Res Voc Ed.

Real Thing. Kurt Andersen. LC 81-7043. 192p. (Orig.). 1982. pap. 5.25 o.p. (ISBN 0-03-060037-5, Owl Bks). H Holt & Co.

Real Thing. Tom Stoppard. 88p. (Orig.). 1984. 14.95 o.p. (ISBN 0-571-13200-6); pap. 5.95 o.p. (ISBN 0-571-11983-2). Faber & Faber.

Real Time Language Design & Development. S. J. Young. (Computers & Their Applications Ser.). 352p. 1982. 91.00 o.p. (ISBN 0-470-27343-7). Halsted Pr.

Real Time Programming, 1977: Proceedings of the IFAC-IFIP Workshop, Eindhoven, The Netherlands, June 1977. Ed. by C. H. Smedema & N. V. Phillips. (Annual Review in Automatic Programming: Vol. 9). 251p. 1978. 80.00 o.p. (ISBN 0-08-022019-3). Pergamon.

Real Time Programming, 1981: Proceedings. IFAC-IFIP Workshop, Kyoto, Japan, Aug. 31-Sept. 2, 1981. Ed. by T. Hasegawa. (Annual Review in Automatic Programming: Vol. 11). (Illus.). 1982. 50.00 o.p. (ISBN 0-08-027613-X). Pergamon.

Real Time Programming, 1983: Proceedings of the IFAC-IFIP Workshop, 12th, Hertford, U. K., March 1983. Ed. by G. M. Bull. 100p. 1983. 35.00 o.p. (ISBN 0-08-030568-7). Pergamon.

Real-Time Ultrasonography. Ed. by Fred Winsberg & Peter L. Cooperberg. (Clinics in Diagnostic Ultrasound Ser.: Vol.10). (Illus.). 1982. 30.00 o.p. (ISBN 0-443-08187-5). Churchill.

Real Tom Thumb. Helen R. Cross. LC 80-11447. (Illus.). 96p. (gr. 3-7). 1980. 8.95 o.s.i. (ISBN 0-02-724600-0, Four Winds). Macmillan.

Real West Marginal Way: A Poet's Autobiography. Richard Hugo. Ed. by Ripley S. Hugo & James Welch. 1986. 16.45 o.p. (ISBN 0-393-02326-5). Norton.

Real World. Christopher Knowlton. LC 83-45505. 256p. 1984. 15.95 o.p. (ISBN 0-689-11439-7, Atheneum). Macmillan.

Real World of the Public Schools. Harry S. Broudy. 271p. 1972. pap. text ed. 9.95 o.p. (ISBN 0-15-575846-2, HC). HarBraceJ.

Realidad y Utopia en el Descubrimiento y Conquista de la America Hispana, 1492-1682. Stelio Cro. (Span.). 1984. 20.50x o.p. (ISBN 0-936968-07-9). Intl Bk Ctr.

Realism. Damian Grant. (Critical Idiom Ser.). 1970. pap. 5.50x o.p. (ISBN 0-416-17820-0, NO. 2216). Routledge Chapman & Hall.

Realism in the Application of ACI Standard 214-65. 1973. pap. 25.90 o.p. (ISBN 0-685-85114-1, SP-37). ACI.

Realism, Reality & the Fictional Theory of Alain Robbe-Grillet & Anais Nin. Patricia A. Deduck. LC 82-13549. 118p. 1982. lib. bdg. 25.50 o.p. (ISBN 0-8191-2719-1); pap. text ed. 10.00 o.p. (ISBN 0-8191-2720-5). U Pr of Amer.

Realistic Illustrations in Japan. (Illus.). 174p. 1986. pap. 25.00 o.p. (ISBN 0-8161-8810-6, Pub. by Graphic-Sha Pub Co Ltd Japan). G K Hall.

Realities & Illusions Eighteen Eighty-Six to Nineteen Thirty-Two. Raymond Moley. Ed. by Frank Freidel. LC 78-13887. (History of the United States 1876-1976: Vol. 13). 1980. lib. bdg. 22.00 o.p. (ISBN 0-8240-9692-4). Garland Pub.

Realities of American Foreign Policy. George F. Kennan. 1966. pap. 2.95 o.p. (ISBN 0-393-00320-5, Norton Lib). Norton.

Realities of American-Palestine Relations. Frank E. Manuel. LC 72-596. 378p. 1975. Repr. of 1949 ed. lib. bdg. 35.00x o.p. (ISBN 0-8371-5999-7, MARA). Greenwood.

Realities of Social Research. Jennifer Platt. LC 75-30275. 223p. 1976. 41.95x o.p. (ISBN 0-470-69119-0). Halsted Pr.

Reality & Other Writings. Richard H. James. 1977. 4.00 o.p. (ISBN 0-682-48917-4). Exposition-Phoenix.

Reality & Scientific Truth: Discussions with Einstein, von Laue, & Planck. Ilse Rosenthal-Schneider. Ed. by Thomas Braun. LC 80-13950. (Illus.). 150p. 1980. 20.00x o.p. (ISBN 0-8143-1650-6). Wayne St U Pr.

Reality & Theatre. Naim Kattan. Tr. by Alan Brown. 152p. 1972. 4.95 o.p. (ISBN 0-88784-710-2, Pub. by Hse Anansi Pr Canada). U of Toronto Pr.

Reality-Centered People Management: Keys to Improved Productivity. Erwin S. Stanton. 160p. 1982. 14.95 o.p. (ISBN 0-8144-5676-6). AMACOM.

Reality Game: A Guide to Humanistic Counselling & Therapy. John Rowan. 204p. (Orig.). 1984. pap. 9.95x o.p. (ISBN 0-7100-9814-6). Routledge Chapman & Hall.

Reality Game & How to Win It: Making the Mysteries of Time & Space Work for You. Brad Steiger. 272p. 1986. pap. 8.95 o.p. (ISBN 0-87877-085-2, Greenbriar Books). Newcastle Pub.

Reality: Glimpses of Life. Lilian L. Schalet. 64p. (Orig.). 1983. pap. 5.00 o.p. (ISBN 0-682-49940-4). Exposition-Phoenix.

Reality in a Looking Glass: Rationality Through an Analysis of Traditional Folly. Anton Zijderveld. 208p. 1982. 26.95x o.p. (ISBN 0-7100-0949-6). Routledge Chapman & Hall.

Reality of Hell & the Goodness of God. Harold T. Bryson. LC 83-51674. 192p. 1984. pap. 4.95 o.p. (ISBN 0-8423-5279-1). Tyndale.

Reality of Retirement: The Inner Experience of Becoming a Retired Person. Jules Z. Willing. LC 80-21919. 1981. 10.95 o.p. (ISBN 0-688-00298-6); pap. 6.95 o.p. (ISBN 0-688-00394-X). Lively Mind Bks.

Reality of the Gospel & the Unreality of the Churches. Douglas J. Hall. LC 75-12852. 1975. pap. 3.45 o.s.i. (ISBN 0-664-24775-X, Westminster). Westminster John Knox.

Realization Theory. Ed. by A. Ruberti. LC 76-21964. 1977. pap. 23.00 o.p. (ISBN 0-08-021276-X). Pergamon.

Realize Your Potential. V. Pekelis. 311p. 1987. 5.95 o.p. (ISBN 0-8285-3475-6, Pub. by Mir Pubs USSR). Imported Pubns.

Realm of Algebra. Isaac Asimov. (Illus.). (gr. 7 up). 1961. 8.95 o.p. (ISBN 0-395-06563-1). HM.

Realm of Feelings. Vera A. Toole. 21p. 1985. 6.95 o.p. (ISBN 0-533-06222-5). Vantage.

Realm of Measure. Isaac Asimov. (Illus.). (gr. 8 up). 1960. 8.95 o.p. (ISBN 0-395-06564-X). HM.

Realm of Spirit & the Realm of Caesar. Nicolaii Berdiaer. Tr. by Donald A. Luurie from Rus. LC 74-1554. 182p. 1975. Repr. of 1953 ed. lib. bdg. 59.50x o.p. (ISBN 0-8371-7395-7, BESC). Greenwood.

Realm of the Universe. 3rd ed. George Abell. 1984. pap. text ed. 28.95 o.p. (CBS C); instr's manual 12.00 o.p. (ISBN 0-03-058506-6). SCP.

Realms of Philosophy. 3rd ed. William S. Sahakian & Mabel L. Sahakian. 640p. 1981. pap. text ed. 10.60 o.p. (ISBN 0-87073-531-4); 29.95 o.p. Schenkman Bks Inc.

Realms of Teaching. David A. Welton. 1980. text ed. 27.95 o.p. (ISBN 0-395-30771-6). HM.

Realtors Guide to Practice Equal Opportunity in Housing. 57p. 1.00 o.p. (ISBN 0-318-15192-8, 111-831); 11-25 copies 0.75 ea. o.p.; 26 or more copies 0.50 ea. o.p. Natl Assoc Realtors.

Realval: IBM Personal Computer Version. Evaluation Consultants, Inc. Staff. 80p. 1984. 275.00 o.p. (ISBN 0-07-021113-2). McGraw.

Realworld Management Deskbook. Auren Uris. 1983. 29.95 o.p. (ISBN 0-442-28809-3). Van Nos Reinhold.

Reanimacion Sin Sensaciones. A. Axelrod. 155p. (Span.). 1977. pap. 2.95 o.p. (ISBN 0-8285-1699-5, Pub. by Mir Pubs USSR). Imported Pubns.

Reap in Tears. Jack Hoffenberg. 1969. pap. 1.95 o.p. (ISBN 0-380-00477-1, 26401). Avon.

Reap, So, & Harvest. Vivian Hunsucker. LC 84-90188. 309p. 1985. 14.95 o.p. (ISBN 0-533-06240-3). Vantage.

Reapportionment: Law & Technology. 90p. 1980. 5.00 o.s.i. (ISBN 1-55516-712-8). Natl Conf State Legis.

Reapportionment of the Oklahoma House of Representatives: Politics & Process. Richard D. Bingham. (Legislative Research Ser: No. 2). 33p. 1972. pap. 1.50 o.p. (ISBN 0-686-20792-0). Univ OK Gov Res.

Rearrangements of Pencillanic Acid Derivatives. R. J. Stoodley. 1976. pap. 15.50 o.p. (ISBN 0-08-020477-5). Pergamon.

Reason & Chance in Scientific Discovery. Taton. 1957. (ISBN 0-8022-1692-7). Philos Lib.

Reason & Genius. Alfred Hock. 144p. 1960. (ISBN 0-8022-0731-6). Philos Lib.

Reason & Genius: Studies in Their Origin. Alfred Hock. LC 70-138150. 1971. Repr. of 1960 ed. lib. bdg. 35.00x o.p. (ISBN 0-8371-5607-6, HORG). Greenwood.

Reason & Human Good in Aristotle. John M. Cooper. LC 74-30852. 224p. 1975. text ed. 20.00x o.p. (ISBN 0-674-74952-9). Harvard U Pr.

Reason & Responsibility: Readings in Some Basic Problems of Philosophy. 6th ed. Ed. by Joel Feinberg. 602p. 1985. text ed. (ISBN 0-534-03873-5). Wadsworth Pub.

Reason & Teaching. Israel Scheffler. LC 72-86641. 1973. 29.50x o.s.i. (ISBN 0-8290-2403-4). Irvington.

Reason & the Nature of Things. Jacob Loewenberg. LC 58-6818. (Paul Carus Lecture Ser.). 399p. 1959. 18.95 o.p. (ISBN 0-87548-105-1). Open Court.

Reason Enough: A Case for the Christian Faith. Clark H. Pinnock. 126p. 1986. pap. 5.95 o.p. (ISBN 0-85364-296-6, Pub. by Paternoster UK). Attic Pr.

Reason in Common Sense. George Santayana. 1980. pap. text ed. 5.00 o.p. (ISBN 0-486-23919-5). Dover.

Reason in Law. 2nd ed. Lief H. Carter. 1984. 19.25 o.p. (ISBN 0-673-39425-5). Scott F.

Reason of State & Statecraft in Spanish Political Thought: 1595-1640. J. A. Fernandez-Santamaria. LC 82-25614. 376p. (Orig.). 1983. text ed. 33.00 o.p. (ISBN 0-8191-3046-X); pap. text ed. 16.75 o.p. (ISBN 0-8191-3047-8). U Pr of Amer.

Reason, Truth & God. Renford Bambrough. (Library Reprints Ser.). 174p. 1979. 45.00x o.p. (ISBN 0-416-72530-9, NO. 2823). Routledge Chapman & Hall.

Reason Why. G. Howard Frost. LC 61-15240. 1962. (ISBN 0-8022-0554-2). Philos Lib.

Reason Why. Cecil Woodham-Smith. LC 81-70067. 1982. pap. 8.95 o.s.i. (ISBN 0-689-70622-7, 275, Atheneum). Macmillan.

Reasonable Doubt: An Investigation into the Assassination of John F. Kennedy. Henry Hurt. LC 85-7571. (Illus.). 531p. 1987. 19.95 o.p. (ISBN 0-03-004059-0); pap. 9.95 o.p. H Holt & Co.

Reasoning & Argument in Psychology. P. B. Bell & P. J. Staines. 228p. (Orig.). 1983. pap. 11.95x o.p. (ISBN 0-7100-0712-4). Routledge Chapman & Hall.

Reasons to Stay. Margaret W. Froehlich. LC 86-10322. 192p. (YA) (gr. 6 up). 1986. 12.70 o.s.i. (ISBN 0-395-41068-1). HM.

Reassessment of the Concept of Criminality: An Analysis of Criminal Behavior in Terms of Individual & Current Environment - the Application of a Stochastic Model. Eggert Petersen. LC 76-51327. 134p. 1977. 57.95x o.p. (ISBN 0-470-99034-1). Halsted Pr.

Rebecca, Margaret, & Nasty Annie. (Platt & Munk Cricket Bks.). (Illus.). 24p. (ps-3). 1978. 2.50 o.p. (ISBN 0-448-46528-0, G&D); PLB 3.59 o.p. (ISBN 0-448-13074-2). Putnam Pub Group.

Rebecca of Sunnybrook Farm. Kate D. Wiggin. (gr. 4-7). 5.95 o.p. (ISBN 0-395-07074-0). HM.

Rebecca West: A Celebration. Rebecca West. 1978. pap. 9.95 o.p. (ISBN 0-14-004912-6). Penguin.

Rebel: Devoted to the Exposition of Anarchist Communism, Nos. 1-6. 1969. Repr. of 1895 ed. lib. bdg. 13.75x o.p. (ISBN 0-8371-9233-1, RE00). Greenwood.

Rebel Gold. Thomas F. Jones. LC 75-9812. 160p. (gr. 8 up). 1975. 5.95 o.s.i. (ISBN 0-664-32571-8, Westminster). Westminster John Knox.

Rebel on the Bridge: A Life of the Decembrist Baron Andrey Rozen, 1800-84. Glynn Barratt. LC 75-21990. (Illus.). xvii, 310p. 1976. 19.00x o.p. (ISBN 0-8214-0217-X). Ohio U Pr.

Rebel Scotland: A History of Democracy in Scotland. Roly Wason. 1976. 4.00 o.p. (ISBN 0-682-48550-0, University). Exposition-Phoenix.

Rebellion, Creativity & Revelation. S. Giora Shoham. Intro. by Albert Cherns. 320p. 1986. 29.95 o.p. (ISBN 0-905927-61-3). Transaction Pubs.

Rebellion in the University. Seymour M. Lipset. LC 76-8801. 1976. pap. text ed. 4.95x o.s.i. (ISBN 0-226-48455-6, P669, Phoen). U of Chicago Pr.

Rebellious Prophet: A Life of Nicolai Berdgaev. Donald A. Lowrie. LC 73-11867. (Illus.). 310p. 1974. Repr. of 1960 ed. lib. bdg. 35.00x o.p. (ISBN 0-8371-7095-8, LORP). Greenwood.

Rebels & Their Causes: Essays in Honour of A. L. Morton. Maurice Cornforth. 1957. pap. 19.95x o.p. (ISBN 0-85315-426-0). Humanities.

Rebel's Return. Edwin Booth. (Orig.). 1981. pap. 1.95 o.s.i. (ISBN 0-505-51686-1, Pub. by Tower Bks). Dorchester Pub Co.

Rebirth & Destiny of Israel. David B. Gurion. 539p. 1953. (ISBN 0-8022-0099-0). Philos Lib.

Rebirth of Ministry: A Study of the Biblical Character of the Church's Ministry. James D. Smart. LC 60-6189. 192p. 1978. pap. 4.95 o.s.i. (ISBN 0-664-24206-5, Westminster). Westminster John Knox.

Rebonding: Preventing & Restoring Damaged Relationships. Donald Joy. 192p. 1986. 11.95 o.p. (ISBN 0-8499-0519-2, 0519-2). Word Bks.

Reborn. Leonard Simon. LC 78-57333. 1979. 9.95 o.p. (ISBN 0-87795-202-7, Arbor Hse). Morrow.

Reborn As Meaning: Panegyrical Biography from Isocrates to Walton. Michael P. Rewa. 140p. (Orig.). 1983. lib. bdg. 25.00 o.p. (ISBN 0-8191-3013-3); pap. text ed. 10.00 o.p. (ISBN 0-8191-3014-1). U Pr of Amer.

Reborn to Multiply. Paul Foust. LC 73-9110. 1973. pap. 2.95 o.p. (ISBN 0-570-03170-2, 12-2573). Concordia.

Recall Methods in Social Surveys. Louis Moss & Harvey Goldstein. (Studies in Education: No. 9). 176p. (Orig.). pap. text ed. 12.00x o.p. (ISBN 0-85473-080-X, 00581, Pub. by U London Inst Ed England). Heinemann Ed.

Recall the Poppies. Marjorie Bryant. (Illus.). 1979. pap. 6.00 o.p. (ISBN 0-931832-14-4). Fithian Pr.

Recapitalizing America: Alternatives to the Corporate Distortion of National Policy. S. M. Miller & Donald Tomaskovic-Devey. 220p. 1983. 16.95x o.p. (ISBN 0-7100-9941-X). Routledge Chapman & Hall.

Recasting Bourgeois Europe: Stabilization in France, Germany, & Italy in the Decade After World War One. Charles S. Maier. LC 73-2488. 700p. 1975. pap. 16.95x LPE o.p. (ISBN 0-691-10025-X). Princeton U Pr.

Receiving Aeriel Systems. I. A. Davidson. (Illus.). 152p. 1957. (ISBN 0-8022-0347-7). Philos Lib.

Receiving the Spirit at Old First Church. Arthur A. Rouner, Jr. LC 81-19959. 96p. (Orig.). 1982. pap. 5.95 o.p. (ISBN 0-8298-0492-7). Pilgrim NY.

Recent Advances in Analytical Spectroscopy: Proceedings of the 9th International Conference on Atomic Spectroscopy & 22nd Colloquium Spectroscopicum Internationale, Tokyo, Japan, 4-8 September 1981. International Conference on Atomic Spectroscopy Staff. Ed. by K. Fuwa. (IUPAC Symposium Ser.). (Illus.). 336p. 1982. 105.00 o.p. (ISBN 0-08-026221-X). Pergamon.

Recent Advances in Aquatic Mycology. E. B. Gareth Jones. LC 74-27179. 748p. 1976. 105.95 o.p. (ISBN 0-470-29176-1). Halsted Pr.

Recent Advances in Blood Coagulation, No. 4. Ed. by L. Poller. LC 76-42237. (Illus.). 320p. 1985. text ed. 72.00 o.p. (ISBN 0-443-03223-8). Churchill.

Recent Advances in Clinical Immunology. Ed. by R. A. Thompson. LC 77-30129. (Illus.). 226p. 1987. text ed. 65.00 o.p. (ISBN 0-443-03494-X). Churchill.

Recent Advances in Clinical Immunology, No. 3. Ed. by R. A. Thompson & Noel R. Rose. LC 77-30129. (Illus.). 318p. 1983. text ed. 62.95 o.p. (ISBN 0-443-02641-6). Churchill.

Recent Advances in Clinical Pharmacology, No. 3. Ed. by Paul Turner & David G. Shand. LC 80-40796. 288p. 1983. text ed. 65.00 o.p. (ISBN 0-443-02649-1). Churchill.

Recent Advances in Clinical Therapeutics, Vol. 1: Selected Topics: Hypertension, Cardiovascular Disease, Analgesics & Endocrine Disorders. Ed. by Jack Yetiv & Joseph Bianchine. LC 81-12670. 1981. 41.00 o.p. (ISBN 0-12-788950-7). Acad Pr.

Recent Advances in Clinical Virology, No. 3. Ed. by A. P. Waterson. LC 80-49993. (Illus.). 278p. 1983. text ed. 64.75 o.p. (ISBN 0-443-02646-7). Churchill.

Recent Advances in Corporate Finance. Edward Altman & Marti G. Subrahmanyam. 1985. 50.00 o.p. (ISBN 0-87094-560-2). Dow Jones-Irwin.

Recent Advances in Corporate Finance. Edward I. Altman & Marti G. Subrahmanyam. 1985. pap. 20.95x o.p. (ISBN 0-256-03279-3). Irwin.

Recent Advances In Depression. C. N. Stefanis. 152p. 1982. 26.00 o.p. (ISBN 0-08-027954-6). Pergamon.

Recent Advances in Endocrinology & Metabolism, No. 2. J. L. O'Riordan. LC 77-30086. (Recent Advances in Endocrinology & Metabolism Ser.). (Illus.). 1982. 46.25 o.p. (ISBN 0-443-02231-3). Churchill.

Recent Advances in Epilepsy, Vol. 3. Ed. by Timothy A. Pedley & Brian S. Meldrum. (Illus.). 315p. 1986. text ed. 62.00 o.p. (ISBN 0-443-03359-5). Churchill.

Recent Advances in Gas Chromatography. Ed. by I. Domsky & J. Perry. 1971. 89.75 o.p. (ISBN 0-8247-1146-7). Dekker.

Recent Advances in Gastroenterology, No. 5. Ed. by Ian A. Bouchier. (Illus.). 293p. 1980. text ed. 40.70 o.p. (ISBN 0-443-02461-8). Churchill.

Recent Advances in Geriatric Medicine, No. 2. Ed. by Bernard Issacs. (Recent Advances in Geriatric Medicine Ser.). (Illus.). 1982. pap. text ed. 32.50 o.p. (ISBN 0-443-02320-4). Churchill.

Recent Advances in Geriatric Medicine, No. 3. Ed. by Bernard Isaacs. (Illus.). 283p. 1985. text ed. 73.00 o.p. (ISBN 0-443-03022-7). Churchill.

Recent Advances in Haemotology, Immunology & Blood Transfusion. Ed. by S. R. Hollan et al. 418p. 1983. text ed. 45.00x o.p. (ISBN 0-471-90164-4, Pub. by Wiley Med). Wiley.

Recent Advances in Hepatology, Vol. 2. Ed. by Howard C. Thomas & E. Anthony Jones. (Illus.). 193p. 1986. text ed. 90.00 o.p. (ISBN 0-443-03200-9). Churchill.

Recent Advances in Holography III: Proceedings of the SPIE Technical Symposium, Los Angeles, 1980. (SPIE Seminar Proceedings: Vol. 215). 208p. 37.00 o.p. (ISBN 0-89252-243-7); 30.00, members o.p. (ISBN 0-317-34750-0). SPIE.

Recent Advances in Infection, No. 2. Ed. by David S. Reeves & A. M. Geddes. (Illus.). 1982. pap. text ed. 33.50 o.p. (ISBN 0-443-02410-3). Churchill.

Recent Advances in Intensive Therapy, No. 1. Ed. by I. Ledingham. (Recent Advances in Intensive Therapy Ser.). (Illus.). 1978. 35.00 o.p. (ISBN 0-443-01432-9). Churchill.

Recent Advances in Leather Conservation: Proceedings of a Refresher Course Sponsored by FAIC, June,1984. Ferry W. Harpers & Sonja Fogle. 15.00 o.p. (ISBN 0-318-18700-0). Am Inst Conser Hist.

Recent Advances in Lifeline Earthquake Engineering in Japan. Ed. by H. Shibata & T. Ariman. (PVP: No. 43). 158p. 1980. 24.00 o.p. (ISBN 0-686-69859-2, H00170). ASME.

Recent Advances in Liquid - Liquid Extraction. C. Hanson. 1971. 150.00 o.p. (ISBN 0-08-015682-7). Pergamon.

Recent Advances in Mining & Processing of Low-Grade Submarginal Mineral Deposits. LC 76-11771. 1977. 50.00 o.p. (ISBN 0-08-021051-1). Pergamon.

Recent Advances in Obesity Research, Vol. 2. George A. Bray. LC 78-64353. 510p. 1978. 29.00 o.p. (ISBN 0-87762-259-0). Technomic.

Recent Advances in Ophthalmology, No. 6. Ed. by Sidney I. Davidson. LC 82-9495. (Illus.). 113p. 1983. pap. text ed. 25.95 o.p. (ISBN 0-443-01660-7). Churchill.

Recent Advances in Phytochemistry: Structure, Biogenesis, Distribution. Phytochemical Society of North America Symposium Staff. Ed. by V. C. Runeckles & T. J. Mabry. 1974. Vol. 7. 56.50 o.p. (ISBN 0-12-612407-8); Vol. 8. 56.50 o.p. (ISBN 0-12-612408-6). Acad Pr.

Recent Advances in Pipe Support Design. Ed. by E. Van Stijgeren. (PVP Ser.: Vol. 68). 115p. 1982. 30.00 o.p. (H00225). ASME.

Recent Advances in Radiology & Medical Imaging, No. 8. Ed. by R. E. Steiner & T. Sherwood. (Illus.). 213p. 1986. text ed. 95.00 o.p. (ISBN 0-443-03108-8). Churchill.

Recent Advances in Renal Medicine, No. 2. Ed. by Norman F. Jones & D. K. Peters. LC 74-33158. (Illus.). 323p. 1983. pap. text ed. 46.25 o.p. (ISBN 0-443-02278-X). Churchill.

Recent Advances in Respiratory Medicine, Vol. 4. David C. Fenley & Thomas L. Petty. (Illus.). 285p. 1986. text ed. 90.00 o.p. (ISBN 0-443-03411-7). Churchill.

Recent Advances in Rheumatology, No. 3. J. Moll & Carson W. Dick. (Illus.). 239p. 1983. text ed. 49.95 o.p. (ISBN 0-443-02681-5). Churchill.

Recent Advances in Sexually Transmitted Diseases, No. 2. Ed. by Harris. 281p. 1981. text ed. 46.25 o.p. (ISBN 0-443-01817-0). Churchill.

Recent Advances in Steroid Biochemistry, Vols. 2-3. Ed. by J. R. Pasqualini. LC 75-4332. 1977. Vol. 3, 1977. 305.00 o.p. (ISBN 0-08-021307-3); Vol. 2, 312p., 1975. pap. 67.00 o.p. (ISBN 0-08-019709-4). Pergamon.

Recent Advances in Surgery, Pt. 12. Ed. by R. C. Russell. (Illus.). 286p. (Orig.). 1986. pap. text ed. 25.95 o.p. (ISBN 0-443-03240-8). Churchill.

Recent Advances in the Analytical Chemistry of the Noble Metals. F. E. Beamish & J. C. Van Loon. LC 77-166010. 527p. 1972. 130.00 o.p. (ISBN 0-08-016751-9). Pergamon.

Recent Advances of Avian Endocrinology: Proceedings of a Satellite Symposium of the 28th International Congress of Physiological Sciences, Budapest, Hungary, 1980. Ed. by G. Pethes et al. LC 80-42007. (Advances in Physiological Sciences: Vol. 33). (Illus.). 450p. 1981. 71.00 o.p. (ISBN 0-08-027355-6). Pergamon.

Recent Contributions to Fluid Mechanics. Ed. by W. Haase. (Illus.). 338p. 1982. 23.20 o.p. (ISBN 0-387-11940-X). Springer-Verlag.

Recent Developments in Accelerated Testing & Maturity of Concrete: Thirteen Reports. (Transportation Research Record Ser.). 121p. 1975. 10.00 o.p. (ISBN 0-309-02466-8). Transport Res Bd.

Recent Developments in Boiling & Condensation: Reprotext. E. R. Winter et al. (Illus.). 106p. 1977. 21.20x o.p. (ISBN 0-89573-000-6). VCH Pubs.

Recent Developments in Bus Transportation. (Transportation Research Record Ser.). 76p. 1978. 4.80 o.p. (ISBN 0-309-02692-X). Transport Res Bd.

Recent Developments in Carbonate Sedimentology in Central Europe. Ed. by G. Mueller & G. M. Friedman. (Illus.). 1969. 37.00 o.p. (ISBN 0-387-04303-9). Springer-Verlag.

Recent Developments in Cardiac Muscle Pharmacology. Ed. by Shoji Shibata & Leslie E. Bailey. LC 82-2948. (Illus.). 136p. 1982. monograph 29.50 o.p. (ISBN 0-89640-071-9). Igaku-Shoin.

Recent Developments in Condensed Matter Physics, Vol. 1: Invited Papers. Ed. by J. T. Devreese et al. LC 80-28067. 874p. 1981. 110.00x o.p. (ISBN 0-306-40646-2, Plenum Pr). Plenum Pub.

Recent Developments in Condensed Matter Physics, Vol. 2: Metals, Disordered Systems, Surfaces & Interfaces. Ed. by J. T. Devreese et al. LC 80-28067. 496p. 1981. 85.00x o.p. (ISBN 0-306-40647-0, Plenum Pr). Plenum Pub.

Recent Developments in Condensed Matter Physics, Vol. 3: Impurities, Excitons, Polarons, & Polaritons. Ed. by J. T. Devreese et al. LC 80-28067. 436p. 1981. 75.00x o.p. (ISBN 0-306-40648-9, Plenum Pr). Plenum Pub.

Recent Developments in Condensed Matter Physics, Vol. 4: Low-Dimensional Systems, Phase Changes, & Experimental Techniques. Ed. by J. T. Devreese et al. LC 80-28067. 464p. 1981. 79.50x o.p. (ISBN 0-306-40649-7, Plenum Pr); Set (Vols. 1-4) 275.00 o.p. Plenum Pub.

Recent Developments in Gauge Theories. Ed. by Thooft et al. LC 80-18528. (NATO ASI Series B, Physics: Vol. 59). 446p. 1980. 79.50x o.p. (ISBN 0-306-40479-6, Plenum Pr). Plenum Pub.

Recent Developments in Georgia Law. 313p. 1983. 12.00 o.p. (ISBN 0-318-02435-7). ICLE Georgia.

Recent Developments in Inventory Theory. Moshe F. Friedman. 74p. 1981. pap. 46.00 o.p. (ISBN 0-08-025844-1). Pergamon.

Recent Developments in Mathematical Physics: Proceedings of the International University Courses on Nuclear Physics, 12th, Schladming, Austria, 1973. International University Courses on Nuclear Physics Staff. Ed. by P. Urban. LC 73-13322. (Acta Physica Austriaca: Suppl. 2). (Illus.). vi, 610p. 1973. 87.40 o.p. (ISBN 0-387-81190-7). Springer-Verlag.

Recent Developments in Particle Symmetries. Ed. by A. Zichlichi. 1966. 71.00 o.p. (ISBN 0-12-780562-1). Acad Pr.

Recent Developments in Regional Science. R. Funck. (Karlsruhe Papers in Regional Science). 153p. 1974. pap. 10.00x o.p. (ISBN 0-85086-034-2, NO. 2912, Pub. by Pion England). Routledge Chapman & Hall.

Recent Developments in Securitites Litigation. Practising Law Institute Staff & Bruce G. Vanyo. LC 84-62195. (Litigation & Administrative Practice Series). (Illus.). 1984. 40.00 o.p. PLI.

Recent Developments in State Constitutional Law, Vol. 277. Practising Law Institute Staff. 277p. 1985. pap. 45.00 o.p. (ISBN 0-317-27581-X, #H4-4963). PLI.

Recent Developments in Switching Theory. Ed. by Amar Mukhopadhyay. (Electrical Science Ser). 1971. 99.00 o.p. (ISBN 0-12-509850-2). Acad Pr.

Recent Developments in the Theory of Polar Continua: Proceedings of CISM, Department for Mechanics of Deformable Bodies, Univ. of Belgarde, 1970. CISM (International Center for Mechanical Sciences), Department for Mechanics for Deformable Bodies Staff. (CISM Publications: No. 27). 345p. 1973. pap. 32.50 o.p. (ISBN 0-387-81144-3). Springer-Verlag.

Recent Developments Transcripts. 1985. 90.00 o.p. (ISBN 0-88124-135-0). Cal Cont Ed Bar.

Recent Discoveries in Chinese Archaeology. Ed. by Foster Stockwell & Tang Bowen. Tr. by Zuo Boyang from Chinese. (Illus.). 107p. 1984. pap. 9.95 o.p. (ISBN 0-8351-1377-9). China Bks.

Recent Ideals of American Art. George W. Sheldon. LC 75-28882. (Art Experience in Late 19th Century America Ser.: Vol. 16). (Illus.). 1976. Repr. of 1890 ed. lib. bdg. 106.00 o.p. (ISBN 0-8240-2240-8). Garland Pub.

Recent Innovations in Cultivation of Pacific Molluscs. D. E. Morse et al. (DIA Ser.: Vol. 14). 1987. Repr. 117.00 o.p. (ISBN 0-317-65944-8). Elsevier.

Recent Orientations of Regional Analysis in French Geography. Ed. by E. Juillard. 1976. pap. 44.00 o.p. (ISBN 0-08-019970-4). Pergamon.

Recent Progress in Andrology. Ed. by A. Fabbrini & E. Steinberger. (Proceedings of the Serono Symposia: Vol. 14). 1979. 91.00 o.p. (ISBN 0-12-247350-7). Acad Pr.

Recent Progress in Pediatric Endocrinology. Ed. by Giuseppe Chiumello & Z. Laron. 1978. 76.00 o.p. (ISBN 0-12-173250-9). Acad Pr.

Recent Readings in Reinforcement & Satisfaction. Ed. by Maynard W. Shelly & Tina Z. Adelberg. 1972. 34.50x o.p. (ISBN 0-8422-5020-4). Irvington.

Recent Sedimentary Carbonates, Part 1: Marine Carbonates. J. D. Milliman et al. LC 73-82359. (Illus.). 375p. 1973. 33.40 o.p. (ISBN 0-387-06116-9). Springer-Verlag.

Recent Southern Economic Development as Revealed by the Changing Structure of Employment. Edgar S. Dunn, Jr. LC 62-63139. (University of Florida Social Sciences Monographs: No. 14). (Illus.). 1962. pap. 3.50 o.p. (ISBN 0-8130-0067-X). U Presses Fla.

Recent Studies on Preimplantation Mammalian Embryos In Vitro, 2 vols, Vol. 1. Shuetu Suzuki et al. 205p. 1972. text ed. 35.50x o.p. (ISBN 0-8422-7039-6). Irvington.

Recent Studies on Preimplantation Mammalian Embryos In Vitro, 2 vols, Vol. 2. Ralph L. Brinster et al. LC 72-6668. 186p. 1972. text ed. 35.50x o.p. (ISBN 0-8422-7038-8). Irvington.

Recent Transportation Literature for Planning & Engineering Librarians (January 1985) Daniel Krummes & Michael Kleiber. (Public Admininntration Ser.: Bibliography P-1598). 55p. 1985. pap. 8.25 o.p. (ISBN 0-89028-248-X). Vance Biblios.

Recent Transportation Literature for Planning & Engineering Librarians (February 1985) Daniel Krummes & Michael Kleiber. (Public Administration Ser.: Bibliography P 1617). 1985. pap. 8.25 o.p. (ISBN 0-89028-287-0). Vance Biblios.

Recent Transportation Literature for Planning & Engineering Librarians (March 1985) Daniel Krummes & Michael Kleiber. (Public Administration Ser.: Bibliography P 1637). 1985. pap. 8.25 o.p. (ISBN 0-89028-327-3). Vance Biblios.

Recent Transportation Literature for Planning & Engineering Librarians: A Selection Based upon the Acquisitions of the Institute of Transportation Studies Library, University of California, Berkeley, (December 1985) Daniel Krummes & Michael Kleiber. (Public Administration Ser.: P 1817). 58p. 1985. 9.00 o.p. (ISBN 0-89028-667-1). Vance Biblios.

Recent Transportation Literature for Planning & Engineering Librarians: A Selection Based upon the Acquisitions of the Institute of Transportation Studies Library, University of California, Berkeley, (November 1985) Daniel Krummes & Michael Kleiber. (Public Administration Ser.: P 1797). 51p. 1985. 7.50 o.p. (ISBN 0-89028-627-2). Vance Biblios.

Recent Transportation Literature for Planning & Engineering Librarians: A Selection Based upon the Acquisitions of the Institute of Transportation Studies Library, University of California, Berkeley, (October 1985) Daniel Krummes & Michael Kleiber. (Public Administration Ser.: P 1777). 63p. 1985. 9.75 o.p. (ISBN 0-89028-577-2). Vance Biblios.

Recent Transportation Literature for Planning & Engineering Librarians: A Selection Based upon the Acquisitions of the Institute of Transportation Studies Library, University of California, Berkeley (September 1985) Daniel Krummes & Michael Kleiber. (Public Administration Ser.: P 1757). 59p. 1985. 9.00 o.p. (ISBN 0-89028-557-8). Vance Biblios.

Recent Transportation Literature for Planning & Engineering Librarians: A Selection Based upon the Acquisitions of the Institute of Transportation Studies Library, University of California, Berkeley (August 1985) Daniel Krummes & Michael Kleiber. (Public Administration Ser.: P 1737). 82p. 1985. 12.00 o.p. (ISBN 0-89028-517-9). Vance Biblios.

Recent Transportation Literature for Planning & Engineering Librarians: A Selection Based upon the Acquisitions of the Institute of Transportation Studies Library, University of California, Berkeley (July 1985) Daniel Krummes & Michael Kleiber. (Public Administration Ser.: P 1718). 67p. 1985. 9.75 o.p. (ISBN 0-89028-488-1). Vance Biblios.

Recent Transportation Literature for Planning & Engineering Librarians: A Selection Based upon the Acquisitions of the Institute of Transportation Studies Library, University of California, Berkeley (June 1985) Daniel Krummes & Michael Kleiber. (Public Administration Ser.: P 1697). 56p. 1985. 8.25 o.p. (ISBN 0-89028-447-4). Vance Biblios.

Recent Transportation Literature for Planning & Engineering Librarians: A Selection Based upon the Acquisitions of the Institute of Transportation Studies Library, University of California, Berkeley (May 1985) Daniel Krummes & Michael Kleiber. (Public Administration Ser.: P 1677). 63p. 1985. 9.75 o.p. (ISBN 0-89028-407-5). Vance Biblios.

Recent Transportation Literature for Planning & Engineering Librarians: A Selection Based upon the Acquisitions of the Institute of Transportation Studies Library, University of California, Berkeley (April 1985) Daniel Krummes & Michael Kleiber. (Public Administration Ser.: P 1657). 57p. 1985. 8.25 o.p. (ISBN 0-89028-367-2). Vance Biblios.

Recent Trends in Graph Theory: Proceedings of the New York City Graph Theory Conference, 1st, 1970. New York City Graph Theory Conference Staff. Ed. by M. Capobianco et al. (Lecture Notes in Mathematics: Vol. 186). (Illus.). 1971. pap. 14.00 o.p. (ISBN 0-387-05386-7). Springer-Verlag.

Recent Trends in Social Learning Theory. Ed. by Ross D. Parke. 1972. 36.50 o.p. (ISBN 0-12-545050-8). Acad Pr.

Recent Trends in Systems Theory. Ed. by S. D. Bedrosian & W. A. Porter. 1976. pap. 40.00 o.p. (ISBN 0-08-020590-9). Pergamon.

Reception: An Ecumenical Opportunity. William G. Rusch. LC 87-20710. 1987. pap. 3.25 o.p. (ISBN 0-8006-2091-7, Fortress). Augsburg Fortress.

Reception of Classical German Literature in England, 1760-1860: A Documentary History from Contemporary Periodicals, 10 vols. Ed. & intro. by John Boening. Incl. Vol. 1. General Introduction & Reviews from 1760 to 1813 (ISBN 0-8240-0990-8); Vol. 2. Reviews from 1813 to 1835 (ISBN 0-8240-0991-6); Vol. 3. Reviews from 1835 to 1860 (ISBN 0-8240-0992-4); Vol. 4. Authors from Bodmer to Klopstock (ISBN 0-8240-0993-2); Vol. 5. Authors from Lavater to Novalis (ISBN 0-8240-0994-0); Vol. 6. The Reception of Early German Romantics: Richter, the Brothers Schlegel, Tieck & Hoffmann (ISBN 0-8240-0995-9); Vol. 7. General Critical Articles on Goethe & Reviews Which Discuss Goethe & Schiller Together, Arranged in Order of Appearance (ISBN 0-8240-0996-7); Vol. 8. Reviews of Werther, Goethe's Early Works, His Poems & Faust (ISBN 0-8240-0997-5); Vol. 9. The Works of Goethe's Midcareer, Wilhelm Meister & Such Works As Dichtung und Wahrheit, Etc (ISBN 0-8240-0998-3); Vol. 10. The English Reception of Specific Works of Schiller, from the Early Plays to the Historical Works (ISBN 0-8240-0999-1). 1977. Set. lib. bdg. 120.00 each o.p. (ISBN 0-686-77265-2). Garland Pub.

Receptionist. Hazel Atkins. 112p. 1981. pap. 14.95x o.p. (ISBN 0-7131-0580-1). Trans-Atl Phila.

Receptivity. Francis K. Nemeck. 135p. 1985. 10.00 o.p. (ISBN 0-533-06057-5). Vantage.

Receptor-Mediated Binding & Internalization of Toxins & Hormones. Ed. by John H. Middlebrook & Leonard D. Kohn. 1981. 29.95 o.p. (ISBN 0-12-494850-2). Acad Pr.

Receptor Regulation see Queues: Receptors & Recognition Series B.

Receptors: A Quantitative Approach. Alexander Levitzki. 1984. 25.95 o.p. (ISBN 0-8053-6410-2). Benjamin Cummings.

Receptors & Cellular Pharmacology: Proceedings of the 6th International Congress of Pharmacology, Helsinki, 1975, Vol. 1. Ed. by E. Klinge. 238p. 1976. 105.00 o.p. (ISBN 0-08-020539-9). Pergamon.

Receptors & Hormone Action, Vol. 1. Ed. by B. W. O'Malley & L. Birnbaumer. 1978. 85.00 o.p. (ISBN 0-12-526301-5). Acad Pr.

Receptors & Hormone Action, Vol. 3. Ed. by B. W. O'Malley & Lutz Birnbaumer. 1978. 92.00 o.p. (ISBN 0-12-526303-1). Acad Pr.

Receptors & Recognition, Series A, 6 vols. Ed. by P. Cuatrecasas & M. F. Greaves. Incl. Vol. 1. (No. 6072). 175p. 1976 (ISBN 0-412-13800-X); Vol. 2. 229p. 1976 (ISBN 0-412-13810-7, NO. 6073); Vol. 3. 166p. 1977 (ISBN 0-412-14310-0, NO. 6074); Vol. 4. 258p. 1977 (ISBN 0-412-14330-5, NO. 6075); Vol. 5. 212p. 1978 (ISBN 0-412-15270-3, NO. 6076); Vol. 6. 199p. 1978 (ISBN 0-412-15290-8, NO. 6077). 85.20 set o.p. (ISBN 0-412-15950-3, NO. 6878, Pub. by Chapman & Hall England); 15.95 ea. o.p. Routledge Chapman & Hall.

Receptors in Pharmacology. Ed. by John R. Smythies & Ronald J. Bradley. (Modern Parmacology-Toxicology Ser.: Vol. 11). 516p. 1978. 95.00 o.p. (ISBN 0-8247-6546-X). Dekker.

Recherche de la Purete. Jean Giono. (Illus.). deluxe ed. 1750.00 o.p. (ISBN 0-685-34174-7). French & Eur.

Recherche-Operation, Application: Deroulement d'un Seminair-Atelier sur la Recherche Operationelle dans le Domaine de la Sante Publique, tenu au Centre Universitaire des Sciences de la Sante a Yaounde, Cameroun, 6-11 Decembre 1976. Ed. by A. Dorozynski. 27p. 1977. pap. 2.00 o.p. (ISBN 0-88936-118-5, IDRC-081F, IDRC). UNIPUB.

Recipe Index, Nineteen Seventy-One: The Eater's Guide to Periodical Literature. Ed. by John Forsman. LC 72-884. 774p. 1972. 52.00x o.p. (ISBN 0-8103-0526-7). Gale.

Recipe Index, Nineteen Seventy: The Eater's Guide to Periodical Literature. Ed. by John Forsman. LC 72-884. 784p. 1972. 52.00x o.p. (ISBN 0-8103-0525-9). Gale.

Recipe Yearbook Annual. Date not set. Knapp Pr.

Recipes for Self-Sufficient Living. Marlynn Phipps et al. LC 84-3117. (Illus.). 160p. (Orig.). 1984. pap. 9.95 o.p. (ISBN 0-87747-640-3, Pub. by Shadow Mountain). Deseret Bk.

Recipes for Starving Actors. Victor Izay. 1964. pap. 3.50 o.p. (ISBN 0-87505-251-7). Borden.

Recipes from Pasquale's Kitchen. Pasquale Carpino. LC 84-10251. (Illus.). 212p. 1985. 17.95 o.p. (ISBN 0-385-19306-8); 9.95 o.p. (ISBN 0-385-19307-6). Doubleday.

Recitatif. Dorothy B. Aspinwall & Jacques Reda. Tr. by Dorothy Aspinwall. (Fr. & Eng.). 1983. 10.00x o.p. (ISBN 0-936968-05-2). Intl Bk Ctr.

Recitations for Children. Ed. by Grace M. Stanistreet. LC 77-20404. (Granger Poetry Library Ser.). 1978. Repr. of 1930 ed. 20.25x o.p. (ISBN 0-89609-076-0). Roth Pub Inc.

Recits de la Demi-brigade. Jean Giono. (Coll. Soleil). 15.75 o.p. (ISBN 0-685-34171-2). Schoenhof.

Reckless Heart. Dee Austin. (Dawn of Love Ser.: No. 1). (gr. 7 up). 1985. pap. 2.50 o.p. (ISBN 0-671-62462-8). Archway.

Reckless Yearning. Victoria Pade. (Avon Romance Ser.). 368p. 1987. pap. 3.95 o.p. (ISBN 0-380-89880-2). Avon.

Reckoning at Arrowhead. W. W. Southard. 1985. 13.95 o.p. (ISBN 0-8161-3800-1, Large Print Bks). G K Hall.

Reclaiming the Bar-V. Thomas A. Taylor. 224p. 1987. 12.50 o.p. (ISBN 0-8062-2956-X). Carlton.

Reclaiming the Old Testament for the Christian Pulpit. Donald E. Gowan. LC 79-87743. 163p. 1980. 13.95 o.p. (ISBN 0-8042-0166-8, John Knox). Westminster John Knox.

Recognition of Air Pollution Injury to Vegetation: A Pictorial Atlas. Air Pollution Control Association. (Illus.). 112p. 1970. 15.00 o.p. (ISBN 0-318-12273-1, ATL); members 10.00 o.p. (ISBN 0-318-12274-X). Air & Waste.

Recognition of Reason. Edward Pols. LC 63-14296. (Philosophical Exploration Ser.). 269p. 1963. 9.95x o.p. (ISBN 0-8093-0111-3). S Ill U Pr.

Recognitions. William Gaddis. 1979. pap. 3.95 o.p. (ISBN 0-380-00030-X, 60921-5, Bard). Avon.

Recognitions. Graddis. 1970. pap. 4.95 o.p. (ISBN 0-15-676105-X, Harv). HarBraceJ.

Recollections of a Lifetime, or Men & Things I Have Seen. Samuel G. Goodrich. LC 67-23886. 1110p. 1967. Repr. of 1857 ed. 43.00x o.p. (ISBN 0-8103-3041-5). Gale.

Recollections of a Longshore Gunner. BB. 216p. 1979. 11.25 o.p. (ISBN 0-85115-067-5, Pub. by Boydell & Brewer). Longwood Pub Group.

Recollections of an Excursion to the Monasteries of Alcobaca & Batalha. William Beckford. 27.50 o.p. (ISBN 0-87556-541-7). Saifer.

Recollections of an Irish Rebel. J. Devoy. 508p. 1979. Repr. of 1929 ed. 30.00x o.p. (ISBN 0-7165-0045-0, BBA 02226, Pub. by Irish Academic Pr Ireland). Biblio Dist.

Recollections of My Immigrant Grandmother. Dorothea A. Gross. 64p. 1987. 7.95 o.p. (ISBN 0-8062-3071-1). Carlton.

Recollections of Seventy Years. Franklin B. Sanborn. LC 67-23889. 621p. 1967. Repr. of 1909 ed. 48.00x o.p. (ISBN 0-8103-3045-8). Gale.

Recollections of the Flathead Mission. Gregory Mengarini. Ed. by Gloria Lothrop. LC 74-27573. (Illus.). 1977. 28.50 o.p. (ISBN 0-87062-111-4). A H Clark.

Recollections of the Golden Triangle: A Novel. Alain Robbe-Grillet. Tr. by J. A. Underwood. 160p. (Orig.). pap. 6.95 o.p. (ISBN 0-394-62275-8). Grove.

Recollections of the Powys Brothers. Ed. by Belinda Humfrey. 1980. text ed. 26.50x o.p. (ISBN 0-7206-0547-4). Humanities.

Recombinant DNA. Ed. by K. J. Denniston & L. W. Enquist. LC 80-14100. (Benchmark Papers in Microbiology Ser.: Vol. 15). 391p. 1982. 62.95 o.p. (ISBN 0-87933-378-2). Van Nos Reinhold.

Recombinant DNA & Genetic Experimentation: Proceedings. Conference on Recombinant DNA, Committee on Genetic Experimentation (COGENE) & the Royal Society of London, Wye College, Kent, UK, April, 1979. Ed. by Joan Morgan & W. J. Whelan. LC 79-40962. (Illus.). 334p. 1979. 99.00 o.p. (ISBN 0-08-024427-0). Pergamon.

Recombinant DNA Lab Manual. Fuchs Hackett & Messing. 1984. pap. text ed. 24.95 o.p. (ISBN 0-8053-3672-9). Benjamin-Cummings.

Recombinant DNA: Proceedings of the Third Symposium on Macromolecules, Cleveland, June 1981. A. G. Walton. 1987. 109.75 o.p. (ISBN 0-317-65948-0). Elsevier.

Recombinant DNA: Readings from Scientific American. D. Freifelder. 147p. 1978. pap. 10.95 o.p. (ISBN 0-317-63604-9). W H Freeman.

Recombination in Semiconductors: Selected Proceedings of the International Conference Held at the University of Southampton, England. 30 August - 1st September 1978. Ed. by P. T. Landsberg & A. F Willoughby. 1979. pap. 63.00 o.p. (ISBN 0-08-024226-X). Pergamon.

Recommendations for Control of Occupational Safety & Health Hazards, Foundries. (DHHS Publication NIOSH Ser.). 199p. 1985. pap. 7.50 o.p. (ISBN 0-318-19922-X, S/N 017-033-00420-0). USGPO.

Recommendations for the Presentation of Infrared Absorption Spectra in Data Collections-A: Condensed Phases. Ed. by D. E. Becker. 1978. pap. 35.00 o.p. (ISBN 0-08-022376-1). Pergamon.

Recommended Country Hotels of Britain 1987. (Illus.). 135p. (Orig.). 1987. pap. 5.95 o.p. (ISBN 0-935161-55-4). Hunter Pub NY.

Recommended Country Hotels of Britain, 1988. (Illus.). 150p. (Orig.). 1988. pap. 6.95 o.p. (ISBN 0-317-57814-6). Hunter Pub NY.

Recommended International Standard for Edible Tallow. (CAC-RS Ser.: No. 31-1969). 18p. 1970. pap. 4.50 o.p. (ISBN 92-5-101776-X, F633, FAO). UNIPUB.

Recommended Practice for Electric Power Distribution for Industrial Plants. Institute of Electrical & Electronics Engineers, Inc. (IEEE) Staff. 388p. 1976. 19.95x o.p. (ISBN 0-471-02686-7). Wiley.

Recommended Practice for Glass Fiber Reinforced Concrete Panels. (PCI Journal Reprints Ser.). 35p. 1985. pap. 8.00 o.p. (ISBN 0-318-19767-7, JR231). P-PCI.

Recommended Reference Books for Small & Medium-Sized Libraries & Media Centers 1986. Ed. by Bohdan S. Wynar. 300p. 1986. 30.00 o.p. (ISBN 0-87287-540-7). Libs Unl.

Recommended Rules for Care & Operation of Heating Boilers. (Boiler & Pressure Vessel Code Ser.: Sec. 6). 1980. 35.00 o.p. (ISBN 0-685-76820-1, P00060); pap. 45.00 loose-leaf o.p. (ISBN 0-685-76821-X, V00060). ASME.

Recommended Wayside Inns of Britain. (Illus.). 135p. (Orig.). 1987. pap. 6.95 o.p. (ISBN 0-935161-45-7). Hunter Pub NY.

Recommended Wayside Inns of Britain, 1988. (Illus.). 150p. (Orig.). 1988. pap. 6.95 o.p. (ISBN 1-55650-022-X). Hunter Pub NY.

Recommunion: A True Story. Whitey Stuart. 145p. (Orig.). 1988. pap. 7.50 o.p. Thundblt Pr NV.

Reconciliation: A Study of Paul's Theology. Ed. by Ralph Martin & Peter Toon. LC 80-16340. (New Foundations Theological Library). 272p. 1981. 12.95 o.p. (ISBN 0-8042-3709-3, John Knox); pap. 11.95 o.p. (ISBN 0-8042-3729-8). Westminster John Knox.

Reconciliation & Liberation: Challenging a One-Dimensional View of Salvation. Jan M. Lochman. LC 80-24060. 160p. (Orig.). 1980. pap. 6.95 o.p. (ISBN 0-8006-1340-6, 1-1340, Fortress). Augsburg Fortress.

Reconciliation, Law & Righteousness: Essays in Biblical Theology. Peter Stuhlmacher. Tr. by Everett R. Kalin. LC 85-45482. 240p. 1986. 24.95 o.p. (ISBN 0-8006-0770-8, 1-770, Fortress). Augsburg Fortress.

Reconciliation Primer. John H. Gerstner. 1981. pap. 2.50 o.p. (ISBN 0-88469-143-8). BMH Bks.

Reconciliations. Elizabeth Klein. 416p. 1982. 14.95 o.p. (ISBN 0-395-32048-8). HM.

Reconciling. Francis J. Buckley. LC 81-68699. 96p. (Orig.). 1981. pap. 2.95 o.p. (ISBN 0-87793-237-9). Ave Maria.

Reconciling. Mary J. McFadyen et al. (Themepaks Ser.). (gr. 1-6). 1977. 4.95 o.p. (ISBN 0-8042-1458-1, John Knox). Westminster John Knox.

Reconditioning Heavy-Duty Freeways. (National Cooperative Highway Research Program Report). 60p. 1978. 6.40 o.p. (ISBN 0-309-02856-6). Transport Res Bd.

Reconstructing Educational Psychology. Ed. by Bill Gillham. 198p. 1978. 25.00 o.p. (ISBN 0-85664-631-8, Pub. by Croom Helm Ltd); pap. 11.50 o.p. (ISBN 0-85664-667-9). Routledge Chapman & Hall.

Reconstructing Psychological Practice. Ed. by Ian McPherson & Andrew Sutton. 202p. 1981. 26.00 o.p. (ISBN 0-7099-0419-3, Pub. by Croom Helm Ltd); pap. 9.75 o.p. (ISBN 0-7099-1709-0). Routledge Chapman & Hall.

Reconstruction of Humanity. P. A. Sorokin. Repr. of 1948 ed. 26.00 o.p. (ISBN 0-527-84826-3). Kraus Repr.

Reconstruction of Morality. Karl Holl. Ed. by James L. Adams & Walter F Bense. Tr. by Fred W. Meuser & Walter E. Wietzke. LC 79-50098. 160p. 1979. pap. 8.50 o.p. (ISBN 0-8066-1720-9, 10-5440, Augsburg). Augsburg Fortress.

Reconstruction of Secondary Education: Theory, Myth & Practice Since the War. A. McPherson & J. Gray. (Routledge Education Bks.). 300p. 1983. 34.95x o.p. (ISBN 0-7100-9265-2); pap. 18.50x o.p. (ISBN 0-7100-9268-7). Routledge Chapman & Hall.

Reconstruction of the Church. Ed. by James B. Jordan. LC 86-80570. (Christianity & Civilization Ser.: No. 4). xiv, 338p. (Orig.). 1986. pap. 12.95 o.p. (ISBN 0-939404-11-7). Geneva Ministr.

Reconstructions: Avant-Garde Art in Japan 1945-1965. Ed. by David Elliott. (Illus.). 96p. 1987. pap. 14.95 o.p. (ISBN 0-87663-507-9). Universe.

Reconstructive Procedures in Surgery. P. Gilroy Bevan. (Illus.). 454p. 1982. text ed. 64.95 o.p. (ISBN 0-632-00602-1, B 0664-0). Mosby.

Reconstructive Surgery of the Arteries. Jorg Vollmar. (Illus.). 447p. 1980. 69.95 o.p. (ISBN 0-913258-87-3). Thieme Med Pubs.

Record Albums Price Guide. 4th ed. Jerry Osbourne & Bruce Hamilton. 1982. pap. 10.95 o.p. (ISBN 0-686-87113-8). Norwalk Pr.

Record & Tape Reviews Index Nineteen Seventy-Four. Antoinette O. Maleady. LC 72-3355. 1975. 32.50 o.p. (ISBN 0-8108-0817-X). Chulainn Press.

Record & Tape Reviews Index Nineteen Seventy-Two. Antoinette O. Maleady. LC 72-3355. 1973. 27.50 o.p. (ISBN 0-8108-0672-X). Chulainn Press.

Record & Tape Reviews Index Nineteen Seventy-Three. Antoinette O. Maleady. LC 72-3355. 1974. 32.50 o.p. Chulainn Press.

Record Houses of 1971. Architectural Record Magazine Editors. (Illus.). 1971. text ed. 3.95 o.p. (ISBN 0-07-002207-0). McGraw.

Record Houses, 1981. Architectural Record Magazine Editors. (Architectural Record Ser.). (Illus.). 224p. 1981. pap. text ed. 6.00 o.p. (ISBN 0-07-002334-4). McGraw.

Record Houses, 1985. Architectural Record Magazine Editors & Walter F. Wagner, Jr. (Illus.). 300p. 1985. pap. text ed. 9.95 o.p. (ISBN 0-07-002433-2). McGraw.

Record Interiors, 1981. Architectural Record Magazine Editors. (Illus.). 224p. 1981. pap. text ed. 6.00 o.p. (ISBN 0-07-002358-1). McGraw.

Record Interiors, 1982. Architectural Record Magazine Editors. (Architectural Record Ser.). (Illus.). 200p. 1982. pap. text ed. 7.95 o.p. (ISBN 0-07-002379-4). McGraw.

Record Interiors, 1983. Architectural Record Magazine Editors. 200p. 1983. pap. text ed. 7.95 o.p. (ISBN 0-07-002391-3). McGraw.

Record Interiors, 1984. Architectural Record Magazine Editors. 250p. 1984. pap. text ed. 8.95 o.p. (ISBN 0-07-002431-6). McGraw.

Record Keeper: The Workbook That Helps You Organize Your Life. Crystal K. Meriwether & Curtis L. Sippel. LC 84-23899. 1985. pap. 14.95 o.p. (ISBN 0-934878-57-9). Dembner Bks.

Record of Geologic Time: A Vicarious Trip. D. Nations. (McGraw-Hill Concepts in Introductory Geology). (Illus.). 80p. 1975. text ed. 22.95 o.p. (ISBN 0-07-012326-8). McGraw.

Record of Singing. Michael Scott. (Illus.). 1978. 27.50 o.s.i. (ISBN 0-684-15528-1, ScribT). Scribner.

Record of the Parish List of Deaths, 1785-1819. William Bentley. 177p. 1882. 5.00 o.p. (ISBN 0-88389-081-X). Essex Inst.

Recordings of Beethoven. High Fidelity Magazins Staff. LC 77-26057. 1978. Repr. of 1971 ed. lib. bdg. 35.00x o.p. (ISBN 0-313-20171-4, HFRB). Greenwood.

Records Interiors, 1987. Architectural Record Magazine Staff. 228p. 1988. text ed. 16.95 o.p. (ISBN 0-07-002452-9). Mcgraw.

Records Management Applications. Violet Thomas et al. 161p. 1983. pap. (ISBN 0-471-89094-4). Wiley.

Records Management for State & Local Government: A Bibliography. Mary E. Huls. (Public Administration Ser.: P 1682). 10p. 1985. 2.00 o.p. (ISBN 0-89028-412-1). Vance Biblios.

Records of a Scottish Village: Lasswade 1650-1750. Rab Houston. 32p. 1982. pap. 125.00x incl. microfiche o.p. (ISBN 0-85964-118-X). Chadwyck-Healey.

Records of Baltimore's Private Organizations: A Guide to Archival Resources. John T. Guertler & Adele M. Newburger. LC 80-8976. 334p. 1981. lib. bdg. 48.00 o.p. (ISBN 0-8240-9360-7). Garland Pub.

Records of California Men in the War of the Rebellion: 1861-1867. Compiled by Richard Orton. LC 78-23517. 888p. 1979. Repr. of 1890 ed. 110.00x o.p. (ISBN 0-8103-3347-3). Gale.

Records of the Columbia Historical Society of Washington D.C. 1957-1974. Ed. by Francis C. Rosenberger. Incl. 1957-1959. (Illus.). 1961. 20.00x (ISBN 0-8139-0493-5); 1960-1962. (Illus.). 1963. 20.00x (ISBN 0-8139-0494-3); 1963-1965. (Illus.). 1966. 20.00x (ISBN 0-8139-0495-1); 1966-1968. (Illus.). 1969. 20.00x (ISBN 0-8139-0496-X); 1969-1970. LC 1-17677. (Illus.). 1971. 20.00x (ISBN 0-8139-0497-8); 1971-1972. 1973. 20.00x (ISBN 0-8139-0501-X); 1973-74. 1976. 20.00x (ISBN 0-8139-0641-5). LC 73-84160. U Pr of Va.

Records of the Trial of Walter Langeton, 1307-12. Ed. by Royal Historical Society Staff. (Camden Fourth Ser.: No. 6). 1970. 27.00 o.p. (ISBN 0-901050-02-4, Pub. by Boydell & Brewer). Longwood Pub Group.

Records of the UNESCO General Conference, Nineteenth, 1976: Vol. 1, Resolutions. UNESCO Staff. pap. 11.50 o.p. (ISBN 92-3-101496-X, M531, UNESCO). UNIPUB.

Records of the UNESCO General Conference, Third Extraordinary Session, Paris, 1973: Resolutions & Proceedings. UNESCO Staff. 334p. (Orig.). 1974. pap. 13.50 o.p. (ISBN 92-3-001170-3, U522, UNESCO). UNIPUB.

Recovering Biblical Sensuousness. William E. Phipps. LC 75-22348. 192p. 1975. 7.95 o.s.i. (ISBN 0-664-20805-3, Westminster). Westminster John Knox.

Recovering Commercial Debts. 1983. 120.00 o.p. (ISBN 0-8002-3422-7). Intl Pubns Serv.

Recovering Silver from Photographic Materials. Kodak. 1979. pap. 4.00 o.p. (ISBN 0-87985-227-5, J-10). Eastman Kodak.

Recovery from Brain Damage. Ed. by Stanley Finger. LC 77-27585. (Illus.). 440p. 1978. 55.00x o.p. (ISBN 0-306-31107-0, Plenum Pr). Plenum Pub.

Recovery of Confidence. John W. Gardner. 1970. 5.00 o.p. (ISBN 0-393-05407-1). Norton.

Recovery of Faith. Sarvepalli Radhakrishnan. Repr. of 1955 ed. lib. bdg. 35.00x o.p. (ISBN 0-8371-0197-2, RARF). Greenwood.

Recovery of Preaching. Henry H. Mitchell. LC 76-62959. 1977. pap. 7.64i o.p. (ISBN 0-06-065763-4, RD 229). HarpR.

Recreation & Leisure: Improving the Quality of Life. 2nd ed. Donald Weiskopf. 400p. 1982. text ed. write for info. o.s.i. (ISBN 0-205-07712-9, 627712); tchr's ed. avail. o.s.i. (ISBN 0-205-07713-7, 6277136L). Allyn.

Recreation & Leisure: Issues in an Era of Change. Ed. by Thomas Goodale & Peter A. Witt. LC 79-92646. 394p. (Orig.). 1980. pap. text ed. 14.95x o.p. (ISBN 0-910251-00-2). Venture Pub PA.

Recreation Guide to Chicago & Suburbs. Museum Publications Staff. LC 80-66754. 1979. pap. 6.95 o.p. (ISBN 0-914090-65-8). Chicago Review.

Recreation Lakes of California. 7th ed. D. J. Dirksen & R. A. Reeves. 240p. 1986. pap. 10.95 o.p. (ISBN 0-943798-08-6). Recreation Sales Pub.

Recreation Ministry: A Guide for all Congregations. Bill Maness. LC 81-85324. 102p. 1983. pap. 9.95 o.p. (ISBN 0-8042-1186-8, John Knox). Westminster John Knox.

Recreation Planning & Management. Ed. by Stanley R. Lieber & Daniel R. Fesenmaier. 400p. (Orig.). 1982. pap. text ed. 15.95x o.p. (ISBN 0-910251-03-7). Venture Pub PA.
Recreation Site Survey Manual. Edinburgh University, Tourism & Recreation Unit Staff. (Illus.). 150p. 1983. 33.00 o.p. (ISBN 0-419-12680-5, NO. 6769, Pub. by Tavistock). Routledge Chapman & Hall.
Recreational Areas. Ed. by Time-Life Books Editors. (Home Repair & Improvement Ser.). (Illus.). 1980. 10.95 o.p. Time-Life.
Recreational Geography of the U. S. S. R. V. Preobrazhensky & V. Krivosheyev. 228p. 1982. 6.45 o.p. (ISBN 0-686-47689-1, Pub. by Progress Pubs U. S. S. R.). Imported Pubns.
Recreational Land Management. C. W. Miles & W. Seabrooke. 1977. 25.00x o.p. (ISBN 0-419-11060-7, NO. 6467, Pub. by E & FN Spon). Routledge Chapman & Hall.
Recreational Management Handbook. Ed. by Institute of Recreation Management Staff. 1980. 40.00x o.p. (ISBN 0-419-11620-6, NO. 6336, Pub. by E & FN Spon England). Routledge Chapman & Hall.
Recreational Planning for New Communities. Stephen B. Barasch. LC 73-86541. 1974. 5.00 o.p. (ISBN 0-682-47775-3, University). Exposition-Phoenix.
Recreational Use of Wild Lands. 3rd ed. C. Frank Brockman & Lawrence C. Merriam, Jr. (M-H Series in Forest Resources). (Illus.). 1979. text ed. 43.95 o.p. (ISBN 0-07-007982-X). McGraw.
Recruiting & Selecting Profitable Sales Personnel. Edgar Ellman. 176p. 1983. ring-bound 22.95 o.p. (ISBN 0-8436-0774-2). Van Nos Reinhold.
Recruiting Evangelism Callers: Enlisting & Coordinating Workers. Walter A. Schmidt. 56p. (Orig.). 1984. pap. 4.95 o.p. (ISBN 0-8066-2069-2, 23-1830, Augsburg). Augsburg Fortress.
Recruiting, Marketing, & Retention in Institutions of Higher Education. Professional Associates Staff et al. LC 83-10310. (Illus.). 362p. (Orig.). 1983. pap. text ed. 15.50 o.p. (ISBN 0-8191-3331-0). U Pr of Amer.
Recruitment & Selection Practices in Oklahoma Police Departments. John Pelissero. (Criminal Justice Policy & Administration Research Ser.). 47p. 1978. 3.00 o.p. (ISBN 0-686-00897-9). Univ OK Gov Res.
Recruitment Handbook. 3rd ed. Ed. by Bernard Ungerson. 354p. 1983. text ed. 47.00x o.p. (ISBN 0-566-02192-7). Gower Pub Co.
Recrystallization in Metals & Alloys. S. S. Gorelik. 479p. 1981. 13.00 o.p. (ISBN 0-8285-2065-8, Pub. by Mir Pubs USSR). Imported Pubns.
Rectified Lunar Atlas. E. A. Whitaker et al. LC 63-17721. (Photographic Lunar Atlas, Suppl: No. 2). (Illus.). 147p. 1964. 50.00x o.p. (ISBN 0-8165-0077-0). U of Ariz Pr.
Rector of Justin. Louis Auchincloss. 1964. 4.95 o.p. (ISBN 0-395-07361-8). HM.
Rector of Justin. Louis Auchincloss. 1980. pap. 3.95 o.p. (ISBN 0-395-29179-8). HM.
Rectory Umbrella & Mischmasch. Lewis Carroll. (Illus.). 1932. pap. 3.50 o.p. (ISBN 0-486-21345-5). Dover.
Recueil d'Articles, 2 vols. Benjamin Constant & Ephraim Harpaz. 1566p. 1972. Set. 99.50 o.p. (ISBN 0-686-54615-6). French & Eur.
Recueil et Parallele des Edifices de Tout Genre Anciens et Modernes. J. N. Durand & Anthony Vidler. (Illus.). 1982. Repr. of 1800 ed. portfolio 150.00 o.p. (ISBN 0-910413-01-0). Princeton Arch.
Recurrent Dislocation of the Shoulder. H. F. Moseley. (Illus.). 176p. 1961. 15.00x o.p. (ISBN 0-7735-0004-9, McGill Canada). U of Toronto Pr.
Recurrent Education: A Revived Agenda. Barry Smith et al. Ed. by Chris Duke. (Research & Policy Studies in Recurrent Education: Vol. 1). 288p. 1986. 29.00 o.p. (ISBN 0-949614-24-6, Pub. by Croom Helm UK). Routledge Chapman & Hall.
Recurrent Themes & Sequences in North American Indian-European Culture Contact. Edward M. Larrabee. LC 76-24257. (Transactions Ser.: Vol. 66, Pt. 7). (Illus.). 1976. pap. 12.00 o.p. (ISBN 0-87169-667-3). Am Philos.
Recurring Miracle. Ed. by Derick R. Marsh. 208p. 1980. pap. 20.00x o.p. (ISBN 0-424-00085-7, Pub. by Sydney U Pr Australia). Intl Spec Bk.
Recurring Mirror. Alain Robbe-Grillet. 1986. pap. 8.95 o.p. (ISBN 0-394-55347-0, Ever). Grove.
Recursive Functions in Computer Theory. Roezsa Peter. LC 80-42072. (Ellis Horwood Series in Computers & Their Applications). 179p. 1982. 69.95 o.p. (ISBN 0-470-27195-7). Halsted Pr.
Recursive Universe: Cosmic Complexity & the Limits of Scientific Knowledge. William Poundstone. LC 84-9045. (Illus.). 320p. 1984. 15.95 o.p. (ISBN 0-688-03975-8). Morrow.
Recycle & Secondary Recovery of Metals. Ed. by P. R. Taylor et al. LC 85-21792. (Illus.). 862p. 1985. 86.00 o.p. (ISBN 0-87339-007-5). Minerals Metals.
Recycled Hallelujahs. James Weekley. 1982. pap. 4.95 o.p. (ISBN 0-89536-532-4, 1814). CSS of Ohio.
Recycling & Disposal of Solid Waste. M. E. Henstock. LC 75-4235. 223p. 1975. pap. 55.00 o.p. (ISBN 0-08-019685-3). Pergamon.
Recycling Berlin Seventy-Nine, 2 vols. Ed. by K. J. Thome-Kozmiensky. 1450p. 1979. Set. 89.70 o.p. (ISBN 0-387-09661-2). Springer-Verlag.
Recycling Materials for Highways. (National Cooperative Highway Research Program Synthesis of Highway Practice). 53p. 1978. 5.60 o.p. (ISBN 0-309-02859-0). Transport Res Bd.
Recycling: Opportunities & Constraints: Proceedings of the Conference Co-Sponsored by the Federation of Materials Science & the U. S. Bureau of Mines, Washington, D. C., U. S. A., 17-19 July 1984. Ed. by M. B. Bever & M. E. Henstock. 136p. 1985. pap. 85.00 o.p. (ISBN 0-08-032635-8, E135, D145, G135, Pub. by PPL). Pergamon.
Recyclopedia. Robin Simons. (Illus.). (gr. 3-7). 1976. 9.95 o.p. (ISBN 0-395-24390-4). HM.
Red & the Black see also Scarlet & the Black.
Red & the Black. Stendhal, pseud. Tr. by C. K. Scott-Moncrieff. (Black & Gold Lib). 1954. 8.95 o.p. (ISBN 0-87140-833-3). Liveright.
Red & the Blue: A Study in Treason & Intelligence. Andrew Sinclair. 1987. 17.95 o.p. (ISBN 0-316-79237-3). Little.
Red & the Green. Richard Dimitt. (Illus., Orig.). (ps-3). 1.75 o.s.i. (ISBN 0-8198-0131-3). Dghtrs St Paul.
Red & the Pumpkins. Jocelyn Stevenson. LC 83-10801. (Fraggle Rock Bks.). (Illus.). 48p. (gr. 1-4). 1983. 6.95 o.s.i. (ISBN 0-03-068679-2). H Holt & Co.
Red Army: The Red Army 1918-1945; The Soviet Army 1946 to the Present. Basil H. Liddell-Hart. (Illus.). 13.25 o.p. (ISBN 0-8446-0774-6). Peter Smith.
Red Badge of Courage. Stephen Crane. 134p. 1983. pap. text ed. 3.95x o.p. (ISBN 0-460-01309-2, Pub. by Evman England). Biblio Dist.
Red Badge of Courage. Stephen Crane. Ed. by Henry Binder. 192p. 1983. pap. 6.95 o.p. (ISBN 0-380-64113-5, 64113). Avon.
Red Badge of Courage. Stephen Crane. LC 82-82814. (Illus.). 176p. 1982. 12.95 o.p. (ISBN 0-89577-155-1). RD Assn.
Red Badge of Courage: An Annotated Text with Critical Essays. rev. ed. Stephen Crane. (Critical Edition Ser.). 1977. text ed. 12.50 o.p. (ISBN 0-393-04435-1, NortonC). Norton.
Red Badge of Courage: An Annotated Text with Critical Essays. Stephen Crane. Ed. by Sculley Bradley et al. (Norton Critical Editions Ser.). 1962. pap. 2.45x o.p. (ISBN 0-393-09543-6, NortonC). Norton.
Red Baron. Manfred Von Richthofen. Ed. by Stanley M. Ulanoff. Tr. by Peter Kilduff from Ger. LC 80-68107. (Illus.). 241p. 1980. Repr. 12.95 o.p. (ISBN 0-8168-7925-7, 27925, TAB-Aero). TAB Bks.
Red Baron. Nicholas Wright. (Illus.). (gr. 6-8). 1977. text ed. 10.95 o.p. (ISBN 0-07-072040-1). McGraw.
Red Bird of Ireland. Sondra G. Langford. LC 82-13897. 192p. (gr. 4-7). 1983. 10.95 o.s.i. (ISBN 0-689-50270-2, M K McElderry). Macmillan.
Red Book on Transportation of Hazardous Materials. Lawrence W. Bierlein. LC 76-44394. 896p. 1983. 94.95 o.p. (ISBN 0-8436-1407-2). Van Nos Reinhold.
Red Car Days: Pacific Electric Memories. Raphael Long. Ed. by Jim Walker. (Special Ser.: No. 90). (Illus.). 64p. 1983. pap. 11.95 o.p. (ISBN 0-916374-63-7). Interurban.
Red Carpet. Joseph Finder. LC 82-18694. (New Republic Bk.). (Illus.). 419p. 1983. 16.95 o.p. (ISBN 0-03-060484-2). H Holt & Co.
Red Cell Structure & Its Breakdown. E. P. Ponder. (Protoplasmatologia: Vol. 10, Pt. 2). (Illus.). 1955. pap. 34.90 o.p. (ISBN 0-387-80388-2). Springer-Verlag.
Red Cell Structure & Metabolism: Proceedings. Ed. by Bracha Ramot. 1971. 55.00 o.p. (ISBN 0-12-577150-9). Acad Pr.
Red Chair Waits. Alice M. Huggins. (Illus.). (gr. 4-6). 1948. 3.95 o.s.i. (ISBN 0-664-32047-3, Westminster). Westminster John Knox.
Red Chameleon. Stuart M. Kaminsky. (Inspector Porfiry Rostnikov Mystery Ser.). 224p. 1985. 13.95 o.s.i. (ISBN 0-684-18424-9, ScribT). Scribner.
Red Coal. Gerald Stern. 96p. 1981. 12.95 o.p. (ISBN 0-395-30541-1); pap. 5.95 o.p. (ISBN 0-395-30542-X). HM.
Red Cross Story. Brian Peachment. 1977. pap. text ed. 1.60 o.s.i. (ISBN 0-08-021036-8). Pergamon.
Red Daniel. Duncan MacNeil. 1977. pap. 1.50 o.s.i. (ISBN 0-8439-0477-1, Pub. by Leisure Bks CT). Dorchester Pub Co.
Red Doll. Juan L. Cebrian. Tr. by Philip W. Silver. LC 87-21060. 224p. 1987. 15.95 o.s.i. (ISBN 1-55584-145-7). Weidenfeld.
Red Dreams. Ken Gerner. 1978. 15.00x o.p.; pap. 5.00 o.p. Copper Canyon.
Red Eagles. David Downing. 256p. 1987. 18.95 o.p. (ISBN 0-02-533380-1). Macmillan.
Red Earth, White Earth. Will Weaver. LC 86-15599. 352p. 1986. 17.45 o.s.i. (ISBN 0-671-61977-2). S&S.
Red Embers. Dorothy Lyons. LC 48-8369. (Illus.). (gr. 7 up). 1948. 4.50 o.p. (ISBN 0-15-266014-3, HJ). HarBraceJ.
Red Emma Speaks. pap. (ISBN 0-8052-0752-X). Random.
Red Flag. Michael Skinner. (Illus.). 144p. pap. 12.95 o.p. Aviation.
Red Flag Seminar. 1984. 25.00 o.p. (ISBN 0-88129-141-2). Wash Bar CLE.
Red for Danger. L. T. Rolt. LC 76-28618. (Illus.). 192p. 1982. 24.95 o.p. (ISBN 0-7153-8362-0). David & Charles.
Red Fox. Anthony Hyde. (Special Editions Ser.). 1986. lib. bdg. 19.95 o.p. (ISBN 0-8161-4056-1, Large Print Bks). G K Hall.
Red Fox. Anthony Hyde. 512p. 1987. pap. 11.95 o.p. (ISBN 0-8161-4057-X, Large Print Bks). G K Hall.
Red Fox. Charles G. Roberts. LC 77-187419. (Illus.). 256p. (gr. 3-7). 1972. 7.95 o.p. (ISBN 0-395-13735-7). HM.
Red Fox: Brigadier-General Stand Watie's Civil War Years in Indian Territory. Wilfred Knight. LC 87-90675. (Illus.). 320p. 1988. 27.50 o.p. (ISBN 0-87062-179-3). A H Clark.
Red Fraggle's Birthday. Jennifer Taubner. LC 84-81840. (Illus.). 12p. (ps-k). 1985. bds. 2.95 o.s.i. (ISBN 0-03-002559-1). H Holt & Co.
Red Giants & White Dwarfs. Robert Jastrow. (Illus.). 1979. 14.95 o.p. (ISBN 0-393-85002-1). Norton.
Red Grooms: Philadelphia Cornucopia. Janet Kardon & Paula Marincola. 1982. 15.00 o.p. (ISBN 0-88454-029-4). U of PA Contemp Art.
Red Hawk. Elizabeth A. Lynn. (Illus.). 72p. 1983. 65.00 o.p. (ISBN 0-941826-04-X) (ISBN 0-941826-05-8). Cheap St.
Red Herrings. Tim Heald. LC 85-25268. (Crime Club Ser.). 192p. 1986. 12.95 o.p. (ISBN 0-385-23354-X). Doubleday.
Red Herrings. Tim Heald. (Lythway Ser.). 1987. lib. bdg. 17.50 o.p. (ISBN 0-7451-0581-5, Pub. by Chivers Pr UK). G K Hall.
Red Horse Hill. Stephen W. Meader. LC 30-23594. (Illus.). (gr. 6 up). 1930. 6.95 o.p. (ISBN 0-15-266193-X, HJ). HarBraceJ.
Red Hot & Dangerous. Michael Geller. (Bud Dugan Ser.: No. 4). 192p. (Orig.). 1982. pap. 2.25 o.s.i. (ISBN 0-505-51773-6, Pub. by Tower Bks). Dorchester Pub Co.
Red Ice. Mary J. Hutchinson. 224p. (Orig.). 1981. pap. 2.25 o.p. (ISBN 0-380-78725-3, 78725-3). Avon.
Red in the Morning. Edith Begner. 1977. pap. 1.75 o.p. (ISBN 0-380-01679-6, 33506). Avon.
Red Jaguar. Alison Prince. LC 72-75280. (gr. 2-5). 1972. 4.95 o.p. (ISBN 0-689-30063-8, Atheneum). Macmillan.
Red Letter Days. Molly Keane & Snaffles. (Illus.). 96p. 1988. 29.95 o.p. (ISBN 0-233-98159-4, Pub. by A Deutsch England). David & Charles.
Red Light, Green Light: The Life of Garrett Morgan & His Invention of the Stoplight. Dovie D. Sweet. (gr. k-4). 1978. 5.00 o.p. (ISBN 0-682-49088-1). Exposition-Phoenix.
Red Man's America: A History of the Indians in the United States. rev. ed. Ruth M. Underhill. LC 79-171345. (Illus.). 1971. lib. bdg. 25.00 o.s.i. (ISBN 0-226-84164-2). U of Chicago Pr.
Red Menace. Michael Anania. 144p. 1986. pap. 3.95 o.p. (ISBN 0-380-70053-0, Bard). Avon.
Red Midnight. Heather X. Graham. (Candlelight Ecstasy Supreme Ser.: No. 17). 288p. (Orig.). 1984. pap. 2.50 o.s.i. (ISBN 0-440-17431-7). Dell.
Red Mittens. Laura Bannon. (Illus.). (gr. k-3). 1974. reinforced bdg. 5.95 o.p. (ISBN 0-395-19863-1). HM.
Red Monarch: Scenes from the Life of Stalin. Yuri Krotkov. Tr. by Tanya E. Mairs. 1979. 10.95 o.p. (ISBN 0-393-08836-7). Norton.
Red Pottage, 1899 see In Deacon's Orders, 1895.
Red Prelude see Alexander Conspiracy: A Life of A. I. Zhelybov.
Red President. Martin Gross. LC 86-13496. 408p. 1987. 17.95 o.s.i. (ISBN 0-385-23490-2). Doubleday.
Red Ribbon on a White Horse. Anzia Yezierska. 226p. 1981. pap. 9.95 o.p. (ISBN 0-89255-053-8). Persea Bks.
Red Riding Hood. Beatrice S. De Regniers. LC 79-175561. (Illus.). 48p. (ps-3). 1972. 5.95 o.p. (ISBN 0-689-30036-0, Atheneum). Macmillan.
Red Saturday. Martin Allen. LC 84-28747. 150p. (Orig.). 1985. pap. 8.95 o.p. (ISBN 0-571-13477-7). Faber & Faber.
Red Scare: A Study in National Hysteria, 1919-1920. Robert K. Murray. 1955. pap. text ed. 4.95 o.p. (ISBN 0-07-044075-1). McGraw.
Red Sea Is Your Blood. Alvin B. Kuhn. 66p. 1976. pap. 5.95 o.s.i. (ISBN 0-88697-007-5). Life Science.
Red Shift. Alan Garner. 1981. pap. 1.95 o.s.i. (ISBN 0-345-30071-8, Del Rey). Ballantine.
Red Shoes. Michael Powell. (Masterworks Collections). 1987. pap. 8.95 o.p. (ISBN 0-8044-6661-0). Ungar.
Red Shoes. Michael Powell & Emeric Pressberger. 1978. pap. 1.95 o.p. (ISBN 0-380-37812-4, 37812-4). Avon.
Red Shoes Ballet & the Tales of Hoffman, Vol. 14. Monk Gibbon. Ed. by Bruce S. Kupelnick. LC 76-52106. (Classics of Film Literature Ser.). 1978. lib. bdg. 47.00 o.p. (ISBN 0-8240-2878-3). Garland Pub.
Red Soil. Rajendra Awasthi. (Vikas Library of Modern Indian Writing: No.27). 136p. 1982. text ed. 17.95x o.p. (ISBN 0-7069-1961-0, Pub. by Vikas India). Advent NY.
Red Sonja, No. 4: Endithor's Daughter. David C. Smith & Richard L. Tierney. 1983. pap. 2.50 o.s.i. (ISBN 0-441-71159-6, Pub. by Ace Science Fiction). Ace Bks.
Red Sox Fever. Ellery H. Clark, Jr. LC 79-88276. (Illus.). 1979. 9.95 o.p. (ISBN 0-682-49397-X, Banner). Exposition-Phoenix.
Red Sox Forever. Ellery H. Clark, Jr. 1977. 7.50 o.p. (ISBN 0-682-48867-4, Banner). Exposition-Phoenix.
Red Star over China. rev. ed. Edgar Snow. 1968. pap. 11.95 o.s.i. (ISBN 0-394-17797-5, E618, Ever). Grove.
Red Tape & Broken Hearts: Tragedy in Veterans Hospitals. Anne M. Hanson. 1975. 7.50 o.p. (ISBN 0-682-48218-8, Banner). Exposition-Phoenix.
Red Velvet Mansion. Margaret Egerton. 1979. 6.00 o.p. (ISBN 0-682-49226-4). Exposition-Phoenix.
Red Virgin: Memoirs of Louise Michel. Ed. by Bullitt Lowry & Elizabeth E. Gunter. 272p. 1981. 21.50 o.p. (ISBN 0-8173-0062-7); pap. 9.95 o.p. (ISBN 0-8173-0063-5). U of Ala Pr.
Red Virgin Soil: Soviet Literature in the Late 1920's. Robert A. Maguire. (Studies of the Russian Institute, Columbia University). 1967. 42.50 o.p. (ISBN 0-691-06111-4). Princeton U Pr.
Red, White, & Blue Paradise: The American Canal Zone. Herbert Knapp & Mary Knapp. 320p. 1985. 16.95 o.p. (ISBN 0-15-176135-3). HarBraceJ.
Red Wine of Youth: A Life of Rupert Brooke. Arthur J. Stringer. LC 72-6211. 287p. 1972. Repr. of 1948 ed. lib. bdg. 22.50x o.p. (ISBN 0-8371-6456-7, STRW). Greenwood.
Red, Yellow, Blue: A Wrinkles Book of Colors. Anita Shevett & Steve Shevett. LC 86-70326. (Illus.). 12p. (ps-k). 1986. 2.95 o.s.i. (ISBN 0-394-88427-2, BYR). Random.
Red Yesterdays. Glenn Sirley. 1976. 9.95 o.p. (ISBN 0-89015-134-2). Eakin Pr.
Redating the New Testament. John A.. Robinson. LC 76-17554. 384p. 1976. 15.00 o.s.i. (ISBN 0-664-21336-7, Westminster). Westminster John Knox.
Rede und Redeszene in der Deutschen Erzahlung Bis Wolfram Von Eschenbach. 18.00 o.p. (ISBN 0-384-54370-7); pap. 13.00 o.p. (ISBN 0-685-02059-2). Johnson Repr.
Rededication of Fondren Library of Rice University. Ed. by Hardin Craig, Jr. (Rice University Studies: Vol. 55, No. 4). 112p. 1969. pap. 10.00x o.p. (ISBN 0-89263-202-X). Rice Univ.
Redeemer. Hugh Fleetwood. LC 79-55598. 1980. 8.95 o.p. (ISBN 0-689-11037-5, Atheneum). Macmillan.
Redeeming the Sin: Social Science & Literature. Audrey Borenstein. LC 78-9332. 269p. 1978. 30.00x o.p. (ISBN 0-231-04430-5). Columbia U Pr.
Redefining Personnel Services. National Association of Women Deans & Counselors. 1972. pap. 3.00 o.p. (ISBN 0-686-09577-4). Natl Assn Women.
Redefining Politics: People, Resources & Power. Adrian Leftwich. 320p. 1983. 32.00 o.p. (ISBN 0-416-73590-8, NO. 3950); pap. 14.95 o.p. (ISBN 0-416-73600-9, NO. 3951). Routledge Chapman & Hall.
Redefining Remedial Education: Policies & Practice in Secondary Schools. Hazel Bines. 200p. 1986. 29.00 o.p. (ISBN 0-7099-3984-1, Pub. by Croom Helm Ltd); pap. 13.50 o.p. (ISBN 0-7099-5028-4). Routledge Chapman & Hall.
Redefining Revolution. 2nd ed. Cornelius Castoriadis. 200p. 1988. 29.95 o.p. (ISBN 0-920057-18-7, Dist. by U of Toronto Pr); pap. 14.95 o.p. (ISBN 0-920057-19-5, Dist. by U of Toronto Pr). Black Rose Bks.
Redefining the Manager's Job: The Proactive Manager in a Reactive World. Merritt Kastens. 256p. 1980. 14.95 o.p. (ISBN 0-8144-5619-7). AMACOM.

Redemption of Elsdon Bird. Noel Virtue. 128p. 1987. 15.95 o.s.i. (ISBN 0-8021-0022-8). Grove.

Redemptive History & Biblical Interpretation. Geerhardus Vos. Ed. by Richard B. Gaffin, Jr. 584p. 1981. 17.50 o.p. (ISBN 0-8010-9286-8). Baker Bk.

Redirecting Farm Policy to Enable Farmers to Do Without Handouts. Joseph C. Genske. 1978. 5.50 o.p. (ISBN 0-682-49135-7). Exposition-Phoenix.

Rediscovered Masterpieces of Mesoamerica: Mexico-Guatemala-Honduras. Ed. by Gerald Berjonneau & Jean-Louis Sonnery. (Illus.). 288p. 1986. 75.00 o.p. (ISBN 0-8478-0709-6). Rizzoli Intl.

Rediscoveries in Art: Some Aspects of Taste, Fashion, & Collecting in England & France. Francis Haskell. (Wrightsman Lectures Ser.). 340p. 1980. Paperback Ser. pap. 16.95 o.p. (ISBN 0-8014-9187-8). Cornell U Pr.

Rediscovering India. (Illus.). 150p. 1983. text ed. 50.00x o.p. (ISBN 0-7069-2277-8, Pub. by Vikas India). Advent NY.

Rediscovering Mathematics. A. H. Hackert. 1982. text ed. 27.95 o.p. (ISBN 0-8053-3660-5); pap. text ed. 4.95 instr' s guide o.p. (ISBN 0-8053-3661-3). Benjamin-Cummings.

Rediscovering Pastoral Care. Alastair V. Campbell. LC 81-7547. 132p. 1981. pap. 7.95 o.s.i. (ISBN 0-664-24381-9, Westminster). Westminster John Knox.

Rediscovering the Person in Medical Care: Patient, Family, Physician, Nurse, Chaplain, Pastor. James B. Nelson. LC 76-3858. (Orig.). 1976. pap. 4.95 o.p. (ISBN 0-8066-1534-6, 10-5450, Augsburg). Augsburg Fortress.

Rediscovering the Sacraments: Approaches to the Sacrament. Brennan Hill. 126p. (Orig.). 1982. 4.95 o.p. (ISBN 0-8215-9882-1). Sadlier.

Rediscovery of Jesus' Eschatological Discourse: Studies in the History of Gospel Traditions. David Wenham. (Gospel Perspectives Ser.: Vol. IV). 406p. pap. text ed. 14.95x o.s.i. (Pub. by JSOT Pr England). Eisenbrauns.

Rediscovery: Three Hundred Years of Stories by & about Women. Ed. by Betzy Dinesen. 272p. 1982. pap. 3.50 o.p. (ISBN 0-380-60756-5, 60756-5, Bard). Avon.

Redistribution Reactions. J. C. Lockhart. 1970. 54.00 o.p. (ISBN 0-12-454450-9). Acad Pr.

Redistributive Effects of Government Programmes: The Chilean Case. A. Foxley et al. (Illus.). 1979. 50.00 o.p. (ISBN 0-08-023130-6). Pergamon.

Redox Indicators: Characteristics & Applications. Ed. by Adam Hulanicki & Stanislaw Glab. 1978. pap. 50.00 o.p. (ISBN 0-08-022383-4). Pergamon.

Redox Properties: Changes Affected by Coordination see Coordinative Interactions.

Reducing Input Subsidies to Livestock Producers in Cyprus: An Economic Analysis. Avishay Braverman et al. (Working Paper: No. 782). 62p. 1986. 5.00 o.p. (ISBN 0-8213-0672-3). World Bank.

Reducing Worker Absenteeism. Ed. by Dallas L. Jones et al. 72p. 1980. 12.00 o.p. (ISBN 0-938654-23-3, ABSENT). Indus Dev Inst Sci.

Reduction of Iron Ores: Scientific Basis & Technology. L. V. Bogdandy & H. J. Engell. LC 77-126891. (Illus.). 1971. 141.60 o.p. (ISBN 0-387-05056-6). Springer-Verlag.

Reduction of Military Budgets. (Disarmament Study Ser.: No. 4). 197p. 1981. pap. 15.00x o.p. (ISBN 0-8002-3457-X). Intl Pubns Serv.

Reductionist Poem. Anthony Cronin. 39p. 1980. pap. 6.95 o.p. (ISBN 0-906897-12-2). Dufour.

Redundancies, Again! Susie Andruk & David O'Connor. (Illus.). 1980. 6.00 o.p. (ISBN 0-682-49693-6). Exposition-Phoenix.

Reed's Nautical Almanac & Coast Pilot: East Coast Edition, 1983. (Illus.). 800p. 1983. 19.70 o.p. (ISBN 0-900335-74-2, Better Boating Assoc). Norton.

Reed's Nautical Almanac & Coast Pilot. (Illus.). 1983. East Coast ed. pap. 19.95 o.p. (ISBN 0-900335-81-5); West Coast ed. pap. 19.95 o.p. (ISBN 0-900335-82-3). Norton.

Reed's Nautical Almanac & Coast Pilot: East Coast. Ed. by Oswald M. Watts. (Illus.). 1981. pap. 17.95 o.p. (ISBN 0-900335-69-6). Norton.

Reed's Nautical Almanac & Coast Pilot: West Coast. Ed. by Oswald M. Watts. (Illus.). 1981. pap. 17.95 o.p. (ISBN 0-900335-70-X). Norton.

Reefer Madness: Marijuana in America. Larry Sloman. (Illus.). 360p. 1983. pap. 8.95 o.s.i. (ISBN 0-394-62446-7, E851, Ever). Grove.

Reefs & Banks of the North Western Gulf of Mexico: Their Geological, Physical & Biological Dynamics. Richard Rezak et al. LC 84-26989. 259p. 1985. 49.95 o.p. (ISBN 0-471-89379-X, Pub. by Wiley-Interscience). Wiley.

Reeney. Molly Cone. (Illus.). (gr. 7-9). 1963. 4.95 o.p. (ISBN 0-395-06710-3). HM.

Refer to Occupational Therapy. 2nd ed. A. J. Shopland. 1979. pap. text ed. 11.00 o.p. (ISBN 0-443-01866-9). Churchill.

Reference Book of Chemistry. J. H. White. 312p. 1967. (ISBN 0-8022-1860-1). Philos Lib.

Reference Book of English Words & Phrases for Foreign Science Students. R. F. Price. 1966. 24.00 o.p. (ISBN 0-08-011750-3); pap. 50.00 o.p. (ISBN 0-08-020381-7). Pergamon.

Reference Books: A Brief Guide. 8th ed. Marion V. Bell & Eleanor A. Swidan. 1978. pap. 5.00 o.p. (ISBN 0-910556-11-3). Enoch Pratt.

Reference Books Bulletin, 1985-1986. Ed. by Sandy Whiteley. LC 73-159565. 200p. 1987. pap. text ed. 22.50x o.p. (ISBN 0-8389-3336-X). ALA.

Reference Encyclopedia for the IBM Personal Computer, 2 vols. 2nd ed. Gary Phillips & Karen Phillips. 700p. 1983. Set. 69.95 o.p. (ISBN 0-912677-01-5). Tate Pub.

Reference Grammar for Students of English. Reg A. Close. (English As a Second Language Bk.). (Illus.). 342p. 1975. pap. text ed. 14.95 o.p. (ISBN 0-582-52277-3). Longman.

Reference Guide to American Science Fiction Films: Vol. I, 1897-1929. A. W. Strickland & Forrest J. Ackerman. LC 81-51748. 400p. 1981. 34.95 o.s.i. (ISBN 0-89917-268-7). TIS Inc.

Reference Guide to Handbooks & Annuals. 1985 ed. Ed. by J. William Pfeiffer. LC 75-14661. 206p. 1985. pap. 14.95 o.p. (ISBN 0-88390-065-3). Univ Assocs.

Reference Guide to the Study of Public Opinion. Harwood L. Childs. LC 73-12777. 118p. Repr. of 1934 ed. 40.00x o.p. (ISBN 0-8103-3704-5). Gale.

Reference Service. 2nd rev. ed. Krishan Kumar. 390p. 1980. text ed. 27.50x o.p. (ISBN 0-7069-0637-3, Pub. by Vikas India). Advent NY.

Reference Service in American Public Libraries Serving Populations of 10,000 or More: Report of the Public Library Reference Survey Committee of the Reference Services Division, American Library Association. (Occasional Papers: No. 61). 21p. 1961. pap. 1.00 o.p. (ISBN 0-317-58843-5). U of Ill Lib Info Sci.

Reference Services & Library Education: Essays in Honor of Frances Neel Cheney. Ed. by Edwin S. Gleaves & John M. Tucker. LC 81-48266. 320p. 1982. 33.00x o.p. (ISBN 0-669-05320-1). Lexington Bks.

Reference Sources in Library & Information Services: A Guide to the Literature. Gary R. Purcell & Gail A. Schlachter. LC 83-19700. 359p. 1984. lib. bdg. 46.75 o.p. (ISBN 0-87436-355-1). ABC-Clio.

Reference to Kinds in English. Greg N. Carlson. Ed. by Jorge Hankamer. LC 79-6619. (Outstanding Dissertations in Linguistics Ser.). 300p. 1985. text ed. 42.00 o.p. (ISBN 0-8240-4551-3). Garland Pub.

Reference Work in the Public Library. Rolland E. Stevens & Joan M. Walton. LC 82-17147. 269p. 1983. 28.50 o.p. (ISBN 0-87287-332-3). Libs Unl.

Referring. Leonard Linsky. 1967. text ed. 12.50x o.p. (ISBN 0-391-01746-2). Humanities.

Refinements of the Nash Equilibrium Concept. E. Van Damme. (Lecture Notes in Economics & Mathematical Systems Ser.: Vol. 219). 151p. 1983. pap. 15.00 o.p. (ISBN 0-387-12690-2). Springer-Verlag.

Refiner's Fire. Mark Helprin. 1985. pap. 4.95 o.p. (ISBN 0-440-37316-6, LE). Dell.

Refiner's Fire. Lee Kingman. (gr. 7 up). 1981. 8.95 o.p. (ISBN 0-395-31606-5). HM.

Refinery-Petrochemical Plant Construction & Maintenance-Plant Operation & Control-Noise & Pollution Control In Refinery-Petrochemical Plants: A Workbook for Engineers. 148p. 1982. 30.00 o.p. (I00154). ASME.

Refining Composition Skills. 2nd ed. Regina L. Smalley & Mary K. Hank. 80p. 1986. pap. text ed. write for info. o.p. (ISBN 0-02-411830-3). Macmillan.

Reflections. A. B. Dow. LC 75-109044. 100.00 o.p. (ISBN 0-87359-020-1). Northwood Inst Pr.

Reflections. Joseph V. Novak. 1978. 6.00 o.p. (ISBN 0-682-49026-1). Exposition-Phoenix.

Reflections - Nineteen Hundred to Nineteen Fifty. Esther C. Schaad & Edna E. Wiese. (Illus.). 219p. 1985. plastic comb., laminated cover 25.00 o.p. (ISBN 0-936195-00-2). Double E Pubs.

Reflections: A Personal Guide for Life's Most Crucial Questions. Paul Tournier. LC 81-21944. 192p. 1982. pap. 7.95 o.s.i. (ISBN 0-664-24420-3, Westminster). Westminster John Knox.

Reflections & Maxims. Baruch Spinoza. Ed. by Dagobert D. Runes. LC 65-20326. 1965. (ISBN 0-8022-1619-6). Philos Lib.

Reflections Books, 4 vols. Daniel Overduin. 1980. Set. pap. 6.95 o.p. (ISBN 0-570-03817-0, 12-2785). Concordia.

Reflections: Essays, Aphorisms, Autobiography Writings. Walter Benjamin. Tr. by Edmond Jephcott. 348p. 1979. 12.95 o.p. (ISBN 0-15-176189-2); pap. 6.95 o.p. (ISBN 0-15-676245-5). HarBraceJ.

Reflections from the Keyboard: The World of the Concert Pianist. David Dubal. (Illus.). 384p. 1984. 19.45 o.s.i. (ISBN 0-671-49240-3). Summit Bks.

Reflections in the Son. Mary Irwin. LC 85-4109. 1985. 6.95 o.p. (ISBN 0-8054-5710-0). Broadman.

Reflections of a Palestinian. Mohammad Tarbush. LC 85-73827. 93p. 1986. pap. 5.95 o.p. (ISBN 0-943182-04-2). Am Arab Affairs.

Reflections of a Physicist. P. W. Bridgman. 588p. 1955. (ISBN 0-8022-0174-1). Philos Lib.

Reflections of Hippo. Paul White. (Jungle Doctor Picture Fable Ser.). 21p. (gr. 1-7). 1986. Set of 8. pap. 26.50 o.p. (ISBN 0-85364-372-5, Pub. by Paternoster UK). Attic Pr.

Reflections of Nazism. Saul Friedlander. 112p. 1986. pap. 3.95 o.p. (ISBN 0-380-70090-5, Discus). Avon.

Reflections of the Past. Montana Ghost Town Preservation Society Staff. 136p. (Orig.). 1984. pap. 11.95 o.p. (ISBN 0-934318-39-5). Falcon Pr MT.

Reflections of the Spirit. Andy Kast. LC 84-90246. 59p. 1985. 6.95 o.p. (ISBN 0-533-06291-8). Vantage.

Reflections on a Century of United States-Korean Relations. Academy of Korean Studies, Wilson Center Staff. LC 83-3644. (Illus.). 382p. (Orig.). 1983. lib. bdg. 39.50 o.p. (ISBN 0-8191-3109-1); pap. text ed. 20.75 o.p. (ISBN 0-8191-3110-5). U Pr of Amer.

Reflections on Africa. Grace L. Chavis. LC 74-21438. 1975. 4.00 o.p. (ISBN 0-682-48127-0, Banner). Exposition-Phoenix.

Reflections on Economic Development & Social Change. Hanumantha Rao et al. 1979. 22.50x o.p. (ISBN 0-8364-0522-6). South Asia Bks.

Reflections on Equestrian Art. Nuno Oliveira. Tr. by Phyllis Fields from Port. (Illus.). 12.25 o.p. (ISBN 0-85131-257-8, Pub. by J A Allen U K). S R Smith Sporting Bks.

Reflections on Espionage. John Hollander. LC 75-338260. 1976. 8.95 o.p. (ISBN 0-689-10704-8, Atheneum). Macmillan.

Reflections on International Administration. Alexander Loveday. LC 74-9168. 334p. 1974. Repr. of 1956 ed. lib. bdg. 35.00x o.p. (ISBN 0-8371-7618-2, LOIA). Greenwood.

Reflections on Man: Readings in Philosophical Psychology from Classical Philosophy to Existentialism. Jesse A. Mann & Gerald F. Kreyche. (Harbrace Ser. in Philosophy). 1966. text ed. 17.95 o.p. (ISBN 0-15-576448-9, HC). HarBraceJ.

Reflections on Samson. Lou Lipsitz. (Illus.). 1977. pap. 5.00 o.p. (ISBN 0-87711-071-9). Story Line.

Reflections on the Brazilian Counterrevolution. Florestan Fernandes. Pref. by Warren Dean. Tr. by Michel Vale & Patrick M. Hughes. LC 80-5456. 200p. 1981. 35.00 o.p. (ISBN 0-87332-177-4). M E Sharpe.

Reflections on the Christ. David Spangler. 138p. 1981. pap. 10.95 o.p. (ISBN 0-905249-52-6). Lorian Pr.

Reflections on the Creed. Daniel Overduin. 1980. pap. 0.75 o.p. (ISBN 0-570-03814-6, 12-2782). Concordia.

Reflections on the Lord's Prayer. Daniel Overduin. 1980. pap. 0.75 o.p. (ISBN 0-570-03815-4, 12-2783). Concordia.

Reflections on the Nature of Leadership. Page Smith. (Fourth George Clark Lecture February 25, 1979 Ser.). (Illus.). 52p. 1985. Repr. of 1982 ed. lib. bdg. 12.75 o.p. (ISBN 0-8191-4870-9, Society of Cincinnati). U Pr of Amer.

Reflections on the Organ Stoplist: Theory & Practice from the Organ Workshop. Hans G. Klais. Tr. by Homer D. Blanchard from Ger. (Illus.). 1975. 17.50 o.p. (ISBN 0-930112-00-8). Organ Lit.

Reflections on the Path. Herbert B. Puryear. (Illus.). 183p. (Orig.). 1979. pap. 3.50 o.p. (ISBN 0-87604-113-6). ARE Pr.

Reflections on the Sacraments. Daniel Overduin. 1980. pap. 0.75 o.p. (ISBN 0-570-03816-2, 12-2784). Concordia.

Reflections on the Ten Commandments. Daniel Overduin. 1980. pap. 0.75 o.p. (ISBN 0-570-03813-8, 12-2781). Concordia.

Reflections with Dream Songs & Other Tales. Wesley L. Apker. 80p. 1982. 6.00 o.p. (ISBN 0-682-49798-3). Exposition-Phoenix.

Reflector Antenna Analysis & Design. P. J. Wood. (IEE Electromagnetic-Waves Series: No. 7). 256p. 1986. Repr. of 1980 ed. 50.00 o.p. (ISBN 0-906048-21-4, EWR07). Inst Elect Eng.

Reflector Antennas. Ed. by A. W. Love. LC 77-94519. 427p. 1978. 47.95x o.p. (ISBN 0-471-04605-1); pap. 31.50x o.p. (ISBN 0-471-04606-X). Wiley.

Reflex Action. Christopher Fitzsimons. LC 79-55615. 1980. 10.95 o.p. (ISBN 0-689-11036-7, Atheneum). Macmillan.

Reflex for the MAC: Database Design & Applications. Mary Johnson. (Illus.). 368p. 1987. pap. 19.95 o.p. (ISBN 0-8306-2901-7, 2901). TAB Bks.

Reflexes & Motor Integration: Sherrington's Concept of Integrative Action. Judith P. Swazey. LC 69-13768. (Monographs in the History of Science Ser). 1969. 18.50x o.s.i. (ISBN 0-674-75240-6). Harvard U Pr.

Reform & Intellectual Debate in Victorian England, 1830-1880. David Skilton & Barbara Dennis. (Volume in the World & Word Ser.). 256p. 1986. 31.00 o.p. (ISBN 0-7099-2375-9, Pub. by Croom Helm UK); pap. 17.00 o.p. (ISBN 0-7099-3315-0, Pub. by Croom Helm UK). Routledge Chapman & Hall.

Reform & Organizational Survival. Ronald G. Corwin. LC 72-10367. 496p. 1973. 29.50 o.p. (ISBN 0-471-17519-6, Pub. by Wiley). Krieger.

Reform of Industrial Relations. Ed. by Hugh M. Pollock. (Issues in Industrial Relations Ser.). 100p. 1982. 14.95 o.p. (ISBN 0-86278-026-8, Pub. by O'Brien Pr Ireland); pap. 7.95 o.p. (ISBN 0-86278-027-6, Pub. by O'Brien Pr Ireland). Irish Bks Media.

Reform of International Institutions. C. Fred Bergsten et al. (Triangle Papers: No. 11). 1978. 15.00 o.s.i. (ISBN 0-318-02786-0); pap. 6.00 o.s.i. (ISBN 0-318-02787-9). Trilateral Comm.

Reform of International Institutions see Trilateral Commission Task Force Reports.

Reform of Teacher Education in the U. K. James Lynch. 211p. 1979. pap. 24.00x o.p. (ISBN 0-900868-68-6, Open Univ Pr). Taylor & Francis.

Reformation: A Picture Story of Martin Luther. Dietrich Steinwede. Tr. by Edward A. Cooperrider from Ger. LC 82-49055. (Illus.). 56p. 1983. pap. 0.95 o.p. (ISBN 0-8006-1710-X, 1-1710, Fortress). Augsburg Fortress.

Reformation & Catholicity. Gustaf E. Aulen. Tr. by Eric H. Wahlstrom from Swedish. LC 78-25981. 1979. Repr. of 1961 ed. lib. bdg. 35.00x o.p. (ISBN 0-313-20809-3, AURC). Greenwood.

Reformation & the Irish Episcopate. 2nd ed. Hugh J. Lawlor. (Church Historical Society, London, Ser.: No. 11). Repr. of 1932 ed. 20.00 o.p. (ISBN 0-8115-3135-X). Kraus Repr.

Reformation Essays. James P. Whitney. (Church Historical Society London N. S. Ser.: No. 38). Repr. of 1939 ed. 40.00 o.p. (ISBN 0-8115-3161-9). Kraus Repr.

Reformation in Poland, Some Social & Economic Aspects. Paul Fox. LC 71-104272. 1971. Repr. of 1924 ed. lib. bdg. 35.00x o.p. (ISBN 0-8371-3924-4, FORP). Greenwood.

Reformation, Then & Now. Charles S. Anderson. (Orig.). 1966. pap. 1.75 o.p. (ISBN 0-8066-9353-3, 10-5462, Augsburg). Augsburg Fortress.

Reformer's Art: Dickens' Picturesque & Grotesque Imagery. Nancy K. Hill. LC 80-23256. (Illus.). xii, 169p. 1981. text ed. 16.95x o.p. (ISBN 0-8214-0586-1); pap. 8.50x o.p. (ISBN 0-8214-0613-2). Ohio U Pr.

Reformers in India, 1793-1833: An Account of the Work of Christian Missionaries on Behalf of Social Reform. Kenneth Ingham. LC 73-16425. xi, 150p. 1973. Repr. of 1956 ed. lib. bdg. 17.00x o.p. (ISBN 0-374-94112-2, Octagon). Hippocrene Bks.

Reformers in the Wings. David C. Steinmetz. (Twin Brooks Ser.). 240p. 1981. pap. 7.95 o.p. (ISBN 0-8010-8208-0). Baker Bk.

Reforming Metropolitan Governments: A Bibliography. Anthony G. White. LC 75-7832. (Garland Ref. Lib. of Humanities). 1979. lib. bdg. 25.00 o.p. (ISBN 0-8240-9994-X). Garland Pub.

Reforming the Long-Term-Care System: Financial & Organizational Options. Ed. by James J. Callahan, Jr. & Stanley S. Wallack. LC 80-8366. (University Health Policy Consortium Ser.). 272p. 1981. pap. 18.00x o.p. (ISBN 0-669-05547-6). Lexington Bks.

Refractory Transition Metal Compounds: High Temperature Cermets. Ed. by G. V. Samsonov. 1964. 61.50 o.p. (ISBN 0-12-617550-0). Acad Pr.

Refrigeration & Air Conditioning. Air Conditioning & Refrigeration Institute Staff. (Illus.). 1979. 37.33 o.p. (ISBN 0-13-770164-0). P-H.

Refrigeration & Air Conditioning. W. F. Stoecker. (Mechanical Engineer's License Examination Library). 1958. text ed. 42.00 o.p. (ISBN 0-07-061615-9). McGraw.

Refrigeration & Air Conditioning. A. R. Trott. 304p. 1981. text ed. 44.50 o.p. (ISBN 0-07-084543-3). McGraw.

Refrigeration & Air Conditioning Technology: Concepts, Procedures & Troubleshooting Techniques. William Whitman & William Johnson. LC 86-16506. 960p. 1986. text ed. 34.95 o.p. (ISBN 0-8273-2416-2); instr's. guide 10.00 o.p. (ISBN 0-8273-3479-6). Delmar.

Refrigeration License Manual. 2nd ed. Sylvan Harfenist. LC 74-24888. (Illus.). 1975. pap. 12.00 o.p. (ISBN 0-668-02726-6). Arco.

Refrigeration on Fishing Vessels. 2nd ed. John Merritt. (Illus.). 164p. 1979. pap. 20.50 o.p. (ISBN 0-85238-095-X, FN24, Pub. by FNB). UNIPUB.

Refrigerator Perry & the Super Bowl Bears. Bill Gutman. (gr. 4 up). 1987. pap. 2.50 o.p. (ISBN 0-671-63127-6). Archway.

Refuge from Darkness: Wilfrid Israel & the Rescue of the Jews. Naomi Shepherd. LC 83-22000. 1984. 18.45 o.p. (ISBN 0-394-52503-5). Pantheon.

Refuge under the Boot. Talvikki Manninen. 233p. 1985. 12.95 o.p. (ISBN 0-533-06515-1). Vantage.

Refugees: Viewpoints, Case Studies & Theoretical Considerations on the Care & Management of Refugees. F. Souza. (Illus.). 136p. 1980. pap. 23.00 o.p. (ISBN 0-08-025460-8). Pergamon.

Refugee's Vision. James A. Miehl, Jr. 1977. 4.00 o.p. (ISBN 0-682-48944-1). Exposition-Phoenix.

Refuse Recycling & Recovery: A Review of the State of the Art. John R. Holmes. LC 80-42145. (Institution of Environmental Sciences Ser.). 200p. 1981. 59.95 o.p. (ISBN 0-471-27902-1); pap. 34.95x o.p. (ISBN 0-471-27903-X). Wiley.

Refusenik: Trapped in the Soviet Union. Mark Y. Azbel. Ed. by Grace P. Forbes. (Illus.). 528p. 1981. 17.95 o.p. (ISBN 0-395-30226-9). HM.

Refutation of the 'Apology for Actors' see Apology for Actors.

Regain: Roman. Jean Giono. (Coll. Soleil). (Fr). 1958. 13.25 o.p. (ISBN 0-685-11524-0). French & Eur.

Regard the Lilies, Regard the Blood: Poems to the Blessed Virgin. John Hart. 79p. 1983. pap. 6.00 o.s.i. (ISBN 0-682-49941-2). Exposition-Phoenix.

Regards sur le Monde Actuel. Paul Valery. (Coll. Soleil). 9.95 o.p. (ISBN 0-685-36624-3). Schoenhof.

Regards to the Man in the Moon. Ezra J. Keats. LC 85-47781. (Illus.). 32p. (gr. k-3). 1985. pap. 4.95 o.s.i. (ISBN 0-02-044130-4, Collier). Macmillan.

Regatta. Douglas Wallop. 1981. 12.95 o.p. (ISBN 0-393-01364-2). PB.

Regeln und Sprache Des Sports, Vol. 1. Mannheim. (Ger.). 7.95 o.p. (ISBN 3-411-01361-3, M-7600, Pub. by Bibliographisches Inst.). French & Eur.

Regency International Directory of Private Investigators, Private Detectives & Debt Collection Agencies, 1985-86. 19th ed. 1985. 51.00 o.p. Intl Pubns Serv.

Regency Lady's Faery Bower. Amelia J. Murray. 14.95 o.p. (ISBN 0-03-006109-1). H Holt & Co.

Regency Style - Eighteen Hundred to Eighteen Thirty. Donald Pilcher. LC 48-7660. 120p. 1947. Repr. 29.00x o.p. (ISBN 0-403-07233-6). Somerset Pub.

Regenerating the Inner City. David Donnison & Alan Middleton. 304p. 1987. (ISBN 0-7102-1116-3, Pub. by Routledge UK); pap. (ISBN 0-7102-1117-1). Routledge Chapman & Hall.

Regeneration. S. A. Weltmer. 44p. 1959. pap. 7.95 o.s.i. (ISBN 0-88697-022-9). Life Science.

Regeneration in Lower Vertebrates & Invertebrates, 3 vols, Vol. 1. James E. Turner et al. LC 72-8249. 1973. 24.50x o.p. (ISBN 0-8422-7046-9). Irvington.

Regeneration in Lower Vertebrates & Invertebrates, 3 vols, Vol. 2. Margaret Egar et al. LC 72-8249. 1973. 24.50x o.p. (ISBN 0-8422-7051-5). Irvington.

Regeneration in Lower Vertebrates & Invertebrates, 3 vols, Vol. 3. Victor Eichler et al. LC 72-8249. 1972. 24.50x o.p. (ISBN 0-8422-7052-3). Irvington.

Regeneration of Selected Tropical Tree Species in Corcovado National Park, Costa Rica. Stanley R. Herwitz. (U.C. Publications in Geography: Vol. 24). 1981. pap. 15.00x o.p. (ISBN 0-520-09631-2). U of Cal Pr.

Regents Competency Tests. Adrienne Forbes & Gloria Debease. LC 80-14348. 250p. (Orig.). 1980. pap. 6.95 o.p. (ISBN 0-668-04815-8, 4815-8). Arco.

Regents Illustrated Classics Series. rev. ed. Ed. by Elaine Kirn. 1982. pap. text ed. 2.25 o.p. (ISBN 0-686-95094-1); 3.95 o.p. (ISBN 0-686-99463-9). Prentice ESL.

Reggae Bloodlines. Stephen Davis & Peter Simon. LC 76-42428. (Illus.). 1977. pap. 10.95 o.s.i. (ISBN 0-385-12330-2, Anch). Doubleday.

Reggie. Reggie Jackson & Mike Lupica. 1985. pap. 3.95 o.s.i. (ISBN 0-345-31216-3). Ballantine.

Reggie Jackson Story. Bill Libby. LC 79-684. (Illus.). (gr. 5 up). 1979. 11.75 o.p. (ISBN 0-688-41889-9). Lothrop.

Regimental Steins. John L. Harrell. (Illus.). 250p. 25.00 o.p. (ISBN 0-317-55241-4). Johnson Ref Bks.

Regina. Leslie Epstein. 288p. 1982. 13.95 o.p. (ISBN 0-698-11203-2, Coward). Putnam Pub Group.

Regina. Leslie Epstein. 256p. 1984. pap. 3.95 o.p. (ISBN 0-380-65540-3, 65540, Bard). Avon.

Reginald Marsh's New York: Paintings, Drawings, Prints & Photographs. Marilyn Cohen. 1984. 18.25 o.p. Peter Smith.

Region, Class & Gender: A European Comparison. P. Cooke. (Illus.). 62p. 1984. pap. 22.00 o.p. (ISBN 0-08-032303-0). Pergamon.

Regional Bus Transportation: Five Reports. (Transportation Research Record Ser.). 58p. 1975. 2.60 o.p. (ISBN 0-309-02451-X). Transport Res Bd.

Regional Compendium of Fisheries Legislation: West Africa (CECAR Region) Norway Funds-in-Trust. (Legislative Studies: No. 27). 530p. (Eng. & Fr.). 1983. pap. text ed. 35.75 o.p. (ISBN 92-5-001307-8, F2434, FAO). UNIPUB.

Regional Cooking of China. Margaret Gin & Alfred Castle. LC 75-15674. (Illus.). 192p. 1975. pap. 5.95 o.p. (ISBN 0-912238-63-1, One Hund One Prods). Ortho.

Regional Costumes of the Netherlands. V. Bing & J. Braet Von Uberfeldt. (Illus.). 1978. 75.00 o.p. (ISBN 0-88431-313-1). E J Brill USA.

Regional Cuisines of Greece. St. Paul's Greek Orthodox Church Women Staff. LC 79-6038. (Illus.). 256p. 1981. 19.95 o.p. (ISBN 0-385-15680-4). Doubleday.

Regional Cults, No. 16. R. P. Werbner. 1977. 55.50 o.p. (ISBN 0-12-744950-7). Acad Pr.

Regional Development at the International Level, Vol. II: African & Canadian Perspectives. Timothy M. Shaw & Yash Tandon. (Illus.). 288p. (Orig.). 1985. lib. bdg. 30.00 o.p. (ISBN 0-8191-4848-2); pap. text ed. 14.25 o.p. (ISBN 0-8191-4849-0). U Pr of Amer.

Regional Development at the International Level, Vol. I: Canadian & African Perspectives. Ed. by Timothy M. Shaw & Yash Tandon. (Illus.). 338p. (Orig.). 1985. lib. bdg. 31.00 o.p. (ISBN 0-8191-4850-4); pap. text ed. 15.25 o.p. (ISBN 0-8191-4851-2). U Pr of Amer.

Regional Development in Western Europe. 2nd ed. Ed. by Hugh D. Clout. LC 80-40852. 417p. 1981. 73.95x o.p. (ISBN 0-471-27846-7); pap. 36.00 o.p. (ISBN 0-471-27845-9). Wiley.

Regional Difference in America: A Statistical Sourcebook. Ed. by Alfred N. Garwood. 640p. 1988. lib. bdg. 47.50x o.p.; pap. 40.00x o.p. Numbers & Concepts.

Regional Dimensions of Industrial Policy. Ed. by Michael E. Bell & Paul S. Lande. LC 80-8994. 224p. 1981. 26.50x o.p. (ISBN 0-669-04491-1). Lexington Bks.

Regional Directory of Minority & Women-Owned Business Firms: North Central Region. Ed. by Pamela G. Osbourne. 250p. 1988. 95.00 o.s.i. (ISBN 0-933527-16-0). Business Research.

Regional Directory of Minority & Women-Owned Business Firms: Southeastern Region. Pamela G. Osbourne. 150p. 1988. 95.00 o.s.i. (ISBN 0-933527-13-6). Business Research.

Regional Directory of Minority & Women-Owned Business Firms: Western Region. Ed. by Pamela G. Osbourne. 300p. 1988. 95.00 o.s.i. (ISBN 0-933527-17-9). Business Research.

Regional Diversity of Political Values: Idaho Political Culture. Robert H. Blank. LC 78-62742. 1978. pap. text ed. 11.00 o.p. (ISBN 0-8191-0590-2). U Pr of Amer.

Regional Economic Cooperation in South Asia. M. R. Aggarwal. 176p. 1979. text ed. 22.00x o.p. Coronet Bks.

Regional Geography: Global Patterns. Pontius-Woodward. 208p. 1985. pap. text ed. 13.95 o.p. (ISBN 0-8403-3768-X). Kendall-Hunt.

Regional History of the Railways of Great Britain: North & Mid Wales, Vol. 11. Peter E. Baughan. LC 79-56255. (Illus.). 208p. 1980. 24.95 o.p. (ISBN 0-7153-7850-3). David & Charles.

Regional History of the Railways of Great Britain: The North East, Vol. 4. K. Hoole. (Illus.). 260p. 1986. 32.95 o.p. (ISBN 0-946537-31-3). David & Charles.

Regional History of the Railways of Great Britain, Vol. 13: Thames & Severn. R. Christiansen. LC 80-68696. (Illus.). 224p. 1981. 32.95 o.p. (ISBN 0-7153-8004-4). David & Charles.

Regional History of the Railways of Great Britain: Vol. 14: The Lake Counties. David Joy. (Illus.). 240p. 1983. 32.95 o.p. (ISBN 0-946537-02-X). David & Charles.

Regional History of the Railways of Great Britain, Vol. 8: South & West Yorkshire. David Joy. (Regional Histories of the Railways of Great Britain Ser.). (Illus.). 304p. 1984. 29.95 o.p. (ISBN 0-946537-11-9). David & Charles.

Regional Housing Assistance Allocations & Regional Housing Needs. John Goodman, Jr. 50p. 1979. pap. text ed. 6.00 o.p. (ISBN 0-87766-263-0). Urban Inst.

Regional Imagination: The South & Recent American History. Dewey W Grantham. LC 78-26556. 1979. 15.95x o.p. (ISBN 0-8265-1207-0). Vanderbilt U Pr.

Regional Impacts of Resource Developments. Ed. by Chris Kissling et al. 285p. 1984. 24.95 o.p. (ISBN 0-949614-08-4, Pub. by Croom Helm Ltd). Routledge Chapman & Hall.

Regional Integration: Theory & Research. Ed. by Leon N. Lindberg & Stuart A. Scheingold. LC 77-139717. (Illus.). 1970. 29.50x o.s.i. (ISBN 0-674-75326-7); pap. 8.95x o.s.i. (ISBN 0-674-75327-5). Harvard U Pr.

Regional Mobility & Resource Development in West Africa. Akin L. Mabogunje. (Keith Callard Lectures Ser.). 160p. 1972. 5.00 o.p. (ISBN 0-7735-0120-7, McGill Canada); pap. 2.50 o.p. (ISBN 0-7735-0129-0, McGill Canada). U of Toronto Pr.

Regional National Econometric Modeling with an Application to the Italian Economy. Ed. by Murray Brown et al. 204p. 1978. 24.00x o.p. (ISBN 0-85086-064-4, NO. 2932, Pub. by Pion England). Routledge Chapman & Hall.

Regional Nuclear Fuel Cycle Centeis: Vol. 1, Sintesis del Informe sobre el Proyecto de Estudio del OIEA (1977) (Illus.). 135p. 1977. pap. 17.25 o.p. (ISP445-1, IAEA). UNIPUB.

Regional Patterns of Intercensal & Lifetime Migration in Sri Lanka. Dayalal Abeyesekera. LC 81-12540. (Papers of the East-West Population Institute: No. 75). v, 46p. (Orig.). 1981. pap. text ed. 1.25 o.p. (ISBN 0-86638-016-7). EW Ctr HI.

Regional Planning in Europe. Ed. by R. Hudson & J. Lewis. 1982. pap. 17.95x o.p. (ISBN 0-85086-097-0, 8008, Pub. by Pion Ltd.). Routledge Chapman & Hall.

Regional Restructuring under Advanced Capitalism. Ed. by Philip O'Keefe. (Geography & Environment Ser.). 134p. 1984. 26.00 o.p. (ISBN 0-7099-1943-3, Pub. by Croom Helm Ltd). Routledge Chapman & Hall.

Regional Science: New Concepts & Old Problems. E. L. Cripps. (London Papers in Regional Science). 210p. 1980. pap. text ed. 15.50x o.p. (ISBN 0-85086-048-2, ?NO. 2958, Pub. by Pion England). Routledge Chapman & Hall.

Regional Statistics: A Guide to Information Sources. Ed. by M. Balachandran. LC 80-14260. (Economics Information Guide Ser.: Vol. 13). 272p. 1980. 68.00x o.p. (ISBN 0-8103-1463-0). Gale.

Regional Studies for Planning & Projection: The Siberian Experience. A. G. Aganbegyan. (Regional Planning Ser.: No. 7). 1979. text ed. 46.25 o.p. (ISBN 90-279-7888-3). Mouton.

Regional Systems: IGU Congress, Moscow, 1976, Proceedings, Pt. 2. Ed. by Yuri Medvedkov. 1977. pap. 23.00 o.p. (ISBN 0-08-021323-5). Pergamon.

Regional Wage Inflation & Unemployment. Ed. by R. L. Martin. 235p. 1981. 25.00x o.p. (ISBN 0-85086-090-3, NO. 8003, Pub. by Pion England). Routledge Chapman & Hall.

Register of International Rivers. United Nations Centre for Natural Resources, Energy & Transport Staff. 1978. 51.00 o.p. (ISBN 0-08-022408-3); 29.00 o.p. (ISBN 0-08-023411-9). Pergamon.

Registered As Disabled. Sally Sainsbury. 205p. 1970. pap. text ed. 6.25x o.p. (ISBN 0-7135-1619-4, Pub. by Bedford England). Gower Pub Co.

Registration & the Military Selective Service Act. 3.50 o.p. Natl Lawyers Guild.

Registry of California Wineries. Leslie K. Brown. (Illus.). 352p. (Orig.). 1988. pap. 14.95 o.p. Colwyn Corp.

Registry of Toxic Effects of Chemical Substances, 1983-84 Cumulative Supplement to the 1981-82 Edition, 2 vols. 13th ed. Ed. by Richard L. Lewis & Doris Sweet. 2112p. 1985. pap. 27.00 o.p. (ISBN 0-318-20138-0, S/N 017-033-00421-8). USGPO.

Regrets Only. Sally Quinn. 525p. 1986. 18.45 o.s.i. (ISBN 0-671-24973-8). S&S.

Regular & Related Solutions: The Solubility of Gases, Liquids & Solids. Joel Hildebrand et al. LC 79-122670. 238p. Repr. of 1970 ed. 19.50 o.p. (ISBN 0-442-15665-0, (JW), VN). Krieger.

Regulars. Stephen Lewis. (Orig.). 1980. pap. 2.50 o.p. (ISBN 0-8439-0735-5, Pub. by Leisure Bks CT). Dorchester Pub Co.

Regulation D Offerings of Limited Partnerships & Corporate Capital Raising: At the Commission & in Practice: ALI-ABA Course of Study Materials. United States Securities & Exchange Commission & Federal Bar Association, Securities Law Committee. LC 85-107864. (Illus.). o.p. Am Law Inst.

Regulation of Aldosterone Biosynthesis. J. Mueller. LC 73-137143. (Monographs on Endocrinology: Vol. 5). (Illus.). 1971. 26.00 o.p. (ISBN 0-387-05213-5). Springer-Verlag.

Regulation of Broadcasting: 1983 Supplement. Douglas H. Ginsburg & Mark D. Director. (American Casebook Ser.). 182p. 1983. pap. text ed. 5.95 o.p. (ISBN 0-314-75957-3). West Pub.

Regulation of Brokers, Dealers & Securities Markets. Nicholas Wolfson & Richard M. Phillips. (Securities Law Ser.). 1977. Cumulative Suppls., annual. 97.50 o.p. (ISBN 0-88262-133-5, 77-23761); 48.00 o.p. Warren Gorham & Lamont.

Regulation of Cell Metabolism: Organizational & Pharmacological Aspects on the Molecular Level. Ed. by Enrico Mihich. 382p. 1971. 84.00 o.p. (ISBN 0-12-495760-9). Acad Pr.

Regulation of Corporate Political Activity. 2nd ed. Frazer F. Hilder & Thomas W. Watkins. LC 83-15321. (Corporate Practice Ser.: No. 16). 1983. 92.00 o.p. BNA.

Regulation of Fluid & Electrolyte Balance: A Programmed Instruction in Clinical Physiology. 2nd ed. Gretchen M. Reed & Vincent F. Sheppard. LC 76-20109. (Illus.). 1977. pap. text ed. (ISBN 0-7216-7513-1). Saunders.

Regulation of Gluconeogenesis. Ed. by H. D. Soling & B. Willms. 1971. 29.50 o.p. (ISBN 0-12-654350-X). Acad Pr.

Regulation of Macromolecular Synthesis by Low Molecular Weight Mediators. Ed. by Gerhard Koch & Dietmar Richter. LC 79-26279. 1979. 42.50 o.p. (ISBN 0-12-417580-5). Acad Pr.

Regulation of Metabolism. E. A. Newsholme & C. Start. LC 72-5721. 349p. 1973. text ed. 54.95x o.p. (ISBN 0-471-63530-8, Pub. by Wiley-Interscience); pap. 41.95x o.p. (ISBN 0-471-63531-6). Wiley.

Regulation of Parasite Populations. Ed. by Gerald W. Esch & Brent B. Nikol. 1977. 56.00 o.p. (ISBN 0-12-241750-X). Acad Pr.

Regulation of Phosphate & Mineral Metabolism. Ed. by Shaul G. Massry et al. LC 82-7602. (Advances In Experimental Medicine & Biology Ser.: Vol. 151). 720p. 1982. 110.00x o.p. (ISBN 0-306-41020-6, Plenum Pr). Plenum Pub.

Regulation of Secondary Product & Plant Hormone Metabolism: Proceedings of the 12th FEBS Meeting, Dresden, 1978. Ed. by K. Schreiber & M. Luckner. (Federation of European Biochemical Society Ser.: Vol. 55). (Illus.). 1979. 87.00 o.p. (ISBN 0-08-023179-9). Pergamon.

Regulation: Process & Politics. Congressional Quarterly, Inc. Staff. LC 82-14292. 184p. 1982. pap. 9.95 o.p. (ISBN 0-87187-243-9). Congr Quarterly.

Regulation, Service Quality, & Market Performance: A Model of Airline Rivalry. John C. Panzar. LC 78-75053. (Outstanding Dissertations in Economics Ser.). 1979. lib. bdg. 20.00 o.p. (ISBN 0-8240-4131-3). Garland Pub.

Regulation V. Compensation in Land Use Control: A Recommended Accommodation, a Critique, & an Interpretation. John J. Costonis et al. LC 77-5939. 1977. pap. 4.50x o.p. (ISBN 0-87772-226-9). UCB IGS.

Regulations Affecting International Banking Operations in Belgium-Luxembourg, France, Germany, the Netherlands, Sweden, Switzerland & the United Kingdom 1980-1981. OECD Staff. 149p. (Orig.). 1981. pap. 9.50x o.p. (ISBN 92-64-12196-X). OECD.

Regulations for Electrical Installations: 15th Edition of the IEE Wiring Regulations. 260p. 1986. pap. 70.00 casebound o.p. (ISBN 0-85296-324-6, WR004). Inst Elect Eng.

Regulatory Aspects of Carcinogenesis & Food Additives: The Delaney Clause. Ed. by Frederick Coulston. (Ecotoxicology & Environmental Quality Ser.). 1979. 64.00 o.p. (ISBN 0-12-192750-4). Acad Pr.

Regulatory Change in an Atmosphere of Crisis: Current Implications of the Roosevelt Years. Ed. by Gary M. Walton. LC 79-23164. 1979. 30.50 o.p. (ISBN 0-12-733950-7). Acad Pr.

Regulatory Control & Standardization of Allergenic Extracts. H. D. Brede & E. A. Stevens. 356p. 1985. pap. 42.00 o.p. (ISBN 0-89574-217-9, Pub. by Gustav Fischer Verlag). VCH Pubs.

Regulatory Environment for Science: A Techical Memorandum. LC 85-600503. (OTA-TM-SET Ser.: No. 34). (Illus.). 154p. (Orig.). 1986. pap. 6.00 o.p. (ISBN 0-318-19921-1, S/N 052-003-01024-1). USGPO.

Regulatory Functions of the CNS - Motion & Organization Principles: Proceedings of the 28th International Congress of Physiological Sciences, Budapest, 1980. J. Szentagothai et al. LC 80-4188. (Advances in Physiological Sciences: Vol. 1). (Illus.). 300p. 1981. 50.00 o.p. (ISBN 0-08-026814-5). Pergamon.

Regulatory Functions of the CNS Subsystems: Proceedings of the 28th International Congress of Physiological Sciences, Budapest, 1980. J. Szentagothai et al. LC 80-41884. (Advances in Physiological Sciences: Vol. 2). (Illus.). 293p. 1981. 50.00 o.p. (ISBN 0-08-027371-8). Pergamon.

Regulatory Genetics of the Immune System. Ed. by Eli Sercarz. 1977. 71.50 o.p. (ISBN 0-12-637160-1). Acad Pr.

Regulatory Mechanism in Lymphocyte Activation. Ed. by D. O. Lucas. 1977. 91.00 o.p. (ISBN 0-12-458050-5). Acad Pr.

Regulatory Mechanisms for Protein Synthesis in Mammalian Cells. Ed. by Anthony San Pietro et al. 1968. 71.50 o.p. (ISBN 0-12-618960-9). Acad Pr.

Regulatory Mechanisms of Synaptic Transmission. Ed. by R. Tapia & C. W. Cotman. 430p. 1981. 69.50x o.p. (ISBN 0-306-40740-X, Plenum Pr). Plenum Pub.

Regulatory Peptides in Digestive, Nervous & Endocrine Systems: Proceedings of the International Symposium on Regulatory Peptides, Mode of Action on Digestive, Nervous & Endocrine Systems held in Gouvieux-Chantilly, France, 9-11 May. 1985. Ed. by M. Lewin & S. Bonfils. (INSERM Symposium Ser.: No. 25). 434p. 1985. 131.75 o.p. (ISBN 0-444-80717-9). Elsevier.

Regulatory Reform & Public Utilities. Ed. by Michael A. Crew. LC 81-47749. 288p. 1982. 31.50x o.p. (ISBN 0-669-04834-8). Lexington Bks.

Regulatory Reform since Nineteen Seventy-Seven: A Bibliographic Overview. Clarence E. Chisholm & Alva W. Stewart. (Public Administration Ser.: Bibliography P 1619). 1985. pap. 2.00 o.p. (ISBN 0-89028-289-7). Vance Biblios.

Regulatory Regimes in Conflict: Problems of Regulation in a Continental Perspective. Ed. by Fred Thompson. LC 84-17316. (Illus.). 170p. 1985. 25.50 o.p. (ISBN 0-8191-4269-7, Pub. by CN Stud Pro Inst); pap. 12.25 o.p. (ISBN 0-8191-4270-0, Pub. by CN Stud Pro Inst). U Pr of Amer.

Regulatory T Lymphocytes. Ed. by Benvenuto Pernis & Henry J. Vogel. (P & S Biomedical Science Ser.). 1980. 77.00 o.p. (ISBN 0-12-551860-9). Acad Pr.

Rehabilitating Historic Buildings. (Real Estate Law & Practice Ser.). 862p. 1983. 45.00 o.p. (ISBN 0-686-80164-4, N4-4414). PLI.

Rehabilitation Approaches to Drug & Alcohol Dependence. International Labour Office Staff & Behrouz Shahandeh. viii, 91p. (Orig.). 1985. pap. 8.95 o.p. (ISBN 92-2-100526-7). Intl Labour Office.

Rehabilitation Medicine & Psychiatry. Jack Meislin. (Illus.). 564p. 1976. 40.00 o.p. (ISBN 0-398-03432-X). C C Thomas.

Rehabilitation of Criminal Offenders: Problems & Prospects. National Research Council. 1979. pap. 15.25x o.p. (ISBN 0-309-02895-7). Natl Acad Pr.

Rehabilitation of Say's Law. W. H. Hutt. LC 74-82499. xiii, 150p. 1974. 10.95x o.p. (ISBN 0-8214-0164-5). Ohio U Pr.

Rehabilitation of the Coronary Patient. 2nd ed. Nanette K. Wenger & Herman K. Hellerstein. LC 83-14664. 563p. 1984. 39.50x o.p. (ISBN 0-471-86330-0). Wiley.

Rehabilitation of the Hand. 4th rev. ed. C. B. Wynn-Parry. LC 80-41761. (Illus.). 1981. text ed. 120.00 o.p. (ISBN 0-407-38503-7). Butterworth.

Rehabilitation of the Head Injured Adult. Mitchell Rosenthal et al. LC 82-23504. 454p. 1983. 45.00 o.p. (ISBN 0-8036-7625-5). Davis Co.

Rehabilitation of the Severely Mentally Retarded Trainable Child. Edna Earle Heyward. 1978. 10.00 o.p. (ISBN 0-682-49044-X). Exposition-Phoenix.

Rehabilitation of the War Injured. Doherty. (ISBN 0-8022-0408-2). Philos Lib.

Rehabilitation Technology Sourcebook. Alexandra Enders & Marion G. Hall. 300p. o.s.i. (ISBN 0-939957-12-4). Demos Pubns Inc.

Rehearsal for Disaster: The Boom & Collapse of 1919-1920. John D. Hicks. LC 61-12136. 1961. 4.00 o.p. (ISBN 0-8130-0110-2). U Presses Fla.

Rehearsal's Off! George Booth. (Illus.). 1977. pap. 3.95 o.p. (ISBN 0-380-01719-9, 60574-0). Avon.

Reich & Nation: The Holy Roman Empire As Idea & Reality, 1763-1806. John G. Gagliardo. LC 79-2170. 384p. 1980. 25.00x o.p. (ISBN 0-253-16773-6). Ind U Pr.

Reich: The March of the Second SS Panzer Division Through France. Max Hastings. LC 81-7208. (Illus.). 272p. 1982. 16.50 o.p. (ISBN 0-03-057059-X). H Holt & Co.

Reign of AntiChrist. R. Gerald Culleton. 1974. pap. 6.00 o.s.i. (ISBN 0-89555-047-4). TAN Bks Pubs.

Reign of Error: Psychiatry, Authority, & Law. Lee Coleman. LC 83-71943. 320p. 1985. 18.95x o.p. (ISBN 0-8070-0481-2); pap. 9.95 o.p. (ISBN 0-8070-0479-0, BP702). Beacon Pr.

Reign of Philip the Fair. Joseph R. Strayer. LC 79-3232. 1980. 48.00 o.p. (ISBN 0-691-05302-2); pap. 19.00 L.P.E. o.p. (ISBN 0-691-10089-6). Princeton U Pr.

Reign of the Fortunate King: Manuel First of Portugal. Elaine Sanceau. 184p. 1970. 21.50 o.p. (ISBN 0-208-00968-X, Archon). Shoe String.

Reigning Cats & Dogs. Sonia Levitin. LC 77-15811. 1978. 7.95 o.p. (ISBN 0-689-10868-0, Atheneum). Macmillan.

Reima Pietila: Architecture, Context & Modernism. Malcolm Quantrill. (Illus.). 248p. 1985. 45.00 o.p. (ISBN 0-8478-0636-7); pap. 29.95 o.p. (ISBN 0-8478-0635-9). Rizzoli Intl.

Reimarus: Fragments. Ed. by Charles H. Talbert & Leander E. Keck. Tr. by Ralph S. Fraser from Ger. LC 74-127527. (Lives of Jesus Ser.). 292p. 1970. pap. 2.00 o.p. (ISBN 0-8006-0152-1, 1-152, Fortress). Augsburg Fortress.

Reimos en Serio. Charles Whitehead et al. 132p. 1984. pap. 6.50 o.p. (ISBN 0-88334-179-4). Ind Sch Pr.

Reincarnation of Bridgett. Joseph F. Coscia. 139p. 1981. 6.00 o.p. (ISBN 0-682-49699-5). Exposition-Phoenix.

Reincarnation: The Best Short Stories of Cunninghame Graham. B. Cunninghame Graham. LC 79-28208. 160p. 1980. 8.95 o.p. (ISBN 0-89919-004-9). Ticknor & Fields.

Reindustrialization: Implications for Voc Ed. James A. Leach. 50p. 1982. 4.95 o.p. (ISBN 0-318-22187-X, IN233). Natl Ctr Res Voc Ed.

Reindustrialization of America. Business Week Magazine Staff. 1982. text ed. 23.50 o.p. (ISBN 0-07-009324-5). McGraw.

Reine Margot. Alexandre Dumas. 1973. 4.95 o.p. (ISBN 0-686-55833-2). Schoenhof.

Reine Morte. Henry de Montherlant. (Folio 12). 1972. 3.95 o.p. (ISBN 0-686-55530-9). Schoenhof.

Reinforced & Prestressed Concrete. 2nd. ed. F. Kong & R. Evans. 1980. pap. 27.95 o.p. (ISBN 0-442-30751-9). Van Nos Reinhold.

Reinforced Concrete Designer's Handbook. 9th ed. Charles E. Reynolds & James C. Steedman. (Viewpoint Ser.). 506p. 1981. text ed. 57.50x o.p. (ISBN 0-7210-1198-5, Pub. by C & CA London); pap. text ed. 45.00x o.p. (ISBN 0-7210-1199-3, Pub. by C & CA London). Scholium Intl.

Reinforced Concrete Detailer's Manual. Brian Boughton. 1979. pap. text ed. 14.75x o.p. (ISBN 0-258-97128-2, Pub. by Granada England). Gower Pub Co.

Reinforced Concrete Detailer's Manual. 3rd ed. Brian Boughton. 136p. 1979. pap. 20.00x o.p. (ISBN 0-246-11336-7, Pub. by Granada England). Sheridan.

Reinforced Concrete Fundamentals. 4th ed. Phil M. Ferguson. LC 78-21555. 724p. 1979. 49.00x o.p. (ISBN 0-471-01459-1). Wiley.

Reinforced Concrete Structures, 2 vols. V. Baikov & E. Sigalov. 664p. 1981. 14.50 o.p. (ISBN 0-8285-1975-7, Pub. by Mir Pubs USSR). Imported Pubns.

Reinforced Plastics Industry. 1982. 950.00 o.p. (ISBN 0-89336-267-0, P 055). BCC.

Reinforcement. Ed. by Jack Tapp. 1969. 79.50 o.p. (ISBN 0-12-683650-7). Acad Pr.

Reinhardt Schuhmann International Symposium on Innovative Technology & Reactor Design in Extraction Metallurgy. Ed. by D. R. Gaskell et al. (Illus.). 1065p. 1986. 95.00 o.p. (ISBN 0-87339-053-9). Minerals Metals.

Reinhold Niebuhr. Bob E. Patterson. LC 76-46783. (Makers of the Modern Theological Mind Series). 1977. 8.95 o.p. (ISBN 0-87680-508-X). Word Bks.

Reino de las Tinieblos. Dallas Witmer. (Span.). pap. 1.25 o.p. (ISBN 0-686-32331-9). Rod & Staff.

Reintegrating the Offender: Assessing the Impact of Community Corrections. John Hylton. LC 80-5730. 334p. 1981. lib. bdg. 30.75 o.p. (ISBN 0-8191-1387-5); pap. text ed. 15.25 o.p. (ISBN 0-8191-1388-3). U Pr of Amer.

Reinventing the Rhetorical Tradition. Ed. by Ariva Freedman & Ian Pringle. 197p. 1981. 13.25 o.p. (ISBN 0-8141-3987-6). NCTE.

Rejoice & Be Exceeding Glad. Mary Light. pap. 1.00 o.p. (ISBN 0-910924-60-0). Macalester.

Rejoice in Me: A Pocket Guide to Daily Spiritual Prayer. David Rossage. 256p. 1987. 7.95 o.p. (ISBN 0-89283-364-5). Servant.

Rejoicing Heart. Joyce M. Smith. 1979. pap. 2.95 o.p. (ISBN 0-8423-5418-2). Tyndale.

Rejoicing with Creation. Tom Malone. pap. 6.95 o.p. (ISBN 0-8042-1420-4, John Knox). Westminster John Knox.

Rejuvenation Strategy: A Medically Approved Fitness Program to Remove the Effects of Aging. Rene Cailliet & Leonard Gross. LC 86-11517. (Illus.). 304p. 1987. 16.95 o.s.i. (ISBN 0-385-19714-4). Doubleday.

Relais & Chateaux, 1988. 200p. (Orig.). 1988. pap. 6.95 o.p. (ISBN 0-317-66607-X). Hunter Pub NY.

Relapse & Recovery in Drug Abuse. Ed. by Frank M. Tims & Carl G. Leukefeld. (DHHS Publication ADM Ser.: No. 86-1473). 205p. 1986. pap. 6.00 o.p. (ISBN 0-318-21638-8, S/N 017-024-01302-1). USGPO.

Relate. Ed. by John C. Souter. 80p. pap. 4.95 o.p. Tyndale.

Relating to Readers in the 'Eighties. Clark, Martire & Bartolomeo, Inc. Staff. 54p. 6.00 o.p. Am News Pubs.

Relationship Between Disarmament & Development. (Disarmament Study Ser.: No. 5). 189p. 1982. pap. 14.00x o.p. Intl Pubns Serv.

Relationship of the Library to Instructional Systems. James Brown et al. Ed. by John T. Corrigan. (Catholic Library Association Studies in Librarianship: No. 2). 1978. pap. 3.00 o.p. (ISBN 0-87507-006-X). Cath Lib Assn.

Relationships Between Physiographic Units & Highway Design Factors. 161p. 1972. 7.20 o.p. Transport Res Bd.

Relative Analgesia in Dental Practice: Inhalation Analgesia & Sedation with Nitrous Oxide. 2nd ed. Harry Langa. LC 76-1223. (Illus.). 1976. text ed. write for info. o.p. (ISBN 0-7216-5621-8). Saunders.

Relative Values for Physicians. Relative Value Studies, Inc. Staff. 368p. 1984. text ed. 75.00 o.p. (ISBN 0-07-073964-1). McGraw.

Relatives. David Plante. (Orig.). 1974. pap. 3.45 o.p. (ISBN 0-380-00103-9, 20685). Avon.

Relativistic Propagation of Light. Wallace Kantor. 1976. 10.00x o.p. (ISBN 0-87291-084-9); pap. 6.95x o.p. (ISBN 0-685-74222-9). Coronado Pr.

Relativistic Thermodynamics, Vol. 1. Richard A. Weiss. LC 76-20068. 1976. 10.00 o.p. (ISBN 0-682-48532-2, University). Exposition-Phoenix.

Relativistic Thermodynamics, Vol. 2. Richard A. Weiss. 1976. 11.00 o.p. (ISBN 0-682-48617-5, University). Exposition-Phoenix.

Relativity & Reality. E. G. Barter. 140p. 1953. (ISBN 0-8022-0071-0). Philos Lib.

Relativity in Man & Society. Arthur F. Bentley. 1967. lib. bdg. 26.00 o.p. (ISBN 0-374-90589-4, Octagon). Hippocrene Bks.

Relativity Reexamined. Leon Brillouin. 1970. 30.50 o.p. (ISBN 0-12-134945-4). Acad Pr.

Relaxation Dynamics: Nine World Approaches to Self-Relaxation. Jonathan C. Smith. LC 85-61470. 350p. (Orig.). 1985. pap. text ed. 18.95 o.p. (ISBN 0-87822-244-8). Res Press.

Relaxation in Magnetic Resonance: Dielectric & Mossbauer Applications. Charles P. Poole et al. 1971. 84.00 o.p. (ISBN 0-12-561450-0). Acad Pr.

Relaxation in Shock Waves. Y. V. Stupochenko et al. Tr. by R. Shao-Lin Lee. LC 67-21459. (Applied Physics & Engineering Ser.: Vol. 1). (Illus.). 1967. 61.60 o.p. (ISBN 0-387-03727-6). Springer-Verlag.

Relaxation of Elementary Excitations: Proceedings. Ed. by S. R. Kubo & E. E. Hanamura. (Springer Ser. in Solid-State Sciences: Vol. 18). (Illus.). 285p. 1980. 48.00 o.p. (ISBN 0-387-10129-2). Springer-Verlag.

Relaxed Body Book: A High-Energy Anti-Tension Program. American Health Magazine Editors et al. Ed. by Daniel Coleman. LC 85-20609. (Illus.). 256p. 1986. pap. 19.95 o.p. (ISBN 0-385-19983-X); pap. 12.95 o.p. (ISBN 0-385-19984-8). Doubleday.

Release of Catecholamines from Adrenergic Neurons. new ed. Ed. by David M. Paton. 1979. 93.00 o.p. (ISBN 0-08-021536-X); pap. 39.00 o.p. (ISBN 0-08-023755-X). Pergamon.

Releasing the Potential of the Older Volunteer. Ed. by Mary M. Seguin & Beatrice O'Brien. (Andrus Gerontology Center Bk.). (Illus.). 96p. 1976. pap. 7.00x o.p. (ISBN 0-317-06886-5, 05749-5). Lexington Bks.

Relevance of Education. Jerome S. Bruner. LC 74-139376. 192p. 1971. 5.95x o.p. (ISBN 0-393-04334-7, Norton Lib.); pap. 4.95x o.p. (ISBN 0-393-00690-5, Norton Lib). Norton.

Relevance of Parasitology to Human Welfare Today. Ed. by Angela E. Taylor & Ralph Muller. (Symposia of the British Society for Parasitology Ser.: Vol. 16). (Illus.). 144p. 1978. pap. 19.75 o.p. (ISBN 0-632-00422-3, B 4884-X, Blackwell). Mosby.

Relevance of Physics. Stanley L. Jaki. LC 66-20583. 1967. lib. bdg. 25.00x o.s.i. (ISBN 0-226-39143-4). U of Chicago Pr.

Relevance of the Old Testament for the Christian Faith: Biblical Theology & Interpretive Methodology. S. M. Mayo. 220p. (Orig.). 1982. lib. bdg. 29.25 o.p. (ISBN 0-8191-2656-X); pap. text ed. 13.25 o.p. (ISBN 0-8191-2657-8). U Pr of Amer.

Releve du Matin. Henry de Montherlant. (Folio 281). 1972. 3.95 o.p. (ISBN 0-686-55531-7). Schoenhof.

Reliability Design for Vibroacoustic Environments: AMD, Vol. 9. Ed. by D. D. Kana & T. G. Butler. 1974. pap. 18.00 o.p. (ISBN 0-685-77460-0, I00047). ASME.

Reliability Engineering Nineteen Seventy-Eight: Proceedings of the SRE Reliability Symposium, Ottawa, Ontario, Canada, October, 1978. Canadian Reliability Engineers Staff. LC 78-10571. 1979. pap. 29.00 o.p. (ISBN 0-08-023228-0). Pergamon.

Reliability Engineering, 1975. Canadian Reliability Engineers Staff. 1976. pap. 35.00 o.p. (ISBN 0-08-019977-1). Pergamon.

Reliability Engineering 1980: Proceedings of the 1980 Canadian SRE Reliability Symposium, Ottawa, Ontario, Canada May 15-16 1980. Canadian Reliabilty Engineers Staff. 170p. 1981. pap. 43.00 o.p. (ISBN 0-08-026163-9). Pergamon.

Reliability for the Technologies. Leonard Doty. LC 85-14423. 242p. 1985. 24.95x o.p. (ISBN 0-8311-1169-0). Indus Pr.

Reliability of Power Supply Systems. Institution of Electrical Engineers (UK) Staff & Peter Peregrinus, Ltd. Staff. (Conference Publications: No. 225). 166p. 1983. pap. 64.00 o.s.i. (ISBN 0-85296-278-9, IC225). Inst Elect Eng.

Reliability Stress Analysis & Failure Prevention Methods in Mechanical Design. Ed. by W. D. Milestone. 328p. 1980. 40.00 o.p. (ISBN 0-317-33607-X, H00165); members 20.00 o.p. (ISBN 0-317-33608-8). ASME.

Reliable Nuclear Power Today: Proceedings, American Nuclear Society Topical Meeting, Charlotte NC, April 10-13, 1978. 172p. softcover 23.00 o.p. (ISBN 0-317-33039-X, 700036). Am Nuclear Soc.

Reliable Production in the Process Industries. Institution of Chemical Engineers. 1982. 52.50 o.s.i. (ISBN 0-08-028764-6). Pergamon.

Reliable Software Through Composite Design. Glenford J. Myers. 159p. 1979. pap. 11.95 o.p. (ISBN 0-442-25620-5). Van Nos Reinhold.

Relief Pitcher. Dick Friendlich. (gr. 7-10). 1965. 4.75 o.s.i. (ISBN 0-664-32324-3, Westminster). Westminster John Knox.

Religion: A Sociological View. Elizabeth K. Nottingham. LC 81-40769. 348p. 1981. pap. text ed. 14.25 o.p. (ISBN 0-8191-1813-3). U Pr of Amer.

Religion among the Unitarian Universalists: Converts in the Step Father's House. Robert B. Tapp. LC 72-82127. (Quantitative Studies in Social Relations Ser). 1973. 46.50 o.p. (ISBN 0-12-785824-5). Acad Pr.

Religion & Art in Conflict: Introduction to a Cross-Disciplinary Task. Samuel Laeuchli. LC 79-23711. 252p. (Orig.). 1980. pap. 9.95 o.p. (ISBN 0-8006-1635-9, 1-1635, Fortress). Augsburg Fortress.

Religion & Culture: An Introduction to Anthropology of Religion. Anne M. Malefijt. 1968. text ed. write for info. o.p. (ISBN 0-02-374920-2). Macmillan.

Religion & Law: Biblical-Judaic & Islamic Perspectives. Ed. by Edwin B. Firmage et al. 450p. 1988. text ed. price not set o.p. (ISBN 0-931464-39-0). Eisenbrauns.

Religion & Law: The First Amendment in Historical Perspective. Harold J. Berman. (Juris Ser.: No. 1). 23p. (Orig.). 1986. pap. text ed. 5.00 o.s.i. (ISBN 0-944561-15-2). Chr Legal.

Religion & Personality in the Spiral of Life. David Belgum. LC 79-66478. 1979. pap. text ed. 15.00 o.p. (ISBN 0-8191-0832-4). U Pr of Amer.

Religion & Pilgrim Taxes Under the Company Raj. LC 87-61956. 207p. 1987. Riverdale Co.

Religion & Politics in Tibet. Bina R. Burman. 1979. text ed. 17.50x o.p. (ISBN 0-7069-0801-5, Pub. by Vikas India). Advent NY.

Religion & Sexism. Rosemary R. Ruether. 1974. pap. 10.70 o.p. (ISBN 0-671-21693-7, Touchstone Bks). S&S.

Religion & Society in North America: An Annotated Bibliography. Ed. by Robert de V. Brunkow. LC 82-24304. (Clio Bibliography Ser.: No. 12). 515p. 1983. lib. bdg. 69.00 o.p. (ISBN 0-87436-042-0). ABC-Clio.

Religion & Society of North-East India. Sujata Miri. 128p. 1980. text ed. 13.95x o.p. (ISBN 0-7069-1136-9, Pub. by Vikas India). Advent NY.

Religion & the American Dream: The Search for Freedom Under God. Christopher F. Mooney. LC 76-54332. 1977. softcover 4.95 o.s.i. (ISBN 0-664-24135-2, Westminster). Westminster John Knox.

Religion & the American Revolution. Ed. by Jerald C. Brauer. LC 76-9718. 96p. 1976. pap. 2.95 o.p. (ISBN 0-8006-1241-8, Fortress). Augsburg Fortress.

Religion & the People, Eight Hundred to Seventeen Hundred. Ed. by James Obelkevich. LC 78-7847. v, 336p. 1979. 32.50x o.p. (ISBN 0-8078-1332-X). U of NC Pr.

Religion & the Unconscious. Ann Ulanov & Barry Ulanov. LC 75-16302. 288p. 1975. 13.95 o.s.i. (ISBN 0-664-20799-5, Westminster). Westminster John Knox.

Religion & Theatre. M. L. Varadpande. 100p. 1982. text ed. 15.00x o.p. (ISBN 0-391-02794-8). Humanities.

Religion & Violence: A Primer for White Americans. Robert M. Brown. LC 73-14710. (Illus.). 128p. 1973. pap. 5.95 o.s.i. (ISBN 0-664-24977-9, Westminster). Westminster John Knox.

Religion at the Polls. Albert J. Menendez. LC 76-30655. 1977. pap. 5.95 o.s.i. (ISBN 0-664-24117-4, Westminster). Westminster John Knox.

Religion: Classic Sociological Approaches. R. O'Toole. 1984. text ed. 12.95 o.p. (ISBN 0-07-548560-5). McGraw.

Religion Game, American Style. Edward Stevens. LC 76-9367. 168p. 1976. pap. 5.95 o.p. (ISBN 0-8091-1951-X). Paulist Pr.

Religion in a Technical Age. Samuel H. Miller. LC 68-17628. 1968. 9.95x o.s.i. (ISBN 0-674-75650-9). Harvard U Pr.

Religion in Action. Jerome Davis. 288p. 1956. (ISBN 0-8022-0359-0). Philos Lib.

Religion in American Life. Conrad Wright. LC 72-180481. (Life in America Ser.). (Illus.). 182p. (gr. 7-12). 1972. pap. 8.48 o.p. (ISBN 0-395-03145-1). HM.

Religion in Chinese Garment. Karl L. Reichelt. 1951. (ISBN 0-8022-1317-0). Philos Lib.

Religion in Modern English Drama. Gerald C. Weales. LC 75-45367. 317p. 1976. Repr. of 1961 ed. lib. bdg. 24.75x o.p. (ISBN 0-8371-8735-4, WEME). Greenwood.

Religion in Modern India. Ed. by Robert D. Baird. 1982. 36.00x o.p. (ISBN 0-8364-0826-8); 19.00x o.p. (ISBN 0-8364-0830-6). South Asia Bks.

Religion in Overalls. William Johnsson. LC 77-22464. (Anvil Ser.). 1977. pap. 8.95 o.p. (ISBN 0-8127-0143-7). Review & Herald.

Religion in Plato & Cicero. John E. Rexine. 96p. 1959. (ISBN 0-8022-1330-8). Philos Lib.

Religion in Prison. J. Arthur Hoyles. 150p. 1955. (ISBN 0-8022-0751-0). Philos Lib.

Religion in the American Novel: The Search for Belief, 1860-1920. Leo F. O'Connor. LC 83-21842. 364p. (Orig.). 1984. lib. bdg. 32.75 o.p. (ISBN 0-8191-3683-2); pap. text ed. 15.25 o.p. (ISBN 0-8191-3684-0). U Pr of Amer.

Religion in the Eighteenth Century. John Browning & Richard Morton. LC 79-17715. (McMaster University Eighteenth Century Studies). 145p. 1979. lib. bdg. 22.00 o.p. (ISBN 0-8240-4005-8). Garland Pub.

Religion in the Rebel Ranks. Sidney J. Romero. (Illus.). 226p. (Orig.). 1983. lib. bdg. 28.50 o.p. (ISBN 0-8191-3327-2); pap. text ed. 13.25 o.p. (ISBN 0-8191-3328-0). U Pr of Amer.

Religion in the Secular City: Toward a Post-Modern Theology. Harvey Cox. 320p. 1984. 16.50 o.p. (ISBN 0-671-45344-0). S&S.

Religion in the Secular City: Toward a Postmodern Theology. Harvey Cox. 304p. 1985. pap. 8.95 o.s.i. (ISBN 0-671-52805-X, Touchstone Bks). S&S.

Religion in the Twentieth Century. Vergilius Ferm. (ISBN 0-8022-0495-3). Philos Lib.

Religion in Wood: A Book of Shaker Furniture. Edward D. Andrews & Faith Andrews. LC 66-12722. (Midland Bks Ser.: No. 286). (Illus.). 128p. 1966. 20.00 o.p. (ISBN 0-253-17360-4); pap. 7.95x o.p. (ISBN 0-253-20286-8). Ind U Pr.

Religion: Innocent or Guilty. Ron Yerman. LC 85-90019. 180p. 1985. 11.95 o.p. (ISBN 0-533-06540-2). Vantage.

Religion of Dostoevsky. A. Boyce Gibson. LC 73-9956. 224p. 1974. 6.95 o.s.i. (ISBN 0-664-20989-0, Westminster). Westminster John Knox.

Religion of Jesus: Christianity's Unclaimed Heritage of Prophetic Religion. Leroy Waterman. LC 78-16405. 1978. Repr. of 1952 ed. lib. bdg. 35.00x o.p. (ISBN 0-313-20586-8, WARJ). Greenwood.

Religion of Negro Protestants. Ruby F. Johnston. 256p. 1956. (ISBN 0-8022-0809-6). Philos Lib.

Religion of the Machine Age. Dora Russell. 232p. 1985. 27.95 o.p. (ISBN 0-7100-9547-3). Routledge Chapman & Hall.

Religion of the Occident. Martin A. Larson. 1959. (ISBN 0-8022-0932-7). Philos Lib.

Religion of the Republic: Is There an American Religion. Ed. by Elwyn A. Smith. LC 70-130326. 1970. 2.00x o.p. (ISBN 0-8006-0049-5, Fortress). Augsburg Fortress.

Religion of Tomorrow. John E. Boodin. Philos Lib.

Religion on Capitol Hill: Myths & Realities. Peter L. Benson et al. 192p. 1982. 11.49i o.p. (ISBN 0-06-060780-7). HarpR.

Religion, Philosophy, & Science. Burham P. Beckwith. 1958. (ISBN 0-8022-0089-3). Philos Lib.

Religion, Philosophy & Science. Burnham Putnam Beckwith. 1957. 6.50 o.p. (ISBN 0-682-47012-0). Exposition-Phoenix.

Religion, Society, & the Homosexual. James R. Brown & N. Butwill. LC 73-10095. 44p. 1973. pap. 2.95 o.p. (ISBN 0-8422-0343-5). Irvington.

Religion Through Reason. Ernest L. Ramer. 1975. 4.50 o.p. (ISBN 0-682-48237-4). Exposition-Phoenix.

Religion Through the Ages. H. F. Bell & C. S. MacFarland. 1948. (ISBN 0-8022-0095-8). Philos Lib.

Religion, Vol. 3 (Incl. 1986-1987 Supplements) Ed. by Eleanor C. Goldstein. 1987. 30.00 o.p. (ISBN 0-89777-085-4). Soc Issues.

Religions. Myrtle Langley. (Book of Beliefs Ser.). 1981. 9.95 o.p. (ISBN 0-89191-478-1, 54783). Cook.

Religions & History: A Textbook for the Enlightenment of 12th Graders in our Tax-Supported Public High Schools. Leslie R. Severinghaus. 1985. 13.95 o.p. (ISBN 0-533-06577-1). Vantage.

Religions in Modern India. Ed. by Giri Raj Gupta. (Main Currents in Indian Sociology Ser.: Vol. 5). 368p. 1983. text ed. 37.50x o.p. (Pub. by Vikas India). Advent NY.

Religions of Primitive Peoples. Daniel G. Brinton. LC 79-88423. 1969. Repr. of 1897 ed. lib. bdg. 22.50x o.p. (ISBN 0-8371-1763-1, BRR&). Greenwood.

Religions of the Ancient Near East. Helmer Ringgren. Tr. by John Sturdy. LC 72-8587. (Illus.). 208p. 1972. 7.50 o.s.i. (ISBN 0-664-20953-X, Westminster). Westminster John Knox.

Religions of the World. George A. Barton. LC 74-90469. Repr. of 1929 ed. lib. bdg. 35.00x o.p. (ISBN 0-8371-2216-3, BARW). Greenwood.

Religious Attitudes of Japanese Men. Fernando M. Basabe. LC 68-57415. 1969. bds. 15.00 o.p. (ISBN 0-8048-0651-9). C E Tuttle.

Religious Belief & Philosophical Thought. William P. Alston. 1963. text ed. 15.95 o.p. (ISBN 0-15-575851-9, HC). HarBraceJ.

Religious Buildings. Architectural Record Magazine Editors. 1980. text ed. 45.50 o.p. (ISBN 0-07-002342-5). McGraw.

Religious Changes in Contemporary Poland: Secularization & Politics. Maciej Pomian-Srzednicki. (International Library of Sociology). 227p. 1982. 27.95x o.p. (ISBN 0-7100-9245-8). Routledge Chapman & Hall.

Religious Concepts in Ancient America & in the Holy Land: As Illustrated by the Sacred Book of the Quiche Mayans & by the Bible. Donald Jackson. 1976. 8.00 o.p. (ISBN 0-682-48503-9, University). Exposition-Phoenix.

Religious Conflict in Fourth Century Rome. B. F. Croke & J. D. Harris. (Sources in Ancient History Ser.). 139p. (Orig.). 1982. pap. 21.00x o.p. (ISBN 0-424-00091-1, Pub. by Sydney U Pr Australia). Intl Spec Bk.

Religious Design of Hemingway's Early Fiction. Larry E. Grimes. Ed. by A. Walton Litz. LC 85-1183. (Studies in Modern Literature: No. 50). 166p. 1985. 34.95 o.p. (ISBN 0-8357-1635-X). UMI Res Pr.

Religious Dimension in Hegel's Thought. Emil L. Fackenheim. 1984. 16.25 o.p. (ISBN 0-8446-5997-5). Peter Smith.

Religious Education in a Pluralistic Society. M. C. Felderhof. 160p. 1985. pap. text ed. 20.95 o.s.i. (ISBN 0-340-35413-5). Princeton Bk Co.

Religious Education: Its Effects, Its Challenges Today. Robert J. Fox. 1972. pap. 0.95 o.s.i. (ISBN 0-8198-0344-8). Dghtrs St Paul.

Religious Experience & Scientific Method. Henry N. Wieman. 1971. Repr. of 1926 ed. lib. bdg. 22.50x o.p. (ISBN 0-8371-4368-3, WIRE). Greenwood.

Religious Experience: Its Nature, Types, & Validity. Alan C. Bouquet. LC 75-40997. 140p. 1976. Repr. of 1968 ed. lib. bdg. 35.00x o.p. (ISBN 0-8371-8714-1, BORL). Greenwood.

Religious Experience of Mankind. 3rd ed. Ninian Smart. (Scribner Press Ser.). (Illus.). 656p. 1984. 30.00 o.s.i. (ISBN 0-684-18077-4, ScribT). Scribner.

Religious Expression. World Religions Development Center. (Illus.). 68p. 1978. pap. 6.95 o.p. (ISBN 0-89505-003-X); pap. 3.95 guide bk. o.p. Tabor Pub.

Religious Expression, Guide. World Religious Development Center. 64p. 1978. pap. 3.75 o.p. (ISBN 0-89505-002-1). Tabor Pub.

Religious Freedom, Nineteen Sixty-Five to Nineteen Seventy-Five: A Symposium on a Historic Document. Ed. by Walter J. Burghardt. LC 76-45938. 1977. pap. 2.95 o.p. (ISBN 0-8091-1993-5). Paulist Pr.

Religious Guidance. Leibowitz. 1958. (ISBN 0-8022-0956-4). Philos Lib.

Religious Heritage of America. Albert M. Shulman. LC 81-3594. (Illus.). 480p. 1982. 25.00 o.s.i. (ISBN 0-498-02162-9). A S Barnes.

Religious Liberty in America: History & Prospects. Glenn T. Miller. LC 75-33000. 1976. pap. 4.75 o.s.i. (ISBN 0-664-24785-7, Westminster). Westminster John Knox.

Religious Liberty in the United States: The Development of Church-State Thought Since the Revolutionary Era. Elwyn A. Smith. LC 70-178093. 400p. 1972. 2.00 o.p. (ISBN 0-8006-0071-1, Fortress). Augsburg Fortress.

Religious Life & the Poor: Liberation Theology Perspectives. Alejandro Cussianovich. Tr. by John Drury from Span. LC 78-16740. Orig. Title: Desde los Pobres de la Tiera. 168p. (Orig.). 1979. pap. 1.74 o.p. (ISBN 0-88344-429-1). Orbis Bks.

Religious Life of Ancient Rome. Jesse B. Carter. 270p. 1972. Repr. of 1911 ed. lib. bdg. 27.50x o.p. (ISBN 0-8154-0429-8). Cooper Sq.

Religious Literature of the West. John R. Whitney & Susan W. Howe. LC 70-158996. (Orig.). 1971. 8.95 o.p. (ISBN 0-8066-1118-9, 10-5467, Augsburg). Augsburg Fortress.

Religious Newspapers in the Old Northwest to 1861: A History, Bibliography, & Record of Opinion. Wesley Norton. LC 75-36983. xi, 196p. 1977. 12.50x o.p. (ISBN 0-8214-0193-9). Ohio U Pr.

Religious Organization: A Trend Report & Bibliography Prepared for the International Sociological Association Under the Auspices of the International Committee for Social Science Documentation. James A. Beckford. (La Sociologie Contemporaine: Vol. 21, No. 2). 1973. pap. 11.60x o.p. (ISBN 90-2797-851-4). Mouton.

Religious Perspectives & Problems: An Introduction to the Philosophy of Religion. Ed. by Allen V. Eikner. LC 80-67265. 368p. 1980. lib. bdg. 29.75 o.p. (ISBN 0-8191-1215-1); pap. text ed. 16.25 o.p. (ISBN 0-8191-1216-X). U Pr of Amer.

Religious Philosophy: A Group of Essays. Harry A. Wolfson. LC 61-16696. 1965. pap. 1.95 o.p. (ISBN 0-689-70211-6, 75, Atheneum). Macmillan.

Religious Philosophy: A Group of Essays. Harry A. Wolfson. LC 61-16696. 1961. 18.50x o.s.i. (ISBN 0-674-75900-1, Belknap Pr). Harvard U Pr.

Religious Publishing & Communications. Judith S. Duke. LC 80-17694. (Communications Library). 274p. 1980. professional 29.95 o.s.i. (ISBN 0-914236-61-X). G K Hall.

Religious Science Book. Parker L. Johnstone. 212p. 1984. 7.95 o.p. (ISBN 0-917802-13-6). Theoscience Found.

Religious Science for Youth. Docia W. Norris. pap. 1.50 o.s.i. (ISBN 0-87516-153-7). DeVorss.

Religious Symbols & Their Functions. Ed. by Haralds Biezais. 178p. (Orig.). 1979. pap. text ed. 22.50 o.p. (ISBN 91-22-00199-9, Pub. by Almqvist & Wiksell). Coronet Bks.

Religious Television: The Experience in America. Peter Horsfield. LC 83-11313. (Communication & Human Values Ser.). (Illus.). 192p. 1984. text ed. 17.95 o.p. (ISBN 0-582-28432-5). Longman.

Religious Thought & the Modern Psychologies: A Critical Conversation in the Theology of Culture. Don S. Browning. LC 86-45205. 288p. 1986. 22.50 o.p. (ISBN 0-8006-0784-8, 1-784, Fortress). Augsburg Fortress.

Religious Thought of H. Richard Niebuhr. Jerry Irish. LC 83-62021. 120p. 1983. pap. 6.95 o.p. (ISBN 0-8042-0680-5, John Knox). Westminster John Knox.

Religious Unbeliever. Milton A. Shaham. 94p. 1982. 5.00 o.p. (ISBN 0-682-49888-2). Exposition-Phoenix.

Religious Writer's Marketplace: The Definitive Sourcebook. rev. & updated ed. Ed. by William H. Gentz. LC 84-27691. 221p. 1985. pap. 17.95 o.p. (ISBN 0-89471-305-1). Running Pr.

Reliving Reincarnation Through Hypnosis. Ralph Grossi. 1975. 7.00 o.p. (ISBN 0-682-48286-2, Banner). Exposition-Phoenix.

Re'lize Whut Ahm Talkin' 'Bout. Steve Chenault. softcover 7.95 o.p. (ISBN 0-912216-24-7). Angel Pr.

Reluctant Dragon. Grahame. (gr. 2-6). 11.50 o.p.; pap. 4.95 o.p. H Holt & Co.

Reluctant Europeans: The Attitudes of the Nordic Countries Towards European Integration. Toivo Miljan. 1977. lib. bdg. 15.00x o.p. (ISBN 0-7735-0293-9, McGill Canada). U of Toronto Pr.

Reluctant Farewell: An American Reporter's Candid Look Inside the Soviet Union. Andrew Nagorski. LC 85-917. 320p. 1987. 16.95 o.p. (ISBN 0-03-005069-3, Co-Pub. by New Republic); pap. 8.95 o.p. H Holt & Co.

Reluctant Guru. R. K. Narayan. 173p. 1975. pap. 2.50 o.s.i. (ISBN 0-88253-729-6). Ind-US Inc.

Reluctant Heiress. Janet Templeton. LC 85-20748. (Starlight Romance Ser.). 192p. 1986. 12.95 o.p. (ISBN 0-385-19989-9). Doubleday.

Reluctant Memory. Dorothy L. Gray. 1977. 4.00 o.p. (ISBN 0-682-48897-6). Exposition-Phoenix.

Reluctant Naturalist: An Unnatural Field Guide to the Natural World. Charles A. Monagan. LC 83-45507. (Illus.). 224p. 1984. 10.95 o.p. (ISBN 0-689-11437-0, Atheneum). Macmillan.

Reluctant Pioneer: Mary Vowell Adams. Beatrice L. Bliss. (Illus.). 233p. 1972. pap. 4.95 o.p. (ISBN 0-9600504-1-8). Binford-Metropolitan.

Reluctant Resister. Jeff Deitrich. (Illus.). 1983. 17.00 o.p. (ISBN 0-87775-156-0); pap. 8.00 o.p. (ISBN 0-87775-157-9). Unicorn Pr.

Reluctant Revolutionary. Edward Teller. LC 64-25274. 85p. 1964. 10.00x o.p. (ISBN 0-8262-0032-X). U of Mo Pr.

Reluctant Vision: An Essay in the Philosophy of Religion. Patrick T. Burke. LC 73-88354. 144p. (Orig.). 1974. pap. 0.50 o.p. (ISBN 0-8006-1068-7, Fortress). Augsburg Fortress.

Reluctant Witness. Kenneth L. Chaffin. LC 74-84548. 1975. 8.50 o.p. (ISBN 0-8054-5550-7). Broadman.

Remaking Cities: Contradictions of the Recent Urban Environment. Alison Ravetz. 375p. 1980. 29.95 o.p. (ISBN 0-85664-293-2, Pub. by Croom Helm Ltd); pap. 13.00 o.p. (ISBN 0-7099-2220-5). Routledge Chapman & Hall.

Remaking of Christian Doctrine. Maurice Wiles. LC 78-5800. 1978. softcover 5.95 o.s.i. (ISBN 0-664-24217-0, Westminster). Westminster John Knox.

Remarkable Birth of Planet Earth. Henry M. Morris. LC 73-166083. 112p. 1972. pap. 3.50 o.p. (ISBN 0-87123-485-8, 200485). Bethany Hse.

Remarkable Birth of Planet Earth. Henry M. Morris. 115p. 1972. pap. 4.50 o.p. (ISBN 0-89051-000-8). Master Bks.

Remarkable Egg. Adelaide Holl. LC 68-24455. (Illus.). (gr. k-3). 1968. PLB 11.88 o.p. (ISBN 0-688-51090-6). Lothrop.

Remarkable Expedition: The Story of Stanley's Rescue of Emin Pasha from Equatorial Africa. Olivia Manning. LC 85-47607. (Illus.). 288p. 1985. 12.95 o.p. (ISBN 0-689-11627-6, Atheneum). Macmillan.

Remarkable Riderless Runaway Tricycle. Bruce McMillan. LC 77-19027. (Illus.). (gr. k-3). 1978. PLB 6.95 o.p. (ISBN 0-395-26496-0). HM.

Remarkable Spaceship Earth. Ron Cottrell. LC 82-70775. (Accent Imperials Ser.). (Illus.). 64p. (Orig.). 1982. gift book 9.95 o.p. (ISBN 0-89636-088-1). Accent Bks.

Remarkable World of John Wesley: Pioneer in Mental Health. Franklin Wilder. (Illus.). 1978. 7.00 o.p. (ISBN 0-682-49129-2). Exposition-Phoenix.

Remarkable Writing Machine. Carol H. Behrman. LC 80-26648. (Illus.). 64p. (gr. 3-5). 1981. lib. bdg. 8.59 o.s.i. (ISBN 0-671-34026-3). Messner.

Remarks During a Journey Through North America in the Years 1819, 1920 & 1921. Adam Hodgson. LC 76-107479. Repr. of 1823 ed. 35.00x o.p. (ISBN 0-8371-3755-1, HRN&). Greenwood.

Rembrandt & Persia. Leonard J. Slatkes. (Illus.). 120p. 1983. 20.00 o.p. (ISBN 0-89835-241-X). Abaris Bks.

Rembrandt & Spinoza. J. M. Balet. LC 61-18686. 232p. 1962. (ISBN 0-8022-0054-0). Philos Lib.

Rembrandt & the Bible. A. Hyatt Mayor. (Illus.). 52p. 1979. 1.00 o.p. (ISBN 0-87099-194-9). Metro Mus Art.

Rembrandt: Paintings from Soviet Museums. V. Lowensohn-Lessing. 184p. 1987. 45.00 o.p. (ISBN 0-8285-3810-7, Pub. by Aurora Pubs USSR). Imported Pubns.

Rembrandt Self-Portraits. Pascal Bonafoux. LC 85-42921. (Illus.). 140p. 1985. 60.00 o.p. (ISBN 0-8478-0629-4). Rizzoli Intl.

Rembrandt: The Nightwatch. E. Haverkamp-Begemann. LC 81-47921. (Illus.). 204p. 1982. cloth 37.00x o.p. (ISBN 0-691-03991-7); pap. 14.50x o.p. (ISBN 0-691-00341-6). Princeton U Pr.

Rembrandt's House. Anthony Bailey. 1978. 13.95 o.p. (ISBN 0-395-25706-9). HM.

Rembrandt's Sacrifice of Manoah. Fritz Saxl. (Warburg Institute Studies: Vol. 9). pap. 13.00 o.p. (ISBN 0-8115-1387-4). Kraus Repr.

Remediating Reading Disabilities: Simple Things That Work. J. E. Cook & Elsie C. Earlley. LC 79-20412. 266p. 1979. text ed. 34.00 o.p. Aspen Pub.

Remediation & Instruction in Language: Oral Language, Reading & Writing. Diana Phelps-Terasaki et al. LC 83-9946. 350p. 1982. 36.00 o.p. (ISBN 0-89443-938-3). Aspen Pub.

Remedies for Breach by Sellers & Buyers under the Uniform Commercial Code. Practising Law Institute Staff & Melvin D. Kraft. LC 84-60431. (Commercial Law & Practice Course Handbook Ser.: No. 323). 1984. pap. 15.00 o.p. (A4-4-84). PLI.

Remember the Rainbow. Jacqueline Mehrabi. (Illus.). 40p. (ps-2). 1985. pap. (ISBN 0-85398-191-4). G Ronald Pub.

Remember the Secret. Elisabeth Kubler-Ross. LC 81-68454. (Illus.). 64p. (gr. 5 up). 1981. 8.95 o.p. (ISBN 0-89087-332-1). Celestial Arts.

Remember This Time. Gloria K. Broder & Bill Broder. LC 83-4249. 336p. o.s.i. (ISBN 0-937858-23-4). Newmarket.

Remember to Kill Me. Hugh Pentecost. (Nightingale Paperbacks). 1985. pap. 10.95 o.p. (ISBN 0-8161-3848-6, Large Print Bks). G K Hall.

Remembered Anger. Martha Albrand. 1973. pap. 0.75 o.p. (ISBN 0-380-01523-4, 14464). Avon.

Remembering. James Campbell et al. (Themepaks Ser.). (gr. 1-6). 1976. 4.95 o.p. (ISBN 0-8042-1459-X, John Knox). Westminster John Knox.

Remembering Made Easy. Arthur L. Logan. LC 65-27668. 1965. pap. 1.95 o.p. (ISBN 0-668-01402-4). Arco.

Remembering Vernon. Juliet Fox-Hutchinson. 112p. (Orig.). 1984. pap. 12.95x o.p. (ISBN 0-85362-209-4, Oriel). Routledge Chapman & Hall.

Remembering with Love. Helen S. Rice. (Illus.). 128p. 1985. 13.95 o.p. (ISBN 0-8007-1434-2). Revell.

Remembrance of Games Past: On Tour with the Tennis Grand Masters. John Sharnik. (Illus.). 384p. 1986. 19.95 o.p. (ISBN 0-02-610040-1). Macmillan.

Remington Bullet Knives. Melvin Brewster & George A. Hoyem. (Illus.). 50p. (Orig.). 1985. pap. 9.95 o.p. (ISBN 0-9604982-5-7). Armory Pubns.

Remington No. Two: Good Day for a Hangin' James C. Boone. 176p. 1987. pap. 2.50 o.p. (ISBN 0-380-75266-2). Avon.

Remington, No. 3: Showdown at Comanche Butte. James C. Boone. 160p. (Orig.). 1987. pap. 2.50 o.p. (ISBN 0-380-75268-9). Avon.

Remington, No. 4: Lawman's Justice. James C. Boone. 160p. 1987. pap. 2.50 o.p. (ISBN 0-380-75269-7). Avon.

Remington, No. 5: Wyoming Blood Trail. James C. Boone. 176p. 1987. pap. 2.75 o.p. (ISBN 0-380-75270-0). Avon.

Remington, No. 9: The Lawless Clan. James C. Boone. 160p. 1988. pap. 2.75 o.p. (ISBN 0-380-75612-9). Avon.

Reminiscences & Memorials of Men of the Revolution. Artemas B. Muzzey. LC 70-142542. 444p. 1971. Repr. of 1883 ed. 51.00x o.p. (ISBN 0-8103-3629-4). Gale.

Reminiscences of Clara Schumann As Found in the Diary of Her Grandson Ferdinand Schumann. Ed. & intro. by June M. Dickinson. (Illus.). 1974. pap. 12.95 o.p. (ISBN 0-913000-49-3). Maestro Scope.

Reminiscences of Literary London from 1779-1853. Thomas Rees. LC 68-24476. 176p. 1969. Repr. of 1896 ed. 35.00x o.p. (ISBN 0-8103-3888-2). Gale.

Reminiscences of Tolstoy. Ed. by Kalpana Sahni. 144p. 1981. text ed. 12.50x o.p. (ISBN 0-391-02021-8). Humanities.

Reminiscences of War Resisters in World War I. Incl. We Did Not Fight, 1914-1918. Ed. by Julian Bell; New Holy Office, or Why I Oppose Conscription. Norman Angell. LC 73-147653. (Library of War & Peace; Conscrip. & Cons. Object.). lib. bdg. 46.00 o.p. (ISBN 0-8240-0418-3). Garland Pub.

Reminiscing with Horace: A Delightful Conversation Between a Man & the Cat Who "Owns" Him. Eldridge Warner. (Illus.). 1979. 5.00 o.p. (ISBN 0-682-49499-2). Exposition-Phoenix.

Remodelers Handbook: A Manual of Professional Practice for Home Improvement Contractors. Ed. by Benjamin Williams. LC 76-53565. (Illus.). 416p. 1977. pap. 18.50 o.p. (ISBN 0-910460-21-3). Nat Assn H Build.

Remodeling Estimators Reference Book. (Illus.). 328p. 1984. 22.95 o.p. Nat Assn H Build.

Remodeling Your Home. 3rd ed. Sunset Magazine & Books Editors. LC 78-53674. (Illus.). 96p. 1978. pap. 5.95 o.p. (ISBN 0-376-01506-3, Sunset Bks.). Sunset-Lane.

Remorse. Alba de Cespedes. Tr. by William Weaver from Ital. LC 78-14003. 1978. lib. bdg. 35.00x o.p. (ISBN 0-313-20731-3, CERE). Greenwood.

Remote Kingdoms. Tertius Chandler. 1976. 7.50 o.p. (ISBN 0-682-48379-6, University). Exposition-Phoenix.

Remote Sensing: Energy Related Studies. Ed. by T. Nejat Veziroglu. LC 75-23018. 491p. 1975. 41.95x o.p. (ISBN 0-470-90665-0). Halsted Pr.

Remote Sensing for Environmental Sciences. Ed. by E. Schanda. (Ecological Studies: Vol. 18). (Illus.). 370p. 1976. 45.00 o.p. (ISBN 0-387-07465-1). Springer-Verlag.

Remote Sensing from Satellites: Proceedings of Workshops I & IX of the COSPAR Interdisciplinary Scientific Commission A (Meetings A2) of the COSPAR 25th Plenary Meeting Held in Graz, Austria 25 June - 7 July 1974. Ed. by W. D. Carter & E. T. Engman. 264p. 1985. pap. 54.00 o.p. (ISBN 0-08-032751-6, Pub. by P P L). Pergamon.

Remote Sensing in Geology. Barry S. Siegal & Alan R. Gillespie. LC 79-17967. 702p. 1980. text ed. write for info. o.p. (ISBN 0-471-79052-4). Wiley.

Remote Sensing of Earth from Space: Role of "Smart Sensors", PAAS67. Ed. by Roger A. Breckenridge. LC 79-18200. (Illus.). 505p. 1979. 69.50 o.p. (ISBN 0-915928-33-7). AIAA.

Remote Sensing of Earth Resources & the Environment: Proceedings of the SPIE Seminar, Palo Alto, 1971, Vol. 27. Society of Photo-Optical Instrumentation Engineers Staff. (SPIE Seminar Proceedings). 168p. 1971. 29.00 o.p. (ISBN 0-89252-037-X). SPIE.

Remote Sensing: Proceedings of an EARSEL-ESA Symposium, Guildford, U. K., April 8-11. Ed. by G. K. Pardoe. (Illus.). 64p. 1985. pap. 39.00 o.p. (ISBN 0-08-032538-6, Pub. by PPL). Pergamon.

Removable Closure of the Interdental Space. Arnold Gaerny. (Illus.). 196p. 1972. 38.00 o.p. (ISBN 0-931386-62-4). Quint Pub Co.

Removable Partial Denture Construction. Bates. 160p. 1978. 21.00 o.p. (ISBN 0-7236-0481-9, Pub. by John Wright UK). Butterworth.

Removal of the Choctaw Indians. Arthur H. DeRosier, Jr. LC 70-111044. (Illus.). 1970. 18.95x o.s.i. (ISBN 0-87049-113-X); pap. text ed. 8.95 o.s.i. (ISBN 0-87049-329-9). U of Tenn Pr.

Remove the Bodies. Elizabeth Ferrars. (Black Dagger Crime Ser.). 192p. 1988. text ed. 14.95x o.p. (ISBN 0-86220-726-6, Pub. by Firecrest Pub Ltd). Prescott Pr NH.

Remove Your Shoes. Jim Hogan. 128p. (Orig.). pap. text ed. 5.95 o.s.i. (ISBN 0-934318-34-4). Falcon Pr MT.

Removing the Obstacles. Institute for Food & Development Policy Staff. Ed. by Brent Millikan & David Kinley. 45p. (Orig.). 1984. pap. 2.95 o.p. (ISBN 0-935028-15-3). Inst Food & Develop.

Renaissance. LC 79-10210. (Living Past Ser.). (Illus.). 64p. (gr. 4 up). 1979. 7.95 o.p. (ISBN 0-668-04787-9, 4787-9). Arco.

Renaissance & Reform: The Italian Contribution. Frances A. Yates. Ed. by J. Trapp. (Collected Essays Ser.: Vol. II). (Illus.). 288p. 1983. 31.50 o.p. (ISBN 0-7100-9530-9). Routledge Chapman & Hall.

Renaissance & Renewal in the Twelfth Century. Ed. by Robert L. Benson & Giles Constable. (Illus.). 832p. 1983. text ed. 70.00x o.p. (ISBN 0-674-76085-9). Harvard U Pr.

Renaissance & Renewal in the Twelfth Century. Ed. by Robert L. Benson & Giles Constable. 816p. 1985. pap. text ed. 17.95x o.p. (ISBN 0-674-76086-7). Harvard U Pr.

Renaissance Architecture. Peter Murray. LC 70-149850. (History of World Architecture). (Illus.). 1971. 50.00 o.p. (ISBN 0-8109-1000-4). Abrams.

Renaissance Bronzes: From Ohio Collections. William D. Wixom. LC 75-30966. (Illus.). 196p. 1975. pap. 15.00x o.p. (ISBN 0-910386-24-2, Pub. by Cleveland Mus Art). Ind U Pr.

Renaissance Cavalier. John S. White. 1959. (ISBN 0-8022-1862-8). Philos Lib.

Renaissance Diplomacy. Garrett Mattingly. 1971. pap. 4.95 o.p. (ISBN 0-395-12687-8, 68, SenEd). HM.

Renaissance Drama, 1 of 7 vols. Intro. by Derek Traversi. (Great Writers Library). 122p. pap. 7.95 o.p. (ISBN 0-312-34702-2). Academy Chi Pubs.

Renaissance Drama. Ed. by James Vinson. (Great Writer's Library). 122p. (Orig.). 1980. pap. 6.95 o.p. (ISBN 0-312-34702-2). St Martin.

Renaissance England. Ed. by Roy Lamson & Hallett Smith. 1956. 15.95x o.p. (ISBN 0-393-09487-1, NortonC). Norton.

Renaissance: Essays in Interpretation. Andre Chastel & Cecil Grayson. 336p. 1982. 46.00 o.p. (ISBN 0-416-31130-X, NO. 3770). Routledge Chapman & Hall.

Renaissance in Cyclooctatetraene Chemistry. Leo A. Paquette. Ed. by Barton et al. 1976. pap. 15.50 o.p. (ISBN 0-08-020479-1). Pergamon.

Renaissance in Japan: A Cultural Survey of the Seventeenth Century. Kenneth P. Kirkwood. LC 72-120389. (Illus.). 1970. Repr. bds. 6.50 o.p. (ISBN 0-8048-0916-X). C E Tuttle.

Renaissance of Wonder: The Fantasy Worlds of J. R. R. Tolkein, C. S. Lewis, George MacDonald, E. Nesbit, & Others. Marion Lochhead. LC 80-7753. 192p. 1980. 8.95i o.p. (ISBN 0-06-250520-3). HarpR.

Renaissance Painting in Manuscripts: Treasures from the British Library. Ed. by Thomas Kren. Janet Backhouse et al. LC 83-12591. (Illus.). 217p. 1983. 39.50 o.p. (ISBN 0-933920-51-2, Co-pub. by Hudson Hill Pr); pap. 25.00 o.p. (ISBN 0-933920-52-0). Hudson Hills.

Renaissance Rhetoric: A Short Title Catalogue. James J. Murphy. LC 80-8501. 375p. 1981. lib. bdg. 61.00 o.p. (ISBN 0-8240-9487-5). Garland Pub.

Renaissance Self-Fashioning: More to Shakespeare. Stephen Greenblatt. LC 80-13837. 272p. 1980. lib. bdg. 25.00x o.s.i. (ISBN 0-226-30653-4). U of Chicago Pr.

Renal & Urologic Disorders. Ed. by Helen Hamilton & Minnie B. Rose. (Nurse's Clinical Library). (Illus.). 192p. 1984. text ed. 19.95 o.p. (ISBN 0-916730-74-3). Springhouse Pub.

Renal Medicine & Urology: Library of General Practice, Vol. 4. David Brooks & Netar Mallick. (Illus.). 294p. 1982. pap. 23.95 o.p. (ISBN 0-443-01718-2). Churchill.

Renal Nursing. Uldall. 1986. 15.00 o.p. (ISBN 0-8016-5172-7). Mosby.

Renal Transport & Diuretics. International Symposium on Renal Transport, West Germany, 1968. Ed. by K. Thurau & H. Jahrmaerker. (Illus.). 1969. 58.50 o.p. (ISBN 0-387-04686-0). Springer-Verlag.

Renata, Whizbrain, & the Ghost. Caron Lee Cohen. LC 86-22330. (Illus.). 32p. (gr. k-3). 1987. 12.95 o.s.i. (ISBN 0-689-31271-7, Atheneum Childrens Bks). Macmillan.

Renaud et Armide see Theatre.

Rencontres. Edward C. Knox. (Illus.). 241p. 1972. pap. text ed. 9.95 o.p. (ISBN 0-15-576602-3, HC). HarBraceJ.

Rendered Infamous: A Book of Political Reality. Stephen Gaskin. Ed. by Matthew McClure. (Illus.). 224p. (Orig.). 1982. 12.00 o.p. (ISBN 0-913990-40-X); pap. 4.95 o.p. (ISBN 0-913990-32-9). Book Pub Co.

Rendering of God in the Old Testament, No. 10. Dale Patrick. Ed. by Walter Brueggemann & John R. Donahue. LC 80-2389. (Overtures to Biblical Theology Ser.). 176p. (Orig.). 1981. pap. 8.95 o.p. (ISBN 0-8006-1533-6, 1-1533, Fortress). Augsburg Fortress.

Rendering Standards. Stephen W. Rich. (Illus.). 352p. 1984. 32.50 o.p. (ISBN 0-442-22670-5). Van Nos Reinhold.

Rendering Standards in Architecture & Design. Stephen Rich. (Illus.). 352p. 1985. pap. 19.95 o.p. (ISBN 0-442-22671-3). Van Nos Reinhold.

Rendez-Vous see Djinn.

Rendezvous with Love. Jane Hinchman. LC 87-6681. (Starlight Romance Ser.). 192p. 1987. 12.95 o.s.i. (ISBN 0-385-24123-2). Doubleday.

Rendezvous with Rama. Arthur C. Clarke. LC 73-3497. 1973. 8.95 o.s.i. (ISBN 0-15-176835-8). HarBraceJ.

Rendezvous with the Unknown. Adolph H. Parr. pap. 0.95 o.p. (ISBN 0-8198-0133-X). Dghtrs St Paul.

Renegade & the Comancheros. Jack Slade. (Sundance Ser.). 1978. pap. 2.25 o.p. (ISBN 0-8439-0569-7, Pub. by Leisure Bks CT). Dorchester Pub Co.

Renegade Player. Dixie Browning. (Nightingale Ser.). 256p. (Orig.). 1985. pap. 9.95 o.p. (ISBN 0-8161-3917-2, Large Print Bks). G K Hall.

Renegotiable Rate: Mortgage Handbook. Financial Publishing Co. Staff. 384p. 1981. pap. 16.50 o.p. (ISBN 0-87600-557-1). Finan Pub.

Renegotiations in International Business Transactions: The Process of Dispute-Resolution Between Multinational Investors & Host Societies. William A. Stoever. LC 79-4727. 400p. 1981. 35.00x o.p. (ISBN 0-669-03057-0). Lexington Bks.

Renew, Parish Book, No. 1. Archdiocese of Newark, Office of Pastoral Renewal Staff. 1980. 75.00 o.p. (ISBN 0-8091-9191-1). Paulist Pr.

Renewable Energy Prospects: Proceedings of the Conference on Non-Fossil Fuel & Non-Nuclear Fuel Energy Strategies, Honolulu, USS, January 1979. Ed. by W. Bach et al. 340p. 1980. 29.00 o.p. (ISBN 0-08-024252-9). Pergamon.

Renewable Energy Technologies. Ed. by M. J. Chadwick & L. A. Kristoferson. 1986. 84.00 o.p. (ISBN 0-08-034061-X, Pub. by PPL). Pergamon.

Renewable Energy: The Power to Choose. Daniel Deudney & Christopher Flavin. 1983. 18.45 o.p. (ISBN 0-393-01710-9). Norton.

Renewable Resources Management: Applications of Remote Sensing - RNRF Symposium. 760p. 1984. pap. 42.00 o.p. (ISBN 0-937294-51-9). ASP & RS.

Renewable Virgin. Barbara Paul. (Nightingale Ser.). 360p. (Orig.). 1985. pap. 9.95 o.p. (ISBN 0-8161-3888-5, Large Print Bks). G K Hall.

Renewal in the Spirit. Pius R. Regamey. 1980. 5.95 o.s.i. (ISBN 0-8198-6402-1); pap. 4.95 o.s.i. (ISBN 0-8198-6403-X). Dghtrs St Paul.

Renewal of American Catholicism. David J. O'Brien. LC 72-85825. 320p. 1974. pap. 4.95 o.p. (ISBN 0-8091-1828-9). Paulist Pr.

Renewal of the Teacher-Scholar: Faculty Development in the Liberal Arts College. William C. Nelsen. vi, 110p. (Orig.). 1981. pap. 7.00 o.s.i. (ISBN 0-911696-06-7). Assn Am Coll.

Renewed Church of the United Brethren, 1722-1930. William G. Addison. (Church Historical Society London Ser.: No. 9). Repr. of 1932 ed. 40.00 o.p. (ISBN 0-8115-3133-3). Kraus Repr.

Renormalization Group Analysis of the Hierarchical Model. P. Collet & J. P. Eckmann. (Lecture Notes in Physics: Vol. 74). 1978. pap. 14.00 o.p. (ISBN 0-387-08670-6). Springer-Verlag.

Renovascular Hypertension. James C. Stanley et al. (Illus.). 400p. 1984. write for info. o.p. (ISBN 0-7216-8551-X). Saunders.

Renovation of a Medium-Sized Public Library Building. Herbert Goldhor & Lawrence A. Sahm. (Occasional Papers: No. 63). 9p. 1961. pap. 1.00 o.p. (ISBN 0-317-58844-3). U of Ill Lib Info Sci.

Rent Control: A Non Solution. 56p. 3.50 o.p. (ISBN 0-318-15193-6, NO. 111-116). Natl Assoc Realtors.

Rent Control: Case Histories. 50p. 8.00 o.p. (ISBN 0-318-15194-4, NO. 186-108). Natl Assoc Realtors.

Rent Stabilization & Control Laws in N. Y. Jeffrey H. Gallet et al. (Supplemented annually). 25.00 o.p. (ISBN 0-87526-082-9). Gould.

Rents of Council Houses. R. A. Parker. 90p. 1967. pap. text ed. 5.00x o.p. (ISBN 0-686-70857-1, Pub. by Bedford England). Gower Pub Co.

Renunciation As a Tragic Focus: A Study of Five Plays. Eugene H. Falk. LC 72-78701. (American Guidebook Ser.). 1954. Repr. 29.00x o.p. (ISBN 0-403-04236-4). Somerset Pub.

Renunciation of War see Origin & Conclusion of the Paris Pact.

Reorganised National Health Service. 2nd ed. Ruth Levitt. 256p. 1979. pap. 9.00 o.p. (ISBN 0-85664-683-0, Pub. by Croom Helm Ltd). Routledge Chapman & Hall.

Reorganised National Health Service. 3rd ed. Ruth Levitt & Andrew Wall. LC 84-12745. 296p. 1984. 31.00 o.p. (ISBN 0-7099-1673-6, Pub. by Croom Helm Ltd); pap. 15.50 o.p. (ISBN 0-7099-1674-4). Routledge Chapman & Hall.

Reoviruses see Echo Viruses.

Repair & Reconstruction in the Orbital Region. 2nd ed. John C. Mustarde. (Illus.). 1980. text ed. 130.00 o.p. (ISBN 0-443-01698-4). Churchill.

Repair & Remodeling Cost Data, 1986. 7th ed. Means, R. S., Company, Inc. Staff. Ed. by Allan Cleveland. (Illus.). 480p. 1985. pap. 42.95 o.p. (ISBN 0-87629-003-9). R S Means.

Repairing Old China & Ceramic Tile. Jeff Oliver. 1986. 9.95 o.p. (ISBN 0-316-65007-2). Little.

Repaso. rev. ed. Ed. by Donald D. Walsh & Harlan Sturm. (Sp). 1971. text ed. 9.95x o.p. (ISBN 0-393-09955-5, NortonC). Norton.

Repaso De Gramatica. 2nd ed. Osvaldo N. Soto. 360p. 1974. pap. text ed. 15.00 o.p. (ISBN 0-15-576617-1, HC). HarBraceJ.

Repeated Exposure: Photographic Imagery in the Print Media. George L. McKenna. LC 81-86054. (Illus.). 104p. (Orig.). 1982. pap. 14.00x o.p. (ISBN 0-942614-07-0). Nelson-Atkins.

Repent & Believe. Derek Prince. (Foundation Ser.: Bk. II). 1965-66. pap. 2.95 o.p. (ISBN 0-934920-01-X, B-11). Derek Prince.

Repent, Lanny Merkel. Faith Sullivan. 228p. 1981. text ed. 9.95 o.p. (ISBN 0-07-062347-3). McGraw.

Repent, O Graduate. Harold T. Toolsie. 1980. 7.50 o.p. (ISBN 0-682-49060-1). Exposition-Phoenix.

Repertoire d'Art et d'Archeologie, Vols. 1-45. 1170.00 o.p. (ISBN 0-317-44527-8); pap. 936.00 o.p. (ISBN 0-317-44528-6). Kraus Repr.

Repertoire: Essais Critiques, 4 vols. Michel Butor. 1960-64. Set. pap. 65.00 o.p. (ISBN 0-685-11526-7). French & Eur.

Repertoire International des Musiques Electroacoustiques. Hugh Davies. 330p. Repr. of 1968 ed. lib. bdg. 49.00 o.p. (Pub. by Am Repr Serv). Reprint Servs.

Repertory of Disarmament Research: 1982. United Nations Institute for Disarmament Research Staff. 1982. 35.00 o.p. (ISBN 92-9045-002-9, GVE.82.0.2). UN.

Repl Pkg Drops Strea. 1971. 37.84 o.p. (ISBN 0-07-521269-2). McGraw.

Replay: Murder. John Logue. 1983. pap. 2.50 o.s.i. (ISBN 0-345-30304-0). Ballantine.

Report from Group Seventeen. Robert C. O'Brien. LC 76-175291. 1972. 5.95 o.s.i. (ISBN 0-689-10445-6, Atheneum). Macmillan.

Report from Peking: Observations of a Western Diplomat on the Cultural Revolution. D. W. Fokkema. 1972. 9.95 o.p. (ISBN 0-7735-0146-0, McGill Canada). U of Toronto Pr.

Report from the Heart. Consuelo S. Baehr. 1977. pap. 1.75 o.p. (ISBN 0-380-01658-3, 33266). Avon.

Report from the Synod: John Paul II & the Battle for Vatican II. Richard Cowden-Guido. 448p. (Orig.). 1986. pap. 12.95 o.p. (ISBN 0-937495-00-X). Trinity Comns.

Report Graphics: Writing the Design Report. Richard Austin. 176p. 1983. 26.95 o.p. (ISBN 0-442-20886-3). Van Nos Reinhold.

Report of an FAO-UNDP International Expert Consultation on the Use of Improved Technology for Food Production in Rainfed Areas of Tropical Asia. 65p. 1976. pap. 7.50 o.p. (ISBN 0-685-66341-8, F1088, FAO). UNIPUB.

Report of an FAO-WHO Joint Conference on Food Additives: Geneva, Sept. 1975. (Nutrition Meetings Reports: No. 11). 14p. (2nd printing). 1974. pap. 5.75 o.p. (ISBN 0-92-802-4, F246, FAO). UNIPUB.

Report of the Ad-Hoc Dean Evaluation Committee. 1978. 5.00 o.p. (ISBN 0-686-83874-2). AACP Alexandria.

Report of the Adjunct Task Force on Antitrust Aspects of Third Party Payment Negotiations. (State Legal Initiatives: Legal Developments Report No. 2). 57p. 1983. 30.00 o.p. (ISBN 0-317-36954-7, C-118912). Am Hospital.

Report of the Commission on the Supply of & Demand for Qualified Librarians. Library Association, London Staff. 72p. (Orig.). 1977. pap. text ed. 10.50x o.p. (ISBN 0-85365-870-6, Pub. by Lib Assn England). Oryx Pr.

Report of the Director General on the Activities of the Organization. Incl. 1969. pap. 9.25 (U546). UNIPUB; 1971. pap. 8.75 (U547). UNIPUB; 1972. pap. 16.50 (U548). UNIPUB; 1973. pap. 14.50 (U549). UNIPUB; 1974. pap. 17.25 (U550). UNIPUB. UNESCO). UNIPUB.

Report of the DOD Commission on Beirut International Airport Terrorist Act, October 23, 1983. (Admiral Long Committee Report). 147p. (Orig.). 1984. pap. 4.75 o.p. (ISBN 0-318-11824-6, S/N 008-000-00400-5). USGPO.

Report of the Eighth Session of the Near East Commission on Agricultural Planning. (Illus.). 26p. 1978. pap. 7.50 o.p. (ISBN 92-5-100354-8, F1251, FAO). UNIPUB.

Report of the Expert Consultation on the Conditions of Access to the Fish Resources of the Exclusive Economic Zones. 205p. 1983. pap. text ed. 15.50 o.p. (ISBN 92-5-101422-1, F2512, FAO). UNIPUB.

Report of the FAO-ADAA Workshop on the Management of Small Scale Fishery Enterprises. (Fisheries Technical Papers: No. 3). 24p. 1977. pap. 7.50 o.p. (ISBN 92-5-100290-8, F1262, FAO). UNIPUB.

Report of the FAO-Australia Workshop on the Management of Penaeid Shrimp-Prawns in the Asia-Pacific Region: Kooralbyn Valley, Queensland, Australia, 29 October - 2 November 1984. (Fisheries Reports: No. 323). 19p. 1985. pap. 7.50 o.p. (ISBN 92-5-102247-X, F2764, FAO). UNIPUB.

Report of the FAO-ECAFE Expert Group on Selected Aspects of Agricultural Planning in Asia & the Far East. (Agricultural Planning Studies: No. 2). 62p. (Eng. & Fr., 5th Printing 1975). 1963. pap. 7.50 o.p. (ISBN 92-5-100003-4, F2059, FAO). UNIPUB.

Report of the FAO Technical Conference on Fish Inspection & Quality Control: Halifax, 1969. (Fisheries Reports: No. 81). 73p. 1969. pap. 7.50 o.p. (ISBN 0-686-93041-X, F1684, FAO). UNIPUB.

Report of the FAO Technical Conference on the Freezing & Irradiation of Fish: Madrid, 1967. (Fisheries Reports: No. 53). 60p. 1968. pap. 7.50 o.p. (ISBN 0-686-93012-6, F1669, FAO). UNIPUB.

Report of the FAO-WHO Symposium on the Use of Anabolic Agents in Animal Production & Its Public Health Aspects. 24p. 1975. pap. 7.50 o.p. (ISBN 0-685-61023-3, F1092, FAO). UNIPUB.

Report of the Fifteenth FAO Regional Conference for the Near East: Rome, 21-25 April 1981. 54p. 1981. pap. 7.50 o.p. (ISBN 92-5-101108-7, F2222, FAO). UNIPUB.

Report of the Fifteenth Session of the Intergovernmental Group on Oilseeds, Oils & Fats to the Committee on Commodity Problems: Rome, March 1981. 12p. (Eng., Fr. & Span.). 1981. pap. 7.50 o.p. (ISBN 92-5-101065-X, F2128, FAO). UNIPUB.

Report of the Fifth Session of the Regional Commission on Land & Water Use in the Near East: Islamabad, Pakistan, 20-22 Oct. 1976. (Land & Water Development Documents: No. 13). 32p. 1976. pap. 7.50 o.p. (ISBN 92-5-100238-X, F2090, FAO). UNIPUB.

Report of the First FAO-SIDA Seminar on Improvement of Nutritional Quality in Barley & Spring Wheat. 1978. pap. 7.50 o.p. (ISBN 92-5-100283-5, F1267, FAO). UNIPUB.

Report of the Fishery Committee for the Eastern Central Atlantic (CECAF), Subcommittee on Fishery Development: 1st Session, Dakar, Senegal, 1974. (Fisheries Reports: No. 145). 40p. 1974. pap. 7.50 o.p. (ISBN 0-686-93973-5, F1713, FAO). UNIPUB.

Report of the Fishery Committee for the Eastern Central Atlantic (CECAF), Working Party on Resource Evaluation: 5th Session, Dakar, Senegal, 1980. (Fisheries Reports: No. 244). 127p. (Eng. & Fr.). 1981. pap. 9.75 o.p. (ISBN 92-5-101061-7, F2169, FAO). UNIPUB.

Report of the Fourteenth FAO Regional Conference for the Near East. 1979. pap. 7.50 o.p. (ISBN 92-5-100688-1, F1555, FAO). UNIPUB.

Report of the Government Consultation on Crop & Post Harvest Protection Needs in the Sahel. (Illus.). 46p. 1978. pap. 7.50 o.p. (ISBN 92-5-100304-1, F1246, FAO). UNIPUB.

Report of the Government Consultation on Codes of Practice for Fish & Fishery Products: Rome, October , 1975. (Fisheries Reports: No. 173). 6p. 1976. pap. 7.50 o.p. (ISBN 0-685-68360-5, F823, FAO). UNIPUB.

Report of the Indian Ocean Fishery Commission Special Working Party on Stock Assessment of Shrimp of the Indian Ocean Area: 1st Session, Bahrain, 1971. (Fisheries Reports: No. 138). 44p. 1973. pap. 7.50 o.p. (ISBN 0-686-93969-7, F781, FAO). UNIPUB.

Report of the International Commission for the Conservation of Atlantic Tunas: 1st Meeting, Rome 1969. (Fisheries Reports: No. 84). 47p. 1970. pap. 7.50 o.p. (ISBN 0-686-93046-0, F1686, FAO). UNIPUB.

Report of the International Symposium on the Early Life History of Fish: Obun, Scotland. (Fisheries Reports: No. 141). 61p. 1973. pap. 7.50 o.p. (ISBN 0-686-93971-9, F786, FAO). UNIPUB.

Report of the Joint ICES-EIFAC Symposium on Eel Research & Management: Helsinki, Finland, 9-11 June 1976 (Anguilla Spp.) (European Inland Fisheries Advisory Commission (EIFAC): Technical Papers: No. 28). 49p. (Eng. & Fr.). 1976. pap. 7.50 o.p. (ISBN 92-5-000121-5, F769, FAO). UNIPUB.

Report of the Joint Session of the Indian Ocean Fisheries Commission (IOFC) (Seventh Session) & the Indo-Pacific Fisheries Commission (IPFC) (Twentieth Session) Bali, Indonesia, November 1982. (Fisheries Reports: No. 281). 198p. (Eng. & Fr.). 1984. pap. 7.90 o.p. (ISBN 92-5-001378-7, F2493, FAO). UNIPUB.

Report of the Meeting for Consultations on Underwater Noise: Rome, 1968. (Fisheries Reports: No. 76). 35p. 1970. pap. 7.50 o.p. (ISBN 0-686-93032-0, F1682, FAO). UNIPUB.

Report of the Native Grievances Inquiry, 1913-1914. South Africa, Commissioner on Native Grievances Inquiry. LC 77-109362. Repr. of 1914 ed. lib. bdg. 35.00x o.p. (ISBN 0-8371-3851-5, NGI&, Pub. by Negro U Pr). Greenwood.

Report of the Presidential Commission on the Space Shuttle Challenger Accident, Vol. 1. (Illus.). 266p. (Orig.). 1986. pap. 18.00 o.p. (S/N 040-000-00496-3). USGPO.

Report of the Second International Training Course in Remote Sensing Applications for Agriculture: Rome, 1977. (Miscellaneous Documents Ser.). 93p. 1978. pap. 7.50 o.p. (ISBN 92-5-100425-0, F1316, FAO). UNIPUB.

Report of the Second Joint FAO-WHO Conference on Food Additives: Rome, June, 1963. (Nutrition Meetings Reports: No. 34). 13p. 1974. pap. 5.00 o.p. (ISBN 92-5-101825-1, F381, FAO). UNIPUB.

Report of the Second Meeting of the Eastern African Sub-Committee for Soil Correlation & Land Evaluation: Addis-Ababa, Ethiopia, 25-30 October 1976. East African Subcommittee for Soil Correlation & Land Evaluation. (World Soil Resources Reports: No. 47). 131p. 1978. pap. 8.50 o.p. (ISBN 92-5-100408-0, F1318, FAO). UNIPUB.

Report of the Seminar on Agricultural Credit for Small Farmers in Latin America: Quito, Ecuador, 1974. (Development Documents: No. 20). 130p. 1975. pap. 11.50 o.p. (ISBN 0-686-92819-9, F683, FAO). UNIPUB.

Report of the Sixteenth FAO Regional Conference for Latin America: Havana, 1-6 Sept. 1980. 109p. (Eng., Fr. & Span.). 1980. pap. 7.50 o.p. (ISBN 92-5-101039-0, F2148, FAO). UNIPUB.

Report of the Twelfth FAO Regional Conference for Europe: Athens, Greece, 22-27 Sept. 1980. 50p. 1980. pap. 7.50 o.p. (ISBN 92-5-101013-7, F2165, FAO). UNIPUB.

Report of the United States Attorney General's National Committee to Study the Antitrust Laws. United States Attorney General's National Committee to Study the Antitrust Laws. LC 76-10980. xiii, 393p. 1976. Repr. of 1955 ed. lib. bdg. 35.00x o.p. (ISBN 0-8371-8822-9, USAL). Greenwood.

Report of the Working Party on the Association of Overseas Territories with the European Economic Community, Including Commodity Trade Studies. (Eng. & Fr.). 1958. pap. 5.50 o.p. (ISBN 0-686-93126-2, G54, GATT). UNIPUB.

Report of World Conference of the United Nations Decade for Women: Proceedings of the World Conference on Equality, Development & Peace, Copenhagen, July 14-30, 1988. World Conference of the United Nations Decade for Women Staff. 18.00 o.p. (ISBN 92-1-130040-1, E.80.IV.3). UN.

Report on Domestic & International Loan Charge-offs, 1985. Ed. by Marlene Granitz. (Illus.). 40p. 1986. pap. text ed. 18.00 o.s.i. (ISBN 0-936742-34-8). Robt Morris Assocs.

Report on Human Rights in Chile. 1986. 5.00 o.p. Natl Lawyers Guild.

Report on Library Networks. Donald D. Hendricks. (Occasional Papers: No. 108). 23p. 1973. pap. 2.00 o.p. (ISBN 0-317-58901-6). U of Ill Lib Info Sci.

Report on Nicaragua. NLG. 5.00 o.p. Natl Lawyers Guild.

Report on Practices of the Electric Power Research Institute: In the Selection & Contracting of Research Projects. 86p. 1984. 7.50 o.p. (ISBN 0-318-17730-7). NARUC.

Report on Quantitative Analysis in Fishery Industries Development: Expert Consultation held at Rome, Italy, 1975. (Fisheries Reports: No. 167). 1975. pap. 7.50 ea. o.p. (F809, FAO); Vol. 1, 22p. pap. o.p. (F809); Vol. 2, 24p. pap. o.p. (F810); Vol. 3, 12p. pap. o.p. (F811); Vol. 4, 14p. pap. o.p. (F812); Vol. 5, 11p. pap. o.p. (F813); Vol. 6, 7p. pap. o.p. (F814). UNIPUB.

Report on the Ad Hoc Consultation on a Scheme for Agricultural Credit Development. (Development Documents: No. 31). 24p. (Eng., Fr. & Span.). 1976. pap. 7.50 o.p. (ISBN 92-5-100087-5, F1150, FAO). UNIPUB.

Report on the British Museum (Natural History) 1978-1980. Trustees of the British Museum (Natural History) (Illus.). x, 167p. 1981. pap. 18.75x o.p. (ISBN 0-565-00842-0, Pub. by Brit Mus Nat Hist England). Sabbot-Natural Hist Bks.

Report on the FAO-RED Workshop on the Effective Use of Marketing for the Development of Small Farmers in Asia: Held in Bangkok, Thailand, 3-7 May 1976. 86p. 1976. pap. 9.75 o.p. (ISBN 92-5-100083-2, F1135, FAO). UNIPUB.

Report on the Greeks: Findings of a Twentieth Century Fund Team Which Surveyed Conditions in Greece in 1947. Twentieth Century Fund Staff. pap. 24.00 o.p. (ISBN 0-527-02839-8). Kraus Repr.

Report on the International Conference on New Musical Notation Organized by the Index of New Musical Notation (New York) & the Seminar of Musicology (Ghent) Ed. by Herman Sabbe et al. 120p. 1975. pap. text ed. 30.00 o.p. (ISBN 90-265-0221-4, Pub. by Swets Pub Serv Holland). Swets North Am.

Report on the Scientific Results of the Voyage of H. M. S. Challenger During the Years 1873-1876, 50 Vols. Great Britain, Challenger Office Staff. (Illus.). 1880-1895. Set. 5000.00 o.p. (ISBN 0-384-19750-7). Johnson Repr.

Report on Trade Conditions in China. Harry Burrill & Raymond F. Crist. LC 78-74353. (Modern Chinese Economy Ser.). 130p. 1980. lib. bdg. 20.00 o.p. (ISBN 0-8240-4265-4). Garland Pub.

Report to Congress & the Secretary by the Task Force on Long-Term Health Care Policies. Daniel P. Bourque. LC 87-2170. (DHHS Publication HCFA). 340p. 1987. pap. 18.00 o.p. (ISBN 0-318-23757-1, 017-060-00202-6). USGPO.

Report to Congress on Alaskan Oil: Section 126 of the Export Administration Amendments Act of 1985. (Illus.). 215p. (Orig.). 1986. pap. 10.00 o.p. (ISBN 0-318-21309-5, S/N 003-009-00480-2). USGPO.

Report to Congress: Waste from the Extraction & Benefication of Metallic Ores, Phosphate Rock, Asbestos, Overburden from Uranium Mining & Oil Shale. (Illus.). 308p. 1985. pap. 11.00 o.p. (ISBN 0-318-19894-0, S/N 055-000-00253-3). USGPO.

Report Writing for Business. 7th ed. Raymond V. Lesikar. 1986. 33.50x o.p. (ISBN 0-256-03332-3). Irwin.

Report Writing in dBASE II. Marilyn McMahon et al. 1985. pap. 15.95 o.p. (ISBN 0-912677-19-8). Tate Pub.

Reporter Finds God Through Spiritual Healing. Emily G. Neal. (Orig.). 1965. pap. 5.95 o.p. (ISBN 0-8192-1057-9). Morehouse Pub.

Reporter Services & Their Use. Ed. by Sanford M. Morse. 126p. 1980. pap. 5.00 o.p. (ISBN 0-87179-340-7). BNA.

Reporting. Lillian Ross. 1964. 6.50 o.s.i. S&S.

Reporting for the Print Media. 2nd ed. Fred Fedler. 342p. 1979. pap. text ed. 14.95 o.p. (ISBN 0-15-576613-9, HC). HarBraceJ.

Reporting for the Print Media. 3rd ed. Fred Fedler. 641p. 1984. pap. text ed. 17.00 net o.p. (ISBN 0-15-576625-2, HC). HarBraceJ.

Reporting for the Print Media: A Workbook. Fred Fedler. (Illus.). 257p. (Orig.). 1973. pap. text ed. 12.95 o.p. (ISBN 0-15-576615-5, HC). HarBraceJ.

Reporting from Moscow: Soviet Successions. David Thomas. Ed. by Walter Laquer & Michael Ledeen. (American Media & Foreign Affairs Ser.). 192p. 1986. 19.95 o.p. Transaction Pubs.

Reporting on Comparative Financial Statements. (Statements on Standards for Accounting & Review Services Ser.: No. 2). 1979. pap. 1.60 o.p. (ISBN 0-686-70247-6). Am Inst CPA.

Reporting on Compiled Financial Statements. (Statements on Standards for Accounting & Review Services Ser.: No. 5). 1982. pap. 1.60 o.p. (ISBN 0-686-84312-6). Am Inst CPA.

Reporting Public Affairs. Schulte. 1981. write for info. o.p. (ISBN 0-02-408040-3). Macmillan.

Reportpack Simplified. Donald C. Scot. 250p. 1983. 44.95 o.p. (ISBN 0-442-28111-0). Van Nos Reinhold.

Reports. Midwest Category Seminar, 3rd. Ed. by M. Barr. LC 70-96694. (Lecture Notes in Mathematics: Vol. 106). 1969. pap. 14.70 o.p. (ISBN 0-387-04625-9). Springer-Verlag.

Reports & Opinions of the Attorney General of the Republic of Liberia: December 1922-July 1930. Liberia, Republic of, Staff. 448p. 1969. 40.00x o.p. (ISBN 0-8014-0530-0). Cornell U Pr.

Reports & Papers on Botany. Ed. by Arthur Henfrey. Repr. of 1849 ed. 37.00 o.p. (ISBN 0-384-22312-5). Johnson Repr.

Reports & Relevant Papers of the Workshop on Controlled Reproduction of Cultivated Fishes. Controlled Reproduction of Cultivated Fishes Workshop Staff. (European Inland Fisheries Advisory Commission (EIFAC): Technical Papers: No. 25). 180p. 1975. pap. 11.75 o.p. (ISBN 0-686-93008-8, F766, FAO). UNIPUB.

Reports of the Cambridge Anthropological Expedition to Torres Straits, 6 vols. Ed. by A. C. Haddon. Incl. General Ethnography. Repr. of 1935 ed. 53.00 o.p. (ISBN 0-685-27602-3); Physiology & Psychology. Repr. of 1901 ed. 35.00 (ISBN 0-685-27603-1); Linguistics. S. H. Ray. Repr. of 1907 ed. 53.00 o.p. (ISBN 0-685-27604-X); Arts & Crafts. Repr. of 1912 ed. Vols. 4-6. 44.00 ea. o.p.; Sociology, Magic & Religion of the Western Islanders. Repr. of 1904 ed. 33.00 o.p. (ISBN 0-685-27606-6); Sociology, Magic & Religion of the Eastern Islanders. Repr. of 1908 ed. 26.00 o.p. (ISBN 0-685-27607-4). (Landmarks in Anthropology Ser). 2242p. Set. 260.00 o.p. (ISBN 0-686-57612-8). Johnson Repr.

Reports of the Midwest Category Seminar, Fourth. Midwest Category Seminar Staff. Ed. by S. MacLane. LC 78-126772. (Lecture Notes in Mathematics: Vol. 137). 1970. pap. 10.90 o.p. (ISBN 0-387-04926-6). Springer-Verlag.

Repossessions: 1982 & 1987 Supplement. LC 82-60508. 141p. 1982. pap. 48.00 o.p. (ISBN 0-943116-09-0). Nat Consumer Law.

Representation & Redistricting Issues. Bernard Grofman et al. LC 81-47783. (Policy Studies Organization Bk.). 304p. 1982. 33.00x o.p. (ISBN 0-669-04718-X). Lexington Bks.

Representation Theory of Finite Groups & Associative Algebras. Charles W. Curtis & Irving Reiner. LC 62-16994. (Pure & Applied Mathematics Ser.). 685p. 1962. 69.50 o.p. (ISBN 0-470-18975-4, Pub. by Wiley-Interscience). Wiley.

Representation Theory of the Symmetric Groups. G. D. James. (Lecture Notes in Mathematics Ser.: Vol. 682). 1978. pap. 15.00 o.p. (ISBN 0-387-08948-9). Springer-Verlag.

Representations of AF-Algebras & of the Group U (Infinity) S. V. Stratila & D. V. Voiculescu. (Lecture Notes in Mathematics: Vol. 486). ix, 169p. 1975. pap. 14.00 o.p. (ISBN 0-387-07403-1). Springer-Verlag.

Representations of Communicative Semitopological Semigroups. C. F. Dunkl & D. E. Ramirez. (Lecture Notes in Mathematics Ser.: Vol. 435). vi, 181p. 1975. pap. 14.00 o.p. (ISBN 0-387-07132-6). Springer-Verlag.

Representations of Finite Chevalley Groups. B. Srinivasan. (Lecture Notes in Mathematics: Vol. 764). 177p. 1979. pap. text ed. 16.00 o.p. (ISBN 0-387-09716-3). Springer-Verlag.

Representations of Permutation Groups, Part 1: Representations of Wreath Products & Applications to the Representations Theory of Symmetric & Alternating Groups. A. Kerber. LC 72-183956. (Lecture Notes in Mathematics: Vol. 240). viii, 192p. 1972. pap. 10.00 o.p. (ISBN 0-387-05693-9). Springer-Verlag.

Representations of Real Numbers by Infinite Series. J. Galambos. LC 75-44296. (Lecture Notes in Mathematics: Vol. 502). 1976. pap. 13.00 o.p. (ISBN 0-387-07547-X). Springer-Verlag.

Representative French Poetry. rev. ed. Ed. by Victor E. Graham. LC 67-55719. 1965. net 45.00 o.p. (ISBN 0-8020-1338-4). U of Toronto Pr.

Representative Government in Ireland: A Study of Dail Eireann, 1919-48. J. L. McCraken. LC 75-31470. (Illus.). 1976. Repr. of 1958 ed. lib. bdg. 22.50x o.p. (ISBN 0-8371-8534-3, MCRG). Greenwood.

Representative Irish Tales. Ed. by William B. Yeats. 1979. pap. text ed. 9.00x o.p. (ISBN 0-391-00988-5). Humanities.

Representative Modern Plays: Ibsen to Tennessee Williams. Robert Warnock. 1964. pap. (ISBN 0-673-05415-2). Scott F.

Representative Works of Contemporary American Artists. Alfred Trumble. Ed. by H. Barbara Weinberg. LC 75-28879. (Art Experience in Late 19th Century America Ser.: Vol. 13). (Illus.). 1976. Repr. of 1887 ed. lib. bdg. 88.00 o.p. (ISBN 0-8240-2237-8). Garland Pub.

Representing Prisoners: A Course Handbook. Alvin J. Bronstein. (Litigation & Adminstrative Practice Ser.). 973p. 1981. softcover 45.00 o.p. (ISBN 0-686-79681-0, C4-4154). PLI.

Representing Residential Landlords & Tenants, 2 vols. Pennsylvania Bar Institute Staff. 498p. 1987. 45.00 o.p. (ISBN 0-318-02179-X, 381). PA Bar Inst.

Representing Small Businesses. Ed. by David O. Stewart. LC 85-12119. (Business Practice Library). 766p. 1986. 75.00 o.p. (ISBN 0-471-81726-0, Pub by Wiley Law Publications). Wiley.

Representing Superdoll. Richard Peck. (gr. 7 up). 1980. pap. 1.50 o.p. (ISBN 0-380-00416-X, 47845). Avon.

Representing the Growing Technology Company. American Law Institute-American Bar Association Committee for Continuing Professional Education. LC 87-107673. (ALI-ABA Course of Study Materials Ser.). 877p. o.p. Am Law Inst.

Representing the Tenant in Commercial Leasing. Massachusetts Continuing Legal Education-New England Law Institute, Inc. Staff. 1983. write for info. o.p. Mass CLE.

Representing Trade Associations, 1985. Practising Law Institute Staff & Roger A. Clark. LC 85-19017. (Commercial Law & Practice Course Handbook Ser.: No. 362). 544p. 1985. 15.00 o.p. (A4 4131). PLI.

Reprints of Articles on Drug Therapy, 6 Vols. Ed. by Jan Koch-Weser. Incl. Vol. 6. (Illus.). 215p. 1980. Repr. of 1980 ed. pap. 7.50 (ISBN 0-910133-12-3); Vol. 5. (Illus.). 232p. 1980. Repr. of 1980 ed. pap. 7.50 (ISBN 0-910133-11-5); Vol. 4. (Illus.). 141p. 1977. Repr. of 1976 ed. pap. 6.00 (ISBN 0-910133-10-7); Vol. 3. (Illus.). 197p. 1976. Repr. of 1975 ed. pap. 6.00 (ISBN 0-910133-09-3); Vol. 2. (Illus.). 167p. 1976. Repr. of 1975 ed. pap. text ed. 6.00 (ISBN 0-910133-08-5); Vol. 1. (Illus.). 163p. 1976. Repr. of 1974 ed. pap. text ed. 6.00 (ISBN 0-910133-07-7). (Orig.). pap. MA Med Soc.

Reprise: The Extraordinary Revival of Early Music. Joel Cohen & Herb Snitzer. 224p. 1985. 25.00 o.p. (ISBN 0-316-15037-1). Little.

Repro Math A Test. (ISBN 0-07- 376819-7). McGraw.

Repro-Math A TG. (ISBN 0-07-376813-8). McGraw.

Repro Math B Test. (ISBN 0-07-376820-0). McGraw.

Repro Math C Test. (ISBN 0-07- 376821-9). McGraw.

Repro-Math C TG. (ISBN 0-07- 376815-4). McGraw.

Repro Math D Test. (ISBN 0-07- 376822-7). McGraw.

Repro-Math D TG. (ISBN 0-07- 376816-2). McGraw.

Repro Math E Test. McGraw.

Repro-Math E TG. (ISBN 0-07- 376817-0). McGraw.

Repro-Math E W-TG. (ISBN 0-07- 376830-8). McGraw.

Repro Math F Test. (ISBN 0-07- 376824-3). McGraw.

Repro-Math F TG. (ISBN 0-07-376818-9). McGraw.

Repro-Math R TG. (ISBN 0-07- 376812-X). McGraw.

Repro-Math 8 TG. (ISBN 0-07- 376814-6). McGraw.

Reproducing Kernel Hilbert Spaces: Applications in Statistical Signal Processing. Ed. by H. L. Weinert. LC 82-9332. (Benchmark Papers in Electrical Engineering & Computer Science: Vol. 25). 655p. 1982. 67.95 o.p. (ISBN 0-87933-434-7). Van Nos Reinhold.

Reproduction & Development: Proceedings of the 28th International Congress of Physiological Sciences, Budapest, 1980. Ed. by B. Flerko et al. LC 80-41877. (Advances in Physiological Sciences: Vol. 15). (Illus.). 200p. 1981. 34.00 o.p. (ISBN 0-08-027336-X). Pergamon.

Reproduction of Marine Invertebrates: Acoelomate & Pseudocoelomate Metazoans, Vol. 1. Ed. by Arthur C. Giese & John S. Pearse. 1974. 93.50 o.p. (ISBN 0-12-282501-2). Acad Pr.

Reproduction Photography for Lithography. Eric Chambers. (Illus.). 340p. 1979. 40.00 o.p. (1504) (ISBN 0-88362-057-X). Graphic Arts Tech Found.

Reproduction: Proceedings of the Society for the Study of Developmental Biology, 24th Symposium. Society for the Study of Developmental Biology Staff. Ed. by Michael Locke. 1966. 69.50 o.p. (ISBN 0-12-454174-7). Acad Pr.

Reproduction Provoquee chez les Poissons: Theorie et Pratique. B. J. Harvey & W. S. Hoar. 48p. 1980. pap. 3.00 o.p. (ISBN 0-88936-254-8, IDRC-TS21F, IDRC). UNIPUB.

Reproductive Anthropology: Descent Through Woman. Donald A. Gebbie. LC 80-42013. 321p. 1981. 75.00x o.p. (ISBN 0-471-27985-4, Dist. by A R Liss). Wiley.

Reproductive Behaviour in Ungulates. Andrew F. Fraser. 1968. 60.00 o.p. (ISBN 0-12-266450-7). Acad Pr.

Reproductive Biology. Ed. by H. Balin & S. Glasser. 1973. 92.00 o.p. (ISBN 0-444-15004-8, Excerpta Medica). Elsevier.

Reproductive Clinical Problems in the Dog. D. Joshua & J. Jones. 206p. 1982. 24.00 o.p. (ISBN 0-7236-0656-0). Butterworth.

Reproductive Development of the Female: A Study in the Comparative Physiology of the Adolescent Organism. 3rd ed. Ashley Montagu. LC 78-55285. (Illus.). 252p. 1979. 26.00 o.p. (ISBN 0-88416-218-4). Year Bk Med.

Reproductive Health Hazards in the Workplace. Ed. by Office of Technology Assessment Task Force Staff. LC 65-20035. 422p. 1987. 39.50 o.p. (ISBN 0-397-53003-X). Hemisphere Pub.

Reproductive Health Hazards in the Workplace. LC 85-600559. (OTA-BA-266 Ser.). (Illus.). 436p. (Orig.). 1985. pap. 15.00 o.p. (ISBN 0-318-19895-9, S/N 052-003-01001-1). USGPO.

Reproductive Physiology of Teleost Fishes: A Review of Present Knowledge & Needs for Future Research. (Agricultural Development & Coordination Programme). 89p. 1981. pap. 7.50 o.p. (ISBN 92-5-101145-1, F2257, FAO). UNIPUB.

Reptile Ecology. Harold Heatwole. (Australian Ecology Ser.). (Illus.). 1985. pap. write for info. o.p. U of Queensland Pr.

Reptiles & Amphibians of Australia. 3rd ed. Harold G. Cogger. (Illus.). 660p. 1983. 59.50 o.p. (ISBN 0-88359-012-3). R Curtis Bks.

Reptiles & Amphibians of Minnesota. Walter J. Breckenridge. (Illus.). 1944. 8.95 o.p. (ISBN 0-8166-0573-4). U of Minn Pr.

Reptilian Lungs: Functional Anatomy & Evolution. S. F. Perry. (Advances in Anatomy, Embryology, & Cell Biology Ser.: Vol. 79). (Illus.). 80p. 1983. pap. 24.00 o.p. (ISBN 0-387-12194-3). Springer-Verlag.

Republic. Plato. Tr. by A. D. Lindsay. 1980. Repr. of 1976 ed. 12.95x o.p. (ISBN 0-460-10064-5, Evman); pap. 7.95x o.p. (ISBN 0-460-11064-0, DEL-04325, Evman). Biblio Dist.

Republic! A Novel of Texas. E. V. Thompson. 448p. 1985. 16.95 o.p. (ISBN 0-531-09795-1). Watts.

Republic: Conversations on Fundamentals. Charles A. Beard. LC 80-12036. xiii, 366p. 1980. Repr. of 1962 ed. lib. bdg. 35.00x o.p. (ISBN 0-313-22411-0, BERP). Greenwood.

Republic of China: A Reference Book. 2nd ed. 1986. 68.00x o.p. (ISBN 0-8002-3981-4). Intl Pubns Serv.

Republic of China: A Reference Book, 1987. 550p. 60.00 o.p. (ISBN 0-8002-4103-7). Intl Pubns Serv.

Republic of Cousins: Women's Oppression in Mediterranean Society. Germaine Tillion. 181p. 1983. text ed. 25.00x o.p. (ISBN 0-86356-100-4); pap. text ed. 9.95x o.p. Humanities.

Republic of India: The Development of its Laws & Constitution. Alan Gledhill. LC 77-98761. xii, 309p. Repr. of 1951 ed. lib. bdg. 35.00x o.p. (ISBN 0-8371-2813-7, GLRI). Greenwood.

Republic of Indonesia. D. Woodman. 435p. 1956. (ISBN 0-8022-1928-4). Philos Lib.

Republic of Vietnam: An In-Depth Study of Indochina's Fortress under Attack & the Roots of U. S. Involvement. Harold R. Moroz. 1978. 5.00 o.p. (ISBN 0-682-49125-X). Exposition-Phoenix.

Republic P-47. Aero Publishers, Inc., Aeronautical Staff. LC 66-19665. (Aero Ser: Vol. 6). 1966. pap. 5.95 o.p. (ISBN 0-8168-0520-2, 20520, TAB-Aero). TAB Bks.

Republican, Vols. 1-14, No. 25. 1970. Repr. of 1819 ed. lib. bdg. 525.00x o.p. (ISBN 0-8371-9234-X, RP00). Greenwood.

Republican Party & Black America: From McKinley to Hoover, 1896-1933. Richard B. Sherman. LC 72-96714. 274p. 1973. 20.00x o.p. (ISBN 0-8139-0467-6). U Pr of Va.

Republican Roosevelt. 2nd ed. John M. Blum. LC 54-5182. 177p. 1954. 13.50x o.p. (ISBN 0-674-76301-7); pap. 6.95x o.p. (ISBN 0-674-76302-5). Harvard U Pr.

Republicans, Negroes, & Progressives in the South, Nineteen Twelve to Nineteen Sixteen. Paul D. Casdorph. LC 80-15398. (Illus.). ix, 262p. 1981. text ed. 19.75 o.p. (ISBN 0-8173-0048-1). U of Ala Pr.

Repurchase & Reverse Repurchase Agreements 1985. 715p. 1985. 15.00 o.p. (A4-4135). PLI.

Repurchase & Reverse Repurchase Agreements Revisited 1984, Vol. 341. Practising Law Institute Staff. 303p. 1984. pap. 40.00 o.p. (ISBN 0-317-27425-2, #A-41045). PLI.

Reputation of Trollope. John C. Olmsted & Jeffrey Welch. LC 76-52683. (Library of Humanities Reference Bks.: No. 88). lib. bdg. 36.00 o.p. (ISBN 0-8240-9885-4). Garland Pub.

Requiem & Poem Without a Hero. Anna Akhmatova. Tr. by D. M. Thomas from Rus. 78p. 1976. 10.00x o.p. (ISBN 0-8214-0350-8); pap. 5.50 o.p. (ISBN 0-8214-0357-5). Ohio U Pr.

Requiem for a Lost Piety: The Contemporary Search for the Christian Life. Edward Farley. 1966. pap. 2.50 o.s.i. (ISBN 0-664-24708-3, Westminster). Westminster John Knox.

Requiem for a Woman's Soul. Omar Rivabella. LC 85-10765. 128p. 1986. 14.45 o.s.i. (ISBN 0-394-54917-1). Random.

Requiem for Astounding. Alva Rogers. LC 64-57082. (Illus.). 1964. pap. 6.00 o.p. (ISBN 0-911682-16-3). Advent.

Requiem Pour une Nonne: Theatre. Albert Camus. 1956. pap. 7.50 o.p. (ISBN 0-685-11527-5). Schoenhof.

Requirements for Certification of Teachers, Counselors, Librarians, Administrators: For Elementary Schools, Secondary Schools & Junior Colleges. 49th, 1984-85 ed. Mary P. Burks. LC 43-1905. 240p. 1984. lib. bdg. 24.00x o.s.i. (ISBN 0-226-08103-6). U of Chicago Pr.

Requirements for Certification of Teachers, Counselors, Librarians, Adminstrators: For Elementary Schools, Secondary Schools & Junior Colleges. 50th ed. Mary P. Burks. 234p. 1985. lib. bdg. 26.00x o.s.i. (ISBN 0-226-08104-4). U of Chicago Pr.

Requirements for Certification of Teachers, Counselors, Librarians, Administrators: For Elementary Schools, Secondary Schools....(Etc) 51st ed. Mary P. Burks. x, 240p. 1986. lib. bdg. 28.00x o.s.i. (ISBN 0-226-08105-2). U of Chicago Pr.

Requirements for Certification of Teachers, Counselors, Librarians, Administrators for Elementary Schools, Secondary Schools, Junior Colleges, 1981-82. 46th ed. Elizabeth H. Woellner. (Illus.). 240p. 1981. lib. bdg. 18.00x o.s.i. (ISBN 0-226-90466-0, A43-1905). U of Chicago Pr.

Requirements for Certification of Teachers, Counselors, Librarians, Administrators for Secondary Schools, Junior Colleges, 1983. 48th ed. Elizabeth H. Woellner. (Illus.). viii, 228p. 1983. lib. bdg. 23.00x o.s.i. (ISBN 0-226-90468-7, A43-1905). U of Chicago Pr.

Requirements for Certification of Teachers, Counselors, Librarians, Administrators: 1980-81. 45th ed. Elizabeth H. Woellner. (LC 43-1905). 1980. lib. bdg. 17.00x o.s.i. (ISBN 0-226-90465-2). U of Chicago Pr.

Requirements of Developed Socialist Society. B. Mochalov. 144p. 1980. pap. 4.45 o.p. (ISBN 0-8285-1815-7, Pub. by Progress Pubs USSR). Imported Pubns.

Requirements of Laws & Regulations Enforced by the U. S. Food & Drug Administration. 85p. 1984. pap. 2.50 o.p. (ISBN 0-318-18826-0, S/N 017-012-00321-4). USGPO.

Res & Ab Lab 1. (Our Nations Heritage Ser.). (ISBN 0-07-375433-1). McGraw.

Res & Ab Lab 2. (Our Nations Heritage Ser.) (ISBN 0-07-375434-X). McGraw.

Rescue. Joseph Conrad. 1968. pap. 1.95 o.p. (ISBN 0-393-00457-0, Norton Lib). Norton.

Rescued from Barry: Locomotive Restoration. Alan M. Warren. (Illus.). 192p. 1983. 24.95 o.p. (ISBN 0-7153-8260-8). David & Charles.

Research Act. 2nd ed. Norman K. Denzin. 1978. text ed. 28.95 o.p. (ISBN 0-07-016361-8). McGraw.

Research Advances In Alcohol & Drug Problems, Vol. 4. Ed. by Y. Israel et al. (Illus.). 512p. 1978. 70.00x o.p. (ISBN 0-306-34424-6, Plenum Pr). Plenum Pub.

Research & American Industrial Development. Harold Vagtborg. LC 75-14439. 1976. 89.00 o.p. (ISBN 0-08-019791-4). Pergamon.

Research & Development in FY Nineteen Eighty-Six: Colloquium Proceedings. Ed. by American Association for the Advancement of Science, Public Sector Staff. 1985. pap. text ed. write for info. o.p. (ISBN 0-87168-280-X). AAAS.

Research & Development in the FY 1984 Budget: A Preliminary Analysis. Intersociety Working Group Staff. Ed. by Shapley & Teich. 237p. 1983. pap. 5.00 o.p. (ISBN 0-87168-261-3). AAAS.

Research & Development Limited Partnerships: Structuring, Financing, & Marketing. Practising Law Institute Staff & M. Carr Ferguson. LC 85-233168. (Tax Law & Estate Planning Ser.). 1985. 45.00 o.p. (J4-3571). PLI.

Research & Development: Project Selection Criteria. rev. ed. Jackson E. Ramsey. Ed. by Richard Farmer. LC 86-16085. (Research for Business Decisions: No. 80). 222p. 1986. 44.95 o.p. (ISBN 0-8357-1708-9). UMI Res Pr.

Research & Experiment in Stuttering. H. R. Beech & F. Fransella. 1968. 55.00 o.p. (ISBN 0-08-012539-5). Pergamon.

Research & Innovation in the Modern Corporation. Edwin Mansfield et al. LC 78-159455. 1972. 13.95x o.p. (ISBN 0-393-09826-5). Norton.

Research & Medical Practice: Their Interaction. Ciba. (Ciba Symposium Ser.: No. 44). 1987. 29.00 o.p. (ISBN 0-317-65930-8). Elsevier.

Research & Service: A Fifty Year Record. Dorothy C. Tompkins. LC 77-169911. 154p. (Orig.). 1971. pap. 3.00x o.p. (ISBN 0-87772-081-9). UCB IGS.

Research & the Library: A Student Guide to Basic Techniques. Alan L. Whipple. 120p. (Orig.). (gr. 8-11). 1974. pap. text ed. 3.95x o.p. (ISBN 0-88334-062-3). Ind Sch Pr.

Research Catalog of the Library of the American Museum of Natural History: Classed Catalog. Reading Catalog of the Library of the American Museum of Natural History Staff. 1978. 1050.00 o.p. (ISBN 0-8161-0238-4, Hall Library). G K Hall.

Research Catalogue of the American Geographical Society: First Supplement, 2 pts. Ed. by American Geographical Society Library, New York Staff. Incl. Pt. 1. Regional Catalogue, 2 vols. 1972. lib. bdg. 260.00 (ISBN 0-8161-0999-0); Pt. 2. Topical Catalogue, 2 vols. 1974. lib. bdg. 265.00 (ISBN 0-8161-1083-2). Hall Library). G K Hall.

Research Center Directory, 2 vols. 12th ed. Ed. by Peter D. Dresser. 2000p. 1987. 365.00x o.p. (ISBN 0-8103-0678-6). Gale.

Research Centers Directory, Nineteen Eighty-Seven, 2 vols. 11th ed. Ed. by Mary M. Watkins. 1770p. 1986. Set. 355.00x o.p. (ISBN 0-8103-0472-4). Gale.

Research, Co-Operation & Evaluation of Educational Programmes in the Third World: Workshops Held by the Development Studies Association-Education in Developing Countries Study Group, University of Leeds, U. K., March 30, 1984 & IDS, University of Sussex, U. K., April 9-13, 1984. Ed. by K. Watson & J. Oxenham. 1985. pap. 26.00 o.p. (ISBN 0-08-033395-8, Pub. by PPL). Pergamon.

Research Conference on Labor Relations: Proceedings, Annual Research Conference, 8th, UCLA, 1965. Annual Research Conference Staff. 2.00 o.p. (ISBN 0-89215-028-9). U Cal LA Indus Rel.

Research Design in Clinical Psychology & Psychiatry. 2nd, enl. & rev. ed. J. B. Chassan. LC 78-23548. 492p. 1979. 21.95x o.p. (ISBN 0-470-26577-9). Halsted Pr.

Research Films in Biology, Anthropology, Psychology & Medicine. Anthony R. Michaelis. 1955. 84.50 o.p. (ISBN 0-12-493350-5). Acad Pr.

Research for Profit. O. A. Battista. LC 74-16902. 1974. pap. 4.95 o.p. (ISBN 0-915074-01-X). Knowledge Bk Pubs.

Research for Social Welfare: Six Case Studies in Cyprus. L. G. Moseley. 143p. 1979. pap. text ed. 9.75x o.p. (ISBN 0-7199-0948-1, Pub. by Bedford England). Gower Pub Co.

Research Guide to Jingji Yanjiu. Ed. by James Nickum. (Chinese Research Aid Ser.: No. 4). 1972. 6.00x o.p. (ISBN 0-912966-44-0). IEAS.

Research Guide to Philosophy. Terrence N. Tice & Thomas P. Slavens. LC 83-11834. (Sources of Information in the Humanities Ser.). xii, 608p. 1983. 49.00x o.p. (ISBN 0-8389-0333-9). ALA.

Research Guide to Science Fiction Studies. Marshall B. Tymn et al. (Reference Library of the Humanities: Vol. 87). (LC 76-052682). 1977. lib. bdg. 28.00 o.p. (ISBN 0-8240-9886-2). Garland Pub.

Research Guidelines: A Handbook for Therapists. Cecily J. Partridge & Rosemary E. Barnitt. 111p. 1986. 25.00 o.p. (ISBN 0-87189-305-3). Aspen Pub.

Research in Archives: The Use of Unpublished Primary Sources. Philip C. Brooks. LC 69-19273. (Midway Reprint Ser.). xii, 128p. 1982. pap. text ed. 8.00x o.s.i. (ISBN 0-226-07576-1). U of Chicago Pr.

Research in Arid Regions at Texas Tech: A Listing of Faculty & Student Studies. 26p. 1967. 0.75 o.s.i. Intl Ctr Arid & Semi-Arid.

Research in General Practice. J. R. Howie. 193p. 1979. 30.00 o.p. (ISBN 0-85664-506-0, Pub. by Croom Helm Ltd); pap. 14.75 o.p. (ISBN 0-7099-1268-4). Routledge Chapman & Hall.

Research in Phenomenology, 4 vols. Ed. by John Sallis et al. LC 72-176038. (Orig.). Vol. 1. 1971. pap. text ed. 6.50x o.p. (ISBN 0-391-00467-0); Vol. 2. 1972. pap. text ed. 7.00x o.p. (ISBN 0-391-00278-3); Vol. 3. 1973. pap. text ed. 6.50x o.p. (ISBN 0-391-00345-3); Vol. 4. 1974. pap. text ed. 6.50x o.p. (ISBN 0-391-00385-2). Humanities.

Research in Phenomenology, Vol. 9. John Sallis. (Orig.). 1979. pap. text ed. 10.50x o.p. (ISBN 0-391-01297-5). Humanities.

Research in Phenomenology, Vol. 12. John Sallis. 247p. 1982. pap. text ed. 10.50x o.p. Humanities.

Research in Phenomenology, Vol. 13. John Sallis. 254p. 1983. pap. text ed. 22.50x o.p. (ISBN 0-317-06291-3). Humanities.

Research in Phenomenology, Vol. 14, 1984. Ed. by John Sallis. 288p. 1984. pap. 22.50x o.p. Humanities.

Research in Phenomenology: 1975, Vol. 5. John Sallis et al. 1975. pap. text ed. 7.95x o.p. (ISBN 0-391-00491-3). Humanities.

Research in Phenomenology: 1976, Vol. 6. John Sallis et al. 1976. pap. text ed. 10.50x o.p. (ISBN 0-391-00708-4). Humanities.

Research in Phenomenology, 1980, Vol. 10. Ed. by John Sallis. 237p. 1980. pap. text ed. 10.50x o.p. (ISBN 0-391-02229-6). Humanities.

Research in Phenomenology, 1985, Vol. 15. Ed. by John Sallis. 304p. 1985. pap. text ed. 22.50x o.p. (ISBN 0-318-20603-X). Humanities.

Research in Protozoology, Vol. 1-3. Ed. by T. T. Chen. 1972. 100.00 o.p. (ISBN 0-08-016437-4). Pergamon.

Research in Service to Society: The First Fifty Years of the Institute for Research in Social Science at the University of North Carolina. Guy B. Johnson & Guion G. Johnson. LC 79-21247. (Institute for Research in Social Science). xv, 442p. 1980. 27.00x o.p. (ISBN 0-8078-1420-2). U of NC Pr.

Research in Support of Motor Truck Brake System Design & Development. Paul S. Fancher. (Illus.). 141p. 1980. 12.00 o.p. (ISBN 0-938654-27-6, BRAKE). Indus Dev Inst Sci.

Research in the Psychobiology of Human Behavior. Eugene Meyer & Joseph V. Brady. LC 78-24710. 1979. text ed. 17.50x o.p. (ISBN 0-8018-2238-6). Johns Hopkins.

Research in the Schizophrenic Disorder, Vol. 1 & Vol. 2: The Stanley R. Dean Award Lectures. Ed. by Robert Cancro & Stanley R. Dean. 667p. 1986. Vol. 1, 291p. 47.50 o.s.i. (ISBN 0-08-035162-X); Vol. 2, 376p. 57.50 o.s.i. (ISBN 0-08-035163-8). Pergamon.

Research in Transportation: Legal-Legislative & Economic Sources & Procedures. Ed. by Kenneth U. Flood. LC 72-118792. (Management Information Guides Ser.: No. 20). 132p. 1970. 68.00x o.p. (ISBN 0-8103-0820-7). Gale.

Research in Verbal Behavior & Some Neuro-Physiological Implications. Ed. by Kurt Salzinger & Suzanne Salzinger. 1967. 78.00 o.p. (ISBN 0-12-617150-5). Acad Pr.

Research in Zoos & Aquariums. Institute of Laboratory Animal Resources Staff. 1975. pap. 11.50x o.p. (ISBN 0-309-02319-X). Natl Acad Pr.

Research into Personal Development: Educational & Vocational Choice. Ed. by Anders Duner. 192p. 1978. pap. text ed. 18.50 o.p. (ISBN 90-265-0284-2, Pub. by Swets & Zeitlinger Netherlands). CJ Hogrefe Pubs.

Research into Teaching Methods in Higher Education. 4th ed. Ruth M. Beard & Donald Bligh. 158p. 1978. pap. 23.00 o.p. (ISBN 0-900868-61-9, Open Univ Pr). Taylor & Francis.

Research Issues in Irrigation Systems in Developing Countries: Proceedings. (Lincoln Institute Monograph: No. 78-6). 1978. pap. 4.00 o.s.i. (ISBN 0-686-23890-7). Lincoln Inst Land.

Research Libraries & Technology. Herman H. Fussler. 1974. lib. bdg. 10.00x o.s.i. (ISBN 0-226-27558-2). U of Chicago Pr.

Research Methodology & Its Application to Nursing. Yvonne M. Williamson. LC 80-22919. 325p. 1981. 24.95 o.p. (ISBN 0-471-03313-8). Wiley.

Research Methods. Patrick McNeill. (Society Now Ser.). 160p. 1985. pap. text ed. 6.50 o.p. (ISBN 0-422-79540-2, 9590, Pub. by Tavistock England). Routledge Chapman & Hall.

Research Methods for Nurses. Winona B. Ackerman & Paul R. Lohnes. (Illus.). 304p. 1981. text ed. 38.95x o.p. (ISBN 0-07-000182-0). McGraw.

Research Methods in Education. Louis Cohen & Lawrence Manion. (Illus.). 328p. 1980. 25.50 o.p. (ISBN 0-85664-917-1, Pub. by Croom Helm Ltd). Routledge Chapman & Hall.

Research Methods in Librarianship: Historical & Bibliographical Methods in Library Research. Ed. by Rolland E. Stevens. LC 79-631732. (Monograph: No. 10). 140p. 1971. 5.00x o.p. (ISBN 0-87845-032-7). U of Ill Lib Info Sci.

Research Methods: Statistical Concepts & Research Practicum. John H. Behling. 1977. pap. text ed. 8.25 o.p. (ISBN 0-8191-0084-6). U Pr of Amer.

Research Needs Associated with Toxic Substances. Michael F. Saunders et al. Ed. by Water Pollution Control Federation Staff. (Illus.). 300p. 1982. pap. 40.00 o.p. (ISBN 0-943244-02-1, P0002LN). Water Pollution.

Research Needs Relating to Performance of Aggregates in Highway Construction. (National Cooperative Highway Research Project Report). 68p. 1970. 3.40 o.p. (ISBN 0-309-01887-0). Transport Res Bd.

Research Needs Report: Design, Materials & Manufacturing Research. 1976. pap. text ed. 5.00 o.p. (ISBN 0-685-72347-X, H00089). ASME.

Research Needs Report: Energy Conversion Research. 129p. 1976. pap. 10.00 o.p. (ISBN 0-685-99210-1, H00090). ASME.

Research on Mathematical Thinking of Young Children. Ed. by Leslie P. Steffe. LC 75-22461. 208p. 1975. pap. 8.00 o.p. (ISBN 0-87353-088-8). NCTM.

Research on Steroids. Ed. by A. Klopper et al. 1979. 67.50 o.p. (ISBN 0-12-416050-6). Acad Pr.

Research on Steroids, Vol. 4. C. Conti et al. 1971. 70.00 o.p. (ISBN 0-08-017573-2). Pergamon.

Research Organization & Science Promotion in the Federal Republic of Germany. Ed. by Hildegard & Reinhold Geimer. 217p. 1981. lib. bdg. 18.00 o.p. (ISBN 3-598-10357-3). K G Saur.

Research Paper. Barbara Gregorich & Therese F. Waldowski. LC 78-730060. (Illus.). 1977. pap. text ed. 159.00 o.s.i. (A323). Soc for Visual.

Research Paper: Process, Form, & Content. 5th ed. Audrey J. Roth. 305p. 1986. pap. text ed. (ISBN 0-534-06090-0). Wadsworth Pub.

Research Paper-the Business Report: A Few Ideas. Sheldon F. Katz. 41p. 1984. pap. text ed. 4.50 o.p. (ISBN 0-89917-435-3, Pub. by College Town Pr). Tichenor Pub.

Research Planning & Action for the Elderly. Ed. by Donald Kent et al. LC 72-140049. 569p. 1972. 49.95 o.p. (ISBN 0-87705-056-2). Human Sci Pr.

Research Practices in the Study of Kinship. Alan Barnard & Anthony Good. (Research Methods in Social Anthropology Ser.). 1984. 38.00 o.p. (ISBN 0-12-078980-9). Acad Pr.

Research Priorities in African Literature. Ed. by Bernth Lindfors. 222p. 1984. lib. bdg. 27.00 o.p. (ISBN 3-598-10570-3). K G Saur.

Research Priorities in Tropical Biology. National Research Council. xii, 116p. 1980. pap. text ed. 9.75x o.p. (ISBN 0-309-03043-9). Natl Acad Pr.

Research Project on Workfare. Arodel Child & Lynn Johnson. 257p. o.s.i. (32,115). NCLS Inc.

Research Results of the National Day Care Study. Jeffrey Travers & Barbara D. Goodson. (National Day Care Study Ser.). (Illus.). 288p. (Orig.). 1981. 35.00x o.p. (ISBN 0-89011-554-0). Abt Bks.

Research Scientist. Educational Research Council of America Staff. Ed. by Theodore N. Ferris & John P. Marchak. (Real People at Work Ser.: Series O). (Illus.). 36p. (Orig.). (gr. 5). 1976. pap. text ed. 2.70 o.p. (ISBN 0-89247-116-6, 9539). Changing Times.

Research Studies in Comparative Sociology. Ed. by Charles Mark. 147p. 1973. pap. text ed. 8.95x o.p. (ISBN 0-8422-0308-7). Irvington.

Research to Education: A Conceptual Introduction. James H. McMillan & Sally Schumacher. 1984. text ed. write for info. o.p. (ISBN 0-673-39167-1). Scott F.

Research Tools for Latin American Historians: A Select, Annotated Bibliography. David P. Werlich. LC 78-68291. 285p. 1980. lib. bdg. 43.00 o.p. (ISBN 0-8240-9762-9). Garland Pub.

Research, Training, Test & Production Reactor Directory. 2nd ed. LC 83-71582. (Handbook Ser.). 1983. 350.00 o.p. (ISBN 0-89448-507-5). Am Nuclear Soc.

Researcher's Guide to Washington Experts see Who Knows: A Guide to Washington Experts.

Researches in Spiritualism. William Crookes. (Illus.). 112p. 1984. Repr. of 1880 ed. photocopy 8.95 o.p. (ISBN 0-915554-18-6). Sourcebook.

Researches on Magnetism, Electricity, Heat, Light, Crystallization & Chemical Attraction in Relation to the Vital Force. Karl Von Reichenbach. Tr. by William Gregory. 1974. 10.00 o.p. (ISBN 0-8216-0216-0, Pub. by Univ Bks). Carol Pub Group.

Reseau Aerien. Michel Butor. pap. 9.95 o.p. (ISBN 0-685-37257-X). French & Eur.

Resena de la Investigacion sobre Efectividad de los Maestros en Africa, America Latina, Filipinas, India, Malasia, Medio Oriente y Tailandia: Sintesis de Resultados. B. Avalos & W. Haddad. 118p. 1981. pap. 10.00 o.p. (ISBN 0-88936-259-9, IDRC-TS23S, IDRC). UNIPUB.

Reservoir Design: A Bibliography. Coppa & Avery Consultants Staff. (Architecture Ser.: Bibliography A 1319). 1985. pap. 2.00 o.p. (ISBN 0-89028-269-2). Vance Biblios.

Resettlement. Arthur J. Demarest. 166p. 1970. 6.50x o.p. (ISBN 0-911038-75-2, New Voices). Noontide.

Reshaping Remedial Education. Geof Sewell. 144p. 1982. 26.00 o.p. (ISBN 0-7099-2348-1, Pub. by Croom Helm Ltd). Routledge Chapman & Hall.

Residence of Twenty-One Years in the Sandwich Islands: A Civil, Religious & Political History. rev. 3rd ed. Hiram Bingham. LC 77-83041. 1981. 27.50 o.p. (ISBN 0-8048-1252-7). C E Tuttle.

Residency & Domicile: Issues after the Tax Reform Act of 1984. 224p. 1985. 15.00 o.p. (J4-3565). PLI.

Resident Care Management System. Erwin Rausch & Menna Perper. 162p. 1983. 21.95 o.p. (ISBN 0-8436-0793-9). Van Nos Reinhold.

Resident Witch. Marian T. Place. (Illus.). (gr. 2-5). 1978. pap. 2.50 o.p. (ISBN 0-380-00852-1, Camelot). Avon.

Residential - Light Commercial Cost Data, 1986. 5th ed. Means, R. S., Company, Inc. Staff. Ed. by Dwayne Lehigh. 425p. 1985. pap. 41.95 o.p. (ISBN 0-87629-007-1). R S Means.

Residential Care: A Reader in Current Theory & Practice. Ed. by R. G. Walton & D. Elliott. LC 79-41182. (Social Work Ser.). (Illus.). 345p. 1980. 87.00 o.p. (ISBN 0-08-024690-7); pap. 28.00 o.p. (ISBN 0-08-024689-3). Pergamon.

Residential Care for the Mentally Retarded. E. Stephen. 64p. 1970. pap. 9.00 o.p. (ISBN 0-08-016106-5). Pergamon.

Residential Carpentry. 2nd ed. Mortimer P. Reed. LC 84-15215. 705p. 1985. (ISBN 0-471-86507-9); pap. 17.95 o.p. (ISBN 0-471-81544-6). Wiley.

Residential Consumption, Economic Opportunity & Race. Franklin D. Wilson. LC 79-51705. (Studies in Population). 1979. 28.50 o.p. (ISBN 0-12-757980-X). Acad Pr.

Residential Cost File. Engelsman. 1985. pap. 41.95 o.p. (ISBN 0-442-26705-3). Van Nos Reinhold.

Residential Cost Manual, 1984. Coert Engelsman. 1983. pap. 29.95 o.p. (ISBN 0-442-26679-0). Van Nos Reinhold.

Residential Development & the Planning System: A Study of the Housing Land System at the Local Level. Y. Rydin. (Illus.). 70p. 1985. pap. 22.00 o.p. (ISBN 0-08-032742-7, Pub. by PPL). Pergamon.

Residential Development Handbook. 2nd ed. W. P. O'Mara et al. LC 77-930497. (Community Builders Handbook Ser.). (Illus.). 338p. 1980. 59.00 o.p. (ISBN 0-87420-580-8, R09). Urban Land.

Residential Education. W. R. Fraser. LC 68-24064. 1968. 80.00 o.p. (ISBN 0-08-012909-9); pap. 80.00 o.p. (ISBN 0-08-012908-0). Pergamon.

Residential Group Therapy for Children. Daphne Lennox. (Residential Social Workers Ser.). 220p. 1982. pap. 10.95 o.p. (ISBN 0-422-77550-9, NO. 3782, Pub. by Tavistock England). Routledge Chapman & Hall.

Residential Homes for the Physically Handicapped. Hampden Inskip. 58p. 1981. pap. 5.50x o.p. (ISBN 0-7199-1067-6, Pub. by Bedford England). Gower Pub Co.

Residential Housing & Nuclear Attack. Diane Diacon. LC 84-17639. 146p. 1984. 23.50 o.p. (ISBN 0-7099-0868-7, Pub. by Croom Helm Ltd). Routledge Chapman & Hall.

Residential Mortgage Foreclosures: Current Developments. Pennsylvania Bar Institute Staff. 252p. 1984. 25.00 o.p. (ISBN 0-318-02181-1, 249). PA Bar Inst.

Residential Psychiatric Treatment of Children. Philip Barker et al: LC 74-7208. 354p. 1974. 51.95x o.p. (ISBN 0-470-04910-3). Halsted Pr.

Residential Real Estate for Those Who More Than Dabble. Massachusetts Continuing Legal Education-New England Law Institute, Inc. Staff. 1983. write for info. o.p. Mass CLE.

Residential Segregation: The State & Constitutional Conflict in American Urban Areas. Ronald J. Johnston. (Special Publication Institute, British Geographers Ser.: No. 17). 1984. 36.50 o.p. (ISBN 0-12-387660-5). Acad Pr.

Residential Wiring: Concepts & Practices. Harry Hawkins. 1983. text ed. 18.00 o.p. (ISBN 0-534-02426-2, PWS-Kent Ser Tech). PWS-Kent Pub.

Residual Gases in Electron Tubes: Proceedings. Ed. by T. A. Giorgi & P. Della Porta. 1972. 66.00 o.p. (ISBN 0-12-285550-7). Acad Pr.

Residual Stress & Stress Relaxation. Ed. by Eric Kula & Volker Weiss. LC 82-9803. (Sagamore Army Materials Research Conference Ser.: Vol. 28). 546p. 1982. 89.50x o.p. (ISBN 0-306-41102-4, Plenum Pr). Plenum Pub.

Residue Reviews, Vol. 50. Ed. by F. A. Gunther. x, 192p. 1974. 43.50 o.p. (ISBN 0-387-90082-9). Springer-Verlag.

Residue Reviews, Vol. 53. T. R. Futuko et al. Ed. by F. A. Gunther. (Illus.). 185p. 1974. 38.00 o.p. (ISBN 0-387-90084-5). Springer-Verlag.

Residue Reviews, Vol. 54. D. B. Peakall. LC 62-18595. (Illus.). x, 190p. 1975. 39.00 o.p. (ISBN 0-387-90099-3). Springer-Verlag.

Residue Reviews, Vol. 55. Ed. by F. A. Gunther & J. Davies Gunther. (Residues of Pesticides & Other Contaminants in the Total Environment Ser.). (Illus.). 180p. 1975. text ed. 43.00 o.p. (ISBN 0-387-90102-7). Springer-Verlag.

Residue Reviews, Vol. 56. E. D. Magallona et al. (Illus.). 160p. 1975. 34.00 o.p. (ISBN 0-387-90115-9). Springer-Verlag.

Residue Reviews, Vol. 57. Ed. by F. A. Gunter & J. Davies Gunter. (Illus.). 160p. 1975. 29.00 o.p. (ISBN 0-387-90118-3). Springer-Verlag.

Residue Reviews, Vol. 59. LC 62-18595. (Illus.). 160p. 1975. 31.90 o.p. (ISBN 0-387-90145-0). Springer-Verlag.

Residue Reviews, Vol. 63. J. M. Desmarchelier et al. LC 62-18595. 1976. 35.80 o.p. (ISBN 0-387-90164-7). Springer-Verlag.

Residue Reviews, Vol. 69. Ed. by F. A. Gunther & J. Davies Gunther. LC 62-18595. 1978. 27.50 o.p. (ISBN 0-387-90306-2). Springer-Verlag.

Residue Reviews, Vol. 70. (Illus.). 1979. 27.50 o.p. (ISBN 0-387-90398-4). Springer-Verlag.

Residue Reviews, Vol. 80. Ed. by F. A. Gunther & J. Davies Gunther. (Illus.). 198p. 1981. 39.60 o.p. (ISBN 0-387-90567-7). Springer-Verlag.

Residue Reviews: Residues of Pesticides & Other Contaminants in the Total Environment, 2 vols. Ed. by F. A. Gunther. LC 62-18595. (Residue Reviews Ser.). (Illus.). viii, 168p. 1973. Vol. 48. 40.00 o.p. (ISBN 0-387-90064-0); Vol. 49. 33.00 o.p. (ISBN 0-387-90068-3). Springer-Verlag.

Residue Reviews: Residues of Pesticides & Other Contaminants in the Total Environment, Vol. 64. Ed. by F. A. Gunther & J. Davies Gunther. LC 62-18595. (Illus.). 1976. 39.00 o.p. (ISBN 0-387-90214-7). Springer-Verlag.

Residue Reviews: Residues of Pesticides & Other Contaminants in the Total Environment, Vol. 65. Ed. by F. A. Gunther & J. Davies Gunther. LC 62-18595. (Illus.). 1977. 27.00 o.p. (ISBN 0-387-90222-8). Springer-Verlag.

Residue Reviews: Residues of Pesticides & Other Contaminants in the Total Environment, Vol. 66. Ed. by F. A. Gunther & J. Davies Gunther. LC 62-18595. 1977. 42.90 o.p. (ISBN 0-387-90251-1). Springer-Verlag.

Residue Reviews: Residues of Pesticides & Other Contaminants in the Total Environment, Vol. 68. Ed. by F. A. Gunther & J. Davies Gunther. LC 62-18595. 1977. 44.00 o.p. (ISBN 0-387-90253-8). Springer-Verlag.

Residue Reviews: Sumithion, Vol. 60. Y. Nishizawa et al. LC 62-18595. (Illus.). 208p. 1976. 33.00 o.p. (ISBN 0-387-90091-8). Springer-Verlag.

Residue Reviews: The Problems of Residues in Meat of Edibles, Vol. 46. K. Kaemmerer & S. Buntenkoetter. Ed. by F. A. Gunther. LC 62-18595. 250p. 1973. 71.00 o.p. (ISBN 0-387-90060-8). Springer-Verlag.

Residue Utilization: Management of Agricultural & Agro-Industrial Wastes. 1978. pap. 7.50 o.p. (ISBN 92-5-100320-3, F1265, FAO). UNIPUB.

Titles

Residues & Duality. R. Hartshorne. (Lecture Notes in Mathematics Ser.: Vol. 20). 1966. pap. 21.90 o.p. (ISBN 0-387-03603-2). Springer-Verlag.

Residues of Pesticides & Other Contaminants in the Total Environment. Ed. by F. A. Gunther & J. Davies Gunther. (Residue Reviews Ser.: Vol. 67). 1977. 29.00 o.p. (ISBN 0-387-90252-X). Springer-Verlag.

Residues of Veterinary Drugs in Food: Report of a Joint FAO-WHO Expert Consultation, Rome, 29 October - 5 November 1984. (Food & Nutrition Papers: No. 32). 54p. (Eng., Fr. & Span.). 1985. pap. 7.50 o.p. (ISBN 92-5-002210-7, F2774, FAO). UNIPUB.

Resilience of Ecosystems. Rene Dubos. (Illus.). 1978. pap. 2.50x o.p. (ISBN 0-87081-107-X). Univ Pr Colo.

Resinography: An Introduction to the Definition, Identification, & Recognition of Resins, Polymers, Plastics, & Fibers. Theodore G. Rochow & Eugene G. Rochow. LC 75-34208. (Illus.). 194p. 1976. 37.50x o.p. (ISBN 0-306-30863-0, Plenum Pr). Plenum Pub.

Resistance & Caribbean Literature. Selwyn R. Cudjoe. LC 76-25616. xii, 319p. 1981. 20.00x o.p. (ISBN 0-8214-0353-2); pap. 8.95x o.p. (ISBN 0-8214-0573-X). Ohio U Pr.

Resistance & Deformation of Solid Media. Daniel Rosenthal. LC 72-10583. 372p. 1974. 36.00 o.p. (ISBN 0-08-017100-1). Pergamon.

Resistance: European Resistance to Nazism 1940-45. M. R. Foot. LC 76-49521. 360p. 1977. text ed. 15.00 o.p. (ISBN 0-07-021475-1). McGraw.

Resistance Fighter: Anti-Nazi Terror Tactics of the Austrian Underground. Kurt Von Steiner. (Illus.). 120p. (Orig.). 1986. pap. text ed. 10.00 o.p. (ISBN 0-87364-349-6). Paladin Pr.

Resistance Through Rituals: Youth Subcultures in Post-War Britain. Ed. by Stuart Hall & Tony Jefferson. 1976. 14.95 o.p. (ISBN 0-8419-6601-X). Holmes & Meier.

Resocializing Sex Roles: A Guide for Educators. Ed. by Elinor Waters. 114p. 1980. pap. text ed. 9.25 o.p. (ISBN 0-911547-64-9, 72199W34). Am Assn Coun Dev.

Resolution, Properties, & Genetic Aspects of Complement. Ed. by Kunio Yonemasu et al. 172p. 1974. text ed. 34.50x o.p. (ISBN 0-8422-7229-1). Irvington.

Resolving Community Conflict: An Annotated Bibliography. Anne O. Kilpatrick. 84p. 1983. pap. 4.00 o.p. (ISBN 0-911847-01-4). U GA Inst Community.

Resolving Faculty Disputes. Jane McCarthy & Irving Ladimer. LC 81-67937. 80p. 1981. pap. 8.00 o.p. (ISBN 0-943001-12-9). Am Arbitration.

Resort Timesharing. Keith Trowbridge. 1982. 10.95 o.p. (ISBN 0-671-43984-7). S&S.

Resort to Murder: A Sam Birge Mystery. William Krasner. 224p. 1985. 13.95 o.s.i. (ISBN 0-684-18328-5). Scribner.

Resource Acquisition in Corporate Growth. David W. Packer. 1964. 12.00x o.p. (ISBN 0-262-16010-2). MIT Pr.

Resource Based Learning for School Governors. Alan George. LC 84-19965. 198p. 1984. 26.50 o.p. (ISBN 0-7099-1184-X, Pub. by Croom Helm Ltd). Routledge Chapman & Hall.

Resource Directory: Organization & Publications That Promote Sex Equity in Postsecondary Education. American Institutes for Research Staff. 73p. 1982. 10.00 o.p. (ISBN 0-911696-32-6). Assn Am Coll.

Resource Guide for Search & Rescue Training Material. Rick LaValla & Gene Fear. 1978. pap. 5.00 o.p. (ISBN 0-913724-17-3). Emerg Response Inst.

Resource Management: An Alternative View of the Management Process. Paul S. Bender. LC 82-13471. (Wiley Series on Systems Engineering & Analysis Ser.). 227p. 1982. 41.95x o.p. (ISBN 0-471-08179-5, Pub. by Wiley-Interscience); 41.95 o.p. Assn Inform & Image Mgmt.

Resource Manual for How to Be a Nurse's Aide in a Nursing Home. Didactic Systems staff. 1983. pap. 49.95 o.p. (ISBN 0-686-62231-6). Van Nos Reinhold.

Resource Notebook on Organization. Duane E. Webster. 147p. 1979. 15.00 o.p. (ISBN 0-318-03474-3, ED 191 475). OMS.

Resource Notebook on Planning. Jeffery J. Gardner. 155p. 1979. 15.00 o.p. (ISBN 0-318-16099-4). OMS.

Resource Notebook on Staff Development. Jane E. Rosenberg & Maureen Sullivan. 309p. 1983. 25.00 o.p. (ISBN 0-318-03475-1). OMS.

Resource Organization in Primary Schools. 2nd. ed. Cecilia Gordon. (Orig.). 1987. pap. text ed. 17.95X o.p. (ISBN 0-86184-164-6). Trans Atl Phila.

Resource Recovery Guide, Vol. 1. Ed. by James G. Abert. 608p. 1983. 51.95 o.p. (ISBN 0-442-20235-0). Van Nos Reinhold.

Resource Recovery Processing Equipment. David Bendersky et al. LC 82-7882. (Pollution Technology Rev. 93). (Illus.). 417p. 1983. 42.00 o.p. (ISBN 0-8155-0911-1). Noyes.

Resource Structure of Agriculture: An Economic Analysis. K. Cowling et al. LC 70-114570. 1970. 36.00 o.p. (ISBN 0-08-015585-5). Pergamon.

Resource Teacher: A Guide to Effective Practices. 2nd ed. J. Lee Wiederholt et al. 1983. text ed. write for info. o.s.i. (ISBN 0-205-07978-4, 247978). Allyn.

Resources & Playing. B. Goodall & A. Kirby. LC 78-40931. (Oxford Geography Ser.). 373p. 1979. 55.00 o.p. (ISBN 0-08-023711-8); pap. 24.00 o.p. (ISBN 0-08-023710-X). Pergamon.

Resources for Electric Vehicles & Their Infrastructure: Proceedings. 156p. 1980. pap. 15.00 o.p. (ISBN 0-906048-22-2, PPL-17). Soc Auto Engineers.

Resources for Social Change: Race in the United States. James S. Coleman. LC 77-152494. 134p. 1971. 12.75 o.p. (ISBN 0-471-16493-3, JW). Krieger.

Resources for the Information Economy see **Understanding U. S. Information Policy.**

Resources for Writing for Publication in Education. Sidney B. Katz et al. LC 79-27127. 1980. pap. text ed. 7.95x o.p. (ISBN 0-8077-2579-X). Tchrs Coll.

Resources Management. R. L. Martino. 1970. text ed. 24.95 o.p. (ISBN 0-07-040652-9). McGraw.

Resources, Regimes, World Order. Anthony J. Dolman. (Pergamon Policy Studies on International Development Ser.). 425p. 1981. 58.00 o.p. (ISBN 0-08-028080-3); pap. 105.00 o.p. (ISBN 0-08-028079-X). Pergamon.

Resources, Society & Future. G. Backstrand. 1980. 63.00 o.p. (ISBN 0-08-023266-3); pap. 24.00 o.p. (ISBN 0-08-023267-1). Pergamon.

Respectable Minority: The Democratic Party in the Civil War Era, 1860-1868. Joel H. Silbey. 1977. 12.95 o.p. (ISBN 0-393-05648-1); pap. 4.95x o.p. (ISBN 0-393-09087-6). Norton.

Respectable Sydney Merchant: A. B. Spark of Tempe. Ed. by Graham Abbott & Geoffrey Little. 1976. 27.00x o.p. (ISBN 0-424-00016-4, Pub. by Sydney U Pr). Intl Spec Bk.

Respective Roles of State & Local Governments in Land Policy & Taxation. Ed. by George Lefcoe. (Lincoln Institute Monograph: No. 80-7). 271p. 1980. pap. text ed. 12.00 o.s.i. (ISBN 0-686-31827-7). Lincoln Inst Land.

Respiration of Amphibious Vertebrates. Ed. by G. M. Hughes. 1976. 97.00 o.p. (ISBN 0-12-360750-7). Acad Pr.

Respiration: Proceedings of the 28th International Congress of Physiological Sciences, Budapest 1980. Ed. by I. Hutas & L. A. Debreczeni. (Advances in Physiological Sciences: Vol. 10). (Illus.). 665p. 1981. 100.00 o.p. (ISBN 0-08-026823-4). Pergamon.

Respiratory Disorders. Ed. by Helen Hamilton & Minnie B. Rose. LC 83-20354. (Nurse's Clinical Library). (Illus.). 192p. 1984. text ed. 19.95 o.p. (ISBN 0-916730-58-1). Springhouse Pub.

Respiratory Distress Syndrome: Based on a Conference at Dedham, Mass., May, 1973. Ed. by Claude A. Villee et al. 1973. 60.50 o.p. (ISBN 0-12-722350-9). Acad Pr.

Respiratory Emergencies. Ed. by Kathy E. Goldberg & Joan E. Mason. (Nursing Now Ser.). (Illus.). 128p. 1984. text ed. 13.95 o.p. (ISBN 0-916730-80-8). Springhouse Pub.

Respiratory Functions of Blood. Ed. by Lars Garby & Jerry H. Meldon. LC 77-21980. (Topics in Hematology Ser.). (Illus.). 300p. 1977. 49.50x o.p. (ISBN 0-306-30998-X, Plenum Med Bk). Plenum Pub.

Respiratory Medicine for Primary Care Physicians. Ed. by Charles Drage. LC 82-6870. 222p. 1983. 39.50 o.p. (ISBN 0-12-788165-4). Acad Pr.

Respiratory Monitoring in Intensive Care. Ed. by Alastair A. Spence. LC 82-1190. (Clinics In Critical Care Medicine Ser.: Vol. 4). (Illus.). 1983. 56.00 o.p. (ISBN 0-443-02062-0). Churchill.

Respiratory Physiology. 4th ed. N. Balfour Slonim. LC 81-11055. (Illus.). 311p. 1981. pap. text ed. 19.95 o.p. (ISBN 0-8016-4668-5). Mosby.

Respiratory Problems, Vol. 5. Ellen K. Boyda. (RN Assessment Ser.). 180p. 1986. pap. 15.95 o.p. (ISBN 0-87489-282-1). Med Economics.

Respiratory Therapy Review: A Workbook & Study Guide. 2nd ed. Neal Kelsey. LC 81-14170. (Illus.). 402p. 1981. pap. text ed. 27.95 o.p. (ISBN 0-8016-2638-2). Mosby.

Responding to Casualties of Ships Bearing Hazardous Cargoes. Marine Board Staff. 1979. pap. 8.75 o.p. (ISBN 0-309-02935-X). Natl Acad Pr.

Responding to the Terrorist Threat: Security & Crisis Management. Ed. by Richard H. Shultz, Jr. & Stephen Sloan. (Policy Studies). 1981. 65.00 o.p. (ISBN 0-08-025106-4). Pergamon.

Response in American Catholic Periodicals to the Crises of the Great Depression, 1930-1935. Lawrence B. DeSaulniers. LC 83-23603. 198p. (Orig.). 1984. lib. bdg. 26.00 o.p. (ISBN 0-8191-3786-3); pap. text ed. 12.50 o.p. (ISBN 0-8191-3787-1). U Pr of Amer.

Response: The Church in Mission to a World in Crisis. James A. Cogswell. (Illus., Orig.). 1971. pap. 2.50 o.p. (ISBN 0-8042-9062-8, John Knox). Westminster John Knox.

Response to Adversity: Higher Education in a Harsh Climate. Gareth Williams & Tessa Blackstone. 153p. 1983. 21.00x o.p. (ISBN 0-8002-3886-9). Taylor & Francis.

Responses of Adolescents While Reading Four Short Stories. James R. Squire. 1964. pap. 5.50 o.p. (ISBN 0-8141-4100-5). NCTE.

Responses of Plants to Environmental Stresses. J. Levitt. (Physiological Ecology Ser.). 1972. 85.00 o.p. (ISBN 0-12-445560-3). Acad Pr.

Responses: Prose Pieces, 1948-1976. Richard Wilbur. LC 76-24903. 238p. 1976. 13.95 o.p. (ISBN 0-15-176930-3). HarBraceJ.

Responses to Elie Wiesel. Ed. by Harry J. Cargas. LC 77-94055. 1978. o. p. 15.00 o.p. (ISBN 0-89255-031-7); pap. 5.95 o.p. (ISBN 0-89255-032-5). Persea Bks.

Responses to Participation at Work. M. Marchington. 232p. 1980. text ed. 37.95x o.p. (ISBN 0-566-02148-X). Gower Pub Co.

Responsibilities of Business Leadership: Talks Presented at the Leadership Conference. General Electric Company Staff. (Management History Ser.: No. 75). (Illus.). 113p. 1975. Repr. of 1954 ed. 15.00 o.s.i. (ISBN 0-87960-112-4). Hive Pub.

Responsibilities of Journalism. Ed. by Robert Schmuhl. LC 83-40596. 160p. 1984. text ed. 13.95x o.s.i. (ISBN 0-268-01623-2). U of Notre Dame Pr.

Responsibilities of Users of Standardized Tests (RUST) write for info. o.p. (72179C). Am Assn Coun Dev.

Responsibility Accounting & Performance Evaluations. Elwood L. Miller. 1981. 25.95 o.p. (ISBN 0-442-28818-2). Van Nos Reinhold.

Responsibility of Peoples & Other Essays in Political Criticism. Dwight Macdonald. LC 74-4659. 240p. 1974. Repr. of 1957 ed. lib. bdg. 22.50x o.p. (ISBN 0-8371-7478-3, MAPC). Greenwood.

Responsible & Effective Communication. Wayne N. Thompson. LC 77-77006. (Illus.). 1978. text ed. 16.50 o.p. (ISBN 0-395-25075-7). HM.

Responsible Before God. John E. Brown. (CPA VVS Jr. High Pupil-Leader Bklet. Ser.). 1975. pap. 1.50 o.s.i. (ISBN 0-664-29761-7, Westminster). Westminster John Knox.

Responsible Faith: Christian Theology in the Light of 20th-Century Questions. Hans Schwarz. LC 85-26657. 448p. 1986. text ed. 25.95 o.p. (ISBN 0-8066-2188-5, 10-5483, Augsburg). Augsburg Fortress.

Responsible Freedom in the Americas. Ed. by Angel Del Rio. Repr. of 1955 ed. lib. bdg. 35.00x o.p. (ISBN 0-8371-0199-9, RIFA). Greenwood.

Responsible Parenthood. Gilbert W. Kliman & Albert Rosenfeld. LC 79-3437. 360p. 1983. pap. 8.95 o.s.i. (ISBN 0-03-063537-3). H Holt & Co.

Responsible Parenthood: The Child's Psyche Through the Six-Year Pregnancy. Gilbert M. Kliman & Albert Rosenfeld. LC 79-3437. (Illus.). 348p. 1980. 14.95 o.s.i. (ISBN 0-03-040951-9). H Holt & Co.

Responsible Parenting among Men & Nations: A Challenge for Uncle Sam & the World. Stephen G. Burrows. 96p. 1981. 6.00 o.p. (ISBN 0-682-49752-5). Exposition-Phoenix.

Responsible with Creation. Ted R. Witt. pap. 6.95 o.p. (ISBN 0-8042-1422-0, John Knox). Westminster John Knox.

Rest Days, the Christian Sunday, the Jewish Sabbath & Their Historical & Anthropological Prototypes. Hutton Webster. LC 68-58165. 344p. 1968. Repr. of 1916 ed. 48.00x o.p. (ISBN 0-8103-3342-2). Gale.

Rest from the Quest. Elissa L. McClain. LC 84-80407. 173p. (Orig.). 1985. pap. 5.95 o.p. (ISBN 0-910311-13-7). Huntington Hse Inc.

Rest of Eighty. Wayne Green Books Editors. Ed. by Sandra Hutchinson. 232p. 1983. spiral bdg. 9.97 o.p. (ISBN 0-88006-062-X, BK7392). Wayne Green Ent.

Rest Rabbit Rest. Jacquelyn Reinach. Ed. by Ruth L. Perle. LC 77-13311. 1978. 2.95 o.p. (ISBN 0-03-042056-3). H Holt & Co.

Rest Without Peace. Elizabeth Byrd. 1975. pap. 1.50 o.p. (ISBN 0-380-00401-1, 26831). Avon.

Restatement Citations. Shepard's Citation, Inc. Staff. (Specialized Citations). 1976. 170.00 o.p. Shepards-McGraw.

Restaurant & Institutional Food Service Industry. Business Communications Staff. 97p. 1985. 1250.00 o.p. (ISBN 0-89336-426-6, GA-039R). BCC.

Restaurant Guide for Lake Tahoe & Vicinity. Mike Parr & Gwen Parr. LC 87-50418. (Illus.). 240p. (Orig.). 1987. pap. 7.95 o.p. (ISBN 0-9618573-0-7). Tahoe Pub.

Restaurant Industry Operations Report, 1986. National Restaurant Association Staff. 80p. 1986. pap. 40.00 o.p. (ISBN 0-317-57913-4, CS956). Natl Restaurant Assn.

Restaurant Industry Operations Report, 1985. National Restaurant Association Staff. 80p. 1985. pap. 38.00 o.p. (ISBN 0-317-57915-0, CS955). Natl Restaurant Assn.

Restaurant Profits Through Advertising & Promotion: The Indispensable Plan. Tom Feltenstein. 156p. 1983. 18.95 o.p. (ISBN 0-8436-2262-8). Van Nos Reinhold.

Restaurants (Architecture) G. Aloi. (Illus.). 1972. 50.00 o.p. E J Brill USA.

Restaurants of New Orleans. Roy F. Guste, Jr. (Illus.). 239p. 1983. 19.95 o.p. (ISBN 0-393-01746-X). Norton.

Restaurants of New York: 1985 Edition. Seymour Britchky. 352p. 1984. pap. 9.95 o.p. (ISBN 0-671-46375-6). S&S.

Restaurants of San Francisco: The Definitive Guide to the Bay Area's Best. rev. ed. Patricia Unterman & Stan Sesser. LC 85-31365. 228p. (Orig.). 1986. pap. 8.95 o.p. (ISBN 0-87701-378-0). Chronicle Bks.

Restaurants U. S. A. Index of Articles, 1982-85. 32p. 1985. pap. 3.00 o.p. (ISBN 0-317-57843-X, NWIND). Natl Restaurant Assn.

Restless Lady & Other Stories. Frances P. Keyes. 1963. 6.95 o.p. (ISBN 0-87140-907-0). Liveright.

Restless Universe. Nigel Henbest & Heather Couper. (Illus.). 214p. 1982. 19.95 o.p. (ISBN 0-540-01069-3, Pub. by G Philip). Sheridan.

Restless Universe: An Introduction to Astronomy. Harry L. Shipman. LC 77-78584. (Illus.). 1978. text ed. 32.50 o.p. (ISBN 0-395-25392-6). HM.

Restoration Adaptations. Ed. by Edward A. Langhans. LC 78-66611. (Eighteenth Century English Drama Ser.). 1980. lib. bdg. 73.00 o.p. (ISBN 0-8240-3575-5). Garland Pub.

Restoration & Eighteenth Century Drama, 1 of 7 vols. Intro. by Arthur H. Scouten. (Great Writers Library). 151p. pap. 7.95 o.p. (ISBN 0-312-34704-9). Academy Chi Pubs.

Restoration & Eighteenth-Century Poetry 1660-1780. Eric Rothstein. (English Poetry Ser.). 256p. pap. 10.95x o.p. (ISBN 0-7102-0552-X). Routledge Chapman & Hall.

Restoration & Revolution: Political, Social & Religious Writings 1660-1700. Ed. by William Myers. LC 85-24274. (World & Word Ser.). 256p. 1985. 34.50 o.p. (ISBN 0-7099-3502-1, Pub. by Croom Helm Ltd); pap. 20.50 o.p. (ISBN 0-7099-3558-7). Routledge Chapman & Hall.

Restoration Comedy of Wit. Thomas H. Fujimura. LC 78-13942. 1979. Repr. of 1952 ed. lib. bdg. 27.50x o.p. (ISBN 0-313-21232-5, FURC). Greenwood.

Restoration Manual: An Illustrated Guide to the Preservation & Restoration of Old Buildings. Orin M. Bullock, Jr. 192p. 1983. pap. 14.95 o.p. (ISBN 0-442-21433-2). Van Nos Reinhold.

Restoration of Habitats Impacted by Oil Spills. John Cairns, Jr. & Arthur L. Buikema, Jr. 192p. 1984. text ed. 44.95 o.p. (ISBN 0-250-40551-2). Butterworth.

Restoration of Motor Function in the Stroke Patient. 2nd ed. Margaret Johnstone. LC 81-67473. (Illus.). 237p. 1983. pap. text ed. 15.75 o.p. (ISBN 0-443-02604-1). Churchill.

Restoration Revivals on the British Stage, 1944-1979: A Critical Survey. Retta M. Taney. 384p. (Orig.). 1985. lib. bdg. 29.00 o.p. (ISBN 0-8191-4695-1); pap. text ed. 16.50 o.p. (ISBN 0-8191-4696-X). U Pr of Amer.

Restoration Theatre Production. Jocelyn Powell. (Theatre Production Ser.). (Illus.). 124p. 1984. 35.00x o.p. (ISBN 0-7100-9321-7). Routledge Chapman & Hall.

Restorative Dental Materials. 7th ed. Robert G. Craig. (Illus.). 492p. 1984. pap. text ed. 39.95 o.p. (ISBN 0-8016-1129-6). Mosby.

Restoring & Flying a Sport Plane on a Budget. Randall Brink. (Illus.). 192p. 1982. pap. 8.95 o.p. (ISBN 0-8306-2319-1, 2319). TAB Bks.

Restoring & Renovating Old Houses. W. W. Parker. LC 72-94859. 1973. 6.00 o.p. (ISBN 0-682-47593-9, Banner). Exposition-Phoenix.

Restrictive Business Practices. (Eng. & Fr.). 1959. pap. 5.00 o.p. (ISBN 0-686-93128-9, G62, GATT). UNIPUB.

Restructuring Hospital Quality Assurance: The New Guide for Health Care Providers. Jean G. Carroll. LC 84-71132. 225p. 1984. 27.50 o.p. (ISBN 0-87094-541-6). Dow Jones-Irwin.

Restructuring of Manufacturing Industry: The Experience of the Textile Industry in Pakistan, Philippines, Portugal & Turkey. Barend A. De Vries & Willem Brakel. (Working Paper: No. 558). 59p. 1983. 5.00 o.p. (ISBN 0-8213-0151-9, WP 0558). World Bank.

Restructuring of Social & Political Theory. Richard J. Bernstein. LC 76-12544. 1976. 17.95 o.p. (ISBN 0-15-176940-0). HarBraceJ.
Restyling Your Wardrobe. Ed. by Time Life Books Staff. LC 76-37283. (Art of Sewing Ser.). (Illus.). (gr. 6 up). 1976. 11.97 o.p. (ISBN 0-8094-1767-7, Pub. by Time-Life). Silver.
Resume & Job Hunting Guide for Present & Future Veterans: How to Make Your Military Training Count in Civilian Job Markets. Caroline S. De Prez & Richard J. De Prez. 176p. 1984. pap. 8.95 o.p. (ISBN 0-668-06129-4, 6129-4). Arco.
Resume Writing: A Comprehensive How-to-Do-It Guide. 2nd ed. Ed. by Burdette E. Bostwick. LC 80-18100. 314p. 1982. 15.95 o.p. (ISBN 0-471-08067-5, Pub. by Wiley-Interscience); pap. 8.95 o.p. (ISBN 0-471-09943-0). Wiley.
Resume Writing Guide. Ed. by Henry B. Stern. 16p. 1981. 3.50 o.p. (ISBN 0-89128-972-0, PVP972). Am Foun Blind.
Resumes for Better Jobs. 3rd ed. Lawrence Brennan et al. (Illus.). 208p. 1987. pap. 6.95 o.p. (ISBN 0-13-774936-8). Monarch Pr.
Resumes for Better Jobs. rev. ed. Stanley Strand & Edward C. Gruber. 1973. pap. 5.95 o.p. (ISBN 0-671-18708-2). Monarch Pr.
Resumes for College Graduates. William Lewis. (Job Finders Ser.). 144p. (Orig.). 1982. pap. 7.95 o.p. (ISBN 0-671-44179-5). Monarch Pr.
Resumes for Engineers. Arthur Pell & George Sadek. (Monarch's Job Finders Ser.). 128p. 1982. pap. 7.95 o.p. (ISBN 0-671-44304-6). Monarch Pr.
Resumes for Job Hunters. 2nd ed. Maury Shykind. LC 75-42763. 1976. pap. 6.00 o.p. (ISBN 0-668-03961-2). Arco.
Resurgent Militarism. Michael T. Klare. 14p. 1978. pap. Transaction Pubs.
Resurrection. Ulrich Wilckens. Tr. by A. M. Stewart from Ger. LC 77-15752. Orig. Title: Auferstehung. 1978. 6.95 o.p. (ISBN 0-8042-0396-2, John Knox). Westminster John Knox.
Resurrection Narratives: A Redactional Study. Grant R. Osborne. 288p. 1984. pap. 11.95 o.p. (ISBN 0-8010-6708-1). Baker Bk.
Resurrection of Jesus of Nazareth. Willi Marxsen. Tr. by Margaret Kohl from Ger. LC 76-120083. 192p. (Orig.). 1970. pap. 4.95 o.p. (ISBN 0-8006-0001-0, 1-1, Fortress). Augsburg Fortress.
Resurrection of the Body. F. Matthias Alexander. Ed. by Edward Maisel. LC 85-27903. 204p. 1986. pap. 8.95 o.p. (ISBN 0-87773-358-9, 74381-4, Dist. by Random). Shambhala Pubns.
Resurrection of the Dead. Derek Prince. (Foundation Ser.: Bk. VI). 1965-66. pap. 2.95 o.p. (ISBN 0-934920-05-2, B-15). Derek Prince.
Resurrection Two. Bo Grady. 80p. (ISBN 0-682-49698-7). Exposition-Phoenix.
Resurrexit. Leona C. Ross. 400p. pap. 4.95 o.p. (ISBN 0-8439-2727-5). Dorchester Pub Co.
Resuscitation Controversial Aspects: Proceedings. European Congress of Anaesthesiology of the World Federation of Societies of Anaesthesiologists, 1st, Vienna, 1962. Ed. by P. Safar. (Anaesthesiology & Resuscitation Ser.: Vol. 1). 1963. pap. 15.40 o.p. (ISBN 0-387-03050-6). Springer-Verlag.
Retail Advertising: Management & Technique. William Haight. 1976. text ed. write for info. o.p. (ISBN 0-673-15299-5). Scott F.
Retail Management: A Marketing Channels Approach. Roger A. Dickinson. 1974. (ISBN 0-534-00318-4). PWS-Kent Pub.
Retail Merchandising: Principles & Applications. Ralph D. Shipp, Jr. LC 75-31040. (Illus.). 352p. 1976. text ed. 28.95 o.p. (ISBN 0-395-20271-X). HM.
Retail Planning in the European Community. Ross Davies. 228p. 1979. text ed. 37.25x o.p. (ISBN 0-566-00308-2). Gower Pub Co.
Retail Sales Tax. 1981. 5.23 o.p. (ISBN 0-317-69881-8). U Va Ctr Pub Serv.
Retail Security: Controlling Loss for Profit. Bob Curtis. (Illus.). 720p. 1983. text ed. 27.95 o.p. (ISBN 0-409-95066-1). Butterworth.
Retailer's Basic Accounting Handbook: A Manual Retail Accounting System. 80p. pap. 15.00 o.p. (ISBN 0-87102-002-5, 26-0150). Natl Ret Merch.
Retailer's Complete Guide to Bigger Sales-Lower Costs-Higher Profits. Phillip M. Perry. LC 82-878. (Illus.). 300p. (Orig.). 1982. pap. 45.00 o.p. (ISBN 0-87624-509-2, Inst Busn Plan). P-H.
Retailing. Richard H. Buskirk & Bruce Buskirk. (Marketing Ser.). (Illus.). 1979. text ed. 32.95 o.p. (ISBN 0-07-009318-0). McGraw.
Retailing. 3rd ed. J. Barry Mason et al. 1988. 38.95 o.p. (ISBN 0-256-02942-3); 13.95 o.p. (ISBN 0-256-02943-1). Irwin.
Retailing: A Professional Approach. Charles A. Bearchell. (Illus.). 288p. 1975. text ed. 12.95 o.p. (ISBN 0-15-576658-9, HC). HarBraceJ.
Retailing & Its Environment. Albert D. Bates. 310p. 1979. 12.95x o.p. (ISBN 0-442-80522-5). PWS-Kent Pub.
Retailing: Challenge & Opportunity. Robert F. Hartley. 1975. text ed. 16.50 o.p. (ISBN 0-395-17073-7). HM.
Retailing: Challenge & Opportunity. 2nd ed. Robert F. Hartley. LC 79-88102. 1980. text ed. 25.95 o.p. (ISBN 0-395-28185-7). HM.
Retailing Job Analysis & Job Evaluation. National Retail Merchant Association Staff. 17.00 o.p. (ISBN 0-87102-032-7, 55-9522). Natl Ret Merch.
Retailing Management. 5th ed. William R. Davidson et al. LC 83-23378. 779p. 1984. text ed. (ISBN 0-471-05717-7). Wiley.
Retailing Today: An Introduction. Don L. James et al. (Illus.). 700p. 1975. text ed. 21.95 o.p. (ISBN 0-15-576670-8, HC). HarBraceJ.
Retaining Adult Students. Gordon G. Darkenwald. 23p. 1981. 2.80 o.p. (ISBN 0-318-22189-6, IN225). Natl Ctr Res Voc Ed.
Retardation of Evaporation by Monolayers. Ed. by Victor K. La Mer. 1962. 65.50 o.p. (ISBN 0-12-435150-6). Acad Pr.
Retarded Child. Inez Bull. LC 72-94851. 1973. 5.00 o.p. (ISBN 0-682-47652-8). Exposition-Phoenix.
Retarded Child. Herta Loewy. 1952. (ISBN 0-8022-0990-4). Philos Lib.
Retention of Title on the Sale of Goods. John Parris. 184p. 1982. text ed. 36.75x o.p. (ISBN 0-246-11612-9, Pub. by Granada England). Gower Pub Co.
Rethinking Australia's Defence. Ross Babbage. (Illus.). 312p. 1981. text ed. 37.50x o.p. (ISBN 0-7022-1486-8). U of Queensland Pr.
Rethinking Educational Change. Eric Hewton. 113p. 1983. 24.00x o.p. (ISBN 0-900868-93-7, Open Univ Pr). Taylor & Francis.
Rethinking Educational Research. W. B. Dockrell & David Hamilton. 224p. 1980. text ed. 39.95 o.s.i. (ISBN 0-340-20548-2). Princeton Bk Co.
Rethinking General Practice: Dilemmas in Primary Care. Margot Jefferys & Bessie Sachs. LC 83-4962. 288p. 1983. pap. 15.95 o.p. (ISBN 0-422-78630-6, NO. 3974). Routledge Chapman & Hall.
Rethinking Liberalism. Walter T. Anderson. 1983. pap. 4.95 o.p. (ISBN 0-380-84848-1, 84848, Discus). Avon.
Rethinking Local Services: Examining Alternative Delivery Approaches. (Management Information Services Special Report). 289p. 1984. pap. 25.00 o.p. (ISBN 0-87326-991-8). Intl City Mgt.
Rethinking People Management: A New Look at the Human Resources Function. James G. Stockard. 1980. 14.95 o.p. (ISBN 0-8144-5576-X). AMACOM.
Rethinking Sisterhood: Unity in Diversity. Ed. by R. Duelli Klein. (Illus.). 100p. 1985. pap. 21.00 o.p. (ISBN 0-08-032679-X, Pub. by PPL). Pergamon.
Rethinking Systems Analysis & Design. Gerald M. Weinberg. 193p. 1982. text ed. (ISBN 0-673-39077-2). Scott F.
Rethinking Teacher Education. Ed. by David Hopkins & Ken Reid. LC 84-28555. 262p. 1985. 31.00 o.p. (ISBN 0-7099-3705-9, Pub. by Croom Helm Ltd). Routledge Chapman & Hall.
Rethinking the Philosophy of Employee Relations in the Public Service see Issues in the Public Employee Relations Library: Series 1.
Reticuloendothelial System. John W. Rebuck et al. LC 79-23857. (International Academy of Pathology Monograph). 344p. 1980. Repr. of 1975 ed. 29.50 o.p. (ISBN 0-89874-101-7, John Wiley). Krieger.
Retief & the Rebels. Keith Laumer. 1980. pap. (ISBN 0-671-81866-X, Timescape). PB.
Retief to the Rescue. Keith Laumer. 256p. 1983. 14.50 o.s.i. (ISBN 0-671-45699-7, Timescape). PB.
Retinoids: New Trends in Research & Therapy. J. Saurat. (Illus.). xii, 516p. 1985. 152.75 o.p. (ISBN 3-8055-4026-4). S Karger.
Retirement & Income: A National Research Report of Behavior & Opinion Concerning Retirement, Pensions, & Social Security. Harris, Louis, & Associates Staff. LC 82-49183. (Refernce Library of Social Science). 148p. 1983. lib. bdg. 23.00 o.p. (ISBN 0-8240-9142-6). Garland Pub.
Retirement Guide for Canadians: Planning Now for a Comfortable Future. 8th ed. Henry S. Hunnisett. 295p. 1988. 9.95 o.p. (ISBN 0-88908-680-X). ISC Pr.
Retirement Income Opportunities in an Aging America: Vol. 1: Coverage & Benefit Entitlement. Sylvester J. Schieber & Patricia M. George. LC 81-5494. 131p. (Orig.). 1981. pap. 15.00 o.p. (ISBN 0-86643-013-X); Set, Vols I, II, III. pap. 25.00 o.p. (ISBN 0-86643-012-1). Employee Benefit.
Retirement Planning for Small Business & Professionals Entering the Top-Heavy & Parity Age: ALI-ABA Video Law Review Study Materials. ALI-ABA Committee on Continuing Professional Education. LC 84-166979. (Illus.). xiv, 290p. o.p. Am Law Inst.
Retirement Policy: Planning for Change. Jennifer L. Warlick et al. Ed. by Kathryn H. Anderson. 58p. 1982. 5.75 o.p. (ISBN 0-318-22190-X, IN242). Natl Ctr Res Voc Ed.
Retirement Threat. Tony Lamb & Dave Duffy. LC 76-62676. 177p. 1977. text ed. 14.95 o.p. (ISBN 0-686-91718-9). Univ Assocs.
Retiring Right: Planning for Your Successful Retirement. Larry Kaplan. 353p. 1986. pap. 12.95 o.p. (ISBN 0-89529-298-X). Avery Pub.
Retouches a mon Retour de l'U.R.S.S. Andre Gide. 128p. 1937. 4.95 o.p. (ISBN 0-686-56055-8). Schoenhof.
Retour a Roissy see Story of O: Part Two, Return to the Chateau.
Retour du Tchad. Andre Gide. pap. 5.50 o.p. (ISBN 0-685-34157-7). Schoenhof.
Retractationum Libri Duo. Saint Aurelius Augustinus. (Corpus Scriptorum Ecclesiasticorum Latinorum Ser: Vol. 36). 34.00 o.p. (ISBN 0-384-02357-6). Johnson Repr.
Retraining for the Elderly Disabled. Margaret Mort. LC 84-23761. 458p. (Orig.). 1985. pap. 26.00 o.p. (ISBN 0-7099-3532-3, Pub. by Croom Helm Ltd). Routledge Chapman & Hall.
Retrato de la Reina: La Historia de Nuestra Senora de Guadalupe. Sr. Mary Amatora. 1972. 7.50 o.p. (ISBN 0-682-47542-4, Lochinvar); pap. 5.00 o.p. (ISBN 0-682-47548-3, Lochinvar). Exposition-Phoenix.
Retrieval of Information in the Humanities & Social Science. Slavens. (Library Science & Information Ser.: Vol. 37). 216p. 1981. 39.75 o.p. (ISBN 0-8247-1542-X). Dekker.
Retrospect. J. C. Kirby. 1979. 5.00 o.p. (ISBN 0-682-49498-4). Exposition-Phoenix.
Retrospect see Fate of French-E in English: The Plural of Nouns Ending in-th.
Retrovirus Genes in Lymphocyte Function & Growth. Ed. by E. Wecker & I. Horack. (Current Topics in Microbiology & Immunology Ser.: Vol. 98). (Illus.). 180p. 1982. 46.00 o.p. (ISBN 0-387-11225-1). Springer-Verlag.
Retroviruses, Vol. I. Ed. by P. K. Vogt & H. Koprowski. (Current Topics in Microbiology Ser.: Vol. 103). (Illus.). 146p. 1983. 40.00 o.p. (ISBN 0-387-12167-6). Springer-Verlag.
Return. Yaw M. Boateng. (African Writers Ser.: No. 186). viii, 120p. (Orig.). 1977. pap. text ed. 6.00 o.p. (ISBN 0-435-90186-9). Heinemann Ed.
Return. Mike Evans. LC 85-31943. 224p. 1986. 12.95 o.p. (ISBN 0-8407-5501-5). Nelson.
Return. Herbert Mitgang. 1973. pap. 0.95 o.p. (ISBN 0-380-00311-2, 23341-X). Avon.
Return Engagement: The Role of American Librarians at the Second International Library Conference, London, 1897. Budd L. Gambee. (Occasional Papers: No. 129). 26p. 1977. pap. 2.00 o.p. (ISBN 0-317-58966-0). U of Ill Lib Info Sci.
Return from Babel. Gerald M. Spring. 1951. (ISBN 0-8022-1627-7). Philos Lib.
Return from Death: An Exploration of the Near-Death Experience. Margot Grey. 224p. (Orig.). 1985. pap. 10.95 o.p. (ISBN 1-85063-019-4, Ark Paperbks). Routledge Chapman & Hall.
Return from the Grave. Ed. by Hugh Lamb. LC 76-28598. 1977. 8.95 o.s.i. (ISBN 0-8008-6782-3). Taplinger.
Return from the Stars. Stanislaw Lem. Tr. by Barbara Marszal & Frank Simpson. LC 79-3358. (Helen & Kurt Wolff Bk.). 312p. 1980. 8.95 o.s.i. (ISBN 0-15-177082-4). HarBraceJ.
Return from the Stars. Stanislaw Lem. 256p. 1982. pap. 2.95 o.p. (ISBN 0-380-58578-2, 58578-2, Bard). Avon.
Return from the U. S. S. R. & Afterthoughts on My Return. Andre Gide. Tr. by Richard Howard from Fr. (Illus.). 192p. 1987. 15.95 o.p. (ISBN 0-374-24950-4). FS&G.
Return from Witch Mountain. Alexander Key. LC 77-26992. 144p. 1981. 9.95 o.p. (ISBN 0-664-32630-7, Westminster). Westminster John Knox.
Return Migration & Regional Economic Problems. Ed. by Russell King. LC 85-24288. 1986. 43.00 o.p. (ISBN 0-7099-1578-0, Pub. by Croom Helm Ltd). Routledge Chapman & Hall.
Return of Halley's Comet. Andrew Fraknoi et al. (Illus.). 36p. 1985. 4.00 o.p. (ISBN 0-937707-05-8, IP 700). Astron Soc Pacific.
Return of Otis. Joseph N. Chappelle. 40p. 1988. 5.75 o.p. (ISBN 0-8062-2943-8). Carlton.
Return of Sherlock Holmes. Arthur Conan Doyle. LC 87-42703. (Illus.). 320p. 1987. 25.00 o.p. (ISBN 0-89296-248-8). Mysterious Pr.
Return of the Dinosaurs. Stephan Wilkinson. Ed. by Ernest Dupuy. (Hammond's Captain Atlas & the Globe Riders Ser.). (Illus.). 48p. (gr. 2 up). 1988. pap. 6.95 o.p. (ISBN 0-8437-3550-3). Hammond Inc.
Return of the Dragon. Jane Zaring. (Illus.). (gr. 5-8). 1981. 7.95 o.p. (ISBN 0-395-30350-8). HM.
Return of the Native. Thomas Hardy. 48p. (Orig.). 1987. pap. 9.95 o.p. (ISBN 1-55651-779-3); audiocassette tape incl. o.p. (ISBN 1-55651-780-7). Cram Cassettes.
Return of the Plague: British Society & the Cholera 1831-32. Michael Durey. 1979. text ed. 39.00x o.p. (ISBN 0-391-01038-7). Humanities.
Return of the Whistler. Blossom Elfman. 160p. 1981. 8.95 o.p. (ISBN 0-395-29464-9). HM.
Return of Try This One. Ed. by Cindy S. Hansen. LC 86-14252. (Illus.). 80p. (Orig.). 1986. pap. 5.95 o.p. (ISBN 0-931529-13-1). Group Pub.
Return to a Chinese Village. Jan Myrdal. (Illus.). 1984. 14.45 o.p. (ISBN 0-394-53774-2); pap. 7.95 o.p. (ISBN 0-394-72453-4). Pantheon.
Return to Arcady. Adelaide N. Baker. LC 73-80849. (Illus.). 192p. 1973. 8.95 o.p. (ISBN 0-88208-018-0). Chicago Review.
Return to Earth. H. M. Hoover. 144p. 1981. pap. 1.95 o.p. (ISBN 0-380-54486-5, 54486). Avon.
Return to Fire Island. Burt Hirschfeld. 320p. 1984. pap. 3.95 o.p. (ISBN 0-380-88088-1, 88088-1). Avon.
Return to Free Market Economics. John Jewkes. 1978. 32.50 o.p. (ISBN 0-8419-5028-8). Holmes & Meier.
Return to God & His Gift of Healing. John Scott-Whiting. 1980. 9.50 o.p. (ISBN 0-682-49545-X). Exposition-Phoenix.
Return to Love. Virginia Smiley. (Silver Bell). 192p. 1982. pap. 1.95 o.p. (ISBN 0-8439-1156-5, Pub. by Leisure Bks CT). Dorchester Pub Co.
Return to Meaningfulness. Robert Powell. LC 80-54613. 176p. 1982. pap. text ed. 8.50 o.p. (ISBN 0-932238-07-6, Pub. by Avant Bks). Slawson Comm.
Return to Reason: An Introduction to Objectivism. Paul Lepanto. 1971. 15.00 o.p. (ISBN 0-682-47204-2). Exposition-Phoenix.
Return to Sender. Raymund Mungo. LC 75-12661. 208p. 1975. 7.95 o.p. (ISBN 0-395-20505-0, Co-Pub. by San Francisco Bk Co). HM.
Return to Sinai: The Arab Offensive 1973. D. K. Palit. LC 74-901203. 172p. 1974. 10.00x o.p. (ISBN 0-88386-291-3). South Asia Bks.
Return to the River. Don Coldsmith. LC 87-6676. (Double D Western Ser.). 192p. 1987. 12.95 o.s.i. (ISBN 0-385-23520-8). Doubleday.
Return to the Sea. William A. Robinson. LC 75-185573. 1972. 10.00 o.p. (ISBN 0-8286-0060-0). J De Graff.
Return to Thrush Green. Miss Read. LC 79-858. 1979. 8.95 o.p. (ISBN 0-395-27627-6). HM.
Return to Vision. 2nd ed. Ed. by Richard L. Cherry et al. Robert J. Conley & Bernard A. Hirsch. 432p. 1975. pap. 12.95 o.p. (ISBN 0-395-17836-3). HM.
Return Trips. Alice Adams. (Large Print Books). 327p. 1986. lib. bdg. 16.95x o.p. (ISBN 0-8161-4086-3, Large Print Bks). G K Hall.
Returning to a Dream. William L. Sieller. 1979. 6.50 o.p. (ISBN 0-8233-0308-X). Golden Quill.
Returning to School: The RN to BSN Handbook. Akemi Hiraki & Pamela Kees Parlocha. 1983. pap. text ed. 11.95 o.p. (ISBN 0-316-36460-6). Little.
Reunion. Fred Uhlman. 112p. 1977. 6.95 o.p. (ISBN 0-374-24951-2). FS&G.
Reunion Handbook: A Guide for Reunion Organizers. Thomas Ninkovich & Eleanor Vincent. LC 82-62767. 62p. 1983. pap. 4.95 o.p. (ISBN 0-9610470-0-3). Reunion Research.
Reutilization of Waste Materials: Selected Papers from the Third Recycling World Congress, Basle, Switzerland, 29 September-1 October 1980. Ed. by M. E. Henstock. 80p. 1981. pap. 29.00 o.p. (ISBN 0-08-028743-3). Pergamon.
Revanche & Revision: The Ligue des Patriotes & the Origins of the Radical Right in France, 1882-1900. Peter M. Rutkoff. LC 80-39575. x, 182p. 1981. text ed. 18.95x o.p. (ISBN 0-8214-0589-6). Ohio U Pr.
Revel. 3rd ed. Junior League of Shreveport, Inc. Staff. LC 79-89035. (Illus.). 385p. 1980. 11.95 o.p. (ISBN 0-9602246-1-0); spiral 7.17 o.p. (ISBN 0-686-58146-6). Jr League Shreveport.
Revelation. Alger M. Fitch, Jr. (Standard Bible Studies). 112p. 1986. pap. 5.95 o.p. (ISBN 0-87403-173-7, 40113). Standard Pub.
Revelation. Frederick A. Tatford. 656p. lib. bdg. 23.95 o.p. (ISBN 0-8254-5246-5). Kregel.
Revelation Expounded. W. Kelly. 5.95 o.p. (ISBN 0-88172-106-9). Believers Bkshelf.
Revelation of Humanity. Jonas Sepetys. LC 73-88709. 233p. 1974. (ISBN 0-8022-2137-8). Philos Lib.

Revelation of Jesus Christ. Donald W. Richardson. 1977. pap. 1.25 o.p. (ISBN 0-8042-3597-X, John Knox). Westminster John Knox.

Revelation of Jesus Christ. Ray F. Robbins. LC 75-1739. 240p. 1976. bds. 6.50 o.p. (ISBN 0-8054-1354-5). Broadman.

Revelation-The Last Book of the Bible. Edwin A. Schick. LC 76-62602. 80p. (Orig.). 1977. pap. 3.95 o.p. (ISBN 0-8006-1253-1, 1-1253, Fortress). Augsburg Fortress.

Revelations: Forerunner of Christ. Herbert H. Ogletree. 1977. 6.50 o.p. (ISBN 0-682-48934-4). Exposition-Phoenix.

Revelations of an Army Nurse. Catherine Hagarty. 1981. 6.75 o.p. (ISBN 0-8062-1591-7). Carlton.

Revelations of Dr. Modesto. Alan Harrington. LC 55-9261. (Library of Contemporary Americana). 256p. 1984. pap. 7.95 o.p. (ISBN 0-87795-652-9, Arbor Hse). Morrow.

Revelations One: Noah's Flood Was a Result of Nuclear War. Kostis Kandias. (Illus.). 202p. 1981. 10.00 o.p. (ISBN 0-682-49672-3). Exposition-Phoenix.

Revelliere-Lepeaux, Citizen Director, 1753-1824. Georgia Robison. LC 72-8923. 308p. 1971. Repr. of 1938 ed. lib. bdg. 19.50x o.p. (ISBN 0-374-96893-4, Octagon). Hippocrene Bks.

Revels History of Drama in English: Medieval Drama, Vol. I. L. Potter. 1983. 59.95 o.p. (ISBN 0-416-13020-8, NO. 6422). Routledge Chapman & Hall.

Revels History of Drama in English, Vol. 7: 1880 to the Present. Hugh Hunt et al. (Revels History of Drama in English Ser.). (Illus.). 1978. 59.95x o.p. (ISBN 0-416-13080-1, NO. 2057); pap. 19.95x o.p. (ISBN 0-416-81390-9, NO. 2058). Routledge Chapman & Hall.

Revenge Is the Best Exercise. David Brenner. (Illus.). 192p. (Orig.). 1984. pap. 9.95 o.p. (ISBN 0-87795-655-3, Arbor Hse). Morrow.

Revenge, My Friend. Robin Legg. 1985. 7.95 o.p. (ISBN 0-533-06580-1). Vantage.

Revenge of the Falcon Knight. Scott Siegel. (Wizards, Warriors & You Ser.: Bk. 6). 112p. (gr. 4 up). 1985. pap. 2.25 o.p. (ISBN 0-380-89524-2). Avon.

Revenge Rides High. G. L. Guthridge. 208p. 1982. pap. 2.25 o.p. (ISBN 0-8439-1159-X, Pub. by Leisure Bks CT). Dorchester Pub Co.

Revenue & Taxation of the Chinese Empire. Joseph Edkins. LC 78-74331. (Modern Chinese Economy Ser.). 240p. 1980. lib. bdg. 32.00 o.p. (ISBN 0-8240-4252-2). Garland Pub.

Revenue Sharing in India. Christine Wallich. 85p. 1982. 5.00 o.p. (ISBN 0-317-59152-5, WP 1523). World Bank.

Revenue Sharing Renewal, No. 15. John T. Marlin. (COMP Papers Ser.). 52p. pap. 7.50 o.p. (ISBN 0-916450-36-8). Nat Civic League.

Reverence for Life. William A. Wait. 39p. (Orig.). 1981. pap. 2.95 o.p. (ISBN 0-938696-03-3, 8660). Pubs Bk Sales.

Reverence for Life & Family Program: Parent-Teacher Resource. John E. Forliti. 1981. pap. 4.50 176 pp o.p. (ISBN 0-697-01789-3); tchr. training tape 9.95 o.p. (ISBN 0-697-01837-7). Wm C Brown.

Reverence of Life. 65-22624 ed. Albert Schweitzer. 1965. Philos Lib.

Reverend Randollph & the Avenging Angel. Charles M. Smith. 192p. 1982. pap. 2.50 o.p. (ISBN 0-380-58933-8, 58933-8). Avon.

Reverend Randollph & the Fall from Grace, Inc. Charles M. Smith. 224p. 1982. pap. 2.50 o.p. (ISBN 0-380-59832-9, 59832-9). Avon.

Reverend Randollph & the Unholy Bible. Charles M. Smith. 304p. 1984. pap. 2.95 o.p. (ISBN 0-380-67660-5, 67660). Avon.

Reverend Randollph & the Wages of Sin. Charles M. Smith. 208p. 1982. pap. 2.50 o.p. (ISBN 0-380-57174-9, 57174-9). Avon.

Reverend Randolph & the Holy Terror. Charles M. Smith. 1982. pap. 2.50 o.p. (ISBN 0-380-60707-7, 60707). Avon.

Reverend Samuel Davies Abroad: The Diary of a Journey to England & Scotland, 1753-55. Ed. by Samuel Davies & George W. Pilcher. LC 67-12991. 191p. 1967. 19.95 o.p. (ISBN 0-252-74547-7). U of Ill Pr.

Reversals: A Personal Account of Victory over Dyslexia. Eileen Simpson. 1979. 12.95 o.p. (ISBN 0-395-27516-4). HM.

Reverse Acronyms, Initialisms & Abbreviations Dictionary. 12th ed. 304p. 1987. 225.00x o.p. (ISBN 0-8103-2507-1). Gale.

Reverse Acronyms, Initialisms & Abbreviations Dictionary, Vol. 3. 13th ed. Ed. by Julie E. Towell. (Acronyms, Initialisms & Abbreviations Dictionary Ser.: Vol. 3). 3300p. 1988. 230.00x o.p. (ISBN 0-8103-2582-9). Gale.

Reverse Discrimination: A Resource Guide. Jim Buchanan. LC 85-233321. (Public Administration Ser.: P 1703). 1985. 3.00 o.p. (ISBN 0-89028-453-9). Vance Biblios.

Reverse Osmosis. P. Hoornaert. (EPO Applied Technology Ser.: Vol. 4). 220p. 1984. 77.00 o.p. (ISBN 0-08-031144-X). Pergamon.

Reversible Sex Roles: The Special Case of Benares Sweepers. Mary Searle-Chatterjee. (Women in Development Ser.). (Illus.). 120p. 1981. 38.00 o.p. (ISBN 0-08-025780-1). Pergamon.

Reversing Earth. Peter Warlow. (Illus.). 213p. 1982. 35.00 o.p. (ISBN 0-460-04478-8). State Mutual Bk.

Review Exercises in Chinese Sentence Structure. Henry C. Fenn. 1.95 o.p. (ISBN 0-88710-078-3). Yale Far Eastern Pubns.

Review Manual for Immunohematology. Neville J. Bryant. 352p. 1982. write for info. o.p. (ISBN 0-7216-2166-X). Saunders.

Review Manual for Operators. William E. Brown & Richard S. Sacks. LC 81-68888. (Illus.). 182p. 1981. pap. text ed. 19.95 o.p. (ISBN 0-250-40501-6). Butterworth.

Review of Annulation. M. Jung. Ed. by D. H. Barton. 1976. pap. 12.75 o.p. (ISBN 0-08-020621-2). Pergamon.

Review of Austrian Economics, Vol. 1. Ed. by Murray N. Rothbard. LC 85-460036. 272p. 1986. 35.00x o.p. (ISBN 0-669-12892-9). Lexington Bks.

Review of Fisheries in OECD Member Countries, 1983. OECD Staff. 250p. (Orig.). 1984. pap. 18.00x o.p. (ISBN 92-64-12638-4). OECD.

Review of German. Sten G. Flygt. 1959. 6.95x o.p. Norton.

Review of Human Physiology. 2nd ed. H. Frank Winter & Melvin L. Shourd. (Illus.). 563p. 1982. write for info. o.p. (ISBN 0-7216-9469-1). Saunders.

Review of Medical Microbiology. 16th ed. Ernest Jawetz et al. LC 60-11336. (Illus.). 557p. 1984. lexotone cover 18.50 o.p. (ISBN 0-87041-057-1, 295725). Appleton & Lange.

Review of Past Research & Test Activities see Monitoring the Outcome of Social Services.

Review of Placement Services Within a Comprehensive Rehabilitation Framework: Technical Report. David Vandergoot & Jessica Swirsky. LC 78-72067. 60p. 1979. 5.25 o.p. (ISBN 0-686-38819-4). Human Res Ctr.

Review of Practical Nursing for State Board Examinations. 2nd ed. Ed. by Sandra F. Smith. 478p. 1983. pap. 15.95 o.p. (ISBN 0-917010-11-6). Natl Nursing.

Review of Research in Social Studies Education: 1976-1983. Ed. by William B. Stanley. (Orig.). 1985. pap. 12.95 o.p. (ISBN 0-89994-303-9). Soc Sci Ed.

Review of Research Methods in Education. M. Clemens Johnson. 1980. text ed. 30.50 o.p. (ISBN 0-395-30641-8). HM.

Review of "Shall We Splinter?" Robert R. Taylor, Jr. 1985. pap. 3.00 o.p. (ISBN 0-934916-08-X). Natl Christian Pr.

Review of the Agricultural Situation in Europe at the End of 1975, 2 Vols. pap. 12.00 o.p. (E.76.II.E.11). UN.

Review of the Agricultural Situation in Europe at the End of 1977, 2 Vols. Set. pap. 14.50 o.p. (E.78.II.E.12). UN.

Review of the Agricultural Situation in Europe at the End of 1979: Volume 1: General Review, Livestock and Meat; Volume 2: Grain and Dairy Products, 2 Vols. (Agricultural Market Reviews: No. 22). Set. pap. 17.00 o.p. (E.80.II.E.13). UN.

Review of the Agricultural Situation in Europe at the End of 1973, 2 Vols. Set. pap. 9.50 o.p. (E.74.II.E.8). UN.

Review of the Agricultural Situation in Europe at the End of 1974, 2 Vols. Set. pap. 14.50 o.p. (E.75.II.E.12). UN.

Review of the Agricultural Situation in Europe at the End of 1981, 2 Vols. pap. 17.00 o.p. (E.82.II.E.8). UN.

Review of the Agricultural Situation in Europe at the End of 1980: Vol. 1: Grain, Livestock & Meat; Vol. 2: Dairy Products & Eggs, 2 Vols. (Agricultural Market Reviews: No. 23). 295p. 1981. Set. pap. 13.00 o.p. (E.81.II.E.15). UN.

Review of the Agricultural Situation in Europe at the End of 1982, Vol. I. (Agricultural Market Reviews: No. 25). 116p. 1983. pap. text ed. 30.00 o.p. (E.83.II.E.15). UN.

Review of the Agricultural Situation in Europe at the End of 1976, 2 Vols. pap. 19.00 o.p. (E.77.II.E.7). UN.

Review of the Agricultural Situation in Europe at the End of 1978, 2 Vols. Set. pap. 20.00 o.p. (E.79.II.E.14). UN.

Review of the Agricultural Situation in Europe at the End of 1983, Agricultural Market Review, 2 vols, No. 26. LC 84-46787. 256p. Volume I: General Review & Grain 109p. 25.00 o.p. (ISBN 92-1-116191-6, E.84.II.E.10); Volume II: Livestock, Meat & Dairy Products 147p. 25.00 o.p. UN.

Review of the Biological Control of Insects & Other Pests in South-East Asia & the Pacific Region. Ed. by V. P. Rao et al. 149p. 1971. text ed. 18.15 o.p. (ISBN 0-85198-114-3). CAB Intl.

Review of the Current State of Radiation Protection Philosophy. LC 74-31940. (NCRP Reports Ser.: No. 43). 1975. 9.00 o.p. (ISBN 0-913392-25-1). NCRP Pubns.

Review of the North & Central American Species of Paravilla Painter (Diptera: Bombyliidae) Jack C. Hall. (UC Publications in Entomology: Vol. 92). 192p. 1981. pap. 16.50x o.p. (ISBN 0-520-09625-8). U of Cal Pr.

Review of the Political Conflict in America, from the Commencement of the Anti-Slavery Agitation to the Close of Southern Reconstruction. Alexander Harris. LC 70-109328. 1970. Repr. of 1876 ed. 35.00x o.p. (ISBN 0-8371-3594-X, HPC&). Greenwood.

Review of United States Competitiveness in Agricultural Trade, a Technical Memorandum. LC 86-600586. (OTA-TM-TET-29 Ser.). (Illus.). 110p. (Orig.). 1986. pap. 5.50 o.p. (ISBN 0-318-21556-X, S/N 052-003-01054-2). USGPO.

Review Outlines & Materials for Business Law & CPA Law Review. William T. Schantz & Janice E. Jackson. LC 80-13096. 985p. 1980. pap. text ed. 18.50 o.p. (ISBN 0-8299-2071-4). West Pub.

Review Papers: International Solar-Terrestrial Physics Symposium, Sao-Paolo, June, 1974. Ed. by S. A. Bowhill. 212p. 1976. pap. 50.00 o.p. (ISBN 0-08-019959-3). Pergamon.

Review Questions in Analytical Toxicology. J. E. Wallace & N. A. Wade. LC 82-70669. 200p. (Orig.). 1982. pap. text ed. 19.00 o.p. (ISBN 0-931890-09-8, Biomed Pubns). Year Bk Med.

Review Questions in Anatomic Pathology. Ed. by A. M. Ring & S. L. Ostrin. LC 83-73100. (Illus.). 432p. (Orig.). 1985. pap. text ed. 32.00 o.p. (ISBN 0-931890-18-7, Biomed Pubns). Year Bk Med.

Review Questions In Clinical Pathology. Samuel Ostrin & Alvin M. Ring. 399p. 1986. 32.00 o.p. (ISBN 0-931890-19-5, Biomed Pubns). Year Bk Med.

Review Questions in General Vascular Surgery, Vol. 1. William H. Brown & Roy L. Tawes. 288p. 1984. 45.00 o.p. (ISBN 0-941022-05-6). Appleton Davies.

Review Text in Health. Bro. Patricius Dougherty & Sr. Carmel Leifer. (gr. 7-12). 1962. pap. text ed. 9.58 o.p. (ISBN 0-87720-161-7). AMSCO Sch.

Review Text in United States History. rev. ed. Paul M. Roberts. (Illus., Orig.). (gr. 7-9). 1967. pap. text ed. 10.83 o.p. (ISBN 0-87720-601-5). AMSCO Sch.

Reviewing Academic Performance Approaches to the Evaluation of Departments & Individuals. Ernest Roe et al. LC 85-21016. (Scholars' Library). (Illus.). 341p. 1987. text ed. 42.50x o.p. (ISBN 0-7022-1967-3). U of Queensland Pr.

Reviewing the Forties. Diana Trilling. LC 78-5182. 1978. 9.95 o.s.i. (ISBN 0-15-177084-0). HarBraceJ.

Reviews of Diagnosis: Oral Medicine, Radiology & Treatment Planning. Norman K. Wood. LC 79-15358. 266p. 1979. pap. 22.95 o.p. (ISBN 0-8016-5614-1). Mosby.

Reviews of Physiology, Vol. 69. Ed. by R. H. Adrian et al. LC 73-14479. (Illus.). 255p. 1974. 57.90 o.p. (ISBN 0-387-06498-2). Springer-Verlag.

Reviews of Physiology, Biochemistry & Pharmacology, Vol. 71. Ed. by R. H. Adrian et al. (Illus.). vi, 175p. 1975. 59.00 o.p. (ISBN 0-387-06939-9). Springer-Verlag.

Reviews of Physiology, Biochemistry & Pharmacology, Vol. 77. Ed. by R. H. Adrian et al. LC 74-3674. (Illus.). 1977. 74.00 o.p. (ISBN 0-387-07963-7). Springer-Verlag.

Reviews of Physiology, Biochemistry & Pharmacology, Vol. 78. Ed. by R. H. Adrian et al. LC 74-3674. 1977. 61.00 o.p. (ISBN 0-387-07975-0). Springer-Verlag.

Reviews of Physiology, Biochemistry, & Pharmacology, Vol. 93. Ed. by R. H. Adrian. (Illus.). 220p. 1982. 53.00 o.p. (ISBN 0-387-11297-9). Springer-Verlag.

Reviews of Plasma Physics. Ed. by M. A. Leontovich. LC 64-23244. Vol. 1, 1965, 326p. 59.50x o.p. (ISBN 0-306-17061-2, Consultants); Vol. 2, 1966, 298p. 59.50x o.p. (ISBN 0-306-17062-0); Vol. 3, 1967, 326p. 59.50x o.p. (ISBN 0-306-17063-9); Vol. 4, 1966, 242p. 55.00x o.p. (ISBN 0-306-17064-7); Vol. 5, 1970, 526p. 85.00x o.p. (ISBN 0-306-17065-5); Vol. 6, 1975, 332p. 59.50x o.p. (ISBN 0-306-17066-3). Plenum Pub.

Reviews of Plasma Physics, Vol. 8. Ed. by M. A. Leontovich. LC 64-23244. 472p. 1980. 79.50x o.p. (ISBN 0-306-17068-X, Consultants). Plenum Pub.

Reviews of Plasma Physics, Vol. 7. Ed. by M. A. Leontovich. LC 64-23244. (Illus.). 390p. 1979. 69.50x o.p. (ISBN 0-306-17067-1, Consultants). Plenum Pub.

Reviews of the World Situation: 1949-50. Ed. by Richard D. Challener. (Legislative Origins of American Foreign Policy Ser.: Vol. 8). 1979. lib. bdg. 67.00 o.p. (ISBN 0-8240-3037-0). Garland Pub.

Revised Basic Cookbook. Marjorie Heseltine & Ula Dow. (Illus.). 1967. 12.95 o.p. (ISBN 0-395-07792-3). HM.

Revised Financial Reporting Model for Municipalities, No. 6-7. John C. Burton. (Government Auditing Ser.). 1980. pap. 6.00 o.p. (ISBN 0-686-70150-X). Nat Civic League.

Revised Transition State Spectrum for Concerted Bimolecular B - Eliminations. D. J. McLennan. 1976. pap. 14.00 o.s.i. (ISBN 0-08-020472-4). Pergamon.

Revising Business Prose. Richard A. Lanham. LC 80-26689. 98p. 1981. pap. text ed. 9.95 o.p. (ISBN 0-684-17018-3). Scribner.

Revising: New Essays for Teachers of Writing. Ed. by Ronald A. Sudol. (Illus.). 187p. 1982. 11.00 o.p. (ISBN 0-8141-4126-9). NCTE.

Revision Gesteinsbewohnender Sippen der Flechtengattung Catillaria Mass in Europa(Lecanorales, Lecideaceae) H. Kilias. (Illus.). 240p. (Ger.). 1981. pap. text ed. 18.00x o.p. (ISBN 3-7682-1318-8). Lubrecht & Cramer.

Revision of the Marine Nematodes of the Superfamily Draconematoidea Filipjev, 1918 (Nematoda: Draconematina) M. W. Allen & Ella M. Noffsinger. (U C Publications in Zoology: Vol. 109). 1978. 17.50x o.p. (ISBN 0-520-09583-9). U of Cal Pr.

Revision of the South American Nematognathi or Catfishes. Carl H. Eignmann. pap. 55.00 o.p. (ISBN 0-384-14040-8). Johnson Repr.

Revisionist. Douglas Crase. 96p. 1981. 10.95 o.p. (ISBN 0-316-16062-8); pap. 5.95 o.p. (ISBN 0-316-16060-1). Little.

Revisionist Bibliography - 1981. Institute for Historical Review Staff. Ed. by Keith Stimely. 70p. (Orig.). 1980. pap. 3.00 o.p. (ISBN 0-911038-97-3). Inst Hist Rev.

Revisions of the Ektopodonitdae (Mammalia, Marsupialia, Phalangeroidea) of the Australian Neogene. Ed. by Michael Woodburne & William A. Clemens. (UC Publications in Geological Sciences: Vol. 131). 1986. 15.95x o.p. (ISBN 0-317-65322-9). U of Cal Pr.

Revisor. Paul Woodbine. 1979. text ed. 7.00 o.p. (ISBN 0-916258-09-2, Colophon Bks). Woodbine Pr.

Revitalizing Neighborhoods & Downtowns: A Selective, Annotated Bibliography on Urban Ecology. Susan C. Marcavage et al. (Public Administration Series: Bibliography: No. P 1767). 47p. 1985. pap. 6.75 o.p. (ISBN 0-89028-567-5). Vance Biblios.

Revival of Metaphysical Poetry. Joseph E. Duncan. LC 79-75991. 1969. Repr. of 1959 ed. lib. bdg. 19.00x o.p. (ISBN 0-374-92394-9, Octagon). Hippocrene Bks.

Revival: The Rain from Heaven. Arthur Wallis. 128p. 1985. pap. 5.95 o.p. (ISBN 0-8007-5204-X). Revell.

Revlon Art of Beauty. Revlon. LC 81-43587. (Illus.). 128p. 1982. pap. 14.95 o.p. (ISBN 0-385-17871-9, Dolp); prepack of 10 149.50 o.p. (ISBN 0-385-18366-6). Doubleday.

Revolt in Athens: The Greek Communist "Second Round", 1944-1945. John O. Iatrides. LC 76-39052. 352p. 1972. 37.00x o.p. (ISBN 0-691-05203-4). Princeton U Pr.

Revolt in Southern Rhodesia 1896-7. T. O. Ranger. (Illus.). 416p. (Orig.). 1978. pap. text ed. 17.50x o.p. (ISBN 0-435-94799-0). Heinemann Ed.

Revolt of American Women. Oliver Jensen. LC 52-9856. (Illus.). 1971. pap. 4.95 o.p. (ISBN 0-15-676605-1, HB200, Harv). HarBraceJ.

Revolt of Ten-X. Joan D. Carris. LC 80-7980. (gr. 4-6). 1980. 7.95 o.p. (ISBN 0-15-266462-9, HJ). HarBraceJ.

Revolting Transaction. Barnaby Conrad. (Illus.). 200p. 1983. 16.95 o.p. (ISBN 0-87795-534-4, Arbor Hse). Morrow.

Revolucion Debe Saber Defenderse. L. Semenenko et al. 223p. (Span.). 1979. pap. 6.45 o.p. (ISBN 0-8285-1491-7, Pub. by Progress Pubs USSR). Imported Pubns.

Revolution & Education in People's Korea: Theses on Socialist Education. Kim Il Sung. 58p. 1.50 o.p. (ISBN 0-89567-025-9). World View Forum.

Revolution & Structural Change in Latin America, 2 Vols. Ronald H. Chilcote. LC 68-28100. (Bibliographical Ser.: No. 40). 1970. Set. 40.00x o.p. (ISBN 0-8179-2401-9). Hoover Inst Pr.

Revolution & Survival: The Foreign Policy of Soviet Russia, 1917-1918. Richard K. Debo. LC 78-9671. 1979. 32.50x o.p. (ISBN 0-8020-5411-0). U of Toronto Pr.

Revolution at Work: Mass Campaigns in China. Ed. by C. P. Cell. (Studies in Social Discontinuity). 1977. 24.95 o.p. (ISBN 0-12-164750-1). Acad Pr.

Revolution in Consciousness. Frederic Lionel. 144p. (Orig.). 1984. pap. 8.95 o.p. (ISBN 0-7102-0066-8). Routledge Chapman & Hall.
Revolution in Cuba. Herbert L. Matthews. LC 73-1362. (Encore Edition). (Illus.). 432p. 1975. 5.95 o.p. (ISBN 0-684-15684-9, ScribT). Scribner.
Revolution in Laos. K. Phomvihane. 255p. 1981. 5.00 o.p. (ISBN 0-8285-2017-8, Pub. by Progress Pubs USSR). Imported Pubns.
Revolution in Perspective: Essays on the Hungarian Soviet Republic. Ed. by Andrew C. Janos & William B. Slottman. LC 74-138510. 1971. 32.00x o.p. (ISBN 0-520-01920-2). U of Cal Pr.
Revolution in Peru: Mariategui & the Myth. John M. Baines. LC 72-148690. 216p. 1972. 14.00 o.s.i. (ISBN 0-8173-4721-6). U of Ala Pr.
Revolution in Tanner's Lane, 1887. William H. White. Ed. by Robert L. Wolff. Bd. with Miriam's Schooling, Eighteen Ninety. LC 75-1515. (Victorian Fiction Ser.). 1975. lib. bdg. 73.00 o.p. (ISBN 0-8240-1588-6). Garland Pub.
Revolution in the Phillipines: The U. S. in Hall of Cracked Mirrors. Fred Poole & Max Vanzi. 368p. 1984. text ed. 18.85 o.p. (ISBN 0-07-050438-5). McGraw.
Revolution in the Schools. Ronald Gross & Judith Murphy. LC 64-24558. (Orig.). 1964. pap. 2.95 o.p. (ISBN 0-15-677086-5, Harv). HarBraceJ.
Revolution in Virginia. Hamilton J. Eckenrode. LC 64-7769. 311p. 1964. Repr. of 1916 ed. 29.50 o.p. (ISBN 0-208-00525-0, Archon). Shoe String.
Revolution of Mary Leary. Susan Shreve. 192p. (YA) (gr. 7 up). 1984. pap. 2.25 o.p. (ISBN 0-380-68494-2, 68494-2, Flare). Avon.
Revolution of the Spirit: Crisis of Value in Russia, Eighteen-Ninety to Nineteen-Eighteen. Martha Chomiak & Bernice Rosenthal. Tr. by Marian Schwarz. 360p. 1982. 27.00 o.p. (ISBN 0-89250-062-X). Orient Res Partners.
Revolution Sans Modele. Francois Chatelet et al. (Archontes Ser: No. 6). 188p. (Fr.). 1975. pap. text ed. 25.00x o.p. (ISBN 90-2797-615-5). Mouton.
Revolution Underway: An Aging Church in an Aging Society. Cedric W. Tilberg. LC 84-8122. 128p. 1984. pap. 5.95 o.p. (ISBN 0-8006-1817-3, Fortress). Augsburg Fortress.
Revolution within a Revolution: Women in Guinea-Bissau. Stephanie Urdang. 20p. 1986. Repr. of 1975 ed. 0.60 o.p. (ISBN 0-317-56003-4). Africa Fund.
Revolutionary Age (Weekly Organ of the Communist Party U. S. A., Majority Group, Vols. 1-3, No. 5. Communist Labor Party of America Staff. 1970. Repr. of 1929 ed. lib. bdg. 180.00x o.p. (ISBN 0-8371-9237-4, RA20). Greenwood.
Revolutionary America: An Interpretive Overview. Robert M. Calhoun. (History of the United States Ser.). (Illus.). 212p. (Orig.). 1976. pap. text ed. 12.00 net o.p. (ISBN 0-15-576712-7, HC). HarBraceJ.
Revolutionary & Dissident Movements: An International Guide. 2nd ed. Ed. by Henry W. Degenhardt. 600p. 1988. 140.00x o.p. (ISBN 0-8103-2056-8, Pub. by Longman). Gale.
Revolutionary Ascetic. Bruce Mazlish. 1977. pap. text ed. 4.95 o.p. (ISBN 0-07-041173-5). McGraw.
Revolutionary Personality: Lenin, Trotsky, Gandhi. E. Victor Wolfenstein. (Center of International Studies Ser.). 1971. 37.00x o.p. (ISBN 0-691-08611-7); pap. 9.95x o.p. (ISBN 0-691-02450-2, 251). Princeton U Pr.
Revolutionary Road. Richard Yates. (Contemporary Classics Ser). 1971. pap. 1.75 o.p. (ISBN 0-440-37412-X). Dell.
Revolutionary Suicide. Huey P. Newton & Herman Blake. LC 72-93749. 1973. 8.95 o.p. (ISBN 0-15-177092-1). HarBraceJ.
Revolutionary Theology in the Making: Barth-Thurneysen Correspondence 1914-1925. Karl Barth & Eduard Thurneysen. Tr. by J. D. Smart. 1964. 3.95 o.p. (ISBN 0-8042-0696-1, John Knox). Westminster John Knox.
Revolutionary Thought from Marx to Mao, 10 vols. 1977. Set. pap. 14.95 o.p. (ISBN 0-8351-0310-2). China Bks.
Revolutionary Vanguard: Battle of Ideologies. M. Basmanov. 318p. 1977. 6.45 o.p. (ISBN 0-8285-1501-8, Pub. by Progress Pubs USSR). Imported Pubns.
Revolutionary War. (Our Nations Heritage Ser.). (ISBN 0-07-375396-3). McGraw.
Revolutionary War Memoir & Selected Correspondence of Philip Van Cortlandt. Philip Van Cortlandt. Ed. by Jacob Judd. LC 75-43654. (Van Cortlandt Family Papers: Vol. 1). (Illus.). 208p. 1976. 12.00 o.s.i. (ISBN 0-912882-27-1). Sleepy Hollow.
Revolutions & Military Rule in the Middle East: The Arab States, Vol. 2. George M. Haddad. 14.95 o.s.i. (ISBN 0-8315-0060-3). Speller.
Revolutions & Revolutionaries. A. J. Taylor. LC 80-66006. 1980. 12.95 o.p. (ISBN 0-689-11069-3, Atheneum). Macmillan.
Revolutions & Revolutionists: A Comprehensive Guide to the Literature. Robert Blackey. LC 82-6653. (War-Peace Bibliography Ser.: No. 17). 488p. 1982. lib. bdg. 58.00 o.p. (ISBN 0-87436-330-6). ABC-Clio.
Revolvers. Ian V. Hogg. (Illus.). 1984. 14.95 o.p. (ISBN 0-85368-674-2, Arms & Armour Pr). Sterling.
Revolving Funds & Business Enterprises of the Government, Exclusive of Lending Agencies. Haskins & Sells. Repr. of 1949 ed. lib. bdg. 35.00x o.p. (ISBN 0-8371-3168-5, HARF). Greenwood.
Revue des Etudes Armeniennes: Vols. 1-11, Paris, 1920-21-1931-33. pap. 446.00 o.p. (ISBN 0-317-44400-X). Kraus Repr.
Reward & Punishment in Human Learning. Joseph Nuttin & Anthony G. Greenwald. 1968. 44.00 o.p. (ISBN 0-12-522950-X). Acad Pr.
Rewrite Man. Brian Forbes. 320p. 1985. 16.45 o.p. (ISBN 0-671-50610-2). S&S.
Rewriting Your Family Drama. Andrew Schwebel et al. 272p. 1989. 17.95 o.p. (ISBN 0-87477-498-5). J P Tarcher.
Rex & the Single Girl. Mary Ann Kelly. 1978. 5.00 o.p. (ISBN 0-682-49150-0). Exposition-Phoenix.
Rex Forrester's True Hunting Adentures. Rex Forrester. (Illus.). 208p. 1986. pap. 14.95 o.p. (ISBN 0-7233-0737-7, Pub. by Whitcoulls NZ). Intl Spec Bk.
Rex Q. C. Illus. by Nicola Smee. (Illus.). (gr. k-3). 1984. 8.70 o.p. (ISBN 0-316-49342-2). Little.
Rex Stout: A Primary & Secondary Bibliography. Guy Townsend et al. LC 80-8507. 210p. 1980. lib. bdg. 36.00 o.p. (ISBN 0-8240-9479-4). Garland Pub.
Reynold's Political Instructor, Nos. 1-27. 1971. Repr. of 1849 ed. lib. bdg. 49.00x o.p. (ISBN 0-8371-9238-2, RY00). Greenwood.
Reynolds Stone. Ruari McLean. (Illus.). 88p. (Orig.). 1984. pap. 5.95 o.p. (ISBN 0-905209-22-2, Pub. by Victoria & Albert Mus UK). Faber & Faber.
Rhapsody. Janine French. LC 86-4424. (Starlight Romance Ser.). 192p. 1986. 12.95 o.p. (ISBN 0-385-23565-8). Doubleday.
Rheological Techniques. R. W. Whorlow. LC 79-40992. (Physics in Medicine & Biology Ser.). 447p. 1980. 112.00 o.p. (ISBN 0-470-26736-4). Halsted Pr.
Rheology of the Circulation. R. L. Whitmore. LC 68-18535. 232p. 1968. 50.00 o.p. (ISBN 0-08-012661-8). Pergamon.
Rhetoric & Literature. P. Joseph Canavan. 352p. (Orig.). 1974. text ed. 21.95 o.p. (ISBN 0-07-009705-4). McGraw.
Rhetoric & Poetic. Ed. by Donald C. Bryant. 96p. 1965. pap. 6.00 o.p. (ISBN 0-87745-007-2). U of Iowa Pr.
Rhetoric & Reality: The Arab Mind Considered. Jack Laffin. LC 78-58319. 1978. pap. 4.95 o.s.i. (ISBN 0-8008-6792-0). Taplinger.
Rhetoric for Argument. Marie Secor & Jeanne Fahnestock. 416p. 1981. text ed. 14.00 o.p. (ISBN 0-394-32416-1, RanC). Random.
Rhetoric for Today. 3rd ed. William F. Smith & Raymond D. Liedlich. 1974. pap. text ed. 7.95 o.p. (ISBN 0-15-577050-0, HC). HarBraceJ.
Rhetoric for Today. 5th ed. William F. Smith & Raymond D. Liedlich. 270p. 1980. pap. text ed. 9.95 o.p. (ISBN 0-15-577054-3, HC). HarBraceJ.
Rhetoric for Today. 4th ed. William F. Smith & Raymond D. Liedlich. (Orig.). 1977. pap. text ed. 8.95 o.p. (ISBN 0-15-577052-7, HC). HarBraceJ.
Rhetoric in Classical Historiography. A. J. Woodman. 224p. 1988. lib. bdg. 37.50 o.p. (ISBN 0-7099-5256-2, Pub. by Croom Helm UK). Routledge Chapman & Hall.
Rhetoric Made Plain. 2nd ed. Jo Ray McCuen & Anthony C. Winkler. 1978. pap. text ed. 10.95 o.p. (ISBN 0-15-577075-6, HC). HarBraceJ.
Rhetoric Made Plain. JoRay McCuen & Anthony C. Winkler. 288p. (Orig.). 1974. pap. text ed. 7.95 o.p. (ISBN 0-15-577073-X, HC). HarBraceJ.
Rhetoric Made Plain. 4th ed. Anthony C. Winkler & Jo R. McCuen. 455p. 1984. text ed. 14.00 o.p. (ISBN 0-15-577079-9, HC). HarBraceJ.
Rhetoric Made Plain. 3rd ed. Anthony C. Winkler & Jo Ray McCuen. 458p. 1981. text ed. 13.95 o.p. (ISBN 0-15-577077-2, HC). HarBraceJ.
Rhetoric of Criticism: From Hobbes to Coleridge. S. Talmor. LC 83-13390. 127p. 1984. 35.00 o.p. (ISBN 0-08-030846-5). Pergamon.
Rhetoric of Western Thought. 3rd ed. James L. Golden et al. 1982. pap. text ed. 18.95 o.p. (ISBN 0-8403-2916-4, 40291601). Kendall Hunt.
Rhetoric, Romance & Technology: Studies in the Interaction of Expression & Culture. Walter J. Ong. LC 74-153722. 358p. 1971. 37.50x o.p. (ISBN 0-8014-0645-5). Cornell U Pr.
Rhetorical Dimensions in Criticism. Donald C. Bryant. LC 72-94149. x, 146p. 1973. 17.50x o.p. (ISBN 0-8071-0214-8). La State U Pr.
Rheumatic Therapeutics. Ed. by S. H. Roth et al. (Illus.). 550p. 1985. text ed. 45.00 o.p. (ISBN 0-07-054010-1). McGraw.
Rheumatic Valvular Disease in Children. Ed. by J. B. Borman & M. S. Gotsman. (Illus.). 240p. 1980. pap. 57.90 o.p. (ISBN 0-387-10079-2). Springer-Verlag.
Rheumatism & Arthritis. Leonard Mervyn. (Lythway Ser.). 1987. lib. bdg. 15.95x o.p. (ISBN 0-7451-0610-2, Pub. by Chivers Pr UK). G K Hall.
Rheumatoid Arthritis. Jerome H. Herman et al. LC 72-14155. (Illus.). 220p. 1973. text ed. 28.50x o.p. (ISBN 0-8422-7108-2). Irvington.
Rheumatoid Arthritis: Pathogenetic Mechanisms & Consequences in Therapeutics. Ed. by W. Muller et al. 1972. 98.50 o.p. (ISBN 0-12-510050-7). Acad Pr.
Rheumatoid Foot: Diagnosis, Pathomechanics, & Treatment. K. Tillman. Tr. by Ian F. Goldie from Ger. (Illus.). 116p. 1979. text ed. 31.50 o.p. (ISBN 0-88416-304-0). Year Bk Med.
Rhiannon. Roberta Gellis. (Roselynde Chronicles Ser.). 1984. lib. bdg. 13.95 o.p. (ISBN 0-8398-2864-0, Gregg). G K Hall.
Rhine Journey. Ann Schlee. LC 80-12265. (Illus.). 176p. 1981. 10.95 o.p. (ISBN 0-03-056894-3). H Holt & Co.
Rhine Pirates. Hans P. Schaad. Tr. by Elizabeth D. Crawford. LC 68-7304. (Illus.). (gr. k-3). 1968. 4.75 o.p. (ISBN 0-15-266680-X, HJ). HarBraceJ.
Rhine Valley Travel Guide. Berlitz Editors. (Berlitz Travel Guides). (Illus.). 1982. pap. 4.95 o.p. (ISBN 0-02-969450-7, Berlitz). Macmillan.
Rhinehart Reader Companion. Grace Eilis. (Illus.). 432p. 1989. pap. text ed. write for info. o.p. (ISBN 0-03-014244-X). HR&W.
Rhinoceros & Other Plays: The Leader, The Future Is in Eggs. Eugene Ionesco. Tr. by Derek Prouse from Fr. 1960. pap. 6.95 o.p. (ISBN 0-394-17226-4, E259, Ever). Grove.
Rhode Island: Agency. suppl. 6.50 o.p. Am Law Inst.
Rhode Island Atlas. Marion I. Wright & Robert J. Sullivan. LC 80-52911. (Illus.). 239p. (Orig., Contains considerable text). 1983. 22.50 o.p. (ISBN 0-917012-52-6); pap. 12.95 o.p. (ISBN 0-917012-19-4). RI Pubns Soc.
Rhode Island: Conflict of Laws. suppl. 6.00 o.p. Am Law Inst.
Rhode Island: Contracts. 9.50 o.p. (ISBN 0-686-90885-6). Am Law Inst.
Rhode Island Directory of Manufacturers, 1986. 268p. 1986. pap. 18.00 o.p. (ISBN 0-318-02868-9). Manufacturers.
Rhode Island Furniture. Joseph K. Ott. (Illus.). 1965. 15.00 o.p. (ISBN 0-917218-01-9). A Mobray Inc.
Rhode Island: Judgements. 8.50 o.p. (ISBN 0-686-90889-9). Am Law Inst.
Rhode Island: Restitution. 8.50 o.p. (ISBN 0-686-90891-0). Am Law Inst.
Rhode Island: Security. 8.50 o.p. (ISBN 0-686-90893-7). Am Law Inst.
Rhode Island Study Manual for Life & Accident & Health Insurance. 1986. pap. 5.95 o.p. (ISBN 0-88462-645-8, 5310-25, Longman Fin Serv Pub). Longman Finan.
Rhode Island Transit Album. D. Scott Molloy. (Illus.). 64p. (Orig.). 1978. pap. 4.95 o.p. (ISBN 0-686-32864-7). Boston St Rwy.
Rhode Island's Ocean Sands: Management Guidelines for Sand & Gravel Extraction in State Waters. M. J. Grant. 51p. write for info. o.p. (P310). Sea Grant Pubns.
Rhodes Travel Guide. Berlitz Editors. (Travel Guides for English Speakers Ser.). 1976. pap. 4.95 o.p. (ISBN 0-02-969460-4, Berlitz). Macmillan.
Rhodesia, the Problem. D. Smith. 1969. Repr. 15.50 o.p. (ISBN 0-08-007094-9). Pergamon.
Rhyme & Reason. Fred S. Baylis. 1978. 4.00 o.p. (ISBN 0-682-49040-7). Exposition-Phoenix.
Rhyme of a Race & Other Poems. Jennie Douglass Moore. 1978. 4.50 o.p. (ISBN 0-682-49068-7). Exposition-Phoenix.
Rhymes. (Preschool Puppet Board Bks.). (Illus.). 7p. (ps-1). 1976. 2.50 o.p. (ISBN 0-448-09743-5, G&D). Putnam Pub Group.
Rhymes Around the Day. Pat Thomson. LC 82-24001. (Illus.). 32p. (ps-1). 1983. 10.25 o.p. (ISBN 0-688-02073-9); lib. bdg. 10.88 o.p. (ISBN 0-688-02074-7). Lothrop.
Rhymes of Boys & Girls. Illus. by Blanche F. Wright. (Real Mother Goose Mini Boxed Set Ser.). (Illus.). (ps-1). 1987. bds. 5.95 o.p. (ISBN 0-02-689015-1, Checkerboard Pr). Macmillan.
Rhymes of the Ranges: A New Collection of the Poems of Bruce Kiskaddon. Bruce Kiskaddon. Intro. by Hal Cannon. (Illus.). 144p. 1987. 14.95 o.p. (ISBN 0-87905-264-3). Gibbs Smith Pub.
Rhymes, Riddles & Research. Lorretta B. Minn. (gr. 4-8). 1981. 5.95 o.p. (ISBN 0-86653-024-X, GA 253). Good Apple.
Rhyming & Reading. Becky Daniel & Charlie Daniel. (gr. 1-4). 1979. 5.95 o.p. (ISBN 0-916456-42-0, GA115). Good Apple.
Rhythm & Tempo: A Study in Music History. Curt Sachs. 391p. Repr. lib. bdg. 49.00 o.p. (Pub. by Am Repr Serv). Reprint Servs.
Rhythm Music & Education. Emile Jaques-Dalcroze. Tr. by Harold F. Rubenstein from Fr. 1973. pap. 5.25 o.p. (ISBN 0-913650-09-9). CPP Belwin.
Rhythmic Activity of Fishes. Ed. by J. E. Thorpe. 1978. 87.00 o.p. (ISBN 0-12-690650-5). Acad Pr.
Rhythms in Dialogue. Joseph Jaffe & Stanley Feldstein. (Personality & Psychopathology Ser.: Vol. 8). 1970. 24.95 o.p. (ISBN 0-12-379850-7). Acad Pr.
Rhytismataceae of the Indian Subcontinent. P. F. Cannon & D. W. Minter. 123p. 1986. pap. text ed. 26.00 o.p. CAB Intl.
RIA Federal Tax Course: Individual Income Tax. 1986 ed. Research Institute of America Staff. 1985. 27.95x o.p. (ISBN 0-256-03202-5). Irwin.
RIA Safety Standard. 79p. 1985. pap. text ed. 34.00 o.p. (ISBN 0-317-18021-5). Robot Inst Am.
Ribbon Flowers, Paper Flowers. Yuri Uchiyama. LC 73-89697. (Illus.). 160p. 1974. 15.50 o.p. (ISBN 0-87011-221-X); pap. 9.50 o.p. (ISBN 0-87011-496-4). Kodansha.
Ribbons of Silver. Katherine Myers. (Avon Romance Ser.). 416p. 1985. pap. 2.95 o.p. (ISBN 0-380-89602-8). Avon.
Rice Diet Report: How I Lost up to 12 Pounds a Week on the World-Famous Weight-Loss Plan. Judy Moscovitz. 234p. 1986. 16.95 o.p. (ISBN 0-399-13141-8). Putnam Pub Group.
Rice Economies: Technology & Development in Asian Societies. Francesca Bray. 272p. 1986. text ed. 39.95x o.p. (ISBN 0-631-14877-9). Basil Blackwell.
Rice Improvement in Eastern, Central & Southern Africa. 159p. 1985. pap. text ed. 8.30 o.s.i. (ISBN 971-104-147-2, Pub. by Intl Rice Res Philippines). Agribookstore.
Rice: Production & Utilization. Bor S. Luh. (Illus.). 1980. 69.95 o.p. (ISBN 0-87055-332-1). AVI.
Riceburner. Richard Hyer. 208p. 1986. 16.95 o.s.i. (ISBN 0-684-18727-2). Scribner.
Rich & the Mighty. Vera Cowie. LC 84-21165. 408p. 1985. 16.95 o.p. (ISBN 0-385-19931-7). Doubleday.
Rich & the Mighty. Vera Cowie. 1986. pap. 3.95 o.p. (ISBN 0-380-69971-0). Avon.
Rich Christians in an Age of Hunger: A Biblical Study. Ronald J. Sider. LC 76-45106. 254p. 1977. pap. 5.95 o.p. (ISBN 0-8091-2015-1). Paulist Pr.
Rich Is Best. Julie Ellis. 1985. 16.95 o.p. (ISBN 0-87795-629-4, Arbor Hse). Morrow.
Rich Is Better: How Women Can Bridge the Gap Between Wanting & Having It All. Tessa A. Warschaw. LC 84-13532. 264p. 1985. 15.95 o.p. (ISBN 0-385-19044-1). Doubleday.
Rich Little Poor Girl. T. J. Feely. 1982. pap. PB.
Rich Man. Georges Simenon. LC 76-151139. (Helen & Kurt Wolff Bk.). 1971. 5.95 o.p. (ISBN 0-15-177162-6). HarBraceJ.
Rich Man, Poor Man. Donald W. Shriver, Jr. LC 71-37003. (Christian Ethics for Modern Man Ser.). (Illus.). 112p. (Orig.). 1972. pap. 1.95 o.p. (ISBN 0-8042-9092-X, John Knox). Westminster John Knox.
Rich Man, Poor Man see Heinemann Guided Readers.
Rich Mitch. Marjorie W. Sharmat. LC 83-5398. (Illus.). 144p. (gr. 3-7). 1983. 10.25 o.p. (ISBN 0-688-02407-6). Morrow.
Richard A. Sol Yurick. 480p. 1983. pap. 3.95 o.p. (ISBN 0-380-62430-3, 62430). Avon.
Richard A. A Novel about Genius Rampant Sol Yurick. LC 80-66497. 446p. 1982. 14.95 o.p. (ISBN 0-87795-272-8, Arbor Hse). Morrow.
Richard & Cosima Wagner: Biography of a Marriage. Geoffrey Skelton. (Illus.). 288p. 1982. 14.95 o.p. (ISBN 0-395-31836-X). HM.
Richard Bentley: A Descriptive, Annotated Bibiography. Robert E. Bourdette. LC 84-45392. 275p. 1985. lib. bdg. 37.00 o.p. (ISBN 0-8240-8849-2). Garland Pub.
Richard Binns' Best of Britain. Richard Binns. LC 84-45570. (Illus.). 144p. 1985. pap. 8.95 o.p. (ISBN 0-689-11522-9, Atheneum). Macmillan.
Richard Brautigan. Marc Chenetier. LC 82-20880. (Contemporary Writers Ser.). 96p. 1983. pap. 4.75 o.p. (ISBN 0-416-32960-8, NO. 3751). Routledge Chapman & Hall.

Richard Brinsley Sheridan: A Reference Guide. Jack D. Durant. 1981. lib. bdg. 36.50 o.p. (ISBN 0-8161-8146-2, Hall Reference). G K Hall.

Richard Coeur De Lion: A Biography. Philip Henderson. (Illus.). 256p. (LC 76-00004). 1976. Repr. of 1959 ed. lib. bdg. 22.50x o.p. (ISBN 0-8371-8724-9, HERI). Greenwood.

Richard Cragun. W. Terry. 1982. 30.00 o.s.i. (ISBN 0-318-03155-8). E J Brill USA.

Richard Henry Dana, 2 Vols. Charles F. Adams. LC 67-23883. 838p. 1968. Repr. of 1890 ed. 43.00x o.p. (ISBN 0-8103-3038-5). Gale.

Richard Lester: A Guide to References & Resources. Diane Rosenfeldt. 1978. lib. bdg. 21.50 o.p. (ISBN 0-8161-8185-3, Hall Reference). G K Hall.

Richard Meier, Architect: A Selected Bibliography. Jamie W. Coniglio. (Architecture Ser.: A 1462). 6p. 1985. 2.00 o.p. (ISBN 0-89028-552-7). Vance Biblios.

Richard Morehead's Texas. Richard Morehead. 1982. 9.95 o.p. (ISBN 0-89015-306-X). Eakin Pr.

Richard Parkes Bonington. Carlos Peacock. LC 79-63955. (Illus.). 1980. 25.00 o.s.i. (ISBN 0-8008-6793-9). Taplinger.

Richard Rogers: RIBA Gold Medallist, 1985. Valerie J. Nurcombe. (Architecture Ser.: A 1496). 24p. 1985. 3.75 o.p. (ISBN 0-89028-626-4). Vance Biblios.

Richard Scarry's Busy Houses. Richard Scarry. LC 81-50713. (Shape Bks.). (Illus.). 24p. (ps-k). 1981. spiral plastic bdg. 2.95 o.p. (ISBN 0-394-84937-X). Random.

Richard Scarry's Great Big Air Book. Richard Scarry. LC 79-146649. (Illus.). (gr. k-3). 1971. 8.95 o.s.i. (ISBN 0-394-82167-X, BYR); lib. bdg. 11.99 o.s.i. (ISBN 0-394-92167-4). Random.

Richard Scarry's Lowly Worm Car & Truck Book. Richard Scarry. LC 82-61012. (Illus.). 16p. (ps-2). 1983. pap. 2.95 o.s.i. (ISBN 0-394-85760-7). Random.

Richard Scarry's Peasant Pig & the Terrible Dragon. Richard Scarry. LC 80-5086. (Illus.). 48p. (ps-3). 1980. bds. 4.95 o.s.i. (ISBN 0-394-84567-6); lib. bdg. 5.99 o.s.i. (ISBN 0-394-94567-0). Random.

Richard Scarry's Stories to Color: With Lowly Worm & Mr. Paint Pig. Richard Scarry. (Illus.). (ps-3). 1978. pap. 2.95 o.s.i. (ISBN 0-394-83961-7, BYR). Random.

Richard Scarry's Toy Book. Richard Scarry. (Illus.). (ps-3). 1978. pap. 2.95 o.s.i. (ISBN 0-394-83962-5, BYR). Random.

Richard Second see also King Richard Second.

Richard Second see also Tragedy of King Richard Second.

Richard Shuttleworth. Kevin Desmond. (Illus.). 192p. 1982. 19.95 o.p. (ISBN 0-86720-629-2). Janes Info Group.

Richard Strauss: A Critical Commentary on His Life & Works, 2 Vols. Norman R. Del Mar. Repr. of 1969 ed. lib. bdg. 108.00 o.p. (Pub. by Am Repr Serv). Reprint Servs.

Richard Strauss: A Critical Study of the Operas. William S. Mann. 402p. Repr. of 1966 ed. lib. bdg. 59.00 o.p. (Pub. by Am Repr Serv). Reprint Servs.

Richard Strauss & Romain Rolland: Correspondence. Romain Rolland. 239p. Repr. of 1968 ed. lib. bdg. 39.00 o.p. (Pub. by Am Repr Serv). Reprint Servs.

Richard Third see also King Richard Third.

Richard Third see also Tragedy of King Richard Third.

Richard Wagner: A Biography. D. Watson. 384p. 1983. pap. text ed. 8.95 o.p. (ISBN 0-07-068479-0). McGraw.

Richard Wagner & His World. Charles Osborne. LC 76-56892. (Encore Edition). (Illus.). 1977. 3.95 o.p. (ISBN 0-684-16915-0, ScribT). Scribner.

Richard Wagner: His Life, Art & Thought. Ronald Taylor. LC 78-63053. 1979. 14.95 o.s.i. (ISBN 0-8008-4792-X, Crescendo). Taplinger.

Richard Wagner: His Life, His Work, His Century, 2 Vols. Martin Gregor-Dellin. Tr. by J. Maxwell Brownjohn from Ger. (Helen & Kurt Wolff Bk.). (Illus.). 592p. 1983. 25.00 o.s.i. (ISBN 0-15-177151-0). HarBraceJ.

Richard Wagner: The Man, His Mind, & His Music. Robert W. Gutman. LC 73-12381. (Illus.). 490p. 1974. pap. 5.95 o.p. (ISBN 0-15-677610-3, Harv). HarBraceJ.

Richard Wagner: The Story of an Artist. Guy De Pourtales. Tr. by Lewis May from Fr. LC 76-138173. (Illus.). 1972. Repr. of 1932 ed. lib. bdg. 35.00x o.p. (ISBN 0-8371-5630-0, PORW). Greenwood.

Richard Wilbur: A Bibliographical Checklist. John P. Field. LC 79-626237. (Serif Ser.: No. 16). 95p. 1971. 10.00x o.p. (ISBN 0-87338-035-5). Kent St U Pr.

Richard's Bicycle Book. rev. ed. Richard Ballantine. 1982. pap. 7.95 o.p. (ISBN 0-345-30242-7). Ballantine.

Richard's Things. Fredrick Raphael. 1976. pap. 1.50 o.p. (ISBN 0-380-00733-9, 30064). Avon.

Richardson the Novelist: The Psychological Patters. Gerald Levin. (Costerus New Ser.: No. 9). 1978. pap. text ed. 17.50x o.p. (ISBN 90-6203-410-1). Humanities.

Richardsoniana, 25 vols. Incl. Vol. 1. lib. bdg. (ISBN 0-8240-1304-2); Vol. 2. lib. bdg. (ISBN 0-8240-1305-0); Vol. 3. lib. bdg. (ISBN 0-8240-1306-9); Vol. 4 & 5. lib. bdg. (ISBN 0-8240-1307-7); Vol. 6. lib. bdg. (ISBN 0-8240-1308-5); Vol. 7. lib. bdg. (ISBN 0-8240-1309-3); Vol. 8. lib. bdg. (ISBN 0-8240-1310-7); Vol. 9. lib. bdg. (ISBN 0-8240-1311-5); Vol. 10. lib. bdg. (ISBN 0-8240-1312-3); Vol. 11. lib. bdg. (ISBN 0-8240-1313-1); Vol. 12. lib. bdg. o.p. (ISBN 0-8240-1314-X); Vol. 13. lib. bdg. (ISBN 0-8240-1315-8); Vol. 14. lib. bdg. o.p. (ISBN 0-8240-1316-6); Vol. 15. lib. bdg. o.p. (ISBN 0-8240-1317-4); Vols. 16-19. Set. lib. bdg. 207.00 (ISBN 0-8240-1318-2); lib. bdg. o.p.; Vols. 20 & 21. Set. lib. bdg. 76.00 (ISBN 0-8240-1319-0); lib. bdg.; Vols. 22-25. Set. lib. bdg. 152.00 (ISBN 0-8240-1320-4); lib. bdg. o.p.. (Life & Times of Seven Major British Writers Ser). 1974. lib. bdg. 57.00 o.p. Garland Pub.

Richelieu & His Age, 3 vols. Carl J. Burckhardt. LC 71-88470. (Helen & Kurt Wolff Bk.). 1972. Vol. 1. 9.95 o.p. (ISBN 0-15-177159-6); Vol. 2. 12.95 o.p. (ISBN 0-15-177160-X); Vol. 3. 12.95 o.p. (ISBN 0-15-177158-8). HarBraceJ.

Richelieu & Reason of State. William F. Church. LC 76-181518. 582p. 1972. 49.00x o.p. (ISBN 0-691-05199-2). Princeton U Pr.

Richelieu & the Councillors of Louis XIII. Orest A. Ranum. LC 76-3762. 211p. 1976. Repr. of 1963 ed. lib. bdg. 22.50x o.p. (ISBN 0-8371-8803-2, RARI). Greenwood.

Richer Living. Ernest Holmes & Raymond C. Barker. 372p. 1973. pap. 9.50 o.p. (ISBN 0-911336-48-6). Sci of Mind.

Riches of Prayer. Olavi Kaukola. Tr. by Bernhard Hillila. LC 85-47716. 80p. 1986. pap. 3.95 o.p. (ISBN 0-8006-1861-0, 1-1861, Fortress). Augsburg Fortress.

Riches under Your Roof: How to Make Your Home Worth Thousands More. Jim Belliveau & Mary Belliveau. LC 82-15420. 256p. 1983. 17.95 o.s.i. (ISBN 0-03-053016-4); pap. 9.95 o.s.i. (ISBN 0-03-053301-5). H Holt & Co.

Richest Hole on Earth: A History of the Bingham Copper Mine. Leonard J. Arrington & Gary B. Hansen. 103p. (Orig.). 1963. pap. 4.50 o.p. (ISBN 0-87421-028-3). Utah St U Pr.

Richest Place on Earth: The Story of Virginia City, Nevada, & the Heyday of the Comstock Lode. Ed. by Warren Hinckle, 3rd & Frederic Hobbs. 1978. 14.95 o.p. (ISBN 0-395-25348-9). HM.

Richleighs of Tantamount. Barbara Willard. LC 67-16229. (Illus.). (gr. 6-8). 1967. 5.50 o.p. (ISBN 0-15-266750-4, HJ). HarBraceJ.

Rich's Business Guide to Silicon Valley & No. CA: 1987-1988. (Illus.). 400p. 1987. 109.50 o.p. (ISBN 0-914189-05-0). Busn Direct CA.

Richthofen: A True History of the Red Baron. William E. Burrows. LC 75-85010. (Illus.). 1969. 8.95 o.p. (ISBN 0-15-177172-3). HarBraceJ.

Rick Elstein's Tennis Kinetics with Martina Navratilova. Mary Carillo. 1985. 17.45 o.p. (ISBN 0-671-55540-5). S&S.

Rick Shannon & the Case of the Missing Pilot. Allan Stewart. (Fingerprint Mystery Ser.). 144p. (gr. 8-12). 1984. pap. 2.95 o.p. (ISBN 0-8423-0212-3). Tyndale.

Rick Shannon & the Secret of the Blue Dragon. Allan Stewart. (Finger Print Mystery Bks.). 160p. (gr. 6-8). 1985. pap. 3.50 o.p. (ISBN 0-8423-5857-9). Tyndale.

Rickenbacker's Luck: An American Life. Finis Farr. 1979. 12.95 o.p. (ISBN 0-395-27102-9). HM.

Rickety Witch. Maggie S. Davis. LC 84-498. (Illus.). 32p. (ps-3). 1984. 10.95 o.p. (ISBN 0-8234-0521-4). Holiday.

Rickover: Controversy & Genius - A Biography. Norman Polmar & Thomas B. Allen. 784p. 1984. pap. 12.95 o.p. (ISBN 0-671-52815-7, Touchstone Bks). S&S.

Rico's Cat. Dana Brookins. LC 76-8841. (Illus.). (gr. 3-6). 1979. 6.95 o.p. (ISBN 0-395-28850-9, Clarion). HM.

Riddle. Dan Sherman. LC 77-79527. 1977. 7.95 o.p. (ISBN 0-87795-164-0, Arbor Hse). Morrow.

Riddle-Master of Hed. Patricia A. McKillip. LC 76-5492. 240p. (gr. 6-12). 1976. 14.95 o.s.i. (ISBN 0-689-30545-1, Atheneum Childrens Bks). Macmillan.

Riddle Monster. Lisl Weil. LC 81-1030. (Illus.). 32p. (ps-3). 1981. 7.95 o.s.i. (ISBN 0-395-31019-9, Clarion). HM.

Riddle of the Bermuda Triangle. Ed. by Martin Ebon. (Orig.). 1975. pap. 1.75 o.p. (E8063, Sig.). NAL.

Riddle of the Didache: Fact or Fiction, Heresy or Catholicism? Frederick E. Vokes. (Church Historical Society London N. S.: No. 32). Repr. of 1938 ed. 40.00 o.p. (ISBN 0-8115-3156-2). Kraus Repr.

Riddle of the Early Academy. Harold Cherniss. LC 78-66594. (Ancient Philosophy Ser.). 111p. 1982. lib. bdg. 18.00 o.p. (ISBN 0-8240-9604-5). Garland Pub.

Riddle of the Future: A Modern Study of Precognition. Andrew MacKenzie. LC 75-8199. 176p. 1975. 8.50 o.s.i. (ISBN 0-8008-6795-5). Taplinger.

Riddle of Violence. Kenneth Kaunda. LC 80-8348. 192p. 1981. 9.95 o.p. (ISBN 0-06-250450-9, HarpR). HarpR.

Riddles: Ancient & Modern. Mark Bryant. LC 83-73464. 208p. 1984. 15.95 o.s.i. (ISBN 0-911745-49-1); pap. 6.95 o.p. (ISBN 0-911745-50-5). P Bedrick Bks.

Riddles in Mathematics: A Book of Paradoxes. Eugene P. Northrop. LC 74-32267. 270p. 1975. pap. 29.50 o.p. (ISBN 0-88275-273-1). Krieger.

Riddles of the Stars: White Dwarfs, Red Giants, & Black Holes. Robert Kraske. LC 79-87520. (Illus.). (gr. 4-7). 1979. 6.95 o.p. (ISBN 0-15-266907-8, HJ). HarBraceJ.

Riddles of Three Oceans. A. Kondratov. 267p. 1974. 4.45 o.p. (ISBN 0-8285-0833-X, Pub. by Progress Pubs USSR). Imported Pubns.

Ride. John Wainwright. 224p. 1986. pap. 2.95 o.p. (ISBN 0-931773-69-5). Critics Choice Paper.

Ride a Crooked Trail. Burt Arthur & Budd Arthur. 1979. pap. 1.25 o.p. (ISBN 0-505-51389-7, Pub. by Tower Bks). Dorchester Pub Co.

Ride a Pale Horse. Helen MacInnes. (Large Print Books (General Ser.)). 1985. lib. bdg. 17.95 o.p. (ISBN 0-8161-3863-X); pap. 9.95 o.p. (ISBN 0-8161-3864-8). G K Hall.

Ride a Proud Horse. Barbara Morgenroth. LC 77-21111. (gr. 6-9). 1978. 8.95 o.p. (ISBN 0-689-30624-5, Atheneum). Macmillan.

Ride a Wild Dream. Lynn Hall. (Illus.). 160p. (gr. 5-9). 1978. pap. 2.25 o.p. (ISBN 0-380-40303-X, 62067-7, Camelot). Avon.

Ride, & Stay Alive. Ed. by Jeff Robinson. (Illus.). 128p. pap. text ed. 4.95 o.s.i. (ISBN 0-89287-024-9, X910). Clymer Pub.

Ride East, Ride West. Anne Powers. 1978. pap. 1.95 o.p. (ISBN 0-505-51300-5, Pub. by Tower Bks). Dorchester Pub Co.

Ride On, Ride On. Sylvia P. Martin. (gr. k-4). 1968. bds. 3.50 o.p. (ISBN 0-8066-0822-6, 10-5514, Augsburg). Augsburg Fortress.

Ride Out the Dark: The Experiences of an Englishwoman in Wartime Germany. Christabel Bielenberg. LC 84-10717. 285p. 1984. pap. 6.95 o.p. (ISBN 0-8398-2853-5, Gregg). G K Hall.

Ride Out the Storm. Aleen Malcolm. (Orig.). 1981. pap. 2.95 o.p. (ISBN 0-440-17399-X). Dell.

Ride the Red-Eyed Wind. M. J. Pearson. LC 78-2206. (Illus.). 176p. (gr. 6 up). 1978. 8.95 o.p. (ISBN 0-87518-157-0). Dillon.

Ride the Thunder. Janet Dailey. (General Ser.). 1984. lib. bdg. 13.95 o.p. (ISBN 0-8161-3666-1, Large Print Bks); pap. 9.95 o.p. (ISBN 0-8161-3709-9). G K Hall.

Ride the West Wind. Barbara Chamberlain. LC 78-73150. (gr. 3-7). 1979. pap. 2.95 o.p. (ISBN 0-89191-133-2). Cook.

Ride When You're Ready. Evelyn Bolton. LC 74-9763. (Evelyn Bolton's Horse Stories Ser.). (Illus.). 32p. (gr. 4 up). 1974. PLB 7.95 o.p. (ISBN 0-87191-373-9). Creative Ed.

Ride with Wings. Maryn Langer. 224p. 1987. pap. 5.95 o.p. (ISBN 0-310-47771-9, 15650P). Zondervan.

Rider Haggard. Norman Etherington. (English Authors Ser.: No. 383). 1984. lib. bdg. 15.95 o.p. (ISBN 0-8057-6869-6, Twayne). G K Hall.

Riders in the Sky. F. Tuglas. 78p. 1986. 5.95 o.p. (ISBN 0-8285-3773-9, Pub. by Perioodika Tallinn). Imported Pubns.

Riding. Robert Owen & John Bullock. (Illus.). 96p. 1985. 12.95 o.p. (ISBN 0-668-06284-3). Arco.

Riding & Jumping. William C. Steinkraus. LC 79-91104. 1969. 11.95 o.p. (ISBN 0-385-04816-5). Doubleday.

Riding Bareback to Las Vegas. Harry A. White. LC 84-90052. (Illus.). 112p. 1985. 10.00 o.p. (ISBN 0-533-06133-4). Vantage.

Riding from A to Z: A Practical Manual of Horsemanship. Peter Churchill. LC 77-88451. (Illus.). 1978. 9.95 o.s.i. (ISBN 0-8008-6796-3). Taplinger.

Riding on a School Bus. Joyce E. Dunn. LC 84-90496. (Illus.). 56p. (gr. 1-3). 1985. 4.95 o.p. (ISBN 0-533-06378-7). Vantage.

Riding the Nightmare. Selma R. Williams. LC 78-6023. (Illus.). (gr. 7 up). 1978. 9.95 o.p. (ISBN 0-689-30633-4, Atheneum). Macmillan.

Riding the Rails: Reminiscences of a Railway Career. John R. Martin. (Illus.). 1985. 12.95 o.p. (ISBN 0-533-06184-9). Vantage.

Riding to Jerusalem. Bettina Selby. LC 85-28697. (Illus.). 232p. 1986. 17.95 o.p. (ISBN 0-87226-074-7). P Bedrick Bks.

Riff, Remember. Lynn Hall. (gr. 3-7). 1975. pap. 0.95 o.p. (ISBN 0-380-00186-1, 21899, Camelot). Avon.

Rifka Bangs the Teakettle. Chaya Burstein. LC 79-91068. (Illus.). (gr. 4-6). 1970. 4.95 o.p. (ISBN 0-15-266944-2, HJ). HarBraceJ.

Rifle River. Roy LeBeau. (Buckskin Ser.: No. 1). 240p. (Orig.). 1982. pap. 2.25 o.p. (ISBN 0-8439-1158-1, Pub. by Leisure Bks CT). Dorchester Pub Co.

Rifle Shooting As a Sport. Ed. by Bernd Klinger. (Illus.). 186p. 1981. 15.00 o.s.i. (ISBN 0-498-02581-0). A S Barnes.

Rifomycin: Chemotherapy. Arthur Vall-Spinosa et al. (Illus.). 220p. 1973. text ed. 34.00x o.p. (ISBN 0-8422-7067-1). Irvington.

Rift Valley: Afro-Arabian. Ed. by Albert M. Quennell. (Benchmark Papers in Geology: Vol. 60). 419p. 1982. 55.95 o.p. (ISBN 0-87933-383-9). Van Nos Reinhold.

Rift Zones of the World Ocean. Ed. by A. P. Vinogradov & G. B. Udintsev. Tr. by N. Kaner. LC 75-16178. 503p. 1975. 118.00 o.p. (ISBN 0-470-90838-6, JW). Krieger.

Rig. Ronald Wilcox. 1978. pap. 1.95 o.p. (ISBN 0-8439-0593-X, Pub. by Leisure Bks CT). Dorchester Pub Co.

Rig Warrior. William W. Johnstone. 288p. 1987. pap. 3.50 o.p. (ISBN 0-8217-2066-X). Zebra.

Riga: A Guide. M. Debrer. 156p. 1982. 6.95 o.p. (ISBN 0-8285-2586-2, Pub. by Progress Pubs USSR). Imported Pubns.

Rigged Hiblert Space & Quantum Mechanics: Lectures in Mathematical Physics at the University of Texas at Austin. A. Boehm. (Lecture Notes in Physics Ser.: Vol. 78). 1978. pap. 10.00 o.p. (ISBN 0-387-08843-1). Springer-Verlag.

Rigging & Boilermaker Safety. Resource Systems International Staff. 1982. pap. text ed. 15.00 o.p. (ISBN 0-8359-6726-3, Reston). P-H.

Rigging: Basic Principles. Resource Systems International Staff. 1982. pap. text ed. 15.00 o.p. (ISBN 0-8359-6723-9, Reston). P-H.

Rigging: Cranes & Other Lifting Equipment. Resource Systems International Staff. 1982. pap. text ed. 15.00 o.p. (ISBN 0-8359-6724-7, Reston). P-H.

Rigging: Equalizing & Distributing Loads. Resource Systems International Staff. 1982. pap. text ed. 15.00 o.p. (ISBN 0-8359-6725-5, Reston). P-H.

Rigging: Ropes. Resource Systems International Staff. 1982. pap. text ed. 15.00 o.p. (ISBN 0-8359-6727-1, Reston). P-H.

Rigging: Tools. Resource Systems International Staff. 1982. pap. text ed. 15.00 o.p. (ISBN 0-8359-6728-X, Reston). P-H.

Right & Left: Essays on Dual Symbolic Classification. Ed. by Rodney Needham. LC 73-82982. 1974. lib. bdg. 12.50x o.s.i. (ISBN 0-226-56995-0); P759. pap. 7.50 o.s.i. (ISBN 0-226-56996-9, Phoen). U of Chicago Pr.

Right & the Power: The Prosecution of Watergate. Leon Jaworski. LC 76-22594. 316p. 1976. 15.00x o.p. (ISBN 0-87201-792-3). Gulf Pub.

Right Brain: A New Understanding of the Unconscious Mind & Its Creative Powers. Thomas R. Blakeslee. LC 79-26209. (Illus.). 288p. 1980. 15.95 o.p. (ISBN 0-385-15099-7, Anchor Pr). Doubleday.

Right from the Start: A Guide to Nonsexist Child Rearing. Selma Greenberg. 1979. pap. 4.95 o.p. (ISBN 0-395-27817-1). HM.

Right from the Start: A Guide to Nonsexist Child Rearing. Selma Greenberg. LC 77-20000. 1978. 8.95 o.p. (ISBN 0-395-25714-X). HM.

Right Horse: An Owner's & Buyers' Guide. Janet W. Macdonald. LC 84-6240. (Illus.). 160p. 1984. 9.95 o.p. (ISBN 0-668-06246-0, 6246-0). Arco.

Right Human Relations: The Only Way to World Peace. Gene H. Lawrence. 110p. 1980. pap. 3.00 o.s.i. (ISBN 0-682-49627-8). Exposition-Phoenix.

Right Image. James D. Horan. 1975. pap. 1.75 o.p. (ISBN 0-380-00220-5, 21790). Avon.

Right Mental Attitude. Jerry Savelle. 138p. (Orig.). 1981. pap. 3.25 o.p. (ISBN 0-89274-159-7). Harrison Hse.

Right Now. David Kherdian. LC 82-21185. (Illus.). 36p. (ps-1). 1983. lib. bdg. 10.99 o.s.i. (ISBN 0-394-95596-X). Knopf.

Right of Possession. Jayne Castle. (Candlelight Ecstasy Ser.: No. 23). (Orig.). pap. 2.25 o.p. (ISBN 0-440-17441-4). Dell.

Right of the Accused to Defence in the U. S. S. R. Y. Stetsovky. 284p. 1982. 6.95 o.p. (ISBN 0-8285-2420-3, Pub. by Progress Pubs U. S. S. R.). Imported Pubns.

Right of the People to Be Secure: An Examination of the Fourth Amendment. rev. 2nd. ed. Charles E. Moylan, Jr. 304p. 1979. 9.50 o.p. (ISBN 0-318-15273-8). Natl Coll DA.

Right on Cue, Andy Capp. Reginald Smythe. (Andy Capp Ser.). (Illus.). 128p. 1979. pap. 1.25 o.s.i. (ISBN 0-449-13589-6, GM). Fawcett.

Right on Time Andy Capp. Reginald Smythe. (Andy Capp Ser.). (Illus.). 1978. pap. 1.25 o.s.i. (ISBN 0-449-14076-8, GM). Fawcett.

Right Path: Abd al Husyan Sharaf al-Din al Musawi. Tr. by Muhammad A. Khan. 515p. 1987. pap. 16.95 o.p. (ISBN 0-7103-0271-1, A0770, Pub. by Routledge UK). Routledge Chapman & Hall.

Right Picture. Ken Heyman & John Durniak. LC 86-3422. (Illus.). 160p. 1986. 27.50 o.p. (ISBN 0-8174-5725-9, Amphoto); pap. 16.95 o.p. (ISBN 0-8174-5726-7). Watson-Guptill.

Right Reason. William F. Buckley, Jr. LC 85-4475. 480p. 1985. 19.95 o.s.i. (ISBN 0-385-15235-3). Doubleday.

Right Stuff. Tom Wolfe. LC 73-85731. 436p. 1979. 15.95 o.p. (ISBN 0-374-25032-4). FS&G.

Right Thinking: Insights for Spiritual Growth. Bill Hull. LC 84-63115. 144p. 1985. pap. 4.95 o.p. (ISBN 0-89109-531-4). NavPress.

Right Time, the Right Place. Joseph S. Salzburg. 1978. 7.00 o.p. (ISBN 0-682-49039-3). Exposition-Phoenix.

Right Time to Love. Ann Ashton. LC 85-27480. (Starlight Romance Ser.). 192p. 1986. 12.95 o.p. (ISBN 0-385-19901-5). Doubleday.

Right Time to Love. Ann Ashton. LC 86-31905. (Starlight Romance Ser.). 336p. 1987. 16.95 o.s.i. (ISBN 0-385-23985-8, GC Large Print). Doubleday.

Right-to-Education Child: A Curriculum for the Severely & Profoundly Mentally Retarded. Donald G. Myers et al. (Illus.). 248p. 1978. 30.00 o.p. (ISBN 0-398-02923-7). C C Thomas.

Right to Fly. I. Egorov. 240p. 1983. pap. 3.95 o.p. (ISBN 0-8285-2469-6, Pub. by Progress Pubs USSR). Imported Pubns.

Right to Innocence: Healing the Trauma of Child Sexual Abuse. Beverly Engel. o.p. J P Tarcher.

Right to Kill. Scott Jansen. 192p. (Orig.). pap. (ISBN 0-505-51711-6, Pub. by Tower Bks). Dorchester Pub Co.

Right to Know: A Review of Advice Services in Rural Areas. National Council of Social Service. 71p. 1978. pap. text ed. 1.90x o.p. (ISBN 0-7199-0954-6, Pub. by Bedford England). Gower Pub Co.

Right to Lifers: Who They Are, How They Operate, Where They Get Their Money. Connie Paige. LC 83-4795. 1983. 14.50 o.s.i. (ISBN 0-671-43180-3). Summit Bks.

Right to Love. Jennifer A. Lawson. 64p. 1980. 5.00 o.p. (ISBN 0-682-49651-0). Exposition-Phoenix.

Right to Meet & Confer: Legislative Enactments see Issues in the Public Employee Relations Library: Series 1.

Right to Remain Silent. Milton Meltzer. LC 72-76366. (Illus.). 128p. (gr. 7 up). 1972. 5.95 o.p. (ISBN 0-15-266990-6, HJ). HarBraceJ.

Right to Song: The Life of John Clare. Edward Storey. (Illus.). 330p. 1982. 38.00 o.p. (ISBN 0-413-39940-0, NO. 3825). Heinemann Ed.

Right to Work. Nels Anderson. LC 70-136835. (Illus.). 152p. 1973. Repr. of 1938 ed. lib. bdg. 22.50x o.p. (ISBN 0-8371-5264-X, ANRW). Greenwood.

Right Way to Play Chess. D. Brine Pritchard. (Illus.). 1977. 11.95 o.p. (ISBN 0-87523-087-3). Emerson.

Right Word: A Concise Thesauras. LC 78-3461. (gr. 9 up). 1978. 3.95 o.p. (ISBN 0-395-26672-6). HM.

Right You Are, Mr. Moto. John P. Marquand. 1986. pap. 4.95 o.p. (ISBN 0-316-54706-9). Little.

Righteous Remnant: The House of David. Robert S. Fogarty. LC 80-84666. (Illus.). 208p. 1981. 17.50 o.p. (ISBN 0-87338-251-X). Kent St U Pr.

Righteousness in the New Testament: Justification in Lutheran-Catholic Dialogue. John Reumann. LC 81-43086. 320p. 1982. pap. 13.95 o.p. (ISBN 0-8006-1616-2, 1-1616, Fortress). Augsburg Fortress.

Righteousness Inside Out: The Heart of the Problem & the Problem of the Heart. Mike Cope. 180p. text ed. o.s.i. (ISBN 0-89225-339-8). Gospel Advocate.

Rights & Duties of Citizens: Practice Materials for Foundations of Citizenship. Eileen L. Corcoran. Bk. 1 1964. pap. 2.75x o.p. (ISBN 0-88323-061-5, 159); Bk. 2 1965. pap. 2.75x o.p. (ISBN 0-88323-062-3, 160); Bk. 3 1970. pap. 2.75x o.p. (ISBN 0-88323-063-1, 161). Pendergrass Pub.

Rights Contracts in the Communictions Media. Richard Wincor. 233p. 1979. 30.00 o.p. (ISBN 0-15-100049-2, H39743). HarBraceJ.

Rights of Aliens. David Carliner. 1977. pap. 1.50 o.p. (ISBN 0-380-00885-8, 44925-0, Discus). Avon.

Rights of Gun Owners. Alan Gottlieb. 216p. (Orig.). 1981. pap. 6.95 o.p. (ISBN 0-89803-056-0). Green Hill.

Rights of Mental Patients. Bruce J. Ennis & Richard D. Emery. 1978. pap. 1.75 o.p. (ISBN 0-380-01859-4, 77024, Discus). Avon.

Rights of Mentally Retarded Persons. Paul Friedman. 1976. pap. 1.50 o.p. (ISBN 0-380-00868-8, 54064-9, Discus). Avon.

Rights of Police Officers. Gilda Brancato & Elliot E. Polebaum. 192p. (Orig.). 1981. pap. 2.95 o.p. (ISBN 0-380-78352-5, 78352-5, Discus). Avon.

Rights of Prisoners. David Rudovsky et al. 1977. pap. 1.50 o.p. (ISBN 0-380-01387-8, 77016, Discus). Avon.

Rights of Reporters. Joel M. Gora. 1981. pap. 1.25 o.p. (ISBN 0-380-00188-8, 38836-7, Discus). Avon.

Rights of Servicemen. Robert S. Rivkin. (ACLU Handbook Ser). (Orig.). 1981. pap. 1.25 o.p. (ISBN 0-380-01526-9, 33365, Discus). Avon.

Rights of Students. Alan H. Levine. 1977. pap. 1.75 o.p. (ISBN 0-380-00945-5, 53702, Discus). Avon.

Rights of Suspects. Oliver Rosengart & Gail Weinheimer. 1981. pap. 0.95 o.p. (ISBN 0-380-01529-3, 28043, Discus). Avon.

Rights of the Poor. Sylvia Law. 1981. pap. 0.95 o.p. (ISBN 0-380-01527-7, 28001-9, Discus). Avon.

Rights of the Victim. Margaret O. Hyde. (Single Title Ser.). 128p. (gr. 7 up). 1983. PLB 11.90 o.p. (ISBN 0-531-04596-X). Watts.

Rights of Veterans. David F. Addlestone et al. 1978. pap. 1.75 o.p. (ISBN 0-380-01838-1, 77008, Discus). Avon.

Rights of Women. Susan D. Ross. 1981. pap. 1.25 o.p. (ISBN 0-380-01528-5, 27953, Discus). Avon.

Rights of Young People. Alan Sussman. 1977. pap. 1.75 o.p. (ISBN 0-380-00935-8, 77032, Discus). Avon.

Rights, Wrongs, & In-Betweens: Guiding Our Children to Christian Maturity. Jim Larson. LC 83-72121. 144p. (Orig.). 1984. pap. 6.95 o.p. (ISBN 0-8066-2065-X, 10-5518, Augsburg). Augsburg Fortress.

Rigid Rods & the Characterization of Polyisozyanides see Polymerization Reactions.

Rigidity of Behavior: A Variational Approach to the Effect of Einstellung. Abraham S. Luchins & Edith Hirsch. LC 59-16826. 1959. 10.00 o.p. (ISBN 0-87114-007-1). U of Oreg Bks.

Rigorous Atomic & Molecular Physics. Ed. by G. Velo & A. S. Wightman. LC 81-12059. (NATO ASI Series B, Physics: Vol. 74). 504p. 1981. 85.00x o.p. (ISBN 0-306-40829-5, Plenum Pr). Plenum Pub.

Rigs of the Nine Principal Types of American Sailing Vessels. Charles G. Davis. (Illus.). pap. 0.95 o.s.i. (ISBN 0-87577-028-2). Peabody Mus Salem.

Rikki-Tikki-Tavi. Chuck Jones. (Good Friends Ser.). (Illus.). 48p. (gr. k-6). 1982. 4.95 o.p. (ISBN 0-8249-8041-7). Ideals.

Rikki-Tikki-Tavi. Rudyard Kipling. LC 85-32568. (Creative's Classic Short Stories Ser.). 48p. (gr. 4 up). 1986. PLB 8.95 o.p. (ISBN 0-88682-002-2). Creative Ed.

Riley's Last Hunt. Frank Calkins. LC 85-25212. (Doubled D Western Ser.). 192p. 1986. 12.95 o.p. (ISBN 0-385-23468-6). Doubleday.

Rilke: Man & Poet. Nora Purtscher. LC 71-169852. (Illus.). 373p. 1972. Repr. of 1950 ed. lib. bdg. 22.50x o.p. (ISBN 0-8371-6247-5, PURI). Greenwood.

Rim of the Unknown. Frank B. Long. 1972. 8.95 o.p. (ISBN 0-87054-060-2). Arkham.

Rime of the Ancient Mariner. Samuel Taylor Coleridge. Ed. by Walter Hallenborg. 1976. pap. 1.75 o.p. (ISBN 0-380-00999-4, 56309, Bard). Avon.

Rimskie Elegii. Joseph Brodsky. LC 82-60519. 20p. (Rus.). 1982. pap. 5.00 o.p. (ISBN 0-89830-062-2). Russica Pubs.

Ring & Categories of Modules. W. Anderson & K. R. Fuller. LC 73-80045. (Graduate Texts in Mathematics Ser.: Vol. 13). 368p. 1974. 28.00 o.p. (ISBN 0-387-90069-1); pap. 24.00 o.p. (ISBN 0-387-90070-5). Springer-Verlag.

Ring: Four Plays for Children. Adapted by Philip Caggiano. 96p. 1982. pap. 2.50 o.p. (ISBN 0-380-79434-9, 79434-9, Bard). Avon.

Ring Lardner's "You Know Me Al" The Comic Strip Adventures of Jack Keefe. Ring Lardner. LC 78-20641. 160p. (Orig.). 1979. pap. 6.95 o.p. (ISBN 0-15-676696-5, Harv). HarBraceJ.

Ring Master. David Gurr. LC 87-10860. 752p. 1987. 25.00 o.p. (ISBN 0-689-11935-6, Atheneum). Macmillan.

Ring of Dancers: Images of Faroese Culture. Jonathan Wylie & David Margolin. (Symbol & Culture Ser.). 1981. text ed. 29.95x o.p. (ISBN 0-8122-7783-X). U of Pa Pr.

Ring of Fire. Shirley R. Murphy. LC 77-1576. (gr. 5-9). 1977. 7.95 o.p. (ISBN 0-689-30594-X, Atheneum). Macmillan.

Ring of Fire. Shirley R. Murphy. 226p. 1979. pap. 1.75 o.p. (ISBN 0-380-47191-4, 47191-4, Flare). Avon.

Ring of Fire. David Ritchie. LC 80-69391. (Illus.). 296p. 1981. 14.95 o.p. (ISBN 0-689-11150-9, Atheneum). Macmillan.

Ring of Jingles. Mitchell B. Carroll. (Illus.). 64p. 1979. 4.00 o.p. (ISBN 0-682-49282-5). Exposition-Phoenix.

Ring of the Nibelung. Ul De Rico. (Illus.). 204p. 1980. 15.00 o.p. (ISBN 0-500-23324-1). Thames Hudson.

Ring of Truth. Vernon Scannell. LC 85-16734. 342p. 1985. 16.95 o.p. (ISBN 0-88186-350-5). Parkwest Pubns.

Ring of Zoraya. Harriet Graham. LC 81-8082. 192p. (gr. k-1). 1982. PLB 9.95 o.p. (ISBN 0-689-30880-9, Atheneum). Macmillan.

Ring Out! A Book of Bells. Jane H. Yolen. LC 74-4043. 128p. (gr. 4-7). 1979. 6.95 o.p. (ISBN 0-395-28886-X, Clarion). HM.

Ring Record Book & Boxing Encyclopedia. Ed. by Bert Sugar. LC 81-66027. 1981. 20.00 o.p. (ISBN 0-689-11190-8, Atheneum). Macmillan.

Ring Transformation of Heterocycles, 2 vols. H. C. Van Der Plas. 1973. Vol. 1. 79.50 o.p.; Vol. 2. 101.50 o.p. (ISBN 0-12-711702-4). Acad Pr.

Ringers in the Tower. Harold Bloom. LC 73-149595. xii, 352p. 1973. pap. text ed. 3.45x o.s.i. (ISBN 0-226-06049-7, P536, Phoen). U of Chicago Pr.

Ringolevio. Emmett Grogan. 1973. pap. 1.50 o.p. (ISBN 0-380-01530-7, 14449). Avon.

Rings & Modules of Quotients. B. Stenstroem. (Lecture Notes in Mathematics: Vol. 237). 136p. 1972. pap. 9.00 o.p. (ISBN 0-387-05690-4). Springer-Verlag.

Rings of Grass. Nancy Hedberg. (Living Bks.). 240p. 1985. pap. 3.50 o.p. (ISBN 0-8423-5605-3). Tyndale.

Rings of Stone: The Prehistoric Stone Circles of Britain & Ireland. Aubrey Burl. LC 79-17741. (Illus.). 280p. 1980. 19.95 o.p. (ISBN 0-89919-000-6). Ticknor & Fields.

Rings, Swings & Climbing Things: Enhancing Your Child's Development with Easy-to-Make Play Equipment. 1985. 10.95 o.p. (ISBN 0-8092-5264-3). Contemp Bks.

Rio Alive. 4th ed. Arnold Greenberg & Harriet Greenberg. (Alive Travel Ser.). (Illus.). 1980. pap. 4.95 o.p. (ISBN 0-935572-00-7). Alive Pubns.

Rio Alive. 5th ed. Arnold Greenberg & Harriet Greenberg. (Alive Travel Ser.). 300p. 1987. pap. 9.95 o.p. (ISBN 0-935572-12-0). Alive Pubns.

Rio Alive. rev. ed. Harriet Greenberg & Arnold Greenberg. 1977. pap. 2.95 o.p. (ISBN 0-686-23067-1). Alive Pubns.

Rio Grande--Ruler of the Rockies. R. C. Farewell & Bill Bradley. (Illus.). 176p. 1987. 34.95 o.p. (ISBN 0-87046-080-3). Interurban.

Rio Grande Glory Days. Gilbert Lathrop. LC 76-45760. (Illus.). 356p. 1976. 16.95 o.p. (ISBN 0-87095-056-8). Gldn West Bks.

Riots, U. S. A. rev. ed. Willard A. Heaps. LC 69-13444. (gr. 6 up). 1979. 6.95 o.s.i. (ISBN 0-395-28907-6, Clarion). HM.

Rip Ford's Texas. John S. Ford. 1963. pap. write for info. o.p. (ISBN 0-292-73354-2). U of Tex Pr.

Rip-Roaring Races & Rallies. Elwood D. Baumann. (Illus.). 128p. (gr. 7 up). 1981. lib. bdg. 8.90 o.p. (ISBN 0-531-04344-4). Watts.

Rip Van Winkle. Sanford Friedman. LC 80-66016. 1980. 12.95 o.p. (ISBN 0-689-11099-5, Atheneum). Macmillan.

Ripening Seed. Colette. Tr. by Roger Senhouse. LC 73-178784. 152p. 1973. Repr. lib. bdg. 24.75x o.p. (ISBN 0-8371-6292-0, CORS). Greenwood.

Rire. Henri Bergson. pap. 8.95 o.p. (ISBN 0-685-37211-1). French & Eur.

Risa. Henri Bergson. pap. 8.95 o.p. (ISBN 0-685-11531-3). French & Eur.

Rise & Decline of Western Liberalism. Anthony Arblaster. 450p. 1984. 45.00x o.p. (ISBN 0-85520-765-5). Basil Blackwell.

Rise & Fall. Milovan Djilas. Tr. by John Loud. LC 84-12972. 352p. 1985. 24.95 o.p. (ISBN 0-15-177572-9). HarBraceJ.

Rise & Fall of American Humor. Jesse Bier. xii, 544p. 1980. Repr. of 1968 ed. lib. bdg. 40.00x o.p. (ISBN 0-374-90632-7, Octagon). Hippocrene Bks.

Rise & Fall of Lin Piao. Jaap Van Ginneken. 1977. pap. 2.50 o.p. (ISBN 0-380-00988-9, 32656, Discus). Avon.

Rise & Fall of Project Camelot: Studies in the Relationship Between Social Science & Practical Politics. rev. ed. Ed. by Irving L. Horowitz. 1974. pap. 7.95x o.p. (ISBN 0-262-58029-2). MIT Pr.

Rise & Fall of Superwoman. Carole Sheron. LC 79-26704. (Orion Ser.). 96p. 1980. pap. 3.95 o.p. (ISBN 0-8127-1270-6). Review & Herald.

Rise & Fall of the CIA: From Wild Bill Donovan to William Casey. John Ranelagh. 1986. 22.45 o.p. (ISBN 0-671-44318-6). S&S.

Rise & Fall of the German Air Force 1933-1945. Intro. by H. A. Probert. 448p. 1987. 29.95 o.p. (ISBN 0-85368-560-6, Pub. by Arms & Armour). Sterling.

Rise & Fall of the Jewish Gangster in America. Albert Fried. LC 79-22568. (Illus.). 352p. 1980. 14.95 o.s.i. (ISBN 0-03-021371-1). H Holt & Co.

Rise & Fall of the Seas: The Story of the Tides. Ruth Brindze. LC 64-11491. (Illus.). (gr. 7 up). 1964. 5.95 o.p. (ISBN 0-15-267380-6, HJ). HarBraceJ.

Rise & Fall of the Third Reich: A History of Nazi Germany. William L. Shirer. (gr. 9 up). 1960. 29.45 o.s.i. (ISBN 0-671-62420-2). S&S.

Rise & Progress of the People Called Quakers. William Penn. 1977. pap. 2.95 o.s.i. (ISBN 0-913408-32-8). Friends United.

Rise of Anthropology in India: A Social Science Orientation, 2 vols. L. P. Vidyarthi. Incl. Vol. I. The Tribal Dimensions; Vol. II. The Rural Urban & Other Dimensions. 1979. Set. 45.00x o.p. (ISBN 0-391-01086-7). Humanities.

Rise of British Colonialism in Southern Nigeria, 1700-1900: A Study of the Bights of Benin and Bonny. Kalu E. Ume. 304p. 1980. 12.50 o.p. (ISBN 0-682-49533-6, University). Exposition-Phoenix.

Rise of Christian Europe. Hugh Trevor-Roper. (History of European Civilization Library). 1966. pap. text ed. 8.95 o.p. (ISBN 0-15-577125-6, HC). HarBraceJ.

Rise of Communist China. Schools Council History 13-16 Project Staff. (Modern World Problems Ser.). (Illus.). 1979. lib. bdg. 12.95 o.p. (ISBN 0-912616-70-9); pap. text ed. 6.95 o.p. (ISBN 0-912616-69-5). Greenhaven.

Rise of English Opera. Eric W. White. 1951. (ISBN 0-8022-1857-1). Philos Lib.

Rise of Guardian Democracy: The Supreme Court's Role in Voting Rights Disputes, 1845-1969. Ward E. Elliott. LC 73-90611. (Political Studies). 368p. 1974. text ed. 27.00x o.p. (ISBN 0-674-77156-7). Harvard U Pr.

Rise of Methodism: A Source Book. Richard M. Cameron. 1954. (ISBN 0-8022-0209-8). Philos Lib.

Rise of Music in the Ancient World. Curt Sachs. (Illus.). 1943. 15.95x o.p. (ISBN 0-393-09718-8, NortonC). Norton.

Rise of Rawlins Lowndes, 1721-1800. Carl J. Vipperman. LC 78-17353. (Tricentennial Studies: No. 12). xiv, 276p. 1978. lib. bdg. 21.95x o.p. (ISBN 0-87249-259-1). U of SC Pr.

Rise of Statistical Thinking, 1820-1900. Theodore Porter. LC 85-43306. 350p. 1986. text ed. 42.50x o.p. (ISBN 0-691-08416-5). Princeton U Pr.

Rise of the Accounting Profession, 2 vols. John L. Carey. 1969. Set. 36.50 o.p. (ISBN 0-685-05617-1). Am Inst CPA.

Rise of the American Chemistry Profession, 1850-1900. Edward H. Beardsley. LC 64-65130. (University of Florida Social Sciences Monographs: No. 23). 1964. pap. 3.50 o.p. (ISBN 0-8130-0014-9). U Presses Fla.

Rise of the Evolution Fraud. Malcolm Bowden. 1982. pap. 8.95 o.p. (ISBN 0-89051-085-7). Master Bks.

Rise of the Feudal Monarchies. Sidney Painter. LC 82-2936. (Development of Western Civilization Ser.). xii, 147p. 1982. Repr. of 1951 ed. lib. bdg. 35.00x o.p. (ISBN 0-313-23560-0, PARF). Greenwood.

Rise of the French Communist Party. Edward Mortimer. 431p. 1984. 65.00 o.p. (ISBN 0-571-09754-5). Faber & Faber.

Rise of the Habsburg Empire: 1526-1815. Victor S. Mamatey. LC 77-15525. (Berkshire Studies). 192p. 1978. pap. text ed. 6.50 o.p. (ISBN 0-88275-639-7). Krieger.

Rise of the New Physics: Its Mathematical & Physical Theories, 2 vols. A. D'Abro. Orig. Title: Decline of Mechanism. 14.50 ea o.p. (ISBN 0-8446-0569-7); Set. 29.00 o.p. Peter Smith.

Rise of the Western Philosophy: The Pre-Socratics. Oscar Olshansky. 1977. 6.00 o.p. (ISBN 0-682-48915-8, University). Exposition-Phoenix.

Rise of Words & Their Meanings. Samuel Reiss. (ISBN 0-8022-1325-1). Philos Lib.

Rise of World Lutheranism: An American Perspective. E. Clifford Nelson. LC 80-2376. 1982. 24.95 o.p. (ISBN 0-8006-0661-2, Fortress). Augsburg Fortress.

Rishis in Indian Art & Literature. C. Sivaramamurti. (Illus.). 258p. 1981. text ed. 55.00 o.p. (ISBN 0-391-02654-2). Humanities.

Rising Damp. Barbara Corcoran. LC 79-22675. (gr. 5-9). 1980. 7.95 o.p. (ISBN 0-689-30736-5, Atheneum). Macmillan.

Rising Generation. LC 87-70805. 1987. pap. 5.95 o.p. (ISBN 0-87579-088-7). Deseret Bk.

Rising Glory of America, 1760-1820. Ed. by Gordon S. Wood. LC 75-151798. (American Culture Ser). (Illus.). 1971. 8.95 o.p. (ISBN 0-8076-0611-1); pap. 4.95 o.p. (ISBN 0-8076-0610-3). Braziller.

Titles

Titles

Rising Moon: Political Change in Sarawak. Michael B. Leigh. LC 72-76423. (Illus.). 304p. 1974. 25.00x o.p. (ISBN 0-424-06580-0, Pub. by Sydney U Pr); pap. 22.00x o.p. (ISBN 0-424-06590-8, Pub by Sydney U Pr). Intl Spec Bk.
Rising of al-Husayn: Its Impact on the Consciousness of Muslim Society. Shaykh M. Al-Din. Tr. by I. K. Howard. 1987. pap. 15.95 o.p. (ISBN 0-7103-0191-X, Kegan Paul). Routledge Chapman & Hall.
Rising Thunder. Carolyn A. Wharton. 224p. 1986. pap. 5.95 o.p. (ISBN 0-310-47701-8, 15623P). Zondervan.
Rising Yen. Richard S. Thorn. 121p. 1987. text ed. 18.00 o.p. (ISBN 9971-988-74-7, Pub. by Inst Southeast Asian Stud). Gower Pub Co.
Risk Analysis Guide to Insurance & Employee Benefits. A. E. Pfaffle & Sal Nicosia. (AMA Management Briefings). 108p. 1986. 10.00 o.p. (ISBN 0-8144-2323-X). AMACOM.
Risk & Aging. Paul C. Brearley & M. R. P. Hall. (Hazards & Helping). 250p. (Orig.). 1982. pap. 9.95x o.p. (ISBN 0-7100-9080-3). Routledge Chapman & Hall.
Risk & Capital Adequacy in Commercial Banks. Ed. by Sherman J. Maisel. LC 81-3324. (Nat'l Bureau of Economic Research Monograph). x, 436p. 1981. lib. bdg. 55.00x o.s.i. (ISBN 0-226-50281-3). U of Chicago Pr.
Risk & Gambling. Cohen & Hansel. 1956. (ISBN 0-8022-0277-2). Philos Lib.
Risk & Its Treatment: Changing Societal Consequences. Ed. by George E. Rejda & Ralph B. Ginsberg. LC 78-72994. (Annals: No. 443). 1979. 15.00 o.p. (ISBN 0-87761-238-2); pap. 7.95 o.p. (ISBN 0-87761-239-0). Am Acad Pol Soc Sci.
Risk & Technology Choice in Developing Countries: The Case of Philippine Sugar Factories. Fred S. Avestruz. (Illus.). 192p. (Orig.). 1985. lib. bdg. 23.25 o.p. (ISBN 0-8191-4774-5); pap. text ed. 11.50 o.p. (ISBN 0-8191-4775-3). U Pr of Amer.
Risk & Uncertainty: Non-Deterministic Decision Making in Engineering Economy. Ed. by G. A. Fleischer. 1985. pap. 19.00 o.p. (ISBN 0-89806-018-4, NO. 105). Inst Indus Eng.
Risk Assessment: A Study Group Report. Royal Society of London Staff. 198p. (Orig.). 1983. pap. text ed. 16.00x o.p. (ISBN 0-85403-208-8, Pub. by Royal Soc London). Scholium Intl.
Risk-Benefit Assessments & Societal Cost of Nuclear & Other Energy Sources. Ed. by R. A. Karam & L. E. Weaver. 120p. 1983. pap. 48.00 o.p. (ISBN 0-08-030543-1). Pergamon.
Risk Control for Churches. M. Douglas Clark. LC 81-86316. (Illus.). 1981. 3-ring binder 39.50 o.s.i. (ISBN 0-88061-007-7). Inst Pub ILCI.
Risk Factors & Multiple Cancers. Ed. by Basil A. Stoll. (New Horizons in Oncology Ser.). 850p. 1984. text ed. 79.95 o.p. (ISBN 0-471-10513-9, Dist. by A R Liss). Wiley.
Risk Management: College Edition. Matthew Lenz. Ed. by Merritt Company Staff. 321p. 1981. 31.25 o.p. (ISBN 0-930868-42-0). Merritt Co.
Risk Management: Concepts & Applications. Robert I. Mehr & Bob A. Hedges. 1974. 34.95x o.p. (ISBN 0-256-01614-3). Irwin.
Risk Management for Librarians: A Bibliographical List. Lorna Peterson. (Public Administration Ser.: P 1706). 8p. 1985. 2.00 o.p. (ISBN 0-89028-456-3). Vance Biblios.
Risk Management in the Public Sector: Recent Writings. Jacqueline Mundell. (Public Administration Ser.: P 1685). 14p. 1985. 2.25 o.p. (ISBN 0-89028-415-6). Vance Biblios.
Risk Theory: The Stochastic Basis of Insurance. 2nd ed. E. Beard et al. (Monographs on Applied Probability & Statistics). 1977. 17.50x o.p. (ISBN 0-412-15100-6, NO.6031, Pub. by Chapman & Hall). Routledge Chapman & Hall.
Risk: Uncertainty & Decision Making in Property Management. P. Bryne & B. D. Cadman. 130p. 1984. 33.00 o.p. (ISBN 0-419-11950-7, 6673, Pub. by E & FN Spon England). Routledge Chapman & Hall.
Risks of Unintentional Nuclear War. Daniel Frei. 255p. 1982. 19.00x o.p. (ISBN 0-8002-3317-4). Intl Pubns Serv.
Risque Technologique Majeur. P. Lagadec. (Fr.). 1982. 160.00 o.p. (ISBN 0-08-027058-1). Pergamon.
Rita Hayworth: The Time, the Place, the Woman. John Kobal. (Illus.). 1978. 12.95 o.p. (ISBN 0-393-07526-5). Norton.
Rita Myers: Rift-Rise, Video Installation. Alternative Museum Staff. LC 87-72178. (Orig.). 1987. pap. 6.00 o.p. (ISBN 0-932075-16-9). Alternative Mus.
Rite of Passage. Gunnard Landers. LC 79-56014. 1980. 10.95 o.p. (ISBN 0-87795-248-5, Arbor Hse). Morrow.
Rite of the Dragon. Janet Gluckman. 352p. 1982. pap. 3.50 o.p. (ISBN 0-8439-1098-4, Pub. by Leisure Bks CT). Dorchester Pub Co.
Rite Thing. Eugene Brand. LC 74-101106. 1970. pap. 3.50 o.p. (ISBN 0-8066-9360-6, 10-5520). Augsburg Fortress.
Rites of Autumn. Cliff Schimmels. 180p. 1985. pap. 4.95 o.p. (ISBN 0-89693-334-2). Victor Bks.
Rites of Passage. Ed. by Garrett Solyom & Bronwen Solyom. LC 79-84170. (Illus.). 48p. 1979. 6.00 o.s.i. (ISBN 0-317-68013-7). Mingei Intl Mus.
Rites of Passage in a Student Culture. Thomas A. Leemon. LC 72-81190. 1972. pap. text ed. 9.95x o.p. (ISBN 0-8077-1673-1). Tchrs Coll.
Rites of Spring: A Student's Guide to Spring Break in Florida. Rollin Riggs. LC 82-72064. (Illus.). 1982. pap. 5.95 o.p. (ISBN 0-87795-426-7, Arbor Hse). Morrow.
Rites of Winter: A Skier's Budget Guide to Making It on the Slopes. Bruce Jacobsen & Rollin Riggs. (Illus.). 224p. (Orig.). 1984. pap. 7.95 o.p. (ISBN 0-87795-640-5, Arbor Hse). Morrow.
Ritsos in Parentheses. Yannis Ritsos. Tr. by Edmund Keeley from Gr. LC 78-70317. (Lockert Library of Poetry in Translation). 1979. 28.50x o.p. (ISBN 0-691-06397-4); pap. 9.50 o.p. (ISBN 0-691-01358-6). Princeton U Pr.
Ritter Von Schulthess-Rechberg'sche Munz-U. Medaillen Sammlung. Julius Erbstein & Albert Erbstein. LC 73-92777. 1120p. 1974. Repr. 50.00x o.p. (ISBN 0-88000-029-5). Quarterman.
Ritual. J. N. Williamson. 320p. 1982. pap. 3.25 o.p. (ISBN 0-8439-1168-9, Pub. by Leisure Bks CT). Dorchester Pub Co.
Ritual & Drama: The Mediaeval Theater. Francis Edwards. (Illus.). 1976. pap. text ed. 11.00x o.p. Coronet Bks.
Ritual Cosmos: The Sanctification of Life in African Religions. Evan M. Zuesse. LC 79-13454. x, 256p. 1980. 21.95x o.p. (ISBN 0-8214-0398-2). Ohio U Pr.
Ritual in the Dark. Colin Wilson. 416p. 1982. pap. 5.95 o.p. (ISBN 0-586-04391-8). Academy Chi Pubs.
Ritual of the Wind: North American Indian Ceremonies, Music & Dance. rev. ed. Jamake Highwater. 1984. pap. 14.95 o.p. (ISBN 0-912383-02-X). HarpR.
Ritual of Wind: North American Indian Ceremonies, Music, & Dance. rev. ed. Jamake Highwater. LC 83-80563. (Illus.). 196p. 1983. pap. 14.95 o.p. (ISBN 0-912383-02-X). Van der Marck.
Rituals of Surgery. Richard Selzer. 1980. pap. 3.95 o.p. (ISBN 0-671-25340-9, Touchstone Bks). S&S.
Rivals: America & Russia Since World War II. Adam B. Ulam. 1987. 14.25 o.p. (ISBN 0-8446-6177-5). Peter Smith.
Rivals of Spring. Cliff Schimmels. 180p. 1986. pap. 4.95 o.p. (ISBN 0-89693-335-0). Victor Bks.
River & Desert: A Bilingual Anthology of Mexican Literature, (Poetry) Tr. by Harry Polkinghorn. 1987. Lat Am Lit Rev Pr.
River & I: A Voyage Down the Missouri River in 1908. John G. Neihardt. (Illus.). 7.75 o.p. (ISBN 0-8446-2641-4). Peter Smith.
River at Green Knowe. Lucy M. Boston. LC 57-8950. (Illus.). (gr. 4-7). 1959. 5.95 o.p. (ISBN 0-15-267446-2, HJ). HarBraceJ.
River at Green Knowe. Lucy M. Boston. LC 59-8950. (Illus.). 153p. (gr. 4-6). 1966. pap. 2.95 o.p. (ISBN 0-15-677701-0, VoyB). HarBraceJ.
River at Green Knowe see Adventures at Green Knowe.
River Basin Planning: Theory & Practice. Suranjit K. Saha & Christopher J. Barrow. 380p. 1981. 76.95 o.p. (ISBN 0-471-09977-5, Pub. by Wiley-Interscience). Wiley.
River Between. Lawrence C. Powell. LC 79-15594. 112p. 1979. 10.00 o.p. (ISBN 0-88496-141-9). Capra Pr.
River Guide One: Maine. (Illus.). 234p. 1980. pap. 7.95 o.p. (ISBN 0-317-33380-1) (ISBN 0-317-33381-X). AMC Books.
River Guide Two: Central & Southern New England. The Appalachian Mountain Club. (Illus.). 362p. 1978. pap. 9.95 o.p. (ISBN 0-317-33382-8). AMC Books.
River in Winter & Other Poems. Esther E. Wick. 1978. 4.00 o.p. (ISBN 0-682-49179-9). Exposition-Phoenix.
River Journeys. Russel Bradon et al. (Illus.). 208p. 1985. 19.95 o.p. (ISBN 0-87052-140-3). Hippocrene Bks.
River Lady. Jude Deveraux. (Large Print Bks (General Ser.)). 431p. 1986. lib. bdg. 17.95 o.p. (ISBN 0-8161-4138-X). G K Hall.
River Management. P. C. Isaac. (Illus.). 258p. 1967. 47.00 o.p. (ISBN 0-85334-460-4, Pub. by Elsevier Applied Sci England). Elsevier.
River Mist & Other Stories. Kunikida Doppo. Tr. by David G. Chibbett from Japanese. LC 82-84515. 182p. 1983. 14.95 o.s.i. (ISBN 0-87011-591-X). Kodansha.
River Morphology. Ed. by Stanley A. Schumm. (Benchmark Papers in Geology Ser.: Vol. 2). 1982. pap. 48.95 o.p. (ISBN 0-87933-139-9). Van Nos Reinhold.
River of Dreams. Gay Courter. (General Ser.). 1984. lib. bdg. 18.95 o.p. (ISBN 0-8161-3768-4, Large Print Bks). G K Hall.
River of Light: Spirituality, Judaism, & the Evolution of Consciousness. Lawrence Kushner. LC 80-7738. 192p. 1981. 12.95 o.p. (ISBN 0-940646-00-5). Rossel Bks.
River of Swans. Don Coldsmith. LC 86-4457. (Spanish Bit Saga Ser.: Bk. 10). 192p. 1986. 12.95 o.s.i. (ISBN 0-385-23228-4). Doubleday.
River of Tears. Charles W. Clark. 64p. 1986. 6.95 o.p. (ISBN 0-8062-2964-0). Carlton.
River People: Adventuring with Otters. Philip Wayre. LC 75-33551. (Illus.). 215p. 1976. 9.95 o.s.i. (ISBN 0-8008-6797-1). Taplinger.
River Piking. John Sidley. 1987. 24.00 o.p. (ISBN 0-85115-466-2, Pub. by Boydell & Brewer). Longwood Pub Group.
River Rat. Hollis C. Powell. 224p. 1982. 10.50 o.p. (ISBN 0-682-49891-2, Banner). Exposition-Phoenix.
River Road to China: The Mekong River Expedition, 1866-73. Milton Osborne. (Illus.). 249p. (Orig.). 1975. 8.95 o.p. (ISBN 0-87140-578-4). Liveright.
River Runaways. David Roth. (gr. 5-9). 1981. 7.95 o.p. (ISBN 0-395-31678-2). HM.
River Runner's Recipes. Patricia Chambers. LC 83-19644. (Illus.). 132p. 1984. pap. 6.95 o.p. (ISBN 0-914718-85-1). Pacific Search.
River Runs Through It. Norman Maclean. LC 82-23759. (Illus.). 128p. 1983. gift ed. 25.00 o.s.i. (ISBN 0-226-50058-6); 50.00 o.s.i. (ISBN 0-226-50059-4). U of Chicago Pr.
River Within: The Search for God in Depth. Christopher Bryant. 160p. 1983. pap. 5.50 o.p. (ISBN 0-8358-0468-2). Upper Room.
Riverine Maya: The Torquegua & Other Chols of the Lower Motagua Valley. Lawrence H. Feldman. LC 75-621315. (Museum Brief: No. 15). (Illus.). 25p. 1975. pap. 1.20x o.p. (ISBN 0-913134-14-7). Mus Anthro Mo.
Rivers. M. Morisawa. 224p. 1985. pap. 29.95 o.p. (ISBN 0-470-20548-2, Co-Pub. with Longman). Wiley.
Rivers. Geoffrey E. Petts. (Sources & Methods in Geography Ser.). (Illus.). 216p. (Orig.). 1983. pap. text ed. 19.95 o.p. (ISBN 0-408-11070-8). Butterworth.
Rivers of Empire: Water, Aridity, & the Growth of the American West. Donald Worster. 1986. 12.95 o.s.i. (ISBN 0-394-51680-X). Pantheon.
Rivers of Living Water. Ruth Paxson. (Moody Classics Ser.). 1984. pap. 3.50 o.p. (ISBN 0-8024-7367-9). Moody.
Rivers of Time. Jean B. Hudson. 1979. pap. 1.95 o.p. (ISBN 0-380-40444-3, 40444). Avon.
River's Way: The Process of Science & the Dreambody. Arnold Mindell. (Illus.). 160p. (Orig.). 1985. pap. 9.95 o.p. (ISBN 0-7102-0631-3). Routledge Chapman & Hall.
Riverside, California. (Panel Advisory Service Report Ser.). 52p. 1983. pap. 10.00 o.p. (ISBN 0-317-06733-8, R-17). Urban Land.
Riverside County Street Atlas 1984. Thomas Brothers Maps. (Illus.). 208p. 1983. pap. 9.50 o.p. (ISBN 0-88130-046-2). Thomas Bros Maps.
Riverside County Street Atlas, 1985. Thomas Bros. Maps. (Illus.). 208p. 1985. pap. 10.50 o.p. (ISBN 0-88130-097-7). Thomas Bros Maps.
Riverside County Street Atlas, 1987. rev. ed. Thomas Bros. Maps Staff. (Illus.). 208p. 1986. pap. 12.95 o.p. (ISBN 0-88130-221-X). Thomas Bros Maps.
Riverside County Thomas Guide, 1988. Thomas Bros. Maps Staff. (Illus.). 218p. 1987. pap. 12.95 o.p. (ISBN 0-88130-251-1). Thomas Bros Maps.
Riversong. Yvonne Kalman. 416p. 1986. pap. 3.95 o.p. (ISBN 0-380-89618-4). Avon.
Riverworld & Other Stories. Philip Jose Farmer. 1981. lib. bdg. 16.95 o.p. (ISBN 0-8398-2618-4, Gregg). G K Hall.
Riza Shah Pahlavi: The Resurrection & Reconstruction of Iran 1878-1944. Donald N. Wilber. LC 74-34518. 1975. 15.00 o.p. (ISBN 0-682-48206-4, University). Exposition-Phoenix.
RLIN II Processing for UC Online Catalog Input: Bibliographic Specifications. Karen Coyle. 1984. 5.00 o.p. (ISBN 0-317-18069-X). UCDLA.
RN Medication Tips. S. White & K. Williamson. 1981. pap. 21.95 o.p. (ISBN 0-87489-251-1). Med Economics.
RN's Sex Q & A: Candid Advice for You & Your Patients. Dorothy DeMoya et al. 1983. pap. 18.95 o.p. (ISBN 0-87489-360-7). Med Economics.
Road & Track Illustrated Auto Dictionary. John Dinkel. (Illus.). 96p. 1981. pap. 3.95 o.p. (ISBN 0-393-00028-1). Norton.
"Road & Track" Illustrated Auto Dictionary. John Dinkel. 1977. 6.95 o.p. (ISBN 0-393-08777-8). Norton.
Road & Track's Used Car Classics. Ed. by Peter Bohr. LC 85-72198. (Illus.). 1987. pap. 12.95 o.p. (ISBN 0-912528-44-3). John Muir.
Road Atlas. 176p. 1988. 4.95 o.p. (ISBN 0-376-09015-4). Sunset-Lane.
Road Atlas America 1983. rev. ed. Ed. by Hammond Staff. (Illus.). 72p. 1983. pap. 4.50 o.p. (ISBN 0-8437-2642-3). Hammond Inc.
Road Atlas America 1987. Ed. by Hammond Staff. LC 82-81118. (Illus.). 96p. 1986. pap. 4.95 o.p. (ISBN 0-8437-2659-8). Hammond Inc.
Road Atlas of Ireland: The Ordinance Survey. (Illus.). 82p. 1985. 12.95 o.p. (ISBN 0-7171-1404-X, Pub. by Gill & MacMillan). Seven Hills Bk Dists.
Road Back. Chester Lynn. 1985. 6.95 o.p. (ISBN 0-533-05321-8). Vantage.
Road Back. 1981. pap. 7.95 o.s.i. (ISBN 0-87306-264-7). Feldheim.
Road Belong Cargo: A Study of the Cargo Movement in the Southern Madang District New Guinea. Peter Lawrence. (Illus.). 1967. pap. text ed. 12.50x o.p. (ISBN 0-7190-0457-8). Humanities.
Road from Hiroshima: A Narrative Poem. Marc Kaminsky. 119p. 1984. 9.70 o.p. (ISBN 0-671-53055-0). S&S.
Road Goes Ever on. 2nd, rev. ed. J. R. R. Tolkien & Donald Swann. 1978. 10.00 o.p. (ISBN 0-395-24758-6). HM.
Road Less Traveled: A New Psychology of Love, Traditional Values & Spiritual Growth. M. Scott Peck. 1978. 15.95 o.s.i. (ISBN 0-671-24086-2). S&S.
Road Not Taken: An Introduction to Robert Frost. Robert Frost. LC 51-9831. (Illus.). (gr. 9 up). 1951. 13.50 o.p. (ISBN 0-03-027150-9, Owl Bks.); pap. 8.95 o.p. (ISBN 0-03-000073-4). H Holt & Co.
Road of a Naturalist. Donald C. Peattie. (Hall Nonfiction Paperbacks). (Illus.). 320p. 1986. pap. 9.95 o.p. (ISBN 0-8398-2890-X). G K Hall.
Road of Life & Death. Paul Radin. (Bollingen Ser.: Vol. 5). 1945. 33.00 o.p. (ISBN 0-691-09819-0). Princeton U Pr.
Road of Propaganda. Karin Dovring. 160p. 1959. (ISBN 0-8022-0415-5). Philos Lib.
Road of the Dashing Commuter. A. J. McNulty. 1980. 6.00 o.p. (ISBN 0-682-49564-6). Exposition-Phoenix.
Road Passenger Transport & Road Goods Transport. Denys Munby & A. H. Watson. Ed. by W. F. Manunder. LC 77-30558. 1978. 57.00 o.p. (ISBN 0-08-022449-0). Pergamon.
Road Pricing & Transit Improvement Program in Berkeley, California: A Preliminary Analysis. Melvyn Cheslow. 73p. 1978. pap. 6.00x o.p. (ISBN 0-87766-233-9, 22300). Urban Inst.
Road Racing. Nicole Puleo. LC 72-5417. (Superwheels & Thrill Sports Bks.). (Illus.). 48p. (gr. 4-9). 1973. PLB 9.95 o.p. (ISBN 0-8225-0404-9). Lerner Pubns.
Road Runners & Other Cuckoos. Aline Amon. LC 78-6648. (Illus.). (gr. 5-9). 1978. 7.95 o.p. (ISBN 0-689-30646-6, Atheneum). Macmillan.
Road to Communism: An International Quarterly, Vols. 1-2, No. 2. 1970. Repr. of 1934 ed. lib. bdg. 28.00x o.p. (ISBN 0-8371-9239-0, RC00). Greenwood.
Road to Dignity. Thomas R. Brooks. LC 81-66446. 1981. 14.95 o.p. (ISBN 0-689-11214-9, Atheneum). Macmillan.
Road to Eleusis: Unveiling the Secret of the Mysteries. Gordon Wasson. LC 77-84399. 120p. 1978. 12.95 o.p. (ISBN 0-15-177872-8). HarBraceJ.
Road to Gdansk: Poland & the U. S. S. R. Daniel Singer. LC 80-39914. 256p. 1982. 15.00 o.p. (ISBN 0-85345-567-8, CL5678); pap. 6.50 o.s.i. (ISBN 0-85345-568-6). Monthly Rev.
Road to Infinity. Isaac Asimov. 256p. 1981. pap. 2.75 o.p. (ISBN 0-380-54155-6, 54155-6, Discus). Avon.
Road to Inner Freedom. Baruch Spinoza. 224p. 1957. (ISBN 0-8022-1623-4). Philos Lib.
Road to Kabul: The Second Afghan War, 1878-1881. Brian Robson. (Illus.). 320p. 1987. 39.95 o.p. (ISBN 0-85368-719-6, Pub. by Arms & Armour). Sterling.
Road to Kadesh: A Historical Interpretation of the Battle Reliefs of King Sety I at Karnak. William J. Murnane. LC 84-62072. (Studies in Ancient Oriental Civilization: No. 42). (Illus.). 1985. pap. 20.00 o.p. (ISBN 0-918986-43-5). Oriental Inst.
Road to Khartoum: A Life of General Charles Gordon. Charles C. Trench. (Illus.). 1979. 15.95 o.p. (ISBN 0-393-01237-9). Norton.
Road to Mingulay. Derek Cooper. (Illus.). 224p. 1985. 25.00 o.p. (ISBN 0-317-30921-8). Routledge Chapman & Hall.

Road to Nationhood: A Chronicle of Dominion-Provincial Relations. Wilfrid Eggleston. LC 70-147218. 337p. 1972. Repr. of 1946 ed. lib. bdg. 22.50x o.p. (ISBN 0-8371-5983-0, EGRN). Greenwood.

Road to Nowhere. Elisabeth Ogilvie. 288p. 1983. text ed. 14.95 o.p. (ISBN 0-07-047700-0). McGraw.

Road to Nowhere see Heinemann Guided Readers.

Road to Paradise Island. Victoria Holt. 384p. 1985. 16.95 o.p. (ISBN 0-385-19110-3). Doubleday.

Road to Peace. Rueben Pearl. 1957. (ISBN 0-8022-1294-8). Philos Lib.

Road to Pearl Harbor: Nineteen Forty-One. Richard Collier. LC 81-66001. 1981. 16.95 o.p. (ISBN 0-689-11154-1, Atheneum). Macmillan.

Road to Self Knowledge. Rudolf Steiner. 1975. 10.95 o.p. (ISBN 0-85440-290-X, Pub by Steinerbooks); pap. 6.95 o. p. o.p. (ISBN 0-85440-291-8). Anthroposophic.

Road to Tara: The Life of Margaret Mitchell. Anne Edwards. LC 82-19520. (Illus.). 384p. 1983. 15.45 o.p. (ISBN 0-89919-169-X). Ticknor & Fields.

Road to Victory. S. Divilkovsky & I. Ognetov. 270p. 1980. pap. 5.45 o.p. (ISBN 0-8285-1841-6, Pub. by Progress Pubs USSR). Imported Pubns.

Road to World War II: A Documentary History. Ed. by Keith Eubank. LC 74-179768. 1973. pap. 12.95x o.s.i. (ISBN 0-88295-734-1). Harlan Davidson.

Road to Xanadu: A Study in the Ways of the Imagination. John L. Lowes. (Illus.). pap. 2.85 o.p. (ISBN 0-395-08390-7, 41, SenEd). HM.

Road Traffic Signalling. Institution of Electrical Engineers (UK) Staff & Peter Peregrinus, Ltd. Staff. (IEE Conference Publication: No. 207). 202p. 1982. pap. 65.00 o.p. (ISBN 0-85296-259-2, IC 207). Inst Elect Eng.

Road Unseen. Peter Jenkins & Barbara Jenkins. LC 85-25952. 224p. 1985. 12.95 o.p. (ISBN 0-8407-5961-4). Nelson.

Road Unseen. Peter Jenkins & Barbara Jenkins. (General Ser.). 406p. 1986. lib. bdg. 18.95 o.p. (ISBN 0-317-46368-3, Large Print Bks). G K Hall.

Road User Information Needs, Pedestrian Movement, & Bicycle Travel Patterns. (Transportation Research Record Ser.). 53p. 1978. 3.40 o.p. (ISBN 0-309-02828-0). Transport Res Bd.

Road User Protection: Selected Papers from the 8th International Conference on Accident & Traffic Medicine, Aarhus, Denmark, 10-13 June 1980. Ed. by Ronald Somers. 70p. 1981. pap. 35.00 o.p. (ISBN 0-08-028099-4). Pergamon.

Road Users & the Police. M. C. Dix & A. D. Layzell. (Illus.). 152p. 1983. 27.00 o.p. (ISBN 0-7099-2059-8, Pub. by Croom Helm Ltd); pap. 13.00 o.p. (ISBN 0-7099-2060-1). Routledge Chapman & Hall.

Roads & Canals in the Eighteenth Century. Marjorie Greenwood. Ed. by Marjorie Reeves. (Then & There Ser.). (Illus.). 92p. (Orig.). (gr. 7-12). 1977. pap. text ed. 4.95 o.p. (ISBN 0-582-20383-X). Longman.

Roads of Earth. Allen Drury. LC 82-45393. 384p. 1984. 16.95 o.s.i. (ISBN 0-385-00219-X). Doubleday.

Roads to Gettysburg. John W. Schildt. 1978. 18.00 o.p. (ISBN 0-87012-295-9). McClain.

Roads to Recovery: A National Directory of Alcohol & Drug Addiction Treatment Centers. Ed. by Jean Moore. LC 85-19538. 480p. 1986. pap. 17.95 o.p. (ISBN 0-02-059470-4, Collier). Macmillan.

Roadshow. William Marshall. LC 85-858. 192p. 1985. 13.95 o.s.i. (ISBN 0-03-001744-0). H Holt & Co.

Roadside Development Evaluation of Research. (National Cooperative Highway Research Program Report). 78p. 1972. 4.20 o.p. (ISBN 0-309-02022-0). Transport Res Bd.

Roadside Hazards & Safety Improvements: Four Reports. (Transportation Research Record Ser.). 52p. 1975. 2.40 o.p. (ISBN 0-309-02396-3). Transport Res Bd.

Roadside History of Colorado. James McTighe. LC 84-80537. (Illus.). 362p. (Orig.). 1984. pap. 9.95 o.p. Johnson Bks.

Roadside Safety Improvement Programs on Freeways: A Cost-Effectiveness Priority Approach. (National Cooperative Highway Research Program Report). 64p. 1974. 4.00 o.p. (ISBN 0-309-02208-8). Transport Res Bd.

Roadway Delineation Systems. (National Cooperative Highway Research Program Report). 349p. 1972. 14.00 o.p. (ISBN 0-309-02011-5). Transport Res Bd.

Roald Dahl's Revolting Rhymes. Roald Dahl. LC 82-15263. (Illus.). 48p. (gr. 3-6). 1983. 9.95 o.s.i. (ISBN 0-394-85422-5); lib. bdg. 9.99 o.s.i. (ISBN 0-394-95422-X). Knopf.

Roaming Free: Wild Horses of the American West. Skylar Hansen. LC 83-61145. (A Western Horizons Bk.). (Illus.). 84p. (Orig.). 1984. pap. 11.95 o.p. (ISBN 0-87358-337-X). Northland.

Roan Colt. Reginald Ottley. LC 67-10209. (Illus.). (gr. 5-7). 1967. 5.50 o.p. (ISBN 0-15-267700-3, HJ). HarBraceJ.

Roanoke. Sonia Levitin. LC 73-76323. (Illus.). 224p. (gr. 5-9). 1973. 7.95 o.p. (ISBN 0-689-30114-6, Atheneum). Macmillan.

Roar Lion Roar. Irvin Faust. 1966. pap. 1.45 o.p. (ISBN 0-380-01532-3, 15396, Bard). Avon.

Roaring Girl. Thomas Middleton. Ed. by Thomas Dekker & A. H. Gomme. (New Mermaid Ser.). 1976. pap. 3.95x o.p. (ISBN 0-393-90024-X). Norton.

Roaring Lead. William C. MacDonald. 1974. pap. 0.75 o.p. (ISBN 0-380-00119-5, 20198). Avon.

Roast of the Town. Joey Adams. (Illus.). 288p. 1986. 15.95 o.p. (ISBN 0-13-781436-4). P-H.

Rob & Smith's Operative Surgery: Paediatric Surgery. 4th ed. Spitz & Nixon. 1986. 99.95 o.p. (ISBN 0-8016-4417-8). Mosby.

Rob & Smith's Operative Surgery: Vascular Surgery. DeWeese. 1985. 110.00 o.p. (ISBN 0-8016-4410-0, C-4410-0). Mosby.

Rob Roy. Walter Scott. 1982. Repr. of 1906 ed. 9.95x o.p. (ISBN 0-460-00142-6, Evman); pap. 7.95x o.p. (ISBN 0-460-01142-1, Evans). Biblio Dist.

Robber Bridegroom. Eudora Welty. LC 42-23596. 1963. pap. 3.95 o.p. (ISBN 0-689-70204-3, 25, Atheneum). Macmillan.

Robber Bridegroom. Eudora Welty. LC 42-23596. 1948. 6.95 o.p. (ISBN 0-15-178317-9). HarBraceJ.

Robber Ghost. Karin Anckarsvard. Tr. by Annabelle MacMillan. LC 61-6307. (Illus.). (gr. 3-7). 1962. 6.50 o.p. (ISBN 0-15-267804-2, HJ). HarBraceJ.

Robber Ghost. Karin Anckarsvard. Tr. by Annabelle MacMillan. LC 61-6307. (Illus.). (gr. 4-6). 1968. pap. 3.95 o.p. (ISBN 0-15-678350-9, VoyB). HarBraceJ.

Robber of a Tither? D. E. Wisner. (Illus.). 8p. (gr. k-4). pap. text ed. o.s.i. CEF Press.

Robber Rocks: Letters & Memories of Hart Crane, 1923-1932. Susan J. Brown. LC 73-82537. (Illus.). 1969. 16.00x o.p. (ISBN 0-8195-4007-2). Wesleyan U Pr.

Robert A. Heinlein. Ed. by Joseph D. Olander & Martin H. Greenberg. LC 76-11054. (Writers of the 21st Century Ser.). (Orig.). 1978. 12.95 o.s.i. (ISBN 0-8008-6801-3); pap. 5.95 o.s.i. (ISBN 0-8008-6802-1). Taplinger.

Robert Aldrich: A Guide to References & Resources. Alain Silver & Elizabeth Ward. 1979. lib. bdg. 20.50 o.p. (ISBN 0-8161-7993-X, Hall Reference). G K Hall.

Robert & James Adams: Birth of Style. Joseph Rykwert & Anne Rykwert. (Illus.). 222p. pap. 25.00 o.p. (ISBN 0-8478-0589-1). Rizzoli Intl.

Robert & the Magic String. Ivan Sherman. LC 72-88174. (Illus.). 32p. (gr. k-3). 1973. 5.50 o.p. (ISBN 0-15-267820-4, HJ). HarBraceJ.

Robert Barnes, Nineteen Fifty-Six to Nineteen Eighty-Four: A Survey. Dennis Adrian. Ed. by Trent Myers. (Illus.). 80p. 1985. exhibition catalog 15.95 o.p. (ISBN 0-913883-14-X). Madison Art.

Robert Benjamin & the Disappearing Act. Jeanette Grise. LC 80-19519. (Illus.). (gr. 3-5). 1980. 8.95 o.s.i. (ISBN 0-664-32673-0, Westminster). Westminster John Knox.

Robert Brady: Ceramic Sculpture. Thomas H. Garver. (Illus.). 1982. 0.50 o.p. (ISBN 0-913883-08-5). Madison Art.

Robert Bridges Recollections see Needed Words.

Robert Buhler. Colin Hayes. (Royal Academy Painters & Sculptors Ser.). (Illus.). 73p. 1987. 16.95 o.p. (ISBN 0-89733-240-7). Academy Chi Pubs.

Robert Burns. Ian Grimble. LC 86-14026. (Illustrated Biographies Ser.). (Illus.). 128p. 1986. 16.95 o.p. (ISBN 0-87226-095-X). P Bedrick Bks.

Robert Burns: Rantin' Dog, Poet of the Common Man. John Lindsey. (Black & Gold Lib). (Illus.). 1947. 6.95 o.p. (ISBN 0-87140-891-0, Co-Pub with Tudor). Liveright.

Robert Carrier's Menu Planner. Robert Carrier. 29.95 o.p. (ISBN 0-316-12977-1). Little.

Robert Creeley: An Inventory. Mary Novik. LC 72-96943. (Serif Ser.: No. 28). 227p. 1973. 12.00x o.p. (ISBN 0-87338-139-4). Kent St U Pr.

Robert Creeley: An Inventory 1945-1970. Mary Novik. 144p. 1973. 6.00x o.p. (ISBN 0-7735-0191-6, McGill Canada). U of Toronto Pr.

Robert E. Sherwood. R. Baird Shuman. (Twayne's United States Authors Ser.). 1964. pap. 10.95 o.p. (ISBN 0-8084-0265-X, T58, Twayne). New Coll U Pr.

Robert Elsmere. Mrs. Humphrey Ward. Ed. by Clyde L. Ryals. 9.00 o.p. (ISBN 0-8446-3135-3). Peter Smith.

Robert Francis: Collected Poems, 1936-1976. Robert Francis. LC 76-8753. (Illus.). 304p. 1976. pap. text ed. 17.50x o.p. (ISBN 0-87023-211-8). U of Mass Pr.

Robert Frost. Philip L. Gerber. (Twayne's United States Authors Ser). 1966. pap. 10.95 o.p. (ISBN 0-8084-0266-8, T107, Twayne). New Coll U Pr.

Robert Frost: A Tribute to the Source. Dewitt Jones & David Bradley. LC 78-10444. (Illus.). 176p. 1979. 22.95 o.s.i. (ISBN 0-03-046326-2). H Holt & Co.

Robert Frost & New England: The Poet As Regionalist. John C. Kemp. LC 78-70301. 1979. 30.50x o.p. (ISBN 0-691-06393-1). Princeton U Pr.

Robert Frost One Hundred. Edward Lathem. LC 74-15258. 1974. 10.00 o.s.i. (ISBN 0-87923-111-4); pap. 4.50 o.p. (ISBN 0-87923-112-2). Godine.

Robert Frost: The Early Years, 1894-1915. Ed. by L. Thompson. LC 66-20523. 1982. 12.50 o.p. (ISBN 0-03-059770-6); pap. 25.00 o.p. H Holt & Co.

Robert Frost: The Years of Triumph, 1915-1938. Ed. by L. Thompson. LC 66-20523. 1970. 15.00 o.s.i. (ISBN 0-03-084530-0). H Holt & Co.

Robert G. Ingersoll: A Checklist. Gordon Stein. LC 78-626234. (Serif Ser.: No. 9). 158p. 1969. 10.00x o.p. (ISBN 0-87338-047-9). Kent St U Pr.

Robert Graves: His Life & Work. Martin Seymour-Smith. (Illus.). 624p. 1983. 22.50 o.s.i. (ISBN 0-03-022171-4). H Holt & Co.

Robert Greene: A Reference Guide. James S. Dean. (Reference Guides to Literature Ser.). 1984. lib. bdg. 61.00 o.s.i. (ISBN 0-8161-7854-2, Hall Reference). G K Hall.

Robert Herrick: A Reference Guide. Elizabeth H. Hageman. 1982. lib. bdg. 35.50 o.p. (ISBN 0-8161-8012-1, Hall Reference). G K Hall.

Robert Leroy Platzman Memorial. H. Hering. 428p. 1976. pap. 69.00 o.p. (ISBN 0-08-019957-7). Pergamon.

Robert Longo. Carter Ratcliff. (Illus.). 120p. pap. 25.00 o.p. (ISBN 0-8478-0602-2). Rizzoli Intl.

Robert Louis Stevenson: A Teller of Tales. Eulalie O. Grover. LC 71-164308. (Illus.). x, 282p. (YA) (gr. 9-12). 1975. Repr. of 1940 ed. 40.00x o.p. (ISBN 0-8103-4080-1). Gale.

Robert McAlmon: Expatriate Publisher & Writer. Robert E. Knoll. LC 57-62784. xiv, 96p. 1959. pap. 2.95x o.p. (ISBN 0-8032-5226-9). U of Nebr Pr.

Robert Marx: Quest for Treasure. Robert F. Marx. Ed. by B. J. Nelson. LC 81-85739. (Illus.). xiv, 286p. (Orig.). 1982. pap. 11.95 o.p. (ISBN 0-9⁚5920-42-5). Ram Pub.

Robert Mondavi of the Napa Valley. Cyril Ray. (Illus.). 208p. 1984. 14.95 o.p. (ISBN 0-89141-233-6). Presidio Pr.

Robert Morris: Revolutionary Financier. Clarence L. Ver Steeg. LC 71-120764. 276p. 1970. Repr. of 1954 ed. lib. bdg. 20.00x o.p. (ISBN 0-374-98078-0, Octagon). Hippocrene Bks.

Robert Musil. Hannah Hickman. 1984. 24.95 o.p. (ISBN 0-87548-419-0). Open Court.

Robert Penn Warren: A Reference Guide. Ed. by Neil Nakadate. 1977. lib. bdg. 36.50 o.p. (ISBN 0-8161-7820-8, Hall Reference). G K Hall.

Robert Pinget: The Novel As Quest. Robert M. Henkels, Jr. LC 74-2815. (Studies in the Humanities: No. 18). 208p. 1979. 17.75 o.p. (ISBN 0-8173-7323-3). U of Ala Pr.

Robert Plant. (Illus.). 32p. (gr. 4-12). 1985. 4.95 o.p. (ISBN 0-88188-341-7, Robus Books). H Leonard Pub Corp.

Robert Redford. Bruce Crowther. (Film Stars Ser.). (Illus.). 96p. 1985. 7.95 o.p. (ISBN 0-87052-119-5). Hippocrene Bks.

Robert Schumann, His Life & His Work. Herbert Bedford. LC 70-106712. 270p. 1971. Repr. of 1933 ed. lib. bdg. 35.00x o.p. (ISBN 0-8371-3442-0, BERS). Greenwood.

Robert Silverberg. Ed. by Joseph D. Olander & Martin H. Greenberg. LC 78-56281. (Writers of the 21st Century Ser.). (ISBN 0-8008-6805-6); pap. (ISBN 0-8008-6806-4). Taplinger.

Robert Smalls. (Black History Illustrated Ser.: No. 9). (Illus.). 1970. pap. 0.59 o.p. (ISBN 0-685-78152-6). Guild Bks.

Robert Southey: The Critical Heritage. Ed. by Lionel Madden. 1984. pap. 15.00 o.p. (ISBN 0-7102-0394-2). Routledge Chapman & Hall.

Robert White. Ed. by P. C. Buck et al. (Tudor Church Music Ser.: Vol. 5). 1963. Repr. of 1926 ed. 85.00x o.p. Broude.

Roberte Ce Soir & The Revocation of the Edict of Nantes. Pierre Klossowski. Tr. by Austryn Wainhouse. 1969. pap. 2.95 o.p. (ISBN 0-394-17257-4, E556, Ever). Grove.

Roberto Clemente: The Pride of Puerto Rico. Irving Gerber. (American Destiny Ser.: Puerto Ricans). (gr. 4). 1978. Set of 10. 12.95 o.p. (ISBN 0-87594-178-8). Book-Lab.

Robin Goodfellow & the Giant Dwarf. M. Jennings & T. DePaola. 48p. 1981. text ed. 9.95 o.p. (ISBN 0-07-032451-4). McGraw.

Robin Hood. J. C. Holt. LC 81-53059. (Illus.). 208p. 1982. 17.95 o.p. (ISBN 0-500-25081-2). Thames Hudson.

Robin Hood. J. C. Holt. LC 81-53059. (Illus.). 1983. pap. 11.95f o.p. (ISBN 0-500-27308-1). Thames Hudson.

Robin Hood see New Method Supplementary Readers: Bestseller Pack.

Robin Yount. Rothaus et al. (Sports Superstars Ser.). (Illus.). 32p. 14.25 o.p.; PLB 9.95 o.p. (ISBN 0-317-31204-9). Creative Ed.

Robinson Crusoe see also Adventures of Robinson Crusoe.

Robinson Crusoe see also Life & Adventures of Robinson Crusoe.

Robinson Crusoe. Daniel Defoe. 1977. Repr. of 1975 ed. 14.95x o.p. (ISBN 0-460-00059-4, Evman); pap. 2.50x o.p. (ISBN 0-460-01059-X, Evman). Biblio Dist.

Robinson Crusoe. Daniel Defoe. (Illus.). (gr. 4-6). 1952-63. 5.95 o.p. (ISBN 0-448-05821-9, G&D); 2.95 o.p. (ISBN 0-448-05467-1); deluxe ed. 12.95 o.p. (ISBN 0-448-06021-3); PLB 3.79 o.p. (ISBN 0-448-03260-0). Putnam Pub Group.

Robinson Crusoe: My Journals & Sketchbooks. Robinson Crusoe. LC 74-2240. 80p. (gr. 3-7). 1974. 6.95 o.p. (ISBN 0-15-267836-0, HJ). HarBraceJ.

Robland. Michael Randolph. 1985. 7.95 o.p. (ISBN 0-533-05284-X). Vantage.

Robot Book. Malone. 1978. pap. 6.95 o.p. (ISBN 0-15-678452-1, VoyB). HarBraceJ.

Robot in Every Home: An Introduction to Personal Robots & Brand-Name Buyer's Guide. Mike Higgins. 192p. (Orig.). 1985. pap. 16.95 o.p. (ISBN 0-317-39392-8). Robot Inst Am.

Robot User Buying Patterns: A National Market Survey. (Illus.). 60p. 1985. pap. 51.95 o.p. (ISBN 0-317-39393-6). Robot Inst Am.

Robot World. (Fact Bks). 96p. (gr. 4-7). pap. 3.50 o.p. (ISBN 0-528-87137-4, Checkerboard Pr). Macmillan.

Robotics. Anne Cardoza & Suzee J. Vlk. (Illus.). 160p. 1985. 16.95 o.p. (ISBN 0-8306-0858-3, 1858); pap. 10.60 o.p. (ISBN 0-8306-1858-9). TAB Bks.

Robotics Age: In the Beginning. Ed. by Carl Helmers. 241p. 1983. pap. 16.95 o.p. (ISBN 0-8104-6325-3). Sams.

Robotics & Manipulators: Theory & Practice. Ed. by A. Morecki. 36p. 1983. pap. 10.00 o.p. (ISBN 0-08-030530-X, 11). Pergamon.

Robotics Bibliography 1970-1981. A. Gomersall & P. Farmer. 190p. 1985. pap. 49.30 o.p. (ISBN 0-387-15016-1). Springer-Verlag.

Robotics: Future Factories, Future Workers. Ed. by Robert J. Miller. (Annals: Vol. 470). 224p. 1983. 15.00 o.p. (ISBN 0-317-06457-6); pap. 7.95 o.p. (ISBN 0-317-06458-4). Am Acad Pol Soc Sci.

Robotics Primer: The What, Why & How of Robots in the Workplace. Robert A. Ullrich. 121p. 1983. pap. text ed. 9.95 o.p. (ISBN 0-317-18019-3). Robot Inst Am.

Robots. Gatland & Jeffries. (World of the Future Ser.). (gr. 5-9). 1979. 6.95 o.p. (ISBN 0-86020-240-2, Usborne-Hayes); PLB 12.96 o.p. (ISBN 0-88110-003-X); pap. 4.95 o.p. (ISBN 0-86020-241-0). EDC.

Robots A Two Z. Thomas H. Metos. LC 80-21004. (Illus.). 80p. (gr. 4 up). 1980. PLB 9.29 o.p. (ISBN 0-671-34027-1). Messner.

Robots & Empire. Isaac Asimov. LC 85-1600. 384p. 1985. 16.95 o.p. (ISBN 0-385-19092-1). Doubleday.

Robots & Robotology. R. H. Warring. (Illus.). 128p. (Orig.). 1984. 13.95 o.p. (ISBN 0-8306-0673-4); pap. 7.95 o.p. (ISBN 0-8306-1673-X, 1673). TAB Bks.

Robots & Telechirs. Meredith W. Thring. LC 83-10685. (Ellis Horwood Series in Engineering Science). 298p. 1983. 58.95x o.p. (ISBN 0-470-27465-4); pap. 39.95 o.p. (ISBN 0-470-20174-6). Halsted Pr.

Robots East Seminar: Proceedings. Robotic Industries Association Staff. 200p. 1985. pap. 42.00 o.p. (ISBN 0-317-39390-1). Robot Inst Am.

Robots Eight Conference Proceedings, Detroit, Michigan, June, 1984, 2 Vols. Robots Eight, Detroit, Mich., June 1984. Incl. Vol. I. Applications for Today; Vol. II. Future Considerations. 1800p. 1984. Set. 113.00 o.p. (ISBN 0-318-01664-8); 67.00 o.p. Robot Inst Am.

Robots: Facts Behind the Fiction. Michael Chester. LC 83-61237. (Illus.). 96p. (gr. 5-9). 1983. 9.95 o.s.i. (ISBN 0-02-718220-7). Macmillan.

Robots in Industry: Applications for the Electronics Industry. Technical Insights, Inc. Staff. 196p. 1983. 95.00 o.p. Tech Insights.

Titles

Robots in Industry: General Applications. Technical Insights, Inc. Staff. LC 82-99925. 219p. 1984. 95.00 o.p. Tech Insights.

Robots, Men & Minds. Ludwig Von Bertalanffy. LC 67-27524. 1969. pap. 4.95 o.p. (ISBN 0-8076-0428-3). Braziller.

Robots Nine Conference Proceedings, 2 vols. 2000p. (Orig.). 1985. Vol. 1 Advancing Applications. pap. 67.00 ea. o.p.; Vol. 2 Current Issues, Future Concerns. pap. 113.00 set o.p. (ISBN 0-317-39397-9). Robot Inst Am.

Robust Statistical Methods. J. J. Rey. (Lecture Notes in Mathematics Ser.: Vol. 690). 1978. pap. 12.00 o.p. (ISBN 0-387-09091-6). Springer-Verlag.

Robustness in Statistics. Ed. by Robert L. Launer & Graham N. Wilkinson. LC 79-13893. 1979. 41.50 o.p. (ISBN 0-12-438150-2). Acad Pr.

Rocannon's World. Ursula K. LeGuin. Ed. by Lester Del Rey. LC 75-419. (Library of Science Fiction). 1975. lib. bdg. 21.00 o.p. (ISBN 0-8240-1424-3). Garland Pub.

Rochester. David Farley-Hills. (Critical Heritage Ser.). 288p. 1985. pap. 15.00 o.p. (ISBN 0-7102-0594-5). Routledge Chapman & Hall.

Rochester's Wife. D. E. Stevenson. LC 40-9317. 1978. 8.95 o.s.i. (ISBN 0-03-042616-2). H Holt & Co.

Rock & Mineral Analysis, Vol.27. 2nd ed. Wesley M. Johnson & John A. Maxwell. LC 81-1659. (Chemical Analysis: A Ser. of Monographs on Analytical Chemistry & its Applications). 489p. 1981. 85.00x o.p. (ISBN 0-471-02743-X, Pub. by Wiley-Interscience). Wiley.

Rock & Roll Retreat Blues. Douglas K. Hall. 1974. pap. 1.50 o.p. (ISBN 0-380-00159-4, 19596). Avon.

Rock Art of East Mexico & Central America: An Annotated Bibliography. rev. ed. Matthias Strecker. (Monograph x). 81p. 1982. pap. 7.00x o.p. (ISBN 0-917956-36-2). UCLA Arch.

Rock Band: Big Men in a Great Big Town. Carolyn Meyer. LC 80-13349. 168p. (gr. 9 up). 1980. 8.95 o.p. (ISBN 0-689-50181-1, Atheneum). Macmillan.

Rock Bolting: A Practical Handbook Describing All Aspects of Rock Bolts & Their Application in Rock Engineering. Norwegian Institute of Rock Schach Blasting Techniques Staff. 1979. 21.00 o.p. (ISBN 0-08-022503-9). Pergamon.

Rock Characterization, Testing & Monitoring: ISRM Suggested Methods. Ed. by E. T. Brown. LC 80-49711. 200p. 1981. 50.00 o.p. (ISBN 0-08-027308-4); pap. 50.00 o.p. (ISBN 0-08-027309-2). Pergamon.

Rock Cried Out. Ellen Douglas. LC 79-87474. 320p. 1979. 10.95 o.p. (ISBN 0-15-178322-5). HarBraceJ.

Rock Day-by-Day. Barry Lazell & Steve Smith. (Illus.). 256p. (Orig.). (YA) (gr. 10 up). 1987. pap. 12.95 o.p. (ISBN 0-85112-825-4, Pub. by Guinness Superlatives). Sterling.

Rock Gardening. Peter McHoy. (Blandford Gardening Handbook Ser.). (Illus.). 128p. 1986. 14.95 o.p. (ISBN 0-7137-1575-8, Pub. by Blandford Pr England); pap. 8.95 o.p. (ISBN 0-7137-1578-2). Sterling.

Rock Is My Home. (Illus.). 224p. 1976. pap. 15.00 o.p. (ISBN 0-89192-299-7, Pub. by Wepf & Co). Interbk Inc.

Rock Mechanics. Alfreds R. Jumikis. (Rock & Soil Mechanics Ser.). (Illus.). 1979. 35.00x o.p. (ISBN 0-87849-026-4, Trans Tech Pubns (BRD)). Gower Pub Co.

Rock Mechanics: Key to Energy Production. Ed. by Howard L. Hartman. LC 86-60959. (U. S. Symposium on Rock Mechanics: No. 27). (Illus.). 976p. 1986. 63.50x o.p. (ISBN 0-87335-059-6, 059-6). SMM&E Inc.

Rock-Mechanics Research in the U. S. National Research Council Staff. (Illus.). 1966. pap. 5.25x o.p. (ISBN 0-309-01466-2). Natl Acad Pr.

Rock Mechanics Symposium: AMD, Vol. 3. Ed. by D. L. Sikarskie. 130p. 1973. 12.50 o.p. (ISBN 0-317-33609-6, I00012); members 6.25 o.p. (ISBN 0-317-33610-X). ASME.

Rock Mechanics Symposium: Proceedings, Vol. 3. Ed. by D. L. Sikarskie. 130p. 1973. pap. text ed. 12.50 o.p. (ISBN 0-685-38865-4, I00012). ASME.

Rock 'n' Roll Confidential. Penny Stallings. (Illus.). 256p. 1984. pap. 14.45i o.p. (ISBN 0-316-80998-5). Little.

Rock 'n' Roll Times: The Style & Spirit of the Early Beatles & Their First Fans. Jurgen Vollmer. LC 82-22240. (Illus.). 180p. (Orig.). 1983. pap. 6.95 o.p. (ISBN 0-87951-173-7). Overlook Pr.

Rock Plants for Small Gardens. Royton E. Heath. (Illus.). 144p. 1982. 17.95 o.p. (ISBN 0-917304-46-2). Timber.

Rock Record. Terry Hounsome & Tim Chambre. 544p. 1981. 17.95 o.p. (ISBN 0-87196-547-X); pap. 9.95 o.p. (ISBN 0-87196-548-8). Facts on File.

Rock Shots. (Illus.). 32p. (gr. 4-12). 1985. pap. 3.95 o.p. (ISBN 0-88188-351-4, Robus Books). H Leonard Pub Corp.

Rock Video Superstars II. Daniel Cohen & Susan Cohen. (Illus.). (gr. 4 up). pap. 2.50 o.p. (ISBN 0-671-63397-X). Archway.

Rock Yearbook 1981. Michael Gross & Maxim Jakubowski. 1981. pap. 11.95 o.p. (ISBN 0-394-17794-0, E774, Ever). Grove.

Rockaby & Other Works. Samuel Beckett. 128p. 1981. pap. 3.95 o.p. (ISBN 0-394-17924-2, E777, Ever). Grove.

Rocket in My Pocket: Rhymes & Chants of Young Americans. Carl A. Withers. LC 48-4881. (Illus.). 214p. (gr. 4-6). 1948. reinforced bdg. 5.95 o.p. (ISBN 0-03-015071-X); pap. 7.95 o.p. H Holt & Co.

Rocket Island. Theodore Taylor. 144p. 1985. pap. 2.50 o.p. (ISBN 0-380-89674-5, Flare). Avon.

Rockhound Trails. Jean Bartenbach. LC 76-25430. (Illus.). (gr. 4-6). 1977. 7.50 o.p. (ISBN 0-689-30547-8, Atheneum). Macmillan.

Rockliffe's Babies. Simon Raby. 160p. 1988. lib. bdg. 19.95x o.s.i. (ISBN 0-7451-0818-0, Pub. by Chivers Pr UK). G K Hall.

Rocks & Minerals. rev. ed. B. Simpson. 1966. text ed. 25.00 o.p. (ISBN 0-08-011744-9); pap. 9.00 o.p. Pergamon.

Rocks & Minerals of Michigan. O. F. Poindexter et al. (Illus.). 49p. (Orig.). 1971. pap. 3.95 o.p. (ISBN 0-910726-73-6). Hillsdale Educ.

Rocks around the Crucifix. Ralph Emerson Fernbaugh. 1977. 5.00 o.p. (ISBN 0-682-48793-7). Exposition-Phoenix.

Rocks, Ice, & Water. David Alt & Donald Hyndman. LC 73-78910. (Roadside Geology Ser.). (Illus.). 104p. 1973. pap. 4.95 o.p. (ISBN 0-87842-041-X). Mountain Pr.

Rocks of the World. 1978. pap. 84.00x o.p. (ISBN 0-08-022920-4). Pergamon.

Rockstore Seventy-Seven: Proceedings of the First International Symposium on Storage in Excavated Rock Caverns, Stockholm, Sweden, Sept. 5-8 1977, 3 vols. Ed. by Magnus Bergman. LC 77-30591. 1978. Set. 405.00 o.p. (ISBN 0-08-022407-5). Pergamon.

Rockwell Kent. Ed. by Fridolf Johnson. LC 81-47477. (Illus.). 352p. 1982. 59.50 o.s.i. (ISBN 0-394-41771-2). Knopf.

Rocky. Julia Sorel. 1979. pap. 1.95 o.s.i. (ISBN 0-345-28652-9). Ballantine.

Rocky Mountain Cache: Western Wild Game Cookbook. Sharon L. Duffala. LC 82-7542. (Illus.). 72p. (Orig.). 1982. pap. 5.95 o.p. (ISBN 0-87108-630-1). Pruett.

Rocky Mountain Horticulture. 3rd ed. George W. Kelly. (Illus.). 1967. pap. 8.95 o.p. (ISBN 0-87108-014-1). Pruett.

Rocky Mountain Medicine: Doctors, Drugs & Disease in Early Colorado. R. H. Shikes. 250p. 1986. 34.95 o.p. (ISBN 1-55566-001-0). Johnson Bks.

Rocky Mountain National Park Hiking Trails: Including Indian Peaks. 6th ed. Kent Dannen & Donna Dannen. LC 84-48887. (Illus.). 288p. 1985. pap. 8.95 o.s.i. (ISBN 0-88742-021-4). Globe Pequot.

Rocky Mountain Trees. 2nd rev. ed. Richard J. Preston, Jr. LC 68-20408. (Illus.). 1968. pap. 5.95 o.p. (ISBN 0-486-21898-8). Dover.

Rocky Mountain Trees: A Handbook of the Native Species, with Plates & Distribution Maps. 3rd rev. ed. Richard J. Preston, Jr. (Illus.). 13.50 o.p. (ISBN 0-8446-2758-5). Peter Smith.

Rococo to Romanticism: Art & Architecture 1700-1850. LC 76-14072. (Garland Library of the History of Art). 1976. lib. bdg. 61.00 o.p. (ISBN 0-8240-2420-6). Garland Pub.

Rod McKuen's Book of Days. Rod McKuen. 1982. gift ed. 24.04i o.p. (ISBN 0-06-250570-X). HarpR.

Rod McKuen's Book of Days: And a Month of Sundays. Rod McKuen. LC 81-47421. (Illus.). 160p. 1981. 9.57 o.p. (ISBN 0-06-250569-6). HarpR.

Rodda Act--One Year Later. Jack Blackburn. (IPA Training Manual). 1977. 8.00 o.p. (ISBN 0-89215-072-6). U Cal LA Indus Rel.

Rodent Control in Agriculture: A Handbook on the Biology & Control of Commensal Rodents as Agricultural Pests. J. H. Greaves. (Plant Production & Protection Papers: No. 40). 95p. 1982. pap. text ed. 7.50 o.p. (ISBN 92-5-101295-4, F2407, FAO). UNIPUB.

Rodent Pests - Biology & Control: Bibliography. (Plant Production & Protection Papers: No. 7). 836p. 1977. pap. 50.00 o.p. (ISBN 92-5-100435-8, F1334, FAO). UNIPUB.

Rodenticides: Analyses, Specifications, Formulations. (Plant Production & Protection Papers: No. 16). 81p. 1979. pap. 7.50 o.p. (ISBN 92-5-100798-5, F1867, FAO). UNIPUB.

Rodeo: An Anthropologist Looks at the Wild & the Tame. Elizabeth A. Lawrence. LC 81-3330. (Illus.). 304p. 1982. 29.95x o.p. (ISBN 0-87049-328-0). U of Tenn Pr.

Roderick D. McKenzie on Human Ecology. Roderick D. McKenzie. Ed. by Amos H. Hawley. LC 68-9728. (Heritage of Sociology Ser.). 1969. pap. text ed. 3.45x o.s.i. (ISBN 0-226-31982-2, P326, Phoen). U of Chicago Pr.

Roderick Hudson. Henry James. 1977. pap. 4.95 o.p. (ISBN 0-395-25353-5, 85, SenEd). HM.

Roderick Random. Tobias G. Smollett. 1982. pap. 5.95x o.p. (ISBN 0-460-01790-X, Evman). Biblio Dist.

Rodin. Ionel Jianou & C. Goldscheider. (Illus.). 25.00 o.p. (ISBN 0-8283-1363-6); pap. 2.50 o.s.i o.p. (ISBN 0-8283-1364-4). Branden Pub Co.

Rodin & Balzac: Bronzes from the Cantor, Fitzgerald Collection, Inc. Cantor, Fitzgerald Collection, Inc. Staff. (Illus.). 72p. 1973. pap. 4.00x o.s.i. (ISBN 0-913060-24-0). Norton Art.

Rodin: Drawings & Watercolors. Ed. by Claudie Judrin. (Illus.). 1983. slipcased 85.00 o.s.i. (ISBN 0-500-23368-3). Thames Hudson.

Rodin Museum. Karel Schampers & Godert Van Colmjon. (Illus.). 96p. 1988. pap. 12.00 o.p. (ISBN 2-85025-080-5, Fernand Hazan). Moyer Bell Limited.

Rodin Museum Handbook. John L. Tancock. LC 70-101487. (Illus.). 108p. 1986. pap. 4.95 o.p. (ISBN 0-87633-008-1). Phila Mus Art.

Rodin: The B. Gerald Cantor Collection. Joan V. Miller & Gary Marotta. (Illus.). 184p. 1986. 40.00 o.p. (ISBN 0-8050-0029-1, Dist. by Henry Holt & Co.); museum ed. 35.00 o.p. (ISBN 0-87099-442-5); pap. 25.00 o.p. (ISBN 0-87099-443-3). Metro Mus Art.

Rods, Bundles & Stiches: A Century of Southern California Indian Basketry. Ed. by R. A. Lopez & C. L. Moser. LC 81-85592. (Illus.). 240p. 1981. 28.50 o.p. (ISBN 0-935661-07-7). Riverside Mus Pr.

Roe Deer. Astrid B. Sucksdorff. Tr. by Alan Tapsell from Swedish. LC 70-1820. (Illus.). 48p. (gr. 3 up). 1969. 5.95 o.p. (ISBN 0-15-268365-8, HJ). HarBraceJ.

Roentgen Diagnosis of Bones. M. Eiken. (Illus.). 1976. pap. 19.95 o.p. (ISBN 0-8151-3027-9). Year Bk Med.

Roentgen-Video-Techniques. Ed. by Paul H. Heintzen & J. H. Bursch. LC 77-99147. (Illus.). 354p. 1978. 33.00 o.p. (ISBN 0-88416-237-0). Year Bk Med.

Roentgenological Studies of Traumatic & Recurrent Anterior & Inferior Dislocations of the Shoulder Joint. Ivan Hermodsson. (Illus.). 1963. 10.00 o.p. (ISBN 0-7735-0008-1, McGill Canada). U of Toronto Pr.

Roger Bacon. Westacott. (ISBN 0-8022-1853-9). Philos Lib.

Roger Caras Dog Book. Roger Caras. LC 79-17757. (Illus.). 304p. 1980. 16.95 o.p. (ISBN 0-275-23540-8). H Holt & Co.

Roger Casement. Brian Inglis. LC 73-15422. 1974. 8.95 o.p. (ISBN 0-15-178327-6). HarBraceJ.

Roger Eberts Movie Home Companion: Full-Length Reviews of 600 Films on Cassette--1989. rev. ed. Roger Ebert. 612p. pap. 11.95 o.p. Andrews & McMeel.

Roger Ebert's Movie Home Companion: 1988 Edition. Roger Ebert. 768p. (Orig.). 1987. pap. 10.95 o.p. (ISBN 0-8362-6212-3). Andrews & McMeel.

Roger Ebert's Movie Home Companion: 400 Films on Cassette, 1980-85. Roger Ebert. 500p. (Orig.). 1985. pap. 9.95 o.p. (ISBN 0-8362-6209-3). Andrews & McMeel.

Roger Fry: An Annotated Bibliography. Donald A. Laing. LC 78-68305. (Garland Reference Library of the Humanities Ser.). 200p. 1979. lib. bdg. 43.00 o.p. (ISBN 0-8240-9838-2). Garland Pub.

Roger Verge's Cuisine of the South of France. Roger Verge. Tr. by Roberta W. Smoler from Fr. LC 85-19164. (Three-Star Chefs of France Ser.). (Illus.). 286p. 1985. pap. 9.95 o.p. (ISBN 0-688-06152-4, Quill). Morrow.

Roger Williams & Mary. Albert Johnson. (Orig.). 1957. pap. 0.95 o.p. (ISBN 0-377-80481-9). Friendship Pr.

Rogue. Janet Dailey. (Hall Large Print Bk.). 1985. lib. bdg. 13.95 o.p. (ISBN 0-8161-3667-X, Large Print Bks); pap. text ed. 9.95 o.p. (ISBN 0-8161-3739-0). G K Hall.

Rogue Bear. Donald Seaman. 224p. 1988. 19.95 o.p. (ISBN 0-241-12363-1, Pub. by Hamish Hamilton). David & Charles.

Rogue Diamond. James B. Lynne. LC 79-55621. 1980. 12.95 o.p. (ISBN 0-689-11048-0, Atheneum). Macmillan.

Rogue Hercules. Dennis Pitts. LC 77-88904. 1978. 6.95 o.p. (ISBN 0-689-10849-4, Atheneum). Macmillan.

Rogue Moon. Algis Budrys. 1978. pap. 2.45 o.p. (ISBN 0-380-00100-4, 38950-9, Equinox). Avon.

Rogue Rancher. Will Travers. (Lythway Ser.). 176p. 1988. lib. bdg. 17.50 o.s.i. (ISBN 0-7451-0672-2, Pub. by Chivers Pr UK). G K Hall.

Rogues & Running Dogs. rev. ed. D. Brian Plummer. (Illus.). 1984. 18.00 o.p. (ISBN 0-85115-166-3, Pub. by Boydell & Brewer). Longwood Pub Group.

Rogue's Daughter. Molly N. Bull. 224p. 1986. pap. 5.95 o.p. (ISBN 0-310-47551-1, 15602P). Zondervan.

Rogue's Masquerade. Margaret Summerville. 1981. pap. 2.25 o.p. (ISBN 0-380-78469-6, 78469). Avon.

Rogues, Royalty & Reporters: The Age of Queen Anne Through Its Newspapers. William B. Ewald, Jr. LC 78-17410. 1978. Repr. of 1956 ed. lib. bdg. 35.00x o.p. (ISBN 0-313-20506-X, EWRR). Greenwood.

ROI: Planning for Profitable Growth. Richard B. Stockton. LC 84-45355. (Better Business Ser.). 150p. 35.00 o.p. (ISBN 0-8019-7555-7); pap. 19.95 o.p. (ISBN 0-8019-7556-5). Chilton.

ROI: Practical Theory & Innovative Application. rev. & enl. ed. Robert A. Peters. 1979. 23.95 o.p. (ISBN 0-8144-5496-8). AMACOM.

Rokudan: A Tale of Love in Six Movements. Pat Burch. LC 80-29375. 192p. 1981. 9.95 o.s.i. (ISBN 0-8008-6818-8). Taplinger.

Roland Harvey's Incredible Book of Almost Everything. Roland Harvey. (Illus.). 160p. (Orig.). (gr. 1-9). 1985. pap. 9.95 o.p. (ISBN 0-86788-024-4, Pub. by Five Mile Pr Australia). Sterling.

Role & Structure of Customs Duties, Exercises, & Sales Taxes. John F. Due. LC 70-119108. 201p. 1970. 24.50x o.p. (ISBN 0-8018-1167-8). Johns Hopkins.

Role des Arbres au Sahel: Compte Rendu du Colloque tenu a Dakar (Senegal) du 5 au 10 Novembre 1979. CRDI, Ottawa. 92p. 1980. pap. 7.00 o.p. (ISBN 0-88936-262-9, IDRC-158F, IDRC). UNIPUB.

Role of Accreditation in Directly Improving Educational Quality. Steven M. Jung. 30p. 1986. 8.00 o.p. (ISBN 0-318-20486-X). Coun Postsecondary Accredit.

Role of Airfreight in Physical Distribution: Including Two Cases by J. D. Steele. H. T. Lewis & J. W. Culliton. 1956. Repr. of 1956 ed. 50.00 o.p. (ISBN 0-08-018744-7). Pergamon.

Role of Animals in Biological Cycling of Forest-Steppe Ecosystems. Ed. by R. I. Zlotin & K. S. Khodashova. Tr. by William Lewus & W. E. Grant. LC 80-12228. 240p. 1982. 31.95 o.p. (ISBN 0-87933-377-4). Van Nos Reinhold.

Role of Chromosomes in Development: Proceedings of the Society for the Study of Developmental Biology, 23rd Symposium. Society for the Study of Developmental Biology Staff. Ed. by Michael Locke. 1964. 57.50 o.p. (ISBN 0-12-454150-X). Acad Pr.

Role of Cities in Attaining a Desirable Population Distribution in the Context of Rapid Urbanization: The Case Study in Bicol, The Philippines. (Working Papers Ser.: No. 74-1). 125p. pap. 6.00 o.p. (ISBN 0-686-78212-7, CRD045, UNCRD). UNIPUB.

Role of Cities in Attaining a Desirable Population Distribution in the Context of Rapid Urbanization: Case Study of Meerut, India. (Working Papers Ser.: No. 74-1). 114p. pap. 6.00 o.p. (ISBN 0-686-78213-5, CRD046, UNCRD). UNIPUB.

Role of Cities in Attaining a Desirable Population Distribution in the Context of Rapid Urbanization: Japan Study, Case Study on the Tokaido Corridor, Pt. 1. (Working Papers Ser.: No. 74-1). 54p. pap. 6.00 o.p. (ISBN 0-686-78235-6, CRD047, UNCRD). UNIPUB.

Role of Cyclic Nucleotides in Carsinogenesis. Ed. by J. Schultz & H. G. Gratzner. 1973. 63.50 o.p. (ISBN 0-12-632750-5). Acad Pr.

Role of Education in National Defense. Alvin Tucker. 15p. o.s.i. (ISBN 0-318- 22194-2, OC86). Natl Ctr Res Voc Ed.

Role of Evaluators in Curriculum Development. Ed. by Pinchas Tamir. LC 84-17610. 232p. 1984. 29.95 o.p. (ISBN 0-7099-2470-4, Pub. by Croom Helm Ltd). Routledge Chapman & Hall.

Role of Government in the United States-Practice & Theory: A Report of a Conference at the College of Public & International Affairs of the American University, Washington, D. C.. March 2-3. 1984. Ed. by Robert E. Cleary. 250p. (Orig.). 1985. lib. bdg 26.75 o.p. (ISBN 0-8191-4798-2); pap. text ed 12.50 o.p. (ISBN 0-8191-4799-0). U Pr of Amer.

Role of History in Religion. Robert Leet Patterson. 1971. 6.50 o.p. (ISBN 0-682-47296 4, University). Exposition-Phoenix.

Role of International Nongovernmental Organizations in World Politics. Werner J. Feld & Roger A. Coate. (CISE Learning Package Ser.: No. 17). (Illus.). 56p. (Orig.). 1976. pap. text ed. 3.00x o.p. (ISBN 0-936876-30-1). LRIS.

Role of Mathematics in the Rise of Science. Salomon Bochner. 1966. 39.50x o.p. (ISBN 0-691-08028-3); pap. 11.50 o.p. (ISBN 0-691-02371-9). Princeton U Pr.

Role of Membranes in Metabolic Regulation: Proceedings of the University of Nebraska Medical School Symposium, Omaha, Neb, May 1972. University of Nebraska Medical School Symposium Staff. Ed. by Myron A. Mehlman & Richard W. Hanson. 1972. 71.50 o.p. (ISBN 0-12-487840-7). Acad Pr.

Role of Nucleotides for the Function & Conformation of Enzymes: Proceedings of the Alfred Benzon Symposium, 1st. Benzon, Alfred, Symposium. Ed. by H. M. Kalckar et al. 1970. 77.00 o.p. (ISBN 0-12-394550-X). Acad Pr.

Role of Outside Counsel in the Business Investigation, Vol. 279. Practising Law Institute Staff. 283p. 1985. pap. 40.00 o.p. (ISBN 0-317-27586-0, #H4-4965). PLI.

Role of Peptides in Neuronal Function. Ed. by J. Barker & T. Smith. 1980. 110.00 o.p. (ISBN 0-8247-6926-0). Dekker.

Role of Pharmacokinetics in Prenatal & Perinatal Toxicology. Ed. by D. Neubert et al. (Illus.). 654p. 1978. text ed. 38.00 o.p. (ISBN 0-88416-293-1). Year Bk Med.

Role of Phoenicians in the Interaction of Mediterranean Civilizations. Ed. by William A. Ward. 1968. 22.95x o.p. (ISBN 0-8156-6011-1, Am U Beirut). Syracuse U Pr.

Role of Probability & Statistics in the Structural Analysis of Pavements: Five Reports. (Transportation Research Record Ser.). 73p. 1976. 3.20 o.p. (ISBN 0-309-02489-7). Transport Res Bd.

Role of Psychiatry in Medical Education: An Appraisal & a Forecast. Sidney L. Werkman. LC 66-10810. (Commonwealth Fund Publications Ser). (Illus.). 1966. 16.00x o.s.i. (ISBN 0-674-77730-1). Harvard U Pr.

Role of RNA in Development & Reproduction: Proceedings of the Second International Symposium April 25-30, 1980. Science Press Staff. 946p. 1981. 71.95 o.p. (ISBN 0-442-20090-0). Van Nos Reinhold.

Role of Rock: A Guide to the Social & Political Consequences of Rock Music. Don Hibbard & Carol Kaleialoha. 216p. 1983. 14.95 o.p. (ISBN 0-13-782458-0); 6.95 o.p. (ISBN 0-13-782441-6). P-H.

Role of Telecommunications in Socio-Economic Development: A Review of the Literature. 50.00 o.p. (ISBN 0-686-32981-3). Info Gatekeepers.

Role of Terrestrial Vegetation in the Global Carbon Cycle: Measurement by Remote Sensing. Ed. by George M. Woodwell. LC 83-10333. (SCOPE Ser.: SCOPE 23). 247p. 1984. 69.95 o.p. (ISBN 0-471-90262-4, 1-409, Pub. by Wiley-Interscience). Wiley.

Role of the Augsburg Confession: Catholic & Lutheran Views. Ed. by Joseph A. Burgess. LC 79-7373. 224p. 1980. 14.95 o.p. (ISBN 0-8006-0549-7, 1-549, Fortress). Augsburg Fortress.

Role of the British Press in the 1976 American Presidential Election. George C. Osborn & Don Martin. LC 80-68861. 187p. 1981. 10.00 o.p. (ISBN 0-682-49667-7). Exposition-Phoenix.

Role of the Congressman. Roger H. Davidson. LC 68-27986. 1969. 29.50x o.p. (ISBN 0-672-53587-4). Irvington.

Role of the European Investment Bank. Sheila Lewenhak. (Illus.). 284p. 1982. 30.00 o.p. (ISBN 0-7099-1613-2, Pub. by Croom Helm Ltd). Routledge Chapman & Hall.

Role of the Faith Mission: A Brazilian Case Study. Fred E. Edwards. LC 79-152406. (Illus.). 139p. 1971. pap. 3.45 o.p. (ISBN 0-87808-406-1). William Carey Lib.

Role of the Library in an Electronic Society: Proceedings of the Clinic on Library Applications of Data Processing 1979. Ed. by F. W. Lancaster. LC 79-19449. 200p. 1980. 9.00 o.p. U of Ill Lib Info Sci.

Role of the Major Histocompatibility Complex in Immunobiology. Martin E. Dorf. LC 80-772. 525p. 1981. lib. bdg. 66.00 o.p. (ISBN 0-8240-7129-8). Garland Pub.

Role of the Mass Media in American Politics. Ed. by L. John Martin & Richard D. Lambert. LC 76-11898. (Annals Ser: No. 427). 200p. 1976. pap. 7.95 o.p. (ISBN 0-87761-205-6). Am Acad Pol Soc Sci.

Role of the Polymeric Matrix in the Processing & Structural Properties Composite Materials. Ed. by James C. Seferis & Luigi Nicolais. LC 82-18895. 696p. 1983. 110.00x o.p. (ISBN 0-306-41134-2, Plenum Pr). Plenum Pub.

Role of the Public Sector in Developing Countries: Bangladesh. Muzaffer Ahmad. (ICPE Country Studies). 146p. 1984. pap. 9.00x o.s.i. (ISBN 92-9038-802-1). Kumarian Pr.

Role of the Public Sector in Developing Countries: Somalia. Abdulkadir H. Deriye. (ICPE Country Studies). 116p. 1983. pap. 9.00x o.s.i. (ISBN 92-9038-801-3). Kumarian Pr.

Role of the Supreme Court: Policymaker or Adjudicator. Sam J. Ervin, Jr. & Ramsey Clark. 85p. 1970. 14.00 o.p. (ISBN 0-8447-2018-6). Am Enterprise.

Role of the Teacher in the Nursery School. Joan E. Cass. 97p. 1975. 35.00 o.p. (ISBN 0-08-018282-8); pap. 35.00 o.p. (ISBN 0-08-018281-X). Pergamon.

Role of the Telephone in Economic Development. Institute for Communication Research, Stanford University Staff. 1980. 50.00 o.s.i. (ISBN 0-686-37965-9). Info Gatekeepers.

Role of Vincent Van Gogh's Copies in the Development of His Art. Charles Chetham. LC 75-23788. (Outstanding Dissertations in the Fine Arts - 19th Century). (Illus.). 1976. lib. bdg. 50.00 o.p. (ISBN 0-8240-1984-9). Garland Pub.

Role of Voluntary Organizations in Social Welfare. Hugh W. Mellor. LC 85-6626. 216p. 1985. 26.00 o.p. (ISBN 0-7099-3581-1, Pub. by Croom Helm Ltd); pap. 12.00 o.p. (ISBN 0-7099-3586-2). Routledge Chapman & Hall.

Role: O'Neill's Cornelius Melody. Lennart Josephson. Tr. by Alan Blair from Swedish. 1978. pap. text ed. 25.00x o.p. (ISBN 0-391-00811-0). Humanities.

Role-Play Technique: A Handbook for Management & Leadership Practice. Norman R. F. Maier et al. LC 74-30943. 290p. 1975. pap. 9.95 o.p. (ISBN 0-88390-104-8). Univ Assocs.

Role Playing: A Practical Manual for Group Facilitators. Malcolm E. Shaw et al. LC 79-67712. 202p. 1980. pap. 10.50 o.p. (ISBN 0-88390-156-0). Univ Assocs.

Role Playing for Managers. J. Towers. 1974. 55.00 o.p. (ISBN 0-08-017827-8); pap. 23.00 o.p. (ISBN 0-08-018984-9). Pergamon.

Role-Playing for Supervisors. J. Maxwell Towers. 1969. pap. text ed. 10.25 o.p. (ISBN 0-08-006711-5). Pergamon.

Role Relationship of Men & Women. George W. Knight, III. 1985. pap. 5.95 o.p. (ISBN 0-8024-7369-5). Moody.

Role Theory. R. C. Hesterman. 320p. 1981. 10.00 o.p. (ISBN 0-682-49812-2). Exposition-Phoenix.

Role Theory: Perspectives for Health Professionals. Ed. by Margaret E. Hardy & Mary Conway. (Illus.). 354p. 1978. 27.50 o.p. (ISBN 0-8385-8471-3). Appleton & Lange.

Roles & Values. R. S. Downie. 1979. pap. 10.95x o.p. (ISBN 0-416-14920-0, NO. 2167). Routledge Chapman & Hall.

Roles of Women & Community Development. Bahir Bilgin. 1978. 4.00 o.p. (ISBN 0-682-49084-9, University). Exposition-Phoenix.

Rolind of Meru. Peter Lyle. 1977. pap. 1.50 o.p. (ISBN 0-380-00981-1, 32581). Avon.

Roll, Justice, Roll! A Salute to Israel. William Richard Simmons. 1978. 4.50 o.p. (ISBN 0-682-49015-6). Exposition-Phoenix.

Roller Skating Book. Lavada Weir. LC 79-19653. (Illus.). 128p. (gr. 4 up). 1979. lib. bdg. 8.29 o.s.i. (ISBN 0-671-33048-9). Messner.

Rolling Files: A Study of the Bible. Cuthbert Melville. 1980. 7.95 o.s.i. (ISBN 0-682-48165-3). Exposition-Phoenix.

Rolling Stone Review 1985: The Year In Rock Music. Ira A. Robbins. (Illus.). 256p. 22.50 o.p. (ISBN 0-684-18333-1, ScribT); pap. 11.95 o.s.i. (ISBN 0-684-18332-3). Scribner.

Rolling Stones A to Z. Sue Weiner & Lisa Howard. LC 83-48291. (Illus.). 256p. 1983. pap. 10.95 o.p. (ISBN 0-394-62000-3, E-879, Ever). Grove.

Rolling Stones in Their Own Words. David Dalton. (Illus.). 128p. 1983. pap. 6.95 o.p. (ISBN 0-399-41007-4, Perigee). Putnam Pub Group.

Rolling Stones: The First Twenty Years. David Dalton. 1982. 24.50 o.p. (ISBN 0-394-52427-6); pap. 13.95 o.p. (ISBN 0-394-70812-1). Knopf.

Rolling Wheels. Carl Framen. 38p. 1985. 6.95 o.p. (ISBN 0-533-06352-3). Vantage.

Rollo Tape's Secret Techniques in Tape Reading & Stock Market Tactics. Rollo Tape. (Illus.). 1977. 145.35 o.p. (ISBN 0-89266-024-4). Am Classical Coll Pr.

Rolls-Royce: The Complete Works-The Best 599 Rolls-Royce Stories. Mike Fox & Steve Smith. 1984. 19.95 o.p. (ISBN 0-571-13363-0); pap. 9.95 o.p. (ISBN 0-571-13364-9). Faber & Faber.

Roly Poly Pudding. Beatrix Potter. (Illus.). (ps-2). 1908. 4.95 o.p. (ISBN 0-7232-0607-4). Warne.

Roman. Roman Polanski. Ed. by Maria D. Guarnaschelli. LC 83-13221. (Illus.). 443p. 1984. 17.95 o.p. (ISBN 0-688-02621-4). Morrow.

Roman Bath Discovered. rev. ed. Barry Cunliffe. 256p. 1984. 30.00x o.p. (ISBN 0-7102-0196-6). Routledge Chapman & Hall.

Roman Britain. Aileen Fox. LC 68-23081. (Illus.). (gr. 7 up). 1968. 13.95 o.p. (ISBN 0-8023-1143-1). Dufour.

Roman by Polanski. Roman Polanski. 448p. 1985. pap. 4.95 o.s.i. (ISBN 0-345-30512-4). Ballantine.

Roman Campagna in Classical Times. Thomas Ashby. LC 78-12509. (Illus.). 1979. Repr. of 1970 ed. lib. bdg. 24.75x o.p. (ISBN 0-313-21115-9, ASRC). Greenwood.

Roman Catholic Theology of Pastoral Care. Regis A. Duffy. LC 83-48006. (Theology & Pastoral Care Ser.). 128p. 1983. pap. 2.50 o.p. (ISBN 0-8006-1727-4, 1-1727, Fortress). Augsburg Fortress.

Roman de Troie, 6 Vols. Benoit de Saint-More. Set. 215.00 o.p. (ISBN 0-384-03915-4); Set. pap. 192.00 o.p. (ISBN 0-384-03916-2). Johnson Repr.

Roman Dynamism: Studies in Ancient Roman Thought Language & Custom. Hendrik Wagenvoort. LC 74-30929. 1976. Repr. of 1947 ed. lib. bdg. 22.50x o.p. (ISBN 0-8371-7887-8, WARD). Greenwood.

Roman Elegists' Attitude Towards Women. Saara Lilja. Ed. by Steele Commager. LC 77-70836. (Latin Poetry Ser.: Vol. 25). 1979. Repr. of 1965 ed. lib. bdg. 37.00 o.p. (ISBN 0-8240-2974-7). Garland Pub.

Roman Empire. Isaac Asimov. (Illus.). (gr. 8-11). 1967. 9.95 o.p. (ISBN 0-395-06577-1). HM.

Roman Engineers. L. A. Hamey & J. A. Hamey. LC 81-13746. (Cambridge Topics Bks.). (Illus.). 52p. (gr. 6 up). 1982. PLB 8.95 o.p. (ISBN 0-8225-1227-0). Lerner Pubns.

Roman England. John Burke. (Illus.). 152p. 1984. 15.45 o.p. (ISBN 0-393-01826-1). Norton.

Roman Imperial Art in Greece & Asia Minor. Cornelius C. Vermeule. LC 67-20886. (Illus.). 1968. 34.50x o.s.i. (ISBN 0-674-77775-1, Belknap Pr). Harvard U Pr.

Roman Lettering. L. C. Evetts. LC 78-72593. 1979. pap. 6.95 o.s.i. (ISBN 0-8008-6822-6, Pentalic). Taplinger.

Roman Life. Mary Johnston. 1957. text ed. write for info. o.p. (ISBN 0-673-05069-6). Scott F.

Roman Magic. Hugh Fleetwood. LC 77-12547. 1978. 7.95 o.p. (ISBN 0-689-10839-7, Atheneum). Macmillan.

Roman Mould of the Australian Catholic Church. J. N. Molony. 1969. 17.50x o.p. (ISBN 0-522-83934-7, Pub by Melbourne U Pr). Intl Spec Bk.

Roman People. Olivia Coolidge. (Illus.). (gr. 7 up). 1959. 3.75 o.p. (ISBN 0-395-06729-4). HM.

Roman Polanski: A Biography. Thomas Kiernan. LC 80-997. (Illus.). 1980. pap. 3.50 o.p. (ISBN 0-394-17945-5, B463, BC). Grove.

Roman Polanski: A Guide to References & Resources. Virginia W. Wexman & Gretchen Bisplinghoff. 1979. lib. bdg. 20.00 o.p. (ISBN 0-8161-7906-9, Hall Reference). G K Hall.

Roman Politics. Frank F. Abbott. LC 63-10295. (Our Debt to Greece & Rome Ser). Repr. of 1930 ed. 15.00 o.p. (ISBN 0-8154-0000-4). Cooper Sq.

Roman Provincial Administration till the Age of the Antonines. George H. Stevenson. LC 75-18364. (Illus.). 182p. 1975. Repr. of 1939 ed. lib. bdg. 22.50x o.p. (ISBN 0-8371-8321-9, STRP). Greenwood.

Roman Republic. Isaac Asimov. (Illus.). (gr. 7 up). 1966. 9.95 o.p. (ISBN 0-395-06576-3). HM.

Roman Satire. Michael Coffey. LC 76-28824. 1976. 16.95x o.p. (ISBN 0-416-85120-7, NO. 2146); pap. 16.95x o.p. (ISBN 0-416-85130-4, NO. 2147). Routledge Chapman & Hall.

Roman Solution. Wallace Henley. (Living Bks.). 128p. 1986. pap. 4.95 o.p. (ISBN 0-8423-5660-6). Tyndale.

Roman Spirit in Religion, Thought & Art. Albert Grenier. Tr. by M. R. Dobie. LC 76-118639. (Illus.). 423p. 1970. Repr. of 1926 ed. lib. bdg. 32.50x o.p. (ISBN 0-8154-0330-5). Cooper Sq.

Roman Stamp: Frame & Facade in Some Forms of Neo-Classicism. Robert M. Adams. LC 72-50241. (Illus.). 1974. 40.00x o.p. (ISBN 0-520-02345-5); pap. 8.95x o.p. (ISBN 0-520-03715-4). U of Cal Pr.

Roman Summer. Jane Arbor. (Nightingale Paperbacks). 1985. pap. 9.95 o.p. (ISBN 0-8161-3872-9, Large Print Bks). G K Hall.

Roman Way. Edith Hamilton. 1981. pap. 2.25 o.p. (ISBN 0-380-01533-1, 51391-9, Discus). Avon.

Roman Way. Edith Hamilton. (gr. 7 up). 1932. 9.25 o.p. (ISBN 0-393-04173-5). Norton.

Romance. Gwen Davis. 1983. 14.50 o.p. (ISBN 0-87795-497-6, Arbor Hse). Morrow.

Romance at Redhaven. Kathleen Yapp. (Chime Romance Ser.: No. 101). 1980. pap. 2.50 o.p. (ISBN 0-89191-292-4). Cook.

Romance in the Roaring Forties & Other Stories. Damon Runyon. LC 85-15788. 324p. (Orig.). 1986. 19.95 o.p. (ISBN 0-688-05421-8, Pub. by Beech Tree Bks). Morrow.

Romance of Architecture. Photos by Roloff Beny. (Illus.). 312p. 1985. 49.50 o.p. (ISBN 0-8109-1589-8). Abrams.

Romance of Dundee. Irma Dupre et al. (Illus.). 360p. 1985. 18.50 o.p. (ISBN 0-916445-12-7). Crossroads Comm.

Romance of London. John Timbs. LC 68-22058. 1004p. 1968. Repr. of 1865 ed. 70.00x o.p. (ISBN 0-8103-3498-4). Gale.

Romance of Money. Duane R. Pappas. (Library of Business Psychology). (Illus.). 119p. 1983. 57.15x o.p. (ISBN 0-86722-024-4). Inst Econ Pol.

Romance of Symbolism & Its Relation to Church Ornament & Architecture. Sidney Heath. LC 70-174054. (Illus.). 282p. 1976. Repr. of 1909 ed. 40.00x o.p. (ISBN 0-8103-4302-9). Gale.

Romance of the Three Kingdoms, 2 Vols. Kuan-Chung Lo. Tr. by C. H. Brewitt-Taylor. LC 59-10407. 1969. Set. boxed 37.50 o.p. (ISBN 0-8048-0726-4). C E Tuttle.

Romance of Tristan & Isolt. Tr. by Norman B. Spector. (Medieval French Texts Ser.). 91p. 1973. text ed. 19.95 o.s.i. (ISBN 0-8101-0405-9). Northwestern U Pr.

Romance of Two Worlds. Marie Corelli. Ed. by Robert L. Wolff. LC 75-484. (Victorian Fiction Ser.). 1975. Repr. of 1886 ed. lib. bdg. 73.00 o.p. (ISBN 0-8240-1561-4). Garland Pub.

Romance of Wine. H. Warner Allen. LC 71-166424. (Illus.). 1971. pap. 3.50 o.p. (ISBN 0-486-21684-5). Dover.

Romances sans Paroles see Bonne Chanson.

Romancing the Stone. Joan Wilder. 1984. pap. 2.95 o.p. (ISBN 0-380-87262-5, 87262). Avon.

Romanesque Art in Europe. Ed. by Gustav Kunstler. (Norton Library Series, N687). (Illus.). 1973. pap. 4.95 o.p. (ISBN 0-393-00687-5, Norton Lib). Norton.

Romanesque Sculpture from the Cathedral of Saint-Etienne, Toulouse. Linda Seidel. LC 76-23646. (Outstanding Dissertations in the Fine Arts). (Illus.). 1977. Repr. of 1965 ed. lib. bdg. 63.00 o.p. (ISBN 0-8240-2729-9). Garland Pub.

Romanesque Sculpture: The Revival of Monumental Stone Sculpture in the Eleventh & the Twelfth Centuries. M. F. Hearn. (Illus.). 365p. 1981. 45.00x o.p. (ISBN 0-8014-1287-0, Pub. by Phaidon England); pap. 19.50x o.p. Cornell U Pr.

Romanian Cook Book. Anisoara Stan. 1969. pap. 2.00 o.p. (ISBN 0-8065-0058-1, Pub. by Citadel Pr). Carol Pub Group.

Romanians in America & Canada: A Guide to Information Sources. Ed. by Vladimir Wertsman. LC 80-191. (Gale Information Guide Library, Ethnic Information Guide Ser.: Vol. 5). 184p. 1980. 68.00x o.p. (ISBN 0-8103-1417-7). Gale.

Romans, Vol. VI. Beacon Bible Expositions Staff. 9.95 o.p. (ISBN 0-8010-0680-5). Baker Bk.

Romans see Word Studies in the Greek New Testament, for the English Reader.

Romans de Jeunesse: Avec: L'Heritiere de Biraque, Jean-Louis ou la Fille Trovee, Clotilde de Lusignan ou le beau Juif, Le Vicaire des Ardennes, 16 vols. facisimile ed. Honore De Balzac. 1964. Set. 395.00 o.p. (ISBN 0-686-53925-7). French & Eur.

Romans Debate: Essays on the Origin & Purpose on the Epistle. Ed. by Karl P. Donfried. LC 77-84082. 1977. pap. 10.95 o.p. (ISBN 0-8066-1607-5, 10-5542, Augsburg). Augsburg Fortress.

Romans et Contes, 10 tomes. Anatole France. Set. 1194.40 o.p. (ISBN 0-685-34116-X). French & Eur.

Romans et Contes, 10 tomes. Anatole France. Incl. Tome I. Thais; Tome II. Lys Rouge; Tome III. Dieux Ont Soif; Tome IV. Crime de Sylvestre Bonnard; Tome V. Rotisserie de la Reine Pedauque; Tome VI. Contes de Jacques Tournebroche, Histoire Contemporaine; Tome VII. Orme du Mail; Tome VIII. Mannequin d'Osier; Tome IX. Anneau d'Amethyste; Tome X. Monsieur Bergeret a Paris. Set. lea. 1623.15 o.p. (ISBN 0-685-34117-8). French & Eur.

Romans, II-Corinthians, Vol. VIII. Beacon Bible Commentary Staff. 15.95 o.p. (ISBN 0-8010-0695-3). Baker Bk.

Romansgrove. Mabel E. Allan. LC 75-9628. (Illus.). 224p. (gr. 5-8). 1975. 6.95 o.p. (ISBN 0-689-30471-4, Atheneum). Macmillan.

Romantic & Classic Cakes. Rose L. Beranbaum. Ed. by Jennifer Sparks. LC 81-68841. (Great American Cooking Schools Ser.). (Illus.). 84p. 1981. pap. 5.95 o.p. (ISBN 0-941034-06-2). I Chalmers.

Romantic Art Theories. August Wiedmann. 192p. 1987. 49.00x o.p. (ISBN 0-946095-24-8, Pub. by Gresham England). State Mutual Bk.

Titles

Romantic Egoists. Louis Auchincloss. LC 73-106666. 1970. Repr. of 1954 ed. lib. bdg. 24.75x o.p. (ISBN 0-8371-3418-8, AUEG). Greenwood.

Romantic Egoists: A Pictorial Autobiography from the Albums of Scott & Zelda Fitzgerald. F. Scott Fitzgerald. Compiled by Scottie F. Smith et al. (Illus.). 1977. Encore Edition. 14.95 o.s.i. (ISBN 0-684-14973-7, ScribT). Scribner.

Romantic Exiles. Edward H. Carr. 391p. 1975. Repr. of 1933 ed. lib. bdg. 27.50x o.p. (ISBN 0-374-91297-1, Octagon). Hippocrene Bks.

Romantic Eye. Photos by Edwin Smith. LC 84-50428. (Illus.). 256p. 1984. 29.95f o.p. (ISBN 0-500-54100-0). Thames Hudson.

Romantic Inns of Mexico: A Selective Guide to Charming Accommodations South of the Border. Toby Smith. LC 85-17153. (Illus.). 144p. 1986. pap. 7.95 o.p. (ISBN 0-87701-333-0). Chronicle Bks.

Romantic Lace Designs. Ondori Publishing Company Staff. (Illus.). 92p. (Orig.). 1984. pap. 6.50 o.p. (ISBN 0-87040-586-1). Japan Pubns USA.

Romantic Movement: A Selective & Critical Bibliography for 1981. David V. Erdman. LC 82-48435. (Romantic Movement Bibliographies Ser.). 417p. 1982. lib. bdg. 55.00 o.p. (ISBN 0-8240-9508-1). Garland Pub.

Romantic Passages in South-Western History: Including Orations, Sketches, & Essays. Alexander B. Meek. LC 74-34423. 336p. 1975. Repr. of 1857 ed. 20.00 o.s.i. (ISBN 0-87152-207-1). Reprint.

Romantic Period: Excluding the Novel, 1 of 7 vols. Intro. by Kenneth Muir. (Great Writers Library). 113p. pap. 7.95 o.p. (ISBN 0-312-34705-7). Academy Chi Pubs.

Romantic Roots in Modern Art. August K. Wiedmann. 304p. 1984. 40.00x o.p. (ISBN 0-905418-51-4, Pub. by Gresham England). State Mutual Bk.

Romantic Vegetarian: A Seasonal Cookbook. Judith Sharlin. (Illus.). 204p. 1984. pap. 9.95 o.p. (ISBN 0-914091-50-6). Chicago Review.

Romantic Ventriloquists: Wordsworth, Coleridge, Keats, Shelley, Byron. rev. ed. Edward E. Bostetter. LC 63-10795. 372p. 1975. 15.00x o.p. (ISBN 0-295-73918-5); pap. 8.00x o.p. (ISBN 0-295-95318-7). U of Wash Pr.

Romanticism & Behavior: Collected Essays, Vol. 2. Morse Peckham. LC 76-29623. x, 390p. 1976. 29.95x o.p. (ISBN 0-87249-328-8). U of SC Pr.

Romanticism & Ideology. David Aers et al. 240p. (Orig.). 1981. pap. 12.95X o.p. (ISBN 0-7100-0781-7). Routledge Chapman & Hall.

Romantics Reviewed: A Collection in Depth of Periodical Reviews (1793-1830, 11 vols. Ed. & intro. by Donald H. Reiman. Incl. Vols. I & II. Pt. A. lib. bdg. 226.00each (ISBN 0-8240-0509-0); Vols. I To V. Pt. B. lib. bdg. 563.00 5 vol. set (ISBN 0-8240-0510-4); Vols. I & II. Pt. C. lib. bdg. 226.00 2 vol. set (ISBN 0-8240-0511-2); Vols. I & II. Bibliography of Literary Reviews in British Periodicals 1798-1820. Ed. by William S. Ward. lib. bdg. 73.00 o.p.. Set. lib. bdg. 740.00 o.p.; lib. bdg. 93.00 o.p. Garland Pub.

Romantik Hotels & Restaurants: Charming Historic Hotels in Europe & the United States. Ed. by The Romantik Hotel & Restaurants Association Staff. (Illus.). 287p. pap. 6.95 o.p. (ISBN 0-916782-91-3, Dist. by Kampmann). Harvard Common Pr.

Rome. Jean Giono et al. 1958. 32.50 o.p. (ISBN 0-686-53988-5). French & Eur.

Rome. Seiyo Kuroda. LC 73-89700. (This Beautiful World Ser.: Vol. 48). (Illus.). 150p. 1974. pap. 4.95 o.p. (ISBN 0-87011-223-6). Kodansha.

Rome. (Berlitz Deluxe Guides). (Illus.). 1988. pap. 10.95 o.p. (ISBN 2-831-50366-3, Berlitz). Macmillan.

Rome. (Berlitz Deluxe Guides). (Illus.). 336p. 1988. 10.95 o.p. (ISBN 0-02-968250-9, Berlitz). Macmillan.

Rome. rev. ed. David Willey. LC 80-50997. (Rand McNally Pocket Guide Ser.). (Illus.). 1985. pap. 5.95 o.p. (ISBN 0-528-84295-1). Rand McNally.

Rome & a Villa. enl. ed. Eleanor Clark. LC 74-5979. (Illus.). 384p. 1982. pap. 8.95 o.p. (ISBN 0-689-70630-8, 1, Atheneum). Macmillan.

Rome & Environs. Alta Macadam. (Blue Guide Ser.). (Illus.). 1982. 24.95 o.p. (ISBN 0-393-01550-5); pap. 14.95 o.p. (ISBN 0-393-30002-1). Norton.

Rome & Jerusalem. Moses Hess. 1958. (ISBN 0-8022-0711-1). Philos Lib.

Rome & Latium Phaidon Cultural Guide. (Phaidon Cultural Guides Ser.). (Illus.). 1987. 17.95 o.p. (ISBN 0-13-782855-1). P-H.

Rome in Rome. Bill Knott. LC 75-44678. 1976. pap. 2.50 o.p. (ISBN 0-913722-07-3, Pub. by Release). Small Pr Dist.

Rome in the Renaissance: The City & the Myth. Ed. by P. A. Ramsey. LC 83-14273. (Medieval & Renaissance Texts & Studies: Vol. 18). (Illus.). 464p. 1982. 22.00 o.p. (ISBN 0-86698-057-1). Medieval & Renaissance NY.

Rome Plenary Meeting of the Trilateral Commission. Trilateral Comm.

Rome 1987-1988. (Frommer's City Guides). 224p. 5.95 o.p. (ISBN 0-671-62362-1). Prentice Hall Pr.

Romeo & Juliet see also Tragedy of Romeo & Juliet.

Romeo & Juliet. William Shakespeare. 48p. (Orig.). 1988. pap. 9.95 o.p. (ISBN 1-55651-781-5); audiocassette tape incl. o.p. (ISBN 1-55651-782-3). Cram Cassettes.

Romewalks. Anya Shetterly. 1984. 9.95 o.s.i. (ISBN 0-03-061913-0). H Holt & Co.

Rommany. Florence Hurd. 1976. pap. 1.95 o.p. (ISBN 0-380-00609-X, 37507). Avon.

Rommel: As Military Commander. Ronald Lewin. 1980. pap. 2.50 o.s.i. (ISBN 0-345-28797-5). Ballantine.

Rommel Papers. Ed. by B. H. Liddell Hart. LC 53-5656. (Illus.). 1953. 17.95 o.p. (ISBN 0-15-178455-8). HarBraceJ.

Rommel the Desert Warrior: The Afrika Korps in World War II. Richard L. Blanco. LC 82-2293. 192p. (gr. 7 up). 1982. PLB 9.79 o.p. (ISBN 0-671-42245-6); pap. 4.95 o.p. (ISBN 0-671-49582-8). Messner.

Romper Room Book of ABC's. Dina Anastasio. LC 84-24651. (Illus.). 32p. (ps-3). 1985. 4.95 o.p. (ISBN 0-385-18313-5). Doubleday.

Romper Room Book of One, Two, Threes. Dina Anastasio. LC 84-24649. (Illus.). 32p. (ps-3). 1985. 4.95 o.p. (ISBN 0-385-18312-7). Doubleday.

Romper Room Book of Shapes. Dina Anastasio. LC 84-24648. (Illus.). 32p. (ps-3). 1985. 4.95 o.p. (ISBN 0-385-18315-1). Doubleday.

Ron. Carl Tiktin. LC 78-57328. 1979. 8.95 o.p. (ISBN 0-87795-198-5, Arbor Hse). Morrow.

Ronald Reagan: Smile, Style & Guile. Harold Jinks. 1986. 16.95 o.p. (ISBN 0-533-06923-8). Vantage.

Ronald Searle in Perspective: The Best of His Work 1938-1985. Ronald Searle. Ed. by Upton Brady & Harold Evans. LC 85-48443. (Illus.). 224p. 1986. 45.00 o.p. (ISBN 0-87113-003-3). Atlantic Monthly.

Ronde. 7.95 o.p. (ISBN 0-317-31486-6, 3635). Routledge Chapman & Hall.

Ronnie & Nancy. Bill Adler. LC 86-5838. 375p. 1986. Repr. of 1985 ed. 15.95 o.p. (ISBN 0-89621-720-5). Thorndike Pr.

Ronnie & Rosey. Judie Angell. LC 77-75362. 269p. (gr. 6-9). 1977. 11.95 o.s.i. (ISBN 0-02-705790-9). Bradbury Pr.

Ronnie & the Great Knitted Robbery. John Antrobus. LC 83-61282. (Illus.). 56p. (gr. 8-10). 1984. 7.50 o.p. (ISBN 0-88186-351-3). Parkwest Pubns.

Ronnie & the Haunted Rolls Royce. John Antrobus. (Illus.). 56p. (gr. 3). 1985. 7.50 o.p. (ISBN 0-88186-352-1). Parkwest Pubns.

Roo! Beverley A. Lewis. LC 85-90123. 155p. 1985. 11.95 o.p. (ISBN 0-533-06625-5). Vantage.

Roof of Africa. David Coulson & James Clarke. LC 84-719. (Illus.). 240p. 1984. 25.00 o.p. (ISBN 0-03-071766-3). H Holt & Co.

Roof of Queensland. Graham Walsh. LC 83-5745. (Illus.). 128p. 1984. 19.95 o.p. (ISBN 0-7022-1833-2). U of Queensland Pr.

Roof over My Head. John Attwood. LC 84-90089. (Illus.). 107p. 1985. 8.95 o.p. (ISBN 0-533-06170-9). Vantage.

Roofing & Waterproofing Manual. 449p. 100.00 o.p. (ISBN 0-317-33666-5); members 85.00 o.p. (ISBN 0-317-33667-3). Assn Phys Plant Admin.

Roofing Ready Reckoner for Timber Roofs of Any Span or Pitch. 2nd ed. Ralph Goss. 75p. 1979. pap. text ed. 11.25x o.p. (ISBN 0-258-96690-4, Pub. by Granada England). Gower Pub Co.

Roofs & Roofing: A Revision of A-557. Mary Vance. (Architecture Ser.: A 1502). 74p. 1985. 11.25 o.p. (ISBN 0-89028-652-3). Vance Biblios.

Rookfleas in the Cellar. Robert Pierik. LC 79-1023. (Illus.). 102p. (gr. 3-6). 1979. 7.95 o.s.i. (ISBN 0-664-32648-X, Westminster). Westminster John Knox.

Rookwood Pottery Potpourri. Virginia R. Cummins. LC 79-92591. (Illus.). 144p. (Orig.). 1980. pap. 26.00 o.p. (ISBN 0-9603818-0-5). C R Leonard & Assocs.

Room Acoustics. Heinrich Kuttruff. LC 73-16149. (Illus.). 298p. 1974. 67.95x o.p. (ISBN 0-470-51105-2). Halsted Pr.

Room for Improvement: Kitchens. Roma Jay & Phyllis Oberman. (Illus.). 120p. 1984. 21.00x o.p. (ISBN 0-572-01269-1). Trans-Atl Phila.

Room Forty: British Naval Intelligence 1914-1918. Patrick Beesley. 1983. 15.95 o.p. (ISBN 0-15-178634-8). HarBraceJ.

Room of Errors. Ladislav Granch. 1985. 15.95 o.p. (ISBN 0-533-06480-5). Vantage.

Room of One's Own. Virginia Woolf. LC 81-47577. (Centenary Editions Ser.). 128p. 1981. 12.95 o.p. (ISBN 0-15-178732-8). HarBraceJ.

Room Outside. John Brookes. LC 84-52803. (Illus.). 448p. 1985. pap. 10.95 o.p. (ISBN 0-500-27137-2). Thames Hudson.

Room to Be People: An Interpretation of the Message of the Bible for Today's World. Jose M. Bonino. Tr. by Vickie Leach from Span. LC 78-14662. 80p. 1979. pap. 4.50 o.p. (ISBN 0-8006-1349-X, 1-1349, Fortress). Augsburg Fortress.

Room to Breathe. Joann B. Guernsey. LC 86-2688. 192p. (gr. 7 up). 1986. 12.70 o.s.i. (ISBN 0-89919-465-6, Pub. by Clarion). Ticknor & Fields.

Room to Move: An Anthology of Australian Women Writers. Ed. by Suzanne Falkiner. 1986. 15.95 o.p. (ISBN 0-531-15019-4). Watts.

Room Upstairs. Norma Levinson. LC 84-5606. 756p. 1984. 15.45 o.p. (ISBN 0-671-52377-5). S&S.

Room with No Number: A Novel. Frank Shingle. 1978. 8.00 o.p. (ISBN 0-682-49182-9, Banner). Exposition-Phoenix.

Room's Dictionary of Confusibles. Adrian Room. 1979. 16.00 o.p. (ISBN 0-7100-0120-7). Routledge Chapman & Hall.

Room's Dictionary of Distinguishables. Adrian Room. 220p. 1981. 13.95 o.p. (ISBN 0-7100-0775-2). Routledge Chapman & Hall.

Room's Dictionary of Distinguishables & Confusibles, 2 vols. Adrian Room. 1981. 23.95 o.p. (ISBN 0-7100-9472-8). Routledge Chapman & Hall.

Roosevelt & Churchill - 1939-1941: The Partnership That Saved the West. Joseph P. Lash. 1976. 12.95 o.p. (ISBN 0-393-05594-9). Norton.

Roosevelt File. Michael Rawcliffe. (Illus.). 96p. (YA) (gr. 9-12). 1980. 17.95 o.p. (ISBN 0-7134-1921-0, Pub. by Batsford England). David & Charles.

Roosevelt: The Lion & the Fox. James M. Burns. LC 56-7920. 1956. 15.00 o.p. (ISBN 0-15-178869-3). HarBraceJ.

Roosevelt: The Lion & the Fox. James M. Burns. Bd. with Roosevelt: The Soldier of Freedom. 1970. boxed set 30.00 o.p. (ISBN 0-15-178872-3). HarBraceJ.

Roosevelt: The Soldier of Freedom. James M. Burns. LC 71-95877. 1970. 15.00 o.p. (ISBN 0-15-178871-5). HarBraceJ.

Roosevelt: The Soldier of Freedom see Roosevelt: The Lion & the Fox.

Root Diseases & Soil-Borne Pathogens. Ed. by T. A. Toussoun et al. LC 73-84531. (Illus.). 1970. 60.00x o.p. (ISBN 0-520-01582-7). U of Cal Pr.

Root of All Evil. E. X. Ferrars. (Large Print Books). 1985. lib. bdg. 14.95 o.p. (ISBN 0-8161-3879-6). G K Hall.

Root of the Vine. A. Fricrichsen et al. 168p. 1953. (ISBN 0-8022-0543-7). Philos Lib.

Rooted Sorrow. Nancy Hedberg. 288p. 1987. pap. 6.95 o.p. (ISBN 0-8423-5713-0). Tyndale.

Rootomom Tree. Margret Elbow. (Illus.). 1978. 5.95 o.p. (ISBN 0-395-26452-9). HM.

Roots & Branches: Current Directions in Slave Studies. Michael Craton. LC 79-22464. 304p. 1980. 75.00 o.p. (ISBN 0-08-025367-9). Pergamon.

Roots & Wings: Talks on Zen. Bhagwan S. Rajneesh. (Orig.). 1979. pap. 9.95 o.p. (ISBN 0-7100-0420-6). Routledge Chapman & Hall.

Roots: Family Histories of Familiar Words. Peter Davies. (Illus.). 224p. 1981. text ed. 24.95 o.p. (ISBN 0-07-015449-X). McGraw.

Roots in the Soil. Johnson D. Hill & Walter E. Stuermann. LC 63-18054. 176p. 1964. (ISBN 0-8022-0719-7). Philos Lib.

Roots of a Black Future: Family & Church. J. Deotis Roberts. LC 80-16788. 152p. 1980. pap. 8.95 o.s.i. (ISBN 0-664-24333-9, Westminster). Westminster John Knox.

Roots of American Loyalty. Merle Curti. LC 68-16409. 1968. pap. 2.75 o.p. (ISBN 0-689-70057-1, 115, Atheneum). Macmillan.

Roots of Anti-Semitism: In the Age of Renaissance & Reformation. Heiko A. Oberman. Tr. by James I. Porter from Ger. LC 83-5695. 163p. 1983. 4.20 o.p. (ISBN 0-8006-0709-0, 1-709, Fortress). Augsburg Fortress.

Roots of Capitalism in Western Civilization. Irving S. Michelman. LC 82-83776. (Illus.). 328p. 1983. 17.95 o.p. (ISBN 0-8119-0486-5). Fell.

Roots of Crime: What You Need to Know about Crime & What You Can Do about It. Eda J. LeShan. LC 85-247. 192p. (YA) (gr. 7 up). 1985. Repr. of 1981 ed. 12.95 o.s.i. (ISBN 0-02-756430-4, Four Winds). Macmillan.

Roots of Crisis in Southern Africa. Ann Seidman. LC 85-72995. 1985. 19.95 o.p. (ISBN 0-86543-025-X); pap. 8.95 o.p. (ISBN 0-86543-026-8). Africa World.

Roots of Evil: Weird Stories of Supernatural Plants. Ed. by Michel Parry. LC 75-29661. 192p. 1976. 7.95 o.s.i. (ISBN 0-8008-6837-4). Taplinger.

Roots of Indian Art. S. P. Gupta. (Illus.). 1980. text ed. 105.00x o.p. (ISBN 0-391-02172-9). Humanities.

Roots of Language. Derek Bickerton. (Illus.). xiii, 351p. 1985. pap. 19.50 o.p. (ISBN 0-89720-044-6). Karoma.

Roots of Life: A Layman's Guide to Genes, Evolution & the Ways of Cells. Mahlon B. Hoagland. 1979. pap. 2.75 o.p. (ISBN 0-380-48041-7, 48041-7, Discus). Avon.

Roots of Life: A Layman's Guide to Genes, Evolution, & the Ways of Cells. Mahlon B. Hoagland. 1977. 11.95 o.p. (ISBN 0-395-25811-1). HM.

Roots of Lomomba: Mongo Land. rev ed. Alexander J. Reid. 1979. 9.00 o.p. (ISBN 0-682-49008-3). Exposition-Phoenix.

Roots of Psychotherapy. Carl A. Whitaker & Thomas P. Malone. LC 80-24437. (Brunner Mazel Classics in Psychoanalysis & Psychotherapy: No. 9). 272p. 1981. Repr. 27.50 o.p. (ISBN 0-87630-265-7). Brunner-Mazel.

Roots of the Reorganization: French Polynesia. F. Edward Butterworth. LC 77-944. (Illus.). 1977. pap. 8.00 o.p. (ISBN 0-8309-0176-0). Herald Hse.

Roots of the Synoptic Gospels. Bo Reicke. LC 85-45485. 224p. 1986. 22.95 o.p. (ISBN 0-8006-0766-X, 1-766, Fortress). Augsburg Fortress.

Roots of Totalitarianism: The Ideological Sources of Fascism, National Socialism, and Communism. J. Lucien Radel. 218p. 1975. text ed. 19.50x o.p. (ISBN 0-8448-0374-X, Pub. by Crane Russak & Co); pap. text ed. 14.50x o.p. (ISBN 0-8448-0600-5). Taylor & Francis.

Roots of Treason: Ezra Pound & the Secret of St. Elizabeth's. E. F. Torrey. 384p. 1983. text ed. 19.95 o.p. (ISBN 0-07-064983-9). McGraw.

Roots of Treason: Ezra Pound & the Secret of St. Elizabeths. E. Fuller Torrey. LC 84-10727. (Illus.). 368p. 1984. pap. 9.95 o.p. (ISBN 0-15-679015-7, Harv). HarBraceJ.

Rope, Twine & Net Making. Anthony Sanctuary. (Shire Album Ser.: No. 51). (Illus.). 32p. 1980. pap. 2.95 o.p. (ISBN 0-85263-502-8, Pub. by Shire Pubns England). Seven Hills Bk Dists.

Ropes of Sand: America's Failure in the Middle East. Wilbur C. Eveland. 1980. 14.95 o.p. (ISBN 0-393-01336-7). Norton.

Rosa: A True Story. Lilian L. Hansen. LC 83-91478. (Illus.). 168p. 1985. 10.95 o.p. (ISBN 0-533-06071-0). Vantage.

Rosa Luxemburg: Her Life & Work. Paul Frolich. Tr. by Johanna Hoornweg from Ger. LC 72-81776. 352p. (Orig.). 1972. pap. 6.95 o.p. (ISBN 0-85345-260-1). Monthly Rev.

Rosa Luxemburg, Women's Liberation & Marx's Philosophy of Revolution. Raya Dunayavskaya. 260p. 1982. text ed. 19.95x o.p. (ISBN 0-391-02569-4); pap. text ed. 10.95x o.p. (ISBN 0-391-02793-X). Humanities.

Rosa May: The Search for a Mining Camp Legend. George Willliams, III. Ed. by Bill Dalton. (Illus.). 240p. 1986. 14.95 o.p. (ISBN 0-935174-21-4); pap. 9.95 o.p. (ISBN 0-935174-22-2). Tree by River.

Rosary Murders. William X. Kienzle. 1979. 9.95 o.p. (ISBN 0-8362-6101-1). Andrews & McMeel.

Rosa's Song: The Life & Ministry of Rosa Page Welch. Rosa P. Welch & Oma L. Myers. LC 84-1882. 224p. 1984. pap. 8.95x o.p. (ISBN 0-8272-3210-1). CBP.

Roscius Anglicanus: An Historical Review of the Stage see Historia Histrionica: An Historical Account of the English Stage.

Rose & the Sword. Joan Mattingly. 352p. (Orig.). 1981. pap. 2.75 o.p. (ISBN 0-8439-0994-3, Pub. by Leisure Bks CT). Dorchester Pub Co.

Rose & the Yew Tree. Mary Westmacott. LC 77-150378. 256p. 1981. pap. 6.95 o.p. (ISBN 0-87795-351-1, Arbor Hse). Morrow.

Rose & the Yew Tree. Mary Westmacott. LC 77-150378. 1971. 5.95 o.p. (ISBN 0-87795-014-8, Arbor Hse). Morrow.

Rose de Sable. Henry De Montherlant. 20.95 o.p. (ISBN 0-685-36985-4). Schoenhof.

Rose de Sable. Henry de Montherlant. 600p. 1968. 12.95 o.p. (ISBN 0-686-55532-5). Schoenhof.

Rose of Dutcher's Coolly. Hamlin Garland. Ed. by Donald Pizer. LC 79-82509. xxxiii, 404p. 1970. pap. 5.95 o.p. (ISBN 0-8032-5071-1, BB 506, Bison). U of Nebr Pr.

Rose of the West. Jaimy Gordon. 1976. 10.00 o.p. (ISBN 0-916258-01-7); pap. 5.00 o.p. (ISBN 0-916258-00-9). Woodbine Pr.

Rose Painting Designs. 27.50x o.p. (ISBN 829-90-7140-2, N606). Vanous.

Roselynde. Roberta Gellis. (Roselynde Chronicles Ser.). 1984. lib. bdg. 13.95 o.p. (ISBN 0-8398-2860-8, Gregg). G K Hall.

Rosenberg File: A Search for the Truth. Ronald Radosh & Joyce Milton. LC 82-15569. 703p. 1983. 22.50 o.p. (ISBN 0-03-049036-7). H Holt & Co.

Rosencrantz & Guildenstern Are Dead. Tom Stoppard. 1967. 10.00 o.s.i. (ISBN 0-394-50380-5, GP817). Grove.

Rosencrantz & Guildenstern Are Dead. Tom Stoppard. (Orig.). 1967. pap. 4.95 o.p. (ISBN 0-394-17260-4, B319, BC). Grove.

Roses. 4th ed. Sunset Magazine & Books Editors. LC 79-90334. (Illus.). 96p. 1980. pap. 6.95 o.p. (ISBN 0-376-03656-7, Sunset Bks). Sunset-Lane.

Rosh Hashanah & Yom Kippur. Howard Greenfeld. LC 79-4818. (Illus.). 32p. (gr. 2-9). 1979. 6.95 o.p. (ISBN 0-03-044756-9). H Holt & Co.

Rosie the Riveter Revisited: Women, the War & Social Change. Sherna B. Gluck. 1987. lib. bdg. 19.95x o.s.i. (ISBN 0-8057-9022-5, Twayne). G K Hall.

Rosie's Birthday Present. Marietta D. Moskin. LC 81-2220. (Illus.). 32p. (ps-2). 1981. PLB 10.95 o.s.i. (ISBN 0-689-30854-X, Atheneum Childrens Bks). Macmillan.

Rosie's Wonderful Dances. Lyndsay Thwaites. LC 84-71671. (Illus.). 32p. (ps-2). 1984. 8.95 o.p. (ISBN 0-233-97632-9). Andre Deutsch.

Ross Forgery. William H. Hallahan. 1975. pap. 1.50 o.p. (ISBN 0-380-00296-5, 23267). Avon.

Ross MacDonald. Matthew J. Bruccoli. (Album Biography Ser.). (Illus.). 1984. 14.95 o.p. (ISBN 0-15-179009-4). HarbraceJ.

Rossetti-Leyland Letters: The Correspondence of an Artist & His Patron. Ed. by Francis L. Fennell, Jr. LC 75-14552. xxxiv, 111p. 1978. 12.00x o.p. (ISBN 0-8214-0207-2). Ohio U Pr.

Rossini a Biography. Herbert Weinstock. 560p. Repr. of 1968 ed. lib. bdg. 69.00 o.p. (Pub. by Am Repr Serv). Reprint Servs.

Roster '87. write for info. o.p. County Super Assn CA.

Rotary Wing Flight. 124p. pap. 14.95 o.p. Av Suppl & Acad.

Rotating Electrical Equipment Testing, 2 vols. Ed. by R. L. Caton et al. (Engineering Craftsmen: No. G22). (Illus.). 1969. Set. spiral bdg. 69.95x o.p. (ISBN 0-85083-072-9). Trans-Atl Phila.

Rotating Electrical Equipment Winding & Building, 2 vols. Ed. by R. T. Anderson et al. (Engineering Craftsmen: No. G2). (Illus.). 1969. Set. spiral bdg. 79.95x o.p. (ISBN 0-85083-030-3). Trans-Atl Phila.

Rotating Fluids in Geophysics. Ed. by P. H. Roberts & A. M. Soward. 1979. 76.00 o.p. (ISBN 0-12-589650-6). Acad Pr.

Rotational Dynamics of Orbiting Gyrostats: Proceedings of CISM, Department for General Mechanics, Dubrovnik, 1971. CISM (International Center for Mechanical Sciences), Department for General Mechanics Staff. Ed. by R. Roberson et al. (CISM Publications: No. 102). (Illus.). 208p. 1974. pap. 23.10 o.p. (ISBN 0-387-81198-2). Springer-Verlag.

Rotational Spectra & Molecular Structure. James E. Wollrab. (Physical Chemistry Ser.: Vol. 13). 1967. 88.50 o.p. (ISBN 0-12-762150-4). Acad Pr.

Rotha on the Film. Paul Rotha. Ed. by Bruce S. Kupelnick. LC 76-52126. (Classics of Film Literature Ser.). 1978. lib. bdg. 23.00 o.p. (ISBN 0-8240-2892-9). Garland Pub.

Rothschilds: A Family Portrait. Frederic Morton. LC 62-7938. (Illus.). (YA) 1962. 10.95 o.p. (ISBN 0-689-10204-6, Atheneum). Macmillan.

Rotisserie de la Reine Pedauque see Romans et Contes.

Rotisserie League Baseball. Rotisserie League Staff. Ed. by Glen Waggoner. 1984. pap. 8.95 o.p. (ISBN 0-553-34081-6). Bantam.

Rotor Dynamical Instability. Ed. by M. L. Adams, Jr. (AMD Ser.: Vol. 55). 100p. 1983. pap. text ed. 24.00 o.p. (ISBN 0-317-02645-3, G00227). ASME.

Rottweiler. Judy Elsden & Lary Elsden. (Illus.). 200p. 1988. 29.95 o.s.i. (ISBN 0-09-171400-1, Pub. by Century Hutchinson). David & Charles.

Rough Guide to Amsterdam. Martin Dunford & Jack Holland. (Rough Guide). 1988. pap. 11.95 o.p. (ISBN 0-7102-1191-0, Pub. by Routledge UK). Routledge Chapman & Hall.

Rough Guide to Amsterdam & Holland. Martin Dunford & Jack Holland. (Routledge Rough Guides Ser.). 192p. (Orig.). 1984. pap. 8.95 o.p. (ISBN 0-7102-0158-3). Routledge Chapman & Hall.

Rough Guide to Brittany & Normandy. Greg Ward. (Rough Guide). 1988. pap. 11.95 o.p. (ISBN 0-7102-1119-8, Pub. by Routledge UK). Routledge Chapman & Hall.

Rough Guide to China. Rhonda Evans et al. (Illus.). 500p. 1987. pap. 12.95 o.p. (ISBN 0-7102-0423-X). Routledge Chapman & Hall.

Rough Guide to France. Kate Baillie et al. 475p. 1986. pap. 11.95 o.p. (ISBN 0-7102-0438-8). Routledge Chapman & Hall.

Rough Guide to Greece. rev. ed. Mark Ellingham et al. (Routledge Rough Guides Ser.). 320p. 1984. pap. 7.95 o.p. (ISBN 0-7102-0311-X). Routledge Chapman & Hall.

Rough Guide to Greece. Mark Ellingham et al. (Rough Guide). 1987. pap. 10.95 o.p. (ISBN 0-7102-1189-9, Pub. by Routledge UK). Routledge Chapman & Hall.

Rough Guide to Kenya. Richard Trillo. (Illus.). 300p. 1987. pap. 12.95 o.p. (ISBN 0-7102-0616-X). Routledge Chapman & Hall.

Rough Guide to Mexico. Jack Fisher. (Routledge Rough Guides Ser.). 232p. (Orig.). 1985. pap. 9.95 o.p. (ISBN 0-7102-0059-5). Routledge Chapman & Hall.

Rough Guide to Morocco. Mark Ellington & Shaun McViegh. (Routledge Rough Guides Ser.). 232p. (Orig.). 1985. pap. 11.95 o.p. (ISBN 0-7102-0153-2). Routledge Chapman & Hall.

Rough Guide to New York. Jack Holland & Martin Dunford. (Illus.). 240p. 1987. pap. 9.95 o.p. (ISBN 0-317-56855-8). Routledge Chapman & Hall.

Rough Guide to Paris. Kate Baillie & Tim Salmon. (Illus.). 240p. 1987. pap. 11.95 o.p. (ISBN 0-7102-0712-3). Routledge Chapman & Hall.

Rough Guide to Peru. Dilwyn Jenkins & Clare Jenkins. (Routledge Rough Guides Ser.). 264p. (Orig.). 1985. pap. 9.95 o.p. (ISBN 0-7102-0058-7). Routledge Chapman & Hall.

Rough Guide to Portugal. rev. ed. Mark Ellingham et al. (Routledge Rough Guides Ser.). 224p. 1984. pap. 7.95 o.p. (ISBN 0-7102-0345-4). Routledge Chapman & Hall.

Rough Guide to Spain. rev. ed. Mark Ellingham & John Fisher. (Routledge Rough Guide Ser.). (Illus.). 250p. (Orig.). 1985. pap. 9.95 o.p. (ISBN 0-7102-0344-6). Routledge Chapman & Hall.

Rough Guide to Tunisia. Peter Morris. (Routledge Rough Guides Ser.). 192p. (Orig.). 1985. pap. 7.95 o.p. (ISBN 0-7102-0148-6). Routledge Chapman & Hall.

Rough Guide to Yugoslavia. John McGhie et al. (Routledge Rough Guides Ser.). 224p. (Orig.). 1985. pap. 9.95 o.p. (ISBN 0-7102-0159-1). Routledge Chapman & Hall.

Rough Justice. LC 79-50482. (Mary Elizabeth Braddon Ser.: Vol. 12). 1980. Repr. of 1898 ed. lib. bdg. 46.00 o.p. (ISBN 0-8240-4361-8). Garland Pub.

Rough Road. Margaret M. MacPherson. LC 65-21701. (Illus.). (gr. 7 up). 1966. 4.75 o.p. (ISBN 0-15-269147-2, HJ). HarbraceJ.

Roughing It in the Bush; Or, Life in Canada, 2 vols. Susannah Moodie. LC 70-104530. 451p. 1986. Repr. of 1852 ed. lib. bdg. 56.50 o.p. (ISBN 0-8290-1929-4). Irvington.

Roughing It with Charlie, "C" Co., 2nd. Ranger Btn. 2nd ed. Edwin M. Sorvisto. LC 78-71271. (Illus.). 1978. pap. 5.95x o.p. (ISBN 0-932572-02-2). Phillips Pubns.

Roughneck: A Novel. Warren P. Garretson. 1985. 12.95 o.p. (ISBN 0-533-06568-2). Vantage.

Roughneck: The Life & Times of Big Bill Haywood. Peter Carlson. (Illus.). 1983. 17.00 o.p. (ISBN 0-393-01621-8). Norton.

Roughneck: The Life & Times of Big Bill Haywood. Peter Carlson. (Illus.). 352p. 1984. pap. 6.70 o.p. (ISBN 0-393-30208-3). Norton.

Roughshod. Thomas W. Shaw. 208p. (Orig.). 1982. pap. 2.25 o.s.i. (ISBN 0-449-14503-4, GM). Fawcett.

Round about & Long Ago. Eileen Colwell. (Illus.). 128p. (gr. 3-7). 1974. 4.95 o.p. (ISBN 0-395-18515-7). HM.

Round about Midnight: A Portrait of Miles Davis. Eric Nisenson. LC 82-2507. (Illus.). 256p. 1982. pap. 10.95 o.p. (ISBN 0-385-27232-4, Dial). Doubleday.

Round Dance Book. Lloyd Shaw. LC 49-7327. (Illus.). 1948. 5.00 o.p. (ISBN 0-87004-154-1). Caxton.

Round Valley Songs. William Oandasan. 64p. (Orig.). 1984. pap. 4.00 o.p. (ISBN 0-931122-35-X). West End.

Roundball Culture: South Carolina Basketball. Dan Klores. LC 79-91433. (College Sports Ser.). (Illus.). 275p. 1980. 9.95 o.p. (ISBN 0-87397-156-6). Strode.

Rounds. Frederick Busch. 244p. 1980. 9.95 o.p. (ISBN 0-374-25258-0). FS&G.

Rous Sarcoma: Current Research I. Peter Duesberg et al. LC 72-10910. (Illus.). 220p. 1973. text ed. 29.00x o.p. (ISBN 0-8422-7063-9). Irvington.

Rous Sarcoma: Current Research II. new ed. Sen-Itiroh Hakomori et al. LC 72-10910. (Illus.). 160p. 1973. text ed. 29.00x o.p. (ISBN 0-8422-7075-2). Irvington.

Rousseau's Political Writings. Jean-Jacques Rousseau. Ed. by Alan Ritter. Tr. by Julia Bondanella. (Critical Editions Ser.). 1987. pap. text ed. 17.95x o.p. (ISBN 0-393-02479-2). Norton.

Routes of Contagion. Andre Siegfried. LC 63-8087. (Illus.). 1965. 3.50 o.p. (ISBN 0-15-179010-8). HarBraceJ.

Routines in Neonatal Care. Cooke. 1986. 35.00 o.p. (ISBN 0-8016-1121-0). Mosby.

Rover 2000 & 2200 '63 - '73. J. H. Haynes & B. L. Chalmers Hunt. (Owners Workshop Manuals Ser.: No. 034). 1978. 15.95 o.p. (ISBN 0-85696-496-4, Pub. by J H Haynes England). Haynes Pubns.

Row of Tigers. Barbara Corcoran. LC 69-13523. 1969. 4.25 o.p. (ISBN 0-689-20070-6, Atheneum). Macmillan.

Rowing Toward Eden. Ted Morgan. 256p. 1981. 10.95 o.p. (ISBN 0-395-29714-1). HM.

Roy Campbell: A Descriptive & Annotated Bibliography. D. S. Parsons. LC 79-7930. (Illus.). 306p. 1980. lib. bdg. 43.00 o.p. (ISBN 0-8240-9526-X). Garland Pub.

Roy Lichtenstein. Ed. by Jack Cowart. (Illus.). 180p. (Ger.). 1983. 50.00 o.p. (ISBN 3-7913-0589-1, Pub. by Prestel). TeNeues.

Roy Lichtenstein: Landscape Sketches 1984-1985. Ed. by Constance Glenn & Jack Glenn. (Abrams Facsimile Reproduction Sketchbook Ser.). (Illus.). 1986. 75.00 o.p. (ISBN 0-8109-1264-3); deluxe ed. 250.00 o.p. (ISBN 0-8109-4997-0). Abrams.

Roy Stryker Papers Nineteen Hundred Twelve to Nineteen Seventy-Two: A Guide to the Microfilm Edition. Ed. by David G. Horvath. 142p. 1982. pap. 75.00 o.p. (ISBN 0-667-00697-4). Chadwyck-Healey.

Royal Abbey of Saint-Denis in the Time of Abbot Suger (1122-1151) Sumner M. Crosby et al. Ed. by Ellen Shultz. LC 80-28849. (Illus.). 128p. 1981. pap. 12.95 o.p. (ISBN 0-87099-261-9). Metro Mus Art.

Royal African Company. K. G. Davies. LC 57-6673. 1970. pap. 3.45 o.p. (ISBN 0-689-70239-6, NL24, Atheneum). Macmillan.

Royal Air Force Between the Wars. Raymond L. Rimell. (Vintage Warbirds Ser.: No. 3). (Illus.). 64p. (Orig.). 1985. pap. 9.95 o.p. (ISBN 0-85368-703-X, Pub. by Arms & Armour). Sterling.

Royal Bastards of Medieval England. C. Given-Wilson & A. Curteis. (Illus.). 200p. 1984. 25.00x o.p. (ISBN 0-7102-0025-0). Routledge Chapman & Hall.

Royal Blood. Alissa Channing. 96p. 1980. pap. 1.95 o.p. (ISBN 0-380-77743-6, 77743). Avon.

Royal Canadian Academy of Arts: Exhibitions & Members, 1880-1979. Ed. by Evelyn McMann. 464p. 1981. 80.00x o.p. (ISBN 0-8020-2366-5). U of Toronto Pr.

Royal College of Physicians & Surgeons of Canada, 1920-1960. D. Sclater Lewis. (Illus.). 266p. 1962. 9.00 o.p. (ISBN 0-7735-9052-8, McGill Canada). U of Toronto Pr.

Royal College of San Carlos: Surgery & Spanish Medical Reform in the Late Eighteenth Century. Michael E. Burke. LC 76-50237. xv, 215p. 1977. 21.75 o.p. (ISBN 0-8223-0382-5). Duke.

Royal Correspondence of the Assyrian Empire. Ed. by Leroy Waterman. Vols. 17, 18. 31.00 ea. o.p. (ISBN 0-384-38817-5); 74.00 o.p. vols. 19 & 20 bound in 1 vol (ISBN 0-384-38819-1). Johnson Repr.

Royal Faces: Nine Hundred Years of British Monarchy. Hugh Clayton. LC 82-80980. (Illus.). 1982. 14.95 o.p. (ISBN 0-500-01287-3). Thames Hudson.

Royal Family Pop-Up. L. Leete-Hodge. 12p. 1984. 9.98 o.s.i. (ISBN 0-517-44650-2, Pub. by Bounty). Outlet Bk Co.

Royal Family: Years of Transition. Theo Aronson. (Illus.). 272p. 1984. 19.95 o.p. (ISBN 0-7195-4084-4). Salem Hse Pubs.

Royal Feud: The Dark Side of the Love Story of the Century. Michael Thornton. 1985. 17.45 o.s.i. (ISBN 0-671-60298-5). S&S.

Royal Flying Corps in World War I. Raymond L. Rimell. (Vintage Warbirds Ser.: No. 1). (Illus.). 64p. (Orig.). 1985. pap. 9.95 o.p. (ISBN 0-85368-693-9, Pub. by Arms & Armour). Sterling.

Royal Handbook. Alan Hamilton. (Illus.). 176p. 1986. 12.95 o.p. (ISBN 0-13-783358-X). P-h.

Royal Heritage: The Treasures of the Kings & Queens of England. J. H. Plumb & Huw Wheldon. LC 77-3832. (Illus.). 1977. 25.00 o.p. (ISBN 0-15-179011-6). HarBraceJ.

Royal House of Stuart: The Descendants of King James VI of Scotland, James I of England, 3 Vols. A. C. Addington. (Illus.). 1976. Set. 175.00 o.p. (ISBN 0-317-27392-2). E J Brill USA.

Royal Hymns of Shulgi, King of Ur: Man's Quest for Immortal Fame. Jacob Klein. LC 81-65929. (Transactions Ser.: Vol. 71, Pt. 7.). 1981. 10.00 o.p. (ISBN 0-87169-717-3). Am Philos.

Royal Kingdom of Egypt Military Decorations & Medals: Pre-1952 (French Version) David V. Olson. 75p. 1987. pap. 10.00 o.p. WW Milit Exch.

Royal London Guide & Streetfinder. o.p. Salem Hse Pubs.

Royal Marines Commandos Fitness & Survival Skills. John Watney. (Illus.). 176p. 1988. 17.95 o.p. (ISBN 0-7153-8716-2). David & Charles.

Royal Mistress. Patricia C. Horton. 1977. pap. 1.95 o.p. (ISBN 0-380-01713-X, 33886). Avon.

Royal Palaces of France. Ian Dunlop. (Illus.). 282p. 1985. 34.50 o.p. (ISBN 0-393-02222-6). Norton.

Royal Parks of London. Guy Williams. (Illus.). 234p. 1985. o.p. (ISBN 0-89733-146-X); pap. 8.95 o.s.i. (ISBN 0-89733-145-1). Academy Chi Pubs.

Royal Priesthood. Nolan P. Howington. LC 85-22376. 1986. pap. 4.95 o.p. (ISBN 0-8054-1622-6). Broadman.

Royal Reach. Lamm. 11.95 o.p. (ISBN 0-87306-133-0). Feldheim.

Royal Review. Tim Graham. 1985. pap. 8.95 o.p. (ISBN 0-03-000133-1, Owl Bks). H Holt & Co.

Royal Service. Stephen P. Barry. (General Ser.). 387p. 1983. lib. bdg. 14.95 o.p. (ISBN 0-8161-3530-4, Large Print Bks). G K Hall.

Royal Singles. Christopher Egerton-Thomas. (Illus.). 176p. (Orig.). 1985. pap. 9.95 o.p. (ISBN 0-671-49634-4, Fireside). S&S.

Royal Society & Its Dining Clubs. T. E. Allibone. LC 75-35793. 1976. 62.00 o.p. (ISBN 0-08-020493-7). Pergamon.

Royal Sunset: The European Dynasties & the Great War. Gordon Brooke-Shepherd. LC 86-19859. (Illus.). 312p. 1987. 19.95 o.s.i. (ISBN 0-385-19849-3). Doubleday.

Royal Touch: Sacred Monarchy & Scrofula in England & France. Marc Bloch. Tr. by J. E. Anderson. (Illus.). 496p. 1973. 25.00x o.p. (ISBN 0-7735-0071-5, McGill Canada). U of Toronto Pr.

Royal Trains: From Queen Victoria to the Present. Patrick Kingston & Geoffrey Kichenside. (Illus.). 192p. 1986. 39.95 o.p. (ISBN 0-7153-8594-1). David & Charles.

Royal Victoria Hospital Eighteen Eighty-Seven to Nineteen Forty-Seven. D. Sclater Lewis. 352p. 1969. 10.00 o.p. (ISBN 0-7735-9073-0, McGill Canada). U of Toronto Pr.

Royal Web: The Story of Princess Victoria & Frederick of Prussia. Ladislas Farago & Andrew Sinclair. (Illus.). 384p. 1982. text ed. 12.95 o.p. (ISBN 0-07-019941-8). McGraw.

Royal Worcester Porcelain. Henry Sandon. (Illus.). 308p. 1979. 45.00 o.p. (ISBN 0-214-20580-0, Pub. by Barrie & Jenkins England). Seven Hills Bk Dists.

Royal Year. Tim Graham. 1983. pap. 7.95 o.s.i. (ISBN 0-03-064168-3). H Holt & Co.

Royalty for Commoners: The Complete Known Ancestry of John of Gaunt, Son of Edward III, King of England, & Queen Phillippa. Roderick W. Stuart. xi, 292p. 1988. 21.50 o.p. (ISBN 1-55613-097-X). Heritage Bk.

Royce on the Human Self. James H. Cotton. LC 69-10080. (Illus.). 1968. Repr. of 1954 ed. lib. bdg. 35.00x o.p. (ISBN 0-8371-0053-4, COHS). Greenwood.

Roycroft Furniture: 1906 Catalog. (Illus.). 52p. 1985. pap. 4.95 o.p. (ISBN 0-87905-413-1). Gibbs Smith Pub.

Rozenburg: Monographie Einer Manufaktur 1883-1917. T. Van Velzen. (Illus.). 224p. (Ger.). 1985. 45.00 o.p. (ISBN 3-921811-32-5, Pub. by Kunst & Antiquitaten West Germany). Seven Hills Bk Dists.

RSVP: The Houghton Mifflin Reading, Study, & Vocabulary Program. James F. Shepherd. LC 80-82698. (Illus.). 352p. 1981. pap. 12.95 o.p. (ISBN 0-395-29342-1). HM.

Rubaiyat of Omar Khayyam. Omar Khayyam. Tr. by Edward Fitzgerald. 1960. pap. 0.70 o.p. (ISBN 0-380-18770-1, Bard). Avon.

Rubella Handicapped Children: The Effects of Bi-Lateral Cataract & Or Hearing Impairment on Behavior & Learning. J. Van Dijk. (Modern Approaches to the Diagnosis & Instructions of Multi-Handicapped Children: Vol. 16). xiv, 254p. 1982. text ed. 25.50 o.p. (ISBN 90-265-0432-2, Pub. by Swets & Zeitlinger Netherlands). CJ Hogrefe Pubs.

Rubens & the Book: Title Pages by Peter Paul Rubens (1977) Ed. by Julius S. Held. (Illus.). 1978. pap. 15.00 o.s.i. (ISBN 0-685-87096-0). E J Brill USA.

Rubens: The Antwerp Altarpieces. Rubens. Ed. by John R. Martin. LC 68-20828. (Critical Studies in Art History Ser). (Illus.). 1969. pap. text ed. 6.95x o.p. (ISBN 0-393-09862-1). Norton.

Rubout at the Onyx. H. Paul Jeffers. LC 81-5709. (Joan Kahn Bk). 192p. 1981. 10.95 o.p. (ISBN 0-89919-046-4). Ticknor & Fields.

Ruby Sweetwater & the Ringo Kid. Sheldon Bart. LC 80-14683. 384p. 1980. text ed. 11.95 o.p. (ISBN 0-07-003872-4). McGraw.

Ruby the Donkey: A Winter Story. Mirabel Cecil. 119p. 1980. text ed. 3.95 o.p. (ISBN 0-07-010321-6). McGraw.

Rude Food. Pierre Le Postre. (Illus.). 48p. 1983. pap. 9.95 o.s.i. (ISBN 0-345-31234-1). Ballantine.

Rudi Gernreich's Black & White Book. (Illus.). 120p. 1989. 50.00 o.p. (ISBN 0-942642-26-0). Twelvetrees Pr.

Rudolf Bultmann. Ian Henderson. Ed. by D. E. Nineham & E. H. Robertson. LC 66-11071. (Makers of Contemporary Theology Ser). 1966. pap. 3.45 o.p. (ISBN 0-8042-0698-8, John Knox). Westminster John Knox.

Rudolf Schwarz: Bibliography & Building List. Edward H. Teague. (Architecture Ser.: A 1451). 9p. 1985. 2.00 o.p. (ISBN 0-89028-541-1). Vance Biblios.

Rudolf Steiner Education: The Waldorf Schools. 2nd ed. Francis Edmonds. 139p. 1982. pap. 9.50 o.p. (ISBN 0-85440-344-2, Pub. by Steinerbooks). Anthroposophic.

Rudolph Focke & the Theory of the Classified Catalog. Gordon Stevenson. (Occasional Papers: No. 145). 30p. 1980. pap. 3.00 o.p. (ISBN 0-317-58995-4). U of Ill Lib Info Sci.

Rudy in Hollywood. William Overgard. 1984. pap. 7.95 o.p. (ISBN 0-03-000087-4, Owl Bks). H Holt & Co.

Rudyard Kipling. Martin Fido. LC 85-28594. (Illustrated Biographies Ser.). (Illus.). 144p. 1986. pap. 9.95 o.p. (ISBN 0-87226-049-6). P Bedrick Bks.

Rufino Tamayo. Jacques Lassaigne. LC 82-50504. (Illus.). 299p. 1982. 75.00 o.p. (ISBN 0-8478-0455-0). Rizzoli Intl.

Rug & Textile Arts: A Periodical Index, 1890-1982. Textile Museum, Washington D. C. 471p. 1983. lib. bdg. 255.00 o.p. (ISBN 0-8161-0426-3, Hall Library). G K Hall.

Rugby League Lions Australia & New Zealand Nineteen Eighty-Four. Ray French. Intro. by David Oxley. LC 84-28769. (Illus.). 160p. 1985. 21.95 o.p. (ISBN 0-571-13525-0); pap. 10.95 o.p. (ISBN 0-571-13526-9). Faber & Faber.

Ruger 1022 Exotic Weapons System. (Exotic Weapons Systems Ser.). (Illus.). 96p. 1983. pap. 15.00 o.p. (ISBN 0-87364-274-0). Paladin Pr.

Rugs. Jeffrey Weiss. (Illus.). 1979. 14.95 o.p. (ISBN 0-393-01290-5); pap. 7.95 o.p. (ISBN 0-393-00944-0). Norton.

Ruined Motel. Reginald Gibbons. 80p. 1981. 10.95 o.p. (ISBN 0-395-31659-6); pap. 5.95 o.p. (ISBN 0-395-31660-X). HM.

Ruining the New Road. William Matthews. LC 72-102333. 1970. sewn in wrappers 4.00 o.p. (ISBN 0-685-79051-7). Small Pr Dist.

Ruins of Isis. Marion Zimmer Bradley. Ed. by Polly Freas & Kelly Freas. LC 78-14268. (Illus.). 1978. pap. 5.95 o.p. (ISBN 0-915442-60-4, Starblaze). Donning Co.

Rule Britannia. Daphne Du Maurier. 1976. pap. 1.50 o.p. (ISBN 0-380-00062-8, 19547). Avon.

Rule Britannia: The Victorian & Edwardian Navy. Peter Padfield. (Illus.). 192p. 1981. 21.95 o.p. (ISBN 0-7100-0774-4). Routledge Chapman & Hall.

Rule Golden & Other Stories. Damon Knight. 1979. pap. 2.25 o.p. (ISBN 0-380-43646-9, 43646). Avon.

Rule Nine: Politics, Administration & Civil Rights. Norman C. Thomas. 7.00 o.p. (ISBN 0-8446-3063-2). Peter Smith.

Rule of Force: Readings on the Totalitarian Challenge to Democracy. Ed. by Erwin R. Steinberg. 7.00 o.p. (ISBN 0-8446-3004-7). Peter Smith.

Rule of Law. Ed. by A. Hutchinson & P. Monahan. 224p. 1987. 35.00 o.p. (Pub. by Carswell-Canada). Transnatl Pubs.

Rule of Walter De Wenlok, Abbot of Westminster. Ed. by Camden Society, Royal Historical Society Staff. (Camden Fourth Ser.: No. 2). 1970. 27.00 o.p. (ISBN 0-901050-63-6, Pub. by Boydell & Brewer). Longwood Pub Group.

Rulers of Empire: The French Colonial Service in Africa. William B. Cohen. LC 76-137405. (Publications Ser.: No. 95). 1971. 11.95x o.p. (ISBN 0-8179-1951-1). Hoover Inst Pr.

Rules for Admission to the Bar in the United States & Territories: 1982 Edition. Ed. by William H. Morris. 95p. 1982. pap. text ed. (ISBN 0-314-66184-0). West Pub.

Rules for Inservice Inspection of Nuclear Power Plant Components: Division 1. (Boiler & Pressure Vessel Code Ser.: Sec. XI). 1980. 80.00 o.p. (ISBN 0-685-76832-5, P00111); pap. 105.00 loose-leaf o.p. (ISBN 0-685-76833-3, V00111). ASME.

Rules of Compensability & Valuation Evidence in Highway Land Acquisition. (National Cooperative Highway Research Program Report). 77p. 1970. 4.40 o.p. (ISBN 0-309-01892-7). Transport Res Bd.

Rules of Procedure of the General Assembly. rev. ed. 86p. 1986. 7.00 o.p. (ISBN 92-1-100270-2, E.85.1.13). UN.

Rules of Procedure of the Industrial Development Board: 1983. 29p. 1983. pap. text ed. 5.00 o.p. (ISBN 0-686-88392-6, UN83/2B2, UNIDO). UNIPUB.

Rules of the Aztec Language: Classical Nahuatl Grammar. Arthur J. Anderson. LC 72-88553. 1973. pap. text ed. 10.00x o.p. (ISBN 0-87480-023-4). U of Utah Pr.

Rules of the Game of Superpower Military Intervention in the Third World: 1975-1980. Neil Matheson. LC 81-43825. 168p. (Orig.). 1982. lib. bdg. 28.25 o.p. (ISBN 0-8191-2495-8); pap. text ed. 12.00 o.p. (ISBN 0-8191-2496-6). U Pr of Amer.

Rules of the U. S. Bankruptcy Court for the Eastern District of Virginia. Michie Company Editorial Staff. 142p. 1985. looseleaf 20.00 o.p. (ISBN 0-87215-899-3). Michie Co.

Ruling Illusions: Philosophy & the Social Order. Anthony Skillen. 1978. pap. text ed. 12.50x o.p. (ISBN 0-391-00775-0). Humanities.

Rumanian-English, English-Rumanian Pocket Dictionary, 2 vols. (Rumanian & Eng.). 1978. Set. pap. 6.50 o.p. (ISBN 0-685-85951-7). E J Brill USA.

Rumanian Folk Music, 5 vols. 1967-1975 ed. Bela Bartok & Benjamin Suchoff. Tr. by E. C. Teodorescu et al from Rumanian. Incl. Vol. 1. Instrumental Melodies. 75.00 o.p. (ISBN 0-685-85187-7); Vol. 2. Vocal Melodies. 75.00 o.p. (ISBN 0-685-85188-5); Vol. 3. Texts. 75.00 o.p. (ISBN 0-685-85189-3); Vol. 4. Carols & Christmas Songs (Colinde) 150.00 o.p. (ISBN 0-685-85190-7); Vol. 5. Maramures County. 85.00 o.p. (ISBN 0-685-85191-5). (Bartok Archives Studies in Musicology.). (Illus.). 1978. 460.00 set o.p. (ISBN 0-685-85186-9). E J Brill USA.

Rumanian Music: 1967-1975, 5 vols. B. Bartok & B. Suchoff. 450.00 set o.p. (ISBN 0-686-91774-X). E J Brill USA.

Rumbeard. Sandra Valerius. LC 84-90154. 76p. (gr. 3-5). 1985. 6.45 o.p. (ISBN 0-533-06211-X). Vantage.

Rumi the Persian. A. R. Arasteh. 1965. 15.00 o.p. (ISBN 0-7100-7859-5). E J Brill USA.

Ruminants: Cattle, Sheep & Goats, Guidelines for Breeding, Care & Management of Laboratory Animals. Institute of Laboratory Animal Resources Staff. (Illus.). 76p. 1974. pap. 6.95 o.p. (ISBN 0-309-02149-9). Natl Acad Pr.

Rumor & Other Stories. James Robison. 151p. 1985. 14.70 o.s.i. (ISBN 0-671-52722-3). Summit Bks.

Rumor of War. Philip Caputo. LC 76-29900. 1977. 10.00 o.s.i. (ISBN 0-03-017631-X). H Holt & Co.

Rumpelstilskin with Benjy & Bubbles. Ruth L. Perle. LC 78-55628. (Read with Me Ser.). (Illus.). (gr. k-3). 1979. 2.95 o.s.i. (ISBN 0-03-044956-1). H Holt & Co.

Rumpelstiltskin. Jacob Grimm & Wilhelm K. Grimm. Ed. & illus. by Jacqueline Ayer. LC 67-20165. (gr. k-3). 1967. 9.95 o.p. (ISBN 0-15-269525-7, HJ). HarBraceJ.

Rumpelstiltskin. Jacob Grimm & Wilhelm K. Grimm. LC 83-90. (Illus.). 32p. (gr. k-3). 1983. reinforced bdg. 10.95 o.p. (ISBN 0-8234-0488-9). Holiday.

Rumrunner & Other Stories. Mary A. Armstrong. 1979. 5.00 o.p. (ISBN 0-682-49334-1). Exposition-Phoenix.

Rumrunners. Eldon W. Eberhard. 1982. 8.50 o.p. (ISBN 0-682-49822-X). Exposition-Phoenix.

Run. William Sleator. (gr. 7 up). 1975. pap. 1.50 o.p. (ISBN 0-380-00270-1, 45302). Avon.

Run Before the Wind: A Novel. Stuart Woods. LC 82-14266. 1983. 16.00 o.p. (ISBN 0-393-01651-X). Norton.

Run: Computer Education. 2nd ed. Dennis O. Harper & James H. Stewart. LC 85-15182. (Computer Science Ser.). 250p. 1985. pap. text ed. 16.50 pub net o.p. (ISBN 0-534-05406-4). Brooks-Cole.

Run for the Money. Scott Corbett. (Illus.). (gr. 4-6). 1973. 10.45 o.p. (ISBN 0-316-15707-4, Pub. by Atlantic Monthly Pr). Little.

Run Sara Run. Anne Worboys. 288p. 1981. 10.95 o.s.i. (ISBN 0-684-16818-9). Scribner.

Run Softly, Go Fast. Barbara Wersba. LC 70-115089. (gr. 7 up). 1970. PLB 7.95 o.p. (ISBN 0-689-20611-9, Atheneum). Macmillan.

Run the Cat Roads: A True Story of Bank Robbers in the Thirties. L. L. Edge. LC 80-25930. 1981. 12.50 o.p. (ISBN 0-934878-01-3). Dembner Bks.

Run-Through. John Houseman. 544p. 1984. pap. 9.95 o.p. (ISBN 0-671-41390-2, Touchstone Bks). S&S.

Run to the Roar. Jim Bakker & Tammy Bakker. LC 80-80656. 142p. 1982. pap. 2.95 o.p. (ISBN 0-89221-104-0). New Leaf.

Run to the Waterfall. Arturo Vivante. 1979. 8.95 o.s.i. (ISBN 0-684-16276-8, ScribT). Scribner.

Run Toward the Nightland: Magic of the Oklahoma Cherokees. Jack F. Kilpatrick & Anna G. Kilpatrick. LC 67-19814. (Illus.). 212p. 1977. pap. 9.95 o.p. (ISBN 0-87074-084-9). SMU Press.

Run with the Ring. Kathryn Vinson. LC 65-22747. (gr. 7 up). 1965. 5.50 o.p. (ISBN 0-15-269793-4, HJ). HarBraceJ.

Run Your Own Retail Store: From Raising the Money to Counting the Profits. Irving Burstinger. (Illus.). 304p. 1981. 19.95 o.p. (ISBN 0-13-784017-9, Spec); pap. 14.95 o.p. (ISBN 0-13-784009-8). P-H.

Runaway! Martin Chadzynski & Carli Lakland. LC 79-14284. (gr. 7 up). 1979. text ed. 9.95 o.p. (ISBN 0-07-010360-7). McGraw.

Runaway. Gilbert Morris. (Living Bks.). 400p. (Orig.). 1987. 4.50 o.p. (ISBN 0-8423-5797-1). Tyndale.

Runaway. Clarissa Watson. LC 84-45633. 250p. 1985. 12.95 o.p. (ISBN 0-689-11521-0, Atheneum). Macmillan.

Runaway Horse. Martin Walser. Tr. by Leila Vennewitz from Ger. LC 79-22749. 128p. 1987. 8.95 o.p. (ISBN 0-03-046501-X); pap. 6.97 o.p. H Holt & Co.

Runaway Maggie. Carol Leith. (Ringling Bros. & Barnum & Bailey Circus Bks.). (Illus.). 16p. (ps-k). 1986. 6.70 o.p. (ISBN 0-316-52035-7). Little.

Runaway Reactions. Institution of Chemical Engineers. 1982. 58.50 o.s.i. (ISBN 0-08-028766-2). Pergamon.

Runaway Road. Stan Mack. LC 79-5265. (Illus.). 48p. (ps-3). 1980. 5.95 o.s.i. (ISBN 0-686-86569-3); PLB 5.95 o.s.i. (ISBN 0-686-91533-X). Parents.

Runaway West. H. A. Everts. 1979. pap. 6.00 o.p. (ISBN 0-682-49379-1, Lochinvar). Exposition-Phoenix.

Runaways & Non-Runaways in an American Suburb: An Exploratory Study of Adolescent & Parental Coping. Albert R. Roberts. 117p. 1981. pap. text ed. (ISBN 0-534-10819-9). Wadsworth Pub.

Runaway's Diary. Marilyn Harris. (gr. 7-10). 1983. pap. 2.25 o.p. (ISBN 0-671-49751-0). Archway.

Rune Games. Marijane Osborn & Stella Longland. (Illus.). 200p. (Orig.). 1982. pap. 11.95 o.p. (ISBN 0-7100-9303-9). Routledge Chapman & Hall.

Runes: An Introduction. R. W. Elliott. (Illus.). 128p. 1960. (ISBN 0-8022-0448-1). Philos Lib.

Runes & Their Origin: Denmark & Elsewhere. Erik Moltke. (Illus.). 554p. (Orig.). 1985. pap. text ed. 87.50x o.p. (ISBN 87-480-0578-9, Pub. by Nationalmuseet Forlaget (Copenhagen Denmark)). Coronet Bks.

Runner. Richard A. Watson. 128p. 1982. 8.95 o.p. (ISBN 0-932298-24-9). Tri-State Pr Corp.

Runner Stumbles. Milan Stitt. 1979. pap. 2.25 o.p. (ISBN 0-380-44719-3, 44719-3, Bard). Avon.

Runner's Book. Raymond Bridge. LC 78-18747. (Encore Editions). (Illus.). 1978. pap. 1.45 o.p. (ISBN 0-684-16698-4, ScribT). Scribner.

Runner's Guide to the U. S. A. Martina D'Alton. LC 78-10315. (Illus.). 1979. 12.95 o.p. (ISBN 0-671-40070-3); pap. 6.95 o.p. (ISBN 0-671-40022-3). Summit Bks.

Runner's Handbook: A Complete Fitness Guide for Men & Women on the Run. Bob Glover & Jack Shepard. (Handbook Ser). 1978. pap. 6.95 o.p. (ISBN 0-14-046325-9). Penguin.

Running. Jim Ramsay. (Illus.). 96p. (Orig.). 1984. pap. 5.95 o.p. (ISBN 0-671-53068-2, Fireside). S&S.

Running a Business Meeting. Gary Holland. (Clear & Simple Ser.). (Orig.). 1984. pap. 3.95 o.p. (ISBN 0-440-57541-9, Dell Trade Pbks). Dell.

Running: A Guide to the Literature, Vol. 1. Bob Wischnia & Marty Post. (Garland Guides to the World We Live In Ser.). 180p. 1983. lib. bdg. 20.00 o.p. (ISBN 0-8240-9105-1). Garland Pub.

Running a Practice: A Manual of Practice Management. 3rd ed. R. V. Jones et al. LC 84-23840. 314p. (Orig.). 1985. pap. 19.00 o.p. (ISBN 0-7099-1455-5, Pub. by Croom Helm Ltd). Routledge Chapman & Hall.

Running & Being. George A. Sheehan. 1978. 9.95 o.p. (ISBN 0-671-22713-0). S&S.

Running Away. Michael Keefe. (McGraw-Hill Paperbacks). (Illus., Orig.). 1979. pap. text ed. 3.95 o.p. (ISBN 0-07-033470-6). McGraw.

Running Back. Robert McKay. LC 79-87523. (gr. 7 up). 1979. 7.95 o.p. (ISBN 0-15-269782-9, HJ). HarBraceJ.

Running in Place. James A. Miller. 1986. 17.45 o.p. (ISBN 0-671-49928-9). S&S.

Running in the Family. Michael Ondaatje. 212p. 1982. 12.95 o.p. (ISBN 0-393-01637-4). Norton.

Running MS-DOS. 2nd ed. Van Wolverton. 448p. (Orig.). 1985. pap. 21.95 o.p. (ISBN 0-914845-68-3). Microsoft.

Running MS-DOS. 3rd ed. Van Wolverton. LC 87-31520. 496p. 1988. 35.00 o.p. (ISBN 1-55615-116-0); pap. 22.95 o.p. (ISBN 1-55615-115-2). Microsoft.

Running MS-DOS: The Microsoft Guide to Getting the Most Out of the Standard Operating System for the IBM PC & 50 Other Personal Computers. Van Wolverton. (Illus.). 384p. 1984. pap. 19.95 o.p. (ISBN 0-914845-07-1). Microsoft.

Running on Empty: The Future of the Automobile in An Oil-Short World. Lester Brown et al. 1979. 9.95 o.p. (ISBN 0-393-01334-0). Norton.

Running Out of Space: What Are the Alternatives? American Library Association, Library Administration Division, Buildings & Equipment Section, Buildings for College & University Libraries Committee. LC 78-1796. 172p. 1978. pap. 15.00x o.p. ALA.

Running Out of Space: What Are the Alternatives? 172p. 1978. pap. 15.00 o.p. (ISBN 0-8389-3215-0). Library Admin.

Running Scared. Jean Thesman. 176p. (Orig.). 1987. pap. 2.50 o.p. (ISBN 0-380-75230-1, Flare). Avon.

Running: The Women's Handbook. Liz Sloan & Ann Kramer. (Illus.). 138p. (Orig.). 1985. pap. 6.95 o.p. (ISBN 0-86358-043-2, Pandora Pr). Routledge Chapman & Hall.

Running Wild. Helen Griffiths. LC 77-3814. (Illus.). 160p. (gr. 5 up). 1977. 6.95 o.p. (ISBN 0-8234-0309-2). Holiday.

Running Wild. Shirley Powell. 192p. 1981. pap. 2.25 o.p. (ISBN 0-380-78170-0, 78170, Flare). Avon.

Running Wild: The Next Industrial Revolution. Adam Osborne. 182p. (Orig.). 1979. pap. text ed. 5.95 o.p. (ISBN 0-07-931028-1). Osborne-McGraw.

Running with God. James C. Hefley. (Orig.). 1975. pap. 1.25 o.p. (ISBN 0-380-00541-7, 26815). Avon.

Running Workshops: A Guide for Trainers in the Helping Professions. The Coping with Crisis Research & Training Group, the Open University Staff. 176p. 1986. 22.95 o.p. (ISBN 0-7099-4809-3, Pub. by Croom Helm UK). Routledge Chapman & Hall.

Running Your Best Race Computerized Edition: IBM-PC Version. Joe Henderson. 224p. 1984. plastic comb 18.95 o.p. (ISBN 0-697-00460-0). Wm C Brown.

Rural Children in Selected Counties of North Carolina. United States Children's Bureau Staff. Ed. by Francis S. Bradley & Margaretta A. Williamson. LC 76-78778. (Illus.). 1969. Repr. of 1918 ed. 35.00x o.p. (ISBN 0-8371-1399-7, RCN&, Pub. by Negro U Pr). Greenwood.

Rural Community Studies in Europe: Trends, Selected & Annotated Bibliographies, Analyses, Vol. I. Ed. by Jean-Louis Durand-Drouhin & Lili-Marie Szwengrub. LC 80-41523. (Publications of the Vienna Centre Ser.). (Illus.). 342p. 1981. 105.00 o.p. (ISBN 0-08-021384-7). Pergamon.

Rural Community Studies in Europe, Vol. II: Trends, Selected & Annotated Bibliographies, Analyses. Ed. by J. L. Durand-Drouhin & L. M. Szwengrub. (Vienna Centre Ser.: No. 6). (Illus.). 271p. 1982. 70.00 o.p. (ISBN 0-08-026094-2, PBL). Pergamon.

Rural Development: A Geographical Perspective. Keith Hoggart & Henry Buller. 352p. 1987. lib. bdg. 49.95x o.p. (ISBN 0-7099-3756-3, Pub. by Croom Helm UK). Routledge Chapman & Hall.

Rural Development & the Changing Countries of the World, Bks. 1 & 2. Ed. by P. Manniche & J. F. Porter. LC 65-14224. 1970. 130.00 o.p. (ISBN 0-08-011155-6). Pergamon.

Rural Development in India Since Independence. Kalipada Dev. 294p. 1986. text ed. 32.50x o.p. (ISBN 81-207-0119-4, Pub. by Sterling Pubs India). Apt Bks.

Rural Development in Pakistan. Shoaib S. Khan. 1980. 15.00x o.p. (ISBN 0-7069-0924-0, Pub. by Vikas India). Advent NY.

Rural Economy & Country Life in the Medieval West. Georges Duby. Tr. by Cynthia Postan. LC 68-20530. Orig. Title: Economie Rurale et la Vie Des Campagnes Dans l'Occident Medieval. (Illus.). xvi, 612p. 1968. pap. 12.95x o.p. (ISBN 0-87249-347-4). U of SC Pr.

Rural Employment & Administration in the Third World. Charles Harvey & Jake Jacobs. 128p. 1979. text ed. 37.95x o.p. (ISBN 0-566-00261-2). Gower Pub Co.

Rural Employment: Trends, Options, Choices. Ian Hodge & Martin Whitby. 272p. 1981. 35.00x o.p. (ISBN 0-416-73080-9, NO. 3537). Routledge Chapman & Hall.

Rural Employment: Trends, Options, Choices. Ian Hodge & Martin Whitby. (Illus.). 262p. 1983. pap. 15.95 o.p. (ISBN 0-416-36280-X, NO.3912). Routledge Chapman & Hall.

Rural Energy & Developing Countries: A Bibliography. Julia M. Rholes et al. (Public Administration Ser.: P 1820). 14p. 1985. 2.25 o.p. (ISBN 0-89028-670-1). Vance Biblios.

Rural England: 1066-1348. H. E. Hallem. 1981. text ed. 28.50x o.p. (ISBN 0-391-02303-9). Humanities.

Rural Enterprise & Nonfarm Employment. Dennis Anderson & Mark Leiserson. (Working Paper). 87p. 1978. 5.00 o.p. (ISBN 0-686-36150-4, PP-7802). World Bank.
Rural Housing. Alwyn Jones. 76p. 1975. pap. text ed. 5.00x o.p. (ISBN 0-7135-1887-1, Pub. by Bedford England). Gower Pub Co.
Rural Industrialization: Problems & Potentials. facsimile ed. North Central Regional Center for Rural Development Staff. 154p. 1974. pap. text ed. 9.20x o.p. (ISBN 0-8138-2465-6). Iowa St U Pr.
Rural Leadership & Population Control in Bangladesh. M. Rashiduzzaman. LC 82-40245. 110p. (Orig.). 1982. lib. bdg. 26.00 o.p. (ISBN 0-8191-2637-3); pap. text ed. 10.00 o.p. (ISBN 0-8191-2638-1). U Pr of Amer.
Rural Local Government & Rural Development in Malaysia. Stephen Chee. (Special Series on Rural Local Government: No. 9). 112p. (Orig.). 1974. pap. text ed. 3.50 o.p. (ISBN 0-86731-095-2). Cornell CIS RDC.
Rural Medicine: Obstacles & Solutions for Self-Sufficiency. Stanley S. Wallack & Sandra E. Kretz. LC 79-48057. (University Health Policy Consortium Ser.). (Illus.). 208p. 1981. 25.50x o.p. (ISBN 0-669-03691-9). Lexington Bks.
Rural Post Offices. Cliff Taylor & David Emerson. 36p. 1981. pap. text ed. 4.00x o.p. (ISBN 0-7199-1056-0, Pub. by Bedford England). Gower Pub Co.
Rural Public Transportation. (Transportation Research Record Ser.). 88p. 1978. 5.00 o.p. (ISBN 0-309-02835-3). Transport Res Bd.
Rural Regional Planning: Towards an Operational Theory. D. Conyers. 66p. 1984. pap. 22.00 o.p. (ISBN 0-08-032351-0). Pergamon.
Rural-Urban Relations in the Bangkok Metropolitan Dominance Subregion. (Country Monographs). 312p. 1979. pap. 8.50 o.p. (ISBN 0-686-78256-9, CRD071, UNCRD). UNIPUB.
Rush & Leafcraft. Germaine Brotherton. 1977. 7.95 o.p. (ISBN 0-395-25787-5). HM.
Rushes. John Rechy. LC 79-2302. 1979. 10.00 o.p. (ISBN 0-394-50861-0). Grove.
Rushes. John Rechy. LC 79-2302. 1979. pap. 4.50 o.s.i. (ISBN 0-394-17883-1, Ever). Grove.
Rusi & Brassey's Defence Yearbook, 1977-78. Ed. by Royal United Services Institute for Defense Studies Staff. LC 75-29923. 1978. lib. bdg. 40.00x o.p. (ISBN 0-89158-823-X). Westview.
Rusi & Brassey's Defence Yearbook 1985. 95th ed. Royal United Services Institute for Defence Studies (RUSI), London Staff. (Rusi & Brassey's Defence Yearbook Ser.). 388p. 1985. 46.00 o.p. (ISBN 0-08-031168-7, Pub. by Aberdeen Scotland); pap. 20.50 o.p. (ISBN 0-08-031169-5, Pub. by Aberdeen Scotland). Pergamon.
Ruskin Spear. Mervyn Levy. (Royal Academy Painters & Sculptors Ser.). 73p. 1986. 16.95 o.p. (ISBN 0-89733-183-4). Academy Chi Pubs.
Russell County. Theodosia Barrett. LC 81-69331. 148p. 1981. 10.95 o.s.i. (ISBN 0-89227-047-0). Commonwealth Pr.
Russell Sturgis: Eighteen Thirty-Six to Nineteen Nine. Lamia Doumato. (Architecture Ser.: Bibliography A 1339). 1985. pap. 2.00 o.p. (ISBN 0-89028-309-5). Vance Biblios.
Russia. Harrison E. Salisbury. LC 65-27494. (New York Times Byline Books). (Orig.). 1965. pap. 3.25 o.p. (ISBN 0-689-10239-9, Atheneum). Macmillan.
Russia, America, the Bomb & the Fall of Western Europe. Brian May. 260p. 1984. 19.95x o.p. (ISBN 0-7100-9757-3). Routledge Chapman & Hall.
Russia & Europe. Reinhard Wittram. (History of European Civilization Library). 1973. pap. text ed. 6.95 o.p. (ISBN 0-15-577963-X, HC). HarBraceJ.
Russia & the Communist Countries: Documents. J. A. Naik. 1980. text ed. 55.00x o.p. (ISBN 0-391-01792-6). Humanities.
Russia & the Mediterranean 1797-1807. Norman E. Saul. LC 72-96755. 1970. lib. bdg. 22.00x o.s.i. (ISBN 0-226-73540-0). U of Chicago Pr.
Russia & the Russians: Inside the Closed Society. Kevin Klose. 384p. 1984. 17.00 o.p. (ISBN 0-393-01786-9). Norton.
Russia & the Weimar Republic. Lionel Kochan. LC 78-17679. 1978. Repr. of 1954 ed. lib. bdg. 35.00x o.p. (ISBN 0-313-20503-5, KORW). Greenwood.
Russia & the West: Documents 1972-1975. Ed. by J. A. Naik. 466p. 1981. text ed. 35.00x o.p. (ISBN 0-391-02295-4). Humanities.
Russia & the Western World: 1946-1971 Documents. J. A. Naik. 227p. 1980. text ed. 29.95x o.p. (ISBN 0-391-01745-4). Humanities.
Russia in Asia & Africa Documents, 1972-75. Ed. by J. A. Naik. 260p. 1981. text ed. 19.95x o.p. (ISBN 0-391-02294-6). Humanities.
Russia: The People & the Power. Robert G. Kaiser. LC 75-34069. 516p. 1976. 12.95 o.p. (ISBN 0-689-10696-3, Atheneum). Macmillan.
Russia under the Last Tsar. Ed. by Theofanis G. Stavrou. LC 74-790447. (Illus., Orig.). 1969. 10.00x o.p. (ISBN 0-8166-0514-9); pap. 4.95x o.p. (ISBN 0-8166-0515-7, MP19). U of Minn Pr.
Russian: A Complete Elementary Course. Peter Rudy et al. 1970. 15.95x o.p. (ISBN 0-393-09871-0, NortonC); text & tape set o.p. 90.00 o.p. (ISBN 0-686-66509-0). Norton.
Russian Architecture. Arthur Voyce. (ISBN 0-8022-1785-0). Philos Lib.
Russian Architecture, Trends in Nationalism & Modernism. Arthur Voyce. Repr. of 1948 ed. lib. bdg. 35.00x o.p. (ISBN 0-8371-2292-9, VORA). Greenwood.
Russian Art, Icons & Decorative Arts from the Origin to the 20th Century. Philippe Verdier. LC 73-8333. (Illus.). 1959. pap. 5.00 o.p. (ISBN 0-911886-17-6). Walters Art.
Russian Beauty & Other Stories. Vladimir Nabokov. Tr. by Dmitri Nabokov & Simon Karlinsky. LC 72-10094. 224p. 1974. pap. text ed. 7.95 o.p. (ISBN 0-07-045711-5). McGraw.
Russian Blue. Helen Griffiths. LC 73-78454. (Illus.). 160p. (gr. 4-6). 1973. 4.50 o.p. (ISBN 0-8234-0233-9). Holiday.
Russian Bride. Marcelle Bernstein. 320p. 1987. 17.45 o.s.i. (ISBN 0-671-63158-6). S&S.
Russian Church & the Soviet State, 1917-1950. John S. Curtiss. 1953. 11.75 o.p. (ISBN 0-8446-1141-7). Peter Smith.
Russian Colonial Expansion to 1917. Ed. by Michael Rywkin. LC 84-71094. (Issue Studies (U. S. S. R. & East Europe): No. 4). 250p. 1987. 25.00 o.p. (ISBN 0-910895-01-5). Assn Study Nat.
Russian Colonization of Kazakhstan, 1896-1916. George J. Demko. LC 67-66166. (Uralic & Altaic Ser.: No. 99). 271p. (Orig.). 1969. pap. text ed. 10.50x o.p. (ISBN 0-87750-082-7). Res Ctr Lang Semiotic.
Russian Communism. William H. Wilbur. LC 64-17829. 1964. 5.95 o.p. (ISBN 0-87004-173-8). Caxton.
Russian Composers. Elsa Z. Posell. LC 67-22172. (Illus.). (gr. 4-6). 1967. 3.50 o.p. (ISBN 0-395-07034-1). HM.
Russian Convoys 1941-1945. (Warships Illustrated Ser.: No. 9). (Illus.). 64p. (Orig.). 1987. pap. 9.95 o.p. (ISBN 0-85368-773-0, Pub. by Arms & Armour). Sterling.
Russian Cooking. Miyo Nagaya. (Golden Cooking Card Bk.). (Illus.). 42p. (Orig.). 1973. pap. 3.95 o.p. (ISBN 4-07-973642-8, Pub. by Shufunmoto Co Ltd Japan). C E Tuttle.
Russian Dialogues. Alexander Blum. 1969. text ed. 16.25 o.p. (ISBN 0-08-012519-0); pap. 7.00 o.p. (ISBN 0-08-012518-2). Pergamon.
Russian Economic History: A Guide to Information Sources. Ed. by Daniel R. Kazmer & Vera Kazmer. LC 73-17588. (Economics Information Guide Ser.: Vol. 4). 536p. 1977. 68.00x o.p. (ISBN 0-8103-1304-9). Gale.
Russian-English Dictionary & Reader in the Cybernetical Sciences. Samuel Kotz. 1966. 54.00 o.p. (ISBN 0-12-422450-4). Acad Pr.
Russian-English Dictionary of Data Processing Terminology. 359p. (Rus. & Eng.). 1971. text ed. 6.95 o.p. (ISBN 0-686-92123-2, M-9127). French & Eur.
Russian-English Polytechnical Dictionary. B. V. Kuznetzov. 723p. (Rus. & Eng.). 1981. 30.00 o.p. (ISBN 0-8285-1851-3, Pub. by Rus Lang Pubs USSR). Imported Pubns.
Russian Enigma. Clive Egleton. LC 82-45170. 256p. 1982. 12.95 o.p. (ISBN 0-689-11303-X, Atheneum). Macmillan.
Russian Fairy Tales. (gr. k-6). 1987. 12.95 o.p. (ISBN 0-8249-8160-X). Ideals.
Russian Folk Tales. Compiled by Alexander Afanasyev. Tr. by Robert Chandler from Rus. LC 80-50746. (Illus.). 80p. 1982. pap. 9.95 o.s.i. (ISBN 0-87773-233-7, 71234-X). Shambhala Pubns.
Russian Folk-Tales with Introduction & Notes. Leonard A. Magnus. LC 74-6486. 366p. 1974. Repr. of 1916 ed. 43.00x o.p. (ISBN 0-8103-3654-5). Gale.
Russian for English-Speaking Learners. V. Wagner. 621p. 1983. 10.95 o.p. (ISBN 0-8285-2738-5, Pub. by Rus Lang Pubs USSR). Imported Pubns.
Russian for Everybody: Introductory Lessons. L. L. Babalova & Z. N. Iyevleva. 103p. 1985. pap. 9.95 o.p. (ISBN 0-8285-3350-4, Pub. by Rus Lang Pubs USSR); write for info. cassette o.p. Imported Pubns.
Russian for Scientists. V. I. Mitrokhina & O. G. Motovilova. 349p. 1981. 10.00 o.p. (ISBN 0-8285-2171-9, Pub. by Rus Lang Pubs USSR). Imported Pubns.
Russian Impact on Art. Mikhail Alpatov. Philos Lib.
Russian in Ten Minutes. Kristine Kershul. 1984. pap. 12.95 o.p. (ISBN 0-916682-89-7). Outdoor Empire.
Russian Jew Cooks in Peru. Violeta Autumn. LC 73-81086. (Illus.). 192p. 1973. 7.95 o.s.i. (ISBN 0-912238-42-9, One Hund One Prods); pap. 4.95 o.s.i. (ISBN 0-912238-41-0). Ortho.
Russian Lacquer, Legends & Fairy Tales, Vol. I. Lucy Maxym. 80p. 1985. 250.00x o.p. (ISBN 0-317-61379-0, Pub. by Collets (UK)). State Mutual Bk.
Russian Lacquer, Legends & Fairy Tales, Vol. II. Lucy Maxym. 80p. 1986. 275.00x o.p. (ISBN 0-317-61382-0, Pub. by Collets (UK)). State Mutual Bk.
Russian Leave. Anthony Stuart. LC 81-66967. 208p. 1981. 12.50 o.p. (ISBN 0-87795-336-8, Arbor Hse). Morrow.
Russian Lexicology. N. M. Shanskii. 1969. 22.00 o.p. (ISBN 0-08-012842-4). Pergamon.
Russian Literature: An Introduction. Robert Lord. LC 79-63625. 214p. 1985. Repr. of 1980 ed. 7.95 o.s.i. (ISBN 0-8008-6941-9). Taplinger.
Russian Museum: A Guide. A. Gubarev. 175p. 1981. 5.95 o.p. (ISBN 0-8285-2298-7, Pub. by Progress Pubs USSR). Imported Pubns.
Russian Music from the Beginning. Boris V. Asaf'ev. 329p. Repr. of 1953 ed. lib. bdg. 49.00 o.p. (Pub. by Am Repr Serv). Reprint Servs.
Russian Poetry, Nineteen Seventeen to Nineteen Fifty-Five. Ed. & tr. by Jack Lindsay. LC 77-13747. 1978. Repr. of 1957 ed. lib. bdg. 35.00x o.p. (ISBN 0-313-20000-9, LIRP). Greenwood.
Russian Professor. Andrew Gilchrist. 224p. 1985. pap. 2.95 o.p. (ISBN 0-931773-22-9). Critics Choice Paper.
Russian Radicals Look to America, 1825-1894. David Hecht. LC 68-9544. (Illus.). 1968. Repr. of 1947 ed. lib. bdg. 35.00x o.p. (ISBN 0-8371-0102-6, HERR). Greenwood.
Russian Science Grammar. A. G. Waring. 1967. 45.00 o.p. (ISBN 0-08-011342-7); pap. 7.75 o.p. (ISBN 0-08-011341-9). Pergamon.
Russian Scientific Reader. E. J. Warne. (Rus.). 1967. pap. 2.95x o.p. (ISBN 0-393-09712-9, NortonC). Norton.
Russian Struggle for Power. C. Jay Smith, Jr. 1956. (ISBN 0-8022-1595-5). Philos Lib.
Russian Struggle for Power, Nineteen Fourteen to Nineteen Seventeen: A Study of Russian Foreign Policy During the First World War. Clarence J. Smith. Repr. of 1956 ed. lib. bdg. 41.50x o.p. (ISBN 0-8371-2282-1, SMRS). Greenwood.
Russian Symphony. Dmitri Shostakovich. (ISBN 0-8022-1565-3). Philos Lib.
Russian Theater & Costume Designs from the Fine Arts Museums of San Francisco. Intro. by John E. Bowlt. LC 79-55788. (Illus.). 64p. 1979. pap. 6.95 o.p. (ISBN 0-88401-033-3). Fine Arts Mus.
Russian War: Nineteen Forty One Nineteen Forty Five. Ed. by Mrazkova & Remes. 152p. 1987. 22.50 o.p. (ISBN 0-88029-084-6, Pub. by Dorset Pr). Hippocrene Bks.
Russian Women: Two Stories. I. Grekova. Tr. by Lynn Visson from Rus. LC 83-8553. 266p. 1984. 17.95 o.p. (ISBN 0-15-179056-6). HarBraceJ.
Russians. Bill Hotchkiss & Judith Shears. 640p. (Orig.). 1984. pap. 4.95 o.p. (ISBN 0-440-07553-X). Dell.
Russia's Children. Herschel Alt & Edith Alt. 1963. 19.95x o.p. (ISBN 0-8084-0383-4). New Coll U Pr.
Russia's Lost Literature of the Absurd: Selected Works of Daniil Kharms & Alexander Vvedensky. Ed. & tr. by George Gibian. 224p. 1974. pap. 2.95x o.p. (ISBN 0-393-00723-5, Norton Lib). Norton.
Russia's Military Way to the West: Origins & Nature of Russian Military Power 1700-1800. Christopher Duffy. 320p. 1985. 37.50x o.p. (ISBN 0-7100-0797-3); pap. 12.95 o.p. (ISBN 0-7102-0535-X). Routledge Chapman & Hall.
Russia's New Religion. Parker L. Johnstone. 208p. 1984. 7.95 o.p. (ISBN 0-917802-11-X). Theoscience Found.
Russkaia Literaturnaia Parodiia. (Rus.). 1981. pap. 6.50 o.p. (ISBN 0-88233-604-5); write for info o.p. Ardis Pubs.
Russkii Iazyk: Grammaticheskoe Uchenie O Slove. V. V. Vinogradov. (Russian Ser.: Vol. 19). 1947. 30.00 o.p. (ISBN 0-87569-021-1). Academic Intl.
Russkii Narodnye Skazkii: (Russian Fairy Tales) A. Kurkin. 72p. 1987. 10.95 o.p. (ISBN 0-8285-3748-8, Pub. by Aurora Pubs USSR). Imported Pubns.
Russo-German War: Autumn 1941. Ed. by W. Victor Madeja. (Battle Situation - East Front Ser.). (Illus.). 80p. (Orig., Ger.). 1988. pap. text ed. 12.95 o.p. (ISBN 0-941052-82-6, 27). Valor Pub.
Russo-Japanese Conflict: Its Causes & Issues. K. Asakawa. (Illus.). 399p. 1972. Repr. of 1904 ed. 37.50x o.p. (ISBN 0-7165-2048-6, BBA 02211, Pub. by Irish Academic Pr Ireland). Biblio Dist.
Rust. Conrad Hilberry. LC 73-92903. 61p. 1974. 6.95x o.p. (ISBN 0-8214-0153-X). Ohio U Pr.
Rust Fungi of Cereals, Grasses & Bamboos. G. B. Cummins. LC 75-147257. (Illus.). 1971. 43.00 o.p. (ISBN 0-387-05336-0). Springer-Verlag.
Rustic Speech & Folklore. Elizabeth M. Wright. LC 68-18011. 368p. 1968. Repr. of 1913 ed. 40.00x o.p. (ISBN 0-8103-3294-9). Gale.
Rustication of Urban Youth in China: A Social Experiment. Ed. by Peter J. Seybolt. LC 76-17395. 232p. 1977. 37.50 o.p. (ISBN 0-87332-082-4). M E Sharpe.
Rustler's Blood. David Everett. 1979. pap. 1.75 o.p. (ISBN 0-8439-0702-9, Pub. by Leisure Bks CT). Dorchester Pub Co.
Ruth Montgomery: Herald of the New Age. Ruth Montgomery. LC 85-25424. 288p. 1986. 16.95 o.s.i. (ISBN 0-385-23311-6, Dolp). Doubleday.
Rutherford B. Hayes State Memorial, Fremont, Ohio. rev. ed. Watt Marchman. (Illus.). 40p. 1962. pap. 1.00 o.p. (ISBN 0-318-00862-9). Ohio Hist Soc.
Rutland Street: The Story of an Educational Experiment for Disadvantaged Children in Dublin. Seamas Holland. (Illus.). 1979. 27.00 o.p. (ISBN 0-08-024264-2). Pergamon.
RV Lawyers' Guide: Selected Franchise & Warranty Laws of the Fifty States Affecting the RV Manufacturer. Recreation Vehicle Industry Association (U.S.) Staff. LC 82-210392. 1983. 150.00 o.p. RV Indus Assn.
RV-Truck-Van Conversion Guide. Four by Four's & Off-Road Vehicles & Travelin' Vans Editors. (Illus.). 304p. 1983. pap. 12.95 o.p. (ISBN 0-8306-2109-1, 2109). TAB Bks.
Rwanda: A Country Study. Ed. by Richard F. Nyrop. LC 72-60689. (DA Pam 550-84, Area Handbook Ser.). 228p. 1986. Repr. of 1974 ed. 9.50 o.p. (ISBN 0-318-20142-9, S/N 008-020-01062-6). USGPO.
Rydberg Series in Atoms & Molecules. A. B. Duncan. (Physical Chemistry Ser, Vol. 23). 1971. 59.00 o.p. (ISBN 0-12-223950-4). Acad Pr.
Rymes of Robyn Hood: An Introduction to the English Outlaw. R. B. Dobson & J. Taylor. LC 75-31564. (Illus.). 1976. 35.95x o.p. (ISBN 0-8229-1126-4). U of Pittsburgh Pr.
Ryrie's Concise Guide to the Bible. Charles Ryrie. LC 83-71924. 163p. (Orig.). 1983. pap. 5.95 o.p. Heres Life.

S

S Corporations. American Institute of Certified Public Accountants. Continuing Professional Education Division Staff & Gregory B. McKeen. LC 85-127112. (Illus.). write for info. o.p. Am Inst CPA.
S. E. M. Atlas of Cells & Tissues. Tsuneo Fujita et al. LC 80-85298. (Illus.). 338p. 1981. 90.00 o.p. (ISBN 0-89640-051-4). Igaku-Shoin.
S. I. O. P. The Secret U. S. Plan for Nuclear War. Peter Pringle & William Arkin. LC 83-42650. 1983. 16.45 o.p. (ISBN 0-393-01798-2). Norton.
S. J. Perelman. Douglas Fowler. (United States Authors Ser.). 1983. lib. bdg. 13.50 o.p. (ISBN 0-8057-7376-2, Twayne). G K Hall.
S. J. Perelman: A Life. Dorothy Herrmann. 1986. 18.95 o.p. (ISBN 0-399-13154-X). Putnam Pub Group.
S. Legend in Applied Probability & Statistics, Vol. I. Rev. ed. V. V. Shvyrkov. LC 81-85204. (Illus.). 224p. 1982. 13.80 o.s.i. (ISBN 0-942004-00-0, 1A). Throwkoff Pr.
S. Legend in Applied Probability & Statistics, Vol. 1. V. V. Shvyrkov. LC 81-52997. (Illus.). 205p. 1981. write for info. o.s.i. Throwkoff Pr.
S-M: The Last Taboo. Gerald Greene & Caroline Greene. LC 74-7680. 1974. pap. 2.95 o.p. (ISBN 0-394-17832-7, B376, BC). Grove.
S-One Hundred Bus Handbook. Dave Bursky. 280p. 1980. pap. 17.50 o.p. (ISBN 0-8104-0897-X). Sams.
S, Portrait of a Spy. Ian Adams. LC 82-731. 192p. 1982. 11.95 o.p. (ISBN 0-89919-087-1). Ticknor & Fields.
S. S. San Pedro. James G. Cozzens. LC 67-19206. 1967. uniform ed. 3.50 o.p. (ISBN 0-15-184837-8). HarBraceJ.
S-V Forty Viruses: Molecular Structure. Hohn M. Lehman et al. (Illus.). 220p. 1973. text ed. 27.50x o.p. (ISBN 0-8422-7066-3). Irvington.
Saab Service Repair Handbook 95, 96, 99, & Sonett 1967-1979. Ed. by Jeff Robinson. (Illus.). pap. 13.95 o.p. (ISBN 0-89287-121-0, A185). Clymer Pub.
Saad Ahaah Sinil: Dual Language. Martha Austin & Regina Lynch. 42p. 1983. 6.00 o.s.i. (ISBN 0-936008-18-0). Navajo Curr.
Saami Religion: Scripta Instituti Donneriani Aboensis XII. Ed. by Tore Ahlback. (Illus.). 294p. (Orig.). 1987. pap. 38.50x o.p. (ISBN 91-22-00863-2, Pub. by Almqvist & Wiksell). Coronet Bks.

Saar Controversy. W. R. Bisschop. (Grotius Society Publication: No. 2). 186p. 1961. 22.00 o.p. (ISBN 0-379-00399-6). Oceana.

Sabbath Breaking & the Death Penalty: A Theological Investigation. James B. Jordan. LC 86-80679. 109p. (Orig.). 1986. pap. 9.95 o.p. (ISBN 0-939404-13-3). Geneva Ministr.

Sabbatical Reflections: The Ten Commandments in a New Day. Brita Stendahl. LC 79-23775. 132p. 1980. 8.95 o.p. (ISBN 0-8006-0643-4, 1-643, Fortress). Augsburg Fortress.

Sabiston Surgery Update. 1989. (ISBN 0-7216-7882-3). Saunders.

Sabre & Lance: An Illustrated History of Cavalry. Peter Newark. (Illus.). 256p. 1987. 29.95 o.p. (ISBN 0-7137-1813-7, Pub. by Blandford Pr England). Sterling.

Sabre Jets over Korea: A Firsthand Account. Douglas K. Evans. (Illus.). 272p. (Orig.). 1984. pap. 15.15 o.p. (ISBN 0-8306-2352-3, 2352). TAB Bks.

Saccharin: Current Status. Ed. by L. Goldberg & D. M. Conning. (Illus.). 148p. 1985. pap. 83.00 o.p. (ISBN 0-08-032009-0, H221, H120, Pub. by PPL). Pergamon.

Sachem. Donald C. Porter. (Reader's Request Ser.). 1983. lib. bdg. 19.95 o.p. (ISBN 0-8161-3449-9, Large Print Bks). G K Hall.

Sachsenspiegel & Bible. Ed. by Guido Kisch. (Mediaeval Studies Ser.: No. 5). 1941. 25.00 o.p. (ISBN 0-268-00238-X). U of Notre Dame Pr.

Sackcloth & Ashes. Jacqueline K. Bridges. LC 84-91345. 99p. 1985. 8.95 o.p. (ISBN 0-533-06442-2). Vantage.

Sacrament. Peter Gzowski. LC 80-51208. 1980. 9.95 o.p. (ISBN 0-689-11114-2, Atheneum). Macmillan.

Sacrament of Peace. Francoise D. Berube & John-Paul Berube. (gr. 2-3). Ages 7-8. childs bk. 2.95 o.p. (ISBN 0-8091-9166-0); Ages 9-12. childs bk. 2.95 o.p. (ISBN 0-8091-9167-9); director's guide 4.95 o.p. (ISBN 0-8091-9169-5). Paulist Pr.

Sacrament of the Present Moment: Self Abandonment to the Divine Providence. Jean-Pierre De Caussade. Tr. by Kitty Muggeridge from Fr. LC 81-48206. 128p. 1982. 8.61i o.p. (ISBN 0-06-061809-4). HarpR.

Sacramento County Including Portions of Placer County Street Guide & Directory, 1988. Thomas Bros. Maps Staff. (Illus.). 170p. 1988. pap. 11.95 o.p. (ISBN 0-88130-270-8). Thomas Bros Maps.

Sacramento County Street Atlas 1985: Including Placer & El Dorado. Thomas Bros. Maps Staff. (Illus.). 144p. pap. 9.95 o.p. (ISBN 0-88130-122-1). Thomas Bros Maps.

Sacramento County Street Atlas: 1987. Thomas Bros. Maps Staff. (Illus.). 170p. 1986. pap. 11.95 o.p. (ISBN 0-88130-201-5). Thomas Bros Maps.

Sacramento, El Dorado, Placer & Yolo Counties Public Schools: How Are They Doing? (1984) Lillian S. Clancy. (How Are They Doing Ser.). 145p. (Orig.). 1984. pap. 13.95 o.p. (ISBN 0-939580-11-X). CA Schl Surveys.

Sacramento-Solano Counties Street Atlas & Directory, 1980. rev. ed. Thomas Bros. Maps Staff. (Illus.). 1988. pap. 18.95 o.p. Thomas Bros Maps.

Sacraments, Liturgy & Prayer. Megan McKenna & Darryl Ducote. LC 78-71531. (Followers of the Way Ser.: Vol. 5). 221p. (gr. 9-12). 1979. 22.50 o.p. (ISBN 0-8091-9546-1). Paulist Pr.

Sacred Calligraphy of the East. John Stevens. LC 80-53446. (Illus.). 224p. (Orig.). 1981. pap. 10.95 o.s.i. (ISBN 0-394-74832-8). Shambhala Pubn.

Sacred Geometry. Nigel Pennick. LC 81-47848. (Library of Spiritual Wisdom). 160p. 1982. pap. 6.68i o.p. (ISBN 0-06-066492-4, CN 4027). HarpR.

Sacred Harp: A Tradition & Its Music. Buell E. Cobb, Jr. LC 76-12680. 256p. 1978. 15.00x o.p. (ISBN 0-8203-0426-3). U of Ga Pr.

Sacred Hoop: Recovering the Feminine in American Indian Traditions. Paula G. Allen. LC 85-47950. 288p. 1986. 24.95 o.p. (ISBN 0-8070-4600-0); pap. 10.95 o.p. (BP758). Beacon Pr.

Sacred India: Hinduism, Buddhism, Jainism. Ann C. Boger & Joellen K. DeOreo. LC 85-19559. (Illus.). 60p. 1986. pap. 7.95 o.p. (ISBN 0-910386-84-6, Pub. by Cleveland Mus Art). Ind U Pr.

Sacred Officials of the Eleusinian Mysteries. Kevin Clinton. LC 73-79573. (Transaction Ser.: Vol. 64, Pt. 3). (Illus.). 1974. pap. 16.00 o.p. (ISBN 0-87169-643-6). Am Philos.

Sacred Places of San Francisco. Joseph A. Baird, Jr. et al. (Illus.). 300p. 1985. 35.00 o.p. (ISBN 0-89141-192-5). Presidio Pr.

Sacred Rage: The Crusade of Modern Islam. Robin Wright. 1985. 17.45 o.s.i. (ISBN 0-671-60113-X, Linden Pr.). S&S.

Sacred Sixty-Six. Rolf E. Aaseng. LC 67-11721. (Orig.). 1967. pap. 5.50 plastic bdg. o.p. (ISBN 0-8066-0706-8, 10-5569, Augsburg). Augsburg Fortress.

Sacred Theory of the Earth. Thomas Burnet. LC 65-10027. (Centaur Classics Ser.). (Illus.). 414p. 1965. 22.50x o.p. (ISBN 0-8093-0186-5). S Ill U Pr.

Sacrifice. Pamela Ferguson. LC 79-55619. 1981. 13.95 o.p. (ISBN 0-689-11035-9, Atheneum). Macmillan.

Sacrifice & the Death of Christ. Frances M. Young. LC 78-2889. 1978. softcover 4.95 o.s.i. (ISBN 0-664-24210-3, Westminster). Westminster John Knox.

Sacrificial Worship of the Old Testament. J. H. Kurtz. Tr. by James Martin. (Twin Brooks Ser.). 454p. 1980. pap. 8.95 o.p. (ISBN 0-8010-5419-2). Baker Bk.

Sacrilege Malais. Pierre Boulle. 1967. 9.95 o.p. (ISBN 0-686-54114-6). French & Eur.

Sadat. David Hirst & Irene Beeson. 384p. 1982. 19.95 o.p. (ISBN 0-571-11690-6). Faber & Faber.

Saddlemakers of Sheridan County, Wyoming. Ann L. Gorzalka. LC 82-23043. 1984. 14.95 o.p. (ISBN 0-87108-634-4). Pruett.

Sadhanas for Spiritual Life. Ed. by Ramakrishna Math Staff. 166p. pap. 2.75 o.p. (ISBN 0-87481-507-X). Vedanta Pr.

Sadist. (Ryker Ser). 1975. pap. 1.25 o.p. (ISBN 0-685-59192-1, LB309ZK, Pub. by Leisure Bks CT). Dorchester Pub Co.

Sadness of Witches. Janice Elliott. 1988. 19.95 o.p. (ISBN 0-340-41657-2, Pub. by Hodder & Stoughton UK). David & Charles.

Sadopaideia. (Victorian Library). 256p. 1984. 14.95 o.p. (ISBN 0-394-54265-7, GP952). Grove.

SAF Forest Policies & Positions, 1985. Society of American Foresters Staff. 68p. 1985. pap. 6.00 o.p. (ISBN 0-939970-30-9). Soc Am Foresters.

Safari South America: The Saki Monkeys of Guyana & Other Wildlife. Christina Wood. LC 73-1764. (Illus.). 224p. 1973. 7.95 o.s.i. (ISBN 0-8008-6945-1). Taplinger.

Safe & Efficient Plant Operation & Maintenance. Chemical Engineering Magazine Editors. LC 80-14762. (Chemical Engineering Ser.). 400p. 1980. text ed. 42.50 o.p. (ISBN 0-07-010707-6). McGraw.

Safe & Sane: The Sensible Way to Protect Yourself, Your Loved Ones, Your Property & Possessions. Joseph D. McNamara. LC 83-22087. 224p. 1984. pap. 7.95 o.p. (ISBN 0-399-50859-7, G&D). Putnam Pub Group.

Safe & Sound: A Parent's Guide to Child Protection. Roderick Townley. 233p. 1985. 16.45 o.p. (ISBN 0-671-54420-9). S&S.

Safe & Sound: A Parent's Guide to Child Protection. Roderick Townley. 256p. 1986. pap. 6.95 o.s.i. (ISBN 0-671-62804-6, Fireside). S&S.

Safe Hockey: How to Survive the Game Intact. Encore ed. Lois Kalchman. 1981. 3.50 o.p. (ISBN 0-684-16979-7, ScribT). Scribner.

Safe Houses. Lynne Alexander. LC 85-47594. 272p. 1985. 13.95 o.p. (ISBN 0-689-11606-3, Atheneum). Macmillan.

Safe in His Arms. Hans E. Wisloff. Tr. by Joel M. Njus. LC 69-14185. (Norwegian). 1969. 7.50 o.p. (ISBN 0-8066-0905-2, 10-5577, Augsburg). Augsburg Fortress.

Safe Roads Act of Nineteen Eighty-Three: A Summary & Compilation of Statutes Amended or Affected by the Act. University of North Carolina at Chapel Hill Institute of Government & James C. Drennan. LC 84-620532. 72p. 1983. 5.00 o.p. Institute Government.

Safe Sally Seat Belt & the Magic Click. Phyllis Gobbell & Jim Laster. (Illus.). 48p. (gr. k-5). 1986. 3.95 o.p. (ISBN 0-8249-8122-7). Ideals.

SAFE: Security Audit & Field Evaluation for Computer Facilities & Information Systems. Leonard I. Krauss. 336p. 1981. 29.95 o.p. (ISBN 0-8144-5526-3). AMACOM.

Safed the Sage. William E. Barton. pap. 3.50 o.p. (ISBN 0-8042-3424-8, John Knox). Westminster John Knox.

Safeguarding the Land. Gloria Skurzynski. LC 80-8805. (Illus.). 162p. (gr. 7 up). 1981. 9.95 o.p. (ISBN 0-15-269956-2, HJ). HarBraceJ.

Safeguarding the Land. Gloria Skurzynski. LC 80-8805. (Illus.). 192p. (gr. 7 up). 1981. pap. 3.95 o.p. (ISBN 0-15-269957-0, VoyB). HarBraceJ.

Safeguards: Proceedings, American Nuclear Society Executive Conference, Cape Cod MA, 16-19 October 1977. 360p. softcover 34.00 o.p. (ISBN 0-317-33077-2, 650005). Am Nuclear Soc.

Safety: A Personal Focus. David L. Bever. (Illus.). 448p. 1984. 24.95 o.p. (ISBN 0-8016-0681-0). Mosby.

Safety & Health - A Guide to Law. 1980. 2.00 o.p. Natl Lawyers Guild.

Safety & Health in Agricultural Work: An ILO Code of Practice. 4th ed. 1983. 12.25 o.p. Intl Labour Office.

Safety & Health in Agricultural Work: ILO Code of Practice. 2nd ed. 1973. 12.25 o.p. (ISBN 92-2-100194-6). Intl Labour Office.

Safety & Health in Building & Civil Engineering Work: ILO Code of Practice. 1981. 28.00 o.p. (ISBN 92-2-100974-2). Intl Labour Office.

Safety & Health in Shipbuilding & Ship Repairing. (An IRO Code of Practice Ser.: No. 27). 1984. 19.25 o.p. (ISBN 92-2-101199-2). Intl Labour Office.

Safety & Health in Shipbuilding & Ship Repairing: ILO Code of Practice. 2nd ed. 1978. 19.25 o.p. (ISBN 92-2-101199-2). Intl Labour Office.

Safety & Health Practices of Multinational Enterprises. International Labour Organisation Staff. viii, 90p. 1984. pap. 12.25 o.p. (ISBN 92-2-103742-8). Intl Labour Office.

Safety & Survival at Sea. E. C. Lee & Kenneth Lee. (Illus.). 1972. 10.00 o.p. (ISBN 0-393-03112-8). Norton.

Safety & Survival at Sea. rev. ed. E. C. Lee & Kenneth Lee. (Illus.). 1980. 17.95 o.p. (ISBN 0-393-03242-6). Norton.

Safety & Survival Education see Individualized Health Incentive Program Modules For Physically Disabled Students.

Safety & the Executive. James V. Findlay. Frwd. by Bette Stephenson & William Hassel. LC 79-54954. (Illus.). 128p. 1979. 18.00 o.p. (ISBN 0-88061-008-5). Inst Pub ILCI.

Safety at Work & the Unions. P. B. Beaumont. (Illus.). 192p. 1983. 25.25 o.p. (ISBN 0-7099-0097-X, Pub. by Croom Helm Ltd). Routledge Chapman & Hall.

Safety, Health & Welfare in the Printing Industry. M. C. Fairley. 1968. pap. 7.75 o.p. (ISBN 0-08-013033-X). Pergamon.

Safety in Construction & Maintenance Work Zones & Transportation of Hazardous Materials. (Transportation Research Record Ser.). 51p. 1978. 3.00 o.p. (ISBN 0-309-02839-6). Transport Res Bd.

Safety in Industry. D. I. Macfarlane. (Illus.). 72p. 1955. (ISBN 0-8022-1028-7). Philos Lib.

Safety in Nuclear Power Plant Operation, Including Commissioning & Decommissioning: A Code of Practice. (Safety Ser.: No. 50-C-O). 40p. (Fr., Eng., Rus. & Span.). 1979. pap. write for info. o.p. (ISP503, IAEA). UNIPUB.

Safety in Working with Chemistry. Michael E. Green & Amos Turk. (Illus.). 1978. pap. text ed. write for info. o.p. (ISBN 0-02-346420-8). Macmillan.

Safety Labels for Padmounted Switchgear & Transformers Sited in Public Areas. 1982. 6.50 o.p. (ISBN 0-318-18031-6, 260-1982). Natl Elec Mfrs.

Safety Management. 4th ed. John V. Grimaldi & Rollin H. Simonds. 1984. 38.95x o.p. (ISBN 0-256-02507-X). Irwin.

Safety Management: A Human Approach. Dan Petersen. LC 74-32008. (Illus.). 395p. 1975. 28.50x o.p. (ISBN 0-913690-04-X). Aloray.

Safety Management Planning Manual. Ted S. Ferry. 1987. looseleaf 287.00x o.p. (ISBN 0-930868-46-3). Merritt Co.

Safety of Computer Control Systems, 1983: Achieving Safe Real Time Computer Systems, Proceedings of the Third IFAC-IFIP Workshop, SAFECOMP 'Eighty-Three, Cambridge, U. K., September 20-22, 1983. Ed. by J. A. Baylis. (IFAC Proceedings Ser.). 233p. 1983. 77.00 o.p. (ISBN 0-08-030563-6, 11/2). Pergamon.

Safety of Computer Control Systems 1985: Proceedings of the 4th IFAC Workshop, Como, Italy, 1-3 October 1985. Ed. by W. J. Quirk. (IFAC Publication Ser.). (Illus.). 190p. 1985. 51.00 o.p. (ISBN 0-08-032570-X, Pub. by PPL). Pergamon.

Safety of Foods. 2nd ed. Horace D. Graham. (Illus.). 1980. 67.95 o.s.i. (ISBN 0-87055-337-2). AVI.

Safety Operations Manual. 250p. 1981. 3-ring binder 18.95 o.p. (ISBN 0-317-57922-3, MG850). Natl Restaurant Assn.

Safety Performance Management. George L. Germain. (Illus.). 38p. Incl. transparency masters. 3-ring binder 57.50 o.s.i. (ISBN 0-88061-019-0). Inst Pub ILCI.

Safety Regulation & Compliance. Ed. by Freddy Homburger & Judith K. Marquis. 129p. 1985. 49.00x o.p. (ISBN 3-8055-3941-X). Transaction Pubs.

Safety Signs & Announcements. (Easy-to-Make Photocopier Bks.). (Orig.). 1983. pap. 14.95 o.p. (ISBN 0-87280-038-5, Asher-Gallant). Caddylak Systs.

Safety Supervision. Dan Petersen. LC 83-26608. 211p. 1984. Repr. 19.50x o.p. (ISBN 0-913690-10-4). Aloray.

Safety-Wise: For Girls (Grade 7-12) & Adults Who Work Directly with Girls. rev. ed. Girl Scouts of the U. S. A. Staff. 1982. pap. 1.40 o.p. (ISBN 0-88441-428-0, 26-206). Girl Scouts USA.

Saga, Legend, Tale, Novella, Fable. George W. Coats. (JSOT Supplement Ser.). 159p. pap. text ed. 8.95x o.s.i. Eisenbrauns.

Saga of a Wayward Sailor. Tristan Jones. 272p. 1980. pap. 3.50 o.p. (ISBN 0-380-52985-8, 62190-8). Avon.

Saga of Aaron Burr. John P. Cohalan, Jr. LC 85-91063. 80p. 1986. text ed. 12.50 o.s.i. (ISBN 0-682-40286-9). Exposition-Phoenix.

Saga of an American Jewish Family since the Revolution: A History of the Family of Jonas Phillips. Samuel Rezneck. LC 79-6725. 1980. text ed. 26.75 o.p. (ISBN 0-8191-0939-8); pap. text ed. 12.25 o.p. (ISBN 0-8191-0940-1). U Pr of Amer.

Saga of Denny McCune. Burt Arthur & Budd Arthur. 1979. pap. 1.25 o.p. (ISBN 0-505-51397-8, Pub. by Tower Bks). Dorchester Pub Co.

Saga of Erik the Viking. (ISBN 0-8052-3876-X). Random.

Saga of Seven Sisters. Hazel S. McCartney. 1985. 12.00 o.p. (ISBN 0-533-06270-5). Vantage.

Saga of Silent Sue. Leigh Williams. LC 85-25721. (Chumble Chums Ser.). (Illus.). 32p. (ps-3). 1987. 5.95 o.s.i. (ISBN 0-394-87849-3, BYR). Random.

Saga of the Bluebird. Katherine M. Braun. (Illus.). 62p. 1982. pap. 7.00 o.s.i. (ISBN 0-682-49913-7). Exposition-Phoenix.

Saga of the Mountain Soldiers: The Story of the Tenth Mountain Division. Curtis W. Casewit. LC 81-9662. (Illus.). 160p. (gr. 7 up). 1981. lib. bdg. 9.79 o.s.i. (ISBN 0-671-41630-8). Messner.

Sagesse see Bonne Chanson.

Saguaro Forest. Peter Wild. LC 86-60514. (Western Horizons Bk.). (Illus.). 96p. (Orig.). 1986. pap. 11.95 o.p. (ISBN 0-87358-405-8). Northland.

Sahara Handbook: Algeria, Lybia, Egypt, Niger, Mali. Rev. 2nd ed. Simon Glen & Jan Glen. (Illus.). 316p. (Orig.). 1986. pap. 29.95 o.p. (ISBN 0-903909-10-3, Roger Lascelles). Bradt Ent.

Sahib: An American Misadventure in India. Carl Pope. 192p. 1972. 6.95 o.p. (ISBN 0-87140-553-9). Liveright.

Sai Baba, the Saint of Shirdi. Mani Sahukar. LC 75-29273. 1977. 3.95 o.s.i. (ISBN 0-913922-11-0). Dawn Horse Pr.

Saigon. Anthony Grey. 825p. 1982. 19.95 o.p. (ISBN 0-316-32822-7). Little.

Sail Before Sunset. Earl Hinz. LC 79-250. (Illus.). 244p. 1979. 12.95 o.p. (ISBN 0-679-51350-7). Western Marine Ent.

Sail Far Away: Reflections on Life Afloat. Robert Carter. (Illus.). 1978. 11.95 o.p. (ISBN 0-393-03214-0). Norton.

Sailboat Auxiliary Engine Maintenance: Atomic, Chrysler, Ford, Perkins, Pisces, Volvo-Penta, Westerbeke, Yanmar. Brick Price. Ed. by Jeff Robinson. (Illus.). 144p. 1975. pap. text ed. 9.00 o.p. (ISBN 0-89287-079-6, B610). Clymer Pub.

Sailboat Maintenance. Ed. by Jeff Robinson. (Illus.). 336p. pap. text ed. 10.00 o.p. (ISBN 0-89287-068-0, B600). Clymer Pub.

Sailing Aerodynamics. John Morwood. (Illus.). 128p. 1954. (ISBN 0-8022-1158-5). Philos Lib.

Sailing Away from Night. John Digby. 1978. pap. 5.00 o.p. (ISBN 0-686-65479-X). Story Line.

Sailing Book. Michael Bartlett & Joanne A. Fishman. LC 81-71663. 1982. 22.95 o.p. (ISBN 0-87795-369-4, Arbor Hse). Morrow.

Sailing: From Jibs to Jibing. Gary Paulsen. LC 81-9627. (Illus.). 192p. (gr. 7 up). 1981. lib. bdg. 9.79 o.s.i. (ISBN 0-671-34057-3). Messner.

Sailing Is for Me. Tom Vandervoort. LC 81-3726. (Sports for Me Bks.). (Illus.). (gr. 2-5). 1981. PLB 7.95 o.p. (ISBN 0-8225-1128-2, AACR2). Lerner Pubns.

Sailing Journal: An Illustrated Notebook with Quotes. Running Press Staff. (Orig.). 1987. pap. 5.95 o.p. (ISBN 0-89471-546-1); lib. bdg. 15.90 o.p. (ISBN 0-89471-547-X). Running Pr.

Sailing Knots. J. Altimiras. Tr. by Tom Willis. 128p. 1984. 12.95 o.p. (ISBN 0-668-06266-5). Arco.

Sailing Lifestyle: A Guide to Sailing & Cruising for Pleasure. John Rousmaniere. (Illus.). 288p. 1985. 16.45 o.p. (ISBN 0-671-50887-3). S&S.

Sailing Primer. Harvey Frommer & Ronald Weinmann. LC 77-13431. 1978. 7.95 o.p. (ISBN 0-689-10841-9, Atheneum). Macmillan.

Sailing Smart: Winning Techniques, Tactics & Strategies. Buddy Melges & Charles Mason. LC 82-15557. (Illus.). 216p. 1983. 16.95 o.s.i. (ISBN 0-03-058579-1). H Holt & Co.

Sailing to Cythera: And Other Anatole Stories. Nancy Willard. LC 74-5602. (Illus.). 80p. (gr. k up). 1974. 5.95 o.p. (ISBN 0-15-269960-0, HJ). HarBraceJ.

Sailing with Paul. H. A. Ironside. pap. 1.35 o.p. (ISBN 0-87213-387-7). Loizeaux.

Sailing Yacht. 2nd ed. Juan Baader. Tr. by Inge Moore. (Illus.). 1979. 32.50 o.p. (ISBN 0-393-03220-5). Norton.

Saint Abroad. Leslie Charteris. (Saint Ser.). 1979. pap. 1.95 o.p. (ISBN 0-441-74896-1). Ace Bks.

St. Agustine's Conversation: An Outline of His Development to the Time of His Ordination. William J. Simpson. (Church Historical Society London N. S. Ser.: No. 1). Repr. of 1930 ed. 40.00 o.p. (ISBN 0-8115-3125-2). Kraus Repr.

Saint & Mr. Teal. Leslie Charteris. (Saint Ser.). 176p. 1981. pap. 2.25 o.s.i. (ISBN 0-441-74911-9). Ace Bks.

Saint & the Happy Highwayman. Leslie Charteris. (Saint Ser.). 224p. 1981. pap. 2.50 o.s.i. (ISBN 0-441-74891-0). Ace Bks.

Saint & the Hapsburg Necklace. Leslie Charteris. 192p. 1979. pap. 1.95 o.p. (ISBN 0-441-74898-8). Ace Bks.

Saint & the People Importers. Leslie Charteris. (Saint Ser.). 1979. pap. 1.95 o.p. (ISBN 0-441-74900-3). Ace Bks.

Saint & the Sizzling Saboteur. Leslie Charteris. (Saint Ser.). 160p. 1981. pap. 2.25 o.p. (ISBN 0-441-74908-9). Ace Bks.

St. Antholin's; or, Old Churches & New: A Tale for the Times, 1841. Francis E. Paget. Ed. by Robert L. Wolff. Bd. with Milford Malvoisin; or, Pews & Pew-Holders, 1842. LC 75-469. (Victorian Fiction Ser.). 1975. lib. bdg. 73.00 o.p. (ISBN 0-8240-1547-9). Garland Pub.

Saint-Blaise-Des-Simples. Jean Cocteau. (Illus.). 32p. 1973. 8.95 o.p. (ISBN 0-686-54560-5). French & Eur.

St. Clair: Three Narratives. John A. Scott. 131p. 1987. 12.50 o.p. (ISBN 0-7022-1907-X). U of Queensland Pr.

St. Croix Boyhood. Ralph L. Henry. LC 72-84771. (Illus.). 107p. 1972. 4.95 o.p. (ISBN 0-685-26839-X). Minn Hist.

St. Croix, St. Thomas, St. John: Danish West Indian Sketchbook & Diary, 1843-44. Henry Morton. (Illus.). 184p. 1975. 27.50x o.p. (ISBN 87-980249-2-2, St. Croix Landmarks Society). U Pr of Va.

Saint Elizabeth. Anne Seesholtz. 1952. (ISBN 0-8022-1532-7). Philos Lib.

Saint Errant. Leslie Charteris. (Saint Ser.). 224p. 1981. pap. 2.25 o.p. (ISBN 0-441-74888-0). Ace Bks.

St. Francis De Sales. Henry Covannier. 1973. Repr. 5.00 o.s.i. (ISBN 0-8198-0512-2). Dghtrs St Paul.

St. George & the Dragon: A Folk Play. Compiled by John Langstaff. LC 73-75437. (gr. 3 up). 1973. PLB 4.95 o.p. (ISBN 0-689-30421-8, Atheneum). Macmillan.

St. George & the Godfather. Norman Mailer. 1983. 16.95 o.p. (ISBN 0-87795-560-3, Arbor Hse); pap. 7.95 o.p. (ISBN 0-87795-563-8). Morrow.

St. Germaine. rev. ed. Louise Cantoni. (gr. 4-8). 1973. 1.75 o.s.i. (ISBN 0-8198-0262-X). Dghtrs St Paul.

Saint Goes on. Leslie Charteris. 1982. pap. 2.50 o.s.i. (ISBN 0-441-74882-1). Ace Bks.

Saint Goes West. Leslie Charteris. 200p. 1982. pap. 2.50 o.s.i. (ISBN 0-441-74883-X). Ace Bks.

Saint in Action. Leslie Charteris. 320p. 1980. pap. 2.25 o.p. (ISBN 0-441-74899-6). Ace Bks.

Saint Intervenes. Leslie Charteris. 304p. 1981. pap. 2.25 o.p. (ISBN 0-441-74887-2). Ace Bks.

Saint Jerome in the Renaissance. Eugene F. Rice, Jr. LC 84-21321. (Symposia in Comparative History Ser.: No. 13). (Illus.). 272p. 1985. text ed. 32.50x o.p. (ISBN 0-8018-2381-1). Johns Hopkins.

Saint Joan. George Bernard Shaw. Ed. by Stanley Weintraub. LC 76-134308. 1971. pap. 8.95 o.p. (ISBN 0-672-61091-4). Odyssey Pr.

Saint Joan. George Bernard Shaw. (Penguin Plays Ser.). (YA) (gr. 9 up). 1950. pap. 2.95 o.p. (ISBN 0-14-048005-6). Penguin.

Saint Joan of Arc. Vita Sackville-West. LC 84-9125. 416p. 1984. pap. 7.95 o.p. (ISBN 0-8398-2856-X, Gregg). G K Hall.

Saint John. John Marsh. LC 77-81619. (Westminster Pelican Commentaries Ser.). 704p. 1978. 19.50 o.s.i. (ISBN 0-664-21346-4, Westminster). Westminster John Knox.

Saint John Chrysostom: A Scripture Index. R. A. Krupp. LC 84-21028. 270p. 1985. lib. bdg. 29.00 o.p. (ISBN 0-8191-4380-4). U Pr of Amer.

Saint John: Two Hundred Years Proud. George W. Schuyler. (Illus.). 208p. 1984. 27.95 o.s.i. (ISBN 0-89781-108-9). Windsor Pubns Inc.

St. Jude & "His People" Antoinette Ancona. LC 85-90095. 124p. 1985. 10.95 o.p. (ISBN 0-533-06604-2). Vantage.

Saint-Just, Colleague of Robespierre. Eugene W. Curtis. LC 73-14540. xi, 402p. 1973. Repr. of 1935 ed. lib. bdg. 31.50x o.p. (ISBN 0-374-92010-9, Octagon). Hippocrene Bks.

St. Leon: A Tale of the Sixteenth Century, 4 vols. William Godwin. (Feminist Controversy in England, 1788-1810 Ser.). 1974. Set. lib. bdg. 242.00 o.p. (ISBN 0-8240-0862-6). Garland Pub.

St. Louis. (Documentary History of American Cities Ser.). 220p. pap. 6.95 o.p. (ISBN 0-8160-1503-1). Facts on File.

St. Louis Cardinals. rev. ed. Martin. (Baseball Today Ser.). 48p. (gr. 4 up). 1982. PLB 11.45 o.p. (ISBN 0-87191-875-7). Creative Ed.

Saint Luke. G. B. Caird. LC 77-81622. (Westminster Pelican Commentaries Ser.). 272p. 1978. 10.95 o.s.i. (ISBN 0-664-21345-6, Westminster). Westminster John Knox.

Saint Margaret of Cortona. Francois Mauriac. Tr. by Bernard Fechtman. 243p. 1948. (ISBN 0-8022-1088-0). Philos Lib.

Saint Mark. D. E. Nineham. LC 77-81621. (Westminster Pelican Commentaries Ser.). 478p. 1978. 14.95 o.s.i. (ISBN 0-664-21344-8, Westminster). Westminster John Knox.

St. Martin de Porres. Richard C. Cushing. LC 62-20203. (Illus.). 75p. 1981. 4.00 o.s.i. (ISBN 0-8198-6818-3, STO280); pap. 2.00 o.s.i. (ISBN 0-8198-6819-1). Dghtrs St Paul.

St. Maximilian Kolbe. Antonio Ricciardi. 1988. 7.95 o.p. (ISBN 0-317-67493-5, ST0283); pap. 6.50 o.p. (ISBN 0-317-67494-3). Dghtrs St Paul.

Saint Meets the Tiger. Leslie Charteris. 320p. 1980. pap. 1.95 o.p. (ISBN 0-441-52411-7). Ace Bks.

Saint of the Day. Ed. by Leonard Foley. (Illus.). 354p. 1981. text ed. 10.95 o.p. (ISBN 0-912228-96-2). St Anthony Mess Pr.

Saint on the Spanish Main. Leslie Charteris. (Saint Ser.). 224p. 1981. pap. 2.25 o.p. (ISBN 0-441-74889-9). Ace Bks.

Saint Overboard. Leslie Charteris. (The Saint Ser.). 288p. 1981. pap. 2.25 o.p. (ISBN 0-441-74895-3). Ace Bks.

St. Paul of the Cross: A Source-Workbook in Paulacrucian Studies. Jude C. Mead. 560p. 1983. pap. 12.95 o.p. (ISBN 0-89944-070-3). Don Bosco Multimedia.

Saint Paul's Journey in the Greek Orient. Henri Metzger. 1956. Philos Lib.

St. Peter's Banker: Michele Sindona. Luigi Difonzo. 288p. 1983. 15.95 o.p. (ISBN 0-531-09889-3). Watts.

St. Peter's Fair. Ellis Peters. 224p. 1984. pap. 2.95 o.p. (ISBN 0-449-20540-1, Crest). Fawcett.

St. Petersburg. Andrei Biely. Tr. & intro. by John Cournos. (Illus., Orig.). (YA) (gr. 9 up). 1959. pap. 12.50 o.p. (ISBN 0-394-17237-X, E331, Ever). Grove.

St. Petersburg, Industrialization & Change. James H. Bater. (Studies in Urban History Ser). 400p. 1976. lib. bdg. 32.00x o.p. (ISBN 0-7735-0266-1, McGill Canada). U of Toronto Pr.

Saint Returns. Leslie Charteris. (Lythway Ser.). 248p. 1988. lib. bdg. 18.50x o.p. (ISBN 0-7451-0714-1, Pub. by Chivers Pr UK). G K Hall.

Saint Steps in. Leslie Charteris. (Saint Ser.). 288p. 1980. pap. 1.95 o.p. (ISBN 0-441-74902-X). Ace Bks.

St. Teresa of Avila. Giorgio Papasogli. LC 58-12223. 1973. Repr. 5.00 o.p. (ISBN 0-8198-0511-4). Dghtrs St Paul.

St. Thomas Aquinas: Scriptum Super Sententiis - An Index of Authorities Cited. Charles H. Lohr. viii, 391p. 1980. 50.00x o.p. (ISBN 0-8232-0103-1). Fordham.

Saint to the Rescue. Leslie Charteris. (Saint Ser.). 256p. 1980. pap. 1.95 o.p. (ISBN 0-441-74903-8). Ace Bks.

St. Vincent & the Grenadines: Economic Situation & Selected Development Issues. 122p. 1985. 5.00 o.p. (ISBN 0-8213-0625-1, BK 0625). World Bank.

Saint vs. Scotland Yard. Leslie Charteris. 288p. 1980. pap. 2.25 o.p. (ISBN 0-441-74907-0). Ace Bks.

Saint Wulstan, Prelate & Patriot: A Study of His Life & Times. John W. Lamb. (Church Historical Society, London, New Ser.: No. 16). Repr. of 1933 ed. 40.00 o.p. (ISBN 0-8115-3139-2). Kraus Repr.

Saints Are People: Church History Through the Saints. Alfred McBride. 144p. (Orig.). 1981. pap. 4.50 o.p. (ISBN 0-697-01785-0). Wm C Brown.

Saints' Craftbook. Margaret L. Sheriff. Tr. by Bette S. Margolis. (Illus., Orig.). 1976. pap. 3.95 o.p. (ISBN 0-8192-1213-X). Morehouse Pub.

Saints for Contemporary Women. Mary H. Valentine. 1987. 12.95 o.p. (ISBN 0-88347-210-4). Thomas More.

Saints for Kids by Kids. Robert Charlebois et al. 80p. 1984. pap. 2.95 o.p. (ISBN 0-89243-223-3). Liguori Pubns.

Saints for Young Christians. Ed Curley. (gr. 4-6). 1983. 9.95 o.p. (ISBN 0-89837-088-4, Pub. by Pflaum Pr). Pflaum Pr.

Saint's Getaway. Leslie Charteris. (Saint Ser.). 256p. 1980. pap. 1.95 o.p. (ISBN 0-441-74905-4). Ace Bks.

Saints: Heroes to Follow. William V. Coleman & Patricia R. Coleman. (Daybreak Ser.). (Illus.). 1976. tchrs. ed. 9.95x o.p. (ISBN 0-89622-038-9). Twenty-Third.

Saints in Art. Clara E. Clement. LC 77-89303. 240p. 1976. Repr. of 1899 ed. 46.00x o.p. (ISBN 0-8103-3030-X). Gale.

Saints of Sage & Saddle: Folklore Among the Mormons. Austin Fife & Alta Fife. 375p. 1980. pap. 14.95 o.p. (ISBN 0-87480-180-X). U of Utah Pr.

Saints of the Atlas. Ernest Gellner. LC 78-89515. (Nature of Human Society Ser.). 1969. lib. bdg. 20.00x o.s.i. (ISBN 0-226-28699-1). U of Chicago Pr.

Saint's Revelation. LC 84-90117. 51p. 1985. 6.95 o.p. (ISBN 0-533-06193-8). Vantage.

Saints Without Halos: The Human Side of Mormon History. Leonard J. Arrington & Davis Bitton. 168p. 1981. 10.95 o.p. (ISBN 0-941214-01-X). Signature Bks.

Salad & Soup Book: More Than Two Hundred & Fifty Delectable Recipes from Annie's Kitchen. Annie Lerman. LC 83-9178. (Illus.). 144p. (Orig.). 1983. lib. bdg. 15.90 o.p. (ISBN 0-89471-236-5); pap. 6.95 o.p. (ISBN 0-89471-235-7). Running Pr.

Salad Book. Geri Harrington. LC 76-53406. 1977. 9.95 o.p. (ISBN 0-689-10789-7, Atheneum). Macmillan.

Salad Crops All Year Round. H. Witham Fogg. (Illus.). 200p. 1983. 19.95 o.p. (ISBN 0-7153-8411-2). David & Charles.

Salad Garden. Elisabeth Arter. 190p. 15.00 o.p. (ISBN 0-7099-0530-0, Pub. by Croom Helm Ltd). Routledge Chapman & Hall.

Saladin in His Time. P. H. Newby. LC 83-20831. 224p. 1984. 23.95 o.p. (ISBN 0-571-13044-5). Faber & Faber.

Salads & Summer Dishes. Maren Lopategui. (Step-by-Step Cooking Ser.). 160p. 1986. 10.95 o.p. (ISBN 0-8120-5683-3). Barron.

Salaries of Engineering Technicians & Technologists: 1981. 225.00x o.p. (ISBN 0-87615-142-X, 304-82). AAES.

Salaries of Engineers in Education 1984. Engineering Manpower Commission. Ed. by P. J. Sheridan. (Illus.). 75p. (Orig.). 1984. pap. 55.00 o.p. (ISBN 0-87615-155-1). AAES.

Salaries of Engineers in Education 1986. Engineering Manpower Commission & R. A. Ellis. (Orig.). 1987. pap. 80.00 o.p. (ISBN 0-87615-156-X). AAES.

Salary Management for the Nonspecialist. Stanley B. Henrici. 256p. 1980. 15.95 o.p. (ISBN 0-8144-5565-4). AMACOM.

Salary Study. 1985. text ed. 10.00 o.p. (ISBN 0-87868-244-9, 2449). Child Welfare.

Sale & Distribution of Books from Seventeen Hundred. Ed. by Robin Myers & Michael Harris. (Publishing Pathways Ser.). (Illus.). 130p. 1986. pap. 10.00 o.p. (ISBN 0-317-47132-5). Chadwyck-Healey.

Salem Chapel. Margaret W. Oliphant. Ed. by Robert L. Wolff. LC 75-1508. (Victorian Fiction Ser.). 1975. Repr. of 1863 ed. lib. bdg. 66.00 o.p. (ISBN 0-8240-1582-7). Garland Pub.

Salem Witchcraft, 2 Vols. Charles W. Upham. LC 59-10887. (American Classics Ser.). (Illus.). 1959. 40.00x o.p. (ISBN 0-8044-1947-7). Ungar.

Sales & Marketing Forms. (Easy-to-Make Photocopier Bks.). (Orig.). 1982. pap. 14.95 o.s.i. (ISBN 0-87280-044-X, Asher-Gallant). Caddylak Systs.

Sales & Promotional Announcements. (Easy-to-Make Photocopier Bks.). (Orig.). 1984. pap. 14.95 o.p. (ISBN 0-87280-031-8, Asher-Gallant). Caddylak Systs.

Sales & Sales Management. 2nd ed. P. Allen. (Illus.). 288p. 1979. pap. 15.95x o.p. (ISBN 0-7121-1962-0, Pub. by Macdonald & Evans England). Trans-Atl Phila.

Sales Budgeting. (PRIME-PRIME 100 Ser). 1969. 35.00 o.p. (ISBN 0-8144-1106-1). AMACOM.

Sales Forecasting for the Field Sales Manager. (PRIME-PRIME 100 Ser). 1973. 35.00 o.p. (ISBN 0-8144-1110-X). AMACOM.

Sales Laws (N. Y.) 1976 ed. Paul Zola. 100p. 1975. 5.00 o.p. (ISBN 0-87526-210-4). Gould.

Sales Management. Chonko & Enis. 1989. 36.95 o.p. (ISBN 0-256-05965-9). Irwin.

Sales Management. Charles M. Futrell. LC 80-65796. 528p. 1981. text ed. 32.95x o.s.i. (ISBN 0-03-049276-9); instr's. manual 10.00 o.s.i. (ISBN 0-03-052201-3). Dryden Pr.

Sales Management. Robert F. Hartley. LC 78-69614. (Illus.). 1979. text ed. 42.36 o.p. (ISBN 0-395-26511-8); test bank 1.50 o.p. HM.

Sales Management: Concepts & Cases. 2nd ed. Douglas J. Dalrymple. LC 84-17226. 635p. 1985. text ed. (ISBN 0-471-87872-3). Halsted Pr.

Sales Management Game. 2nd ed. Louis E. Boone et al. 1978. pap. text ed. write for info. o.p. (ISBN 0-02-312170-X). Macmillan.

Sales Manager's Handbook. Ed. by Edwin E. Bobrow & Larry Wizenberg. LC 82-71068. 576p. 1983. 55.00 o.p. (ISBN 0-87094-240-9). Dow Jones-Irwin.

Sales of Real Property. Samuel A. Goldberg. 605p. 1971. 17.50 o.p. (ISBN 0-317-30765-7, B253). Am Law Inst.

Salesman in the Field: Conditions of Work & Employment of Commercial Travellers & Representatives. Michael Bell. Ed. by International Labour Office, Geneva Staff. viii, 108p. (Orig.). 1980. pap. 10.50 o.p. (ISBN 92-2-102308-7). Intl Labour Office.

Salesman Review Outline. 9th ed. George Gaines, Jr. & David S. Coleman. 168p. 1985. pap. 12.95 o.p. (ISBN 0-88462-528-1, 1610-03, Real Estate Ed). Longman Finan.

Salesman Review Outline & Exam Guide. 11th ed. George Gaines, Jr. & David S. Coleman. (G & C Learning Ser.). 194p. 1987. pap. 12.95 o.p. (ISBN 0-88462-671-7, Real Estate Ed); pap. text ed. 7.95 o.p. (ISBN 0-317-57653-4, Real Estate Ed). Longman Finan.

Salesman's Laugh. 2.00 o.p. (ISBN 0-936672-48-X). Aerial Photo.

Salesmanship: A Contemporary Approach. Ferdinand F. Mauser. 1973. text ed. 15.95 o.p. (ISBN 0-15-578042-5, HC). HarBraceJ.

Salespersons Guide to Merchandising. Carol A. Cardella. 44p. 1978. pap. 6.50 o.p. (ISBN 0-86718-041-2). Nat Assn H Build.

Saliva & Salivation: Proceedings of a Satellite Symposium to the 28th International Congress of Physiological Held at Szekesfehervar, Hungary, 1980. Ed. by T. Zelles. LC 80-41878. (Advances in Physiological Sciences: Vol. 28). (Illus.). 500p. 1981. 87.00 o.p. (ISBN 0-08-027349-1). Pergamon.

Salivary Gland Tumors. Ed. by Ludwika Sikorowa et al. LC 80-14975. 200p. 1983. 14.75 o.p. (ISBN 0-08-025557-4). Pergamon.

Salivary Glands & Their Secretions. Ed. by L. M. Sreebny & J. Meyer. 1964. 100.00 o.p. (ISBN 0-08-010546-7). Pergamon.

Sally Wister's Journal. Sarah Wister. 96p. 1988. pap. 7.95 o.p. (ISBN 1-55709-114-5). Applewood.

Sally's Calendar Book. Gloria G. Morrell. (gr. 1-3). 1986. pap. 3.95 o.p. (ISBN 0-8054-4337-1). Broadman.

Salmagundi Reader. Ed. by Robert Boyers & Peggy Boyers. LC 82-49294. 640p. 1984. 25.00x o.p. (ISBN 0-253-35060-3). Ind U Pr.

Salmon. Atsushi Sakurai. LC 83-47941. (Illus.). 1984. 18.45 o.s.i. (ISBN 0-394-53397-6). Knopf.

Salmon for Simon. Betty Waterton. LC 79-55187. (Illus.). 32p. (ps-3). 1980. 8.95 o.p. (ISBN 0-689-50169-2, Atheneum). Macmillan.

Salmon: Their Fight for Survival. Anthony Netboy. (Illus.). 1974. 17.95 o.p. (ISBN 0-395-14013-7). HM.

Salonica Travel Guide. Berlitz Editors. (Travel Guides Ser.). 1980. pap. 4.95 o.p. (Berlitz). Macmillan.

Salons of the "Independants", 1884 to 1891. Ed. by Theodore Reff. (Modern Art in Paris 1855 to 1900 Ser.). 253p. 1981. lib. bdg. 53.00 o.p. (ISBN 0-8240-4709-5). Garland Pub.

Salons of the "Independants", 1892 to 1895. Ed. by Theodore Reff. (Modern Art in Paris 1855 to 1900 Ser.). 320p. 1981. lib. bdg. 53.00 o.p. (ISBN 0-8240-4710-9). Garland Pub.

Salons of the "Refuses" Ed. by Theodore Reff. (Modern Art in Paris 1855 to 1900 Ser.). 133p. 1981. lib. bdg. 53.00 o.p. (ISBN 0-8240-4722-2). Garland Pub.

Saloon Survival. Andy Kane. LC 83-6414. (Illus.). 112p. 1983. pap. 6.00 o.p. (ISBN 0-87364-267-8). Paladin Pr.

SALT. Duncan Bush. LC 86-70095. 70p. 1986. pap. 9.95 o.p. (ISBN 0-907476-55-4, Pub. by Poetry Wales Pr UK). Dufour.

Salt & Hypertension: Proceedings of the Lewis K. Dahl Symposium. Ed. by Junichi Iwai. LC 82-1090. (Illus.). 320p. 1982. monograph 32.50 o.p. (ISBN 0-89640-072-7). Igaku-Shoin.

Salt & Light: Talks & Writings of the Sermon on the Mount. Eberhard Arnold. LC 77-1204. 1977. pap. 6.00 o.p. (ISBN 0-87486-170-5). Plough.

Salt & Light: Talks & Writings on the Sermon on the Mount. Eberhard Arnold. LC 67-18009. 1967. 8.00 o.p. (ISBN 0-87486-105-5). Plough.

Salt Boy. new ed. Mary Perrine. 32p. (gr. k-3). 1973. pap. 0.95 o.p. (ISBN 0-395-17450-3, Sandpiper). HM.

Salt Deposits, Their Origin & Composition. O. Braitsch. Tr. by P. J. Burek & A. E. Nairn. LC 74-132576. (Minerals, Rock & Inorganic Materials: Vol. 4). (Illus.). 1971. 42.00 o.p. (ISBN 0-387-05206-2). Springer-Verlag.

Salt-Free Herb Cookery. Edith Stovel. (Illus.). 32p. 1986. pap. 1.95 o.p. (ISBN 0-88266-342-9, Garden Way Pub). Storey Comm Inc.

Salt: The Complete Brand Name Guide to Sodium Content. Michael F. Jacobson et al. LC 82-40505. 320p. 1983. pap. 5.95 o.p. (ISBN 0-89480-361-1, 361). Workman Pub.

SALT: The Primary Cause of Disease? James H. Johnson. pap. 3.00 o.s.i. (ISBN 0-317-55120-5). Truth Seeker.

Salt-Water Aquarium in the Home. Robert P. Straughan. (Illus.). 384p. 1959. 19.95 o.s.i. (ISBN 0-498-01531-9). A S Barnes.

Saltbound: A Winter on Block Island. Chip Williamson. LC 79-26330. (Illus.). 1980. 10.95 o.p. (ISBN 0-416-00501-2, 0166). Routledge Chapman & Hall.

Salted Lemons. Doris B. Smith. LC 80-66250. 240p. (gr. 3-7). 1980. 9.95 o.s.i. (ISBN 0-02-778060-0, Four Winds). Macmillan.

Saltmarsh Ecology. S. P. Long & C. F. Mason. (Tertiary Level Biology Ser.). 1983. 35.00 o.p. (ISBN 0-412-00301-5, NO. 5034, Pub. by Chapman & Hall); pap. 16.95 o.p. (ISBN 0-412-00311-2, NO. 5035). Routledge Chapman & Hall.

Salts & Brines Nineteen Eighty-Five. Ed. by W. Joseph Schlitt. LC 84-52557. (Illus.). 209p. 1985. pap. 40.00 o.p. (ISBN 0-89520-434-7, 434-7). SMM&E Inc.

Salutations see Hunger & Thirst & Other Plays.

Salvador. Joan Didion. 1983. 12.50 o.p. (ISBN 0-671-47024-8). S&S.

Salvador Allende. J. Lavretski. 294p. (Span.). 1978. 6.45 o.p. (ISBN 0-8285-1445-3, Pub. by Progress Pubs USSR). Imported Pubns.

Salvador Witness: The Life & Calling of Jean Donovan. Ana Carrigan. 320p. 1984. 16.45 o.p. (ISBN 0-671-47992-X). S&S.

Salvagers. Harvey Benham. (Illus.). 212p. 1980. 14.00 o.p. (ISBN 0-9505944-2-3, Pub. by Boydell & Brewer). Longwood Pub Group.

Salvation. Robert Hicks & Richard Bewes. (Understanding Bible Truth Ser.). (Orig.). 1981. pap. 0.95 o.p. (ISBN 0-89840-019-8). Heres Life.

Salvation & Health: The Interlocking Processes of Life. James N. Lapsley. LC 79-188383. 174p. 1972. 5.95 o.s.i. (ISBN 0-664-20936-X, Westminster). Westminster John Knox.

Salvation & the Church. ARCIC II Staff. (Lambeth Study Papers). 32p. 1987. pap. 1.40 o.s.i. (ISBN 0-88028-063-8). Forward Movement.

Salvation Comes from the Lord. Arnold V. Wallenkampf. Ed. by Gerald Wheeler. LC 83-3297. 128p. (Orig.). 1983. pap. 5.95 o.s.i. (ISBN 0-8280-0210-X). Review & Herald.

Salvation of the Nations. Jean Danielou. 1962. pap. 2.95x o.p. (ISBN 0-268-00244-4). U of Notre Dame Pr.

Salvation Patrol. Winifred Gearing. 152p. (Orig.). 1981. 6.50 o.p. (ISBN 0-86544-018-2). Salv Army Suppl South.

Salzburg Connection. Helen MacInnes. LC 68-24394. 1968. 9.50 o.s.i. (ISBN 0-15-179253-4). HarBraceJ.

Sam & Violet Are Twins. Nicole Rubel. (Illus.). 32p. (gr. 1-3). 1981. pap. 1.95 o.p. (ISBN 0-380-76919-0, 76919-0, Camelot). Avon.

Sam & Violet Go Camping. Nicole Rubel. (Illus.). 32p. (gr. 1-3). 1981. pap. 1.95 o.p. (ISBN 0-380-76927-1, 76927-1, Camelot). Avon.

Sam & Violet's Bedtime Mystery. Nicole Rubel. (gr. k-3). 1985. pap. 2.50 o.p. (ISBN 0-380-89820-9, Camelot). Avon.

Sam & Violet's Birthday Book. Nicole Rubel. (Snuggle & Read Story Bks.). (Illus.). 32p. (Orig.). (ps-3). 1982. pap. 1.95 o.p. (ISBN 0-380-79095-5, 79095-5, Camelot). Avon.

Sam & Violet's Christmas Story. Nicole Rubel. (Illus.). 32p. (Orig.). (ps-3). 1981. pap. 1.95 o.p. (ISBN 0-380-78063-1, 78063, Camelot). Avon.

Sam Crockers Boats: A Design Catalog. Sturgis Crocker. LC 84-48687. (Illus.). 320p. 1985. 18.95 o.p. (ISBN 0-87742-195-1). Intl Marine.

Sam Et Violet Sont Jumeaux. Nicole Rubel. (Illus.). 32p. (Fr.). (ps-3). 1982. pap. 1.95 o.p. (ISBN 0-380-81281-9, 81281, Camelot). Avon.

Sam Francis. rev. ed. Peter Selz. Ed. by Susan Einstein & Jan Butterfiled. 1985. write for info. o.p. (ISBN 0-8109-0928-6). Abrams.

Sam Houston: Mid Muddle & Mud. D. B. Hiatt. (Illus.). 200p. 1980. 8.95 o.p. (ISBN 0-89015-272-1). Eakin Pr.

Sam Myers (Eighteen Five to Eighteen Eighty-Three) & Lydia Horner (Eighteen Thirty-Three to Nineteen Seven) Their Ancestors & Descendants. Forrest D. Myers. LC 78-71401. (Illus., Orig.). 1979. 15.00x o.s.i. (ISBN 0-9602156-0-3). A E Myers.

Sam Shepard. Don Shewey. 1985. pap. 3.95 o.p. (ISBN 0-440-17581-X). Dell.

Sam Shepard, Arthur Kopit, & the Off-Broadway Theater. Doris Auerbach. (United States Authors Ser.). 1982. lib. bdg. 14.50 o.p. (ISBN 0-8057-7371-1, Twayne). G K Hall.

Sam Shue & the Seven Satchels. LC 76-1480. (Illus.). 64p. (ps-4). 1977. 4.95 o.p. (ISBN 0-915998-02-5). Lime Rock Pr.

Sam, Sipe, & Company: The History of the Cleveland Browns. Bill Levy. (Illus.). 324p. 13.95 o.p. (ISBN 0-939738-04-X). Zubal Inc.

Sam Snead: Teaches You His Simple "Key Approach" to Golf. Sam Snead & Larry Sheehan. (Illus.). 1975. 9.95 o.p. (ISBN 0-689-10657-2, Atheneum). Macmillan.

Samadhi: The Superconsciousness of the Future. Mouni Sadha. (Unwin Paperbacks). 1977. pap. 8.95 o.p. (ISBN 0-04-149039-8). Unwin Hyman.

Samaras, Pastels & Bronzes. Donald Kuspit. (Illus.). 44p. (Orig.). 1982. pap. 15.00 o.p. (ISBN 0-938608-06-1). Pace Pubns.

Samaria. Parrot. 1958. (ISBN 0-8022-1274-3). Philos Lib.

Samaritans & Jews: The Origins of Samaritanism Reconsidered. R. J. Coggins. LC 74-3712. (Growing Points in Theology Ser.). 176p. 1974. pap. 3.49 o.p. (ISBN 0-8042-0109-9, John Knox). Westminster John Knox.

Samarkand. Z. Finitskaya. 108p. 1982. 5.45 o.p. (ISBN 0-8285-2353-3, Pub. by Progress Pubs USSR). Imported Pubns.

Same-Day Surgical & Medical Care. Earleen H. Cook & Joseph L. Cook. (Public Administration Ser.: P 1738). 18p. 1985. 3.00 o.p. (ISBN 0-89028-518-7). Vance Biblios.

Same River Twice. Corinne D. Bliss. LC 82-45169. 288p. 1982. 13.95 o.p. (ISBN 0-689-11296-3, Atheneum). Macmillan.

Sammy the Sloth. Alice L. Mason. (Illus.). 16p. (gr. k-6). 1984. pap. 1.50 o.p. (ISBN 0-8249-8064-6). Ideals.

Sammy's Missing Blanket. Roxanne D. Cote. 32p. 1986. 6.75 o.p. (ISBN 0-8062-2923-3). Carlton.

Samoan Tangle: A Study in Anglo-German-American Relations 1878-1900. Paul M. Kennedy. 342p. 1972. 35.00x o.p. (ISBN 0-7165-2150-4, BBA 03053, Pub. by Irish Academic Pr). Biblio Dist.

Samovnushenie I Ego Vliianie Na Organizm Cheloveka see Self-Suggestion & Its Influence on the Human Organism.

Sampled-Data Control Systems. Eliahu I. Jury. LC 76-57949. 476p. 1977. Repr. of 1958 ed. 29.50 o.p. (ISBN 0-88275-529-3). Krieger.

Sampler of Forms for Special Libraries. SLA, Social Science Group, Washington DC Chapter Staff. LC 81-8747. (Illus.). 212p. 1982. spiral bdg. 26.00 o.p. (ISBN 0-87111-262-0). SLA.

Sampler of New England Land Use. Aubrey W. Birkelbach. 1975. pap. 2.00 o.s.i. (ISBN 0-686-17294-9). Lincoln Inst Land.

Samplers: Four Centuries of a Gentle Craft. Anne Sebba. (Illus.). 1979. 12.98 o.s.i. (ISBN 0-500-23300-4). Thames Hudson.

Sampling & Statistics Handbook for Research in Education. Chester H. McCall, Jr. 368p. 1980. 15.00 o.p. (ISBN 0-8106-3089-3). NEA.

Sampling of Particulate Materials. 2nd ed. P. M. Gy. LC 79-16075. (Developments in Geomathematics Ser.: Vol. 4). 432p. 1982. 84.25 o.p. (ISBN 0-444-42079-7). Elsevier.

Sampling with Unequal Probabilities. K. R. Brewer & M. Hanif. (Lecture Notes in Statistics Ser.: Vol. 15). (Illus.). 164p. 1982. pap. 16.50 o.p. (ISBN 0-387-90807-2). Springer-Verlag.

Sams Hookup Book: Do-It-Yourself Connections for Your VCR. 104p. 1986. pap. 4.95 o.p. (ISBN 0-672-22248-5). Sams.

Sam's Place. Lilian Moore. LC 73-76325. (Illus.). 32p. (gr. 1 up). 1973. 4.25 o.p. (ISBN 0-689-30116-2, Atheneum). Macmillan.

Sam's System: A Guide to Computers. Rosemary Court. (Computer Bk.). (Illus.). 48p. (gr. 4 up). 1983. PLB 11.93 o.p. (ISBN 0-516-00591-X). Childrens.

Samson: A Secret Betrayed, a Vow Ignored. James L. Crenshaw. LC 77-15748. 1978. 7.95 o.p. (ISBN 0-8042-0170-6, John Knox). Westminster John Knox.

Samson Strike. Tony Williamson. LC 79-55594. 1980. 9.95 o.p. (ISBN 0-689-11061-8, Atheneum). Macmillan.

Samuel Barber. Nathan Broder. 111p. Repr. of 1954 ed. lib. bdg. 39.00 o.p. (Pub. by Am Repr Serv). Reprint Servs.

Samuel Beckett. Dierdre Bair. 1978. 19.95 o.p. (ISBN 0-15-179256-9). HarBraceJ.

Samuel Beckett. Ed. by Lawrence Graver & Raymond Federman. (Critical Heritage Ser.). 1979. 27.00x o.p. (ISBN 0-7100-8948-1). Routledge Chapman & Hall.

Samuel Beckett. Charles Lyons. LC 82-47989. (Grove Press Modern Dramatists Ser.). (Illus.). 196p. 1983. pap. 9.95 o.s.i. (ISBN 0-394-62411-4, E815, Ever). Grove.

Samuel Beckett. John Pilling. 1976. 21.95x o.p. (ISBN 0-7100-8323-8). Routledge Chapman & Hall.

Samuel Beckett: A Biography. Dierdre Bair. LC 79-24485. (Illus.). 736p. 1980. pap. 7.95 o.p. (ISBN 0-15-679241-9, Harv). HarBraceJ.

Samuel Beckett: A Checklist. J. F. Tanner & J. Don Vann. LC 70-626232. (Serif Ser.: No. 8). 91p. 1969. 10.00x o.p. (ISBN 0-87338-051-7). Kent St U Pr.

Samuel Daniel & Michael Drayton: A Reference Guide. James L. Harner. 1980. lib. bdg. 40.50 o.p. (ISBN 0-8161-8322-8, Hall Reference). G K Hall.

Samuel Gompers: A Selected List of References about the Man & His Times. David R. Myers. LC 86-600163. (Illus.). 63p. 1986. pap. 2.00 o.p. (ISBN 0-8444-0539-6, S/N 030-000-00177-0). USGPO.

Samuel Gompers: American Statesman. Florence C. Thorne. 192p. 1957. (ISBN 0-8022-1720-6). Philos Lib.

Samuel Greenberg, Hart Crane & the Lost Manuscripts. Marc Simon. 1978. text ed. 17.50x o.p. (ISBN 0-391-00558-8). Humanities.

Samuel Griswold Goodrich, Creator of Peter Parley. Daniel Roselle. LC 68-19534. 1968. 44.50x o.p. (ISBN 0-87395-033-X). State U Ny Pr.

Samuel Johnson. John Wain. 336p. 1976. pap. text ed. 4.95 o.p. (ISBN 0-07-067715-8). McGraw.

Samuel Johnson the Moralist. Robert B. Voitle, Jr. LC 61-8842. 1961. 15.00x o.s.i. (ISBN 0-674-78766-8). Harvard U Pr.

Samuel Milton Jones Papers: An Inventory to the Microfilm Edition. Morgan J. Barclay & Jean W. Strong. 95p. 1978. 5.95 o.p. (ISBN 0-318-03217-1). Ohio Hist Soc.

Samuel R. Delany: A Primary & Secondary Bibliography, 1962-1979. Michael W. Peplow & Robert S. Bravard. 1980. lib. bdg. 30.50 o.p. (ISBN 0-8161-8054-7, Hall Reference). G K Hall.

Samuel Richardson. Austin Dobson. LC 67-23877. 224p. 1968. Repr. of 1902 ed. 35.00x o.p. (ISBN 0-8103-3055-5). Gale.

Samuel Smith & the Politics of Business, 1752-1839. John S. Pancake. LC 72-4061. 248p. 1972. 16.50 o.p. (ISBN 0-8173-5161-2). U of Ala Pr.

Samuel Terry: The Botany Bay Rothschild. Gwyneth M. Dow. (Illus.). 256p. 1975. 23.00x o.p. (ISBN 0-424-06820-6, Pub. by Sydney U Pr). Intl Spec Bk.

Samuel Wilderspin & the Infant School Movement. Phillip McCann & Francis A. Young. (Illus.). 314p. 1983. 34.50 o.p. (ISBN 0-7099-2903-X, Pub. by Croom Helm Ltd). Routledge Chapman & Hall.

Samurai. Jean Mabire & Yves Breheret. (Corps d'Elite Ser.). 1979. pap. 2.25 o.p. (ISBN 0-441-74950-X). Ace Bks.

Samurai. George MacBeth. LC 75-2234. 240p. 1975. 6.95 o.p. (ISBN 0-15-179270-4). HarBraceJ.

Samurai: A Military History. S. R. Turnbull. (Illus.). 304p. 1983. Repr. of 1977 ed. 29.95 o.p. (ISBN 0-85045-097-7, Pub. by Osprey Pub UK). Seven Hills Bk Dists.

Samurai, the Invincible Warriors. F. Brinkley. Ed. by Charles Lucas. LC 75-42567. (Series 316). 1975. pap. text ed. 6.95 o.p. (ISBN 0-89750-043-1). Ohara Pubns.

San Agustin Acasaguastlan Archaeological Project: Report on the 1979 Field Season. Garry R. Walters. (Museum Briefs Ser.: No.25). 1980. pap. 2.30 o.p. (ISBN 0-913134-25-2). Mus Anthro Mo.

San Andreas. Alistair MacLean. LC 85-4395. 320p. 1985. 16.95 o.p. (ISBN 0-385-23152-0). Doubleday.

San Antone. V. J. Banis. 349p. 1985. 15.95 o.p. (ISBN 0-87795-683-9, Arbor Hse). Morrow.

San Antonio Spurs. Jim Moore. (NBA Today Ser.). (Illus.). 48p. (gr. 4 up). 1984. PLB 10.45 o.p. (ISBN 0-87191-988-5). Creative Ed.

San Antonio: The Texas Monthly Guidebook. Nancy H. Foster & Ben Fairbank. Ed. by Barbara Rodriguez. (Texas Monthly Guidebooks Ser.). 320p. (Orig.). 1983. pap. 9.95 o.p. (ISBN 0-932012-62-0). Texas Month Pr.

San Bernadino County Street Guide & Directory, 1988. Thomas Bros. Maps Staff. (Illus.). 232p. 1987. pap. 12.95 o.p. (ISBN 0-88130-252-X). Thomas Bros Maps.

San Bernardino County: Land of Contrasts. Walter C. Schuiling. (Illus.). 207p. 1984. 22.95 o.p. (ISBN 0-89781-116-X). Windsor Pubns Inc.

San Bernardino County: Prototype Courtroom Design. National Center for State Courts Staff. 18p. 1975. manuscript 1.08 o.s.i. (MAB-109). Natl Ctr St Courts.

San Bernardino County Public Schools: How Are They Doing? (1984) Lillian S. Clancy. (How Are THey Doing Ser.). 90p. 1984. pap. 13.95 o.p. (ISBN 0-939580-14-4). CA Schl Surveys.

San Bernardino County Street Atlas 1984. Thomas Brothers Maps. (Illus.). 240p. 1983. pap. 9.50 o.p. (ISBN 0-88130-045-4). Thomas Bros Maps.

San Bernardino County Street Atlas, 1985. Thomas Bros. Maps. (Illus.). 140p. 1985. pap. 9.50 o.p. (ISBN 0-88130-096-9). Thomas Bros Maps.

San Bernardino County Street Atlas, 1987. Thomas Bros. Maps Staff. (Illus.). 140p. 1986. pap. 12.95 o.p. (ISBN 0-88130-222-8). Thomas Bros Maps.

San Bernardino-Riverside Counties Census Tract. Thomas Bros. Maps Staff. 1988. 39.95 o.p. (ISBN 0-88130-340-2). Thomas Bros Maps.

San Bernardino-Riverside Counties Street Atlas & Directory with Zip Codes, 1987. rev. ed. Thomas Bros. Maps Staff. (Illus.). 455p. 1987. pap. 26.95 o.p. Thomas Bros Maps.

San Bernardino-Riverside Counties Street Atlas & Directory, 1987. rev. ed. Thomas Bros. Maps Staff. (Illus.). 448p. 1986. pap. 19.95 o.p. Thomas Bros Maps.

San Bernardino-Riverside Counties Street Atlas, 1985. Thomas Bros. Maps. (Illus.). 448p. 1985. pap. 17.00 o.p. (ISBN 0-88130-100-0). Thomas Bros Maps.

San Bernardino-Riverside Counties Street Atlas, 1986. Thomas Bros. Maps Staff. (Illus.). 448p. 1987. pap. 19.95 o.p. (ISBN 0-88130-223-6). Thomas Bros Maps.

San Bernardino-Riverside Counties Street Atlas 1984. Thomas Brothers Maps. (Illus.). 448p. 1983. pap. 17.00 o.p. (ISBN 0-88130-047-0). Thomas Bros Maps.

San Bernardino-Riverside Counties Street Guide & Directory 1989. Thomas Bros. Maps Staff. (Illus.). 450p. 1988. pap. 21.95 o.p. (ISBN 0-88130-305-4). Thomas Bros Maps.

San Bernardino-Riverside Zip Code Atlas: 1987. Thomas Bros. Maps Staff. (Illus.). 455p. 1986. pap. 26.95 o.p. (ISBN 0-88130-233-3). Thomas Bros Maps.

San Diego - Street Guide & Directory Including Imperial County, 1988. Thomas Bros. Maps Staff. (Illus.). 216p. 1988. pap. 12.95 o.p. (ISBN 0-88130-255-4). Thomas Bros Maps.

San Diego & the Southland: Just the Facts. Joan C. Tucker. Ed. by Elizabeth Rand. LC 84-61288. (Illus.). 168p. (Orig.). 1984. pap. 7.95 o.p. (ISBN 0-914488-31-7). Rand-Tofua.

San Diego Chargers. Julian May. (NFL Today Ser.). (gr. 4-8). 1980. PLB 10.45 o.p. (ISBN 0-87191-733-5); pap. 4.25 o.p. (ISBN 0-89812-236-8). Creative Ed.

San Diego Clippers. Jim Moore. (NBA Today Ser.). (Illus.). 48p. (gr. 4 up). 1984. PLB 10.45 o.p. (ISBN 0-87191-989-3). Creative Ed.

San Diego County Public Schools: How Are They Doing? (1984) Lillian S. Clancy. (How Are They Doing Ser.). 125p. (Orig.). 1984. pap. 13.95 o.p. (ISBN 0-939580-15-2). CA Schl Surveys.

San Diego County Street Atlas & Directory, 1987. rev. ed. Thomas Bros. Maps Staff. (Illus.). 208p. 1986. pap. 12.95 o.p. (ISBN 0-88130-224-4). Thomas Bros Maps.

San Diego County Street Atlas 1984. Thomas Brothers Maps. (Illus.). 208p. 1983. pap. 10.95 o.p. (ISBN 0-88130-051-9). Thomas Bros Maps.

San Diego County Street Atlas, 1987: Including Imperial County. Thomas Bros. Maps Staff. (Illus.). 208p. 1986. pap. 11.95 o.p. Thomas Bros Maps.

San Diego County Zip Code Atlas 1986. Thomas Bros. Maps Staff. (Illus.). 302p. 1987. 15.95 o.p. Thomas Bros Maps.

San Diego County Zip Code Street Atlas & Directory, 1987. rev. ed. Thomas Bros. Maps Staff. (Illus.). 302p. 1986. pap. 15.95 o.p. (ISBN 0-88130-227-9). Thomas Bros Maps.

San Diego County, 1985. (Illus.). 216p. 1985. pap. 10.95 o.p. (ISBN 0-88130-094-2). Thomas Bros Maps.

San Diego-Orange Counties Combination Street Atlas, 1986. Thomas Bros. Maps Staff. (Illus.). 352p. 1986. pap. 18.95 o.p. (ISBN 0-88130-173-6). Thomas Bros Maps.

San Diego-Orange Counties Combination Street Atlas 1987. Thomas Bros Maps, Staff. (Illus.). 352p. 1986. pap. 19.95 o.p. (ISBN 0-88130-225-2). Thomas Bros Maps.

San Diego Padres. rev. ed. Hinz. LC 82-239847. (Baseball Today Ser.). 48p. (gr. 4 up). 1982. PLB 11.45 o.p. (ISBN 0-87191-872-2). Creative Ed.

San Diego Zoo Picture Books, 4 vols. (San Diego Zoo Ser.). (Illus.). 12p. (ps-7). Set. deluxe ed. 23.50 o.s.i. (ISBN 0-89346-242-X). Heian Intl.

San Francisco. Paul C. Johnson. LC 78-117381. (This Beautiful World Ser.: Vol. 17). (Illus., Orig.). 1970. pap. 4.95 o.p. (ISBN 0-87011-120-5). Kodansha.

San Francisco Access. rev. ed. Richard S. Wurman. (Access Guidebooks). (Illus.). 144p. 1985. pap. 9.95 o.p. (ISBN 0-915461-09-9). Access Pr.

San Francisco-Access. Ed. by Richard S. Wurman. (Access Guidebook Ser.). (Illus.). 144p. 1982. pap. 9.95 o.p. (ISBN 0-9604858-3-X). Access Pr.

San Francisco & North Bay Counties Public Schools: How Are They Doing? (1984) Lillian S. Clancy. (How Are They Doing Ser.). 160p. (Orig.). 1984. pap. 13.95 o.p. (ISBN 0-939580-09-8). CA Schl Surveys.

San Francisco by Cable Car. George Young & Bill Henkin. (Illus.). 196p. (Orig.). 1983. pap. 7.95 o.p. (ISBN 0-914728-46-6). Wingbow Pr.

San Francisco Calamity by Earthquake. 1983. 12.98 o.p. (ISBN 0-517-40548-2). Crown.

San Francisco Celebrity Chef. Sam Bronfman. Ed. by Sheila Hosner. (Celebrity Chef Ser.). 240p. (Orig.). 1987. pap. 9.95 o.p. (ISBN 0-89716-164-5). Peanut Butter.

San Francisco County Street Atlas 1987. Thomas Bros. Maps Staff. (Illus.). 90p. pap. 10.95 o.p. Thomas Bros Maps.

San Francisco County Street Guide & Directory 1988. Thomas Bros. Maps Staff. (Illus.). 98p. 1988. pap. 10.95 o.p. (ISBN 0-88130-277-5). Thomas Bros Maps.

San Francisco Dinner Party Cookbook. rev. ed. Judith Ets-Hokin. LC 81-68589. 256p. 1982. pap. 9.95 o.s.i. (ISBN 0-89087-338-0). Celestial Arts.

San Francisco Dinner Party Cookbook. Judith Ets-Hokin. LC 74-30116. (San Francisco Book Co. Bk.). (Illus.). 192p. 1975. 7.95 o.p. (ISBN 0-395-20287-6). HM.

San Francisco Forty Niners. Julian May. (NFL Today Ser.). (Illus.). (gr. 3-6). 1977. PLB 10.45 o.p. (ISBN 0-87191-599-5); pap. 4.25 o.p. (ISBN 0-686-67474-X). Creative Ed.

San Francisco Giants. rev. ed. Brannon. LC 82-16177. (Baseball Today Ser.). 48p. (gr. 4 up). 1982. PLB 11.45 o.p. (ISBN 0-87191-873-0). Creative Ed.

San Francisco: Marin Counties Street Guide & Directory Census Tract Edition, 1987. Thomas Bros. Maps Staff. (Illus.). 174p. 1987. pap. 39.95 o.p. (ISBN 0-88130-241-4). Thomas Bros Maps.

San Francisco Museum of Modern Art: The Painting & Sculpture Collection. Diana DuPont et al. LC 84-11844. (Illus.). 404p. 1985. 75.00 o.p. (ISBN 0-933920-59-8, Dist. by Rizzoli); pap. 32.50 museum distribution only o.p. (ISBN 0-933920-60-1). Hudson Hills.

San Francisco on a Shoestring: The Intelligent Traveller's (& Natives) Guide to Budget Living in San Francisco. 4th ed. Louis E. Madison. (Illus.). 160p. 1987. pap. 5.95 o.p. (ISBN 0-912125-02-0). A M Zimmermann.

San Francisco Scenes. Greg Frazier. (City Scenes Ser.). (Illus.). 32p. 1972. pap. 3.95 o.p. (ISBN 0-912300-29-9, 29-9). Troubador Pr.

San Francisco Symphony: Music, Maestros & Musicians. David Schneider. (Illus.). 336p. 1983. 15.95 o.p. (ISBN 0-89141-181-X). Presidio Pr.

San Francisco Underground Gourmet. 4th ed. R. B. Read. 1977. pap. 3.95 o.p. (ISBN 0-671-22770-X, Fireside). S&S.

San Francisco Works Out. Corbin Young. 1985. 6.95 o.p. (ISBN 0-87795-691-X, Arbor Hse). Morrow.

San Juan Islands. facs. ed. Homer Wilhelm. (Shorey Historical Ser.). 42p. pap. 4.95 o.p. (ISBN 0-8466-0125-7, S125). Shorey.

San Juan Islands: Afoot & Afloat. Marge Mueller. LC 78-54424. (Illus.). 224p. (Orig.). 1979. pap. 9.95 o.p. (ISBN 0-916890-63-5). Mountaineers.

San Luis Obispo County: Looking Backward into the Middle Kingdom. Daniel Krieger. 144p. 1988. 27.95 o.s.i. (ISBN 0-89781-233-6, 5266). Windsor Pubns Inc.

San Martin. John C. Metford. 1951. (ISBN 0-8022-1108-9). Philos Lib.

San Mateo County Street Atlas & Directory, 1986. rev. ed. Thomas Bros. Maps Staff. (Illus.). 72p. 1987. pap. 10.95 o.p. Thomas Bros Maps.

San Mateo County Street Atlas 1987. 2nd ed. Thomas Bros. Maps Staff. (Illus.). 72p. pap. 10.95 o.p. (ISBN 0-88130-198-1). Thomas Bros Maps.

San Mateo County Street Guide & Directory 1988. Thomas Bros. Maps Staff. (Illus.). 74p. 1988. pap. 10.95 o.p. (ISBN 0-88130-282-1). Thomas Bros Maps.

San Mateo, Santa Clara & Santa Cruz Counties Public Schools: How Are They Doing? (1984) Lillian S. Clancy. (How Are They Doing Ser.). 180p. (Orig.). 1984. pap. 13.95 o.p. (ISBN 0-939580-10-1). CA Schl Surveys.

San Quentin Story, As Told to Dean Jennings. Clinton T. Duffy. LC 68-54417. (Illus.). 1968. Repr. of 1950 ed. lib. bdg. 22.50x o.p. (ISBN 0-8371-0395-9, DUSQ). Greenwood.

San Xavier Altarpiece. Robert C. Goss. LC 73-87715. (Illus.). 94p. 1974. pap. 4.95 o.p. (ISBN 0-8165-0323-0). U of Ariz Pr.

Sancta Sanctorum. W. E. Orchard. 210p. 1955. (ISBN 0-8022-1241-7). Philos Lib.

Sancti Filastrii Episcopi Brixiensis Diversarum Hereseon Liber. St. Philastrius Bishop of Brescia. Repr. of 1898 ed. 50.00 o.p. (ISBN 0-384-46225-1). Johnson Repr.

Sanctuary Legal Resource Packet. 50.00 o.p. Natl Lawyers Guild.

Sand County Almanac Illustrated. new ed. Aldo Leopold. LC 77-22656. (Illus.). 1977. 25.00 o.p. (ISBN 0-915024-15-2). WI Trails.

Sand Creatures & Castles: How to Build Them. Bob Reed & Pat Reed. LC 75-32250. (Illus.). 64p. (gr. 5-12). 1976. reinforced bdg. 5.95 o.s.i. (ISBN 0-03-014366-7). H Holt & Co.

Sand in Her Shoes. Mildred Lawrence. LC 49-10407. (Illus.). (gr. 4-7). 1949. 4.95 o.p. (ISBN 0-15-270129-X, HJ). HarBraceJ.

Sand, Sea, Shells & Sky. Harry Bornstein. (Signed English Ser.). 36p. 1974. pap. 5.95 o.p. (ISBN 0-913580-32-5, Clerc Bks). Gallaudet Univ Pr.

Sand Trap. Caroline B. Cooney. 192p. 1983. pap. 2.50 o.p. (ISBN 0-380-83295-X, 83295). Avon.

Sandbar Sinister. Phoebe A. Taylor. 1968. 4.95 o.p. (ISBN 0-393-08523-6). Norton.

Sandburg: Photographers View Carl Sandburg. Ed. by Edward Steichen. LC 65-19070. (Illus.). 1966. 10.75 o.p. (ISBN 0-15-179280-1). HarBraceJ.

Sandcatcher. Stuart Jackman. LC 79-23239. 1980. 10.95 o.p. (ISBN 0-689-11026-X, Atheneum). Macmillan.

Sandglass. Danilo Kis. Tr. by Ammiel Alcalay & Klara Alcalay. 304p. 18.95 o.p. (ISBN 0-374-25386-2). FS&G.

Sandi Patti: The Book of Words. (Illus.). 80p. (Orig.). 1986. pap. 9.95 o.p. (ISBN 0-88188-463-4, HL00183671). H Leonard Pub Corp.

Sanditon. Jane Austen et al. LC 74-20584. 1975. 8.95 o.p. (ISBN 0-395-20284-1). HM.

Sandlot Peanuts. Charles M. Schulz. LC 77-71363. (Illus.). 1977. 11.95 o.p. (ISBN 0-03-022621-X). H Holt & Co.

Sandman. Bob Shepperson. (Illus.). 32p. (ps up). 12.95 o.p. (ISBN 0-374-36405-2). FS&G.

Sandman's Dust. Melvin J. Bukist. 256p. 1986. 14.95 o.p. (ISBN 0-87795-731-2). Morrow.

Sandor Petofi. Eniko M. Basa. (World Authors Ser.). 1980. lib. bdg. 16.95 o.p. (ISBN 0-8057-6429-1, Twayne). G K Hall.

Sandra Smith's Review for NCLEX-RN. 4th ed. Sandra F. Smith. 704p. 1986. 21.95 o.p. (ISBN 0-917010-21-3). Natl Nursing.

Sandra Smith's Review of Nursing for State Board Examinations. 3rd ed. Ed. by Sandra F. Smith. 608p. 1982. pap. 18.95 o.p. (ISBN 0-917010-07-8). Natl Nursing.

Sandscreen. Ian Stuart. LC 86-16222. (Crime Club Ser.). 192p. 1987. 12.95 o.s.i. (ISBN 0-385-23799-5). Doubleday.

Sandtiquity. Connie Simo et al. LC 78-20696. (Illus.). 1980. pap. 10.95 o.p. (ISBN 0-8008-6989-3). Taplinger.

Sandwich Glass: The History of the Boston & Sandwich Glass Company. Ruth W. Lee. (Illus.). 590p. 35.00 o.s.i. (ISBN 0-317-55000-4). Apollo.

Sandy, the Talking Cat. Esther M. Newhall. (Illus.). 1977. 5.00 o.p. (ISBN 0-682-48932-8). Exposition-Phoenix.

Sane Society. Erich Fromm. 1955. pap. 5.95 o.s.i. (ISBN 0-03-025540-6). H Holt & Co.

Sang Des Autres. Simone De Beauvoir. 1945. 6.50 o.p. (ISBN 0-685-11555-0). Schoenhof.

Sang Thong: A Dance-Drama from Thailand. King Rama, 2nd. Tr. by Fern S. Ingersoll. LC 72-88097. (Illus.). 1972. 6.00 o.p. (ISBN 0-8048-1002-8). C E Tuttle.

Sanguinet's Crown. Patricia Veryan. (General Ser.). 517p. 1986. lib. bdg. 15.95x o.p. (ISBN 0-8161-4028-6, Large Print Bks). G K Hall.

Sanitary Engineering: Problems & Calculations for the Professional Engineer. Harry Harbold. LC 79-88898. (Illus.). 1980. 32.95 o.p. (ISBN 0-250-40319-6). Butterworth.

Sanitary Landfill. (ASCE Manual & Report on Engineering Practice Ser.: No. 39). 105p. 1976. 27.00x o.p. (ISBN 0-87262-215-0). Am Soc Civil Eng.

Sanitation, Hydrology, Hydraulics. 20.00 o.p. Am Consul Eng.

Sanity, Insanity & Common Sense. E. M. Suarez et al. 1987. 16.45 o.s.i. (ISBN 0-449-90244-7, Columbine). Fawcett.

Sanskrit Grammar, with Comparative Indo-European Explanations. Manfred Mayrhofer. Tr. by Gordon Ford, Jr. from Ger. LC 68-13738. (Alabama Linguistic & Philological Ser: Vol. 20). 115p. 1972. 10.75 o.p. (ISBN 0-8173-0353-7). U of Ala Pr.

Sanskrit Vocabulary Arranged According to Word Families with Meanings in English, German & Spanish. B. Schlerath. 1980. 25.00 o.p. (ISBN 90-04-06108-8). E J Brill USA.

Santa Barbara & Ventura Counties Public Schools: How Are They Doing? (1984) Lillian S. Clancy. (How Are They Doing Ser.). 100p. (Orig.). pap. 13.95 o.p. (ISBN 0-939580-16-0). CA Schl Surveys.

Santa Barbara County, Including Portions of San Luis Obispo County Thomas Guide 1988. Thomas Bros. Maps Staff. (Illus.). 214p. 1988. pap. 12.95 o.p. (ISBN 0-88130-272-4). Thomas Bros Maps.

Santa Barbara County, Including Portions of San Luis Obispo County & Ventura County Thomas Guide 1988. Thomas Bros. Maps Staff. (Illus.). 311p. 1988. pap. 19.95 o.p. (ISBN 0-88130-273-2). Thomas Bros Maps.

Santa Barbara County Street Atlas 1985: Including San Luis Obispo. Thomas Bros. Maps Staff. (Illus.). 112p. pap. 9.50 o.p. (ISBN 0-88130-107-8). Thomas Bros Maps.

Santa Barbara County Street Atlas: 1987 (Including San Luis Obispo) Thomas Bros. Maps Staff. (Illus.). 114p. 1987. pap. 12.95 o.p. (ISBN 0-88130-214-7). Thomas Bros Maps.

Santa Barbara History Makers. Walker A. Tompkins. Ed. by Barbara H. Tompkins. LC 83-17591. (Illus.). 440p. 25.00 o.p. (ISBN 0-87461-053-2). McNally & Loftin.

Santa Barbara-Ventura Counties Street Atlas 1985, Including San Luis Obispo County. Thomas Bros. Maps Staff. (Illus.). 200p. pap. 16.50 o.p. (ISBN 0-88130-108-6). Thomas Bros Maps.

Santa Barbara-Ventura Counties Street Atlas: 1987 (Including San Luis Obispo County) Thomas Bros. Maps Staff. (Illus.). 210p. 1987. pap. 19.95 o.p. (ISBN 0-88130-213-9). Thomas Bros Maps.

Santa Clara - San Mateo Counties Street Guide & Directory 1988. Thomas Bros. Maps Staff. (Illus.). 218p. 1988. pap. 18.95 o.p. (ISBN 0-88130-280-5). Thomas Bros Maps.

Santa Clara County Street Atlas & Directory, 1986. rev. ed. Thomas Bros. Maps Staff. (Illus.). 144p. 1986. pap. 10.95 o.p. (ISBN 0-88130-178-7). Thomas Bros Maps.

Santa Clara County Street Atlas 1987. Thomas Bros. Maps Staff. (Illus.). 72p. pap. 10.95 o.p. (ISBN 0-88130-230-9). Thomas Bros Maps.

Santa Clara County Street Guide & Directory 1988. Thomas Bros. Maps Staff. (Illus.). 144p. 1988. pap. 10.95 o.p. (ISBN 0-88130-279-1). Thomas Bros Maps.

Santa Clara-San Mateo Counties Street Atlas & Directory 1987. rev. ed. Thomas Bros. Maps Staff. (Illus.). 144p. 1987. pap. 18.95 o.p. (ISBN 0-88130-197-3). Thomas Bros Maps.

Santa Clara-San Mateo Counties Street Atlas 1985. Thomas Bros. Maps Staff. (Illus.). 144p. pap. 16.45 o.p. (ISBN 0-88130-127-2). Thomas Bros Maps.

Santa Claus Killer. A. H. Garnet. LC 81-1255. (Joan Kahn Bk). 384p. 1981. 12.95 o.p. (ISBN 0-89919-029-4). Ticknor & Fields.

Santa Claus the Movie: Patch & the Evil Toymaker. Daisy Miller. (Illus.). 24p. (ps-1). 1985. pap. 1.95 o.p. (ISBN 0-448-10278-1, G&D). Putnam Pub Group.

Santa Claus the Movie: The Boy Who Didn't Believe in Christmas. Michael Teitelbaum. (Illus.). 24p. (ps-1). 1985. pap. 1.95 o.p. (ISBN 0-448-10277-3, G&D). Putnam Pub Group.

Santa Claus Visits the Thinggumajigs. Dick Keller & Irene Keller. (Illus.). 48p. (gr. k-6). 1982. 2.95 o.p. (ISBN 0-8249-8045-X). Ideals.

Santa Fe. Hank Mitchum. (Nightingale Paperbacks ser.). 302p. 1987. pap. 12.95 o.p. (ISBN 0-8161-4332-3, Large Print Bks). G K Hall.

Santa Fe Trail. H. M. Powell. 1979. ltd. ed. cancelled 195.00 o.p. (ISBN 0-87140-634-9). Liveright.

Santanic Condition. David Thoreau. LC 80-66499. 1981. 13.95 o.p. (ISBN 0-87795-274-4, Arbor Hse). Morrow.

Santa's Christmas Journey. Roger Brooke. LC 85-61188. (Illus.). 32p. (ps-3). 1985. 5.95 o.p. (ISBN 0-528-82688-3, Checkerboard Pr). Macmillan.

Santayana's Aesthetics: A Critical Introduction. Irving Singer. LC 72-12317. 235p. 1973. Repr. of 1957 ed. lib. bdg. 22.50x o.p. (ISBN 0-8371-6696-9, SISB). Greenwood.

Santeria: Bronx. Judith Gleason. LC 74-19493. 224p. (gr. 8 up). 1975. PLB 7.95 o.p. (ISBN 0-689-30447-1, Atheneum). Macmillan.

Santi Di Tito. Jack Spalding. LC 79-57494. (Outstanding Dissertations in the Fine Arts Ser.: No. 5). 527p. 1985. lib. bdg. 80.00 o.p. (ISBN 0-8240-3944-0). Garland Pub.

Santiago's Silver Mine. Eleanor Clymer. LC 72-86930. 72p. (gr. 3-5). 1973. 4.50 o.p. (ISBN 0-689-30081-6, Atheneum). Macmillan.

Santorini. Alistair MacLean. LC 86-19804. 256p. 1987. 16.95 o.p. (ISBN 0-385-23153-9). Doubleday.

Sanyo MBC 550-555 Beginners & Intermediate Guide. Fred Blechman. LC 85-772. 360p. 1985. pap. text ed. 17.45 o.p. (ISBN 0-03-000187-0, HoltC). HR&W.

Sappho: A Play in Verse. Lawrence Durrell. 96p. 1967. pap. 4.95 o.p. (ISBN 0-571-08161-4). Faber & Faber.

Saqt Al Zand (the Spark from the Flint) Abu Ala Al Ma'Arri. Tr. by Arthur Wormhoudt. (Arab Translation Ser.: No. 2). 1972. pap. 6.50x o.p. (ISBN 0-916358-52-6). Wormhoudt.

Sara & Gerald: Villa America & After. Honoria M. Donnelly & Richard N. Billings. 1984. pap. 7.95 o.p. (ISBN 0-03-069831-6, Owl Bks.). H Holt & Co.

Sara & the Pinch. Carla Stevens. (Illus.). 48p. (gr. k-3). 1980. 6.95 o.p. (ISBN 0-395-29435-5, Clarion). HM.

Sara Summer. Mary D. Hahn. 160p. (gr. 3-6). 1979. 7.95 o.p. (ISBN 0-395-28968-8, Clarion). HM.

Saraband of Lost Time. Richard Grant. 336p. 1985. pap. 2.95 o.p. (ISBN 0-380-89533-1). Avon.

Saracen Archery. Ed. by J. D. Latham. W. F. Paterson. (Illus.). 35.00 o.p. (ISBN 0-87556-143-8). Saifer.

Sarada Devi, the Holy Mother: Her Life & Conversations. Swami Tapasyananda & Swami Nikhilananda. (Illus.). 6.50 o.p. (ISBN 0-87481-435-9). Vedanta Pr.

Sarah & Joshua. J. J. McKenna. 1979. pap. 2.50 o.p. (ISBN 0-380-41053-2, 41053). Avon.

Sarah Bernhardt: The Art Within the Legend. Gerda Taranow. LC 70-90962. (Illus.). 1972. 38.00x o.p. (ISBN 0-691-06181-5). Princeton U Pr.

Sarah Winnemucca. Katherine Gehm. LC 75-12600. 185p. 1975. 8.95 o.p. (ISBN 0-89019-030-5). Norwalk Pr.

Saranac: America's Magic Mountain. Robert Taylor. LC 85-24911. (Illus.). 308p. 1986. 17.45 o.p. (ISBN 0-395-37905-9). HM.

Saratoga Hot. Hortense Calisher. LC 84-24695. 288p. 1985. 16.95 o.s.i. (ISBN 0-385-19975-9). Doubleday.

Saratoga Swimmer. Stephen Dobyns. LC 81-66003. 1981. 12.95 o.p. (ISBN 0-689-11193-2, Atheneum). Macmillan.

Sarcoidosis & Other Granulomatous Disorders: International Conference, 9th, Paris, 31 August - 4 September 1981. Ed. by J. Chretien & J. Marsac. (Illus.). 950p. 1983. 145.00 o.p. (ISBN 0-08-027088-3). Pergamon.

Sarcophaga & Allies of North America see Thomas Say Foundation Publications.

Sarcoplasmic Reticulum: Transport & Energy Transduction. Leopoldo DeMeis. LC 81-2325. 182p. 1981. 52.50 o.p. (ISBN 0-471-05025-3, Pub. by John Wiley). Krieger.

Sartre. Peter Caws. (Arguments of the Philosophers Ser.). (Hlus.). 1979. 26.95x o.p. (ISBN 0-7100-0314-5). Routledge Chapman & Hall.

Sartre et la Mise en Signe. Ed. by Michael Issacharoff & Jean-Claude Vilquin. LC 81-68003. (French Forum Monographs: No. 30). 167p. (Orig.). 1982. pap. 12.95x o.p. (ISBN 0-917058-29-1). French Forum.

Sartre on Theater. Jean-Paul Sartre. Ed. by Michel Contat & Michel Rybalka. Tr. by Frank Jellinek from Fr. 1978. pap. 5.95 o.p. (ISBN 0-394-73312-6). Pantheon.

SAS Applications Guide, 1980 Edition. SAS Institute, Inc. Staff. (Illus.). 204p. (Orig.). 1980. pap. 9.95 o.p. (ISBN 0-917382-16-1). SAS Inst.

SAS Basic Video Course: Coordinator's Guide. rev. ed. SAS Institute, Inc. Staff. 1985. pap. 14.95 o.p. (ISBN 0-917382-61-7). SAS Inst.

SAS Companion for the VSE Operating System, 1983. SAS Institute Inc. 103p. (Orig.). 1983. pap. 6.95 o.p. (ISBN 0-917382-44-7). SAS Inst.

SAS-ETS User's Guide, 1982 Edition. SAS Institute, Inc. Staff. (Orig.). 1983. pap. text ed. 14.95 o.p. (ISBN 0-917382-38-2). SAS Inst.

SAS-FSP User's Guide, 1982 Edition. SAS Institute, Inc. Staff. (Illus.). 81p. 1982. pap. 9.95 o.p. (ISBN 0-917382-32-3). SAS Inst.

SAS-GRAPH User's Guide, 1980 Edition. SAS Institute, Inc. Staff. (Illus.). 72p. (Orig.). 1980. pap. 9.95 o.p. SAS Inst.

SAS-GRAPH User's Guide, 1981 Edition. 2nd ed. Ed. by SAS Institute, Inc. Staff. (Illus.). 126p. (Orig.). 1981. pap. 9.95 o.p. (ISBN 0-917382-18-8). SAS Inst.

SAS Language Guide for Personal Computers, Version 6. SAS Institute Inc. Staff. 429p. 1985. pap. 14.95 o.p. (ISBN 0-917382-80-3). SAS Inst.

SAS-OR User's Guide, 1983 Edition. SAS Institute, Inc. Staff. 164p. 1983. pap. 9.95 o.p. (ISBN 0-917382-45-5). SAS Inst.

SAS Procedures Guide for Personal Computers, Version 6. SAS Institute Inc. Staff. 373p. 1985. pap. 14.95 o.p. (ISBN 0-917382-79-X). SAS Inst.

SAS Technical Report: Changes & Enhancements to Base SAS Software for Personal Computers, Release 6.03. SAS Institute Inc. 383p. 1987. pap. 12.95 o.p. (ISBN 1-55544-071-1). SAS Inst.

SAS User's Guide: Basics, 1982 Edition. SAS Institute, Inc. Staff. 923p. (Orig.). 1982. pap. 14.95 o.p. (ISBN 0-917382-36-6). SAS Inst.

SAS User's Guide: Statistics, 1982 Edition. SAS Institute, Inc. Staff. 584p. (Orig.). 1982. pap. 14.95 o.p. (ISBN 0-917382-37-4). SAS Inst.

SAS Video Training Basics 100-Series Instructional Guide, 1981. rev. ed. SAS Institute, Inc. Staff. (Orig.). 1981. pap. 7.95 o.p. (ISBN 0-917382-26-9). SAS Inst.

SAS Views: Introduction to SAS, 1982 Edition. SAS Institute, Inc. Staff. 130p. 1982. pap. 40.00 o.p. (ISBN 0-917382-34-X). SAS Inst.

SAS Views: Procedure Writing, 1981 Edition. 2nd ed. SAS Institute, Inc. Staff. 178p. 1981. pap. 40.00 o.p. (ISBN 0-917382-27-7). SAS Inst.

SAS Views: Regression & ANOVA, 1981. SAS Institute, Inc. Staff. (Illus.). 350p. (Orig.). 1981. pap. 40.00 o.p. (ISBN 0-917382-23-4). SAS Inst.

SAS Views: SAS Color Graphics, 1983 Edition. SAS Institute, Inc. Staff. (Orig.). 1983. pap. 40.00 o.p. (ISBN 0-917382-47-1). SAS Inst.

Sasakawa, the Warrior for Peace: Global Philanthropist. Paula Daventry. (Illus.). 143p. 1981. pap. 9.00 o.p. (ISBN 0-08-028126-5). Pergamon.

Sasha, My Friend. Barbara Corcoran. LC 69-18968. 208p. (gr. 5-9). 1969. 7.95 o.p. (ISBN 0-689-20582-1, Atheneum). Macmillan.

Sasha the Cheetah. (Zoo Babies Ser.). 16p. (gr. k-6). 1982. pap. 1.25 o.p. (ISBN 0-8249-8037-9). Ideals.

Sasha the Silly. Marjorie W. Sharmat. LC 83-18357. (Illus.). 32p. (gr. k-3). 1984. reinforced bdg 12.95 o.p. (ISBN 0-8234-0503-6). Holiday.

SAT Success: Peterson's Study Guide to English & Math Skills for College Entrance Examinations: SAT, ACT and PSAT. Joan D. Carris & Michael R. Crystal. LC 82-16165. 386p. (Orig.). 1982. pap. 9.95 o.p. (ISBN 0-87866-208-1). Petersons Guides.

Satan in the Woods. Moses J. Steiner. LC 78-54567. 1978. 10.95 o.p. (ISBN 0-88400-057-5). Shengold.

Satan Sleeps with the Holy: Word Paintings. Carolyn M. Kleefeld. LC 82-80785. 110p. 1982. 11.95 o.p. (ISBN 0-9602214-9-2); pap. 7.95 o.p. (ISBN 0-9602214-8-4). Jalmar Pr.

Satanic Rituals. Anton S. LaVey. 1976. pap. 4.50 o.p. (ISBN 0-380-01392-4). Avon.

Satanic Rituals. Anton S. LaVey. 7.95 o.p. (ISBN 0-8216-0171-7, Pub. by Univ Bks). Carol Pub Group.

Satan's Death Blast. Grant Stockbridge. (Spider Ser.: No. 1). 192p. 1984. pap. 2.95 o.p. (ISBN 0-89300-009-4). Blazing Pubns.

Satan's Manor. Mark Andrews. 288p. 1982. pap. 3.25 o.p. (ISBN 0-8439-1175-1, Pub. by Leisure Bks CT). Dorchester Pub Co.

Satanstoe. James Fenimore Cooper. LC 62-9515. xviii, 425p. 1962. pap. 6.95x o.p. (ISBN 0-8032-5036-3, BB 138, Bison). U of Nebr Pr.

Satellite & Cable TV: Scrambling & Descrambling. Frank Baylin & Brent Gale. 272p. (Orig.). 1986. pap. text ed. 19.95 o.p. (ISBN 0-917893-07-7, Baylin Gale). Consol.

Satellite Beacons, Observations from 1964 to 1970. G. K. Hartmann et al. (Mitteilungen Aus Dem Max-Planck Institut Fuer Aeronomie: Vol. 48). 93p. 1972. pap. 17.70 o.p. (ISBN 0-387-05893-1). Springer-Verlag.

Satellite Communications. Stan Prentiss. (Illus.). 288p. 1983. 16.95 o.p. (ISBN 0-8306-0632-7); pap. 12.95 o.p. (ISBN 0-8306-1632-2, 1632). TAB Bks.

Satellite Communications. Ed. by Harry L. Van Trees. LC 78-65704. (Volume in the IEEE Press Selected Reprint Ser.). 1980. 56.95x o.p. (ISBN 0-471-06101-8, Pub. by Wiley-Interscience); pap. 37.00x o.p. (ISBN 0-471-06100-X, Pub. by Wiley-Interscience). Wiley.

Satellite Communications-An Introduction. Robert M. Gagliardi. (Engineering Ser.). (Illus.). 475p. 1983. 49.65 o.s.i. (ISBN 0-534-02976-0, Lifetime Learn). Van Nos Reinhold.

Satellite Communications: Proceedings of the Canadian Domestic & International Conference, 1st, June 15-17, Ottawa, Canada. Ed. by K. Feher. 670p. 1983. 121.00 o.p. (ISBN 0-444-86690-6, North-Holland). Elsevier.

Satellite Communications Services & Equipment Markets. International Resource Development, Inc. Staff. 322p. 1983. write for info. o.p. (ISBN 0-88694-581-X). Intl Res Dev.

Satellite Generals: A Study of Military Elites in the Soviet Sphere. Ithiel Pool. LC 75-26779. (Hoover Institute Studies, Series B: No. 5). 165p. 1975. Repr. of 1955 ed. lib. bdg. 24.75x o.p. (ISBN 0-8371-8372-3, POSG). Greenwood.

Satellite of the Sun: The Science of the Earth & Its Surroundings. Athelstan Spilhaus. LC 58-10605. (Illus.). 1964. pap. 1.25 o.p. (ISBN 0-689-70186-1, 57, Atheneum). Macmillan.

Satellite Perturbations & Orbital Determination. Ed. by P. Lala. (Advances in Space Research: Vol. 1, No. 6). (Illus.). 95p. 1981. pap. 14.50 o.p. (ISBN 0-08-028380-2). Pergamon.

Satellite Systems for Mobile Communications & Navigation: Related Conference Proceedings. Ed. by J. E. Flood & C. J. Hughes. (IEE Conference Publication: No. 222). 224p. 1983. pap. 72.00 o.s.i. (ISBN 0-85296-273-8, IC222). Inst Elect Eng.

Satellite Tech Talk. Ruth Radlauer et al. LC 83-21059. (Tech Talk Bks.). (Illus.). 64p. (gr. 4 up). 1984. lib. bdg. 14.60 o.p. (ISBN 0-516-08253-1). Childrens.

Satellites Today: The Complete Guide to Satellite Television. Frank Baylin & Amy Toner. (Illus.). 163p. (Orig.). 1985. pap. 11.95 o.p. (ISBN 0-917893-01-8). ConSol.

Satire, Burlesque, Protest & Ridicule 1. Ed. by Walter H. Rubsamen. (Ballad Opera Ser.). 1975. lib. bdg. 61.00 o.p. (ISBN 0-8240-0904-5). Garland Pub.

Satire, Burlesque, Protest, & Ridicule 2. Ed. by Walter H. Rubsamen. (Ballad Opera Ser.). 1974. lib. bdg. 61.00 o.p. (ISBN 0-8240-0905-3). Garland Pub.

Satire in the Eighteenth Century. John D. Browning. LC 82-49148. (McMaster Studies in the 18th Century). 231p. 1983. lib. bdg. 36.00 o.p. (ISBN 0-8240-4009-0). Garland Pub.

Satires. Persius. Ed. by J. R. Jenkinson. 49.00 o.s.i. (ISBN 0-86516-109-7); pap. 16.50 o.s.i. (ISBN 0-86516-110-0). Bolchazy Carducci.

Satiric Catharsis in Shakespeare: A Theory of Dramatic Structure. Alice L. Birney. LC 79-185976. 1973. 33.00x o.p. (ISBN 0-520-02214-9). U of Cal Pr.

Satisfaction Guaranteed: The Ultimate Guide to Consumer Self-Defense. Ralph Charell. 1985. 14.70 o.p. (ISBN 0-671-49804-5, Linden Pr). S&S.

Satori in Paris. Jack Kerouac. 1966. pap. 2.25 o.p. (ISBN 0-394-17437-2, B135, BC). Grove.

Satori in Paris & Pic. Jack Kerouac. LC 85-81781. 1986. pap. 4.95 o.p. (ISBN 0-394-62173-5, BC). Grove.

Saturday Always Comes: The Relaxed Way to Sales Success. Irwin B. Meisel. 180p. 1984. pap. 9.95 o.p. (ISBN 0-87863-222-0, Farnsworth Pub Co). Longman Finan.

Saturday Evening Post Norman Rockwell Book. Saturday Evening Post Editors. (Illus.). 160p. 1983. pap. 3.95 o.p. (ISBN 0-89387-073-0). Curtis Pub Co.

Saturday Evening Post Vegetable Primer. Saturday Evening Post Editors. LC 80-70885. (Illus.). 144p. (Orig.). 1982. pap. 5.95 o.p. (ISBN 0-89387-045-5, Co-Pub. by Sat Eve Post). Curtis Pub Co.

Saturday Morning. Kent Mackenzie & Gary Goldsmith. 160p. 1971. pap. 0.95 o.p. (ISBN 0-380-01393-2, 08235). Avon.

Saturday Night & Sunday Morning. Alan Sillitoe. 192p. 1951. pap. 3.50 o.p. (ISBN 0-451-13590-3, AE2162, Sig). NAL.

Saturday Night at Daisy's. Jeff Cohn. LC 77-92055. 1978. 8.95 o.p. (ISBN 0-15-179412-X). HarBraceJ.

Saturday Night at San Marcos. William Packard. LC 86-80909. 240p. 1987. pap. 7.95 o.s.i. (ISBN 0-394-62273-1). Grove.

Saturday Night Live. Ed. by Anne Beatts & John Head. (Illus.). 1977. pap. 7.95 o.p. (ISBN 0-380-01801-2, 51342). Avon.

Saturday Notebook: A Diary for Children & Adults to Use Together. Thomas Moore & Norris Frederick. (Illus.). 112p. (ps up). 1983. concealed wire binding 8.95 o.p. (ISBN 0-914788-72-8). Globe Pequot.

Saturday's Child. Clell Edgar Bowman. 1976. 10.00 o.p. (ISBN 0-682-48520-9). Exposition-Phoenix.

Saturdays in the City. Ann S. Bond. (gr. 3-6). 1979. 8.95 o.s.i. (ISBN 0-395-28376-0). HM.

Satyagrahas in Bengal, Nineteen Twenty-One to Nineteen Thirty-Nine. Buddhadeva Bhattacharyya. 1977. 15.00x o.p. (ISBN 0-88386-901-2). South Asia Bks.

Satyr Candidate. Richard M. Rose. 1979. 7.50 o.p. (ISBN 0-682-49383-X). Exposition-Phoenix.

Satyricon. Petronius Arbiter. Tr. by W. C. Firebaugh. 1943. 6.95 o.p. (ISBN 0-87140-861-9, Co-Pub with Tudor). Liveright.

Satz-Lexikon des Englischen Geschaeftsbriefes. Burfeindt-Moral & H. H. Zacher. 400p. (Ger.). 1972. 20.95 o.p. (ISBN 3-468-39120-X). Langenscheidt.

Sauce Book. Pepita Aris. 176p. 1984. text ed. 15.95 o.p. (ISBN 0-07-002189-9). McGraw.

Saucer Hill. Paul Adler. (YA) (gr. 7 up). 1979. pap. 1.95 o.p. (ISBN 0-380-47613-4, 47613). Avon.

Saudi. Laurie Devine. 520p. 1985. 17.45 o.p. (ISBN 0-671-47453-7). S&S.

Saudi Arabia. 2nd ed. Middle East Economic Digest Staff. Ed. by Trevor Mostyn. (MEED Practical Guides Ser.). (Illus.). 350p. (Orig.). 1985. pap. 16.95x o.p. (ISBN 0-946510-00-8). Lynne Rienner.

Saudi Arabia: A Case Study in Development. Fouad Al-Farsy. 224p. (Orig.). 1982. pap. 17.50x o.p. (ISBN 0-7103-0005-0). Routledge Chapman & Hall.

Saudi Arabia: Post Report. rev. ed. (State Department Publication: No. 9009). 28p. 1986. pap. 1.50 o.p. (S/N 044-000-02128-5). USGPO.

Saudi Arabia Travel Guide. 1985. 4.95 o.p. (ISBN 0-02-969840-5, Berlitz). MacMillan.

Saudi Arabia's Development Potential: Application of an Islamic Growth Model. Robert E. Looney. LC 79-2274. 384p. 1981. 40.00x o.p. (ISBN 0-669-03083-X). Lexington Bks.

Saudis: Inside the Desert Kingdom. Sandra Mackey. 1987. 19.45 o.s.i. (ISBN 0-395-41165-3). HM.

Saul. Andre Gide. pap. 3.95 o.p. (ISBN 0-685-23910-1, 2586). Schoenhof.

Saul & Morris, Worlds Apart. James Yaffe. LC 81-13304. 240p. 1982. 15.50 o.p. (ISBN 0-03-059432-4). H Holt & Co.

Saul Bellow. Malcolm Bradbury. (Contemporary Writers Ser.). 96p. 1982. pap. 5.95x o.p. (ISBN 0-416-31650-6, NO. 3559). Routledge Chapman & Hall.

Saul Steinberg: Still Life & Architecture. Italo Calvino. (Illus.). 40p. (Orig.). 1982. pap. 15.00 o.p. (ISBN 0-938608-07-X). Pace Pubns.

Sauna: The Finnish Bath. Stephen Greene Press (Illus.) Staff & H. J. Viherjuvri. 96p. 10.00 o.p. (ISBN 0-470-50223-1). Sauna Soc.

Sauternes: A Study of the Great Sweet Wines of Bordeaux. Jeffrey Benson & Alastair Mackenzie. (Illus.). 184p. 26.00 o.p. (ISBN 0-85667-062-6). Sotheby Pubns.

Sauve Qui Peut. Lawrence Durrell. (Illus.). 82p. 1979. pap. 4.95 o.p. (ISBN 0-571-09224-1). Faber & Faber.

Savage Autumn. Constance Obanyon. 1984. pap. 3.50 o.p. (ISBN 0-8217-1457-0). Zebra.

Savage Conquest. Janelle Taylor. 1985. pap. 3.75 o.p. (ISBN 0-8217-1533-X). Zebra.

Savage Grace. Natalie Robins & Steven M. Aronson. LC 85-7117. (Illus.). 500p. 1985. 17.95 o.p. (ISBN 0-688-04373-9). Morrow.

Savage Heroes: Tales of Magical Fantasy. Ed. by Michel Parry. LC 79-66645. (Illus.). 190p. 1980. 9.95 o.s.i. (ISBN 0-8008-6996-6). Taplinger.

Savage Holiday. Richard Wright. 220p. 1975. Repr. of 1954 ed. 8.50x o.p. (ISBN 0-911860-54-1). Chatham Bkseller.

Savage Kingdom. Zane Grey. 1978. pap. 1.50 o.s.i. (ISBN 0-505-51293-9, Pub. by Tower Bks). Dorchester Pub Co.

Savage Life & Scenes in Australia & New Zealand: Being an Artist's Impressions of Countries & People at the Antipodes, 2 Vols. in 1. 2nd ed. George F. Angas. (Illus.). 28.00 o.p. (ISBN 0-384-01465-8). Johnson Repr.

Savage Mind. Claude Levi-Strauss. LC 66-28197. (Nature of Human Society Ser). (Chicago Collector's ed.). 1968. 10.00 o.s.i. (ISBN 0-226-47485-2). U of Chicago Pr.

Savage Obsession. Cassie Edwards. 1983. pap. 3.50 o.p. (ISBN 0-8217-1269-1). Zebra.

Savage Spirit. Meg Cameron. (Dawn of Love Ser.: No. 3). (YA) (gr. 7 up). pap. 2.25 o.p. (ISBN 0-671-55155-8). Archway.

Savage State of Grace. Donald MacKenzie. LC 87-17112. (Crime Club Ser.). 192p. 1988. pap. 12.95 o.p. (ISBN 0-385-24317-0). Doubleday.

Savage Surrender. Lindsey Hanks. (Avon Romance Ser.). 1986. pap. 3.50 o.p. (ISBN 0-380-75021-X). Avon.

Savage Web. Sharon Whitby. 190p. 1986. pap. 2.95 o.p. (ISBN 0-931773-68-7). Critics Choice Paper.

Savages & Shakespeare Wallah. James Ivory. 1973. pap. 3.95 o.p. (ISBN 0-394-17799-1, E604, Ever). Grove.

Savate: Martial Art of France. rev. ed. Philip Reed & Richard Muggeridge. (Illus.). 72p. 1986. pap. text ed. 12.00 o.p. (ISBN 0-87364-379-8). Paladin Pr.

Save: Hockey's Brave Goalies. Hal Bock. 1974. pap. 1.25 o.p. (ISBN 0-380-00135-7, 20669). Avon.

Save That Raccoon! Gloria D. Miklowitz. LC 77-12031. (Illus.). (ps-3). 1978. 5.95 o.p. (ISBN 0-15-270241-5, HJ). HarBraceJ.

Save the Whale. Michael Koepf. 1978. text ed. 8.95 o.p. (ISBN 0-07-035280-1). McGraw.

Saving America's Birds. Paula Hendrich. LC 81-15624. (Illus.). 160p. (gr. 6 up). 1982. 11.75 o.p. (ISBN 0-688-00417-2). Lothrop.

Saving Grace. Ken Hartnett. 356p. 1986. pap. 3.75 o.p. (ISBN 0-931773-55-5). Critics Choice Paper.

Saving Money Through Ten-Year Trusts. William A. Hancock. (Illus.). 1979. text ed. 24.95 o.p. (ISBN 0-07-025983-6). McGraw.

Saving Old Buildings. Sherban Cantacuzino & Susan Brandt. (Illus.). 240p. 1981. 67.50 o.p. (ISBN 0-85139-498-1). Nichols Pub.

Saving Social Security. Robert Schuettinger. 1977. pap. 15.00 o.p. (ISBN 0-930690-07-9). Coun Soc Econ.

Saving the Appearances: A Study in Idolatry. Owen Barfield. LC 65-23538. 190p. 1965. pap. 4.95 o.p. (ISBN 0-15-679490-X, Harv). HarBraceJ.

Saving the Housing Assistance Plan: Improving Incentives to Local Governments. Raymond J. Struyk. 36p. 1979. pap. text ed. 7.00 o.p. (ISBN 0-87766-270-3). Urban Inst.

Saving Time & Taxes in Planning & Preparing Estate, Gift, & Fiduciary Returns. George M. Schain. LC 84-28702. 1985. 75.00 o.p. (ISBN 0-8240-7292-8). Garland Pub.

Savings & Loan Associations: Ohio Laws & Regulations. 587p. 1985. 40.00 o.p.; Suppl. 1984. 25.00 o.p. Anderson Pub Co.

Savings Banking: An Industry in Change. 350p. 1985. 36.00 o.p. (ISBN 0-318-04773-X, 116). Bank Admin Inst.

Savior for All Seasons. William P. Barker. 192p. 1986. 10.95 o.p. (ISBN 0-8007-1485-7). Revell.

Saviors. Helen Yglesias. 1987. 17.45 o.s.i. (ISBN 0-395-35419-6). HM.

Savoir Partage: Semiotique it Theorie de la Connaissance Dans l'Oeuvre de Marcel Proust. Jacques Fontanille. LC 87-30929. (Actes Semiotiques Ser.: Vol. 4). 227p. (Orig.). 1987. pap. 33.00x o.p. (Hades-Benjamins). Benjamins North Am.

Savory Shellfish of North America. Sandra Romashko. LC 77-74610. (Illus.). 1977. pap. 4.95 o.s.i. (ISBN 0-89317-015-1). Windward Pub.

Savoy, 5 vols. Ed. by Arthur Symonds. 1967. Repr. of 1896 ed. 265.00x set o.p. (ISBN 0-7146-2115-3, F Cass Co). Biblio Dist.

Savoy Heritage: Sixteen Twenty-One to the Present. Louis G. Savoy. (Illus.). 144p. 1983. 8.00 o.p. (ISBN 0-682-49955-2). Exposition-Phoenix.

Saxon England. John Hamilton & Alan Sorrell. LC 68-25985. (Illus.). (gr. 6-9). 1968. 13.95 o.p. (ISBN 0-8023-1149-0). Dufour.

Say: An Experiment in Learning. Simon Stuart. LC 72-95963. (Illus.). 220p. 1973. 7.95x o.p. (ISBN 0-87586-039-7). Agathon.

Say "Cheese"! Looking at Snapshots in a New Way. Graham King. LC 83-20828. (Illus.). 216p. 1984. pap. 13.95 o.p. (ISBN 0-396-08354-4). Dodd.

Say Hello, Vanessa. Majorie W. Sharmat. LC 79-1511. (Illus.). 32p. (gr. k-3). 1979. reinforced bdg. 7.95 o.p. (ISBN 0-8234-0354-8). Holiday.

Say Hi to Jesus for Me: The Story of Young Todd & His Battle Against Cancer. Gabriele Monson. LC 78-66951. 1979. pap. 6.95 o.p. (ISBN 0-8066-1690-3, 10-5593, Augsburg). Augsburg Fortress.

Say-It-Faith. Elmer L. Towns. 1983. pap. 5.95 o.p. (ISBN 0-8423-5825-0). Tyndale.

Say It in Another Language: Phrases in Spanish, French, Japanese, Swahili, & German. Lore S. Bonar et al. 16p. (YA) (gr. 7 up). 1976. pap. text ed. 3.75 pkg. of 20 o.p. (ISBN 0-88441-414-0, 26-814). Girl Scouts USA.

Say It in French. Leon J. Cohen. LC 55-13819. 1962. lib. bdg. 8.50x o.p. (ISBN 0-88307-555-5). Gannon.

Say It in Modern Greek. George Pappageotes. LC 57-804. 1956. lib. bdg. 8.50x o.p. (ISBN 0-88307-559-8). Gannon.

Say It in Spanish. Leon J. Cohen. LC 56-20451. 1960. lib. bdg. 8.50x o.p. (ISBN 0-88307-561-X). Gannon.

Say it, Spirit. Geraldine B. Sheard. 128p. 1987. 8.95 o.p. (ISBN 0-8062-2917-9). Carlton.

Say It with Love. Howard G. Hendricks. LC 72-77011. 143p. 1972. pap. 5.95 o.p. (ISBN 0-88207-050-9). Victor Bks.

Say Yes to Your Potential. Skip Ross & Carole C. Carlson. 166p. 1985. pap. 6.95 o.p. (ISBN 0-8499-3014-6, 3014-6). Word Bks.

Say You Want Me. Richard Cohen. 268p. 1988. 17.95 o.p. (ISBN 0-317-67033-6). Soho Press.

Saying What You Mean: A Commonsense Guide to American Usage. Robert Claiborne. 1986. 16.45 o.p. (ISBN 0-393-02312-5). Norton.

Saying Yes to Change. Barbara M. Johnson. LC 81-65649. 128p. (Orig.). 1981. pap. 4.95 o.p. (ISBN 0-8066-1885-X, 10-5594, Augsburg). Augsburg Fortress.

Sayings & Doings of Pai-Chang. Tr. by Thomas Cleary. LC 78-21228. (Zen Writings Ser.: Vol. 6). 1979. pap. 5.95 o.p. (ISBN 0-916820-10-6). Center Pubns.

Sayings of Jesus. 5.95 o.p. (ISBN 0-88088-351-0). Peter Pauper.

Sayings Parallels: A Workbook for the Jesus Tradition. John D. Crossan. LC 85-16220. (Foundations & Facets Ser.). 256p. 1986. 24.95 o.p. (ISBN 0-8006-2109-3, 1-2109, Fortress); pap. 14.95 o.p. (ISBN 0-8006-1909-9, 1-1909). Augsburg Fortress.

Says Who?--Authority & Old Adam. Otis Dunbar Richardson. 1978. 7.00 o.p. (ISBN 0-682-49010-5). Exposition-Phoenix.

Sayula Popoluca Texts. Lawrence Clark. (Publications in Linguistics & Related Fields Ser.: No. 6). 216p. 1961. pap. 2.00 o.p. (ISBN 0-88312-616-8); microfiche (3) 6.00x o.p. (ISBN 0-88312-508-0). Summer Inst Ling.

Sbornik P'es Dlia Zhizni Solo: Stikhi. Aleksei Tsvetkov. 1978. 18.50 o.p. (ISBN 0-88233-347-X); pap. 4.00 o.p. (ISBN 0-88233-348-8). Ardis Pubs.

Scaffold. Chinghiz Aitmatov. Tr. by Natasha Ward from Rus. 352p. 1989. 18.95 o.p. Grove.

Scale Coordinate & Its Geometry: The Quantization of Riemannian Geometry. William Bender. LC 76-9498. 1975. text ed. 10.00 o.p. (ISBN 0-682-48567-5, University). Exposition-Phoenix.

Scale in Production Systems: Based on an IIASA Workshop June 26-29, 1979. Ed. by J. A. Buzacott et al. (IIASA Proceedings: Vol. 15). (Illus.). 256p. 1982. 73.00 o.p. (ISBN 0-08-028725-5). Pergamon.

Scale, Innovation, Merger & Monopoly. H. Townsend. LC 68-24069. 1968. text ed. 11.00 o.p. (ISBN 0-08-012942-0); pap. text ed. 5.50 o.p. (ISBN 0-08-012941-2). Pergamon.

Scale Model Electric Tramways & How to Model Them. E. Jackson Stevens. (Illus.). 196p. 1986. 24.95 o.p. (ISBN 0-7153-8632-8). David & Charles.

Scale Models in Plastic. Ed. by Roger Chesneau. (Encore Edition). (Illus.). 1979. 3.75 o.s.i. (ISBN 0-684-16250-4, ScribT). Scribner.

Scale Studies for Violin: Appendix to H. Schradieck's Scales. H. Sitt. (Carl Fischer Music Library: No. 346). 1903. pap. 4.95 o.p. (ISBN 0-8258-0043-9, L346). Fischer Inc NY.

Scales & Balances. J. T. Graham. (Shire Album Ser.: No. 55). (Illus.). 32p. (Orig.). 1981. pap. 2.95 o.p. (ISBN 0-85263-547-8, Pub. by Shire Pubns England). Seven Hills Bk Dists.

Scales & Chords for Piano. F. A. Schultz. (Carl Fischer Music Library: No. 176). 1900. pap. 4.50 o.p. (ISBN 0-8258-0097-8, L176). Fischer Inc NY.

Scales, Intervals, Keys & Triads: A Self-Instruction Program. John Clough. (Orig., Prog. Bk.). 1964. pap. 8.95x o.p. (ISBN 0-393-09625-4, NortonC). Norton.

Scaling in Two-Phase Flow. Ed. by P. Saha. (HTD: Vol. 14). 53p. 1980. 12.00 o.p. (ISBN 0-686-69860-6, G00187). ASME.

Scandal of Christianity: The Gospel as Stumbling Block to Modern Man. Emil Brunner. LC 65-12729. 1965. pap. 5.95 o.p. (ISBN 0-8042-0708-9, John Knox). Westminster John Knox.

Scandal of Father Brown. G. K. Chesterton. 1986. pap. 10.95 o.p. (ISBN 0-8161-3930-X, Large Prints Bks). G K Hall.

Scandal of Lent: Themes for Lenten Preaching in the Gospel of John. Robert Kysar. LC 81-52267. 112p. (Orig.). 1982. pap. 5.95 o.p. (ISBN 0-8066-1899-X, 10-5597, Augsburg). Augsburg Fortress.

Scandalous Lady: The Life & Times of Madame Restell. Allan Keller. LC 81-66008. 1981. 12.95 o.p. (ISBN 0-689-11213-0, Atheneum). Macmillan.

Scandinavia. Sylvie Nickels. LC 82-61196. (Pocket Guide Ser.). (Illus.). 1987. pap. 5.95 o.p. (ISBN 0-528-84893-3). Rand McNally.

Scandinavia. (AA Road Map Ser.). (Illus.). (ISBN 0-86145-144-9, Pub. by Auto Assn England). Salem Hse Pubs.

Scandinavia. Time-Life Books Editors. (Library of Nations). (Illus.). 160p. (YA) (gr. 7 up). 1986. lib. bdg. 23.93 o.p. Time-Life.

Scandinavia: A New Geography. B. S. John. 256p. 1984. pap. 29.95 o.p. (ISBN 0-470-20507-5, Co-Pub. with Longman). Wiley.

Scandinavia on Thirty-Five Dollars a Day. Darwin Porter. 480p. 1985. pap. 9.95 o.p. (ISBN 0-671-52437-2). Prentice Hall Pr.

Scandinavia on Twenty-Five Dollars a Day, 1983-84. 336p. 1982. pap. 7.95 o.p. (ISBN 0-671-44916-8). Prentice Hall Pr.

Scandinavia Revisited: A Norwegian-American Tours Her Homeland. Bergljot Abrahamson. 1958. 3.50 o.p. (ISBN 0-682-40002-5). Exposition-Phoenix.

Scandinavian Social-Democracy Today. O. K. Timashkova. 271p. 1981. 7.00 o.p. (ISBN 0-8285-2170-0, Pub. by Progress Pubs USSR). Imported Pubns.

Scandium: Its Occurence, Chemistry, Physics, Metallurgy, Biology & Technology. C. T. Horovitz et al. 1975. 132.00 o.p. (ISBN 0-12-355850-6). Acad Pr.

Scandium, Yttrium, Lanthanum & Lanthanide Nitrates. Ed. by S. Siekierski & M. Salomon. LC 83-8145. (Solubility Data Ser.: Vol. 13). 514p. 1983. 110.00 o.p. (ISBN 0-08-026192-2). Pergamon.

Scanners & Imagery Systems for Earth Observation: Proceedings, Vol. 51. Society of Photo-Optical Instrumentation Engineers Staff. 1975. 28.00 o.p. (ISBN 0-89252-063-9). SPIE.

Scanning Electron Microscope Atlas of Mammalian Reproduction. Ed. by E. S. Hafez. LC 73-33562. 1976. 106.00 o.p. (ISBN 0-387-91129-4). Springer-Verlag.

Scanning Electron Microscope: Atlas of Periodontal Biology & Pathology. Carranza et al. (Illus.). 250p. 1989. 42.50 o.p. Ishiyaku Euro.

Scanning Electron Microscopy. 2nd ed. J. Ohnsorge & R. Holm. LC 77-99145. (Illus.). 168p. 1978. pap. 35.00 o.p. (ISBN 0-88416-235-4). Year Bk Med.

Scanning Electron Microscopy in Biology: A Students' Atlas of Biological Organization. R. G. Kessel & C. Y. Shih. (Illus.). x, 345p. 1976. 42.00 o.p. (ISBN 0-387-06724-8). Springer-Verlag.

Scapegoat. Mary L. Settle. 288p. 1982. pap. 3.95 o.s.i. (ISBN 0-345-29802-0). Ballantine.

Scapegoat: Ritual & Literature. Ed. by John B. Vickery & J'nan M. Sellery. LC 70-166472. (Myth & Dramatic Form Ser). (Orig.). 1972. pap. 9.95 o.p. (ISBN 0-395-11256-7, 3-57680). HM.

Scaramouche. Rafael Sabatini. 10.95 o.p. (ISBN 0-395-08142-4). HM.

Scareboy. Jeanne M. Hart. LC 57-8067. (Illus.). (gr. 1-4). 1957. PLB 5.95 o.p. (ISBN 0-395-27660-8, Pub. by Parnassus). HM.

Scarecrow. Floyd Collins. LC 79-19491. 1980. pap. 3.95 o.p. (ISBN 0-918518-06-7). Ion Books.

Scared Stiff: Tales of Sex & Death. Ramsey Campbell. 1987. 25.00 o.p. (ISBN 0-910489-17-3). Scream Pr.

Scaremongers: The Advocacy of War & Rearmament 1896-1914. A. J. Morris. 400p. 1984. 49.95x o.p. (ISBN 0-7102-0162-1). Routledge Chapman & Hall.

Scarf Book. (Illus.). o.p. Stewart Tabori & Chang.

Scarlet Letter. Nathaniel Hawthorne. 1971. pap. 2.50x o.p. (ISBN 0-460-01122-7, Evman, Evman). Biblio Dist.

Scarlet Letter. Nathaniel Hawthorne. Ed. by H. Levin. (Riverside Library). 5.95 o.p. (ISBN 0-395-08128-9). HM.

Scarlet Letter. Nathaniel Hawthorne. Ed. by Sculley Bradley et al. (Critical Editions). (Annotated). (gr. 9-12). 1966. text ed. 5.50 o.p. (ISBN 0-393-05318-0); pap. text ed. 2.45x o.p. (ISBN 0-393-09562-2, 9562). Norton.

Scarlet Letter. 2nd ed. Nathaniel Hawthorne. Ed. by Sculley Bradley et al. (Norton Critical Edition Ser.). 1978. 12.95 o.p. (ISBN 0-393-04495-5); pap. 7.95x o.p. (ISBN 0-393-09073-6). Norton.

Scarlet Letter. Nathaniel Hawthorne. LC 84-60093. (Illus.). 256p. 1984. 12.95 o.p. (ISBN 0-89577-184-5). RD Assn.

Scarlet Letter: A Reading. Nina Baym. 152p. 1986. 17.95 o.s.i. (Twayne); pap. 6.95 o.s.i. (ISBN 0-8057-8001-7). G K Hall.

Scarlet Letter by Nathaniel Hawthorne. 48p. (Orig.). 1988. pap. 9.95 o.p. (ISBN 1-55651-827-7); cassette o.p. (ISBN 1-55651-828-5). Cram Cassettes.

Scarlet Letter: Text, Sources, Criticism. Nathaniel Hawthorne. Ed. by Kenneth S. Lynn. 1961. pap. text ed. 7.95 o.p. (ISBN 0-15-578167-7, HC). HarBraceJ.

Scarlet Mansion. Allan W. Eckert. 480p. 1985. 19.95 o.p. (ISBN 0-316-20883-3). Little.

Scarlet Night. Dorothy S. Davis. 1980. 9.95 o.p. (ISBN 0-684-16492-2). Scribner.

Scarlet Royal. Anne Emery. LC 76-23407. 1976. 6.50 o.s.i. (ISBN 0-664-32604-8, Westminster). Westminster John Knox.

Scarlet Ruse. John D. MacDonald. (Travis McGee Ser.). 1985. pap. 3.50 o.p. (ISBN 0-449-13040-1, GM). Fawcett.

Scarlet Shield of Shalimar. Barbara Siegel & Scott Siegel. (Wizards, Warriors & You: No. 12). 112p. 1986. pap. 2.95 o.p. (ISBN 0-380-89949-3). Avon.

Scarlet Thread. Mary H. Weik. LC 68-18462. (Illus.). (gr. 6 up). 1968. 4.50 o.p. (ISBN 0-689-20463-9, Atheneum); PLB 4.13 o.p. (ISBN 0-689-20464-7). Macmillan.

Scarne's Complete Guide to Gambling. John Scarne. (Illus.). 900p. 1974. 24.00 o.p. (ISBN 0-671-21734-8). S&S.

Scarne's Guide to Casino Gambling. John Scarne. 1978. 13.95 o.p. (ISBN 0-671-24219-9). S&S.

Scarne's Guide to Modern Poker. John Scarne. 1980. 11.95 o.p. (ISBN 0-671-24796-4). S&S.

Scarpa, Planet of the Mindless Ones. Ruth Norman & Charles Spaegel. 500p. 1989. text ed. 17.95 o.p. (ISBN 0-932642-91-8). Unarius Pubns.

Scars. Richard C. Matheson. (Illus.). 224p. 1986. 15.00 o.p. (ISBN 0-910489-15-7); deluxe ed. 15.00 o.p. (ISBN 0-317-20266-9). Scream Pr.

Scarsdale Nutritionist's Weight Loss Cookbook. Judith R. Corlin & Mary S. Miller. 192p. 1982. pap. 7.75 o.p. (ISBN 0-671-45794-2, Fireside). S&S.

Scarsdale Nutritionist's Weight-Loss Program for Teenagers. Judith R. Corlin & Mary S. Miller. 208p. 1983. pap. 8.50 o.p. (ISBN 0-671-46262-8, Fireside). S&S.

Scattering & Localization of Classical Wave in Random Media. P. Sheng. (World Scientific Series on Directions in Condensed Matter Physics: Vol. 8). 300p. 1989. 60.00 o.p. (ISBN 9971-50-539-8); pap. 37.00 o.p. (ISBN 9971-50-540-1). World Scientific Pub.

Scavenger's Son. Thakazhi S. Pillai. Tr. by R. E. Asher from Malayalam. 143p. 1975. pap. 2.50 o.s.i. (ISBN 0-89253-025-1). Ind-US Inc.

Scene de Ballet Fantasia for Violin & Piano Op.100 Beriot. Ed. by Jules Centano. (Carl Fischer Music Library: No. 64). 1912. pap. 6.00 o.p. (ISBN 0-8258-0012-9, L64). Fischer Inc NY.

Scenes & Characters of the Middle Ages. Edward L. Cutts. LC 67-27866. (Social History Reference Ser.). (Illus.). 560p. 1968. Repr. of 1872 ed. 40.00x o.p. (ISBN 0-8103-3257-4). Gale.

Scenes from Married Life & Scenes from Later Life. William Cooper. 528p. 1985. pap. 5.95 o.p. (ISBN 0-380-69896-X, Bard). Avon.

Scenes from Provincial Life & Scenes from Metropolitan Life. William Cooper. 432p. 1984. pap. 4.95 o.p. (ISBN 0-380-69302-X, Bard). Avon.

Scenes from the Nineteenth-Century Stage in Advertising Woodcuts. Ed. by Stanley Appelbaum. 13.25 o.p. (ISBN 0-8446-5552-X). Peter Smith.

Scenic Great Smoky Mountains National Park Address Book. (Illus.). 2.50 o.p. (ISBN 0-936672-64-1). Aerial Photo.

Scenic North Carolina Address Book: From Mountains to the Sea. (Illus.). 4.50 o.p. (ISBN 0-936672-63-3). Aerial Photo.

Scenic Wonders of Canada. (Illus.). 1979. 24.95 o.p. (ISBN 0-393-01289-1, Pub. by Reader's Digest). Norton.

Scentual Touch: A Personal Guide to Aromatherapy Massage. Judith Jackson. LC 85-27164. (Illus.). 224p. 1986. pap. 14.95 o.p. (ISBN 0-03-006763-4). H Holt & Co.

Scepter of Egypt: A Background for the Study of Egyptian Antiquities in the Metropolitan Museum of Art. William C. Hayes. Incl. Vol. 1. From the Earliest Times to the End of the Middle Kingdom. 25.00 o.s.i. (ISBN 0-87099-072-1); pap. 18.50 o.s.i.; Vol. 2. Hyksos Period & the New Kingdom (1675-1080 B.C.) 16.95 o.p. (ISBN 0-87099-074-8); pap. 18.50 o.s.i. (ISBN 0-87099-191-4). LC 52-7286. (Illus.). 1959. Metro Mus Art.

Sceptical Sociology. John Carroll. 256p. 1980. 26.00x o.p. (ISBN 0-7100-0587-3). Routledge Chapman & Hall.

Scepticism & Animal Faith. George Santayana. 14.75 o.p. (ISBN 0-8446-2863-8). Peter Smith.

Scepticism & Poetry: An Essay on the Poetic Imagination. David G. James. LC 80-21749. 274p. 1980. Repr. of 1960 ed. lib. bdg. 35.00x o.p. (ISBN 0-313-22840-X, JASP). Greenwood.

Schaum's Outline of Accounting I. 2nd ed. James A. Cashin & Joel J. Lerner. (Schaum's Outline Ser.). 1980. pap. text ed. 8.95 o.p. (ISBN 0-07-010251-1). McGraw.

Schaum's Outline of Child Psychology. Terry Faw. (Illus., Orig.). 1980. pap. text ed. 7.95 o.p. (ISBN 0-07-020110-2). McGraw.

Schaum's Outline of Programming with BASIC. 2nd ed. Byron S. Gottfried. (Schaum's Outline Ser.). 1982. pap. text ed. 9.95 o.p. (ISBN 0-07-023855-3). McGraw.

Schaum's Outline of Psychology of Learning. Arno F. Wittig. (Schaum's Outline Ser.). (Illus.). 1981. pap. text ed. 7.95 o.p. (ISBN 0-07-071192-5). McGraw.

Scheme of Things. Allen Wheelis. LC 80-7949. (Helen & Kurt Wolff Bk.). 204p. 1980. 9.95 o.p. (ISBN 0-15-179573-8). HarBraceJ.

Schindler's List. Thomas Keneally. 1982. 17.50 o.p. (ISBN 0-671-44977-X). S&S.

Schindler's List. Thomas Keneally. (Large Print Books). 1985. lib. bdg. 18.95 o.p. (ISBN 0-8161-3854-0). G K Hall.

Schirra's Space. Walter M. Schirra & Richard N. Billings. LC 87-43312. 1988. 16.95 o.p. (ISBN 1-55770-034-6). Quinlan Pr.

Schismatrix. Bruce Sterling. Ed. by Robert Silverberg. 1985. 15.95 o.p. (ISBN 0-87795-645-6, Arbor Hse). Morrow.

Schistomiasis III: Abstracts of the Complete Literature 1963-1974, 2 vols. Kenneth S. Warren & Donald B. Hoffman. LC 76-16052. 673p. 1977. 95.00x o.p. (ISBN 0-470-15204-4). Halsted Pr.

Schistosomiasis: Epidemiology, Treatment & Control. P. Jordan & G. Webbe. (Illus.). 376p. 1982. text ed. 35.00x o.p. (ISBN 0-433-17581-8, Pub. by W Heinemann Med Bks). Sheridan Med Bks.

Schistosomiasis IV: Condensations of the Selected Literature 1963-1975, 2 vols. Ed. by Donald B. Hoffman, Jr. & Kenneth S. Warren. LC 77-11864. (Illus.). 538p. 1978. Set. text ed. 119.00 o.p. (ISBN 0-89116-164-3). Hemisphere Pub.

Schizoid. Joseph Stagnitto. 1978. 7.00 o.p. (ISBN 0-682-49216-7). Exposition-Phoenix.

Schizophrenia. John M. Neale & Thomas F. Oltmanns. LC 80-10169. 554p. 1980. 43.95 o.p. (ISBN 0-471-63086-1). Wiley.

Schizophrenia. Manfred Sakel. 352p. 1958. (ISBN 0-8022-1468-1). Philos Lib.

Schizophrenia: A Source of Social Insight. Brian W. Grant. LC 74-32084. 1975. 10.00 o.s.i. (ISBN 0-664-20722-7, Westminster). Westminster John Knox.

Schizophrenia & Human Value: Chronic Schizophrenia, Science & Society. Peter Barham. 232p. 1985. 34.95x o.p. (ISBN 0-631-13474-3). Basil Blackwell.

Schizophrenia & Madness. Andrew C. Smith. 176p. 1982. text ed. 27.95x o.p. (ISBN 0-04-157008-1); pap. 8.95 o.p. (ISBN 0-04-157009-X). Unwin Hyman.

Schizophrenia: Medical Diagnosis or Moral Verdict? Theodore R. Sarbin & James C. Mancuso. (Pergamon General Psychology Ser.). 1981. 70.00 o.p. (ISBN 0-08-024613-3); pap. 70.00 o.p. (ISBN 0-08-024612-5). Pergamon.

Schizophrenia, Paranoid Conditions, Depression see Teaching Program in Psychiatry.

Schizophrenia: Theory, Diagnoses & Treatment. Ed. by Herman Denber. 1978. 65.00 o.p. (ISBN 0-8247-6711-X). Dekker.

Schleiermacher: Life & Thought. Martin Redeker. Tr. by John Wallhausser from Ger. LC 72-91526. 224p. 1973. pap. 1.00 o.p. (ISBN 0-8006-0149-1, Fortress). Augsburg Fortress.

Schleiermacher the Theologian: The Construction of the Doctrine of God. Robert R. Williams. LC 77-78650. 214p. 1978. 11.95 o.p. (ISBN 0-8006-0513-6, 1-513, Fortress). Augsburg Fortress.

Schluessel Fuer Die Ggattung Hygrophorus Nach Exsikkatenmerkmalen. A. Bresinsky & J. Huber. (Illus.). 1967. 12.00x o.p. (ISBN 3-7682-0536-3). Lubrecht & Cramer.

Schmuck, Seventeen Eighty to Eighteen Fifty. Brigitte Marquardt. (Illus.). 332p. (Ger.). 1984. 45.00 o.p. (ISBN 3-921811-26-0, Pub. by Kunst & Antiquitaten West Germany). Seven Hills Bk Dists.

Schnitzer-Intensive Nutrition, Schnitzer-Normal Nutrition: 14 Day Menu Plan for Both Nutrition Forms. 10th, rev. ed. J. G. Schnitzer & Mechthilde Schnitzer. (Illus.). 186p. 19.95 o.s.i. (ISBN 3-922894-75-5). Medicina Bio.

Schock's Abc's of Telling & Remembering Stories. Al Schock. 1978. pap. 4.95 o.p. (ISBN 0-685-26401-7). Exposition-Phoenix.

Schock's Emceeing & Unrelated Items. Al Schock. 1978. 9.95 o.p. (ISBN 0-685-26402-5). Exposition-Phoenix.

Schoenberg. Malcolm MacDonald. (Master Musicians Ser.). (Illus.). 304p. 1976. 17.95x o.p. (ISBN 0-460-03143-0, Pub. by J M Dent England). Biblio Dist.

Schoenberg & His School. Rene Leibowitz. (ISBN 0-8022-0955-6). Philos Lib.

Scholar Collects: Selections from the Anthony Morris Clark Bequest. Ed. by Ulrich W. Hiesinger & Ann Percy. LC 80-82234. (Illus.). 171p. (Orig.). 1980. pap. 14.95 o.p. (ISBN 0-87633-036-7). Phila Mus Art.

Scholars, Saints & Sufis: Muslim Religious Institutions since 1500. Ed. by Nikki R. Keddie. 1983. 14.50 o.p. (ISBN 0-8446-5970-3). Peter Smith.

Scholarship Book: The Complete Guide to Private Sector Scholarships, Grants, & Loans for Undergraduates. Ed. by Daniel J. Cassidy & Michael J. Alves. LC 84-11683. 391p. 1984. 29.95 o.p. (ISBN 0-13-792342-2, Busn); pap. 21.95 o.p. (ISBN 0-13-792334-1). P-H.

Scholarship Guide to Commonwealth Universities, 1985-87. 35.00 o.p. (ISBN 0-8002-3996-2). Intl Pubns Serv.

Scholarships & Grants for Study or Research in U. S. A. A Scholarship Handbook for Foreign Nationals. Ed. by Walter Wickremasinghe. 146p. (Orig.). 1986. pap. 21.95x o.p. (ISBN 0-940937-00-X). Amer Coll Serv.

Scholarships & Loans for Nursing Education 1986-1987. 65p. (Orig.). 1986. pap. 8.95 o.p. (41-1964). Natl League Nurse.

Scholarships for International Students: A Complete Guide to U. S. Colleges & Universities. Ed. by Anna Leider. (Illus.). 248p. (Orig.). 1986. pap. 14.95 o.p. (ISBN 0-917760-84-0). Octameron Assocs.

Scholastic Aptitude Test (SAT) Preparation for the College Entrance Examination. Ed. by Brigitte Saunders et al. LC 80-88. 512p. (Orig.). 1980. lib. bdg. 12.00 o.p. (ISBN 0-668-04916-2, 4916); pap. 6.95 o.p. (ISBN 0-668-04920-0, 4920-0). Arco.

Scholasticism. Josef Pieper. 1964. pap. text ed. 5.95 o.p. (ISBN 0-07-049930-6). McGraw.

Scholasticism & Welfare Economics. Stephen T. Worland. 1967. 21.95 o.p. (ISBN 0-268-00246-0). U of Notre Dame Pr.

School. A. Gaidar. 159p. 1982. pap. 3.50 o.p. (ISBN 0-8285-2427-0, Pub. by Progress Pubs USSR). Imported Pubns.

School Acres: An Adventure in Rural Education. Rossa B. Cooley. LC 71-106853. (Illus.). Repr. of 1930 ed. 35.00x o.p. (ISBN 0-8371-3475-7, CSC&). Greenwood.

School & Community. C. Lindsay. 1970. pap. text ed. 7.00 o.p. (ISBN 0-08-016043-3). Pergamon.

School & Community in Less Developed Areas. Ed. by Kevin M. Lillis. LC 85-6678. 281p. 1985. 31.00 o.p. (ISBN 0-7099-1655-8, Pub. by Croom Helm Ltd). Routledge Chapman & Hall.

School & Community in the Third World. M. E. Sinclair & Kevin Lillis. 188p. 1980. 28.50 o.p. (ISBN 0-7099-0323-5, Pub. by Croom Helm Ltd). Routledge Chapman & Hall.

School & Me. Nancy Lindenauer & Edythea G. Selman. LC 79-11522. (Illus.). (gr. 1-3). 1979. pap. 3.95 o.p. (ISBN 0-03-052171-8). H Holt & Co.

School Consultation: Readings about Preventive Techniques for Pupil Personnel Workers. Joel Meyers et al. (Illus.). 368p. 1977. spiral bdg. 48.00x o.p. (ISBN 0-398-03485-0). C C Thomas.

School Curriculum Planning. Denis Lawton. (Studies in Teaching & Learning). 122p. (Orig.). 1986. pap. text ed. 16.95 o.s.i. (ISBN 0-340-38249-X). Princeton Bk Co.

School Dictionary. A. E. Anderson. 384p. (ISBN 0-8022-0031-1). Philos Lib.

School Discipline: A Socially Literate Solution. Alfred S. Alschuler. 1980. text ed. 19.95 o.p. (ISBN 0-07-001127-3). McGraw.

School Discipline Policies & Procedures: A Practical Guide. 1984. pap. 10.00 o.p. (ISBN 0-88364-104-6). Natl Sch Boards.

School Effectiveness: A Reassessment of the Evidence. George F. Madaus et al. 1980. text ed. 23.25 o.p. (ISBN 0-07-039378-8). McGraw.

School Finance Reform in the Nineteen Eighties: Social Needs & the New Federalism. League of Women Voters Education Fund. 64p. 1982. pap. 3.50 o.p. (ISBN 0-89959-327-5, 523). LWV US.

School Foodservice. 3rd ed. Dorothy VanEgmond-Pannell. (Illus.). 1985. 26.95 o.s.i. (ISBN 0-87055-463-8). AVI.

School for Community Action: Serving the Many Faces of Families in the Eighties, No. 7. pap. 4.75 o.p. (ISBN 0-941840-04-2). NCJW.

School for Murder. Robert Barnard. 192p. 1984. 12.95 o.p. (ISBN 0-684-18113-4, ScribT). Scribner.

School Governing Bodies. Ed. by Maurice Kogan et al. 220p. (Orig.). 1984. pap. text ed. 20.00x o.p. (ISBN 0-435-82512-7). Heinemann Ed.

School Guidance Systems: Objectives, Functions, Evaluation, & Change. Merville C. Shaw. LC 72-5248. 400p. 1973. text ed. 16.75 o.p. (ISBN 0-395-14058-7). HM.

School Labor Strife: Rebuilding the Team see Communication Alert Series.

School Law, Georgia. 292p. 1981. 4.50 o.p. (ISBN 0-318-02437-3). ICLE Georgia.

School Law, Georgia. 444p. 1984. 9.00 o.p. (ISBN 0-318-02438-1). ICLE Georgia.

School Librarianship. James E. Herring. 116p. 1982. 16.50 o.p. (ISBN 0-85157-347-9, Pub. by Bingley England). ALA.

School Library Materials Center: Its Resources & Their Utilization. Ed. by Alice Lohrer. (Allerton Park Institute Ser.: No. 10). 109p. 1964. 5.00x o.p. (ISBN 0-87845-005-X). U of Ill Lib Info Sci.

School Library Media Annual 1984. 2nd., 2nd Annual Vol. ed. Ed. by Shirley L. Aaron & Pat R. Scales. 528p. 1984. lib. bdg. 35.00 o.p. (ISBN 0-87287-434-6). Libs Unl.

School Library Media Center. 3rd ed. Emanuel T. Prostano & Joyce S. Prostano. LC 82-7193. (Library Science Text). 200p. 1982. 28.00 o.p. (ISBN 0-87287-286-6); pap. text ed. 20.00 o.p. (ISBN 0-87287-334-X). Libs Unl.

School Library Media Center Taxonomy. David V. Loertscher. 1986. 10.00x o.p. (ISBN 0-931510-20-1). Hi Willow.

School Life in Paris & Lovely Nights of Young Girls. 288p. 1984. pap. 8.95 o.p. (ISBN 0-394-62348-7, E-968, Ever). Grove.

School of Bowing for Violin, 2 bks, Op. 2. Otakar Sevcik. (Carl Fischer Music Library: Nos. 291 & 292). 1904. Bk. 1. pap. 4.00 o.p. (ISBN 0-8258-0038-2, L291); Bk. 2, 42p. pap. 4.00 o.p. (ISBN 0-8258-0039-0, L292). Fischer Inc NY.

School of Technic for Violin, Op. 1, Pt. 3. O. Sevcik. (Carl Fischer Music Library: No. 284). pap. 7.00 o.p. (ISBN 0-8258-0036-6, L284). Fischer Inc NY.

School of Technic for Violin, Op. 1, Pt. 4: Exercises in Double Stops. O. Sevcik. (Carl Fischer Music Library: No. 285). 1964. pap. 7.00 o.p. (ISBN 0-8258-0037-4, L285). Fischer Inc NY.

School of Velocity for Piano, 2 bks, Op. 299. Carl Czerny. (Carl Fischer Music Library: Nos. 341 & 399). 1903. Bk. 1. pap. 4.00 o.p o.p. (ISBN 0-8258-0109-5, L-339); Bk. 2, 23p. pap. 1.00 o.p. (ISBN 0-8258-0110-9, L-341). Fischer Inc NY.

School Psychology: Perspectives & Issues. Ed. by Gary D. Phye & Daniel J. Reschly. (Educational Psychology Ser.). 1979. 24.95 o.p. (ISBN 0-12-554250-X). Acad Pr.

School Reading Program: A Handbook for Teachers, Supervisors, & Specialists. Richard J. Smith et al. LC 77-77993. (Illus.). 1978. text ed. 32.95 o.p. (ISBN 0-395-25452-3). HM.

School Science for Tomorrow's Citizens. M. Bassey. 1963. pap. 35.00 o.p. (ISBN 0-08-009797-9). Pergamon.

School Subjects & Curriculum Change: Case Studies in the Social History of Curriculum. Ivor F. Goodson. (Curriculum Policy & Research Ser.). 212p. 1983. 29.95 o.p. (ISBN 0-7099-1104-1, Pub. by Croom Helm Ltd); pap. 12.50 o.p. (ISBN 0-7099-1158-0). Routledge Chapman & Hall.

School Survival Junior-Senior High: You're It-It's Up to You. Albert Frigone. Ed. by S. Michele McFadden. (Illus.). 31p. (Orig.). (gr. 7-12). 1981. pap. text ed. 1.25 o.p. (ISBN 0-89262-052-8); 30 copy pack 37.50 o.p. (ISBN 0-686-78760-9). Career Pub.

School Suspensions: Are They Helping Children? Children's Defense Fund Staff et al. LC 75-26436. 257p. 1975. pap. 5.50 o.s.i. (ISBN 0-938008-12-9). Children's Defense.

School Teacher in England & the United States. R. K. Kelsall & H. M. Kelsall. 1969. 50.00 o.p. (ISBN 0-08-006519-8); pap. 50.00 o.p. (ISBN 0-08-006518-X). Pergamon.

School Ties: Two Screenplays. William Boyd. Ed. by Maria D. Guarnaschelli. LC 86-2523. 1986. 12.95 o.p. (ISBN 0-688-06568-6). Morrow.

School Transfer & Curriculum Continuity. Brian T. Gorwood. LC 85-22423. 256p. 1985. 31.00 o.p. (ISBN 0-7099-1177-7, Pub. by Croom Helm Ltd). Routledge Chapman & Hall.

School Upon a Hill: Education & Society in Colonial New England. James Axtell. 320p. 1976. pap. 4.95x o.p. (ISBN 0-393-00824-X). Norton.

School, Vol. 3 (incl. 1984-1987 Supplements) Ed. by Eleanor C. Goldstein. (Social Issues Resources Ser.). 1987. 60.00 o.p. (ISBN 0-89777-079-X). Soc Issues.

School Years: Current Issues in the Socialization of Young People. Ed. by John C. Coleman. (Psychology in Progress Ser.). 180p. 1979. 25.00x o.p. (ISBN 0-416-71190-1, NO. 2898); pap. 12.95x o.p. (ISBN 0-416-71200-2, NO. 2899). Routledge Chapman & Hall.

Schooling, Academic Attainment & Occupational Attainment in a Non-Industrialized Society. Stephen P. Heyneman & Janice K. Currie. LC 79-63564. 1979. pap. text ed. 11.50 o.p. (ISBN 0-8191-0729-8). U Pr of Amer.

Schooling for Women's Work. Ed. by Rosemary Deem. 160p. (Orig.). 1980. pap. 18.00x o.p. (ISBN 0-7100-0576-8). Routledge Chapman & Hall.

Schooling in America: A Social Philosophical Perspective. Charles A. Tesconi. 1975. text ed. 15.25 o.p. (ISBN 0-395-18614-5). HM.

Schooling in the Asean Region: Primary & Secondary Education in Indonesia, Malaysia, the Philippines, Singapore & Thailand. Ed. by T. N. Postlethwaite & R. M. Thomas. LC 79-41357. (Illus.). 348p. 1980. 40.00 o.p. (ISBN 0-08-024289-8). Pergamon.

Schooling in Turmoil. Ed. by Geoffrey Walford. LC 85-4101. 273p. 1985. 31.00 o.p. (ISBN 0-7099-3618-4, Pub. by Croom Helm Ltd). Routledge Chapman & Hall.

Schools Abroad of Interest to Americans. 6th ed. Ed. by Porter Sargent Staff. (Handbook Ser.). (Illus.). 464p. 1985. 29.00 o.p. (ISBN 0-87558-111-0). Porter Sargent.

Schools & Churches in American Democracy: In Defense of Public Schools. H. Leo Eddleman. 135p. 1983. pap. 4.00 o.p. (ISBN 0-682-40144-7). Exposition-Phoenix.

Schools & Meaning: Essays on the Moral Nature of Schooling. Ed. by David E. Purpel & Svi Shapiro. 278p. (Orig.). 1985. lib. bdg. 29.00 o.p. (ISBN 0-8191-4438-X); pap. text ed. 13.50 o.p. (ISBN 0-8191-4439-8). U Pr of Amer.

Schools & Society: A Reader in Education & Sociology. Jeanne A. Ballantine. 576p. (Orig.). 1985. pap. text ed. 19.95 o.p. (ISBN 0-87484-707-9). Mayfield Pub.

Schools of the Future: Education into the Twenty-First Century. Marvin Cetron et al. 176p. 1985. text ed. 12.95 o.p. (ISBN 0-07-010350-X). McGraw.

Schools of Thought in the Christian Tradition. Ed. by Patrick Henry. LC 84-47924. 208p. 1984. 3.95 o.p. (ISBN 0-8006-0730-9, 1-730, Fortress). Augsburg Fortress.

Schools, Parents & Governors: A New Approach to Accountability. Joan Sallis. 256p. 1988. lib. bdg. 35.00x o.p. (ISBN 0-7099-4420-9, Pub. by Croom Helm UK). Routledge Chapman & Hall.

Schools, Pupils, & Special Educational Needs. David Galloway. LC 84-23077. 186p. 1985. 26.00 o.p. (ISBN 0-7099-1160-2, Pub. by Croom Helm Ltd); pap. 12.00 o.p. (ISBN 0-7099-1175-0). Routledge Chapman & Hall.

Schooner Bay. Jack Neilson. 1977. 7.50 o.p. (ISBN 0-682-48930-1). Exposition-Phoenix.

Schopenhauer. David W. Hamlyn. (Arguments of the Philosophers Ser.). 224p. 1980. 26.95x o.p. (ISBN 0-7100-0522-9). Routledge Chapman & Hall.

Schopenhauer: His Philosophical Achievement. Ed. by Michael Fox. 276p. 1980. 29.50x o.p. (ISBN 0-389-20097-2). B&N Imports.

Schrodinger Operators. Ed. by H. L. Cycon et al. (Texts & Monographs in Physics). (Illus.). 335p. 1987. 58.10 o.p. (ISBN 0-387-16759-5). Springer-Verlag.

Schroeder's Antiques Price Guide. 4th ed. 608p. 1986. pap. 9.95 o.p. (ISBN 0-89145-314-8). Collector Bks.

Schroeder's Antiques Price Guide. 6th ed. (Illus.). 608p. 1988. pap. 11.95 o.p. (ISBN 0-89145-358-X, 1847). Collector Bks.

Schubert. Arthur Hutchings. (Master Musicians Ser.). (Illus.). 233p. 1978. Repr. of 1978 ed. 17.95x o.p. (ISBN 0-460-03139-2, Pub. by J. M. Dent England). Biblio Dist.

Schubert & the Symphony. Brian Newbould. (Illus.). 350p. 45.00 o.s.i. (ISBN 0-907689-26-4, Pub. by Toccata Pr UK); pap. 22.95 o.s.i. (ISBN 0-907689-27-2, Pub. by Toccata Pr UK). David & Charles.

Schubert: Memoirs by His Friends. Otto E. Deutsch. 501p. Repr. of 1958 ed. lib. bdg. 69.00 o.p. (Pub. by Am Repr Serv). Reprint Servs.

Schubert Reader: A Life of Franz Schubert in Letters & Documents. Otto E. Deutsch. 1039p. Repr. of 1947 ed. lib. bdg. 108.00 o.p. (Pub. by Am Repr Serv). Reprint Servs.

Schubert Songs, by Maurice J. E. Brown. Maurice J. E. Brown. 62p. Repr. of 1967 ed. lib. bdg. 39.00 o.p. (Pub. by Am Repr Serv). Reprint Servs.

Schubert, the Man. Oskar Bie. LC 76-109710. (Illus.). xvii, 215p. 1971. Repr. of 1928 ed. lib. bdg. 35.00x o.p. (ISBN 0-8371-4201-6, BISM). Greenwood.

Schubert: The Master Musicians. John Reed. (Illus.). 315p. 1987. 29.95 o.p. (ISBN 0-460-03183-X, Pub. by J M Dent England). Biblio Dist.

Schumann. Andre Boucourechliev. Tr. by Arthur Boyars. LC 75-28923. (Illus.). 192p. 1976. Repr. of 1959 ed. lib. bdg. 26.50x o.p. (ISBN 0-8371-8475-4, BOSC). Greenwood.

Sci-Fi. William Marshall. LC 80-27264. (Yellowthread Street Mystery Ser.). 192p. 1981. 10.95 o.s.i. (ISBN 0-03-047486-8). H Holt & Co.

Sci Fi. William Marshall. 1984. pap. 3.95 o.s.i. (ISBN 0-03-071063-4). H Holt & Co.

Science--Who Needs It? Ben Bova. LC 74-18053. (Illus.). (gr. 7 up). 1975. 5.95 o.s.i. (ISBN 0-664-32557-2, Westminster). Westminster John Knox.

Science & Contemporary Society. Ed. by Frederick J. Crosson. 1967. 19.95x o.p. (ISBN 0-268-00247-9). U of Notre Dame Pr.

Science & Engineering Literature: A Guide to Reference Sources. 3rd ed. H. Robert Malinowsky & Jeanne M. Richardson. LC 80-21290. (Library Science Text Ser.). 342p. 1980. lib. bdg. 33.00x o.p. (ISBN 0-87287-230-0); pap. text ed. 21.00 o.p. (ISBN 0-87287-245-9). Libs Unl.

Science & Engineering Programs: Apple II Edition. Ed. by John Heilborn. 223p. 1981. pap. text ed. 15.95 o.p. (ISBN 0-07-931063-X). Osborne-McGraw.

Science & Man's Behavior. Burrow. 1954. (ISBN 0-8022-0198-9). Philos Lib.

Science & Medicine to Eighteen-Seventy: Pamphlets in the Library. S. J. Crowther & Marion Fawcett. 200p. 1968. 2.00 o.p. (ISBN 0-317-33133-7, NO.1). Am Philos.

Science & Metaphysics: Variations on Kantian Themes. Wilfrid Sellars. 246p. 1982. pap. text ed. 15.00x o.p. (ISBN 0-391-02621-6). Humanities.

Science & Modern Life. E. John Russell. 106p. 1956. (ISBN 0-8022-1417-7). Philos Lib.

Science & Other Matters. Victor Weisskopf. 1988. 17.95 o.p.; pap. 12.95 o.p. W H Freeman.

Science & Our Troubled Conscience. J. Robert Nelson. LC 80-8045. 192p. (Orig.). 1980. pap. 8.95 o.p. (ISBN 0-8006-1398-8, 1-1398, Fortress). Augsburg Fortress.

Science & Politics in Canada. G. Bruce Doern. 1972. 13.75 o.p. (ISBN 0-7735-0108-8, McGill Canada). U of Toronto Pr.

Science & Rationalism in the Government of Louis Fourteenth, 1661-1683. James E. King. LC 74-159202. 337p. 1971. Repr. of 1950 ed. lib. bdg. 23.00x o.p. (ISBN 0-374-94585-3, Octagon). Hippocrene Bks.

Science & Secrets of Early Medicine: Egypt-Babylonia-India-China-Mexico-Peru. Jurgen Thorwald. LC 63-15319. (Helen & Kurt Wolff Bk.). 1963. 12.00 o.p. (ISBN 0-15-179585-1). HarBraceJ.

Science & Sensations of Vocal Tone. Edgar F. Herbert-Caesari. 1968. 7.50 o.s.i. (ISBN 0-8008-7003-4, Crescendo). Taplinger.

Science & Singing. Ernest G. White. LC 68-59104. 1970. 6.95 o.s.i. (ISBN 0-8008-7006-9, Crescendo). Taplinger.

Science & Society in Modern Japan. Ed. by Shigeru Nakayama et al. 1974. 45.00x o.p. (ISBN 0-262-14022-5). MIT Pr.

Science & Society in the Sixteenth & Seventeenth Centuries. Alan G. Smith. (History of European Civilization Library). (Illus.). 216p. (Orig.). 1972. pap. text ed. 9.50 o.p. (ISBN 0-15-578399-8, HC). HarBraceJ.

Science & Starvation. D. J. Hughes. 1968. 15.50 o.p. (ISBN 0-08-012327-9); pap. 14.25 o.p. (ISBN 0-08-012326-0). Pergamon.

Science & Strategy of Squash. John O. Truby, Jr. (Illus.). 1985. pap. 12.50 o.s.i. (ISBN 0-684-14260-0). Scribner.

Science & Technology: A Reader. Eleanor Lander. 176p. 1983. pap. text ed. 9.25 o.p. (ISBN 0-88377-257-4). Newbury Hse.

Science & Technology: Biennial Report to the Congress, 1983-1984, (NSF 86-12) (Illus.). 147p. 1986. 7.00 o.p. (ISBN 0-318-23637-0, S/N 038-000-00567-7). USGPO.

Science & Technology in India. B. R. Nanda. 169p. 1986. text ed. 22.50x o.p. (Pub. by Vikas India). Advent NY.

Science & Technology in the World of the Future. Arthur B. Bronwell. LC 74-114914. 394p. 1970. 24.50 o.p. (ISBN 0-471-10594-5, Pub. by Wiley). Krieger.

Science & Technology of Surface Coatings. Ed. by Brian N. Chapman & J. C. Anderson. 1974. 86.00 o.p. (ISBN 0-12-168350-8). Acad Pr.

Science & Technology of Tributyl Phosphate: Selected Technical & Industrial Uses, Vol. II. Ed. by Wallace W. Schultz & James D. Navratil. 295p. 1987. 2 part set 190.00 o.p. (ISBN 0-317-61081-3). CRC Pr.

Science & Technology Policy: Priorities of Governments. F. Tisdell. LC 80-41228. 210p. 1981. 33.00x o.p. (ISBN 0-412-23320-7, NO. 6552, Pub. by Chapman & Hall). Routledge Chapman & Hall.

Science & the Car. C. E. Jones. Ed. by R. W. Thomas & R. S. Lowrie. (gr. 7-12). 1975. pap. 2.75 o.p. (ISBN 0-08-018283-6). Pergamon.

Science & the Cure of Diseases: Letters to Members of Congress. Efriam Racker. LC 79-84012. 1979. 22.50x o.p. (ISBN 0-691-08243-X); pap. 8.50x o.p. (ISBN 0-691-02363-8). Princeton U Pr.

Science & the Detection of Crime. C. R. Cuthbert. 1958. (ISBN 0-8022-0330-2). Philos Lib.

Science and the Paranormal. Ed. by George O. Abell & Barry Singer. (Illus.). 432p. 1981. 17.95 o.s.i. (ISBN 0-684-16655-0, ScribT). Scribner.

Science & the Second Renaissance of Europe. A. Danzin. 1979. pap. 33.00 o.p. (ISBN 0-08-022442-3). Pergamon.

Science & the Sociology of Knowledge. Michael Mulkay. (Controversies in Sociology Ser.: No. 8). 1979. text ed. 19.95x o.p. (ISBN 0-04-301093-8); pap. text ed. 11.95x o.p. (ISBN 0-04-301094-6). Unwin Hyman.

Science as Inquiry. Ed. by John Penick. 1983. pap. 7.00 o.p. (ISBN 0-317-65989-8). Natl Sci Tchrs.

Science at War. J. G. Crowther & R. Whiddington. (ISBN 0-8022-0322-1). Philos Lib.

Science de la Paix. Louis Bara. LC 78-147448. (Library of War & Peace; Problems of the Organized Peace Movement: Selected Documents). lib. bdg. 46.00 o.p. (ISBN 0-8240-0238-5). Garland Pub.

Science Digest Book of Halley's Comet. John Tullius. 122p. 1985. pap. 9.95 o.p. (ISBN 0-380-89527-7). Avon.

Science Education & Ethical Values: Introducing Ethics & Religion into the Classroom & Laboratory. Ed. by David Gosling & Bert Musschenga. 1985. pap. 8.95 o.p. (ISBN 0-317-18104-1, Fortress). Augsburg Fortress.

Science et Technologie pour le Developpement: Rapport Comparatif Principal du Project "Instruments de Politique Scientifique et Technique" F. Sagasti. 124p. 1979. pap. 8.50 o.p. (ISBN 0-88936-218-1, IDRC-109F, IDRC). UNIPUB.

Science Fiction A to Z. Ed. by Isaac Asimov & Martin H. Greenberg. 1982. 22.95 o.p. (ISBN 0-395-31285-X). HM.

Science Fiction As Literature. John Aquino. 64p. 1976. pap. 5.95 o.p. (ISBN 0-8106-1804-4). NEA.

Science Fiction Book Review Index, 1923-1973. Ed. by H. W. Hall. LC 74-29085. 456p. 1975. 185.00x o.p. (ISBN 0-8103-1054-6). Gale.

Science Fiction Book Review Index, 1974 to 1979. Ed. by H. W. Hall. 416p. 1981. 185.00x o.p. (ISBN 0-8103-1107-0). Gale.

Science Fiction by Gas Light. Sam Moskowitz. LC 73-15074. (Classics of Science Fiction Ser.). (Illus.). 364p. 1986. 25.25 o.p. (ISBN 0-88355-128-4); pap. 10.00 o.p. (ISBN 0-88355-157-8). Hyperion Conn.

Science Fiction Gold: Classic Films of the 50's. Dennis Saleh. (Illus.). 1979. pap. text ed. 7.95 o.p. (ISBN 0-07-054467-0). McGraw.

Science Fiction Hall of Fame, 2 vols. (YA) (gr. 9 up). 1981. Boxed set. pap. 8.85 o.p. (ISBN 0-380-30411-2, 55947). Avon.

Science Fiction Hall of Fame, Vol. 2A. Ed. by Ben Bova. 1976. pap. 2.95 o.p. (ISBN 0-380-00038-5, 58750-5). Avon.

Science Fiction Hall of Fame, Vol. 2B. Ed. by Ben Bova. 1981. pap. 2.95 o.p. (ISBN 0-380-00054-7, 60194-X). Avon.

Science Fiction Hall of Fame, Vol. 3: The Nebula Winners. Ed. by Arthur C. Clarke & George Proctor. 688p. 1982. pap. 3.95 o.p. (ISBN 0-380-79335-0, 79335-0). Avon.

Science Fiction Handbook: How to Write & Sell Imaginative Stories. rev. ed. L. Sprague De Camp & Catherine C. De Camp. 1977. pap. text ed. 3.95 o.p. (ISBN 0-07-016198-4). McGraw.

Science Fiction in the Cinema. John Baxter. LC 69-14896. pap. 4.95 o.s.i. (ISBN 0-498-07416-1). A S Barnes.

Science Fiction in the Thirties. Damon Knight. 1977. pap. 4.95 o.p. (ISBN 0-380-00904-8, 31708-7). Avon.

Science Fiction: Its Criticism & Teaching. Patrick Parrinder. 1980. 25.00 o.p. (ISBN 0-416-71390-4, NO. 6356); pap. 10.95x o.p. (ISBN 0-416-71400-5, NO. 6393). Routledge Chapman & Hall.

Science Fiction of the Fifties. Martin H. Greenberg & Joseph Olander. 1979. pap. 4.95 o.p. (ISBN 0-380-46409-8, 46409-8). Avon.

Science Fiction of the Forties. Ed. by Frederick Pohl. 1978. pap. 4.95 o.p. (ISBN 0-380-40097-9, 40097-9). Avon.

Science Fiction: The Future. Dick Allen. 345p. (Orig.). 1971. pap. text ed. 10.95 o.p. (ISBN 0-15-578650-4, HC). HarBraceJ.

Science Fictional Solar System. Ed. by Isaac Asimov et al. 336p. 1982. pap. 4.95 o.p. (ISBN 0-586-05228-3, Pub. by Granada England). Academy Chi Pubs.

Science for Chemical Process Operators. C. A. Colman-Porter. 1972. pap. text ed. 7.25 o.p. (ISBN 0-08-015725-4). Pergamon.

Science for the Citizen. 4th ed. Lancelot Hogben. (Illus.). 1957. 15.00x o.p. (ISBN 0-393-06324-0, NortonC). Norton.

Science: Good, Bad & Bogus. Martin Gardner. 432p. 1983. pap. 3.95 o.p. (ISBN 0-380-61754-4, 61754-4, Discus). Avon.

Science-Hobby Book of Archaeology. rev. ed. Virginia J. Fortiner. LC 62-11633. (Science Hobby Bks.). (Illus.). (gr. 5-10). 1968. PLB 4.95 o.p. (ISBN 0-8225-0552-5). Lerner Pubns.

Science-Hobby Book of Boating. rev. ed. Maxwell R. Garret. LC 68-28032. (Science Hobby Bks.). (Illus.). (gr. 5-10). 1968. PLB 4.95 o.p. (ISBN 0-8225-0554-1). Lerner Pubns.

Science-Hobby Book of Shell Collecting. rev. ed. Miriam Gilbert. LC 67-17404. (Science Hobby Bks.). (gr. 5-10). 1968. PLB 4.95 o.p. (ISBN 0-8225-0557-6). Lerner Pubns.

Science, Ideology & Development-Three Essays on Development Theory. Archie Mafeje. 86p. 1978. pap. 9.50 o.s.i. (ISBN 0-8419-9731-4, Africana). Holmes & Meier.

Science in Your Own Back Yard. Elizabeth K. Cooper. LC 58-5705. (Illus.). (gr. 4-7). 1958. 6.95 o.p. (ISBN 0-15-270664-X, HJ). HarBraceJ.

Science in Your Own Back Yard. Elizabeth K. Cooper. LC 58-5705. (gr. 4-7). 1965. pap. 1.35 o.p. (ISBN 0-15-679596-5, AVB4, VoyB). HarBraceJ.

Science Indicators: The Nineteen Eighty-Five Report. 7th ed. (Illus.). 330p. 1985. pap. 15.00 o.p. (ISBN 0-318-20143-7, S/N 038-000-00563-4). USGPO.

Science Looks at Mysterious Monsters. Thomas G. Aylesworth. LC 82-2304. (gr. 5 up). 1982. lib. bdg. 9.79 o.s.i. (ISBN 0-671-43657-0). Messner.

Science, Man, & Morals. William H. Thorpe. LC 76-14962. (Illus.). 1976. Repr. of 1965 ed. lib. bdg. 35.00x o.p. (ISBN 0-8371-8143-7, THSMM). Greenwood.

Science Now. P-H.

Science Objectives. National Assessment of Educational Progress Staff. 56p. 1972. 1.40 o.p. (ISBN 0-318-13998-7, ED 072 976, Natl Assessment Ed Progress). Ed Comm States.

Science Objectives: Third Assessment, 1976-77. National Assessment of Educational Progress Staff. 68p. 1.75 o.p. (ISBN 0-318-13999-5, ED-179-402, Natl Assessment Ed Progress). Ed Comm States.

Science of Animals That Serve Mankind. 2nd ed. John R. Campbell & John F. Lasley. (Agricultural Science Ser.). (Illus.). 736p. 1975. text ed. 42.95 o.p. (ISBN 0-07-009696-1). McGraw.

Science of Coexistence. Ambrose Ryder. LC 68-23352. 1968. 5.95 o.p. (ISBN 0-8022-1422-3). Philos Lib.

Science of Cycling. Edmund R. Burke. LC 86-10246. (Illus.). 223p. 1986. text ed. 18.00x o.p. (ISBN 0-87322-048-X, BBUR0048). Human Kinetics.

Science of Education, 3 vols. Caleb Gattegno. Bd. with Facts of Awareness (ISBN 0-87825-125-1); Affectivity & Learning (ISBN 0-87825-073-5); Awareness of Awareness (ISBN 0-87825-126-X). 1977. 3.00 ea. o.p. Ed Solutions.

Science of Experience: A Direction for Psychology. Stanton Peele. LC 81-48555. 160p. 1983. 25.00x o.p. (ISBN 0-669-05420-8). Lexington Bks.

Science of Folklore. Alexander H. Krappe. 1964. pap. 4.25x o.p. (ISBN 0-393-00282-9, Norton Lib). Norton.

Science of Food & Cooking. 3rd ed. Allan Cameron. (Illus.). 1973. pap. 19.95x o.p. (ISBN 0-7131-1791-5). Trans-Atl Phila.

Science of Historical Theology: Elements of a Definition, Vol. 1. John F. McCarthy. 195p. (Orig.). 1976. pap. 6.00 o.p. (ISBN 0-912103-01-9). Stella Maris Bks.

Science of Hitting. Ted Williams. (Illus.). (gr. 7 up). 1971. 9.95 o.p. (ISBN 0-671-20892-6). S&S.

Science of Hitting. Ted Williams & John Underwood. (Illus.). 1982. pap. 8.50 o.s.i. (ISBN 0-671-44913-3). PB.

Science of Human Regeneration (Postgraduate Orthopathy) see Secret of Regeneration.

Science of Law According to the American Theory of Government. E. L. Campbell. viii, 375p. 1981. Repr. of 1887 ed. lib. bdg. 32.50x o.p. (ISBN 0-8377-0433-2). Rothman.

Science of Photobiology. Ed. by K. C. Smith. LC 77-2130. 442p. 1977. 55.00x o.p. (ISBN 0-306-31051-1, Plenum Pr.); pap. 29.50x o.p. (ISBN 0-306-20029-5). Plenum Pub.

Science of Politics: An Introduction to Hypothesis Formation & Testing. William H. Coogan & Oliver H. Woshinsky. 242p. (Orig.). 1982. lib. bdg. 29.75 o.p. (ISBN 0-8191-2652-7); pap. text ed. 13.00 o.p. (ISBN 0-8191-2653-5). U Pr of Amer.

Science of Religion & the Sociology of Knowledge: Some Methodological Questions. Ninian Smart. LC 72-12115. 176p. 1973. 22.00x o.p. (ISBN 0-691-07191-8); pap. 9.50x o.p. (ISBN 0-691-01997-5). Princeton U Pr.

Science of Society. Messner. 256p. 1959. (ISBN 0-8022-1107-0). Philos Lib.

Science of Spying. Daniel Cohen. (gr. 7-12). 1977. text ed. 9.95 o.p. (ISBN 0-07-011578-8). McGraw.

Science of Teaching Art. Mitchell Terry. 1986. 20.00x o.p. (ISBN 0-931510-14-7). Hi Willow.

Science of the Culture of Freshwater Fish Species in China, 17 Microfiches. IDRC, Ottawa Staff. 1981. Set. UNIPUB.

Science on the Shores & Banks. Elizabeth K. Cooper. (Illus.). (gr. 5 up). 1960. 4.95 o.p. (ISBN 0-15-270843-X, HJ). HarBraceJ.

Science on the Shores & Banks. Elizabeth K. Cooper. LC 60-8411. (Illus.). (gr. 7 up). 1966. pap. 1.50 o.p. (ISBN 0-15-679609-0, AVB38, VoyB). HarBraceJ.

Science Policy Perspectives U. S. A.: The U. S. & Japan (Symposium) Ed. by Arthur Gerstenfeld. LC 82-18159. 1982. 34.50 o.p. (ISBN 0-12-281280-8). Acad Pr.

Science, Politics & the Great Deception, Religion. Ruth Norman. 530p. (Orig.). text ed. 14.95 o.p. (ISBN 0-932642-93-4). Unarius Pubns.

Science Projects Ser. Mirrors. Hy Ruchlis. (Science-Math Projects Ser.). (Illus.). (gr. 4-9). pap. 3.50 o.p. (ISBN 0-87594-014-5). Book-Lab.

Science Readings for Students of English As a Second Language, with Exercises for Vocabulary Development. K. Croft. 1968. text ed. 2.75 o.p. (ISBN 0-07-013883-4). McGraw.

Science, Reason & Religion. Derek Stanesby. 210p. 1985. 34.50 o.p. (ISBN 0-7099-3360-6, Pub. by Croom Helm Ltd). Routledge Chapman & Hall.

Science, Scripture & the Young Earth. Henry M. Morris. LC 83-81187. 1983. pap. 5.00 pkg of 5 o.p. (ISBN 0-932766-06-4, Inst Creation). Master Bks.

Science: Suggestions for Teaching. Philadelphia Suburban School Study Council, Group C Staff. 1958. pap. 2.50x o.p. (ISBN 0-8134-0495-9, 495). Inter Print Pubs.

Science, Technology & Development in the Muslim World. Ziauddin Sardar. LC 77-12756. 1977. text ed. 28.50x o.p. (ISBN 0-391-00771-8). Humanities.

Science, Technology, & Freedom. Willis H. Truitt & T. W. Solomons. 432p. 1974. pap. 15.50 o.p. (ISBN 0-395-17685-9). HM.

Science, Technology & Global Problems, 4 vols. 1980. Set. 250.00 o.p. (ISBN 0-08-025235-4, PBL). Pergamon.

Science, Technology & Global Problems: Proceedings of the Symposium on the Role of Science & Technology in Solving Global Problems, Tallinn, U. S. S. R., Jan 1979. Ed. by J. Gvishiani. LC 79-40546. 1979. 125.00 o.p. (ISBN 0-08-024469-6). Pergamon.

Science Technology & Global Problems-Views from the Developing World. Ed. by S. Radhakrishna. (Illus.). 1980. 69.00 o.p. (ISBN 0-08-024489-0). Pergamon.

Science, Technology & the Future: Soviet Scientists Analysis of the Problems of & Prospects for the Development of Science & Technology & Their Role in Society. Ed. by E. P. Velikhov et al. LC 79-40113. (Illus.). 480p. 1980. 52.00 o.p. (ISBN 0-08-024743-1). Pergamon.

Science under Sail: The Story of Oceanography. Lois McCoy & Floyd McCoy. LC 82-3003. (Illus.). 128p. (gr. 4-7). 1985. 12.50 o.s.i. (ISBN 0-03-060236-X). H Holt & Co.

Science Update. Ed. by H. Messel. (Illus.). 336p. 1984. pap. text ed. 19.75 o.p. (ISBN 0-08-029842-7, 02/32:9, 17/47:2,10). Pergamon.

Science v Philosophy. F. G. Connolly. 1957. (ISBN 0-8022-0288-8). Philos Lib.

Science Year: The World Book Science Annual. 2nd, 1985 ed. Ed. by World Book, Inc. Staff. (Illus.). 400p. (YA) (gr. 7-12). 1985. PLB write for info. o.p. (ISBN 0-7166-0586-4). World Bk.

Sciences see Comprehensive Dissertation Index, 1974: Supplement, 1975.

Sciences & Theology in the Twentiety Century. A. R. Peacocke. (Oxford International Symposia Ser.). 320p. 1981. 25.00x o.p. (ISBN 0-85362-188-8). Routledge Chapman & Hall.

Sciences de L'education-Sciences of Education: Catalogues et Inventaires. Ed. by Diana Richet. (Maison des Sciences De L'homme, Service D'echange D'informations Scientifiques: No. 6). 1975. pap. 28.00x o.p. (ISBN 0-686-21809-4). Mouton.

Scientific Adventure. Herbert Dingle. (Illus.). 380p. 1953. (ISBN 0-8022-0399-X). Philos Lib.

Scientific American Book: Bibliography. LC 84-21099. 1985. 21.95 o.p. (ISBN 0-7167-1711-5); pap. 13.95 o.p. (ISBN 0-7167-1712-3). W H Freeman.

Scientific American Book of Mathematical Puzzles & Diversions. Ed. by Martin Gardner. 1963. pap. 5.75 o.p. (ISBN 0-671-63652-9, Fireside). S&S.

Scientific American Cumulative Index 1948-1978. Scientific American, Inc. Staff. 1979. 45.00 o.p. (ISBN 0-89454-002-5). Scientific Am Inc.

Scientific & Humorous Revelations of God. 2nd rev. ed. Paul J. Raabe. 1981. 4.00 o.p. (ISBN 0-682-49415-1). Exposition-Phoenix.

Scientific & Technical Books & Serials in Print, 1988, 3 vols. Ed. by Bowker, R. R., Staff. 4490p. 1987. 175.00 o.p. (ISBN 0-8352-2362-0). Bowker.

Scientific & Technical Revolution: Economic Aspects. S. A. Heinman. 342p. 1981. 8.00 o.p. (ISBN 0-8285-2074-7, Pub. by Progress Pubs USSR). Imported Pubns.

Scientific & Technological Cooperation among Industrialized Countries: The Role of the United States. National Research Council. 259p. 1984. pap. text ed. 20.95x o.p. (ISBN 0-309-03487-6). Natl Acad Pr.

Scientific & Technological Revolution: Its Role in Today's World. N. Dryakhlov. 264p. 1984. pap. 2.95 o.p. (ISBN 0-8285-2780-6, Pub. by Progress Pubns USSR). Imported Pubns.

Scientific Approach to Homeopathy. George R. Henshaw. 1980. 10.00 o.p. (ISBN 0-682-49518-2, University). Exposition-Phoenix.

Scientific Autobiography. Max Planck. 1949. (ISBN 0-8022-1986-1). Philos Lib.

Scientific Ballooning-II. Ed. by W. Riedler & M. Friedrich. (Advances in Space Research: Vol. 1, No. 11). (Illus.). 274p. 1981. pap. 42.00 o.p. (ISBN 0-08-028390-X). Pergamon.

Scientific Ballooning: Proceedings of Symposium 7 of the COSPAR Twenty-Fifth Plenary Meeting Held in Graz, Austria, 25 June -7 July 1984, No. IV. Ed. by W. Riedler & K. Torkar. (Illus.). 140p. 1985. pap. 54.00 o.p. (ISBN 0-08-032753-2, Pub. by P P L). Pergamon.

Scientific Basis for Nuclear Waste Management, Vol. 1. Ed. by Gregory J. McCarthy. LC 79-12440. 582p. 1979. 79.50x o.p. (ISBN 0-306-40181-9, Plenum Pr). Plenum Pub.

Scientific Basis for Nuclear Waste Management, Vol. 2. Ed. by Clyde J. Northrup, Jr. et al. LC 79-12440. 956p. 1980. 110.00x o.p. (ISBN 0-306-40550-4, Plenum Pr). Plenum Pub.

Scientific Basis for Nuclear Waste Management, Vol. 3. Ed. by John G. Moore. LC 81-10663. 650p. 1981. 89.50x o.p. (ISBN 0-306-40803-1, Plenum Pr). Plenum Pub.

Scientific Basis of Medical Imaging. Ed. by P. N. Wells. (Illus.). 284p. 1982. text ed. 72.00 o.p. (ISBN 0-443-01986-X). Churchill.

Scientific Basis of Obstetrics & Gynecology. 3rd ed. Ed. by Ronald R. MacDonald. LC 84-9451. (Illus.). 520p. 1985. text ed. 68.50 o.p. (ISBN 0-443-02399-9). Churchill.

Scientific Betting. pap. 2.25 o.p. (ISBN 0-685-19497-3). Powner.

Scientific Books, Libraries, & Collectors: Supplement to the Third Edition. J. L. Thornton & R. I. Tully. 1979. 17.75x o.p. (ISBN 0-85365-920-6, Pub. by the Library Assn). Nichols Pub.

Scientific Case for Creation. Henry M. Morris. LC 77-78019. (Illus.). 1977. pap. 2.95 o.p. (ISBN 0-89051-037-7). Master Bks.

Scientific Communism: A Textbook. 334p. 1982. 5.95 o.p. (ISBN 0-8285-2475-0, Pub. by Progress Pubs USSR). Imported Pubns.

Scientific Creationism: Public School Edition. Henry M. Morris et al. LC 74-14159. 1974. 8.95 o.p. (ISBN 0-89051-002-4); pap. 7.95 o.p. (ISBN 0-89051-001-6). Master Bks.

Scientific Death Investigation: Proceedings, 47th Annual Anatomic Pathology Slide Seminar. Charles S. Petty et al. LC 83-12272. (Proceedings of AP Slide Seminar Ser.). (Illus.). 145p. 1983. pap. 28.00 o.p. (ISBN 0-89189-175-7, 50-1-048-00). Am Soc Clinical.

Scientific Evidence of the Existence of the Soul. Benito F. Reyes. LC 70-122432. 259p. 10.00 o.p. World Univ Amer.

Scientific Exercise Training. Zebas-Thomas. 160p. 1984. pap. text ed. 12.95 o.p. (ISBN 0-8403-3373-0). Kendall-Hunt.

Scientific Forecasting & Human Needs: Trends, Methods & Message. Ed. by UNESCO Staff. LC 83-25046. (Illus.). 228p. 1984. 34.00 o.p. (ISBN 0-08-027970-8); pap. 5.50 o.p. (ISBN 0-08-030867-8). Alemany Pr.

Scientific Humanism & Christian Thought. Dubarle. 120p. 1956. (ISBN 0-8022-0420-1). Philos Lib.

Scientific Illustration: A Guide for the Beginning Artist. Zbigniew T. Jastrzebski. (Illus.). 336p. 1985. 49.95 o.p. (ISBN 0-13-795949-4); pap. 24.95 o.p. (ISBN 0-13-795931-1). P H.

Scientific Karatedo: Spiritual Development of Individuality in Mind & Body. Masayuki Hisatake. (Illus.). 256p. 1976. 26.00 o.p. (ISBN 0-87040-362-1). Japan Pubns USA.

Scientific Papers of Tjalling Koopmans. Ed. by M. Beckmann. LC 76-95566. (Illus.). 1970. 41.00 o.p. (ISBN 0-387-05009-4). Springer-Verlag.

Scientific Principles & Methods of Strength Fitness. 2nd ed. John P. O'Shea. LC 75-18158. (Physical Education Ser.). (Illus.). 160p. 1976. pap. text ed. 12.00 o.p. (ISBN 0-394-34892-3, RanC). Random.

Scientific Productivity: The Effectiveness of Research Groups in Six Countries. Ed. by Frank M. Andrews. 469p. (Co-published with Cambridge University Press). 1979. pap. 29.95 o.p. (ISBN 92-3-101599-0, UM42, UNESCO). UNIPUB.

Scientific Program & Abstracts: International CODATA Conference, 10th, July 14-17, 1986, Ottawa, Canada. Ed. by CODATA. (CODATA Bulletin Ser.). 102p. 1986. pap. 15.00 o.p. (ISBN 0-08-032529-7, PBL). Pergamon.

Scientific Revelations of God. Paul John Raabe. 1972. 3.00 o.p. (ISBN 0-682-47458-4). Exposition-Phoenix.

Scientific Revolution. Ed. by Vern L. Bullough. LC 77-21207. (European Problem Studies). 136p. 1978. pap. text ed. 6.50 o.p. (ISBN 0-88275-635-4). Krieger.

Scientific Revolution. P. M. Harman. (Lancaster Pamphlet Ser.). 48p. 1983. pap. 3.95 o.p. (ISBN 0-416-35040-2, NO. 3851). Routledge Chapman & Hall.

Scientific Strategies in Human Affairs: To Tell the Truth. Irwin D. Bross. LC 74-80672. 1975. 6.50 o.p. (ISBN 0-682-48028-2, University). Exposition-Phoenix.

Scientific Stream Pollution Analysis. Nemerov. 358p. 1974. 37.50 o.p. (ISBN 0-89116-519-3). Hemisphere Pub.

Scientific Studies in Behavioral Development. Ed. by Lu Hsien. 105p. 1971. text ed. 19.50x o.p. (ISBN 0-8290-1604-X); pap. text ed. 7.95x o.p. (ISBN 0-8290-1096-3). Irvington.

Scientific Study of Religion. J. Milton Yinger. (Illus.). 1970. text ed. write for info. o.p. (ISBN 0-02-430900-1). Macmillan.

Scientific Study of Social Behavior. Michael Argyle. (Illus.). 240p. 1957. (ISBN 0-8022-0037-0). Philos Lib.

Scientific Temperaments. Philip J. Hilts. 1982. 15.50 o.p. (ISBN 0-671-22533-2). S&S.

Scientific Temperaments: Three Lives in Contemporary Science. Philip J. Hilts. 1984. pap. 7.75 o.s.i. (ISBN 0-671-50590-4, Touchstone Bks). S&S.

Scientific Thought. Charles D. Broad. (Quality Paperback: No. 208). 555p. 1959. pap. 4.95 o.p. (ISBN 0-8226-0208-3). Littlefield.

Scientific Use of Factor Analysis in Behavioral & Life Sciences. Ed. by Raymond B. Cattell. LC 77-10695. (Illus.). 640p. 1978. 65.00x o.p. (ISBN 0-306-30939-4, Plenum Pr). Plenum Pub.
Scientific Value of the First Chapter of Genesis. Beth Green. 1978. 4.50 o.p. (ISBN 0-682-48987-5). Exposition-Phoenix.
Scientist at the Seashore. James S. Trefil. LC 84-14112. (Illus.). 208p. 1985. 16.95 o.p. (ISBN 0-684-18235-1, ScribT). Scribner.
Scientist Looks at the Sasquatch II. Ed. by Roderick Sprague & Grover S. Krantz. LC 79-63536. (Gembook & Anthropological Monograph). (Illus.). 195p. 1979. 7.95 o.p. (ISBN 0-89301-061-8). U of Idaho Pr.
Scientist-Technician As Expert Witness: A Bibliography. Frederick Frankena. (Public Administration Ser.: P 1828). 11p. 1985. 2.00 o.p. (ISBN 0-89028-678-7). Vance Biblios.
Scientist vs. the Humanist. Ed. by George Levine & Owen P. Thomas. (Orig.). 1963. pap. 3.95x o.p. (ISBN 0-393-09588-6, NortonC). Norton.
Scientists & Inventors. Anthony Feldman & Peter Ford. (Horizons of Knowledge Ser.). (Illus.). 352p. 1979. 29.95 o.p. (ISBN 0-87196-410-4). Facts on File.
Scientists Confront Creationism. Ed. by Laurie R. Godfrey. LC 82-12500. (Illus.). 288p. 1983. 19.00 o.p. (ISBN 0-393-01629-3). Norton.
Scientists in Search of Their Conscience: Proceedings. Symposium on the Impact of Science on Society, Brussels, 1971. Ed. by A. Michaelis & H. Harvey. LC 72-90441. (Illus.). 240p. 1973. 27.20 o.p. (ISBN 0-387-06026-X). Springer-Verlag.
Scintilla & the Fall of the Children of Seth. Frederick Jevsevar. 1978. 7.50 o.p. (ISBN 0-682-49092-X). Exposition-Phoenix.
Scintillation Counters in High Energy Physics. Yu K. Akimov. 1965. 54.00 o.p. (ISBN 0-12-047450-6). Acad Pr.
Scio Syndrome. Helmut Fessl. LC 84-91343. 99p. 1985. 8.95 o.p. (ISBN 0-533-06443-0). Vantage.
Scipione Africano. Francesco Cavalli. Ed. by Howard M. Brown. LC 76-20963. (Italian Opera 1640-1770 Ser.). 1978. lib. bdg. 77.00 o.p. (ISBN 0-8240-2604-7). Garland Pub.
Scissor Magic. Ethel T. Jordan. (ps-4). 1982. 6.95 o.p. (ISBN 0-86653-097-5, GA 424). Good Apple.
Scoliosis. Ed. by Gordon Robin. 1973. 36.50 o.p. (ISBN 0-12-589850-9). Acad Pr.
Scoop. Agatha Christie et al. Bd. with Behind the Screen. 208p. 1984. pap. 2.95 o.s.i. (ISBN 0-441-75505-4, Pub. by Charter Bks). Ace Bks.
Scoop. Evelyn Waugh. 1985. 13.95 o.p. (Large Print Bks). G K Hall.
Scope of Collective Bargaining in the Public Sector see Issues in the Public Employee Relations Library: Series 4.
Scopophilia: The Love of Looking. Ed. by Gerard Malanga. LC 85-40103. (Illus.). 128p. 1985. 19.95 o.p. (ISBN 0-912383-15-1). Van der Marck.
Score. Richard Stark. 1981. lib. bdg. 11.50 o.p. (ISBN 0-8398-2711-3, Gregg). G K Hall.
Score & Podium: A Complete Guide to Conducting. Frederick Prausnitz. 1983. 24.95x o.p. (ISBN 0-393-95154-5). Norton.
Scored for Listening: A Guide to Music. 2nd ed. Guy A. Bockmon & William J. Starr. (Illus.). 213p. (Orig.). 1972. pap. text ed. 12.75 o.p. (ISBN 0-15-579055-2, HC). HarBraceJ.
Scoring High on Reading Tests. 4th ed. LC 77-28477. 1978. pap. 5.00 o.p. (ISBN 0-668-00731-1). Arco.
Scoring High on the Armed Forces Test. E. P. Steinberg. LC 83-21395. 288p. (Orig.). 1984. pap. 3.95 o.p. (ISBN 0-668-05930-3). Arco.
Scorpion. Peter McCurtin. (Sundance Ser.: No. 32). 1980. pap. 1.75 o.p. (ISBN 0-8439-0756-8, Pub. by Leisure Bks CT). Dorchester Pub Co.
Scorpion God. William Golding. LC 70-174508. 178p. 1972. 5.95 o.p. (ISBN 0-15-136410-9). HarBraceJ.
Scorpion: The CVR(T) Range. Simon Dunstanx. (Tanks Illustrated Ser.: No. 22). (Illus.). 72p. (Orig.). 1986. pap. 9.95 o.p. (ISBN 0-85368-747-1, Pub. by Arms & Armour). Sterling.
Scorpions. (Metal Mania Ser.). (Illus.). 48p. (gr. 4-12). 1984. 6.95 o.p. (ISBN 0-88188-330-1, Robus Books). H Leonard Pub Corp.
Scorpion's Tail. Antony Sharples. LC 75-26100. 194p. 1976. 8.95 o.s.i. (ISBN 0-8008-7004-2). Taplinger.
Scot Free. Ivy Strick. LC 78-66809. 1979. 8.95 o.s.i. (ISBN 0-8008-7012-3). Taplinger.
Scotch. John Kenneth Galbraith. 1964. 6.95 o.p. (ISBN 0-395-07715-X). HM.
Scotch Reels: Scotland in Cinema & Television. Ed. by Colin McArthur. (Illus.). 96p. 1982. pap. 7.95 o.p. (ISBN 0-85170-121-3, Pub. by British Film Inst England). U of Ill Pr.
Scotch Verdict: Dame Gordon vs. Pirie & Woods. Lillian Faderman. LC 83-7989. (Illus.). 388p. 1983. 17.50 o.p. (ISBN 0-688-01559-X). Morrow.
Scotch Verdict: Dame Gordon vs. Pirie & Woods. Lillian Faderman. LC 83-8620. (Illus.). 388p. 1983. pap. 8.45 o.p. (ISBN 0-688-02054-2, Quill NY). Morrow.
Scotland. John Tomes. (Blue Guides Ser.). (Illus.). 1984. 24.95 o.p. (ISBN 0-393-01551-3); pap. 17.95 o.p. (ISBN 0-393-30003-X). Norton.
Scotland: A New Study. Ed. by Chalmers Clapperton. (Illus.). 344p. 1983. 18.95 o.p. (ISBN 0-7153-8489-9). David & Charles.
Scotland: An Anthology. Ed. by Paul Harris. 1986. 19.95 o.p. (ISBN 0-316-34830-9). Little.
Scotland Bed & Breakfast, '88. (ISBN 0-85419-330-8). Salem Hse Pubs.
Scotland for the Motorist. Salem Hse Pubs.
Scotland Hotels & Guesthouses. (ISBN 0-85419-329-4). Salem Hse Pubs.
Scotland, One Thousand One Things to See. (ISBN 0-85419-267-0). Salem Hse Pubs.
Scotland Road Atlas. (ISBN 0-86145-625-4, Pub. by Auto Assn England). Salem Hse Pubs.
Scotland: Self Catering Accommodation. Scottish Tourist Board Publication Staff. 366p. (Orig.). 1984. pap. 3.95 o.p. (ISBN 0-85419-233-6, Pub. by Automobile Assn Brit). Salem Hse Pubs.
Scotland: Shaping of a Nation. rev. ed. Gordon Donaldson. 272p. 1980. 32.95 o.p. (ISBN 0-7153-6904-0). David & Charles.
Scotland Touring Map. (ISBN 0-85419-325-1). Salem Hse Pubs.
Scotland Yard Scientist: My Thirty Years in Forensic Science. H. J. Walls. LC 73-1763. 1973. 6.95 o.s.i. (ISBN 0-8008-7010-7). Taplinger.
Scotland Yesterday. C. S. Minto. (Illus.). 128p. 1989. 24.95 o.p. (ISBN 0-7134-6005-9, Pub. by Batsford England). David & Charles.
Scots. Jane Toombs. 608p. (Orig.). 1984. pap. 3.95 o.p. (ISBN 0-440-07610-2, Dell Trade Pbks). Dell.
Scots Abroad: Labour, Capital, Enterprise, 1750-1914. Ed. by R. A. Cage. LC 84-19985. 288p. 1984. 31.00 o.p. (ISBN 0-7099-0833-4, Pub. by Croom Helm Ltd). Routledge Chapman & Hall.
Scots Concise Dictionary. Ed. by Mairi Robinson. xli, 820p. 1985. 40.00 o.p. (ISBN 0-08-028491-4, Pub. by Aberdeen U Pr). E J Brill USA.
Scots in Australia: A Study of New South Wales, Victoria & Queensland, 1788-1900. Malcolm D. Prentis. (Illus.). 304p. 1983. 39.50x o.p. (ISBN 0-424-00100-4, Pub. by Sydney U Pr Australia). Intl Spec Bk.
Scott. new ed. Christopher. (Orig.). 1978. pap. 3.95 o.p. (ISBN 0-87243-078-2). Templegate.
Scott & Amundsen: The Race to the South Pole. Roland Huntford. LC 83-6393. (Illus.). 576p. 1984. pap. 12.95 o.p. (ISBN 0-689-70656-1, 300, Atheneum). Macmillan.
Scott, Foresman Advanced Dictionary. rev. ed. Ed. by Clarence L. Barnhart. 1978. 19.95 o.p. (ISBN 0-385-14852-6). Doubleday.
Scott Madsen Poster Book. Photos by Aaron Jones & Lis DeMarco. (Illus.). 36p. (Orig.). 1984. pap. 11.95 o.p. (ISBN 0-671-54431-4, Fireside). S&S.
Scott Nineteen Eighty-One Stamp Catalogue: United States-United Nations-Canada. Ed. by Scott Publishing Company Staff. 1980. pap. 2.95 o.p. (ISBN 0-15-679672-4, Harv). HarBraceJ.
Scott of the Antarctic. Elspeth Huxley. LC 77-23662. 1978. 12.95 o.p. (ISBN 0-689-10861-3, Atheneum). Macmillan.
Scott Postage Stamp Catalogue & Inventory Checklist 1984. 208p. 1986. pap. 2.95 o.s.i. (ISBN 0-06-465153-3). Scott Pub Co.
Scott Specialized Catalogue of Canadian Stamps & Covers, 1984. Ed. by Edmund Wright. (Illus.). 168p. 1983. pap. 3.50 o.s.i. (ISBN 0-89487-059-9). Scott Pub Co.
Scott Specialized Catalogue of Canadian Stamps & Covers: 1985 Edition. Ed. by Edmund H. Wright et al. (Illus.). 170p. 1984. pap. 3.95 o.s.i. (ISBN 0-89487-067-X). Scott Pub Co.
Scott Specialized Catalogue of United States 1988. Ed. by Richard L. Sine & William W. Cummings. (Illus.). 1000p. 1987. 29.95 o.s.i. (ISBN 0-89487-101-3); pap. 20.00 o.s.i. (ISBN 0-89487-094-7). Scott Pub Co.
Scott Specialized Catalogue of United States Stamps, 1987. rev. ed. Ed. by Richard L. Sine & William W. Cummings. (U. S. Specialized Catalogue Ser.). (Illus.). 976p. 1986. pap. 20.00 o.s.i. (ISBN 0-89487-083-1). Scott Pub Co.
Scott Standard Postage Catalogue, 1985, Vol. I. Ed. by William Cummings. (Illus.). 1000p. 1984. 20.00 o.s.i. (ISBN 0-89487-062-9). Scott Pub Co.
Scott Standard Postage Stamp Catalogue Nineteen Eighty Eight: United States, Canada, Great Britain & the Commonwealth United Nations. rev. ed. Ed. by Richard L. Sine & William W. Cummings. (Vol. 1). (Illus.). 1207p. 1987. pap. 20.00 o.s.i. (ISBN 0-89487-090-4). Scott Pub Co.
Scott Standard Postage Stamp Catalogue, 1985, Vol. IV. Ed. by William Cummings. (Illus.). 1000p. 1984. pap. 20.00 o.s.i. (ISBN 0-89487-065-3). Scott Pub Co.
Scott Standard Postage Stamp Catalogue, 1985, Vol. III. Ed. by William Cummings. (Illus.). 1000p. 1984. pap. 20.00 o.s.i. (ISBN 0-89487-064-5). Scott Pub Co.
Scott Standard Postage Stamp Catalogue, 1985, Vol. II. Ed. by William Cummings. (Illus.). 1000p. 1984. pap. 20.00 o.s.i. (ISBN 0-89487-063-7). Scott Pub Co.
Scott Standard Postage Stamp Catalogue 1984, Vol. IV. Ed. by William W. Cummings & Barbara A. Weinfield. (Illus.). 1000p. 1983. softcover 20.00 o.s.i. (ISBN 0-89487-056-4). Scott Pub Co.
Scott Standard Postage Stamp Catalogue 1984, Vol. III. Ed. by William W. Cummings & Barbara A. Weinfield. (Illus.). 1983. softcover 20.00 o.s.i. (ISBN 0-89487-055-6). Scott Pub Co.
Scott Standard Postage Stamp Catalogue, 1984, Vol. 1. Ed. by William W. Cummings & Barbara A. Weinfield. (Illus.). 900p. 1983. softcover 20.00 o.s.i. (ISBN 0-89487-053-X). Scott Pub Co.
Scott Standard Postage Stamp Catalogue, 1984, Vol. 2. Ed. by William W. Cummings & Barbara A. Weinfeld. (Illus.). 1100p. 1983. softcover 20.00 o.s.i. (ISBN 0-89487-054-8). Scott Pub Co.
Scott Standard Postage Stamp Catalogue, 1988: Countries of the World A-F, Vol. 2. rev. ed. Ed. by Richard L. Sine & William W. Cummings. (Scott Standard Postage Stam Catalogue Ser.). (Illus.). 1184p. 1987. pap. 20.00 o.s.i. (ISBN 0-89487-091-2). Scott Pub Co.
Scott Standard Postage Stamp Catalogue, 1987, Vol. 1: U. S. Canada, G.B., & the Commonwealth, U. N. rev. ed. Ed. by Richard L. Sine & William W. Cummings. (Illus.). 1168p. 1986. pap. 20.00 o.s.i. (ISBN 0-89487-079-3). Scott Pub Co.
Scott Standard Postage Stamp Catalogue 1988, Vol. 1-4. rev. ed. Ed. by Richard L. Sine & William W. Cummings. (Scott Standard Postage Stamp Catalogue Ser.). (Illus.). 1987. 119.95 o.s.i. (ISBN 0-89487-103-X); pap. 80.00 o.s.i. (ISBN 0-89487-102-1). Scott Pub Co.
Scott Standard Postage Stamp Catalogue 1987, Vol. 3: Countries of the World G-O. rev. ed. Ed. by Richard L. Sine & William W. Cummings. (Standard Postage Stamp Catalogue Ser.). (Illus.). 1986. pap. 20.00 o.s.i. (ISBN 0-89487-081-5). Scott Pub Co.
Scott Standard Postage Stamp Catalogue 1988, Vol. 3: Countries of the World G-O. rev. ed. Ed. by Richard L. Sine & William W. Cummings. (Standard Postage Stamp Catalogue Ser.). (Illus.). 1246p. 1987. pap. 20.00 o.s.i. (ISBN 0-89487-092-0). Scott Pub Co.
Scott Standard Postage Stamp Catalogue 1988, Vol. 4: Countries of the World P-Z. rev. ed. Ed. by Richard L. Sine & William W. Cummings. (Scott Standard Postage Stamp Catalogue Ser.). (Illus.). 1120p. 1987. pap. 20.00 o.s.i. (ISBN 0-89487-093-9). Scott Pub Co.
Scott Standard U. S. Coin Catalogue 1984. Ed. by Joseph H. Rose & Harry Miller. (Illus.). 202p. 1983. pap. 2.95 o.s.i. (ISBN 0-06-465151-7). Scott Pub Co.
Scott U. S. Coin Catalog. Scott. 1981. pap. 1.75 o.p. (ISBN 0-89487-030-0). HarBraceJ.
Scott U. S. First Day Cover Catalogue & Checklist, 1988. rev. ed. (Illus.). 1988. pap. 4.95 o.s.i. (ISBN 0-89487-119-6). Scott Pub Co.
Scott U. S. Pocket Catalogue & Checklist 1988. Ed. by William W. Cummmings. 1987. pap. 3.95 o.s.i. (ISBN 0-89487-095-5). Scott Pub Co.
Scottie Showcase: A Pictorial Introduction to Scottie Dog Collectibles. Donna J. Newton. (Illus.). 144p. 1988. pap. 15.00 o.p. (ISBN 0-9620064-0-8). Country Scottie.
Scottish Ballad Operas, One: Pastoral Comedies. Ed. by Walter H. Rubsamen. (Ballad Opera Ser.). 1974. lib. bdg. 61.00 o.p. (ISBN 0-8240-0923-1). Garland Pub.
Scottish Ballad Operas, Three: Farce & Satire. Ed. by Walter H. Rubsamen. (Ballad Opera Ser.). 1974. lib. bdg. 61.00 o.p. (ISBN 0-8240-0925-8). Garland Pub.
Scottish Ballad Operas, Two: History & Politics. Ed. by Walter H. Rubsamen. (Ballad Opera Ser.). 1974. lib. bdg. 61.00 o.p. (ISBN 0-8240-0924-X). Garland Pub.
Scottish Burgh & County Heraldry. R. M. Urquhart. LC 72-12491. (Illus.). 272p. 1973. 38.00x o.p. (ISBN 0-8103-2005-3). Gale.
Scottish East Coast Potteries, 1750-1840. Patrick McVeigh. (Illus.). 1979. text ed. 49.95x o.p. (ISBN 0-85976-038-3). Humanities.
Scottish Educational System. 2nd rev. ed. S. Leslie Hunter. 296p. 1972. 70.00 o.p. (ISBN 0-08-016667-9); pap. text ed. 7.75 o.p. (ISBN 0-08-016668-7). Pergamon.
Scottish Enlightenment & Early Victorian English Society. Anand C. Chitnis. LC 85-22379. 224p. 1986. 34.50 o.p. (ISBN 0-85664-580-X, Pub. by Croom Helm Ltd). Routledge Chapman & Hall.
Scottish Fiddlers & Their Music. Mary A. Alburger. (Illus.). 224p. 1983. 35.95 o.s.i. (ISBN 0-575-03174-3, Pub. by Gollancz England). David & Charles.
Scottish Highlands. (AA Ordinance Survey Leisure Guides Ser.). (Illus.). 120p. 1986. pap. 18.95 o.p. (ISBN 0-86145-235-6, Pub. by Automobile Assn Brit); bds. 22.95 laminated o.p. (ISBN 0-86145-236-4). Salem Hse Pubs.
Scottish Metrical Psalter (1650) A Revision. Nichol Grieve. 183p. 1940. pap. 3.75 o.p. (ISBN 0-567-02127-0). Attic Pr.
Scottish Proverbs. Andrew Henderson. LC 70-75962. 230p. 1969. Repr. of 1881 ed. 40.00x o.p. (ISBN 0-8103-3894-7). Gale.
Scottish Short Stories. Ed. by James Campbell. 240p. pap. 5.95 o.p. (Pub. by Granada England). Academy Chi Pubs.
Scottish Tradition: A Collection of Scottish Folklore. David Buchan. 288p. 1984. 25.00 o.p. (ISBN 0-7100-9531-7). Routledge Chapman & Hall.
Scottish Travel Books: List of Travels, Tours, Journeys - Relating to Scotland. A. Mitchell. 207p. 1983. Repr. of 1901 ed. 25.00 o.p. (ISBN 0-87556-658-8). Saifer.
Scottish Vernacular Literature: A Succinct History. 3rd. ed. Thomas F. Henderson. LC 70-75473. 480p. 1969. Repr. of 1910 ed. 46.00x o.p. (ISBN 0-8103-3884-X). Gale.
Scottish Weapons & Fortifications, 1100-1800. Ed. by David Caldwell. (Illus.). 1980. text ed. 45.00x o.p. (ISBN 0-85976-047-2). Humanities.
Scotty & the Kittens. Mary H. Manoni. Ed. by Susan Mahoney. (Raggedy Ann's & Raggedy Andy's Friends Book Cassettes). (Illus.). 16p. (gr. k-3). 1979. pap. text ed. 24.95 o.p. (ISBN 0-89290-066-0). Soc for Visual.
Scourge of the Steel Mask: G-8 & His Battle Aces, No. 1. Robert J. Hogan. 192p. 1985. pap. 2.95 o.p. (ISBN 0-89300-240-2). Blazing Pubns.
Scrabble. Ann L. Rodiger. (Educational Dance Score Registry Ser.). (Illus.). 21p. 1980. dance score 15.00 o.s.i. (ISBN 0-932582-35-4). Dance Notation.
Scrabble Brand Puzzle Book. Gyles Brandreth. (Illus.). 240p. 1984. pap. 7.70 o.p. (ISBN 0-671-50536-X, Fireside). S&S.
Scramble: A Narrative History of the Battle of Britain. Norman Gelb. LC 85-8720. (Illus.). 400p. 1985. 22.95 o.p. (ISBN 0-15-179615-7). HarBraceJ.
Scramble: Sunshine, Rainfall, Sunshine-Such Is Life. Trena T. Nelson. 1979. pap. 4.00 o.p. (ISBN 0-682-49231-0). Exposition-Phoenix.
Scrambled Chickens & Seventy Four Other Eccentric How-To's. Jim Erskine & Craig Boldman. LC 81-6904. (Illus., Orig.). 1982. pap. 4.95 o.p. (ISBN 0-03-059908-3, Owl Bks). H Holt & Co.
Scrambles Amongst the Alps. Edward Whymper. (Illus.). 262p. 1986. 24.95 o.p. (ISBN 0-87905-239-2). Gibbs Smith Pub.
Scramblings. John C. Karl. 1976. 4.00 o.p. (ISBN 0-682-48640-X). Exposition-Phoenix.
Scrap Art. Tony Hart. (Tony Hart Fun Bks.). (Illus.). 32p. (gr. 1-4). 1984. 5.95 o.p. (ISBN 0-7182-2952-5, Pub. by Kaye & Ward). David & Charles.
Scrap Saver's Stitchery Book: A Farm Journal Book. Sandra L. Foose. (Illus.). 1978. 14.95 o.p. (ISBN 0-385-13437-1). Doubleday.
Scratch. Archibald MacLeish. 1971. 5.95 o.p. (ISBN 0-395-12346-1). HM.
Screaming High. David Line. 176p. (gr. 6 up). 1985. 12.95 o.p. (ISBN 0-316-52682-7). Little.
Screen of Time: A Study of Luchino Visconti. Monica Stirling. LC 78-22273. 1979. 14.95 o.p. (ISBN 0-15-179684-X). HarBraceJ.
Screen Printing Techniques. Silvie Turner. LC 75-18636. (Illus.). 1979. pap. 7.95 o.s.i. (ISBN 0-8008-7008-5, Pentalic). Taplinger.
Screening Deep Test of Articulation. Eugene T. McDonald. 69p. (Orig.). 1976. pap. text ed. 35.00 o.p. (ISBN 0-88450-912-5, 7230-B). Communication Skill.
Screening for Children with Special Needs: Multidisciplinary Approaches. Ed. by Geoff Lindsay. 202p. 1984. 25.00 o.p. (ISBN 0-7099-1636-1, Pub. by Croom Helm Ltd); pap. 15.50 o.p. (ISBN 0-7099-4130-7). Routledge Chapman & Hall.

Screenplay. MacDonald Harris. LC 82-45175. 255p. 1982. 12.95 o.p. (ISBN 0-689-11306-4, Atheneum). Macmillan.

Screenplay: The Foundations of Screenwriting. rev. ed. Syd Field. 224p. 1982. pap. 6.95 o.s.i. (ISBN 0-385-28915-4, Delta). Dell.

Screenplays. Werner Herzog. Tr. by Alan Greenberg from Ger. 208p. 1980. 12.95 o.p. (ISBN 0-934378-02-9); pap. 5.95 osi o.p. Tanam Pr.

Screens. Jean Genet. Tr. by Bernard Frechtman from Fr. 1962. pap. 4.95 o.p. (ISBN 0-394-17245-0, E374, Ever). Grove.

Screwtape Letters. C. S. Lewis. LC 80-18591. (Illus.). 136p. 1980. Repr. of 1979 ed. 9.95 o.p. (ISBN 0-8006-0650-7, 1-650, Fortress). Augsburg Fortress.

Scribble Monster. Jack Kent. LC 81-47533. (Illus.). 32p. (gr. 4-8). 1981. 6.95 o.p. (ISBN 0-15-271031-0, HJ). HarBraceJ.

Scribe: A Handbook of Classroom Ideas to Motivate the Teaching of Handwriting. (Spice Ser.). 1976. 8.95 o.s.i. (ISBN 0-89273-122-2). Educ Serv.

Scribes & Sources. Ed. by A. S. Osley. LC 79-88418. (Illus.). 272p. 1980. 35.00x o.s.i. (ISBN 0-87923-297-8). Godine.

Scribner Book of Embroidery Designs. Ed. by Muriel L. Baker. (Illus.). 1981. encore ed. 9.95 o.p. (ISBN 0-684-17570-3, ScribT); pap. 12.95 o.p. (ISBN 0-684-16944-4). Scribner.

Scribner Companion to the Brontes. Gareth L. Evans & Barbara L. Evans. (Illus.). 448p. 1982. 22.50 o.s.i. (ISBN 0-684-17662-9, ScribT). Scribner.

Scribner Desk Dictionary of American History. LC 84-14019. 608p. 1984. 24.95 o.s.i. (ISBN 0-684-18154-1). Scribner.

Scribner Guide to Orchestral Instruments. The Diagram Group Staff. LC 83-179512. (Illus.). 119p. 1983. 11.95 o.s.i. (ISBN 0-684-17951-2, ScribT). Scribner.

Scripps College Annual Treasury of Ceramic Art. (Illus.). 25p. 1965. folder catalogue 1.00 o.s.i. Galleries Coll.

Script Letter: Its Form, Construction & Application. Tommy Thompson. 13.50 o.p. (ISBN 0-8446-3068-3). Peter Smith.

Scriptorium of Bury St. Edmunds in the Twelfth Century. Elizabeth P. McLachlan. LC 83-48695. (Theses from the Courtauld Institute of Art Ser.). (Illus.). 515p. 1984. lib. bdg. 60.00 o.p. (ISBN 0-8240-5983-2). Garland Pub.

Scripts People Live. Claude M. Steiner. 1974. 8.95 o.p. (ISBN 0-394-49267-6, GP748). Grove.

Scriptual Dramas for Children. Denis O'Gorman. LC 77-70632. 232p. 1977. pap. 8.95 o.p. (ISBN 0-8091-2021-6). Paulist Pr.

Scriptural Cloning. H. Laurence Crowell. 1979. 4.00 o.p. (ISBN 0-682-49192-6). Exposition-Phoenix.

Scriptural Holiness. Noel Brooks. 3.95 o.p. (ISBN 0-911866-53-1); pap. 2.95 o.p. (ISBN 0-911866-54-X). Advocate.

Scriptural Signs of the Second Coming. James J. Unopulus. 1979. pap. 1.50 o.p. (ISBN 0-89036-072-3). Hawkes Pub Inc.

Scriptural Treasury of Eternal Life. Mary E. Mathis. 1981. pap. 0.10 o.p. (ISBN 0-570-08357-5, 12-2937). Concordia.

Scriptural Treasury of Forgiveness. Mary E. Mathis. 1981. pap. 0.10 o.p. (12-2935). Concordia.

Scriptural Treasury of Guidance. Mary E. Mathis. 1981. pap. 0.10 o.p. (ISBN 0-570-08350-8, 12-2930). Concordia.

Scriptural Treasury of Hope. Mary E. Mathis. LC 12-2931. 1981. pap. 0.10 o.p. (ISBN 0-570-08351-6). Concordia.

Scriptural Treasury of Joy. Mary E. Mathis. 1981. pap. 0.10 o.p. (ISBN 0-570-08353-2, 12-2933). Concordia.

Scriptural Treasury of Love. Mary E. Mathis. 1981. pap. 0.10 o.p. (ISBN 0-570-08356-7, 12-2936). Concordia.

Scriptural Treasury of Peace. Mary E. Mathis. 1981. pap. 0.10 o.p. (ISBN 0-570-08352-4, 12-2932). Concordia.

Scripture & Tradition in Judaism. 2nd rev. ed. Geza Vermes. (Studia Post Biblica: No. 4). 1973. text ed. 9.95x o.p. (ISBN 90-040-3626-1). Humanities.

Scripture Index to the New International Dictionary of New Testament Theology: And Index to Selected Extrabiblical Literature. David Townsley & Russell Bjork. Ed. by Brown & Colin. 208p. 1985. pap. 19.95 o.p. (ISBN 0-310-44501-9, 11315P). Zondervan.

Scripture Today. Durstan McDonald et al. LC 80-81100. 102p. (Orig.). 1981. pap. 4.95 o.p. (ISBN 0-8192-1271-7). Morehouse Pub.

Scriptures, Sects & Visions: A Profile of Judaism from Ezra to the Jewish Revolts. Michael E. Stone. LC 78-54151. 160p. 1980. 5.95 o.p. (ISBN 0-8006-0641-8, 1-641, Fortress). Augsburg Fortress.

Scrolls of Edessa. Robert L. Wise. 216p. 1987. pap. 7.95 o.p. (ISBN 0-89693-343-1). Victor Bks.

Scrub Fire. Ann De Roo. LC 80-12267. 120p. (gr. 4-7). 1980. 9.95 o.p. (ISBN 0-689-30775-6, Atheneum). Macmillan.

Scrubber Strategy: The How & Why of Flue Gas Desulfurization. Mary A. Baviello & Alexandra Bowie. LC 82-81547. 180p. 1982. 37.50x o.p. (ISBN 0-918780-19-5). INFORM.

SCSS Short Guide: An Introduction to the SCSS Conversational System. Keith J. Sours. 144p. 1982. text ed. 11.95 o.p. (ISBN 0-07-046539-8). McGraw.

Scuba Diving. Joan Deakin. (Illus.). 160p. 1981. 16.95 o.s.i. (ISBN 0-7153-7952-6). David & Charles.

Scuba Safe & Simple. John Reseck, Jr. 1976. pap. 7.95 o.p. (ISBN 0-13-796680-6, Parker). P-H.

Scuderia Ferrari. Luigi Orsini. (Illus.). 1981. 99.00 o.p. (ISBN 0-85045-378-X, Pub. by Osprey England). Motorbooks Intl.

Scuff Marks on the Ceiling: Surviving & Enjoying Your Child's Early Years. Denise Turner. 192p. 1986. 11.95 o.p. (ISBN 0-8499-0513-3). Word Bks.

Scuffler. Harvey Orkin. 1974. 6.95 o.p. (ISBN 0-15-179700-5). HarBraceJ.

Sculpting in Clay. Janice Lovoos. pap. 9.95 o.p. (ISBN 0-8306-1344-7, 1344). TAB Bks.

Sculptor's Daughter. Tove Jansson. (Illus.). 1976. pap. 3.95 o.p. (ISBN 0-380-00751-7, 30254). Avon.

Sculptors' Drawings over Six Centuries. Colin Eisler. (Agrinde Bk.). (Illus.). 1981. pap. 20.00 o.p. (ISBN 0-9601068-7-1). Dodd.

Sculptors of the West Portals of Chartres Cathedral. Whitney S. Stoddard. (Illus.). 1987. 64.50 o.p. (ISBN 0-393-02365-6). Norton.

Sculptors on Paper: New York. Rene P. Barilleaux. (Illus.). 48p. (Orig.). 1987. pap. 19.95 o.p. (ISBN 0-913883-16-6). Madison Art.

Sculpture Gardens: A Bibliography of Periodical Literature. Edward H. Teague. (Architecture Ser.: A 1429). 4p. 1985. 2.00 o.p. (ISBN 0-89028-479-2). Vance Biblios.

Sculpture in Stone: Museum of Fine Arts Boston. M. B. Comstock & C. C. Vermeule. (Illus.). 296p. 35.00 o.p. (ISBN 0-686-47011-7). Apollo.

Sculpture of Africa. Eliot Elisofon & William Fagg. LC 76-50293. (Illus.). 1978. Repr. of 1958 ed. lib. bdg. 50.00 o.p. (ISBN 0-87817-210-6). Hacker.

Sculpture of Giovanni & Bartolomeo Bon & Their Workshop. Anne Schulz. LC 78-50190. (Transactions Ser.: Vol. 68, Pt. 3). (Illus.). 1978. pap. 12.00 o.p. (ISBN 0-87169-683-5). Am Philos.

Sculpture of Tullio Lombardo: Studies in Sources & Meaning. Sarah B. Wilk. LC 77-94723. (Outstanding Dissertations in the Fine Arts Ser.). 1978. lib. bdg. 55.00x o.p. (ISBN 0-8240-3256-X). Garland Pub.

Scuola Grande di San Marco, Nineteen Thirty-Seven to Fifteen Fifty: The Architecture of a Venetial Lay Confraternity. Philio L. Sohm. LC 79-57495. (Outstanding Dissertation in the Fine Arts Ser.: No. 5). 480p. 1982. lib. bdg. 67.00 o.p. (ISBN 0-8240-3943-2). Garland Pub.

Scurvy: Past & Present. Alfred F. Hess. LC 81-69886. (Nutrition Foundations Reprints Ser.). 288p. 1982. 35.00 o.p. (ISBN 0-12-345280-5). Acad Pr.

Scuttle the Computer Pirates: Software Protection Schemes. Richard H. Baker. 208p. (Orig.). 1984. 21.95 o.p. (ISBN 0-8306-0718-8, 1718); pap. 15.50 o.p. TAB Bks.

Scythian Art. George Charriere. (Illus.). 1979. 45.00 o.p. (ISBN 0-686-65987-2, Pub. by Alpine Bk Co). Eastview.

Sea & Sky in Watercolour. Leslie Worth. (Leisure Arts Ser.: Bk. 8). (Illus.). 32p. 1984. pap. 2.95 o.p. (ISBN 0-89134-090-4, Pub. by North Light Pub). Writers Digest.

Sea & the Ice: A Naturalist in Antarctica. Louis J. Halle. 1973. 10.95 o.p. (ISBN 0-395-15470-7). HM.

Sea at Montauk & Other Poems. Marion H. Lee. 1977. 4.00 o.p. (ISBN 0-682-48881-X). Exposition-Phoenix.

Sea Bed Mechanics. J. F. Sleath. LC 84-2179. (Ocean Engineering Ser.: 1-194). 335p. 1984. 47.50x o.p. (ISBN 0-471-89091-X, Pub. by Wiley-Interscience). Wiley.

Sea Chest: A Yachtsman's Reader. Ed. by Critchell Rimington. 355p. 1975. 14.95 o.p. (ISBN 0-393-03183-7). Norton.

Sea for Sam. rev. ed. W. Maxwell Reed & Wilfrid S. Bronson. Ed. by Paul F. Brandwein. LC 59-12826. (gr. 7 up). 1960. 7.95 o.p. (ISBN 0-15-271380-8, HJ). HarBraceJ.

Sea-Grape Tree. Lehmann. 1977. 7.95 o.p. (ISBN 0-15-179720-X). HarBraceJ.

Sea Gull. Anton Chekhov. Ed. by Henry Popkin. Tr. by Ann Jellicoe. (Orig.). 1975. pap. 0.95 o.p. (ISBN 0-380-00364-3, 24638, Bard). Avon.

Sea-Hunters. Edouard A. Stackpole. LC 72-6845. (Illus.). 510p. 1973. Repr. of 1953 ed. lib. bdg. 32.50x o.p. (ISBN 0-8371-6498-2, STSH). Greenwood.

Sea in Soviet Strategy. Bryan Ranft & Geoffrey Till. 275p. 1983. 21.95 o.p. (ISBN 0-87021-957-X). Naval Inst Pr.

Sea Lions. James Fenimore Cooper. Ed. by Warren S. Walker. LC 65-18416. (Illus.). 1965. pap. 2.45x o.p. (ISBN 0-8032-5037-1, BB 306, Bison). U of Nebr Pr.

Sea Marine Atlas: Southern California. rev. ed. William P. Crawford. (Illus.). 1979. 19.95 o.p. (ISBN 0-393-03219-1). Norton.

Sea of Death. Jorge Amado. Tr. by Gregory Rabassa from Port. 288p. 1984. pap. 4.50 o.p. (ISBN 0-380-88559-X, Bard). Avon.

Sea of Glass. Barry B. Longyear. 320p. 1986. cancelled 18.95 o.s.i. (ISBN 0-312-94402-0). Bluejay Bks.

Sea of Slaughter. Farley Mowat. LC 84-72722. 438p. 1985. 24.95 o.p. (ISBN 0-87113-013-0). Atlantic Monthly.

Sea of Thought. George Henry Woodward. 1977. 4.00 o.p. (ISBN 0-682-48747-3). Exposition-Phoenix.

Sea of Troubles. J. J. McCoy. LC 74-22474. (Illus.). 192p. (gr. 6 up). 1979. 7.95 o.p. (ISBN 0-395-28916-5, Clarion). HM.

Sea Otters: A Natural History & Guide. Roy Nickerson. LC 84-19955. (Illus.). 112p. (Orig.). 1984. pap. 7.95 o.p. (ISBN 0-87701-309-8). Chronicle Bks.

Sea Robbers. Robert Kraske. LC 77-76439. (Illus.). 147p. (gr. 5 up). 1977. 6.95 o.p. (ISBN 0-15-271170-8, HJ). HarBraceJ.

Sea Runners. Ivan Doig. LC 82-45174. (Illus.). 288p. 1982. 13.95 o.p. (ISBN 0-689-11302-1, Atheneum). Macmillan.

Sea Sailing. Ed. by Wang Tuoming. (Illus.). 18p. (ps). 1986. pap. 1.95 o.p. (ISBN 0-8351-1569-0). China Bks.

Sea, Sails & Shipwreck: The Career of the Four Masted Schooner Purnell T. White. Robert H. Burgess. LC 73-124313. (Illus.). 144p. 1970. 6.00 o.p. (ISBN 0-87033-147-7). Tidewater.

Sea Shells of the West Indies: A Guide to the Marine Molluscs of the Caribbean. Michael Humfrey. LC 74-20213. (Illus.). 352p. 1975. 19.95 o.s.i. (ISBN 0-8008-7014-X). Taplinger.

Sea Shepherd: One Man's Crusade for Whales & Seals. Paul Watson & Warren Rogers. (Illus.). 1981. 14.95 o.p. (ISBN 0-393-01499-1). Norton.

Sea Siege. Andre Norton. LC 57-8586. (gr. 5-8). 1957. 5.50 o.p. (ISBN 0-15-271738-2, HJ). HarBraceJ.

Sea, Sky & Stars: An Illustrated History of Grumman Aircraft. M. J. Hardy. (Illus.). 160p. 1987. 29.95 o.p. (ISBN 0-85368-832-X, Pub. by Arms & Armour). Sterling.

Sea Slang of the Twentieth Century. W. Granville. 271p. 1950. (ISBN 0-8022-0618-2). Philos Lib.

Sea Story. Ronald Johnston. LC 79-55622. 1980. 11.95 o.p. (ISBN 0-689-11046-4, Atheneum). Macmillan.

Sea Stranger. Kevin C. Crossley-Holland. (Illus.). 48p. 1979. 4.95 o.p. (ISBN 0-395-28853-3). HM.

Sea Surveying. Ed. by A. E. Ingham. LC 74-3066. 539p. 1975. 183.00x o.p. (ISBN 0-471-42729-2, Pub. by Wiley-Interscience). Wiley.

Sea Treasure. Kathleen Y. Johnstone. (Illus.). (gr. 5-12). 1957. 5.00 o.p. (ISBN 0-395-06845-2). HM.

Sea Urchin Development: Cellular & Molecular Aspects. Louis W. Stearns. LC 73-18054. 352p. 1982. 58.95 o.p. (ISBN 0-87933-026-0). Van Nos Reinhold.

Sea Urchin Embryo: Biochemistry & Morphogenesis. Ed. by G. Czihak & R. Peter. LC 74-16245. (Illus.). 720p. 1975. text ed. 82.00 o.p. (ISBN 0-387-06931-3). Springer-Verlag.

Sea War: The Story of the United States Merchant Marine in World War II. Felix Riesenberg, Jr. LC 74-4660. (Illus.). 320p. 1974. Repr. of 1956 ed. lib. bdg. 22.50x o.p. (ISBN 0-8371-7479-1, RISW). Greenwood.

Sea War 1939-1945. Janusz Piekalkiewicz. (Illus.). 354p. 1987. 29.95 o.p. (ISBN 0-7137-1665-7, Pub. by Blandford Pr England). Sterling.

Sea Wolves. Wolfgang Frank. 224p. 1981. pap. 2.50 o.s.i. (ISBN 0-345-29504-8). Ballantine.

Sea World Alphabet Book. Sea World Press Staff & Alan Sloan, Inc. LC 79-65202. (Sea World Press Ser.). (Illus.). 32p. (ps-3). 1980. 4.95 o.p. (ISBN 0-15-271946-6, HJ). HarBraceJ.

Sea World Book of Sharks. Eve Bunting. LC 79-63920. (Sea World Press Ser.). (Illus.). 80p. (gr. 4-6). 1980. 12.95 o.s.i. (ISBN 0-15-271947-4, HJ). HarBraceJ.

Seaboard Parish. George MacDonald. 240p. 1985. pap. 5.95 o.p. (ISBN 0-89693-329-6). Victor Bks.

Seacoast Fortifications of the United States: An Introductory History. Emmanuel R. Lewis. (Illus.). 147p. 1985. pap. 9.95 o.p. (ISBN 0-89141-257-3). Presidio Pr.

Seafire. Karen Robards. 416p. 1983. pap. 3.75 o.p. (ISBN 0-8439-1084-4, Pub. by Leisure Bks CT). Dorchester Pub Co.

Seafloor Spreading Centers: Hydrothermal Systems. P. A. Rona & R. P. Lowell. LC 79-18265. (Bench Papers in Geology: Vol. 56). 424p. 1982. 61.95 o.p. (ISBN 0-87933-363-4). Van Nos Reinhold.

Seafood. Bon Appetit Magazine Editors. LC 83-9828. (Cooking with Bon Appetit Ser.). (Illus.). 144p. 1984. 12.95 o.p. (ISBN 0-89535-120-X). Knapp Pr.

Seafood Cookbook. Shirley Ross. 1978. text ed. 12.95 o.p. (ISBN 0-07-053881-6). McGraw.

Seafood Creations by an Italian Gourmet. Nicholas T. Castellucci. 1978. 7.95 o.p. (ISBN 0-682-49141-1, Banner). Exposition-Phoenix.

Seafood Favorites: Recipes from Authors & Staff of International Marine Publishing Company. LC 83-49419. (Illus.). 128p. 1984. pap. 4.95 o.p. (ISBN 0-87742-180-3, S630). Intl Marine.

Seafood of South-East Asia. Alan Davidson. (Illus.). 366p. 1985. 15.95x o.p. (ISBN 0-8139-1073-0). U Pr of Va.

Seafood Primer: A Practical Book of Fish Cookery. Shirley LaMere. LC 84-45101. (Illus.). 64p. (Orig.). 1984. pap. 4.50 o.p. (ISBN 0-916870-78-2). Creative Arts Bk.

Seagull. Yashar Kemal. 1981. 11.95 o.p. (ISBN 0-394-51856-X). Pantheon.

Seal-Woman. Ronald Lockley. (gr. 7 up). 1977. pap. 1.50 o.p. (ISBN 0-380-00797-5, 38778). Avon.

Seal Woman. Ronald Lockley. 232p. 1988. lib. bdg. 19.95x o.s.i. (ISBN 0-7451-0815-6, Pub. by Chivers Pr UK). G K Hall.

Seals & Sealing. R. H. Warring. 272p. 1981. 79.50x o.p. (ISBN 0-85461-072-3, Pub by Trade & Tech England). Gower Pub Co.

SEALS No. 3: Rescue! Steve MacKenzie. 176p. (Orig.). 1987. pap. 2.50 o.p. (ISBN 0-380-75191-7). Avon.

Seals, No. 5: Breakout. Steve MacKenzie. 176p. 1988. pap. 2.95 o.p. (ISBN 0-380-75194-1). Avon.

Seals No. 6: Desert Rain. Steve Mackenzie. 176p. 1988. pap. 2.95 o.p. (ISBN 0-380-75195-X). Avon.

Seaman. rev. ed. Educational Research Council of America Staff. Ed. by Jack R. Braverman & John P. Marchak. (Real People at Work Ser.: B). (Illus.). 36p. 1977. pap. text ed. 2.70 o.p. (ISBN 0-89247-016-X, 9226). Changing Times.

Seamanship. (ISBN 0-671-60979-3). P-H.

Seamanship. T. F. Wickham. 192p. 1956. (ISBN 0-8022-1875-X). Philos Lib.

Seamanship Handbook for Basic Studies. 6th, rev. ed. G. J. Bonwick. (Illus.). 1978. 17.50 o.s.i. (ISBN 0-686-77961-4). E J Brill USA.

Sean O'Casey. James Simmons. LC 83-49384. (Modern Dramatists Ser.). 224p. 1984. 19.50 o.s.i. (ISBN 0-394-53859-5, GP 903). Grove.

Sean O'Casey. James Simmons. LC 83-49384. (Modern Dramatists Ser.). 224p. 1984. pap. 9.95 o.s.i. (ISBN 0-394-62042-9, E922, Ever). Grove.

Sean O'Casey & His World. David Krause. LC 76-7182. (Encore Edition). (Illus.). 128p. 1976. 3.95 o.p. (ISBN 0-684-16547-3, ScribT). Scribner.

Sean the Sea Gull. Vel Randolph. (Illus.). 25p. (gr. 3-5). 1985. 4.95 o.p. (ISBN 0-533-06351-5). Vantage.

Seance. Joan L. Nixon. LC 79-90031. (gr. 6 up). 1980. 12.95 o.p. (ISBN 0-15-271158-9, HJ). HarBraceJ.

Seaport Systems & Spatial Change: Technology, Industry & Development Strategies. Ed. by B. S. Hoyle & D. Hilling. LC 83-16987. 481p. 1984. 67.95x o.p. (ISBN 0-471-90354-X, Pub. by Wiley-Interscience). Wiley.

Search A Picture Puzzles. Tony Tallarieo. (Puzzlebacks Ser.). 64p. (gr. 3-7). 1981. pap. 1.50 o.s.i. (ISBN 0-671-42656-7). Wanderer Bks.

Search-a-Word Shapes, Nos. 11 & 12. Dawn Gerger. 96p. (Orig.). (gr. 5-6). 1974. pap. 0.75 ea. o.p. (Tempo); No. 11. pap. (ISBN 0-685-49144-7, 5768); No. 12. pap. (ISBN 0-685-49145-5, 5769). Ace Bks.

Search & Discovery: A Tribute to Albert Szent Gyorgy. B. Kaminer. 1977. 61.00 o.p. (ISBN 0-12-395150-X). Acad Pr.

Search & Rescue: The Team & the Missions. Margaret Poynter. LC 79-22375. (Illus.). 176p. (gr. 4-8). 1980. 8.95 o.s.i. (ISBN 0-689-30756-X, Atheneum Childrens Bks). Macmillan.

Search & Research. Noel C. Stevenson. LC 77-21845. 222p. 1984. pap. 6.95 o.p. (ISBN 0-87747-660-8). Deseret Bk.

Search & Seizure: A Treatise on the Fourth Amendment, 1985 Pocket Parts to Vols. 1-3. Wayne R. LaFave. 948p. 29.95 o.p. West Pub.

Search for a New Europe, 1919-1971. A. Burke et al. 1971. pap. text ed. 6.95x o.p. (ISBN 0-8290-1186-2). Irvington.

Titles

Search for an Eternal Norm: As Represented by Three Classics. Louis J. Halle. LC 80-5793. 220p. 1981. lib. bdg. 28.25 o.p. (ISBN 0-8191-1444-8); pap. text ed. 12.50 o.p. (ISBN 0-8191-1445-6). U Pr of Amer.

Search for Common Ground. Ed. by P. Gould & G. Olsson. 270p. 1982. 26.50x o.p. (ISBN 0-85086-093-8, NO. 8006, Pub by Pion England). Routledge Chapman & Hall.

Search for Criminal Man. Ysabel Rennie. LC 77-3109. (Dangerous Offenders Project Ser.). 368p. 1978. pap. 18.00x o.p. (ISBN 0-669-07626-0). Lexington Bks.

Search for Delicious. Natalie Babbitt. (gr. 3-7). 1980. pap. 1.25 o.p. (ISBN 0-380-01541-2, 42085, Camelot). Avon.

Search for Extraterrestrial Intelligence. NASA Staff. Ed. by Philip Morrison et al. 13.75 o.p. (ISBN 0-8446-5797-2). Peter Smith.

Search for Freedom: America & Its People. William J. Jacobs. (ISBN 0-02- 645180-8, 64518); (ISBN 0-02- 645190-5, 64519); (ISBN 0-02- 645220-0, 64522). Glencoe.

Search for God. Hans Schwarz. LC 74-14187. 288p. 1978. pap. 6.95 o.p. (ISBN 0-8066-1672-5, 10-5601, Augsburg). Augsburg Fortress.

Search for God. David M. White. 448p. 1983. 24.95 o.p. (ISBN 0-02-627110-9); deluxe ed. 75.00 o.p. (ISBN 0-686-48308-1). Macmillan.

Search for Human Values. Cornelius J. Van Der Poel. LC 75-161445. 192p. 1973. pap. 3.95 o.p. (ISBN 0-8091-1781-9, Deus). Paulist Pr.

Search for Jewish Theology. new ed. Bernard J. Bamberger. LC 77-28457. 1978. 7.95x o.p. (ISBN 0-87441-295-1); pap. 4.95x o.p. (ISBN 0-87441-300-1). Behrman.

Search for Joseph Tully. William H. Hallahan. 1977. pap. 1.95 o.p. (ISBN 0-380-01696-6, 33712). Avon.

Search for Life on Mars. Henry S. Cooper, Jr. LC 79-20061. 276p. 1980. 10.95 o.s.i. (ISBN 0-03-046166-9). H Holt & Co.

Search for Life on Mars. Henry S. Cooper, Jr. LC 81-2440. 264p. 1981. pap. 6.95 o.s.i. (ISBN 0-03-059818-4, Owl Bk). H Holt & Co.

Search for Love. Matthew O. Emiohe. 224p. 1983. 11.00 o.s.i. (ISBN 0-682-49954-4). Exposition-Phoenix.

Search for Maggie Hare. Elizabeth Byrd. (Orig.). 1977. pap. 1.50 o.p. (ISBN 0-380-00925-0, 31872). Avon.

Search for Maturity. Charles C. Kao. LC 75-15805. 176p. 1975. 7.50 o.s.i. (ISBN 0-664-20828-2, Westminster). Westminster John Knox.

Search for Neotiques - Values to Shape the Future. Marguerite E. Buttner. 1978. 7.50 o.p. (ISBN 0-682-49171-3, Banner). Exposition-Phoenix.

Search for Quality & Coherence in Baccalaureate Education. Project on Redefining the Meaning & Purpose of Baccalaureate Degrees Staff. 44p. 1982. pap. 3.00 o.p. (ISBN 0-317-06220-4). Assn Am Coll.

Search for Sara: A Novel. Martin Russell. 184p. 1986. pap. 3.95 o.p. (ISBN 0-394-62331-2, BC). Grove.

Search for Security in the Pacific, 1901-14, Vol. 1. Neville Meaney. (A History of Australian Defense & Foreign Policy 1901-50). (Illus.). 272p. 1975. 36.00x o.p. (ISBN 0-424-00006-7, Pub by Sydney U Pr). Intl Spec Bk.

Search for Solutions. Horace F. Judson. LC 79-22054. (Illus.). 224p. 1980. 16.95 o.s.i. (ISBN 0-03-043771-7). H Holt & Co.

Search for Spock. Vonda N. McIntyre. (Star Trek Ser.). 1984. lib. bdg. 12.95 o.p. (ISBN 0-8398-2839-X, Gregg). G K Hall.

Search for the Ancient Order, Vol. 1. Earl I. West. 18.95 o.s.i. (ISBN 0-89225-154-9). Gospel Advocate.

Search for the Atocha. rev., 2nd ed. Eugene Lyon. LC 75-25049. (Florida Classics Ser.). (Illus.). 288p. (Orig.). 1985. pap. 9.95 o.p. (ISBN 0-912451-15-7). Florida Classics.

Search for the Beloved: A Clinical Investigation of the Trauma of Birth & Pre-Natal Conditioning. Nandor Fodor. 1972. 7.95 o.p. (ISBN 0-8216-0148-2, Pub. by Univ Bks). Carol Pub Group.

Search for the Crescent Moon. Eth Clifford. (Illus.). 256p. (gr. 7-12). 1974. 5.95 o.p. (ISBN 0-395-16035-9). HM.

Search for the Holy. William F. Kraft. LC 72-152336. 184p. 1971. pap. 4.95 o.s.i. (ISBN 0-664-24923-X, Westminster). Westminster John Knox.

Search for the "Manchurian Candidate" The CIA & Mind Control. John Marks. 252p. 1980. pap. text ed. 4.95 o.p. (ISBN 0-07-040397-X). McGraw.

Search for the Past: An Introduction to Archaeology. Michael Avi-Yonah. LC 72-10791. (Lerner Archaeology Ser.). (Illus.). 96p. (gr. 5 up). 1974. PLB 8.95 o.p. (ISBN 0-8225-0826-5). Lerner Pubns.

Search for Two Bad Mice. Eleanor Clymer. LC 80-12789. (Illus.). 80p. (gr. 2-5). 1980. 9.95 o.s.i. (ISBN 0-689-30771-3, Atheneum Childrens Bks). Macmillan.

Search for Understanding: Lutheran Conversations with Reformed, Anglican, & Roman Catholic Churches. Warren A. Quanbeck. LC 72-90259. 112p. 1972. pap. 2.95 o.p. (ISBN 0-8066-1306-8, 10-5610, Augsburg). Augsburg Fortress.

Search Heaven & Hell. Mark Donnelly & Nina Fenton. Ed. by Jon Rappaport. LC 86-81968. 500p. 1986. pap. 10.95 o.p. (ISBN 1-55666-001-4). Authors Unltd.

Search Warrants in North Carolina. Michael Crowell. 118p. 1976. 2.00 o.p. (ISBN 0-686-39458-5). Institute Government.

Search Within. Humphreys. pap. 10.50 o.p. (ISBN 0-8356-5143-6). Theos Pub Hse.

Search Within. D. Gaynell Lawson. 1979. 7.00 o.p. (ISBN 0-682-49350-3). Exposition-Phoenix.

Searches & Seizures: Three Novellas. Stanley Elkin. LC 78-58499. 320p. 1978. pap. 10.95 o.s.i. (ISBN 0-87923-253-6, Nonpareil Bks). Godine.

Searching for Aboriginal Languages: Memoirs of a Field Worker. Bob Dixon. LC 83-5919. (Illus.). 330p. 1984. text ed. 32.50 o.p. (ISBN 0-7022-1713-1); pap. 14.95 o.p. (ISBN 0-7022-1933-9). U of Queensland Pr.

Searching for Cultural Foundations. Philip McShane. LC 83-23594. 224p. (Orig.). 1984. lib. bdg. 26.75 o.p. (ISBN 0-8191-3727-8); pap. text ed. 13.00 o.p. (ISBN 0-8191-3728-6). U Pr of Amer.

Searching for God. George B. Hume. 1978. pap. 4.95 o.p. (ISBN 0-8192-1240-7). Morehouse Pub.

Searching for the Core. Keith J. Shapiro & Bruce A. James. 126p. 1988. 35.00 o.p. PES Inc WI.

Searching for the Real China. David Ng. (Orig.). 1978. pap. 2.25 o.p. (ISBN 0-377-00073-6). Friendship Pr.

Searching for You. Ulrich Schaffer. LC 77-20458. 1978. pap. 9.57i o.p. (ISBN 0-06-067083-5, RD 259). HarpR.

Searching Spirit: Joy Adamson's Autobiography. Joy Adamson. LC 78-23764. 256p. 1979. 12.95 o.p. (ISBN 0-15-179919-9). HarBraceJ.

Searching the Chemical Literature. Ed. by T. E. Singer. LC 61-11330. (Advances in Chemistry Ser: No. 30). 1961. 29.95 o.p. (ISBN 0-8412-0031-9). Am Chemical.

Searching the Law: The States. Francis R. Doyle. 500p. 1988. 65.00 o.p. Transnatl Pubs.

Searching Writing. Ken Macrorie. LC 86-16064. 352p. 1980. pap. 14.00x o.p. (ISBN 0-86709-141-X). Boynton Cook Pubs.

Searie Dearie. Luella Bennett. 28p. 1973. pap. 1.50 o.p. (ISBN 0-89036-005-7). Hawkes Pub Inc.

Sears, Roebuck Catalogue: 1902 Edition. (Bounty Bks.). (Illus.). 1970. 6.98 o.p. (ISBN 0-517-00982-X); pap. 7.98 o.p. (ISBN 0-517-00922-6). Crown.

Seascape. Edward A. Albee. LC 73-91622. 1975. 7.95 o.p. (ISBN 0-689-10539-8, Atheneum). Macmillan.

Seascapes by Alexa. Alexa Von Tempsky. (Illus.). 34p. 1974. soft bdg. 2.00 o.p. (ISBN 0-930492-11-0). Hawaiian Serv.

Seashells & Laughing Gulls. Patricia Leonard. LC 84-60342. (Illus.). 74p. 1984. 5.95 o.p. (ISBN 0-938232-38-X). Winston-Derek.

Seashells of Brazil. Eliezer Rios. 328p. 1986. pap. 30.50 o.s.i. (ISBN 0-915826-19-4). Am Malacologists.

Seashells of the Arabian Gulf. Kathleen Smythe. (Natural History of the Arabian Gulf Ser.). (Illus.). 180p. 1982. text ed. 24.95x o.p. (ISBN 0-04-594001-0). Unwin Hyman.

Seashore Animals of the Pacific Coast. Myrtle E. Johnson & Harry J. Snook. (Illus.). pap. 7.95 o.p. (ISBN 0-486-21819-8). Dover.

Seashore Entertaining. Naomi Black. LC 86-28051. (Illus.). 128p. 1987. 22.50 o.p. (ISBN 0-89471-506-2). Running Pr.

Seashore Life. Gerald Cox. (Illus.). pap. o.s.i. (ISBN 0-935576-31-2). Kesend Pub Ltd.

Seaside & Lakeside Domestic Architecture: A Bibliography. Mary E. Huls. (Architecture Ser.: A 1486). 6p. 1985. 2.00 o.p. (ISBN 0-89028-616-7). Vance Biblios.

Season: A Candid Look at Broadway. William Goldman. LC 69-14851. 1969. 8.95 o.p. (ISBN 0-15-179923-7). HarBraceJ.

Season for Love. Heather X. Graham. (Candlelight Ecstasy Ser.: No. 154). (Orig.). 1983. pap. 1.95 o.s.i. (ISBN 0-440-18041-4). Dell.

Season in Heaven. William Gibson. LC 74-77624. 192p. 1974. 6.95 o.p. (ISBN 0-689-10615-7, Atheneum). Macmillan.

Season in Hell. A. Michael Edwardes. LC 72-11088. (Illus.). 326p. 1973. 12.95 o.s.i. (ISBN 0-8008-7015-8). Taplinger.

Season in Monte Carlo. Edwin Gilbert. LC 75-40512. 1976. 8.95 o.p. (ISBN 0-87795-131-4, Arbor Hse). Morrow.

Season in Purgatory. Thomas Keneally. LC 76-24458. 1977. 8.95 o.p. (ISBN 0-15-179922-9). HarBraceJ.

Season of Birds. Dion Henderson. LC 76-21044. (Illus.). 1976. 7.95 o.p. (ISBN 0-915024-07-1). WI Trails.

Season of Calm Weather. Michael Collings. 68p. 1974. 2.00 o.p. (ISBN 0-89036-030-8). Hawkes Pub Inc.

Season of Delight. Joanne Greenberg. LC 80-20421. 240p. 1981. 12.95 o.s.i. (ISBN 0-03-057627-X). H Holt & Co.

Season of Delight. Joanne Greenberg. 256p. 1982. pap. 2.95 o.p. (ISBN 0-380-60285-7, 60285-7). Avon.

Season of Hard Desires. Shirley Schoonover. 240p. 1981. pap. 2.50 o.p. (ISBN 0-380-77149-7, 77149). Avon.

Season of Secrets. Alison C. Herzig & Jane L. Mali. LC 82-47909. 192p. (gr. 5-7). 1982. 14.95 o.p. (ISBN 0-316-35889-4). Little.

Season of Silence. Mary F. Shura. LC 75-23194. (Illus.). 144p. (gr. 5-9). 1976. 6.95 o.p. (ISBN 0-689-30513-3, Atheneum). Macmillan.

Season of Yellow Leaf. Douglas C. Jones. LC 83-117. (Illus.). 323p. 1983. 15.95 o.p. (ISBN 0-03-060042-1). H Holt & Co.

Season Sarcophagus in Dumbarton Oaks. George M. Hanfmann. LC 71-146800. (Dumbarton Oaks Studies: Vol. 2). (Illus.). 518p. 1951. Repr. 35.00x o.p. (ISBN 0-88402-001-0). Dumbarton Oaks.

Seasonal Guide to Indoor Gardening. Jack Kramer. LC 76-22192. 1976. pap. 5.95 o.p. (ISBN 0-395-24975-9). HM.

Seasonal Hearth: The Woman at Home in Early America. rev. ed. Adelaide Hechtlinger. LC 86-12681. (Illus.). 256p. 1986. 19.95 o.p. (ISBN 0-87951-258-X). Overlook Pr.

Seasonal Star Charts. James S. Sweeney, Jr. 24p. (Orig.). 1972. pap. text ed. 9.95 o.p. (ISBN 0-8331-1802-1). Hubbard Sci.

Seasonal Variations of the Eskimo: A Study in Social Morphology. Marcel Mauss & Henri Beuchat. Tr. by James J. Fox from Fr. (Illus.). 1979. 21.95x o.p. (ISBN 0-7100-0205-X). Routledge Chapman & Hall.

Seasons. Illus. by Aurelius Battaglia. LC 76-43128. (Cricket Bk.). (Illus.). (ps-1). 1978. 2.50 o.p. (ISBN 0-448-46514-0, G&D). Putnam Pub Group.

Seasons. Suzanne Green. LC 86-16193. (Perlorians Ser.). (Illus.). 32p. (ps-3). 1987. pap. 5.95 o.p. (ISBN 0-385-23506-2); pap. 5.95 o.p. (ISBN 0-385-24007-4). Doubleday.

Seasons Change. Helen Cannon. 320p. 1981. pap. 2.50 o.p. (ISBN 0-380-77164-0, 77164). Avon.

Seasons Come Spring. Paul A. Giffin. 1979. 5.00 o.p. (ISBN 0-682-49491-7). Exposition-Phoenix.

Seasons in Flight. Brian W. Aldiss. LC 84-24329. 160p. 1986. 10.95 o.p. (ISBN 0-689-11538-5, Atheneum). Macmillan.

Seasons of Life. Paul Tournier. Tr. by John S. Gilmour. LC 63-8709. 1976. 4.95 o.p. (ISBN 0-8042-2160-X, John Knox); pap. 2.95 o.p. (ISBN 0-8042-3651-8). Westminster John Knox.

Seasons of Our Joy: A Handbook of Jewish Festivals. Arthur I. Waskow. 1986. 17.45 o.s.i. (ISBN 0-671-61865-2). Summit Bks.

Seasons of Passion see Danielle Steel.

Seasons of Strength: New Visions of Adult Christian Maturing. Evelyn E. Whitehead & James D. Whitehead. LC 84-4199. 240p. 1984. pap. 13.95 o.p. (ISBN 0-385-19635-0). Doubleday.

Seasons of the Heart. Ramona Stewart. (Orig.). 1981. pap. 2.50 o.p. (ISBN 0-505-51714-0, Pub. by Tower Bks). Dorchester Pub Co.

Seats in All Parts: Life at the Movies. Leslie L. Halliwell. (Illus.). 224p. 1985. 15.95 o.p. (ISBN 0-684-18386-2, ScribT). Scribner.

Seats, Votes & the Spatial Organization of Elections. Graham Gudgin & Peter J. Taylor. 254p. 1979. 27.00x o.p. (ISBN 0-85086-073-3, NO. 6380, Pub. by Pion England). Routledge Chapman & Hall.

Seattle Celebrity Chefs. Bill Schwartz & Mike McCormick. 200p. (Orig.). 1986. pap. 9.95 o.p. (ISBN 0-89716-149-1). Peanut Butter.

Seattle Epicure. 14th ed. Richard Kinssies. Ed. by Sheila Hosner. (Epicure Ser.). 151p. (Orig.). 1987. pap. 7.95 o.p. (ISBN 0-89716-165-3). Peanut Butter.

Seattle Green. Jane Adams. (Illus.). 527p. 1987. Repr. lib. bdg. 18.95 o.p. (ISBN 0-89621-847-3). Thorndike Pr.

Seattle Mariners. rev. ed. Hinz. LC 82-239163. (Baseball Today Ser.). 48p. (gr. 4 up). 1982. PLB 11.45 o.p. (ISBN 0-87191-874-9). Creative Ed.

Seattle Supersonics. Don Ward. (NBA Today Ser.). (Illus.). 48p. (gr. 4 up). 1984. PLB 10.45 o.p. (ISBN 0-87191-990-7). Creative Ed.

Seattle Times Cookbook. Ed. by Sharon Lane et al. (Illus.). 436p. 1985. 18.95 o.p. (ISBN 0-89716-144-0). Peanut Butter.

Seaward Margin of Belize Barrier & Atoll Reefs. N. P. James & R. N. Ginsburg. (International Association of Sedimentologists & the Societas Internationalis Limnologiae Symposium Proceedings Ser.: No. 3). 191p. 1980. pap. 56.95x o.p. (ISBN 0-470-26928-6). Halsted Pr.

Seaweeds & Their Uses. V. J. Chapman & D. J. Chapman. 1980. 60.00x o.p. (ISBN 0-412-15740-3, NO. 6362, Pub. by Chapman & Hall England). Routledge Chapman & Hall.

Seawise. Donald M. Street, Jr. (Illus.). 1980. 17.50 o.p. (ISBN 0-393-03232-9). Norton.

Sebastian (SuperSleuth) & the Santa Claus Caper. Mary B. Christian. LC 84-4424. (Illus.). 64p. (gr. 2-6). 1984. 8.95 o.s.i. (ISBN 0-02-718460-9). Macmillan.

SEC & the Public Interest. Susan M. Phillips & J. Richard Zecher. (Illus.). 184p. 1981. text ed. 32.50x o.p. (ISBN 0-262-16080-3). MIT Pr.

SEC Enforcement Issues: An Advanced Seminar. Securities & Exchange Commission, United States & Practising Law Institute Staff. LC 82-61806. (Corporate Law & Practice Course Handbook Ser.: No. 404). 568p. 1982. 40.00 o.p. PLI.

Secluded Islands of the Atlantic Coast. David Yeadon. 1984. 14.95 o.p. (ISBN 0-517-54364-8); pap. 8.95 o.p. (ISBN 0-517-54365-6). Crown.

Second Annual Corporate & Banking Law Institute. 527p. 1983. 21.00 o.p. (ISBN 0-318-02381-4). ICLE Georgia.

Second Annual Eastern Regional Ground Water Conference: Proceedings. 1985. 43.75 o.p. (ISBN 0-318-23023-2). Natl Water Well.

Second Annual Educational Conference on Prepaid Legal Services: November Nineteen Eighty-Two. 512p. 1982. 105.00 o.p. (ISBN 0-317-40261-7, 3-014); 9 tapes avail. o.p. Am Prepaid.

Second Annual Family Law Institute. 187p. 1984. 11.00 o.p. (ISBN 0-318-02390-3). ICLE Georgia.

Second Assessment of Mathematics, 1977-78: Released Exercise Set. National Assessment of Educational Progress Staff. 362p. 1979. 22.60 o.p. (ISBN 0-318-14000-4). Ed Comm States.

Second Banana. Dottie Lamm. (Illus.). 248p. (Orig.). 1983. pap. 8.95 o.p. (ISBN 0-933472-79-X). Johnson Bks.

Second Black Lizard Anthology of Crime Fiction. Ed. by Ed Gorman. 1988. 15.95 o.s.i. (Blk Lizard). Creative Arts Bk.

Second Book in English. rev ed. Robert J. Dixson. (Illus., Orig.). (gr. 9-12). 1971. pap. text ed. 3.50 o.p. (ISBN 0-88345-143-3, 17975). Prentice ESL.

Second Book of Electronics Projects. John E. Traister. pap. 4.50 o.p. (ISBN 0-8306-1317-X, 1317). TAB Bks.

Second Book of Ugg. L. M. Fallow. 1959. (ISBN 0-8022-0473-2). Philos Lib.

Second Canadian-American Conference on Hydrogeology: Proceedings. 1986. 43.75 o.p. (ISBN 0-318-23039-9). Natl Water Well.

Second Chance. Walter J. Adams, Jr. 40p. 1987. 7.95 o.p. (ISBN 0-8062-3070-3). Carlton.

Second Chance. Syd Banks. 1987. pap. 6.95 o.s.i. (ISBN 0-449-90243-9, Columbine). Fawcett.

Second Chance: The Triumph of Internationalism in America During World War II. Robert A. Divine. LC 67-14101. 1967. pap. text ed. 3.45x o.s.i. (ISBN 0-689-70267-1, 175, Atheneum). Macmillan.

Second Chronicle of Thomas Covenant, 3 vols. Stephen R. Donaldson. Boxed Set. pap. 10.95 o.p. (ISBN 0-345-32088-3, Del Rey). Ballantine.

Second City. Donna McCrohan. (Illus.). 272p. 1987. pap. 9.95 o.p. (ISBN 0-399-51339-6, Perigee). Putnam Pub Group.

Second Collection. Bernard J. Lonergan. LC 74-14798. 314p. 1975. 12.00 o.s.i. (ISBN 0-664-20721-9, Westminster). Westminster John Knox.

Second Coming Bible Commentary. William E. Biederwolf. (Paperback Reference Library). 728p. 1985. pap. 17.95 o.p. (ISBN 0-8010-0887-5). Baker Bk.

Second Coming: More Computing Projects Which Failed. Robert L. Glass. 1980. 9.00 o.p. (ISBN 0-686-26939-X). Computing Trends.

Second Coming of Jesus. G. F. Taylor. 3.95 o.p. (ISBN 0-911866-63-9); pap. 2.00 o.p. (ISBN 0-911866-62-0). Advocate.

Second Common Reader. Virginia Woolf. LC 32-31590. 245p. 1956. pap. 4.95 o.p. (ISBN 0-15-679973-1, Harv). HarBraceJ.

Second Complete Home Decorating Catalogue. rev. ed. Jose Wilson & Arthur Leaman. LC 80-26201. (Illus.). 224p. 1981. 19.95 o.p. (ISBN 0-03-055941-3); pap. 11.95 o.p. (ISBN 0-03-055936-7). H Holt & Co.

Second Concerto for Piano & Orchestra, Op. 18. S. Rachmaninoff. (Carl Fischer Music Library: No. 1060). 63p. pap. 7.50 o.p. (ISBN 0-8258-0180-X, L1060). Fischer Inc NY.

Second Course in Calculus. Harley Flanders & Justin J. Price. 1974. text ed. 6.00 o.p. (ISBN 0-12-259662-5); instrs' manual 3.50 o.p. (ISBN 0-12-259663-3). Acad Pr.
Second Creation: Makers of the Revolution in Twentieth Century Physics. Robert P. Crease & Charles C. Mann. 475p. 1985. 25.00 o.p. (ISBN 0-02-521440-3). Macmillan.
Second Daughter: Growing up in China 1930-1949. Katherine Wei & Terry Quinn. 256p. 1984. 16.95 o.p. (ISBN 0-316-92811-9). Little.
Second Daughter: Growing up in China, 1930 to 1949. Katherine Wei & Terry Quinn. LC 85-8413. (Illus.). 256p. 1985. pap. 7.95 o.p. (ISBN 0-03-005628-4, Owl Bks). H Holt & Co.
Second Day. I. Ehrenburg. 366p. 1985. pap. 4.00 o.p. (ISBN 0-8285-2793-8, Pub. by Raduga Pubs USSR). Imported Pubns.
Second Death of Samuel Auer. Bernard Packer. LC 78-10728. 1979. 10.95 o.p. (ISBN 0-15-179955-5). HarBraceJ.
Second Flight of the Starfire. Edwin Mumford. 1972. 4.00 o.p. (ISBN 0-682-47462-2). Exposition-Phoenix.
Second Great Awakening in Connecticut. Charles R. Keller. LC 68-26923. ix, 275p. 1968. Repr. of 1942 ed. 25.00 o.p. (ISBN 0-208-00662-1, Archon). Shoe String.
Second Greatest Commandment. William Fletcher. LC 83-62501. 156p. 1983. pap. 4.95 o.p. (ISBN 0-89109-502-0). NavPress.
Second Hand Is Better. Douglas Matthews et al. LC 74-80710. 1975. 9.95 o.p. (ISBN 0-87795-089-X, Arbor Hse); pap. 4.50 o.p. (ISBN 0-87795-095-4). Morrow.
Second Heaven. Judith Guest. 1983. pap. 8.95 o.p. (ISBN 0-8161-3559-2, Large Print Bks). G K Hall.
Second Homes: Curse or Blessing. Ed. by J. T. Coppock. 1977. 31.00 o.p. (ISBN 0-08-021371-5); pap. 11.25 o.p. (ISBN 0-08-021370-7). Pergamon.
Second India Studies: Overview. H. Ezekiel. 1978. 4.50x o.p. (ISBN 0-8364-0251-0). South Asia Bks.
Second International Symposium on Metallurgical Slags & Fluxes. Ed. by H. A. Fine & D. R. Gaskell. LC 84-62011. 1984. 72.00 o.p. (ISBN 0-89520-483-5). Minerals Metals.
Second Jungle Book. Rudyard Kipling. (gr. 7-11). 1923. 4.50 o.s.i. (ISBN 0-385-07483-2). Doubleday.
Second LACUS Forum: Proceedings. Linguistic Association of Canada & the U. S. Staff. Ed. by Peter A. Reich. 1975. pap. text ed. 12.95 o.s.i. (ISBN 0-917496-05-1). Hornbeam Pr.
Second Letter to the Corinthians. Rudolf Bultmann. Tr. by Roy A. Harrisville. LC 83-70517. 272p. 1985. 19.95 o.p. (ISBN 0-8066-2023-4, 10-5633, Augsburg). Augsburg Fortress.
Second Life. Stephanie Cook. 384p. 1982. pap. 3.95 o.s.i. (ISBN 0-345-30675-9). Ballantine.
Second Marriage. Frederick Barthelme. 204p. 1984. 15.45 o.p. (ISBN 0-671-47441-3). S&S.
Second Marriage. Denise Robins. 1979. pap. 1.95 o.p. (ISBN 0-380-45492-0, 45492). Avon.
Second Marriage: The Promise & the Challenge. Darlene McRoberts. LC 77-84087. 1978. pap. 6.95 o.p. (ISBN 0-8066-1612-1, 10-5635, Augsburg). Augsburg Fortress.
Second Math Helper. Evelyn Farmer. (Classroom Pairing: Math Tutorial Program Ser.). 64p. (gr. k-1). 1975. 2.95 o.p. (ISBN 0-87594-141-9). Book-Lab.
Second-Mile People. Isobel Kuhn. 1982. pap. 3.50 o.p. (ISBN 0-85363-145-X). OMF Bks.
Second National Ground Water Quality Symposium: Proceedings. 43.75 o.p. (ISBN 0-318-23003-8). Natl Water Well.
Second Official I Hate Cats Book. Skip Morrow. LC 81-47461. (Illus.). 64p. 1981. pap. 3.95 o.p. (ISBN 0-03-059359-X, Owl Bks). H Holt & Co.
Second Opinion Handbook: A Guide for Medical Self Defense. Eugene McCarthy et al. (Illus.). 96p. (Orig.). 1987. pap. 5.95 o.p. (ISBN 0-941130-25-8). Lyons & Burford.
Second-Order Phase Transitions & the Irreducible Representation of Space Groups. H. F. Franzen. (Lecture Notes in Chemistry Ser.: Vol. 32). 98p. 1982. pap. 11.20 o.p. (ISBN 0-387-11958-2). Springer-Verlag.
Second Person. Lehman Strauss. 1951. 7.95 o.s.i. (ISBN 0-87213-826-7). Loizeaux.
Second Quiltmaker's Handbook. Michael James. (Creative Handcrafts Ser.). 208p. 1981. 19.95 o.p. (ISBN 0-13-797795-6, Spec); pap. 12.95 o.p. (ISBN 0-13-797787-5). P-H.
Second Ring of Power. Carlos Castaneda. 1978. 11.95 o.s.i. (ISBN 0-671-22942-7). S&S.
Second Season: Lent, Easter, Ascension. Wayne Saffen. LC 72-87064. (Illus.). 96p. 1973. pap. 0.50x o.p. (ISBN 0-8006-0144-0, Fortress). Augsburg Fortress.
Second Seed. Mary L. Polan. 288p. 1987. 17.95 o.p. (ISBN 0-684-18735-3). Scribner.
Second Self: Computers & the Human Spirit. Sherry Turkle. 352p. 1984. 17.45 o.p. (ISBN 0-671-46848-0). S&S.
Second Shopper's Guide to Museum Stores. Compiled by Shelley Hodupp. LC 78-52191. (Illus.). 1978. pap. 7.95 o.p. (ISBN 0-87663-983-X). Universe.
Second Sight for Tommy. Regina J. Woody. LC 70-182540. 160p. (gr. 5-9). 1972. 4.75 o.s.i. (ISBN 0-664-32511-4, Westminster). Westminster John Knox.
Second Skin. Rochelle Dubois. 1978. 1.00 o.p. (ISBN 0-686-15526-2). Merging Media.
Second Skin. 2nd ed. Marilyn J. Horn. 1975. text ed. 20.90 o.p. (ISBN 0-395-18552-1). HM.
Second Special Conference Issue. Ed. by P. J. McEwan. 144p. 1983. pap. 22.00 o.p. (ISBN 0-08-027937-6). Pergamon.
Second Stage. Betty Friedan. 352p. 1982. pap. 8.95 o.s.i. (ISBN 0-671-45951-1). Summit Bks.
Second Star to the Right. Deborah Hautzig. 160p. 1982. pap. 2.25 o.p. (ISBN 0-380-60343-8, 60105-2, Flare). Avon.
Second Start: A Widow's Guide to Financial Survival at a Time of Emotional Crisis. Judith N. Brown & Christine Baldwin. 1986. 16.45 o.p. (ISBN 0-671-60349-3). S&S.
Second Step: Baccalaureate Education for Registered Nurses. Mary Searight. LC 76-3499. (Illus.). 252p. 1976. text ed. 16.50x o.p. (ISBN 0-8036-7780-4). Davis Co.
Second Sun. Bill Tremblay. LC 84-26102. (Poetry Ser.). 84p. (Orig.). 1986. pap. 6.95 o.p. (ISBN 0-934332-42-8). L'Epervier Pr.
Second Sun. 2nd ed. Bill Tremblay. LC 84-26102. (Poetry Ser.). 84p. 1989. pap. 9.95 o.p. L'Epervier Pr.
Second Thoughts on the Dead Sea Scrolls. F. F. Bruce. 157p. 1986. pap. 8.95 o.p. (ISBN 0-85364-017-3, Pub. by Paternoster UK). Attic Pr.
Second Tongue: An Anthology of Poetry from Malaysia & Singapore. Ed. by Edwin Thumboo. (Writing in Asia Ser.). 1976. pap. text ed. 6.50x o.p. (ISBN 0-686-60465-2). Heinemann Ed.
Second Touch. Keith Miller. LC 67-31340. 1982. 7.95 o.p. (ISBN 0-8499-0338-6, 80036). Word Bks.
Second Touring Guide to Britain. British Tourist Authority Staff. 192p. 1987. pap. 18.95 o.p. (ISBN 0-86145-080-9, Pub. by British Tour). Salem Hse Pubs.
Second Treasury of Christmas Music. Ed. by Will L. Reed. LC 68-16193. (gr. 9 up). 1968. 15.95 o.p. (ISBN 0-87523-165-9). Emerson.
Second Trimester Abortion: Perspectives after a Decade of Experience. Ed. by Gary S. Berger et al. 364p. 1981. text ed. 42.00 o.p. (ISBN 0-88416-256-7). Year Bk Med.
Second Try: Labour & the EEC. U. Kitzinger. 1969. 33.00 o.p. (ISBN 0-08-012961-7); pap. 13.25 o.p. (ISBN 0-08-012960-9). Pergamon.
Second View. Rephotographic Survey Project Staff. LC 84-3600. (Illus.). 223p. 1984. 65.00 o.p. (ISBN 0-8263-0751-5). U of NM Pr.
Second Voyage of Seventh Carrier. Peter Albano. 1986. pap. 3.50 o.p. (ISBN 0-8217-1774-X). Zebra.
Second World War: Chartwell Edition, 6 Vols. Winston S. Churchill. 1983. 294.00 set o.s.i. (ISBN 0-395-34929-X). HM.
Secondary Analysis in Social Research: A Guide to Data Services & Methods with Examples. Catherine Hakim. (Contemporary Social Research Ser.: No. 5). 224p. 1982. text ed. 28.50x o.p. (ISBN 0-04-312015-6); pap. text ed. 12.50x o.p. (ISBN 0-04-312016-4). Unwin Hyman.
Secondary Attachments. Greg Herriges. 243p. 1986. 15.95 o.p. (ISBN 0-688-06171-0). Morrow.
Secondary Education: School & Community. William Van Til. LC 77-76861. (Illus.). 1978. text ed. 27.95 o.p. (ISBN 0-395-25751-4). HM.
Secondary Glaucomas. Robert Ritch & M. Bruce Shields. LC 81-18686. (Illus.). 429p. 1982. text ed. 60.00 o.p. (ISBN 0-8016-4195-0). Mosby.
Secondary Ion Mass Spectrometry SIMS IV: Proceedings of the International Conference, 4th, Minoo-Kanko Hotel, Osaka, Japan, November 13-19, 1984. International Conference on Secondary Ion Mass Spectrometry Staff. Ed. by A. Benninghoven et al. (Springer Series in Chemical Physics: Vol. 36). (Illus.). 495p. 1984. 49.50 o.s.i. (ISBN 0-387-13316-X). Springer Verlag.
Secondary Metabolism of Plants & Animals. Martin Luckner. 1972. 82.50 o.p. (ISBN 0-12-459050-0). Acad Pr.
Secondary School Graduation: University Entrance Qualification in Socialist Countries. new ed. Wolfgang Mitter. LC 77-30471. 1979. 36.00 o.p. (ISBN 0-08-022237-4); pap. 22.00 o.p. (ISBN 0-08-022238-2). Pergamon.
Secondary School Mathematics for the Learning Disabled. Ed. by John F. Cawley. LC 84-16946. 327p. 1984. 36.50 o.p. (ISBN 0-89443-597-3). Aspen Pub.
Secondary School Reading Instruction: The Content Areas. 2d ed. Betty D. Roe et al. LC 82-83290. 1983. text ed. 32.25 o.p. (ISBN 0-395-32783-0). HM.
Secondary School Reading: Process-Program-Procedure. Walter R. Hill. 1978. text ed. 38.00 o.p. (ISBN 0-205-06129-X, 2361299). Allyn.
Secondary Spread of Cancer. Ed. by R. W. Baldwin. 1978. 66.00 o.p. (ISBN 0-12-076850-X). Acad Pr.
Secondary Teaching Methods. Kenneth T. Henson. 384p. 1981. text ed. 19.50 o.p. (ISBN 0-669-03316-2). Heath.
Secondary Worlds. W. H. Auden. 127p. 1985. pap. 6.95 o.p. (ISBN 0-571-13221-9). Faber & Faber.
Secrecy & Democracy: The CIA in Transition. Stansfield Turner. 306p. 1985. 16.45 o.p. (ISBN 0-395-35573-7). HM.
Secret Agent. Joseph Conrad. 1953. pap. 4.95 o.s.i. (ISBN 0-385-09352-7, Anch). Doubleday.
Secret Band of Brothers: A Full & True Exposition of All the Various Crimese, Villainies, & Misdeeds of This Powerful Organization in the United States. Jonathan H. Green. (Illus.). 1980. 9.50 o.p. (ISBN 0-682-49368-6, University). Exposition-Phoenix.
Secret Battle. A. P. Herbert. LC 81-66448. 1981. 9.95 o.p. (ISBN 0-689-11156-8, Atheneum). Macmillan.
Secret Behind the Blue Door. Frances C. Matranga. (Voyager Ser.). 96p. (Orig.). (gr. 4-9). 1981. pap. 3.45 o.p. (ISBN 0-8010-6121-0). Baker Bk.
Secret Britain. (Pub. by Auto Assn England). Salem Hse Pubs.
Secret Chambers & Hiding-Places. rev. ed. 3rd ed. Allan Fea. LC 79-155739. 320p. 1971. Repr. of 1901 ed. 43.00x o.p. (ISBN 0-8103-3385-6). Gale.
Secret Cross of Lorraine. Thea J. Brow. (gr. 5-8). 1981. 8.95 o.p. (ISBN 0-395-30344-3). HM.
Secret Destiny of America. M. P. Hall. 1959. (ISBN 0-8022-0661-1). Philos Lib.
Secret Fallout: Low-Level Radiation from Hiroshima to Three-Mile Island. rev. ed. Ernest Sternglass. (McGraw-Hill Paperbacks Ser.). 300p. (Orig.). 1981. pap. text ed. 5.95 o.p. (ISBN 0-07-061242-0). McGraw.
Secret Fire: How Women Live Their Sexual Fantasies. Rosemarie Santini. LC 81-48538. 320p. 1982. pap. 3.95 o.s.i. (ISBN 0-394-17979-X, B-469, BC). Grove.
Secret Garden see New Method Supplementary Readers: Bestseller Pack.
Secret Gardens: A Study of the Golden Age of Children's Literature. Humphrey Carpenter. (Illus.). 235p. 1985. 16.45 o.p. (ISBN 0-395-35293-2). HM.
Secret Go the Wolves. R. D. Lawrence. LC 79-22709. 276p. 1980. 10.95 o.p. (ISBN 0-03-052436-9). H Holt & Co.
Secret Gospel: The Discovery & Interpretation of the Secret Gospel According to Mark. Morton Smith. LC 82-73215. 157p. pap. 7.95 o.s.i. (ISBN 0-913922-55-2). Dawn Horse Pr.
Secret Hiding-Places: The Origins, Histories & Descriptions of English Secret Hiding-Places Used by Priests, Cavaliers, Jacobites, & Smugglers. Granville Squiers. LC 70-157499. (Tower Bks). (Illus.). 288p. 1971. Repr. of 1934 ed. 43.00x o.p. (ISBN 0-8103-3920-X). Gale.
Secret History: An Eyewitness Expose of the Rise of Mormonism. John Ahmanson. Tr. by Gleason L. Archer from Danish. 1984. 9.95 o.p. (ISBN 0-8024-0277-1). Moody.
Secret House: Twenty-Four Hours in the Strange & Unexpected World in Which We Spend Our Nights & Days. David Bodanis. (Illus.). 224p. 1986. 19.45 o.s.i. (ISBN 0-671-60032-X). S&S.
Secret in Miranda's Closet. Sheila Greenwald. LC 76-62499. (Illus.). (gr. 4-7). 1977. 6.95 o.p. (ISBN 0-395-25152-4). HM.
Secret in the Hills. (Horse Stories Gift Set Ser.). (gr. 3-9). write for info. o.p. Cook.
Secret in the Stlalakum Wild. Christie Harris. LC 72-175554. (Illus.). (gr. 4-6). 1972. 1.29 o.s.i. (ISBN 0-689-30027-1, Atheneum Childrens Bks). Macmillan.
Secret Ingredients: Inactive Ingredients in Drugs. Jeffrey Brown. 1988. 15.95 o.p. (ISBN 0-8016-0865-1). Mosby.
Secret Isaac. Jerome Charyn. LC 78-57326. 1978. 9.95 o.p. (ISBN 0-87795-196-9, Arbor Hse). Morrow.
Secret Kingdom. Pat Robertson & Bob Slosser. 1983. pap. 4.95 leader's guide o.p. (ISBN 0-8407-5877-4); study guide 2.95 o.p. (ISBN 0-8407-5854-5). Nelson.
Secret Life of the Reindeer-Cat. Albert Lazan. LC 81-51894. 91p. (gr. 7 up). 1981. pap. 5.95 o.p. (ISBN 0-89917-315-2). TIS Inc.
Secret Life of the Unborn Child. Thomas Verny & John Kelly. 256p. 1981. 13.95 o.s.i. (ISBN 0-671-25312-3). Summit Bks.
Secret Life of Toys. R. G. Austin. (Which Way Secret Door Bks.). (Illus.). (gr. 1-3). 1983. pap. 1.95 o.p. (ISBN 0-671-46982-7). Archway.
Secret Lives: And Other Stories. Ngugi Wa Thiong O. LC 75-23931. 160p. 1975. 6.95 o.p. (ISBN 0-88208-058-X). Chicago Review.
Secret Lives of Fat People. Mildred Klingman. 156p. 1981. 8.95 o.p. (ISBN 0-395-31006-7). HM.
Secret Look: Poems. Jessamyn West. LC 73-15428. 96p. 1974. 9.95 o.s.i. (ISBN 0-15-179985-7). HarBraceJ.
Secret Name. Barbara Williams. LC 75-187858. (Illus.). 123p. (gr. 3-7). 1972. 6.50 o.p. (ISBN 0-15-272227-0, HJ). HarBraceJ.
Secret of Awen Castle. Florence Hurd. 1974. pap. 0.95 o.p. (ISBN 0-380-01542-0, 18853). Avon.
Secret of Effective Prayer. Helen S. Shoemaker. LC 67-19306. 1976. pap. 1.95 o.p. (ISBN 0-87680-869-0, 91004, Key Word Bks). Word Bks.
Secret of Happiness. rev. & enl. ed. Billy Graham. 160p. 1985. 11.95 o.p. (ISBN 0-8499-0508-7). Word Bks.
Secret of Haunted Mesa. Phyllis A. Whitney. LC 75-4617. 144p. (gr. 6 up). 1975. 5.75 o.s.i. (ISBN 0-664-32568-8, Westminster). Westminster John Knox.
Secret of Healing. Frederick Bailes. pap. 1.00 o.p. (ISBN 0-87516-163-4). DeVorss.
Secret of Health. Richard Lynch. 6.95 o.p. (ISBN 0-87159-143-X). Unity School.
Secret of Humor. Leonard Feinberg. 1978. pap. text ed. 25.00x o.p. (ISBN 90-6203-370-9). Humanities.
Secret of Life. Marvin H. Jackson. 1985. 6.95 o.p. (ISBN 0-533-06406-6). Vantage.
Secret of Meditation. Rieker. 176p. 1957. (ISBN 0-8022-1342-1). Philos Lib.
Secret of Quarry House. Claire Lorrimer. 1976. pap. 1.25 o.p. (ISBN 0-380-00497-6, 27540). Avon.
Secret of Regeneration. Hilton Hotema. Orig. Title: Science of Human Regeneration (Postgraduate Orthopathy) (Illus.). 900p. 1963. pap. 59.95 o.s.i. (ISBN 0-88697-019-9). Life Science.
Secret of Rejuvenation: Professor Brown Squad's Great Discovery of the Fountain of Youth. Raymond Bernard. 39p. 1956. pap. 7.95 o.s.i. (ISBN 0-88697-036-9). Life Science.
Secret of Stone House Farm. Miriam Young. LC 63-15405. (Illus.). (gr. 5-7). 1966. pap. 0.60 o.p. (ISBN 0-15-679994-4, AVB48, VoyB). HarBraceJ.
Secret of the Bats: The Exploration of Carlsbad Caverns. John Stewart. LC 75-168541. (Illus.). (gr. 4 up). 1972. 4.75 o.s.i. (ISBN 0-664-32504-1, Westminster). Westminster John Knox.
Secret of the Chateau see House of Illusions.
Secret of the Crazy Quilt. Florence Hightower. LC 72-184247. (Illus.). 240p. (gr. 5-9). 1973. 6.95 o.p. (ISBN 0-395-13729-2). HM.
Secret of the Diamond Fireside. Ann Terry. (Illus.). 161p. (YA) (gr. 11 up). 1981. pap. 2.95 o.p. (ISBN 0-942241-19-3, 8678). Pubs Bk Sales.
Secret of the Disappearing Sultan. Margery Warner. LC 74-33121. (Illus.). 160p. (gr. 3-7). 1975. 5.95 o.p. (ISBN 0-395-20504-2). HM.
Secret of the Emerald Star. Phyllis A. Whitney. LC 64-16345. (Illus.). (gr. 5-9). 1964. 4.95 o.s.i. (ISBN 0-664-32337-5, Westminster). Westminster John Knox.
Secret of the Invisible City. Dale Carlson. LC 84-80178. (Jenny Dean Mystery Ser.). (Illus.). (gr. 3-7). 1984. pap. 2.95 o.p. (ISBN 0-448-19004-4, G&D). Putnam Pub Group.
Secret of the Lost Lake. Carolyn Keene. (Dana Girls Ser.: Vol. 11). (gr. 4-7). 2.95 o.p. (ISBN 0-448-09091-0, G&D). Putnam Pub Group.
Secret of the Lost Tunnel. rev. ed. Franklin W. Dixon. (Hardy Boys Ser: Vol. 29). (Illus.). (gr. 5-9). 1950. 4.50 o.p. (ISBN 0-448-08929-7, G&D). Putnam Pub Group.
Secret of the Minstrel's Guitar. Carolyn Keene. (Dana Girls Ser.: Vol. 5). (Illus.). 192p. (gr. 4-7). 1972. 2.95 o.p. (ISBN 0-448-09085-6, G&D). Putnam Pub Group.
Secret of the Poison Ring. Dorothy Y. Croman. (Outlands Adventure Ser.). 128p. (Orig.). (gr. 3-6). 1986. 3.50 o.p. (ISBN 0-8423-5898-6). Tyndale.
Secret of the Seven Crows. Wylly F. St. John. (Illus.). (gr. 3-5). 1976. pap. 1.75 o.p. (ISBN 0-380-00433-X, 55244-2, Camelot). Avon.
Secret of the Stone Face. Phyllis A. Whitney. LC 77-1261. 144p. (gr. 5-9). 1977. 8.95 o.s.i. (ISBN 0-664-32612-9, Westminster). Westminster John Knox.
Secret of the Strawbridge Place. Helen P. Jacob. LC 75-23199. (Illus.). 224p. (gr. 4-6). 1976. 7.95 o.p. (ISBN 0-689-30504-4, Atheneum). Macmillan.
Secret of the Target. Jackson S. Morisawa. 144p. 1988. pap. 14.95 o.p. (ISBN 0-415-00194-3, Pub. by Routledge UK). Routledge Chapman & Hall.

Secret of the Unknown Powers. Buchanan. 1985. 7.95 o.p. (ISBN 0-317-28941-1). Vantage.

Secret of Wildcat Swamp. Franklin W. Dixon. (Hardy Boys Ser: Vol. 31). (gr. 5-9). 1952. 4.50 o.p. (ISBN 0-448-08931-9, G&D). Putnam Pub Group.

Secret of Wing Chun Butterfly Knives Form. rev. ed. Austin Goh. (Illus.). 88p. 1986. pap. text ed. 12.00 o.p. (ISBN 0-87364-380-1). Paladin Pr.

Secret Papers of Julia Templeton. Peter Cooper. 160p. (gr. 4-7). 1985. pap. 7.95 o.p. (ISBN 0-89272-197-9). Down East.

Secret Report on the Cuban Revolution. Carlos A. Montaner. Tr. by Eduardo Zayas-Bazan from Span. LC 79-66693. 292p. 1981. 14.95 o.p. (ISBN 0-87855-300-2); pap. 6.95 o.p. (ISBN 0-87855-720-2). Transaction Pubs.

Secret Revelations of Tibetan Thangkas. Detlef-Ingo Lauf. (Illus.). 1979. 40.00 o.p. (ISBN 3-591-08025-X, Pub. by Aurum Verlag Germany). Hunter Hse.

Secret Spinner: Tales of Rav Gedalia. Howard Cushnir. LC 85-5782. (Illus.). 48p. (gr. 2-5). 1985. pap. 5.95 o.p. (ISBN 0-930494-47-4). Kar Ben.

Secret Strength... for Those Who Search. Joni E. Tada. 1988. 14.95 o.p. Multnomah.

Secret Symmetry: Sabina Spielrein Between Jung & Freud. Aldo Carotenuto. Commentary by Bruno Bettelheim. Tr. by Arno Pomerans et al. 1984. pap. 8.95 o.p. (ISBN 0-394-72295-7). Pantheon.

Secret Trees. Luci Shaw. LC 76-1342. (Wheaton Literary Ser.). (Illus.). 78p. 1976. cloth 6.95 o.p. (ISBN 0-87788-909-0). Shaw Pubs.

Secret Understandings. abr. ed. Morris Philipson. 384p. 1983. 16.50 o.p. (ISBN 0-671-46619-4). S&S.

Secret Visitor. Grace Patterson. (Illus.). 96p. (YA) (gr. 7up). 1982. 6.00 o.p. (ISBN 0-682-49860-2). Exposition-Phoenix.

Secret Wars of CIA. Parakal Pauly. 138p. 1984. text ed. 15.00x o.p. (ISBN 0-86590-311-5, Pub. by Sterling Pubs India). Apt Bks.

Secret Weapon & Other Stories. Azriel Eisenberg & Leah A. Globe. 200p. 1966. 9.95 o.p. (ISBN 0-900689-76-5). Soncino Pr.

Secret Weapon in Africa. Oleg Ignatyev. (Illus.). 189p. 1977. 5.45 o.p. (ISBN 0-8285-3230-3, Pub. by Progress Pubs USSR). Imported Pubns.

Secret Weapon in Africa. Oleg Ignatyev. 190p. 1977. 10.00x o.p. (Pub. by Collets (UK)). State Mutual Bk.

Secret World of Underground Creatures. Dorothy Leon. LC 82-8185. (Illus.). 64p. (gr. 4-6). 1982. lib. bdg. 8.79 o.s.i. (ISBN 0-671-42403-3). Messner.

Secret Zodiac: The Hidden Art in Medieval Astrology. Fred Gettings. (Illus.). 224p. 1987. 39.95 o.p. (ISBN 0-7102-1147-3, Pub. by Routledge UK). Routledge Chapman & Hall.

Secreta: Three Methods of Laying Gold Leaf. Joyce Grafe. (Illus.). 112p. 1986. pap. 9.95 o.s.i. (ISBN 0-8008-7023-9). Taplinger.

Secretarial Dental Assistant. Mary A. Douglas. 304p. 1981. 19.95 o.p. (ISBN 0-442-21860-5). Van Nos Reinhold.

Secretarial Management. Josephine Shaw. 256p. (Orig.). 1978. pap. text ed. 16.95x o.p. Trans-Atl Phila.

Secretarial Office Procedures. D. E. Lee & Walter A. Brower. 1976. text ed. 27.75 o.p. (ISBN 0-07-037035-4). McGraw.

Secretaries of Defense: A Brief History, 1947-1985. Roger R. Trask. (Illus.). 75p. (Orig.). 1985. pap. 3.00 o.p. (ISBN 0-318-18830-9, S/N 008-001-00147-9). USGPO.

Secretary Mechanisms of Exocrine Glands. Ed. by N. A. Thorn. 1975. 97.50 o.p. (ISBN 0-12-690450-2). Acad Pr.

Secretary Set. Grossman. (Illus.). 1985. pap. 20.95 o.p. (ISBN 0-471-82908-0). Wiley.

Secretary's Administrative Handbook: Tactics for Taking Charge of Your Career, the Secretacial Profession. Anne Montgomery. LC 83-21759. 368p. 1984. 19.95 o.p. (ISBN 0-471-02089-3). Wiley.

Secretary's Handbook. rev ed. Doris H. Whalen. 1973. pap. text ed. 7.50 o.p. (ISBN 0-15-579297-0, HC). HarBraceJ.

Secretary's Handbook: A Manual for Office Personnel. 4th ed. Doris H. Whalen. 326p. 1983. pap. text ed. 14.00 net o.p. (ISBN 0-15-579301-2, HC). HarBraceJ.

Secretary's Handbook: A Manual for Office Personnel. 3rd ed. Doris H. Whalen. 1978. 9.95 o.p. (ISBN 0-15-579299-7). HarbraceJ.

Secretory Diarrhea. Ed. by M. Field & J. S. Fordtran. (Clinical Physiology Ser.). 237p. 1980. 30.00 o.p. (ISBN 0-318-12932-9). Am Physiological.

Secretory Mechanisms of Salivary Glands. International Conference on Mechanisms of Salivary Secretion & Their Regulation-2nd-Birmingham-Ala.-1966. Ed. by Leon H. Schneyer & Charlotte A. Schneyer. 1967. 84.50 o.p. (ISBN 0-12-627950-0). Acad Pr.

Secrets. Danielle Steel. (Special Editions Ser.). 1986. lib. bdg. 18.95x o.p. (ISBN 0-8161-4013-8, Large Print Bks). G K Hall.

Secrets. Paul Tournier. LC 65-13442. 1976. 5.50 o.p. (ISBN 0-8042-2165-0, John Knox); pap. 2.95 o.p. (ISBN 0-8042-3655-0). Westminster John Knox.

Secrets Not Meant to Be Kept. Gloria D. Miklowitz. LC 85-46073. 144p. (gr. 7 up). 1987. pap. 13.95 o.p. (ISBN 0-385-29491-3). Delacorte.

Secrets Not Meant to Be Kept. Date not set. (ISBN 0-385-29491-3). Delacorte.

Secrets of a Corporate Headhunter. John Wareham. LC 79-55603. 1980. 10.95 o.s.i. (ISBN 0-689-11059-6, Atheneum). Macmillan.

Secrets of a Private Eye: Or, How to Be Your Own Private Investigator. Irwin Blye & Ardy Friedberg. LC 86-14942. 1987. 16.95 o.s.i. (ISBN 0-8050-0370-3). H Holt & Co.

Secrets of a Silent Stranger. Ruth Hallman. LC 76-13598. (Hiway Bk.: A High Interest-Low Reading Level Book). 1976. 6.95 o.s.i. (ISBN 0-664-32598-X, Westminster). Westminster John Knox.

Secrets of Ego Power & Control. Kenneth W. Willoughby. LC 73-77588. 1973. 6.50 o.p. (ISBN 0-682-47697-8, Banner). Exposition-Phoenix.

Secrets of Harry Bright. Joseph Wambaugh. LC 85-10453. 329p. 1985. 17.95 o.p. (ISBN 0-688-05958-9). Morrow.

Secrets of Health That Many Doctors & Dentists May Not Know. Joseph Aaron Zinman. 1977. 6.50 o.p. (ISBN 0-682-48732-5). Exposition-Phoenix.

Secrets of Hidden Creek. Wylly F. St. John. (Illus.). (gr. 3-7). 1976. pap. 1.50 o.p. (ISBN 0-380-00746-0, 51359, Camelot). Avon.

Secrets of Life Extension. John A. Mann. (Illus.). 256p. (Orig.). 1980. 14.00 o.p. (ISBN 0-936602-06-6); pap. 7.95 o.p. Kampmann.

Secrets of MacWrite, MacPaint, & MacDraw. David D. Busch. (Microcomputer Bookshelf Ser.). 225p. (Orig.). 1986. pap. 15.95 o.p. (ISBN 0-673-39098-5). Scott F.

Secrets of Management Excellence. John J. McCarthy. LC 84-29381. 248p. 1984. 50.00 o.p. (ISBN 0-932648-60-6). Boardroom.

Secrets of Our National Literature: Chapters in the History of the Anonymous & Pseudonymous Writings of Our Countrymen. William P. Courtney. LC 68-21761. 264p. 1968. Repr. of 1908 ed. 43.00x o.p. (ISBN 0-8103-3140-3). Gale.

Secrets of Salt-Free Cooking: A Complete Low Sodium Cookbook. Jeanne Jones. LC 79-343. (Illus.). 1979. pap. 7.95 o.p. (ISBN 0-89286-147-9, One Hund One Prods). Ortho.

Secrets of Smart Airline Travelers. Richard A. Bodner. LC 86-18837. (Illus.). 128p. (Orig.). 1986. pap. 4.95 o.p. (ISBN 0-932620-65-5). Betterway Pubns.

Secrets of Strong Families. Nick Stinnett & John DeFrain. 288p. 1986. 16.95 o.p. (ISBN 0-316-81630-2). Little.

Secrets of Successful Humor. Rusty Wright & Linda R. Wright. 256p. 1985. 13.95 o.p. (ISBN 0-89840-086-4). Heres Life.

Secrets of Successful Speaking. Maureen Hanigan. LC 84-111243. 176p. 1984. pap. 5.95 o.p. (ISBN 0-02-012420-1, Collier). Macmillan.

Secrets of Successful Writing, Speaking, & Listening. David V. Lewis. 200p. 1982. 16.95 o.p. (ISBN 0-8144-5685-5). AMACOM.

Secrets of Syndication: How to Make Money Using Other People's Money. Richard H. Beguelin. 1985. 18.45i o.p. (ISBN 0-316-08783-1). Little.

Secrets of the Blood. Felix Jackson. LC 80-66002. 1980. 10.95 o.p. (ISBN 0-689-11076-6, Atheneum). Macmillan.

Secrets of the Deep. Gordon Dickson. 192p. (Orig.). 1985. pap. 2.95 o.p. (ISBN 0-931773-29-6). Critics Choice Paper.

Secrets of the Gnomes. Rien Poortvliet & Wil Huygen. (Illus.). 200p. 1984. pap. 12.95 o.p. (ISBN 0-345-30861-1, Del Rey). Ballantine.

Secrets of the Hand. Maria Gardini. (Illus.). 160p. 1985. pap. 12.95 o.p. (ISBN 0-02-011450-8, Collier). Macmillan.

Secrets of the Heart. Cassie Edwards. 400p. (Orig.). 1982. pap. 3.50 o.p. (ISBN 0-8439-1142-5, Pub. by Leisure Bks CT). Dorchester Pub Co.

Secrets of the Heart. Kahlil Gibran. 128p. 1971. Repr. of 1947 ed. (ISBN 0-8022-2080-0) (ISBN 0-8022-0581-X). Philos Lib.

Secrets of the Mighty Sioux. F. Edward Butterworth. 1982. pap. 4.99 o.p. (ISBN 0-8309-0352-6). Ind Pr MO.

Secrets of the Mummies. Joyce Milton. LC 84-1963. (Step-up Bks). (Illus.). 72p. (gr. 2-5). 1984. 4.95 o.s.i. (ISBN 0-394-86769-6, Pub. by BYR); lib. bdg. 8.99 o.s.i. (ISBN 0-394-96769-0). Random.

Secrets of the Pirate Inn. Wylly Folk St. John. (gr. 2-7). 1976. pap. 1.50 o.p. (ISBN 0-380-00629-4, 51979, Camelot). Avon.

Secrets of the Tax Revolt. James R. Adams. LC 84-3765. 416p. 1984. 16.95 o.p. (ISBN 0-15-179998-9). HarBraceJ.

Secrets of the Temple: How the Federal Reserve Runs the Country. William Greider. 816p. 1988. 24.45 o.s.i. (ISBN 0-671-47989-X). S&S.

Secrets of the Video Game Superstars. Len Albin. (Illus.). 1982. pap. 2.50 o.p. (ISBN 0-380-80614-2). Avon.

Secrets Parents Should Know about Public Schools. G. Terry Frith. LC 85-14555. 253p. 1985. 15.45 o.p. (ISBN 0-671-55845-5). S&S.

Secrets Parents Should Know about Public Schools. Terry Frith. 256p. 1986. pap. 6.95 o.p. (ISBN 0-671-62791-0, Fireside). S&S.

Section Three Hundred & Three Stock Redemptions Buy the Numbers. Stephan R. Leimberg. LC 85-244354. Date not set. (Pub. by Farnsworth Pub Co). Longman Finan.

Sectional Human Anatomy: Correlated with CT & MRI. Man-Chung Han & Chu-Wan Kim. (Illus.). 235p. 1985. 65.00 o.p. (ISBN 0-89640-118-9). Igaku-Shoin.

Secular Choral Music in Print: 1982 Supplement. Ed. by Nancy K. Nardone. LC 82-8131. (Music-In-Print Ser.). 179p. 1982. lib. bdg. 75.00 o.p. (ISBN 0-88478-013-9). Musicdata.

Secular Music in America Eighteen One to Eighteen Twenty-Five: A Bibliography, 3 Vols. Richard J. Wolfe. Repr. of 1964 ed. lib. bdg. 177.00 o.p. (Pub. by Am Repr Serv). Reprint Servs.

Secular Outlook: Wages & Prices. John T. Dunlop. 1957. 2.00 o.p. (ISBN 0-89215-046-7). U Cal LA Indus Rel.

Secular Relevance of the Church. Gayraud S. Wilmore. (Orig.). 1962. pap. 1.25 o.s.i. (ISBN 0-664-24410-6, Westminster). Westminster John Knox.

Secure Communication Systems: Related Conference Proceedings. Ed. by J. E. Flood & C. J. Hughes. (IEE Conference Publication: No. 231). 78p. 1984. pap. 41.00 o.s.i. (ISBN 0-85296-288-6, IC231). Inst Elect Eng.

Secure Executive: The Secret of Becoming One, Being One, Staying One. Steven Kahn. 128p. 1986. 10.00 o.p. (ISBN 0-399-13213-9, Putnam); 10-copy counterpack 129.50 o.p. (ISBN 0-399-13217-1). Putnam Pub Group.

Secured Creditor in Court 1985. Practising Law Institute Staff. 560p. 1985. pap. 15.00 o.p. (A4-411 4). PLI.

Secured Creditors & Lessore under the Bankruptcy Reform Act 1985. 477p. 1985. 15.00 o.p. (A4-4129). PLI.

Secured Transactions in a Nutshell. 2nd ed. Henry J. Bailey, III. LC 81-7404. (Nutshell Ser.). 391p. 1981. pap. text ed. 9.95 o.p. (ISBN 0-314-59846-4). West Pub.

Securing the Revolution: Ideology in American Politics, 1789-1815. Richard Buel, Jr. LC 74-38120. 403p. (Orig.). 1974. pap. 14.95x o.p. (ISBN 0-8014-9147-9). Cornell U Pr.

Securities Activities of Commercial Banks. Ed. by Arnold Sametz. LC 80-8339. 208p. 1981. 33.00x o.p. (ISBN 0-669-04031-2). Lexington Bks.

Securities Acts: Federal & Pennsylvania. Pennsylvania Bar Institute Staff. 349p. 1985. 60.00 o.p. (ISBN 0-318-19074-5, 309). PA Bar Inst.

Securities Filings: Review & Update, 1983. Practising Law Institute Staff & Peter E. Yaeger. LC 83-221891. (Corporate Law & Practice Course Handbook Ser.: No. 424). (Illus.). 672p. 1983. 35.00 o.p. PLI.

Securities Law Handbook, 1985. Harold S. Bloomenthal. (Securities Law Ser.). (Orig.). 1987-1988. pap. 85.00 o.p. (ISBN 0-87632-518-5). Clark Boardman.

Securities Law Review, 1986. LC 72-96215. (Securities Law Ser.). 1986. 70.00 o.p. (ISBN 0-87632-503-7). Clark Boardman.

Securities Regulation in a Nutshell. 2nd ed. David L. Ratner. LC 82-11108. (Nutshell Ser.). 312p. 1982. pap. text ed. 9.95 o.p. (ISBN 0-314-66864-0). West Pub.

Securities Regulation: The Law of 1987 Pocket Part. Thomas L. Hazen. 196p. 1986. pap. 8.95 o.p. (ISBN 0-314-33810-1). West Pub.

Security & Disarmament. Mitchell Sharp et al. Trilateral Comm.

Security & Loss Control. 1st ed. Norman R. Bottom & John Kostanoski. 352p. 1983. write for info. o.p. (ISBN 0-02-312700-7). Macmillan.

Security Challenge in Northeast Asia: Report of a Conference. Ed. by John W. Lewis. (Special Report of the Northeast Asia-United States Forum on International Policy, Stanford University). 77p. 1982. pap. 7.00 o.p. (ISBN 0-935371-06-0). ISIS.

Security Dictionary. Richard Hofmeister & David Prince. LC 83-61093. 8.95 o.p. (ISBN 0-672-22020-2). Sams.

Security for All & Free Enterprise. Henry Wachtel. 1955. (ISBN 0-8022-1786-9). Philos Lib.

Security Gamble: Deterrence Dilemmas in the Nuclear Age. Ed. by Douglas MacLean. LC 84-15080. (Maryland Studies in Public Philosophy). 190p. 1984. 29.95x o.p. (ISBN 0-8476-7329-4, Rowman & Allanheld); pap. 14.95x o.s.i. (ISBN 0-8476-7337-5). Rowman.

Security in Disarmament. Ed. by Richard J. Falk & Richard J. Barnet. (Center of International Studies). 1965. 47.50x o.p. (ISBN 0-691-07520-4); pap. 14.50x o.p. (ISBN 0-691-02158-9, 80). Princeton U Pr.

Security in the 1980's. Harold Brown et al. Trilateral Comm.

Security Investigator's Handbook. Paul Fuqua & Jerry Wilson. LC 78-62615. 232p. 1979. 19.00x o.p. (ISBN 0-87201-398-7). Gulf Pub.

Security Manual. 4th ed. Eric Oliver & John Wilson. 244p. (Orig.). 1983. pap. text ed. 12.50x o.p. (ISBN 0-566-02415-2). Gower Pub Co.

Security of Englishmen's Lives, or the Trust Power & Duty of Grand Juries. John Somers. (Civil Liberties in American History Ser.). 1974. Repr. of 1681 ed. lib. bdg. 12.50 o.p. (ISBN 0-306-70604-0). Da Capo.

Security of Personal Computer Systems: A Management Guide. Dennis D. Steinauer. LC 84-601156. (Computer Science & Technology Ser.). 68p. (Orig.). 1985. pap. 3.00 o.p. (S/N 003-003-02627-1). USGPO.

Security of Salvation. Richard C. Nies. LC 78-17523. (Waymark Ser.). 1978. pap. 2.50 o.p. (ISBN 0-8127-0187-9). Review & Herald.

Security Risk Management: A Practitioners Guide. Mosler Anti-Crime Bureau Staff. Ed. by Robert Rosberg. LC 80-66648. (Illus.). 192p. 1980. 10.95 o.p. (ISBN 0-916752-42-9). Longman Trade.

Security Safeguards in Computer Operations. Charles F. Hemphill, Jr. & Robert D. Hemphill. 1979. pap. 7.50 o.p. (ISBN 0-8144-2232-2). AMACOM.

Security, Strategy, & the Logic of Chinese Foreign Policy. Jonathan D. Pollack. LC 82-80971. (Research Papers & Policy Studies (Rpps): No. 5). 66p. 1981. 2.50x o.p. (ISBN 0-912966-34-3). IEAS.

Security Systems: Considerations, Layout, Performance. William J. Cook, Jr. LC 82-50653. 144p. 1983. pap. 10.95 o.p. (ISBN 0-672-21949-2, 21953). Sams.

Sediment Dynamics on the Changjiang Estuary & the Adjacent East China Sea: A Selection of Edited Papers from the International Symposium Held in Hangzhou, People's Republic of China, April 1983. Ed. by J. D. Milliman & J. Qingming. 236p. 1985. pap. 44.00 o.p. (ISBN 0-08-030257-2, Pub. by Aberdeen Scotland). Pergamon.

Sedimentary Carbonate Minerals. F. Lippmann. LC 72-90186. (Minerals, Rocks & Inorganic Materials Ser.: Vol. 6). (Illus.). 300p. 1973. 39.80 o.p. (ISBN 0-387-06011-1). Springer-Verlag.

Sedimentation in Submarine Canyons, Fans & Trenches. Ed. by D. J. Stanley & G. Kelling. LC 77-19163. 395p. 1982. 67.95 o.p. (ISBN 0-87933-313-8). Van Nos Reinhold.

Sedimentation of the Modern Carbonate Tidal Flats of Northwest Andros Island, Bahamas. Lawrence A. Hardie. LC 76-47389. (Johns Hopkins University Studies in Geology: No. 22). (Illus.). 232p. 1977. 32.00x o.p. (ISBN 0-8018-1895-8). Johns Hopkins.

Seduction? A Biblical Response. rev. ed. Thomas F. Reid et al. Ed. by Florence K. Biros & Carole Williams. (Illus.). 1986. pap. 6.95 o.p. (ISBN 0-936369-02-7). Son-Rise Pubns.

Seduction & Betrayal: Women & Literature. Elizabeth Hardwick. 1983. 14.00 o.p. (ISBN 0-8446-6036-1). Peter Smith.

Seduction & Other Stories. Joyce Carol Oates. LC 75-4541. 275p. (Orig.). 1976. 14.00 o.p. (ISBN 0-87685-229-0). Black Sparrow.

Seduction of Lucy. Dell McLaren. 1977. pap. 1.50 o.p. (ISBN 0-505-51179-7, Pub. by Tower Bks). Dorchester Pub Co.

Seduction of the Spirit. Harvey Cox. 1985. pap. 8.95 o.p. (ISBN 0-671-21728-3, Touchstone Bks). S&S.

Seductions of Natalie Bach. William Luvaas. 1986. 18.95 o.p. (ISBN 0-316-53768-3); pap. 8.95 o.p. (ISBN 0-316-53769-1). Little.

See & Say. Antonio Frasconi. LC 55-8675. (Illus.). (gr. 1 up). 1972. pap. 1.35 o.p. (ISBN 0-15-680350-X, VoyB). HarBraceJ.

See & Say: A Picture Book in Four Languages. Antonio Frasconi. LC 55-8675. (Illus.). (gr. k-3). 1955. 6.95 o.p. (ISBN 0-15-272454-0, HJ). HarBraceJ.

See Cyprus. Paul Watkins. 96p. 1985. 19.00x o.p. (ISBN 0-903372-10-X, Pub. by P Watkins-Format Bks England). State Mutual Bk.

See Dave Run. Jeannette Eyerly. (gr. 7-9). 1979. pap. 2.50 o.p. (ISBN 0-671-62067-3). Archway.

See Dave Run. Jeannette Eyerly. (gr. k up). 1986. o.p. Archway.

See How They Run: Suzy Prudden's Running Book for Kids. Suzy Prudden. LC 78-71308. (Illus.). (gr. 3 up). 1979. lib. bdg. 5.99 o.p. (ISBN 0-448-13126-9, G&D); pap. 3.95 o.p. (ISBN 0-448-16828-6). Putnam Pub Group.

See Inside a Space Station. rev. ed. Robin Kerrod. Ed. by Warwick Press. 32p. (gr. 4-9). 1988. 11.90 o.p. (ISBN 0-531-19031-5, Warwick). Watts.

See Inside a Submarine. Jonathan Rutland. Ed. by Warwick Press. 32p. (gr. 4-9). 1988. 11.90 o.p. (Warwick). Watts.

See Inside an Airport. Jonathan Rutland. Ed. by JV-Warwick Press Staff. (See Inside Ser.). (Illus.). 32p. (gr. 4-9). 1988. 10.40 o.p. (Warwick). Watts.

See Inside an Oil Rig & Tanker. Jonathan Rutland. Ed. by JV-Warwick Press Staff. (See Inside Ser.). (Illus.). 32p. (gr. 4-9). 1988. 9.90 o.p. (Warwick). Watts.

See It! Do It! Your Faith in Action. David Ng. (Orig.). (gr. 9-12). 1972. pap. 2.50 o.p. (ISBN 0-377-02401-5). Friendship Pr.

See Madeira & the Canaries. Annette Pink. 144p. 19.00x o.p. (ISBN 0-903372-06-1, Pub. by P Watkins-Format Bks England). State Mutual Bk.

See Malta & Gozo. Inge Severin. 144p. 1985. 19.00x o.p. (ISBN 0-903372-08-8, Pub. by P Watkins-Format Bks England). State Mutual Bk.

See Me More Clearly: Career & Life Planning for Teens with Physical Disabilities. Joyce S. Mitchell. LC 79-3768. (gr. 7 up). 1980. 8.95 o.p. (ISBN 0-15-272460-5, HJ). HarBraceJ.

See My Lovely Poison Ivy. Lilian Moore. LC 75-8581. 48p. (gr. 1-5). 1975. 7.95 o.p. (ISBN 0-689-30468-4, Atheneum). Macmillan.

See No Evil. Geoffrey Cowan. 1980. pap. 4.95 o.p. (ISBN 0-671-25411-1, Touchstone). S&S.

See Sicily. Paul Watkins. 192p. 1985. 19.00x o.p. (ISBN 0-903372-05-3, Pub. by P Watkins-Format Bks England). State Mutual Bk.

See-Sound Show: A Multimedia Kit. Mary O'Hara. (Orig.). (gr. 1-6). 1970. pap. 5.95 o.p. (ISBN 0-377-58069-4). Friendship Pr.

See You at the Match. Margaret Joy. LC 85-6874. (Illus.). 68p. (gr. 6-9). 1985. pap. 11.95 o.p. (ISBN 0-571-13663-X). Faber & Faber.

See You Later, Alligator. William F. Buckley, Jr. LC 84-18813. 312p. 1985. 16.95 o.p. (ISBN 0-385-19442-0). Doubleday.

Seeburg Jukebox Service Manual, Brochure & Trouble-Shooting Guide for 1957 Models KS200, KD200 & L100. Seeburg Company Staff. Ed. by Frank Adams. 210p. 1984. Repr. of 1957 ed. 36.50 o.p. (ISBN 0-913599-36-0, R-266). AMR Pub Co.

Seed Has Life in It. (Feelings & Growth Development Coloring Bks.). (Illus.). (ps-k). 0.75 o.p. (ISBN 0-8091-6545-7). Paulist Pr.

Seed Identification Manual. Alexander C. Martin & William D. Barkely. 1973. 35.00x o.p. (ISBN 0-520-00814-6). U of Cal Pr.

Seed Legislation. Luis M. Bombin-Bombin. (Legislative Studies: No. 16). 121p. (Eng., Fr. & Span.). 1978. pap. 8.25 o.p. (ISBN 92-5-100832-9, F2083, FAO). UNIPUB.

Seedlin' Poems of Poet Tree. Doris J. Drinnon. 1985. 6.95 o.p. (ISBN 0-533-06579-8). Vantage.

Seeds of Anger: Revolts in America, 1670-1771. Sally S. Booth. 1977. 10.95 o.p. (ISBN 0-8038-6742-5). Hastings.

Seeds of Change. Kerry Livgren & Kenneth Boa. LC 82-83636. 180p. 1983. pap. 7.95 o.p. (ISBN 0-89107-265-9, Crossway Bks). Good News.

Seeds of Consciousness: The Wisdom of Sri Nisargadatta Maharaj. Ed. by Jean Dunn. LC 81-47636. 224p. 1982. pap. 9.95 o.p. (ISBN 0-394-17939-0, E785, Ever). Grove.

Seeds of Disaster: A Report on South Africa. John Laurence. LC 68-20088. 1968. 5.95 o.s.i. (ISBN 0-8008-7025-5). Taplinger.

Seeds of Liberty: The Genesis of the American Mind. Max Savelle. LC 81-792. (Illus.). xvii, 618p. 1981. Repr. of 1965 ed. lib. bdg. 50.00x o.p. (ISBN 0-313-22880-9, SASL). Greenwood.

Seeds of Movement: Philosophy of Movement with Techniques Applied to the Beginner. Genevieve Jones. (Illus.). 1971. spiral bdg. 12.00 o.p. (ISBN 0-913650-10-2). CPP Belwin.

Seeds to the Wind: Poems, Songs, Meditations. Mark Allen. LC 79-10662. (Illus.). 119p. 1979. 10.00 o.p. (ISBN 0-931432-05-7); pap. 5.95 o.p. (ISBN 0-931432-04-9). New Wrld Lib.

Seedtime of the Republic. Clinton Rossiter. LC 53-5647. 1953. 14.95 o.p. (ISBN 0-15-180111-8). HarBraceJ.

Seeing Red. Roger Ormerod. 208p. 1985. 12.95 o.p. (ISBN 0-684-18366-8, ScribT). Scribner.

Seeing Through Stone: A Teacher's Guide to Lessons in Studio Poetry. Dennie L. Smith & Lana J. Smith. 48p. 1984. wkbk. 4.95 o.p. (ISBN 0-918518-33-4, St Luke TN). Peachtree Pubs.

Seeing Through the Dark: Blind & Sighted, Vision Shared. Malcolm E. Weiss. LC 76-17015. (Illus.). 1976. 5.95 o.p. (ISBN 0-15-272815-5, HJ). HarBraceJ.

Seeing What Plants Do. Joan E. Rahn. LC 70-175559. (Illus.). (gr. 3-5). 1972. 4.95 o.p. (ISBN 0-689-30034-4, Atheneum). Macmillan.

Seeing with a Painter's Eye. (ISBN 0-671-60789-8). P-H.

Seeing Writing. Lewis Meyers. 226p. 1980. pap. text ed. 11.00 net o.p. (ISBN 0-15-579420-5, HC). HarBraceJ.

Seek-A-Word, No. 4. 128p. 1982. pap. 1.50 o.p. (ISBN 0-505-51830-9, Pub. by Tower Bks). Dorchester Pub Co.

Seeker after Truth: A Handbook of Sufi Tales & Teachings. Adries Shah. LC 82-48401. 232p. (Orig.). 1982. pap. 7.64 o.p. (ISBN 0-06-067257-9, CN-4049). HarpR.

Seekers. Philip Kime. LC 84-90215. 61p. 1985. 6.95 o.p. (ISBN 0-533-06269-1). Vantage.

Seekers & Saviors. Time-Life Books Editors. (Enchanted World Ser.). (Illus.). 144p. (YA) (gr. 7 up). 1986. 19.93 o.p.; lib. bdg. 23.93 o.p. Time-Life.

Seeking a New Accommodation in World Commodity Markets. Carl E. Beigie et al. (Triangle Papers: No. 10). 1976. 15.00 o.p. (ISBN 0-318-02784-4); pap. 6.00 o.p. (ISBN 0-318-02785-2). Trilateral Comm.

Seeking a New Accommodation in World Commodity Markets see Trilateral Commission Task Force Reports.

Seeking Change: Early Childhood Education for the Disadvantaged in South Africa. Ann Short. (Bernard Van Leer International Education Ser.). (Illus.). 317p. (Orig.). 1985. pap. 12.00 o.p. (ISBN 0-931114-29-2). High Scope.

Seeking the Elephant, Eighteen Forty-Nine: James Mason Hutchings' Journal of His Overland Trek to California. James M. Hutchings. Ed. by Shirley Sargent. LC 80-67777. (American Trail Ser.: No. XII). (Illus.). 210p. 1981. 30.00 o.p. (ISBN 0-87062-136-X). A H Clark.

Seething African Pot, a Study of Black Nationalism, 1882-1935. Daniel Thwaite. 1970. Repr. of 1936 ed. 35.00x o.p. (ISBN 0-8371-3757-8, TSP&). Greenwood.

Segmentation of the Primitive Neural Tube in Chick Embryos: A Morphological, Histochemical & Autoradiographical Investigation. S. Vaage. (Advances in Anatomy, Embryology & Cell Biology: Vol. 41, Pt. 3). (Illus.). 1969. pap. 26.00 o.p. (ISBN 0-387-04460-4). Springer-Verlag.

Segmented Society: An Introduction to the Meaning of America. Robert H. Wiebe. 1983. 13.25 o.p. (ISBN 0-8446-6017-5). Peter Smith.

Segments I: Brent Riley Drawings. Sarah Rogers-Lafferty. (Illus., Orig.). 1984. pap. 5.00 o.s.i. (ISBN 0-917562-30-5). Contemp Arts.

Segregation Factor in the Florida Democratic Gubernatorial Primary of 1956. Helen L. Jacobstein. LC 72-3302. (University of Florida Social Sciences Monographs: No. 47). 1972. pap. 3.50 o.p. (ISBN 0-8130-0359-8). U Presses Fla.

Seifert Manifolds. P. Orlik. LC 72-90184. (Lecture Notes in Mathematics: Vol. 291). 155p. 1972. pap. 7.00 o.p. (ISBN 0-387-06014-6). Springer-Verlag.

Seigneurs De Nesle En Picardie (12e Siecle a 1286) Leurs Chartes et leur Histoire. William M. Newman. (Memoirs Ser.: Vol. 91). 1971. 32.00 o.p. (ISBN 0-87169-091-8). Am Philos.

Seismic Design for the Professional Engineering Examination. 3rd ed. Michael R. Lindeburg. LC 80-81796. (Engineering Review Manual Ser.). (Illus.). 104p. 1980. 13.95 o.p. (ISBN 0-932276-32-6). Prof Pubns CA.

Seismic Risk & Engineering Decisions. C. Lomnitz & E. Rosenblueth. (Developments in Geotechnical Engineering Ser.: Vol. 15). 426p. 1976. 110.75 o.p. (ISBN 0-444-41494-0). Elsevier.

Seizure of Political Power. Feliks Gross. 1958. (ISBN 0-8022-0635-2). Philos Lib.

Sejanus: His Fall. Ben Jonson. Ed. by W. F. Bolton. (New Mermaid Ser.). 1976. pap. 1.95x o.p. (ISBN 0-393-90016-9). Norton.

Selchie's Seed. Shulamith Oppenheim. (Illus.). (gr. 8-12). 1977. pap. 1.25 o.p. (ISBN 0-380-01727-X, 34165, Camelot). Avon.

Select Annotated Bibliography on Women & the Ethnic Minorities of Color in Social Work Education. Houda S. Abdul-Baki. 1985. 10.00 o.p. (ISBN 0-533-05934-8). Vantage.

Select Bibliography of East Asian Foods & Nutrition Arranged According to Subject Matter & Area. pap. 19.50 o.p. (F1438, FAO). UNIPUB.

Select Collection of Scarce & Valuable Tracts & Other Publications on the National Debt & the Sinking Fund. Ed. by John R. McCulloch. LC 65-16989. xx, 703p. 1966. Repr. of 1857 ed. 50.00x o.s.i. (ISBN 0-678-00148-0). Kelley.

Selected Abstracts on Translocation & Amplification of Oncogenes. (Oncology Overview Ser.). 113p. 1987. pap. 6.00 o.p. (ISBN 0-318-22944-7, S/N 017-042-00198-6). USGPO.

Selected Addresses of Gordon W. Blackwell, President of Florida State University, Sept. 16, 1960 to Jan. 31, 1965. Gordon W. Blackwell. LC 65-64028. (Florida State U. Studies: No. 43). 1965. 6.95 o.p. (ISBN 0-8130-0481-0). U Presses Fla.

Selected Agricultural Statistics on Spain, 1970-82. Natalie Tawil & Athena Hyson. (Agriculture Dept. Statistical Bulletin: 742). (Illus.). 152p. 1986. pap. 7.50 o.p. (ISBN 0-318-21353-2, S/N 001-019-00472-0). USGPO.

Selected Architecture Books Published in Canada 1974-1984. Mary Vance. (Architecture Ser., Bibliography: A 1478). 62p. 1985. pap. 9.00 o.p. (ISBN 0-89028-608-6). Vance Biblios.

Selected Articles from the Real Property Law Reporter. 223p. 1985. 25.00 o.p. (ISBN 0-88124-140-7). Cal Cont Ed Bar.

Selected Articles on Local Government Law. 394p. 1984. 10.00 o.p. (ISBN 0-318-02419-5). ICLE Georgia.

Selected Bibliography of Natal Maps. C. E. Merrett. 1979. lib. bdg. 53.00 o.p. (Hall Reference). G K Hall.

Selected Bibliography on the Aging, & on the Role of the Library in Serving Them. Mollie Kramer. (Occasional Papers: No. 107). 39p. 1973. pap. 2.00 o.p. (ISBN 0-317-58893-1). U of Ill Lib Info Sci.

Selected Bibliography on the Economic Geography of Canada: Agriculture, Land Use, Resources, Energy, Development, Recreation & Tourism. Thomas A. Rumney. (Public Administration Ser.: P 1761). 25p. 1985. 3.75 o.p. (ISBN 0-89028-561-6). Vance Biblios.

Selected Bibliography on the Economic Geography of Canada: Industry, Transportation, Urban, & Tertiary Systems. Thomas A. Rumney. (Public Administration Ser.: P 1762). 25p. 1985. 3.75 o.p. (ISBN 0-89028-562-4). Vance Biblios.

Selected Black American, African & Caribbean Authors: A Bio-Bibliography. Ed. by James A. Page & Jae M. Roh. LC 85-5225. 402p. 1985. lib. bdg. 55.00 o.p. (ISBN 0-87287-430-3). Libs Unl.

Selected Commercial Statutes: 1987. 1987. pap. write for info. o.p. West Pub.

Selected Constants: Oxidation & Reduction Potentials of Inorganic Substances in Aqueous Solutions. Ed. by G. Charlot et al. 78p. 1976. 35.00 o.p. (ISBN 0-08-020836-3). Pergamon.

Selected Contributions to the History of Cartography & Scientific Instruments. Marcel Destombes. 1988. 150.00x o.p. (ISBN 90-6194-485-6, Pub. by Hes Pubs Netherlands). Benjamins North Am.

Selected Corporation & Partnership Statutes, Rules & Forms: 1987. 1987. pap. write for info. o.p. West Pub.

Selected Environmental Law Statutes. 1985 ed. West Publishing Co. Editorial Staff. 786p. 1985. pap. text ed. 10.95 o.p. (ISBN 0-314-94145-2). West Pub.

Selected Environmental Law Statutes: 1987. 1987. pap. write for info. o.p. West Pub.

Selected Epigrams. Martial. Tr. by Ralph Marcellino from Lat. LC 68-14043. 1968. pap. text ed. 4.25x o.p. (ISBN 0-672-60330-6). Irvington.

Selected Essays of Ahad Ha-'Am. Ed. by Leon Simon. LC 62-20752. 1970. pap. 8.95 o.p. (ISBN 0-689-70246-9, T20, Atheneum). Macmillan.

Selected Essays of Fredrik Barth: Process & Form in Social Life. Fredrik Barth. (International Library of Anthropology). 1981. 35.00x o.p. (ISBN 0-7100-0720-5). Routledge Chapman & Hall.

Selected Federal Taxation, Statutes & Regulations, 1988. Ed. by Michael D. Rose. 1988. pap. text ed. write for info. o.p. (ISBN 0-314-73122-9). West Pub.

Selected Federal Taxation Statutes & Regulations: 1987 Edition. Ed. by Michael D. Rose. 1576p. 1987. pap. text ed. 16.95 o.p. (ISBN 0-314-38236-4). West Pub.

Selected Lectures, 3 Vols. Royal Society Staff. 1968-1970. Vol. 1. 43.50 o.p. (ISBN 0-12-573650-9); Vol. 2. 43.50 o.p. (ISBN 0-12-573652-5); Vol. 3. 43.50 o.p. (ISBN 0-12-573653-3). Acad Pr.

Selected Letters of e. e. Cummings. e. e. Cummings. Ed. by F. W. Dupee & George Stade. LC 69-12032. (Illus.). 1969. 8.95 o.p. (ISBN 0-15-180575-X). HarBraceJ.

Selected Letters of Edmund Burke. Ed. by Edmund Burke & Harvey C. Mansfield, Jr. 32.50x o.p. U of Chicago Pr.

Selected Letters of Eugene O'Neill. Ed. by Travis Bogard & Jackson R. Bryer. 1988. price not set o.p. Yale U Pr.

Selected Letters of Friedrich Nietzsche. Friedrich Nietzsche. Tr. by Christopher Middleton. LC 69-20453. 1969. lib. bdg. 15.00x o.s.i. (ISBN 0-226-58410-0). U of Chicago Pr.

Selected Letters of Robert Frost. Robert Frost. Ed. by L. Thompson. LC 64-10767. 1964. 10.00 o.s.i. (ISBN 0-03-043155-7). H Holt & Co.

Selected Love Poems. Michael J. Phillips. LC 80-18275. 120p. 1980. 18.50 o.p. (ISBN 0-915144-87-5); pap. 6.95 o.p. (ISBN 0-915144-88-3). Hackett Pub.

Selected Medieval & Renaissance Manuscript Collections in Microform. Peter P. Olevnik. (Occasional Papers: No. 133). 24p. 1978. pap. 2.00 o.p. (ISBN 0-317-58972-5). U of Ill Lib Info Sci.

Selected Microcomputer Applications for Teachers: A Hands-on Approach with the Apple. Richard D. Howell & Patrick B. Scott. 112p. (Orig.). 1985. pap. 28.00x o.p. (ISBN 0-89787-411-0). Gorsuch Scarisbrick.

Selected Paintings by Fan Zeng. Ed. by Xu Zhongmin & Zhou Daguang. Tr. by Miao Ling from Chinese. (Illus.). 56p. 1985. pap. 14.95 o.p. (ISBN 0-8351-1564-X). China Bks.

Selected Paintings of Wu Zuoren & Xiao Shufang. Wu Zuoren & Xiao Shufang. 1982. 65.00 o.p. (ISBN 0-08-027950-3). Pergamon.

Selected Papers. William A. Heidel. Ed. by Leonardo Taran. LC 78-66566. (Ancient Philosophy Ser.). 460p. 1982. lib. bdg. 53.00 o.p. (ISBN 0-8240-9594-4). Garland Pub.

Selected Papers. Paul Shorey. LC 78-66645. (Ancient Philosophy Ser.). 875p. 1980. lib. bdg. 94.00 o.p. (ISBN 0-8240-9586-3). Garland Pub.

Selected Papers from the English Institute 1982-83. Ed. by Walter B. Michaels & Donald E. Pease. LC 84-47940. (New Series: No. 9). 208p. 1985. text ed. 19.50x o.p. (ISBN 0-8018-2542-3). Johns Hopkins.

Selected Papers in Optical Computing: Supplement to Proceedings of the SPIE International Optical Computing Conference, Italy, 1976. 84p. 8.00 o.p. (ISBN 0-317-34755-1); members 6.00 o.p. (ISBN 0-317-34756-X). SPIE.

Selected Poems. Mirella Aquila. 120p. 1981. pap. 5.00 o.p. (ISBN 0-682-49666-9). Exposition-Phoenix.

Selected Poems. Alain Bosquet. Tr. by Samuel Beckett et al from Fr. & Eng. LC 71-181687. 189p. 1972. 12.95 o.p. (ISBN 0-8214-0111-4); pap. 7.95 o.p. (ISBN 0-8214-0112-2). Ohio U Pr.

Selected Poems. Bertolt Brecht. Tr. by H. R. Hays. LC 59-13887. 1971. pap. 4.95 o.s.i. (ISBN 0-15-680646-0, Harv). HarBraceJ.

Selected Poems. Robert Creeley. LC 76-10608. 1976. pap. 8.95 o.p. (ISBN 0-684-14810-2, SL688, ScribT). Scribner.

Selected Poems. dual language ed. R. Gamzatov. 347p. 1974. text ed. 3.95 o.p. (ISBN 0-8285-0628-0, Pub. by Progress Pubs USSR). Imported Pubns.

Selected Poems. Karen Gershon. LC 66-23803. 1966. 3.95 o.p. (ISBN 0-15-180648-9). HarBraceJ.

Selected Poems. Gunter Grass. LC 66-31902. (Helen & Kurt Wolff Bk.). 1966. 9.95 o.p. (ISBN 0-15-180655-1). HarBraceJ.

Selected Poems. Rodney Hall. 1978. 17.50x o.p. (ISBN 0-7022-0994-5); pap. 9.95x o.p. (ISBN 0-7022-0995-3). U of Queensland Pr.

Selected Poems. Howard Moss. LC 70-139321. 1971. pap. 3.95 o.p. (ISBN 0-689-10561-4, Atheneum). Macmillan.

Selected Poems. Richard Murphy. 64p. (Orig.). 1983. pap. 5.95 o.p. (ISBN 0-571-11357-5). Faber & Faber.

Selected Poems. Janos Pilinszky. Tr. by Ted Hughes & Janos Csokits. LC 76-52273. (Poetry in Translation Ser.). 1977. o. p. 8.95 o.p. (ISBN 0-89255-017-1); pap. 4.95 o.s.i. (ISBN 0-89255-018-X). Persea Bks.

Selected Poems. 3rd rev. ed. John C. Ransom. LC 69-14732. (American Poetry Ser.: No. 16). 1978. pap. 4.95 o.p. (ISBN 0-912946-54-7). Ecco Pr.

Selected Poems. Theodore Roethke. 72p. 1969. pap. 4.95 o.p. (ISBN 0-571-09164-4). Faber & Faber.

Selected Poems. Carl Sandburg. Ed. by Rebecca West. LC 26-15796. 1926. 8.95 o.p. (ISBN 0-15-180663-2). HarBraceJ.

Selected Poems. (ISBN 0-8052-0718-X). Random.

Selected Poems. Jon Silkin. 224p. 1988. pap. text ed. 13.95 o.p. (ISBN 0-415-00219-2, Pub. by Routledge UK). Routledge Chapman & Hall.

Selected Poems. R. A. Simpson. 164p. 1982. text ed. 17.50 o.p. (ISBN 0-7022-1647-X); pap. 7.50 o.p. (ISBN 0-7022-1648-8). U of Queensland Pr.

Selected Poems. Stephen Spender. 80p. 1965. pap. 4.95 o.p. (ISBN 0-571-06358-6). Faber & Faber.

Selected Poems. Mark Strand. LC 80-66013. 1980. 10.95 o.p. (ISBN 0-689-11088-X, Atheneum); pap. 7.95 o.p. (ISBN 0-689-11089-8). Macmillan.
Selected Poems. E. Vinokurov. 295p. 1979. 6.95 o.p. (ISBN 0-8285-1622-7, Pub. by Progress Pubs USSR). Imported Pubns.
Selected Poems. Sandor Weores & Fernec Juhasz. Tr. by Davis Wevill & Edward Morgan. 12.00 o.p. (ISBN 0-8446-0290-6). Peter Smith.
Selected Poems. rev. & enl. ed. William Carlos Williams. LC 69-11993. 1969. pap. 4.95 o.p. (ISBN 0-8112-0236-4, NDP131). New Directions.
Selected Poems: Alexander Prokofiev. Ed. by V. Bakhtin. 277p. 1980. 6.45 o.p. (ISBN 0-8285-1982-X, Pub. by Progress Pubs USSR). Imported Pubns.
Selected Poems & Prose. Arnold. 1978. 14.95x o.p. (ISBN 0-460-10951-0, Evman); pap. 3.50x o.p. (ISBN 0-460-11951-6, Evman). Biblio Dist.
Selected Poems from Moods. Theodore Dreiser. Ed. by Robert Palmer Saalbach. 1969. 7.50 o.p. (ISBN 0-682-46914-9, University). Exposition-Phoenix.
Selected Poems: In Five Sets. Laura Riding. 96p. 1973. 6.95 o.p. (ISBN 0-393-04378-9); pap. 1.95 o.p. (ISBN 0-393-00701-4). Norton.
Selected Poems, Nineteen Forty to Nineteen Eighty-Two. Normon Nicholson. 272p. 1983. 12.95 o.p. (ISBN 0-571-11949-2); pap. 6.95 o.p. (ISBN 0-571-11950-6). Faber & Faber.
Selected Poems Nineteen Sixty to Nineteen Eighty. Andrew Taylor. 182p. 1982. text ed. 17.95 o.p. (ISBN 0-7022-1661-5); pap. 6.95 o.p. (ISBN 0-7022-1662-3). U of Queensland Pr.
Selected Poems of Ai Qing. Ai Qing. Ed. by Eugene C. Eoyang et al. LC 82-47956. (Midland Bks Ser.: No. 302). 476p. (Orig., Chinese.). 1983. 27.50x o.p. (ISBN 0-253-34519-7); pap. 10.95x o.p. (ISBN 0-253-20302-3). Ind U Pr.
Selected Poems of H. D. H. D. 1957. pap. 8.95 o.p. (ISBN 0-394-17329-5, E71, Ever). Grove.
Selected Poems of Osip Mandelstam. Tr. by Clarence Brown & W. S. Merwin. LC 73-81725. 1974. 6.25 o.p. (ISBN 0-689-10583-5, Atheneum). Macmillan.
Selected Poems of Samuel Johnson & Oliver Goldsmith. Ed. by Alan Rudrum & Peter Dixon. LC 76-116468. (English Library). 146p. (Orig.). 1970. pap. text ed. 5.95x o.p. (ISBN 0-87249-151-X). U of SC Pr.
Selected Poems of Thomas Gray & William Collins. Ed. by Arthur Johnston. LC 72-116475. (English Library). 222p. (Orig.). 1970. pap. 5.95x o.p. (ISBN 0-87249-163-3). U of SC Pr.
Selected Poetry. S. Esenin. 383p. 1981. 8.45 o.p. (ISBN 0-8285-2518-8, Pub. by Progress Pubs USSR). Imported Pubns.
Selected Poetry. Patrick Gallagher. 1979. pap. 4.00 o.p. (ISBN 0-682-49339-2). Exposition-Phoenix.
Selected Poetry & Prose of Robert Louis Stevenson. Robert Louis Stevenson. Ed. by Bradford A. Booth. LC 68-7088. 503p. 1968. pap. 3.95 o.p. (ISBN 0-395-05206-8, B111, RivEd). HM.
Selected Population, Housing & Economic Characteristics in Kalamazoo County by Tracts: 1960-1970. Katherine Ford & Phyllis Buskirk. 63p. 1973. pap. 0.50 o.p. (ISBN 0-911558-46-2). W E Upjohn.
Selected Problems in Yavapai Syntax: The Verde Valley Dialect. Martha B. Kendall. LC 75-25118. (American Indian Linguistics Ser.). 1976. lib. bdg. 51.00 o.p. (ISBN 0-8240-1969-5). Garland Pub.
Selected Prose & Poetry. Mikhail Kuzmin. Ed. by Michael Green. 1980. 22.50 o.p. (ISBN 0-88233-417-4); pap. 6.50 o.p. (ISBN 0-88233-418-2). Ardis Pubs.
Selected Readings for Casework Supervisors in Public Agencies. A. Arcaro et al. 1970. pap. text ed. 7.95x o.p. (ISBN 0-8290-1187-0). Irvington.
Selected Readings for Introductory Anthropology. Ed. by Charles H. Ainsworth. LC 74-11102. 150p. 1974. pap. text ed. 5.95x o.p. (ISBN 0-8422-0409-1). Irvington.
Selected Readings for Introductory Sociology. 2nd ed. Ed. by Charles H. Ainsworth. 176p. 1974. pap. text ed. 6.00x o.p. (ISBN 0-8422-0460-1). Irvington.
Selected Readings for Marriage & the Family. Ed. by Charles H. Ainsworth. LC 72-11042. 1973. 39.50x o.p. (ISBN 0-8422-5123-5). Irvington.
Selected Readings from Military Thought: 1963-1973, Vol. 5, Pt. 1. Ed. by Joseph D. Douglass, Jr. Amoretta M. Hoeber. 258p. (Orig.). 1982. pap. 7.50 o.p. (ISBN 0-318-21895-X, S/N 008-070-00471-2). USGPO.
Selected Readings in Behavior Modification. Ed. by Robert S. Ruskin. LC 72-86360. 142p. 1972. text ed. 8.95x o.p. (ISBN 0-8422-0235-8). Irvington.
Selected Readings in Chemical Kinetics. Ed. by M. Back & K. J. Laidler. 1967. 45.00 o.p. (ISBN 0-08-012344-9); pap. 45.00 o.p. (ISBN 0-08-012343-0). Pergamon.
Selected Readings in Chromatography. R. J. Magee. (Selected Readings in Analytical Chemistry). (Illus.). 1970. pap. text ed. 6.00 o.p. (ISBN 0-08-015851-X). Pergamon.
Selected Readings in Education Adminstration. Ed. by Stuart Chilton. 141p. 1970. pap. text ed. 9.95x o.p. (ISBN 0-8290-1094-7). Irvington.
Selected Readings in Image Evaluation. Ed. by Rodney Shaw. 509p. 1976. 45.00 o.p. (ISBN 0-317-34757-8); members 35.00 o.p. (ISBN 0-317-34758-6). SPIE.
Selected Readings in Modern Language Teaching. Ed. by Vincent J. Colimore. 92p. 1969. pap. text ed. 6.95x o.p. (ISBN 0-8290-1091-2). Irvington.
Selected Readings in Modern World History. E. R. Bradley. 1970. pap. text ed. 9.95 o.p. (ISBN 0-8290-1188-9). Irvington.
Selected Readings in Neuropsychology. N. Butters. 1972. text ed. 29.50x o.p. (ISBN 0-8422-5006-9); pap. text ed. 8.50x o.p. (ISBN 0-8422-0221-8). Irvington.
Selected Readings in Quantitative Urban Analysis. Samuel J. Bernstein & W. Giles Mellon. LC 77-30458. 1978. 45.00 o.p. (ISBN 0-08-019593-8); pap. 29.00 o.p. (ISBN 0-08-019592-X). Pergamon.
Selected Readings in Sociobiology. James Hunt. (Illus.). 464p. 1980. pap. text ed. 21.95x o.p. (ISBN 0-07-031308-3). McGraw.
Selected Readings in the Philosophy of Education. 4th ed. Joe Park. (Illus.). 367p. 1974. pap. text ed. (ISBN 0-02-391650-8). Macmillan.
Selected Readings on American Industry. T. J. Morrisey. 249p. 1974. text ed. 29.50x o.p. (ISBN 0-8422-5199-5); pap. text ed. 7.25x o.p. (ISBN 0-8422-0440-7). Irvington.
Selected Reports in Ethnomusicology: Essays in Honour of Peter Crossley-Holland on His 65th Birthday, Vol. IV. Ed. by Nazir A. Jairazbhoy & Nicole Marzac-Holland. LC 76-640181. xxv, 300p. 1983. pap. text ed. 12.95 o.p. (ISBN 0-88287-016-5). UCLA Dept Ethnom.
Selected Short Stories. M. Gorky. 410p. 1974. 6.45 o.p. (ISBN 0-8285-0981-6, Pub. by Progress Pubs USSR). Imported Pubns.
Selected Short Stories of John O'Hara. John O'Hara. Ed. by Lionel Trilling. LC 56-8834. 1956. 6.95 o.s.i. (ISBN 0-394-60494-6, 9976P). Modern Lib.
Selected Short Stories of Thein Pe Myint. Tr. by Patricia M. Milne. 105p. 1973. 4.00 o.p. (ISBN 0-87727-091-0, DP 91). Cornell SE Asia.
Selected Speeches & Writings. Konstantin Chernenko. (Illus.). 250p. 1982. text ed. 30.00 o.p. (ISBN 0-08-025848-4). Pergamon.
Selected Speeches of Robert M. Strozier. Robert M. Strozier. LC 60-63743. (Florida State U. Studies: No. 35). 1960. 6.00 o.p. (ISBN 0-8130-0475-6). U Presses Fla.
Selected Stories. Vsevolod Ivanov. Tr. by Keith Hammond et al. 398p. 1983. pap. 4.00 o.p. (ISBN 0-8285-2619-2, Pub. by Raduga Pubs USSR). Imported Pubns.
Selected Stories. V. Korolenko. 391p. 1978. 5.45 o.p. (ISBN 0-686-98354-8, Pub. by Progress Pubs USSR). Imported Pubns.
Selected Stories by American Authors *see* **Graded Readers for Students of English As a Second Language.**
Selected Stories of Sean O'Faolain. Sean O'Faolain. LC 78-5780. 1978. 14.95 o.p. (ISBN 0-316-63285-6, Pub. by Atlantic Monthly Pr.). Little.
Selected Stories of Xiao Hong. Xiao Hong. Tr. by Howard Goldbratt from Chinese. 220p. 1982. pap. 4.95 o.p. (ISBN 0-8351-1049-4). China Bks.
Selected Tales. Nikolai Leskov. Tr. by David Magarshack from Rus. 300p. pap. o.s.i. FS&G.
Selected Tales of Laiozhai. Pu Songling. (Panda Bks.). 151p. (Orig.). 1981. pap. 4.95 o.p. (ISBN 0-8351-0943-7). China Bks.
Selected Team Sports for Men. John H. Shaw et al. Repr. of 1952 ed. lib. bdg. 35.00x o.p. (ISBN 0-8371-2498-0, SHTS). Greenwood.
Selected Terms of Irrigation. (Terminology Bulletins: No. 34). 94p. (Eng., Fr., Span. & Arabic.). 1978. pap. 9.00 o.p. (ISBN 92-5-000668-3, F1544, FAO). UNIPUB.
Selected to Live. Johanna R. Dobschiner. 192p. 1973. 5.95 o.p. (ISBN 0-8007-0613-7). Revell.
Selected Topics in Environmental Biology. Ed. by B. Bhatia et al. LC 76-47082. 1977. 305.00 o.p. (ISBN 0-08-021210-7). Pergamon.
Selected Topics in Information Theory: Proceedings of CISM, Department of Hydro & Gas Dynamics, 1970. CISM (International Center for Mechanical Sciences), Department of Automation & Information Staff. Ed. by G. Longo. (CISM International Center for Mechanical Sciences Ser.: No. 18). (Illus.). 111p. 1974. pap. 16.10 o.p. (ISBN 0-387-81166-4). Springer-Verlag.
Selected Topics in Particle Physics. Ed. by J. Steinberger. (Italian Physical Society: Course 41). 1968. 71.50 o.p. (ISBN 0-12-368841-8). Acad Pr.
Selected Topics in Preventive Cardiology. Ed. by A. Raineri & J. J. Kellerman. LC 83-8989. (Ettore Majorana International Science Series, Life Sciences: Vol. 12). 286p. 1983. 65.00x o.p. (ISBN 0-306-41375-2, Plenum Pr). Plenum Pub.
Selected Topics of the Theory of Chemical Elementary Processes. E. E. Nikitin & L. Zuelicke. (Lecture Notes in Chemistry Ser.: Vol. 8). (Illus.). 1978. pap. 14.00 o.p. (ISBN 0-387-08768-0). Springer-Verlag.
Selected Topics on Elementary Particle Physics. Ed. by M. Conversi. (Italian Physical Society: Course 26). 1964. 82.50 o.p. (ISBN 0-12-368826-4). Acad Pr.
Selected Verse. S. Narovchatov. 181p. 1979. 6.45 o.p. (ISBN 0-8285-1561-1, Pub. by Progress Pubs USSR). Imported Pubns.
Selected Water Problems in Islands & Coastal Waters: Proceedings, Malta, 1978. United Nations Economic Commission for Europe, Committee on Water Problems. (ECE Seminars & Symposia). (Illus.). 1979. 145.00 o.p. (ISBN 0-08-024447-5). Pergamon.
Selected Works. A. Issahakian. 133p. 1976. 2.95 o.p. (ISBN 0-8285-0988-3, Pub. by Progress Pubs USSR). Imported Pubns.
Selected Works. Vladimir I. Lenin. LC 75-175177. 800p. 1971. pap. 5.75 o.p. (ISBN 0-7178-0300-7). Intl Pubs Co.
Selected Works. K. Ushinsky. 256p. 1975. 5.45 o.p. (ISBN 0-8285-0428-8, Pub. by Progress Pubs USSR). Imported Pubns.
Selected Works in Organic Chemistry. A. N. Nesmeyanov. 1964. 285.00 o.p. (ISBN 0-08-010158-5). Pergamon.
Selected Works: Konstantin Stanislavsky. O. Korneva. 310p. 1985. 9.95 o.p. (ISBN 0-8285-2908-6, Pub. by Raduga Pubs USSR). Imported Pubns.
Selected Works of Deng Xiaoping, 1975-1982. Deng Xiaoping. 418p. 1984. text ed. 14.95 o.p. (ISBN 0-8351-1302-7); pap. 11.95 o.p. (ISBN 0-8351-1305-1). China Bks.
Selected Works of Nikolai S. Gumilev. Ed. by Burton Raffel & Alla Burago. LC 74-161442. 1972. 39.50x o.p. (ISBN 0-87395-098-4). State U NY Pr.
Selected Writings. Thomas B. Macaulay. Ed. by John Clive & Thomas Pinney. LC 78-171350. (Classics of British Historical Literature Ser.). 1973. pap. text ed. 4.25x o.s.i. (ISBN 0-226-49997-9, P455, Phoen). U of Chicago Pr.
Selected Writings. James A. Michener. LC 57-6493. 1957. 6.95 o.s.i. (ISBN 0-394-60467-9). Modern Lib.
Selected Writings. Edgar Allan Poe. Ed. by David Galloway. (English Library). (Orig.). (YA) (gr. 9 up). 1968. pap. 2.95 o.p. (ISBN 0-14-043028-8). Penguin.
Selected Writings. Iosif Stalin. 1970. Repr. of 1942 ed. lib. bdg. 45.00x o.p. (ISBN 0-8371-4482-5, STWR). Greenwood.
Selected Writings of A. R. Luria. Ed. by Michael Cole. LC 78-64342. 320p. 1978. 40.00 o.p. (ISBN 0-87332-127-8). M E Sharpe.
Selected Writings of Artaud. Antonin Artaud. Ed. by Susan Sontag. Tr. by Helen Weaver from Fr. LC 79-143303. 661p. 1976. 20.00 o.p. (ISBN 0-374-26048-6); pap. 9.95 o.p. (ISBN 0-374-51399-6). FS&G.
Selected Writings of Benjamin Rush. Dagobert D. Runes. 1947. (ISBN 0-8022-1448-7). Philos Lib.
Selected Writings of E.T.A. Hoffmann, 2 Vols. E. T. Hoffmann. Ed. by Elizabeth C. Knight & Leonard J. Kent. LC 73-88790. (Illus.). 1969. Set. boxed 30.00 o.s.i. (ISBN 0-226-34788-5). U of Chicago Pr.
Selected Writings of Sir Thomas Browne. Thomas Browne. Ed. by Geoffrey Keynes. LC 68-55536. (Illus.). 1970. pap. text ed. 3.25x o.s.i. (ISBN 0-226-07636-9, P347, Phoen). U of Chicago Pr.
Selected Writings of Truman Capote. Truman Capote. LC 83-42946. 1963. 6.95 o.p. (ISBN 0-394-60495-4). Modern Lib.
Selecting a Preschool. Turnbull et al. LC 83-7020. (Illus.). 261p. 1984. pap. 18.00x o.p. (ISBN 0-8391-1890-2, 1257). Pro Ed.
Selecting American School Principals: A Sourcebook for Educators. D. Catherine Baltzell & Robert A. Dentler. 71p. 1983. pap. 2.50 o.p. (ISBN 0-318-11826-2, S/N 065-000-00195-1). USGPO.
Selecting, Analyzing, & Displaying Planning Information. Harold Starr et al. 164p. 1979. 9.75 o.p. (ISBN 0-318-15555-9, RD164). Natl Ctr Res Voc Ed.
Selecting & Developing Media for Instruction. 2nd ed. Ronald H. Anderson. 192p. 1983. 27.95 o.p. (ISBN 0-442-20976-2). Van Nos Reinhold.
Selecting & Ordering Populations: A New Statistical Methodology. Jean D. Gibbons et al. LC 77-3700. 592p. 1977. 55.50 o.p. (ISBN 0-317-54512-4, Pub. by John Wiley). Krieger.
Selecting, Developing & Retaining Women Executives. Helen J. McLane. 256p. 1982. pap. 16.95 o.p. (ISBN 0-442-26320-1). Van Nos Reinhold.
Selecting, Developing & Retaining Women Executives: A Corporate Strategy for the Eighties. Helen J. McLane. 256p. 1980. 26.95 o.p. (ISBN 0-442-20165-6). Van Nos Reinhold.
Selecting Interventions for Nutritional Improvement - A Manual. (Nutrition in Agriculture Ser.: No. 3). 85p. 1984. pap. 7.50 o.p. (ISBN 92-5-101402-7, F2489, FAO). UNIPUB.
Selecting Materials for Process Equipment. Chemical Engineering Magazine Editors. (Chemical Engineering Ser.). 280p. 1980. text ed. 36.50 o.p. (ISBN 0-07-010692-4). McGraw.
Selecting the Right Data Base Software for the IBM PC. Kathleen McHugh & Veronica Corchado. LC 84-50992. 96p. 1984. pap. 9.95 o.p. (ISBN 0-89588-174-8). SYBEX.
Selecting the Right Spreadsheet Software for the IBM PC. Kathleen McHugh & Veronica Corchado. LC 84-50993. 96p. 1984. pap. 9.95 o.p. (ISBN 0-89588-178-0). SYBEX.
Selecting the Right Word Processing Software for the IBM PC. Veronica Corchado & Kathleen McHugh. LC 84-50991. 96p. 1984. pap. 9.95 o.p. (ISBN 0-89588-177-2). SYBEX.
Selection of European Folk Dances, 5 vols. J. F. Richardson. 1978. Vol. 1. pap. text ed. 4.40 flexi-cover o.p. (ISBN 0-08-010833-4); Vol. 2. pap. text ed. 4.40 flexi-cover o.s.i. (ISBN 0-08-010842-3); Vol. 3. pap. text ed. 4.40 flexi-cover o.s.i. (ISBN 0-08-011926-3); Vol. 4. pap. text ed. 4.40 flexi-cover o.s.i. (ISBN 0-08-016190-1); Vol. 5, A Selection of Israeli Folk Dances. pap. text ed. 4.40 flexi-cover o.s.i. (ISBN 0-08-021589-0). Pergamon.
Selection of Patients for X-Ray Examinations: Denial Radiographic Examinations. 40p. 1987. pap. 2.00 o.p. (ISBN 0-318-23843-8, 017-015-00236-5). USGPO.
Selection of State Roadside Cross Sections. (National Cooperative Highway Research Program Report). 57p. 1975. 4.40 o.p. (ISBN 0-309-02335-1). Transport Res Bd.
Selection of Teachers & Supervisors in Urban School Systems: A Transcript of the Public Hearings Held before the New York City Commission on Human Rights, January 25-29, 1971. Ed. by Paul Tractenberg. LC 72-81915. 1972. 25.00x o.p. (ISBN 0-87988-001-5). Agathon.
Selection of the Vice President. new ed. Dorothy C. Tompkins. LC 74-600. (Public Policy Bibliographies: No. 6). 1974. 3.75x o.p. (ISBN 0-87772-198-X). UCB IGS.
Selection: The Stress Theory of Evolution. Richard de C. Studdert. (Illus.). 160p. 1983. 8.00 o.p. (ISBN 0-682-49927-7, University). Exposition-Phoenix.
Selections from Early Middle English, 1130-1250. Joseph Hall. 1972. Repr. of 1920 ed. lib. bdg. 47.50x o.p. (ISBN 0-8371-4233-4, HAME). Greenwood.
Selections from Pushkin. Aleksandr Pushkin. 458p. 1985. 8.95 o.p. (ISBN 0-8285-3065-3, Pub. by Rus Lang Pubs USSR). Imported Pubns.
Selections from Records of the Historian. Sima Qian. (Illus.). 1980. text ed. 15.95 o.p. (ISBN 0-8351-0617-9); pap. 9.95 o.p. (ISBN 0-8351-0618-7). China Bks.
Selections from the Collection of Marion & Gustave Ring. Ed. by Virginia Wageman. LC 85-600125. (Illus.). 60p. (Orig.). 1985. pap. 10.00 o.p. (ISBN 0-318-18833-3, S/N 047-001-00162-1). USGPO.
Selections from the New American Commonwealth: American Values Projected Abroad. Louis Heren. (Exxon Ser.: Vol. XVI). 180p. (Orig.). 1984. lib. bdg. 27.50 o.p. (ISBN 0-8191-4003-1); pap. text ed. 11.25 o.p. (ISBN 0-8191-4004-X). U Pr of Amer.
Selections from the Norton Simon Museum of Art. Ed. by David W. Steadman. LC 72-77426. (Publications of the Art Museum Ser). (Illus.). 240p. 1972. 58.50x o.p. (ISBN 0-691-03887-2). Princeton U Pr.
Selections from the Permanent Collection. Whitney Museum of American Art Staff. LC 76-19074. 1977. lib. bdg. 25.00 2 color fiches incl. o.s.i. (ISBN 0-226-69818-1, Chicago Visual Lib). U of Chicago Pr.

Selections from the Writings of Lord Dunsany. Dunsany. 124p. 1971. Repr. of 1912 ed. 10.00x o.p. (ISBN 0-7165-1343-9, Pub. by Cuala Press Ireland). Biblio Dist.
Selective Bibliography in Science & Engineering. Northeastern University, Dodge Library, Boston Staff. 1964. 78.00 o.s.i. (ISBN 0-8161-0701-7, Hall Library). G K Hall.
Selective Bibliography of California Labor History. Mitchell Slobodek. 265p. 1964. 8.00 o.p. (ISBN 0-89215-045-9). U Cal LA Indus Rel.
Selective Inhibitors of Viral Functions. Ed. by W. A. Carter. LC 73-81479. (Uniscience Ser). 377p. 1973. 70.50 o.p. (ISBN 0-87819-027-9). CRC Pr.
Selective Music Lists, 1979: Instrumental Solos & Ensembles. Music Educators National Conference Staff. LC 72-75840. 176p. 1979. pap. 6.25 o.p. (ISBN 0-940796-17-1, 1042). Music Ed Natl.
Selective Oxidation of Hydrocarbons. D. J. Hucknall. 1974. 63.00 o.p. (ISBN 0-12-358950-9). Acad Pr.
Selective Studies in Health & Social Services. Ed. by A. G. McDonald. (OMEGA Special Issue Ser.: Vol. 9, No. 5). 104p. 1981. pap. 35.00 o.p. (ISBN 0-08-023620-0). Pergamon.
Selective Trout. Doug Swisher & Carl Richards. LC 83-60676. (Illus.). 184p. 1983. pap. 17.95 o.p. (ISBN 0-8329-0336-1). Lyons & Burford.
Selectric Interface. George Young. Ed. by Nan McCarthy. (Illus.). 124p. 1982. pap. 12.97 o.p. (ISBN 0-88006-051-4, BK 7388). Wayne Green Ent.
Selena. Ernest Brawley. LC 78-65199. 1979. 10.95 o.p. (ISBN 0-689-10951-2, Atheneum). Macmillan.
Selenium. 2nd ed. Irene Rosenfeld & O. A. Beath. 1964. 80.00 o.p. (ISBN 0-12-597550-3). Acad Pr.
Selenium & Selenides. V. Chizhikov & T. Shchastlivyi. 403p. 1968. 63.00x o.p. (ISBN 0-569-03528-7, Pub. by Collets (UK)). State Mutual Bk.
Selenium in Biology & Medicine: Second International Symposium. J. E. Spallholz et al. (Illus.). 1981. 67.95 o.p. (ISBN 0-87055-379-8). AVI.
Self-Adhesive Business Labels. (Photocopier Bks.). (Orig.). 1984. pap. 19.95 o.p. (ISBN 0-87280-020-2, Asher-Gallant). Caddylak Systs.
Self & the Other in the Ontologies of Sartre & Buber. Sylvain Boni. LC 82-20130. 202p. (Orig.). 1983. lib. bdg. 29.00 o.p. (ISBN 0-8191-2852-X); pap. text ed. 13.25 o.p. (ISBN 0-8191-2853-8). U Pr of Amer.
Self & World: Readings in Philosophy. James A. Ogilvy. 1973. 11.95 o.p. (ISBN 0-15-579629-1). HarbraceJ.
Self-Assessment in Basic Sciences for Dentists. Ed. by R. L. Speirs. (Illus.). 288p. 1986. 8.95 o.p. (ISBN 0-317-55842-0). Mosby.
Self-Assessment in Dentistry. Speirs. (Illus.). 288p. 1986. pap. 16.50 o.p. (ISBN 0-632-01424-5, B-4733-9). Mosby.
Self-Assessment in Histological Techniques. John D. Bancroft & Brian T. Chalk. LC 84-27488. (Illus.). 214p. 1985. pap. text ed. 22.00 o.p. (ISBN 0-443-03104-5). Churchill.
Self-Assessment in Radiology. Mendelson & Whitehouse. 200p. 1987. 16.50 o.p. (ISBN 0-8016-3395-8, B-33958). Mosby.
Self-Assessment in Radiology 2: Gastro-Intestinal Radiology. Michael Berger. 174p. 1985. 18.50 o.p. (ISBN 0-471-83802-0). Wiley.
Self-Assessment of Current Knowledge in Nuclear Medicine. 2nd ed. John B. Selby & Donald G. Frey. 1982. spiral bdg. 34.00 o.p. (ISBN 0-87488-239-7). Med Exam.
Self-Assessment of Current Knowledge in Ophthalmology. 2nd ed. Timothy Van Scott & Sidney J. Weiss. 1981. 34.00 o.p. (ISBN 0-87488-255-9). Med Exam.
Self-Assessment of Current Knowledge in Obstetrics & Gynecology. 4th ed. David Charles. 1984. pap. text ed. 30.75 o.p. (ISBN 0-87488-265-6). Med Exam.
Self-Assessment of Current Knowledge in Rheumatology. 2nd ed. Robert E. Pieroni. 1976. spiral bdg. 29.25 o.s.i. (ISBN 0-87488-258-3). Med Exam.
Self-Assessment of Current Knowledge in Therapeutic Radiology. 3rd ed. Ned B. Hornback. 1984. pap. text ed. 34.00 o.p. (ISBN 0-87488-394-6). Med Exam.
Self-Change: Strategies for Solving Personal Problems. Michael J. Mahoney. 224p. 1981. pap. 4.95 o.p. (ISBN 0-393-00067-2). Norton.
Self-Change: Strategies for Solving Personal Problems. Michael J. Mahoney. 1979. 12.95 o.p. (ISBN 0-393-01176-3). Norton.
Self-Chosen: "Our Crowd" Is Dead--Long Live "Our Crowd" Jean Baer. (Illus.). 1984. pap. 7.95 o.p. (ISBN 0-87795-536-0, Arbor Hse). Morrow.
Self-Chosen: Our Crowd Is Dead-Long Live Our Crowd! Jean Baer. LC 81-66962. (Illus.). 345p. 1982. 15.95 o.p. (ISBN 0-87795-330-9, Arbor Hse). Morrow.
Self-Concept in Education: Selected Readings for Educational Psychology. F. Vitro et al. 1971. pap. text ed. 8.95x o.p. (ISBN 0-8290-1189-7). Irvington.
Self-Concept of Black Americans. Vivian V. Gordon. 118p. 1977. pap. text ed. 9.25 o.p. (ISBN 0-8191-0151-6). U Pr of Amer.
Self Consistency: A Theory of Personality. Prescott Lecky. 144p. 1973. Repr. 7.95 o.p. (ISBN 0-87208-027-7). Island Pr Pubs.
Self Control. Mary Brunton. (Mothers of the Novel Reprints Ser.). 448p. 1986. pap. 7.95 o.p. (ISBN 0-86358-084-X, Pandora Pr). Routledge Chapman & Hall.
Self Creation. George Weinberg. 1979. pap. 2.50 o.p. (ISBN 0-380-43521-7, 65680-9). Avon.
Self-Deception & Morality. Mike W. Martin. LC 86-5467. x, 182p. 1988. pap. 9.95 o.p. (ISBN 0-7006-0353-0). U Pr of KS.
Self-Defense for Gentle People. Rolf Cahn. LC 73-88701. (Illus.). 183p. (Orig.). pap. 6.00 o.p. (ISBN 0-912528-07-9). John Muir.
Self-Destruction: The Disintegration & Decay of the U. S. Army During the Vietnam Era. Cincinnatus. (Illus.). 1981. 15.95 o.p. (ISBN 0-393-01346-4). Norton.
Self-Discipline. Louis C. Schroeter. 1978. 7.50 o.p. (ISBN 0-682-49001-6). Exposition-Phoenix.
Self Disclosure: An Experimental Analysis of the Transparent Self. Sidney Jourard. LC 78-10576. 264p. 1979. Repr. of 1971 ed. lib. bdg. 21.50 o.p. (ISBN 0-88275-767-9). Krieger.
Self-Education-Self Assessment in Thoracic Surgery. Coordinating Committee for Continuing Education in Thoracic Surgery. LC 80-84130. 232p. 1983. 100.00 o.p. (ISBN 0-8403-3156-8, 40315601). Kendall-Hunt.
Self-Esteem Passport. Michael Krawetz. 1984. pap. 2.95 o.s.i. (ISBN 0-03-069846-4). H Holt & Co.
Self-Esteem: The New Reformation. Robert H. Schuller. 144p. 1982. 4.99 o.p. (ISBN 0-8499-4172-5). Word Bks.
Self-Evaluation Checklists, 1972, 16 vol. LC 72-87101. (OSHA Occupational Standards). 3-ring notebooks 365.00 o.p. (ISBN 0-87912-105-X, 115-01). Natl Safety Coun.
Self-Evaluation Checklists, 1973, 9 vol. LC 72-75201. (OSHA Construction Standards). 3-ring notebooks 300.00 o.p. (ISBN 0-87912-106-8, 118-01). Natl Safety Coun.
Self-Evaluation for Primary Schools. I. A. Rodger & J. A. Richardson. (Studies in Teaching & Learning). 216p. (Orig.). 1985. pap. text ed. 20.95 o.s.i. (ISBN 0-340-36933-7). Princeton Bk Co.
Self-Funding of Welfare Benefits. Carlton Harker. 169p. (Orig.). 1981. pap. 15.00 o.p. (ISBN 0-89154-162-4). Intl Found Employ.
Self-Government at the King's Command. Albert B. White. LC 74-5927. 130p. 1974. Repr. of 1933 ed. lib. bdg. 35.00x o.p. (ISBN 0-8371-7526-7, WHKC). Greenwood.
Self Government in Russia. Paul Vinogradoff. LC 78-14148. (Russian Studies). 118p. Repr. of 1915 ed. o.s.i.(ISBN 0-88355-821-1). Hyperion Conn.
Self Healing. Meir Schneider. 224p. 1987. pap. 9.95 o.p. (ISBN 0-7102-1084-1, Pub. by Routledge UK). Routledge Chapman & Hall.
Self-Health: The Lifelong Fitness Book. Nathaniel Lande. LC 79-14671. (Illus.). 192p. 1980. 9.95 o.s.i. (ISBN 0-03-048316-6). H Holt & Co.
Self-Hypnosis: The Key to Health & Happiness. A. B. King. 128p. (Orig.). 1986. pap. 5.95 o.p. (ISBN 0-7137-1787-4, Pub. by Javelin England). Sterling.
Self-Image of a Christian: Humility & Self-Esteem. Mark Kinzer. (Living As a Christian Ser.). 106p. (Orig.). 1980. pap. 2.95 o.s.i. (ISBN 0-89283-088-3). Servant.
Self-Knowledge & Self-Identity. Sydney Shoemaker. LC 63-13910. (Contemporary Philosophy Ser.). (Illus.). 273p. 1963. 28.50x o.p. (ISBN 0-8014-0383-9). Cornell U Pr.
Self-Love. Robert H. Schuller. 160p. 1975. pap. 2.95 o.p. (ISBN 0-8007-8195-3, Spire Bks). Revell.
Self-Made Woman: Biography of Nobel-Prize-Winner Grazia Deledda. Carolyn Balducci. 256p. (gr. 7 up). 1975. 6.95 o.p. (ISBN 0-395-21914-0). HM.
Self-Management & Behavior Change: From Theory to Practice. Ed. by Paul Karoly & Frederick H. Kanfer. (General Psychology Ser.). 400p. 1982. 59.00 o.p. (ISBN 0-08-025987-1); pap. 22.00 o.p. (ISBN 0-08-025986-3). Pergamon.
Self-Paced Business Mathematics. Nanci L. Dummett. 410p. 1979. pap. text ed. 17.85x o.p. (ISBN 0-534-00616-7). PWS-Kent Pub.
Self Paced Business Mathematics. 3rd ed. Nanci Lee. 448p. (gr. 11-12). 1986. pap. text ed. 20.25 o.p. (ISBN 0-534-06222-9). PWS-Kent Pub.
Self-Paced Instructor Training Modules, 4 modules. (Illus.). 176p. 1985. pap. text ed. 49.50 o.p. (ISBN 0-87683-693-7). GP Pub.
Self-Possession. Marion Halligan. 285p. 1988. 15.95 o.p. (ISBN 0-7022-2035-3). U of Queensland Pr.
Self-Reflection in the Arts & Sciences. A Blum & P. McHugh. 159p. 1984. text ed. 15.00x o.p. (ISBN 0-391-02877-4). Humanities.
Self Reliant Potter. (ISBN 0-671-61193-3). P-H.
Self-Renewal. rev. ed. John W. Gardner. 1981. 12.95 o.p. (ISBN 0-393-01486-X). Norton.
Self-Report Methods of Estimating Drug Use: Meeting Current Challenges of Validity. Ed. by Beatrice A. Rouse. 189p. 1985. pap. 4.25 o.p. (ISBN 0-318-18834-1, S/N 017-024-01246-7). USGPO.
Self-Steering for Sailboats. Gerard Dijkstra. (Illus.). 1979. 11.95 o.p. (ISBN 0-393-03238-8). Norton.
Self Study Books in Electrical & Semiconductor Engineering: PI-16 Three-Phase Power & Its Measurements. Programmed Instruction Staff. (Siemens Programmed Instruction "pi" Self-Study Bks.: No. 16). 67p. 1979. 4.95 o.p. (ISBN 0-471-25985-3, Wiley Heyden). Wiley.
Self-Sufficient House. Frank Coffee. LC 80-13434. (Illus.). 1981. 17.95 o.p. (ISBN 0-03-053611-1); pap. 9.95 o.p. (ISBN 0-03-059171-6). H Holt & Co.
Self-Suggestion & Its Influence on the Human Organism. A. S. Romen. Ed. by A. S. Lewis & V. Forsky. LC 80-28703. Orig. Title: Samovnushenie I Ego Vliianie Na Organizm Cheloveka. (Illus.). 456p. 1981. 40.00 o.p. (ISBN 0-87332-195-2). M E Sharpe.
Self-Teaching Process in Higher Education. P. J. Hills. 160p. 1976. 21.25 o.p. (ISBN 0-85664-288-6, Pub. by Croom Helm Ltd). Routledge Chapman & Hall.
Self-Validating Numerics For Function Space Problems: Computation With Guarantees For Differential & Integral Equations. Monograph ed. Edgar W. Kaucher & Willard L. Miranker. (Notes & Reports in Computer Science & Applied Mathematics Ser.). 1984. 39.50 o.p. (ISBN 0-12-402020-8). Acad Pr.
Selfish Giant. Oscar Wilde. (Illus.). (gr. k-3). 1978. 8.95 o.p. (ISBN 0-458-93420-8, NO. 0062). Routledge Chapman & Hall.
Selichoth Night. Gershon Kranzler. saddle-stitched 5.00 o.p. (ISBN 0-87559-132-9). Shalom.
Sell & Re-Sell Your Photos. Rohn Engh. LC 81-1877. (Illus.). 323p. 1981. 15.95 o.p. (ISBN 0-89879-046-8). Writers Digest.
Sell Like an Ace...Live Like a King. John Wolfe. 1976. 9.95 o.p. (ISBN 0-13-804211-X, Reward); pap. 5.95 o.p. (ISBN 0-13-804203-9). P-H.
Selling: A Managerial & Behavioral Science Analysis. 2nd ed. Joseph W. Thompson. (Illus.). 600p. 1973. text ed. 28.95 o.p. (ISBN 0-07-064378-4). McGraw.
Selling: A Self-Management Approach. Ferdinand F. Mauser. (Illus.). 1977. text ed. 16.50 o.p. (ISBN 0-15-579630-5, HC). HarbraceJ.
Selling & Today's Consumer: Buying? Selling? Then Do It Right! T. L. Chamberlin. 1978. 10.00 o.p. (ISBN 0-682-49127-6). Exposition-Phoenix.
Selling by Mail: An Entrepreneurial Guide to Direct Marketing. John W. Graham & Susan K. Jones. 1985. 24.95 o.s.i. (ISBN 0-684-18215-7). Scribner.
Selling by Seminar. Michael J. Enzer. 225p. 1986. 25.00 o.p. (ISBN 0-87094-762-1). Dow Jones-Irwin.
Selling: Concepts & Techniques for Today. Enis & Chonko. 1989. 35.95 o.p. (ISBN 0-256-05964-0). Irwin.
Selling Death: Cigarette Smoking & Advertising. Thomas Whiteside. LC 75-162434. 1971. 5.95 o.p. (ISBN 0-87140-541-5). Liveright.
Selling Money. S. C. Gwynne. LC 86-9143. 192p. 1986. 16.95 o.s.i. (ISBN 1-55584-005-1). Weidenfeld.
Selling of Jesus. Victor V. Bryditzki. LC 85-+012. (Illus.). 128p. (Orig.). 1985. pap. 4.25 o.p. (ISBN 0-937958-22-0). Chick Pubns.
Selling of the Royal Family: The Mystique of the British Monarchy. John Pearson. (Illus.). 319p. 1986. 17.45 o.p. (ISBN 0-671-49749-9). S&S.
Selling of the South: The Southern Crusade for Industrial Development, 1936 - 1980. James C. Cobb. LC 81-18594. 293p. 1982. text ed. 27.50 o.p. (ISBN 0-8071-0994-0). La State U Pr.
Selling of the Welfare State: The Privatisation of Council Housing. Ray Forest & Alan Murie. 192p. 1987. 43.00 o.p. (ISBN 0-7099-1081-9, Pub. by Croom Helm UK). Routledge Chapman & Hall.
Selling Out. Dan Wakefield. 352p. 1985. 16.95 o.p. (ISBN 0-316-91774-5). Little.
Selling Science: How the Press Covers Science & Technology. Dorothy Nelkin. LC 86-25820. 225p. 1988. pap. 9.95 o.p. (ISBN 0-7167-1988-6). W H Freeman.
Selling to NASA. (Illus.). 44p. (Orig.). 1986. pap. 3.25 o.p. (ISBN 0-318-22432-1, S/N 033-000-00995-0). USGPO.
Selling Your Home Sweet Home. Sloan Bashinsky. 160p. 1985. 10.95 o.p. (Dist. by Prentice Hall). Menasha Ridge.
Sell's Directory of Products & Services, 1986. 101st ed. 1986. 77.00 o.p. (ISBN 0-85499-512-9). Intl Pubns Serv.
Selma, Nineteen Sixty-Five: The March That Changed the South. Charles Fager. LC 85-35221. (Illus.). 271p. 1985. pap. 10.95 o.p. (ISBN 0-8070-0405-7, BP 695). Beacon Pr.
Selves: Drama in Perspective. Ed. by Irving Deer & Harriet A. Deer. (Illus.). 512p. 1975. pap. text ed. 8.95 o.p. (ISBN 0-15-579633-X, HC). HarBraceJ.
Selves in Relation: An Introduction to Psychotherapy & Groups. Keith Oatley. Ed. by Peter Herriot. LC 83-19525. (New Essential Psychology Ser.). 175p. 1984. pap. 6.50x o.p. (ISBN 0-416-33630-2, NO. 4057). Routledge Chapman & Hall.
Semantics of Concurrent Computation. Ed. by G. Kahn. (Lecture Notes in Computer Science Ser.: Vol. 70). 1979. pap. 22.00 o.p. (ISBN 0-387-09511-X). Springer-Verlag.
Semantics of Data Types: International Symposium, Sophia-Antipolis, France, June 27-29, 1984 Proceedings. Ed. by G. Kahn et al. (Lecture Notes in Computer Science Ser.: Vol. 173). vi, 391p. 1984. pap. 19.50 o.p. (ISBN 0-387-13346-1). Springer-Verlag.
Semantics of New Testament Greek. J. P. Louw. LC 81-67308. (Semeia Studies). 176p. 1982. pap. 12.95 o.p. (ISBN 0-8006-1511-5, Fortress). Augsburg Fortress.
Semantics of Scope in English. Anthony S. Kroch. Ed. by Jorge Hankamer. LC 78-66559. (Outstanding Dissertations in Linguistics Ser.). 1985. 38.00 o.p. (ISBN 0-8240-9681-9). Garland Pub.
Semantics of the Modal Auxiliaries. Jennifer Coates. (Illus.). 272p. 1982. 39.95 o.p. (ISBN 0-7099-0735-4, Pub. by Croom Helm Ltd). Routledge Chapman & Hall.
Semi-Groups of Operators & Approximation. P. L. Butzer & H. Berens. LC 68-11980. (Grundlehren der Mathematischen Wissenschaften: Vol. 145). 1968. 39.00 o.p. (ISBN 0-387-03832-9). Springer-Verlag.
Semi-Official Dallas Cowboys Haters' Handbook. Mark Nelson & Miller Bonner. (Illus.). 128p. 1984. pap. 4.95 o.p. (ISBN 0-02-029440-9, Collier). Macmillan.
Semi-Quadratic Poetry Quaverly Quipped in Quatrain: The Q Volume. Gene Powell. 1985. 7.95 o.p. (ISBN 0-533-06656-5). Vantage.
Semiconductor & Microprocesor Technology 1979: Proceedings of the Seminex Technical Seminar & Exhibition, London, England, March 26-30, 1979. SEMINEX Staff. Ed. by G. W. A. Dummer. (Illus.). 252p. 1980. pap. 61.00 o.p. (ISBN 0-08-026134-5). Pergamon.
Semiconductor & Microprocessor Technology 1980: Selected Papers Presented at the Annual SEMINEX Technical Seminar & Exhibition, London, U. K. Ed. by G. W. Dummer & Malvern Wells. 190p. 1981. pap. 48.00 o.p. (ISBN 0-08-028674-7). Pergamon.
Semiconductor & Microprocessor Technology 1981: Selected Papers Presented at the 1981 Annual Seminex Technical Seminar & Exhibition, London, U. K. Ed. by G. W. A. Dummer. 144p. 1982. pap. 47.00 o.p. (ISBN 0-08-028722-0). Pergamon.
Semiconductor Circuit Design: For A.C. & D.C. Amplification Switching. 3rd ed. J. Watson. 536p. 1978. 31.95x o.p. (ISBN 0-470-99236-0). Halsted Pr.
Semiconductor Circuits: Theory, Design & Experiment. J. R. Abrahams & G. J. Pridham. 1966. 65.00 o.p. (ISBN 0-08-011652-3). Pergamon.
Semiconductor Detectors in the Future of Nuclear Medicine. P. B. Hoffer et al. LC 77-159479. (Illus.). 1971. 7.50 o.p. (ISBN 0-685-76505-9). Year Bk Med.
Semiconductor Heterojunctions. B. L. Sharma & R. K. Purohit. LC 73-18449. 1974. 55.00 o.p. (ISBN 0-08-017747-6). Pergamon.
Semiconductor Physics. P. S. Kireev. 672p. 1978. 10.80 o.p. (ISBN 0-8285-0802-X, Pub. by Mir Pubs USSR). Imported Pubns.
Semiconductor Power Devices: Physics of Operation & Fabrication Technology. Sorab K. Ghandhi. LC 77-8019. 329p. 1977. 45.95x o.p. (ISBN 0-471-02999-8, Pub by Wiley-Interscience). Wiley.
Semiconductor Technology 1975. Geoffrey W. Dummer. 1976. pap. 35.00 o.p. (ISBN 0-08-019976-3). Pergamon.
Semiconductor Technology 1976. Ed. by Geoffrey W. Dummer. 1977. pap. 35.00 o.p. (ISBN 0-08-020983-1). Pergamon.
Semiconductor Technology 1977. Geoffrey W. Dummer. 1977. pap. 43.00 o.p. (ISBN 0-08-022148-3). Pergamon.

Semiconductor Technology 1978. Geoffrey W. Dummer. 1979. pap. 57.00 o.p. (ISBN 0-08-024205-7). Pergamon.

Semiconductors. Ed. by Robert A. Smith. (Italian Physical Society: Course 22). 1963. 99.50 o.p. (ISBN 0-12-368822-1). Acad Pr.

Semigroups. Ed. by T. E. Hall et al. LC 80-23748. 1980. 44.50 o.p. (ISBN 0-12-319450-4). Acad Pr.

Semimetals & Narrow-Bandgap Semiconductors. D. R. Lovett. 1977. 29.00x o.p. (ISBN 0-85086-060-1, NO. 2939, Pub. by Pion England). Routledge Chapman & Hall.

Seminar for Murder. B. M. Gill. 224p. 1986. 13.95 o.s.i. (ISBN 0-684-18651-9). Scribner.

Seminar Material, Filing & Administering a Chapter 13 Proceeding. Institute for Continuing Legal Education (New Jersey) Staff. LC 83-182218. 0.00 o.p. NJ Inst CLE.

Seminar Material for Settlement Techniques. New Jersey Institute for Continuing Legal Education Staff & Herman L. Breitkopf. LC 83-187456. (Illus.). 128p. 0.00 o.p. NJ Inst CLE.

Seminar Materials for ICLE's Second Annual Symposium on Residential Real Estate Law & Practice. Residential Real Estate Law & Practice Symposium Staff et al. LC 83-186193. 0.00 o.p. NJ Inst CLE.

Seminar Materials for Local Property Taxes & the New Jersey Tax Court. Institute for Continuing Legal Education (New Jersey) Staff & Lawrence L. Lasser. LC 83-181740. (Illus.). ii, 167p. 0.00 o.p. NJ Inst CLE.

Seminar on Childhood Poisoning. Ed. by G. D. Maragos. (Journal: Paediatrician Ser.: Vol. 6, No. 3-5). (Illus.). 1978. 62.00 o.p. (ISBN 3-8055-2863-9). S Karger.

Seminar on Office Pediatrics, Part I. Ed. by G. D. Maragos. (Journal: Paediatrician: Vol. 7, No. 6). (Illus.). 1979. pap. 20.75 o.p. (ISBN 3-8055-3010-2). S Karger.

Seminary: A Search. Paul Hendrickson. 320p. 1983. 14.50 o.s.i. (ISBN 0-671-42030-5). Summit Bks.

Seminary: A Search. Paul Hendrickson. 320p. 1987. pap. 6.95 o.s.i. (ISBN 0-671-63586-7). Summit Bks.

Semiology. Pierre Guiraud. 1975. 18.00x o.p. (ISBN 0-7100-8005-0); pap. 7.95x o.p. (ISBN 0-7100-8011-5). Routledge Chapman & Hall.

Semiology, Symbolism & Architecture: A Selected & Partially Annotated Bibliography. William Gwin & Mary M. Gwin. (Architecture Ser.: Bibliography A 1346). 1985. pap. 3.00 o.p. (ISBN 0-89028-316-8). Vance Biblios.

Semiotics & Legal Theory. Bernard S. Jackson. 350p. 1985. 27.50x o.p. (ISBN 0-7100-9719-0). Routledge Chapman & Hall.

Semiotics 1980. Ed. by Michael Herzfeld & Margot D. Lenhart. LC 81-23386. 606p. 1982. 85.00x o.p. (ISBN 0-306-40827-9, Plenum Pr). Plenum Pub.

Semiramis see Poesies.

Semisynthetic Peptides & Proteins. Ed. by R. E. Offord & C. Dibello. 1978. 54.50 o.p. (ISBN 0-12-524350-2). Acad Pr.

Semisynthetic Proteins. R. E. Offord. LC 79-40521. 235p. 1980. 104.00x o.p. (ISBN 0-471-27615-4, Pub. by Wiley-Interscience). Wiley.

Semitic Background of the Term, Mystery in the New Testament. Raymond E. Brown. Ed. by John Reumann. LC 68-56269. (Facet Bks. Biblical Ser). (Orig.). 1968. pap. 1.00 o.p. (ISBN 0-8006-3047-5, Fortress). Augsburg Fortress.

Semka, The Sammy Skobel Story. Skobel & McDonald. 1982. 10.95 o.p. (ISBN 0-89803-108-7, Dist. by Kampmann). Green Hill.

Semper Fi Mac: Living Memories of the U. S. Marines in World War II. Henry Berry. LC 81-71664. (Illus.). 370p. 1982. 16.95 o.p. (ISBN 0-87795-370-8, Arbor Hse). Morrow.

Senate Rubberstamp Machine. 150p. 1977. 1.00 o.p. (ISBN 0-914389-09-2). Common Cause.

Senate vs. Governor, Alabama 1971: Referents for Opposition in a One-Party Legislature. Harold W. Stanley. LC 74-23369. (Illus.). 126p. 1975. 9.75 o.s.i. (ISBN 0-8173-4827-1). U of Ala Pr.

Senator Gerald P. Nye & American Foreign Relations. Wayne S. Cole. LC 80-17370. (Illus.). 293p. 1980. Repr. of 1962 ed. lib. bdg. 35.00x o.p. (ISBN 0-313-22660-1, COSN). Greenwood.

Senator Joe McCarthy. Rovere. 1959. 4.95 o.p. (ISBN 0-15-180801-5). HarBraceJ.

Senator John Slidell & the Community He Represented in Washington, 1853-1861. A. L. Diket. LC 81-43676. 278p. (Orig.). 1982. lib. bdg. 30.50 o.p. (ISBN 0-8191-2547-4); pap. text ed. 14.00 o.p. (ISBN 0-8191-2548-2). U Pr of Amer.

Senator Robert F. Wagner & the Rise of Urban Liberalism. J. Joseph Huthmacher. LC 68-16869. (Illus.). 1971. pap. text ed. 3.45x o.p. (ISBN 0-689-70259-0, 167, Atheneum). Macmillan.

Senators from Georgia. Josephine Mellichamp. LC 75-32113. 1976. 12.95 o.p. (ISBN 0-87397-082-9). Strode.

Send in the Lions. Eric Clark. LC 80-69371. 1981. 10.95 o.p. (ISBN 0-689-11125-8, Atheneum). Macmillan.

Send These to Me: Jews & Other Immigrants in Urban America. John Higham. LC 74-77844. 1975. pap. text ed. 4.95x o.p. (ISBN 0-689-70527-1, 216, Atheneum). Macmillan.

Senderos de Comunion. Francisco E. Estrello. 1.75 o.p. (ISBN 0-8358-0416-X). Upper Room.

Sending Messages. John W. Stewig. LC 77-26110. (Illus.). (gr. 3-7). 1978. PLB 6.95 o.p. (ISBN 0-395-24387-4). HM.

Senile Retinoschisis: Morphological Relationship of the Formation of Spaces Within the Peripheral Retina to Senile Retinochisis & to Schisis Detachment. W. Gottinger. Tr. by J. W. Bayo. LC 77-93498. (Illus.). 66p. 1978. pap. 20.00 o.p. (ISBN 0-88416-243-5). Year Bk Med.

Senior Citizens' Cartoons. 2nd ed. William Armstrong. (Armstrong Cartoon Ser.). (Illus.). 48p. (Orig.). (ps up). 1971. pap. 1.00 o.p. (ISBN 0-913452-12-2). Jesuit Bks.

Senior Dropout. James L. Summers. (gr. 7-10). 1965. 5.50 o.s.i. (ISBN 0-664-32356-1, Westminster). Westminster John Knox.

Senior Examiner-Social Services. Jack Rudman. (Career Examination Ser.: C-2139). (Cloth bdg. avail. on request). 1988. pap. 14.00 o.p. (ISBN 0-8373-2139-5). Natl Learning.

Senior High School Principalship: The Effective Principal, Vol. II. Richard A. Gorton & Kenneth E. McIntyre. Ed. by Thomas F. Koerner. 1978. pap. 9.00 o.p. (ISBN 0-88210-094-7). Natl Assn Principals.

Senior High School Principalship: The National Survey, Vol. I. Ed. by Thomas F. Koerner. 1978. pap. 9.00 o.p. (ISBN 0-88210-091-2). Natl Assn Principals.

Senior High School Principalship: The Summary Report, Vol. III. Lloyd McCleary & Scott Thomson. Ed. by Thomas Koerner. 1979. pap. text ed. 6.75 o.p. (ISBN 0-88210-098-X). Natl Assn Principals.

Senior Personnel Examiner. Jack Rudman. (Career Examination Ser.: C-1017). (Cloth bdg. avail. on request). pap. 10.00 o.p. (ISBN 0-8373-1017-2). Natl Learning.

Senior Principal Supervising Cashier-TA. Jack Rudman. (Career Examination Ser.: C-2005). (Cloth bdg. avail. on request). pap. 12.00 o.p. (ISBN 0-8373-2005-4). Natl Learning.

Senior Year. Anne Emery. (Illus.). (gr. 5-9). 1949. 4.95 o.s.i. (ISBN 0-664-32051-1, Westminster). Westminster John Knox.

Sensation & Perception. 2nd ed. Stanley Coren et al. 606p. 1984. text ed. 30.00 net o.p. (ISBN 0-15-579634-8, COREN2, HC, HC). HarBraceJ.

Sensation & Perception. 2nd ed. E. Bruce Goldstein. 481p. 1984. text ed. (ISBN 0-534-03035-1). Wadsworth Pub.

Sensation & Perception in the History of Experimental Psychology. Edwin G. Boring. (Century Psychology Ser). 1977. Repr. of 1942 ed. 49.50x o.p. (ISBN 0-89197-491-1). Irvington.

Sensational Vegetarian Salads - Crisp, Colorful & Delicious: Dishes for All Seasons. Desda Crockett. (Illus.). 128p. (Orig.). pap. (ISBN 0-7225-1527-8, Pub. by Thorsons (England)). Sterling.

Sense & Sensibility in Childbirth: A Guide to Supportive Obstetrical Care. Judith Herzfeld. (Illus.). 176p. 1987. pap. 6.70 o.p. (ISBN 0-393-30381-0). Norton.

Sense & Sensuality. Rosalind Brackenbury. 256p. 1987. 14.95 o.s.i. (ISBN 0-8008-7062-X). Taplinger.

Sense of Biblical Narrative II: Stuctural Analyses in the Hebrew Bible. David Jobling. (JSOT Supplement Ser.: No. 39). 152p. pap. text ed. 8.95x o.s.i. (Pub. by JSOT Pr England). Eisenbrauns.

Sense of Grace: Celebrating the Life of the Honorable Grace Olivier Peck. Thomas Vaughan et al. LC 80-84479. (Illus.). 72p. 1981. pap. 25.00 o.p. (ISBN 0-87595-096-5). Oregon Hist.

Sense of History: The Best Writing from the Pages of American Heritage. Ed. by American Heritage Staff. LC 85-7516. 832p. 1985. 29.95 o.p. (ISBN 0-8281-1175-8, Dist. by H M). Am Heritage.

Sense of Life, a Sense of Sin. Eugene C. Kennedy. 200p. 1976. pap. 3.50 o.p. (ISBN 0-385-12070-2, Im). Doubleday.

Sense of Mission: Guidance from the Gospel of John. Albert C. Winn. LC 80-28000. 118p. 1981. pap. 6.95 o.s.i. (ISBN 0-664-24365-7, Westminster). Westminster John Knox.

Sense of Performance in the Post-Art Theatre. S. Tharu. 210p. 1983. text ed. 12.50x o.p. (ISBN 0-391-03050-7). Humanities.

Sense of Shadow. Kate Wilhelm. 1981. 9.95 o.p. (ISBN 0-395-30545-4). HM.

Sense of the Cosmos: The Encounter of Modern Science with Ancient Truth. Jacob Needleman. 192p. 1988. pap. text ed. 12.95 o.p. (ISBN 1-85063-105-0). Routledge Chapman & Hall.

Sense of the Past. Graeme Garden. (Illus.). 124p. 1988. 18.95 o.p. (ISBN 0-7063-6345-0, Pub. by Ward Lock). David & Charles.

Sense of Touch. Tr. by E. H. Weber. (Experimental Psychology Ser.). 1978. 73.00 o.p. (ISBN 0-12-740550-X). Acad Pr.

Sense of Warning. Barry N. Kaufman. 320p. (Orig.). 1984. pap. 3.50 o.p. (ISBN 0-440-17923-8). Dell.

Senseless. J. Douglas Burtt. (Orig.). 1981. pap. 1.95 o.p. (ISBN 0-505-51637-3, Pub. by Tower Bks). Dorchester Pub Co.

Senses Considered As Perceptual Systems. James J. Gibson. LC 66-7132. 1972. text ed. 34.50 o.p. (ISBN 0-395-04494-4). HM.

Senses of Animals & Men. Lorus Milne & Margery Milne. LC 62-9411. (Illus.). 1962. pap. 3.25 o.p. (ISBN 0-689-70333-3, 192, Atheneum). Macmillan.

Sensing. James Campbell et al. (Themepaks Ser.). (gr. 1-6). 1977. 4.95 o.p. (ISBN 0-8042-1460-3, John Knox). Westminster John Knox.

Sensing & Communication Between Vehicles. (National Cooperative Highway Research Program Report). 105p. 1968. 5.00 o.p. (ISBN 0-317-36104-X, 1585). Transport Res Bd.

Sensing: Letting Yourself Live. Betty W. Keane. LC 78-4753. 1979. 12.95i o.p. (ISBN 0-06-250470-3). HarpR.

Sensitive Man & the Christ. Robert K. Hudnut. LC 72-135268. (Orig.). 1972. pap. 2.50 o.p. (ISBN 0-8006-0160-2, Fortress). Augsburg Fortress.

Sensitive Thoughts for the New Wave Soul. Denise A. Reynolds. 1984. 6.95 o.p. (ISBN 0-8062-2291-3). Carlton.

Sensitives. Herbert Burkholz. LC 86-2645. 288p. 1987. 18.95 o.p. (ISBN 0-689-11842-2, Atheneum). Macmillan.

Sensitivity & Optimization. R. Spence & R. Brayton. (Computer Aided Design of Electrical Circuits Ser.: Vol. 2). 1977. 105.25 o.p. (ISBN 0-444-41929-2). Elsevier.

Sensitivity Methods in Control Theory. Ed. by L. Radanovic. 1966. 110.00 o.p. (ISBN 0-08-011827-5); pap. 110.00 o.p. (ISBN 0-08-013784-9). Pergamon.

Sensitivity to Social Change. National Association for Women Deans, Administrators & Counselors. 1977. pap. 3.00 o.p. (ISBN 0-686-17827-0). Natl Assn Women.

Sensor Design Using Computer Tools: Proceedings of SPIE Seminar on Sensor Design Using Computer Tools, Los Angeles, California, Jan., 1982. SPIE - International Society for Optical Engineering Staff. Ed. by John A. Jamieson. (SPIE Seminar Proceedings: Vol. 327). 208p. 1982. 40.00 o.p. (ISBN 0-89252-362-X); 34.00, members o.p. (ISBN 0-317-34759-4). SPIE.

Sensory Aids for the Hearing Impaired. Ed. by Harry Levitt & James M. Pickett. LC 76-28875. 566p. 1980. 56.95 o.p. (ISBN 0-471-08436-0, Pub. by Wiley-Interscience); pap. 33.95x o.p. (ISBN 0-471-08437-9). Wiley.

Sensory Analysis of Food. Ed. by John R. Piggott. 396p. 1984. 88.25 o.p. (ISBN 0-85334-272-5, I-263-84, Pub. by Elsevier Applied Sci England). Elsevier.

Sensory Deprivation: Fifteen Years of Research. Ed. by John P. Zubek. LC 69-12143. (Century Psychology Ser.). (Illus.). 1969. 47.50x o.p. (ISBN 0-89197-400-8); pap. text ed. 24.95x o.p. (ISBN 0-89197-401-6). Irvington.

Sensory Functions of the Skin with Special Reference to Man. Ed. by Yngve Zotterman. LC 76-20572. 1976. 120.00 o.p. (ISBN 0-08-021208-5). Pergamon.

Sensory Functions: Proceedings of the 28th International Congress of Physiological Sciences, Budapest, 1980. Ed. by E. Grastyan & P. Molnar. LC 80-41852. (Advances in Physiological Sciences). (Illus.). 350p. 1981. 57.00 o.p. (ISBN 0-08-027337-8). Pergamon.

Sensory Integration: Handbook of Behavioral Neurobiology, Vol 1. Ed. by R. Bruce Masterton. LC 78-17238. 600p. 1978. 85.00x o.p. (ISBN 0-306-35191-9, Plenum Pr). Plenum Pub.

Sensory Mechanisms of the Spinal Cord. Ed. by W. D. Willis & R. E. Coggeshall. LC 78-15764. 494p. 1978. 69.50x o.p. (ISBN 0-306-40083-9, Plenum Pr). Plenum Pub.

Sensory Physiology of Aquatic Lower Vertebrates: Proceedings of a Satellite Symposium of the 28th International Congress of Physiological Sciences, Budapest, Hungary, 1980. Ed. by T. Szabo & C. Czeh. LC 80-42204. (Advances in Physiological Sciences Ser.: Vol. 31). (Illus.). 280p. 1981. 50.00 o.p. (ISBN 0-08-027352-1). Pergamon.

Sensory Reception: Cytology, Molecular Mechanisms & Evolution. Y. A. Vinnikov. LC 74-412. (Molecular Biology, Biochemistry & Biophysics Ser.: Vol. 17). (Illus.). x, 392p. 1974. 71.00 o.p. (ISBN 0-387-06674-8). Springer-Verlag.

Sensory Systems of Primates. Ed. by Charles R. Noback. LC 78-15383. (Advances In Primatology Ser.). (Illus.). 220p. 1978. 49.50x o.p. (ISBN 0-306-31127-5, Plenum Pr). Plenum Pub.

Sensual Pleasure: A Woman's Guide. Eva L. Margolies. 192p. (Orig.). 1981. pap. 5.95 o.p. (ISBN 0-380-78006-2, 83592-4). Avon.

Sensuality of Strength. Gayle Olinekova. (Illus.). 128p. 1984. pap. 9.50 o.p. (ISBN 0-671-49187-3, Fireside). S&S.

Sensuous Angel. Heather X. Graham. (Candlelight Ecstasy Ser.: No. 359). 192p. 1985. pap. 2.25 o.p. (ISBN 0-440-17636-0). Dell.

Sent from the Father: Meditations on the Fourth Gospel. Jose Comblin. Tr. by Carl Kabat from Port. LC 78-16750. Orig. Title: O Enviado do Pai. 115p. (Orig.). 1979. pap. 2.48 o.p. (ISBN 0-88344-453-4). Orbis Bks.

Sentence Book. Lee A. Jacobus. 1976. pap. text ed. 8.95 o.p. (ISBN 0-15-579640-2, HC). HarBraceJ.

Sentence Book. 2nd ed. Lee A. Jacobus. 223p. 1980. pap. text ed. 10.00 o.p. (ISBN 0-15-579645-3, HC). HarBraceJ.

Sentence Combing & Paragraph Construction. Katie Davis. 244p. 1983. pap. text ed. write for info. o.p. (ISBN 0-02-327880-3). Macmillan.

Sentence Sense: A Basic Grammar. Enno Klammer. LC 76-49780. 437p. 1977. pap. text ed. 10.95 o.p. (ISBN 0-15-579670-4, HC). HarBraceJ.

Sentence Skills: A Workbook for Writers. John Langan. 1979. pap. text ed. 16.95 o.p. (ISBN 0-07-036255-6). McGraw.

Sentence Structure. Philip Lutgendorf & Mary Jane Gray. LC 77-730353. (Illus.). (gr. 7-9). 1977. pap. text ed. 209.00 o.s.i. (ISBN 0-89290-119-5, A144). Soc for Visual.

Sentencing Guidelines & Policy Statements, 3 Bks. 215p. (Orig.). 1987. pap. 16.00 o.p. (ISBN 0-318-22948-X, S/N 052-070-06305-0). USGPO.

Sentencing in Washington. David Boerner. 833p. 1985. 120.00 o.p. Butterworth WA.

Sentencing: The Decision As to Type, Length, & Conditions of Sentence. Robert O. Dawson. 428p. 1969. pap. 7.95 o.p. (ISBN 0-316-17739-3). Little.

Sententiae Petri Pictaviensis 1. Philip S. Moore & Marthe Dulong. (Mediaeval Studies Ser.: No. 7). (Lat). 1943. 40.00 o.p. (ISBN 0-268-00250-9). U of Notre Dame Pr.

Sententiae Petri Pictaviensis 2. Philip S. Moore et al. (Mediaeval Studies Ser: No. 11). (Lat). 1950. pap. 20.00 o.p. (ISBN 0-268-00391-2). U of Notre Dame Pr.

Sentimental Education. Gustave Flaubert. 448p. pap. 3.95 o.p. (ISBN 0-452-00719-4, CE 1692, Sig Classics). NAL.

Sentinel. Jeffrey Konvitz. 1981. pap. 2.50 o.s.i. (ISBN 0-345-30437-3). Ballantine.

Sentinels of Peace: The Soviet Armed Forces. 175p. 1980. 22.50 o.p. (ISBN 0-8285-2072-0, Pub. by Progress Pubs USSR). Imported Pubns.

Sentinels of Solitude: West Coast Lighthouses. Photos by Chad Ehlers. LC 81-81324. (Illus.). 88p. (Orig., Text by James Gibbs). 1981. pap. 9.95 o.s.i. (ISBN 0-912856-72-6). Gr Arts Ctr Pub.

Sentinels of the North Pacific. James A. Gibbs. (Illus.). 1955. 10.95 o.p. (ISBN 0-8323-0011-X). Binford-Metropolitan.

Separable Algebras over Commutative Rings. F. DeMeyer & E. Ingraham. LC 70-151404. (Lecture Notes in Mathematics: Vol. 181). 1971. pap. 8.20 o.p. (ISBN 0-387-05371-9). Springer-Verlag.

Separate & Unequal: Public School Campaigns & Racism in the Southern Seaboard States, 1901-1915. Louis R. Harlan. LC 68-16414. (Studies in American Negro Life). 1968. pap. 2.75 o.p. (ISBN 0-689-70088-1, NL2, Atheneum). Macmillan.

Separate Development. Christopher Hope. 180p. 1981. 10.95 o.s.i. (ISBN 0-684-17308-5, ScribT). Scribner.

Separate Development. Christopher Hope. 208p. 1983. pap. 4.95 o.s.i. (ISBN 0-684-17835-4, ScribT). Scribner.

Separate Peace. John Knowles. 48p. (Orig.). 1988. pap. 9.95 o.p. (ISBN 1-55651-829-3); audiocassette tape incl. o.p. (ISBN 1-55651-830-7). Cram Cassettes.

Separate Vacations. Eric Weber. 1979. pap. 2.50 o.p. (ISBN 0-380-47266-X, 47266-X). Avon.

Separate Worlds. Sharon Conrad. 40p. 1988. 6.95 o.p. (ISBN 0-8062-3059-2). Carlton.

Separation & Divorce in North Carolina: How to Do It with or Without a Lawyer. Michael H. McGee. LC 84-48036. 144p. 1984. pap. 9.95 o.p. (ISBN 0-88742-011-7). Globe Pequot.

Separation & Purification of Materials. R. Hammond. (Illus.). 320p. (ISBN 0-8022-0671-9). Philos Lib.

Separation Methods in Organic Chemistry & Biochemistry. E. J. Wolf. 1969. 29.95 o.p. (ISBN 0-12-761650-0). Acad Pr.

Separation of Cells & Subcellular Elements. Ed. by H. Peeters. (Illus.). 1979. 34.00 o.p. (ISBN 0-08-024957-4). Pergamon.

Separation Techniques I: Liquid-Liquid Systems. Chemical Engineering Magazine Editors. (Chemical Engineering Book). 384p. 1980. text ed. 39.95 o.p. (ISBN 0-07-010711-4). McGraw.

Separation Techniques II: Gas-Liquid-Solid Systems. Chemical Engineering Magazine Editors. (Chemical Engineering Book). 400p. 1980. text ed. 36.50 o.p. (ISBN 0-07-010717-3). McGraw.

Sephardic Jews of Bordeaux: Assimilation & Emancipation in Revolutionary & Napoleonic France. Frances Malino. LC 77-22659. (Judaic Studies: Vol. 7). 200p. 1978. 15.75 o.p. (ISBN 0-8173-6903-1). U of Ala Pr.

Sept Femmes de Gilbert le Mauvais. Michel Butor. (Coll. Scholies). 10.95 o.p. (ISBN 0-685-37260-X). French & Eur.

September Echoes: A Study of the Maryland Campaign of 1862. John W. Schildt. (Illus.). 140p. (Orig.). 1984. pap. 6.95 o.p. (ISBN 0-932751-01-6). Beidel Printing Hse.

Septimus Bean & His Amazing Machine. Janet Quin-Harkin. LC 79-163. (Illus.). 48p. (ps-3). 1980. 5.95 o.s.i. (ISBN 0-8193-0999-0); PLB 5.95 o.s.i. (ISBN 0-8193-1000-X). Parents.

Sequence: A Basic Writing Course. Rory D. Stephens. 1982. pap. text ed. 14.95 o.p. (ISBN 0-03-055256-7). HR&W.

Sequencing Theory. S. Ashour. LC 72-83014. (Lecture Notes in Economics & Mathematical Systems: Vol. 69). (Illus.). 138p. 1972. pap. 6.30 o.p. (ISBN 0-387-05877-X). Springer-Verlag.

Sequential Development of Reading Abilities. Helen M. Robinson. LC 60-14354. (Supplementary Educational Monographs; Midway Reprint Ser.). (Illus.). 1977. pap. text ed. 11.00x o.s.i. (ISBN 0-226-72188-4, SEM 90). U of Chicago Pr.

Sequential Methods in Statistics. 2nd ed. G. Barrie Wetherill. (Monographs in Applied Probability & Statistics). 1975. pap. 17.95x o.p. (ISBN 0-412-21810-0, NO. 6317, Pub. by Chapman & Hall). Routledge Chapman & Hall.

Sequential Transmission of Digital Information. D. A. Klousky. 215p. 1978. 4.95 o.p. (ISBN 0-8285-0694-9, Pub. by Mir Pubs USSR). Imported Pubns.

Sequestree de Poitiers. Andre Gide. 145p. 1977. 3.95 o.p. (ISBN 0-686-56056-6). Schoenhof.

Sequestres d'Altona. Jean-Paul Sartre. (Coll. Soleil). 1960. 14.50 o.p. (ISBN 0-685-11559-3). Schoenhof.

Ser y el Mesias see Being & the Messiah: The Message of St. John.

Seraffyn's European Adventures. Lin Pardey & Larry Pardey. (Illus.). 1979. 17.50 o.p. (ISBN 0-393-03231-0). Norton.

Seraffyn's Mediterranen Adventure. Lin Pardey & Larry Pardey. (Illus.). 1981. 18.95 o.p. (ISBN 0-393-03266-3). Norton.

SERB Official Reporter. 1987. 155.00 o.p. (ISBN 0-8322-0235-5). Banks-Baldwin.

Serbo-Croat for Foreigners. 4th ed. S. Babic. (Illus.). 1977. pap. 7.50 o.s.i. (ISBN 0-685-58560-3). E J Brill USA.

Serbo-Croatian, English: English-Serbo Croatian Dictionary, 2 vols. Morton Benson. 1373p. 1987. 55.00 ea. o.p. (ISBN 0-87052-399-6) (ISBN 0-87052-398-8). Hippocrene Bks.

Serbo-Croatian for Foreigners. Slauna Babic. 240p. 1987. 9.95 o.p. (ISBN 0-87052-397-X). Hippocrene Bks.

Serbo-Croatian Reading Passages, with Comments, Exercises, Vocabulary. S. Babic. 1975. 10.00 o.p. (ISBN 0-88431-623-8). E J Brill USA.

Serena' Magic. Heather X. Graham. (Candlelight Ecstasy Ser.: No. 271). 192p. (Orig.). 1984. pap. 1.95 o.s.i. (ISBN 0-440-17860-6). Dell.

Serenade: The Stories of Joseph A. L. Poitras. Joseph A. Poitras. 130p. 1985. 10.95 o.p. (ISBN 0-533-06213-6). Vantage.

Serendipity in St. Helena. I. Shine. 1970. 51.00 o.p. (ISBN 0-08-012794-0). Pergamon.

Serendipity New Testament for Groups: New International Version. Lyman Coleman. 9.95 o.p. (ISBN 0-8091-2863-2). Paulist Pr.

Serene Thoughts of a Poet. Neagu Vulcanescu. 1979. pap. 5.00 o.p. (ISBN 0-682-49357-0). Exposition-Phoenix.

Serge Koussevitsky, the Boston Symphony Orchestra & the New American Music. Hugo Leichtentritt. 199p. Repr. of 1946 ed. lib. bdg. 39.00 o.p. (Pub. by Am Repr Serv). Reprint Servs.

Serge Lifar Collection of Ballet & Costume Design. (Illus.). 84p. 1965. pap. 5.00 o.p. (ISBN 0-317-13580-5). Wadsworth Atheneum.

Sergeant Getulio. Joao U. Ribeiro. 1977. 7.95 o.p. (ISBN 0-395-25705-0). HM.

Sergeant Hawk: Under Attack. Patrick Clay. (Sergeant Hawk: No. 3). 256p. 1981. pap. 2.25 o.p. (ISBN 0-8439-0962-5, Pub. by Leisure Bks CT). Dorchester Pub Co.

Sergeant's Colonel. Walter C. Krause. LC 85-91003. (Illus.). 224p. 1985. 13.50 o.p. (ISBN 0-682-40241-9). Exposition-Phoenix.

Sergei Prokofiev: A Soviet Tragedy. Victor Seroff. LC 78-73657. 1979. 14.95 o.s.i. (ISBN 0-8008-7067-0, Crescendo); pap. 7.95 o.s.i. (ISBN 0-8008-7068-9, Crescendo). Taplinger.

Sergei Witte & the Industrialization of Russia. Theodore Von Laue. LC 63-10520. (Illus.). 1969. pap. text ed. 4.95x o.p. (ISBN 0-689-70196-9, 141, Atheneum). Macmillan.

Sergei Yesenin: The Man, the Verse, the Age. Y. Prokushev. 309p. 1979. 9.45 o.p. (ISBN 0-8285-1567-0, Pub. by Progress Pubs USSR). Imported Pubns.

Serial Arrangement of Chinese Characters. George A. Kennedy. 2.00 o.p. (ISBN 0-88710-087-2). Yale Far Eastern Pubns.

Serial Dissections of the Human Brain. Carlton G. Smith. LC 81-2540. (Illus.). 100p. 1981. text ed. 17.00 o.p. (ISBN 0-8067-1811-0). Urban & S.

Serial Publications in Large Libraries. Ed. by Walter C. Allen. LC 74-629637. (Allerton Park Institute Ser.: No. 16). 194p. 1970. 6.00x o.p. (ISBN 0-87845-011-4). U of Ill Lib Info Sci.

Serials in Selected European Languages: The Language Problem. Jeanne H. Shedd. (Occasional Papers: No. 132). 51p. 1978. pap. 2.00 o.p. (ISBN 0-317-58970-9). U of Ill Lib Info Sci.

Serials: Past, Present & Future. Clara D. Brown & Lynn S. Smith. LC 80-81267. 1980. 19.50x o.p. (ISBN 0-913956-05-8). EBSCO Ind.

Series III: Nineteen Seventy-Eight Revenue Act Forward. (Primary Sources Ser.). write for info. o.p. BNA.

Series in Mathematics Modules, 5 Modules. Leon Ablon et al. 1981. pap. Module 1. pap. 8.95 o.p. (ISBN 0-8053-0131-3); Module 2. pap. 8.95 o.p. (ISBN 0-8053-0132-1); Module 3. pap. 8.95 o.p. (ISBN 0-8053-0133-X); Module 4. pap. 8.95 o.p. (ISBN 0-8053-0134-8); Module 5. pap. 8.95 o.p. (ISBN 0-8053-0135-6). Benjamin-Cummings.

Series in Mathematics Modules: Practical Mathematics, Module 2A. Helen B. Siner. Ed. by Leon J. Ablon. LC 75-12083. 1975. Module 2A. pap. text ed. 7.95 o.p. (ISBN 0-8465-6714-8). Benjamin-Cummings.

Series of Elementary Exercises upon Geological Maps. John Platt. 1974. pap. text ed. 6.95x o.p. (ISBN 0-04-550019-3). Unwin Hyman.

Series TV: How a Show Is Made. Malka Drucker & Elizabeth James. LC 83-2119. (Illus.). 112p. (gr. 4up). 1983. 11.45 o.p. (ISBN 0-89919-142-8, Clarion). HM.

Serious Call to a Contemplative Lifestyle. E. Glenn Hinson. LC 74-9658. 120p. 1974. pap. 3.95 o.s.i. (ISBN 0-664-24992-2, Westminster). Westminster John Knox.

Serious Call to Holy Living. Abriged by ed. William Law. 96p. 1985. pap. 3.95 o.p. (ISBN 0-8423-5861-7). Tyndale.

Serious Programming in BASIC. Henry Simpson. (Illus.). 224p. 1986. 21.95 o.p. (ISBN 0-8306-0350-6, 2650); pap. 14.60 o.p. (ISBN 0-8306-2650-6, 2650P). Tab Bks.

Serious Reduction of Hazardous Waste for Pollution Prevention & Industrial Efficiency. LC 86-600571. (OTA-ITE-317 Ser.). 264p. (Orig.). 1986. pap. 12.00 o.p. (ISBN 0-318-21557-8, S/N 052-003-01048-8). USGPO.

Serious Stories for Children. Michael Oswald. 1978. 4.00 o.p. (ISBN 0-682-48786-4). Exposition-Phoenix.

Seris. David Burckhalter. LC 75-44915. 80p. 1976. pap. 7.50 o.p. (ISBN 0-8165-0517-9). U of Ariz Pr.

Serizawa: A Living Treasure of Japan. Commentary by Martha Longenecker. LC 79-90086. (Illus.). 45p. 1979. 7.50 o.s.i. (ISBN 0-317-68014-5). Mingei Intl Mus.

Sermon on the Mount. Joachim Jeremias. Ed. by John Reumann. Tr. by Norman Perrin from Ger. LC 63-17882. (Facet Bks.). (Orig.). 1963. pap. 2.50 o.p. (ISBN 0-8006-3002-5, 1-3002, Fortress). Augsburg Fortress.

Sermon on the Mount. Eduard Thurneysen. LC 64-12625. 1964. pap. 1.95 o.p. (ISBN 0-8042-3448-5, John Knox). Westminster John Knox.

Sermon Outlines on the Person & Work of Christ. George W. Lockaby. LC 80-67916. 1981. pap. 2.95 o.p. (ISBN 0-8054-2238-2). Broadman.

Sermons for Special Occasions. 1981. pap. 5.95 o.p. (ISBN 0-570-03825-1, 12-2790). Concordia.

Sermons of Athens Clay Pullias. Athens C. Pullias. Ed. by J. D. Thomas. (Great Preachers Ser). 1962. 11.95 o.p. (ISBN 0-89112-203-6). Abilene Christ U.

Sermons of B. C. Goodpasture. B. C. Goodpasture. Ed. by J. D. Thomas. (Great Preachers Ser). 1967. 11.95 o.p. (ISBN 0-89112-212-5). Abilene Christ U.

Sermons of Jim Bill McInteer. Ed. by J. D. Thomas. (Great Preachers Ser). 1966. 9.95 o.p. (ISBN 0-89112-210-9). Abilene Christ U.

Sermons of M. Norvel Young. Ed. by J. D. Thomas. (Great Preachers Ser). 1963. 11.95 o.p. (ISBN 0-89112-204-4). Abilene Christ U.

Sermons of Willard Collins. Ed. by J. D. Thomas. (Great Preachers Ser). 1964. 9.95 o.p. (ISBN 0-89112-206-0). Abilene Christ U.

Serologic Analysis of Human Cancer Antigens. Ed. by Steven A. Rosenberg. LC 79-19361. 1980. 77.00 o.p. (ISBN 0-12-597160-5). Acad Pr.

Serological Epidemology. Ed. by John R. Paul & Colin White. 1973. 58.50 o.p. (ISBN 0-12-547550-0). Acad Pr.

Serotonin & Behavior. Jack Barchas. Ed. by Earl Usdin. 1973. 75.00 o.p. (ISBN 0-12-078150-6). Acad Pr.

Serpent & the Rainbow. E. Wades Davis. 288p. 1986. 17.45 o.p. (ISBN 0-671-50247-6). S&S.

Serpent & the Satellite. F. A. Morin. 1953. (ISBN 0-8022-1149-6). Philos Lib.

Serpent & the Stag: The Saga of England's Powerful & Glamourous Cavendish Family from the Age of Henry the Eighth to the Present. John Pearson. 1984. 19.95 o.s.i. (ISBN 0-03-055431-4, William Abrahams Bk). H Holt & Co.

Serpentine Assassin. Flint Dille & David Marconi. LC 86-52198. (Agent 13 (the Midnight Avenger) Ser.: Bk. 2). 192p. (Orig.). 1986. pap. 2.95 o.p. (ISBN 0-88038-282-1). TSR Inc.

Serpentine Futures. Lewis Packer. LC 85-14139. 63p. 1987. 12.50 o.p. (ISBN 0-7022-1906-1). U of Queensland Pr.

Serpent's Teeth: The Story of Cadmus. Penelope Farmer & Chris Connor. LC 76-137760. (Illus.). 48p. (gr. 2-4). 1972. 5.95 o.p. (ISBN 0-15-272904-6, HJ). HarBraceJ.

Serpico. Peter Maas. 320p. 1974. pap. 2.95 o.s.i. (ISBN 0-553-20449-1, 13424-8). Bantam.

Serre's Conjecture. T. Y. Lam. (Lecture Notes in Mathematics: Vol. 635). 1978. pap. 18.00 o.p. (ISBN 0-387-08657-9). Springer-Verlag.

Servant & Son: Jesus in Parable & Gospel. J. Ramsey Michaels. LC 80-84651. 322p. 1982. pap. 9.95 o.s.i. (ISBN 0-8042-0409-8, John Knox). Westminster John Knox.

Servant of the Word. Dawn De Vries. LC 86-45902. 240p. 1987. pap. 14.95 o.p. (ISBN 0-8006-3203-6, Fortress). Augsburg Fortress.

Servant of the Word. Herbert H. Farmer. LC 64-20405. 128p. (Orig.). 1964. pap. 3.95 o.p. (ISBN 0-8006-4001-2, 1-4001, Fortress). Augsburg Fortress.

Servants of Post-Industrial Power: Sociologie Du Travail in Modern France. Michael Rose. LC 78-65594. 244p. 1979. 40.00 o.p. (ISBN 0-87332-130-8). M E Sharpe.

Serve: Key to Winning Tennis. Tony Trabert & Jim Hook. (Illus.). 128p. 1984. 12.95 o.p. (ISBN 0-396-08298-X); pap. 7.95 o.p. (ISBN 0-396-08299-8). Dodd.

Service & Education in Medical Genetics. Ed. by Ian H. Porter & Ernest B. Hook. (Birth Defects Institute Symposium VIII Ser.). 1979. 50.00 o.p. (ISBN 0-12-562650-9). Acad Pr.

Service Book & Hymnal of the Lutheran Church in America. 1958. 5.75 o.p. (ISBN 0-685-10952-6, 3-600, Fortress). Augsburg Fortress.

Service Imperative for Libraries: Essays in Honor of Margaret E. Monroe. Ed. by Gail A. Schlachter. LC 82-8991. 215p. 1982. text ed. 28.50 o.p. (ISBN 0-87287-272-6). Libs Unl.

Services, Pt. 1. Thomas Tomkins. Ed. by P. C. Buck. (Tudor Music Ser.: Vol.8). 1963. Repr. of 1928 ed. 85.00x o.p. Broude.

Services for Children & Their Families. T. Stroud. 1973. 41.00 o.p. (ISBN 0-08-016604-0); pap. 65.00 o.p. (ISBN 0-08-016605-9). Pergamon.

Services for the Mentally Handicapped in Britain. Nigel Malin et al. 266p. 1980. 30.00 o.p. (ISBN 0-85664-869-8, Pub. by Croom Helm Ltd); pap. 11.50 o.p. (ISBN 0-85664-870-1, Pub. by Croom Helm Ltd). Routledge Chapman & Hall.

Servicing Home VCR's. Date not set. (ISBN 0-8104-0652-7). Sams.

Servicio De Alimentacion (Food Service Worker) Hospital Research & Educational Trust of the AHA. 1972. pap. 5.50 o.p. (ISBN 0-87618-337-2); instructor's guide 5.50 o.p. (ISBN 0-87618-338-0). Brady Bks.

Serving Children & Adolescents with Developmental Disabilities in the Special Education Classroom: Proven Methods. Sebastian Striefel & Mary J. Cadez. LC 83-3632. (Illus.). 276p. (Orig.). 1983. pap. text ed. 18.95 o.p. (ISBN 0-933716-32-X, 32X). P H Brookes.

Serving God with Mammon: The Economic Ministry of the Family. Roger H. Crook. (Orig.). 1965. pap. 1.50 o.p. (ISBN 0-8042-9633-2, John Knox). Westminster John Knox.

Serving Successful Salads: A Merchandising Cookbook. Helen M. Albert. LC 75-33339. 192p. 1983. 19.95 o.p. (ISBN 0-8436-2068-4). Van Nos Reinhold.

Serving the Few: Corporate Capitalism & the Bias of Government Policy. Edward S. Greenberg. LC 79-10104. 275p. 1974. pap. write for info. o.p. (ISBN 0-02-346630-8). Macmillan.

Servol Village: A Caribbean Experience in Education & Community. Gerard Pantin. (Bernard Van Leer International Education Ser.). (Illus.). 85p. (Orig.). 1984. pap. 6.00 o.p. (ISBN 0-931114-27-6). High Scope.

Sesame Street Mother Goose. Sesame Street Staff. LC 75-39341. (Sesame Street Pop-up Ser.: No. 9). (Illus.). (ps-3). 1976. 6.95 o.s.i. (ISBN 0-394-83256-6, BYR). Random.

Sesame Street Pop-up Riddle Book. Sesame Street Staff. LC 77-70852. (Sesame Street Pop-up: No. 11). (Illus.). (ps-3). 1977. bds. 6.95 o.s.i. (ISBN 0-394-83546-8, BYR). Random.

Session d'Aix-en-Provence Nineteen Fifty-Four. Ed. by Institut de Droit International Staff. (Institut de Droit International Annuaire: Vol. 45, Nos. 1-2). lxxvi, 975p. 1954. pap. 80.00 o.p. (ISBN 3-8055-1510-3). S Karger.

Session d'Amsterdam Nineteen Fifty-Seven. Ed. by Institut de Droit International Staff. (Institut de Droit International Annuaire: Vol. 47, Nos. 1-2). lxxxiv, 1212p. 1957. pap. 96.00 o.p. (ISBN 3-8055-1515-4). S Karger.

Session de Bath Nineteen-Fifty. Ed. by Institut de Droit International Staff. (Institut de Droit International Annuaire: Vol. 43, Nos.1-2). lxvi, 1180p. 1950. pap. 48.00 o.p. (ISBN 3-8055-1503-0). S Karger.

Sessions on Remote Sensing 1980. Ed. by A. B. Kahle et al. (Advances in Space Research: Vol. 1, No. 10). (Illus.). 314p. 1981. pap. 48.00 o.p. (ISBN 0-08-028388-8). Pergamon.

Set Microgardening. (ISBN 0-07-079834-6). McGraw.

Set of Four Trauma Books. LC 12-2823. (Trauma Bks.: No. 2). 1983. Set. pap. 9.95 o.p. (ISBN 0-570-08260-9). Concordia.

Set on Edge. Bernice Rubens. 224p. 1987. 19.95 o.p. (ISBN 0-241-12123-X, Pub. by Hamish Hamilton). David & Charles.

Set One. (Story-Go-Round Bks.). 1983. pop-up 7.50 o.p. (ISBN 0-8431-0917-3). Price Stern.

Set Pendulums. (ISBN 0-07-079840-0). McGraw.

Set Small Things. (ISBN 0-07-079832-X). McGraw.

Set Steps to Engl 1. Kernan. (ISBN 0-07-079332-8). McGraw.

Set-Theoretic Topology. Ed. by G. M. Reed. 1977. 52.50 o.p. (ISBN 0-12-584950-8). Acad Pr.

Set Theory & Hierarchy Theory. Ed. by W. Marek & M. Srebrny. (Lecture Notes in Mathematics: Vol. 537). 1976. 20.00 o.p. (ISBN 0-387-07856-8). Springer-Verlag.

Set Theory & Hierarchy Theory 5: Bierutowice, Poland 1976. Ed. by A. Lachlan et al. (Lecture Notes in Mathematics: Vol 619). 1977. pap. 22.00 o.p. (ISBN 0-387-08521-1). Springer-Verlag.

Set Two. (Story-Go-Round Bks.). 1983. pop-up 7.50 o.p. (ISBN 0-8431-0918-1). Price Stern.

Set-Up: A Novel of Disinformation. Vladimir Volkoff. 1985. 16.95 o.p. (ISBN 0-87795-660-X, Arbor Hse). Morrow.

Set up Your Home Studio. (Kodak Library of Creative Photography). 1988. 11.95 o.p. (ISBN 0-86706-236-3). Time-Life.

Setting Limits: Medical Goals in an Aging Society. Daniel Callahan. LC 87-13029. 256p. 1987. 18.45 o.s.i. (ISBN 0-671-22477-8). S&S.

Setting Out: A Guide for Site Engineers. S. G. Brightly. 262p. 1975. pap. text ed. 17.50x o.p. (ISBN 0-258-96929-6, Pub. by Granada England). Gower Pub Co.

Setting the East Ablaze: Lenin's Dream of an Empire in Asia. Peter Hopkirk. (Illus.). 1985. 17.45 o.p. (ISBN 0-393-01943-8). Norton.

Setting the Mould: The United States & Britain, 1945-50. Robin Edmonds. 1987. 22.45 o.p. (ISBN 0-393-02382-6). Norton.

Setting the Tone: Essays & a Diary. Ned Rorem. LC 82-14427. 384p. 1983. 18.95 o.p. (ISBN 0-698-11234-2, Coward). Putnam Pub Group.

Setting up Shop: The Do's & Dont's of Starting a Small Business. R. B. Smith. LC 81-8146. 256p. 1982. text ed. 29.95 o.p. (ISBN 0-07-058531-8). McGraw.

Settle West. (Our Nations Heritage Ser.). Date not set. (ISBN 0-07-375423-4). McGraw.

Settle Your Fidgets. Carol J Farley. LC 77-1650. (Illus.). (gr. 4-6). 1977. 6.95 o.p. (ISBN 0-689-30604-0, Atheneum). Macmillan.

Settlement: The Most Important Productive Medium of Economic Man. Ed. by W. Tietze. 92p. 1975. pap. 23.00 o.p. (ISBN 0-08-019671-3). Pergamon.

Settlements Including Deferred Payments. 206p. 1984. pap. 15.00 o.p. (ISBN 0-317-27558-5, #H4-4953). PLI.

Settlers. William S. Long. (Australians Ser.: Vol. II). 1984. lib. bdg. 12.95 o.p. (ISBN 0-8398-2825-X, Gregg). G K Hall.

Settling Down. Ira Sadoff. LC 74-20848. 1978. pap. 3.95 o.p. (ISBN 0-395-20361-9). HM.

Settling the West. (Our Nations Heritage Ser.). Date not set. (ISBN 0-07-375402-1). McGraw.

Seurat & the Evolution of the La Grande Jatte. Daniel C. Rich. LC 35-32753. (Illus.). 1970. Repr. of 1935 ed. lib. bdg. 22.50x o.p. (ISBN 0-8371-2361-5, RISE). Greenwood.

Seven Ages of Man: A Survey of Human Development. Ed. by Robert R. Sears & S. Shirley Feldman. LC 73-12029. 155p. 1973. pap. 6.95x o.p. (ISBN 0-913232-06-8). W Kaufmann.

Seven Caves: Archaeological Explorations in the Middle East. Carleton S. Coon. LC 80-24503. (Illus.). xx, 354p. 1981. Repr. of 1957 ed. lib. bdg. 35.00x o.p. (ISBN 0-313-22824-8, COSCA). Greenwood.

Seven Clam Sisters. Xia Qing. (Illus.). 18p. (Orig.). (gr. 5-7). 1982. pap. 1.95 o.p. (ISBN 0-8351-1143-1). China Bks.

Seven Contemporary Chinese Women Writers. Gladys Yang. (Panda Ser.). (Illus.). 280p. (Orig.). 1982. pap. 5.95 o.p. (ISBN 0-8351-0962-3). China Bks.

Seven Daily Sins & What to Do about Them. Cecil Murphey. 112p. (Orig.). 1981. pap. 2.95 o.p. (ISBN 0-89283-101-4). Servant.

Seven Daughters & Seven Sons. Barbara Cohen & Bahija Lovejoy. LC 81-8092. 216p. (gr. 5-9). 1982. 12.95 o.s.i. (ISBN 0-689-30875-2, Atheneum Childrens Bks). Macmillan.

Seven Detective Stories see New Method Supplementary Readers: Bestseller Pack.

Seven Dramatic Moments in the Life of Christ: Plays for Church Events. Kenneth Barker. LC 78-52443. 1978. pap. 3.49 o.p. (ISBN 0-8042-1432-8, John Knox). Westminster John Knox.

Seven Eleven. Douglas M. Holly. 270p. 1982. 12.50 o.p. (ISBN 0-682-49895-5). Exposition-Phoenix.

Seven Feet Four & Growing. H. Alton Lee. LC 77-13923. 96p. (gr. 6-9). 1978. 8.95 o.s.i. (ISBN 0-664-32623-4, Westminster). Westminster John Knox.

Seven Footprints to Satan. Abraham Merritt. 1976. pap. 1.25 o.p. (ISBN 0-380-00690-1, 28209). Avon.

Seven Gothic Tales. Isak Dinesen. 1972. pap. 4.95 o.p. (ISBN 0-394-71807-0, V807, Vin). Random.

Seven-Headed Serpent. Ali Ghanem. Tr. by Alan Sheridan. 352p. 1986. 17.95 o.p. (ISBN 0-15-181200-4). HarBraceJ.

Seven Last Words of the Church. Ralph W. Neighbour, Jr. LC 79-51937. 1979. pap. 4.95 o.p. (ISBN 0-8054-5527-2). Broadman.

Seven Letters: The Securities Market & You. Clarence Wolf, Jr. LC 81-66095. 64p. 1981. pap. 1.95 o.p. (ISBN 0-916224-62-7). Banyan Bks.

Seven Mysteries of Life: An Exploration in Science & Philosophy. Guy Murchie. (Illus.). 1978. 18.95 o.p. (ISBN 0-395-26310-7). HM.

Seven Novellas. Marsden Dillenback & John C. Schweitzer. 1966. pap. text ed. 4.45 o.p. (ISBN 0-684-51510-5, ScribC). Scribner.

Seven Popular Games of Backgammon. Nicholas Frantzis. 1979. 6.00 o.p. (ISBN 0-682-49295-7). Exposition-Phoenix.

Seven Puccini Librettos. Tr. by William Weaver. (Eng. & Ital.). 1981. 25.00 o.p. (ISBN 0-393-01221-2); pap. 9.95 o.p. (ISBN 0-393-00930-0). Norton.

Seven Ravens. Jacob Grimm & Wilhelm K. Grimm. LC 63-2506. (Illus.). (gr. k-3). 1963. 6.95 o.p. (ISBN 0-15-272920-8, HJ). HarBraceJ.

Seven Ravens. Jacob Grimm & Wilhelm K. Grimm. LC 83-61777. (Illus.). 22p. (gr. 1 up). 1983. Repr. of 1981 ed. pap. 5.95 o.p. (ISBN 0-907234-47-X). Picture Bk Studio.

Seven Rivers West. Edward Hoagland. 320p. 1986. 18.45 o.s.i. (ISBN 0-671-60753-7). Summit Bks.

Seven Roads to Moscow. W. G. Jackson. (Illus.). 344p. 1958. (ISBN 0-8022-0783-9). Philos Lib.

Seven Sermons Before Edward VI, Fifteen Forty-Nine. Hugh Latimer. Ed. by Edward Arber. 1985. pap. 17.50 o.p. Saifer.

Seven Serpents & Seven Moons. Demetrio Aguilera-Malta. Tr. by Gregory Rabassa. 320p. 1981. pap. 3.50 o.p. (ISBN 0-380-54767-8, 54767-8, Bard). Avon.

Seven Sexes. William Tenn. 240p. 1980. pap. 2.25 o.s.i. (ISBN 0-345-28956-0). Ballantine.

Seven Shades. Valerie P. Brown. 1985. 7.95 o.p. (ISBN 0-317-38098-2). Vantage.

Seven Shares in a Gold Mine. Margaret Larkin. (Illus.). 1959. 3.95 o.p. S&S.

Seven Silent Men. Noel Behn. 356p. 1984. 16.95 o.p. (ISBN 0-87795-499-2, Arbor Hse). Morrow.

Seven Sister-Folk Tales, No. 6. (Chinese Folk Tales' Ser.). (Illus.). 122p. 1982. pap. 2.95 o.p. (ISBN 0-8351-1037-0). China Bks.

Seven Skinny Goats. Victor G. Ambrus. LC 70-11257. (Illus.). (gr. k-2). 1970. 5.95 o.p. (ISBN 0-15-272926-7, HJ); 5.95 o.p. (ISBN 0-15-272927-5). HarBraceJ.

Seven Sloppy Days of Phineas Pig. Mitchell Sharmat. LC 81-6954. (Illus.). 48p. (ps-3). 1983. 12.95 o.p. (ISBN 0-15-272936-4, HJ). HarBraceJ.

Seven Songs about Armenia. G. Emin. 232p. 1981. 6.95 o.p. (ISBN 0-8285-2343-6, Pub. by Progress Pubs USSR). Imported Pubns.

Seven Soviet Arts. Kurt London. 1970. Repr. of 1937 ed. lib. bdg. 41.50x o.p. (ISBN 0-8371-4263-6, LOSA). Greenwood.

Seven Sparrows & the Motor Car Picnic. Joan Hickson. (Illus.). 32p. (ps-2). 1982. 9.95 o.p. (ISBN 0-233-97363-X). Andre Deutsch.

Seven Spells to Farewell. Betty Baker. LC 81-19305. 123p. (gr. 5-9). 1982. 8.95 o.s.i. (ISBN 0-02-708150-8). Macmillan.

Seven Stars for Catfish Bend. Ben L. Burman. (Illus.). 88p. (gr. 3-5). 1981. pap. 1.95 o.p. (ISBN 0-380-53488-6, 53488-6, Camelot). Avon.

Seven Stars for Catfish Bend see Three from Catfish Bend.

Seven Strategies for Wealth & Happiness: Power Ideas from America's Foremost Business Philosopher. Jim Rohn. 160p. 1988. pap. 8.95 o.p. (ISBN 0-914629-73-5, Dist. by St. Martins). Prima Pub Comm.

Seven Things Children Need. John M. Drescher. LC 76-2879. 152p. 1976. pap. 3.50 o.p. (ISBN 0-8361-1798-0). Herald Pr.

Seven Thousand Years of Pottery & Porcelain. M. Wykes-Joyce. (Illus.). 240p. 1958. (ISBN 0-8022-1938-1). Philos Lib.

Seven Was the Padre's Number. Henry James. 1973. 6.00 o.p. (ISBN 0-682-47784-2). Exposition-Phoenix.

Seven Ways Jesus Heals. Norvel Hayes. 142p. (Orig.). 1982. pap. 4.95 o.p. (ISBN 0-89274-235-6, HH-235). Harrison Hse.

Seven Winters. Elizabeth Bowen. 72p. 1971. Repr. of 1942 ed. 15.00x o.p. (ISBN 0-7165-1397-8, BBA 02047, Pub. by Cuala Press Ireland). Biblio Dist.

Seven Witches. George MacBeth. LC 77-92539. 1978. 7.95 o.p. (ISBN 0-15-181370-1). HarBraceJ.

Seventeen-Seventy-Six: Year of Illusions. Thomas Fleming. (Illus.). 525p. 1975. 12.50 o.p. (ISBN 0-393-05542-6). Norton.

Seventeenth Annual Employee Benefits Institute. (Tax Law & Estate Planning Ser.). 299p. 1987. 45.00 o.p. (J4-3603). PLI.

Seventeenth Annual Institute on Securities Regulation, 2 vols. 1088p. 1985. 40.00 o.p. (B4-6730). PLI.

Seventeenth Century. 2nd ed. George N. Clark. LC 80-27737. (Illus.). xix, 378p. 1981. Repr. of 1947 ed. lib. bdg. 39.25x o.p. (ISBN 0-313-22765-9, CLSC). Greenwood.

Seventeenth-Century American Poetry. Ed. by Harrison T. Meserole. 1972. pap. 4.95 o.p. (ISBN 0-393-00620-4, Norton Lib). Norton.

Seventeenth Century Art in Flanders & Holland. LC 76-14071. (Garland Library of the History of Art). 1976. lib. bdg. 61.00 o.p. (ISBN 0-8240-2419-2). Garland Pub.

Seventeenth Century Background Studies in the Thought of the Age in Relation to Poetry & Religion. Basil Wiley. 288p. 1986. pap. 9.95 o.p. (ISBN 0-7448-0041-2, 0041W, Ark Paperbks). Routledge Chapman & Hall.

Seventeenth Century Italian Drawings in the Metropolitan Museum of Art. Jacob Bean. LC 78-21502. (Illus.). 300p. 1979. 28.50 o.p. (ISBN 0-87099-183-3, MPLE1930); pap. 8.95 o.p. (ISBN 0-87099-184-1). Metro Mus Art.

Seventeenth Century Prose & Poetry. 2nd ed. Alexander M. Witherspoon & Frank J. Warnke. 1963. 20.00 o.p. (ISBN 0-15-580235-6). HarbraceJ.

Seventeenth Degree. Mary McCarthy. LC 74-1065. 1974. 7.95 o.p. (ISBN 0-15-181355-8). HarBraceJ.

Seventh. Richard Stark. 1981. lib. bdg. 11.50 o.p. (ISBN 0-8398-2737-7, Gregg). G K Hall.

Seventh Babe. Jerome Charyn. LC 78-73866. 1979. 9.95 o.p. (ISBN 0-87795-220-5, Arbor Hse). Morrow.

Seventh-Day Adventism in a Nutshell. D. M. Canright. 2.75 o.p. (ISBN 0-89225-162-X). Gospel Advocate.

Seventh-Day Adventism Renounced. D. M. Canright. 1982. 9.50 o.p. (ISBN 0-89225-163-8); pap. 5.95 o.p. Gospel Advocate.

Seventh Lacus Forum: Proceedings. Linguistic Association of Canada & the U. S. Staff. Ed. by J. E. Copeland & P. W. Davis. 1980. pap. text ed. 12.95 o.s.i. (ISBN 0-917496-19-1). Hornbeam Pr.

Seventh National Ground Water Quality Symposium. 1984. 43.75 o.p. (ISBN 0-318-23006-2). Natl Water Well.

Seventh Royale. Donald Stanwood. LC 83-45495. 395p. 1987. 19.95 o.p. (ISBN 0-689-11449-4, Atheneum). Macmillan.

Seventh Secret. Irving Wallace. (Large Print Bks (Special Editions)). 515p. 1986. lib. bdg. 19.95 o.p. (ISBN 0-8161-4148-7). G K Hall.

Seventrees. Janice Y. Brooks. 1981. pap. 3.95 o.p. (ISBN 0-451-14592-5, Sig). NAL.

Seventy-Fifth American Exhibition. A. James Speyer & Neal Benezra. LC 85-73683. 72p. 1986. pap. 12.95 o.p. (ISBN 0-86559-062-1). Art Inst Chi.

Seventy-Fifth Anniversary Projects: Girl Scout Leaders' Guide, 27-201. (Illus.). 20p. 1986. 1.25 o.p. (ISBN 0-317-47672-6). Girl Scouts USA.

Seventy-Five Melodious & Progressive Studies for Violin, 2 bks, Op. 36. F. Mazas. Ed. by G. Saenger. (Carl Fischer Music Library: Nos. 100 & 101). 1901. Bk. 1. pap. 7.00 o.p. (ISBN 0-8258-0015-3, L100); Bk. 2. pap. 7.00 o.p. (ISBN 0-8258-0016-1, L101). Fischer Inc NY.

Seventy-Five Writers of the Colonial South: A Reference Guide. Jack D. Wages. 1979. lib. bdg. 34.50 o.p. (ISBN 0-8161-7979-4, Hall Reference). G K Hall.

Seventy-Five Years of Chromatography: A Historical Dialogue. L. S. Ettre & A. Zlatkis. (Journal of Chromatography Ser.: Vol. 17). 502p. 1979. 79.00 o.p. (ISBN 0-444-41754-0). Elsevier.

Seventy Five Years of Dentistry: The Diamond Jubilee Volume of the Florida State Dental Society. Helen S. Haines & Robert Thoburn. LC 60-10225. 1960. 10.00 o.p. (ISBN 0-8130-0092-0). U Presses Fla.

Seventy Five Years of Pontiac-Oakland. John Gunnell. Ed. by George H. Dammann. LC 81-71489. (Automotive Ser.). (Illus.). 528p. 1982. 34.95 o.p. (ISBN 0-912612-20-7). Crestline.

Seventy-Fourth American Exhibition. A. James Speyer & Anne Rorimer. (Illus.). 64p. 1982. pap. 8.95 o.p. (ISBN 0-86559-050-8). Art Inst Chi.

Seventy Modern Business Letters. (Letter Bks.). (Orig.). 1983. pap. 14.95 o.s.i. (ISBN 0-87280-148-9, Asher-Gallant). Caddylak Systs.

Seventy-One Creative Bible Story Projects: Patterns for Crafts, Visuals, & Learning Centers. Helen Gramelsbach. (Illus.). 64p. 1983. pap. 4.95 o.p. (ISBN 0-87239-607-X, 2103). Standard Pub.

Seventy-Second & Rodeo. Roz Avrett. 200p. 1984. 15.50 o.p. (ISBN 0-87795-535-2, Arbor Hse). Morrow.

Seventy-Seven for Engineers & Scientists. Larry R. Nyhoff & Sanford Leestma. 100p. 1985. write for info. solns. manual o.p. (ISBN 0-02-388630-7). Macmillan.

Seventy-Six Hours: The Invasion of Tarawa. Eric Hammel & John Lane. 1980. pap. 2.25 o.s.i. (ISBN 0-505-51464-8, Pub. by Tower Bks). Dorchester Pub Co.

Seventy-Six Psychic Techniques: A Primer in Parapsychology. Sheila Ostrander & Lynn Schroeder. Ed. by John O'Quinn. 8p. 1980. pap. text ed. 3.95 o.s.i. (ISBN 0-9609802-5-3). Life Science.

Seventy-Six Ways to Save Our Nation. Natasha Decker. 1977. 2.95 o.p. (ISBN 0-89036-063-4). Hawkes Pub Inc.

Seventy-Third American Exhibition: The Art Institute of Chicago. A. James Speyer & Anne Rorimer. LC 52-40306. (Illus.). 51p. (Orig.). 1979. pap. 4.00 o.p. (ISBN 0-86559-034-6). Art Inst Chi.

Seventy-Three Poems. e. e. Cummings. LC 63-20271. 92p. 1963. 6.95 o.s.i. (ISBN 0-15-181360-4). HarBraceJ.

Seventy Years & Never a Dull Moment. Celia Bloom. 1980. 5.00 o.p. (ISBN 0-682-49561-1). Exposition-Phoenix.

Seventy Years of Life & Labour, 2 vols. Samuel Gompers. LC 66-21674. 1967. Repr. of 1925 ed. Set. 87.50x o.s.i. (ISBN 0-678-00213-4). Kelley.

Several Complex Variables. H. Grauert & K. Fritzsche. Ed. by F. W. Gehring & C. C. Moore. Tr. by H. J. Mumaw from Ger. LC 75-46503. (Graduate Texts in Mathematics: Vol. 38). (Illus.). 1976. 29.95 o.p. (ISBN 0-387-90172-8). Springer-Verlag.

Several Complex Variables 1: Proceedings. International Mathematical Conference, College Park, 1970. Ed. by J. Horvath. (Lecture Notes in Mathematics: Vol. 155). 1970. pap. 12.00 o.p. (ISBN 0-387-05183-X). Springer-Verlag.

Severe & Unusual Weather. Joe R. Eagleman. 250p. 1982. 38.95 o.p. (ISBN 0-442-26195-0). Van Nos Reinhold.

Severe Weather Flying. Dennis W. Newton. (McGraw-Hill Aviation Ser.). (Illus.). 160p. 1983. text ed. 32.50 o.p. (ISBN 0-07-046402-2). McGraw.

Severed Ties. George E. Simpson & Neal R. Burger. (Orig.). 1983. pap. 3.50 o.p. (ISBN 0-440-17705-7). Dell.

Severn Bore. Fred Rowbotham. (Illus.). 108p. 1983. 14.95 o.p. (ISBN 0-7153-8508-9). David & Charles.

Sevres Egyptian Service: 1810-12. Charles Truman. (Orig.). pap. 7.95 o.p. (ISBN 0-905209-24-9, Pub. by Victoria & Albert Mus UK). Faber & Faber.

Sew & Save Source Book: Your Guide to Supplies for Creative Sewing. Margaret A. Boyd. LC 83-11888. (Illus.). 216p. (Orig.). 1984. pap. 9.95 o.p. (ISBN 0-932620-23-X). Betterway Pubns.

Sewage Sludge Stabilization & Disinfection. A. M. Bruce. LC 84-4608. (Water & Wastewater Technology Ser.: No. 1-714). 624p. 1984. text ed. 78.95x o.p. (ISBN 0-470-20080-4). Halsted Pr.

Sewanee. William A. Percy. 14p. 1968. pap. 15.00 o.p. (ISBN 0-918769-04-3). Univ South.

Sewanee in Ruins. Richard Tillinghast. 39p. 1983. pap. 15.00 o.p. (ISBN 0-918769-05-1). Univ South.

Sewing Accessories: An Illustrated History. Victor Houart. (Illus.). 128p. 1985. 16.95 o.s.i. (ISBN 0-285-62629-9, Pub. by Souvenir Pr Ltd Uk); pap. 12.95 o.s.i. (ISBN 0-285-62634-5, Pub. by Souvenir Pr Ltd UK). Seven Hills Bk Dists.

Sewing Easy Garments Without a Pattern. Carol Handley Little. (Illus.). 160p. 1985. 18.95 o.p. (ISBN 0-9613962-1-0). Cal Creative Pubns.

Sewing for the Home. LC 84-42638. 17.45 o.p. (ISBN 0-394-54052-2); pap. 10.95 o.p. (ISBN 0-394-72756-8). Random.

Sewing Sculpture: Sewn Art in Three Dimensions. Charlene Kinser. LC 76-56736. (Illus.). 144p. 1977. 12.50 o.p. (ISBN 0-87131-215-8); pap. 6.95 o.p. (ISBN 0-87131-236-0). M Evans.

Sex: A User's Manual. The Diagram Group Staff. (Illus.). 196p. 1981. pap. 9.95 o.p. (ISBN 0-399-50517-2, Perigee). Putnam Pub Group.

Sex & Behavior: Status & Prospect. T. E. McGill et al. LC 77-17840. (Illus.). 458p. 1978. 55.00x o.p. (ISBN 0-306-31084-8, Plenum Pr). Plenum Pub.

Sex & Fantasy: Patterns of Male & Female Development. Robert May. 1980. 12.95 o.p. (ISBN 0-393-01316-2). Norton.

Sex & Infertility. R. G. Harrison & C. H. DeBoer. 1977. 30.50 o.p. (ISBN 0-12-327850-3). Acad Pr.

Sex & Money. John D. Spooner. 1986. pap. 3.95 o.p. (ISBN 0-440-17717-0). Dell.

Sex & Sensibility: Ideal & Erotic Love from Milton to Mozart. Jean H. Hagstrum. LC 79-20657. (Illus.). 1980. lib. bdg. 30.00x o.s.i. (ISBN 0-226-31289-5). U of Chicago Pr.

Sex & Sunsets. Tim Sandlin. LC 86-18454. 1987. 16.95 o.p. (ISBN 0-8050-0168-9). H Holt & Co.

Sex & the Brain. Jo Durden-Smith & Diane DeSimone. (Illus.). 1983. 16.95 o.p. (ISBN 0-87795-484-4, Arbor Hse). Morrow.

Sex & the Mentally Handicapped. Rev. ed. Ann Craft & Michael Craft. 1982. pap. 8.95 o.p. (ISBN 0-7100-9293-8). Routledge Chapman & Hall.

Sex & the Spiritual Path. Herbert B. Puryear. 225p. (Orig.). 1980. pap. 3.95 o.p. (ISBN 0-87604-129-2). ARE Pr.

Sex & You: The Emotional & Physical Aspects of Growing Up. Alexander Gunn. (Illus.). 128p. (YA) (gr. 7 up). 1986. 22.95x o.p. (ISBN 0-356-10926-7, Pub. by MacD & Co). Trans-Atl Phila.

Sex As Bait: Eve, Casanova & Don Juan. S. Giora Shoham. LC 82-17386. (Illus.). 226p. 1984. 25.00 o.p. (ISBN 0-7022-1703-4). U of Queensland Pr.

Sex-Based Discrimination: Cases & Materials, 1986 Supplement. 2nd ed. Herma H. Kay. (American Casebook Ser.). 260p. 1985. pap. text ed. 8.95 o.p. (ISBN 0-314-97400-8). West Pub.

Sex-Based Discrimination: Text, Cases & Materials. 2nd ed. Herma H. Kay. LC 81-11657. (American Casebook Ser.). 1045p. 1981. text ed. 33.95 o.p. (ISBN 0-314-60377-8). West Pub.

Sex Chromosomes. Ursula Mittwoch. 1967. 64.50 o.p. (ISBN 0-12-501050-8). Acad Pr.

Sex Chromosomes & Sex-Linked Genes. S. Ohno. (Monographs on Endocrinology: Vol. 1). (Illus.). 1977. 35.00 o.p. (ISBN 0-387-03934-1). Springer-Verlag.

Sex Contract: The Evolution of Human Behavior. Helen E. Fisher. LC 81-11120. (Illus.). 256p. 1982. 13.50 o.p. (ISBN 0-688-00640-X). Morrow.

Sex, Culture & Myth. Malinowski. 1962. 6.95 o.p. (ISBN 0-15-180900-3). HarBraceJ.

Sex Cure. Dana Lloyd. 192p. (Orig.). 1981. pap. 2.50 o.p. (ISBN 0-380-78477-7, 78477-7). Avon.

Sex Differences in Human Communication. Barbara Eakins & R. Gene Eakins. LC 77-77660. (Illus.). 1978. pap. 14.50 o.p. (ISBN 0-395-25510-4). HM.

Sex Differentiation & Schooling. Ed. by Michael Marland. (Organization in Schools Ser.). vi, 250p. 1984. text ed. 27.50x o.p. (ISBN 0-435-80592-4). Heinemann Ed.

Sex Discrimination & Law: A Selected Bibliography. Dittakavi N. Rao. (Public Administration Series: Bibliography: No. P 1830). 1985. pap. 3.75 o.p. (ISBN 0-89028-680-9). Vance Biblios.

Sex Discrimination in Employment. William F. Pepper & Florynce R. Kennedy. 337p. 1982. 30.00x o.p. (ISBN 0-87215-331-2, 65775). Michie Co.

Sex During Pregnancy & after Childbirth. Sylvia Close. 144p. 1985. pap. 7.95 o.p. (ISBN 0-7225-0929-4). Newcastle Pub.

Sex Education: Issues & Directives. Wade Baskin & Pat Powers. LC 68-54971. 1969. (ISBN 0-8022-2263-3). Philos Lib.

Sex Equity Strategies. 2nd ed. Louise Vetter et al. 192p. 1980. 11.00 o.p. (ISBN 0-318-22198-5, RD144). Natl Ctr Res Voc Ed.

Sex Etiquette: Should I? Can I? May I? Must I? Or, the Modern Woman's Guide to Mating Manners. Marilyn Hamel. 1986. pap. 3.95 o.p. (ISBN 0-440-17656-5). Dell.

Sex Fair Career Counseling. Peggy Hawley. 58p. 1980. pap. text ed. 6.25 o.p. (ISBN 0-911547-66-5, 72195W34). Am Assn Coun Dev.

SEX-I-CON! Poetry. Philip L. Sherrod. 81p. (Orig.). 1985. pap. 7.95 o.s.i. (ISBN 0-317-18741-4). Carrousel Pubns.

Sex: If I Didn't Laugh, I'd Cry. Jess Lair. 1983. pap. 3.95 o.p. (ISBN 0-449-20283-6, Crest). Fawcett.

Sex in the Bible. Tom Horner. LC 73-87676. 1974. 8.50 o.p. (ISBN 0-8048-1124-5). C E Tuttle.

Sex Life of the Animals. Herbert Wendt. (Illus.). 1965. 7.95 o.p. (ISBN 0-671-64850-0). S&S.

Sex Lure: Cartoons. Ja Roma. 1977. 4.50 o.p. (ISBN 0-682-48221-8). Exposition-Phoenix.

Sex Manual for People over Thirty. Ira Alterman. 96p. 1984. pap. 3.95 o.p. (ISBN 0-8092-5354-2). Contemp Bks.

Sex Outside of Marriage. Jean C. Lipke. LC 76-104895. (Being Together Bks.). (Illus.). (YA) (gr. 7-12). 1971. PLB 5.95 o.p. (ISBN 0-8225-0599-1). Lerner Pubns.

Sex Outside of Marriage see Marriage.

Sex Problems in Practice. 81p. 1982. pap. 10.00x o.p. (ISBN 0-7279-0087-0, Pub. by British Med Assoc UK). Taylor & Francis.

Sex Role Stereotyping in the Schools. 2nd rev. ed. Ed. by Elizabeth H. Weiner. 120p. 1980. 8.95 o.p. (ISBN 0-8106-1490-1). NEA.

Sex-Role System: Psychological & Sociological Perspectives. Ed. by Jane Chetwynd & Oonagh Hartnett. (Orig.). 1978. pap. 8.95x o.p. (ISBN 0-7100-8722-5). Routledge Chapman & Hall.

Sex, Science Fiction, Stage, Screen, Soccer & Other Educational Matters: The Uncensored Letters of a Prep School Freshman. Jack Lee. Ed. by Travis Jefferson. 1978. 6.00 o.p. (ISBN 0-682-49190-X). Exposition-Phoenix.

Sex Stereotyping in Advertising. Alice E. Courtney & Thomas W. Whipple. 256p. 1983. 32.00x o.p. (ISBN 0-669-03955-1). Lexington Bks.

Sex Straight up with a Twist of Lemon. Wendy Darling. 128p. (Orig.). 1986. pap. 7.50 o.p. (ISBN 0-682-40282-6). Exposition-Phoenix.

Sex Studies Index: 1980. Kinsey, Alfred C., Institute for Sex Research, Indiana University Staff. 1982. lib. bdg. 80.00 o.s.i. (ISBN 0-8161-0386-9, Hall Library). G K Hall.

Sex Tax: A Political Fantasy. W. E. Dunn. 1979. 6.00 o.p. (ISBN 0-682-49463-1). Exposition-Phoenix.

Sex Therapy Today. Patricia Gillan & Richard Gillan. LC 77-78402. 1977. pap. 4.95 o.p. (ISBN 0-394-17024-5, E702, Ever). Grove.

Sex, with Love: A Guide for Young People. Eleanor Hamilton. LC 77-75442. (Illus.). (gr. 7-10). 1978. 12.95x o.p. (ISBN 0-8070-2580-1); pap. 6.95 o.p. (ISBN 0-8070-2581-X, BP563). Beacon Pr.

Sexbombs: The Life & Death of Jayne Mansfield. Guus Luitjters & Gerard Timmer. Tr. by Josh Pachter. (Illus.). 164p. (Dutch.). 1987. pap. 12.95 o.p. (Pub. by Citadel Pr). Carol Pub Group.

Sexism, Racism & Oppression. Arthur Brittan & Mary Maynard. 220p. 1984. 29.95x o.s.i. (ISBN 0-85520-674-8); pap. 14.95 o.p. (ISBN 0-85520-675-6). Basil Blackwell.

Sexpionage: The Exploitation of Sex by Soviet Intelligence. David Lewis. LC 76-2534. (Illus.). 192p. 1976. 8.95 o.p. (ISBN 0-15-181380-9). HarBraceJ.

Sexual Abuse: Incest Victims & Their Families. Jean M. Goodwin. LC 81-16300. (Illus.). 224p. 1982. text ed. 23.00 o.p. (ISBN 0-7236-7012-9). Butterworth.

Sexual Addiction. Patrick J. Carnes. LC 83-8137. 215p. 1983. 12.95 o.p. (ISBN 0-89638-058-0); pap. 8.95 o.p. (ISBN 0-89638-066-1). CompCare.

Sexual Assault: A Guide for Community Action. Barbara J. Rodabaugh & Melanie Austin. 1981. lib. bdg. 33.00 o.p. (ISBN 0-8240-7197-2). Garland Pub.

Sexual Behavior in the Human Male. Alfred C. Kinsey et al. LC 48-5195. (Illus.). 1948. write for info. o.p. (ISBN 0-7216-5445-2). Saunders.

Sexual Behavior: Pharmacology & Biochemistry. Ed. by M. Sandler & G. Gessa. 1975. 32.75 o.p. (ISBN 0-7204-7545-7, North Holland). Elsevier.

Sexual Behaviour in Canada: Patterns & Problems. Benjamin Schlesinger. 1977. pap. 8.95 o.p. (ISBN 0-8020-6314-4). U of Toronto Pr.

Sexual Compatibility: A Practical Approach to Solving Problems. John F. O'Connor. 1985. 8.95 o.p. (ISBN 0-317-17527-0, Perigee). Putnam Pub Group.

Sexual Confidence. Debora Phillps & Robert Judd. 240p. 1980. 9.95 o.p. (ISBN 0-395-29479-7). HM.

Sexual Connection. John Sparks. 1978. text ed. 8.95 o.p. (ISBN 0-07-059908-4). McGraw.

Sexual Difficulties in Marriage. David Mace. Ed. by William E. Julme. LC 72-75652. (Pocket Counsel Bks.). 64p. (Orig.). 1972. pap. 1.75 o.p. (ISBN 0-8006-1108-X, 1-1108, Fortress). Augsburg Fortress.

Sexual Divisions: Patterns & Processes. Ed. by Mary Evans & Clare Ungerson. 224p. 1983. pap. 13.50 o.p. (ISBN 0-422-78440-0, NO. 3835, Pub. by Tavistock). Routledge Chapman & Hall.

Sexual Dysfunction. Ben N. Ard, Jr. LC 73-17735. 300p. 1975. 30.00x o.p. (ISBN 0-87668-113-5). Aronson.

Sexual Dysfunction: A Behavioral Approach to Causation, Assessment & Treatment. Derek Jehu. LC 79-40582. 304p. 1979. 98.95x o.p. (ISBN 0-471-99756-0, Pub. by Wiley-Interscience); pap. 48.95x o.p. (ISBN 0-471-27597-2, Pub. by Wiley-Interscience). Wiley.

Sexual Enhancement for Women. Judith Silverstein. LC 78-51452. (Illus.). 96p. (Orig.). 1982. pap. 10.00 o.p. (ISBN 0-940050-02-1). Sun Rose.

Sexual Fiction. Maurice Charney. 200p. 1981. 22.00x o.p. (ISBN 0-416-31930-0, NO. 6519); pap. 8.95 o.p. (ISBN 0-416-31940-8, NO. 6518). Routledge Chapman & Hall.

Sexual Fix. Date not set. (ISBN 0-8052-3860-3). Random.

Sexual Imprisonment. Partick G. Oh. 1979. 8.50 o.p. (ISBN 0-682-49274-4, Banner). Exposition-Phoenix.

Sexual Interactions. Elizabeth Allgeier & Albert Allgeier. LC 87-80888. (Illus.). 632p. 1984. text ed. 25.50 o.p. (ISBN 0-669-03536-X). Heath.

Sexual Intimacy. Andrew Greeley. 200p. 1982. pap. 9.95 o.p. (ISBN 0-88347-143-4). Thomas More.

Sexual Inversion: The Questions-with Catholic Answers. Herbert F. Smith. 1979. 2.95 o.p. (ISBN 0-8198-0612-9); pap. 1.95 o.p. (ISBN 0-8198-0613-7). Dghtrs St Paul.

Sexual Life in Ancient China. Robert H. Van Gulik. 1974. Repr. of 1961 ed. text ed. 75.00x o.p. (ISBN 9-0040-3917-1). Humanities.

Sexual Life in Ancient Greece. Hans Licht, pseud. Ed. by Lawrence Dawson. Tr. by J. H. Freese from Gr. LC 75-27675. (Illus.). 556p. 1976. Repr. of 1953 ed. lib. bdg. 36.25x o.p. (ISBN 0-8371-8464-9, BRSLG). Greenwood.

Sexual Life of Savages in North-Western Melanesia. Bronislaw Malinowski. (Illus.). 1962. pap. 6.95 o.p. (ISBN 0-15-680810-2, HB48, Harv). HarBraceJ.

Sexual Perspective: Homosexuality & Art in the Last 100 Years in the West. Emmanuel Cooper. (Illus.). 320p. 1986. 35.00 o.p. (96356, Pub. by Routledge UK); pap. 18.95 o.p. (ISBN 0-7102-0902-9, 09029). Routledge Chapman & Hall.

Sexual Politics, Sexual Communities: The Making of a Homosexual Minority in the United States, 1940-1970. John D'Emilio. LC 82-16000. 262p. 1983. 20.00x o.s.i. (ISBN 0-226-14265-5). U of Chicago Pr.

Sexual Problems in Medical Practice. LC 81-7947. 1981. 26.00 o.p. (ISBN 0-89970-098-5, OP-120). AMA.

Sexual Revolution. C. Antonio Provost. LC 84-90221. 110p. 1985. 10.00 o.p. (ISBN 0-533-06274-8). Vantage.

Sexual Static: How Men Are Confusing the Women They Love. Morton H. Shaevitz. 1987. 14.95 o.p. (ISBN 0-316-77292-5). Little.

Sexual Style: Facing & Making Choices About Sex. Robert Meyners & Claire Wooster. 1979. 10.00 o.p. (ISBN 0-15-181399-X). HarBraceJ.

Sexual Unfolding: Sexual Development & Sex Therapies in Late Adolescence. Lorna J. Sarrel & Philip M. Sarrel. 1979. text ed. 19.95 o.p. (ISBN 0-316-77100-7). Little.

Sexuality & Homosexuality: A New View. Arno Karlen. 1971. 15.00 o.p. (ISBN 0-393-01087-2). Norton.

Sexuality & Marriage. James F. Moore. LC 87-12626. 160p. (Orig.). 1987. pap. 8.95 o.p. (ISBN 0-8066-2282-2, 10-5729, Augsburg). Augsburg Fortress.

Sexuality & the Counseling Pastor. Herbert W. Stroup, Jr. & Norma S. Wood. LC 73-88344. 136p. 1974. 5.95 o.p. (ISBN 0-8006-0264-1, 1-264, Fortress). Augsburg Fortress.

Sexuality & the Genetics of Bacteria. rev. ed. Francois Jacob & E. Wollman. 1961. 39.95 o.p. (ISBN 0-12-379450-1). Acad Pr.

Sexuality, Love & Immorality. J. P. Grip. 1957. (ISBN 0-8022-0632-8). Philos Lib.

Sexuality, the Bible & Science. Stephen Sapp. LC 76-62617. 160p. 1977. 4.00 o.p. (ISBN 0-8006-0503-9, 1-503, Fortress). Augsburg Fortress.

Sexuality: The Human Perspective. Gary Kelly. LC 79-23962. 1980. 14.95 o.p. (ISBN 0-8120-5360-5); pap. 9.95 o.p. (ISBN 0-8120-0931-2). Barron.

Sexuality Today: The Human Perspective. Gary F. Kelly. LC 88-703137. (Illus.). 512p. 1988. pap. text ed. 15.95 o.p. Dushkin Pub.

Sexually Aggressive Woman. 1976. pap. 2.75 o.p. (ISBN 0-451-09859-5, E9859, Sig). NAL.

Sexually Transmitted Disease: Guidelines for Physicians & Health Workers. Alan S. Meltzer. 86p. (Orig.). 1981. handbook 6.95 o.p. (ISBN 0-88831-126-5). Eden Pr.

Sexually Transmitted Diseases. Ed. by R. D. Catterall. 1976. 76.00 o.p. (ISBN 0-12-164150-3). Acad Pr.

Sexually Transmitted Diseases: Diagnosis & Treatment. Elizabeth B. Connell & Howard J. Tatum. LC 85-70298. 1985. pap. 8.65 o.p. Creative Infomatics.

Sexus. Henry Miller. LC 86-33723. (Rosy Crucifixion Ser.: Bk. 1). 640p. 1987. pap. 9.95 o.s.i. (ISBN 0-394-62371-1, BC). Grove.

Sexy Legs in Twenty Days: Spot Reducing the Aerobics Way. Deborah Frichman-McKenzie. (Illus.). 64p. 1983. 2.95 o.p. (ISBN 0-399-50780-9, Perigee). Putnam Pub Group.

Seychelles. Hildebrand Editorial Staff. (Hildebrand's Travel Guides Ser.). (Illus.). 127p. 1985. pap. 8.95 o.s.i. (ISBN 0-87052-017-2). Hippocrene Bks.

Seymore Snake & Friends: Chester Does His Chores Speech Reinforcement for the Ch Sound. Katherine T. McAvoy. (gr. 3-6). 1981. pap. text ed. 9.95 o.p. (ISBN 0-86703-034-8). Opportunities Learn.

Seymore Snake & Friends: Freddy the Frog Speech Reinforcement for the R Sound. Katherine T. McAvoy. (gr. 3-6). 1981. pap. text ed. 9.95 o.p. (ISBN 0-86703-032-1). Opportunities Learn.

Seymore Snake & Friends-Liam the Leprechaun: Speech Reinforcement for the L Sound. Katherine T. McAvoy. (gr. 3-6). pap. text ed. 9.95 o.p. (ISBN 0-86703-033-X). Opportunities Learn.

Seymore Snake & Friends: S Sound Reinforcement. Katherine T. McAvoy. (gr. 3-6). 1981. pap. text ed. 9.95 o.p. (ISBN 0-86703-031-3). Opportunities Learn.

Seymore Snake & Friends: Shadra O'Shay: Speech Reinforcement for the Sh Sound. Katherine T. McAvoy. (gr. 3-6). 1981. pap. text ed. 9.95 o.p. (ISBN 0-86703-035-6). Opportunities Learn.

Seymore Snake & Friends: Theodore Throughly: Speech Reinforcement for the Th Sound. Katherine T. McAvoy. (gr. 3-6). 1981. pap. text ed. 9.95 o.p. (ISBN 0-86703-036-4). Opportunities Learn.

Seymour, a Gibbon: About Apes & Other Animals & How You Can Help to Keep Them Alive. Phyllis Borea. LC 73-75431. (Illus.). (gr. 4-7). 1973. PLB 5.25 o.p. (ISBN 0-689-30415-3, Atheneum). Macmillan.

S.F. Robot Plastic Model, Vols. 1-4. 1984. T.V. Land 1 Pack 5.30 ea. o.p. Bks Nippan.

Sgt. Hawk. Patrick Clay. 1979. pap. 1.75 o.p. (ISBN 0-8439-0640-5, Pub. by Leisure Bks CT). Dorchester Pub Co.

Shackleton: His Antarctic Writings Selected & Introduced by Christopher Ralling. Ed. by Christopher Ralling. LC 86-3335. (Illus.). 264p. 1986. 22.50 o.p. (ISBN 0-87226-082-8). P Bedrick Bks.

Shackleton's Boat Journey. F. A. Worsley. (Illus.). 1977. 8.95 o.p. (ISBN 0-393-08759-X). Norton.

Shades. Betty Brock. (gr. 3-5). 1983. pap. 0.95 o.p. (ISBN 0-380-01545-5, 27888, Camelot). Avon.

Shadow. Arthur Tress. (Illus.). 1975. pap. 5.45 o.p. (ISBN 0-380-01546-3, 23424). Avon.

Shadow & Whispers: Power Politics Inside the Knowledge from Brezhnev to Gorbachev. Dusko Doder. LC 86-10135. (Illus.). 352p. 1986. 19.45 o.s.i. (ISBN 0-394-54998-8). Random.

Shadow Applique. 5.98 o.p. (ISBN 0-317-38602-6). Gick.

Shadow Behind the Curtain. Velda Johnston. 1985. 14.95 o.p. (ISBN 0-8161-3921-0, Large Print Bks). G K Hall.

Shadow Book. Beatrice S. De Regniers & Isabel Gordon. LC 60-10244. (Illus.). 32p. (gr. k-3). 1960. 5.95 o.p. (ISBN 0-15-272991-7, HJ). HarBraceJ.

Shadow Box. Michael Cristofer. 1978. pap. 2.25 o.p. (ISBN 0-380-01865-9, 46839, Bard). Avon.

Shadow Cabinet. W. T. Tyler. 353p. 1986. pap. 3.95 o.p. (ISBN 1-55547-108-0). Critics Choice Paper.

Shadow Dancers. Jane L. Curry. LC 83-3733. 204p. (gr. 7 up). 1983. 10.95 o.s.i. (ISBN 0-689-50276-1, M K McElderry). Macmillan.

Shadow Falls. Claire Lorrimer. 1974. pap. 0.95 o.p. (ISBN 0-380-00185-3, 21444). Avon.

Shadow Hawk. Andre Norton. LC 60-10247. 1960. 5.50 o.p. (ISBN 0-15-273170-9, HJ). HarBraceJ.

Shadow in the Cave: The Broadcaster, His Audience, & the State. Anthony Smith. LC 73-18146. 351p. 1973. Repr. 34.95 o.p. (ISBN 0-252-00442-6). U of Ill Pr.

Shadow in the Sun. Bernice Grohskopf. LC 74-19490. 224p. (gr. 6 up). 1975. PLB 6.95 o.p. (ISBN 0-689-30448-X, Atheneum). Macmillan.

Shadow in the Weave. Michael Humfrey. LC 86-18075. 176p. 1987. 15.95 o.p. (ISBN 0-87951-265-2). Overlook Pr.

Shadow Man. Clare Barroll. 192p. (Orig.). 1984. pap. 2.95 o.p. (ISBN 0-380-89235-9). Avon.

Shadow Man: The Life of Dashiell Hammett. Richard Layman. LC 80-8752. 352p. 1981. 14.95 o.p. (ISBN 0-15-181459-7). HarBraceJ.

Shadow Network: Espionage Ss an Instrument of Soviet Policy. Edward Van Der Rhoer. 368p. 1984. 17.95 o.s.i. (ISBN 0-684-17960-1, ScribT). Scribner.

Shadow Nose. Elizabeth Levy. LC 83-7925. (Illus.). 64p. (gr. 2-5). 1983. 10.25 o.p. (ISBN 0-688-02410-6); lib. bdg. 10.88 o.p. (ISBN 0-688-02411-4). Morrow.

Shadow of a Dream & an Imperative Duty. William Dean Howells. LC 71-79475. (Selected Edition of W. D. Howells: Center for Editions of American Authors: Vol. 17). 272p. 1969. 15.00x o.p. (ISBN 0-253-35190-1). Ind U Pr.

Shadow of a Man. Allan Nixon. 1979. pap. 2.50 o.p. (ISBN 0-380-46060-2, 46060). Avon.

Shadow of Desire. Fela D. Scott. (Avon Romance Ser.). 1986. pap. 3.50 o.p. (ISBN 0-380-89981-7). Avon.

Shadow of Keynes: Understanding Keynes, Cambridge, & Keynesian Economics. Elizabeth S. Johnson & Harry G. Johnson. LC 78-56338. 1982. 15.00 o.s.i. (ISBN 0-226-40148-0); pap. text ed. 8.95x o.s.i. (ISBN 0-226-40149-9, Phoen). U of Chicago Pr.

Shadow of the Flame. Jean Canavan. 304p. 1984. pap. 2.95 o.p. (ISBN 0-380-86504-1, 86504). Avon.

Shadow of the Hawk & Other Stories. Marie De France. Ed. by James Reeves. LC 76-28949. (gr. 6 up). 1979. 7.95 o.p. (ISBN 0-395-28820-7, Clarion). HM.

Shadow of the Hunter: Stories of Eskimo Life. Richard K. Nelson. LC 80-11091. 272p. 1980. 12.50x o.s.i. (ISBN 0-226-57179-3). U of Chicago Pr.

Shadow of the Mountain. Sylvia Wilkinson. 1977. 8.95 o.p. (ISBN 0-395-25170-2). HM.

Shadow of the Palms. Janice Law. 1980. 8.95 o.p. (ISBN 0-395-28591-7). HM.

Shadow of the Plantation. Charles S. Johnson. LC 53-3592. (Midway Reprint Ser.). 1979. pap. text ed. 10.00x o.s.i. (ISBN 0-226-40159-6). U of Chicago Pr.

Shadow of the Rock. Patricia Wright. 384p. 1980. pap. 2.50 o.p. (ISBN 0-380-49064-1, 49064). Avon.

Shadow of the Ship. Robert W. Franson. 288p. (Orig.). 1983. pap. 2.75 o.s.i. (ISBN 0-345-30688-0, Del Rey). Ballantine.

Shadow over the Earth. Philip Wilding. 160p. 1956. (ISBN 0-8022-1878-4). Philos Lib.

Shadow Prices for Economic Appraisal of Projects: An Application to Thailand. Sadiq Ahmed. (Working Paper: No. 609). 90p. 1984. 5.00 o.p. (ISBN 0-8213-0244-2, WP 0609). World Bank.

Shadow Prices for Trade Strategy & Investment Planning in Egypt. John Page, Jr. LC 82-8594. (World Bank Staff Working Papers: No. 521). 212p. (Orig.). 1982. pap. 10.00 o.p. (ISBN 0-8213-0009-1, WP0521). World Bank.

Shadow Quilting: A Leading Designer Introduces a Beautiful New Craft. Majorie Puckett. (Illus.). 176p. 1986. 24.95 o.p. (ISBN 0-684-18339-0). Scribner.

Shadow Scrapbook. Walter Gibson. LC 78-22277. (Orig.). 1979. pap. 8.95 o.p. (ISBN 0-15-681475-7, Harv). HarBraceJ.

Shadow Spy. Nicholas Luard. LC 78-22264. 1979. 7.95 o.p. (ISBN 0-15-125712-4). HarBraceJ.

Shadow Stealers. R. G. Austin. (Which Way Bk.: No. 16). 128p. (Orig.). (gr. 3-6). 1984. pap. 1.95 o.p. (ISBN 0-671-52635-9). Archway.

Shadow Taker. Blaine M. Yorgason & Carl J. Eaton. LC 85-20593. 133p. 1985. 8.95 o.p. (ISBN 0-87579-018-6). Deseret Bk.

Shadow Weaver. David Lee. 1984. pap. 8.00 o.p. (ISBN 0-918116-25-2). Brooding Heron Pr.

Shadowed Lullabies. Morton Reed. (Orig.). 1989. pap. 4.50 o.p. Pinnacle MO.

Shadowed Path. Barbara Corcoran. (Moonstone Novels Ser.: No. 2). 160p. (Orig.). (gr. 5 up). 1985. pap. 2.25 o.p. (ISBN 0-671-50781-8). Archway.

ShadowPlay. Norman Hartley. LC 81-69237. 288p. 1982. 12.95 o.p. (ISBN 0-689-11249-1, Atheneum). Macmillan.

Shadows. Douglas Scott. 256p. 1988. 19.95 o.p. (ISBN 0-436-44444-5, Pub. by Secker Warburg UK). David & Charles.

Shadows & Light. Francesca Stanfill. 1984. 16.45 o.p. (ISBN 0-671-53256-1). S&S.

Shadows & the Crosses. John D. Ballam. LC 85-62907. 90p. (Orig.). 1985. pap. 5.95 o.p. (ISBN 0-938232-58-4). Winston-Derek.

Shadows Eight. Charles L. Grant. (Science Fiction Ser.). 192p. 1985. 12.95 o.p. (ISBN 0-385-19823-X). Doubleday.

Shadows in Paradise. Erich M. Remarque. 1972. 6.95 o.p. (ISBN 0-15-181480-5). HarBraceJ.

Shadows Nine. Charles L. Grant. LC 85-643084. (Science Fiction Ser.). 192p. 1986. 12.95 o.s.i. (ISBN 0-385-23486-4). Doubleday.

Shadows of Heaven: Religion & Fantasy in the Writing of C. S. Lewis, Charles Williams & J. R. R. Tolkien. Gunnar Urang. LC 73-153998. 208p. 1971. 7.95 o.p. (ISBN 0-8298-0197-9). Pilgrim NY.

Shadows of Splendor. Jillian Hunter. (Avon Romance Ser.). 384p. 1987. pap. 3.95 o.p. (ISBN 0-380-75170-4). Avon.

Shadows of the Buffalo: A Family Odyssey among the Indians. Adolph Hungry Wolf & Beverly Hungry Wolf. LC 83-61365. (Illus.). 288p. 1983. 12.95 o.p. (ISBN 0-688-01680-4). Morrow.

Shadows of the Heart. Florence Hurd. 400p. 1980. pap. 2.50 o.p. (ISBN 0-380-76406-7, 76406). Avon.

Shadows of the Rising Sun: A Critical View of the Japanese Miracle. Jared Taylor. LC 83-9915. 1983. 14.95 o.p. (ISBN 0-688-02455-6). Morrow.

Shadows of the Storm. National Historical Society Staff. Ed. by William C. Davis & Bell I. Wiley. LC 80-1659. (Image of War Ser. 1861-1865: Vol. 1). (Illus.). 464p. 1981. pap. 19.95 o.p. (ISBN 0-385-15466-6). Doubleday.

Shadows of Turning. Paul J. Bartholomew. LC 84-90202. 81p. 1985. 7.95 o.p. (ISBN 0-533-06253-5). Vantage.

Shadows on Little Reef Bay. C. S. Adler. LC 83-15207. 180p. (gr. 6 up). 1984. 10.45 o.p. (ISBN 0-89919-217-3, Clarion). HM.

Shadows on Our Skin. Jennifer Johnston. 1979. pap. 2.50 o.p. (ISBN 0-380-44347-3, Bard). Avon.

Shadows on the Grass. Isak Dinesen. 160p. 1961. pap. 3.95 o.p. (ISBN 0-394-71062-2, Vin). Random.

Shadows over Nordmaar. Dezra D. Phillips. LC 87-51252. (Advanced Dungeons & Dragons Gamebook Ser.: No. 16). (Illus.). 192p. (Orig.). (gr. 7-12). 1988. pap. 2.95 o.p. (ISBN 0-88038-541-3). TSR Inc.

Shadows over Paradise. Hope Goodwin. LC 87-19058. (Starlight Romance Ser.). 192p. 1987. 12.95 o.p. (ISBN 0-385-24337-5). Doubleday.

Shadows over the Sunshine Act. 73p. 1977. 1.00 o.p. (ISBN 0-914389-11-4). Common Cause.

Shadows Ten. Charles L. Grant. (Science Fiction Ser.). 192p. 1987. 12.95 o.p. (ISBN 0-385-23893-2). Doubleday.

Shady Lady. Ruth Gordon. LC 81-70029. 1982. 12.95 o.p. (ISBN 0-87795-364-3, Arbor Hse). Morrow.

Shaggy Dog Riddles. Lori Miescke. Ed. by Ann Fay. LC 83-16743. (Illus.). 32p. (gr. 1-5). 1983. PLB 7.75 o.p. (ISBN 0-8075-7329-9). A Whitman.

Shaggy Dog Story. Eric Partridge. 110p. 1955. (ISBN 0-8022-1279-4). Philos Lib.

Shaggy Dogs & Spotty Dogs & Shaggy & Spotty Dogs. Seymour Leichman. LC 73-75322. (Illus.). (gr. k-1). 1973. 5.50 o.p. (ISBN 0-15-278020-3, HJ). HarBraceJ.

Shags Finds a Kitten. Gyo Fujikawa. (Illus.). 32p. (ps-1). 1983. pap. 3.95 o.p. (ISBN 0-448-16465-5, G&D). Putnam Pub Group.

Shaitan. Max Ehrlich. LC 80-66498. 320p. 1982. 13.95 o.p. (ISBN 0-87795-273-6, Arbor Hse). Morrow.

Shake-Speare: The Mystery. George E. Sweet. 1985. 13.95 o.p. (ISBN 0-533-06203-9). Vantage.

Shakedown. Jonathan Kwitny. 1978. pap. 1.95 o.p. (ISBN 0-380-01957-4, 38380). Avon.

Shakespeare. Martin Fido. LC 85-9637. (Illustrates Biographies Ser.). (Illus.). 144p. 1985. pap. 9.95 o.p. (ISBN 0-87226-031-3). P Bedrick Bks.

Shakespeare. Illus. by Patricia Machin. (Pocket Poets Ser.). (Illus.). 52p. 1985. 4.95 o.p. (ISBN 0-86350-049-8). Salem Hse Pubs.

Shakespeare: A Celebration Fifteen Sixty-Four to Nineteen Sixty-Four. Ed. by T. J. Spencer. 1964. 16.00x o.p. (ISBN 0-88307-255-6). Gannon.

Shakespeare an Elizabethian Culture. Date not set. (ISBN 0-8052-3902-2). Random.

Shakespeare & His Theatre. Jim Bradbury. Ed. by Marjorie Reeves. (Then & There Ser.). (Illus.). 95p. (Orig.). (gr. 7-12). 1977. pap. text ed. 4.95 o.p. (ISBN 0-582-20539-5). Longman.

Shakespeare & His World. F. E. Halliday. (And His-Her World Ser.). (Illus.). 1980. Encore Edition. 4.95 o.p. (ISBN 0-684-16898-7, ScribT). Scribner.

Shakespeare & the Confines of Art. Philip Edwards. (Methuen Library Reprint Ser.). 176p. 1981. 32.00x o.p. (ISBN 0-416-32200-X, NO. 3581). Routledge Chapman & Hall.

Shakespeare & the Faerie Queene. Abbie F. Potts. 1970. Repr. of 1958 ed. lib. bdg. 35.00 o.p. (ISBN 0-8371-1156-0, POSF). Greenwood.

Shakespeare & the Supernatural. Cumberland Clark. 346p. Repr. of 1931 ed. 29.00 o.p. (ISBN 0-403-04266-6). Somerset Pub.

Shakespeare at Work, Fifteen Ninety-Two to Sixteen Three. George B. Harrison. LC 80-11668. 325p. 1980. Repr. of 1958 ed. lib. bdg. 41.50x o.p. (ISBN 0-313-22426-9, HASH). Greenwood.

Shakespeare Bibliography: The Catalogue of the Birmingham Shakespeare Library, 7 vols. Compiled by Birmingham Shakespeare Library Staff. 4311p. 1971. Set. 445.00x o.p. (ISBN 0-7201-0180-8); pap. 191.00 o.p. Mansell.

Shakespeare Companion. Gareth Lloyd Evans & Barbara Lloyd Evans. (Encore Edition). (Illus.). 1978. encore ed 5.95 o.p. (ISBN 0-684-16908-8, ScribT). Scribner.

Shakespeare Criticism: Dryden to Morgann. S. Homchaudhuri. 1979. text ed. 19.00x o.p. Coronet Bks.

Shakespeare Garden: With Numerous Illustrations from Photographs & Reproductions of Old Wood Cuts. Esther Singleton. LC 74-8203. 444p. 1974. Repr. of 1922 ed. 46.00x o.p. (ISBN 0-8103-4048-8). Gale.

Shakespeare Handbook. facsimile ed. Raymond M. Alden. 315p. Repr. of 1932 ed. lib. bdg. 21.00 o.p. (ISBN 0-8290-0787-3). Irvington.

Shakespeare in His Own Time. D. C. Biswas. 1979. text ed. 12.50x o.p. (ISBN 0-391-01762-4). Humanities.

Shakespeare in Sable: A History of Black Shakespearean Actors. Errol Hill. LC 83-18106. (Illus.). 217p. 1984. 20.00 o.p. (ISBN 0-87023-426-9). U of Mass Pr.

Shakespeare Plain: The Making & Performing of Shakespeare's Plays. William Leary. (McGraw-Hill Paperbacks). 1977. text ed. 7.95 o.p. (ISBN 0-07-036947-X); pap. text ed. 4.95 o.p. (ISBN 0-07-036946-1). McGraw.

Shakespeare: Seven Tragedies: the Dramatist's Manipulation of Response. E. A. Honigmann. LC 79-54988. 215p. 1978. Repr. of 1976 ed. 26.50x o.p. (ISBN 0-06-492965-5); pap. 13.95x o.p. (ISBN 0-06-492967-1). B&N Imports.

Shakespeare, Spenser, Donne. Frank Kermode. Penguin USA.

Shakespeare under Elizabeth. George B. Harrison. Repr. of 1933 ed. 29.00 o.p. (ISBN 0-403-04273-9). Somerset Pub.

Shakespearean Metaphor: Studies in Language & Form. Ralph Berry. 128p. 1978. 19.50x o.s.i. (ISBN 0-8476-6047-8). Rowman.

Shakespearean Plant Names: Identifications & Interpretations. Mats Ryden. (Stockholm Studies in English: No. 43). (Illus.). 1978. pap. text ed. 17.50 o.p. (ISBN 91-22-00139-5). Humanities.

Shakespeare's Audience. Alfred Harbage. 20.00 o.p. (ISBN 0-8446-2203-6). Peter Smith.

Shakespeare's Biblical Knowledge & Use of the Book of Common Prayer. Richmond Noble. 1970. lib. bdg. 20.00x o.p. (ISBN 0-374-96115-8, Octagon). Hippocrene Bks.

Shakespeare's Comedy of Love. Alexander Leggatt. 1974. pap. 13.95x o.p. (ISBN 0-416-79130-1, NO. 2294). Routledge Chapman & Hall.

Shakespeare's Drama. Una Ellis-Fermor. Ed. by Kenneth Muir. 1980. 29.95x o.p. (ISBN 0-416-74090-1, NO. 2044); pap. 13.95x o.p. (ISBN 0-416-74100-2, NO. 2043). Routledge Chapman & Hall.

Shakespeare's Dramatic Art. Wolfgang Clemen. (Methuen Library Reprints). 1981. 45.00x o.p. (ISBN 0-416-30580-6, NO. 2218). Routledge Chapman & Hall.

Shakespeare's Dramatic Structures. Anthony Brennan. 224p. 1986. text ed. 34.95 o.p. (ISBN 0-7102-0450-7). Routledge Chapman & Hall.

Shakespeare's Early Tragedies. Nicholas Brooke. 214p. 1973. pap. 12.95x o.p. (ISBN 0-416-77560-8, NO. 2114). Routledge Chapman & Hall.

Shakespeare's English see Society's Work.

Shakespeare's Favorite Novel: A Study of the Golden Asse As Prime Source. J. J. Tobin. LC 84-5135. 218p. (Orig.). 1984. lib. bdg. 27.50 o.p. (ISBN 0-8191-3896-7); pap. text ed. 13.00 o.p. (ISBN 0-8191-3897-5). U Pr of Amer.

Shakespeare's Grammatical Style: A Computer-Assisted Analysis of "Richard II" & "Antony & Cleopatra" Dolores M. Burton. LC 73-6795. 382p. 1973. 20.00x o.p. (ISBN 0-292-77504-0). U of Tex Pr.

Shakespeare's Heroical Histories: Henry Six & Its Literary Tradition. David Riggs. LC 75-152701. 1971. 16.00x o.s.i. (ISBN 0-674-80400-7). Harvard U Pr.

Shakespeare's Life & Times: A Pictorial Record. Roland M. Frye. LC 67-11031. (Illus.). 1967. 37.00x o.p. (ISBN 0-691-06119-X); pap. 13.95x o.p. (ISBN 0-691-01318-7). Princeton U Pr.

Shakespeare's Mature Tragedies. Bernard McElroy. LC 72-5389. 268p. 1973. 27.50 o.p. (ISBN 0-691-06247-1). Princeton U Pr.

Shakespeare's "Merry Wives of Windsor" William Green. 1962. 26.00x o.p. (ISBN 0-691-06120-3). Princeton U Pr.

Shakespeare's Othello: The Harbrace Theater Edition. John R. Brown. (Illus.). 108p. 1973. pap. text ed. 8.00 o.p. (ISBN 0-15-567678-4, HC). HarBraceJ.

Shakespeare's Plays Today: Some Customs & Conventions of the Stage. Arthur C. Sprague & J. C. Trewin. LC 73-133842. (Illus.). 158p. 1971. lib. bdg. 14.95x o.p. (ISBN 0-87249-205-2). U of SC Pr.

Shakespeare's Political Drama: The History Plays & the Roman Plays. Alexander Leggatt. 320p. 1988. lib. bdg. 45.00 o.p. (ISBN 0-415-00655-4). Routledge Chapman & Hall.

Shakespeare's Pronunciation. Helge Kokeritz. 1953. 75.00x o.p. (ISBN 0-686-83738-X). Elliots Bks.

Shakespeare's Romances & the Royal Family. David M. Bergeron. LC 85-689. xiv, 256p. 1985. 25.00x o.p. (ISBN 0-7006-0271-2). U Pr of KS.

Shakespeare's Sexual Comedy: A Mirror for Lovers. Hugh M. Richmond. LC 77-155437. Repr. of 1971 ed. (ISBN 0-8290-2141-8). Irvington.

Shakespeare's Sonnets. Kenneth Muir. (Unwin Critical Library). 1979. text ed. 22.95 o.p. (ISBN 0-04-821042-0). Unwin Hyman.

Shakespeare's Theatre. Peter Thomson. (Theatre Production Ser.). (Illus.). 190p. 1985. pap. 12.95x o.p. (ISBN 0-7102-0382-9); 19.95x o.p. (ISBN 0-7100-9480-9). Routledge Chapman & Hall.

Shakespeare's Use of Dream & Vision. John Arthos. 208p. 1977. 19.50x o.p. (ISBN 0-87471-912-7). Rowman.

Shakespeare's Wordplay. M. M. Mahood. 1968. pap. 10.95x o.p. (ISBN 0-416-29560-6, NO. 2836). Routledge Chapman & Hall.

Shall We Amend the Fifth Amendment? Lewis Mayers. LC 78-6206. 341p. 1978. Repr. of 1959 ed. lib. bdg. 35.00x o.p. (ISBN 0-313-20394-6, MASH). Greenwood.

Shall We Dance? Brian H. Edwards. 1984. pap. 4.95 o.p. (ISBN 0-87552-970-4, Evangel Pr UK). Presby & Reformed.

Shallow Waters: A Year on Cape Cod's Pleasant Bay. Bill Sargent. (Illus.). 144p. 1981. 17.95 o.p. (ISBN 0-395-29481-9). HM.

Shallow Waters: A Year on Cape Cod's Pleasant Bay. William Sargent. (Illus.). 168p. 1985. pap. 12.95 o.p. (ISBN 0-940160-28-5). Parnassus Imprints.

Shallows. Tim Winton. LC 85-48146. 235p. 1986. 14.95 o.p. (ISBN 0-689-11806-6, Atheneum). Macmillan.

Shalom, My Marty... Helen McPeck. 1978. 6.50 o.p. (ISBN 0-682-48994-8). Exposition-Phoenix.

Shalom Woman. Margaret Wold. LC 75-2828. 128p. 1975. pap. 6.95 o.p. (ISBN 0-8066-1475-7, 10-5740, Augsburg). Augsburg Fortress.

Shaman & the Magician. Nevill Drury. 130p. 1987. pap. 11.95 o.p. (ISBN 1-85063-085-2, Pub. by Routledge UK). Routledge Chapman & Hall.

Shaman & the Magician: Journeys Between the Worlds. Nevill Drury. 156p. (Orig.). 1982. pap. 8.95 o.p. (ISBN 0-7100-0910-0). Routledge Chapman & Hall.

Shamanism: The Foundations of Magic. (ISBN 0-85030-453-9, Pub. by Thorsons UK). Weiser.

Shamans, Lamas & Evangelicals: The English Missionaries in Siberia. C. R. Bawden. (Illus.). 400p. 1985. 50.00x o.p. (ISBN 0-7102-0064-1). Routledge Chapman & Hall.

Shame & Guilt. Gerhart Piers & Milton B. Singer. 112p. 1972. pap. 1.95x o.p. (ISBN 0-393-00649-2, Norton Lib). Norton.

Shamu, Sea World Star. Sea World, Inc. Staff. (Bathtime Bks.). (Illus.). (ps). 1982. 2.95 o.p. (ISBN 0-394-85404-7). Random.

Shan. Eric Van Lustbader. LC 86-10027. 608p. 1986. 18.45 o.s.i. (ISBN 0-394-55640-2). Random.

Shanghai. Christopher New. 1985. 19.45 o.s.i. (ISBN 0-671-42197-2). Summit Bks.

Shanghai Honeymoon. Maurice Dekobra. (ISBN 0-8022-0373-6). Philos Lib.

Shanghai, Nineteen Twenty-five: Urban Nationalism & the Defense of Foreign Privilege. Nicholas R. Clifford. LC 79-14469. (Michigan Monographs in Chinese Studies: No. 37). (Orig.). 1979. pap. text ed. 6.00 o.p. (ISBN 0-89264-037-5). U of Mich Ctr Chinese.

Shaniko: From Wool Capital to Ghost Town. Helen G. Rees. LC 81-70285. (Illus.). 1982. 8.95 o.s.i. (ISBN 0-8323-0398-4); pap. 6.50 o.p. (ISBN 0-8323-0399-2). Binford-Metropolitan.

Shank's Mare. Ikku Jippensha. LC 60-14370. (Illus.). 1960. pap. 8.25 o.p. (ISBN 0-8048-0524-5). C E Tuttle.

Shanties from the Seven Seas. Stan Hugill. 1980. Repr. of 1961 ed. 30.00 o.p. (ISBN 0-7100-1573-9). Routledge Chapman & Hall.

Shanty Town City: The Case of Poona. Bapat. (Progress in Planning Ser.: Vol. 15, Pt. 3). 85p. 1981. pap. 16.25 o.p. (ISBN 0-08-026811-0). Pergamon.

Shape & Form of Puget Sound. Robert E. Burns. LC 84-15354. (Pugest Sound Bks.). (Illus.). 114p. (Orig.). 1985. pap. 8.95 o.p. (ISBN 0-295-96184-8). U of Wash Pr.

Shape & Style of Proust's Novel. John P. Houston. LC 81-16171. 141p. 1982. 19.95x o.p. (ISBN 0-8143-1698-0). Wayne St U Pr.

Shape Memory Effects in Alloys. Ed. by Jeff Perkins. LC 75-31928. (Illus.). 584p. 1975. 95.00x o.p. (ISBN 0-306-30891-6, Plenum Pr). Plenum Pub.

Shape of Scriptural Authority. David L. Bartlett. LC 83-48009. 176p. 1983. pap. 1.00 o.p. (ISBN 0-8006-1713-4, 1-1713, Fortress). Augsburg Fortress.

Shape of the Past. John W. Montgomery. LC 75-26651. 400p. 1975. pap. 9.95 o.p. (ISBN 0-87123-535-8, 210535). Bethany Hse.

Shape of the Question: The Mission of the Church in a Secular Age. Kent S. Knutson. LC 72-78558. 128p. (Orig.). 1972. pap. 3.50 o.p. (ISBN 0-8066-1225-8, 10-5750, Augsburg). Augsburg Fortress.

Shape of Utopia: Studies in a Literary Genre. Robert C. Elliott. LC 78-103136. 1970. lib. bdg. 15.00x o.s.i. (ISBN 0-226-20500-2). U of Chicago Pr.

Shape Shifters: Fantasy & Science Fiction Tales About Humans Who Can Change Their Shapes. Compiled by Jane H. Yolen. LC 77-13646. (gr. 6 up). 1979. 8.95 o.p. (ISBN 0-395-28933-5, Clarion). HM.

Shape Shifters: Shaman Women in Contemporary Society. Ed. by Michele Jamal. 260p. (Orig.). 1987. pap. 12.95 o.p. (ISBN 1-85063-060-7, Pub. by Routledge UK). Routledge Chapman & Hall.

Shape Up. Harold Albert. 1975. 4.40 o.p. (ISBN 0-89536-212-0, 1914). CSS of Ohio.

Shape Up. O. Quentin Hyder. (Illus.). 160p. 1979. 4.95 o.p. (Power Bks); pap. 4.95 o.p. (ISBN 0-8007-0975-6). Revell.

Shape Up. (Purse Books). 1974. pap. 0.49 o.p. (ISBN 0-440-67962-1). Dell.

Shape-up & Hiring Hall. Charles P. Larrowe. LC 75-46614. (Illus.). 250p. 1976. Repr. of 1955 ed. lib. bdg. 35.00x o.p. (ISBN 0-8371-8750-8, LASU). Greenwood.

Shape up for Sex. Dan Liberatore & Judy Davis. 1979. pap. 1.95 o.p. (ISBN 0-380-44982-X, 44982). Avon.

Shape up from the Inside Out. John R. Throop. (Living Bks.). 128p. (Orig.). 1986. pap. 2.95 o.p. (ISBN 0-8423-5899-4). Tyndale.

Shape Your Body, Shape Your Life: The Weight Training Ways to Total Fitness. Tony Lycholat. (Illus.). 128p. (Orig.). 1987. pap. 6.99 o.p. (ISBN 0-85059-869-9, Pub. by PSL P Stephens). Sterling.

Shapes. Jan Pienkowski. (Concept Bks.). (Illus.). 32p. (ps-k). 1981. 3.95 o.s.i. (ISBN 0-671-44455-7, Little Simon). S&S.

Shapes & Perceptions: An Intuitive Approach to Geometry. Gail Konkle. LC 74-2464. 1974. text ed. write for info. o.p. (ISBN 0-87150-164-3, PWS 1361, Prindle). PWS-Kent Pub.

Shapes of Change. Marcia B. Siegel. 400p. 1981. pap. 3.95 o.p. (ISBN 0-380-53892-X, 53892-X, Discus). Avon.

Shapes of Change: Images of American Dance. Marcia B. Siegel. 1979. 15.00 o.p. (ISBN 0-395-27090-1). HM.
Shaping a Library: William L. Clements As Collector. M. Maxwell. (Illus.). 1973. 32.50 o.p. (ISBN 9-0607-2631-6). E J Brill USA.
Shaping College Writing: Paragraph & Essay. 2nd ed. Joseph D. Gallo & Henry W. Rink. (Orig.). 1973. pap. text ed. 6.95 o.p. (ISBN 0-15-580859-1, HC). HarBraceJ.
Shaping College Writing: Paragraph & Essay. 3rd ed. Joseph D. Gallo & Henry W. Rink. 165p. 1979. pap. text ed. 10.95 o.p. (ISBN 0-15-580861-3, HC). HarBraceJ.
Shaping of America: A People's History of the Young Republic. Page Smith. LC 79-13592. 870p. 1980. text ed. 20.00 o.p. (ISBN 0-07-059017-6). McGraw.
Shaping of America's Heartland: The Landscape of the Middle West. Betty F. Thomson. (Naturalist's America Ser.: Vol. 4). 1977. 11.95 o.p. (ISBN 0-395-24760-8). HM.
Shaping of France. Isaac Asimov. LC 72-75604. (Illus.). 288p. (gr. 7 up). 1972. 5.95 o.p. (ISBN 0-395-13891-4). HM.
Shaping of North America: From Earliest Times to 1763. Isaac Asimov. LC 72-7931. (Illus.). 272p. (gr. 7-12). 1973. 9.95 o.p. (ISBN 0-395-15493-6). HM.
Shaping of Southern England. Ed. by David Jones. LC 80-40888. (Special Publications of the Institute of British Geographers: Vol.2). 1981. 41.00 o.p. (ISBN 0-12-388950-2). Acad Pr.
Shaping of the Earth. William F. Smith. (Illus.). 128p. 1981. 7.00 o.p. (ISBN 0-682-49715-0). Exposition-Phoenix.
Shaping of Western Civilization. Ludwig F. Schaefer et al. 1970. pap. 5.95x study guide o.p. (ISBN 0-03-081102-3). Irvington.
Shaping the Body Politic. American Alliance for Health, Physical Education, Recreation & Dance Staff. 9.95x o.p. (ISBN 0-317-06643-9). AAHPERD.
Shaping the Future: The Ethics of Dietrich Bonhoeffer. James Burtness. LC 85-47723. 208p. 1985. pap. 16.95 o.p. (ISBN 0-8006-1869-6, 1-1869, Fortress). Augsburg Fortress.
Shaping Your Child into an Athlete. Faye S. Blake. 144p. 1986. 8.95 o.p. (ISBN 0-8062-2930-6). Carlton.
Sharad: Camel Driver for the Kings. Russell Q. Chilcote. 1978. pap. 1.75x o.p. (ISBN 0-8358-0379-1). Upper Room.
Shards. John F. Hubickey. 1978. 4.50 o.p. (ISBN 0-682-49017-2). Exposition-Phoenix.
Share My Thoughts, Pretty Please. Joyce M. Bagley. 1976. 4.00 o.p. (ISBN 0-682-48544-6). Exposition-Phoenix.
Shared Space: The Two Circuits of the Urban Economy in Underdeveloped Countries. Milton Santos. xii, 266p. 1979. 14.95x o.p. (ISBN 0-416-79660-5, NO. 2874); pap. 14.95x o.p. (ISBN 0-416-79670-2, NO. 2875). Routledge Chapman & Hall.
Shareholder Meetings & Shareowner Control in Today's Securities Markets. 566p. 1985. 15.00 o.p. (B4-6732). PLI.
Sharing. Marian Bennett. (Wipe-Clean Bks.). (Illus.). 12p. (ps). 1985. pap. 1.39 o.p. (ISBN 0-87239-959-1, 3519). Standard Pub.
Sharing. Sy Cook & Martha Moffett. 224p. (Orig.). 1984. pap. 2.95 o.p. (ISBN 0-380-86538-6, 86538). Avon.
Sharing. Taro Gomi. (Fun Time Ser.). (Illus.). 22p. (ps-1). 1981. 3.50 o.p. (ISBN 0-89346-198-9). Heian Intl.
Sharing Birth: A Father's Guide to Giving Support During Labor. Carl Jones. LC 84-15990. (Illus.). 192p. (Orig.). 1985. pap. 7.95 o.p. (ISBN 0-688-04164-7, Quill). Morrow.
Sharing Global Resources. Uzi B. Arad et al. LC 78-13233. (Council on Foreign Relations 1980's Project). (Illus.). 1979. text ed. 14.95 o.p. (ISBN 0-07-002150-3); pap. text ed. 6.95 o.p. (ISBN 0-07-002151-1). McGraw.
Sharing Possessions: Mandate & Symbol of Faith. Luke T. Johnson. Ed. by Walter Brueggemann & John R. Donahue. LC 80-2390. (Overtures to Biblical Theology Ser.: No. 9). 176p. (Orig.). 1981. pap. 2.50 o.p. (ISBN 0-8006-1534-4, 1-1534, Fortress). Augsburg Fortress.
Sharing Resources: Post Secondary Education & Industry Cooperation. Catherine P. Warmbrod & Jon J. Persavich. 175p. 1981. 10.00 o.p. (ISBN 0-318-15558-3, RD203). Natl Ctr Res Voc Ed.
Sharing the Risk: How the Nation's Businesses, Homes & Autos Are Insured. rev. ed. 192p. 1985. pap. 6.95 o.p. (ISBN 0-932387-10-1). Insur Info.
Sharing the Same Bowl: A Socioeconomic History of Women & Class in Accra, Ghana. Claire C. Robertson. LC 83-48112. (Illus.). 320p. 1984. 22.50x o.p. (ISBN 0-253-35205-3). Ind U Pr.
Sharing the Sun, Vols. 1-10. Ed. by K. W. Boer. Incl. Vol. 1. International & U. S. Programs Solar Flux. 1977. pap. 72.00 (ISBN 0-08-021686-2); Vol. 2. Solar Collectors. 1977. pap. 72.00 (ISBN 0-08-021687-0); Vol. 3. Solar Heating & Cooling Buildings. 1977. pap. 105.00 o.p. (ISBN 0-08-021688-9); Vol. 4. Solar System, Simulation, Design. 1977. pap. 80.00 (ISBN 0-08-021689-7); Vol. 5. Solar Thermal & Ocean Thermal. 1977. pap. 94.00 (ISBN 0-08-021690-0); Vol. 6. Photovoltaics & Materials. 1977. pap. 90.00 o.p. (ISBN 0-08-021691-9); Vol. 7. Agriculture, Biomass, Wind, New Developments. 1977. pap. 100.00 o.p. (ISBN 0-08-021692-7); Vol. 8. Storage, Water Heater, Data Communication, Education. 1977. pap. 72.00 (ISBN 0-08-021693-5); Vol. 9. Socio - Economics & Cultural. 1977. pap. 61.00 (ISBN 0-08-021694-3); Vol. 10. Business & Commercial Implications. 1977. pap. 48.00 (ISBN 0-08-021695-1). 1977. Set. pap. 965.00 o.p. (ISBN 0-08-021696-X). Pergamon.
Shariyat-Ki-Sugmad: Buch Eins, Vol. 1. Paul Twitchell. Tr. by Steve DeWitt et al from Ger. 186p. (Orig.). 1980. pap. 8.95 o.p. (ISBN 0-914766-56-2, 0538). Illum Way Pub.
Shariyat Ki Sugmad: Buch Zwei, Vol. 2. Paul Twitchell. Tr. by Steve Dewitt & Uli Sacchet. 204p. (Orig., Ger.). 1981. pap. 8.95 o.p. (ISBN 0-914766-70-8, 0539). Illum Way Pub.
Shariyat-Ki-Sugmad: Premier Livre, Vol. 1. Paul Twitchell. Tr. by Yves D. Martin from Fr. 190p. (Orig.). 1980. pap. 8.95 o.p. (ISBN 0-914766-34-1, 0338). Illum Way Pub.
Shark: A Photographer's Story. Jeremy Stafford-Deitsch. LC 87-4798. (Illus.). 200p. 1987. 19.95 o.s.i. (ISBN 0-87156-776-8). Sierra.
Shark Hunter. William E. Young. 1978. pap. 1.50 o.p. (ISBN 0-8439-0563-8, Pub. by Leisure Bks CT). Dorchester Pub Co.
Shark Man: Master Hunter of the Deep. Robert F. Boggs. 1977. 7.95 o.p. (ISBN 0-89328-007-0). Lorenz Corp.
Sharks. Rhonda Blumberg. 1980. pap. 2.25 o.p. (ISBN 0-380-49247-4, 64980-2, Camelot). Avon.
Sharks. Ann McGovern. LC 76-17122. (Illus.). 48p. (gr. k-3). 1976. 9.95 o.s.i. (ISBN 0-02-765740-X, Four Winds). Macmillan.
Sharks & Little Fish. Wolfgang Ott. 1982. pap. 2.95 o.s.i. (ISBN 0-345-30390-3). Ballantine.
Sharks, Wrecks, & Movie Stars: The Adventures of an Underwater Photographer. rev. ed. Jack McKenney. Orig. Title: Dive to Adventure. (Illus.). 1990. pap. o.s.i. (ISBN 0-89732-082-4). Menasha Ridge.
Sharon's Pic-A-Story. (gr. 6-8). 1984. pap. 4.95 o.p. (ISBN 0-317-05538-0). Sharon Pubns.
Sharon's UFO Code for Outer Space. I. W. Whiteside. (Illus.). 49p. (Orig.). 1983. pap. 4.00 o.p. (ISBN 0-682-49969-2). Exposition-Phoenix.
Sharp End. John Ellis. 1980. encore ed. 4.50 o.p. (ISBN 0-684-16728-X, ScribT). Scribner.
Sharp Focus Watercolor Painting: Techniques for Hot-Pressed Surfaces. Georg Shook & Gary Witt. 144p. 1981. 27.50 o.p. (ISBN 0-8230-4794-6). Watson-Guptill.
Sharpe's Sword: The Salamanca Campaign. Bernard Cornwell. 336p. 1984. pap. 5.95 o.p. (ISBN 0-14-007024-9). Penguin.
Sharpshooter. John Reese. 224p. 1982. pap. write for info. o.p. (ISBN 0-8439-1092-5, Pub. by Leisure Bks CT). Dorchester Pub Co.
Shatterday. Harlan Ellison. 320p. 1980. 12.95 o.p. (ISBN 0-395-28587-9). HM.
Shattered Chain. Marion Zimmer Bradley. 1979. lib. bdg. 12.50 o.p. (ISBN 0-8398-2502-1, Gregg). G K Hall.
Shattered Dream: Herbert Hoover & the Great Depression. Gene Smith. 288p. 1984. pap. text ed. 7.95 o.p. (ISBN 0-07-058474-5). McGraw.
Shattered Mask. D. G. Devon. 1983. pap. 2.75 o.s.i. (ISBN 0-345-29849-7). Ballantine.
Shattered Self: E. T. A. Hoffmann's Tragic Vision. Horst Daemmrich. LC 72-11451. 144p. 1973. text ed. 17.95x o.p. (ISBN 0-8143-1493-7). Wayne St U Pr.
Shattered Silk. Barbara Michaels. LC 86-47658. 369p. 1986. 15.95 o.p. (ISBN 0-689-11620-9, Atheneum). Macmillan.
Shattered Stone. Robert Newman. LC 75-6834. 256p. (gr. 4-7). 1975. 6.95 o.p. (ISBN 0-689-30481-1, Atheneum). Macmillan.
Shattering the German Night. Jud Newborn & Annette E. Dumbach. LC 85-10288. 1986. 17.95 o.p. (ISBN 0-316-60413-5). Little.
Shavian Guide to the Intelligent Woman. Barbara B. Watson. 256p. 1972. pap. 2.45x o.p. (ISBN 0-393-00640-9). Norton.
Shavian Playground: An Exploration of the Art of George Bernard Shaw. Margery M. Morgan. (Illus.). 1974. pap. 13.95x o.p. (ISBN 0-416-82500-1, NO. 2327). Routledge Chapman & Hall.
Shaw & Ibsen: Bernard Shaw's 'The Quintessence of Ibsenism' & Related Writings. J. L. Wisenthal. LC 79-14858. 1979. 25.00x o.p. (ISBN 0-8020-5454-4). U of Toronto Pr.
Shawls, Crinolines & Filigree: Dress & Adornment of the Women of New Mexico. Carmen G. Espinosa. LC 72-138042. (Illus.). 80p. 1970. 8.00 o.p. (ISBN 0-87404-026-4). Tex Western.
Shawno: Large Print Books. George Dennison. 1985. lib. bdg. 11.95 o.p. (ISBN 0-8161-3876-1). G K Hall.
Shaw's Dramatic Criticism from the Saturday Review 1895-1898. George Bernard Shaw. Ed. by John F. Matthews. 5.00 o.p. (ISBN 0-8446-2930-8). Peter Smith.
Shaw's Textbook of Operative Gynaecology. 5th ed. John Howkins & Christopher N. Hudson. (Illus.). 1983. 138.75 o.p. (ISBN 0-443-02150-3). Churchill.
She & the Dubious Three. Dorothy Crayder. LC 74-75559. (Illus.). 192p. (gr. 4-6). 1974. 6.95 o.p. (ISBN 0-689-30407-2, Atheneum). Macmillan.
She Never Looked Back: Margaret Mead in Samoa. Samuel Epstein & Beryl Epstein. LC 78-31821. (Science Discovery Ser.). (Illus.). (gr. 3-7). 1980. PLB 6.99 o.p. (ISBN 0-698-30715-1, Coward). Putnam Pub Group.
She, the Adventuress. Dorothy Crayder. LC 72-86931. 192p. (gr. 4-6). 1973. 5.95 o.p. (ISBN 0-689-30082-4, Atheneum). Macmillan.
She Walks in Beauty. Stephen Longstreet. LC 77-81017. 1970. 6.95 o.p. (ISBN 0-87795-004-0, Arbor Hse). Morrow.
She Woke Me Up So I Killed Her. Tr. by Paul Bowles. LC 82-71550. 100p. 1986. 25.00 o.p. (ISBN 0-317-02696-8); pap. 7.95 o.p. Cadmus Eds.
Shea Lectures: Solving General Chemistry Problems. Richard Shea. 160p. 1982. 15.00 o.p. (ISBN 0-682-49871-8, University). Exposition-Phoenix.
Shear Strength of Reinforced Concrete Members. 84p. 1979. 16.95 o.p. (ISBN 0-317-32089-0, 426.1R-77). ACI.
Shear Zones in Rocks: Papers Presented at the International Conference Held at the University of Barcelona, May 1979. J. Carreras et al. 200p. 1980. pap. 48.00 o.p. (ISBN 0-08-026244-9). Pergamon.
Sheaves: Poems & Songs. Rabindrath Tagore. 1951. (ISBN 0-8022-1684-6). Philos Lib.
Shedding Light on Benefits Issues: Educational Conference Proceedings 1984 Annual, Vol. 26. Ed. by Mary E. Brennan. 342p. 1985. text ed. 35.00 o.p. (ISBN 0-89154-281-7). Intl found Employ.
Sheep among Wolves. Don R. Pegram. 1982. pap. 1.25 o.p. (ISBN 0-89265-084-2). Randall Hse.
Sheep & Goat Handbook see International Stockman's School Handbooks, 1984.
Sheep & the Rowan Tree. Julia Butcher. LC 83-26423. (Illus.). 32p. (gr. k-2). 1984. 12.50 o.s.i. (ISBN 0-03-071602-0). H Holt & Co.
Sheep Book: A Handbook for the Modern Shepherd. Ronald B. Parker. (Illus.). 384p. 1983. 19.95 o.p. (ISBN 0-684-17871-0, ScribT). Scribner.
Sheep on the Farm. Cliff Moon. LC 83-71628. (Down on the Farm Bks.). (Illus.). 33p. (ps-2). 1983. PLB 8.90 o.p. (ISBN 0-531-04698-2). Watts.
Sheepherders. Michael Mathers. (Illus.). 1975. 5.95 o.p. (ISBN 0-395-20723-1, Pub. by Montana Bks). Madrona Pubs.
Sheer Delight. Cora Kenyon & Cory Kenyon. (Candlelight Ecstasy Ser.: No. 407). 1986. pap. 2.25 o.p. (ISBN 0-440-17596-8). Dell.
Sheet Metal Drafting. 2nd ed. Melvin L. Betterley. (Illus.). 1978. text ed. 36.95 o.p. (ISBN 0-07-005126-7). McGraw.
Sheet Metalwork. R. E. Smith. pap. 5.28 o.p. (ISBN 0-87345-111-2). Glencoe.
Sheetfed Pressroom Manager's Training Guide. Frank Drazan. 1987. write for info. o.p. F Drazan.
Sheldon's Lunch. Bruce Lemerise. LC 80-10449. (Illus.). 48p. (ps-3). 1980. 5.95 o.s.i. (ISBN 0-686-86572-3); PLB 5.95 o.s.i. (ISBN 0-686-91534-8). Parents.
Sheldon's Retail Directory, 1988. 104th ed. Ed. by Kenneth W. Phelon, Jr. 730p. 1989. pap. 100.00 o.p. (ISBN 0-942239-02-4). P S & M Inc.
Shelf List of the Union Theological Seminary Library (New York), 10 vols. Union Theological Seminar Library Staff. 1960. Set. lib. bdg. 990.00 o.p. (ISBN 0-8161-0499-9, Hall Library). G K Hall.
Shell & Tube Heat Exchangers. Ed. by William R. Apblett, Jr. 1982. 82.00 o.p. (ISBN 0-87170-145-6). ASM.
Shell Art: A Handbook for Making Flowers, Mosaics, Jewelry & Other Ornaments. Helen Krauss. 14.00 o.p. (ISBN 0-8446-5473-6). Peter Smith.
Shell Auto Care Guide. Ross R. Olney. 304p. 1986. 17.45 o.s.i. (ISBN 0-671-61083-X, Fireside); pap. 8.95 o.s.i. (ISBN 0-671-62788-0). S&S.
Shell Beach Mystery. Frances Priddy. (gr. 7-10). 1963. 3.25 o.s.i. (ISBN 0-664-32319-7, Westminster). Westminster John Knox.
Shell Bed to Shell Midden. Betty Meehan. (AIAS New Ser.: No. 37). 187p. 1982. text ed. 22.50x o.p. (ISBN 0-391-02243-1); pap. text ed. 15.00x o. p. o.p. Humanities.
Shell Book of Beachcombing. Tony Soper. LC 73-5276. (Illus.). 128p. 1973. 5.50 o.s.i. (ISBN 0-8008-7177-4). Taplinger.
Shell Classification Research. Richard Hyman. (Occasional Papers: No. 146). 60p. 1980. pap. 3.00 o.p. (ISBN 0-317-58996-2). U of Ill Lib Info Sci.
Shell Collecting. Jerry G. Walls. (Illus.). 96p. 1981. 5.95 o.p. (ISBN 0-87666-631-4, KW-130). TFH Pubns.
Shell Craft. Glen Pownall. (E. G. New Crafts Bks.). 72p. 1980. 8.25 o.p. (ISBN 0-85467-021-1, Pub. by Viking Sevenseas New Zealand). Intl Spec Bk.
Shell Dredging & Its Influence on Gulf Coast Environments. Ed. by Arnold H. Bouma. LC 75-39416. 464p. 1976. 50.00x o.p. (ISBN 0-87201-805-9). Gulf Pub.
Shell Game. Douglas Terman. 448p. 1985. 16.45 o.s.i. (ISBN 0-671-53292-8, Pub. by Poseidon). S&S.
Shell: Gift of the Sea. Hugh Stix et al. (Illus.). 164p. 1985. 14.98 o.p. (ISBN 0-8109-8058-4). Abrams.
Shellbby Rumford: The Story of a Happy Rabbit. Bernice D. Smith. (Illus.). 64p. (ps-2). 1984. 5.50 o.p. (ISBN 0-682-40177-3). Exposition-Phoenix.
Shelley. Illus. by Patricia Machin. (Pocket Poets Ser.). (Illus.). 52p. 1985. 4.95 o.p. (ISBN 0-86350-046-3). Salem Hse Pubs.
Shelley. Percy Bysshe Shelley. (Plain Texts of the Poets Ser). 1968. pap. 2.50x o.p. (ISBN 0-7022-0676-8). U of Queensland Pr.
Shelley Potteries: The History & Production of a Staffordshire Family of Potters. Chris Watkins et al. (Illus.). 176p. 1983. 35.00 o.p. (ISBN 0-09-143270-7, Pub. by Barrie & Jenkins England). Seven Hills Bk Dists.
Shelley's Critical Prose. Percy Bysshe Shelley. Ed. by B. R. McElderry, Jr. LC 66-19856. (Regents Critics Ser.). xxiv, 183p. 1967. 16.50x o.p. (ISBN 0-8032-0461-2); pap. 2.95x o.p. (ISBN 0-8032-5462-8). U of Nebr Pr.
Shelley's Later Poetry. Milton T. Wilson. LC 74-12952. 332p. 1974. Repr. of 1959 ed. lib. bdg. 22.50x o.p. (ISBN 0-8371-7774-X, WISH). Greenwood.
Shellfish Heritage Cookbook. Robert Robinson. (Illus.). 120p. (Orig.). 1982. pap. 6.95 o.s.i. (ISBN 0-911145-02-8). Chapter & Cask.
Shells from Cape Cod to Cape May: With Special Reference to the New York City Area. M. K. Jacobson & W. K. Emerson. Orig. Title: Shells of the New York City Area. (Illus.). 10.25 o.p. (ISBN 0-8446-0155-1). Peter Smith.
Shells of the New York City Area see Shells from Cape Cod to Cape May: With Special Reference to the New York City Area.
Shelter. Marty Asher. 1986. 12.95 o.p. (ISBN 0-87795-772-X). Morrow.
Shelter Provision in Developing Countries: The Influence of Standards & Criteria. Ed. by C. Ian Jackson & A. L. Mabogunje. LC 77-14301. (SCOPE Ser. (Scientific Committee on Problems of the Environment): SCOPE Report 11). 94p. 1978. pap. 24.95 o.p. (ISBN 0-471-99581-9, Pub. by Wiley-Interscience). Wiley.
Shelter What You Make; Minimize the Take: Tax Shelters for Financial Planning. Beverly Tanner et al. 265p. 1982. 14.95 o.p. (ISBN 0-936602-45-7). Kampmann.
Sheltered Life. Ellen Glasgow. LC 85-14081. 408p. 1985. pap. 8.95 o.s.i. (ISBN 0-15-681690-3, Harv). HarBraceJ.
Shelters, Shacks, & Shanties. Daniel C. Beard. (Encore Edition). (Illus.). 1976. pap. 0.98 o.p. (ISBN 0-684-17407-3, SL632, ScribT). Scribner.
Shemittah: What It's All About. Eliezer Gewirtz & Yaakov Fruchter. (Illus.). 56p. (gr. 1-12). 1987. pap. text ed. 5.00 o.p. (ISBN 0-914131-78-8). Torah Umesorah.
Shenandoah Saga: A Narrative History of the U. S. Navy's Pioneering Large Rigid Airship. 3rd rev Large Format ed. Thom Hook. Ed. by T. G. Settle. LC 73-86973. (Famous Airships Ser.). (Illus.). 208p. 1981. pap. 8.95 o.p. (ISBN 0-9601506-3-3). Airshow Pubs.
Shenanigans of Mr. B. Eleanor Archer-Lofton. 32p. 1986. 6.50 o.p. (ISBN 0-8062-2968-3). Carlton.
Shepard's Atlantic Reporter Citations: A Compilation of Citations to all Cases Reported in the Atlantic Reporter. The Citations...Include Affirmances, Reversals & Dismissals by Higher State Courts & by the United States Supreme Court. 2nd ed. Shepard's Citation, Inc. Staff. LC 57-4936. 1957-78. supplement 55.00 o.p. (ISBN 0-686-89932-6). Shepards-McGraw.

Shepard's Bankruptcy Citations: Cases & Statutes, a Compilation of Citations to United States Supreme Court Decisions. Shepard's Citation, Inc. Staff. LC 85-1937. 1980. Supplements available. 150.00 o.p. Shepards-McGraw.

Shepard's California Citations. 8th ed. Shepard's McGraw-Hill Staff. LC 85-10803. write for info. o.p. Shepards-McGraw.

Shepard's Connecticut Case Names Citator: A Compilation of Case Names & Citations of Connecticut Cases Decided From 1935 to the Present. Shepard's McGraw-Hill Staff. LC 85-10872. write for info. o.p. Shepards-McGraw.

Shepard's Indiana Citations Cases: A Compilation of Citations Which Include Affirmances, Reversals, & Dismissals by the Indian Courts & the United States Supreme Court.., 2 vols. 6th ed. Shepard's Citation, Inc. Staff. LC 78-21127. 1978. 74.00 o.p. (ISBN 0-686-89807-9). Shepards-McGraw.

Shepard's Missouri Citations, Statutes. Shepard's Citation, Inc. Staff. Supplements available. 220.00 o.p. (ISBN 0-686-89817-6). Shepards-McGraw.

Shepard's Nevada Citations, Cases & Statutes: A Compilation of Citations to Nevada Cases Reported in the Nevada Reports & in the Pacific Reporter, the United States Constitution & Statutes, & the Nevada Constitution, Codes, Statutes, Ordinances, & Court Rules. Shepard's Citation, Inc. Staff. LC 79-12188. Supplements available. 165.00 o.p. (ISBN 0-686-89830-3). Shepards-McGraw.

Shepard's New Mexico Citations, Cases & Statutes: A Compilation of Citations to New Mexico Cases Reported in the New Mexico Reports & in the Pacific Reporter, to the United States Constitution & Statutes, New Mexico Constitution, Statutes, Laws, Charters, Ordinances, Court Rules, & Jury Instructions. 3rd ed. Shepard's Citation, Inc. Staff. LC 76-25869. 1976. Supplements available. 150.00 o.p. (ISBN 0-686-89839-7). Shepards-McGraw.

Shepard's North Carolina Citations, Cases, 2 Vols. Shepard's Citation, Inc. Staff. LC 81-8955. Supplements available. 225.00 o.p. Shepards-McGraw.

Shepard's Ohio Citations, Cases. Shepard's Citation, Inc. Staff. 233p. Supplements available. 255.00 o.p. (ISBN 0-686-90105-3). Shepards-McGraw.

Shepard's Oklahoma Citations: A Compilation of Citations to Oklahoma Cases Reported in the Various Seriers of Oklahoma Reports & Southwestern Reporter. Shepard's Citation, Inc. Staff. LC 78-18787. Supplements available. 190.00 o.p. (ISBN 0-686-90108-8). Shepards-McGraw.

Shepard's Restatement of the Law Citations: A Compilation of Citations to the American Law Institute's Restatement of the Law. Shepard's Citation, Inc. Staff & American Law Institute Staff. LC 76-53554. 1976. Supplements available. 165.00 o.p. (ISBN 0-686-90220-3). Shepards-McGraw.

Shepard's South Carolina Citations Cases: A Compilation of Citations Which Include Affirmances, Reversals, & Dismissals by the South Carolina Courts & the United States Supreme Court. Shepard's Citation, Inc. Staff. LC 57-2534. 1982. 95.00 o.p. (ISBN 0-686-90224-6). Shepards-McGraw.

Shepard's Texas Case Names Citator: A Compilation of Case Names & Citations of Texas Cases Decided from 1940 to the Present. Shepard's Citation, Inc. Staff. LC 83-20175. 76.00 o.p. Shepards-McGraw.

Shepard's Vermont Citations: Cases & Statutes. Shepard's Citation, Inc. Staff. LC 85-581. 1985. 145.00 o.p. Shepards-McGraw.

Shepard's Washington Case Names Citator: A Compilation of Case Names & Citations of Washington Cases Decided from 1940 to the Present. Shepard's Citation, Inc. Staff. LC 85-1941. 1985. write for info. o.p. Shepards-McGraw.

Shepherd Avenue. Charles Carillo. Ed. by Melanie Kroupa & Amy Meeker. LC 85-20066. 324p. 1985. 15.95 o.p. (ISBN 0-87113-043-2). Atlantic Monthly.

Shepherd Kings. Peter Danielson. (Children of the Lion Ser.: Bk. 2). 1985. lib. bdg. 13.95 o.p. (ISBN 0-8398-2870-5, Gregg). G K Hall.

Shepherd Looks at Psalm 23. Phillip Keller. (Illus.). 160p. 1987. gift ed. 19.95 o.p. (ISBN 0-310-35670-9, 6780G). Zondervan.

Sheppard's Book Dealers in the British Isles, 1987. 12th ed. 500p. 1987. 40.00 o.p. (ISBN 0-946653-24-0, Pub. by Europa England). Intl Pubns Serv.

Sheppard's International Directory of Print & Map Sellers. 1987. 42.00x o.p. (ISBN 0-946653-25-9, Pub. by Europa England). Intl Pubns Serv.

Sherborne; or, the House at the Four Ways, 1875. Edward H. Dering. Ed. by Robert L. Wolff. LC 75-457. (Victorian Fiction Ser.). 1976. lib. bdg. 73.00 o.p. (ISBN 0-8240-1536-3). Garland Pub.

Sherca. Syndey B. Smith. (Short Play Ser.). 1979. pap. 1.95x o.p. (ISBN 0-912262-57-5). Proscenium.

Sheriff & the Panhandle Murders. D. R. Meredith. 224p. 1985. pap. 2.95 o.p. (ISBN 0-380-69929-X). Avon.

Sherlock Holmes & the Case of Doctor Freud. Michael Shepherd. (Illus.). 32p. 1985. pap. 5.95 o.p. (ISBN 0-422-79990-4, 9621, Pub. by Tavistock England). Routledge Chapman & Hall.

Sherlock Holmes: My Life & Crimes. Michael Hardwick. LC 84-8054. (Illus.). 208p. 1984. 16.95 o.p. (ISBN 0-385-19654-7). Doubleday.

Sherlock Holmes: The Published Apocrypha. Arthur Conan Doyle. Ed. by Jack W. Tracy. 1980. 11.95 o.p. (ISBN 0-395-29454-1). HM.

Sherlock Slept Here: A Brief History of the Singular Adventures of Sir Arthur Conan Doyle in America, with Some Observations upon the Exploits of Mr. Sherlock Holmes. Howard Lachtman. (Illus.). 176p. (Orig.). 1985. pap. 9.95 o.p. (ISBN 0-88496-227-X). Capra Pr.

Sherlock Slept Here: Being a Brief History of the Singular Adventures of Sir Arthur Conan Doyle in America, with Some Observations Upon the Exploits of Mr. Sherlock Holmes. Howard Lachtman. 160p. 1988. Repr. lib. bdg. 24.95x o.p. (ISBN 0-8095-4047-9). Borgo Pr.

Shermans of Mannerville. Jack Ansell. LC 77-139295. 1971. 6.95 o.p. (ISBN 0-87795-008-3, Arbor Hse). Morrow.

Sherry: The Golden Wine of Spain. Cork Millner. LC 84-14615. (Illus.). xiii, 153p. 1984. 18.95 o.p. (ISBN 0-932620-37-X). Betterway Pubns.

Sherwood Anderson. Rex J. Burbank. (United States Authors Ser.). 1964. lib. bdg. 17.95 o.s.i. (ISBN 0-8057-0020-X, Twayne). G K Hall.

Sherwood Anderson's Notebook 1926. Sherwood Anderson. LC 72-105299. 1970. 10.00x o.p. (ISBN 0-911858-03-2). Appel.

Sherwood Ring. Elizabeth M. Pope. (Illus.). (gr. 7 up). 1958. 7.95 o.p. (ISBN 0-395-07033-3). HM.

Sherwood Walks Home. James Flora. LC 66-16004. (Illus.). (gr. 1-3). 1966. 6.95 o.p. (ISBN 0-15-273735-9, HJ). HarBraceJ.

Sheryl. Ralph Hayes. 1980. pap. 2.25 o.p. (ISBN 0-505-51452-4, Pub. by Tower Bks). Dorchester Pub Co.

She's Called Tootsie. Margaret A. Farkas. 64p. 1987. 7.95 o.p. (ISBN 0-8062-2944-6). Carlton.

She's Nobody's Baby: A History of American Women in the 20th Century. Ed. by Suzanne Levine. (Illus.). 224p. 1983. pap. 12.50 o.p. (ISBN 0-671-49247-0, Fireside). S&S.

Shetland. rev. ed. James R. Nicholson. LC 79-52367. (Illus.). 1979. 22.95 o.s.i. (ISBN 0-7153-8518-6). David & Charles.

Sheza Joy. Norma C. Ash. 1985. 6.95 o.p. (ISBN 0-533-06563-1). Vantage.

Shielding the Flame: An Intimate Conversation with Merek Edelman, One of the Last Surviving Leaders of the Warsaw Ghetto Uprising. Hanna Krall. Tr. by Joanna Stasinska & Lawrence Weschler. LC 86-210. 124p. 1986. 13.95 o.p. (ISBN 0-03-006002-8). H Holt & co.

Shifting Cultivation in Latin America. (Forestry Development Papers: No. 17). (Span.). pap. 17.00 o.p. (F1300, FAO). UNIPUB.

Shifting Gears. Nena O'Neill & George O'Neill. 1975. pap. 2.25 o.p. (ISBN 0-380-00281-7, 50518). Avon.

Shi'ite Anthology. Allamah Tabataba'I. Ed. by William C. Chittick. 152p. 1986. text ed. 25.00 o.p. (ISBN 0-7103-0159-6); pap. text ed. 12.95 o.p. (ISBN 0-317-40555-1). Routledge Chapman & Hall.

Shilling for Candles. Josephine Tey. (Portway Ser.). 304p. 1988. lib. bdg. 18.50x o.s.i. (ISBN 0-7451-7114-1, Pub. by Chivers Pr UK). G K Hall.

Shin Tzu Heritage. Jon Ferrante et al. (Illus.). 1988. write for info. o.p. (ISBN 0-87714-132-0). Denlingers.

Shingle Style & the Stick Style: Architectural Theory & Design from Richardson to the Origins of Wright. rev. ed. Vincent Scully. (Publications in the History of Art Ser.: No. 20). (Illus.). 1971. 32.50x o.p. (ISBN 0-300-01434-1); pap. 17.95x o.p. (ISBN 0-300-01519-4). Yale U Pr.

Shining Armour. Kenneth Wood. (Julia MacRae Bks.). 144p. (gr. 7). 1982. 9.95 o.p. (ISBN 0-531-04434-3, MacRae). Watts.

Shining Day. Frank Ross. LC 80-69394. 1981. 13.95 o.p. (ISBN 0-689-11111-8, Atheneum). Macmillan.

Shining Sword. Charles G. Coleman. LC 56-31266. (YA) (gr. 7 up). 1956. pap. 3.95 o.s.i. (ISBN 0-87213-086-X). Loizeaux.

Shinkansen High-Speed Rail Network of Japan: Proceedings of a IIASA Conference, June 27-30 1977. Ed. by A. Straszak & R. Tuch. (IIASA Proceedings Ser.: Vol. 7). 1980. 195.00 o.p. (ISBN 0-08-024444-0). Pergamon.

Shino & Oribe Kiln Sites. R. J. Faulkner & O. R. Impey. (Illus.). 96p. (Orig.). 1981. pap. 17.50 o.p. (ISBN 0-903697-11-4, Pub. by R G Sawers UK). C E Tuttle.

Shinto: Japan's Spiritual Roots. Stuart D. Picken. LC 79-91520. (Illus.). 80p. 1980. 22.95 o.p. (ISBN 0-87011-410-7). Kodansha.

Ship Construction. 2nd ed. D. J. Eyres. (Illus.). 340p. 1978. pap. 24.50x o.p. (ISBN 0-434-90556-9). Sheridan.

Ship of Gold. Norman Polmar & Thomas Allen. 288p. 1986. 17.95 o.p. (ISBN 0-02-597980-9). Macmillan.

Ship of Ishtar. Abraham Merritt. 1977. pap. 1.25 o.p. (ISBN 0-380-00929-3, 41129-6). Avon.

Ship Stability for Masters & Mates. 3rd ed. D. R. Derrett. 1977. 20.00 o.s.i. (ISBN 0-540-01403-6). E J Brill USA.

Ship Structural Design: A Rationally-Based, Computer Aided, Optimization Approach. Owen F. Hughes. LC 83-1110. (Ocean Engineering Ser.). 566p. 1983. 77.95x o.p. (ISBN 0-471-03241-7, 1-194). Wiley.

Ship That Changed the World: The Escape of the Goeben to the Dardenelles in 1914. Dan Van der Vat. LC 85-28637. (Illus.). 252p. 1986. 17.95 o.p. (ISBN 0-917561-13-9). Adler & Adler.

Shipboard Antennas. 2nd ed. Preston Law. (Artech Radar Library). (Illus.). 575p. 1986. 61.00 o.p. (ISBN 0-89006-123-8). Artech Hse.

Shiphandling for the Mariner. Daniel H. MacElrevey. LC 83-71314. 254p. 1983. 20.00x o.p. (ISBN 0-87033-301-1). Cornell Maritime.

Shipmaster's Handbook on Ship's Business. Ben Martin. LC 68-20976. 318p. 1969. 17.50x o.p. (ISBN 0-87033-098-5). Cornell Maritime.

Shipping & Craft in Silhouette. Charles G. Davis. LC 70-162509. (Tower Bks.). (Illus.). 100p. 1972. Repr. of 1929 ed. 40.00x o.p. (ISBN 0-8103-3945-5). Gale.

Ships & Naval Architecture (S. I. Units) R. Munro-Smith. (Illus.). 1977. pap. 22.50x o.p. (ISBN 0-900976-68-3, Pub. by Inst Marine Eng). Intl Spec Bk.

Ship's Doctor. Stephen Kerry. LC 74-164018. 1972. 6.50 o.s.i. (ISBN 0-8008-7179-0). Taplinger.

Ship's Gear: A Review of Deck Machinery. D. H. Beattie & W. M. Somerville. (Marine Engineering Practice Ser.: Vol. 2, Pt. 16). 1979. pap. 9.00x o.p. (ISBN 0-900976-78-0, Pub. by Inst Marine Eng). Intl Spec Bk.

Ship's Gear: Technical Symposium. pap. 24.25 o.p. (FN71, FNB). UNIPUB.

Ships that Pass. Frank A. Weaner. 160p. 1987. 9.95 o.p. (ISBN 0-317-60465-1). Carlton.

Shirley Ann Grau. Paul Schlueter. (United States Authors Ser.: No. 382). 1981. lib. bdg. 14.50 o.p. (ISBN 0-8057-7316-9, Twayne). G K Hall.

Shirley Busbee, 3 vols. 1983. Set. pap. 10.95 o.p. (ISBN 0-380-84921-6). Avon.

Shirley Maclaine. Roy Pickard. (Film Stars Ser.). (Illus.). 96p. 1985. 7.95 o.p. (ISBN 0-87052-122-5). Hippocrene Bks.

Shirley Temple Scrapbook. Loraine Burdick. 1982. pap. 8.95 o.p. (ISBN 0-8246-0277-3). Jonathan David.

Shirt-Sleeves Management. James F. Evered. 160p. 1981. 14.95 o.p. (ISBN 0-8144-5636-7). AMACOM.

Shmittah: What It's All About. Eliezer Gevirtz. (Orig.). 1987. 5.00 o.p. Torah Umesorah.

Shock. Ed. by Katherine Carey & Alice Perkins. LC 83-20068. (Nursing Now Ser.). 136p. 1984. text ed. 13.95 o.p. (ISBN 0-916730-63-8). Springhouse Pub.

Shock & Vibration Control Handbook. 2nd ed. Cyril M. Harris & Charles E. Crede. 1976. text ed. 69.50 o.p. (ISBN 0-07-026799-5). McGraw.

Shock of Motherhood: The Unexpected Challenge for the New Generation of Mothers. Beppie Harrison. 256p. 1986. 17.95 o.p. (ISBN 0-684-18485-0). Scribner.

Shock Waves in Chemistry. Lifshitz. 400p. 1980. 75.00 o.p. (ISBN 0-8247-1331-1). Dekker.

Shock Waves in Collisionless Plasmas. D. A. Tidman. Ed. by N. A. Krali. LC 74-13711. 187p. (Orig.). 1971. 18.50 o.p. (ISBN 0-471-86785-3, JW). Krieger.

Shocking Truth about Water. 24th, rev. ed. Paul C. Bragg & Patricia Bragg. (Illus.). pap. 4.95 o.p. (ISBN 0-87790-000-0). Health Sci.

Shoe for All Seasons. Jeff MacNelly. 128p. 1983. pap. 6.95 o.p. (ISBN 0-03-061657-3). H HOlt & Co.

Shoe Must Go On. Jeff MacNelly. 128p. 1985. pap. 6.95 o.s.i. (ISBN 0-03-000737-2, Owl Bks). H Holt & Co.

Shoe Time. Aimee Liu & Meg Rottmamn. 1986. pap. 8.95 o.p. (ISBN 0-87795-737-1). Morrow.

Shoelace Solution. Ray Broekel. LC 79-52409. (Carolrhoda Mini-Mysteries Ser.). (Illus.). (gr. 1-4). 1980. PLB 5.95 o.p. (ISBN 0-87614-115-7). Carolrhoda Bks.

Shoeless Joe. W. P. Kinsella. 288p. 1982. 11.95 o.p. (ISBN 0-395-32047-X). HM.

Shoemaker: The Anatomy of a Psychopath. Flora R. Schreiber. 1983. 16.50 o.p. (ISBN 0-671-22652-5). S&S.

Shoemaker's Gift. Lyndell Ludwig. LC 82-73196. (Illus.). 36p. (ps-1). 1983. pap. 4.95 o.p. (ISBN 0-916870-53-7). Creative Arts Bk.

Shoes That Danced & Other Poems. Anna H. Branch. LC 77-89722. (One-Act Plays in Reprint Ser.). 1977. Repr. of 1905 ed. 19.50x o.p. (ISBN 0-8486-2027-5). Roth Pub Inc.

Shoestring. Paul Abelman. LC 83-61259. 224p. 1984. 9.95 o.p. (ISBN 0-88186-376-9); pap. 3.50 o.p. (ISBN 0-88186-875-2). Parkwest Pubns.

Shogun. James Clavell. LC 74-77840. 1975. 19.95 o.p. (ISBN 0-689-10565-7, Atheneum). Macmillan.

Sholokhov: A Critical Appreciation. L. Yakimenko. 371p. 1973. 6.45 o.p. (ISBN 0-8285-1090-3, Pub. by Progress Pubs USSR). Imported Pubns.

Shoot-Out at Buffalo Gulch. Bernard Palmer. (Living Books). 304p. 1985. pap. 3.95 o.p. (ISBN 0-8423-5849-8). Tyndale.

Shoot! (Si Gura) The Notebook of Serafino Gubbio Cinematograph Operator. Luigi Pirandello. Ed. by Bruce S. Kupelnick. LC 76-52123. (Classics of Film Literature Ser.). 1978. lib. bdg. 22.00 o.p. (ISBN 0-8240-2889-9). Garland Pub.

Shooter's Bible, No. 77: 1986. Ed. by William S. Jarrett. 576p. (Orig.). 1985. pap. 12.95 o.p. (ISBN 0-88317-128-7). Stoeger Pub Co.

Shooter's Bible: 1984 Edition, No. 75. Robert F. Scott. 576p. (Orig.). 1983. pap. 11.95 o.p. (ISBN 0-88317-117-1). Stoeger Pub Co.

Shooter's Bible: 1985 Edition, No. 76. Ed. by William S. Jarrett. (Illus.). 576p. (Orig.). 1985. pap. 12.95 o.p. (ISBN 0-88317-124-4). Stoeger Pub Co.

Shooters Bible, 1988, No. 79. Ed. by W. S. Jarrett. 576p. 1987. pap. 14.95 o.p. Stoeger Pub Co.

Shooting: A Complete Guide for Beginners. John Marchington. (Illus.). 184p. (Orig.). 1982. pap. 6.95 o.p. (ISBN 0-571-11932-8). Faber & Faber.

Shooting for the Gold: A Portrait of America's Olympic Athletes. Walter Iooss, Jr. & Dave Anderson. LC 85-150626. 144p. 1984. 29.95 o.p. (ISBN 0-915463-03-2, Pub. by Jameson Bks, Dist. by Kampmann). Green Hill.

Shooting from Scratch. Michael Paulet. (Illus.). 256p. 1987. 17.95 o.p. (ISBN 0-907675-64-6, Pub. by Buchan & Enright UK). Seven Hills Bk Dists.

Shooting in the Dark: A Novel. Carolyn Hougan. 256p. 1984. 15.45 o.p. (ISBN 0-671-46722-0). S&S.

Shooting Ourselves in the Foot. Bernard J. O'Keefe. LC 85-7651. 294p. 1985. 15.45 o.p. (ISBN 0-395-38511-3). HM.

Shooting Star. David Brierley. 224p. 1983. 12.95 o.s.i. (ISBN 0-684-17899-0, ScribT). Scribner.

Shooting Time Guide to Ferretting. Fred Taylor. 1987. pap. 8.50 o.p. (ISBN 0-907675-11-5, Pub. by Buchan & Enright England). Seven Hills Bk Dists.

Shooting Trail. Jack Bassett. 1986. 12.50 o.p. (ISBN 0-8166-0249-2, Large Print Bks). G K Hall.

Shop & Dine. Jo Kitchen & Rebecca Davidson. LC 76-22514. (Illus.). pap. (ISBN 0-915864-03-7). Academy Chi Pubs.

Shop Boy: An Autobiography. J. B. Thomas. 182p. 1983. 15.95 o.p. (ISBN 0-7100-9347-0). Routledge Chapman & Hall.

Shop by Mail Worldwide. Anne Flato & Marilyn Schiff. LC 86-40159. 224p. 1987. pap. 9.95 o.s.i. (ISBN 0-394-74667-8, Vin). Random.

Shop Made Easy. Frank Cattaneo. (Illus.). 134p. 1971. pap. text ed. 4.25x o.p. (ISBN 0-88323-064-X, 188). Pendergrass Pub.

Shop of the Crafters: At Cincinnati. (Illus.). 72p. 1985. pap. 6.95 o.p. (ISBN 0-87905-414-X). Gibbs Smith Pub.

Shop on High Street: Toys & Games of Early America. John J. Loeper. LC 77-24737. (Illus.). (gr. 3-6). 1978. 7.95 o.p. (ISBN 0-689-30622-9, Atheneum). Macmillan.

Shop Theory. National Machine Tool Builders Association Staff. LC 83-6903. (NMTBA Shop Practice Ser.). 176p. 1983. pap. 13.95 o.p. (ISBN 0-471-07839-5, 1-472). Wiley.

Shop Toons. James Kost. (Illus.). 126p. (Orig.). 1979. pap. 4.95 o.p. (ISBN 0-89100-109-3, EA-FUN). IAP.

Shopacheck's Rugby League Review, Nineteen Eighty-Four to Nineteen Eighty-Five. Paul Fitzpatrick. (Illus.). 144p. 1985. 23.95 o.p. (ISBN 0-571-13687-7); pap. 13.95 o.p. (ISBN 0-571-13690-7). Faber & Faber.

Shopkeepers & Master Artisans in Nineteenth-Century Europe. Ed. by Geoffrey Crossick. 304p. 1984. 39.95 o.p. (ISBN 0-416-35660-5, NO. 4153). Routledge Chapman & Hall.

Shopkeeper's Daughter. George MacDonald. 288p. 1986. pap. 5.95 o.p. (ISBN 0-89693-270-2). Victor Bks.

Shopper's Guide to the Best Buys in England, Scotland & Wales. (Frommer's Special Interest Guides Ser.). pap. 10.95 o.p. (ISBN 0-671-55625-8). P-H.

Shopping. Sue Tarsky. (Time to Talk Ser.). (Illus.). 32p. (ps-2). 1983. 1.50 o.s.i. (ISBN 0-671-47110-4, Little Simon). S&S.

Shopping Center Development & Investment. Mary A. Hines. LC 83-6540. (Real Estate for Professional Practitioners Ser.). 376p. 1983. 55.00x o.p. (ISBN 0-471-86851-5, 1-242). Wiley.

Shopping Center Zoning. J. Ross McKeever. LC 73-88224. (Illus.). 73p. 1973. pap. 11.50 o.p. (ISBN 0-87420-069-5, S07). Urban Land.

Shopping Centers & Malls. Ed. by Retail Reporting Association Staff. (Illus.). 192p. 1986. 44.95 o.p. R Silver.

Shopping Centre Management. P. G. Martin. 328p. 1982. 42.00 o.p. (ISBN 0-419-11870-5, NO. 6674, Pub. by E & FN Spon England). Routledge Chapman & Hall.

Shopwell Dairy Lover's Cookbook. 1981. write for info. o.p. (ISBN 0-916752-10-0). Longman Trade.

Shore Road Mystery. Franklin W. Dixon. (Hardy Boys Ser: Vol. 6). (Illus.). (gr. 5-9). 1964. 4.50 o.p. (ISBN 0-448-08906-8, G&D); PLB 3.29 o.p. (ISBN 0-448-18906-2). Putnam Pub Group.

Shorelines: Birds at the Water's Edge. Michael Warren. LC 84-40104. (Illus.). 128p. 1984. 25.00 o.p. (ISBN 0-8129-1133-4). Times Bks.

Short Bike Rides in Connecticut. 2nd, rev. ed. Edwin Mullen & Jane Griffith. LC 75-1924. (Illus.). 128p. 1983. pap. 6.95 o.s.i. (ISBN 0-87106-930-X). Globe Pequot.

Short Bike Rides in Rhode Island. 2nd, rev. ed. Howard Stone. LC 78-73547. (Illus.). 248p. 1984. pap. 8.95 o.s.i. (ISBN 0-87106-948-2). Globe Pequot.

Short Circuit: Inside the World of Professional Tennis. Michael Mewshaw. LC 82-48699. 320p. 1983. 13.95 o.s.i. (ISBN 0-689-11384-6, Atheneum). Macmillan.

Short Commentary on Kant's Critique of Pure Reason. 2nd ed. Alfred C. Ewing. LC 39-13499. 1967. pap. text ed. 9.00x o.s.i. (ISBN 0-226-22778-2, P265, Phoen). U of Chicago Pr.

Short Course in Calculus. Bodh R. Gulati. LC 79-67409. 536p. 1981. text ed. 36.95x o.p.; solutions manual 20.00 o.p. (ISBN 0-03-057434-X). Dryden Pr.

Short Course in Minolta Photography. Barbara London. (Illus.). 144p. 1983. pap. 12.50 o.p. (ISBN 0-930764-53-6, Co.-Pub. by Van Nos Reinhold). Curtin & London.

Short Course in Modern Organic Chemistry. John F. Leffler. Ed. by James Smith. 366p. 1973. text ed. write for info. o.p. (ISBN 0-02-369320-7). Macmillan.

Short Course in Photography. Barbara London. (Illus.). 144p. 1983. pap. 12.50 o.p. (ISBN 0-930764-51-X). Curtin & London.

Short Course in Remedial English Composition. Renee C. Crauder & Gwendolyn E. Etter-Lewis. 1977. pap. 3.95x o.p. (ISBN 0-8134-1938-7, 1938); instructor's manual 1.00 o.p. (ISBN 0-8134-1939-5, 1939). Inter Print Pubs.

Short Course in Sheet Metal Shop Theory: Including 25 Practical Projects. Richard S. Budzik. LC 79-93131. (Illus.). (gr. 7-12). 1979. 17.95 o.p. (ISBN 0-912914-05-X). Practical Pubns.

Short Course on Error Correcting Codes. N. J. Sloane. (CISM International Centre for Mechanical Sciences Ser.: Vol. 188). (Illus.). 76p. 1982. pap. 12.00 o.p. (ISBN 0-387-81303-9). Springer-Verlag.

Short Cut to Winning Bridge. Alfred Sheinwold. 1979. 3.00 o.p. (ISBN 0-87980-366-5). Wilshire.

Short Cuts: Styling & Caring for Short Hair. Olivier Casanova & Patrice Casanova. 1985. pap. 7.95 o.p. (ISBN 0-671-55375-5, Pub. by Fireside). S&S.

Short Cuts to Affective on the Job Writing. Lynn Lamphear. 179p. 1982. 14.95 o.p. (ISBN 0-13-809145-5); pap. 6.95 o.p. (ISBN 0-13-809137-4). P-H.

Short Dictionary of Classical Word Origins. Harry E. Wedeck. (ISBN 0-8022-1839-3). Philos Lib.

Short Dictionary of Weaving. M. E. Pritchard. (Illus.). 200p. 1956. (ISBN 0-8022-2018-5). Philos Lib.

Short-Distance Phenomena in Nuclear Physics. Ed. by David H. Boal & Richard M. Woloshyn. (NATO ASI Series B, Physics: Vol. 104). 438p. 1983. 72.50x o.p. (ISBN 0-306-41494-5, Plenum Pr). Plenum Pub.

Short Essays. 4th ed. Gerald Levin. 416p. 1986. pap. text ed. 13.00 net o.p. (ISBN 0-15-580918-0, Pub. by HC). HarBraceJ.

Short Essays: Models for Composition. 2nd ed. Gerald Levin. 334p. 1980. pap. text ed. 9.95 o.p. (ISBN 0-15-580914-8, HC). HarBraceJ.

Short Essays: Models for Composition. 3rd ed. Gerald Levin. 361p. 1983. pap. text ed. 8.75 o.p. (ISBN 0-15-580916-4, HC). HarBraceJ.

Short Essays: Models for Composition. Ed. by Gerald Levin. (Orig.). 1977. pap. text ed. 7.95 o.p. (ISBN 0-15-580912-1, HC). HarBraceJ.

Short Guide to Reading & Writing Poetry. William E. Taylor. 1976. pap. 4.50 o.p. (ISBN 0-912112-33-6). Everett-Edwards.

Short Guide to the High Plains. Tom Clark. signed, ltd. ed. o.p. (ISBN 0-932274-18-8). Cadmus Eds.

Short Guide to Traditional Grammar. J. R. Bernard. 88p. 1975. pap. 9.00x o.p. (ISBN 0-424-06950-4, Pub. by Sydney U Pr). Intl Spec Bk.

Short Guide to Writing a Critical Review. new rev. ed. Eliot D. Allen & Ethel B. Colbrunn. 1975. pap. 2.00 o.p. (ISBN 0-912112-20-4). Everett-Edwards.

Short Guide to Writing a Research Paper: Manuscript Form & Documentation. rev. ed. Eliot D. Allen & Ethel B. Colbrunn. 1975. pap. 2.50 o.p. (ISBN 0-912112-19-0). Everett-Edwards.

Short Guide to Writing about Art. 2nd ed. Sylvan Barnet. 1985. pap. write for info. o.p. (ISBN 0-673-39195-7). Scott F.

Short Guide to Writing Better Themes. 4th ed. Ann Morris. 1973. pap. 3.50 o.p. (ISBN 0-912112-23-9). Everett-Edwards.

Short History International Language Movement. Guerard. LC 78-14124. 1988. Repr. of 1922 ed. 23.00 o.s.i. (ISBN 0-88355-796-7). Hyperion Conn.

Short History of a Small Place: A Novel. T. R. Pearson. 1986. 17.45 o.s.i. (ISBN 0-671-54352-0, Pub. by Linden Pr). S&S.

Short History of Air Power. James L. Stokesbury. LC 85-43431. 352p. 1986. 18.95 o.p. (ISBN 0-688-05061-1). Morrow.

Short History of Anatomy & Physiology: From the Greeks to Harvey. Charles Singer. Orig. Title: Evolution of Anatomy. (Illus.). 1957. pap. text ed. 4.95 o.p. (ISBN 0-486-20389-1). Dover.

Short History of Anti-Semitism. Vamberto Morais. 1976. 11.95x o.p. (ISBN 0-393-05567-1). Norton.

Short History of Chinese Art. Hugo Munsterberg. (ISBN 0-8022-1170-4). Philos Lib.

Short History of Christianity. Ed. by Archibald G. Baker. LC 40-34185. (Midway Reprints Ser.). 1983. pap. text ed. 11.00x o.s.i. (ISBN 0-226-03527-1). U of Chicago Pr.

Short History of Christianity. Martin E. Marty. LC 80-8042. 384p. 1980. pap. 9.95 o.p. (ISBN 0-8006-1427-5, 1-1427, Fortress). Augsburg Fortress.

Short History of Existentialism. Jean Wahl. (ISBN 0-8022-1789-3). Philos Lib.

Short History of French Literature. I. C. Thimann. 1967. 19.75 o.p. (ISBN 0-08-012011-3); pap. 55.00 o.p. (ISBN 0-08-012010-5). Pergamon.

Short History of Ireland. Martin Wallace. 96p. (Orig.). 1986. pap. 5.95 o.p. (ISBN 0-86281-171-6, Pub. by Appletree Pr). Irish Bks Media.

Short History of Latin America. Benjamin Keen & Mark Wasserman. 1980. pap. 17.95 o.p. (ISBN 0-395-27838-4). HM.

Short History of Literary English. 2nd ed. W. F. Bolton. (Quality Paperback: No. 266). 86p. 1973. pap. 1.50 o.p. (ISBN 0-8226-0266-0). Littlefield.

Short History of Observatories. Marian Donnelly. LC 73-175209. 1973. 7.50 o.p. U of Oreg Bks.

Short History of Paper Money & Banking in the United States. William M. Gouge. LC 65-26366. 1968. Repr. of 1833 ed. 45.00x o.s.i. (ISBN 0-678-00307-6). Kelley.

Short History of Russia. rev. ed. Benedict H. Sumner. LC 43-17185. (Maps). 1962. pap. 5.95 o.p. (ISBN 0-15-682319-5, Harv). HarBraceJ.

Short History of Sex. Richard Armour. 1970. text ed. 4.95 o.p. (ISBN 0-07-002263-1). McGraw.

Short History of Shakespearean Criticism. Arthur M. Eastman. 418p. 1974. pap. 4.95x o.p. (ISBN 0-393-00705-7, Norton Lib). Norton.

Short History of the British Army. Eric W. Sheppard. LC 74-23642. (Illus.). 505p. 1975. Repr. of 1950 ed. lib. bdg. 45.50x o.p. (ISBN 0-8371-7567-4, SHBA). Greenwood.

Short History of the CPSU. B. N. Ponomaryov et al. 390p. 1970. 4.45 o.p. (ISBN 0-8285-0495-4, Pub. by Progress Pubs USSR). Imported Pubns.

Short History of the First Liberian Republic. Ed. by Joseph S. Guannu. 1985. pap. 10.00 o.p. (ISBN 0-682-40267-2). Exposition-Phoenix.

Short History of the Movies. 3rd ed. Gerald Mast. (Illus.). 1981. 20.00 o.p. (ISBN 0-226-50982-6). U of Chicago Pr.

Short History of the Papacy in the Middle Ages. Walter Ullmann. 1974. pap. 16.95x o.p. (ISBN 0-416-74970-4, NO. 2562). Routledge Chapman & Hall.

Short History of the World, Vol. I. Ed. by A. Z. Manfred. 600p. 1974. 9.95 o.p. (ISBN 0-8285-0497-0, Pub. by Progress Pubs USSR). Imported Pubns.

Short History of the World, Vol. II. Ed. by A. Z. Manfred. 519p. 1974. 7.95 o.p. (ISBN 0-8285-0498-9, Pub. by Progress Pubs USSR). Imported Pubns.

Short Introduction to Modern Growth Theory. Ching-yao Hsieh et al. LC 78-61916. 1978. pap. text ed. 12.00 o.p. (ISBN 0-8191-0628-3). U Pr of Amer.

Short Introduction to Philosophy. Robert G. Olson. (Orig.). 1967. pap. text ed. 12.95 o.p. (ISBN 0-15-580974-1, HC). HarBraceJ.

Short Letter, Long Farewell. Peter Handke. Tr. by Ralph Manheim from Ger. 167p. 1974. 7.95 o.p. (ISBN 0-374-26318-3). FS&G.

Short Life: A Novel. Aharon Megged. Tr. by Miriam Arad from Hebrew. LC 80-13001. Orig. Title: Ha-Hayim ha-Ketsarim. 288p. 1980. 10.95 o.s.i. (ISBN 0-8008-7180-4). Taplinger.

Short Novels of Jack Schaefer. Jack Schaefer. 1967. 6.95 o.p. (ISBN 0-395-08153-X). HM.

Short Poems. John Berryman. 120p. 1967. 4.95 o.p. (ISBN 0-374-26328-0). FS&G.

Short Season: The Hard Work & High Times of Baseball in the Spring. David Falkner. LC 85-40830. 288p. 1986. 16.45 o.s.i. (ISBN 0-8129-1266-7, Dist. by Random House). Times Bks.

Short Stories. Rafaela Contreras de Dario. LC 65-21263. (Hispanic-American Studies Ser: No. 20). (Orig., Span.). 1965. pap. 2.00 o.p. (ISBN 0-87024-040-4). U of Miami Pr.

Short Stories. Silvinia Ocampo. Tr. by Jason Weiss. 1987. Lat Am Lit Rev Pr.

Short Stories. Theresa Vu. LC 84-91268. 58p. 1985. 8.95 o.p. (ISBN 0-533-06346-9). Vantage.

Short Stories: A Critical Anthology. Ensaf Thune & Ruth Prigozy. Ed. by D. Anthony English. 544p. 1973. pap. text ed. write for info. o.p. (ISBN 0-02-420790-X). Macmillan.

Short Stories for Insight. Ed. by Teresa F. Glazier. (Orig.). 1967. pap. text ed. 7.95 o.p. (ISBN 0-15-580990-3, HC). HarBraceJ.

Short Stories of Ernest Hemingway: Critical Essays. Ed. by Jackson J. Benson. LC 74-75815. xv, 375p. 1975. pap. 23.25 o.p. (ISBN 0-8223-0320-5). Duke.

Short Story. Ian Reid. (Critical Idiom Ser.). 1977. 9.95x o.p. (ISBN 0-416-56060-1, NO. 2402); pap. 5.50x o.p. (ISBN 0-416-56070-9, NO. 2403). Routledge Chapman & Hall.

Short Studies on Great Subjects. James A. Froude. 1964. Repr. of 1906 ed. 8.95x o.p. (ISBN 0-460-00013-6, Evman). Biblio Dist.

Short Synopsis of the Most Essential Points in Hawaiian Grammar. W. C. Alexander. LC 68-13866. pap. 2.95 o.p. (ISBN 0-8048-0528-8). C E Tuttle.

Short-Term Bioassays in the Analysis of Complex Environmental Mixtures, Pt. 1. Ed. by Michael D. Waters et al. LC 79-22240. (Environmental Science Research Ser.: Vol. 15). 602p. 1979. 95.00x o.p. (ISBN 0-306-40319-6, Plenum Pr). Plenum Pub.

Short-Term Bioassays In the Analysis of Complex Environmental Mixtures, Pt. 2. Ed. by Michael D. Waters et al. LC 81-17839. (Environmental Science Research Ser.: Vol. 22). 540p. 1981. 89.50x o.p. (ISBN 0-306-40890-2, Plenum Pr). Plenum Pub.

Short-Term Energy Outlook Annual 1985: Methodology. (EIA-0202 (86) M Ser.). 44p. 1986. pap. 2.25 o.p. (ISBN 0-318-21601-9, S/N 061-003-00493-8). USGPO.

Short-Term Mutagenicity Test Systems for Detecting Carcinogens. Ed. by K. H. Norpoth & R. C. Garner. 400p. 1980. 42.50 o.p. (ISBN 0-387-09203-X). Springer-Verlag.

Short Term Skill Training: Alternative Approaches for Vocational Education. Russell Paulsen. 20p. 1981. 2.35 o.p. (ISBN 0-318-22199-3, IN222). Natl Ctr Res Voc Ed.

Short Term Transit Policies & Downtown Revitalization. F. Ulrich. 29p. 1979. pap. 6.00x o.p. (28500). Urban Inst.

Short-Term Visual Information Forgetting. A. H. Van Der Heijden. (International Library of Psychology). 224p. 1982. 29.95x o.p. (ISBN 0-7100-0851-1). Routledge Chapman & Hall.

Short View of Mobile's Ancient Money. Cameron Plummer & Mary F. Plummer. (Illus.). 24p. 1961. pap. o.p. (ISBN 0-940882-09-4). HB Pubns.

Short Visit to Ergon. E. M. Osborn. 192p. 1982. 8.50 o.p. (ISBN 0-682-49873-4). Exposition-Phoenix.

Short Voyages. Stephen Jones. 1985. 19.45 o.p. (ISBN 0-393-03303-1). Norton.

Short Walk. Alice Childress. 336p. 1981. pap. 3.50 o.p. (ISBN 0-380-54239-0, 64790-7, Bard). Avon.

Short Walks on Cape Cod & the Vineyard. 2nd, rev. ed. Hugh Sadlier & Heather Sadlier. LC 75-34252. (Illus.). 128p. 1983. pap. 5.95 o.p. (ISBN 0-87106-921-0). Globe Pequot.

Short-Wave Mystery. rev. ed. Franklin W. Dixon. (Hardy Boys Ser: Vol. 24). (gr. 5-9). 1928. 4.50 o.p. (ISBN 0-448-08924-6, G&D); PLB 3.29 o.p. (ISBN 0-448-18924-0). Putnam Pub Group.

Short Wave Radiation Problems in Homogeneous Media: Asymptotic Solutions. C. O. Bloom & N. D. Kazarinoff. (Lecture Notes in Mathematics: Vol. 522). 1976. 13.00 o.p. (ISBN 0-387-07698-0). Springer-Verlag.

Shortchanged Update: Minorities & Women in Banking. CEP Staff & Tina L. Simich. Ed. by Wendy C. Schwartz. LC 76-50522. 1976. pap. 39.95 o.p. (ISBN 0-87871-005-1). CEP.

Shortcut to the Italian Language. Rigal. LC 60-13639. 292p. 1960. (ISBN 0-8022-1345-6). Philos Lib.

Shortcuts. Elizabeth Franklin. 256p. 1984. 15.95 o.p. (ISBN 0-8119-0703-1). Fell.

Shortened CPA Law Review. 5th ed. George C. Thompson & Gerald P. Brady. (Business Ser.). 560p. 1980. text ed. 22.95x o.p. (ISBN 0-686-69155-5). PWS-Kent Pub.

Shortened CPA Law Review. 4th ed. George C. Thompson & Gerald P. Brady. 1977. (ISBN 0-534-00496-2). PWS-Kent Pub.

Shortest Shorter: A Distillation of the Shorter Oxford English Dictionary A - M. Susanna Cuyler. (Illus.). 15p. (Orig.). 1985. pap. 5.00 o.p. (ISBN 0-9612018-2-7). B Rugged.

Shorthand Fashion Sketching. 4th ed. Patricia L. Rowe. LC 60-6848. 1964. 17.50 o.p. (ISBN 0-87005-068-0). Fairchild.

Shosha. Isaac Bashevis Singer. 1979. lib. bdg. 15.95 o.p. (ISBN 0-8161-6710-9, Large Print Bks). G K Hall.

Shostakovich: The Man & His Work. Ivan Martynov. (ISBN 0-8022-1074-0). Philos Lib.

Shotcrete for Ground Support. 776p. 1977. 45.25 o.p. (ISBN 0-317-32090-4, SP-54). ACI.

Shotgun in Combat. T. Lesce. (Weaponry Ser.). lib. bdg. cancelled o.s.i. (ISBN 0-8490-3725-5). Gordon Pr.

Shotokan Karate: Free Fighting Techniques. rev. ed. C. Mack & K. Enoeda. (Illus.). 96p. 1985. pap. text ed. 12.00 o.p. (ISBN 0-87364-365-8). Paladin Pr.

Shots of Style: Great Fashion Photographs Chosen by David Bailey. David Bailey & Martin Harrison. (Illus.). 224p. 1986. 60.00 o.p. (ISBN 0-948107-26-X); pap. 25.00 o.p. Faber & Faber.

Should Evolution Be Taught? John N. Moore. 1977. pap. 1.00 o.p. (ISBN 0-89051-043-1). Master Bks.

Should Government Encourage Homeownership? Raymond J. Struyk. 85p. 1977. pap. 6.50 o.p. (ISBN 0-87766-192-8, 18700). Urban Inst.

Should I Have an Abortion? Eldon Weisheit. 96p. 1976. pap. 1.75 o.p. (ISBN 0-570-03725-5, 12-2627). Concordia.

Should Land Have Selling Value? John C. Lincoln. 1972. pap. 0.75 o.s.i. (ISBN 0-686-17295-7). Lincoln Inst Land.

Should Trees Have Standing? Toward Legal Rights for Natural Objects. Christopher D. Stone. 1975. pap. 1.50 o.p. (ISBN 0-380-00400-3, 255693, Discus). Avon.

Should You Be Psychoanalyzed? Samuel Lowry. 1967. pap. 2.45 o.p. (ISBN 0-8065-0068-9, 245, Pub. by Citadel Pr). Carol Pub Group.

Shoulder Surgery. J. I. Bayley & L. Kessel. (Illus.). 320p. 1982. 67.00 o.p. (ISBN 0-387-11040-2). Springer-Verlag.

Shoulders of Atlas. Mary E. Wilkins Freeman. Date not set. pap. (ISBN 0-89733-281-4). Academy Chi Pubs.

Shoulders to the Wheel: Energy-Related College-Business Cooperative Agreements. Mary J. Jackman & James R. Mahoney. 64p. (Orig.). 1982. pap. 6.00 o.p. (ISBN 0-87117-117-1). Am Assn Comm Jr Coll.

Shout Across the River. Stephen Poliakoff. 56p. 1979. pap. 4.95 o.p. (ISBN 0-413-46230-7, NO. 3002). Heinemann Ed.

Show & Tell With Charlie: A Picture-Word Book. (Learning Curves Bks.). (Illus.). 16p. (ps-1). 1987. pap. 4.95 o.p. (ISBN 0-553-18361-3). Bantam.

Show Business Is Murder. Carol-Lynn R. Waugh et al. 256p. (Orig.). 1983. pap. 2.75 o.p. (ISBN 0-380-81554-0, 81554-0). Avon.

Show Jumping Records, Facts & Champions. Judith Draper. (Illus.). 240p. 1988. 24.95 o.p. (ISBN 0-85112-473-9, Pub. by Guinness Superlatives England). Sterling.

Show Me, Lord. Evelyn Ramsey. 180p. 1982. pap. 4.95 o.p. (ISBN 0-8341-0781-3). Beacon Hill.

Show Must Go On -- Even for Children. Carroll Atkinson. (Illus.). 224p. 1977. 7.50 o.p. (ISBN 0-682-48769-4). Exposition-Phoenix.

Show of Force. Charles D. Taylor. 352p. 1985. pap. 3.50 o.s.i. (ISBN 0-441-76195-X, Pub. by Charter Bks). Ace Bks.

Show Songs from the Black Crook to the Red Mill: Original Sheet Music for 60 Songs from 50 Shows, 1866-1906. Ed. by Stanley Applebaum. (Illus.). 15.25 o.p. (ISBN 0-8446-5152-4). Peter Smith.

Showa: An Inside History of Hirohito's Japan. Tessa Morris-Suzuki. LC 84-10521. 344p. 1985. 18.45 o.s.i. (ISBN 0-8052-3944-8). Schocken.

Showdown & Other Poems. MacPhelan Reese. 1985. 10.00 o.p. (ISBN 0-533-06483-X). Vantage.

Showdown in the Middle East. G. Vandeman. (Stories That Win Ser.). pap. 1.25 o.p. (ISBN 0-8163-0392-4). Pacific Pr Pub Assn.

Showers of Blessing. Matilda Nordtvedt & Pearl Steinkuehler. LC 19-764. 96p. (Orig.). 1980. pap. 4.95 o.p. (ISBN 0-8024-0434-0). Moody.

Showing-Off: The Lighter Side of Show-Jumping. Julian Seaman. (Illus.). 124p. 1988. 12.95 o.p. (ISBN 0-86051-397-1, Pub. by Robson UK). Parkwest Pubns.

Showing Ponies. Anne Bullen. (Illus.). 48p. pap. (ISBN 0-85131-106-7, NL51, Pub. by J A Allen U K). S R Smith Sporting Bks.

Showings, Healing & the Ordinary Person. Ann Hargrove. (Illus.). 225p. (Orig.). 1987. pap. 6.95 o.p. (ISBN 0-89638-128-5). CompCare.

Showroom Design in the United States: A Bibliography of Articles, 1978-1983. Carole Cable. (Architecture Ser.: A 1368). 16p. 1985. 2.25 o.p. (ISBN 0-89028-358-3). Vance Biblios.

Shrapnel & the Poet's Year. George MacBeth. LC 74-81284. 160p. 1974. 7.50 o.p. (ISBN 0-689-10638-6, Atheneum). Macmillan.

Shreveport, the Beginnings. Holice H. Henrici. 89p. (Orig.). 1986. pap. 6.95 o.p. (ISBN 0-940984-28-8). U of SW LA Ctr LA Studies.

Shrewbetinna's Birthday. John S. Goodall. LC 73-224238. (Illus.). 1971. 7.95 o.p. (ISBN 0-15-274080-5, HJ). HarBraceJ.

Shrine & Other Stories. Mary Lavin. 1977. 6.95 o.p. (ISBN 0-395-25773-5). HM.

Shrines of Power: The Grand Tour, Vol. 2. Flavio Conti. Tr. by Patrick Creagh. LC 77-90863. 1979. 15.95 o.p. (ISBN 0-15-182321-9). HarBraceJ.

Shrinking of America: Myths of Psychological Change. Bernie Zilbergeld. 1983. 17.00i o.p. (ISBN 0-316-98794-8). Little.

Shrinking the Federal Government. Irene S. Rubin. 256p. 1985. pap. text ed. 15.95 o.p. (ISBN 0-582-28473-2). Longman.

Shropshire Lad. Alfred E. Housman. LC 80-13329. 126p. 1980. Repr. of 1946 ed. lib. bdg. 22.50x o.p. (ISBN 0-313-22456-0, HOSH). Greenwood.

Shrubs & Small Trees. P-H.

Shrubs & Trees for Australian Gardens. Ernest E. Lord. (Illus.). 1979. 59.95x o.p. (ISBN 0-85091-104-4, Pub. by Lothian). Intl Spec Bk.

Shubuhat Haul al-Islam. Muhammad Qutb. 203p. (Orig., Arabic.). 1977. pap. 4.75x o.s.i. (ISBN 0-939830-15-9, Pub. by IIFSO Kuwait). New Era Pubns MI.

Shufflebrain. Paul Pietsch. (Illus.). 288p. 1981. 10.95 o.p. (ISBN 0-395-29480-0). HM.

Shura. Alexander A. Cooper. 64p. 1986. 6.95 o.p. (ISBN 0-8062-3009-6). Carlton.

Shutterbugs & Car Thieves. Hilary Milton. 144p. (Orig.). (gr. 3-7). 1981. pap. 2.50 o.s.i. (ISBN 0-671-44415-8). Wanderer Bks.

Shuttered Windows. Florence C. Means. (Illus.). (gr. 7-9). 6.95 o.p. (ISBN 0-395-06936-X). HM.

Shuttle to the Next Space Age. (Illus.). 131p. 18.00 o.p. (ISBN 0-317-32189-7). AIAA.

Shy Child: A Parent's Guide to Preventing & Overcoming Shyness from Infancy to Adulthood. Philip G. Zimbardo & Shirley L. Radl. LC 80-28570. 272p. 1981. text ed. 11.95 o.p. (ISBN 0-07-072827-5). McGraw.

Shy Ones. Lynn Hall. (Illus.). 192p. (YA) (gr. 9-12). 1977. pap. 1.75 o.p. (ISBN 0-380-01723-7, 63263-2, Camelot). Avon.

Si le Gran ne Meurt: Memoires. Andre Gide. (Coll. Folio). pap. 4.50 o.p. (ISBN 0-685-34158-5). Schoenhof.

Si-Sio2 System. Ed. by P. Balk. 1984. write for info. o.p. Elsevier.

Siamese Cat Owners Encyclopedia. Date not set. (ISBN 0-87605-813-6). Howell Bk.

Siamese Cats. Mary Dunnill. (Pet Care Ser.). 1984. pap. 6.50 o.p. (ISBN 0-8120-2924-0). Barron.

Siamese Cats. Louise B. Van Der Meid. (Orig.). pap. 2.95 o.p. (ISBN 0-87666-183-5, M-509). TFH Pubns.

Siberia: Epic of the Century. V. Sansone. 1980. 6.45 o.p. (ISBN 0-8285-1918-8, Pub. by Progress Pubs USSR). Imported Pubns.

Siberia Today & Tomorrow. Violet Conolly. LC 75-26327. (Illus.). 260p. 1976. 20.00 o.s.i. (ISBN 0-8008-7182-0). Taplinger.

Siberian Intervention. John A. White. 1970. Repr. of 1950 ed. lib. bdg. 38.50x o.p. (ISBN 0-8371-1976-6, WHIS). Greenwood.

Siberian Stories. S. Sartakov. 607p. 1979. 9.45 o.p. (ISBN 0-8285-1621-9, Pub. by Progress Pubs USSR). Imported Pubns.

Siblings. Robert J. Burger. 256p. 1984. 13.00 o.p. (ISBN 0-682-40188-9). Exposition-Phoenix.

Sicilian. Mario Puzo. 448p. 1984. 17.45 o.p. (ISBN 0-671-43564-7, Linden Pr). S&S.

Sicilian Defence, Bk. 1. S. Gligoric & V. Sokolov. 1972. pap. 100.00 o.p. (ISBN 0-08-017276-8). Pergamon.

Sicilian Specialist. Norman Lewis. 288p. 1986. pap. 3.50 o.p. (ISBN 1-55547-132-3). Critics Choice Paper.

Sicily Enough. Claire Rabe. (Illus.). 1976. pap. 3.75 o.p. (ISBN 0-88496-070-6). Capra Pr.

Sicily Travel Guide. (Berlitz Travel Guides). (Illus.). 1982. pap. 4.95 o.p. (ISBN 0-02-969510-4, Berlitz). Macmillan.

Sick & Tired of Being Sick & Tired. Neil Solomon & Mark Lipton. 352p. 1989. 18.95 o.p. (ISBN 0-922066-02-7). Wynwood Pr.

Sickle Cell Hemoglobinopathies: A Comprehensive Bibliography 1910-1972. Charles W. Triche & Diane S. Triche. LC 73-85959. v, 434p. 1974. 18.00x o.p. (ISBN 0-87875-048-7). Whitston Pub.

Sickness & Health: A Novel. Colin Douglas. LC 80-28316. 200p. (ISBN 0-8008-7178-2). Taplinger.

Side-Lights on English Society: Sketches from Life, Social & Satirical. rev ed. E. C. Murray. LC 75-83371. (Illus.). xii, 452p. 1969. Repr. of 1885 ed. 43.00x o.p. (ISBN 0-8103-3285-X). Gale.

Sidekicks: Or a Merger of Marvelous Magnitude. Anne Croswell. LC 83-40033. (Illus.). 128p. 1983. pap. 5.95 o.p. (ISBN 0-89480-589-4, 589). Workman Pub.

Sidelights on Christology: Did Jesus Die on the Cross? F. Charles Schwarz. 1977. 5.50 o.p. (ISBN 0-682-48912-3). Exposition-Phoenix.

Sidewalk Psalms... & Some from Country Lanes. Wilma Burton. LC 79-92015. 119p. 1980. 8.95 o.p. (ISBN 0-89107-165-2). Good News.

Sidewalk Racer & Other Poems of Sports & Motion. Lillian Morrison. LC 77-907. (Illus.). (gr. 6 up). 1977. 11.75 o.p. (ISBN 0-688-41805-8); PLB 11.88 o.p. (ISBN 0-688-51805-2). Lothrop.

Sidewalk Story. Sharon B. Mathis. (gr. 2-4). 1981. pap. 0.95 o.p. (ISBN 0-380-00851-3, 31146, Camelot). Avon.

Sidney. Susan Jeschke. LC 74-13188. (Illus.). (ps-3). 1975. reinforced bdg. o.p. 4.95 o.s.i. (ISBN 0-03-013536-2); pap. 2.95 o.s.i. (ISBN 0-03-048966-0). H Holt & Co.

Sidney Lanier, Henry Timrod & Paul Hamilton Hayne: A Reference Guide. Ed. by Jack De Bellis. 1978. lib. bdg. 29.00 o.p. (ISBN 0-8161-7967-0, Hall Reference). G K Hall.

Sidney Lumet: A Guide to References & Resources. Stephen E. Bowles. (Reference Books). 1979. lib. bdg. 20.50 o.p. (ISBN 0-8161-7938-7, Hall Reference). G K Hall.

Sidney Sime: Master of the Mysterious. Simon Heneage & Henry Ford. 1980. pap. 8.95 o.p. (ISBN 0-500-27154-2). Thames Hudson.

Siecle des Lumieres en Province: Academies et Academiciens Provinciaux, 1680-1789, 2 tomes. Daniel Roche. (Ecole des Hautes Etudes en Sciences Sociales. Centre de Recherches Historiques, Civilsations et Societes: No. 62). (Illus.). 1978. pap. 50.40x set o.p. (ISBN 90-279-7634-1). Mouton.

Siecus Circle. Claire Chambers. LC 75-41650. 1977. pap. 6.95 o.p. (ISBN 0-88279-119-2). Western Islands.

Siege of Charleston, by the British Fleet & Army Under the Command of Admiral Arbuthnot & Sir Henry Clinton, Which Terminated with the Surrender of That Place on the 12th of May, 1780. Franklin B. Hough. LC 74-34458. (Illus.). 224p. 1975. Repr. of 1867 ed. 12.50 o.s.i. (ISBN 0-87152-192-X). Reprint.

Siege of Krishnapur. J. G. Farrell. LC 74-1228. 352p. 1974. 7.95 o.p. (ISBN 0-15-182323-5). HarBraceJ.

Siege of Silent Henry. Lynn Hall. (YA) (gr. 7 up). 1977. pap. 1.50 o.p. (ISBN 0-380-01744-X, 49445). Avon.

Siege of the Dragonriders. Eric Affabee. (Wizards, Warriors & You Ser.: Bk. 2). (Illus.). 112p. 1984. pap. 2.50 o.p. (ISBN 0-380-88054-7, 88054-7). Avon.

Siege of Trapp's Mill. Annabel Farjeon. LC 73-84826. 136p. (gr. 5-9). 1974. 4.95 o.p. (ISBN 0-689-30136-7, Atheneum). Macmillan.

Siege: The Saga of Israel & Zionism. Conor C. O'Brien. 200p. 1986. 24.45 o.s.i. (ISBN 0-671-60044-3). S&S.

Siege Warfare: The Fortress in the Early Modern World, 1494-1660. Christopher Duffy. (Illus.). 1979. 30.00 o.p. (ISBN 0-7100-8871-X). Routledge Chapman & Hall.

Siegel's Modular Forms & Dirichlet Series. H. Maass. LC 73-171870. (Lecture Notes in Mathematics Ser.: Vol. 216). 1971. pap. 18.00 o.p. (ISBN 0-387-05563-0). Springer-Verlag.

Siegfried's Silent Night. Brad Bluth & Toby Bluth. 32p. (Orig.). (gr. k-6). 1983. 3.95 o.p. (ISBN 0-8249-8059-X). Ideals.

Siena: A City & Its History. Judith Hook. (Illus.). 258p. 1980. 30.95 o.p. (ISBN 0-241-10297-9, Pub. by Hamish Hamilton England). David & Charles.

Siena Baptistry Font: A Study of an Early Renaissance Collaborative Program, 1416-1434. John T. Paoletti. LC 78-74374. (Fine Arts Dissertations, Fourth Ser.). (Illus.). 1980. lib. bdg. 40.00 o.p. (ISBN 0-8240-3961-0). Garland Pub.

Sierra Club Naturalist's Guide to the Deserts of the Southwest. Peggy Larson & Lane Larson. LC 76-24835. (Naturalist's Guide Ser). (Illus.). 288p. 1977. pap. 9.95 o.p. (ISBN 0-87156-186-7). Sierra.

Sierra Gold Mystery. new ed. Carolyn Keene. (Dana Girls Ser.: Vol. 10). (Illus.). 192p. (gr. 4-7). 1973. 2.95 o.p. (G&D). Putnam Pub Group.

Sierra Nevada. Verna Johnston. (Naturalist's America Ser.). 1970. 11.95 o.p. (ISBN 0-395-10949-3). HM.

Sierra Sunrise. Lynn Wilson & Jim Wilson. Ed. by Vicki Leon. (Illus.). 64p. (Orig.). 1985. pap. 8.95 o.p. (ISBN 0-918303-05-2). Blake Pub.

Sieve Methods. H. Halberstam & H. E. Richert. 1975. 86.00 o.p. (ISBN 0-12-318250-6). Acad Pr.

Sigemi: A Japanese Village Girl. Ruth Kirk. LC 65-21699. (Illus.). (gr. 3-5). 1965. 5.95 o.p. (ISBN 0-15-274152-6, HJ). HarBraceJ.

Sight, Sound, & Sense. Ed. by Thomas A. Sebeok. LC 77-21520. (Advances in Semiotics Ser.). 320p. 1978. 20.00x o.p. (ISBN 0-253-35230-4). Ind U Pr.

Sights & Sounds of Ophthamology: Occular & Periocular Trauma. Vol. 5 ed. Hirst & Illiff. 1983. pap. 225.00 U.S. o.p. (ISBN 0-8016-2208-5). Mosby.

Sights & Sounds of the City: Vistas y Sonidos de la Ciudad. Hope R. Warriner. LC 76-20523. (Illus., Eng. & Span.). (gr. k-3). 1976. 5.95 o.p. (ISBN 0-87917-054-9). Ethridge.

Sigma & PI Electrons in Organic Compounds. W. Kutzelnigg et al. LC 51-5497. (Topics in Current Chemistry: Vol. 22). (Illus.). 1971. pap. 36.60 o.p. (ISBN 0-387-05473-1). Springer-Verlag.

Sigmund Freud: A New Appraisal. Maryse Choisy. LC 62-18553. 150p. 1963. (ISBN 0-8022-0242-X). Philos Lib.

Sigmund Freud: The World Within. Anne E. Neimark. LC 76-18713. (Illus.). (gr. 7 up). 1976. 6.95 o.p. (ISBN 0-15-274164-X, HJ). HarBraceJ.

Sigmund's Birthday Surprise. (Tales from Fern Hollow Ser.). (Illus.). 22p. (ps-1). 1985. 1.98 o.p. (ISBN 0-517-44571-9). Outlet Bk Co.

Sign & Billboard Design: An Architectural Approach. Coppa & Avery Consultants Staff. (Architecture Ser.: A 1409). 8p. 1985. 2.00 o.p. (ISBN 0-89028-439-3). Vance Biblios.

Sign & Guiding for Libraries: A Practical Guide to Design & Production. Linda Reynolds & Stephen Barret. 158p. 1981. 32.50 o.p. (ISBN 0-85157-312-6, Pub. by Bingley England). ALA.

Sign & Symbol Communication for Mentally Handicapped People. Philip R. Jones & Ailsa Cregan. (Illus.). 200p. 1985. 29.00 o.p. (ISBN 0-7099-1431-8, Pub. by Croom Helm Ltd); pap. 15.50 o.p. (ISBN 0-7099-1479-2). Routledge Chapman & Hall.

Sign Carving. Garrit D. Lydecker. (Illus.). 304p. (Orig.). 1983. 19.95 o.p. (ISBN 0-8306-0101-5); pap. 14.60 o.p. (ISBN 0-8306-0601-7, 1601). TAB Bks.

Sign Design. Signs of the Times Magazine Editors. LC 85-12134. (Illus.). 256p. 1985. 55.00 o.p. (ISBN 0-86636-013-1). PBC Intl Inc.

Sign in Sidney Brustein's Window see Raisin in the Sun.

Sign Language Among North American Indians Compared with That among Other Peoples & Deaf Mutes. (with Articles by A. L. Kroeber & C. F. Vogelin) D. Garrick Mallery. (Approaches to Semiotics Ser: No. 14). (Illus.). 552p. 1972. Repr. of 1881 ed. text ed. 40.80x o.p. (ISBN 0-686-22538-4). Mouton.

Sign Languages Used by Deaf People, & Psycholinguistics. 128p. (Orig.). 1986. pap. 20.00 o.p. (ISBN 9-02650-701-1). CJ Hogrefe Pubs.

Sign of the Chrysanthemum. Katherine Paterson. (Illus.). 132p. (gr. 6 up). 1980. pap. 2.25 o.p. (ISBN 0-380-49288-1, Camelot). Avon.

Sign of the Crescent Moon. Thomas J. Saunders. LC 76-56040. 1977. 7.00 o.p. (ISBN 0-682-48762-7). Exposition-Phoenix.

Sign of the Eighties. Gail Parent. 320p. 1987. 17.95 o.p. (ISBN 0-399-13262-7, Putnam). Putnam Pub Group.

Sign of the Praying Tiger. Ben L. Burman. 4.95 o.s.i. (ISBN 0-685-02657-4). Taplinger.

Sign of the Twisted Candles. rev. ed. Carolyn Keene. (Nancy Drew Ser: Vol. 9). (Illus.). (gr. 4-7). 1959. 2.95 o.p. (G&D); PLB 3.29 o.p. (ISBN 0-448-19509-7). Putnam Pub Group.

Sign Painter. Barbara M. Sutryn. (Living Bks.). 352p. 1985. 3.95 o.p. (ISBN 0-8423-5894-3). Tyndale.

Signal-Close Action. Alexander Kent. 352p. 1984. pap. 3.50 o.s.i. (ISBN 0-515-07437-3). Jove Pubns.

Signal Processing: Proceedings. Ed. by J. W. Griffiths et al. 790p. 1973. 110.50 o.p. (ISBN 0-12-303450-7). Acad Pr.

Signal Routing in Integrated Circuit Layout. Chi-Ping Hsu. Ed. by Harold Stone. LC 86-1382. (Computer Science: Very Large Systems Integration: No. 1). 126p. 1986. 44.95 o.p. (ISBN 0-8357-1744-5). UMI Res Pr.

Signers of the Declaration. John Bakeless. LC 69-14723. (Illus.). (gr. 7 up). 1969. 6.95 o.p. (ISBN 0-395-06581-X). HM.

Signet Book of Inexpensive Wine. rev. ed. Susan Lee. 1979. pap. 1.95 o.p. (J8980, Sig). NAL.

Significance of Jesus. Joyce Marie Smith. 1976. pap. 2.95 o.p. (ISBN 0-8423-5887-0). Tyndale.

Significance of the Bible for the Church. Anders Nygren. Ed. by John Reumann. Tr. by Carl C. Rasmusen. LC 63-17879. (Facet Bks.). 56p. (Orig.). 1963. pap. 2.50 o.p. (ISBN 0-8006-3000-9, Fortress). Augsburg Fortress.

Significant NASA Inventions Available for Licensing in Foreign Countries. LC 86-7898. (NASA SP-7038(08)). 180p. (Orig.). 1986. pap. 5.00 o.p. (ISBN 0-318-20385-5, S/N 033-000-00986-1). USGPO.

Significant State Appellate Decisions. National Judicial College (U. S.) Staff. (Series 1850). 1980. pap. 7.50 o.p. (ISBN 0-686-08770-4). Natl Judicial Coll.

Signifying Animal: The Grammar of Language & Experience. Ed. by Irmengard Rauch & Gerald F. Carr. LC 79-3624. (Advances in Semiotics). 304p. 1980. 24.95x o.p. (ISBN 0-253-18496-7). Ind U Pr.

Signpost-Middle East. Anne C. Stephens. (Orig.). (gr. 4-6). 1979. pap. 2.95 o.p. (ISBN 0-377-00087-6). Friendship Pr.

Signposts to Freedom: The Ten Commandments of Christian Ethics. Jan M. Lochman. Tr. by David Lewis. LC 81-52283. 192p. (Orig.). 1982. pap. 10.95 o.p. (ISBN 0-8066-1915-5, 10-5767, Augsburg). Augsburg Fortress.

Signposts to the Past: Placenames & the History of England. Margaret Gelling. (Illus.). 256p. 1978. 17.50x o.p. (ISBN 0-460-04264-5, Pub. by J. M. Dent England). Biblio Dist.

Signs & Omens. Bruce Forester. 264p. 1986. pap. 2.95 o.p. (ISBN 0-931773-67-9). Critics Choice Paper.

Signs & Portents. Al Hines. 1973. pap. 1.25 o.p. (ISBN 0-380-01549-8, 14845). Avon.

Signs & Symbols of the Sun. Elizabeth S. Helfman. LC 73-20121. (Illus.). 192p. (gr. 4-7). 1979. 8.95 o.p. (ISBN 0-395-28860-6, Clarion). HM.

Signs & Symptoms of Chemical Exposure. J. Bradford Block. 164p. 1980. spiral bdg. 23.00x o.p. (ISBN 0-398-03958-5). C C Thomas.

Signs & Wonders. Mary Light. 1968. pap. 1.00 o.p. (ISBN 0-910924-66-X). Macalester.

Signs in Contemporary Culture. Arthur A. Berger. (Annenberg Communication Ser.). (Illus.). 224p. 1984. text ed. 35.95 o.p. (ISBN 0-582-28487-2). Longman.

Signs, Language & Behavior. Charles Morris. 1955. 7.95 o.p. (ISBN 0-8076-0020-2). Braziller.

Signs of an Apostle. C. K. Barrett. Ed. by John Reumann. LC 72-75646. 160p. (Orig.). 1972. pap. 1.50x o.p. (ISBN 0-8006-0116-5, 1-116, Fortress). Augsburg Fortress.

Signs of His Coming: Dramas & Meditations for Advent, Christmas & Epiphany. W. A. Poovey. LC 73-78261. 1973. pap. 3.50 o.p. (ISBN 0-8066-1326-2, 10-5780, Augsburg). Augsburg Fortress.

Signs of Life. Sumner L. Elliott. LC 80-21914. 288p. 1981. 11.95 o.p. (ISBN 0-89919-022-7). Ticknor & Fields.

Signs of Love: The Sacraments of Christ. Leonard Foley. (Illus.). 1976. pap. 1.95 o.p. (ISBN 0-912228-32-6). St Anthony Mess Pr.

Signs of the Stars. Frederick Davies. (Illus.). 224p. 1987. 24.95 o.p. (ISBN 0-13-842410-1); pap. 12.95 o.p. (ISBN 0-13-842808-5). P-H.

Signs of the Times. H. L. Willmington. 1981. pap. 5.95 o.p. (ISBN 0-8423-5888-9). Tyndale.

Signs, Songs & Stories. Ed. by Virginia Sloyan. (Illus.). 160p. 1982. pap. 8.50 o.p. (ISBN 0-8146-1285-7). Liturgical Pr.

Sikh Symposium 1985. Jarnail Singh. 121p. 1986. 8.00 o.p. (ISBN 0-8364-1840-9). South Asia Bks.

Sikhgurus: Their Lives & Teachings. K. S. Duggal. write for info. o.p. (ISBN 0-89389-106-1). Himalayan Pubs.

Sikhs. Khushwant Singh & Raghu Rai. LC 85-22359. 144p. 1985. Repr. lib. bdg. 44.95x o.p. (ISBN 0-89370-891-7). Borgo Pr.
Silas & Con. A. C. Stewart. LC 77-23318. 132p. (gr. 4-7). 1977. 5.95 o.p. (ISBN 0-689-50086-6, Atheneum). Macmillan.
Silas Marner. George Eliot. LC 86-60831. (Illus.). 208p. 1986. 12.95 o.p. (ISBN 0-89577-248-5). RD Assn.
Silas Marner. George Eliot. 48p. (Orig.). 1989. pap. 9.95 o.p. (ISBN 1-55651-831-5); audiocassette tape incl. o.p. (ISBN 1-55651-832-3). Cram Cassettes.
Silas Marner: The Weaver of Raveloe. George Eliot. 1978. Repr. of 1977 ed. 11.95x o.p. (ISBN 0-460-00121-3, Evman); pap. 2.95x o.p. (ISBN 0-460-01121-9). Biblio Dist.
Silence de la Mer. Jean Vercors. Ed. by Henri Peyre & Marguerite Peyre. LC 51-33178. (Orig., Fr). 1944. 3.95 o.p. (ISBN 0-394-44545-7). Pantheon.
Silence of Snakes. Lewis Green. LC 84-16804. 350p. 1984. 5.98 o.p. (ISBN 0-89587-040-1). Blair.
Silencer Patents, Vol. III: European Patents 1901-1978. Donald G. Thomas. (Illus.). 253p. 1978. pap. 20.00 o.p. (ISBN 0-87364-102-7). Paladin Pr.
Silences. Tillie Olsen. 320p. 1986. pap. 4.50 o.p. (ISBN 0-440-38337-4, LE). Dell.
Silent Epidemic: We Can Stop Teenage Suicide. Mary A. Wilder. LC 85-90257. 94p. 1986. 10.00 o.p. (ISBN 0-533-06682-4). Vantage.
Silent in Court. Susanne Dell. 64p. 1971. pap. text ed. 5.00 o.p. (ISBN 0-7135-1576-7, Pub. by Bedford England). Gower Pub Co.
Silent Issues of the Church. Carl H. Lundquist. 156p. 1985. pap. 6.50 o.p. (ISBN 0-89693-721-6). Victor Bks.
Silent Liars. Michael Underwood. (Nightingales Ser.). 318p. 1987. pap. 12.95x o.p. (ISBN 0-8161-4223-8, Large Print Bks.). G K Hall.
Silent Life. Thomas Merton. 1983. 12.75 o.p. (ISBN 0-8446-5986-X). Peter Smith.
Silent Murder. Mildred Evelyn Flagg. 1977. 5.50 o.p. (ISBN 0-682-48758-9). Exposition-Phoenix.
Silent Myocardial ISC-INFR. Cohn. (Basic & Clinical Cardiology Ser.). 256p. 1986. 49.75 o.p. (ISBN 0-8247-7469-8). Dekker.
Silent Night, Holy Night. Paul Rosel. (Illus.). 1969. 3.25 o.p. (ISBN 0-8066-0928-1, 11-9388, Augsburg). Augsburg Fortress.
Silent Ones. Elisabeth Ogilvie. 304p. 1981. text ed. 11.95 o.p. (ISBN 0-07-047679-9). McGraw.
Silent Path to God. James E. Griffiss. LC 79-8903. 112p. 1980. pap. 4.95 o.p. (ISBN 0-8006-1384-8, 1-1384, Fortress). Augsburg Fortress.
Silent Scream. Martha Janssen. LC 83-5714. 112p. 1983. pap. 4.95 o.p. (ISBN 0-8006-1722-3, 1-1722, Fortress). Augsburg Fortress.
Silent Sea. Harry Homewood. 1981. text ed. 12.95 o.p. (ISBN 0-07-029695-2). McGraw.
Silent September. Joyce Landorf. 1984. pap. 10.00 o.p. (ISBN 0-317-14051-5). Word Bks.
Silent Siege: Japanese Attacks Against North America in World War II. Bert Webber. (Illus.). 397p. 1985. o.s.i 22.50 o.s.i. (ISBN 0-87770-315-9); pap. 16.95 o.s.i. (ISBN 0-87770-318-3). Ye Galleon.
Silent Spring. Rachael L. Carson. 304p. 1981. pap. 2.95 o.p. (ISBN 0-449-23871-7, Crest). Fawcett.
Silent Spring. Rachel L. Carson. (Illus.). 1962. 17.45 o.p. (ISBN 0-395-07506-8). HM.
Silent Studio. David D. Duncan. (Illus.). 1976. 12.50 o.p. (ISBN 0-393-04442-4). Norton.
Silent Surrender. Kari Levitt. 1971. pap. 2.75 o.p. (ISBN 0-87140-254-8). Liveright.
Silent Tears. Jeanette Black. 1985. 11.95 o.p. (ISBN 0-533-06497-X). Vantage.
Silent Traveller in Japan. Chiang Yee. (Illus.). 1972. 15.00 o.p. (ISBN 0-393-08642-9). Norton.
Silent Traveller in Paris. Chiang Yee. (Illus.). 1962. 7.50 o.p. (ISBN 0-393-08449-3). Norton.
Silent Twins. Marjorie Wallace. (Illus.). 256p. 1986. 16.95 o.p. (ISBN 0-13-810276-7). Prentice Hall Pr.
Silent Voices. Jared Angira. (African Writers Ser.). 1972. pap. text ed. 5.50 o.p. (ISBN 0-435-90111-7). Heinemann Ed.
Silent Word. new ed. Francis Brabazon. 1978. text ed. 9.95 o.p. (ISBN 0-913078-34-4); pap. text ed. 6.95 o.p. (ISBN 0-913078-35-2). Sheriar Pr.
Silhouette Crafts. Romilda Dilley. (Illus.). 24p. (YA) (gr. 9-12). 1987. wkbk. 2.95 o.p. (ISBN 0-87403-238-5, 2148). Standard Pub.
Silhouette in Scarlet. Elizabeth Peters. 288p. 1985. pap. 3.50 o.p. (ISBN 0-931773-03-2). Critics Choice Paper.
Silhouettes: How to Make & Use Them. Jack Kramer. LC 76-44873. 1977. 7.95 o.p. (ISBN 0-395-25060-9). HM.
Silhouettes of Charles S. Thomas, Colorado Governor & United States Senator. Sewell Thomas. LC 59-7608. (Illus.). 228p. 1959. 7.50 o.p. (ISBN 0-87004-167-3). Caxton.
Silhouettes of Thought. Jessie Turner. (Illus.). 80p. pap. 2.95 o.p. (ISBN 0-89036-150-9). Hawkes Pub Inc.
Silhouetting Halftones & Making Dropout Masks. 38p. 1981. 16.00 o.s.i. (ISBN 0-88362-029-4, 0431). Graphic Arts Tech Found.
Silicon Carbide-1968. H. K. Henisch & R. Roy. 1974. 95.00 o.p. (ISBN 0-08-006768-9). Pergamon.
Silicon Idol. Date not set. (ISBN 0-8052-3927-8). Random.
Silicon Reagents for Organic Synthesis. William P. Weber. (Reactivity & Structure: Vol. 14). 450p. 1983. 140.00 o.p. (ISBN 0-387-11675-3). Springer-Verlag.
Silicon Semiconductor Data. H. F. Wolf. 1969. 170.00 o.p. (ISBN 0-08-013019-4). Pergamon.
Silicon Valley. Michael Rogers. 1982. 15.50 o.p. (ISBN 0-671-41030-X). S&S.
Silicones. Fordham. (Illus.). 256p. 1961. (ISBN 0-8022-0518-6). Philos Lib.
Silk & Satin. Marcia Wolfson. 320p. 1986. 18.95 o.p. (ISBN 0-399-13192-2, Putnam). Putnam Pub Group.
Silk & Steel. Stephen Alter. 327p. 1980. 11.95 o.p. (ISBN 0-374-26411-2). FS&G.
Silk Pictures of Thomas Stevens. Wilma Sinclar LeVan Baker. 1957. 50.00x o.p. (ISBN 0-682-40006-8, Banner). Exposition-Phoenix.
Silk Screen Printing. rev. ed. James Eisenberg & Francis J. Kafka. (Illus.). (gr. 9 up). 1957. pap. 6.00 o.p. (ISBN 0-87345-205-4). Glencoe.
Silks. Roberta Spear. LC 79-19210. (National Poetry Ser.). 96p. (Orig.). 1980. 8.95 o.p. (ISBN 0-03-056117-5); pap. 4.95 o.p. (ISBN 0-03-056116-7). H Holt & Co.
Silkworms & Science: The Story of Silk. Elizabeth K. Cooper. (Illus.). (gr. 5 up). 1961. 4.95 o.p. (ISBN 0-15-274241-7, HJ). HarBraceJ.
Silva Mind Control Method. Jose Silva & Philip Miele. 1977. 9.95 o.p. (ISBN 0-671-22427-1). S&S.
Silver Apples, Golden Apples: Best-Loved Irish Verse. Frank Delaney. (Illus.). 1987. pap. 15.95 o.p. (ISBN 0-85640-391-1, Pub. by Blackstaff Ireland). Irish Bks Media.
Silver Azide, Cyanide, Cyanamides, Cyanate, Selenocyanate & Thiocyanate: Solubilities of Solids. M. Salomon. (Solubility Data Ser.: Vol. 3). 1979. 110.00x o.p. (ISBN 0-08-022350-8). Pergamon.
Silver Christmas Ornaments: A Collector's Guide. Clara J. Scroggins. LC 79-15323. (Illus.). 208p. 1980. 25.00 o.s.i. (ISBN 0-498-02385-0). A S Barnes.
Silver Crest: My Russian Boyhood. Kornei Chukofky. Tr. by Beatrice Stillman from Rus. LC 75-32248. 192p. (gr. 5 up). 1976. 6.95 o.s.i. (ISBN 0-03-014241-5). H Holt & Co.
Silver Dove. Andrey Biely. Tr. by George Reavey from Rus. LC 73-21039. 1974. pap. 7.95 o.p. (ISBN 0-394-17859-9, E637, Ever). Grove.
Silver Ghost. Chuck Kinder. 1979. 8.95 o.p. (ISBN 0-15-124067-1). HarBraceJ.
Silver-Glass Mirrors for Solar Thermal Systems. Al Czanderna. (Illus.). 71p. (Orig.). 1985. pap. 2.50 o.p. (ISBN 0-318-18835-X, S/N 061-000-00660-5). USGPO.
Silver: Its History & Romance. Benjamin White. LC 71-174144. (Illus.). xxviii, 362p. 1972. Repr. of 1920 ed. 48.00x o.p. (ISBN 0-8103-3930-7). Gale.
Silver Lobby: A Guide to Advocacy for Older Persons. Clinton W. Hess & Paul A. Kerschner. LC 78-61804. 1978. pap. 4.00x o.p. (ISBN 0-88474-075-7, 05735-5). Lexington Bks.
Silver Matzoth. Gershon Kranzler. saddle-stitched 5.00 o.p. (ISBN 0-87559-131-0). Shalom.
Silver Mezzuzah. Gershon Kranzler. saddle-stitched 5.00 o.p. (ISBN 0-87559-133-7). Shalom.
Silver New Nothing. Sybil Marshall. 1987. 22.00 o.p. (ISBN 0-85115-461-1, Pub. by Boydell & Brewer). Longwood Pub Group.
Silver Palate Gift Set, 2 vols. Julee Rosso. 22.90 o.p. (ISBN 0-89480-011-6). Workman Pub.
Silver Rose. David A. Kaufelt. 272p. (Orig.). 1983. pap. 3.50 o.p. (ISBN 0-440-17592-5). Dell.
Silver Shores. Yvonne Kalman. LC 82-72069. 352p. 1982. 14.95 o.p. (ISBN 0-87795-432-1, Arbor Hse). Morrow.
Silver Shores. Yvonne Kalman. 416p. 1984. pap. 3.95 o.p. (ISBN 0-380-68676-7). Avon.
Silver: The Restless Metal. Roy W. Jastram. LC 80-28361. 224p. 1981. 44.95x o.p. (ISBN 0-471-03912-8, Pub. by Wiley-Interscience). Wiley.
Silver Tip, My Crippled Coyote. Lee Templeton. 112p. 1983. 6.95 o.p. (ISBN 0-89015-371-X). Eakin Pr.
Silver Touch. Rosalind Laker. LC 86-24199. 360p. 1987. 16.95 o.s.i. (ISBN 0-385-23745-6). Doubleday.
Silver Vessels of the Sansanian Period: Royal Imagery, Vol. 1. Prudence O. Harper & Pieter Meyers. Ed. by Anne M. Preuss & Polly Cone. (Illus.). 272p. 1981. 35.00 o.p. (ISBN 0-87099-248-1). Metro Mus Art.
Silver Web. Jean Nash. (Orig.). 1980. pap. 2.25 o.p. (ISBN 0-505-51473-7, Pub. by Tower Bks). Dorchester Pub Co.
Silver Wings, Santiago Blue. Janet Dailey. 480p. 1984. 15.45 o.s.i. (ISBN 0-671-50405-3, Pub. by Poseidon); 40.00 o.s.i. (ISBN 0-671-50906-3). S&S.
Silver Wings, Santiago Blue. Janet Dailey. (General Ser.). 1984. lib. bdg. 15.95 o.s.i. (ISBN 0-8161-3725-0, Large Print Bks); pap. 10.95 o.s.i. (ISBN 0-8161-3762-5). G K Hall.
Silver Woven in My Hair. Shirley R. Murphy. LC 76-25578. (Illus.). (gr. 4-6). 1977. 6.95 o.p. (ISBN 0-689-30558-3, Atheneum). Macmillan.
Silverleaf Syndrome. Eleanor Robinson. (Orig.). 1980. pap. text ed. 1.95 o.p. (ISBN 0-505-51556-3, Pub. by Tower Bks). Dorchester Pub Co.
Silvernail. Jim Morris. 256p. 1986. pap. 3.50 o.p. (ISBN 0-440-18046-5). Dell.
Silverstreet. Thomas E. Williams. (Illus.). 240p. 1983. 15.00 o.p. (ISBN 0-682-49929-3). Exposition-Phoenix.
Silverthorn. Raymond E. Feist. LC 83-27471. 360p. 1985. 15.95 o.p. (ISBN 0-385-19210-X). Doubleday.
Silverwood. Joanna Barnes. 432p. 1985. 16.45 o.p. (ISBN 0-671-45940-6, Linden Pr). S&S.
Silverwood. Joanna Barnes. (Large Print Books (General Ser.)). 558p. 1985. lib. bdg. 18.95 o.p. (ISBN 0-8161-3936-9). G K Hall.
Silverwork & Jewelery. Henry Wilson. 1978. pap. 9.95 o.p. (ISBN 0-8008-7192-8, Pentalic). Taplinger.
Simba Gold. Donald Courtney. (Orig.). 1985. pap. 3.50 o.p. (ISBN 0-440-18052-X). Dell.
Similarity Methods for Differential Equations. G. W. Bluman & J. D. Cole. LC 74-20838. (Applied Mathematical Sciences Ser.: Vol. 13). (Illus.). 1974. pap. 16.50 o.p. (ISBN 0-387-90107-8). Springer-Verlag.
Similes: As Gentle As a Lamb, Spin Like a Top, & Other "Like" or "As" Comparisons Between Unlike Things. Joan Hanson. LC 76-22433. (Joan Hanson Word Bks.). (Illus.). (ps-3). 1976. PLB 4.95 o.p. (ISBN 0-8225-1108-8). Lerner Pubns.
Simon. Molly Cone. LC 74-115449. (Illus.). (gr. 5-9). 1970. 3.50 o.p. (ISBN 0-395-06706-5). HM.
Simon & Schuster Book of Cryptic Crossword Puzzles, No. 4. Ed. by Eugene T. Maleska. 64p. 1986. pap. 5.95 o.s.i. (ISBN 0-671-55752-1, Fireside). S&S.
Simon & Schuster Book of Cryptic Crossword Puzzles, No. 5. Ed. by Eugene T. Maleska. (Illus.). 64p. 1987. pap. 5.95 o.s.i. (ISBN 0-671-61816-4, Fireside). S&S.
Simon & Schuster Book of Cryptic Puzzles, No. 3. Ed. by Eugene T. Maleska. 1984. pap. 5.70 o.s.i. (ISBN 0-671-50213-1, Fireside). S&S.
Simon & Schuster Book of the Opera. 1985. pap. 14.95 o.s.i. (ISBN 0-671-60438-4, Fireside). S&S.
Simon & Schuster Crossword Book of Quotations. Ed. by Eugene T. Maleska. (Series 12). (Orig.). 1980. pap. 4.80 o.s.i. (ISBN 0-671-24090-0, Fireside). S&S.
Simon & Schuster Crossword from the Times, Series 36: A Daily Collection. Ed. by Margaret P. Farrar. 1979. pap. 5.75 o.s.i. (ISBN 0-671-24795-6, Fireside). S&S.
Simon & Schuster Crossword Puzzle Book, No. 120. Margaret P. Farrar & Eugene T. Maleska. 1979. pap. 5.75 o.s.i. (ISBN 0-671-24099-4, Fireside). S&S.
Simon & Schuster Crossword Puzzle Treasury, No. 27. Margaret P. Farrar & Eugene T. Maleska. 1985. pap. 6.95 o.s.i. (ISBN 0-671-55753-X). S&S.
Simon & Schuster Crosswords from the Times, Series 35: A Sunday Collection. Ed. by Margaret P. Farrar. 1979. pap. 5.75 o.s.i. (ISBN 0-671-24778-6, Fireside). S&S.
Simon & Schuster Crostics, No. 90. Thomas H. Middleton. (Simon & Schuster Crostics Ser.). (Orig.). 1983. pap. 6.95 o.s.i. (ISBN 0-671-49435-X, Fireside). S&S.
Simon & Schuster Crostics, No. 72. Ed. by Thomas H. Middleton. 1974. pap. 2.95 spiral bound o.s.i. (ISBN 0-671-21866-2, Fireside). S&S.
Simon & Schuster Crostics, No. 80. Ed. by Thomas H. Middleton. 1978. pap. 4.95 spiral bound o.s.i. (ISBN 0-671-24412-4). S&S.
Simon & Schuster Picture Dictionary of Phonics from A to Zh. Linda Hayward. (Illus.). (ps-5). 1984. pap. 10.95 o.s.i. (ISBN 0-671-43102-1, Little Simon). S&S.
Simon & Schuster Pocket Art Museum Guide. Helen Langdon. (Illus.). 1981. pap. 6.95 o.p. (ISBN 0-671-42007-0). S&S.
Simon & Schuster Pocket Companion to Shakespeares' Plays. J. C. Trewin. 1981. pap. 5.95 o.p. (ISBN 0-671-42006-2). S&S.
Simon & Schuster Pocket Encyclopedia of Prescription & Nonprescription Drugs. Samuel W. Perry. (Illus.). 1982. pap. 5.95 o.p. (ISBN 0-671-42398-3). S&S.
Simon & Schuster Pocket Guide to Antiques. Bevis Hillier. (Illus.). 1981. pap. 7.95 o.p. (ISBN 0-671-25250-X). S&S.
Simon & Schuster Pocket Guide to Cheese. Sandy Carr. (Illus.). 1981. pap. 5.95 o.p. (ISBN 0-671-42475-0). S&S.
Simon & Schuster Pocket Guide to Italian Wines. Burton Anderson. 1982. pap. 5.95 o.p. (ISBN 0-671-45234-7). S&S.
Simon & Schuster Question & Answer Book. Kathleen N. Daly. Ed. by Wendy Barish. (Illus.). 320p. (gr. 3 up). 1982. pap. 8.50 o.s.i. (ISBN 0-671-44427-1). Wanderer Bks.
Simon & Schuster Sports Question & Answer Book. Edward F. Dolan, Jr. Ed. by Diane Arico. (Illus.). 256p. (gr. 3 up). 1984. 6.95 o.s.i. (ISBN 0-671-47749-8). Wanderer Bks.
Simon & Schuster United States Question & Answer Book. Larry Lorimer. (Simon & Schuster Question & Answer Book Ser.). (gr. 2-7). 1984. 7.95 o.s.i. (ISBN 0-671-52588-3). Wanderer Bks.
Simon & Schuster's Concise International Dictionary: English-Spanish, Spanish-English. new abr. ed. Tana De Ganiez. LC 74-33235. 1408p. (Eng. & Span.). 1975. text ed. 12.95 o.p. (ISBN 0-671-22020-9). S&S.
Simon & Schuster's Crossword Puzzle Book: Series No. 136. Ed. by Eugene T. Maleska. 1985. pap. 5.95 o.s.i. (ISBN 0-671-50206-9). S&S.
Simon & Schuster's Crostic Omnibus, No. 13. Ed. by Thomas H. Middleton. 96p. 1984. pap. 6.95 o.s.i. (ISBN 0-671-54194-3, Fireside). S&S.
Simon & Schuster's Crostics, No. 91. Thomas H. Middleton. 1984. pap. 6.95 o.s.i. (ISBN 0-671-50647-1, Fireside). S&S.
Simon & Schuster's Crostics No. 93. Ed. by Thomas H. Middleton. 1985. pap. 6.95 o.s.i. (ISBN 0-671-55671-1). S&S.
Simon & Schuster's Crostics Omnibus, No. 9. Thomas H. Middleton. 1979. pap. 5.75 o.s.i. (ISBN 0-671-24794-8, Fireside). S&S.
Simon & Schuster's Illustrated Young Reader's Dictionary. 1983. pap. 4.80 o.s.i. (ISBN 0-671-47144-9). Wanderer Bks.
Simon & Schuster's Large-Type Crosswords, No. 6. Ed. by Margaret P. Farrar. 96p. (Orig.). 1982. pap. 5.95 o.s.i. (ISBN 0-671-43644-9, Fireside). S&S.
Simon de Montfort: Reformer & Rebel. Luckock. 1970. 3.38 o.p. (ISBN 0-08-008757-4). Pergamon.
Simon Pure. Julian F. Thompson. 336p. (YA) (gr. 7 up). 1987. pap. 2.50 o.p. (ISBN 0-590-40508-X, Point). Scholastic Inc.
Simon Says. Bill Morrison. LC 83-9431. (Illus.). 32p. (gr. k-3). 1983. PLB 12.95 o.p. (ISBN 0-316-58475-4). Little.
Simon Says: The Best of Roger Simon. Roger Simon. 320p. 1986. pap. 8.95 o.p. (ISBN 0-8092-4853-0). Contemp Bks.
Simon the Snake. Alice L. Mason. (Illus.). 16p. (gr. k-6). 1984. pap. 1.50 o.p. (ISBN 0-8249-8069-7). Ideals.
Simon Wiesenthal Center Annual, Vol. 5. Ed. by Henry Friedlander & Sybil Milton. 320p. 1988. 30.00 o.p. (ISBN 0-527-96492-1). Kraus Intl.
Simone Weil: An Introduction to Her Thought. John Hellman. LC 83-48917. 120p. 1984. pap. 6.95 o.p. (ISBN 0-8006-1763-0, 1-1763, Fortress). Augsburg Fortress.
Simon's Night. Jon Hassler. LC 79-10900. 1979. 9.95 o.p. (ISBN 0-689-10981-4, Atheneum). Macmillan.
Simple Astronomy. Iain Nicolson. LC 73-11573. (Encore Edition). (Illus.). 1974. 2.95 o.p. (ISBN 0-684-15429-3, ScribT). Scribner.
Simple Chinese Stories. George A. Kennedy. 3.95 o.p. (ISBN 0-88710-088-0). Yale Far Eastern Pubns.
Simple Cobler of Aggawam in America. Nathaniel Ward. Ed. by Paul M. Zall. LC 69-19107. xviii, 81p. 1969. 7.50x o.p. (ISBN 0-8032-0188-5). U of Nebr Pr.
Simple Embroidery Designs. Ondori Publishing Company Staff. (Illus.). 103p. (Orig.). 1985. pap. 7.95 o.p. Japan Pubns USA.
Simple Feasts: Appetizers, Main Dishes & Desserts. Ed. by Marilee Matteson. (Illus.). 200p. 1983. 21.95 o.p. (ISBN 0-395-33102-1). HM.
Simple Geological Structures. John Platt & John Challinor. 1974. pap. text ed. 7.95x o.p. (ISBN 0-04-550020-7). Unwin Hyman.
Simple Gifts. Joanne Greenberg. LC 86-323. 208p. 1987. 15.95 o.p. (ISBN 0-8050-0034-8); pap. 7.95 o.p. H Holt & Co.
Simple Gifts, Vols. 1&2. Ed. by Gabe Huck. 1974. pap. 6.50 o.p. (ISBN 0-918208-65-3). Liturgical Conf.

Titles

Simple Joys of Womanhood. Betty J. Busch. 32p. 1988. 7.95 o.p. Carlton.

Simple Machines & How We Use Them. Tillie S. Pine & Joseph Levine. (Illus.). (gr. 3-5). 1965. text ed. 8.95 o.p. (ISBN 0-07-050067-3). McGraw.

Simple Matter of Justice: The Phyllis Wheatly YWCA Story. Florence J. Radcliffe. 304p. 1985. 13.00 o.p. (ISBN 0-682-40199-4). Exposition-Phoenix.

Simple Minds: An Illustrated Biography. 96p. 1985. 1.95 o.s.i. (ISBN 0-7119-0617-3). Cherry Lane.

Simple Pictures Are Best. Nancy Willard. LC 76-4923. (Illus.). (gr. 1-4). 1977. 7.95 o.p. (ISBN 0-15-274958-6, HJ). HarBraceJ.

Simple Plant Propagation. R. C. Wright. LC 77-70396. (Illus.). 1978. pap. 5.95 o.p. (ISBN 0-8120-0795-6). Barron.

Simple Program Schemes & Formal Languages. J. Engelfriet. (Lecture Notes in Computer Science Ser.: Vol. 20). vii, 254p. 1974. pap. 18.00 o.p. (ISBN 0-387-06953-4). Springer-Verlag.

Simple Propagation. encore ed. Noel J. Prockter. LC 77-71046. (Illus.). 1977. 1.95 o.p. (ISBN 0-684-16365-9, ScribT). Scribner.

Simple Relaxation. Laura Mitchell. LC 78-73069. 1979. 8.95 o.p. (ISBN 0-689-10961-X, Atheneum). Macmillan.

Simple Subs Book. L. Sellers. 1968. text ed. 25.00 o.p. (ISBN 0-08-013042-9); pap. text ed. 14.00 o.p. (ISBN 0-08-013041-0). Pergamon.

Simple's Uncle Sam. Langston Hughes. (American Century Ser.). 180p. 1965. pap. 7.95 o.p. (ISBN 0-8090-0087-3). Hill & Wang.

Simplest Explanation of God Ever Explained. Nam U. Detacuden. 230p. 1983. 13.50 o.p. (ISBN 0-682-49951-X). Exposition-Phoenix.

Simplicity of Prayer: A Discussion of the Methods & Results of Christian Prayer. H. A. Williams. LC 77-78649. 80p. 1977. pap. 0.75 o.p. (ISBN 0-8006-1315-5, 1-1315, Fortress). Augsburg Fortress.

Simplicius Simplicissimus. Hans J. C. Von Grimmelshausen. Tr. by Lesley Weissenborn & Helmut Weissenborn. (Orig.). 1982. pap. 10.95 o.s.i. (ISBN 0-7145-3910-4). Riverrun NY.

Simplified Accounting for Non-Accountants. Rick S. Hayes & C. Richard Baker. LC 81-85174. 304p. 1984. pap. 3.50 o.s.i. (ISBN 0-515-07140-4). Playboy Pbks.

Simplified ANSI FORTRAN IV Programming. 2nd ed. Gerald A. Silver & Joan B. Silver. (Illus.). 335p. 1976. pap. text ed. 15.00 o.p. (ISBN 0-15-581040-5, HC). HarBraceJ.

Simplified Apple Bookkeeping. Larry D. Peel. (Orig.). 1984. spiral bdg. 24.95 o.p. (ISBN 0-88006-090-5, CC7417). Wayne Green Ent.

Simplified Boatbuilding: Flat Bottom. Harry V. Sucher. (Illus.). 1973. 24.95 o.p. (ISBN 0-393-03173-X). Norton.

Simplified Boatbuilding: The V-Bottom Boat. Harry V. Sucher. LC 73-22340. (Illus.). 458p. 1974. 24.95 o.p. (ISBN 0-393-03180-2). Norton.

Simplified Design of Structural Wood. 3rd ed. Harry Parker & Harold D. Hauf. LC 78-9888. 269p. 1979. 33.00 o.p. (ISBN 0-471-66630-0, Pub. by Wiley-Interscience). Wiley.

Simplified Drugs & Solutions for Nurses, Including Arithmetic. 8th ed. Norma Dison. (Illus.). 169p. 1983. pap. text ed. 12.95 o.p. (ISBN 0-8016-1313-2). Mosby.

Simplified FORTRAN IV Programming. Gerald A. Silver. (Illus.). 1971. pap. text ed. 14.95 o.p. (ISBN 0-15-581049-9, HC). HarBraceJ.

Simplified Guide to Construction Management for Architects & Engineers. James E. Gorman. LC 75-34480. 288p. 1983. 24.95 o.p. (ISBN 0-8436-0160-4). Van Nos Reinhold.

Simplified Low-Cost Maintenance Control. rev. ed. W. Colebrook Cooling. 128p. 1983. 24.95 o.p. (ISBN 0-8144-5657-X). AMACOM.

Simplified LRP for Faster Business Growth & Profit. Ed. by William A. Spooner. LC 83-4354. 211p. 1983. 109.00 o.p. (ISBN 0-317-03970-9, Inst Busn Plan). P-H.

Simplified Medical Dictionary. R. Franks & H. Swartz. 276p. 1977. casebound 27.50 o.s.i. (ISBN 0-87489-054-3). Med Economics.

Simplified Methods in Pressure Vessel Analysis, PVP-PB-029. Ed. by R. S. Barsoum. (Pressure Vessel & Piping Division Ser.: Bk. No. G00137). 1978. 18.00 o.p. (ISBN 0-685-37581-1). ASME.

Simplified Statistics for Students in Education & Psychology. Robert H. Koenker. (Quality Paperback Ser.: No. 251). 171p. 1974. pap. 6.95 o.p. (ISBN 0-8226-0251-2). Littlefield.

Simplified Swahili. Peter M. Wilson. 328p. (Orig.). 1981. pap. text ed. 13.25 o.p. (ISBN 0-582-62358-8). Longman.

Simplis. Karl G. Joreskog & Dag Sorbom. looseleaf binder 20.00 o.p. Sci Ware.

Simply Italian. Paul A. Smiroldo. 116p. (Orig.). pap. 9.95 o.p. (ISBN 0-931494-84-2). Brunswick Pub.

Simpson's dBASE III Library. Alan Simpson. LC 85-63326. 362p. (Orig.). 1985. pap. 18.95 o.p. (ISBN 0-89588-300-7). Sybex.

Simulated Worlds: A Computer Model of National Decision-Making. Stuart A. Bremer. LC 76-3244. 1976. 34.00x o.p. (ISBN 0-691-05661-7). Princeton U Pr.

Simulating the Housing Allowance Program in Green Bay & South Bend: A Comparison of the Urban Institute Housing Model with the Supply Experiment. Jean Vanski & Larry Ozanne. 93p. 1978. pap. 10.00x o.p. (ISBN 0-87766-236-3, 23800). Urban Inst.

Simulating the Urban Economy. P. Smith & W. I. Morrison. (Monographs in Spatial & Environmental Analysis). 152p. 1975. 17.95x o.p. (ISBN 0-85086-046-6, NO. 2957, Pub. by Pion England). Routledge Chapman & Hall.

Simulation Games for Religious Education. Richard Reichert. LC 75-142. 1977. pap. 5.95 o.p. (ISBN 0-8042-1436-0, John Knox). Westminster John Knox.

Simulation in Higher Education: Papers from the Denison Simulation Center, Denison University, Granville, Ohio. Ed. by Esther Thorson. 1979. 15.00 o.p. (ISBN 0-682-49122-5, University). Exposition-Phoenix.

Simulation of Field Water Use & Crop Yield. R. A. Feddes et al. LC 78-10697. (Simulation Monographs Ser.). 188p. 1979. pap. 37.95x o.p. (ISBN 0-470-26463-2). Halsted Pr.

Simulation of Infectious Disease Epidemics. Eugene Ackerman et al. (Illus.). 210p. 1984. 32.75x o.p. (ISBN 0-398-04900-9). C C Thomas.

Simulation of Metal Forming Processes by the Finite Element Method (SIMOP-I) Ed. by K. Lange. (IFU Ser.: Vol. 85). (Illus.). 316p. 1986. pap. 32.60 o.p. (ISBN 0-387-16592-4). Springer-Verlag.

Simulation of the Water Balance of Arable Land & Pastures. G. F. Makkink & H. D. Van Heemst. (Illus.). 85p. 1975. pap. 15.50 o.p. (ISBN 90-220-0566-6, PDC87, PUDOC). UNIPUB.

Simulation: Statistical Foundations & Methodology. G. Arthur Mihram. (Mathematics in Science & Engineering Ser: Vol. 92). 1972. 95.00 o.p. (ISBN 0-12-495950-4). Acad Pr.

Simulation Technology & Traffic Accident Record Systems. (Transportation Research Record Ser.). 76p. 1979. 3.00 o.p. (ISBN 0-309-02952-X). Transport Res Bd.

Simulator Training of Nuclear Reactor Operators. Ed. by Albert E. Hickey. 151p. 1980. 15.00 o.p. (ISBN 0-89785-974-X). Am Inst Res.

Simulators. Ed. by M. Sage et al. (IEE Conference Publication: No. 226). 344p. 1983. pap. 99.00 o.s.i. (ISBN 0-85296-279-7, IC226). Inst Elect Eng.

Simuliation of Operations in Space: Capabilities & Requirements. 1988. 36.00 o.p. (ISBN 0-89883-995-5, SP724). Soc Auto Engineers.

Sin & Confession on the Eve of the Reformation. T. Tentler. 1977. 46.50x o.p. (ISBN 0-691-07219-1). Princeton U Pr.

Sin & Madness: Studies in Narcissism. Shirley Sugerman. LC 76-26033. 1976. softcover 5.95 o.s.i. (ISBN 0-664-24125-5, Westminster). Westminster John Knox.

Sin Comes of Age. Duncan E. Littlefair. LC 75-23277. 192p. 1975. 6.50 o.s.i. (ISBN 0-664-20807-X, Westminster). Westminster John Knox.

Sin of Obedience. Willard Beecher & Marguerite Beecher. 88p. (Orig.). 1982. pap. 4.75 o.p. (ISBN 0-942350-00-6). Beecher Found.

Sinai Tapestry. Edward Whittemore. 1978. pap. 1.95 o.p. (ISBN 0-380-37853-1, 37853). Avon.

Sinai Tapestry. Edward Whittemore. LC 76-28604. 1977. 8.95 o.s.i. (ISBN 0-03-018536-X). H Holt & Co.

Since Nineteen Hundred: A History of the United States in Our Times. 5th ed. Oscar T. Barck & Nelson M. Blake. 1974. write for info. o.p. (ISBN 0-02-305930-3, 30593). Macmillan.

Since O'Casey: And Other Essays on Irish Drama. Robert Hogan. LC 82-22813. (Irish Literary Studies: No. 15). 176p. 1983. text ed. 28.50x o.p. (ISBN 0-389-20346-7). B&N Imports.

Sincere Ideal: Studies on Sincerity in Eighteenth Century English Literature. Leon Guilhamet. 320p. 1974. 15.00x o.p. (ISBN 0-7735-0189-4, McGill Canada). U of Toronto Pr.

Sinclair Lewis: A Reference Guide. Robert E. Fleming & Esther Fleming. 1980. lib. bdg. 21.00 o.p. (ISBN 0-8161-8094-6, Hall Reference). G K Hall.

Sinclair Library: Dictionary Catalog of the Hawaiian Collection, 4 vols. University of Hawaii, Honolulu Staff. 1963. Set. lib. bdg. 355.00 o.p. (ISBN 0-8161-0650-9, Hall Library). G K Hall.

Sind or Float Replac. 1971. 28.88 o.p. (ISBN 0-07-521274-9). McGraw.

Sinfully Good Cookbook. Gayle E. Salvatore. 256p. (Orig.). 1986. pap. text ed. 10.00 o.p. (ISBN 0-87507-035-3). Cath Lib Assn.

Sinfulness of American Slavery, 2 vols. Charles Elliott. Ed. by Benjamin F. Tefft. LC 68-58055. 1969. Repr. of 1850 ed. Set. 33.00x o.p. (ISBN 0-8371-0407-6, ELS&). Vol. 2. 18.25 o.s.i. (ISBN 0-8371-0980-9, ELU&). Greenwood.

Sing. Ed. by American Camping Association Publications Committee. 95p. 1978. pap. 2.50 o.p. (ISBN 0-87603-037-1, SO 01). Am Camping.

Sing a New Song. Andrea J. Shepard. 96p. (Orig.). 1986. pap. 5.95 o.p. (ISBN 0-310-34302-X, 12352P). Zondervan.

Sing a Song for Me. Margo Wheaton. 64p. 1980. 5.00 o.p. (ISBN 0-682-49614-6). Exposition-Phoenix.

Sing a Song of Sixpence. Illus. by Margaret Chamberlain. LC 83-22510. (Nursery Rhyme Press-Out Bks.). (Illus.). 8p. (gr. k-2). 1984. bds. 4.95 o.p. (ISBN 0-911745-29-7, Bedrick Blackie). P Bedrick Bks.

Sing a Song of Sixpence. Ray Marshall & Korky Paul. Ed. by Kate Klimo. (Chubby Pop-Ups Ser.). (Illus.). 10p. (ps-k). 1983. 3.80 o.s.i. (ISBN 0-671-46237-7, Little Simon). S&S.

Sing a Song of Software: Verse & Images for the Computer-Literate. Leonard J. Soltzberg. (Illus.). 88p. pap. 9.95 o.p. (ISBN 0-86576-073-X). W Kaufmann.

Sing & Dance. Dora Dubsky. 1977. 4.25 o.p. (ISBN 0-913650-51-X). CPP Belwin.

Sing for Your Supper. Yvonne Horn. LC 79-87519. (gr. 7 up). 1979. 6.95 o.p. (ISBN 0-15-274959-4, HJ). HarBraceJ.

Sing Hey for Christmas Day! Ed. by Lee B. Hopkins. LC 75-6612. (Illus.). 32p. (gr. 1-5). 1975. 7.95 o.p. (ISBN 0-15-274960-8, HJ). HarBraceJ.

Sing Loose. Lillian Pohlmann. LC 68-19639. 160p. (YA) (gr. 9 up). 1968. 3.95 o.s.i. (ISBN 0-664-32424-X, Westminster). Westminster John Knox.

Sing Me a Song. Joyce S. Whitcomb. 64p. 1982. 4.00 o.p. (ISBN 0-682-49849-1). Exposition-Phoenix.

Sing Me No Songs: A Novel. Kusum Ansal. (Vikas Library of Modern Indian Writing: No. 22). 1982. text ed. 17.95x o.p. (ISBN 0-7069-1771-5, Pub. by Vikas India). Advent NY.

Sing Out: For the Reader Who Loves to Explore Life. Annie R. Napier. 40p. 1986. 7.00 o.p. (ISBN 0-8062-2561-0). Carlton.

Sing Praises! Management of Church Hymns. Dale E. Ramsey. 30p. (Orig.). 1983. pap. 3.50 o.p. (ISBN 0-8272-3300-0). CBP.

Singapore Economy. P. S. You & C. Y. Lim. 1971. 15.00 o.s.i. (ISBN 0-685-36181-0). E J Brill USA.

Singapore Wink. Ross Thomas. 224p. 1987. pap. 3.95 o.p. (ISBN 0-445-40558-9). Mysterious Pr.

Singer in the Stone. John Willett. (gr. 5-8). 1981. 6.95 o.p. (ISBN 0-395-30374-5). HM.

Singer of Tales. Albert B. Lord. LC 60-10038. 1965. pap. text ed. 3.95x o.p. (ISBN 0-689-70129-2, 76, Atheneum). Macmillan.

Singing & Dancing Games for the Very Young. Esther L. Nelson. LC 77-79513. (Illus.). (ps). 1982. 11.95 o.p. (ISBN 0-8069-4568-0); lib. bdg. 14.49 o.p. (ISBN 0-8069-4569-9); pap. 8.95 o.p. (ISBN 0-8069-7572-5). Sterling.

Singing & the Gold. A. B. Matthiessen. 1979. pap. 2.25 o.p. (ISBN 0-380-46102-1, 46102). Avon.

Singing Bone. R. Austin Freeman. LC 75-44972. (Crime Fiction Ser.). 1976. Repr. of 1912 ed. lib. bdg. 21.00 o.p. (ISBN 0-8240-2367-6). Garland Pub.

Singing Creek Where the Willows Grow: The Rediscovered Diary of Opal Whiteley. Benjamin Hoff. 384p. 1988. pap. 9.95 o.s.i. (ISBN 0-446-38676-6). Warner Bks.

Singing Creek Where the Willows Grow: The Rediscovered Diary of Opal Whiteley. Ed. by Benjamin Hoff. 288p. 1986. 16.45 o.s.i. (ISBN 0-89919-444-3). Ticknor & Fields.

Singing Detective. Dennis Potter. 300p. 1986. 22.95 o.p. (ISBN 0-571-14631-7); pap. 9.95 o.p. (ISBN 0-571-14590-6). Faber & Faber.

Singing for My Echo: Memories of a Native Healer of Santa Fe. Gregorita Rodriguez & Edith Powers. (Cota Editions: No. 2). (Illus.). 96p. (Orig.). 1987. pap. 6.95 o.s.i. (ISBN 0-943734-22-3). Ocean Tree Bks.

Singing Heart. N. M. Gohagan. LC 85-91001. 96p. 1985. 10.00 o.p. (ISBN 0-682-40272-9). Exposition-Phoenix.

Singing in A Dark Language. Terri Drake. 1986. 3.00 o.p. (ISBN 0-317-61626-9). New Collage.

Singing Rabbit. G. Menovschchikov. 12p. 1984. pap. 1.99 o.p. (ISBN 0-8285-2939-6, Pub. by Raduga Pubs USSR). Imported Pubns.

Singing Soldiers. John J. Niles. LC 68-26595. 192p. 1968. Repr. of 1927 ed. 35.00x o.p. (ISBN 0-8103-3416-X). Gale.

Singing Swan: An Account of Anna Seward & Her Acquaintance with Doctor Johnson, Boswell & Others of Their Time. Margaret E. Ashmun. LC 68-57589. (Illus.). 1969. Repr. of 1931 ed. lib. bdg. 35.00x o.p. (ISBN 0-8371-0287-1, ASSS). Greenwood.

Singing Wind. Marjorie K. Lawrence. 1985. 6.95 o.p. (ISBN 0-533-06632-8). Vantage.

Singing Word: Youth with a Mission Songbook. enl &rev. 2nd ed. Youth with a Mission Staff. (Illus.). 288p. 1974. plastic spiral bd. 5.95 o.p. (ISBN 0-87123-505-6, 280505). Bethany Hse.

Single. Harriet Frank, Jr. 1977. 8.95 o.p. (ISBN 0-395-25778-6). HM.

Single After Fifty: How to Have the Time of Your Life. Adeline P. McConnell & Beverly Anderson. 1978. text ed. 10.95 o.p. (ISBN 0-07-044873-6). McGraw.

Single But Not Alone. Mary Strebeck. (Illus.). 80p. (Orig.). 1982. pap. 4.95 o.s.i. (ISBN 0-939298-16-3, 163); pap. 2.95 leader's guide, 38pgs. o.s.i. (252). J M Prods.

Single-Camera Video Production Handbook: Techniques, Equipment, & Resources for Producing Quality Video Programs. Barry Fuller et al. (Illus.). 252p. 1982. 26.95 o.p. (ISBN 0-13-810762-9); pap. 18.95 o.p. (ISBN 0-13-810754-8). P-H.

Single Case Experimental Designs: Strategies for Studying Behavior Change. Michel Hersen & David H. Barlow. Ed. by A. P. Goldstein & L. Krasner. 1976. text ed. 47.00 o.p. (ISBN 0-08-019512-1); pap. text ed. 16.00 o.p. (ISBN 0-08-019511-3). Pergamon.

Single Cell Protein--Safety for Animal & Human Feeding: Proceedings of the Protein-Calorie Advisory Group of the United Nations System Symposium, Milan, Italy, March-April 1977. S. Garattini et al. LC 78-40993. (Illus.). 220p. 1979. 48.00 o.p. (ISBN 0-08-023765-7); pap. 18.75 o.p. (ISBN 0-08-023764-9). Pergamon.

Single Dose Treatment of Urinary Tract Infection. Ed. by Ross R. Bailey. 1982. text ed. 17.50 o.p. (ISBN 0-86792-007-6, Pub by Adis Pr Australia). Year Bk Med.

Single Handed: Devices & Aids for One Handers & Sources of These Devices. 3.50 o.p. (1480). Cheever Pub.

Single in America. J. L. Barkas. LC 79-55599. 1980. 10.95 o.p. (ISBN 0-689-11029-4, Atheneum). Macmillan.

Single Lens Reflex Camera Handbook. Michael Langford. LC 79-3473. (Illus.). 1980. 8.95 o.s.i. (ISBN 0-394-51090-9). Knopf.

Single Level & Underground Home Plans. L. F. Garlinghouse Co., Inc. LC 81-81751. (Illus.). 116p. (Orig.). 1981. pap. 2.95 o.s.i. (ISBN 0-938708-01-5). L F Garlinghouse Co.

Single Man. Christopher Isherwood. 1978. pap. 1.95 o.p. (ISBN 0-380-37689-X, 60251-2, Bard). Avon.

Single Mother's Handbook. Elizabeth S. Greywolf. LC 83-17350. (Orig.). 1984. 12.95 o.p. (ISBN 0-688-02260-X); pap. 6.70 o.p. (ISBN 0-688-02261-8). Morrow.

Single Nature's Double Name: The Collectedness of the Conflicting in British & American Romanticism. Raymond Benoit. (De Proprietatibus Litterarum Ser.: No. 26). 1973. text ed. 16.00x o.p. (ISBN 90-2792-599-2). Mouton.

Single Parent Experience. Carole Klein. 1978. pap. 2.50 o.p. (ISBN 0-380-01551-X, 47456-5). Avon.

Single Parent Housing Guide. Ruth Rejnis. 216p. 1984. pap. 9.95 o.p. (ISBN 0-87131-448-7). M Evans.

Single Speckled Egg. Sonia Levitin. (Illus.). 40p. (gr. k-3). 1976. Repr. PLB 6.95 o.p. (ISBN 0-395-27658-6). HM.

Single Ticket to China. Douglas Hare. 1974. pap. text ed. 1.85 o.s.i. (ISBN 0-08-017839-1). Pergamon.

Single-Whip Method of Taxation in China. Liang Fang-Chung. LC 56-4991. (East Asian Monographs: No. 1). 1956. pap. 11.00x o.p. (ISBN 0-674-80895-9). Harvard U Pr.

Single Woman of Today. M. B. Smith. 1952. (ISBN 0-8022-1600-5). Philos Lib.

Single's Almanac. Jeffrey Ullman. 1986. pap. 8.95 o.s.i. (ISBN 0-345-32633-4). Ballantine.

Singles: The New Americans. Jacqueline Simenaver & David Carroll. 1982. 15.95 o.p. (ISBN 0-671-25052-3). S&S.

Singlet Molecular Oxygen. Ed. by A. P. Schaap. LC 76-3496. (Benchmark Papers in Organic Chemistry Ser.: Vol. 5). 400p. 1976. 82.50 o.p. (ISBN 0-12-787415-1). Acad Pr.

Singlet Oxygen. Ed. by Harry H. Wasserman & Robert W. Murray. LC 77-25737. (Organic Chemistry Ser.). 1979. 85.00 o.p. (ISBN 0-12-736650-4). Acad Pr.

Singletusk. Bjorn Kurten. 195p. 1986. 14.95 o.p. (ISBN 0-394-55352-7). Pantheon.

Singular & Degenerate Cauchy Problems. R. W. Carroll & R. E. Showalter. 1976. 52.50 o.p. (ISBN 0-12-161450-6). Acad Pr.

Singular Generation. Wanda Urbanska. LC 86-4553. 264p. 1986. 16.95 o.p. (ISBN 0-385-19264-9). Doubleday.

Singular Integrals. U. Neri. LC 76-166077. (Lecture Notes in Mathematics: Vol. 200). 1971. pap. text ed. 12.00 o.p. (ISBN 0-387-05502-9). Springer-Verlag.

Singular Man. J. P. Donleavy. 1973. pap. 1.50 o.p. (ISBN 0-440-37941-5, LE). Dell.

Singular Optimal Control: The Linear-Quadratic Problem. D. J. Clements & B. D. Anderson. (Lecture Notes in Control & Information Science: Vol. 5). 1978. pap. 12.00 o.p. (ISBN 0-387-08694-3). Springer-Verlag.

Singular Voices: American Poetry Today. Ed. by Stephen Berg. 240p. 1985. pap. 9.95 o.p. (ISBN 0-380-89876-4). Avon.

Singularity Theory & Introduction to Catastrophe Theory. Y. C. Lu. LC 76-48307. (Illus.). 1980. soft cover 21.00 o.p. (ISBN 0-387-90221-X). Springer-Verlag.

Sinister Affair. Eric Rhodin. (gr. 7 up). 1973. 4.75 o.s.i. (ISBN 0-664-32530-0, Westminster). Westminster John Knox.

Sinister Airfield. Alison Prince. LC 82-18877. (Illus.). 128p. (gr. 4-6). 1983. 10.25 o.p. (ISBN 0-688-01741-X). Morrow.

Sinister Sign Post. Franklin W. Dixon. (Hardy Boys Ser: Vol. 15). (gr. 5-9). 1936. 4.50 o.p. (ISBN 0-448-08915-7, G&D); PLB 3.29 o.p. (ISBN 0-448-18915-1). Putnam Pub Group.

Sinkholes - Their Geology, Engineering & Environmental Impact: First Multidisciplinary Conference on Sinkholes, Orlando, Florida, 15-17 October 1984. Ed. by F. B Beck. 440p. 1984. text ed. 76.50 o.p. (ISBN 90-6191-570-8, Pub. by A A Balkema). Gower Pub Co.

Sinking of Clay City. Robert Wrigley. 1979. 12.00 o.p.; pap. 5.00 o.p. (ISBN 0-914742-42-6). Copper Canyon.

Sinking of the Titanic: A Poem. Hans M. Enzensberger. 99p. 1980. 11.95 o.p. (ISBN 0-395-29120-8); pap. 5.95 o.p. (ISBN 0-395-29121-6). HM.

Sinners & Saints. George W. Walter. 1983. 7.95 o.s.i. (ISBN 0-932052-31-2). North Country.

Sinning Against the Holy Spirit. Don R. Pegram. 1982. pap. 1.25 o.p. (ISBN 0-89265-085-0). Randall Hse.

Sins of New York As "Exposed" by the Police Gazette. Edward Vanevery. LC 70-174130. (Illus.). 318p. 1976. Repr. of 1930 ed. 43.00x o.p. (ISBN 0-8103-4038-0). Gale.

Sins of Omission. Catherine Lanigan. 432p. 1986. pap. 3.95 o.p. (ISBN 0-380-89582-X). Avon.

Sins of Saints. Herbert Lockyer. LC 75-108378. 1970. pap. 5.95 o.p. (ISBN 0-87213-532-2). Loizeaux.

Sinusoidal Analysis & Modeling of Weakly Nonlinear Circuits: With Application to Nonlinear Interference Effects. Donald D. Weiner & John F. Spina. (Electrical-Computer Science & Engineering Ser.). 304p. 1980. 32.95 o.p. (ISBN 0-442-26093-8). Van Nos Reinhold.

Sioux. Irene Handl. Ed. by Robert Gottlieb. LC 84-48795. 1985. 15.45 o.s.i. (ISBN 0-394-54444-7). Knopf.

Sioux: A Critical Bibliography. Herbert T. Hoover. LC 79-2167. (Newberry Library D'Arcy McNiclke Center for the History of the American Indian Bibliographical Ser.). 96p. 1980. pap. 4.95x o.p. (ISBN 0-253-34972-9). Ind U Pr.

Sioux Are Coming. Walter O'Meara. (Illus.). (gr. 3-7). 1971. 6.95 o.p. (ISBN 0-395-12759-9). HM.

Sir Alfred Munnings Eighteen Seventy-Eight to Nineteen Fifty-nine. Stanley Booth. LC 87-61924. (Illus.). 66p. 1988. 29.95 o.p. (ISBN 0-318-23734-2, Pub. by P Wilson Pubs). Sotheby Pubns.

Sir Alfred Munnings 1878-1959: An Appreciation of the Artist & a Selection of His Paintings. Stanley Booth. (Illus.). 218p. 1978. 65.00 o.p. (ISBN 0-85667-043-X). Sotheby Pubns.

Sir Arthur Keith: An Autobiography. 1951. (ISBN 0-8022-0838-X). Philos Lib.

Sir Arthur Pinero's Plays & Players. Henry H. Fyfe. LC 78-6207. (Illus.). 1978. Repr. of 1930 ed. lib. bdg. 35.00x o.p. (ISBN 0-313-20391-1, FYSR). Greenwood.

Sir Arthur Sullivan. Percy M. Young. 304p. Repr. of 1972 ed. lib. bdg. 49.00 o.p. (Pub. by Am Repr Serv). Reprint Servs.

Sir Arthur Sullivan His Life Letters & Diaries. Herbert Sullivan. 306p. Repr. of 1950 ed. lib. bdg. 49.00 o.p. (Pub. by Am Repr Serv). Reprint Servs.

Sir Charles Arden-Clarke. David Rooney. 236p. 1982. text ed. 12.50 o.p. (ISBN 0-89874-598-5). Krieger.

Sir Charles Eastlake & the Victorian Art World. David Robertson. LC 75-43797. (Illus.). 1978. text ed. 90.50x o.p. (ISBN 0-691-03902-X). Princeton U Pr.

Sir Donald Cameron: Colonial Governor. Harry A. Gailey. LC 74-7301. (Publications Ser.: No. 139). 181p. 1974. 10.95x o.p. (ISBN 0-8179-6391-X). Hoover Inst Pr.

Sir Edward Appleton, C.B.E., K.C.B., F.R.S. Ronald Clark. 256p. 1972. 65.00 o.p. (ISBN 0-08-016093-X). Pergamon.

Sir Edwin Landseer. Richard Ormond. LC 81-81916. (Illus.). 224p. (Orig.). 1981. pap. 8.50 o.p. (ISBN 0-87633-044-8). Phila Mus Art.

Sir Eldon Gorst: The Overshadowed Proconsul. Peter Mellini. LC 76-51878. (Publication Ser: No. 178). (Illus.). 1977. 12.95x o.p. (ISBN 0-8179-6781-8). Hoover Inst Pr.

Sir Francis Drake. Julian S. Corbett. LC 69-13865. 1970. Repr. of 1890 ed. lib. bdg. 35.00x o.p. (ISBN 0-8371-4086-2, COFD). Greenwood.

Sir Francis Drake. James A. Williamson. LC 74-30930. (Illus.). 160p. 1975. Repr. of 1951 ed. lib. bdg. 22.50x o.p. (ISBN 0-8371-7886-X, WIFD). Greenwood.

Sir Frederic Madden: A Bibliography & Biographical Sketch. Robert W. Ackerman & Gretchen P. Ackerman. LC 78-68237. 150p. 1979. lib. bdg. 22.00 o.p. (ISBN 0-8240-9819-6). Garland Pub.

Sir Gibbie. Date not set. (ISBN 0-8052-3730-5). Random.

Sir Hans Sloane & the British Museum. G. R. De Beer. (Illus.). 1953. text ed. 11.50x o.p. (ISBN 0-565-00644-4, Pub. by Brit Mus Nat Hist England). Sabbot-Natural Hist Bks.

Sir John Harington. D. H. Craig. (English Authors Ser.: No. 386). 1985. lib. bdg. 19.95 o.p. (ISBN 0-8057-6872-6, Twayne). G K Hall.

Sir John Sloane: Seventeen Fifty-Three to Eighteen Thirty-Seven. John N. Summerson. LC 52-11842. 96p. 1952. Repr. 29.00 o.p. (ISBN 0-403-07225-5). Somerset Pub.

Sir John Soane, Architect. Dorothy Stroud. LC 83-11488. (Illus.). 288p. 1984. 73.00 o.p. (ISBN 0-571-13050-X). Faber & Faber.

Sir Philip Sidney. John A. Symonds. LC 67-23878. 216p. 1968. Repr. of 1886 ed. 35.00x o.p. (ISBN 0-8103-3056-3). Gale.

Sir Philip Sidney As a Literary Craftsman. Kenneth Myrick. LC 35-13065. x, 362p. 1966. pap. 6.95x o.p. (ISBN 0-8032-5140-8, BB 312, Bison). U of Nebr Pr.

Sir Philip Sidney's Defense of Poesy. Philip Sidney. Ed. by Lewis Soens. LC 74-108900. (Regents Critics Ser). xlii, 95p. 1970. 13.95x o.p. (ISBN 0-8032-0464-7). U of Nebr Pr.

Sir Thomas Elyot & Roger Ascham: A Reference Guide. Jerome S. Dees. 1981. 31.50 o.p. (ISBN 0-8161-8353-8, Hall Reference). G K Hall.

Sir Thomas Wyatt & Henry Howard, Earl of Surrey: A Reference Guide. Clyde W. Jentoft. 1980. lib. bdg. 28.00 o.p. (ISBN 0-8161-8176-4, Hall Reference). G K Hall.

Sir Walter Scott, an Index, Placing the Short Poems in His Novels & His Long Poems & Dramas. Ed. by Allston Burr. LC 76-148632. vi, 130p. Repr. of 1936 ed. lib. bdg. 35.00x o.p. (ISBN 0-8371-5994-6, BUSW). Greenwood.

Sir William & the Pumpkin Monster. Cuyler. (gr. 2-6). 9.95 o.p. (ISBN 0-03-064032-6); pap. 4.95 o.p. H Holt & Co.

Sir William Blackstone. David A. Lockmiller. 11.75 o.p. (ISBN 0-8446-0776-2). Peter Smith.

Sirenoid Ganoids, Vol. 2. L. C. Mial. Repr. of 1907 ed. 70.00 o.p. (ISBN 0-384-38760-8). Johnson Repr.

Sirens. Eric Van Lustbader. LC 81-1482. 480p. 1981. 13.95 o.p. (ISBN 0-87131-346-4). M Evans.

Sires of Runners of 1978: Supplement. Thoroughbred Owners & Breeders Association Staff. 1978. lib. bdg. 15.00 o.p. (ISBN 0-936032-17-0); pap. 10.00 o.p. (ISBN 0-936032-18-9). Blood-Horse.

Sires of Runners of 1979. Ed. by Blood-Horse, Inc. Staff. (Annual Supplement). 1980. lib. bdg. 20.00 o.p. (ISBN 0-936032-19-7); pap. 10.00 o.p. (ISBN 0-936032-20-0). Blood-Horse.

Sirius & Saba. Deborah King. (Illus.). 32p. (gr. 3-6). 1982. 13.95 o.p. (ISBN 0-241-10599-4, Pub. by Hamish Hamilton England). David & Charles.

Sistema Generalizado de Preferencial De Estados Unidos: Cobertura Y Procedimientos Administrativos Vignetes en 1980. OAS, General Secretariat, International Trade & Export Development Program Staff. (International Trade Ser.). 58p. pap. text ed. 5.00 o.p. (ISBN 0-8270-1125-3). OAS.

Sister Arts: The Tradition of Literary Pictorialism & English Poetry from Dryden to Gray. Jean H. Hagstrum. LC 59-11948. (Midway Reprint Ser). (Illus.). xxii, 338p. 1975. pap. text ed. 21.00x o.s.i. (ISBN 0-226-31294-1). U of Chicago Pr.

Sister Celebrations: Nine Worship Experiences. Ed. by Arlene Swidler. LC 74-80414. 96p. (Orig.). 1974. pap. 0.50 o.p. (ISBN 0-8006-1084-9, 1-1084, Fortress). Augsburg Fortress.

Sister D'Aranyi. Joseph Macleod. 1972. 7.50 o.s.i. (ISBN 0-8008-7223-1, Crescendo). Taplinger.

Sister Death: Leader's Guide. O'Kelly Whitaker. 1976. pap. 1.95 o.p. (ISBN 0-8192-4072-9). Morehouse Pub.

Sister Satan. Dana Reed. 400p. (Orig.). 1984. pap. 3.75 o.s.i. (ISBN 0-8439-2152-8, Pub. by Leisure Bks CT). Dorchester Pub Co.

Sister X & the Victims of Foul Play. Carlene H. Polite. 145p. 1975. 8.95 o.p. (ISBN 0-374-26521-6). FS&G.

Sisters. Dale V. Atkins. 140p. 1984. 15.95 o.p. (ISBN 0-87795-597-2, Arbor Hse). Morrow.

Sisters. Pamela Hill. (Nightingale Ser.). 252p. 1988. pap. 12.95x o.p. (ISBN 0-8161-4416-8). G K Hall.

Sisters. Margaret H. Wright. 80p. 1986. 7.95 o.p. (ISBN 0-8062-2911-X). Carlton.

Sisters, Brothers, & Others. Suzanne Szasz & Elizabeth Taleporos. LC 83-42642. (Illus.). 1984. 17.45 o.p. (ISBN 0-393-01810-5). Norton.

Sisters of Sacred Song: Selected Listing of Women Hymnodists in Great Britain & America. Samuel J. Rogal. LC 80-8482. 180p. 1981. lib. bdg. 28.00 o.p. (ISBN 0-8240-9482-4). Garland Pub.

Sisters: The Story of Olivia de Havilland & Joan Fontaine. Charles Higham. (Illus.). 1984. 15.95 o.p. (ISBN 0-698-11268-7, Coward). Putnam Pub Group.

Sita. Kate Millett. 1985. pap. 3.50 o.s.i. (ISBN 0-345-33066-8). Ballantine.

Site Engineering for Developers & Builders. Thomas L. Brown. LC 88-62223. 184p. 1988. pap. 38.00 o.p. (ISBN 0-86718-320-9). Nat Assn H Build.

Site Investigation Practice. M. Joyce. (Illus.). 300p. 1982. 49.95 o.p. (ISBN 0-419-12260-5, NO. 6733, Pub. by E & FN Spon England). Routledge Chapman & Hall.

Site Planning Standards. Joseph De Chiara. LC 77-9440. (Illus.). 1977. text ed. 54.50 o.p. (ISBN 0-07-016216-6). McGraw.

Site Selection for Health Care Facilities. James Lifton & Owen B. Hardy. LC 82-13745. 64p. (Orig.). 1982. pap. 18.75 o.s.i. (ISBN 0-87258-382-1, 127200). AHPI.

Site Work. 20.00 o.p. (ISBN 0-317-65068-8). Am Consul Eng.

Sitt Marie-Rose. Etel Adnan. Tr. by Georgina Kleege from Fr. 116p. (Orig.). 1982. pap. 7.50 o.p. (ISBN 0-942996-02-X, Dist. by Three Continents). Post Apollo Pr.

Sitting by My Laughing Fire. Ruth B. Graham. LC 77-75457. 1977. 10.95 o.p. (ISBN 0-8499-2933-4). Word Bks.

Sitting for the Psalms: A Historical Study. (Church Historical Society, London, New Ser.: No. 6). Repr. of 1931 ed. 20.00 o.p. (ISBN 0-8115-3130-9). Kraus Repr.

Sitting on the Blue-Eyed Bear: Navajo Myths & Legends. Gerald Hausman. LC 75-23930. (Illus.). 144p. (gr. 7 up). 1976. 10.00 o.p. (ISBN 0-88208-061-X). Chicago Review.

Situation Analyst: Stategic Manager. James F. Moore. 1985. pap. 19.95x o.p. (ISBN 0-256-03536-9). Irwin.

Situation Ethics Debate. Ed. by Harvey Cox & Joseph Fletcher. LC 68-11991. 286p. 1968. pap. 2.65 o.s.i. (ISBN 0-664-24814-4, Westminster). Westminster John Knox.

Situation of Poetry. Jacques Maritain & Raissa Maritain. 1955. (ISBN 0-8022-1061-9). Philos Lib.

Situation Tragedy. Simon Brett. 192p. 1981. 9.95 o.s.i. (ISBN 0-684-17268-2, ScribT). Scribner.

Situational Chinese. Beverly Hong. (Illus.). 335p. (Orig.). 1983. pap. 8.95 o.p. (ISBN 0-8351-1386-8). China Bks.

Situations & Attitudes. Jon Barwise & John Perry. 256p. 1983. 27.50x o.s.i. (ISBN 0-262-02189-7). MIT Pr.

Situations in Marketing: A Collection of Marketing Cases & Questions. James H. Sood. 1976. pap. 4.95x o.p. (ISBN 0-256-01856-1). Irwin.

Sitwells: A Family's Biography. John Pearson. 1979. 15.00 o.p. (ISBN 0-15-182703-6). HarBraceJ.

Six & Silver. Joan Phipson. LC 70-152696. (Illus.). 190p. (gr. 4-6). 1971. 5.95 o.p. (ISBN 0-15-275330-3, HJ). HarBraceJ.

Six Answers to the Problem of Taste. Ronald Suter. LC 79-84279. 1979. pap. text ed. 8.25 o.p. (ISBN 0-8191-0726-3). U Pr of Amer.

Six Approaches to Child Rearing: Models from Psychological Theory. D. Eugene Mead. LC 76-19040. 1976. pap. 5.95x o.p. (ISBN 0-8425-0327-7). Brigham.

Six Aspects of African History see Tarikh.

Six Characters in Search of a Republic: Studies in the Political Thought of the American Colonies. Clinton Rossiter. LC 64-54742. 1964. pap. 2.95 o.p. (ISBN 0-15-682740-9, Harv). HarBraceJ.

Six Chinese Brothers: An Ancient Tale. Cheng Hou-tien. LC 79-1218. (Illus.). (gr. k-5). 1979. 5.95 o.s.i. (ISBN 0-03-048311-5). H Holt & Co.

Six Days of the Condor. James Grady. LC 73-22258. 192p. 1974. 9.95 o.p. (ISBN 0-393-08692-5). Norton.

Six Days to Saturday: Joe Paterno & Penn State. Jack Newcombe. LC 74-11207. (Illus.). 128p. (gr. 7 up). 1974. 6.95 o.p. (ISBN 0-374-36975-5). FS&G.

Six Demons of Love: A Book about Men & Love. Steve Berman. 144p. 1984. pap. text ed. 6.95 o.p. (ISBN 0-07-004915-7). McGraw.

Six Faces of Lent: Dramas. William A. Poovey. LC 73-88599. 96p. (Orig.). 1974. pap. 3.95 o.p. (ISBN 0-8066-1403-X, 10-5805, Augsburg). Augsburg Fortress.

Six-Figure Tables of Trigonometric Functions. L. S. Khrenov. 1964. 50.00 o.p. (ISBN 0-08-010101-1). Pergamon.

Six Figure Woman. Lois Wyse. 192p. 1983. 11.50 o.p. (ISBN 0-671-47764-1, Linden Pr). S&S.

Six Great Overtures in Full Score. Ludwig van Beethoven. (Music Scores to Play & Study Ser.). 288p. 1985. pap. 9.95 o.p. (ISBN 0-486-24789-9). Dover.

Six Great Poets: Chaucer, Pope, Wordsworth, Shelley, Tennyson, the Brownings. Aubrey De Selincourt. Repr. of 1956 ed. 26.00x o.p. (ISBN 0-403-04283-6). Somerset Pub.

Six-Gun Melody. William C. MacDonald. 1974. pap. 0.75 o.p. (ISBN 0-380-00068-7, 19745). Avon.

Six-Gun Mystique. John G. Cawelti. 148p. 1970. 7.95 o.p. (ISBN 0-87972-007-7); pap. 4.95 o.p. (ISBN 0-87972-008-5). Bowling Green Univ.

Six Hundred & One Words You Need to Know for the SAT. Liebb Bromberg. 1981. pap. text ed. 6.95 o.p. (ISBN 0-8120-2409-5). Barron.

Six Hundred & Thirty-Eight Olympic Champions. Valeri Steinbach. Tr. by Y. Kopytkin & A. Timofeyev. 271p. 1984. pap. 4.95 o.p. (ISBN 0-8285-2790-3, Pub. by Raduga Pubs USSR). Imported Pubns.

Six Hundred Bible Gems & Outlines. S. R. Briggs & J. H. Elliott. LC 75-42955. 200p. 1976. pap. 5.95 o.p. (ISBN 0-8254-2255-8). Kregel.

Six Hundred Fifth More Individual Open Salts Illustrated. Allan B. Smith & Helen B. Smith. (Illus.). 1973. pap. 7.00 o.p. (ISBN 0-940554-05-4). Country Hse.

Six Hundred More Things to Make for the Farm & Home. G. C. Cook & Lloyd J. Phipps. (Illus.). (gr. 9-12). 1952. 22.60 o.p. (ISBN 0-8134-0198-4); text ed. 16.95x o.p. Inter Print Pubs.

Six Hundred School. Jack Rudman. (Teachers License Examination Ser.: S-7). (Cloth bdg. avail. on request). pap. 19.95 o.p. Natl Learning.

Six Key Cut. Max Crawford. LC 85-48130. 288p. 1986. 14.95 o.p. (ISBN 0-689-11778-7, Atheneum). Macmillan.

Six Language Traveler's Dictionary. (Pocket Professor Ser.). 1985. pap. 5.95 o.p. (ISBN 0-946913-19-6, Pub. by College Lane Pubs). Kampmann.

Six Medieval Men & Women. Henry S. Bennett. LC 55-14637. 1962. pap. text ed. 3.95x o.p. (ISBN 0-689-70009-1, 3, Atheneum). Macmillan.

Six-Million-Dollar Cucumber. Richard E. Churchill. (Illus.). 96p. 1977. pap. 1.25 o.s.i. (ISBN 0-440-97973-0, LFL). Dell.

Six-Million Huit-Cent Dix Mille Litres D'eau Par Seconde. Michel Butor. 12.50 o.p. (ISBN 0-685-37259-6). Schoenhof.

Six Million Swindle. Austin J. App. 39p. 1986. pap. 1.50 o.p. (ISBN 0-317-53004-6). Noontide.

Six Months in the West Indies in Eighteen Twenty-Five. Henry N. Coleridge. LC 72-100284. Repr. of 1826 ed. 35.00x o.p. (ISBN 0-8371-2948-6, CSM&). Greenwood.

Six Months with an Older Woman. David A. Kaufelt. 1982. pap. 2.95 o.p. (ISBN 0-440-18313-8). Dell.

Six Novelists Look at Society. John Atkins. (Orig.). 1980. 11.95 o.p. (Pub. by Journeyman Pr England); pap. 7.95 o.p. (ISBN 0-7145-3863-9). Riverrun NY.

Six Plays for Children: Biography & Play Analyses by Coleman A. Jennings. Aurand Harris. LC 77-655. (Illus.). 390p. (ps up). 1977. 14.50x o.p. (ISBN 0-292-70325-2). U of Tex Pr.

Six Poets of the San Francisco Renaissance: Portraits & Checklists. David Kherdian. 17.50 o.p. (ISBN 0-87791-000-6). Giligia.

Six Prophets for Today: Dramas on Jonah, Obadiah, Amos, Habakkuk, Hosea, Micah. W. A. Poovey. LC 77-84079. 1977. pap. 3.50 o.p. (ISBN 0-8066-1604-0, 10-5815, Augsburg). Augsburg Fortress.

Six Seventeen Squadron: The Dambusters at War. Tom Bennett. (Illus.). 272p. (Orig.). 1988. pap. 12.95 o.p. (ISBN 1-85260-041-1, Pub. by PSL P Stephens England). Sterling.

Six-Shooter Sod-Buster. Russ Kidd. (Lythway Ser.). 176p. 1988. lib. bdg. 17.50 o.s.i. (ISBN 0-7451-0647-1, Pub. by Chivers Pr UK). G K Hall.

Six Strike Stories see Issues in the Public Employee Relations Library: Series 2.
Six Stud Kit Senior BA. Date not set. (ISBN 0-07-017590-X). McGraw.
Six Studies in Quarrelling. Vincent Brome. LC 72-6176. 197p. 1973. Repr. of 1958 ed. lib. bdg. 35.00x o.p. (ISBN 0-8371-6484-2, BRSQ). Greenwood.
Six Thousand Five Hundred & Two Applications. Rodnay Zaks. LC 78-73740. (Six Thousand Five Hundred & Two Ser.: No. 2). (Illus.). 278p. 1979. pap. 14.95 o.p. (ISBN 0-89588-015-6, D302). SYBEX.
Six Times True. Mae H. Ashworth. 48p. (Orig.). (gr. 7-9). 1973. pap. 1.95 o.p. (ISBN 0-377-03601-3). Friendship Pr.
Six Weeks. Fred M. Stewart. LC 76-8637. 1976. 7.95 o.p. (ISBN 0-87795-136-5, Arbor Hse). Morrow.
Six Wheel Drive. Ronald T. Martin. 64p. 1986. 6.95 o.p. (ISBN 0-8062-3022-3). Carlton.
Six World Religions. L. Aletrino. Tr. by Mary Foran. (Orig.). (gr. 12 up). 1969. pap. 4.95 o.p. (ISBN 0-8192-2000-0). Morehouse Pub.
Sixteen Hundred & Three to Present Day see Plymouth: A New History.
Sixteen Modern American Authors: A Survey of Research & Criticism. Ed. by Jackson R. Bryer. LC 73-97454. xx, 673p. 1973. 40.00 o.p. (ISBN 0-8223-0297-7). Duke.
Sixteenth Annual Institute on Securities Regulation, 2 vols. (Corporate Law & Practice Course Handbooks Ser.: Vol. 464 & 465). 1229p. 1984. Set. 40.00 o.p. (ISBN 0-317-11418-2, B4-6694). PLI.
Sixth & Seventh Symphonies in Full Orchestral Score. Ludwig van Beethoven. 328p. 1976. pap. 9.95 o.p. (ISBN 0-486-23379-0). Dover.
Sixth Annual Microcomputers in Education Conference: Ethics & Excellence in Computer Education: Choice or Mandate? Ed. by Janie Hydrick. (Computers in Education Ser.). 385p. 1986. text ed. 35.00 o.p. (ISBN 0-88175-130-8, Computer Sci Pr). W H Freeman.
Sixth-Century Athens: The Sources. A. French. 92p. (Orig.). 1987. pap. 10.00 o.p. (ISBN 0-424-00123-3, Pub. by Sydney U Pr). Intl Spec Bk.
Sixth International Conference on Computers & the Humanities. Sarah K. Burton & Douglas D. Short. LC 83-7479. (Computers in Education Ser.). 781p. 1983. 40.00 o.p. (ISBN 0-914894-96-X, Computer Sci Pr). W H Freeman.
Sixth International Conference on Numerical Methods in Fluid Dynamics: Proceedings of the Conference, Tbilisi, (U. S. S. R.) June 21-24, 1978. Ed. by H. Cabannes et al. (Lecture Notes in Physics: Vol. 90). 1979. pap. 33.00 o.p. (ISBN 0-387-09115-7). Springer-Verlag.
Sixth International Tin Agreement. United Nations Conference on Trade & Development Staff. LC 81-214523. 61p. 6.00 o.p. (ISBN 92-1-112012-8, E.82.II.D.16). UN.
Sixth LACUS Forum Proceedings, Linguistic Association of Canada & the U. S. Ed. by William G. McCormack & Herbert J. Izzo. 1979. pap. text ed. 12.95 o.s.i. (ISBN 0-917496-16-7). Hornbeam Pr.
Sixth National Ground Water Quality Symposium. 1983. 31.25 o.p. (ISBN 0-318-23007-0). Natl Water Well.
Sixth National Symposium & Exposition on Aquifer Restoration: Proceedings. LC 86-18198. 1986. 43.75 o.p. (ISBN 0-318-23015-1). Natl Water Well.
Sixth Report of the United States Geographic Board: 1890-1932. United States Geographic Board Staff. LC 67-8571. 844p. 1967. Repr. of 1933 ed. 48.00x o.p. (ISBN 0-685-11676-X). Gale.
Sixth Sense. Larry Kettelkamp. (Illus.). (gr. 5-9). 1970. PLB 11.88 o.p. (ISBN 0-688-31463-5). Morrow.
Sixth Sense of Animals. Maurice Burton. LC 72-6622. (Illus.). 192p. 1973. 7.95 o.s.i. (ISBN 0-8008-7232-0). Taplinger.
Sixties Going on Seventies. Nora Sayre. LC 72-87048. 1973. 9.95 o.p. (ISBN 0-87795-054-7, Arbor Hse). Morrow.
Sixty American Poets, Eighteen Ninety-Six to Nineteen Forty-Four. rev. ed. U. S. Library of Congress, General Reference & Bibliography Division Staff. LC 73-5993. xii, 168p. Repr. of 1954 ed. 35.00x o.p. (ISBN 0-8103-3365-1). Gale.
Sixty-Eight Great Ideas: The Library Awareness Handbook. Ed. by Peggy Barber. LC 82-11518. 66p. 1982. pap. 7.50x o.p. (ISBN 0-8389-0376-2). ALA.
Sixty-Eight Thousand Microprocessor Handbook. 2nd ed. William Cramer & Gerry Kane. 176p. 1985. pap. text ed. 14.95 o.p. (ISBN 0-07-881205-4). Osborne-McGraw.
Sixty-Eight Thousand Microprocessor Handbook. G. Kane. 118p. 1981. pap. text ed. 10.95 o.p. (ISBN 0-07-931041-9, Osborne-McGraw). McGraw.
Sixty-Eight Thousand: Principles & Programming. Leo Scanlon. LC 81-51553. 240p. 1981. pap. 16.95 o.p. (ISBN 0-672-21853-4, 21853). Sams.
Sixty Fifth Tape. Frank Ross. LC 78-20367. 1979. 10.95 o.p. (ISBN 0-689-10965-2, Atheneum). Macmillan.
Sixty-Five Buttercream Flowers. Richard V. Snyder. (Illus.). 1957. 8.50 o.p. (ISBN 0-682-40089-0, Banner). Exposition-Phoenix.
Sixty Minutes: The Power & the Politics. Axel Madsen. 261p. 1984. 16.95 o.p. (ISBN 0-396-08401-X). Dodd.
Sixty-Nine Images...Below the Belt! Poetry. Philip L. Sherrod. LC 84-72169. (Illus.). 79p. (Orig.). 1984. pap. 7.95 o.s.i. Carrousel Pubns.
Sixty Scenic Wonders in China. 1981. 6.95 o.p. (ISBN 0-8351-0771-X). China Bks.
Sixty-Second Christian. Gary R. Collins. 64p. 1984. 5.95 o.p. (ISBN 0-8499-0450-1, 0450-1). Word Bks.
Sixty-Six Etudes in All the Major & Minor Keys. Anton Slama. (Illus.). 1922. pap. 7.00 o.p. (ISBN 0-8258-0248-2, 0-498). Fischer Inc NY.
Sixty-Six Family Handyman Wood Projects. Family Handyman Magazine Editors. Ed. by Richard Newton. (Illus.). 208p. 1985. 21.95 o.p. (ISBN 0-8306-0464-2, 2632); pap. 14.60 o.p. (ISBN 0-8306-1164-9, 2632P). TAB Bks.
Sixty Six Portland Place: The London Headquarters of the Royal Institute of British Architects. Ed. by Royal Institute of British Architects Staff. (Illus.). 48p. pap. 6.95 o.p. (ISBN 0-900630-90-6, Pub. by RIBA). Intl Spec Bk.
Sixty-Two Hiking Trails, Northern Oregon Cascades. Don Lowe & Roberta Lowe. Ed. by Thomas K. Worcester. (Illus.). 144p. (Orig.). 9.95 o.p. (ISBN 0-317-65201-X). Touchstone Oregon.
Sixty Ways, Sixty Days & Twenty Four Ways to Greater Business Productivity, Vol. 1. Charles R. Macdonald. 450p. 1981. 79.50 o.p. (ISBN 0-87624-516-5, Inst Busn Plan). P-H.
Sixty Years at the Bar: Anecdotes of a Corporation Lawyer. Harold D. Burgess. 167p. 1981. 8.95 o.p. (ISBN 0-682-49781-9). Exposition-Phoenix.
Sixty Years of the Oscar: The Official History of the Academy of Motion Picture Arts & Sciences. Robert Osborne. (Illus.). 384p. 1988. 44.95 o.p. (ISBN 0-89659-952-3). Abbeville Pr.
Sixty Years on the Frontier in the Pacific Northwest. Andrew Pambrun. 158p. 1979. 19.95 o.s.i. (ISBN 0-87770-183-0). Ye Galleon.
Size of the Sheet in America: Paper-Moulds Manufactured by N & D Sellers of Philadelphia. John Bidwell. (Illus.). 1978. pap. 4.00x o.p. (ISBN 0-912296-31-3, Dist. by U Pr of Va). Am Antiquarian.
Size, Structure, & Future of Farms. Ed. by A. Gordon Ball. Earl O. Heady. LC 78-153163. (Illus.). 1972. 11.95x o.p. Iowa St U Pr.
Sizes. Jan Pienkowski. Ed. by Kate Klimo. (Pienkowski Concept Bks.). (Illus.). 32p. (ps-k). 1983. 4.80 o.s.i. (ISBN 0-671-46244-X, Little Simon). S&S.
Skara House at the Mediaeval University of Paris. Astrik L. Gabriel. (Mediaeval Texts & Studies Ser.: No. 9). 1960. 25.00 o.p. (ISBN 0-268-00255-X). U of Notre Dame Pr.
Skateboard Book. rev. ed. Ben Davidson. (Illus.). 1979. pap. 4.95 o.p. (ISBN 0-448-12484-X, G&D). Putnam Pub Group.
Skateboarder's Bible: Technique, Equipment, Stunts, Terms, Etc. Albert Cassorla. LC 76-28511. (Illus.). 128p. (Orig.). (gr. 6 up). 1976. lib. bdg. 12.90 o.p. (ISBN 0-914294-59-8); pap. 4.95 o.p. (ISBN 0-914294-60-1). Running Pr.
Skateboards & Skateboarding: The Complete Beginner's Guide. LaVada Weir. (Illus.). (gr. 4-6). 1977. pap. 1.75 o.p. (ISBN 0-671-41136-5). Archway.
Skater's Handbook. John M. Petkevich. LC 83-16514. (Illus.). 210p. 1984. 15.95 o.p. (ISBN 0-684-18016-2, ScribT). Scribner.
Skater's Waltz: A Novel. Philip Norman. 1985. 15.45 o.p. (ISBN 0-671-50379-0, Linden Pr). S&S.
Skating Heidens. Mary V. Fox. LC 80-23066. (Illus.). 128p. (gr. 5-12). 1981. PLB 13.95 o.p. (ISBN 0-89490-046-3). Enslow Pubs.
Skating Party. Marina Warner. LC 82-73007. 192p. 1983. 10.95 o.p. (ISBN 0-689-11368-4, Atheneum). Macmillan.
SKCALB. Lee O. Lewis. LC 84-91442. 48p. 1985. 6.95 o.p. (ISBN 0-533-06510-0). Vantage.
Skeezer: Dog with a Mission. Elizabeth Yates. 1974. pap. 1.25 o.p. (ISBN 0-380-00105-5, 48223). Avon.
Skeletal Injury in the Child. John A. Ogden. LC 81-8384. (Illus.). 656p. 1982. text ed. 115.00 o.p. (ISBN 0-8121-0809-4). Lea & Febiger.
Skeletal Muscle Pathology. F. L. Mastaglia & John Walton. LC 81-21701. (Illus.). 648p. 1983. text ed. 145.00 o.p. (ISBN 0-443-02028-0). Churchill.
Skellig: Island Outpost of Europe. Des Lavelle. 1976. 10.95 o.p. (ISBN 0-7735-0276-9, McGill Canada). U of Toronto Pr.
Skenes Yacht Design. Francis Kinney. 1983. 22.95 o.p. (ISBN 0-396-07968-7). Dodd.
Sketch of Chinese Geography (in Characters) Charles Chu. 3.95 o.p. (ISBN 0-88710-089-9); tapes avail. o.p. (ISBN 0-88710-090-2). Yale Far Eastern Pubns.
Sketch of the History of South Carolina to the Close of the Proprietary Government by the Revolution of 1719. William J. Rivers. LC 77-187372. 470p. 1972. Repr. of 1856 ed. 25.00 o.p. (ISBN 0-87152-100-8). Reprint.
Sketch of the Laws Relating to Slavery in the Several States of the United States of America. George M. Stroud. LC 68-55917. 1969. Repr. of 1956 ed. lib. bdg. 22.50x o.p. (ISBN 0-8371-0673-7, STS&, Pub. by Negro U Pr). Greenwood.
Sketchbook of Birds. Charles Tunnicliffe. LC 79-1920. (Illus.). 144p. 1979. 19.95 o.s.i. (ISBN 0-03-052326-5). H Holt & Co.
Sketchbook 1946-1949. Max Frisch. Tr. by Geoffrey Skelton. LC 76-54706. (Helen & Kurt Wolff Bk.). 1977. 12.95 o.p. (ISBN 0-15-182893-8). HarBraceJ.
Sketchbook 1966 to 1971. Max Frisch. Tr. by Geoffrey Skelton. LC 73-19649. (Helen & Kurt Wolff Bk.). 1974. 10.00 o.p. (ISBN 0-15-182892-X). HarBraceJ.
Sketches of Haiti: From the Expulsion of the French to the Death of Christophe. William W. Harvey. LC 77-111578. 1971. Repr. of 1827 ed. 35.00x o.p. (ISBN 0-8371-4604-6, HSH&). Greenwood.
Sketches of Nebraska. Robert Hanna. LC 84-3722. (Illus.). xx, 124p. 1984. 16.95 o.p. (ISBN 0-8032-2328-5); pap. 11.95 o.p. U of Nebr Pr.
Sketches of the Life & Correspondences of Nathanael Green, 2 vols. William Johnson. LC 78-119063. 516p. 1973. Repr. of 1822 ed. Set. lib. bdg. 65.00 o.p. (ISBN 0-306-71953-3). Da Capo.
Sketching Interior Architecture. Norman Diekman & John Pile. (Illus.). 176p. 1985. 32.50 o.p. (ISBN 0-8230-7450-1, Whitney Lib); pap. 19.95 o.p. (ISBN 0-8230-7459-5). Watson-Guptill.
Skew Distributions & Sizes of Business Firms. Y. Ijiri & H. A. Simon. (Studies in Mathematical & Managerial Economics: Vol. 24). 232p. 1977. 58.00 o.p. (ISBN 0-7204-0518-1, North-Holland). Elsevier.
Ski Book. Morten Lund & Bob Gillen. LC 82-72066. (Illus.). 1982. 22.95 o.p. (ISBN 0-87795-430-5, Arbor Hse). Morrow.
Ski-Doo Snowmobile Service-Repair: 1970-1979. Ed. by Eric Jorgensen. (Illus.). pap. 8.95 o.p. (ISBN 0-89287-178-4, X953). Clymer Pub.
Ski Europe: Winter 1987. rev. ed. Charles Leocha & William Walker. LC 85-51209. 280p. (Orig.). 1986. pap. 8.95 o.p. (ISBN 0-915009-07-2). World Leis Corp.
Ski Europe: Winter 1987-88. rev. ed. Charles Leocha & William Walker. LC 87-50899. (Illus.). 392p. 1987. pap. 11.95 o.p. (ISBN 0-915009-08-0). World Leis Corp.
Ski Europe: Winter 1989. Charles Leocha & William Walker. 1988. pap. 11.95 o.p. (ISBN 0-915009-09-9). World Leis Corp.
Ski Maintenance & Repair Handbook. Seth Masia. (Illus.). 192p. 1982. pap. 7.95 o.p. (ISBN 0-8092-5737-8). Contemp Bks.
Ski Trails & Old Timers' Tales in Idaho & Montana. Ron Watters. LC 78-62074. (Illus.). 272p. 1978. pap. 7.95 o.p. (ISBN 0-932722-05-9). Solstice Pr.
Ski with Nitka. Louis Nitka. LC 72-82134. (Illus.). 64p. 1972. pap. 1.25 o.p. (ISBN 0-88208-006-7). Chicago Review.
Skid Resistance. (National Cooperative Highway Research Program Synthesis of Highway Practice). 66p. 1972. 4.00 o.p. (ISBN 0-309-02024-7). Transport Res Bd.
Skid Resistance, 16 reports. (Transportation Research Record Ser.). 152p. 1974. 6.60 o.p. (ISBN 0-309-02368-8). Transport Res Bd.
Skidding Accidents: Ancillary Papers. 150p. 1976. 6.40 o.p. (ISBN 0-309-02580-X). Transport Res Bd.
Skidding Accidents: Pavement Characteristics. (Transportation Research Record Ser.). 110p. 1976. 4.60 o.p. (ISBN 0-309-02575-3). Transport Res Bd.
Skidding Accidents: Tires, Vehicles & Vehicle Components. (Transportation Research Record Ser.). 171p. 1976. 7.00 o.p. (ISBN 0-309-02574-5). Transport Res Bd.
Skidding Accidents: Wet-Weather, Accident Experience, Human Factors, & Legal Aspects. (Transportation Research Record Ser.). 87p. 1976. 3.60 o.p. (ISBN 0-309-02576-1). Transport Res Bd.
Skidmore, Owings & Merrill: Architecture & Urbanism 1973-1983. Albert Bush-Brown & Oswald W. Grube. LC 83-16955. (Illus.). 400p. 1984. 60.95 o.s.i. (ISBN 0-442-21169-4). Van Nos Reinhold.
Skiiers Directory & Almanac: 1983. Thomas & Leeds Staff. 1982. pap. 3.95 o.p. (ISBN 0-686-82385-0). Dell.
Skiing America: Winter 1989. Charles Leocha. 1988. pap. 11.95 o.p. (ISBN 0-915009-10-2). World Leis Corp.
Skiing to Win. Harvey Edwards. LC 73-5239. (Illus.). (gr. 7 up). 1973. 5.95 o.p. (ISBN 0-15-275400-8, HJ). HarBraceJ.
Skill in Counterattacks. Pu Gill Gwon. LC 79-56538. (Ser. 135). 1979. pap. 10.95 o.p. (ISBN 0-89750-067-9). Ohara Pubns.
Skills Development in Reading, Writing & Quantatitive. Beryl B. Blain et al. Rev. by Angelica Braestrup & Aftab Hassan. (Complete Preparation for the MCAT Ser.: Vol. 2). 1985. pap. text ed. 17.00 o.p. (ISBN 0-941406-10-5). Betz Pub Co Inc.
Skills of Management. W. David Rees. 199p. 1984. 25.00 o.p. (ISBN 0-7099-2267-1, Pub. by Croom Helm Ltd); pap. 12.00 o.p. (ISBN 0-7099-2266-3). Routledge Chapman & Hall.
Skills of Management. A. N. Welsh. 240p. 1981. 15.95 o.p. (ISBN 0-8144-5670-7). AMACOM.
Skills Vital to Successful Managers. Chemical Engineering Magazine Editors. 1979. text ed. 34.50 o.p. (ISBN 0-07-010737-8). McGraw.
Skillstuff-Reasoning. Imogene Forte & Joy MacKenzie. LC 80-81737. (Skillstuff Set). (Illus.). 240p. (gr. 2-6). 1981. pap. text ed. 12.95 o.p. (ISBN 0-913916-81-1, IP 81-1). Incentive Pubns.
Skillstuff Set, 3 bks. 1980. 35.95 o.s.i. (ISBN 0-86530-008-9, IP08-9). Incentive Pubns.
Skin & Bone. Gwynne Vevers. LC 83-18757. (Your Body Ser.). (Illus.). 24p. (gr. 1-4). 1984. 8.25 o.p. (ISBN 0-688-02820-9); lib. bdg. 7.63 o.p. (ISBN 0-688-02821-7). Lothrop.
Skin & Scuba Diving. Albert A. Tillman. (Physical Education Activities Ser.). 78p. 1966. pap. text ed. write for info. o.p. (ISBN 0-697-07022-0). Wm C Brown.
Skin Care for Men Only: A Complete Guide. Zia Wesley-Hosford. 1987. pap. 4.95 o.p. (ISBN 0-15-682749-2, Harv). HarBraceJ.
Skin Deep. Helene Geutary & Patrice Casanova. (Illus.). 1984. 24.95 o.p. (ISBN 0-394-53812-9, GP 911). Grove.
Skin Disease in the Dog & Cat: The Library of Veterinary Practice. Grant. 1986. 12.50 o.p. (ISBN 0-8016-1959-9). Mosby.
Skin Sense: The Complete Guide to Skin Care for Men. Nance Mitchell. (Orig.). 1987. pap. 8.95 o.p. (ISBN 0-449-90189-0, Columbine). Fawcett.
Skinflick. Joseph Hansen. LC 79-11077. (Rinehart Suspense Novel). 192p. 1980. 8.95 o.s.i. (ISBN 0-03-048931-8); pap. 3.95 o.s.i. H Holt & Co.
Skinflick. Joseph Hansen. LC 79-11077. 192p. 1980. pap. 3.50 o.s.i. (ISBN 0-03-057641-5). H Holt & Co.
Skinny Island: More Tales of Manhattan. Louis Auchincloss. 1987. 17.45 o.s.i. (ISBN 0-395-43295-2). HM.
Skinnybones. Barbara Park. 112p. (gr. 2-5). 1983. pap. 2.25 o.p. (ISBN 0-380-64832-6, Camelot). Avon.
Skins on the Earth. Primus St. John. LC 75-14652. 74p. 1975. 16.00x o.p. (ISBN 0-685-52614-3); pap. 7.00 o.p. (ISBN 0-914742-07-8). Copper Canyon.
Skip to My Lou: For Brownies, Juniors, Cadettes, Seniors & Leaders. Girl Scouts of the U. S. A. Staff. 32p. (gr. 1-8). 1958. pap. 1.50 o.p. (ISBN 0-88441-307-1, 20-199). Girl Scouts USA.
Skipper. Paige Dixon. LC 79-10420. 132p. (gr. 5-9). 1979. 8.95 o.s.i. (ISBN 0-689-30706-3, Atheneum). Macmillan.
Skopas in Malibu. Andrew Stewart. LC 28-81304. (Illus.). 90p. 1982. 16.00 o.p. (ISBN 0-89236-054-2); pap. 9.00 o.p. (ISBN 0-89236-036-4). J P Getty Trust.
Skorpion's Death: A Novel. David Brierly. 256p. 1986. 13.70 o.s.i. (ISBN 0-671-47755-2). Summit Bks.
Skulduggery. William Marshall. LC 79-1935. (Rinehart Suspense Novel). 192p. 1980. 8.95 o.s.i. (ISBN 0-03-047491-4). H Holt & Co.
Skulduggery. William Marshall. 1984. pap. 3.95 o.p. (ISBN 0-03-071064-2). H Holt & Co.
Skull Beneath the Skin. P. D. James. 352p. 1982. 13.95 o.s.i. (ISBN 0-684-17773-0, ScribT). Scribner.
Skulls along the River. Quincy Troupe. 144p. (Orig.). 1984. pap. 5.95 o.s.i. (ISBN 0-918408-22-9). Reed & Cannon.
Skunk & Possum. Graham Tether. (Illus.). (gr. k-3). 1979. PLB 6.95 o.p. (ISBN 0-395-28270-5). HM.
Sky. Yvonne Yaw. 1977. 7.95 o.p. (ISBN 0-395-25693-3). HM.

Sky & Water in Pastel, Bk. 21. Aubrey Phillips. (Leisure Arts Ser.). (Illus.). 32p. (Orig.). 1984. pap. 2.95 o.p. (ISBN 0-89134-088-2). North Light Bks.

Sky Children. Donald Olson. (Orig.). 1975. pap. 1.25 o.p. (ISBN 0-380-00427-5, 26781). Avon.

Sky Dancer: The Secret Life & Songs of the Lady Yeshe Tsogyel. Ed. by Keith Dowman. (Illus.). 350p. (Orig.). 1984. pap. 14.95 o.p. (ISBN 0-7100-9576-7). Routledge Chapman & Hall.

Sky Hook. Dan Jorgensen. LC 85-14983. (Pennypinchers Ser.). 128p. (gr. 4-9). 1985. pap. 3.95 o.p. (ISBN 0-89191-682-2, 56820, Chariot Bks). Cook.

Sky Is Falling. Anne Emery. LC 79-113472. (gr. 8 up). 1970. 4.50 o.s.i. (ISBN 0-664-32475-4, Westminster). Westminster John Knox.

Sky Jumps Into Your Shoes at Night. Jasper Tomkins. Date not set. pap. 7.95 o.p. (ISBN 0-310-57111-1, 16111P). Zondervan.

Sky Man on the Totem Pole. Christie Harris. LC 74-19496. (Illus.). 176p. (gr. 4-7). 1975. PLB 7.95 o.p. (ISBN 0-689-30450-1, Atheneum). Macmillan.

Sky on Fire: The First Battle of Britain. Raymond H. Fredette. LC 75-33909. 290p. 1976. pap. 5.25 o.p. (ISBN 0-15-682750-6, HB329, Harv). HarBraceJ.

Sky Pilot. Frank Connor. 1973. pap. 0.95 o.p. (ISBN 0-380-01552-8, 17905). Avon.

Sky Prints Aviation Enroute Atlas. annual 27th ed. Sky Prints Corp. Staff. 1988. 69.50 o.p. (ISBN 0-911720-64-2, Pub. by FR). Aviation.

Skye. Derek Cooper. (Illus.). 242p. 1983. pap. 11.95 o.p. (ISBN 0-7100-9565-1). Routledge Chapman & Hall.

Skye O'Malley. Bertrice Small. 1984. pap. 4.95 o.p. (ISBN 0-345-32364-5). Ballantine.

Skyfall. Harry Harrison. LC 76-23433. 1977. 8.95 o.p. (ISBN 0-689-10764-1, Atheneum). Macmillan.

Skyfire. Frank Asch. LC 83-16165. (Illus.). 32p. 1984. 12.95 o.s.i. (ISBN 0-13-812389-6). P-H.

Skylark of Space. Edward E. Smith & Lee H. Garby. Ed. by Lester Del Rey. LC 75-427. (Library of Science Fiction). 1975. lib. bdg. 21.00 o.p. (ISBN 0-8240-1432-4). Garland Pub.

Skylark Three. Edward E. Smith. Ed. by Lester Del Rey. LC 75-429. (Library of Science Fiction). 1975. lib. bdg. 21.00 o.p. (ISBN 0-8240-1433-2). Garland Pub.

Skylights: A Revision of A-621. Mary Vance. (Architecture Ser.: A 1503). 9p. 1985. 2.00 o.p. (ISBN 0-89028-653-1). Vance Biblios.

Skyscraper. Robert Byrne. LC 83-45514. 288p. 1984. 14.95 o.p. (ISBN 0-689-11430-3, Atheneum). Macmillan.

Skyscrapers: A Revision of A-577. Mary Vance. (Architecture Ser.: A 1501). 62p. 1985. 9.00 o.p. (ISBN 0-89028-651-5). Vance Biblios.

Skysurfing: A Guide to Hang Gliding. Eddie Paul. 1975. pap. 3.95 o.p. (ISBN 0-8306-2234-9, 2234). TAB Bks.

Skytrap: An Adventure Novel. John Smith. 1984. 12.45 o.p. (ISBN 0-393-01860-1). Norton.

Skywalking: The Life & Films of George Lucas. George Pollack. 1984. pap. 3.50 o.s.i. (ISBN 0-345-31419-0). Ballantine.

Skywatch: The Western Weather Guide. Richard A. Keen. (Illus.). 190p. 1987. 13.95 o.p. (ISBN 1-55591-019-X). Fulcrum Inc.

Skyway Typology. Bernard Jacob & Carol Morphew. 1984. 14.00 o.p. (ISBN 0-317-06678-1). Am Inst Arch.

Skyway Typology Minneapolis. Bernard Jacob & Carol Morphew. 1984. pap. 19.50 o.p. (ISBN 0-913962-66-X, M620). Am Inst Arch.

SLA Triennial Salary Survey. Special Libraries Association Staff. LC 86-1847. 74p. 1986. pap. 25.00 o.p. (ISBN 0-87111-316-3). SLA.

Slab Boys. John Byrne. (Paisley Patterns Trilogy). 44p. 1983. pap. 5.95 o.p. (ISBN 0-907540-20-1, NO.3990). Routledge Chapman & Hall.

Slade's Wells Fargo Colt. John B. McClernan. 1977. 5.00 o.p. (ISBN 0-682-48925-5). Exposition-Phoenix.

Slag. David Hare. 78p. 1971. pap. 5.95 o.p. (ISBN 0-571-09643-3). Faber & Faber.

Slammer. Ben Greer. LC 74-20351. 1975. 8.95 o.p. (ISBN 0-689-10649-1, Atheneum). Macmillan.

Slang Today & Yesterday: With a Short Historical Sketch & Vocabularies of English, American & Australian Slang. 4th ed. Eric Partridge. 1970. 30.00 o.p. (ISBN 0-7100-6922-7). Routledge Chapman & Hall.

Slanguage II. John Artman. (Illus.). 80p. (gr. 4-8). 1983. wkbk. 7.95 o.p. (ISBN 0-86653-146-7, GA 474). Good Apple.

Slattery Stands Alone. Steven C. Lawrence. (Slattery Ser.). (Orig.). 1976. pap. 0.95 o.p. (ISBN 0-685-64017-5, LB337NK, Pub. by Leisure Bks CT). Dorchester Pub Co.

Slattery's Gun Says No. Steven C. Lawrence. 1975. pap. 0.95 o.p. (ISBN 0-685-52942-8, LB258NK, Pub. by Leisure Bks CT). Dorchester Pub Co.

Slaughter Zone. Frank Garrett. (Killsquad Ser.: No. 8). 176p. 1987. pap. 2.50 o.p. (ISBN 0-380-75364-2). Avon.

Slave. William Malliol. 1986. 16.45 o.p. (ISBN 0-393-02268-4). Norton.

Slave Society in the British Leeward Islands at the End of the Eighteenth Century. Elsa V. Goveia. LC 80-13. (Caribbean Ser.: No. 8). (Illus.). ix, 370p. 1980. Repr. of 1965 ed. lib. bdg. 32.50x o.p. (ISBN 0-313-22156-1, GOSL). Greenwood.

Slave Songs of the Georgia Sea Islands. Lydia A. Parrish. 256p. Repr. of 1942 ed. lib. bdg. 39.00 o.p. (Pub. by Am Repr Serv). Reprint Servs.

Slave States of America, 2 Vols. James S. Buckhingham. LC 68-55873. (Illus.). Repr. of 1842 ed. 45.00x o.p. (ISBN 0-8371-0330-4, BUS&). Greenwood.

Slave Trade. Herbert Gold. LC 78-73862. 1979. 8.95 o.p. (ISBN 0-87795-217-5, Arbor Hse). Morrow.

Slavery & the Numbers Game: A Critique of Time on the Cross. Herbert G. Gutman. LC 75-15899. (Blacks in the New World Ser.). (Illus.). 183p. 1975. pap. 5.95 o.p. (ISBN 0-252-00565-1). U of Ill Pr.

Slavery in the Union. Gilman M. Ostrander. 1970. pap. text ed. 3.25x o.s.i. (ISBN 0-88273-224-2). Forum Pr IL.

Slaves of Sleep. L. Ron Hubbard. 1979. pap. 2.75 o.p. (ISBN 0-440-17646-8). Dell.

Slaves of the White Myth: The Psychology of Neocolonialism. Thomas Gladwin & Ahmad Saidin. LC 80-14939. 1981. text ed. 15.00x o.p. (ISBN 0-391-01936-8). Humanities.

Slave's Tale. Erik C. Haugaard. (Illus.). (gr. 7 up). 1965. 7.95 o.p. (ISBN 0-395-06804-5). HM.

Slaves Uprooted & the Mau Mau Massacre. John P. Sykes. 1978. 4.50 o.p. (ISBN 0-682-49035-0). Exposition-Phoenix.

Slavic Community on Strike: Immigrant Labor in Pennsylvania Anthracite. Victor R. Greene. 1968. 15.95x o.p. (ISBN 0-268-00256-8). U of Notre Dame Pr.

Slavonic Encyclopedia. Joseph S. Roucek. (ISBN 0-8022-1393-6). Philos Lib.

Slayboys. Philip Kirk. (Butler Ser.: No. 3). pap. 1.75 o.p. (ISBN 0-8439-0683-9, Pub. by Leisure Bks CT). Dorchester Pub Co.

Slaying of the Dragon: Modern Tales of the Playful Imagination. Ed. by Franz Rottensteiner. LC 83-26542. 320p. 1984. 14.95 o.p. (ISBN 0-15-182975-6). HarbraceJ.

Sleep. Marie G. Stopes. 160p. 1956. (ISBN 0-8022-1656-0). Philos Lib.

Sleep & Dreaming: Origin, Nature & Functions. David Cohen. 1979. text ed. 51.00 o.p. (ISBN 0-08-021467-3). Pergamon.

Sleep & Sleep Disordery, 1986. Ed. by H. Lechner & E. Korner. (Journal, European Neurology: Vol. 25, Suppl. 2). 160p. 1986. pap. 37.50 o.p. (ISBN 3-8055-4443-X). S Karger.

Sleep & Wakefulness. rev. ed. Nathaniel Kleitman. LC 63-17854. 1963. lib. bdg. 40.00x o.s.i. (ISBN 0-226-44071-0). U of Chicago Pr.

Sleep, Divine & Human, in the Old Testament. Thomas H. McAlpine. (JSOT Supplement Ser.: No. 38). 232p. pap. text ed. 16.95x o.s.i. (Pub. by JSOT Pr England). Eisenbrauns.

Sleep Mechanisms. Ed. by A. Borbely & J. Valatx. (Experimental Brain Research Ser.: Suppl. 8). (Illus.). 330p. 1984. 35.00 o.p. (ISBN 0-387-13146-9). Springer-Verlag.

Sleep: Physiology, Biochemistry, Psychology, Pharmacology, Clinical Implications, Proceedings of the European Congress of Sleep Research, 1st, Basel, October 1972. European Congress of Sleep Research Staff. Ed. by W. P. Koella et al. (Illus.). 1973. 121.50 o.p. (ISBN 3-8055-1604-5). S Karger.

Sleep: The Mysterious Third of Your Life. Jonathan Kastner & Marianna Kastner. LC 67-22392. (Curriculum Related Bks.). (Illus.). (gr. 7 up). 1968. 5.75 o.p. (ISBN 0-15-275911-5, HJ). HarBraceJ.

Sleep Tight, Alex Pumpernickel. Fernando Krahn. 32p. (ps up). 1982. 9.95 o.p. (ISBN 0-316-50312-6, Joy St Bks). Little.

Sleep Two, Three, Four. John Neufeld. 1977. pap. 0.75 o.p. (ISBN 0-380-01443-2, 04580). Avon.

Sleep Well, Christine. Alice Brennan. 1973. pap. 0.75 o.p. (ISBN 0-380-01554-4, 17491). Avon.

Sleeper. Eric Clark. LC 79-55569. 1980. 11.95 o.p. (ISBN 0-689-11032-4, Atheneum). Macmillan.

Sleeping Beauty. Ed. by Warren Chappell. (Illus.). (gr. k up). 1987. pap. 5.95 o.s.i. (ISBN 0-8052-0683-3). Schocken.

Sleeping Beauty. Jacob Grimm & Wilhelm K. Grimm. 1960. 4.95 o.p. (ISBN 0-15-275672-8, HJ). HarBraceJ.

Sleeping Beauty with Benjy & Bubbles. Ruth L. Perle. LC 78-55625. (Read with Me Ser.). (Illus.). 32p. (gr. k-3). 1979. 2.95 o.s.i. (ISBN 0-03-044966-9). H Holt & Co.

Sleeping Dog. Dick Lochte. 288p. 1985. 15.95 o.p. (ISBN 0-87795-738-X, Arbor Hse). Morrow.

Sleeping Dogs. Frank Ross. LC 77-88911. 1978. 8.95 o.p. (ISBN 0-689-10850-8, Atheneum). Macmillan.

Sleeping Giant & Other Stories. Eleanor Estes. LC 48-9223. (Illus.). (gr. 1-5). 1948. 4.50 o.p. (ISBN 0-15-275851-8, HJ). HarBraceJ.

Sleeping Pills, Insomnia, & Medical Practice. Institute of Medicine Staff. 1979. pap. text ed. 7.50x o.p. (ISBN 0-309-02881-7). Natl Acad Pr.

Sleeping Spy. Herbert Burkholtz & Clifford Irving. 1984. pap. 2.95 o.s.i. (ISBN 0-345-31465-4). Ballantine.

Sleeping with Soldiers: In Search of the Macho Man. Rosemary Daniell. LC 84-6701. 288p. 1985. 14.95 o.p. (ISBN 0-03-062431-2). H Holt & Co.

Sleeping with the Enemy. Nancy Price. 320p. 1987. 17.45 o.s.i. (ISBN 0-671-62967-0). S&S.

Sleepless Days. Jurek Becker. Tr. by Leila Vennewitz. Ed. by Helen Wolff. LC 79-1811. (Helen & Kurt Wolff Bk.). 1979. 7.95 o.p. (ISBN 0-15-182982-9). HarBraceJ.

Sleepside Story. Greg Bear. (Illus.). 84p. 1988. signed numbered slipcased 95.00x o.p. (ISBN 0-941826-18-X). Cheap St.

Sleepwalker. David Combs. 320p. 1983. pap. 2.95 o.p. (ISBN 0-380-85183-0, 85183-0). Avon.

Sleepwalker's Moon. Ella T. Ellis. LC 79-22665. 252p. (gr. 7 up). 1980. 9.95 o.p. (ISBN 0-689-30739-X, Atheneum). Macmillan.

Sleepwalking. Meg Wolitzer. 224p. 1984. pap. 2.25 o.p. (ISBN 0-380-68221-4, 68221, Flare). Avon.

Sleepy Owl. Marcus Pfister. LC 85-63305. (Illus.). 32p. (gr. k-2). 1986. 10.95 o.p. (ISBN 0-03-008023-1, North South Bks.). H Holt & Co.

Sleepy Ronald. Jack Gantos. (Illus.). (gr. k-3). 1976. PLB 6.95 o.p. (ISBN 0-395-24743-8). HM.

Sleepytime. (Platt & Munk Peggy Cloth Bks). (Illus.). 8p. (ps). 1979. 2.50 o.p. (ISBN 0-448-46836-0, G&D); PLB 4.95 o.s.i. (ISBN 0-448-11921-8). Putnam Pub Group.

Sleeve Puppets. Brenda Morton. LC 77-92754. (Illus.). 1978. 8.50 o.s.i. (ISBN 0-8008-7237-1). Taplinger.

Sleighs, the Gentle Transportation: Or, Sleighs of Old Montreal. Carlo Italiano. (Illus.). 1978. 2.95 o.p. (ISBN 0-88776-105-4); pap. 5.95 o.p. (ISBN 0-88776-103-8). Tundra Bks.

Sleightly Deceived. Patrick A. Kelley. 224p. (Orig.). 1987. pap. 2.95 o.p. (ISBN 0-380-75231-X). Avon.

Sleightly Invisible. Patrick A. Kelley. 224p. (Orig.). 1986. pap. 2.95 o.p. (ISBN 0-380-75116-X). Avon.

Sleightly Lethal. Patrick A. Kelley. (Harry Colderword Ser.: No. 2). 224p. 1986. pap. 2.95 o.p. (ISBN 0-380-89727-X). Avon.

Sleightly Murder. Patrick A. Kelley. (Harry Colderwood Ser.: No. 1). 208p. 1985. pap. 2.75 o.p. (ISBN 0-380-89511-0). Avon.

Slice of Snow: A Book of Poems. Joan W. Anglund & Joan Walsh. LC 70-11830. (gr. 1-5). 1970. 3.95 o.p. (ISBN 0-15-183015-0, HJ). HarBraceJ.

Slide. Gerald A. Browne. LC 75-40510. 1976. 8.95 o.p. (ISBN 0-87795-099-7, Arbor Hse). Morrow.

Slide Atlas of Immunology. Roitt et al. 1985. 750.00 o.p. (ISBN 0-8016-4285-X). Mosby.

Slide Presentation & Script for Word Information Processing. 2nd ed. Marly Bergerud & Jean Gonzalez. 36p. 1984. pap. 195.00 o.p. (ISBN 0-471-80577-7). Wiley.

Slight Mourning. Catherine Aird. 192p. 1986. pap. 2.95 o.p. (ISBN 0-553-25631-9). Bantam.

Slillful Hands. Raymond Brown. 1972. pap. 2.95 o.p. (ISBN 0-87508-035-9). Chr Lit.

Slim Chance in a Fat World: Behavioral Control of Obesity. professional ed. Richard B. Stuart & Barbara Davis. (Illus., Orig.). 1972. pap. 13.95 incl. program materials o.p. (ISBN 0-87822-060-7, 0607); (bk. alone) 11.95 o.p. (ISBN 0-87822-064-X, 0608); (materials alone) 2.95 o.p. (ISBN 0-87822-061-5, 0615). Res Press.

Slim Down Camp. Stephen Manes. 192p. (gr. 4-6). 1981. 8.95 o.p. (ISBN 0-395-30170-X, Clarion). HM.

Slim Goodbody: The Inside Story. John Burstein. (Illus.). (gr. k-6). 1977. 9.95 o.p. (ISBN 0-07-009240-0); pap. text ed. 4.95 o.p. (ISBN 0-07-009241-9). McGraw.

Slim Goodbody's Healthy Days Diary: Activity Book. John Burstein. (Illus.). 64p. (ps-5). 1983. spiral 5.95 o.p. (ISBN 0-89845-056-X, B056X). Caedmon.

Slime. John Halkin. 252p. 1986. pap. 2.95 o.p. (ISBN 0-931773-74-1). Critics Choice Paper.

Slimer. Harry A. Knight. 224p. (Orig.). 1989. pap. 3.50 o.s.i. (ISBN 1-55785-076-3). Bart Books.

Slimmer's Microwave Cookbook. Margaret Weale. (Illus.). 120p. (Orig.). 1983. 16.95 o.p. (ISBN 0-7153-8392-2). David & Charles.

Slipped Disc. James Cyriax. (Encore Edition). 252p. 1981. encore ed. 5.95 o.p. (ISBN 0-684-17745-5, ScribT); pap. 7.95 o.p. (ISBN 0-684-17274-7). Scribner.

Slipping Down Life. Anne Tyler. 1985. lib. bdg. 14.95 o.p. (ISBN 0-8161-3711-0, Large Print Bks). G K Hall.

Slither. John Halkin. 256p. 1986. pap. 2.95 o.p. (ISBN 0-931773-63-6). Critics Choice Paper.

Slope Morphology. Ed. by Stanley A. Schumm & M. Paul Mosley. (Benchmark Papers in Geology: Vol. 6). 454p. 1982. 59.95 o.p. (ISBN 0-87933-024-4). Van Nos Reinhold.

Slopes: Form & Process. D. Brunsden. (Special Publication of the Institute of British Geographers Ser.: No. 3). 1980. 28.50 o.p. (ISBN 0-12-137980-9). Acad Pr.

Sloppy Kisses. Elizabeth Winthrop. LC 80-13673. (Illus.). 32p. (gr. k-3). 1980. 8.95 o.s.i. (ISBN 0-02-793210-9). Macmillan.

Slovak-English, English-Slovak Concise Technical Dictionary. rev. 3rd ed. J. Novak & R. Binder. (Slovak & Eng.). 1971. 15.00 o.p. (ISBN 0-685-39855-2). E J Brill USA.

Slovenia: A Portrait. I. Bratko & F. Stele. (Illus.). 1973. 25.00 o.s.i. (ISBN 0-685-58567-0). E J Brill USA.

Slow Brain Potentials & Behavior. Rockstroh et al. LC 82-1939. 271p. 1982. text ed. 39.00 o.p. (ISBN 0-8067-0291-5). Urban & S.

Slow Learner. M. F. Cleugh. (Illus.). 1957. (ISBN 0-8022-0264-0). Philos Lib.

Slow Learner. J. S. Roucek. LC 79-81816. 1970. (ISBN 0-8022-2305-2). Philos Lib.

Slow Learner in Mathematics: 35th Yearbook. National Council of Teachers of Mathematics Staff. LC 72-8350. (Illus.). 528p. 1972. 24.00 o.p. (ISBN 0-87353-015-2). NCTM.

Slow Speed Diesel Engines. S. H. Henshall & G. G. Jackson. (Marine Engineering Practice Ser.: Vol. 2, Pt. 17). 1979. pap. 9.00x o.p. (ISBN 0-900976-79-9, Pub. by Inst Marine Eng). Intl Spec Bk.

Slow Transmissible Diseases of the Nervous System: Clinical, Epidemiological, Genetic & Pathological Aspects of the Spongiform Encephalopathie, Vol. 1. Ed. by Stanley B. Prusiner & William J. Hadlow. LC 79-18087. 1980. 60.00 o.p. (ISBN 0-12-566301-3). Acad Pr.

Slow Transmissible Diseases of the Nervous System: Pathogenesis, Immunology, Virology & Molecular Biology of the Spongiform Encephalopathies, Vol. 2. Ed. by Stanley B. Prusiner & William J. Hadlow. LC 79-18087. 1979. 60.00 o.p. (ISBN 0-12-566302-1). Acad Pr.

Slowly, Slowly I Raise the Gun. Jay Bennett. 128p. 1983. pap. 2.25 o.p. (ISBN 0-380-84426-5, 84426-5, Flare). Avon.

Slowly, Slowly in the Wind. Patrick Highsmith. 192p. (Orig.). 1987. pap. 8.95 o.p. (ISBN 0-89296-910-5). Mysterious Pr.

SLR Photographer's Handbook. Carl Shipman. LC 77-10176. (Illus.). 1977. pap. 10.95 o.p. (ISBN 0-912656-59-X). Price Stern.

Slugger Heart & Other Stories. Joseph Campos-De Metro. LC 83-18533. 208p. 1984. 12.95 o.p. (ISBN 0-15-183100-9). HarBraceJ.

Slums of Baltimore, Chicago, New York & Philadelphia. U. S. Bureau of Labor Staff. LC 73-89065. 1969. Repr. of 1894 ed. 33.00 o.p. (ISBN 0-8371-1922-7, WRS&, Pub. by Negro U Pr). Greenwood.

Sm Student Balance P. (ISBN 0-07-521025-8). McGraw.

Small Arms of the World. 11th ed. Edward C. Ezelle & W. H. Smith. (Illus.). 672p. 1979. Repr. of 1943 ed. 29.95 o.p. (ISBN 0-8117-1558-2). Stackpole.

Small Arms of the World: A Basic Manual of Small Arms. 12th, rev. ed. W. H. Smith. (Illus.). 896p. 49.95 o.s.i. (ISBN 0-317-55095-0). Apollo.

Small Business: A Novel. Tom Parker. 1986. 14.45 o.p. (ISBN 0-393-02254-4). Norton.

Small Business Course Training Tools Directory. 1985. 35.00 o.p. (ISBN 0-317-40618-3). Am Assn Comm Jr Coll.

Small Business Financing. Shepard's Citation, Inc. Staff et al. (Commercial Law Publications). 398p. 1983. 80.00 o.p. (ISBN 0-07-010676-2). Shepards-McGraw.

Small Business Handbook: Comprehensive Guide to Starting & Running Your Own Business. Irving Burstinger. (Illus.). 1979. text ed. 22.95 o.p. (ISBN 0-13-814202-5, Spec); pap. text ed. 15.95 o.p. (ISBN 0-13-814194-0). P-H.

Small Business Legal Advisor. William A. Hancock. 288p. 1982. text ed. 36.95 o.p. (ISBN 0-07-025979-8). McGraw.

Small Business Management. 2nd ed. Hailes & Hubbard. LC 76-3945. 1977. pap. 16.95 o.p. (ISBN 0-8273-1400-0); instr's. guide 3.30 o.p. (ISBN 0-8273-1401-9). Delmar.

Small Business Management. 3rd ed. William D. Hailes, Jr. & Raymond T. Hubbard. LC 82-46006. 416p. 1983. pap. text ed. 18.95 o.p. (ISBN 0-8273-2108-2). Delmar.

Titles

Small Business Management. Paul Harmon. LC 78-62923. 362p. 1979. text ed. 19.95x o.p. (ISBN 0-442-20970-3). PWS-Kent Pub.
Small Business Management. 2nd ed. Nicholas C. Siropolis. LC 81-82561. 1982. text ed. 29.95 o.p. (ISBN 0-395-31732-0). HM.
Small Business Management: A Guide to Entrepreneurship. Nicholas C. Siropolis. LC 76-13799. (Illus.). 1977. text ed. 21.95 o.p. (ISBN 0-395-24475-7). HM.
Small Business Management Principles. Stanley R. Sondeno. 1985. 35.95x o.p. (ISBN 0-256-03168-1). Irwin.
Small Business Management Training Tool Directory. 1985. 8.95 o.p. (ISBN 0-317-40622-1). Am Assn Comm Jr Coll.
Small Business Sourcebook. 2nd ed. Ed. by Robert J. Elster. 1837p. 1986. 185.00x o.p. (ISBN 0-8103-1597-1). Gale.
Small Business Specialists. 63p. 1986. pap. 3.25 o.p. (ISBN 0-318-21658-2, S/N 008-000-00462-5). USGPO.
Small Business Survival Guide: A Handbook. Bob Coleman. LC 83-42678. 1984. 18.45 o.p. (ISBN 0-393-01768-0). Norton.
Small Business: Theory & Policy. Ed. by Cyril Levicki. 152p. (Orig.). 1984. pap. 12.00 o.p. (ISBN 0-7099-3327-4, Pub. by Croom Helm Ltd). Routledge Chapman & Hall.
Small Busted Women Have Big Hearts. Herbert I. Kavet. 96p. 1984. pap. 3.95 o.p. (ISBN 0-8092-5353-4). Contemp Bks.
Small Ceremonies. Carol Shields. 1976. text ed. 7.95 o.p. (ISBN 0-07-082340-5). McGraw.
Small Change. Francois Truffaut. LC 76-44660. (Illus.). 1977. pap. 1.95 o.p. (ISBN 0-394-17921-8, B399, BC). Grove.
Small Claims. Jill Ciment. LC 86-5643. 208p. 1986. 14.95 o.s.i. (ISBN 1-55584-000-0). Weidenfeld.
Small Community As Educator & Human Scale in Schools. Griscom Morgan & Arthur Morgan. 1970. pap. 1.00 o.p. (ISBN 0-910420-14-9). Comm Serv OH.
Small Computer Systems for Solicitors, 2 Pts. C. T. Edge. 152p. (Orig.). 1983. pap. text ed. 38.50x o.p. (ISBN 0-566-03442-5). Gower Pub Co.
Small Computers for Business & Industry. Dermot McKeone. 209p. 1979. text ed. 34.25x o.p. (ISBN 0-566-02096-3). Gower Pub Co.
Small Computers in Business. Small Computers in Business Seminar, London. 37p. 1981. pap. 28.60x o.p. (ISBN 0-686-97777-7, Pub. by Online Conference England). Gower Pub Co.
Small Country Houses of Today. Ed. by Lawrence Weaver. (Illus.). 224p. 1983. Repr. of 1911 ed. 49.50 o.p. (ISBN 0-907462-34-0). Antique Collect.
Small Cruiser Navigation. R. M. Tetley. (Illus.). 144p. 1984. 22.95 o.p. (ISBN 0-7153-8520-8). David & Charles.
Small Engines: Operation & Maintenance. William H. Crouse. (Automotive Technology Ser.). (Illus.). 448p. 1973. text ed. 22.85 o.p. (ISBN 0-07-014691-8). McGraw.
Small Escapes under the Sun. John Sinor. 1981. pap. 4.95 o.p. (ISBN 0-935572-10-4). Alive Pubns.
Small Farms--Livestock Buildings & Equipment. Midwest Plan Service Engineers Staff & Northeast Regional Agricultural Engineering Service Staff. LC 83-23697. (Illus.). 1984. pap. 6.00 o.s.i. (ISBN 0-89373-060-2, NRAES-6-MWPS-27). Midwest Plan Serv.
Small Fatigue Cracks. Ed. by R. O. Ritchie & J. Lankford. (Illus.). 666p. 1986. 99.00 o.p. (ISBN 0-87339-052-0). Minerals Metals.
Small Fruit Culture. 5th ed. James S. Shoemaker. (Illus.). 1978. 26.95 o.p. (ISBN 0-87055-248-1). AVI.
Small Futures: Children, Inequality & the Limits of Liberal Reform. Carnegie Council Staff & Richard DeLone. LC 77-92536. 288p. 1979. 12.95 o.p. (ISBN 0-15-183128-9). HarBraceJ.
Small Group Communication: A Reader. 4th ed. Robert S. Cathcart et al. 520p. 1984. pap. text ed. write for info o.p. (ISBN 0-697-04189-1). Wm C Brown.
Small-Group Cultures. Tom McFeat. 1974. 29.00 o.p. (ISBN 0-08-017073-0); pap. text ed. 16.00 o.p. (ISBN 0-08-017770-0). Pergamon.
Small Home Plans. 2nd ed. Ed. by Garlinghouse, L. F., Co., Staff. (Illus.). 112p. 1986. pap. 2.95 o.p. (ISBN 0-938708-16-3). L F Garlinghouse Co.
Small Home Plans. Ed. by L. F. Garlinghouse Co., Staff. LC 82-81518. (Illus.). 116p. (Orig.). 1982. pap. 2.50 o.s.i. (ISBN 0-938708-04-X). L F Garlinghouse Co.
Small Homes for Pleasant Living. 35th ed. W. D. Farmer. (Illus.). 40p. (Orig.). 1980. pap. 2.50 o.p. (ISBN 0-931518-12-1). W D Farmer.
Small Hotels of California: A Selective Guide to the Best of California's Most Charming Small Hotels & Inns. Bill Gleeson. LC 83-27306. (Illus.). 128p. (Orig.). 1984. pap. 7.95 o.p. (ISBN 0-87701-293-8). Chronicle Bks.
Small House in the Sun. Samuel Chamberlain. 1936. pap. 14.95 o.p. (ISBN 0-8038-9281-0). Hastings.
Small Hydroelectric Projects for Rural Development: Planning & Management. Ed. by Louis J. Goodman & Ralph N. Love. (Pergamon Policy Studies). 250p. 1981. 30.00 o.p. (ISBN 0-08-025966-9). Pergamon.
Small Industry in the Eighties. Ram K. Vepa. 450p. 1983. text ed. 35.00x o.p. (ISBN 0-7069-1964-5, Pub. by Vikas India). Advent NY.
Small Investor's Guide to Large Profits in the Stock Market. Justin W. Heatter. 192p. 1983. 15.95 o.s.i. (ISBN 0-684-17864-8, ScribT). Scribner.
Small Nation Survival. V. V. Sveics. 1970. 8.50 o.p. (ISBN 0-682-47163-1, University). Exposition-Phoenix.
Small Nuclear Forces & U. S. Security Policy: Threats & Potential Conflicts in the Middle East & South Asia. Ed. by Rodney W. Jones. LC 83-47790. 304p. 1984. 30.00x o.p. (ISBN 0-669-06736-9). Lexington Bks.
Small Paintings of the Masters, 3 vols. Egbert Haverkamp-Begemann et al. Ed. by Leslie Shore. LC 80-51389. (Illus.). 270p. 1980. Set. 3600.00 o.p. (ISBN 0-934516-34-0). Vol. 1 (ISBN 0-934516-35-9). Vol. 2 (ISBN 0-934516-36-7). Vol. 3 (ISBN 0-934516-37-5). Shorewood Fine Art.
Small People in Colorado Places. Susan Kaye. LC 88-18713. (Illus.). 150p. 1988. pap. 8.95 o.p. (ISBN 0-87108-702-2). Pruett.
Small Plays for You & a Friend. Sue Alexander. LC 74-4019. (Illus.). 48p. (gr. 1-4). 1979. 6.95 o.s.i. (ISBN 0-395-28762-6, Clarion). HM.
Small Prayers for Small Children About Big & Little Things. Paul Schreivogel. LC 76-135226. (Illus.). 32p. (ps-2). 1971. 4.50 o.p. (ISBN 0-8066-1109-X, 10-5835, Augsburg). Augsburg Fortress.
Small Public Libraries & the Planning Process. 58p. 1981. 7.00x o.p. (ISBN 0-8389-6512-1); members 6.30x o.p. ALA.
Small-Sample Reactivity Measurements in Nuclear Reactors. Wesley K. Foell. LC 74-144051. (ANS Monographs). 272p. 1972. 27.00 o.p. (ISBN 0-89448-003-0, 300005). Am Nuclear Soc.
Small-Scale Enterprises in Korea & Taiwan. Sam P. S. Ho. (Working Paper: No. 384). vi, 151p. 1980. 8.00 o.p. (ISBN 0-686-36187-3, WP-0384). World Bank.
Small Scale Industry: Problems & Prospects. (UNIDO Monographs on Industrialization of Developing Countries: Problems & Prospects: Vol. 11). pap. 4.00 o.p. (ISBN 92-1-106026-5, E.69.II.B.39 VOL.II). UN.
Small-Scale Manufacture of Footwear. (Technology Ser.: No. 2). xvi, 207p. 1982. 11.40 o.p. (ISBN 92-2-103079-2). Intl Labour Office.
Small-Scale Oil Extraction from Groundnuts & Copra: Technical Memorandum, No. 5. International Labour Office Staff. (Technology Ser.). xi, 111p. (Orig.). 1983. pap. 12.25 o.p. (ISBN 92-2-103503-4). Intl Labour Office.
Small-Scale Weaving: Technical Memorandum No. 4. International Labour Office Staff. (Technology Ser.). viii, 129p. (Orig.). 1983. pap. 14.00 o.p. (ISBN 92-2-103419-4). Intl Labour Office.
Small Solar Buildings in Cool Northern Climates. David Oppenheim. (Illus.). 144p. 1981. 32.50 o.p. (ISBN 0-85139-596-1). Nichols Pub.
Small Sound of the Trumpet: Women in Medieval Life. Margaret W. Labarge. LC 86-47509. (Illus.). 288p. 1986. 21.95 o.p. (ISBN 0-8070-5626-X). Beacon Pr.
Small Space Design. (ISBN 0-671-61198-4). P-H.
Small Store Planning for Growth. (Small Business Management Ser.: No. 33). (Illus.). 102p. 1984. pap. text ed. 5.50 o.p. (ISBN 0-318-21696-5, S/N 045-000-00152-1). USGPO.
Small Time Operator. Computer ed. Bernard Kamoroff & Emil Krause. LC 83-72091. 240p. 1984. pap. 19.95 o.s.i. (ISBN 0-89708-117-X). And Bks.
Small Time Operator: How to Start Your Own Small Business, Keep Your Books, Pay Your Taxes & Stay Out of Trouble. rev. ed. Bernard Kamoroff. (Illus.). 192p. 1987. pap. 10.95 o.p. Bell Springs Pub.
Small Town. Shelby Hearon. LC 85-47603. 356p. 1985. 15.95 o.p. (ISBN 0-689-11583-0, Atheneum). Macmillan.
Small Town. Sloan Wilson. LC 77-79550. 1978. 10.95 o.p. (ISBN 0-87795-172-1, Arbor Hse). Morrow.
Small Town America: A Narrative History Sixteen Twenty to the Present. Richard Lingeman. 544p. 1981. pap. 8.95 o.p. (ISBN 0-395-31540-9). HM.
Small Town Children's Christmas. P. K. Hallinan. 24p. (gr. k-6). 1987. 2.95 o.p. (ISBN 0-8249-8165-0). Ideals.
Small Town Girl. Ellen Cooney. LC 82-23379. 208p. (gr. 7 up). 1983. 9.70 o.p. (ISBN 0-395-33881-6). HM.
Small Town in American Drama. Ima H. Herron. LC 69-11729. (Illus.). 1969. 17.95x o.p. (ISBN 0-87074-077-6). SMU Press.
Small Town Sourcebook & Guide. Old Sturbridge Village Staff. (Illus.). 96p. 1979. saddlewire bdg 10.00 o.p. (ISBN 0-913387-00-2); guide, 128p. 4.50 o.p. (ISBN 0-913387-01-0). Old Sturbridge.
Small Towns in China. Fei H. Tung et al. (China Studies). 374p. 1986. pap. 7.95 o.p. (ISBN 0-8351-1529-1). China Bks.
Small Towns of Natal, a Socioeconomic Sample Survey. University of Natal - Pietermaritzburg - Department of Sociology & Social Work Staff. LC 71-97410. (Illus.). 1970. Repr. of 1953 ed. 17.50 o.p. (ISBN 0-8371-2653-3, SMT&). Greenwood.
Small TV Studio: Equipment & Facilities. Alan Bermingham et al. (Media Manual Ser.). (Illus.). 164p. 1976. pap. 18.95 o.p. (ISBN 0-240-50869-6). Focal Pr.
Small Voices & Great Trumpets: Minorities & the Media. Ed. by Bernard Rubin. LC 80-12427. 308p. 1980. 35.95 o.p. (ISBN 0-03-056973-7); pap. 18.95 o.p. (ISBN 0-275-91504-2, B1504). Praeger.
Small Wind Turbines Systems Conference, 1981. Ed. by Rocky Flats Wind Energy Research Center Staff. 439p. 1984. pap. 85.00 o.s.i. (ISBN 0-88016-048-9). Windbks.
Small Woman: The Story of Gladys Aylward of China. Alan Burgess. 266p. 1985. pap. 5.95 o.p. (ISBN 0-89283-232-0, Pub. by Vine Books). Servant.
Small World. David Lodge. 400p. 1986. pap. 4.50 o.s.i. (ISBN 0-446-34143-6). Warner Bks.
Small World Vegetable Gardening. John E. Bryan. LC 76-58364. (Illus.). 144p. 1977. 4.95 o.s.i. (ISBN 0-912238-79-8, One Hund One Prods); pap. 4.95 o.s.i. (ISBN 0-912238-78-X). Ortho.
Smalltalk-Eighty: The Language & Its Implementation. Adele Goldberg & David Robson. (Illus.). 544p. 1983. text ed. 46.25 o.s.i. (ISBN 0-201-11371-6). Addison-Wesley.
Smart As the Devil. Felice Picano. LC 74-82235. 1975. 7.95 o.p. (ISBN 0-87795-097-0, Arbor Hse). Morrow.
Smart BASIC for the Adam. W. Searle & D. Jones. (Illus.). 384p. 1984. pap. 12.95 o.p. (ISBN 0-89303-846-6). Brady Bks.
Smart Bombs. Philip Kirk. (Butler Ser.: No. 2). 1979. pap. 1.75 o.p. (ISBN 0-8439-0676-6, Pub. by Leisure Bks CT). Dorchester Pub Co.
Smart Dads I Know. Charlie W. Shedd. 1978. pap. 1.75 o.p. (ISBN 0-380-39388-3, 39388-3). Avon.
Smart Investers Guide to Real Estate. Robert Bruss. 1983. 13.95 o.p. (ISBN 0-517-55095-4, CROWN). Crown.
Smart Investors Guide to Real Estate. Robert Bruss. 1981. 13.95 o.p. (ISBN 0-517-54232-3). Crown.
Smart Money Real Estate for the 80's: New Profits in Big Properties. Robert Irwin. 240p. 1982. 14.00 o.p. (ISBN 0-936602-41-4). Kampmann.
Smart Shopper's Guide to Food Buying & Preparation. Joan Bingham & Dolores Riccio. (Illus.). 288p. 1982. 14.95 o.s.i. (ISBN 0-684-17464-2, ScribT). Scribner.
Smart Shopper's Guide to Food Buying & Preparation. Joan Bingham & Dolores Riccio. 320p. 1983. pap. 6.95 o.s.i. (ISBN 0-684-17822-2, ScribT). Scribner.
Smartest Person in the World. Sandy Clifford. LC 79-14138. (Illus.). (gr. k-3). 1979. pap. 4.95 o.p. (ISBN 0-395-28411-2, Pub. by Parnassus). HM.
Smashing the Communal Pot. Wang Guichen et al. (China Studies). 200p. 1985. pap. 6.95 o.p. (ISBN 0-8351-1687-5). China Bks.
SME-AIME Cumulative Index, 1936-1968. 1972. 25.00x o.p. (ISBN 0-89520-012-0). SMM&E Inc.
Smell of Hay. Giorgio Bassani. LC 75-16222. (Helen & Kurt Wolff Bk.). 193p. 1975. 7.95 o.p. (ISBN 0-15-183146-7). HarBraceJ.
Smell of It & Other Stories. Sonallah Ibrahim. (African Writers Ser.). 1971. pap. text ed. 6.50 o.p. (ISBN 0-435-90095-1). Heinemann Ed.
Smelly Jelly Smelly Fish. Michael Rosen. (Illus.). 24p. (ps-4). 1987. 10.95 o.s.i. (ISBN 0-13-814567-9). P-H.
Smetana. Brian Large. 473p. Repr. of 1970 ed. lib. bdg. 59.00 o.p. (Pub. by Am Repr Serv). Reprint Servs.
SMGP Rd-Sp Cht, Set 8. Kottmeyer. Date not set. (ISBN 0-07-033714-0). McGraw.
SMGP Rd-Sp Tm, Set A. Kottmeyer. Date not set. (ISBN 0-07-033713-6). McGraw.
SMGP Rd-Sp Tm, Set B. Kottmeyer. Date not set. (ISBN 0-07-033716-0). McGraw.
SMGP Rd-Sp Web, Set B. Kottmeyer. Date not set. (ISBN 0-07-033715-2). McGraw.
Smile & the Cry: Memoirs of a Lithuanian Woman. Julia M. Urban. (Illus.). 1979. 6.50 o.p. (ISBN 0-682-49409-7). Exposition-Phoenix.
Smile God Loves You: 59 Gospel Talks for Children to See & Hear. Lavern G. Franzen. LC 72-90257. 128p. (Orig.). 1973. pap. 5.50 o.p. (ISBN 0-8066-1304-1, 10-5840, Augsburg). Augsburg Fortress.
Smile in His Lifetime. Joseph Hansen. LC 80-21420. 312p. 1981. 13.95 o.p. (ISBN 0-03-056064-0). H Holt & Co.
Smile! Jesus Is Lord: Fifty Messages for Children to See & Hear. Lavern G. Franzen. LC 74-14175. 112p. (Orig.). (gr. 3 up). 1975. pap. 5.50 o.p. (ISBN 0-8066-1458-7, 10-5842, Augsburg). Augsburg Fortress.
Smile of Blazing Wings & Other Plays. Sid Sondergard. 1978. 5.00 o.p. (ISBN 0-682-49023-7). Exposition-Phoenix.
Smile Worm - Who Am I? What Will I Be? Betty S. Hinson. 48p. 1987. 6.95 o.p. (ISBN 0-8062-3036-3). Carlton.
Smiles Make Fewer Wrinkles. Lousie G. Doughty. 58p. 1985. 5.95 o.p. (ISBN 0-533-06214-4). Vantage.
Smith Agama Collection: Sanskrit Books & Manuscripts Relating to Pancaratra Studies-a Descriptive Catalog. H. Daniel Smith. LC 78-9149. (Foreign & Comparative Studies Program, South Asian Special Publications Ser.: No. 2). 1978. pap. text ed. 9.00x o.p. (ISBN 0-915984-79-2). Syracuse U Foreign Comp.
Smith, Marx & After: Ten Essays in the Development of Economic Thought. Ronald L. Meek. 1977. 27.00 o.p. (ISBN 0-412-14360-7, NO. 6199, Pub. by Chapman & Hall). Routledge Chapman & Hall.
Smithereened Apart: A Critique of Hart Crane. Samuel Hazo. LC 62-22179. (Illus.). x, 146p. 1977. 10.00x o.p. (ISBN 0-8214-0373-7); pap. 4.95x o.p. (ISBN 0-8214-0383-4). Ohio U Pr.
Smith's Review of Torts. 4th ed. Myron G. Hill, Jr. et al. LC 83-6847. (Smith's Review Ser.). 320p. 1983. pap. text ed. 13.95 o.p. (ISBN 0-314-71911-3). West Pub.
Smithsonian Book of Flight for Young People. LC 87-35912. (Illus.). 128p. (gr. 3-7). 1988. PLB 16.95 o.p. (ISBN 0-689-31422-1, Atheneum Childrens Bks). Macmillan.
Smithsonian Collection of Classic Jazz. Ed. by Martin Williams. 48p. 1973. records & booklet 45.00x o.p. (ISBN 0-393-09300-X). Norton.
Smithy of Burgwald. Gershon Kranzler. saddle-stitched 5.00 o.p. (ISBN 0-87559-135-3). Shalom.
SMM6 Handbook: Guidelines for Architects, Quantity Surveyors, Estimators, Contractors. Dearle Practice & Henderson Practice. 150p. 1979. pap. 12.00x o.p. (ISBN 0-246-11406-1, Pub by Granada England). Sheridan.
Smoke Away! May Wilson. 1981. pap. 1.15 o.p. (ISBN 0-85363-138-7). OMF Bks.
Smoke Control in Fire Safety Design. D. G. Butcher & A. C. Parnell. 1979. 45.00x o.p. (ISBN 0-419-11190-5, Pub. by E & FN Spon, NO. 6558). Routledge Chapman & Hall.
Smoke Detector. Eric Wright. (Nightingale Paperbacks). 1985. pap. 10.95 o.p. (ISBN 0-8161-3900-8, Large Print Bks). G K Hall.
Smoke Detector: An Inspector Charlie Salter Mystery. Eric Wright. 192p. 1984. 12.95 o.p. (ISBN 0-684-18191-6). Scribner.
Smoke Detectors: A Bibliographical Overview. Coppa & Avery Consultants Staff. (Architecture Ser.: A 1510). 9p. 1985. 2.00 o.p. (ISBN 0-89028-660-4). Vance Biblios.
Smoke of London: Two Prophecies. Ed. by James P. Lodge, Jr. Incl. Fumifugium or, The Inconvenience of the Aer-Smoake of London Dissipated. John Evelyn; The Doom of London. Robert Barr. 7.50 o.s.i. (ISBN 0-08-022309-5). Pergamon.
Smoke on the Mountain: An Interpretation of the Ten Commandments. Joy Davidman. LC 85-7622. 140p. 1970. pap. 5.95 o.s.i. (ISBN 0-664-24919-1, Westminster). Westminster John Knox.
Smoke Ring. Larry Niven. 1987. 16.45 o.p. (ISBN 0-345-30256-7, Del Rey). Ballantine.
Smoke Ring: Tobacco, Money & Multinational Politics. Peter Taylor. 352p. 1984. 18.45 o.p. (ISBN 0-394-53213-9). Pantheon.
Smoke Rings over the Valley. Ray Gallinger. 1983. 7.95 o.s.i. (ISBN 0-932052-32-0). North Country.
Smokers' Humour. Joel Rothman. 78p. 1985. pap. 2.95 o.p. (ISBN 0-86051-218-5). Parkwest Pubns.
Smokey the Shark & Other Fishy Tales. Charles Keller. (Illus.). 48p. (gr. 3-7). 1984. pap. 4.95 o.s.i. (ISBN 0-13-814690-X). P-H.
Smoking & Aging. Raymond Bosse & Charles L. Rose. LC 81-48002. 272p. 1984. 37.00x o.p. (ISBN 0-669-05230-2). Lexington Bks.

Smoking & Health: A Report of the British Medical Association Professional Division. British Medical Association. LC 85-2641. 192p. 1986. pap. 14.50 o.p. (ISBN 0-471-90937-8, Dist. by A R Liss). Wiley.

Smoking Gun: How the American Tobacco Industry Gets Away with Murder. Elizabeth Whelan. LC 84-50685. 224p. 1984. 15.95 o.p. (ISBN 0-89313-039-7). G F Stickley Co.

Smoky Mountain Dreams: The Life Story of Edith Wilson Heston. Brenda P. Russell. 192p. 1987. 11.95 o.p. (ISBN 0-8062-3072-X). Carlton.

Smooth Muscle Contractions. Stephens. 744p. 1984. 89.75 o.p. (ISBN 0-8247-1727-9). Dekker.

Smudge. Illus. by Mike Dickinson. (Illus.). 32p. 1988. 12.95 o.p. (ISBN 0-89659-818-7). Abbeville Pr.

Smuggler see Heinemann Guided Readers.

Smut: True Experiences from "Straight to Hell" Boyd McDonald. pap. 12.00 o.s.i. Gay Pr NY.

SN Distribution of Grocery Store Sales, 1987. 10th ed. Fairchild Special Projects Division Staff. 320p. 1987. pap. 45.00 o.p. (ISBN 0-87005-565-8). Fairchild.

SN Distribution Study of Grocery Store Sales. Fairchild Special Projects Division Staff. 310p. 1985. pap. 45.00 o.p. (ISBN 0-87005-501-1). Fairchild.

Snack Food Technology. 2nd ed. Samuel A. Matz. (Illus.). 1984. 49.95 o.p. (ISBN 0-87055-460-3). AVI.

Snail. Richard Miller. LC 83-13020. (Illus.). 320p. 1984. 16.95 o.p. (ISBN 0-03-063311-7, Owl Bks.). H Holt & Co.

Snail. Richard Miller. LC 83-13020. 304p. 1985. pap. 7.95 o.p. (ISBN 0-03-063309-5, Owl Bks.). H Holt & Co.

Snake in the Sandtrap: And Other Misadventures on the Pro Golf Tour. Lee Trevino & Sam Blair. LC 85-8463. (Illus.). 192p. 1985. 13.95 o.p. (ISBN 0-03-002889-2). H Holt & Co.

Snake Tales Pencil Puzzle Book. 48p. (gr. k-3). 1984. pap. 1.50 o.p. (ISBN 0-448-23377-0, G&D); pap. 36.00 set of 24 o.p. (ISBN 0-448-81724-1, G&D). Putnam Pub Group.

Snake: The Candid Autobiography of Football's Most Outrageous Renegade. Ken Stabler & Berry Stainback. LC 86-2115. (Illus.). 256p. 1986. 15.95 o.p. (ISBN 0-385-23450-3). Doubleday.

Snake Versus Man. Johan Marais. 102p. 1985. 7.95 o.p. (ISBN 0-86954-267-2, Pub. by Macmillan S Africa). Intl Spec Bk.

Snakes. Nina Leen. LC 77-13917. (Illus.). (gr. 5 up). 1978. 7.95 o.p. (ISBN 0-03-039926-2). H Holt & Co.

Snakes of South America. Marcos A. Freiberg. (Illus.). 192p. 1982. 14.95 o.p. (ISBN 0-87666-912-7, PS-758). TFH Pubns.

Snap! Photography. Miriam Cooper. LC 81-88. (Illus.). 64p. (gr. 3 up). 1981. 8.59 o.p. (ISBN 0-671-34021-2). Messner.

Snapshot. Ed. by Jonathan Green. LC 74-18754. (Illus.). 128p. 1974. 20.00 o.p. (ISBN 0-912334-67-3); pap. 12.50 o.p. (ISBN 0-912334-68-1). Aperture.

Snare of the Hunter. Helen MacInnes. LC 73-15427. 1974. 7.50 o.s.i. (ISBN 0-15-183180-7). HarBraceJ.

Snares of the Enemy. Pauline King. 208p. 1986. 13.95 o.p. (ISBN 0-684-18442-7, ScribT). Scribner.

Snarkout Boys & the Baconburg Horror. Daniel Pinkwater. LC 83-19544. 160p. (gr. 5 up). 1984. 11.75 o.p. (ISBN 0-688-02670-2). Lothrop.

Snatched by a Killer Wave. Glen Wright. Ed. by Carol Murphy. (Illus.). (gr. 3-6). 1981. PLB 6.95 o.p. (ISBN 0-89868-114-6, Read Res); pap. text ed. 4.95 o.p. (ISBN 0-89868-121-9, Read Res). ARO Pub.

Sneakers. Karen Markoe & Louis Phillips. (Funnybones Ser.). (Illus.). 64p. (gr. 3-7). 1981. pap. 1.50 o.s.i. (ISBN 0-671-42117-4). Wanderer Bks.

Sneaking Through Sociology: An Instructional System for the Introductory Course. T. W. Craighead. 1970. pap. text ed. 9.50x o.p. (ISBN 0-8290-1190-0). Irvington.

Sniff in Time. Susan Saunders. LC 81-10763. (Illus.). 32p. (ps-3). 1982. 10.95 o.s.i. (ISBN 0-689-30890-6, Atheneum Childrens Bks). Macmillan.

Snippy & Snappy. Wanda Gag. (Illus.). (gr. 1-3). 1960. PLB 5.99 o.p. (ISBN 0-698-30319-9, Coward). Putnam Pub Group.

Snoggle. J. B. Priestley. LC 74-188966. (Illus.). 160p. (gr. 4-7). 1972. 5.95 o.p. (ISBN 0-15-276430-5, HJ). HarBraceJ.

Snohomish County Street Atlas & Directory, 1987. rev. ed. Thomas Bros. Maps Staff. (Illus.). 100p. 1986. pap. 11.95 o.p. (ISBN 0-88130-193-0). Thomas Bros Maps.

Snohomish County Street Atlas, 1986. Thomas Bros. Maps Staff. (Illus.). 100p. 1987. pap. 11.95 o.p. (ISBN 0-88130-141-8). Thomas Bros Maps.

Snookered. Donald Trelford. 208p. (Orig.). 1986. pap. 11.95 o.p. (ISBN 0-571-13640-0). Faber & Faber.

Snoopy Collection. J. C. Suares. 1982. pap. 9.95 o.s.i. (ISBN 0-345-30340-7). Ballantine.

Snoopy on Wheels. Charles M. Schulz. LC 82-60878. (Chunky Bks.). (Illus.). 28p. (ps). 1983. 2.95 o.p. (ISBN 0-394-85630-9). Random.

Snout to Snout. Daniel Kaminsky. 26p. 1974. pap. 2.50 o.p. (ISBN 0-914946-49-8). Cleveland St Univ Poetry Ctr.

Snow. Jennifer Levin. 416p. 1984. 15.50 o.s.i. (ISBN 0-671-47314-X, Poseidon). PB.

Snow & the Sun: A South American Folk Rhyme in Two Languages. Antonio Frasconi. LC 61-12342. (gr. k-3). 1961. 6.95 o.p. (ISBN 0-15-276565-4, HJ). HarBraceJ.

Snow Ball. A. R. Gurney. LC 84-10971. 1984. 15.95 o.p. (ISBN 0-87795-621-9, Arbor Hse). Morrow.

Snow Country, Autumn, Winter & Spring in Yellowstone. Steven Fuller & Jeremy Schmidt. (Illus.). 48p. o.p. (ISBN 0-934948-03-8). Yellowstone Assn.

Snow Gods. Herbert Burkholz. LC 84-45612. 512p. 1985. 19.95 o.p. (ISBN 0-689-11509-1, Atheneum). Macmillan.

Snow on Snow. Maura Stanton. (Younger Poets Ser.: No. 70). 96p. 1975. 14.95t o.p. (ISBN 0-300-01866-5); pap. 7.95x o.p. (ISBN 0-300-01867-3). Yale U Pr.

Snow Papers: A Memoir of Illusion, Power-Lust & Cocaine. Richard Smart. Ed. by Joyce Johnson. LC 85-47996. 320p. 1985. 16.95 o.p. (ISBN 0-87113-030-0). Atlantic Monthly.

Snow Queen. Hans Christian Andersen. LC 68-18440. (Illus.). (gr. 3-7). 1968. 6.95 o.p. (ISBN 0-689-30018-2, Atheneum). Macmillan.

Snow Queen. Marcia Brown & Hans Christian Andersen. LC 72-168499. (Illus.). 96p. (gr. 1-5). 1972. 6.95 o.s.i. (ISBN 0-684-12611-7, Pub. by Scribner). Macmillan.

Snow Queen. Joan D. Vinge. 560p. 1984. pap. 3.95 o.p. (ISBN 0-440-17749-9). Dell.

Snow Removal & Ice Control Techniques at Interchanges. (National Cooperative Highway Research Project Report). 90p. 1971. 5.20 o.p. (ISBN 0-309-02007-7). Transport Res Bd.

Snow Toward Evening: Poems. Melville Cane. LC 74-13258. 117p. (Orig.). 1974. pap. 3.50 o.p. (ISBN 0-15-683400-6, Harv). HarBraceJ.

Snow White. Donald Barthelme. LC 67-14324. 1967. pap. 6.95 o.s.i. (ISBN 0-689-70331-7, 191, Atheneum). Macmillan.

Snow White & Rose Red. Ed McBain. 1985. 14.95 o.p. (ISBN 0-03-002603-2). H Holt & Co.

Snow White & the Seven Dwarfs. Illus. by Nicky Marsh. (Children's Classics Ser.). 32p. (gr. k-3). 1988. 5.95 o.p. (ISBN 0-8249-8263-0). Ideals.

Snow White Syndrome: All about Envy. Betsy Cohen. 256p. 1987. 15.95 o.p. (ISBN 0-02-526970-4). Macmillan.

Snowball. Jimmy Sangster. (Rinehart Suspense Novel Ser.). 224p. 1986. 15.95 o.p. (ISBN 0-8050-0063-1). H Holt & Co.

Snowball Fight in the White House. Louise L. Davis. LC 73-15782. (Illus.). 64p. (gr. 6-9). 1974. 3.50 o.s.i. (ISBN 0-664-32539-4, Westminster). Westminster John Knox.

Snowblind. Robert Sabbag. 1978. pap. 3.50 o.p. (ISBN 0-380-01868-3, 60116-8). Avon.

Snowblind Moon: A Novel of the West. John B. Cooke. 687p. 1985. 18.45 o.p. (ISBN 0-671-45089-1). S&S.

Snowed-in Book. Albert B. Paine. Ed. by Thom Roberts. (Illus.). (gr. 2-6). 1974. pap. 1.25 o.p. (ISBN 0-380-00149-7, 18960, Camelot). Avon.

Snowflakes in the Desert. Gerald D. Coverdale. 1977. 6.00 o.p. (ISBN 0-682-48706-6). Exposition-Phoenix.

Snowmobile Service. 1985. pap. 11.95 o.p. (ISBN 0-87288-034-6). Intertec Pub.

Snowshoe. Monte Miller. LC 82-83035. (Illus.). 32p. (Orig.). (ps). 1983. pap. 3.95 o.p. (ISBN 0-914766-88-0, 0266). Illum Way Pub.

Snowshoe Book. William Osgood & Leslie Hurley. LC 75-4769. (Illus.). 160p. 1975. (ISBN 0-8289-0222-4); pap. 7.95 o.p. (ISBN 0-8289-0221-6). Greene.

Snowshoeing. 2nd ed. Gene Prater. LC 80-21452. (Illus.). 176p. (Orig.). 1980. pap. 8.95 o.p. (ISBN 0-916890-98-8). Mountaineers.

Snowthrower Service. 1985. pap. 6.95 o.p. (ISBN 0-87288-016-8). Intertec Pub.

Snubber Design Applications & Minimization Methods. Ed. by F. M. Frederickson. (PVP Ser.: Vol. 55). 75p. 1981. 14.00 o.p. (ISBN 0-686-34515-0, H00191). ASME.

Snuff Bottles & Other Stories. Deng Youmei et al. Tr. by Gladys Yang from Chinese. 220p. (Orig.). 1987. pap. 5.95 o.p. (ISBN 0-8351-1607-7). China Bks.

Snug Little House. Eils M. Lewis. LC 80-24282. (Illus.). 32p. (ps-3). 1981. 9.95 o.p. (ISBN 0-689-50177-3, Atheneum). Macmillan.

Snuggle & Read, 6 vols. 1983. Boxed Set. pap. 13.50 o.s.i. (ISBN 0-380-84905-4, Camelot). Avon.

Snyder's Walk. Thomas B. Morgan. LC 86-16224. 360p. 1987. pap. 17.95 o.p. (ISBN 0-385-23637-9, Dolp). Doubleday.

So Big! Harriet Ziefert. LC 86-61785. (Look-at-Me Bks). (Illus.). 14p. (ps). 1987. 2.95 o.s.i. (ISBN 0-394-88555-4, BYR). Random.

So Busy! Harriet Ziefert. LC 86-61787. (Look-at-Me Books). (Illus.). 14p. (ps). 1987. 2.95 o.s.i. (ISBN 0-394-88557-0, BYR). Random.

So Call It a Mitzvah. Walter Weiner. 1978. 6.00 o.p. (ISBN 0-682-49116-0). Exposition-Phoenix.

So Called Historical Jesus & the Historic Biblical Christ. Martin Kahler. Tr. by Carl E. Braaten from Ger. LC 64-12994. 168p. 1964. pap. 3.75 o.p. (ISBN 0-8006-1960-9, 1-1960, Fortress). Augsburg Fortress.

So Clean! Harriet Ziefert. LC 86-61786. (Look-at-Me Books). (Illus.). 14p. (ps). 1987. 2.95 o.s.i. (ISBN 0-394-88556-2, BYR). Random.

So Dangerous My Love. Carol Gaye. (Lythway Ser.). 256p. 1988. lib. bdg. 19.50x o.p. (ISBN 0-7451-0683-8, Pub. by Chivers Pr UK). G K Hall.

So Dear to Me. Winifred A. Mole. 1985. 11.95 o.p. (ISBN 0-533-06486-4). Vantage.

So Far, So Good, So What? Women's Studies in the U. K. Ed. by R. Duelli-Klein. 100p. 1984. pap. 19.25 o.p. (ISBN 0-08-030816-3). Pergamon.

So Grand. Christopher Logan. 416p. (Orig.). 1985. pap. 3.95 o.s.i. (ISBN 0-449-12713-3, GM). Fawcett.

So Help Me God: A Calendar of Quick Prayers for Half-Skeptics. J. Geddes MacGregor. LC 72-97263. 1970. 3.95 o.p. (ISBN 0-8192-1104-4). Morehouse Pub.

So High the Price. P. J. Kelley. LC 68-28104. (St. Paul Editions). 1968. 3.00 o.p. (ISBN 0-8198-0148-8). Dghtrs St Paul.

So I Was a Sergeant: Memoirs of an Occupation Soldier. Walter C. Krause. 1978. 10.00 o.p. (ISBN 0-682-49139-X). Exposition-Phoenix.

So ist es! A Contemporary Reader. Kimberly Sparks & Edith Reichmann. (Illus.). 90p. 1972. pap. text ed. 7.95 o.p. (ISBN 0-15-581382-X, HC). HarBraceJ.

So Little! Harriet Ziefert & Mavis Smith. LC 86-61788. (Look-at-Me-Books). (Illus.). 14p. (ps). 1987. 2.95 o.s.i. (ISBN 0-394-88558-9, BYR). Random.

So Little Cause for Caroline. Eric Bercovici. LC 81-65999. 1981. 10.95 o.p. (ISBN 0-689-11176-2, Atheneum). Macmillan.

So Long, Scout, & Other Stories of Maine. Gerald E. Lewis. (Illus.). 224p. (Orig.). 1987. pap. text ed. 9.90 o.p. (ISBN 0-916153-03-7). Ten Thirty Pr.

So Many Kingdoms. Jeanne Williams. 384p. 1986. pap. 3.95 o.p. (ISBN 0-380-75091-0). Avon.

So Many Raccoons. Jan Wahl. LC 85-7779. (Illus.). 42p. (gr. 2-3). lib. bdg. 9.45 o.s.i. Caedmon.

So Much That Is New: Baldwin Spencer. D. J. Mulvaney & J. H. Calaby. 492p. 1985. 35.00 o.p. (ISBN 0-522-84169-4, Melbourne U Pr). Intl Spec Bk.

So Near, Yet So Far Away. Mary R. Dees. Ed. by Mary Penoi. LC 85-90849. (Illus.). 191p. 1985. hdbk. 14.95 o.p. (ISBN 0-942316-10-X). Pueblo Pub Pr.

So, Nothing Is Forever. Adrienne Jones. LC 74-9381. (Illus.). 256p. (gr. 7 up). 1974. 6.95 o.p. (ISBN 0-395-19499-7). HM.

So Now You're a Principal. rev. ed. Mel Heller. Ed. by T. Koerner. 48p. 1982. pap. 5.75 o.p. (ISBN 0-88210-068-8). Natl Assn Principals.

So Send I You. Ralph M. Riggs. 128p. 1965. 1.25 o.p. (ISBN 0-88243-587-6, 02-0587). Gospel Pub.

So Short a Time. Barbara Gelb. LC 73-6630. (Illus.). 288p. 1973. 7.95 o.p. (ISBN 0-393-07478-1). Norton.

So That It Flower: A Gathering of Poems. Melville Cane. LC 66-15015. 1966. 9.95 o.p. (ISBN 0-15-183850-X). HarBraceJ.

So the Witch Won't Eat Me: Fantasy & the Child's Fear of Infanticide. Dorothy Bloch. 1978. 9.95 o.p. (ISBN 0-395-26290-9). HM.

So What About History. Edmund S. Morgan. LC 69-13533. (Illus.). (gr. 7 up). 1969. PLB 5.95 o.p. (ISBN 0-689-20663-1, Atheneum). Macmillan.

So What If I'm a Sore Loser? Barbara Williams. LC 80-24783. (Illus.). 48p. (ps-3). 1981. 8.95 o.p. (ISBN 0-15-277260-X, HJ). HarBraceJ.

So Who Hasn't Got Problems? Marjorie Franco. 160p. (gr. 7 up). 1979. 6.95 o.p. (ISBN 0-395-27814-7). HM.

So You Are Looking for a New Job... Now What? George D. Moffett, Jr. 109p. 1983. 6.00 o.p. (ISBN 0-682-49953-6). Exposition-Phoenix.

So You Have a Retinal Detachment: A Guide for Patients. Fred M. Wilson. (Illus.). 136p. 1978. spiral bdg. 18.25 o.p. (ISBN 0-398-03700-0). C C Thomas.

So You Think You Know Your Boyfriend-Girlfriend? Bruce Nash. Ed. by Meg Schneider. (Flip-Overs Ser.). 64p. (Orig.). (gr. 3-7). 1982. pap. 2.85 o.s.i. (ISBN 0-671-45548-6). Wanderer Bks.

So You Think You Know Your Brother-Sister? Bruce Nash. Ed. by Meg Schneider. (Flip-Overs Ser.). 64p. (Orig.). (gr. 3-7). 1982. pap. 2.85 o.s.i. (ISBN 0-671-45549-4). Wanderer Bks.

So You Think You've Got Problems: Twelve Stubborn Saints & Their Pushy Parents. Sharon Nastick. LC 81-85454. (Illus.). 96p. (Orig.). (gr. 5 up). 1982. pap. 3.95 o.p. (ISBN 0-87973-661-5, 661). Our Sunday Visitor.

So You Want a Successful HERO Program. Margaret V. Rourke & Christine A. Gentry. Ed. by Elizabeth Simpson. (Careers in Home Economics Ser.). 1979. text ed. 19.60 o.p. (ISBN 0-07-023176-1). McGraw.

So You Want to Be a Dancer. William E. Thomas. LC 78-26247. (Illus.). 128p. (gr. 4 up). 1979. lib. bdg. 8.79 o.s.i. (ISBN 0-671-32993-6). Messner.

So You Want to Be a Leader. Kenneth O. Gangel. pap. 3.45 o.p. (ISBN 0-87509-131-8); leaders guide 2.95 o.p. (ISBN 0-87509-298-5). Chr Pubns.

So You Want to Be a Rock & Roll Star. Rev. ed. S. Lawrence. 224p. 1983. pap. text ed. 6.95 o.p. (ISBN 0-07-036723-X). McGraw.

So You Want to Build a House. Peter Hotton. (Illus.). 256p. (Orig.). 1976. pap. 13.45i o.p. (ISBN 0-316-37386-9). Little.

So You Want to Buy a Word Processor? Helen Harris & Ela Chauhan. 147p. (Orig.). 1982. pap. text ed. 24.90x o.p. (ISBN 0-09-150351-5, Pub. by Busn Bks England). Gower Pub Co.

So You Want to Go Back to School. Marjorie Lenz & Marjorie Shaevitz. (Illus.). 1977. pap. text ed. 14.95 o.p. (ISBN 0-07-037178-4). McGraw.

So You Want to Go to Law School. John F. Dobbyn. LC 76-19202. 1976. pap. 6.95 o.p. (ISBN 0-685-71466-7). West Pub.

So You Want to Grow. Luis Palau. LC 86-80720. 1986. pap. 4.95 o.p. (ISBN 0-89081-554-2). Harvest Hse.

So You Want to Plan a Birthday Party. Catherine A. Durkin et al. LC 79-22279. (Illus.). (gr. 4 up). 1980. 11.95 o.p. (ISBN 0-689-30760-8, Atheneum); pap. 6.95 o.p. Macmillan.

So You Want to Start a Restaurant? rev. ed. Dewey A. Dyer. 160p. 1983. 19.95 o.p. (ISBN 0-8436-2199-0). Van Nos Reinhold.

Soap Opera Babylon. Jason Bonderoff. (Illus.). 128p. 1987. pap. 8.95 o.p. (ISBN 0-399-51291-8, Perigee). Putnam Pub Group.

Soap Opera Encyclopedia. Christopher Schemering. (Orig.). 1985. pap. 8.95 o.p. (ISBN 0-345-32459-5). Ballantine.

Soap World. Robert LaGuardia. (Illus.). 1983. 22.95 o.p. (ISBN 0-87795-482-8, Arbor Hse). Morrow.

Soap World. Robert LaGuardia. LC 83-72889. (Illus.). 408p. 1984. pap. 12.95 o.p. (ISBN 0-87795-639-1, Arbor Hse). Morrow.

SOAR: A Program for the Gifted - Parent's Guidebook. Charlotte Reid & John D. Reid. Ed. by Janet Lovelady. (Illus.). 40p. (Orig.). 1982. pap. 4.95 o.p. (ISBN 0-935266-11-9, GI-228). Jalmar Pr.

SOAR: A Program for the Gifted Using Bloom's Taxonomy - Student's Workbook. Janet Lovelady. (Illus.). 40p. (Orig.). 1982. pap. 4.95 o.p. (ISBN 0-935266-10-0, GI-227). Jalmar Pr.

SOAR: A Program for the Gifted Using Bloom's Taxonomy - Teacher's Guidebook. Charlotte Reid & John D. Reid. Ed. by Janet Lovelady. (Illus.). 40p. (Orig.). 1982. pap. 4.95 o.p. (ISBN 0-935266-09-7, GI-226). Jalmar Pr.

Sobek Adventure Vacations. 4th ed. Ed. by Sobek's International Explorers Society Staff. (Illus.). 160p. 1986. lib. bdg. 24.80 o.p. (ISBN 0-89471-429-5); pap. 12.95 o.p. (ISBN 0-89471-428-7). Running Pr.

Sobibor: Martyrdom & Revolt. Ed. by Miriam Novitch. LC 79-57354. (Illus.). 168p. (Orig.). 1980. pap. 10.95 o.p. (ISBN 0-89604-016-X). Holocaust Pubns.

Sobriquets & Nicknames. Albert R. Frey. LC 66-22671. 488p. 1966. Repr. of 1888 ed. 40.00x o.p. (ISBN 0-8103-3003-2). Gale.

Sobs That Bloom: A Novel. Mridula Sinha. 132p. 1986. text ed. 15.95x o.p. (ISBN 0-7069-3105-X, Pub. by Vikas India). Advent NY.

Soccer. Mike Yaxley. (Competitive Sports Ser.). (Illus.). 64p. (YA) (gr. 5 up). 1982. 17.95 o.s.i. (ISBN 0-7134-3980-7, Pub. by Batsford England). David & Charles.

Soccer for Young Champions. 7th ed. Robert J. Antonacci. (Young Champions Ser.). (Illus.). (gr. 4-6). 1978. text ed. 10.95 o.p. (ISBN 0-07-002147-3). McGraw.

Soccer Is for Me. Lowell A. Dickmeyer. LC 77-92294. (Sports for Me Bks.). (Illus.). (gr. 2-5). 1978. PLB 7.95 o.p. (ISBN 0-8225-1076-6). Lerner Pubns.

Soccer: Techniques & Tactics. European Syndicate of Soccer Experts Staff. Ed. by Jeff Cross. Tr. by Wendy Gill from Ger. Orig. Title: Fussball Perfekt. (Illus.). 1978. pap. 5.95 o.p. (ISBN 0-89149-028-0). Jolex.
Social Administration: The Management of the Social Services. Ed. by Simon Slavin. Date not set. 15.00 o.s.i. Coun Soc WK Ed.
Social & Economic Characteristics of the Population in Metro & Nonmetro Counties, 1970-80. David A. McGranahan et al. (Agriculture Department Rural Development Research Report 58). (Illus.). 74p. 1986. pap. 3.75 o.p. (ISBN 0-318-21607-8, S/N 001-019-00442-8). USGPO.
Social & Economic Environment of Black Farmers. Robert A. Hoppe. (Agriculture A Department Rural Developement Research Report 61 Ser.). (Illus.). 23p. 1986. pap. 1.25 o.p. (ISBN 0-318-21572-1, S/M 001-019-00463-1). USGPO.
Social & Economic Factors in Transportation Planning. (Transportation Research Record Ser.). 72p. 1976. 3.20 o.p. (ISBN 0-309-02596-6). Transport Res Bd.
Social & Economic Perspectives on Irrigation. Ed. by Ian Carruthers. 100p. 1981. pap. 26.00 o.p. (ISBN 0-08-026780-7). Pergamon.
Social & Foreign Affairs in Iraq. Saddam Hussein. Tr. by Khalid W. Kishtainy. 123p. 1979. 25.00 o.p. (ISBN 0-7099-0061-9, Pub. by Croom Helm Ltd). Routledge Chapman & Hall.
Social & Personality Development. David R. Shaffer. LC 78-12032. (Psychology Ser.). (Illus.). 1979. text ed. 28.75 pub net o.p. (ISBN 0-8185-0289-4). Brooks-Cole.
Social & Political Conflict in Prussia, 1858-1864. Eugene N. Anderson. 1968. lib. bdg. 31.50x o.p. (ISBN 0-374-90266-6, Octagon). Hippocrene Bks.
Social & Political History of the German 1848 Revolution. Rudolph Stadelmann. Tr. by James G. Chastain from Ger. LC 74-27711. Orig. Title: Soziale und Politis Che Geschichet der Revolution Von 1848. xvi, 218p. 1975. 15.00x o.p. (ISBN 0-8214-0177-7). Ohio U Pr.
Social & Political Ideas of Some English Thinkers of the Augustan Age, A.D. 1650-1750. A Series of Lectures Delivered at King's College University of London during the Session 1927-28. Ed. by F. J. Hearnshaw. LC 83-1518. 246p. 1983. Repr. of 1950 ed. lib. bdg. 35.00x o.p. (ISBN 0-313-23860-X, HAUG). Greenwood.
Social & Political Ideas of Some Representative Thinkers of the Revolutionary Era: A Series of Lectures Delivered at King's College University of London during the Session 1929-30. Ed. by F. J. Hearnshaw. LC 83-1519. 251p. 1983. Repr. of 1950 ed. lib. bdg. 35.00x o.p. (ISBN 0-313-23863-4, HREV). Greenwood.
Social & Political Perspectives in the Thought of Soren Kierkegaard. David B. Fletcher. LC 81-43716. 88p. 1983. lib. bdg. 24.25 o.p. (ISBN 0-8191-2689-6); pap. text ed. 8.75 o.p. (ISBN 0-8191-2690-X). U Pr of Amer.
Social & Religious Heretics in Five Centuries. Carl Heath. LC 78-147622. (Library of War & Peace; Non-Resis. & Non-Vio.). 1972. lib. bdg. 46.00 o.p. (ISBN 0-8240-0397-7). Garland Pub.
Social & Religious Themes in English Art, 1840-1860. Lindsay Errington. LC 83-48701. (Theses from the Courtauld Institute of Art Ser.). (Illus.). 584p. 1984. lib. bdg. 70.00 o.p. (ISBN 0-8240-5977-8). Garland Pub.
Social & Vocational Rehabilitation Resources: Africa, Vol. 1. x, 230p. (Orig., Eng. & Fr.). 1984. pap. 14.00 o.p. (ISBN 92-2-003776-9). Intl Labour Office.
Social Anthropology & Law. I. Hamnett. 1977. 44.00 o.p. (ISBN 0-12-322350-4). Acad Pr.
Social Anthropology of North American Tribes. enl. ed. Fred Eggan et al. LC 55-5123. 574p. 1972. pap. 3.95 o.s.i. (ISBN 0-226-19074-9, P473, Phoen). U of Chicago Pr.
Social Area Analysis. Eshref Shevky & Wendell Bell. LC 75-147222. (Illus.). 70p. 1972. Repr. of 1955 ed. lib. bdg. 22.50x o.p. (ISBN 0-8371-5987-3, SHAA). Greenwood.
Social Auditing: Evaluating the Impact of Corporate Programs. David H. Blake et al. LC 76-2901. (Illus.). 176p. 1976. 18.95 o.p.; pap. text ed. 16.95 o.p. (ISBN 0-275-91466-6, B1466). Praeger.
Social Basis of Criminal Justice: Ethical Issues for the Eighty's. Frank Schmalleger & Robert Gustafson. LC 80-6175. 328p. (Orig.). 1981. lib. bdg. 29.75 o.p. (ISBN 0-8191-1685-8); pap. text ed. 14.50 o.p. (ISBN 0-8191-1686-6). U Pr of Amer.
Social Basis of Religion. Simon Patten. (Neglected American Economists Ser.). 1974. lib. bdg. 61.00 o.p. (ISBN 0-8240-1028-0). Garland Pub.
Social Behavior & Organization Among Vertebrates. Ed. by William Etkin. LC 64-13974. (Illus.). 1964. lib. bdg. 15.00x o.s.i. (ISBN 0-226-22036-2). U of Chicago Pr.
Social Behavior: Its Elementary Forms. rev. ed. George C. Homans. 386p. 1974. text ed. 16.00 o.p. (ISBN 0-15-581417-6, HC). HarBraceJ.
Social Biology of the Bushy-Tailed Woodrat, Neotoma Cinerea. Peter Escherich. (UC Publications in Zoology: Vol. 110). 1982. pap. 17.50x o.p. (ISBN 0-520-09595-2). U of Cal Pr.
Social Care Research. Jack Barnes. 163p. 1978. pap. text ed. 12.15x o.p. (ISBN 0-7199-0947-3, Pub. by Bedford England). Gower Pub Co.
Social Change. Roberta A. Gardner. 1977. pap. 16.50 o.p. (ISBN 0-395-30599-3). HM.
Social Change. Steven Vago. 1980. text ed. 27.95 o.p. (ISBN 0-03-040771-0). HR&W.
Social Change & New Profiles of Educational Personnel: National Studies: India, Nepal, Philippines, Republic of Korea. Asian Programme of Educational Innovation for Development. 44p. 1981. pap. 5.00 o.p. (ISBN 0-686-81854-7, UB100, UB). UNIPUB.
Social Change & Political Development in Weimar Germany. Ed. by Richard Bessel & E. J. Feuchtwanger. LC 80-41179. 298p. 1981. 28.50x o.p. (ISBN 0-389-20176-6, 06952). B&N Imports.
Social Change & Rural Development: Intervention or Participation - A Zambian Case Study. M. Nelson-Richards. LC 80-5686. 162p. 1982. lib. bdg. 25.50 o.p. (ISBN 0-8191-2291-2); pap. text ed. 10.00 o.p. (ISBN 0-8191-2292-0). U Pr of Amer.
Social Change & the Aged: Recent Trends in the United States. Fred C. Pampel. LC 79-4752. (Illus.). 240p. 1981. 25.00x o.p. (ISBN 0-669-02928-9). Lexington Bks.
Social Change & the Growth of British Power in the Gold Coast: The Fante States Eighteen Hundred & Seven to Eighteen Seventy-Four. Mary McCarthy. LC 83-7019. 208p. (Orig.). 1983. lib. bdg. 27.50 o.p. (ISBN 0-8191-3148-2); pap. text ed. 13.25 o.p. (ISBN 0-8191-3149-0). U Pr of Amer.
Social Change & the Individual: Japan Before & After Defeat in World War II. Kazuko Tsurumi. 1970. 50.00x o.p. (ISBN 0-691-09347-4). Princeton U Pr.
Social Change & Training of Educational Personnel. 94p. 1983. pap. text ed. 6.50 o.p. (ISBN 0-686-88391-8, UB130, UNESCO Regional Office). UNIPUB.
Social Change at Work: The ICI Weekly Staff Agreement. Joe Roeber. LC 75-11849. 342p. 1975. 49.95x o.p. (ISBN 0-470-73000-5). Halsted Pr.
Social Change in a Hostile Environment: The Crusaders' Kingdom of Jerusalem. Aharon Ben-Ami. (Princeton Studies on the Near East Ser.). (Illus.). 1969. 28.50x o.p. (ISBN 0-691-09344-X). Princeton U Pr.
Social Change in Indian Society. R. Sinha. 1980. 12.50 o.p. (ISBN 0-391-02184-2). Humanities.
Social Change in the Twentieth-Century. Daniel Chirot. 1977. pap. text ed. 14.50 o.p. (ISBN 0-15-581420-6, HC). HarBraceJ.
Social Changes in a Peripheral Society: The Creation of a Balkan Colony. Ed. by Daniel Chirot. 1976. 38.00 o.p. (ISBN 0-12-173150-2). Acad Pr.
Social Class in the Contemporary United States. Ed. by Gerald Erickson & Harold L. Schwartz. LC 77-92856. (Studies in Marxism: Vol. 2). 101p. 1977. pap. 7.95x o.p. (ISBN 0-930656-04-0). MEP Pubns.
Social Class, Language & Education. Denis Lawton. (International Library of Sociology). 192p. 1968. pap. 9.95x o.p. (ISBN 0-7100-6895-6). Routledge Chapman & Hall.
Social Classes in Marxist Theory. Allin Cottress. 330p. 1985. 39.50x o.p. (ISBN 0-7100-9906-1). Routledge Chapman & Hall.
Social Cognition & Depression. Ed. by Nicholas A. Kuiper. E. Tory Higgins. LC 86-18453. 142p. 1985. pap. text ed. 10.00 o.p. (ISBN 0-89862-575-0). Guilford Pr.
Social Conditions in the United States: Materials Published 1980-1984. Mary Vance. (Public Administration Ser.: P 1700). 45p. 1985. 6.75 o.p. (ISBN 0-89028-450-4). Vance Biblios.
Social Construction of Communities. Gerald D. Suttles. LC 74-177310. (Studies of Urban Society). 1973. pap. text ed. 2.95x o.s.i. (ISBN 0-226-78190-9, P543, Phoen). U of Chicago Pr.
Social Context of Paul's Ministry: Tentmaking & Apostleship. Ronald F. Hock. LC 79-7381. 112p. 1980. 8.95 o.p. (ISBN 0-8006-0577-2, 1-577, Fortress). Augsburg Fortress.
Social Context of the New Testament: A Sociological Analysis. Derek Tidball. 160p. 1984. pap. 9.95 o.p. (ISBN 0-310-45391-7, 12602P). Zondervan.
Social Control. 2nd ed. Joseph S. Roucek. LC 70-111497. 606p. 1970. Repr. of 1956 ed. lib. bdg. 27.50x o.p. (ISBN 0-8371-4640-2, ROSO). Greenwood.
Social Control & Education. Brian Davies. 1976. pap. 7.50x o.p. (ISBN 0-416-55810-0, NO. 6369). Routledge Chapman & Hall.
Social Cost-Benefit Analysis: A Guide for Country & Project Economists to the Derivation & Application of Economic & Social Accounting Prices. Colin Bruce. (Working Paper: No. 239). iii, 143p. 1976. 8.00 o.p. (ISBN 0-8213-9191-7, WP-0239). World Bank.
Social Costs of Solar Energy: A Study of Photovoltaic Energy Systems. Thomas L. Neff. LC 80-23732. (Pergamon Policy Studies on Science & Technology). (Illus.). 110p. 1981. 24.00 o.p. (ISBN 0-08-026315-1). Pergamon.
Social Criticism & Nineteenth-Century American Fictions. Robert Shulman. LC 87-5933. 344p. 1987. text ed. 30.00 o.p. (ISBN 0-8262-0648-4). U of Mo Pr.
Social Criticism of Stephen Leacock: The Unsolved Riddle of Social Justice & Other Essays. Stephen Leacock. LC 73-78960. (Social History of Canada Ser.). 1973. pap. 6.95 o.p. (ISBN 0-8020-6201-6). U of Toronto Pr.
Social Development in Youth. Ed. by John A. Meacham & Nicolas R. Santilli. 184p. 1981. pap. 43.95 o.p. Transaction Pubs.
Social Development of Handicapped Children & Adolescents. Patrick J. Schloss. LC 83-11786. 1983. 34.00 o.p. (ISBN 0-89443-886-7). Aspen Pub.
Social Deviancy among Youth. Ed. by William W. Wattenberg. LC 66-2248. (National Society for the Study of Education Yearbooks Ser.: No. 65, Pt. 1). 1966. lib. bdg. 8.00x o.s.i. (ISBN 0-226-60081-5). U of Chicago Pr.
Social Dynamics of Development. David Pitt. 1976. text ed. 29.00 o.p. (ISBN 0-08-020533-X); pap. text ed. 14.00 o.p. (ISBN 0-08-020530-5). Pergamon.
Social, Economic, & Environmental Implications in Transportation Planning: Nine Reports. (Transportation Research Record Ser.). 95p. 1976. 4.00 o.p. (ISBN 0-309-02497-8). Transport Res Bd.
Social, Economic, Behavioral & Urban Growth Considerations, 9 reports. (Transportation Research Record Ser.). 65p. 1974. 4.20 o.p. (ISBN 0-309-02351-3). Transport Res Bd.
Social England under the Regency. John Ashton. LC 67-23940. 450p. 1968. Repr. of 1899 ed. 30.00x o.p. (ISBN 0-8103-3253-1). Gale.
Social Exchange in Developing Relationships. Ed. by Robert L. Burgess & Ted L. Huston. LC 79-6934. 1979. 39.00 o.p. (ISBN 0-12-143550-4). Acad Pr.
Social Exchange Theory: Structure & Influence in Social Psychology. J. K. Chadwick-Jones. (European Monographs in Social Psychology). 1976. 75.00 o.p. (ISBN 0-12-166350-7). Acad Pr.
Social Forces Influencing American Education. Ralph W. Tyler. LC 61-1759. (National Society for the Study of Education Yearbooks Ser: No. 60, Pt. 2). 1961. lib. bdg. 6.00x o.s.i. (ISBN 0-226-60061-0); pap. text ed. 4.50x o.s.i. (ISBN 0-226-60062-9). U of Chicago Pr.
Social Function of Art. Radhakamal Mukerjee. 1954. (ISBN 0-8022-1168-2). Philos Lib.
Social Functioning Framework: An Approach to the Human Behavior & Social Environment Sequence. Ruth M. Butler. 3.00 o.s.i. (70-320-01). Coun Soc WK Ed.
Social Hierarchy & Dominance. Ed. by Martin W. Schein. LC 74-26937. (Benchmark Papers in Animal Behavior, Ser. 3). 401p. 1975. 69.50 o.p. (ISBN 0-12-787419-4). Acad Pr.
Social History of England, Eighteen Fifty-One to Nineteen Eighty-Six. Francois Bedarida. Tr. by A. S. Forster. 448p. 1988. pap. text ed. 17.95 o.p. (ISBN 0-317-67351-3). Routledge Chapman & Hall.
Social History of England, Eighteen Fifty-One to Nineteen Seventy-Five. Francois Bedarida. 448p. 1979. 15.95x o.p. (ISBN 0-416-85910-0, NO. 2833); pap. 14.95x o.p. (ISBN 0-416-85920-8, NO. 2834). Routledge Chapman & Hall.
Social History of Housing, Eighteen Fifteen to Nineteen Eighty-Five. John Burnett. 384p. 1986. 39.95 o.p. (ISBN 0-416-36770-4, 1024). Routledge Chapman & Hall.
Social History of Housing Eighteen Fifteen to Nineteen Seventy. John Burnett. 352p. (Orig.). 1985. pap. 13.95 o.p. (ISBN 0-416-73720-X, NO. 9343). Routledge Chapman & Hall.
Social History of Music: From the Middle Ages to Beethoven & Music & Society since 1815. Henry Raynor. LC 78-58318. 1978. pap. 7.95 o.s.i. (ISBN 0-8008-7238-X, Crescendo). Taplinger.
Social History of Occupational Health. Ed. by Paul Weindling. LC 85-21286. 288p. 1985. 31.00 o.p. (ISBN 0-7099-3606-0, Pub. by Croom Helm Ltd). Routledge Chapman & Hall.
Social History of Scottish Dance: Ane Celestial Recreatioun. George S. Emmerson. (Illus.). 352p. 1972. 17.50 o.p. (ISBN 0-7735-0087-1, McGill Canada). U of Toronto Pr.
Social History of the French Revolution. Norman Hampson. 228p. 1987. pap. text ed. 11.95 o.p. (ISBN 0-7100-6525-6, Pub. by Routledge UK). Routledge Chapman & Hall.
Social History of the United States: A Guide to Information Sources. Ed. by Donald F. Tingley. LC 78-13196. (American Government & History Information Guide Ser.: Vol. 3). 272p. 1979. 68.00x o.p. (ISBN 0-8103-1366-9). Gale.
Social Idealism & the Problem of Objectivity. Tronn Overend. LC 82-17359. (Scholars' Library). 215p. 1983. text ed. 34.50x o.p. (ISBN 0-7022-1712-3). U of Queensland Pr.
Social Images & Process in Urban New Guinea: A Study of Port Moresby. Alan Rew. LC 74-17389. (AES Ser). 262p. 1974. text ed. 25.95 o.p. (ISBN 0-8299-0024-1). West Pub.
Social Impact Assessment, Monitoring, & Management by the Electric Energy Industry: State-of-the-Practice (AIF-NESP-012) Energy Impact Associates, Inc. Staff. (National Environmental Studies Project: NESP Reports). 150p. 1977. 45.00 o.p. (ISBN 0-318-13592-2); to NESP sponsors 15.00 o.p. (ISBN 0-318-13593-0). US Coun Energy Awareness.
Social Impact of Computers. Gerald A. Silver. 342p. 1979. pap. text ed. 12.00 o.p. (ISBN 0-15-581427-3, HC). HarBraceJ.
Social Impact of Oil: The Case of Peterhead. Robert Moore. 176p. 1982. 27.50x o.p. (ISBN 0-7100-0903-8). Routledge Chapman & Hall.
Social Implications of Industrialization & Urbanization in Africa South of the Sahara. International African Institute Staff. LC 72-12557. (Illus.). 743p. 1973. Repr. of 1956 ed. lib. bdg. 35.00x o.p. (ISBN 0-8371-6720-5, SIIU). Greenwood.
Social Indicators: An Annotated Bibliography of Current Literature. Kevin J. Gilmartin et al. LC 78-67062. (Library of Social Science). 137p. 1979. lib. bdg. 28.00 o.p. (ISBN 0-8240-9755-6). Garland Pub.
Social Influence & Social Change. Serge Moscovici. (European Monographs in Social Psychology Ser.). 1977. 55.50 o.p. (ISBN 0-12-508450-1). Acad Pr.
Social Information & Regulation of Social Development. V. Afanasyev. 363p. 1978. 5.95 o.p. (ISBN 0-8285-0437-7, Pub. by Progress Pubs USSR). Imported Pubns.
Social Innovations for Development. Ed. by C. G. Heden & A. King. (Illus.). 173p. 1984. 24.00 o.p. (ISBN 0-08-025770-4). Pergamon.
Social Insects. O. W. Richards. (Illus.). 212p. 1953. (ISBN 0-8022-1335-9). Philos Lib.
Social Integration of Migrant Workers & Other Ethnic Minorities: A Documentation of Current Research. Ed. by M. Herfurth et al. (Vienna Centre Ser.: No. 7). 290p. 1982. 35.00 o.p. (ISBN 0-08-028957-6). Pergamon.
Social Interaction & Ethnic Segregation. Ed. by Peter Jackson & Susan Smith. LC 81-67914. (Special Publications of the Institute of British Geographers Ser.: No. 12). 1982. 36.00 o.p. (ISBN 0-12-379080-8). Acad Pr.
Social Intercourse: From Greeting to Goodbye. Mark L. Knapp. 1978. pap. text ed. 18.00 net o.p. (4859618). Allyn.
Social Issues in Computing. C. C. Gotlieb & A. Borodin. (Computer Science & Applied Mathematics Ser.). 1973. 17.00 o.p. (ISBN 0-12-293750-3). Acad Pr.
Social Knowledge: An Essay on the Nature & Limits of Social Science. Paul Mattick, Jr. LC 84-27723. 144p. 1986. 25.00 o.p. (ISBN 0-87332-333-5). M E Sharpe.
Social Life of a Modern Community. William L. Warner. 1941. 20.00x o.p. (ISBN 0-686-83769-X). Elliots Bks.
Social Life of Britain's Five-Year Olds: A Report on the Child Health & Education Study. A. F. Osborn et al. (Routledge Educations Books). 272p. 1984. 29.95x o.p. (ISBN 0-7100-9618-6). Routledge Chapman & Hall.
Social Life of Monkeys & Apes. 2nd ed. S. Zuckerman. (Illus.). 496p. 1981. 39.95x o.p. (ISBN 0-7100-0691-8). Routledge Chapman & Hall.
Social Logics Conversations & Groups in Everyday Life: A Model for the Social Sciences. James H. Parker. LC 85-9111. 208p. (Orig.). 1985. text ed. 26.75 o.p. (ISBN 0-8191-4750-8); pap. text ed. 12.50 o.p. (ISBN 0-8191-4751-6). U Pr of Amer.
Social Mobility in Industrial Society: A Study of Political Sociology. Seymour M. Lipset & Reinhard Bendix. (Institute of Industrial Relations, UC Berkeley). 1959. pap. 5.95 o.p. (ISBN 0-520-00756-5). U of Cal Pr.
Social Mobility in Traditional China. W. Eberhard. 1962. 35.00 o.s.i. (ISBN 0-685-00396-5). E J Brill USA.

Social Movements of the Sixties & Seventies. Ed. by Jo Freeman. LC 81-18586. (Illus.). 480p. (Orig.). 1982. pap. text ed. 20.95 o.p. (ISBN 0-582-28091-5). Longman.

Social Order & the Limits of Law: A Theoretical Essay. Iredell Jenkins. LC 79-3216. 1980. 44.50x o.p. (ISBN 0-691-07241-8); pap. 12.95x o.p. (ISBN 0-691-02007-8). Princeton U Pr.

Social Origins of the Irish Land War. Samuel Clark. LC 79-83980. (Rural Social Structure & Collective Action in 19th Century Ireland). 1979. 42.00x o.p. (ISBN 0-691-05272-7); pap. 17.50x LPE o.p. (ISBN 0-691-10068-3). Princeton U Pr.

Social Philosophy of Martin Buber: The Social World as a Human Dimension. John W. Murphy. LC 82-21779. 176p. (Orig.). 1983. lib. bdg. 27.75 o.p. (ISBN 0-8191-2940-2); pap. text ed. 12.25 o.p. (ISBN 0-8191-2941-0). U Pr of Amer.

Social Planning for Canada. League for Social Reconstruction Staff. LC 72-94917. (Social History of Canada Ser.). 1975. pap. 9.95c o.p. (ISBN 0-8020-6178-8). U of Toronto Pr.

Social Plays in Primates. Euclid O. Smith. 1978. 43.00 o.p. (ISBN 0-12-652750-4). Acad Pr.

Social Policy & Its Administration. J Monie & A. Wise. 1977. 145.00 o.p. (ISBN 0-08-021943-8). Pergamon.

Social Problems. Michael S. Bassis et al. Ed. by Robert K. Merton. 586p. 1982. text ed. 24.00 net o.p. (ISBN 0-15-581430-3, HC). HarBraceJ.

Social Problems. 2nd ed. Eitzen. 1983. text ed. 34.30 o.p. (ISBN 0-205-07916-4, 817916); instr's. manual avail. o.p. Allyn.

Social Problems. 3rd ed. Eitzen. 1985. text ed. 37.00 o.p. (ISBN 0-205-08584-9). Allyn.

Social Problems. 3rd ed. Howard E. Freeman & Wyatt C. Jones. 1980. text ed. 27.50 o.p. (ISBN 0-395-30594-2). HM.

Social Problems. Jon M. Shepard & Harwin L. Voss. (Illus.). 1978. pap. text ed. write for info. o.p. (ISBN 0-02-409670-9). Macmillan.

Social Problems & Criminal Justice. Emilio Viano & Alvin W. Cohn. LC 73-92238. (Nelson-Hall Law Enforcement Ser.). 288p. 1975. 22.95x o.s.i. (ISBN 0-88229-115-7). Nelson-Hall.

Social Problems & Public Policy: Inequality & Justice. Ed. by Lee Rainwater. LC 72-97244. 464p. 1974. 27.95x o.p. (ISBN 0-202-30246-6); pap. text ed. 23.95x o.p. (ISBN 0-202-30247-4). Aldine de Gruyter.

Social Problems: Divergent Perspectives. Thomas J. Sullivan et al. LC 79-20676. 728p. 1980. (ISBN 0-02-418430-6). Macmillan.

Social Problems: Impact, Process & Solution. John Stimson et al. 346p. 1985. pap. 11.50 o.p. (ISBN 0-02-417490-4). Macmillan.

Social Problems in American Society. Melvin L. DeFleur. LC 82-81108. 640p. 1983. text ed. 29.50 o.p. (ISBN 0-395-32567-6). HM.

Social Problems of Man's Environment: Where We Live & Work. P. Fedoseyev & T. Timofeyev. 334p. 1981. 8.50 o.p. (ISBN 0-8285-2273-1, Pub. by Progress Pubs USSR). Imported Pubns.

Social Problems 1988-89. 16th, rev. ed. Ed. by LeRoy W. Barnes. LC 73-78577. (Annual Editions Ser.). (Illus.). 256p. 1988. pap. text ed. 9.95x o.p. (ISBN 0-87967-723-6). Dushkin Pub.

Social Processes of Scientific Development. Ed. by Richard Whitley. 1974. 24.50x o.p. (ISBN 0-7100-7705-X). Routledge Chapman & Hall.

Social Program Implementation. Ed. by Walter Williams & Richard F. Elmore. (Quantitative Studies in Social Relations Ser.). 1976. 24.95 o.p. (ISBN 0-12-756850-6). Acad Pr.

Social Protest from the Left in Canada Eighteen Seventy to Nineteen Seventy. Peter H. Weinrich. 750p. 1982. 65.00x o.p. (ISBN 0-8020-5567-2). U of Toronto Pr.

Social-Psychological Analysis of Police Assailants. C. Kenneth Meyer et al. (Criminal Justice Policy & Administration Research Ser.). 1978. 3.00 o.p. (ISBN 0-686-04910-1). Univ OK Gov Res.

Social Psychology. 3rd ed. James V. Zanden. 512p. 1983. text ed. 23.00 o.p. (ISBN 0-394-33020-X, RanC). Random.

Social Psychology: A Sociology Perspective. Arthur G. Neal. 544p. 1983. text ed. 25.00 o.p. (ISBN 0-394-34843-5, RanC). Random.

Social Psychology: A Symbolic Interaction Perspective. Jerry D. Cardwell. LC 75-158650. pap. 6.95x o.s.i. (ISBN 0-88295-203-X). Harlan Davidson.

Social Psychology & Discretionary Law. Lawrence E. Abt & Irving R. Stuart. 1979. 27.95 o.p. (ISBN 0-442-27907-8). Van Nos Reinhold.

Social Psychology & Intergroup Relations. M. Billig. (European Monographs in Social Psychology). 1976. 90.00 o.p. (ISBN 0-12-097950-0). Acad Pr.

Social Psychology in the Eighties. 4th ed. Kay Deaux & Lawrence C. Wrightsman. LC 83-7379. (Psychology Ser.). 700p. 1983. text ed. 25.00 pub net o.p. (ISBN 0-534-02926-4). Brooks-Cole.

Social Psychology of Civil Defense. Ronald W. Perry. (Batelle Human Affairs Research Centers Ser.). 144p. 1982. 21.50x o.p. (ISBN 0-669-05963-3). Lexington Bks.

Social Psychology of Education: Theory & Research. Daniel Bar-Tal & Leonard Saxe. LC 77-28746. 384p. 1978. text ed. 19.95x o.p. (ISBN 0-470-26306-7). Halsted Pr.

Social Psychology of Industry: Human Relations in the Factory. J. A. Brown. 320p. 1954. pap. 4.95 o.p. (ISBN 0-14-020296-X, Pelican). Penguin.

Social Psychology of Organizations. Frederick Glen. (Essential Psychology Ser.). 1976. pap. 4.50x o.p. (ISBN 0-416-84050-7, 2735). Routledge Chapman & Hall.

Social Psychology of Religion. Michael Argyle & Benjamin Beit-Hallahmi. 1975. 25.00x o.p. (ISBN 0-7100-7997-4); pap. 10.95X o.p. (ISBN 0-7100-8043-3). Routledge Chapman & Hall.

Social Psychology of Schooling. Colin Roger. (Routledge Education Bks.). 190p. 1982. 25.00x o.p. (ISBN 0-7100-9012-9); pap. 12.95x o.p. (ISBN 0-7100-9013-7). Routledge Chapman & Hall.

Social Psychology of Sport: An Experiential Approach. Albert V. Carron. 1981. pap. text ed. 11.95 o.p. (ISBN 0-932392-09-1). Mouvement Pubns.

Social Psychology of Telecommunications. John Short et al. LC 75-44335. 195p. 1976. 63.95 o.p. (ISBN 0-471-01581-4, Pub. by Wiley-Interscience). Wiley.

Social Psychology of Tourist Behaviour. P. L. Pearce. (International Series in Experimental Social Psychology: Vol. 3). 142p. 1982. 40.00 o.p. (ISBN 0-08-025794-1). Pergamon.

Social Psychology: The Theory & Application of Symbolic Interactionism. Robert H. Lauer & Warren H. Handel. LC 76-10895. 512p. 1977. text ed. 20.95 o.p. (ISBN 0-395-24333-5). HM.

Social Reform & Reaction in America: An Annotated Bibliography. Ed. by Carl Degler. LC 82-24294. (Clio Bibliography Ser.: No. 13). 375p. 1984. lib. bdg. 65.50 o.p. (ISBN 0-87436-048-X). ABC-Clio.

Social Rehabilitation & Poverty: The Cleveland Inner-City Project. Ed. by James E. Trela. 135p. 1974. pap. text ed. 4.95x o.p. (ISBN 0-8422-0455-5). Irvington.

Social Responsibility & the Responsible Society. Bruce Allsopp. 208p. (Orig.). 1985. pap. 19.95x o.p. (ISBN 0-85362-220-5, Oriel). Routledge Chapman & Hall.

Social Roles: A Focus for Social Studies in the Nineteen Eighty's. Douglas P. Superka & Sharryl Hawke. LC 82-5813. (Project SPAN Reports Ser.). 85p. (Orig.). 1982. pap. 11.95 o.p. (ISBN 0-89994-274-1). Soc Sci Ed.

Social Science & Medicine: Seventh International Conference Background Papers. Ed. by Peter J. McEwan. (Journal of Social Science & Medicine Ser.: Vol. 15A, No. 3). 100p. 1981. pap. 18.00 o.p. (ISBN 0-08-028130-3). Pergamon.

Social Science & Social Welfare. Ed. by John M. Romanyshyn. Date not set. 4.50 o.p. (74-650-06). Coun Soc WK Ed.

Social Science Education: A Book of Readings. Henry Olsen et al. LC 72-86195. 369p. 1972. text ed. 29.00x o.p. (ISBN 0-8422-5029-8); pap. text ed. 8.95x o.p. (ISBN 0-8422-0215-3). Irvington.

Social Science Practitioner As Expert Witness: A Bibliography. Frederick Frankena. (Public Administration Ser.: P 1825). 8p. 1985. 2.00 o.p. (ISBN 0-89028-675-2). Vance Biblios.

Social Science Research in the Dry Lands. Otis W. Templer. 75p. 1976. 3.50 o.p. (ISBN 0-318-14560-X, 76-6). Intl Ctr Arid & Semi-Arid.

Social Sciences & Humanities see Comprehensive Dissertation Index, 1974: Supplement, 1975.

Social Sciences & Public Policy in the Developing World. Ed. by Laurence D. Stifel et al. LC 81-47748. 384p. 1982. 26.50x o.p. (ISBN 0-669-04824-0). Lexington Bks.

Social Scientist Investigates Women of the Ancient World. Henry J. Brun. (Illus.). 152p. (gr. 7-12). 1976. PLB 10.97 o.p. (ISBN 0-8239-0361-3). Rosen Group.

Social Security & Medicare. 1984. (ISBN 0-88129-147-1). Wash Bar CLE.

Social Security & National Policy: Sweden, Yugoslavia, Japan. David E. Woodsworth. 1977. lib. bdg. 8.50x o.p. (ISBN 0-7735-0282-3, McGill Canada); pap. 3.95 o.p. (ISBN 0-7735-0283-1). U of Toronto Pr.

Social Security Claims & Procedures: 1986 P.P, Vols. 1 & 2. 3rd ed. Harvey L. McCormick. 520p. 1986. write for info. o.p. (ISBN 0-314-24869-2). West Pub.

Social Security Disability Claims. (Litigation & Administrative Practice Course Handbook Ser.: Vol. 131). 321p. 1984. 45.00 o.p. (ISBN 0-317-11453-0, C4-4165). PLI.

Social Security Disability Programs: An International Perspective. Ed. by Barbara Duncan & Diane Woods. (Monograph: No. 41). 1987. pap. 6.00 o.p. World Rehab Fund.

Social Security Law. 363p. 1984. 16.00 o.p. (ISBN 0-318-02442-X). ICLE Georgia.

Social Security Law of the European Communities. Ed. by Philippa Watson. 292p. 1980. text ed. 31.00x o.p. (ISBN 0-7201-0926-4). Mansell.

Social Security Manual. 1987 ed. Advanced Sales Reference Service Department Staff. 190p. 1987. pap. 6.50 o.p. (ISBN 0-87218-445-5). Natl Underwriter.

Social Security Manual. Advanced Sales Reference Service Department Editorial Staff. 191p. 1988. pap. 7.00 o.p. (ISBN 0-87218-458-7). Natl Underwriter.

Social Security, Medicare & Pensions: A Sourcebook for Older Americans. 3rd ed. Joseph L. Matthews & Dorothy M. Berman. Orig. Title: Source Book for Older Americans-Income, Rights & Benefits. 275p. 1987. pap. 14.95 o.p. (ISBN 0-87337-038-4). Nolo Pr.

Social Security Programs Throughout the World, Nineteen Eighty-Three. 307p. 1984. pap. 9.00 o.p. (ISBN 0-318-11829-7, S/N 017-070-00408-3). USGPO.

Social Security, Savings Plans & Other Retirement Arrangements: Answers to Questions on Subject Matter, CEBS Course 3. 5th ed. 104p. (Orig.). 1984. pap. 15.00 o.p. (ISBN 0-89154-257-4). Intl Found Employ.

Social Security, Savings Plans & Other Retirement Arrangements: Learning Guide CEBS Course Three. 5th ed. 1984. Spiral bdg. 18.00 o.p. (ISBN 0-89154-256-6). Intl Found Employ.

Social Self. R. C. Ziller. 320p. 1973. pap. 55.00 o.p. (ISBN 0-08-017250-4). Pergamon.

Social Self: Group Influences on Personal Identity. Elisha Y. Babad & Max Birnbaum. LC 82-21553. (Sage Library of Social Research: Vol. 144). (Illus.). 267p. 35.00 o.p. (ISBN 0-8039-1938-7); pap. 16.95 o.p. (ISBN 0-8039-1939-5). Sage.

Social Service for All? Ed. by Peter Townsend. 126p. 1968. pap. (ISBN 0-7163-4000-3). Transaction Pubs.

Social Services: Federal Legislation vs. State Implemention. Bill Benton et al. 157p. 1978. pap. 7.95x o.p. (ISBN 0-87766-237-1, 23700). Urban Inst.

Social Services in Early Education: Head Start, Day Care & Early Education Schools. Ed. by Jeanne Mueller & Harry Morgan. 114p. 1974. pap. text ed. 8.95x o.p. (ISBN 0-685-55784-7). Irvington.

Social Situation of Women in the Novels of Ellen Glasgow. Elizabeth Gallup Myer. 1978. 5.00 o.p. (ISBN 0-682-49165-9, University). Exposition-Phoenix.

Social Skills & Personal Problem Solving: A Handbook of Methods. Philip Priestley et al. (Illus.). 1979. 28.00x o.p. (ISBN 0-422-76540-6, NO.2394, Pub. by Tavistock England); pap. 15.95x o.p. (ISBN 0-422-76550-3, NO.3797). Routledge Chapman & Hall.

Social Skills in Prison & the Community: Problem-Solving for Offenders. Philip Priestley et al. 224p. (Orig.). 1984. pap. 14.95x o.p. (ISBN 0-7100-9272-5). Routledge Chapman & Hall.

Social Skills Training & Psychiatric Nursing. Owen Hargie & Patrick J. McCartan. 288p. (Orig.). 1986. pap. 19.00 o.p. (ISBN 0-7099-3749-0, Pub. by Croom Helm Ltd). Routledge Chapman & Hall.

Social Stratification & Mobility in the U. S. S. R. Ed. by Murray Yanowitch & Wesley A. Fisher. LC 72-77202. (Illus.). 402p. 1973. text ed. 30.00 o.p. (ISBN 0-87332-008-5). M E Sharpe.

Social Structure of Modern Britain. 2nd ed. E. A. Johns. 212p. 1972. text ed. 12.65 o.p. (ISBN 0-08-016869-8); pap. text ed. 6.05 o.p. (ISBN 0-08-016870-1). Pergamon.

Social Studies Exercise Set. National Assessment of Educational Progress Staff. (Exercise or Items). 373p. 18.00 o.p. (ISBN 0-318-14001-2, Natl Assessment Ed Progress). Ed Comm States.

Social Studies in Early Childhood: An Interactionist Point of View. Ed. by Alicia L. Pagano. LC 78-57997. (Bulletin Ser.: No. 58). (Illus.). 96p. (Orig.). 1978. pap. text ed. 8.35 o.p. (ISBN 0-87986-022-7, 498-15276). Nat Coun Soc Studies.

Social Studies in the Elementary School. Ed. by Ralph C. Preston. LC 57-631. (National Society for the Study of Education Yearbooks Ser: No. 56, Pt. 2). 1957. lib. bdg. 6.50x o.s.i. (ISBN 0-226-60042-4); pap. text ed. 4.50x o.s.i. (ISBN 0-226-60043-2). U of Chicago Pr.

Social Studies Strategies for Today's Learners. W. P. McLemore. 1976. pap. text ed. 9.95x o.p. (ISBN 0-8422-0537-3). Irvington.

Social Studies Student Investigates American Law. Edward Muir. (Social Studies Student Ser.). (Illus.). (YA) (gr. 7-12). 1977. lib. bdg. 10.97 o.p. (ISBN 0-8239-0396-6). Rosen Group.

Social Studies Student Investigates Business in the American Economy. Joseph Wolfson. (Illus.). 116p. (gr. 7-12). 1977. PLB 10.97 o.p. (ISBN 0-8239-0369-9). Rosen Group.

Social Studies Student Investigates Modern Wars. Arnold Rosenberg. 151p. (YA) (gr. 7-12). 1977. PLB 10.97 o.p. (ISBN 0-8239-0379-6). Rosen Group.

Social Studies Student Investigates Money. Allen Argoff. (gr. 7-12). 1977. PLB 10.97 o.p. (ISBN 0-8239-0375-3). Rosen Group.

Social Studies Student Investigates the Retreat from Imperialism. Henry J. Brun. 179p. (YA) (gr. 7-12). 1978. PLB 10.97 o.p. (ISBN 0-8239-0414-8). Rosen Group.

Social System: A Treatise on the Principle of Exchange. John Gray. LC 73-73. xvi, 374p. 1973. Repr. of 1831 ed. 45.00x o.s.i. (ISBN 0-678-00962-7). Kelley.

Social System & Culture of Modern India: A Research Bibliography. Danesh A. Chekki. LC 74-19226. (Reference Library of Social Science: No. 1). 873p. 1974. lib. bdg. 103.00 o.p. (ISBN 0-8240-1056-6). Garland Pub.

Social Teaching of Vatican II: Its Origin & Development. Catholic Social Ethics-an Historical & Comparative Study. Rodger Charles. LC 81-83567. (Illus.). 597p. 1982. 30.00 o.p. (ISBN 0-89870-013-2). Ignatius Pr.

Social Texts & Contexts: Literature & Social Psychology. Jonathan Potter et al. 250p. 1984. 15.00x o.p. (ISBN 0-7100-9553-8). Routledge Chapman & Hall.

Social Theory & Social Welfare. Peter Taylor-Gooby & Jennifer Dale. 256p. 1981. pap. text ed. 22.50x o.p. (ISBN 0-7131-6332-1). Trans-Atl Phila.

Social Theory & the Urban Question. Peter Saunders. LC 80-21654. 302p. 1981. text ed. 35.00 o.p. (ISBN 0-8419-0622-X); pap. text ed. 16.75 o.p. (ISBN 0-8419-0623-8). Holmes & Meier.

Social Therapy in Psychiatry. 2nd ed. Clark. 1981. pap. text ed. 10.00 o.p. Churchill.

Social Treatment: An Approach to Interpersonal Helping. James K. Whittaker. LC 71-172856. 1974. lib. bdg. 34.95x o.p. (ISBN 0-202-36011-3); pap. text ed. 16.95x o.p. (ISBN 0-202-36012-1). Aldine de Gruyter.

Social Uses of Social Science. Robert Redfield. Ed. by Margaret P. Redfield. (Papers Ser: Vol. 2). 1963. lib. bdg. 12.00x o.s.i. (ISBN 0-226-70636-2). U of Chicago Pr.

Social Welfare Forum Nineteen Seventy-Nine. Ed. by National Conference on Social Welfare Staff. LC 8-85377. 1980. 35.00x o.p. (ISBN 0-231-04990-0). Columbia U Pr.

Social Welfare Forum: Official Proceedings. National Conference on Social Welfare Staff. Incl. Ninety Fourth Annual Forum. 1967 (ISBN 0-231-03136-X); Ninety Fifth Annual Forum. 1968 (ISBN 0-231-03232-3); Ninety Sixth Annual Forum. 1969 (ISBN 0-231-03390-7); Nintey Seventh Annual Forum. 1970 (ISBN 0-231-03473-3); Nintey Eighth Annual Forum. 1971 (ISBN 0-231-03587-X). LC 8-85377. 35.00x ea. o.p. Columbia U Pr.

Social Welfare: Help or Hindrance. Ed. by Carol Foster et al. (Information Plus Ser.). 104p. 1988. pap. 16.95 o.p. (ISBN 0-936474-63-7). Info Plus TX.

Social Welfare in the Nineteen Eighties & Beyond. Eveline M Burns. LC 77-17818. 20p. 1978. pap. 4.00x o.p. (ISBN 0-87772-251-X). UCB IGS.

Social Welfare Spending: Accounting for Changes from Nineteen Fifty to Nineteen Seventy-Eight. Robert J. Lampman. (Institute of Research on Poverty Policy Analysis Ser.). 1984. 32.50 o.p. (ISBN 0-12-435260-X). Acad Pr.

Social Work & Human Problems: Casework, Consultation & Other Topics. Elizabeth E. Irvine. (International Series in Social Work). 1979. 63.00 o.p. (ISBN 0-08-023128-4); pap. 25.00 o.p. (ISBN 0-08-023127-6). Pergamon.

Social Work & Medical Practice. H. A. Prins & M. B. Whyte. LC 71-184453. 94p. 1972. 23.00 o.p. (ISBN 0-08-016847-7). Pergamon.

Social Work & Social Living. Reynolds. 2.50 o.p. (ISBN 0-8065-0332-7, Pub. by Citadel Pr). Carol Pub Group.

Social Work & Social Philosophy: A Guide for Practice. Chris L. Clark & Stewart Asquith. 160p. 1985. 22.95x o.p. (ISBN 0-7102-0610-0); pap. 12.95x o.p. (ISBN 0-7100-9630-5). Routledge Chapman & Hall.

Social Work Day-to-Day: The Experience of Generalist Social Practice. Carolyn W. Konle. LC 81-14303. 224p. 1982. pap. text ed. 15.95 o.p. (ISBN 0-582-28345-0). Longman.

Social Work in Context. Jim Black & Ric Bowl. 1983. 33.00 o.p. (ISBN 0-422-78270-X, NO. 3964, Pub. by Tavistock). Routledge Chapman & Hall.

Social Work in Focus: Clients' & Social Workers' Perception in Long Term Social Work. Eric Sainsbury & David Phillips. (Library of Social Work). 220p. (Orig.). 1982. pap. 10.95x o.p. (ISBN 0-7100-9068-4). Routledge Chapman & Hall.

Social Work in Long-Term Care Facilities. Shirley Conger & Kay Moore. 160p. 1984. pap. 24.95 o.p. (ISBN 0-442-21898-2). Van Nos Reinhold.

Social Work Practice: Proceedings. National Conference on Social Welfare Staff. Incl. Ninety-Third Annual Meeting. 1966 (ISBN 0-231-03032-0); Ninety-Fourth Annual Meeting. 1967 (ISBN 0-231-03154-8); Ninety-Fifth Annual Meeting. 1968 (ISBN 0-231-03247-1); Ninety-Sixth Annual Meeting. 1969 (ISBN 0-231-03389-3); Ninety-Seventh Annual Meeting. 1970 (ISBN 0-231-03474-1); Ninety-Eighth Annual Meeting. 1971 (ISBN 0-231-03588-8). LC 5-85377. 35.00x ea. o.p. Columbia U Pr.

Social Work Processes. 3rd ed. Beulah R. Compton & Burt Galaway. 609p. 1984. pap. text ed. (ISBN 0-534-10509-2). Wadsworth Pub.

Social Work Research & Evaluation. 2nd ed. Richard M. Grinnell, Jr. LC 83-63543. 550p. 1984. text ed. 27.95 o.p. (ISBN 0-87581-303-8). Peacock Pubs.

Social Work Research & the Analysis of Social Data. J. W. McCulloch et al. LC 74-32369. 252p. 1975. 60.00 o.p. (ISBN 0-08-018213-5); pap. 60.00 o.p. (ISBN 0-08-018212-7). Pergamon.

Social Work Review: Approaches to Evaluation & Analysis of Patient Care, QRB Special Edition. Intro. by Helen Rehr. LC 82-81564. 80p. 1982. pap. 20.00 o.s.i. (ISBN 0-86688-052-6). Joint Comm Hlthcare.

Social Work Supervision in Practice. B. Kent. 1969. pap. text ed. 4.95 o.p. (ISBN 0-08-006363-2). Pergamon.

Social Work Values: An Inquiry. Noel Timms. 200p. (Orig.). 1983. pap. 11.50x o.p. (ISBN 0-7100-9404-3). Routledge Chapman & Hall.

Social Work with Mentally Handicapped People. Christopher Hanvey. (Community Care Practice Handbook Ser.). (Orig.). 1981. pap. text ed. 6.50x o.p. (ISBN 0-435-82403-1). Gower Pub Co.

Social Worker. Barry Malzberg. 1977. pap. 1.50 o.s.i. (ISBN 0-8439-0511-5, Pub. by Leisure Bks CT). Dorchester Pub Co.

Social World of Imprisoned Girls. Rose Giallombardo. LC 80-22340. 328p. 1981. Repr. of 1974 ed. text ed. 24.50 o.p. (ISBN 0-89874-239-0). Krieger.

Socialism & Affluence. Ed. by William Rodgers. 94p. 1970. pap. (ISBN 0-7163-4002-X). Transaction Pubs.

Socialism & Social Science: Selected Writings of Ervin Szabo. Ervin Szabo. Ed. by Gyorgy Litvan & Janos Bak. 288p. 1982. 28.95x o.p. (ISBN 0-7100-9007-2). Routledge Chapman & Hall.

Socialism & the Individual: Notes on Joining the Labour Party. William A. Sinclair. LC 77-18930. 1978. Repr. of 1955 ed. lib. bdg. 35.00x o.p. (ISBN 0-313-20199-4, SISO). Greenwood.

Socialism & the Newly Independent Nations. R. A. Ulyanovsky. 562p. 1974. 5.95 o.p. (ISBN 0-8285-0317-6, Pub. by Progress Pubs USSR). Imported Pubns.

Socialism & War. Louis B. Boudin. LC 73-147507. (Library of War & Peace; Labor, Socialism & War). 1972. lib. bdg. 46.00 o.p. (ISBN 0-8240-0302-0). Garland Pub.

Socialism as a Social System. T. M. Jaroszewski & P. S. Ignatovsky. 448p. 1981. pap. 2.95 o.p. (ISBN 0-8285-2401-7, Pub. by Progress Pubs USSR). Imported Pubns.

Socialism: Foreign Policy in Theory & Practice. Sh. P. Sanakoyev & N. E. Kapachenko. 182p. 1976. 4.45 o.p. (ISBN 0-8285-0318-4, Pub. by Progress Pubs USSR). Imported Pubns.

Socialism: From Utopia to Science. 5th ed. Frederick Engels. Tr. by Edward Aveling. 1974. pap. text ed. 0.75 o.p. (ISBN 0-935534-27-X). NY Labor News.

Socialism: Its Role in History. V. Zagladin. 175p. 1983. pap. 3.95 o.p. (ISBN 0-8285-2735-0, Pub. by Progress Pubs USSR). Imported Pubns.

Socialism Looks Forward. John Strachey. (ISBN 0-8022-1664-1). Philos Lib.

Socialismo Real y Su Significacion Internacional. B. N. Ponomareov. 99p. (Span.). 1979. pap. 1.45 o.p. (ISBN 0-8285-1433-X, Pub. by Progress Pubs USSR). Imported Pubns.

Socialist, Nos. 1-9. 1970. Repr. of 1919 ed. lib. bdg. 38.00x o.p. (ISBN 0-8371-9244-7, SO00). Greenwood.

Socialist Appeal: An Organ of Revolutionary Socialism, Vols. 1-3, No. 3. 1968-37. Repr. of 1937 ed. lib. bdg. 30.00x o.p. (ISBN 0-8371-9245-5, S100). Greenwood.

Socialist Ideology. N. B. Bikkenin. 1980. pap. 5.95 o.p. (ISBN 0-8285-1771-1, Pub. by Progress Pubs USSR). Imported Pubns.

Socialist Internationalism: Theory & Practice of International Relations of a New Type. S. Anghelov. 507p. 1982. pap. 2.95 o.p. (ISBN 0-8285-2299-5, Pub. by Progress Pubs USSR). Imported Pubns.

Socialist Life Style & the Family. V. Yazkova. 212p. 1984. pap. 3.95 o.p. (ISBN 0-8285-2730-X, Pub. by Progress Pubs USSR). Imported Pubns.

Socialist Literature: Problems of Development. D. Markov. 224p. 1984. 7.95 o.p. (ISBN 0-8285-2794-6, Pub. by Raduga Pubs USSR). Imported Pubns.

Socialist Models of Development. Ed. by C. K. Wilber & K. P. Jameson. 240p. 1982. 48.00 o.p. (ISBN 0-08-027921-X). Pergamon.

Socialist Ownership & Political Systems under Socialism. Wlodzimierz Brus. 256p. 1975. 26.95x o.p. (ISBN 0-7100-8247-9). Routledge Chapman & Hall.

Socialist Population Politics: The Political Implications of Demographic Trends in the U. S. S. R. & Eastern Europe. John Besemeres. LC 80-65260. 320p. 1980. 35.00 o.p. (ISBN 0-87332-154-5). M E Sharpe.

Socialist Propaganda in the Twentieth-Century British Novel. David Smith. 203p. 1978. 21.50x o.p. (ISBN 0-8476-6023-0). Rowman.

Socialist Register: Annuals: Nineteen Sixty-Eight to Nineteen Seventy-Eight. Ed. by Ralph Milliband & J. Saville. 17.50 ea. o.p. (ISBN 0-87556-440-2). Saifer.

Socialist Spirit, Vols. 1-2, No. 6. 1970. Repr. of 1903 ed. lib. bdg. 41.00x o.p. (ISBN 0-8371-9247-1, SS00). Greenwood.

Socialization after Childhood: Two Essays. Orville G. Brim, Jr. & Stanton Wheeler. 116p. 1966. pap. text ed. write for info. o.p. (ISBN 0-02-314860-8). Macmillan.

Socialization, Sexism & Stereotyping, Women's Issues in Nursing. Janet Muff. LC 81-18690. (Illus.). 434p. 1982. pap. text ed. 19.95 o.p. (ISBN 0-8016-3581-0). Mosby.

Socially Disadvantaged. Ed. by Earl J. Ogletree. LC 73-17001. 1974. Vol. 1. 39.50x o.p. (ISBN 0-8422-5142-1); pap. text ed. 18.50x o.p. (ISBN 0-8422-0349-4); Vol. 2. 39.50x o.p. (ISBN 0-8422-5156-1); pap. text ed. 14.50x o.p. (ISBN 0-8422-0380-X). Irvington.

Societal Crises & Educational Response: A Book of Readings. R. H. Wagoner et al. 1969. pap. text ed. 6.95x o.p. (ISBN 0-8290-1191-9). Irvington.

Societe International De Chirurgie Orthopedique et de Traumatology: Fifty Years of Achievement. Ed. by E. Vander Elst. (Illus.). 1978. 18.90 o.p. (ISBN 0-387-08968-3). Springer-Verlag.

Society & Drugs, Social & Cultural Observations. Richard H. Blum et al. Incl. Vol. 2. Students & Drugs, College & High School Observations. LC 73-75936. (Social & Behavioral Science Ser.). 1969. 2 vol. set 65.00x o.p. (ISBN 0-87589-424-0); Vol. 1. (ISBN 0-87589-033-4); Vol. 2. (ISBN 0-87589-034-2). Jossey-Bass.

Society & Education. 6th ed. Daniel U. Levine & Robert J. Havighurst. 1984. text ed. 39.00 o.p. (ISBN 0-205-08084-7, 238084). Allyn.

Society & Education. 7th ed. Daniel U. Levine & Robert J. Havighurst. 1989. text ed. 40.00 casebd. o.p. (238084). Allyn.

Society & Medication: Conflicting Signals for Prescribers & Patients. Ed. by John P. Morgan & Doreen V. Kagan. LC 81-48145. 400p. 1983. 40.00x o.p. (ISBN 0-669-05290-6). Lexington Bks.

Society & Nature. I. Novik. 301p. 1981. 6.00 o.p. (ISBN 0-8285-2049-6, Pub. by Progress Pubs USSR). Imported Pubns.

Society & Religion During the Age of Industrialization: Christianity in Victorian England. Lee E Grugel. LC 78-65844. (Illus.). 1979. pap. text ed. 10.00 o.p. (ISBN 0-8191-0671-2). U Pr of Amer.

Society & the Healthy Homosexual. George Weinberg. 160p. 1973. 1.95 o.p. (ISBN 0-385-05083-6, Anch). Doubleday.

Society, Culture & Change in the Middle East. Raphael Patai. LC 70-84742. (Illus.). 1971. pap. 16.95x o.p. (ISBN 0-8122-1009-3, Pa Paperbks); 18.00 o.p. (ISBN 0-8122-7289-7). U of Pa Pr.

Society in Colonial North Carolina. Alan D. Watson. (Illus.). x, 93p. 1982. pap. 2.00 o.p. (ISBN 0-86526-103-2). NC Archives.

Society in Revolutionary North Carolina. Alice E. Mathews. (Illus.). viii, 91p. 1976. pap. 3.00 o.p. (ISBN 0-86526-117-2). NC Archives.

Society of American Foresters Ethics Guide. Society of American Foresters. 1985. pap. 5.00 o.s.i. (ISBN 0-939970-29-5). Soc Am Foresters.

Society of Automotive Engineers Proceedings. Incl. 22p. 1975. 30.00 o.p. (ISBN 0-89883-171-7, SP-397); members o.p. 19.75 (ISBN 0-317-35777-8); 325p. 1977. pap. 45.00 (P-70); 175p. 1978. pap. 45.00 (ISBN 0-89883-046-X, P76); 314p. 1979. pap. 45.00 (ISBN 0-85296-210-X, P-84); 270p. 1977. 30.00 (ISBN 0-89883-042-7, P-71). Soc Auto Engineers.

Society of Friends. George Gorman. 1978. pap. text ed. 3.15 o.s.i. (ISBN 0-08-021412-6). Pergamon.

Society of Mind. Marvin Minsky. 1987. 22.45 o.s.i. (ISBN 0-671-60740-5). S&S.

Society of Publication Designers Twenty Second Publication Design Annual. (Illus.). 256p. 1988. 39.95 o.p. (ISBN 0-8230-4887-X). Madison Square.

Society of Women: A Study of a Women's Prison. Rose Giallombardo. LC 66-14132. 244p. 1970. pap. text ed. write for info. o.p. (ISBN 0-02-341840-0). Macmillan.

Society, Religion & Art of the Kushana India: A Historico-Symbiosis. Kanchan Chakraberti. (Illus.). 116p. 1981. text ed. 32.50x o.p. (ISBN 0-391-02501-5). Humanities.

Society, Schools & Progress in Australia. P. H. Partridge. LC 68-24067. 1968. text ed. 29.00 o.p. (ISBN 0-08-012919-6); pap. text ed. 16.00 o.p. (ISBN 0-08-012918-8). Pergamon.

Society, Schools & Progress in Canada. J. Katz. 1969. text ed. 21.00 o.p. (ISBN 0-08-006374-8); pap. text ed. 9.25 o.p. (ISBN 0-08-006373-X). Pergamon.

Society, Schools & Progress in China. Chiu-Sam Tsang LC 68-21109. 1968. text ed. 24.00 o.p. (ISBN 0-08-012844-0); pap. 85.00 o.p. (ISBN 0-08-012843-2). Pergamon.

Society, Schools & Progress in England. G. Baron. 1966. 29.00 o.p. (ISBN 0-08-011594-2); pap. 14.25 o.p. (ISBN 0-08-011593-4). Pergamon.

Society, Schools & Progress in India. J. Sargent. LC 68-21106. 1968. 65.00 o.p. (ISBN 0-08-012840-8); pap. 65.00 o.p. (ISBN 0-08-012839-4). Pergamon.

Society, Schools & Progress in Israel. A. F. Kleinberger. LC 73-92460. 1969. 90.00 o.p. (ISBN 0-08-006494-9); pap. 90.00 o.p. (ISBN 0-08-006493-0). Pergamon.

Society, Schools & Progress in Japan. Tetzuya Kobayashi. 222p. 1976. 55.00 o.p. (ISBN 0-08-019936-4); pap. 55.00 o.p. (ISBN 0-08-019935-6). Pergamon.

Society, Schools & Progress in Nigeria. L. J. Lewis. 1965. 29.00 o.p. (ISBN 0-08-011340-0); pap. 40.00 o.p. (ISBN 0-08-011339-7). Pergamon.

Society, Schools & Progress in Peru. Roland G. Paulston. 336p. 1971. 85.00 o.p. (ISBN 0-08-016428-5). Pergamon.

Society, Schools & Progress in Scandinavia. C. W. Dixon. 1965. 38.00 o.p. (ISBN 0-08-011405-9); pap. 18.50 o.p. (ISBN 0-08-011404-0). Pergamon.

Society, Schools & Progress in Tanzania. J. Cameron & W. A. Dodd. 1970. 65.00 o.p. (ISBN 0-08-015564-2); pap. 65.00 o.p. (ISBN 0-08-015563-4). Pergamon.

Society, Schools & Progress in the West Indies. John J. Figueroa. 1971. 60.00 o.p. (ISBN 0-08-016174-X). Pergamon.

Society, State & Schooling. Ed. by Michael Young. 284p. 1980. text ed. 27.00x o.p. (ISBN 0-905273-02-8, Falmer Pr); pap. 15.00x o.p. (ISBN 0-905273-01-X). Taylor & Francis.

Society, the City & the Space-Economy of Urbanism. D. Harvey. LC 72-77212. (CCG Resource Papers: No. 18). (Illus.). 1972. pap. text ed. 5.00 o.p. (ISBN 0-89291-065-8). Assn Am Geographers.

Society with Tears. Sarnoff. 6.00 o.p. (ISBN 0-8065-0333-5, Pub. by Citadel Pr). Carol Pub Group.

Society's Work. Robert Bridges et al. Ed. by Steele Commager. Incl. Nature of Human Speech; English Handwriting; Notes on Relative Clauses; On Some Disputed Points in English Grammar; English Vowel Sounds; Study of American English; English Handwriting; Shakespeare's English; American Pronunciation. (Society for Pure English: Vol. 3). 1979. lib. bdg. 50.00 o.p. (ISBN 0-8240-3667-0). Garland Pub.

Socio-Economic Models in Geography. R. J. Chorley & P. Haggett. 468p. 1968. pap. 12.95x o.p. (ISBN 0-416-29630-0, NO.2137). Routledge Chapman & Hall.

Socio - Economics & Cultural see Sharing the Sun.

Socio-Political Complex. A. Khoshkish. 1979. 72.00 o.p. (ISBN 0-08-023391-0); pap. 22.00 o.p. (ISBN 0-08-024722-9). Pergamon.

Socio-Political Thought in African Literature. Gideon-Cyprus Mutiso. 1974. text ed. 10.50x o.p. (ISBN 0-333-15556-4). Humanities.

Socio-Psychological Dimensions of Education: Teaching & Learning. A. Lightfoot. 1971. pap. text ed. 8.50x o.p. (ISBN 0-8290-1192-7). Irvington.

Sociobiology & Human Nature: An Interdisciplinary Critique & Defense. Ed. by Michael S. Gregory et al. LC 78-62559. (Social & Behavioral Science Ser.). (Illus.). 1978. text ed. 29.95x o.p. (ISBN 0-87589-384-8). Jossey-Bass.

Socioeconomic Characteristics of Medical Practice. 147p. 1985. pap. 25.00 o.p. (ISBN 0-89970-201-5, OP-228-5). AMA.

Socioeconomic Characteristics of Medical Practice, 1986. pap. 40.00 o.p. (ISBN 0-89970-232-5, OP-228-6). AMA.

Sociological Concepts & Research: Acquisition, Analysis, & Interpretation of Social Information. Ralph Thomlinson. LC 81-40782. 192p. 1981. pap. text ed. 10.00 o.p. (ISBN 0-8191-1805-2). U Pr of Amer.

Sociological Footprints: Introductory Readings in Sociology. Leonard Cargan & Jeanne H. Ballantine. LC 78-69541. (Illus.). 1979. pap. 10.50 o.p. (ISBN 0-395-26718-8). HM.

Sociological Formalism & Structural-Functional Analysis: The Nature of the "Social" Reality Sui Generis? Form? System? Daniel De Sousa. 1975. 7.50 o.p. (ISBN 0-682-48346-X, University). Exposition-Phoenix.

Sociological Health Problems see Individualized Health Incentive Program Modules For Physically Disabled Students.

Sociological Method. 3rd ed. Stephen Cole. 1980. pap. 14.95 o.p. (ISBN 0-395-30857-7). HM.

Sociological Methodology 1970. Ed. by Edgar F. Borgatta & George W. Bohrnstedt. LC 74-110635. (Social & Behavioral Science Ser.). 1970. 39.95x o.p. (ISBN 0-87589-070-9). Jossey-Bass.

Sociological Methodology 1976. Ed. by David R. Heise. LC 68-54940. (Social & Behavioral Science Ser.). (Illus.). 1975. 39.95x o.p. (ISBN 0-87589-262-0). Jossey-Bass.

Sociological Methods: A Sourcebook. 2nd ed. Norman K. Denzin. 1978. text ed. 27.95 o.p. (ISBN 0-07-016366-9); pap. 14.95 o.p. (ISBN 0-07-016365-0). McGraw.

Sociological Orientation. 2nd ed. Stephen Cole. 1980. pap. 21.95 o.p. (ISBN 0-395-30579-9). HM.

Sociological Perspectives. Ed. by Jeremy Tunstall & Kenneth Thompson. (Education Ser). 1972. pap. 4.95 o.p. (ISBN 0-14-080608-3). Penguin.

Sociological Realities: A Guide to the Study of Society. 2nd ed. Ed. by Irving L. Horowitz. Mary S. Strong. 551p. 1971. pap. Transaction Pubs.

Sociological Research, Vol. 2. Ed. by Matilda W. Riley & Robert K. Merton. 195p. 1963. pap. text ed. 13.95 o.p. (ISBN 0-15-582313-2). HarBraceJ.

Sociological Self-Images. I. L. Horowitz. 1970. text ed. 28.00 o.p. (ISBN 0-08-016400-5). Pergamon.

Sociological Theory. 5th ed. Lewis A. Coser & Bernard Rosenberg. 1982. text ed. (ISBN 0-02-325220-0). Macmillan.

Sociological Theory. 2nd ed. S. Mennell. 1980. 42.95 o.p. (ISBN 0-442-30697-0). Van Nos Reinhold.

Sociological Theory. George Ritzer. 486p. 1982. text ed. 24.00 o.p. (ISBN 0-394-32516-8, KnopfC). Knopf.

Sociological Theory in Use. Ken Menzies. (Illus.). 220p. 1982. 24.95x o.p. (ISBN 0-7100-0892-9); pap. 10.95x o.p. (ISBN 0-7100-0893-7). Routledge Chapman & Hall.

Sociologie Des Communications De Masse: Tendences Actuelles De la Recherche et Bibliographie. Alphons Silbermann. (Current Sociology-la Sociologie Contemporaine: No. 18-3). 1973. pap. 10.00x o.p. (ISBN 90-2797-175-7). Mouton.

Sociologie Du Developpement Africain: Tendances Actuelles De la Recherche et Bibliographie. Abdelwahab Boudhiba. (Current Sociology: No. 18/2). 1972. pap. 7.20x o.p. (ISBN 90-2796-948-5). Mouton.

Sociologie Du Developpement Latino-Americain: Tendances Actuelles De la Recherche et Bibliographie, 2 pts. Ed. by Pablo G. Casanova. Incl. Pt. 1. Etudes Generales. (No. 18). 1971. pap. 7.20x (ISBN 0-686-22179-6); Pt. 2. Etudes Sectorielles. (No. 19). 1973. pap. 12.00x (ISBN 90-2797-218-4). (La Sociologie Contemporaine). pap. Mouton.

Sociologists, Economists & Democracy. Brian Barry. LC 78-55039. (Illus.). vi, 202p. 1978. pap. text ed. 8.00x o.s.i. (ISBN 0-226-03823-8). U of Chicago Pr.

Sociology. David B. Brinkerhoff & Lynn K. White. (Illus.). 624p. 1985. text ed. 37.00 o.p. (ISBN 0-314-85220-4). West Pub.

Sociology. 3rd ed. Paul B. Horton & Chester L. Hunt. (Illus.). 560p. 1972. text ed. 29.95 o.p. (ISBN 0-07-030425-4, C). McGraw.

Sociology. 2nd ed. Rodney Stark. 619p. 1987. text ed. (ISBN 0-534-06834-0). Wadsworth Pub.

Sociology: A Brief but Critical Introduction. Anthony Giddens. 182p. 1982. pap. text ed. 9.50 o.p. (ISBN 0-15-505554-2, HC). HarBraceJ.

Sociology: A Liberating Perspective. Liazos. 1985. 24.00 o.p. (ISBN 0-205-08359-5, 818359). Allyn.
Sociology: An Introduction. J. Ross Eshleman & Barbara G. Cashion. 1984. text ed. write for info. o.p. (ISBN 0-673-39573-1); tchr's. manual avail. o.p.; study guide 12.00 o.p. (ISBN 0-673-39574-X); test bank avail. o.p. Scott F.
Sociology & American Social Issues. Leonard Gordon. LC 77-78577. (Illus.). 1978. text ed. 30.50 o.p. (ISBN 0-395-25369-1). HM.
Sociology & Politics of Development: A Theoretical Study. Baidya N. Varma. (International Library of Sociology). 1980. 26.95x o.p. (ISBN 0-7100-0428-1). Routledge Chapman & Hall.
Sociology & Social Work. B. J. Heraud. LC 79-119894. 1970. text ed. 19.25 o.p. (ISBN 0-08-015855-2); pap. text ed. 8.50 o.p. (ISBN 0-08-015854-4). Pergamon.
Sociology & Socialism in Contemporary China. Siu-Lun Wong. (International Library of Sociology). 1979. 21.95x o.p. (ISBN 0-7100-0089-8). Routledge Chapman & Hall.
Sociology & Society in Contemporary China, 1979-1983: A Special Issue of Chinese Sociology & Anthropology. Ed. by David S. Chu. 224p. 1984. pap. 16.95 o.p. (ISBN 0-87332-278-9). M E Sharpe.
Sociology & the School: An Interactionist Viewpoint. Peter Woods. 210p. (Orig.). 1983. pap. 10.50x o.p. (ISBN 0-7100-9342-X). Routledge Chapman & Hall.
Sociology as Disenchantment: The Evolution of the Work of George Gurvitch. Richard Swedberg. 201p. 1982. text ed. 17.50x o.p. (ISBN 0-391-02397-7). Humanities.
Sociology: Concepts & Characteristics. 6th ed. Judson R. Landis. 417p. 1986. pap. text ed. (ISBN 0-534-06438-8). Wadsworth Pub.
Sociology of Aging. Diana K. Harris & William E. Cole. LC 79-89741. (Illus.). 1980. text ed. 26.95 o.p. (ISBN 0-395-28528-3). HM.
Sociology of America: A Guide to Information Sources. Ed. by Charles Mark & Paula F. Mark. LC 73-17560. (American Studies Information Guide Ser.: Vol. 1). 468p. 1976. 68.00x o.p. (ISBN 0-8103-1267-0). Gale.
Sociology of Communism. Jules Monnerot. Tr. by Jane Degras & Richard Rees. LC 76-46469. 1977. Repr. of 1953 ed. lib. bdg. 35.00x o.p. (ISBN 0-8371-9309-5, MOSO). Greenwood.
Sociology of Contemporary Quebec Nationalism: A Annotated Bibliography & Review. Ronald D. Lambert. LC 80-8506. 250p. 1981. lib. bdg. 36.00 o.p. (ISBN 0-8240-9480-8). Garland Pub.
Sociology of Corrections: A Book of Readings. Robert G. Leger & John R. Stratton. LC 76-51462. 557p. 1977. pap. write for info. o.p. (ISBN 0-02-369050-X). Macmillan.
Sociology of Crime. Ed. by Joseph S. Roucek. 1970. Repr. of 1961 ed. lib. bdg. 23.75 o.p. (ISBN 0-8371-2105-1, ROSC). Greenwood.
Sociology of Dissent. Serge R. Denisoff. (Orig.). 1974. pap. text ed. 11.95 o.p. (ISBN 0-15-582364-7, HC). HarBraceJ.
Sociology of Education. Mark A. Chesler & William Cave. (Illus.). 1981. text ed. (ISBN 0-02-322150-X). Macmillan.
Sociology of Education: An Introduction. 2nd ed. Sarane S. Boocock. LC 79-88445. (Illus.). 1980. text ed. 26.95 o.p. (ISBN 0-395-28524-0). HM.
Sociology of Gender. Laurie Davidson & Laura K. Gordon. 1984. pap. 19.50 o.p. (ISBN 0-395-30588-8). HM.
Sociology of Housework. Ann Oakley. LC 75-4668. 264p. 1975. pap. 5.95 o.p. (ISBN 0-394-73088-7). Pantheon.
Sociology of Knowledge in the United States of America. Kurt H. Wolff. (Current Sociology: Vol. 15, No. I). 1967. pap. 6.00x o.p. (ISBN 90-2796-572-2). Mouton.
Sociology of Law. Georges Gurvitch. (ISBN 0-8022-0647-6). Philos Lib.
Sociology of Law: A Trend Report & Bibliography Prepared for the International Sociological Assoc. Under the Auspices of the International Committee for Social Sciences Documentation. Manfred Rehbinder. (Current Sociology-la Sociologie Conteporaine: Vol. XX, 3). 1975. pap. 10.00x o.p. (ISBN 90-2797-305-9). Mouton.
Sociology of Marriage & Family Behavior 1957-1968: A Trend Report & Bibliography. Ed. by John Mogey. 364p. 1971. text ed. 27.60x o.p. (ISBN 0-686-22483-3). Mouton.
Sociology of Marriage & Family: Gender, Love & Property. Randall Collins & Geraldine Markel. LC 84-25453. (Illus.). 527p. 1984. text ed. 26.95x o.s.i. (ISBN 0-8304-1072-4); instr's. resource manual avail. o.s.i. (ISBN 0-8304-1133-X); student study guide 8.95 o.s.i. (ISBN 0-8304-1132-1). Nelson-Hall.
Sociology of Organizational Change. E. A. Johns. LC 73-8972. 182p. 1973. 45.00 o.p. (ISBN 0-08-017601-1); pap. 45.00 o.p. (ISBN 0-08-017602-X). Pergamon.
Sociology of Political Praxis: An Introduction to Gramsci's Theory. Leonardo Salamini. 256p. 1981. 28.95x o.p. (ISBN 0-7100-0928-3). Routledge Chapman & Hall.
Sociology of Religion. George Simmel. 96p. 1960. (ISBN 0-8022-1572-6). Philos Lib.
Sociology of Religion. Joachim Wach. 1944. lib. bdg. 12.00x o.s.i. (ISBN 0-226-86707-2). U of Chicago Pr.
Sociology of School Organization. Ronald King. LC 83-11366. (Contemporary Sociology of the School Ser.). 120p. 1983. pap. 8.95 o.p. (ISBN 0-416-34220-5, NO. 3960). Routledge Chapman & Hall.
Sociology of Science in Europe. Ed. by Robert K. Merton & Jerry Gaston. LC 77-2996. (Perspectives in Sociology). 397p. 1977. 22.95x o.p. (ISBN 0-8093-0633-6). S Ill U Pr.
Sociology of the Arts. Ed. by Mildred Weil & Duncan Hartley. LC 75-7162. 1975. pap. text ed. 4.40x o.p. (ISBN 0-8134-1731-7, 1731). Inter Print Pubs.
Sociology of the Social Sciences: A Trend Report & Bibliography. Elisabeth T. Crawford. (Current Sociology-la Sociologie Contemporaine: No. 19-2). 1973. pap. 8.40x o.p. (ISBN 90-2797-655-4). Mouton.
Sociology of Youth Culture & Youth Subcultures. Mike Brake. 1980. pap. 25.00x o.p. (ISBN 0-7100-0363-3); pap. 12.95x o.p. (ISBN 0-7100-0364-1). Routledge Chapman & Hall.
Sociology: Readings. John E. Owen. LC 80-39729. 1981. pap. text ed. 8.00 o.p. (ISBN 0-394-33292-X, RanC). Random.
Sociology Sampler. Ed. by Julie E. White. 325p. 1971. pap. text ed. 9.75x o.p. (ISBN 0-8422-0147-5). Irvington.
Sociology-Technology: The Foundations of Postacademic Social Science. Jay Weinstein. LC 80-24637. 290p. 1982. 39.95 o.p. (ISBN 0-87855-404-1). Transaction Pubs.
Sociology: The Basic Concepts. Edward E. Sagarin. LC 76-41969. 1978. pap. 15.95 o.p. (ISBN 0-275-50330-5, HoltC). HR&W.
Sociology: The Study of Social Systems, Vol. 2. Ronald Fletcher. 224p. 1981. 20.00 o.s.i. (ISBN 0-684-16998-3, ScribT). Scribner.
Sociology: Understanding Social Behavior. Alan P. Bates & Joseph Julian. (Instructors guide written by Patricia Harvey). 1975. text ed. 39.96 o.p. (ISBN 0-395-18652-8); instr's. guide & resource manual 2.36 o.p. (ISBN 0-395-18794-X). HM.
Sociology, Work & Industry. Tony Watson. 272p. 1980. 30.00x o.p. (ISBN 0-7100-0542-3); pap. 12.95x o.p. (ISBN 0-7100-0543-1). Routledge Chapman & Hall.
Sociology 1988-89. 17th, rev. ed. Ed. by Kurt Finsterbusch. LC 72-76876. (Annual Editions Ser.). (Illus.). 256p. 1988. pap. text ed. 9.95x o.p. (ISBN 0-87967-711-2). Dushkin Pub.
Sociopolitical Aspects of Canal Irrigation in the Valley of Oaxaca. Susan Lees. Ed. by Kent V. Flannery. (Memoirs No. 6, Prehistory & Human Ecology of the Valley of Oaxaca Ser.: Vol. 2). (Illus.). 1973. pap. 6.00x o.p. (ISBN 0-932206-70-0). U Mich Mus Anthro.
Sociotechnics: A Trend Report & Bibliography. Ed. by Adam Podgorecki. (La Sociologie Contemporaine: Vol.23, No. 1). 1977. pap. 14.40x o.p. (ISBN 90-2797-692-9). Mouton.
Sociotherapy & Psychotherapy. Marshall Edelson. LC 73-94997. 1970. lib. bdg. 20.00x o.s.i. (ISBN 0-226-18430-7). U of Chicago Pr.
Socrates, the Snowman. Doris L. Gasser. (Illus.). (gr. k-4). 1980. 5.00 o.p. (ISBN 0-682-49446-1). Exposition-Phoenix.
Socrates to Sartre. 2nd ed. Samuel E. Stumpf. 544p. 1974. text ed. 28.95 o.p. (ISBN 0-07-062326-0). McGraw.
Socratic: Comtemporary Philosophy & Christian Faith. John Wisdom. 1952. (ISBN 0-8022-1912-8). Philos Lib.
Sod-House Frontier, 1854-1890: A Social History of the Northern Plains from the Creation of Kansas & Nebraska to the Admission of the Dakotas. Everett Dick. LC 78-24204. (Illus.). xxii, 612p. 1979. pap. 12.95 o.p. (ISBN 0-8032-6551-4, BB 700, Bison). U of Nebr Pr.
Sodium & Potassium in Foods & Drugs. LC 79-27938. pap. 7.00 o.p. (ISBN 0-89970-007-1, OP-080). AMA.
Sodium Hydroxide, No. 10. (ISBN 0-07-521006-1). McGraw.
Sods I Have Cut on the Turf. Jack Leach. (Illus.). 4.50 o.p. (ISBN 0-85131-190-3, Pub. by J A Allen U K). S R Smith Sporting Bks.
Soft Aerobics: The New Low-Impact Workout for Injury Free Exercise. Nancy Burstein. (Illus.). 96p. 1987. pap. 4.95 o.p. (ISBN 0-399-51360-4, Perigee). Putnam Pub Group.
Soft As the Wind. Edith Eckblad. LC 74-79365. (Illus.). 32p. (gr. 1 up). 1974. 3.95 o.p. (ISBN 0-8066-1428-5, 10-5850, Augsburg). Augsburg Fortress.
Soft Crafts for Special Occasions: A Wrights Idea Book. Stephanie Wargo. LC 81-69075. (Illus.). 144p. 1982. 11.95 o.p. (ISBN 0-916752-51-8). Longman Trade.
Soft Drink, Hard Labor: Coca-Cola Workers in Guatemala. Miguel A. Reyes. 60p. (Orig.). 1987. pap. 4.00 o.p. (ISBN 0-85345-749-2, Pub. by Lat Am Bur UK). Monthly Rev.
Soft Exercise. Arthur S. Balaskas & John L. Stirk. (Illus.). 160p. 1983. pap. 9.95 o.p. (ISBN 0-684-17508-8, ScribT). Scribner.
Soft Gold: The Fur Trade & Cultural Exchange on the Northwest Coast of America. Annotations by Bill Holm. LC 82-81739. (Illus.). 312p. (Orig.). 1982. 29.95 o.p. (ISBN 0-87595-107-4, Western Imprints); pap. 19.95 o.p. Oregon Hist.
Soft-Hackled Fly: A Trout Fisherman's Guide. Sylvester Nemes. LC 75-25235. 128p. 1975. 9.95 o.p. (ISBN 0-85699-124-4); pap. 4.95 o.s.i. (ISBN 0-85699-125-2). Chatham Pr.
Soft Machine. William S. Burroughs. 1966. pap. 2.45 o.s.i. (ISBN 0-394-17115-2, B131, BC). Grove.
Soft of Pisces. Allen Dale. 1977. 4.00 o.p. (ISBN 0-682-48875-5). Exposition-Phoenix.
Soft Pretzels with Mustard. David Brenner. (Illus.). 324p. 1983. 14.95 o.p. (ISBN 0-87795-442-9, Arbor Hse). Morrow.
Soft Skull Sam. Syd Hoff. LC 80-24590. (Let Me Read Ser.). (Illus.). 32p. (gr. 4-6). 1981. 6.95 o.p. (ISBN 0-15-277062-3, HJ). HarBraceJ.
Soft Skull Sam. Syd Hoff. LC 80-24590. (Let Me Read Ser.). (Illus.). 32p. (ps-3). 1981. pap. 2.95 o.p. (ISBN 0-15-277063-1, VoyB). HarBraceJ.
Soft Tissue Pain & Disability. Rene Cailliet. LC 77-22612. (Illus.). 313p. 1977. pap. text ed. 14.95x o.p. (ISBN 0-8036-1630-9). Davis Co.
Soft Tissue Sarcomas. Herman D. Suit & Karl H. Proppe. (Illus.). 253p. 1983. pap. 120.00 o.p. (ISBN 0-08-027468-4, H210, H230). Pergamon.
Soft Tissue Tumors. Franz M. Enzinger & Sharon W. Weiss. LC 82-3402. (Illus.). 864p. 1982. text ed. 154.00 o.p. (ISBN 0-8016-1499-6). Mosby.
Soft X-Ray Band Spectra & the Electronic Structures of Metals & Materials. Ed. by Derek J. Fabian. 1969. 99.00 o.p. (ISBN 0-12-247450-3). Acad Pr.
Softball Is for Me. Rosemary G. Washington. LC 81-15562. (Sports for Me Bks.). (Illus.). 48p. (gr. 2-5). 1982. PLB 7.95 o.p. (ISBN 0-8225-1130-4). Lerner Pubns.
Softener. Melvin Bolton. 1986. 14.95 o.p. (ISBN 0-531-15015-1). Watts.
Softness in the Wind. Esther B. Gates. 1975. 4.00 o.p. (ISBN 0-682-48251-X). Exposition-Phoenix.
Softwar. Thierry Breton & Denis Beneich. Tr. by Mark Howson. LC 85-16340. 256p. (Fr.). 1986. pap. 15.95 o.p. (ISBN 0-03-004998-9). H Holt & Co.
Software Aids & Tools Survey. (OIT-FSMC-86-002 Ser.). 638p. 1985. pap. 22.00 o.p. (ISBN 0-318-19903-3, S/N 022-001-00140-6). USGPO.
Software Buyer's Guide. Tony Webster. (BYTE Book). (Illus.). 1984. pap. text ed. 19.95 o.p. (ISBN 0-07-068967-9). McGraw.
Software Buyer's Guidebook: Strategies for Selecting Business Software. Allan F. Froehlich. (Data Processing Ser.). 200p. 1983. 35.95 o.p. (ISBN 0-534-02702-4, Lifetime Learn). Van Nos Reinhold.
Software Catalog: Business Software. International Software Database Staff. 1984. 35.00 o.p. (ISBN 0-444-00934-5). Elsevier.
Software Catalog for Home Builders, 1986. 3rd ed. National Association of Home Builders Staff. Ed. by Robert C. Stroh. 181p. 1987. pap. 12.00 o.p. (ISBN 0-317-43444-6). Nat Assn H Build.
Software Catalog: Minicomputers, 1985. International Software Database Staff. 1450p. 1985. 125.00 o.p. (ISBN 0-444-00982-5). Elsevier.
Software Catalog: Science & Engineering. 2nd ed. International Software Database Staff. 512p. 1985. 45.00 o.p. (ISBN 0-444-00977-9). Elsevier.
Software Configuration Management. William B Bryan et al. LC 80-83084. (Tutorial Texts Ser.). 452p. 1980. 25.00 o.p. (ISBN 0-8186-0309-7, Q309). IEEE Comp Soc.
Software Cost Estimating & Life-Cycle Control: Getting the Software Numbers. Lawrence H. Putnam. LC 80-83083. (Tutorial Texts Ser.). 349p. 1980. 25.00 o.p. (ISBN 0-8186-0314-3, Q314). IEEE Comp Soc.
Software Design Strategies. 2nd ed. Glen D. Bergland & Ronald D. Gordon. LC 81-84179. (Tutorial Texts Ser.). 479p. 1981. 30.00 o.p. (ISBN 0-8186-0389-5, Q389). IEEE Comp Soc.
Software Development Tools. W. E. Riddle & R. E. Fairley. (Illus.). 280p. 1980. pap. 22.00 o.p. (ISBN 0-387-10326-0). Springer-Verlag.
Software Encyclopedia, 1988, 2 vols. Ed. by Bowker, R. R., Co. Staff. 2100p. 1988. 149.95 o.p. (ISBN 0-8352-2410-4). Bowker.
Software Engineering, Vols. 1-2. Julius Tou. 1971. Vol. 1. 67.50 o.p. (ISBN 0-12-696201-4); Vol. 2. 67.50 o.p. (ISBN 0-12-696202-2). Acad Pr.
Software Engineering for Telecommunication Switching Systems. Institution of Electrical Engineers (UK) Staff & Peter Peregrinus, Ltd. Staff. (IEE Conference Publication Ser.: No. 223). 234p. 1983. pap. 74.00 o.p. (ISBN 0-85296-276-2, IC223). Inst Elect Eng.
Software Engineering Standards. 1985. 24.95 o.p. (ISBN 0-471-82802-5). Wiley.
Software Engineering with Ada. Grady Booch. 1983. text ed. 31.25 o.p. (ISBN 0-8053-0600-5); transparency masters o.p. 50.00 o.p. (ISBN 0-8053-0601-3). Benjamin-Cummings.
Software for Amateur Radio. Joe Kasser. (Illus.). 352p. (Orig.). 1984. 21.95 o.p. (ISBN 0-8306-0360-3); pap. 15.95 o.p. (ISBN 0-8306-0260-7, 1560). TAB Bks.
Software Maintenance Management. James A. McCall et al. LC 85-600596. (National Bureau of Standards Special Publication. Computer Science & Technology Ser.: No. 500-129). (Illus.). 67p. (Orig.). 1985. pap. 2.75 o.p. (ISBN 0-318-18838-4, S/N 003-003-02681-6). USGPO.
Software Marketplace: Where to Sell What You Program. S. D. Prince. 224p. 1984. pap. text ed. 16.95 o.p. (ISBN 0-07-050859-3). McGraw.
Software Portability & Standards. Ingemar Dahlstrand. (Computers & Their Applications Ser.: No. 1403). 150p. 1984. 28.95x o.p. (ISBN 0-470-20083-9). Halsted Pr.
Software Proctection & Marketing: Computer Programs & Data Bases, Video Games & Motion Pictures 1983, 2 vols. Practising Law Institute Staff & Morton D. Goldberg. (Patents, Copyrights, Trademarks, & Literacy Course Handbook Ser.). 1983. vols. 159, 160 40.00 o.p. (G6-3723). PLI.
Software Project Management: Step-by-Step. Milton D. Rosenau & Marsha D. Lewin. (Illus.). 314p. 1984. 39.95 o.p. Van Nos Reinhold.
Software Publishing & Distribution. International Resource Development, Inc. Staff. 215p. 1983. 1850.00x o.p. (ISBN 0-88694-574-7). Intl Res Dev.
Software Reference Guide. 2nd ed. Christine Ulrich & Milou Carolan. 287p. (Orig.). 1988. pap. 35.00 o.p. (ISBN 0-87326-938-1, 38511). Intl City Mgt.
Software Reference Guide, 1986-87. Dennis M. Kouba. (Special Report Ser.). 278p. (Orig.). 1987. pap. 29.50 o.p. (ISBN 0-87326-943-8). Intl City Mgt.
Software Sourcebook. Alan J. Lewis. LC 83-73590. 269p. 1984. looseleaf o.p.(ISBN 0-916187-00-4); retail 49.95 o.p. Datatext.
Software Testing & Validation Techniques. 2nd rev. ed. Edward Miller & William E. Howden. LC 81-81431. (Tutorial Texts Ser.). 499p. 1981. 27.00 o.p. (ISBN 0-8186-0365-8, Q365). IEEE Comp Soc.
Software Tools for the IBM PC. Richard W. Brightman & Jeffrey M. Dimsdale. 512p. 1987. pap. text ed. 26.95 o.p. (ISBN 0-8273-2945-8); instr's. guide 6.00 o.p. (ISBN 0-8273-2946-6); diskette 12.95 o.p. (ISBN 0-8273-2947-4). Delmar.
Sogoshosha: Engines of Export-Based Growth. Y. Tsurumi. 91p. 1984. pap. text ed. 9.95x o.p. (ISBN 0-920380-58-1, Pub. by Inst Res Pub Canada). Gower Pub Co.
Soho: A Picture Portrait by Carl Glassman. Intro. by John Leonard. LC 84-8507. (Illus.). 96p. 1985. pap. 10.95 o.p. (ISBN 0-87663-566-4). Universe.
Soho Madonna. Ellen A. Conley. 1980. pap. 2.25 o.p. (ISBN 0-380-75614-5, 75614). Avon.
Soie Sauvage. Olga Broumas. 1979. 22.00 o.p.; pap. 5.00 o.p. (ISBN 0-914742-46-9). Copper Canyon.
Soil & Health. (ISBN 0-8052-0334-6). Random.
Soil & Plant Testing As a Basis of Fertilizer Recommendations. A. Cottenie. (Soils Bulletins: No. 38-2). 120p. 1980. pap. 8.50 o.p. (ISBN 92-5-100956-2, F2034, FAO). UNIPUB.
Soil & Rock Mechanics, Culverts, & Compaction, 9 reports. (Transportation Research Record Ser.). 105p. 1975. 4.60 o.p. (ISBN 0-309-02453-6). Transport Res Bd.
Soil Animals. Keith McE. Keven. (Illus.). 1962. (ISBN 0-8022-0846-0). Philos Lib.
Soil-Cement Construction Handbook. 45p. 1969. pap. 4.25 o.p. (ISBN 0-89312-114-2, EB003S). Portland Cement.
Soil-Cement Slope Protection for Embankments: Field Inspection & Control. 1976. pap. 3.70 o.p. (ISBN 0-89312-155-X, IS168W). Portland Cement.
Soil Components, Vol. One: Organic Components. Ed. by J. E. Gieseking. LC 73-14742. (Illus.). x, 538p. 1975. 88.00 o.p. (ISBN 0-387-06861-9). Springer-Verlag.

Titles

Soil Components, Vol. Two: Inorganic Components. Ed. by J. E. Gieseking. (Illus.). 770p. 1975. 102.00 o.p. (ISBN 0-387-06862-7). Springer-Verlag.

Soil Conditions & Plant Growth. 10th ed. E. W. Russell. 840p. 1986. 54.95 o.p. (ISBN 0-470-20582-2, Co-Pub. with Longman). Wiley.

Soil Conservation. Helmut Kohnke & A. R. Bertrand. (Agricultural Ser.). 1959. text ed. 45.95 o.p. (ISBN 0-07-035285-2). McGraw.

Soil Conservation & Management in the Humid Tropics. Ed. by D. J. Greenland & R. Lal. LC 76-8908. 283p. 1977. 108.00 o.p. (ISBN 0-471-99473-1). Wiley.

Soil Geography. James Cruikshank. (Illus.). 265p. 16.95 o.p. (ISBN 0-686-74073-4); pap. 12.95 o.p. (ISBN 0-7153-5847-2). David & Charles.

Soil Grass & Cancer. Andre Voisin. (Illus.). 300p. 1959. Philos Lib.

Soil Mechanics. 3rd ed. R. F. Craig. 1984. 34.95 o.p. (ISBN 0-442-30567-2); pap. 19.95 o.p. (ISBN 0-442-30568-0). Van Nos Reinhold.

Soil Mechanics, 7 reports. (Transportation Research Record Ser.). 92p. 1974. 3.80 o.p. (ISBN 0-309-02354-8). Transport Res Bd.

Soil Mechanics & Foundation Engineering: Proceedings of the 4th Regional Conference for Africa, Cape Town, 1967. Ed. by A. Burges & J. S. Cregg. 437p. 1968. text ed. 102.00 o.p. (ISBN 0-317-64993-0, Pub. by A A Balkema). Gower Pub Co.

Soil Mechanics Laboratory Manual. Braja M. Das. LC 82-1451. 250p. 1982. pap. text ed. 13.95x o.p. (ISBN 0-910554-36-6). Engineering.

Soil Mechanics: Rutting in Asphalt Pavements, Embankments on Varved Clays, & Foundations. (Transportation Research Record Ser.). 106p. 1976. 4.40 o.p. (ISBN 0-309-02595-8). Transport Res Bd.

Soil Mechanics, SI Version. T. William Lambe & Robert V. Whitman. LC 77-14210. (Geotechnical Engineering Ser.). 553p. 1979. 52.50x o.p. (ISBN 0-471-02491-0). Wiley.

Soil Processes. B. J. Knapp. (Process in Physical Geography Ser.: No. 2). (Illus.). 1979. pap. text ed. 12.95x o.p. (ISBN 0-04-631011-8). Unwin Hyman.

Soil Stabilization, 6 reports. (Transportation Research Record Ser.). 59p. 1974. 2.60 o.p. (ISBN 0-309-02291-6). Transport Res Bd.

Soil Survey & Land Evaluation. Anthony Young & David Dent. (Illus.). 304p. 1981. text ed. 45.00x o.p. (ISBN 0-04-631013-4); pap. text ed. 24.95x o.p. (ISBN 0-04-631014-2). Unwin Hyman.

Soil Taxonomy: A Basic System of Soil Classification for Making & Interpreting Soil Surveys. Usda et al. (Selected Government Publications, A Wiley Reprint Ser.: 1-698). 768p. 1983. 49.95x o.p. (ISBN 0-471-80009-0, Pub. by Wiley-Interscience). Wiley.

Soil Taxonomy & Soil Properties. (Transportation Research Record Ser.). 81p. 1977. 5.20 o.p. (ISBN 0-309-02671-7). Transport Res Bd.

Soil Warming by Electricity. R. H. Coombes. (Illus.). 128p. (ISBN 0-8022-0293-4). Philos Lib.

Soil, Water & Crop Production. Marlowe D. Thorne & D. Wynne Thorne. (Illus.). 1979. 29.95 o.p. (ISBN 0-87055-281-3). AVI.

Soils: An Australian View Point. Ed. by Commonwealth Scientific & Industrial Research Organization, Australia Staff. 1983. 110.00 o.p. (ISBN 0-12-654240-6). Acad Pr.

Soils & Soil Fertility. 4th ed. Louis M. Thompson & Frederick Troeh. (Ag Ser.). (Illus.). 1977. text ed. 43.95 o.p. (ISBN 0-07-064411-X). McGraw.

Soils of Canada, 2 vols. (Illus., Report & inventory). 1977. Set. pap. 35.00x o.p. (ISBN 0-660-00502-6). Gower Pub Co.

Soils of Cumra Area, Turkey: Cumra Bolgesinin Topraklari Turkiye. (Agricultural Research Reports: No. 720). 1969. pap. 11.75 o.p. (ISBN 90-220-0186-5, PDC177, PUDOC). UNIPUB.

Soils of the Kucuk Menderes Valley, Turkey. (Agricultural Research Reports: 785). (Illus.). 1972. pap. 40.00 o.p. (ISBN 90-220-0421-X, PDC91, PUDOC). UNIPUB.

Soils, Their Nature, Classes, Distribution, Uses, & Care. rev. 2nd ed. J. W. Batten & J. Sullivan Gibson. LC 76-40302. (Illus.). 314p. 1977. 14.50 o.p. (ISBN 0-8173-2876-9). U of Ala Pr.

Sojourn in America: An Encounter & Reverbration. Som P. Ranchan. 130p. 1985. text ed. 20.00x o.p. (ISBN 0-7069-2709-5, Pub. by Vikas India). Advent NY.

Sojourn in Mosaic. Robert A. Elfers. (Orig.). 1979. pap. 2.95 o.p. (ISBN 0-377-00089-2). Friendship Pr.

Sojourn on This Sable Earth. Faraz Tyebjee. LC 84-90200. 95p. 1985. 7.95 o.p. (ISBN 0-533-06249-7). Vantage.

Sojourners: A Narrative of the Human Adventure As Lived by Some Historic Dreamers & Sufferers. Philip McFarland. LC 79-63630. (Illus.). 1979. 22.50 o.p. (ISBN 0-689-11003-0, Atheneum). Macmillan.

Sol LeWitt. Ed. by Alicia Legg. LC 77-15309. (Illus.). 1978. 30.00 o.p. (ISBN 0-87070-427-3); pap. 12.50 o.p. (ISBN 0-87070-428-1). Museum Mod Art.

Sol y Sombra. 2nd ed. Paul Pimsleur et al. 1977. 10.95 o.p. (ISBN 0-15-582411-2). HarbraceJ.

Sol y Sombra: Lectures de Hoy. Paul Pimsleur. (Illus.). 1972. pap. 6.95 o.p. (ISBN 0-15-582410-4, HC). HarBraceJ.

Solano County Street Atlas: 1988 (Plus the Cities of Woodland, Davis & Napa) Thomas Bros. Maps Staff. (Illus.). 1988. pap. 10.95 o.p. (ISBN 0-88130-184-1). Thomas Bros Maps.

Solano-Sonoma Counties Street Atlas & Directory, 1988. rev. ed. Thomas Bros. Maps Staff. (Illus.). 228p. 1988. pap. 18.95 o.p. Thomas Bros Maps.

Solar Active Regions. Ed. by Frank Orrall. LC 79-565371. (Skylab Solar Workshop Ser.: No. 3). 1981. 25.00x o.p. (ISBN 0-87081-085-5). Univ Pr Colo.

Solar Business Experience. Ed. by Rick Schwolsky & John Hayes. (Solar Realities Forum: Learning from Experience Ser.). 1982. pap. text ed. 30.00x o.s.i. (ISBN 0-89553-047-3). Am Solar Energy.

Solar Cell Array Design Handbook: The Principles & Technology of Photovoltaic Energy Conversion. Hans S. Rauschenbach. 560p. 1980. 54.95 o.p. (ISBN 0-442-26842-4). Van Nos Reinhold.

Solar Church. Jennifer A. Adams. Ed. by Douglas R. Hoffman. LC 82-11281. 288p. (Orig.). 1982. pap. 9.95 o.p. (ISBN 0-8298-0482-X). Pilgrim NY.

Solar Collectors see Sharing the Sun.

Solar Collectors: A Revision of A-560. Mary Vance. (Architecture Ser.: A 1504). 84p. 1985. 12.75 o.p. (ISBN 0-89028-654-X). Vance Biblios.

Solar Concentrating Mirrors. P. M. Heggen. (Illus.). 100p. 1988. text ed. 80.00x o.s.i. (ISBN 0-937041-14-9); pap. text ed. 50.00x o.s.i. (ISBN 0-937041-15-7). Systems Co.

Solar Cooling & Dehumidifying: Proceedings of the First International Solar Cooling & Dehumidifying Conference (Solar 80), Held in Caracas, 3-6 August 1980. Ed. by A. R. Martinez. (Illus.). 260p. 1981. 53.00 o.p. (ISBN 0-08-027571-0). Pergamon.

Solar Cooling & Heating: Proceedings of the Solar Cooling & Heating Forum, Miami Beach, Dec. 13-15, 1976, 3 vols. new ed. Solar Cooling & Heating Forum Staff. Ed. by T. N. Veziroglu. LC 77-28813. (Illus.). 1066p. 1978. Set. text ed. 255.00 o.p. (ISBN 0-89116-165-1). Hemisphere Pub.

Solar Crop Drying, 2 Vols. Mahendra S. Sodha et al. 1987. 165.00 set o.p. (ISBN 0-317-60692-1). Vol. I 208 p. Vol II 196 p. CRC Pr.

Solar Energy Almanac. Martin McPhillips. (Illus.). 256p. 1983. pap. 10.95 o.p. (ISBN 0-89696-152-4, Everest House Book). Dodd.

Solar Energy Computer Models Directory. 136p. 1985. pap. 4.75 o.p. (ISBN 0-318-19593-3, S/N 061-000-00661-3). USGPO.

Solar Energy Conversion: An Introductory Course. Solar Energy Conversion Course, 5th, University of Waterloo, Ontario, August 6-19, 1978. Ed. by A. E. Dixon & J. D. Leslie. LC 79-41159. (Illus.). 1979. 320.00 o.p. (ISBN 0-08-024744-X). Pergamon.

Solar Energy Conversion: Solid-State Physics Aspects. Ed. by B. O. Seraphin. (Topics in Applied Physics: Vol. 31). (Illus.). 1979. 60.00 o.p. (ISBN 0-387-09224-2). Springer-Verlag.

Solar Energy for Domestic Heating & Cooling. A. Eggers-Lura. 1979. 120.00 o.p. (ISBN 0-08-022152-1). Pergamon.

Solar Energy for Homes Current Status. National Association of Home Builders Staff. 72p. 1980. pap. 6.25 o.p. (ISBN 0-86718-043-9). Nat Assn H Build.

Solar Energy for the Northeast. Mark Uhran. (Illus.). 176p. (Orig.). 1980. pap. 6.95 o.p. (ISBN 0-933614-04-7). Peregrine Pr Pubs.

Solar Energy Fundamentals & Design: With Computer Applications. William B. Stine & Raymond W. Harrigan. LC 84-22207. (Alternate Energy Ser.). 536p. 1985. 39.95 o.p. (ISBN 0-471-88718-8). Wiley.

Solar Energy: Fundamentals in Building Design. Bruce N. Anderson. LC 76-45467. (Illus.). 1977. text ed. 43.50 o.p. (ISBN 0-07-001751-4). McGraw.

Solar Energy in Buildings. Charles Chauliaguet et al. LC 8-27031. 174p. 1979. 61.95 o.p. (ISBN 0-471-27570-0, Pub. by Wiley-Interscience). Wiley.

Solar Energy in Developing Countries. A. Eggers-Lura. 1979. 93.00 o.p. (ISBN 0-08-023253-1). Pergamon.

Solar Energy Index. Arizona State University Library Staff. 1980. 240.00 o.p. (ISBN 0-08-023888-2). Pergamon.

Solar Energy Index: Supplement I. Arizona State University Library Staff. 250p. 1982. 145.00 o.p. (ISBN 0-08-028832-4). Pergamon.

Solar Energy, International Progress: Proceedings of the International Symposium-Workshop on Solar Energy, 16-22 June 1978, Cairo, Egypt, 4 vols. Ed. by T. Nejat Veziroglu. 1980. 540.00 o.p. (ISBN 0-08-025077-7). Pergamon.

Solar Energy: The Awakening Science. Daniel Behrman. 1980. pap. 7.95 o.p. (ISBN 0-316-08772-6). Little.

Solar Energy Update: A Select Guide to Federal & State Government Agencies, Trade & Professional Associations Information Systems, Centers & Publications. Ed. by Claire Mencke. LC 74-79869. 1977. 25.00 o.p. (ISBN 0-89947-009-2, EIC Intell). Bowker.

Solar Energy-Utility Interface. Ed. by A. B Cambel et al. 190p. 1982. pap. 26.00 o.p. (ISBN 0-08-028695-X). Pergamon.

Solar Energy Utilization. Timothy I. Michels. 1979. 34.95 o.p. (ISBN 0-442-25368-0). Van Nos Reinhold.

Solar Engineering, 1982. Ed. by W. D. Turner. 603p. 1982. 85.00 o.p. (H00212). ASME.

Solar Flare Prediction. Constance Sawyer et al. 1986. 32.50 o.p. (ISBN 0-87081-159-2). Univ Pr Colo.

Solar Flares. Ed. by Peter Sturrock. LC 78-73437. (Skylab Solar Workshop Ser.: No. 2). 1979. 32.50 o.p. (ISBN 0-87081-076-6). Univ Pr Colo.

Solar Heating & Cooling Buildings see Sharing the Sun.

Solar Heating Design Process: Active & Passive. Jan F. Kreider. (Illus.). 432p. 1982. text ed. 37.50x o.p. (ISBN 0-07-035478-2). McGraw.

Solar Houses: A Bibliography. Mary Vance. (Architecture Ser.: A 1505). 31p. 1985. 4.50 o.p. (ISBN 0-89028-655-8). Vance Biblios.

Solar Houses for a Cold Climate. Dean Carriere & Fraser Day. (Illus.). 1982. pap. 4.50 Encore o.p. (ISBN 0-684-17424-3, ScribT). Scribner.

Solar Houses: Vol. 17, Facts & Pictures About Authors & Illustrators of Books for Young Peoples. Louis Gropp. LC 78-51802. (Illus.). 1978. 17.95 o.p. (ISBN 0-394-50089-X); pap. 9.95 o.p. (ISBN 0-394-73543-9). Pantheon.

Solar-Hydrogen Energy System: An Authoritative Review of Water-Splitting Systems by Solar Beam & Solar Heat; Hydrogen Production, Storage & Utilization. Ed. by T. Ohta. LC 79-40694. (Illus.). 1979. 73.00 o.p. (ISBN 0-08-022713-9). Pergamon.

Solar Maximum Analysis: Proceedings of Symposium 2 of the COSPAR 25th Plenary Meeting, Graz, Austria, 25 June-7 1984. Ed. by P. A. Simon. (Illus.). 412p. 1985. pap. 54.00 o.p. (ISBN 0-08-032735-4, Pub. by PPL). Pergamon.

Solar Noise Storms. O. Elgaroy. Ed. by D. Ter Harr. 1977. 95.00 o.p. (ISBN 0-08-021039-2). Pergamon.

Solar Output & Its Variation. Ed. by O. R. White et al. LC 76-15773. (Illus.). 1977. 25.00x o.p. (ISBN 0-87081-071-5). Univ Pr Colo.

Solar Power Satellites: Proceedings of the International Symposium, Toulouse, France, June 1980. Ed. by J. W. Freeman. 200p. 1981. pap. 43.00 o.p. (ISBN 0-08-027592-3). Pergamon.

Solar Radiation Data Directory. 154p. 1983. pap. 8.50 o.p. (ISBN 0-318-11830-0, S/N 061-000-00619-2). USGPO.

Solar Radiation Measurements in Developing Countries. Ed. by B. Goldberg. 135p. 1983. pap. 25.00 o.p. (ISBN 0-08-030547-4). Pergamon.

Solar-Space Observations & Stellar Prospects: Proceedings of the Topical Meeting of the COSPAR Interdisciplinary Scientific Commission E (Meetings E1, E2 & E6) of the COSPAR 25th Plenary Meeting, Graz, Austria, 25 June-7 July 1984. Ed. by J. W. Harvey et al. (Illus.). 184p. 1985. pap. 54.00 o.p. (ISBN 0-08-032743-5, Pub. by PPL). Pergamon.

Solar System & Its Strange Objects. Ed. by Brian J. Skinner. LC 81-21156. (Earth & Its Inhabitants: Selected Readings from American Scientist Ser.). (Illus.). 197p. (Orig.). 1982. pap. 11.95x o.p. (ISBN 0-913232-84-X). W Kaufmann.

Solar System Log. Andrew Wilson. 128p. 1987. pap. 14.95 o.p. (ISBN 0-7106-0444-0). Janes Info Group.

Solar System, Simulation, Design see Sharing the Sun.

Solar Terrestrial Physics. J. W. King & W. S. Newman. 1967. 86.00 o.p. (ISBN 0-12-407850-8). Acad Pr.

Solar-Terrestrial Physics: Proceedings of an International Symposium, Innsbruck, Austria, 1978. Ed. by Granville Beynon. (Illus.). 240p. 1979. pap. 52.00 o.p. (ISBN 0-08-025054-8). Pergamon.

Solar Thermal & Ocean Thermal see Sharing the Sun.

Solar Thermal Technical Information Guide. (Illus.). 181p. 1985. pap. 7.00 o.p. (ISBN 0-318-19904-1, S/N 061-000-00659-1). USGPO.

Solar Variability, Weather & Climate. National Research Council Staff. 106p. 1982. pap. text ed. 11.95x o.p. (ISBN 0-309-03284-9). Natl Acad Pr.

Solaraust Microcomputer Solar Analysis Package. E. Baker. 1985. 41.50 o.s.i. (ISBN 0-08-029860-5, Pub. by PPA). Pergamon.

Solarman: The Beginning. David Oliphant & Alison Bellack. (Pendulum Illustrated Originals Ser.). (Illus.). (gr. 4-12). 1979. pap. text ed. 2.45 o.p. (ISBN 0-88301-425-4); wkbk. 1.25 o.p. (ISBN 0-88301-435-1). Pendulum Pr.

Soldier & the State: The Theory & Politics of Civil Military Relations. Samuel P. Huntington. LC 57-6349. 1957. 29.50x o.p. (ISBN 0-674-81735-4, Belknap Pr). Harvard U Pr.

Soldier Boy. Michael French. LC 85-19167. 173p. (gr. 8 up). 1986. 13.95 o.p. (ISBN 0-448-47768-8, G&D). Putnam Pub Group.

Soldier: His Daily Life Through the Ages. Philip Warner. LC 75-10062. (Illus.). 176p. 1975. 8.95 o.s.i. (ISBN 0-8008-7248-7). Taplinger.

Soldier of God. 1.00 o.p. (NCR 465). Paulist Pr.

Soldier of Liberty: Casimir Pulasky. Clarence Manning. (ISBN 0-8022-1048-1). Philos Lib.

Soldier of the Queen. Max Hennessy. LC 80-65993. 1980. 9.95 o.p. (ISBN 0-689-11074-X, Atheneum). Macmillan.

Soldier, Sage, Saint. Robert C. Neville. LC 77-75798. 1978. 20.00 o.p. (ISBN 0-8232-1035-9); pap. 10.00 o.p. (ISBN 0-8232-1036-7). Fordham.

Soldier's Duty. K. Rokossovsky. 341p. 1985. 9.95 o.p. (ISBN 0-317-47698-X, Pub. by Progress Pubs USSR). Imported Pubns.

Soldier's Life. D. Dragunsky. 280p. 1977. 4.95 o.p. (ISBN 0-8285-1569-7, Pub. by Progress Pubs USSR). Imported Pubns.

Soldiers of Forty-Four. William P. McGivern. LC 78-72919. 1979. 10.95 o.p. (ISBN 0-87795-208-6, Arbor Hse). Morrow.

Soldiers of the Cross: Notes on the Ecclesiastical History of New Mexico, Arizona, & Colorado. J. B. Salpointe. LC 67-29317. 299p. 1982. lib. bdg. 44.95x o.p. (ISBN 0-89370-733-3). Borgo Pr.

Sole Prints: A Reference Guide for Law Enforcement Personnel. Don A. Myers. (Illus.). 180p. 1982. ref. manual 24.95 o.s.i. (ISBN 0-9608626-0-9). S O L E Pubns.

Sole Solution. I. Zelig Josephson. Ed. by Melvin H. Naiman. 1979. 6.00 o.p. (ISBN 0-682-49438-0). Exposition-Phoenix.

Solicitors' & Barristers' Directory & Diary 1985. Ed. by Waterlow Publishers, Ltd. Staff. 1472p. 1985. 44.00 o.p. (ISBN 0-08-039241-5, Pub. by Aberdeen Scotland). Pergamon.

Solicitors' & Barristers' Directory & Diary: 1984 Edition, 2 vols. Ed. by Waterlows Publishers Staff. 2000p. 1984. Set. 84.60 o.s.i. (ISBN 0-08-039171-0). Pergamon.

Solid Clues: Quantum Physics, Molecular Biology & the Future of Science. Gerald Feinberg. 304p. 1985. 17.45 o.p. (ISBN 0-671-45608-3). S&S.

Solid Clues: Quantum Physics, Molecular Biology, & the Future of Science. Gerald Feinberg. 1986. pap. 8.95 o.p. (ISBN 0-671-62252-8, Touchstone Bks). S&S.

Solid Earth Geophysics & Geotechnology. Ed. by J. L. Swedlow. 95p. 1982. 18.00 o.p. (ISBN 0-317-33615-0, G00175); members 9.00 o.p. (ISBN 0-317-33616-9). ASME.

Solid Electrolytes: Proceedings of the International Meeting on Solid Electrolytes, 2nd, University of St. Andrews, Sept. 20-22, 1978. International Meeting on Solid Electrolytes Staff. Ed. by R. D. Armstrong. (Illus.). 68p. 1979. pap. 33.00 o.p. (ISBN 0-08-025267-2). Pergamon.

Solid-Gas Interface, Vols. 1 & 2. Ed. by E. A. Flood. 1967. Vol. 1. 125.00 o.p. (ISBN 0-8247-1200-5); Vol. 2. 125.00 o.p. (ISBN 0-8247-1201-3). Dekker.

Solid Ionic & Ionic-Electronic Conductors. Ed. by R. D. Armstrong. LC 77-747. 1977. 40.00 o.p. (ISBN 0-08-021592-0). Pergamon.

Solid-Liquid Equilibrium. T. Haase & H. Schonert. 1969. 70.00 o.p. (ISBN 0-08-012663-4). Pergamon.

Solid: Nine Vital Lessons on Settling, Saving & Solidifying the Black Marriage. Walter A. McCray. 72p. (Orig.). 1981. pap. 3.95 o.p. (ISBN 0-933176-05-8). Black Light Fellow.

Solid State Circuits. G. J. Pridham. 196p. 1973. 50.00 o.p. (ISBN 0-08-016932-5); pap. 12.75 o.p. (ISBN 0-08-016933-3). Pergamon.

Solid State Devices, 1985. Ed. by P. Balk & O. G. Folberth. (Studies in Electrical & Electronic Engineering: No. 23). 242p. 1986. 87.00 o.p. (ISBN 0-444-42600-0). Elsevier.

Solid-State Electronic Circuits for Engineering Technology. Anthony S. Manera. (Illus.). 672p. 1973. text ed. 39.95 o.p. (ISBN 0-07-039871-2). McGraw.

Titles

Solid State Electronics Concepts. J. L. Matthews. 1972. text ed. 40.95 o.p. (ISBN 0-07-040960-9). McGraw.

Solid State Maser. D. H. Orton et al. LC 74-101374. 1970. 75.00x o.p. (ISBN 0-08-006819-7); pap. 75.00 o.p. (ISBN 0-08-006818-9). Pergamon.

Solid State Nuclear Track Detectors: Proceedings of the 12th International Conference, Mexico, 4-10 September 1983. Ed. by G. Espinosa et al. LC 84-201795. 651p. 1984. 165.00 o.p. (ISBN 0-08-031420-1). Pergamon.

Solid-State Physics. Ed. by G. Hohler. LC 76-18956. (Tracts in Modern Physics: Vol. 78). (Illus.). 1976. 52.90 o.p. (ISBN 0-387-07774-X). Springer-Verlag.

Solid State Physics see Physics Programs.

Solid State Plasmas. M. F. Hoyaux. 1970. 15.95x o.p. (ISBN 0-85086-011-3, NO.2914, Pub. by Pion England); pap. 9.50x o.p. (ISBN 0-85086-012-1, NO.2907). Routledge Chapman & Hall.

Solid State Power Rectifiers. R. Wells. 186p. 1982. text ed. 24.50 o.p. (ISBN 0-246-11751-6, Pub. by Granada England). Gower Pub Co.

Solid State Quantum Chemistry: The Chemical Bond & Energy Bands in Tetrahedral Semiconductors. Alexander A Levin. 1977. text ed. 43.95 o.p. (ISBN 0-07-037435-X). McGraw.

Solid Surface Physics. J. Hoelzl et al. (Springer Tracts in Modern Physics: Vol. 85). (Illus.). 1979. 43.00 o.p. (ISBN 0-387-09266-8). Springer-Verlag.

Solid Waste As a Resource. Ed. by M. E. Henstock & M. W. Biddulph. LC 77-24726. 1978. 37.00 o.p. (ISBN 0-08-021571-8). Pergamon.

Solid Wastes, Vol. II. Ed. by Stanton S. Miller. LC 73-87146. 1973. 8.50 o.p. (ISBN 0-8412-0184-6); pap. 6.95 o.p. (ISBN 0-8412-0238-9). Am Chemical.

Solidaridad de los Pueblos con la Republica Espanola 1936-1939. Commision International de Redaccion & Dolores Ibarruri. 415p. (Span.). 1974. 5.45 o.p. (ISBN 0-8285-1443-7, Pub. by Progress Pubs USSR). Imported Pubns.

Solidification & Casting of Metals. 574p. 1979. text ed. 72.00x o.p. (ISBN 0-904357-16-3, Pub. by Inst Metals). Gower Pub Co.

Solids Handling. Chemical Engineering Magazine Editors. Ed. by Kenneth J. McNaughton. (Illus.). 263p. 1981. text ed. 35.50 o.p. (ISBN 0-07-010781-5). McGraw.

Solids Separation Processes. Institution of Chemical Engineers Staff. 1982. 79.00 o.s.i. (ISBN 0-08-028757-3). Pergamon.

Soliloquies. William Shakespeare. 1960. 5.95 o.p. (ISBN 0-88088-493-2). Peter Pauper.

Soliloquy & Other Poems. Ramona R. Newton. (Illus.). 64p. 1981. 5.00 o.p. (ISBN 0-682-49774-6). Exposition-Phoenix.

Solitary in the Ranks: Lawrence of Arabia As Airman & Private Soldier. H. Montgomery Hyde. LC 77-88903. 1978. 11.95 o.p. (ISBN 0-689-10848-6, Atheneum). Macmillan.

Solitary Secret. Patricia Hermes. LC 84-22572. 135p. (gr. 6 up). 1985. 11.95 o.p. (ISBN 0-15-277190-5, HJ). HarBraceJ.

Solitons & Polarons in Solid State Physics. D. Baeriswyl & A. Bishop. 300p. 1989. 63.00 o.p. (ISBN 9971-50-407-3); pap. 35.00 o.p. (ISBN 9971-50-408-1). World Scientific Pub.

Solitude & Privacy. Paul Halmos. 200p. 1953. (ISBN 0-8022-0665-4). Philos Lib.

Solitudes. R. G. Vliet. 1977. 8.95 o.p. (ISBN 0-15-183669-8). HarBraceJ.

Solitude's Lawman. Ray Hogan. LC 87-17111. (Double D Western Ser.). 192p. 1988. pap. 12.95 o.p. (ISBN 0-385-24431-2). Doubleday.

Solitudes: Short Stories. Goffredo Parise. Tr. by Isabel Quigly from Ital. LC 84-40551. 173p. (Orig.). 1985. pap. 7.95 o.s.i. (ISBN 0-394-72994-3, Vin). Random.

Solo Blues. Paula Gosling. 256p. 1982. pap. 2.50 o.s.i. (ISBN 0-345-30643-0). Ballantine.

Solo Song, Fifteen Eighty to Seventeen Thirty. Carol MacClintock. 1980. 17.50x o.p. (ISBN 0-393-02141-6); pap. 9.95x o.p. (ISBN 0-393-09982-2). Norton.

Solo: The Story of the African Wild Dog. Hugo Van Lawick. LC 73-19747. 1974. 6.95 o.p. (ISBN 0-395-18321-9). HM.

Solomon's Children: Exploding the Myths of Divorce. Glynnis Walker. 1985. 16.95 o.p. (ISBN 0-87795-748-7, Arbor Hse). Morrow.

Solomon's New Men. E. W. Heaton. LC 74-13412. (Illus.). 216p. 1975. 15.00x o.p. (ISBN 0-87663-714-4, Pica Pr). Universe.

Solomon's Words of Wisdom. Solomon Alter. 48p. 1985. 6.95 o.p. (ISBN 0-533-06504-6). Vantage.

Soloviev - History of Russia, Vol. 14. Ed. by Edward G. Orchard. 1988. 31.00 o.p. (ISBN 0-317-66681-9). Academic Intl.

Solubilities on Inorganic & Organic Compounds, Vol 3. Stephen. 1979. 720.00 o.p. (ISBN 0-08-023570-0). Pergamon.

Solubility of Gases & Liquids: A Graphic Approach. W. Gerrard. LC 76-10676. (Illus.). 276p. 1976. 55.00x o.p. (ISBN 0-306-30866-5, Plenum Pr). Plenum Pub.

Solution Equilibria. F. R. Hartley et al. LC 79-42956. 361p. 1980. 113.95 o.p. (ISBN 0-470-26880-8). Halsted Pr.

Solution Manual for Operating Systems: Design & Implementation. Raymond W. Turner. 159p. 1986. text ed. write for info. o.p. (ISBN 0-02-421830-8). Macmillan.

Solution Mining Symposium. Ed. by F. F. Aplan & A. D. Pernichele. 469p. 1974. 15.00 o.p. (ISBN 0-317-35843-X, 025-2); members 10.00 o.p. (ISBN 0-317-35844-8); student members 6.00 o.p. (ISBN 0-317-35845-6). SMM&E Inc.

Solution of the Inverse Problem in Geophysical Interpretation. Ed. by R. Cassinis. LC 81-4067. 392p. 1981. 75.00x o.p. (ISBN 0-306-40735-3, Plenum Pr). Plenum Pub.

Solutions for the Major Problems That Face America Today & Beyond. John Carroll, Jr. 1984. 7.50 o.p. (ISBN 0-533-05414-1). Vantage.

Solutions Manual for Introduction to Digital Control Systems. Hugh F. Vanlandingham. 99p. 1985. pap. write for info. o.p. (ISBN 0-02-422620-3). Macmillan.

Solutions Manual to Accompany Petrucci's General Chemistry. 4th ed. Ralph H. Petrucci & Robert K. Wismer. 420p. 1985. write for info. solutions manual o.p. (ISBN 0-02-394540-0). Macmillan.

Solutions to Inflation. Ed. by David C. Colander. 220p. 1979. pap. text ed. 8.00 o.p. (ISBN 0-15-582450-3, HC). HarBraceJ.

Solve Your Child's Sleep Problems. Richard Ferber. 212p. 1985. 16.45 o.p. (ISBN 0-671-46027-7). S&S.

Solvent Effects in Organic Chemistry. Christian Reichardt. (Monographs in Modern Chemistry: Vol. 3). (Illus.). 355p. 1979. 69.00 o.p. (ISBN 0-89573-011-1). VCH Pubs.

Solvent Effects on Chemical Phenomena. Edward S. Amis & James F. Hinton. 1973. Vol. 1. 91.50 o.p. (ISBN 0-12-057301-6). Acad Pr.

Solvent Effects on Reaction Rates & Mechanisms. Edward S. Amis. 1966. 81.00 o.p. (ISBN 0-12-057350-4). Acad Pr.

Solvent Extraction & Ion Exchange in the Nuclear Fuel Cycle. Ed. by D. H. Logsdail & A. L. Mills. (Industrial Chemistry Ser.). 223p. 1985. 66.95 o.p. (ISBN 0-470-20241-6). Halsted Pr.

Solvent Extraction Reviews, Vol. 1. Ed. by Y. Marcus. 1971. 69.75 o.p. (ISBN 0-8247-1438-5). Dekker.

Solving Business Problems: All About Spreadsheet Software, One Point. 1985. 16.95 o.p. (ISBN 0-8104-6777-1). Sams.

Solving Business Problems with Calculators. 5th ed. Richard R. McCready. 1977. 16.95x o.p. (ISBN 0-534-00495-4). PWS-Kent Pub.

Solving Cash Flow Problems Using 1-2-3 & Symphony. David O. Olson et al. LC 84-45693. 300p. 1985. pap. 19.95 o.p. (ISBN 0-8019-7604-9). Chilton.

Solving Cipher Secrets. M. E. Ohaver. 160p. 1983. lib. bdg. 26.80 o.p. (ISBN 0-89412-117-0); pap. 18.80 o.p. (ISBN 0-89412-057-3). Aegean Park Pr.

Solving in Style. John Nunn. 220p. 1985. 16.95 o.p. (ISBN 0-04-794020-4). Unwin Hyman.

Solving Local Government Problems: Practical Applications of Operations Research in Cities & Regions. Charles E. Pinkus & Anne Dixson. (Illus.). 304p. 1981. text ed. 37.50x o.p. (ISBN 0-04-658232-0); pap. text ed. 29.95x o.p. (ISBN 0-04-658233-9). Unwin Hyman.

Solving Mathematical Word Problems. Betty S. Lawing. LC 81-68876. (General Mathematics Ser.). (Illus.). 128p. (Orig.). 1983. pap. text ed. 13.95 o.p. (ISBN 0-8273-1587-2). Delmar.

Solving People-Problems. Peter Honey. 137p. 1981. text ed. 25.95 o.p. (ISBN 0-07-084544-1). McGraw.

Solving Plant Problems: Design, Operation, Maintenance. Ed. by William O'Keefe & Thomas C. Elliott. LC 84-12605. (Illus.). 272p. 1984. text ed. 34.50 o.p. (ISBN 0-07-050585-3). McGraw.

Solving Problems Together. Hogie Wyckoff. LC 80-1003. 272p. 1980. pap. 7.95 o.s.i. (ISBN 0-394-17739-8, E 767, Ever). Grove.

Solving Publishing's Toughest Problems. Jim Mann. 1982. 49.95 o.p. (ISBN 0-918110-07-6). Hanson Pub Grp.

Solving the Riddle of the Universe. Arthur A. Walty. 1952. (ISBN 0-8022-1804-0). Philos Lib.

Solving Your Career Mystery. rev. ed. Muriel S. Karlin. LC 75-12718. (Careers in Depth Ser.). (Illus.). 190p. (gr. 7-12). 1982. lib. bdg. 10.97 o.p. (ISBN 0-8239-0322-2). Rosen Group.

Solzhenitsyn: Creator & Heroic Deed. Leonid D. Rzhevsky. Tr. by Sonja Miller from Rus. LC 77-13643. 144p. 1978. 10.75 o.p. (ISBN 0-8173-7900-2). U of Ala Pr.

Soma: Divine Mushroom of Immortality. R. Gordon Wasson. LC 68-11197. (Illus.). 1972. pap. 8.95 o.p. (ISBN 0-15-683800-1, Harv). HarBraceJ.

Somatic Cell Genetics. Ed. by C. Thomas Caskey & D. Christopher Robbins. LC 82-7604. (NATO ASI Series A, Life Sciences: Vol. 50). 226p. 1982. 49.50x o.p. (ISBN 0-306-41018-4, Plenum Pr). Plenum Pub.

Somatosensory System. Ed. by H. H. Kornhuber. LC 75-16098. (Illus.). 344p. 1975. 30.00 o.p. (ISBN 0-88416-129-3). Year Bk Med.

Some American Men. Gloria Emerson. 1985. 17.45 o.s.i. (ISBN 0-671-24588-0). S&S.

Some Aspects of Earth-Moving Machines As Used in Agriculture. (Agricultural Services Bulletins: No. 27). (Illus.). 56p. (2nd Printing 1976). 1975. pap. 7.50 o.p. (ISBN 92-5-101887-1, F716, FAO). UNIPUB.

Some Aspects of Queueing & Storage Systems. Amitaval Ghosal. LC 78-114016. (Lecture Notes in Operations Research & Mathematical Systems: Vol. 23). 1970. pap. 10.70 o.p. (ISBN 0-387-04947-9). Springer-Verlag.

Some Aspects of Shakespeare's Sonnets. S. P. Sengupta. 1966. text ed. 20.00 o.p. Coronet Bks.

Some Aspects of Vacuum Ultraviolet Radiation Physics. Boris Vodar & J. Romand. LC 73-20163. 1974. 71.00 o.p. (ISBN 0-08-016984-8). Pergamon.

Some Basic Theory for Statistical Inference. E. J. Pitman. LC 78-11921. (Monographs on Applied Probability & Statistics). 105p. 1979. 21.00x o.p. (ISBN 0-412-21720-1, 6221, Pub. by Chapman & Hall England). Routledge Chapman & Hall.

Some Case Studies in Latin America. Ed. by P. McEwan. 88p. 1983. pap. 25.00 o.p. (ISBN 0-08-030843-0, 27). Pergamon.

Some Characteristics of Poverty-U. S. A. pap. cancelled o.s.i. (ISBN 0-8395-3632-1, 3632). BSA.

Some Comm TRS 80. (ISBN 0-07-931054-0). McGraw.

Some Common Crutches. Shirley Schwarzrock & C. Gilbert Wrenn. (Coping with Ser.). (Illus.). 43p. (gr. 7-12). pap. text ed. 3.00 o.p. (ISBN 0-913476-15-3). Am Guidance.

Some Considerations for Counselors. National Association for Women Deans, Administrators & Counselors. 1974. pap. 3.00 o.p. (ISBN 0-686-09581-2). Natl Assn Women.

Some Conventions of Standard Written English. 3rd ed. William H. Pixton. 1979. pap. text ed. 7.95 o.p. (ISBN 0-8403-2643-2). Kendall-Hunt.

Some Dimensions of the Formal Organization. Ed. by Ben Dowd. 121p. 1972. pap. text ed. 7.95x o.p. (ISBN 0-8422-0205-6). Irvington.

Some Discourse, Sermons & Remains. Joseph Glanville. Ed. by Rene Wellek. LC 75-11221. (British Philosophers & Theologians of the 17th & 18th Centuries Ser.). 1979. lib. bdg. 51.00 o.p. (ISBN 0-8240-1775-7). Garland Pub.

Some Distance. Douglas Messerli. 42p. (Orig.). 1983. pap. text ed. 4.00 o.p. (ISBN 0-937804-09-6). Segue NYC.

Some Effects of Technological Change on New England Fishermen. Carl Gersuny et al. (Marine Technical Report Ser.: No. 42). 1975. pap. 1.00 o.p. (ISBN 0-938412-14-0). Sea Grant Pubns.

Some Emerging Issues in Legal Liability of Children's Agencies. Carol M. Rose. LC 77-88236. 68p. 1978. pap. 5.00 o.p. (ISBN 0-87868-173-6, 1736). Child Welfare.

Some English Books with Coloured Plates. Ronald V. Tooley. LC 75-162521. 308p. 1971. Repr. of 1935 ed. 44.00x o.p. (ISBN 0-8103-3762-2). Gale.

Some Factors Affecting Attainment at 18: A Study of Examination Performance in British Schools. H. B. Miles. (Illus.). 1979. 34.00 o.p. (ISBN 0-08-024678-8). Pergamon.

Some Feet Have Noses. Anita Gustafson. LC 81-15573. (Illus.). 96p. (gr. 4 up). 1983. 13.00 o.p. (ISBN 0-688-00925-5); PLB 12.88 o.p. (ISBN 0-688-00926-3). Lothrop.

Some Few Hints in Defence of Dramatical Entertainments see Mr. Law's Unlawfulness of the Stage Entertainment Examin'd.

Some Glad Morning. Faye Gibbons. LC 81-22549. 240p. (gr. 4-6). 1982. 11.75 o.p. (ISBN 0-688-01068-7). Morrow.

Some Improperly Posed Problems of Mathematical Physics. M. M. Lavrentiev. Tr. by R. J. Sacker. (Springer Tracts in Natural Philosophy: Vol. 11). (Illus.). 1967. 20.00 o.p. (ISBN 0-387-03984-8). Springer-Verlag.

Some Issues in Joint Union-Management Quality of Worklife Improvement Efforts. Paul D. Greenberg & Edward M. Glaser. LC 80-14044. 85p. 1980. pap. 4.95 o.p. (ISBN 0-911558-70-5). W E Upjohn.

Some Just Clap Their Hands: Raising a Handicapped Child. Margaret Mantle. 264p. 1987. 16.95 o.p. (Dist. by Watts); pap. 12.95 o.p. (ISBN 0-915361-74-4, Dist. by Watts). Adama Pubs Inc.

Some Key Issues for the World Periphery: Selected Essays. Miguel S. Wionczek. 480p. 1981. 110.00 o.p. (ISBN 0-08-025783-6). Pergamon.

Some Like It Hotter. Geraldine Duncann. LC 85-334. (Illus.). 192p. (Orig.). 1985. pap. 9.95 o.p. (ISBN 0-89286-245-9, One Hund One Prods). Ortho.

Some Lose Their Way. Frederick J. Lipp. LC 80-13510. 132p. (gr. 5-9). 1980. 8.95 o.p. (ISBN 0-689-50178-1, Atheneum). Macmillan.

Some Modern Cults, Sects, Movements & World Religions. Ed. by Thomas B. Warren & Garland Elkins. 1981. 13.00 o.p. (ISBN 0-934916-46-2). Natl Christian Pr.

Some Network Models in Management Science. S. E. Elmaghraby. (Lecture Notes in Operations Research & Mathematical Systems: Vol. 29). 1974. pap. 14.00 o.p. (ISBN 0-387-04952-5). Springer-Verlag.

Some Notes on H. P. Lovecraft. August Derleth. 50p. (Orig.). 1982. pap. 3.95 o.p. (ISBN 0-318-04720-9). Necronomicon.

Some Notes on Wampum. Edwin S. Welles. 26p. Repr. of 1924 ed. 2.00 o.p. (ISBN 0-940748-48-7). Conn Hist Soc.

Some of My Friends Have Tails. Virginia McKenna. LC 76-17730. 1970. 5.50 o.p. (ISBN 0-15-183745-7, HJ). HarBraceJ.

Some of Snooksie's Sayings, Stories & Pictures: Words of Wisdom. Edwin Mumford. (Illus.). 101p. 1980. pap. 7.50 o.p. (ISBN 0-682-49639-1). Exposition-Phoenix.

Some of the Best from Kilobaud Microcomputing. Ed. by Emily A. Gibbs & Jim Perry. 223p. 1980. 10.95 o.p. (BK7311). Wayne Green Ent.

Some of the Best from Kilobaud Microcomputing. Ed Juge et al. Ed. by Emily A. Gibbs & Jim Perry. (Illus.). 223p. 1980. pap. text ed. 10.95 o.p. (ISBN 0-88006-019-0, BK 7311). Wayne Green Ent.

Some Outstanding Clocks over Seven Hundred Years 1250-1950: 1250-1950. H. Alan Lloyd. (Illus.). 216p. 1981. ltd. ed. 69.50 o.p. (ISBN 0-907462-04-9). Antique Collect.

Some Paradoxes of Paul. Edmund B. Keller. LC 74-75085. 276p. 1974. (ISBN 0-8022-2144-0). Philos Lib.

Some People. Harold Nicolson. LC 82-71254. 256p. 1982. pap. 6.95 o.p. (ISBN 0-689-70627-8, 280, Atheneum). Macmillan.

Some Pleasure There to Find. Elizabeth Rossiter. 1977. pap. 1.50 o.p. (ISBN 0-380-01640-0, 32979). Avon.

Some Practical Laws of Learning. B. R. Bugelski. LC 77-84042. (Fastback Ser.: No. 96). 1977. pap. 0.90 o.p. (ISBN 0-87367-096-5). Phi Delta Kappa.

Some Recent Government Publications of Professional Interest to School Librarians: A Bibliographic Essay. Marilyn A. Lester. (Occasional Papers: No. 100). 31p. 1971. pap. 1.00 o.p. (ISBN 0-317-58877-X). U of Ill Lib Info Sci.

Some Social Aspects of Dentistry. Ed. by W. R. Ayer. 100p. 1981. pap. 18.00 o.p. (ISBN 0-08-028132-X). Pergamon.

Some Sort of Epic Grandeur: The Life of F. Scott Fitzgerald. Matthew J. Bruccoli. LC 80-8740. 640p. 1981. 25.00 o.s.i. (ISBN 0-15-183242-0). HarBraceJ.

Some Spanish-American Poets. 2nd ed. Tr. by Alice S. Blackwell. LC 68-23276. (Illus.). 1968. Repr. of 1937 ed. lib. bdg. 35.00x o.p. (ISBN 0-8371-0022-4, BLSP). Greenwood.

Some Special Problems of Children Aged 2-5. Nina Ridenour & Isabel Johnson. 1976. pap. 1.75 o.p. (ISBN 0-686-12268-2). Jewish Bd Family.

Some Strike It Rich: Memoirs & Tales of a Native Son of California. Frank L. Tarleton. (Illus.). 1979. 7.50 o.p. (ISBN 0-682-49275-2, Lochinvar). Exposition-Phoenix.

Some Successive Approximation Methods in Control & Oscillation Theory. P. L. Falb & J. L. De Jong. (Mathematics in Science & Engineering Ser.: Vol. 59). 1969. 77.00 o.p. (ISBN 0-12-247950-5). Acad Pr.

Some Sweet Day. Bryan Woolley. (Southern Writers Ser.). 1985. pap. 2.95 o.p. (ISBN 0-380-69916-8). Avon.

Some Taoist Alchemical Legends. Gustav Meyrink. 1986. pap. 3.95 o.p. (ISBN 0-916411-52-4, Pub. by Alchemical Pr). Holmes Pub.

Some Things Dark & Dangerous. Ed. by Joan Kahn. 224p. 1976. pap. 2.25 o.p. (ISBN 0-380-01556-0, 61168-6, Flare). Avon.

Some Things Fierce & Fatal. Ed. by Joan Kahn. 176p. 1976. pap. 2.25 o.p. (ISBN 0-380-00388-0, 61176-7, Flare). Avon.

Some Things of Value: Micronesian Customs as Seen by Micronesians. Micronesian Community College Students Staff. Ed. by Gene Ashby. LC 82-60520. (Illus.). 200p. (Orig.). 1983. pap. 7.95 o.p. (ISBN 0-931742-12-9). Rainy Day Oreg.

Some Things Strange & Sinister. Ed. by Joan Kahn. 224p. 1976. pap. 2.25 o.p. (ISBN 0-380-00084-9, 61184-8, Flare). Avon.

Some Versions of Silence. Robert Dana. (Orig.). 1967. 4.50 o.p. (ISBN 0-393-04145-X); pap. 1.95 o.p. (ISBN 0-393-04246-4). Norton.

Some Versions of the Fall: The Myth of the Fall of Man in English Literature. Eric Smith. LC 75-185025. (Illus.). 1973. 22.95x o.p. (ISBN 0-8229-1107-8). U of Pittsburgh Pr.

Some Women Dance. Helene Mansfield. 416p. 1985. pap. 3.95 o.p. (ISBN 0-380-89629-X). Avon.

Somebody Knows I'm Alive. Cecil B. Murphey. LC 76-44967. 1978. 4.95 o.p. (ISBN 0-8042-2206-1, John Knox). Westminster John Knox.

Somebody That Nobody Knows. Lenora F. Edwards. 1977. 4.00 o.p. (ISBN 0-682-48768-6). Exposition-Phoenix.

Somebody to Kill. Richard Reinsmith. (Bodyguard Ser.: No. 4). 224p. (Orig.). pap. (ISBN 0-505-51798-1, Pub. by Tower Bks). Dorchester Pub Co.

Somebody to Kill. Richard Reinsmith. (Bodyguard Ser.: No. 4). 224p. (Orig.). 1982. pap. 2.50 o.p. (ISBN 0-8439-1177-8, Pub. by Leisure Bks CT). Dorchester Pub Co.

Somebody's Hero. Bluth Brothers Staff. (Buddies Ser.). (Illus.). 48p. (gr. k-6). 1984. 5.95 o.p. (ISBN 0-8249-8063-8). Ideals.

Someday You Will Understand. Ruth S. Brown. 1979. 5.00 o.p. (ISBN 0-682-49320-1). Exposition-Phoenix.

Someone at the Door. Caroline Crane. LC 84-21193. 196p. 1985. 12.95 o.p. (ISBN 0-396-08601-2). Dodd.

Someone Else's Grave. Alison Smith. 184p. 1986. pap. 2.95 o.p. (ISBN 0-931773-86-5). Critics Choice Paper.

Someone in the House. Barbara Michaels. LC 81-5572. 320p. 1981. 10.95 o.p. (ISBN 0-396-08022-7). Dodd.

Someone Is Killing the Great Chefs of Europe. Nan Lyons & Ivan Lyons. LC 75-45140. 240p. 1976. 7.95 o.p. (ISBN 0-15-183760-0). HarBraceJ.

Someone Special, Just Like You. Brown. (gr. 2-6). 1984. 12.95 o.p. (ISBN 0-8050-0481-5). H Holt & Co.

Someone Was Here: Profiles in the AIDS Epidemic. George Whitmore. 1988. 17.95 o.p. (ISBN 0-317-66210-4). Grove.

Someplace Safe. Greg Herriges. 272p. 1985. pap. 2.75 o.p. (ISBN 0-380-69897-8, Flare). Avon.

Something Beautiful from God. Susan S. Macaulay. LC 80-67388. (Illus.). 1980. pap. 7.95 o.p. (ISBN 0-89107-186-5, Crossway Bks). Good News.

Something Evil. Caroline Crane. LC 84-8171. 224p. 1984. 12.95 o.p. (ISBN 0-396-08419-2). Dodd.

Something in Common. Robert Robin. 245p. 1985. 16.45 o.p. (ISBN 0-671-54769-0). S&S.

Something More. Catherine Marshall. 276p. 1976. pap. 3.50 o.p. (ISBN 0-8007-8266-6, Spire Bks). Revell.

Something Overheard: An Invitation to the New Testament. A. E. Harvey. LC 78-71045. 1979. pap. 3.50 o.p. (ISBN 0-8042-0417-9, John Knox). Westminster John Knox.

Something, Somehow, Somewhere, Someday. Sri Chinmoy. 70p. (Orig.). 1973. pap. 2.00 o.p. (ISBN 0-88497-025-6). Aum Pubns.

Something Special. Beatrice S. De Regniers & Irene Haas. LC 58-9745. (Illus.). (gr. k-3). 1958. 5.95 o.p. (ISBN 0-15-277101-8, HJ). HarBraceJ.

Something the Cat Dragged In. Charlotte MacLeod. (Nightingale Paperbacks Ser.). 1984. pap. 10.95 o.p. (ISBN 0-8161-3710-2, Large Print Bks). G K Hall.

Something to Crow About. Dorothy Van Woerkom. Ed. by Kathleen Tucker. LC 84-24001. (Illus.). 32p. (gr. 1-4). 1982. PLB 10.25 o.p. (ISBN 0-8075-7534-8). A Whitman.

Something to Love. Denise Robins. (Nightingale Paperbacks Ser.). 344p. 1987. pap. 11.95 o.p. (ISBN 0-8161-4323-4, Large Print Bks). G K Hall.

Something to Sing about, for Young Voices. Sally E. Schott & Lois B. Land. (Illus.). 352p. (gr. 7-9). 1984. pap. text ed. 25.95 o.p. (ISBN 0-911320-05-9); wkbk. for levels 1-3 2.95 o.p. (ISBN 0-911320-06-7). Schirmer Bks.

Something Wicked. E. X. Ferrars. (Nightingale Large Print Ser.). 1985. pap. text ed. 9.95 o.p. (ISBN 0-8161-3763-3, Large Print Bks). G K Hall.

Something Wicked This Way Comes. Ray Bradbury. 1962. 9.95 o.p. (ISBN 0-671-67960-0). S&S.

Something Wonderful Happened. Janet E. Givens & Susan E. Dodge. LC 81-10780. (Illus.). 32p. (ps-2). 1982. PLB 8.95 o.s.i. (ISBN 0-689-30904-X, Atheneum Childrens Bks). Macmillan.

Something Wonderful Right Away. Jeffrey Sweet. 432p. 1978. pap. 2.95 o.p. (ISBN 0-380-01884-5, 79707-0, Discus). Avon.

Something Worth Saving. Myrna Marshall. (Living Bks). 192p. (Orig.). 1987. 3.50 o.p. (ISBN 0-8423-6068-9). Tyndale.

Something's Wrong with My Child: A Parents' Book About Children with Learning Disabilities. Milton Brutten et al. LC 73-5876. 1973. 8.95 o.p. (ISBN 0-15-183737-6). HarBraceJ.

Something's Wrong with My Child: A Parent's Handbook about Children with Learning Disabilities. Milton Brutten et al. LC 79-10285. 284p. 1979. pap. 6.95 o.p. (ISBN 0-15-683805-2, Harv). HarBraceJ.

Sometimes I Feel. Rochelle Barsuhn. LC 85-10351. (Illus.). 32p. (gr. 1-2). 1985. PLB 4.95 o.p. (ISBN 0-89693-228-1). Dandelion Hse.

Sometimes I Wonder about Me: Teen-Agers & Mental Health. Marion Howard. 200p. 1983. 14.95 o.p. (ISBN 0-8264-0199-6). Continuum.

Sometimes in the Dead of Night. D. J. Arneson. Ed. by Meg Schneider. (Chiller Ser.). (gr. 3-7). 1983. pap. 3.80 o.s.i. (ISBN 0-671-45593-1). Wanderer Bks.

Sometimes in the Dead of Night. D. J. Arneson & Bernard Brett. LC 82-10514. (Chiller Ser.). 128p. (gr. 8-12). 1983. lib. bdg. 8.79 o.s.i. (ISBN 0-671-46782-4). Messner.

Sometimes It's OK to Tell Secrets. Amy C. Bahr. LC 85-80576. (It's OK to Say No Picture Bks.). (Illus.). 32p. (ps-2). 1986. 4.95 o.p. (ISBN 0-448-15325-4, G&D). Putnam Pub Group.

Sometimes of Children. Enid L. Huelsberg. (gr. k-2). 1976. pap. 3.00 o.p. (ISBN 0-89039-172-6). Ann Arbor Pubs.

Sometimes Sad, Sometimes Glad. Mary O'Hara. 32p. (Orig.). (gr. 6-10). 1973. pap. 1.75 o.p. (ISBN 0-377-03701-X). Friendship Pr.

Sometimes the Books Froze: Wyoming's Economy & Its Banks. L. Milton Woods. LC 85-70773. 1985. 25.00x o.p. (ISBN 0-87081-153-3). Univ Pr Colo.

Sometimes They Bite. Lawrence Block. 304p. 1983. 14.50 o.p. (ISBN 0-87795-485-2, Arbor Hse). Morrow.

Sometimes When It Rains: Short Stories by South African Women. Ann Oosthuizen. LC 86-25490. 1987. 25.00 o.p. (ISBN 0-86358-107-2, 81072, Pub. by Pandora Pr); pap. 9.95 o.p. (ISBN 0-86358-198-6, 81986). Routledge Chapman & Hall.

Somewhere in New Guinea. Frank Clune. 1952. (ISBN 0-8022-0268-3). Philos Lib.

Somewhere Is Such a Kingdom: Poems, 1952-1971. Geoffrey Hill. LC 75-11949. 1975. 6.95 o.p. (ISBN 0-395-20712-6); pap. 3.95 o.p. (ISBN 0-395-20706-1). HM.

Son: A Psychopath & His Victims. Jack Olsen. LC 83-45082. (Illus.). 436p. 1983. 17.95 o.p. (ISBN 0-689-11408-7, Atheneum). Macmillan.

Son & Heir. Edith Begner. 1977. pap. 1.75 o.p. (ISBN 0-380-01787-3, 35311). Avon.

Son Is Given. Ed. by Virginia Sutch. LC 73-16915. (Illus.). 128p. (gr. 1-2). 1974. pap. 3.50 o.p. (ISBN 0-8042-9457-7, John Knox). Westminster John Knox.

Son of Charlemagne: A Contemporary Life of Louis the Pious. Ed. by Allen Cabaniss. LC 61-1398. 1961. 16.95x o.p. (ISBN 0-8156-2031-4). Syracuse U Pr.

Son of Cheap Video. Don Lancaster. LC 80-51714. 224p. 1980. pap. 10.95 o.p. (ISBN 0-672-21723-6, 21723); Set. 15.95 o.p. (21766). Sams.

Son of God: The Origin of Christology & the History of Jewish-Hellenistic Religion. Martin Hengel. Tr. by John Bowden from Ger. LC 75-37151. 112p. 1976. pap. 5.50 o.p. (ISBN 0-8006-1227-2, 1-1227, Fortress). Augsburg Fortress.

Son of Man in Myth & History. Frederick H. Borsch. (New Testament Library). 1967. 8.50 o.s.i. (ISBN 0-664-20794-4, Westminster). Westminster John Knox.

Son of Man: The Story of Jesus. Emil Ludwig. (Black & Gold Lib). (Illus.). 1945. 7.95 o.p. (ISBN 0-87140-882-1). Liveright.

Son of Muscle Car Mania. Mitch Frumkin. LC 82-3527. (Illus.). 176p. 1983. pap. 14.95 o.p. (ISBN 0-87938-154-X). Motorbooks Intl.

Son of the Great American Novel. James Fritzhand. 1978. pap. 1.95 o.p. (ISBN 0-380-01962-0, 38448). Avon.

Son of the Middle Border. Hamlin Garland. LC 78-26593. xxvi, 467p. 1979. 29.95x o.p. (ISBN 0-8032-2102-9); pap. 6.95 o.p. (ISBN 0-8032-7000-3, BB 694, Bison). U of Nebr Pr.

Son of the Wolf. Jack London. 1900. 39.00x o.p. (ISBN 0-403-00613-2). Somerset Pub.

Son Who Left Home see What the Bible Tells Us: Third Series.

Sonata. Rosamond T. Albert. LC 84-90297. 214p. 1986. 13.95 o.p. (ISBN 0-533-06342-6). Vantage.

Sonata Forms. Charles Rosen. (Illus.). 1980. 18.95x o.p. (ISBN 0-393-01203-4). Norton.

Sonata in the Baroque Era. 3rd ed. William S. Newman. 1972. pap. 6.95 o.p. (ISBN 0-393-00622-0, Norton Lib). Norton.

Sonata in the Classic Era. 2nd ed. William S. Newman. 1972. pap. 8.95 o.p. (ISBN 0-393-00623-9, Norton Lib.). Norton.

Sonata Principle. Wilfred H. Mellers. 232p. Repr. of 1969 ed. lib. bdg. 39.00 o.p. (Pub. by Am Repr Serv). Reprint Servs.

Sonata Since Beethoven. 2nd ed. William S. Newman. 1972. pap. 9.95 o.p. (ISBN 0-393-00624-7, Norton Lib). Norton.

Sonata since Beethoven. 3rd ed. William S. Newman. 1983. 22.50x o.p. (ISBN 0-393-95290-8). Norton.

Soncino Haggadah. Cecil Roth. 4.95x o.p. (ISBN 0-685-01039-2). Bloch.

Sone Que la Nieve Ardia. Antonio Skarmeta. 242p. (Span.). 1981. pap. 8.00 o.s.i. (ISBN 84-85594-03-7, 3003). Ediciones Norte.

Song Called Hope. Arthur Gordon. 48p. 1985. 6.95 o.p. (ISBN 0-8378-5081-9). Gibson.

Song Celestial or Bhaggvad-Gita: From the Mahabharata, Being a Discourse Between Arjuna, Prince of India, & the Supreme Being under the Form of Krishna. Tr. by Edwin Arnold. 1967. pap. 5.00 o.p. (ISBN 0-7100-6268-0). Routledge Chapman & Hall.

Song Ceramics. Mary Tregear. (Illus.). 262p. 50.00 o.p. (ISBN 0-317-55045-4). Apollo.

Song for Gilgamesh. Elizabeth J. Hodges. LC 70-115070. (Illus.). (gr. 4-8). 1971. PLB 5.25 o.p. (ISBN 0-689-20657-7, Atheneum). Macmillan.

Song: I Want a Witness. Michael S. Harper. LC 72-81793. (Pitt Poetry Ser). 1972. 15.95 o.p. (ISBN 0-8229-3254-7); pap. 8.95 o.p. (ISBN 0-8229-5231-9). U of Pittsburgh Pr.

Song of Fourteen Songs. Michael D. Goulder. (JSOT Supplement Ser.: No. 36). viii, 94p. pap. text ed. 7.50x o.s.i. (Pub. by JSOT Pr England). Eisenbrauns.

Song of Hero. Stephen Du Vall. 1977. 4.00 o.p. (ISBN 0-682-48860-7). Exposition-Phoenix.

Song of Heyoehkah. Hyemyohsts Storm. LC 80-8359. (Native American Publishing Program). (Illus.). 224p. 1981. 3.50 o.p. (ISBN 0-06-452000-5). HarpR.

Song of Joy. Elaine L. Schulte. 224p. 1987. pap. 5.95 o.p. (ISBN 0-310-47281-4, 15574P). Zondervan.

Song of Love. Betty Headapohl. (Living Books). 224p. 1985. pap. 3.50 o.p. (ISBN 0-8423-6072-7). Tyndale.

Song of Love: A Biblical Understanding of Sex. Helmut Gollwitzer. Tr. by Keith Crim from Ger. LC 78-14667. 80p. 1979. pap. 3.95 o.p. (ISBN 0-8006-1360-0, 1-1360, Fortress). Augsburg Fortress.

Song of Man. Aaron Nissenson. 1964. 14.95x o.p. (ISBN 0-8084-0046-0). New Coll U Pr.

Song of Songs: Love Poems from the Bible. Marcia Falk. LC 77-73049. (Illus.). 1977. 4.95 o.p. (ISBN 0-15-183770-8). HarBraceJ.

Song of the Birds: Sayings, Stories & Impressions of Pablo Casals. Julian L. Webber. 120p. 1987. 14.95 o.p. (ISBN 0-86051-305-X). Parkwest Pubns.

Song of the Cheyenne. Jory Sherman. LC 86-29245. (Double D Western Ser.). 192p. 1987. 12.95 o.s.i. (ISBN 0-385-23251-9). Doubleday.

Song of the Clyde: A History of Clyde Shipbuilding. Fred M. Walker. (Illus.). 1985. 24.50 o.p. (ISBN 0-393-01948-9). Norton.

Song of the Dark Druid. Josepha Sherman. LC 86-91555. (Endless Quest Bks.: No. 36). 160p. (Orig.). (gr. 3-8). 1987. pap. 2.25 o.p. (ISBN 0-88038-442-5). TSR Inc.

Song of the Self Supreme: Astavakra Gita. Tr. by Radhakamal Mukerjee. LC 74-24308. 293p. 1981. 9.95 o.s.i. (ISBN 0-913922-14-5). Dawn Horse Pr.

Song of the Shepherd. Ruth Overholtzer. (Illus.). 19p. (gr. k-4). pap. text ed. cancelled o.s.i. CEF Press.

Song of the Vineyard: A Guide Through the Old Testament. rev. ed. Davie Napier. LC 78-14672. 360p. 1981. pap. 5.95 o.p. (ISBN 0-8006-1352-X, 1-1352, Fortress). Augsburg Fortress.

Song of the Wild. Allan W. Eckert. 252p. 1980. 14.95 o.p. (ISBN 0-316-20877-9). Little.

Song of the Wolf. Scott C. Stone. 1985. 15.95 o.p. (ISBN 0-87795-678-2, Arbor Hse). Morrow.

Song of Zion. M. Wohlgemuth. 1977. 5.00 o.p. (ISBN 0-682-48946-8). Exposition-Phoenix.

Songs after Lincoln. Paul Horgan. 74p. 1965. 4.95 o.p. (ISBN 0-374-26664-6). FS&G.

Songs along the Mahantonga: Pennsylvania Dutch Folksongs. Walter E. Boyer et al. 232p. 1964. Repr. of 1951 ed. 35.00x o.p. (ISBN 0-8103-5002-5). Gale.

Songs & Ballads of Dundee. N. Gatherer. (Illus.). 176p. 1985. pap. text ed. 15.00x o.p. (ISBN 0-85976-146-0, Pub. by John Donald Pub UK). Humanities.

Songs & Ballads of the Maine Lumberjacks. Ed. by Roland P. Gray. LC 73-75944. 216p. 1969. Repr. of 1924 ed. 35.00x o.p. (ISBN 0-8103-3835-1). Gale.

Songs & Lyrics from the English Masques & Light Operas. Ed. by Frederick S. Boas. LC 77-14508. 1977. Repr. of 1949 ed. lib. bdg. 35.00x o.p. (ISBN 0-8371-9842-9, BOMO). Greenwood.

Songs & Poems. Alexander Galich. Tr. by Gerry Smith from Rus. 188p. 1983. 25.00 o.p. (ISBN 0-88233-784-X). Ardis Pubs.

Songs & Sonnets from Laura's Lifetime. Francis Petrarch. Tr. by Nicholas Kilmer from Ital. LC 80-28300. 144p. 1981. 15.00 o.p. (ISBN 0-86547-027-8); pap. 7.50 o.p. (ISBN 0-86547-028-6). N Point Pr.

Songs for a Son. Robert L. Peters. (Orig.). 1967. pap. 2.75 o.p. (ISBN 0-393-04288-X). Norton.

Songs for Language Learning. Sandra J. Shanin. 40p. (Orig.). 1984. pap. text ed. 49.95 o.p. (ISBN 0-88450-899-4, 4633-B). Communication Skill.

Songs for Silent Moments: Prayers for Daily Living. Lois W. Johnson. LC 79-54115. 128p. (Orig.). 1980. pap. 4.95 o.p. (ISBN 0-8066-1765-9, 10-5851, Augsburg). Augsburg Fortress.

Songs for the Space Age Child. Marian K. Richardson & Mary B. Stover. (Illus.). 32p. (Orig.). (ps-4). 1973. pap. 1.95 o.p. (ISBN 0-8192-1159-1). Morehouse Pub.

Songs from the Baltic Coast. A. Luur et al. 88p. 1987. 20.00 o.p. (ISBN 0-8285-3775-5, Pub. by Perioodika Tallinn). Imported Pubns.

Songs from the Stars. Norman Spinard. 1981. pap. 2.50 o.s.i. (ISBN 0-671-82826-6, Timescape). PB.

Songs from Vagabondia. Bliss Carman & Richard Hovey. LC 68-57593. Repr. of 1895 ed. lib. bdg. 35.00x o.p. (ISBN 0-8371-1800-X, CASO). Greenwood.

Songs in Action. P. Gelineau. (Illus.). 320p. (Orig.). 1974. text ed. 29.95 o.p. (ISBN 0-07-023071-4). McGraw.

Songs of a Worker. Arthur O'Shaughnessy. Ed. by Ian Fletcher & John Stokes. LC 76-20159. (Decadent Consciousness Ser.). 1978. lib. bdg. 46.00 o.p. (ISBN 0-8240-2782-5). Garland Pub.

Songs of Armenia. G. Emin. 206p. 1979. 4.95 o.p. (ISBN 0-8285-1641-3, Pub. by Progress Pubs USSR). Imported Pubns.

Songs of Gods, Songs of Humans: The Epic Tradition of the Ainu. Tr. by Donald Philippi from Ainu. LC 81-83970. 432p. 1982. pap. 16.75 o.p. (ISBN 0-86547-063-4). N Point Pr.

Songs of Innocence & of Experience. William Blake. (Orig.). 1971. pap. 0.70 o.p. (ISBN 0-380-01557-9, 18762, Bard). Avon.

Songs of Irish Rebellion: Political Street Ballads & Rebel Songs, 1780-1900. Georges D. Zimmermann. LC 67-21410. 344p. Repr. of 1967 ed. 35.00x o.p. (ISBN 0-8103-5025-4). Gale.

Songs of Mririda. Mririda. Tr. by Daniel Halpern & Paula Paley. LC 74-82761. (Keepsake Ser: Vol. 6). (Illus.). 52p. 1974. 10.00 o.p. (ISBN 0-87775-062-9); pap. 4.00 o.p. (ISBN 0-87775-065-3). Unicorn Pr.

Songs of Oscar Hammerstein II. Oscar Hammerstein. LC 74-21637. (Illus.). 1975. 14.95 o.s.i. (ISBN 0-02-871020-7); pap. 9.95 o.s.i. (ISBN 0-02-871010-X). Schirmer Bks.

Songs of the Bards of Bengal. Tr. & intro. by Deben Bhattacharya. 1970. pap. 4.95 o.p. (ISBN 0-394-17385-6, E543, Ever). Grove.

Songs of the Dream People: Chants & Images from the Indians & Eskimos of North America. Ed. & illus. by James Houston. LC 72-77130. (gr. 4 up). 1972. 5.95 o.p. (ISBN 0-689-30306-8, Atheneum). Macmillan.

Songs of the Synagogue of Florence, 2 vols. Ed. by Fernando D. Belgrado. Incl. Vol. 1. The Three Festivals (ISBN 0-87203-108-X); Vol. 2. The High Holy Days. 0p (ISBN 0-87203-109-8). (Illus.). 60p. 1982. 32.95 ea. o.p. Hermon.

Songs of the Vaisnava Acaryas. Ed. by Swami Acyutananda. 1979. pap. 6.95 o.p. (ISBN 0-912776-56-0). Bhaktivedanta.

Songs of Thomas D'Urfey. Thomas D'Urfey. Ed. by Cyrus L. Day. (Harvard Studies in English). 1969. Repr. of 1933 ed. 23.00 o.p. (ISBN 0-384-11020-7). Johnson Repr.

Songwriter's Market, 1983. Ed. by Barbara N. Kuroff. 432p. 1982. 13.95 o.p. (ISBN 0-89879-086-7). Writers Digest.

Songwriter's Market, 1984. Ed. by Barbara N. Kuroff. 432p. 1983. 13.95 o.p. (ISBN 0-89879-123-5). Writers Digest.

Songwriter's Market, 1985. Rand Ruggeberg. 432p. 1984. 14.95 o.p. (ISBN 0-89879-154-5). Writers Digest.

Songwriter's Market '86. Ed. by Rand Ruggeberg. 432p. 1985. 15.95 o.p. (ISBN 0-89879-201-0, 2071). Writers Digest.

Songwriter's Market '87. Ed. by Julie Whaley. 448p. 1986. 15.95 o.p. (ISBN 0-89879-247-9). Writers Digest.

Songwriter's Market 88. Ed. by Julie Whaley. 480p. 1987. 16.95 o.p. (ISBN 0-89879-276-2). Writers Digest.

Songwriter's Rhyming Dictionary. Sammy Cahn. (Illus.). 216p. 1983. 17.95 o.p. (ISBN 0-87196-765-0). Facts on File.

Sonnet. John Fuller. (Critical Idiom Ser.). 1972. pap. 5.50x o.p. (ISBN 0-416-65690-0, NO.2205). Routledge Chapman & Hall.

Sonnets for an Analyst. Gladys Schmitt. LC 72-95670. 1973. 5.95 o.p. (ISBN 0-15-183780-5). HarBraceJ.

Sonnets from the Interior Life & Other Autobiographical Verse. Kenneth E. Boulding. LC 75-289. 176p. 1975. pap. 15.00x o.p. (ISBN 0-87081-064-2). Univ Pr Colo.

Sonnets from the Portuguese. Elizabeth Barrett Browning. 1966. pap. 0.75 o.p. (ISBN 0-380-01558-7, 19836, Bard). Avon.

Sonnets from the Portuguese. Elizabeth Barrett Browning. (Classics Ser.). (gr. 9 up). slip case 4.95 o.p. (ISBN 0-442-82509-9). Peter Pauper.

Sonnets of Here & Now. Jay R. Reist. 1985. 5.95 o.p. (ISBN 0-533-06573-9). Vantage.

Sonnets of Wordsworth: A Critical Study. P. P. Chauhan. 1981. text ed. 20.00x o.p. Coronet Bks.

Sonoma County Street Atlas, 1988. Thomas Bros. Maps Staff. (Illus.). 156p. 1988. pap. 10.95 o.p. (ISBN 0-88130-179-5). Thomas Bros Maps.

Sonoma-Marin Counties Street Atlas, 1984. Thomas Bros. Maps Staff. (Illus.). 228p. 1984. pap. 16.45 o.p. (ISBN 0-88130-080-2). Thomas Bros Maps.

Sonoma-Marin Counties Street Atlas 1988. Thomas Brothers Maps Staff. (Illus.). 228p. 1988. pap. 18.95 o.p. (ISBN 0-88130-180-9). Thomas Bros Maps.

Sonomammography: An Atlas of Comparative Breast Ultrasound. P. B. Guyer & K. C. Dewbury. 1987. (ISBN 0-471-91342-1, Dist. by A R Liss). Wiley.

Sonora Mutation. Albert J. Elias. 1978. pap. 1.95 o.p. (ISBN 0-380-01963-9, 38463). Avon.

Sons & Daughters of God: Our New Identity in Christ. Ken Wilson. (Living As a Christian Ser.). 80p. (Orig.). 1981. pap. 2.50 o.p. (ISBN 0-89283-097-2). Servant.

Sons & Daughters of Mystical Creatures Coloring Book. Ed. by Jim Sorenson. (Orig.). 1983. pap. 3.95 o.s.i. (ISBN 0-89716-134-3). Peanut Butter.

Sons & Lovers: Text & Criticism. D. H. Lawrence. 1968. 10.00 o.p. Penguin USA.

Sons of Africa. Georgina A. Gollock. LC 75-89001. 1969. Repr. of 1928 ed. 35.00x o.p. (ISBN 0-8371-1746-1, GSA&). Greenwood.

Sons of Chong. March K. Eu. Ed. by S. Michele McFadden. (Illus.). (gr. 3 up). 1978. pap. 6.95 o.p. (ISBN 0-89262-022-6). Career Pub.

Sons of Mosiah. Mark E. Petersen. LC 83-73652. 125p. 1984. 6.95 o.p. (ISBN 0-87747-297-1). Deseret Bk.

Sons of Saintly Women. Bernard Packer. LC 81-66447. 1981. 14.95 o.p. (ISBN 0-689-11177-0, Atheneum). Macmillan.

Sons of the Pioneers. John Givens. LC 77-73052. 1977. 10.00 o.p. (ISBN 0-15-183775-9); pap. 3.95 o.p. (ISBN 0-15-683815-X, Harv). HarBraceJ.

Sons of the Prophets: Leaders in Protestantism from Princeton Seminary. Ed. by Hugh T. Kerr. 1963. 29.50x o.p. (ISBN 0-691-07136-5). Princeton U Pr.

Sonya's Mommy Works. Arlene Alda. Ed. by Kate Klimo. (Illus.). 48p. (ps-3). 1982. 7.75 o.s.i. (ISBN 0-671-45157-X, Little Simon). S&S.

Soon She Must Die. Anna Clarke. (Nightingale Paperbacks Ser.). 1984. pap. 9.95 o.p. (ISBN 0-8161-3703-X, Large Print Bks). G K Hall.

Soon to Be a Major Motion Picture. Theodore Gershuny. LC 81-4710. 384p. 1982. pap. 8.95 o.p. (ISBN 0-03-059819-2, Owl Bks). H Holt & Co.

Sooner or Later. Bruce Hart & Carole Hart. (YA) (gr. 7 up). 1983. pap. 2.50 o.p. (ISBN 0-380-64717-6, 64717-6, Flare). Avon.

Sooner or Later: The Timing of Parenthood in Adult Lives. Pamela Daniels & Kathy Weingarten. 1982. 14.95 o.p. (ISBN 0-393-01484-3). Norton.

Sooner or Later: The Timing of Parenthood in Adult Lives. Pamela Daniels & Kathy Weingarten. 384p. 1983. pap. 6.70 o.p. (ISBN 0-393-30132-X). Norton.

Soonie & the Dragon. Shirley R. Murphy. LC 79-11728. (Illus.). (gr. 4-6). 1979. 7.95 o.p. (ISBN 0-689-30720-9, Atheneum). Macmillan.

Sophia Scarlotti & Ceecee. Anita M. Feagles. LC 78-12630. (gr. 5-9). 1979. 8.95 o.p. (ISBN 0-689-30680-6, Atheneum). Macmillan.

Sophie & Gussie. Marjorie W. Sharmat. LC 72-85188. (Ready-to-Read Ser). (Illus.). 64p. (gr. 1-3). 1973. 6.95 o.p. (ISBN 0-02-782310-5). Macmillan.

Sophie Kay's Microwave. Sophie K. Petros. (Illus.). 80p. (Orig.). 1984. pap. 4.95 o.p. (ISBN 0-8249-3022-3). Ideals.

Sophisticated Estate Planning Techiques: ALI-ABA Course of Study Materials. Massachusetts Continuing Legal Education-New England Law Institute, Inc. Staff & American Law Institute-American Bar Association Committee on Continuing Professional Education. LC 84-227296. 624p. write for info. o.p. Am Law Inst.

Sophisticated Signals & the Uncertainty Principle in Radar. D. E. Vakman. Ed. by Ernest Jacobs. Tr. by K. N. Trirogoff. (Applied Physics & Engineering Ser.: Vol. 4). 1968. 52.00 o.p. (ISBN 0-387-04050-1). Springer-Verlag.

Sophisticated Traveler: Winter: Love It or Leave It. Ed. by A. M. Rosenthal et al. LC 84-40173. (Illus.). 519p. 1984. 14.95 o.p. (ISBN 0-394-53696-7, Pub. by Villard Bks). Random.

Sophists. Untersteiner. 1954. (ISBN 0-8022-1755-9). Philos Lib.

Sophists, Socratics & Cynics. H. D. Rankin. LC 83-12206. 264p. 1983. 28.50x o.p. (ISBN 0-389-20421-8). B&N Imports.

Sopping Thursday. Edward Gorey. (Illus.). 72p. (Orig.). 1971. pap. 4.95 o.p. (ISBN 0-88496-176-1). Capra Pr.

Sopwith Fighters. J. M. Bruce. (Vintage Warbirds Ser.: No. 5). (Illus.). 64p. (Orig.). 1986. pap. 9.95 o.p. (ISBN 0-85368-790-0, Pub. by Arms & Armour). Sterling.

Sor Juana Ines de la Cruz o las Trampas de la Fe. Octavio Paz. 658p. (Span.). 1982. 12.50 o.s.i. (ISBN 968-16-1211-6, 3008). Ediciones Norte.

Sorcerer's Apprentice. Charles Johnson. LC 85-47776. 256p. 1986. 9.95 o.p. (ISBN 0-689-11653-5, Atheneum). Macmillan.

Sorcery. J. Finley Hurley. 256p. 1985. 25.00x o.p. (ISBN 0-7102-0292-X). Routledge Chapman & Hall.

Sore Loser. Genevieve Gray. LC 73-22056. (Illus.). 128p. (gr. 2-6). 1974. 5.95 o.p. (ISBN 0-395-18589-0). HM.

Sore Throats & Sonnets of Love & Opposition. Howard Brenton. 47p. 1979. pap. 4.95 o.p. (ISBN 0-413-46580-2, 3012). Routledge Chapman & Hall.

Soren Kierkegaard. Elmer H. Duncan. Ed. by Bob E. Patterson. LC 76-2862. (Markers of the Modern Theological Mind Ser.). 1976. 8.95 o.p. (ISBN 0-87680-463-6, 80463). Word Bks.

Soren Kierkegaard. Robert L. Perkins. Ed. by Dennis E. Nineham & E. H. Robertson. LC 69-14337. (Makers of Contemporary Theology Ser). (Orig.). 1969. pap. 3.45 o.p. (ISBN 0-8042-0710-0, John Knox). Westminster John Knox.

Sorrow & Joy. J. D. Thomas et al. 1963. 11.95 o.p. (ISBN 0-89112-025-4). Abilene Christ U.

Sorrow Beyond Dreams. Peter Handke. Tr. by Ralph Manheim from Ger. 70p. 1975. 6.95 o.p. (ISBN 0-374-26680-8). FS&G.

Sorrowful & Immaculate Heart of Mary: Message of Berthe Petit, Franciscan Tertiary (1870-1943) Pref. by T. Cadoux. 110p. 1966. pap. 3.00 o.s.i. (ISBN 0-913382-02-7, 101-2). Prow Bks-Franciscan.

Sorry So Sloppy: A Teacher's Portfolio. Deanne Davila Burt. 1977. 5.50 o.p. (ISBN 0-682-48895-X). Exposition-Phoenix.

Sort of a Saga. Bill Mauldin. LC 72-8412. (Illus.). 192p. 1973. 6.95 o.p. (ISBN 0-393-07363-7). Norton.

Sort of Life. Graham Greene. LC 77-156146. 1971. 7.95 o.p. (ISBN 0-671-21010-6). S&S.

Sostoianie Sna. Alexei Tsvetkov. 115p. (Rus.). 1981. 18.50 o.p. (ISBN 0-88233-710-6); pap. 4.00 o.p. (ISBN 0-88233-711-4). Ardis Pubs.

Sotheby's Guide to Buying & Selling at Auction. C. Hugh Hildesley. (Illus.). 223p. 1984. 17.45 o.p. (ISBN 0-393-01782-6). Norton.

Sotheby's: Portrait of an Auction House. Frank Herrmann. (Illus.). 468p. 1981. 29.95 o.p. (ISBN 0-393-01424-X). Norton.

Soucie's Fishing Databook. Gary Soucie. LC 85-6347. 128p. (Orig.). 1985. pap. 10.95 o.p. (ISBN 0-8329-0375-2). Lyons & Burford.

Souffles, Mousses, Jellies & Creams. Robert Ackart. LC 79-55606. 224p. 1982. 0.00 o.p. (ISBN 0-689-11028-6, 284, Atheneum); pap. 6.95 o.p. (ISBN 0-689-70631-6). Macmillan.

Soul Brothers & Sister Lou. Kristin Hunter. (YA) (gr. 7 up). 1976. pap. 1.75 o.p. (ISBN 0-380-00686-3, 59717-9, Flare). Avon.

Soul Butter & Hog Wash & Other Essays on the American West. Ed. by Thomas G. Alexander. LC 77-89974. (Charles Redd Monographs in Western History Ser.: No. 8). 1978. pap. 4.95 o.p. (ISBN 0-8425-1232-2). Brigham.

Soul Food. Tr. by Kenneth N. Taylor. 1973. pap. 5.95 o.p. (ISBN 0-8423-6100-6). Tyndale.

Soul of America. Esquire Magazine Editors. (Scribner-Esquire Press Bks.). 256p. 1986. 16.95 o.p. (ISBN 0-684-18638-1). Scribner.

Soul of Fire. John Uhlmann & Peggy Heinrich. 170p. 1987. text ed. 19.95 o.p. (ISBN 0-317-58721-8). Exposition-Phoenix.

Soul of the Black Preacher. Johnson. 4.95 o.p. Pilgrim NY.

Soul of the City. Ethel S. Creighton. (Illus.). 1944. o.p. (ISBN 0-940882-01-9). HB Pubns.

Soul of the Night: An Astronomical Pilgrimage. Chet Raymo. LC 85-6480. (Illus.). 208p. 1985. 15.95 o.p. (ISBN 0-13-822883-3). P-H.

Soul of the Wolf. Michael W. Fox. (Illus.). 144p. 1980. 12.95 o.p. (ISBN 0-316-29109-9). Little.

Soul Search: Spiritual Growth Through a Knowledge of Past Lifetimes. Glenn Williston & Judith Johnstone. 256p. (Orig.). 1983. pap. 9.99 o.p. (ISBN 0-85500-161-5, Turnstone Pr). Sterling.

Soulforge: A Dragonlance Adventure. Terry Phillips. LC 85-90158. (Dragonlance Adventure Gamebooks). (Illus.). 187p. (Orig.). (gr. 6 up). 1985. pap. 2.50 o.p. (ISBN 0-88038-254-6). TSR Inc.

Soulmate. Charles W. Runyon. 1974. pap. 0.95 o.p. (ISBN 0-380-01560-9, 18028). Avon.

Souls of Lambs: A Fable. Dan Mitchell. 1979. 7.95 o.p. (ISBN 0-395-27572-5). HM.

Soulwinning: Out Where the People Are. rev. ed. T. L. Osborn. (Illus.). 218p. (Orig.). 1982. pap. 3.95 o.p. (ISBN 0-317-44699-1). Harrison Hse.

Sound & Sense: An Introduction to Poetry. 4th ed. Laurence Perrine. 1973. pap. text ed. 7.50 o.p. (ISBN 0-15-582602-6, HC). HarBraceJ.

Sound & Sense: An Introduction to Poetry. 6th ed. Laurence Perrine. LC 76-58774. 345p. (Orig.). 1982. pap. text ed. 12.00 o.p. (ISBN 0-15-582606-9, HC). HarBraceJ.

Sound & Sense: An Introduction to Poetry. 5th ed. Laurence Perrine. 1977. 8.75 o.p. (ISBN 0-15-582604-2). HarbraceJ.

Sound & the Fury *32490. William Faulkner. 1966. 14.00 o.p. (ISBN 0-394-44640-2). Random.

Sound Barrier. Neville Duke & Edward Lanchberry. (Illus.). 140p. 1955. (ISBN 0-8022-0422-8). Philos Lib.

Sound Control & Thermal Insulation of Buildings. Paul D. Close. LC 65-28400. 510p. 1966. 34.50 o.p. (ISBN 0-442-35058-9, Pub. by Van Nostrand). Krieger.

Sound Evidence. June Thomson. 295p. 1986. pap. 10.95x o.p. (ISBN 0-8161-3986-5, Large Print Bks). G K Hall.

Sound Friendships: The Story of Willa & Her Hearing Ear Dog. Elizabeth Yates. LC 86-29110. 96p. 1987. 12.95 o.s.i. (ISBN 0-88150-080-1). Countryman.

Sound: In Eight Languages. Ed. by R. W. Stephens. LC 74-16209. (International Dictionaries of Science & Technology Ser.). 853p. 1975. 79.95x o.p. (ISBN 0-470-82200-7). Halsted Pr.

Sound of Dreams. Herman Weiss. 288p. 1981. pap. 2.50 o.p. (ISBN 0-380-76976-X, 76976-X). Avon.

Sound of Light. Irina Starr. LC 69-20335. 140p. 1969. (ISBN 0-8022-2301-X). Philos Lib.

Sound of Our Own Voices: Women's Study Clubs, 1860-1900. Theodora P. Martin. LC 87-47535. (Illus.). 256p. 1987. 25.00 o.p. (ISBN 0-8070-6710-5). Beacon Pr.

Sound of the Bell. Penny S. Anderson. LC 83-7453. (Illus.). 32p. (gr. 3-4). 1983. PLB 4.95 o.p. (ISBN 0-89693-217-6). Dandelion Hse.

Sound Pleasure: A Prelude to Active Listening. 2nd ed. Donald Ivey. LC 75-30287. (Illus., Orig.). 1977. pap. text ed. 15.00 o.p. (ISBN 0-02-870900-4); record package 15.00 o.p. (ISBN 0-02-870870-9). Schirmer Bks.

Sound Production in Fishes. Ed. by William N. Tavolga. LC 76-28352. (Benchmark Papers in Animal Behavior: Vol. 9). 1977. 72.50 o.p. (ISBN 0-12-787515-8). Acad Pr.

Sound Reception in Fishes, 2 vols. Ed. by W. N. Tavolga. LC 76-13525. (Benchmark Papers in Animal Behavior: Vol. 7). 1976. 72.50 o.p. (ISBN 0-12-787516-6). Acad Pr.

Sound Recording. 2nd ed. John Eargle. 320p. 1980. 26.95 o.p. (ISBN 0-442-22557-1). Van Nos Reinhold.

Sound Thinking - Basic Learning, the Making & Sharing of Music. Catherine H. Kiernan. 1987. 9.95 o.p. (ISBN 0-8062-2238-7). Carlton.

Sound to Remember. Sonia Levitin. LC 79-87522. (Illus.). (ps-3). 1979. 6.95 o.p. (ISBN 0-15-277248-0, HJ). HarBraceJ.

Sound Waves in Solids. H. F. Pollard. 1977. 33.00x o.p. (ISBN 0-85086-053-9, NO.2933, Pub. by Pion England). Routledge Chapman & Hall.

Sounding Right. Robbins Burling. 160p. 1982. pap. text ed. 14.50 o.p. (ISBN 0-88377-216-7). Newbury Hse.

Soundings: A Thematic Guide for Daily Scripture Prayer. Christopher Aridas. LC 83-16509. 224p. 1984. pap. 4.50 o.s.i. (ISBN 0-385-19157-X, Im). Doubleday.

Soundings at Sea Level. Henry B. Hough. 1980. 10.95 o.p. (ISBN 0-395-29165-8). HM.

Sounds All Around. Joy T. Friedman. LC 80-83935. Orig. Title: Look Around & Listen. (Illus.). 80p. (gr. k-2). 1981. PLB 10.15 o.p. (ISBN 0-448-13945-6, G&D); pap. 3.95 o.p. (ISBN 0-448-14755-6). Putnam Pub Group.

Sounds & Scores. Henry Mancini. 244p. 1973. Repr. 19.95 o.s.i. (ISBN 0-89524-060-2, 4001). Cherry Lane.

Sounds & Signals: How We Communicate. Charles T. Meadow. LC 75-2133. (Franklin Institute Bk). (Illus.). (gr. 3-6). 1975. 6.50 o.s.i. (ISBN 0-664-32566-1, Westminster); pap. 4.50 o.s.i. (ISBN 0-664-34008-3, Westminster). Westminster John Knox.

Sounds of English & Italian. Frederick B. Agard & Robert J. Di Pietro. LC 65-25118. (Midway Reprint Ser). 76p. 1974. pap. text ed. 6.00x o.s.i. (ISBN 0-226-01020-1). U of Chicago Pr.

Sounds of My Soul. Willadeene & Joan. (Illus.). 64p. 1981. pap. 4.00 o.s.i. (ISBN 0-682-49811-4). Exposition-Phoenix.

Sounds of the Passion: Meditations on Jesus' Journey to the Cross. David M. Owen. LC 87-28996. 112p. (Orig.). 1975. pap. 5.95 o.p. (ISBN 0-8066-2298-9, 10-5950, Augsburg). Augsburg Fortress.

Sounds Real: Radio in Everyday Life. C. S. Higgins & P. D. Moss. LC 81-21808. (Illus.). 237p. 1983. text ed. 27.50 o.p. (ISBN 0-7022-1900-2); pap. 14.95 o.p. (ISBN 0-7022-1910-X). U of Queensland Pr.

Soup. rev. ed. Coralie Castle. LC 81-11277. (Illus.). 192p. 1981. pap. 7.95 o.p. (ISBN 0-89286-195-9, One Hund One Prods). Ortho.

Soup, Beautiful Soup. Felipe Rojas-Lombardi. (Illus.). 1985. 17.45 o.s.i. (ISBN 0-394-53886-2). Random.

Soups & Salads. Bon Appetit Magazine Editors. LC 82-23295. (Cooking with Bon Appetit Ser.). (Illus.). 144p. 1984. 12.95 o.p. (ISBN 0-89535-116-1). Knapp Pr.

Soups & Salads. Sandi Cooper. Ed. by Betsy Lawrence. LC 81-70441. (Great American Cooking Schools Ser.). (Illus.). 84p. 1982. pap. 5.95 o.p. (ISBN 0-941034-13-5). I Chalmers.

Soups & Sandwiches. Sue Deeming & Bill Deeming. LC 83-80967. (Illus.). 160p. 1983. pap. 6.95 o.p. (ISBN 0-89586-216-6). Price Stern.

Soups, Chowders & Stews. Georgia Orcutt. Ed. by Sandra Taylor. LC 80-53728. (Flavor of New England Ser.). 144p. 1981. pap. 8.95 o.p. (ISBN 0-911658-17-3). Yankee Bks.

Soups of Hakafri Restaurant: Original Version. Rena Franklin. LC 82-2678. (Illus.). 144p. 1982. 12.95 o.p. (ISBN 0-937404-12-8). Triad Pub FL.

Source Book for Food Scientists. Herbert W. Ockerman. (Illus.). 1978. 92.95 o.p. (ISBN 0-87055-228-7). AVI.

Source Book for Older Americans-Income, Rights & Benefits see Social Security, Medicare & Pensions: A Sourcebook for Older Americans.

Source Book for the Disabled. Ed. by Glorya Hale. 1982. pap. 14.95 o.s.i. (ISBN 0-03-057654-7, Owl Bks). H Holt & Co.

Source Book in Medieval Science. Edward Grant. LC 70-183977. (Source Books in the History of Science Ser). 896p. 1974. text ed. 49.50x o.p. (ISBN 0-674-82360-5). Harvard U Pr.

Source Book of Food Enzymology. Sigmund Schwimmer. (Illus.). 1981. 99.95 o.s.i. (ISBN 0-87055-369-0). AVI.

Source Book of Franchise Opportunities. Robert E. Bond. LC 84-71569. 250p. 1984. 19.95 o.p. (ISBN 0-87094-475-4). Dow Jones-Irwin.

Source Book of World War Two Aircraft. John M. Emory. (Illus.). 160p. 1987. 39.95 o.p. (ISBN 0-7137-1722-X, Pub. by Blandford Pr England). Sterling.

Source Book on Applications of the Laser in Metalworking. E. Metzbower. 1981. 55.00 o.p. (ISBN 0-87170-117-0). ASM.

Source Book on Brazing & Brazing Technology. M. M. Schwartz. 1980. 55.00 o.p. (ISBN 0-87170-099-9). ASM.

Source Book on Electron Beam & Laser Welding. M. M. Schwartz. 1981. 55.00 o.p. (ISBN 0-87170-104-9). ASM.

Source Book on Innovative Welding Processes. M. M. Schwarta. 1981. 55.00 o.p. (ISBN 0-87170-105-7). ASM.

Source Coding Theory. CISM (International Center for Mechanical Sciences), Department of Automation & Information Staff. Ed. by G. Longo. (CISM Publications: No. 32). (Illus.). 83p. 1973. pap. 12.40 o.p. (ISBN 0-387-81090-0). Springer-Verlag.

Source of Light. Reynolds Price. LC 80-69650. 1981. 13.95 o.p. (ISBN 0-689-11136-3, Atheneum). Macmillan.

Source of Supply (SOS) 3rd, rev. ed. Global Engineering Documents Staff. Ed. by Carla J. Hook. 588p. 1987. write for info. perfect bdg. o.s.i. (ISBN 0-912702-41-9). Global Eng.

Source of the Swastika. Lord Russell. 1954. (ISBN 0-8022-1411-8). Philos Lib.

Source Problems in American History. Armin Rappaport & Richard Traina. 416p. 1972. pap. text ed. write for info. o.p. (ISBN 0-02-398410-4). Macmillan.

Sourcebook for Programmable Calculators. Texas Instruments Staff. 1979. text ed. 44.50 o.p. (ISBN 0-07-063746-6). McGraw.

Sourcebook for the Biological Sciences. 2nd ed. Evelyn Morholt et al. (Teaching Science Ser.). 795p. 1966. text ed. 20.75 o.p. (ISBN 0-15-582850-9, HC). HarBraceJ.

Sourcebook for the Disabled. Glorya Hale. 1979. 4.95 o.p. (ISBN 0-318-23308-8). Phoenix Soc.

Sourcebook in Marriage & the Family. 4th ed. Ed. by Marvin B. Sussman. 432p. 1974. pap. 15.50 o.p. (ISBN 0-395-17538-0). HM.

Sourcebook of Aid for the Mentally & Physically Handicapped. Ed. by Judith Norback. 528p. 1983. pap. 33.95 o.p. (ISBN 0-442-21205-4). Van Nos Reinhold.

Sourcebook of Articulation Learning Activities. William J. Worthley. 1981. 22.00 o.p. (ISBN 0-316-95458-6). Little.

Sourcebook of Electronic Circuits. John Markus. 1967. text ed. 76.50 o.p. (ISBN 0-07-040443-7). McGraw.

Sourcebook of Sex & Sex Therapy. Ed. by Judith Norback & Patricia Weitz. 344p. 1983. pap. 35.95 o.p. (ISBN 0-442-21204-6). Van Nos Reinhold.

Sourcebook on Clinical Pharmacy. 2nd ed. American Society of Hospital Pharmacists. LC 79-24069. (Illus.). 404p. 1980. text ed. 20.00 o.p. (ISBN 0-88416-303-2). Year Bk Med.

Sourcebook on New Immigration. Ed. by Roy S. Bryce-Laporte. LC 78-64477. 511p. 1979. 29.95 o.p. (ISBN 0-87855-305-3). Transaction Pubs.

Sourcebook on the Environment: The Scientific Perspective. Charles S. ReVelle & Penelope L. ReVelle. 1974. pap. 16.50 o.p. (ISBN 0-395-17018-4). HM.

Sources for the Early History of Ireland: Ecclesiastical. James F. Kenney. 1967. lib. bdg. 57.50x o.p. (ISBN 0-374-94560-8, Octagon). Hippocrene Bks.

Sources for the History of Irish Civilization: Articles in Irish Periodicals, 9 vols. National Library of Ireland Staff, Dublin. 1970. Set. 990.00 o.p. (ISBN 0-8161-0858-7, Hall Library). G K Hall.

Sources in Modern East Asian History & Politics. Ed. by Theodore McNelly. LC 67-18502. (Illus., Orig.). 1967. pap. text ed. 19.95x o.p. (ISBN 0-89197-419-9). Irvington.

Sources of Information in Librarianship & Information Science. R. J. Prytherch. 208p. 1983. 26.00x o.p. (ISBN 0-566-03436-0, 06087-9, Pub. by Gower Pub Co England). Lexington Bks.

Sources of Information in Librarianship & Information Science: A Grafton Book. Ray Prytherch. 212p. 1983. 26.00x o.p. (ISBN 0-317-03078-7, 06087-9). Lexington Bks.

Sources of Information in Transportation: Part 1, General Transportation. 3rd ed. Mary J. Burke et al. (Public Administration Ser.: Bibliography P-1599). 71p. 1985. pap. 10.50 o.p. (ISBN 0-89028-249-8). Vance Biblios.

Sources of Information in Transportation: Part 2, Air Transportation. 3rd ed. Jane M. Janiak & Marty H. Lovelock. (Public Administration Ser.: Bibliography P-1600). 40p. 1985. pap. 6.00 o.p. (ISBN 0-89028-250-1). Vance Biblios.

Sources of Information in Transportation: Part 3, Shipping. 3rd ed. George J. Billy et al. (Public Administration Ser.: Bibliography P-1601). 49p. 1985. pap. 7.50 o.p. (ISBN 0-89028-251-X). Vance Biblios.

Sources of Information in Transportation: Part 4, Railroads. 3rd ed. Gilda Martinello. (Public Administration Ser.: Bibliography P-1602). 20p. 1985. pap. 3.00 o.p. (ISBN 0-89028-252-8). Vance Biblios.

Sources of Information in Transportation: Part 5, Trucking. 3rd ed. Linda Rothbart et al. (Public Administration Ser.: Bibliography P-1603). 67p. 1985. pap. 9.75 o.p. (ISBN 0-89028-253-6). Vance Biblios.

Sources of Information in Transportation: Part 6, Inland Water Transportation. 3rd ed. Mary L. Roy. (Public Administration Ser.: Bibliography P-1604). 39p. 1985. pap. 6.00 o.p. (ISBN 0-89028-254-4). Vance Biblios.

Sources of Information in Transportation: Part 7, Pipelines. 3rd ed. Marie Tilson & Jane Law. (Public Administration Ser.: Bibliography P-1605). 34p. 1985. pap. 5.25 o.p. (ISBN 0-89028-255-2). Vance Biblios.

Sources of Information in Transportation: Part 8, Highways. 3rd ed. Daniel C. Krummes et al. (Public Administration Ser.: Bibliography P-1606). 68p. 1985. pap. 10.50 o.p. (ISBN 0-89028-256-0). Vance Biblios.

Sources of Information in Transportation: Part 9, Urban Transportation. 3rd ed. Michael C. Kleiber & Sylvie Hetu. (Public Administration Ser.: Bibliography P-1607). 23p. 1985. pap. 3.75 o.p. (ISBN 0-89028-257-9). Vance Biblios.

Sources of Invention. 2nd ed. John Jewkes et al. LC 79-90986. (Illus.). 1971. pap. 6.95x o.p. (ISBN 0-393-00502-X, Norton Lib). Norton.

Sources of Organizational & Personal Power in the U. S. Senate: A Test of Alternative Models. Samuel A. Kirkpatrick & Lawrence K. Pettit. (Legislative Research Ser: No. 7). 29p. 1973. pap. 1.50 o.p. (ISBN 0-686-20793-9). Univ OK Gov Res.

South. rev. ed. Jerry E. Jennings & Marion H. Smith. LC 78-70052. (United States Ser). (Illus.). 288p. (gr. 5 up). 1979. text ed. 9.93 ea. 1-4 copies o.p. (ISBN 0-88296-064-4); 5 or more copies 7.94 ea. o.p.; tchrs' annotated ed. 13.68 o.p. (ISBN 0-88296-347-3). Gateway Pr MI.

South Africa. Hildebrand Editorial Staff. (Hildebrand's Travel Guides Ser.). (Illus.). 127p. 1985. pap. 9.95 o.p. (ISBN 0-87052-018-0). Hippocrene Bks.

South Africa & U. S. Multinational Corporations. Ann Seidman & Neva Seidman. LC 77-99205. 256p. 1978. 10.00 o.p. (ISBN 0-88208-084-9); pap. 6.95 o.s.i. (ISBN 0-88208-085-7). Chicago Review.

South Africa: Civilizations in Conflict. Jim Hoagland. LC 76-177533. 1972. 10.95 o.p. (ISBN 0-395-13646-6). HM.

South Africa: Foreign Investment & Apartheid. Lawrence Litvak et al. 100p. 1978. pap. 3.95 o.p.; bulk prices o.p. Inst Policy Stud.

South Africa Review Service Company Reports. 25p. 1985. 25.00 ea. o.p. IRRC Inc DC.

South Africa Review Service Company Reports. 20p. 1984. 25.00 ea. o.p. IRRC Inc DC.

South Africa: Time Running Out. U. S. Policy Toward Southern Africa Study Commission. LC 81-2742. (Perspectives on Southern Africa: No. 29). (Illus.). 1981. 29.95x o.p. (ISBN 0-520-04504-1); pap. 14.95 o.p. (ISBN 0-520-04547-5). U of Cal Pr.

South Africa Today: No Easy Path to Peace. Graham Leach. 256p. 1986. text ed. 24.95 o.p. (ISBN 0-7102-0848-0). Routledge Chapman & Hall.

South Africa Year Book 1978 (State of) Economic, Financial & Statistical Year-Book for the Republic of South Africa. 1978. 35.00 o.s.i. (ISBN 0-685-81373-8). E J Brill USA.

South Africa: Years of Lost Opportunities. Frank J. Parker. LC 78-20633. 304p. 1983. 33.00x o.p. (ISBN 0-669-02750-2). Lexington Bks.

South African Bibliography. Conrad Reitz. (Occasional Papers: No. 90). 17p. 1967. pap. 1.00 o.p. (ISBN 0-317-58868-0). U of Ill Lib Info Sci.

South African Communists Speak, 1915-1980. Y. M. Dadoo et al. 474p. 1981. pap. 25.00x o.p. (ISBN 0-686-83901-3, Pub. by Inkuleko). Imported Pubns.

South African Dialogue: Contrasts in South African Thinking on Basic Race Issues. Ed. by N. J. Rhoodie. LC 73-4205. (Illus.). 640p. 1973. 12.50 o.s.i. (ISBN 0-664-20979-3, Westminster). Westminster John Knox.

South African Novel in English Since 1950: An Information & Resource Guide. G. E. Gorman. 1978. 40.50 o.p. (ISBN 0-8161-8178-0, Hall Reference). G K Hall.

South African Women Speak. Ed. by Jane Barrett et al. LC 86-45005. 268p. 1986. pap. 11.95 o.p. (ISBN 0-394-62201-4, Ever). Grove.

South Africa's National Bibliography, 1983. Intl Pubns Serv.

South Africa's Plan & Capability in Nuclear Field. (Disarmament Studies: No. 2). 40p. 5.00x o.p. (ISBN 0-8002-3315-8). Intl Pubns Serv.

South America. rev. ed. Raymond Fideler & Carol Kvande. LC 76-17680. (World Cultures Ser). (Illus.). (gr. 5 up). 1978. text ed. 11.20 1-4 copies o.s.i. (ISBN 0-88296-103-9); text ed. 8.96 5 or more o.s.i. (ISBN 0-88296-103-9); tchrs' ed 6.96 o.s.i. (ISBN 0-88296-353-8). Gateway Pr MI.

South America, Central America & the Caribbean, 1986. 90.00x o.p. (ISBN 0-317-44262-7, Pub. by Europa). Intl Pubns Serv.

South America, Central America & the Caribbean, 1986: First Edition of a Survey & Directory of the Countries of the Region. 582p. 1986. pap. 90.00 o.p. (EUR55, Europa). UNIPUB.

South America, Nineteen Eighty-One. Steve Birnbaum. (Get 'em & Go Travel Guides). 1980. pap. 9.95 o.p. (ISBN 0-395-29757-5). HM.

South America, Nineteen Eighty-Two. Steve Birnbaum. (Get 'em & Go Travel Guide Ser.). 672p. 1981. pap. 10.95 o.p. (ISBN 0-395-31537-9). HM.

South America on a Shoestring. Geoff Crowther. (Illus.). 516p. 1983. pap. 12.95 o.p. (ISBN 0-908086-08-3). Hippocrene Bks.

South America on Twenty-Five Dollars a Day. Arnold Greenberg. 432p. 1985. pap. 9.95 o.p. (ISBN 0-671-53156-5). Prentice Hall Pr.

South America on Twenty-Five Dollars a Day: 1983-84 Edition. Arnold Greenberg & Harriet Greenberg. (Illus.). 400p. 1983. 7.75 o.p. (ISBN 0-671-45613-X). Prentice Hall Pr.

South America, 1980. Steve Birnbaum. (Get 'em & Go Travel Guides Ser.). 1979. 15.00 o.p. (ISBN 0-395-27772-8); pap. 9.95 o.p. (ISBN 0-395-27773-6). HM.

South America 1983. Steve Birnbaum. 1986. pap. 11.45 o.p. (ISBN 0-395-32874-8). HM.

South America 1984. Steve Birnbaum. 1983. pap. 11.45 o.p. (ISBN 0-395-34633-9). HM.

South America, 1985. Steve Birnbaum. (Get 'em & Go Travel Guides). 1984. pap. 11.70 o.p. (ISBN 0-395-36519-8). HM.

South America, 1987. Steve Birnbaum. (Illus.). 784p. 1986. pap. 12.70 o.s.i. (ISBN 0-395-42335-X). HM.

South American Handbook, 1984. Ed. by John Brooks. (Illus.). 24.95 o.p. (ISBN 0-528-84770-8). Rand McNally.

South American Handbook, 1986. 62nd ed. 1985. 41.00 o.p. (ISBN 0-900751-24-X). Intl Pubns Serv.

South American Handbook, 1988. rev. ed. Ed. by John Brooks. (Illus.). 1472p. 28.95 o.p. (ISBN 0-528-88271-6). Rand McNally.

South American Indian Narrative Theoretical & Analytical Approaches: An Annotated Bibliography. Susan A. Niles. LC 80-9020. 205p. 1985. lib. bdg. 31.00 o.p. (ISBN 0-8240-9308-9). Garland Pub.

South American Species of the Subgenus Anistosarsus Chaudoir (Genus Notiobia Party: Carabidae: Coleoptera) Part II: Evolution & Biogeography. Gerald R. Noonan. (Contributions in Biology & Geology Ser.: No. 45). 118p. 1981. 6.75 o.p. (ISBN 0-89326-072-X). Milwaukee Pub Mus.

South American Species of the Subgenus "Anistosarsus" Chaudoir (Genus "Notiobia" Party-Carabidae-Coleoptera) Part I: Taxonomy & Natural History. Gerald R. Noonan. (Contributions in Biology & Geology Ser.: No. 44). 1981. 5.75 o.p. (ISBN 0-89326-071-1). Milwaukee Pub Mus.

South & North & Other Poems. Lyall Wilkes. 48p. 1984. 8.95 o.p. (ISBN 0-85362-208-6, Oriel). Routledge Chapman & Hall.

South & Southeast Wind Atlas. De Harpporte. 1983. 24.95 o.p. (ISBN 0-442-21822-2). Van Nos Reinhold.

South Asia. 2nd ed. B. L. Johnson. 1981. text ed. 22.50x o.p. (ISBN 0-435-35488-4). Heinemann Ed.

South Asian History, Seventeen Fifty to Nineteen Fifty: A Guide to Periodicals, Dissertations & Newspapers. C. M. Case. 1967. 66.00x o.p. (ISBN 0-691-03059-6). Princeton U Pr.

South Asian Microform Project (SAMP) Catalog: 1980 Cumulative Education. 246p. 12.50 o.p. (ISBN 0-932486-33-9). Ctr Res Lib.

South Besieged. National Historical Society Staff. Ed. by William C. Davis & Bell I. Wiley. LC 82-45399. (Image of War 1861-1865 Ser.: Vol. V). (Illus.). 464p. 1983. 39.95 o.p. (ISBN 0-385-18281-3). Doubleday.

South Carolina Colonial Land Policies. Robert K. Ackerman. LC 74-16184. (Tricentennial Studies: No. 9). 1977. 19.95x o.p. (ISBN 0-87249-254-0). U of SC Pr.

South Carolina Criminal Law. 600p. 1985. looseleaf 12.95 o.p. Gould.

South Carolina Highway Department, 1917-1987. John H. Moore. 350p. 1987. text ed. 9.95x o.p. (ISBN 0-87249-528-0). U of SC Pr.

South Carolina Hiking Trails. Allen DeHart. LC 83-49035. (Illus.). 288p. 1984. pap. 8.95 o.s.i. (ISBN 0-88742-009-5). Globe Pequot.

South Carolina Imprints, 1731-1800: A Descriptive Bibliography. Christopher Gould & Richard P. Morgan. LC 84-21662. 325p. 1985. lib. bdg. 75.00 o.p. (ISBN 0-87436-415-9). ABC-Clio.

South Carolina Industrial Directory, 1988. 600p. 1988. pap. 60.00 o.p. (ISBN 0-318-02870-0). Manufacturers.

South Carolina Motor Vehicles Code. 600p. 1985. 11.95 o.p. (ISBN 0-87526-305-4). Gould.

South Carolina: Trusts. 8.50 o.p. (ISBN 0-686-90895-3). Am Law Inst.

South Carolina Women: They Dared to Lead. Idella Bodie. LC 78-64858. (Illus.). 160p. 1978. Clothbound 9.95 o.p. (ISBN 0-87844-044-5). Sandlapper Pub Co.

South Central California Counties Public Schools: How Are They Doing? 1985. Lillian S. Clancy. (California Public Schools: How Are They Doing?: Vol. 3). 415p. (Orig.). 1984. pap. 23.95 o.p. (ISBN 0-939580-21-7). CA Schl Surveys.

South Central California Counties Public Schools, 1986, Vol. 3. Lillian S. Clancy. (California Public Schools Ser.: How Are They Doing?). 400p. (Orig.). 1985. pap. 24.95 o.p. (ISBN 0-939580-30-6). CA Schl Surveys.

South Central California Counties Public Schools, 1987, Vol. 3. Lillian S. Clancy. (California Public Schools: How Are They Doing? Ser.). 400p. (Orig.). 1987. pap. 24.95 o.p. (ISBN 0-939580-39-X). CA Schl Surveys.

South Central California Counties Public Schools, 1988, Vol. 3. Lillian S. Clancy. (California Public Schools: How Are They Doing? Ser.). 400p. (Orig.). 1988. pap. 25.95 o.p. (ISBN 0-939580-47-0). CA Schl Surveys.

South Dakota: Conflict of Laws. 8.50 o.p. (ISBN 0-686-90897-X). Am Law Inst.

South Dakota: Contracts. 9.50 o.p. (ISBN 0-686-90899-6). Am Law Inst.

South Dakota: Torts, Vols. 1-2. Set. 8.50 o.p. (ISBN 0-686-90901-1). Am Law Inst.

South Dakota: Trusts. 8.50 o.p. (ISBN 0-686-90903-8). Am Law Inst.

South East Asia. rev. ed. Milton Osborne. 208p. (Orig.). 1983. pap. text ed. 9.95x o.p. (ISBN 0-86861-269-3). Unwin Hyman.

South-East Asia on a Shoestring. 5th ed. Tony Wheeler. 574p. (Orig.). 1985. pap. 9.95 o.p. (ISBN 0-908086-67-9). Lonely Planet.

South East Europe. (AA Road Map Ser.). (Illus.). Date not set. (ISBN 0-86145-072-8, Pub. by Auto Assn England). Salem Hse Pubs.

South East to AD 1000: A Regional History of England. Drewett. (Illus.). 384p. 1988. text ed. 39.95 o.p. (ISBN 0-582-49271-8). Longman.

South Korea. Dieter Rumpf. (Hildebrand Travel Guides Ser.). (Illus.). 255p. 1987. pap. 11.95 o.p. (ISBN 0-87052-366-X, Pub by Hildebrand). Hippocrene Bks.

South of Tiburon. Robert Lewis. 1977. 7.50 o.p. (ISBN 0-682-48933-6). Exposition-Phoenix.

South on the Sound: An Illustrated History of Tacoma & Pierce County. Murray Morgan & Rosa Morgan. (Illus.). 199p. 1984. 22.95 o.s.i. (ISBN 0-89781-074-0). Windsor Pubns Inc.

South Pacific Handbook. 2nd ed. David Stanley. (Illus.). 578p. (Orig.). 1983. pap. 12.95 o.p. (ISBN 0-9603322-3-5). Moon Pubns CA.

South Sea Supercargo. Louis Becke. Ed. by A. Grove Day. LC 68-18937. 200p. (YA) (gr. 9 up). 1967. Repr. 10.00x o.p. (ISBN 0-87022-060-8). UH Pr.

South Shore: America's Last Interurban. William Middleton. LC 70-131244. 186p. 22.95 o.p. (ISBN 0-87095-003-7). Gldn West Bks.

South-Siberian Oral Literature Turkic Texts, Vol. 1. V. V. Radloff. LC 66-64926. (Uralic & Altaic Ser: Vol. 79, Bk. 1). 419p. (Repr of 1866 ed). 1967. pap. text ed. 19.95x o.p. (ISBN 0-87750-075-4). Res Ctr Lang Semiotic.

South Star. Betsy G. Hearne. LC 77-3166. (Illus.). 96p. (gr. 3-7). 1977. 7.95 o.s.i. (ISBN 0-689-50091-2, M K McElderry). Macmillan.

South Street: A Photographic Guide to New York City's Historic Seaport. Edmund V. Gillon, Jr. 11.25 o.p. (ISBN 0-8446-5578-3). Peter Smith.

South Texas Garden Book. Bob Webster. (Illus.). 140p. (Orig.). 1980. pap. 11.95 o.p. (ISBN 0-931722-03-9); lib. bdg. 18.95 o.p. (ISBN 0-931722-12-8). Corona Pub.

South Texas Mexican Cookbook. Lucy M. Garza. (Illus.). 96p. 1982. 8.95 o.p. (ISBN 0-89015-344-2). Routledge Chapman & Hall.

South to the Caribbean: How to Carry Out the Dream of Sailing Your Own Boat to the Caribbean. Bill Robinson. (Illus.). 1981. 18.95 o.p. (ISBN 0-393-03265-5). Norton.

South West Africa & the United Nations. Faye Carroll. LC 75-3984. 123p. 1975. Repr. of 1967 ed. lib. bdg. 35.00x o.p. (ISBN 0-8371-7441-4, CASWA). Greenwood.

South-West Wales: Pembrokeshire & Carmarthenshire. Vyvyan Rees. (Shell Guide Ser.). (Illus.). 90p. (ISBN 0-571-04810-2). Intl Pubns Serv.

South Wind. Ester J. Neely. 1979. pap. 2.25 o.p. (ISBN 0-8439-0666-9, Pub. by Leisure Bks CT). Dorchester Pub Co.

Southeast & Southern England. David K. C. Jones. (Geomorphology of the British Isles Ser.). 1980. 25.00x o.p. (ISBN 0-416-84550-9, NO.6506). Routledge Chapman & Hall.

Southeast Asia. Tillman Durdin. LC 65-27529. (New York Times Byline Books). (Orig.). 1966. pap. 2.25 o.p. (ISBN 0-689-10075-2, Atheneum). Macmillan.

Southeast Asia. Mountbattan. 1951. (ISBN 0-8022-1159-3). Philos Lib.

Southeast Asia. Time-Life Books Editors. (Library of Nations). (Illus.). 160p. (YA) (gr. 7 up). 1987. lib. bdg. 23.93 o.p. (ISBN 0-8094-5318-5). Time-Life.

Southeast Asia: A Bibliography for Undergraduate Libraries. University of the State of New York, Foreign Area Materials Center Staff. Ed. by Donald C. Johnson. LC 73-122457. (Occasional Publications Ser: No. 13). 59p. 1970. 8.95 o.s.i. (ISBN 0-87272-015-2). Brodart.

Southeast Asia Collection: Checklist of Southeast Asian Serials. Yale University Staff. 1968. 78.00 o.p. (ISBN 0-8161-0819-6, Hall Library). G K Hall.

Southeast Asia Field Trip for the Library of Congress, Nineteen Seventy to Nineteen Seventy-One. Cecil Hobbs. 94p. 1971. pap. 3.50 o.p. (ISBN 0-87727-085-6, DP 85). Cornell SE Asia.

Southeast Asia Handbook: Singapore, Burma, Brunei, Borneo, Malaysia, Thailand. S. Loose & R. Ramb. (Illus.). 550p. 1983. pap. 13.95 o.p. (ISBN 3-922025-07-2). Bradt Ent.

Southeast Asia Politics: Malayasia & Indonesia. G. P. Bhattacharjee. 1977. 11.00x o.p. (ISBN 0-88386-841-5). South Asia Bks.

Southeast Asia Subject Catalog, 6 vols. Library of Congress Staff. 1972. Set. lib. bdg. 595.00 o.p. (ISBN 0-8161-0857-9, Hall Library). G K Hall.

Southeast Asian Affairs, 1984. Ed. by Pushpa Thambipillai. 384p. 1985. text ed. 45.00 o.p. (ISBN 0-566-00875-0). Gower Pub Co.

Southern Africa: The Continuing Crisis. 2nd ed. Ed. by Gwendolen M. Carter & Patrick O'Meara. LC 81-48324. (Midland Bks.: No. 280). (Illus.). 416p. 1982. 35.00x o.p. (ISBN 0-253-35400-5); pap. 12.95x o.p. (ISBN 0-253-20280-9). Ind U Pr.

Southern African History Before 1900: A Select Bibliography of Articles. Leonard Thompson et al. LC 70-143322. (Bibliographical Ser.: No. 49). 1971. 9.95x o.p. (ISBN 0-8179-2491-4). Hoover Inst Pr.

Southern Baptist in the White House. James T. Baker. LC 77-8926. 1977. pap. 3.95 o.s.i. (ISBN 0-664-24144-1, Westminster). Westminster John Knox.

Southern Bed & Breakfast Book. rev. ed. Corinne M. Ross. LC 85-45690. (Illus.). 192p. 1986. pap. 8.95 o.p. (ISBN 0-88742-062-1). Globe Pequot.

Southern Cal Football see Trojans: A Story of Southern California Football.

Southern California Anthology. Ed. by McLaughlin & Westphal. 1985. pap. 9.95 o.p. (ISBN 0-915520-81-8). Ross-Erikson.

Southern California Counties Public Schools, 1986, Vol. I. Lillian S. Clancy. (California Public Schools Ser.: How Are They Doing?). 400p. (Orig.). 1985. pap. 24.95 o.p. (ISBN 0-939580-28-4). CA Schl Surveys.

Southern California Counties Public Schools, 1987, Vol. 1. Lillian S. Clancy. (California Public Counties Public Schools: How Are They Doing? Ser.). 400p. (Orig.). 1987. pap. 24.95 o.p. (ISBN 0-939580-37-3). CA Schl Surveys.

Southern California Counties Public Schools, 1988, Vol. 1. Lillian S. Clancy. (California Public Schools: How Are They Doing? Ser.). 400p. (Orig.). 1987. pap. 25.95 o.p. (ISBN 0-939580-45-4). CA Schl Surveys.

Southern California Counties Public Schools: How Are They Doing? Lillian S. Clancy. (California Public Schools: How Are They Doing? 1985 Ser.: Vol. 1). 370p. (Orig.). 1984. pap. 23.95 o.p. (ISBN 0-939580-19-5). CA Schl Surveys.

Southern California Public Schools: How Are They Doing? (1984) Lillian S. Clancy. (How Are They Doing Ser.). 1185p. (Orig.). 1984. pap. 40.00 o.p. (ISBN 0-939580-06-3). CA Schl Surveys.

Southern Childhood. Jerry L. Messec. Ed. by Jean McConochie. 64p. 1984. pap. text ed. 1.95 o.p. (ISBN 0-88345-495-5, 20812). Prentice ESL.

Southern Cooking to Remember. Kathryn T. Windham. LC 76-19963. 1978. 9.95 o.p. (ISBN 0-87397-098-5). Strode.

Southern Dreams & Trojan Women. Leo Snow. LC 85-11069. 329p. 1985. 16.50 o.p. (ISBN 0-89587-047-9). Blair.

Southern Dreams & Trojan Women. Leo Snow. 400p. 1986. pap. 4.50 o.p. (ISBN 0-380-70149-9). Avon.

Southern Editorials on Secession. Ed. by Dwight L. Dumond. 1964. 16.50 o.p. (ISBN 0-8446-1162-X). Peter Smith.

Southern Gardener's Soil Handbook. William Peavy. LC 78-58245. (Illus.). 96p. (Orig.). 1979. pap. 6.95x o.p. (ISBN 0-88415-817-9, Pub. by Pacesetter Pr). Gulf Pub.

Southern Heritage All Pork Cookbook. LC 84-60634. (Illus.). 144p. 1985. 9.95 o.p. (ISBN 0-8487-0611-0). Oxmoor Hse.

Southern Heritage Beef, Veal & Lamb Cookbook. LC 83-61838. (Southern Heritage Cookbook Library). (Illus.). 143p. 1984. 9.95 o.p. (ISBN 0-8487-0608-0). Oxmoor Hse.

Southern Heritage Breads Cookbook. LC 82-62139. (Southern Heritage Cookbook Library). (Illus.). 144p. 1983. 9.95 o.p. (ISBN 0-8487-0602-1). Oxmoor Hse.

Southern Heritage Breakfast & Brunch Cookbook. (Southern Heritage Cookbook Library). (Illus.). 144p. 1985. 9.95 o.p. (ISBN 0-8487-0613-7). Oxmoor Hse.

Southern Heritage Cakes Cookbook. LC 82-62141. (Southern Heritage Cookbook Library). (Illus.). 143p. 1983. 9.95 o.p. (ISBN 0-8487-0601-3). Oxmoor Hse.

Southern Heritage Celebrations Cookbook. LC 83-60430. (Southern Heritage Cookbook Library). (Illus.). 143p. 1983. 9.95 o.p. (ISBN 0-8487-0607-2). Oxmoor Hse.

Southern Heritage Company's Coming Cookbook. LC 82-62140. (Southern Heritage Cookbook Library). (Illus.). 144p. 1983. 9.95 o.p. (ISBN 0-8487-0603-X). Oxmoor Hse.

Southern Heritage Cookie Jar Cookbook. (Southern Heritage Cookbook Library). (Illus.). 144p. 1985. 9.95 o.p. (ISBN 0-8487-0616-1). Oxmoor Hse.

Southern Heritage Family Gatherings Cookbook. LC 83-62574. (Southern Heritage Cookbook Library). (Illus.). 144p. 1984. 9.95 o.p. (ISBN 0-8487-0610-2). Oxmoor Hse.

Southern Heritage Gift Receipts Cookbook. (Southern Heritage Cookbook Library). (Illus.). 144p. 1986. 9.95 o.p. (ISBN 0-8487-0615-3). Oxmoor Hse.

Southern Heritage Just Desserts Cookbook. LC 83-82156. (Illus.). 144p. 1985. 9.95 o.p. (ISBN 0-8487-0606-4). Oxmoor Hse.

Southern Heritage Pies & Pastries Cookbook. LC 83-62573. (Southern Heritage Cookbook Library). (Illus.). 144p. 1984. 9.95 o.p. (ISBN 0-8487-0609-9). Oxmoor Hse.

Southern Heritage Plain & Fancy Poultry. LC 82-62142. (Southern Heritage Cookbook Library). (Illus.). 144p. 1983. 9.95 o.p. (ISBN 0-8487-0604-8). Oxmoor Hse.

Southern Heritage Sea & Stream Cookbook. LC 84-61240. (The Southern Heritage Cookbook Library). (Illus.). 144p. 1985. 9.95 o.p. (ISBN 0-8487-0612-9). Oxmoor Hse.

Southern Heritage Socials & Soirees Cookbook. (Southern Heritage Cookbook Library). (Illus.). 144p. 1985. 9.95 o.p. (ISBN 0-8487-0617-X). Oxmoor Hse.

Southern Heritage Soups & Stews Cookbook. (Southern Heritage Cookbook Library). (Illus.). 144p. 1985. 9.95 o.p. (ISBN 0-8487-0614-5). Oxmoor Hse.

Southern Heritage Sporting Scene Cookbook. (Southern Heritage Cookbook Library). (Illus.). 144p. 1986. 9.95 o.p. (ISBN 0-8487-0618-8). Oxmoor Hse.

Southern Heritage Vegetables Cookbook. LC 83-60429. (The Southern Heritage Cookbook Library Ser.). (Illus.). 144p. 1984. 9.95 o.p. (ISBN 0-8487-0605-6). Oxmoor Hse.

Southern Italy. enl. & rev. ed. Paul Blanchard. (Illus.). 1982. 29.95 o.p. (ISBN 0-393-01553-X); pap. 16.95 o. p. o.p. (ISBN 0-393-30005-6). Norton.

Southern Italy: From Rome to Calabria. 4th, rev. ed. Paul Blanchard. (Blue Guides Ser.). (Illus.). 1984. pap. 16.70 o.p. (ISBN 0-393-30065-X). Norton.

Southern King Arthur Family. O. S. Nock. LC 76-2885. (Illus.). 96p. 1976. 19.95 o.p. (ISBN 0-7153-7156-8). David & Charles.

Southern Landscape Tradition in Texas. John B. Jackson. LC 80-65249. (Anne Burnett Tandy Lectures in Amercian Civilization Ser.: No. 1). 37p. 1980. pap. 9.50 o.p. (ISBN 0-88360-035-8, Dist. by Univ. of Texas Pr). Amon Carter.

Southern Lights & Shadows. Frank Fowler. 1976. 16.00x o.p. (ISBN 0-424-00017-2, Pub. by Sydney U Pr). Intl Spec Bk.

Southern Literary Study: Problems & Possibilities. Ed. by Louis D. Rubin, Jr. & C. Hugh Holman. LC 75-11553. xiii, 235p. 1975. 22.50x o.p. (ISBN 0-8078-1252-8). U of NC Pr.

Southern Living Annual Recipes, 1980. Southern Living Magazine Food Editors. LC 79-88364. (Illus.). 352p. 1981. 17.95 o.p. (ISBN 0-8487-0516-5). Oxmoor Hse.

Southern Living Garden Guide. Southern Living Magazine Gardening Editors & John A. Floyd, Jr. LC 80-84409. (Illus.). 224p. 1981. 19.95 o.p. (ISBN 0-8487-0518-1). Oxmoor Hse.

Southern Living 1984 Annual Recipes. Southern Living Magazine Food Editors. LC 83-60428. (Illus.). 368p. 1984. 17.95 o.p. (ISBN 0-8487-0638-2). Oxmoor Hse.

Southern Nights & City Lights. Ron Hudspeth. LC 82-61870. 179p. 1982. 1.98 o.p. (ISBN 0-931948-41-X). Peachtree Pubs.

Southern Ocean, CCAMLR Convention Area, Fighting Areas 48, 58 & 88, Vol. II. Ed. by W. Fischer & J. C. Hureau. (FAO Species Identificaion Sheets for Fishery Purposes Ser.). (Illus.). 470p. (Orig.). 1986. pap. text ed. 45.00 o.p. (ISBN 92-5-102358-1, F2935, FAO). UNIPUB.

Southern Photographs. William Christenberry. (Illus.). 136p. (Orig.). 1988. pap. 19.95 o.p. (ISBN 0-89381-336-2). Aperture.

Southern Plantation Overseer As Revealed in His Letters. Ed. by John S. Bassett. LC 68-55870. (Illus.). 1969. Repr. of 1925 ed. lib. bdg. 22.50x o.p. (ISBN 0-8371-0297-9, BAO&). Greenwood.

Southern Redneck: A Phenomenological Class Study. Julian B. Roebuck & Mark L. Hickson, III. LC 82-9831. 222p. 1984. pap. 13.95 o.p. (ISBN 0-275-91796-7, B1796). Praeger.

Southern Regional Ground Water Conference, 1985: Proceedings. LC 85-29851. 1986. 43.75 o.p. (ISBN 0-318-23025-9). Natl Water Well.

Southern Regions of the United States. Howard Odum. LC 73-76846. 678p. 1969. Repr. of 1936 ed. 48.00x o.p. (ISBN 0-87586-015-X). Agathon.

Southwest Job Bank: A Comprehensive Guide to Major Local Employers. Adams, Robert Lang, & Associates Staff & J. Michael. (Job Bank Ser.). 224p. (Orig.). 1983. pap. 9.95 o.p. (ISBN 0-937860-15-8). Adams Inc MA.

Southwest Pacific & the War. California University Committee on International Relations. LC 74-3750. 168p. 1974. Repr. of 1944 ed. lib. bdg. 35.00x o.p. (ISBN 0-8371-7473-2, CUSP). Greenwood.

Southwest Review Reader. Ed. by Margaret L. Hartley. LC 74-28267. (Illus.). 256p. 1974. 12.95 o.p. (ISBN 0-87074-147-0). SMU Press.

Southwest: South or West? Frank E. Vandiver. LC 75-16448. (Illus.). 48p. 1975. 4.00 o.p. (ISBN 0-89096-003-8). Tex A&M Univ Pr.

Southwestern Indian Drypainting. Leland C. Wyman. LC 82-23891. (School of American Research Southwest Indian Art Ser.). (Illus.). 343p. 1983. 55.00x o.p. (ISBN 0-8263-0640-3). U of NM Pr.

Souvenirs De Guerre see Memoirs of War, 1914-15.

Souvenirs Fresh & Rancid. Alfred Adler. LC 83-81147. 224p. 1982. 14.95 o.s.i. (ISBN 0-394-53218-X, GP868). Grove.

Souvenirs Fresh & Rancid. Alfred Adler. 224p. 1982. pap. 6.95 o.p. (ISBN 0-394-62467-X, Ever). Grove.

Sovereign Ghost: Studies in Imagination. Denis Donoghue. LC 75-27923. 1977. 25.00x o.p. (ISBN 0-520-03134-2). U of Cal Pr.

Sovereignty: An Inquiry into the Political Good. Bertrand De Jouvenel. Tr. by J. F. Huntington. LC 57-9548. 1957. 20.00x o.p. (ISBN 0-226-14161-6). U of Chicago Pr.

Sovereignty & Intervention. Richard N. Gardner & Andre Glucksmann. Trilateral Comm.

Soviet Achievement. J. P. Nettl. LC 68-10825. (History of European Civilization Library). (Illus.). 288p. 1967. pap. text ed. 8.95 o.p. (ISBN 0-15-582901-7, HC). HarBraceJ.

Soviet Almanac. Novosti Press Editors. LC 80-7938. (Illus.). 228p. 1981. 19.95 o.p. (ISBN 0-15-184601-4). HarBraceJ.

Soviet & East European Law & the Scientific-Technical Revolution. Ed. by Gordon B. Smith et al. (Pergamon Policy Studies on International Politics). (Illus.). 330p. 1981. 85.00 o.p. (ISBN 0-08-027195-2). Pergamon.

Soviet & Russian Newspapers at the Hoover Institution: A Catalog. Karol Maichel. LC 66-26281. (Bibliographical Ser.: No. 24). 235p. 1966. 10.95x o.p. (ISBN 0-8179-2241-5); pap. 7.95x o.p. (ISBN 0-8179-2242-3). Hoover Inst Pr.

Soviet & Western Perspectives in Social Psychology. Ed. by L. H. Strickland. LC 79-40311. 1979. 63.00 o.p. (ISBN 0-08-023389-9). Pergamon.

Soviet Approach to National Security. Gloria C. Duffy & Jennifer Scheck. 144p. 1987. pap. 12.95 o.p. (ISBN 0-88738-712-8). Transaction Pubs.

Soviet Armed Forces: Books in English, 1950-1967. Michael Parrish. LC 71-128167. (Bibliographical Ser.: No. 48). 1970. 9.95x o.p. (ISBN 0-8179-2481-7). Hoover Inst Pr.

Soviet Armed Forces Review Annual, 1977-1985, Vols. 1-9. Ed. by David R. Jones. (SAFRA Ser.). 69.50 ea. o.p. Academic Intl.

Soviet Armed Forces Review Annual 1986-1987, Vol. 10. Ed. by David Jones. 1988. 71.00 o.p. (ISBN 0-87569-100-5); pap. 91.00 o.p. Academic Intl.

Soviet Armenia. K. S. Demirchian. Tr. by Percy Ludwick. 98p. 1984. 5.95 o.p. (ISBN 0-8285-2839-X, Pub. by Progress Pubns USSR). Imported Pubns.

Soviet Army Uniforms in World War II. Steven J. Zaloga. (Uniforms Illustrated Ser.: No. 9). (Illus.). 64p. (Orig.). 1985. pap. 9.95 o.p. (ISBN 0-85368-678-5, Pub. by Arms & Armour). Sterling.

Soviet Ballet. Juris Slonimsky. (ISBN 0-8022-1587-4). Philos Lib.

Soviet Chess. Ed. by R. G. Wade. 1976. pap. 3.00 o.p. (ISBN 0-87980-311-8). Wilshire.

Soviet Colossus: A History of the U. S. S. R. Michael G. Kort. (Illus.). 350p. 1985. 19.95 o.p. (ISBN 0-684-18178-9). Scribner.

Soviet Conduct in World Affairs. Compiled by Alexander Dallin. LC 75-31359. 318p. 1976. Repr. of 1960 ed. lib. bdg. 38.50x o.p. (ISBN 0-8371-8511-4, DASCW). Greenwood.

Soviet Court. V. Terebilov. 182p. 1973. 4.95 o.p. (ISBN 0-8285-0282-X, 131647, Pub. by Progress Pubs USSR). Imported Pubns.

Soviet-East European Dialogue: Relations of a New Type? Nish Jamgotch, Jr. LC 68-29991. (Studies: No. 21). 1968. 8.95x o.p. (ISBN 0-8179-3211-9); pap. 5.95 o.p. (ISBN 0-8179-3212-7). Hoover Inst Pr.

Soviet-East European Dilemmas. Ed. by Karen Dawisha & Philip Hanson. LC 80-28573. 226p. 1981. 32.50 o.p. (ISBN 0-8419-0697-1); pap. 14.95 o.p. (ISBN 0-8419-0698-X). Holmes & Meier.

Soviet Economic Policy: Income Differentials in the U. S. S. R. Vinod Mehta. LC 77-70009. 1977. text ed. 12.50x o.p. (ISBN 0-391-00750-5). Humanities.

Soviet Economic Thought & Political Power in the U. S. S. R. Aron Katsenelinboigen. LC 78-17552. (Pergamon Policy Studies). 1980. 55.00 o.p. (ISBN 0-08-022467-9). Pergamon.

Soviet Economy. rev. ed. Nicolas Spulber. 1969. 12.95x o.p. (ISBN 0-393-09860-5, NortonC). Norton.

Soviet Economy Nineteen Forty to Nineteen Sixty-Five. Vladimir Katkoff. LC 73-11750. 559p. 1973. Repr. of 1961 ed. lib. bdg. 59.50x o.p. (ISBN 0-8371-7085-0, KASE). Greenwood.

Soviet Family of Nations: A Latvian Journey. Darshan Singh. 110p. 1984. text ed. 13.95x o.p. (ISBN 0-86590-212-7, Pub. by Sterling Pubs India). Apt Bks.

Soviet Foreign-Policy Aims: Neutralism & Finlandism. George Schwab. (Anvil Ser.). 1989. pap. write for info. o.p. (ISBN 0-89874-575-6). Krieger.

Soviet Foreign Policy in the 1980's. Ed. by Roger E. Kanet. LC 81-22654. 378p. 1982. 33.95 o.p. (ISBN 0-03-059314-X); pap. 16.95 o.p. (ISBN 0-275-91539-5, B1539). Praeger.

Soviet Foreign Policy: Objectives & Principles. F. Peterenko & V. Popov. 310p. 1985. 5.95 o.p. (ISBN 0-8285-3060-2, Pub. by Progress Pubs USSR). Imported Pubns.

Soviet Foreign Policy since World War II: Imperial & Global. 2nd ed. Alvin Z. Rubinstein. 1985. pap. text ed. write for info. o.p. (ISBN 0-673-39476-X). Scott F.

Soviet Foreign Policy Since World War II. Joseph L. Nogee & Robert H. Donaldson. (Pergamon Policy Studies on International Politics). 300p. 1981. text ed. 43.00 o.p. (ISBN 0-08-025997-9); pap. text ed. 12.00 o.p. (ISBN 0-08-025996-0). Pergamon.

Soviet Foreign Policy since World War II. 2nd ed. Joseph L. Nogee & Robert H. Donaldson. 400p. 1984. text ed. 47.00 o.p. (ISBN 0-08-030152-5); pap. text ed. 13.95 o.p. (ISBN 0-08-030151-7). Pergamon.

Soviet Foreign Propaganda. Frederick C. Barghoorn. 1964. 41.00x o.p. (ISBN 0-691-08713-X). Princeton U Pr.

Soviet Foreign Relations & World Communism: A Selected, Annotated Bibliography of 7,000 Books in 30 Languages. Ed. by Thomas T. Hammond. 1965. 105.00x o.p. (ISBN 0-691-08714-8). Princeton U Pr.

Soviet Foreign Trade: Today & Tomorrow. V. I. Klochek. 278p. 1985. 6.95 o.p. (ISBN 0-8285-3091-2, Pub. by Progress pubs USSR). Imported Pubns.

Soviet Geography Today: Physical Geography. N. Gvozdetsky. 280p. 1982. 6.95 o.p. (ISBN 0-8285-2352-5, Pub. by Progress Pubs USSR). Imported Pubns.

Soviet Government: A Selection of Official Documents on Internal Policies. Ed. by Mervyn Matthews. LC 73-14369. 472p. 1974. text ed. 30.00x o.s.i. (ISBN 0-8008-7334-3). Taplinger.

Soviet Helicopters: Design, Development & Tactics. John Everett-Heath. 1983. 24.95 o.p. (ISBN 0-86720-662-4). Janes Info Group.

Soviet High Command. Richard Woff. (Illus.). 256p. 1988. 3-ring binder 825.00x o.p. (ISBN 0-7106-0557-9). Janes Info Group.

Soviet Humor: The Best of Krokodil. Krokodil Editors. (Illus.). 208p. (Orig.). 1980. pap. 12.95 o.p. Andrews & McMeel.

Soviet Imperialism. G. A. Tokaev. 76p. 1956. (ISBN 0-8022-1728-1). Philos Lib.

Soviet International Behavior & U. S. Policy Options. Ed. by Dan Caldwell. LC 84-48047. 304p. 1985. text ed. 16.95x o.p. (ISBN 0-669-09125-1); pap. text ed. 0.00 o.p. Lexington Bks.

Soviet Journey. Louis Fischer. LC 72-136529. (Illus.). 308p. 1973. Repr. of 1935 ed. lib. bdg. 35.00x o.p. (ISBN 0-8371-5450-2, FISJ). Greenwood.

Soviet Land Legislation. N. Sryodoyev. 147p. 1975. 3.95 o.p. (ISBN 0-8285-0345-1, 232836, Pub. by Progress Pubs USSR). Imported Pubns.

Soviet Land Power. Mark Urban. (Illus.). 128p. 1985. 19.95 o.p. (ISBN 0-87052-027-X). Hippocrene Bks.

Soviet Legal Philosophy. V. I. Lenin et al. Tr. by Hugh W. Babb. 1951. 37.00 o.p. (ISBN 0-384-56790-8). Johnson Repr.

Soviet Literature: Yesterday, Today & Tomorrow. Yuri Kuzmenko. Tr. by Jan Butler. 328p. 1983. 9.95 o.p. (ISBN 0-8285-2617-6, Pub. by Raduga Pubs USSR). Imported Pubns.

Soviet Local & Republic Elections. Max E. Mote. LC 65-26268. (Studies: No. 10). 123p. 1965. pap. 6.95x o.p. (ISBN 0-8179-3102-3). Hoover Inst Pr.

Soviet Military Doctrine, 1960 to the Present. Alfred L. Monks. LC 82-15273. 357p. 1984. text ed. 39.50x o.s.i. (ISBN 0-8290-0726-1). Irvington.

Soviet Military Power, 1987. 6th ed. 1987. pap. 7.50 o.p. (ISBN 0-318-22593-X, S/N 008-000-00464-1). USGPO.

Soviet Military Strategy in Europe. Joseph D. Douglass, Jr. LC 79-19320. (Pergamon Policy Studies. An Institute for Foreign Policy Analysis Bk.). 270p. 1980. 90.00 o.p. (ISBN 0-08-023702-9). Pergamon.

Soviet Muntinational State. Ed. by Martha B. Olcott et al. Tr. by Michel Vale & Anthony Olcott. 400p. Date not set. text ed. 49.95 o.p. (ISBN 0-87332-389-0). M E Sharpe.

Soviet Navy Today. Milan Vego. (Warships Illustrated Ser.: No. 6). (Illus.). 68p. (Orig.). 1986. pap. 9.95 o.p. (ISBN 0-85368-763-3, Pub. by Arms & Armour). Sterling.

Soviet Peace Efforts on Eve of World War Two. Ed. by A. A. Groymko et al. 68p. 1976. 8.95 o.p. (ISBN 0-8285-0500-4, Pub. by Progress Pubs USSR). Imported Pubns.

Soviet Perceptions of War & Peace. Ed. by Graham D. Vernon. 201p. (Orig.). 1981. pap. 6.00 o.p. (ISBN 0-318-20148-8, S/N 008-020-00862-1). USGPO.

Soviet Perspectives of Contemporary Asia. Bhabani Sen Gupta. 187p. 1984. text ed. 18.50x o.p. (ISBN 0-391-03026-4). Humanities.

Soviet Perspectives on International Relations, 1956-1967. William Zimmerman. LC 68-56326. (Studies of the Russian Inst. Columbia Univ). 1969. 26.00 o.p. (ISBN 0-691-07525-5); pap. 13.50x o.p. (ISBN 0-691-02168-6). Princeton U Pr.

Soviet Philosophy. John Somerville. (ISBN 0-8022-1609-9). Philos Lib.

Soviet Planned Economic Order. William H. Chamberlin. LC 77-95088. Repr. of 1931 ed. lib. bdg. 35.00x o.p. (ISBN 0-8371-2544-8, CHSE). Greenwood.

Soviet Policies Toward the Developing World during the 1980s: The Dilemmas of Power & Presence. Daniel S. Papp. (Illus.). 433p. (Orig.). 1986. pap. 16.00 o.p. (ISBN 0-318-22742-8, S/N 008-070-00588-3). USGPO.

Soviet Policy & Practice Towards Third-World Conflicts. Steven T. Hosmer & Thomas W. Wolfe. 336p. 1982. 35.00x o.p. (ISBN 0-669-06054-2). Lexington Bks.

Soviet-Polish Relations, 1917-1921. Piotr S. Wandycz. LC 69-18047. (Russian Research Center Studies: No. 59). (Illus.). 1969. 29.50x o.s.i. (ISBN 0-674-82780-5). Harvard U Pr.

Soviet Political Agenda: Problems & Priorities, 1950-1970. Daniel Tarschys. LC 78-53821. 256p. 1979. 35.00 o.p. (ISBN 0-87332-119-7). M E Sharpe.

Soviet Political Elite: Brief Biographies. Borys Levytsky. LC 78-157887. (Special Project). 640p. 1970. 70.00x o.p. (ISBN 0-8179-4161-4). Hoover Inst Pr.

Soviet Political Posters. G. Pavlov. 35p. 1986. pap. 30.00 o.p. (ISBN 0-8285-3261-3, Pub. by Aurora Pubs USSR). Imported Pubns.

Soviet Politics - The Dilemma of Power: The Role of Ideas in Social Change. Barrington Moore, Jr. LC 76-19137. 1977. pap. 14.95 o.p. (ISBN 0-87332-088-3). M E Sharpe.

Soviet Power: The Kremlin's Foreign Policy-Brezhnev to Andropov. Jonathan Steele. 276p. 1983. 19.25 o.p. (ISBN 0-671-49209-8). S&S.

Soviet Power: The Kremlin's Foreign Policy-Brezhnev to Andropov. rev. ed. Jonathan Steele. 304p. 1984. pap. 7.95 o.p. (ISBN 0-671-52813-0, Touchstone Bks). S&S.

Soviet Prefects: The Local Party Organs in Industrial Decision-Making. Jerry F. Hough. LC 69-18033. (Russian Research Center Studies: No. 58). 1969. 29.50x o.s.i. (ISBN 0-674-82785-6). Harvard U Pr.

Soviet Psychoprisons. Harvey Fireside. 224p. 1982. pap. 4.95 o.p. (ISBN 0-393-00065-6). Norton.

Soviet Psychoprisons. Harvey Fireside. (Illus.). 1979. 17.50 o.p. (ISBN 0-393-01266-2). Norton.

Soviet Public International Law: Doctrines & Diplomatic Practice. Kazimierz Grzybowski. LC 74-107954. xx, 544p. 1987. lib. bdg. 46.75 o.p. (ISBN 0-8223-0264-0). Duke.

Soviet Reality in the Seventies. W. J. Pomeroy. 222p. 1981. 5.60 o.p. (ISBN 0-8285-2068-2, Pub. by Progress Pubs USSR). Imported Pubns.

Soviet Regional Policy: A Quantitative Inquiry into the Social & Political Development of the Soviet Republics. Jan-Ake Dellenbrant. 208p. 1980. pap. text ed. 32.50x o.p. (ISBN 0-391-01797-7). Humanities.

Soviet Road to Olympus: Theory & Practice of Soviet Physical Culture & Sports. 1976. 79.95 o.p. (ISBN 0-686-57136-3, M-6191). French & Eur.

Soviet Russia Since the War. Hewlett Johnson. LC 78-21070. 1979. Repr. of 1947 ed. lib. bdg. 35.00x o.p. (ISBN 0-313-20865-4, JOSR). Greenwood.

Soviet Russian Literature: Selected Reading. Y. Andreyev. 879p. 1980. 17.00 o.p. (Pub. by Progress Pubs USSR). Imported Pubns.

Soviet Russian Poetry of the Nineteen Fifties to Nineteen Seventies. A. Ahkmatova. 254p. 1981. 7.00 o.p. (ISBN 0-8285-2063-1, Pub. by Progress Pubs USSR). Imported Pubns.

Soviet Russian Stories of the 1960's & 1970's. Y. Bochkarev. 419p. 1977. 7.45 o.p. (ISBN 0-8285-0949-2, Pub. by Progress Pubs USSR). Imported Pubns.

Soviet Science of Interstellar Space. S. Pikelner. LC 63-13348. 256p. 1963. (ISBN 0-8022-1977-2). Philos Lib.

Soviet Security Concept. V. Petrovsky. 76p. 1986. pap. 1.95 o.p. (ISBN 0-8285-3209-5, Pub. by Progress Pubs USSR). Imported Pubns.

Soviet Short Stories. Ed. by Avrahm Yarmolinsky. LC 75-17467. 301p. 1975. Repr. of 1960 ed. lib. bdg. 35.00x o.p. (ISBN 0-8371-8310-3, YASS). Greenwood.

Soviet Soldier. V. Drozdov & A. Korkeshkin. 180p. 1980. pap. 4.45 o.p. (ISBN 0-8285-1666-9, Pub. by Progress Pubs USSR). Imported Pubns.

Soviet Staff Officer. Ivan Krylov. 1951. (ISBN 0-8022-0899-1). Philos Lib.

Soviet State & Its Inception. Harry Best. (ISBN 0-8022-0120-2). Philos Lib.

Soviet Submarine Fleet: A Photographic Survey. Ed. by John Berg. (Illus.). 80p. 1986. 19.95x o.p. (ISBN 0-7106-0361-4). Janes Info Group.

Soviet Syndrome. Besancon. 1978. 8.95 o.p. (ISBN 0-15-184603-0). HarBraceJ.

Soviet-Type Economic Systems: A Guide to Information Sources. Z. Edward O'Relley. LC 73-17583. (Economics Information Guide Ser.: Vol. 12). 240p. 1978. 68.00x o.p. (ISBN 0-8103-1306-5). Gale.

Soviet-Type Economies: Performance & Evolution. 3rd ed. Robert W. Campbell. 272p. 1974. pap. 15.95 o.p. (ISBN 0-395-17231-4). HM.

Soviet Union. rev. ed. Douglas W. Jackson. LC 83-80051. (World Cultures Ser). (Illus.). 176p. (gr. 6 up). 1983. text ed. 13.70 o.p. (ISBN 0-88296-197-7); tchr's. guide 8.96 o.p. (ISBN 0-88296-387-2); skills manual incl. o.p. Gateway Pr MI.

Soviet Union. Time-Life Books Editors. (Library of Nations). (Illus.). 160p. (YA) (gr. 7 up). 1984. lib. bdg. 23.93 o.p. (ISBN 0-8094-5302-9). Time-Life.

Soviet Union after Stalin. Helen Lazareff & Pierre Lazareff. (Illus.). 256p. 1956. (ISBN 0-8022-0940-8). Philos Lib.

Soviet Union: Facts, Figures, Data. Ed. by Borys Lewytzkyj. 614p. 1979. lib. bdg. 60.00 o.p. (ISBN 3-598-07040-3). K G Saur.

Soviet Union: The Fifty Years. Ed. by Harrison E. Salisbury. LC 67-26001. (New York Times Bks.). (Illus.). 1967. 10.00 o.p. (ISBN 0-15-184605-7). HarBraceJ.

Soviet Union: The Incomplete Superpower. 2nd ed. Paul Dibb. 320p. (Orig.). 1988. pap. 12.95 o.p. (ISBN 0-252-06017-2). U of Ill Pr.

Soviet Union Today: An Interpretive Guide. James Cracraft. LC 83-1916. (Illus.). x, 348p. 1983. pap. 9.95 o.s.i. (ISBN 0-226-03875-0, 03875-0). U of Chicago Pr.

Soviet Uzbekistan. S. Rashidov. 104p. 1982. 4.95 o.p. (ISBN 0-8285-2317-7, Pub. by Progress Pubs USSR). Imported Pubns.

Soviet Volunteers in China, Nineteen Twenty-Five to Nineteen Forty-Five. Y. V. Chudodeyev et al. 320p. 1980. 8.95 o.p. (ISBN 0-8285-1932-3, Pub. by Progress Pubs USSR). Imported Pubns.

Soviet Women. Y. Z. Danilova et al. 184p. 1975. 2.95 o.p. (ISBN 0-8285-0290-0, Pub. by Progress Pubs USSR). Imported Pubns.

Soviet Women: A Portrait. N. Vishneva-Sarafanova. 158p. 1981. 5.80 o.p. (ISBN 0-8285-2113-1, Pub. by Progress Pubs USSR). Imported Pubns.

Soviet-Yugoslav Relations, 1948-1972: A Bibliography of Soviet, Western & Yugoslav Comment & Analysis. Brian Hunter. LC 75-24104. (Reference Library of Social Science: Vol. 18). 200p. 1976. lib. bdg. 30.00 o.p. (ISBN 0-8240-9971-0). Garland Pub.

Sovieticus: American Myths & Soviet Realities. Stephen F. Cohen. LC 85-2949. 1985. 12.45 o.p. (ISBN 0-393-01981-0). Norton.

Soviets Begin War in the Middle East-U. S. Counters. R. C. Miller. 86p. 1983. pap. 5.00 o.p. (ISBN 0-682-49967-6). Exposition-Phoenix.

Soviets in Central Asia. A. P. Coates & Zelda K. Coates. 1952. (ISBN 0-8022-0270-5). Philos Lib.

Soviets, Organos Del Poder Popular. M. Shafir. 314p. (Span.). 1979. 7.45 o.p. (ISBN 0-8285-1730-4, Pub. by Progress Pubs USSR). Imported Pubns.

Sovremennaia Russkaia Proza. Alexandr Genis & Peter Vail. LC 82-18213. (Illus.). 180p. (Rus.). 1982. pap. 8.50 o.s.i. (ISBN 0-938920-28-6). Hermitage.

Sow the Seeds of Hemp. Gary Jennings. 272p. 1982. pap. 2.75 o.p. (ISBN 0-380-57794-1, 57794). Avon.

Sow the Seeds of Hemp. Gary Jennings. 288p. 1976. 7.95 o.p. (ISBN 0-393-08733-6). Norton.

Soya Foods Cookery. Leah Leneman. (Illus.). 128p. 1988. pap. 9.95 o.p. (ISBN 0-7102-1028-0, Pub. by Kegan Paul). Routledge Chapman & Hall.

Soybean Physiology, Agronomy, & Utilization. Ed. by Geoffrey A. Norman. 1978. 47.00 o.p. (ISBN 0-12-521160-0). Acad Pr.

Soziale und Politis Che Geschichet der Revolution Von 1848 see Social & Political History of the German 1848 Revolution.

Space. Robin Kerrod et al. LC 83-51804. (Encyclopedia of Transport Ser.). 64p. 1985. 14.95 o.p. (ISBN 0-382-06776-2); 9.95 o.p. (ISBN 0-382-06991-9). Silver.

Space Age Terrors! Hilary Milton. Ed. by Betty Schwartz. (Plot Your Own Horror Stories Ser.: No. 3). (Illus.). 128p. (Orig.). 1983. pap. 2.85 o.s.i. (ISBN 0-671-49248-9). Wanderer Bks.

Space & Terrestrial Biotechnology. A. Fiechter. (Advances in Biochemical Engineering Ser.: Vol. 22). (Illus.). 230p. 1982. 48.40 o.p. (ISBN 0-387-11464-5). Springer-Verlag.

Space & Time in Special Relativity. N. David Mermin. LC 67-30052. (Illus.). 1968. pap. text ed. 21.95 o.p. (ISBN 0-07-041499-8). McGraw.

Space Between: Literature & Politics. Jay Cantor. LC 81-47600. 160p. 1982. text ed. 20.00x o.p. (ISBN 0-8018-2672-1). Johns Hopkins.

Space Biospheres. John Allen & Mark Nelson. (Illus.). 96p. 1986. pap. 6.95 o.p. (ISBN 0-907791-05-0). Synerg AZ.

Space Careers. Charles Sheffield & Carol Rosin. LC 84-60210. 267p. 1984. 16.95 o.p. (ISBN 0-688-03182-X). Morrow.

Space Cats. Steven Kroll. (Illus.). 48p. (gr. 1-4). 1981. pap. 1.95 o.p. (ISBN 0-380-53371-5, 53371-5, Camelot). Avon.

Space Circus. Alex Raymond. (Flash Gordon Ser.: No. 3). 1974. pap. 0.95 o.p. (ISBN 0-380-00064-4, 19696). Avon.

Space-Crafting: Invent Your Own Flying Spaceships. Mary Dewey. LC 86-422. (Illus.). 64p. (gr. 2-6). 1986. 11.95 o.s.i. (ISBN 0-13-823998-3). P-H.

Space Debris, Asteroids & Satellite Orbits: Proceedings of Workshop IV & XIII & of the COSPAR Interdisciplinary Scientific Commission P (Meeting Pl) of the COSPAR Twenty-fifth Plenary Meeting Held i n Graf, Austria, 25 June-7 July 1984. Ed. by D. J. Kessler. LC 83-645550. (Illus.). 236p. 1985. pap. 54.00 o.p. (ISBN 0-08-033189-0, Pub. by PPL). Pergamon.

Space Developments: Applications of Space & Energy: Selected Proceedings of the XXXI International Astronautical Congress, Tokyo, Japan, 21-28 September 1980. Ed. by L. G. Napolitano. 360p. 1981. 99.00 o.p. (ISBN 0-08-026729-7). Pergamon.

Space Developments for the Future of Mankind. L. G. Napolitano. 1980. 180.00 o.p. (ISBN 0-08-025454-3). Pergamon.

Space Developments for the Future of Mankind-II: Proceedings of the Thirtieth International Astronautical Congress, Munich, FRG. September 16-23 1979. Ed. by L. G. Napolitano. 228p. 1980. pap. 58.00 o.p. (ISBN 0-08-026159-0). Pergamon.

Space Exploration & the Solar System. Ed. by B. Rossi. (Italian Physical Society: Course 24). 1964. 71.50 o.p. (ISBN 0-12-368824-8). Acad Pr.

Space Flight: The Records. Tim Furniss. (Illus.). 176p. 1985. 14.95 o.p. (ISBN 0-85112-435-6, Pub. by Guinness Superlatives England); pap. 12.95 o.p. (ISBN 0-85112-451-8, Pub. by Guinness Superlatives England). Sterling.

Space Freighter - Future Supply Ship: A Complete Kit in a Book. Wayne McLoughlin. (Build-It-Yourself Ser.). 40p. 1982. pap. 8.95 o.p. (ISBN 0-316-56215-7). Little.

Space Garbage: Comets, Meteors & Other Solar-System Debris. Jack Meadows. (Illus.). 160p. 1985. pap. 17.95 o.p. (ISBN 0-540-01087-1, Pub. by G Philip UK). Sheridan.

Space in Time (A Few Fragments in an on-Going Dilemma) Orazio Monaco. 1979. 7.00 o.p. (ISBN 0-682-49149-7). Exposition-Phoenix.

Space Location & Regional Development. Ed. by M. Chatterji. 240p. 1976. pap. 18.95x o.p. (ISBN 0-85086-054-7, 2943, Pub. by Pion England). Routledge Chapman & Hall.

Space, Mankind's Fourth Environment: Selected Proceedings of the XXXII IAF Congress, Rome, September 6-12, 1981. Ed. by L. G. Napolitano. (Astronautical Research Ser.). 450p. 1982. 135.00 o.p. (ISBN 0-08-028708-5, A140). Pergamon.

Space Observations for Climate Studies: Proceedings of Symposium 4 of the COSPAR Twenty-Fifth Plenary Meeting Held in Graz Austria, 25 June-7 July 1984. Ed. by G. Ohring & H. J. Bolle. (Illus.). 404p. 1985. pap. 54.00 o.p. (ISBN 0-08-033195-5, Pub. by PPL). Pergamon.

Space Observations of Aerosols & Ozone: Proceedings of the Topical Meeting of the COSPAR Interdisciplinary Scientific Commission A (Meetings A1 & A2) of the COSPAR 24th Plenary Meeting held in Ottawa, Canada, 16 May-2 June, 1982, Vol. 2/5. Ed. by M. P. McCormick & J. E. Lovill. (Illus.). 120p. 1983. pap. 50.00 o.p. (ISBN 0-08-030427-3). Pergamon.

Space on Earth: Architecture: People & Buildings. Charles Knevitt. 232p. 1986. pap. 19.95 o.p. (ISBN 0-423-01440-4, 1027). Routledge Chapman & Hall.

Space Opera. Jack Vance. 192p. 1984. Repr. of 1965 ed. lib. bdg. 15.95 o.p. (ISBN 0-934438-99-4). Underwood-Miller.

Space Panorama. P. D. Lowman, Jr. (Illus.). 1968. 50.00 o.p. E J Brill USA.

Space Power Systems Engineering, PAAS16. Ed. by G. C. Szego & J. E. Taylor. LC 66-16539. (Illus.). 1302p. 1966. 94.50 o.p. (ISBN 0-317-36822-2). AIAA.

Space Radiation Biology & Related Topics. Ed. by Cornelius A. Tobias & Paul Todd. (U. S. Atomic Energy Commission Monograph Ser.). 1973. 52.25 o.p. (ISBN 0-12-691850-3). Acad Pr.

Space Relativity: Selected Papers Presented at the 4th, 5th & 6th International Sympodia on Space Relativity. Ed. by W. Wrigley. 80p. 1983. pap. 40.00 o.p. (ISBN 0-08-029339-5, A140). Pergamon.

Space Research: Directions for the Future. National Research Council, Space Science Board Staff. 1966. pap. 8.75x o.p. (ISBN 0-309-01403-4). Natl Acad Pr.

Space Search. Mack Reynolds. (Orig.). 1984. pap. 2.75 o.p. (ISBN 0-440-08095-9, Emerald). Dell.

Space Shuttle. Bill Yenne. 1988. 12.98 o.p. (ISBN 0-8317-7989-6, Gallery Bks). Smith Pubs.

Space Shuttle: A Quantum Leap. George J. Torres. (Illus.). 144p. 1986. 12.95 o.p. (ISBN 0-89141-253-0). Presidio Pr.

Space Shuttle: Its Story & How to Make a Flying Paper Model. Frank Ross, Jr. LC 79-12155. (Illus.). (gr. 5 up). 1979. 10.25 o.p. (ISBN 0-688-41882-1); PLB 10.88 o.p. (ISBN 0-688-51882-6). Lothrop.

Space Shuttle Log. Tim Furniss. 1986. pap. 14.95 o.p. (ISBN 0-7106-0360-6). Janes Info Group.

Space Shuttle Story. Andrew Wilson, 1986. 7.98 o.p. (ISBN 0-517-49953-3). Crown.

Space Systems Economics: Cost Reductions in Space Operations. Ed. by D. E. Koelle. 60p. 1985. pap. 45.00 o.p. (ISBN 0-08-032800-8, PBL). Pergamon.

Space Time & Self. rev. ed. E. Norman Pearson. LC 71-1546. (Illus.). pap. 5.95 o.s.i. (ISBN 0-8356-0409-8, Quest). Theos Pub Hse.

Space-Time Concepts in Urban & Regional Models. Ed. by E. L. Cripps. (London Papers in Regional Science). 238p. 1974. pap. 15.50x o.p. (ISBN 0-85086-044-X, NO.2955, Pub. by Pion England). Routledge Chapman & Hall.

Space-Time Nuclear Reactor Kinetics. W. H. Stacey, Jr. (Nuclear Science & Technology Ser: Vol. 5). 1969. 60.50 o.p. (ISBN 0-12-662050-4). Acad Pr.

Space to Breathe, Room to Grow: The Hows & Whys of Loving, Intimate Relationships. Jill Briscoe & Judy Golz. 176p. 1985. pap. 6.95 o.p. (ISBN 0-8407-9528-9). Nelson.

Space Tracking & Data Systems, AAS8. Ed. by Jerry Grey. LC 81-19080. (Illus.). 236p. 1981. 20.00 o.p. AIAA.

Space Trajectories. Ed. by T. C. Helvey. 1960. 53.00 o.p. (ISBN 0-12-340450-9). Acad Pr.

Space Transportation Systems: 1980-2000, AAS1. Christopher J. Cohan & Walter B. Olstad. LC 78-24171. (Illus.). 91p. 1978. 20.00 o.p. (ISBN 0-915928-27-2). AIAA.

Space Two Thousand-Activities to Be Performed for the Next Decade: Selected Papers from the 33rd IAF Congress, Paris, France, 27 September - 2 October 1982. Ed. by L. Napolitano. 150p. 1983. pap. 91.00 o.p. (ISBN 0-08-031106-7). Pergamon.

Space Voyager. (First Adventures Ser.). (ps-5). 1984. 5.70 o.s.i. (ISBN 0-671-50765-6, Little Simon). S&S.

Spacefaring People: Perspectives on Early Spaceflight. Alex Roland. LC 84-979. (NASA SP Ser.: No. 4405). (Illus.). 164p. (Orig.). 1985. pap. 3.50 o.p. (ISBN 0-318-18840-6, S/N 033-000-00933-0). USGPO.

Spaceflight-Venus. Philip Wilding. 192p. 1955. Philos Lib.

Spacelab: An International Short-Stay Orbiting Laboratory. Walter Froehlich. (NASA EP Ser.: No. 165). 82p. 1983. pap. 7.00 o.p. (ISBN 0-318-11750-9, S/N 033-000-00895-3). USGPO.

Spaces & Places: Views of Montgomery's Built Environment. Montgomery Museum of Fine Arts Staff & Diane J. Gingold. LC 78-58339. (Illus.). 48p. 1978. pap. 4.00 o.s.i. (ISBN 0-89280-010-0). Montgomery Mus.

Spaces of Sleep in Midsummer. Karin Lessing. (Illus.). 1982. 35.00 o.p. (ISBN 0-915316-95-1). Pentagram.

Spade Coin Types of the Chou Dynasty. Arthur B. Coole. LC 76-86803. (Encyclopedia of Chinese Coins Ser.: Vol. 3). (Illus.). 1973. 35.00x o.p. (ISBN 0-88000-011-2). Quarterman.

Spain. R. A. Dixon. LC 79-89189. (Rand McNally Pocket Guide). (Illus., Orig.). 1980. pap. 5.95 o.p. (ISBN 0-528-84292-7). Rand McNally.

Spain. Dana Facaros & Michael Pauls. (Cadogan Guides Ser.). (Illus.). 350p. (Orig.). 1987. pap. 12.95 o.s.i. (ISBN 0-87106-833-8). Globe Pequot.

Spain. Time-Life Books Editors. (Library of Nations). (Illus.). 160p. (YA) (gr. 7 up). 1986. lib. bdg. 23.93 o.p. Time-Life.

Spain: A Brief History. 2nd ed. Pierre Vilar. 1977. text ed. 18.25 o.s.i. (ISBN 0-08-021462-2, 2199); pap. text ed. 6.25 o.s.i. (ISBN 0-08-021461-4, 2199). Pergamon.

Spain: A Phaidon Cultural Guide. Phaidon Press Limited Staff. (Illus.). 600p. 1985. 16.95 o.p. (ISBN 0-13-824145-7). P-H.

Spain & Defense of the West: Ally & Liability. Arthur P. Whitaker. LC 79-25194. (Publication of the Council on Foreign Relations). (Illus.). 408p. 1980. Repr. of 1961 ed. lib. bdg. 37.50x o.p. (ISBN 0-313-22145-6, WHSD). Greenwood.

Spain & Morocco (Plus the Canary Islands) on Twenty-Five Dollars a Day. Darwin Porter. 504p. 1985. pap. 9.95 o.p. (ISBN 0-671-52436-4). Prentice Hall Pr.

Spain & Morocco (Plus the Canary Islands) on Twenty-Five Dollars a Day. 464p. 1983. pap. 12.95 o.p. (ISBN 0-671-44792-0). Prentice Hall Pr.

Spain & Portugal. (AA Road Map Ser.). (Illus.). Date not set. (ISBN 0-86145-016-7, Pub. by Auto Assn England). Salem Hse Pubs.

Spain & Portugal in Twenty-Two Days. Rick Steves. (Illus.). 104p. (Orig.). 1986. pap. 4.95 o.p. (ISBN 0-912528-51-6). John Muir.

Spain & Portugal in Twenty-Two Days. rev. ed. Rick Steves. (Twenty-Two Days Ser.). (Illus.). 136p. 1987. pap. 6.95 o.p. (ISBN 0-912528-63-X). John Muir.

Spain & the American Civil War: Relations at Mid-Century, 1855 to 1868, Vol. 70, Pt. 4. James W. Cortada. (Transactions Ser.: Vol. 70, pt. 4.). 1980. 10.00 o.p. (ISBN 0-87169-704-1). Am Philos.

Spain & the Empire: 1519-1643. Bohdan Chudoba. LC 71-84177. 1969. Repr. of 1952 ed. lib. bdg. 23.00x o.p. (ISBN 0-374-91559-8, Octagon). Hippocrene Bks.

Spain in Transition: Franco's Regime. Arnold Hottinger. (Washington Papers: Vol. II, No. 18). 68p. (Orig.). 1974. pap. text ed. 7.95 o.p. (ISBN 0-8191-5975-1, Pub. by CSIS). U Pr of Amer.

Spain: The Mainland. Ian Robertson. (Blue Guides Ser.). (Illus.). 29.95 o.p. (ISBN 0-393-01554-8); pap. 17.95 o.p. (ISBN 0-393-30006-4). Norton.

Spain: The Struggle for Democracy Today. Constantine C. Menges. (Washington Papers: Vol. VI, No. 58). 80p. (Orig.). 1978. pap. text ed. 7.95 o.p. (ISBN 0-8191-6007-5, Pub. by CSIS). U Pr of Amer.

Spalding Guide to Fitness for the Weekend Athlete. Gary Rosenthal. LC 76-9107. (Illus.). 128p. 1976. 7.95 o.p. (ISBN 0-916752-01-1). Longman Trade.

Spaniards in Their History. Ramon Menendez Pidal. Tr. by Walter Starkie. 1966. pap. 3.95x o.p. (ISBN 0-393-00353-1, Norton Lib). Norton.

Spaniels for Sport. Talbot Radcliffe. 1969. 15.95 o.s.i. (ISBN 0-87605-802-0). Howell Bk.

Spanish America: Tradition & Social Innovation. Frederick B. Pike. (Library of World Civilization Ser.). 1973. 7.95x o.p. (ISBN 0-393-05488-8); pap. 4.95x o.p. (ISBN 0-393-09340-9). Norton.

Spanish-American Blanketry: Its Relationship to Aboriginal Weaving in the Southwest. H. P. Mera. (Illus.). 96p. 1988. 29.95 o.p. (ISBN 0-295-96614-9); pap. 14.95 o.p. (ISBN 0-295-96615-7). U of Wash Pr.

Spanish American Modernista Poets. Ed. by G. Brotherston. LC 68-31793. 1968. text ed. 18.25 o.s.i. (ISBN 0-08-012858-0); pap. text ed. 8.00 o.s.i. (ISBN 0-08-012857-2). Pergamon.

Spanish American Revolutions, 1808-1862. John Lynch. (Revolutions in the Modern World Ser). (Illus.). 352p. 1974. text ed. 15.00x o.p. (ISBN 0-393-05388-1); pap. text ed. 6.95x o.p. (ISBN 0-393-09411-1). Norton.

Spanish-American Women Writers: A Bibliographical Research Checklist. Lynn E. Cortina. LC 82-48281. 304p. 1983. lib. bdg. 39.00 o.p. (ISBN 0-8240-9247-3). Garland Pub.

Spanish & Mexican Land Grants in New Mexico & Colorado. Ed. by John R. Van Ness & Christine M. Van Ness. (Illus.). 119p. (Orig.). 1980. pap. 9.95x o.p. (ISBN 0-317-47102-3). Sunflower U Pr.

Spanish Civil War. Antony Beevor. LC 83-71475. (Illus.). 384p. 1983. 19.95x o.s.i. (ISBN 0-911745-11-4). P Bedrick Bks.

Spanish Civil War: 1936-1939. Paul Preston. (Illus.). 192p. 1986. 20.00 o.s.i. (ISBN 0-394-55565-1). Grove.

Spanish Cooking. Ediciones Danae. (Golden Cooking Card Bks.). (Illus.). 42p. (Orig.). 1973. pap. 3.95 o.p. (ISBN 4-07-973636-3, Pub. by Shufunmoto Co Ltd Japan). C E Tuttle.

Spanish Drama Before Lope de Vega. James P. Crawford. LC 74-15215. 223p. 1982. Repr. of 1967 ed. lib. bdg. 90.50 o.p. (ISBN 0-8371-7814-2, AECRSD). Greenwood.

Spanish Elizabethans: The English Exiles at the Court of Philip II. Albert J. Loomie. LC 83-10691. xii, 280p. 1983. Repr. of 1963 ed. lib. bdg. 41.50x o.p. (ISBN 0-313-24083-3, LOSE). Greenwood.

Spanish-English & English-Spanish Medical Dictionary. 3rd ed. F. Ruiz Torres. (Span. & Eng.). 1965. 25.00 o.p. (ISBN 8-4205-0455-6). E J Brill USA.

Spanish-English, English-Spanish Dictionary of Banking Accounting & Related Fields, 2 Vols. Luisa G. Ruitenbeek et al. Set. pap. 30.00x o.p. Span.-Eng (ISBN 84-85198-02-6). Eng.-Span (ISBN 84-85198-05-0). E J Brill USA.

Spanish-English, English-Spanish Dictionary of Chemistry & Chemical Products. 2nd rev. & enl. ed. G. S. Hawley. (Span. & Eng.). 1968. pap. 15.00 o.s.i. (ISBN 0-686-91766-9). E J Brill USA.

Spanish-English, English-Spanish Dictionary of Maritime & Shipbuilding Terms. Ed. by Juan A. Perez. (Span. & Eng.). 50.00 o.p. (ISBN 8-4707-9081-1). E J Brill USA.

Spanish-English Handbook. rev. ed. Grace Howell & Jesus Perez Y Sabido. 158p. 1977. pap. 19.95 o.p. (ISBN 0-87489-073-X). Med Economics.

Spanish Grammar in Review: Patterns for Communication. Kenneth Chastain. 1979. pap. 23.50 o.p. (ISBN 0-395-30966-2). HM.

Spanish-Guarani Relations in Early Colonial Paraguay. Elman R. Service. LC 76-106699. (Illus.). 106p. 1971. Repr. of 1954 ed. lib. bdg. 35.00x o.p. (ISBN 0-8371-3373-4, SESP). Greenwood.

Spanish Inquisition: Its Rise. Jean Plaidy. 1966. pap. 4.95 o.p. (ISBN 0-8065-0056-5, Pub. by Citadel Pr). Carol Pub Group.

Spanish Made Simple. Eugene Jackson & Antonio Rubio. pap. 4.95 o.p. (ISBN 0-385-01212-8, Made). Doubleday.

Spanish Main. Peter Wood & Time-Life Books Editors. (Seafarer Ser.). (Illus.). 1980. 13.95 o.p. (ISBN 0-8094-2719-2). Time-Life.

Spanish Marriage. Madeleine Robins. 192p. (Orig.). 1984. pap. 2.25 o.s.i. (ISBN 0-449-20124-4, Crest). Fawcett.

Spanish Missions in Texas. Charlotte W. Pevoto. (Architecture Ser.: A 1483). 9p. 1985. 2.00 o.p. (ISBN 0-89028-613-2). Vance Biblios.

Spanish Moon. Beverly W. Hull. (Supreme Ser.: No.105). (Orig.). 1986. pap. 2.75 o.p. (ISBN 0-440-17822-3). Dell.

Spanish Now! 4th ed. Ruth Silverstein et al. Ed. by Nathan Quinones. (Illus.). 480p. (gr. 7-12). 1977. text ed. 14.95 o.p. (ISBN 0-8120-5202-1); pap. text ed. 8.95 o.p. (ISBN 0-8120-0928-2). Barron.

Spanish One-Two-One, Bk. 1. Juan Estarellas. 382p. (gr. 9 up). 1974. 5.95 o.p. (ISBN 0-88345-228-6); cassettes & filmstrips 300.00 o.p. (ISBN 0-685-53168-6). Prentice ESL.

Spanish One-Two-One, Bk. 2. Juan Estarellas. 402p. (gr. 9 up). 1974. 5.95 o.p. (ISBN 0-88345-229-4); cassettes & filmstrips 300.00 o.p. (ISBN 0-685-53169-4). Prentice ESL.

Spanish One Two-One: From Sound to Letter. Juan Estarellas. (gr. 9-12). 1975. pap. 6.95 o.p. (ISBN 0-88345-239-1); cassettes o.p. 105.00 o.p. (ISBN 0-685-65048-0); 110.00 o.p. tapes (ISBN 0-686-77136-2). Prentice ESL.

Spanish Orthography, Morphology & Syntax for Bilingual Educators. Richard V. Teschner. LC 85-11130. 252p. (Orig.). 1985. lib. bdg. 28.75 o.p. (ISBN 0-8191-4781-8); pap. text ed. 13.50 o.p. (ISBN 0-8191-4782-6). U Pr of Amer.

Spanish Painting from the Primitives to Ribera. Marianne Haraszti-Takacs. Tr. by Lili Halapy. (Illus.). 63p. 25.00 o.s.i. (ISBN 963-13-1355-7). Newbury Bks.

Spanish Painting from Zurbaran to Goya. Marianna Haraszti-Takacs. write for info. o.s.i. Newbury Bks.

Spanish Phonology & Morphology: A Generative View. William W. Cressey. LC 78-23327. 169p. 1978. pap. text ed. 7.95 o.s.i. (ISBN 0-87840-045-1). Georgetown U Pr.

Spanish Poetry of the Grupo Poetico de 1927. G. Connell. 1978. 60.00 o.p. (ISBN 0-08-016950-3). Pergamon.

Spanish Readings for Conversation. Ed. by Walter A. Dobrian & Coleman R. Jeffers. (Orig., Prog. Bk., Span). 1972. pap. 11.50 o.p. (ISBN 0-395-04367-0). HM.

Spanish Red: An Ethnogeographical Study of Cochineal & the Opuntia Cactus. R. A. Donkin. LC 77-76426. (Transactions Ser.: Vol. 67, Pt. 5). (Illus.). 1977. pap. 10.00 o.p. (ISBN 0-87169-675-4). Am Philos.

Spanish Revolution. Stanley G. Payne. (Revolutions in the Modern World Ser). (Illus.). 1969. pap. text ed. 6.95x o.p. (ISBN 0-393-09885-0, NortonC). Norton.

Spanish Revolution, Vols. 1-2, No. 12. United Libertarian Organization Staff. 1968. Repr. of 1938 ed. lib. bdg. 44.00x o.p. (ISBN 0-8371-9249-8, SP00). Greenwood.

Spanish Revolution, Vols. 1-2, No. 9. Worker's Party of Marxist Unification, U.S.A. Staff. 1936-37. Repr. lib. bdg. 16.50x o.p. (ISBN 0-8371-9250-1, SP10). Greenwood.

Spanish Royal Corps of Engineers in the Western Borderlands: Instrument of Bourbon Reform, 1764-1815. Janet R. Fireman. LC 75-25210. (Spain in the West: Vol. 12). (Illus.). 1977. 25.00 o.p. (ISBN 0-87062-116-5). A H Clark.

Spanish War: An American Epic 1898. G. J. O'Toole. (Illus.). 440p. 1984. 19.45 o.p. (ISBN 0-393-01839-3). Norton.

Spanish 1-2-1: Level 3. Juan Estarellas. (gr. 9-12). 1976. pap. text ed. 5.95 o.p. (ISBN 0-88345-269-3); cassettes & filmstrips 300.00 o.p. (ISBN 0-685-75084-1). Prentice ESL.

Spanish 1-2-1: Level 4. Juan Estarellas. 1977. pap. text ed. 5.95 o.p. (ISBN 0-88345-231-6); cassettes 150.00 o.p. (ISBN 0-685-82027-0). Prentice ESL.

Spanish...Without A6. Mikhail Yudovich. (Macmillan Chess Library). (Illus.). 128p. 1986. pap. 8.95 o.p. (ISBN 0-02-029060-8, Collier). Macmillan.

Spanking the Maid. Robert Coover. 256p. 1981. pap. 4.95 o.p. (ISBN 0-394-17971-4, E804, Ever). Grove.

Spanning the Decades: A Spiritual Pilgrimage. Bertha P. Wyker. (Illus.). 224p. 1981. 8.50 o.p. (ISBN 0-682-49746-0). Exposition-Phoenix.

Spanning Two Centuries: Historic Bridges of Australia. Colin O'Connor. 1986. 39.50 o.p. (ISBN 0-317-46038-2). U of Queensland Pr.

Sparkling Wine. Sheldon Wasserman & Pauline Wasserman. LC 84-1923. (Illus.). 288p. 1984. 27.95 o.p. (ISBN 0-8329-0366-3). New Century.

Sparkplug of the Hornets. Stephen W. Meader. LC 53-7868. (Illus.). (gr. 7 up). 1968. pap. 0.75 o.p. (ISBN 0-15-684710-8, VoyB). HarBraceJ.

Sparks of Light: Counseling in the Hasidic Tradition. Zalman M. Schachter & Edward Hoffman. LC 83-42804. 208p. (Orig.). 1983. pap. 9.95 o.p. (ISBN 0-394-72188-8). Shambhala Pubns.

Sparrows of Paris. Mario Pei. 1958. (ISBN 0-8022-1959-4). Philos Lib.

Sparse Matrix Techniques. Ed. by V. A. Barker. LC 77-1128. (Lecture Notes in Mathematics: Vol. 572). 1977. pap. 10.10 o.p. (ISBN 0-387-08130-5). Springer-Verlag.

Sparta & Lakonia: A Regional History Thirteen Hundred to Three Sixty-Two B.C. Paul Cartledge. (States & Cities of Ancient Greece Ser.). 1979. 30.00x o.p. (ISBN 0-7100-0377-3). Routledge Chapman & Hall.

Spartans: A Story of Michigan State Football. Fred. W Stabley. LC 75-12206. (College Sports Ser.). 1975. 9.95 o.p. (ISBN 0-87397-067-5). Strode.

Spatial Analysis, Industry & the Industrial Environment: Progress in Research & Applications, 3 vols. Ed. by F. E. Hamilton & G. J. R. Linge. Incl. Vol. 1. Industrial Systems. 289p. 1979. 91.95 o.p. (ISBN 0-471-99738-2); Vol. 2. International Industrial Systems. 672p. 1981. 100.00 o.p. (ISBN 0-471-27918-8); Vol. 3. Regional Economies & Industrial Systems. Ed. by F. E. Hamilton & G. J. Linge. 652p. 1984. 122.00 o.p. (ISBN 0-471-10271-7). LC 80-41418. 1654p. 1984. Set. 313.00 o.p. (ISBN 0-471-90431-7). Wiley.

Spatial Aspects of Influenza Epidemics. A. D. Cliff et al. 256p. 1987. text ed. 52.50 o.p. (ISBN 0-85086-103-9, Pub. by Pion England). Routledge Chapman & Hall.

Spatial Autocorrelation. A. D. Cliff & J. K. Ord. (Monographs in Spatial & Environmental Analysis). (Illus.). 178p. 1974. 17.95x o.p. (ISBN 0-85086-036-9, MNO.2954, Pub. by Pion England). Routledge Chapman & Hall.

Spatial Diffusion: The Spread of Ideas & Innovations in Geographic Space. Peter Gould. (CISE Learning Package Ser.: No. 11). (Illus.). 55p. (Orig.). 1975. pap. text ed. 3.00x o.p. (ISBN 0-936876-26-3). LRIS.

Spatial Dimensions of Public Policy. J. T. Coppock & W. D. Sewell. 200p. 1976. 31.00 o.p. (ISBN 0-08-020629-8). Pergamon.

Spatial Distribution of Urban Populations: A Bibliography. Dale E. Casper. (Public Administration Ser.: Bibliography P-1609). 15p. 1985. pap. 2.25 o.p. (ISBN 0-89028-259-5). Vance Biblios.

Spatial Divisions of Labour: Social Structures & the Geography of Production. Doreen Massey. 372p. (Orig.). 1985. text ed. 29.95x o.p. (ISBN 0-416-01041-5, 9408); pap. text ed. 12.95x o.p. (ISBN 0-416-01051-2, 9409). Routledge Chapman & Hall.

Spatial, Environmental, & Resource Policy in the Developing Countries. Ed. by Manas Chatterji et al. LC 83-16448. 448p. 1984. text ed. 41.95x o.p. (ISBN 0-566-00650-2). Gower Pub Co.

Spatial Interaction: The Geography of Movement. John C. Lowe & S. Moryadas. 1975. text ed. 30.50 o.p. (ISBN 0-395-18584-X). HM.

Spatial Organisation of Culture. Ed. by Ian Hodder. LC 78-1354. 1978. 29.95x o.p. (ISBN 0-8229-1134-5). U of Pittsburgh Pr.

Spatial Patterns of Office Growth & Location. Ed. by P. W. Daniels. LC 78-8386. 414p. 1979. 78.95 o.p. (ISBN 0-471-99675-0). Wiley.

Spatial Pricing & Differentiated Markets. George Norman. 185p. 1987. pap. text ed. 24.95 o.p. (ISBN 0-85086-121-7, 1161, Pub. by Pion England). Routledge Chapman & Hall.

Spatial Processes: Models & Applications. A. D. Cliff & J. K. Ord. 1980. 30.00x o.p. (ISBN 0-85086-081-4, NO.2225, Pub. by Pion). Routledge Chapman & Hall.

Spatial Time Series Analysis-Forecasting-Control. R. J. Bennett. 674p. 1979. 87.50x o.p. (ISBN 0-85086-069-5, NO.2935, Pub. by Pion England). Routledge Chapman & Hall.

Spatiality of the Novel. Joseph A. Kestner. LC 78-14377. 230p. 1979. 22.50x o.p. (ISBN 0-8143-1612-3). Wayne St U Pr.

Spawn of Dragonspear. Steve Perrin. LC 87-51259. (Advanced Dungeons & Dragons Gamebook Ser.: No. 17). (Illus.). 192p. (Orig.). (YA) (gr. 7-12). 1988. pap. 2.95 o.p. (ISBN 0-88038-570-7). TSR Inc.

Spawn of Hell. William Schoell. 400p. 1984. pap. 3.75 o.s.i. (ISBN 0-8439-2112-9, Pub. by Leisure Bks CT). Dorchester Pub Co.

Spawning Problem Fishes. Willy Jocher. Incl. Book 1 (ISBN 0-87666-146-0, PS-302); Book 2 (ISBN 0-87666-147-9, PS-302). (Illus.). 1972. pap. 4.95 ea. o.p. TFH Pubns.

Speak, Angel. Mary E. Robertson. LC 82-73015. 256p. 1983. 12.95 o.p. (ISBN 0-689-11362-5, Atheneum). Macmillan.

Speak, Angele. Robertson. (Atheneum). Macmillan.

Speak Chinese by Singing. Charlie Ling & Betty Ling. 1978. 7.50 o.p. (ISBN 0-682-49016-4, Banner). Exposition-Phoenix.

Speak Chinese: Selections for Memorization. Linda Hsia & Y. C. Wang. 1.95 o.p. (ISBN 0-88710-102-X); tapes avail. o.p. (ISBN 0-88710-103-8). Yale Far Eastern Pubns.

Speak Chinese: Translation Exercises. 2.95 o.p. (ISBN 0-88710-106-2). Yale Far Eastern Pubns.

Speak Easy: How to Talk Your Way to the Top. Sandy Linver. LC 78-10612. 222p. 1979. 14.95 o.s.i. (ISBN 0-671-40020-7). Summit Bks.

Speak Out: Speeches, Open Letters, Commentaries. Gunter Grass. Tr. by Ralph Manheim. LC 69-12035. (Helen & Kurt Wolff Bk). 142p. 1969. 9.95 o.s.i. (ISBN 0-15-184704-5). HarBraceJ.

Speak Out! Speeches, Open Letters, Commentaries. Gunter Grass. Tr. by Ralph Manheim. LC 69-12035. (Helen & Kurt Wolff Bk.). 142p. 1969. pap. 2.45 o.s.i. (ISBN 0-15-684716-7, Harv). HarBraceJ.

Speak Roughly to Your Little Boy: A Collection of Parodies & Burlesques. Ed. by Myra C. Livingston. LC 71-140779. (Illus.). (gr. 3 up). 1971. 8.50 o.p. (ISBN 0-15-277859-4, HJ). HarBraceJ.

Speak Softly of Christmas. John Campbell. 1973. 6.95 o.p. (ISBN 0-682-47899-7). Exposition-Phoenix.

Speak with Confidence. 4th ed. Albert J. Vasile & Harold K. Mintz. 1986. pap. text ed. (ISBN 0-673-39316-X). Scott F.

Speaker of Mandarin. Ruth Rendell. 1983. 12.45 o.s.i. (ISBN 0-394-52272-9). Pantheon.

Speaker's Bible. 2nd ed. Jacob W. Spatz. 288p. 1986. pap. 10.00 o.p. (ISBN 0-938033-00-X). Alert Pubs.

Speaker's Handbook. Jo Sprague & Douglas Stuart. 389p. 1984. text ed. 14.00 o.p. (ISBN 0-15-583175-5, HC). HarBraceJ.

Speaking Aids Through the Grades. Ruth K. Carlson. LC 74-14719. 1975. pap. text ed. 4.95x o.p. (ISBN 0-8077-2421-1). Tchrs Coll.

Speaking & Listening: A Contemporary Approach. Wayne A. Shrope. 1970. pap. text ed. 9.95 o.p. (ISBN 0-15-583180-1, HC). HarBraceJ.

Speaking of Chaucer. E. Talbot Donaldson. 1972. pap. 3.95 o.p. (ISBN 0-393-00633-6, Norton Lib). Norton.

Speaking of God Today: Jews & Lutherans in Conversation. Ed. by Paul D. Opsahl & Marc H. Tanenbaum. LC 73-89083. 192p. 1974. 0.50x o.p. (ISBN 0-8006-0275-7, Fortress). Augsburg Fortress.

Speaking of Jesus: Finding the Words for Witness. Richard Lischer. LC 81-70556. 144p. 1982. pap. 1.95 o.p. (ISBN 0-8006-1631-6, 1-1631, Fortress). Augsburg Fortress.

Speaking of Maine: A Selection from the Writings of Virginia Chase. Virginia Chase. Ed. by Margaret Shea. (Illus.). 128p. (Orig.). 1983. pap. 8.95 o.p. (ISBN 0-89272-170-7). Down East.

Speaking of Science Seventy-Seven: Proceedings of the Royal Institution, Vol. 50. 300p. 1978. 32.00x o.p. (ISBN 0-85066-135-8). Taylor & Francis.

Speaking of Selling. T. Anastasi. 1983. cassette & wkbk. 59.95 o.p. (ISBN 0-8436-0877-3). Van Nos Reinhold.

Speaking with an Audience. 2nd ed. John J. Makay. 128p. 1984. pap. text ed. 10.95 o.p. (ISBN 0-8403-2230-5). Kendall-Hunt.

Spear of Azzurra. Megan Stine & H. William Stine. Ed. by Stephanie Spinner. LC 85-19571. (Thundercats Thriller Series). (Illus.). 64p. (gr. 2-6). 1986. pap. 1.95 o.s.i. (ISBN 0-394-87879-5). Random.

Special Accounting Procedures see Accounting Ten-Twelve.

Special Applications & Techniques: Applications & Techniques. Resource Systems International Staff. 1982. pap. text ed. 15.00 o.p. (ISBN 0-8359-8622-5, Reston). P-H.

Special Circumstances. Brian Lysaght. 224p. 1984. pap. 2.50 o.p. (ISBN 0-380-68643-0, 68643-0). Avon.

Special Day Prayers for the Very Young Child. M. Grenier. LC 56-1719. (gr. 1-4). 1983. 5.57 o.p. (ISBN 0-570-04076-0). Concordia.

Special Education: A New Look. Ed. by Bob M. Van Osdol & Patricia Perryman. 350p. 1974. text ed. 29.50x o.p. (ISBN 0-8422-5181-2); pap. text ed. 8.75x o.p. (ISBN 0-8422-0417-2). Irvington.

Special Education & Pediatrics: A New Relationship. Special Issue of Exceptional Children. Ed. by M. Thomas Thomas. 1982. pap. 7.00 o.p. (ISBN 0-86586-130-7). Coun Exc Child.

Special Education & Social Control: Invisible Disasters. Julienne Ford et al. 192p. 1982. pap. 19.95x o.p. (ISBN 0-7100-0951-8). Routledge Chapman & Hall.

Special Education in America: Its Legal & Governmental Foundations. Ed. by Joseph Ballard et al. 112p. 1982. pap. 16.50 o.p. (ISBN 0-86586-133-1). Coun Exc Child.

Special Education Index to Assessment Materials. National Information Center for Special Education Materials (NICSEM) Staff. LC 79-84457. (Orig.). 1980. pap. 10.00 o.p. (ISBN 0-89320-026-3). Natl Info Ctr NM.

Special Education Index to Parent Materials. National Information Center for Special Education Materials (NICSEM) Staff. LC 79-84456. (Orig.). 1979. pap. 10.00 o.p. (ISBN 0-89320-025-5). Natl Info Ctr NM.

Special Education Telephone Directory. 32p. (Orig.). 1987. pap. 1.50 o.s.i. (ISBN 0-937925-30-6). Capitol VA.

Special Education Yearbook 1986. Ed. by June B. Jordan & Bruce A. Ramirez. 96p. 1987. 15.00 o.p. (ISBN 0-86586-168-4). Coun Exc Child.

Special Educator: Stress & Survival. Barbara R. DeShong. LC 81-1743. 230p. 1981. text ed. 34.00 o.p. (ISBN 0-89443-358-X). Aspen Pub.

Special Educator's Consultation Handbook. Lorna Idol-Maestas, LC 82-18455. 372p. 1982. 36.00 o.p. (ISBN 0-89443-926-X). Aspen Pub.

Special Effects. Harriet Frank, Jr. 1979. 8.95 o.p. (ISBN 0-395-27219-X). HM.

Special Effects in Motion Picture: Some Methods for Producing Mechanical Special Effects. Frank P. Clark. (Illus.). 238p. 7.50 o.s.i. (ISBN 0-318-16592-9). Soc Motion Pic & TV Engrs.

Special English for Hotel Personnel, Bk. 1: Office Managers, Clerks, Cashiers, Telephone Operators. Vivien Worsdall. 1971. pap. 6.40 o.p. (ISBN 0-02-976040-2). Macmillan.

Special Fleet: The History of the Presidential Yachts. Fred E. Crockett. LC 84-51558. (Illus.). 112p. (Orig.). 1985. pap. 10.95 o.p. (ISBN 0-89272-171-5). Down East.

Special Forces Operational Techniques: Unconventional Warfare, Counter Insurgency, Improvised Weapons, Intelligence, Logistics, Infiltration. 1986. lib. bdg. 79.95 o.p. (ISBN 0-8490-3673-9). Gordon Pr.

Special Gift. Marica L. Simon. LC 78-4329. (gr. 3-7). 1978. 6.95 o.p. (ISBN 0-15-277865-9, HJ). HarBraceJ.

Special Kids' Stuff. Cherrie Farnette et al. LC 76-505. (Illus.). 312p. (gr. 4-8). 1976. 12.95 o.p. (ISBN 0-913916-20-X, IP 20-X). Incentive Pubns.

Special Kind of Love: Care for the Dying Child. Robert W. Buckingham. LC 82-22073. 192p. 1983. 12.95 o.p. (ISBN 0-8264-0229-1). Continuum.

Special Legacy: An Oral History of Soviet Jewish Emigres in the United States. Sylvia Rothchild. 1985. 17.45 o.p. (ISBN 0-671-47325-5). S&S.

Special Legacy: An Oral History of Soviet Jewish Emigres in the United States. Sylvia Rothchild. 336p. 1986. pap. 8.95 o.p. (ISBN 0-671-62817-8, Touchstone). S&S.

Special Look. Karen Koch. 1973. pap. 1.25x o.p. (ISBN 0-88323-115-8, 220). Pendergrass Pub.

Special Multi-Peril Guide: A Sales Tool for Explaining the SMP Policy to Prospects. 10.00 o.p. (ISBN 0-942326-29-6, 30150). Rough Notes.

Special National Proceedures Concerning Non-Discrimination in Employment: With Particular Reference to the Private Sector. (Practical Guides). 65p. (Eng., Fr. & Span., 2nd Impression). 1981. pap. 10.50 o.p. (ILO35, ILO). UNIPUB.

Special Occasion Announcements & Invitations. (Photocopier Bks.). (Orig.). 1984. pap. 14.95 o.p. (ISBN 0-87280-021-0, Asher-Gallant). Caddylak Systs.

Special Occasion Cake Decorating. Vi Wittington. (Illus.). 80p. (Orig.). 1984. pap. 4.95 o.p. (ISBN 0-8249-3028-2). Ideals.

Special Occasion Desserts. Bon Appetit Magazine Editors. LC 85-14659. (Bon Appetit Ser.). (Illus.). 144p. 12.95 o.p. (ISBN 0-89535-170-6). Knapp Pr.

Special Places: For the Discerning Traveler in Oregon, Washington, Idaho, Montana, British Columbia & California Wine Country. Fred Nystrom & Mardi M. Nystrom. LC 86-82839. (Illus.). 216p. 1986. pap. 13.95 o.p. (ISBN 0-932575-25-0). Gr Arts Ctr Pub.

Special Problems in Gyrodynamics: Proceedings of CISM, Department for Genaeral Mechanics, 1970. CISM (International Center for Mechanical Sciences), Department for General Mechanics Staff. Ed. by P. C. Muller. (CISM Publications: No. 63). (Illus.). 96p. 1973. pap. 14.20 o.p. (ISBN 0-387-81085-4). Springer-Verlag.

Special Problems in High Energy Physics: Proceedings. International University Courses on Nuclear Physics, 6th, Schladming, Austria, 1967. Ed. by P. Urban. (Illus.). 1967. 42.50 o.p. (ISBN 0-387-80836-1). Springer-Verlag.

Special-Purpose Steam Turbines for Refinery Services. 2nd ed. 50p. 1979. 11.00 o.p. (ISBN 0-317-33100-0, 822-61200). Am Petroleum.

Special-Purpose Steam Turbines for Refinery Services. 3rd ed. 1987. 25.00 o.p. Am Petroleum.

Special Report Number Thirty-Nine: Ogallala Aquifer Symposium, 1979. Ed. by R. B. Matox & W. D. Miller. 242p. 20.00 o.p. Intl Ctr Arid & Semi-Arid.

Special Reports on Educational Subjects, 28 vols. Her Majesty's Stationery Office, Office of Special Inquiries & Reports Staff. (Incl. 2 suppls.). Repr. of 1914 ed. Set. 1850.00 o.p. (ISBN 0-384-57015-1). Johnson Repr.

Special Senses. 2nd ed. George J. McKenzie et al. (Penguin Library of Nursing Ser.). (Illus.). 215p. (Orig.). 1986. pap. text ed. 17.00 o.p. (ISBN 0-443-03081-2). Churchill.

Special Services in Hospitals: Monographs. Mary Vance. (Public Administration Ser.: P 1678). 17p. 1985. 2.25 o.p. (ISBN 0-89028-408-3). Vance Biblios.

Special Theory of Relativity. C. W. Kilmister. 1970. 75.00 o.p. (ISBN 0-08-006996-7); pap. 75.00 o.p. (ISBN 0-08-006995-9). Pergamon.

Special World of the Artisan. Fred Pratson. LC 75-21724. (Illus.). 128p. (gr. 3-7). 1974. 5.95 o.p. (ISBN 0-395-18510-6). HM.

Specialisation & Cooperation of the Socialist Economies. Yu. Kormov. 217p. 1980. 7.95 o.p. (ISBN 0-8285-1869-6, Pub. by Progress Pubs USSR). Imported Pubns.

Specialized Methods of Teaching Reading. Florence Shankman. 1970. pap. text ed. 9.50x o.p. (ISBN 0-8290-1193-5). Irvington.

Specialties of the House. Compiled by Our Lady of Grace Montessori School of Manhasset Staff. 486p. 10.00 o.p. (ISBN 0-918544-96-3). Wimmer Bks.

Specialty & Hi Performance Fiber: Update. Business Communications Staff. 311p. 1987. pap. 1950.00 o.p. (ISBN 0-89336-526-2, GB-069R). BCC.

Specialty Nursing Courses: OR. 78p. 1976. 5.00 o.p. (ISBN 0-939583-18-6). Assn Oper Rm Nurses.

Specialty Steels & Hard Materials: Proceedings of the International Conference (Materials Development '82), Pretoria, South Africa, 9-12 November 1982. Ed. by N. R. Comins & J. B. Clark. 450p. 1983. 130.00 o.p. (ISBN 0-08-029358-1). Pergamon.

Species Groups of South American Frogs of the Genus Eleutherodactylus: (Leptodactylidae) John D. Lynch. (Occasional Papers: No. 61). 24p. 1976. 1.50 o.p. (ISBN 0-317-04878-3). U of KS Mus Nat Hist.

Species Muscorum Frondosorum. J. Hedwig. (Illus.). 1960. Repr. of 1801 ed. 48.00x o.p. (ISBN 3-7682-7055-6). Lubrecht & Cramer.

Specific & Non-Specific Factors in Psychopharmacology. Max Rinkel. LC 62-18546. 192p. 1963. (ISBN 0-8022-1351-0). Philos Lib.

Specific Duties, Inflation & Floating Currencies. (Studies in International Trade: No. 4). 24p. 1978. pap. 10.50 o.p. (ISBN 0-685-25469-0, G103, GATT). UNIPUB.

Specification Analysis in the Linear Model. Ed. by Maxwell King & David Giles. (International Library of Economics). 416p. 1987. text ed. 42.50 o.p. (ISBN 0-7102-0614-3). Routledge Chapman & Hall.

Specification & Estimation of Multiple-Output Functions. G. Hasenkamp. 1976. pap. 11.00 o.p. (ISBN 0-387-07625-5). Springer-Verlag.

Specification Clauses for Rehabilitation & Conversion Work. Levitt Bernstein & Anthony Richardson. (Illus.). 128p. 1982. 27.50 o.s.i. (ISBN 0-85139-582-1). Nichols Pub.

Specification Writing for Architects & Surveyors. 8th ed. Arthur J. Willis & Christopher J. Willis. 98p. 1983. pap. text ed. 24.50x o.p. (ISBN 0-246-12228-5, Pub. by Granada England). Gower Pub Co.

Specifications & Applications of Industrial Robots in Japan 1984. Ed. by Japan Industrial Robot Association Staff. (Illus.). 780p. 1984. softbound 125.00x o.p. (ISBN 0-87936-016-X). Scholium Intl.

Specifications & Criteria for Biochemical Compounds. 3rd ed. Division of Chemistry & Chemical Technology. 224p. 1972. 22.25x o.p. (ISBN 0-309-01917-6). Natl Acad Pr.

Specifications for Commercial Interiors: Professional Liabilities, Regulations, & Performance Criteria. S. C. Reznikoff. (Illus.). 304p. 1979. 37.50 o.p. (ISBN 0-8230-7353-X, Whitney Lib). Watson-Guptill.

Specificity & Action of Animal, Bacterial & Plant Toxins see Queues: Receptors & Recognition Series B.

Specificity of Embryological Interactions see Queues: Receptors & Recognition Series B.

Speciman Preparation in Materials Science. P. J. Goodhew. (Practical Methods in Electron Microscopy: Vol. 1, No. 1). 1983. 24.75 o.p. (ISBN 0-444-10412-7, North-Holland). Elsevier.

Specimens of Bantu Folk-Lore from Northern Rhodesia. J. Torrend. LC 72-78777. (Illus.). 1969. Repr. of 1921 ed. 35.00x o.p. (ISBN 0-8371-1398-9, TOB&, Pub. by Negro U Pr). Greenwood.

Specimens of Type, Brass Rulers & Dashes, Ornaments & Borders, Society Emblems, Check Lines, Cuts, Initials & Other Productions of the American Type Founders Co. American Type Founders Co. Staff. Ed. by John Bidwell. (Nineteenth Century Book Arts & Printing History Ser.). 80.00 o.p. (ISBN 0-8240-3889-4). Garland Pub.

Speck in the Sky. Peter Moran. (Illus.). 96p. 1987. 14.95 o.p. (ISBN 0-7137-1902-8, Pub. by Blandford Pr England). Sterling.

Specs: The Comprehensive Foodservice Purchasing & Specification Manual. Ray Peddersen. LC 76-56460. 1200p. 1983. 99.95 o.p. (ISBN 0-8436-2084-6). Van Nos Reinhold.

Spectacle. Jacques Prevert. 1960. 11.95 o.p. (ISBN 0-685-23896-2). Schoenhof.

Spectacles. Ann Beattie. LC 85-15088. (Goblin Tales Ser.). (Illus.). 48p. (gr. 4-6). 1985. 10.95 o.p. (ISBN 0-89480-926-1). Workman Pub.

Spectacles for Specialists. Lewis W. Britton. LC 84-91333. 185p. 1985. 10.95 o.p. (ISBN 0-533-06416-3). Vantage.

Spectacular Helmets of Japan: 16th-19th Century. Japan Society Staff. LC 86-45181. (Illus.). 193p. 1986. Repr. 60.00 o.s.i. (ISBN 0-87011-784-X). Kodansha.

Specter! A Chrestomathy of "Spookery" Bill Pronzini. LC 81-71682. 1982. 13.95 o.p. (ISBN 0-87795-391-0, Arbor Hse); pap. 6.95 o.p. (ISBN 0-87795-403-8). Morrow.

Spectra of Diatomic Molecules see Molecular Spectra & Molecular Structure.

Spectra-Structure Correlation. John P. Phillips. (Illus.). 1964. 52.50 o.p. (ISBN 0-12-553450-7). Acad Pr.

Spectral Analysis of Nonlinear Operators. S. Fucik et al. (Lecture Notes in Mathematics: Vol. 346). 340p. 1973. pap. 19.00 o.p. (ISBN 0-387-06484-2). Springer-Verlag.

Spectral Atlas of Nitrogen Dioxide: 5530a to 6480a. Donald K. Hsu et al. 1978. 69.00 o.p. (ISBN 0-12-357950-3). Acad Pr.

Spectral Methods in Econometrics. George S. Fishman. LC 72-78517. (Rand Corporation Research Studies). 1969. text ed. 16.00x o.s.i. (ISBN 0-674-83191-8). Harvard U Pr.

Spectral Problems in Organic Chemistry. R. Davis & C. H. J. Wells. (Illus.). 200p. 1984. pap. text ed. 10.95 o.p. (ISBN 0-412-00561-1, 9019, Pub. by Chapman & Hall England). Routledge Chapman & Hall.

Spectral Properties of Disordered Chains & Lattices. J. Hori. 1969. 60.00 o.p. (ISBN 0-08-012359-7). Pergamon.

Spectral Properties of Hamiltonian Operators. K. Joergens & J. Weidmann. LC 72-97678. (Lecture Notes in Mathematics Ser.: Vol. 313). 140p. 1973. pap. 12.00 o.p. (ISBN 0-387-06151-7). Springer-Verlag.

Spectral, Spatial, & Temporal Properties of Lasers. A. M. Ratner. LC 76-167677. (Optical Physics & Engineering Ser.). 220p. 1972. 49.50x o.p. (ISBN 0-306-30542-9, Plenum Pr). Plenum Pub.

Spectral Techniques & Fault Detection. Mark G. Karpovsky. 1985. 49.50 o.p. (ISBN 0-12-400060-6). Acad Pr.

Spectral Theory & Differential Equations: Proceedings of the Symposium, Dundee, 1974. Symposium, Dundee Staff. Ed. by W. N. Everitt. LC 75-6605. (Lecture Notes in Mathematics Ser.: Vol. 448). xii, 321p. 1975. pap. 20.00 o.p. (ISBN 0-387-07150-4). Springer-Verlag.

Spectral Theory of Linear Operators. H. R. Dowson. 1978. 108.00 o.p. (ISBN 0-12-220950-8). Acad Pr.

Spectral Theory of Operators in Hilbert Space. rev. ed. K. O. Friedrichs. LC 73-13721. (Applied Mathematical Sciences: Vol. 9). x, 246p. 1981. pap. 23.95 o.p. (ISBN 0-387-90076-4). Springer-Verlag.

Spectre of Phillip. R. D. Milns & J. R. Ellis. (Sources in Ancient History Ser). 1970. pap. 15.00x o.p. (ISBN 0-424-06120-1, Pub. by Sydney U Pr). Intl Spec Bk.

Spectrochemical Analysis by X-Ray Fluorescence. Rudolf O. Muller. LC 70-107540. 350p. 1972. 55.00x o.p. (ISBN 0-306-30436-8, Plenum Pr). Plenum Pub.

Spectrochemical Analysis in the U. S. S. R. Ed. by S. L. Mandelstam. 112p. 1982. pap. 19.25 o.p. (ISBN 0-08-028747-6). Pergamon.

Spectrophysics. Anne P. Thorne. 380p. (Orig.). 1988. pap. text ed. 35.00 o.p. (ISBN 0-412-27470-1). Routledge Chapman & Hall.

Spectroscopic Analysis of Gaseous Mixtures. O. P. Bochkova & E. Y. Shreyder. 1966. 82.00 o.p. (ISBN 0-12-109450-2). Acad Pr.

Spectroscopic Methods in Organic Chemistry. 3rd ed. D. H. Williams & I. Fleming. (Illus.). 1980. text ed. 39.95 o.p. (ISBN 0-07-084108-X). McGraw.

Spectroscopy at Radio & Microwave Frequency. J. E. Ingram. 320p. 1956. (ISBN 0-8022-0777-4). Philos Lib.

Spectroscopy of Flames. 2nd ed. A. G. Gaydon. 1974. 49.95x o.p. (ISBN 0-412-12870-5, 6120, Pub. by Chapman & Hall). Routledge Chapman & Hall.

Spectroscopy of Shallow Centers in Semiconductors: Selected Proceedings of the International Conference, 1st, Berkeley, CA, Aug. 2-3, 1984. Ed. by K. K. Bajaj et al. 120p. 1985. pap. 28.00 o.p. (ISBN 0-08-032569-6, Pub. by PPL). Pergamon.

Spectrum. Theodore N. Ferris. 64p. 4.00 o.p. (ISBN 0-682-49638-3). Exposition-Phoenix.

Spectrum: A Guide to the Independent Press & Informative Organizations. 17th, rev. ed. Compiled by Bayliss Corbett. LC 81-642893. 81p. 1987. pap. 15.00x o.p. (ISBN 0-933152-09-4). Bayliss Corbett.

Spectrum in Chemistry. J. E. Crooks. 1978. 44.00 o.p. (ISBN 0-12-195550-8); pap. 44.00 o.p. (ISBN 0-12-195552-4). Acad Pr.

Spectrum Management Techniques. Donald M. Jansky. Ed. by Donald R. White. LC 76-52508. (Illus.). 187p. 1977. text ed. 32.00 o.p. (ISBN 0-932263-11-9). White Consult.

Speculation in Reality. Irving F. Laucks. 1953. (ISBN 0-8022-0934-3). Philos Lib.

Speculations. Ed. by Isaac Asimov & Alice Laurance. 312p. 1982. 13.95 o.p. (ISBN 0-395-32065-8). HM.

Speech Analysis. Ed. by R. W. Schafer & J. D. Markel. LC 78-65706. (IEEE Press Selected Reprint Ser.). 469p. 1979. 44.95x o.p. (ISBN 0-471-05830-0); pap. 29.50x o.p. (ISBN 0-471-05832-7, Pub. by Wiley-Interscience). Wiley.

Speech & Brain-Mechanisms. Wilder Penfield & Lamar Roberts. LC 59-5602. (Illus.). 1966. pap. text ed. 4.95x o.p. (ISBN 0-689-70152-7, 88, Atheneum). Macmillan.

Speech & Drama Club Activities. Gerald L. Ratcliff. (Theatre Student Ser.). 108p. 1982. lib. bdg. 14.95 o.p. (ISBN 0-8239-0565-9). Rosen Group.

Speech & Facsimile Scrambling & Decoding: Basic Text on Speech Scrambling. (Cryptographic Ser.). 1981. lib. bdg. 30.80 o.p. (ISBN 0-89412-119-7); pap. 22.80 o.p. (ISBN 0-89412-046-8). Aegean Park Pr.

Speech & Hearing Problems in the Classroom. Phyllis P. Phillips. LC 74-78838. (Speech & Hearing Ser.). (Illus.). 159p. (Orig.). 1984. pap. text ed. 5.95 o.p. (ISBN 0-8220-1807-1). Cliffs.

Speech & Language: Vol. 11: Advances in Basic Research & Theory. Ed. by Norman J. Lass. (Serial Publication). 1984. 65.00 o.p. (ISBN 0-12-608611-7). Acad Pr.

Speech & Lipreading Instructional Program. Mary A. Shurina. 1977. pap. text ed. 10.95 o.p. (ISBN 0-8134-1840-2, 1840); instructor's booklet 1.00x o.p. (ISBN 0-8134-1839-9, 1839). Inter Print Pubs.

Speech: Code, Meaning, & Communication. John W. Black & Wilbur E. Moore. LC 72-6686. (Illus.). 430p. 1973. Repr. of 1955 ed. lib. bdg. 35.00x o.p. (ISBN 0-8371-6493-1, BLSC). Greenwood.

Speech Communication & Human Interaction. 2nd ed. Thomas M. Scheidel. 1976. text ed. write for info. o.p. (ISBN 0-673-15005-4). Scott F.

Speech Communication for the Classroom Teacher. 2nd ed. Pamela J. Cooper. 296p. 1984. pap. text ed. 19.00x o.p. (ISBN 0-89787-319-X). Gorsuch Scarisbrick.

Speech Communication: Foundation & Challenges. J. D. Hughey & Arlee W. Johnson. 1975. pap. write for info. o.p. (ISBN 0-02-358230-8). Macmillan.

Speech Communication: Principles & Contexts. Richard F. Whitman & Paul H. Boase. 480p. 1983. text ed. write for info. o.p. (ISBN 0-02-427370-8). Macmillan.

Speech Communication: Theory & Practice. Albert Tepper. 1978. pap. text ed. 7.95 o.p. (ISBN 0-8403-1931-2). Kendall-Hunt.

Speech Disorders in Children. C. E. Renfrew. 78p. 1972. text ed. 8.75 o.p. (ISBN 0-08-016828-0). Pergamon.

Speech-Hearing Pathology & Surgery. Richard B. Yules et al. LC 79-51131. (Cliffs Speech & Hearing Ser.). (Illus., Orig.). 1980. pap. text ed. 4.95 o.p. (ISBN 0-8220-1828-4). Cliffs.

Speech in the Pulpit. P. E. Sangster. 64p. 1958. (ISBN 0-8022-1480-0). Philos Lib.

Speech, Language & Reading Worksheets: Fun with Language. Margaret F. Smith. 90p. 1983. wkbk. 24.95 o.p. (ISBN 0-88450-851-X, 4636-B). Communication Skill.

Speech News. Rev. ed. Dianne S. Barad. (gr. 7-12). 1983. manual 18.95 o.p. (ISBN 0-88450-733-5, 3135-B). Communication Skill.

Speech One Hundred & Three Handbook. rev. ed. Catherine M. Cummings & B. R. Smith. 1985. pap. text ed. 5.85 o.s.i. (ISBN 0-89917-449-3). Tichenor Pub.

Speech Pathology: An Introduction. Oliver Bloodstein. LC 78-69600. (Illus.). 1979. text ed. 24.95 o.p. (ISBN 0-395-27048-0). HM.

Speech Retarded & Deaf Children: Their Psychological Development. Ed. by Trian Fundudis et al. LC 78-75264. 1980. 73.00 o.p. (ISBN 0-12-270150-X). Acad Pr.

Speech Sounds & Features. Gunnar Fant. (Current Studies in Linguistics Ser: No. 4). 224p. 1974. 30.00x o.p. (ISBN 0-262-06051-5). MIT Pr.

Speech Synthesis. Ed. by J. L. Flanagan & L. R. Rabiner. LC 73-9728. (Benchmark Papers in Acoustics: Vol. 3). 511p. 1982. 58.95 o.p. (ISBN 0-87933-044-9). Van Nos Reinhold.

Speech Training. A. Musgrave Horner. 1952. (ISBN 0-8022-0745-6). Philos Lib.

Speeches & Writings. Xiaoping Deng. (Leaders of the World Ser.). (Illus.). 115p. 1984. 19.25 o.p. (ISBN 0-08-028165-6); pap. 9.75 o.p. (ISBN 0-08-028166-4). Pergamon.

Speedy Trial: Practice & Procedure. California Continuing Education of the Bar Staff et al. LC 80-70118. (California Criminal Law Practice Ser.). xi, 158p. 1981. 30.00 o.p. Cal Cont Ed Bar.

Spell Bound, Vol. 5. Jennifer Rabin. (Avon Young Adult Ser.). 192p. (YA) (gr. 5-9). 1987. pap. 2.50 o.p. (ISBN 0-380-75132-1). Avon.

Spell It Fast! The Quick Way to Spell 25,000 Easily Misspelled Words Using Sixty Stimulating Word Lists. Robert C. Gilboy. LC 81-1146. 286p. 1981. pap. 5.95 o.p. Acropolis.

Spell It Right! Ray C. Meyers & Dale Goodban. 1979. pap. text ed. 11.95x o.p. (ISBN 0-917962-61-3). T H Peek.

Spell Me a Witch. Barbara Willard. LC 81-47536. 142p. (gr. 8-12). 1981. 8.95 o.p. (ISBN 0-15-277902-7, HJ). HarBraceJ.

Spell of the Northern Lights. Lucy J. Sypher. LC 74-19130. (gr. 4-6). 1975. 7.95 o.p. (ISBN 0-689-30460-9, Atheneum). Macmillan.

Spell of Words: Studies in Language Bearing on Custom. Lina Eckenstein. LC 68-23153. 312p. 1969. Repr. of 1932 ed. 30.00x o.p. (ISBN 0-8103-3892-0). Gale.

Spellcoats. Diana W. Jones. LC 79-10421. 1979. 7.95 o.p. (ISBN 0-689-30712-8, Atheneum). Macmillan.

Spelling. C. D. Buchanan. (gr. 1). 1972. pap. text ed. 2.25 each incl. 8 texts (bk. 3 cancelled o.p. (ISBN 0-8449-2800-3); 2.25 o.p.; 1.00 o.p. Carroll CA.

Spelling: Caught or Taught? A New Look. Margaret Peters. 144p. (Orig.). 1985. pap. 9.95x o.p. (ISBN 0-7102-0359-4). Routledge Chapman & Hall.

Spelling the Easy Way. (Easy Way Ser.). 1982. 8.95 o.p. (ISBN 0-8120-2502-4). Barron.

Spelling Your Way to Success. rev. ed. Joseph Mersand & Francis Griffith. LC 73-16791. (gr. 9 up). 1982. text ed. 8.50 o.p. (ISBN 0-8120-5414-8); pap. text ed. 6.95 o.p. (ISBN 0-8120-2339-0). Barron.

Spelling 1500: A Program. 2nd ed. J. N. Hook. LC 76-9569. 300p. 1976. pap. text ed. 11.25 o.p. (ISBN 0-15-583211-5, HC). HarBraceJ.

Spells & Bindings. Time-Life Books Editors. (Enchanted World Ser.). (Illus.). 144p. (YA) (gr. 7 up). 1985. 19.93 o.p.; lib. bdg. 23.93 o.p. Time-Life.

Spence Makes Circles. Christa Chevalier. Ed. by Kathy Tucker. LC 82-11017. (Just For Fun Bks.). (Illus.). 32p. (ps-1). 1982. 10.25 o.p. (ISBN 0-8075-7570-4). A Whitman.

Spend Game. Jonathan Gash. LC 80-26266. (Joan Kahn Bk.). 204p. 1981. 9.95 o.p. (ISBN 0-89919-030-8). Ticknor & Fields.

Spend It Foolishly. Mary Gallagher. LC 77-23661. 1978. 10.95 o.p. (ISBN 0-689-10859-1, Atheneum). Macmillan.

Spend It Foolishly. Mary Gallagher. 1979. pap. 2.25 o.p. (ISBN 0-380-46011-4, 46011). Avon.

Spenser's Allegory of Justice in Book Five of "The Faerie Queene" T. K. Dunseath. LC 78-14441. 1979. Repr. of 1968 ed. lib. bdg. 35.00x o.p. (ISBN 0-313-21047-0, DUSA). Greenwood.

Spenser's Allegory: The Anatomy of Imagination. Isabel G. MacCaffrey. 1976. 55.00x o.p. (ISBN 0-691-06306-0); pap. 18.50x o.p. (ISBN 0-691-10043-8). Princeton U Pr.

Spenser's "Fierce Warres & Faithfull Loves" Martial & Chivalric Symbolism in "The Faerie Queene" Michael Leslie. LC 83-14929. (Illus.). 224p. 1983. 45.00x o.p. (ISBN 0-389-20465-X, 08026). B&N Imports.

Spent Fuel Policy & Its Implications: Proceedings, American Nuclear Society Executive Conference. 276p. softcover 28.00 o.p. (ISBN 0-317-33078-0, 650006). Am Nuclear Soc.

Sperm Capacitation. Charles E. Hamner et al. 228p. text ed. 29.50x o.p. (ISBN 0-8422-7083-3). Irvington.

Spermatozoon: Maturation, Motility, Surface Properties & Comparative Aspects. Ed. by Don W. Fawcett & Michael J. Bedford. LC 79-9196. (Illus.). 464p. 1979. text ed. 60.00 o.p. (ISBN 0-8067-0601-5). Urban & S.

Spermiogenesis. David M. Phillips. 1974. 32.50 o.p. (ISBN 0-12-553650-X). Acad Pr.

Sphere: The Form of a Motion. A. R. Ammons. 80p. 1974. pap. 2.95 o.p. (ISBN 0-393-04393-2). Norton.

Spice for Life. Walt Schmidt. 48p. 1985. 6.95 o.p. (ISBN 0-8378-5075-4). Gibson.

Spider Book. rev ed. John H. Comstock. Ed. by W. J. Gertsch. (Handbooks of American Natural History Ser. - Comstock Bk). (Illus.). 740p. 1948. 42.50x o.p. (ISBN 0-8014-0084-8). Cornell U Pr.

Spider-Man: The Secret Story of Marvel's World Famous Wall Crawler. Roger Stern. LC 81-10022. (Secret Stories of the Sensational Super Heroes Ser.). (Illus.). 64p. (gr. 3 up). 1981. PLB 13.27 o.p. (ISBN 0-516-02414-0). Childrens.

Spider Webs. Margaret Millar. LC 86-5425. 320p. 1986. 16.95 o.p. (ISBN 0-688-06593-7). Morrow.

Spider's Touch. Janice W. Goggans & Myrtle Beavers. (Illus.). 1980. 5.00 o.p. (ISBN 0-682-49513-1). Exposition-Phoenix.

Spider's Web: Problems in Regulatory Biology. Peter N. Witt et al. LC 68-54832. (Illus.). 1969. 19.70 o.p. (ISBN 0-387-04390-X). Springer-Verlag.

SPIE Annual Technical Symposium, 13th, Washington, DC, 1968: Proceedings. 486p. 8.00 o.p. (ISBN 0-89252-086-8); 5.00, members o.p. (ISBN 0-317-34741-1). SPIE.

SPIE Annual Technical Symposium, 14th, San Francisco, 1969: Proceedings. 550p. 8.00 o.p. (ISBN 0-89252-087-6); members 5.00 o.p. (ISBN 0-317-34740-3). SPIE.

SPIE European Electro-Optics Conference, Geneva, 1976: Proceedings. (SPIE Seminar Proceedings). 352p. 40.00 o.p. (ISBN 0-89252-126-0); members 24.00 o.p. (ISBN 0-317-34742-X). SPIE.

SPIE European Electro-Optics Markets & Technology Conference, 2nd, Switzerland, 1974: Proceedings. 440p. 35.00 o.p. (ISBN 0-317-34743-8); members 19.00 o.p. (ISBN 0-317-34744-6). SPIE.

Spies in the Sky. John W. Taylor & David Monday. LC 72-5709. (Encore Edition). (Illus.). 176p. 1973. 2.95 o.p. (ISBN 0-684-15959-7, ScribT). Scribner.

Spik in Glyph? Alurista. LC 81-65312. 64p. (Orig.). 1981. pap. 5.00 o.p. (ISBN 0-934770-09-3). Arte Publico.

Spiky the Hedgehog. Mirabel Cecil. LC 79-26358. (Illus.). 32p. (gr. k-3). 1980. text ed. 3.95 o.p. (ISBN 0-07-010322-4). McGraw.

Spilites & Spilitic Rocks. Ed. by G. C. Amstutz. (International Union of Geological Sciences: Ser. A, No. 4). (Illus.). 450p. 1974. 46.00 o.p. (ISBN 0-387-06448-6). Springer-Verlag.

Spill. Chester Aaron. LC 76-28467. (gr. 5 up). 1977. 7.95 o.p. (ISBN 0-689-50069-6, Atheneum). Macmillan.

Spilt Emotions. Robert H. Stone. 1979. 5.00 o.p. (ISBN 0-682-49466-6). Exposition-Phoenix.

Spilt Milk. John Daniel. 1977. pap. 1.00 o.p. (ISBN 0-931832-09-8). Fithian Pr.

Spin Labeling in Pharmacology. Jordan L. Holtzman. 1984. 44.00 o.p. (ISBN 0-12-354050-X). Acad Pr.

Spin the Spin. S. Tomonaya. 300p. 1989. 51.00 o.p. (ISBN 9971-50-330-1). World Scientific Pub.

Spina Bifida: Problems & Management. Stark. 1977. 25.50 o.p. (ISBN 0-632-00158-5, B-4640-5). Mosby.

Spinal Angiomas: Advances in Diagnosis & Therapy. Ed. by H. W. Pia & R. Djindjian. (Illus.). 1978. 71.00 o.p. (ISBN 0-387-08369-3). Springer-Verlag.

Spinal Cord Injuries. Hardy & Rossier. LC 75-18933. (Illus.). 108p. 1975. lib. bdg. 20.00 o.p. (ISBN 0-88416-056-4). Year Bk Med.

Spinal Cord Injuries: Psychological, Social & Vocational Adjustment. (Pergamon General Psychology Ser.). (Illus.). 1980. 26.50 o.p. (ISBN 0-08-024661-3). Pergamon.

Spinal Specialist's Guide to Exercise, Fitness & Health. F. Michael Blair. LC 85-1234. (Illus.). 188p. 1985. 19.95 o.p. (ISBN 0-932620-47-7); pap. 12.95 o.p. (ISBN 0-932620-41-8). Betterway Pubns.

Spine Chillers. John Galsworthy et al. Ed. by A. G. Eyre. (Longman Simplified English Ser.). 82p. 1980. pap. 3.95 o.p. (ISBN 0-582-52672-8). Longman.

Spinning & Plug Fishing: An Illustrated Textbook. Barrie Rickards & Ken Whitehead. (Illus.). 27.00 o.p. (ISBN 0-85115-462-X, Pub. by Boydell & Brewer). Longwood Pub Group.

Spinning for Trout. Bob Gooch. (Illus.). 192p. 1981. 14.95 o.s.i. (ISBN 0-684-16843-X, ScribT). Scribner.

Spinning Tables. Elementary Science Study Staff. 1971. tchr's guide 7.60 o.p. (ISBN 0-07-017699-X). McGraw.

Spinoza. Karl Jaspers. Ed. by Hannah Arendt. Tr. by Ralph Manheim from Ger. LC 74-4336. (From the Great Philosophers Ser.). 120p. 1974. pap. 2.95 o.p. (ISBN 0-15-684730-2, Harv). HarBraceJ.

Spinoza & Grammatical Tradition. A. J. Klijnsmit. (Mededeingen vanwege het Spinozahuis Ser.: No. 49). 16p. 1986. 4.25 o.p. (ISBN 90-04-08095-3, Pub. by E J Brill). E J Brill USA.

Spinoza Bibliography. Columbia University Staff. Compiled by Adolph S. Oko. 1964. lib. bdg. 79.00 o.p. (ISBN 0-8161-0699-1, Hall Library). G K Hall.

Spinoza Dictionary. Runes. 320p. 1951. (ISBN 0-8022-1450-9). Philos Lib.

Spinoza: Dictionary. Ed. by Dagobert D. Runes. LC 76-43957. 1976. Repr. of 1951 ed. lib. bdg. 35.00x o.p. (ISBN 0-8371-9293-5, RUSO). Greenwood.

Spinoza of Market Street. Isaac Bashevis Singer. 256p. 1981. pap. 2.95 o.p. (ISBN 0-449-24311-7, Crest). Fawcett.

Spinoza, Portrait of a Spiritual Hero. R. Kayser. (ISBN 0-8022-0833-9). Philos Lib.

Spins in Chemistry. R. McWeeny. (Current Chemical Concepts Ser). 1970. 47.00 o.p. (ISBN 0-12-486750-2). Acad Pr.

Spinster. Sylvia Ashton-Warner. 256p. 1986. pap. 7.95 o.p. (ISBN 0-671-61767-2, Touchstone). S&S.

Spinster & Her Enemies: Feminism & Sexuality, 1880 to 1930. Sheila Jeffreys. 252p. (Orig.). 1986. pap. 9.95 o.p. (ISBN 0-86358-050-5, Pandora Pr). Routledge Chapman & Hall.

Spiral. David L. Lindsey. LC 86-47655. 320p. (Orig.). 1986. 16.95 o.p. (ISBN 0-689-11625-X, Atheneum). Macmillan.

Spiral Man T-A Micro. (ISBN 0-07-852146-7). McGraw.

Spiralian Embryology. George Taylor et al. 222p. 1972. text ed. 26.50x o.p. (ISBN 0-8422-7010-8). Irvington.

Spirit Aflame: Luis Palau's Mission to London. Susan Holton & David L. Jones. 258p. 1985. 7.95 o.p. (ISBN 0-8010-4293-3). Baker Bk.

Spirit & His Gifts. George T. Montague. LC 74-77425. 72p. (Orig.). 1974. pap. 1.95 o.p. (ISBN 0-8091-1829-7, Deus). Paulist Pr.

Spirit & Power of Christian Secularity. Ed. by Albert L. Schlitzer. LC 75-75154. 1969. 19.95 o.p. (ISBN 0-268-00321-1). U of Notre Dame Pr.

Spirit & Ritual: The Morse Collection of Ancient Chinese Art. Virginia Bower & Robert L. Thorp. (Illus.). 96p. 1982. pap. 1.00 o.p. (ISBN 0-87099-304-6). Metro Mus Art.

Spirit & the Congregation: Studies in I Corinthians 12-15. Ralph P. Martin. 160p. (Orig.). 1984. 11.95 o.p. (ISBN 0-8028-3608-9). Eerdmans.

Spirit & the Flesh: Sexual Diversity in American Indian Culture. Walter L. Williams. LC 86-47505. 312p. 1986. 21.95 o.p. (ISBN 0-8070-4602-7). Beacon Pr.

Spirit & the Word. Z. T. Sweeny. 1982. pap. 3.95 o.p. (ISBN 0-89225-264-2). Gospel Advocate.

Spirit-Baptism: A Pentecostal Alternative. Harold D. Hunter. LC 83-10500. 322p. (Orig.). 1983. lib. bdg. 30.00 o.p. (ISBN 0-8191-3323-X); pap. text ed. 15.25 o.p. (ISBN 0-8191-3324-8). U Pr of Amer.

Spirit Bible. Compiled by Eugene S. Geissler. LC 73-88004. 272p. 1973. pap. 2.25 o.p. (ISBN 0-87793-062-7). Ave Maria.

Spirit, Faith, & Church. Pannenberg et al. 1970. 4.50 o.s.i. (ISBN 0-664-20880-0, Westminster). Westminster John Knox.

Spirit Filled Church in Action. A. B. Simpson. 112p. 1975. 3.45 o.p. (ISBN 0-87509-037-0). Chr Pubns.

Spirit-Filled Life. Verla A. Mooth. 1978. 6.00 o.p. (ISBN 0-682-49113-6). Exposition-Phoenix.

Spirit in My Life. James Alberione. 1977. pap. 0.95 o.s.i. (ISBN 0-8198-0460-6). Dghtrs St Paul.

Spirit in the Church. Megan McKenna & Darryl Ducote. LC 78-71531. (Followers of the Way Ser.: Vol. 4). (gr. 9-12). 1979. 22.50 o.p.; cassette 7.50 o.p. (ISBN 0-8091-7669-6). Paulist Pr.

Spirit of Barbizon: France & America. Text by Daniel Rosenfeld. 88p. 1989. pap. 17.95 o.p. Moyer Bell Limited.

Spirit of Buddhism Today. Koin Takada. Tr. by Philip Yampolsky. (Illus.). 1973. 9.95 o.p. (ISBN 0-89346-095-8); pap. 2.95 o.p. (ISBN 0-89346-043-5). Heian Intl.

Spirit of Democratic Capitalism. Michael Novak. 433p. 1982. 19.25 o.p. (ISBN 0-671-43154-4). S&S.

Spirit of Enterprise. George Gilder. 1984. 17.45 o.p. (ISBN 0-671-45482-X). S&S.

Spirit of Findhorn. Eileen Caddy. LC 75-36747. (Illus.). 1979. pap. 7.95 o.p. (ISBN 0-06-061291-6, RD 296). HarpR.

Spirit of Flame: A Study of St. John of the Cross. E. A. Peers. 1979. pap. 4.95 o.p. (ISBN 0-8192-1262-8). Morehouse Pub.

Spirit of God. Thomas Hopko. 1976. pap. 4.25 o.p. (ISBN 0-8192-1217-2). Morehouse Pub.

Spirit of May. Jean-Jacques Servan-Schreiber. 1969. pap. text ed. 4.95 o.p. (ISBN 0-07-056315-2). McGraw.

Spirit of Military Institutions. Auguste F. Marmont. Tr. by Frank Schaller. Repr. of 1864 ed. lib. bdg. 35.00x o.p. (ISBN 0-8371-5018-3, MAMI). Greenwood.

Spirit of Mornese. Carlo Colli. 198p. (Orig.). 1982. pap. 4.95 o.p. (ISBN 0-89944-064-9, P-064-9). Don Bosco Multimedia.

Spirit of Ole Brant Lake: Or, up at BLC. Robert Gersten. 1985. 8.95 o.p. (ISBN 0-533-06602-6). Vantage.

Spirit of Revolution in Seventeen Eighty-Nine: A Study of Public Opinion As Revealed in the Political Songs & Other Popular Literature. Cornwell B. Rogers. 1970. Repr. of 1949 ed. lib. bdg. 35.00x o.p. (ISBN 0-8371-1632-5, ROSR). Greenwood.

Spirit of St. Louis. Charles A. Lindbergh. 544p. 1985. pap. 5.95 o.p. (ISBN 0-380-69855-2, Discus). Avon.

Spirit of Solidarity. Joseph Tischner. Tr. by Marek B. Zaleski & Benjamin Fiori. LC 83-48988. 128p. 1984. 10.53 o.p. (ISBN 0-06-068271-X). HarpR.

Spirit of the Letter: Essays in European Literature. Renato Poggioli. LC 65-22064. 1965. 24.50x o.s.i. (ISBN 0-674-83310-4). Harvard U Pr.

Spirit of the Santee. Ethel F. Bull. LC 84-90124. 218p. 1985. 12.95 o.p. (ISBN 0-533-06207-1). Vantage.

Spirit of the Winding Water: A Novel of the Epic 1877 Wilderness Plight of the Nez Perce Indians. Judy B. Hanson. 1979. 7.50 o.p. (ISBN 0-682-49345-7, Lochinvar). Exposition-Phoenix.

Spirit of Your Marriage. David Ludwig. LC 79-50088. 1979. pap. 7.95 o.p. (ISBN 0-8066-1721-7, 10-5890, Augsburg). Augsburg Fortress.

Spirit of Zen: A Way of Life, Work & Art in the Far East. Alan W. Watts. 1958. pap. 7.95 o.p. (ISBN 0-394-17418-6, E219, Ever). Grove.

Spirit-Paraclete in the Fourth Gospel. Hans Windisch. Ed. by John Reumann. Tr. by James W. Cox from Ger. LC 68-12330. (Facet Bks.). 64p. (Orig.). 1968. pap. 1.00 o.p. (ISBN 0-8006-3046-7, 1-3046, Fortress). Augsburg Fortress.

Spirit Woman. Stan Steiner. LC 79-3001. (Harper Native American Publishing Program Ser.). (Illus.). 256p. 1980. 12.95i o.p. (ISBN 0-06-451975-9). HarpR.

Spirit Wrestler. James Houston. 288p. 1981. pap. 2.75 o.p. (ISBN 0-380-56911-6, 56911-6). Avon.

Spirit Wrestler. James Houston. LC 79-1829. 320p. 1980. 12.50 o.p. (ISBN 0-15-184755-X). HarBraceJ.

Spirited Cooking: An Introduction to Wines in the Kitchen. Robert Ackart. LC 84-45059. 384p. 1984. 17.95 o.p. (ISBN 0-689-11471-0, Atheneum). Macmillan.

Spirits Rebellious. Kahlil Gibran. 128p. 1946. (ISBN 0-8022-0582-8). Philos Lib.

Spirits (1976), Ghosts (1971) see White House Ghosts.

Spiritual Advice from the Early Christian Ascetics: Selections from the Lausaic History of Palladius. Palladius. pap. 2.95 o.p. (ISBN 0-317-60815-0). Eastern Orthodox.

Spiritual & Demonic Magic from Ficino to Campanella. D. P. Walker. (Warburg Institute Studies: Vol. 22). Repr. of 1958 ed. 44.00 o.p. (ISBN 0-8115-1394-7). Kraus Repr.

Spiritual Automobile. James W. Cuffee. Ed. by Charles Knickerbocker. 44p. 1980. 4.75 o.p. (ISBN 0-682-48997-2). Exposition-Phoenix.

Spiritual Breakthrough. Wilmer M. Zuehlke. LC 76-40870. 1977. 10.00 o.p. (ISBN 0-682-48642-6). Exposition-Phoenix.

Spiritual Discernment & Politics: Guidelines for Religious Communities. J. B. Libanio. Tr. by Theodore Morrow from Port. LC 82-2257. Orig. Title: Discernment E politica. 144p. (Orig.). 1982. pap. 1.74 o.p. (ISBN 0-88344-463-1). Orbis Bks.

Spiritual Disciplines. Anne Ortlund. 160p. 1987. 11.95 o.p. (ISBN 0-8499-0565-6). Word Bks.

Spiritual Disciplines: Growth Through the Practice of Prayer, Fasting, Dialogue, & Worship. rev. ed. James E. Massey. Ed. by Joseph D. Allison. 112p. 1985. pap. 6.95 o.p. (ISBN 0-310-37151-1, 12410P). Zondervan.

Spiritual Dryness. Walter Trobisch. pap. 0.75 o.p. (ISBN 0-87784-138-1). Inter-Varsity.

Spiritual Dynamics of Howard Thurman's Theology. Mozella G. Mitchell. LC 85-1227. 225p. (Orig.). 1985. pap. 14.95x o.p. (ISBN 0-932269-42-7). Wyndham Hall.

Spiritual Exercise for New Parents. Elwyn A. Smith. LC 85-47714. 64p. 1985. pap. 1.00 o.p. (ISBN 0-8006-1863-7, 1-1863, Fortress). Augsburg Fortress.

Spiritual Exercises of St. Ignatius: A Literal Translation & a Contemporary Reading. David L. Fleming. Ed. by George E. Ganss. LC 77-93429. (Study Aids on Jesuit Topics Ser.: No. 7). 290p. 1978. 12.00 o.p. (ISBN 0-912422-32-7); smyth sewn 9.00 o.p. (ISBN 0-912422-31-9); pap. 7.00 o.p. (ISBN 0-912422-28-9). Inst Jesuit.

Spiritual Exercises of St. Ignatius of Loyola. St. Ignatius. Tr. by Lewis Delmage. 1978. 4.00 o.s.i. (ISBN 0-8198-0557-2); pap. 2.25 o.s.i. (ISBN 0-8198-0558-0). Dghtrs St Paul.

Spiritual Journey of Joel S. Goldsmith. Lorraine Sinkler. 1977. pap. 5.95i o.p. (ISBN 0-686-77830-8, RD 243). HarpR.

Spiritual Leadership: Leader's Guide. J. Oswald Sanders & Dana Gould. (Orig.). 1987. pap. 4.95 o.p. (ISBN 0-8024-8226-0). Moody.

Spiritual Nuggets: A Devotional Book. Ryburn T. Stancil. 1975. 5.00 o.p. (ISBN 0-682-48316-8). Exposition-Phoenix.

Spiritual Power. rev ed. Don Basham. 92p. 1976. pap. 2.25 o.s.i. (ISBN 0-88368-075-0). Whitaker Hse.

Spiritual Rock. Clarence L. Tedder. 1979. 8.50 o.p. (ISBN 0-682-49249-3). Exposition-Phoenix.

Spiritual Survival in the Last Days. Greg Laurie. LC 82-81919. Orig. Title: Occupy Till I Come. 144p. (Orig.). 1985. pap. 3.95 o.p. (ISBN 0-317-54453-5). Harvest Hse.

Spiritual Thoughts & Prayers. Thomas W. Wersell. LC 74-76920. 80p. (Orig.). 1974. pap. 0.50x o.p. (ISBN 0-8006-1305-8, Fortress). Augsburg Fortress.

Spirituality & Analogia Entis According to Erich Przywara, S. J. Metaphysics & Religious Experience, the Ignation Exercises, the Balance in 'Similarity' & 'Greater Dissimilarity' According to Lateran IV. James V. Zeitz. LC 82-17588. 358p. (Orig.). 1983. lib. bdg. 34.75 o.p. (ISBN 0-8191-2783-3); pap. text ed. 16.75 o.p. (ISBN 0-8191-2784-1). U Pr of Amer.

Spirituality & Human Emotion. Robert C. Roberts. 134p. 1983. pap. 6.95 o.p. (ISBN 0-8028-1939-7). Eerdmans.

Spirituality & Pastoral Care. Nelson S. Thayer. LC 84-48716. (Theology & Pastoral Care Ser.). 128p. 1985. pap. 3.50 o.p. (ISBN 0-8006-1734-7, 1-1734, Fortress). Augsburg Fortress.

Spirituality for the Long Haul: Biblical Risk & Moral Stand. Robert S. Bilheimer. LC 83-48918. 176p. 1984. pap. 8.95 o.p. (ISBN 0-8006-1760-6, 1-1760, Fortress). Augsburg Fortress.

Spirituality of John Calvin. Lucien J. Richard. LC 73-16920. 352p. 1974. pap. 5.00 o.p. (ISBN 0-8042-0711-9, John Knox). Westminster John Knox.

Spirituelle Aufzeichnungen. Paul Twitchel. Tr. by Institutue Lanfranco et al. 256p. (Orig., Ger.). 1980. pap. 3.95 o.p. (ISBN 0-914766-53-8, 0528). Illum Way Pub.

Spiritus Contra Spiritum: The Struggle of an Alcoholic Pastor. Greg Martin. LC 76-46355. 1977. pap. 5.65 o.s.i. (ISBN 0-664-24131-X, Westminster). Westminster John Knox.

Spiro Mound, Vol. 14. Henry W. Hamilton & Charles C. Willoughby. Ed. by Carl H. Chapman. (Missouri Archaeologist). (Illus.). 276p. 1981. pap. 10.00 o.s.i. (ISBN 0-943414-06-7). MO Arch Soc.

Spiro Mound Copper. Henry Hamilton et al. Ed. by Carl H. Chapman. LC 74-31740. (Memoir Ser.: No. 11). (Illus.). 212p. (Orig.). 1974. pap. 5.00 o.s.i. (ISBN 0-943414-27-X). MO Arch Soc.

Spitballs & Holy Water. James F. Donohue. 1977. pap. 1.75 o.p. (ISBN 0-380-01655-9, 33233). Avon.

Spitfire Story. Alfred Price. (Illus.). 256p. 1982. 29.95 o.p. (ISBN 0-86720-624-1). Janes Info Group.

Spits & Bars. Ed. by M. L. Schwartz. LC 72-88983. (Benchmark Papers in Geology: Vol. 3). 452p. 1982. 63.95 o.p. (ISBN 0-87933-012-0). Van Nos Reinhold.

Spivey Assignment. Philip Rosenberg. LC 79-10085. 320p. 1979. 10.95 o.p. (ISBN 0-03-044371-7). H Holt & Co.

Splash & Flow. Ruth R. Howell. LC 73-76318. (Illus.). 48p. (gr. k-3). 1973. 4.95 o.p. (ISBN 0-689-30101-4, Atheneum). Macmillan.

Splash of Red. Antonia Fraser. 1982. 12.95 o.p. (ISBN 0-393-01511-4). Norton.

Splash the Dolphin. Cynthia Overbeck. Tr. by Dyan Hammarberg from Fr. LC 76-1218. (Animal Friends Bks). (Illus.). 24p. (gr. k-4). 1976. PLB 5.95 o.p. (ISBN 0-87614-061-4). Carolrhoda Bks.

Splendid Art of Opera: A Concise History. Ethan Mordden. (Illus.). 448p. 1980. 19.95 o.p. (ISBN 0-416-00731-7, NO.0152). Routledge Chapman & Hall.

Splendid Murder. Reynolds H. Hayden. 1977. 11.50 o.p. (ISBN 0-682-48675-2). Exposition-Phoenix.

Splendid Symbols: Textiles & Tradition in Indonesia. Mattiebelle Gittinger. LC 79-50373. (Illus.). 240p. (Orig.). 1979. pap. 20.00 o.p. (ISBN 0-87405-011-1). Textile Mus.

Splendor of Dresden: Five Centuries of Art Collecting. LC 78-6542. 229p. 1978. 20.00 o.p. (ISBN 0-8076-0901-3). Braziller.

Splendor of the Faith: Meditations on the Credo of the People of God. Anton Morgenroth. 206p. (Orig.). 1983. pap. 7.95 o.p. (ISBN 0-931888-14-X). Christendom Coll Pr.

Splendor of the Gods: The Grand Tour, Vol. IV. Flavio Conti. LC 78-51424. 1980. 15.95 o.p. (ISBN 0-15-184774-6). HarBraceJ.

Splendor That Was Egypt. Margaret A. Murray. (ISBN 0-8022-1178-X). Philos Lib.

Splendours of Tamilnadu. 1981. 35.00x o.p. (ISBN 0-8364-0762-8, Pub. by Marg India). South Asia Bks.

Splendours of the Vijayanagara. 1981. 30.00x o.p. (ISBN 0-8364-0792-X, Pub. by Marg India). South Asia Bks.

Splintered Moon. Leslie Davis. (Velvet Glove Ser.: No. 19). 224p. 1985. pap. 2.25 o.p. (ISBN 0-380-89785-7). Avon.

Split & Dalmatia. Berlitz Editors. (Travel Guides Ser.). 1977. pap. 4.95 o.p. (ISBN 0-317-12275-4, Berlitz). Macmillan.

Split Images. Elmore Leonard. LC 81-67524. 288p. 1981. 12.50 o.p. (ISBN 0-87795-354-6, Arbor Hse). Morrow.

Split Images. Elmore Leonard. (Large Print Bks (General Ser.)). 362p. 1986. lib. bdg. 16.95 o.p. (ISBN 0-8161-3949-0). G K Hall.

Split Infinitive see Metaphor.

Split Second: A Lennox Kemp Mystery. M. R. Meek. 170p. 1987. 13.95 o.p. (ISBN 0-684-18734-5). Scribner.

Split Vision: The Portrayal of Arabs in the American Media. rev & exp. ed. Ed. by Edmund Ghareeb. LC 83-71909. 397p. 1983. 12.95 o.p. (ISBN 0-943182-00-X); pap. 6.95 o.p. (ISBN 0-943182-01-8). Am-Arab Affairs.

Spoiled Sport: A Fan's Notes on the Troubles of Spectator Sports. John Underwood. 312p. 1984. 16.45i o.p. (ISBN 0-316-88733-1). Little.

Spoilers. David Hooks. 1985. 15.95 o.p. (ISBN 0-87795-628-6, Arbor Hse). Morrow.

Spoils of Ararat. Robert Katz. 1978. 8.95 o.p. (ISBN 0-395-25702-6). HM.

Spoken Arabic: The Language of Lebanon. Emile Karam. LC 82-5513. 1982. pap. 8.95 o.p. (ISBN 0-932506-18-6); pap. 16.50 with cassette (90 min.) o.p. St Bedes Pubns.

Spoken French in Review. 3rd ed. Quentin M. Hope. 1974. write for info. o.p. (ISBN 0-02-356950-6); write for info. o.p. (ISBN 0-02-357090-3). Macmillan.

Spoken Yoruba. E. W. Stevick & Odaleye Aremu. (Spoken Language Ser.). 381p. 1980. pap. 15.00x o.p. (ISBN 0-87950-708-X); cassettes, 34 dual track 185.00x o.p. (ISBN 0-87950-710-1); text & cassettes 200.00x o.p. (ISBN 0-87950-712-8). Spoken Lang Serv.

Spokesmen for God. Edith Hamilton. 1962. pap. 3.95 o.p. (ISBN 0-393-00169-5, Norton Lib). Norton.

Spontaneous & Virus Induced Transformation in Cell Culture. Jan Ponten. LC 75-137784. (Virology Monographs: Vol. 8). (Illus.). 1971. 42.00 o.p. (ISBN 0-387-80991-0). Springer-Verlag.

Spontaneous Hypertension: Its Pathogenesis & Complications. Ed. by K. Okamoto. LC 72-86725. (Illus.). xiv, 266p. 1972. 30.70 o.p. (ISBN 0-387-05942-3). Springer-Verlag.

Spook Birds. Eve Bunting. Ed. by Kathleen Tucker. LC 81-686. (Illus.). 40p. (gr. 3-7). 1981. PLB 7.50 o.p. (ISBN 0-8075-7587-9). A Whitman.

Spook Crooks: Exposing the Secrets of the Propheteers Who Conduct Our Wickedest Industry. Julien J. Proskauer. LC 70-162517. (Illus.). 302p. 1971. Repr. of 1932 ed. 40.00x o.p. (ISBN 0-8103-3760-6). Gale.

Spoon River Anthology. new ed. Edgar L. Masters. 1962. pap. 4.95 o.p. (ISBN 0-02-070010-5, Collier). Macmillan.

Spoonbread & Strawberry Wine. Norma Jean & Carole Darden. 1981. pap. 2.75 o.p. (ISBN 0-449-24264-1, Crest). Fawcett.

Spoonbread & Strawberry Wine: Recipes & Reminiscences of a Family. Norma J. Darden & Carole Darden. LC 77-82620. 1978. 15.95 o.p. (ISBN 0-385-12468-6, Anchor Pr). Doubleday.

Spore Research. Ed. by A. N. Barker et al. 1974. 76.00 o.p. (ISBN 0-12-078752-0). Acad Pr.

Spore Research. Ed. by A. N. Barker et al. 1978. Vol. 1. 91.50 o.p. (ISBN 0-12-078701-6); Vol. 2. 109.00 o.p. (ISBN 0-12-078702-4). Acad Pr.

Spore Research 1971. Ed. by A. N. Barker & G. W. Gould. 1972. 84.00 o.p. (ISBN 0-12-078750-4). Acad Pr.

Spore Seven. Clancy Carlile. 288p. 1980. pap. 2.25 o.p. (ISBN 0-380-49031-5, 49031). Avon.

Sport. Dick Schaap. LC 75-13407. 1975. 8.95 o.p. (ISBN 0-87795-122-5, Arbor Hse). Morrow.

Sport Administration: Learning Designs for Administrators of Sport, Physical Education, & Recreation. John J. Jackson. (Illus.). 416p. 1981. 41.25x o.p. (ISBN 0-398-04440-6). C C Thomas.

Sport Americana Alphabetical Baseball Card Checklist, No. 2. 224p. 1983. 8.95 o.p. (ISBN 0-937424-17-X). Edgewater.

Sport Americana Baseball Address List. 160p. 1982. 8.95 o.p. (ISBN 0-937424-14-5). Edgewater.

Sport Americana Baseball Card Price Guide & Checklist-Pocket Edition. 256p. 2.50 o.p. (ISBN 0-937424-15-3). Edgewater.

Sport Americana Baseball Card Price Guide, No. 6. 528p. 1984. 9.95 o.p. (ISBN 0-937424-23-4). Edgewater.

Sport Americana Baseball Card Price Guide, No. 7. 528p. 1985. 11.95 o.p. (ISBN 0-937424-26-9). Edgewater.

Sport Americana Baseball Card Price Guide, No.8. 512p. 1986. 11.95 o.p. (ISBN 0-937424-29-3). Edgewater.

Sport Americana Football, Hockey, Basketball & Boxing Card Price Guide, No. 3. 360p. 1984. 9.95 o.p. (ISBN 0-937424-22-6). Edgewater.

Sport Americana Football, Hockey, Basketball & Boxing Card Price Guide, No. 4. 416p. 1985. 12.95 o.p. (ISBN 0-937424-27-7). Edgewater.

Sport Americana Price Guide to the Non-Sports Cards, No. 2. 360p. 1983. 9.95 o.p. (ISBN 0-937424-20-X). Edgewater.

Sport Americana Team Baseball Card Checklist, No. 1. 128p. 1983. 7.95 o.p. (ISBN 0-937424-19-6). Edgewater.

Sport Americana Team Baseball Card Checklist, No. 2. 160p. 1985. 8.95 o.p. (ISBN 0-937424-28-5). Edgewater.

Sport in Art: A Guide for Beginning Illustrators. Robert Henkes. (Art & Design Ser.). (Illus.). 224p. (Orig.). 1986. pap. 17.95 o.p. (ISBN 0-13-835513-4). P-H.

Sport in History. Ed. by Richard Cashman & Michael McKernan. 1979. 25.00x o.p. (ISBN 0-7022-1355-1); pap. 14.95 o.p. (ISBN 0-7022-1356-X). U of Queensland Pr.

Sport Management in Schools & Colleges. Harold J. Vanderzwaag. 320p. 1983. text ed. write for info. o.p. (ISBN 0-02-422500-2). Macmillan.

Sport Parachuting Manual. 5th ed. R. A. Gunby. Ed. by Jeppesen Sanderson Staff. (Illus.). 162p. 1974. pap. text ed. 5.49 o.p. (ISBN 0-88487-008-1, RE314751). Jeppesen Sanderson.

Sport with Terriers. Patricia A. Lent. LC 73-85940. (Illus.). 1973. 13.95 o.p. (ISBN 0-914124-01-3). Arner Pubns.

Sporting Injuries: A Trainer's Guide. Peter Dornan. (Illus.). 69p. 1980. pap. 5.00 o.p. (ISBN 0-7022-1448-5). U of Queensland Pr.

Sporting News American League Red Book, 1987. 104p. 1987. pap. 9.95 o.p. (ISBN 0-89204-254-0). Sporting News.

Sporting News Best Sports Stories. 288p. 1987. pap. 10.95 o.p. (ISBN 0-317-65370-9). Sporting News.

Sporting News Complete Baseball Record Book. 300p. 1986. pap. 12.95 o.p. (ISBN 0-89204-210-9). Sporting News.

Sporting News Complete Baseball Record Book, 1987. 368p. 1987. pap. 12.95 o.p. (ISBN 0-89204-239-7). Sporting News.

Sporting News Football Register, 1985. 488p. 1985. pap. 9.95 o.p. (ISBN 0-89204-188-9). Sporting News.

Sporting News Football Register, 1987. 480p. 1987. pap. 10.95 o.p. (ISBN 0-89204-248-6). Sporting News.

Sporting News Hockey Guide, 1985-1986. 240p. 1985. pap. 9.95 o.p. (ISBN 0-89204-198-6). Sporting News.

Sporting News Hockey Guide 1987-1988. 1987. pap. 10.95 o.p. (ISBN 0-89204-258-3). Sporting News.

Sporting News Hockey Register 1987-1988. 1987. pap. 10.95 o.p. (ISBN 0-89204-259-1). Sporting News.

Sporting News Hockey Register 1987-88. 1987. 10.95 o.p. Sporting News.

Sporting News National League Green Book, 1987. 104p. 1987. pap. 9.95 o.p. (ISBN 0-89204-255-9). Sporting News.

Sporting News Official Baseball Guide, 1986. 496p. 1986. pap. 9.95 o.p. (ISBN 0-89204-209-5). Sporting News.

Sporting News Official Baseball Guide, 1987. 496p. 1987. pap. 10.95 o.p. (ISBN 0-89204-237-0). Sporting News.

Sporting News Official Baseball Register, 1986. 576p. 1986. pap. 9.95 o.p. (ISBN 0-89204-208-7). Sporting News.

Sporting News Official Baseball Register, 1987. 592p. 1987. pap. 10.95 o.p. (ISBN 0-89204-238-9). Sporting News.

Sporting News Official Baseball Rules, 1986. 104p. 1986. pap. 2.50 o.p. (ISBN 0-89204-211-7). Sporting News.

Sporting News Official Baseball Rules, 1987. 104p. 1987. pap. 2.95 o.p. (ISBN 0-89204-240-0). Sporting News.

Sporting News Official NBA Guide, 1985-1986. 480p. 1985. pap. 9.95 o.p. (ISBN 0-89204-194-3). Sporting News.

Sporting News Official NBA Guide, 1987-1988. 1987. pap. 10.95 o.p. (ISBN 0-89204-251-6). Sporting News.

Sporting News Official NBA Register, 1985-1986. 352p. 1985. pap. 9.95 o.p. (ISBN 0-89204-193-5). Sporting News.

Sporting News Official NBA Register, 1987-1988. 1987. pap. 10.95 o.p. (ISBN 0-89204-252-4). Sporting News.

Sporting News Pro Football Guide, 1985. 392p. 1985. pap. 9.95 o.p. (ISBN 0-89204-189-7). Sporting News.

Sporting News Pro Football Guide, 1987. 400p. 1987. pap. 10.95 o.p. (ISBN 0-89204-247-8). Sporting News.

Sporting News Super Bowl Book, 1987. 368p. 1987. pap. 10.95 o.p. (ISBN 0-89204-249-4). Sporting News.

Sporting News: Take Me out to the Ball Park. (Illus.). 288p. 1985. 29.95 o.s.i. (ISBN 0-89204-101-3); pap. text ed. 15.95 o.s.i. (ISBN 0-89204-205-2). Sporting News.

Sports & Recreational Activities for Men & Women. 8th ed. Dale Mood et al. LC 82-8302. (Illus.). 442p. 1982. pap. text ed. 17.95 o.p. (ISBN 0-8016-0290-4). Mosby.
Sports & Recreational Programs for the Child & Young Adult with Physical Disability: Proceedings of Winter Park Seminar. 101p. 1984. 10.00 o.p. (ISBN 0-89203-001-1, 4000025). Amer Acad Ortho Surg.
Sports at Random: Q & A. Jerome Agel. 1984. pap. 6.95 o.p. (ISBN 0-87795-541-7, Arbor Hse). Morrow.
Sports Bestiary. George Plimpton. LC 82-10002. (Illus.). 112p. 1982. text ed. 14.95 o.p. (ISBN 0-07-050290-0). McGraw.
Sports Cards: Collecting, Trading & Playing. Margo McLoone & Alice Siegel. LC 78-13790. (Illus.). (gr. 4-8). 1979. 8.95 o.s.i. (ISBN 0-03-042696-0); pap. 4.95 o.s.i. (ISBN 0-03-049311-0). H Holt & Co.
Sports Classics: American Writers Choose Their Best. H. Siner. (Paperbacks Ser.). 324p. 1984. pap. text ed. 7.95 o.p. (ISBN 0-07-057298-4). McGraw.
Sports Collectibles. William Ketchum. LC 85-80130. 96p. pap. 7.95 o.p. (ISBN 0-89586-249-2). Price Stern.
Sports Collectors' Digest Baseball Cards Price Guide. Dan Albaugh & Bob Lemke. LC 87-80033. (Illus.). 500p. 1987. pap. 10.95 o.s.i. (ISBN 0-87341-094-7). Krause Pubns.
Sports Collectors Digest Baseball Price Card Guide. 2nd ed. Dan Albaugh & Bob Lemke. LC 87-80033. 1988. pap. text ed. 12.95 o.s.i. (ISBN 0-87341-105-6). Krause Pubns.
Sports Encyclopedia: Pro Football the Modern Era, 1960 to the Present. David S. Neft & Richard M. Cohen. 416p. 1982. pap. 13.50 o.p. (ISBN 0-671-45066-2, Fireside). S&S.
Sports Illusion, Sports Reality: A Reporter's View of Sports, Journalism, & Society. Leonard Koppett. 288p. 1981. 13.95 o.p. (ISBN 0-395-31297-3). HM.
Sports Injuries Manual. Donald F. Featherstone. 1956. (ISBN 0-8022-0479-1). Philos Lib.
Sports Lingo: A Dictionary of the Language of Sports. Harvey Frommer. LC 82-12130. 312p. 1983. 9.95o.p. (ISBN 0-689-10939-3, Atheneum); pap. 7.95 o.s.i. (ISBN 0-689-70640-5, 289). Macmillan.
Sports Medicine: Fitness, Training, Injuries. 2nd ed. Ed. by Otto Appenzeller & Ruth A. Atkinson. LC 83-3471. (Illus.). 460p. 1983. pap. text ed. 26.50 o.p. (ISBN 0-8067-0132-3). Urban & S.
Sports Performance Factors. William Southmayd & James Rippe. 1986. pap. 10.95 o.p. (ISBN 0-399-51188-1, Perigee). Putnam Pub Group.
Sports Photography. Bill Hurter. LC 78-70044. (Photography How-to Ser.). (Illus.). 1978. pap. 3.95 o.p. (ISBN 0-8227-4026-5). Petersen Pub.
Sports Places Rated. Richard Whittingham. (Illus.). 240p. 1986. pap. 12.95 o.p. (ISBN 0-528-88051-9). Rand McNally.
Sports Roots: How Nicknames, Namesakes, Trophies, Competitions & Expressions Came to Be in the World of Sports. Harvey Frommer. LC 79-7313. (Illus.). 1979. 8.95 o.p. (ISBN 0-689-10980-6, Atheneum). Macmillan.
Sports Skills: A Conceptual Approach to Meaningful Movement. 2nd ed. Beverly L. Seidel et al. 592p. 1980. text ed. write for info. o.p. (ISBN 0-697-07168-5). Wm C Brown.
Sports Star: Bob Griese. S. H. Burchard. LC 75-11779. (Sports Star Ser.). (Illus.). 64p. (gr. 1-5). 1975. 5.25 o.p. (ISBN 0-15-277997-3, HJ). HarBraceJ.
Sports Star: Bob Griese. S. H. Burchard. LC 75-11779. (Sports Star Ser.). (Illus.). (gr. 1-5). 1975. pap. 2.50 o.p. (ISBN 0-15-278002-5, VoyB). HarBraceJ.
Sports Star: Brad Park. S. H. Burchard. LC 75-11778. (Sports Star Ser.). (Illus.). 64p. (gr. 1-5). 1975. 4.95 o.p. (ISBN 0-15-277998-1, HJ). HarBraceJ.
Sports Star: Brad Park. S. H. Burchard. LC 75-11778. (Sports Star Ser.). (Illus.). (gr. 1-5). 1975. pap. 2.95 o.p. (ISBN 0-15-278003-3, VoyB). HarBraceJ.
Sports Star: Chris Evert Lloyd. S. H. Burchard. LC 76-18156. (Sports Star Ser.). (Illus.). (gr. 1-5). 1976. 5.25 o.p. (ISBN 0-15-278007-6, HJ). HarBraceJ.
Sports Star: Chris Evert Lloyd. S. H. Burchard. LC 76-18156. (Sports Star Ser.). (Illus.). (gr. 1-5). 1976. pap. 2.95 o.p. (ISBN 0-15-278008-4, VoyB). HarBraceJ.
Sports Star: Dorothy Hamill. S. H. Burchard. LC 77-88960. (Sports Star Ser.). (Illus.). 64p. (gr. 1-5). 1978. 4.95 o.p. (ISBN 0-15-278014-9, VoyB). HarBraceJ.
Sports Star: Earl Campbell. S. H. Burchard. LC 80-7979. (Sports Star Ser.). (Illus.). 64p. (gr. 1-5). 1980. 6.95 o.p. (ISBN 0-15-278019-X, HJ). HarBraceJ.
Sports Star: Earl Campbell. S. H. Burchard. LC 80-7979. (Sports Star Ser.). (Illus.). 64p. (gr. 1-5). 1980. pap. 2.95 o.p. (ISBN 0-15-278021-1, VoyB). HarBraceJ.
Sports Star: Elvin Hayes. S. H. Burchard. LC 79-24286. (Sports Star Ser.). (Illus.). 64p. (gr. 1-5). 1980. 5.95 o.p. (ISBN 0-15-278018-1, HJ). HarBraceJ.
Sports Star: Elvin Hayes. S. H. Burchard. LC 79-24286. (Sports Star Ser.). (Illus.). 64p. (gr. 1-5). 1980. pap. 2.50 o.p. (ISBN 0-15-684828-7, VoyB). HarBraceJ.
Sports Star: Fernando Valenzuela. S. H. Burchard. LC 82-47932. (Sports Star Ser.). (Illus.). 64p. (ps-3). 1982. pap. 2.95 o.p. (ISBN 0-15-278045-9, VoyB). HarBraceJ.
Sports Star: Franco Harris. S. H. Burchard. LC 75-35527. (Sports Star Ser.). (Illus.). 64p. (gr. 1-5). 1976. 6.95 o.p. (ISBN 0-15-278000-9, HJ). HarBraceJ.
Sports Star: Franco Harris. S. H. Burchard. LC 75-35527. (Sports Star Ser.). (Illus.). (gr. 1-5). 1976. pap. 3.95 o.p. (ISBN 0-15-278005-X, VoyB). HarBraceJ.
Sports Star: George Brett. S. H. Burchard. LC 81-13293. (Sports Star Ser.). (Illus.). 64p. (gr. 1-5). 1982. 7.95 o.p. (ISBN 0-15-278040-8, HJ). HarBraceJ.
Sports Star: George Brett. S. H. Burchard. LC 81-13293. (Sports Star Ser.). (Illus.). 64p. (gr. 1-5). 1982. pap. 2.95 o.p. (ISBN 0-15-278041-6, VoyB). HarBraceJ.
Sports Star: Herschel Walker. S. H. Burchard. LC 83-22674. (Sports Star Ser.). (Illus.). 64p. (gr. 1-5). 1984. pap. 5.95 o.p. (ISBN 0-15-278053-X, VoyB). HarBraceJ.
Sports Star: Herschel Walker. S. H. Burchard. LC 83-22674. (Sports Star Ser.). (Illus.). 64p. (gr. 1-5). 1984. 11.95 o.p. (ISBN 0-15-278052-1, HJ). HarBraceJ.
Sports Star: Jim "Catfish" Hunter. S. H. Burchard. LC 75-35525. (Sports Star Ser.). (Illus.). 64p. (gr. 1-5). 1976. 4.95 o.p. (ISBN 0-15-278175-7, HJ). HarBraceJ.
Sports Star: Jim "Catfish" Hunter. S. H. Burchard. LC 75-35525. (Sports Star Ser.). (Illus.). (gr. 1-5). 1976. pap. 2.50 o.p. (ISBN 0-15-278176-5, VoyB). HarBraceJ.
Sports Star: John McEnroe. S. H. Burchard. LC 79-87509. (Sports Star Ser.). (Illus.). 64p. (gr. 1-5). 1979. 5.95 o.p. (ISBN 0-15-278017-3, HJ). HarBraceJ.
Sports Star: John McEnroe. S. H. Burchard. LC 79-87509. (Sports Star Ser.). (Illus.). (gr. 1-5). 1979. pap. 4.95 o.p. (ISBN 0-15-684787-6, VoyB). HarBraceJ.
Sports Star: Larry Bird. S. H. Burchard. LC 83-81264. (Sports Star Ser.). (Illus.). 64p. (gr. 1-5). 1983. 10.95 o.p. (ISBN 0-15-278050-5, HJ). HarBraceJ.
Sports Star: Larry Bird. S. H. Burchard. LC 83-81264. (Sports Star Ser.). (Illus.). 64p. (ps-3). 1983. pap. 4.95 o.p. (ISBN 0-15-278051-3, VoyB). HarBraceJ.
Sports Star: Mark "The Bird" Fidrych. S. H. Burchard. LC 77-4685. (Sports Star Ser.). (Illus.). 64p. (gr. 1-5). 1977. 4.95 o.p. (ISBN 0-15-278012-2, HJ). HarBraceJ.
Sports Star: Mark "The Bird" Fidrych. S. H. Burchard. LC 77-4685. (Sports Star Ser.). (Illus.). (gr. 1-5). 1977. pap. 2.95 o.p. (ISBN 0-15-684826-0, VoyB). HarBraceJ.
Sports Star: "Mean" Joe Greene. S. H. Burchard. LC 76-18130. (Sports Star Ser.). (Illus.). (gr. 1-5). 1976. 5.95 o.p. (ISBN 0-15-278009-2, HJ). HarBraceJ.
Sports Star: "Mean" Joe Greene. S. H. Burchard. LC 76-18130. (Sports Star Ser.). (Illus.). (gr. 1-5). 1976. pap. 3.95 o.p. (ISBN 0-15-278031-9, VoyB). HarBraceJ.
Sports Star: Nadia Comaneci. S. H. Burchard. LC 77-3967. (Sports Star Ser.). (Illus.). 64p. (gr. 1-5). 1977. 4.95 o.p. (ISBN 0-15-278013-0, HJ). HarBraceJ.
Sports Star: Nadia Comaneci. S. H. Burchard. LC 77-3967. (Sports Star Ser.). (Illus.). (gr. 1-5). 1977. pap. 2.95 o.p. (ISBN 0-15-684827-9, VoyB). HarBraceJ.
Sports Star: Pele. S. H. Burchard. LC 75-33707. (Sports Star Ser.). (Illus.). 64p. (gr. 1-5). 1976. 4.95 o.p. (ISBN 0-15-278001-7, HJ). HarBraceJ.
Sports Star: Pele. S. H. Burchard. LC 75-33707. (Sports Star Ser.). (Illus.). (gr. 1-5). 1976. pap. 2.95 o.p. (ISBN 0-15-278006-8, VoyB). HarBraceJ.
Sports Star: Reggie Jackson. S. H. Burchard. LC 78-20567. (Sports Star Ser.). (Illus.). 64p. (gr. 1-4). 1979. 6.95 o.p. (ISBN 0-15-278016-5, HJ). HarBraceJ.
Sports Star: Reggie Jackson. S. H. Burchard. LC 78-20567. (Sports Star Ser.). (Illus.). (gr. 1-5). 1979. pap. 2.95 o.p. (ISBN 0-15-684791-4, VoyB). HarBraceJ.
Sports Star: Sugar Ray Leonard. S. H. Burchard. LC 82-48764. (Sports Star Ser.). 64p. (gr. 1-5). 1983. 11.95 o.p. (ISBN 0-15-278048-3, HJ). HarBraceJ.
Sports Star: Sugar Ray Leonard. S. H. Burchard. LC 82-48764. (Sports Star Ser.). (Illus.). 64p. (gr. 1-5). 1983. pap. 4.95 o.p. (ISBN 0-15-278049-1, VoyB). HarBraceJ.
Sports Star: The Book of Baseball Greats. S. H. Burchard. LC 82-48763. (Sports Star Ser.). 64p. (gr. 1-5). 1983. 10.95 o.p. (ISBN 0-15-278060-2, HJ). HarBraceJ.
Sports Star: The Book of Baseball Greats. S. H. Burchard. LC 82-48763. (Sports Star Ser.). (Illus.). 64p. (gr. 1-5). 1983. pap. 4.95 o.p. (ISBN 0-15-278061-0, VoyB). HarBraceJ.
Sports Star: Tom Seaver. Marshall Burchard & S. H. Burchard. LC 74-7265. (Sports Star Ser.). (gr. 1-5). 1974. 4.95 o.p. (ISBN 0-15-277996-5, HJ). HarBraceJ.
Sports Star: Tom Seaver. Marshall Burchard & S. H. Burchard. LC 74-7265. (Sports Star Ser.). (Illus.). (gr. 1-5). 1974. pap. 3.95 o.p. (ISBN 0-15-278011-4, VoyB). HarBraceJ.
Sports Star: Tommy John. S. H. Burchard. LC 80-8794. (Sports Star Ser.). (Illus.). 64p. (gr. 1-5). 1981. 6.95 o.p. (ISBN 0-15-278038-6, HJ). HarBraceJ.
Sports Star: Tommy John. S. H. Burchard. LC 80-8794. (Sports Star Ser.). (Illus.). 64p. (gr. 1-5). 1981. pap. 3.95 o.p. (ISBN 0-15-278039-4, VoyB). HarBraceJ.
Sports Star: Tony Dorsett. S. H. Burchard. LC 78-52808. (Sports Star Ser.). (Illus.). (gr. 1-5). 1978. 5.25 o.p. (ISBN 0-15-278015-7, HJ). HarBraceJ.
Sports Star: Tony Dorsett. S. H. Burchard. LC 78-52808. (Sports Star Ser.). (Illus.). (gr. 1-5). 1978. pap. 4.95 o.p. (ISBN 0-15-684792-2, VoyB). HarBraceJ.
Sports Star: Tracy Austin. S. H. Burchard. LC 81-84215. (Sports Star Ser.). (Illus.). 64p. (gr. 1-5). 1982. 7.95 o.p. (ISBN 0-15-278042-4, HJ). HarBraceJ.
Sports Star: Tracy Austin. S. H. Burchard. LC 81-84215. (Sports Star Ser.). (Illus.). 64p. (gr. 1-5). 1982. pap. 2.95 o.p. (ISBN 0-15-278043-2, VoyB). HarBraceJ.
Sports Star: Walt Frazier. S. H. Burchard. LC 75-11781. (Sports Star Ser.). (Illus.). 64p. (gr. 1-5). 1975. 4.95 o.p. (ISBN 0-15-277999-X, HJ). HarBraceJ.
Sports Star: Walt Frazier. S. H. Burchard. LC 75-11781. (Sports Star Ser.). (Illus.). 64p. (gr. 1-5). 1975. pap. 3.95 o.p. (ISBN 0-15-278004-1, VoyB). HarBraceJ.
Sports Star: Wayne Gretzky. S. H. Burchard. LC 82-47931. (Sports Star Ser.). (Illus.). 64p. (gr. 1-5). 1982. 8.95 o.p. (ISBN 0-15-278046-7, HJ). HarBraceJ.
Sports Star: Wayne Gretzky. S. H. Burchard. LC 82-47931. (Sports Star Ser.). (Illus.). 64p. (ps-3). 1982. pap. 2.95 o.p. (ISBN 0-15-278047-5, VoyB). HarBraceJ.
Sports Trivia Puzzler, No. 4. Robert Kelly. (Orig.). 1981. pap. 1.95 o.p. (ISBN 0-440-07807-5). Dell.
Sports, Vol. 3 (incl. 1986-1987 Supplements) Ed. by Eleanor C. Goldstein. 1987. 30.00 o.p. (ISBN 0-89777-087-0). Soc Issues.
Sportsbeauty. Kathryn Lance. 208p. 1984. pap. 5.95 o.p. (ISBN 0-380-85696-4, 85696). Avon.
Sportscience: Physical Laws & Optimum Performance. Peter J. Brancazio. LC 83-20152. 400p. 1984. 18.25 o.s.i. (ISBN 0-671-45584-2). S&S.
Sportset: A Math Practice Set. Jerry Funk. 100p. 1981. pap. text ed. 12.00 o.p. (ISBN 0-205-07670-X, 177670); instr's manual avail. o.p. (ISBN 0-205-07671-8). Allyn.
Sportsfashion. France-Michele Adler. 192p. 1980. pap. 7.95 o.p. (ISBN 0-380-76075-4, 76075-4). Avon.
Sportshape: Body Conditioning for Women & Men-from the Daily Jogger to the Weekend Athlete. Helane Royce. (Illus.). 1983. pap. 6.95 o.p. (ISBN 0-87795-538-7, Arbor Hse). Morrow.
Sportsmen & Gamesmen: American Sporting Life in the Age of Jackson. John Dizikes. 1981. 15.00 o.p. (ISBN 0-395-27776-0). HM.
Sportswear, Casual Wear, Separates, Jeans: Women's, Misses', Juniors' 6th ed. Fairchild Market Research Division Staff. (Fairchild Fact Files Ser.). (Illus.). 50p. 1986. pap. 20.00 o.p. (ISBN 0-87005-555-0). Fairchild.
SPOT Simulation Applications Handbook. 293p. 1984. pap. 70.00 o.p. (ISBN 0-937294-60-8). ASP & RS.
Spot: The Rise of Political Advertising on Television. Edwin Diamond & Stephen Bates. 432p. 1986. pap. 9.95 o.p. (ISBN 0-262-54043-6). MIT Pr.
Spotlight Heroes: Two Decades of Rock & Roll Superstars As Seen Through the Camera of John Rowlands. John Rowlands. 160p. 1981. pap. text ed. 9.95 o.p. (ISBN 0-07-054159-0). McGraw.
Spotlight on Scott Baio, Clark Brandon, Leif Garret & John Schneider. L. B. Taylor, Jr. Ed. by Wendy Barish. (Illus.). 144p. (gr. 3 up). 1982. pap. 2.85 o.s.i. (ISBN 0-671-45212-6). Wanderer Bks.
Spotlight to Fame. Patti Beckman. (Silhouette Romances Ser.). 1984. lib. bdg. 8.95 o.p. (ISBN 0-8398-2804-7, Gregg). G K Hall.
Spots & Splashes & a Million Butterflies see Magga Birds of Ranatan.
Spots & Stripes. Ed. by San Diego Zoological Society Staff. (San Diego Zoo Series of Picture Bks.). (Illus.). 12p. (ps-2). 1985. bds. 2.95 o.p. (ISBN 0-89346-236-5). Heian Intl.
Spots Are Special. Kathryn O. Galbraith. LC 75-28179. (Illus.). 32p. (ps-3). 1976. 5.95 o.p. (ISBN 0-689-50038-6, Atheneum). Macmillan.
Spotted Flower & the Ponokomita. K. Follis Cheatham. LC 77-7253. (Illus.). 92p. (gr. 5-8). 1977. 7.95 o.s.i. (ISBN 0-664-32617-X, Westminster). Westminster John Knox.
Spotted Sphinx. Joy Adamson. LC 77-85008. (Helen & Kurt Wolff Bk.). (Illus.). 313p. 1969. 9.50 o.p. (ISBN 0-15-184795-9). HarBraceJ.
Spotty the Goat see There's a Skunk in My Trunk.
Spraakkunst Van Het Marind. P. Drabbe. 1955. 28.00 o.p. (ISBN 0-384-12595-6). Johnson Repr.
Sprache und Stil in Waelschen Gast Des Thomasin Von Circlaria. Friedrich Ranke. (Ger). 18.00 o.p.; pap. 13.00 o.p. (ISBN 0-685-02141-6). Johnson Repr.
Sprachlabor-Cassetten II mit Sprechuebungen see Deutsch X 3.
Sprachlabor-Cassetten, Saemtliche Sprechuebungen, Doppelspur Mitnachsprechpausen, 10 Casetten see Deutsch X 3.
Sprachlabor-Tonbaender II mit Sprechuebungen see Deutsch X 3.
Sprachlabor-Tonbaender saemtliche Sprechuebungen, Vollspur mit Nachsprechpausen, 10 Tonbaender see Deutsch X 3.
Spray It Loud. Jill Posener. (Illus.). 96p. 1987. pap. 9.95 o.p. (ISBN 0-86358-100-5, 81005, Pub. by Pandora Pr). Routledge Chapman & Hall.
Spread. Barry Malzberg. 1977. pap. 1.50 o.p. (ISBN 0-505-51180-0, Pub. by Tower Bks). Dorchester Pub Co.
Spreading Deserts: The Hand of Man. Erik Eckholm & Lester R. Brown. LC 77-81479. (Institute Papers). 1977. pap. 4.00 o.p. (ISBN 0-916468-12-7). Worldwatch Inst.
Sprechuebungem I - Textheft see Deutsch X 3.
Sprechuebungen II see Deutsch X 3.
Sprichworter und Lieder Aus der Gegend Von Turfan. Albert V. Le Coq. Repr. of 1911 ed. 16.00 o.p. (ISBN 0-384-32000-7). Johnson Repr.
Spring & Asura. Kenji Miyazawa. Tr. by Hiroaki Sato. LC 73-85173. 104p. 1975. 6.00 o.p. (ISBN 0-914090-00-3); pap. 3.50 o.p. (ISBN 0-914090-01-1). Chicago Review.
Spring Comes Riding. Betty Cavanna. (Illus.). (gr. 5-9). 1950. 5.50 o.s.i. (ISBN 0-664-32069-4, Westminster). Westminster John Knox.
Spring Green. Valrie M. Selkowe. LC 84-11202. (Illus.). 32p. (ps-1). 1985. 11.75 o.p. (ISBN 0-688-04055-1); PLB 11.88 o.p. (ISBN 0-688-04056-X). Lothrop.
Spring in October: The Story of the Polish Revolution 1956. Konrad Syrop. LC 75-35032. (Illus.). 207p. 1976. Repr. of 1958 ed. lib. bdg. 22.50x o.p. (ISBN 0-8371-8574-2, SYSO). Greenwood.
Spring in Washington. Louis J. Halle. LC 42-30273. (Illus.). 1963. pap. 1.25 o.p. (ISBN 0-689-70084-9, 22, Atheneum). Macmillan.
Spring Laughter. Christina Rainsford. LC 80-66877. 103p. 1980. 5.50 o.p. (ISBN 0-8233-0316-0). Golden Quill.
Spring of Love. Celia Dale. 1977. pap. 1.50 o.p. (ISBN 0-8439-0479-8, Pub. by Leisure Bks CT). Dorchester Pub Co.
Spring of the Tiger. Victoria Holt. LC 78-22814. 1979. 13.95 o.s.i. (ISBN 0-385-15261-2). Doubleday.
Spring Remembered: A Scottish Jewish Childhood. Evelyn Cowan. LC 78-66450. 1979. 8.50 o.s.i. (ISBN 0-8008-7367-X). Taplinger.
Spring Tide. Mary Ray. (Illus.). 174p. (gr. 5-9). 1979. pap. 2.95 o.p. (ISBN 0-571-11331-1). Faber & Faber.
Spring 1985: An Annual of Archetypal Psychology & Jungian Thought. Ed. by James Hillman. 185p. (Orig.). 1985. pap. 15.00 o.p. (ISBN 0-88214-021-3). Spring Pubns.
Springboard for Overlord, Hampshire & the D-Day Landings. Anthony Kemp. (Down Memory Lane, Old Hampshire Ser.). (Illus.). 70p. (Orig.). 1987. pap. 4.95 o.p. (ISBN 0-903852-42-X, Pub. by Milestone Pubns UK). Seven Hills Bk Dists.
Springboard to Discovery. Mary L. Lacy. 1976. 1.25 o.p. (ISBN 0-8042-3595-3, John Knox). Westminster John Knox.
Springfield & Clark County: An Illustrated History. William A. Kinnison. 152p. 1985. 22.95 o.s.i. (ISBN 0-89781-146-1). Windsor Pubns Inc.
Springfield Carbine on the Western Frontier. Kenneth Hammer. (Illus.). 1970. pap. 2.00 o.p. (ISBN 0-88342-214-X). Old Army.
Springfield Forty-Five Seventy. John Reese. 192p. 1982. pap. 1.95 o.p. (ISBN 0-505-51789-2, Pub. by Tower Bks). Dorchester Pub Co.

Springhouse Drug Reference. Ed. by Donna Hilton. 1393p. 1988. pap. 29.95 o.p. (ISBN 0-87434-107-8). Springhouse Pub.

Springs in the Valley see Streams in the Desert.

Springs of Love. Anna B. Mow. LC 79-11186. 1979. pap. 1.95 o.p. (ISBN 0-87178-810-1). Brethren.

Springsteen. Robert Hilburn. LC 85-14195. (Illus.). 256p. 1985. 32.50 o.p. (ISBN 0-684-18456-7, ScribT). Scribner.

Springsteen. Robert Hilburn. 256p. 1986. pap. 17.95 o.p. (ISBN 0-684-18703-5). Scribner.

Springsteen Back in the U. S. A. Marty Monroe. 64p. 1984. 7.95 o.p. (ISBN 0-88188-325-5, Pub. by Robus Bks). H Leonard Pub Corp.

Springtime in Fraggle Rock. Dennis Hockerman. (Illus.). (ps-k). 1985. 0.99 o.s.i. (ISBN 0-03-004442-1). H Holt & Co.

Sprint Cars. Sylvia Wilkinson. LC 81-6165. (World of Racing Ser.). (Illus.). 48p. (gr. 4 up). 1981. PLB 11.93 o.p. (ISBN 0-516-04717-5); pap. 3.95 o.p. (ISBN 0-516-44717-3). Childrens.

Sprite--MG Midget Service--Repair Handbook: All Models, 1958-1979. Ed. by Jeff Robinson. (Illus.). pap. 11.95 o.p. (ISBN 0-89287-164-4, A205). Clymer Pub.

Sprite MG Midget Handbook & Service Manual: 1958-1968. (Illus.). pap. 5.00 o.p. (ISBN 0-89287-252-7, A188). Clymer Pub.

Sprocket's Christmas Tale. Louise Gikow. LC 84-6526. (Fraggle Rock Bks.). (Illus.). (gr. 1-4). 1984. 7.95 o.s.i. (ISBN 0-03-000708-9). H Holt & Co.

Sprouse's Income Tax Handbook, 1986. Mary L. Sprouse. (Handbooks Ser.). 592p. 1985. pap. 7.95 o.p. Penguin.

Sprouse's Income Tax Handbook, 1987. Mary L. Sprouse. 384p. 1986. pap. 9.95 o.p. (ISBN 0-14-046774-2). Penguin.

Sprout & the Helicopter. Jennifer Wayne. (Illus.). 96p. (gr. 4-6). 1977. text ed. 8.95 o.p. (ISBN 0-07-068698-X). McGraw.

Sprouter's Cookbook: For Fast Kitchen Crops. Marjorie Blanchard. LC 74-83147. (Illus.). 144p. 1975. pap. 5.95 o.p. (ISBN 0-88266-041-1, Garden Way Pub). Storey Comm Inc.

Sprung Time: Seasons of the Christian Year. Robert G. Hamerton-Kelly. LC 79-56162. 144p. (Orig.). 1980. pap. 4.50 o.p. (ISBN 0-8358-0397-X). Upper Room.

SPSS-Eleven: The SPSS Batch System for the DEC PDP-11. 2nd rev. ed. Norman H. Nie & C. Hadlai Hull. 1982. text ed. 16.95x o.p. (ISBN 0-07-046546-0). McGraw.

SPSS Guide to Data Analysis. Marija J. Norusis. LC 86-60306. 402p. (Orig.). 1986. pap. 10.95 o.p. (ISBN 0-918469-24-4). SPSS Inc.

SPSS-PCplus. SPSS, Inc. Staff & Marija Norusis. LC 85-14553. 656p. (Orig.). 1985. pap. 29.95x o.p. (ISBN 0-918469-14-7). SPSS Inc.

SPSS-PCplus Advanced Statistics. SPSS, Inc. Staff & Marija Norusis. LC 85-14552. 320p. (Orig.). 1985. pap. 19.95x o.p. (ISBN 0-918469-15-5). SPSS Inc.

SPSS-PCplus Tables. SPSS, Inc. Staff. LC 85-14551. 224p. (Orig.). 1985. pap. 14.95x o.p. (ISBN 0-918469-16-3). SPSS Inc.

SPSS-X Advanced Statistical Guide. Marija J. Norusis. 820p. 1985. text ed. 15.95 o.p. (ISBN 0-07-046548-7). McGraw.

SPSS-X Graphics. SPSS, Inc. Staff. 320p. 1985. text ed. 37.95 o.p. (ISBN 0-07-046554-1). McGraw.

SPSS-X Introducing Statistics Guide. Marija J. Norusis. 1983. text ed. 15.95 o.p. (ISBN 0-07-046549-5). McGraw.

SPSS-X Tables. SPSS, Inc. Staff. 176p. 1985. text ed. 15.95 o.p. (ISBN 0-07-046558-4). McGraw.

SPSS-X User's Guide. SPSS, Inc. Staff. 864p. 1983. text ed. 30.95 o.p. (ISBN 0-07-046550-9). McGraw.

SPSS-X User's Guide. 2nd ed. SPSS, Inc. Staff. 1000p. 1986. text ed. 34.95 o.p. (ISBN 0-07-046553-3). McGraw.

Spurs for Suzanna. Betty Cavanna. (Illus.). 224p. (gr. 5-9). 1947. 5.50 o.s.i. (ISBN 0-664-32026-0, Westminster). Westminster John Knox.

Spy. Norman Garbo. 1980. 10.95 o.p. (ISBN 0-393-01321-9). Norton.

Spy: A Tale of the Neutral Ground. facsimile ed. James Fenimore Cooper. (Library of Classics Ser: No. 18). (Illus.). pap. text ed. 3.95 o.s.i. (ISBN 0-02-843130-8). Hafner.

Spy Case Built for Two. Amelia Walden. LC 69-15249. (gr. 7 up). 1969. 3.95 o.s.i. (ISBN 0-664-32433-9, Westminster). Westminster John Knox.

Spy: Dr. Bancroft, America's First Double Agent. Arthur Mullin. 400p. 1987. 18.95 o.s.i. (ISBN 0-88496-268-7). Capra Pr.

Spy in the Deuce Court. Frank Deford. LC 85-28200. 256p. 1986. 17.95 o.p. (ISBN 0-399-13134-5). Putnam Pub Group.

Spy in the Ointment. Donald E. Westlake. 208p. 1987. pap. 3.95 o.p. (ISBN 0-445-40617-8). Mysterious Pr.

Spy Lady & the Muffin Man. Sesyle Joslin. LC 74-137757. (Illus.). (gr. 4-6). 1971. 4.75 o.p. (ISBN 0-15-278182-X, HJ). HarBraceJ.

Spy on Danger Island. Amelia Walden. (gr. 7-10). 1965. 3.50 o.s.i. (ISBN 0-664-32364-2, Westminster). Westminster John Knox.

Spy on Spider. John N. Chance. (Lythway Ser.). 176p. 1988. lib. bdg. 17.50x o.s.i. (ISBN 0-7451-0713-3, Pub. by Chivers Pr UK). G K Hall.

Spy Story. Len Deighton. LC 74-3124. 1974. 6.95 o.p. (ISBN 0-15-184838-6). HarBraceJ.

Spy Unmasked: Or, the Memoirs of Enoch Crosby, Alias Harvey Birch, the Hero of James Fenimore Cooper's "the Spy" facsimile ed. H. L. Barnum. LC 75-29452. (Illus.). 264p. 1975. Repr. of 1828 ed. 11.50 o.p. (ISBN 0-916346-15-3). Harbor Hill Bks.

Spy Wednesday: A Novel. William Hood. 1986. 14.45 o.p. (ISBN 0-393-02250-1). Norton.

Spy Who Barked in the Night. Marc Lovell. LC 85-13176. (Crime Club Ser.). 192p. 1986. 12.95 o.p. (ISBN 0-385-23261-6). Doubleday.

Spy Who Never Was. Sheila Martin. 192p. (Orig.). 1982. pap. 2.25 o.p. (ISBN 0-8439-1036-4, Pub. by Leisure Bks CT). Dorchester Pub Co.

Spymaster. Donald Freed. LC 78-72922. 1980. 12.95 o.p. (ISBN 0-87795-211-6, Arbor Hse). Morrow.

Squandering Eden: Africa at the Edge. Mort Rosenblum & Doug Williamson. 1987. 19.95 o.p. (ISBN 0-15-184860-2). HarbraceJ.

Squanto. Matthew G. Grant. LC 73-12813. (We the People Ser.). 1974. PLB 7.95 o.p. (ISBN 0-87191-270-8). Creative Ed.

Square & the Circle of the Indian Arts. K Vatsyayan. (Illus.). 159p. 1983. text ed. 65.00x o.p. (ISBN 0-391-02686-0). Humanities.

Square Crib. Graham Jackson. 122p. 1982. 16.95 o.p. (ISBN 0-7022-1640-2); pap. 9.75 o.p. (ISBN 0-7022-1650-X). U of Queensland Pr.

Squarehead & Me. Henry L. Haynes. LC 79-25523. (gr. 4-7). 1980. pap. 8.95 o.s.i. (ISBN 0-664-32663-3, Westminster). Westminster John Knox.

Squarely Behind the Beavers. Philbrook Paine. (Illus.). 1963. 3.95 o.p. (ISBN 0-393-08470-1). Norton.

Squash. Rachel Bard & Caroline Kellogg. LC 77-3917. (Edible Garden Ser.). (Illus.). 1977. pap. 2.50 o.s.i. (ISBN 0-89286-113-4, One Hund One Prods). Ortho.

Squash: The Ambitious Player's Guide. Alan Colburn. 112p. 1984. pap. 9.95 o.p. (ISBN 0-571-13361-4). Faber & Faber.

Squat Pyramid: Canadian Studies in the United States. Richard A. Preston. (Occasional Papers: No. 9). 70p. 1980. 8.00 o.p. (ISBN 0-916994-23-6). Ctr Intl Stud Duke.

Squatter, Selector, & Storekeeper. D. Waterson. 1968. 22.00x o.p. (ISBN 0-424-05740-9, Pub by Sydney U Pr). Intl Spec Bk.

Squatter Settlements: Monographs. Mary Vance. (Public Administration Ser.: P 1765). 13p. 1985. 2.00 o.p. (ISBN 0-89028-565-9). Vance Biblios.

Squaw Man's Son. Evelyn S. Lampman. LC 77-17503. 192p. (gr. 5-9). 1978. 7.95 o.p. (ISBN 0-689-50102-1, Atheneum). Macmillan.

Squeeze. James D. Davidson. 1980. 11.95 o.s.i. (ISBN 0-671-40084-3). S&S.

Squeeze Play. Paul Benjamin. 208p. 1984. pap. 2.50 o.p. (ISBN 0-380-67686-9, 67686). Avon.

Squib. Nina Bawden. LC 82-75. (Illus.). 160p. (gr. 5 up). 1982. Repr. 11.75 o.p. Lothrop.

Squire's Bride: A Norwegian Folk Tale. P. C. Asbjornsen. LC 74-19316. (Illus.). 32p. (gr. k-2). 1975. 6.95 o.p. (ISBN 0-689-30463-3, Atheneum). Macmillan.

Sri Aurobindo on the Tantra. Sri Aurobindo. Compiled by Sri M. P. Pandit. 47p. (Orig.). 1979. pap. 2.00 o.p. (ISBN 0-941524-17-5). Lotus Light.

Sri Chinmoy Family Cookbook. Ed. by Sri Chinmoy Centre Staff. (Illus.). 230p. 1980. pap. 5.95 o.p. (ISBN 0-88497-505-3). Aum Pubns.

Sri Chinmoy Speaks, 10 pts. Sri Chinmoy. Incl. Pt. 1. 55p (ISBN 0-88497-282-8); Pt. 2. 58p (ISBN 0-88497-285-2); Pt. 3. 65p (ISBN 0-88497-286-0); Pt. 4. 62p (ISBN 0-88497-288-7); Pt. 5. 56p (ISBN 0-88497-289-5); Pt. 6. 57p (ISBN 0-88497-290-9); Pt. 7. 58p (ISBN 0-88497-294-1); Pt. 8. 56p (ISBN 0-88497-295-X); Pt. 9. 51p (ISBN 0-88497-296-8); Pt. 10. 62p (ISBN 0-88497-335-2). 1976-77. pap. 2.00 ea. o.p. Aum Pubns.

Sri Lanka. Nigel Palmer. LC 84-50340. (Illus.). 24p. 1984. 29.95f o.s.i. (ISBN 0-500-24120-1). Thames Hudson.

Sri Lanka. Akira Uchiyama. LC 73-79761. (This Beautiful World Ser.: Vol. 44). (Illus.). 150p. (Orig.). 1973. pap. 4.95 o.p. (ISBN 0-87011-209-0). Kodansha.

Sri Lanka: A Travel Survival Kit. 3rd ed. Tony Wheeler. (Illus.). 208p. (Orig.). 1984. pap. 7.95 o.p. (ISBN 0-908086-62-8). Lonely Planet.

Sri Lanka Travel Guide. Berlitz Editors. (Travel Guides Ser.). 1982. pap. 4.95 o.p. (ISBN 0-317-12282-7, Berlitz). Macmillan.

Sri Lanka Travel Survival Kit. Tony Wheeler. pap. 6.95 o.p. (ISBN 0-908086-32-6). Lonely Planet.

Sri Lanka: Unrest in Paradise. Pranay Gupte. 224p. 1988. 17.95 o.p. (ISBN 0-87131-529-7). M Evans.

Sri Lankan Fishermen: Rural Capitalism & Peasant Society. Paul Alexander. (South Asia Monograph Ser.). 1982. pap. 22.00x o.p. (ISBN 0-908070-06-3, Pub. by Australian Nat Univ). South Asia Bks.

Sri Lanka's Foreign Policy: A Study in Non-Alignment. H. S. Nissanka. 400p. 1984. text ed. 35.00x o.p. (ISBN 0-7069-2608-0, Pub. by Vikas India). Advent NY.

Srimad Bhagavatam: Eighth Canto, 3 vols. Swami A. C. Bhaktivedanta. LC 73-169353. (Illus.). 1976. 12.95 ea. o.p. Vol. 1 (ISBN 0-912776-90-0). Vol. 2 (ISBN 0-912776-91-9). Vol. 3 (ISBN 0-912776-92-7). Bhaktivedanta.

Srimad Bhagavatam: Eleventh Canto, 4 Vols. Bhaktivedanta Swami. (Illus.). 416p. 1983. 12.95 ea. o.p. (ISBN 0-89213-125-X). Bhaktivedanta.

Srimad-Bhagavatam: Eleventh Canto, Vol. 1. Hridayananda dasa Goswami Acaryadeva. (Illus.). 450p. 1982. 12.95 o.p. (ISBN 0-89213-112-8); text ed. 9.95 o.p. (ISBN 0-686-98021-2). Bhaktivedanta.

Srimad Bhagavatam: Fifth Canto, 2 vols. Swami A. C. Bhaktivedanta. LC 73-169353. (Illus.). 1976. 12.95 ea. o.p. (ISBN 0-686-85716-X). Vol. 1 (ISBN 0-912776-78-1). Vol. 2 (ISBN 0-912776-79-X). Bhaktivedanta.

Srimad Bhagavatam: First Canto, 3 vols. Swami A. C. Bhaktivedanta. LC 73-169353. (Illus.). 1972. 12.95 ea. o.p. Vol. 1 (ISBN 0-912776-27-7). Vol. 2 (ISBN 0-912776-29-3). Vol. 3 (ISBN 0-912776-34-X). Bhaktivedanta.

Srimad Bhagavatam: Fourth Canto, 4 vols. Swami A. C. Bhaktivedanta. LC 73-169353. (Illus.). 1974. 12.95 ea. o.p. Vol. 1 (ISBN 0-912776-38-2). Vol. 2 (ISBN 0-912776-47-1). Vol. 3 (ISBN 0-912776-48-X). Vol. 4 (ISBN 0-912776-49-8). Bhaktivedanta.

Srimad Bhagavatam: Ninth Canto, 3 vols. Swami A. C. Bhaktivendanta. LC 73-169353. (Illus., Sanskrit & Eng.). 1977. 12.95 ea. o.p. Vol. 1 (ISBN 0-912776-94-3). Vol. 2 (ISBN 0-912776-95-1). Vol. 3 (ISBN 0-912776-96-X). Bhaktivedanta.

Srimad Bhagavatam: Second Canto, 2 vols. Swami A. C. Bhaktivedanta. LC 73-169353. (Illus.). 1972. 12.95 ea. o.p. Vol. 1 (ISBN 0-912776-28-5). Vol. 2 (ISBN 0-912776-35-8). Bhaktivedanta.

Srimad Bhagavatam: Seventh Canto, 3 vols. Swami A. C. Bhaktivedanta. LC 73-169353. (Illus.). 1976. 12.95 ea. o.p. Vol. 1 (ISBN 0-912776-86-2). Vol. 2 (ISBN 0-912776-87-0). Vol. 3 (ISBN 0-912776-89-7). Bhaktivedanta.

Srimad Bhagavatam: Sixth Canto, 3 vols. Swami A. C. Bhaktivedanta. LC 73-169353. (Illus.). 1976. 12.95 ea. o.p. Vol. 1 (ISBN 0-912776-81-1). Vol. 2 (ISBN 0-912776-82-X). Vol. 3 (ISBN 0-912776-83-8). Bhaktivedanta.

Srimad-Bhagavatam: Tenth Canto, Vol 1. Swami Prabhupada A. C. Bhaktivedanta. LC 73-169353. 1977. 12.95 o.p. (ISBN 0-912776-97-8). Bhaktivedanta.

Srimad-Bhagavatam: Tenth Canto, Vol 2. Swami Prabhupada A. C. Bhaktivedanta. 1977. 12.95 o.p. (ISBN 0-912776-98-6). Bhaktivedanta.

Srimad-Bhagavatam: Tenth Canto, Vol. 3. Swami Prabhupada A. C. Bhaktivedanta. (Illus.). 112p. 1980. 12.95 o.p. (ISBN 0-89213-107-1). Bhaktivedanta.

Srimad Bhagavatam: Third Canto, 4 vols. Swami A. C. Bhaktivedanta. LC 73-169353. (Illus.). 1974. 12.95 ea. o.p. Vol. 1 (ISBN 0-912776-37-4). Vol. 2 (ISBN 0-912776-44-7). Vol. 3 (ISBN 0-912776-46-3). Vol. 4 (ISBN 0-912776-75-7). Bhaktivedanta.

Srimad Bhagavatam: 11th Canto, Vol. 5. Bhaktivedanta Swami. 1985. 12.95 o.p. (ISBN 0-89213-126-8). Bhaktivedanta.

Srimad Bhagavatam: 12th Canto, Vol. 1. Bhaktivedanta Swami & Hridayananda Das Goswami. 1985. 12.95 o.p. (ISBN 0-89213-129-2). Bhaktivedanta.

Srimad Bhagavatam: 12th Canto, Vol. 2. Bhaktivedanta Swami. 1985. 12.95 o.p. (ISBN 0-89213-130-6). Bhaktivedanta.

SSB..the Misunderstood Mode. James B. Wilson. 96p. 1978. pap. 5.50 o.p. (ISBN 0-88006-009-3, BK 7351). Wayne Green Ent.

Stab in the Back. Malcolm Gray. LC 86-11491. (Crime Club Ser.). 192p. 1986. 12.95 o.p. (ISBN 0-385-23474-0). Doubleday.

Stab in the Dark. Lawrence Block. LC 81-66971. 192p. 1981. 10.95 o.p. (ISBN 0-87795-340-6, Arbor Hse). Morrow.

Stabilitatsaussagen uber Klassen Von Matrizen mit Verschwindenden Zeilensummen. G. A. Aschinger. (Lecture Notes in Economics & Mathematical Systems: Vol. 113). 112p. 1975. pap. 13.00 o.p. (ISBN 0-387-07414-7). Springer-Verlag.

Stability & Flexibility: An Analysis of Natural Systems. 1980. 34.00 o.p. (ISBN 0-08-024683-4). Pergamon.

Stability & Switching in Cellular Differentiation. Ed. by R. M. Clayton & D. E. Truman. LC 83-18053. (Advances In Experimental Medicine & Biology Ser.: Vol. 158). 496p. 1982. 85.00x o.p. (ISBN 0-306-41181-4, Plenum Pr). Plenum Pub.

Stability Constants of Metal Complexes: Critical Survey of Stability Constants of EDTA Complexes, Vol. 14. International Union of Pure & Applied Chemistry Staff. Ed. by G. Anderegg. 1977. pap. 17.25 o.p. (ISBN 0-08-022009-6). Pergamon.

Stability in Coal Mining: Proceedings of the International Symposium, 1st, Vancouver, B. C., Canada 1978. International Symposium on Stability in Coal Mining Staff. Ed. by C. O. Brawner & Ian P. Dorling. LC 78-73842. (World Coal Bk.). (Illus.). 496p. 1979. 55.00 o.p. (ISBN 0-87930-108-2). Miller Freeman.

Stability in Underground Mining II. Ed. by A. B. Szwilski & C. O. Brawner. LC 84-71630. (International Conferences on Stability in Underground Mining Ser.). (Illus.). 606p. 1984. 45.00x o.p. (ISBN 0-89520-430-4, 430-4). SMM&E Inc.

Stability of Adaptive Controllers. B. Egardt. Ed. by A. V. Balakrishnan & M. Thoma. (Lecture Notes in Control & Information Sciences: Vol. 20). (Illus.). 1979. pap. 14.00 o.p. (ISBN 0-387-09646-9). Springer-Verlag.

Stability of Biological Communities. Y. Svirezhev. 319p. 1983. 9.95 o.p. (ISBN 0-8285-2371-1, Pub. by Mir Pubs USSR). Imported Pubns.

Stability of Elastic Structures. Ed. by H. H. Leipholz. (CISM-International Center for Mechanical Sciences Courses & Lectures: Vol. 238). (Illus.). 1979. 28.40 o.p. (ISBN 0-387-81473-6). Springer-Verlag.

Stability of Elastic Systems. S. J. Britvec. 480p. 1973. 120.00 o.p. (ISBN 0-08-016859-0). Pergamon.

Stability of Fluid Motions 1. D. D. Joseph. (Springer Tracts in Natural Philosophy: Vol. 27). 1976. 57.00 o.p. (ISBN 0-387-07514-3). Springer-Verlag.

Stability of Heavy Minerals in Sediments. Ed. by Gretchen Luepke. 1984. 41.95 o.p. (ISBN 0-442-25925-5). Van Nos Reinhold.

Stability of Industrial Organisms. Ed. by B. E. Kirsop. 57p. 1980. pap. text ed. 5.75 o.p. (ISBN 0-85198-470-3). CAB Intl.

Stability of Motion. W. Hahn. Tr. by A. P. Baartz. (Grundlehren der Mathematischen Wissenschaften: Vol. 138). (Illus.). 1968. 40.20 o.p. (ISBN 0-387-03829-9). Springer-Verlag.

Stability of the Differentiated State. Ed. by H. Ursprung. (Results & Problems in Cell Differentiation Ser.: Vol. 1). (Illus.). 1969. 42.00 o.p. (ISBN 0-387-04315-2). Springer-Verlag.

Stability Theory & Existence of Periodic Solutions & Almost Periodic Solutions. T. Yoshizawa. LC 74-28140. (Applied Mathematical Sciences Ser.: Vol. 14). vii, 233p. 1975. pap. 21.50 o.p. (ISBN 0-387-90112-4). Springer-Verlag.

Stability Theory by Liapunov's Direct Method. LC 77-7285. (Applied Mathematical Sciences: Vol. 22). (Illus.). 1977. 27.50 o.p. (ISBN 0-387-90258-9). Springer-Verlag.

Stability Theory of Dynamical Systems. N. P. Bhatia & G. P. Szegoe. LC 70-126892. (Grundlehren der Mathematischen Wissenschaften: Vol. 161). (Illus.). 1970. 34.50 o.p. (ISBN 0-387-05112-0). Springer-Verlag.

Stabilization, 8 reports. (Transportation Research Record Ser.). 81p. 1976. 6.00 o.p. (ISBN 0-309-02470-6). Transport Res Bd.

Stabilization of Local Government in New South Wales, 1858-1906. F. A. Larcombe. (History of Local Government in New South Wales Ser.: Vol. 2). 352p. 1975. 33.00x o.p. (ISBN 0-424-00001-6, Pub. by Sydney U Pr). Intl Spec Bk.

Stabilization of Soils. (Transportation Research Record Ser.). 66p. 1977. 4.40 o.p. (ISBN 0-309-02670-9). Transport Res Bd.

Stable & Random Motions in Dynamical Systems: With Special Emphasis on Celestial Mechanics. Jurgen Moser. LC 73-2481. (Annals of Mathematics Studies: No. 77). 1973. 25.00x o.p. (ISBN 0-691-08132-8). Princeton U Pr.

Stable Homotopy. J. M. Cohen. LC 77-139950. (Lecture Notes in Mathematics: Vol. 165). 1970. pap. 11.00 o.p. (ISBN 0-387-05192-9). Springer-Verlag.

Stable Isotopes: Proceedings of the Third International Conference. Ed. by E. Roseland Klein & Peter D. Klein. 1979. 64.00 o.p. (ISBN 0-12-413650-8). Acad Pr.

Stable Organic Cation Salts: Ion Pair Equilibria & Use in Cationic Polymerization see Polymerization Reactions.

Staff Development in Libraries: Bibliography. 49p. 1983. 7.50 o.p. (ISBN 0-8389-6758-2). Library Admin.

Staff Management in University & College Libraries. Peter Durey. Ed. by C. Chandler. 144p. 1976. 23.00 o.p. (ISBN 0-08-019718-3). Pergamon.

Staff Relations in the Civil Service: The Canadian Experience. Saul J. Frankel. 344p. 1962. 8.50 o.p. (ISBN 0-7735-0002-2, McGill Canada). U of Toronto Pr.

Staff Support & Staff Training. T. Collins & T. Bruce. (Residential Social Work Ser.). 168p. 1984. pap. 11.95 o.p. (ISBN 0-422-76920-7, 4003, Pub. by Tavistock England). Routledge Chapman & Hall.

Staff Training in Mental Handicap. Ed. by James Hogg. 224p. 1986. 27.50 o.p. (ISBN 0-7099-3728-8, Pub. by Croom Helm UK). Routledge Chapman & Hall.

Staffan. Tr. by Ross Shideler. LC 78-123608. (Illus.). (gr. 1-5). 1970. 3.95 o.p. (ISBN 0-395-27670-5, Pub. by Parnassus). HM.

Staffing of Congress: A Selected Bibliography. Jamie W. Coniglio. (Public Administration Ser.: P 1749). 5p. 1985. 2.00 o.p. (ISBN 0-89028-529-2). Vance Biblios.

Staffing Organizations. Benjamin Schneider. Ed. by Lyman W. Porter. LC 75-20584. (Management & Organizations Ser.). (Illus.). 200p. 1976. text ed. 16.50x o.p. (ISBN 0-673-16148-X); pap. text ed. write for info. o.p. (ISBN 0-673-16147-1). Scott F.

Staffordshire. Arthur Mee. (King's England Ser.). (ISBN 0-340-15030-0). Intl Pubns Serv.

Staffordshire Pottery: The Tribal Art of England. Anthony Oliver. (Illus.). 192p. 1980. 65.00 o.p. (ISBN 0-434-54392-6, Pub. by W Heinemann Ltd). David & Charles.

Staffs of Life. E. J. Kahn, Jr. 288p. 1985. 19.95 o.p. (ISBN 0-316-48192-0). Little.

Stag Boy. William Rayner. LC 72-91232. (gr. 7 up). 1973. 4.25 o.p. (ISBN 0-15-278400-4, HJ). HarBraceJ.

Stage Coach & Tavern Tales of the Old Northwest. Harry E. Cole. Ed. by Louise P. Kellogg. LC 77-137353. 376p. 1972. Repr. of 1930 ed. 46.00x o.p. (ISBN 0-8103-3073-3). Gale.

Stage Costumes for Girls. Jean Greenhowe. LC 75-23205. (Illus.). 1976. 10.95 o.p. (ISBN 0-8238-0196-9). Plays.

Stage Directions. John Gielgud. LC 78-23580. 1979. Repr. of 1963 ed. lib. bdg. 35.00x o.p. (ISBN 0-313-21035-7, GISD). Greenwood.

Stage for Poets: Studies in the Theatre of Hugo & Musset. Charles Affron. LC 75-153847. (Princeton Essays in Literature Ser.). 1972. 29.50x o.p. (ISBN 0-691-06201-3). Princeton U Pr.

Stage in the Eighteenth Century. 1981. lib. bdg. 31.00 o.p. (ISBN 0-8240-4008-2). Garland Pub.

Stage Makeup. 6th ed. Richard Corson. (Illus.). 464p. 1981. text ed. 37.33 o.p. (ISBN 0-13-840512-3). P-H.

Stage Management Forms & Formats. Barbara Dilker. LC 79-16689. (Illus.). 192p. (Orig.). 1982. pap. text ed. 14.95x o.s.i. (ISBN 0-910482-85-3). Drama Bk.

Stage Managers Directory, 1988. rev ed. Ed. by David Rodger. 180p. 1987. pap. 15.00 o.p. (ISBN 0-911747-08-7). Broadway Pr.

Stage-Screen Debate: A Study in Popular Aesthetics. Gregory A. Waller. Ed. by Garth S. Jowett. LC 81-48353. (Dissertations on Film Ser.). 426p. 1983. lib. bdg. 61.00 o.p. (ISBN 0-8240-5111-4). Garland Pub.

Stage Struck. Simon Gray. LC 80-25312. 64p. 1981. 9.95 o.p. (ISBN 0-394-51804-7); pap. 4.95 o.p. (ISBN 0-394-17882-3). Seaver Bks.

Stagecoach. Ed. by Richard J. Anobile. 1975. pap. 6.45 o.p. (ISBN 0-380-00291-4, 22913-7, Flare). Avon.

Stagecraft & Scene Design. Herbert Philippi. LC 53-6010. 1953. text ed. 21.50 o.p. (ISBN 0-395-05053-7). HM.

Stagecraft for Nonprofessionals. 3rd ed. F. A. Buerki. (Illus.). 144p. (Orig.). 1972. pap. 9.95 o.p. (ISBN 0-299-06234-1). U of Wis Pr.

Stages in Writing. K. Taylor. 1973. text ed. 20.95 o.p. (ISBN 0-07-062995-1). McGraw.

Stages: Understanding How You Make Your Moral Decisions. Nathaniel Lande & Afton Slade. LC 78-195000. 1979. 10.00 o.p. (ISBN 0-06-250510-6). HarpR.

Stagewise & Mass Transfer Operations. Ed. by J. M. Calo & E. J. Henley. (Modular Instruction Series B: Vol. 3). 61p. 1983. pap. 30.00 o.p. (ISBN 0-317-05081-8). Am Inst Chem Eng.

Staggerford. Jon Hassler. LC 76-57757. 1977. 8.95 o.p. (ISBN 0-689-10793-5, Atheneum). Macmillan.

Stagnation & Growth in the American Economy, 1784-1792. Gordon C. Bjork. Ed. by Stuart Bruchey. LC 84-48304. (American Economic History Ser.). 186p. 1985. lib. bdg. 30.00 o.p. (ISBN 0-8240-6652-9). Garland Pub.

Stain. Rikki Ducornet. LC 84-48117. 192p. 1984. 12.95 o.p. (ISBN 0-394-54284-3, GP-955). Grove.

Stain of Circumstance: Selected Poems. Lloyd Frankenberg. LC 73-85448. 237p. 1974. 12.95 o.p. (ISBN 0-8214-0138-6). Ohio U Pr.

Staining Methods for Sectioned Material. P. R. Lewis & D. P. Knight. (Practical Methods in Electron Microscopy: Vol. 5, Pt. 1). 1977. 27.00 o.p. (ISBN 0-7204-0606-4, North-Holland). Elsevier.

Stairs. G. Aloi. (Illus.). 1973. 30.00 o.s.i. (ISBN 0-685-36171-3). E J Brill USA.

Stairway C. Elvire Murail. Tr. by M. L. Linden. 192p. 1986. pap. 3.95 o.p. (ISBN 0-380-89678-8, Bard). Avon.

Stairway to Heaven: Religion in Rock. Davin Seay & Mary Neely. 384p. 1986. pap. 9.95 o.s.i. (ISBN 0-345-33022-6, Pub. by Ballantine Epiphany). Ballantine.

Stakes Winners of 1978: Supplement. Throughbred Owners & Breeders Association Staff. 1978. lib. bdg. 15.00 o.p. (ISBN 0-936032-21-9); pap. 10.00 o.p. (ISBN 0-936032-22-7). Blood-Horse.

Stakes Winners of 1981. Ed. by Blood-Horse, Inc. Staff. (Annual Supplement Ser.). 800p. 1982. lib. bdg. 30.00 o.p. (ISBN 0-936032-48-0); pap. 20.00 o.p. (ISBN 0-936032-49-9). Blood-Horse.

Stakes Winners of 1983: Annual Supplement to The Blood Horse. 900p. (Orig.). 1984. 30.00 o.p. (ISBN 0-936032-69-3); pap. 21.50 o.p. (ISBN 0-936032-70-7). Blood Horse.

Stalin & German Communism. Ruth Fischer. 1981. 34.95 o.p. (ISBN 0-87855-391-6). Transaction Pubs.

Stalin File. Martin McCauley. (World Leaders Ser.). 1979. 17.95 o.p. (ISBN 0-7134-1918-0, Pub. by Batsford England). David & Charles.

Stalin's Failure in China, 1924-1927. Conrad Brandt. 1966. pap. 3.95x o.p. (ISBN 0-393-00352-3, Norton Lib). Norton.

Stalin's Secret War. Nikolai Tolstoy. LC 81-47458. 496p. 1982. 18.50 o.p. (ISBN 0-03-047266-0). H Holt & Co.

Stalk a Stranger. Rachel Scott. (Velvet Glove Ser.: No. 22). 1985. pap. 2.25 o.p. (ISBN 0-380-89787-3). Avon.

Stalker: A Mystery. Liza Cody. 168p. 1985. 11.95 o.s.i. (ISBN 0-684-18234-3, ScribT). Scribner.

Stalker Affair. Frank Doherty. 120p. (Orig.). 1986. pap. 6.95 o.p. (ISBN 0-85342-795-X, Pub. by Mercier Pr Ireland). Irish Bks Media.

Stalker Trilogy, 3 vol. James M. Stalker. 1986. Set. pap. 23.95 o.p. (ISBN 0-310-44178-1, 12619P). Zondervan.

Stalkers. Luke Short. (Nightingale Ser.). 227p. 1988. pap. 12.95 o.p. (ISBN 0-8161-4425-7, Large Print Bks). G K Hall.

Stalking Horse. James Pattinson. 208p. 1986. pap. 2.95 o.p. (ISBN 0-931773-62-8). Critics Choice Paper.

Stalking the Headhunter: The Smart Job-Hunter's Guide to Executive Recruiters. Stonesong Press Staff & John J. Tarrant. LC 86-47579. 288p. (Orig.). 1986. 17.95 o.p. (ISBN 0-553-05181-4). Bantam.

Stalking the Perfect Tan. G. B. Trudeau. 1988. pap. 5.95 o.p. H Holt & Co.

Stall Buddies. Penny Pollock. (Illus.). 64p. (gr. 3-7). 1984. 9.95 o.p. (ISBN 0-399-21118-7, Putnam). Putnam Pub Group.

Stallion Register, 1981. Ed. by Blood Horse Staff. (Illus.). 900p. 1980. 20.00 o.p. (ISBN 0-936032-33-2); pap. 10.00 o.p. (ISBN 0-936032-34-0). Blood-Horse.

Stallion Register, 1983: Annual Supplement to the Blood-Horse. Ed. by Blood-Horse Staff. (Illus.). 1200p. 1982. 20.00 o.p. (ISBN 0-936032-54-5); pap. 10.00 o.p. (ISBN 0-936032-55-3). Blood-Horse.

Stallion Register, 1987. (Annual Supplement to the Blood-Horse). 1300p. 1986. text ed. 35.00 o.p. (ISBN 0-939049-00-7); pap. 26.50 o.p. (ISBN 0-939049-01-5). Blood Horse.

Stallone! Jeff Rovin. 1985. pap. 3.95 o.s.i. (ISBN 0-671-61872-5). PB.

Stamp Collecting A-Z. Walter J. Young. LC 80-27181. (Illus.). 240p. 1981. 15.00 o.s.i. (ISBN 0-498-02479-2). A S Barnes.

Stamp Collector's Encyclopedia. R. J. Sutton. (Illus.). 344p. 1966. (ISBN 0-8022-1676-5). Philos Lib.

Stamp Curiosities. R. J. Sutton. (Illus.). 292p. 1958. (ISBN 0-8022-1675-7). Philos Lib.

Stamps Are Money. R. J. Sutton. (Illus.). 196p. 1960. (ISBN 0-8022-1674-9). Philos Lib.

Stan & Jan Berenstain's It's All in the Family. Stan Berenstain & Janice Berenstain. (Orig.). 1985. pap. 5.95 o.s.i. (ISBN 0-345-32693-8). Ballantine.

Stan DeFreitas Complete Guide to Florida Gardening. Stan DeFreitas' (Illus.). 312p. 1984. 19.95 o.p. (ISBN 0-87833-341-X). Taylor Pub.

Stan Smith's Six Tennis Basics. Stan Smith. Ed. by Larry Sheehan. LC 74-81265. (Illus.). 48p. (Orig.). 1974. pap. 3.95 o.p. (ISBN 0-689-10636-X, Atheneum). Macmillan.

Stand & Deliver. Andre Norton. 320p. (Orig.). 1984. pap. 3.25 o.p. (ISBN 0-440-08233-1, Emerald). Dell.

Stand Bold in Grace: An Exposition of Hebrews. Robert G. Gromacki. 1984. pap. 8.95 o.p. (ISBN 0-8010-3804-9). Baker Bk.

Stand to Horse. Andre Norton. LC 56-8354. (gr. 7 up). 1968. pap. 0.75 o.p. (ISBN 0-15-684890-2, VoyB). HarBraceJ.

Stand Tough. Powell. 1983. 4.50 o.p. (ISBN 0-88207-592-6). Victor Bks.

Stand Up, Friend, with Me. Edward Field. 1964. pap. 3.95 o.p. (ISBN 0-394-17336-8, E671, Ever). Grove.

Stand Up, Lucy. Elizabeth Hall. LC 73-142823. (Illus.). (gr. 3-7). 1971. 5.95 o.p. (ISBN 0-395-12365-8). HM.

Stand We At Last. Zoe Fairbairns. 624p. 1984. pap. 3.95 o.p. (ISBN 0-380-65565-9, 65565). Avon.

Standard Aircraft Workers' Manual. 14th ed. Fletcher Aircraft Company Staff. 190p. 1985. spiral bdg. 7.50x o.p. (ISBN 0-911721-29-0, Pub. by Fletcher). Aviation.

Standard & Poor's Rating Guide. Standard & Poor's Research Dept. Staff. Incl. Corporate Bonds; Commercial Paper; Municipal Bonds; International Securities. (Illus.). 1979. text ed. 38.95 o.p. (ISBN 0-07-051883-1). McGraw.

Standard Basic Math & Applied Plant Calculations. Stephen M. Elonka. 1977. text ed. 33.00 o.p. (ISBN 0-07-019297-9). McGraw.

Standard Boiler Operators' Questions & Answers. Stephen M. Elonka & Anthony L. Kohan. 1969. text ed. 43.75 o.p. (ISBN 0-07-019275-8, P&RB). McGraw.

Standard Catalog of American Cars, 1805-1942. 2nd ed. Beverly R. Kimes. LC 85-50390. 1536p. (Orig.). 1985. pap. 29.95 o.s.i. (ISBN 0-87341-045-9). Krause Pubns.

Standard Catalog of U. S. Paper Money. 5th, rev. ed. Chester L. Krause & Robert F. Lemke. LC 81-81876. (Illus.). 1985. pap. 18.95 o.s.i. (ISBN 0-87341-078-5). Krause Pubns.

Standard Catalog of United States Paper Money. 6th ed. Robert Lemke & Cheste Krause. Ed. by Bob Wilhite. LC 81-81876. (Illus.). 192p. 18.95 o.s.i. (ISBN 0-87341-102-1). Krause Pubns.

Standard Catalog of World Coins. 13th ed. Chester Krause & Clifford Mishler. LC 79-640940. (Illus.). 1536p. 1986. pap. 29.95 o.s.i. (ISBN 0-87341-086-6). Krause-Pubns.

Standard Catalog of World Gold Coins. Chester Krause & Clifford Mishle. LC 85-61548. (Illus.). 704p. 1985. pap. 39.95 o.s.i. (ISBN 0-87341-031-9). Krause Pubns.

Standard Catalog of World Paper Money: Specialized, Vol. 1. 5th ed. Albert Pick. Ed. by Colin Bruce & Neil Shafer. (Illus.). 100p. 1986. 45.00 o.s.i. (ISBN 0-317-47019-1). Krause Pubns.

Standard Catalog World Coins. 14th ed. Chester Krause & Clifford Mishler. LC 79-640940. (Illus.). 1600p. 1987. pap. 29.95 o.s.i. (ISBN 0-87341-095-5). Krause Pubns.

Standard Catalogue of British Coins, Vol. One: Coins of England & the United Kingdom. rev. ed. H. A. Seaby. Ed. by Stephen Mitchell & Brian Reeds. (Illus.). 340p. 1988. 20.00 o.p. (ISBN 1-85264-006-5, Pub. by Seaby UK). Numismatic Fine Arts.

Standard Details for Fire-Resistive Building Construction. Louis Przetak. (Illus.). 1977. text ed. 44.50 o.p. (ISBN 0-07-050910-7). McGraw.

Standard Dictionary of Librarianship: Standardworterbuch fur das Bibliothekswen, Vol. 2. Ed. by Eberhard Sauppe. 428p. (Ger. & Eng.). 1989. lib. bdg. 90.00 o.p. (ISBN 3-598-10620-3). K G Saur.

Standard Dictionary of Meteorological Sciences: English-French - French-English. Gerard J. Proulx. 320p. 1971. 22.00 o.p. (ISBN 0-7735-0066-9, McGill Canada). U of Toronto Pr.

Standard Directory of Advertisers: Classified Edition. National Register Publishing Co. Staff. LC 5-21147. 1984. 397.00 o.p. (ISBN 0-87217-000-4). Natl Register.

Standard Directory of Advertisers: Geographical Edition. National Register Publishing Co. Staff. LC 15-21147. 1984. 397.00 o.p. Natl Register.

Standard Directory of Worldwide Marketing. National Register Publishing Co. Staff. LC 84-62414. 1987. 197.00 o.p. (ISBN 0-87217-075-6). Natl Register.

Standard Dreaming. Hortense Calisher. 1983. 13.95 o.p. (ISBN 0-87795-043-1, Arbor Hse); pap. 5.95 o.p. (ISBN 0-87795-556-5). Morrow.

Standard Easter Program Book, No. 36. Compiled by Laurie Hoard. 48p. 1985. pap. 1.95 o.p. (ISBN 0-87239-870-6, 8706). Standard Pub.

Standard for the Visual Inspection of Casting Surfaces. 3.00 o.s.i. (ISBN 0-686-44991-6). Steel Founders.

Standard FORTRAN: A Problem-Solving Approach. Laura G. Cooper & Marilyn Z. Smith. LC 72-4395. 288p. (Orig.). 1973. pap. 29.16 o.p. (ISBN 0-395-14028-5). HM.

Standard Guide to Horse & Pony Breeds. Ed. by Elwyn H. Edwards. LC 79-23921. (Illus.). 352p. 1980. text ed. 24.95 o.p. (ISBN 0-07-019035-6). McGraw.

Standard Guide to South Asian Coins & Paper Money Since 1556, A. D. Colin R. Bruce, II & Nicholas Rhodes. LC 82-81657. 1982. 42.50 o.s.i. Krause Pubns.

Standard Handbook for Electrical Engineers. 11th ed. Donald G. Fink & H. Wayne Beaty. (Illus.). 1978. text ed. 85.00 o.p. (ISBN 0-07-020974-X). McGraw.

Standard Handbook Modern Paper Money. O'Donnell. 15.00 o.s.i. (ISBN 0-87341-068-8). Krause Pubns.

Standard Handbook of Fastening & Joining. Robert O. Parmley. 1977. text ed. 63.00 o.p. (ISBN 0-07-048511-9). McGraw.

Standard International Trade Classification, Revision 2. pap. 10.00 o.p. (ISBN 92-1-161133-4, E.75.XVII.6). UN.

Standard Mathematical Tables. 26th ed. Ed. by William H. Beyer. 624p. 1981. 24.95 o.p. (ISBN 0-8493-0626-4). CRC Pr.

Standard Methods for the Examination of Water & Wastewater: Laboratory Texts. 15th ed. 1134p. 1981. 60.00 o.p. (ISBN 0-318-16855-3, S0025); 48.00, to members o.p. (ISBN 0-318-16856-1). Water Pollution.

Standard Methods of Chemical Analysis: Vol. IIIA, Instrumental Methods. 6th ed. Ed. by Frank J. Welcher et al. LC 74-23465. 996p. 1975. Repr. of 1966 ed. 70.00 o.p. Krieger.

Standard Methods of Clinical Chemistry. Ed. by Miriam Reiner et al. Incl. Vol. 1. Ed. by Miriam Reiner. 1953. 39.00 (ISBN 0-12-609101-3); Vol. 2. Ed. by David Seligson. 1958. 41.50 (ISBN 0-12-609102-1); Vol. 3. 1961. o.p. (ISBN 0-12-609103-X); Vol. 4. 1964. 41.50 (ISBN 0-12-609104-8); Vol. 5. Ed. by S. Meites. 1965. 41.50 (ISBN 0-12-609105-6); Vol. 6. Ed. by R. P. MacDonald. 1970. 55.00 (ISBN 0-12-609106-4); Vol. 7. 1972. 59.50 (ISBN 0-12-609107-2). Acad Pr.

Standard Musical Repertoire with Accurate Timings. William J. Reddick. Repr. of 1947 ed. lib. bdg. 35.00x o.p. (ISBN 0-8371-2692-4, REMR). Greenwood.

Standard Nomenclature of Athletic Injuries. Ed. by American Medical Association, Subcommittee on Classification of Sports in Injuries et al. (Orig.). 1968. pap. 2.00 o.p. (ISBN 0-89970-079-9, OP-43). AMA.

Standard Postcard Catalog. 2nd ed. James L. Lowe. LC 82-70056. (Illus.). 288p. (Orig.). 1982. pap. text ed. 21.95 o.p. (ISBN 0-913782-10-6). Deltiologists Am.

Standard Practices for Import & Export Restrictions & Exchange Controls. (Available from the International Trade Center). pap. 5.00 o.p. (G48, GATT). UNIPUB.

Standard Refrigeration & Air Conditioning: Questions & Answers. 2nd ed. Stephen M. Elonka & Quaid W. Minich. 1973. text ed. 34.50 o.p. (ISBN 0-07-019291-X, P&RB). McGraw.

Standard Siddur-Prayerbook. 1974. 8.95 o.s.i. (ISBN 0-87306-990-0). Feldheim.

Standard Specifications for Construction of Roads & Bridges on Federal Highway Projects: FP-85. 702p. 1985. fabricoid 10.00 o.p. (ISBN 0-318-19905-X, S/N 050-001-00299-0). USGPO.

Standard Teachers Guide for Beauty Culture. C. Sidney. 1976. 18.95 o.p. (ISBN 0-87350-066-0). Milady Pub.

Standard Terms of Energy Economy: Ruttley. World Energy Conference Staff. 1978. 120.00 o.p. (ISBN 0-08-022445-8). Pergamon.

Standard Trade Index of Japan. Japan Chamber of Commerce & Industry Staff. 1986. 174.00x o.s.i. (ISBN 0-8002-3881-8). Intl Pubns Serv.

Standard Trade Index of Japan, 1982-83. 26th ed. Japan Chamber of Commerce & Industry Staff. LC 55-36368. (Illus.). 1500p. 1982. 135.00x o.p. (ISBN 0-8002-2879-0). Intl Pubns Serv.

Standard Trade Index of Japan, 1983-84. 27th ed. Japan Chamber of Commerce & Industry Staff. LC 55-36368. 1500p. 1983. 135.00x o.p. (ISBN 0-8002-3006-X). Intl Pubns Serv.

Standard Trade Index of Japan: 1987-88. 31st ed. 1445p. 1987. 227.00 o.p. (ISBN 0-8002-4096-0). Intl Pubns Serv.

Standard-Vacuum Oil Company & United States East Asian Policy, 1933-1941. Irvine H. Anderson. 280p. 1975. 32.00x o.p. (ISBN 0-691-04629-8). Princeton U Pr.

Standardization in Immunofluorescence. Holborow. (Illus.). 282p. 1970. 15.75 o.p. (ISBN 0-632-06200-2, B-2234-4). Mosby.

Standardizing Foodservice for Quality & Efficiency. Arthur Tolve. (Illus.). 1984. 35.95 o.s.i. (ISBN 0-87055-437-9). AVI.

Standards & Colors of the American Revolution. Edward W. Richardson. (Illus.). 350p. 1982. 33.95 o.p. (ISBN 0-8122-7839-9). U of Pa Pr.

Standards & Practices for Instrumentation. 8th ed. (Standards & Practices Reference Ser.). 1400p. 1986. text ed. 194.50x o.p. (ISBN 0-87664-900-2). Instru Soc.

Standards & Procedures for Systems Documentation. Andrew W. Poschmann. LC 83-45207. 288p. 1984. pap. 55.00x comb bdg. o.p. (ISBN 0-8144-7015-7). AMACOM.

Standards for Child-Support Payments: Intra-Family Transfers. Judith Cassetty. LC 81-47441. cancelled o.s.i. (ISBN 0-669-04592-6). Lexington Bks.

Standards for Critical Care. 2nd ed. Brenda C. Johanson. (Illus.). 600p. 1984. pap. text ed. 27.95 o.p. (ISBN 0-8016-2526-2). Mosby.

Standards for Petroleum & Its Products: Methods for Analysis & Testing, 2 Vols, Pt. 1. 45th ed. 1986. 160.00 o.p. (ISBN 0-471-90998-X). Wiley.

Standards in Absorption Spectrometry. C. Burgess & A. Knowles. (Techniques in Visible & Ultraviolet Spectrometry Ser.). 1981. 29.95x o.p. (ISBN 0-412-22470-4, 2230, Pub. by Chapman & Hall). Routledge Chapman & Hall.

Standards, Principles & Techniques in Quality Food Production. 3rd. ed. Lendal Kotschevar. 1983. 29.95 o.p. (ISBN 0-8436-0583-9). Van Nos Reinhold.

Standing & Understanding. Stanley B. Frost. 1969. 5.00 o.p. (ISBN 0-7735-0059-6, McGill Canada). U of Toronto Pr.

Standing By. Juanita Ryan. LC 83-51593. 192p. (Orig.). 1984. pap. 6.95 o.p. (ISBN 0-8423-6601-6). Tyndale.

Standing for Their Faith. William Woodson. 1979. 8.95 o.p. (ISBN 0-317-39803-2). Gospel Advocate.

Standing Ground: Sculpture by American Women. Sarah R. Lafferty. (Illus.). 1987. 12.95 o.s.i. (ISBN 0-917562-47-X). Contemp Arts.

Standing Out: Being Real in an Unreal World. Charles R. Swindoll. LC 82-24595. Orig. Title: Home: Where Life Makes Up Its Mind. 105p. 1983. pap. 9.95 o.p. (ISBN 0-88070-014-9). Multnomah.

Standing Stones: And Other Monuments of Early Ireland. 2nd ed. Kenneth McNally. (Illus.). 128p. 1988. pap. 16.95 o.p. (ISBN 0-86281-201-1, Pub. by Appletree Pr). Irish Bks Media.

Stanger's Partnership Performance Yearbook: Oil & Gas, 1985. Stranger, Robert A., & Co., Staff. 329p. 1985. 75.00 o.p. (ISBN 0-943570-06-9). R A Stanger.

Stanger's Tax Shelter Yearbook, 1984. Stranger, Robert A., & Co., Staff. LC 83-70914. 400p. 1984. 75.00 o.p. (ISBN 0-87094-574-2). Dow Jones-Irwin.

Stanhope: A Study in Eighteenth-Century War & Diplomacy. Basil Williams. LC 78-26687. (Illus.). 1979. Repr. of 1932 ed. lib. bdg. 42.50x o.p. (ISBN 0-313-20918-9, WISW). Greenwood.

Stanislavsky, a Life. David Magarshack. LC 74-2558. (Illus.). 414p. 1975. Repr. of 1950 ed. lib. bdg. 39.75x o.p. (ISBN 0-8371-7416-3, MASU). Greenwood.

Stanislavsky on the Art of the Stage. Konstantin Stanislavsky. Tr. & intro. by David Magarshack. 1986. pap. 9.95 o.p. (ISBN 0-8090-0532-8). FS&G.

Stanislaw Lem. J. Madison Davis. Ed. by Roger C. Schlobin. (Reader's Guides to Contemporary Science Fiction & Fantasy Authors Ser.: Vol. 32). (Illus., Orig.). 1988. 17.95x o.p. (ISBN 0-930261-21-6); pap. 9.95x o.p. (ISBN 0-930261-20-8). Starmont Hse.

Stanislaw Lem. Ed. by Joseph D. Olander & Martin H. Greenberg. LC 78-56276. (Writers of the 21st Century Ser.). (ISBN 0-8008-7372-6); pap. (ISBN 0-8008-7373-4). Taplinger.

Stanley Kubrick: A Guide to Reference & Resources. Wallace Coyle. 1980. lib. bdg. 30.50 o.p. (ISBN 0-8161-8058-X, Hall Reference). G K Hall.

Stanley Kubrick Directs. enl. ed. Alexander Walker. LC 77-153692. (Illus.). 304p. 1972. pap. 8.95 o.p. (ISBN 0-15-684892-9, Harv). HarBraceJ.

Stanwyck. Jane E. Wayne. (Illus.). 224p. 1986. 15.95 o.p. (ISBN 0-87795-750-9, Arbor Hse). Morrow.

Stanza. Ernst Haublein. (Critical Idiom Ser.). 1978. 5.50x o.p. (ISBN 0-416-84600-9, NO.2222); pap. 5.50x o.p. (ISBN 0-416-84610-6, NO.2743). Routledge Chapman & Hall.

"Stanze" of Angelo Poliziano. Angelo Poliziano. Ed. by David Quint. LC 78-53180. 128p. 1979. 11.00x o.p. (ISBN 0-87023-145-6). U of Mass Pr.

"Stanze" of Angelo Poliziano. Ed. by David Quint. Date not set. price not set o.p. U of Mass Pr.

Stapeley Book of Water Gardens. Stanley Russell. (Illus.). 160p. 1986. 25.95 o.p. (ISBN 0-7153-8649-2). David & Charles.

Staphylococci. Jay O. Cohen. LC 72-3482. 548p. 1972. 48.50 o.p. (ISBN 0-471-16426-7, Pub. by Wiley). Krieger.

Staphylococci & Staphylococcal Infections: Proceedings of the Inernational Symposium, Warsaw, Sept., 1971. International Symposium on Staphylococci & Staphylococcal Infections Staff. Ed. by J. Jeljaszewicz. (Contributions to Microbiology & Immunology Ser.: Vol. 1). (Illus.). 1973. 123.50 o.p. (ISBN 3-8055-1634-7). S Karger.

Stapp Car Crash Conference: Proceedings of the conference, 28th. 1984. 45.00 o.p. (ISBN 0-89883-711-1, P152). Soc Auto Engineers.

Star Address Book. Curtis Marlow. 160p. 1985. 2.95 o.p. (ISBN 0-317-40079-7). Sharon Pubns.

Star Beams. Etta M. Gibbany. 24p. pap. 2.00 o.p. (ISBN 0-88053-323-4, S-304). Macoy Pub.

Star Child. Fred M. Stewart. LC 74-80712. 1974. 6.95 o.p. (ISBN 0-87795-093-8, Arbor Hse). Morrow.

Star-Crossed: The Story of Robert Walker & Jennifer Jones. Beverly Linet. (Illus.). 320p. 1986. 17.95 o.p. (ISBN 0-399-13194-9, Putnam). Putnam Pub Group.

Star Diaries. Stanislaw Lem. Tr. by Michael Kandel. LC 83-26385. (Illus.). 286p. 1985. pap. 4.95 o.s.i. (ISBN 0-15-684905-4, Harv). HarBraceJ.

Star Dreams. June F. Singer. 464p. 1984. pap. 4.75 o.p. (ISBN 0-380-68031-9, 68031). Avon.

Star Eternal. Ka-Tzetnik. LC 75-141639. 1971. 4.95 o.p. (ISBN 0-87795-009-1, Arbor Hse). Morrow.

Star Evolution. Ed. by Livio Gratton. (Italian Physical Society Ser.: Course 28). (Illus.). 1964. 85.50 o.p. (ISBN 0-12-368828-0). Acad Pr.

Star for a Day see Heinemann Guided Readers.

Star Ghosts. Hans Holzer. 1979. pap. 1.75 o.p. (ISBN 0-8439-0686-3, Pub. by Leisure Bks CT). Dorchester Pub Co.

Star Girl. Henry Winterfield. (gr. 2-7). 1976. pap. 1.25 o.p. (ISBN 0-380-00659-6, 28506, Camelot). Avon.

Star Griffin. Michael Kurland & Randall Garrett. LC 86-19869. 192p. 1987. 12.95 o.s.i. (ISBN 0-385-19395-5). Doubleday.

Star Guard. Andre Norton. LC 55-7612. 1955. 4.95 o.p. (ISBN 0-15-279068-3, HJ). HarBraceJ.

Star Guide (Nineteen Eighty-Eight to Nineteen Eighty-Nine) Where to Reach Movie Stars, TV Stars, Rock Stars, Sports Stars, & Other Famous Celebrities. Terry Robinson. 191p. 1987. pap. 9.95 o.p. Axiom Info Res.

Star Hawks, No. 2. United Media Syndicate Staff. 160p. (Orig.). (gr. 7-12). 1981. pap. 1.50 o.s.i. (ISBN 0-448-17272-0, Pub. by Tempo). Ace Bks.

Star Ka'ats & the Winged Warriors. Andre Norton & Dorothy Madlee. (Star Ka'ats Ser.). (Illus.). (gr. 3-5). 1983. pap. 1.95 o.p. (ISBN 0-671-45289-4). Archway.

Star Light, Star Bright. Stephanie Foster. (Leisure First Romance Ser.: No. 4). 192p. (YA) (gr. 6-12). 1982. pap. 1.95 o.p. (ISBN 0-8439-1144-1, Pub. by Leisure Bks CT). Dorchester Pub Co.

Star Maps for Beginners. I. M. Levitt & Roy K. Marshall. (Illus.). 64p. 1983. pap. 7.95 o.s.i. (ISBN 0-671-47258-5, Fireside). S&S.

Star Myths & Stories: From Andromeda to Virgo. Percy M. Proctor. (Illus.). 1972. 8.50 o.p. (ISBN 0-682-47470-3, Banner). Exposition-Phoenix.

Star of Danger. Marion Zimmer Bradley. 1979. lib. bdg. 11.95 o.p. (ISBN 0-8398-2512-9, Gregg). G K Hall.

Star of Danger. Jane W. Levin. LC 66-10075. (Illus.). (gr. 7 up). 1966. 5.50 o.p. (ISBN 0-15-279380-1, HJ). HarBraceJ.

Star Rangers. Andre Norton. LC 53-7869. (gr. 7 up). 1953. 5.95 o.p. (ISBN 0-15-279426-3, HJ). HarBraceJ.

Star Rangers. Andre Norton. 224p. 1985. pap. 2.50 o.s.i. (ISBN 0-345-32308-4, Dey Rey). Ballantine.

Star Showers. Jean Low. 64p. 1982. 5.00 o.p. (ISBN 0-682-49817-3). Exposition-Phoenix.

Star Signs. Leonard E. Fisher. LC 83-305. (Illus.). 32p. (gr. 1-4). 1983. reinforced bdg. 13.95 o.p. (ISBN 0-8234-0491-9). Holiday.

Star Spangled Retirement Dream: Why It's Going to Sour & What You Can Do About It. James Gollin. 224p. 1981. encore ed. 4.95 o.p. (ISBN 0-684-16866-9, ScribT). Scribner.

Star Speak: Your Body Language from the Stars. Sybil Leek. LC 75-1151. 1975. 8.95 o.p. (ISBN 0-87795-118-7, Arbor Hse). Morrow.

Star Trails: Reproducible Carryover Worksheets for R, S, L, TH, SH, CH. rev. & Combined ed. Valeda Blockcolsky & Joan M. Frazer. 258p. (gr. k-8). 1983. pap. 19.95 o.p. (ISBN 0-88450-862-5, 7029-B). Communication Skill.

Star Trek. James A. Lely. (TV & Movie Tie-Ins Ser.). (Illus.). (gr. 4 up). 1979. PLB 8.95 o.p. (ISBN 0-87191-718-1). Creative Ed.

Star Trek, No. 12. James Blish & J. A. Lawrence. (gr. 6-12). 1977. pap. 2.95 o.s.i. (ISBN 0-553-25252-6). Bantam.

Star Warriors. William J. Broad. 256p. 1986. pap. 8.95 o.s.i. (ISBN 0-671-62820-8, Touchstone). S&S.

Star Warriors: A Penetrating Look into the Lives of the Young Scientists Behind Our Space Age Weaponry. William J. Broad. 236p. 1985. 16.45 o.p. (ISBN 0-671-54566-3). S&S.

Star Wars. George Lucas. 1977. 6.95 o.p. (ISBN 0-345-27476-8). Ballantine.

Star Wars: Delusions & Dangers. U. S. S. R. Ministry of Defense Staff. 56p. 1985. pap. 1.75 o.p. (ISBN 0-8285-9142-3, Pub by Progress Pubs USSR). Imported Pubns.

Star Wars Intergalactic Passport. Lucasfilm, Ltd. Staff. 32p. 1983. pap. 2.50 o.s.i. (ISBN 0-345-31053-5). Ballantine.

Star Wars: Suicide or Survival? Alan Chalfont. 1986. 16.95 o.p. (ISBN 0-316-13607-7). Little.

Star Wave: Mind, Consciousness, & Quantum Physics. Fred A. Wolf. (Illus.). 400p. 1985. 19.95 o.p. (ISBN 0-02-630860-6). Macmillan.

Star Web. Joan Cox. 336p. 1980. pap. 2.50 o.p. (ISBN 0-380-75697-8, 75697). Avon.

Star Woman & Other Shawnee Tales. Retold by James A. Clifton. 94p. (Orig.). 1984. lib. bdg. 20.75 o.p. (ISBN 0-8191-3712-X); pap. text ed. 7.00 o.p. (ISBN 0-8191-3713-8). U Pr of Amer.

Starch: Chemistry & Technology, 2 vols. 2nd ed. Ed. by Roy L. Whistler & Eugene F. Paschall. Incl. Vol. 1. Fundamental Aspects. 1965. 81.00 o.p. (ISBN 0-12-746261-9); Vol. 2. Industrial Aspects. 1967. 99.00 o.p. (ISBN 0-12-746262-7). 1984. 98.00 o.p. Acad Pr.

Starch Industry. J. W. Knight. 1969. text ed. 19.50 o.p. (ISBN 0-08-013044-5). Pergamon.

Starett. Arthur V. Deutcsh. LC 78-57329. 1978. 8.95 o.p. (ISBN 0-87795-199-3, Arbor Hse). Morrow.

Starfire. Judith E. French. 352p. 1987. pap. 3.95 o.p. (ISBN 0-380-75241-7). Avon.

Starflight & Other Improbabilities. Ben Bova. LC 72-7332. (Illus.). 128p. (gr. 7 up). 1973. 4.75 o.s.i. (ISBN 0-664-32520-3, Westminster). Westminster John Knox.

Starforce Red Alert. Chris Spencer. LC 84-71418. 144p. (gr. 9-12). 1984. pap. 3.95 o.p. (ISBN 0-89107-321-3, Crossway Bks). Good News.

Starless Night. Ruby M. Ayers. (Lythway Ser.). 232p. 1988. lib. bdg. 18.50 o.s.i. (ISBN 0-7451-0641-2, Pub. by Chivers Pr UK). G K Hall.

Starlife! Lynda R. Stephenson. LC 85-10766. 140p. (Orig.). 1985. pap. 5.95 o.p. (ISBN 0-8307-1053-1, 5900163). Regal.

Starlight. Scott Ely. LC 86-19058. 208p. 1987. 15.95 o.s.i. (ISBN 1-55584-047-7). Weidenfeld.

Starlight. Thomas E. Kipp. (Illus.). 55p. 1983. 5.50 o.p. (ISBN 0-682-49946-3). Exposition-Phoenix.

Starlight Furnace: An Historical Novel. Clifford T. Stafford. 1979. 10.00 o.p. (ISBN 0-682-49289-2). Exposition-Phoenix.

Starlight Rider. Ernest Haycox. (Large Print Books (General Ser.)). 343p. 1985. lib. bdg. 15.95 o.p. (ISBN 0-8161-3883-4). G K Hall.

Starlord: The Conquest of Earth. Stuart D. Waymire. (Illus.). 1988. 17.95 o.p. Thundblt Pr NV.

Starlore among the Navaho. Berard Haile. LC 76-53085. 1977. lib. bdg. 15.00x o.p. (ISBN 0-88307-532-6); pap. 7.95 o.p. (ISBN 0-88307-533-4). Gannon.

Starring. James Fritzhand. 1977. pap. 1.95 o.p. (ISBN 0-380-01653-2, 33118). Avon.

Stars. Daphne Davis. 280p. 1984. pap. 14.70 o.p. (ISBN 0-671-53083-6, Fireside). S&S.

Stars & Other Korean Short Stories. Sun-won Hwang. Tr. by Edward W. Poitrass. (Writing in Asia Ser.). 227p. (Orig., Korean.). 1980. pap. text ed. 9.00x o.p. (ISBN 0-686-98153-7). Heinemann Ed.

Stars & Outer Space Made Easy. Carlos S. Mundt. LC 74-6491. (Illus.). 95p. (gr. 4 up). 1963. 11.95 o.p. (ISBN 0-911010-71-8); pap. 5.95 o.p. (ISBN 0-911010-70-X). Naturegraph.

Stars & Telescopes for the Beginner. Roy Worvill. LC 79-14034. (Illus.). 1980. 7.95 o.s.i. (ISBN 0-8008-4464-5). Taplinger.

Stars & the Bible. Clyde L. Ferguson. 1978. 8.95 o.p. (ISBN 0-682-49042-3). Exposition-Phoenix.

Stars & Your Baby. Michael Colmer. (Illus.). 256p. (Orig.). 1987. pap. 7.95 o.p. (ISBN 0-7137-1946-X, Pub. by Javelin England). Sterling.

Stars for Sam. rev. ed. W. Maxwell Reed. Ed. by Paul F. Brandwein. LC 59-12827. (Illus.). (gr. 7 up). 1960. 7.95 o.p. (ISBN 0-15-279784-X, HJ). HarBraceJ.

Stars of Country Music. Ed. by Bill Malone & Judith McCulloh. 1976. pap. 2.50 o.p. (ISBN 0-380-00867-X, 31344). Avon.

Stars of the American Musical Theater in Historic Photographs. Ed. by Stanley Applebaum & James Camner. 1983. 16.50 o.p. (ISBN 0-8446-5933-9). Peter Smith.

Stars over Texas. Beverly C. Warren. LC 87-20171. (Starlight Romance Ser.). 192p. 1988. 12.95 o.s.i. (ISBN 0-385-24339-1). Doubleday.

Stars Principal. J. D. McClatchy. 80p. 1986. 16.95 o.p. (ISBN 0-02-582960-2, Collier); pap. 9.95 o.p. (ISBN 0-02-070030-X, Collier). Macmillan.

Stars, Spells, Secrets & Sorcery: A Do It Yourself Guide to the Occult. Barbara Haislip. (Illus.). 320p. (gr. 5 up). 1976. 14.95 o.p. (ISBN 0-316-33820-6). Little.

Stars Were Ours: The Best from Paperback Quarterly I. Ed. by R. Reginald & Billy Lee. (Starmont Popular Culture Studies: No. 4). (Illus., Orig.). 1988. 19.95x o.p. (ISBN 0-930261-83-6); pap. text ed. 9.95x o.p. (ISBN 0-930261-82-8). Starmont Hse.

Starseed Transmissions: An Extraterrestrial Report. Raphael. (Illus.). 96p. (Orig.). 1986. pap. 6.95 o.p. (ISBN 0-912949-00-7). Uni-Sun.

Starship. Brian Aldiss. 1985. pap. 1.25 o.p. (ISBN 0-380-00226-4, 55152). Avon.

Starship Troopers. Robert A. Heinlein. 208p. (gr. 5-10). 1986. pap. 2.95 o.s.i. (ISBN 0-425-09144-9). Berkley Pub.

Starskimmer. John G. Betancourt. LC 85-50155. (Amazing Stories Ser.: Bk. 5). 222p. (Orig.). 1986. pap. 2.95 o.p. (ISBN 0-88038-262-7). TSR Inc.

Start & Run a Profitable Beauty Salon: A Complete Step-by-Step Business Plan. Paul Poque. 158p. (Orig.). 1983. pap. 14.95 o.p. (ISBN 0-88908-568-4, 9521). ISC Pr.

Start & Run a Profitable Consulting Business. Douglas Gray. pap. 12.95 o.s.i. (ISBN 0-88908-598-6, 9532). TAB Bks.

Start & Run a Profitable Craft Business. William G. Hynes. 154p. (Orig.). 1984. pap. 10.95 o.s.i. (ISBN 0-88908-579-X, 9526). TAB Bks.

Start & Run a Profitable Home Typing Business. Barbara Aliaga. 94p. 1984. pap. 9.95 o.p. (ISBN 0-88908-585-4). ISC Pr.

Start & Run a Profitable Video Stores: A Complete Step-by-Step Business Plan. Stan Loh. 168p. (Orig.). 1983. pap. 10.95 o.p. (ISBN 0-88908-571-4, 9522). ISC Pr.

Start English for Science. G. D. Nogas & A. R. Bolitho. 29p. (Orig.). 1982. pap. text ed. 6.95 o.p. (ISBN 0-582-74819-4); tchrs. ed. 4.50 o.p. (ISBN 0-582-74820-8). Longman.

Start Point: Six Studies in Violence. Otis D. Richardson. 1973. 8.00 o.p. (ISBN 0-682-47672-2). Exposition-Phoenix.

Start to Win. Eric Twiname. (Illus.). 1974. 12.50 o.p. (ISBN 0-393-03158-6). Norton.

Start-Up Money: How to Finance Your New Small Business. 2nd, rev. ed. Michael McKeever. LC 84-61578. (Illus.). 220p. 1986. pap. 12.95 o.p. (ISBN 0-87337-023-6). Nolo Pr.

Start Well! A Guide to Healthy Eating for You & Your Baby. Michael Schwab & Inke Schwab. (Family Handbooks Ser.). 96p. (Orig.). 1984. pap. 9.95 o.p. (ISBN 0-86683-846-5). HarpR.

Starting a Church-Sponsored Weekday Preschool Program: A Manual of Guidance. Ed. by Thomas H. Sauerman & Linda Schomaker. LC 80-14160. 128p. (Orig.). 1980. pap. 6.95 o.p. (ISBN 0-8006-1377-5, 1-1377, Fortress). Augsburg Fortress.

Starting a Mini-Business: A Guidebook for Seniors & Others Who Dream of Having Their Own Part-Time, Home-Based Business. Nancy Olsen. LC 86-71743. (Illus.). 144p. (Orig.). 1986. pap. 8.95 o.p. (ISBN 0-933271-01-8). Fair Oaks CA.

Starting a Successful Business on the West Coast. Douglas L. Clark. 208p. 1983. pap. 12.95 o.p. (ISBN 0-88908-910-8, 9513). ISC Pr.

Starting & Succeeding in Your Own Photography Business. Jeanne C. Thwaites. LC 84-2336. 343p. 1984. 19.95 o.p. (ISBN 0-89879-112-X). Writers Digest.

Starting Anew after Seventy: The Story of Ida Ella Jones, Primitive Artist. Ida J. Williams. (Illus.). 1980. 5.50 o.p. (ISBN 0-682-49544-1). Exposition-Phoenix.

Starting FORTH: An Introduction to the FORTH Language & Operating Systems for Beginners & Professionals. Forth, Inc. Staff & Leo Brodie. LC 81-11837. (Software Ser.). (Illus.). 384p. 1982. text ed. 26.67 o.p. (ISBN 0-13-842930-8); pap. text ed. 21.95 o.p. (ISBN 0-13-842922-7). P-H.

Starting from Scratch: Our Island for Ocelots. Jeanette Travers. LC 75-37390. (Illus.). (YA) (gr. 9 up). 1976. 8.95 o.s.i. (ISBN 0-8008-7369-6). Taplinger.

Starting from Seeds. Elementary Science Study Staff. 1971. tchr's. guide 13.52 o.p. (ISBN 0-07-017726-0). McGraw.

Starting Right, Staying Strong: A Guide to Effective Ministry. Daniel L. Johnson. LC 82-22383. 108p. (Orig.). 1983. pap. 5.95 o.p. (ISBN 0-8298-0648-2). Pilgrim NY.

Starting Small, Investing Smart: What to Do with 5 to 5,000 Dollars. Donald R. Nichols. LC 83-73715. 196p. 1984. 16.95 o.p. (ISBN 0-87094-509-2). Dow Jones-Irwin.

Starting Teaching. R. Honeyford. 178p. 1982. 24.00 o.p. (ISBN 0-7099-1226-9, Pub. by Croom Helm Ltd); pap. 8.25 o.p. (ISBN 0-7099-1227-7). Routledge Chapman & Hall.

Starting to Paint in Oils. John Raynes. LC 79-56681. (Start to Paint Ser.). (Illus.). 104p. 1980. pap. 3.95 o.s.i. (ISBN 0-8008-7386-6, Pentalic). Taplinger.

Starting to Paint Portraits. Bernard Dunstan. LC 79-63840. (Start to Paint Ser.). (Illus.). 1979. pap. 3.95 o.s.i. (ISBN 0-8008-7382-3, Pentalic). Taplinger.

Starting to Paint Still Life. Bernard Dunstan. LC 79-63841. (Start to Paint Ser.). (Illus.). 1979. pap. 3.95 o.s.i. (ISBN 0-8008-7383-1, Pentalic). Taplinger.

Starting to Paint with Acrylics. John Raynes. LC 79-56682. (Start to Paint Ser.). (Illus.). 104p. 1980. pap. 3.95 o.s.i. (ISBN 0-8008-7385-8, Pentalic). Taplinger.

Starting to Sail. 2nd ed. D. Cobb. (Illus.). 1973. pap. 5.00 o.s.i. (ISBN 0-540-07132-3). E J Brill USA.

Starting with Poetry. Ann C. Colley & Judith K. Moore. 1973. pap. text ed. 8.00 o.p. (ISBN 0-15-583757-5, HC). HarBraceJ.

Starting with Watercolour. Rowland Hilder. LC 79-63842. (Start to Paint Ser.). (Illus.). 1979. pap. 3.95 o.s.i. (ISBN 0-8008-7384-X, Pentalic). Taplinger.

Starting Your Own Veterinary Practice. Ed. by Veterinary Medicine Publishing Co. Staff. LC 84-52837. 78p. 1985. pap. 18.95 o.s.i. (ISBN 0-935078-31-2). Veterinary Med.

Starving in the Shadow of Plenty. L. Schwartz-Nobel. 240p. 1982. pap. text ed. 5.95 o.p. (ISBN 0-07-055776-4). McGraw.

STAT: Special Techiques in Assertiveness Training for Women in the Health Professions. 2nd ed. Melodie Chenevert. LC 82-22857. (Illus.). 130p. 1983. pap. text ed. 12.95 o.p. (ISBN 0-8016-1135-0). Mosby.

State Against Blacks. W. E. Williams. (New Press Ser.). 208p. 1982. text ed. 14.95 o.p. (ISBN 0-07-070378-7). McGraw.

State Against Blacks. W. E. Williams. 208p. 1984. pap. text ed. 6.95 o.p. (ISBN 0-07-070379-5). McGraw.

State & Local Government. 3rd ed. Bruce Stinebrickner. (Annual Editions Ser.). (Illus.). 288p. 1987. pap. text ed. 9.95 o.p. (ISBN 0-87967-686-8). Dushkin Pub.

State & Local Taxation Cases & Materials. 4th ed. Jerome R. Hellerstein & Walter Hellerstein. LC 78-2418. (American Casebook Ser.). 1041p. 1978. Includes 1982 supplement. text ed. 32.95 o.p. (ISBN 0-8299-2000-5); tchr's. manual avail. o.p. West Pub.

State & Nations in the U. S. S. R. V. S. Shevtsov. 208p. 1982. 6.45 o.p. (ISBN 0-8285-2419-X, Pub. by Progress Pubs USSR). Imported Pubns.

State & Opposition in Military Brazil. Maria H. Alves. (Latin American Monographs: No. 63). 368p. 1985. 22.50x o.p. (ISBN 0-292-77598-9). U of Tex Pr.

State & Society in Europe 1550-1650. V. G. Kiernan. 320p. 1987. pap. text ed. 17.95x o.p. (ISBN 0-631-13043-8). Basil Blackwell.

State & Society in Roman Galilee, A. D. 132-212. Martin Goodman. (Publications in the Oxford Centre for Postgraduate Hebrew Studies: Vol. 4). 318p. 1983. text ed. 36.95x o.s.i. (ISBN 0-86598-089-6, Rowman & Allanheld). Rowman.

State & Urban Policy Analysis: An Annotated Bibliography. T. R. Carr & Stephanie Colston. 1975. 3.50 o.p. (ISBN 0-686-18643-5). Univ OK Gov Res.

State-Approved Schools of Nursing LPN-LVN 1986. 1986. pap. 15.95 o.p. (ISBN 0-88737-335-6). Natl League Nurse.

State-Approved Schools of Nursing LPN-LVN 1987. 1987. pap. 15.95 o.p. (ISBN 0-88737-376-3). Natl League Nurse.

State-Approved Schools of Nursing RN, 1986. 44th ed. 98p. 1986. pap. 15.95 o.p. (19-2161). Natl League Nurse.

State-Approved Schools of Nursing RN 1987. 1987. pap. 15.95 o.p. (ISBN 0-88737-375-5). Natl League Nurse.

State, Bureaucracy & Civil Society: A Critical Discussion of the Political Theory of Karl Marx. Victor M. Perez-Diaz. (New Studies in Sociology Ser.). 1978. text ed. 15.25x o.p. (ISBN 0-333-23788-9); pap. text ed. 9.95x o.p. (ISBN 0-391-00555-3). Humanities.

State by State Guide to Budget Motels: 1984-85. 2nd ed. Ed. by Loris G. Bree. 226p. (Orig.). 1984. pap. 6.95 o.p. (ISBN 0-943400-03-1). Mar Lor Pr.

State by State Guide to Budget Motels: Spring 1987 to Spring 1988. Ed. by Loris G. Bree. (Affordable Travel Ser.). 280p. 1987. pap. 8.95 o.p. (ISBN 0-943400-15-5). Mar Lor Pr.

State By State Guide to Budget Motels: 1985-1986 Edition. Ed. by Loris Bree. (MarLor Press Bk.). 264p. 6.95 o.s.i. (ISBN 0-943400-05-8). Contemp Bks.

State Child Care Fact Book 1986. Helen Blank & Amy Wilkins. Ed. by Children's Defense Fund Staff. 142p. (Orig.). 1988. pap. 5.95 o.s.i. (ISBN 0-938008-62-5). Children's Defense.

State Commission Regulation & Monitoring of the Fuel Adjustment Clauses, Purchased Gas Adjustment Clause, & Electric & Gas Utility Fuel Procurement Practices. 258p. 1978. 15.00 o.p. (ISBN 0-318-15029-8). NARUC.

State Constitutional & Statutory Restrictions upon the Structural, Functional, & Personnel Powers of Local Government. United States Advisory Commission on Intergovernmental Relations. LC 78-13964. 1979. Repr. of 1962 ed. lib. bdg. 35.00x o.p. (ISBN 0-313-20674-0, ACSC). Greenwood.

State Courts: Options for the Future. Victoria S. Cashman & Theodore J. Fetter. 58p. 1980. 4.00 o.p. Natl Ctr St Courts.

State Debt & Public Liability in Oklahoma. Ed. by Bureau of Government Research Staff. 22p. 1982. 2.00 o.p. (ISBN 0-318-01378-9). Univ OK Gov Res.

State Demographics: Population Profiles of the 50 States. Ed. by American Demographics Magazine Staff. LC 83-70909. 300p. 1984. 59.50 o.p. (ISBN 0-87094-451-7). Dow Jones-Irwin.

State Economic Policies of the Ch'ing Government: 1840-1895. Jerome Chen. LC 78-24797. (Modern Chinese Economy Ser.: Vol. 2). 250p. 1980. lib. bdg. 33.00 o.p. (ISBN 0-8240-4251-4). Garland Pub.

State Emblems. Compiled by Ethel M. Ramsey & William H. Ramsey, Jr. 1983. pap. 3.50 o.p. (ISBN 0-686-40183-2). Basin Pub.

State Executive Reorganization since 1940: A Selected Bibliography. Alva W. Stewart. (Public Administration Ser.: P 1683). 12p. 1985. 2.00 o.p. (ISBN 0-89028-413-X). Vance Biblios.

State Fiscal Conditions Entering 1984. (Legislative Finance Papers Ser.). 28p. 1984. 15.00 o.s.i. (ISBN 1-55516-042-5). Natl Conf State Legis.

State Fiscal Indicators. Steven Gold. (Legislative Finance Paper Ser.). 107p. 1982. 10.00 o.s.i. (ISBN 1-55516-534-6). Natl Conf State Legis.

State, France, & the Sixteenth Century. Howell Lloyd. (Early Modern Europe Today Ser.). 256p. 1983. text ed. 34.95x o.p. (ISBN 0-04-940066-5). Unwin Hyman.

State Functions & Linear Control Systems. Donald Schultz & J. Melsa. (Electronic Systems Ser.). 1967. text ed. 39.00 o.p. (ISBN 0-07-055655-5). McGraw.

State Government Influence in U. S. International Economic Policy. John M. Kline. LC 82-48473. 288p. 1983. 33.00x o.p. (ISBN 0-669-06141-7). Lexington Bks.

State in the Making: Myth, History, & Social Transformation in Pre-Colonial Ufipa. Roy Willis. LC 80-8155. (African Systems of Thought Ser.). (Illus.). 352p. 1981. 32.50x o.p. (ISBN 0-253-19537-3). Ind U Pr.

State Income Differentials, 1919-1954. Frank A. Hanna. LC 76-39841. 1977. Repr. of 1959 ed. lib. bdg. 35.00x o.p. (ISBN 0-8371-9352-4, HASD). Greenwood.

State Income Tax Consequences of Retirement Plan Distributions. Anthony P. Curatola. 20p. 1986. 9.00 o.p. (ISBN 0-89154-324-4). Intl Found Employ.

State, Industrialization & Class Formations in India: A Neo-Marxist Perspective on Colonialism, Underdevelopment & Development. Anupam Sen. 330p. 1982. 30.00x o.p. (ISBN 0-7100-0888-0). Routledge Chapman & Hall.

State Law of the Socialist Countries. A. Kh. Makhrenko. 438p. 1976. 6.45 o.p. (ISBN 0-8285-0346-X, 232111, Pub. by Progress Pubs USSR). Imported Pubns.

State Legal Initiatives Reports 1-4. 222p. 90.00 o.p. (ISBN 0-317-36960-1, C-118900). Am Hospital.

State Legislative Control of Federal Aid Funds: The Case of Oklahoma. Larry Walker. (Legislative Research Ser.: No. 13). 1978. 4.00 o.p. (ISBN 0-686-04911-X). Univ OK Gov Res.

State Legislative Sourcebook, 1986: A Resource Guide to Legislative Information in the Fifty States. Lynn Hellebust. 500p. 1989. 105.00 o.p. (ISBN 0-9615227-3-9). Govt Res Serv.

State Legislative Summary 1985: Children & Youth Issues. Ed. by Joan M. Smith. 139p. (Orig.). pap. text ed. 15.00 o.p. (ISBN 1-55516-617-2). Natl Conf State Legis.

State Legislatures in American Politics. Ed. by Alexander Heard. LC 66-23439. 1966. 3.95 o.p. (ISBN 0-936904-03-8). Am Assembly.

State Map Library. Ed. by Cartographic Editors of Gousha. (Illus.). 40p. 1983. folded maps in carton file 39.95 o.p. (ISBN 0-88098-037-0). H M Gousha.

State-Monopoly Capitalism & the Labour Theory of Value. Y. Pevsner. 390p. 1982. 7.95 o.p. (Pub. by Progress Pubs USSR). Imported Pubns.

State of Corruption. Paul Geddes. LC 85-24830. 1986. 14.45 o.p. (ISBN 0-03-008164-5). H Holt & Co.

State of Drama Study. John L. Styan. (Kathleen Robinson Lectures on the Drama & the Theatre, University of Sydney, Trinity Term 1983 Ser.). (Illus.). 64p. (Orig.). 1984. pap. 8.25x o.p. (ISBN 0-424-00110-1, Pub. by Sydney U Pr). Intl Spec Bk.

State of Emergency, A Novel. Basil Jackson. 1982. 13.95 o.p. (ISBN 0-393-01605-6). Norton.

State of Fear. Menan Du Plessis. 1987. 25.00 o.p. (ISBN 0-86358-167-6, Pub. by Routledge UK); pap. 9.95 o.p. (ISBN 0-86358-168-4, Pub. by Routledge UK). Routledge Chapman & Hall.

State of Food Agriculture, 1980. (ISBN 0-317-12260-6). Intl Pubns Serv.

State of Grace. Joy Williams. (Signature Editions Ser.). 264p. 1986. pap. 6.95 o.p. (ISBN 0-684-18645-4). Scribner.

State of Ming Coin Knives & Minor Knife Coins. Arthur B. Coole. LC 72-86802. (Encyclopedia of Chinese Coins Ser.: Vol. 6). (Illus.). 1977. 35.00x o.p. (ISBN 0-88000-013-9). Quarterman.

State of New York Law Revision Committee Reports, 1954-1956, 6 vols. Joel V. Burstein. LC 79-90809. 1980. Repr. of 1954 ed. Set. lib. bdg. 220.00 o.p. (ISBN 0-89941-030-8). W S Hein.

State of North Carolina Extradition Manual. Ed. by Michael Crowell. 55p. 1980. 5.00 o.p. (ISBN 0-686-39459-3). Institute Government.

State of Play. INDECS Economics Staff. 144p. (Orig.). 1980. text ed. 17.50x o.p. (ISBN 0-86861-042-9); pap. text ed. 8.95x o.p. (ISBN 0-86861-050-X). Unwin Hyman.

State of the Art. Arthur C. Danto. (Illus.). 240p. 1987. 19.95 o.p. (ISBN 0-13-770868-8). P-H.

State of the Art: A Photographic History of the Integrated Circuit. Stan Augarten. LC 83-669. (Illus.). 90p. 1983. 17.45 o.p. (ISBN 0-89919-206-8); pap. 9.70 o.p. (ISBN 0-89919-195-9). Ticknor & Fields.

State of the Art of Ecological Modelling: Proceedings of the Conference on Ecological Modelling, Copenhagen, 28 August 2, September 1978. S. E. Jorgensen. LC 78-41208. (Environmental Sciences & Applications Ser.: Vol. 7). 1979. pap. 195.00 o.p. (ISBN 0-08-023443-7). Pergamon.

State-of-the-Art of Ground Control in Longwall Mining & Mining Subsidence. Intro. by Y. P. Chugh. LC 82-71991. (Illus.). 271p. (Orig.). 1982. pap. text ed. 38.00x o.p. (ISBN 0-89520-400-2, 400-2). SMM&E Inc.

State-of-the-Art Robot Catalog: Robots for Fun, Show, Personal & Home Use & Industry. Phil Berger. LC 83-20838. (Illus.). 148p. 1984. pap. 12.95 o.p. (ISBN 0-396-08361-7). Dodd.

State of the Baltic. G. Kullenberg. (Marine Pollution Bulletin Ser.: Vol. 12, No. 6). 48p. 1981. pap. 6.00 o.p. (ISBN 0-08-026283-X). Pergamon.

State of the Nation: Presidential Addresses to Parliament from Dr. Rajendra Prasad to Neelam Sanjiva Reddy. R. L. Handa. 1983. text ed. 35.00x o.p. (ISBN 0-86590-162-7, Pub. by Sterling Pubs India). Apt Bks.

State of the Planet: A Report Prepared by the International Federation of Institutes for Advanced Study, Stockholm. Alexander King. (Illus.). 1980. text ed. 35.00 o.p. (ISBN 0-08-024717-2); pap. text ed. 16.00 o.p. (ISBN 0-08-024716-4). Pergamon.

State of the Union of Europe: Report of the CADMOS Group to the European People. Ed. by Denis De Rougemont. 1979. 18.75 o.p. (ISBN 0-08-024483-1); pap. 12.75 o.p. (ISBN 0-08-024476-9). Pergamon.

State of the World Atlas. Pluto Press Staff et al. 1981. 16.95 o.s.i. (ISBN 0-671-42438-6, Touchstone); pap. 9.95 o.s.i. (ISBN 0-671-42439-4). S&S.

State Parks of Arizona. John V. Young. LC 85-20690. (Coyote Bks.). (Illus.). 212p. 1986. pap. 11.95 o.p. (ISBN 0-8263-0842-2). U of NM Pr.

State Policies & Migration: Studies in Latin America & the Caribbean. Ed. by Peter Peek & Guy Standing. 603p. 1982. 32.50 o.p. (ISBN 0-7099-2028-8, Pub. by Croom Helm Ltd). Routledge Chapman & Hall.

State Policies, Party Politics, & Regional Change. Ray Hudson. (Studies in Society & Space). (Illus.). 400p. 1988. text ed. 79.95 o.p. (ISBN 0-85086-125-X, Pub. by Pion England). Routledge Chapman & Hall.

State Politics & Redistricting, 2 Pts. Congressional Quarterly, Inc. Staff. LC 82-7261. (Orig.). 1982. Pt. I, 199 pp., Pt. II, 231pp. pap. 16.00 set o.p. (ISBN 0-87187-233-1). Congr Quarterly.

State Property in the U. S. S. R. R. Khalfina. 168p. 1980. pap. 3.45 o.p. (ISBN 0-8285-1970-6, Pub. by Progress Pubs USSR). Imported Pubns.

State Rate-Setting Legislation: Legal Issues in the Negotiation & Implementation of a Statute. (State Legal Initiatives: Legal Developments Report Ser.: No. 3). 61p. 1984. 30.00 o.p. (ISBN 0-317-36956-3, C-118913). Am Hospital.

State Regulation of Capital Formation & Securities Transactions. Practising Law Institute Staff et al. LC 83-61006. (Corporate Law & Practice Course Handbook Ser.: No. 415). (Illus.). 848p. 1983. 40.00 o.p. (ISBN 0-317-12900-7). PLI.

State Regulation of Health Service Utilization: Lessons from Michigan. Bruce Stuart. 94p. 1979. pap. text ed. 6.00 o.p. (ISBN 0-87766-256-8). Urban Inst.

State Regulation of Preferred Provider Organizations: A Survey of State Statutes. (State Legal Initiatives: Legal Development Report Ser.: No. 4). 90p. 1984. 25.00 o.p. (ISBN 0-317-36958-X, C-118914). Am Hospital.

State Regulation of Prepaid Legal Services in Brief. 3rd ed. 55p. 1986. 20.00 o.p. (ISBN 0-317-64336-3). Am Prepaid.

State Scarlet. David Aaron. 352p. 1987. 18.95 o.p. (ISBN 0-399-13243-0, Putnam). Putnam Pub Group.

State, the Family, & Education. Miriam E. David. (Radical Social Policy Ser.). 304p. (Orig.). 1980. pap. 17.50x o.p. (ISBN 0-7100-0601-2). Routledge Chapman & Hall.

State, the Investor, & the Railroad: The Boston & Albany, 1825-1867. Stephen Salsbury. LC 67-20881. (Center for the Study of the History of Liberty in America Ser.). (Illus.). 1967. 29.50x o.s.i. (ISBN 0-674-83580-8). Harvard U Pr.

State, the Law & the Family: Critical Perspectives. Michael Freeman. 328p. (Orig.). 1985. pap. 16.95 o.p. (ISBN 0-422-79080-X, 9332, Pub. by Tavistock England). Routledge Chapman & Hall.

State Trooper: Highway Patrolman, Ranger. Ed. by Hy Hammer. LC 81-471. 128p. (Orig.). 1981. pap. 8.00 o.p. (ISBN 0-668-05234-1, 5234). Arco.

State Veterans' Laws: Digests of State Laws Regarding Rights, Benefits, & Privileges of Veterans & Their Dependents (Revised to February 1, 1984) 324p. 1984. 8.00 o.p. (ISBN 0-318-23087-9, 052-070-05914-1). USGPO.

Statecraft As Soulcraft: What Government Does. George F. Will. 192p. 1983. 13.50 o.p. (ISBN 0-671-42733-4). S&S.

Statecraft As Soulcraft: What Government Does. George F. Will. 1984. pap. 7.95 o.s.i. (ISBN 0-671-42734-2, Touchstone). S&S.

Stateline. John Van der Zee. LC 75-33627. 216p. 1976. 7.95 o.p. (ISBN 0-15-184905-6). HarBraceJ.

Statement before the House Committee on the Judiciary Subcommittee on Civil & Constitutional Rights, April 3, 1985. Jules Lobel & Barbara Wolvovitz. 3.50 o.p. Natl Lawyers Guild.

States, Microstates & Islands. Ed. by Edward Dommen & Philippe Hein. LC 85-11336. 216p. 1985. 34.50 o.p. (ISBN 0-7099-0862-8, Pub. by Croom Helm Ltd). Routledge Chapman & Hall.

States of Grace: Eight Plays. Ed. by Brendan Gill. LC 75-12532. (Illus.). 655p. 1975. 19.95 o.s.i. (ISBN 0-15-184910-2). HarBraceJ.

States under Stress: A Report on the Finances of Massachusetts, Michigan, Texas, & California: California Policy Seminar Conference Report. California Policy Seminar Staff & Peggy B. Musgrave. LC 85-622290. (Illus.). vii, 60p. 6.00 o.p. UCB IGS.

Static. Jim R. Lane. 240p. (Orig.). 1984. pap. 3.50 o.p. (ISBN 0-380-89243-X). Avon.

Static Electrical Equipment Testing. Ed. by D. R. Adams et al. (Engineering Craftsmen Ser.: No. G21). (Illus.). 1969. spiral bdg. 45.00x o.p. (ISBN 0-89563-021-4). Trans-Atl Phila.

Static Electrical Equipment Winding & Building, 2 vols. Ed. by Engineering Industry Training Board, London Staff. (Engineering Craftsmen: No. G1). (Illus.). 1968. Set. spiral bdg. 69.95x o.p. (ISBN 0-89563-022-2). Vol. 2 (ISBN 0-85083-128-8). Trans-Atl Phila.

Static Electrification. Leonard B. Loeb. (Illus.). 1958. 44.90 o.p. (ISBN 0-387-02322-4). Springer-Verlag.

Static Elimination. T. Horvath & I. Berta. LC 82-4791. (Electrostatics & Electrostatic Applications Ser.: 1-617). 118p. 1982. text ed. 42.95 o.p. (ISBN 0-471-10405-1). Wiley.

Static Steam: Locomotives on Display in Nebraska. James J. Reisdorff. (Illus.). 60p. 1985. pap. 7.50 o.p. (ISBN 0-9609568-4-0). South Platte.

Statics & Strength of Materials. 3rd ed. Alfred E. Jensen & Harry H. Chenoweth. LC 75-8820. (Illus.). 608p. 1975. text ed. 42.95 o.p. (ISBN 0-07-032472-7). McGraw.

Statics of Granular Media. Sokolovskill. 1965. pap. 70.00 o.p. (ISBN 0-08-013624-9). Pergamon.

Station Gehenna. Andrew Weiner. (Isaac Asimov Presents Ser.). 192p. 1987. 15.95 o.p. (ISBN 0-86553-191-9). Congdon & Weed.

Station, No. 22: Devil's Canyon. Hank Mitchum. (Stagecoach Ser.). 192p. 1986. pap. 2.75 o.p. (ISBN 0-553-25421-9). Bantam.

Stationary Ark. Gerald Durrell. (Illus.). 1977. 8.95 o.p. (ISBN 0-671-22878-1). S&S.

Stationary Ark. Gerald Durrell. 1984. pap. 6.75 o.p. (ISBN 0-671-50758-3, Touchstone). S&S.

Stationary Processes & Prediction Theory. H. Furstenberg. (Annals of Mathematics Studies, Vol. 44). (Orig.). 1960. pap. 34.00x o.p. (ISBN 0-691-08041-0). Princeton U Pr.

Statistical Abstract of East-West Trade & Finance: Staff Report. 2nd ed. Ronald C. Oechsler & Leyla Woods. (Illus.). 49p. 1986. pap. 2.75 o.p. (ISBN 0-318-20384-7, S/N 003-009-00475-6). USGPO.

Statistical Abstract of the United States, 1986: National Data Book & Guide to Sources. 106th ed. (Illus.). 1013p. 1986. 27.00 o.p. (ISBN 0-318-19907-6, S/N 003-024-06369-7). USGPO.

Statistical Abstract of the United States, 1987, National Data Book & Guide to Sources. 107th ed. LC 4-18089. (Illus.). 990p. 1987. 29.00 o.p. (ISBN 0-318-22591-3, 003-024-06573-8); pap. 22.00 o.p. (ISBN 0-318-22592-1, 003-024-06572-0). USGPO.

Statistical Analysis: A Computer Oriented Approach. A. A. Afifi & S. P. Azen. 1972. text ed. 20.50 o.p. (ISBN 0-12-044450-X). Acad Pr.

Statistical Analysis for Business & Economics. Leonard J. Kazmier. (Illus.). 1978. text ed. 25.00 o.p. (ISBN 0-07-033439-0). McGraw.

Statistical Analysis for Decision Making. Morris Hamburg. 1970. text ed. 19.95 o.p. (ISBN 0-15-583760-5, HC). HarBraceJ.

Statistical Analysis for Decision Making. 2nd ed. Morris Hamburg. (Illus.). 801p. 1977. text ed. 25.95 o.p. (ISBN 0-15-583747-8, HC). HarBraceJ.

Statistical Analysis for Decision Making. 3rd ed. Morris Hamburg. 829p. 1983. 24.75 o.p. (ISBN 0-15-583450-9, HC). HarBraceJ.

Statistical Analysis in Geology. Ed. by J. M. Cubitt & S. Henley. LC 78-17368. (Benchmark Papers in Geology: Vol. 37). 340p. 1982. 57.95 o.p. (ISBN 0-87933-335-9). Van Nos Reinhold.

Statistical Analysis of Social Data. Richard A. Zeller & Edward G. Carmines. 1980. text ed. 36.76 o.p. (ISBN 0-395-30777-5); pap. 11.95 o.p. (ISBN 0-395-30778-3). HM.

Statistical Analysis of Spatial Dispersion. A. Rogers. (Monographs in Spatial & Environmental Systems Analysis). 164p. 1974. 19.95x o.p. (ISBN 0-85086-045-8, NO.2959, Pub. by Pion England). Routledge Chapman & Hall.

Statistical Analysis of Spatial Pattern. M. S. Bartlett. (Monographs in Applied Probability & Statistics). 1976. 22.00x o.p. (ISBN 0-412-14290-2, NO.6030, Pub. by Chapman & Hall). Routledge Chapman & Hall.

Statistical Applications in the Spatial Sciences. N. Wrigley. 310p. 1980. 33.00x o.p. (ISBN 0-85086-075-X, 3021, Pub. by Pion England). Routledge Chapman & Hall.

Statistical Computation. Ed. by R. C. Milton & J. A. Nelder. 1969. 65.00 o.p. (ISBN 0-12-498150-X). Acad Pr.

Statistical Decision Theory & Related Topics: Proceedings. Ed. by Shanti S. Gupta & James Yackel. 1971. 76.50 o.p. (ISBN 0-12-307550-5). Acad Pr.

Statistical Decision Theory in Adaptive Control Systems. Yoshikazu Sawaragi et al. (Mathematics in Science & Engineering Ser: Vol. 39). 1967. 66.00 o.p. (ISBN 0-12-620350-4). Acad Pr.

Statistical Design & Analysis of Experiments. P. W. John. 1971. write for info. o.p. (ISBN 0-02-360820-X). Macmillan.

Statistical Guidelines for Contributors to Medical Journals. 1983. pap. 5.00x o.p. (ISBN 0-8002-3869-9, Pub. by British Med Assoc UK). Taylor & Francis.

Statistical Indicators for Asia & the Pacific, March, 1983, Vol. XIII, No. 1. 83p. 1983. pap. text ed. 9.00 o.p. (E.83.II.F.9). UN.

Statistical Indicators for Asia & the Pacific: March, 1984, Vol. 14, No. 1. 84p. 1984. pap. 9.50 o.p. (ISBN 92-1-119227-7, E.84.II.F.9). UN.

Statistical Indicators for Asia & the Pacific: September 1984, Vol. XIV, No. 3. United Nations Economic Commission for Asia & the Pacific. 84p. 1985. pap. 9.50 o.p. (ISBN 92-1-119230-7, E.84.II.F.18). UN.

Statistical Indicators for Asia & the Pacific: September 1983, Vol. 13, No. 3. 85p. (Orig.). 1984. pap. 9.00 o.p. (E.83.II.F.18). UN.

Statistical Inference for Markov Processes. Patrick Billingsley. LC 61-8646. (Midway Reprint Ser.). 84p. 1975. pap. text ed. 5.50x o.s.i. (ISBN 0-226-05077-7). U of Chicago Pr.

Statistical Inference in Random Coefficient Regression Models. P. A. Swamy. LC 75-173909. (Lecture Notes in Operations Research & Mathematical Systems: Vol. 55). viii, 209p. 1971. pap. 14.70 o.p. (ISBN 0-387-05603-3). Springer-Verlag.

Statistical Literacy: A Guide to Interpretation. Dennis G. Haack. (Illus.). 1978. pap. text ed. (ISBN 0-87872-183-5, Duxbury Pr). PWS-Kent Pub.

Statistical Measures of Corporate Bond Financing Since 1900. W. B. Hickman. (National Bureau of Economics Research, E.V.3). 1960. 48.50x o.p. (ISBN 0-691-04178-4). Princeton U Pr.

Statistical Mechanics. Kerson Huang. LC 63-11437. 470p. 1963. (ISBN 0-471-41760-2). Wiley.

Statistical Mechanics. R. Kubo. 426p. 1971. text ed. 53.25 o.p. (ISBN 0-7204-0090-2, North-Holland). Elsevier.

Statistical Mechanics & Its Chemical Applications. M. H. Everdell. 1975. 55.00 o.p. (ISBN 0-12-244450-7). Acad Pr.

Statistical Mechanics & Mathematical Problems. Ed. by A. Lenard. (Lecture Notes in Physics: Vol. 20). (Illus.). viii, 246p. 1973. pap. 14.70 o.p. (ISBN 0-387-06194-0). Springer-Verlag.

Statistical Mechanics & the Foundations of Thermodynamics. A. Martin-Loef. (Lecture Notes in Physics Ser.: Vol. 101). 1979. pap. 13.00 o.p. (ISBN 0-387-09255-2). Springer-Verlag.

Statistical Mechanics, Kinetic, Theory & Stochastic Process. C. V. Heer. 1972. 27.50 o.p. (ISBN 0-12-336550-3). Acad Pr.

Statistical Mechanics of the Liquid Surface. Clive A. Croxton. LC 79-40819. 345p. 1980. 116.00 o.p. (ISBN 0-471-27663-4, Pub. by Wiley-Interscience). Wiley.

Statistical Methods for Building Price Data. D. T. Beeston. 1983. 38.00x o.p. (ISBN 0-419-12270-2, NO. 6795, Pub. by E & FN Spon); pap. 21.00 o.p. (NO. 6794, Pub. by Chapman & Hall). Routledge Chapman & Hall.

Statistical Methods for Digital Computers. Ed. by Kurt Enslein et al. LC 60-6509. (Mathematical Methods for Digital Computers Ser.: Vol. 3). 454p. 1977. 59.95 o.p. (ISBN 0-471-70690-6, Pub. by Wiley-Interscience). Wiley.

Statistical Methods for Food & Agriculture. Filmore E. Bender et al. (Illus.). 1982. 33.95 o.p. (ISBN 0-87055-391-7). AVI.

Statistical Methods for Psychology. David C. Howell. 608p. 1982. text ed. write for info. o.p. (ISBN 0-87872-269-6, 8025, Duxbury Pr). PWS-Kent Pub.

Statistical Methods for Survival Data Analysis. Elisa T. Lee. LC 80-24720. 557p. 1981. 38.95 o.p. (ISBN 0-534-97987-4, Lifetime Learn). Van Nos Reinhold.

Statistical Methods in Agriculture & Experimental Biology. R. Mead & R. N. Curnow. 300p. 1983. 55.00 o.p. (ISBN 0-412-24230-3, NO. 6767); pap. 27.00 o.p. (ISBN 0-412-24240-0, NO. 6768). Routledge Chapman & Hall.

Statistical Methods in Experimental Physics. Eadie. 1971. Repr. 42.50 o.p. (ISBN 0-7204-0239-5). Elsevier.

Statistical Methods in Sonar. V. V. Ol'shevskii. LC 78-18196. 262p. 1978. 75.00x o.p. (ISBN 0-306-10947-6, Consultants). Plenum Pub.

Statistical Methods: (New Quality Philosophy) 6th ed. V. Shvyrkov. LC 87-51571. (Illus.). 285p. 1988. wkbk. 32.55 o.p. (ISBN 0-942004-21-3). Throwkoff Pr.

Statistical Package for the Social Sciences Bibliography: Selected SPSS Manuals & Research Articles Using SPSS. Patrick H. Kellough. (Public Administration Ser.: P 1671). 8p. 1985. 2.00 o.p. (ISBN 0-89028-381-8). Vance Biblios.

Statistical Papers Series. Incl. Pt. 4. Handbook of Population & Housing Censuses. (Series F). pap. 6.00 o.p. (E.70.XVII.7); Yearbook of World Energy Statistics. (No. 23, Series J). pap. 60.00 o.p. (E.80.XVII.7); Methods used in Compiling the U. N. Price Indexes for Basic Commodities in International Trade. (Series M). pap. 3.00 o.p. (UN70/17/17). UN.

Statistical Physics. A. Isihara. 1971. 49.50 o.p. (ISBN 0-12-374650-7). Acad Pr.

Statistical Physics & Chaos in Fusion Plasmas. Ed. by C. W. Horton, Jr. & L. E. Reichl. LC 83-19649. (Nonequilibrium Problems in the Physical Science & Biology Ser.: 1-479). 361p. 1984. 105.00 o.p. (ISBN 0-471-88310-7, Pub. by Wiley-Interscience). Wiley.

Statistical Power Analysis for the Behavioral Sciences. rev. ed. Jacob Cohen. 1977. 39.95 o.p. (ISBN 0-12-179060-6). Acad Pr.

Statistical Reasoning. Smith. 1985. 28.50 o.p. (ISBN 0-205-08295-5, 168295). Allyn.

Statistical Reasoning in Sociology. 3rd ed. John H. Mueller et al. LC 76-13097. (Illus.). 1977. text ed. 32.95 o.p. (ISBN 0-395-24417-X). HM.

Statistical Reasoning in the Behavioral Sciences. Richard J. Shavelson. 1980. text ed. write for info. o.p. (ISBN 0-205-06933-9, 7969333); instr's. manual avail. o.p. (ISBN 0-205-06934-7). Allyn.

Statistical Records of the First Bank of the United States. James O. Wettereau. Ed. by Stuart Bruchey. LC 84-48319. (American Economic History Ser.). 317p. 1985. lib. bdg. 58.00 o.p. (ISBN 0-8240-6667-7). Garland Pub.

Statistical Report, Rural Electric Borrowers, 1986. (Rural Electrification Admininstration Bulletin: 1-1). 253p. 1987. pap. 12.00 o.p. (ISBN 0-318-23529-3, S/N 001-010-00097-2). USGPO.

Statistical Reporting in Home & Community Health Services. 49p. 1977. 12.95 o.p. (ISBN 0-88737-114-0, 21-1652). Natl League Nurse.

Statistical Sampling Software for Auditing & Accounting. H. Arkin & R. Arkin. 160p. 1985. 275.00 o.p. (ISBN 0-07-079119-8). McGraw.

Statistical Science in Economic Forecasting. V. V. Shvyrkov. LC 83-70153. (Illus.). 206p. (Orig.). 1983. pap. 18.30 wkbk. o.s.i. (ISBN 0-942004-04-3). Throwkoff Pr.

Statistical Services in Ten Years' Time. J. W. Duncan. 1978. 69.00 o.p. (ISBN 0-08-022416-4). Pergamon.

Statistical Sources & Methods: Consumer Price Indices, Vol. 1. vii, 281p. 1984. pap. 22.75 o.p. (ISBN 92-2-103774-6). Intl Labour Office.

Statistical Studies of Historical Social Structure. Kenneth W. Wachter et al. (Studies in Anthropology Ser.). 1978. 29.50 o.p. (ISBN 0-12-729150-4). Acad Pr.

Statistical Summary Report of the 1979 University of California Union Catalog Data Base. Blanche Grosswald. (Working Paper: No. 10). 1980. 5.00 o.p. (ISBN 0-686-87251-7). UCDLA.

Statistical Techniques in Geographical Analysis. Gareth Shaw & Dennis Wheeler. LC 84-12003. 364p. 1985. 54.95 o.p. (ISBN 0-471-10317-9). Wiley.

Statistical Theories of Mental Test Scores. Frederic M. Lord & Melvin R. Novick. (Illus.). 568p. 1968. text ed. 28.00 o.p. (ISBN 0-394-34771-4, RanC). Random.

Statistical Theories of Spectra: Fluctuations. Ed. by Charles E. Porter. (Perspectives in Physics Ser.). (Illus., Orig.). 1965. pap. 50.50 o.p. (ISBN 0-12-562356-9). Acad Pr.

Statistical Theory. rev. ed. Lancelot Hogben. (Illus.). 1968. 15.00x o.p. (ISBN 0-393-06305-4). Norton.

Statistical Theory & Inference in Research. Bancroft & Chein-Pai Han. (Statistics: Textbooks & Monographs Ser.: Vol. 40). 432p. 1981. 59.75 o.p. (ISBN 0-8247-1400-8). Dekker.

Statistical Theory of Non-Equilibrium Processes in a Plasma. Yu L. Klimontovich. 1967. 63.00 o.p. (ISBN 0-08-011966-2). Pergamon.

Statistical Theory of Signal Detection. 2nd ed. C. W. Helmstrom. 1969. 120.00 o.p. (ISBN 0-08-013265-0). Pergamon.

Statistical Theory with Engineering Applications. A. Hald. (Probability & Mathematical Statistics Ser.). 783p. 1952. 71.95x o.p. (ISBN 0-471-34056-1, Pub. by Wiley-Interscience). Wiley.

Statistical Thermodynamics. Rev. ed. Chang L. Tieu & John H. Lienhard. LC 84-27910. (Illus.). 397p. 1985. text ed. 45.00 o.p. (ISBN 0-89116-048-5). Hemisphere Pub.

Statistical Treatment of Fatigue Experiments. L. G. Johnson. 116p. 1964. 47.50 o.p. (ISBN 0-444-40322-1). Elsevier.

Statistical Yearbook for Asia & the Pacific: 1981. Incl. 1973. pap. 24.00 o.p. (ISBN 0-686-93828-3, UN74/2F11); 1974. 24.00 o.p. (ISBN 0-686-93829-1, UN75/2F15); Suppl. pap. 6.00 o.p. (ISBN 0-686-99185-0, UN76/2F19); 1975. pap. 30.00 o.p. (ISBN 0-686-93831-3, UN76/2F17); 1976. pap. 34.00 o.p. (ISBN 0-686-93832-1, UN77/2F8); 1977. 492p. pap. 34.00 o.p. (E.78.II.F.14); 1978. pap. 34.00 o.p. (ISBN 0-686-93834-8, UN79/2F4); 1979. pap. 30.00 o.p. (UN80/2F11); 1980. pap. text ed. 33.00 o.p. (EF.81.II.F.7); 1981. 563p. 1983. pap. text ed. 48.00 o.p. (EF.83.II.F.2, UN). (Eng. & Fr.). UN.

Statistical Yearbook for Latin America. Incl. 1975. pap. 34.00 o.p. (ES.77.II.G.4); 1976. pap. 35.00 o.p. (ES.78.II.G.2); 1977 & 1978. pap. 32.00 o.p. (ISBN 0-686-93827-5); 1979. 45p. 1981. pap. 26.00 o.p. (ES.80.II.G.4); 1980. 1980. pap. 29.00 o.p. (ES.81.II.G.5). (Latin American Ser.). (Eng. & Span.). UN.

Statistical Yearbook for Latin America, 1984. 40.00 o.p. (ISBN 92-1-021022-0). Intl Pubns Serv.

Statistical Yearbook for Latin America, 1979. United Nations Staff. LC 75-645451. (Illus.). 471p. (Orig.). 1982. pap. 26.00x o.p. (ES.80.11.G.4). UN.

Statistical Yearbook for Latin America, 1980. United Nations Staff. LC 75-645451. (Illus.). 617p. 1983. 29.00x o.p. (ISBN 0-8002-1089-1). Intl Pubns Serv.

Statistical Yearbook (UNESCO) 1981. 17th ed. UNESCO-United Nations Educational, Scientific & Cultural Organization (Paris) Staff. LC 65-3517. 1280p. 1981. 104.00x o.p. (ISBN 92-3-001965-8). Intl Pubns Serv.

Statistical Yearbook 1978. 30th ed. United Nations Staff. LC 50-2746. 966p. 1979. 50.00x o.p. (ISBN 0-8002-2332-2); pap. 41.00x o.s.i. (ISBN 0-8002-1077-8). Intl Pubns Serv.

Statistical Yearbook, 1979-1980. United Nations Staff. cloth 60.00 o.p. (E/F.81.XVII.1). UN.

Statistical Yearbook, 1979-80. 31st ed. United Nations Staff. LC 50-2746. (Illus.). 952p. 1981. 60.00x o.p.; pap. 52.00 o.p. (E.81.XVII.1). UN.

Statistical Yearbook, 1983-1984. 34th ed. LC 50-2746. 1070p. 1986. 70.00x o.p. (ISBN 0-8002-3156-2); pap. 60.00x o.p. (ISBN 0-8002-3157-0). Intl Pubns Serv.

Statistics. 2nd ed. Norma Gilbert. 1981. text ed. 32.95 o.p. (ISBN 0-03-058091-9, CBS C); instr's manual 9.95 o.p. (ISBN 0-03-058093-5). SCP.

Statistics. S. Letchford. 1981. pap. 14.95 o.p. (ISBN 0-85258-189-0). Van Nos Reinhold.

Statistics. 2nd ed. Robert S. Witte. 448p. 1985. text ed. 28.95 o.p. (ISBN 0-03-063593-4, HoltC). HR&W.

Statistics: A Fresh Approach. 2nd ed. Donald H. Sanders et al. (Illus.). 1979. text ed. 30.95 o.p. (ISBN 0-07-054667-3). McGraw.

Statistics: A Microcomputer Approach with Utility Supporting Software. Freeman F. Elzey. 256p. 1984. pap. write for info. o.p. Brooks-Cole.

Statistics, Africa: Sources for Social, Economic, & Market Research. 2nd ed. Ed. by Joan M. Harvey. 1978. 80.00x o.p. (ISBN 0-900246-26-X, Pub. by CBD Research Ltd.). Gale.

Statistics America: Sources for Social, Economic, & Marketing Research. 2nd ed. Joan M. Harvey. 300p. 1980. 185.00x o.p. (ISBN 0-900246-16-2, Pub. by CBD Res Ltd.). Gale.

Statistics: An Introduction. Mason et al. 626p. 1983. text ed. 26.00 o.p. (ISBN 0-15-583525-4, HC). HarBraceJ.

Statistics & Comp MTH in BAS. 1982. 33.95 o.p. (ISBN 0-442-30474-9). Van Nos Reinhold.

Statistics & Econometrics: A Guide to Information Sources. Ed. by Joseph Zaremba. (Economics Information Guide Ser.: Vol. 15). 720p. 1980. 68.00x o.p. (ISBN 0-8103-1466-5). Gale.

Statistics & Economic Policy. Ewan Clague. 39p. 1966. 2.00 o.p. (ISBN 0-89215-049-1). U Cal LA Indus Rel.

Statistics & Experimental Design for Toxicologists. Shayne Gad & Carrol S. Weil. 380p. 1986. 42.50 o.p. (ISBN 0-936923-01-6); pap. 25.50 o.p. (ISBN 0-936923-00-8). Telford Pr.

Statistics & Probability in Modern Life. 3rd ed. Joseph Newmark. 1983. text ed. 33.95 o.p. (ISBN 0-03-058407-8, CBS C); instr's manual 19.95 o.p. (ISBN 0-03-058408-6). SCP.

Statistics for Analytical Chemistry. J. C. Miller & J. N. Miller. LC 84-19271. (Ellis Horwood Series in Analytical Chemistry). 202p. 1985. 39.95 o.p. (ISBN 0-470-20128-2). Halsted Pr.

Statistics for Business & Economics: Methods & Applications. 2nd ed. Edwin Mansfield. 1983. text ed. 31.95x o.p. (ISBN 0-393-95293-2). Norton.

Statistics for Business & Economics. Heitzman & Mueller. 1980. text ed. 43.00 o.s.i. (ISBN 0-205-06753-0, 106753-2); solutions manual avail. o.s.i. (ISBN 0-205-06754-9, 1067540); study guide 16.00 o.s.i. (ISBN 0-205-06756-5, 1067567). Allyn.

Statistics for Business & Economics. Heinz Kohler. 1985. text ed. write for info. o.p. (ISBN 0-673-15822-5). Scott F.

Statistics for Business & Economics. Edwin Mansfield. (Illus.). 1980. text ed. 21.95x o.p. (ISBN 0-393-95057-3); Readings & Case Studies. pap. 8.95x o.p. (ISBN 0-393-95066-2); Problems, Exercises & Case Studies. pap. 6.95x o.p. (ISBN 0-393-95062-X). Norton.

Statistics for Business & Economics. 3rd ed. Susan L. Reiland. 336p. 1985. pap. text ed. write for info. study guide o.p. (ISBN 0-02-378780-5). Macmillan.

Statistics for Business & Economics. Joseph G. Van Matre & Glenn H. Gilbreath. 1980. text ed. 19.50x o.p. (ISBN 0-256-02276-3); study guide & wkbk. 6.50x o.p. (ISBN 0-256-02357-3). Irwin.

Statistics for Engineers. Richard Scheaffer & James McClave. 480p. 1982. text ed. write for info. o.p. (ISBN 0-87872-298-X, 6950, Duxbury Pr). PWS-Kent Pub.

Statistics for Experimentalists. B. E. Cooper. 1969. 90.00 o.p. (ISBN 0-08-012600-6). Pergamon.

Statistics for Great Britain, Germany & France, 1867-1909. National Monetary Commission. LC 82-48211. (Gold, Money, Inflation & Deflation Ser.). 354p. 1983. lib. bdg. 44.00 o.p. (ISBN 0-8240-5274-9). Garland Pub.

Statistics for Management & Economics. 4th ed. William Mendenhall & James Reinmuth. 1982. write for info. o.p. (ISBN 0-87150-411-1, Duxbury Pr). PWS-Kent Pub.

Statistics for Management & Economics. 4th ed. William Mendenhall & James E. Reinmuth. 928p. 1982. text ed. write for info. o.p. (ISBN 0-87872-296-3, 8015, Duxbury Pr). PWS-Kent Pub.

Statistics for Management Decisions. rev. ed. Donald R. Plane & Edward B. Oppermann. 1981. 30.95 o.p. (ISBN 0-256-02438-3). Irwin.

Statistics for Modern Business Decisions. 2nd ed. Laurence L. Lapin. 1978. 24.95 o.p. (ISBN 0-15-583775-3). HarbraceJ.

Statistics for Modern Business Decisions. Lawrence L. Lapin. (Illus.). 1973. text ed. 17.95 o.p. (ISBN 0-15-583764-8, HC). HarBraceJ.

Statistics for Modern Business Decisions. 3rd ed. Lawrence L. Lapin. (Illus.). 877p. 1982. text ed. 24.75 o.p. (ISBN 0-15-583743-5, HC). HarBraceJ.

Statistics for Nurses: An Introductory Text. Frederick J. Kviz & Kathleen A. Knafl. 313p. 1980. pap. text ed. 13.95 o.p. (ISBN 0-316-50750-4). Little.

Statistics for Physicists. B. R. Martin. 1971. 47.50 o.p. (ISBN 0-12-474750-7). Acad Pr.

Statistics for Psychology. 2nd ed. William Mendenhall & James T. McClave. LC 77-23194. 1977. write for info. o.p. (ISBN 0-87872-045-6, Duxbury Pr). PWS-Kent Pub.

Statistics for Public Policy & Management. Matlack. LC 79-11886. 1980. text ed. write for info. o.p. (ISBN 0-87872-226-2, Duxbury Pr). PWS-Kent Pub.

Statistics for Social Data Analysis. George W. Bohrnstedt & David Knoke. LC 81-82889. 530p. 1982. text ed. 35.00 o.p. (ISBN 0-87581-275-9). Peacock Pubs.

Statistics for the Behavioral Sciences: A First Course for Students of Psychology & Education. Frederick J. Gravetter & Larry B. Wallanu. 705p. 1985. text ed. 38.25 o.p. (ISBN 0-314-85241-7). West Pub.

Statistics for the Behavioral Sciences. James Jaccard. 384p. 1983. text ed. (ISBN 0-534-01247-7). Wadsworth Pub.

Statistics for the Teacher. 2nd ed. D. M. McIntosh. 1967. 35.00 o.p. (ISBN 0-08-012254-X); pap. text ed. 35.00 o.p. (ISBN 0-08-012255-8). Pergamon.

Statistics: Meaning & Method. Lawrence L. Lapin. 576p. 1975. text ed. 19.95 o.p. (ISBN 0-15-583772-9, HC). HarbraceJ.

Statistics: Methods & Analyses. 2nd ed. L. Chao. 1974. text ed. 41.95 o.p. (ISBN 0-07-010525-1). McGraw.

Statistics of Communications Common Carriers: Year Ended December 31, 1984. 172p. 1986. pap. 7.00 o.p. (S/N 004-000-00448-5). USGPO.

Statistics of Income: 1982, Corporation Income Tax Returns. (Internal Revenue Service Publication Ser.: No. 16). (Illus.). 156p. 1985. pap. 6.00 o.p. (ISBN 0-318-21890-9, S/N 048-004-01886-1). USGPO.

Statistics of Income, 1983: Corporation Income Tax Returns. LC 61-37568. (Internal Revenue Service Publication Ser.: No. 16). (Illus.). 151p. 1986. pap. 8.00 o.p. (ISBN 0-318-21817-8, S/N 048-004-01930-2). USGPO.

Statistics of Income, 1984: Corporation Income Tax Returns. LC 61-37568. (IRS Publication: No. 16). (Illus.). 168p. 1987. pap. 8.50 o.p. (ISBN 0-318-23847-0, 048-004-02256-7). USGPO.

Statistics of Natural Selection. Brian F. Manly. (Population & Community Biology Ser.). 450p. 1985. text ed. 55.00 o.p. (ISBN 0-412-25630-4, 9673, Pub. by Chapman & Hall England). Routledge Chapman & Hall.

Statistics of Public Libraries Serving Populations of Less Than Thirty-Five Thousand, 1962. (Monograph: No. 3). 237p. 1967. 5.00x o.s.i. (ISBN 0-87845-025-4); pap. 3.00x o.p. (ISBN 0-87845-062-9). U of Ill Lib Info Sci.

Statistics of Public Libraries, 1974 (LIBGIS I) Helen M. Eckard. (Monograph No. 15). 88p. 1978. pap. 2.50x o.p. (ISBN 0-87845-063-7, NCES 77-200). U of Ill Lib Info Sci.

Statistics of Public School Library Media Centers, 1974 (LIBGIS I) Nicholas Osso. (Monograph No. 14). 59p. 1978. pap. 2.50x o.p. (ISBN 0-87845-064-5, NCES 77-203). U of Ill Lib Info Sci.

Statistics of Road Traffic Accidents in Europe: 1973-1980, 1983. Incl. 1973. pap. 7.00 o.p. (EFR.74.II.E.19); 1974. pap. 7.00 o.p. (EFR.75.II.E.20); 1975. pap. 8.50 o.p. (EFR.76.II.E.24); 1976. pap. 8.50 o.p. (EFR.77.E.21); 1977. pap. 8.50 o.p. (EFR,78.II.E.24); 1978. 106p. 1979. pap. 9.00 o.p. (EFR.79.II.E.27); 1980. pap. 10.00 o.p. (EFR.81.II.E.27); 1983. pap. text ed. 12.50 o.p. (EFR.82.II.E.21); Vol. 29. 1982. 107p. 1984. pap. text ed. 13.50 o.p. (EFR.83.II.E.30). (Eng., Fr. & Rus.). UN.

Statistics of World Trade in Steel: 1973-1981. Incl. 1966. pap. 2.00 o.p. (ISBN 0-686-93814-3, UN67/2E7); 1967. pap. 2.00 o.p. (ISBN 0-686-93815-1, UN69/2E6); 1968. pap. 2.00 o.p. (ISBN 0-686-93816-X, UN69/2E/17); 1969. pap. 2.00 o.p. (ISBN 0-686-93817-8, UN70/2E/12); 1971. pap. 3.00 (ISBN 0-686-93818-6, UN72/2E/8); 1972. pap. 3.00 o.p. (ISBN 0-686-93819-4, UN73/2E/15); 1973. pap. 5.00 (EFR.74.II.E.15); 1974. pap. 5.00 (EFR.75.II.E.15); 1975. pap. 6.00 (EFR.76.II.E.19); 1976. pap. 6.00 (EFR.77.II.E.16); 1977. pap. 6.00 (EFR.78.II.E.18); 1978. 75p. 1980. pap. 6.00 (EFR.79.II.E.19, UN); 1979. 69p. 1980. pap. 6.00 (EFR.80.II.E.18, UN); 1980. 71p. 1982. pap. 7.00 (EFR.81.II.E.23); 1981. 75p. (Eng., Fr. & Rus.). 1982. pap. 8.00 (EFR.82.II.E.15). (Eng., Fr. & Rus.). UN.

Statistics of World Trade in Steel, 1982. 73p. 1983. pap. text ed. 9.50 o.p. (ISBN 92-1-016005-3, E.83.II.E.24). UN.

Statistics of World Trade in Steel, 1985. 75p. 1986. pap. 8.50 o.p. (ISBN 92-1-016192-0, E-F-R.86.II.E.9). UN.

Statistics on Narcotic Drugs Furnished by Governments in Accordance with the International Treaties & Maximum Levels of Opium Stock: 1973-1981. Incl. 1971. pap. 3.50 o.p. (ISBN 0-686-93652-3, UN72/11/8); 1972. pap. 6.00 o.p. (ISBN 0-686-93653-1, UN73/11/11); 1973. pap. 6.00 (E.75.XI.2); 1974. pap. 7.00 (E.75.XI.5); 1975. pap. 8.50 (E.76.XI.7); 1976. pap. 9.50 (E.77.XI.5); 1977. pap. 9.50 (ISBN 0-686-93658-2, E.78.XI.5); 1978. 1980. pap. 9.00 (E.80.XI.4); 1979. pap. 9.00 (E.80.XI.7); 1980. pap. 11.00 (EES.81.XI.3); 1981. pap. text ed. 12.00 (EFS.82.XI.6). 95p. (Eng., Fr. & Span.). 1980. UN.

Statistics on Psychotropic Substances. Incl. 1977. 88p. 1979. 9.00 (EFS.79.XI.4); 1978. pap. 10.00 (EFS.80.XI.3); 1979. 97p. 1980. pap. 10.00 (EFS.80.XI.6); 1980. 72p. 1981. pap. 10.00 (EFS.81.XI.4); 1981. 86p. 1983. pap. 10.00 (ISBN 0-686-46334-X, EFS.80.XI.5); 1982. 86p. 1984. pap. 11.00 (ISBN 92-1-048003-1, EFS.83.XI.8); 1983. 89p. 1985. pap. text ed. 12.50 (EFS.84.XI.7). (Orig., Eng., Fr. & Span.). UN.

Statistics on Psychotropic Substances for 1983. 89p. 1985. pap. 12.50 o.s.i. (EFS.84.7). UN.

Statistics on Spheres, Vol. 6. Geoffrey S. Watson. LC 83-1328. (Canadian Mathematical Society Series of Monographs & Advanced Texts). 238p. 1983. pap. 29.95 o.p. (ISBN 0-471-88866-4). Wiley.

Statistics Sources. 11th ed. Ed. by Steven Wasserman & Jacqueline W. O'Brien. 1550p. 1987. 280.00 o.p. (ISBN 0-8103-4398-3). Gale.

Statistics Tables. H. R. Neave. 1977. pap. text ed. 6.95x o.p. (ISBN 0-04-001001-5). Unwin Hyman.

Statmaster: Exploring & Computing Statistics. C. Michael Levy & William J. Froming. 1983. 8.95 o.p. (ISBN 0-686-46634-9); write for info. o.p. (ISBN 0-673-39522-7); IBM demonstration package o.p. (ISBN 0-673-49245-1); Apple demonstration package o.p. (ISBN 0-673-49246-X); write for info. IBM instr's. disc o.p. (ISBN 0-673-49243-5); write for info. Apple instr's. disc o.p. (ISBN 0-673-49244-3). Scott F.

Statue of Liberty. Michael George. (Illus.). 56p. (Orig.). 1985. pap. 14.95 o.p. (ISBN 0-8109-2294-0). Abrams.

Statue of Liberty Enlightening the World. Rodman Gilder. 1986. pap. 5.95 o.p. (ISBN 0-918222-75-3). Morrow.

Statue of Liberty: Heritage of America. Paul Weinbaum. LC 78-78122. (Illus.). 48p. 1979. 8.95 o.p. (ISBN 0-916122-64-6); pap. 4.50 o.p. (ISBN 0-916122-63-8). KC Pubns.

Statue of Liberty Is Cracking Up: A Guide to Loving, Leaving, & Living Again. Jan Curran et al. LC 78-22247. 1979. 8.95 o.p. (ISBN 0-15-184916-1). HarBraceJ.

Statue of Liberty: The First Hundred Years. Bernard A. Weisberger. LC 85-9182. (Illus.). 192p. 1985. 29.95 o.p. (ISBN 0-8281-1189-8, Dist. by H M). Am Heritage.

Status Integration & Suicide: A Sociological Study. Jack P. Gibbs & Walter T. Martin. LC 64-3173. (Illus.). 1964. 8.00 o.p. (ISBN 0-87114-009-8). U of Oreg Bks.

Status of Biomedical Research & Related Technology for Tropical Diseases. Intro. by John T. Gibbons. LC 85-600508. (OTA-H-258). (Illus.). 300p. (Orig.). 1985. pap. 11.00 o.p. (ISBN 0-318-18844-9, S/N 052-003-00987-1). USGPO.

Status of Guidance & Counseling in the Nation's Schools. Joseph Hollis. 250p. pap. text ed. 5.75 o.p. (ISBN 0-911547-70-3, 72133W34). Am Assn Coun Dev.

Status of Probation & Parole. (Series 2: No. 3). 30p. (Orig.). 1981. pap. 3.50 o.p. (ISBN 0-942974-23-9). Am Correctional.

Statutory Supplement to Cases & Materials on Labor Law. Douglas L. Leslie. 1979. pap. 6.95 o.p. (ISBN 0-316-52158-2). Little.

Stave Churches in Norway. Roggenkamp. 24.00 o.p. (ISBN 0-85440-205-5). Anthroposophic.

Stay Alive in the Desert. 2nd ed. K. E. Melville. (Illus.). 136p. 1981. pap. 10.95 o.p. (ISBN 0-903909-11-1, Pub. by Roger Lascelles England). Bradt Ent.

Stay on Your Toes, Maggie Adams! Karen S. Dean. LC 85-91176. 153p. (YA) (gr. 6-8). 1986. pap. 2.50 o.p. (ISBN 0-380-89711-3, Flare). Avon.

Stay Tuned: A Concise History of American Broadcasting. Christopher H. Sterling & John M. Kittross. 562p. 1978. text ed. (ISBN 0-534-00514-4). Wadsworth Pub.

Stay Tuned: A Guide to Selective Viewing. J. Brent Bill. 144p. 1985. pap. 5.95 o.p. (ISBN 0-8007-5202-3). Revell.

Staying Alive. William Rotsler. Ed. by Wendy Barish. (Plot-Your-Own Adventure Stories). 128p. (gr. 3 up). 1983. pap. 2.85 o.s.i. (ISBN 0-671-49541-0). Wanderer Bks.

Staying Hard. Charles Gaines & George Butler. (Orig.). 1980. pap. 10.75 o.p. (ISBN 0-671-41265-5). S&S.

Staying in Love. William J. Diehm. LC 85-28681. 128p. (Orig.). 1986. pap. 6.95 o.p. (ISBN 0-8066-2191-5, 10-5996, Augsburg). Augsburg Fortress.

Staying in the Game: How to Keep Young & Active. Ray Siegener. 1980. 9.95 o.p. (ISBN 0-395-27596-2). HM.

Staying Off the Beaten Track. 6th ed. Elizabeth Gundrey. (Illus.). 416p. (Orig.). 1987. pap. 12.95 o.p. (ISBN 0-09-949670-4, Pub. by Automobile Assn Brit). Salem Hse Pubs.

Staying off the Beaten Track. Date not set. Salem Hse Pubs.

Staying on Top When Things Go Wrong. Linda R. Wright. 120p. 1983. pap. 2.95 o.p. (ISBN 0-8423-6623-7). Tyndale.

Staying Power. P. Fryer. 595p. 1984. text ed. 39.95x o.p. (ISBN 0-391-03167-8). Humanities.

Staying Solvent: A Comprehensive Guide to Equal Credit for Women. Emily Card. LC 84-4537. 256p. 1985. 15.95 o.p. (ISBN 0-03-062954-3). H Holt & Co.

STD: A Common Sense Guide to Sexually Transmitted Diseases. Maria Corsaro & Carole Korzeniowsky. (Illus.). 144p. 1982. pap. 5.25 o.p. (ISBN 0-03-059914-8, Owl Bks). H Holt & Co.

STD Bus Interfacing. Christopher A. Titus et al. LC 82-50652. 286p. 1982. pap. 13.95 o.p. (ISBN 0-672-21888-7, 21888). Sams.

STD: Sexually Transmitted Diseases. Stephen Zinner. 1985. 16.45 o.s.i. (ISBN 0-671-49957-2). Summit Bks.

Steadfast Tin Soldier. Hans Christian Andersen. LC 78-122493. (Illus.). (ps-2). 1971. 4.95 o.p. (ISBN 0-689-20661-5, Atheneum). Macmillan.

Steadfast Tin Soldier. Hans Christian Andersen. LC 83-9360. (Illus.). 32p. (gr. 1-3). 1983. 14.95 o.p. (ISBN 0-316-03949-7). Little.

Steady Work: Essays in the Politics of Democratic Radicalism, 1953-1966. Irving Howe. LC 66-22275. 1967. pap. 2.45 o.s.i. (ISBN 0-15-684930-5, Harv). HarBraceJ.

Stealing the Language: The Emergence of Women's Poetry in America. Alicia S. Ostriker. LC 85-47949. 291p. 1986. 19.95 o.p. (ISBN 0-8070-6302-9). Beacon Pr.

Stealing the Language: The Emergence of Women's Poetry in America. Alicia S. Ostriker. LC 85-73368. 336p. 1987. pap. 10.95 o.p. (ISBN 0-8070-6303-7, BP 763). Beacon Pr.

Steam & Gas Tables with Computer Equations. Thomas F. Irvine, Jr. 1984. 42.50 o.p. Acad Pr.

Steam British Isles: Minor & Miniature Railway Preservation. Terry Kirtland & Roger Cromblehome. 368p. 1985. 24.95 o.s.i. (ISBN 0-7153-8673-5). David & Charles.

Steam from Waterloo. H. C. Rogers. (Illus.). 160p. 1985. 19.95 o.p. (ISBN 0-7153-8617-4). David & Charles.

Steam Launch. Richard M. Mitchell. LC 81-83863. (Illus.). 256p. 1982. 39.95 o.p. (ISBN 0-87742-117-X). Intl Marine.

Steam Locomotive. W. A. Tuplin. 1980. text ed. 20.75x o.p. (ISBN 0-239-00198-2). Humanities.

Steam Locomotive. W. A. Tuplin. 1974. 10.00 o.s.i. (ISBN 0-684-13749-6, ScribT). Scribner.

Steam Locomotive Directory of North America. J. David Conrad. 1986. Transport Res Bd.

Steam Navy of the United States. Frank M. Bennett. LC 70-98814. 1972. Repr. of 1896 ed. lib. bdg. 56.25x o.p. (ISBN 0-8371-2949-4, BESN). Greenwood.

Steam Pig. James McClure. (International Crime Ser.). 1982. pap. 2.95 o.p. (ISBN 0-394-71021-5). Pantheon.

Steam Storage Installations. W. Goldstern. 1970. 55.00 o.p. (ISBN 0-08-015560-X). Pergamon.

Steam Tables. Date not set. 115.00 o.p. Hemisphere Pub.

Stedman's Medical Dictionary: Fifth Unabridged Lawyers' Edition. William H. L. Dornette. 1678p. 1982. 55.00 o.p. Anderson Pub Co.

Steel & Style: The Story of Alessi Household Ware. Patrizia Scarzella. 187p. 45.00 o.s.i. (ISBN 0-317-66854-4). Princeton Arch.

Steel Construction: A Bibliography. Mary Vance. (Architecture Ser.: A 1447). 31p. 1985. 4.50 o.p. (ISBN 0-89028-537-3). Vance Biblios.

Steel for the User. R. E. Rolfe. 400p. 1956. (ISBN 0-8022-1367-7). Philos Lib.

Steel in the United States: Restructuring to Compete. William T. Hogan. LC 83-49519. 176p. 1984. 29.00x o.p. (ISBN 0-669-08234-1). Lexington Bks.

Steel Industry in Brief: Continuous Casting Installations World-Wide. 114p. 1982. 75.00 o.p. (ISBN 0-317-40459-8). Iron & Steel.

Steel Industry in Brief: Japan. Ed. by R. L. Deily. 156p. 1977. pap. 75.00 o.p. (ISBN 0-317-34776-4). Iron & Steel.

Steel Structures: Practical Design Studies. T. J. MacGinley. 300p. 1981. 39.95x o.p. (ISBN 0-419-12560-4, NO. 6631, E & FN Spon England); pap. 17.95x o.p. (ISBN 0-419-11710-5, NO. 6598). Routledge Chapman & Hall.

Steel Trap in North America: The Illustrated Story of Its Design, Production, & Use with Furbearing & Predatory Animals, from Its Colorful Past to the Present Controversy. Richard Gerstell. (Illus.). 352p. 1985. 44.95 o.p. (ISBN 0-8117-1698-8). Stackpole.

Steele Rudd Selection, 3 vols. Steele Rudd. 2470p. 1985. boxed set 45.00 o.p. (ISBN 0-7022-1687-9). U of Queensland Pr.

Steelhead. Mel Marshall. LC 72-96089. (Illus.). 186p. 1973. 15.95 o.p. (ISBN 0-8329-0932-7, Pub. by Winchester Pr). New Century.

Steelmaking Conference: Proceedings of the 66th Conference. LC 83-111773. 650p. 1983. 60.00 o.p. (ISBN 0-89520-155-0). Iron & Steel.

Steelmaking Conference: Proceedings of the 68th Conference. 510p. 1985. 60.00 o.p. (ISBN 0-932897-02-9). Iron & Steel.

Steely Blue. Dennis Smith. 256p. 1984. 15.45 o.p. (ISBN 0-671-44019-5). S&S.

Steeple People & the World: Planning for Mission Through the Church. John Killinger. (Orig.). 1977. pap. 2.50 o.p. (ISBN 0-377-00059-0). Friendship Pr.

Steer North. Kathrene S. Pinkerton. LC 62-8346. (gr. 7 up). 1962. 4.95 o.p. (ISBN 0-15-280210-X, HJ). HarBraceJ.

Steering Clear: Helping Your Child Through the High-Risk Drug Years. Dorothy Cretcher. 112p. (Orig.). 1982. pap. 4.95 o.p. (ISBN 0-86683-689-6). HarpR.

Steering the Economy: The British Experiment. Samuel Brittan. LC 71-152814. 505p. 1971. 22.95 o.p. (ISBN 0-912050-05-5, Library Pr). Open Court.

Steering the Modern State: Changes in Central Coordination in Three Australian State Governments. Martin Painter. 208p. (Orig.). 1987. pap. 25.00 o.p. (ISBN 0-424-00126-8, Pub. by Sydney U Pr). Intl Spec Bk.

Stefanie Powers: Superlife! Stephanie Powers & Judith B. Quine. 224p. 1985. 17.45 o.p. (ISBN 0-671-50616-1). S&S.

Steinbrenner! Dick Schaap. 320p. 1983. pap. 3.95 o.p. (ISBN 0-380-62752-3, 62752-3). Avon.

Steinbrenner's Yankees: An Inside Account. Ed Linn. LC 82-1002. 322p. 1982. 14.95 o.s.i. (ISBN 0-03-060416-8). H Holt & Co.
Steindler's New Firearms Dictionary. R. A. Steindler. (Illus.). 320p. 1985. 24.95 o.p. (ISBN 0-8117-1675-9). Stackpole.
Stellar Atmospheres. Ed. by Jesse L. Greenstein. LC 61-9045. (Stars & Stellar Systems Ser: Vol. 6). (Illus.). 1961. lib. bdg. 50.00x o.s.i. (ISBN 0-226-45958-6). U of Chicago Pr.
Stellar Formation. V. C. Reddish. 225p. 1978. 69.00 o.p. (ISBN 0-08-018062-0); pap. 28.00 o.p. (ISBN 0-08-023053-9). Pergamon.
Stellar Science Fiction Stories, No. 7. Ed. by Judy-Lynn Del Rey. 224p. (Orig.). 1981. pap. 2.50 o.p. (ISBN 0-345-29473-4, Del Rey). Ballantine.
Stello: A Session with Doctor Noir. Alfred De Vigny. Tr. by Irving Massey. 1963. 5.50 o.p. (ISBN 0-7735-0006-5, McGill Canada). U of Toronto Pr.
Stem Cells: Their Identification & Characterization. Ed. by C. S. Potten. LC 82-9493. (Illus.). 304p. 1983. text ed. 64.75 o.p. (ISBN 0-443-02451-0). Churchill.
Stems Cells: Renewing Cell Population. Ed. by A. B. Cairnie. 1976. 63.50 o.p. (ISBN 0-12-155050-8). Acad Pr.
Stencil Book. (ISBN 0-671-60929-7). Arco.
Stenciled Quilt. Marie Sturmer. Ed. by Cathryn Baskin. LC 86-50090. (Illus.). 160p. 1986. pap. 15.95 o.p. (ISBN 0-89909-103-2). Yankee Bks.
Stendhal Fichier, 3 Vols. Compiled by Francois Michel. 1964. Set. 298.00 o.s.i. (ISBN 0-8161-0583-9, Hall Library). G K Hall.
Stengel: His Life & Times. Robert W. Creamer. (Illus.). 336p. 1984. 16.50 o.p. (ISBN 0-671-22489-1). S&S.
Stenographer-Typist: U. S. Government Positions GS2 & GS7. 8th ed. Ed. by Hy Hammer. LC 81-17675. (Illus.). 224p. (Orig.). 1983. pap. 8.00 o.p. (ISBN 0-668-05412-3). Arco.
Step by Step: College Writing. 3rd ed. Randy DeVillez. 328p. 1984. pap. text ed. 15.95 o.p. (ISBN 0-8403-3306-4, 40330601). Kendall-Hunt.
Step-by-Step Guide: Carburetor Tuneup & Overhaul. Herschel Whittington & Ray Whittington. (Illus.). 224p. 1982. pap. 9.70 o.p. (ISBN 0-8306-4814-3, 814). TAB Bks.
Step-By-Step Guide to Gardening Techniques. Alan Titchmarsh. (Step-by-Step Encyclopedia of Gardening). (Orig.). 1982. 8.95 o.s.i. (ISBN 0-671-42255-3). S&S.
Step-by-Step Guide to Landscaping & Gardening. Leo L. Bailey. LC 74-84421. (Illus.). 1974. 12.50 o.p. (ISBN 0-682-48084-3, Banner). Exposition-Phoenix.
Step-by-Step Guide to Plant Propagation. Phillip M. Browse. 1979. pap. 9.95 o.s.i. (ISBN 0-671-24832-4, Fireside). S&S.
Step-by-Step Guide to Pruning. Christopher Brickell. 1979. pap. 9.95 o.s.i. (ISBN 0-671-24831-6, Fireside). S&S.
Step by Step Microwave Cooking for Boys & Girls. Bonnie Aeschliman. (Illus.). 64p. (Orig.). (gr. k-7). 1985. pap. 3.95 o.p. (ISBN 0-8249-3049-5). Ideals.
Step-by-Step Microwave Cooking for Boys & Girls. Bonnie Aeschliman. (Illus.). 64p. (gr. 3-6). 1986. PLB 13.27 o.p. (ISBN 0-516-09165-4). Childrens.
Step-by-Step Sugar Artistry. Peggy Ann Barton. LC 74-75055. 1974. 6.00 o.p. (ISBN 0-682-47741-9, Banner). Exposition-Phoenix.
Step by Step We Climb to Freedom, Vol. 2. LC 88-18011. (Step by Step Ser.). 192p. 1989. pap. 9.95 o.p. (ISBN 0-9619770-2-7). Pearl Publishing.
Step by Step We Climb to Freedom & Victory, Vol. 3. Pearl Dorris. LC 88-18013. (Step by Step Ser.). 208p. 1989. pap. 9.95 o.p. (ISBN 0-9619770-3-5). Pearl Publishing.
Step into Sales: Six Weeks to Successful Direct Selling from Your Home. Claire M. Cleaver. (Illus.). 256p. 1983. pap. 8.95 o.p. (ISBN 0-380-65391-5, 65391). Avon.
Step on It, Andrew. Barbara S. Hazen. LC 80-12522. (Illus.). 32p. (ps-2). 1980. 8.95 o.s.i. (ISBN 0-689-30792-6, Atheneum). Macmillan.
Step One: The Gospel & the Ghetto. Harv Oostdyk. 342p. 1983. pap. 8.95 o.p. (ISBN 0-89221-094-X). New Leaf.
Step to Energy Independence: Gasohol. Ed. by T. P. Lyons. LC 81-68334. (Illus.). 346p. 1982. 45.00x o.p. (ISBN 0-412-00241-8, NO. 6710, Pub. by Chapman & Hall). Routledge Chapman & Hall.
Stepchild. Joanne Fluke. (Orig.). 1980. pap. 2.25 o.p. (ISBN 0-440-18408-8). Dell.
Stepfamilies: Making Them Work. Erna Paris. 240p. 1985. pap. 2.95 o.p. (ISBN 0-380-89670-2). Avon.
Stephanie the Emperor's Agent. Marceline Gobineau. 1977. pap. 1.75 o.p. (ISBN 0-380-01822-5, 36129). Avon.
Stephen: A Singular Saint. Martin N. Scharkemann. 207p. 1968. Concordia Schl Grad Studies.
Stephen Crane. James B. Colvert. LC 84-3805. (Album Biographies Ser.). (Illus.). 352p. 1984. 24.95 o.p. (ISBN 0-15-184958-7). HarBraceJ.
Stephen Crane. James B. Colvert. LC 84-3805. (Album Biographies Ser.). (Illus.). 352p. 1984. pap. 12.95 o.p. (ISBN 0-15-684946-1, Harv). HarBraceJ.
Stephen Crane at Brede: An Anglo-American Literary Circle of the Eighteen Nineties. Gordon Milne. LC 80-8126. 69p. 1980. lib. bdg. 19.75 o.p. (ISBN 0-8191-1139-2); pap. text ed. 8.25 o.p. (ISBN 0-8191-1140-6). U Pr of Amer.
Stephen Crane: The Critical Heritage. Ed. by Richard Weatherford. (Critical Heritage Ser.). 1984. pap. 15.00 o.p. (ISBN 0-7102-0397-7). Routledge Chapman & Hall.
Stephen Crane: The Critical Heritage. Ed. by Richard M. Weatherford. (Critical Heritage Ser.). 362p. 1973. 30.00x o.p. (ISBN 0-7100-7636-3). Routledge Chapman & Hall.
Stephen Crane's The Red Badge of Courage see Graded Readers for Students of English As a Second Language.
Stephen Morris. Nevil Shute. 1980. 23.95 o.p. (ISBN 0-434-69932-2, Pub. by W Heinemann Ltd). David & Charles.
Stephen Vincent Benet. Parry Stroud. (Twayne's United States Authors Ser). 1962. pap. 10.95 o.p. (ISBN 0-8084-0285-4, T27, Twayne). New Coll U Pr.
Stephen Yan Seafood Wokbook. Stephen Yan. (Illus.). 176p. Date not set. spiral bdg. 9.95 o.p. (ISBN 0-919493-87-4, Pub. by Key Porter Canada). U of Toronto Pr.
Stephensons' Britain. Derrick Beckett. (Illus.). 240p. 1984. 24.95 o.p. (ISBN 0-7153-8269-1). David & Charles.
Steppenwolf. rev. ed. Hermann Hesse. LC 63-12171. 1970. 9.95 o.s.i. (ISBN 0-03-085318-4). H Holt & Co.
Stepping from the Shadows. Patricia McKillip. LC 81-69151. 1982. 12.95 o.p. (ISBN 0-689-11211-4, Atheneum). Macmillan.
Stepping Lightly: An A to Z Guide for Stepparents. Cynthia Lewis-Steere. LC 81-15224. (Illus.). 213p. (Orig.). 1981. pap. 7.95 o.p. (ISBN 0-89638-051-3). CompCare.
Stepping Out. Carolyn Stoloff. LC 70-168608. 1971. 5.00 o.p. (ISBN 0-87775-085-8); pap. 2.00 o.p. (ISBN 0-87775-026-2). Unicorn Pr.
Stepping Out: A Love Story. Rolaine Hochstein. 1977. 7.95 o.p. (ISBN 0-393-08787-5). Norton.
Stepping Out, Sharing Christ in Everyday Circumstances. Margaret Rockwell. LC 84-47804. 134p. 1984. pap. 5.95 o.p. (ISBN 0-89840-072-4). Heres Life.
Stepping Out: Short Stories on Friendships Between Women. Ed. by Ann Oosthuizen. (Pandora Fiction Ser.). 192p. 1986. pap. 8.95 o.p. (ISBN 0-86358-048-3, 80483). Routledge Chapman & Hall.
Stepping Over: Personal Encounters with Young Extremists. Malcolm McConnell. LC 83-19095. 358p. 1984. 17.45 o.p. (ISBN 0-88349-166-4, Pub. by RD Assn). Random.
Stepping Stones to Further Jewish Relations. Ed. by Helga Croner. 7.95 o.p. Paulist Pr.
Stepping up: How to Fight Your Boss & Win. Jonathan Kramer. 233p. 1985. pap. 8.95 o.p. (ISBN 0-87795-702-9, Arbor Hse). Morrow.
Steppping into CAD Professional Edition. Mark Merickel. (Illus.). 288p. 1987. pap. 29.95 o.p. (ISBN 0-317-61773-7). New Riders Pub.
Steps along the Way: A Governor's Scrapbook. Lamar Alexander. LC 86-18184. 160p. 1986. 19.95 o.p. (ISBN 0-8407-4215-0). Nelson.
Steps in Mathematics Modules I-V. Leon Ablon et al. 1981. pap. 30.95 o.p. (ISBN 0-8053-0140-2). Benjamin-Cummings.
Steps in Time. Fred Astaire. LC 79-9148. (Series in Dance). 1979. Repr. of 1959 ed. 32.50 o.p. (ISBN 0-306-79575-2). Da Capo.
Steps in Time. Fred Astaire. LC 80-28725. (Quality Paperbacks Ser.). (Illus.). 327p. 1981. pap. 9.95 o.p. (ISBN 0-306-80141-8). Da Capo.
Steps Out of Time. Eric Houghton. LC 80-13611. 128p. (gr. 5-8). 1980. 10.25 o.p. (ISBN 0-688-41970-4); PLB 10.88 o.p. (ISBN 0-688-51970-9). Lothrop.
Steps to My Best Friends House. Evelyn W. Minshull. LC 79-25954. (Illus.). 144p. 1980. 8.95 o.s.i. (ISBN 0-664-32659-5, Westminster). Westminster John Knox.
Steps to Nuclear Power: A Guidebook. (Technical Reports Ser.: No. 164). (Illus.). 106p. 1975. pap. 14.50 o.p. (ISBN 92-0-155175-4, IDC164, IAEA). UNIPUB.
Steps to Writing Well: A Concise Guide to Composition. 2nd ed. Jean Wyrick. 263p. 1984. pap. text ed. 17.95 o.p. (ISBN 0-03-062207-7). HR&W.
Stepsister Sally. Helen F. Daringer. LC 52-7083. (Illus.). (gr. 3-7). 1966. pap. 1.45 o.p. (ISBN 0-15-684951-8, VoyB). HarBraceJ.
Stepsisters. Joan L. Oppenheimer. (gr. 12 up). 1983. pap. 2.25 o.p. (ISBN 0-671-52526-3). Archway.
Stereo & Theoretical Chemistry. Ed. by F. Boschke. LC 51-5497. (Topics in Current Chemistry Ser.: Vol. 31). (Illus.). 160p. 1972. pap. 27.90 o.p. (ISBN 0-387-05841-9). Springer-Verlag.
Stereochemistry & Conformational Analysis. Johannes Dale. (Illus.). 230p. 1978. pap. 20.60x o.p. (ISBN 0-89573-101-0). VCH Pubs.
Stereochemistry: Basic Concepts & Applications. M. Nogradi. 250p. 1980. 75.00 o.p. (ISBN 0-08-021161-5). Pergamon.
Stereochemistry One: In Memory of van't Hoff. Ed. by F. Boschke. LC 51-5497. (Topics in Current Chemistry Ser.: Vol. 47). (Illus.). 150p. 1974. 39.00 o.p. (ISBN 0-387-06648-9). Springer-Verlag.
Stereochemistry Two: In Memory of van't Hoff. Ed. by F. Boschke. LC 51-5497. (Topics in Current Chemistry Ser.: Vol. 48). (Illus.). 160p. 1974. 33.00 o.p. (ISBN 0-387-06682-9). Springer-Verlag.
Stereodynamics of Molecular Systems. Ramaswamy H. Sarma. 1979. 110.00 o.p. (ISBN 0-08-024629-X). Pergamon.
Stereoelectronic Control in the Cleavage of Tetrahedral Intermediates in the Hydrolysis of Esters & Amides. Pierre Deslongchamps. Ed. by Barton et al. 1976. pap. 14.00 o.s.i. (ISBN 0-08-020480-5). Pergamon.
Stereoscopic Atlas of Macular Diseases: Diagnosis & Treatment. 2nd ed. J. Donald Gass. LC 76-57176. (Illus.). 424p. 1977. cloth 77.50 o.p. (ISBN 0-8016-1754-5). Mosby.
Stereoselective Reductions. Ed. by M. P. Doyle & C. T. West. (Benchmark Papers in Organic Chemistry: Vol. 6). 1976. 84.50 o.p. (ISBN 0-12-786368-0). Acad Pr.
Stereotactic Treatment of Epilepsy. Ed. by F. J. Gillingham et al. LC 76-25838. 1976. pap. 82.60 o.p. (ISBN 0-387-81374-8). Springer-Verlag.
Stereotypes, Distortions & Omissions in U. S. History Textbooks: A Content Analysis Instrument for Detecting Racism & Sexism. Council on Interracial Books for Children, Inc. Staff. 143p. (gr. 11-12). 1977. pap. 8.95x o.s.i. (ISBN 0-930040-03-1). CIBC.
Sterile Cuckoo. John Nichols. 1976. pap. 1.50 o.p. (ISBN 0-380-00481-X, 26419). Avon.
Sterilization & Fertility Decline in Puerto Rico. Harriet B. Presser. LC 76-4775. (Population Monograph Ser.: No. 13). 1976. Repr. of 1973 ed. lib. bdg. 29.75x o.p. (ISBN 0-8371-8834-2, PRSF). Greenwood.
Sterling & the Tariff, Nineteen Twenty-Nine to Nineteen Twenty-Two. Barry J. Eichengreen. LC 81-6673. (Princeton Studies in International Finance: No. 48). 1981. pap. text ed. 6.50x o.p. (ISBN 0-88165-219-9). Princeton U Int Finan Econ.
Sterling in Decline. Alec Cairncross & Barry Eichengreen. 270p. 1985. 45.00x o.p. (ISBN 0-631-13368-2); pap. 12.95x o.p. (ISBN 0-631-13938-9). Basil Blackwell.
Sterling's Managed Float: The Operations of the Exchange Equalisation Account, 1932-39. Susan Howson. LC 80-23197. (Princeton Studies in International Finance Ser.: No. 46). 1980. pap. text ed. 6.50x o.p. (ISBN 0-88165-217-2). Princeton U Int Finan Econ.
Stern. Bruce J. Friedman. 1983. 14.95 o.p. (ISBN 0-87795-554-9, Arbor Hse); pap. 6.95 o.p. (ISBN 0-87795-555-7). Morrow.
Stern Drive Service-Repair Handbook: OMC, MerCruiser, Stern-Powr, Berkeley, Jacuzzi. Clymer Publications Staff. (Illus.). pap. 10.00 o.p. (ISBN 0-89287-186-5, B641). Clymer Pub.
Steroid Biochemistry. E. Heftmann. 1969. 60.50 o.p. (ISBN 0-12-336650-X). Acad Pr.
Steroid Hormone Regulation of the Brain: Proceedings of an International Symposium, 27-28 October 1980, Wenner-Gren Center, Stockholm, Sweden. K. Fuxe et al. (Wenner-Gren Ser.: Vol. 34). (Illus.). 428p. 1981. 105.00 o.p. (ISBN 0-08-026864-1). Pergamon.
Steroid-Protein Interactions. U. Westphal. LC 79-146234. (Monographs on Endocrinology: Vol. 4). (Illus.). 1971. 63.00 o.p. (ISBN 0-387-05312-3). Springer-Verlag.
Steroids & Brain Edema. Ed. by K. Schuermann & H. J. Reulen. LC 72-91334. (Illus.). 350p. 1973. pap. 32.00 o.p. (ISBN 0-387-05958-X). Springer-Verlag.
Steroids & Peptides: Selected Chemical Aspects for Biology, Biochemistry & Medicine. Joseph B. Dence. LC 79-21236. 432p. 1980. 74.95 o.p. (ISBN 0-471-04700-7, Pub. by Wiley-Interscience). Krieger.
Steroids in Nonmammalian Vertebrates. Ed. by David R. Idler. 1972. 86.00 o.p. (ISBN 0-12-370350-6). Acad Pr.
Steroids: The Keys to Life. Rupert F. Witzmann. 288p. 1981. 37.95 o.p. (ISBN 0-442-29590-1). Van Nos Reinhold.
Sterospecific Polymerization of Isoprene. E. Ceausescu. (Illus.). 300p. 1983. 85.00 o.p. (ISBN 0-08-029987-3). Pergamon.
Steve Biko: I Write What I Like. Stephen Biko. Ed. by Adrian Stubbs. LC 78-19499. 1979. 10.95i o.p. (ISBN 0-06-250052-X). HarpR.
Steve Birnbaum Brings You the Best of Walt Disney World. Steve Birnbaum. 192p. 1985. pap. 7.95 o.p. (ISBN 0-395-39404-X). HM.
Steve Ciarcia's Ask Byte. Steve Ciarcia. 200p. (Orig.). 1985. pap. text ed. 14.95 o.p. (ISBN 0-07-881200-3). Osborne-McGraw.
Steve Rieschl's Ski Touring for the Fun of It. Cortlandt Freeman. LC 73-13891. (Sports Illustrated Bk.). (Illus.). 1974. 7.95 o.p. (ISBN 0-316-74561-8); pap. 6.95 o.p. (ISBN 0-316-74562-6). Little.
Stevie Smith: A Selection. Pref. by Hermione Lee. (Illus.). 224p. 1985. 16.95 o.p. (ISBN 0-571-13029-1); pap. 6.95 o.p. (ISBN 0-571-13030-5). Faber & Faber.
Stevie Wonder: The Illustrated Discography. 96p. 1985. pap. 7.95 o.s.i. (ISBN 0-7119-0616-5). Cherry Lane.
Stewardess. Julia Percival & Pixie Burger. 1973. pap. 1.75 o.p. (ISBN 0-380-01562-5, 24539). Avon.
Steward's Manual. 2nd ed. Student Buyers' Association Staff. 51p. 1978. 2.50 o.p. (ISBN 0-318-17888-5, H01B). NASCO.
Stewards of the Mysteries: Sermons for Festivals & Special Occasions. Carl E. Braaten. LC 82-72639. 128p. (Orig.). 1983. pap. 5.95 o.p. (ISBN 0-8066-1945-7, 10-6004, Augsburg). Augsburg Fortress.
Stewardship in the New Testament Church. Holmes Rolston. pap. 2.95 o.p. (ISBN 0-317-06442-8, 2172-3, John Knox). Westminster John Knox.
Stewardship Preaching. Mark Gravrock. (Ser. B). 56p. (Orig.). 1984. pap. 5.95 o.p. (ISBN 0-8066-2076-5, 10-6002, Augsburg). Augsburg Fortress.
Stewardship Preaching. Stephen O. Swanson. (Series A). 56p. 1983. pap. 5.95 o.p. (ISBN 0-8066-2029-3, 10-6001, Augsburg). Augsburg Fortress.
Stewardship: Taking Care of God's World. Sarah Fletcher. (Illus.). (gr. k-4). 1984. pap. 3.95 o.p. (ISBN 0-570-04106-6, 56-1498). Concordia.
Stewed Goose. James Flora. LC 73-75434. (Illus.). 32p. (ps-4). 1973. 4.95 o.p. (ISBN 0-689-30417-X, Atheneum). Macmillan.
Stichija: Poems. Inna Bogachinskaya. 1983. 4.00 o.s.i. RWCPH.
Stick. Elmore Leonard. LC 82-72073. 1983. 14.50 o.p. (ISBN 0-87795-436-4, Arbor Hse). Morrow.
Stick. Elmore Leonard. 1985. lib. bdg. 15.95 o.p. (ISBN 0-8161-3908-3, Large Print Bks). G K Hall.
Stick-Carrier. Veronica Maz. 1975. 6.00 o.p. (ISBN 0-682-48423-7). Exposition-Phoenix.
Stick It, Stitch It & Stuff It Toybook. Penelope Frith. LC 74-32476. (Illus.). 114p. 1975. 5.95 o.p. (ISBN 0-87131-178-X). M Evans.
Sticky Child. Malcolm Bird. LC 81-4071. (Illus.). 32p. (gr. 4-8). 1981. 6.95 o.p. (ISBN 0-15-280338-6, HJ). HarBraceJ.
Stig of the Dump. Clive King. 1986. 11.95 o.p. (Large Print Bks). G K Hall.
Stigma. Robert M. Page. (Concepts in Social Policy Ser.). 156p. (Orig.). 1984. pap. 13.95x o.p. (ISBN 0-7100-9786-7). Routledge Chapman & Hall.
Stikhotvoreniya. Henri Volokhonsky. LC 83-20488. 160p. (Rus.). 1983. pap. 8.00 o.s.i. (ISBN 0-938920-45-6). Hermitage.
Still Close to the Island. Cyril Dabydeen. 111p. 1980. pap. 8.00 o.p. (ISBN 0-88970-036-2, Pub. by Commoner's Pub Canada). Three Continents.
Still Glides the Stream. D. E. Stevenson. 1979. 9.95 o.s.i. (ISBN 0-03-052086-X). H Holt & Co.
Still Going Bananas. Charles Keller. (Illus.). 48p. (gr. 3-7). 1982. pap. 3.95 o.s.i. (ISBN 0-13-846840-0, Pub. by Treehouse). P-H.
Still Life. Antonia Byatt. 376p. 16.95 o.p. (ISBN 0-684-18577-6, ScribT). Scribner.
Still Life with Pistol. Roger Ormerod. 176p. 1986. 13.95 o.s.i. (ISBN 0-684-18728-0). Scribner.
Still Lives. Rob Swigart. 1976. pap. 3.00 o.p. (ISBN 0-931832-03-9). Fithian Pr.
Still Living? Yeti, Sasquatch & the Neanderthal Enigma. Myra Shackley. (Illus.). 1986. pap. 9.95 o.p. (ISBN 0-500-27406-1). Thames Hudson.
Still Missing. Beth Gutcheon. 384p. pap. 3.50 o.s.i. (ISBN 0-440-17864-9, Dell Trade Pbks). Dell.
Still More Antonyms: Together & Apart & Other Words That Are As Different in Meaning As Rise & Fall. Joan Hanson. LC 76-22421. (Joan Hanson Word Bks.). (Illus.). (gr. k-3). 1976. PLB 4.95 o.p. (ISBN 0-8225-1106-1). Lerner Pubns.

Still More Homonyms: Night & Knight & Other Words That Sound the Same but Look As Different As Ball & Bawl. Joan Hanson. LC 76-22427. (Joan Hanson Word Bks.). (Illus.). (ps-3). PLB 4.95 o.p. (ISBN 0-8225-1107-X). Lerner Pubns.

Still More Wandering Thoughts. Thomas Smyth. 80p. 1981. 5.50 o.p. (ISBN 0-682-49743-6). Exposition-Phoenix.

Still River. Hal Clement. LC 86-26603. 1987. 16.45 o.s.i. (ISBN 0-345-32916-3). Ballantine.

Still Time to Pray. Catharine Brandt. LC 82-72648. 96p. (Orig.). 1983. pap. 5.50 o.p. (ISBN 0-8066-1955-4, 10-6007, Augsburg). Augsburg Fortress.

Still Time to Sing: Prayers & Praise for Late in Life. Catharine Brandt. LC 80-65547. 96p. (Orig.). 1980. pap. 5.50 o.p. (ISBN 0-8066-1792-6, 10-6010, Augsburg). Augsburg Fortress.

Still under the Thumb. Brian Burch. 1988. pap. 1.00 o.p. Samisdat.

Still's Disease: Juvenile Chronic Polyarthritis. Ed. by Malcoln Jayson. 1976. 67.50 o.p. (ISBN 0-12-381250-X). Acad Pr.

Stillwatch. Mary H. Clark. 1984. 14.70 o.p. (ISBN 0-671-46952-5). S&S.

Stillwater Smith. Frank Roderus. LC 85-20420. (Double D Western Ser.). 192p. 1986. 12.95 o.p. (ISBN 0-385-23066-4). Doubleday.

Stimulating Poetry II. Paul E. Crowl. 1979. 4.50 o.p. (ISBN 0-682-49291-4). Exposition-Phoenix.

Stimulation in Early Infancy: Proceedings. Centre for Advanced Study in the Developmental Sciences. Ed. by Anthony Ambrose. 1970. 46.50 o.p. (ISBN 0-12-055950-1). Acad Pr.

Stinkerbelle the Nark: An Otter's Story. Marna Fyson. LC 75-37458. (Illus.). (YA) (gr. 7 up). 1976. 9.95 o.s.i. (ISBN 0-8008-7421-8). Taplinger.

Stir Up the Precipitable World. Keiko M. Gibson. 1985. 8.00 o.p. (ISBN 0-934834-69-5). White Pine.

Stirling Engines. G. T. Reader & C. Hooper. (Illus.). 400p. 1982. 65.00x o.p. (ISBN 0-419-12400-4, NO. 6577, Pub. by E & FN Spon England). Routledge Chapman & Hall.

Stirrings in Sheffield on Saturday Night. Allen Cullen. 1981. pap. 4.95 o.p. (ISBN 0-413-31340-9, NO.6475). Heinemann Ed.

Stitch. Richard Stern. 205p. 1986. pap. 5.95 o.p. (ISBN 0-87795-837-8). Morrow.

Stitch by Stitch: Needlework for Beginners. Carolyn Meyer. LC 77-117618. (gr. 4-6). 1970. 5.50 o.p. (ISBN 0-15-280350-5, HJ). HarBraceJ.

Stitch in Time: Victorian & Edwardian Needlecraft. Geoffrey Warren. LC 76-12187. (Illus.). 1976. 9.95 o.s.i. (ISBN 0-8008-7435-8). Taplinger.

Stitch with Style. Beverly Rush. LC 79-14559. (Connecting Threads Ser.). (Illus.). 98p. 1979. pap. 9.95 o.p. (ISBN 0-914842-39-0). Madrona Pubs.

Stitches & Samplers. Ondori Publishing Company Staff. (Ondori Embroidery Ser: Vol. 2). (Illus.). 104p. 1979. pap. 5.50 o.p. (ISBN 0-87040-357-5). Japan Pubns USA.

Stochastic Abundance Models: With Emphasis on Biological Communities & Species Diversity. S. Engen. 126p. 1978. 19.95x o.p. (ISBN 0-412-15240-1, NO.6102, Pub. by Chapman & Hall England). Routledge Chapman & Hall.

Stochastic Analysis. Ed. by Avner Friedman & Mark Pinsky. 1978. 59.50 o.p. (ISBN 0-12-268380-3). Acad Pr.

Stochastic Control by Functional Analysis Methods. A. Bensoussan. (Studies in Mathematics & Its Applications: Vol. 11). 410p. 1982. 79.00 o.p. (ISBN 0-444-86329-X, North-Holland). Elsevier.

Stochastic Control Theory & Stochastic Differential Systems. Ed. by M. Kohlman & W. Vogel. (Lecture Notes in Control & Information Science Ser.: Vol. 16). (Illus.). 1979. pap. 41.00 o.p. (ISBN 0-387-09480-6). Springer-Verlag.

Stochastic Differential Equations & Applications, 2 vols. Avner Friedman. (Probability & Mathematical Statistics Ser.). Vol. 1,1975. 59.00 o.p. (ISBN 0-12-268201-7); Vol. 2, 1976. 76.50 o.p. (ISBN 0-12-268202-5). Acad Pr.

Stochastic Differential Equations & Diffusion Processes. N. Ikeda & S. Watanabe. (North-Holland Mathematical Library: Vol. 24). 464p. 1981. 116.00 o.p. (ISBN 0-444-86172-6, North-Holland). Elsevier.

Stochastic Differential Systems One Filtering & Control: A Function Space Approach. A. V. Balakrishnan. LC 73-79363. (Lecture Notes in Economics & Mathematical Systems: Vol. 84). 252p. 1973. pap. 14.00 o.p. (ISBN 0-387-06303-X). Springer-Verlag.

Stochastic Economics: With Applications of Stochastic Processes, Control & Programming. Gerhard Tintner & Jati K. Sengupta. 1972. 66.00 o.p. (ISBN 0-12-691650-0). Acad Pr.

Stochastic Linear Programming. P. Kall. (Econometrics & Operations Research: Vol. 21). 120p. 1975. 26.00 o.p. (ISBN 0-387-07491-0). Springer-Verlag.

Stochastic Methods in Mechanics of Granular Bodies. J. Litwiniszyn. (CISM - International Centre for Mechanical Sciences, Courses & Lectures: Vol. 93). (Illus.). 93p. 1975. pap. 13.30 o.p. (ISBN 0-387-81310-1). Springer-Verlag.

Stochastic Methods in the Dynamics of Satellites. P. Sagirow. (CISM - International Centre for Mechanical Sciences, Courses & Lectures Ser.: Vol. 57). 132p. 1975. pap. 17.20 o.p. (ISBN 0-387-81092-7). Springer-Verlag.

Stochastic Models in Biology. Narendra Goel & Nira Richter-Dyn. 1974. 62.50 o.p. (ISBN 0-12-287460-9). Acad Pr.

Stochastic Models in Population Genetics. Ed. by Wen-Hsiung Li. (Benchmark Papers in Genetics: Vol. 7). 1977. 76.50 o.p. (ISBN 0-12-786955-7). Acad Pr.

Stochastic Population Models in Ecology & Epidemology. M. S. Bartlett. (Monographs in Applied Probability & Statistics). 1960. 10.95x o.p. (ISBN 0-416-52330-7, NO.6429). Routledge Chapman & Hall.

Stochastic Process: Proceedings. Ed. by D. Williams. (Lecture Notes in Mathematics Ser.: Vol. 851). 540p. 1981. pap. 29.00 o.p. (ISBN 0-387-10690-1). Springer-Verlag.

Stochastic Processes. Maurice Girault. (Econometrics & Operations Research Ser.: Vol. 3). (Illus.). 1966. 22.50 o.p. (ISBN 0-387-03629-6). Springer-Verlag.

Stochastic Processes. K. Ito. (Tata Institute Lectures on Mathematics Ser.). vi, 233p. 1984. pap. 7.10 o.p. (ISBN 0-387-12873-5). Springer-Verlag.

Stochastic Processes & Applications in Biology & Medicine, Pt. 2: Models. M. Iosifescu & P. Tautu. LC 73-77733. (Biomathematics, Ser.: Vol. 4). 337p. 1973. 43.00 o.p. (ISBN 0-387-06271-8). Springer-Verlag.

Stochastic Processes & Related Topics: Proceedings, Vol. 1. Ed. by M. L. Puri. 1975. 60.50 o.p. (ISBN 0-12-568001-5). Acad Pr.

Stochastic Theory of Service Systems. L. Kosten. LC 72-10124. 180p. 1973. 35.00 o.p. (ISBN 0-08-016948-1). Pergamon.

Stock Cars. Sylvia Wilkinson. LC 80-27729. (World of Racing Ser.). (Illus.). 48p. (gr. 4 up). 1981. PLB 11.93 o.p. (ISBN 0-516-04715-9); pap. 3.95 o.p. (ISBN 0-516-44715-7). Childrens.

Stock Exchange Official Yearbook 1985-1986. London Stock Exchange Staff. 1100p. 1987. 195.00x o.p. (Stockton Pr). Groves Dict Music.

Stock Exchange Official Yearbook, 1986-87. London Stock Exchange Staff. 1100p. 1987. 195.00 o.p. (ISBN 0-935859-12-8, Stockton Pr). Groves Dict Music.

Stock Exchange Official Yearbook, 1986-87. 1000p. 1987. text ed. 225.00 o.p. (ISBN 0-333-39703-7). Intl Pubns Serv.

Stock Index Futures. Ed. by Frank J. Fabozzi & Gregory Kipnis. LC 83-70863. 225p. 1984. 37.50 o.p. (ISBN 0-87094-424-X). Dow Jones-Irwin.

Stock Market. Marc Rosenblum. LC 76-84418. (Real World of Economics Ser.). (Illus.). (gr. 5-11). 1970. PLB 4.95 o.p. (ISBN 0-8225-0615-7). Lerner Pubns.

Stock Market. 4th ed. Richard J. Teweles & Edward S. Bradley. LC 82-8535. (Professional Banking & Finance Ser.). 474p. 1982. 24.95 o.p. (ISBN 0-471-08588-X). Wiley.

Stock Market & Inflation. Ed. by J. Anthony Boeckh & Richard T. Coghlan. LC 81-82913. 225p. 1982. 19.95 o.p. (ISBN 0-87094-272-7). Dow Jones-Irwin.

Stock Market Arithmetic: A Primer for New Investors. Charles Caes. LC 81-85563. 112p. 1982. pap. 6.95 o.p. (ISBN 0-89526-868-X). Regnery Gateway.

Stock Market Forecasting for Entrepreneurs. Michael Hayes. 1980. pap. 6.95 o.p. AMACOM.

Stock Market Theory of the Circulation of the Classes: How to Apply & Interpret it Properly for the Maximization of Profits. Rodolfo V. Damiani. (Illus.). 113p. 1984. 147.75 o.p. (ISBN 0-86654-270-1). Inst Econ Finan.

Stock of Whales. pap. 12.00 o.p. (ISBN 0-85238-039-9, FN19, FNB). UNIPUB.

Stock Options Manual. 2nd ed. Gary L. Gastineau. (Illus.). 1979. text ed. 32.95 o.p. (ISBN 0-07-022970-8). McGraw.

Stock Photo & Assignment. 2nd ed. Ed. by Fred W. McDarrah. 320p. 1985. pap. 29.95 o.p. (ISBN 0-913069-01-9). Photo Arts Ctr.

Stockholm Plus Ten: Promises, Promises? The Decade since the 1972 U. N. Environment Conference. 1982. 5.50 o.p. (ISBN 0-905347-30-7). C I D E.

Stockholm School & the Development of Dynamic Method. Bjorn A. Hansson. 286p. 1982. 29.50 o.p. (ISBN 0-7099-1225-0, Pub. by Croom Helm Ltd). Routledge Chapman & Hall.

Stocking Up. Organic Gardening Editors & Carol H. Stoner. (Illus.). 552p. 1985. pap. 10.95 o.p. (ISBN 0-87857-541-3). Rodale Pr Inc.

Stocking Up. rev. ed. Carol H. Stoner. LC 77-3942. 1977. 19.95 o.p. (ISBN 0-87857-167-1). Rodale Pr Inc.

Stockmarket Encyclopedia of the Fortune. Standard's & Poor's Staff. 1982. pap. text ed. 27.50 o.p. (ISBN 0-07-051886-6). McGraw.

Stocks & Shares. 2nd ed. B. J. Millard. 1980. 32.95x o.p. (ISBN 0-471-25907-1, Wiley Heyden); pap. 10.95 o.p. (ISBN 0-471-90910-6). Wiley.

Stockton International Business Reports: Egypt. InterMatrix Ltd. Staff. (Stockton International Business Reports Ser.). 100p. 1985. Looseleaf within ring binder, cancelled 250.00x o.p. (ISBN 0-943818-30-3, Stockton Pr). Groves Dict Music.

Stockton International Business Reports: Malaysia. InterMatrix Ltd. Staff. (Stockton International Business Reports Ser.). 100p. 1985. Looseleaf within ring binder, cancelled 250.00x o.p. (ISBN 0-943818-27-3, Stockton Pr). Groves Dict Music.

Stockton International Business Reports: Brazil. InterMatrix Ltd. Staff. (Stockton International Business Reports Ser.). 100p. 1985. cancelled 250.00x o.p. (ISBN 0-943818-24-9, Stockton Pr). Groves Dict Music.

Stockton International Business Reports: Indonesia. InterMatrix Ltd. Staff. (Stockton International Business Reports Ser.). 100p. 1985. Looseleaf within ring binder, cancelled 250.00x o.p. (ISBN 0-943818-22-2, Stockton Pr). Groves Dict Music.

Stockton International Business Reports: Thailand. InterMatrix Ltd. Staff. (Stockton International Business Reports Ser.). 100p. 1985. loose leaf, cancelled 250.00x o.p. (ISBN 0-943818-32-X, Stockton Pr). Groves Dict Music.

Stockton International Business Reports: India. InterMatrix Ltd. Staff. (Stockton International Business Reports Ser.). 100p. 1985. looseleaf, cancelled 250.00x o.p. (ISBN 0-943818-34-6, Stockton Pr). Groves Dict Music.

Stockton International Business Reports: Mexico. InterMatrix Ltd. Staff. (Stockton International Reports Ser.). 100p. 1985. looseleaf, cancelled 250.00x o.p. (ISBN 0-943818-35-4, Stockton Pr). Groves Dict Music.

Stockton International Business Reports: Saudi Arabia. InterMatrix Ltd. Staff. (Stockton International Business Reports Ser.). 100p. 1985. cancelled 250.00x o.p. (ISBN 0-943818-26-5, Stockton Pr). Groves Dict Music.

Stockton International Business Reports: South Korea. InterMatrix Ltd. Staff. (Stockton International Business Reports Ser.). 100p. 1985. Looseleaf within ring binder, cancelled 250.00x o.p. (ISBN 0-943818-23-0, Stockton Pr). Groves Dict Music.

Stoics. F. H. Sandbach. Ed. by M. I. Finley. (Ancient Culture & Society Ser). 1975. 7.95x o.p. (ISBN 0-393-04411-4). Norton.

Stole Patterns. Jeff Wedge. 90p. 1985. pap. 8.95 o.p. (ISBN 0-8192-1373-X). Morehouse Pub.

Stolen Jew. Jay Neugeboren. 336p. 1981. 14.95 o.p. (ISBN 0-03-056223-6). H Holt & Co.

Stolen Legacy. George G. James. 1954. (ISBN 0-8022-0790-1). Philos Lib.

Stolen Moments: Conversations with Contemporary Musicians. Tom Schnabel. (Illus.). 220p. 19.95 o.s.i. (ISBN 0-918226-17-1); pap. 13.95 o.s.i. (ISBN 0-918226-22-8). Acrobat.

Stolen Paintings. Wolfgang Ecke. (Illus.). (gr. 5-9). 1981. 9.95 o.s.i. (ISBN 0-13-846865-6). P-H.

Stolen Past. John Knowles. LC 82-15472. 211p. 1983. 14.95 o.p. (ISBN 0-03-062209-3). H Holt & Co.

Stolen Spring. Hans Scherfig. Tr. by Jack Brondum from Danish. (Illus.). 160p. 1982. pap. 8.00 o.p. Fjord Pr.

Stoletov Dossier. Vil Lipatov. Tr. by Alex Miller. 443p. 1983. 12.95 o.p. (ISBN 0-8285-2667-2, Pub. by Raduga Pubs USSR). Imported Pubns.

Stone Age Archaeology of Southern Africa. C. Garth Sampson. 1974. 39.95 o.p. (ISBN 0-12-785759-1). Acad Pr.

Stone & the Violets. Milovan Djilas. LC 76-174507. 1972. 6.95 o.s.i. (ISBN 0-15-185100-X). HarBraceJ.

Stone Arrow. Richard Herley. LC 84-22705. 209p. 1985. 12.95 o.p. (ISBN 0-688-02920-5). Morrow.

Stone Collection: The Origins, Migrations & Growth of an Illustrious Family. Robert H. Stone. (Illus.). 272p. 1981. 14.50 o.p. (ISBN 0-682-49592-1). Exposition-Phoenix.

Stone Five Eighty-Eight. Gerald A. Browne. 1985. 17.95 o.p. (ISBN 0-87795-539-5, Arbor Hse). Morrow.

Stone Five Eighty-Eight. Gerald A. Browne. (Large Print Bks.). 688p. 1986. lib. bdg. 18.95 o.p. (ISBN 0-8161-4139-8, Large Print Bks); pap. 10.95 o.p. (ISBN 0-8161-4140-1). G K Hall.

Stone God Awakens. Philip Jose Farmer. 192p. 1975. pap. 2.25 o.p. (ISBN 0-441-78654-5). Ace Bks.

Stone of Destiny. Robert De Maria. 384p. 1985. pap. 3.95 o.s.i. (ISBN 0-345-28625-1). Ballantine.

Stone, Properties, Durability in Man's Environment. 2nd & rev. ed. E. M. Winkler. LC 72-8059. (Applied Mineralogy Ser.: Vol. 4). (Illus.). 230p. 1975. 53.70 o.p. (ISBN 0-387-81313-6). Springer-Verlag.

Stone Soup. Ann McGovern. (Illus.). (gr. 2-3). 1971. pap. 1.95 o.p. (ISBN 0-590-33818-8); pap. 3.95 o.p. bk. & record (ISBN 0-590-04393-5). Scholastic Inc.

Stone Villages of Britain. Geoffrey Wright. (Illus.). 224p. 1985. 39.95 o.p. (ISBN 0-7153-8312-4). David & Charles.

Stone Virgin. Barry Unsworth. LC 85-24897. 309p. 1986. 17.45 o.s.i. (ISBN 0-395-35412-9). HM.

Stone Walls & Sugar Maples: An Ecology for Northeasterners. Marjorie Holland & John Burk. (Illus.). 192p. 1979. pap. 5.95 o.p. (ISBN 0-910146-22-5). AMC Books.

Stoneflies. Carl Richards et al. LC 80-18317. (Illus.). 192p. 1980. 27.95 o.p. (ISBN 0-8329-3273-6). Lyons & Burford.

Stoneflies. Doug Swisher et al. (Illus.). 192p. 1988. 27.95 o.p. Lyons & Burford.

Stones & the Scriptures. Edwin Yamauchi. 1981. pap. 5.95 o.p. (ISBN 0-8010-9916-1). Baker Bk.

Stones: Eighteenth Century Scottish Gravestones. Betty Willsher & Doreen Hunter. LC 78-62268. (Illus.). 128p. 1979. 14.95 o.p. (ISBN 0-8008-7447-1); pap. 7.95 o.s.i. (ISBN 0-8008-7017-4). Taplinger.

Stones of Bau. Nicholas Wollaston. 228p. 1988. 19.95 o.p. (ISBN 0-241-12041-1, Pub. by Hamish Hamilton). David & Charles.

Stones of Green Knowe. L. M. Boston. LC 75-44143. (Illus.). 128p. (gr. 5-9). 1976. 7.95 o.p. (ISBN 0-689-50058-0, Atheneum). Macmillan.

Stones of the Abbey. Fernand Pavillon. 1976. pap. 1.95 o.p. (ISBN 0-380-00737-1, 30106, Bard). Avon.

Stones of the Abbey. Fernand Pouillon. Tr. by Edward Gillott. LC 70-95858. (Helen & Kurt Wolff Bk.). 1970. 5.95 o.p. (ISBN 0-15-185075-5). HarBraceJ.

Stonor Eagles. William Horwood. 704p. 1982. 15.95 o.p. (ISBN 0-531-09873-7). Watts.

Stony the Road: Essays from the Hampton Institute Archives. Ed. by Keith L. Schall. LC 76-56224. (Illus.). 183p. 1977. 14.95x o.p. (ISBN 0-8139-0720-9). U Pr of Va.

Stop Insomnia: How to Sleep Well Through Bed Exercises. Richard R. Fuller. (Illus.). 1980. 5.00 o.p. (ISBN 0-682-49582-4). Exposition-Phoenix.

Stop Legal Stealing. John C. Lincoln. 1972. pap. 0.75 o.p. (ISBN 0-686-17296-5). Lincoln Inst Land.

Stop Making Yourself Sick. Harold Adolph & David L. Bourne. 132p. 1986. pap. 5.50 o.p. (ISBN 0-89693-325-3). Victor Bks.

Stop Me Before I Plan Again. Richard Hedman. LC 77-73251. (Illus.). 112p. (Orig.). 1977. pap. 9.95 o.s.i. (ISBN 0-918286-10-7). Planners Pr.

Stop Me Before I Plan Again. Richard Hedman. 112p. 1977. pap. 9.95 o.p. (ISBN 0-318-13083-1). Am Plan Assn.

Stop Nuclear War! A Handbook. David P. Barash & Judith E. Lipton. LC 82-48162. 396p. 1982. pap. 7.95 o.p. (ISBN 0-394-62433-5, E835, Ever). Grove.

Stop Procrastinating--Do It! James R. Sherman. LC 80-82893. (Orig.). 1981. pap. 2.25 o.p. (ISBN 0-935538-01-1). Pathway Bks.

Stop Smoking Activity Book. Edward Boggs. LC 84-28465. (Illus.). 96p. (Orig.). 1985. pap. 7.95 o.p. (ISBN 0-87879-464-6, Pub. by Arena Pr). Acad Therapy.

Stop Smoking Diet. Jane Ogle. LC 81-3181. 168p. 1983. pap. 5.95 o.p. (ISBN 0-87131-410-X). M Evans.

Stop Stress & Aging Now: The Methuselah Manual. David C. Gardner & Grace J. Beatty. LC 84-72980. (Illus.). 353p. (Orig.). 1985. pap. 12.95 o.p. (ISBN 0-9613999-9-6). ATRA.

Stopout! Working Ways to Learn. Joyce S. Mitchell. (YA) 1979. pap. 2.95 o.p. (ISBN 0-380-44727-4, 44727). Avon.

Stopping & Range of Ions in Matter, Volumes 1-4. Ed. by J. F. Ziegler. 1985. 140.00 o.s.i. (ISBN 0-08-022053-3). Pergamon.

Stopping Out: A Guide to Leaving College & Getting Back In. Judi R. Kesselman. LC 76-1906. 228p. 1976. 8.95 o.p. (ISBN 0-87131-199-2); pap. 3.95 o.p. (ISBN 0-87131-209-3). M Evans.

Storage & Piped Distribution of Heating Oil Safety Code, Vol. 10. Institute of Petroleum Staff. 1971. 16.75 o.p. (ISBN 0-444-39962-3). Elsevier.

Storage of Energy. W. Hassenzahl. 1983. 92.95 o.p. (ISBN 0-87933-093-7). Van Nos Reinhold.

Storage, Water Heater, Data Communication, Education see Sharing the Sun.

Store Fronts & Facades. Ed. by Martin M. Pegler. (Illus.). 176p. 1986. 39.95 o.p. (ISBN 0-934590-14-1). R Silver.

Stored Data Description & Data Translation: A Model & Language. R. W. Taylor. 1977. pap. 25.00 o.p. (ISBN 0-08-021624-2). Pergamon.

Storehouses of the Snow. Woodard & Bischoff. 1980. pap. 1.95 o.p. (ISBN 0-8439-0746-0, Pub. by Leisure Bks CT). Dorchester Pub Co.

Stores of the World Directory. 10th, enl. ed. 1978-79. 85.00 o.s.i. (ISBN 0-7079-6910-7). E J Brill USA.

Stores of the World Directory, 1984-1985, 2 vols. 13th ed. 1984. 175.00 o.p. (ISBN 0-7079-6932-8). E J Brill USA.

Stores, Shops Hypermarkets Retail Directory of the U. K., 1986. 40th ed. 1986. 180.00x o.p. (ISBN 0-7079-6936-0). Intl Pubns Serv.

Stories. M. Garshin. 383p. 1982. pap. 4.00 o.p. (ISBN 0-8285-2486-6, Pub. by Progress Pubs USSR). Imported Pubns.

Stories About Birds & Bird Watchers: From Bird Watcher's Digest. Ed. by Mary B. Bowers. LC 80-7925. (Illus.). 192p. 1981. 12.95 o.p. (ISBN 0-689-11093-6, Atheneum). Macmillan.

Stories about Lenin & the Revolution. Z. Vosresentskaya et al. 175p. 1982. 5.95 o.p. (ISBN 0-8285-2348-7, Pub. by Progress Pubs USSR). Imported Pubns.

Stories about Magnitka. S. Alexeyev. Tr. by Natalia Belskaya. 102p. 1983. pap. 3.95 o.p. (ISBN 0-8285-2771-7, Pub. by Raduga Pubs USSR). Imported Pubns.

Stories about Workers. Benjamin Piltch. (Illus.). 1983. pap. 3.75 o.p. (ISBN 0-88323-197-2, 208). Pendergrass Pub.

Stories & Parables of the Hafetz Hayyim. David Zaretsky & Charles Wengrov. Orig. Title: Hayyim. 1976. 9.95 o.p. (ISBN 0-87306-132-2). Feldheim.

Stories & Texts for Nothing. Samuel Beckett. 1967. pap. 6.95 o.p. (ISBN 0-394-17268-X, E466, Ever). Grove.

Stories by Edgar Allan Poe see Graded Readers for Students of English As a Second Language.

Stories by Edith Wharton see Graded Readers for Students of English As a Second Language.

Stories by Jack London see Graded Readers for Students of English As a Second Language.

Stories by O. Henry see Graded Readers for Students of English As a Second Language.

Stories by Washington Irving see Graded Readers for Students of English As a Second Language.

Stories California Indians Told. Anne B. Fisher. LC 57-8065. (Illus.). (gr. 3-7). 1957. 5.95 o.p. (ISBN 0-395-27723-X, Pub. by Parnassus). HM.

Stories California Indians Told. Anne B. Fisher. 1957. 6.95 o.p. (ISBN 0-395-27664-0). HM.

Stories for a Prince. (Illus.). 48p. (ps-1). 1985. 12.95 o.p. (ISBN 0-241-11052-1, Pub. by Hamish Hamilton England). David & Charles.

Stories for Around the Campfire. Ray Harriot. (Illus.). 138p. (Orig.). (gr. 5-10). 1986. pap. 4.95 o.p. (ISBN 0-9617653-0-5). Campfire Pub.

Stories for Special Days: Messages for Children on the Lesser Festivals. Michael L. Sherer. LC 78-51342. 1978. pap. 3.95 o.p. (ISBN 0-8066-1667-9, 10-6020, Augsburg). Augsburg Fortress.

Stories for the Children's Hour. rev. ed. Kenneth N. Taylor. LC 68-26408. (Illus.). (gr. k-6). 5.95 o.p. (ISBN 0-8024-8326-7); pap. 3.95 o.p. (ISBN 0-8024-0063-9). Moody.

Stories for the Sophisticated. Lionel A. Canaan. 1981. 7.95 o.p. (ISBN 0-533-04871-0). Vantage.

Stories from a Snowy Meadow. Carla Stevens. LC 76-3542. 48p. (gr. 2-5). 1979. 6.95 o.p. (ISBN 0-395-28883-5, Clarion). HM.

Stories from Ancient Canaan. Ed. by Michael D. Coogan. LC 77-20022. 120p. 1978. pap. 7.95 o.s.i. (ISBN 0-664-24184-0, Westminster). Westminster John Knox.

Stories from Carleton. William Carleton. 1973. Repr. of 1889 ed. text ed. 15.00x o.p. (ISBN 0-87696-040-9). Humanities.

Stories from Old-Fashioned Children's Books, Brought Together & Introduced to the Reader. Andrew W. Tuer. LC 68-31438. 456p. 1968. Repr. of 1899 ed. 34.00x o.p. (ISBN 0-8103-3489-5). Gale.

Stories from the Bible. Walter De la Mare. (Illus.). 418p. (gr. 3). 1985. pap. 6.95 o.p. (ISBN 0-571-11086-X). Faber & Faber.

Stories from the Twilight Zone. Rod Serling. LC 86-47578. 432p. (Orig.). 1986. pap. 9.95 o.p. (ISBN 0-553-34329-7, Spectra). Bantam.

Stories from Three Islands: Haiti, Jamaica, Puerto Rico. Ruth Montgomery & Edna Mc Guire. (gr. 1-7). 1977. 3.25 o.p. (ISBN 0-377-00064-7). Friendship Pr.

Stories in the Sky. Paul Thigpen. LC 85-29109. 160p. (gr. 4-6). 1986. pap. 7.95 o.p. (ISBN 0-89191-361-0). Cook.

Stories Jesus Told. Norman J. Bull. LC 76-75402. (Illus.). (gr. 3-7). 1969. 3.50 o.p. (ISBN 0-8066-0924-9, 10-6031, Augsburg). Augsburg Fortress.

Stories Jesus Told. Heather Dyer. Incl. The Good Samaritan (ISBN 0-89191-286-X); The Good Shepherd (ISBN 0-89191-283-5); The Great Feast (ISBN 0-89191-284-3); The House Built on Sand (ISBN 0-89191-288-6); The Prodigal Son (ISBN 0-89191-285-1); The Rich Man (ISBN 0-89191-287-8). (Illus.). (gr. 1-4). 1980. Repr. 2.50 ea. o.p. Cook.

Stories Jesus Told. Patricia Mahany. (Standard's Coloring Bks.). (Illus.). 16p. (Orig.). (gr. k-3). 1982. pap. 0.89 o.p. (ISBN 0-87239-601-0, 2390). Standard Pub.

Stories Made of Bible Stories. Abraham Cronbach. 1961. 17.95x o.p. (ISBN 0-8084-0386-9). New Coll U Pr.

Stories Never Heard Before. Ruth N. Edwards. LC 85-90144. 62p. 1985. 5.95 o.p. (ISBN 0-533-06634-4). Vantage.

Stories of an Expatriate. Otakar Machotka. 1985. 8.95 o.p. (ISBN 0-533-06479-1). Vantage.

Stories of Light. Edmund Wilson. 1952. 9.95 o.p. (ISBN 0-374-51045-8). FS&G.

Stories of Men & Rats. Sam Spiller. 1982. 10.00 o.p. (ISBN 0-682-49882-3). Exposition-Phoenix.

Stories of Old Lahaina. Inez Ashdown. soft bdg. 1.50 o.p. (ISBN 0-930492-12-9). Hawaiian Serv.

Stories of Our Favorite Hymns. Christopher Idle. (Illus.). 80p. 1980. 14.95 o.p. (ISBN 0-8028-3535-X). Eerdmans.

Stories of the American West see Graded Readers for Students of English As a Second Language.

Stories of the Greeks. Rex Warner. 480p. 1978. 15.00 o.p. (ISBN 0-374-27056-2); pap. 9.95 o.p. (ISBN 0-374-50728-7). FS&G.

Stories of the Trees. S. L. Dyson. LC 78-175735. (Illus.). 274p. 1974. Repr. of 1890 ed. 40.00x o.p. (ISBN 0-8103-3033-4). Gale.

Stories of Wales: Told for Children. Elisabeth Sheppard-Jones. (Illus.). (gr. 3-6). 1978. pap. 5.95 o.p. (ISBN 0-902375-41-5). Academy Chi Pubs.

Stories the Animals Tell Me. Beatrice Lydecker. LC 79-1777. (Illus.). 1979. 7.95i o.p. (ISBN 0-06-250550-5). HarpR.

Stories to Dramatize. Winifred Ward. 1952. 12.50 o.p. (ISBN 0-87602-011-2). Anchorage.

Stories to Tell to Children: A Selected List. Ed. by Laura E. Cathon et al. LC 73-13317. (Illus.). 168p. 1974. pap. 5.95 o.p. (ISBN 0-8229-5246-7). U of Pittsburgh Pr.

Stork Is Dead. Charlie W. Shedd. LC 68-36991. 1982. pap. 4.95 o.p. (ISBN 0-8499-2956-3, 91014, Key Word Bks). Word Bks.

Stork Spills the Beans. Richard Hefter. LC 76-44020. (Sweet Pickles Ser.). (Illus.). (gr. k-2). 1977. 2.95 o.p. (ISBN 0-03-018076-7). H Holt & Co.

Stork Tracks. Paul Wadden. (Haiku Ser.: No. 14). 1983. pap. 2.50 o.p. (ISBN 1-55780-084-7). Juniper Pr WI.

Storm. A. B. Whipple. (Planet Earth Ser.). (Illus.). 176p. (YA) (gr. 7 up). 1982. 18.60 o.p. (ISBN 0-8094-4314-7); lib. bdg. 22.60 o.p. Time-Life.

Storm & Other Poems. William P. Root. (Orig.). 1969. pap. 2.45 o.p. (ISBN 0-689-10234-8, Atheneum). Macmillan.

Storm from the West. Barbara Willard. LC 64-17089. (Illus.). 189p. (gr. 7 up). 1964. 5.95 o.p. (ISBN 0-15-280480-3, HJ). HarBraceJ.

Storm of Passion. Virginia Brown. (Avon Romance Ser.). 352p. 1986. pap. 3.95 o.p. (ISBN 0-380-89933-7). Avon.

Storm over Paris. Blanche Lempel. 1954. (ISBN 0-8022-0958-0). Philos Lib.

Storm Petrels. Gordon Brook-Shepherd. (Ballantine Espionage-Intelligence Library: No. 11). 224p. 1981. pap. 2.75 o.s.i. (ISBN 0-345-30164-1). Ballantine.

Storm Petrels: The Flight of the First Soviet Defectors. Gordon Brook-Shepherd. LC 77-84386. 288p. 1978. 8.95 o.p. (ISBN 0-15-185223-5). HarBraceJ.

Storm Treasure. Robert M. Packie. LC 81-66266. (Illus.). 160p. (Orig.). (gr. 6). 1981. 8.95 o.p. (ISBN 0-89272-082-4). Down East.

Stormqueen! Marion Zimmer Bradley. 1979. lib. bdg. 11.95 o.p. (ISBN 0-8398-2504-8, Gregg). G K Hall.

Storms. Amy H. Scott. 48p. 1987. 6.95 o.p. (ISBN 0-8062-2794-X). Carlton.

Storms Brewed in Other Men's Worlds: The Confrontation of Indians, Spanish, & French in the Southwest, 1540-1795. Elizabeth A. H. John. LC 75-9996. (Illus.). 840p. 1975. 24.50 o.p. (ISBN 0-89096-000-3). Tex A&M Univ Pr.

Stormswift. Madeleine Brent. LC 84-8128. 336p. 1985. 15.95 o.p. (ISBN 0-385-19047-6). Doubleday.

Story. Gail E. Haley. LC 69-18961. (Illus.). (gr. k-3). 1970. pap. 4.95 o.p. (Aladdin). Macmillan.

Story & Promise: A Brief Theology of the Gospel About Jesus. Robert W. Jenson. LC 72-87060. 208p. 1973. pap. 3.95 o.p. (ISBN 0-8006-0143-2, Fortress). Augsburg Fortress.

Story & Structure. 5th ed. Laurence Perrine. 549p. 1978. pap. text ed. 10.95 o.p. (ISBN 0-15-583786-9, HC). HarBraceJ.

Story & Structure. 6th. ed. Laurence Perrine & Thomas R. Arp. 527p. 1983. pap. text ed. 12.75 o.p. (ISBN 0-15-583788-5, HC). HarBraceJ.

Story & Structure. 4th ed. Ed. by Laurence Perrine. 1970. pap. text ed. 6.95 o.p. (ISBN 0-15-583782-6, HC). HarBraceJ.

Story Key to Geographic Names. Oscar Dedrich Von Engeln & Jane M. Urquhart. LC 74-13855. 298p. 1976. Repr. of 1924 ed. 43.00x o.p. (ISBN 0-8103-4062-3). Gale.

Story, Myth & Celebration in Old French Narrative Poetry 1050-1200. Karl D. Uitti. LC 72-4048. 272p. 1973. 34.00x o.p. (ISBN 0-691-06242-0). Princeton U Pr.

Story of a Country Medical College: A History of the Clinical School of Medicine & the Vermont Medical College, Woodstock, Vermont, 1827-1856. Frederick C. Waite. (Illus.). 213p. 1945. 2.00x o.p. (ISBN 0-934720-12-6). VT Hist Soc.

Story of a Fierce Bad Rabbit. Beatrix Potter. (ps-2). 1906. 4.95 o.p. (ISBN 0-7232-0611-2). Warne.

Story of a Great Pioneer in Black Education: Bennie Carl Elmore, 1909-1973. Inez K. Elmore. 1975. 5.00 o.p. (ISBN 0-682-48194-7). Exposition-Phoenix.

Story of Adele H. Francois Truffaut. LC 75-42798. (Illus.). 1975. pap. 2.45 o.p. (ISBN 0-394-17908-0, B395, BC). Grove.

Story of America. rev. ed. Hendrik W. Van Loon. 1942. 7.95 o.p. (ISBN 0-87140-828-7). Liveright.

Story of Archaeology. A. Allen. (Illus.). 256p. 1958. (ISBN 0-8022-0019-2). Philos Lib.

Story of Astrology. Manly P. Hall. 1957. (ISBN 0-8022-0662-X). Philos Lib.

Story of Atlantis & the Lost Lemuria. Scott Elliott. 9.75 o.p. (ISBN 0-8356-5509-1). Theos Pub Hse.

Story of Australia. Meredith Hooper. LC 76-8056. (Illus.). (ps-5). 1976. 7.50 o.s.i. (ISBN 0-8008-7452-8). Taplinger.

Story of Ballet. Joan Lawson. LC 76-17368. (Illus.). 1979. pap. 8.95 o.s.i. (ISBN 0-8008-7455-2). Taplinger.

Story of Befana: An Italian Christmas Tale. Ilse Plume. LC 81811. (Illus.). 32p. 1987. 12.95 o.p. Godine.

Story of Big Creek. David H. Redinger. Ed. by Bill Myers. (Illus.). 252p. 1987. 32.95 o.p. (ISBN 0-87046-070-6, Pub. by Trans-Anglo). Interurban.

Story of Biochemistry. Alice E. Corrall & Justine Glass. LC 62-20871. (Illus.). 232p. 1964. (ISBN 0-8022-0596-8). Philos Lib.

Story of Blood. Kenneth Walker. (Illus.). 213p. 1963. (ISBN 0-8022-1795-8). Philos Lib.

Story of Burnt Njal. Tr. by George W. Dasent. 1971. Repr. of 1911 ed. 13.95x o.p. (ISBN 0-460-00558-8, Evman); pap. 3.50x o.p. (ISBN 0-460-01558-3, Evman). Biblio Dist.

Story of Chanukah for Children. (gr. k-5). 2.95 o.p. (ISBN 0-8249-8020-4). Ideals.

Story of Chemistry. Georg Lockemann. pap. 1.45 o.p. (ISBN 0-685-19414-0, 61, Pub. by Citadel Pr). Carol Pub Group.

Story of Chemistry. George Lockerman. (Illus.). 160p. 1960. (ISBN 0-8022-0986-6). Philos Lib.

Story of Christmas. Date not set. incl. cassette 9.95 o.p. Ideals.

Story of Computers. Roger Piper. LC 64-20226. (Illus.). (gr. 7 up). 1964. 4.95 o.p. (ISBN 0-15-280847-7, HJ). HarBraceJ.

Story of Dance Music. Paul Nettl. (ISBN 0-8022-1197-6). Philos Lib.

Story of Dissection. Jack Kevorkian. 1960. (ISBN 0-8022-0848-7). Philos Lib.

Story of Dragons & Other Monsters. Thomas G. Aylesworth. LC 79-21550. (Illus.). 96p. (gr. 5-8). 1980. text ed. 9.95 o.p. (ISBN 0-07-002646-7). McGraw.

Story of Easter for Children. 1988. pap. 3.95 o.p. (ISBN 0-8249-8183-9). Ideals.

Story of Easter for Children. Beverly Wiersum. Ed. by James A. Kuse. (Illus.). (ps-3). 1979. pap. 2.95 o.p. (ISBN 0-89542-452-5). Ideals.

Story of Ellen: How Love Transforms a Troubled Child. Elizabeth D. Satre. LC 78-66952. 1979. pap. 3.95 o.p. (ISBN 0-8066-1691-1, 10-6045, Augsburg). Augsburg Fortress.

Story of English Literature. R. F. Patterson. (ISBN 0-8022-1289-1). Philos Lib.

Story of Felicity. Anna Aragno. (Illus.). 64p. (gr. 2 up). 1980. 5.00 o.p. (ISBN 0-682-49633-2). Exposition-Phoenix.

Story of How the Easter Bunny Got His Wife. William E. Avant. 30p. (gr. k-4). 1987. 6.75 o.p. (ISBN 0-8062-2842-3). Carlton.

Story of Human Emotions. George M. Lott. 1958. (ISBN 0-8022-0997-1). Philos Lib.

Story of Idaho. rev. ed. Virgil Young. LC 84-50204. (Illus.). 270p. 1984. text ed. 16.95 o.p. (ISBN 0-89301-096-0). U of Idaho Pr.

Story of Job. Adapted by & illus. by Beverley Brodsky. LC 85-24303. (Illus.). 40p. (ps-4). 14.95 o.p. (ISBN 0-8076-1142-5). Braziller.

Story of John Rice Irwin's Museum of Appalachia. John R. Irwin. (Illus.). 96p. 1987. pap. 4.95 o.p. (ISBN 0-88740-102-3). Schiffer.

Story of Judaism. rev. ed. Bernard J. Bamberger. 1970. 9.95 o.p. (ISBN 0-8074-0193-5, 959291). UAHC.

Story of Mankind. rev. ed. Hendrik W. Van Loon. LC 72-167290. 642p. (gr. 7 up). 1972. 16.95 o.p. (ISBN 0-87140-547-4). Liveright.

Story of Maryland Politics: An Outline History of the Big Political Battles of the State from 1864 to 1910, with Sketches & Incidents of the Men & Measures That Figured As Factors, & the Names of Most of Those Who Held Office in That Period. Frank R. Kent. LC 68-31444. xiv, 454p. Repr. of 1911 ed. 40.00x o.p. (ISBN 0-8103-5035-1). Gale.

Story of Minstrelsy. Edmondstoune Duncan. LC 69-16802. (Music Story Ser). 358p. 1968. Repr. of 1907 ed. 40.00x o.p. (ISBN 0-8103-4240-5). Gale.

Story of Miss Moppet. Beatrix Potter. (Illus.). (ps-2). 1906. 4.95 o.p. (ISBN 0-7232-0612-0). Warne.

Story of Mr. & Mrs. Vinegar. Stephen Gammell. LC 81-12347. (Illus.). 32p. (ps-3). 1982. 10.25 o.p. (ISBN 0-688-00887-9); PLB 10.88 o.p. (ISBN 0-688-00889-5). Lothrop.

Story of Motown. Peter Benjaminson. LC 79-2332. (Illus.). 1979. pap. 8.95 o.p. (ISBN 0-394-17554-9, E745, Ever). Grove.

Story of Music. Evelyn Porter. (ISBN 0-8022-2003-7). Philos Lib.

Story of Musical Organizations. Robert W. Surplus. LC 62-20805. (Musical Books for Young People). (Illus.). (gr. 5-11). 1963. PLB 4.95 o.p. (ISBN 0-8225-0060-4). Lerner Pubns.

Story of My Life. Date not set. (ISBN 0-8052-3814-X); pap. (ISBN 0-8052-0721-X). Random.

Story of Nigeria. 4th ed. Michael Crowder. 432p. 1978. pap. 9.95 o.p. (ISBN 0-571-04947-8). Faber & Faber.

Story of Notation. C. Abdy Williams. LC 69-16797. 280p. 1968. Repr. of 1903 ed. 40.00x o.p. (ISBN 0-8103-3557-3). Gale.

Story of O: Part Two, Return to the Chateau. Pauline Reage. Tr. by Sabine D'Estree from Fr. LC 77-155130. Orig. Title: Retour a Roissy. 158p. 1980. pap. 3.95 o.s.i. (ISBN 0-394-17658-8, B364, BC). Grove.

Story of Old Abe. Malcolm Rosholt & Margaret Rosholt. LC 87-90548. (Illus.). 104p. (gr. 4 up). 1987. 15.95 o.p. (ISBN 0-317-64459-9). Rosholt Hse.

Story of Opera. Ernest M. Lee. LC 69-16803. (Music Story Ser). 292p. 1968. Repr. of 1909 ed. 30.00x o.p. (ISBN 0-8103-3359-7). Gale.

Story of Oregon, Illinois: Eighteen Eighty-Six to Nineteen Eighty-Six. Ed. by Charles Mongan, Sr. (Illus.). 300p. (YA) 1988. 25.00 o.s.i. (ISBN 0-9617730-0-6). Oregon Sesqui Celeb.

Story of Organ Music. C. Abdy Williams. LC 69-16789. 314p. 1968. Repr. of 1905 ed. 35.00x o.p. (ISBN 0-8103-3558-1). Gale.

Story of Paul. James Kallas. LC 66-19206. (Orig.). 1966. pap. 7.95 o.p. (ISBN 0-8066-0608-8, 10-6055, Augsburg). Augsburg Fortress.

Story of Philosophy. rev. ed. Will Durant. 1961. 14.95 o.p. (ISBN 0-671-69500-2). S&S.

Story of Pop see Heinemann Guided Readers.

Story of Poppyseed. Bargi Sargent. (Illus.). 48p. (gr. k-2). 6.95 o.p. (ISBN 0-448-18966-6, G&D). Putnam Pub Group.

Story of Pygmalion. Pamela Espeland. LC 80-15792. (Myths for Modern Children Ser.). (Illus.). 32p. (gr. 1-4). 1981. PLB 7.95 o.p. (ISBN 0-87614-127-0, AACR1). Carolrhoda Bks.

Story of Quakerism. rev. ed. Elfrida Vipont. LC 77-71638. (Illus.). 1977. pap. 9.95 o.s.i. (ISBN 0-913408-31-X). Friends United.

Story of Santa Claus, Junior. James V. Cagle. (Illus.). 1979. 5.00 o.p. (ISBN 0-682-49464-X). Exposition-Phoenix.

Story of Seven Maidens: Classics of the Victorian Imagination. 192p. 1987. pap. 7.95 o.p. (ISBN 0-394-62299-5, Ever). Grove.

Story of Steel. Brenda Thompson & Rosemary Giesen. LC 76-22464. (Lerner First Fact Bks.). (Illus.). (gr. k-3). 1977. PLB 4.95 o.p. (ISBN 0-8225-1362-5). Lerner Pubns.
Story of Story Magazine. Martha Foley. 1980. 12.95 o.p. (ISBN 0-393-01348-0). Norton.
Story of Symphony. Ernest M. Lee. LC 69-16804. (Illus.). 260p. 1968. Repr. of 1916 ed. 38.00x o.p. (ISBN 0-8103-3568-9). Gale.
Story of the American Lutheran Church. Alvin N. Rogness. LC 80-65555. 96p. (Orig.). 1980. pap. 4.95 o.p. (ISBN 0-8066-1800-0, 10-6038, Augsburg). Augsburg Fortress.
Story of the Amulet. E. Nesbit. 288p. (gr. 4 up). 1959. pap. 2.95 o.p. (ISBN 0-14-030130-5, Puffin). Penguin.
Story of the Bicycle. John Woodforde. (Illus.). 1977. pap. 7.95 o.p. (ISBN 0-7100-8644-X). Routledge Chapman & Hall.
Story of the Church. L. C. Rudolph. (Illus., Orig.). (gr. 5-7). 1967. pap. 3.95 o.p. (ISBN 0-8042-9441-0, John Knox). Westminster John Knox.
Story of the Davis Cup. Alan Trengove. (Illus.). 577p. 1986. 24.95 o.s.i. (ISBN 0-09-159860-5, Pub. by Century Hutchinson). David & Charles.
Story of the Dictionary. Robert Kraske. LC 74-23177. (Illus.). (gr. 5 up). 1975. 6.50 o.p. (ISBN 0-15-280850-7, HJ). HarBraceJ.
Story of the Four World Centres: For Girls & Leaders. rev. ed. World Association of Girl Guides & Girl Scouts Staff. (Illus.). 51p. (gr. 4-8). 1982. pap. 2.25 o.p. (ISBN 0-900827-27-0, 23-123). Girl Scouts USA.
Story of the Gypsies. Konrad Bercovici. LC 78-164051. (Illus.). 310p. 1975. Repr. of 1928 ed. 37.00x o.p. (ISBN 0-8103-4042-9). Gale.
Story of the Jew. rev. ed. Harry Gersh et al. LC 64-22514. (Illus.). (gr. 8-11). 1965. 5.95x o.p. (ISBN 0-87441-019-3). Behrman.
Story of the Jubilee Singers, with Their Songs. rev. ed. J. B. Marsh. LC 79-78583. (Illus.). 1969. Repr. of 1881 ed. lib. bdg. 22.50x o.p. (ISBN 0-8371-1424-1, MAJ&, Pub. by Negro U Pr). Greenwood.
Story of the Law. Rene A. Wormser. 1972. pap. 6.95 o.p. (ISBN 0-671-21333-4, Touchstone Bks). S&S.
Story of the Mary Rose. Ernie Bradford. (Illus.). 1982. 24.95 o.p. (ISBN 0-393-01620-X). Norton.
Story of the Mass. 1.00 o.p. (NCR 457). Paulist Pr.
Story of the Mine. Charles H. Shinn. LC 79-23102. (Vintage Nevada Ser.). Orig. Title: Story of the Mine. (Illus.). xiv, 277p. 1980. pap. 6.50 o.p. (ISBN 0-87417-059-1). U of Nev Pr.
Story of the Mine see Story of the Mine.
Story of the Motor Car. David Carey. (Illus.). (gr. 4 up). cancelled o.s.i. (ISBN 0-7214-0135-X). Merry Thoughts.
Story of the Negro: The Rise of the Race from Slavery, 2 vols. Booker T. Washington. LC 69-16564. (Illus.). 1970. Repr. of 1909 ed. Vol. 1. lib. bdg. 15.00 o.p. (ISBN 0-8371-1172-2, WSO&, Pub. by Negro U Pr); Vol. 2. lib. bdg. 15.00 o.p. (ISBN 0-8371-1173-0, WSP&, Pub. by Negro U Pr). Greenwood.
Story of the Old Testament Simply Told. Florence E. Waggener. (Illus.). 1979. 5.50 o.p. (ISBN 0-682-49375-9). Exposition-Phoenix.
Story of the Organ. C. F. Williams. LC 78-90250. (Illus.). 342p. 1972. Repr. of 1903 ed. 40.00x o.p. (ISBN 0-8103-3067-9). Gale.
Story of the Other Wise Man. Henry van Dyke. LC 83-47885. (Illus.). 96p. 1983. 8.61 o.p. (ISBN 0-06-068855-6). HarpR.
Story of the Pennsylvania Germans: Embracing an Account of Their Origin, Their History, Their Dialect. William Beidelman. LC 70-81759. 262p. 1969. Repr. of 1898 ed. 43.00x o.p. (ISBN 0-8103-3571-9). Gale.
Story of the Pilgrims & Their Indian Friends: A Thanksgiving Story for Children. 4th ed. Eunice Cauper. (Illus.). 16p. (gr. k). 1988. pap. 4.95 o.p. (ISBN 0-8283-1899-9). Branden Pub Co.
Story of the Plant Kingdom. 3rd ed. rev ed. Merle C. Coulter. LC 64-10093. (Illus.). 1964. lib. bdg. 17.50x o.s.i. (ISBN 0-226-11621-2). U of Chicago Pr.
Story of the Ukraine. Clarence A. Manning. (ISBN 0-8022-1049-X). Philos Lib.
Story of the Wise Men & the Child. Lisl Weil. LC 81-2561. (Illus.). 32p. (ps-2). 1981. 9.95 o.s.i. (ISBN 0-689-30860-4, Atheneum Childrens Bks). Macmillan.
Story of the World's Literature. John Macy. 1961. 7.95 o.p. (ISBN 0-87140-876-7). Liveright.
Story of Two Johns. Phyllis Tickle. (Illus.). 36p. (gr. 5 up). 1976. 5.95 o.p. (ISBN 0-918518-01-6, St Luke TN). Peachtree Pubs.
Story of Watches. T. P. Cuss. (Illus.). 172p. 1952. Philos Lib.
Story of Werewolves. Thomas G. Aylesworth. 1978. text ed. 9.95 o.p. (ISBN 0-07-002645-9). McGraw.
Story with No End. Jose Forner et al. (Illus.). (gr. 6). 1988. 12.95 o.p. (ISBN 0-317-68089-7). Herald Pr.
Story with No End. Sampedro Forner et al. (Illus.). 176p. (Orig.). (YA) (gr. 8-12). 1988. 14.95 o.p. (ISBN 0-8361-3469-9). Herald Pr.
Storybooks for Caring Parents. Dave Jackson. 1985. pap. 3.95 o.p. (ISBN 0-317-18164-5). Cook.
Storyteller: A Novel. Harold Robbins. 1985. 17.45 o.p. (ISBN 0-671-55749-1). S&S.
Stout-Hearted Seven. Neta L. Frazier. LC 73-5240. (gr. 4-6). 1973. 5.95 o.p. (ISBN 0-15-281450-7, HJ). HarBraceJ.
Stowboaters. Hervey Benham. (Illus.). 49p. 1977. 9.00 o.p. (ISBN 0-9505944-0-7, Pub. by Boydell & Brewer). Longwood Pub Group.
Strabismus & Amblyopia. Frank W. Newell. LC 75-12028. (Clinical Studies in Ophthalmology). (Illus.). 324p. 1975. 25.00 o.p. (ISBN 0-88416-035-1). Year Bk Med.
Stradivari-Cremona Mystery Disclosed. Pete Molenaar. LC 85-91055. (Illus.). 64p. 1986. pap. 25.00 o.p. (ISBN 0-682-40283-4). Exposition-Phoenix.
Straight Cut. Madison S. Bell. 240p. 1986. 15.45 o.p. (ISBN 0-89919-438-9). Ticknor & Fields.
Straight Talk About American Education. Theodore M. Black. LC 81-48513. 288p. 1982. 14.95 o.p. (ISBN 0-15-185584-6). HarBraceJ.
Straight Talk About Death with Young People. Richard G. Watts. LC 75-12551. (Illus.). 1975. pap. 3.95 o.s.i. (ISBN 0-664-24765-2, Westminster). Westminster John Knox.
Straight Talk About Teaching in Today's Church. Locke E. Bowman, Jr. (Orig.). 1967. pap. 2.95 o.s.i. (ISBN 0-664-24752-0, Westminster). Westminster John Knox.
Straight-White-Male. Ed. by Glenn R. Bucher. LC 75-13039. 160p. 1976. pap. 1.00 o.p. (ISBN 0-8006-1209-4, 1-1209, Fortress). Augsburg Fortress.
Strain Gage Primer. 2nd ed. C. C. Perry & H. R. Lissner. 1962. text ed. 58.50 o.p. (ISBN 0-07-049461-4). McGraw.
Strain Patterns in Rocks. Ed. by S. H. Treagus. 250p. 1984. 44.00 o.s.i. (ISBN 0-08-030273-4, 2302). Pergamon.
Strained Relations. Alison Cairns. 199p. 1986. pap. 2.95 o.p. (ISBN 0-931773-97-0). Critics Choice Paper.
Strange & Scary Ghosts. Mark Mills. (Illus.). 96p. (Orig.). (gr. 4-8). 1987. pap. 2.25 o.s.i. (ISBN 0-87406-269-1). Willowisp Pr.
Strange Animals I Have Known. Raymond L. Ditmars. (Illus.). 1939. 6.95 o.p. (ISBN 0-15-185631-1). HarBraceJ.
Strange Animals I Have Known. Raymond L. Ditmars. 1966. pap. 0.60 o.p. (ISBN 0-15-685632-8, HPL3). HarBraceJ.
Strange Appearance of Howard Cranebill Jr. Henrik Drescher. (Illus.). (ps-3). 1982. 11.75 o.p. (ISBN 0-688-00961-1); PLB 11.88 o.p. (ISBN 0-688-00962-X). Lothrop.
Strange Artifacts: A Sourcebook on Ancient Man, Vol. M1. William R. Corliss. LC 74-75256. (Illus.). 268p. 1974. 8.95x o.p. (ISBN 0-9600712-2-9). Sourcebook.
Strange But True Basketball Stories. Howard Liss. LC 82-13138. (Random House Sports Library). (Illus.). 144p. (gr. 5-10). 1983. pap. 1.95 o.p. (ISBN 0-394-85631-7). Random.
Strange but Wonderful Cosmic Awareness of Duffy Moon. Jean Robinson. LC 73-15526. (Illus.). 144p. (gr. 3-6). 1979. 6.95 o.p. (ISBN 0-395-28880-0, Clarion). HM.
Strange Death of Franklin D. Roosevelt. Emanuel Josephson. 294p. Date not set. pap. 3.75 o.p. (ISBN 0-317-53233-2). Noontide.
Strange Destiny of Rupert Brooke. John Lehmann. LC 80-13822. (Illus.). 228p. 1981. 12.95 o.p. (ISBN 0-03-057479-X). H Holt & Co.
Strange Empire, a Narrative of the Northwest. Joseph K. Howard. LC 73-19575. (Illus.). 601p. 1974. Repr. of 1952 ed. lib. bdg. 36.25x o.p. (ISBN 0-8371-7290-X, HOSE). Greenwood.
Strange Encounters: Mysteries of the Air. David Beaty. LC 83-45497. (Illus.). 160p. 1984. 13.95 o.p. (ISBN 0-689-11447-8, Atheneum). Macmillan.
Strange Enthusiasm: A Life of Thomas Wentworth Higginson, 1823-1911. Tilden G. Edelstein. LC 68-27752. (Studies in American Negro Life). 1970. pap. 3.95 o.p. (ISBN 0-689-70241-8, NL25, Atheneum). Macmillan.
Strange Felony. Elizabeth Linington. LC 85-20590. (Crime Club Ser.). 192p. 1986. 12.95 o.p. (ISBN 0-385-23265-9). Doubleday.
Strange Felony. Elizabeth Linington. LC 86-24082. 360p. 1987. 16.95 o.s.i. (ISBN 0-385-23983-1, GC Large Print). Doubleday.
Strange Invasion of Catfish Bend. Ben L. Burman. 156p. (gr. 3-5). 1981. pap. 1.95 o.p. (ISBN 0-380-53520-3, 53520-3, Camelot). Avon.
Strange Life: A Sourcebook on the Mysteries of Organic Nature. William R. Corliss. LC 75-6128. (Strange Life Ser.: Vol. B1). (Illus.). 275p. 1975. 8.95x o.p. (ISBN 0-9600712-8-8). Sourcebook.
Strange Life of Ivan Osokin. P. D. Ouspensky. 166p. 1986. pap. 6.95 o.p. (ISBN 0-7100-9419-1). Routledge Chapman & Hall.
Strange Life of Ivan Osokin. P. D. Ouspensky. (Arkana Fiction Ser.). 166p. 1987. pap. 9.95 o.p. (ISBN 1-85063-083-6, Pub. by Routledge UK). Routledge Chapman & Hall.
Strange Necessity: Essays. Rebecca West. Repr. of 1928 ed. 19.00 o.p. (ISBN 0-403-08958-1). Somerset Pub.
Strange New World Across the Street. Nan Gilbert. (gr. 5-9). 1979. pap. 1.50 o.p. (ISBN 0-380-45922-1, 45922-1, Camelot). Avon.
Strange Phenomena: A Sourcebook of Unusual Natural Phenomena, Vol. G2. William R. Corliss. LC 73-9148. 1974. 8.95x o.p. (ISBN 0-9600712-5-3). Sourcebook.
Strange Relations. Philip Jose Farmer. 1978. pap. 2.45 o.p. (ISBN 0-380-00095-4, 41418). Avon.
Strange Stories of UFOs. Len Ortzen. LC 77-76726. 1977. 7.95 o.s.i. (ISBN 0-8008-7468-4). Taplinger.
Strange Story of False Teeth. John Woodforde. 152p. 1983. pap. 8.95 o.p. (ISBN 0-7100-9307-1). Routledge Chapman & Hall.
Strange Story of the Quantum. 2nd ed. Banesh Hoffman. 14.50 o.p. (ISBN 0-8446-0702-9). Peter Smith.
Strange Sunlight. Peter LaSalle. Ed. by Scott Lubeck. 288p. 1984. 15.95 o.p. (ISBN 0-932012-87-6). Texas Month Pr.
Strange Survivals, Some Chapters in the History of Man. Sabine Baring-Gould. LC 67-23909. (Illus.). 296p. 1968. Repr. of 1892 ed. 35.00x o.p. (ISBN 0-8103-3422-4). Gale.
Strange Tales About Jesus: A Survey of Unfamiliar Gospels. Per Beskow. LC 82-16001. 144p. 1983. pap. 9.95 o.p. (ISBN 0-8006-1686-3, 1-1686, Fortress). Augsburg Fortress.
Strange Tales of 'Gone with the Wind' Norman Shavin & Austin Mcdermott. (Illus.). 52p. 1985. pap. 3.50 o.s.i. (ISBN 0-910719-06-3). Capricorn Corp.
Strange Things Happen Here: Twenty-Six Short Stories & a Novel. Luisa Valenzuela. LC 78-22274. 264p. 1979. 9.95 o.p. (ISBN 0-15-185782-2). HarBraceJ.
Strange Tunes. Kamala Sanders. 1979. 7.50 o.p. (ISBN 0-682-49213-2). Exposition-Phoenix.
Strange White Doves. Alexander Key. (Illus.). (gr. 4 up). 1972. 4.25 o.s.i. (ISBN 0-664-32508-4, Westminster). Westminster John Knox.
Strangeness. Ed. by Thomas M. Disch & Charles Naylor. 1978. pap. 2.50 o.p. (ISBN 0-380-41434-1, 41434). Avon.
Stranger & Brother: A Portrait of C. P. Snow. Philip Snow. (Illus.). 256p. 1983. 14.95 o.s.i. (ISBN 0-684-17801-X, ScribT). Scribner.
Stranger & Friend: The Way of an Anthropologist. Hortense Powdermaker. 1966. 7.50x o.p. (ISBN 0-393-07442-0). Norton.
Stranger at Green Knowe see Adventures at Green Knowe.
Stranger Beside Me. Ann Rule. (Illus.). 1980. 14.95 o.p. (ISBN 0-393-01399-5). Norton.
Stranger in Gloucester. Clive Murphy. 288p. 1987. 34.95 o.p. (ISBN 0-436-29670-5, Pub. by Secker & Warburg UK). David & Charles.
Stranger in My Bed. Beverly Slater. (Illus.). 208p. 1984. 16.95 o.p. (ISBN 0-87795-587-5, Arbor Hse). Morrow.
Stranger in My Grave. Margaret Millar. 1973. pap. 1.25 o.p. (ISBN 0-380-01563-3, 17426). Avon.
Stranger in My House: Jews & Arabs in the West Bank. Walter Reich. LC 84-10833. 112p. 1984. 12.95 o.p. (ISBN 0-03-000752-6). H Holt & Co.
Stranger in the Pines. May McNeer. LC 74-142826. (Illus.). (gr. 5-9). 1971. 7.95 o.p. (ISBN 0-395-12367-4). HM.
Stranger in Two Worlds. Jean Harris. LC 86-103. 320p. 1986. 18.95 o.p. (ISBN 0-02-548330-7). Macmillan.
Stranger on the Road. Linda Markstein & Dorien Grunbaum. 1985. pap. text ed. 7.25 o.p. (ISBN 0-88377-289-2). Newbury Hse.
Strangers. Barbara Ewing. LC 77-15348. 1978. 6.95 o.p. (ISBN 0-689-10855-9, Atheneum). Macmillan.
Strangers. Rosie Thomas. 324p. 1987. 17.45 o.s.i. (ISBN 0-671-62875-5). S&S.
Strangers. Bill Van Horn. 1983. 4.00 o.p. (ISBN 0-89536-587-1, 1926). CSS of Ohio.
Strangers All Are Gone. Anthony Powell. (Anthony Powell's Memoirs Ser.: Vol. IV). (Illus.). 208p. 1983. 18.50 o.s.i. (ISBN 0-03-063279-X). H Holt & Co.
Strangers Among Us: Enlightened Beings from a World to Come. Ruth Montgomery. LC 79-10574. 1979. 9.95 o.p. (ISBN 0-698-10992-9, Coward). Putnam Pub Group.
Strangers & Brothers: Omnibus Edition, 3 vols. C. P. Snow. LC 74-37229. 1979. Set. 67.50 o.s.i. (ISBN 0-684-12865-9, ScribT). Scribner.
Strangers & Pilgrims. Ann Cornelisen. (McGraw-Hill Paperbacks Ser.). 324p. 1981. pap. text ed. 5.95 o.p. (ISBN 0-07-013192-9). McGraw.
Strangers & Pilgrims: The Last Italian Migration. Ann Cornelisen. LC 79-3429. 320p. 1980. 12.95 o.s.i. (ISBN 0-03-044285-0). H Holt & Co.
Strangers & Sojourners at Port Royal. Ruth Clark. 1972. lib. bdg. 26.00x o.p. (ISBN 0-374-91664-0, Octagon). Hippocrene Bks.
Stranger's Bread. Nancy Willard. LC 75-41361. (Illus.). 32p. (gr. k-3). 1977. 4.95 o.s.i. (ISBN 0-15-281750-6, HJ). HarBraceJ.
Strangers Dark & Gold. Norma Johnston. LC 74-19463. (Illus.). 256p. (gr. 6 up). 1975. PLB 7.95 o.p. (ISBN 0-689-30451-X, Atheneum). Macmillan.
Strangers From the Stars. Nancy Etchemendy. (Illus.). 154p. (Orig.). (gr. 3-6). 1983. pap. 2.25 o.p. (ISBN 0-380-83568-1, 83568-1, Camelot). Avon.
Strangers in Eden. Peggy Mercer. (Velvet Glove Ser.: No. 13). 192p. 1985. pap. 2.25 o.p. (ISBN 0-380-89664-8). Avon.
Strangers in Paradise: The Hollywood Emigres, 1933-1950. John R. Taylor. LC 82-21312. 256p. 1983. 16.95 o.s.i. (ISBN 0-03-061944-0). H Holt & Co.
Strangers Outside the Feast: A Choral Reading. Warren Mild. (gr. 9 up). 1966. pap. 0.75 o.p. (ISBN 0-377-80081-3). Friendship Pr.
Strangers' Sky see Celebration in Darkness.
Strangers to These Shores: Race & Ethnic Relations in the United States. Vincent M. Parrillo. LC 79-87856. 1980. text ed. 26.95 o.p. (ISBN 0-395-28562-3). HM.
Strangers to This Ground: Cultural Diversity in Contemporary American Writing. Wilbur M. Frohock. LC 61-17183. 192p. 1961. 12.95x o.p. (ISBN 0-87074-055-5). SMU Press.
Strangling of Persia: Story of the European Diplomacy & Oriental Intrigue That Resulted in the Denationalization of Twelve Million Mohammedans, a Personal Narrative. William M. Shuster. LC 69-10154. 1968. Repr. of 1912 ed. lib. bdg. 24.50x o.p. (ISBN 0-8371-0224-3, SHSP). Greenwood.
Strasbourg in Transition, 1648-1789. Franklin L. Ford. (Illus.). 1966. pap. 1.85x o.p. (ISBN 0-393-00321-3, Norton Lib). Norton.
Strategic Alternatives: Selection, Development & Implementation. William E. Rothschild. 1979. 16.95 o.p. (ISBN 0-8144-5514-X). AMACOM.
Strategic Analysis, Selection, & Management of R & D Projects. D. Bruce Merrifield. LC 77-14599. 1977. 7.50 o.p. (ISBN 0-8144-2212-8). AMACOM.
Strategic & Long-Range Planning for Public Administrators: A Selective Bibliography. Lorna Peterson. (Public Administration Ser.: P 1805). 5p. 1985. 2.00 o.p. (ISBN 0-89028-635-3). Vance Biblios.
Strategic & Product Planning for the Automotive Industry. Ed. by David E. Cole et al. 1981. 12.00 o.p. (ISBN 0-938654-30-6). Indus Dev Inst Sci.
Strategic Behavior in Business & Government. Charles E. Summer. (Little, Brown Ser. in Strategy & Policy). 369p. 1980. pap. text ed. 16.50 o.p. (ISBN 0-316-82197-7). Little.
Strategic Bombers & Conventional Weapons: Airpower Options. Thomas A. Keaney. (National Security Affairs Monograph: No. 84-4). 85p. (Orig.). 1984. pap. 2.50 o.p. (ISBN 0-318-20150-X, S/N 008-020-00988-1). USGPO.
Strategic Bombers, 1945-1985. Michael J. Taylor. (Warbirds Illustrated Ser.: Vol. 30). (Illus.). 68p. (Orig.). pap. 9.95 o.p. (ISBN 0-85368-664-5, Pub. by Arms & Armour). Sterling.
Strategic Bombing in World War II: The Story of the United States Strategic Bombing Survey. David MacIsaac. LC 75-27037. 1976. 31.00 o.p. (ISBN 0-8240-2025-1). Garland Pub.
Strategic Defense Initiative. David Baker. 1988. price not set o.p. (ISBN 0-89464-015-1). Orbit Bk Co.
Strategic Evaluation & Management of Capital Expenditures. Robert E. Pritchard & Thomas J. Hindelang. 304p. 1981. 29.95 o.p. (ISBN 0-8144-5656-1). AMACOM.
Strategic Goal Analysis of Options for Tuna Longline Joint Ventures in Southeast Asia: Indonesia-Japan Case Study. Gerald Marten & Yoshiaki Matsuda. LC 81-3263. (East-West Environment & Policy Institute Research Report: No. 3). viii, 74p. (Orig.). 1981. pap. text ed. 3.00 o.s.i. (ISBN 0-86638-025-6). EW Ctr HI.
Strategic Intervention for Hyperactive Children. Ed. by Martin Gittelman. LC 81-14407. 244p. 1981. 40.00 o.p. (ISBN 0-87332-202-9). M E Sharpe.

Strategic Investing: How to Profit from the Coming Inflationary Depression. Douglas R. Casey. 1982. 15.50 o.p. (ISBN 0-671-43885-9). S&S.

Strategic Management. Frank T. Paine & Carl R. Anderson. 368p. 1983. text ed. 31.95x o.p. (ISBN 0-03-061828-2); pap. 17.95x o.p. (ISBN 0-03-070778-1). Dryden Pr.

Strategic Management & Business Policy. William F. Glueck. (Management Ser.). (Illus.). 288p. 1980. text ed. 19.95 o.p. (ISBN 0-07-023506-6, C). McGraw.

Strategic Management: Concepts, Decisions & Cases. Lester A. Digman. 1986. 39.95 o.p. (ISBN 0-256-03256-4). Irwin.

Strategic Management of Development Programmes: Guidelines for Action. Samuel Paul. Ed. by International Labour Office Staff. (Management Development Ser.: No. 19). vii, 137p. (Orig.). 1984. pap. 14.00 o.p. (ISBN 92-2-103252-3). Intl Labour Office.

Strategic Market Management. David A. Aaker. LC 83-21694. 336p. 1984. pap. 22.95 o.p. (ISBN 0-471-87110-9, Pub by Wiley). Wiley.

Strategic Marketing Management. Gordon R. Foxall. LC 81-6828. 273p. 1981. pap. 26.95x o.p. (ISBN 0-470-27265-1). Halsted Pr.

Strategic Marketing: Techniques, Technologies & Realities in the Electronic Information Marketplace. Ed. by Leslie R. Chase & Robert Landers. 1985. pap. 59.95 o.p. (ISBN 0-942774-20-5). Info Indus.

Strategic Metals Investment Handbook. Philip Goldberg & Mitchell J. Posner. LC 82-1052. (Illus.). 360p. 1983. 19.95 o.p. (ISBN 0-03-059489-8). H Holt & Co.

Strategic Military Deception. Ed. by Donald C. Daniel & Katherine L. Herbig. LC 81-14364. (Pergamon Policy Studies on Security Affairs). (Illus.). 400p. 1982. 95.00 o.p. (ISBN 0-08-027219-3). Pergamon.

Strategic Perspectives on Social Policy. Ed. by John E. Tropman et al. LC 74-14737. 1976. 95.00 o.p. (ISBN 0-08-018227-5); pap. 95.00 o.p. (ISBN 0-08-018226-7). Pergamon.

Strategic Planning. Cuns. 64p. 1987. saddle stitch 10.95 o.p. (ISBN 0-8403-4210-1). Kendall-Hunt.

Strategic Planning: Concepts & Implementation Text, Readings & Cases. John K. Ryans, Jr. & William L. Shanklin. (Illus.). 240p. 1984. pap. text ed. 14.00 o.p. (ISBN 0-394-33946-0, RanC). Random.

Strategic Planning: Contemporary Viewpoints. Marie Ensign & Laurie N. Adler. LC 85-1342. (Dynamic Organization Ser.). 231p. 1985. lib. bdg. 39.00 o.p. (ISBN 0-87436-448-5). ABC-Clio.

Strategic Planning for Workplace Drug Abuse Programs. Thomas E. Backer. LC 87-1538. (DHHS Publication ADM Ser.). 68p. 1987. pap. 3.25 o.p. (ISBN 0-318-23762-8, 017-024-01337-4). USGPO.

Strategic Planning in London: The Rise & Fall of the Primary Road Network. Douglas Hart. Ed. by Urban & Regional Planning Advisory Committee. 239p. 1976. 26.00 o.p. (ISBN 0-08-019780-9). Pergamon.

Strategic Planning in South East England 1968-78: A Case Study. B. E. Linders. (Illus.). 83p. 1985. pap. 22.00 o.p. (ISBN 0-08-032720-6, Pub. by Aberdeen Scotland). Pergamon.

Strategic Planning Process for Hospitals. Joseph P. Peters. 200p. 1985. pap. 34.95 o.s.i. (ISBN 0-939450-46-1, 127126). AHPI.

Strategic Planning Process: 1986 Small Cities Goodall Award Winning Program. Madlyn Barnett. cancelled o.s.i. Coun Jewish Feds.

Strategic Survey 1986-1987. 240p. 1987. pap. 16.00x o.p. (ISBN 0-86079-125-4). Janes Info Group.

Strategic Survey, 1987-88. 240p. 1988. pap. 18.00x o.p. (ISBN 0-86079-148-3). Janes Info Group.

Strategic Terminology. Urs Schwarz & Laszlo Hadik. 160p. (Ger., Eng. & Fr.). 12.50 o.p. (ISBN 0-686-57217-3, M-6509). French & Eur.

Strategie Pour Deux Jambons see Death Sty: A Pig's Tale.

Strategies: A Rhetoric & Reader. 2nd ed. Charlene Tibbetts & A. M. Tibbetts. 1984. pap. text ed. write for info. o.p. (ISBN 0-673-15897-7). Scott F.

Strategies for Administrative Reform. Gerald E. Caiden & Heinrich Siedentopf. LC 81-48070. (Policy Studies Organization Bk.). 272p. 1982. 36.00x o.p. (ISBN 0-669-05241-8). Lexington Bks.

Strategies for Business & Technical Writing. Kevin J. Harty. 285p. 1980. pap. text ed. 11.95 o.p. (ISBN 0-15-583924-1, HC). HarBraceJ.

Strategies for Business & Technical Writing. 2nd ed. Kevin J. Harty. 287p. 1985. pap. text ed. 12.00 net o.p. (ISBN 0-15-583925-X, HC). HarBraceJ.

Strategies for Consumer Counselor Training. 2nd ed. Institute of Financial Education Staff. 230p. 1980. pap. 13.00 o.p. (ISBN 0-912857-10-2). Inst Finan Educ.

Strategies for Economic Development in Africa: Theory & Policies. Fidelis S. Akagha. LC 84-90090. 149p. 1985. 13.95 o.p. (ISBN 0-533-06174-1). Vantage.

Strategies for Educational Change. Walter Marks & Raphael O. Nystrand. (Illus.). 1980. text ed. write for info. o.p. (ISBN 0-02-376180-6). Macmillan.

Strategies for Effective Desegregation: Lessons from Research. Ed. by Willis D. Hawley. LC 82-47968. 224p. 1982. pap. 14.00x o.p. (ISBN 0-669-06376-2). Lexington Bks.

Strategies for Implementing Work Experience Programs. Grady Kimbrell & Ben S. Vineyard. 400p. 1975. text ed. 44.00 o.p. (ISBN 0-87345-528-2). Glencoe.

Strategies for Improving Reading in Social Studies. Fred Green et al. 1979. pap. text ed. 9.95 o.p. (ISBN 0-8403-2098-1). Kendall-Hunt.

Strategies for Increasing the Use of Statistical Data. Alice Robbin. (Occasional Papers: No. 158). 31p. 1983. pap. 3.00 o.p. (ISBN 0-317-59005-7). U of Ill Lib Info Sci.

Strategies for Managing Nuclear Proliferation: Economic & Political Issues. Ed. by Dagobert Brito & Michael D. Intriligator. LC 82-49525. 336p. 1983. 39.00x o.p. (ISBN 0-669-06442-4). Lexington Bks.

Strategies for Postsecondary Education. Peter G. Scott. LC 75-8372. 161p. 1975. 37.95x o.p. (ISBN 0-470-76860-6). Halsted Pr.

Strategies for Public Health: Promoting Health & Preventing Disease. Ed. by Lorenz K. Ng & Devra Davis. 416p. 1980. 29.95 o.p. (ISBN 0-442-24428-2). Van Nos Reinhold.

Strategies for Real-Time System Specification. Derek J. Hatley & Imtiaz A. Pirhai. (Illus.). 400p. (Orig.). 1987. pap. 45.00 o.p. (ISBN 0-932633-04-8). Dorset Hse Pub Co.

Strategies for Reducing Gasoline Consumption Through Improved Motor Vehicle Efficiency. (Special Report). 51p. 1976. 2.40 o.p. (ISBN 0-309-02557-5). Transport Res Bd.

Strategies for Second Language Acquisition. Florence Stevens. 256p. (Orig.). 1984. pap. 18.95 o.p. (ISBN 0-920792-39-1). Eden Pr.

Strategies for Stopping Shopping Centers: A Guidebook on Minimizing Excessive Shopping Center Growth. Ed. by Laurence A. Alexander. LC 80-65968. (Orig.). 1980. pap. 21.00 o.p. (ISBN 0-915910-17-9). Downtown Res.

Strategies for Vertical Integration. Kathryn R. Harrigan. LC 83-47513. 400p. 1983. 35.00x o.p. (ISBN 0-669-06694-X). Lexington Bks.

Strategies for Women's Studies in the Eighties. G. Bowles. 100p. 1984. pap. 19.25 o.p. (ISBN 0-08-031320-5). Pergamon.

Strategies in Cold: Natural Torpidity & Thermogenesis. Ed. by Lawrence Wang & Jack W. Hudson. 1978. 68.00 o.p. (ISBN 0-12-734550-7). Acad Pr.

Strategies of Ethics. Bernard Rosen. LC 77-77431. (Illus.). 1978. text ed. 22.95 o.p. (ISBN 0-395-25077-3). HM.

Strategies of Immune Regulation. Ed. by Eli E. Sercarz & Alastair J. Cunningham. LC 79-28392. 1980. 65.50 o.p. (ISBN 0-12-637140-7). Acad Pr.

Strategies of Microbial Life in Extreme Environments, LSRR 13. Ed. by Moshe Shilo. (Dahlem Workshop Reports Ser.). 514p. 1979. 42.40x o.p. (ISBN 0-89573-082-0). VCH Pubs.

Strategies of the Major Oil Companies. William N. Greene. Ed. by Richard Farmer. LC 84-24076. (Research for Business Decisions Ser.: No. 70). 362p. 1985. 49.95 o.p. (ISBN 0-8357-1606-6). UMI Res Pr.

Strategy & Policy. rev. ed. Arthur A. Thompson, Jr. & A. J. Strickland, III. 1981. text ed. 20.95x o.p. (ISBN 0-256-02385-9). Irwin.

Strategy & Politics. Edward N. Luttwak. LC 79-65224. 1980. text ed. 19.95 o.p. (ISBN 0-87855-346-0). Transaction Pubs.

Strategy & the Defense Dilemma. Gerald Garvey. LC 83-48737. 160p. 1984. 29.00x o.p. (ISBN 0-669-07508-6). Lexington Bks.

Strategy for Financial Mobility. Gordon Donaldson. LC 73-94406. 1969. 21.95x o.p. (ISBN 0-87584-078-7). Harvard Busn.

Strategy for Leadership. Edward R. Dayton & Ted W. Engstrom. 240p. 1979. pap. 7.95 o.p. (ISBN 0-8007-0994-2). Revell.

Strategy for Plenty: The Indicative World Plan for Agricultural Development. (World Food Problems Ser.: No. 11). 63p. (Orig.). 1970. pap. 5.00 o.p. (ISBN 92-5-101670-4, F451, FAO). UNIPUB.

Strategy for Terminating a Nuclear War. Clark C. Abt. (Special Study Ser.). 200p. 1985. pap. 19.85x o.p. (ISBN 0-8133-7050-7). Westview.

Strategy Formulation & Implementation. 3rd ed. Ed. by Strickland & Thompson. 1986. 22.95 o.p. (ISBN 0-256-03173-8). Irwin.

Strategy Formulation & Implementation: Tasks of the General Manager. 2nd ed. Arthur A. Thompson, Jr. & A. J. Strickland, 3rd. 1983. pap. 18.95x o.p. (ISBN 0-256-02884-2). Irwin.

Strategy Management: How to Plan, Execute & Control Strategic Plans for Your Business. Kevin Tourangeau. 256p. 1981. text ed. 27.50 o.p. (ISBN 0-07-065043-8). McGraw.

Strategy Memo on Legal Issues & Strategies in Plant Closings. Milwaukee Labor Committee & National Labor Law Center. 5.90 o.p. Natl Lawyers Guild.

Strategy of Combat. P-H.

Strategy of Economic Development. Albert O. Hirschman. 1978. pap. 3.95x o.p. (ISBN 0-393-00900-9, N900, Norton Lib). Norton.

Strategy of Survival. Bhagwat S. Goyal. 244p. 1975. text ed. 15.00x o.p. (ISBN 0-391-02714-X, Pub. by U B S Pub India). Humanities.

Stratigraphical Atlas of Fossil Foraminifera. Ed. by D. Graham Jenkins & John W. Murray. (British Micropalaeontological Society Series). 310p. 1981. 89.95x o.p. (ISBN 0-470-27191-4). Halsted Pr.

Stratigraphy. Roy R. Lemon. 640p. 1988. 37.95 o.p. (ISBN 0-675-20537-9). Merrill.

Stratigraphy & Glacial-Marine Sediments of the Amerasian Basin, Central Arctic Ocean. David L. Clark et al. LC 80-65270. (Special Paper: No. 181). (Illus., Orig.). 1980. pap. 13.00 o.p. (ISBN 0-8137-2181-4). Geol Soc.

Stratigraphy: Foundation & Concepts. Barbara M. Conkin & James E. Conkin. 1984. 47.95 o.p. (ISBN 0-442-21747-1). Van Nos Reinhold.

Stratospheric Circulation. Ed. by Willis L. Webb. (Progress in Astronautics & Aeronautics: Vol. 22). 1969. 24.00 o.p. (ISBN 0-12-535122-4). Acad Pr.

Stratospheric Circulation, PAAS22. Ed. by W. L. Webb. LC 64-103. (Illus.). 600p. 1969. 49.50 o.p. (ISBN 0-317-36812-5). AIAA.

Strauss & Welt's Diseases of the Kidney, 2 vols. 3rd ed. Lawrence E. Earley & Carl W. Gottschalk. 1979. text ed. 25.00 o.p. (ISBN 0-316-20314-9). Little.

Stravinsky. Francis Routh. (Master Musicians Ser.: M-172). (Illus.). 1978. pap. 7.95 o.p. (ISBN 0-8226-0702-6). Littlefield.

Stravinsky: A New Appraisal of His Work. Ed. by Paul H. Lang. 1963. pap. 3.45 o.p. (ISBN 0-393-00199-7, Norton Lib). Norton.

Stravinsky: His Life & Work. Eric W. White. (ISBN 0-8022-1858-X). Philos Lib.

Stravinsky Scrapbook. Robert Craft. LC 83-50016. (Illus.). 180p. 1984. 24.95f o.s.i. (ISBN 0-500-01310-1). Thames-Hudson.

Strawberries. Maggie Waldron. LC 77-2126. (Edible Garden Ser.). (Illus.). 1977. pap. 2.50 o.s.i. (ISBN 0-89286-112-6, One Hund One Prods). Ortho.

Strawberries in the Sea. Elisabeth Ogilvie. 1977. pap. 1.75 o.p. (ISBN 0-380-00732-0, 30056). Avon.

Strawberry Fairies. (ps-3). plastic bdg. 2.00 o.p. (ISBN 0-8198-0202-6); pap. 1.25 o.p. (ISBN 0-8198-0203-4). Dghtrs St Paul.

Strawberry Statement. James S. Kunen. 1970. pap. 1.25 o.p. (ISBN 0-380-01447-5, 091917). Avon.

Stray Cow. Meyer Llewellyn. 1971. pap. 2.15 o.p. (ISBN 0-08-015697-5). Pergamon.

Stream, Lake, Estuary, Ocean Pollution. Nemerow. 1985. 46.95 o.p. (ISBN 0-442-26720-7). Van Nos Reinhold.

Stream of Consciousness: Scientific Investigations into the Flow of Human Experience. Ed. by K. S. Pope & J. L. Singer. LC 78-2003. (Emotions, Personality, & Psychotherapy Ser.). (Illus.). 392p. 1978. 39.50x o.p. (ISBN 0-306-31117-8, Plenum Pr). Plenum Pub.

Streaming: An Educational System in Miniature. Brian Jackson. 156p. 1964. pap. 8.95x o.p. (ISBN 0-7100-3926-3). Routledge Chapman & Hall.

Streamline Your Bidding. Victor Mollo. 192p. 1979. 16.95 o.p. (ISBN 0-571-11441-5); pap. 6.95 o.p. (ISBN 0-571-11516-0). Faber & Faber.

Streamliners & War Horses. Richard M. Wagner & Roy J. Wright. (Cincinnati Streetcar Ser.: No. 9). 52p. 1984. 12.95 o.p. (ISBN 0-914196-22-7). Trolley Talk.

Streamlining Land Use Regulation: A Guidebook for Local Governments. John Vranicar et al. 74p. 1982. Repr. of 1980 ed. 16.00 o.s.i. Planners Pr.

Streams in the Desert, 5 Vols. Mrs. Charles E. Cowman. 1986. Set. 48.75 o.p. (ISBN 0-310-37668-8, 6882); Vol. 5. 10.95 o.p. (ISBN 0-310-22480-2, 6905). Zondervan.

Streams in the Desert, Vol. 3. Mrs. Charles E. Cowman. Orig. Title: Springs in the Valley. 1986. 10.95 o.p. (ISBN 0-310-22440-3, 6903). Zondervan.

Streams in the Desert, Vol. 4. Mrs. Charles E. Cowman. Orig. Title: Traveling Toward Sunrise. 1986. 10.95 o.p. (ISBN 0-310-22470-5, 6904). Zondervan.

Street Cars of Boston: Closed Horse & Electric Cars to 1900, Vol. 1. O. R. Cummings. (Illus.). 92p. (Orig.). 1973. pap. 6.00 o.p. (ISBN 0-911940-18-9). Cox.

Street Cop. 10/1986 ed. Michael C. Macdonald & John Bane, Jr. LC 86-60374. 200p. 16.95 o.s.i. (ISBN 0-933341-35-0). Quinlan Pr.

Street Directory of the Principal Cities of the United States: Embracing Letter-Carrier Offices Established to April 30, 1908. 5th ed. U. S. Post Office Department Staff. LC 76-179692. 912p. Repr. of 1908 ed. 75.00x o.p. (ISBN 0-8103-3072-5). Gale.

Street Furniture. Henry Aaron. (Shire Album Ser.: No. 47). (Illus.). 32p. 1980. pap. 2.95 o.p. (ISBN 0-85263-498-6, Pub. by Shire Pubns England). Seven Hills Bk Dists.

Street Life: Afro-American Culture in Urban Trinidad. Michael Lieber. 1981. lib. bdg. 17.00 o.p. (ISBN 0-8161-9033-X, Univ Bks). G K Hall.

Street of the Laughing Camel. Ben L. Burman. 4.95 o.s.i. (ISBN 0-685-20506-1). Taplinger.

Street or Pulpit? The Witness of Activist Monsignor Charles Owen Rice of Pittsburgh. Kenneth K. McNulty, Sr. (Answers Ser.). 288p. (Orig.). 1985. pap. 9.95 o.p. (ISBN 0-935025-00-6). Data & Res Tech.

Street Smart Investing: A Price-Value Approach to Stock Market Profits. George B. Clairmont & Kiril Sokoloff. 1984. pap. 8.95 o.p. (ISBN 0-394-72424-0, Vin). Random.

Street-Smart: The Guardian Angel Guide to Safe Living. Alliance of Guardian Angels, Inc. Staff & Curtis Sliwa. LC 82-16238. (Illus.). 192p. 1982. pap. 5.95 o.p. (ISBN 0-201-07789-2). Addison-Wesley.

Street Soldier's Handbook of Poetry. Rita C. Cordoze. 40p. 1987. 7.50 o.p. (ISBN 0-8062-3060-6). Carlton.

Street Where I Live. Alan J. Lerner. (Illus.). 336p. 1980. pap. 5.95 o.p. (ISBN 0-393-00970-X). Norton.

Street Where I Live. Alan J. Lerner. (Illus.). 1978. 12.95 o.p. (ISBN 0-393-07532-X). Norton.

Streetcops. Stephen F. Coleman. 355p. (Orig.). 1986. pap. text ed. 11.95X o.p. (ISBN 0-88133-226-7). Sheffield Wisc.

Street's Cruising Guide to the Eastern Caribbean, Vol. 2. Ed. by Donald M. Street, Jr. (Illus.). 1980. 24.95 o.p. (ISBN 0-393-03247-7). Norton.

Street's Cruising Guide to the Eastern Caribbean, Vol. 3. Donald J. Street, Jr. (Illus.). 1980. 25.95 o.p. (ISBN 0-393-03254-X). Norton.

Streets of East London. William J. Fishman & N. Breach. (Illus.). 1980. pap. 22.50 o.p. (ISBN 0-7156-1416-9). E J Brill USA.

Streetwise. Mary E. Mark. (Illus.). 104p. (Orig.). 1988. pap. 24.95 o.p. (ISBN 0-8122-1268-1). U of Pa Pr.

Strega Nona. Tomie De Paola. LC 75-11565. (Illus.). (ps-3). 1979. 13.95x o.s.i. (ISBN 0-13-851600-6, Pub. by Treehouse); pap. 6.95 o.s.i. (ISBN 0-13-851592-1). P-H.

Strength & Failure of Visco-Elastic Materials. G. M. Bartenev & Yu. S. Zuyev. 1968. 110.00 o.p. (ISBN 0-08-012183-7). Pergamon.

Strength Fitness: Physiological Principles Training Techniques. 2nd, expanded ed. Wescott. 207p. 1987. text ed. 30.95 o.p. (ISBN 0-205-10493-2, Pub. by Longwood Div). Wm C Brown.

Strength for the Soul: Wisdom from Past & Present. Dorothy M. Fuller. LC 75-13037. 128p. 1975. 0.50x o.p. (ISBN 0-8006-0417-2, Fortress). Augsburg Fortress.

Strength of Biological Materials. Hiroshi Yamada. LC 75-110279. 308p. 1973. Repr. of 1970 ed. 22.50 o.p. (ISBN 0-88275-119-0). Krieger.

Strength of Government. McGeorge Bundy. LC 68-54016. (Godkin Lectures: 1968). 1968. 9.95x o.s.i. (ISBN 0-674-84300-2). Harvard U Pr.

Strength of Materials. P. Black. 1966. 115.00 o.p. (ISBN 0-08-011555-1). Pergamon.

Strength of Materials. A. A. Ilyushin & V. S. Lenskii. Ed. by L. C. Redshaw. Tr. by J. K. Loshor. 1967. 115.00 o.p. (ISBN 0-08-011461-X). Pergamon.

Strength of Materials for Civil Engineers. T. Megson. 1982. 34.50 o.p. (ISBN 0-442-30755-1). Van Nos Reinhold.

Strength of Materials: Theory & Examples. R. C. Stephens. (Illus.). 1970. pap. text ed. 23.50x o.p. (ISBN 0-7131-3211-6). Trans-Atl Phila.

Strength of Structural Materials: Understanding Basic Structural Design. Giuseppe DeCampoli. LC 84-3569. 461p. 1984. text ed. 36.95 o.p. (ISBN 0-471-89082-0). Wiley.

Strength of Tradition: Stories of the Immigrant Presence in Australia. Ed. by R. F. Holt. LC 82-10874. 288p. 1983. 19.50 o.p. (ISBN 0-7022-1691-7); pap. 8.95 o.p. (ISBN 0-7022-1701-8). U of Queensland Pr.

Strength to Dream: Literature & the Imagination. Colin Wilson. LC 73-2876. 277p. 1973. Repr. of 1962 ed. lib. bdg. 22.50x o.p. (ISBN 0-8371-6819-8, WISD). Greenwood.

Strength Training for Football: The Penn State Way. 2nd ed. Daniel P. Riley. LC 81-84784. (Illus.). 144p. 1982. pap. 8.95 o.p. (ISBN 0-88011-042-2, PRIL0042). Leisure Pr.

Strengthening Humanities in Community Colleges. Ed. by Roger Yarrington. (Orig.). 1980. pap. 5.00 o.p. (ISBN 0-87117-094-9). Am Assn Comm Jr Coll.

Strengthening Intergovernmental Management: An Agenda for Reform, a Special Report. 1980. 5.00 o.s.i. (ISBN 0-317-06623-4). Am Soc Pub Admin.

Strengthening School Leadership. Illinois Principals Association Staff. LC 76-29805. 1976. pap. text ed. 3.50x o.p. (ISBN 0-8134-1854-2, 1854). Inter Print Pubs.

Strengthening the United Nations. Organization of Peace Commission & Arthur N. Holcombe. LC 74-7536. 276p. 1976. Repr. of 1957 ed. lib. bdg. 35.00x o.p. (ISBN 0-8371-7579-8, HOUN). Greenwood.

Strengthening Your Grip. Charles R. Swindoll. 236p. 1982. 12.95 o.p. (ISBN 0-8499-0312-2). Word Bks.

Stresemann & the Rearmament of Germany. Hans W. Gatzke. 1969. pap. 2.65x o.p. (ISBN 0-393-00486-4, Norton Lib). Norton.

Stress. 3rd ed. Elleen B. Curns. (Illus.). 34p. 1981. 7.00 o.p. ACCORD IL.

Stress Analysis of Pressure Vessels & Pressure Vessel Components. S. S. Gill. 1970. 150.00 o.p. (ISBN 0-08-006729-8). Pergamon.

Stress Analysis Problems in SI Units. D. F. Mallows & W. J. Pickering. LC 71-171465. 1972. 80.00 o.p. (ISBN 0-08-016293-2); pap. 12.75 o.p. (ISBN 0-08-016292-4). Pergamon.

Stress & Anxiety, Vol. 1. Ed. by C. D. Spielberger & I. G. Sarason. LC 74-28292. (Clinical Psychology Ser). 335p. 1975. 37.95x o.p. (ISBN 0-470-81605-8). Halsted Pr.

Stress & Anxiety, Vol. 7. Irwin G. Sarason & Charles D. Spielberger. 1981. text ed. 34.50 o.p. (ISBN 0-07-054722-X). McGraw.

Stress & Anxiety, Vol. 7. Ed. by Irwin G. Sarason & Charles D. Spielberger. LC 74-28292. (Clinical & Community Psychology, Stress & Anxiety Ser.). (Illus.). 384p. 1980. text ed. 36.50 o.p. (ISBN 0-89116-183-X). Hemisphere Pub.

Stress & Anxiety, Vol. 8. Ed. by Charles D. Spielberger et al. LC 74-28292. (Clinical & Community Psychology, Stress & Anxiety Ser.). (Illus.). 456p. 1982. text ed. 39.95 o.p. (ISBN 0-89116-184-8). Hemisphere Pub.

Stress & Frustration. Irving L. Janis. 215p. 1971. pap. text ed. 8.75 o.p. (ISBN 0-15-583942-X, HC). HarBraceJ.

Stress & the Bottom Line: A Guide to Personal Well-Being & Corporate Health. E. M. Gherman. 352p. 1981. 16.95 o.p. (ISBN 0-8144-5696-0). AMACOM.

Stress & the Teaching Profession. Sheldon F. Greenberg. LC 84-6379. 188p. (Orig.). 1984. pap. text ed. 15.95 o.p. (ISBN 0-933716-39-7, 397). P H Brookes.

Stress at Work. Ed. by C. L. Cooper & R. Payne. (Studies in Occupational Stress). 293p. 1978. 71.95 o.p. (ISBN 0-471-99547-9, Pub. by Wiley-Interscience). Wiley.

Stress, Diet, & Your Heart. Dean Ornish. LC 81-24003. (Illus.). 400p. 1982. 16.95 o.s.i. (ISBN 0-03-049011-1). H Holt & Co.

Stress, Drugs & Health - Recent Brain-Behavior Research. F. Campbell & G. Singer. (Illus.). 136p. 1983. pap. text ed. 15.00 o.p. (ISBN 0-08-024838-1). Pergamon.

Stress for Success. Donald R. Morse & M. Lawrence Furst. 400p. 1981. pap. 14.95 o.p. (ISBN 0-442-26228-0). Van Nos Reinhold.

Stress in Israel. Shlomo Breznitz. 304p. 1982. 29.95 o.p. (ISBN 0-442-24422-3). Van Nos Reinhold.

Stress Management: A Comprehensive Guide to Wellness. Edward A. Charlesworth & Ronald G. Nathan. LC 84-45060. 292p. 1984. 17.95 o.p. (ISBN 0-689-11503-2, Atheneum). Macmillan.

Stress Management Workshop. Carol Hartman. Ed. by Dan Jones. 175p. (Orig.). 1985. spiral bound 24.50 o.p. (ISBN 0-936352-23-X). U of KS Cont Ed.

Stress Physiology in Crop Plants. Harry Mussell & Richard C. Staples. LC 78-27567. 510p. 1979. 67.50x o.p. (ISBN 0-471-03809-1, Pub. by Wiley-Interscience). Wiley.

Stress Point in Marriage. Bill Blackburn & Deana Blackburn. 160p. 1985. 9.95 o.p. (ISBN 0-8499-0388-2, 0388-2). Word Bks.

Stressed Ecosystems. John Cairns. (Illus.). 350p. 1989. 49.95 o.p. (ISBN 0-87371-038-X). Lewis Pubs Inc.

Stressed for Success. Cathy Guisewite. 1986. pap. 2.95 o.p. (ISBN 0-449-21017-0, Crest). Fawcett.

Stressless Home: A Step-by-Step Guide to Turning Your Home into the Haven You Deserve. Robert M. Bramson & Susan Bramson. LC 82-45390. (Illus.). 240p. 1985. 15.95 o.p. (ISBN 0-385-18289-9, Anchor Pr). Doubleday.

StressMap: Finding Your Pressure Points. C. Michele Haney & Edmond W. Boenisch, Jr. LC 82-15391. 160p. (Orig.). 1982. pap. 6.95 o.p. (ISBN 0-915166-19-4). Impact Pubs Cal.

Stretching a Point. Mitch Struble. (Franklin Institute Bk). (Illus.). (gr. 5 up). 1971. 4.95 o.s.i. (ISBN 0-664-32499-1, Westminster); pap. 2.95 o.s.i. (ISBN 0-664-34002-4, Westminster). Westminster John Knox.

Stretching Fence. Sonya Dorman. LC 75-14550. 61p. 1975. 8.95 o.p. (ISBN 0-8214-0188-2, 82-81891); pap. 4.95 o.p. (ISBN 0-8214-0209-9). Ohio U Pr.

Stretching the Limits: Breakthroughs in Sports Science That Create Super Athletes. Lee Torrey. LC 85-15866. (Illus.). 288p. 1985. 18.95 o.p. (ISBN 0-396-08585-7). Dodd.

Striated Muscle. Ed. by Carl M. Pearson & F. K. Mostofi. LC 73-6903. 518p. 1973. 41.50 o.p. Krieger.

Strict Vegetarian Cookbook. Lorine Tadej. LC 84-61271. 160p. pap. 7.95 o.p. (ISBN 0-912145-02-1). MMI Pr.

Strictly Personal & Confidential: The Letters That Harry Truman Never Mailed. Monte E. Poen. 1982. pap. 7.70 o.p. (ISBN 0-316-71222-1). Little.

Stride Toward Freedom. Martin Luther King, Jr. LC 58-7099. 1958. 13.45 o.p. (ISBN 0-06-064690-X). HarpR.

Strife of Interests: Politics & Policies in Australian Health Services. Sidney Sax. 350p. 1985. text ed. 34.95x o.p. (ISBN 0-86861-484-X). Unwin Hyman.

Strike. Yvonne Burgess. LC 79-23680. 219p. 1980. 9.95 o.s.i. (ISBN 0-8008-7471-4). Taplinger.

Strike! Patricia Larkin. (R. N. Ser.: Bk. 4). 240p. (Orig.). 1989. pap. 2.95 o.p. (ISBN 1-55802-062-4). Lynx Bks.

Strike: A Current Assessment. Benjamin Aaron. 1967. 1.00 o.p. (ISBN 0-89215-052-1). U Cal LA Indus Rel.

Strike a Giant Bell. John Davis. 1980. 3.00 o.p. (ISBN 0-8198-6815-9); pap. 2.00 o.p. (ISBN 0-8198-6816-7). Dghtrs St Paul.

Strike for Freedom! The Story of Lech Walesa & Polish Solidarity. Robert Eringer. LC 82-12978. 320p. 1982. 12.95 o.p. (ISBN 0-396-08065-0). Dodd.

Strike Through the Mask: New Lyrical Poems. Peter R. Viereck. LC 77-178793. 70p. 1972. Repr. of 1950 ed. lib. bdg. 22.50x o.p. (ISBN 0-8371-6283-1, VIST). Greenwood.

Strike Two. Ron Luciano & David Fisher. (Illus.). 326p. (Orig.). 1984. 14.95 o.p. (ISBN 0-553-05049-4). Bantam.

Strikes. K. G. Knowles. (Illus.). 340p. 1953. (ISBN 0-8022-0875-4). Philos Lib.

Strikes & Solutions see Issues in the Public Employee Relations Library: Series 1.

Striking a Balance: Dancers Talk About Dancing. Barbara Newman. (Illus.). 416p. 1982. 17.95 o.p. (ISBN 0-395-31325-2); pap. 10.95 o.p. (ISBN 0-395-32194-8). HM.

String of Amber: The Heritage of the Mennonites. B. Davies. (Illus.). 1973. 15.00 o.s.i. (ISBN 0-685-47308-2). E J Brill USA.

String of Chances. Phyllis R. Naylor. LC 82-1790. 252p. (gr. 6 up). 1982. 11.95 o.s.i. (ISBN 0-689-30935-X, Atheneum Childrens Bks). Macmillan.

String of Chinese Peach-Stones. W. Arthur Cornaby. LC 70-175730. (Illus.). 502p. 1974. Repr. of 1895 ed. 43.00x o.p. (ISBN 0-8103-3125-X). Gale.

String of Pearls. Mary Crowley. 160p. 1985. 9.95 o.p. (ISBN 0-8499-0499-4, 0499-4). Word Bks.

String of Pearls. 2nd enlarged ed. Portia Conrad LePage. 1978. 4.50 o.p. (ISBN 0-682-49007-5). Exposition-Phoenix.

String of Pearls: An Abbreviated Poetic Version of Holy Scripture. John Roberts. 64p. 1987. 6.75 o.p. (ISBN 0-8062-2836-9). Carlton.

Stringed Instruments of the Middle Ages, Their Evolution & Development. Hortense Panum. Ed. by Jeffrey Pulver. 1970. Repr. of 1939 ed. lib. bdg. 35.00x o.p. (ISBN 0-8371-4307-1, PASI). Greenwood.

Strings on a Kite: The Poetry of Max Hart. Max Hart. 78p. 1983. pap. 5.95 o.p. (ISBN 0-682-49994-3). Exposition-Phoenix.

Strip Mining for Coal. Dorothy C. Tompkins. LC 73-919. (Public Policy Bibliographies: No. 4). 86p. (Orig.). 1973. pap. 5.00x o.p. (ISBN 0-87772-166-1). UCB IGS.

Striped Horses: The Story of a Zebra Family. Betty Dineen. LC 82-7786. (Illus.). 96p. (gr. 4-6). 1982. 9.95 o.s.i. (ISBN 0-02-732200-9). Macmillan.

Stripping: The Assembly of Film Images. Harold L. Peck. LC 83-82330. 304p. 1984. 40.00 o.p. (ISBN 0-88362-049-9, 1507). Graphic Arts Tech Found.

Striving After Wind. Norma Johnston. LC 76-4473. 272p. (gr. 7-12). 1976. 8.95 o.p. (ISBN 0-689-30540-0, Atheneum). Macmillan.

Stroke. Nexhat Thaqi. 144p. 1987. 8.95 o.p. (ISBN 0-8062-1846-0). Carlton.

Stroke: A Doctor's Personal Story of His Recovery. Charles C. Dahlberg & Joseph Jaffe. (Illus.). 1977. 12.95 o.p. (ISBN 0-393-08720-4). Norton.

Stroke: A Self-Help Manual for Stroke Sufferers & Their Relatives. R. M. Youngson. 144p. (Orig.). 1988. pap. 9.95 o.p. (ISBN 0-7153-8945-9, Pub. by David & Charles Pub England). Sterling.

Stroke Patient: Principles of Rehabilitation. 2nd ed. Margaret Johnstone. (Illus.). 1982. pap. text ed. 10.00 o.p. (ISBN 0-443-02544-4). Churchill.

Strong & Weak Interactions. Ed. by A. Zichichi. 1967. 104.00 o.p. (ISBN 0-12-780545-1). Acad Pr.

Strong Brown God: The Story of the Niger River. Sanche De Gramont. LC 75-33298. 356p. 1976. 12.50 o.p. (ISBN 0-395-19782-1). HM.

Strong Brown God: The Story of the Niger River. Sanche De Gramont. 1977. pap. 5.95 o.p. (ISBN 0-395-25224-5). HM.

Strong Interactions. Ed. by L. W. Alvarez. (Italian Physical Society Ser.: Course 33). 1966. 82.50 o.p. (ISBN 0-12-368833-7). Acad Pr.

Strong Land & a Sturdy England in the Middle Ages. Richard Barber. LC 75-43895. (Illus.). 128p. (gr. 6 up). 1979. 8.95 o.p. (ISBN 0-395-28888-6, Clarion). HM.

Strong Opinions. Vladimir Nabokov. (McGraw-Hill Paperbacks Ser.). 348p. 1981. pap. text ed. 6.95 o.p. (ISBN 0-07-045725-5). McGraw.

Strong Opinions. Vladimir Nabokov. LC 73-6604. 352p. 1973. text ed. 8.95 o.p. (ISBN 0-07-045737-9). McGraw.

Strong Poison. Dorothy L. Sayers. 1978. pap. 2.75 o.p. (ISBN 0-380-01567-6, 69401-8). Avon.

Stronger Than Steel: The Wayne Alderson Story. R. C. Sproul. LC 80-7746. 244p. 1980. 11.95i o.p. (ISBN 0-06-067502-0). HarpR.

Stronghold: History Military. Date not set. (ISBN 0-8052-3938-3). Random.

Strongholds. Lucy M. Boston. LC 68-24383. 1969. 4.95 o.p. (ISBN 0-15-185988-4, HJ). HarBraceJ.

Strongly Interacting Particles. Riccardo Levi-Setti & Thomas Lasinski. (Chicago Lectures in Physics Ser). 1973. pap. text ed. 8.00x o.s.i. (ISBN 0-226-47445-3). U of Chicago Pr.

Stroop Report: The Jewish Quarter of Warsaw Is No More! Jurgen Stroop. LC 79-1900. 1979. 10.00 o.p. (ISBN 0-394-50443-7). Pantheon.

Structopathic Children, 2 pts. J. F. W. Kok. Incl. Pt. 1. Description of Disturbance Type & Strategies. 1126p (ISBN 90-237-4109-9); Pt. 2. Results of Experimental Research of Structuring Group Therapy. 122p (ISBN 90-237-4110-2). (Modern Approaches to the Diagnosis & Instruction of Multi-Handicapped Children Ser.: Vols. 9 & 10). 1972. text ed. 30.00 ea. o.p. (Pub. by Swets & Zeitlinger Netherlands). CJ Hogrefe Pubs.

Structural. 25.00 o.p. Am Consul Eng.

Structural Analysis. 2nd ed. R. Coates et al. 1980. pap. 43.95 o.p. (ISBN 0-442-30757-8). Van Nos Reinhold.

Structural Analysis. Russell C. Hibbeler. 107p. 1985. pap. solutions manual avail. o.p. (ISBN 0-02-354470-8). Macmillan.

Structural Analysis: A Matrix Approach. G. S. Pandit & S. P. Gupta. 592p. 1981. text ed. 12.20 o.p. (ISBN 0-07-096554-4). McGraw.

Structural Analysis of Narrative. Jean Calloud. Ed. by William A. Beardslee. Tr. by Daniel Patte from Fr. LC 75-37158. (Semeia Studies). 128p. 1976. pap. 3.95 o.p. (ISBN 0-8006-1503-4, 1-1503, Fortress). Augsburg Fortress.

Structural Analysis of the Rabbit Kidney. B. Kaissling & W. Kriz. (Advances in Anatomy, Embryology & Cell Biology: Vol. 56). (Illus.). 1979. pap. 33.00 o.p. (ISBN 0-387-09145-9). Springer-Verlag.

Structural Analysis Using Virtual Work. F. Thompson & G. G. Hayward. (Illus.). 320p. 1985. 59.95 o.p. (ISBN 0-412-22280-9, NO. 9128, Pub. by Chapman & Hall); 31.00 o.p. (ISBN 0-412-22290-6, NO. 9128, Pub. by Chapman & Hall). Routledge Chapman & Hall.

Structural & Functional Aspects of Phytochemistry see Symposia.

Structural & Kinetic Approach to Plasma Membrane Functions: Proceedings,Grignon, September 6-9, 1976. Ed. by C. Nicolau & A. Paraf. (Proceedings in Life Sciences Ser.). (Illus.). 1977. 37.00 o.p. (ISBN 0-387-08265-4). Springer-Verlag.

Structural Approach in Psychological Testing. M. L. Kaplan et al. LC 70-93755. 1971. 34.00 o.p. (ISBN 0-08-006867-7). Pergamon.

Structural Basis of Membrane Function. Ed. by D. Hatefi. 1976. 60.50 o.p. (ISBN 0-12-332450-5). Acad Pr.

Structural Brickwork. A. W. Hendry. LC 80-26993. 209p. 1981. 64.95x o.p. (ISBN 0-470-27109-4). Halsted Pr.

Structural Change & Prospects for Urbanization in Asian Countries. Gavin W. Jones. LC 83-16373. (Papers of East-West Population Institute: No. 88). vi, 46p. (Orig.). 1983. pap. 1.75 o.p. (ISBN 0-86638-047-7). EW Ctr HI.

Structural Change in a Developing Economy. Richard R. Nelson & T. P. Schultz. LC 79-148168. (Rand Corporation Research Study). 1971. 38.50x o.p. (ISBN 0-691-04163-6). Princeton U Pr.

Structural Change in the U. S. Automobile Industry. Ed. by Jeffrey A. Hunker. LC 82-48529. 288p. 1983. 34.00x o.p. (ISBN 0-669-06267-7). Lexington Bks.

Structural COBOL Programming. Morris Pollock & Harry Geist. 340p. 1982. pap. text ed. write for info. o.p. (ISBN 0-02-384150-8). Macmillan.

Structural Communication. Kieran Egan. LC 74-83215. 1976. pap. text ed. 7.95 o.p. (ISBN 0-8224-6550-7). D S Lake Pubs.

Structural Concrete Elements. E. W. Bennett. (Illus.). 1973. 21.95x o.p. (ISBN 0-412-09020-1, 6034, Pub. by Chapman & Hall). Routledge Chapman & Hall.

Structural Crashworthiness: Proceedings of the Structural Crashworthiness Conference, Liverpool University, 14-16 September 1983. Ed. by N. Jones. 100p. 1983. pap. 46.00 o.p. (ISBN 0-08-031136-9). Pergamon.

Structural Crystallography in Chemistry & Biology. Ed. by Jenny P. Glusker. LC 80-13858. (Benchmark Papers in Physical Chemistry & Chemical Physics: Vol. 4). 421p. 1982. 56.95 o.p. (ISBN 0-87933-368-5). Van Nos Reinhold.

Structural Design of Asphalt Concrete Pavement Systems. (Special Report). 217p. 1971. 10.00 o.p. (ISBN 0-309-01972-9); pap. 8.00 o.p. Transport Res Bd.

Structural Design of Nuclear Plant Facilities: Proceedings, American Nuclear Society Conference, New Orleans, December 8-10, 1975, 3 vols. 1668p. softcover 84.00 o.p. (ISBN 0-317-33012-8, 700014). Am Nuclear Soc.

Structural Design of Nuclear Plant Facilities: Proceedings, American Nuclear Society Conference, Chicago, December 17-18, 1973, 3 vols. 1240p. 60.00 o.p. (ISBN 0-317-33013-6, 700009). Am Nuclear Soc.

Structural Dynamics Heat Conduction. CISM (International Center for Mechanical Sciences) Staff. Ed. by B. F. De Veubeke et al. (CISM Publications: No. 126). (Illus.). 256p. 1974. pap. 25.60 o.p. (ISBN 0-387-81201-6). Springer-Verlag.

Structural Econometric Model of the Saudi Arabian Economy: Nineteen Sixty to Nineteen Seventy. Faisal Safooq Al-Bashir. LC 77-441. 144p. 1977. text ed. 36.50 o.p. (ISBN 0-471-02177-6). Krieger.

Structural Elements in Particle Physics & Statistical Mechanics. Ed. by J. Honerkamp & J. Pohlmeyer. (NATO ASI Series B, Physics: Vol. 82). 470p. 1983. 75.00x o.p. (ISBN 0-306-41038-9, Plenum Pr). Plenum Pub.

Structural Engineering, 2 vols. in 1. 2nd, Combined ed. Richard N. White et al. LC 76-202. 670p. 1976. Vol. 1: Introduction to Design Concepts & Analysis, 2nd ed. text ed. (ISBN 0-471-94067-4). Vol. 2: Intermediate Structures, rev. ed. Wiley.

Structural Engineering Design Programs: Software Project. N. Morton. 1985. 350.00 o.p. (ISBN 0-07-079572-X). McGraw.

Structural Exegesis - from Theory to Practice: Exegesis of Mark 15 & 16 Hermeneutical Implications. Daniel Patte & Aline Patte. LC 78-54557. 144p. 1978. 8.95 o.p. (ISBN 0-8006-0524-1, 1-524). Augsburg Fortress.

Structural Linguistics & Human Communication. B. Malmberg. LC 63-12931. (Kommunikation und Kybernetik in Einzeldarstellungen: Band 2). (Illus.). 1976. 33.10 o.p. (ISBN 0-387-03888-4). Springer-Verlag.

Structural Masonry Designer's Manual. W. G. Curtin et al. (Illus.). 448p. 1982. text ed. 95.00x o.p. (ISBN 0-246-11208-5). Sheridan.

Structural Mechanics & Analysis. James Michalos & E. N. Wilson. 1965. text ed. write for info. o.p. (ISBN 0-02-381330-X). Macmillan.

Structural Mechanics Software Series, 5 vols. Ed. by Nicholas Perrone & Walter D. Pilkey. (Software Ser.). (Illus.). 1985. 30.00x ea. o.p. Vol. 1 (ISBN 0-8139-0735-7). Vol. 2 (ISBN 0-8139-0781-0). Vol. 3, 344p (ISBN 0-8139-0857-4). Vol. 4, 467p (ISBN 0-8139-0918-X). Vol. 5, 342p (ISBN 0-8139-1032-3). U Pr of Va.

Structural Modeling & Optimization. D. G. Carmichael. (Engineering Science Ser.). 306p. 1981. 81.95 o.p. (ISBN 0-470-27114-0). Halsted Pr.

Structural Models & African Poetics: Towards a Pragmatic View of Literature. Sunday O. Anozie. 220p. 1981. 37.50x o.p. (ISBN 0-7100-0467-2). Routledge Chapman & Hall.

Structural Phase Transitions. A. D. Bruce & R. A. Cowley. 325p. 1981. 35.00x o.p. (NO.6589, Pub by Pion England). Routledge Chapman & Hall.

Structural Radii, Electron-Cloud Radii, Ionic Radii & Solvation see Coordinative Interactions.

Structural Safety & Reliability: Proceedings of the International Conference. Ed. by Alfred M. Freudenthal et al. 1972. 170.00 o.p. (ISBN 0-08-016566-4). Pergamon.

Structural Stability, the Theory of Catastrophes, & Applications in the Sciences: Proceedings. Conference Held at Battelle Seattle Research Center, 1975. Ed. by P. Hilton et al. (Lecture Notes in Mathematics: Vol. 525). 1977. soft cover 24.00 o.p. (ISBN 0-387-07791-X). Springer-Verlag.

Structural Steel Designer's Handbook. Ed. by Frederick S. Merritt. (Illus.). 1000p. 1972. text ed. 84.00 o.p. (ISBN 0-07-041507-2). McGraw.

Structural Theorems & Their Applications. B. G. Neal. 1964. text ed. 21.00 o.p. (ISBN 0-08-010872-5); pap. text ed. 9.75 o.p. (ISBN 0-08-010871-7). Pergamon.

Structural Theory of Organic Chemistry. N. D. Epiotis et al. LC 76-57966. (Topics in Current Chemistry: Vol. 70). 1977. 59.00 o.p. (ISBN 0-387-08099-6). Springer-Verlag.

Structuralism & Education. Rex Gibson. (Studies in Teaching & Learning). 166p. (Orig.). 1984. pap. text ed. 14.95 o.s.i. (ISBN 0-340-33975-6). Princeton Bk Co.

Structuralism & Marxism. A. Schaff. LC 77-30331. 256p. 1978. 46.00 o.p. (ISBN 0-08-020505-4). Pergamon.

Structure-Activity Relationships & Theory. Ed. by C. J. Cavallito. LC 72-13533. 1973. 115.00 o.p. (ISBN 0-08-016890-6). Pergamon.

Structure Analysis by Electron Diffraction. B. K. Vainshtein. 1964. 110.00 o.p. (ISBN 0-08-010241-7). Pergamon.

Structure & Action of Proteins. Richard E. Dickerson & Irving Geis. LC 69-11112. 1969. pap. text ed. 21.95 o.p. (ISBN 0-8053-2391-0). Benjamin-Cummings.

Structure & Agency in the Formation of National Urban Policy in the U. S. A., 1976-1980. D. Wilmoth. 48p. 1986. pap. 22.00 o.p. (ISBN 0-08-034147-0, Pub. by PPL). Pergamon.

Structure & Application of Galvanomagnetic Devices. H. Weiss. 1969. 93.00 o.p. (ISBN 0-08-012597-2). Pergamon.

Structure & Approximation in Physical Theories. Ed. by A. Hartkamper & H. J. Schmidt. LC 81-15846. 264p. 1981. text ed. 55.00x o.p. (ISBN 0-306-40882-1, Plenum Pr). Plenum Pub.

Structure & Bonding, Vol. 17. Ed. by Dunitz et al. LC 67-11280. (Illus.). 260p. 1973. 43.00 o.p. (ISBN 0-387-06458-3). Springer-Verlag.

Structure & Bonding in Solid State Chemistry. M. F. Ladd. (Chemical Science Ser.). 326p. 1986. pap. 19.95 o.p. (ISBN 0-470-20321-8). Halsted Pr.

Structure & Chemistry of the Aging Heart. H. F. Gey et al. 238p. 1974. text ed. 24.00x o.p. (ISBN 0-8422-7168-6). Irvington.

Structure & Control of State Economy. W. L. L'Esperance. 198p. 1981. 23.00x o.p. (ISBN 0-85086-082-2, NO.8000, Pub. by Pion England). Routledge Chapman & Hall.

Structure & Crystallization of Glasses. W. Vogel. 1971. 71.00 o.p. (ISBN 0-08-006998-3). Pergamon.

Structure & Dynamics of Socioeconomic Systems, Cybernetics in Organization & Management, Engineering Systems Methodology, Systems Research on Science & Technology: Proceedings of the European Meeting on Cybernetics & Systems Research, Linz, Austria, March 1978, Vol. 10. Cybernetics & Systems Research Staff. LC 75-6641. (Illus.). 562p. 1982. text ed. 125.00 o.p. (ISBN 0-89116-239-9). Hemisphere Pub.

Structure & Evolution of the Continental Lithosphere. Ed. by H. N. Pollack & V. Rama Murthy. (Illus.). 210p. 1984. 83.00 o.p. (ISBN 0-08-030023-5). Pergamon.

Structure & Function in Cilia & Flagella. P. Satir. Ed. by M. Alfert et al. Bd. with Trichocystoides. Corps Trichocytoides. Cnidocystes & Colloblastes. R. Horvasse. (Illus.). 57p. 1965. (Protoplasmatologia: Vol. 3, Pt. E). (Illus.). iv, 52p. 1965. pap. 34.90 o.p. (ISBN 0-387-80732-2). Springer-Verlag.

Structure & Function of Animal Cell Components. P. N. Campbell. 1966. 34.00 o.p. (ISBN 0-08-011819-4); pap. 13.00 o.p. (ISBN 0-08-011818-6). Pergamon.

Structure & Function of Biological Membranes. Ed. by Lawrence I. Rothfield. (Molecular Biology Ser.). 1971. 85.50 o.p. (ISBN 0-12-598650-5). Acad Pr.

Structure & Function of Chloroplasts. Ed. by M. Gibbs. LC 79-130575. (Illus.). 1972. 38.00 o.p. (ISBN 0-387-05258-5). Springer-Verlag.

Structure & Function of Haemocyanin: Proceedings in Life Sciences. European Molecular Biology International Workshop, Fifth, Marine Biological Laboratory of the University of Malta, Malta, August 2-4, 1976. Ed. by J. V. Bannister. (Illus.). 1977. 48.00 o.p. (ISBN 0-387-08284-0). Springer-Verlag.

Structure & Function of Inhibitory Neuronal Mechanisms. Ed. by U. S. Von Euler et al. 1968. 140.00 o.p. (ISBN 0-08-012414-3). Pergamon.

Structure & Function of Muscle. 2nd ed. Geoffrey H. Bourne. Vol. 1, 1972. 105.00 o.p. (ISBN 0-12-119101-X); Vol. 2, 1973. 114.00 o.p. (ISBN 0-12-119102-8); Vol. 3, 1973. 105.00 o.p. (ISBN 0-12-119103-6); Vol. 4, 1974. 105.00 o.p. (ISBN 0-12-119104-4); 349.00 set o.p. (ISBN 0-685-36103-9). Acad Pr.

Structure & Function of Oxidation Reduction Enzymes. A. Akeson & A. Ehrenburg. 788p. 1972. 210.00 o.p. (ISBN 0-08-016874-4). Pergamon.

Structure & Function of Plant Cells in Saline Habitats. B. P. Strogonov et al. Ed. by B. Gollak. Tr. by A. Mercado from Rus. LC 73-13609. (Illus.). 284p. 1973. 64.95x o.p. (ISBN 0-470-83406-4). Halsted Pr.

Structure & Function of Proprioceptors in the Invertebrates. P. J. Mill. 686p. 1976. 54.50x o.p. (ISBN 0-412-12890-X, NO.6201, Pub. by Chapman & Hall England). Routledge Chapman & Hall.

Structure & Function of Sarcoplasmic Reticulum (Symposium) Sidney Fleischer & Yuji Tonomura. LC 83-21556. 1985. 64.50 o.p. (ISBN 0-12-260380-X). Acad Pr.

Structure & Function of the Body. 7th ed. Catherine P. Anthony & Gary A. Thibodeau. (Illus.). 320p. 1983. text ed. 18.95 o.p. (ISBN 0-8016-0296-3); study guide 10.95 o.p. (ISBN 0-8016-2943-8). Mosby.

Structure & Function of the Cell. 2nd ed. Gary Parker. (Programmed Biology S tudies). 1977. 6.95 o.s.i. (ISBN 0-88462-006-9, 3304-05, Ed Methods). Longman Finan.

Structure & Function of the Endoplasmic Reticulum in Animal Cells. Ed. by F. C. Gran & F. C. Gran. 1968. 29.00 o.p. (ISBN 0-12-295056-9). Acad Pr.

Structure & Function of the Gonadotropins. Ed. by Kenneth W. McKerns. LC 78-12372. (Biochemical Endocrinology Ser.). (Illus.). 646p. 1978. 85.00x o.p. (ISBN 0-306-40097-9, Plenum Pr). Plenum Pub.

Structure & Function Relationships in Biochemical Systems. Ed. by Francesco Bossa et al. LC 82-9139. (Advances In Experimental Medicine & Biology Ser.: Vol. 148). 394p. 1982. 69.50x o.p. (ISBN 0-306-41034-6, Plenum Pr). Plenum Pub.

Structure & Functions of Contractile Proteins. Boris F. Poglazov. 1966. 68.50 o.p. (ISBN 0-12-559150-0). Acad Pr.

Structure & Governance of Higher Education. Ed. by Michael Shattock. 1983. 21.00x o.p. (ISBN 0-900868-91-0, Open Univ Pr). Taylor & Francis.

Structure & Meaning: An Introduction to Literature. Anthony Dube et al. LC 75-31038. (Illus.). 1152p. 1976. text ed. 18.95 o.p. (ISBN 0-395-21967-1). HM.

Structure & Mechanism in Organo-Phosphorus Chemistry. R. F. Hudson. (Organic Chemistry Ser.: Vol. 6). 1966. 82.50 o.p. (ISBN 0-12-360250-5). Acad Pr.

Structure & Metabolism of the Pancreatic Islets - a Centennial of Paul Langerhan's Discovery. S. Falkmer et al. 1970. 170.00 o.p. (ISBN 0-08-015844-7). Pergamon.

Structure & Metabolism of the Pancreatic Islets. Ed. by S. E. Brolin. 1964. 95.00 o.p. (ISBN 0-08-010758-3). Pergamon.

Structure & Process in Speech Perception: Proceedings of the Dynamic Aspects of Speech Perception Symposium, I. P. O. Eindhoven, the Netherlands, Aug. 4-6, 1975. Dynamic Aspects of Speech Perception Symposium Staff. Ed. by A. Cohen & S. G. Nooteboom. (Communications & Cybernetics: Vol. II). (Illus.). 370p. 1976. 38.00 o.p. (ISBN 0-387-07520-8). Springer-Verlag.

Structure & Properties of Dual-Phase Steels: Proceedings of the AIME Annual Meeting, New Orleans, 1979. AIME Annual Meeting Staff. Ed. by R. A. Kot & J. W. Morris. (Illus.). 362p. 40.00 o.p. (ISBN 0-89520-357-X); members 26.00 o.p. (ISBN 0-317-34894-9); student members 14.00 o.p. (ISBN 0-317-34895-7). ASM.

Structure & Properties of Inorganic Solids. F. S. Galasso. LC 70-104123. 1970. 75.00 o.p. (ISBN 0-08-006873-1). Pergamon.

Structure & Properties of Polymers. LC 61-642. (Advances in Polymer Science: Vol. 29). (Illus.). 1978. 54.00 o.p. (ISBN 0-387-08886-5). Springer-Verlag.

Structure & Reactivity of Cycloimmonium Ylides. J. P. Surpateanu et al. 1977. pap. 14.00 o.p. (ISBN 0-08-021585-8). Pergamon.

Structure & Transformations of Organic Molecules. Ed. by F. Boschke et al. (Topics in Current Chemistry: Vol. 32). (Illus.). 110p. 1972. pap. 30.30 o.p. (ISBN 0-387-05936-9). Springer-Verlag.

Structure & Ultrastructure of Microorganisms. E. M. Brieger. 1963. 66.00 o.p. (ISBN 0-12-134350-2). Acad Pr.

Structure, Extractives, & Utilization of Bark. Jack Weiner & Vera Pollack. (Bibliographic Ser.: No. 191). 446p. 1960. 23.00 o.p. (ISBN 0-317-34450-1). Inst Paper Chem.

Structure in Thought & Feeling. Susan Aylwin. 320p. 1985. 49.95 o.p. (ISBN 0-416-35990-6, 9466). Routledge Chapman & Hall.

Structure, Interaction & Social Theory. Derek Layder. 200p. 1981. 25.00x o.p. (ISBN 0-7100-0762-0). Routledge Chapman & Hall.

Structure of Ammon's Horn. Santiago Ramon Y Cajal. Tr. by Lisbeth M. Kraft. (Illus.). 100p. 1968. 15.25 o.p. (ISBN 0-398-01543-0). C C Thomas.

Structure of Attractors in Dynamical Systems: Proceedings, North Dakota, June 20-24, 1977. Ed. by N. G. Markley et al. LC 78-13670. (Lecture Notes in Mathematics: Vol. 668). 1978. pap. 20.00 o.p. (ISBN 0-387-08925-X). Springer-Verlag.

Structure of Crystalline Polymers. Hiroyuki Tadokoro. LC 78-15024. 465p. 1979. 68.50 o.p. (ISBN 0-471-02356-6). Krieger.

Structure of Disadvantage. Ed. by Muriel Brown. (SSRC-DHSS Studies in Deprivation & Disadvantages: No. 12). viii, 210p. 1983. pap. text ed. 12.50x o.p. (ISBN 0-435-82093-1). Gower Pub Co.

Structure of Factors. new ed. Salvatore Anastasia & Paul M. Willig. LC 72-78469. 1974. 30.00x o.p. Algorithmics.

Structure of French. Edgar N. Mayer. 1969. pap. 10.00x o.p. (ISBN 0-87081-074-X). Univ Pr Colo.

Structure of Geology. David B. Kitts. LC 77-7395. 200p. 1977. pap. 9.95x o.p. (ISBN 0-87074-162-4). SMU Press.

Structure of Metallic Catalysts. J. R. Anderson. 1975. 81.50 o.p. (ISBN 0-12-057150-1). Acad Pr.

Structure of Metals: A Modern Conception. Institution of Metallurgists Staff. 1959. 8.25x o.p. (ISBN 0-677-60580-3). Gordon & Breach.

Structure of Modernist Poetry. Theo Hermans. 264p. 1982. 27.50 o.p. (ISBN 0-7099-0002-3, Pub. by Croom Helm Ltd). Routledge Chapman & Hall.

Structure of Molecules & Internal Rotation. San-Ichiro Mizushima. (Physical Chemistry Ser.: Vol. 2). 1954. 66.00 o.p. (ISBN 0-12-501750-2). Acad Pr.

Structure of Planets. G. H. Cole & W. G. Watton. LC 77-18646. (Wykeham Science Ser.: No. 45). 232p. 1977. 19.50x o.p. (ISBN 0-8448-1309-5, Pub. by Crane Russak & Co). Taylor & Francis.

Structure of Science: Problems in the Logic of Scientific Explanation. Ernest Nagel. 1961. text ed. 16.95 o.p. (ISBN 0-15-584665-5, HC). HarBraceJ.

Structure of Social Science. Michael Lessnoff. (Studies in Sociology Ser.). 1978. pap. text ed. 14.95 o.p. (ISBN 0-04-300046-0). Unwin Hyman.

Structure of Socialist Society. Andras Hegedus. 1977. 15.95x o.p. (ISBN 0-09-459400-7, Pub. by Constable Pubs UK). Trans-Atl Phila.

Structure of Stratification in Thailand. Moshe Lissak. 1973. 4.95 o.p. (ISBN 0-87855-265-0); pap. text ed. 2.95x o.p. (ISBN 0-87855-672-9). Transaction Pubs.

Structure of Television. P. Gould et al. (Illus.). 178p. 1984. 29.95 o.p. (ISBN 0-85086-110-1, 9195, Pub. by Pion England). Routledge Chapman & Hall.

Structure of the Autonomic Nervous System. G. Gabella. 1976. 75.00x o.p. (ISBN 0-412-13620-1, 6114, Pub. by Chapman & Hall). Routledge Chapman & Hall.

Structure of the Book of Job: A Form-Critical Analysis. Claus Westermann. Tr. by Charles A. Muenchow from Ger. LC 80-2379. 160p. 1981. 14.95 o.p. (ISBN 0-8006-0651-5, 1-651, Fortress). Augsburg Fortress.

Structure of the Canyon Mountain (Oregon) Ophiolite & Its Implication for Sea-Floor Spreading. Hans G. Lallemant. LC 75-41702. (Special Paper: No. 173). (Illus., Orig.). 1976. pap. 5.60 o.p. (ISBN 0-8137-2173-3). Geol Soc.

Structure of the Eye. Ed. by George K. Smelser. 1961. 85.00 o.p. (ISBN 0-12-648950-5). Acad Pr.

Structure of the Legal Environment: Law, Ethics & Business. Bill Shaw & Arthur D. Wolfe. LC 86-7510. 880p. Date not set. price not set o.p. (ISBN 0-534-06252-0). PWS-Kent Pub.

Structure of the Novel. Edwin Muir. LC 29-3271. 1969. pap. 1.65 o.p. (ISBN 0-15-685688-3, Harv). HarBraceJ.

Structure of the Retina. Santiago Ramon Y Cajal. Tr. by Sylvia A. Thorpe & Mitchell Glickstein. (Illus.). 224p. 1972. 28.75 o.p. (ISBN 0-398-02385-9). C C Thomas.

Structure of the Stratosphere & Mesosphere. Willis L. Webb. (International Geophysics Ser.: Vol. 9). 1966. 63.00 o.p. (ISBN 0-12-739850-3). Acad Pr.

Structure of the Universe. E. L. Schatzman. (Illus., Orig.). 1968. pap. text ed. 3.95 o.p. (ISBN 0-07-055172-3). McGraw.

Structure of Time. W. H. Newton-Smith. (International Library of Philosophy & Scientific Method Ser.). (Illus.). 1980. 32.50x o.p. (ISBN 0-7100-0362-5). Routledge Chapman & Hall.

Structure of U. S. Business. Jay M. Gould & Bentley H. Paykin. Ed. by Trinet, Inc. Staff. LC 81-65730. 250p. 1981. pap. 100.00 o.p. (ISBN 0-86692-003-X). Trinet.

Structure of Water & Aqueous Solutions. Werner A. Luck. (Illus.). 247p. 1974. 67.50x o.p. (ISBN 3-527-25588-5). VCH Pubs.

Structured Analysis & Design of Information Systems. K. Wigander et al. 288p. 1984. text ed. 36.95 o.p. (ISBN 0-07-015061-3). McGraw.

Structured Approach to FORTRAN 77 Programming: With WATFIV. C. Joseph Sass. 350p. 1983. scp 23.00 o.p. (ISBN 0-205-07918-0, 207918). Wm C Brown.

Structured COBOL: A Problem-Solving Approach. Gerard A. Paquette. 624p. 1984. pap. text ed. 22.00 o.p. (ISBN 0-87150-697-1, 8300). PWS-Kent Pub.

Structured COBOL for Microcomputers. D. Keith Carver. 150p. 1983. pap. write for info. o.p. Brooks-Cole.

Structured COBOL Library. Ruth Ashley & Judi N. Fernandez. 1986. 125.00 o.p. (ISBN 0-471-62448-9). Wiley.

Structured COBOL Programming. John C. Molluzzo. 730p. 1987. pap. text ed. (ISBN 0-534-07188-0). Wadsworth Pub.

Structured COBOL Programming. 4th ed. Nancy Stern & Robert A. Stern. LC 84-17282. 848p. 1985. pap. text ed. 36.25 o.p. (ISBN 0-471-87150-8). Wiley.

Structured COBOL: Programming & Problem Solving. Pat Fenton & Brian Williams. 704p. 1988. pap. 31.95 o.p. (ISBN 0-8016-1662-X). Irwin.

Structured Experiences for Integration of Handicapped Children. Karen Anderson & Alan Milliren. LC 83-9949. 416p. 1983. 36.00 o.p. (ISBN 0-89443-877-8). Aspen Pub.

Structured FORTRAN 77 for Business & General Applications. Harice L. Seeds. LC 81-125. 512p. 1981. pap. 30.95 o.p. (ISBN 0-471-07836-0). Wiley.

Structured FORTRAN 77 for Engineers & Scientists. D. M. Etter. 1982. 26.95 o.p. (ISBN 0-8053-2520-4); instr's. guide 4.95 o.p. (ISBN 0-8053-2521-2); software supplement package 50.00 o.p. (ISBN 0-8053-2517-4). Benjamin-Cummings.

Structured Mortgage & Receivable Financing. Practising Law Institute Staff & Rodney S. Dayan. LC 85-72525. (Real Estate Law & Practice Course Handbook Ser.: No. 264). 752p. 1985. 15.00 o.p. (N4-4443). PLI.

Structured PL-1 Programming: An Introduction. John Xenakis. 1979. pap. text ed. write for info. o.p. (ISBN 0-87872-190-8, Duxbury Pr). PWS-Kent Pub.

Structured Settlements. Pennsylvania Bar Institute Staff. 101p. 1983. 20.00 o.p. (ISBN 0-318-02167-6, 233). PA Bar Inst.

Structured Walkthroughs. 2nd ed. Edward Yourdon. 152p. (Orig.). 1978. pap. 15.00 o.p. (ISBN 0-917072-09-X, Yourdon). P-H.

Structures & Environment Handbook. rev. ed. Midwest Plan Service Engineers Staff. LC 76-27983. (Illus.). 658p. 1983. pap. text ed. 25.00 o.p. (ISBN 0-89373-057-2, MWPS-1). Midwest Plan Serv.

Structures & Sequences in Clastic Rocks. (Short Course Notes Ser.). 249p. 1982. 20.00 o.p. (9). SEPM.

Structures: Basic Theory with Worked Examples. K. Logie. 1982. pap. 14.95 o.p. (ISBN 0-442-30760-8). Van Nos Reinhold.

Structures for Business & Professional Speech: A Working Resource Manual. 2nd ed. Lawrence W. Hugenberg, Sr. & Alfred W. Owens, II. 144p. 1985. pap. text ed. 11.95 o.p. (ISBN 0-8403-3484-2). Kendall-Hunt.

Structures of Thinking. Karl Mannheim. Ed. by David Kettler et al. Tr. by Jeremy Shapiro & Shierry Weber. (International Library of Sociology). 240p. 1982. 32.00x o.p. (ISBN 0-7100-0936-4). Routledge Chapman & Hall.

Structures Technology for Large Radio & Radar Telescope Systems. Ed. by James W. Mar. 1969. 50.00x o.p. (ISBN 0-262-13046-7). MIT Pr.

Structuring of Experience. Ed. by I. C. Uzgiris & F. Weizman. LC 76-45357. (Illus.). 464p. 1977. 55.50x o.p. (ISBN 0-306-30961-0, Plenum Pr). Plenum Pub.

Structuring Speech: A How-to-Do-It Book About Public Speaking. Gerald M. Phillips & J. Jerome Zolten. 274p. 1976. pap. text ed. write for info. o.p. (ISBN 0-02-395690-9). Macmillan.

Structuring the Therapeutic Process: Compromise with Chaos - a Therapist's Response to the Individual & the Group. Murray Cox. LC 77-4181. 1978. 55.00 o.s.i. (ISBN 0-08-020403-1); pap. text ed. 16.75 o.s.i. (ISBN 0-08-020402-3). Pergamon.

Struggle & Fulfillment: The Inner Dynamics of Religion & Morality. Donald Evans. LC 80-8050. 256p. 1981. pap. 8.95 o.p. (ISBN 0-8006-1426-7, 1-1426, Fortress). Augsburg Fortress.

Struggle for a Free Europe. Dean Acheson. 1971. pap. text ed. 3.95x o.p. (ISBN 0-393-09983-0). Norton.

Struggle for Afghanistan. Nancy P. Newell & Richard S. Newell. LC 80-69829. (Illus.). 236p. 1981. 26.95x o.p. (ISBN 0-8014-1389-3). Cornell U Pr.

Struggle for Cyprus. Charles Foley & W. I. Scobie. LC 74-10837. (Publications Ser.: No. 137). 187p. 1975. 9.95x o.p. (ISBN 0-8179-6371-5). Hoover Inst Pr.

Struggle for Development: National Strategies in an International Context. Ed. by Manfred A. Bienefeld & E. Martin Godfrey. LC 81-19821. 352p. 1982. 85.00 o.p. (ISBN 0-471-10152-4). Wiley.

Struggle for Freedom. Knofel Staton. LC 76-18381. 96p. 1977. pap. 2.25 o.p. (ISBN 0-87239-063-2, 40034). Standard Pub.

Struggle for Freedom: The History of Black Americans. Daniel S. Davis. LC 71-187857. (Illus.). 256p. 1972. 6.50 o.p. (ISBN 0-15-281815-4, HJ). HarBraceJ.

Struggle for Inner Peace. rev. ed. Henry R. Brandt. 136p. 1984. pap. 5.50 o.p. (ISBN 0-88207-245-5). Victor Bks.

Struggle for Justice. 1971. pap. 4.95 o.p. (ISBN 0-686-95388-6). Am Fr Serv Comm.

Struggle for Justice: A Report on Crime & Punishment in America. American Friends Service Committee. 186p. 1971. 4.50 o.p. (ISBN 0-8090-8927-0); pap. 4.95 o.p. (ISBN 0-8090-1363-0). Hill & Wang.

Struggle for Madrid: The Central Epic of the Spanish Conflict, 1936-1937. Robert G. Colodny. 256p. 1958. 9.50 o.p. (ISBN 0-87855-034-8). Transaction Pubs.

Struggle for the American Curriculum 1893-1958. Herbert M. Kliebard. 293p. 1986. text ed. 24.95 o.p. (ISBN 0-7102-0055-2). Routledge Chapman & Hall.

Struggle for the Ministry of Health. Frank Honigsbaum. 80p. 1970. pap. text ed. 5.00x o.p. (ISBN 0-7135-1836-7, Pub. by Bedford England). Gower Pub Co.

Struggle for Transcaucasia. Firuz Kazemzadeh. 1952. (ISBN 0-8022-0834-7). Philos Lib.

Struggle Is a Name for Hope. Renny Golden & Shelia Collins. (Worker Writer Ser.: No. 3). 48p. (Orig.). 1982. pap. 3.00 o.p. (ISBN 0-931122-24-4). West End.

Struggle of a Hong Kong Girl. Lily Chan. 1986. 12.95 o.p. (ISBN 0-533-06593-3). Vantage.

Struggle of Prayer. Donald G. Bloesch. LC 79-3589. 192p. 1980. 10.95i o.p. (ISBN 0-06-060797-1). HarpR.

Struggle over Eritrea, 1962-1978: War & Revolution in the Horn of Africa. Haggai Erlich. (Publication Ser.: No. 260). 176p. 1982. pap. 10.95x o.p. (ISBN 0-8179-7602-7). Hoover Inst Pr.

Struggling with Sex: Serious Call to Marriage-Centered Sexual Life. Arthur A. Rouner, Jr. LC 86-32028. 112p. (Orig.). 1987. pap. 6.95 o.p. (ISBN 0-8066-2243-1, 10-6096, Augsburg). Augsburg Fortress.

Struwwelpeter. Heinrich Hoffmann. (Illus.). (gr. 1-5). 1909. 7.95 o.p. (ISBN 0-7100-1534-8). Routledge Chapman & Hall.

Stryker's Children. Joyce A. Schneider. 1984. 15.95 o.p. (ISBN 0-87795-610-3, Arbor Hse). Morrow.

Stryker's Kingdom. W. A. Harbinson. 410p. 1986. pap. 3.95 o.p. (ISBN 0-931773-79-2). Critics Choice Paper.

Stu Apte's Fishing in the Florida Keys & Flamingo. 3rd ed. Stuart C. Apte. LC 76-360969. (Illus.). 96p. 1982. pap. 4.95 o.p. (ISBN 0-89317-006-2). Windward Pub.

Stubborn Child. Mark Devlin. LC 84-45053. 288p. 1985. 14.95 o.p. (ISBN 0-689-11476-1, Atheneum). Macmillan.

Stubborn Faith: Papers on Old Testament & Related Subjects Presented to Honor William Andrew Irwin. Ed. by Edward C. Hobbs. LC 56-12567. 184p. 1956. 13.95x o.p. (ISBN 0-87074-079-2). SMU Press.

Stubb's Run. Peter L. Sandberg. 1979. 7.95 o.p. (ISBN 0-395-28423-6). HM.

Stuckenschmid. Tr. by H. H. Schoenberg from Ger. 400p. (Orig.). 1985. pap. 5.95 o.s.i. (ISBN 0-7145-0091-7). Riverrun NY.

Stud Farm Diary. Humphrey S. Finney. Repr. (ISBN 0-85131-194-6, NL51, Dist. by Miller). S R Smith Sporting Bks.

Studebaker: The Complete Story. William A. Cannon & Fred K. Fox. (Illus.). 368p. 1982. 39.95 o.p. (ISBN 0-8306-2064-8, 2064). TAB Bks.

Student Access to Libraries & Library Resources in Secondary Schools. Lawrence H. McGrath. (Occasional Papers: No. 97). 28p. 1969. pap. 1.00 o.p. (ISBN 0-317-58875-3). U of Ill Lib Info Sci.

Student Activities in Secondary Schools: A Bibliography. Compiled by Jackson et al. Battiste. 86p. 1980. pap. 7.00 o.p. (ISBN 0-88210-109-9). Natl Assn Principals.

Student Advocate, Vols. 1-3, No. 1. 1969. Repr. of 1938 ed. lib. bdg. 24.75x o.p. (ISBN 0-8371-9251-X, S300). Greenwood.

Student Aid & Public Higher Education: A Progress Report. Jacob O. Stampen & Roxanne W. Reeves. 1983. 5.00 o.p. (ISBN 0-317-40624-8). Am Assn Comm Jr Coll.

Student Body Workbook. 32p. Date not set. 8.95 o.p. (ISBN 0-318-23894-2). Future Home.

Student Chemist Explores Computations. Julian May. LC 74-8140. (Student Scientist Ser.). 140p. (YA) (gr. 7-12). 1975. PLB 10.97 o.p. (ISBN 0-8239-0301-X). Rosen Group.

Student Chemist Explores Organic Compounds. Ted Charney. LC 75-12904. (YA) (gr. 7-12). 1976. PLB 10.97 o.p. (ISBN 0-8239-0326-5). Rosen Group.

Student Council Handbook. National Association of Secondary School Principals Staff. 1982. pap. 8.00 o.p. Natl Assn Principals.

Student Developement in Tomorrow's Higher Education. Robert Brown. 56p. 1972. pap. text ed. 4.00 o.p. (ISBN 0-911547-72-X, 72157W34). Am Assn Coun Dev.

Student Development in Higher Education. Don Creamer. 1980. 16.00 o.p. (ISBN 1-55620-029-3, 72608C). Am Assn Coun Dev.

Student Earth Scientist Explores Changing Earth. Constantine Constant. LC 75-8906. (Student Scientist Ser.). (YA) (gr. 7-12). 1976. PLB 10.97 o.p. (ISBN 0-8239-0330-3). Rosen Group.

Student Earth Scientist Explores Weather. Constantine Constant. LC 74-13746. (Student Scientist Ser.). (Illus.). 133p. (gr. 7-12). 1975. PLB 10.97 o.p. (ISBN 0-8239-0303-6). Rosen Group.

Student Experience of Higher Education. Ian Lewis. LC 84-45557. 180p. 1984. 27.50 o.p. (ISBN 0-7099-1666-3, Pub. by Croom Helm Ltd). Routledge Chapman & Hall.

Student Guide American Government I. 3rd ed. 304p. 1985. pap. 9.95 o.p. (ISBN 0-8403-3649-7). Kendall-Hunt.

Student Guide for Canadian, Pt. 3. Ed. by Life Office Management Association Staff. (FLMI Insurance Education Program Ser.). 1976. pap. 8.00 workbook o.p. (ISBN 0-915322-20-X). LOMA.

Student Guide for Management Principles. 3rd ed. Ed. by Life Office Management Association Staff. (FLMI Insurance Education Program Ser.). 200p. 1981. pap. 4.50 workbook o.p. (ISBN 0-915322-43-9). LOMA.

Student Guide to Accounting for Life Insurance Companies. Ed. by Life Office Management ASsociation Staff. (FLMI Insurance Education Program Ser.). 94p. 1980. pap. 5.00 workbook o.p. (ISBN 0-915322-42-0). LOMA.

Student Guide to American Government II. 3rd ed. 320p. 1985. pap. 9.95 o.p. (ISBN 0-8403-3651-9). Kendall-Hunt.

Student Guide to American Government Survey. 3rd ed. 400p. 1985. pap. 14.95 o.p. (ISBN 0-8403-3658-6). Kendall-Hunt.

Student Guide to New York. Leslie Gourse. (Illus.). 1984. pap. 8.95 o.p. (ISBN 0-88254-895-6). Hippocrene Bks.

Student Involvement Manual for Personnel Management. William F. Glueck & Jerry A. Wall. 1979. pap. 6.95x o.p. (ISBN 0-256-02253-4). Irwin.

Student Journalist & Broadcasting. John R. Rider. LC 68-12132. (Student Journalist Ser.). (Illus., Photos). (gr. 7-12). 1968. PLB 10.97 o.p. (ISBN 0-8239-0114-9). Rosen Group.

Student Journalist & Creative Photography. Bill Ward. LC 75-30781. (gr. 7-12). 1976. PLB 10.97 o.p. (ISBN 0-8239-0335-4). Rosen Group.

Student Journalist & Depth Reporting. Bill G. Ward. LC 70-163427. (Student Journalist Ser.). (gr. 7 up). 1972. PLB 10.97 o.p. (ISBN 0-8239-0251-X). Rosen Group.

Student Journalist & Designing the Opinion Pages. William G. Ward. LC 69-14235. (Student Journalist Ser.). (Illus.). (gr. 7 up). 1969. PLB 10.97 o.p. (ISBN 0-8239-0116-5). Rosen Group.

Student Journalist & Editing. Charles Garven. Ed. by Ruth C. Rosen. LC 68-11055. (Student Journalist Ser.). (Illus.). (gr. 7 up). 1968. PLB 10.97 o.p. (ISBN 0-8239-0117-3). Rosen Group.

Student Journalist & Editing the Yearbook. Edmund C. Arnold. LC 72-94929. (YA) (gr. 7-12). 1973. PLB 10.97 o.p. (ISBN 0-8239-0279-X). Rosen Group.

Student Journalist & Editorial Leadership. William G. Ward. LC 68-22157. (Student Journalist Ser.). (gr. 7 up). PLB 10.97 o.p. (ISBN 0-8239-0118-1). Rosen Group.

Student Journalist & Effective Writing Style. Bryan Reddick. LC 75-44487. (gr. 7 up). 1976. PLB 10.97 o.p. (ISBN 0-8239-0352-4). Rosen Group.

Student Journalist & Free-Lance Writing. Emalene Sherman. LC 67-14525. (Student Journalist Ser). (gr. 7 up). 1969. PLB 10.97 o.p. (ISBN 0-8239-0120-3). Rosen Group.

Student Journalist & Interviewing. rev. ed. Hazel Presson. LC 67-10292. (Student Journalist Ser.). (gr. 7 up). 1982. PLB 10.97 o.p. (ISBN 0-8239-0488-1). Rosen Group.

Student Journalist & Layout. Hazel Presson. LC 72-163949. (Illus.). 116p. (YA) (gr. 7 up). 1972. PLB 10.97 o.p. (ISBN 0-8239-0253-6). Rosen Group.

Student Journalist & Making Advertising Pay for the School Publication. Glen Wright. Ed. by Ruth C. Rosen. LC 68-10818. (Student Journalist Ser.). (Illus.). (gr. 7 up). 1968. PLB 10.97 o.p. (ISBN 0-8239-0123-8). Rosen Group.

Student Journalist & Mass Communication. Julian Adams. (Illus.). 190p. 1981. lib. bdg. 10.97 o.p. (ISBN 0-8239-0499-7); workbook 2.50 o.p. (ISBN 0-8239-0538-1). Rosen Group.

Student Journalist & Photographing Sports. Bill Ward. (gr. 7-12). 1981. PLB 12.50 o.p. (ISBN 0-8239-0520-9). Rosen Group.

Student Journalist & Photojournalism. Herb Germar. LC 67-15471. (Student Journalist Ser.). 188p. (gr. 7 up). 1967. PLB 10.97 o.p. (ISBN 0-8239-0125-4). Rosen Group.

Student Journalist & Reviewing the Performing Arts. Samuel L. Singer. LC 73-80359. (Student Journalist Ser.). (Illus.). 182p. (gr. 7 up). 1974. PLB 10.97 o.p. (ISBN 0-8239-0287-0). Rosen Group.

Student Journalist & Staff Management. John Reque. (gr. 7-12). 1979. PLB 10.97 o.p. (ISBN 0-8239-0442-3). Rosen Group.

Student Journalist & the Newsmagazine Format. Elaine Pritchett. LC 75-35664. (gr. 7 up). 1976. PLB 10.97 o.p. (ISBN 0-8239-0340-0). Rosen Group.

Student Journalist & Thinking Editorials. William G. Ward. Ed. by Ruth C. Rosen. LC 74-79745. (Student Journalist Ser.). (Illus.). (gr. 7 up). 1969. PLB 10.97 o.p. (ISBN 0-8239-0129-7). Rosen Group.

Student Journalist & Twenty-One Keys to News Reporting. Hazel Presson. (Student Journalist Ser.). 1982. lib. bdg. 10.97 o.p. (ISBN 0-8239-0519-5). Rosen Group.

Student Journalist's Proofreader's Manual. Marion McCullo. LC 69-11852. (Student Journalist Ser.). (gr. 7 up). PLB 9.97 o.p. (ISBN 0-8239-0126-2). Rosen Group.

Student Kit Equip SM. Date not set. (ISBN 0-07-019371-1). McGraw.

Student Leadership Programs in Higher Education. Dennis Roberts. 1981. 17.00 o.p. (ISBN 1-55620-030-7, 72604C). Am Assn Coun Dev.

Student Learning Styles & Brain Behavior. Ed. by Thomas F. Koerner. 256p. (Orig.). 1982. pap. text ed. 9.00 o.p. (ISBN 0-88210-142-0). Natl Assn Principals.

Student Life in a Class Society. J. Abbott. 1971. 160.00 o.p. (ISBN 0-08-015654-1). Pergamon.

Student Merit Awards: High School. Ed. by Leroy Sachs. (Illus.). 160p. (Orig.). (gr. 9-12). 1984. pap. 9.00 o.p. (ISBN 0-87353-214-7). NCTM.

Student Merit Awards: Middle School. Ed. by Leroy Sachs. (Illus.). 120p. (gr. 6-8). 1984. pap. 6.00 o.p. (ISBN 0-87353-215-5). NCTM.

Student Movement see Radical Probe: The Logic of Student Rebellion.

Student Paraprofessionals: A Working Model for Higher Education. Ursula Delworth et al. (ACPA Student Personnel Monograph: No. 17). 80p. 1974. pap. 4.00 a non member o.p. (ISBN 0-911547-73-8, 72158W34); pap. 3.00 members o.p. (ISBN 0-686-34306-9). Am Assn Coun Dev.

Student Resource Book, No. 1. (Our Nations Heritage Ser.). Date not set. (ISBN 0-07-375431-5). McGraw.

Student Resource Book, No. 2. (Our Nations Heritage Ser.). Date not set. (ISBN 0-07-375432-3). McGraw.

Student Review, Vols. 1-5, No. 1. 1970. Repr. of 1935 ed. lib. bdg. 53.00x o.p. (ISBN 0-8371-9252-8, S400). Greenwood.

Student Scientist Explores Energy & Fuels. rev. ed. William L. Kaplan & Melvyn Lebowitz. LC 74-34077. (gr. 7-12). 1981. PLB 10.97 o.p. (ISBN 0-8239-0338-9). Rosen Group.

Student Teaching: The Entrance to Professional Physical Education. John B. Woods et al. 1973. pap. text ed. 11.00 o.p. (ISBN 0-12-763050-3). Acad Pr.

Student Team Learning: An Overview & Practical Guide. Robert E. Slavin. 56p. 1983. 8.95 o.p. (ISBN 0-8106-1827-3). NEA.

Student Unrest in India: A Comparative Approach. Aileen Ross. 1969. 13.75 o.p. (ISBN 0-7735-0041-3, McGill Canada). U of Toronto Pr.

Student Workbook for Introduction to the Administration of Justice. Martin Carlsen et al. 1978. pap. text ed. 10.95 o.p. (ISBN 0-8403-1921-5). Kendall-Hunt.

Student Writer's Guide. 5th ed. Eliot D. Allen & Ethel B. Colbrunn. 1976. pap. text ed. 5.00 o.p. (ISBN 0-912112-18-2). Everett-Edwards.

Students' Accounting Vocabulary. Diane Houghton & Ralph G. Wallace. 278p. 1980. pap. text ed. 15.00x o.p. (ISBN 0-566-00330-9). Gower Pub Co.

Students & Drugs, College & High School Observations see Society & Drugs, Social & Cultural Observations.

Student's Career Guide to a Future in the Allied Health Professions. Craig R. Ilk. LC 81-10887. (Illus.). 208p. 1982. 9.95 o.p. (ISBN 0-668-04913-8); pap. 7.95 o.p. (ISBN 0-668-04921-9). Appleton & Lange.

Students Concerto No. 4 in D Major for Violin & Piano, Op. 15. F. Seitz. (Carl Fischer Music Library: No. 593). 1904. pap. 5.00 o.p. (ISBN 0-8258-0080-3, L593). Fischer Inc NY.

Student's Cookbook. Jenny Baker. LC 85-1544. 144p. (Orig.). 1985. pap. 6.95 o.p. (ISBN 0-571-13522-6). Faber & Faber.

Student's Dictionary of Synonyms & Antonyms. 1983. pap. 2.95 o.p. (ISBN 0-89531-033-3). Sharon Pubns.

Student's Grammar of English. Jan A. Van Ek & Nico J. Robat. 384p. 1985. 45.00x o.p. (ISBN 0-631-90050-0); pap. 15.95 o.p. (ISBN 0-631-90060-8). Basil Blackwell.

Student's Guide Through the Talmud. Chajes. 19.95 o.p. (ISBN 0-87306-089-X). Feldheim.

Student's Guide to Piaget. D. J. Boyle. LC 77-94056. 1969. text ed. 12.00 o.p. (ISBN 0-08-006407-8); pap. 5.75 o.p. (ISBN 0-08-006406-X). Pergamon.

Student's Guide to Western Calligraphy: An Illustrated Survey. Joyce I. Whalley. LC 83-42805. (Illus.). 200p. 1984. pap. 14.95 o.p. (ISBN 0-394-72189-6). Shambhala Pubns.

Student's Manual of Auditing. 2nd ed. V. Cooper. 1983. pap. 34.95 o.p. (ISBN 0-85258-175-0). Van Nos Reinhold.

Students Must Write: A Guide to Better Writing in Course Work & Examinations. Robert Barrass. LC 82-8237. (Illus.). 120p. 1982. pap. 7.95 o.p. (ISBN 0-416-33620-5, NO. 3650). Routledge Chapman & Hall.

Students, My Friends: A Personal Journal of Experiences with Young People, Pt. 2. Don J. Black. 168p. (Orig.). (YA) (gr. 11 up). 1979. pap. 5.50 o.p. (ISBN 0-942241-20-7, 8709). Pubs Bk Sales.

Students Older Than Average. National Association for Women Deans, Administrators & Counselors. 1975. pap. 3.00 o.p. (ISBN 0-686-13305-6). Natl Assn Women.

Students Protest. Ed. by Philip G. Altbach & Robert Laufer. LC 72-160738. (Annals Ser: No. 395). 1971. pap. 7.95 o.p. (ISBN 0-87761-138-6). Am Acad Pol Soc Sci.

Student's Values in Drugs & Drug Abuse. Mary V. Sztorc. 1976. pap. 2.00 o.p. (ISBN 0-87507-000-0). Cath Lib Assn.

Students View the Campus Culture. National Association of Women Deans & Counselors. 1973. pap. 3.00 o.p. (ISBN 0-686-09578-2). Natl Assn Women.

Student's Webster Dictionary. Ed. by Jess Stein. (Illus.). 48p. 1984. pap. 2.95 o.p. (ISBN 0-89531-075-9, 0114-72). Sharon Pubns.

Student's World Atlas. Vahe Movsessian. (Illus.). 48p. (Orig.). (gr. 2 up). 1981. pap. 3.95 o.p. (ISBN 0-89531-022-8, 0115-72). Sharon Pubns.

Studien Zur Geschichte der Alteren Arabischen Furstenspiegel. Gustav Richter. (Ger.). 1932. pap. 12.00 o.p. (ISBN 0-384-50770-0). Johnson Repr.

Studien Zur Kulturkunde, Vols. 1-8. 1933-43. 165.00 o.p. (ISBN 0-384-58680-5). Johnson Repr.

Studies & Issues in Smoking Behavior. Ed. by Salvatore V. Zagona. 263p. 1967. 7.50x o.p. (ISBN 0-8165-0089-4). U of Ariz Pr.

Studies for Student Pilots. Michael Royce. 1956. (ISBN 0-8022-1403-7). Philos Lib.

Studies for Violin, Op. 32. Hans Sitt. Ed. by Gustav Saenger. (Carl Fischer Music Library: No. 112). pap. 6.00 o.p. (ISBN 0-8258-0019-6, L112). Fischer Inc NY.

Studies in American Politics. Ed. by Kenneth T. Palmer & James F. Horan. 192p. 1974. text ed. 29.00x o.p. (ISBN 0-8422-5209-6); pap. text ed. 6.95x o.p. (ISBN 0-8422-0331-1). Irvington.

Studies in Analysis. Ed. by Gian-Carlo Rota. (Advances in Mathematics Supplementary Studies Ser.: Vol. 4). 1979. 83.00 o.p. (ISBN 0-12-599150-9). Acad Pr.

Studies in Ancient Technology, 9 vols. 2nd, rev. ed. R. J. Forbes. Incl. Vols. 1-7. 1964-66. 40.00 ea. o.p.; Vols. 8-9. Metallurgy in Antiquity. (Illus.). 1971-72. Set. 95.00 o.p. (ISBN 90-04-03487-0). E J Brill USA.

Studies in Arabic Philology. As-Sayyid Bakr. (Arabic.). 1969. 15.00x o.s.i. (ISBN 0-86685-055-4). Intl Bk Ctr.

Studies in Bamidbor (Numbers) 1982. 12.95 o.s.i. (ISBN 0-686-76263-0). Feldheim.

Studies in Bereshis (Genesis) 1982. 12.95 o.s.i. (ISBN 0-686-76261-4). Feldheim.

Studies in Byzantine History & Modern Greek Folklore, Vol. 1. Constance N. Tsirpanlis. 180p. 1980. pap. 9.95 o.p. (ISBN 0-686-36330-2). EO Pr.

Studies in Chinese Literary Genres. Ed. & intro. by Cyril Birch. LC 77-157825. 1975. 32.00x o.p. (ISBN 0-520-02037-5). U of Cal Pr.

Studies in Chinese Thought. Ed. by Arthur F. Wright. LC 53-13533. (Midway Reprint Ser). (Illus.). xiv, 318p. 1976. pap. text ed. 12.00x o.s.i. (ISBN 0-226-90800-3). U of Chicago Pr.

Studies in Christian Existentialism. John Macquarrie. 1966. 10.00x o.p. (ISBN 0-7735-0024-3, McGill Canada). U of Toronto Pr.

Studies in Comparative Criminal Law. E. M. Wise & G. O. Mueller. (Illus.). 338p. 1975. 43.25 o.p. (ISBN 0-398-03168-1). C C Thomas.

Studies in Convection: Theory Measurement & Applications, Vol. 2. Ed. by B. E. Launder. 1978. 61.00 o.p. (ISBN 0-12-438002-6). Acad Pr.

Studies in Cross-Cultural Psychology, Vol. 1. Ed. by Neil Warren. 1977. 43.50 o.p. (ISBN 0-12-609201-X). Acad Pr.

Studies in Daniel's Prophecies. Charles H. Wright. 368p. lib. bdg. 14.95 o.p. (ISBN 0-8254-5275-9). Kregel.

Studies in Dante, First Series: Scriptures & Classical Authors in Dante. Edward Moore. LC 68-57627. (Illus.). 1969. Repr. of 1896 ed. lib. bdg. 35.00 o.p. (ISBN 0-8371-0909-4, MODF). Greenwood.

Studies in Dante, Third Series: Miscellaneous Essays. Edward Moore. LC 68-57629. (Illus.). 1969. Repr. of 1903 ed. lib. bdg. 35.00 o.p. (ISBN 0-8371-0917-5, MODT). Greenwood.

Studies in East African Geography & Development. Ed. by S. H. Ominde. (Illus.). 1971. 44.00x o.p. (ISBN 0-520-02073-1). U of Cal Pr.

Studies in Educational Evaluation. A. Lewy. (Pergamon Reviews in Educational Evaluation: Vol. 6, No. 2). (Illus.). 116p. 1980. pap. 21.00 o.p. (ISBN 0-08-026760-2). Pergamon.

Studies in Elizabethan Literature. P. S. Shastry. 1972. text ed. 25.00x o.p. Coronet Bks.

Studies in English Puritanism from the Restoration to the Revolution, 1660-1688. Charles E. Whiting. (Church Historical Society London, N. S. Ser.: No. 5). Repr. of 1931 ed. 95.00 o.p. (ISBN 0-8115-3129-5). Kraus Repr.

Studies in French. Madeleine Alcover et al. (Rice University Studies: Vol. 63, No. 1). 133p. 1977. pap. 10.00x o.p. (ISBN 0-89263-231-3). Rice Univ.

Studies in French in Honor of Andre Bourgeois. Catharine S. Brosman et al. (Rice University Studies: Vol. 59, No. 3). 100p. 1973. pap. 10.00x o.p. (ISBN 0-89263-217-8). Rice Univ.

Studies in French Literature. Andre Bourgeois et al. (Rice University Studies: Vol. 57, No. 2). 127p. 1971. pap. 10.00x o.p. (ISBN 0-89263-208-9). Rice Univ.

Studies in German in Memory of Andrew Louis. Ed. by Robert L. Kahn. (Rice University Studies: Vol. 55, No. 3). 250p. 1969. pap. 10.00x o.p. (ISBN 0-89263-201-1). Rice Univ.

Studies in German in Memory of Robert L. Kahn. Ernst Behler et al. Ed. by Hans Eichner & Lisa Kahn. (Rice University Studies: Vol. 57, No. 4). 134p. 1971. pap. 10.00x o.p. (ISBN 0-89263-210-0). Rice Univ.

Studies in Hakka Folktales, 2 vols. Wolfram Eberhard. (Asian Folklore & Social Life Monograph: No. 61). 290p. 1974. photocopy 42.00x o.p. (ISBN 0-89986-056-7). Oriental Bk Store.

Studies in Heat Transfer: A Festschrift for E.R.G. Eckert. James P. Hartnett et al. LC 79-15633. (Illus.). 1979. text ed. 62.95 o.p. (ISBN 0-07-026962-9). McGraw.

Studies in Hegelian Cosmology. John McTaggart & Ellis McTaggart. LC 83-48513. (Philosophy of Hegel Ser.). 312p. 1984. lib. bdg. 38.00 o.p. (ISBN 0-8240-5636-1). Garland Pub.

Studies in History. Katherine F. Drew et al. (Rice University Studies: Vol. 58, No. 4). 155p. 1972. pap. 10.00x o.p. (ISBN 0-89263-214-3). Rice Univ.

Studies in Honor of Everett W. Hesse. Ed. by William McCrary & Jose A. Madrigal. LC 80-53824. 180p. (Orig.). 1981. pap. 25.00 o.p. (ISBN 0-89295-014-5). Society Sp & Sp-Am.

Studies in Honour of Arthur Dale Trendal. Alexander Cambitoglou. (Illus.). 1979. 40.00x o.p. (ISBN 0-424-00063-6, Pub. by Sydney U Pr). Intl Spec Bk.

Studies in Human Sexual Behavior: The American Scene. Ed. by Ailon Shiloh. (Illus.). 488p. 1970. 25.50 o.p. (ISBN 0-398-01746-8). C C Thomas.

Studies in Italian Art & Architecture: 15th Through 18th Centuries. Ed. by Henry Millon. (American Academy in Rome Studies in Art History). (Illus.). 1980. 70.00x o.p. (ISBN 0-262-13156-0). MIT Pr.

Studies in Jazz Discography. Institute for Jazz Studies. 112p. 1972. pap. 5.00x o.p. (ISBN 0-87855-594-3). Transaction Pubs.

Studies in Jewish Ethnopoetry. Heda Jason. (Asian Folklore & Social Life Monograph: No. 72). 1975. 19.00x o.p. (ISBN 0-89986-068-0). Oriental Bk Store.

Studies in Jocular Literature. William C. Hazlitt. LC 67-24352. 240p. 1969. Repr. of 1890 ed. 35.00x o.p. (ISBN 0-8103-3529-8). Gale.

Studies in Joshua-Job. William R. Newell. LC 83-19899. (Old Testament Studies). 222p. 1983. kivar 7.95 o.p. (ISBN 0-8254-3314-2). Kregel.

Studies in Judaism. Solomon Schechter. LC 58-11934. (Temple Bks). 1970. pap. 3.45 o.p. (ISBN 0-689-70233-7, T14, Atheneum). Macmillan.

Studies in Linear Programming. Ed. by H. M. Salkin & J. Saha. LC 74-28998. (Studies in Management Science & Systems: Vol. 2). 322p. 1975. 66.00 o.p. (ISBN 0-444-10884-X, North-Holland). Elsevier.

Studies in Linguistics in Honor of Raven I. McDavid Jr. Lawrence M. Davis et al. LC 77-156749. 461p. 1972. 26.75 o.p. (ISBN 0-8173-0010-4). U of Ala Pr.

Studies in Luke-Acts. Ed. by Leander E. Keck & J. Louis Martyn. LC 79-8886. 324p. 1980. pap. 1.50 o.p. (ISBN 0-8006-1379-1, 1-1379, Fortress). Augsburg Fortress.

Studies in Lutheran Hermeneutics. Ed. by John Reumann et al. LC 78-14673. 352p. 1979. 15.95 o.p. (ISBN 0-8006-0534-9, 1-534, Fortress). Augsburg Fortress.

Studies in Medieval & Renaissance Music. Manfred F. Bukofzer. (Illus.). 1964. pap. 5.95 o.p. (ISBN 0-393-00241-1, Norton Lib.). Norton.

Studies in New Guinea Linguistics. Alex Vincent et al. 148p. 1962. pap. 1.50 o.p. (ISBN 0-88312-645-1). Summer Inst Ling.

Studies in Numerical Analysis. B. K. Scaife. 1974. 60.50 o.p. (ISBN 0-12-621150-7). Acad Pr.

Studies in Paleo-Oceanography. 218p. 1974. 14.00 o.p. (ISBN 0-918985-02-1, 20); members 11.00 o.p. SEPM.

Studies in Parasitology in Memory of Clark P. Read. C. Arme et al. Ed. by J. E. Byram & George Stewart. (Rice University Studies: Vol. 62, No. 4). 236p. 1977. pap. 10.00x o.p. (ISBN 0-89263-230-5). Rice Univ.

Studies in Paul. Nils A. Dahl. LC 77-84083. 1977. pap. 10.95 o.p. (ISBN 0-8066-1608-3, 10-6100, Augsburg). Augsburg Fortress.

Studies in Philosophy: A Symposium on Gilbert Ryle. Ed. by Konstantin Kolenda. (Rice University Studies: No. 58, No. 3). 134p. 1972. pap. 10.00x o.p. (ISBN 0-89263-213-5). Rice Univ.

Studies in Physiology Presented to John C. Eccles. Ed. by D. R. Curtis & A. K. McIntyre. (Illus.). 1965. 25.00 o.p. (ISBN 0-387-03411-0). Springer-Verlag.

Studies in Pizzicato & Harmonics. Gaylord Yost. 1951. 2.50 o.p. (ISBN 0-913650-21-8). CPP Belwin.

Studies in Public Regulation. Ed. by Gary Fromm. (Regulation of Economic Activity Ser.). (Illus.). 400p. 1981. 60.00x o.p. (ISBN 0-262-06074-4). MIT Pr.

Studies in Pure Mathematics. Ed. by L. Mirsky. 1971. 45.50 o.p. (ISBN 0-12-498450-9). Acad Pr.

Studies in Recent Australian Novel. Ed. by K. G. Hamilton. 257p. 1979. 34.50x o.p. (ISBN 0-7022-1247-4). U of Queensland Pr.

Studies in Renaissance & Baroque Music in Honor of Arthur Mendel. Ed. by Robert L. Marshall. 1974. 37.00 o.p. (ISBN 0-913574-26-0, EAMARS). Eur-Am Music.

Studies in Roman Literature, Culture & Religion. Hendrik Wagenvoort. Ed. by Steele Commager. LC 77-70817. (Latin Poetry Ser.: Vol. 31). 1978. lib. bdg. 40.00 o.p. (ISBN 0-8240-2981-X). Garland Pub.

Studies in Ruskin: Essays in Honor of Van Akin Burd. Ed. by Robert E. Rhodes & Del Ivan Janik. LC 81-16883. (Illus.). xx, 244p. 1982. lib. bdg. 22.95x o.p. (ISBN 0-8214-0627-2). Ohio U Pr.

Studies in Seventeenth Century Imagery, 2 vols. in 1. Manrio Praz. LC 40-3654. Repr. 79.00x o.p. (ISBN 0-403-07208-5). Somerset Pub.

Studies in Sir Thomas Browne. Robert Cawley & George Yost. LC 65-29995. 1965. 5.00 o.p. (ISBN 0-87114-011-X). U of Oreg Bks.

Studies in State Taxation with Particular Reference to the Southern States. J. H. Hollander. 1973. Repr. of 1900 ed. 26.00 o.p. (ISBN 0-384-23971-4). Johnson Repr.

Studies in Subjective Probability. H. E. Kyburg. 1969. pap. 7.50 o.p. (ISBN 0-471-51128-5). Krieger.

Studies in the American Jewish Experience II: Contributions from the Fellowship Programs of the American Jewish Archives. Ed. by Jacob R. Marcus & Abraham J. Peck. 228p. (Orig.). 1984. lib. bdg. 26.75 o.p. (ISBN 0-8191-3714-6); pap. text ed. 13.00 o.p. (ISBN 0-8191-3715-4). U Pr of Amer.

Studies in the Archaeology & Palaeoanthropology of South Asia. Ed. by K. Kennedy & G. Possehl. 144p. 1984. text ed. 22.50x o.p. (ISBN 0-391-03049-3). Humanities.

Studies in the Eighteenth Century Background of Hume's Empiricism. Mary S. Kuypers. LC 82-48337. (Philosophy of David Hume Ser.). 148p. 1983. lib. bdg. 28.00 o.p. (ISBN 0-8240-5413-X). Garland Pub.

Studies in the Gospel of Mark. Martin Hengel. Tr. by John Bowden. LC 85-4508. 216p. 1985. pap. 12.95 o.p. (ISBN 0-8006-1881-5, Fortress). Augsburg Fortress.

Studies in the History of Art, 1973, Vol. 5. Wolfgang Stechow et al. LC 72-600309. (Illus.). 79p. pap. 12.50x o.p. (ISBN 0-89468-023-4, Dist. by U Pr of New Eng). Natl Gallery Art.

Studies in the Intellectual History of Tokugawa Japan. Masao Maruyama. Tr. by Mikiso Hane from Japanese. LC 70-90954. 350p. 1975. 42.00x o.p. (ISBN 0-691-07566-2). Princeton U Pr.

Studies in the Lankavatara Sutra: An Elucidation & Analysis of One of the Most Important Texts of Mahayana Buddhism, in Which Almost All Its Principal Tenets Are Presented Including the Teaching of Zen. Daisetz T. Suzuki. 1968. Repr. of 1930 ed. 31.00 o.p. (ISBN 0-7100-6330-X). Routledge Chapman & Hall.

Studies in the Lateglacial of North-West Europe: Including Papers Presented at a Symposium of the Quaternary Research Association Held at University College London, January 1979. Ed. by J. J. Lowe et al. (Illus.). 215p. 1980. 69.00 o.p. (ISBN 0-08-024001-1). Pergamon.

Studies in the Life & Works of Petrarch. Ernest H. Wilkins. LC 55-8492. 1977. Repr. of 1955 ed. 12.00 o.p. (ISBN 0-910956-37-5). Medieval Acad.

Studies in the Lutheran Confessions. rev. ed. Willard D. Allbeck. LC 68-11139. 336p. 1968. 6.50 o.p. (ISBN 0-8006-0095-9, 1-95, Fortress). Augsburg Fortress.

Studies in the Organization of Conversational Interaction. Ed. by James N. Schenkein. 1978. 29.95 o.p. (ISBN 0-12-623550-3). Acad Pr.

Studies in the Paranoid. 52p. 1988. 5.00 o.p. Spevack.

Studies in the Perception of Language. Ed. by Willem J. Levelt & Giovanni B. D'Arcais. LC 78-2548. 1979. 91.95 o.p. (ISBN 0-471-99633-5, Pub. by Wiley-Interscience). Wiley.

Studies in the Phonology of Colloquial English. Ken Lodge. 160p. 1984. 27.50 o.p. (ISBN 0-7099-1631-0, Pub. by Croom Helm Ltd). Routledge Chapman & Hall.

Studies in the Psychology of the Mystics. Joseph Marechal. LC 65-1694. 1964. lib. bdg. 12.95x o.p. (ISBN 0-87343-044-1); pap. 6.00x o.p. (ISBN 0-87343-014-X). Magi Bks.

Studies in the Romance Verb. Nigel Vincent & Martin Harris. 200p. 1982. 32.00 o.p. (ISBN 0-7099-2602-2, Pub. by Croom Helm). Routledge Chapman & Hall.

Studies in the Scope & Method of "The Authoritarian Personality" Ed. by Richard Christie & Marie Jahoda. LC 81-584. (Continuities in Social Research Ser.). 279p. 1981. Repr. of 1954 ed. lib. bdg. 35.00x o.p. (ISBN 0-313-22444-7, CHSS). Greenwood.

Studies in the Scottish Lateglacial Environment. Ed. by J. M. Gray & J. J. Lowe. 1977. 46.00 o.p. (ISBN 0-08-020498-8). Pergamon.

Studies in the Sermon on the Mount. Oswald Chambers. 1973. pap. 5.95 o.p. Chr Lit.

Studies in the Shakespeare Apocrypha. Baldwin Maxwell. 1969. Repr. of 1956 ed. lib. bdg. 35.00x o.p. (ISBN 0-8371-1857-3, MAAP). Greenwood.

Studies in the Shemoth, 2 vols. Leibowitz. 1976. 17.50 o.s.i. (ISBN 0-685-71930-8). Feldheim.

Studies in the Structure of Hebrew Narrative. Robert C. Culley. LC 75-37159. (Semeia Studies). 128p. 1976. pap. 3.95 o.p. (ISBN 0-8006-1504-2, 1-1504, Fortress). Augsburg Fortress.

Studies in the Theory of Numbers. Leonard E. Dickson. LC 61-13494. 13.95 o.p. (ISBN 0-8284-0151-9). Chelsea Pub.

Studies in Topology. Ed. by Nick Stavrakas & Keith Allen. 1975. 79.50 o.p. (ISBN 0-12-663450-5). Acad Pr.

Studies in Tourism, Wildlife Parks & Conservation. Tej Vir Singh et al. (Illus.). 300p. 1982. 30.00 o.p. (ISBN 0-935638-07-5). Travel & Tourism.

Studies in Type Design: Alphabets with Random Quotations. Rudolph Ruzicka. 1968. boxed portfolio 25.00x o.p. (ISBN 0-317-02690-9, 777-7). U Pr of New Eng.

Studies in Uto-Aztecan Grammar, 4 vols. Ed. by Ronald W. Langacker. (Publications in Linguistics Ser.: No. 56). Set. pap. 54.00 o.p. (ISBN 0-88312-069-0); microfiche (3) 6.00 o.p. (ISBN 0-88312-469-6). Summer Inst Ling.

Studies in Uto-Aztecan Grammar: Southern Uto-Aztecan Grammatical Sketches, Vol. 4. Ed. by Ronald W. Langacker. LC 84-51054. (Publications in Linguistics Ser.: No. 56). 459p. (Orig.). 1984. pap. 18.00 o.p. (ISBN 0-88312-098-4); 18.00 o.p. (ISBN 0-88312-402-5); pap. 18.00x o.p. Summer Inst Ling.

Studies in Vayikra. 1982. 8.95 o.s.i. (ISBN 0-686-76262-2). Feldheim.

Studies in Verbal Behavior: An Empirical Approach. Kurt Salzinger & Richard S. Feldman. LC 76-179073. 474p. 1973. 42.00 o.p. (ISBN 0-08-016926-0). Pergamon.

Studies in Vocabulary see Word Studies in the Greek New Testament, for the English Reader.

Studies in World Literature. M. I. Kuruvilla. 249p. 1984. text ed. 27.50x o.p. (ISBN 0-86590-271-2, Pub. by Sterling Pubs India). Apt Bks.

Studies in Zen. Suzuki. 1955. (ISBN 0-8022-1678-1). Philos Lib.

Studies of British Newspapers & Periodicals from Their Beginning to 1800. Katherine K. Weed & Richmond P. Bond. Repr. of 1946 ed. 12.00 o.p. (ISBN 0-384-66370-2). Johnson Repr.

Studies of Mineral Deposits. Ed. by V. Smirnov. 288p. 1983. 11.95 o.p. (ISBN 0-8285-2763-6, Pub. by Mir Pubs USSR). Imported Pubns.

Studies of Narcotic Drugs: 26th International Congress of Physiological Sciences, New Delhi, October 1974. Ed. by P. B. Bradley & E. Costa. 1976. pap. 35.00 o.p. (ISBN 0-08-020565-8). Pergamon.

Studies of Relief & Rehabilitation in China. Owen L. Dawson. LC 78-74350. (Modern Chinese Economy Ser.). 126p. 1980. lib. bdg. 20.00 o.p. (ISBN 0-8240-4285-9). Garland Pub.

Studies of the Modern World System. Ed. by Albert Bergesen. LC 80-10871. (Studies in Social Discontinuity). 1980. 38.50 o.p. (ISBN 0-12-090550-7). Acad Pr.

Studies on Botel Tobago & Yap. Inez De Beauclair. (Asian Folklore & Social Life Monograph: No. 19). (Eng. & Ger.). 1971. 19.00 o.p. (ISBN 0-89986-021-4). Oriental Bk Store.

Studies on Greek & Roman History & Literature. B. Baldwin. (London Studies in Classical Philology: Vol. 15). 604p. 1985. 75.00x o.p. (ISBN 90-70265-09-5, Pub. by Gieben Holland). Humanities.

Studies on the Anatomy & Function of Bone & Joints. Ed. by Frances G. Evans. (Illus.). 1966. 36.00 o.p. (ISBN 0-387-03677-6). Springer-Verlag.

Studies on the Cantigas de Santa Maria: Art, Music & Poetry. Ed. by Israel J. Katz & John E. Keller. 529p. 1987. 30.00 o.p. (ISBN 0-317-61793-1). Hispanic Seminary.

Studies on the Diencephalon. Santiago Ramon y Cajal. Tr. by Enrique Ramon-Moliner. (Illus.). 248p. 1966. 30.00 o.p. (ISBN 0-398-01542-2). C C Thomas.

Studies on the Society of Aborigines in Kweichow, China. Ch'en Kou-chun. (Asian Folklore & Social Life Monograph: No. 46). 400p. (Chinese.). 1973. 20.00x o.p. (ISBN 0-89986-044-3). Oriental Bk Store.

Studies on the Synthesis of Corrins and Related Ligands. Robert V. Stevens. 14p. 1976. pap. 12.75 o.p. (ISBN 0-08-021333-2). Pergamon.

Studies on the Tea in Modern Taiwan. Wu Chen-Tau. (Asian Folklore & Social Life Ser.: Vol. 94). 1977. 17.00x o.p. (ISBN 0-89986-326-4). Oriental Bk Store.

Studs Lonigan. James T. Farrell. 1979. pap. 2.75 o.p. (ISBN 0-380-00934-X, 59758-6, Bard). Avon.

Study & Like It. John J. Vogel. 1977. 9.00 o.p. (ISBN 0-682-48771-6, University). Exposition-Phoenix.

Study & Practice of Yoga. Ed. by University Books. 5.00 o.p. (ISBN 0-8216-0156-3, Pub. by Univ Bks). Carol Pub Group.

Study English for Science. A. R. Bolitho & P. L. Sandler. (English As a Second Language Bk.). 104p. 1980. pap. text ed. 6.95 o.p. (ISBN 0-582-55248-6). Longman.

Study Guide & Review Manual of Human Embryology. 2nd ed. Keith L. Moore. 304p. 1982. pap. 22.95 o.p. (ISBN 0-7216-6476-8). Saunders.

Study Guide for Advanced Life: Problem Solving in Cardiac Arrest. Grauer. 1984. pap. 19.95 o.p. (ISBN 0-8016-1878-9). Mosby.

Study Guide for Auerbach Money, Banking, & Financial Markets. 2nd ed. David C. Klingaman. 126p. 1986. write for info. o.p. (ISBN 0-02-364780-9). Macmillan.

Study Guide for California Drivers Handbook. Charles Pearce. Incl. Adapted N.Y. State Drivers Handbook. pap. 3.95. 1973. pap. 1.50 o.p. (ISBN 0-89036-823-6); study guide pap. o.p. 2.95 o.p. (ISBN 0-89036-824-4); vocabulary o.p. 1.95 o.p. (ISBN 0-89036-825-2); sample tests o.p. 1.95 o.p. (ISBN 0-89036-828-7); study guide for official N.Y. state driver's manual pap. 2.50, sample tests 1.00 o.p. (ISBN 0-89036-827-9). Hawkes Pub Inc.

Study Guide for General Physics. John J. Merrill. 314p. 1975. 7.95x o.p. (ISBN 0-471-59626-4). Wiley.

Study Guide to Accompany an Introduction to Data Processing for business & Management. Robert J. Thierauf & John F. Niehaus. LC 79-20568. 366p. 1980. 45.50 o.p. (ISBN 0-471-03439-8); tchrs' manual 9.00 o.p. (ISBN 0-471-03440-1). Wiley.

Study Guide to Accompany Management Accounting see Management Accounting: A Decision Emphasis.

Study Guide to the Multiple Choice Examinations for Third & Second Mates. 4th ed ed. Richard James & Richard M. Plant. LC 82-2438. 1982. pap. 24.50x o.p. (ISBN 0-87033-289-9). Cornell Maritime.

Study in Methodist Discipline. C. R. Nichol. Date not set. pap. 1.95 o.p. (ISBN 0-915547-50-3). Abilene Christ U.

Study in Radicalism & Dissent. William S. Fowler. LC 72-11684. (Illus.). 192p. 1973. Repr. of 1961 ed. lib. bdg. 35.00x o.p. (ISBN 0-8371-6673-X, FOSR). Greenwood.

Study in Scarlet. Arthur Conan Doyle. Bd. with Houi 1 of the Baskervilles. LC 86-61761. (Illus.). 336p. (gr. 7-12). 1986. 12.95 o.p. (ISBN 0-895' 7-?54-X). RD Assn.

Study in the Theor, of Inflation. Bent Hansen. LC 68-4112. x, 262p. Repr. of 1951 ed. 39.50x o.s.i. (ISBN 0-678-06019-3). Kelley.

Study Notes for Technicians: Electrical & Electronic Principles, Vol. 1. J. B. Pratley. 96p. 1982. text ed. 7.00 o.p. (ISBN 0-07-084661-8). McGraw.

Study of a Recordkeeping System for Inprocessing of Transient Workers at Nuclear Power Plants: AIF-NESP-025. (National Environmental Studies Project: NESP Reports). 1982. 50.00 o.p. (ISBN 0-318-02233-8). US Coun Energy Awareness.

Study of Adverbs. Shuan-Fan Huang. (Janua Linguarum, Ser. Minor: No. 213). 96p. (Orig.). 1975. pap. text ed. 13.50x o.p. (ISBN 90-2793-363-4). Mouton.

Study of American English see Society's Work.

Study of American Folklore: An Introduction. Jan H. Brunvand. 1968. 8.95x o.p. (ISBN 0-393-09803-6, NortonC). Norton.

Study of American Folklore: An Introduction. 2nd ed. Jan H. Brunvand. 1978. 19.95x o.p. (ISBN 0-393-09048-5, NortonC). Norton.

Study of American History. James Bryce. LC 72-136056. 1971. Repr. of 1922 ed. lib. bdg. 35.00x o.p. (ISBN 0-8371-5206-2, BRAH). Greenwood.

Study of American History, 2 vols. Dushkin Publishing Group Staff. LC 73-85201. (Illus.). 1368p. 1974. Vol. 2. pap. text ed. 8.95 o.p. Dushkin Pub.

Study of Bossuet. William J. Simpson. (Church Historical Society London N. S. Ser.: No. 22). pap. 40.00 o.p. (ISBN 0-8115-3146-5). Kraus Repr.

Study of Data Base Processor Technology. Laura A. Gregory. LC 79-66678. (Data Base Monograph: No. 8). (Illus.). 77p. (Orig.). pap. 15.00x o.s.i. (ISBN 0-89435-035-8). QED Info Sci.

Study of Early Christianity. Joseph B. Tyson. Ed. by Kenneth J. Scott. (Illus.). 448p. 1973. text ed. write for info. o.p. (ISBN 0-02-421900-2). Macmillan.

Study of Economics. Turley Mings. (gr. 11 up). 1976. pap. text ed. 8.95 o.p. (ISBN 0-685-54574-1); tchr's guide, test bk, wkbk 4.50 o.p. (ISBN 0-685-54575-X). Dushkin Pub.

Study of Economics: Principles, Concepts & Applications. Turley Mings. LC 83-16992. (Illus.). 472p. 1983. 21.95 o.p. (ISBN 0-87967-323-0). Dushkin Pub.

Study of Franz Brentano. Antos C. Rancurello. LC 68-14641. 1968. 42.00 o.p. (ISBN 0-12-577050-2). Acad Pr.

Study of Fugue. Alfred Mann. (Illus.). 1966. pap. 5.95x o.p. (ISBN 0-393-09675-0, NortonC). Norton.

Study of History, 2 vols. Arnold Toynbee. Abridged by D. C. Somervell. 1149p. 1979. Boxed Set. pap. 1.95 o.p. (ISBN 0-440-38374-9, LE). Dell.

Study of Home-Economics Education in Teacher-Training Institutions for Negroes. United States Federal Board for Vocational Education Staff. LC 75-82094. (Illus.). 1969. Repr. of 1923 ed. 22.50 o.p. (ISBN 0-8371-2047-0, HOE&, Pub. by Negro U Pr). Greenwood.

Study of Human Communication. Nan Lin. 260p. 1973. pap. text ed. write for info. o.p. (ISBN 0-02-371090-X). Macmillan.

Study of Jazz. 5th ed. Paul Tanner & Maurice Gerow. 256p. 1983. pap. text ed. write for info. o.p. (ISBN 0-697-03567-0); instr's. manual avail. o.p. (ISBN 0-697-03568-9). Wm C Brown.

Study of Kant. James Ward. Ed. by Lewis W. Beck. Bd. with Immanual Kant (Seventeen Twenty-Four to Eighteen Hundred Four) The British Academy Annual Philosophical Lecture. LC 75-32045. (Philosophy of Immanuel Kant Ser.: Vol. 9). 1976. Repr. of 1922 ed. lib. bdg. 29.00 o.p. (ISBN 0-8240-2333-1). Garland Pub.

Study of Lorenzo De'Medici's Villa at Poggio a Caiano, 2 vols. Philip E. Foster. LC 77-94695. (Outstanding Dissertations in the Fine Arts Ser.). 776p. 1978. lib. bdg. 88.00 Set o.p. (ISBN 0-8240-3227-6). Garland Pub.

Study of Music in the Elementary School: A Conceptual Approach. Music Educators National Conference Staff. Ed. by Flavis Evenson & Charles L. Gary. LC 67-31352. 182p. (Orig.). 1967. pap. 5.00 o.p. (ISBN 0-940796-19-8, 1048). Music Ed Natl.

Study of Old English Literature. Charles L. Wrenn. 1967. pap. 3.95x o.p. (ISBN 0-393-09768-4, NortonC). Norton.

Study of Play: Problems & Prospects. Ed. by David F. Lancy & B. Allan Tindall. LC 76-27948. (Association for the Anthropological Study of Play Ser.: Vol. 1). 255p. (Orig.). 1977. pap. text ed. 18.00x o.p. (ISBN 0-918438-06-3, PLAN0006). Leisure Pr.

Study of Psychology. Joseph Rubinstein. 640p. (gr. 11 up). 1975. text ed. 11.50 o.p. (ISBN 0-87967-105-X); tchr's. guide & tchr's. guide testbook avail. o.p. (ISBN 0-685-51785-3); wkbk. 3.95 o.p. (ISBN 0-685-51786-1). Dushkin Pub.

Study of Samurai Income & Entrepreneurship. Kozo Yamamura. LC 73-87378. (East Asian Ser.: No. 76). 256p. 1974. text ed. 19.50x o.s.i. (ISBN 0-674-85322-9). Harvard U Pr.

Study of the Early Development of Mongols. V. Cowie. LC 75-99554. 1970. 35.00 o.p. (ISBN 0-08-006828-6). Pergamon.

Study of the Effects of Reduced Occupational Radiation Exposure Limits on the Nuclear Power Industry (AIF-NESP-017) Catalytic, Inc. Staff. (National Environmental Studies Project: NESP Reports). 62p. 1980. 45.00 o.p. (ISBN 0-318-13594-9); NESP sponsors 15.00 o.p. (ISBN 0-318-13595-7). US Coun Energy Awareness.

Study of the Indian & the American Mind. Ed. by Roy Harvey Pearce & J. Hillis Miller. LC 53-6486. 272p. 1967. pap. 9.95x o.p. (ISBN 0-8018-0525-2). Johns Hopkins.

Study of the Isolation System for Geologic Disposal of Radioactive Wastes. Waste Isolation Systems Panel, Board on Radioactive Waste Management, National Research Council Staff. 1983. pap. text ed. 24.95x o.p. (ISBN 0-309-03384-5). Natl Acad Pr.

Study of the Revelation. John A. Copeland. 1971. pap. 4.50 o.p. (ISBN 0-89137-702-6). Quality Pubns.

Study of the Standard of Living of Working Families in Shanghai. Simon Yang & L. K. Tao. Ed. by Ramon H. Myers. LC 80-8826. (China During the Interregnum 1911-1949, The Economy & Society Ser.). 142p. 1982. lib. bdg. 22.00 o.p. (ISBN 0-8240-4681-1). Garland Pub.

Study of Theology. Gerhard Ebeling. Tr. by Duane A. Priebe from Ger. LC 78-5393. 216p. 1978. 9.95 o.p. (ISBN 0-8006-0529-2, 1-529, Fortress). Augsburg Fortress.

Study of Time I: Ist Conference of the International Society for the Study of Time. Ed. by J. T. Fraser et al. LC 72-80472. (Illus.). 558p. 1972. 33.00 o.p. (ISBN 0-387-05824-9). Springer-Verlag.

Study of Variables That Affect the Corrosion of Sour Water Strippers. 70p. 1976. 8.00 o.p. (ISBN 0-317-33101-9, 82294800). Am Petroleum.

Study of Workmen's Compensation In Relation To Sheltered Workshops. Henry Viscardi, Jr. & Irving M. Friedman. 68p. 1971. 1.50 o.p. (ISBN 0-686-38807-0). Human Res Ctr.

Study on Cotton Textiles. (Fr.). 1966. pap. 8.00 o.p. (ISBN 0-686-93131-9, G112, GATT). UNIPUB.

Study on Inflation & Unemployment. Hak-Un Kim. LC 80-8618. (Outstanding Dissertations in Economics Ser.). 1984. lib. bdg. 24.00 o.p. (ISBN 0-8240-4175-5). Garland Pub.

Study on Planning for Basic Needs: Workshop on Improving the Methods of Planning for Comprehensive Regional Developments, 16 May-12 June 1978. (Working Papers Ser.: No. 78-26). 25p. 1978. pap. 6.00 o.p. (ISBN 0-686-75494-8, CRD064, UNCRD). UNIPUB.

Study Outline & Workbook in the Elements of Music. 8th ed. Frank W. Hill & Roland Searight. 224p. 1984. write for info. wire coilbinding o.p. (ISBN 0-697-03608-1); instr's. manual avail. o.p. (ISBN 0-697-03622-7). Wm C Brown.

Study Skills Shop. Cherrie Farnette. (Choose-a-Card Ser.). (Illus.). 64p. (gr. 2-6). 1980. pap. text ed. 6.95 o.p. (ISBN 0-913916-69-2, IP 69-2). Incentive Pubns.

Study War No More: A Selection of Alternatives. Joe W. Haldeman. 1978. pap. 2.95 o.p. (ISBN 0-380-40519-9, 59337-8). Avon.

Studying Literature. G. A. Wilkes. 96p. 1986. pap. 6.95 o.p. (ISBN 0-424-00116-0). Intl Spec Bk.

Stuff of Sleep & Dreams: Experiments in Literary Psychology. Leon Edel. 368p. 1983. pap. 4.95 o.p. (ISBN 0-380-63719-7, 63719, Discus). Avon.

Stuffed Feet. Mike Thaler. (Illus.). 107p. (Orig.). (gr. k up). 1983. pap. 2.50 o.p. (ISBN 0-380-84673-X, 84673, Camelot). Avon.

Stuka at War. rev. ed. Peter C. Smith. (Illus.). 128p. 1980. encore ed. 7.95 o.p. (ISBN 0-684-16701-8, ScribT). Scribner.

Stumbling Block. Francois Mauriac. 1952. (ISBN 0-8022-1089-9). Philos Lib.

Sturgis Standard Code of Parliamentary Procedure. 2nd ed. Alice F. Sturgis. 1966. text ed. 32.50 o.p. (ISBN 0-07-062272-8); text ed. 19.95 o.p. (ISBN 0-07-062268-X). McGraw.

Sturt: The Chipped Idol. Edgar Beale. LC 80-670049. (Illus.). 1980. 33.00x o.p. (ISBN 0-424-00069-5, Pub. by Sydney U Pr). Intl Spec Bk.

Stuttering: A New Look at an Old Problem Based on Neurophysiological Aspects. Charles P. Overstake. (Illus.). 160p. 1979. 21.25 o.p. (ISBN 0-398-03896-1). C C Thomas.

Stuttering & Behavior Therapy: Current Status & Experimental Foundations. Roger J. Ingham. (Illus.). 500p. 1984. pap. 46.50 o.p. College-Hill.

Stuttering: Integrating Theory & Practice. Tr. by S. Richard Silverman. LC 82-13818. 228p. 1982. 29.50 o.p. (ISBN 0-89443-665-1). Aspen Pub.

Stuttering: What It Is & What to Do About It. Stanley Ainsworth. LC 74-76252. (Speech & Hearing Ser.). 101p. (Orig.). 1975. pap. text ed. 4.95 o.p. (ISBN 0-8220-1805-5). Cliffs.

Style & Civilizations. Alfred L. Kroeber. LC 73-8560. 191p. 1973. Repr. of 1957 ed. lib. bdg. 22.50x o.p. (ISBN 0-8371-6966-6, KRSC). Greenwood.

Style & Idea. Arnold Schoenberg. 1950. (ISBN 0-8022-1506-8). Philos Lib.

Style & Idea. Arnold Schonberg. 244p. Repr. of 1950 ed. lib. bdg. 39.00 o.p. (Pub. by Am Repr Serv). Reprint Servs.

Style & Structure in Shakespeare. Henry Wells & H. H. Gowda. 1979. text ed. 14.95x o.p. (ISBN 0-7069-0711-6). Humanities.

Style & Substance. Judith Martin. LC 86-47672. 320p. 1986. 15.95 o.p. (ISBN 0-689-11514-8, Atheneum). Macmillan.

Style As Argument: Contemporary American Nonfiction. Chris Anderson. 19.95 o.p. (ISBN 0-317-59143-6); pap. 10.95 o.p. (ISBN 0-317-59144-4). S Ill U Pr.

Style As Structure & Meaning: William Bradford's "Of Plymouth Plantation" Floyd Ogburn, Jr. LC 80-5879. 169p. 1981. lib. bdg. 24.25 o.p. (ISBN 0-8191-1590-8); pap. text ed. 11.50 o.p. (ISBN 0-8191-1591-6). U Pr of Amer.

Style in History. Peter Gay. LC 76-25490. (McGraw-Hill Paperbacks). 1976. pap. text ed. 3.95 o.p. (ISBN 0-07-023063-3). McGraw.

Style of Palestrina & the Dissonance. Knud Jeppesen. 306p. Repr. of 1970 ed. lib. bdg. 49.00 o.p. (Pub. by Am Repr Serv). Reprint Servs.

Style: Ten Lessons in Clarity & Grace. 2nd ed. Joseph M. Williams. 1985. pap. text ed. (ISBN 0-673-18058-1). Scott F.

Styles. Paul V. Carter. Ed. by Kathy R. Aszkenas. 224p. 1987. 15.95 o.p. (ISBN 0-682-40354-7). Exposition-Phoenix.

Styles for Writing: A Brief Rhetoric. Gerald Levin. 242p. 1972. pap. text ed. 5.50 o.p. (ISBN 0-15-584760-0, HC). HarBraceJ.

Styles of Acting: A Scenebook for the Advanced Acting Student. Elaine Novak. LC 85-6407. 240p. 1985. 17.95 o.p. (ISBN 0-13-858804-X); pap. 8.95 o.p. (ISBN 0-13-858796-5). P H.

Styles of Learning & Teaching: An Integrative Outline of Educational Psychology for Students, Teachers & Lecturers. Noel J. Entwistle. LC 80-41172. 293p. 1981. 77.95x o.p. (ISBN 0-471-27901-3); pap. 37.00x o.p. (ISBN 0-471-10013-7). Wiley.

Styles of Thinking: Strategies for Asking Questions, Making Decisions & Solving Problems. Allen F. Harrison & Robert M. Bramson. LC 80-1095. (Illus.). 216p. 1982. 14.95 o.p. (ISBN 0-385-15763-0, Anchor Pr). Doubleday.

Stylistic Analysis of Arshile Gorky's Art from 1943-1948. Robert F. Reiff. LC 76-23679. (Outstanding Dissertations in the Fine Arts-American). (Illus.). 345p. 1977. Repr. of 1961 ed. lib. bdg. 63.00 o.p. (ISBN 0-8240-2719-1). Garland Pub.

Stylistics & Psychology: Investigations of Foregrounding. Willie Van Peer. 224p. 1986. 43.00 o.p. (ISBN 0-7099-2604-9, Pub. by Croom Helm Ltd). Routledge Chapman & Hall.

Su Tung-P'o: Selections from a Sung Dynasty Poet. Tr. by Burton Watson. LC 65-13619. 1965. 25.00x o.p. (ISBN 0-231-02798-2); pap. 12.00x o.p. (ISBN 0-231-02799-0). Columbia U Pr.

Sub-Clinical Lead Poisoning. D. Stofen & H. A. Walsren. 1974. 85.00 o.p. (ISBN 0-12-671650-1). Acad Pr.

Sub-Regional Planning Studies: An Evaluation. T. M. Cowling & G. C. Steeley. LC 73-4476. 1973. text ed. 21.00 o.p. (ISBN 0-08-017019-6). Pergamon.

Sub Rosa: The O.S.S. & American Espionage. Stewart Alsop & Thomas Branden. LC 64-57431. 272p. 1964. pap. 1.65 o.p. (ISBN 0-15-686300-6, Harv). HarBraceJ.

Sub-Saharan Africa: A Guide to Information Sources. Ed. by W. A. Skurnik. LC 73-17513. (International Relations Information Guide Ser.: Vol. 3). 144p. 1977. 68.00x o.p. (ISBN 0-8103-1391-X). Gale.

Subaltern. Duncan Macneil. 1977. pap. 1.50 o.p. (ISBN 0-505-51148-7, Pub. by Tower Bks). Dorchester Pub Co.

Subaru 1970-84: RTUG. Chilton Automotives Editorial Staff. LC 83-45314. 312p. 1984. pap. 12.50 o.p. (ISBN 0-8019-7479-8). Chilton.

Subchapter S Revisions of 1982. Pennsylvania Bar Institute Staff. 21p. 1983. incl. audiocassettes 30.00 o.p. (ISBN 0-318-02162-5, 219). PA Bar Inst.

Subcontracting Policy in the Airframe Industry. J. S. Day. 1956. 60.00 o.p. (ISBN 0-08-018745-5). Pergamon.

Subdrainage & Soil Moisture. (Transportation Research Record Ser.). 76p. 1979. 4.00 o.p. (ISBN 0-309-02951-1). Transport Res Bd.

Subduction Zone Metamorphism. Ed. by W. G. Ernst. LC 74-25224. (Benchmark Papers in Geology Ser: No. 19). 1975. 85.50 o.p. (ISBN 0-12-786448-2). Acad Pr.

Subhas Chandra Bose & the Indian National Movement. Hari H. Das. text ed. 37.50x o.p. (ISBN 0-86590-104-X, Pub. by Sterling Pubs India). Apt Bks.

Subject & Object in Modern English. Barbara H. Partee. Ed. by Jorge Hankamer. LC 78-66576. (Outstanding Dissertations in Linguistics Ser.). 1985. 20.00 o.p. (ISBN 0-8240-9679-7). Garland Pub.

Subject & Topic: Proceedings of the Symposium, University of California, Santa Barbara, Mar. 1975. Symposium, University of California, Santa Barbara Staff. Ed. by Charles N. Li. 1976. 68.00 o.p. (ISBN 0-12-447350-4). Acad Pr.

Subject Area Reading in the Middle School. David Bishop. 45p. 1982. 4.25 o.p. (ISBN 0-318-18691-8). Natl Middle Schl.

Subject Bibliography of the Social Sciences & Humanities. B. M. Hale. LC 78-113358. 1970. text ed. 22.00 o.p. (ISBN 0-08-015791-2). Pergamon.

Subject Catalog of the Baker Library, 10 vols. Harvard University, Graduate School of Business Administration Staff. 1971. Set. 1065.00 o.p. (ISBN 0-8161-0186-8, Hall Library). G K Hall.

Subject Catalog of the Baker Library: First Supplement. Harvard University, Graduate School of Business Administration Staff. 1974. 120.00 o.p. (ISBN 0-8161-1180-4, Hall Library). G K Hall.

Subject Catalog of the Department Library, 20 Vols. Ed. by U. S. Department of Health, Education & Welfare, Washington, D. C. Staff. 1965. Set. 1875.00 o.p. (ISBN 0-8161-0234-1, Hall Library). G K Hall.

Subject Catalog of the Department Library: First Supplement, 7 vols. Ed. by U. S. Department of Health, Education & Welfare, Washington, D. C. Staff. 1973. Set. 765.00 o.p. (Hall Library). G K Hall.

Subject Catalog of the Ibero-American Institute in Berlin, Prussian Cultural Heritage Foundation. Ibero-American Institute Staff, in Berlin. 1977. lib. bdg. 2810.00 o.p. (ISBN 0-8161-0068-3, Hall Library). G K Hall.

Subject Catalog of the Library of the Cornell University School of Hotel Administration, 2 vols. 1981. Set. lib. bdg. 210.00 o.p. (ISBN 0-8161-0421-2, Hall Library). G K Hall.

Subject Catalog of the Library of the New York Academy of Medicine, 34 Vols. New York Academy of Medicine Staff. 1969. Set. lib. bdg. 3225.00 o.p. (ISBN 0-8161-0826-9, Hall Library). G K Hall.

Subject Catalog of the Library of the New York Academy of Medicine, 1st Supplement, 4 vols. New York Academy of Medicine Staff. 1974. Set. lib. bdg. 495.00 o.p. (ISBN 0-8161-0184-1, Hall Library). G K Hall.

Subject Catalog of the World War One Collection, 4 Vols. New York Public Library, Research Libraries Staff. 1961. Set. 295.00 o.p. (ISBN 0-8161-0559-6, Hall Library). G K Hall.

Subject Catalogue Film, Vol. 1: Individual Holding as of July 1981. Ed. by Stadt und Universitatsbucherei & Frankfurt am Main. 397p. 1982. lib. bdg. 40.00 o.p. (ISBN 3-598-10414-6). K G Saur.

Subject Catalogue of the Arthur Lakes Library of the Colorado School of Mines. Colorado School of Mines Editors. 1977. lib. bdg. 595.00 o.p. (ISBN 0-8161-0072-1, Hall Library). G K Hall.

Subject Directory of Special Libraries & Information Centers 1988, 5 vols. 11th ed. Ed. by Brigitte T. Darnay. 1987. Set. 685.00x o.p. (ISBN 0-8103-4342-8). Gale.

Subject Directory of Special Libraries & Information Centers 1988: Business & Law Libraries, Vol. 1. 11th ed. Ed. by Brigitee T. Darnay. 381p. 1987. 160.00x o.p. (ISBN 0-8103-4343-6). Gale.

Subject Directory of Special Libraries & Information Centers 1988: Education & Information Science Libraries, Vol. 2. 11th ed. Ed. by Brigitte T. Darnay. 279p. 1987. 160.00x o.p. (ISBN 0-8103-4344-4). Gale.

Subject Directory of Special Libraries & Information Centers 1988: Health Sciences Libraries, Vol. 3. 11th ed. Ed. by Brigitte T. Darnay. 348p. 1987. 160.00x o.p. (ISBN 0-8103-4345-2). Gale.

Subject Directory of Special Libraries & Information Centers 1988: Social Sciences & Humanities Libraries, Vol. 4. 11th ed. Ed. by Brigitte T. Darnay. 794p. 1987. 160.00x o.p. (ISBN 0-8103-4346-0). Gale.

Subject Directory of Special Libraries & Information Centers 1988: Science & Engineering Libraries, Vol. 5. 11th ed. Ed. by Brigitte T. Darnay. 609p. 1987. 160.00x o.p. (ISBN 0-8103-4347-9). Gale.

Subject Guide to Books in Print, 1987-88, 4 vols. Ed. by Bowker, R. R., Staff. 7524p. 1987. 179.95 o.p. (ISBN 0-8352-2355-8); microfiche full year sub. 350.00 o.p. (ISBN 0-8352-2405-8). Bowker.

Subject Guide to Children's Books in Print, 1987-88. Ed. by Bowker, R. R., Staff. 527p. 1987. 75.00 o.p. (ISBN 0-8352-2361-2). Bowker.

Subject Guide to Microforms in Print, 1987. Ed. by Microforms in Print Staff. 1987. lib. bdg. 149.50x o.p. (ISBN 0-88736-182-X). Meckler Corp.

Subject Headings, 5 Vols. New York Public Library, Research Libraries Staff. 1960. Set. lib. bdg. 340.00 o.p. (ISBN 0-8161-0368-2, Hall Library). G K Hall.

Subject Index of Bulletins Published by the Bureau of Labor Statistics: Consisting of "Subject Index of the Publications of the United States Bureau of Labor Statistics up to May 1, 1915" (Issued in 1915) & "Subject Index of Bulletins Published by the Bureau of Labor Statistics, 1915-1959" (Issued in 1960, 2 vols. in 1. United States Bureau of Labor Statistics Staff. LC 78-10739. 1979. Repr. of 1915 ed. lib. bdg. (ISBN 0-313-20688-0, USSI). Greenwood.

Subject Index to the Holy Koran. Kamran Fani & Baha Khoramshahi. lib. bdg. 19.00x o.p. (ISBN 0-939214-52-0). Mazda Pubs.

Subjective Meaning & Culture: An Assessment Through Word Associations. Lorand B. Szalay & James Deese. LC 78-15561. 166p. 1978. 16.95x o.p. (ISBN 0-470-26486-1). Halsted Pr.

Subjects & Sources for Research Writing, Second Ser. Ed. by Raymond W. Short & Robert DeMaria. (Second Series). (Orig.). 1963. pap. 3.95x o.p. (ISBN 0-393-09602-5, NortonC). Norton.

Subjunctives see Metaphor.

Submerge: The Story of Divers & Their Crafts. Anabel Dean. LC 75-33917. (Franklin Institute Bk). (Illus.). (gr. 6-9). 1976. 6.50 o.s.i. (ISBN 0-664-32569-6, Westminster); pap. 4.50 o.s.i. (ISBN 0-664-34009-1, Westminster). Westminster John Knox.

Submicroscopic Cytochemistry, 2vols. Ed. by Isidore Gersh. Incl. Vol. 1. Protein & Nucleic Acids. 1974. 73.50 o.p. (ISBN 0-12-281401-0); Vol.2. Membranes,Mitochondria, & Connective Tissue. 1974. 54.00 (ISBN 0-12-281402-9). Acad Pr.

Submicroscopic Cytodifferentiation. M. Dvorak. LC 75-177565. (Advances in Anatomy, Embryology, & Cell Biology: Vol. 45, Pt. 4). (Illus.). 120p. 1971. 45.50 o.p. (ISBN 0-387-05622-X). Springer-Verlag.

Submicroscopic Ortho- & Patho-Morphology of the Liver. H. David. 1964. 320.00 o.p. (ISBN 0-08-010903-9). Pergamon.

Submillimetre Spectroscopy. G. W. Chantry. 1972. 66.50 o.p. (ISBN 0-12-170550-1). Acad Pr.

Submillimetre Waves & Their Applications: Proceedings of the International Conference, 3rd, 1978. International Conference on Submillimetre Waves & Their Applications Staff. LC 79-40065. (Illus.). 1979. 71.00 o.p. (ISBN 0-08-023817-3). Pergamon.

Subnational Politics: Readings in State & Local Government. David C. Saffell & Terry Gilbreth. (Political Science Ser.). (Illus.). 320p. 1981. pap. text ed. 9.75 o.p. (ISBN 0-394-34939-3, RanC). Random.

Subnuclear Phenomena, Pts. A-B. Ed. by A. Zichichi. 1971. 80.00 ea. o.p. Pt. A (ISBN 0-12-780580-X). Pt. B (ISBN 0-12-780582-6). Acad Pr.

Subnuclear Resonance Science Unification Key: Old Data-New Concepts. Harold H. Belcher. 1977. 14.50 o.p. (ISBN 0-682-48884-4, University). Exposition-Phoenix.

Subnuclear Zoo. Sylvia L. Engdahl & Rick Roberson. LC 77-1686. (Illus.). (gr. 6-9). 1977. 6.95 o.p. (ISBN 0-689-30582-6, Atheneum). Macmillan.

Subordination or Liberation? The Development & Conflicting Theories of Black Education in Nineteenth Century Alabama. Robert G. Sherer. LC 75-44050. 224p. 1977. 18.75 o.p. (ISBN 0-8173-9111-8). U of Ala Pr.

Subsidence Over Mines & Caverns, Moisture & Frost Actions & Classification. (Transportation Research Record Ser.). 83p. 1976. 3.60 o.p. (ISBN 0-309-02588-5). Transport Res Bd.

Subsidised Public Transport & the Demand for Travel. Bailey Goodwin et al. 234p. 1983. text ed. 33.95x o.p. (ISBN 0-566-00654-5). Gower Pub Co.

Subsidized Housing Information File. Metropolitan Washington Council of Governments Staff & Scott W. Reilly. LC 83-166809. (Housing Technical Report Ser.). 538p. 1983. 25.00 o.p. (ISBN 0-317-12895-7). Metro Wash Lib.

Substance Abuse & Psychiatric Illness: Proceedings of the Second Annual Coatesville--Jefferson Conference on Addiction. Ed. by Edward Gottheil et al. LC 79-25407. 224p. 1980. 36.50 o.p. (ISBN 0-08-025547-7). Pergamon.

Substance Abuse: Bibliography. 7.50 o.p. (ISBN 0-317-59914-3, 72509C). Am Assn Coun Dev.

Substance Abuse Disorders in Clinical Practice. Edward C. Senay. (Senay Ser.). 256p. 1983. text ed. 25.50 o.p. (ISBN 0-7236-7024-2). Butterworth.

Substance P, Vol. 2. Petr Skrabanek & David Powell. Ed. by D. F. Horrobin. LC 80-646426. (Annual Research Reviews Ser.). 175p. 1980. 26.00 o.p. (ISBN 0-88831-073-0). Eden Pr.

Substoichiometry in Radiochemical Analysis. J. Ruzicka & J. Stary. 1968. 40.00 o.p. (ISBN 0-08-012442-9). Pergamon.

Substrates & Supports for Separations & Immobilizations. Business Communications Staff. 1988. 1950.00 o.p. (C-089). BCC.

Subsurface Exploration & Sampling of Soils for Civil Engineering Purposes. M. Juul Hvorslev. 533p. 1949. pap. 24.00x o.p. (ISBN 0-87262-169-3). Am Soc Civil Eng.

Subsurface Space--Environment Protection, Low Cost Storage, Energy Savings: Proceedings of the International Symposium, Stockholm, Sweden, June 23-27, 1980, 3 vols. Ed. by M. Bergman. (Illus.). 1500p. 1981. 365.00 o.p. (ISBN 0-08-026136-1). Pergamon.

Subterranean Horses. Yannis Ritsos. Tr. by Minas Savvas from Gr. LC 80-83220. (International Poetry: Vol. 3). (Illus.). xii, 63p. 1980. 12.95x o.p. (ISBN 0-8214-0579-9); pap. 6.95 o.p. (ISBN 0-8214-0580-2). Ohio U Pr.

Subterranean Termites: Their Prevention & Control in Buildings. rev. ed. Raymond H. Beal et al. (Home & Garden Bulletin Ser.: No. 64). (Illus.). 36p. 1986. pap. 1.25 o.p. (ISBN 0-318-22437-2, S/N 001-000-04481-8). USGPO.

Subtle Brains & Lissom Fingers. 3rd ed. Andrew Wynter. LC 67-27868. (Social History Reference Ser.). (Illus.). 456p. 1968. Repr. of 1863 ed. 35.00x o.p. (ISBN 0-8103-3267-1). Gale.

Subtle Psychology of Selling & of Business Relations. Armand C. Montgomery. (Illus.). 157p. 1989. 77.75 o.p. (ISBN 0-86654-278-7). Inst Econ Finan.

Subtraction 20-10, Levels 1 & 2. Reusable ed. Kitty Wehrli. (Michigan Arithmetic Program Ser.). (gr. 2-3). 1976. Level 1. wkbk 8.50 ea. o.p. (ISBN 0-89039-178-5). Level 2 (ISBN 0-89039-220-X). Ann Arbor Pubs.

Suburban Gardener & Villa Companion. J. C. Loudon. Ed. by John D. Hunt. LC 79-56971. (English Landscape Garden Ser.). 766p. 1982. lib. bdg. 100.00 o.p. (ISBN 0-8240-0177-X). Garland Pub.

Suburban Geology: An Introduction to the Common Rocks & Minerals of Your Back Yard & Local Park. Richard Headstrom. (Illus.). 160p. 1985. 16.95 o.p. (ISBN 0-13-859240-3); pap. 8.95 o.p. (ISBN 0-13-859232-2). P-H.

Suburbanization Dynamics & the Future of the City. James W. Hughes. 300p. 1974. (ISBN 0-87855-108-5). Transaction Pubs.

Suburbia: A Guide to Information Sources. Ed. by Joseph Zikmund & Deborah E. Dennis. LC 78-10523. (Urban Studies Information Guide Ser: Vol. 9). 160p. 1979. 68.00x o.p. (ISBN 0-8103-1435-5). Gale.

Suburbs of Hell. Randolph Stow. LC 83-51575. 176p. 1984. 13.95 o.s.i. (ISBN 0-8008-7487-0). Taplinger.

Subversion of Women As Practiced by Churches, Witch-Hunters, & Other Sexists. Nancy Van Vuuren. LC 73-5874. 1973. 5.95 o.s.i. (ISBN 0-664-20972-6, Westminster). Westminster John Knox.

Subversive. Jose Rizal. Tr. by Leon M. Guerrero. Orig. Title: Filibusterismo. 1968. pap. 1.95x o.p. (ISBN 0-393-00449-X, Norton Lib). Norton.

Subversive Family: An Alternative History of Love & Marriage. Ferdinand Mount. (Counterpoint Ser.). 282p. 1983. pap. 9.95 o.p. (ISBN 0-04-942180-8). Unwin Hyman.

Subversive Science: Essays Toward an Ecology of Man. Ed. by Paul Shepard & Daniel McKinley. LC 69-15029. (Illus., Orig.). 1969. pap. 16.50 o.p. (ISBN 0-395-05399-4). HM.

Subway Design: An Architectural Guide. Coppa & Avery Consultants Staff. (Architecture Ser.: Bibliography A-1310). 11p. 1985. pap. 2.00 o.p. (ISBN 0-89028-240-4). Vance Biblios.

Succeed with Math: Every Student's Guide to Conquering Math Anxiety. Sheila Tobias. 272p. 1987. pap. 12.95 o.p. (ISBN 0-87447-259-8, 51295). College Bd.

Succeeding on the Job: A Self-Study Guide for Students. Patricia M Rath. 1970. pap. text ed. 8.00x o.p. (ISBN 0-8134-1167-X, 1167). Inter Print Pubs.

Success! Michael Korda. 1978. 3.50 o.s.i. (ISBN 0-345-32577-X); pap. 3.50 o.s.i. (ISBN 0-345-27741-4). Ballantine.

Success & Failure in Learning to Read. Ronald Morris. 176p. (ISBN 0-8022-1153-4). Philos Lib.

Success & Survival in the Family Owned Business. Pat Alcorn. 256p. 1981. text ed. 26.95 o.p. (ISBN 0-07-000961-9). McGraw.

Success Book for Landlords: A Money-Making Guide for Property Owners, Managers & Investors. David N. Siegel. (Illus.). 272p. 1983. 13.00 o.p. (ISBN 0-682-49992-7). Exposition-Phoenix.

Success Control: Positive Thinking. Enoch A. Gyamfi. 1985. 6.50 o.p. (ISBN 0-8062-2464-9). Carlton.

Success Handbook for Salespeople. Paul J. Micali. 208p. 1983. pap. 12.95 o.p. (ISBN 0-8436-0853-6). Van Nos Reinhold.

Success Is a Way of Life. Christopher Hills. LC 83-19417. 96p. (Orig.). 1983. 3.95 o.p. (ISBN 0-916438-49-X). Univ of Trees.

Success Is the Quality of Your Journey. Jennifer James. 1988. pap. 8.95 o.p. Newmarket.

Success of Modern Private Enterprise. Roland W. Bartlett. LC 70-106133. 1970. 7.95 o.p. (ISBN 0-8134-1148-3, 1148); text ed. 5.95x o.p. Inter Print Pubs.

Success over Sixty. Albert Myers & Christopher Andersen. 1984. 15.45 o.s.i. (ISBN 0-671-49460-0). Summit Bks.

Success over Sixty. Albert Myers & Christopher P. Andersen. 1986. pap. 8.95 o.s.i. (ISBN 0-671-62013-4). Summit Bks.

Success over Sixty. Albert Myers & Christopher Anderson. (General Ser.). 1985. lib. bdg. 16.95 o.p. (ISBN 0-8161-3801-X, Large Print Bks). G K Hall.

Success Strategies for the New Sales Manager. Mack Hanan et al. 1982. pap. 8.95 o.p. (ISBN 0-8144-7566-3). AMACOM.

Success: The Glenn Bland Method. 1975. pap. 4.95 o.p. (ISBN 0-8423-6690-3). Tyndale.

Success with Sentences. Helen R. Kocher & Alec Ross. (Orig.). 1966. pap. text ed. write for info. o.p. (ISBN 0-02-365490-2). Macmillan.

Successful Activities of Hale Pickett. Hale Pickett. LC 84-90121. (Illus.). 56p. 1985. 6.95 o.p. (ISBN 0-533-06199-7). Vantage.

Successful Air Conditioning & Refrigeration Repair. Roger A. Fischer. pap. 9.70 o.p. (ISBN 0-8306-1281-5, 1281P). TAB Bks.

Successful American Urban Plans. W. G. Roeseler. LC 81-47028. 224p. 1981. 35.00x o.p. (ISBN 0-669-04540-3). Lexington Bks.

Successful Business English. Norman B. Sigband et al. 1983. pap. text ed. (ISBN 0-673-15589-7). Scott F.

Successful Business Writing: How to Write Successful Letters, Proposals, Resumes, & Speeches. Lassor A. Blumenthal. 80p. 1976. pap. 3.95 o.p. (ISBN 0-399-50798-1, G&D). Putnam Pub Group.

Successful Cold Call Selling. Lee Boyan. LC 83-45211. 208p. 1983. 15.95 o.p. (ISBN 0-8144-5771-1). AMACOM.

Successful Community Fundraising: A Complete How-to Guide. Sheila Petersen. LC 79-83688. (Illus.). 1979. pap. 7.95 o.p. (ISBN 0-89803-003-X, Dist. by Kampmann). Green Hill.

Successful Cross-Examination. Noel Stevenson. 1972. text ed. 59.50 o.p. (ISBN 0-13-194837-7). P-H.

Successful Deer Hunting. Sam Fadala. LC 83-72342. (Illus.). 288p. (Orig.). 1983. pap. 12.95 o.p. (ISBN 0-910676-64-X). DBI.

Successful Dieting Tips. Bruce Lansky. Ed. by Kathe Grooms. LC 81-11028. (Illus.). 132p. 1981. pap. 4.95 o.p. (ISBN 0-671-54492-6). Meadowbrook.

Successful Direct Selling: How to Plan, Launch, Promote, & Maintain a Profitable Direct Selling Company. Ronald A. Bernstein. (Illus.). 240p. 1984. 21.95 o.p. (ISBN 0-13-860726-5). P-H.

Successful Elementary Teacher. Ed. by James L. Kelly & Mary J. Kelly. (Illus.). 164p. (Orig.). 1985. lib. bdg. 26.25 o.p. (ISBN 0-8191-4533-5); pap. text ed. 9.25 o.p. (ISBN 0-8191-4532-7). U Pr of Amer.

Successful Face. Amy Greene & Molly Pomerance. LC 85-14672. (Illus.). 1985. 14.70 o.s.i. (ISBN 0-671-54772-0). Summit Bks.

Successful Financial Planning. George Hardisty & Margaret Hardisty. 1978. 25.00 o.p. (ISBN 0-915262-62-2). Revell.

Successful Flea Market Selling. pap. 9.95 o.p. (ISBN 0-8306-1207-6, 1207). TAB Bks.

Successful Fundraising. William K Grasty & Kenneth Sheinkopf. 1983. 17.95 o.s.i. (ISBN 0-684-17493-6). Scribner.

Successful Handling of Casualty Claims. Pat Magarick. LC 73-91720. 1974. 47.50 o.p. (ISBN 0-87632-168-6). Clark Boardman.

Successful Handling of the DWI Case. 392p. 1983. 25.00 o.p. (ISBN 0-88129-118-8). Wash Bar CLE.

Successful Industrial Real Estate Brokerage. 3rd. ed. Real Estate Education Company Staff & Grubb & Ellis Staff. LC 84-4746. 322p. 1984. pap. 29.95 o.p. (ISBN 0-88462-492-7, 1922-03, Real Estate Ed). Longman Finan.

Successful Investing. rev. ed. Ed. by United Business Service Staff. 1983. pap. 12.95 o.s.i. (ISBN 0-671-46734-4). S&S.

Successful Job Hunting for Managers, Professionals & Graduates. R. C. Miller. 127p. 1983. pap. text ed. 9.95x o.p. (ISBN 0-631-13398-4). Basil Blackwell.

Successful Leasing & Selling of Office Property. 2nd ed. Real Estate Education Company Staff & Grubb & Ellis Staff. LC 83-19050. 250p. 1983. pap. 29.95 o.p. (ISBN 0-88462-493-5, 1922-02, Real Estate Ed). Longman Finan.

Successful Leasing & Selling of Retail Property. 2nd ed. Real Estate Education Company Staff & Grubb & Ellis Staff. LC 84-3447. 246p. 1984. pap. 29.95 o.p. (ISBN 0-88462-494-3, 1922-01, Real Estate Ed.). Longman Finan.

Successful Life. George Wood. Ed. by Jo Anne Sekowsky. 64p. 1984. pap. text ed. 3.25 o.p. (ISBN 0-930756-82-7, 531017). Aglow Pubns.

Successful Management of Large Clerical Operations: A Guide to Improving Service Transaction Systems. Martin F. Stankard, Jr. LC 80-11991. (Illus.). 288p. 1980. text ed. 28.50 o.p. (ISBN 0-07-060831-8). McGraw.

Successful Mangement Information Systems. rev. ed. Helen H. Ligon. Ed. by Richard Farmer. LC 86-6979. (Research for Business Decisions Ser.: No. 78). 224p. 1986. 49.95 o.p. (ISBN 0-8357-1703-8). UMI Res Pr.

Successful Marketing for Small Business. William A. Cohen & Marshall E. Reddick. 288p. 1981. 17.95 o.p. (ISBN 0-8144-5611-1). AMACOM.

Successful Marketing of Schools. Melvyn Hornick. 90p. 1980. softcover 8.95 o.p. (ISBN 0-932930-38-7). Pilgrimage Inc.

Successful Outdoor Writing. Jack Samson. LC 79-11854. 244p. 1979. 11.95 o.p. (ISBN 0-911654-66-6). Writers Digest.

Successful Parties: Simple & Elegant. Martin Johner & Gary Goldberg. Ed. by Jean Atcheson. LC 83-71040. (Great American Cooking School Ser.). (Illus.). 84p. 1983. pap. 5.95 o.p. (ISBN 0-941034-19-4). I Chalmers.

Successful Pension Design for the Small to Medium Size Business. Robert F. Slimmon. LC 80-13148. (Illus.). 396p. 1980. 69.50 o.p. (ISBN 0-87624-524-6, Inst Busn Plan). P-H.

Successful Project Management. 2nd. ed. W. J. Taylor & T. F. Watling. 269p. 1979. text ed. 36.75x o.p. (ISBN 0-220-67004-8, Pub. by Busn Bks England). Gower Pub Co.

Successful Responses to Financial Difficulty. Ed. by Carol Frances. LC 81-48570. (Higher Education Ser.: No. 38). 1982. 11.95x o.p. (ISBN 0-87589-896-3). Jossey-Bass.

Successful Sandy Soil Gardening. Bette G. Wahlfeldt. (Illus.). 1979. pap. 6.95 o.p. (ISBN 0-8306-1068-5, 1068). TAB Bks.

Successful Secrets to Smart Retailing. Philip M. Perry. 300p. 1982. 34.50 o.p. (ISBN 0-87624-528-9, Inst Busn Plan). P-H.

Successful Selling Strategies. David El Fattal. 56p. (Orig.). 1988. pap. 6.00 o.p. El Fattal Enterprises.

Successful Settlement of Large Liabilities: How Annuity Policies Will Work for You. George Haufler. 1985. 25.00 o.p. (ISBN 0-682-40259-1). Exposition-Phoenix.

Successful Sewing: A Modern Guide. Nesta Hollis. LC 76-84974. (Illus.). (gr. 8 up). 8.75 o.s.i. (ISBN 0-8008-7490-0). Taplinger.

Successful Small Business Management. 4th ed. Curtis E. Tate, Jr. et al. 1985. 36.95 o.p. (ISBN 0-256-03278-5). Irwin.

Successful Small Business Management. Leon A. Wortman. (Illus.). 1976. 12.95 o.p. (ISBN 0-8144-5394-5). AMACOM.

Successful Strategies for Recruiting Family Day Care Providers. Tom Copeland & Megan Roach. Ed. by Jill Hix. (Illus.). 110p. (Orig.). 1986. pap. text ed. 17.95 o.p. (ISBN 0-934140-32-4). Toys 'n Things.

Successful Supervision. James R. White. 1976. text ed. 34.50 o.p. (ISBN 0-07-084458-5). McGraw.

Successful Team Building Through TA. Dudley Bennett. 1980. 14.95 o.p. (ISBN 0-8144-5607-3). AMACOM.

Successful Techniques That Multiply Profits & Personal Payoff in the Closely - Held Corporation. 4th ed. IBP Research & Editorial Staff. LC 80-16143. (Illus.). 500p. 1980. 79.50 o.p. (ISBN 0-87624-532-7, Inst Busn Plan). P-H.

Successful Techniques That Multiply Profits & Personal Payoff in the Closely-Held Corporation. 3rd ed. IBP Research & Editorial Staff. LC 75-9004. 1977. 39.50 o.p. (ISBN 0-87624-531-9, Inst Busn Plan). P-H.

Successful Transitions: A Guide Through the Employment Process. 1982. 8.95 o.p. (ISBN 0-940428-03-2). Ed Assocs KY.

Successful Transitions: A Guide Through the Employment Process. 1982. pap. 7.95 o.p. (ISBN 0-940428-02-4). Ed Assocs KY.

Successful Waterfowling. Zack Taylor. LC 80-39811. 288p. (Orig.). 1981. pap. 15.95 o.s.i. (ISBN 0-8117-2147-7). Stackpole.

Successful Writing: A Rhetoric for Advanced Composition. Maxine C. Hairston. 284p. 1981. text ed. 16.95x o.p. (ISBN 0-393-95148-0). Norton.

Successfully Ever After: A Young Woman's Guide to Career Happiness. Shirley S. Fader. (McGraw-Hill Paperback Ser.). 300p. 1982. text ed. 15.95 o.p. (ISBN 0-07-019890-X); pap. text ed. 6.95 o.p. (ISBN 0-07-019889-6). McGraw.

Succession: A Novel of Elizabeth & James. George Garrett. LC 84-18163. 552p. 1985. Repr. of 1983 ed. 11.95 o.p. (ISBN 0-688-03915-4, Quill). Morrow.

Succulent Plants. A. Bertrand. (Illus.). 128p. 1959. (ISBN 0-8022-0119-9). Philos Lib.

Succulents & Their Cultivation. Margaret J. Martin & Peter Chapman. LC 77-83777. (Illus.). 1978. 19.95 o.s.i. (ISBN 0-684-15514-1, ScribT). Scribner.

Succulents of Southern Africa. B. Barkuizen. 1980. 60.00x o.p. (ISBN 0-686-69985-8, Pub. by Bailey Bros & Swinfen Ltd). State Mutual Bk.

Such a Pretty Face: Being Fat in America. Marcia Millman. (Illus.). 1980. 12.95 o.p. (ISBN 0-393-01317-0). Norton.

Such a Strange Lady. Janet Hitchman. 1976. pap. 1.95 o.p. (ISBN 0-380-00807-6, 30825). Avon.

Such a Vision of the Street: Mother Teresa; The Spirit & The Work. Eileen Egan. LC 81-43570. (Illus.). 456p. 1985. 16.95 o.s.i. (ISBN 0-385-17490-X). Doubleday.

Such As Us: Southern Voices of the Thirties. Ed. by Tom E. Terrill & Jerrold Hirsch. (Illus.). 1979. pap. 5.95 o.p. (ISBN 0-393-00927-0). Norton.

Such As Us: Southern Voices of the Thirties. Ed. by Tom E. Terrill & Jerrold Hirsch. LC 77-14248. (Illus.). xxvi, 302p. 1978. 22.50x o.p. (ISBN 0-8078-1318-4). U of NC Pr.

Such Sweet Thunder: Forty-Nine Pieces on Jazz. Whitney Balliett. 366p. Repr. of 1966 ed. lib. bdg. 49.00 o.p. (Pub. by Am Repr Serv). Reprint Servs.

Sudan. M. W. Daly. (World Bibliographical Ser.: No. 40). 175p. 1983. lib. bdg. 26.75 o.p. (ISBN 0-903450-70-4). ABC-Clio.

Sudanna, Sudanna. Brian Herbert. 239p. 1985. 15.95 o.p. (ISBN 0-87795-657-X, Arbor Hse). Morrow.

Sudba Faini: A Novel. Alexander Skachinsky. 1983. 8.95 o.s.i. RWCPH.

Sudbury Region: An Illustrated History. Graeme S. Mount. LC 86-5653. (Illus.). 144p. 1986. 24.95 o.p. (ISBN 0-89781-177-1). Windsor Pubns Inc.

Sudden Death. William X. Kienzle. (Large Print Bks.). 445p. 1986. lib. bdg. 16.95 o.p. (ISBN 0-8161-3965-2). G K Hall.

Sudden Door. Madeline Benedict. 1960. 2.75 o.p. (ISBN 0-8233-0005-6). Golden Quill.

Sudden Land. Dale Oldham. (Orig.). 1980. pap. 1.75 o.p. (ISBN 0-505-51480-X, Pub. by Tower Bks). Dorchester Pub Co.

Sudden View: A Traveller's Tale from Mexico. Sybille Bedford. LC 63-797. 1963. pap. 1.45 o.p. (ISBN 0-689-70008-3, 18, Atheneum). Macmillan.

Suddenly Poor: A Guide for the Downwardly Mobile. Timothy & Suares. (Illus.). 1983. 5.70 o.p. (ISBN 0-316-93607-3, Atlantic Monthly Pr Bk). Little.

Sudeten-German Tragedy. Austin J. App. (Illus.). 84p. (Orig.). 1979. pap. 3.00x o.p. (ISBN 0-911038-66-3, Inst Hist Rev). Noontide.

Sudina. Jessie Schell. (YA) (gr. 7 up). 1977. pap. 1.50 o.p. (ISBN 0-380-01763-6, 34967). Avon.

Sue Ellen. Edith F. Hunter. LC 77-90274. (Illus.). (gr. 3-7). 1969. 7.95 o.p. (ISBN 0-395-06836-3). HM.

Sue the B-St-Rds: The Victim's Handbook. Douglas Matthews. LC 72-97686. 1973. 6.95 o.p. (ISBN 0-87795-059-8, Arbor Hse); pap. 2.95 o.p. (ISBN 0-87795-125-X). Morrow.

Sue the B-st-rds: The Victim's Handbook. rev. ed. Douglas Matthews. LC 80-52011. 1981. pap. 7.95 o.p. (ISBN 0-87795-288-4, Arbor Hse). Morrow.

Sueno de una Noche de Agosto. Gregorio Martinez Sierra. Ed. by Donald Walsh. (Span). 1952. pap. 3.95x o.p. (ISBN 0-393-09477-4, NortonC). Norton.

Suez Canal in World Affairs. Hugh J. Schonfield. (Illus.). 180p. 1953. (ISBN 0-8022-1513-0). Philos Lib.

Suffer the Little Children: The Battle Against Childhood Cancer. Jocelyn Demers. Tr. by James Parry from Fr. 192p. 1986. pap. 10.95 o.s.i. (ISBN 0-920792-62-6). Eden Pr.

Suffolk Churches. 5th ed. H. Munro Cautley. (Illus.). 448p. 1982. 45.00 o.p. (ISBN 0-85115-143-4, Pub. by Boydell & Brewer). Longwood Pub Group.

Suffragettes: Sally. Gertrude Colmore. 320p. (Orig.). 1984. pap. 8.95 o.p. (ISBN 0-86358-041-6, Pandora Pr). Routledge Chapman & Hall.

Sufi: Expressions of the Mystic Quest. Laleh Bakhtiar. (Illus.). 1976. pap. 5.95 o.p. (ISBN 0-380-00691-X, 29546). Avon.

Sufi Teachings. Hazrat Inayat Khan. (Sufi Message of Hazrat Inayat Khan Ser.: Vol. 8). 332p. 1979. 14.95 o.s.i. (ISBN 90-6077-954-1, Pub. by Servire BV Netherlands). Hunter Hse.

Sugar. University of Glasgow Staff & George Abbott. 304p. 1988. lib. bdg. 65.00 o.p. (ISBN 0-7099-0531-9, Pub. by Croom Helm UK). Routledge Chapman & Hall.

Sugar & Mr. Duck. Martha M. Moran. (Illus.). (gr. k-2). 1973. 4.50 o.p. (ISBN 0-682-47763-X). Exposition-Phoenix.

Sugar Country. J. Carlyle Sitterson. LC 73-10738. (Illus.). 414p. 1973. Repr. of 1953 ed. lib. bdg. 22.50x o.p. (ISBN 0-8371-7027-3, SISC). Greenwood.

Sugar Factory. Robert Carter. LC 87-12625. 144p. 1987. 14.95 o.p. (ISBN 0-689-11926-7, Atheneum). Macmillan.

Sugar Gets the Skunk. Martha M. Moran. (Illus.). (gr. k-4). 1977. 4.50 o.p. (ISBN 0-682-48778-3). Exposition-Phoenix.

Sugar Maple Research: Sap Production, Processing, & Marketing of Maple Syrup. Robert A. Gregory. 112p. 1982. pap. 4.50 o.p. (ISBN 0-318-11834-3, S/N 001-001-00598-3). USGPO.

Sugar Trap & How to Avoid It. Beatrice T. Hunter. LC 81-20110. 245p. 1982. 10.95 o.p. (ISBN 0-395-31824-6). HM.

Sugarless Baking Book: The Natural Way to Prepare America's Favorite Breads, Pies, Cakes, Puddings & Desserts. Patricia T. Mayo. LC 82-42757. (Illus.). 116p. (Orig.). 1983. pap. 5.95 o.p. (ISBN 0-87773-227-2). Shambhala Pubns.

Sugarless Cookery for the Gourmet: Delectable Dietetic Dishes for Sugar-Restricted Diets. Elsie M. Peckham. 1976. 12.50 o.p. (ISBN 0-682-48359-1, Banner). Exposition-Phoenix.

Suggestions for Self-Evaluation of Geography Programs with Self-Study Data Forms. AAG Consulting Services Panel Staff. 1974. pap. 2.50 o.p. (ISBN 0-89291-141-7). Assn Am Geographers.

SUGI Supplemental Library User's Guide, 1983 Edition. SAS Institute, Inc. Staff. 402p. (Orig.). 1983. pap. 11.95 o.p. (ISBN 0-917382-48-X). SAS Inst.

Suicidal Behavior. J. W. McCulloch & A. E. Philip. LC 72-188140. 133p. 1972. 45.00 o.p. (ISBN 0-08-016855-8). Pergamon.

Suicidal Impulse of the Business Community. Milton Friedman. pap. 1.00 o.p. Hoover Inst Pr.

Suicidal Patient: Recognition, Intervention, Management. Victor Victoroff. 280p. 1983. casebound 31.95 o.p. (ISBN 0-87489-261-9). Med Economics.

Suicide. Nicolai Erdman. 52p. (Orig.). 1981. pap. 5.95 o.p. (ISBN 0-86104-203-4, NO. 4125). Routledge Chapman & Hall.

Suicide Academy. Daniel Stern. 192p. 1985. 5.95 o.p. (ISBN 0-87795-759-2, Arbor Hse). Morrow.

Suicide among Young Adults. A. Morgan Parker, Jr. LC 73-92852. (Illus.). 1974. 8.00 o.p. (ISBN 0-682-47886-5, University). Exposition-Phoenix.

Suicide & Ethics. Ed. by Margaret P. Battin & Ronald Maris. (Special Issue S Ser.: Vol. 13, No. 3). 112p. 1984. pap. 9.95 o.p. Guilford Pr.

Suicide & Grief. Howard W. Stone. LC 70-171506. 144p. 1972. pap. 3.50 o.p. (ISBN 0-8006-1402-X, 1-402, Fortress). Augsburg Fortress.

Suicide Course. Roy Brown. 128p. (gr. 6 up). 1980. 7.95 o.p. (ISBN 0-395-29436-3, Clarion). HM.

Suicide of Christian Theology. John W. Montgomery. LC 70-270170. 528p. 1970. 12.95 o.p. (ISBN 0-87123-521-8, 210521). Bethany Hse.

Suicide: Prevention, Intervention, Postvention. Ed. by Earl A. Grollman. LC 79-141873. (Illus.). 1971. pap. 7.95 o.p. (ISBN 0-8070-2775-8, BP392). Beacon Pr.

Suicide Prevention: Proceedings of the International Congress for Suicide Prevention, 7th, Amsterdam, August 27-30, 1973. International Congress for Suicide Prevention Staff et al. 677p. 1974. pap. text ed. 33.25 o.p. (ISBN 90-265-0186-2, Pub. by Swets & Zeitlinger Netherlands). CJ Hogrefe Pubs.

Suicide Syndrome. Ed. by Richard D. T. Farmer & Steven R. Hirsch. 256p. 1980. 29.95 o.p. (ISBN 0-85664-868-X, Pub. by Croom Helm Ltd). Routledge Chapman & Hall.

Suicide Thoughts & Reflections: 1960-1980. Edwin S. Shneidman. 172p. 1981. pap. 19.95 o.p. Guilford Pr.

Suiciders. J. T. McIntosh. 1973. pap. 0.75 o.p. (ISBN 0-380-01569-2, 17889). Avon.

Suicide's Wife. David Madden. 1979. pap. 1.95 o.p. (ISBN 0-380-47522-7, 47522). Avon.

Suing in North Carolina Small Claims Court: A Practical Guide. David A. Guth. 370p. 1983. 25.00x o.p. (ISBN 0-87215-623-0). Michie Co.

Suitability of Hen Eggs for Incubation in the Fresh State & After Storage. V. V. Rol'nik. 1978. pap. 9.75 o.p. (ISBN 90-220-0609-3, PDC94, PUDOC). UNIPUB.

Suitable Design: How to Organize Your Writing. John Harrington & Michael Wenzl. (Illus.). 176p. 1983. pap. text ed. write for info. o.p. (ISBN 0-02-350280-0). Macmillan.

Suite from the Ivory Rooming House. Roger Finch. (Orig.). 1988. 15.00 o.p. (ISBN 0-944550-07-X); pap. text ed. 5.00 o.p. (ISBN 0-944550-06-1). Pygmy Forest Pr.

Suitor. George E. Hatvary. 192p. 1981. pap. 2.25 o.p. (ISBN 0-380-78188-3, 78188). Avon.

Suitor to Spare. Janet Templeton. LC 86-16787. (Starlight Romance Ser.). 192p. 1987. 12.95 o.p. (ISBN 0-385-23390-6). Doubleday.

Sul Ross State University: The Cultural Center of Trans-Pecos Texas 1917-1975. Clifford B. Casey. (Illus.). 416p. 1976. 9.50 o.p. (ISBN 0-933512-25-2). Pioneer Bk Tx.

Sulfer Ylides: Emerging Synthetic Intermediates. Barry M. Trost & Lawrence S. Melvin, Jr. (Organic Chemistry Ser.). 1975. 82.50 o.p. (ISBN 0-12-701060-2). Acad Pr.

Sulfonation & Related Reactions. Everett E. Gilbert. LC 76-52491. 542p. 1977. Repr. of 1965 ed. lib. bdg. 35.00 o.p. (ISBN 0-88275-528-5). Krieger.

Sulfur Dioxide, Chlorine, Fluorine & Chlorine Oxides. A. S. Young. 1983. 110.00x o.p. (ISBN 0-08-026218-X). Pergamon.

Sulla: The Last Republican. Arthur Keaveney. 256p. 1983. 33.00 o.p. (ISBN 0-7099-1507-1, Pub. by Croom Helm Ltd). Routledge Chapman & Hall.

Sulphide Catalysts, Their Properties & Applications. Otto Weisser & S. Landa. Tr. by Ota Sofr. 506p. 1973. 86.00 o.p. (ISBN 0-08-017556-2). Pergamon.

Sulphide Silver Pattern & Cytoarchitectonics of Parahippocampal Areas in the Rat. F. M. Haug. (Advances in Anatomy, Embryology & Cell Biology: Vol. 52, Pt. 4). (Illus.). 1976. soft cover 21.30 o.p. (ISBN 0-387-07850-9). Springer-Verlag.

Sulphone Molecular Structures: Conformation & Geometry from Electron Diffraction & Microwave Spectroscopy; Structural Variations. I. Hargittai. (Lecture Notes in Chemistry: Vol. 6). (Illus.). 1978. pap. 18.00 o.p. (ISBN 0-387-08654-4). Springer-Verlag.

Sulphur in Australasian Agriculture. K. D. McLachlan. (Illus.). 256p. 1975. 36.00x o.p. (ISBN 0-424-06850-8, Pub by Sydney U Pr). Intl Spec Bk.

Sulphur, Sulphur Dioxide, Sulphuric Acid. Ed. by U. Sander et al. Tr. by A. I. More. 428p. 1984. Repr. of 1982 ed. text ed. 45.00x o.p. (ISBN 0-902777-64-5). VCH Pubs.

Sultana. Michael Prince of Greece. 448p. 1984. pap. 3.95 o.p. (ISBN 0-380-68502-7, 68502). Avon.

Sum of Things. Olivia Manning. LC 80-7924. 1981. 10.95 o.s.i. (ISBN 0-689-11096-0, Atheneum). Macmillan.

Sumerian King List. Thorkild Jacobsen. LC 39-19328. 1939. pap. text ed. 12.00x o.s.i. (ISBN 0-226-62273-8, AS11). U of Chicago Pr.

Sumerians: Their History, Culture & Character. Samuel N. Kramer. LC 63-11398. (Illus.). 1963. lib. bdg. 25.00x o.s.i. (ISBN 0-226-45237-9). U of Chicago Pr.

Suministro de Medicamentos: La Seleccion, Adquisicion, Distribucion y Uso de Productos Farmaceuticos en la Atencion Primaria de Salud. Management Sciences for Health Staff et al. Ed. by Jonathan D. Quick & Margaret L. Hume. Tr. by Jan D. Gibboney & Adrian M. Petit. Orig. Title: Managing Drug Supply in Selection, Procurement, Distribution & Use of Pharmaceuticals in Primary Health Care. (Illus.). 632p. (Orig., Span.). 1984. pap. text ed. 7.50 o.p. (ISBN 0-913723-07-X). Mgmt Sci Health.

Summa Contra Haereticos. Ed. by James A. Corbett & Joseph N. Garvin. (Mediaeval Studies Ser.: No. 15). (Lat). 1968. 35.00 o.p. (ISBN 0-268-00268-1). U of Notre Dame Pr.

Summary of Research in Science Education 1979. D. P. Butts. 130p. 1981. pap. 29.95 o.p. (ISBN 0-471-86587-7). Wiley.

Summary of Research on the Reading Interests & Habits of College Graduates. Brewster Porcella. (Occasional Papers: No. 74). 41p. 1964. pap. 1.00 o.p. (ISBN 0-317-58856-7). U of Ill Lib Info Sci.

Summary of the Colloquium on Public Law 94-210. Ed. by John H. Davis. (Lincoln Institute Monograph: No. 77-3). 1977. pap. text ed. 1.00 o.s.i. (ISBN 0-686-20039-X). Lincoln Inst Land.

Summary of the Eighth APCA Government Affairs Seminar. Air Pollution Control Association Government Affairs Seminar, 8th Washington, D.C. 1980. 56p. 1980. pap. 5.00 o.p. (ISBN 0-318-12275-8, SP-34). Air & Waste.

Summary of the Seventh APCA Government Affairs Seminar. Air Pollution Control Association Government Affairs Seminar, 7th, Washington, D.C., 1979. 68p. 1979. pap. 5.00 o.p. (ISBN 0-318-12276-6, SP-31). Air & Waste.

Summer. Jack Ansell. LC 73-82179. 1973. 7.95 o.p. (ISBN 0-87795-063-6, Arbor Hse). Morrow.

Summer. Edward Bond. 1982. pap. 5.95 o.p. (ISBN 0-413-49320-2, NO. 3639). Heinemann Ed.

Summer at Fairacre. Miss Read. (Illus.). 256p. 1985. 14.45 o.p. (ISBN 0-395-38016-2). HM.

Summer Birds. Penelope Farmer. LC 62-12822. (Illus.). (gr. 4-6). 1962. 4.95 o.p. (ISBN 0-15-282485-5, HJ). HarBraceJ.

Summer Break. Victoria Althoff. 112p. (gr. 6-8). 1987. 2.25 o.s.i. (ISBN 0-87406-196-2). Willowisp Pr.

Summer Cabin Cartoons. 2nd ed. Wm. Armstrong. (Armstrong Cartoon Ser.). (Illus.). 48p. (gr. 1-6). 1972. pap. 1.00 o.p. (ISBN 0-913452-11-4). Jesuit Bks.

Summer Dreams. Bill Gutman. (Going for it Ser.: No. 3). 144p. 1985. pap. 2.50 o.p. (ISBN 0-380-89901-9, Flare). Avon.

Summer Dreams. Dorothy Oxley. LC 84-71420. Orig. Title: Wheelchair Summer. 144p. (gr. 6-10). 1984. pap. 3.95 o.p. (ISBN 0-89107-319-1, Crossway Bks). Good News.

Summer Employment Directory of the U. S., 1988. Ed. by Pat Beusterien. 256p. (Orig.). 1987. pap. 9.95 o.p. (ISBN 0-89879-280-0). Writers Digest.

Summer Employment Directory of the U. S., 1986. Ed. by Rand Ruggeberg. 256p. (Orig.). 1985. pap. 9.95 o.p. (ISBN 0-89879-205-3). Writers Digest.

Summer Employment Directory of the U. S. 1984. Barbara N. Kuroff. 213p. 1983. pap. 8.95 o.p. (ISBN 0-89879-119-7). Writers Digest.

Summer Employment Directory of the U. S. 1985. Rand Ruggeberg. 256p. (Orig.). 1984. pap. 8.95 o.p. (ISBN 0-89879-156-1, 3085). Writers Digest.

Summer Employment Directory of the U. S. 1987. Ed. by Julie Whaley. 256p. (Orig.). 1987. pap. 9.95 o.p. (ISBN 0-89879-224-X). Writers Digest.

Summer Ends Now. John Emery. 164p. 1980. 15.95x o.p. (ISBN 0-7022-1467-1); pap. 7.95 o.p. (ISBN 0-7022-1468-X). U of Queensland Pr.

Summer Ends Too Soon. Mort Grossman. LC 75-20418. (gr. 6 up). 1975. 6.50 o.s.i. (ISBN 0-664-32580-7, Westminster). Westminster John Knox.

Summer Feasts. Molly Finn. 1985. pap. 6.95 o.p. (ISBN 0-671-55453-0, Fireside). S&S.

Summer Fires: New Poetry of Africa. Ed. by Angus Calder et al. (African Writers Ser.: No. 257). xii, 116p. 1984. pap. text ed. 7.00 o.p. (ISBN 0-435-90257-1). Heinemann Ed.

Summer Fling: Candlelight Ecstasy 288. Natalie Stone. (Candlelight Ecstasy Ser.: No. 288). (Orig.). 1984. pap. 1.95 o.p. (ISBN 0-440-18350-2). Dell.

Summer Food. Judith Olney. LC 77-15870. 1978. 10.95 o.p. (ISBN 0-689-10882-6, Atheneum). Macmillan.

Summer Fun with the Fraggles. Dean Yeagle. (Illus.). 48p. (ps-1). 1985. 0.99 o.s.i. (ISBN 0-03-004443-X). H Holt & Co.

Summer Games Access, 1988: A Viewer's Guide to the Sports, Athletes, Records & Sites. Created by Richard S. Wurman. (Illus.). 108p. 1988. pap. 6.95 o.p. (ISBN 0-13-875840-9). P-H.

Summer Garden, Winter Kitchen. Geri Harrington. 1976. 9.95 o.p. (ISBN 0-689-10720-X, Atheneum). Macmillan.

Summer Ghost. Ruth Tomalin. (gr. 5-9). 1986. 15.95 o.p. (ISBN 0-571-13826-8). Faber & Faber.

Summer Home. Cynthia Grant. LC 81-1921. 156p. (gr. 4-8). 1981. PLB 9.95 o.p. (ISBN 0-689-30872-8, Atheneum). Macmillan.

Summer House Cookbook. Chris C. Madden. LC 78-71062. 192p. 1979. pap. 5.95 o.p. (ISBN 0-15-686302-2, Harv). HarBraceJ.

Summer Hunt. Joseph Monninger. LC 82-71062. 288p. 1983. 14.95 o.p. (ISBN 0-689-11325-0, Atheneum). Macmillan.

Summer in Sodom with Kitchen Privileges. Florence Holland. 1977. 6.50 o.p. (ISBN 0-682-48968-9). Exposition-Phoenix.

Summer in the Enchanted Forest. (Enchanted Forest Ser.). (Illus.). (ps-1). 1985. 2.98 o.s.i. (ISBN 0-517-46981-2). Outlet Bk Co.

Summer Jobs in Britain. Ed. by Susan Griffith. 174p. (Orig.). 1988. pap. 9.95 o.p. (ISBN 0-907638-84-8, Pub. by Vacation-Work England). Writers Digest.

Summer Jobs in Britain 1985. Ed. by Susan Griffith. 167p. (Orig.). 1985. pap. 8.95 o.p. (ISBN 0-907638-33-3, 3085, Pub. by Vacation Work Pub). Writers Digest.

Summer Jobs in Britain 1987. Ed. by Susan Griffith. 174p. 1987. pap. 8.95 o.p. (ISBN 0-907638-68-6, Pub. by Vacation-Work England). Writers Digest.

Summer of a Million Wings: Arctic Quest for the Sea-Eagle. Hugh Brandon-Cox. LC 74-10365. (Illus.). 184p. 1975. 8.95 o.s.i. (ISBN 0-8008-7492-7). Taplinger.

Summer of the Stallion. June A. Hanson. LC 78-24212. (Illus.). 128p. (gr. 5-9). 1979. 9.95 o.s.i. (ISBN 0-02-742620-3). Macmillan.

Summer of the Swans. Betsy Byars. 1978. pap. 1.50 o.p. (ISBN 0-380-00098-9, 50526, Camelot). Avon.

Summer of the White Goat. Paige Dixon. LC 76-25848. (Illus.). 128p. (gr. 3-7). 1977. 5.95 o.s.i. (ISBN 0-689-30552-4, Atheneum). Macmillan.

Summer Opportunities for Kids & Teenagers, 1984. Ed. by Diane Conley. 294p. 1983. pap. 9.95 o.p. (ISBN 0-87866-223-5). Petersons Guides.

Summer Opportunities for Kids & Teenagers 1985. 2nd ed. Ed. by Diane Conley. (Annual Guides Ser.). (Illus.). 499p. (Orig.). 1984. pap. 9.95 o.p. (ISBN 0-87866-275-8). Petersons Guides.

Summer Opportunities for Kids & Teenagers 1987. 4th ed. (Peterson's Annual Guides Ser). 603p. (Orig.). 1986. pap. 12.95 o.p. (ISBN 0-87866-444-0). Petersons Guides.

Summer Opportunities for Kids & Teenagers 1988. 5th ed. (Peterson's Annual Guides Ser.). 677p. (Orig.). 1987. lib. bdg. 19.95 o.p. (ISBN 0-87866-657-5); pap. 14.95 o.p. (ISBN 0-87866-558-7). Petersons Guides.

Summer Pioneers: Memories of Old Field. Hanford Twitchell. 1977. 4.50 o.p. (ISBN 0-682-48979-4). Exposition-Phoenix.

Summer Pony. Jean S. Doty. LC 74-20802. (Illus.). 128p. (gr. 3-7). 1976. pap. 1.95 o.s.i. (ISBN 0-02-042950-9, Collier). Macmillan.

Summer School: A New Look. John W. Dougherty. LC 81-80016. (Fastback Ser.: No. 158). 1981. pap. 0.90 o.p. (ISBN 0-87367-158-9). Phi Delta Kappa.

Summer Song. Pamela Oldfield. 416p. 1988. 19.95 o.s.i. (ISBN 0-7126-0313-1, Pub. by Century Hutchinson). David & Charles.

Summer Stars. Alexis H. Jordan. (Candlelight Ecstasy Ser.: No. 373). (Orig.). 1985. pap. 2.25 o.p. (ISBN 0-440-18352-9). Dell.

Summer Sweaters. Nihon Vogue Staff. (Illus.). 78p. (Orig.). 1985. pap. 7.95 o.p. Japan Pubns USA.

Summer to Remember. Bonnie Towne. 128p. (gr. 5-8). 1985. 2.25 o.s.i. (ISBN 0-87406-009-5). Willowisp Pr.

Summer Winds. Cliff Schimmels. 180p. 1986. pap. 4.95 o.p. (ISBN 0-89693-262-1). Victor Bks.

Summerdog Comes Home: The Previous Adventures of Hobo. George A. Zabriskie. (Illus.). 128p. (Orig.). (gr. 1 up). 1983. pap. 2.25 o.p. (ISBN 0-380-75259-X, 83709-9, Camelot). Avon.

Summerisch-Akkadische Parallelen Zum Aufbau Alttestamentlicher Psalmen. Friedrich Stummer. Repr. of 1922 ed. 15.00 o.p. (ISBN 0-384-58710-0). Johnson Repr.

Summermaker: An Ojibway Indian Myth. Margery Bernstein & Janet Kobrin. LC 76-14875. (Encore Editions: Myths You Can Read by Yourself). 48p. (gr. 1-3). 1977. 1.19 o.s.i. (ISBN 0-684-17356-5, ScribJ). Scribner.

Summers on the Saranacs. Maitland C. De Sormo. LC 80-81853. (Illus.). 1980. 30.00 o.s.i. (ISBN 0-9601158-6-2). North Country.

Summersea. Samantha Harte. 1989. pap. 3.95 o.p. (ISBN 0-7701-1052-5). PaperJacks US.

Summit Conference. Robert D. MacDonald. (Illus.). 64p. 1983. pap. 4.00 o.p. (ISBN 0-88145-009-X). Broadway Play.

Summits to Reach: Report on the Topography of the San Juan Country. Franklin Rhoda. Ed. by Mike Foster. LC 84-15135. (Illus.). 168p. 1984. pap. 7.95 o.p. (ISBN 0-87108-667-0). Pruett.

Summitt. William P. McGivern. LC 79-57078. 1981. 14.95 o.p. (ISBN 0-87795-251-5, Arbor Hse). Morrow.

Sumner Today. William G. Sumner. Ed. by Maurice Davie. 1940. 49.50x o.p. (ISBN 0-686-83794-0). Elliots Bks.

Sun Also Rises. Ernest Hemingway. 1984. pap. 3.95 o.p. (ISBN 0-684-18260-2). Scribner.

Sun & Earth. Herbert Friedman. LC 85-14295. (Scientific American Library). (Illus.). 256p. 1985. 32.95 o.p. (ISBN 0-7167-5012-0, Dist. by W H Freeman). Sci Am Bks.

Sun & Shadow. Jean-Pierre Aumont. 1977. 9.95 o.p. (ISBN 0-393-07511-7). Norton.

Sun & Steel. Yukio Mishima. Tr. by John Bester from Japanese. 176p. 1972. pap. 4.95 o.p. (ISBN 0-394-17765-7, E583, Ever). Grove.

Sun & the Moon & Other Fictions. P. K. Page. (Found Books: No. 1). 204p. 1973. 11.95 o.p. (ISBN 0-88784-429-4, Pub. by Hse Anansi Pr Canada); pap. 6.95 o.p. (ISBN 0-88784-327-1). U of Toronto Pr.

Sun Bear's Book of the Vision Quest: Personal Transformation in the Wilderness. Steven Foster & Meredith Little. (Illus.). 172p. (Orig.). 1987. pap. 9.95 o.p. (ISBN 0-13-080110-0). P-H.

Sun Behind the Sun Behind the Sun. Bhagwan Shree Rajneesh. Ed. by Ma Prem Maneesha. LC 83-181209. (Initiation Talks Ser.). (Illus.). 648p. (Orig.). 1980. 21.95 o.p. (ISBN 0-88050-138-3). Chidvilas Inc.

Sun City. Tove Jansson. 1977. pap. 1.95 o.p. (ISBN 0-380-00955-2, 32318, Bard). Avon.

Sun Dance Religion: Power for the Powerless. Joseph G. Jorgensen. LC 70-182089. 1972. lib. bdg. 12.50x o.s.i. (ISBN 0-226-41085-4). U of Chicago Pr.

Sun Dials & Roses of Yesterday. Alice M. Earle. LC 79-75790. 488p. 1969. Repr. of 1902 ed. 37.00x o.p. (ISBN 0-8103-3830-0). Gale.

Sun, Earth, & Man. George P. Bischof & Eunice S. Bischof. LC 56-8352. (Illus.). (gr. 5 up). 1957. 4.50 o.p. (ISBN 0-15-282643-2, HJ). HarBraceJ.

Sun in His Belly. Raymond Roseliep. 40p. 1977. 10.00 o.p. (ISBN 0-913719-01-3); pap. 3.50 o.p. (ISBN 0-913719-00-5). High-Coo Pr.

Sun: Mankind's Future Source of Energy, 3 vols. Ed. by F. De Winter. 1979. 505.00 o.p. (ISBN 0-08-022725-2). Pergamon.

Sun Place. Ray Connolly. 368p. 1981. pap. 2.95 o.p. (ISBN 0-380-78816-0, 78816-0). Avon.

Sun Placed in the Abyss & Other Texts. Francis Ponge. Tr. by Serge Gavronsky from Fr. LC 77-3631. 1977. pap. 8.00 o.p. (ISBN 0-915342-22-7). SUN.

Sun Rain. Niki Yektai. LC 83-20792. (Illus.). 32p. (ps-1). 1984. 11.95 o.s.i. (ISBN 0-02-793690-2, Four Winds Pr). Macmillan.

Sun Rhythm Form. Ralph Knowles. (Illus.). 304p. 1982. pap. 12.50 o.p. (ISBN 0-262-61040-X). MIT Pr.

Sun Shines Bright. Isaac Asimov. 256p. 1983. pap. 2.95 o.p. (ISBN 0-380-61390-5, 61390-5, Discus). Avon.

Sun Shines over the Sanggan River. Ding Ling. Tr. by Yang Xianyi & Gladys Yang. 379p. (Orig.). 1984. pap. 7.95 o.p. (ISBN 0-8351-1008-7). China Bks.

Sun Signs. L. Goodman. 1986. 44.75X o.p. (ISBN 0-245-50457-5, Pub. by Harrap Ltd England). State Mutual Bk.

Sunbeams & Shadows. Rev. Fielding T. Howard. 1978. 4.50 o.p. (ISBN 0-682-48993-X). Exposition-Phoenix.

Sunbonnet Family of Quilt Patterns. P-H.

Sundance: The Marauders. Peter McCurtin. (Orig.). 1980. pap. 1.75 o.p. (Pub. by Leisure Bks CT). Dorchester Pub Co.

Sunday. Thomas Lux. 1979. 8.95 o.p. (ISBN 0-395-28349-3); pap. 4.95 o.p. (ISBN 0-395-28350-7). HM.

Sunday. Georges Simenon. Tr. by Nigel Ryan. (Helen & Kurt Wolff Bk.). 1976. pap. 2.50 o.p. (ISBN 0-15-686301-4, Harv). HarBraceJ.

Sunday after Sunday: Preaching the Homily as a Story. Robert Waznak. LC 82-62922. 128p. (Orig.). 1983. pap. 4.95 o.p. (ISBN 0-8091-2540-4). Paulist Pr.

Sunday Between Wars. Ben Maddow. (Illus.). 1979. 17.95 o.p. (ISBN 0-393-05698-8). Norton.

SUNDAY Documentation & User's Manual. Davis Straub. 220p. 1982. ringbinder 35.00 o.p. (ISBN 0-934478-31-7). Ecotope.

Sunday Driver. Brock Yates. (Illus.). 258p. 1972. 7.95 o.p. (ISBN 0-374-27183-6). FS&G.

Sunday Hangman. James McClure. 1985. pap. 2.95 o.p. (ISBN 0-394-72992-7). Pantheon.

Sunday Naturalist. Anthony Sobin. LC 82-6316. xii, 75p. 1982. text ed. 14.95x o.p. (ISBN 0-8214-0636-1); pap. 7.95 o.p. (ISBN 0-8214-0637-X). Ohio U Pr.

Sunday Punch. Edwin Newman. 1979. 9.95 o.p. (ISBN 0-395-28050-8). HM.

Sunday Readers Lectionary: For Lay Ministers. Oswald Hirmer & Fritz Lobinger. 672p. (Orig.). 1986. pap. 8.95 o.p. (ISBN 0-00-599921-9). HarpR.

Sunday Telegraph Business Finance Directory 1985-86: The Guide to Sources of Corporate Finance in Britain. Ed. by G. Bricault & J. Carr. 340p. 1985. 77.00 o.p. (ISBN 0-86010-609-8); pap. 61.00 o.p. (ISBN 0-86010-610-1). Graham & Trotman.

Sunday Times Crossword Omnibus. Ed. by Margaret P. Farrar. 1982. pap. 5.75 o.p. (ISBN 0-671-21917-0, Fireside). S&S.

Sunday Whirling. Alberta Eiseman. LC 77-2000. 1977. 5.95 o.p. (ISBN 0-689-30581-8, Atheneum). Macmillan.

Sunday Woman. Carl Fruttero & Franco Lucentini. 1976. pap. 1.75 o.p. (ISBN 0-380-00865-3, 31328). Avon.

Sunday Woman. Carlo Fruttero & Franco Lucentini. Tr. by William Weaver from Ital. LC 73-6981. (Helen & Kurt Wolff Bk.). 1973. 7.50 o.p. (ISBN 0-15-186720-8). HarBraceJ.

Sunday's Scriptures: An Interpretation. rev. ed. William Syndor. 160p. (Orig.). 1980. pap. 5.95 o.p. (ISBN 0-8192-1215-6). Morehouse Pub.

Sundiata: An Epic of Old Mali. D. T. Naine. (Forum Ser). (Orig.). 1965. pap. text ed. 7.95x o.p. (ISBN 0-582-64024-5). Humanities.

Sundowners. Jon Cleary. LC 67-14015. 382p. 1984. pap. 7.95 o.s.i. (ISBN 0-684-13364-4, ScribT). Scribner.

Sunflower Splendor. Ed. by Wu-Chi Liu & Irving Yucheng Lo. LC 74-25136. (Anchor Literary Library). 696p. 1975. pap. 8.95 o.p. (ISBN 0-385-09716-6, Anch). Doubleday.

Sunflowers for Van Gogh. David D. Duncan. LC 86-42729. (Illus.). 148p. 1986. 25.00 o.p. (ISBN 0-8478-0764-9). Rizzoli Intl.

Sunlight to Electricity: Prospects for Solar Energy Conversion by Photovoltaics. Joseph A. Merrigan. LC 75-6933. 192p. (Orig.). 1975. 15.00x o.p. (ISBN 0-262-13116-1); pap. 6.95 o.p. (ISBN 0-262-63072-9). MIT Pr.

Sunne in Splendour. Sharon K. Penman. 1982. 19.95 o.s.i. (ISBN 0-03-061368-X). H Holt & Co.

Sunny Side of F.D.R. M. S. Venkataramani. LC 75-181688. 292p. 1973. 16.00x o.p. (ISBN 0-8214-0107-6). Ohio U Pr.

Sunny-side Up. Beatrice B. Wille. (Illus.). 112p. 1982. pap. 5.95 o.p. (ISBN 0-682-49877-7). Exposition-Phoenix.

Sunrise on the Mohican. Everett E. Eckstein. (Illus.). 62p. 1982. 6.00 o.p. (ISBN 0-682-49918-8). Exposition-Phoenix.

Sunrise with Seamonsters: Travels & Discoveries 84. Paul Theroux. 365p. 1985. 18.45 o.p. (ISBN 0-395-38221-1). HM.

Sunrising. David Cook. LC 85-31045. 248p. 1986. 16.95 o.p. (ISBN 0-87951-253-9). Overlook Pr.

Sunrising. David Cook. 248p. 1989. pap. 8.95 o.p. (ISBN 0-87951-338-1). Overlook Pr.

Sunset: A History of Parisian Drama in the Last Years of Louis XIV, 1701-1715. Henry C. Lancaster. LC 76-29737. 1976. Repr. of 1945 ed. lib. bdg. 35.00x o.p. (ISBN 0-8371-9278-1, LASH). Greenwood.

Sunset Bomber. D. Kincaid. 1986. 16.45 o.s.i. (ISBN 0-671-60444-9, Pub. by Linden Pr). S&S.

Sunset in Biafra. Elechi Amadi. (African Writers Ser.). 1973. pap. text ed. 6.50 o.p. (ISBN 0-435-90140-0). Heinemann Ed.

Sunset Road Atlas. (Illus.). 128p. 1986. Deluxe 5.95 o.p. (ISBN 0-376-09010-3); Standard, 80 p. 4.95 o.p. (ISBN 0-376-09011-1); Pocket, 64 p. 1.95 o.p. (ISBN 0-376-09012-X). Sunset-Lane.

Sunshine Country. Cristina Roy. 160p. (YA) 5.60 o.p. (ISBN 0-686-05594-2); pap. 4.35 o.p. (ISBN 0-686-05595-0). Rod & Staff.

Sunshine Family & the Pony. Sharron Loree. LC 71-171859. (Illus.). 48p. (ps-2). 1979. 5.95 o.p. (ISBN 0-395-28816-9, Clarion). HM.

Sunshine Tree: And Other Tales From Around the World. Wendy Heller. (Illus.). 96p. 11.50 o.p. (ISBN 0-85398-153-1). G Ronald Pub.

Sunspot. Desmond Lowden. LC 80-24994. (Suspense Novel Ser.). 224p. 1982. 12.95 o.p. (ISBN 0-03-047616-X). H Holt & Co.

Suntanned Days. (Follow Your Heart Ser.: No. 9). (YA) (gr. 7 up). pap. 2.25 o.p. (ISBN 0-671-55824-2). Archway.

Sunward I've Climbed. Howard A. Craig. LC 74-80106. 1975. 10.00 o.p. (ISBN 0-87404-049-3). Tex Western.

Super Bowl II: Green Bay Packers vs. Oakland Raiders. Ward. (Super Bowl Champions Ser.). (Illus.). 32p. (gr. 3-8). PLB 8.95 o.p. Creative Ed.

Super Champ. David R. Collins. 1982. 6.95 o.p. (ISBN 0-89015-349-3). Eakin Pr.

Super Chief: Train of the Stars. Stan Repp. LC 80-18725. (Illus.). 19.95 o.s.i. (ISBN 0-87095-081-9). Gldn West Bks.

Super-Colossal Book of Puzzles, Tricks & Games. Sheila A. Barry. LC 77-93325. (Illus.). 640p. (gr. 3 up). 1985. Repr. 6.98 o.p. (ISBN 0-8069-4720-9). Sterling.

Super Eight Book. rev. ed. Jean B. Fages & Christian Pagano. 364p. (Fr.). 1971. pap. 19.95 o.p. (ISBN 0-686-57183-5, M-6251). French & Eur.

Super Eight Book. Lenny Lipton. 1975. pap. 9.50 o.p. (ISBN 0-671-22082-9, Fireside). S&S.

Super Executive's Guide to Getting Things Done. Charles H. Ford. 272p. 1983. 14.95 o.p. (ISBN 0-8144-5724-X). AMACOM.

Super-Fluid Helium. J. F. Allen. 1966. 53.00 o.p. (ISBN 0-12-051150-9). Acad Pr.

Super-Heavy Elements: Theoretical Predictions & Experimental Generation-(Proceedings of the 27th Nobel Symposium) Ed. by Sven Nilsson & Nils Nilsson. 184p. (Orig.). 1974. pap. text ed. 27.50x o.p. (Pub. by Almqvist & Wiksell). Coronet Bks.

Super Natural Dessert Cookbook. Lois Fishkin & Susan DiMarco. LC 84-45095. (Illus.). 132p. (Orig.). 1984. pap. 6.95 o.p. (ISBN 0-916870-61-8). Creative Arts Bk.

Super People: Will They Replace Us? Jeanne Bendick. LC 79-14486. (Illus.). (gr. 7 up). 1980. text ed. 9.95 o.p. (ISBN 0-07-004503-8). McGraw.

Super Plastic Model Manual: Macross, Vol. 1. (Illus.). 1984. 8.95 o.p. (ISBN 0-318-02677-5). Bks Nippan.

Super Plastic Model Manual: Macross & Orguss, Vol. 2. (Illus.). 1984. 8.95 o.p. (ISBN 0-318-02678-3). Bks Nippan.

Super Power Steam Locomotives. Richard J. Cook. LC 66-29787. (Illus.). 144p. 1966. 20.95 o.p. (ISBN 0-87095-010-X). Gldn West Bks.

Super Self: The Art & Science of Self-Management: A Practical Guide to Getting the Most Out of Your Life. Robert Heller. LC 78-20365. 1979. 9.95 o.p. (ISBN 0-689-10971-7, Atheneum). Macmillan.

Super Stitches: A Book of Superstitions. Ann Nevins. LC 82-15875. (Illus.). 64p. (gr. 1-4). 1983. 9.95 o.p. (ISBN 0-8234-0476-5). Holiday.

Super Tenant: New York City Tenant Handbook. 2nd ed. John M. Striker & Andrew O. Shapiro. LC 77-72336. 1978. 8.95x o.s.i. (ISBN 0-03-021101-8); pap. 4.95x o.s.i. (ISBN 0-03-021096-8). H Holt & Co.

Super Traveler: The Complete Handbook of Essential Facts, Regulations, Rights & Remedies for Trouble-Free International Travel. Saul Miller. LC 79-1934. 400p. (Orig.). 1980. 14.95 o.s.i. (ISBN 0-03-049571-7); pap. 6.95 o.s.i. (ISBN 0-03-049576-8). H Holt & Co.

Superabrasives 1985: Proceedings. Society of Manufacturing Engineers Staff. 1985. 58.00 o.p. (ISBN 0-87263-183-4). SME.

Superalloys. Ed. by Chester T. Sims & William C. Hagel. LC 72-5904. (Science & Technology of Materials Ser.). 614p. 1972. 79.95x o.p. (ISBN 0-471-79207-1). Wiley.

Superbill: Guide to a Uniform Billing & Claims System. Medical Group Management Association Staff. (Illus.). 60p. 1974. 10.00 o.p. (ISBN 0-933948-02-6); members 5.00 o.p.; corresp. subscr. 8.00 o.p. Med Group Mgmt.

Superbowl Sunday. Mitch Gelman. (gr. 4 up). pap. 2.25 o.p. (ISBN 0-317-13577-5). Archway.

SuperCalc: Home & Office Companion. Elna Tymes & Peter Antoniak. 192p. (Orig.). 1983. pap. text ed. 15.95 o.p. (ISBN 0-07-881113-9). Osborne-McGraw.

SuperCalc Program Made Easy. Chris Wood. 250p. (Orig.). 1984. pap. text ed. 15.95 o.p. (ISBN 0-07-931088-5). Osborne-McGraw.

SuperCalc 3 Models. Gilbert Held. LC 84-29129. (Application Software Ser.). 250p. (Orig.). 1985. pap. 17.95 o.p. (ISBN 0-938862-28-6). Weber Systems.

Supercharging MS-DOS (Software Version) Van Wolverton. LC 86-21775. 320p. 1987. pap. 34.95 incl. 5.25-inch disk o.p. (ISBN 1-55615-119-5); disk incl. o.p. Microsoft.

Supercharging MS-DOS: The Microsoft Guide to High Performance Computing for the Experienced PC User. Van Wolverton. LC 86-21775. 320p. (Orig.). 1986. pap. 18.95 o.p. (ISBN 0-914845-95-0). Microsoft.

Supercharging WordStar. Ed. by Arthur Naiman & Kelly Horan. (Illus.). 348p. 1987. pap. 18.00 o.p. (ISBN 0-940235-10-2). Goldstein & Blair.

Supercomputers - Design & Applications. Kai Hwang. LC 84-81316. (Tutorial Text Ser.). 640p. 1984. 36.00 o.p. (ISBN 0-8186-0581-2, EZ581). IEEE Comp Soc.

Superconductivity & Quantum Fluids. Z. M. Galasiewicz. 1970. 50.00 o.p. (ISBN 0-08-013089-5). Pergamon.

Superconductor Materials Science: Metallurgy, Fabrication, & Applications. Ed. by Simon Foner & Brian B. Schwartz. LC 81-8669. (NATO ASI Series B, Physics: Vol. 68). 1000p. 1981. 150.00x o.p. (ISBN 0-306-40750-7, Plenum Pr). Plenum Pub.

Superconscious World. Peter Reveen. 160p. 1987. 19.95 o.p. (ISBN 0-920792-86-3). Eden Pr.

Supercritical Wing Sections: A Handbook. F. Bauer et al. LC 74-34333. (Lecture Notes in Economics & Mathematical Systems: Vol. 108). (Illus.). v, 296p. 1975. pap. 17.00 o.p. (ISBN 0-387-07029-X). Springer-Verlag.

Supercritical Wing Sections III. F. Bauer et al. (Lecture Notes in Economics & Mathematical Systems Ser: Vol. 150). 1977. pap. 12.00 o.p. (ISBN 0-387-08533-5). Springer-Verlag.

Superforce: The Search for a Grand Unified Theory of Nature. Paul Davies. LC 84-5473. 288p. 1984. 17.45 o.s.i. (ISBN 0-671-47685-8). S&S.

Superfund Environmental Liability Update. James F. Bycott & Nicholas C. Gladding. 124p. 1988. manual 35.00 o.p. (00369). PES Inc WI.

Superfund Manual: Legal & Management Strategies. Ridgway M. Hall, Jr. et al. 224p. 1985. pap. text ed. 46.00 o.p. (ISBN 0-86587-047-0). Gov Insts.

Superfund Manual: Legal & Management Strategies. 2nd ed. Ridgway M. Hall, Jr. et al. (Superfund Manual Ser.). 506p. 1987. pap. text ed. 87.00 o.p. (ISBN 0-86587-704-1). Gov Insts.

Supergravity Theory: A Geometric Perspective, 2 vols. L. Castellani et al. 1200p. 1989. 88.00 o.p. (ISBN 9971-50-037-X); pap. 58.00 o.p. (ISBN 9971-50-038-8). World Scientific Pub.

Supergrowth: Buying & Selling Agencies for Profit. Miller, Russell, Inc. Staff. LC 81-82012. 1981. text ed. 32.50 o.p. (ISBN 0-87218-311-4). Natl Underwriter.

Superheavy Elements: Proceedings. International Symposium on Superheavy Elements, March 9-11, 1978, Lubbock, Texas. Ed. by M. A. Lodhi. 604p. 1979. 150.00 o.p. (ISBN 0-08-022946-8). Pergamon.

Superhelical DNA. (Landmark Ser.). 1979. 22.50x o.p. (ISBN 0-8422-4125-6). Irvington.

Superintendent. Date not set. (ISBN 0-8052-3893-X). Random.

Superintendent Plans His Work. Idris W. Jones. 1956. pap. 4.95 o.p. (ISBN 0-8170-0172-7). Judson.

Superior Court Judicial Profiles. Massachusetts Continuing Legal Education-New England Law Institute, Inc. Staff. LC 85-107910. 252p. write for info. o.p. Mass CLE.

Supermanagers: Managing for Success, the Movers & the Doers, & the Reasons Why. Robert Heller. 1985. pap. text ed. 9.95 o.p. (ISBN 0-07-028309-5). McGraw.

Supermarine Spitfire. Aero Publishers, Inc., Aeronautical Staff. LC 66-22653. (Aero Ser: Vol. 10). 1966. pap. 5.95 o.p. (ISBN 0-8168-0536-9, 20536, TAB-Aero). TAB Bks.

Supermarket News Distribution Study of Grocery Store Sales, 1986. Fairchild Books Special Projects Division Staff. 300p. 1986. pap. 45.00 o.p. (ISBN 0-87005-535-6). Fairchild.

Supermarriage: Overcoming the Predictable Crises of Married Life. Harvey L. Ruben. LC 85-48236. 261p. 1986. 14.95 o.p. (ISBN 0-553-05121-0). Bantam.

Supermouse. Jean Ure. LC 83-22022. (Illus.). 160p. (gr. 4-8). 1984. 10.25 o.p. (ISBN 0-688-02742-3). Morrow.

Supernatural in Modern Fiction. Dorothy Scarborough. 1967. lib. bdg. 20.50 o.p. (ISBN 0-374-97049-1, Octagon). Hippocrene Bks.

Supernatural Short Stories of Robert Louis Stevenson. 188p. (Orig.). 1986. pap. 11.95 o.p. (ISBN 0-7145-3550-8). Riverrun NY.

Supernatural Solution: Chilling Stories of Spooks & Sleuths. Ed. by Michel Parry. LC 75-27979. 224p. 1976. 8.95 o.s.i. (ISBN 0-8008-7497-8). Taplinger.

Supernaturalism of New England. John Greenleaf Whittier. Ed. by Edward Wagenknecht. LC 69-10628. 1969. Repr. of 1847 ed. 12.95x o.p. (ISBN 0-8061-0824-X). U of Okla Pr.

Superplanes. John G. Navarra. LC 77-16936. (gr. 3-7). 1979. 8.95a o.p. (ISBN 0-385-12561-5); PLB o.p. (ISBN 0-385-12562-3). Doubleday.

Superplastic Forming of Structural Alloys. Ed. by N. E. Paton & C. H. Hamilton. 440p. 1982. (Reproduction on Demand - UMI) 36.00 o.p. (ISBN 0-89520-389-8). Minerals Metals.

Superplastic Forming: Proceedings of 1984 Symposium. 92p. 58.00 o.p. (6436L). ASM.

Superplastic Forming: Proceedings. San Diego, 1982. Ed. by N. E. Paton & C. H. Hamilton. (Illus.). 440p. 50.00 o.p. (ISBN 0-89520-389-8); members 24.00 o.p. (ISBN 0-317-36261-5); student members 12.00 o.p. (ISBN 0-317-36262-3). ASM.

Superplasticity. K. A. Padmanabham & G. J. Davies. (Materials Research & Engineering: Vol. 2). (Illus.). 292p. 1980. pap. 39.00 o.p. (ISBN 0-387-10038-5). Springer-Verlag.

Superplasticizers in Concrete. 1979. 47.75 o.p. (ISBN 0-686-71034-7, SP-62) (ISBN 0-686-71035-5). ACI.

Superpower Confrontation on the Seas: Naval Development & Strategy Since 1945. Jurgen Rohwer. (Washington Papers: Vol. III, No. 26). 96p. 1975. pap. text ed. 7.95 o.p. (ISBN 0-8191-5982-4, Pub by CSIS). U Pr of Amer.

Superspill. James Dawson. (Illus.). 128p. 1981. 18.95 o.p. (ISBN 0-86720-588-1). Janes Info Group.

Superstars: How Stellar Explosions Shape the Destiny of Our Universes. David H. Clark. (Illus.). 224p. 1984. text ed. 17.95 o.p. (ISBN 0-07-011152-9). McGraw.

Superstition in All Ages. Jean Meslier. Tr. by Anna Knopp. 346p. 1974. pap. 13.95 o.s.i. (ISBN 0-88697-008-5). Life Science.

Superstitions. May Wong. LC 77-92541. 1978. 7.95 o.p. (ISBN 0-15-186798-4). HarBraceJ.

Superstitions from North Carolina, 2 vols, Vols. 6-7. Wayland D. Hand. LC 58-10967. (Frank C. Brown Collection of North Carolina Folklore Ser.). Vol. 6. 32.50 o.p. (ISBN 0-8223-0258-6); Vol. 7. 32.50 o.p. (ISBN 0-8223-0259-4). Duke.

Superstitions of Sailors. Angelo S. Rappoport. LC 71-158207. 290p. 1971. Repr. of 1928 ed. 43.00x o.p. (ISBN 0-8103-3739-8). Gale.

Superstitions of the Highlands & Islands of Scotland. John G. Campbell. 344p. 1970. 43.00x o.p. (ISBN 0-8103-3589-1). Gale.

Superstitious? Here's Why! Julie F. Batchelor & Claudia De Lys. LC 54-566. (Illus.). (gr. 5 up). 1954. 5.95 o.p. (ISBN 0-15-283179-7, HJ). HarBraceJ.

Superstitious? Here's Why! Julie F. Batchelor & Claudia De Lys. LC 54-8566. (Illus.). (gr. 5 up). 1966. pap. 1.25 o.p. (ISBN 0-15-686793-1, VoyB). HarBraceJ.

Superstrategists: Great Captains, Theorists, & Fighting Men Who Have Shaped the History of Warfare. John R. Elting. 320p. 1985. 22.95 o.p. (ISBN 0-684-18353-6, ScribT). Scribner.

Superstrings 1987: Proceedings of the Trieste Spring School on Superstrings, 1987. Ed. by L. Alvarez-Gaume et al. 432p. (Orig.). 1988. 64.00 o.p.; pap. 44.00 o.p. (ISBN 9971-50-518-5). World Scientific Pub.

Supertuning Your Firebird Trans-Am. Joe Oldham. (Illus.). 288p. 1981. pap. 12.60 o.p. (ISBN 0-8306-2088-5, 2088P). TAB Bks.

Supertuning Your Z-28 Camaro. Joe Oldham. LC 84-980. (Illus.). 160p. (Orig.). 1984. pap. 5.95 o.p. (ISBN 0-87938-184-1). Motorbooks Intl.

Supervised Occupational Experience Manual. 2nd ed. Merle A. Carwin. 242p. 1982. pap. text ed. 5.50x o.p. (ISBN 0-8134-2228-0, 2228). Inter Print Pubs.

Supervising Clerk-Stenographer. 4th ed. Arco Editorial Board. LC 67-25272. 1977. lib. bdg. 9.00 o.p. (ISBN 0-668-01705-8); pap. 8.00 o.p. (ISBN 0-668-04309-1). Arco.

Supervising on the Job: A Self-Study Guide for Students. Patricia M Rath et al. 1971. pap. text ed. 8.00x o.p. (ISBN 0-8134-1238-2, 1238). Inter Print Pubs.

Supervision. Charles M. Ray & Charles L. Eison. 396p. 1983. text ed. 30.95x o.p. (ISBN 0-03-054556-0); instr's manual 19.95 o.p. (ISBN 0-03-054561-7). Dryden Pr.

Supervision: An Applied Behavioral Science Approach to Managing People. Jerry L. Gray. LC 83-22224. 544p. 1984. text ed. write for info. o.p. (ISBN 0-534-03129-3). PWS-Kent Pub.

Supervision & Team Support. Ed. by Sheila Martel. 104p. 1981. pap. text ed. 8.75 o.p. (ISBN 0-7199-1066-8, Pub. by Bedford England). Gower Pub Co.

Supervision Can Be Easy. David K. Lindo. (Illus.). 1979. 14.95 o.p. (ISBN 0-8144-5548-4). AMACOM.

Supervision Decision! Employee Guide to Choosing a Supervisory Position. Paul O. Radde. LC 81-1116. (Illus.). 100p. 1981. vinyl binder 26.50 o.p. (ISBN 0-89384-060-2); wkbk. to counsel employees incl. o.p. Univ Assocs.

Supervision Decision! Employee Workbook for Choosing a Supervisory Position. Paul O. Radde. (Illus.). 73p. 1981. pap. 8.50 o.p. (ISBN 0-89384-061-0). Univ Assocs.

Supervision for Today's Schools. 2nd ed. Peter F. Oliva. LC 83-5417. 480p. pap. text ed. 29.95 o.p. (ISBN 0-582-28420-1). Longman.

Supervision in the Administration of Justice: Police, Corrections, Courts. 2nd ed. Paul B. Weston. (Illus.). 224p. 1978. 31.25 o.p. (ISBN 0-398-03762-0). C C Thomas.

Supervision of Employees in Libraries. Ed. by Rolland E. Stevens. LC 79-10860. (Allerton Park Institute Ser: No. 24). 113p. 1979. 9.00 o.p. (ISBN 0-87845-051-3). U of Ill Lib Info Sci.

Supervision: Principles of Professional Management. 2nd ed. Robert M. Fulmer & Steven C. Franklin. 1982. text ed. write for info. o.p. (ISBN 0-02-479660-3). Macmillan.

Supervision: The Direction of People at Work. 4th ed. W. Richard Plunkett. 416p. 1986. net 34.00 o.p. (ISBN 0-205-11562-4, H1562-1); instr's. manual avail. o.p. Allyn.

Supervision: The Reluctant Profession. Ralph L. Mosher et al. LC 72-158636. (Orig.). 1903. pap. 18.95 o.p. (ISBN 0-395-12509-X). HM.

Supervisor Development Programmes: Role Handbook. C. Turney & L. G. Cairns. (Illus.). 278p. (Orig.). 1983. pap. 25.50x o.p. (ISBN 0-424-00098-9, Pub. by Sydney U Pr). Intl Spec Bk.

Supervisor 2 (Child Welfare) Jack Rudman. (Career Examination Ser.: C-1807). (Cloth bdg. avail. on request). pap. 10.00 o.p. (ISBN 0-8373-1807-6). Natl Learning.

Supervisor's Handbook. Edwin B. Feldman & George B. Wright. LC 82-71741. 420p. 1982. 29.95 o.p. (ISBN 0-8119-0449-0). Fell.

Supervisor's Problem Solver. W. H. Weiss. 240p. 1983. 15.95 o.p. (ISBN 0-8144-5754-1). AMACOM.

Supervisors Resource Set. Olson. 1986. pap. 29.85 o.p. (ISBN 0-471-85669-X). Wiley.

Supervisors Safety Manual. 5th ed. LC 78-58304. 436p. 1978. 29.25 o.p. (ISBN 0-87912-064-9, 151.28). Natl Safety Coun.

Supervisory Control of Absenteeism. James V. Findlay & Richard G. Morrison. LC 77-77275. (Illus.). 62p. 1977. Incl. transparency masters. 3-ring binder 69.50 o.s.i. (ISBN 0-88061-018-2). Inst Pub ILCI.

Supervisory Library. Broadwell. 1986. 29.90 o.p. (ISBN 0-471-62399-7). Wiley.

Supervisory Safety Promotion. M. Douglas Clark & George L. Germain. (Illus.). 1978. Incl. transparency masters. 3-ring binder 57.00 o.s.i. (ISBN 0-88061-020-4). Inst Pub ILCI.

Superwives. Jeanne Parr. 1977. pap. 1.75 o.p. (ISBN 0-380-01641-9, 32995). Avon.

Suplemento a la Segunda Edicion del Diccionario Pornua de Historia, Biografia y Geografia de Mexico. 496p. (Span.). 17.50 o.p. (ISBN 0-686-56693-9, S-12280). French & Eur.

Suppertime for Baby Ben. Harriet Ziefert. LC 84-61324. (Baby Ben Bks.). (Illus.). 16p. (ps). 1985. 3.95 o.s.i. (ISBN 0-394-87024-7, BYR). Random.

Supplement au Dictionnaire de la Noblesse Francaise. Etienne de Sereville & Fernand de Saint-Simon. 668p. (Fr.). 1977. 65.00 o.p. (ISBN 0-686-56752-8, M-6514). French & Eur.

Supplement to Corporations 1986: Law & Policy, Materials & Problems, 1982. Lewis D. Solomon et al. (American Casebook Ser.). 345p. 1986. pap. 10.95 o.p. (ISBN 0-314-26047-1). West Pub.

Supplement to Dodson-Dotson Family of Southwest Virginia. (Illus.). 125p. 1965. 15.00 o.p. (ISBN 0-89308-025-X, FH 8). Southern Hist Pr.

Supplement to Edward S. Corwin's Constitution & What It Means Todays. Edward S. Corwin. Ed. by Harold W. Chase & Craig R. Ducat. 1981. pap. 3.50x o.p. (ISBN 0-691-02761-7). Princeton U Pr.

Supplement to Inservice Guides. 1978. 6.00 o.s.i. (ISBN 0-938846-09-4). Ebenezer Ctr.

Supplement to Judicial Remedies in the European Communities. L. J. Brinkhorst & H. G. Schermers. xii, 183p. 1972. pap. text ed. 10.00x o.p. (ISBN 90-268-0641-8). Rothman.

Supplement to Let's Make It Happen. 32p. 1983. pap. 2.25 o.p. (ISBN 0-88441-333-0, 20-817). Girl Scouts USA.

Supplement to the Bibliography of Walter Gropius see American Association of Architectural Bibliographers' Papers.

Supplement to the Handbook of Magazine Publishing, 1978. 1978. 20.00 o.p. (ISBN 0-918110-03-3). Hanson Pub Grp.

Supplement to the Handbook of Middle American Indians, Vol. 4: Ethnohistory. Ed. by Victoria R. Bricker & Ronald Spores. (Illus.). 240p. 1986. text ed. 40.00x o.p. (ISBN 0-292-77604-7). U of Tex Pr.

Supplement to the New English-Russian Dictionary: Supplement. I. R. Galperin. 432p. (Eng. & Rus.). 1980. 10.00 o.p. (ISBN 0-8285-1901-3, Pub. by Rus Lang Pubs USSR). Imported Pubns.

Supplement to the Standard Textbook of Cosmetology. Milady Editors. (Illus.). 1978. 4.65 o.p. (ISBN 0-87350-077-6); 4.95 o.p. spanish ed. (ISBN 0-87350-075-X). Milady Pub.

Supplement to Wigmore on Evidence, 1985. Walter A. Reiser, Jr. LC 61-10756. 784p. 1985. pap. write for info. o.p. (ISBN 0-316-73971-5). Little.

Supplement to World Economic Survey, 1978: The Expansion of Exports from Developing Countries & Policies of Structural Adjustment in Developed Countries see World Economic Survey.

Supplemental Audio Cassettes: For Adults with Neurogenic Communicative Disorders. Anne P. Bedwinek. 1981. 24.95 o.p. (ISBN 0-88450-732-7, 3136-B). Communication Skill.

Supplemental Tables of Molecular Orbital Calculations, 2 vols. A. Streitwieser, Jr. & J. I. Brauman. 1965. Set. 400.00 o.p. (ISBN 0-08-010219-0). Pergamon.

Supplemental Ways for Improving International Stability: Proceedings of the IFAC Workshop, Laxenburg, Austria, 13-15, September, 1983. Ed. by H. Chestnut et al. (IFAC Publication Ser.). 304p. 1984. 91.00 o.p. (ISBN 0-08-031631-X). Pergamon.

Supplementary English Glossary. Thomas L. Davies. LC 68-23468. 756p. 1968. Repr. of 1881 ed. 53.00x o.p. (ISBN 0-8103-3245-0). Gale.

Supplications (Du'a) Amir Al-Muminin. Tr. by William C. Chittick from Arabic & Eng. 63p. 1986. text ed. 24.95 o.p. (ISBN 0-7103-0156-1). Routledge Chapman & Hall.

Supplies & Office Maintenance, Vol. 8. A. Ziegler. (Illus.). 1982. pap. 21.95 o.p. (ISBN 0-87489-157-4). Med Economics.

Supplies for Pendulu. Date not set. (ISBN 0-07-017571-3). McGraw.

Supplies Management for Health Service. Stanley Hyman. 244p. 1979. 30.00x o.p. (ISBN 0-85664-707-1, Pub. by Croom Helm Ltd). Routledge Chapman & Hall.

Supply Management. 163p. 1981. 24.50 o.p. (ISBN 92-2-102365-6). Intl Labour Office.

Supplying Washington's Army. Erna Risch. LC 80-607092. (Special Studies). (Illus.). 484p. 1981. 15.00 o.p. (ISBN 0-318-21920-4, S/N 008-029-00115-2). USGPO.

Support for School Management. A. J. Bailey. 192p. 1987. 31.00 o.p. (ISBN 0-7099-5033-0, Pub. by Croom Helm UK). Routledge Chapman & Hall.

Support for Secession: Lancashire & the American Civil War. Mary Ellison. LC 72-80158. 276p. 1973. lib. bdg. 17.00x o.s.i. (ISBN 0-226-20593-2). U of Chicago Pr.

Support for Social Work Education. Date not set. 1.10 o.s.i. Coun Soc Wk Ed.

Supported Self-Study in Secondary Education. Philip Waterhouse. (Orig.). 1983. pap. text ed. 21.00x o.p. (ISBN 0-86184-112-3). Trans Atl Phila.

Supporting Innovations in Education: Preparing Administrators, Supervisors and Other Key Personnel: Report of a Technical Working Group Meeting, Seoul, September 29-October 11, 1980. 86p. 1981. pap. 5.00 o.p. (ISBN 0-686-81853-9, UB103, UB). UNIPUB.

Supporting the Learning Teacher: A Source Book for Teacher Centers. Marilyn Hapgood. LC 73-82073. 1975. 10.00x o.p. (ISBN 0-87586-044-3). Agathon.

Suppression. Francisco H. Mosti. 64p. 1981. 9.00 o.p. (ISBN 0-682-49691-X). Exposition-Phoenix.

Suppression of Experimental Allergic Encephalomyelitis & Multiple Sclerosis. Ed. by A. N. Davison & M. L. Cuzner. LC 79-41796. 1980. 76.00 o.p. (ISBN 0-12-206660-X). Acad Pr.

Supramolecular Structure & Function. Ed. by Greta Pifat & Janok N. Herak. LC 82-24604. 374p. 1983. 69.50x o.p. (ISBN 0-306-41257-8, Plenum Pr). Plenum Pub.

Suprasegmental Phonology. William Leben. Ed. by Jorge Hankamer. (Outstanding Dissertation in Linguistics Ser.). 33.00 o.p. (ISBN 0-8240-4556-4). Garland Pub.

Supreme Champions. Peter Alliss. (Illus.). 240p. 1986. 22.50 o.p. (ISBN 0-684-18320-X). Scribner.

Supreme Court. 2nd ed. Lawrence Baum. LC 84-23864. 270p. 1985. pap. 17.95 o.p. (ISBN 0-87187-327-3); 19.95 o.p. (ISBN 0-87187-343-5). Congr Quarterly.

Supreme Court Activism & Restraint. Stephen C. Halpern & Charles M. Lamb. LC 81-47764. (Illus.). 448p. 1982. 36.00x o.p. (ISBN 0-669-04855-0); pap. 18.00x o.p. (ISBN 0-669-09848-5). Lexington Bks.

Supreme Court & Individual Rights. Congressional Quarterly, Inc. Staff. LC 79-26967. 303p. (Orig.). 1980. pap. 10.95 o.p. (ISBN 0-87187-195-5). Congr Quarterly.

Supreme Court & the Constitution: Readings in American Constitutional History. 2nd ed. Ed. by Stanley I. Kutler. LC 77-934. 1977. pap. text ed. 12.95x o.p. (ISBN 0-393-09140-6). Norton.

Supreme Court Cases Affecting the Legal Rights of Women. 5.00 o.p. (ISBN 0-317-17484-3). Women's Legal Defense.

Supreme Court in Crisis: A History of Conflict. Robert J. Steamer. LC 74-123544. 1971. 12.95x o.p. (ISBN 0-87023-080-8); pap. 11.95x o.p. (ISBN 0-87023-077-8). U of Mass Pr.

Supreme Court, Justice & the Law. 3rd ed. Congressional Quarterly, Inc. Staff. LC 83-2120. 194p. 1983. pap. 10.95 o.p. (ISBN 0-87187-253-6). Congr Quarterly.

Supreme Court Rules of the State of Delaware. Michie Company Editorial Staff. 97p. 1984. 5.00 o.p. (ISBN 0-87215-894-2). Michie Co.

Supreme Doctrine: Discourses on the Kenopanishad. Bhagwan S. Rajneesh. 356p. (Orig.). 1980. pap. 12.95 o.p. (ISBN 0-7100-0572-5). Routledge Chapman & Hall.

Supreme Labor Court in Nazi Germany. Marc Linder. 290p. 1987. write for info. o.p. (Pub. by Vittorio Klostermann W. Germany). Transnatl Pubs.

Sur Fischer: Initiation Aux Echecs. Fernando Arrabal. (Illus.). 180p. 1973. 14.95 o.p. (ISBN 0-686-54462-5). French & Eur.

Surangini Tales. Partap Sharma. LC 72-88173. (Illus.). 128p. (gr. 4-7). 1973. 5.75 o.p. (ISBN 0-15-283200-9, HJ). HarBraceJ.

Suretyship & the Builder. National Association of Home Builders Staff. 37p. 1979. pap. 10.00 o.p. (ISBN 0-86718-044-7). Nat Assn H Build.

Surf City-Drag City. Rob Burt. (Illus.). 128p. 1986. 17.95 o.p. (Pub. by Blandford Pr England); pap. 12.95 o.p. (ISBN 0-7137-1891-9). Sterling.

Surface Active Chemicals. H. E. Garrett. 177p. 1972. 45.00 o.p. (ISBN 0-08-016422-6). Pergamon.

Surface Active Ethylene Oxide Adducts. N. Schonfeldt. LC 69-19089. 1970. 235.00 o.p. (ISBN 0-08-012819-X). Pergamon.

Surface & Borehole Geophysical Methods & Ground Water: Proceedings. LC 86-31154. 1987. 43.75 o.p. (ISBN 0-318-23038-0). Natl Water Well.

Surface & Colloid Science, Vol. 10. Ed. by Egon Matijevic. LC 67-29459. (Illus.). 360p. 1978. 59.50x o.p. (ISBN 0-306-38260-1, Plenum Pr). Plenum Pub.

Surface Chemistry: Proceedings. Ed. by Per Ekwall et al. 1966. 45.00 o.p. (ISBN 0-12-237050-3). Acad Pr.

Surface Chic. James Charlton. 64p. (Orig.). 1984. pap. 7.95 o.p. (ISBN 0-380-87478-4). Avon.

Surface Effects in Adhesion, Friction, Wear & Lubrication. D. H. Buckley. (Tribiology Ser.: Vol. 5). 1987. 153.75 o.p. (ISBN 0-317-65927-8). Elsevier.

Surface Freight: Rail, Truck, & Intermodal. (Transportation Research Record Ser.). 92p. 1980. 5.40 o.p. (ISBN 0-309-03073-0). Transport Res Bd.

Surface Mining. LC 68-24169. 1968. 30.00x o.p. (ISBN 0-89520-002-3). SMM&E Inc.

Surface Mining: Soil, Coal, & Society. National Research Council Commission on Natural Resources. 1981. pap. 11.50x o.p. (ISBN 0-309-03140-0). Natl Acad Pr.

Surface Mobilities on Solid Materials: Fundamental Concepts & Applications. Ed. by Vu T. Binh. (NATO ASI Series B, Physics: Vol. 86). 598p. 1983. 95.00x o.p. (ISBN 0-306-41125-3, Plenum Press). Plenum Pub.

Surface Mount Technology Equipment Trends. Date not set. write for info. o.p. (ISBN 0-914405-25-X). Electronic Trend.

Surface Phenomena in Enhanced Oil Recovery. Ed. by D. O. Shah. LC 81-8704. 886p. 1981. 135.00x o.p. (ISBN 0-306-40757-4, Plenum Pr). Plenum Pub.

Surface Physics. (Tracts in Modern Physics: Vol. 77). (Illus.). 130p. 1976. 35.00 o.p. (ISBN 0-387-07501-1). Springer-Verlag.

Surface Preparation & Finishes for Metals. Society of Manufacturing Engineers Staff & J. A. Murphy. 1971. text ed. 52.00 o.p. (ISBN 0-07-059557-7). McGraw.

Surface Properties of Materials: Proceedings from the Conference on Surface Properties of Materials, Held at the University of Missouri, Rolla, June 24-27, 1974. Ed. by L. L. Levenson. (Journal of Surface Science: Vol. 48). 294p. 1975. Repr. of 1975 ed. 47.50 o.p. (ISBN 0-444-10846-7, North-Holland). Elsevier.

Surface Roughness Effects in Hydrodymanic & Mixed Lubrication. Ed. by S. M. Rohde & H. S. Cheng. 218p. 1980. 30.00 o.p. (ISBN 0-686-69862-2, G00193). ASME.

Surface Topology. P. A. Firby & C. F. Gardiner. (Mathematics & Its Applications Ser.). 216p. 1982. 54.95X o.p. (ISBN 0-470-27528-6). Halsted Pr.

Surface Transportation Regulation & Railroad Planning. (Transportation Research Record Ser.). 58p. 1978. 3.40 o.p. (ISBN 0-309-02832-9). Transport Res Bd.

Surface Treatments for Improved Performance & Properties. Ed. by John J. Burke & Volker Weiss. (Sagamore Army Materials Research Conference Proceedings Ser.: Vol. 26). 226p. 1982. 49.50x o.p. (ISBN 0-306-40897-X, Plenum Pr). Plenum Pub.

Surface Treatments for Protection. 343p. 1978. pap. text ed. 30.40x o.p. (ISBN 0-318-20352-9, Pub. by Inst Metals). Gower Pub Co.

Surface Water Treatment for Communities in Developing Countries. Christopher R. Schulz & Daniel A. Okun. LC 84-3570. 299p. 1984. text ed. 44.95x o.p. (ISBN 0-471-80261-1, Pub. by Wiley Interscience). Wiley.

Surfaces & Planar Discontinuous Groups: Revised & Expanded Translation. H. Zieschang et al. (Lecture Notes in Mathematics Ser.: Vol. 835). 334p. 1980. pap. 21.00 o.p. (ISBN 0-387-10024-5). Springer-Verlag.

Surfaces of a Diamond, Novel. Louis D. Rubin, Jr. LC 81-6034. 232p. 1981. 16.95 o.p. (ISBN 0-8071-0897-9). La State U Pr.

Surfactants, Detergents & Sequestrants: Developments since 1979. Ed. by J. I. DiStasio. LC 81-38360. (Chem. Tech. Rev. 192). 353p. 1981. 48.00 o.p. (ISBN 0-8155-0856-5). Noyes.

Surfing Subcultures of Australia & New Zealand. Kent Pearson. (Illus.). 1980. 34.50x o.p. (ISBN 0-7022-1398-5); pap. 14.95x o.p. (ISBN 0-7022-1487-6). U of Queensland Pr.

Surgeon of His Honour. Pedro Calderon de la Barca. Tr. by Roy Campbell from Span. LC 77-13711. 1978. Repr. of 1960 ed. lib. bdg. 35.00x o.p. (ISBN 0-8371-9871-2, CASU). Greenwood.

Surgeon on Safari. Paul J. Jorden & James R. Adair. (Living Bks.). 192p. (Orig.). 1985. pap. 3.95 o.p. (ISBN 0-8423-6686-5). Tyndale.

Surgeon: The Making of an Inner-City Doctor. Richard Caleel & John Littell. LC 85-43091. 256p. 1986. 15.95 o.p. (ISBN 0-89256-307-9). Rawson Assocs.

Surgeons All. Harvey Graham. (Illus.). 460p. 1957. (ISBN 0-8022-0616-6). Philos Lib.

Surgeon's Mate, Sixteen Hundred Seventeen. John Woodall. 1977. text ed. 18.00x o.p. (ISBN 0-906230-15-2). State Mutual Bk.

Surgeon's Turn. George H. Rawls. 1985. 7.95 o.p. (ISBN 0-533-06664-6). Vantage.

Surgery: A Textbook for Students. R. M. Kirk et al. (Illus.). 1974. text ed. 24.00x o.p. (ISBN 0-8464-0901-1); pap. text ed. 29.95 o.p. (ISBN 0-8464-0902-X). Beekman Pubs.

Surgery & Life: The Extraordinary Career of Alexis Carrel. Theodore Malinin. 1979. 12.95 o.p. (ISBN 0-15-186882-4). HarBraceJ.

Surgery Annual, 1985, Vol. 17. Ed. by Lloyd M. Nyhus. 400p. 1984. 59.95 o.p. (ISBN 0-8385-8723-2). Appleton & Lange.

Surgery Annual, 1986, Vol. 18. Lloyd Nyhus. 416p. 1985. 59.95 o.p. (ISBN 0-8385-8725-9). Appleton & Lange.

Surgery Examination Review. Simon Wapnick & Nino Carnevale. LC 81-20503. (Medical Review Ser.). (Illus.). 112p. (Orig.). 1982. pap. 17.95 o.p. (ISBN 0-668-05107-8). Appleton & Lange.

Surgery in the Aged. Lazar J. Greenfield. LC 75-8177. (Major Problems in Clinical Surgery Ser.: Vol. 17). pap. cancelled o.s.i. (ISBN 0-317-26435-4, 2024990). Bks Demand UMI.

Surgery of Kidney & Ureteral Anomalies. M. D. Dzhavad-Zade. 1980. 12.75 o.p. (ISBN 0-8285-1872-6, Pub. by Mir Pubs USSR). Imported Pubns.

Surgery of the Facial Nerve. 2nd ed. Adolf Miehlke. Tr. by L. S. Michaelis. LC 72-85770. (Illus.). 255p. 1973. text ed. write for info. o.p. (ISBN 0-7216-6318-4). Saunders.

Surgery: PreTest Self-Assessment & Review. 3rd ed. PreTest Services, Inc Staff et al. (Clinical Science Ser.). 272p. 1985. text ed. 13.95 o.p. (ISBN 0-07-051005-9). McGraw.

Surgical Care I: A Physiologic Approach to Clinical Management. Ed. by Robert E. Condon & Jerome J. De Cosse. LC 79-21864. (Illus.). 474p. 1980. text ed. 37.50 o.p. (ISBN 0-8121-0643-1). Lea & Febiger.

Surgical Correction of Dentofacial Deformities, 3 vols. William H. Bell et al. LC 76-27050. 1980. Set. text ed. 395.00 o.p. (ISBN 0-7216-1671-2); Vol. 1. 135.00 o.p. (ISBN 0-7216-1675-5); Vol. 2. 135.00 o.p. (ISBN 0-7216-1707-7); Vol. 3. 135.00 o.p. Saunders.

Surgical Instruments in Greek & Roman Times. John S. Milne. LC 70-95630. (Illus.). xi, 187p. 1970. Repr. of 1907 ed. 29.50x o.p. (ISBN 0-678-03755-8). Kelley.

Surgical Nursing. C. Humphrey. 399p. 1983. text ed. 23.00 o.p. (ISBN 0-07-072993-X). McGraw.

Surgical Physiology. John F. Burke. (Illus.). 592p. 1983. write for info. o.p. (ISBN 0-7216-2183-X). Saunders.

Surgical Problems in the Aged. K. Vowles. (Illus.). 208p. 1979. 29.00 o.p. (ISBN 0-7236-0510-6, Pub. by John Wright UK). Butterworth.

Surgical Rehabilitation in Leprosy. Frank McDowell et al. LC 74-1279. 448p. 1974. 40.00 o.p. (ISBN 0-683-05853-3). Krieger.

Surgical Versus Conservative Treatment of Intracranial Arteriovenous Malformations. L. Pellettieri. (Acta Niurochirurgica Supplementum: Vol. 29). (Illus.). 86p. 1980. pap. 34.90 o.p. (ISBN 0-387-81561-9). Springer-Verlag.

Surprise. Z. Voskrenskaya. 32p. 1974. pap. 0.99 o.p. (ISBN 0-8285-1236-1, Pub. by Progress Pubs USSR). Imported Pubns.

Surprise at Muddy Creek. Leone C. Anderson. LC 84-7072. (Illus.). 32p. (gr. 1-2). 1984. lib. bdg. 4.95 o.p. (ISBN 0-89693-222-2). Dandelion Hse.

Surprise Me, Jesus. Herbert F. Brokering. LC 73-83785. 96p. 1973. pap. 6.95 o.p. (ISBN 0-8066-1338-6, 10-6150, Augsburg). Augsburg Fortress.

Surprise Party. William Katz. 1984. text ed. 12.95 o.p. (ISBN 0-07-033371-8). McGraw.

Surprised by Light. Ulrich Schaffer. LC 80-7751. (Illus.). 80p. 1980. 10.53i o.p. (ISBN 0-06-067086-X); pap. 11.49i o.p. (ISBN 0-06-067087-8, RD 335). HarpR.

Surprising Years: Understanding Your Changing Adolescent. Cliff Schimmels & Hank Resnik. (Illus.). 140p. (Orig.). 1985. pap. 7.50 o.p. (ISBN 0-933419-08-2). Quest Intl.

Surrealism. Ed. by Herbert E. Read. LC 37-1497. 251p. 1936. Repr. 49.00x o.p. (ISBN 0-403-07248-4). Somerset Pub.

Surrealism & Its Affinities: The Mary Reynolds Collection. 2nd ed. Hugh Edwards. LC 73-132025. (Illus.). 147p. pap. 1.50 o.p. (ISBN 0-86559-003-6). Art Inst Chi.

Surrealists Look at Art. Andre Breton et al. Ed. by Pontus Hulten. LC 85-81092. (Illus.). 96p. (Orig.). 1988. price not set o.p. (ISBN 0-932499-08-2); pap. price not set o.p. (ISBN 0-932499-09-0). Lapis Pr.

Surrender & Other Poems. Cosmo E. Damiani. 96p. 1987. 8.95 o.p. (ISBN 0-8062-3074-6). Carlton.

Surreptitious Printing in England, 1550-1640. Denis B. Woodfield. LC 75-185916. (Illus.). 203p. 1973. 17.50x o.p. (ISBN 0-8139-0940-6, Bibliographical Society of America). U Pr of Va.

Surrogate. David Combs. 208p. 1982. pap. 2.50 o.p. (ISBN 0-380-81133-2, 81133). Avon.

Surrogate Mother. Noel P. Keane & Dennis L. Breo. 256p. 1981. 14.95 o.p. (ISBN 0-89696-113-3, Everest House Book); pap. 8.95 o.p. (ISBN 0-686-85939-1). Dodd.

Sursis see Chemins de la liberte.

Surveillance Methods & Ways & Means of Communicating with Drivers. (National Cooperative Highway Research Program Report). 66p. 1966. 2.60 o.p. (ISBN 0-317-36106-6, 1473). Transport Res Bd.

Surveillant Science: Remote Sensing of the Environment. 2nd ed. Robert K. Holz. LC 84-7508. 413p. 1985. pap. text ed. 23.50x o.p. (ISBN 0-471-08638-X). Wiley.

Surveillant Science: Remote Sensing of the Environment. Ed. by Robert K. Holz. LC 72-7922. (Illus.). 300p. (Orig.). 1973. pap. 19.95 o.p. (ISBN 0-395-14041-2). HM.

Survey & Critique of World Bank Supported Research in International Comparisons of Real Product. Robin Marris. (Working Paper: No. 365). ii, 56p. 1979. 6.95 o.p. (ISBN 0-8213-9234-4, WP-0365). World Bank.

Survey & Evaluation of Handling & Disposing of Solid Low-Level Nuclear Fuel Cycle Wastes (AIF-NESP-008) NUS Corporation Staff. (National Environmental Studies Project: NESP Reports). 125p. 1976. 24.00 o.p. (ISBN 0-318-13596-5); to NESP sponsors 12.00 o.p. (ISBN 0-318-13597-3). US Coun Energy Awareness.

Survey & Public Opinion Research: Grades Five to Twelve. Lois S. Roets. 120p. tchrs.' ed. 14.00 o.p. (ISBN 0-911943-04-8). Leadership Pubs.

Survey of Accountants' Views on the Desirability & Method of Inflation Accounting. Rosalie C. Hallbauer & Surendra P. Agrawal. LC 83-6900. (Illus.). 350p. (Orig.). 1983. lib. bdg. 34.25 o.p. (ISBN 0-8191-3212-8); pap. text ed. 17.75 o.p. (ISBN 0-8191-3213-6). U Pr of Amer.

Survey of Afro-American Experience in the U. S. Economy. Martin O. Ijere. 1978. 8.50 o.p. (ISBN 0-682-49029-6, University). Exposition-Phoenix.

Survey of American Genealogical Periodicals & Periodical Indexes. Ed. by Kip Sperry. LC 78-55033. (Genealogy & Local History Ser.: Vol. 3). 216p. 1978. 68.00x o.p. (ISBN 0-8103-1401-0). Gale.

Survey of American History Since 1865 see American Past: A Survey of American History.

Survey of American History to 1877 see American Past: A Survey of American History.

Survey of American Law. Elmer C. Johnson. LC 78-98957. 1970. text ed. 9.95 o.p. (ISBN 0-682-47032-5, University). Exposition-Phoenix.

Survey of Arts Administration Training: 1985-86. 5th ed. Ed. by E. Arthur Prieve. LC 84-21593. 86p. (Orig.). 1984. pap. 7.50 o.p. (ISBN 0-915400-49-9). Am Council Arts.

Survey of Arts Administration Training: 1987-88. 6th ed. Ed. by E. Arthur Prieve. 87p. (Orig.). 1987. pap. 8.95 o.p. (ISBN 0-915400-55-3, 7275). Am Council Arts.

Survey of Basic Accounting. 4th ed. R. F. Salmonson et al. 1985. 33.95 o.p. (ISBN 0-256-03203-3); workbook 12.95 o.p. (ISBN 0-256-03204-1). Irwin.

Survey of Binary Systems. 3rd ed. R. H. Bruck. LC 79-143906. (Ergebnisse der Mathematik und Ihrer Grenzebiete: Vol. 20). 1971. 22.00 o.p. (ISBN 0-387-03497-8). Springer-Verlag.

Survey of Clinical Pediatrics. 7th ed. Edward Wasserman & Donald S. Gromisch. (Illus.). 560p. 1981. text ed. 37.00 o.p. (ISBN 0-07-068431-6). McGraw.

Survey of Contemporary Toxicology, Vol. 1. Ed. by Anthony T. Tu. LC 79-25224. 357p. 1980. 74.00x o.p. (ISBN 0-471-04085-1, Pub. by Wiley-Intersience). Wiley.

Survey of Contemporary Toxicology, Vol. 2. Ed. by Anthony T. Tu. LC 79-25224. 248p. 1982. 73.00 o.p. (ISBN 0-471-06352-5, Pub. by Wiley-Interscience). Wiley.

Survey of Documentary Sources for Property Holding in London Before the Great Fire. Compiled by Derek Keene & Vanessa Harding. (Illus.). 248p. 1986. lib. bdg. 35.00 o.p. (ISBN 0-900952-22-9). Chadwyck-Healey.

Survey of Embryology. Francis G. Gilchrist. 1968. text ed. 51.95 o.p. (ISBN 0-07-023208-3). McGraw.

Survey of Financial Reporting & Accounting Developments in the Hospital Industry. Price Waterhouse Staff. (Illus.). 51p. (Orig.). 1984. pap. text ed. 25.00 o.s.i. (ISBN 0-930228-24-3). Healthcare Fin Mgmt Assn.

Survey of French Literature, 2 Vols. Morris Bishop. 1955. Vol. 1. 6.75 o.p. (ISBN 0-15-584961-1); Vol. 2. 6.75 o.p. (ISBN 0-15-584962-X). HarbraceJ.

Survey of Fusion Reactor Technology: Definition of Problems. EURATOM Advisory Group on Fusion Reactor Technology, 1972. 1975. pap. 23.00 o.p. (ISBN 0-08-020453-8). Pergamon.

Survey of Hidden Variables Theories. F. J. Belinfante. 376p. 1973. text ed. 54.00 o.p. (ISBN 0-08-017032-3). Pergamon.

Survey of Information Systems Interests Report July 1987. American Trucking Associations. 29p. 1987. pap. 125.00 o.p. (ISBN 0-88711-109-2). Am Trucking Assns.

Survey of International Affairs, Indexes, 1920-1930. Repr. of 1932 ed. 50.00, incl. suppl. vols o.p. (ISBN 0-384-58817-4). Johnson Repr.

Survey of International Arbitration Sites. American Arbitration Association Staff. LC 84-81526. 107p. 1984. pap. 15.00 o.p. (ISBN 0-943001-09-9); pap. 10.00 members o.p. Am Arbitration.

Survey of International Arbitrations, 1794-1970. Alexander M. Stuyt. LC 72-79626. 587p. 1972. lib. bdg. 32.50 o.p. (ISBN 0-379-00008-3). Oceana.

Survey of Living Primates & Their Anatomy. Friderun Ankel-Simons. 288p. 1983. pap. text ed. write for info. o.p. (ISBN 0-02-303500-5). Macmillan.

Survey of London. John Stow. 1987. Repr. of 1956 ed. 14.95x o.p. (ISBN 0-460-00589-8, Evman); pap. 12.95 o.p. (ISBN 0-460-11589-8). Biblio Dist.

Survey of Management Audits of Utility Operating Performance & Efficiency. 49p. 1976. 3.50 o.p. (ISBN 0-318-15031-X). NARUC.

Survey of Management Audits of Utility Operating Performance & Efficiency. 49p. 1976. 3.50 o.p. NARUC.

Survey of Negro Colleges & Universities. United States Office of Education Staff. LC 72-82096. (Illus.). 1969. Repr. of 1929 ed. 44.00x o.s.i. (ISBN 0-8371-1878-6, SNC&, Pub. by Negro U Pr). Greenwood.

Survey of New Guinea Languages. A. Capell. LC 68-21925. (Illus.). 158p. 1971. 27.00x o.p. (ISBN 0-424-05420-5, Pub. by Sydney U Pr). Intl Spec Bk.

Survey of Persian Handicraft. Jay Gluck & Sumi Gluck. (Illus.). 416p. 125.00 o.p. (ISBN 0-317-55043-8). Apollo.

Survey of Progress in Chemistry, Vols. 1-9. Ed. by Arthur F. Scott. Incl. Vol. 1. 1963. 59.50 o.p. (ISBN 0-12-610501-4); Vol. 2. 1965. 59.50 o.p. (ISBN 0-12-610502-2); Vol. 3. 1966. 59.50 o.p. (ISBN 0-12-610503-0); Vol. 4. 1968. 59.50 o.p. (ISBN 0-12-610504-9); Vol. 5. 1969. 59.50 o.p. (ISBN 0-12-610505-7); Vol. 6. 1973. 75.00 o.p. (ISBN 0-12-610506-5); Vol. 7. 1976. 59.50 o.p. (ISBN 0-12-610507-3); lib. bdg. 70.00 o.p. (ISBN 0-12-610574-X); Vol. 8. 1978. 65.00 o.p. (ISBN 0-12-610508-1); lib. bdg. 75.00 o.p. (ISBN 0-12-610576-6); Vol. 9. 1980. 49.50 o.p. (ISBN 0-12-610509-X); lib. bdg. 65.00 o.p. (ISBN 0-12-610578-2); Vol. 10. 1983. 65.00. Acad Pr.

Survey of Russian Music. M. D. Calvocoressi. LC 73-6208. (Illus.). 142p. 1974. Repr. of 1944 ed. lib. bdg. 35.00x o.p. (ISBN 0-8371-6888-0, CARM). Greenwood.

Survey of Spousal Violence Against Women in Kentucky. Louis Harris. (Louis Harris Publications Ser.). 1981. lib. bdg. 24.00 o.p. (ISBN 0-8240-9373-9). Garland Pub.

Survey of State Library Agencies, 1977: For the National Center for Educational Statistics. Barratt Wilkins. (Occasional Papers: No. 142). 46p. 1979. pap. 2.00 o.p. (ISBN 0-317-58992-X). U of Ill Lib Info Sci.

Survey of the Electronic Funds Transfer Transaction System, 1986. 66p. 1986. 90.00 o.p. (685). Bank Admin Inst.

Survey of the New Testament. W. W. Sloan. LC 61-10614. 1961. (ISBN 0-8022-1586-6). Philos Lib.

Survey of User Attitudes Toward Selected Services Offered by the Colorado State University Libraries. Robert W. Burns, Jr. & Ronald W. Hasty. (Occasional Papers: No. 121). 51p. 1975. pap. 2.00 o.p. (ISBN 0-317-58943-1). U of Ill Lib Info Sci.

Survey Research & Public Attitudes in Eastern Europe & the Soviet Union. Ed. by William Welsh. LC 79-27902. (Pergamon Policy Studies on International Politics). (Illus.). 506p. 1981. 145.00 o.p. (ISBN 0-08-025958-8). Pergamon.

Survey Research Methods. Floyd J. Fowler. (Applied Social Research Methods Ser.: Vol. 1). 160p. 1984. text ed. 19.95 o.p. (ISBN 0-8039-2347-3); pap. text ed. 9.95 o.p. (ISBN 0-8039-2348-1). Sage.

Surveying Instrumentation, & the Global Positioning System, Vol. II: ASPRS-ACSM Annual Convention, Washington, DC. American Congress on Surveying & Mapping & American Society for Photogrammetry & Remote Sensing Staff. 317p. 1986. 10.00 o.p. (ISBN 0-317-59917-8, T667). Am Congrs Survey.

Surveyors of the Liguasan Marsh. Antonio R. Enriquez. (Asian & Pacific Writing Ser.). 131p. 1981. text ed. 22.50 o.p. (ISBN 0-7022-1532-5); pap. 9.75 o.p. (ISBN 0-7022-1533-3). U of Queensland Pr.

Surveys of African Economies, 7 vols. International Monetary Fund Staff. Incl; Vol. 4. Democratic Republic of Congo, (Zaire), Malagasy Republic, Malawi, Mauritius & Zambia. 1971; Vol. 5. Botswana, Lesotho, Swaziland, Burundi, Equatorial Guinea, & Rwanda. 1973; Vol. 7. Algeria, Mali, Morocco, & Tunisia. 1977. (Eng. & Fr.). 5.00 ea. o.p. Intl Monetary.

Surveys of Australian Political Science. Ed. by Don Aitkin. 372p. 1985. text ed. 32.00x o.p. (ISBN 0-86861-548-X); pap. text ed. 16.00x o.p. (ISBN 0-86861-556-0). Unwin Hyman.

Surveys of Migration in Developing Countries: A Methodological Review. Sidney Goldstein & Alice Goldstein. LC 81-4285. (Papers of the East-West Population Institute: No. 71). v, 120p. (Orig.). 1981. pap. text ed. 2.50 o.p. (ISBN 0-86638-021-3). EW Ctr HI.

Survival-A Sequential Program for College Writing. 3rd; rev. ed. Robert Frew et al. 350p. 1985. pap. 16.95x o.p. (ISBN 0-917962-50-8). T H Peek.

Survival! Air Force Manual 64-5. Department of the Air Force. (Illus.). 144p. 1979. pap. 8.00 o.p. (ISBN 0-87364-167-1). Paladin Pr.

Survival & Disembodied Existence. Terence Penelhum. (Studies in Philosophical Psychology). 1970. text ed. 10.50x o.p. (ISBN 0-391-00054-3); pap. text ed. 6.00x o.p. (ISBN 0-391-01751-9). Humanities.

Survival & Mission for the City Church. Gaylord B. Noyce. LC 74-23160. 1975. pap. 3.95 o.s.i. (ISBN 0-664-24813-6, Westminster). Westminster John Knox.

Survival: Black & White. Florence Halpern. 225p. 1973. text ed. 31.00 o.p. (ISBN 0-08-016994-5); pap. 13.25 o.p. (ISBN 0-08-017193-1). Pergamon.

Survival: Body, Mind & Death in the Light of Psychic Experience. David Lorimer. 288p. (Orig.). 1984. pap. 12.95 o.p. (ISBN 0-7102-0003-X). Routledge Chapman & Hall.

Survival Family. new ed. Mary Bergman. (Illus.). 1977. pap. 3.95 o.p. (ISBN 0-89036-091-X). Hawkes Pub Inc.

Survival Guide to Computer Systems: A Primer for Executives. William E. Perry. 249p. 1983. 21.95 o.p. (ISBN 0-8436-0880-3). Van Nos Reinhold.

Survival Handbook. William K. Merrill. LC 76-188594. (Illus.). 1972. 15.95 o.p. (ISBN 0-8329-0681-6, Pub. by Winchester Pr). New Century.

Survival in Antarctica NSF 84-55. (Illus.). 106p. 1984. 4.00 o.p. (ISBN 0-318-19689-1, S/N 038-000-00549-9). USGPO.

Survival in Toxic Environments. Ed. by M. A. Khan & John Bederka. 1974. 65.50 o.p. (ISBN 0-12-406050-1). Acad Pr.

Survival Is Not Enough. Richard Pipes. 288p. 1984. 16.45 o.p. (ISBN 0-671-49535-6). S&S.

Survival Kit for Apple Computer Games. Ray Spangenburg & Dian Moser. LC 82-17912. (Illus.). 162p. 1983. pap. (ISBN 0-534-01432-1). Brooks-Cole.

Survival Kit Series: Educational Software. Spangenburg & Moser. 1984. write for info. o.p. (ISBN 0-534-03329-6). Brooks-Cole.

Survival: My Life in Love & War. Rafael Alberto Rivas. 1977. 8.50 o.p. (ISBN 0-682-48942-5). Exposition-Phoenix.

Survival of Helga Braun: A Memoir. Helga Braum. 1985. 11.95 o.p. (ISBN 0-317-28953-5). Vantage.

Survival of Mechanical Systems in Transient Environments. Ed. by T. L. Geers & P. Tong. LC 79-954424. (Applied Mechanics Division Ser.: Vol. 36). 196p. 1979. 24.00 o.p. (ISBN 0-686-62963-9, G00153). ASME.

Survival of the Chinese Jews: The Jewish Community of Kaifeng. Donald D. Leslie. (Illus.). 270p. 1973. text ed. 59.95 o.p. (ISBN 90-040-3413-7). Humanities.

Survival of the Historic Vestments in the Lutheran Church after Fifteen Fifty-Five. Arthur Carl Piepkorn. 120p. 1956. Concordia Schl Grad Studies.

Survival of the Small Firm. John Stanworth et al. 1986. text ed. 42.00x o.p. (ISBN 0-566-00725-8). Gower Pub Co.

Survival on Atlantis. Patrick D. Mulcahy. 176p. 1986. 9.95 o.p. (ISBN 0-8062-2967-5). Carlton.

Survival Prayers for Young Mothers. Deborah A. Holmes. 6.95 o.s.i. (ISBN 0-8042-2195-2, John Knox). Westminster John Knox.

Survival Probabilities: The Goal of Risk Theory. Hilary L. Seal. LC 78-8599. (Probability & Mathematical Statistics Ser.). 103p. 1978. 64.95 o.p. (ISBN 0-471-99683-1, Pub. by Wiley-Interscience). Wiley.

Survival Sense for Pilot & Passengers. R. Stoffel & Patrick Lavalla. LC 80-70906. (Illus.). 224p. (Orig.). 1980. pap. 7.95 o.p. (ISBN 0-913724-24-6). Emerg Response Inst.

Survival Training & Techniques. John Muston. (Illus.). 128p. 1987. flexibind 12.95 o.p. (ISBN 0-85368-811-7, Pub. by Arms & Armour). Sterling.

Survival-Unite to Live. Jim Bakker. LC 80-84504. 1980. 7.95 o.p. (ISBN 0-89221-081-8). New Leaf.

Survivals of Roman Religion. Gordon Laing. LC 63-10280. (Our Debt to Greece & Rome Ser). 257p. 1963. Repr. of 1930 ed. 25.00x o.p. (ISBN 0-8154-0130-2). Cooper Sq.

Survive the Savage Sea. Dougal Robertson. 217p. 1985. pap. 6.95 o.p. (Pub. by Granada England). Academy Chi Pubs.

Survive, Thrive & Be Happy - While You Work: A Manual for Working Women. Dana Britton. 92p. (Orig.). 1989. pap. 6.00 o.p. (ISBN 0-944478-03-4). Dock Pub Co.

Surviving Adolescence: A Handbook for Adolescents & Their Parents. Peter Bruggen & Charles O'Brian. 1986. pap. 9.95 o.p. (ISBN 0-571-13936-1). Faber & Faber.

Surviving As a Middle Manager. Michael Broussine & Yvonne Guerrier. (Illus.). 224p. 1983. 27.25 o.p. (ISBN 0-7099-1137-8, Pub. by Croom Helm Ltd). Routledge Chapman & Hall.

Surviving in College. David J. Yarington. 166p. 1977. pap. text ed. write for info. o.p. (ISBN 0-02-430780-7). Macmillan.

Surviving Retirement. John H. Graves. 64p. 1987. 7.95 o.p. (ISBN 0-8062-3082-7). Carlton.

Surviving Sisters. Gail Pass. LC 80-69373. 1981. 12.95 o.p. (ISBN 0-689-11134-7, Atheneum). Macmillan.

Surviving the Flood. Stephen Minot. LC 81-66006. 1981. 14.95 o.p. (ISBN 0-689-11180-0, Atheneum). Macmillan.

Survivor. James Forman. LC 76-2478. 288p. (gr. 7 up). 1976. 11.95 o.p. (ISBN 0-374-37312-4). FS&G.

Survivor. Herbert James. 1979. pap. 2.50 o.p. (ISBN 0-451-11395-0, Sig). NAL.

Survivor. George MacBeth. LC 77-92539. 1978. 7.95 o.p. (ISBN 0-15-187046-2). HarBraceJ.

Survivor: Cadwallader Colden II in Revolutionary America. Eugene R. Fingerhut. LC 82-20092. (Illus.). 200p. (Orig.). 1983. lib. bdg. 29.00 o.p. (ISBN 0-8191-2868-6); pap. text ed. 13.00 o.p. (ISBN 0-8191-2869-4). U Pr of Amer.

Survivors. Georges Simenon. Tr. by Stuart Gilbert from Fr. LC 84-22385. (Helen & Kurt Wolff Bk.). 180p. 1985. 14.95 o.s.i. (ISBN 0-15-187047-0). HarBraceJ.

Survivors: Documentary Account of the Victims of Northern Ireland. Alf McCreary. 1977. 24.95 o.p. (ISBN 0-8464-0904-6). Beekman Pubs.

Survivors: Enduring Animals of North America. Jack D. Scott. LC 75-10132. (Illus.). 128p. (gr. 5 up). 1975. 7.50 o.p. (ISBN 0-15-283257-2, HJ). HarBraceJ.

Susan Comes Through the Fire. Lois Eddy McDonnell. LC 68-56619. (Orig.). (gr. 1-3). 1969. pap. 1.75 o.p. (ISBN 0-377-09701-2). Friendship Pr.

Susan Hayward: Portrait of a Survivor. Beverly Linet. LC 80-66003. 1980. 12.95 o.p. (ISBN 0-689-11079-0, Atheneum). Macmillan.

Susannah & the Blue House Mystery. Patricia Elmore. (Orig.). (gr. 4-6). 1984. pap. 1.95 o.p. (ISBN 0-671-43493-4). Archway.

Susie in the Algrave or Susie the Tail-Wagger. Reev. 1977. 5.00 o.p. (ISBN 0-682-48842-9). Exposition-Phoenix.

Suspended Sentence: A Guide for Writers. Roscoe C. Born. 160p. 1986. 13.95 o.s.i. (ISBN 0-684-18672-1). Scribner.

Susquehanna: NYS&W. Krause & Crist. (Carstens Hobby Bks.: No. C38). (Illus.). 1980. pap. 12.00 o.p. (ISBN 0-911868-38-0). Carstens Pubns.

Sustainable Food Systems. Dietrich Knorr. (Illus.). 1983. 35.95 o.p. (ISBN 0-87055-398-4). AVI.

Sustainable Society: Ethics & Economic Growth. Robert L. Stivers. LC 75-40049. 1976. soft cover 5.25 o.s.i. (ISBN 0-664-24789-X, Westminster). Westminster John Knox.

Sustainable Society: Implications for Limited Growth. Barry Buxton. LC 76-24365. (Special Studies). 1977. text ed. 29.95 o.p. (ISBN 0-275-23890-3); pap. 19.95 o.p. (ISBN 0-275-91472-0, B1472). Praeger.

Sustaining Love: Healing & Growth in the Passages of Marriage. David Augsburger. Ed. by Earl Roe. LC 88-18656. 196p. 1989. 14.95 o.s.i. (ISBN 0-8307-1318-2, 5111782). Regal.

Sustaining Power of Hope. Leslie B. Flynn. 132p. 1985. pap. 5.50 o.p. (ISBN 0-89693-600-7). Victor Bks.

Susy in a Movie? David N. Bruskin. (Pocketbook Bks.). (Illus.). 10p. (ps-2). 1988. bds. 12.95 o.p. Bound Fun Inc.

Susy's Free Shopping Spree. David N. Bruskin. (Pocketbook Bks.). (Illus.). 10p. (ps-2). 1988. bds. 12.95 o.p. Bound Fun Inc.

Suye Mura: A Japanese Village. John F. Embree. LC 40-1477. (Illus.). 1964. pap. 3.25 o.s.i. (ISBN 0-226-20632-7, P173, Phoen). U of Chicago Pr.

Suzdal: A Guide. A. Milovsky. 139p. 1981. 7.45 o.p. (ISBN 0-8285-2485-8, Pub. by Progress Pubs USSR). Imported Pubns.

Suzuki A50P, A50 & AS50: '69-'77. Jim Hammond. pap. 13.50 o.p. (ISBN 0-85696-328-3, 328). Haynes Pubns.

Suzuki B100 P, B120 Student '66 - '77. Stewart Wilkins. (Owners Workshop Manuals Ser.: No. 298). 1979. 13.50 o.p. (ISBN 0-85696-298-8, Pub. by J H Haynes England). Haynes Pubns.

Suzuki DS80-250 Singles, 1978-1980: Service, Repair, Maintenance. Eric Jorgensen. (Illus., Orig.). pap. text ed. 13.95 o.p. (ISBN 0-89287-316-7, M363). Clymer Pub.

Suzuki Education in Action: A Story of Talent Training from Japan. Clifford A. Cook. LC 74-136977. 1970. 7.50 o.p. (ISBN 0-682-47192-5, University). Exposition-Phoenix.

Suzuki FZ50 Suzy '79 - '80. Martyn Meek. pap. 11.50 o.p. (ISBN 0-85696-575-8, 575). Haynes Pubns.

Suzuki GS1000 Chain Drive Fours: 1978-1979 Service-Repair-Performance. Ed. by Eric Jorgensen. (Illus., Orig.). pap. text ed. 13.95 o.p. (ISBN 0-89287-315-9, M375). Clymer Pub.

Suzuki GT 380, 550 '72 - '77. George Collett. (Owners Workshop Manuals Ser.: No. 216). 1979. 13.50 o.p. (ISBN 0-85696-216-3, Pub. by J H Haynes England). Haynes Pubns.

Suzuki GT750 (3-cyl) Models '71 - '77. Mansur Darlington. (Owners Workshop Manuals Ser.: No. 302). 1979. 13.50 o.p. (ISBN 0-85696-302-X, Pub. by J H Haynes England). Haynes Pubns.

Suzuki Owners Workshop Manual: Five Hundred Twins '68 Thru '76. David Rabone. (Owners Workshop Manuals Ser.: No. 135). 1979. 13.50 o.p. (ISBN 0-85696-135-3, Pub. by J H Haynes England). Haynes Pubns.

Suzuki RM Series '79-'80. Pete Shoemark. pap. 13.50 o.p. (ISBN 0-85696-534-0, 534). Haynes Pubns.

Suzuki SP-DR 370 & 400 Singles, 1978-1980: Service, Repair, Performance. Ed. by Eric Jorgensen. (Illus., Orig.). pap. text ed. 11.95 o.p. (ISBN 0-89287-327-2, M374). Clymer Pub.

Suzuki 100, 125, 185, & 250 Trail Bikes '79-'81. Chris Rogers. pap. 13.50 o.p. (ISBN 0-85696-797-1, 797). Haynes Pubns.

Suzuki: 50-120cc Singles 1964-1981-Service, Repair, Maintenance Handbook. 3rd ed. Ed. by Eric Jorgensen. (Illus.). pap. 13.95 o.p. (ISBN 0-89287-292-6, M367). Clymer Pub.

Suzy Prudden's I Can Exercise Anywhere Book. Suzy Prudden & Jeffrey Sussman. LC 81-40507. (Illus.). 160p. 1981. pap. 4.95 o.p. (ISBN 0-89480-186-4, 468). Workman Pub.

Svenska Fur Nyborjaae, Vol. 1. E. Heider et al. 1978. 22.00x ea. o.p. (ISBN 0-89918-212-7, S212); Vanous.

Svetoten: Poems. Elena Kluyeva. 1984. 4.95 o.s.i. RWCPH.

Swahili-English Dictionary. Charles W. Rechenbach. LC 67-31438. (Publications in the Languages of Africa Ser.: No. 1). 641p. (Swahili & Eng.). 1968. 36.95 o.p. (ISBN 0-8132-0406-2). Cath U Pr.

Swahili Grammar. 2nd ed. E. O. Ashton. 1976. pap. text ed. 6.50x o.p. (ISBN 0-582-62701-X). Longman.

Swami & Sam: A Yoga Book. Brandt Dayton. (Illus.). 95p. (Orig.). pap. 0.95 o.p. (ISBN 0-89389-014-6). Himalayan Pubs.

Swampbusting: Wetland Conversion & Farm Programs. Ralph E. Heimlich & Linda L. Langner. (Agriculture Economic Report 551). (Illus.). 36p. 1986. pap. 2.00 o.p. (ISBN 0-318-21574-8, S/N 001-019-00459-2). USGPO.

Swampland Flowers: The Letters & Lectures of Zen Master Ta Hui. Ta Hui. Tr. by Christopher Cleary. LC 77-77853. 1977. pap. 3.95 o.p. (ISBN 0-394-17011-3, E696, Ever). Grove.

Swan Lake. Pam Kennedy. (Illus.). 48p. (gr. k-5). 1986. 5.95 o.p. (ISBN 0-8249-8151-0). Ideals.

Swan Lake. Anne Nugent. (Stories of the Ballets Ser.). (Illus.). 48p. 1985. 8.95 o.p. (ISBN 0-8120-5674-4). Barron.

Swan Prince. Mikhail Baryshnikov & Peter Anastos. LC 87-47574. 80p. 1987. 16.95 o.p. (ISBN 0-553-05218-7). Bantam.

Swan Song. Edmund Crispin. 192p. 1982. pap. 2.50 o.p. (ISBN 0-380-55145-4, 70020). Avon.

Swann. Dan Sherman. LC 78-57325. 1978. 8.95 o.p. (ISBN 0-87795-195-0, Arbor Hse). Morrow.

Swan's Island. Elizabeth Spires. 1985. pap. 8.95 o.p. (ISBN 0-03-004423-5, Owl Bks). H Holt & Co.

Swans of the World. Sylvia B. Wilmore. LC 74-3669. (Illus.). 224p. 1974. 14.95 o.s.i. (ISBN 0-8008-7524-9). Taplinger.

Swans of the World. Sylvia B. Wilmore. LC 74-3669. (Illus.). 1979. pap. 8.50 o.s.i. (ISBN 0-8008-7523-0). Taplinger.

Swansong. Richard Francis. LC 86-47661. 304p. 1986. 15.95 o.p. (ISBN 0-689-11843-0, Atheneum). Macmillan.

Swap Finance Service. 394p. 1986. pap. 240.00 o.p. (ISBN 0-8002-4073-1). Intl Pubns Serv.

Swapping Boy. John Langstaff et al. (Illus.). (gr. k-3). 1960. 6.50 o.p. (ISBN 0-15-283358-7, HJ). HarBraceJ.

Swastika. Robert Kail. 1979. pap. 2.25 o.p. (ISBN 0-505-51422-2, Pub. by Tower Bks). Dorchester Pub Co.

Swastika on the Synagogue Door. J. Leonard Romm. LC 83-27263. (Lazarus Family Mystery Ser.). 180p. (Orig.). (gr. 3-10). 1984. pap. 6.95 o.p. (ISBN 0-940646-53-6). Rossel Bks.

Swastika Outside Germany. Donald M. McKale. LC 77-22304. 288p. 1977. 19.00x o.p. (ISBN 0-87338-209-9). Kent St U Pr.

S.W.A.T Team Manual. R. Cappel. lib. bdg. cancelled o.s.i. (ISBN 0-8490-3669-0). Gordon Pr.

Swatting Flies. Robert Young & LaVonne Klohn. (Illus.). 96p. (gr. 4-8). 1984. wkbk 7.95 o.p. (ISBN 0-86653-175-0). Good Apple.

Sweat Equity: What it Really Takes to Build America's Best Small Companies - By the Guys Who Did It. Geoffrey Smith & Paul B. Brown. 246p. 1986. 17.45 o.s.i. (ISBN 0-671-55210-4). S&S.

Sweden. Brian McIlroy. (World Cinema Ser.: No. 2). (Illus.). 1988. 24.95 o.s.i. (ISBN 0-948911-48-4, Pub. by Flicks Books England). U of Ill Pr.

Sweden in the Nineteen Eighty's. Michael Stevenson. (Public Administration Ser.: P 1664). 13p. 1985. 2.00 o.p. (ISBN 0-89028-374-5). Vance Biblios.

Sweden in World Society: Thoughts about the Future. Future Studies, Secretariat, Stockholm, Sweden. LC 80-40321. (Illus.). 228p. 1980. 48.00 o.p. (ISBN 0-08-025456-X); pap. 23.00 o.p. (ISBN 0-08-025455-1). Pergamon.

Swedish America, 1914-1932. Sture Lindmark. 360p. 1971. 7.50 o.p. (ISBN 0-318-16622-4). Swedish-Am.

Swedish Arbetshafte. A. Svenssons. 116p. 1978. pap. 22.00x o.p. (ISBN 91-738-2449-6, S-211). Vanous.

Swedish Contributions to the Polish Resistance Movement During World War II. J. Lewandowski. 114p. (Orig.). 1979. pap. text ed. 16.50x o.p. (ISBN 0-317-46423-X, Pub. by Almqvist & Wiksell). Coronet Bks.

Swedish-English Dictionary of Technical Terms Used in Business, Industry, Administration, Education & Research. 2nd rev. & enl. ed. Ingvar E. Gullberg. (Swedish & Eng.). 150.00 o.p. (ISBN 91-1-775052-0). E J Brill USA.

Swedish-English Fact Ordbok (Technical Terms) 2nd ed. Ingvar E. Gullberg. (Swedish & Eng.). 1977. 225.00x o.p. (ISBN 91-177-5052-0, S-207). Vanous.

Swedish-English Technical Dictionary. Gullberg. 1722p. 225.00 o.p. (ISBN 91-177-5052-0, SW207). Vanous.

Swedish Export Directory, 1982. 63rd ed. Ed. by Swedish Trade Council Staff. LC 72-623267. 800p. (Orig.). 1982. 54.00x o.p. (ISBN 0-8002-3028-0). Intl Pubns Serv.

Sweeneys from 9D. Ethel Kessler & Leonard Kessler. LC 84-20156. (Illus.). 56p. (gr. 1-4). 1985. 9.95 o.s.i. (ISBN 0-02-750230-9). Macmillan.

Sweet Abandon. Wendy Lozano. 272p. 1980. pap. 2.25 o.p. (ISBN 0-380-75416-9, 75416). Avon.

Sweet Anarchy. Nathaniel Benchley. 304p. 1981. pap. 2.50 o.p. (ISBN 0-380-53777-X, 53777-X). Avon.

Sweet & Deadly. Charlaine Harris. 180p. 1981. 8.95 o.p. (ISBN 0-395-30532-2). HM.

Sweet & Hard Cider: Making It, Using It, & Enjoying It. rev. ed. Annie Proulx & Lew Nichols. LC 80-19701. (Illus.). 188p. 1984. pap. 9.95 o.p. (ISBN 0-88266-352-6, Garden Way Pub). Storey Comm Inc.

Sweet & Sour Hippo. Paul White. (Jungle Doctor Picture Fable Ser.). 21p. (gr. 1-7). 1986. Set of 8. pap. 26.50 o.p. (ISBN 0-85364-376-8, Pub. by Paternoster UK). Attic Pr.

Sweet Country. Caroline Richards. LC 78-14078. 1979. 9.95 o.p. (ISBN 0-15-187332-1). HarBraceJ.

Sweet Country. Caroline Richards. 1986. pap. 7.95 o.p. (ISBN 0-671-62285-4, Fireside). S&S.

Sweet Familiarity. Daoma Winston. LC 81-66963. 256p. 1981. 11.95 o.p. (ISBN 0-87795-331-7, Arbor Hse). Morrow.

Sweet Land of Liberty. O. Z. Tyler, Jr. LC 86-91399. (Illus.). 288p. 1987. text ed. 17.50 o.p. (ISBN 0-682-40315-6). Exposition-Phoenix.

Sweet Language: The Adventures of a Roman Lover. Roberto Costa. LC 83-90925. 191p. 1985. 10.95 o.p. (ISBN 0-533-05935-6). Vantage.

Sweet Life! Macrobiotic Desserts. Marcea Weber. (Illus.). 1981. pap. 12.50 o.p. (ISBN 0-87040-493-8). Japan Pubns USA.

Sweet Lou. Lou Pinella & Maury Allen. (Illus.). 1986. 16.95 o.p. (ISBN 0-399-13142-6). Putnam Pub Group.

Sweet Lucy. Players Magazine Staff. (Orig.). 1976. pap. 1.50 o.p. (ISBN 0-87067-813-2, BH813). Holloway.

Sweet Nutcracker. David Kossoff. LC 86-60935. (Illus.). 50p. (gr. 5-9). 1986. 8.95 o.p. (ISBN 0-88186-378-5, Pub. by Tarquin). Parkwest Pubns.

Sweet Pea. Jill Krementz. 1969. 5.95 o.p. (ISBN 0-15-283536-9, HJ). HarbraceJ.

Sweet Pea's Thank-You Book. (Antioch Little Shape Bks.). (Illus.). 22p. (ps-3). 1984. 2.50 o.p. (ISBN 0-89954-238-7). Antioch Pub Co.

Sweet Rome. Audrey Stainton. LC 81-7026. 320p. 1982. 15.50 o.p. (ISBN 0-03-059579-7). H Holt & Co.

Sweet Sounds of Life. Janelle C. Lapaglia. 1979. 5.00 o.p. (ISBN 0-682-49332-5). Exposition-Phoenix.

Sweet Talk. Michael Abbensetts. 1981. pap. 6.95 o.p. (ISBN 0-413-31470-7, 6473, Pub. by Eyre Methuen). Heinemann Ed.

Sweet Thunder. Lynn Scott-Drennan. LC 86-24222. (Starlight Romance Ser.). 192p. 1987. 12.95 o.p. (ISBN 0-385-23531-3). Doubleday.

Sweet Touch in Family Cooking. Sylvia Schur. LC 77-89548. 1978. 7.95 o.p. (ISBN 0-916752-19-4). Longman Trade.

Sweet Valley High, 4 vols, No. 1. Boxed Set. pap. 9.00 o.p. (ISBN 0-553-30853-X). Bantam.

Sweet Whispers, Brother Rush. Virginia Hamilton. 220p. (gr. 5 up). 1983. pap. 2.25 o.p. (ISBN 0-380-64824-5, Camelot). Avon.

Sweet William. Beryl Bainbridge. LC 75-43672. 192p. 1976. 7.95 o.s.i. (ISBN 0-8076-0816-5). Braziller.

Sweetbriar. Jude Deveraux. (Gregg Hardcovers Ser.). 1985. lib. bdg. 12.95 o.p. (ISBN 0-8398-2874-8, Gregg). G K Hall.

Sweetheart & Others. Seymour Chwast. 1975. pap. 3.25 o.p. (ISBN 0-380-00351-1, 23572-2). Avon.

Sweetheart, Don't Ask Me to Fix It. Lewis Kearns. (Illus.). 128p. 1987. text ed. 12.50 o.p. (ISBN 0-682-40342-3). Exposition-Phoenix.

Sweetly Sings the Donkey: Animal Rounds for Children to Sing or Play on Recorders. Ed. by John Langstaff. LC 76-9530. (Illus.). 32p. (gr. 3 up). 1976. 6.95 o.p. (ISBN 0-689-50063-7, Atheneum). Macmillan.

Sweets for Saints & Sinners. Janice Feuer. LC 80-21934. (Illus.). 144p. 1980. pap. 5.95 o.p. (ISBN 0-89286-180-0, One Hund One Prods). Ortho.

Sweets Without Guilt. Minuha Cannon. LC 80-18133. (Illus.). 150p. (Orig.). 1980. pap. 5.95 o.p. (ISBN 0-914788-30-2). Globe Pequot.

Swept Away No. 8: All Shook Up. Fran Lantz. 160p. (Orig.). 1987. pap. 2.50 o.p. (ISBN 0-380-75136-4, Flare). Avon.

Swept Away: Why Women Fear their Own Sexuality. Carol Cassell. 224p. 1984. 14.70 o.p. (ISBN 0-671-45238-X). S&S.

Swept Away: Why Women Fear Their Own Sexuality. Carol Cassell. 208p. 1985. pap. 3.95 o.p. (ISBN 0-553-25182-1). Bantam.

Swept in the Wave of Terror. Gloria Skurzynski. LC 85-4278. 160p. (gr. 4-7). 1985. 10.25 o.p. (ISBN 0-688-05820-5). Lothrop.

Swift & the Satirist's Art. Edward W. Rosenheim, Jr. LC 36-11400. (Midway Reprint Ser.). xii, 244p. 1982. pap. text ed. 14.00x o.s.i. (ISBN 0-226-72794-7). U of Chicago Pr.

Swift Corridor: Espionage Networks in Switzerland During World War II. Jozef Garlinski. (Illus.). 252p. 1981. 24.00x o.p. (ISBN 0-460-04351-X, Pub. by J. M. Dent England). Biblio Dist.

Swift to Hear, Slow to Speak. Jerry Butler. 1975. pap. 4.75 o.p. (ISBN 0-89137-511-2). Quality Pubns.

Swiftly Now. Carolyn Stoloff. LC 81-11150. 52p. 1982. lib. bdg. 13.95x o.p. (ISBN 0-8214-0646-9); pap. 6.95 o.p. (ISBN 0-8214-0647-7). Ohio U Pr.

Swift's Poetry 1900-1980: An Annotated Bibliography of Studies. David M. Vieth. (British Literature Ser.). 275p. 1982. lib. bdg. 43.00 o.p. (ISBN 0-8240-9393-3). Garland Pub.

Swim for Fitness. Marianne Brems. LC 78-32033. (Illus.). 1979. pap. 6.95 o.p. (ISBN 0-87701-124-9). Chronicle Bks.

Swimming Chickens & Other Half-Breasted Accounts of the Animal World. Colin McEnroe. 144p. 1987. 14.95 o.s.i. (ISBN 0-385-23993-9, Dolp). Doubleday.

Swimming Is for Me. Lowell A. Dickmeyer. LC 80-15366. (Sports for Me Bks.). (Illus.). (gr. 2-5). 1980. PLB 7.95 o.p. (ISBN 0-8225-1084-7). Lerner Pubns.

Swimming Pool Season. Rose Tremain. LC 85-2781. 1985. 16.45 o.s.i. (ISBN 0-671-50464-9). Summit Bks.

Swimmy. Leo Lionni. (Pinwheel Bks). (ps). 1963. pap. 2.95 o.s.i. (ISBN 0-394-82620-5). Pantheon.

Swinburne: The Critical Heritage. Ed. by Clyde K. Hyder. (Critical Heritage Ser.). 1984. pap. 15.00 o.p. (ISBN 0-7102-0398-5). Routledge Chapman & Hall.

Swine Production. 4th ed. J. L. Krider & W. E. Carroll. 1970. text ed. 45.95 o.p. (ISBN 0-07-035502-9, C). McGraw.

Swine Production & Nutrition. Wilson G. Pond & Jerome H. Maner. (Illus.). 733p. 1984. 64.95 o.s.i. (ISBN 0-87055-450-6). AVI.

Swineherd. Hans Christian Andersen. 1958. 3.25 o.p. (ISBN 0-15-283715-9, HJ). HarBraceJ.

Swing of the Gate. Roy Brown. LC 78-6422. 112p. (gr. 6 up). 1979. 6.95 o.p. (ISBN 0-395-28895-9, Clarion). HM.

Swingin' Texas Fiddlin' Moore et al. pap. 6.95 o.p. (ISBN 0-318-19423-6, Pub. by Peer-Southern). CPP Belwin.

Swiss Architecture: A General Sourcelist. Anthony G. White. (Architecture Ser.: A 1384). 9p. 1985. 2.00 o.p. (ISBN 0-89028-394-X). Vance Biblios.

Swiss Bank Accounts: Investments Through Swiss Banks. William Von Graz. LC 88-92323. 64p. (Orig.). 1988. pap. 15.95 o.p. H W Parker.

Swiss Capital Market. Henri M. Neier. 130p. 1983. 120.00 o.p. (ISBN 0-8002-3403-0). Intl Pubns Serv.

Swiss Civil Code: English Version, with Vocabularies & Notes, 4 vols. Ivy Williams. 1976. Repr. of 1923 ed. Set. lib. bdg. 100.00x o.p. (ISBN 0-686-81316-2); Vol. 1. (ISBN 3-85856-000-6); Vol. 2. (ISBN 3-85856-002-2); Vol. 3. (ISBN 3-85856-003-0); Vol. 4. (ISBN 3-85856-004-9). Rothman.

Swiss Conspiracy. Michael Stanley. 1976. pap. 1.95 o.p. (ISBN 0-380-00492-5, 34082). Avon.

Swiss Country Inns & Chalets. Karen Brown & Clare Brown. LC 83-51721. (Country Inns Travel Guide Ser.). (Illus., Orig.). 1984. pap. 9.95 o.p. (ISBN 0-930328-04-3). Travel Pr.

Swiss Export Products & Services Directory, 1983-85. 14th ed. Swiss Office for the Development of Trade, Geneva Staff. LC 53-19872. 920p. 1982. 82.00x o.s.i. (ISBN 0-8002-3059-0). Intl Pubns Serv.

Swiss Family Robinson. Johann Wyss. (Illus.). (gr. 4-6). PLB 3.79 o.p. (ISBN 0-448-13454-3, G&D); deluxe ed. 12.95 o.p. (ISBN 0-448-06022-1). Putnam Pub Group.

Switch. William Bayer. 1984. 14.70 o.p. (ISBN 0-671-49424-4, Linden Pr). S&S.

Switch. William Bayer. (General Ser.). 420p. 1986. lib. bdg. 17.95 o.p. (ISBN 0-8161-4037-5, Large Print Bks). G K Hall.

Switchgear & Control Handbook. R. W. Smeaton. 1977. text ed. 65.00 o.p. (ISBN 0-07-058439-7). McGraw.

Switching & Linear Power Supply, Power Converter Design. Abraham I. Pressman. (Illus.). 1977. text ed. 25.95 o.p.; net solutions manual 1.95 o.p. (ISBN 0-8104-5827-6). Sams.

Switching & Linear Power Supply, Power Converter Design. Raytheon Company Staff & Abraham I. Pressman. 384p. 1986. 39.95 o.p. (ISBN 0-8104-5847-0). Sams.

Switzerland a Phaidon Cultural Guide. Phaidon Press Limited Staff. 480p. 1985. 17.95 o.p. (ISBN 0-13-879774-1). P-H.

Switzerland: An International Banking & Financial Center. Max Ikle. Tr. by Eric Schiff from Ger. LC 72-76544. 156p. 1982. 41.95 o.p. (ISBN 0-87933-002-3). Van Nos Reinhold.

Switzerland Country Travel Guide. Berlitz Editors. (Travel Guides Ser.). 1985. pap. 7.95 o.p. (ISBN 0-317-12283-5, Berlitz). Macmillan.

Switzerland for Beginners. George Mikes. (Illus.). 86p. 1975. 9.95 o.p. Andre Deutsch.

Switzerland French Speaking Travel Guide. Berlitz Editors. (Travel Guides Ser.). 1979. pap. 4.95 o.p. (ISBN 0-317-12281-9, Berlitz). Macmillan.

Switzerland Travel Guide. Berlitz Editors. (Travel Guides for German Speakers Ser.). 1978. pap. 4.95 o.p. (ISBN 0-02-969540-6, Berlitz). Macmillan.

Sword & the Centuries: Or Old Sword Days & Old Sword Ways. Alfred Hutton. LC 72-130411. (Illus.). 392p. 1970. 14.50 o.p. (ISBN 0-8048-0943-7). C E Tuttle.

Sword & the Sundial. Phyllis Prokop. (gr. 5 up). 1981. pap. 2.95 o.p. (ISBN 0-89191-376-9, 53769). Cook.

Sword Hunters of the Hamran Arabs see Nile Tributaries of Abyssinia, & the Sword Hunters of the Hamran Arabs.

Sword Is Forged. Evangeline Walton. 347p. 1983. 15.50 o.s.i. (ISBN 0-671-46490-6, Timescape). PB.

Sword of Aldones. Marion Zimmer Bradley. LC 77-4513. (Darkover Ser.). 1977. Repr. of 1962 ed. lib. bdg. 11.50 o.p. (ISBN 0-8398-2367-3, Gregg). G K Hall.

Sword of Aldones see Planet Savers.

Sword of Aradel. Alexander Key. LC 76-54893. (gr. 5-9). 1977. 7.50 o.s.i. (ISBN 0-664-32609-9, Westminster). Westminster John Knox.

Sword of Gnosis: Metaphysics, Cosmology, Tradition, Symbolism. Ed. by John Needleman. 448p. 1986. pap. 10.95 o.p. (ISBN 0-317-40557-8). Routledge Chapman & Hall.

Sword of His Mouth. Robert C. Tannehill. Ed. by William A. Beardslee. LC 75-18948. (Semeia Studies). 236p. 1976. pap. 7.95 o.p. (ISBN 0-8006-1501-8, 1-1501, Fortress). Augsburg Fortress.

Sword of Laban, 2 vols. rev. ed. F. Edward Butterworth. 1985. Vol. 1. 30.00 o.p. (ISBN 0-8309-0422-0). Vol. 2. Herald Hse.

Sword of No-Sword: Life of the Master Warrior Tesshu. John Stevens. LC 84-5468. (Illus.). 184p. 1984. 14.95 o.p. (ISBN 0-87773-284-1, 72770-3). Shambhala Pubns.

Sword of Winter. Marta Randall. 288p. 1983. 14.50 o.s.i. (ISBN 0-671-47543-6, Timescape). PB.

Swords of WWII Germany. Thomas M. Johnson & John R. Omsby. (Illus.). 66p. pap. 5.00 o.p. (ISBN 0-317-55220-1). Johnson Ref Bks.

Swordwield. Aedric. 240p. 1987. 10.95 o.p. (ISBN 0-8062-3046-0). Carlton.

Sybelle. Roberta Gellis. (Roselynde Chronicles Ser.). 1984. lib. bdg. 13.95 o.p. (ISBN 0-8398-2865-9, Gregg). G K Hall.

SYBEX Computer Blue Book. National Association of Computer Dealers (NACD) Staff. 421p. (Orig.). 1987. pap. 9.95 o.p. (ISBN 0-89588-460-7). Sybex.

SYBEX Computer Blue Books. National Association of Computer Dealers (NACD) Staff. 354p. (Orig.). 1988. pap. 9.95 o.p. (ISBN 0-89588-526-3). Sybex.

SYBEX Personal Computer Dictionary. Sybex Staff & Rodnay Zaks. LC 83-51824. 121p. (Eng., Ger., Span., Ital., Fr. & Pol.). 1984. pap. 3.95 o.p. (ISBN 0-89588-199-3). SYBEX.

SYBEX WordPerfect Study Guide. Milano et al. 175p. (Orig.). 1987. pap. 10.95 o.p. (ISBN 0-89588-434-8). Sybex.

Sycamore Steeple. Suzanne P. Ellison. 224p. 1987. pap. 5.95 o.p. (ISBN 0-310-47721-2, 15625P). Zondervan.

Sycamore Stories. Jerome Koch. pap. 3.50 o.p. (ISBN 0-8006-1945-5, 1-1945). Augsburg Fortress.

Sycamore Year. Mildred Lee. LC 74-6409. 160p. (gr. 6 up). 1974. 11.75 o.p. (ISBN 0-688-41643-8); PLB 11.88 o.p. (ISBN 0-688-51643-2). Lothrop.

Sydney Micro Skills Redeveloped: Series One Handbook. Ed. by Cliff Turney. (Teaching Skills Development Project Ser.). 140p. (Orig.). 1983. pap. text ed. 11.00x o.p. (ISBN 0-424-00102-0, Pub. by Sydney U Pr Australia). Intl Spec Bk.

Sydney Micro Skills Redeveloped: Series Two Handbook. Ed. by Cliff Turney. (Teaching Skills Development Project Ser.). 162p. (Orig.). 1983. pap. text ed. 11.00x o.p. (ISBN 0-424-00104-7, Pub. by Sydney U Pr Australia). Intl Spec Bk.

Sydney Micro Skills, Series 3 Handbook: Classroom Management & Discipline. C. Turney & L. C. Cairns. (Illus.). 1976. pap. 10.00x o.p. (ISBN 0-424-00025-3, Pub. by Sydney U Pr). Intl Spec Bk.

Sydney Micro Skills, Series 4 Handbook: Guiding Small Group Discussion, Small Group Teaching & Individualized Instruction. C. Turney et al. (Illus.). 1976. pap. 10.00x o.p. (ISBN 0-424-00026-1, Pub. by Sydney U Pr). Intl Spec Bk.

Sydney Micro Skills Series 5 Handbook: Guiding Discovery Learning & Fostering Creativity. C. Turney et al. (Illus.). 1977. pap. 10.00x o.p. (ISBN 0-424-00042-3, Pub. by Sydney U Pr). Intl Spec Bk.

Sydney Smith. George W. E. Russell. LC 79-156929. 254p. 1971. Repr. of 1905 ed. 35.00x o.p. (ISBN 0-8103-3720-7). Gale.

Sydney the Koala. (Zoo Babies Ser.). 16p. (gr. k-6). 1982. pap. 1.25 o.p. (ISBN 0-8249-8033-6). Ideals.

Syllabus of Problem Oriented Patient Care. Francis A. Neelon & George Ellis. 1974. spiral binding 12.00 o.p. (ISBN 0-316-59980-8). Little.

Sylvan Beach, New York. Jack Henke. (Illus.). 226p. 1983. 11.95 o.s.i. (ISBN 0-932052-18-5). North Country.

Sylvester & the Magic Pebble. William Steig. LC 69-14484. (Illus.). 30p. (gr. 1 up). 1979. pap. 4.95 o.s.i. (ISBN 0-671-96022-9). Windmill Bks.

Sylvia Plath & Ted Hughes. Margaret D. Uroff. LC 79-74. 245p. 1979. 22.95 o.p. (ISBN 0-252-00734-4). U of Ill Pr.

Sylvia Plimack Mangold Paintings: 1965-1982. (Illus.). 48p. 1983. 11.95 o.p. (ISBN 0-913883-05-0). Madison Art.

Sylvia Porter's Income Tax Book, 1982. Sylvia Porter. 184p. (Orig.). 1981. pap. 3.95 o.p. (ISBN 0-380-77925-0, 77925). Avon.

Sylvia Porter's Income Tax Book, 1983. Sylvia Porter. 176p. 1982. pap. 3.95 o.p. (ISBN 0-380-81687-3, 81687-3). Avon.

Sylvia Porter's Income Tax Book, 1984. Sylvia Porter. 192p. 1983. pap. 4.95 o.p. (ISBN 0-380-85555-0, 85555). Avon.

Sylvia Porter's Income Tax Book, 1985. Sylvia Porter. 192p. 1984. pap. 5.95 o.p. (ISBN 0-380-89496-3). Avon.

Sylvia Porter's Money Book. Sylvia Porter. 1976. pap. 6.95 o.p. (ISBN 0-380-00638-3, 40089). Avon.

Sylvia Porter's Personel 1987 Income Tax Book. Sylvia Porter. 200p. 1986. pap. 5.95 o.p. (ISBN 0-380-89994-9). Avon.

Sylvia Porter's Tax Book, 1981. Sylvia Porter. 1981. pap. 3.95 o.p. (ISBN 0-380-76752-X, 76752). Avon.

Sylvia Porter's Tax Guide, 1986. Sylvia Porter. 1985. pap. 5.95 o.p. (ISBN 0-380-89993-0). Avon.

Sylvia Porter's Three Hundred & Eighty Five Tax-Saving Tips: How to Profit from the New Tax Law. Sylvia Porter. 1987. pap. 6.95 o.p. (ISBN 0-380-89995-7). Avon.

Sylvia Porter's Your Own Money. Sylvia Porter. 768p. 1983. pap. 12.95 o.p. (ISBN 0-380-83527-4, 83527-4). Avon.

Symbiotic Imperative: A Blueprint for Living Together Campatibly. W. D. Taylor. 165p. 1981. 9.50 o.p. (ISBN 0-682-49675-8). Exposition-Phoenix.

Symbol & Politics in Communal Ideology: Cases & Questions. Ed. by Sally F. Moore & Barbara G. Myerhoff. LC 75-16810. (Symbol, Myth & Ritual Ser.). (Illus.). 240p. 1975. 24.50x o.p. (ISBN 0-8014-0988-8); pap. 9.95x o.p. (ISBN 0-8014-9157-6). Cornell U Pr.

Symbol of Man. G. Wilson Knight. LC 81-40003. (Illus.). 194p. 1981. lib. bdg. 25.50 o.p. (ISBN 0-8191-1588-6); pap. text ed. 11.50 o.p. (ISBN 0-8191-1589-4). U Pr of Amer.

Symbol Sourcebook: An Authoritative Guide to International Graphic Symbols. Ed. by Henry Dreyfuss. LC 71-172261. (Illus.). 320p. 1972. text ed. 71.50 o.p. (ISBN 0-07-017837-2). McGraw.

Symbol, Status, & Personality. Samuel I. Hayakawa. LC 63-1772. 1963. 7.50 o.p. (ISBN 0-15-187610-X). HarBraceJ.

Symbolic & Algebraic Computation: EUROSAM Seventy-Nine: an International Symposium. Ed. by E. W. Ng. (Lecture Notes in Computer Science: Vol. 72). 1979. pap. 30.00 o.p. (ISBN 0-387-09519-5). Springer-Verlag.

Symbolic Domination: Cultural Symbols & Historical Change in Morocco. Paul Rabinow. LC 74-7565. (Midway Reprint). 1978. pap. text ed. 10.00x o.s.i. (ISBN 0-226-70149-2). U of Chicago Pr.

Symbolic Images: Studies in the Art of the Renaissance, No. II. E. H. Gombrich. LC 84-28111. (Illus.). xii, 356p. 1985. pap. 14.95 o.s.i. (ISBN 0-226-30217-2). U of Chicago Pr.

Symbolic Life. C. G. Jung. 1985. 10.00x o.p. (ISBN 0-317-62191-2, Guild of Pastoral Psych). State Mutual Bk.

Symbolic Method of Coleridge, Baudelaire, & Yeats. Anca Vlasopolos. LC 82-20079. 232p. 1983. 24.95x o.p. (ISBN 0-8143-1730-8). Wayne St U Pr.

Symbolic Process & Its Integration in Children: A Study in Social Psychology. John F. Markey. LC 78-56924. (Midway Reprint Ser.). 1978. pap. text ed. 9.00x o.s.i. (ISBN 0-226-50585-5). U of Chicago Pr.

Symbolic Profile. Ruth T. Fry & Joyce Hall. LC 76-5085. 94p. 1976. 16.00x o.p. (ISBN 0-87201-815-6). Gulf Pub.

Symbolic Prophecy of the Great Pyramid. 16th ed. H. Spencer Lewis. LC 37-3808. 192p. 1982. 8.95 o.p. (ISBN 0-912057-13-0, G-514). AMORC.

Symbolic Sit-Ins: Protest Occupations at the California Capitol. John Lofland & Michael Fink. LC 81-40725. 128p. (Orig.). 1982. PLB 26.25 o.p. (ISBN 0-8191-2503-2); pap. text ed. 9.75 o.p. (ISBN 0-8191-2504-0). U Pr of Amer.

Symbolicarum Quaestionum de Universo Genere. Achille Bocchi. Ed. by Stephen Orgel. LC 78-68188. (Philosophy of Images Ser: Vol. 5). 1979. lib. bdg. 80.00 o.p. (ISBN 0-8240-3679-4). Garland Pub.

Symbolism in Greek Mythology: Human Desire & Its Transformations. Paul Diel. Tr. by Vincent Stuart et al from Fr. LC 79-67686. 240p. 1980. 20.00 o.p. (ISBN 0-87773-178-0, 51083-6). Shambhala Pubns.

Symbolism in Poland: Collected Essays. Commentary by Wieslaw Juszczak et al. (Illus.). 64p. 1984. Set only. pap. 20.00 o.p. (ISBN 0-89558-107-8). Detroit Inst Arts.

Symbolism in Polish Painting 1890-1914. Intro. by Patrice Marandel. (Illus.). 164p. 1984. pap. 8.00 o.p. (ISBN 0-89558-104-3). Detroit Inst Arts.

Symbolism of the East & West. Harriet G. Murray-Aynsley. LC 77-141748. (Illus.). 238p. 1971. Repr. of 1900 ed. 43.00x o.p. (ISBN 0-8103-3395-3). Gale.

Symbolism: The Universal Language. J. C. Cooper. LC 86-18838. 128p. 1986. lib. bdg. 19.95x o.p. (ISBN 0-8095-7001-7). Borgo Pr.

Symbols & Civilization: Science, Religion, Morals, Art. Ralph Ross. LC 62-21848. 1963. pap. 3.25 o.p. (ISBN 0-15-687605-1, Harv). HarBraceJ.

Symbols & the Self. rev. ed. Violet M. Shelley. 1976. pap. 3.95 o.p. (ISBN 0-87604-092-X). ARE Pr.

Symbols & Their Meaning. Rolf Myller. LC 77-17015. (Illus.). (gr. 4-6). 1978. 9.95 o.p. (ISBN 0-689-30638-5, Atheneum). Macmillan.

Symbols Around Us. Sven T. Achen. 240p. 1981. pap. 14.95 o.p. (ISBN 0-442-28261-3). Van Nos Reinhold.

Symbols of Religious Faith. Ben F. Kimpel. 1954. (ISBN 0-8022-0861-4). Philos Lib.

Symbols of Sovereignty. Brian Barker. (Illus.). 254p. 1979. 21.50x o.p. (ISBN 0-8476-6192-X). Rowman.

Symbols of the Faith. Warner L. Hall. (Illus., Orig.). (gr. 7-11). 1965. pap. 1.50 o.p. (ISBN 0-8042-9343-0, John Knox). Westminster John Knox.

Symbols of Transformation in Poetry. Alan Hobson. 1985. 10.00x o.p. (ISBN 0-317-62198-X, Guild of Pastoral Psych). State Mutual Bk.

Symmetric Generalized Topological Structures. C. J. Mozzochi et al. LC 76-15121. 1976. text ed. 7.50 o.p. (ISBN 0-682-48584-5, University). Exposition-Phoenix.

Symmetric Hilbert Spaces & Related Topics. A. Guichardet. LC 72-76390. (Lecture Notes in Mathematics: Vol. 261). 102p. 1972. pap. 15.00 o.p. (ISBN 0-387-05803-6). Springer-Verlag.

Symmetries in Elementary Particle Physics. Ed. by A. Zichichi. 1965. pap. 43.00 o.p. (ISBN 0-12-780556-7). Acad Pr.

Symmetries in Nuclear Structure. Ed. by K. Abrahams et al. LC 83-2455. (NATO ASI Series B, Physics: Vol. 93). (Illus.). 312p. 1983. 57.50x o.p. (ISBN 0-306-41341-8, Plenum Pr). Plenum Pub.

Symmetries In Science I. Ed. by Bruno Gruber & Richard S. Millman. LC 80-18665. 506p. 1980. 75.00x o.p. (ISBN 0-306-40541-5, Plenum Pr). Plenum Pub.

Symmetry & Chirality. C. A. Mead. LC 51-5497. (Topics in Current Chemistry: Vol. 49). (Illus.). 90p. 1974. 22.00 o.p. (ISBN 0-387-06705-1). Springer-Verlag.

Symmetry & Function of Biological Systems at the Macromolecular Level: Proceedings of the Eleventh Nobel Symposium. Ed. by Arne Engstrom & Bror Strandberg. (Illus.). 436p. 1969. text ed. 37.50x o.p. (Pub. by Almqvist & Wiksell). Coronet Bks.

Symmetry in Chemistry. H. H. Jaffe & Milton M. Orchin. LC 76-7534. 206p. 1977. pap. text ed. 8.50 o.p. (ISBN 0-88275-414-9). Krieger.

Symmetry in Coordination Chemistry. John P. Fackler, Jr. 1971. 9.00 o.p. (ISBN 0-12-247540-2); pap. 7.25 o.p. (ISBN 0-12-247550-X). Acad Pr.

Symmetry of Many Electron Systems. I. G. Kaplan. 1975. 85.50 o.p. (ISBN 0-12-397150-0). Acad Pr.

Sympathetic History of Jonestown: The Moore Family Involvement in Peoples Temple. Rebecca Moore. LC 85-11632. (Studies in Religion & Society: Vol. 14). (Illus.). 448p. 1985. lib. bdg. 69.95x o.p. (ISBN 0-88946-860-5). E Mellen.

Symphonie Pastorale: Roman. Andre Gide. 1953. pap. 7.95 o.p. (ISBN 0-685-11579-8). Schoenhof.

Symphonies of Havergal Brian. Malcolm MacDonald. LC 78-110357. (Illus.). 1978. Vol. 1. symphonies 1 to 12 11.95 o.s.i. (ISBN 0-8008-7527-3, Crescendo); Vol. 2. symphonies 13 to 29 13.95 o.s.i. (ISBN 0-8008-7528-1). Taplinger.

Symphonies of Havergal Brian, Vol.3. Malcolm MacDonald. LC 78-110357. 256p. 1984. 13.95 o.s.i. (ISBN 0-8008-7530-3, Crescendo). Taplinger.

Symphonies of Ralph Vaughan Williams. Elliot S. Schwartz. Date not set. price not set o.p. U of Mass Pr.

Symphony. Louise Cuyler. (History of Musical Forms Ser). 1973. pap. text ed. 6.95 o.p. (ISBN 0-15-585076-8, HC). HarBraceJ.

Symphony Encore: Program Notes. Dick Andersen. LC 84-72623. (Illus.). 281p. 1984. 21.95 o.p. (ISBN 0-89588-247-7). SYBEX.

Symphony Encore: Program Notes see Andersen's Symphony Tips & Tricks.

Symphony for the Devil: The Rolling Stones Story. Philip Norman. (Illus.). 448p. 1984. 17.45 o.p. (ISBN 0-671-44975-3, Linden Pr). S&S.

Symphony: Structure & Style. Roland Nadeau. 1974. pap. 7.50 o.s.i. (ISBN 0-8008-7526-5, Crescendo). Taplinger.

Symphony User's Handbook. Weber Systems, Inc. Staff. 1985. pap. 14.95 o.p. (ISBN 0-345-32376-9). Ballantine.

Symposia, Vols. 5 & 6. Phytochemical Society of North America Staff. Ed. by V. C. Runeckles & T. C. Tso. Incl. Vol. 5. Structural & Functional Aspects of Phytochemistry. 1972. 67.00 (ISBN 0-12-612405-1); Vol. 6. Terpenoids: Structure, Biogenesis, Distribution. 1973. 51.00 (ISBN 0-12-612406-X). Acad Pr.

Symposium on Aspirin & Related Drugs: Their Action & Uses. Ed. by K. D. Rainsford et al. (Illus.). pap. cancelled o.s.i. (ISBN 3-7643-0902-4). Adlers Foreign Bks.

Symposium on Cataract Surgery. New Orleans Academy of Ophthalmology Staff. 1984. 67.00 o.p. (ISBN 0-8016-3821-6). Mosby.

Symposium on Computer Applications in Medical Care, 9th 1985: Proceedings. 913p. 1985. 88.00 o.p. (ISBN 0-8186-0647-9, Q647); microfiche 88.00 o.p. (ISBN 0-8186-4647-0). IEEE Comp Soc.

Symposium on Ethics: The Role of Moral Values in Contemporary Thought. Bernard D. Ouden. 104p. (Orig.). 1983. lib. bdg. 25.25 o.p. (ISBN 0-8191-2763-9); pap. text ed. 9.75 o.p. (ISBN 0-8191-2764-7). U Pr of Amer.

Symposium on Free Radicals in Biological Systems. Ed. by M. S. Blois. 1961. 82.50 o.p. (ISBN 0-12-107550-8). Acad Pr.

Symposium on Frontiers in Reconstructive Microsurgery, Vol. 24. Buncke & Furnas. 1984. cloth 88.95 o.p. (ISBN 0-8016-1714-6). Mosby.

Symposium on Idiopathic Low Back Pain. American Academy of Orthopedic Surgeons Staff. Ed. by Agustus A. White & Stephen L. Gordon. (Illus.). 448p. 1982. text ed. 65.00 o.p. (ISBN 0-8016-0059-6). Mosby.

Symposium on Materials Review for 1972: Proceedings of a Meeting Held April 11-13, 1972, Los Angeles, California, Vol. 17. 322p. 1972. 20.00 o.p. (ISBN 0-938994-16-6). SAMPE.

Symposium on Medical & Surgical Diseases of the Retina & Vitreous. New Orleans Academy of Ophthalmology Staff. 1983. 65.00 o.p. (ISBN 0-8016-3672-8). Mosby.

Symposium on Photomorphogenesis. Ed. by Song Pill-Soon. 1978. pap. 21.00 o.p. (ISBN 0-08-022677-9). Pergamon.

Symposium on Surface Area Determination: Proceedings, Additional Publication, Bristol, U. K., 16-18 July 1969. International Union of Pure & Applied Chemistry. Ed. by R. H. Ottewill. 416p. 1976. 110.00 o.p. (ISBN 0-08-020818-5). Pergamon.

Symposium on the Foot & Ankle. American Academy of Orthopaedic Surgeons Staff. Ed. by Richard H. Kiene & Kenneth A. Johnson. LC 82-21716. (Illus.). 250p. 1983. text ed. 57.00 o.p. (ISBN 0-8016-0133-9). Mosby.

Symposium on the Foot & Leg in Running Sports. American Academy of Orthopaedic Surgeons Staff. LC 82-8188. (Illus.). 208p. 1982. text ed. 50.00 o.p. (ISBN 0-8016-0054-5). Mosby.

Symposium on the Numerical Treatment of O.D.E. Integral & Integro-Differential Equations. Rome 1960. 680p. 1961. 36.95x o.p. (ISBN 0-8176-0378-6). Birkhauser.

Symposium on the Thermal & Hydraulic Aspects of Nuclear Reactor Safety - Light Water Reactors, Vol. 1. Ed. by O. C. Jones, Jr. & S. G. Bankoff. 1977. pap. text ed. 25.00 o.p. (ISBN 0-685-86878-8, G00127). ASME.

Symposium on Vascular Malformations & Melanotic Lesions, Vol. 22. H. Bruce Williams. LC 82-6422. (Illus.). 421p. 1982. text ed. 86.95 o.p. (ISBN 0-8016-5602-8). Mosby.

Symptoms & Illness. David Locker. 1981. 29.95x o.p. (ISBN 0-422-77460-X, NO.6498, Pub. by Tavistock). Routledge Chapman & Hall.

Symptoms & Signs in Clinical Medicine. 10th ed. C. Ogilvie. (Illus.). 1980. 38.00 o.p. (ISBN 0-7236-0530-0, Pub. by John Wright UK). Butterworth.

Symptoms: The Complete Home Medical Encyclopedia. Ed. by Sigmund S. Miller. 672p. 1978. pap. 9.95 o.p. (ISBN 0-380-01896-9, 69617-7). Avon.

Synagogue Havurot: A Comparative Study. Gerald B. Bubis & Harry Wasserman. LC 82-23912. 160p. (Orig.). 1983. lib. bdg. 27.00 o.p. (ISBN 0-8191-2969-0, Co-pub. by Ctr Jewish Comm Studies); pap. text ed. 11.25 o.p. (ISBN 0-8191-2970-4). U Pr of Amer.

Synapse. rev. ed. E. G. Gray. Ed. by J. J. Head. LC 76-53173. (Carolina Biology Readers Ser.: No. 35). (Illus.). 16p. (gr. 10 up). 1977. pap. 1.80 o.p. (ISBN 0-89278-235-8, 45-9635). Carolina Biological.

Synaptic Constituents in Health & Disease: Proceedings of the Third Meeting of the European Society for Neurochemistry, Bled, August 31st-Sept, 5th, 1980. Ed. by M. Brzin et al. (Illus.). 760p. 1980. 180.00 o.p. (ISBN 0-08-025921-9). Pergamon.

Synchronization of EEG Activity in Epilepsies: Proceedings of the Austrian Academy of Sciences Symposium, Vienna, 1971. Austrian Academy of Sciences Symposium Staff. Ed. by H. Petsche & Mary A. Brazier. LC 72-75730. (Illus.). 440p. 1973. 95.00 o.p. (ISBN 0-387-81064-1). Springer-Verlag.

Synchrotron Radiation. A. A. Sokolov. 1969. 70.00 o.p. (ISBN 0-08-012945-5). Pergamon.

Syncretic Society. Felipe G. Casals. Ed. by Alfred G. Meyer. Tr. by Guy Daniels from Fr. LC 80-5455. 100p. 1980. 35.00 o.p. (ISBN 0-87332-176-6). M E Sharpe.

Syndicalist, Vols. 1-3. 1970. Repr. lib. bdg. 64.50x o.p. (ISBN 0-8371-9386-9, SY00). Greenwood.

Syndicated Loans. Robert P. McDonald. 240p. 1983. 120.00 o.p. (ISBN 0-8002-3424-3). Intl Pubns Serv.

Syndrome. Barbara Pronin. 304p. 1986. pap. 3.50 o.p. (ISBN 0-380-89623-0). Avon.

Synergetics-A Workshop: Proceedings of the International Workshop on Synergetics at Schloss Elmau, Bavaria, Germany, May 2-7,1977. Ed. by H. Haken. (Illus.). 1981. 36.00 o.p. (ISBN 0-387-08483-5). Springer-Verlag.

Synergistic Management: Creating the Climate for Superior Performance. Michael Doctoroff. (Illus.). 1978. 13.95 o.p. (ISBN 0-8144-5445-3). AMACOM.

Synergists. Ed. by Dorothy Walters. (Illus.). 269p. 1984. 16.95 o.p. (ISBN 0-934344-14-0, Pub. by Royal CBS). Fell.

Synfuels Engineering. Chemical Engineering Magazine Editors. (Illus.). 300p. 1982. text ed. 46.50 o.p. (ISBN 0-07-010698-3). McGraw.

Synfuels Industry Development. Richard F. Hill. LC 80-65895. (Illus.). 168p. 1980. pap. text ed. 25.00 o.p. (ISBN 0-86587-083-7). Gov Insts.

Synfuels Industry Opportunities. Ed. by Richard F. Hill et al. Elliot B. Boardman & Martin L. Heavner. LC 80-84730. 178p. 1981. text ed. 32.50 o.p. (ISBN 0-86587-088-8). Gov Insts.

Synge: Complete Plays. 3.95 o.p. (ISBN 0-317-31487-4, 3502). Routledge Chapman & Hall.

Synopsis of American History: Complete Volume. 5th ed. Charles Sellers et al. 1981. pap. 18.95 o.p. (ISBN 0-395-30735-X); Vol. 1. pap. 14.50 o.p. (ISBN 0-395-30736-8); Vol. 2. pap. 14.50 o.p. (ISBN 0-395-30737-6). HM.

Synopsis of Anaesthesia. 9th ed. R. S. Atkinson et al. (Illus.). 976p. 1982. pap. text ed. 42.00 o.p. (ISBN 0-7236-0621-8). Butterworth.

Synopsis of Biological Data on Saccorhiza Polyschides. T. A. Norton. (Fisheries Synopses: No. 83). 28p. 1970. pap. 7.50 o.p. (ISBN 92-5-101899-5, F1766, FAO). UNIPUB.

Synopsis of Biological Data on the Norway Lobster: Nephrops Norvegicus (Linnaeus, 1758) A. S. Farmer. (Fisheries Synopses: No. 112). (Illus.). 97p. 1975. pap. 7.50 o.p. (ISBN 92-5-101906-1, F845, FAO). UNIPUB.

Synopsis of California Stalk - Eyed Crustacea. Samuel J. Holmes. (California Academy of Sciences, Occasional Papers: No. 7). (Illus.). 262p. 1900. 37.00 o.p. (ISBN 0-384-24040-2). Johnson Repr.

Synopsis of Cardiology. S. C. Jordan. (Illus.). 352p. 1979. pap. 22.00 o.p. (ISBN 0-7236-0533-5, Pub. by John Wright UK). Butterworth.

Synopsis of Children's Diseases. 5th ed. Rendle-Short & Gray. 806p. 1978. 32.50 o.p. (ISBN 0-7236-0416-9, Pub. by John Wright UK). Butterworth.

Synopsis of Endocrinology & Metabolism. 2nd ed. I. Ramsay. 224p. 1980. pap. 20.00 o.p. (ISBN 0-7236-0485-1, Pub. by John Wright UK). Butterworth.

Synopsis of Gastroenterology. R. H. Salter. 176p. 1980. pap. 35.00 o.p. (ISBN 0-7236-0536-X, Pub. by John Wright UK). Butterworth.

Synopsis of Gynecologic Oncology. 2nd ed. C. Paul Morrow & Duane E. Townsend. LC 80-22384. (Clinical Monographs in Obstetrics & Gynecology). 488p. 1981. 40.00 o.p. (ISBN 0-471-06504-8, Pub. by Wiley-Med). Wiley.

Synopsis of Occupational Medicine. Tyrer & Lee. 192p. 1979. pap. 19.50 o.p. (ISBN 0-7236-0513-0, Pub. by John Wright UK). Butterworth.

Synopsis of Ophthalmology. J. Martin-Doyle. (Illus.). 300p. 1975. 22.50 o.p. (ISBN 0-7236-0446-0, Pub. by John Wright UK). Butterworth.

Synopsis of Opthamology: The Opthamology Book. 6th ed. Havener. 1984. pap. 34.95 o.p. (ISBN 0-8016-2121-6). Mosby.

Synopsis of Otolaryngology. 3rd ed. Ballantyne & Groves. 614p. 1978. 41.50 o.p. (ISBN 0-7236-0460-6, Pub. by John Wright UK). Butterworth.

Synopsis of Renal Diseases. Alex M. Davison. (Illus.). 192p. 1981. pap. text ed. 21.00 o.p. (ISBN 0-7236-0569-6, Pub. by John Wright UK). Butterworth.

Synopsis of Surgery. 5th ed. Richard D. Liechty & Robert T. Soper. LC 80-12884. (Illus.). 716p. 1985. pap. text ed. 41.95 o.p. (ISBN 0-8016-3099-1). Mosby.

Synopsis of Surgical Anatomy. 11th ed. D. DuPlessis. (Illus.). 900p. 1975. 36.00 o.p. (ISBN 0-7236-0384-7, Pub. by John Wright UK). Butterworth.

Synopsis of the Biology of the Middle American Highland Frog Rana Maculata Brocchi. Jaime Villa. (Contributions in Biology & Geology Ser.: No. 21). 1979. 1.00 o.p. (ISBN 0-89326-037-1). Milwaukee Pub Mus.

Synopsis: Past-Present-Future. Worth S. Rough. LC 84-90177. 84p. 1984. 17.95 o.p. (ISBN 0-533-06227-6). Vantage.

Synoptic Abstract. Joseph B. Tyson & Thomas R. W. Longstaff. Ed. by J. Arthur Baird & David Noel Freedman. (The Computer Bible Ser.: Vol. XV). 1978. pap. 15.00 o.p. (ISBN 0-935106-05-7). Biblical Res Assocs.

Synoptic Classification of Living Organisms. R. S. Barnes. LC 84-1237. (Illus.). 276p. (Orig.). pap. text ed. 16.95x cancelled o.s.i. (ISBN 0-87893-048-5). Sinauer Assocs.

Synoptic Climatology: Methods & Applications. R. G. Barry & A. H. Perry. 500p. 1973. 66.00x o.p. (ISBN 0-416-08500-8, 2078). Routledge Chapman & Hall.

Syntactic Derivation of Tagalog Verbs. Videa P. DeGuzman. LC 78-11029. (Oceanic Linguistic Special Publication: No. 16). 1978. pap. text ed. 15.00x o.p. (ISBN 0-8248-0627-1). UH Pr.

Syntax & Semantics of Questions in Navajo. Ellen Schauber. Ed. by Jorge Hankamer. LC 78-66568. (Outstanding Dissertations in Linguistics Ser.). 1979. lib. bdg. 43.00 o.p. (ISBN 0-8240-9676-2). Garland Pub.

Syntax of Spoken Brazilian Portuguese. Earl W. Thomas. LC 69-11280. (Eng. & Port.). 1969. 12.95x o.p. (ISBN 0-8265-1130-9). Vanderbilt U Pr.

Syntax of Spoken Brazilian Portuguese. Earl W. Thomas. (Vanderbilt University Press Bks.). 363p. 1969. 12.95 o.p. U of Ill Pr.

Syntax Oriented Translator. Peter Z. Ingerman. 1966. 24.50 o.p. (ISBN 0-12-370850-8). Acad Pr.

Syntaxe de l'Haitien. Claire Lefebvre. Ed. by Helene Magloire-Holly & Nanie Piou. xiv, 251p. (Fr.). 1982. pap. 15.00 o.p. (ISBN 0-89720-055-1). Karoma.

Syntheses & Physical Studies of Inorganic Compounds. C. F. Bell. LC 79-178772. 253p. 1972. 65.00 o.p. (ISBN 0-08-016651-2). Pergamon.

Syntheses of Natural Products. Ed. by F. L. Boschke. (Topics in Current Chemistry Ser.: Vol. 91). 118p. 1980. 45.00 o.p. (ISBN 0-387-09827-5). Springer-Verlag.

Synthesis & Analysis Methods for Safety & Reliability Studies. Ed. by G. Apostolakis et al. LC 79-21315. 474p. 1980. 79.50x o.p. (ISBN 0-306-40316-1, Plenum Pr). Plenum Pub.

Synthesis & Properties of Mestastable Phases: Proceedings. TMS-AIME Fall Meeting in Pittsburgh, 1980. Ed. by E. S. Machlin & T. J. Rowland. (Illus.). 197p. 32.00 o.p. (ISBN 0-89520-372-3); members 20.00 o.p. (ISBN 0-317-36263-1); student members 11.00 o.p. (ISBN 0-317-36264-X). ASM.

Synthesis & Technique in Inorganic Chemistry. 2nd ed. Robert J. Angelici. 1977. text ed. 32.95 o.p. (ISBN 0-7216-1281-4, CBS C). SCP.

Synthesis of Feedback Systems. Isaac M. Horowitz. 1963. text ed. 27.00 o.p. (ISBN 0-12-355950-2). Acad Pr.

Synthesis of Life. Ed. by Charles C. Price. (Benchmark Papers in Organic Chemistry: Vol. 1). 391p. 1982. 61.95 o.p. (ISBN 0-87933-131-3). Van Nos Reinhold.

Synthesis of Passive Networks: Theory & Methods Appropriate to the Realization & Approximation Problems. Ernest A. Guillemin. LC 76-50044. 760p. 1977. Repr. of 1957 ed. 46.00 o.p. (ISBN 0-88275-481-5). Krieger.

Synthesis of Philosophy. Harold J. Dumain. LC 74-29555. 1975. (ISBN 0-8022-2159-9). Philos Lib.

Synthetic & Mechanistic Organic Chemistry. F. Minisci et al. (Topics in Current Chemistry: Vol. 62). 1976. 53.00 o.p. (ISBN 0-387-07525-9). Springer-Verlag.

Synthetic Aperture Radar. Ed. by John J. Kovaly. LC 76-42314. (Artech Radar Library). 329p. 1976. 40.00 o.p. (ISBN 0-89006-056-8). Artech Hse.

Synthetic Aperture Radar Systems Theory & Design. R. O. Harger. (Electrical Science Ser). 1969. 40.00 o.p. (ISBN 0-12-325050-1). Acad Pr.

Synthetic Fuels. R. F. Probstein & R. E. Hicks. (Chemical Engineering Ser.). 576p. 1982. text ed. 43.50x o.p. (ISBN 0-07-050908-5). McGraw.

Synthetic Organic Chemicals: United States Production & Sales, 1984. 68th ed. Edmund Cappuccilli et al. (United States International Trade Commission Publication: No. 1745). 323p. 1985. pap. 12.00 o.p. (ISBN 0-318-18847-3, S/N 049-000-00060-0). USGPO.

Synthetic Organic Chemistry-1: Proceedings of the First International Conference, Louvain, Belgium, 1974. Ed. by A. Bruylants. 1976. 150.00 o.p. (ISBN 0-08-020990-4). Pergamon.

Synthetic Procedures in Nucleic Acid Chemistry: Vol. 1. Ed. by W. Werner Zorbach & R. Stuart Tipson. 570p. (Orig.). 1968. 34.00 o.p. (ISBN 0-470-98415-5). Krieger.

Synthetic Uses of Anodic Substitution Reactions. Lennart Eberson & Klas Nyberg. 1977. pap. 14.00 o.p. (ISBN 0-08-021583-1). Pergamon.

Syria & Egypt: From the Tell El Amarna Letters. Flinders Petrie. 196p. 1978. 12.50 o.p. (ISBN 0-89005-234-4). Ares.

Syst-O-Color, Vier-Kleurensysteem, 2 vols. Paul Schuitema. (Illus.). 1966. loose-leaf bdg. 106.00x o.p. (ISBN 0-686-21790-X). Mouton.

System Analysis & Design Projects. Jack D. Harpool et al. 1986. pap. 24.95 o.p. (ISBN 0-8016-2068-6). Irwin.

System & Function: Toward a Theory of Society. Piotr Sztompka. 1974. 19.95 o.p. (ISBN 0-12-681850-9). Acad Pr.

System & Theory of Geosciences, 2 pts. Ed. by H. Uhlig. 103p. 1975. Vol. 1. pap. 23.00 o.p. (ISBN 0-08-019664-0); Pt. 2. pap. 23.00 o.p. (ISBN 0-08-019670-5). Pergamon.

System Design Guide, Featuring dBASE II. Ron Freshman. 183p. 1984. pap. 18.50 o.p. (ISBN 0-912677-12-0). Tate Pub.

System Developments Standards. C. Candullo. 544p. 1985. text ed. 54.95 o.p. (ISBN 0-07-009724-0). McGraw.

System for Assessing Affectivity. Robert E. Bills. LC 73-22712. 240p. 1975. 21.75 o.s.i. (ISBN 0-8173-9107-X). U of Ala Pr.

System for Development Planning & Budgeting. Arie Beenhakker. 200p. 1980. text ed. 37.95x o.p. (ISBN 0-566-00326-0). Gower Pub Co.

System Identification: Advances & Case Studies. Ed. by Raman K. Mehra & Dmitri G. Lainiotis. 1976. 69.50 o.p. (ISBN 0-12-487950-0). Acad Pr.

System Identification Tutorials. Ed. by R. Isermann. (Automatica: Vol. 16, No. 5). (Illus.). 88p. 1981. pap. 7.00 o.p. (ISBN 0-08-027302-5); pap. text ed. 12.50 o.p. (ISBN 0-08-027583-4). Pergamon.

System of Metaphysics. George S. Fullerton. LC 68-23290. Repr. of 1968 ed. lib. bdg. 35.00x o.p. (ISBN 0-8371-0079-8, FUSM). Greenwood.

System of Physical Education in the U. S. S. R. G. I. Kukushkin. 231p. 1983. 7.95 o.p. (ISBN 0-8285-2608-7, Pub. by Raduga Pubs USSR). Imported Pubns.

System Sensitivity Analysis. Ed. by J. B. Cruz, Jr. LC 72-93263. (Benchmark Papers in Electrical Engineering & Computer Science Ser: Vol. 1). 428p. 1982. 58.95 o.p. (ISBN 0-87933-020-1). Van Nos Reinhold.

System Theory: A Unified State-Space Approach to Continuous & Discrete Systems. Louis Padulo & Michael A. Arbib. LC 73-77941. (Illus.). 1974. text ed. 37.95 o.p. (ISBN 0-7216-7035-0). Hemisphere Pub.

System 1022 Host Language Interface User's Reference Manual. 2nd ed. Andrew Garland et al. 142p. 1981. looseleaf 21.50x o.p. (ISBN 0-912055-01-4). CompuServe Data Tech.

System 1032 Host Language Interface User's Guide. rev. ed. Joshua Goldman & Nina Zolotow. (Illus.). 126p. 1985. looseleaf 21.50x o.p. (ISBN 0-912055-11-1). CompuServe Data Tech.

System-370 Job Control Language. Gary D. Brown. LC 77-24901. 297p. 1977. pap. 24.95x o.p. (ISBN 0-471-03155-0). Wiley.

Systema Mycologicum, Sistens Fungorum Ordines, Genera et Species, 6 vols. in 4. Elias M. Fries. 160.00 o.p. (ISBN 0-384-16960-0). Johnson Repr.

Systematic Analog Computer Programming. 2nd ed. A. S. Charlesworth & J. R. Fletcher. 1975. 24.95 o.p. (ISBN 0-8464-0905-4). Beekman Pubs.

Systematic & Regional Biogeography. Stanley Morain. 300p. 1984. 37.95 o.s.i. (ISBN 0-442-26186-1). Van Nos Reinhold.

Systematic Approach to Advertising Creativity. Stephen Baker. 288p. 1983. pap. text ed. 10.95 o.p. (ISBN 0-07-003353-6). McGraw.

Systematic Approach to Commercial & Clerical Training. K. Oakley & W. Richmond. 1970. pap. 8.50 o.p. (ISBN 0-08-015722-X). Pergamon.

Systematic Bibliography in England, 1850-1895. W. Boyd Rayward. (Occasional Papers: No. 84). 50p. 1967. pap. 1.00 o.p. (ISBN 0-317-58865-6). U of Ill Lib Info Sci.

Systematic Identification of Flavonoids. T. J. Mabry et al. LC 72-95565. 1970. 35.00 o.p. (ISBN 0-387-04964-9). Springer-Verlag.

Systematic Materials Analysis. J. H. Richardson & R. V. Peterson. 1974. Vol. 2. 71.50 o.p. (ISBN 0-12-587802-8); Vol. 3. 84.00 o.p. (ISBN 0-12-587803-6). Acad Pr.

Systematic Materials Analysis. Ed. by J. H. Richardson & R. V. Peterson. (Materials Science Ser.: Vol. 1). 1974. 79.00 o.p. (ISBN 0-12-587801-X). Acad Pr.

Systematic Materials Analysis, Vol. 4. Ed. by J. H. Richardson & R. V. Peterson. (Materials Science & Technology Ser). 1978. 85.00 o.p. (ISBN 0-12-587804-4). Acad Pr.

Systematic Medication Profile Review. Q. M. Srnka & Tim Self. 1982. pap. text ed. 12.00 o.s.i. (ISBN 0-910769-03-6). Am Coll Apothecaries.

Systematic Nursing Care. Rosemary Long. (Illus.). 96p. 1981. 21.00 o.p. (ISBN 0-571-11616-7); pap. 7.95 o.p. Faber & Faber.

Systematic Philosophy: An Overview of Metaphysics Showing the Development from the Greeks to the Contemporaries with Specified Directions & Projections. John E. Van Hook. (Illus.). 1979. 8.50 o.p. (ISBN 0-682-49398-8, University). Exposition-Phoenix.

Systematic Sociology. Karl Mannheim. 176p. 1958. (ISBN 0-8022-1046-5). Philos Lib.

Systematic Sociology of Australian Education. R. J. King & R. E. Young. 204p. 1986. text ed. 29.95x o.p. (ISBN 0-86861-897-7). Unwin Hyman.

Systematics of the Colletidae Based on Mature Larvae with Phenetic Analysis of Apoid Larvae (Hymenoptera, Apoidea) Ronald J. McGinley. (UC Publications in Entomology: Vol. 91). 332p. 1981. pap. 20.50x o.p. (ISBN 0-520-09623-1). U of Cal Pr.

Systeme Interactif sur Mini-Ordinateur pour la Recherche Documentaire et la Gestion de Bibliotheques. F. A. Daneliuk. 19p. 1979. pap. 2.00 o.p. (ISBN 0-88936-192-4, IDRC-TS14F, IDRC). UNIPUB.

Systeme monetaire international face aux Desequilibres: Report & Proceedings of a Seminar Held in Paris, November 23-25, 1981. Ed. by Paul Coulbois. 165p. (Fr.). 1982. text ed. 5.00 o.s.i. (ISBN 2-7178-0578-8). Intl Monetary.

Systemic Lupus Erythematosis. Ed. by Robert Lahita. LC 86-11007. 1056p. 1986. (ISBN 0-471-87388-8, Pub. by Wiley Med). Wiley.

Systemic Pathology, Vol. 5. 2nd ed. W. St. C. Symmers. LC 75-3574. 1979. 102.00 o.p. (ISBN 0-443-01333-0). Churchill.

Systemic Pathology, Vol. 6. 2nd ed. W. St. C. Symmers. LC 75-3574. 1980. 120.00 o.p. (ISBN 0-443-01831-6). Churchill.

Systemic Sclerosis: Current Research, Vol. 1. Ed. by Richard K. Winkelmann et al. 212p. 1974. text ed. 28.50x o.p. (ISBN 0-8422-7202-X). Irvington.

Systemic Sclerosis: Current Research, Vol. 2. I. Capusan et al. 1974. text ed. 29.50x o.p. (ISBN 0-8422-7203-8). Irvington.

Systemic Sclerosis, Scleroderma. Ed. by Malcolm I. Jayson & Carol M. Black. LC 87-37122. 1988. (ISBN 0-471-90846-0). Wiley.

Systems Analysis & Design: A Foundation for the 1980's. Ed. by W. W. Cotterman et al. 553p. 1981. 78.00 o.p. (ISBN 0-444-00642-7, North-Holland); pap. 44.75 o.p. (ISBN 0-444-00758-X). Elsevier.

Systems Analysis & Design Methods. 2nd ed. Whitten & Bentley. (Illus.). 880p. 1989. 42.95 o.p. (ISBN 0-8016-5460-2). Mosby.

Systems Analysis & Design Methods. Whitten et al. 1985. 42.95 o.p. (ISBN 0-8016-5464-5); pap. 12.95 casebook o.p. (ISBN 0-8016-5465-3). Mosby.

Systems Analysis & Design Methods: International Edition. Whitten & Bentley. 880p. 1989. 23.95 o.p. (ISBN 0-8016-5497-1). Mosby.

Systems Analysis & Design: Traditional Structured & Advanced Concepts & Techniques. 2nd ed. James C. Wetherbe. (Illus.). 401p. 1984. text ed. 33.25 o.p. (ISBN 0-314-77858-6). West Pub.

Systems Analysis & Simulation, 1985: Proceedings of the 2nd International Symposium on Systems Analysis & Simulation, Berlin, GDR, 26-31 August, 1985. Ed. by A. Sydow et al. 1986. 84.00 o.p. (ISBN 0-08-034024-5, Pub. by PPL). Pergamon.

Systems Analysis for Business Data Processing. 3rd ed. H. D. Clifton. 242p. 1978. text ed. 30.75x o.p. (ISBN 0-220-66369-6, Pub. by Busn Bks England). Gower Pub Co.

Systems & Circuits for Electrical Engineering Technology. new ed. Charles Belove & Melvyn Drossman. (Illus.). 1976. text ed. 45.00 o.p. (ISBN 0-07-004430-9). McGraw.

Systems & Data Processing in Insurance Companies: Student Guide. rev. ed. Charles H. Cissley. LC 82-80670. (FLMI Insurance Education Program Ser.). 287p. 1982. text ed. 12.00 o.p. (ISBN 0-915322-55-2); wkbk. 7.00 o.p. (ISBN 0-915322-56-0). LOMA.

Systems & Procedures Including Office Management Information Sources. Ed. by Chester Morrill, Jr. LC 67-31261. (Management Information Ser.: No. 12). 380p. 1967. 68.00x o.p. (ISBN 0-8103-0812-6). Gale.

Systems Approach to Conservation Tillage. F. M. Di'Itri. LC 85-12855. (Illus.). 345p. 1985. 39.95 o.p. (ISBN 0-87371-024-X). Lewis Pubs Inc.

Systems Approach to Social Foundation of American Education. Ed. by Moses Stambler. 618p. 1969. pap. text ed. 19.50x o.p. (ISBN 0-8290-1084-X). Irvington.

Systems Approach to Water Management. Ed. by Asit K. Biswas. (Illus.). 1976. text ed. 48.00 o.p. (ISBN 0-07-005480-0). McGraw.

Systems Building for Bridges. (Special Report). 76p. 1972. 2.40 o.p. (ISBN 0-309-02063-8). Transport Res Bd.

Systems Contracting. Ralph Bolton. 1979. pap. 7.50 o.p. (ISBN 0-8144-2236-5). AMACOM.

Systems Design with Advanced Microprocessors. John Freer. 288p. 1987. pap. 26.95 o.p. (ISBN 0-672-22595-6). Sams.

Systems Documentation Manual. 3rd ed. National Computing Centre, Ltd. Staff. LC 72-97127. (Illus.). 160p. 1973. 40.00x o.p. (ISBN 0-85012-101-9). Intl Pubns Serv.

Systems Engineering: Methodology & Applications. Ed. by Andrew P. Sage. LC 77-82294. 408p. 1977. 36.95 o.p. (ISBN 0-87942-097-9, PP00950). Inst Electrical.

Systems for Study. 2nd ed. Alton L. Raygor & David M. Wark. (McGraw-Hill Basic Skills Ser.). (Illus.). 1979. text ed. 21.95 o.p. (ISBN 0-07-044419-6). McGraw.

Systems Laboratory for Information Management. James F. Courtney, Jr. & Ronald Jensen. 1981. pap. 13.95x o.p. (ISBN 0-256-02574-6). Irwin.

Systems of Ethics & Value Theory. William Sahakian. LC 63-11487. 470p. 1963. Philos Lib.

Systems of Linear Inequalities. A. S. Solodovnikov. 123p. 1979. pap. 3.95 o.p. (ISBN 0-8285-1515-8, Pub. by Mir Pubs USSR). Imported Pubns.

Systems Research II: Methodological Problems. Ed. by J. M. Gvishiani. (Advances in Systems Research Ser.). (Illus.). 280p. 1985. 52.00 o.p. (ISBN 0-08-030556-3, Pub. by PPL). Pergamon.

Systems Safety: Technology & Application. Sol Malasky. 300p. 1982. lib. bdg. 41.00 o.p. (ISBN 0-8240-7280-4). Garland Pub.

Systems Selling Strategies: How to Justify Premium Prices for Commodity Products. Mack Hanan et al. 1978. 14.95 o.p. (ISBN 0-8144-5460-7). AMACOM.

Systems Specifications for a Micro-or Mini-Computer Based Accountant's Client Write-up Systems. Gordon E. Louvau et al. 128p. 1983. pap. 34.95 o.p. Van Nos Reinhold.

Systems Theory & Biology: Proceedings of the Systems Symposium 3rd, Case Western Reserve University, Institute of Technology. Systems Symposium Staff. Ed. by M. D. Mesavoric. (Illus.). 1968. 58.30 o.p. (ISBN 0-387-04356-X). Springer-Verlag.

Systems Theory & Regional Integration: The "Market Model" of International Politics. James P. O'Leary. LC 78-66420. 1978. pap. text ed. 13.25 o.p. (ISBN 0-8191-0500-7). U Pr of Amer.

Systems Theory: Philosophical & Methodological Problems. I. V. Blauberg et al. 318p. 1977. 5.95 o.p. (ISBN 0-8285-0440-7, Pub. by Progress Pubs USSR). Imported Pubns.

Systems Thinking in Action. Ed. by M. C. Jackson & P. Keys. 1985. pap. 25.00 o.p. (ISBN 0-08-033413-X, Pub. by PPL). Pergamon.

Systems View of Planning: Towards a Theory of the Urban & Regional Planning Process. 2nd ed. George Chadwick. (Urban and Regional Planning Series: Vol. 2). 404p. 1975. text ed. 19.80 o.p. (ISBN 0-08-016799-3); pap. 13.20 o.p. (ISBN 0-08-018232-1). Pergamon.

Szivarvany, No. 18. 128p. 1986. pap. 9.00 o.s.i. (ISBN 0-936398-36-1). Framo Pub.

Szivarvany, No. 19. 128p. 1986. pap. 9.00 o.s.i. (ISBN 0-936398-37-X). Framo Pub.

T

T & B Cell Cooperation. Fernando Morgado et al. 200p. 1973. text ed. 24.50x o.p. (ISBN 0-8422-7116-3). Irvington.

T & B Lymphocytes: Proceedings of the ICN-UCLA Symposia on Molecular & Cellular Biology, 1979, Vol. XVI. ICN-UCLA Symposia Staff. Ed. by Fritz H. Bach et al. LC 79-26438. (Recognition & Function Ser.). 1979. 83.00 o.p. (ISBN 0-12-069850-1). Acad Pr.

T. E. Lawrence: A Bibliography. Jeffrey Meyers. LC 74-11361. (Reference Library of the Humanities: No. 5). 50p. 1975. lib. bdg. 19.00 o.p. (ISBN 0-8240-1052-3). Garland Pub.

T. E. Lawrence to His Biographers, Robert Graves & Liddell Hart. Thomas E. Lawrence. LC 76-25030. 260p. 1976. Repr. of 1963 ed. lib. bdg. 27.25x o.p. (ISBN 0-8371-9006-1, GRLB). Greenwood.

T. H. O'Sullivan Photographer. Beaumont Newhall & Nancy Newhall. LC 66-25971. (Illus.). 43p. 1966. pap. 5.95 o.p. (Dist by Univ. of Texas Pr). Amon Carter.

T. L. Yuan Bibliography of Western Writings on Chinese Art & Archaeology. Ed. by Harrie A. Vanderstappen. LC 76-356246. 606p. 1975. 106.00x o.p. (ISBN 0-7201-0521-8). Mansell.

T. Lucreti Cari de Rerum Natura Libri Sex. Ed. by Karl Lachmann. (Latin Poetry Ser.). 439p. 58.00 o.p. (ISBN 0-8240-2956-9). Garland Pub.

T. S. Eliot: A Life. Peter Ackroyd. (Illus.). 338p. 1984. 24.45 o.p. (ISBN 0-671-53043-7). S&S.

T. S. Eliot: A Life. Peter Ackroyd. 1985. pap. 12.95 o.p. (ISBN 0-671-60572-0, Touchstone Bks.). S&S.

T. S. Eliot: Aesthetics & History. Lewis Freed. LC 61-11289. 251p. 1962. pap. 7.95 o.p. (ISBN 0-87548-011-X). Open Court.

T. S. Eliot: The Longer Poems. Derek Traversi. LC 76-18793. 1976. 10.00 o.p. (ISBN 0-15-191380-3). HarBraceJ.

T. S. Eliot: The Longer Poems. Derek T. Traversi. LC 76-18793. 1976. pap. 3.95 o.p. (ISBN 0-15-692020-4, Harv). HarBraceJ.

T. S. Eliot: The Metaphysical Perspective. Eric Thompson. LC 62-16697. (Crosscurrents-Modern Critiques Ser.). 208p. 1963. 7.95x o.p. (ISBN 0-8093-0089-3). S Ill U Pr.

T. S. Eliot's Concept of Language: A Study of its Development. Harry T. Antrim. LC 76-634405. (University of Florida Humanities Monographs: No. 35). 75p. 1971. pap. 3.50 o.p. (ISBN 0-8130-0326-1). U Presses Fla.

T. S. Eliot's Intellectual Development, 1922-1939. John D. Margolis. LC 71-171071. 1972. lib. bdg. 21.00x o.s.i. (ISBN 0-226-50518-9). U of Chicago Pr.

T. S. Eliot's Social Criticism. Roger Kojecky. 255p. 1972. 7.95 o.p. (ISBN 0-374-27243-3). FS&G.

T V see also Television.

TA & the Manager. Dudley Bennett. (AMACOM Executive Bks). 1978. pap. 5.95 o.p. (ISBN 0-8144-7511-6). AMACOM.

TA & the Manager. Dudley Bennett. (Illus.). 1976. 13.95 o.p. (ISBN 0-8144-5422-4). AMACOM.

TA K Vam Pridu. Stanislav Lesnevskii. 368p. 1982. 39.00x o.p. (Pub. by Collets UK). State Mutual Bk.

Taamim Lakorim. 1982. pap. 7.50 o.s.i. (ISBN 0-686-76267-3); cassette 7.50 o.s.i. (ISBN 0-686-76268-1); book & cassette 12.00 o.s.i. (ISBN 0-686-76269-X). Feldheim.

TAB Handbook of Hand & Power Tools. Rudolf F. Graf & George J. Whalen. (Illus.). 512p. (Orig.). 1984. 26.95 o.p. (ISBN 0-8306-0638-6, 1638); pap. 17.60 o.p. (ISBN 0-8306-1638-1, 1638P). TAB Bks.

Tabellenbuch zur Umrechnung metrischer Masse in englische Masse; Tables for the Conversion Metric System of Measurement to the British System. Hans W. Schleiden. (Technischer Verlag Herbert Cram). (Ger.-Eng.). 1961. 23.75x o.p. (ISBN 3-11-005632-1). De Gruyter.

Taber's Cyclopedic Medical Dictionary. 14th ed. Ed. by Clayton L. Thomas. LC 80-16588. (Illus.). 1818p. 1981. 15.95x o.p. (ISBN 0-8036-8307-3); Thumb-indexed Edition. text ed. 18.95x o.p. (ISBN 0-8036-8306-5). Davis Co.

Taber's Cyclopedic Medical Dictionary. 15th ed. Ed. by Clayton L. Thomas. LC 62-8364. (Illus.). 2207p. 1985. text ed. 21.95 thumb-indexed o.p. (ISBN 0-8036-8308-1); text ed. 19.50 o.p. (ISBN 0-8036-8309-X). Davis Co.

Tabitha Fffoulkes. John Linssen. LC 78-57319. 1978. 8.95 o.p. (ISBN 0-87795-192-6, Arbor Hse). Morrow.

Table & Chair. Sue Tarsky. (Look & Say Ser.). (Illus.). 32p. 1983. 1.50 o.s.i. (ISBN 0-671-47657-2, Little Simon). S&S.

Table Before Me. John W. Rilling. LC 76-7859. 1977. pap. 1.95 o.p. (ISBN 0-8006-1230-2, Fortress). Augsburg Fortress.

Table Book, 2 Vols. William Hone. LC 67-12946. 454p. Repr. of 1827 ed. Set. 54.00x o.p. (ISBN 0-8103-3006-7). Gale.

Table Constants Tables of V17. Inte. 1971. 230.00 o.p. (ISBN 0-08-016546-X). Pergamon.

Table Number Seven. Victor Canning. 178p. 1988. 19.95 o.p. (ISBN 0-434-10749-2, Pub. by W Heinemann Ltd). David & Charles.

Table of Earth Satellites, Nineteen Fifty-Seven to Nineteen Eighty. Royal Aircraft Establishment Staff. 680p. 75.00x o.p. (ISBN 0-87196-599-2). Facts on File.

Table of Integrals, Series & Products. I. S. Gradshteyn & I. M. Ryshik. 1966. 21.50 o.p. (ISBN 0-12-294750-9). Acad Pr.

Table of the Lord: Holy Communion in the Life of the Church. Alvin N. Rogness. LC 82-72640. 96p. (Orig.). 1983. pap. 4.95 o.p. (ISBN 0-8066-1946-5, 10-6182, Augsburg). Augsburg Fortress.

Table Tennis. David Philip & Joel Cohen. 1975. 7.95 o.p. (ISBN 0-689-10684-X, Atheneum). Macmillan.

Tables & Formulas see World Book Desk Reference Set.

Tables for Statisticians. John White et al. 61p. 1984. pap. text ed. 5.00x o.p. (ISBN 0-7022-1146-X). U of Queensland Pr.

Tables of All Primitive Roots of Odd Primes Less Than 1,000. Roger Osborn. 70p. 1961. 6.00x o.p. (ISBN 0-292-73394-1). U of Tex Pr.

Tables of Antenna Characteristics. Ronald W. King. LC 74-157425. 400p. 1971. 95.00x o.p. (ISBN 0-306-65154-8, IFI Plenum). Plenum Pub.

Tables of Co-efficients for the Analysis of Triple Angular Correlations of Gamma-Rays from Aligned Nuclei. G. Kaye et al. 1969. 55.00 o.p. (ISBN 0-08-012260-4). Pergamon.

Tables of Laplace, Heaviside, Fourier & Z Transforms. M. Healy. 78p. 1972. 10.50 o.p. (ISBN 0-470-36663-X, Pub. by John Wiley). Krieger.

Tables of Ordinary & Extraordinary Refractive Indices, Group Refractive Indices & - H-Sub-Ox - F Curves for Standard Ionospheric Layer Models. Walter Becker. 1960. 7.10 o.p. (ISBN 0-387-02580-4). Springer-Verlag.

Tabletop & Giftwares. Fairchild Market Research Division Staff. (Fairchild Fact Files Ser.). (Illus.). 50p. 1986. pap. 17.50 o.p. (ISBN 0-87005-557-7). Fairchild.

Tablets of Baha'u'llah Revealed after the Kitab-i-Aqdas. Baha'u'llah. Tr. by Shoghi Effendi & Habib Taherzadeh. LC 79-670079. 1978. 17.95 o.p. (ISBN 0-85398-077-2, 103-021, Pub. by Universal Hse. of Justice); pap. 7.95 o.p. (ISBN 0-85398-137-X). Baha'i.

Taboo. Franz B. Steiner. 200p. 1956. (ISBN 0-8022-1640-4). Philos Lib.

Taboo Love. Joseph A. Ngongwikuo. (Illus.). 1980. 10.00 o.p. (ISBN 0-682-49507-7). Exposition-Phoenix.

Tabulation of Infrared Spectral Data. David Dolphin & Alexander Wick. LC 76-48994. 566p. 1977. 37.50 o.p. (ISBN 0-471-21780-8). Krieger.

TAC-USA Directory. 1988. 8.00 o.p. (ISBN 0-317-65148-X). Athletics Cong.

Tachycardias: Mechanisms, Diagnosis, Treatment. Ed. by Mark E. Josephson & Hein J. J. Wellens. LC 84-3949. (Illus.). 553p. 1984. text ed. 57.50 o.p. (ISBN 0-8121-0899-X). Lea & Febiger.

Tackle Craft. C. Boyd Pfeiffer. (ISBN 0-8329-0241-1). Lyons & Burford.

Tacoma: The City of Destiny, 1884-1984. Ann Roush. 24p. (Orig.). 1984. pap. 5.00 o.p. (ISBN 0-9603666-9-5). R & M Pr WA.

Tactical Air Command. Don Linn & Don Spering. (Warbirds Illustrated Ser.: No. 39). (Illus.). 64p. (Orig.). 1986. pap. 9.95 o.p. (ISBN 0-85368-752-8, Pub. by Arms & Armour). Sterling.

Tactics & Strategies of Classroom Discipline. Brian D. Rude. 1979. 6.00 o.p. (ISBN 0-682-49307-4). Exposition-Phoenix.

Tactics of Christian Resistance. Ed. by Gary North. LC 83-81783. (Christianity & Civilization Ser.: No. 3). 528p. 1983. pap. 14.95 o.p. (ISBN 0-939404-07-9). Geneva Ministr.

Tactics on Bass: How to Fish the 23 Most Common Bass "Hotspots" Ray Ovington. (Illus.). 320p. 1983. 19.95 o.p. (ISBN 0-684-17860-5, ScribT). Scribner.

Tafsir-ul-Quran, Vol. I-IV. A. Majid Daryabadi. 75.00 o.p. (ISBN 0-317-14641-6). Kazi Pubns.

Tagalog-English-English-Tagalog Dictionary. rev. ed. Maria O. Guzman. (Tagalog & Eng.). pap. 22.50 o.s.i. (ISBN 0-686-68939-9). E J Brill USA.

Tagget. Irving A. Greenfield. LC 78-72920. 1979. 9.95 o.p. (ISBN 0-87795-209-4, Arbor Hse). Morrow.

Tagore Testament. Rabindrath Tagore. Tr. by Indu Dutt. 132p. 1955. (ISBN 0-8022-1685-4). Philos Lib.

Tahiti & French Polynesia: A Travel Survival Kit. Rob Kay. (Illus.). 136p. (Orig.). 1985. pap. 7.95 o.p. (ISBN 0-908086-80-6). Lonely Planet.

Tahiti: Complete Travel Guide to All of the Islands. Vicki Poggioli. (Illus.). 216p. (Orig.). 1987. pap. 9.95 o.p. (ISBN 0-87052-363-5). Hippocrene Bks.

Tahitians: Mind & Experience in the Society Islands. Robert I. Levy. LC 73-77136. (Illus.). 1973. lib. bdg. 14.00x o.s.i. (ISBN 0-226-47605-7). U of Chicago Pr.

Tahitians: Mind & Experience in the Society Islands. Robert I. Levy. LC 73-77136. (Illus.). xxviii, 548p. 1975. pap. text ed. 8.95x o.s.i. (ISBN 0-226-47607-3, P649, Phoen). U of Chicago Pr.

Tai-Pan. James Clavell. LC 66-16356. 1966. 17.50 o.p. (ISBN 0-689-11068-5, Atheneum). Macmillan.

Tailed Amphibians of Europe. J. W. Steward. LC 79-97191. (Illus.). 1970. 8.50 o.s.i. (ISBN 0-8008-7540-0). Taplinger.

Tailing Disposal Today: Proceedings of the International Tailing Symposium, 2nd, Denver, Colorado, 1978, Vol. 2. International Tailing Symposium Staff. Ed. by George O. Argall, Jr. LC 73-78129. (World Mining Book). (Illus.). 600p. 1979. 37.50 o.p. (ISBN 0-87930-106-6). Miller Freeman.

Tailor-Made Teaching in the Church School. Mary Duckert. LC 73-21904. 128p. 1974. pap. 2.85 o.s.i. (ISBN 0-664-24985-X, Westminster). Westminster John Knox.

Tailoring Software for Multiple Processor Systems. Karsten Schwan. Ed. by Harold Stone. LC 84-28081. (Computer Science: Distributed Database Systems Ser.: No. 16). 202p. 1985. 44.95 o.p. (ISBN 0-8357-1645-7). UMI Res Pr.

Tailoring Vocational Education to Adult Needs. Norma B. Brewer. 30p. 1981. 2.80 o.p. (ISBN 0-318-22206-X, IN226). Natl Ctr Res Voc Ed.

Tailor's Pattern Book: From Spain in the Year 1589. Juan De Alcega. 279p. limited ed 50.00x o.s.i. (ISBN 0-318-01133-6). Robin & Russ.

Tainted Gold. Lynn Michaels. (Velvet Glove Ser.: No. 15). 192p. 1985. pap. 2.25 o.p. (ISBN 0-380-89666-4). Avon.

Tainted Lilies. Becky L. Wayrich. 1984. pap. 3.50 o.s.i. (ISBN 0-449-12528-9, GM). Fawcett.

Taiwan. Hildebrand Editorial Staff. (Travel Guide Ser.). (Illus.). 196p. 1986. pap. 9.95 o.p. (ISBN 0-87052-164-0, Pub. by Hildebrand). Hippocrene Bks.

Taiwan Buyer's Guide, 1986-87. 1986. 180.00x o.p. (ISBN 0-8002-3993-8). Intl Pubns Serv.

Taize Picture Bible. Ed. by Eric De Suassure. LC 69-11860. (Illus.). 298p. 1968. 9.95 o.p. (ISBN 0-8006-0005-3, 1-5, Fortress). Augsburg Fortress.

Takamiyama: The World of Sumo. Jesse Kuhaulua & John Wheeler. LC 72-96129. (Illus.). 176p. 1973. 15.95 o.p. (ISBN 0-87011-195-7). Kodansha.

Take a Bow, Andy Capp. Reginald Smythe. (Andy Capp Ser.). 1978. pap. 1.25 o.s.i. (ISBN 0-449-13629-9, GM). Fawcett.

Take a Chance on Love. Jan Gelman. (Follow Your Heart Romance Ser.: No. 6). 128p. (Orig.). (gr. 5 up). 1984. pap. 1.95 o.p. (ISBN 0-671-52408-9). Archway.

Take Another Look at the Keyboard. William L. Fowler. LC 82-90364. (Illus.). 100p. 1982. pap. text ed. 12.00 o.p. (ISBN 0-943894-00-X). Fowler Music.

Take Back the Night: Women on Pornography. Ed. by Laura Lederer. LC 80-17084. 352p. 1980. 14.95 o.p. (ISBN 0-688-03728-3). Morrow.

Take Care. C. W. Brister. LC 76-51022. 1979. pap. 3.95 o.p. (ISBN 0-8054-5578-7). Broadman.

Take Charge of Your Finances & Win Financial Freedom. Justin W. Heatter. 256p. 1984. 14.95 o.p. (ISBN 0-684-18236-X). Scribner.

Take Fire. Margaret Honton. LC 80-69778. 64p. (Orig.). 1980. pap. 4.00 o.p. (ISBN 0-936014-09-1). Dawn Valley.

Take Him to the Streets. rev. ed. Jonathan Gainsbrugh. LC 84-62779. 236p. 1985. pap. 5.95 o.p. (ISBN 0-910311-26-9). Huntington Hse Inc.

Take Hold of Your Future: Leader's Manual. JoAnn Harris-Bowlsbey et al. 152p. (Orig.). 1982. pap. text ed. 6.95 o.p. (ISBN 0-937734-03-9). Am Coll Testing.

Take It Again from the Top. Debra Jarvis. 128p. 1986. pap. 4.95 o.p. (ISBN 0-7459-1138-2). Lion USA.

Take It Easy. Ray Ashford. LC 75-36443. 96p. (Orig.). 1976. pap. 1.50 o.p. (ISBN 0-8006-1219-1, Fortress). Augsburg Fortress.

Take It to the Lord: Prayer Laments for the Afflicted. Wendell W. Frerichs. LC 81-52273. 80p. (Orig.). 1982. pap. 4.95 o.p. (ISBN 0-8066-1905-8, 10-6191, Augsburg). Augsburg Fortress.

Take Me Home. Bonnie Jamison. (Living Books). 176p. 1986. pap. 3.50 o.p. (ISBN 0-8423-6901-5). Tyndale.

Take Me Where the Good Times Are. Robert Cormier. 176p. 1981. pap. 2.25 o.p. (ISBN 0-380-52662-X, 52662-X). Avon.

Take My Waking Slow. Gunilla B. Norris. LC 72-115084. (Illus.). (gr. 5-9). 1970. PLB 4.25 o.p. (ISBN 0-689-20608-9, Atheneum). Macmillan.

Take off with the Electron & BBC Micro. Audrey Bishop & Owen Bishop. (Illus.). 144p. (Orig.). 1984. pap. 11.95 o.p. (ISBN 0-246-12356-7, Pub. by Granada England). Sheridan.

Take Two: A Life in Movies & Politics. Philip Dunne. (Illus.). 1980. text ed. 14.95 o.p. (ISBN 0-07-018306-6). McGraw.

Take Your Choice-Separation or Mongrelization. Theodore G. Bilbo. 330p. 1986. pap. 9.00 o.p. (ISBN 0-317-53018-6). Noontide.

Take Your Life Off Hold. Ted Dreier. (Illus.). 225p. 1987. 15.95 o.p. (ISBN 1-55591-020-3). Fulcrum Inc.

Takeoffs & Landings. Leighton Collins. 1981. 19.95 o.s.i. (ISBN 0-440-08503-9, E Friede). Delacorte.

Takeoffs from Tension. Mary J. Irion et al. (Orig.). 1969. pap. 0.85 o.p. (ISBN 0-377-80571-8). Friendship Pr.

Takeover Madness: Corporate America Fights Back. Allen Michel & Israel Shaked. LC 85-32315. 397p. 1986. 22.95 o.p. (ISBN 0-471-01079-0). Wiley.

Takeover Time. Arthur R. Solmssen. 1986. 17.95 o.p. (ISBN 0-316-80370-7). Little.

Takestock: Worship. Don M. Wardlaw. 37.50 o.p. (ISBN 0-8042-4034-5, John Knox). Westminster John Knox.

Taking a Chance. Anna Hudson. (Candlelight Ecstasy Ser.: No. 240). (Orig.). 1984. pap. 1.95 o.s.i. (ISBN 0-440-18482-7). Dell.

Taking Action in the Community. (Leadership Pamphlet Ser.: No. 3). 1955. 1.40 o.p. (ISBN 0-88379-016-5). A A A C E.

Taking & Defending Depositions in Personal Injury Cases. Practising Law Institute Staff & David G. Miller. LC 83-62545. (Litigation Course & Administrative Practice Handbook Ser.: No. 236). 240p. 1983. 15.00 o.p. PLI.

Taking Better Travel Photos. (Kodak Library of Creative Photography). 1988. 11.95 o.p. (ISBN 0-86706-220-7). Time-Life.

Taking Care. Fanny Howe. 1985. pap. 2.50 o.p. (ISBN 0-380-89864-0). Avon.

Taking Care of Outdoor Gear. Ed. by Stackpole Books, Inc. Staff. (Illus.). 320p. 1983. 14.95 o.p. (ISBN 0-8117-0841-1); pap. 9.95 o.p. (ISBN 0-8117-2148-5). Stackpole.

Taking Care of Your Child: A Parents' Guide to Medical Care. Robert Pantell et al. LC 77-81635. 1977. 12.95 o.p. (ISBN 0-201-08122-9); pap. 10.95 o.p. (ISBN 0-201-08123-7). Addison-Wesley.

Taking Cash Out of the Closely-Held Corporation. Lawrence C. Silton. LC 79-25961. 330p. 1980. 59.50 o.p. (ISBN 0-87624-534-3, Inst Busn Plan). P-H.

Taking Cash Out of the Closely-Held Corporation. 2nd ed. Lawrence C. Silton. 330p. 1983. 89.50 o.p. (ISBN 0-87624-535-1, Inst Busn Plan). P-H.

Taking Chances: Lessons in Putting Passion & Creativity into Your Work Life. Dale Dauten. LC 85-43240. 192p. 1986. 15.00 o.p. (ISBN 0-937858-69-2). Newmarket.

Taking Chances: The Psychology of Losing & How to Profit from It. Robert T. Lewis. 1979. 7.95 o.p. (ISBN 0-395-27606-3). HM.

Taking Charge. Compiled by Dale Dieleman. (Good Things for Youth Leaders Ser.). pap. 3.45 o.p. (ISBN 0-8010-2911-2). Baker Bk.

Taking Charge: The/Dynamics of Taking Charge. John J. Gabarro. 208p. 1987. text ed. 22.95 o.p. Harvard Busn.

Taking Control Counter Display. Garfield. 1988. pap. 49.75 o.p. (ISBN 0-471-61363-0). Wiley.

Taking Darwin Seriously: A Naturalistic Approach to Philosophy. Michael Ruse. 250p. 1986. 39.95x o.p. (ISBN 0-631-14145-6). Basil Blackwell.

Taking Lives: Genocide & State Power. 3rd ed. Irving L. Horowitz. (Issues in Contemporary Civilization Ser.). 1980. 12.95x o.p. (ISBN 0-87855-353-3); pap. text ed. 5.95x o.p. (ISBN 0-87855-751-2). Transaction Pubs.

Taking Off. Pixie Burger & Julie Percivall. 1981. pap. 1.25 o.p. (ISBN 0-380-00212-4, 20800). Avon.

Taking off with BASIC on the IBM PCjr. Nancy R. Watson. (Illus.). 224p. 1985. pap. 14.95 o.p. (ISBN 0-89303-869-5). Brady Bks.

Taking on the World: Empowering Strategies for Parents of Children with Disabilities. Joyce S. Mitchell. LC 81-47537. 288p. 1982. 12.95 o.p. (ISBN 0-15-187864-1). HarBraceJ.

Taking on Tomorrow. Ned White. 26p. 1980. 2.35 o.p. (ISBN 0-318-22208-6, SN25). Natl Ctr Res Voc Ed.

Taking Pictures. Nina Leen. (Illus.). 48p. (ps-5). 1980. pap. 1.75 o.p. (ISBN 0-380-49205-9, 49205-9, Camelot). Avon.

Taking Pictures. Ed. by Nina Leen. LC 76-41156. (Illus.). (gr. k-3). 1977. reinforced bdg. 6.95 o.p. (ISBN 0-03-018701-X). H Holt & Co.

Taking Root: Israeli Settlement in the West Bank, the Golan & Gaza-Sinai, 1967-1980, Vol. 1. William W. Harris. LC 80-40953. (Geographical Research Studies). 223p. 1980. 79.95 o.p. (ISBN 0-471-27863-7, Pub. by Res Stud Pr). Wiley.

Taking Sides. Norma Klein. 144p. 1976. pap. 2.25 o.p. (ISBN 0-380-00528-X, 60054-4, Flare). Avon.

Taking Sides: America's Secret Relations with a Militant Israel. Stephen Green. LC 83-61736. 320p. 1984. 14.95 o.p. (ISBN 0-688-02643-5). Morrow.

Taking Sides: Clashing Views on Controversial Bioethical Issues. Carol Levine. 312p. 1984. casebound 11.95 o.p. (ISBN 0-87967-490-3); pap. 8.95 o.p. Dushkin Pub.

Taking Sides: Clashing Views on Controversial Bioethical Issues. 2nd ed. Carol Levine. LC 86-71775. (Illus.). 372p. 1987. pap. text ed. 9.95 o.p. Dushkin Pub.

Taking Sides: Clashing Views on Controversial Environmental Issues. Theodore Goldfarb. LC 83-70926. 324p. 1984. casebound 11.95x o.p. (ISBN 0-87967-477-6); pap. 8.95x o.p. (ISBN 0-317-43446-2). Dushkin Pub.

Taking Sides: Clashing Views on Controversial Environmental Issues. 2nd ed. Theodore Goldfarb. LC 86-71776. (Illus.). 336p. 1987. pap. text ed. 9.95 o.p. (ISBN 0-87967-656-6). Dushkin Pub.

Taking Sides: Clashing Views on Controversial Educational Issues. 3rd ed. James W. Noll. LC 85-71102. 360p. 1985. casebound 11.95 o.p. (ISBN 0-87967-597-7); pap. 8.95 o.p. (ISBN 0-317-43445-4). Dushkin Pub.

Taking Sides: Clashing Views on Controversial Educational Issues. 4th ed. James W. Noll. LC 86-48003. (Illus.). 384p. 1987. pap. text ed. 9.95 o.p. (ISBN 0-87967-660-4). Dushkin Pub.

Taking Sides: Clashing Views on Controversial Economic Issues. 2nd ed. Thomas R. Swartz & Frank J. Bonello. LC 81-69170. 360p. 1984. casebound 11.95 o.p. (ISBN 0-87967-488-1); pap. 8.95 o.p. (ISBN 0-317-43443-8). Dushkin Pub.

Taking Sides: Clashing Views on Controversial Issues in American History, Vol. I. Eugene Kuzirian & Larry Madaras. LC 85-70820. 276p. 1985. pap. 8.95 o.p. (ISBN 0-87967-562-4). Dushkin Pub.

Taking Sides: Clashing Views on Controversial Issues in American History, Vol. II. Eugene Kuzirian & Larry Madaras. LC 85-70821. 300p. 1985. pap. 8.95 o.p. (ISBN 0-87967-568-3). Dushkin Pub.

Taking Sides: Clashing Views on Controversial Issues in American History, Vol. I. 2nd ed. Larry Madaras. LC 86-48001. (Illus.). 396p. 1987. pap. text ed. 9.95 o.p. (ISBN 0-87967-658-2). Dushkin Pub.

Taking Sides: Clashing Views on Controversial Issues in American History, Vol. II. 2nd ed. Larry Madaras. LC 86-48004. (Illus.). 396p. 1987. pap. text ed. 9.95 o.p. (ISBN 0-87967-659-0). Dushkin Pub.

Taking Sides: Clashing Views on Controversial Issues in Human Sexuality. Robert T. Francoeur. LC 86-48002. (Illus.). 360p. (Orig.). 1987. pap. text ed. 9.95 o.p. (ISBN 0-87967-661-2). Dushkin Pub.

Taking Sides: Clashing Views on Controversial Issues in World Politics. John T. Rourke. LC 87-72264. (Illus.). 336p. (Orig.). 1988. pap. text ed. 9.95 o.p. (ISBN 0-87967-737-6). Dushkin Pub.

Taking Sides: Clashing Views on Controversial Legal Issues. 2nd ed. Ethan Katsh. LC 83-72061. 396p. 1986. pap. text ed. 9.95 o.p. (ISBN 0-87967-614-0). Dushkin Pub.

Taking Sides: Clashing Views on Controversial Political Issues. 5th ed. George McKenna. LC 86-71774. (Illus.). 372p. 1987. pap. text ed. 9.95 o.p. (ISBN 0-87967-655-8). Dushkin Pub.

Taking Sides: Clashing Views on Controversial Political Issues. 4th ed. George McKenna & Stanley Feingold. LC 84-71885. 396p. 1985. pap. 8.95x o.p. (ISBN 0-87967-546-2). Dushkin Pub.

Taking Sides: Clashing Views on Controversial Psychological Issues. 3rd ed. Joseph Rubinstein & Brent D. Slife. LC 84-65111. 396p. 1984. casebound 11.95 o.p. (ISBN 0-317-43447-0); pap. 8.95 o.p. (ISBN 0-317-43448-9). Dushkin Pub.

Taking Sides: Clashing Views on Controversial Social Issues. 3rd ed. Kurt Finsterbusch & George McKenna. LC 84-65113. 396p. 1984. casebound 11.95 o.p. (ISBN 0-87967-534-9); pap. 8.95 o.p. (ISBN 0-317-43449-7). Dushkin Pub.

Taking Sides: The Education of a Militant Mind. Michael Harrington. LC 85-7607. 264p. 1985. 16.95 o.p. (ISBN 0-03-004429-4). H Holt & Co.

Taking the Red Eye. (Danger Mouse Lift-the-Flap Bks.). 16p. (gr. k-3). 1986. 5.70i o.p. (ISBN 0-316-14711-7). Little.

Taking Time for Marriage. Ray Jenkins. 1977. pap. 2.95 o.p. (ISBN 0-89225-182-4). Gospel Advocate.

Taking to Water. Roberta Spear. 64p. 1985. pap. 7.95 o.p. (ISBN 0-03-000509-4, Owl Bks). H Holt & Co.

Talanta-Scandinavian Honour Issue: Special Issue of Talanta, Vol. 22 No. 12. Ed. by R. A. Chalmers. 1976. pap. 55.00 o.p. (ISBN 0-08-020879-7). Pergamon.

Talbot-Booth's Merchant Ships, Vol. 2. E. C. Talbot-Booth. 1978. 25.00x o.p. (ISBN 0-89397-046-8); 27.50 o.p. (ISBN 0-89397-030-1). Nichols Pub.

Talbot-Booth's Merchant Ships, Vol. 3. E. C. Talbot-Booth. 1979. 47.50x o.p. (ISBN 0-89397-047-6). Nichols Pub.

Talcott Parsons & the Conceptual Dilemma. Hans P. Adriaansens. (International Library of Sociology). (Illus.). 224p. 1980. 29.95x o.p. (ISBN 0-7100-0519-9). Routledge Chapman & Hall.

Tale of a Tub & Other Satires. Jonathan Swift. Ed. by Kathleen Williams. 1975. 14.95x o.p. (ISBN 0-460-10347-4, Evman); pap. 5.95x o.p. (ISBN 0-460-11347-X, Evman). Biblio Dist.

Tale of Admiral Mouse. Bernard Stone. LC 81-6998. (Illus.). 24p. (gr. k-3). 1982. 10.95 o.p. (ISBN 0-03-061221-7). H Holt & Co.

Tale of Ancient Egypt. Frederick C. Heckel. LC 62-20872. 132p. 1963. (ISBN 0-8022-0699-9). Philos Lib.

Tale of Benjamin Bunny. Beatrix Potter. (Illus.). (ps-2). 1981. 4.95 o.p. (ISBN 0-7232-0595-7); pap. 2.25 o.p. (ISBN 0-7232-6228-4). Warne.

Tale of Fearsome Fritz. Jeanne Willis. LC 82-23348. (Illus.). 24p. (gr. k-3). 1983. 11.95 o.s.i. (ISBN 0-03-063519-5). H Holt & Co.

Tale of Genji-One. Lady Murasaki. LC 50-47132. 1953. pap. 4.95 o.p. (ISBN 0-385-09275-X, Anch). Doubleday.

Tale of Georgie Grub. Jeanne Willis. LC 81-13194. (Illus.). 32p. (gr. k-3). 1982. 9.95 o.s.i. (ISBN 0-03-061222-5). H Holt & Co.

Tale of Jeremy Fisher. Beatrix Potter. 1983. pap. 5.95 with cassette o.p. (ISBN 0-89845-502-2, TBC5022). Caedmon.

Tale of Johnny Townmouse. Beatrix Potter. (Illus.). (ps-2). 1918. 4.95 o.p. (ISBN 0-7232-0604-X). Warne.

Tale of Little Pig Robinson. Beatrix Potter. (ps-2). 1930. 4.95 o.p. (ISBN 0-7232-0610-4). Warne.

Tale of Mr. Jeremy Fisher. Beatrix Potter. (Illus.). (ps-2). 1906. 4.95 o.p. (ISBN 0-7232-0598-1); pap. 2.25 o.p. (ISBN 0-7232-6231-4). Warne.

Tale of Mister Tod. Beatrix Potter. (Illus.). (ps-2). 1912. 4.95 o.p. (ISBN 0-7232-0605-8). Warne.

Tale of Mrs. Tiggy-Winkle. Beatrix Potter. (Illus.). (ps-2). 1982. 4.95 o.p. (ISBN 0-7232-0597-3); pap. 2.25 o.p. (ISBN 0-7232-6230-6). Warne.

Tale of Mrs. Tittlemouse. Beatrix Potter. (Illus.). (ps-2). 1910. 4.95 o.p. (ISBN 0-7232-0602-3); pap. 2.25 o.p. (ISBN 0-7232-6235-7). Warne.

Tale of One January. Albert Maltz. (Orig.). pap. 2.95 o.p. (ISBN 0-7145-0544-7). Riverrun NY.

Tale of Peter Rabbit. Beatrix Potter. (Illus.). (ps-2). 1981. 4.95 o.p. (ISBN 0-7232-0592-2); pap. 2.25 o.p. (ISBN 0-7232-6225-X). Warne.

Tale of Peter Rabbit. Beatrix Potter. (Talking Bookworm Ser.). 1983. pap. 5.95 incl. cassette o.p. (ISBN 0-89845-500-6, TBC5006). Caedmon.

Tale of Peter Rabbit. Beatrix Potter. 1986. pap. 2.25 o.p. (ISBN 0-7232-2938-4). Warne.

Tale of Pigling Bland. Beatrix Potter. (Illus.). (ps-2). 1913. 4.95 o.p. (ISBN 0-7232-0606-6). Warne.

Tale of the Dark Crystal. Donna Bass et al. LC 82-11676. (Illus.). 48p. (gr. k-3). 1982. 9.95 o.s.i. (ISBN 0-03-062414-2). H Holt & Co.

Tale of the Flopsy Bunnies. Beatrix Potter. (Illus.). (gr. k-2). 1909. 4.95 o.p. (ISBN 0-7232-0601-5); pap. 2.25 o.p. (ISBN 0-7232-6234-9). Warne.

Tale of the Porcelain God. Lafcadio Hearn. 1973. 30.00 o.p. (ISBN 0-686-23324-7). Rochester Folk Art.

Tale of Timmy Tiptoes. Beatrix Potter. (Illus.). (ps-2). 1911. 4.95 o.p. (ISBN 0-7232-0603-1); pap. 2.25 o.p. (ISBN 0-7232-6236-5). Warne.

Tale of Tom Kitten. Beatrix Potter. (Illus.). (ps-2). 1907. 4.95 o.p. (ISBN 0-7232-0599-X); pap. 2.25 o.p. (ISBN 0-7232-6232-2). Warne.

Tale of Traveling Matt. Michaela Muntean. LC 83-23711. (Illus.). 32p. (gr. k-2). 1984. 5.95 o.s.i. (ISBN 0-03-071092-8). H Holt & Co.

Tale of Two Bad Mice. Beatrix Potter. (Illus.). (ps-2). 1904. 4.95 o.p. (ISBN 0-7232-0596-5); pap. 2.25 o.p. (ISBN 0-7232-6229-2). Warne.

Tale of Two Cities. Charles Dickens. LC 83-63341. (Illus.). 400p. 1984. 12.95 o.p. (ISBN 0-89577-179-9). RD Assn.

Tale of Two Cities by Charles Dickens. 48p. (Orig.). 1988. pap. 9.95 o.p. (ISBN 1-55651-875-7); cassette o.p. (ISBN 1-55651-876-5). Cram Cassettes.

Tale of Two Towns. Doris C. Bracey. (Illus.). 64p. 1984. 5.50 o.p. (ISBN 0-682-40168-4). Exposition-Phoenix.

Tale Type & Motif Indexes: An Annotated Bibliography. David S. Azzolina. (Folklore Ser.). 250p. 1985. lib. bdg. 33.00 o.p. (ISBN 0-8240-8788-7). Garland Pub.

Talent Education School of Shinichi Suzuki - An Analysis: The Application of the Suzuki Philosophy & Methods to All Areas of Instruction. 3rd, rev. ed. Ray Landers. (Illus.). 64p. 1984. 13.95 o.p. (ISBN 0-682-40154-4, Banner); pap. 8.95 o.p. (ISBN 0-682-40155-2). Exposition-Phoenix.

Talent for Destruction. Sheila Radley. 1984. pap. 2.50 o.s.i. (ISBN 0-345-31250-3). Ballantine.

Talent to Amuse: A Biography of Noel Coward. Sheridan Morley. (Illus.). 400p. 1985. 24.95 o.p. (ISBN 0-316-58371-5). Little.

Tales. Edgar Allan Poe. (Great Illustrated Classics Ser.). (gr. 9 up). 1979. 10.95 o.s.i. (ISBN 0-396-07759-5). Dodd.

Tales & Traditions of Scottish Castles. Nigel Tranter. (Illus.). 112p. 1983. 40.00x o.p. (ISBN 0-904265-69-2, Pub. by Macdonald Pub UK). State Mutual Bk.

Tales & Traditions of the Eskimo. Henrik Rink. (Illus.). 480p. 1975. Repr. of 1875 ed. 27.50x o.p. (ISBN 0-7735-0218-1, McGill Canada). U of Toronto Pr.

Tales for a Stormy Night. Dorothy S. Davis. 1985. pap. 3.25 o.p. (ISBN 0-380-69882-X). Avon.

Tales for My Brothers' Keepers. Thomas Flynn. 112p. 1976. 6.95 o.p. (ISBN 0-393-07502-8). Norton.

Tales from Peking Opera. (Illus.). 232p. (Orig.). 1985. pap. 6.95 o.p. (ISBN 0-8351-1399-X). China Bks.

Tales from the Blue Stacks. Robert Bernen. LC 78-3742. 1978. 8.95 o.s.i. (ISBN 0-684-15540-0, ScribT). Scribner.

Tales from the Levee: The Folklore of St. John the Baptist Parish. Marcia G. Gaudet. (Louisiana Folklife Ser.). 116p. 1984. 10.95 o.p. (ISBN 0-940984-21-0). U of SW LA Ctr LA Studies.

Tales from the Midwest. Gladys L. Luke. 1985. 6.95 o.p. (ISBN 0-533-06127-X). Vantage.

Tales from the Shawangunk Mountains: A Naturalist's Musings, a Bushwhacker's Guide. Marc B. Fried. LC 81-8017. (Illus.). 112p. 1981. 10.95 o.p. (ISBN 0-935272-17-8); pap. 6.95 o.p. (ISBN 0-935272-18-6). ADK Mtn Club.

Tales from the White Hart. Arthur C. Clarke. LC 76-95870. 1970. 5.75 o.s.i. (ISBN 0-15-187979-6). HarBraceJ.

Tales from Tibetan Opera. Wang Yao. (Illus.). 214p. 1986. pap. 6.95 o.p. (ISBN 0-8351-1657-3). China Bks.

Tales in Rhyme. Sue Palmer. (Illus.). 1978. 4.00 o.p. (ISBN 0-682-48904-2). Exposition-Phoenix.

Tales of a Dalai Lama. Pierre Delattre. LC 74-153958. (Fiction Ser.). 160p. 1978. pap. 5.95 o.p. (ISBN 0-916870-10-3). Creative Arts Bk.

Tales of a Hoosier Village: A History of Bristol, Indiana. Ed. by Jean A. Young. LC 88-40028. (Illus.). 250p. (Orig.). 1988. text ed. 24.95x o.p. (ISBN 1-55605-037-2). Wyndham Hall.

Tales of a Rat-Hunting Man. D. Brian Plummer. (Illus.). 1978. 18.00 o.p. (ISBN 0-85115-097-7, Pub. by Boydell & Brewer). Longwood Pub Group.

Tales of an All-Night Town. Elin Schoen. LC 79-1841. 1979. 9.95 o.p. (ISBN 0-15-184993-5). HarBraceJ.

Tales of An Old Ocean. Tjeerd Van Andel. (Illus.). 1978. pap. 8.95 o.p. (ISBN 0-393-03213-2, Norton Lib); pap. 3.95 o.p. (ISBN 0-393-00883-5). Norton.

Tales of Atlantis & the Enchanted Islands. Thomas W. Higginson. (Newcastle Mythology Library: Vol. 3). (Illus.). 260p. 1977. pap. 5.95 o.p. (ISBN 0-87877-042-9, M-42). Newcastle Pub.

Tales of Edisto. Nell S. Graydon. (Illus.). 166p. 1983. Repr. of 1955 ed. 12.95 o.p. (ISBN 0-87844-053-4). Sandlapper Pub Co.

Tales of Human Frailty & the Gentleness of God. Kenneth G. Phifer. LC 73-16914. (Orig.). 1974. pap. 1.00 o.p. (ISBN 0-8042-2197-9, John Knox). Westminster John Knox.

Tales of King Arthur. Thomas Malory. Ed. by Michael Senior. LC 81-40412. (Illus.). 322p. 1982. pap. 15.95 o.s.i. (ISBN 0-8052-0719-8). Schocken.

Tales of Maritime Maine: The Vanished Years of the Maine Coast Brought to Life in Three Absorbing Tales. Bruce Clark. Ed. by Jill Mason. LC 86-51015. 168p. 1987. 12.95 o.p. (ISBN 0-89909-122-9). Yankee Bks.

Tales of Mean Streets. Arthur Morrison. 175p. pap. 6.95 o.s.i. (ISBN 0-85115-221-X, Pub. by Boydell & Brewer). Academy Chi Pubs.

Tales of Pirx the Pilot. Stanislaw Lem. 224p. 1981. pap. 2.95 o.p. (ISBN 0-380-55665-0, 55665-0, Bard). Avon.

Tales of Pirx the Pilot. Stanislaw Lem. Ed. by Helen Wolff. Tr. by Louis Iribarne. LC 79-1832. (Helen & Kurt Wolff Bk.). 1979. 8.95 o.s.i. (ISBN 0-15-187978-8). HarBraceJ.

Tales of Poultney. Elton Haynes. 1977. 3.95 o.p. (ISBN 0-682-48935-2). Exposition-Phoenix.

Tales of Power. Carlos Castaneda. 287p. 1975. pap. 4.95 o.s.i. (ISBN 0-671-22144-2, Touchstone Bks). S&S.

Tales of Pudding Hill: True Animal Stories from New Hampshire. James E. Frazer. 1975. 5.00 o.p. (ISBN 0-682-48096-7). Exposition-Phoenix.

Tales of Racing & Chasing. Terry Biddlecombe. (Illus.). 96p. 1986. 20.95 o.s.i. (ISBN 0-09-162690-0, Pub. by Century Hutchinson). David & Charles.

Tales of Suspense. Edgar Allan Poe. LC 85-63065. (Illus.). 272p. (gr. 7-12). 1986. 12.95 o.p. (ISBN 0-89577-225-6). RD Assn.

Tales of Ten Worlds. Arthur C. Clarke. LC 62-16730. 1962. 6.95 o.s.i. (ISBN 0-15-187980-X). HarBraceJ.

Tales of the Big Bend. Elton Miles. LC 76-17977. (Illus.). 200p. 1976. 11.50 o.p. (ISBN 0-89096-021-6). Tex A&M Univ Pr.

Tales of the Great Western. O. S. Nock. (Illus.). 176p. 1984. 22.95 o.p. (ISBN 0-7153-8347-7). David & Charles.

Tales of the Mountains & the Steppes. C. Aitmatov. 280p. 1973. 6.95 o.p. (ISBN 0-8285-0937-9, Pub. by Progress Pubs USSR). Imported Pubns.

Tales of the Vikings: Saga Translations & Their Histories. Jeffrey R. Redmond. (Illus.). 1982. 19.95 o.p. (ISBN 0-682-49799-1, Banner). Exposition-Phoenix.

Tales of the Witchworld, Vol. 1. Ed. by Andre Norton. 288p. 1987. 18.95 o.s.i. (ISBN 0-312-94475-6); pap. 8.95 cancelled o.s.i. (ISBN 0-312-94466-7). Bluejay Bks.

Tales of Torture. 84p. 1977. pap. 2.00 o.s.i. (ISBN 0-686-95469-6). Ananda Marga.

Tales of Wonder. Jane Yolen. LC 82-62359. 272p. 1987. 14.45 o.s.i. (ISBN 0-8052-3843-3). Schocken.

Tales Out of School. Roger White & Dave Brockington. (Routledge Education Bks.). 148p. 1983. pap. 8.95x o.p. (ISBN 0-7100-9446-9). Routledge Chapman & Hall.

Taliesin & King Arthur. Ruth Robbins. LC 75-129540. (Illus.). (gr. 2-5). 1970. 4.75 o.p. (ISBN 0-395-27721-3, Pub. by Parnassus); PLB 4.59 o.p. (ISBN 0-87466-027-0). HM.

Talislantan Handbook. Stephan M. Sechi. (Illus.). 88p. 1987. pap. 12.00 o.p. (ISBN 0-9610770-8-5). Bard Games.

Talk Never Dies: The Language of Huli Disputes. Laurence Goldman. LC 83-18294. 352p. 1984. 49.95x o.p. (ISBN 0-422-78210-6, NO. 4009). Routledge Chapman & Hall.

Talk Show Guest Directory. Mitchell P. Davis. 104p. 1985. pap. 30.00 o.p. (ISBN 0-934333-00-9). Broadcast Inter.

Talk to the Deaf see **Joy of Signing: The New Illustrated Guide for Mastering Sign Language & the Manual Alphabet.**

Talk to Yourself: Experiencing Intrapersonal Communication. Genelle Austin-Lett & Janet Sprague. LC 75-31037. (Illus.). 160p. 1976. pap. 9.50 o.p. (ISBN 0-395-18576-9). HM.

Talk Two: Children Using English as a Second Language. Joan Tough. vii, 216p. pap. text ed. 16.50x o.p. (ISBN 0-906383-27-7, 00588, Pub. by Onyx Pr UK). Heinemann Ed.

Talkin' about Us: Writing by Students in the Upward Bound Program. Ed. by Bill Wertheim & Irma Gonzalez. (Illus.). 1970. pap. 9.95x o.p. (ISBN 0-89197-436-9). Irvington.

Talkin' & Testifyin' The Language of Black America. Geneva Smitherman. 1977. 13.95 o.p. (ISBN 0-395-25355-1). HM.

Talking About Cakes with an Irish & Scottish Accent. Margaret Bates. 1964. text ed. 16.25 o.p. (ISBN 0-08-010004-X). Pergamon.

Talking about God: Doing Theology in the Context of Modern Pluralism. David Tracy & John B. Cobb, Jr. 144p. 1983. 6.95 o.p. (ISBN 0-8164-2458-6). HarpR.

Talking about Relationships. 2nd ed. Herbert J. Hess & Charles O. Tucker. 80p. 1980. pap. text ed. 4.50x o.p. (ISBN 0-917974-47-6). Waveland Pr.

Talking Christmas Tree: Family Doings for Christmas Time. Robert G. Konzelman. (Orig.). 1966. pap. 1.75 o.p. (ISBN 0-8066-0628-2, 10-6193, Augsburg). Augsburg Fortress.

Talking E. T. Wordbook. Universal City Studios, Inc. Staff. (Texas Insruments Magic Wand Speaking Library). (Illus.). 32p. (ps-3). 1982. text ed. 7.30 o.p. (ISBN 0-89512-065-8). Tex Instr Inc.

Talking Heads. David Gans. 1985. pap. 9.95 o.p. (ISBN 0-380-89954-X). Avon.

Talking Medicine: America's Doctors Tell Their Stories. Ed. by Peter M. Rabinowitz. 1981. 14.95 o.p. (ISBN 0-393-01397-9). Norton.

Talking Sex with Your Kids. Lois B. Morris. (Orig.). 1984. pap. 6.95 o.p. (ISBN 0-671-50022-8, Fireside). S&S.

Talking Tech: A Conversational Guide to Science & Technology. Howard Rheingold & Howard Levine. LC 82-21537. (Illus.). 324p. 1983. pap. 6.45 o.p. (ISBN 0-688-01603-0, Quill NY). Morrow.

Talking with Employees: A Guide for Managers. Marion S. Kellogg. LC 79-50242. 162p. 1979. 19.00x o.p. (ISBN 0-87201-825-3). Gulf Pub.

Talking with You. Ralph J. Orlando, Sr. 104p. 1987. 6.95 o.p. (ISBN 0-8062-2026-0). Carlton.

Talks on Religion. H. F. Bell. 1958. (ISBN 0-8022-0094-X). Philos Lib.

Talks on Soviet Democracy. M. A. Krutogolov. 1980. 6.95 o.p. (ISBN 0-8285-1773-8, Pub. by Progress Pubs USSR). Imported Pubns.

Talks with a Devil. P. D. Ouspensky. 160p. 1988. pap. 9.95 o.p. (ISBN 1-85063-096-8). Routledge Chapman & Hall.

Tall Are the Hills. Bert G. Boss. 1972. 7.50 o.p. (ISBN 0-682-47448-7). Exposition-Phoenix.

Tall, Skinny, Towheaded & Miserable. Lillian Pohlmann. LC 74-22398. (gr. 6 up). 1975. 5.75 o.s.i. (ISBN 0-664-32564-5, Westminster). Westminster John Knox.

Tall Stance. Elois S. Sampson. 1979. 5.50 o.p. (ISBN 0-682-49434-8). Exposition-Phoenix.

Tall Trees, Tough Men. Robert E. Pike. (Illus.). 1967. 14.95 o.p. (ISBN 0-393-07351-3). Norton.

Tall Truths from Short Stories. Crate H. Jones. (Orig.). 1987. pap. 6.95 o.p. (ISBN 0-8054-5729-1). Broadman.

Tallest Tower. Frank Pozmantier. 1952. (ISBN 0-8022-2011-8). Philos Lib.

Tallest Tower: Eiffel & the Belle Epoque. Joseph Harriss. LC 74-31279. 256p. 1975. 10.00 o.p. (ISBN 0-395-20435-6). HM.

Talleyman. John James. 247p. 1988. 18.95 o.p. (ISBN 0-575-03791-1, Pub. by Gollancz England). David & Charles.

Tallgrass Prairie: The Inland Sea. Patricia D. Duncan. LC 78-60177. (Illus.). 1979. 20.00 o.p. (ISBN 0-913504-44-0); pap. 12.95 o.s.i. (ISBN 0-913504-56-4). Lowell Pr.

Tallinn: A Guide Book. 67p. 1980. 6.95 o.p. (ISBN 0-8285-1710-X, Pub. by Progress Pubs USSR). Imported Pubns.

Talmud of Jerusalem. Tr. by H. Polano. 160p. (ISBN 0-8022-1996-9). Philos Lib.

Taman Budiman: Memoirs of an Unorthodox Civil Servant. Mubin Sheppard. 278p. (Orig.). 1979. pap. text ed. 17.50x o.p. Heinemann Ed.

Tamar & the Tiger. Susan Jeschke. LC 79-22591. (Illus.). 40p. (gr. k-2). 1980. 8.95 o.s.i. (ISBN 0-03-052176-9). H Holt & Co.

Tamara. John Krizanc. 1988. (Pub. by Eyre Methuen England). Routledge Chapman & Hall.

Tamarack Tree. Betty Underwood. (gr. 5-9). 1971. 5.95 o.p. (ISBN 0-395-12761-0). HM.

Tamarind: Twenty-Five Years. Text by Marjorie Devon. 98p. Date not set. pap. 14.00 o.p. Moyer Bell Limited.

Tamarisk Tree: My Quest for Liberty & Love, Vol. 1. Dora Russell. (Illus.). 304p. 1983. pap. 7.50 o.p. (ISBN 0-86068-001-0, Pub. by Virago Pr). Salem Hse Pubs.

Tambia Bourri. Evelyn F. Update. 224p. 1987. text ed. 16.00 o.p. (ISBN 0-682-40306-7). Exposition-Phoenix.

Tame Fundamental Group of a Formal Neighbourhood of a Divisor with Normal Crossing on a Scheme. A. Grothendieck & J. P. Murre. (Lecture Notes in Mathematics: Vol. 208). 1971. pap. 11.00 o.p. (ISBN 0-387-05499-5). Springer-Verlag.

Tamerlano. George F. Handel & Howard M. Brown. LC 76-21083. (Italian Opera 1640-1770 Ser.). 1978. lib. bdg. 77.00 o.p. (ISBN 0-8240-2626-8). Garland Pub.

Taming of a Dream. Agustin Lopez. LC 86-913600. 256p. 1987. text ed. 17.50 o.p. (ISBN 0-682-40320-2). Exposition-Phoenix.

Taming of the Shrew. Berger. 1986. lib. bdg. 54.00 o.p. (ISBN 0-8240-8892-1). Garland Pub.

Taming Tension Through Total Health. Leo R. Van Dolson. Ed. by Richard W. Coffen. LC 83-23028. (Illus.). 96p. (Orig.). 1984. pap. 6.50 o.p. (ISBN 0-8280-0224-X). Review & Herald.

Taming the Giant Corporation. Ralph Nader & Mark Green. 1977. 10.50 o.p. (ISBN 0-393-08753-0, N872, Norton Lib); pap. 3.95 o.p. (ISBN 0-393-00872-X). Norton.

Taming the Tongue: Why Christians Should Care about What They Say. Mark Kinzer. (Living as a Christian Ser.). 1982. pap. 3.95 o.p. (ISBN 0-89283-165-0). Servant.

Taming the TV Habit. Kevin Perrotta. 162p. (Orig.). 1982. pap. 6.95 o.p. (ISBN 0-89283-155-3). Servant.

Tammy & Dolls You Love to Dress. John Axe. (Illus.). 81p. pap. 5.95 o.p. (ISBN 0-87588-155-6, 2186). Hobby Hse.

Tammy Camps in the Rocky Mountains. Elizabeth Baker. (gr. 2-5). 1970. 3.95 o.p. (ISBN 0-395-06589-5); PLB 4.95 o.p. (ISBN 0-395-06590-9). HM.

Tampa Bay Buccanners. James R. Rothaus. (NFL Today Ser.). 48p. (gr. 4 up). 1986. PLB 10.45 o.p. (ISBN 0-88682-050-2). Creative Ed.

Tamsen. David Galloway. 448p. 1983. 14.95 o.p. (ISBN 0-15-187992-3). HarBraceJ.

Tan & Sandy Silence. John D. MacDonald. 256p. 1985. pap. 3.50 o.p. (ISBN 0-449-12969-1, GM). Fawcett.

Tana Maguire. Diana Saunders. 300p. 1987. pap. 3.95 o.p. (ISBN 1-55547-159-5). Critics Choice Paper.

Tandava Laksanam or the Fundamentals of Ancient Hindu Dancing. V. N. Naidu. (Illus.). 1971. 20.00 o.s.i. (ISBN 0-685-25498-4). E J Brill USA.

Tangled Bank. Stanley Edgar Hyman. LC 62-11682. 1974. pap. text ed. 4.25x o.p. (ISBN 0-689-70513-1, 204, Atheneum). Macmillan.

Tangled Butterfly. Marion D. Bauer. LC 79-23405. 162p. (gr. 6 up). 1980. 12.70 o.p. (ISBN 0-395-29110-0, Clarion). HM.

Tangled Wing: Biological Constraints on the Human Spirit. Melvin Konner. LC 81-47464. 1982. 19.95 o.s.i. (ISBN 0-03-057062-X). H Holt & Co.

Tangles Mesh. Lee Karr. (Velvet Glove Ser.: No. 23). 1985. pap. 2.25 o.p. (ISBN 0-380-89789-X). Avon.

Tanglewood. Herbert Kupferberg. LC 76-11772. 1977. pap. text ed. 9.95 o.p. (ISBN 0-07-035644-0). McGraw.

Tanglewood Tales see Wonder-Book.

Tango. Slawomir Mrozek. Tr. by Ralph Manheim & Teresa Dzieduszycka. (Orig.). 1969. pap. 3.95 o.p. (ISBN 0-394-17264-7, E433, Ever). Grove.

Tango November. John Howlett. LC 76-53950. 1977. 8.95 o.p. (ISBN 0-689-10794-3, Atheneum). Macmillan.

Tangrams. Elementary Science Study Staff. 1975. tchr's guide 8.72 o.p. (ISBN 0-07-018587-5). McGraw.

Tank Pioneers. Kenneth Macksey. (Illus.). 224p. 1981. 18.95 o.p. (ISBN 0-86720-563-6). Janes Info Group.

Tank Sergeant. Ralph Zumbro. (Illus.). 264p. pap. 3.95 o.p. (ISBN 0-671-63945-5). Archway.

Tank War Nineteen Thirty-Nine to Nineten Forty-Five. Janusz Piekalkiewicz. (Illus.). 332p. 1986. 24.95 o.p. (ISBN 0-7137-1666-5, Pub. by Blandford Pr England). Sterling.

Tank War Vietnam. Simon Dunstan. (Tanks Illustrated Ser.: Vol. 6). (Illus.). 68p. (Orig.). 1985. pap. 9.95 o.p. (ISBN 0-85368-603-3, Pub. by Arms & Armour). Sterling.

Tanker Register, 1986. 26th ed. 1986. 275.00x o.p. (ISBN 0-8002-3998-9). Intl Pubns Serv.

Tanner Lectures on Human Values, Vol. I: 1980. Ed. by Sterling M. McMurring. Joel Feinberg & R. M. Hare. 1980. 20.00x o.p. (ISBN 0-87480-178-8). U of Utah Pr.

Tanner Lectures on Human Values, Vol. III: 1982. Sterling M. McMurrin et al. 1982. 20.00x o.p. (ISBN 0-87480-202-4). U of Utah Pr.

Tantalus. Amanda Hemingway. 1984. 14.95 o.p. (ISBN 0-87795-595-6, Arbor Hse). Morrow.

Tanzanian Doctor. Leader Stirling. (Illus.). 1977. 10.95 o.p. (ISBN 0-7735-0305-6, McGill Canada). U of Toronto Pr.

Tao of Health. Date not set. (ISBN 0-8052-0596-9). Random.

Tao of Health: The Way of Total Well-Being. Michael Blate. (Illus., Orig.). 1978. pap. 6.95 o.s.i. (ISBN 0-916878-05-8). Falkynor Bks.

Tao of Symbols. James N. Powell. 1982. 11.50 o.p. (ISBN 0-688-01351-1). Morrow.

Tao Te Ching. Lao Tsu. Tr. by Richard Wilhelm. 224p. 1985. pap. 10.95 o.p. (ISBN 1-85063-011-9). Routledge Chapman & Hall.

Tao: The Pathless Path, 2 vols. Bhagwan Shree Rajneesh. Ed. by Ma Prem Asha & Ma Prema Veena. LC 82-232884. (Tao Ser.). (Illus.). 1979. Vol. I, 432 pgs. 17.95 ea. o.p. (ISBN 0-88050-148-0). Vol. II, 540 pgs (ISBN 0-88050-149-9). Vol. I, 440p. pap. 15.95 o.p. (ISBN 0-88050-648-2); Vol. II, 1978, 542p. pap. write for info. o.p. (ISBN 0-88050-649-0). Chidvilas Inc.

Taoism & the Rite of Cosmic Renewal. Michael R. Saso. (Illus.). 1972. pap. 8.00x o.p. (ISBN 0-87422-011-4). Wash St U Pr.

Taoist Ways of Healing: The Chinese Art of Pa Chin Hsien. Chee Soo. 144p. (Orig.). 1986. pap. 7.95 o.p. (ISBN 0-85030-475-X, Pub. by Aquarian Pr England). Sterling.

Taoist Yoga: The Chinese Art of K'ai Men. Chee Soo. (Illus.). 160p. (Orig.). 1983. pap. 6.99 o.p. (ISBN 0-85030-332-X, Pub. by Aquarian Pr England). Sterling.

Taormina. Wilhelm Von Gloeden. (Illus.). 32p. (Orig.). 1985. pap. 6.50 o.p. (ISBN 0-907040-75-6, Pub. by GMP England). Alyson Pubns.

Taormina. Photos by Wilhelm Von Gloeden. (Illus.). 112p. 1986. 50.00 o.p. (ISBN 0-942642-22-8). Twelvetrees Pr.

Taos Indians. Blanche C. Grant. LC 76-40917. (Beautiful Rio Grande Classics Ser). 1976. lib. bdg. 10.00 o.p. (ISBN 0-87380-137-7). Rio Grande.

Tap City. Ron Abell. 256p. 1985. 15.45i o.p. (ISBN 0-316-00200-3). Little.

Tap Dancing: Techniques, Routines, Terminology. Constance Atwater. LC 75-158799. (Illus.). (YA) (gr. 9 up). 1971. 13.50 o.p. (ISBN 0-8048-0671-3). C E Tuttle.

Tape for the Turn of the Year. A. R. Ammons. 1972. 6.95 o.p. (ISBN 0-393-04464-5, 00659, Norton Lib); pap. 3.95 o.p. (ISBN 0-393-00659-X). Norton.

Tapestry. Ed. by Wilfred Bockelman. 128p. (Orig.). 1985. pap. 4.95 o.p. (ISBN 0-8066-2177-X, 10-6201, Augsburg). Augsburg Fortress.

Tapestry. Edith Schaeffer. 640p. 1985. pap. 10.95 o.p. (ISBN 0-8499-3016-2, 3016-2). Word Bks.

Tapestry Maker: Poems by Ted Malone. E. T. Malone. LC 73-179907. 96p. 1971. 1.98 o.p. (ISBN 0-910244-64-2). Blair.

Tapestry: Monographs. Mary Vance. (Architecture Ser.: A 1358). 37p. 1985. 5.25 o.p. (ISBN 0-89028-348-6). Vance Biblios.

Tapestry of Childhood. Bettye V. Colburn. (Illus.). 230p. 1979. 9.00 o.p. (ISBN 0-682-49297-3). Exposition-Phoenix.

Tapestry of Eternity. Nellie E. Friend. 1951. (ISBN 0-8022-0547-X). Philos Lib.

Tapestry of the North. Amelia B. Kesling. 159p. 1986. 8.75 o.p. (ISBN 0-8062-2628-5). Carlton.

Tapestry Warriors. Cherry Wilder. LC 82-16279. 276p. (gr. 8up). 1983. pap. 12.95 o.s.i. (ISBN 0-689-30966-X, Atheneum). Macmillan.

Taps for a Jim Crow Army: Letters from Black Soldiers in World War II. Phillip McGuire. LC 82-22689. 278p. 1983. lib. bdg. 23.50 o.p. (ISBN 0-87436-024-2); pap. text ed. 12.75 o.p. (ISBN 0-87436-041-2). ABC-Clio.

Tar Heel Sights: Guide to North Carolina's Heritage. Marguerite Schumann. LC 82-59030. (Illus.). 192p. 1983. pap. 8.95 o.p. (ISBN 0-914788-64-7). Globe Pequot.

Tarahumaras. Antonin Artaud. 160p. 1974. 8.95 o.p. (ISBN 0-686-53838-2). Schoenhof.

Tara's Healing. Janice H. Giles. (General Ser.). 313p. 1986. lib. bdg. 16.95x o.p. (ISBN 0-8161-4050-2, Large Print Bks). G K Hall.

Tara's Song. Barbara F. Johnson. 1978. pap. 3.50 o.p. (ISBN 0-380-39123-6, 60062-5). Avon.

Tardive Dyskinesia & Related Involuntary Movement Disorders. Joseph DeVeaugh-Geiss. (Illus.). 224p. 1982. text ed. 39.00 o.p. (ISBN 0-7236-7006-4). Butterworth.

Tardive Dyskinesia, Task Force Report Eighteen. American Psychiatric Association Staff. LC 80-65372. (Monographs). (Illus.). 212p. 1980. 12.00x o.p. (ISBN 0-89042-218-4, 42-218-4). Am Psychiatric.

Target America: The Influence of Communist Propaganda on U. S. Media. James L. Tyson. (Christian Activist Ser.). 1985. pap. 5.95 o.p. (ISBN 0-89526-816-7). Regnery Gateway.

Target Berlin: Mission Two Hundred Fifty: Sixth of March Nineteen Forty-Four. Jeffrey Ethell & Alfred Price. (Illus.). 224p. 1982. 19.95 o.p. (ISBN 0-86720-551-2). Janes Info Group.

Target Mayflower. Richard C. Hirschhorn. LC 77-73056. 1977. 8.95 o.p. (ISBN 0-15-187995-8). HarBraceJ.

Target Tokyo: The Story of the Sorge Spy Ring. Gordon W. Prange et al. LC 84-3866. (Illus.). 640p. 1985. text ed. 24.95 o.p. (ISBN 0-07-050677-9). McGraw.

Targeting Food Subsidies for the Needy: The Use of Cost-Benefit Analysis & Institutional Design. Abel Mateus. (Working Paper: No. 617). 88p. 1983. 5.00 o.p. (ISBN 0-8213-0295-7, WP 0617). World Bank.

Targeting of Drugs. Ed. by Gregory Gregoriadis et al. LC 82-3822. (NATO ASI Series A, Life Sciences: Vol. 47). 440p. 1982. 75.00x o.p. (ISBN 0-306-41001-X, Plenum Pr). Plenum Pub.

Targeting the Top. Nancy Lee. 352p. 1981. pap. 2.95 o.s.i. (ISBN 0-345-29643-5). Ballantine.

Targum & Testament: Aramaic Paraphrases of the Hebrew Bible: a Light on the New Testament. Martin McNamara. 226p. 1972. 17.50x o.p. (ISBN 0-7165-0619-X, BBA 02203, Pub. by Irish Academic Pr Ireland). Biblio Dist.

Tariff Schedules & Protocols: Final Act Adopted at the 9th Session of the Contracting Parties & Protocols Amending the General Agreement. (Eng. & Fr.). 1955. pap. 5.00 o.p. (ISBN 0-686-93110-6, G128, GATT). UNIPUB.

Tarikh. Incl. Vol. 1, No. 1. Leadership in Nineteenth Century Africa. Ed. by J. B. Webster. 1965. pap. 5.00x (ISBN 0-582-60855-4); Vol. 1, No. 2. African Leadership & European Domination. Ed. by J. B. Webster. 1965. pap. text ed. 5.00x (ISBN 0-582-60856-2); Vol. 1, No. 3. Man in Africa: From the Earliest Beginnings to the Coming of Metal. Ed. by J. B. Webster. 1966. pap. text ed. 5.00x o.p. (ISBN 0-582-60857-0); Vol. 1, No. 4. Modernisers in Africa. Ed. by J. B. Webster. 1967. pap. text ed. 5.00x (ISBN 0-582-60858-9); Vol. 2, No. 1. Early African Christianity. Ed. by J. B. Webster & O. Ikime. 1967. pap. text ed. 5.00x o.p. (ISBN 0-582-60859-7); Vol. 2, No. 2. African Achievement & Tragedy. Ed. by J. B. Webster & O. Ikime. 1968. pap. text ed. 5.00x (ISBN 0-582-60860-0); Vol. 2, No. 3. Six Aspects of African History. Ed. by Obaro Ikime & Segun Osoba. 1968. pap. text ed. 5.00x (ISBN 0-582-60861-9); Vol. 2, No. 4. France in Africa. Segun Osoba & Obaro Ikime. 1969. pap. text ed. 5.00x (ISBN 0-582-60862-7); Vol. 3, No. 1. Christianity in Modern Africa. Ed. by Segun Osoba & Obaro Ikime. 1969. pap. text ed. 5.00x (ISBN 0-582-60863-5); Vol. 3, No. 2. People of Uganda in the 19th Century. Ed. by Segun Osoba & Obaro Ikime. 1970. pap. text ed. 5.00x (ISBN 0-582-60864-3); Vol. 3, No. 3. Indirect Rule in British Africa. Ed. by Obaro Ikime & Segun Osoba. 1970. pap. text ed. 5.00x (ISBN 0-582-60865-1); Vol. 3, No. 4. Independence Movements in Africa, Pt. 1. Ed. by Obaro Ikime. 1971. pap. text ed. 5.00x (ISBN 0-582-60866-X); Vol. 4, No. 1. Independence Movements in Africa, Pt. 2. Ed. by Obaro Ikime & Segun Osoba. 1971. pap. text ed. 5.00x (ISBN 0-582-60867-8); Vol. 4, No. 2. Government in Pre-Colonial Africa. Ed. by Obaro Ikime & Segun Osoba. 1973. pap. text ed. 5.00x (ISBN 0-582-60868-6); Vol. 4, No. 3-4. European Conquest & African Resistance, Pts. 1-2. Ed. by Obaro Ikime & Segun Osoba. 1973-74. pap. text ed. 5.00x (ISBN 0-582-60316-1). Vol. 4, No. 3 (ISBN 0-582-60869-4). Vol. 4, No. 4. pap. 5.00x o.p. (ISBN 0-582-60870-8). Humanities.

Tarikh: Historical Method, Vol. 6, No. 1. Ed. by Robert Smith. 1978. pap. text ed. 5.00x o.p. (ISBN 0-582-60357-9). Humanities.

Tarnished Crown: The Quest for a Racetrack Champion. Carol Flake. LC 86-19878. 384p. 1987. 18.95 o.p. (ISBN 0-385-19775-6). Doubleday.

Tarnished Star. Lee F. Wells. 1976. pap. 1.25 o.p. (ISBN 0-380-00853-X, 31229). Avon.

Tarnished Victory. Created by Rosemary Joyce. (Dream Girls Ser.: No. 3). (YA) (gr. 7 up). pap. 2.50 o.p. (ISBN 0-671-62112-2). Archway.

Tarot Path to Self-Development. Micheline Stuart. LC 77-6016. (Illus.). 57p. 1977. pap. 5.95 o.p. (ISBN 0-87773-110-1). Shambhala Pubns.

Tartans: Their Art & History. Ann Sutton & Richard Carr. LC 84-6488. (Illus.). 192p. 1984. 19.95 o.p. (ISBN 0-668-06189-8, 6189-8). Arco.

Tarzan Alive. Philip Jose Farmer. LC 81-80084. 352p. 1981. pap. 2.75 o.s.i. (ISBN 0-87216-876-X). Playboy Pbks.

Tasha: Her Middle Name Is Mischief. Louise Kantenwein. (Illus.). (gr. k-5). 1981. 5.00 o.p. Exposition-Phoenix.

Tashkent: A Guide. V. Tyurikov. 94p. 1985. 7.95 o.p. (ISBN 0-8285-2800-4, Pub. by Raduga Pubs USSR). Imported Pubns.

Task Analysis for the Sheetfed Offset Press. LC 88-80679. 110p. 1987. text ed. 350.00 o.p. (ISBN 0-88362-115-0). Graphic Arts Tech Found.

Task & Organization. Ed. by Eric J. Miller. LC 75-12606. (Individuals, Groups & Organizations Ser.). 379p. 1976. 86.00x o.p. (ISBN 0-471-60605-7, Pub. by Wiley-Interscience). Wiley.

Task-Centered Management in Human Services. Bageshwari Parihar. (Illus.). 190p. 1984. 24.00 o.p. (ISBN 0-398-04920-3). C C Thomas.

Task Force Report: The Courts. United States Task Force on the Administration of Justice. LC 77-28367. (Illus.). x, 178p. 1978. Repr. of 1967 ed. lib. bdg. 35.00x o.p. (ISBN 0-313-20225-7, USTF). Greenwood.

Task of Nations. Herbert V. Evatt. LC 79-152595. 279p. 1972. Repr. of 1949 ed. lib. bdg. 35.00x o.p. (ISBN 0-8371-6028-6, EVTN). Greenwood.

Task-Related Norms in a State Legislature: The Case of Oklahoma. Lelan E. McLemore. (Legislative Research Ser.: No. 5). 1973. pap. 2.00 o.p. (ISBN 0-686-18647-8). Univ OK Gov Res.

Task-Specific Problem Solving Architectures. B. Chandrasekaran & Tom Bylander. (Illus.). 100p. 1988. pap. text ed. 12.00 o.p. (ISBN 0-929280-10-5). Amer Artificial.

Tasks to Jobs: Developing a Modular System of Training for Hotel Occupations. International Labour Office Staff. (Hotel & Tourism Management Ser.: No. 3). 302p. 1984. text ed. 21.00 o.p. (ISBN 92-2-102148-3). Intl Labour Office.

Tassajara Bread Book. Edward E. Brown. LC 75-143877. (Illus.). 145p. (Orig.). 1977. pap. 5.95 o.p. (ISBN 0-87773-025-3, 73003-8). Shambhala Pubns.

Tassajara Bread Book. Edward E Brown. 1974. pap. 5.95 o.p. (ISBN 0-394-73003-8). Random.

Tassajara Cooking. Edward E Brown. 1974. pap. 8.95 o.p. (ISBN 0-394-70949-7). Random.

Tassajara Cooking: A Vegetarian Cooking Book. Edward E. Brown. LC 73-86144. (Illus.). 256p. 1974. pap. 8.95 o.p. (ISBN 0-87773-047-4, 70949-7). Shambhala Pubns.

Taste & See. William O. Paulsell. LC 76-5634. 1976. pap. 2.50x o.p. (ISBN 0-8358-0347-3). Upper Room.

Taste of Carrot. William Hoest. LC 67-28287. (Illus.). (gr. 1 up). 1967. pap. 1.95 o.p. (ISBN 0-689-20168-0, Atheneum). Macmillan.

Taste of Chaucer: Selections from the Canterbury Tales. Ed. by Anne Malcolmson. LC 64-11493. (Illus.). 184p. (gr. 7 up). 1964. 5.95 o.p. (ISBN 0-15-284270-5, HJ). HarBraceJ.

Taste of China. James Ballingall. (Illus.). 208p. 1984. 13.95 o.p. (ISBN 0-531-09768-4). Watts.

Taste of France. Fay Sharmon & Klaus Boehm. 1982. pap. 10.95 o.p. (ISBN 0-395-32561-7). HM.

Taste of Hate. Lisa Muro. LC 85-90224. 98p. 1985. 7.95 o.p. (ISBN 0-533-06722-7). Vantage.

Taste of Ireland. Theodora FitzGibbon. LC 78-80422. (Illus.). 1969. 5.95 o.p. (ISBN 0-395-07681-1). HM.

Taste of Morocco: A Culinary Journey. Robert Carrier. 1987. 30.00 o.p. (ISBN 0-317-61085-6). Crown.

Taste of New Wine. Keith Miller. 1982. pap. 10.95 o.p. (ISBN 0-8499-0151-0, 4111-3). Word Bks.

Taste of Paradise. Margaret Mayo. (Lythway Ser.). 232p. 1988. lib. bdg. 18.50x o.p. (ISBN 0-7451-0687-0, Pub. by Chivers Pr UK). G K Hall.

Taste of Provence. Leslie Forbes. 1987. 19.95 o.s.i. (ISBN 0-316-28877-2). Little.

Taste of Rabbit Tracks: Expedition into a Frozen Wilderness. Mike Shields. 1978. 10.50 o.p. (ISBN 0-682-49082-2, Banner). Exposition-Phoenix.

Taste of Steel. Robert W. Marsh. 224p. 1982. pap. 2.50 o.p. (ISBN 0-8439-1155-7, Pub. by Leisure Bks CT). Dorchester Pub Co.

Taste of Texas. Jane Trahey. 1949. 14.45 o.p. (ISBN 0-394-40176-X). Random.

Taste of Thailand. David Scott & Kristiaan Inwood. (Illus.). 138p. 1987. pap. 15.95 o.s.i. (ISBN 0-7126-1291-2, Pub. by Century Hutchinson). David & Charles.

Taste of the West: Essays in Honor of Robert G. Athearn. Duane A. Smith. Ed. by Duane A. Smith. LC 82-21548. 1983. 17.95 o.p. (ISBN 0-87108-641-7). Pruett.

Taste of the West from Coors. Ed. by Anita Krajeski. (Illus.). 100p. 5.95 o.p. (ISBN 0-914091-20-4). Chicago Review.

Taste of Time. Ferol Egan. LC 76-48209. 1977. text ed. 9.95 o.p. (ISBN 0-07-019050-X). McGraw.

Taste of Tuscany: Classic Recipes from the Heart of Italy. Compiled by & illus. by Leslie Forbes. (Illus.). 1985. 16.95 o.p. (ISBN 0-316-28876-4). Little.

Taste of Wine: The Art & Science of Wine Appreciation. Emile Peynaud. Tr. by Michael Schuster from Fr. (Illus.). 258p. 1987. 27.50x o.p. (ISBN 0-356-14911-0, Pub. by MacD & Co). Trans-Atl Phila.

Taste of Yiddish. Lillian M Feinsilver. LC 70-88260. 480p. 1980. 14.95 o.p. (ISBN 0-498-02427-X); pap. 6.95 o.p. (ISBN 0-498-02515-2). A S Barnes.

Tasteful Interlude: American Interiors Through the Camera's Eye, 1860 to 1917. William Seale. LC 80-27341. (Illus.). 288p. 1981. pap. 17.50 o.p. (ISBN 0-910050-49-X). AASLH Pr.

Tastemakers: The Shaping of American Popular Taste. Russell Lynes. 16.25 o.p. (ISBN 0-8446-5786-7). Peter Smith.

Tasty Treats. Zokeisha. (Puffies Ser.). (Illus.). 8p. (ps). 1982. pap. 3.40 o.s.i. (ISBN 0-671-44847-1, Little Simon). S&S.

TAT-8 Fiber Optics Undersea Cable. 1984. 75.00 o.p. (ISBN 0-317-11964-8). Info Gatekeepers.

Tatsinda. Elizabeth Enright. LC 63-7888. (Illus.). (gr. 4-6). 1963. 6.95 o.p. (ISBN 0-15-284276-4, HJ). HarBraceJ.

Tattooed Potato & Other Clues. Ellen Raskin. (Illus.). 172p. (gr. 4-7). 1981. pap. 1.95 o.p. (ISBN 0-380-55558-1, 63875-4, Camelot). Avon.

Taurine In Nutrition & Neurology. Ed. by Ryan J. Huxtable & Herminia Pasantes-Morales. LC 81-15699. (Advances in Experimental Medicine & Biology: Vol. 139). 564p. 1981. 89.50x o.p. (ISBN 0-306-40839-2, Plenum Pr). Plenum Pub.

Tavern Cartoons. 2nd ed. William Armstrong. (Armstrong Cartoon Ser.). (Illus.). 48p. (Orig.). (ps up). 1972. pap. 1.00 o.p. (ISBN 0-913452-09-2). Jesuit Bks.

Tax Advisor: A Magazine of Tax Planning Trends & Techniques. 55.00 o.p. (ISBN 0-686-89546-0); 36.00 o.p. (ISBN 0-686-89547-9). Am Inst CPA.

Tax & Estate Planner's Complete Guide for Servicing the Professional Client. R. Sam Rea. 237p. 1982. 59.50 o.p. (ISBN 0-87624-566-1, Inst Busn Plan). P-H.

Tax & Expenditure Limitation by Constitutional Amendment: Four Perspectives on the California Initiative. William A. Niskanen et al. LC 73-9974. 69p. 1973. pap. 2.50x o.p. (ISBN 0-87772-170-X). UCB IGS.

Tax & Expenditure Limitations. Ed. by Ladd & Tideman. 232p. 1981. pap. 12.00x o.p. (ISBN 0-87766-293-2, 30200). Urban Inst.

Tax Aspects of Municipal Finance. Practising Law Institute Staff. 298p. 1985. pap. 45.00 o.p. (ISBN 0-317-27690-5, #N4-4434). PLI.

Tax Aspects of Real Estate Transactions. Massachusetts Continuing Legal Education, Inc. Staff. LC 84-61750. 250p. 1985. 35.00 o.p. Mass CLE.

Tax, Attacks, & Counterattacks: Your Indispensable Guide to Long-Range Tax Strategy. Richard A. Westin & Alan H. Neff. LC 83-4353. 153p. 1983. 8.95 o.p. (ISBN 0-15-188082-4). HarBraceJ.

Tax Audit Answer Book. Panel Publishers, Inc. Staff. 1985. 45.00 o.p. (ISBN 0-916592-56-1). Panel Pubs.

Tax Companion, 1986. LC 80-65410. 656p. 1986. pap. 12.95 o.p. (ISBN 0-88462-643-1, 5606-01, Longman Fin Serv Pub). Longman Finan.

Tax Compliance after TEFRA: Dealing with the New Reporting Requirements & Penalties. Arthur H. Kroll. LC 83-61750. (Tax Law & Estate Planning Ser.: No. 187). 248p. 1983. 45.00 o.p. (ISBN 0-317-01783-7, J43529). PLI.

Tax Desk Book for Farming & Ranching. 2nd ed. Jon D. Wheeler. LC 78-55900. 1978. 39.50 o.p. (ISBN 0-87624-556-4, Inst Busn Plan). P-H.

Tax Desk Book for the Closely-Held Corporation. Albert M. Lehrman. LC 76-18500. 1978. 29.95 o.p. (ISBN 0-87624-540-8, Inst Busn Plan). P-H.

Tax Desk Book for the Small Business. 3rd ed. IBP Research & Editorial Staff. 1979. 39.50 o.p. (ISBN 0-87624-560-2, Inst Busn Plan). P-H.

Tax Desk Book for the Small Business. 2nd ed. IBP Research & Editorial Staff. LC 75-17121. 1977. 29.95 o.p. (ISBN 0-87624-559-9, Inst Busn Plan). P-H.

Tax Effective Total Compensation: Using 401(K) & 125 Plans. James P. Klein. LC 86-103705. (Tax Law & Planning Ser.). 368p. 1985. 45.00 o.p. (J43578). PLI.

Tax-Exempt Financing of Housing Investment. George E. Peterson. 196p. 1979. pap. text ed. 11.75 o.p. (ISBN 0-87766-251-7). Urban Inst.

Tax-Exempt Financing of Non-Governmental Projects. Henry S. Klaiman & Richard Chirls. LC 86-155516. (Tax Law & Estate Planning Ser.). 266p. 1986. 45.00 o.p. (ISBN 0-317-59748-5). PLI.

Tax-Exempt Industrial Development Financing. Pennsylvania Bar Institute Staff. 320p. 1985. 55.00 o.p. (ISBN 0-318-19075-3, 290). PA Bar Inst.

Tax-Exempt Property: A Case Study of Hartford, Connecticut. Gregory H. Wassall. 1974. pap. 3.00 o.s.i. (ISBN 0-686-17297-3). Lincoln Inst Land.

Tax Facts on Investments. 1987 ed. Advanced Sales Reference Service Dept. Staff. (Tax Facts Ser.: No. 2). 439p. 1987. pap. 10.00 o.p. (ISBN 0-87218-449-8). Natl Underwriter.

Tax Facts on Life Insurance. 1987 ed. Advanced Sales Reference Service Dept. Staff. (Tax Facts Ser.: No. 1). 627p. 1987. pap. 10.00 o.p. (ISBN 0-87218-444-7). Natl Underwriter.

Tax Facts on Life Insurance, No. 1. Advanced Sales Reference Service Department Staff. 675p. 1988. pap. 10.75 o.p. (ISBN 0-87218-455-2). Natl Underwriter.

Tax Fighters Guide, 1982. Philip Storrer & Brian Williams. 192p. 1981. pap. 7.95 o.p. (ISBN 0-936602-28-7). Kampmann.

Tax-Free & Tax-Sheltered Investments for the 1980's. IBP Research & Editorial Staff. 624p. 1981. 59.50 o.p. (ISBN 0-87624-569-6, Inst Busn Plan). P-H.

Tax Havens Around the World. Lawrence Owens. Ed. by Rachel Owens & Anne Owens. 40p. 1982. pap. 5.95 o.p. (ISBN 0-940454-00-9, McGill Canada). U of Toronto Pr.

Tax Havens for Corporations. Adam Starchild. LC 79-9325. 176p. 1979. 29.00x o.p. (ISBN 0-87201-818-0). Gulf Pub.

Tax Havens in the Caribbean. lib. bdg. cancelled o.s.i. (ISBN 0-8490-3563-5). Gordon Pr.

Tax in Blood. Benjamin M. Schutz. 240p. 1987. 14.95 o.p. (ISBN 0-317-60879-7, Dist. by Warner Pub Serv & St Martin Pr). Tor Bks.

Tax Law. Albert K. Francisco & Kenneth A. Smith. (C.P.A. Examination Review Ser.). 72p. 1988. pap. text ed. 7.95 o.p. (ISBN 0-932276-83-0). Prof Pubns CA.

Tax Navigation. Ed. by Robert H. Morrison. 265p. 1977. 19.95 o.p. (ISBN 0-930566-22-X). Morrison Peterson Pub.

Tax Planner: User's Guide & Documentation to Accompany Hoffman & Willis West's Federal Taxation. Andrew Rosenberg. 66p. 1985. 11.25 o.p. (ISBN 0-314-95013-3). West Pub.

Tax Planning for Closely Held Businesses: University of Akron School of Law Institute Symposium III: ALI-ABA Course of Study Materials. University of Akron, School of Law Staff & American Law Institute-American Bar Association Committee on Continuing Professional Education. LC 85-179257. Date not set. price not set o.p. Am Law Inst.

Tax Planning for the Marital Dissolution. Practising Law Institute Staff & Carlyn S. McCaffery. LC 86-60313. (Tax Law & Estate Planning Ser.). 152p. 1986. 15.00 o.p. (D45184). PLI.

Tax Planning for the Troubled Business 1987. Grant W. Newton & Gilbert D. Bloom. 448p. 1987. 49.95 o.p. (ISBN 0-471-62800-X). Wiley.

Tax Rates in Virginia's Cities, Counties, & Selected Towns: 1983. Virginia Municipal League Staf. 1983. 15.00 o.p. (ISBN 0-318-02775-5). Va Muni League.

Tax Reduction Strategies for Small Business: Planning Techniques for Wealth Accumlation in the Eighties. Richard Ellerbach. (Illus.). 145p. 1982. 17.95 o.p. (ISBN 0-13-885228-6); 8.95 o.p. (ISBN 0-13-885210-3). P-H.

Tax Reform Act of 1984, Vol. 213. Practising Law Institute Staff. 590p. 1984. pap. 45.00 o.p. (ISBN 0-317-27507-0, J4-3559). PLI.

Tax Reform 1984: The Law, Reports, Hearings, Debates & Related Documents, 20 vols. Bernard D. Reams, Jr. LC 85-45437. Set. lib. bdg. 945.00 o.p. (ISBN 0-89941-430-3). W S Hein.

Tax-saving Plans for Self-employed. 72p. 1985. 6.00 o.p. (22); members 3.00 o.p. Am Consul Eng.

Tax SEC & Accounting Aspects of Corporate Acquisitions 1984. (Tax Law & Practice Course Handbook Ser., 1983-84: Vol. 444). 1984. pap. 45.00 o.p. (ISBN 0-685-85325-X, B4-6674). PLI.

Tax Shelter Answer Book. Jonathan W. Skiba & Joseph P. Sullivan. LC 84-22653. 1984. 39.95 o.p. (ISBN 0-916592-51-0). Panel Pubs.

Tax Shelter Desk Book. Lewis Mosberg. LC 78-57937. 1978. 39.50 o.p. (ISBN 0-87624-578-5, Inst Busn Plan). P-H.

Tax Shelters. 1984. (ISBN 0-88129-143-9). Wash Bar CLE.

Tax Shelters: A Guide for Investors & Their Advisors. Robert E. Swanson & Barbara M. Swanson. LC 81-82990. 450p. 1982. 37.50 o.p. (ISBN 0-87094-276-X). Dow Jones-Irwin.

Tax Shelters: Advanced Planning Techniques, Vol. 222. Practising Law Institute Staff. 290p. 1985. pap. 45.00 o.p. (ISBN 0-317-27527-5, J4-3563). PLI.

Tax Shelters in Canada: Choose with Care. 12th ed. William E. McLeod. 144p. 1987. 6.95 o.p. (ISBN 0-88908-678-8). ISC Pr.

Tax Shelters in Trouble: Private & Public Litigation. James C. Garahan & Jeffrey B. Rudman. LC 82-81734. (Tax Law & Estate Planning Ser.). 501p. 1985. 45.00 o.p. (J4-3573). PLI.

Tax Tactics for Salespersons. Terry K. Schandel. LC 81-66894. (Tax Tactics Ser.). 1982. pap. 4.95 o.p. (ISBN 0-689-11230-0, Atheneum). Macmillan.

Tax Tactics for Teachers. rev. ed. Terry K. Schandel. LC 81-66897. (Tax Tactics Ser.). 1982. pap. 4.95 o.p. (ISBN 0-689-11229-7, Atheneum). Macmillan.

Tax Tactics for the Retired. Terry K. Schandel. LC 81-66895. (Tax Tactics Ser.). 1982. pap. 4.95 o.p. (ISBN 0-689-11231-9, Atheneum). Macmillan.

Tax Tactics for the Singled & Divorced. Terry K. Schandel. LC 81-66896. (Tax Tactics Ser.). 1982. pap. 4.95 o.p. (ISBN 0-689-11232-7, Atheneum). Macmillan.

Tax Tested Strategies in Securities & Options Investments. Rolf Auster. LC 80-24880. 226p. 1980. 49.50 o.p. (ISBN 0-87624-582-3, Inst Busn Plan). P-H.

Tax Workbook 1987. Tom Copeland. (Family Day Care Business Ser.). 48p. (Orig.). (ps). 1987. pap. text ed. 5.50 o.p. (ISBN 0-934140-43-X). Toys 'n Things.

Taxable Sales in Virginia, 1985. (Statistical Ser.). 1986. 3.14 o.p. (ISBN 0-317-69891-5). U Va Ctr Pub Serv.

Taxation see Taxes.

Taxation & Social Policy. Cedric Sandford. 1981. text ed. 30.50x o.p. (ISBN 0-435-82789-8). Gower Pub Co.

Taxation for the General Practitioner. 195p. 1983. 5.00 o.p. (ISBN 0-318-02445-4). ICLE Georgia.

Taxation in Common Transactions: Pennsylvania Legal Practice Course Materials. Pennsylvania Bar Institute & Pennsylvania Bar Institute Staff. 50p. 1985. 25.00 o.p. (ISBN 0-318-02183-8, PLP-85). PA Bar Inst.

Taxation, U. S. A. Willard A. Heaps. LC 71-146653. (gr. 6 up). 1979. 6.95 o.p. (ISBN 0-395-28908-4, Clarion). HM.

Taxes. Kenneth H. Smith. LC 79-84416. (Real World of Economics Ser.). Orig. Title: Taxation. (Illus.). (gr. 5-11). 1970. PLB 4.95 o.p. (ISBN 0-8225-0613-0). Lerner Pubns.

Taxidermy Step by Step. Waddy F. McFall. LC 82-62602. (Illus.). 256p. 1975. 15.95 o.s.i. (ISBN 0-8329-2099-1, Pub. by Winchester Pr). New Century.

Taxing California Property. 2nd ed. Kenneth Ehrman & Sean Flavin. 1979. 75.00 o.s.i. (ISBN 0-915950-31-6); 1986 supplement incl. o.s.i. Bull Pub.

Taxing Insurers: The Revolution Ahead. Carolyn Bowers. Ed. by Richard D. Hadley. 508p. pap. text ed. cancelled o.s.i. (ISBN 0-914176-24-2); pap. text ed. cancelled o.s.i. Wash Busn Info.

Taxis & Behavior see Queues: Receptors & Recognition Series B.

Taxonomia de Suelos. 2nd ed. Soil Survey Staff. Tr. by Walter L. Leighton from Eng. (SMSS Technical Monograph: No. 5). (Span.). 1986. pap. text ed. 8.00 o.s.i. (ISBN 0-932865-04-6). Cornell U Dept.

Taxonomic Studies of the Encyrtidae with the Descriptions of New Species & a New Genus: Hymenoptera: Chalcidoidea. Gordon Gordh & V. Trjapitzin. (Publications in Entomology: Vol. 93). 1982. pap. 11.00x o.p. (ISBN 0-520-09629-0). U of Cal Pr.

Taxonomic Study of the Ranunculus Hispidus: Complex in the Western Hemisphere. Thomas Duncan. (U. C. Publications in Botany: Vol. 77). 1980. pap. 20.00x o.p. (ISBN 0-520-09617-7). U of Cal Pr.

Taxonomy of Critical Tasks for Evaluating Student Teaching. Kuehl. 1979. 2.50 o.p. (ISBN 0-686-38070-3). Assn Tchr Ed.

Taxonomy of Vascular Plants. George H. Lawrence. (Illus.). 1951. text ed. write for info. o.p. (ISBN 0-02-368190-X). Macmillan.

Taxpayers Survival Manual. Howard Fishkin. 1979. pap. 2.95 o.p. (ISBN 0-933586-06-X). Book Promo Pr.

Taxwise Investing. Vernon K. Jacobs. 1985. 24.95 o.p. (ISBN 0-913864-88-9). Enterprise Del.

Taylors of Ongar: An Analytical Bio-Bibliography. Christina D. Stewart. LC 74-23641. (Reference Library of the Humanities: No. 7). (Illus.). 1200p. 1975. lib. bdg. 152.00 o.p. (ISBN 0-8240-1063-9). Garland Pub.

Tchaikovsky: A Self-Portrait. Vladimir Volkoff. LC 73-84133. 1975. 15.00 o.s.i. (ISBN 0-8008-7552-4, Crescendo). Taplinger.

Tchekov the Man. Beatrice Saunders. 15.00x o.p. (ISBN 0-87556-310-4). Saifer.

Tchekov the Man. Beatrice Saunders. (Illus.). 196p. 1987. 39.95x o.p. (ISBN 0-317-61303-0). Dufour.

Tea. (Commodity Reports: No. 1). pap. 5.75 o.p. (F459, FAO). UNIPUB.

Tea Ceremony. Sen'o Tanaka. LC 73-79766. (Illus.). 214p. 1983. pap. 12.95 o.p. (ISBN 0-87011-578-2). Kodansha.

Tea Leaves: Being a Collection of Letters & Documents Relating to the Shipment of Tea to the American Colonies in the Year 1773, by the East India Tea Company. Francis S. Drake. LC 77-95778. (Illus.). 382p. 1970. Repr. of 1884 ed. 40.00x o.p. (ISBN 0-8103-3577-8). Gale.

Tea Lover's Treasury. James N. Pratt. LC 82-3472. (Illus.). 240p. (Orig.). 1982. pap. 8.95 o.p. (ISBN 0-89286-191-6, One Hund One Prods). Ortho.

Tea Party of Miss Moon: From GrandMama's Tales. Mary Thurn-Taxis. (Illus.). 23p. (gr. 1-4). 1984. 11.95 o.p. (ISBN 0-233-97483-0, Pub. by A Deutsch England). David & Charles.

Tea with Demons. Carol Allen & Herbert Lustig. LC 85-5066. 275p. 1985. 17.95 o.p. (ISBN 0-688-05093-X). Morrow.

Tea with George Ohsawa: Selected Writings by the Father of Modern Macrobiotics. George Ohsawa. Tr. by Marc Van Cauweberghe. LC 87-80494. (Illus.). 450p. 1987. 19.95 o.p. (ISBN 0-87040-694-9). Japan Pubns USA.

Teach Me, Lord: Devotions on Basic Christian Teachings. large print ed. Alvin G. Lewis. LC 76-3879. 160p. (Orig.). 1976. pap. 4.95 o.p. (ISBN 0-8066-1535-4, 10-6225, Augsburg). Augsburg Fortress.

Teach Me Now 2. 8p. (ps). 4.95 o.p. (ISBN 0-318-21954-9, 8100101); kit 20.95 o.p. (ISBN 0-318-21955-7, 1640020). CEF Press.

Teach Us To Outgrow Our Madness. Kenzaburo Oe. Tr. & intro. by John Nathan. LC 76-54582. 1977. pap. 9.95 o.s.i. (ISBN 0-394-17002-4, E687, Ever). Grove.

Teach Your Baby. Genevieve Painter. LC 73-139653. 1971. 9.95 o.p. (ISBN 0-671-20860-8). S&S.

Teach Your Child to Read in Sixty Days. Sidney Ledson. (Illus.). 207p. 1975. 7.95 o.p. (ISBN 0-393-08709-3). Norton.

Teach Your TRS-80 to Program Itself. David Busch. (Illus.). 238p. 1984. 16.95 o.p. (ISBN 0-8306-0798-6); pap. 11.15 o.p. (ISBN 0-8306-1798-1, 1798). TAB Bks.

Teach Yourself Afrikaans. H. J. Terblanche. 270p. 1976. 20.00x o.s.i. (ISBN 0-7964-0010-5). E J Brill USA.

Teach Yourself Calligraphy: For Beginners from Eight to Eighty. Ed. by Ellen Korn. (Illus.). 96p. (gr. 8 up). 1982. pap. 6.95 comb binding o.p. (ISBN 0-688-01994-3, Morrow Junior Books). Morrow.

Teach Yourself Needlepoint. Jo I. Christensen. LC 78-838. (Creative Handcrafts Ser.). (Illus.). 1978. 18.95 o.p. (ISBN 0-13-888024-7, Spec); 12.95 o.p. (ISBN 0-13-888016-6, Spec). P-H.

Teach Yourself Painting & Drawing. Carole Vincent. (Illus.). 176p. 1985. pap. 12.95 o.p. (ISBN 0-7137-1580-4, Pub. by Blandford Pr England). Sterling.

Teach Yourself To Write. Evelyn Stenbock. 340p. (Orig.). 1985. pap. 9.95 o.p. (ISBN 0-89879-195-2, 2207). Writers Digest.

Teach Yourself Transatlantic. Robert Hobbs. 238p. 1986. text ed. 9.95 o.p. (ISBN 0-87484-689-7). Mayfield Pub.

Teacher & the Drug Scene. John Eddy. (Fastback Ser.: No. 26). (Orig.). 1973. pap. 0.90 o.p. (ISBN 0-87367-026-4). Phi Delta Kappa.

Teacher & the Needs of Society in Evolution. E. J. King. 1971. 85.00 o.p. (ISBN 0-08-016102-2); pap. text ed. 85.00 o.p. (ISBN 0-08-016103-0); xerox copyflo o.p. Pergamon.

Teacher As Learner: Highlights of Work at the Center & Summer Institutes. Ed. by Ruth Dropkin. (Illus.). 1977. pap. 3.50 o.s.i. (ISBN 0-918374-15-4). City Coll Wk.

Teacher-Centered In-Service Education: Planning & Products. Robert A. Luke. 72p. 1980. 9.95 o.p. (ISBN 0-8106-1624-6). NEA.

Teacher Centers: Where, What, Why? Roy A. Edelfelt & Tamar Orvell. LC 78-61321. (Fastback Ser.: No. 117). 1978. pap. 0.90 o.p. (ISBN 0-87367-117-1). Phi Delta Kappa.

Teacher Education. Ed. by Kevin Ryan. LC 6-16938. (National Society for the Study of Education Yearbooks Ser: 74th Yearbook, Pt. 2). xvi, 336p. 1975. lib. bdg. 10.00x o.s.i. (ISBN 0-226-60118-8). U of Chicago Pr.

Teacher Education at Salve Regina College. W. Burrell. 1970. pap. text ed. 3.40x o.p. (ISBN 0-8290-1194-3). Irvington.

Teacher Education in the Classroom: Initial & In-Service. Patricia M. E. Ashton et al. 144p. 1983. 22.50 o.p. (ISBN 0-7099-1248-X, Pub. by Croom Helm Ltd). Routledge Chapman & Hall.

Teacher Fairs: Counterpoint to Criticism. Sara Ingrassia & Sue Foley. LC 83-83086. (Fastback Ser.: No. 204). 50p. 1984. pap. 0.90 o.p. (ISBN 0-87367-204-6). Phi Delta Kappa.

Teacher in Fiction, Non-Fiction, Films & Drama: An Annotated Bibliography. Mariann P. Winick. (Reference Library of the Humanities: Vol. 69). (LC 76-024749). lib. bdg. cancelled o.s.i. (ISBN 0-8240-9928-1). Garland Pub.

Teacher in the Urban Community. Leonard Covello & Guido D'Agnostino. (Quality Paperback Ser.: No. 242). 275p. 1970. pap. 5.95 o.p. (ISBN 0-8226-0242-3). Littlefield.

Teacher Learning. Ed. by Gwyneth Dow. (Routledge Education Bks.). 110p. 1982. pap. 12.95x o.p. (ISBN 0-7100-9020-X). Routledge Chapman & Hall.

Teacher Practitioner in Nursing, Midwifery & Health Visiting. Peter Jarvis & Sheila Gibson. LC 85-5950. 119p. (Orig.). 1985. pap. 13.50 o.p. (ISBN 0-7099-1437-7, Pub. by Croom Helm Ltd). Routledge Chapman & Hall.

Teacher Resourcebook GR3 ERS. Date not set. (ISBN 0-07-368264-0). McGraw.

Teacher Strategies: Explorations in the Sociology of the School. Peter Woods. 288p. 1980. 28.00 o.p. (ISBN 0-7099-0115-1, Pub. by Croom Helm Ltd); pap. 13.50 o.p. (ISBN 0-7099-0178-X). Routledge Chapman & Hall.

Teacher Strikes: Boon or Bane? A Bibliographic Review. Alva W. Stewart. (Public Administration Ser.: P 1679). 10p. 1985. 2.00 o.p. (ISBN 0-89028-409-1). Vance Biblios.

Teacher Training & Special Educational Needs. Ed. by John Sayer & Neville Jones. LC 85-21340. 208p. 1985. 29.00 o.p. (ISBN 0-7099-3379-7, Pub. by Croom Helm Ltd). Routledge Chapman & Hall.

Teacher, Twist Your Head Around! Gertrude M. Clark. 32p. 1986. 5.75 o.p. (ISBN 0-8062-2857-1). Carlton.

Teachers. Louis Bogart. 199p. 1984. pap. 5.95 o.p. (ISBN 0-317-11799-8). Ramparts.

Teachers & Classes. Kevin Harris. (Education Bks.). 190p. 1982. pap. 10.95x o.p. (ISBN 0-7100-0865-1). Routledge Chapman & Hall.

Teachers & Power. Robert J. Braun. 1973. pap. 2.95 o.p. (ISBN 0-671-21615-5, Touchstone Bks). S&S.

Teachers & Texts. Michael W. Apple. 224p. 1987. 19.95 o.p. (ISBN 0-7102-0774-3, Pub. by Routledge UK). Routledge Chapman & Hall.

Teacher's Choice: Ideas & Activities for Teaching Basic Skills. Sandra Kaplan et al. 1978. 12.95 o.p. (ISBN 0-673-16447-0); pap. 14.95 o.p. (ISBN 0-673-16448-9). Scott F.

Teacher's Experience. S. Shatsky. 342p. 1981. 8.00 o.p. (ISBN 0-8285-2158-1, Pub. by Progress Pubs USSR). Imported Pubns.

Teachers Guide for Teaching Educable Mental Retardates How to Read. Mamie T. Wilson. LC 77-171717. 1974. 4.00 o.p. (ISBN 0-682-47274-3). Exposition-Phoenix.

Teacher's Guide to Current Issues: 1988. 9.00 o.p. (ISBN 0-932765-19-X). Close Up Foun.

Teacher's Guide to Elementary School Physical Education. 3rd ed. Norman A. Cochran et al. 1982. wire coil bdg. 24.95 o.p. (ISBN 0-8403-3456-7, 40345602). Kendall-Hunt.

Teacher's Guide to Elijah: Prophet of God. Wallace Alcorn. (Illus.). 1974. pap. 1.50 o.p. (ISBN 0-87227-022-X). Reg Baptist.

Teachers Handbook of Diagnostic Inventories: Spelling, Reading, Handwriting, Arithmetic -- a Practical Guide with Duplicator Masters. Philip H. Mann et al. 367p. 1979. pap. text ed. 51.95 o.p. (ISBN 0-205-06625-9, 246625, Pub. by Longwood Div). Allyn.

Teachers Have Rights, Too: What Educators Should Know About School Law. Leigh Stelzer & Joanna Banthin. LC 80-70053. 182p. (Orig.). 1981. pap. 7.95 o.p. (ISBN 0-89994-249-0). Soc Sci Ed.

Teachers Library. Ed. by Phyllis M. Hill. 151p. 1977. pap. 8.75 o.p. (ISBN 0-686-63702-X, 1512-6-06). NEA.

Teacher's Manual for the Man for All Time. John Thomsen & Helen Thomsen. pap. 2.25 o.p. (ISBN 0-8192-4035-4). Morehouse Pub.

Teacher's Needs & Concerns Regarding Reading Instruction: Findings, Strategies, & Applications. Ed. by Roger J. De Santi. LC 83-10219. 166p. (Orig.). 1983. lib. bdg. 26.25 o.p. (ISBN 0-8191-3365-5); pap. text ed. 12.00 o.p. (ISBN 0-8191-3366-3). U Pr of Amer.

Teachers of Fulfillment. 2nd ed. Israel Regardie. LC 83-81834. 256p. (Orig.). 1983. pap. 8.95 o.s.i. (ISBN 0-941404-26-9). Falcon Pr AZ.

Teachers of Mad Dog Swamp. Khonkhai Khammaan. Tr. by Gehan Wijeyewardene from Thai. LC 81-14783. (Asian & Pacific Writing 18). 263p. 1982. text ed. 19.95 o.p. (ISBN 0-7022-1641-0); pap. 9.50 o.p. (ISBN 0-7022-1651-8). U of Queensland Pr.

Teachers of Young Children. 3rd ed. Robert D. Hess & Doreen J. Croft. LC 80-81928. (Illus.). 528p. 1980. text ed. 31.95 o.p. (ISBN 0-395-29172-0). HM.

Teachers of Young Children. 2nd ed. Robert D. Hess & Robert J. Croft. 1975. text ed. 17.95 o.p. (ISBN 0-395-18711-7). HM.

Teacher's Pet. Domini Taylor. LC 87-14656. 288p. 1987. 18.95 o.p. (ISBN 0-689-11933-X, Atheneum). Macmillan.

Teacher's Planning Pak & Guide to Individualized Instruction. LC 78-52671. (Learning Center Set). (Illus.). 180p. 1978. pap. 7.95 o.p. (ISBN 0-913916-56-0, IP 56-0). Incentive Pubns.

Teachers' Script A: Numbers & Numerals, Addition 0-10, Addition 10-20, Multiplication 1&2. Kitty Wehrli. (Michigan Arithmetic Program). 162p. 1974. 5.00 o.p. (ISBN 0-89039-115-7). Ann Arbor Pubs.

Teachers' Script B: Subtraction 10-0, Subtraction 20-10, Division. Kitty Wehrli. (Michigan Arithmetic Program). 146p. 1974. tchrs. ed 5.00 o.p. (ISBN 0-89039-116-5). Ann Arbor Pubs.

Teachers' Treasury of Useful Lists & Facts. Catharine S. Bush. 248p. (Orig.). 1984. pap. text ed. 18.95 o.p. (ISBN 0-88450-877-3, 4602-B). Communication Skill.

Teachers Versus Technocrats: An Educational Innovation in Anthropological Perspective. Harry F. Wolcott. LC 77-75138. 1977. 8.95 o.p. (ISBN 0-936276-06-1). Ctr Educ Policy Mgmt.

Teacher's Voice: A Study of Teacher Participation in Educational Decision-Making in Three Alberta Communities. John W. Friesen et al. LC 83-12502. (Illus.). 148p. 1983. lib. bdg. 23.50 o.p. (ISBN 0-8191-3417-1); pap. text ed. 9.25 o.p. (ISBN 0-8191-3418-X). U Pr of Amer.

Teachers with Children: Curriculum in Open Classrooms. Ed. by Ruth Dropkin. (Illus.). 68p. 1976. pap. 3.50 o.s.i. (ISBN 0-918374-16-2). City Coll Wk.

Teachers' Word Book of Thirty Thousand Words. Edward L. Thorndike & Irving Lorge. 1944. text ed. 14.95x o.p. (ISBN 0-8077-2266-9). Tchrs Coll.

Teaching a Literature-Centered English Program. J. Knapton & B. Evans. 11.25 o.p. (ISBN 0-8446-2389-X). Peter Smith.

Teaching about Colorado & Community History. Gary R. Smith. (Illus.). 91p. (Orig.). (gr. 4-12). 1978. pap. 12.95 o.p. (ISBN 0-943804-05-1). U of Denver Teach.

Teaching about Diversity: Latin America. rev. ed. Kenneth A. Switzer & Charlotte A. Redden. (Cultural Studies Ser.). (Illus.). 165p. (gr. 9-12). 1982. pap. 15.95 o.p. (ISBN 0-943804-19-1). U of Denver Teach.

Teaching about Food & Hunger. George G. Otero & Gary R. Smith. (Illus.). 227p. (Orig.). (gr. 6-12). 1978. pap. 14.95 o.p. (ISBN 0-943804-35-3). U of Denver Teach.

Teaching about New Mexico History & Culture. George G. Otero. (Illus.). 108p. (gr. 1-8). 1978. pap. 12.95 o.p. (ISBN 0-943804-04-3). U of Denver Teach.

Teaching about Peace & Nuclear War: A Balanced Approach. John Zola & Jaye Zola. 114p. (Orig.). 1985. pap. 10.95 o.p. (ISBN 0-89994-305-5). Soc Sci Ed.

Teaching about Perception: The Arabs. George G. Otero, Jr. (Orig.). (gr. 5-12). 1978. pap. 15.95 o.p. (ISBN 0-943804-20-5). U of Denver Teach.

Teaching About Race Relations: Problems & Effects. Lawrence Stenhouse & Verna K. Gajendra. (Routledge Education Books). 260p. 1982. 26.95x o.p. (ISBN 0-7100-9036-6). Routledge Chapman & Hall.

Teaching about Spaceship Earth: A Role-Playing Experience for the Middle Grades. (Illus.). 1972. 1.95 o.p. (ISBN 0-685-84002-6). ACEI.

Teaching AIDS: A Resource Guide on Acquired Immune Deficiency Syndrome. Marcia Quackenbush & Pamela Sargent. 124p. 1986. pap. text ed. 14.95 o.p. (ISBN 0-941816-25-7). Network Pubns.

Teaching American History: Structured Inquiry Approaches. Ed. by Glenn M. Linden & Matthew T. Downey. 110p. 1976. 12.95 o.p. (ISBN 0-89994-185-0). Soc Sci Ed.

Teaching American History: The Quest for Relevancy. Ed. by Allan O. Kownslar. LC 74-81013. (Yearbook Ser.: No. 44). (Illus.). 237p. 1974. pap. text ed. 3.50 o.p. (ISBN 0-87986-035-9, 490-15280). Nat Coun Soc Studies.

Teaching an Infant to Swim. Virginia H. Newman. LC 67-11972. (Illus.). 1967. 5.95 o.p. (ISBN 0-15-188110-3). HarBraceJ.

Teaching an Infant to Swim. Virginia H. Newman. LC 67-11972. (Illus.). 1971. pap. 2.95 o.p. (ISBN 0-15-688241-8, Harv). HarBraceJ.

Teaching an Infant to Swim. Virginia H. Newman. LC 82-23395. (Illus.). 128p. 1983. pap. 7.95 o.p. (ISBN 0-15-688242-6, Harv, Harv). HarBraceJ.

Teaching & Development: A Soviet Investigation. L. V. Zankov et al. Ed. by Beatrice B. Szekely. Tr. by Arlo Schultz. LC 77-82338. (Illus.). 296p. (Orig., Rus.). 1977. 40.00 o.p. (ISBN 0-87332-109-X). M E Sharpe.

Teaching & Learning about Aging. Richard O. Ulin. 92p. 1982. 7.95 o.p. (ISBN 0-8106-1826-5). NEA.

Teaching & Learning in the Model Classroom: The Conditions, Relationships & Instructional Specifics. Arlynne Lake Cheers & Lamore J. Carter. LC 73-82083. 1974. text ed. 5.00 o.p. (ISBN 0-682-47757-5, University). Exposition-Phoenix.

Teaching & Learning the Language Arts. 2nd ed. Edna P. DeHaven. 1983. text ed. write for info. o.p. (ISBN 0-673-39148-5). Scott F.

Teaching & Research in the California Desert. Robert C. Stebbins et al. LC 77-29266. (Research Report Ser.: No. 78-1). 26p. 1978. pap. 3.00x o.p. (ISBN 0-87772-253-6). UCB IGS.

Teaching & Television: ETV Explained. Ed. by G. Moir. 1967. text ed. 29.00 o.p. (ISBN 0-08-012355-4); pap. text ed. 10.75 o.p. (ISBN 0-08-012354-6). Pergamon.

Teaching Aphasics & Other Language Deficient Children: Theory & Application of the Association Method. rev. ed. Etoile Dubard. LC 83-1284. (Illus.). 1983. 20.00x o.p. (ISBN 0-87805-182-1); pap. 12.50x o.p. (ISBN 0-87805-053-1). U Pr of Miss.

Teaching As a Lively Art. rev. ed. Marjorie Spock. 145p. 1986. pap. 8.95 o.p. (ISBN 0-88010-127-X). Anthroposophic.

Teaching Autistic Children to Communicate. Paige S. Hinerman. LC 83-10016. 224p. 1983. 32.00 o.p. (ISBN 0-89443-884-0). Aspen Pub.

Teaching Bioethics: Strategies, Problems & Resources. K. Danner Clouser. LC 80-10492. (Teaching of Ethics Ser.: Vol. IV). 77p. 1980. pap. 4.00 o.p. (ISBN 0-916558-07-X). Hastings Ctr.

Teaching Business Writing. Ed. by Jeanne Halpern. 1983. pap. 9.95 o.p. (ISBN 0-931874-13-0). Assn Busn Comm.

Teaching Children Joy. Linda Eyre & Richard Eyre. 203p. pap. 9.95 o.p. (ISBN 0-87747-888-0, Pub. by Shadow Mountain). Deseret Bk.

Teaching Children Music: Fundamentals of Music & Method. 2nd ed. Grant Newman. 424p. 1984. write for info. plastic comb binding o.p. (ISBN 0-697-03616-2); study guide avail. o.p. (ISBN 0-697-03620-0); instr's. manual avail. o.p. (ISBN 0-697-03632-4). Wm C Brown.

Teaching Children Responsibility. Linda Eyre & Richard Eyre. LC 82-12842. (Illus.). 253p. 1982. 9.95 o.p. (ISBN 0-87747-918-6). Deseret Bk.

Teaching Children Through the Environment. Pamela Mays. 256p. 1985. pap. text ed. 19.95 o.s.i. (ISBN 0-340-35902-1). Princeton Bk Co.

Teaching Children to Care. Dorothy Dixon. LC 81-51428. (Illus.). 306p. (Orig.). (gr. k-3). tchrs. ed. 19.95x o.p. (ISBN 0-89622-144-X). Twenty-Third.

Teaching Children to Pray. Johanna Klink. LC 74-34591. 80p. 1975. pap. 1.95 o.s.i. (ISBN 0-664-24766-0, Westminster). Westminster John Knox.

Teaching Children with Severe Difficulties: A Radical Reappraisal. Barbara Shears & Susan Wood. Ed. by Len Barton. (Series on Special Education Needs: Policy, Practice & Social Issues). 200p. 1986. 25.50 o.p. (ISBN 0-7099-4446-2, Pub. by Croom Helm UK); pap. 11.95 o.p. (ISBN 0-7099-4450-0, Pub. by Croom Helm UK). Routledge Chapman & Hall.

Teaching Communication Skills. Ed. by P. J. Hills & Margaret McLaren. (Communication Ser.). 240p. 1986. 39.00 o.p. (ISBN 0-7099-4761-5, Pub. by Croom Helm UK). Routledge Chapman & Hall.

Teaching Craft, Design & Technology Five to Thirteen. Peter H. Williams. LC 84-72700. (Teaching 5-13 Ser.). 152p. 1985. 26.00 o.p. (ISBN 0-7099-2775-4, Pub. by Croom Helm Ltd); pap. 12.00 o.p. (ISBN 0-7099-2776-2). Routledge Chapman & Hall.

Teaching Critical Television Viewing Skills: An Integrated Approach. Milton E. Ploghoft & James A. Anderson. (Illus.). 208p. 1982. 25.50 o.p. (ISBN 0-398-04616-6). C C Thomas.

Teaching Elementary Reading: Principles & Strategies. 2nd ed. Robert Karlin. (Illus.). 1975. text ed. 17.95 o.p. (ISBN 0-15-588002-0, HC). HarBraceJ.

Teaching Elementary Reading: Principles & Strategies. 3rd ed. Robert Karlin. 488p. 1980. 20.00 o.p. (ISBN 0-15-588003-9, HC). HarBraceJ.

Teaching Elementary School Mathematics: An Active Learning Approach. Harold H. Lerch. (Illus.). 416p. 1981. text ed. 27.95 o.p. (ISBN 0-395-29762-1). HM.

Teaching Elementary School Science: A Competency-Based Approach. Clifford H. Edwards & Robert L. Fisher. 1977. text ed. 29.95 o.p. (ISBN 0-275-22510-0). HR&W.

Teaching Elementary Science. 4th ed. William K. Esler & Mary K. Esler. 540p. 1984. text ed. (ISBN 0-534-03408-X). Wadsworth Pub.

Teaching Elementary Science Through Investigation & Colloquium. Brenda Lansdown et al. (Illus.). 1971. pap. text ed. 10.95 o.p. (ISBN 0-15-588013-6, HC). HarBraceJ.

Teaching Emotionally Disturbed Children. Peter Knoblock. LC 82-83370. 448p. 1982. text ed. 35.96 o.p. (ISBN 0-395-29708-7); instr's. manual 2.36 o.p. (ISBN 0-395-29709-5). HM.

Teaching English. Tricia Evans. (Illus.). 212p. 1982. pap. 11.95 o.p. (ISBN 0-7099-0902-0, Pub. by Croom Helm Ltd). Routledge Chapman & Hall.

Teaching English As a Second Language: An Annotated Bibliography. Wallace L. Goldstein. LC 75-17987. (Reference Library of the Humanities Ser.: Vol. 23). 218p. 1975. lib. bdg. 41.00 o.p. (ISBN 0-8240-9991-5). Garland Pub.

Teaching English As a Second Language. John Bright & Gordon McGregor. (English As a Second Language Bk.). 1975. text ed. 13.95x o.p. (ISBN 0-582-54003-8). Longman.

Teaching English Through English. Jane Willis. (Handbooks for Language Teachers). (Illus.). 192p. 1981. pap. text ed. 13.95 o.p. (ISBN 0-582-74608-6). Longman.

Teaching English to Speakers of English. Bradford Arthur. 1973. pap. text ed. 8.95 o.p. (ISBN 0-15-588211-2, HC). HarBraceJ.

Teaching English Today. Dwight L. Burton et al. 1975. text ed. 23.50 o.p. (ISBN 0-395-18616-1). HM.

Teaching English with Video. Margaret Allan. (English As a Second Language Bk.). (Orig.). 1985. pap. 13.95 o.p. (ISBN 0-582-74616-7). Longman.

Teaching for Craft Retailers. Florence Nelson. 8p. 1984. 3.50 o.s.i. (ISBN 0-918328-12-8). Carma.

Teaching for Effective Study. Bernard Chibnall. Ed. by P. J. Hills. (New Patterns of Learning Ser.). 160p. 1986. 29.95 o.p. (ISBN 0-7099-3457-2, Pub. by Croom Helm UK). Routledge Chapman & Hall.

Teaching for Health: The Nurse As Health Educator. Lyn C. Coutts & Leslie K. Hardy. LC 84-11365. (Illus.). 225p. 1985. pap. text ed. 17.50 o.p. (ISBN 0-443-02751-X). Churchill.

Teaching for Learning. 2nd ed. Myron Dembo. 1981. pap. text ed. write for info. o.p. (ISBN 0-673-16450-0). Scott F.

Teaching for the Two-Sided Mind: A Guide to Right Brain-Left Brain Education. Linda V. Williams. (Illus.). 213p. 1983. 13.95 o.p. (ISBN 0-13-892554-2); pap. 7.95 o.p. (ISBN 0-13-892547-X). P-H.

Teaching for Transfer: A Perspective. Nina Selz & William L. Ashley. 19p. 1978. 2.35 o.p. (ISBN 0-318-22210-8, IN141). Natl Ctr Res Voc Ed.

Teaching Foreign Language Skills. Wilga M. Rivers. LC 68-26761. 1968. lib. bdg. 16.00x o.s.i. (ISBN 0-226-72096-9). U of Chicago Pr.

Teaching Global Awareness: An Approach for Grades 1-6. Junelle P. Barrett et al. (Illus.). 217p. (Orig.). (gr. 1-6). pap. 19.95 o.s.i. (ISBN 0-943804-13-2). U of Denver Teach.

Teaching Good Behavior. Time-Life Books Editors. (Successful Parenting Ser.). 144p. 1987. 17.27 o.p.; lib. bdg. 21.17 o.p. Time-Life.

Teaching Handicapped Students in the English Classroom. Ed. by Jane Price. 64p. 1981. 8.95 o.p. (ISBN 0-8106-3176-8). NEA.

Teaching Handicapped Students in the Mathematics Classroom. Ellen-Mary Brockmann. 64p. 1981. 8.95 o.p. (ISBN 0-8106-3177-6). NEA.

Teaching Health Education in the Elementary School. Ruth Engs & Molly Wantz. LC 77-79371. (Illus.). 1978. text ed. 37.16 o.p. (ISBN 0-395-25483-3). HM.

Teaching High School Science: A Source Book for the Physical Sciences. Alexander Joseph et al. (Illus.). 1961. text ed. 13.95 o.p. (ISBN 0-15-587029-7, HC). HarBraceJ.

Teaching in a Multicultural Society: The Task for Teacher Education. Ed. by Maurice Craft. LC 82-135236. 192p. (Orig.). 1981. pap. 13.00x o.p. (ISBN 0-905273-28-1, Falmer Pr). Taylor & Francis.

Teaching in Physical Education. Ed. by Thomas J. Templin & Janice K. Olson. LC 83-81455. (Big Ten Body of Knowledge Symposium Ser.: Vol. 14). 384p. 1983. text ed. 30.00x o.p. (ISBN 0-931250-48-X, BTEM0048). Human Kinetics.

Teaching Kids Math: Problem-Solving Activities to Help Young Children Learn & Enjoy Mathematics. Carne S. Barnett & Sharon Young. (Illus.). 163p. 1982. 14.95 o.p. (ISBN 0-13-893537-8); 7.95 o.p. (ISBN 0-13-893529-7). P-H.

Teaching Language & Literature: Grades Seven to Twelve. 2nd ed. Walter Loban et al. 1969. text ed. 17.95 o.p. (ISBN 0-15-588801-3, HC). HarBraceJ.

Teaching Language Arts Creatively. Mimi B. Chenfeld. (Illus.). 359p. 1978. pap. text ed. 12.00 o.p. (ISBN 0-15-588807-2, HC). HarBraceJ.

Teaching Language Through Sight & Sound - Set 1. Joan M. Sayre. 1980. 34.95x o.p. (ISBN 0-8134-2077-6). Inter Print Pubs.

Teaching, Learning, & the Mind. Young Pai. LC 72-3512. 250p. (Orig.). 1973. pap. 12.75 o.p. (ISBN 0-395-12663-0, 3-42835). HM.

Teaching Literature Overseas: Language-Based Approaches. Ed. by C. J. Brumfit. (English Language Teaching Documents Ser.: Vol. 115). 128p. 1983. pap. text ed. 7.50 o.s.i. (ISBN 0-08-030341-2, 67, Dist. by Alemany Pr). Pergamon.

Teaching Literature to Adolescents: Poetry. Stephen Dunning. 1966. pap. write for info. o.p. (ISBN 0-673-05544-2). Scott F.

Teaching Luther's Catechism, Vol. II. Herbert Girgensohn. Tr. by John W. Doberstein from Ger. LC 59-8463. 1960. 6.00 o.p. (ISBN 0-8006-0866-6, 1-866, Fortress). Augsburg Fortress.

Teaching Manual for Tutor-Librarians. David Finn et al. 1978. 12.00 o.p. (ISBN 0-85365-830-7). Nichols Pub.

Teaching Mathematics. Ed. by Michael Cornelius. LC 82-6404. (Illus.). 248p. 1982. 27.50 o.p. (ISBN 0-89397-137-5); pap. 16.95 o.p. Nichols Pub.

Teaching Mathematics, Five to Thirteen. D. Lumb. (A Volume in the Croom Helm Teaching 5 to 13 Ser.). 224p. 1987. 31.00 o.p. (ISBN 0-7099-4118-8, Pub. by Croom Helm UK); pap. 13.50 o.p. (ISBN 0-7099-4128-5, Pub. by Croom Helm UK). Routledge Chapman & Hall.

Teaching Mathematics in the Elementary School: Selected Readings. F. Smith et al. 1969. pap. text ed. 5.75x o.p. (ISBN 0-8290-1195-1). Irvington.

Teaching Mathematics: Methods & Content. 2nd ed. Fredericka K. Reisman. 1981. text ed. 30.50 o.p. (ISBN 0-395-30706-6). HM.

Teaching Mathematics to the Learning Disabled. Nancy S. Bley & Carol A. Thornton. LC 81-3569. 421p. 1981. text ed. 37.00 o.p. (ISBN 0-89443-357-1). Aspen Pub.

Teaching Mathematics to Young Children: A Basic Guide. Rosalie S. Jensen & Deborach C. Spector. (Illus.). 224p. 1984. 17.95 o.p. (ISBN 0-13-894212-9); pap. 8.95 o.p. (ISBN 0-13-894204-8). P-H.

Teaching Methods for the BI Librarian. 60p. 15.00 o.p. (ISBN 0-8389-6751-5). Assn Coll & Res Libs.

Teaching Methods for the Bibliographic Instruction Librarian. Marilla D. Svinicki. 54p. 1981. 15.00x o.p. (ISBN 0-8389-6751-5); members 10.00x o.p. (ISBN 0-317-37027-8). ALA.

Teaching Morphology Developmentally: Methods & Materials for Teaching Bound Morphology. Kenneth G. Shipley & Carolyn S. Banis. 1981. 99.00 o.p. (ISBN 0-88450-728-9, 3137-B). Communication Skill.

Teaching Music in Urban Schools. Otis D. Simmons. LC 75-2549. 1975. pap. 6.50 o.s.i. (ISBN 0-8008-7554-0, Crescendo). Taplinger.

Teaching Nursing: A Self-Instructional Handbook. Christine Ewan & Ruth White. LC 84-16980. 250p. (Orig.). 1984. pap. 15.00 o.p. (ISBN 0-7099-0936-5, Pub. by Croom Helm Ltd). Routledge Chapman & Hall.

Teaching of Arithmetic. Guy T. Buswell. LC 51-9871. (National Society for the Study of Education Yearbooks Ser: No. 50, Pt. 2). 1951. lib. bdg. 6.50x o.s.i. (ISBN 0-226-60015-7); pap. text ed. 4.50x o.s.i. (ISBN 0-226-60016-5). U of Chicago Pr.

Teaching of Buddha: Pocket Edition. 244p. 1970. pap. 5.00 o.s.i. (ISBN 0-89346-168-7, Bukkyo Dendo Kyokai Japan). Heian Intl.

Teaching of Business Communication. Ed. by G. H. Douglas. 1978. pap. 5.60 o.p. (ISBN 0-931874-00-9). Assn Busn Comm.

Teaching of Chemistry. N. F. Newbury. (Illus.). 294p. 1961. (ISBN 0-8022-1201-8). Philos Lib.

Teaching of Employability Skills: Who's Responsible? Nina Selz. 31p. 1980. 2.80 o.p. (ISBN 0-318-22212-4, SN29). Natl Ctr Res Voc Ed.

Teaching of English as a Foreign Language in Ten Countries. E. G. Lewis & C. E. Massad. 300p. (Orig.). 1975. pap. text ed. 15.75x o.p. (ISBN 91-22-00020-8, Pub. by Almqvist & Wiksell). Coronet Bks.

Teaching of Ethics & the Social Sciences. Donald P. Warwick. LC 80-10154. (Teaching of Ethics Ser.). 69p. 1980. pap. 4.00 o.p. (ISBN 0-916558-11-8). Hastings Ctr.

Teaching of History. Dennis Gunning. 197p. 1978. pap. 11.50 o.p. (ISBN 0-85664-762-4, Pub. by Croom Helm Ltd); 22.00 o.p. (ISBN 0-85664-326-2). Routledge Chapman & Hall.

Teaching of Practice Skills in Undergraduate Programs in Social Welfare & Other Helping Services. Frank Loewenberg & Ralph Dolgoff. Date not set. 3.00 o.s.i. (70-310-70). Coun Soc WK Ed.

Teaching of Saint Gregory: An Early Armenian Catechism. Gregory. Tr. by Robert W. Thomson et al from Armenian. LC 78-115482. (Armenian Texts & Studies: No. 3). 1971. 16.00x o.s.i. (ISBN 0-674-87038-7). Harvard U Pr.

Teaching of Sciences in African Universities: Report of the Rabat Seminar, 1962. Rabat Seminar Staff. (Development of Higher Education Ser.). 112p. 1964. pap. 5.00 o.p. (ISBN 0-686-94191-8, U659, UNESCO). UNIPUB.

Teaching of Secondary School Mathematics, 33rd Yearbk. National Council of Teachers of Mathematics Staff. LC 27-7119. (Illus.). 433p. 1970. 15.75 o.p. (ISBN 0-87353-013-6). NCTM.

Teaching of Social Studies in British Universities. Kathleen Jones. 87p. 1964. pap. text ed. 3.75x o.p. (ISBN 0-686-70858-X, Pub. by Bedford England). Gower Pub Co.

Teaching of Writing: The Eighty-Fifth Yearbook of the National Society for the Study of Education, Pt. II. Ed. by Anthony Petrosky & David Bartholomae. LC 85-62666. x, 212p. 1986. lib. bdg. 18.00x o.s.i. (ISBN 0-226-60142-0, Pub. by Natl Soc Stud Educ). U of Chicago Pr.

Teaching Oral Communication in Elementary Schools. M. L. Willbrand & Richard D. Rieke. 288p. 1983. text ed. write for info. o.p. (ISBN 0-02-427750-9). Macmillan.

Teaching Part Two: Life Company Operations. Ed. by Life Office Management Association Staff. (FLMI Insurance Education Program Ser.). 1975. pap. 10.00 o.p. (ISBN 0-915322-09-9). LOMA.

Teaching Phonetic Skills through Body Movement. B. M. Van Osdol et al. 1975. pap. text ed. 4.75x o.p. (ISBN 0-8422-0503-9). Irvington.

Teaching Physical Education: A Systems Approach. 2nd ed. Robert M. Singer & Walter Dick. 1980. text ed. 25.50 o.p. (ISBN 0-395-28359-0). HM.

Teaching Physical Education: A Systems Approach. Robert N. Singer & Walter Dick. 400p. 1974. text ed. 17.25 o.p. (ISBN 0-395-17770-7). HM.

Teaching Physical Education in Elementary Schools. 6th ed. Maryhelen Vannier & David L. Gallahue. LC 77-80752. (Illus.). 1978. pap. 31.95 o.p. (ISBN 0-7216-8979-5). HR&W.

Teaching Physical Education in the Secondary School. Franklin A. Lindeburg. 237p. 1978. text ed. write for info. o.p. (ISBN 0-02-370670-8). Macmillan.

Teaching Physics for the Inquiring Mind. E. M. Rogers. 1962. pap. 10.50x o.p. (ISBN 0-691-08002-X). Princeton U Pr.

Teaching Poor Readers in the Secondary School. Christine Cassell. (Special Education Ser.). (Illus.). 72p. 1982. pap. 13.00 o.p. (ISBN 0-7099-0294-8, Pub. by Croom Helm Ltd). Routledge Chapman & Hall.

Teaching Practical Criticism: An Introduction. Margaret Mathieson. LC 85-3772. 158p. (Orig.). 1985. pap. 14.95 o.p. (ISBN 0-7099-3504-8, Pub. by Croom Helm Ltd). Routledge Chapman & Hall.

Teaching Practical Social Work. Hazel Danbury. 85p. 1979. pap. text ed. 7.25x o.p. (ISBN 0-7199-0953-8, Pub. by Bedford England). Gower Pub Co.

Teaching Program in Psychiatry, 3 vols. Incl. Vol. 1. Schizophrenia, Paranoid Conditions, Depression. Peter G. Beckett & Thomas H. Bleakley. 244p. 1968. text ed. 8.95x o.p. (ISBN 0-8143-1335-3); pap. 9.95x (ISBN 0-8143-1336-1); Vol. 2. Psychoneurosis, Organic Brain Disease, Psychopharmacology. Peter G. Beckett et al. 270p. 1969. text ed. 9.95x o.p. (ISBN 0-8143-1392-2); pap. text ed. 9.95x (ISBN 0-8143-1393-0); Vol. 3. Personality Development in Preschool Years, Latency, & Adolescence. Leonard R. Piggott & Joseph Fischoff. LC 67-64750. 185p. text ed. 9.95x o.p. (ISBN 0-8143-1532-1); pap. text ed. 9.95x (ISBN 0-8143-1533-X). LC 67-64750. 1975. Wayne St U Pr.

Teaching Reading. Ivan J. Quandt. 1977. text ed. 31.95 o.p. (ISBN 0-395-30700-7). HM.

Teaching Reading & Mathematics. Richard A. Earle. LC 76-2020. 88p. 1976. pap. text ed. 6.00 o.p. (ISBN 0-87207-219-3). Intl Reading.

Teaching Reading Comprehension: Theory & Practice. William D. Page & Gay S. Pinnell. LC 79-4162. 1979. pap. text ed. 11.00 o.p. (ISBN 0-8141-5190-6). NCTE.

Teaching Reading in Compensatory Classes. Ed. by Robert C. Calfee & Priscilla A. Drum. (Orig.). 1979. pap. text ed. 6.50 o.p. (ISBN 0-87207-725-X, 725). Intl Reading.

Teaching Reading in the Social Studies. John P. Lunstrum & Bob L. Taylor. 102p. 1976. 9.95 o.p. (ISBN 0-89994-198-2). Soc Sci Ed.

Teaching Reading in Today's Elementary Schools. 2nd ed. Paul C. Burns & Betty D. Roe. LC 81-80804. 544p. 1981. text ed. 23.50 o.p. (ISBN 0-395-30568-3). HM.

Teaching Reading to Bilingual Children: A Step-by-Step Guide That Guarantees Reading Success. Ellen C. Henderson. LC 78-186481. 1972. pap. text ed. 5.00 o.p. (ISBN 0-682-47437-1, University). Exposition-Phoenix.

Teaching Reading to Mentally Handicapped Children. James Thatcher. (Special Education Ser.). 64p. 1984. pap. 15.00 o.p. (ISBN 0-7099-2408-9, Pub. by Croom Helm Ltd). Routledge Chapman & Hall.

Teaching Reading to Slow & Disabled Learners. Samuel A. Kirk et al. LC 77-77655. (Illus.). 1978. text ed. 30.95 o.p. (ISBN 0-395-25821-9). HM.

Teaching Science As Continuous Inquiry: A Basic 2-E. 2nd ed. Mary B. Rowe. (Illus.). 1978. text ed. 36.95 o.p. (ISBN 0-07-054116-7). McGraw.

Teaching Science to the Ordinary Pupil. Laybourne. (Illus.). 415p. 1958. (ISBN 0-8022-0939-4). Philos Lib.

Teaching Science with Everyday Things. Victor E. Schmidt & Verne N. Rockcastle. 1968. pap. text ed. 22.95 o.p. (ISBN 0-07-055351-3, C). McGraw.

Teaching Secondary Mathematics Through Applications. 2nd ed. Herbert Fremont. 1979. write for info. o.p. (ISBN 0-87150-256-9, PWS 2111, Prindle). PWS-Kent Pub.

Teaching Secondary Students with Mild Learning & Behavior Problems: Methods, Materials, Strategies. Lowell F. Masters & Allen A. Mori. 326p. 1985. 35.50 o.p. (ISBN 0-87189-234-0). Aspen Pub.

Teaching Social Skills to Children. Ed. by Gwendolyn Cartledge & JoAnne F. Milburn. (Pergamon General Psychology Ser.). 1980. 40.00 o.p. (ISBN 0-08-024654-0); pap. text ed. 12.00 o.p. (ISBN 0-08-024653-2). Pergamon.

Teaching Spanish Guitar: In Advanced Modern Style. Victor J. Lawrence. 1942. 3.50 o.p. (ISBN 0-913650-31-5). CPP Belwin.

Teaching Special Children. Norris G. Haring & E. L. Phillips. (Special Education Ser.). 1976. text ed. 38.95 o.p. (ISBN 0-07-026430-9). McGraw.

Teaching Speech Communication in the Secondary School. William D. Brooks & Gustav W. Friedrich. 368p. 1973. text ed. 23.50 o.p. (ISBN 0-395-12629-0, 3-06400). HM.

Teaching Students with Behavior Disorders: Techniques for Classroom Instruction. Patricia A. Gallagher. 300p. 1979. text ed. 22.95 o.p. (ISBN 0-89108-091-0). Love Pub Co.

Teaching the Basic Skills in English: The Role of Spelling, Punctuation & Grammar in Secondary English. Don Smedley. (Teaching Secondary English Ser.). 182p. 1983. 21.00x o.p. (ISBN 0-416-34140-3, NO. 3864); pap. 10.95x o.p. (ISBN 0-416-34150-0, NO. 3865). Routledge Chapman & Hall.

Teaching the Bible to Change Lives. Kathy Hyde. LC 84-47801. 143p. (Orig.). 1984. pap. 6.95 o.p. (ISBN 0-89840-064-3). Heres Life.

Teaching the Black Experience: Methods & Materials. James A. Banks. LC 74-126641. 1970. pap. 5.95 o.p. (ISBN 0-8224-6885-9). D S Lake Pubs.

Teaching the Exceptional Child. Luciano L'Abate & Leonard T. Curtis. LC 74-4575. (Bks. in Psychology Ser). (Illus.). 495p. 1975. text ed. 18.95 o.p. (ISBN 0-7216-5588-2). HR&W.

Teaching the Gifted & Talented in the Science Classroom. William D. Romey. 64p. 1980. 6.95 o.p. (ISBN 0-8106-0736-0). NEA.

Teaching the Gifted-Learning Disabled Child. Paul R. Daniels. LC 82-22775. 240p. 1983. 34.00 o.p. (ISBN 0-89443-928-6). Aspen Pub.

Teaching the Language Arts in the Elementary School. 3rd ed. Martha Dallman. 380p. 1976. text ed. write for info. o.p. (ISBN 0-697-06158-2). Wm C Brown.

Teaching the Learning-Disabled Adolescent. Lester Mann et al. LC 77-74377. (Illus.). 1978. text ed. 24.50 o.p. (ISBN 0-395-25434-5). HM.

Teaching the Magic of Dance. Jaques D'Amboise et al. (Illus.). 1983. 17.25 o.p. (ISBN 0-671-46077-3); pap. 10.75 o.p. (ISBN 0-671-49401-5). S&S.

Teaching the Media: An Introduction to Media Education. Len Masterman. (Illus.). 220p. 1987. 15.00 o.p. (ISBN 0-906890-53-5); pap. 11.00 o.p. (ISBN 0-906890-52-7). M Boyars Pubs.

Teaching the Old Testament in English Classes. James S. Ackerman et al. LC 72-93907. (English Curriculum Study Ser.). 512p. 1973. 20.00x o.p. (ISBN 0-253-35785-3); pap. 7.95x o.p. (ISBN 0-253-28850-9). Ind U Pr.

Teaching the Retarded Visually Handicapped: Indeed They Are Children. Donna L. Bluhm. LC 68-23679. (Illus.). Repr. of 1968 ed. cancelled o.s.i. (ISBN 0-8357-9560-8, 2013063). Bks Demand UMI.

Teaching the Severely Mentally Retarded: Adaptive Skills Training. Allen A. Mori & Lowell F. Masters. LC 79-27489. 407p. 1980. text ed. 36.00 o.p. (ISBN 0-89443-173-0). Aspen Pub.

Teaching the Text. Ed. by Susanne Kappeler & Norman Bryson. 200p. (Orig.). 1983. pap. 10.95x o.p. (ISBN 0-7100-9412-4). Routledge Chapman & Hall.

Teaching the Universe of Discourse. James Moffett. LC 82-83368. 215p. 1982. text ed. 18.95 o.p. (ISBN 0-395-32827-6). HM.

Teaching the Young Child: A Handbook of Open Classroom Practice. Susan Rounds. LC 74-9315. (Illus.). 236p. 1975. 15.00x o.p. (ISBN 0-87586-048-6). Agathon.

Teaching Them to Read. 4th ed. Dolores Durkin. 1983. text ed. 39.00 o.p. (ISBN 0-205-07933-4, 2379333). Allyn.

Teaching Thinking Skills: Social Studies. Karen Rosenblum Cale. 48p. 1987. 6.95 o.p. (ISBN 0-8106-0680-1). NEA.

Teaching Through Research. A. R. Arasteh. 1966. 30.00 o.p. (ISBN 90-04-00108-5). E J Brill USA.

Teaching Today: Tasks & Challenges. J. Michael Palardy. (Illus.). 480p. 1975. pap. text ed. write for info. o.p. (ISBN 0-02-390410-0). Macmillan.

Teaching Today: The Church's First Ministry. Locke E. Bowman, Jr. LC 79-25901. 212p. 1980. pap. 8.95 o.s.i. (ISBN 0-664-24303-7, Westminster). Westminster John Knox.

Teaching under Attack. Walter Roy. (Illus.). 130p. 1983. 29.00 o.p. (ISBN 0-7099-2212-4, Pub. by Croom Helm Ltd); pap. 11.50 o.p. (ISBN 0-7099-2213-2). Routledge Chapman & Hall.

Teaching Values in College: Facilitating Development of Ethical, Moral & Value Awareness in Students. Richard L. Morrill. LC 80-8003. (Higher Education Ser.). 1980. text ed. 23.95x o.p. (ISBN 0-87589-475-5). Jossey-Bass.
Teaching with a Purpose. 7th ed. James M. McCrimmon. 1980. pap. 2.00 instr's. manual o.p. (ISBN 0-395-28254-3). HM.
Teaching with Charisma. Duck. 364p. 1980. text ed. 30.00 o.p. (ISBN 0-205-07256-9, 2372568). Allyn.
Teaching Without Tears: The Classroom Teachers Survival Book. Charles O. Preece. LC 88-80829. 124p. 1988. 14.95 o.s.i. (ISBN 0-9619349-2-1). C O Preece.
Teaching Word Attack Skills. 3rd ed. Lee-Ann Rinsky. 203p. 1984. pap. text ed. 16.00x o.p. (ISBN 0-89787-512-5). Gorsuch Scarisbrick.
Teaching Writing in the Content Areas: Middle School-Junior High. Stephen N. Tchudi & Margie C. Huerts. 64p. 1983. 7.25 o.p. (ISBN 0-8141-3157-3). NCTE.
Teaching Writing in the Content Areas: College. Stephen N. Tchudi. 128p. 1986. pap. 8.50 o.p. (ISBN 0-8141-0728-1). NCTE.
Teaching Writing in the Content Areas: Elementary. Stephen N. Tchudi & Susan J. Tchudi. 64p. 1983. 7.00 o.p. (ISBN 0-8141-1314-1). NCTE.
Teaching Writing in the Content Areas: Senior High School. Stephen N. Tchudi & Joanne Yates. 64p. 1983. 8.50 o.p. (ISBN 0-8141-2116-0). NCTE.
Teaching Writing to Learning Disabled Students. Gerard Giordano. LC 83-25753. 176p. 1984. spiral bdg. 36.00 o.p. (ISBN 0-89443-580-9). Aspen Pub.
Teaching Young Children at School & Home. Edythe Margolin. 448p. 1982. text ed. (ISBN 0-02-375980-1). Macmillan.
Teaching Young Children to Read at Home. Wood Smethurst. 1975. text ed. 16.95 o.p. (ISBN 0-07-058443-5). McGraw.
Teaching Young Children to Swim & Dive. Virginia H. Newman. LC 72-76370. (Illus.). 1969. 5.95 o.p. (ISBN 0-15-188116-2). HarBraceJ.
Teaching Your Child about Sex. Terrance Drake & Marvia Drake. LC 83-71726. 60p. 1983. 6.95 o.p. (ISBN 0-87747-951-8). Deseret Bk.
Teaching Your Computer to Talk: A Manual of Command & Response. Edward R. Teja. (Illus.). 208p. 16.95 o.p. (ISBN 0-8306-0019-1); pap. 8.95 o.p. (ISBN 0-8306-1330-7, 1330). TAB Bks.
Teachings from the American Earth: Perspectives on the Religion, Philosophy, & Spirituality of the American Indian. Ed. by Dennis Tedlock & Barbara Tedlock. (Illus.). 280p. 1975. 9.95x o.p. (ISBN 0-87140-599-7). Liveright.
Teachings of Don Juan. Carlos Castaneda. 1983. pap. 3.95 o.s.i. (ISBN 0-671-49965-3). PB.
Teachniques: Creative Designs for Teaching. Jack R. Presseau. LC 81-85331. 80p. 1982. pap. 6.95 o.s.i. (ISBN 0-8042-1414-X, John Knox). Westminster John Knox.
Teacup Full of Roses. Sharon B. Mathis. (YA) (gr. 7 up). 1979. pap. 1.50 o.p. (ISBN 0-380-00780-0, 54312). Avon.
Team. Dody Donnelly. LC 77-74584. 168p. (Orig.). 1977. pap. 5.95 o.p. (ISBN 0-8091-2013-5). Paulist Pr.
Team Spirit. John Syer. 208p. 1987. 30.95 o.p. (ISBN 0-434-98096-X, Pub. by W Heinemann Ltd). David & Charles.
Team Teaching & Flexible Scheduling for Tomorrow. N. C. Polos. 1969. pap. text ed. 3.50x o.p. (ISBN 0-8290-1196-X). Irvington.
Team Teaching at the College Level. H. M. La Fauci & P. Richter. LC 73-88573. 1971. 45.00 o.p. (ISBN 0-08-006946-0). Pergamon.
Team That Runs Your Hospital. Mary P. Lee. LC 80-36762. 90p. 1980. 9.50 o.s.i. (ISBN 0-664-32669-2, Westminster). Westminster John Knox.
Teamwork: A Prepared Approach to Childbirth. Debra Reiss. LC 85-90986. (Illus.). 192p. 1985. 15.00 o.p. (ISBN 0-682-40268-0). Exposition-Phoenix.
TEAPACK Users' Manual. R. L. Johnston. 118p. 1982. pap. 15.95 o.p. (ISBN 0-471-86443-9). Wiley.
Teapot Dome: Oil & Politics in the 1920's. Burl Noggle. 1965. pap. 5.95 o.p. (ISBN 0-393-00297-7, Norton Lib). Norton.
Teardrops to Diamonds: How God's Love Turns Sorrow into Joy. Carl W. Berner. LC 83-70505. 96p. (Orig.). 1983. pap. 5.50 o.p. (ISBN 0-8066-2011-0, 10-6228, Augsburg). Augsburg Fortress.
Tears & Laughter. Kahlil Gibran. 96p. 1946. pap. (ISBN 0-8022-0583-6). Philos Lib.
Tears & Laughters in My Poetry. Emma S. Mazor. 183p. 1981. 7.50 o.p. (ISBN 0-682-49708-8). Exposition-Phoenix.
Tears for Fears. Philip Kamin. (Illus.). 32p. (gr. 3 up). 1985. pap. 4.95 o.p. (ISBN 0-88188-406-5, Pub. by Robus Bks). H Leonard Pub Corp.
Tears in the Rainbow: The Fannie Korsun Story. David R. Mann. 1985. 7.95 o.p. (ISBN 0-533-06373-6). Vantage.
Tears of Lady Meng: A Parable of People's Political Theology. Choan-Seng Song. LC 82-2295. (Illus.). 80p. (Orig.). 1982. pap. 4.95 o.p. (ISBN 0-88344-505-0). Orbis Bks.
Tears of the Singers. Melinda Snodgrass. (Gregg Press Science Fiction - Star Trek Ser.). 252p. 1986. lib. bdg. 11.95x o.p. (ISBN 0-8398-2932-9, Gregg). G K Hall.
Teasers & Appeasers: Essay & Studies on Themes of Slavic Philology. George Y. Shevelov. 336p. cancelled o.s.i. (ISBN 3-7705-0638-3). Adlers Foreign Bks.
Teatro de Federico Garcia Lorca y Otros Ensayos Sobre Literatura Espanola e Hispanoamericana. Luis Gonzalez-del-Valle. LC 79-66656. 250p. 1980. pap. 30.00 o.p. (ISBN 0-89295-015-3). Society Sp & Sp-Am.
Tech. Staff Anal, 3 vols. TMI Kemeny Commission. 1981. Repr. 385.00 o.p. (ISBN 0-08-026121-3). Pergamon.
Tech Tran Special Report: Machine Vision Systems. 2nd ed. Tech Tran Consultants Staff. 224p. 1986. text ed. 53.95 o.p. (ISBN 0-07-063243-X). McGraw.
Technetium Ninety-Nine-M: Generators, Chemistry, & Preparation of Radiopharmaceuticals. Ed. by W. C. Eckelman. (Illus.). 168p. 1983. pap. 28.00 o.p. (ISBN 0-08-029144-9). Pergamon.
Technic of the Bow Op. 50 for Violin. Casorti. (Carl Fischer Music Library Ser.: No. L-345). (Ger. & Fr.). pap. 6.00 o.p. (ISBN 0-8258-0042-0, L-345). Fischer Inc NY.
Technical Algebra with Applications. C. E. Goodson & S. L. Miertschin. 572p. 1985. 26.95 o.p. (ISBN 0-471-08241-4). Wiley.
Technical Analysis Explained: An Illustrated Guide for the Investor. Martin J. Pring. 1979. text ed. 39.95 o.p. (ISBN 0-07-050871-2). McGraw.
Technical & Business Communication in Two-Year Programs. Ed. by W. Keats Sparrow & Nell Ann Pickett. 205p. (Orig.). 1983. pap. 10.30 o.p. (ISBN 0-8141-5298-8). NCTE.
Technical & Business Writing. Clarence A. Andrews. 1975. text ed. 15.40 o.p. (ISBN 0-395-18603-X). HM.
Technical & Realistic Illustrations of Japan. (Graphic-Sha Bks.). (Illus.). 1984. 32.95 o.p. (ISBN 4-7661-0245-2). Bks Nippan.
Technical & Realistic Illustrations of Japan. (Illus.). 160p. 1986. pap. 25.00 o.p. (ISBN 0-8161-8809-2, Pub. by Graphic-Sha Pub Co Ltd Japan). G K Hall.
Technical & Vocational Education in Asia & Oceania. (Bulletin of the UNESCO Regional Office for Education in Asia & Oceania: Vol.21). 316p. 1980. pap. 19.95 o.p. (ISBN 0-686-69912-2, UB87, UB). UNIPUB.
Technical Assessment of Nuclear Power & Its Alternatives: Proceedings, American Nuclear Society Topical Meeting, Los Angeles, 27-29 February 1980. 374p. pap. 46.00 o.p. (ISBN 0-89448-107-X, 700045). Am Nuclear Soc.
Technical Assessment of Specific Aspects of EPA Proposed Environmental Radiation Standard for the Uranium Fuel Cycle (40CFR 190) & Its Association Documentation (AIF-NESP-011) NUS Corporation Staff. (National Environmental Studies Project: NESP Reports). 150p. 1976. 10.00 o.p. (ISBN 0-318-13598-1); NESP sponsors 5.00 o.p. (ISBN 0-318-13599-X). US Coun Energy Awareness.
Technical Basis for a Size-Specific Particulate Standard, 2 pts. Air Pollution Control Association Specialty Conference, Danvers, MA & Seattle, WA, 1980. 336p. 1980. Air & Waste.
Technical Correspondence: A Handbook & Reference Source for the Technical Professional. Herman M. Weisman. LC 67-30919. 265p. 1968. 17.50 o.p. (ISBN 0-471-92640-X, Pub. by Wiley). Krieger.
Technical Data on Fuel: S. I. Units. 7th rev. ed. Ed. by J. W. Rose & J. R. Cooper. LC 77-24872. 343p. 1978. 113.95x o.p. (ISBN 0-470-99239-5). Halsted Pr.
Technical Dictionary of Production Engineering, 2 vols. Rudolph Walther. 856p. 1973. Vol. 1: English-German. 125.00 o.p. (ISBN 0-08-016959-7); Vol 2: German-English. 85.00 o.p. (ISBN 0-08-016960-0). Pergamon.
Technical Dictionary of Vacuum Physics & Vacuum Technology (English, French, German, Russian) Karl Hurrle et al. 1973. 60.00 o.p. (ISBN 0-08-016957-0). Pergamon.
Technical Digest-Symposium on Optical Fiber Measurements. U. S. Department of Commerce Staff. 1980. pap. 50.00 o.p. (ISBN 0-918435-82-X). Info Gatekeepers.
Technical Documentation Standards for Computer Programs & Computer-Based Systems Used in Engineering. National Computing Centre, Ltd. Staff. (Illus.). 180p. 1980. 72.50x o.s.i. (ISBN 0-85012-247-3). Intl Pubns Serv.
Technical Drawing. 4th ed. W. Abbott. (Illus.). 1976. pap. 23.50x o.p. (ISBN 0-216-90210-X). Trans-Atl Phila.
Technical Guideline for Maize Seed Technology. (AGP-SIDP Ser.: No. 82-1). 211p. 1982. pap. 14.00 o.p. (ISBN 92-5-101190-7, F2323, FAO). UNIPUB.
Technical Issues in Infared Detectors & Arrays, Vol. 409. Ed. by E. Kikrorian. 136p. 42.00 o.p. (ISBN 0-89252-444-8). SPIE.
Technical Manual for ELSA: English Language Skills Assessment in a Reading Context. Cecelia Doherty & Donna Ilyin. (ELSA Tests Ser.). 1981. pap. 4.50 o.p. (ISBN 0-88377-226-4). Newbury Hse.
Technical Mathematics. 3rd ed. Jacqueline Austin & Margarita S. Isern. LC 82-60533. 1983. pap. text ed. 25.95 o.s.i. (ISBN 0-03-061234-9). HR&W.
Technical Mathematics. Al H. Chew et al. LC 75-25011. (Illus.). 576p. 1976. text ed. 23.50 o.p. (ISBN 0-395-24009-3). HM.
Technical Mathematics. Linda Davis. 736p. 1988. 36.95 o.p. (ISBN 0-675-20338-4). Merrill.
Technical Papers. 470p. 6.00 o.p. (ISBN 0-317-32490-X, T651). Am Congrs Survey.
Technical Papers: Fiftieth Meeting of the American Society of Photogrammetry, 2 vols. 894p. 1984. pap. 17.00 o.p. (ISBN 0-937294-57-8). ASP & RS.
Technical Papers: Forty-Ninth Meeting of the Americal Society of Photogrammetry. 411p. 1983. pap. 15.00 o.p. (ISBN 0-937294-47-0). ASP & RS.
Technical Papers of the ASP Fall Technical Meeting: October 1980. 7.00 o.p. (ISBN 0-937294-32-2); pap. 5.00 member o.p. ASP & RS.
Technical Papers of the Measurement, Mapping & Management in the Coastal Zone from Virginia to Maine Symposium, New York, 1979. Measurement, Mapping, & Management in the Coastal Zone from Virginia to Maine Symposium Staff. 272p. 1980. 11.00 o.p. (ISBN 0-317-32496-9, G420). Am Congrs Survey.
Technical Papers of the 46th Annual Meeting of the American Society of Photogrammetry. 552p. 1980. pap. 7.00 o.p. (ISBN 0-937294-27-6); pap. 5.00 members o.p. ASP & RS.
Technical Papers: Proceedings of the ACSM-ASP Fall Convention, September 1982. ACSM-ASP Fall Convention Staff. pap. 15.00 o.p. (ISBN 0-937294-39-X); pap. 7.00 members o.p. ASP & RS.
Technical Program Abstracts & Bibiographies, 1987. 923p. (Orig.). 1987. pap. text ed. 45.00 o.p. (ISBN 0-317-67222-3). Soc Expl Geophys.
Technical Program Abstracts & Biographies, 1986. (Illus.). 640p. (Orig.). pap. text ed. 60.00 o.p. (ISBN 0-931830-44-3). Soc Expl Geophys.
Technical Reference Dictionary. Ed. by E. Burger. 571p. 1979. 95.00 o.p. (ISBN 0-686-92324-3, M-9890). French & Eur.
Technical Report Writing Today. 2nd ed. Steven E. Pauley. LC 78-69557. (Illus.). 1979. text ed. 23.95 o.p. (ISBN 0-395-27111-8). HM.
Technical Report Writing Today. Steven E. Pauley. LC 72-7923. 400p. 1973. text ed. 12.95 o.p. (ISBN 0-395-12664-9, 3-43325). HM.
Technical Sources for Conducting Personal Injury Action. 5th ed. Harry Philo et al. LC 74-18580. 1975. 40.00 o.p. (ISBN 0-686-14527-5). Lawyers Co-Op.
Technical Terms, Symbols & Definitions in English, French, German, Italian, Portuguese, Russian, Spanish & Swedish Used in Soil Mechanics & Foundation. 5th ed. 256p. 1981. text ed. 82.00 o.p. (ISBN 0-317-65974-X, Pub. by A A Balkema). Gower Pub Co.
Technical Trigonometry with Applications. C. E. Goodson & S. L. Miertschin. LC 85-6344. 448p. 1985. 25.95 o.p. (ISBN 0-471-08240-6). Wiley.
Technical Writing. 3rd ed. John M. Lannon. 1984. pap. text ed. write for info. o.p. (ISBN 0-673-39274-0). Scott F.
Technical Writing for Beginners. Winston Smock. (Illus.). 204p. 1984. 13.95 o.p. (ISBN 0-13-898452-2); pap. 6.95 o.p. (ISBN 0-13-898445-X). P-H.
Technically Speaking: Oral Communication for Engineers, Scientists & Technical Personnel. Harold Weiss & J. B. McGrath. 1963. text ed. 35.00x o.p. (ISBN 0-07-069085-5). McGraw.
Technicians Guide To Programmable Controllers. Richard A. Cox. LC 84-7715. 160p. 1984. pap. text ed. 18.50 o.p. (ISBN 0-8273-2420-0); instr's. guide 6.00 o.p. (ISBN 0-8273-2421-9). Delmar.
Technician's Handbook of Plastics. Peter A. Grandilli. 272p. 1981. 29.95 o.s.i. (ISBN 0-442-23870-3). Van Nos Reinhold.
Technicians of Death. Tony Williamson. LC 78-55426. 1978. 8.95 o.p. (ISBN 0-689-10920-2, Atheneum). Macmillan.
Technics & Human Development: The Myth of the Machine, Vol. 1. Lewis Mumford. LC 67-16088. (Illus.). 342p. 1970. 24.95 o.p. (ISBN 0-15-163975-2). HarBraceJ.
Technique of Byrd's Vocal Polyphony. Herbert K. Andrews. LC 79-25357. 306p. 1980. Repr. of 1966 ed. lib. bdg. 45.50x o.p. (ISBN 0-313-22252-5, ANTB). Greenwood.
Technique of Clear Writing. rev. ed. Robert Gunning. 1968. text ed. 16.95 o.p. (ISBN 0-07-025206-8). McGraw.
Technique of Decorative Stained Glass. Paul San Casciani. (Illus.). 120p. 1985. 34.95 o.p. (ISBN 0-7134-4269-7, Pub. by Batsford England). David & Charles.
Technique of Electroorganic Synthesis: Scale-up & Engineering Aspects, Vol. 5, Pt. 3. Ed. by N. L. Weissberger & B. V. Tilak. LC 73-18447. (Techniques of Chemistry Ser.). 536p. 1982. 140.00 o.p. (ISBN 0-471-06359-2, Pub. by Wiley-Interscience). Wiley.
Technique of Jewelry. Rod Edwards. (Illus.). 1977. 17.50 o.s.i. (ISBN 0-684-15309-2, ScribT). Scribner.
Technique of Organic Chemistry: Vol. 9, Pt. 2, Microwave Molecular Spectra. Ed. by W. Gordy & L. Cook. LC 80-16243. 747p. 1970. 67.50 o.p. (ISBN 0-471-93161-6). Krieger.
Technique of Radio Production. Robert McLeish. (Library of Communication Techniques Ser.). (Illus.). 304p. 1978. 29.95x o.p. (ISBN 0-240-51008-9). Focal Pr.
Technique of Solar Returns. new ed. Alexandre Volguine. Tr. by John Broglio from Fr. LC 76-17892. 1976. 15.95 o.p. (ISBN 0-88231-011-9). ASI Pubs Inc.
Techniques & Components of Analogue Computation. Raymond W. Williams. 1962. 52.50 o.p. (ISBN 0-12-756250-8). Acad Pr.
Techniques & Concepts of High-Energy Physics I. Ed. by Thomas Ferbel. LC 81-13767. (NATO ASI Series B, Physics: Vol. 66). 554p. 1981. 89.50x o.p. (ISBN 0-306-40721-3, Plenum Pr). Plenum Pub.
Techniques & Concepts of High-Energy Physics II. Ed. by Thomas Ferbel. (NATO ASI Series B, Physics: Vol. 99). 350p. 1983. 59.50x o.p. (ISBN 0-306-41385-X, Plenum Pr). Plenum Pub.
Techniques & Experiments for Organic Chemistry. Ralph J. Fessenden & Joan S. Fessenden. 480p. 1983. text ed. 24.00 pub net o.p. (ISBN 0-87150-755-2). Brooks-Cole.
Techniques & Materials in Biology. Marjorie P. Behringer. LC 80-12458. 602p. 1982. Repr. of 1973 ed. lib. bdg. 41.50 o.p. (ISBN 0-89874-175-0). Krieger.
Techniques & Materials of Tonal Music: With an Introduction to Twentieth-Century Techniques. 2nd ed. Thomas E. Benjamin et al. LC 78-69578. (Illus.). 1979. text ed. 26.50 o.p. (ISBN 0-395-27066-9). HM.
Techniques & Problems of Assessment for Teachers. Ed. by H. G. Macintosh. 1974. pap. 18.95x o.p. (ISBN 0-7131-1816-4). Trans-Atl Phila.
Techniques du Reboisement dans les Zones Subdesertiques d'Afrique. Guy R. Ferlin. 48p. 1981. pap. 3.50 o.p. (ISBN 0-88936-295-5, IDRC-169F, IDRC). UNIPUB.
Techniques for Culture of Vertebrate Embryos. D. A. New. 1966. 64.50 o.p. (ISBN 0-12-516950-7). Acad Pr.
Techniques for Producing Visual Instructional Media. 2nd ed. Edward O. Minor & H. R. Fyre. 1977. text ed. 37.95 o.p. (ISBN 0-07-042406-3). McGraw.
Techniques for Reducing Roadway Occupancy During Routine Maintenance Activities. (National Cooperative Highway Research Project Report). 55p. 1975. 4.40 o.p. (ISBN 0-309-02340-8). Transport Res Bd.
Techniques for Surgeons. Ed. by J. Patrick O'Leary & Eugene A. Woltering. LC 84-22209. 442p. 1985. 29.95 o.p. (ISBN 0-471-88957-1). Wiley.
Techniques for the Study of Mixed Populations. Ed. by D. W. Lovelock & R. Davies. (Society for Applied Bacteriology Technical Ser.). 1979. 55.50 o.p. (ISBN 0-12-456650-2). Acad Pr.
Techniques for Writing: Composition. Rev. ed. Milton Wohl. LC 78-646. 1985. pap. text ed. 11.50 o.p. (ISBN 0-317-57098-6). Newbury Hse.
Techniques in Aesthetic Rhinoplasty. George C. Peck. (Illus.). 135p. 1983. 85.00 o.p. (ISBN 0-86577-110-3). Thieme Med Pubs.
Techniques in Clinical Immunology. 2nd. ed. R. A. Thompson. (Illus.). 352p. 1981. pap. text ed. 35.75 o.p. (ISBN 0-632-00723-0, B 4948-X). Mosby.
Techniques in Diagnosing Skin & Hair Disease. David M. Pariser & William H. Eaglestein. (Illus.). 224p. 1986. pap. text ed. 38.95 o.p. (ISBN 0-317-42803-9). Thieme Med Pubs.
Techniques in Endocrine Research. Ed. by P. Eckstein & F. Knowles. 1963. 54.50 o.p. (ISBN 0-12-230150-1). Acad Pr.

Titles

Techniques in Experimental Virology. Ed. by Robert J. Harris. 1964. 72.00 o.p. (ISBN 0-12-327190-8). Acad Pr.
Techniques in Fast Reactor Critical Experiments. W. G. Davey & W. C. Redman. LC 79-119375. 314p. 1970. 23.00 o.p. (ISBN 0-677-02680-3, 450006). Am Nuclear Soc.
Techniques in Indian Mural Painting. Jayanta Chakrabarti. (Illus.). 134p. 1981. text ed. 28.50x o.p. (ISBN 0-391-02499-X). Humanities.
Techniques in Opthalmic Plastic Surgery. Ed. by Ralph E. Wesley. LC 85-17813. 482p. 1986. 45.00 o.p. (ISBN 0-471-80439-8). Wiley.
Techniques in Protein Biosynthesis, 3 vols. Peter N. Campbell. Vol. 2. 43.50 o.p. (ISBN 0-12-158162-4); Vol. 3 1973. 48.00 o.p. (ISBN 0-12-158163-2). Acad Pr.
Techniques in Skin Surgery. Ed. by Ervin Epstein & Ervin Epstein, Jr. LC 79-11457. (Illus.). 203p. 1979. text ed. 18.00 o.p. (ISBN 0-8121-0677-6). Lea & Febiger.
Techniques of Abortion. 2nd ed. Neubardt & Harold Schulman. 180p. 1977. 21.50 o.p. (ISBN 0-316-60371-6). Little.
Techniques of Asymptotic Analysis. Lawrence Sirovich. LC 70-149141. (Applied Mathematical Sciences Ser.: Vol. 2). (Illus.). 1971. pap. 21.95 o.p. (ISBN 0-387-90022-5). Springer-Verlag.
Techniques of Attitude Scale Construction. Allen L. Edwards. (Century Psychology Ser.). (Illus.). 1982. Repr. of 1962 ed. text ed. 39.00x o.p. (ISBN 0-8290-0067-4). Irvington.
Techniques of Combined Gas Chromatography - Mass Spectrometry: Applications in Organic Analysis. W. H. McFadden. LC 73-6916. 463p. 1973. 70.00x o.p. (ISBN 0-471-58388-X). Wiley.
Techniques of Crocheted & Openwork Lace. Ena Maidens. (Illus.). 144p. 1982. 24.95 o.s.i. (ISBN 0-7134-2568-7, Pub. by Batsford England). David & Charles.
Techniques of Fire Hydraulics. Lawrence W. Erven. (Fire Science Ser). 1972. text ed. write for info. o.p. (ISBN 0-02-473000-9, 47300). Macmillan.
Techniques of Mediation in Labor Disputes. Walter A. Maggiolo. LC 70-166000. 192p. 1971. lib. bdg. 15.00 o.p. (ISBN 0-379-00112-8). Oceana.
Techniques of Optimization. Ed. by A. V. Balakrishnan & L. W. Neustadt. 1972. 65.00 o.p. (ISBN 0-12-076960-3). Acad Pr.
Techniques of Population Analysis. George W. Barclay. LC 58-59899. 31p. 1958. write for info. o.p. (ISBN 0-02-305900-1). Macmillan.
Techniques of Program & System Maintenance. 2nd ed. Ed. by Garish Parikh. 300p. 1988. 34.50x o.p. (ISBN 0-89435-245-8). QED Info Sci.
Techniques of Reading: An Integrated Program for Improved Comprehension & Speed. 3rd ed. Horace Judson & William S. Schaill. 487p. 1972. pap. text ed. 13.95 o.p. (ISBN 0-15-589690-3, HC). HarBraceJ.
Techniques of Rug Weaving. Peter Collingwood. LC 68-24486. (Illus.). 480p. 1987. 50.00 o.p. (ISBN 0-8230-5200-1). Watson-Guptill.
Techniques of Safety Management. 2nd ed. Daniel C. Petersen. (Illus.). 1978. text ed. 41.50 o.p. (ISBN 0-07-049596-3). McGraw.
Techniques of Sample Preparation for Liquid Scintillation Counting. Ed. by B. W. Fox. (Laboratory Techniques in Biochemistry & Molecular Biology: Vol. 5, Pt. 1). 1976. pap. 37.00 o.p. (ISBN 0-444-11056-9, North-Holland). Elsevier.
Techniques of Scenario Planning. John Chandler & Paul Cockle. (Illus.). 192p. 1982. text ed. 36.50 o.p. (ISBN 0-07-084570-0). McGraw.
Techniques of Small Boat Racing. Ed. by Stuart H. Walker. (Illus.). 1960. 11.95 o.p. (ISBN 0-393-03152-7). Norton.
Techniques of Structured Problem Solving. Arthur B. Van Gundy. 320p. 1980. 29.95 o.p. (ISBN 0-442-21223-2). Van Nos Reinhold.
Techniques of Value Analysis & Engineering. 2nd ed. Lawrence D. Miles. LC 74-157484. (Illus.). 320p. 1972. text ed. 53.95 o.p. (ISBN 0-07-041926-4). McGraw.
Techniques of Writing. 3rd ed. Paul L. Kinsella. 364p. 1981. pap. text ed. 11.95 o.p. (ISBN 0-15-589728-4, HC). HarBraceJ.
Techniques of Writing. 2nd ed. Paul L. Kinsella. 1975. pap. text ed. 9.95 o.p. (ISBN 0-15-589726-8, HC). HarBraceJ.
Techno-Economic Trends in Airborne Equipment for Agriculture & Other Selected Areas: Proceedings of a Seminar Organized by the United Nations Economic Commission for Europe, Warsaw, Poland, 18-22 September 1978. (ECE Seminars & Symposia). (Illus.). 294p. 1980. 89.00 o.p. (ISBN 0-08-022425-3). Pergamon.
Technocratic Illusion: A Study of Managerial Power in Italy. Flavia Derossi. Tr. by Susan LoBello from Ital. LC 81-14341. 284p. 1982. 40.00 o.p. (ISBN 0-87332-185-5). M E Sharpe.
Technological Basis of Radiation Therapy: Practical Clinical Applications. Ed. by Seymour H. Levitt & Norah Tapley. LC 83-9889. (Illus.). 336p. 1984. text ed. 45.00 o.p. (ISBN 0-8121-0898-1). Lea & Febiger.
Technological Change. abr. ed. Edwin Mansfield. (Illus.). 1970. pap. text ed. 3.95x o.p. (ISBN 0-393-09973-3, NortonC). Norton.
Technological Change & Regional Development. Ed. by A. Gillespie. (Pion London Papers in Regional Science Ser.: No. 12). (Illus.). 171p. 1984. pap. 15.00x o.p. (ISBN 0-85086-107-1, NO. 5072). Routledge Chapman & Hall.
Technological Change, Industrial Restructuring & Regional Development. Ash Amin & John Goddard. 192p. 1986. text ed. 39.95x o.p. (ISBN 0-04-338131-6). Unwin Hyman.
Technological Change: Its Impact on Man & Society. Emanuel G. Mesthene. LC 76-106960. (Studies in Technology & Society). 1970. 11.00 o.s.i. (ISBN 0-674-87235-5). Harvard U Pr.
Technological Dependence, Monopoly & Growth. M. Merhav. 1969. 27.00 o.p. (ISBN 0-08-012754-1). Pergamon.
Technological Development Strategies for Developing Countries: A Review for Policy Makers. Maximo Halty-Carrere. 155p. 1979. pap. text ed. 12.95x o.p. (ISBN 0-920380-24-7, Pub. by Inst Res Pub Canada). Gower Pub Co.
Technological Innovation & Industrial Development in Telecommunications: The Role of Public Buying in the Telecommunications Sector in the Nordic Countries. Ed. by Ove Granstrand & Jon Sigurdson. xvi, 254p. (Orig.). 1985. pap. text ed. 39.50x o.p. (ISBN 91-86002-56-2). Coronet Bks.
Technological Innovation & the Decorative Arts. Ed. by Ian M. Quimby & Polly A. Earl. xiv, 373p. 1984. pap. text ed. 14.95X o.p. (ISBN 0-8139-0569-9, Pub. by Winterhur Museum). U Pr of Amer.
Technological Innovation for a Dynamic Economy. Ed. by Christopher T. Hill & James M. Utterback. (Policy Studies). 1979. 90.00 o.p. (ISBN 0-08-025104-8); pap. 90.00 o.p. (ISBN 0-08-025103-X). Pergamon.
Technological Progress & Industrial Leadership: The Growth of the U. S. Steel Industry, 1900-1965. Ed. by Bela Gold et al. LC 83-48756. 832p. 1984. 65.00x o.p. (ISBN 0-669-07535-3). Lexington Bks.
Technological System. Jacques Ellul. 384p. 1980. 19.50x o.p. (ISBN 0-8264-0002-7). Continuum.
Technologies for NATO's Follow-On Forces Attack Concept: A Special Report of OTA's Assessment on Improving NATO's Defense Response. (OTA-ISC-312 Ser.). (Illus.). 46p. 1986. pap. 2.75 o.p. (ISBN 0-318-21314-1, S/N 052-003-01045-3). USGPO.
Technologies in the Laboratory Handling of Motion Picture & Other Long Films. Ed. by Frank P. Clark. (Illus.). 223p. 1971. 1.00 o.p. (ISBN 0-318-16593-7). Soc Motion Pic & TV Engrs.
Technologies of Freedom. Ithiel de Sola Pool. (Illus.). 344p. 1983. 21.00x o.p. (ISBN 0-674-87232-0, Belknap Pr). Harvard U Pr.
Technology Activity Guides, 2 pts. Glenn S. Listar. LC 86-24319. 1987. pap. text ed. 10.00 o.p. (ISBN 0-8273-2739-0); instr's. guide 5.00 o.p. (ISBN 0-8273-2738-2). Delmar.
Technology & Agricultural Policy. National Research Council. 300p. 1988. 32.50x o.p. (ISBN 0-309-03834-0); pap. text ed. 22.50x o.p. (ISBN 0-309-03833-2). Natl Acad Pr.
Technology & Development. Ed. by Konenigsber. 332p. 1981. pap. 39.00 o.p. (ISBN 0-08-028146-X). Pergamon.
Technology & Employment in Industry: A Case Study Approach. 2nd rev. & enl. ed. International Labour Office Staff. Ed. by A. Bhallas. xv, 389p. (Orig.). 1981. 25.65 o.p. (ISBN 92-2-102469-5); pap. 21.40 o.p. (ISBN 92-2-102466-0). Intl Labour Office.
Technology & Employment Practices in Developing Countries. Hubert Schmitz. LC 85-6640. 254p. 1985. 32.50 o.p. (ISBN 0-7099-3301-0, Pub. by Croom Helm Ltd). Routledge Chapman & Hall.
Technology & Energy Choice. Ed. by John Byrne & Daniel Rich. 160p. 1983. pap. 12.95 o.p. (ISBN 0-87855-812-8). Transaction Pubs.
Technology & Social Change. H. Russell Bernard & Pertti J. Pelto. (Illus.). 352p. 1972. text ed. write for info. o.p. (ISBN 0-02-309010-3, 30901). Macmillan.
Technology & Social Institutions. Ed. by Kan Chen. LC 74-77658. 224p. cancelled o.s.i. (ISBN 0-87942-035-9, PC00315). Inst Electrical.
Technology & Social Progress. R. A. Buchanan. 1966. text ed. 11.25 o.p. (ISBN 0-08-011141-6); pap. text ed. 6.25 o.p. (ISBN 0-08-011140-8). Pergamon.
Technology & State: Monographs. Mary Vance. (Public Administration Ser., Bibliography: P 1808). 68p. 1985. pap. 10.50 o.p. (ISBN 0-89028-638-8). Vance Biblios.
Technology & the Changing Family. William F. Ogburn & Meyer Nimkoff. LC 76-44366. 1977. Repr. of 1955 ed. lib. bdg. 22.50x o.p. (ISBN 0-8371-9311-7, OGTC). Greenwood.
Technology & the Character of Contemporary Life: A Philosophical Inquiry. Albert Borgman. LC 84-8639. 342p. 1985. 25.00x o.s.i. (ISBN 0-226-06628-2). U of Chicago Pr.
Technology & the Rural Community: The Social Impact. Ed. by M. J. Campbell. Orig. Title: New Technology & Rural Development. 432p. 1988. lib. bdg. 55.00x o.p. (ISBN 0-7099-4864-6, Pub. by Croom Helm UK). Routledge Chapman & Hall.
Technology & Work: East West Comparisons. Ed. by Peter Grootings. 256p. 1986. 39.00 o.p. (ISBN 0-7099-3801-2, Pub. by Croom Helm Ltd). Routledge Chapman & Hall.
Technology As a Social & Political Phenomenon. Philip L. Bereano. LC 76-18723. 544p. 1976. text ed. 49.95x o.p. (ISBN 0-471-06875-6). Wiley.
Technology Choice & Employment Creation: A Case Study of Three Multinational Enterprises in Singapore. Linda Lim & Pang E. Fong. Ed. by International Labour Office Staff. (Multinational Enterprieses Programe. Research on Employment Effects of Multinational Enterprises. Working Paper: No. 16). iv, 65p. (Orig.). 1981. pap. 8.55 o.p. (ISBN 92-2-102838-0). Intl Labour Office.
Technology Dependent Children: Hospital Versus Home Care, A Technical Memorandum. 115p. (Orig.). 1987. pap. 4.75 o.p. (ISBN 0-318-22955-2, S/N 052-003-01065-8). USGPO.
Technology, Development & the Environment: A Re-Appraisal. A. K. Reddy. (Illus.). 60p. 1980. pap. 9.75 o.p. (ISBN 0-08-025693-7). Pergamon.
Technology Edge: Opportunities for America in World Competition. Gerard K. O'Neill. 256p. 1984. 16.50 o.p. (ISBN 0-671-44766-1). S&S.
Technology, Employment & Basic Needs - ILO Overview Paper: United Nations Conference on Science & Technology for Development. 3rd ed. United Nations Conference on Science & Technology for Development Staff. 27p. 1977. pap. 4.50 o.p. (ISBN 92-2-101928-4, ILO106, ILO). UNIPUB.
Technology for a Changing World. John Davis. Compiled by Roger England. (Illus.). 58p. (Orig.). 1978. pap. 4.25x o.p. (ISBN 0-903031-56-6, Pub. by Intermed Tech England). Intermediate Tech.
Technology for Career Information Delivery: Conference Proceedings. Ed. by Karen S. Kimmel & Joan C. Blank. 109p. 1981. 7.25 o.p. (ISBN 0-318-22214-0, SN34). Natl Ctr Res Voc Ed.
Technology for Management of Hazardous Waste. Business Communications Staff. 1988. pap. 1950.00 o.p. (ISBN 0-89336-462-2, C-059). BCC.
Technology for Ujamaa Village Development in Tanzania. David J. Vail. LC 74-25876. (Foreign & Comparative Studies Program, Eastern African Ser.: No. 18). 64p. 1975. pap. 4.50x o.p. (ISBN 0-915984-15-6). Syracuse U Foreign Comp.
Technology, Invention & Industry. Joan Solomon. (Science in a Social Context Ser.). 1986. pap. text ed. 6.95x o.p. (ISBN 0-631-91980-5). Basil Blackwell.
Technology: Its Promise & Its Problems. Russell Peterson. (Illus.). 1979. pap. 2.50x o.p. (ISBN 0-87081-123-1). Univ Pr Colo.
Technology Management Handbook 1984. Robert Goldscheider. 1984. 47.50 o.p. (ISBN 0-87632-334-4). Clark Boardman.
Technology Mathematics Handbook. Jan J. Tuma. LC 74-26962. 384p. 1975. text ed. 35.50 o.p. (ISBN 0-07-065431-X). McGraw.
Technology of Carbon & Graphite Fiber Composites. John Delmonte. 464p. 1981. 38.95 o.p. (ISBN 0-442-22072-3). Van Nos Reinhold.
Technology of Carbon & Graphite Fiber Composites. John Delmonte. (Illus.). 464p. 1981. 47.00 o.p. (ISBN 0-686-48237-9, 0213). T-C Pubns CA.
Technology of Efficient Energy Utilization: Report, Nato Science Committee Conference, les Arcs, France, Oct. 1973. Ed. by E. G. Kovach. LC 74-19839. 82p. 1974. pap. 35.00 o.p. (ISBN 0-08-018314-X). Pergamon.
Technology of Food Preservation. 4th ed. Norman W. Desrosier & John N. Desrosier. (Illus.). 1977. lib. bdg. 37.50 o.p. (ISBN 0-87055-232-5); pap. 25.95 o.p. (ISBN 0-87055-286-4). AVI.
Technology of Inorganic Compounds: Chemical Engineers' Handbook. B. D. Mel'nik & F. B. Mel'nikov. 252p. 1970. text ed. 50.00x o.p. (ISBN 0-7065-1004-6, Pub. by Keter Pub Jerusalem). Coronet Bks.
Technology of Machine Tools. 2nd ed. Stephen F. Krar et al. LC 77-3663. (Illus.). 1977. text ed. 42.95 o.p. (ISBN 0-07-035383-2). McGraw.
Technology of Man: A Visual History. Carlo M. Cipolla & Derek Birdsall. (Illus.). 288p. 1980. 39.95 o.s.i. (ISBN 0-03-057792-6). H Holt & Co.
Technology, Public Policy, & the Changing Structure of American Agriculture. (OTA-F Ser.: No. 285). (Illus.). 380p. (Orig.). 1986. pap. 13.00 o.p. (ISBN 0-318-20154-2, S/N 052-003-01018-6). USGPO.
Technology: The God That Failed. D. M. Slusser & Gerald H. Slusser. 1971. pap. 2.95 o.s.i. (ISBN 0-664-24909-4, Westminster). Westminster John Knox.
Technology-the Key to Better Environment: Values, Profits, & Growth in Post Industrial Society. Donald C. Blaisdell. LC 73-77582. 1973. 5.50 o.p. (ISBN 0-682-47713-3, University). Exposition-Phoenix.
Technology, the University, & the Community. Ed. by George Bugliarello & H. A. Simon. 1976. 65.00 o.p. (ISBN 0-08-017872-3). Pergamon.
Technology Transfer, 3 vols. Sagafi-Nejad. (Pergamon Policy Studies on International Development). 1983. Set. 145.00 o.p. (ISBN 0-08-028070-6). Pergamon.
Technology Transfer: A Realistic Approach. Silvere Seurat. LC 78-62608. 174p. 1979. 19.00x o.p. (ISBN 0-87201-822-9). Gulf Pub.
Technology Transfer & Change in the Arab World: Proceedings of a Seminar, Beirut, Oct. 1977. United Nations Economic Commission for Western Asia, Natural Resources, Science & Technology Division. Ed. by A. B. Zahlan. 1979. 110.00 o.p. (ISBN 0-08-022435-0). Pergamon.
Technology Transfer, the Research Process, & Creating a Productive Environment. (Record). 51p. 1979. 3.00 o.p. (ISBN 0-309-02993-7). Transport Res Bd.
Technology Unbound. S. Rivkin. 1969. text ed. 12.25 o.p. (ISBN 0-08-006424-8); pap. text ed. 6.25 o.p. (ISBN 0-08-006391-8). Pergamon.
Technology, Vol. 2 (incl. 1983-1987 Supplements) Ed. by Eleanor C. Goldstein. (Social Issues Resources Ser.). 1987. 75.00 o.p. (ISBN 0-89777-060-9). Soc Issues.
Technology's Future: The Hague Congress Technology Assessment. Thomas J. Knight. LC 80-22193. 264p. 1982. text ed. 14.50 o.p. (ISBN 0-89874-283-8). Krieger.
Technomics: The Economics of Technology & the Computer Industry. William H. Inmon. 200p. 1985. 35.00 o.p. (ISBN 0-87094-688-9). Dow Jones-Irwin.
Technophobia: Getting Out of the Technology Trap. Hal Hellman. LC 75-44372. 324p. 1976. 8.95 o.p. (ISBN 0-87131-206-9). M Evans.
Technopolis. Nigel Calder. LC 79-101867. 1971. pap. 3.95 o.p. (ISBN 0-671-21062-9, Touchstone Bks). S&S.
Tecnicas Modernas De Archivo. M. Uribe. (Span). 1970. text ed. 8.95 o.p. (ISBN 0-07-066079-4). McGraw.
Tecnologia de la Contracepcion: Segunda Edicion en Espanol. Robert A. Hatcher et al. Tr. by Eduardo Montana from Eng. (Illus.). 280p. (Span.). 1982. text ed. 19.95x o.p. (ISBN 0-8290-1025-4); pap. text ed. 16.95x o.p. (ISBN 0-8290-1026-2). Irvington.
Tectonic Geomorphology. Ed. by J. T. Hack & M. Morisawa. (Binghamton Symposia in Geomorphology International Ser.: No. 15). 400p. 1985. text ed. 50.00 o.p. (ISBN 0-04-551098-9). Unwin Hyman.
Tectonics: A Selection of Papers. Ed. by J. F. Dewey et al. 150p. 1981. pap. 25.00 o.p. (ISBN 0-08-028742-5). Pergamon.
Tectonics & Sedimentation. Ed. by W. M. Dickinson. (Special Publication Ser.: No. 22). 204p. 1974. 16.00 o.p. (ISBN 0-918985-03-X); members 13.00 o.p. SEPM.
Ted E. Bear Finds Xmas. Date not set. incl. cassette 9.95 o.p. Ideals.
Ted E. Bear Rescues Santa Claus. (gr. k-5). 1985. 2.95 o.p. (ISBN 0-8249-8115-4). Ideals.
Ted Hughes. Thomas West. 96p. 1985. pap. 5.95 o.p. (ISBN 0-416-35400-9, NO. 9032). Routledge Chapman & Hall.
Ted Hughes: A Critical Study. Terry Gifford & Neil Roberts. 288p. 1986. pap. 17.95 o.p. (ISBN 0-571-13932-9). Faber & Faber.
Ted Hughes: A Critical Study. Neil Roberts & Terry Gifford. 288p. 1981. 25.00 o.p. (ISBN 0-571-11701-5); pap. 17.95 o.p. Faber & Faber.
Ted Kautzky Pencil Book: Combined Edition. (ISBN 0-671-60818-5). P-H.
Teddy at the Seashore. Amanda Davidson. LC 83-22745. (Illus.). 24p. (gr. k-2). 1984. 7.95 o.p. (ISBN 0-03-071026-X). H Holt & Co.
Teddy Bear & Friends Price Guide. 2nd ed. Compiled by Helen Sieverling. (Illus.). 200p. 1985. pap. 8.95 o.p. (ISBN 0-87588-255-2, 3105). Hobby Hse.
Teddy Bear Book. Marsha E. Moore. 1985. pap. 9.95 o.p. (ISBN 0-671-54787-9, Fireside). S&S.

Teddy Bear Catalog. Peggy Bialosky & Alan Bialosky. LC 80-51616. (Illus.). 224p. 1980. pap. 5.95 o.p. (ISBN 0-89480-133-3). Workman Pub.
Teddy Bear Catalog. rev. ed. Peggy Bialosky & Alan Bialosky. LC 83-40040. (Illus.). 224p. 1983. pap. 6.95 o.p. (ISBN 0-89480-607-6, 607). Workman Pub.
Teddy Bear Craft Book. Carolyn V. Hall. (Illus.). 160p. 1986. pap. 14.95 o.p. (ISBN 0-13-902222-8). P-H.
Teddy Bear Lovers Catalog: A Treasury of Bearfaced Pleasure. Ted Menten. LC 85-13311. (Illus.). 160p. 1985. 7.98 o.p. (ISBN 0-89471-413-9, Pub. by Courage Bks). Running Pr.
Teddy Bear Postman. Phoebe Worthington & Selby Worthington. (Illus.). (ps-k). 1982. 6.95 o.p. (ISBN 0-7232-2768-3). Warne.
Teddy Bears' Moving Day. Susanna Gretz. LC 81-2299. (Illus.). 32p. (gr. k-3). 1981. 9.95 o.s.i. (ISBN 0-02-737320-7, Four Winds). Macmillan.
Teddy Bears' Picnic. Jimmy Kennedy. (Illus.). Date not set. 14.95 o.p. (ISBN 0-310-57130-8, 16113). Zondervan.
Teddy Bears' Picnic. (Chubby Panoramas Ser.). (Illus.). 1983. 2.85 o.s.i. (ISBN 0-671-47666-1, Little Simon). S&S.
Teddy Beddy Bears Bedtime Book. LC 84-61626. (Baby Fingers Ser.). (Illus.). 14p. (ps). 1985. pap. 2.95 o.s.i. (ISBN 0-394-87052-2, BYR). Random.
Teddy Cleans the House. Amanda Davidson. LC 85-60281. (Illus.). 12p. (ps-k). 1985. 3.95 o.p. (ISBN 0-03-005003-0). H Holt & Co.
Teddy Goes Outside. Amanda Davidson. LC 85-60279. (Illus.). 12p. (ps-k). 1985. 3.95 o.p. (ISBN 0-03-005004-9). H Holt & Co.
Teddy Goes Shopping. Amanda Davidson. LC 85-60278. (Illus.). 12p. (ps-k). 1985. 3.95 o.p. (ISBN 0-03-004999-7). H Holt & Co.
Teddy in the Garden. Amanda Davidson. LC 85-27194. (Illus.). 32p. (ps-2). 1986. 8.95 o.p. (ISBN 0-03-008502-0). H Holt & Co.
Teddy Jo & the Stolen Ring, No. 3. Hilda Stahl. 128p. (gr. 3-9). 1982. pap. 2.95 o.p. (ISBN 0-8423-6945-7). Tyndale.
Teddy Jo & the Strange Medallion, No. 5. Hilda Stahl. 128p. (gr. 4-7). 1983. pap. 2.95 o.p. (ISBN 0-8423-6947-3). Tyndale.
Teddy's Birthday. Amanda Davidson. LC 84-19298. (Illus.). 24p. (ps-2). 1985. 7.95 o.p. (ISBN 0-03-002887-6). H Holt & Co.
Teddy's Favorite Food. Amanda Davidson. LC 85-60280. (Illus.). 12p. (ps-k). 1985. 3.95 o.s.i. (ISBN 0-03-005002-2). H Holt & Co.
Teen-Age Space Adventures. Ed. by Abraham L. Furman. 192p. (YA) (gr. 7 up). 1972. PLB 6.19 o.p. (ISBN 0-8313-1595-4). Lantern.
Teen-Age Underwater Adventure. Ed. by Thomas. (Illus.). (gr. 6-10). 1962. PLB 6.19 o.p. (ISBN 0-8313-0091-4). Lantern.
Teen-Ager, the Bible Speaks to You. W. Riess. 104p. 1987. pap. 3.95 o.p. (ISBN 0-570-06610-7, 12HH2102). Concordia.
Teen-Ager You're Dating. Walter Riess. LC 12-2650. (Orig.). 1964. pap. 3.95 o.p. (ISBN 0-570-06615-8, 12-2650). Concordia.
Teen-Agers at Work. rev. ed. Yvette Dogin. 1983. pap. 3.75 o.p. (ISBN 0-88323-184-0, 164). Pendergrass Pub.
Teen Angels. Sonia Pilcer. 1979. pap. 2.25 o.p. (ISBN 0-380-47662-2, 61689-0). Avon.
Teenage Body Book. Kathy McCoy & Charles Wibbelsman. (gr. 9-12). 1979. pap. 9.95 o.p. (ISBN 0-671-79012-9, Wallaby). PB.
Teenage Employment Guide. Rev. ed. Allan B. Goldenthal. (Illus.). 208p. (Orig.). (gr. 9-12). 1983. pap. 9.95 o.p. (ISBN 0-671-43542-6). Monarch Pr.
Teenage Motherhood: Social & Economic Consequences. Kristin A. Moore et al. 50p. 1979. pap. text ed. 8.50 o.p. (ISBN 0-87766-243-6). Urban Inst.
Teendreams. David Edgar & Susan Todd. 50p. 1979. pap. 4.95 o.p. (ISBN 0-413-46410-5, NO. 3011). Heinemann Ed.
Teens Talk about Alcohol & Alcoholism. Ed. by Paul Dolmetsch & Gail Mauricette. LC 86-16616. 1986. 12.95 o.s.i. (ISBN 0-385-23085-0). Doubleday.
Teetering on the Tightrope. Carol Amen. LC 79-18718. (Orion Ser.). 1979. pap. 3.95 o.p. (ISBN 0-8127-0250-6). Review & Herald.
Teeth 'n' Smiles. David Hare. 92p. 1976. pap. 5.95 o.p. (ISBN 0-571-10995-0). Faber & Faber.
Teeth of the Wolf. Alain Paris. Tr. by Martin Sokolinsky. 252p. 1983. 15.95 o.s.i. (ISBN 0-03-059899-0). H Holt & Co.
Teetoncey. Theodore Taylor. (Illus.). (gr. 3-7). 1984. pap. 1.25 o.p. (ISBN 0-380-00346-5, 52118-0, Camelot). Avon.
Tefuga. Peter Dickinson. 1986. 14.45 o.p. (ISBN 0-394-55180-X). Pantheon.
Teilhard. Mary Lukas & Ellen Lukas. LC 80-26353. (McGraw-Hill Paperbacks Ser.). 360p. 1981. pap. text ed. 6.95 o.p. (ISBN 0-07-039047-9). McGraw.
Teilhard & the Unity of Knowledge. Ed. by Thomas M. King & James F. Salmon. LC 82-60590. 1983. pap. 6.95 o.p. (ISBN 0-8091-2491-2). Paulist Pr.
Teilhard de Chardin. Bernard Towers. Ed. by D. E. Nineham & E. H. Robertson. LC 66-15515. (Makers of Contemporary Theology Ser). (Orig.). 1966. pap. 3.95 o.p. (ISBN 0-8042-0723-2, John Knox). Westminster John Knox.
Teksty, Nineteen Fifty-Five to Nineteen Seventy-Seven. Vladimir Ufliand. (Rus.). 1979. 12.00 o.p. (ISBN 0-88233-379-8); pap. 3.00 o.p. (ISBN 0-88233-380-1). Ardis Pubs.
Tektites. Ed. by Virgil Barnes & Mildred Barnes. LC 72-95942. (Benchmark Papers in Geology Ser: Vol. 4). 445p. 1982. 61.95 o.p. (ISBN 0-87933-027-9). Van Nos Reinhold.
Tela Ignea Satanae, 2 vols. Joh. Chr. Wagenseil. 1631p. Date not set. Repr. of 1681 ed. text ed. 207.00x o.p. (ISBN 0-576-80110-0, Pub. by Gregg Intl Pubs England). Gregg Intl.
Tele-Robotics: The New Medium for Marketing, Sales, & Politics. Richard L. Corbeil, Sr. (Illus.). 112p. 1984. 10.00 o.p. (ISBN 0-682-40137-4). Exposition-Phoenix.
Telecare Ministry: Using the Telephone in a Care Ministry. Harald Grindal. 32p. 1984. pap. 4.95 o.p. (ISBN 0-8066-2099-4, 23-1899, Augsburg). Augsburg Fortress.
Telecom Bypass Markets. International Resource Development, Inc. Staff. 193p. 1984. 985.00x o.p. (ISBN 0-88694-612-3). Intl Res Dev.
Telecom Library Guide to Key Systems & Mini-PBXs. Telecom Library Research Group Staff. 156p. 1981. 75.00 o.p. (ISBN 0-686-98036-0). Telecom Lib.
Telecommunication Principles. J. O'Reilly. 1984. pap. 20.95 o.p. (ISBN 0-442-30592-3). Van Nos Reinhold.
Telecommunication Traffic Engineering. rev. ed. Ed. by D. Bear. 244p. 1980. pap. 33.00 o.p. (ISBN 0-906048-36-2, TE002). Inst Elect Eng.
Telecommunications. (SPEC Kit & Flyer Ser.: No. 98). 129p. 1983. 20.00 o.p. (ISBN 0-318-03458-1). OMS.
Telecommunications & Economic Development. Robert J. Saunders et al. LC 82-49065. (World Bank Ser.). 384p. 1983. text ed. 32.50x o.p. (ISBN 0-8018-2828-7); pap. 16.95x o.p. (ISBN 0-8018-2829-5). Johns Hopkins.
Telecommunications Circuits Data Book. Ed. by Texas Instruments Engineering Staff. (Illus., Orig.). 1986. pap. 9.95 o.p. (ISBN 0-89512-194-8). Tex Instr Inc.
Telecommunications Engineering. J. Dunlop & D. G. Smith. 1984. pap. 19.95 o.p. (ISBN 0-442-30586-9). Van Nos Reinhold.
Telecommunications Function of the British Post Office. Douglas C. Pitt. 208p. 1980. text ed. 37.95 o.p. (ISBN 0-566-00273-6). Gower Pub Co.
Telecommunications in China. 130.00 o.p. (ISBN 0-686-33028-5). Info Gatekeepers.
Telecommunications Planning. Chantico-QED Staff. (Chantico Technical Management Ser.). 364p. 1988. 39.95 o.p. (ISBN 0-89435-254-7). Qed Info Sci.
Telecommunications Principles. J. J. O'Reilly. (Illus.). 152p. 1984. 19.95 o.p. (ISBN 0-442-30591-5). Van Nos Reinhold.
Telecommunications, Radio & Information Technology (Communications 84) (IEE Conference Publications Ser.: No. 235). 179p. 1984. pap. 76.00 o.s.i. (ISBN 0-85296-292-4, IC235). Inst Elect Eng.
Telecommunications: Today & Tomorrow. Ed. by Eli M. Noam. 350p. 1983. 55.00 o.p. (ISBN 0-15-100053-0, H42949, Pub. by Law & Business). HarBraceJ.
Telecommunications-Transportation Tradeoff: Options for Tomorrow. Jack M. Nilles et al. LC 76-18107. 208p. 1976. text ed. 44.50 o.p. (ISBN 0-471-01507-5, JW). Krieger.
Telecommuting: The Organizational & Behavioral Effects of Working at Home. Reagan M. Ramsower. Ed. by Richard Farmer. LC 84-28095. (Research for Business Decisions Ser.: No. 75). 208p. 1985. 39.95 o.p. (ISBN 0-8357-1628-7). UMI Res Pr.
Teleconferencing. K. Ramamohan Rao & Ram Srinivasan. (Illus.). 272p. 1985. 52.95 o.p. (ISBN 0-442-27826-8). Van Nos Reinhold.
Teleconsumers & the Future: A Manual on the AT&T Divestiture. rev. ed. Samuel A. Simon & Michael Whalen. 1983. 3-ring text binder 25.00 o.s.i. (ISBN 0-943444-01-2). T R A C.
Telecourse Student Survey, 1984. Ron Brey & Charles Grigsby. 60p. (Orig.). 1985. pap. 5.00 o.p. (ISBN 0-87117-153-8). Am Assn Comm Jr Coll.
Teleguide: A Handbook for Video Teleconferencing. Public Service Satellite Consortium Staff. 92p. 1981. 34.50 o.p. (ISBN 0-686-98115-4). Telecom Lib.
Telemaco. Alessandro Scarlatti. Ed. by Howard M. Brown. LC 76-21061. (Italian Opera 1640-1770 Ser.). 1978. lib. bdg. 77.00 o.p. (ISBN 0-8240-2622-5). Garland Pub.
Telemedicine: Explorations in the Use of Telecommunications in Health Care. Rashid L. Bashshur et al. (Illus.). 376p. 1975. pap. pap. 57.50x spiral bdg. o.p. (ISBN 0-398-03311-0). C C Thomas.
Telemetry Computer Systems: An Introduction. O. J. Strock. LC 82-49001. 380p. 1983. text ed. 48.50x o.p. (ISBN 0-87664-711-5). Instru Soc.
Telephone Marketing Techniques. Murray Roman. LC 78-32000. 1979. pap. 7.50 o.p. (ISBN 0-8144-2231-4). AMACOM.
Telephones for the Elderly. Peter Gregory. 128p. 1973. pap. text ed. 7.50x o.p. (ISBN 0-7135-1888-X, Pub. by Bedford England). Gower Pub Co.
Teleports & the Intelligent City. Ed. by Andrew D. Lipman et al. 450p. 1986. 55.00 o.p. (ISBN 0-87094-706-0). Dow Jones-Irwin.
Telescope. Louis Bell. (Illus.). 13.25 o.p. (ISBN 0-8446-5877-4). Peter Smith.
Telescopes for the Nineteen Eighties. Ed. by G. Burbidge & A. Hewitt. (Illus.). 1981. text ed. 27.00 o.s.i. (ISBN 0-8243-2902-3). Annual Reviews.
Telescopes: Stars & Stellar Systems, Vol. I. Ed. by Gerald P. Kuiper & Barbara Middlehurst. LC 60-14356. (Midway Reprint Ser.). (Illus.). 1977. pap. text ed. 21.00x o.s.i. (ISBN 0-226-45962-4). U of Chicago Pr.
Telescopic Prosthetic Therapy: Peridontal Prosthesis - Fixed & Removable. I. L. Yalisove & J. B. Dietz, Jr. (Illus.). 367p. 1977. text ed. 48.50x o.p. (ISBN 0-89313-005-2). G F Stickley Co.
Televising Terrorism: Political Violence in Popular Culture. Philip Eliot et al. (Comedia Ser.). 160p. 1984. 15.00 o.p. (ISBN 0-906890-38-1, Scribner Book Co); pap. 8.95 o.p. (ISBN 0-906890-39-X). M Boyars Pubs.
Television see also T V.
Television & Cable Factbook 1982-83, No. 51. 1982. 173.00 set o.p. (ISBN 0-911486-10-0). Stations (ISBN 0-911486-12-7). Cable & Services (ISBN 0-911486-11-9). Eighty-Four Stations Vol (ISBN 0-911486-15-1). Warren Pub Inc.
Television & Children. Michael J. Howe. LC 76-28991. 157p. 1977. 19.50 o.p. (ISBN 0-208-01537-X, Linnet). Shoe String.
Television & Radio Announcing. 2nd ed. Stuart W. Hyde. LC 71-132527. 1972. text ed. 16.50 o.p. (ISBN 0-395-04666-1, 3-26892). HM.
Television & Radio Announcing. 3rd ed. Stuart W. Hyde. LC 78-69615. (Illus.). 1979. text ed. 22.50 o.p. (ISBN 0-395-27108-8). HM.
Television & Radio Announcing. 4th ed. Stuart W. Hyde. LC 82-83204. 528p. 1983. text ed. 29.50 o.p. (ISBN 0-395-32618-4). HM.
Television Engineering, 4 vols. Amos & Birkinshaw. Vol. I. (ISBN 0-8022-0027-3); Vol. II, 1956. (ISBN 0-8022-0028-1); Vol. III, 1957, 224pp, illus. (ISBN 0-8022-0029-X); Vol. IV, illus. (ISBN 0-8022-0030-3). Philos Lib.
Television Engineering. Arvind M. Dhake. (Illus.). 1980. text ed. 4.10 o.p. (ISBN 0-07-096389-4). McGraw.
Television in Community & Junior Colleges: An Overview & Guidelines. James J. Zigerell et al. 44p. 1980. 6.00 o.s.i. (IR-51). ERIC Clear.
Television Marketing. McGraw.
Television Marketing: Network, Local & Cable. D. P. Poltrack. 384p. 1983. text ed. 39.95 o.p. (ISBN 0-07-050406-7). McGraw.
Television Mythologies: Stars, Shows & Signs. Elizabeth Wilson et al. Ed. by Len Masterman. (Comedia Ser.). 144p. 1985. 14.50 o.p. (ISBN 0-906890-55-1); pap. 5.50 o.p. (ISBN 0-906890-56-X). M Boyars Pubs.
Television Nineteen Seventy to Nineteen Eighty. Vincent Terrace. LC 81-3580. (Illus.). 318p. 1981. 22.50 o.p. (ISBN 0-498-02577-2); pap. 14.95 o.s.i. (ISBN 0-498-02539-X). A S Barnes.
Television Plays. Chayefsky. 1971. pap. 9.50 o.p. (ISBN 0-671-21133-1, Touchstone Bks). S&S.
Television Simplified. 7th ed. Kiver & Kaufman. LC 72-11273. 630p. 1973. pap. 31.95 o.p. (ISBN 0-8273-0492-7); instr's. guide o.s.i. 1.70 o.p. (ISBN 0-8273-0493-5). Delmar.
Television Symptom Diagnosis. 2nd ed. Richard W. Tinnell. LC 77-83679. 176p. 1977. pap. 15.95 o.p. (ISBN 0-672-21460-1). Sams.
Television: The Business Behind the Box. Les Brown. LC 77-153684. 1971. 9.50 o.p. (ISBN 0-15-188450-1). HarBraceJ.
Television: The Business Behind the Box. Les Brown. LC 77-153684. 374p. 1973. pap. 4.95 o.p. (ISBN 0-15-688440-2, Harv). HarBraceJ.
Television: The Medium & Its Manners. Ed. by Peter Conrad. 180p. 1982. 14.95x o.p. (ISBN 0-7100-9040-4); pap. 7.95x o.p. (ISBN 0-7100-9041-2). Routledge Chapman & Hall.
Television's Transformation, the Next Twenty-Five Years. Stuart M. De Luca. LC 80-15254. 1980. 14.95 o.s.i. (ISBN 0-498-02474-1). A S Barnes.
Telex: Iran. Photos by Gilles Peress. LC 83-71376. (Illus.). 104p. 1984. pap. 20.00 o.p. (ISBN 0-89381-118-1). Aperture.
Tell It Like It Was: A Conceptual Framework for Financial Accounting. Robert N. Anthony. (Anthony-Graham Series in Accounting). 313p. 1983. pap. 19.95 o.p. (ISBN 0-256-03090-1). Irwin.
Tell It to the Church. Lynn R. Buzzard & Laurence Eck. 192p. (Orig.). 1985. pap. 6.95 o.p. (ISBN 0-8423-6986-4). Tyndale.
Tell It to Washington. rev. ed. League of Women Voters Education Fund Staff. 32p. 1987. pap. 1.00 o.p. (ISBN 0-89959-373-9). LWV US.
Tell Me a Story: Stories for Your Grandchildren & the Art of Telling Them. Charlie W. Shedd & Martha Shedd. LC 83-45568. (Illus.). 144p. 1984. 12.95 o.p. (ISBN 0-385-19004-2). Doubleday.
Tell Me about Your Picture. P-H.
Tell Me Grandma, Tell Me Grandpa. Shirlee Newman. (Illus.). (ps-2). 1979. PLB 6.95 o.p. (ISBN 0-395-27815-5). HM.
Tell Me I'm Allowed to Love. J. Henry. 1979. 5.50 o.p. (ISBN 0-682-49500-X). Exposition-Phoenix.
Tell Me Why: A Guide to Children's Questions about Faith & Life. Marilyn F. Holm. LC 85-7355. 144p. (Orig.). 1985. pap. 7.95 o.p. (ISBN 0-8066-2160-5, 10-6230, Augsburg). Augsburg Fortress.
Tell Thirty-Eight. Rolf Hochhuth. 192p. 1984. 15.45i o.p. (ISBN 0-316-36766-4). Little.
Tell Time. Stanley Rice. LC 63-15403. (Illus.). (gr. 2-5). 1963. 3.50 o.p. (ISBN 0-15-284380-9, HJ). HarBraceJ.
Tell Us the Reason Why. Dorothy Gilliham. 96p. 1986. 8.50 o.p. (ISBN 0-8062-2892-X). Carlton.
Teller Difference Rates: A Study of Factors Affecting Teller Performance. 18p. 1976. 15.00 o.p. (700). Bank Admin Inst.
Telling How Texts Talk: Essays on Reading & Ethnomethodology. A. W. McHoul. (International Library of Phenomenology & Moral Sciences). 1982. 21.95x o.p. (ISBN 0-7100-9047-1). Routledge Chapman & Hall.
Telling Lies: Clues to Deceit in the Marketplace, Politics & Marriage. Paul Ekman. 320p. 1985. 17.45 o.p. (ISBN 0-393-01931-4). Norton.
Telling Lies for Fun & Profit: A Manual for Fiction Writers. Lawrence Block. LC 81-66965. 240p. 1981. 13.95 o.p. (ISBN 0-87795-334-1, Arbor Hse). Morrow.
Telling Time Board Shape Book. (Board Shape Bks.). (Illus.). (ps). 1985. bds. 1.00 o.p. (ISBN 0-517-46321-0). Outlet Bk Co.
Telltale Summer of Tina C. Lila Perl. LC 75-9518. 160p. (gr. 4-8). 1979. 6.95 o.p. (ISBN 0-395-28872-X, Clarion). HM.
Tellurium & Tellurides. T. Chizhikov & J. Shchastlivyi. 320p. 1970. 72.00x o.p. (ISBN 0-569-05560-1, Pub. by Collets (UK)). State Mutual Bk.
Temas y Dialogos. 3rd ed. Altabe. (Span.). 1980. pap. text ed. 13.95 o.p. (ISBN 0-03-051271-9). HR&W.
Temas y Dialogos. 4th ed. David F. Altabe. LC 83-22669. 232p. (Span.). 1984. pap. 14.95 o.p. (ISBN 0-03-063564-0). HR&W.
Tempeh Primer. 2nd ed. Robin Clute & Sigrid Andersen. (Illus.). 64p. pap. 3.95 o.p. Creative Arts Bk.
Tempel in Ankara. Daniel Krencker & Martin Schede. (Denkmaler antiker Architektur, Vol. 3). (Illus.). viii, 62p. (Ger.). 1974. Repr. of 1936 ed. 90.00 o.p. (ISBN 3-11-004987-2). De Gruyter.
Temperament Discussed: Temperament & Development in Infancy & Childhood. Ed. by Geldolph Kohnstamm. 180p. 1987. pap. text ed. 15.30 o.p. (ISBN 90-265-0783-6, Pub. by Swets & Zeitlinger (Netherlands)). CJ Hogrefe Pubs.
Temperature, 2 pts. Ed. by Theodore H. Benziger. Incl. Pt. 1. Arts & Concept. 66.00 (ISBN 0-12-786141-6); Pt. 2. Thermal Homeostasis. 73.00 (ISBN 0-12-786142-4). (Benchmark Papers in Human Physiology: Vols. 9 & 10). 1977. Acad Pr.
Tempest. Ed. by G. A. Wilkes. (Challis Shakespeare Ser.). 1981. pap. 9.00x o.p. (ISBN 0-424-00083-0, Pub. by Sydney U Pr Australia). Intl Spec Bk.
Tempest of the Heart. Nancy Moulton. (Avon Romance Ser.). 384p. 1987. pap. 3.95 o.p. (ISBN 0-380-89957-4). Avon.
Tempestuous Eden. Heather X. Graham. (Candlelight Ecstasy Supreme Ser.: No. 1). 288p. (Orig.). 1983. pap. 2.50 o.s.i. (ISBN 0-440-18646-3). Dell.
Tempestuous Heights. Kamala Sanders. 176p. 1981. 8.50 o.p. (ISBN 0-682-49741-X). Exposition-Phoenix.
Temple. Robert Greenfield. 480p. 1982. 16.50 o.s.i. (ISBN 0-671-44735-1). Summit Bks.
Temple Kent. D. G. Devon. 288p. 1982. pap. 2.75 o.s.i. (ISBN 0-345-29848-9). Ballantine.
Temple of Jerusalem. Andre Parrot. 128p. 1957. (ISBN 0-8022-1275-1). Philos Lib.

Titles

Temple on a Hill. Anne Rockwell. LC 71-75520. (Illus.). (gr. 5-8). 1969. 5.95 o.p. (ISBN 0-689-20619-4, Atheneum). Macmillan.

Temple Scroll: An Introduction, Translation & Commentary. Johann Maier. (No. 34). xii, 147p. pap. text ed. 14.95x o.s.i. (Pub. by JSOT Pr England). Eisenbrauns.

Temples, Churches & Mosques: A Guide to the Appreciation of Religious Architecture. J. G. Davies. LC 82-13130. (Illus.). 256p. 1982. 27.50 o.p. (ISBN 0-8298-0634-2). Pilgrim NY.

Temples of Democracy. Henry-Russell Hitchcock & William Seale. LC 75-35973. 1976. 29.95 o.p. (ISBN 0-15-188536-2). HarBraceJ.

Tempo: Golf's Master Key: How to Find It, How to Keep It. Al Geiberger & Larry Dennis. (Illus.). 160p. 1987. pap. 8.95 o.p. (ISBN 0-671-63532-8). S&S.

Tempo: Life, Work & Leisure. Ed. by Donald W. Cummings & John Herum. (Illus.). 336p. 1974. pap. 21.16 o.p. (ISBN 0-395-17839-8). HM.

Tempo-Patterns of Shakespeare's Plays. John W. Draper. 163p. cancelled o.s.i. (ISBN 3-533-00958-0). Adlers Foreign Bks.

Tempomatic IV: A Management Simulation. 2nd ed. Charles R. Scott, Jr. & Alonzo J. Strickland, III. LC 79-89182. (Illus.). 1980. pap. 14.95 o.p. (ISBN 0-395-28731-6). HM.

Temporal Logic. N. Rescher & A. J. Urquhart. LC 74-141565. (Library of Exact Philosophy: Vol. 3). (Illus.). 1971. 39.00 o.p. (ISBN 0-387-80995-3). Springer-Verlag.

Temporal Organization in Cells. Brian C. Goodwin. 1963. 34.00 o.p. (ISBN 0-12-289350-6). Acad Pr.

Temporary Life. David Storey. 1975. pap. 1.75 o.p. (ISBN 0-380-00513-1, 26542). Avon.

Temporary Shelter. Mary Gordon. LC 86-31672. 224p. 1987. 16.45 o.s.i. (ISBN 0-394-55520-1). Random.

Temporary Times, Temporary Places. Barbara Robinson. 128p. 1983. pap. 2.25 o.p. (ISBN 0-380-63958-0, 63958-0, Flare). Avon.

Temporomandibular Joint Problems: Biologic Diagnosis & Treatment. William K. Solberg & Glenn T. Clark. 177p. 1980. 44.00 o.p. (ISBN 0-931386-18-7). Quint Pub Co.

Temps Uoulu see Our Share of Time.

Temptation: How Christians Can Deal with It. Frances L. Carroll. 192p. 1984. 13.95 o.p. (ISBN 0-13-903229-0); pap. 5.95 o.p. (ISBN 0-13-903211-8). P-H.

Temptation of Archer Watson. Laurence Snelling. 240p. 1974. 6.95 o.p. (ISBN 0-393-08698-4). Norton.

Temptation of Wilfred Malachey. William F. Buckley, Jr. LC 85-40526. (Goblin Tales Ser.). (Illus.). 44p. (gr. 4-6). 1985. 10.95 o.p. (ISBN 0-89480-923-7). Workman Pub.

Tempter. Harriet Lewis. LC 84-91461. 182p. 1985. 12.95 o.p. (ISBN 0-533-06528-3). Vantage.

Temptress. Jude Deveraux. 374p. 1987. lib. bdg. 18.95 o.p. (ISBN 0-8161-4259-9, Large Print Bks). G K Hall.

Ten Best Ways to Save Taxes. G. Cantor & R. Franklin. LC 78-18112. (Estate Planning Ser.). (Illus.). 1978. 39.50 o.p. (ISBN 0-87624-593-9, Inst Busn Plan). P-H.

Ten Black People Who Helped to Build America. Patricia Callow et al. 1977. pap. 3.00 o.p. (ISBN 0-682-48774-0). Exposition-Phoenix.

Ten British Pictures, 1740-1840. Robert R. Wark. LC 74-169905. (Illus.). 137p. 1971. 10.00 o.p. (ISBN 0-87328-048-2); pap. 5.00 o.p. (ISBN 0-87328-049-0). Huntington Lib.

Ten Canadian Poets: A Group of Biographical & Critical Essays. Desmond Pacey. LC 76-23269. 1976. Repr. of 1958 ed. lib. bdg. 27.50x o.p. (ISBN 0-8371-9014-2, PATC). Greenwood.

Ten Cats & Their Tales. Martin Leman. LC 82-6050. (Illus.). 24p. (gr. k-2). 1982. 9.95 o.p. (ISBN 0-03-062176-3). H Holt & Co.

Ten Dharma Realms Are Not Beyond a Single Thought. Tripitaka Master Hua. Tr. by Buddhist Text Translation Society. (Illus.). 72p. (Orig., Eng.). 1976. pap. 4.00 o.p. (ISBN 0-917512-12-X). Buddhist Text.

Ten-Dollar Bill. Dougald B. MacEachen. (Illus.). 128p. 1984. pap. 8.00 o.p. (ISBN 0-682-40181-1). Exposition-Phoenix.

Ten Faces of Ministry: Perspectives on Pastoral & Congregational Effectiveness Based on Survey of 5000 Lutherans. Milo L. Brekke et al. LC 78-66956. 1979. pap. 10.95 o.p. (ISBN 0-8066-1692-X, 10-6238, Augsburg). Augsburg Fortress.

Ten Good Things I Know about Retirement. J. Winston Pearce. LC 82-71668. 1982. 8.95 o.p. (ISBN 0-8054-5429-2). Broadman.

Ten Hands for God. J. Harry Haines. 80p. (Orig.). 1983. pap. 3.50 o.p. (ISBN 0-8358-0449-6). Upper Room.

Ten Mile Treasure. Andre Norton. (Illus.). (gr. 4-6). 1981. pap. 1.95 o.p. (ISBN 0-671-56102-2). Archway.

Ten Million Photoplay Plots. W. Aber Hill. Ed. by Bruce S. Kupelnick. LC 76-52108. (Classics of Film Literature Ser.). 1978. lib. bdg. 18.00 o.p. (ISBN 0-8240-2879-1). Garland Pub.

Ten Modern Irish Playwrights: A Comprehensive Annotated Bibliography. Kimball King. LC 78-68289. (Reference Library of Humanities). 1979. lib. bdg. 22.00 o.p. (ISBN 0-8240-9789-0). Garland Pub.

Ten Nights of Dream, Hearing Things, the Heredity of Taste. Soseki Natsume. Tr. by Aiko Ito & Graeme Wilson. LC 73-86136. 1974. 6.95 o.p. (ISBN 0-8048-1136-9). C E Tuttle.

Ten Pennies for Jesus. Alton Ward. (Illus.). 24p. (Orig.). (ps-1). 1986. pap. 3.50 o.p. (ISBN 0-570-04132-5, 56-1560). Concordia.

Ten SATs. 2nd ed. 304p. (Orig.). 1986. pap. 8.95 o.p. (ISBN 0-87447-246-6). College Bd.

Ten SATs: Scholastic Aptitude Tests of the College Board. 304p. (Orig.). (gr. 11-12). 1983. pap. 8.95 o.p. (ISBN 0-87447-161-3, 001613). College Bd.

Ten Spanish Farces of the Sixteenth, Seventeenth & Eighteenth Centuries. Ed. by George T. Northup. LC 71-137069. (Illus.). 231p. 1974. Repr. of 1922 ed. lib. bdg. 22.50x o.p. (ISBN 0-8371-5532-0, NOSF). Greenwood.

Ten Symphonies of Gorka Konig. Ian Dallas. 128p. 1989. 25.00 o.p. (ISBN 0-7103-0325-4). Routledge Chapman & Hall.

Ten Thousand Ideas for Term Papers, Projects & Reports. Kathryn Lamm. LC 83-5982. 441p. (Orig.). 1984. pap. 6.95 o.p. (ISBN 0-668-05598-7, 5598). Arco.

Ten Thousand Medical Words. Edward E. Byers. 1983. pap. text ed. 8.95 o.p. (ISBN 0-07-009502-7). McGraw.

Ten Thousand Wonderful Things. Ed. by Edmund F. King. LC 75-124587. 700p. 1970. Repr. of 1860 ed. 44.00x o.p. (ISBN 0-8103-3009-1). Gale.

Ten-Ton Monster. R. G. Austin. (Which Way Bks.: No. 21). (Illus.). (gr. 3-6). pap. 2.25 o.p. (ISBN 0-671-55820-X). Archway.

Ten Year Index to Periodical Articles Related to Law (1959-1968) Ed. by Roy M. Mersky & J. Myron Jacobstein. LC 65-29677. 1970. 35.00 o.p. (ISBN 0-87802-050-0). Glanville.

Ten Years Digging in Egypt. Flinders Petrie. (Illus.). 204p. 1976. pap. 10.00 o.p. (ISBN 0-89005-107-0). Ares.

Ten Years in Japan: A Contemporary Record Drawn from the Diaries & Private & Official Papers of Joseph C. Grew, United States Ambassador to Japan, 1932-1942. Joseph C. Grew. LC 72-12556. (Illus.). 554p. 1973. Repr. of 1944 ed. lib. bdg. 23.50x o.p. (ISBN 0-8371-6723-X, GRTY). Greenwood.

Ten Years Inside. Tom Scott. (Illus.). 152p. 1985. pap. 18.95 o.p. (ISBN 0-7233-0738-5, Pub. by Whitcoulls NZ). Intl Spec Bk.

Tenants. Bernard Malamud. 160p. 1981. pap. 2.95 o.p. (ISBN 0-380-53538-6, 58792-0). Avon.

Tenants. Bernard Malamud. 230p. 1971. 10.00 o.p. (ISBN 0-374-27290-5). FS&G.

Tenants Rights: California Tenants' Handbook. 9th ed. Myron Moskovitz & Ralph Warner. 150p. 1986. 14.95 o.p. (ISBN 0-87337-024-4). Nolo Pr.

Tender Betrayal. (Velvet Glove Ser.: No. 11). 176p. 1984. pap. 2.25 o.p. (ISBN 0-380-89474-2). Avon.

Tender Deception. Heather X. Graham. (Candlelight Ecstasy Ser.: No. 214). 192p. (Orig.). 1984. pap. 1.95 o.s.i. (ISBN 0-440-18591-2). Dell.

Tender Fortune. Judith E. French. (Avon Romance Ser.). 368p. 1986. pap. 3.75 o.p. (ISBN 0-380-75034-1). Avon.

Tender Fury. Connie Mason. 400p. (Orig.). 1984. pap. 3.75 o.p. (ISBN 0-8439-2173-0, Pub. by Leisure Bks CT). Dorchester Pub Co.

Tender Is the Storm. Johanna Lindsey. 415p. 1986. lib. bdg. 17.95x o.p. (ISBN 0-8161-3995-4, Large Prints Bks). G K Hall.

Tender Melody. Dorothy Abel. 192p. 1984. 2.95 o.s.i. (ISBN 0-89081-428-7). Harvest Hse.

Tender Offer: A Novel. Nora Johnson. 288p. 1986. 17.45 o.p. (ISBN 0-671-55666-5). S&S.

Tender Offers: Defenses, Responses, & Planning, 3 vols. 2nd ed. Arthur Fleischer, Jr. 1200p. 1983. 210.00 o.p. (ISBN 0-15-100055-7, H39492, Pub. by Law & Business). HarBraceJ.

Tender Prey. Patricia Roberts. 1985. 13.95 o.p. (Large Print Bks). G K Hall.

Tender Reflection. Rosa F. Biggs. 1985. 10.95 o.p. (ISBN 0-533-06660-3). Vantage.

Tender Taming. Heather X. Graham. (Candlelight Ecstasy Ser.: No. 125). (Orig.). 1983. pap. 1.95 o.s.i. (ISBN 0-440-18803-2). Dell.

Tenderfoot. Zane Grey. 208p. 1982. pap. 2.25 o.p. (ISBN 0-505-51813-9, Pub. by Tower Bks). Dorchester Pub Co.

Tenderfoot's Guide to Word Processing. Barbara Chirlan. 1.95 o.p. (ISBN 0-918398-58-4). Weber Systems.

Tenderness & Technique: Nursing Values in Transition. Genevieve R. Meyer. (Monograph & Research Ser.: No. 6). 160p. 1960. 5.00 o.p. (ISBN 0-89215-008-4). U Cal LA Indus Rel.

Tenders & Contracts for Building. The AQUA Group Staff. 100p. 1982. pap. text ed. 14.50x o.p. (ISBN 0-246-11838-5, Pub. by Granada England). Gower Pub Co.

Tending the Family Tree: A Family-Centered, Bible-Based Experience for Church Groups. Mary Y. Nilsen. 80p. (Orig.). 1982. pap. 7.95 o.p. (ISBN 0-86683-169-X). HarpR.

Tendre comme le Souvenir. Guillaume Apollinaire. 11.95 o.p. (ISBN 0-685-37176-X). French & Eur.

Tenebrae. Geoffrey Hill. 1979. 7.95 o.p. (ISBN 0-395-27610-1); pap. 4.50 o.p. (ISBN 0-395-27938-0). HM.

Tenerife & Western Canary Islands. Mary Tisdall & Archie Tisdall. (Illus.). 200p. (Orig.). 1984. pap. 10.95 o.p. (ISBN 0-903909-26-X, Pub. by Roger Lascelles England). Bradt Ent.

Tennessee. Wilma Dykeman. (Illus.). 1977. pap. 1.95 o.p. (ISBN 0-393-05637-6, Co-Pub by AASLH). Norton.

Tennessee Boy. Gloria R. Savoldi. LC 76-185927. 160p. (gr. 5 up). 1972. 4.75 o.s.i. (ISBN 0-664-32513-0, Westminster). Westminster John Knox.

Tennessee Business Directory, 1987-88. American Directory Publishing Co., Inc. Staff. 1317p. (Orig.). 1987. pap. 85.00 o.p. (ISBN 0-944316-03-4). Amer Directory.

Tennessee Court Rules Annotated. Ed. by Tennessee. Supreme Court Staff & Michie Company Staff. Richard W. Walter & Bonnie C. Cole. 640p. 1985. 25.00 o.p. (ISBN 0-87215-891-8). Michie Co.

Tennessee: Cry of the Heart. Dotson Rader. LC 84-28556. (Illus.). 360p. 1985. 16.95 o.p. (ISBN 0-385-19136-7). Doubleday.

Tennessee Directory of Manufacturers, 1988. 576p. 1988. pap. 75.00 o.p. (ISBN 0-318-02872-7). Manufacturers.

Tennessee Sampler. Peter Jenkins. 288p. 1985. pap. 12.95 o.p. (ISBN 0-8407-5964-9). Nelson.

Tennessee Strings: The Story of Country Music in Tennessee. Charles K Wolfe. LC 77-8052. (Tennessee Three Star Bks. Ser.). (Illus.). 1977. lib. bdg. 9.95x o.s.i. (ISBN 0-87049-295-0); pap. 3.50 o.s.i. (ISBN 0-87049-224-1). U of Tenn Pr.

Tennessee: The Old River, Frontier to Secession. Donald Davidson. (Rivers of American Ser). (Illus.). 1946. 4.50 o.p. (ISBN 0-03-028870-3). H Holt & Co.

Tennessee Williams: An Intimate Biography. Dakin Williams & Shepherd Mead. 356p. 1983. 16.95 o.p. (ISBN 0-87795-488-7, Arbor Hse). Morrow.

Tennessee Williams' Letters to Donald Windham: 1940-1965. Tennessee Williams. Ed. by Donald Winham. LC 77-73863. 1977. 10.00 o.s.i. (ISBN 0-03-022636-8). H Holt & Co.

Tennessee Williams: Memoirs. Tennessee Williams. LC 74-1523. (Illus.). 288p. 1975. 14.95 o.s.i. (ISBN 0-385-00573-3); ltd. ed. 75.00 o.s.i. (ISBN 0-385-11436-2). Doubleday.

Tennessee Williams: Memoirs. Tennessee Williams. LC 74-1523. 288p. 1983. pap. 8.95 o.p. (ISBN 0-385-19186-3, Anch). Doubleday.

Tennessee Writers. Thomas D. Young. LC 81-2206. (Tennessee Three Star Ser.). (Illus.). 132p. 1981. lib. bdg. 9.95x o.p. (ISBN 0-87049-319-1); pap. 3.50 o.p. (ISBN 0-87049-320-5). U of Tenn Pr.

Tennis. 4th ed. Joan D. Johnson & Paul Xanthos. (Pysical Education Activities Ser.). 144p. 1980. pap. text ed. write for info. o.p. (ISBN 0-697-07174-X). Wm C Brown.

Tennis & the Mind. Barry Tarshis. LC 77-76789. 1977. 7.95 o.p. (ISBN 0-689-10749-8, Atheneum). Macmillan.

Tennis, Anyone? Stephen Kessler & Jack Barth. (Illus.). 96p. 1985. pap. 5.95 o.p. (ISBN 0-671-50021-X, Pub. by Fireside). S&S.

Tennis Book. Ed. by Michael Barlett & Bob Gillen. (Illus.). 1983. pap. 9.95 o.p. (ISBN 0-87795-542-5, Arbor Hse). Morrow.

Tennis Bum. Margaret Ogan & George Ogan. LC 76-8008. (Hiway Bks.: A High Interest-Low Reading Level Book). 1976. 6.95 o.s.i. (ISBN 0-664-32593-9, Westminster). Westminster John Knox.

Tennis Champion: Billie Jean King. A. R. Morse. (Allstars Ser.). (Illus.). (gr. 2-6). 1976. PLB 6.95 o.p. (ISBN 0-87191-479-4); pap. 3.95 o.p. (ISBN 0-89812-202-3). Creative Ed.

Tennis Medic. Steven R. Levisohn & Harvey B. Simon. (Illus.). 260p. 1984. 14.95 o.p. (ISBN 0-8016-4669-3). Mosby.

Tennis Origins & Mysteries. Malcolm D. Whitman. LC 68-58970. 262p. 1968. Repr. of 1932 ed. 40.00x o.p. (ISBN 0-8103-3542-5). Gale.

Tennyson. Illus. by Patricia Machin. (Pocket Poets Ser.). (Illus.). 52p. 1985. 4.95 o.p. (ISBN 0-86350-044-7). Salem Hse Pubs.

Tennyson. Alfred Tennyson. (Plain Texts of the Poets Ser). 1968. pap. 2.50x o.p. (ISBN 0-7022-0649-0). U of Queensland Pr.

Tennyson: The Growth of a Poet. Jerome H. Buckley. (YA) (gr. 9 up). 1965. pap. 5.75 o.p. (ISBN 0-395-04244-5, 3-07630, RivSL). HM.

Tennyson: The Unquiet Heart. Robert B. Martin. LC 83-1655. (Illus.). 656p. 1983. pap. 12.95 o.p. (ISBN 0-571-11842-9). Faber & Faber.

Tension at the Cell Surface see Enzymology of the Cell Surface.

Tensions Can Be Reduced to Nuisances. Edmund Bergler. 1979. 12.95 o.p. (ISBN 0-87140-976-3); pap. 3.95 o.p. (ISBN 0-87140-123-1). Liveright.

Tensions: Necessary Conflicts in Life & Love. H. A. Williams. 1976. 6.95 o.p. (ISBN 0-87243-070-7). Templegate.

Tent Book. E. M. Hatton. 1980. 18.95 o.p. (ISBN 0-395-27613-6); pap. 9.95 o.p. (ISBN 0-395-28264-0). HM.

Tent Life in Siberia. George Kennan. 448p. 1986. pap. 14.95 o.p. (ISBN 0-87905-254-6, Peregrine Smith). Gibbs Smith Pub.

Tentative Service Requirements for Bridge Rail Systems. (National Cooperative Highway Research Program Report). 62p. 1970. 3.20 o.p. (ISBN 0-309-01784-X). Transport Res Bd.

Tentative Skid-Resistance Requirements for Main Rural Highways. (National Cooperative Highway Research Program Report). 96p. 1967. 3.60 o.p. (ISBN 0-317-36107-4, 1541). Transport Res Bd.

Tenth. MacDonald Harris. LC 83-45125. 320p. 1984. 15.95 o.p. (ISBN 0-689-11417-6, Atheneum). Macmillan.

Tenth Lacus Forum: Proceedings. Linguistic Association of Canada & the U. S. Staff. Ed. by Alan Manning et al. 1983. pap. text ed. 12.95 o.s.i. (ISBN 0-917496-24-8). Hornbeam Pr.

Tenth Man. Graham Greene. 192p. 1985. 14.70 o.p. (ISBN 0-671-50794-X). S&S.

Tenth Muse: The Pursuit of Earth Science. Ronald B. Parker. 240p. 1986. 14.95 o.s.i. (ISBN 0-684-18608-X). Scribner.

Teoria y Practica de la Reproduccion Inducida en los Peces. B. J. Harvey & W. S. Hoar. 48p. 1980. pap. 3.00 o.p. (ISBN 0-88936-253-X, IDRC-TS21S, IDRC). UNIPUB.

Teoriia Literatury Poetika. 4th ed. Boris V. Tomashevskii. Repr. of 1928 ed. 24.00 o.p. (ISBN 0-384-60930-9). Johnson Repr.

Tera Beyond. Malcolm MacCloud. LC 80-36728. 192p. (gr. 5-9). 1981. PLB 9.95 o.p. (ISBN 0-689-30817-5, Atheneum). Macmillan.

Teratocarcinoma & Embryonic Cell Interactions. Ed. by Takashi Muramatsu et al. 1982. 53.50 o.p. (ISBN 0-12-511180-0). Acad Pr.

Teratomas & Differentiation: Proceedings of the Roche Institute of Molecular Biology Symposium, Nutley, NJ, May 1975. Roche Institute of Molecular Biology Symposium Staff. Ed. by Michael I. Sherman & Davor Solter. 1975. 53.50 o.p. (ISBN 0-12-638550-5). Acad Pr.

Terence Conran's New House Book. Terence Conran. 1985. 39.50 o.s.i. (ISBN 0-394-54633-4, Pub. by Villard Bks). Random.

Terence Coran's Decorating with Plants. Susan Conder. 1986. 19.95 o.p. (ISBN 0-316-15324-9). Little.

Terence: The Brothers (Adelphoi) Ed. & tr. by A. S. Gratwick. (BC-AP Classical Texts). 250p. (Orig., Lat. & Eng.). 1986. text ed. 49.00 o.s.i. (ISBN 0-86516-134-8); pap. 16.50 o.s.i. (ISBN 0-86516-133-X). Bolchazy-Carducci.

Terence: The Self-Tormentor (Heaton Timoroumenos) Ed. & tr. by A. J. Brothers. (BC-AP Classical Texts). 250p. (Orig., Lat. & Eng.). 1986. 49.00 o.s.i. (ISBN 0-86516-132-1); pap. 16.50 o.s.i. (ISBN 0-86516-131-3). Bolchazy-Carducci.

Teresa Tendon, Podiatrist: Computerized Accounting Practice Set. Christine Sprenger et al. 1986. Apple. pap. 17.95x o.p. (ISBN 0-256-03532-6); IBM. pap. 17.95x o.p. (ISBN 0-256-03533-4). Irwin.

Term Paper: Step by Step. Donald J. Mulkerne & Gilbert Kahn. LC 82-454871. 1983. pap. 5.95 o.p. (ISBN 0-385-18231-7, Anchor Pr). Doubleday.

Terminal. Colin Forbes. LC 85-47601. 320p. 1985. 14.95 o.p. (ISBN 0-689-11589-X, Atheneum). Macmillan.

Terminal Airport Financing & Management. L. L. Bollinger et al. 1946. Repr. of 1946 ed. 100.00 o.p. (ISBN 0-08-018746-3). Pergamon.

Terminal Man. Michael Crichton. 320p. 1982. pap. 3.50 o.p. (ISBN 0-380-56960-4). Avon.

Terminal Paradox: The Novels of Milan Kundera. Maria N. Banerjee. 256p. 1989. 18.95 o.p. (ISBN 0-8021-1127-0). Grove.

Terminal Transfer. Trevor Martin. 272p. 1984. pap. 3.75 o.p. (ISBN 0-380-88450-X). Avon.

Terminal Transferase In Immunobiology & Leukemia. Ed. by Umberto Bertazzoni & Fred J. Bollum. LC 82-3691. (Advances in Experimental Medicine & Biology: Vol. 145). 406p. 1982. 69.50x o.p. (ISBN 0-306-40989-5, Plenum Pr). Plenum Pub.

Terminals & Network Products for the 3270 Environment. International Resource Development, Inc. Staff. 199p. 1983. write for info o.p. (ISBN 0-88694-580-1). Intl Res Dev.

Terminals & Printers Buyer's Guide. Tony Webster. LC 84-883. (Illus.). 345p. 1984. pap. text ed. 19.95 o.p. (ISBN 0-07-068968-7, BYTE Bks). McGraw.

Termination & Relocation: Federal Indian Policy, 1945-1960. Donald L. Fixico. LC 86-16057. (Illus.). 286p. 1986. 27.50x o.p. (ISBN 0-8263-0908-9). U of NM Pr.

Termination of Employment at the Initiative of the Employer: 65th Session of the International Labour Conference, 1981, Report 8. iii, 107p. (Eng., Fr., Span., Ger. & Rus., Part 1: Preliminary report and questionnaire; Part 2: Replies of governments). 1982. pap. 18.55 o.p. (ISBN 92-2-102411-3, ILO219, ILO) (ISBN 92-2-102412-1, ILO67/8/2). UNIPUB.

Terminological Data Banks: Proceedings of the First Conference Convened 2 & 3 April, 1979 by Infoterm. Ed. by Christian Galiuski. 207p. 1980. pap. 20.00 o.p. (ISBN 3-598-21365-4). K G Saur.

Terminologies of the Eighties: With a Special Section: 10 Years of Infoterm, Convened by Helmut Felber & Others. (Infoterm Ser.: No. 7). 412p. 1982. pap. 35.00 o.p. (ISBN 3-598-21367-0). K G Saur.

Terminology for the Theory of Machines & Mechanisms. Ed. by G. Bogelsack et al. 30p. 1984. pap. 11.00 o.p. (ISBN 0-08-031140-7). Pergamon.

Termpaper. Robert Fuller & Scott Stevens. Date not set. write for info. o.p. (ISBN 0-02-340180-X). Macmillan.

Terms of Endearment. Larry McMurtry. (General Ser.). 1984. lib. bdg. 18.95 o.p. (ISBN 0-8161-3708-0, Large Print Bks). G K Hall.

Terms of Surrender. Janet Dailey. (Nightingale Ser.). 1985. pap. 9.95 o.p. (ISBN 0-8161-3698-X, Large Print Bks). G K Hall.

Terms Used in Music. Peter Gammond. 64p. 1959. (ISBN 0-8022-0559-3). Philos Lib.

Ternary Chalcopyrite Semiconductors: Growth, Electronic Properties & Applications. J. L. Shay & J. H. Wernick. LC 74-5763. 1975. 65.00 o.p. (ISBN 0-08-017883-9). Pergamon.

Terpenoids: Structure, Biogenesis, Distribution see Symposia.

Terpsichore in Sneakers: Post-Modern Dance. Sally Banes. 1980. 17.95 o.p. (ISBN 0-395-28212-8); pap. 7.95 o.p. (ISBN 0-395-28689-1). HM.

Terra. Faber B. Lang. 1953. Philos Lib.

Terra & the Tornado. Mary W. Bell. (Orig.). (gr. 4). 1984. pap. 2.95 o.p. (ISBN 0-8024-8589-8). Moody.

Terra Ceia Site, Manatee County, Florida. Ripley P. Bullen. pap. 7.00 o.p. (ISBN 0-384-06299-7). Johnson Repr.

Terra Infirma. Rodger Kamenetz. LC 85-8761. 136p. 1985. o. p. 14.00x o.p. (ISBN 0-938626-54-X); pap. 9.00 o.p. (ISBN 0-938626-55-8). U of Ark Pr.

Terra Nostra. Carlos Fuentes. Tr. by Margaret S. Peden. 1987. pap. 14.95 o.p. (ISBN 0-374-51414-3). FS&G.

Terrace & Row Houses in Architectural Design: A Selected Bibliography. Bibliographic Research Library Staff. (Architecture Ser.: Bibliography A-1311). 6p. 1985. pap. 2.00 o.p. (ISBN 0-89028-241-2). Vance Biblios.

Terraced Hell: A Japanese Memoir of Defeat & Death in Northern Luzon, Philippines. Tetsuro Ogawa. LC 72-79021. 1972. 7.50 o.p. (ISBN 0-8048-1001-X). C E Tuttle.

Terracotta Art Manual of Bengal. Biswas. (Illus.). 277p. 1982. text ed. 65.00x o.p. (ISBN 0-391-02666-6). Humanities.

Terrain Analysis: A Guide to Site Selection Using Aerial Photographic Interpretation. 2nd ed. Douglas S. Way. (Community Development Ser.: Vol. 1). (Illus.). 1982. 48.95 o.p. (ISBN 0-87933-318-9). Van Nos Reinhold.

Terrain Analysis & Remote Sensing. Ed. by J. R. Townshend. (Illus.). 240p. (Orig.). 1981. text ed. 60.00x o.p. (ISBN 0-04-551036-9); pap. text ed. 34.95x o.p. (ISBN 0-04-551037-7). Unwin Hyman.

Terre des Hommes. Antoine De Saint-Exupery. (Coll. Soleil). 1954. 13.50 o.p. (ISBN 0-685-11584-4). Schoenhof.

Terre Haute: Wabash River City. Dorothy J. Clark. (Illus.). 112p. 1983. 19.95 o.s.i. (ISBN 0-89781-089-9). Windsor Pubns Inc.

Terrestrial Astrology: Divination by Geomancy. Stephen Skinner. (Illus.). 352p. 1980. 39.50 o.p. (ISBN 0-7100-0553-9). Routledge Chapman & Hall.

Terrible Gustave Dore. Hellmut Lehmann-Haupt. LC 76-27880. 1976. Repr. of 1943 ed. lib. bdg. 35.00x o.p. (ISBN 0-8371-9098-3, LHTG). Greenwood.

Terrible, Horrible Edie. Elizabeth C. Spykman. LC 60-8412. (gr. 5 up). 1960. 6.50 o.p. (ISBN 0-15-284788-X, HJ). HarBraceJ.

Terrible, Horrible Edie. Elizabeth C. Spykman. LC 60-8412. 1966. pap. 2.95 o.p. (ISBN 0-15-688650-2, VoyB). HarBraceJ.

Terrible Secret: Suppression of the Truth about Hitlers' Final Solution. Walter Laqueur. 276p. 1980. 16.95 o.p. (ISBN 0-316-51474-8). Little.

Terrible Tales of the Happy Days School. Lois Duncan. (Illus.). 32p. (gr. 3-6). 1983. 10.95 o.s.i. (ISBN 0-316-19541-3). Little.

Terrible Teague Bunch. Gary Jennings. 224p. (Orig.). 1982. pap. 2.50 o.p. (ISBN 0-380-57927-8, 57927-8). Avon.

Terrible Teague Bunch. Gary Jennings. (Illus.). 256p. 1975. 7.95 o.p. (ISBN 0-393-08706-9). Norton.

Terriers of the World: Their History & Characteristics. Tom Horner. LC 83-20745. (Illus.). 352p. 1984. 32.00 o.p. (ISBN 0-571-13145-X). Faber & Faber.

Territorial Imperative: A Personal Inquiry into the Animal Origins of Property & Nations. Robert Ardrey. LC 66-23572. (Illus.). 1966. 10.95 o.s.i. (ISBN 0-689-10015-9, Atheneum). Macmillan.

Territorial Power Domains, Southeast Asia, & China: The Geo-Strategy of an Overarching Massif. Lim Joo-Jock. 252p. 1985. text ed. 28.50x o.p. (ISBN 9-971902-85-0, Pub. by Inst Southeast Asian Stud). Gower Pub Co.

Territory. Ed. by Allen W. Stokes. LC 73-18327. (Benchmark Papers in Animal Behavior Ser.). 416p. 1982. 55.95 o.p. (ISBN 0-87933-113-5). Van Nos Reinhold.

Territory of the Historian. Emmanuel Le Roy-Ladurie. LC 78-31362. 1979. Repr. of 1973 ed. lib. bdg. 26.00x o.s.i. (ISBN 0-226-47327-9). U of Chicago Pr.

Terror Alliance. Jack Hunter. 1980. pap. 2.75 o.p. (ISBN 0-8439-0808-4, Pub. by Leisure Bks CT). Dorchester Pub Co.

Terror at Dark Harbor. Clarissa Ross. (Orig.). 1975. pap. 1.25 o.p. (ISBN 0-380-00368-6, 26500). Avon.

Terror by Gaslight: More Victorian Tales of Terror. Ed. by Hugh Lamb. LC 75-27980. 222p. 1976. 8.95 o.s.i. (ISBN 0-8008-7559-1). Taplinger.

Terror in Cairo. Annette Smith. LC 79-87528. (Illus.). (gr. 4-7). 1979. 2.95 o.p. (ISBN 0-15-284812-6, HJ). HarBraceJ.

Terror in Taormina. Alice Hesse. 1978. 5.00 o.p. (ISBN 0-682-49151-9). Exposition-Phoenix.

Terror on Highway Fifty-Nine. Steve Sellers. 288p. 1984. 14.95 o.p. (ISBN 0-932012-06-X). Texas Month Pr.

Terrorism. Walter Laqueur. LC 77-4872. 1979. 15.00 o.p. (ISBN 0-316-51470-5); pap. 10.45i o.p. (ISBN 0-316-51471-3). Little.

Terrorism in the Late Victorian Novel. Barbara A. Melchiori. LC 85-14923. 257p. 1985. 29.00 o.p. (ISBN 0-7099-3583-8, Pub. by Croom Helm Ltd). Routledge Chapman & Hall.

Terrorism: Interdisciplinary Perspectives. Ed. by Yonah Alexander & Seymour M. Finger. LC 77-7552. 1977. 17.50 o.p. (ISBN 0-89444-004-7). John Jay Pr.

Terrorism Survival Guide: 101 Travel Tips on How Not to Become a Victim. Andy Lightbody. 1987. pap. 2.95 o.p. (ISBN 0-317-56759-4). Dell.

Terrorists of Tomorrow. Paul Anderson. 192p. (Orig.). 1985. pap. 3.50 o.p. (ISBN 0-931773-54-7). Critics Choice Paper.

Terry & the Pirates (1935-1936, Vol. 2. Milton Caniff. Ed. by Bill Blackbeard. LC 84-60900. 224p. 1984. Repr. 32.50x o.p. (ISBN 0-918348-07-2, Pub. by Flying Buttress Classics). NBM.

Terry & the Pirates (1936-1937, Vol. 3. Milton Caniff. Ed. by Bill Blackbeard. LC 84-60900. 288p. 1985. Repr. 32.50x o.p. (ISBN 0-918348-08-0, Pub. by Flying Buttress Classics). NBM.

Terry & the Pirates (1938-1939, Vol. 5. Milton Caniff. Ed. by Bill Blackbeard. LC 84-60900. 288p. 1985. Repr. 34.50x o.p. (ISBN 0-918348-10-2, Pub by Flying Buttress Classics). NBM.

Terry & the Pirates (1939-1940, Vol. 6. Milton Caniff. Ed. by Bill Blackbeard. LC 84-60900. 288p. 1985. Repr. 34.50x o.p. (ISBN 0-918348-12-9, Pub. by Flying Buttress Classics). NBM.

Terry's Turn-Around. Jane B. Moncure. LC 82-7467. (Illus.). (gr. 1-3). 1982. lib. bdg. 4.95 o.p. Dandelion Hse.

Tesoros de la Cocina Mexicana. Hoteles Camiro Real Chefs. (Illus.). 176p. 1985. 19.95 o.p. (ISBN 0-914373-03-X). Wieser & Wieser.

Tess of the D'Urbervilles. Thomas Hardy. Ed. by Scott Elledge. (Critical Edition Ser.). (gr. 9-12). 1966. 10.00x o.p. (ISBN 0-393-05325-3, NortonC); pap. text ed. 3.45x o.p. (ISBN 0-393-09653-X). Norton.

Tess of the D'Urbervilles. Thomas Hardy. LC 85-61119. (Illus.). 368p. 1985. 12.95 o.p. (ISBN 0-89577-215-9). RD Assn.

Tess of the D'Urbervilles. Thomas Hardy. 48p. (Orig.). 1988. pap. 9.95 o.p. (ISBN 1-55651-879-X); audiocassette tape incl. o.p. (ISBN 1-55651-880-3). Cram Cassettes.

Tessa of Destiny. Leigh Ellis. 1980. pap. 2.50 o.p. (ISBN 0-380-75028-7, 75028-7). Avon.

Tessie C. Price. Jean Heyn. LC 79-9442. (Illus.). 210p. 1979. 3.98 o.p. (ISBN 0-89587-010-X). Blair.

Test Bank for an American Portrait. 2nd ed. David Burner et al. 96p. 1985. write for info o.p. (ISBN 0-02-371290-2). Macmillan.

Test Bank for College Algebra. 2nd ed. Bernard Kolman & Arnold Shapiro. 1985. text ed. 10.00 o.p. (ISBN 0-12-417899-5). Acad Pr.

Test Bank to Accompany General Chemistry. Robert Balahura. Ed. by LC LW & GLH. 214p. 1984. pap. write for info. o.p. (ISBN 0-7167-1696-8). W H Freeman.

Test: De Gaulle & Algeria. C. L. Sulzberger. LC 74-6097. 228p. 1974. Repr. of 1962 ed. lib. bdg. 22.50x o.p. (ISBN 0-8371-7492-9, SUTT). Greenwood.

Test Examples for Nonlinear Programming Codes. W. Hock & K. Schittkowski. (Lecture Notes in Economics & Mathematical Systems Ser.: Vol. 187). 177p. 1981. pap. 17.00 o.p. (ISBN 0-387-10561-1). Springer-Verlag.

Test Item Construction in the Cognitive Domain. K. B. Green. 2.00 o.p. (ISBN 0-317-52229-9, A261-08442). Home Econ Educ.

Test of English As a Foreign Language: TOEFL. 2nd ed. Harriet N. Moreno et al. LC 77-13180. 1978. lib. bdg. 12.00 o.p. (ISBN 0-668-04446-2); pap. text ed. 10.95 o.p. (ISBN 0-668-04450-0). Arco.

Test Preparation Guide for Course 1. Susan E. Garrett. (FLMI Insurance Education Program Ser.). 1986. 4.75 o.p. (ISBN 0-915322-89-7). LOMA.

TEST RECORD: No update today. (When wuz the last time youzz brushed your teeth Ser.). 10.00 o.p. (1ZZZ). CAB Intl.

Test the Spirits. C. S. Butler. 1985. pap. 4.95 o.p. (ISBN 0-87552-754-X, Evangel Pr UK). Presby & Reformed.

Test-Tube Women: What Future for Motherhood? Ed. by Rita Arditti et al. Renate D. Klein & Shelley Minden. 350p. (Orig.). 1984. pap. 8.95 o.p. (ISBN 0-86358-030-0, Pandora Pr). Routledge Chapman & Hall.

Test Your Baby's I. Q. Marcia Rosen & Henry Harris. 96p. 1986. pap. 6.95 o.p. (ISBN 0-13-906843-0). P-H.

Test Your Computer I. Q. Alfred Munzert. (Test Yourself Ser.). (Orig.). 1983. pap. 5.95 o.p. (ISBN 0-671-47171-6). Monarch Pr.

Test Your E. S. P. Alfred W. Munzert. (Test Yourself Ser.). 1980. pap. 3.95 o.p. (ISBN 0-671-34039-5). Monarch Pr.

Test Your I. Q. Alfred W. Munzert. (Test Yourself Ser.). 1980. pap. 4.95 o.p. (ISBN 0-671-34035-2). Monarch Pr.

Test Your Management I. Q. Marvelle S. Colby. 128p. 1984. 5.95 o.p. (ISBN 0-671-49366-3). Monarch Pr.

Test Your Marriage I. Q. Marcia Rosen & Joanna M. Polenz. 96p. 1984. pap. 5.95 o.p. (ISBN 0-671-49973-4). Monarch Pr.

Test Your Match Play. H. W. Kelsey. LC 83-20746. 192p. (Orig.). 1984. pap. 7.95 o.p. (ISBN 0-571-13244-8). Faber & Faber.

Test Your Parenting Potential. William Gerin & Jim Johnson. 128p. 1987. pap. 6.95 o.p. (ISBN 0-13-906884-8). P-H.

Test Your Safety Play. Hugh Kelsey. (Master Bridge Ser.). 80p. 1984. pap. 8.95 o.p. (ISBN 0-575-03465-3, Pub. by Gollancz England). David & Charles.

Test Your Sex Appeal. Karen K. Elskamp & Alfred W. Munzert. LC 80-85277. (Test Yourself Ser.). 64p. 1981. pap. 3.95 o.p. (ISBN 0-671-42627-3). Monarch Pr.

Test Your Success I. Q. Joanna M. Polenz & Marcia Rosen. 64p. (Orig.). 1985. pap. 4.95 o.p. (ISBN 0-399-51163-6, Perigee). Putnam Pub Group.

Testament of Alchemy: Being the Revelations of Morienus, Ancient Adept & Hermit of Jerusalem, to Khalid ibn Yazid ibn Mu'awiyya, King of the Arabs, of the Divine Secrets of the Magisterium & Accomplishment of the Alchemical Art. Morienus. Ed. & tr. by Lee Stavenhagen. LC 73-91752. (Illus.). 86p. 1974. 12.00x o.p. (ISBN 0-87451-095-3). U Pr of New Eng.

Testament of Faith. A. K. Brohi. 25.00 o.p. (ISBN 0-317-60630-1). Kazi Pubns.

Testament of Intent. J. D. Lee. 1977. 10.00 o.p. (ISBN 0-682-48885-2, Banner). Exposition-Phoenix.

Testament of Jesus: A Study of the Gospel of John in the Light of Chapter 17. Ernst Kasemann. LC 78-104781. 96p. (Orig.). 1978. pap. 3.95 o.p. (ISBN 0-8006-1399-6, 1-1399, Fortress). Augsburg Fortress.

Testament Perhaps. Yaron Zamir. Ed. by David Altshuler. Tr. by Dan Leon from Hebrew. (Illus.). 160p. 1985. write for info o.p. (ISBN 0-940646-13-7); pap. write for info o.p. (ISBN 0-940646-14-5). Rossel Bks.

Tested by Temptation. W. Graham Scroggie. LC 79-2559. (W. Graham Scroggie Library). 76p. 1980. pap. 4.50 o.p. (ISBN 0-8254-3732-6). Kregel.

Tested Practices: Organizing a School Counseling Program - the Priority: Career Counseling Program. James Wiggins. (NVGA Bk.). 80p. 1974. pap. 3.60 nonmembers o.p. (ISBN 0-911547-76-2, 72208W34); pap. 2.75 members o.p. Am Assn Coun Dev.

Tested Techniques for Teachers of Adults. Ed. by National Association for Public Continuing & Adult Education Publications Committee. LC 72-86720. 53p. 1972. pap. text ed. 2.00x o.p. (ISBN 0-686-01896-6, 751-01384). A A A C E.

Testifying in Court. 2nd ed. Jack E. Horsley & John Carlova. LC 83-863. 154p. 1983. casebound 29.50 o.p. (ISBN 0-87489-315-1). Med Economics.

Testimony & Demeanor: Stories. John Casey. (Shoreline Bks.). 1986. pap. 6.70 o.p. (ISBN 0-393-30393-4). Norton.

Testimony of Richard V. Secord, Joint Hearings, May 5-8, 1987. 701p. 1987. pap. 19.00 o.p. (S/N 052-070-06331-9). USGPO.

Testing & Analysis of Safety-Relief Value Performance. Ed. by A. Singh & M. D. Bernstein. 95p. 1983. pap. text ed. 24.00 o.p. (ISBN 0-317-02650-X, H00266). ASME.

Testing ESL Composition: A Practical Approach. Holly Jacobs et al. 152p. 1981. pap. 14.50 o.p. (ISBN 0-88377-225-6). Newbury Hse.

Testing for Effects of Chemicals on Ecosystems. National Research Council Commission on Natural Resources. 128p. 1981. pap. 8.50x o.p. (ISBN 0-309-03142-7). Natl Acad Pr.

Testing Procedures for Automotive AC & DC Charging Systems. J. D. Grevich. 1972. text ed. 26.90 o.p. (ISBN 0-07-024673-4). McGraw.

Testing the Current. William McPherson. 1984. 15.45 o.p. (ISBN 0-671-25251-8). S&S.

Testing the Field of Vision. Douglas R. Anderson. LC 81-14045. (Illus.). 312p. 1981. text ed. 49.95 o.p. (ISBN 0-8016-0207-6). Mosby.

Tests & Drills in English Grammar, 2 bks. rev. ed. Robert J. Dixson. (Orig.). (gr. 7 up). 1972. Bk. 1. pap. text ed. 3.75 o.p. (ISBN 0-88345-159-X, 18007); Bk. 2. pap. text ed. 3.75 o.p. (ISBN 0-88345-160-3, 18008). Prentice ESL.

Tests & Drills in Spanish Grammar, 2 bks. Juvenal L. Angel & Robert J. Dixson. (Orig., Span. & Eng., Lessons correlated to Conversacion en Espanol). (gr. 9 up). 1973. Bk. 1. pap. text ed. 3.50 o.p. (ISBN 0-88345-161-1, 18100); Bk. 2. pap. text ed. 3.50 o.p. (ISBN 0-88345-162-X, 18101). Prentice ESL.

Tests for Evaluating Degradation of Base Course Aggregates. (National Cooperative Highway Research Project Report). 92p. 1970. 5.00 o.p. (ISBN 0-309-01885-4). Transport Res Bd.

Tests of Musical Ability & Appreciation. Herbert Wing. LC 68-23919. 98p. 1968. Repr. text ed. 7.50x o.p. (ISBN 0-521-07251-4). U of Iowa Pr.

Tethered. David Martin. LC 79-4368. 272p. 1979. 9.95 o.p. (ISBN 0-03-048241-0). H Holt & Co.

Tethys: The Ancestral Mediterranean. Ed. by Peter Sonnenfeld. LC 80-13974. (Benchmark Papers in Geology Ser.: Vol. 53). 352p. 1982. 51.95 o.p. (ISBN 0-87933-355-3). Van Nos Reinhold.

Tetrahedron Reports on Organic Chemistry, Vols. 1 & 4. Derek Barton et al. LC 76-16352. 1978. Vol. 1. 115.00 o.p. (ISBN 0-08-021154-2); Vol. 4. 115.00 o.p. (ISBN 0-08-022093-2). Pergamon.

Tetralin. (American Petroleum Institute Monograph Ser.). 50p. 1978. 8.00 o.p. (ISBN 0-317-33102-7, 82270500). Am Petroleum.

Tetraphenylborates. Popouych. (IUPAC Solubility Data Ser.). 260p. 1981. 110.00 o.p. (ISBN 0-08-023928-5). Pergamon.

Tevye the Dairyman & the Railroad Stories. Date not set. (ISBN 0-8052-4026-8). Random.

Tewa World: Space, Time, Being, & Becoming in a Pueblo Society. Alfonso Ortiz. LC 72-94079. 1969. lib. bdg. 8.75x o.s.i. (ISBN 0-226-63306-3). U of Chicago Pr.

Texan Came Riding. Frank O'Rourke. Bd. with Desperate Rider. pap. (Sig). NAL.

Texan Statecraft, Eighteen Thirty-Six to Eighteen Forty-Five. Joseph W. Schmitz. (Perspectives in American History Ser.: No. 53). xii, 528p. Repr. of 1941 ed. lib. bdg. 49.50x o.p. (ISBN 0-87991-111-5). Porcupine Pr.

Texans, Politics & the New Deal. Lionel V. Patenaude. Ed. by Robert E. Burke & Frank Freidel. LC 82-49075. (Modern American History Ser.). 1983. 33.00 o.p. (ISBN 0-8240-5659-0). Garland Pub.

Texas. Photos by Robert Reynolds. LC 73-75619. (Belding Imprint Ser.). (Illus.). 192p. 1973. 32.50 o.s.i. (ISBN 0-912856-10-6). Gr Arts Ctr Pub.

Texas. Lon Tinkle. LC 73-5198. 1976. 17.95 o.s.i. (ISBN 0-684-13415-2, ScribT); pap. 14.95 o.s.i. (ISBN 0-684-14643-6, ScribT). Scribner.

Texas: A Picture Tour. Intro. by Lon Tinkle. 160p. 1986. pap. 17.95 o.p. (ISBN 0-684-18631-4). Scribner.

Texas: A Salute from Above. T. R. Fehrenbach. 280p. 1985. 34.95 o.p. (ISBN 0-940672-28-6). Shearer Pub.

Texas: A Self-Portrait. Jon Holmes. (Illus.). 240p. 1983. 45.00 o.p. (ISBN 0-8109-1660-6). Abrams.

Texas & Oklahoma: World Travel Guide, 1989. (Illus.). cancelled o.s.i. Wrld Travel.

Texas Archeology: Essays Honoring R. King Harris. Ed. by Kurt House. LC 78-10491. (Institute for the Study of Earth & Man Reports of Investigations: No. 3). (Illus.). 192p. 1978. 12.50 o.p. (ISBN 0-87074-170-5). SMU Press.

Texas Blue Laws. William G. Harper. LC 74-80678. 1974. 7.00 o.p. (ISBN 0-682-48015-0, University). Exposition-Phoenix.

Texas Collections Manual. State Bar of Texas, Professional Efficiency & Economic Research Committee. Ed. by Firmin A. Hickey, Jr. LC 79-620047. 1136p. 1980. 95.00 o.p. (ISBN 0-938160-23-0, 6301). State Bar TX.

Texas: Conflict of Laws. 8.50 o.p. (ISBN 0-686-90906-2). Am Law Inst.

Texas Conservation Guide for Municipal Services. Jacilyn G. Walker & Martha L. DeHaven. 133p. 1977. 6.00 o.p. (ISBN 0-936440-18-X). Inst Urban Studies.

Texas: Contracts. 9.50 o.p. (ISBN 0-686-90908-9). Am Law Inst.

Texas Fact Book, 1982. rev. ed. Joseph E. Pluta et al. 210p. 1982. pap. 6.00 o.p. (ISBN 0-87755-278-9). Bureau Busn UT.

Texas Football see Hook'em Horns: A Story of Texas Football.

Texas Gold. John Reese. 1976. pap. 0.95 o.p. (ISBN 0-505-50973-3, BT50973, Pub. by Tower Bks). Dorchester Pub Co.

Texas Graveyards: A Cultural Legacy. Terry G. Jordan. (Elma Dill Russell Spencer Ser.: No. 13). (Illus.). 160p. 1982. pap. 19.95 o.p. (ISBN 0-292-78044-3). U of Tex Pr.

Texas in Eighteen Thirty-Seven. Ed. by Andrew F. Muir. 1958. pap. write for info. o.p. (ISBN 0-292-73398-4). U of Tex Pr.

Texas Instruments BASIC Manual. Lynne Mass & Thomas M. Kemnitz. LC 85-433. (Kids Working with Computers Ser.). (Illus.). 48p. (gr. 2 up). 1985. lib. bdg. 11.27 o.p. (ISBN 0-516-08428-3). Childrens.

Texas Instruments LOGO Manual. Lynne Mass & Thomas M. Kemnitz. LC 85-451. (Kids Working with Computers Ser.). (Illus.). 48p. (gr. 2 up). 1985. lib. bdg. 11.27 o.p. (ISBN 0-516-08429-1). Childrens.

Texas Job Bank: A Comprehensive Guide to Major Local Employers. Adams, Robert Lang, & Associates Staff. Ed. by John H. Noble. (Job Bank Ser.). 245p. (Orig.). 1982. pap. 9.95 o.p. (ISBN 0-937860-06-9). Adams Inc MA.

Texas Life & Health Insurance. Ed. by Merritt Company Staff. 202p. 1985. write for info. o.p. (ISBN 0-930868-40-4). Merritt Co.

Texas Local Recording Agent's Licensing Course. 1985. write for info. o.p. Merritt Co.

Texas Manufacturers Register, 1988. 1040p. 1988. 114.00 o.p. (ISBN 0-318-04034-4). Manufacturers.

Texas National Energy Modeling Project: An Experience in Large-Scale Model Transfer & Evaluation. Ed. by Milton L. Holloway. 1980. 29.00 o.p. (ISBN 0-12-352950-6). Acad Pr.

Texas Night Riders. Ray Slater. 176p. 1982. pap. 1.95 o.p. (ISBN 0-8439-1063-1, Pub. by Leisure Bks CT). Dorchester Pub Co.

Texas Panhandle Frontier. Frederick W. Rathjen. LC 73-7602. (M. K. Brown Range Life Ser.: No. 12). (Illus.). 298p. 1973. pap. 14.95 o.p. (ISBN 0-292-78007-9). U of Tex Pr.

Texas Pattern Jury Charges, Vol. 1. 2nd ed. Committee on Pattern Jury Charges of the State Bar of Texas. LC 87-62226. 144p. 1987. 85.00 o.p. (ISBN 0-938160-47-8, 6281). State Bar TX.

Texas Pattern Jury Charges: (Workmen's Compensation), 1976 Cumulative Supplement, Vol. 2. Committee on Pattern Jury Charges. LC 78-13954. 45p. 1976. pap. 5.00 o.p. (ISBN 0-938160-03-6, 6306). State Bar TX.

Texas Pattern Jury Charges: 1973 Cumulative Supplement, Vol. 1. Ed. by State Bar of Texas, Pattern Jury Charges Committee. LC 78-13954. 91p. 1973. pap. 6.50 o.p. (ISBN 0-938160-01-X, 6316). State Bar TX.

Texas Politics. 2nd ed. Richard Kraemer & Charldean Newell. (Illus.). 450p. 1983. pap. text ed. 21.00 o.p. (ISBN 0-314-78007-6). West Pub.

Texas Politics: Economics, Power & Policy. 2nd ed. James W. Lamare. (Illus.). 267p. 1984. pap. text ed. 17.75 o.p. (ISBN 0-314-84091-5). West Pub.

Texas Press Women's Cookbook. Texas Press Women's Assn. LC 75-26425. (Illus.). 190p. (Orig.). 1976. pap. 4.95 o.p. (ISBN 0-914872-05-2, Co-Pub Lone Star Publishers). Austin Pr.

Texas Pride. Jeanne Williams. 352p. 1987. pap. 3.95 o.p. (ISBN 0-380-75202-6). Avon.

Texas Rangers. rev. ed. Shaw. LC 82-240245. (Baseball Today Ser.). 48p. (gr. 4 up). 1982. PLB 11.45 o.p. (ISBN 0-87191-876-5). Creative Ed.

Texas Real Estate Finance. 2nd ed. Tom J. Morton. 1985. text ed. write for info. o.p. (ISBN 0-673-16656-2); instr's. manual & test items incl. o.p. Scott F.

Texas Rhythm, Texas Rhyme. Larry Willoughby. Ed. by Barbara Rodriguez. (Illus.). 208p. 1984. 16.95 o.p. (ISBN 0-932012-73-6). Texas Month Pr.

Texas Rich: The Hunt Dynasty from the Early Oil Days Through the Silver Crash. Harry Hurt, III. (Illus.). 1981. 16.95 o.p. (ISBN 0-393-01391-X). Norton.

Texas Rules of Evidence Manual. Hulen D. Wendorf & David A. Schlueter. (State Practice Publications Ser.). 540p. 1983. 60.00x o.p. (ISBN 0-87215-649-4, 68535); 1986 Supplement 20.00x o.p. (ISBN 0-87215-901-9). Michie Co.

Texas Show Caves. Jerry Sinise & Dorothy Sinise. (Illus.). 120p. 1983. pap. 5.95 o.p. (ISBN 0-89015-377-9). Eakin Pr.

Texas Six Man Football. C. H. Underwood. (Illus.). 107p. 1974. pap. 6.95 o.p. (ISBN 0-89015-078-8). Eakin Pr.

Texas State Directory. 28th ed. Scott Sayers. Ed. by Julie Sayers. 640p. (Orig.). 12.95 o.p. (ISBN 0-934367-00-0). TX St Direct.

Texas Station. Christopher Leach. LC 82-21338. 256p. 1983. 14.95 o.p. (ISBN 0-15-188762-4). HarBraceJ.

Texas-Texas A & M Joke Book. S. C. Lee. LC 75-15218. 1975. pap. 2.95 o.p. (ISBN 0-87397-084-5). Strode.

Texas the Beautiful Cookbook. Ed. by Elizabeth Germaine et al. LC 86-50444. 208p. 1986. 29.95 o.s.i. (ISBN 0-940672-39-1). Shearer Pub.

Texas Tradition. Ross Phares. LC 54-11350. (Illus.). 239p. 1975. Repr. of 1954 ed. 7.95 o.p. (ISBN 0-88289-064-6). Pelican.

Texas Trilogy. Preston Jones. (Mermaid Dramabook Ser.). 338p. 1976. pap. 9.50 o.p. (ISBN 0-8090-1236-7). Hill & Wang.

Texas: Trusts. 8.50 o.p. (ISBN 0-686-90910-0). Am Law Inst.

Texas Wildlife: Photographs from Texas Parks & Wildlife Magazine. Intro. by David Baxter. LC 77-99281. (Louise Lindsey Merrick Texas Environment Ser.: No. 1). (Illus.). 196p. 1982. 24.95 o.p. (ISBN 0-89096-047-X). Tex A&M Univ Pr.

Texas Wines & Wineries. Frank Giordano. Ed. by Scott Lubeck. (Illus.). 171p. 1984. 19.95 o.p. (ISBN 0-932012-86-8). Texas Month Pr.

Text & Image in Fifteenth-Century Illustrated Dutch Bibles (1977) Sandra Hindman. (Corpus Sacrae Scripturae Neerlandicae Medii Aevi Ser.: Miscellanea: Vol. 1). (Illus.). 35.00 o.p. (ISBN 90-04-04901-0). E J Brill USA.

Text & Reality. Bernard Lategan & Willem Vorster. (Society of Biblical Literature Semeia Studies). 1985. 14.95 o.p. (ISBN 0-89130-822-9, 06-06-14, Fortress); pap. 9.95 o.p. (ISBN 0-89130-823-7). Augsburg Fortress.

Text & Reality: Aspects of Reference in Biblical Texts. Bernard C. Lategan & Willem S. Vorster. LC 85-47735. 144p. 1985. pap. 1.95 o.p. (ISBN 0-8006-1514-X, Fortress). Augsburg Fortress.

Text-Cassette II mit ausgewaehlten Lektionstexten see Deutsch X 3.

Text of the Agreement of 20 July 1978 Between Guatemala & the Agency for the Application of Safeguards in Connection with the Treaty for the Prohibition of Nuclear Weapons in Latin America & the Treaty on the Non-Proliferation of Nuclear Weapons. International Atomic Energy Agency. (Information Circular Series of the IAEA). 33p. 1983. write for info. o.p. (IAEA). UNIPUB.

Text of the New Testament: An Introduction to the Critical Editions & to the Theory & Practice of Modern Textual Criticism. Kurt Aland & Barbara Aland. (Illus.). xviii, 338p. Date not set. 34.00 o.p. (ISBN 90-04-08367-7, Pub. by E J Brill). E J Brill USA.

Text, Play, & Story, 1983: The Construction & Reconstruction of Self & Society. Ed. by Edward M. Bruner. (Proceedings of the American Ethnological Society Ser.). 1984. 20.00 o.s.i. (ISBN 0-942976-05-3). Am Anthro Assn.

Text Processing Computer System Comparison Charts: 1985 Edition. Harold Durbin. 1985. pap. 25.00 o.s.i. (ISBN 0-936786-04-3). Durbin Assoc.

Text Retrieval: A Directory of Software. Ed. by Catherine D. Hamilton et al. LC 84-22284. 180p. 1985. text ed. 34.50 o.p. (ISBN 0-566-03527-8). Gower Pub Co.

Textbook for Dental Assistants. Virginia Park et al. LC 73-80978. pap. cancelled o.s.i. (ISBN 0-317-26118-5, 2025170). Bks Demand UMI.

Textbook for Employee Benefit Plan Trustees, Administrators & Advisors 1980: Proceedings, Vol. 22. Ed. by Elizabeth A. Hieb. 589p. 1981. text ed. 30.00 o.p. (ISBN 0-89154-150-0). Intl Found Employ.

Textbook for Employee Benefit Plan Trustees, Administrators & Advisors 1981: Proceedings, Vol. 23. Ed. by Elizabeth A. Hieb. 322p. 1982. text ed. 30.00 o.p. (ISBN 0-89154-187-X). Intl Found Employ.

Textbook for Ward Clerks & Unit Secretaries. 6th ed. Willson. 1979. pap. 16.95 o.p. (ISBN 0-8016-5593-5). Mosby.

Textbook in American Education. James B. Edmonson. (National Society for the Study of Education Yearbooks Ser: No. 30, Pt. 2). 1931. 5.00x o.s.i. (ISBN 0-226-59957-4); pap. text ed. 3.00x o.s.i. (ISBN 0-226-59958-2). U of Chicago Pr.

Textbook of Anatomy & Physiology. 11th ed. Catherine P. Anthony & Gary A. Thibodeau. LC 82-12555. (Illus.). 887p. 1983. text ed. 38.95 o.p. (ISBN 0-8016-0289-0); study guide, 348p. 2nd edition 13.95 o.p. (ISBN 0-8016-4011-3). Mosby.

Textbook of Anatomy & Physiology. 2nd ed. Edward J. Reith et al. (Illus.). 1978. text ed. 34.00 o.p. (ISBN 0-07-051873-4). McGraw.

Textbook of Applied Thermodynamics: Steam & Thermal Engineering. S. K. Kulshrestha. (Illus.). xi, 443p. 1983. text ed. 37.50x o.p. (ISBN 0-7069-2158-5, Pub. by Vikas India). Advent NY.

Textbook of Cost Accountancy. M. N. Arora. 750p. 1984. text ed. 45.00x o.p. (ISBN 0-7069-2538-6, Pub. by Vikas India); pap. text ed. 25.00x o.p. (ISBN 0-7069-2539-4, Pub. by Vikas India). Advent NY.

Textbook of Dairy Chemistry. Edgar R. Ling. (Illus.). Vol. I, 230pp. (ISBN 0-8022-0981-5). Vol. II, 140pp, illus. Philos Lib.

Textbook of Diagnostic Ultrasonography. 2nd ed. Sandra L. Hagen-Ansert. LC 82-8190. (Illus.). 800p. 1983. text ed. 68.00 o.p. (ISBN 0-8016-2016-3). Mosby.

Textbook of Disturbances of the Mental Life, or Disturbances of the Psyche & Their Treatment. Johann C. Heinroth. 235p. 1975. text ed. 69.00x o.p. (Pub. by Keter Pub Jerusalem). Coronet Bks.

Textbook of Echocardiography. Vincent E. Friedewald. LC 76-4247. pap. cancelled o.s.i. (ISBN 0-317-07788-0, 2016663). Bks Demand UMI.

Textbook of Economics. Murray Wolfson. 1978. pap. 15.95x o.p. (ISBN 0-416-77090-8, NO. 2856). Routledge Chapman & Hall.

Textbook of Epilepsy. 2nd ed. John P. Laidlaw & Alan Richens. 1982. text ed. 69.00 o.p. (ISBN 0-443-02039-6). Churchill.

Textbook of Health Education. L. Ramachandran & T. Dharmalingam. 278p. 1983. o. p. 20.00x o.p. (ISBN 0-7069-2327-8, Pub. by Vikas India); pap. text ed. 8.95x o.p. (ISBN 0-7069-2328-6, Pub. by Vikas India). Advent NY.

Textbook of Human Anatomy. 3rd ed. Roger C. Crafts. LC 84-19707. 906p. 1985. 39.95 o.p. (ISBN 0-471-88624-6). Wiley.

Textbook of Human Biology. 2nd rev. ed. J. K. Inglis. LC 73-21696. 1974. text ed. 15.50 o.p. (ISBN 0-08-017846-4); pap. text ed. 8.25 o.p. (ISBN 0-08-017847-2). Pergamon.

Textbook of Immunology: An Introduction to Immunochemistry & Immunobiology. 4th ed. James T. Barrett. LC 77-16208. (Illus.). 520p. 1983. pap. text ed. 32.95 o.p. (ISBN 0-8016-0504-0). Mosby.

Textbook of Inorganic Chemistry: General Principles, Vol. 1. K. N. Upadhyaya. (Illus.). 262p. 1985. text ed. 25.00x o.p. (ISBN 0-7069-2613-7, Pub. by Vikas India). Advent NY.

Textbook of Inorganic Chemistry: The Representative Elements, Vol. 2. K. N. Upadhyaya. 256p. 1985. text ed. 25.00x o.p. (ISBN 0-7069-2666-8, Pub. by Vikas India). Advent NY.

Textbook of Inorganic Chemistry: The Transition Elements, Vol. 3. K. N. Upadhyaya. 264p. 1986. text ed. 25.00x o.p. (Pub. by Vikas India). Advent NY.

Textbook of Limnology. 3rd ed. Gerald A. Cole. LC 82-10607. (Illus.). 414p. 1983. text ed. 28.95 cloth o.p. (ISBN 0-8016-1004-4). Mosby.

Textbook of Magnetohydrodynamics. J. A. Shercliff. 1965. text ed. 19.25 o.p. (ISBN 0-08-010661-7); pap. text ed. 7.75 o.p. (ISBN 0-08-010660-9). Pergamon.

Textbook of Medical Practice. J. Fry et al. LC 76-28609. (Illus.). 1977. 27.50 o.p. (ISBN 0-88416-183-8). Year Bk Med.

Textbook of Neonatology. Ed. by N. R. Roberton. (Illus.). 962p. 1986. text ed. 165.00 o.p. (ISBN 0-443-02716-1). Churchill.

Textbook of Nuclear Medicine, Vol. 2: Clinical Applications. 2nd ed. Ed. by John Harbert et al. LC 83-25594. (Illus.). 724p. 1984. text ed. 98.50 o.p. (ISBN 0-8121-0928-7). Lea & Febiger.

Textbook of Obstetrics. V. I. Bodyazhina. 400p. 1984. 12.00 o.p. (ISBN 0-8285-2574-9, Pub. by Mir Pubs USSR). Imported Pubns.

Textbook of Occupational Therapy. Eamon O'Sullivan. 93p. 1955. (ISBN 0-8022-1252-2). Philos Lib.

Textbook of Ophthalmology. 9th ed. Harold G. Scheie & Daniel M. Alert. LC 75-19856. (Illus.). 1977. text ed. write for info. o.p. (ISBN 0-7216-7951-X). Saunders.

Textbook of Oral & Maxillofacial Surgery. 6th ed. Gustav O. Kruger. (Illus.). 896p. 1983. 55.95 o.p. (ISBN 0-8016-2793-1). Mosby.

Textbook of Oral Biology. James H. Shaw et al. LC 76-14687. pap. cancelled o.s.i. (ISBN 0-317-26105-3, 2025172). Bks Demand UMI.

Textbook of Otolaryngology. 6th ed. David F. DeWeese & William H. Saunders. LC 81-14162. (Illus.). 495p. 1982. text ed. 41.95 cloth o.p. (ISBN 0-8016-1273-X). Mosby.

Textbook of Paediatrics, 2 vols. 3rd ed. John O. Forfar & Gavin C. Arneil. (Illus.). 1984. text ed. 194.25 o.p. (ISBN 0-443-02426-X); pap. text ed. 139.00 o.p. (ISBN 0-443-02400-6). Churchill.

Textbook of Pain. Ed. by Patrick D. Wall & Ronald Melzack. (Illus.). 888p. 1984. text ed. 150.00 o.p. (ISBN 0-443-02715-3). Churchill.

Textbook of Pediatric Rheumatology. 2nd ed. Cassidy. 1988. (ISBN 0-471-60031-8). Churchill.

Textbook of Pediatric Rheumatology. Ed. by James T. Cassidy. LC 82-4951. 684p. 1982. 55.00 o.p. (ISBN 0-471-09925-2). Wiley.

Textbook of Physical Chemistry. 2nd ed. Arthur Adamson. 953p. 1979. 44.50 o.p. (ISBN 0-12-044260-4). Acad Pr.

Textbook of Quantum Mechanics. P. M. Mathews & K. Venkatesan. 1979. pap. text ed. 6.20x o.p. (ISBN 0-07-096510-2). McGraw.

Textbook of Rheumatology, 2 vols. 2nd ed. William N. Kelley et al. (Illus.). 2121p. 1985. Set. 210.00 o.p. (ISBN 0-7216-5365-0); Vol. 1. 115.00 o.p. (ISBN 0-7216-5363-4); Vol. 2. 105.00 o.p. (ISBN 0-7216-5362-6). Saunders.

Textbook of Soil Physics. M. C. Oswal. (Illus.). vii, 214p. 1983. text ed. 22.50x o.p. (ISBN 0-7069-2347-2, Pub. by Vikas India). Advent NY.

Textbook of Uncommon Cancer. Williams et al. 1988. (ISBN 0-471-90968-8). Wiley.

Textbook of Venereal Diseases. V. N. Sehgal. (Illus.). 1979. text ed. 15.00x o.p. (ISBN 0-7069-0639-X, Pub. by Vikas India). Advent NY.

Textbook of Veterinary Clinical Pathology. William Medway et al. LC 69-13696. 536p. 1969. 27.50 o.p. Krieger.

Textbook Production & Distribution in the Pacific: Report of a Sub-Regional Seminar on the Production & Distribution of Textbooks & Other Related Teaching-Learning Materials (Nuku'alofa, Tonga, 26 August - 5 September, 1985. 69p. (Orig.). 1986. pap. text ed. 7.50 o.p. (ISBN 0-318-21273-0, UB211, UB). UNIPUB.

Texte der Handel-Oratorien. Elisabeth Bredenforder. pap. 9.00 o.p. (ISBN 0-384-05595-8). Johnson Repr.

Textedit. Irwin Rappaport. 90p. (Orig.). 1982. incl. software 24.95 o.p. (ISBN 0-88006-075-1, CC7387). Wayne Green Ent.

Textedit: A Complete Word Processing System in Kit Form. Irwin Rappaport. 90p. (Orig.). 1982. pap. 9.95 o.p. (ISBN 0-88006-050-6, BK7387). Wayne Green Ent.

Textile-Apparel Industries. Fairchild Market Research Division Staff. (Fairchild Fact Files Ser.). (Illus.). 55p. 1985. pap. 17.50 o.p. (ISBN 0-87005-531-3). Fairchild.

Textile Arts. Date not set. (ISBN 0-8052-0390-7). Random.

Textile Auxiliaries. J. W. Batty. 1967. pap. text ed. 5.75 o.p. (ISBN 0-08-012381-3). Pergamon.

Textile Crafts. Constance Howard. (Illus.). 1978. encore edition 4.95 o.s.i. (ISBN 0-684-15507-9, ScribT). Scribner.

Titles

Textile Dictionary. G. Velco. (Eng., Fr., Ger., Rus. & Bulgarian.). 1977. 70.00x o.p. (ISBN 0-686-44749-2, Pub. by Collets (UK)). State Mutual Bk.
Textile Dyes, Finishes & Auxiliaries. Michael Bogle. LC 76-25746. (Reference Library of Science & Technology Ser.: Vol. 8). (Illus.). 1977. lib. bdg. 24.00 o.p. (ISBN 0-8240-9902-8). Garland Pub.
Textile Glossary. Marvin Klapper. LC 72-88888. 120p. 1973. pap. 1.95 o.p. (ISBN 0-87005-116-4). Fairchild.
Textile Industry: A Case Study of Industrial Development in the Philippines. Laurence D. Stifel. 199p. 1963. pap. 3.00 o.p. (ISBN 0-87727-049-X, DP 49). Cornell SE Asia.
Textile Industry Information Sources. Ed. by Joseph V. Kopycinski. LC 64-25644. (Management Information Guide Ser.: No. 4). 194p. 1964. 68.00x o.p. (ISBN 0-8103-0804-5). Gale.
Textile Marketing Management. Gordon A. Berkstresser, III. LC 83-22096. (Illus.). 135p. 1984. 32.00 o.p. (ISBN 0-8155-0975-8). Noyes.
Textile Products: Selection, Use & Care. Patsy R. Alexander. LC 76-11955. (Illus.). 416p. 1977. text ed. 17.75 o.p. (ISBN 0-395-20358-9). HM.
Textile Sculptures. Irene Waller. LC 77-71688. (Illus.). 1977. 17.50 o.s.i. (ISBN 0-8008-7579-6). Taplinger.
Textile Yarns: Technology, Structure & Applications. B. C. Goswami et al. LC 77-398. 482p. 1977. 72.50x o.p. (ISBN 0-471-31900-7). Wiley.
Textiles Designs of Japan, Vol. III: Okinawan, Ainu, & Foreign Designs. Japan Textile Color Design Center Staff. LC 79-89347. (Illus.). 400p. 1981. 195.00 o.p. (ISBN 0-87011-404-2). Kodansha.
Texts in Transit. Graydon Snyder & Kenneth Shaffer. (Orig.). 1976. pap. 3.95 o.s.i. (ISBN 0-685-61334-8). Brethren.
Texts of Festival. Mick Farren. 1975. pap. 1.25 o.p. (ISBN 0-380-00444-5, 27011). Avon.
Texts of the Songs. Ed. by Elise B. Jorgens. (English Song Ser.: 1600-1675). 300p. 1987. lib. bdg. 75.00 o.p. (ISBN 0-8240-8242-7). Garland Pub.
Textual Criticism of the Old Testament: The Septuagint After Qumran. Ralph W. Klein. Ed. by Gene M. Tucker. LC 74-80420. (Guides to Biblical Scholarship: Old Testament Ser.). 96p. (Orig.). 1974. pap. 4.95 o.p. (ISBN 0-8006-1087-3, 1-1087, Fortress). Augsburg Fortress.
Textures in Research & Practice: Proceedings. International Symposium Clausthal - Zellerfeld, 1968. Ed. by J. Grewen & G. Wassermann. (Illus.). 1969. 34.30 o.p. (ISBN 0-387-04733-6). Springer-Verlag.
Textures of Materials: Proceedings of the 5th Int'l. Conf. on Texture of Materials, March 29-April 1, 1978, Aachen, Germany, 2 vols. Ed. by G. Gottstein & K. Luecke. 1979. pap. 116.90 o.p. (ISBN 0-387-09220-X). Springer-Verlag.
T.F.H. Book of Budgerigars. Evelyn Miller. (Illus.). 80p. 6.95 o.p. (ISBN 0-87666-849-X, HP-004). TFH Pubns.
T.F.H. Book of Gerbils. Marshall Ostrow. (Illus.). 64p. 1981. 6.95 o.p. (ISBN 0-87666-824-4, HP-009). TFH Pubns.
T.F.H. Book of Guinea Pigs. William Ritter. (Illus.). 80p. 1982. 6.95 o.p. (ISBN 0-87666-823-6, HP-008). TFH Pubns.
T.F.H. Book of Hamsters. Mervin F. Roberts. (Illus.). 80p. 1981. 6.95 o.p. (ISBN 0-87666-848-1, HP-003). TFH Pubns.
T.F.H. Book of Kittens. Marjorie F. Schrody. (Illus.). 96p. 6.95 o.p. (ISBN 0-87666-817-1, HP-012). TFH Pubns.
T.F.H. Book of Pet Rabbits. Bob Bennett. (Illus.). 80p. 1982. 6.95 o.p. (ISBN 0-87666-815-5, HP-014). TFH Pubns.
TG las Mujeres. Date not set. (ISBN 0-07-020446-2). McGraw.
Thachers: Island of the Twin Lights. Eleanor C. Parsons. LC 85-9544. (Illus.). 160p. (Orig.). 1985. pap. 9.95 o.p. (ISBN 0-914659-14-6). Phoenix Pub.
Thackeray. Anthony Trollope. LC 67-23880. 224p. 1968. Repr. of 1879 ed. 34.00x o.p. (ISBN 0-8103-3060-1). Gale.
Thackeray & His Twentieth Century Critics: An Annotated Bibliography of British & American Criticism, 1900-1975. John C. Olmsted. LC 76-24394. (Reference Library of the Humanities Ser.: Vol. 62). 1977. lib. bdg. 43.00 o.p. (ISBN 0-8240-9915-X). Garland Pub.
Thaddeus Stevens, Scourge of the South. Fawn Brodie. (Illus.). 1966. pap. 7.95x o.p. (ISBN 0-393-00331-0, Norton Lib). Norton.
Thai Cultural Reader, Bk. II. Robert B. Jones & Ruchira C. Mendiones. (Bk. II). 791p. 1969. 8.25 o.p. (ISBN 0-317-12564-8). Cornell SE Asia.
Thai Values & Behavior Patterns. Robert L. Mole. LC 71-130419. (Illus.). 1971. 4.75 o.p. (ISBN 0-8048-0947-X). C E Tuttle.
Thailand. Insight Guides Staff. (Illus.). 320p. 1983. 18.95 o.p. (ISBN 0-13-912618-X); pap. 16.95 o.p. (ISBN 0-13-912600-7). P-H.
Thailand: A Travel Survival Kit. 2nd ed. Joe Cummings. (Illus.). 216p. (Orig.). 1984. pap. 7.95 o.p. (ISBN 0-908086-52-0). Lonely Planet.
Thailand & Burma. (Hildebrand's Travel Guides Ser.). (Illus.). 210p. pap. 9.95 o.p. (ISBN 0-87052-022-9). Hippocrene Bks.
Thailand: Industrial Development Strategy in Thailand. Bela Balassa. x, 59p. 1980. pap. 5.00 o.p. (ISBN 0-686-39672-3, BK-9155). World Bank.
Thailand Travel Guide. (Berlitz Travel Guides). (Illus.). 1982. pap. 4.95 o.p. (ISBN 0-02-969030-7, Berlitz). Macmillan.
Thais see Romans et Contes.
Thames & Hudson Manual of Architectural Ceramics. David Hamilton. (Illus.). 1978. 18.95 o.s.i. (ISBN 0-500-68014-0). Thames Hudson.
Thames & Hudson Manual of Direct Metal Sculpture. Trevor Faulkner. (Illus.). 1978. 18.95 o.p. (ISBN 0-500-67015-3). Thames Hudson.
Thames & Hudson Manual of Film Editing. Roger Crittenden. (Illus.). 1982. 18.95 o.p. (ISBN 0-500-67023-4); pap. 10.95f o.p. (ISBN 0-500-68023-X). Thames Hudson.
Thames & Hudson Manual of Typography. Ruari McLean. (Illus.). 192p. 1980. 18.95 o.p. (ISBN 0-500-67022-6). Thames Hudson.
Thames & Hudson Manual of Wood Engraving. Walter Chamberlain. (Illus.). 1979. 18.95 o.p. (ISBN 0-500-67018-8). Thames Hudson.
Thank God for Circles. Joanne Marxhausen. LC 75-159012. (ps-2). 1971. 4.50 o.p. (ISBN 0-8066-1135-9, 10-6240, Augsburg). Augsburg Fortress.
Thank God for Circles. Joanne Marxhaussen. LC 75-159012. 32p. 1980. pap. 3.50 o.p. (ISBN 0-8066-1805-1, 10-6241, Augsburg). Augsburg Fortress.
Thank God I'm a Teenager. Charles S. Mueller & Donald R. Bardill. LC 76-3854. (gr. 7-9). 1976. pap. 6.95 o.p. (ISBN 0-8066-1536-2, 10-6242, Augsburg). Augsburg Fortress.
Thank God It's Monday: How to Turn Work into an Adventure. Robert M. Randolph. LC 82-11926. (Illus.). 249p. 1982. 15.95 o.p. (ISBN 0-87624-623-4, Inst Busn Plan). P-H.
Thank You Davey; Thank You, God. Marilyn Worswick & Robert Selle. LC 77-84089. 1978. pap. 4.50 o.p. (ISBN 0-8066-1614-8, 10-6244, Augsburg). Augsburg Fortress.
Thank You for My Grandchild. Betty Isler. 1983. pap. 2.08 o.p. (ISBN 0-570-03915-0, 12-2850). Concordia.
Thank You, God: Prayers for Young Children. Ron Klug & Lyn Klug. LC 80-67800. 32p. (Orig.). (ps-1). 1980. pap. 4.95 o.p. (ISBN 0-8066-1862-0, 10-6243, Augsburg). Augsburg Fortress.
Thank You, Lord, for Little Things. Annice H. Brown. 3.95 o.p. (ISBN 0-8042-2580-X, John Knox). Westminster John Knox.
Thank You, Mr. Moto. John P. Marquand. 288p. 1985. pap. 3.95 o.p. (ISBN 0-316-54698-4). Little.
Thanks for the Mountain. Erling Wold & Marge Wold. LC 74-14178. 112p. (Orig.). 1975. pap. 3.95 o.p. (ISBN 0-8066-1461-7, 10-6245, Augsburg). Augsburg Fortress.
Thanks to the Saint. Leslie Charteris. (Saint Ser.). 160p. 1982. pap. 2.50 o.p. (ISBN 0-441-80493-4). Ace Bks.
Thanksgiving Day. Gail Gibbons. LC 83-175. (Illus.). (ps-3). 1985. pap. 5.95 o.p. (ISBN 0-8234-0576-1). Holiday.
That All Children May Learn We Must Learn: Looking Forward to Teaching. 2nd,1971 ed. Mabel Anderson et al. LC 78-165217. (Illus.). 1972. pap. 4.00 o.p. (ISBN 0-87173-032-4). ACEI.
That Amazing Book-Genesis! Harold Snider. 1977. 4.50 o.p. (ISBN 0-682-48779-1). Exposition-Phoenix.
That Championship Season. Jason Miller. LC 72-87905. 1972. pap. 3.95 o.p. (ISBN 0-689-10538-X, Atheneum). Macmillan.
That Crazy April. Lila Perl. LC 73-14812. 192p. (gr. 4-8). 1979. 7.95 o.p. (ISBN 0-395-28869-X, Clarion). HM.
That Every Man Be Armed: The Evolution of a Constitutional Right. Stephen P Halbrook. LC 84-13127. 286p. 1985. 19.95 o.p. (ISBN 0-8263-0764-7); pap. 11.95 o.p. U of NM Pr.
That Hilarious First Year. Bea Boynton. LC 75-109541. (Illus.). 1971. pap. 2.50 o.p. (ISBN 0-87004-203-3). Caxton.
That Lass O'Lowries. Frances H. Burnett. 224p. 1985. pap. 5.95 o.s.i. (ISBN 0-85115-239-2, Pub. by Boydell England). Academy Chi Pubs.
That Man from Smyrna. Martin. LC 78-17641. 1978. 9.95 o.p. (ISBN 0-8246-0237-4). Jonathan David.
That Noble Cabinet: A History of the British Museum. Edward Miller. LC 73-85452. (Illus.). 400p. 1974. 22.95x o.p. (ISBN 0-8214-0139-4). Ohio U Pr.
That One Mistake. Ferenc Kormendi. (ISBN 0-8022-0884-3). Philos Lib.
That Other Realm of Freedom. Barry Nonweiler. 324p. (Orig.). 1983. pap. 8.50 o.p. (ISBN 0-317-62485-7, Pub. by GMP England). Alyson Pubns.
That Prosser Kid. Lloyd Pye. LC 77-79528. 1977. 8.95 o.p. (ISBN 0-87795-165-9, Arbor Hse). Morrow.
That Quail Robert. Margaret A. Stanger. 1983. pap. 2.50 o.p. (ISBN 0-449-20388-3, Crest). Fawcett.
That Reminds Me. Girault M. Jones. (Illus.). xiv, 211p. (Orig.). 1984. pap. 10.00 o.p. (ISBN 0-918769-08-6). Univ South.
That the Door May Open. Robert W. Uphoff. 1979. 5.00 o.p. (ISBN 0-682-49388-0). Exposition-Phoenix.
That the World May Know. Howard G. Hageman & Ruth D. See. (Illus., Orig.). (gr. 9-11). 1965. pap. 3.75 o.p. (ISBN 0-8042-9250-7, John Knox). Westminster John Knox.
That Was the Life. Dora J. Hamblin. (Illus.). 1977. 10.00 o.p. (ISBN 0-393-08764-6). Norton.
That Wonderful Word Shalom: Dramas on the Biblical Concept of Peace. W. A. Poovey. LC 75-22717. 88p. 1975. pap. 2.50 o.p. (ISBN 0-8066-1517-6, 10-6280, Augsburg). Augsburg Fortress.
Thatcher Government. 2nd ed. Peter Riddell. 270p. 1986. pap. text ed. 14.95x o.p. (ISBN 0-631-14519-2). Basil Blackwell.
That's a Good Idea! new ed. Alan E. Miner. 128p. 1975. pap. 2.95 o.p. (ISBN 0-89036-051-0). Hawkes Pub Inc.
That's Not Chester! Carol Nicklaus. (Illus.). 32p. (ps-3). 1983. pap. 2.25 o.p. (ISBN 0-380-63073-7, 63073-7, Camelot). Avon.
That's Not Fair. Gyo Fujikawa. (Illus.). 32p. (ps-2). 1983. pap. 3.95 o.p. (ISBN 0-448-16466-3, G&D). Putnam Pub Group.
That's Not My Style. Mary Anderson. LC 82-13772. 168p. (gr. 7 up). 1983. 11.95 o.s.i. (ISBN 0-689-30968-6, Atheneum Childrens Bks). Macmillan.
That's the Lawyer. Stephen G. E. Burrows. 256p. 1980. 10.00 o.p. (ISBN 0-682-49594-8). Exposition-Phoenix.
That's What T. J. Says. Betty Bates. LC 82-80815. 160p. (gr. 5-7). 1982. 10.95 o.p. (ISBN 0-8234-0465-X). Holiday.
The Citizen Bee Guide to American Studies: The Citizen Bee Sourcebook of American Studies. rev. ed. Close Up Foundation Staff. (Illus.). 152p. (YA) (gr. 11-12). 1986. pap. text ed. 12.00 o.p. (ISBN 0-932765-06-8); pap. 10.00 o.p. Close Up Foun.
Theater & Its Double. Antonin Artaud. Tr. by Mary C. Richards from Fr. (Illus.). 1958. pap. 7.95 o.p. (ISBN 0-394-17213-2, E127, Ever). Grove.
Theater Experience. 2nd ed. Edwin Wilson. (Illus.). 1980. text ed. 28.95 o.p. (ISBN 0-07-070667-0); pap. text ed. 25.95 o.p. (ISBN 0-07-070668-9). McGraw.
Theater of God: Story in Christian Doctrine. Robert P. Roth. LC 84-48725. 208p. 1985. pap. 1.95 o.p. (ISBN 0-8006-1841-6, 1-1841, Fortress). Augsburg Fortress.
Theater of Spontaneity. 2nd ed. J. L. Moreno. 10.00 o.s.i. (ISBN 0-685-30847-2); pap. 8.00 o.s.i. (ISBN 0-685-30848-0). Beacon Hse.
Theaterbauten von Fellner und Helmer. Hans-Christoph Hoffmann. (Illus.). 308p. (Ger.). 1966. 114.00 o.p. (ISBN 3-7913-0128-4, Pub. by Prestel). TeNeues.
Theatre, Tome I. Jean Cocteau. Incl. Antigone; Maries de la Tour Eiffel; Chevaliers de la Table Ronde; Parents Terribles. (Fr.). 1948-49. pap. 11.75 o.p. (ISBN 0-685-36056-3). French & Eur.
Theatre, Tome II. Jean Cocteau. Incl. Monstres Sacres; Machine a Ecrire; Renaud et Armide; Aigle a Deux Tetes. 1948-49. pap. 10.95 o.p. (ISBN 0-685-36059-8). French & Eur.
Theatre. Robert Cohen. LC 80-84012. (Illus.). 433p. 1981. pap. text ed. 22.95 o.p. (ISBN 0-87484-459-2). Mayfield Pub.
Theatre, 5 vols. Michel De Ghelderode. 328p. 1952-70. Vol. 1. 12.95 o.p. (ISBN 0-686-56047-7); Vols. 2 & 3. 16.95 ea. o.p.; Vol. 4. 8.95 o.p. (ISBN 0-686-56048-5); Vol. 5. 10.95 o.p. (ISBN 0-686-56049-3). Schoenhof.
Theatre, Vol. 4. Jacques Audiberti. 16.50 o.p. (ISBN 0-686-54507-9). French & Eur.
Theatre & National Awakening. Edith C. Malyusz. Tr. by Thomas Szendrey. LC 79-89134. 349p. 1980. 22.50 o.p. (ISBN 0-914648-10-1). Hungarian Cultural.
Theatre & Stage: An Encyclopedic Guide to the Performance of All Amateur Dramatic, Operatic, & Theatrical Work, 2 vols. Ed. by Harold Downs. LC 77-28803. (Illus.). 1979. Repr. of 1951 ed. lib. bdg. 137.50x o.p. (ISBN 0-313-20222-2, DOTS); Vol. 1. lib. bdg. 82.50 o.p. (ISBN 0-313-20223-0, DOTS1); Vol. 2. lib. bdg. 82.50 o.p. (ISBN 0-313-20224-9, DOTS2). Greenwood.
Theatre Art. Ed. by Lee Simonson. LC 74-79205. (Illus.). 1969. Repr. of 1934 ed. 23.50x o.p. (ISBN 0-8154-0289-9). Cooper Sq.
Theatre at Work. Jim Hiley. (Illus.). 220p. 1981. 26.95x o.p. (ISBN 0-7100-0815-5). Routledge Chapman & Hall.
Theatre: Avec: Le Barbier de Seville, Le Marriage de Figaro, La Mere Coupable. Pierre de Beaumarchais & Maurice Rat. (Illus.). 320p. 10.95 o.p. (ISBN 0-686-54085-9). French & Eur.
Theatre: Brief Edition. Robert Cohen. 239p. 1983. pap. text ed. 17.95 o.p. (ISBN 0-87484-585-8). Mayfield Pub.
Theatre Business: From Auditions Through Opening Night. Jan W. Greenberg. LC 80-20295. 1981. 10.95 o.p. (ISBN 0-03-051451-7). H Holt & Co.
Theatre Complet. Georges Courteline. 1961. 19.95 o.p. (ISBN 0-686-54638-5). French & Eur.
Theatre Complet: Paris, Eighteen Sixty-Nine to Eighteen Seventy-One, 4 vols. Pierre de Beaumarchais. 1967. 250.00 o.p. (ISBN 0-686-54087-5). French & Eur.
Theatre Dictionary. W. Granville. 1952. (ISBN 0-8022-0619-0). Philos Lib.
Theatre Directory 1987-88. Ed. by John Istel. 70p. 1987. pap. 4.95 o.p. (ISBN 0-930452-75-5). Theatre Comm.
Theatre Nurse & the Law. Eileen Dixon. 144p. (Orig.). 1984. pap. 14.50 o.p. (ISBN 0-7099-0818-0, Pub. by Croom Helm Ltd). Routledge Chapman & Hall.
Theatre of Aristophanes. Kenneth McLeish. LC 79-3142. (Illus.). 183p. 1980. 11.95 o.s.i. (ISBN 0-8008-7630-X). Taplinger.
Theatre of Commitment. Eric Bentley. LC 67-29961. 1967. 5.00 o.p. (ISBN 0-689-10034-5, Atheneum). Macmillan.
Theatre of the Absurd. 3rd ed. Martin Esslin. 424p. 1983. pap. 7.95 o.p. (ISBN 0-14-020929-8, Pelican). Penguin.
Theatre of the French & German Enlightenment: Five Essays. Ed. by S. S. B. Taylor. 86p. 1979. Repr. of 1978 ed. text ed. 21.50x o.p. (ISBN 0-06-496777-8). B&N Imports.
Theatre on a Shoestring. Adrian Waller. (Quality Paperback: No. 295). 158p. (Orig.). 1975. pap. 3.95 o.p. (ISBN 0-8226-0295-4). Littlefield.
Theatre Student: Diary of Producing a Play. Peter Kline. (Theatre Student Ser.). (Illus.). 140p. 1981. lib. bdg. 14.95 o.p. (ISBN 0-8239-0523-3). Rosen Group.
Theatre Student: Gilbert & Sullivan Production. Peter Kline. LC 74-170281. (Theatre Student Ser.). (gr. 7 up). 1972. PLB 14.95 o.p. (ISBN 0-8239-0252-8). Rosen Group.
Theatre Student: You Can Write a Play. Milton Polsky. (Theatre Stucent Ser.). (Illus.). 170p. 1983. lib. bdg. 14.95 o.p. (ISBN 0-8239-0558-6). Rosen Group.
Theatre Year. 4th ed. Photos by Donald Cooper. (Illus.). 129p. 1984. pap. 11.95 o.p. (ISBN 0-9507578-3-7, NO. 3996). Routledge Chapman & Hall.
Theatres & Auditoriums Architecture. R. Aloi. (Illus.). 1972. 50.00 o.s.i. (ISBN 0-685-30575-9). E J Brill USA.
Theatrical Designs of Charles Ricketts. Eric Binnie. Ed. by Bernard Beckerman. LC 84-23921. (Theater & Dramatic Studies: No. 23). 200p. 1985. 39.95 o.p. (ISBN 0-8357-1584-1). UMI Res Pr.
Theatrical Manager in Britain & America. Ed. by Joseph W. Donohue, Jr. LC 72-154992. (Illus.). 1972. 24.00x o.p. (ISBN 0-691-06188-2). Princeton U Pr.
Theatrical Space in Ibsen, Chekhov & Strindberg: Public Forms of Privacy. Freddie Rokem. Ed. by Oscar Brockett. LC 85-16415. (Theater & Dramatics Studies: No. 32). (Illus.). 106p. 1985. 39.95 o.p. (ISBN 0-8357-1707-0). UMI Res Pr.
Theatrum Redivivum: In Answer to Mr. Pryn's Histrio-Mastix see Mr. William Prynn-His Defence of Stage-Plays: Retraction of a Former Book of His Called 'Histrio-Mastix'.
Thebes in the Fifth Century. Nancy H. Demand. (States & Cities of Ancient Greece Ser.). 208p. 1983. 21.95x o.p. (ISBN 0-7100-9288-1). Routledge Chapman & Hall.
Their Blood Runneth Orange: Inside Clemson Football. Donald F. Barton. LC 83-80727. (Illus.). 192p. 1983. 7.95 o.p. (ISBN 0-88011-174-7). Scribner.
Their New Life in the United States. Language & Orientation Resource Center Staff. 220p. 1981. pap. 9.95 o.p. (ISBN 0-15-599115-9). Ctr Appl Ling.

Their Story-Our Story. Forrest W. Jackson. LC 85-6623. (YA) (gr. 7-12). 1985. pap. 4.95 o.p. (ISBN 0-8054-3618-9, 4236-18). Broadman.

Their Turf. Bernard Livingston. LC 73-82188. (Illus.). 1973. 12.50 o.p. (ISBN 0-87795-068-7, Arbor Hse). Morrow.

Theism & Cosmology. Laird. (ISBN 0-8022-0904-1). Philos Lib.

Theismann. Joe Theismann & Dave Kindred. 1987. 17.95 o.p. (ISBN 0-8092-4843-3). Contemp Bks.

Thekla. D. Lucinda Wicke. 104p. 1987. 12.75 o.p. (ISBN 0-8062-3088-6). Carlton.

Thematic Catalog of the Sacred Works of Giacomo Carissimi. Iva M. Buff. LC 80-142011. 157p. 1979. 39.00 o.p. (ISBN 0-913574-15-5). Eur Am Music.

Thematic Dialogue: Mathematics. Y. A. Kuzman. 96p. 1985. pap. 1.95 o.p. (ISBN 0-8285-3024-6, Pub. by Rus Lang Pubs USSR). Imported Pubns.

Thematic Locator for Mozart's Works, As Listed in Koechel's Chronologisch Thematisches Verzeichnis. 6th ed. George R. Hill & Murray Gould. (Music Indexes & Bibliographies: No. 1). 1970. pap. 7.50 o.p. (ISBN 0-913574-01-5). Eur-Am Music.

Thematic Map Design, Vol. 6. Laboratory for Computer Graphics & Spatial Analysis, Harvard University Graduate School of Design Staff. (Harvard Library of Computer Graphics, Mapping Collection). (Illus.). 134p. 1979. pap. 15.95 o.p. (ISBN 0-8122-1186-3). U of Pa Pr.

Thematic Origins of Scientific Thought: Kepler to Einstein. Gerald Holton. LC 72-83467. 300p. 1973. 19.50x o.p. (ISBN 0-674-87745-4); pap. 10.95 o.p. (ISBN 0-674-87746-2). Harvard U Pr.

Theme & Paragraph. Phillip Burnham & Richard Lederer. Orig. Title: Basic Composition. (Illus.). 1976. pap. text ed. 4.25x o.p. (ISBN 0-88334-078-X). Ind Sch Pr.

Theme & Variations: A Behavior Therapy Casebook. Joseph Wolpe. 200p. 1976. 70.00 o.p. (ISBN 0-08-020422-8); pap. 70.00 o.p. (ISBN 0-08-020421-X). Pergamon.

Themes from Acts. Paul E. Pierson. LC 82-80153. (Bible Commentary for Laymen Ser.). (Orig.). 1982. pap. 3.95 o.s.i. (ISBN 0-8307-0819-7, S361107). Regal.

Themes from Isaiah. Ronald Youngblood. LC 83-19128. (Bible Commentary for Laymen Ser.). 1983. pap. text ed. 3.95 o.s.i. (ISBN 0-8307-0906-1, S373106). Regal.

Themes in American Literature. Philip J. McFarland et al. (Literature Ser.). (Illus.). 815p. (gr. 11). 1972. text ed. 17.40 o.p. (ISBN 0-395-11201-X, 2-26548). HM.

Themes in Economic Anthropology. Ed. by Raymond Firth. (Illus.). 1970. pap. 13.95x o.p. (ISBN 0-422-72540-4, NO. 2198, Pub by Tavistock England). Routledge Chapman & Hall.

Themes in World Literature. Philip J. McFarland et al. (Literature Ser.). 1970. text ed. 23.40 o.p. (ISBN 0-395-02875-2, 2-26380). HM.

Then Again. Sue McCauley. 352p. 1988. 22.95 o.p. (ISBN 0-340-40101-X, Pub. by Hodder & Stoughton UK). David & Charles.

Then Some Other Stuff Happened. Ed. by Bill Lawrence. LC 83-45518. 128p. 1984. pap. 5.95 o.p. (ISBN 0-689-70670-7, 312, Atheneum). Macmillan.

Theo Tobiasse: Artist in Exile. Chaim Potok. (Illus.). 200p. 1986. 50.00 o.p. (ISBN 0-8478-0778-9). Rizzoli Intl.

Theoderich Und Iustinian. Berthold Rubin. pap. 8.00 o.p. (ISBN 0-384-52465-6). Johnson Repr.

Theodicy in the Old Testament. Ed. by James L. Crenshaw. LC 83-8885. (Issues in Religion & Theology Ser.). 176p. 1983. pap. 2.50 o.p. (ISBN 0-8006-1764-9, 1-1764, Fortress). Augsburg Fortress.

Theodor Fontane und der Roman Vom Markischen Junker. Hans G. Wegner. (Ger). 18.00 o.p. (ISBN 0-384-66447-4); pap. 13.00 o.p. Johnson Repr.

Theodore D. A. Cockerell: Letters from West Cliff, Colorado, 1887-1889. William A. Weber. LC 76-15775. 1978. pap. 10.00x o.p. (ISBN 0-87081-122-3). Univ Pr Colo.

Theodore Dreiser: A Checklist. Ed. by Hugh C. Atkinson. LC 77-626231. (Serif Ser.: No. 15). 104p. 1971. 10.00x o.p. (ISBN 0-87338-048-7). Kent St U Pr.

Theodore Dreiser: Our Bitter Patriot. Charles Shapiro. LC 62-16696. (Crosscurrents-Modern Critiques Ser.). 146p. 1962. 6.95x o.p. (ISBN 0-8093-0070-2). S Ill U Pr.

Theodore Dreiser: Sister Carrie. Ed. by Jack Salzman. 418p. 1970. pap. text ed. write for info o.p. (ISBN 0-02-405390-2). Macmillan.

Theodore Herzl: A Biography of the Founder of Modern Zionism. Alex Bein. Tr. by Maurice Samuel from Ger. LC 62-20753. (Temple Bk). 1970. pap. 4.75 o.p. (ISBN 0-689-70244-2, T18, Atheneum). Macmillan.

Theodore Parker: A Descriptive Bibliography. Joel Myerson. LC 81-43354. 238p. 1981. lib. bdg. 33.00 o.p. (ISBN 0-8240-9279-1). Garland Pub.

Theodore Roethke's Career: An Annotated Bibliography. Keith R. Moul. 1978. lib. bdg. 29.00 o.p. (ISBN 0-8161-7892-5, Hall Reference). G K Hall.

Theodore Roosevelt. Aloysius A. Norton. (United States Authors Ser.). 1980. lib. bdg. 13.50 o.p. (ISBN 0-8057-7309-6, Twayne). G K Hall.

Theodore Spencer: Selected Essays. Ed. by A. C. Purves. 1967. 40.00x o.p. (ISBN 0-8135-0539-9). Rutgers U Pr.

Theodore Sturgeon: A Primary & Secondary Bibliography. Lahna Diskin. 1979. lib. bdg. 20.00 o.p. (ISBN 0-8161-8046-6, Hall Reference). G K Hall.

Theodore Winthrop: Portrait of an American Author. Eugene T. Woolf. LC 81-40124. 280p. (Orig.). 1982. lib. bdg. 29.75 o.p. (ISBN 0-8191-1772-2); pap. text ed. 14.25 o.p. (ISBN 0-8191-1773-0). U Pr of Amer.

Theodore's Rival. Edward Ormondroyd. (Illus.). (gr. k-3). 1971. Repr. PLB 5.95 o.p. (ISBN 0-395-27684-5). HM.

Theologians under Hitler: Gerhard Kittel, Paul Althaus, & Emmanuel Hirsch. Robert P. Ericksen. 1987. pap. 8.95 o.p. (ISBN 0-317-59962-3). Yale U Pr.

Theological Outlines. Francis J. Hall. 1895. 7.95 o.p. (ISBN 0-8192-1037-4). Morehouse Pub.

Theology & Pastoral Care. John B. Cobb, Jr. Ed. by Howard J. Clinebell & Howard W. Stone. LC 76-7862. (Creative Pastoral Care & Counseling Ser.). 96p. 1977. pap. 4.50 o.p. (ISBN 0-8006-0557-8, 1-557, Fortress). Augsburg Fortress.

Theology & the Future. Eric L. Mascall. (Orig.). 1968. pap. 3.75 o.p. (ISBN 0-8192-1054-4). Morehouse Pub.

Theology for the Nineteen-Eighties. John Carmody. LC 80-19349. 192p. 1980. pap. 9.50 o.s.i. (ISBN 0-664-24345-2, Westminster). Westminster John Knox.

Theology in Red, White & Black. Benjamin A. Reist. LC 74-27936. 1975. 7.50 o.s.i. (ISBN 0-664-20723-5, Westminster). Westminster John Knox.

Theology of Abraham Bibago: A Defense of the Divine Will, Knowledge, & Providence in Fifteenth-Century Spanish-Jewish Philosophy. Allan Lazaroff. LC 77-10611. (Judaic Studies Ser.). 192p. 1981. text ed. 17.50 o.p. (ISBN 0-8173-6906-6). U of Ala Pr.

Theology of Auschwitz: The Christian Faith & the Problem of Evil. Ulrich Simon. LC 78-71046. 1979. pap. 3.95 o.p. (ISBN 0-8042-0724-0, John Knox). Westminster John Knox.

Theology of Christian Education. Lawrence O. Richards. 320p. 1975. 22.95 o.p. (ISBN 0-310-31940-4, 18135). Zondervan.

Theology of Church Growth. George Peters. 283p. 1981. pap. 11.95 o.p. (ISBN 0-310-43101-8, 11285P). Zondervan.

Theology of Church Leadership. Lawrence O. Richards & Clyde Hoeldtke. (Illus.). 352p. 1980. 22.95 o.p. (ISBN 0-310-31960-9, 18136). Zondervan.

Theology of Conflict: & Other Writings on Nonviolence. Dominique Barbe. 1989. pap. 11.95 o.p. (546). Orbis Bks.

Theology of Exile: Judgment-Deliverance in Jeremiah & Ezekiel. Thomas M. Raitt. LC 76-62610. 288p. 1977. 3.95 o.p. (ISBN 0-8006-0497-0, 1-497, Fortress). Augsburg Fortress.

Theology of Generosity: Principles & Practice of Giving Based on Bible Teaching. W. W. Berrie. 32p. 1982. pap. 2.50 o.p. (ISBN 0-8192-1293-8). Morehouse Pub.

Theology of Grace of Theodore of Mopsuestia. Joanne Dewart. LC 65-18319. (Studies in Christian Antiquity: Vol. 16). 160p. 1971. 12.95x o.p. (ISBN 0-8132-0523-9). Cath U Pr.

Theology of Liberation: History, Politics, & Salvation. rev. ed. Gustavo Gutierrez. Tr. by Caridad Inda & John Eagleson. 272p. 1988. 24.95 o.p. (ISBN 0-88344-543-3); pap. 12.95 o.p. (ISBN 0-88344-542-5). Orbis Bks.

Theology of Personal Ministry. Lawrence Richards & Gib Martin. 272p. 1981. 22.95 o.p. (ISBN 0-310-31970-6, 18137). Zondervan.

Theology of Praise: The Kingdom, the Power, & the Glory. Jan M. Lochman. LC 81-82370. 96p. 1982. pap. 6.50 o.p. (ISBN 0-8042-0730-5, John Knox). Westminster John Knox.

Theology of Q: Eschatology, Prophecy & Wisdom. Richard A. Edwards. LC 75-13042. 192p. 1975. 11.95 o.p. (ISBN 0-8006-0432-6, 1-432, Fortress). Augsburg Fortress.

Theology of the Book of Ruth. Ronald M. Hals. LC 69-12996. (Orig.). 1969. pap. 1.00 o.p. (ISBN 0-8006-3050-5, Fortress). Augsburg Fortress.

Theology of the Epistles. Harry A. Kennedy. LC 20-15157. (Studies in Theology: No. 13). 1919. 6.00x o.p. (ISBN 0-8401-6013-5). A R Allenson.

Theology of the Love of God. George Newlands. LC 80-22547. 224p. 1981. 3.15 o.p. (ISBN 0-8042-0726-7, John Knox); pap. 1.75 o.p. (ISBN 0-8042-0727-5). Westminster John Knox.

Theology of Things. Conrad Bonifazi. LC 76-7549. 1976. Repr. of 1967 ed. lib. bdg. 22.50x o.p. (ISBN 0-8371-8838-5, BOTT). Greenwood.

Theology of Wolfhart Pannenberg. E. Frank Tupper. LC 73-6662. 320p. 1973. 10.95 o.s.i. (ISBN 0-664-20973-4, Westminster). Westminster John Knox.

Theology Primer. John J. Davis. LC 81-67093. 128p. (Orig.). 1981. pap. 5.95 o.p. (ISBN 0-8010-2912-0). Baker Bk.

Theology to Live By. Herman A. Preus. 1977. pap. 7.95 o.p. (ISBN 0-570-03739-5, 12-2643). Concordia.

Theonomy in Christian Ethics. exp. ed. Greg L. Bahnsen. 1984. 17.95 o.p. (ISBN 0-87552-117-7). Presby & Reformed.

Theophilus North. Thornton Wilder. 352p. 1984. pap. 1.75 o.p. (ISBN 0-380-00160-8, 53108-9, Bard). Avon.

Theophoric Personal Names in Ancient Hebrew: A Comparative Study. Jeaneane D. Fowler. (JSOT Supplement Ser.: No. 49). 400p. pap. text ed. 18.95x o.s.i. (Pub. by JSOT Pr England). Eisenbrauns.

Theopoetic: Theology & the Religious Imagination. Amos N. Wilder. LC 75-36458. 112p. 1976. 5.95 o.p. (ISBN 0-8006-0435-0, 1-435, Fortress). Augsburg Fortress.

Theoretical & Clinical Hemorheology: Proceedings. International Society of Hemorheology, 2nd International Conference, Heidelberg, 1969. Ed. by H. Hartert & A. L. Copley. (Illus.). 440p. 1971. 85.00 o.p. (ISBN 0-387-05351-4). Springer-Verlag.

Theoretical & Empirical Foundations of Rational-Emitive Therapy. Albert Ellis & John M. Whiteley. 1979. 8.95 o.p. (ISBN 1-55620-031-5, 71002C). Am Assn Coun Dev.

Theoretical Approaches to Non-Numerical Problem Solving: Proceedings. Systems Symposium - 4th - Case Western Reserve University, Institute of Technology. Ed. by R. B. Banerji & M. D. Mesarovic. LC 79-121996. (Lecture Notes in Operations Research & Mathematical Systems: Vol. 28). 1970. pap. 21.90 o.p. (ISBN 0-387-04900-2). Springer-Verlag.

Theoretical Chemistry: Advances & Perspectives, Vol. 3. Ed. by Douglas Henderson & Henry Eyring. 1978. 65.50 o.p. (ISBN 0-12-681903-3). Acad Pr.

Theoretical Chemistry: Advances & Perspectives, Vol. 5. Ed. by A. R. Katritzky & A. J. Boulton. LC 75-21963. 1980. 71.00 o.p. (ISBN 0-12-681905-X). Acad Pr.

Theoretical Chemistry: Advances & Perspectives, Vol. 4: Periodicities in Chemistry & Biology. Ed. by Henry Eyring & Douglas Henderson. 1978. 85.50 o.p. (ISBN 0-12-681904-1). Acad Pr.

Theoretical Chemistry: Advances in Perspectives, Vol. 2. Ed. by Henry Eyring & Douglas Henderson. 1976. 71.50 o.p. (ISBN 0-12-681902-5). Acad Pr.

Theoretical Chemistry: Theory of Scattering-Papers in Honor of Henry Eyring, Vol. 6a. Ed. by Douglas Henderson. (Serial Publication). 1981. 70.50 o.p. (ISBN 0-12-681906-8). Acad Pr.

Theoretical Chemistry: Theory of Scattering: Papers in Honor of Henry Eyring, Vol. 6B. Ed. by Douglas Henderson. (Serial Publications). 1981. 69.50 o.p. (ISBN 0-12-681907-6). Acad Pr.

Theoretical Developments in Marketing: Proceedings of the Theory Conference, Phoenix, Arizona, February, 1980. Theory Conference Staff. Ed. by Charles W. Lamb, Jr. & Patrick M. Dunne. LC 80-12436. (Illus.). 269p. (Orig.). 1980. pap. text ed. 24.00 o.p. (ISBN 0-87757-138-4). Am Mktg.

Theoretical Ecology. 2nd, rev. ed. Ed. by Robert M. May. LC 80-19344. (Illus.). 500p. text ed. 31.50x cancelled o.s.i. (ISBN 0-87893-514-2); pap. text ed. 31.50x o.s.i. (ISBN 0-87893-515-0). Sinauer Assocs.

Theoretical Electrochemistry. L. Antropov. 568p. 1972. 8.95 o.p. (ISBN 0-8285-0667-1, Pub. by Mir Pubs USSR). Imported Pubns.

Theoretical Foundations of Modern Chemical Analysis. Y. S. Lyalikov & Y. A. Klyachko. 1980. 8.45 o.p. (ISBN 0-8285-1777-0, Pub. by Mir Pubs USSR). Imported Pubns.

Theoretical Inorganic Chemistry. C. K. Jorgensen et al. LC 75-5565. (Topics in Current Chemistry Ser.: Vol. 56). (Illus.). 160p. 1975. text ed. 36.00 o.p. (ISBN 0-387-07226-8). Springer-Verlag.

Theoretical Inorganic Chemistry: No. 2. K. Brenauer et al. (Topics in Current Chemistry: Vol. 65). 1976. 34.00 o.p. (ISBN 0-387-07637-9). Springer-Verlag.

Theoretical Issues in Dakota Phonology & Morphology. Patricia A. Shaw. Ed. by Jorge Hankamer. LC 79-55856. (Outstanding Dissertations in Linguistics Ser.). 404p. 1985. 56.00 o.p. (ISBN 0-8240-4562-9). Garland Pub.

Theoretical Kinematics. O. Bottema & B. Roth. (Applied Mathematics & Mechanics: Vol. 24). 558p. 1979. 147.50 o.p. (ISBN 0-444-85124-0, North-Holland). Elsevier.

Theoretical Magnetofluid-Dynamics. Henri Cabannes. LC 75-117095. (Applied Mathematics & Mechanics Ser.: Vol. 13). 1970. 77.00 o.p. (ISBN 0-12-153750-1). Acad Pr.

Theoretical Methods in Social History. Arthur L. Stinchcombe. (Studies in Social Discontinuity). 1978. 14.95 o.p. (ISBN 0-12-672250-1). Acad Pr.

Theoretical Nuclear Physics. J. Blatt & V. F. Weisskopf. LC 79-4268. 1979. pap. 44.00 o.p. (ISBN 0-387-90382-8). Springer-Verlag.

Theoretical Perspective of Violence Against Police. Daniel C. Kieselhorst. (Criminal Justice Policy & Administration Research Ser.: No. 2). 1974. pap. 3.00 o.p. (ISBN 0-686-18639-7). Univ OK Gov Res.

Theoretical Physics: Applications of Vectors, Matrices, Tensors & Quaternions. A. Kyrala. LC 67-12810. (Studies in Physics & Chemistry: No. 5). pap. cancelled o.s.i. (ISBN 0-317-08733-9, 2051978). Bks Demand UMI.

Theoretical Principles in Astrophysics & Relativity. Ed. by Norman Lebovitz et al. LC 76-25636. (Illus.). 1978. lib. bdg. 25.00x o.s.i. (ISBN 0-226-46989-1). U of Chicago Pr.

Theoretische Grundlagen und die Praktische Verwendbarkeit der Gerichtlich-Medizinischen Alkoholbestimmung (1932) see Principles & Applications of Medicolegal Alcohol Determination.

Theorie Cinetique des Gaz a Repartition Descrete De Vitesses. T. Gatignol. 206p. 1975. pap. 14.70 o.p. (ISBN 0-387-07156-3). Springer-Verlag.

Theorie der Geometrishen Konstruktionen. L. Bierberbach. (Mathematische Rehihe Ser.: No. 13). (Illus.). 162p. (Ger.). 1952. 23.95x o.p. (ISBN 0-8176-0030-2). Birkhauser.

Theories & Approaches to International Politics. 2nd ed. Patrick M. Morgan. LC 79-66439. 310p. 1975. text ed. 12.95 o.p. (ISBN 0-87855-127-1). Transaction Pubs.

Theories of Adolescence. 4th ed. Rolf E. Muuss. 336p. 1982. pap. text ed. 9.00 o.p. (ISBN 0-394-32424-2, RanC). Random.

Theories of Homosexuality. Martin Dannecker. 123p. 1981. pap. 3.95 o.p. (ISBN 0-317-62488-1, Pub. by GMP England). Alyson Pubns.

Theories of Human Communication. 2nd ed. Stephen W. Littlejohn. 340p. 1983. text ed. (ISBN 0-534-01280-9). Wadsworth Pub.

Theories of Learning: A Comparative Approach. George M. Gazda & Raymond J. Corsini. LC 79-91101. 483p. 1980. text ed. 32.50 o.p. (ISBN 0-87581-253-8). Peacock Pubs.

Theories of Learning & Instruction. Ed. by Ernest R. Hilgard. LC 64-3324. (National Society for the Study of Education Yearbooks Ser: No. 63, Pt. 1). 1973. lib. bdg. 6.00x o.s.i. (ISBN 0-226-60073-4); pap. text ed. 4.50x o.s.i. (ISBN 0-226-60074-2). U of Chicago Pr.

Theories of Motivation. Bernard Weiner. 1972. text ed. 27.50 o.p. (ISBN 0-395-30768-6). HM.

Theories of Poverty & Underemployment. David M. Gordon. 1973. pap. text ed. 14.00 o.p. (ISBN 0-669-89268-8). Heath.

Theories of Revelation. H. D. McDonald. 1979. pap. 10.95 o.p. (ISBN 0-8010-6081-8). Baker Bk.

Theories of Social Change. Richard P. Appelbaum. LC 81-80801. 1970. pap. 14.50 o.p. (ISBN 0-395-30558-6). HM.

Theories of Trade Unionism: A Sociology of Industrial Relations. Michael Poole. 280p. 1981. 35.00x o.p. (ISBN 0-7100-0695-0). Routledge Chapman & Hall.

Theories of Trade Unionism: A Sociology of Industrial Relations. Michael Poole. 280p. 1984. pap. 14.95x o.p. (ISBN 0-7102-0020-X). Routledge Chapman & Hall.

Theories of Welfare. Anthony Forder et al. 256p. (Orig.). 1984. pap. 14.95x o.p. (ISBN 0-7100-9625-9). Routledge Chapman & Hall.

Theories on the Nature of Life. Giovanni Blandino. LC 66-24445. 1969. 6.95 o.p. (ISBN 0-8022-2251-X). Philos Lib.

Theory. Ed. by X. Chapuisat et al. (Topics in Current Chemistry Ser: Vol. 68). 1976. 34.00 o.p. (ISBN 0-387-07932-7). Springer-Verlag.

Theory & Application of Information Research: Proceedings of the Second International Research Forum of Information Science, 2nd Royal School Librarianship, Copenhagen, Aug. 1977. Ed. by Ole Harbo & Leif Kajberg. 272p. 1980. 37.00x o.p. (ISBN 0-7201-1513-2). Mansell.

Theory & Applications of Graphs: Proceedings, Michigan, May 11-15, 1976. Ed. by Y. Alavi & D. R. Lick. (Lecture Notes in Mathematics: Vol. 642). 1978. pap. 31.00 o.p. (ISBN 0-387-08666-8). Springer-Verlag.

Theory & Applications of Moment Methods in Many-Fermion Systems. Ed. by B. J. Dalton et al. LC 80-21054. 520p. 1980. 85.00x o.p. (ISBN 0-306-40463-X, Plenum Pr). Plenum Pub.

Theory & Applications of Variable Structure Systems with Emphasis on Modeling & Identification. R. R. Mohler & A. Ruberti. 1972. 51.00 o.p. (ISBN 0-12-504160-8). Acad Pr.

Theory & Design of Broadband Matching Networks. Chen Wai-Kai. 360p. 1976. 110.00 o.p. (ISBN 0-08-019702-7); pap. 110.00 o.p. (ISBN 0-08-019918-6). Pergamon.

Theory & Design of Cryogenic Systems. A. Arkharov. 430p. 1981. 11.60 o.p. (ISBN 0-8285-1974-9, Pub. by Mir Pubs USSR). Imported Pubns.

Theory & Design of Steel Structures. Giulio Ballio & Federico Mazzolani. 664p. 1983. 66.00x o.p. (ISBN 0-412-23660-5, NO. 6886, Pub. by Chapman & Hall England). Routledge Chapman & Hall.

Theory & Evidence. Clark Glymour. LC 79-3209. 352p. 1980. 44.50x o.p. (ISBN 0-691-07240-X); pap. 16.00x LPE o.p. (ISBN 0-691-10077-2). Princeton U Pr.

Theory & Experience of Economic Development: Essays in Honor of Sir W. Arthur Lewis. Ed. by Mark Gersovitz et al. 416p. 1982. text ed. 45.00x o.p. (ISBN 0-04-330323-4). Unwin Hyman.

Theory & Explanation in Archaeology: The Southampton Conference. Colin Renfrew et al. 1982. 29.95 o.p. (ISBN 0-12-586960-6). Acad Pr.

Theory & Management of Systems. 3rd ed. Richard A. Johnson et al. (Management Ser). (Illus.). 544p. 1973. text ed. 40.95 o.p. (ISBN 0-07-032634-7). McGraw.

Theory & Method in a Study of Argentine Fertility. A. V. Cicourel. LC 73-14985. 212p. 1974. lib. bdg. 17.50 o.p. (ISBN 0-471-15793-7). Krieger.

Theory & Method in Urban & Regional Analysis. P. W. Batey. (London Papers in Regional Science). 184p. 1978. pap. 16.00x o.p. (ISBN 0-85086-066-0, NO. 2928, Pub. by Pion England). Routledge Chapman & Hall.

Theory & Phenomenology in Particle Physics, 2 pts. Ed. by A. Zichichi. 1969. Pt. A. 85.00 o.p. (ISBN 0-12-780571-0); Pt. B. 97.00 o.p. (ISBN 0-12-780572-9); Set. 126.00 o.p. Acad Pr.

Theory & Practice: An Introduction to Philosophy. Gerald Runkle. 640p. 1985. text ed. 27.95 o.p. (ISBN 0-03-061757-X, HoltC). HR&W.

Theory & Practice in Affinity Techniques. Ed. by P. V. Sundaram & F. Eckstein. 1979. 87.50 o.p. (ISBN 0-12-677150-2). Acad Pr.

Theory & Practice in Education. R. F. Dearden. 192p. 1984. 19.95x o.p. (ISBN 0-7100-9910-X). Routledge Chapman & Hall.

Theory & Practice in Health Education. Helen S. Ross & Paul Mico. LC 80-82564. (Illus.). 338p. 1980. text ed. 23.95 o.p. (ISBN 0-87484-406-1). Mayfield Pub.

Theory & Practice in Regional Science. I. Masser. (London Papers in Regional Science). 166p. 1976. pap. 12.50x o.p. (ISBN 0-85086-051-2, NO. 2947, Pub. by Pion England). Routledge Chapman & Hall.

Theory & Practice of African Politics. Christian P. Potholm. (Illus.). 302p. 1985. pap. text ed. 15.50 o.p. (ISBN 0-8191-4734-6). U Pr of Amer.

Theory & Practice of Body Massage. Frank Nichols. 1979. 11.35 o.p. (ISBN 0-87350-088-1). Milady Pub.

Theory & Practice of Corporate Mergers, 2 vols. The Economic Conference. (Illus.). 336p. 1989. Set. 237.75 o.p. (ISBN 0-86654-285-X). Inst Econ Finan.

Theory & Practice of Counselling Psychology. Richard Nelson-Jones. 544p. 1984. pap. 22.50 o.p. (ISBN 0-275-91620-0, B1620). Praeger.

Theory & Practice of Histotechnology. 2nd ed. Denza C. Sheehan & Barbara B. Hrapchak. LC 80-11807. 462p. 1980. text ed. 46.95 o.p. (ISBN 0-8016-4573-5). Mosby.

Theory & Practice of Medicine. Hippocrates & Crosby Kelly. LC 64-13308. (Illus.). 384p. 1964. (ISBN 0-8022-0727-8). Philos Lib.

Theory & Practice of Proletarian Internationalism. M. S. Junusov et al. 307p. 1976. 5.45 o.p. (ISBN 0-8285-0413-X, Pub. by Progress Pubs USSR). Imported Pubns.

Theory & Practice of Propellers for Auxiliary Sailboats. John R. Stanton. LC 75-31778. (Illus.). 79p. 1975. pap. 4.00x o.p. (ISBN 0-87033-213-9). Cornell Maritime.

Theory & Practice of Robots & Manipulators, III: Proceedings of the 3rd Symposium. Ed. by A. Morecki & G. Bianchi. 596p. 1980. 155.25 o.p. (ISBN 0-444-99772-5). Elsevier.

Theory & Practice of Thermally Stimulated Luminescence & Related Phenomena: Proceedings of the National Symposium Held in Ahmedabad, India, 8-10 February 1984. Ed. by A. K. Singhvi et al. (Illus.). 250p. 1986. pap. 62.00 o.p. (ISBN 0-08-032618-8, Pub. by PPL). Pergamon.

Theory & Practice of Tone-Relations. Percy Goetschius. LC 72-109968. 187p. 1973. Repr. of 1931 ed. lib. bdg. 35.00x o.p. (ISBN 0-8371-6182-7, GOTR). Greenwood.

Theory & Practice of Transport. David Stewart-David. 1980. pap. 13.95 o.p. (ISBN 0-434-91864-4, Pub. by W Heinemann Ltd). David & Charles.

Theory & Practice of Vocational Guidance. B. Hopson & J. Hayes. 1969. 130.00 o.p. (ISBN 0-08-013284-7); pap. 130.00 o.p. (ISBN 0-08-013391-6). Pergamon.

Theory & Principles of Electrode Processes. B. E. Conway. LC 65-17090. 302p. 1965. 22.50 o.p. (JW). Krieger.

Theory & Problems of International Economics. Dominick Salvatore. (Schaum's Outline Ser). (Illus.). 224p. (Orig.). 1975. pap. 6.95 o.p. (ISBN 0-07-054496-4, SP). McGraw.

Theory & Research in Criminal Justice: Current Perspectives. Ed. by John A. Conley. 150p. 1979. softcover 5.00 o.p. (ISBN 0-87084-014-2). Anderson Pub Co.

Theory & Research in Marriage & the Family. S. T. Habel. 1970. pap. text ed. 8.95x o.p. (ISBN 0-8422-0037-1). Irvington.

Theory & Taste: Four Studies in Aesthetics. Teddy Brunius. 119p. (Orig.). 1969. pap. text ed. 15.95x o.p. (Pub. by Almqvist & Wiksell). Coronet Bks.

Theory & the Meaning of the Lines of the Hand with Special Emphasis on the Life & the Anticipation of One's Life Span. D. Saint Germain. (Illus.). 136p. 1983. 117.85 o.p. (ISBN 0-89901-124-1). Found Class Reprints.

Theory of Alloy Phase Formation: Proceedings of the AIME Annual Meeting, New Orleans, 1979. AIME Staff. Ed. by L. H. Bennett. (Illus.). 525p. 45.00 o.p.; members 30.00 o.p. (ISBN 0-317-34896-5); student members 16.00 o.p. (ISBN 0-317-34897-3). ASM.

Theory of Approximation: With Applications. Ed. by Alan G. Law & Badri N. Sahney. 1976. 69.50 o.p. (ISBN 0-12-438950-3). Acad Pr.

Theory of Auger Transitions. Dipankar Chattarji. 1976. 49.50 o.p. (ISBN 0-12-169850-5). Acad Pr.

Theory of Autodeism. Alberto C. Cernuschi. LC 69-15948. 1969. (ISBN 0-8022-2264-1). Philos Lib.

Theory of Automatic Control. Ed. by A. Netushil. 806p. 1978. 15.00 o.p. (ISBN 0-8285-0698-1, Pub. by Mir Pubs USSR). Imported Pubns.

Theory of Beauty. Harold Osborne. 228p. 1953. (ISBN 0-8022-1249-2). Philos Lib.

Theory of Bernouilli Shifts. Paul Shields. (Chicago Lectures in Mathematics Ser). 1973. pap. text ed. 6.00x o.s.i. (ISBN 0-226-75297-6). U of Chicago Pr.

Theory of Beta-Decay. C. Strachan. LC 72-86202. 1969. 29.00 o.p. (ISBN 0-08-006509-0); pap. 44.00 o.p. (ISBN 0-08-006508-2). Pergamon.

Theory of Bilinear Dynamical Systems: Proceedings of CISM, Department of Automation & Information, 1972. CISM (International Center for Mechanical Sciences), Department of Automation & Information Staff. Ed. by A. Isidori et al. (CISM Publications: No. 158). (Illus.). 69p. 1974. pap. 10.70 o.p. (ISBN 0-387-81206-7). Springer-Verlag.

Theory of Binocular Vision. Ewald Hering. LC 76-30836. (Illus.). 218p. 1977. 49.50x o.p. (ISBN 0-306-31016-3, Plenum Pr). Plenum Pub.

Theory of Business Enterprise. Thorstein Veblen. 420p. 1978. 29.95 o.p. (ISBN 0-87855-311-8); pap. 9.95 o.p. (ISBN 0-87855-699-0). Transaction Pubs.

Theory of Capitalist Regulation: The U. S. Experience. Michel Aglietta. 1979. 24.50 o.p. (ISBN 0-8052-7066-3, Pub. by Verso England). Schocken.

Theory of Cataloguing. P. J. Quigg. 88p. 1966. (ISBN 0-8022-2024-X). Philos Lib.

Theory of Celestial Influence: Man, The Universe, & Cosmic Mystery. Rodney Collin. LC 83-20286. (Illus.). 392p. (Orig.). 1984. pap. 10.95 o.p. (ISBN 0-87773-267-1, 72391-0). Shambhala Pubns.

Theory of Chemical Reaction Dynamics, Vol. 1. Ed. by Michael Baer. 248p. 1985. 137.50 o.p. (ISBN 0-8493-6114-1). CRC Pr.

Theory of Communism. George H. Hampsch. LC 64-21471. 262p. 1965. (ISBN 0-8022-0672-7). Philos Lib.

Theory of Complementation in English Syntax. Joan W. Bresnan. Ed. by Jorge Hankamer. LC 78-66551. (Outstanding Dissertations in Linguistics Ser.). 1985. 46.00 o.p. (ISBN 0-8240-9689-4). Garland Pub.

Theory of Complex Nuclei. V. G. Soloviev. 1976. 105.00 o.p. (ISBN 0-08-018053-1). Pergamon.

Theory of Computer Science: A Programming Approach. J. M. Brady. 1977. pap. 12.95 o.p. (ISBN 0-412-15040-9, NO. 6040, Pub. by Chapman & Hall). Routledge Chapman & Hall.

Theory of Couple-Stresses in Bodies with Constrained Rotations: Proceedings of CISM, Department for MEchanics of Deformable Bodies, 1970. CISM (International Center for Mechanical Sciences), Department for Mechanics of Deformable Bodies Staff. Ed. by M. Sokolowski. (CISM International Centre for Mechanical Sciences Ser.: No. 26). (Illus.). 143p. 1974. pap. 14.90 o.p. (ISBN 0-387-81143-5). Springer-Verlag.

Theory of Cross-Spaces. Robert Schatten. (Annals of Math Studies). 1950. pap. 13.00 o.p. (ISBN 0-527-02742-1). Kraus Repr.

Theory of Economic Growth. W. Arthur Lewis. 1955. pap. text ed. 17.95 o.p. (ISBN 0-04-330054-5). Unwin Hyman.

Theory of Economic Systems. David Conn. LC 80-8619. (Outstanding Dissertations in Economics Ser.). 1984. lib. bdg. 24.00 o.p. (ISBN 0-8240-4176-3). Garland Pub.

Theory of Elasticity with Microstructure for Directionally Reinforced Composites. J. D. Achenbach. (International Centre for Mechanical Sciences Courses & Lectures: No. 167). (Illus.). 1976. pap. 24.00 o.p. (ISBN 0-387-81234-2). Springer-Verlag.

Theory of Electrical Transport in Semi-Conductors. B. R. Nag. 238p. 1972. 70.00 o.p. (ISBN 0-08-016802-7). Pergamon.

Theory of Electromagnetic Field. K. Polivanov. 271p. 1983. 8.95 o.p. (ISBN 0-8285-2747-4, Pub. by Mir Pubs USSR). Imported Pubns.

Theory of Eternal Life. Rodney Collin. LC 83-20288. (Illus.). 132p. (Orig.). 1984. 5.95 o.s.i. (ISBN 0-87773-273-6, 72399-6). Shambhala Pubns.

Theory of Experiments in Paramagnetic Resonance. J. Talpe. LC 79-137411. 272p. 1971. 70.00 o.p. (ISBN 0-08-016157-X). Pergamon.

Theory of Financial Decisions. 2nd ed. Charles W. Haley & Lawrence D. Schall. (Illus.). 1979. text ed. 43.95 o.p. (ISBN 0-07-025568-7). McGraw.

Theory of Finitely Generated Commutative Semigroups. L. Redei. (International Series in Pure & Applied Mathematics: Vol. 82). (Illus.). 1966. text ed. 45.00 o.p. (ISBN 0-08-010520-3). Pergamon.

Theory of Flight. Richard Von Mises. 17.00 o.p. (ISBN 0-8446-2599-X). Peter Smith.

Theory of Fully Ionized Plasmas. Gunter Ecker. 1972. 99.50 o.p. (ISBN 0-12-229750-4). Acad Pr.

Theory of Groups & Its Application to Physical Problems. S. Bhagavantam & T. Venkatarayudu. 1969. 38.50 o.p. (ISBN 0-12-095460-5). Acad Pr.

Theory of Heat. 2nd. ed. R. Becker. Tr. by G. Leibfried. (Illus.). 1967. 44.00 o.p. (ISBN 0-387-03730-6). Springer-Verlag.

Theory of Helix Coil Transitions in Biopolymers. D. Poland & H. A. Scheraga. (Molecular Biology). 1970. 82.50 o.p. (ISBN 0-12-559550-6). Acad Pr.

Theory of Hopf Algebras Attached to Group Schemes. H. Yanagihara. (Lecture Notes in Mathematics: Vol. 614). 1977. pap. text ed. 22.00 o.p. (ISBN 0-387-08444-4). Springer-Verlag.

Theory of Idle Resources. W. H. Hutt. LC 76-26326. 1977. Repr. of 1975 ed. 8.95 o.p. (ISBN 0-913966-19-3, Liberty Clas). Liberty Fund.

Theory of Instruction: Principles & Applications. Siegfried Engelmann & Douglas Carnine. (Illus.). 385p. 1982. text ed. 49.50x o.p. (ISBN 0-8290-0977-9); pap. text ed. 29.95x o.p. (ISBN 0-8290-2040-3). Irvington.

Theory of Knowledge. D. W. Hamlyn. (Modern Introductions to Philosophy Ser.). 308p. 1980. pap. text ed. 15.00x o.p. (ISBN 0-333-11548-1). Humanities.

Theory of Knowledge of Giambattista Vico: On the Method of the New Science Concerning the Common Nature of the Nations. Richard Manson. xiii, 84p. 1969. 16.50 o.p. (ISBN 0-208-00899-3, Archon). Shoe String.

Theory of Lengthwise Rolling. A. I. Tselikov. 342p. 1981. 10.00 o.p. (ISBN 0-8285-2181-6, Pub. by Mir Pubs USSR). Imported Pubns.

Theory of Lie Superalgebras: An Introduction. M. S. Scheunert. (Lecture Notes in Mathematics Ser.: Vol. 716). 1979. pap. 19.00 o.p. (ISBN 0-387-09256-0). Springer-Verlag.

Theory of Linear Economic Models. David Gale. 1960. text ed. 41.50 o.p. (ISBN 0-07-022728-4). McGraw.

Theory of Linear Induction Motors. 2nd ed. Sakae Yamamura. LC 78-21550. 235p. 1979. 48.95x o.p. (ISBN 0-470-26583-3). Halsted Pr.

Theory of Linear Systems. J. E. Rubio. (Electrical Science Ser). 1971. 71.00 o.p. (ISBN 0-12-601650-X). Acad Pr.

Theory of Machines & Computations: International Symposium on the Theory of Machines & Computations. Ed. by Zvi Kohavi & Azaria Paz. 1971. 71.50 o.p. (ISBN 0-12-417750-6). Acad Pr.

Theory of Magnetically Confined Plasmas: Proceedings. Ed. by B. Coppi. (Commission of the European Communities Ser.: Eur 5737). (Illus.). 1979. pap. 145.00 o.p. (ISBN 0-08-023434-8). Pergamon.

Theory of Melody: A Complete General Presentation of the Practical Materials, Resources, & Phenomena. Paul R. Narveson. (Illus.). 380p. 1984. lib. bdg. 33.00 o.p. (ISBN 0-8191-3833-9); pap. text ed. 16.25 o.p. (ISBN 0-8191-3834-7). U Pr of Amer.

Theory of Meson Interactions with Nuclei. Judah M. Eisenberg & Daniel S. Koltun. LC 79-24653. 403p. 1980. 71.95x o.p. (ISBN 0-471-03915-2, Pub. by Wiley-Interscience). Wiley.

Theory of Metallurgical Processes. S. Filippov. 296p. 1975. 10.00 o.p. (ISBN 0-8285-2231-6, Pub. by Mir Pubs USSR). Imported Pubns.

Theory of Molecular Excitations. A. S. Davydov. LC 72-75767. 314p. 1971. 55.00x o.p. (ISBN 0-306-30440-6, Plenum Pr). Plenum Pub.

Theory of Morals. Edgar F. Carritt. LC 73-3021. 144p. 1974. Repr. of 1928 ed. lib. bdg. 22.50 o.p. (ISBN 0-8371-6827-9, CATM). Greenwood.

Theory of Natural Philosophy. Roger J. Boscovich. (Illus.). 1966. pap. 8.95x o.p. (ISBN 0-262-52003-6). MIT Pr.

Theory of Nuclear Magnetic Resonance. I. V. Aleksandrov. 1966. 49.50 o.p. (ISBN 0-12-049850-2). Acad Pr.

Theory of Numbers. Institute, Boulder, Colorado, 1959 Staff. 372p. 53.40 o.p. (ISBN 0-317-32979-0, OP43952); pap. 48.40 members o.p. (ISBN 0-317-32980-4). Am Math.

Theory of Objective Self Awareness. Shelley Duval & Robert A. Wicklund. (Social Psychology Ser). 1972. 42.00 o.p. (ISBN 0-12-225650-6). Acad Pr.

Theory of Optimal Experiments. V. V. Fedorov. (Probability & Mathematical Statistics Ser.). 1972. 67.00 o.p. (ISBN 0-12-250750-9). Acad Pr.

Theory of Oscillators. Alexander Andronov et al. (Illus.). 1966. 205.00 o.p. (ISBN 0-08-009981-5). Pergamon.

Theory of Particulate Processes. Alan D. Randolph & Maurice A. Larson. 1971. 68.00 o.p. (ISBN 0-12-579650-1). Acad Pr.

Theory of Planetary Atmospheres: An Introduction to Their Physics & Chemistry. Joseph W. Chamberlain. (International Geophysics Ser.). 1978. 35.00 o.p. (ISBN 0-12-167250-6). Acad Pr.

Theory of Plasma Instabilities, 2 vols. A. B. Mikhailovskii. Incl. Vol. 1. Instabilities of a Homogeneous Plasma. 308p. 1974 (ISBN 0-306-17181-3, Consultants); Vol. 2. Instabilities of an Inhomogeneous Plasma. 332p. 1974 (ISBN 0-306-17182-1, Consultants). LC 73-83899. (Studies in Soviet Science - Physical Sciences Ser.). 1974. 59.50x ea. o.p. (Consultants). Plenum Pub.

Theory of Possibility: A Constructivistic & Conceptualistic Account of Possible Individuals & Possible Worlds. Nicholas Rescher. LC 75-10540. 1975. 25.95x o.p. (ISBN 0-8229-1122-1). U of Pittsburgh Pr.

Theory of Practical Reason. Arthur E. Murphy. Ed. by A. I. Melden. LC 64-20840. (Paul Carus Lecture Ser.). 458p. 1965. 13.95 o.p. (ISBN 0-87548-110-8). Open Court.

Theory of Probability: An Inquiry into the Logical & Mathematical Foundations of the Calculus of Probability. Hans Reichenbach. (California Library Reprint Series: No. 23). 1971. Repr. of 1949 ed. 42.50x o.p. (ISBN 0-520-01929-6). U of Cal Pr.

Theory of Programming Language Semantics, 2 vols. R. Milne & C. Strachey. 1976. Set. 88.00x o.p. (ISBN 0-412-14260-0, NO. 6320, Pub. by Chapman & Hall). Routledge Chapman & Hall.

Theory of Psychological Scaling. Clyde H. Coombs. LC 75-41413. (Illus.). 94p. 1976. Repr. of 1951 ed. lib. bdg. 22.50x o.p. (ISBN 0-8371-8646-3, COPS). Greenwood.

Theory of Quantum Fluids. E. Feenberg. (Pure & Applied Physics Ser.: Vol. 31). 1969. 69.50 o.p. (ISBN 0-12-250850-5). Acad Pr.

Theory of Random Functions. V. S. Pugachev. 1965. 51.00 o.p. (ISBN 0-08-010421-5). Pergamon.

Theory of Relativity. 2nd ed. R. K. Pathria. 1974. 70.00 o.p. (ISBN 0-08-018032-9); pap. text ed. 80.00 o.p. (ISBN 0-08-018995-4). Pergamon.

Theory of Semiconductor Junction Devices. J. H. Leck. 1967. text ed. 7.70 o.p. (ISBN 0-08-012173-X). Pergamon.

Theory of Simple Liquids. J. P. Hansen & I. R. McDonald. 1977. 75.00 o.p. (ISBN 0-12-323850-1). Acad Pr.

Theory of Social Choice. Peter C. Fishburn. LC 72-1985. (Illus.). 300p. 1973. 30.50x o.p. (ISBN 0-691-08121-2). Princeton U Pr.

Theory of Stochastic Processes I. I. I. Gihman & A. V. Skorohod. (Grundlehren der Mathematischen Wissenschaften: Vol. 210). 570p. 1980. 71.00 o.p. (ISBN 0-387-06573-3). Springer-Verlag.

Theory of Stochastic Processes II. L. I. Gihman & A. V. Skorohod. (Die Grunglehren der Mathematischen Wissenschaften Ser.: Vol. 218). 441p. 1983. 68.00 o.p. (ISBN 0-387-07247-0). Springer-Verlag.

Theory of Superconductivity. Max Von Laue. 1952. 44.00 o.p. (ISBN 0-12-726556-2). Acad Pr.

Theory of Supercritical Wing Sections, with Computer Programs & Examples. F. Bauer et al. LC 72-79583. (Lecture Notes in Economics & Mathematical Systems: Vol. 66). (Illus.). 216p. 1972. pap. 9.00 o.p. (ISBN 0-387-05807-9). Springer-Verlag.

Theory of Symbolic Transformations: A Humanistic Scientific Psychology. Louis Carini. LC 83-1049. (Illus.). 176p. (Orig.). 1983. lib. bdg. 27.50 o.p. (ISBN 0-8191-3053-2); pap. text ed. 12.25 o.p. (ISBN 0-8191-3054-0). U Pr of Amer.

Theory of the Earth's Gravity Field. M. Pick et al. 538p. 1973. 147.50 o.p. (ISBN 0-444-40939-4). Elsevier.

Theory of the Innate Ideas & Their Correlation with the Eternity of the Being. School of Philosophy Editorial Committee. 79p. 1986. 37.50 o.p. (ISBN 0-89266-566-1). Am Classical Coll Pr.

Theory Workbook for Practice & Science of Standard Barbering. Milady Editors. (Illus.). 1984. 12.95 o.p. (ISBN 0-318-22643-X). Milady Pub.

Theosophy Simplified. new ed. Irving S. Cooper. LC 78-64905. 1979. pap. 3.25 o.s.i. (ISBN 0-8356-0519-1, Quest). Theos Pub Hse.

Therapeutic Activities Programming with the Elderly. 1978. 15.00 o.s.i. (ISBN 0-938846-11-6). Ebenezer Ctr.

Therapeutic Communication. Jurgen Ruesch. 496p. 1973. pap. 5.95 o.p. (ISBN 0-393-00672-7). Norton.

Therapeutic Community. Elly Jansen. 400p. 1980. pap. 11.50 o.p. (ISBN 0-7099-0359-6, Pub. by Croom Helm Ltd). Routledge Chapman & Hall.

Therapeutic Drug Monitoring. Ed. by B. Widdop. (Contemporary Issues in Clinical Biochemistry Ser.). (Illus.). 359p. 1985. text ed. 89.00 o.p. (ISBN 0-443-02686-6). Churchill.

Therapeutic Electricity & Ultraviolet Radiation. 2nd ed. Ed. by Sidney Licht. LC 67-14433. 434p. 1967. 28.50 o.p. (ISBN 0-686-65365-3, Pub. by Williams & Wilkins). Krieger.

Therapeutic Plasma Exchange. Ed. by H. J. Gurland et al. (Illus.). 250p. 1981. pap. 22.90 o.p. (ISBN 0-387-10590-5). Springer-Verlag.

Therapeutic Systems: Pattern-Specific Drug Delivery: Concept & Development. Klaus Heilmann. (Illus.). 156p. 1978. pap. text ed. 20.00 o.p. (ISBN 0-88416-285-0). Year Bk Med.

Therapeutic Value of Yoga. Himalayan International Institute Staff. 108p. (Orig.). pap. 3.95 o.p. (ISBN 0-89389-054-5). Himalayan Pubs.

Therapeutics. 3rd ed. J. G. Lewis. LC 77-79678. (Illus.). 304p. 1977. pap. 16.00 o.p. (ISBN 0-88416-207-9). Year Bk Med.

Therapies for Psychosomatic Disorders in Children. Charles E. Schaefer et al. LC 79-88111. (Social & Behavioral Science Ser.). 1979. text ed. 28.95x o.p. (ISBN 0-87589-417-8). Jossey-Bass.

Therapies, Myths & Cosmic Powers. Cyril A. Brathwaite. 1985. 6.95 o.p. (ISBN 0-533-06522-4). Vantage.

Therapy Made Fun! Set 2. Linda Newton. 1982. text ed. 18.95x o.p. (ISBN 0-8134-2232-9). Inter Print Pubs.

Therapy Under Analysis. Ed. by Allen Hammond. 52p. 1986. pap. 2.25 o.p. AAAS.

Theravada Meditation: The Buddhist Transformation of Yoga. Winston L. King. LC 79-25856. 192p. 1980. 22.75x o.s.i. (ISBN 0-271-00254-9). Pa St U Pr.

There & Back Again. Harold Jones. LC 77-3474. (Illus.). 32p. (ps-3). 1977. 5.95 o.p. (ISBN 0-689-50095-5, Atheneum). Macmillan.

There Goes My Aching Back. John Burak. LC 74-21437. 1975. 8.50 o.p. (ISBN 0-682-48134-3, Banner). Exposition-Phoenix.

There is a Better Way to Manage. Hugh A. McLean. 336p. 1982. 19.95 o.p. (ISBN 0-8144-5713-4). AMACOM.

There Is a Bull on My Balcony. Sesyle Joslin & Katharina Barry. LC 66-11202. (Illus.). (gr. 1-6). 1966. 5.95 o.p. (ISBN 0-15-285057-0, HJ). HarBraceJ.

There Is a Dragon in My Bed. Sesyle Joslin & Irene Haas. LC 61-6118. (Illus.). (gr. k-3). 1961. 5.95 o.p. (ISBN 0-15-285146-1, HJ). HarBraceJ.

There Is a Fountain: The Autobiography of a Civil Rights Lawyer. Conrad Lynn. LC 78-19854. 256p. 1979. 12.00 o.p. (ISBN 0-88208-098-9). Chicago Review.

There is Music in the Street. F. R. Parkinson. (ISBN 0-8022-1266-2). Philos Lib.

There Is No Balm in Birmingham. Ann Deagon. LC 75-41623. (Third Godine Poetry Chapbook Ser.). 1978. 5.00 o.s.i. (ISBN 0-87923-177-7). Godine.

There Is No Happiness Without a Feeling. Edward J. Smith. 119p. 1984. 20.00 o.p. (ISBN 0-682-40130-7). Exposition-Phoenix.

There Is No Rhyme for Silver. Eve Merriam. (Illus.). (gr. 2-6). 1962. PLB 3.07 o.p. (ISBN 0-689-20272-5, Atheneum). Macmillan.

There Is Still Love. Malachi Martin. 208p. 1985. pap. 2.95 o.s.i. (ISBN 0-345-30406-3). Ballantine.

There May Be Heaven. Elisabeth Ogilvie. 1976. pap. 1.50 o.p. (ISBN 0-380-00640-5, 27557). Avon.

There Must Be a Lone Ranger: The American West in Film & in Reality. Jenni Calder. LC 74-20216. (Illus.). 256p. 1975. 8.95 o.s.i. (ISBN 0-8008-7636-9). Taplinger.

There Must Be a Lone Ranger: The American West in Myth & Reality. Jenni Calder. (McGraw-Hill Paperbacks). 1977. pap. text ed. 3.95 o.p. (ISBN 0-07-009607-4). McGraw.

There Must Be a Pony. James Kirkwood. 1976. pap. 2.75 o.p. (ISBN 0-380-00689-8, 56317-7). Avon.

There Never Was a Better Brother. M. Ibragimbekov. 414p. 1982. pap. 4.00 o.p. (ISBN 0-8285-2425-4, Pub. by Progress Pubs USSR). Imported Pubns.

There Ought to Be a Law: How Laws Are Made & Work. Ellen Switzer. (Illus.). (gr. 5 up). 1972. 6.95 o.p. (ISBN 0-689-30068-9, Atheneum). Macmillan.

There Really Is Sound. (Leisure Reading Ser.). 56p. 1979. 1.50 o.p. (ISBN 0-88336-701-7). New Readers.

There She Blows: A Narrative of a Whaling Voyage, in the Indian & South Atlantic Oceans. Ben-Ezra S. Ely. Ed. by Curtis Dahl. LC 76-142726. (American Maritime Library: Vol. 3). (Illus.). xxxiii, 208p. 1971. 10.00 o.p. (ISBN 0-8195-4032-3); ltd. ed. 15.00 o.p. (ISBN 0-8195-4033-1). Mystic Seaport.

There Was a Little Girl. Eileen Dewhurst. LC 85-13177. (Crime Club Ser.). 192p. 1986. 12.95 o.p. (ISBN 0-385-23230-6). Doubleday.

There Were Giants in those Days. Gerald Eskenazi. 1987. pap. 9.95 o.p. (ISBN 0-13-914680-6). P-H.

There's a Crocodile under My Bed. I. Schubert & D. Schubert. 1981. text ed. 9.95 o.p. (ISBN 0-07-055614-8). McGraw.

There's a Job for You In: Advertising, Commercial Art, Fashion, Films, Public Relations & Publicity, Publishing, Television & Radio, Travel & Tourism. Leonard Corwen. LC 83-8349. (Illus.). 192p. (Orig.). 1983. pap. 9.95 o.p. (ISBN 0-8329-0273-X). New Century.

There's a Monster Eating My House. Art Cumings. LC 80-25378. (Illus.). 48p. (ps-3). 1981. 5.95 o.s.i. (ISBN 0-8193-1053-0); PLB 5.95 o.p. (ISBN 0-8193-1054-9). Parents.

There's a Party at Mona's Tonight. Harry Allard. (Snuggle & Read Story Bks.). (Illus.). 32p. (ps-3). 1985. pap. 2.50 o.p. (ISBN 0-380-69920-6, Camelot). Avon.

There's a Skunk in My Trunk. Donald W. Kruse. Ed. by May Davenport. Bd. with Spotty the Goat. Robert W. Walker; Christopher C. Cat. Edith Cutting; Night Dancers. Jan Pendleton. LC 81-71555. 58p. (Orig.). (gr. 3-5). 1984. pap. 3.50x o.p. (ISBN 0-943864-32-1). Davenport.

There's Always Another Windmill. Ogden Nash. LC 68-25903. (Illus.). 1968. 6.95 o.p. (ISBN 0-316-59839-9). Little.

There's Always Been a Women's Movement This Century. Dale Spender. (Illus.). 200p. (Orig.). 1983. pap. 5.95 o.p. (ISBN 0-86358-002-5, Pandora Pr). Routledge Chapman & Hall.

There's Fifty Thousand Dollars on My Head. William R. Geraway. 1976. 7.50 o.p. (ISBN 0-682-48465-2). Exposition-Phoenix.

There's Nothing That I Wouldn't Do If You Would Be My POSSLQ. Charles Osgood. LC 81-47460. 204p. 1981. 10.95 o.s.i. (ISBN 0-03-057667-9). H Holt & Co.

There's Nothing to Do, So Let Me Be You. large type ed. Jean H. Berg. (Illus.). (gr. k-3). 1966. 5.50 o.s.i. (ISBN 0-664-32366-9, Westminster). Westminster John Knox.

There's the Sea. Eben M. Anderson. LC 84-90214. (Illus.). 61p. 1985. 6.95 o.p. (ISBN 0-533-06265-9). Vantage.

Therese. Gerard Manley Hopkins. Tr. by Francois Mauriac from Fr. 383p. 1951. pap. 8.95 o.p. (ISBN 0-374-50333-8). FS&G.

Therese Desqueyroux. Francois Mauriac. Ed. by Jean Collignon. (Fr). 1963. pap. text ed. write for info. o.p. (ISBN 0-02-377480-0). Macmillan.

Thermal Accommodation & Adsorption Coefficients of Gases, Vol. II-1. 1st ed. Y. S. Touloukian & C. Y. Ho. (McGraw-Hill-CINDAS Data Ser. on Material Properties). 448p. (Orig.). 1981. text ed. 59.95 o.p. (ISBN 0-07-065031-4). McGraw.

Thermal Analysis, 2 Vols. Robert F. Schwenker, Jr. & Paul Garn. 1969. Vol. 1. 80.00 o.p. (ISBN 0-12-633201-0); Vol. 2. 80.00 o.p. (ISBN 0-12-633202-9); Set. 130.00 o.p. Acad Pr.

Thermal Analysis. Vol. I: Theory Instrumentation-Applied Sciences Industrial-Applications. Hans G. Wiedemann. 628p. 1980. 99.95x o.p. (ISBN 0-8176-1085-5). Birkhauser.

Thermal Behaviour of Textiles. K. Slater. 147p. 1976. 70.00x o.p. (ISBN 0-686-63807-7). State Mutual Bk.

Thermal Computation for Electrical Equipment. Gordon N. Ellison. 1984. 44.95 o.p. (ISBN 0-442-21923-7). Van Nos Reinhold.

Thermal Conductivity, 2 Vols. Ed. by R. P. Tye. 1969. Vol. 1. 67.00 o.p. (ISBN 0-12-705401-4); Vol. 2. 90.00 o.p. (ISBN 0-12-705402-2). Acad Pr.

Thermal Conductivity of Solids. J. E. Parrott & Audrey D. Stuckes. 1975. 17.95x o.p. (ISBN 0-85086-047-4, NO. 2942, Pub. by Pion England). Routledge Chapman & Hall.

Thermal Degradation of Cellulose. (Bibliographic Ser.: No. S45). 55p. 1969. 8.00 o.p. (ISBN 0-317-34461-7). Inst Paper Chem.

Thermal Design Principles of Spacecraft & Entry Bodies. Ed. by Jerry T. Bevans. (Progress in Astronautics & Aeronautics Ser.: Vol. 21). 1969. 28.00 o.p. (ISBN 0-12-535121-6). Acad Pr.

Thermal Design Principles, PAAS21. Ed. by Jerry T. Bevans. LC 64-103. (Illus.). 855p. 1969. 79.50 o.p. (ISBN 0-317-36814-1). AIAA.

Thermal Energy Storage. Ed. by E. G. Kovach. LC 77-71233. 1977. pap. 14.75 o.p. (ISBN 0-08-021724-9). Pergamon.

Thermal Energy Storage & Regeneration. Frank W. Schmidt & A. John Willmott. (Illus.). 352p. 1981. text ed. 56.50 o.p. (ISBN 0-07-055346-7). McGraw.

Thermal Expansion of Crystals. R. S. Krishnan et al. LC 77-30620. (International Ser. in the Science of the Solid State: Vol. 12). 1980. 63.00 o.p. (ISBN 0-08-021405-3). Pergamon.

Thermal-Hydraulics in Nuclear Power Technology. Ed. by K. H. Sun et al. (HTD Ser.: Vol. 15). 86p. 1981. 16.00 o.p. (ISBN 0-686-34492-8, G00204). ASME.

Thermal Insulation. S. D. Probert & D. R. Hub. (Illus.). 121p. 1968. 34.25 o.p. (ISBN 0-444-20025-8, Pub. by Elsevier Applied Sci England). Elsevier.

Thermal Insulation Handbook. William C. Turner & John F. Malloy. 624p. 1981. text ed. 79.00 o.p. (ISBN 0-07-039805-4). McGraw.

Thermal Neutron Scattering. Ed. by P. A. Egelstaff. 1966. 89.00 o.p. (ISBN 0-12-232950-3). Acad Pr.

Thermal Radiation Heat Transfer. 2nd ed. Robert Siegel & John R. Howell. LC 79-17242. (Thermal & Fluids Engineering Hemisphere Ser.). (Illus.). 928p. 1981. text ed. 50.95 o.p. (ISBN 0-07-057316-6); write for info. o.p. (ISBN 0-07-057317-4). McGraw.

Thermal Reactor Safety International Ans-ENS Topical Marketing: Proceedings in San Diego, CA February 2-6, 1986. 1604p. Date not set. 125.00 o.p. (ISBN 0-89448-121-5, 700106). Am Nuclear Soc.

Thermal Stress Analysis. D. J. Johns. 1965. text ed. 17.25 o.p. (ISBN 0-08-011153-X); pap. text ed. 7.75 o.p. (ISBN 0-08-011152-1). Pergamon.

Thermal Stresses in Severe Environments. Ed. by D. P. Hasselman & R. A. Heller. LC 80-17767. 750p. 1980. 105.00x o.p. (ISBN 0-306-40544-X, Plenum Pr). Plenum Pub.

Thermally Stimulated Processes in Solids - New Prospects: Proceedings of an International Workshop, Montpellier, June, 1976. Ed. by J. P. Fillard & J. Van Turnhout. 302p. 1977. 100.00 o.p. (ISBN 0-444-41652-8). Elsevier.

Thermobiology. Ed. by Anthony H. Rose. 1967. 118.50 o.p. (ISBN 0-12-596450-1). Acad Pr.

Thermochemical Properties of Inorganic Substances. I. Barin & O. Knacke. LC 72-95058. (Illus.). 980p. 1973. 129.80 o.p. (ISBN 0-387-06053-7, 0-387-06053-7). Springer-Verlag.

Thermochemical Properties of Inorganic Substances: Supplement. I. Barin et al. (Illus.). 1977. 116.90 o.p. (ISBN 0-387-08031-7). Springer-Verlag.

Thermodynamic Databases: Selected Papers from the First CODATA Symposium on Chemical Thermodynamic & Thermophysical Properties Databases, Paris, France, September 1985. Ed. by CODATA Staff. (CODATA Bulletin Ser.). 1986. pap. 15.00 o.p. (ISBN 0-08-032487-8, Pub. by PPL). Pergamon.

Thermodynamic Diagrams for High Temperature Plasmas of Air-Carbon, Carbon-Hydrogen Mixtures & Argon. H. Kroepelin et al. 1971. 75.00 o.p. (ISBN 0-08-017581-3). Pergamon.

Thermodynamic Effects in Wave Propogation. CISM (International Center for Mechanical Sciences), Department for Mechanics of Rigid Bodies Staff. Ed. by P. Chen. (CISM Publications: No. 72). 33p. 1973. pap. 7.70 o.p. (ISBN 0-387-81176-1). Springer-Verlag.

Thermodynamic Properties & Reduced Correlations for Gases. Lawrence Canjar & Francis Manning. LC 66-30022. 222p. 1967. 21.95x o.p. (ISBN 0-87201-867-9); pap. text ed. 15.00x abridged student o.p. (ISBN 0-87201-868-7). Gulf Pub.

Thermodynamic Properties of Organic Compounds. rev. ed. George J. Janz. (Physical Chemistry Ser.: Vol. 6). 1967. 77.00 o.p. (ISBN 0-12-380451-5). Acad Pr.

Thermodynamic Properties of Selected Metal Sulfates & Their Hydrates. Carroll W. Dekock. LC 86-600060. (Mines Bureau Information Circular Ser.: No. 9081). 61p. 1986. pap. 3.25 o.p. (ISBN 0-318-21640-X, S/N 024-004-02168-3). USGPO.

Thermodynamic Theory of Domain Structures. I. Privorotskii. 129p. 1975. text ed. 39.50 o.p. (ISBN 0-7065-1520-X, Pub. by Keter Pub Jerusalem). Coronet Bks.

Thermodynamics & Electrode Processes in Solid State Electronics see Physics of Electrolytes.

Thermodynamics for Engineers. Jesse S. Doolittle & Francis J. Hale. LC 82-7052. 588p. 1983. text ed. 45.95 o.p. (ISBN 0-471-05805-X, Pub. by Wiley Press). Wiley.

Thermodynamics for Engineers, SI Version. Jesse S. Doolittle & Francis J. Hale. LC 83-10316. 582p. 1983. 38.25 o.p. (ISBN 0-471-87384-5). Wiley.

Thermodynamics in Contemporary Dynamics. CISM (International Center for Mechanical Sciences), Department of Mechanics of Solids Staff. Ed. by P. Glansdorff. (CISM Publications: No. 74). (Illus.). 120p. 1973. pap. 14.80 o.p. (ISBN 0-387-81177-X). Springer-Verlag.

Thermodynamics of Electrical Phenomena in Metals & a Condensed Collection of Thermodynamic Formulas. P. W. Bridgman. (Illus.). 12.00 o.p. (ISBN 0-8446-1737-7). Peter Smith.

Thermodynamics of Materials with Memory. CISM (International Center for Mechanical Sciences), Department of Mechanics of Solids Staff. Ed. by B. D. Coleman. (CISM Publications: No. 73). iii, 47p. 1973. pap. 8.90 o.p. (ISBN 0-387-81125-7). Springer Verlag.

Thermodynamics of Minerals & Melts, Vol. 1. Ed. by R. C. Newton et al. (Advances in Physical Geochemistry Ser.). (Illus.). 272p. 1981. 46.00 o.p. (ISBN 0-387-90530-8). Springer-Verlag.

Thermodynamics of One-Component Systems. William N. Lacey & Bruce H. Sage. 1957. 75.50 o.p. (ISBN 0-12-432550-5). Acad Pr.

Thermodynamics of the Polymerization of Protein. Fumio Oosawa & Sho Asakura. 1976. 54.50 o.p. (ISBN 0-12-527050-X). Acad Pr.

Thermodynamics of the Stepwise Formation of Metal-Ion Complexes in Aqueous Solution see Coordinative Interactions.

Thermodynamics Problem Solver. Research & Education Association Staff. LC 84-61810. (Illus.). 992p. 1988. pap. text ed. 28.85 o.p. (ISBN 0-87891-555-9). Res & Educ.

Thermography: A New Way to Profit from the Energy Crisis. Richard H. Munis. 1976. 5.00 o.p. (ISBN 0-682-48462-8). Exposition-Phoenix.

Thermohydraulics of Two-Phase Systems for Industrial Design & Nuclear Engineering. J. M. Delhaye et al. LC 80-14312. (Hemisphere Series in Thermal & Fluids Engineering). (Illus.). 544p. 1981. text ed. 62.95 o.p. (ISBN 0-07-016268-9). McGraw.

Thermomagnetic Effects in Semiconductors. I. M. Tsidil'Kovskii. Ed. by H. J. Goldsmid et al. Tr. by A. Tybulewicz. 1963. 68.50 o.p. (ISBN 0-12-701850-6). Acad Pr.

Thermomechanical Processing of Aluminum Alloys: Proceedings of the TMS-AIME Fall Meeting, St. Louis, 1978. TMS Staff & AIME Staff. Ed. by James G. Morris. (Illus.). 233p. 28.00 o.p. (ISBN 0-89520-354-5); members 18.00 o.p. (ISBN 0-317-34898-1); student members 10.00 o.p. (ISBN 0-317-34899-X). ASM.

Thermomechanical Processing of Aluminum Alloys. Ed. by James G. Morris. 233p. 1978. (Reproduction on Demand - UMI) 28.00 o.p. (ISBN 0-89520-354-5). Minerals Metals.

Thermomechanical Processing of Microalloyed Austenite: Proceedings. Pittsburgh, 1981. A. J. DeArdo & G. A. Ratz. (Illus.). 680p. 45.00 o.p. (ISBN 0-89520-398-7); members 30.00 o.p. (ISBN 0-317-36286-0); student members 15.00 o.p. (ISBN 0-317-36287-9). ASM.

Thermomechanics. J. C. Gibbings. 1970. text ed. 23.00 o.p. (ISBN 0-08-006334-9); pap. 9.75 o.p. (ISBN 0-08-006333-0). Pergamon.

Thermomechanics of Magnetic Fluids: Theory & Applications Proceedings of the International Advanced Course & Workshop on Thermomechanics of Magnetic Fluids, Udine, Italy, Oct. 3-7, 1977. new ed. International Advanced Course & Workshop on Thermomechanics of Magnetic Fluids Participants. Ed. by Boris Berkovsky. LC 78-15126. 318p. 1978. text ed. 95.00 o.p. (ISBN 0-89116-143-0). Hemisphere Pub.

Thermometer Calibration: A Model for State Calibration Laboratories. Jacqueline A. Wise & Robert J. Soulen, Jr. (NBS Monograph Ser.: No. 174). (Illus.). 94p. 1986. pap. 3.50 o.p. (ISBN 0-318-19908-4, S/N 003-003-02707-3). USGPO.

Thermometric Titrimetry. L. S. Bark & S. M. Bark. 1968. 35.00 o.p. (ISBN 0-08-013047-X). Pergamon.

Thermomicroscopy in the Analysis of Pharmaceuticals. M. Kuhnert-Brandstatter. 424p. 1971. 105.00 o.p. (ISBN 0-08-006990-8). Pergamon.

Thermophysical Properties of Fluids: Proceedings of the Symposium, 8th, 2 Vols, Vol. 1. Thermophysical Properties Symposium Staff. 1981. 65.00 o.p. (I00151). ASME.

Thermophysical Properties of Some Key Solids: Heat Capacity, Thermal Expansion, Electrical Resistivity, Thermal Conductivity & Absolute Thermopower. Ed. by CODATA Staff. (CODATA Bulletin). (Illus.). 52p. 1986. pap. 15.00 o.p. (ISBN 0-08-032488-6, Pub. by PPL). Pergamon.

Thermophysics & Temperature Control of Spacecraft & Entry Vehicles, PAAS18. Ed. by Gerhard B. Heller. LC 66-26844. (Illus.). 865p. (J). 1966. 79.50 o.p. (ISBN 0-317-36818-4). AIAA.

Thermophysics: Applications to Thermal Design of Spacecraft, PAAS23. Ed. by Jerry T. Bevans. LC 64-103. (Illus.). 580p. 1970. 49.50 o.p. (ISBN 0-317-36810-9). AIAA.

Thermoregulation. Ed. by E. Satinoff. LC 79-10267. (Benchmark Papers in Behavior: Vol. 13). 400p. 1982. 59.95 o.p. (ISBN 0-87933-349-9). Van Nos Reinhold.

Thermosense I: Proceedings. Intro. by Thomas M. Lillesand. 244p. 1978. pap. 10.00 o.p. (ISBN 0-937294-13-6). ASP & RS.

Thermosense II: Proceedings. Pref. by Stanley A. Morain. 264p. 1979. pap. 14.00 o.p. (ISBN 0-937294-17-9). ASP & RS.

Thermosense II: Proceedings, American Society of Photogrammetry, November 1979. (Illus.). 264p. 13.00 o.p. (ISBN 0-318-13362-8). ASP & RS.

Thesaurus of Computing Terms. 8th ed. Ed. by National Computing Centre, Ltd. Staff. 1977. pap. 82.50x o.s.i. (ISBN 0-85012-169-8). Intl Pubns Serv.

Thesaurus of Hebrew Oriental Melodies, 10 vols. in 4. Abraham Z. Idelsohn. 150.00x o.p. Ktav.

Thesaurus of Psychological Index Terms. 4th ed. Lois Granick. 263p. (Orig.). 1985. pap. 45.00 o.p. (ISBN 0-912704-68-3, 3100040). Am Psychol.

Thesaurus of Scales & Melodic Patterns. Nicolas Slonimsky. 1947. 49.50 o.s.i. (ISBN 0-684-10551-9, ScribT). Scribner.

Thesaurus Philosophicus Linguae Hebraica, 4 pts. in 2 vols. Klatzkin. (Hebrew.). 50.00x o.s.i. (ISBN 0-87306-118-7). Feldheim.

These & Those. Simon Schwab. 3.50 o.p. (ISBN 0-87306-076-8). Feldheim.

These Beautiful Hills: A Natural History of the U. S. Air Force Academy. Thomas N. James. (Illus.). 56p. (Orig.). 1972. pap. 2.00 o.p. (ISBN 0-910584-30-3). Filter.

These Green-Going-to-Yellow. Marvin Bell. LC 81-66013. 1981. 10.95 o.p. (ISBN 0-689-11228-9, Atheneum); pap. 6.95 o.p. (ISBN 0-689-11227-0). Macmillan.

These Holy Sparks: The Rebirth of the Jewish People. Arthur I. Waskow. LC 83-47737. 256p. 1982. 11.49i o.p. (ISBN 0-06-069263-4). HarpR.

These Men She Gave: Civil War Diary of Athens, Georgia. John F. Stegeman. LC 64-14674. (Illus.). 188p. 1964. 14.00 o.p. (ISBN 0-8203-0179-5). U of Ga Pr.

These Modern Women: Autobiographical Essays from the Twenties. Ed. by Elaine Showalter. 160p. (Orig.). 1989. pap. 8.95 o.p. (ISBN 0-912670-46-0). Feminist Pr.

These Primal Years. John Bowen. 213p. 1981. 10.00 o.p. (ISBN 0-682-49719-3). Exposition-Phoenix.

These Special Ones. Lillia Dean. 1977. 4.50 o.p. (ISBN 0-682-48896-8). Exposition-Phoenix.

These Strange Ashes. Elisabeth Elliot. LC 84-47435. 144p. 1985. pap. text ed. 6.68 o.p. (ISBN 0-06-062229-6). HarpR.

These We Honor. (Illus.). 50p. Date not set. pap. 7.95 o.p. Aviation.

Thessalonians, Titus, Vol. X. Beacon Bible ExpositionsStaff. 6.95 o.p. (ISBN 0-8010-0743-7). Baker Bk.

Theta Functions of Riemann Surfaces. J. D. Fay. (Lecture Notes in Mathematics: Vol. 352). 137p. 1973. pap. 10.00 o.p. (ISBN 0-387-06517-2). Springer-Verlag.

They Blew Our Weather. Frederick Clare. (Illus.). 192p. 1982. 20.00 o.p. (ISBN 0-682-49824-6). Exposition-Phoenix.

They Built Clipper Ships in Their Back Yard. Admont G. Clark. 32p. 1963. pap. 1.95 o.p. (ISBN 0-940160-00-5). Parnassus Imprints.

They Call Me Boober Fraggle. Illus. by Lisa McCue. (Fraggle Rock Bks.). (Illus.). 48p. (gr. 1-4). 1983. 6.95 o.s.i. (ISBN 0-03-068677-6). H Holt & Co.

They Came to Praise I. C. C. Englebert D. Schnotzelhorst. 74.98 o.p. (ISBN 0-317-58499-5). Schirmer Bks.

They Came to Stay: North Americans in the U. S. S. R. Paula Garb. 195p. 1987. 7.95 o.p. (ISBN 0-8285-3579-5, Pub. by Progress Pubs USSR). Imported Pubns.

They Chose Minnesota: A Survey of the State's Ethnic Groups. Ed. by June D. Holmquist. (Illus.). 614p. 1981. 45.00 o.p. (ISBN 0-87351-155-7). Minn Hist.

They Do Things Right in Albern. Jurg Obrist. LC 78-6598. (Illus.). (ps-3). 1978. 6.95 o.p. (ISBN 0-689-30671-7, Atheneum). Macmillan.

They Found Their Voice. Ed. by E. Imbovitz. 256p. 1977. 3.95 o.p. (ISBN 0-8285-0985-9, Pub. by Progress Pubs USSR). Imported Pubns.

They Gave Us Shakespeare: John Heminge & Henry Condell. Charles Connell. (Illus.). 110p. 1982. 15.95x o.p. (ISBN 0-85362-193-4, Oriel). Routledge Chapman & Hall.

They Have to Be Carefully Taught. 161p. 1981. 8.10x o.p. (ISBN 0-88314-191-4). AAHPERD.

They Never Came Home. Lois Duncan. 192p. 1979. pap. 2.50 o.p. (ISBN 0-380-50229-1, 60045-5, Flare). Avon.

They of Rome. Lois Parker. 128p. 1980. pap. 6.95 o.p. (ISBN 0-8127-0308-1). Review & Herald.

They Paved the Way: A History of N. H. Women. Olive Tardiff. (Illus.). vi, 98p. (Orig.). (gr. 9-12). 1980. pap. text ed. 3.95 o.p. (ISBN 0-917890-22-1). Heritage Bk.

They Shoot Canoes, Don't They? Patrick F. McManus. (Large Print Bks.). 323p. 1988. lib. bdg. 17.95x o.s.i. (ISBN 0-8161-4390-0, Large Print Bks). G K Hall.

They Shoot to Slay. Leonard Gribble. (Lythway Ser.). 232p. 1988. lib. bdg. 18.50x o.p. (ISBN 0-7451-0674-9, Pub. by Chivers Pr UK). G K Hall.

They Tell a Story. Martha Lupton. LC 74-167052. vi, 560p. 1972. Repr. of 1940 ed. 43.00x o.p. (ISBN 0-8103-3112-8). Gale.

They Think Again: Restoring Cognitive Abilities Through Teaching. Carl Frankenstein. 320p. 1981. pap. 18.95 o.p. (ISBN 0-442-22549-0). Van Nos Reinhold.

They, Too, Were Flesh & Blood. Evelyn Stough. 80p. 1987. 6.75 o.p. (ISBN 0-8062-2812-1). Carlton.

They Were Dreamers: A Saga of the Irish in North America. James F. Murphy, Jr. LC 81-69138. 1983. 14.95 o.p. (ISBN 0-689-11250-5, Atheneum). Macmillan.

They Were Expendable. William L. White. LC 42-36303. 1966. pap. 0.50 o.p. (ISBN 0-15-689496-3, HPL11, Harv). HarBraceJ.

They Were There. R. Andersen & R. Barlag. 1977. pap. 1.75 o.p. (ISBN 0-570-03769-7, 12-2704). Concordia.

They Were Women Like Me. P-H.

They Who Would Be Free: The Blacks' Search for Freedom. Jane Pease & William H. Pease. LC 74-77620. (Studies in American Negro Life). 1974. pap. text ed. 4.95x o.p. (ISBN 0-689-70517-4, NL33, Atheneum). Macmillan.

They Wrote on Clay: The Babylonian Tablets Speak Today. Edward Chiera. Ed. by George G. Cameron. LC 38-27631. (Illus.). 1938. lib. bdg. 11.00x o.s.i. (ISBN 0-226-10424-9). U of Chicago Pr.

They're Playing Our Song. Max Wilk. LC 72-94250. 1973. 10.00 o.p. (ISBN 0-689-10554-1, Athenuem). Macmillan.

They've Killed Anna. Nathan Hollander. (Harker File Ser.: No. 3). 160p. (Orig.). 1989. pap. text ed. 3.50 o.p. (ISBN 1-55802-198-1). Lynx Bks.

Thick Plate Working, Vol. 1. (Engineering Craftsmen: No. D1). (Illus.). 1969. spiral bdg. 37.50x o.p. (ISBN 0-85083-025-7). Trans-Atl Phila.

Thick Plate Working, Vol. 2. Ed. by J. M. Rowney et al. (Engineering Craftsmen: No. D21). (Illus.). 1969. spiral bdg. 37.50x o.p. Trans-Atl Phila.

Thicker Than Water. Richard Dorso. LC 79-3357. 288p. 1980. 10.95 o.p. (ISBN 0-15-189586-4). HarBraceJ.

Thicket. Patricia Gallagher. 1977. pap. 1.25 o.p. (ISBN 0-380-01578-1, 33316-3). Avon.

Thidwick, the Big-Hearted Moose. Dr. Seuss. LC 48-8129. (Dr. Seuss Paperback Classics Ser.). (Illus.). 48p. (gr. k-3). 1980. pap. 3.95 o.s.i. (ISBN 0-394-84540-4, XBYR). Random.

Thief of Hearts. Jan Mathews. (Second Chance at Love Ser.: No. 273). 192p. 1985. pap. 2.25 o.s.i. (ISBN 0-425-08204-0). Berkley Pub.

Thief Who Hugged a Moonbeam. Harold Berson. LC 70-190382. (Illus.). 40p. (ps-3). 1979. 7.95 o.p. (ISBN 0-395-28767-7, Clarion). HM.

Thief's Journal. Jean Genet. Tr. by Bernard Frechtman from Fr. LC 64-24077. 1982. pap. 9.95 o.p. (ISBN 0-394-62437-8, E837, Ever). Grove.

Thieves. Thomas A. Norton. 259p. 1983. pap. 3.50 o.p. (ISBN 0-8423-6966-X). Tyndale.

Thieves' Kitchen: The Regency Underworld. Donald A. Low. (Illus.). 208p. 1982. 17.95x o.p. (ISBN 0-460-04438-9, Pub. by J M Dent England). Biblio Dist.

Thieves Like Us. Edward Anderson. 1974. pap. 1.25 o.p. (ISBN 0-380-01579-X, 18416). Avon.

Thieves Like Us. Edward Anderson. 1987. pap. 5.95 o.p. (ISBN 0-87795-842-4). Morrow.

Thin Air. William Marshall. LC 77-20786. 1978. 6.95 o.p. (ISBN 0-03-021071-2). H Holt & Co.

Thin Game: Dieting Scams & Dieting Sense. Edwin Bayrd. 1979. pap. 2.25 o.p. (ISBN 0-380-47142-6). Avon.

Thin Ice. E. M. Rees. (Going for It Ser.: No. 6). 1986. pap. 2.50 o.p. (ISBN 0-380-89904-3, Flare). Avon.

Thin Men of Haddam. C. W. Smith. 1980. pap. 1.50 o.p. (ISBN 0-380-00422-4, 24943). Avon.

Thin Plate Working, Vol. 1. 2nd ed. Ed. by H. Dickson et al. (Illus.). 1977. 37.50x o.p. (ISBN 0-686-65561-3) (ISBN 0-85083-387-6). Trans-Atl Phila.

Thin Plate Working, Vol. 2. Ed. by H. Dickson et al. (Engineering Craftsmen: No. D22). (Illus.). 1969. spiral bdg. 37.50x o.p. Trans-Atl Phila.

Thin Red Line. James Jones. 1975. pap. 1.95 o.p. (ISBN 0-380-00309-0, 41095). Avon.

Thin Red Line. James Jones. 1985. pap. 5.95 o.s.i. (ISBN 0-440-38876-7, LE). Dell.

Thin Seam Coal Mining Technology. J. Clark et al. LC 82-7968. (Energy Tech. Rev. 80). (Illus.). 385p. 1983. 36.00 o.p. (ISBN 0-8155-0909-X). Noyes.

Thin Shells: Computing & Theory. J. E. Gibson. (International Series in Structure & Solid Body Mechanics). (Illus.). 1980. 63.00 o.p. (ISBN 0-08-023275-2); pap. 22.00 o.p. (ISBN 0-08-024204-9). Pergamon.

Thine Forever. Ed. by A. G. Suechting. LC 75-6245. 1950. pap. 3.75 o.p. (ISBN 0-8066-1491-9, 10-6386, Augsburg). Augsburg Fortress.

Thine Is the Glory. Samuel A. Schreiner, Jr. LC 74-18163. 1975. 8.95 o.p. (ISBN 0-87795-101-2, Arbor Hse). Morrow.

Thing. J. J. Madison. 1978. pap. 1.50 o.p. (ISBN 0-505-51235-1, Pub. by Tower Bks). Dorchester Pub Co.

Thing of Beauty: Art Nouveau, Art Deco, Arts & Crafts Movement, & Aesthetic Movement Objects in Atlanta Collections. Roy Frangiamore & James Grady. Ed. by Kelly Morris. (Illus.). 91p. 1980. pap. 10.50 o.p. (ISBN 0-939802-04-X). High Mus Art.

Thing You Love Most. Wade G. Harding. 192p. 1987. 11.95 o.p. (ISBN 0-8062-3084-3). Carlton.

Things Divine & Supernatural Conceived by Analogy with Things Natural & Human. Peter Browne. Ed. by Rene Wellek. LC 75-11203. (British Philosophers & Theologians of the 17th & 18th Centuries: Vol. 9). 1976. Repr. of 1733 ed. lib. bdg. 51.00 o.p. (ISBN 0-8240-1758-7). Garland Pub.

Things Fall Apart. Simplified ed. Chinua Achebe. Ed. by John Dabey. (Guided Readers Ser.). (Orig.). 1981. pap. text ed. 2.00x o.p. (ISBN 0-435-27010-9). Heinemann Ed.

Things I Did... & Things I Think I Did. Jean Negulesco. 305p. 1984. 18.45 o.p. (ISBN 0-671-50734-6, Linden Pr). S&S.

Things in the Driver's Seat. Harry R. Huebel. 1972. pap. 15.50 o.p. (ISBN 0-395-30633-7). HM.

Things Not Generally Known. John Timbs. Ed. by David A. Wells. LC 68-30584. 432p. 1968. Repr. of 1857 ed. 48.00x o.p. (ISBN 0-8103-3101-2). Gale.

Things of the Spirit: Pope John Paul II. Pope John Paul II. Ed. by Kathryn Spink. LC 82-47793. 96p. 1982. 7.64i o.p. (ISBN 0-06-064185-1). HarpR.

Things That Go. Illus. by Tadasu Izawa. (My First Puppet Picture Bks.). (Illus.). 48p. (ps-1). 1984. 4.95 o.p. (ISBN 0-448-09776-1, G&D). Putnam Pub Group.

Things That Go: A First-Look-It-Up Book. (Learning Curves Bks.). (Illus.). 12p. (ps-1). 1987. pap. 5.95 o.p. (ISBN 0-553-18358-3). Bantam.

Things That Go Bump in the Flight: A Reassuring Guide to Air Travel. Robert Welch. LC 87-1418. (Illus.). 156p. (Orig.). 1987. pap. 5.95 o.p. (ISBN 0-932620-75-2). Betterway Pubns.

Things That Go Bump in the Night, & Other Fears. Bob Donahue & Marilyn Donahue. (YA) (gr. 7 up). 1983. pap. 3.95 o.p. (ISBN 0-8423-7083-8). Tyndale.

Things That Make for Peace: A Personal Search for a New Way of Life. John Schramm & Mary Schramm. LC 76-3861. 96p. (Orig.). 1976. pap. 5.95 o.p. (ISBN 0-8066-1537-0, 110-6400, Augsburg). Augsburg Fortress.

Things Themselves: Essays & Scenes. Reynolds Price. LC 79-190398. (Illus.). 288p. 1972. 8.95 o.p. (ISBN 0-689-10505-3, Atheneum). Macmillan.

Things to Make & Do for Christmas. Ellen Weiss. (Things to Make & Do Bks.). (gr. k-3). 1980. PLB 10.90 o.p. (ISBN 0-531-02293-5, C02); pap. 3.95 o.p. (ISBN 0-531-02145-9). Watts.

Things to Make & Do for Halloween. Gail Gibbons. LC 75-19396. (Things to Make & Do Ser.). (Illus.). 48p. (gr. k-2). 1976. PLB 10.90 o.p. (ISBN 0-531-01103-8). Watts.

Things to Make & Do for Thanksgiving. (Things to Make & Do Ser.). (gr. 1-3). 1977. lib. bdg. 10.90 o.p. (ISBN 0-531-01324-3). Watts.

Things to Make & Do for Valentine's Day. Tomie De Paola. (Things to Make & Do Ser.). (Illus.). 48p. (gr. k-3). 1976. PLB 10.90 o.p. (ISBN 0-531-01187-9). Watts.

Things We Know: Fourteen Essays on Problems of Knowledge. Frank B. Ebersole. LC 68-63599. 1968. 7.50 o.p. (ISBN 0-87114-016-0). U of Oreg Bks.

Things Won't Be the Same. Kathryn Ewing. LC 80-7982. (gr. 4-6). 1980. 8.95 o.p. (ISBN 0-15-285663-3, HJ). HarBraceJ.

Thingumajig Book of Do's & Don'ts. Irene Keller. (Illus.). 32p. (Orig.). (gr. k-6). 1983. 3.95 o.p. (ISBN 0-8249-8050-6). Ideals.

Thingumajig Book of Health & Safety. 32p. (gr. k-6). 1982. pap. 3.95 o.p. (ISBN 0-8249-8031-X). Ideals.

Thingumajig Book of Manners. Irene Keller. (Illus.). 32p. (gr. k-6). 1981. 3.95 o.p. (ISBN 0-8249-8010-7). Ideals.

Think about It Series, 3 bks. 1981. Set. 19.95 o.p. (IP29-1). Incentive Pubns.

Think Fast, Mr. Moto. John P. Marquand. LC 85-7044. 1986. pap. 3.95 o.p. (ISBN 0-316-54703-4). Little.

Think First, Read Later! Piagetian Prerequisites for Reading. T. Gary Waller. Ed. by Frank B. Murray. (Ira Series on the Development of the Reading Process Ser.). 1978. pap. text ed. 3.00 o.p. (ISBN 0-87207-522-2). Intl Reading.

Think Good Thoughts about a Pussycat. George Booth. (Illus.). 1976. pap. 5.95 o.p. (ISBN 0-380-00762-2, 60582-1). Avon.

Think It Through. George Howard. 48p. (Orig.). 1984. pap. 2.95 o.p. (ISBN 0-89109-163-7). NavPress.

Think Persian. 2nd ed. John Kollock. LC 83-51800. (Illus.). 96p. 1985. pap. 4.95 o.p. (ISBN 0-931948-71-1). Peachtree Pubs.

Think Thin Today. Timoux Thomas. 1983. pap. 3.95 o.p. (ISBN 0-938936-08-5). Daring Bks.

Think Twice Before You Accept That Job. Richard J. Thain. 150p. 1986. pap. 15.00 o.p. (ISBN 0-87094-898-9). Dow Jones-Irwin.

Thinkers of the Twentieth Century: A Biographical, Bibliographical & Critical Dictionary. Ed. by Elizabeth Devine et al. 643p. 1984. 75.00 o.p. (ISBN 0-8103-1516-5). Gale.

Thinking about Art. Lucie-Smith. 1985. 11.95 o.p. Riverrun NY.

Thinking about Faith: An Introductory Guide to Philosophy & Religion. David Cook. 1986. pap. 9.95 o.p. (ISBN 0-310-44131-5, 18401P). Zondervan.

Thinking about Public Policy: A Problem Solving Approach. M. J. Dubnick & B A. Bardes. LC 82-21782. 283p. 1983. pap. 14.00 o.p. (ISBN 0-02-330660-2). Macmillan.

Thinking about Religion. Max Schoen. (ISBN 0-8022-1505-X). Philos Lib.

Thinking about Retirement. John Wallis. LC 72-652. 120p. 1975. text ed. 21.00 o.p. (ISBN 0-08-018269-0); pap. text ed. 8.75 o.p. (ISBN 0-08-018268-2). Pergamon.

Thinking about the Unthinkable in the 1980's. Herman Kahn. LC 84-1432. 229p. 1984. 16.45 o.s.i. (ISBN 0-671-47544-4). S&S.

Thinking about TLC LOGO. 2nd ed. John R. Allen et al. 236p. 1984. pap. 17.45 o.p. (ISBN 0-03-064116-0). HR&W.

Thinking & Language. Judith Greene. (Essential Psychology Ser.). 1975. pap. 4.95x o.p. (ISBN 0-416-81880-3, NO. 2736). Routledge Chapman & Hall.

Titles

Thinking & Perceiving. John W. Yolton. LC 61-11288. 175p. 1962. pap. 4.95 o.p. (ISBN 0-87548-067-5). Open Court.

Thinking Big: The Education of a Gambler. Sol Fox. LC 84-45620. 320p. 1985. 15.95 o.s.i. (ISBN 0-689-11551-2, Atheneum). Macmillan.

Thinking: Directed, Undirected & Creative. K. J. Gilhooly. 1982. 33.00 o.p. (ISBN 0-12-283480-1); pap. 18.00 o.p. (ISBN 0-12-283482-8). Acad Pr.

Thinking in Sentences: A Guide to Clear Writing. Nancy M. Cavender & Leonard A. Weiss. LC 81-82572. 1981. pap. 19.56 o.p. (ISBN 0-395-31690-1); instr's. manual 1.16 o.p. (ISBN 0-395-31691-X). HM.

Thinking in Writing. 2nd ed. Donald McQuade & Robert Atwan. 544p. 1982. pap. text ed. 13.00 o.p. (ISBN 0-394-32819-1, KnopfC). Knopf.

Thinking Investor's Guide to the Stock Market. Kiril Sokoloff. (Illus.). 1978. text ed. 25.95 o.p. (ISBN 0-07-059615-8). McGraw.

Thinking Is Child's Play. Evelyn Sharp. 1982. pap. 1.75 o.p. (ISBN 0-380-01580-3, 41103, Discus). Avon.

Thinking on Paper. Priscilla B. Adams. 120p. 1985. pap. text ed. 3.95 o.p. (ISBN 0-88334-185-9). Ind Sch Pr.

Thinking Physics Is Gedanken Physics. 2nd, enl. ed. Lewis C. Epstein. (Illus.). 600p. 1983. 14.95x o.p. (ISBN 0-935218-04-1). Insight Pr CA.

Thinking Skills: Research & Practice. Barbara Z. Presseisen. 32p. 1986. 2.50 o.p. (ISBN 0-8106-0688-7). NEA.

Thinking Thursdays: Language Arts in the Reading Lab. Ed. by Donna M. Cleary. 1978. pap. text ed. 8.25 o.p. (ISBN 0-87207-223-1). Intl Reading.

Thinking Tools. Curtis Miles & Jane Rauton. Ed. by Doree Pitkin. (Illus.). 358p. 1985. pap. text ed. 18.95x o.p. (ISBN 0-943202-24-8). H & H Pub.

Thinking with the Teachable Machine. John H. Andreae. 1978. 47.50 o.p. (ISBN 0-12-060050-1). Acad Pr.

Thinking Woman's Beauty Book. Jennifer Anderson. 1979. pap. 4.95 o.p. (ISBN 0-380-46375-X). Avon.

Thinner. Richard Bachman. 440p. 1986. 16.95 o.p. (ISBN 0-8161-4020-0, Large Print Bks); pap. 9.95 o.p. (ISBN 0-8161-4021-9, Large Print Bks). G K Hall.

Third Annual Educational Conference on Prepaid Legal Services: November Nineteen Eighty-Three. 800p. 1983. 55.00 o.p. (ISBN 0-317-40260-9, 3-014). Am Prepaid.

Third Arab-Israeli War. Edgar O'Ballance. LC 72-1059. 288p. 1972. 25.00 o.p. (ISBN 0-208-01292-3, Archon). Shoe String.

Third Arm. Ed. by Kenneth Royce. 300p. 1980. text ed. 9.95 o.p. (ISBN 0-07-054169-8). McGraw.

Third Assessment of Science, 1976-1977: Released Exercise Set. National Assessment of Educational Progress Staff. (Exercises or Items). 337p. 1978. 20.65 o.p. (ISBN 0-318-14003-9, ED-161-686, Natl Assessment Ed Progress); technical appendix 2.75 o.p. (ISBN 0-318-14004-7). Ed Comm States.

Third Betrayal. Michael Hartland. 208p. 1987. 16.95 o.p. (ISBN 0-02-548610-1). Macmillan.

Third Blonde: A Novel of Suspense. M. S. Craig. 196p. 1985. 14.95 o.p. (ISBN 0-396-08418-4). Dodd.

Third Book about Achim. Uwe Johnson. LC 67-12273. (Helen & Kurt Wolff Bk.). 1967. 5.75 o.p. (ISBN 0-15-189901-0). HarBraceJ.

Third Book of Criticism. Randall Jarrell. 334p. 1969. 7.50 o.p. (ISBN 0-374-27504-1). FS&G.

Third Book of Individual Open Salts Illustrated. Allan B. Smith & Helen B. Smith. (Illus.). 1976. pap. 7.50 o.p. (ISBN 0-940554-06-2). Country Hse.

Third Breeders' Cup: Annual Supplement. The Blood Horse Staff. (Illus.). 115p. 1986. pap. 6.00 o.p. (ISBN 0-939049-03-1). Blood Horse.

Third Certification of Changes to Schedules to the General Agreement on Tariffs & Trade. (Rectifications and Modifications of Schedules Ser.). 1974. pap. 15.00 o.p. (G25, GATT). UNIPUB.

Third Certification Relating to Rectifications & Modifications of Schedules. General Agreement on Tariffs & Trade Staff. (Orig., Eng. & Fr.). 1967. pap. 14.00 o.p. (ISBN 0-685-11724-3, G45, GATT). UNIPUB.

Third City: Philosophy at War with Positivism. Borna Bebek. 352p. 1983. 29.95x o.p. (ISBN 0-7100-9042-0). Routledge Chapman & Hall.

Third Congress of Lao People's Revolutionary Party. 117p. 1985. pap. 2.95 o.p. (Pub. by Progress Pubs USSR). Imported Pubns.

Third Eastern Regional Ground Water Conference, 1986: Proceedings. LC 86-23602. 1986. 43.75 o.p. (ISBN 0-318-23036-4). Natl Water Well.

Third Experiment: Is There Life on Mars? David E. Fisher. LC 84-21548. 192p. (gr. 7 up). 1985. 12.95 o.s.i. (ISBN 0-689-31080-3, Atheneum Childrens Bks). Macmillan.

Third Flight of the Starfire. Edwin Mumford. 1972. 4.00 o.p. (ISBN 0-682-47503-3). Exposition-Phoenix.

Third Force in Canada: The Cooperative Commonwealth Federation,1932-1948. Dean E. McHenry. LC 76-2061. 351p. 1976. Repr. of 1950 ed. lib. bdg. 25.00x o.p. (ISBN 0-8371-8767-2, MCTF). Greenwood.

Third from the Sun. Guy De Marco. 265p. 1981. 10.00 o.p. (ISBN 0-682-49670-7, Banner). Exposition-Phoenix.

Third Gift. Jan Carew. (Illus.). 32p. (gr. k-3). 1974. 12.45i o.p. (ISBN 0-316-12847-3). Little.

Third Globe: Symposium for the Reconstruction of the Globe Playhouse, Wayne State University. Reconstruction of the Globe Playhouse Symposium Staff. Ed. by C. Walter Hodges et al. LC 81-3362. (Illus.). 268p. 1981. 25.00x o.p. (ISBN 0-8143-1680-8). Wayne St. U Pr.

Third Helpings. Calvin Trillin. LC 82-19517. 192p. 1983. 12.95 o.p. (ISBN 0-89919-173-8). Ticknor & Fields.

Third Industrial Age: Strategy for Business Survival. Charles Tavel. LC 79-40199. (Illus.). 356p. 1980. 85.00 o.p. (ISBN 0-08-022506-3). Pergamon.

Third International Conference on Occupant Protection. Incl. 420p. 1974. 30.00 (ISBN 0-89883-029-X, P-53); members 25.00 (ISBN 0-317-37268-8); 344p. 1966. 8.00 (ISBN 0-89883-012-5, P-12); 488p. 1967. 10.00 (P-20); 462p. 35.00 (ISBN 0-89883-018-4, P-28); 835p. 1971. 35.00 (ISBN 0-89883-025-7, P-39). Soc Auto Engineers.

Third International Congress of Atomic Absorption & Atomic Fluorescence Spectrometry: Proceedings. Ed. by Maurice Pinta. LC 73-3959. 923p. 1973. 64.95x o.p. (ISBN 0-470-68995-1). Halsted Pr.

Third Jewish Catalog: Creating Community. Ed. by Sharon Strassfeld & Michael Strassfeld. LC 80-19818. (Illus.). 416p. 1980. 9.95 o.s.i. (ISBN 0-8276-0183-2, 466). JPS Phila.

Third Life of Grange Copeland. Alice Walker. LC 79-117577. 1970. 7.95 o.p. (ISBN 0-15-189905-3). HarBraceJ.

Third Life of Grange Copeland. Alice Walker. LC 77-3427. 247p. 1977. pap. 4.95 o.p. (ISBN 0-15-689960-4, Harv). HarBraceJ.

Third Line Medicine: Modern Treatment for Persistent Systems. Melvyn R. Werbach. 232p. 1986. pap. 8.95 o.p. (ISBN 1-85063-041-0, 30410). Routledge Chapman & Hall.

Third Math Helper. Eva Pollack. (Math Tutorial Program Ser.). 64p. (gr. k-2). 1975. 3.95 o.p. (ISBN 0-87594-142-7). Book-Lab.

Third Mind. William S. Burroughs. (Illus.). 194p. 1982. pap. 7.95 o.p. (ISBN 0-8050-0184-0). Seaver Bks.

Third National Symposium on Aquifer Restoration & Ground: Proceedings. 1983. 43.75 o.p. (ISBN 0-318-23017-8). Natl Water Well.

Third or Eighteen-Twenty Land Lotteries of Georgia. Silas E. Lucas, Jr. (Seven Land Lotteries of Georgia & Other Land Records Ser.). 412p. 1984. Repr. of 1973 ed. 35.00 o.p. (ISBN 0-89308-021-7, GA 26). Southern Hist Pr.

Third Pagoda & Other Legends of China. J. Frank Bucher. 176p. 1984. 9.00 o.p. (ISBN 0-682-40129-3, Banner). Exposition-Phoenix.

Third Part of the Countess of Pembroke's Yvychurch see Golden Booke of the Leaden Gods.

Third Party Maintenance of PCs. International Resource Development, Inc. Staff. 169p. 1984. 1650.00x o.p. (ISBN 0-88694-588-7). Intl Res Dev.

Third Person. Lehman Strauss. 1954. 7.95 o.s.i. (ISBN 0-87213-827-5). Loizeaux.

Third Person Rural: Further Essays of a Sometime Farmer. large print ed. Noel Perrin. LC 84-135. 240p. 1984. Repr. of 1983 ed. 13.95 o.p. (ISBN 0-89621-527-X). Thorndike Pr.

Third Planet. Paul D. Lowman, Jr. LC 77-128348. (Illus.). 170p. 1972. 45.00x o.p. (ISBN 0-8139-0577-X). U Pr of Va.

Third Reich at War: A Historical Bibliography. LC 83-27168. (ABC-Clio Research Guides Ser.: No. 11). 270p. 1984. lib. bdg. 34.00 o.p. (ISBN 0-87436-393-4). ABC-Clio.

Third Reich, 1933-39: A Historical Bibliography. LC 83-21527. (Research Guides: No. 10). 239p. 1984. lib. bdg. 34.00 o.p. (ISBN 0-87436-379-9). ABC-Clio.

Third Soviet Generation. M. Davidow. 221p. 1983. 6.95 o.p. (ISBN 0-8285-2685-0, Pub. by Progress Pubs USSR). Imported Pubns.

Third Testament of the Holy Bible. S. Joseph Iannarelli. 1985. 5.95 o.p. (ISBN 0-533-06645-X). Vantage.

Third World: Africa. 2nd ed. David Wiley & Marylee Crofts. LC 84-93315. (Illus.). 176p. 1984. pap. text ed. 6.95 o.p. (ISBN 0-87967-500-4). Dushkin Pub.

Third World Countries & Development Options: Zambia. Jonathan H. Chileshe. 220p. 1986. text ed. 30.00x o.p. (ISBN 0-7069-2873-3, Pub. by Vikas India). Advent NY.

Third World in Perspective. H. A. Reitsma & J. M. Kleinpenning. (Illus.). 444p. 1986. pap. 22.95x o.s.i. (ISBN 0-8476-7481-9, Rowman & Allanheld). Rowman.

Third-World Poverty: New Strategies for Measuring Development Progress. Ed. by William P. McGreevey. LC 78-75318. (Human Affairs Research Center Ser.). 240p. 1980. 29.00x o.p. (ISBN 0-669-02839-8). Lexington Bks.

Third World: Premises of U. S. Policy. 2nd rev. ed. Ed. by W. Scott Thompson. LC 83-8426. 319p. 1983. text ed. 22.95 o.p. (ISBN 0-917616-58-8); pap. text ed. 8.95 o.p. (ISBN 0-917616-57-X). ICS Pr.

Third World Resource Directories. Compiled by Thomas P. Fenton & Mary J. Heffron. 160p. Date not set. pap. 119.40 o.p. (ISBN 0-88344-647-2). Orbis Bks.

Third World Tomorrow: A Report from the Battlefront in the War Against Poverty. Paul Harrison. LC 82-19095. 416p. (Orig.). 1983. pap. 7.95 o.p. (ISBN 0-8298-0646-6). Pilgrim NY.

Third World, Vol. 2 (incl. 1983-1986 Supplements) Ed. by Eleanor C. Goldstein. (Social Issues Resources Ser.). 1987. 75.00 o.p. (ISBN 0-89777-063-3). Soc Issues.

Third World War. Harry Welton. 336p. 1949. (ISBN 0-8022-1849-0). Philos Lib.

Third Year of the Nixon Watch. John Osborne. (Illus.). 1972. 6.95 o.p. (ISBN 0-87140-551-2). Liveright.

Thirteen Alabama Ghosts & Jeffrey. Kathryn T. Windham & Margaret G. Figh. LC 71-94443. 1969. 8.95 o.p. (ISBN 0-87397-008-X). Strode.

Thirteen Clues for Miss Marple. Agatha Christie. 1983. pap. 2.95 o.p. (ISBN 0-440-18755-9). Dell.

Thirteen Danish Tales. Mary C. Hatch. LC 49-10046. (Illus.). (gr. 3-6). 1947. 4.50 o.p. (ISBN 0-15-285683-8, HJ). HarBraceJ.

Thirteen Georgia Ghosts & Jeffrey. Kathryn T. Windham. LC 73-87004. 1973. 8.95 o.p. (ISBN 0-87397-041-1). Strode.

Thirteen Horrors of Halloween. Ed. by Carol-Lynn R. Waugh & Martin H. Greenberg. 176p. 1983. pap. 2.95 o.p. (ISBN 0-380-84814-7, 84814). Avon.

Thirteen Mississippi Ghosts & Jeffrey. Kathryn T. Windham. LC 74-15509. 1974. 8.95 o.p. (ISBN 0-87397-047-0). Strode.

Thirteen Pragmatisms, & Other Essays. Arthur O. Lovejoy. LC 83-12578. xi, 290p. 1983. Repr. of 1963 ed. lib. bdg. 41.50x o.p. (ISBN 0-313-24125-2, LOTH). Greenwood.

Thirteen Thirty-Nine or So: Being an Apology for a Pedlar. Nicholas Seare. LC 75-11732. (Illus.). 184p. 1975. 7.95 o.p. (ISBN 0-15-189935-5). HarBraceJ.

Thirteenth International Conference on Defects in Semiconductors. Ed. by L. C. Kimerling & J. M. Parsey, Jr. LC 85-62228. (Illus.). 1252p. 1985. 10.00 o.p. (ISBN 0-89520-485-1). Minerals Metals.

Thirteenth Party Congress & China's Reform. (Illus.). 113p. (Orig.). 1987. pap. 3.95 o.p. (ISBN 0-8351-1835-5). China Bks.

Thirties: From Notebooks & Diaries of the Period. Edmund Wilson. Ed. by Leon Edel. LC 79-28700. 800p. 1980. 17.50 o.p. (ISBN 0-374-27572-6). FS&G.

Thirtieth Institute for City & County Attorneys. 343p. 1983. 12.50 o.p. (ISBN 0-318-02417-9). ICLE Georgia.

Thirty Computer Programs for the Homeowner, in BASIC. David Chance. (Illus.). 364p. 1982. pap. 16.95 o.p. (ISBN 0-8306-0050-7, 1380). TAB Bks.

Thirty Customized Microprocessor Projects. Delton T. Horn. (Illus.). 322p. 1986. 22.95 o.p. (ISBN 0-8306-0705-6); pap. 14.60 o.p. (ISBN 0-8306-2705-7, NO. 2705). TAB Bks.

Thirty-Day Experiment in Prayer. Robert Wood. LC 78-65160. 1978. pap. 3.75 o.p. (ISBN 0-8358-0380-5). Upper Room.

Thirty Days Are Not Enough: More Images for Meditative Journaling. Robert Wood. 112p. (Orig.). 1983. pap. 3.75 o.p. (ISBN 0-8358-0445-3). Upper Room.

Thirty Days Hath July. Alice Brennan. (Orig.). 1975. pap. 0.95 o.p. (ISBN 0-380-00379-1, 25247). Avon.

Thirty Days to More Powerful Writing. Jonathan Price. 192p. (Orig.). 1981. pap. 6.95 o.s.i. (ISBN 0-449-90047-9, Columbine). Fawcett.

Thirty Days to More Powerful Writing. Jonathan Price. 1984. pap. 6.95 o.s.i. (ISBN 0-449-90137-8, Columbine). Fawcett.

Thirty Degrees North, One Sixty Fifth East. Paul J. Stam. 1978. pap. 1.75 o.p. (ISBN 0-380-01965-5, 38489). Avon.

Thirty-Five Amazing Games for Your Commodore 128. John Mihalik. LC 85-81856. 112p. pap. 9.95 o.p. (ISBN 0-89586-398-7). Price Stern.

Thirty Five-Cent Thrills, Vol. 1. Joyce Thompson. LC 78-62952. (Lynx House Press Fiction Ser.). 1978. pap. 6.00 o.p. (ISBN 0-89924-014-3). Lynx Hse.

Thirty Five Hiking Trails, Columbia River Gorge. 2nd ed. Don Lowe & Roberta Lowe. Ed. by Oral Bullard. (Illus.). 80p. (Orig.). 1988. pap. 7.95 o.p. (ISBN 0-911518-77-0). Touchstone Oregon.

Thirty-Five Millimeter Photographer's Handbook. rev. updated ed. Julian Calder et al. 1983. pap. 11.95 o.p. (ISBN 0-517-55124-1). Crown.

Thirty-Five mm Microfilming for Drawing Offices. W. J. Barrett. (Illus.). 135p. 1970. 8.95 o.p. (ISBN 0-240-50698-7). Focal Pr.

Thirty-Five MM Panorama. Roger Hicks. (Illus.). 176p. 1988. pap. 12.95 o.p. (ISBN 0-7153-9292-1, Pub. by David & Charles Pub England). Sterling.

Thirty-Five MM Panorama. Roger W. Hicks. (Illus.). 176p. 1987. 24.95 o.p. (ISBN 0-7153-8930-0, Pub. by David & Charles Pub England). Sterling.

Thirty-Five MM Photographer's Handbook. Julian Calder & John Garrett. (Illus.). 1979. 14.95 o.p. (ISBN 0-517-53917-9); pap. 11.95 o.p. (ISBN 0-517-53918-7). Crown.

Thirty-Five Years in the Frying Pan. B. Hosokawa. 1978. text ed. 10.95 o.p. (ISBN 0-07-030435-1). McGraw.

Thirty-Four MORE Tested, Ready-To-Run Game Programs in BASIC. Delton T. Horn. (Illus.). 224p. 14.95 o.p. (ISBN 0-8306-9654-7, 1228); pap. 8.95 o.p. (ISBN 0-8306-1228-9). TAB Bks.

Thirty-Fourth International Instrumentation Symposium: Proceedings, May 2-5, 1988 - Albuquerque, New Mexico. 762p. 1988. pap. 95.00 o.p. (ISBN 1-55617-106-4, A106-4). Instru Soc.

Thirty Instruction Units in Basic Electricity. slow learner ed. Carl E. Matson. (gr. 9-12). 1961. pap. 4.60 o.p. (ISBN 0-87345-254-2). Glencoe.

Thirty Most Common Problems in Management & How to Solve Them. W. Delaney. 1982. pap. 14.95 o.p. (ISBN 0-8144-5536-0). AMACOM.

Thirty-Odd Boats. Philip C. Bolger. LC 82-80403. (Illus.). 304p. 1982. 22.50 o.p. (ISBN 0-87742-152-8). Intl Marine.

Thirty-One Banana Leaves. Winifred K. Vass. LC 74-7617. 64p. 1975. 3.95 o.p. (ISBN 0-8042-2582-6, John Knox). Westminster John Knox.

Thirty-One Letters & Thirteen Dreams: Poems. Richard Hugo. 1977. 7.95 o.p. (ISBN 0-393-04481-5); pap. 2.95 o.p. (ISBN 0-393-04490-4). Norton.

Thirty-Second State: A Pictorial History of Minnesota. rev. ed. Bertha L. Heilbron. LC 54-14431. (Illus.). 306p. 1966. Repr. of 1958 ed. pap. 8.95 o.p. (ISBN 0-87351-130-1). Minn Hist.

Thirty Six Biggest Mistakes Salesmen Make & How to Correct Them. George N. Kahn. 1963. 9.95 o.p. (ISBN 0-13-918979-3); pap. 6.95 o.p. (ISBN 0-13-918961-0). P-H.

Thirty-Six French Poems. Ed. by Albert Sonnenfeld. 1960. pap. 4.75 o.p. (ISBN 0-395-05420-6). HM.

Thirty-Six German Poems. Ed. by Karl S. Weimar. LC 50-14279. 1950. pap. 5.25 o.p. (ISBN 0-395-05524-5, 3-59405). HM.

Thirty-Six Spanish Poems. E. L. Rivers. LC 57-13596. 1957. pap. 5.00 o.p. (ISBN 0-395-05099-5). HM.

Thirty Thousand Kicks: What's It Like to Be a Rockette? Judith Anne Love. (Illus.). 1980. 7.50 o.p. (ISBN 0-682-49456-9, Banner). Exposition-Phoenix.

Thirty-Three Games of Skill & Chance for the IBM PC. Robert J. Traister. (Illus.). 256p. 1983. 18.95 o.p. (ISBN 0-8306-0126-0, 1526HB); pap. 12.95 o.p. (ISBN 0-8306-1526-1, 1526). TAB Bks.

Thirty-Three Programs for the TI 99-4A. Brian Flynn. 199p. (Orig.). 1984. pap. 12.95 o.p. (ISBN 0-942386-42-6). Compute Pubns.

Thirty-Three Sardonics. Tiffany Thayer. (ISBN 0-8022-1708-7). Philos Lib.

Thirty Two Basic Programs for the IBM-PC Jr. Tom Rugg. 5.95 o.p. (ISBN 0-88056-306-0). Weber Systems.

Thirty Years of Smoke, Heat & Hell. Battalion Chief Warren W. Abriel. 1976. 6.00 o.p. (ISBN 0-682-48661-2). Exposition-Phoenix.

Thirty Years of the American Neptune. Ed. by Ernest S. Dodge. LC 72-82988. 1972. 24.50x o.s.i. (ISBN 0-674-88465-5). Harvard U Pr.

Thirty Years' War. Sigfrid H. Steinberg. (Foundations of Modern History Ser.). (Illus.). 1967. pap. 3.95x o.p. (ISBN 0-393-09752-8, NortonC). Norton.

This Band of Gold. Georgia Dallas. 224p. 1987. pap. 5.95 o.p. (ISBN 0-310-47321-7, 15578P). Zondervan.

This Blessed Earth: New & Selected Poems 1927-1977. John H. Wheelock. LC 78-3844. 1978. 7.95 o.p. (ISBN 0-684-15727-6, ScribT). Scribner.

This Business of Art. Diane Cochrane. 256p. 1978. 17.95 o.p. (ISBN 0-8230-5360-1). Watson-Guptill.

This Business of Music. 4th ed. Sidney Shemel & M. William Krasilovsky. 1979. 18.50 o.p. (ISBN 0-8230-7753-5, Billboard Bks). Watson-Guptill.

This Can't Be Me. David S. Tindall. 1985. 13.95 o.p. (ISBN 0-533-06194-6). Vantage.

This Company of New Men. B. Frank Hall. (Orig., For leaders of gr. 10-12). 1967. pap. 2.95 o.p. (ISBN 0-8042-9851-3, John Knox). Westminster John Knox.

This Cruel Beauty. Trevor Meldal-Johnsen. 368p. (Orig.). 1983. pap. 3.95 o.p. (ISBN 0-380-81851-5, 81851-5). Avon.

This Day. Doris R. Fleming. 80p. 1986. 7.75 o.p. (ISBN 0-8062-2789-3). Carlton.

This Day Is Ours. Jacques Leclercq. Tr. by Dinah Livingstone from Fr. LC 80-50314. Orig. Title: Jour de L'Homme. 128p. (Orig.). 1980. pap. 1.74 o.p. (ISBN 0-88344-504-2). Orbis Bks.

This Day Is the Lord's. Corrie Ten Boom. 1982. pap. 2.75 o.s.i. (ISBN 0-515-06734-2). Jove Pubns.

This Dialogue of One: The Songs & Sonnets of John Donne. Patricia G. Pinka. LC 81-16116. 1982. 18.75 o.p. (ISBN 0-8173-0104-6). U of Ala Pr.

This Difficult Business of Helping. Alan Keith-Lucas. (Orig.). (gr. 9-12). 1965. pap. 1.25 o.p. (ISBN 0-8042-9344-9, John Knox). Westminster John Knox.

This English Language. E. Denison Ross. LC 73-167147. 296p. 1973. Repr. of 1939 ed. 40.00x o.p. (ISBN 0-8103-3184-5). Gale.

This Great Land. Photos by David Muench. 160p. 1983. 40.00 o.p. (ISBN 0-528-81120-7). Rand McNally.

This Hebrew Lord. John S. Spong. 1976. pap. 4.95 o.p. (ISBN 0-8164-2133-1). HarpR.

This House of Sky: Landscapes of a Western Mind. Ivan Doig. LC 78-53897. 1978. 9.95 o.p. (ISBN 0-15-190054-X). HarBraceJ.

This I Believe-Thank You, Billy Sunday, for the Goodness & Mercy Which I Know. Leslie A. Outterson. 1977. 7.00 o.p. (ISBN 0-682-48685-X). Exposition-Phoenix.

This I Saw: The Life & Times of Goya. Antonina Vallentin. Tr. by Katherine W. Woods from Fr. LC 78-152612. (Illus.). 371p. Repr. of 1949 ed. lib. bdg. 35.00x o.p. (ISBN 0-8371-6047-2, VATI). Greenwood.

This Is a Recording. Barbara Corcoran. LC 73-154751. (gr. 5-8). 1971. PLB 5.95 o.p. (ISBN 0-689-20675-5, Atheneum). Macmillan.

This Is Cape Breton. Alice Seward. LC 83-91474. 112p. 1985. 8.95 o.p. (ISBN 0-533-06063-X). Vantage.

This Is English. Lauri E. Lee & Roger E. Olsen. (Illus.). 84p. 1983. tchrs. ed. 9.95X o.p. (ISBN 0-88084-129-X). Alemany Pr.

This Is Home Now. Floyd A. Robinson. 230p. 1983. 14.95 o.p. (ISBN 0-8138-1776-5). Iowa St U Pr.

This Is Israel. Theodore Huebner & Carl Voss. 1956. (ISBN 0-8022-0754-5). Philos Lib.

This Is It, Our Bountiful America. O. F. Brusha. 1978. 10.00 o.p. (ISBN 0-682-49118-7). Exposition-Phoenix.

This Is Karate. rev. ed. Masutatsu Oyama. LC 65-17218. (Illus.). 368p. 1973. boxed 33.50 o.p. (ISBN 0-87040-254-4). Japan Pubns USA.

This Is My Song of Songs. Genevieve W. Syverud. (Orig.). 1966. pap. 2.95 o.p. (ISBN 0-8066-0613-4, 11-9495, Augsburg). Augsburg Fortress.

This Is My Story. Dora M. Ware. 112p. 1984. pap. 6.50 o.p. (ISBN 0-682-40182-X). Exposition-Phoenix.

This Is My Story, This Is My Song. Mary Bramer. 1984. pap. 2.25 o.p. (ISBN 0-570-03923-1, 12-2857). Concordia.

This Is Our Hope. R. E. Orchard. LC 26-784. 150p. 1966. 3.95 o.p. (ISBN 0-88243-617-1, 02-0617). Gospel Pub.

This Is PR: The Realities of Public Relations. 3rd ed. Doug Newsom & Alan Scott. 518p. 1985. text ed. (ISBN 0-534-04287-2). Wadsworth Pub.

This Is Racing. Richard Creagh-Osborne. 1977. 16.95 o.p. (ISBN 0-393-03206-X). Norton.

This Is Sailing. 2nd, rev. ed. Richard Creagh-Osborne. LC 84-62460. 1985. 17.95 o.p. (ISBN 0-688-05429-3, Pub. by Hearst Marine Bks). Morrow.

This Is Sailing. Richard Osborne-Creigh. 1973. 15.95 o.p. (ISBN 0-393-03178-0). Norton.

This Is Southeast Asia Today. Addison Eastman. (Orig.). (YA) (gr. 9 up). 1968. pap. 0.85 o.p. (ISBN 0-377-83101-8). Friendship Pr.

This Is the Day: Selected Sermons. 2nd ed. Theodore P. Ferris. LC 76-39640. 368p. 1980. pap. 10.00 o.p. (ISBN 0-911658-16-5). Yankee Bks.

This Is the Irish Setter. Joan McD. Brearley. (Illus.). 480p. 1975. 19.95 o.p. (ISBN 0-87666-655-1, H-952). TFH Pubns.

This Is the Puzzle of Poverty. Jeanette Struchen. (Illus.). (gr. 9 up). 1966. pap. 0.85 o.p. (ISBN 0-377-83081-X). Friendship Pr.

This Is the Way My Garden Grows: And Comes Into My Kitchen. Barbara D. Borland. (Illus.). 158p. 1986. 13.45 o.p. (ISBN 0-393-02298-6). Norton.

This Is the Way the World Ends. James Morrow. LC 85-24773. (Illus.). 1986. 18.95 o.p. (ISBN 0-03-008037-1). H Holt & Co.

This Is VIC: 20 BASIC. Robert F. Sutherland & Gilman. 1984. text ed. write for info. o.p. (ISBN 0-02-418380-6). Macmillan.

This Island Now. Peter Abrahams. 256p. 1985. pap. 8.95 o.p. (ISBN 0-571-13439-4). Faber & Faber.

This Jockey Drives Late Nights. Henry Livings. 1981. pap. 6.95 o.p. (ISBN 0-413-29490-0, NO. 6478). Heinemann Ed.

This Land Was Theirs: A Study of the North American Indian. 3rd ed. Wendell H. Oswalt. 569p. 1978. text ed. 26.00 o.p. (ISBN 0-394-34413-8, RandC). Random.

This Lie Called Evil. Denise Breton. LC 82-80906. 130p. (Orig.). 1983. pap. 8.50 o.p. (ISBN 0-942958-02-0). Kappeler Inst Pub.

This Little Pig: A Mother Goose Favorite. Illus. by Leonard B. Lubin. LC 84-10021. (Illus.). 32p. (ps-2). 1985. 11.75 o.p. (ISBN 0-688-04088-8); PLB 11.88 o.p. (ISBN 0-688-04089-6). Lothrop.

This Long Disease, My Life: Alexander Pope & the Sciences. Marjorie Nicolson & G. S. Rousseau. LC 68-20874. 1968. 36.50x o.p. (ISBN 0-691-06091-6). Princeton U Pr.

This Loving Torment. Valerie Sherwood. (Gregg Hardcovers Ser.). 1985. lib. bdg. 14.95 o.p. (ISBN 0-8398-2873-X, Gregg). G K Hall.

This Man & Music. Anthony Burgess. 192p. 1985. pap. 3.95 o.p. (ISBN 0-380-69852-8, Discus). Avon.

This Mess We're In! Fred J. Wall. 112p. 1985. pap. 4.95 o.p. (ISBN 0-682-40176-5). Exposition-Phoenix.

This Modern World. 2nd ed. Derek Wood. (gr. 7-12). 1980. pap. text ed. 10.00x o.p. (ISBN 0-435-31951-5). Heinemann Ed.

This 'n That. Bette Davis & Michael Herskowitz. (Illus.). 208p. 1987. 17.95 o.p. (ISBN 0-399-13246-5, Putnam). Putnam Pub Group.

This Narrow Place: Sylvia Townsend Warner & Valentine Ackland-Life, Letters & Politics, 1930-1951. Wendy Mulford. (Life & Times Ser.). (Illus.). 470p. 1988. text ed. (ISBN 0-86358-056-4, Pub. by Pandora Pr); pap. (Pub. by Pandora Pr). Routledge Chapman & Hall.

This Old Bill. Loren D. Estleman. LC 85-12599. 442p. 1985. Repr. of 1984 ed. 13.95 o.p. (ISBN 0-89621-652-7). Thorndike Pr.

This Other Eden. Marilyn Harris. 1978. pap. 3.50 o.p. (ISBN 0-380-01840-3, 58784-X). Avon.

This Place. Andrea Freud-Loewenstein. 544p. 1984. 14.95 o.p. (ISBN 0-86358-039-4). Routledge Chapman & Hall.

This Remarkable Continent: An Atlas of U. S. & Canadian Society & Cultures. Ed. by John F. Rooney, Jr. et al. LC 80-6113. (Illus.). 324p. 1982. 45.00x o.p. (ISBN 0-89096-111-5). Tex A&M Univ Pr.

This River Is in the South. Philip Mead. LC 83-21634. 50p. 1984. 10.95 o.p. (ISBN 0-7022-1695-X); pap. 5.95 o.p. (ISBN 0-7022-1696-8). U of Queensland Pr.

This Rolling Land. Sandy Dengler. (Serenade Saga Ser.: No. 30). 1986. pap. 2.50 o.p. (ISBN 0-310-46872-8, 15546P). Zondervan.

This Rough Magic. Mary Stewart. 1964. 9.95 o.p. (ISBN 0-688-02614-1). Morrow.

This Running Life. George A. Sheehan. 1981. pap. 8.50 o.p. (ISBN 0-671-25609-2, Fireside). S&S.

This Sacred Trust: American Nationality, Seventeen Ninety-Eight to Eighteen Ninety-Eight. Paul C. Nagel. LC 80-18183. xvi, 376p. 1980. Repr. of 1971 ed. lib. bdg. 35.00x o.p. (ISBN 0-313-22657-1, NATS). Greenwood.

This Savage Heart. Patricia Hagan. 384p. (Orig.). 1984. pap. 3.95 o.p. (ISBN 0-380-87759-7). Avon.

This Singing World: Junior Edition. Ed. by Louis Untermeyer. LC 23-17203. (Illus.). (gr. 7 up). 1923. 9.50 o.p. (ISBN 0-15-286041-X, HJ). HarBraceJ.

This Soldier Still at War. John Bryan. LC 74-5528. (Illus.). 352p. 1975. 9.95 o.p. (ISBN 0-15-190060-4). HarBraceJ.

This Song Remembers: Self-Portraits of Native Americans in the Arts. Jane Katz. (gr. 7 up). 1980. 8.95 o.p. (ISBN 0-395-29522-X). HM.

This Space Blank. Gary Hotham. (Haiku Ser.: No. 16). 1984. pap. 2.50 o.p. (ISBN 1-55780-085-5). Juniper Pr WI.

This Splendid Land. Chet Cunningham. 1979. pap. 1.95 o.p. (ISBN 0-8439-0638-3, Pub. by Leisure Bks CT). Dorchester Pub Co.

This Sporting Life. David Storey. 256p. 1982. pap. 1.50 o.p. (ISBN 0-380-00254-X, 58024-1, Bard). Avon.

This Star Shall Abide. Sylvia L. Engdahl. LC 79-175553. (Illus.). (gr. 5-9). 1972. 6.95 o.p. (ISBN 0-689-30026-3, Atheneumx). Macmillan.

This, the House We Live In. Eleanor T. Lincoln & John A. Pinto. (Illus.). 188p. (Orig.). 1983. pap. 9.50 o.p. (ISBN 0-87391-030-3). Smith Coll.

This Triumphant Fire. Anne Carsley. 352p. 1982. pap. 2.95 o.p. (ISBN 0-380-79632-5, 79632). Avon.

This Trivial Harp. Elwood Dudley. 1979. 4.00 o.p. (ISBN 0-682-49369-4). Exposition-Phoenix.

This Vast External Realm. new ed. Dean Acheson. 356p. 1973. 9.95 o.p. (ISBN 0-393-05495-0). Norton.

This Very Body the Buddha. Bhagwan Shree Rajneesh. Ed. by Ma Ananda Vandana. LC 79-904227. (Zen Ser.). (Illus.). 360p. (Orig.). 1978. 16.95 o.p. (ISBN 0-88050-157-X). Chidvilas Inc.

This View of Life: The World of an Evolutionist. George G. Simpson. LC 64-14636. 1966. pap. 2.15 o.p. (ISBN 0-15-690070-X, Harv). HarBraceJ.

This War Without an Enemy. Richard Ollard. (Illus.). 248p. 1976. 15.95 o.p. (ISBN 0-689-10759-5, Atheneum). Macmillan.

This Was My Life. Joseph C. Smith. 1985. 8.95 o.p. (ISBN 0-533-06505-4). Vantage.

This Was the Son of God. Helen S. Thomsen. (Orig.). (gr. 7). 1975. pap. text ed. 2.25x o.p. (ISBN 0-8192-4059-1); tchr's guide 2.25x o.p. (ISBN 0-8192-4060-5). Morehouse Pub.

This Wasn't Supposed to Happen: Single Women over Thirty Talk Frankly about Their Lives. Susan C. Bakos. 224p. 1985. 15.95 o.p. (ISBN 0-8264-0360-3). Continuum.

This We Believe. 2nd ed. Arnold T. Olson. LC 61-18801. 1965. Repr. of 1961 ed. 6.95 o.p. (ISBN 0-911802-01-0). Free Church Pubns.

This Whole Human Rights Business. V. Bolshakov. 327p. 1985. pap. 2.95 o.p. (ISBN 0-8285-2973-6, Pub. by Progress Pubs USSR). Imported Pubns.

This World of Ours. Abram Glaser. 512p. 1955. (ISBN 0-8022-0595-X). Philos Lib.

Thistle Brilliant Morning. Shiki et al. Tr. by William J. Higginson from Japanese. (Xtras Ser.: No. 1). 24p. (Orig.). 1975. pap. 1.50 o.p. (ISBN 0-89120-000-2). From Here.

Thomas Alva Edison: An American Myth. Wyn Wachorst. (Illus.). 256p. 1981. 30.00x o.p. (ISBN 0-262-23108-5). MIT Pr.

Thomas Aquinas Dictionary. Ed. by M. Stockhammer. LC 64-21468. 1965. 7.50 o.p. (ISBN 0-8022-1652-8). Philos Lib.

Thomas B. Turtle. Lisa Brooks. (Illus.). (ps-3). 1978. 10.00 o.p. (ISBN 0-682-49034-2). Exposition-Phoenix.

Thomas Barnes of the Times. Derek Hudson. Ed. by Harold Child. LC 70-138623. (Illus.). 196p. 1972. Repr. of 1943 ed. lib. bdg. 35.00x o.p. (ISBN 0-8371-5735-8, HUTB). Greenwood.

Thomas Bewick & His Pupils. Austin Dobson. LC 69-17340. 252p. 1968. Repr. of 1884 ed. 35.00x o.p. (ISBN 0-8103-3523-9). Gale.

Thomas Carlyle: A Bibliography of English-Language Criticism, 1824-1974. Rodger L. Tarr. LC 76-10837. xiv, 295p. 1976. 20.00x o.p. (ISBN 0-8139-0645-4, Bibliographic Soc. of Amer.). U Pr of Va.

Thomas Carlyle's Life in London at the End of the 19th Century, 2 vols. James A. Froude. (Illus.). 316p. 1985. Repr. of 1909 ed. 237.50 set o.p. Found Class Reprints.

Thomas Chatterton's Art: Experiments in Imagined History. Donald S. Taylor. LC 78-51200. 1978. 34.50x o.p. (ISBN 0-691-06375-3). Princeton U Pr.

Thomas Chippendale, 1718-1779: A Bibliography. Mary Vance. (Architecture Ser.: A 1398). 11p. 1985. 2.00 o.p. (ISBN 0-89028-428-8). Vance Biblios.

Thomas Clarkson: The Friend of Slaves. Earl L. Griggs. LC 75-107476. 1970. Repr. of 1936 ed. 35.00x o.p. (ISBN 0-8371-3754-3, GRC&). Greenwood.

Thomas De Quincey: A Reference Guide. Ed. by H. O. Dendurent. 1978. lib. bdg. 24.00 o.p. (ISBN 0-8161-7840-2, Hall Reference). G K Hall.

Thomas E. Dewey & His Times. Richard Norton-Smith. 672p. 1982. 21.75 o.p. (ISBN 0-671-41741-X). S&S.

Thomas E. Dewey & His Times. Richard N. Smith. 720p. 1984. pap. 11.95 o.p. (ISBN 0-671-41742-8, Touchstone Bks). S&S.

Thomas Eakins: Artist of Philadelphia. Darrel Sewell. LC 82-7509. (Handbooks in American Art: No. 1). (Illus.). 152p. (Orig.). 1982. pap. 12.95 o.p. (ISBN 0-87633-047-2). Phila Mus Art.

Thomas Eakins Collection. Theodor Siegl. LC 76-58647. (Handbooks in American Art: No. 1). (Illus.). 178p. (Orig.). 1978. pap. 11.95 o.p. (ISBN 0-87633-031-6). Phila Mus Art.

Thomas Gage's Travels in the New World. J. Eric Thompson. LC 81-2948. (Illus.). x, 379p. 1981. Repr. of 1958 ed. lib. bdg. 45.50x o.p. (ISBN 0-313-23015-3, THTN). Greenwood.

Thomas George Lawson: African Historian & Administrator in Sierra Leone. David E. Skinner. LC 78-70393. (Publications Ser, No. 222: Hoover Colonial Studies). 254p. 1980. pap. 10.95x o.p. (ISBN 0-8179-7221-8). Hoover Inst Pr.

Thomas H. Mawson, 1861-1933: A Selected Bibliography. Jo N. Beglo. (Architecture Ser.: A 1427). 12p. 1985. 2.00 o.p. (ISBN 0-89028-477-6). Vance Biblios.

Thomas Hardy. Norman Page. 212p. (Orig.). 1981. pap. 10.00 o.p. (ISBN 0-7100-8615-6). Routledge Chapman & Hall.

Thomas Hardy: A Biography. Michael Millgate. 1982. 24.50 o.p. (ISBN 0-394-48802-4). Random.

Thomas Hardy Annual, No. 1. Norman Page. (Literary Annual - Hardy Annual: No. 1). 240p. 1982. text ed. 32.50x o.p. (ISBN 0-391-02649-6). Humanities.

Thomas Hardy-Poet of Tragic Vision: A Study of Hardy's Poetic Sensibility. Manas M. Das. 160p. 1983. text ed. 12.50x o.p. (ISBN 0-391-02805-7). Humanities.

Thomas Hardy's English. Ralph W. Elliott. Ed. by David Crystal. (Language Library). 384p. 1984. 34.95x o.p. (ISBN 0-631-13659-2). Basil Blackwell.

Thomas Heywood. Frederick S. Boas. Repr. of 1950 ed. 19.00 o.p. (ISBN 0-403-02292-4). Somerset Pub.

Thomas Hill Green & the Development of Liberal-Democratic Thought. I. M. Greengarten. 194p. 1981. 22.50x o.p. (ISBN 0-8020-5503-6). U of Toronto Pr.

Thomas Hornsby Ferril. A. Thomas Trusky. LC 73-8335. (Western Writers Ser: No. 6). 1973. pap. 2.95x o.p. (ISBN 0-88430-005-6). Boise St Univ.

Thomas in Dorf see In the Village.

Thomas Jefferson: A Well-Tempered Mind. Carl Binger. LC 69-14694. 1970. 6.95 o.p. (ISBN 0-393-01085-6). Norton.

Thomas Jefferson among the Arts. Eleanor Berman. (ISBN 0-8022-0111-3). Philos Lib.

Thomas Jefferson: An Intimate History. Fawn M. Brodie. (Illus.). 800p. 1974. 24.95 o.p. (ISBN 0-393-07480-3). Norton.

Thomas Jefferson & the Declaration of Independence. Encore ed. James Munves. LC 75-39299. (Illus.). (gr. 5-9). 1978. reinforced bdg. encore ed. 4.19 o.p. (ISBN 0-684-17385-9, ScribT). Scribner.

Thomas Jefferson: The Apostle of Liberty. Marguerite E. Wilbur. 416p. 1962. 6.95 o.p. (ISBN 0-87140-809-0). Liveright.

Thomas Jefferson Versus Religious Oppression. Frank Swancara. 160p. 1970. 5.95 o.p. (ISBN 0-8216-0103-2, Pub. by Univ Bks). Carol Pub Group.

Thomas Johnson Botanical Journeys in Kent & Hampstead. Ed. by J. S. Gilmour. (Illus.). 1972. 16.00x o.p. (ISBN 0-913196-13-4). Hunt Inst Botanical.

Thomas Lyster. David Wurtzel. 224p. 1987. pap. 3.95 o.p. (ISBN 0-380-70180-4). Avon.

Thomas McKean: The Shaping of an American Republicanism. G. S. Rowe. LC 77-94085. (Illus.). 1978. text ed. 25.00x o.p. (ISBN 0-87081-100-2). Univ Pr Colo.

Thomas Mann & Italy. Ilsedore B. Jonas. Tr. by Betty Crouse. LC 79-9779. 208p. 1979. 17.75 o.p. (ISBN 0-8173-8063-9). U of Ala Pr.

Thomas Merton. Victor A. Kramer. (United States Authors Ser.: No. 462). 1984. lib. bdg. 17.95 o.p. (ISBN 0-8057-7402-5, Twayne). G K Hall.

Thomas Merton: A Bibliography. rev. ed. Frank Dell'Isola. LC 74-79148. (Serif Ser.: No. 31). 200p. 1975. 13.50x o.p. (ISBN 0-87338-156-4). Kent St U Pr.

Thomas Merton: A Pictorial Biography. James H. Forest. LC 80-82249. (Illus.). 112p. (Orig.). 1980. pap. 5.95 o.p. (ISBN 0-8091-2284-7). Paulist Pr.

Thomas Merton's Dark Path. rev. ed. William H. Shannon. 260p. 1987. pap. 8.95 o.p. (ISBN 0-374-52019-4). FS&G.

Thomas Merton's Dark Path: The Inner Experience of a Contemplative. William H. Shannon. LC 80-28091. 256p. 1981. 15.00 o.p. (ISBN 0-374-27636-6); pap. 8.95 o.p. (ISBN 0-374-52019-4). FS&G.

Thomas Middleton: A Reference Guide. Sara J. Steene. (Reference Guides to Literature Ser.). 1984. lib. bdg. 61.00 o.s.i. (ISBN 0-8161-8340-6, Hall Reference). G K Hall.

Thomas Moran: Watercolors of the American West. Carol Clark. LC 80-13459. (Illus.). 192p. 1980. 27.50 o.p. (ISBN 0-292-75059-5). U of Tex Pr.

Titles

Thomas More Engagement Calendar, 1989. Ed. by Andrew Costello. 1989. 7.95 o.p. (ISBN 0-88347-230-9). Thomas More.

Thomas Robert Malthus: Critical Assessments, 4 Vols. Ed. by John C. Wood. LC 85-22412. (Croom Helm Critical Assessments of Leading Economists Ser.). 1986. Set. 495.00 o.p. (ISBN 0-7099-3650-8, Pub. by Croom Helm Ltd). Routledge Chapman & Hall.

Thomas Say Foundation Publications. Incl. Vol. 2. Plecoptera or Stoneflies of America North of Mexico. J. G. Needham & P. W. Claassen. (Illus.). 397p. 1925. 12.50 o.p. (ISBN 0-686-11692-5); Vol. 3. Plecoptera Nymphs of North America. P. W. Claassen. (Illus.). 199p. 1931. 10.90 o.p. (ISBN 0-686-11693-3); Vol. 4. Blow Flies of North America. D. G. Hall. (Illus.). 477p. 1948. 15.00 o.p. (ISBN 0-686-11694-1); Vol. 5. Aphids of the Rocky Mountain Region. Miriam A. Palmer. (Illus.). 452p. 1952. 21.70 o.p. (ISBN 0-686-11695-X); Vol. 6. Catalog of the Mosquitoes of the World. Alan Stone et al. 358p. 20.90 o.p. (ISBN 0-686-11696-8); suppl. o.p. 3.35 ea. o.p.; Vol. 7. Monograph of Cimicidae. Robert L. Usinger. (Illus.). 588p. 1966. 21.70 o.p. (ISBN 0-686-11698-4); Vol. 8. Anopheline Names: Their Derivations & Histories. James B. Kitzmiller. LC 82-83331. 639p. 1982. 26.50 o.p. (ISBN 0-938522-17-5). LC 66-22730. Entomol Soc.

Thomas Say Foundation Publications. Incl. Vol. 1. Sarcophaga & Allies of North America. J. M. Aldrich. (Illus.). 301p. 1916. pap. 11.70 o.p. (ISBN 0-686-11699-2). pap. Entomol Soc.

Thomas Sheridan of Smock-Alley, 1719-1788. Esther Sheldon. 1967. 52.50x o.p. (ISBN 0-691-06131-9). Princeton U Pr.

Thomas Tallis. Thomas Tallis et al. Ed. by P. C. Buck. (Tudor Church Music Ser.: Vol. 6). 1963. Repr. of 1928 ed. Broude.

Thomas Telford, 1757-1834: A Select Bibliography. Valerie J. Nurcombe. (Architecture Ser.: A 1389). 19p. 1985. 3.00 o.p. (ISBN 0-89028-399-0). Vance Biblios.

Thomas, West Virginia, 1906. T. Nutter. (Illus.). 1969. Repr. 8.00 o.p. (ISBN 0-87012-073-5). McClain.

Thomas Wolfe. H. J. Muller. Repr. of 1947 ed. 35.00 o.p. (ISBN 0-527-65790-5). Kraus Repr.

Thomas Wolfe: A Bibliography. George R. Preston, Jr. LC 74-12760. (Illus.). 1979. Repr. of 1943 ed. lib. bdg. 35.00x o.p. (ISBN 0-8371-7750-2, PRTW). Greenwood.

Thomas Wolfe Undergraduate. Richard Walser. LC 77-74768. (Illus.). ix, 166p. 1977. 14.95 o.p. (ISBN 0-8223-0387-6). Duke.

Thomasina. Paul Gallico. 256p. (gr. 5 up). 1981. pap. 2.25 o.p. (ISBN 0-380-51524-5, 59980-5, Flare). Avon.

Thompson Chain Reference Bible Survey. Howard Hanke. 1981. 19.95 o.p. (ISBN 0-8499-0272-X). Word Bks.

Thompson Twins: The Official Biography. Rose Rouse. (Illus.). 128p. 1985. pap. 9.95 o.p. (ISBN 0-88188-382-4, Robus Bks). H Leonard Pub Corp.

Thor Heyerdahl: Across the Seas of Time. Paul Westman. LC 82-1431. (Taking Part Ser.). (Illus.). 48p. (gr. 3 up). 1982. PLB 9.95 o.p. (ISBN 0-87518-225-9). Dillon.

Thoracotomy Exercise Manual. 1983. 5.00 o.p. (ISBN 0-940876-07-8). City Hope.

Thorburn's Birds. Ed. by James Fisher. LC 75-34531. (Illus.). 186p. 1976. 27.95 o.s.i. (ISBN 0-87951-044-7). Overlook Pr.

Thore-Buerger & the Art of the Past. Frances S. Jowell. LC 76-23632. (Outstanding Dissertations in the Fine Arts - 19th Century). (Illus.). 1977. Repr. of 1971 ed. lib. bdg. 76.00 o.p. (ISBN 0-8240-2701-9). Garland Pub.

Thoreau. William Condry. 144p. 1954. (ISBN 0-8022-0287-X). Philos Lib.

Thoreau: People, Principles, & Politics. Henry David Thoreau. Ed. by Milton Meltzer. 235p. 1963. 4.50 o.p. (ISBN 0-8090-9350-2). Hill & Wang.

Thoreau: People, Principles & Politics. Henry David Thoreau. Ed. by Milton Meltzer. (American Century Ser.). 235p. (Orig.). 1963. pap. 4.95 o.p. (ISBN 0-8090-0064-4). Hill & Wang.

Thoreau Profile. Milton Meltzer & Walter A. Harding. (Illus.). 13.25 o.p. (ISBN 0-8446-0797-5). Peter Smith.

Thoreau: The Complete Individualist-His Relevance, & Lack of It, for Our Time. Robert Dickens. LC 73-91092. 1974. 6.00 o.p. (ISBN 0-682-47863-6, University). Exposition-Phoenix.

Thorium & Gas Cooled Reactors. J. P. Howe & G. Melese-D'Hospital. 1978. pap. 63.00 o.p. (ISBN 0-08-024208-1). Pergamon.

Thorium: Its Industrial Hygiene Aspects. Roy E. Albert. (U. S. Atomic Energy Commission Monographs). 1966. 25.00 o.p. (ISBN 0-12-048656-3). Acad Pr.

Thorn Birds. Colleen McCullough. 540p. 1978. pap. 6.95 o.p. (ISBN 0-380-56390-8, 56390-8). Avon.

Thorns & Thistles: Juvenile Delinquents in the United States, 1825-1940. Robert M. Mennel. LC 72-95187. 259p. 1973. 20.00x o.p. (ISBN 0-87451-070-8); pap. 8.95x o.p. (ISBN 0-87451-273-5). U Pr of New Eng.

Thornton the Worrier. Marjorie W. Sharmat. LC 78-1286. (Illus.). 32p. (gr. k-3). 1978. 9.95 o.p. (ISBN 0-8234-0328-9). Holiday.

Thornton Wilder. Rex Burbank. (Twayne's United States Authors Ser.). 1961. pap. 10.95 o.p. (ISBN 0-8084-0300-1, T5, Twayne). New Coll U Pr.

Thornton Wilder & His Public. Amos N. Wilder. LC 79-26564. 104p. 1980. 9.95 o.p. (ISBN 0-8006-0636-1, 1-636, Fortress). Augsburg Fortress.

Thorold Dickinson: The Man & His Films. Jeffrey Richards. 224p. 1986. 39.00 o.p. (ISBN 0-7099-2293-0, Pub. by Croom Helm Ltd). Routledge Chapman & Hall.

Thoroughbass Method. Hermann Keller. Tr. by Carl Parrish. 1965. 10.95x o.p. (ISBN 0-393-09744-7, NortonC). Norton.

Thoroughbred Business. Jocelyn de Moubray. (Illus.). 192p. 1988. 29.95 o.p. (ISBN 0-241-12379-8, Pub. by Hamish Hamilton). David & Charles.

Thoroughbred Field Hunter. Christian T Goeldner. LC 75-20593. (Illus.). 184p. 1976. 9.95 o.p. (ISBN 0-498-01767-2). A S Barnes.

Thoroughbreds. Michael Geller. 1981. pap. 2.75 o.p. (ISBN 0-8439-0901-3, Pub. by Leisure Bks CT). Dorchester Pub Co.

Thoroughly Married. Dennis Guernsey. 145p. 1984. pap. text ed. 5.95 o.p. (ISBN 0-8499-3000-6, 3000-6). Word Bks.

Thor's Hammer: Essays on John Gardner. Ed. by Jeff Henderson & Robert E. Lowrey. (Illus.). 210p. (Orig.). 1985. pap. text ed. 12.95 o.p. (ISBN 0-9615143-0-2). Univ Central AR Pr.

Thorstein Veblen & the Institutionalists: A Study in the Philosophy of Economics. David Seckler. LC 73-91642. 175p. 1975. text ed. 15.00x o.p. (ISBN 0-87081-055-3). Univ Pr Colo.

Those Curious New Cults in the Eighties. rev. ed. Bill Petersen. LC 72-93700. 1982. pap. text ed. 3.95 o.p. (ISBN 0-87983-317-3). Keats.

Those Dark Eyes. E. M. Brez. 224p. 1986. pap. 2.95 o.p. (ISBN 0-931773-43-1). Critics Choice Paper.

Those Fabulous Flying Machines: A History of Flight in Three Dimensions with Punch-Out Plane Model. Seymour Reit. (Illus.). 12p. (gr. 4-7). 1985. 17.95 o.s.i. (ISBN 0-02-776020-0). Macmillan.

Those Four & Plenty More. Eleanor Dewees. Ed. by Bobbie J. Van Dolson. (gr. 2-5). 1981. pap. 6.95 o.p. (ISBN 0-8280-0092-1). Review & Herald.

Those Frightened Years. Con Sellers. 368p. (Orig.). 1988. pap. 3.95 o.p. (ISBN 0-553-26939-9). Bantam.

Those Happy Golden Years. Miriam Wood. 1980. 6.95 o.p. (ISBN 0-8280-0062-X, 20380-2). Review & Herald.

Those Incomparable Bonanzas,1944-1972. Larry A. Ball. 1971. 24.95x o.p. (ISBN 0-911720-52-9, Pub. by Ball). Aviation.

Those Powerful Years: The South Coast & Los Angeles 1887-1917. Joseph S. O'Flaherty. (Illus.). 1978. 12.00 o.p. (ISBN 0-682-49103-9, Lochinvar). Exposition-Phoenix.

Those Superstitions. Charles Igglesden. LC 73-12798. 237p. 1974. Repr. of 1932 ed. 40.00x o.p. (ISBN 0-8103-3621-9). Gale.

Those Traver Kids. Bianca Bradbury. LC 72-2759. (Illus.). 208p. (gr. 3-7). 1972. 5.95 o.p. (ISBN 0-395-14330-6). HM.

Those Tremendous Mountains: The Story of the Lewis & Clark Expedition. David F. Hawke. (Illus.). 1980. 12.95 o.p. (ISBN 0-393-01305-7). Norton.

Those Von Tallien Women. Utta Danella. 352p. 1980. pap. 2.75 o.p. (ISBN 0-380-47506-5, 47506). Avon.

Those Who Can, Teach. 2nd ed. Kevin Ryan & James M. Cooper. (Illus.). 500p. 1975. text ed. 14.95 o.p. (ISBN 0-395-18622-6). HM.

Those Who Can, Teach. 3rd ed. Kevin Ryan & James M. Cooper. LC 79-89788. (Illus.). 1980. text ed. 22.95 o.p. (ISBN 0-395-28495-3). HM.

Those Who Can, Teach: Learning Guide. 2nd ed. H. Jerome Freiberg. (Illus.). 1977. pap. 7.25 o.p. (ISBN 0-395-19859-3). HM.

Those Who Fall from the Sun. Josephine R. Stone. LC 78-5139. (gr. 6 up). 1978. 6.95 o.p. (ISBN 0-689-30615-6, Atheneum). Macmillan.

Those Who Stayed Behind. Eleanor Hyde. 1981. pap. 2.95 o.p. (AE1109, Sig). NAL.

Thou Shalt Not Kill. Robert W. Meals. LC 84-90002. 131p. 1985. 10.00 o.p. (ISBN 0-533-06098-2). Vantage.

Thought & Statement. 3rd ed. William G. Leary et al. 1969. text ed. 9.95 o.p. (ISBN 0-15-592051-0, HC). HarBraceJ.

Thought Control in the U. S. A. Hollywood Arts Science & Professions Council. Ed. by Bruce S. Kupelnick. LC 76-52131. (Classics of Film Literature Ser.). 1978. lib. bdg. 31.00 o.p. (ISBN 0-8240-2895-3). Garland Pub.

Thought Reform & the Psychology of Totalism. Robert J. Lifton. 1963. pap. 9.95 o.p. (ISBN 0-393-00221-7, Norton Lib). Norton.

Thoughtfully I Read the Smoke. I. Ziedonis. 1980. 6.45 o.p. (ISBN 0-8285-1805-X, Pub. by Progress Pubs USSR). Imported Pubns.

Thoughts-a-Fleeting. W. Kacy. LC 84-90051. 43p. 1985. 6.95 o.p. (ISBN 0-533-06131-8). Vantage.

Thoughts about Life. Felix Friedberg. 1954. (ISBN 0-8022-0544-5). Philos Lib.

Thoughts for Buffets. Institute Publishing Company Staff. 1958. 17.45 o.p. (ISBN 0-395-07825-3). HM.

Thoughts for Men on the Move. Warren Wiersbe. 1970. pap. 3.50 o.p. (ISBN 0-8024-0132-5). Moody.

Thoughts for Reflection. new ed. Rhea C. Hardy. 96p. (Orig.). pap. 2.00 o.p. (ISBN 0-89036-055-3). Hawkes Pub Inc.

Thoughts for the Quiet Hour. D. L. Moody. pap. 3.50 o.p. (ISBN 0-8024-8729-7). Moody.

Thoughts for Times Like These. S. Ralph Harlow. 192p. 1957. (ISBN 0-8022-0680-8). Philos Lib.

Thoughts in the Atomic Age. Sonja Neborak. 1952. (ISBN 0-8022-1186-0). Philos Lib.

Thoughts in Time, Whispers & Roars. Irene Z. Jimenez. 1985. 6.95 o.p. (ISBN 0-533-06111-3). Vantage.

Thoughts of Giants & Other Poems. Shirley Scott. 60p. (Orig.). 1980. pap. 2.50 o.p. (ISBN 0-931846-16-1). Wash Writers Pub.

Thoughts of Life. M. Rosser Lunsford. LC 87-43128. 110p. (Orig.). 1988. pap. 6.50 o.p. (ISBN 0-935834-65-6). Rainbow Books.

Thoughts of Mine. Joyce J. Shiner. 1985. 5.95 o.p. (ISBN 0-317-28959-4). Vantage.

Thoughts of the Great. Marion Parker. 96p. 1960. (ISBN 0-8022-1263-8). Philos Lib.

Thousand Camps. Mary Waldorf. (gr. 5-9). 1982. 8.95 o.p. (ISBN 0-395-31866-1). HM.

Thousand Days: John F. Kennedy in the White House. Arthur M. Schlesinger, Jr. 1965. 24.50 o.p. (ISBN 0-395-08158-0); limited ed. 50.00 o.p. (ISBN 0-395-08157-2). HM.

Thousand Fires. Anne Powers. 1978. pap. 2.25 o.s.i. (ISBN 0-505-51291-2, Pub. by Tower Bks). Dorchester Pub Co.

Thousand Marriages: A Medical Study of Sex Adjustment. Robert L. Dickinson & Lura Beam. LC 76-95093. Repr. of 1931 ed. lib. bdg. 35.00x o.p. (ISBN 0-8371-3085-9, DIMA). Greenwood.

Thousand Miles up the Nile. Amelia B. Edwards. 528p. 1983. pap. 11.95 o.p. (ISBN 0-7126-0038-8). Hippocrene Bks.

Thousand Pieces of Gold: A Biographical Novel. Ruthanne L. McCunn. 304p. 1983. pap. 3.95 o.p. (ISBN 0-440-38883-X, LE). Dell.

Thousand Quotations: Olympic Edition, Bk. 1. John Newlander. 1977. 4.00 o.p. (ISBN 0-682-48955-7). Exposition-Phoenix.

Thousand Reasons for Living. Dom H. Camara. Ed. by Jose De Brouker. Tr. by Alan Neame from Fr. LC 81-43070. 128p. 1981. 6.95 o.p. (ISBN 0-8006-0664-7, 1-664). Augsburg Fortress.

Thousand Years & a Day. Claus Westermann. LC 62-8544. 292p. 1982. pap. 8.95 o.p. (ISBN 0-8006-1913-7, 1-1913, Fortress). Augsburg Fortress.

Th'overthrow of Stage-Players. John Rainoldes et al. LC 70-170414. (English Stage Ser.: Vol. 11). lib. bdg. 61.00 o.p. (ISBN 0-8240-0594-5). Garland Pub.

Thread of Ariadne. Charles F. Herberger. LC 72-78167. (Illus.). 1972. (ISBN 0-8022-2089-4). Philos Lib.

Thread of Ariadne: A Study of Ancient Greek Dress. Elsa Gullberg & Paul Astrom. (Studies in Mediterranean Archaeology Ser.: No. XXI). (Illus.). 1970. pap. text ed. 19.95x o.p. (ISBN 91-85058-34-3). Humanities.

Threat of Japanese Multinationals: How the West Can Respond. Lawrence G. Franko. LC 83-10599. (IRM Series on Multinationals: I-659). 148p. 1983. 37.00x o.p. (ISBN 0-471-90232-2). Wiley.

Threat to the Barkers. Joan Phipson. LC 65-10962. (Illus.). (gr. 4-6). 1965. 4.95 o.p. (ISBN 0-15-286310-9, HJ). HarBraceJ.

Threats to Security in East Asia-Pacific: National & Regional Perspectives. Charles E. Morrison. LC 82-48632. 256p. 1983. 32.00x o.p. (ISBN 0-669-06369-X). Lexington Bks.

Three. Donna D. Guyer. 176p. 1987. text ed. 16.95 o.p. (ISBN 0-682-40340-7). Exposition-Phoenix.

Three-Acylcyclopentenes & Five-Acylbiyclo (2.1.0) Pentanes: Photochemical & Thermal Isomerizations. Kenneth F. Schaffner. 1976. pap. 15.50 o.p. (ISBN 0-08-020476-7). Pergamon.

Three Adventures of Sherlock Holmes see New Method Supplementary Readers: Bestseller Pack.

Three Alexander Calders: A Family Memoir. Margaret Calder Hayes. LC 77-79244. (Illus.). 1977. 15.00 o.p. (ISBN 0-8397-8017-6). Eriksson.

Three American Painters: Kenneth Noland, Jules Olitski, Frank Stella see Exhibition Catalogues from the Fogg Art Museum.

Three American Travellers in England: James Russell Lowell, Henry Adams, Henry James. Robert C. Le Clair. LC 77-19341. 1978. Repr. of 1945 ed. lib. bdg. 35.00x o.p. (ISBN 0-313-20190-0, LETA). Greenwood.

Three Approaches to Classroom Management: Views From a Psychological Perspective. Jerry D. Lehman. LC 81-43843. 130p. (Orig.). 1982. lib. bdg. 25.50 o.p. (ISBN 0-8191-2572-5); pap. 10.00 o.p. (ISBN 0-8191-2573-3). U Pr of Amer.

Three Argentine Thinkers. Solomon Lipp. LC 68-56191. 192p. 1969. (ISBN 0-8022-2273-0). Philos Lib.

Three Aspects of Crisis in Colonial Kenya. Bismarck Myrick & David L. Easterbrook. LC 75-30552. (Foreign and Comparative Studies Program, Eastern Africa Ser.: No. 21). 91p. 1975. pap. text ed. 5.50x o.p. (ISBN 0-915984-18-0). Syracuse U Foreign Comp.

Three Aspects of Labor Dynamics. Wladimir S. Woytinsky. LC 73-16650. (Illus.). 249p. 1974. Repr. of 1942 ed. lib. bdg. 35.00 o.p. (ISBN 0-8371-7215-2, WOLD). Greenwood.

Three Big Hogs. Manus Pinkwater. LC 75-4780. (Illus.). 40p. (ps-3). 1979. 6.95 o.p. (ISBN 0-395-28819-3, Clarion). HM.

Three Billy Goats Gruff. Marcia Brown. LC 57-5265. (Illus.). (gr. 1-4). 1972. pap. 2.95 o.p. (ISBN 0-15-690150-1, VoyB). HarBraceJ.

Three Billy Goats Gruff. Ed. & illus. by Marcia Brown. LC 57-5265. (Illus.). (gr. k-3). 1957. 10.95 o.p. (ISBN 0-15-286399-0, HJ). HarBraceJ.

Three British Revolutions: 1641, 1688, 1776. Ed. by J. G. Pocock. LC 79-27572. (Folger Institute Essays, Published for the Folger Shakespeare Library). 456p. 1980. 48.50x o.p. (ISBN 0-691-05293-X); pap. 18.95x L.P.E. o.p. (ISBN 0-691-10087-X). Princeton U Pr.

Three by Peter Handke. Peter Handke. 1977. pap. 3.95 o.p. (ISBN 0-380-00968-4, 60303-9, Bard). Avon.

Three Caravans to Yuma: The Untold Story of Bactrian Camels in Western America. Harlan D. Fowler. LC 80-66268. (Illus.). 173p. 1980. 25.00 o.p. (ISBN 0-87062-131-9). A H Clark.

Three-Cent Stamp of the United States, 1851-1857 Issue. Carroll Chase. LC 75-18277. (Illus.). 384p. 1976. Repr. 35.00x o.p. (ISBN 0-88000-070-8). Quarterman.

Three Centuries of Harvard, 1636-1936. facsim. ed. Samuel E. Morison. LC 36-14160. 1936. 27.00x o.p. (ISBN 0-674-88890-1, Belknap Pr). Harvard U Pr.

Three Centuries of Peace Treaties & Their Teachings, 1582-1913. Walter G. Phillimore. LC 73-147602. (Library of War & Peace; International Law). 1975. lib. bdg. 46.00 o.p. (ISBN 0-8240-0363-2). Garland Pub.

Three Centuries of Scientific Hydrology, 1674-1974: Papers, Paris, 1974. Tercentenary of Scientific Hydrology Staff. 123p. (Eng., Fr., Span. & Rus.). 1974. pap. 9.50 o.p. (ISBN 0-686-94189-6, U680, UNESCO). UNIPUB.

Three Children of the Holocaust. Sol Chaneles. (YA) 1974. pap. 1.50 o.p. (ISBN 0-380-00118-7, 39545-2). Avon.

Three Children's Plays: The Poet & the Rent; The Frog Prince & the Revenge of the Space Pandas or Binky Rudich & the Two-Speed Clock. David Mamet. 144p. (gr. 3-7). 1986. 18.95 o.s.i. (ISBN 0-394-55302-0). Grove.

Three Clean Fuels from Coal-Technology & Economics: Synthetic Natural Gas, Methanol, & Medium Btu Gas. Ed. by A. Kasem. 1979. 495.00 o.p. (ISBN 0-8247-6923-6). Dekker.

Three Clinical Faces of Childhood. E. J. Anthony. Ed. by D. C. Gilpin. LC 76-18701. 255p. 1976. 16.95x o.p. (ISBN 0-470-15150-1). Halsted Pr.

Three Coffins for Nino Lencho. Armando B. Rico. LC 84-50242. 1984. pap. 10.95 o.s.i. (ISBN 0-89229-013-7). TQS Pubns.

Three Contemporary Novelists: An Annotated Bibliography of Works by & About John Hawkes, Joseph Heller & Thomas Pynchon. Robert M. Scotto. LC 75-42889. (Reference Library of the Humanities Ser.: Vol. 52). 1977. lib. bdg. 25.00 o.p. (ISBN 0-8240-9948-6). Garland Pub.

Three Critical Years, 1904-05-06. Maurice Paleologue. 12.95 o.s.i. (ISBN 0-8315-0015-8). Speller.

Three-D Machine Vision. Technical Insights, Inc. Staff. 215p. 1984. 190.00 o.p. (ISBN 0-317-14659-9). Tech Insights.

Three-D Maze Art. Larry Evans. LC 80-16987. (Illus.). (gr. 1-12). 1980. pap. 4.95 o.p. (ISBN 0-89844-012-2). Troubador Pr.

Three-D Monster Mazes. Larry Evans. (Illus.). 40p. 1976. pap. 2.95 o.p. (ISBN 0-8431-1745-1). Troubador Pr.

Three Daughters. Waltraud A. Mitgutsch. Tr. by Lisel Mueller. (Helen & Kurt Wolff Book Ser.). 1987. 15.95 o.p. (ISBN 0-15-175298-2). HarBraceJ.

Three-Day Collision Course. Lachlan Patterson. 1985. 7.95 o.p. (ISBN 0-533-06026-5). Vantage.

Three Decades to Doom. David A. Oxley. 1985. 12.95 o.p. (ISBN 0-533-06552-6). Vantage.

Three Dimensional Poe. Haldeen Braddy. LC 73-75915. 1973. 10.00 o.p. (ISBN 0-87404-045-0). Tex Western.

Three-Dimensional Structure of Wood. B. G. Butterfield & B. Meylan. 1980. 25.00 o.p. (ISBN 0-412-16320-9, NO. 6403, Pub by Chapman & Hall England). Routledge Chapman & Hall.

Three Dimensional Turbulent Shear Flows. Ed. by F. Peterson & S. Carmi. 160p. 1982. 30.00 o.p. (G00211). ASME.

Three Essays. Albrecht Ritschl. Tr. by Philip Hefner from Ger. LC 72-75654. 304p. 1972. 10.95 o.p. (ISBN 0-8006-0224-2, Fortress). Augsburg Fortress.

Three Essays on a Sri Lanka Household Survey. Angus Deaton. (LSMS Working Paper: No. 11). 87p. 1981. 5.00 o.p. (ISBN 0-317-59168-1, BK 0038). World Bank.

Three Essays on Thucydides. John H. Finley, Jr. LC 67-17308. (Loeb Classical Monographs Ser). 1967. 16.00x o.s.i. (ISBN 0-674-88935-5). Harvard U Pr.

Three Essays, Seventeen Ninety-Three to Seventeen Ninety-Five: The Tubingen Essay, Berne Fragments, The Life of Jesus. G. W. Hegel. Ed. by Peter Fuss & John Dobbins. LC 83-40599. 192p. 1984. text ed. 18.95x o.s.i. (ISBN 0-268-01854-5, 85-18540). U of Notre Dame Pr.

Three Europeans Look at America: Welfare Policy, Social Trends & Foreign Affairs. Wilhelm Nolling et al. LC 77-22691. 1977. pap. 3.00x o.p. (ISBN 0-87772-246-3). UCB IGS.

Three Exposures. John Guare. LC 82-47922. 256p. 1982. 16.95 o.p. (ISBN 0-15-190178-3). HarBraceJ.

Three Fighters for Freedom. Brian Peachment. 1974. pap. text ed. 1.60 o.s.i. (ISBN 0-08-017617-8). Pergamon.

Three for Revolution. Burke Davis. LC 74-24320. (gr. 7 up). 1975. 6.25 o.p. (ISBN 0-15-286653-1, HJ). HarBraceJ.

Three from Catfish Bend. Ben L. Burman. Incl. High Water at Catfish Bend; Seven Stars for Catfish Bend; Owl Hoots Twice at Catfish Bend. LC 67-12490. (Illus.). (gr. 6 up). 6.95 o.s.i. (ISBN 0-8008-7676-8). Taplinger.

Three from Galilee. Marjorie Holmes. (General Ser.). 1986. lib. bdg. 15.95 o.p. (ISBN 0-8161-4047-2, Large Print Bks). G K Hall.

Three Gay Tales from Grimm. Wanda Gag. (Illus.). 63p. (gr. 1-5). 1982. pap. 2.50 o.p. (ISBN 0-571-11272-2). Faber & Faber.

Three Go Back. J. L. Mitchell. 254p. 1986. 15.00 o.p. (ISBN 0-947898-26-3). Kraus Repr.

Three Guns North. Burt Arthur & Budd Arthur. 1979. pap. 1.25 o.p. (ISBN 0-505-51349-8, Pub. by Tower Bks). Dorchester Pub Co.

Three Hear the Bells. new ed. Alice L. Humphreys. LC 78-52449. 4.95 o.p. (ISBN 0-8042-2586-9, John Knox). Westminster John Knox.

Three Hundred Best Hotels in the World. Rene Lecler. 220p. 1985. pap. 7.95 o.p. (ISBN 0-13-920216-1). P H.

Three Hundred Best Selling Home Plans. Ed. by Garlinghouse, L. F., Co., Staff. LC 85-90952. (Illus.). 224p. (Orig.). 1985. pap. 6.95 o.p. (ISBN 0-938708-15-5). L F Garlinghouse Co.

Three Hundred Eminent Personalities: A Psychosocial Analysis of the Famous. Mildred G. Goertzel et al. LC 78-1149. (Social & Behavioral Science & Higher Education Ser.). 1978. text ed. 39.95x o.p. (ISBN 0-87589-370-8). Jossey-Bass.

Three Hundred Five East. Paul Gillette. LC 72-94017. 1977. 9.50 o.p. (ISBN 0-87795-082-2, Arbor Hse). Morrow.

Three Hundred Great Families of Ireland. Irish Genealogical Foundation Staff. (Irish Genealogical Ser.). (Illus.). 380p. 1985. Repr. text ed. 28.00 o.s.i. (ISBN 0-940134-11-X). Irish Genealog.

Three Hundred Pound Cat. Rosamond Dauer. (Illus.). 32p. (gr. k-3). 1983. pap. 2.25 o.p. (ISBN 0-380-62745-0, 62745-0, Camelot). Avon.

Three Hundred Sixty-Five Days Out in Britain. Date not set. (ISBN 0-86145-765-X, Pub. by Auto Assn England). Salem Hse Pubs.

Three Hundred Thirty-Four. Thomas M. Disch. 1981. pap. 1.65 o.p. (ISBN 0-380-01633-8, 42630). Avon.

Three Hundred Ways to Say No to Your Man. Erica Heller & Vicki Levites. 64p. 1983. pap. 4.80 o.p. (ISBN 0-671-49534-8, Fireside). S&S.

Three Kings of Israel. Mark E. Petersen. LC 80-36697. 179p. 1980. 6.95 o.p. (ISBN 0-87747-829-5). Deseret Bk.

Three Knocks on the Wall. Evelyn S. Lampman. LC 79-23264. 192p. (gr. 5-9). 1980. 8.95 o.p. (ISBN 0-689-50167-6, Atheneum). Macmillan.

Three Lectures on Modern Art. Dreier et al. (ISBN 0-8022-0418-X). Philos Lib.

Three Literary Friendships: Byron & Shelley, Rimbaud & Verlaine, Robert Frost & Edward Thomas. John Lehmann. LC 83-22658. (Illus.). 184p. 1984. 17.95 o.s.i. (ISBN 0-03-061593-3, William Abrahams Bk). H Holt & Co.

Three Little Kittens. Illus. by Lilian Obligado. LC 73-16858. (Illus.). 32p. (gr. 1-2). 1974. pap. 1.95 o.s.i. (ISBN 0-394-82771-6, BYR). Random.

Three Little Kittens. Zokeisha. (Puppet Story Board Bks.). (Illus.). 12p. (ps-2). 1981. 2.95 o.s.i. (ISBN 0-671-42641-9, Little Simon). S&S.

Three Lives of Joseph Conrad. Olivia Coolidge. LC 72-75603. (Illus.). 240p. (gr. 5 up). 1972. 5.95 o.p. (ISBN 0-395-13890-6). HM.

Three Marias. Rachel De Queiroz. 1963. pap. write for info. o.p. (ISBN 0-292-73407-7). U of Tex Pr.

Three Masks of Gaba. Paul Twitchell. LC 82-84578. 199p. 1983. pap. text ed. 3.95 o.p. (ISBN 0-914766-98-8). Illum Way Pub.

Three-Membered Rings. Ed. by A. Davison et al. LC 51-5497. (Topics in Current Chemistry: Vol. 40). (Illus.). iv, 149p. 1973. 33.00 o.p. (ISBN 0-387-06265-3). Springer-Verlag.

Three Men Came to Heidelberg. Thea Van Halsema. (Christian Biography Ser.). 96p. 1982. pap. 3.95 o.p. (ISBN 0-8010-9289-2). Baker Bk.

Three Mozart Operas: Figaro, Don Giovanni, the Magic Flute. Robert B. Moberly. 303p. Repr. of 1968 ed. lib. bdg. 49.00 o.p. (Pub. by Am Repr Serv). Reprint Servs.

Three Neo-Tech Papers. Frank R. Wallace. 1986. 17.50 o.p. (ISBN 0-911752-50-1). I & O Pub.

Three New England Watercolor Painters. Gail Savage et al. LC 74-21601. (Illus.). 72p. (Orig.). 1974. pap. 1.50x o.p. (ISBN 0-86559-016-8). Art Inst Chi.

Three New York Poets. Mark Ameen et al. (Gay Verse Ser.). 94p. 1987. pap. 7.95 o.p. (ISBN 0-85449-052-3, Pub. by GMP England). Alyson Pubns.

Three of Us. Joyce Elbert. LC 72-94016. 1973. 7.95 o.p. (ISBN 0-87795-052-0, Arbor Hse). Morrow.

Three on the Trail. Max Brand. (Large Print Books (General Ser.)). 1985. lib. bdg. 13.95 o.p. (ISBN 0-8161-3851-6). G K Hall.

Three Passions of Countess Natalya. Alan Fisher. 352p. 1986. pap. 3.95 o.p. (ISBN 0-380-75105-4). Avon.

Three Philosophers: Political Prisoners in the Soviet Union. Ed. by Taras Zakydalsky. (Documents of Ukrainian Samveydav: No. 4). 1976. 1.00 o.s.i. (ISBN 0-686-58234-9). Smoloskyp.

Three Philosophies of Education. Henry J. Boettcher. LC 66-26963. 248p. 1967. (ISBN 0-8022-0146-6). Philos Lib.

Three Plays. Nissim Ezekiel. (Writers Workshop Bluebird Ser.). 95p. 1975. cancelled o.s.i. (ISBN 0-88253-660-5); pap. text ed. 4.00 o.s.i. (ISBN 0-88253-659-1). Ind-US Inc.

Three Plays. Horton Foote & William Faulkner. Incl. Roots in a Parched Ground; Old Man; Tomorrow. LC 62-9435. 145p. 1962. pap. 1.45 o.p. (ISBN 0-15-691275-9, Harv). HarBraceJ.

Three Plays. Thomas Middleton. Ed. by Kenneth Muir. (Rowman & Littlefield University Library). 217p. 1975. 9.50x o.p. (ISBN 0-87471-555-5); pap. 4.75x o.p. (ISBN 0-87471-556-3). Rowman.

Three Plays: Absurd Person Singular, Absent Friends, & Bedroom Farce. Alan Ayckbourn. LC 78-20339. 1979. pap. 6.95 o.s.i. (ISBN 0-394-17083-0, B423, BC). Grove.

Three Plays by Thornton Wilder. Thornton Wilder. 1976. pap. 2.50 o.p. (ISBN 0-380-00527-1, 69005-5, Bard). Avon.

Three Plots for Asey Mayo. Phoebe A. Taylor. 1969. 5.95 o.p. (ISBN 0-393-08534-1). Norton.

Three Plus One Equals Billions: The Bendix-Martin Marietta War. Allan Sloan. (Illus.). 356p. 1983. 15.95 o.p. (ISBN 0-87795-504-2, Arbor Hse). Morrow.

Three Political Plays. Ed. by Arlene Sykes. (Contemporary Australian Plays Ser.: No. 9). 156p. 1980. 24.50x o.p. (ISBN 0-7022-1439-6); pap. 12.00x o.p. (ISBN 0-7022-1449-3). U of Queensland Pr.

Three Poor Tailors. Victor G. Ambrus. LC 66-11196. (Illus.). (gr. k-3). 1966. 6.50 o.p. (ISBN 0-15-286847-X, HJ). HarBraceJ.

Three Prefaces on Linnaeus & Robert Brown. W. T. Stearn. (Illus.). 1962. pap. 11.50x o.p. (ISBN 3-7682-0099-X). Lubrecht & Cramer.

Three Prophetic Voices: Studies in Joel, Amos & Hosea. Herbert F. Stevenson. 158p. 1971. 5.95 o.p. (ISBN 0-551-05266-X). Attic Pr.

Three Psychologies: Perspectives from Freud, Skinner & Rogers. 2nd ed. Robert D. Nye. LC 80-25716. 170p. (Orig.). 1981. pap. text ed. 10.75 pub net o.p. (ISBN 0-8185-0438-2). Brooks-Cole.

Three Robbers. Tomi Ungerer. LC 62-7367. (Illus.). (ps-3). 1962. PLB 7.43 o.p. (ISBN 0-689-20452-3, Atheneum). Macmillan.

Three Romes. Russell A. Fraser. LC 84-12946. 352p. 1985. 17.95 o.p. (ISBN 0-15-190186-4). HarBraceJ.

Three Rs of Investing: Return, Risk & Relativity. Austin S. Donnelly. LC 84-72830. 1985. 25.00 o.p. (ISBN 0-87094-557-2). Dow Jones-Irwin.

Three Sectional Staff. Kam Yuen. LC 79-87639. (Weapons Ser.). (Illus.). 1979. pap. 7.95 o.p. (ISBN 0-89750-064-4, 332). Ohara Pubns.

Three Sisters. Anton Chekhov. 1965. pap. 0.75 o.p. (ISBN 0-380-01582-X, 19844, Bard). Avon.

Three-Sixty-Three-Seventy Programming in Assembly Language. Ned Chapin. 1973. text ed. 47.95 o.p. (ISBN 0-07-010552-9). McGraw.

Three Solid Stones. Martha Mvungi. (African Writers Ser.). 1975. pap. 6.50 o.p. Heinemann Ed.

Three Steps to the Essay: An Expository Handbook. John Lindberg. LC 80-69031. 320p. 1981. pap. text ed. 14.50 o.p. (ISBN 0-8191-1714-5). U Pr of Amer.

Three Strikes, but Not Out: Perspectives on Modern Education. Eva M. Walters. 87p. 1985. 7.95 o.p. (ISBN 0-533-06036-2). Vantage.

Three Suitors: One Husband & Until Further Notice. Guillaume Oyono-Mbia. 1981. pap. 6.95 o.p. (ISBN 0-413-32680-2, NO. 6480). Heinemann Ed.

Three Thirty-One Last Processes in Radiation Chemistry: International Symposium on Fast Processes in Radiation Chemistry. Y. Tabata. 1983. pap. 50.00 flexi-cover o.p. (ISBN 0-08-029155-4). Pergamon.

Three Twins: The Telling of a South Indian Folk Epic. Brenda E. Beck. LC 80-8841. (Illus.). 256p. 1982. 22.50x o.p. (ISBN 0-253-36014-5). Ind U Pr.

Three Victorian Travel Writers: An Annotated Bibliography of Criticism on Mrs. Frances Milton Trollope, Samuel Butler, & Robert Louis Stevenson. Frederick J. Bethke. 1978. lib. bdg. 29.00 o.p. (ISBN 0-8161-7852-6, Hall Reference). G K Hall.

Three Virginia Writers: A Reference Guide. Ed. by George C. Longest. 1978. lib. bdg. 31.50 o.p. (ISBN 0-8161-7841-0, Hall Reference). G K Hall.

Three Weeks in Spring. Joan H. Parker & Robert B. Parker. LC 77-12396. 1978. 7.95 o.p. (ISBN 0-395-26282-8). HM.

Three Winds of Death: The Saga of the 503rd Parachute Regimental Combat Team in the South Pacific. Bennett M. Guthrie. (Illus.). 272p. 1984. 13.50 o.p. (ISBN 0-682-40169-2). Exposition-Phoenix.

Three Wishes. Paul Galdone. (Illus.). (gr. k-3). 1961. text ed. 8.95 o.p. (ISBN 0-07-022714-4). McGraw.

Three Wishes: A Collection of Puerto Rican Folktales. Ed. by Ricardo E. Alegria. Tr. by Elizabeth Culbert. LC 69-13770. (Illus.). (gr. 4-6). 1969. 6.75 o.p. (ISBN 0-15-286871-2, HJ). HarBraceJ.

Three with a Bullet. Arthur Lyons. LC 84-4598. (Rinehart Suspense Novel Ser.). 240p. 1986. 13.95 o.p. (ISBN 0-03-059617-3); pap. 3.95 o.p. H Holt & Co.

Three Worlds of Christian Marxist Encounters. Ed. by Nicolas Piediscalzi & Robert G. Thobaben. LC 84-48724. 240p. 1985. pap. 4.95 o.p. (ISBN 0-8006-1840-8, 1-1840, Fortress). Augsburg Fortress.

Three Writers of the Far West: A Reference Guide. Ray C. Longtin. 1980. lib. bdg. 40.50 o.p. (ISBN 0-8161-7832-1, Hall Reference). G K Hall.

Three Years in Chile. Mrs. George B. Merwin. Ed. by Harvey C. Gardiner. LC 65-27286. (Latin American Travel Ser.). 128p. 1966. 4.50x o.p. (ISBN 0-8093-0226-8). S Ill U Pr.

Three Years with Grant: As Recalled by War Correspondent Sylvanus Cadwallader. Sylvanus Cadawallader. Ed. by Benjamin P. Thomas. LC 80-21191. (Illus.). xiv, 361p. 1980. Repr. of 1955 ed. lib. bdg. 35.00x o.p. (ISBN 0-313-22576-1, CATY). Greenwood.

Threepersons Hunt. Brian Garfield. LC 73-87704. 264p. 1974. 6.95 o.p. (ISBN 0-87131-140-2). M Evans.

Threshold Approach in Urban, Regional & Environmental Planning: Theory & Practice. Jerzy Kozlowski. (Illus.). 262p. 1987. text ed. 37.50x o.p. (ISBN 0-7022-1929-0); pap. text ed. 16.50x o.p. (ISBN 0-7022-2020-5). U of Queensland Pr.

Threshold Logic: A Synthesis Approach. Michael Dertouzos. (Press Research Monographs: No. 32). 1965. 27.50x o.p. (ISBN 0-262-04009-3). MIT Pr.

Threshold Logic & Its Applications. Saburo Muroga. LC 76-165830. 494p. 1971. 37.50 o.p. (ISBN 0-471-62530-2, JW). Krieger.

Threshold to Nursing. Jillian MacGuire. 271p. 1969. pap. text ed. 5.00x o.p. (Pub. by Bedford England). Gower Pub Co.

Thresholds of Existence. Upton Ewing. 304p. 1956. (ISBN 0-8022-0463-5). Philos Lib.

Thrift. Katharine E. Cobey. LC 78-5146. (Ser. Three). (Illus.). 1978. pap. 2.00 o.p. (ISBN 0-931846-06-4). Wash Writers Pub.

Thrift Industry in 1985. 1026p. 1985. 15.00 o.p. (A4-4134). PLI.

Thrift Institution Automation Survey. 300p. 1982. 200.00 o.p. (ISBN 0-318-14107-8); members 50.00 o.p. (ISBN 0-318-14108-6). Finan Mgrs Soc.

Thrift Shop Decorating. Adele Williams. LC 75-31071. 1976. 9.95 o.p. (ISBN 0-87795-127-6, Arbor Hse); pap. 3.95 o.p. (ISBN 0-87795-132-2). Morrow.

Throbbing Drums: The Story of James H. Robinson. Amy Lee. (Orig.). 1968. pap. 0.95 o.p. (ISBN 0-377-84141-2). Friendship Pr.

Thromboembolism: A New Approach to Therapy. Ed. by J. R. Mitchell & J. G. Domenet. 1978. 43.00 o.p. (ISBN 0-12-500050-2). Acad Pr.

Thrombosis & Bleeding Disorders: Theory & Methods. Ed. by N. U. Bang. 1971. 60.00 o.p. (ISBN 0-12-077750-9). Acad Pr.

Thrombosis & Urokinase. R. Paoletti & S. Sherry. 1977. 69.00 o.p. (ISBN 0-12-544960-7). Acad Pr.

Throme of the Erril of Sherill. Patricia A. McKillip. LC 73-76324. (Illus.). 80p. (gr. 5 up). 1973. 4.95 o.p. (ISBN 0-689-30115-4, Atheneum). Macmillan.

Throne of Saturn. Allen Drury. 736p. 1981. pap. 1.95 o.p. (ISBN 0-380-00792-4, 22996). Avon.

Through a Brief Darkness. Richard Peck. (YA) (gr. 7 up). 1981. pap. 1.25 o.p. (ISBN 0-380-00161-6, 42093-7). Avon.

Through a Child's Eyes. Donalyn Powell. (Illus.). 48p. (Orig.). 1987. 6.95 o.p. (ISBN 0-87788-812-4). Shaw Pubs.

Through a Child's Looking Glass. Ruth Marion. (Illus.). 36p. (Orig.). 1984. pap. 5.95 o.s.i. (ISBN 0-934318-41-7). Falcon Pr MT.

Through Clouds & Sunshine. Don J. Black. LC 75-3765. 102p. (Orig.). 1975. pap. 4.50 o.p. (ISBN 0-942241-21-5, 8743). Pubs Bk Sales.

Through Darkest America. Neal Barrett, Jr. (Isaac Asimov Presents Ser.). 320p. 1987. 15.95 o.p. (ISBN 0-86553-184-6). Congdon & Weed.

Through Ferrengi Eyes: The Diary of a Peace Corps Volunteer in Ethiopia, 1974-1976. Henry Klein. (Illus.). 1979. 9.00 o.p. (ISBN 0-682-49303-1). Exposition-Phoenix.

Through France to the Med: By Canal to the Sea. Mike Harper. (Illus.). 216p. 1983. 11.95 o.p. (ISBN 0-85614-034-1). Hippocrene Bks.

Through My Eyes. Yvonne A. Miller. (Illus.). 48p. 1983. 5.50 o.p. (ISBN 0-682-49971-4). Exposition-Phoenix.

Through My Memory's Window. Robbie Marquez. 1978. 4.00 o.p. (ISBN 0-682-49005-9). Exposition-Phoenix.

Through Other Eyes: Vivid Narratives of Some of the Bible's Most Notable Characters. Carl E. Price. 144p. (Orig.). 1987. pap. 6.95 o.p. (ISBN 0-8358-0555-7). Upper Room.

Through Prayer to Reality. Douglas A. Rhymes. LC 74-81813. 1976. pap. 3.95 o.p. (ISBN 0-88489-088-0). St Mary's.

Through Russian Eyes: President Kennedy's One Thousand Thirty-Six Days. Anatolii A. Gromyko. Ed. by Philip A. Garon. LC 73-75637. 239p. 1973. 15.95 o.s.i. (ISBN 0-914250-00-0). Intl Lib.

Through the Ages: A History of the Christian Church. Ernest T. Thompson. (Orig.). 1965. pap. 4.95 o.p. (ISBN 0-8042-9040-7, John Knox). Westminster John Knox.

Through the Broken Mirror with Alice. Maia Wojciechowska. LC 74-183848. (gr. 5 up). 1972. 5.95 o.p. (ISBN 0-15-286950-6, HJ). HarBraceJ.

Through the Curtain. Viola P. Neal & Shafica Karagulla. LC 83-71171. 368p. 1983. 14.95 o.p. (ISBN 0-87516-517-6). DeVorss.

Through the Forest of Twisted Dreams. R. L. Stine. (Wizards, Warriors & You Ser.: Bk. 1). (Illus.). 112p. 1984. pap. 2.50 o.p. (ISBN 0-380-88047-4, 88047-4). Avon.

Through the Grecourt Gates. Eleanor T. Lincoln. (Illus.). 118p. 1978. pap. 3.50 o.p. (ISBN 0-87391-025-7). Smith Coll.

Through the Hidden Door. Rosemary Wells. Date not set. price not set o.p. (Point). Scholastic Inc.

Through the Kaleidoscope. Cozy Baker. LC 85-71412. (Illus.). 144p. 1985. 15.00 o.p. (ISBN 0-9608930-1-6). Beechcliff Bks.

Through the Looking Glass. Anthony Verrier. 1983. 18.00 o.p. (ISBN 0-393-01648-X). Norton.

Through the Looking Glass see Alice's Adventures in Wonderland.

Titles

Through the Looking-Glass: And What Alice Found There. Lewis Carroll. LC 68-21827. (Illus.). 176p. (ps up). 1987. 16.95 o.s.i. (ISBN 0-8052-4036-5). Schocken.

Through the Micromaze: A Visual Guide from Ashton-Tate. Wayne Creekmore. (Through the Micromaze Ser.: Vol. 1). 250p. 1983. pap. 9.95 o.p. (ISBN 0-912677-02-3). Tate Pub.

Through the MicroMaze: A Visual Guide to Getting Organized. W. Creekmore & S. Behasa. 1985. pap. text ed. 9.95 o.p. (ISBN 0-07-912618-9). McGraw.

Through the Moongate. Leonard Wolcott & Carolyn Wolcott. (Orig.). (gr. 4-6). 1978. pap. 4.00 o.p. (ISBN 0-377-00074-4). Friendship Pr.

Through the Valley. Arthur W. Mielke. 1977. pap. 1.25 o.p. (ISBN 0-380-01759-8, 34827). Avon.

Through the Valley of Love. Shirley Cook. 224p. 1987. pap. 5.95 o.p. (ISBN 0-310-47381-0, 15584P). Zondervan.

Through the Years in Genesee: An Illustrated History. Alice Lethbridge. 144p. 1985. 22.95 o.p. (ISBN 0-89781-161-5). Windsor Pubns Inc.

Through These Eyes I Saw. James J. Jackson. 30p. 1985. 4.95 o.p. (ISBN 0-533-06221-7). Vantage.

Through Unexplores Texas. W. B. Parker. LC 84-80800. 256p. 1984. ltd. ed. 50.00 o.p. (ISBN 0-87611-073-1); pap. 8.95 o.p. (ISBN 0-87611-065-0). Tex St Hist Assn.

Throwing Shadows. E. L. Konigsburg. (gr. 7 up). 1981. pap. 3.95 o.p. (Aladdin). Macmillan.

Throwing the Sticks: Occult Self-Therapy - The Arts of Self-Transcendence in Post-Freudian Modes of Thought. John C. Cooper. LC 85-51340. 175p. (Orig.). 1985. pap. 9.95x o.p. (ISBN 0-932269-49-4). Wyndham Hall.

Thru' the Turnstile: Tales of My Two Centuries. Alice C. Williams. LC 76-15977. 1976. 6.95 o.p. (ISBN 0-395-24404-8). HM.

Thruway West see Naked Range.

Thunder at Dawn. Jack Hoffenberg. 1978. pap. 1.25 o.p. (ISBN 0-380-01583-8, 37226). Avon.

Thunder from Heaven: The Story of the 17th Airborne Division in WW II. Don Pay. LC 80-69273. (Airborne Ser.: No. 4). (Illus.). 179p. 1980. Repr. 25.00 o.p. (ISBN 0-89839-037-0). Battery Pr.

Thunder in the Mountains. Hank Johnston. LC 70-170098. 128p. 1989. 24.95 o.s.i. (ISBN 0-87046-017-X, Pub. by Trans-Anglo). Interurban.

Thunder on Forbidden Mountain. Theodore W. Munch & Robert D. Winthrop. LC 75-35852. (gr. 5-9). 1976. 6.95 o.s.i. (ISBN 0-664-32588-2, Westminster). Westminster John Knox.

Thunder Pup. Janet Hickman. LC 81-2614. 144p. (gr. 3-7). 1981. 8.95 o.s.i. (ISBN 0-02-743770-1). Macmillan.

Thunderbird Song. Carl M. Beall. 1970. 5.50 o.p. (ISBN 0-682-47055-4). Exposition-Phoenix.

Thunderbolt: A Documentary History of the Republic P-47. Roger Freeman. (Illus.). 1980. encore ed 6.95 o.p. (ISBN 0-684-17573-8, ScribT). Scribner.

Thunderbolt-Champ of the Patowmack. James Percival Haynes. 288p. 1980. 11.00 o.p. (ISBN 0-682-49589-1). Exposition-Phoenix.

Thundercats & the Ghost Warrior: A Find Your Fate Fantasy. Megan Stine & H. William Stine. LC 85-60157. (Illus.). 80p. (gr. 9-12). 1985. pap. 1.95 o.s.i. (ISBN 0-394-87419-6, BYR). Random.

Thundercats & the Snowmen of Hook Mountain: A Find Your Fate Fantasy. Megan Stine & H. William Stine. LC 85-60502. (Illus.). 80p. (gr. 9-12). 1985. pap. 1.95 o.s.i. (ISBN 0-394-87420-X, BYR). Random.

Thundergate, Book III: The Story of Canada. Dennis Adair. 1982. pap. 4.25 o.p. (ISBN 0-380-80952-4, 80952). Avon.

Thurber: A Biography. Burton Bernstein. 1985. 10.95 o.p. (ISBN 0-87795-690-1, Arbor Hse). Morrow.

Thursday Woman. Muriel Davidson. LC 77-18387. 1979. 9.95 o.p. (ISBN 0-689-10884-2, Atheneum). Macmillan.

Thursday's Child. Faith Baldwin. LC 75-18668. 1976. 7.95 o.p. (ISBN 0-03-014916-9). H Holt & Co.

Thursdays 'til Nine. Jane Trahey. LC 79-3366. 230p. 1980. 8.95 o.p. (ISBN 0-15-190261-5). HarBraceJ.

Thurston House. Danielle Steel. (General Ser.). 725p. 1983. lib. bdg. 19.95 o.p. (ISBN 0-8161-3580-0, Large Print Bks). G K Hall.

Thurston House. Danielle Steele. 512p. (YA) pap. 7.95 o.p. (ISBN 0-440-58655-0, Dell Trade Pbks). Dell.

Thus Spake the Kings. Walter H. Marx. (Illus.). 1978. pap. text ed. 6.95x o.p. (ISBN 0-88334-106-9). Ind Sch Pr.

Thwaites' Jesuit Relations, Errata & Addenda. Joseph P. Donnelly. LC 66-27701. (American West Ser). 1967. 6.95 o.p. (ISBN 0-8294-0025-7). Loyola.

Thy Father's House. Monique R. High. LC 86-32975. 384p. 1987. pap. 17.95 o.p. (ISBN 0-385-29558-8). Delacorte.

Thy Father's House. Date not set. (ISBN 0-385-29558-8). Delacorte.

Thy Kingdom Come. Peter Bart. 1981. 13.95 o.p. (ISBN 0-671-41912-9, Linden Pr). S&S.

Thy Rod & Thy Creel. Odell Shepard. LC 84-60996. 128p. 1984. pap. 12.95 o.p. (ISBN 0-8329-0364-7, Pub. by Winchester Pr). New Century.

Thyestes. Jasper Heywood. Ed. by Joost Daalder. (New Mermaids Ser.). 1984. pap. 5.95x o.p. (ISBN 0-393-95237-1). Norton.

Thyristor Control of A. C. Motors. J. M. Murphy. 212p. 1973. text ed. 46.00 o.p. (ISBN 0-08-016943-0). Pergamon.

Thyristor Discontinued Devices. Ed. by Jim Fitzgerald. 448p. 1987. 70.00 o.p. (ISBN 0-317-53936-1). DATA Busn Pub.

Thyristors: Theory & Applications. 2nd ed. Krishna K. Sugandhi & Rajendra K. Sughandi. 315p. 1984. 31.95x o.p. (ISBN 0-470-20015-4). Halsted Pr.

Thyroid & Its Diseases. 5th ed. Leslie J. DeGroot et al. LC 83-27411. 907p. 1984. 65.00 o.p. (ISBN 0-471-88688-2, Pub. by Wiley Med). Wiley.

Thyroid Hormone Metabolism. Ed. by W. A. Harland & J. S. Orr. 1975. 68.00 o.p. (ISBN 0-12-325650-X). Acad Pr.

Thyroid Research III: Eighth International Thyroid Congress 3-5 February 1980, Sydney, Australia. Ed. by J. R. Stockkigt et al. 800p. 1980. 185.00 o.p. (ISBN 0-08-026361-5). Pergamon.

Thyroiditis & Thyroid Function: Clinical, Morphological, & Physiopathological Studies. Paul A. Bastenie & A. M. Ermans. 360p. 1972. 125.00 o.p. (ISBN 0-08-016628-8). Pergamon.

Thyrza: A Tale. George Gissing. Ed. by Jacob King. 528p. (Orig.). 1985. pap. 7.95 o.p. (NO. 9280). Routledge Chapman & Hall.

TI BASIC Computer Programs for the Home. Date not set. (ISBN 0-8104-6402-0). Sams.

TI Games for Kids. Robert Ingalls. 178p. 1984. pap. 12.95 o.p. (ISBN 0-942386-39-6). Compute Pubns.

TI LOGO. Hal Abelson. (Illus.). 1984. pap. text ed. 19.95 o.p. (ISBN 0-07-038459-2, BYTE Bks). McGraw.

Tibet & Its History. 2nd, rev. ed. Hugh E. Richardson. LC 84-5469. (Illus.). 327p. (Orig.). 1984. 19.95 o.p. (ISBN 0-87773-292-2, 54072-7). Shambhala Pubns.

Tibetan Buddhist Chant: Musical Notations & Interpretations of a Song Book by the Bkah Brgyud Pa & Sa Skya Pa Sects. Walter Kaufmann. Tr. by Thubten Jigme Norbu. LC 72-85606. (Humanities Ser.: No. 70). 578p. 1975. 25.00x o.p. (ISBN 0-253-36017-X). Ind U Pr.

Tibetan Folk Tales. Fredrick Hyde-Chambers & Audrey Hyde-Chambers. LC 81-50970. (Illus.). 186p. (Orig.). 1981. 8.95 o.s.i. (ISBN 0-87773-215-9). Shambhala Pubns.

Tibetan Mandalas: The Ngor Collection. Ngor Tharttse mKhanpo bSodnams rgyamtsho. Ed. by Musashi Tachikawa. (Illus., Tibetan, Sanskrit, Japanese & Eng.). 1985. Set. write for info. o.s.i. (ISBN 0-87773-800-9). Shambhala Pubns.

Tibetan Medicine & Other Holistic Health-Care Systems. Tom Dummer. 288p. 1988. pap. 13.95 o.p. (ISBN 0-415-01278-3). Routledge Chapman & Hall.

Tibetan Paintings: A Study of Tibetan Thankas, 11th-19th Centuries. Pratapaditya Pal. LC 84-51458. (Illus.). 235p. 1985. 85.00 o.p. (ISBN 0-85667-189-4). Sotheby Pubns.

Tibetan Thangka Painting: Methods & Materials. David Jackson & Janice Jackson. LC 84-5565. (Illus.). 186p. 1984. 32.50 o.p. (ISBN 0-87773-301-5, 54205-3). Shambhala Pubns.

TIBs of Bill Caudill: CRSS. 206p. 1985. pap. 5.00 o.p. (ISBN 0-317-57031-5). Am Inst Arch.

Ticket Out. Lucy Rosenthal. 368p. 1983. 14.95 o.p. (ISBN 0-15-190282-8). HarBraceJ.

Ticket That Exploded. William S. Burroughs. 1967. pap. 2.95 o.s.i. (ISBN 0-394-17128-4, B164, BC). Grove.

Ticket That Exploded. William S. Burroughs. LC 86-33486. 224p. 1987. pap. 6.95 o.s.i. (ISBN 0-394-62364-9, BC). Grove.

Tickle Tree. Fran Manushkin. (Illus.). 32p. (gr. 3-6). 1982. 10.00 o.p. (ISBN 0-89919-077-4, Clarion). HM.

Tickleoctopus. Audrey Wood. (Illus.). (ps-2). 1980. 7.95 o.p. (ISBN 0-395-29083-X). HM.

Tickling Tails. Scheherazade Shrew. LC 84-90497. 98p. (gr. 3-5). 1985. 6.95 o.p. (ISBN 0-533-06381-7). Vantage.

Tidal Deposits: A Case Book of Recent Examples & Fossil Counterparts. Ed. by R. N. Ginsburg. LC 75-28228. (Illus.). xiii, 421p. 1975. 52.00 o.p. (ISBN 0-387-06823-6). Springer-Verlag.

Tidal Energy. Roger H. Charlier. 1982. 36.95 o.p. (ISBN 0-442-24425-8). Van Nos Reinhold.

Tidal Friction & the Earth's Rotation. Ed. by P. Brosche & J. Suendermann. (Illus.). 1979. 27.00 o.p. (ISBN 0-387-09046-0). Springer-Verlag.

Tidal Wave. Spencer Nordyke. 33p. (Orig.). 1985. pap. text ed. 1.95 o.s.i. (ISBN 0-914307-44-4). R Tilton Ministries.

Tide Flowing. Joan Phipson. LC 80-24375. 168p. (gr. 7 up). 1981. 8.95 o.p. (ISBN 0-689-50196-X, Atheneum). Macmillan.

Tide of Empires: Decisive Naval Campaigns in the Rise of the West, Vol. 1. Peter Padfield. (Illus.). 268p. 1979. 19.95 o.p. (ISBN 0-7100-0150-9). Routledge Chapman & Hall.

Tide of Empires: Decisive Naval Campaigns in the Rise of the West, 1654-1763, Vol. 2. Peter Padfield. 232p. 1982. 27.50 o.p. (ISBN 0-7100-9215-6). Routledge Chapman & Hall.

Tides of Empire: Discursions on the Expansion of Britain Overseas. G. S. Graham. 1972. 7.00 o.p. (ISBN 0-7735-0137-1, McGill Canada). U of Toronto Pr.

Tides of Love. Patricia Matthews. (Gregg Hardcovers Ser.). 1985. lib. bdg. 13.95 o.p. (ISBN 0-8398-2877-2, Gregg). G K Hall.

Tie-Dyed Paper: An Easy New Craft. Anne Maile. LC 74-21644. (Illus.). 136p. (gr. 9-12). 1975. 12.95 o.s.i. (ISBN 0-8008-7702-0). Taplinger.

Tie That Binds. Kent Haruf. 224p. 1984. 13.95 o.p. (ISBN 0-03-071979-8). H Holt & Co.

Tied up in Tinsel. Ngaio Marsh. 1986. 13.95 o.p. (ISBN 0-317-53158-1, Large Print Bks). G K Hall.

Tiepolo: A Bicentenary Exhibition, 1770-1970 see Exhibition Catalogues from the Fogg Art Museum.

Tiepolo Drawings. George Knox. (Illus.). 316p. (Orig.). pap. 15.95 o.p. (ISBN 0-901486-63-9, Pub. by Victoria & Albert Mus UK). Faber & Faber.

Tierra & Libertad! Photographs of Mexico, 1900-1935. Ed. & pref. by David Elliott. (Illus.). 104p. (Orig.). 1986. pap. 14.95 o.p. (ISBN 0-87663-891-4). Universe.

Tiffany Table Manners. W. Hoving. 1980. pap. 2.95 o.s.i. (ISBN 0-679-24108-6). McKay.

Tiger by the Tail: A Marionette Play. 8.00 o.p. (ISBN 0-686-23326-3). Rochester Folk Art.

Tiger Game. William E. Knight. LC 86-6223. 1987. 15.95 o.p. (ISBN 0-934878-79-X). Dembner Bks.

Tiger Island. Patrick Clay. (Sgt. Hawk Ser.: No. 4). 240p. 1982. pap. 2.50 o.p. (ISBN 0-8439-1104-2, Pub. by Leisure Bks CT). Dorchester Pub Co.

Tiger-Skin Rug. Gerald Rose. (Illus.). 30p. (ps-1). 1984. 8.95 o.p. (ISBN 0-571-11278-1). Faber & Faber.

Tiger Watch. Jan Wahl. LC 82-964. (Illus.). 32p. (ps-3). 1982. 12.95 o.p. (ISBN 0-15-287674-X, HJ). HarBraceJ.

Tiger Who Lost His Stripes. Anthony Paul. LC 81-83987. (Illus.). 32p. (ps-3). 1982. 11.95 o.p. (ISBN 0-15-287681-2, HJ). HarBraceJ.

Tigers & Other Lilies. Howard Moss & Frederick Belli. LC 77-1998. (Illus.). (gr. 4-7). 1977. 5.95 o.p. (ISBN 0-689-30592-3, Atheneum). Macmillan.

Tiger's Whisker & Other Tales & Legends from Asia & the Pacific. Harold Courlander. LC 59-10172. (Illus.). (gr. 4-6). 1959. 5.25 o.p. (ISBN 0-15-287652-9, HJ). HarBraceJ.

Tight Case. Edward Hogan. 288p. 1987. 18.95 o.p. (ISBN 0-02-553330-4). Macmillan.

Tightrope Walker. Dorothy Gilman. 224p. 1980. pap. 2.95 o.p. (ISBN 0-449-24305-2, Crest). Fawcett.

Tigran Petrosian - World Champion. A. O. O'Kelly De Galway. 1965. 35.00 o.p. (ISBN 0-08-011013-4); pap. text ed. 35.00 o.p. (ISBN 0-08-011012-6). Pergamon.

Tikta'liktak: An Eskimo Legend. James Houston. LC 65-21696. (Illus.). (gr. 2-4). 1965. 9.95 o.p. (ISBN 0-15-287745-2, HJ). HarBraceJ.

Tile: Remodeling with. Sunset Magazine & Books Editors. LC 77-90719. (Illus.). 80p. 1978. pap. 5.95 o.p. (ISBN 0-376-01674-4, Sunset Bks). Sunset-Lane.

Tiles: A Collector's Guide. Hans Van Lemmen. (Illus.). 143p. 1985. 12.95 o.s.i. (ISBN 0-285-62408-3, Pub. by Souvenir Pr Ltd Uk). Seven Hills Bk Dists.

Tiles: Monographs. Mary Vance. (Architecture Ser.: A 1360). 14p. 1985. 2.25 o.p. (ISBN 0-89028-350-8). Vance Biblios.

Till Armageddon. Billy Graham. 224p. 1984. pap. 6.95 o.p. (ISBN 0-8499-2998-9, 2998-9). Word Bks.

Till Death Do Us Part. John D. Carr. 200p. 1985. pap. 4.95 o.p. (ISBN 0-930330-21-8). Intl Polygonics.

Till Death Do Us Part. Phil Lenhart. 104p. 1987. 8.95 o.p. (ISBN 0-8062-3079-7). Carlton.

Till Death Do Us Part: Bendix vs. Martin Marietta. Hope Lampert. LC 83-8546. 288p. 1983. 12.95 o.p. (ISBN 0-15-190310-7). HarBraceJ.

Till Death Do Us Part or Something Else Comes up. Zane Alexander. LC 76-16851. 1976. pap. 4.50 o.s.i. (ISBN 0-664-24750-4, Westminster). Westminster John Knox.

Till the Break of Day. Maia Wojciechowska. LC 72-79145. 156p. (gr. 7 up). 1972. 5.95 o.p. (ISBN 0-15-287800-9, HJ). HarBraceJ.

Till We Have Faces: A Myth Retold. C. S. Lewis. LC 56-71300. (Illus.). 1957. 9.95 o.p. (ISBN 0-15-190323-9). HarBraceJ.

Tilly. Frank E. Peretti. 126p. Date not set. price not set o.p. (Crossway Bks). Good News.

Tilly's House. Faith Jaques. LC 78-31105. (Illus.). 32p. (ps-4). 1979. 9.95 o.p. (ISBN 0-689-50138-2, Atheneum). Macmillan.

Tilt! Burt Hirschfeld. pap. 2.95 o.p. (ISBN 0-440-08817-8, Emerald). Dell.

Tim: A Baby's Odyssey. Ruth Lucier. (Illus.). 80p. (ps). 1982. 5.50 o.p. (ISBN 0-682-49843-2). Exposition-Phoenix.

Timber Design & Construction Handbook. Timber Engineering Company staff. 1956. text ed. 59.50 o.p. (ISBN 0-07-064606-6). McGraw.

Timber Designer's Manual. E. C. Ozelton & J. A. Baird. (Illus.). 1976. 29.95x o.p. (ISBN 0-8464-0927-5). Beekman Pubs.

Timber-Frame House in England. Trudy West. 12.95 o.p. (ISBN 0-8038-0245-5). Architectural.

Timber-Frame Housing in Britain. Valerie J. Nurcombe. (Architecture Ser.: A 1443). 20p. 1985. 3.00 o.p. (ISBN 0-89028-513-6). Vance Biblios.

Timber in Excavations. 2nd ed. Timber Research & Development Association Staff. 76p. 1984. 26.00 o.p. (ISBN 0-7277-0869-4, Pub. by T Telford UK). Am Soc Civil Eng.

Time. Jan Pienkowski. Ed. by Kate Klimo. (Pienkowski Concept Bks.). (Illus.). 32p. (ps-k). 1983. 4.80 o.s.i. (ISBN 0-671-46247-4, Little Simon). S&S.

Time after Time. Molly Keane. LC 83-47966. 247p. 1984. 13.45 o.s.i. (ISBN 0-394-53280-5). Knopf.

Time & Clocks: A Description of Ancient & Modern Methods of Measuring Time. Henry H. Cunynghame. LC 77-78127. (Illus.). 208p. 1970. Repr. of 1906 ed. 35.00x o.p. (ISBN 0-8103-3576-X). Gale.

Time & Clocks for the Space Age. James Jespersen & Jane Fitz-Randolph. LC 79-14578. (Illus.). (gr. 6 up). 1979. 10.95 o.p. (ISBN 0-689-30710-1, Atheneum). Macmillan.

Time & the Calendars. W. M. O'Neil. (Illus.). 224p. 1978. Repr. of 1975 ed. 23.00 o.p. (ISBN 0-424-00003-2, Pub by Sydney U Pr). Intl Spec Bk.

Time & the Riddle: Thirty-One Zen Stories. Howard Fast. (Orig.). 1980. pap. 6.95 o.p. (ISBN 0-395-29180-1). HM.

Time & Tide Wait for No Man. Ed. by Dale Spender. 212p. (Orig.). 1984. pap. 10.95 o.p. (ISBN 0-86358-024-6). Routledge Chapman & Hall.

Time & Time Again: Autobiographies. Dan Jacobson. Ed. by Peter Davison. LC 85-47787. 214p. 1985. 15.95 o.p. (ISBN 0-87113-027-0). Atlantic Monthly.

Time & Timelessness in Virginia Woolf. Jill Morris. LC 77-71590. 1977. 6.00 o.p. (ISBN 0-682-48805-4, University). Exposition-Phoenix.

Time & Times & Half a Time. James W. Gunn. pap. 1.25 o.p. (ISBN 0-8042-9371-6, John Knox). Westminster John Knox.

Time at the Top. Edward Ormondroyd. LC 63-10140. (Illus.). (gr. 4-7). 1963. 8.95 o.p. (ISBN 0-395-27698-5, Pub. by Parnassus). HM.

Time Bomb: A Veteran Journalist Assesses Today's China from the Inside. Norman Barrymaine. LC 76-164415. (Illus.). 1971. 6.50 o.s.i. (ISBN 0-8008-7730-6). Taplinger.

Time Capsule: The Year 1983 in Photographs. Patrick Robin & Remy Haddad. (Illus.). 1984. 24.95 o.p. (ISBN 0-394-53811-0, GP 912). Grove.

Time Capsule: The Year 1984 in Photographs. (Illus.). 192p. 1984. pap. 14.95 o.p. (ISBN 0-394-62357-6, E966, Ever). Grove.

Time Cat. Lloyd Alexander. (Illus.). 192p. (gr. 4-7). 1976. pap. 1.25 o.p. (ISBN 0-380-00195-0, 57422-5, Camelot). Avon.

Time Counts. Harold Watkins. (Illus.). 1954. Philos Lib.

Time for a Change: A Guide to Careers for Women in Nontraditional Fields. 81p. 1981. 8.95 o.p. (ISBN 0-317-59456-7). Garrett Pk.

Time for Choice. Harold Bassage. (Orig.). 1970. pap. 0.95 o.p. (ISBN 0-377-80601-3). Friendship Pr.

Time for Every Purpose. Betty Isler. 80p. (Orig.). 1986. pap. 4.95 o.p. (ISBN 0-570-03986-X, 12-3013). Concordia.

Time for Everything Under the Sun. Ruth S. Whittenburg. LC 79-84856. 1980. 17.50 o.p. (ISBN 0-8022-2351-6). Philos Lib.

Time for Pagans. Jack Hoffenberg. 1977. pap. 1.95 o.p. (ISBN 0-380-00876-9, 31435). Avon.

Time for Questions: Messages for Lent & Easter. Harris W. Lee. LC 75-22716. 96p. 1976. pap. 2.95 o.p. (ISBN 0-8066-1518-4, 10-6480, Augsburg). Augsburg Fortress.
Time for Reflection. 5.95 o.p. (ISBN 0-88088-528-9). Peter Pauper.
Time for Remembering: The Ruth Graham Bell Story. Patricia D. Cornwell. LC 82-48922. (Illus.). 320p. 1983. 13.45 o.p. (ISBN 0-06-061685-7). HarpR.
Time for Truth. William E. Simon. 1980. pap. 2.95 o.s.i. (ISBN 0-425-05025-4). Berkley Pub.
Time: Fourth Dimension of the Mind. Robert Wallis. LC 68-12603. 192p. (YA) (gr. 7 up). 1968. 6.95 o.p. (ISBN 0-15-190443-X). HarBraceJ.
Time Frames: The Re-thinking of Darwinian Evolution & the Theory of Punctuated Equilibria. Niles Eldredge. 1985. 16.45 o.p. (ISBN 0-671-49555-0). S&S.
Time Frames: The Rethinking of Darwinian Evolution & the Theory of Punctuated Equilibria. Niles Eldridge. 1986. pap. 8.95 o.s.i. (ISBN 0-671-62245-5, Touchstone Bks). S&S.
Time Garden. Edward Eager. LC 58-5707. (Illus.). (gr. 3-7). 1958. 6.50 o.p. (ISBN 0-15-288189-1, HJ). HarBraceJ.
Time Gate. John Jakes. LC 72-175546. (gr. 5-9). 1972. 4.75 o.s.i. (ISBN 0-664-32510-6, Westminster). Westminster John Knox.
Time in, Time Out, Time Enough: A Time Management Guide for Women. Pat R. Materka. LC 81-12106. 222p. 1982. 11.95 o.p. (ISBN 0-13-921726-6); pap. 5.95 o.p. (ISBN 0-13-921718-5). P-H.
Time Inc. The Intimate History of a Publishing Enterprise, 1923-1941. Robert T. Elson. LC 68-16868. (Illus.). 500p. 1968. 10.00 o.p. (ISBN 0-689-10077-9, Atheneum). Macmillan.
Time Is the Simplest Thing. Clifford D. Simak. 1977. pap. 1.50 o.p. (ISBN 0-8439-0480-1, Pub. by Leisure Bks CT). Dorchester Pub Co.
Time-Lapse Cinemicroscopy. Peter Riddle. (Biological Techniques Ser.). 1979. 32.50 o.p. (ISBN 0-12-588060-X). Acad Pr.
Time-Life Book of Annuals. James U. Crocket & Oliver E. Allen. LC 85-27287. 176p. 1986. pap. 12.95 o.s.i. (ISBN 0-03-008524-1, Owl Bks). H Holt & Co.
Time-Life Book of Perennials. James U. Crocket & Time-Life Books Editors. LC 85-27327. 160p. 1986. pap. 12.95 o.s.i. (ISBN 0-03-008523-3, Owl Bks). H Holt & Co.
Time-Life Book of Pruning & Grafting. James U. Crocket & Oliver E. Allen. LC 85-27286. (Illus.). 160p. 1986. pap. 12.95 o.s.i. (ISBN 0-03-008528-4, Owl Bks). H Holt & Co.
Time-Life Book of Shade Gardens. James U. Crocket & Oliver E. Allen. LC 85-27289. (Illus.). 160p. 1986. pap. 12.95 o.s.i. (ISBN 0-03-008519-5, Owl Bks). H Holt & Co.
Time-Life Book of Vegetables & Fruits. James U. Crocket & Oliver E. Allen. LC 85-27326. 1986. pap. 12.95 o.s.i. (ISBN 0-03-008527-6, Owl Bks). H Holt & Co.
Time-Life Book of Wildflower Gardening. James U. Crocket & Oliver E. Allen. LC 85-27290. (Illus.). 160p. 1986. pap. 12.95 o.s.i. (ISBN 0-03-008522-5, Owl Bks). H Holt & Co.
Time Management Checklists & Worksheets. (Checklists Bks.). (Orig.). 1984. pap. 14.95 o.s.i. (ISBN 0-87280-129-2, Asher-Gallant). Caddylak Systs.
Time Management for Executives. Lauren R. Januz & Susan K. Jones. (Illus.). 240p. 1982. pap. 6.95 o.p. (ISBN 0-684-17841-9, ScribT). Scribner.
Time Management for Executives: A Handbook from the Editors of Execu-Time. Lauren R. Januz & Susan K. Jones. 256p. 1982. 15.95 o.s.i. (ISBN 0-684-17290-9, ScribT). Scribner.
Time of Death. Dobrica Cosic. Tr. by Muriel Heppell. LC 77-73047. 1978. 10.95 o.p. (ISBN 0-15-190448-0). HarBraceJ.
Time of Flight Mass Spectrometer. D. Price & J. E. Williams. 1969. 65.00 o.p. (ISBN 0-08-013444-0). Pergamon.
Time of Her Life. Robb F. Dew. (General Ser.). 1985. lib. bdg. 14.95 o.p. (ISBN 0-8161-3816-8, Large Print Bks). G K Hall.
Time of Hunting. Wayne Dodd. LC 75-4779. 128p. (gr. 6 up). 1979. 6.95 o.p. (ISBN 0-395-28903-3, Clarion). HM.
Time of Miracles. Borislav Pekic. Tr. by Lovett F. Edwards. LC 76-21876. 1976. 10.95 o.p. (ISBN 0-15-190464-2). HarBraceJ.
Time of Passage: SF Stories About Death & Dying. Ed. by Joseph D. Olander & Martin H. Greenberg. LC 77-76727. 1978. 9.95 o.s.i. (ISBN 0-8008-7733-0). Taplinger.
Time of Silence. Martinsant. Tr. by George Leeson. 256p. 1964. 4.50 o.p. (ISBN 0-15-190465-0). HarBraceJ.
Time of the Assassins. Claire Sterling. LC 83-18382. 264p. 1984. 14.95 o.s.i. (ISBN 0-03-063554-3). H Holt & Co.
Time of the Assassins: Anatomy of an Investigation. updated ed. Claire Sterling. 1985. pap. 4.95 o.s.i. (ISBN 0-03-003683-6, Owl Bks). H Holt & Co.
Time of the Doves. Merce Rodoreda. Tr. by David Rosenthall. LC 79-9652. 1980. 8.95 o.s.i. (ISBN 0-8008-7731-4). Taplinger.
Time of Their Dying. Stephen S. Rosenfeld & Rosary Sidney. 1977. 7.95 o.p. (ISBN 0-393-08771-9). Norton.
Time on the Cross, 2 vols. Robert W. Fogel & Stanley L. Engerman. Incl. Vol. 1. The Economics of American Negro Slavery. LC 73-18347. 8.95 o.p.; Vol. 2. Evidence & Methods-a Supplement. 12.50 o.p. (ISBN 0-316-28700-8). 1974. Little.
Time on the Cross: The Economics of Negro Slavery, 2 vols. Robert W. Fogel & Stanley L. Engerman. Incl. Economics of American Negro Slavery. 286p. pap. text ed. 9.95; Vol. 2. Evidence & Methods, a Supplement. 288p. 12.50 o.p. (ISBN 0-316-28702-4). 1974. Repr. Vol. 1. pap. text ed. 9.95 o.p. (ISBN 0-316-28701-6); Vol. 2. pap. text ed. 8.95 o.p. (ISBN 0-316-28699-0). Little.
Time out. Al Bryant. pap. 6.95 o.p. (ISBN 0-310-22121-8, 9293P). Zondervan.
Time Out for Grief: A Practical Guide to Passing Through Grief to Happiness. Jean G. Jones. LC 81-85051. 228p. 1982. pap. 4.50 o.p. (ISBN 0-87973-654-2, 654). Our Sunday Visitor.
Time Out for Murder. Alwyn Marston. 1986. 8.95 o.p. (ISBN 0-533-06817-7). Vantage.
Time Out of Joint. Philip K. Dick. 1977. pap. 1.25 o.p. (ISBN 0-505-51143-6, Pub. by Tower Bks). Dorchester Pub Co.
Time Pattern of Ionizing Radiation in Balloon Altitudes in High Latitudes, 2 Pts in 1. G. Pfotzer et al. 1962. pap. 8.90 o.p. (ISBN 0-387-02880-3). Springer-Verlag.
Time, Place & Music: An Anthology of Ethnomusicological Observation, C. 1550 to C. 1800. F. Harrison. (Illus.). 1973. pap. 45.00 o.s.i. (ISBN 0-685-79105-X). E J Brill USA.
Time Returns. Alexandra Ripley. 432p. 1987. pap. 4.50 o.p. (ISBN 0-380-70162-6). Avon.
Time Returns: A Novel of Friends & Mortal Enemies in Fifteenth Century Florence. Alexandra Ripley. LC 85-4613. 360p. 1985. 16.95 o.p. (ISBN 0-385-19408-0). Doubleday.
Time Series. Norbert Wiener. 1964. pap. 9.95x o.p. (ISBN 0-262-73005-7). MIT Pr.
Time: Space & Designs for Actors. Maxine Klein. 1975. pap. 30.36 o.p. (ISBN 0-395-18612-9). HM.
Time Steps. Charlotte V. Allen. LC 85-48138. 384p. 1986. 19.95 o.p. (ISBN 0-689-11773-6, Atheneum). Macmillan.
Time Stream. John Taine, pseud. Ed. by Lester Del Ray. LC 75-437. (Library of Science Fiction). 1975. lib. bdg. 21.00 o.p. (ISBN 0-8240-1439-1). Garland Pub.
Time to Choose. Janine Boissard. Tr. by Mary Feeney. 196p. 1985. 15.95 o.p. (ISBN 0-316-10102-8). Little.
Time to Greez! Incantations from the Third World. Ed. by Janice Mirikitani et al. LC 75-355. (Illus.). 224p. (Orig.). 1975. pap. 4.95 o.p. (ISBN 0-912078-44-8). Volcano Pr.
Time to Heal. William Goldfarb et al. LC 69-17281. 148p. 1969. text ed. 20.00x o.s.i. (ISBN 0-8236-6550-X). Intl Univs Pr.
Time to Kill-A Time to Die. Jack Pearl. LC 78-155326. 1971. 5.95 o.p. (ISBN 0-393-08648-8). Norton.
Time to Mourn: Judaism & Psychology of Bereavement. rev. ed. 1985. pap. 8.95x o.p. Bloch.
Time to Mourn: Judaism & the Psychology of Bereavement. Jack D. Spiro. 1968. 8.95 o.p. (ISBN 0-8197-0185-8). Bloch.
Time to Murder & Create. Lawrence Block. 192p. 1985. pap. 2.95 o.s.i. (ISBN 0-515-08159-0). Jove Pubns.
Time to Reap. Michael T. Hinkemeyer. 1982. pap. 2.95 o.p. (ISBN 0-931773-19-9). Critics Choice Paper.
Time to Stop Pretending. Luis Palau. 156p. 1985. pap. 5.95 o.p. (ISBN 0-89693-332-6). Victor Bks.
Time to Swim. Craig McKee & Margaret Holland. LC 84-52560. (Predictable Reading Bks.). (Illus.). 24p. (gr. k-3). 1985. 7.95 o.s.i. (ISBN 0-87406-003-6). Willowisp Pr.
Time to Swim. Craig McKee & Margaret Holland. (Illus.). 32p. (gr. k-2). 1984. 1.95 o.p. (ISBN 0-87406-076-1). Willowisp Pr.
Time to Take Sides. Sharlya Gold. LC 76-8265. 176p. (gr. 6 up). 1979. 6.95 o.p. (ISBN 0-395-28905-X, Clarion). HM.
Time Together. Marian Seldes. 288p. 1981. 12.95 o.p. (ISBN 0-395-31264-7). HM.
Time Trap. R. Alec Mackenzie. LC 72-82874. 208p. 1972. 11.95 o.p. (ISBN 0-8144-5308-2). AMACOM.
Time Trap of Ming the 13th. Alex Raymond. (Flash Gordon Ser.: No. 4). 1974. pap. 0.95 o.p. (ISBN 0-380-00111-X, 20446). Avon.
Time Travel & Papa Joe's Pipe: Essays on the Human Side of Science. Alan P. Lightman. (Illus.). 192p. 1984. 12.95 o.s.i. (ISBN 0-684-18112-6, ScribT). Scribner.
Time Trip. Rob Swigart. 1979. 8.95 o.p. (ISBN 0-395-27756-6); pap. 4.95 o.p. (ISBN 0-395-27757-4). HM.
Time Warp & a Time to Speak. C. D. Ingram. 1985. 7.95 o.p. (ISBN 0-533-06503-8). Vantage.
Time Wounds All Heels. Lee A. Fitzgerald. 182p. 1980. 10.00 o.p. (ISBN 0-682-49621-9). Exposition-Phoenix.
Timeframe. Enabling Technology Staff & Ashton-Tate Staff. 130p. (Orig.). 1986. pap. 39.95 o.p. (ISBN 0-912677-69-4). Tate Pub.
Timeless Issues. Daniel W. Wynn. LC 66-20219. 1967. (ISBN 0-8022-1942-X). Philos Lib.
Timely & Profitable Help for Troubled Americans. Hans J. Schneider. Orig. Title: Help for Troubled Americans. 1977. 3.95 o.p. (ISBN 0-89036-066-9). Hawkes Pub Inc.
Time's Arrows: Scientific Attitudes Toward Time in Western Culture. Richard Morris. 234p. 1985. 18.45 o.p. (ISBN 0-671-50158-5). S&S.
Times Atlas of the Oceans. Ed. by Alastair Couper. (Illus.). 256p. 1983. 29.95 o.p. (ISBN 0-442-21661-0). Van Nos Reinhold.
Times Atlas of the World. rev. ed. 512p. 1980. 139.95 o.p. (ISBN 0-8129-0906-2). Times Bks.
Times Atlas of World History. rev. ed. Ed. by Geoffrey Barraclough. LC 84-675088. 360p. 85.00 o.p. (ISBN 0-7230-0261-4). Hammond Inc.
Times They Used to Be. Lucille Clifton. LC 73-21859. (Illus.). 64p. (gr. 3-7). 1974. reinforced bdg. 4.95 o.p. (ISBN 0-03-012171-X). H Holt & Co.
Times to Remember: A Dynamic Autobiography. Inez K. Elmore. 1979. 6.00 o.p. (ISBN 0-682-49172-1). Exposition-Phoenix.
Times to Treasure. Mary Micallef. (Illus.). 80p. (gr. 4-8). 1983. wkbk. 6.95 o.p. (ISBN 0-86653-125-4, GA 479). Good Apple.
Timescales in Geomorphology. R. A. Cullingford et al. LC 79-40517. 360p. 1980. 134.95 o.p. (ISBN 0-471-27600-6, Pub. by Wiley-Interscience). Wiley.
Timeservers. Russell M. Griffin. 240p. 1985. pap. 3.50 o.p. (ISBN 0-380-89525-0). Avon.
Timesharing: Concept, Reality & Regulation. Jim Buchanan. (Public Administration Ser.: P 1756). 15p. 1985. pap. 2.25 o.p. (ISBN 0-89028-536-5). Vance Biblios.
Timetable Planning. John Brookes. (Organization in Schools Ser.). 1980. text ed. 18.00x o.p. (ISBN 0-435-80150-3). Heinemann Ed.
Timex-Sinclair 1000: Programs, Games, & Graphics. Robin Jones & Ian Stewart. 100p. 1982. pap. 10.95 o.p. (ISBN 0-8176-3080-5). Birkhauser.
Timing of Biological Clocks. Arthur T. Winfree. LC 86-15602. (Illus.). 199p. 1986. text ed. 32.95 o.p. (ISBN 0-7167-5018-X). W H Freeman.
Timmy Greenthumb. Eileen Lomasney. LC 82-72646. 32p. (Orig.). (gr. 3-6). 1983. pap. 3.95 o.p. (ISBN 0-8066-1953-8, 10-6487, Augsburg). Augsburg Fortress.
Timon of Athens see also Life of Timon of Athens.
Timothy Principle. Roy Robertson. 120p. 1986. pap. 4.95 o.p. (ISBN 0-89109-550-0). NavPress.
Timothy Turtle. Alice V. Davis. LC 40-32634. (Illus.). (gr. k-3). 1940. 5.95 o.p. (ISBN 0-15-288368-1, HJ). HarBraceJ.
Timothy Turtle. Alice V. Davis. LC 40-32634. (Illus.). (gr. 1-4). 1972. pap. 3.95 o.p. (ISBN 0-15-690450-0, VoyB). HarBraceJ.
Timothy's Forest. Freya Littledale & Harold Littledale. (Illus.). (gr. k-3). 1969. PLB 6.87 o.p. (ISBN 0-87460-123-1). Lion Bks.
Timpetoo. Margit Raedal. LC 70-103604. (Illus.). (gr. k-3). 1971. PLB 3.95 o.p. (ISBN 0-87614-010-X). Carolrhoda Bks.
Tin Craft of the Southwest: A Workbook. rev. ed. Fern-Rae Abraham. (Illus.). 32p. 1987. pap. 4.95 o.p. (ISBN 0-86534-098-6). Sunstone Pr.
Tin-Glaze Pottery. Alan Craiger-Smith. 1973. 45.00 o.p. (ISBN 0-571-09349-3). Faber & Faber.
Tin Pan Alley. John Shepherd. (Routledge Popular Music Ser.). 154p. 1982. 14.95x o.p. (ISBN 0-7100-0904-6). Routledge Chapman & Hall.
Tin-Pot Foreign General & the Old Iron Woman. Raymond Briggs. (Illus.). 48p. (gr. k up). 1985. 9.95 o.s.i. (ISBN 0-316-10801-4). Little.
Tin Toy Cars. (Wonderland of Toys Bks.: Vol. 3). (Illus.). 1984. 18.00 o.p. (ISBN 0-318-02771-2). Bks Nippan.
Tin Toy Robots. (Wonderland of Toys Bks.: Vol. 2). (Illus.). 1984. 16.20 o.p. (ISBN 0-318-02770-4). Bks Nippan.
Tin Wife. Joseph Flaherty. 256p. 1984. 16.45 o.p. (ISBN 0-671-47280-1). S&S.
Tina Turner. Philip Kamin. (Illus.). 32p. (gr. 4-12). 1985. pap. 4.95 o.p. (ISBN 0-88188-416-2, Pub. by Robus Bks). H Leonard Pub Corp.
Tina's Eighteenth Summer, No. 6. Hilda Stahl. 1982. pap. 2.95 o.p. (ISBN 0-8423-7219-9). Tyndale.
Tina's Reluctant Friend, No. 3. Hilda Stahl. (gr. 4-7). 1981. pap. 2.95 o.p. (ISBN 0-8423-7216-4). Tyndale.
Tina's Secret Rival, No. 5. Hilda Stahl. 1981. pap. 2.95 o.p. (ISBN 0-8423-7215-6). Tyndale.
Tinkers & Travellers. Sharon Gmelch. 144p. 1976. 12.50 o.p. (ISBN 0-7735-0271-8, McGill Canada). U of Toronto Pr.
Tinker's Wedding. John Millington Synge. 2.00 o.p. (ISBN 0-8283-1578-7). Branden Pub Co.
Tinnitus - Symposium No. 85. CIBA Foundation Symposium. 336p. 1986. 47.50 o.p. (ISBN 0-471-91054-6). Wiley.
Tinnitus & Its Management: A Clinical Text for Audiologists. John G. Clark & Paul Yanick, Jr. (Illus.). 206p. 1984. 30.00x o.p. (ISBN 0-398-05043-0). C C Thomas.
Tinsel Town. Catherine Mann. 416p. 1986. pap. 3.95 o.p. (ISBN 0-380-70142-1). Avon.
Tinsel Town: A Novel. Catherine Mann. 1985. 16.45 o.p. (ISBN 0-671-55262-7). S&S.
Tintinnabulations of Boos & Applause. David Kalugin. (Illus.). 1979. pap. 4.95 o.p. (ISBN 0-933586-05-1). Book Promo Pr.
Tiny Alice. Edward A. Albee. LC 65-15904. 1965. 4.50 o.p. (ISBN 0-685-06640-1, 689-00004-2, Atheneum). Macmillan.
Tiny Little Tow Truck. Alvera. (Illus.). 1980. 5.00 o.p. (ISBN 0-682-49542-5). Exposition-Phoenix.
Tiny Tales from Happywood. Marjory Arr. (gr. 1-3). 1985. pap. 4.95 o.p. (ISBN 0-533-05659-4). Vantage.
Tiny Word Book. Gyo Fujikawa. (Tiny Board Bks.). (Illus.). 14p. (ps). 1981. 2.25 o.p. (ISBN 0-448-15083-2, G&D). Putnam Pub Group.
Tiny's Big Umbrella. Mabel G. LaRue. (Illus.). (gr. k-3). 1964. 6.95 o.p. (ISBN 0-395-06876-2). HM.
Tioconazole: A New Antifungal in Dermatology. Ed. by M. O'Neill East. (Journal: Dermatologica: Vol. 166, Suppl. 1). (Illus.). vi, 34p. 1983. pap. 18.75 o.p. (ISBN 3-8055-3733-6). S Karger.
Tioconazole: A New Antifungal in Gynecology. Ed. by J. T. Henderson. (Journal: Gynaekologische Rundschau: Vol. 23, Suppl. 1). viii, 62p. 1983. pap. 28.00 o.p. (ISBN 3-8055-3709-3). S Karger.
Tips for Junior Pianists. Margaret Dee. 1956. 1.00 o.p. (ISBN 0-913650-38-2). CPP Belwin.
Tips for Pianists. Margaret Dee. 1956. 1.25 o.p. (ISBN 0-913650-39-0). CPP Belwin.
Tips from the Garden Hotline. Ralph Snodsmith. LC 84-1. (Illus.). 224p. 1984. 12.95 o.s.i. (ISBN 0-87833-380-0). Taylor Pub.
Tips from the Tour: Professional Lessons from Today's Top Golfers. Golf Digest Editors. 160p. 1986. 16.45 o.p. (ISBN 0-671-61290-5). S&S.
Tire Tracks & Tread Marks. Bruce Given et al. LC 77-78931. 88p. 1977. 14.00x o.p. (ISBN 0-87201-869-5). Gulf Pub.
Tissue Culture in Medical Research (II) Second International Symposium on Tissue Culture in Medical Research, 1-3 April 1980, Cardiff, Wales. Ed. by R. J. Richards & K. T. Rajan. (Illus.). 281p. 1980. 73.00 o.p. (ISBN 0-08-025924-3). Pergamon.
Tissue Culture: Methods & Applications. Ed. by Paul Kruse, Jr. & M. K. Patterson. 1973. 75.00 o.p. (ISBN 0-12-427150-2). Acad Pr.
Tissue Culture of Trees. Dodds. 147p. 1983. 29.95 o.p. (ISBN 0-87055-444-1, Pub. by AVI Pub.). AVI.
Tissue Interactions & Development. Norman K. Wessells. LC 76-42696. 1977. pap. text ed. 21.95 o.p. (ISBN 0-8053-9620-9). Benjamin-Cummings.
Tissue Management in Restorative Dentistry. Ed. by William F. Malone. (Illus.). 344p. 1982. 38.00 o.p. (ISBN 0-88416-154-4). Year Bk Med.
Tissue Typing & Organ Transplantation. Edmond J. Yunis et al. 1973. 64.00 o.p. (ISBN 0-12-775160-2). Acad Pr.
Titan. Fred M. Stewart. 509p. 1985. 18.45 o.p. (ISBN 0-671-50689-7). S&S.
Titanic. Archibald Gracie. 323p. 1986. pap. 8.95 o.s.i. (ISBN 0-89733-207-5). Academy Chi Pubs.
Titanium & Titanium Alloys: Scientific & Technological Aspects, 3 vols. Ed. by J. C. Williams & A. F. Belov. LC 79-9156. 2500p. 1982. 295.00x o.p. (ISBN 0-306-40191-6, Plenum Pr). Plenum Pub.
Titanium for Energy & Industrial Applications. Ed. by Daniel Eylon. (Illus.). 403p. 36.00 o.p. (ISBN 0-89520-386-3); members 24.00 o.p. (ISBN 0-317-36266-6); student members 12.00 o.p. (ISBN 0-317-36267-4). ASM.
Titans: A Three-Generation Biography of the Dumas. Gerard Manley Hopkins. Tr. by Andre Maurois from Fr. LC 78-156201. (Illus.). 1971. Repr. of 1957 ed. lib. bdg. 27.50x o.p. (ISBN 0-8371-6151-7, MATI). Greenwood.

Titan's Daughter. James Blish. 128p. 1981. pap. 1.95 o.p. (ISBN 0-380-76929-8, 76929). Avon.

Titans of the Soil: Great Builders of Agriculture. Edward J. Dies. LC 76-49613. (Illus.). 1977. Repr. of 1949 ed. lib. bdg. 35.00x o.p. (ISBN 0-8371-9329-X, DITS). Greenwood.

Titantia's Lodestone. Gail Hamilton. LC 74-19491. 240p. (gr. 5-9). 1975. PLB 7.95 o.p. (ISBN 0-689-30449-8, Atheneum). Macmillan.

Tithing in the Early Church. Lukas Vischer. Ed. by Clarence L. Lee. Tr. by Robert C. Schultz from Ger. LC 66-24858. (Facet Bks.). 42p. 1966. pap. 0.50 o.p. (ISBN 0-8006-3032-7, 1-3032, Fortress). Augsburg Fortress.

Titian's Assistants During the Later Years. M. Roy Fisher. LC 76-23618. (Outstanding Dissertations in the Fine Arts Ser.). 1977. lib. bdg. 68.00 o.p. (ISBN 0-8240-2689-6). Garland Pub.

Titius-Bode Law of Planetary Distance. M. Nieto. 173p. 1972. 40.00 o.p. (ISBN 0-08-016784-5). Pergamon.

Title. Christopher Franke. 32p. 1975. pap. 2.50 o.p. (ISBN 0-914946-50-1). Cleveland St Univ Poetry Ctr.

Title Bibliography of English Language Fiction in the Library of Congress Through 1950, 9 vols. 1976. Set. lib. bdg. 795.00 o.p. (ISBN 0-8161-0020-9, Hall Library). G K Hall.

Title Insurance, 1983: Beyond Basics. (Real Estate Law & Practice Course Handbook Ser.). 731p. 1983. 40.00 o.p. (ISBN 0-686-79988-7, N4-4413). PLI.

Title Insurance 1984 Course Handbook. (Real Estate Law & Practice Course Handbook, 1984-85: Vol. 251). 1984. pap. 35.00 o.p. (ISBN 0-685-59706-7, N4-4432). PLI.

Titles of English Books & of Foreign Books Printed in England: An Alphabetical Finding-List by Title of Books Published Under the Author's Name, Pseudonym, or, Initials, Volume Two, 1641-1700. A. F. Allison & V. F. Goldsmith. 318p. 1977. 42.50 o.p. (ISBN 0-208-01625-2, Archon). Shoe String.

Titles of English Books & of Foreign Books Printed in England: An Alphabetical Finding-List by Title of Books Published Under the Author's Name, Pseudonym, or Initials, 1475-1640, Vol. 1. A. F. Allison & V. F. Goldsmith. 176p. 1976. 30.00 o.p. (ISBN 0-208-01619-8, Archon). Shoe String.

Tito. George Bilainkin. (ISBN 0-8022-0127-X). Philos Lib.

Tito: The Story from Inside. Milovan Djilas. LC 80-23040. 192p. 1980. 9.95 o.s.i. (ISBN 0-15-190474-X). HarBraceJ.

Titus Andronicus see also Life of Titus Andronicus.

Titus Andronicus. Hardis. 1985. lib. bdg. 29.00 o.p. (ISBN 0-8240-9074-8). Garland Pub.

TK! Solver the Easy Way. R. Labenski & L. Labenski. 160p. 1985. pap. text ed. 21.95 o.p. (ISBN 0-07-035726-9). McGraw.

TM: Discovering Inner Energy & Overcoming Stress. H. H. Blumfield et al. 1987. pap. 3.50 o.p. (ISBN 0-440-36048-X). Dell.

TM Management Tactics. (ISBN 0-07-067964-9). McGraw.

TM Technique & the Art of Learning. Stephen Truch. (Quality Paperback Ser: No. 329). 250p. 1977. pap. 4.95 o.p. (ISBN 0-8226-0329-2). Littlefield.

TMS32010 User's Guide. 400p. 1984. 14.95 o.p. (SPRU001B). Tex Instr Inc.

To Absent Friends. Red Smith. LC 89-69143. 320p. 1982. 17.95 o.s.i. (ISBN 0-689-11200-9, Atheneum). Macmillan.

To America. Eleanor B. Tripp. LC 69-11493. (Curriculum Related Bks.). (Illus.). 1969. 5.95 o.p. (ISBN 0-15-289040-8, HJ). HarBraceJ.

To Arm a Nation: Rebuilding America's Endangered Defenses. Richard Halloran. LC 86-8717. 396p. 1986. 21.95 o.p. (ISBN 0-02-547540-1). Macmillan.

To Baby with Love: Your Pre-Natal Nutrition Diary. Marilyn Hanson & Robert Segura. (Illus.). 340p. (Orig.). 1982. pap. 9.95 o.s.i. (ISBN 0-915950-55-3). Bull Pub.

To Be a Unicorn. Robert Vavra & Fleur Cowles. LC 86-8572. (Illus.). 48p. 1986. 15.95 o.p. (ISBN 0-688-06598-8). Morrow.

To Be Human: An Introduction to Cultural Anthropology. Alexander Alland, Jr. 657p. 1980. text ed. 21.00 o.p. (ISBN 0-394-34402-2, RanC). Random.

To Be in England. Richard D. Altick. LC 68-20813. (Illus.). 1969. 6.95 o.p. (ISBN 0-393-04302-9). Norton.

To Be or Not to Be: A Question of Survival. Duncan Williams. (International Library Ser.). 1975. pap. 11.75 o.p. (ISBN 0-08-019934-8). Pergamon.

To Be Worthy. Donna F. Crow. 204p. 1986. pap. 5.95 o.p. (ISBN 0-89693-512-4). Victor Bks.

To Become a Racehorse Trainer. Joe Hartigan. Repr. (ISBN 0-85131-234-9, NL51, Pub. by J A Allen U K). S R Smith Sporting Bks.

To Become Somebody: Growing up Against the Grain of Society. John B. Simon. 256p. 1982. 12.95 o.p. (ISBN 0-395-32052-6). HM.

To Bedlam & Part Way Back. Anne Sexton. 1960. pap. 3.95 o.p. (ISBN 0-395-08178-5). HM.

To Bee or Not to Bee. John Penberthy. (Illus.). 96p. 1987. pap. 6.95 o.p. (ISBN 0-911777-15-6). Leadership Dyn.

To Belize with Love. Hannah B. Lapp. LC 86-70999. 380p. (Orig.). (YA) (gr. 10-12). 1986. pap. 14.95 o.p. (ISBN 0-931494-94-X). Brunswick Pub.

To Boldly Go. Eric Delve. 132p. 1986. pap. 5.50 o.p. (ISBN 0-89693-275-3). Victor Bks.

To Build a Fire: Recent Poems & a Prose Piece. Melville Cane. LC 64-14640. 80p. 1964. 9.95 o.p. (ISBN 0-15-190478-2). HarBraceJ.

To Catch a Golden Ring. Marilyn Donahue. LC 80-68312. (gr. 4-9). 1980. pap. 2.95 o.p. (ISBN 0-89191-330-0). Cook.

To Catch a Golden Ring. rev. ed. Marilyn Donahue. LC 80-68312. (Pennypinchers Ser.). 127p. (gr. 5-10). 1984. pap. 2.95 softcover o.p. (ISBN 0-89191-831-0). Cook.

To Catch a Spy. Amelia Walden. LC 64-11048. (gr. 7-10). 1964. 5.50 o.s.i. (ISBN 0-664-32329-4, Westminster). Westminster John Knox.

To Chain the Dog of War: The War Power of Congress in History & Law. Francis D. Wormuth & Edwin B. Firmage. LC 85-14249. 360p. 1987. Repr. of 1986 ed. lib. bdg. 27.50 o.p. (ISBN 0-87074-206-X). SMU Press.

To Cherish All Life: A Buddhist Case for Becoming Vegetarian. Phillip Kapleau. LC 82-47746. (Illus.). 112p. 1982. pap. 5.72 o.p. (ISBN 0-06-250440-1, CN4044). HarpR.

To Comfort You. Laurel Lee. Ed. by Cheryl M. Phillips & Bonnie C. Harvey. (Illus.). 32p. (Orig.). 1984. pap. 0.98 o.p. (ISBN 0-937420-11-5). Stirrup Assoc.

To Control the Stars. Robert Hoskins. LC 76-56166. 1983. pap. 1.95 o.s.i. (ISBN 0-345-31191-4). Ballantine.

To Dad: Written by Children. Ed. by Richard Exley & Helen Exley. 1978. pap. 2.95 o.p. (ISBN 0-395-26472-3). HM.

To Dance. Valery Panov & George Feifer. 1979. pap. 3.95 o.p. (ISBN 0-380-47233-3, 47233-3, Discus). Avon.

To Die Elsewhere. Theodore Wilden. LC 76-21748. 1976. 7.95 o.p. (ISBN 0-15-190480-4). HarBraceJ.

To Die in Beverly Hills. Gerald Petievich. 256p. 1983. 14.50 o.p. (ISBN 0-87795-487-9, Arbor Hse). Morrow.

To Die is Gain. Neal Carlson. (Solace Ser.). 1983. pap. 1.50 o.p. (ISBN 0-8010-2487-0). Baker Bk.

To Die Is Gain: The Experience of One's Own Death. Johann C. Hampe. LC 79-601. 1979. pap. 4.95 o.p. (ISBN 0-8042-2588-5, John Knox). Westminster John Knox.

To Escape the Stars. Robert Hoskins. 1983. pap. 2.50 o.s.i. (ISBN 0-345-31190-6, Del Rey Bks). Ballantine.

To Fathoms in Hell & Back. William W. Bartlett. 208p. 1981. 9.00 o.p. (ISBN 0-682-49790-8). Exposition-Phoenix.

To Find My Son. Ron Putterman. 192p. (Orig.). 1981. pap. 2.50 o.p. (ISBN 0-380-78980-9, 78980). Avon.

To Frighten a Storm. Gladys Cardiff. (Copperhead Chapbook Ser.). 24p. (Orig.). 1975. pap. 5.00 o.p. (ISBN 0-914742-13-2). Copper Canyon.

To Get Rich Is Glorious: China in the Eighties. Orville Schell. LC 84-42697. 210p. 1984. 15.45 o.p. (ISBN 0-394-53952-4). Pantheon.

To Grandma & Grandpa. Ed. by Richard Exley & Helen Exley. 1979. pap. 3.95 o.p. (ISBN 0-395-27502-4). HM.

To Grow in Spirit. Joe J. Christensen. 81p. 1983. 7.95 o.p. (ISBN 0-87747-968-2). Deseret Bk.

To Have & to Hold. Mary Johnston. 1969. 5.95 o.p. (ISBN 0-395-07835-0). HM.

To Hear the River. Kenneth McClane. (Orig.). 1981. pap. 3.00 o.p. (ISBN 0-931122-23-6). West End.

To Heaven on Horseback. Lyman Haverfield. 1977. 5.00 o.p. (ISBN 0-682-48641-8). Exposition-Phoenix.

To Hell with Male Chauvinism! Marjorie M. Booker. 1985. 7.95 o.p. (ISBN 0-533-05707-8). Vantage.

To Inform or to Control? The New Communications Networks. Oswald H. Ganley & Gladys D. Ganley. LC 81-20748. 1982. text ed. 15.95 o.p. (ISBN 0-07-022761-6). McGraw.

To Kill A Mockingbird. Harper Lee. 48p. (Orig.). 1988. pap. 9.95 o.p. (ISBN 1-55651-881-1); audiocassette tape incl. o.p. (ISBN 1-55651-882-X). Cram Cassettes.

To Kill a Shadow. D. B. Drumm. (Traveler Ser.: No. 4). (Orig.). 1984. pap. 2.25 o.p. (ISBN 0-440-18705-2). Dell.

To Kill a Witch. Drew G. Myers. LC 84-91299. 166p. 1985. 11.95 o.p. (ISBN 0-533-06391-4). Vantage.

To Kill the Devil: The Attempts on the Life of Adolph Hitler. Herbert M. Mason, Jr. (Illus.). 1978. 9.95 o.p. (ISBN 0-393-05682-1). Norton.

To Know Christ Jesus. F. J. Sheed. 1980. pap. 4.95 o.p. (ISBN 0-89283-080-8). Servant.

To Leave the Standing Grain. Michael Corr. (Illus.). 1977. 25.00 o.p. (ISBN 0-914742-27-2); pap. 5.00 o.p. Copper Canyon.

To Leisure: An Introduction. John Neulinger. 275p. pap. 16.95 o.p. (ISBN 0-317-30660-X). Venture Pub PA.

To Live & Die in L. A. Gerald Petievich. 1984. 14.95 o.p. (ISBN 0-87795-533-6, Arbor Hse). Morrow.

To Live & to Die: When, Why, & How. Ed. by R. H. Williams. LC 73-2868. (Illus.). 1974. 16.00 o.p. (ISBN 0-387-90097-7). Springer-Verlag.

To Look at Any Thing. Ed. by Lee B. Hopkins. LC 77-88962. (Illus.). (gr. 1 up). 1978. 6.95 o.p. (ISBN 0-15-289083-1, HJ). HarBraceJ.

To Love Again. Keith Terry & Ann Terry. 180p. 1979. 6.95 o.p. (ISBN 0-942241-22-3, 8746). Pubs Bk Sales.

To Love & Be Loved. John Tormey. 1979. pap. 1.95 o.p. (ISBN 0-89243-093-1). Liguori Pubns.

To Love & to Dream. Elizabeth N. Dubus. 320p. 1986. 17.95 o.p. (ISBN 0-399-13172-8, Putnam). Putnam Pub Group.

To Love Each Other: A Woman's Workshop on First Corinthians. Latayne C. Scott. (Woman's Workshop Ser.). 112p. (Orig.). 1985. pap. 4.50 o.p. (ISBN 0-310-38921-6, 10454P). Zondervan.

To Love Is Not to Lose. Lauren Randall. (Illus.). 96p. 1981. pap. 1.95 o.p. (ISBN 0-380-78337-1, 78337). Avon.

To Love Is to Be Happy With. Barry N. Kaufman. 1981. pap. 2.95 o.p. (ISBN 0-449-23475-4, Crest). Fawcett.

To Mom: Written by Children. Ed. by Richard Exley & Helen Exley. 1978. pap. 2.95 o.p. (ISBN 0-395-26478-2). HM.

To Move, to Learn. Date not set. (ISBN 0-8052-0602-7). Random.

To Myself: The Story of a Foster Child. Galila Ron-Feder. Tr. by Miriam Arad from Hebrew. (Illus.). 140p. (gr. 4 up). 1987. 12.95 o.p. (ISBN 1-55774-003-8, Dist. by Watts). Adama Pubs Inc.

To Own a Racehorse. Joe Hartigan. pap. (ISBN 0-85131-233-0, NL51, Pub. by J A Allen U K). S R Smith Sporting Bks.

To Play Man Number One. Ed. by Sara Hannum & John T. Chase. LC 73-75518. (Illus.). (gr. 8 up). 1969. 5.95 o.p. (ISBN 0-689-30016-6, Atheneum). Macmillan.

To Play the Fox. M. S. Craig. 185p. 1986. pap. 2.95 o.p. (ISBN 0-931773-83-0). Critics Choice Paper.

To Pray As Jesus. George Martin. 1978. pap. 2.50 o.p. (ISBN 0-89283-054-9). Servant.

To Pray or Not to Pray. John B. Cobb, Jr. 1974. pap. 1.25x o.p. (ISBN 0-8358-0310-4). Upper Room.

To Read Literature: Fiction, Poetry, Drama. Ed. by Donald Hall. 1983. pap. text ed. 21.95 o.p. (ISBN 0-03-062851-2). HR&W.

To Resist or Surrender. Paul Tournier. LC 64-16248. 1977. 4.95 o.p. (ISBN 0-8042-2232-0, John Knox); pap. 0.95 o.p. (ISBN 0-8042-3663-1). Westminster John Knox.

To Run & Not Be Weary. Stan Cottrell. (Illus.). 192p. 1985. 12.95 o.p. (ISBN 0-8007-1444-X). Revell.

To Sail a Ship of Treasures. Lisl Weil. LC 84-3025. (Illus.). 32p. (gr. k-4). 1984. PLB 10.95 o.s.i. (ISBN 0-689-31059-5, Atheneum Childrens Bks). Macmillan.

To Sail Beyond the Sunset. Robert A. Heinlein. 448p. 1987. 18.95 o.p. (ISBN 0-399-13267-8). Putnam Pub Group.

To Save a Boy: The Story of Boys Home, North Carolina. Edward Uhlan & A. D. Peacock. (Illus.). 1971. 6.00 o.p. (ISBN 0-682-47313-8, Banner). Exposition-Phoenix.

To See His Face. Michael Wilcox. LC 84-70072. 224p. 1984. 7.95 o.p. (ISBN 0-87747-462-1). Deseret Bk.

To See the Dream. West. 3.95 o.p. (ISBN 0-15-190599-1). HarBraceJ.

To See the Dream. Jessamyn West. 1974. pap. 1.25 o.p. (ISBN 0-380-00008-3, 19174). Avon.

To See the World Afresh. Compiled by Lilian Moore. Judith Thurman. LC 73-84831. 120p. (gr. 6 up). 1974. 5.95 o.p. (ISBN 0-689-30141-3, Atheneum). Macmillan.

To See, to Take. Mona Van Duyn. LC 75-103828. (Orig.). 1970. pap. 3.95 o.p. (ISBN 0-689-10312-3, Atheneum). Macmillan.

To Seek America: A History of Ethnic Life in the United States. Maxine S. Seller. LC 77-8248. 1977. lib. bdg. 15.95x o.p. (ISBN 0-89198-117-9); pap. text ed. 13.95x o.p. (ISBN 0-89198-118-7). Ozer.

To Seek Where Shadows Are. Miriam Benedict. 1973. pap. 0.95 o.p. (ISBN 0-380-01587-0, 17756). Avon.

To Set at Liberty: Christian Faith & Human Freedom. Delwin Brown. LC 80-21783. 144p. (Orig.). 1981. pap. 6.95 o.p. (ISBN 0-88344-501-8). Orbis Bks.

To Set the Record Straight: The Break-in, the Tapes, the Conspirators, the Pardon. John J. Sirica. (Illus.). 1979. 17.50 o.p. (ISBN 0-393-01234-4). Norton.

To Set Things Right: The Bible Speaks on Faith & Justice. Justin Vander Kolk. 48p. 1971. pap. 1.25 o.p. (ISBN 0-377-02001-X). Friendship Pr.

To Share with God's Poor: Sister among the Outcasts. Emmanuelle Cinquin. LC 83-47735. (Illus.). 458p. 1983. pap. 5.95 o.p. (ISBN 0-06-061392-0, RD-485). HarpR.

To Smile in Autumn. Gordon Parks. (Illus.). 1979. 14.95 o.p. (ISBN 0-393-01272-7). Norton.

To Speak True: A Study of Poetry As a Spoken Art. B. Mulcahy. 1969. 4.40 o.p. (ISBN 0-08-006444-2). Pergamon.

To Spin Is Miracle Cat. Roger Zelazny. 68p. 1982. lib. bdg. 9.95 o.p. (ISBN 0-934438-50-1). Underwood-Miller.

To Spoil the Sun. Joyce Rockwood. LC 76-10568. (gr. k-3). 1976. 6.95 o.s.i. (ISBN 0-03-018066-X); 12.95 o.s.i. H Holt & Co.

To Stand Alone. George E. White. 1979. 6.00 o.p. (ISBN 0-682-49485-2). Exposition-Phoenix.

To Stay Alive. Denise Levertov. LC 72-159739. (Orig.). 1971. 5.95 o.p. (ISBN 0-8112-0304-2); pap. 4.95 o.p. (ISBN 0-8112-0087-6, NDP325). New Directions.

To Strive to Search, to Find. Marie Shepherd-Moore. 1976. 6.50 o.p. (ISBN 0-682-48568-3). Exposition-Phoenix.

To Succeed in Business, Get There, Honestly If You Can, but Get There. Frank D. Singewald. (Illus.). 64p. 1982. pap. 4.00 o.p. (ISBN 0-682-49863-7). Exposition-Phoenix.

To Talk of Many Things. Pasadena Art Alliance Staff. 1977. pap. 5.95 o.p. (ISBN 0-937042-01-3). Pasadena Art.

To the Best of My Ability: The President & the Constitution. Donald L. Robinson. 1987. 22.00 o.p. (ISBN 0-393-02426-1). Norton.

To the Bitter End. Hans B. Gisevius. Tr. by Richard Winston & Clara Winston. LC 74-29633. 632p. 1975. Repr. of 1947 ed. lib. bdg. 31.25x o.p. (ISBN 0-8371-7983-1, GIBE). Greenwood.

To the City of the Dead: An Account of Travels in Mexico. George Woodcock. LC 74-31872. (Illus.). 271p. 1975. Repr. of 1957 ed. lib. bdg. 35.00 o.p. (ISBN 0-8371-7946-7, WOCI). Greenwood.

To the Ends of the Earth: A General History of the Congregation of the Holy Ghost. Henry J. Koren. LC 82-17682. 656p. 1982. text ed. 18.50x o.p. (ISBN 0-8207-0157-2). Duquesne.

To the Ends of the Earth: Four Expeditions to the Arctic, the Congo, the Gobi, & Siberia. American Museum of Natural History Staff & John Perkins. LC 81-47209. (Illus.). 184p. 1981. 27.00 o.p. (ISBN 0-394-50900-5). Pantheon.

To the Ends of the Earth: The Transglobe Expedition, the First Pole-to Pole Circumnavigation of the Globe. Ranulph Fiennes. (Illus.). 1983. 17.95 o.p. (ISBN 0-87795-490-9, Arbor Hse); pap. 12.95 o.p. (ISBN 0-87795-614-6). Morrow.

To the Foot of the Rainbow. Clyde M. Kluckhohn. LC 80-12317. (Beautiful Rio Grande Classics Ser.). (Illus.). 412p. lib. bdg. 25.00 o.p.; pap. 15.00 o.p. Rio Grande.

To the Frontier. Geoffrey Moorhouse. LC 84-19177. 1985. 17.95 o.p. (ISBN 0-03-000454-3). H Holt & Co.

To the Harbor Light. Henry B. Hough. 1976. 10.95 o.p. (ISBN 0-395-24774-8). HM.

To the Heart of a Bear. Dennis Kyte. 1985. pap. 12.95 o.s.i. (ISBN 0-671-54781-X). S&S.

To the Honor of the Fleet. Robert H. Pilpel. LC 78-3215. 1979. 12.95 o.p. (ISBN 0-689-10932-6, Atheneum). Macmillan.

To the Islands. rev. ed. Randolph Stow. LC 81-21407. 126p. 1982. 9.95 o.s.i. (ISBN 0-8008-7739-X). Taplinger.

To the Kwai -& Back: War Drawings, 1939 - 1945. Ronald Searle. LC 85-73390. (Illus.). 192p. 1985. 35.00 o.p. (ISBN 0-87113-073-4). Atlantic Monthly.

To the Land of the Cattails. Aharon Appelfeld. LC 86-9076. 160p. 1986. 14.95 o.s.i. (ISBN 1-55584-007-8). Weidenfeld.

To the Last Man. William E. Barrett. 1980. pap. 0.95 o.p. (ISBN 0-380-01588-9, 16543). Avon.

To the Lighthouse. Virginia Woolf. LC 81-47579. (Centenary Editions Ser.). 224p. 1981. 17.95 o.p. (ISBN 0-15-190736-6). HarBraceJ.

To the Miner Born: Life in a Mining Village 1918-1945, from a Woman's Point of View. Mary Wade. (Illus.). 200p. (Orig.). 1985. pap. 14.95x o.p. (ISBN 0-85362-219-1, Oriel). Routledge Chapman & Hall.

To the North Magnetic Pole & Through the Northwest Passage. facs. ed. Roald Amundsen. 36p. pap. 3.95 o.s.i. (ISBN 0-8466-0149-4, S149). Shorey.

To the South Seas: The Cruise of the Schooner Mary Pinchot to the Galapogos, the Marquesas, the Tuamotu Islands & Tahiti. Gifford Pinchot. LC 70-174094. (Illus.). xiv, 378p. 1972. Repr. of 1930 ed. 48.00x o.p. (ISBN 0-8103-3933-1). Gale.

To the Top of the Mountain: The Life of Father Umberto Olivieri, "Padre of the Otomis" William N. Abeloe. LC 76-7187. 1976. 8.00 o.p. (ISBN 0-682-48558-6). Exposition-Phoenix.

To Those Concerned Citizens. Gopi Krishna. (Illus.). 16p. 1978. pap. 3.95 o.s.i. (ISBN 0-88697-002-4). Life Science.

To Understand Each Other. Paul Tournier. 1976. pap. 1.25 o.p. (ISBN 0-8042-3673-9, John Knox). Westminster John Knox.

To Wear a City's Crown: The Beginnings of Urban Growth in Texas, 1836-1865. Kenneth W. Wheeler. LC 68-28698. (Illus.). 1968. 17.50x o.s.i. (ISBN 0-674-89340-9). Harvard U Pr.

To Where Streets Are Made of Gold: The Story of a Filipino Immigrant. Dorian Sikat. 1982. 7.50 o.p. (ISBN 0-682-49405-4). Exposition-Phoenix.

To Whom It May Concern or Hello, Someone's Darling. Orelia Benskina. 1978. 4.00 o.p. (ISBN 0-682-49065-2). Exposition-Phoenix.

To Whom the Land of Palestine Belongs. Christopher C. Hong. 1979. 6.50 o.p. (ISBN 0-682-49161-6). Exposition-Phoenix.

To Whom the Wilderness Speaks. Louise D. Lawrence. (Illus.). 208p. 1980. text ed. 14.95 o.p. (ISBN 0-07-092400-7). McGraw.

To Will One Thing: Reflections on Kierkegaard's Purity of Heart. Jeremy Walker. 1972. 11.00 o.p. (ISBN 0-7735-0084-7, Pub. by McGill Canada). U of Toronto Pr.

To Win the Money Game. Venita VanCaspel. 1981. 1.50 o.p. (ISBN 0-8359-8692-6, Reston). P-H.

To You from Me, Folk Verse. Melba Hughes. LC 86-63961. 64p. (Orig.). 1987. pap. 6.95 o.p. (ISBN 0-935834-56-7). Rainbow Books.

To Your Scattered Bodies Go. Philip Jose Farmer. 1980. lib. bdg. 13.50 o.p. (ISBN 0-8398-2620-6, Gregg). G K Hall.

Toad of Toad Hall. A. A. Milne. (gr. k-3). 1982. pap. 2.95 o.p. (ISBN 0-380-58115-9, Bard). Avon.

Toast to Sober Spirits & Joyous Juices: A Collection of Non-Alcoholic Beverage Recipes. rev. ed. Jan Blexrud. LC 76-55449. (Illus.). pap. 6.95 o.p. (ISBN 0-89638-041-6, X1979). CompCare.

Toaster Oven Cook Book. Better Homes & Gardens Editors. (Illus.). 96p. 1982. 6.95 o.p. (ISBN 0-696-01175-1). BH&G.

Tobacco. Rob Stepney. (Triumph Ser.). (Illus.). 64p. 1987. lib. bdg. 11.90 o.p. (ISBN 0-531-10438-9). Watts.

Tobacco & Tobacco Smoke. Ed. by Ernest L. Wynder & Dietrich Hoffman. 1967. 99.00 o.p. (ISBN 0-12-767450-0). Acad Pr.

Tobacco Dictionary. Raymond Jahn. 224p. 1954. (ISBN 0-8022-0788-X). Philos Lib.

Tobacco, Snuff Boxes & Pipes. Lutz Libert. (Illus.). 148p. 1986. 28.50x o.p. (ISBN 0-85613-918-1, Pub. by MacD & Co). Trans-Atl Phila.

Tobago. David L. Niddrie. 1981. 8.50x o.p. (ISBN 0-416-60311-4, NO. 3447). Routledge Chapman & Hall.

Toby Alone. Robbie Branscum. 96p. 1980. pap. 1.75 o.p. (ISBN 0-380-50781-1, 50781-1, Flare). Avon.

Toby & Johnny Joe. Robbie Branscum. 80p. 1981. pap. 1.75 o.p. (ISBN 0-380-52670-0, 52670-0, Flare). Avon.

Tock Book: Poetry for the Last Days. Ira M. Lewis. 25p. 1985. 5.95 o.p. (ISBN 0-533-05908-9). Vantage.

Tocqueville Review - La Revue Tocqueville, 1985-86. Ed. by Jesse R. Pitts & Olivier Zunz. 400p. 1986. text ed. 35.00x o.p. (ISBN 0-8139-1108-7). U Pr of Va.

Tocqueville Review - La Revue Tocqueville, 1986-87, Vol. 8. Jesse R. Pitts. 500p. 1987. text ed. 35.00x o.p. (ISBN 0-8139-1143-5). U Pr of Va.

Tod in Venedig. Thomas Mann. Ed. by A. W. Hornsey. 1971. pap. 7.50 o.p. (ISBN 0-395-11925-1, 3-34397). HM.

Today: A Text-Workbook for English & Composition, Level F. Hans P. Guth & Edgar H. Schuster. 1972. text ed. 5.84 o.p. (ISBN 0-07-025266-1, W). McGraw.

Today: A Text-Workbook for English Language & Composition, Level B. Hans P. Guth. (Illus.). 128p. (gr. 8). 1972. text ed. 5.84 o.p. (ISBN 0-07-025262-9); tchr's ed. 3.80 o.p. (ISBN 0-07-025245-9). McGraw.

Today & Tomorrow. Neville W. Scott. 64p. 1987. 6.95 o.p. (ISBN 0-8062-2976-4). Carlton.

Today I Am a Woman? Linda Lee. LC 79-52914. softcover 2.95 o.p. (ISBN 0-912216-17-4). Angel Pr.

Today Is Saturday. Zilpha K. Snyder. LC 69-13534. (Illus.). (gr. 3-7). 1969. PLB 4.50 o.p. (ISBN 0-689-20629-1, Atheneum). Macmillan.

Today Is Yesterday, Tomorrow! Nancy Martin & David Hand. (Illus.). (gr. 2 up). 1978. pap. 2.95 o.p. (ISBN 0-87516-246-0). DeVorss.

Today Nineteen Eighty-Six: A Personal Record & Reference Book. Ed. by World Book, Inc. Staff. LC 76-27228. (World Book Today Yearly Diaries Ser.). (Illus.). 192p. 1985. write for info. o.p. (ISBN 0-7166-0786-7). World Bk.

Today 1988: A Personal Record & Reference Book. Ed. by World Book, Inc. Staff. LC 76-27228. (World Book Today Yearly Diaries Ser.). (Illus.). 192p. 1987. lib. bdg. (ISBN 0-7166-0788-3). World Bk.

Today's Architectural Mirror: Interiors, Buildings, & Solar Designs. Pamela Heyne. LC 81-10375. (Illus.). 225p. 1981. 34.95 o.p. (ISBN 0-442-23424-4). Van Nos Reinhold.

Today's Business Law. 4th ed. Kennard E. Goodman et al. LC 74-15662. (gr. 10-12). text ed. cancelled o.s.i. (ISBN 0-02-831060-8); cancelled o.s.i. (ISBN 0-02-831090-X); cancelled o.s.i. (ISBN 0-02-831070-5); cancelled o.s.i. (ISBN 0-02-831080-2). Glencoe.

Today's Business Math: A Text Workbook. Burton S. Kaliski. 1975. pap. text ed. 16.95 o.p. (ISBN 0-15-592160-6, HC). HarBraceJ.

Today's Child: A Modern Guide to Baby Care & Child Training. Elizabeth C. Robertson & Margaret I. Wood. LC 71-37204. 288p. 1972. 7.95 o.s.i. (ISBN 0-684-12727-X, ScribT). Scribner.

Today's Curriculum: An Integrative Approach. Ed. by Janice V. Kristo & Phillip A. Heath. LC 81-43666. 90p. (Orig.). 1982. pap. text ed. 8.25 o.p. (ISBN 0-8191-2149-5). U Pr of Amer.

Today's Elementary Social Studies. Dorothy G. Hennings & George Hennings. 1980. text ed. 31.95 o.p. (ISBN 0-395-30626-4). HM.

Today's Father: A Guide to Understanding, Enjoying & Making Things for the Growing Family. Michael Goldsmith et al. (Winston Family Handbooks). 96p. (Orig.). 1984. pap. 9.95 o.p. (ISBN 0-86683-849-X, AY8494). HarpR.

Today's Fleet Maintainance: A Reader for Fleet Executives. Today's Transport International Staff. LC 75-21975. 1975. 12.95 o.p. (ISBN 0-917408-02-0). Bergano Bk Co.

Today's Game. Martin Quigley. 1965. 3.95 o.p. (ISBN 0-670-71845-9). Penguin USA.

Today's Sects. M. C. Burrell & J. S. Wright. pap. 4.50 o.p. (ISBN 0-8010-0855-7). Baker Bk.

Today's Woman in Search of Freedom. Ruthe White. 176p. (Orig.). 1985. pap. 4.95 o.p. (ISBN 0-89081-473-2). Harvest Hse.

Toddler & the New Baby. Sylvia Close. 128p. 1980. pap. 7.95 o.p. (ISBN 0-7100-0523-7). Routledge Chapman & Hall.

Toddler in the Family: A Practical Australian Guide for Parents. Jean Ferguson & Rowena Solomon. LC 84-3499. (Illus.). 137p. 1985. pap. 15.95 o.p. (ISBN 0-7022-1737-9). U of Queensland Pr.

Todor Zhivkov: Statesman & Builder of New Bulgaria. 2nd ed. T. Zhivkov. (Leaders of the World Ser.: Vol. 5). (Illus.). 438p. 1985. 130.00 o.p. (ISBN 0-08-033371-0). Pergamon.

Toffee Apple Tree. Gillian Lindsay. (Illus.). 48p. (gr. 2-5). 1984. 5.95 o.p. (ISBN 0-241-10985-X, Pub. by Hamish Hamilton England). David & Charles.

Tofu Gourmet. Linda L. Barber & Junko Lampert. (Illus.). 128p. 1984. 14.95 o.p. (ISBN 0-87040-589-6). Japan Pubns USA.

Tofu Primer: A Beginner's Book of Bean Cake Cookery. Juel Andersen. LC 84-71565. (Illus.). 64p. (Orig.). 1981. pap. 4.50 o.p. (ISBN 0-916870-33-2). Creative Arts Bk.

Together: Communicating Interpersonally. 2nd ed. John Stewart & Gary A. D'Angelo. 432p. 1980. pap. text ed. 15.00 o.p. (ISBN 0-394-34989-X, RanC). Random.

Together in Peace: Priest's Edition. Joseph M. Champlin. (Illus.). 272p. 1975. pap. 3.95 o.p. (ISBN 0-87793-094-5). Ave Maria.

Together We Can Deal with Life in the 80's. Ronald Jenson & Chuck MacDonald. LC 81-86296. 176p. 1982. pap. 5.95 o.p. (ISBN 0-86605-001-9). Heres Life.

Togetherness Is Love: A Manual of Creative Teaching Ideas. Esther Lee Millett. 1977. 5.50 o.p. (ISBN 0-682-48726-0). Exposition-Phoenix.

Togo under Imperial Germany 1884-1914: A Case Study in Colonial Rule. Arthur J. Knoll. LC 77-83122. (Publications Ser.: No. 190). 1978. 10.95x o.p. (ISBN 0-8179-6901-2). Hoover Inst Pr.

Toiletries, Cosmetics, Fragrances & Beauty Aids. 5th ed. Fairchild Market Research Division Staff. (Fairchild Facts Files). (Illus.). 50p. 1986. pap. 20.00 o.p. (ISBN 0-87005-550-X). Fairchild.

Tokyo-Access. Richard S. Wurman. (Access Guidebooks). (Illus.). 232p. (Orig.). 1984. pap. 11.95 o.p. (ISBN 0-915461-05-6). Access Pr.

Tokyo-Access. Richard S. Wurman. (Access Guides Ser.). pap. 11.95 o.p. (ISBN 0-671-60342-6). S&S.

Tokyo National Museum. Gakuji Hasebe & Seizo Hayashiya. LC 80-82645. (Oriental Ceramics Ser.: Vol. 1). (Illus.). 191p. 1982. 68.00 o.p. (ISBN 0-87011-440-9). Kodansha.

Tokyo National Museum see Oriental Ceramics: The World's Great Collections.

Tokyo Puzzles. Kobon Fujimura. Ed. by Martin Gardner. (Illus.). 1979. pap. 1.50 encore ed o.p. (ISBN 0-684-17749-8, SL 772, ScribT). Scribner.

Tokyo Round: Results & Implications for Developing Countries. Ria Kemper. (Working Paper: No. 372). iii, 35p. 1980. pap. 3.50 o.p. (ISBN 0-8213-9239-5, WP-0372). World Bank.

Tole Technique & Decorative Arts, 4 Vols. Jackie Shaw. (Illus., Orig.). 1974. Vol. 1. pap. 3.95 o.p. (ISBN 0-941284-01-8); Vol. 2. pap. 3.95 o. p. (ISBN 0-941284-02-6); Vol. 3. pap. 3.95 o. p. (ISBN 0-941284-03-4); Vol. 4. pap. 3.95 o.p. (ISBN 0-941284-04-2). Deco Design Studio.

Tole'n. rev. ed. Bob Embry. (Illus.). 84p. 1982. pap. 7.95 o.p. (ISBN 0-917119-10-X, 45-1028). Priscillas Pubns.

Tolerable Movement of Bridge Foundations, Sand Drains, K-Test, Slopes & Culverts. (Transportation Research Record Ser.). 66p. 1978. 4.00 o.p. (ISBN 0-309-02823-X). Transport Res Bd.

Tolkien: A Biography. Humphrey Carpenter. 1977. 10.00 o.p. (ISBN 0-395-25360-8). HM.

Tolkien & the Silmarils. Randel Helms. 128p. 1981. 8.95 o.p. (ISBN 0-395-29469-X). HM.

Tolkien Companion. J. E. Tyler. 1977. pap. 4.95 o.p. (ISBN 0-380-00901-3, 31674-9). Avon.

Tolkien Quest: The Mines of Moria. 160p. 1986. pap. 3.50 o.s.i. (ISBN 0-425-08993-2). Berkley Pub.

Tolkien Scrapbook. Ed. by Alida Becker. LC 79-11435. (Illus.). 192p. (gr. 5 up). 1979. lib. bdg. 19.80 o.p. (ISBN 0-89471-083-4); pap. 9.95 o.p. (ISBN 0-89471-082-6). Running Pr.

Toll. Michael Mewshaw. 1975. pap. 1.75 o.p. (ISBN 0-380-00409-7, 25072). Avon.

Toll Call. Stephen Greenleaf. LC 86-40351. 1987. 16.45 o.s.i. (ISBN 0-394-54116-2, Pub. by Villard Bks). Random.

Toll House Treasury Cookbook. 1989. 4.98 o.s.i. (ISBN 0-517-68014-9). Crown.

Tolstoi in the Sixties. Boris Eikhenbaum. Tr. by White from Rus. 1982. 25.00 o.p. (ISBN 0-88233-470-0). Ardis Pubs.

Tolstoy. Romain Rolland. LC 71-147457. (Library of War & Peace; Peace Leaders: Biographies & Memoirs). 1972. lib. bdg. 46.00 o.p. (ISBN 0-8240-0316-0). Garland Pub.

Tolstoy & Gandhi. Kalidas Nag. (ISBN 0-8022-1181-X). Philos Lib.

Tolstoys: Twenty Generations of Russian History 1353 to 1983. Nikolai Tolstoy. LC 83-61738. (Illus.). 352p. 1983. FPT 22.50 o.p. (ISBN 0-688-02341-X). Morrow.

Tom & the Redcoats. Barnett Spratt. cancelled o.s.i. (ISBN 0-87844-090-9). Sandlapper Pub Co.

Tom B. & the Joyful Noise. Jerome Cushman. LC 70-99444. (Illus.). (gr. 4-7). 1970. 4.25 o.s.i. (ISBN 0-664-32467-3, Westminster). Westminster John Knox.

Tom Horn Autobiography. Tom Horn. 1985. pap. 15.00 o.p. (ISBN 0-87380-145-8). Rio Grande.

Tom Jones see also History of Tom Jones, a Foundling.

Tom Pilgrims Progress. Marie Dubsky. (Illus.). 64p. 1983. pap. 9.95 o.p. (ISBN 0-907040-09-8, Pub. by GMP England). Alyson Pubns.

Tom Sawyer see also Adventures of Tom Sawyer.

Tom Sawyer Fires. Laurence Yep. 144p. (gr. 5 up). 1984. 10.75 o.p. (ISBN 0-688-03861-1, Morrow Junior Books). Morrow.

Tom Seaver's All-Time Baseball Greats. Tom Seaver & Martin Appel. Ed. by Wendy Barish. LC 83-21823. (Illus.). 128p. (Orig.). (gr. 8 up). 1984. 8.50 o.s.i. (ISBN 0-671-49524-0). Wanderer Bks.

Tom Seaver's Baseball Card Book. Tom Seaver & Alice Seigel. 1985. 6.95 o.s.i. (ISBN 0-671-49525-9). Wanderer Bks.

Tom Stoppard. Thomas Whitaker. LC 83-48296. (Modern Dramatists Ser.). (Illus.). 180p. 1984. 17.50 o.s.i. (ISBN 0-394-53507-3, GP-885). Grove.

Tom Stoppard. Thomas Whitaker. LC 83-48296. (Modern Dramatists Ser.). (Illus.). 180p. 1984. pap. 9.95 o.s.i. (ISBN 0-394-62499-8, E878, Ever). Grove.

Tom Stoppard's Plays. Jim Hunter. LC 82-47988. 258p. 1983. pap. 12.50 o.p. (ISBN 0-394-62414-9, E825, Ever). Grove.

Tom Swift & Company: "Boys' Books" by Stratemeyer & Others. John T. Dizer, Jr. LC 81-1559. (Illus.). 192p. 1982. lib. bdg. 19.95x o.p. (ISBN 0-89950-024-2). McFarland & Co.

Tom, the Poet & Gadgetmaker. Tom Serpico. 86p. 1980. 6.00 o.p. (ISBN 0-682-49622-7). Exposition-Phoenix.

Tom Thumb. Jacob Grimm & Wilhelm K. Grimm. Ed. & illus. by Felix Hoffmann. LC 72-85915. 32p. (ps-3). 1973. 7.95 o.p. (ISBN 0-689-30318-1, Atheneum). Macmillan.

Tom Tit Tot. Edward Clodd. LC 67-23907. 264p. 1968. Repr. of 1898 ed. 35.00x o.p. (ISBN 0-8103-3459-3). Gale.

Tomahawk. Buck Bradshaw. (Lythway Ser.). 168p. 1988. lib. bdg. 17.50x o.p. (ISBN 0-7451-0679-X, Pub. by Chivers Pr UK). G K Hall.

Tomahawks & Trombones. Barbara Mitchell. LC 81-21661. (Carolrhoda On My Own Bks.). (Illus.). 56p. (gr. 1-4). 1982. lib. bdg. 8.95 o.p. (ISBN 0-87614-191-2). Carolrhoda Bks.

Tomahawks & Trouble. William O. Steele. (Illus.). (gr. 3-6). 1955. 5.50 o.p. (ISBN 0-15-289084-X, HJ). HarBraceJ.

Tomahawks to Hatpins. Catharine B. Rowles. 228p. 1975. 8.95 o.p. (ISBN 0-932052-12-6). North Country.

Tomas Transtromer: Selected Poems. Tomas Transtromer. Ed. by Robert Hass. Tr. by Robin Fulton et al from Swedish. 160p. 1987. 18.00 o.p. (ISBN 0-88001-105-X). Ecco Pr.

Tomaszewski's Mime Theatre. Andrzej Hausbrandt. (Illus.). 1975. 15.00 o.s.i. (ISBN 0-685-79994-8). E J Brill USA.

Tomato Production, Processing & Quality Evaluation. 2nd ed. Wilbur A. Gould. (Illus.). 1983. 64.95 o.s.i. (ISBN 0-87055-426-3). AVI.

Tomatoes. Margaret Gin. LC 77-3481. (Edible Garden Ser.). (Illus.). 1977. pap. 2.50 o.s.i. (ISBN 0-89286-111-8, One Hund One Prods). Ortho.

Tomb & Other Tales. H. P. Lovecraft. 1982. pap. 2.25 o.p. (ISBN 0-345-30230-3, Del Rey). Ballantine.

Tomb for Boris Daviovch. Kis. 1978. 6.95 o.p. (ISBN 0-15-190486-3). HarBraceJ.

Tomb of Tjanefer at Thebes. Keith C. Seele. LC 59-14285. (Oriental Institute Pubns. Ser: No. 86). (Illus.). 1959. 22.00x o.p. (ISBN 0-226-62187-1, OIP86). U of Chicago Pr.

Tomb Robbers. Daniel Cohen. LC 79-22760. (Illus.). 96p. (gr. 5-8). 1980. text ed. 10.95 o.p. (ISBN 0-07-011566-4). McGraw.

Tombstone Story: The Biography of an Arizona Pioneer. A. Daniel Hughes. 1979. cancelled 10.00 o.p. (ISBN 0-682-49394-5, Lochinvar). Exposition-Phoenix.

Tomiki Aikido: Book One: Randori. rev. ed. Lee A. Loi. (Illus.). 88p. 1985. pap. text ed. 12.00 o.p. (ISBN 0-87364-371-2). Paladin Pr.

Tommaso Campanella: Renaissance Pioneer of Modern Thought. Bernardino M. Bonansea. LC 78-76125. 421p. 1969. 19.95x o.p. (ISBN 0-8132-0263-9). Cath U Pr.

Tommy Builds a House. Gunilla Wolde. LC 70-157101. (Illus.). (ps-1). 1971. 1.25 o.p. (ISBN 0-395-12601-0). HM.

Tommy Cleans His Room. Gunilla Wolde. LC 77-157099. (Illus.). (ps-1). 1971. 1.25 o.p. (ISBN 0-395-12602-9). HM.

Tommy Goes Out. Gunilla Wolde. LC 77-157100. (Illus.). (ps-1). 1971. 1.25 o.p. (ISBN 0-395-12603-7). HM.

Tommy Knockers. Alan Leisk. 72p. 1986. 6.95 o.p. Carlton.

Tommy Takes a Bath. Gunilla Wolde. LC 73-157098. (Illus.). (ps-1). 1971. 1.25 o.p. (ISBN 0-395-12604-5). HM.

Tomo-Chi-Chi. Sara G. Harrell. LC 77-8936. (Story of an American Indian Ser.). (Illus.). 64p. (gr. 5 up). 1977. PLB 7.95 o.p. (ISBN 0-87518-146-5). Dillon.

Tomographic Imaging in Nuclear Medicine. G. S. Freedman. LC 73-82572. (Illus.). 1973. 12.00 o.p. (ISBN 0-88416-036-X). Year Bk Med.

Tomorrow & Forever. Francesca Macklem. 256p. (Orig.). pap. (ISBN 0-505-51839-2, Pub. by Tower Bks). Dorchester Pub Co.

Tomorrow at Dawn. J. G. De Beus. 1980. 12.95 o.p. (ISBN 0-393-01263-8). Norton.

Tomorrow Connection. T. Ernesto Bethancourt. LC 84-47836. 144p. (YA) (gr. 7 up). 1984. 10.95 o.p. (ISBN 0-8234-0543-5). Holiday.

Tomorrow, Inc. SF Stories about Big Business. Ed. by Martin H. Greenberg & Joseph D. Olander. LC 76-11057. (YA) (gr. 10 up). 1976. 9.95 o.s.i. (ISBN 0-8008-7746-2). Taplinger.

Tomorrow Is So Far from Now. David Kalugin. (Illus.). 1979. pap. 4.95 o.p. (ISBN 0-933586-01-9). Book Promo Pr.

Tomorrow Morning, Faustus. I. A. Richards. LC 62-14468. 1962. 4.50 o.p. (ISBN 0-15-190490-1). HarBraceJ.

Tomorrow, New Worlds of Science Fiction. Ed. by Roger Elwood. LC 75-17783. 228p. (gr. 7 up). 1975. 5.95 o.p. (ISBN 0-87131-185-2). M Evans.

Titles

Tomorrow, Night Will Come Again. Clyde Owen Jackson. 1977. 5.00 o.p. (ISBN 0-682-48621-3). Exposition-Phoenix.

Tomorrow's Community-the Development of Neighborhood Organisations. Maurice Broady. 86p. 1979. pap. text ed. 7.25x o.p. (ISBN 0-7199-0966-X, Pub. by Bedford England). Gower Pub Co.

Tomorrow's Education: The French Experience. J. Capelle. 1967. text ed. 31.00 o.p. (ISBN 0-08-012517-4); pap. text ed. 17.50 o.p. (ISBN 0-08-012516-6). Pergamon.

Tomorrow's Workers. Michael E. Borus. LC 82-17154. 208p. 1982. 28.50x o.p. (ISBN 0-669-06090-9). Lexington Bks.

Tomorrow's World: Energy. Malcolm Brinkworth. (Illus.). 128p. 1986. 18.95 o.p. (ISBN 0-88186-402-1); pap. 9.95 o.p. (ISBN 0-563-20347-1). Parkwest Pubns.

Tomorrow's World: Food. Caroline Van Den Brul & Susan Spindler. (Illus.). 128p. 1986. 18.95 o.p. (ISBN 0-88186-401-3); pap. 9.95 o.p. (ISBN 0-563-20305-6). Parkwest Pubns.

Tomorrow's World: Medicine. Fiona Holmes. (Illus.). 128p. 1986. 18.95 o.p. (ISBN 0-88186-403-X); pap. 9.95 o.p. (ISBN 0-563-20346-3). Parkwest Pubns.

Tomorrow's World: Space Technology. Max Whitby. (Illus.). 128p. 1987. 18.95 o.p. (ISBN 0-88186-404-8, Pub. by BBC); pap. 9.95 o.p. (ISBN 0-563-20378-1, Pub. by BBC). Parkwest Pubns.

Tom's Tale. Judith Stinto. (Illus.). (gr. k-3). 5.95 o.p. (ISBN 0-531-04606-0, A Julia Macrae Blackbird Book). Watts.

Ton & Pon: Big & Little. Kazuo Iwamura. LC 83-22350. Orig. Title: Ton to Pon: Okii Shiisai. (Illus.). 48p. (ps-2). 1984. 8.95 o.s.i. (ISBN 0-02-747480-1). Bradbury Pr.

Ton to Pon: Okii Shiisai see Ton & Pon: Big & Little.

Tonal Grammar of Etsako. Baruch Elimelech. (UC Publications in Linguistics: Vol. 87). 1979. pap. 22.00x o.p. (ISBN 0-520-09576-6). U of Cal Pr.

Tongues of Flame. Tim Parks. 144p. 1987. Repr. of 1985 ed. 14.95 o.s.i. (ISBN 0-394-55299-7). Grove.

Tongues of the Moon. Philip Jose Farmer. 1978. pap. 1.50 o.s.i. (ISBN 0-515-04595-0). Jove Pubns.

Tonight on This Late Road. Christine Swanberg. (Illus.). 44p. 1984. pap. 3.00 o.p. (ISBN 0-942582-06-3). Erie St Pr.

Tonight's the Night. Jim Aylesworth. Ed. by Ann Fay. (Self-Starter Bks.). (Illus.). 32p. (ps-1). 1981. PLB 9.75 o.p. (ISBN 0-8075-8020-1). A Whitman.

Toning Your Body: A Bodybuilding Program for Women. Stacey Bentley & Fred Hatfield. LC 82-14119. (Illus.). 160p. (Orig.). 1982. pap. 12.95 o.p. (ISBN 0-8329-0148-2, Pub. by Winchester Pr). New Century.

Tons of Fun: Training Elephants. Martin Hintz. LC 82-3486. (Illus.). 96p. (gr. 4-6). 1982. lib. bdg. 9.29 o.s.i. (ISBN 0-671-44248-1). Messner.

Tony & Me. Alfred Slote. (gr. 3-5). 1976. pap. 1.75 o.p. (ISBN 0-380-00438-0, 52472-4, Camelot). Avon.

Tony: Our Journey Together. Carolyn Koons. LC 83-48432. (Illus.). 320p. 1984. 11.49i o.p. (ISBN 0-06-064762-0). HarpR.

Tony Smith, Ten Elements & Throwback. Sam Hunter. Ed. by Pace Gallery Publications Staff. (Illus.). 48p. (Orig.). 1979. pap. text ed. 9.00 o.p. (ISBN 0-938608-37-1). Pace Pubns.

Tony's Tunnel. Ann S. McGrath. LC 81-2009. (Illus.). 40p. (gr. k-3). 1981. 8.95 o.p. (ISBN 0-03-059878-8). H Holt & Co.

Too Big to Spank. Jay Kesler. LC 77-90580. 160p. 1978. pap. 5.95 o.s.i. (ISBN 0-8307-0623-2, 5409306). Regal.

Too Bright to See. Linda Gregg. LC 80-67983. 72p. 1981. 9.00 o.s.i. (ISBN 0-915308-27-4). Graywolf.

Too Busy to Cook 1985 Datebook & Organizer. (Illus.). 144p. 1984. note pad incl. 19.95 o.p. (ISBN 0-89535-140-4). Knapp Pr.

Too Few Happy Endings: The Dilemma of the Humane Societies. Margaret Poynter. LC 81-2239. (Illus.). 144p. (gr. 4 up). 1981. 9.95 o.s.i. (ISBN 0-689-30864-7, Atheneum Childrens Bks). Macmillan.

Too-Good-to-Be Leftovers Cookbook. 1975. pap. 1.25 o.p. (ISBN 0-380-01585-4, 18325). Avon.

Too-Long Trunk. Regina Sauro. (Illus.). (ps-2). 4.25 o.p. (ISBN 0-8313-0085-X). Lantern.

Too-Loose the Chocolate Moose. Stewart Moskowitz. LC 82-7918. (Illus.). 32p. (gr. k-3). 1982. lib. bdg. 8.79 o.s.i. (ISBN 0-671-45886-8). Messner.

Too Many Cooks. Rex Stout. LC 75-46002. (Crime Fiction Ser.). 1976. Repr. of 1938 ed. lib. bdg. 21.00 o.p. (ISBN 0-8240-2394-3). Garland Pub.

Too Many Cooks. Rex Stout. (Nightingale Paperbacks Large Print Ser.). 1985. pap. 10.95 o.p. (ISBN 0-8161-3868-0). G K Hall.

Too Many Mice! David N. Bruskin. (Story Bus Subseries: School Bus). (Illus.). 10p. (ps-2). 1988. bds. 14.95 o.p. (ISBN 1-55929-012-9). Bound Fun Inc.

Too Many Pastors? The State of the Clergy Job Market. Jackson Carroll & Robert Wilson. LC 80-16037. 1980. pap. 6.95 o.p. (ISBN 0-8298-0405-6). Pilgrim NY.

Too Many Promises: The Uncertain Future of Social Security. Michael J. Boskin. 175p. 1986. 22.50 o.p. (ISBN 0-87094-779-6). Dow Jones-Irwin.

Too Much. Date not set. (ISBN 0-385-29482-4). Delacorte.

Too Much of Water. Bruce Hamilton. LC 82-48242. 288p. 1983. pap. 2.84i o.p. (ISBN 0-06-080635-4, P 635). HarpR.

Too Much Order with Too Little Law. Frank Brennan. LC 82-19956. (Illus.). 303p. 1983. text ed. 27.95 o.p. (ISBN 0-7022-1842-1); pap. 14.50 o.p. (ISBN 0-7022-1852-9). U of Queensland Pr.

Too Much T. J. Jacqueline Shannon. LC 86-1989. 192p. (gr. 7 up). 1986. pap. 14.95 o.p. (ISBN 0-385-29482-4). Delacorte.

Too Much Tenderness: An Autobiography of Childhood & Youth. Christopher Elliot-Binns. 224p. 1983. 17.95 o.p. (ISBN 0-7100-9418-3). Routledge Chapman & Hall.

Too Much Too Soon. Jacqueline Briskin. 1986. lib. bdg. 19.95x o.p. (ISBN 0-8161-3984-9, Large Print Bks); pap. 11.95 o.p. (ISBN 0-8161-3987-3). G K Hall.

Too Rapid Rural Development: Perceptions & Perspectives from Southeast Asia. Ed. by Colin MacAndrews & Chia Lin Sien. LC 82-60405. xiv, 370p. 1982. lib. bdg. 22.95x o.p. (ISBN 0-8214-0668-X); pap. 12.00x o.p. (ISBN 0-8214-0669-8). Ohio U Pr.

Too Short Fred. Susan Meddaugh. (Illus.). (gr. k-3). 1978. reinforced bdg. 5.95 o.p. (ISBN 0-395-27155-X). HM.

Too Short Fred. Susan Meddaugh. 1985. pap. 3.95 o.s.i. (ISBN 0-395-38313-7). HM.

Too Young to Die. Alphonzo Travis. LC 84-91312. 46p. 1985. 5.95 o.p. (ISBN 0-533-06403-1). Vantage.

Too Young to Die. Alida E. Young. 60p. (gr. 5-8). 1987. 2.95 o.s.i. (ISBN 0-87406-236-5). Willowisp Pr.

Tool Book. Gail Gibbons. LC 81-13386. (Illus.). 32p. (gr. k-3). pap. 5.95 o.p. (ISBN 0-8234-0694-6). Holiday.

Tool for Tomorrow: New Knowledge about Genes. Sylvia L. Engdahl & Rick Roberson. LC 78-13777. (Illus.). (gr. 5 up). 1979. 6.95 o.p. (ISBN 0-689-30679-2, Atheneum). Macmillan.

Tooloose the Chocolate Moose. Stewart Moskowitz. Ed. by Kate Klimo. (Moskowitz Bks.). (Illus.). 32p. 1982. 6.75 o.s.i. (ISBN 0-671-45329-7, Little Simon). S&S.

Tools & Techniques for Electronics. A. A. Wicks. 73p. 1979. pap. 4.95 o.p. (ISBN 0-88006-008-5, BK7348). Wayne Green Ent.

Tools & Techniques of Estate Planning. Stephan R. Leimberg et al. LC 87-60896. 535p. 1987. pap. 29.75 o.p. (ISBN 0-87218-446-3). Natl Underwriter.

Tools for Agriculture: A Buyer's Guide to Low-Cost Agricultural Implements. 2nd ed. Compiled by John Boyd. (Illus.). 173p. (Orig.). 1976. pap. 17.50x o.p. (ISBN 0-903031-22-1, Pub. by Intermed Tech England). Intermediate Tech.

Tools for Financial Management: Emphasis on Inflation. Leon Shashua & Yaaqov Goldschmidt. LC 82-47951. 448p. 1983. 40.00x o.p. (ISBN 0-669-05720-7). Lexington Bks.

Tools of the Trade. new ed. R. Bruce McQuigg. (gr. 7-12). 1979. pap. 6.00 o.p. (ISBN 0-88210-096-3). Natl Assn Principals.

Tools of Their Trade: The Book of Professional Fiascos. Hilary MacLeod & Robin Boden. (Illus.). 144p. 1986. pap. 9.95 o.p. (ISBN 0-920792-66-9). Eden Pr.

Toone, Tune & Toon of America: A Family History. Lavern Toone. (Illus.). 450p. (Orig.). 1987. pap. 19.95 o.p. (ISBN 1-55618-017-9). Brunswick Pub.

Tooni, the Elephant Boy. Astrid B. Sucksdorff. LC 73-137762. (Illus.). 48p. (gr. 3 up). 1971. 5.95 o.p. (ISBN 0-15-289426-8, HJ). HarBraceJ.

Tooth-Gnasher Superflash. Daniel M. Pinkwater. LC 80-69996. (Illus.). 32p. (gr. k-3). 1981. 9.95 o.s.i. (ISBN 0-02-774660-7, Four Winds). Macmillan.

Tooth Trip. Eva Eriksson. LC 84-28477. (Victor & Rosalie Bks.). (Illus.). 32p. (ps-3). 1985. PLB 8.95 o.p. (ISBN 0-87614-236-6). Carolrhoda Bks.

Tootle. AISLIN Staff & Johan Sarrazin. (Illus.). 24p. (ps up). 1984. 2.95 o.p. (ISBN 0-88776-168-2). Tundra Bks.

Top Country & Western Records Nineteen Forty-Nine to Nineteen Seventy-One. Compiled by Joel Whitburn. LC 72-6752. 184p. 1972. soft bdg. 25.00x o.p. (ISBN 0-686-81470-3, Pub. by Record Research). Gale.

Top Country & Western Records, 1976. Joel Whitburn. 40p. (Orig.). pap. text ed. 10.00 o.p. (ISBN 0-89820-019-9). Record Research.

Top Dollars for Technical Scholars: A Guide to Engineering, Math, Computer Science & Science Scholarships. Clark Z. Robinson. 88p. (Orig.). 1986. pap. 4.25 o.p. (ISBN 0-917760-78-6). Octameron Assocs.

Top-Down Assembly Language for Your VIC-20 & Commmodore 64. Kenneth Skier. 1984. pap. text ed. 19.95 o.p. (ISBN 0-07-057864-8). McGraw.

Top-Down Assembly Language Programming for Your VIC-20 & Commodore-64. Kenneth Skier. 434p. 1983. pap. text ed. 21.95 o.p. (ISBN 0-07-057863-X, BYTE Bks). McGraw.

Top Executive Compensation: 1985 Edition. Harland Fox. (Report Ser.: No. 854). 73p. 1984. 125.00 o.p. (ISBN 0-8237-0296-0). Conference Bd.

Top Executive Performance: Eleven Keys to Success & Power. William A. Cohen & Nurit Cohen. LC 83-21775. 254p. 1984. 19.95 o.p. (ISBN 0-471-89687-X). Wiley.

Top Gun Fighters & America's Jet Power. George Hall. 1988. 12.98 o.p. (ISBN 0-517-65580-2). Crown.

Top One Hundred: How Are They Doing? 1985. Lillian S. Clancy. (California Public Schools Ser.). 75p. (Orig.). 1984. pap. 5.95 o.p. (ISBN 0-939580-27-6). CA Schl Surveys.

Top One Hundred, 1986. Lillian S. Clancy. (California Public Schools Ser.: How Are They Doing?). 80p. (Orig.). 1985. pap. 12.95 o.p. (ISBN 0-939580-36-5). CA Schl Surveys.

Top One Hundred, 1987. Lillian S. Clancy. (California Public Schools: How Are They Doing? Ser.). 80p. 1987. pap. 12.95 o.p. (ISBN 0-939580-44-6). CA Schl Surveys.

Top One-Hundred, 1988. Lillian S. Clancy. (California Public Schools: How Are They Doing? Ser.). 80p. (Orig.). 1988. pap. 13.95 o.p. (ISBN 0-939580-52-7). CA Schl Surveys.

Top Secret: A Clandestine Operator's Glossary of Terms. Bob Burton. 136p. (Orig.). 1986. pap. text ed. 10.00 o.p. (ISBN 0-87364-350-X). Paladin Pr.

Top Secret Ultra, No. 10. Peter Calvacorlessi. 160p. 1981. pap. 2.75 o.s.i. (ISBN 0-345-30069-6). Ballantine.

Top Ten: Nineteen Fifty-Six to Present. Bob Gilbert & Gary Theroux. LC 82-10478. (Illus.). 320p. 1982. pap. 12.50 o.p. (ISBN 0-671-43215-X, Fireside). S&S.

Top Three Thousand Directories & Annuals 1986-1987. 7th ed. Ed. by Mark Rasdall. 360p. 1986. (ISBN 0-946291-14-4). A Armstrong.

Top Three Thousand Directories & Annuals 1987-1988. 8th ed. Ed. by Mark Rasdall. 360p. 1987. A Armstrong.

Topical & Nautical Operas. Ed. by Walter H. Rubsamen. (Ballad Opera Ser.). 1974. lib. bdg. 61.00 o.p. (ISBN 0-8240-0913-4). Garland Pub.

Topical Index & Digest of the Bible. Harold E. Monser & A. T. Robertson. (Paperback Reference Library). 688p. 1983. pap. 14.95 o.p. (ISBN 0-8010-6160-1). Baker Bk.

Topical Reviews in Accident Surgery, Vol. 1. N. Tubbs & P. S. London. (Topical Reviews Ser.). (Illus.). 240p. 1980. text ed. 34.00 o.p. (ISBN 0-7236-0534-3, Pub. by John Wright UK). Butterworth.

Topical Steroids for Skin Disorders. Clement & Du Viver. 1986. pap. 14.25 o.p. (ISBN 0-8016-1305-1). Mosby.

Topics Aids: Biology: A Catalog of Instructional Media. Robert S. Egan. LC 77-13587. 296p. 1977. pap. 5.00x o.p. (ISBN 0-89096-042-9). Tex A&M Univ Pr.

Topics: Computer Education for Colleges of Education. Ed. by Jean Rogers. 111p. 1983. 9.00 o.p. (ISBN 0-924667-18-4). Intl Council Comp.

Topics in Analytic Number Theory. H. Rademacher. LC 72-79326. (Grundelehren der Mathematischen Wissenschaften: Vol. 169). (Illus.). 340p. 1973. 54.00 o.p. (ISBN 0-387-05447-2). Springer-Verlag.

Topics in Antibiotic Chemistry: Aminoglyosides & Ansamycins, Vol. I. P. G. Sammes. 217p. 1977. 62.95 o.p. (ISBN 0-470-99066-X). Halsted Pr.

Topics in Applied Quantum Electrodynamics. P. Urban. LC 71-98304. (Illus.). 1970. 40.20 o.p. (ISBN 0-387-80962-7). Springer-Verlag.

Topics in Approximation Theory. H. S. Shapiro. LC 73-151323. (Lecture Notes in Mathematics: Vol. 187). 1971. pap. 14.00 o.p. (ISBN 0-387-05376-X). Springer-Verlag.

Topics in Artificial Intelligence. Ed. by A. Marzollo. (CISM-International Centre for Mechanical Sciences Courses & Lectures: Vol. 256). (Illus.). 1979. pap. 24.00 o.p. (ISBN 0-387-81466-3). Springer-Verlag.

Topics in Atomic Collision Theory. Sydney Geltman. (Pure & Applied Physics Ser: Vol. 32). 1969. 89.00 o.p. (ISBN 0-12-279650-0). Acad Pr.

Topics in Automatic Chemical Analysis, Vol. 1. Ed. by J. K. Foreman & P. B. Stockwell. LC 79-40239. (Series in Analytical Chemistry). 313p. 1979. 89.95x o.p. (ISBN 0-470-26600-7). Halsted Pr.

Topics in Basic Immunology. Ed. by M. Sela & M. Prywes. 1969. 57.50 o.p. (ISBN 0-12-635550-9). Acad Pr.

Topics in Child Psychology. S. S. Brown. 1970. pap. text ed. 7.25x o.p. (ISBN 0-8290-1198-6). Irvington.

Topics in Combinatorial Optimization. Ed. by S. Rinaldi. (International Centre for Mechanical Sciences: No. 17). 1977. pap. 25.00 o.p. (ISBN 0-387-81339-X). Springer-Verlag.

Topics in Dietary Fiber Research. Ed. by Gene A. Spiller. LC 77-26883. 234p. 1978. 39.50x o.p. (ISBN 0-306-31126-7, Plenum Pr). Plenum Pub.

Topics in Functional Analysis: Essays Dedicated to M. G. Krein on the Occasion of His 70th. Birthday. Ed. by I. Gohberg & M. Kal. (Adv. in Mathematics Supplementary Studies: Vol. 3). 1978. 99.00 o.p. (ISBN 0-12-287150-2). Acad Pr.

Topics in Information Theory. I. Csiszar & P. Elias. (Colloquia Mathematica Societatis Janos Bolyai Ser.: Vol. 16). 592p. 1977. 142.00 o.p. (ISBN 0-7204-0699-4, North Holland). Elsevier.

Topics in Management Information Systems. Ed. by Steve Teglovic & Robert Lynch. LC 73-3315. 295p. 1973. text ed. 29.50x o.p. (ISBN 0-8422-5092-1); pap. text ed. 8.50x o.p. (ISBN 0-8422-0277-3). Irvington.

Topics in Mathematical Analysis for Economists. Knut Sydsaeter. LC 81-66692. 1981. 46.50 o.p. (ISBN 0-12-679980-6). Acad Pr.

Topics in Mathematical Physics. Halis Odabasi & O. Akyuz. LC 77-84853. (Illus.). 1977. text ed. 29.95 o.p. (ISBN 0-87081-072-3). Univ Pr Colo.

Topics in Metallurgical Thermodynamics. Owen F. Devereux. LC 83-1115. 494p. 1983. 49.95x o.p. (ISBN 0-471-86963-5). Krieger.

Topics in Modern Logic. D. C. Makinson. (University Paperback Ser.). 107p. 1973. pap. 5.95x o.p. (ISBN 0-416-78100-4, NO. 2309). Routledge Chapman & Hall.

Topics in Modern Physics: Tribute to E. U. Condon. Ed. by Wesley E. Brittin & Halis Odabasi. LC 70-135286. 1971. 22.50x o.p. (ISBN 0-87081-010-3). Univ Pr Colo.

Topics in Non-Ferrous Extractive Metallurgy. Ed. by A. R. Burkin. LC 80-17435. (Critical Reports on Applied Chemistry Ser.: Vol. 1). 134p. 1980. 37.95 o.p. (ISBN 0-470-27016-0). Halsted Pr.

Topics in Nonlinear Physics: Proceedings of the Physics Session. International School Of Nonlinear Mathematics & Physics-Munich-1966. Ed. by N. J. Zabusky & M. D. Kruskal. LC 67-20647. 1968. 24.50 o.p. (ISBN 0-387-04363-2). Springer-Verlag.

Topics in Numerical Analysis II. Ed. by J. J. Miller. 1976. 68.00 o.p. (ISBN 0-12-496952-6). Acad Pr.

Topics in Numerical Analysis III. Ed. by J. H. Miller. 1978. 99.00 o.p. (ISBN 0-12-496953-4). Acad Pr.

Topics in Ocean Engineering, 3 vols. Charles L. Bretschneider. Incl. Vol. 1. 428p. 1969 (ISBN 0-87201-598-X); Vol. 2. (Illus.). 229p. 1970 (ISBN 0-87201-599-8); Vol. 3. LC 78-87230. 328p. 1976. 32.00x ea. (ISBN 0-87201-600-5). LC 78-87230. 32.00x ea. o.p. Gulf Pub.

Topics in Pharmaceutical Sciences II: Proceedings of the 43rd International Congress of the F.I.P., Montreux, Switzerland September 5-9,1983. Ed. by D. D. Breimer & P. Speiser. 1984. 112.00 o.p. (ISBN 0-444-80549-4, I-009-84, Biomedical Pr). Elsevier.

Topics in Ring Theory. I. N. Herstein. LC 69-17035. (Chicago Lectures in Mathematics Ser). 1969. pap. text ed. 6.00x o.s.i. (ISBN 0-226-32802-3). U of Chicago Pr.

Topics in Romance Syntax. Osvaldo Jaeggli. 196p. 1981. 27.50x o.p. (ISBN 90-70176-34-3); pap. 19.75x o.p. (ISBN 90-70176-23-8). Foris Pubns.

Topics in Solid State & Quantum Electronics. W. D. Hershberger. LC 75-169163. 522p. 1972. 41.50 o.p. (ISBN 0-471-37350-8, Pub. by John Wiley). Krieger.

Topics in Stereochemistry, Vol. 13. Norman Allinger et al. LC 61-13943. 489p. 1982. 120.00 o.p. (ISBN 0-471-05680-4, Pub. by Wiley-Interscience). Wiley.

Topics in Topology. S. Lefschetz. (Annals of Math Studies). 1942. 14.00 o.p. (ISBN 0-527-02726-X). Kraus Repr.

Topics in Universal Algebra. B. Jonsson. (Lecture Notes in Mathematics: Vol. 250). (Illus.). 220p. 1972. pap. 7.90 o.p. (ISBN 0-387-05722-6). Springer-Verlag.
Topics of Radiofrequency Spectroscopy. Ed. by A. Gozzini. (Italian Physical Society: Course 17). 1962. 82.50 o.p. (ISBN 0-12-368817-5). Acad Pr.
Topics on Contamination in Hydraulic Systems. Society of Automotive Engineers Staff. LC 79-67067. 60p. 1979. Eight papers. pap. 18.00 o.p. (ISBN 0-89883-218-7, SP447). Soc Auto Engineers.
TOPO 72: General Topology & Its Applications. Ed. by R. A. Alo et al. LC 74-390. (Lecture Notes in Mathematics: Vol. 378). xiv, 651p. 1974. pap. 31.00 o.p. (ISBN 0-387-06741-8). Springer-Verlag.
Topographic Terms: English & Spanish. John V. Dobbin. 1971. (G426). Am Congrs Survey.
Topography & Other Poems. Ruth Stone. LC 77-142098. 1971. 5.95 o.p. (ISBN 0-15-190495-2). HarBraceJ.
Topological Embeddings. T. Benny Rushing. (Pure & Applied Mathematics Ser., Vol. 52). 1973. 89.00 o.p. (ISBN 0-12-603550-4). Acad Pr.
Topological Methods in Walrasian Economics. E. Dierker. (Lecture Notes in Economics & Mathematical Systems Ser.: Vol. 92). 130p. 1974. pap. 8.70 o.p. (ISBN 0-387-06622-5). Springer-Verlag.
Topological Spaces. Hans J. Kowalsky. Tr. by Jay Strum. 1965. 65.50 o.p. (ISBN 0-12-423150-0). Acad Pr.
Topological Stability of Smooth Mappings. C. G. Gibson & K. Wirthmuller. (Lecture Notes in Mathematics: Vol. 552). 1976. soft cover 13.00 o.p. (ISBN 0-387-07997-1). Springer-Verlag.
Topological Vector Spaces & Algebras. L. Waelbroeck. (Lecture Notes in Mathematics: Vol. 230). 158p. 1971. pap. 11.00 o.p. (ISBN 0-387-05650-5). Springer-Verlag.
Topological Vector Spaces: The Theory Without Convexity Conditions. N. Adasch et al. (Lecture Notes in Mathematics: Vol. 639). 1978. pap. 14.00 o.p. (ISBN 0-387-08662-5). Springer-Verlag.
Topology. 2nd ed. Solomon Lefschetz. LC 56-11513. 16.95 o.p. (ISBN 0-8284-0116-0). Chelsea Pub.
Topology & Normed Spaces. G. J. Jameson. (Mathematics Ser.). 1974. 21.95x o.p. (ISBN 0-412-12340-1, NO. 6165, Pub. by Chapman & Hall). Routledge Chapman & Hall.
Topology of a Phantom City. Alain Robbe-Grillet. Tr. by J. A. Underwood from Fr. LC 77-77854. 1977. 8.95 o.s.i. (ISBN 0-394-42196-5, GP801). Grove.
Topology of a Phantom City. Alain Robbe-Grillet. Tr. by J. A. Underwood from Fr. LC 77-77854. 1977. pap. 3.95 o.s.i. (ISBN 0-394-17012-1, E698, Ever). Grove.
Topology of CW Complexes. A. T. Lundell & S. Weingram. LC 68-26689. (Illus.). vii, 216p. 1969. 29.00 o.p. (ISBN 0-387-90128-0). Springer-Verlag.
Topos Theory. P. T. Johnstone. 1978. 96.00 o.p. (ISBN 0-12-387850-0). Acad Pr.
Toposes, Algebraic Geometry & Logic. Ed. by F. W. Lawvere. LC 72-86101. (Lecture Notes in Mathematics: Vol. 274). 189p. 1972. pap. 7.00 o.p. (ISBN 0-387-05920-2). Springer-Verlag.
Torah: From Scroll to Symbol in Formative Judaism. Jacob Neusner. LC 84-45190. (Foundations of Judaism Trilogy Ser.). 208p. 1985. 24.95 o.p. (1-734, Fortress). Augsburg Fortress.
Torah with Love: A Guide for Strengthening Jewish Values Within the Family. David Epstein & Suzanne Stutman. (Illus.). 208p. 1986. 14.70 o.p. (ISBN 0-13-925371-8). P-H.
Toral: A Modern Commentary: Genesis. W. Gunther Plaut. (Pardes Torah; Jewish Commentary on the Torah Ser.). 1974. 20.00 o.p. (ISBN 0-8074-0001-7, 381611); pap. 10.00 o.p. (ISBN 0-685-48959-0, 381601). UAHC.
Torch to the Enemy. Martin Caidin. 1979. pap. 1.95 o.s.i. (ISBN 0-345-28304-X). Ballantine.
Torches Together: The Beginning & Early Years of the Bruderhof Communities. Emmy Arnold. LC 63-23426. 1971. 8.95 o.p. (ISBN 0-87486-109-8). Plough.
Tormented Master: A Life of Rabbi Nahman of Bratslav. Arthur Green. LC 78-16674. (Judaic Studies: No. 9). (Illus.). 400p. 1979. 30.00 o.p. (ISBN 0-8173-6907-4). U of Ala Pr.
Torn Lace Curtains. Frank Saunders & James Southwood. LC 82-9194. 1982. 13.95 o.p. (ISBN 0-03-060046-4). H Holt & Co.
Tornado. Michael J. Gething. (Warbirds Illustrated Ser.: No. 42). (Illus.). 72p. (Orig.). 1987. pap. 9.95 o.p. (ISBN 0-85368-788-9, Pub. by Arms & Armour). Sterling.
Tornado. Francis K. Mason. (Illus.). 216p. 1987. 19.95 o.p. (ISBN 0-85059-772-2, Pub. by PSL P Stephens England). Sterling.
Tornadoes over Texas: Waco & San Antonio in Disaster. Harry E. Moore. 1958. write for info. o.p. (ISBN 0-292-73410-7). U of Tex Pr.
Toroidal Embeddings 1. G. Kempf et al. LC 73-11598. (Lecture Notes in Mathematics Ser.: Vol. 339). 209p. 1973. pap. 16.00 o.p. (ISBN 0-387-06432-X). Springer-Verlag.
Toronto Blue Jays. rev. ed. Shaw. LC 82-240252. (Baseball Today Ser.). 48p. (gr. 4 up). 1982. PLB 11.95 o.p. (ISBN 0-87191-877-3). Creative Ed.
Toronto Lampoon. Ed. by Wayne Grigsby. (Illus.). 160p. (Orig.). 1984. pap. 9.95 o.p. (ISBN 0-920792-38-3). Eden Pr.
Torpedo! Harry Homewood. 272p. 1982. text ed. 12.95 o.p. (ISBN 0-07-029698-7). McGraw.
Torpedoes Away. Gordon D. Shirreffs. (gr. 6-8). 1967. 3.75 o.s.i. (ISBN 0-664-32407-X, Westminster). Westminster John Knox.
Torques & Attitude Sensing in Earth Satellites. Ed. by S. Fred Singer. (Applied Mathematics & Mechanics Ser.: Vol. 7). 1964. 71.50 o.p. (ISBN 0-12-646850-8). Acad Pr.
Torre: Herida Por el Rayo. F. Arrabel. 1986. write for info. o.p. Penguin USA.
Torrents of Spring. Ernest Hemingway. 90p. 1972. 5.95 o.s.i. (ISBN 0-684-13088-2, ScribT). Scribner.
Torres Strait: People & History. John Singe. (Illus.). 1980. 25.00x o.p. (ISBN 0-7022-1417-5). U of Queensland Pr.
Torsion of Structural Concrete: Uniformly Prestressed Rectangular Members Without Web Reinforcement. (PCI Journal Reprints Ser.). 48p. pap. 8.00 o.p. (ISBN 0-686-40002-X, JR63). P-PCI.
Tortoise & the Hare, the Lion & the Mouse. (Preschool Puppet Board Bks.). (Illus.). 7p. (ps-1). 1976. 2.50 o.p. (ISBN 0-448-09742-7, G&D). Putnam Pub Group.
Tortoise the Trickster: And Other Folktales from Cameroon. Loreto Todd. (Illus.). 121p. 1985. pap. 4.95 o.p. (ISBN 0-7102-0740-9). Routledge Chapman & Hall.
Tortoise Trickster. Date not set. (ISBN 0-8052-3725-9). Random.
Torture Doctor. David Franke. 1976. pap. 1.75 o.p. (ISBN 0-380-00730-4, 30031). Avon.
Tory's. William Snyder. 384p. 1981. pap. 2.75 o.p. (ISBN 0-380-76547-0, 76547-0). Avon.
Tosh "le Vengeur" Paul Kannady. 1978. 4.50 o.p. (ISBN 0-682-49222-1). Exposition-Phoenix.
Total Banana. Alex Abella. LC 79-1855. 1979. pap. 6.95 o.p. (ISBN 0-15-690475-6, Harv). HarBraceJ.
Total Breathing. Philip Smith. (McGraw-Hill Paperbacks Ser.). 1980. pap. text ed. 6.95 o.p. (ISBN 0-07-058989-5). McGraw.
Total Church Life. Darrell W. Robinson. LC 85-7900. 1985. 8.95 o.p. (ISBN 0-8054-6250-3). Broadman.
Total Couple. Albert Lee & Carol A. Lee. 1977. 7.95 o.p. (ISBN 0-89328-010-0). Lorenz Corp.
Total Development: Essays Toward an Integration of Marxian & Gandhian Perspectives. K. J. Charles. 1983. text ed. 30.00x o.p. (ISBN 0-7069-2075-9, Pub. by Vikas India). Advent NY.
Total Energy. R. M. Diamant. 1970. 29.00 o.p. (ISBN 0-08-006918-5). Pergamon.
Total Fitness for Men. J. Tillman Hall. 1980. pap. text ed. write for info. o.p. (ISBN 0-673-16206-0). Scott F.
Total Geostrophic South Pacific: Flow Patterns, Tracers & Transports. J. L. Reid. 1985. pap. 50.00 o.p. (ISBN 0-08-034011-3, Pub. by PPL). Pergamon.
Total Parenteral Nutrition. Ed. by Philip L. White & Margarita E. Nagy. LC 73-84169. (Illus.). 300p. 1974. 12.00 o.p. (ISBN 0-88416-005-X). Year Bk Med.
Total Sex. Dan Abelow. LC 76-27127. (Illus.). 96p. 1977. pap. 6.95 o.p. (ISBN 0-448-12851-9, G&D). Putnam Pub Group.
Total Tote Bag Book: Designer Totes to Craft & Carry. Joyce Aiken & Jean Ray Laury. LC 76-11058. (Illus.). 128p. 1977. 12.50 o.s.i. (ISBN 0-8008-7793-4); pap. 5.95 o.s.i. (ISBN 0-8008-7794-2). Taplinger.
Totalaction: Ideas & Activities for Teaching Children Ages 5 to 8. Pat Short & Billee Davidson. 1979. pap. 11.95 o.p. (ISBN 0-673-16452-7). Scott F.
Totalitarian Threat. Eugene J. Roesch. 224p. 1963. (ISBN 0-8022-1366-9). Philos Lib.
Totally Outrageous Bumper-Snickers. Mark Not-Twain & Kent Clark. 1988. 2.95 o.p. CCC Pubns.
Totally Topiary. Barbara Gallup & Deborah Reich. (Illus.). 256p. (Orig.). 1987. pap. 10.95 o.p. (ISBN 0-89480-318-2). Workman Pub.
Totila. Giovanni Legrenzi. Ed. by Howard M. Brown. LC 76-20984. (Italian Opera 1640-1770 Ser.). 1978. lib. bdg. 77.00 o.p. (ISBN 0-8240-2608-X). Garland Pub.
Touch. Patricia Rae. (Orig.). 1980. pap. 2.75 o.p. (ISBN 0-505-51580-6, Pub. by Tower Bks). Dorchester Pub Co.
Touch & Go. Cyril N. Parkinson. LC 77-7665. 1977. 8.95 o.p. (ISBN 0-395-25592-9). HM.
Touch for Health. John F. Thie et al. LC 73-86019. (Illus.). 107p. (Orig.). 1973. pap. 13.95 o.p. (ISBN 0-87516-180-4). DeVorss.
Touch for Love. Wataru Ohashi & Mary Hoover. 112p. (Orig.). 1985. pap. 7.95 o.p. (ISBN 0-345-30090-4). Ballantine.
Touch Me. Suzanne Somers. LC 80-51893. (Illus.). 64p. 1980. pap. 3.95 o.p. (ISBN 0-89480-141-4, 443). Workman Pub.
Touch Me Again, Lord. Ruthe White. LC 82-84453. 136p. (Orig.). 1983. pap. 5.95 o.p. (ISBN 0-89840-038-4). Heres Life.
Touch Me in the Morning. Herman L. Mason. LC 84-90265. 210p. 1985. 10.95 o.p. Vantage.
Touch of Healing: Speeches by Sir Zelman Cowen As Governor General, 1977-1982, 3 vols. Zelman Cowen. Ed. by W. G. Walker. LC 85-22501. (Illus.). 1986. Set. text ed. 98.50X o.p. (ISBN 0-7022-1915-0). Vol. I, 153p. Vol. II, 143p. Vol. III, 145p. U of Queensland Pr.
Touch of Heaven Here. Evan Welsh. 96p. 1985. pap. 3.95 o.p. (ISBN 0-8423-7294-6). Tyndale.
Touch of His Love: Devotions for Every Season. Alvin N. Rogness. LC 73-88602. 112p. (Orig.). 1974. pap. 4.50 o.p. (ISBN 0-8066-1405-6, 10-6670, Augsburg). Augsburg Fortress.
Touch of Innocence. Katherine Dunham. LC 59-10256. 312p. 1969. pap. 1.45 o.s.i. (ISBN 0-15-690771-2, Harv). HarBraceJ.
Touch of Light: The Story of Louis Braille. Anne E. Neimark. LC 75-96319. (gr. 4-6). 1970. 6.95 o.p. (ISBN 0-15-289605-8, HJ). HarBraceJ.
Touch of Magic. Betty A. Cavanna. (Illus.). (gr. 6-9). 1961. 5.75 o.s.i. (ISBN 0-664-32253-0, Westminster). Westminster John Knox.
Touch of Poetry. Lawrence J. Paladino. 1985. 5.95 o.p. (ISBN 0-533-06715-4). Vantage.
Touch of Scandal. Leslie Davis. (Velvet Glove Ser.: No. 16). 192p. 1985. pap. 2.25 o.p. (ISBN 0-380-89667-2). Avon.
Touch of Wildness: A Maine Woods Journal. Lew Dietz. 1981. pap. 4.25 o.p. (ISBN 0-89272-021-2). Down East.
Touch Technique for Every Pianist. Margaret Dee. 1955. 1.50 o.p. (ISBN 0-913650-40-4). CPP Belwin.
Touch the Water, Touch the Wind. Amos Oz. Tr. by Nicholas DeLange from Hebrew. LC 74-12178. (Helen & Kurt Wolff Bk.). 192p. 1974. 9.95 o.p. (ISBN 0-15-190873-7). HarBraceJ.
Touch the Wind. Janet Dailey. (General Ser.). 1985. lib. bdg. 13.95 o.p. (ISBN 0-8161-3812-5, Large Print Bks); pap. 9.95 o.s.i. (ISBN 0-8161-3838-9, Large Print Bks). G K Hall.
Touche Ross Guide to Personal Financial Planning. W. Thomas Porter. LC 83-21110. 200p. 1984. 3-ring binder 79.95 o.p. (ISBN 0-13-925701-2, Busn); pap. 19.95 o.p. (ISBN 0-13-925685-7). P-H.
Touched by Diamonds. Colette Collins. 192p. 1984. pap. 2.95 o.p. (ISBN 0-89081-427-9). Harvest Hse.
Touched by Fire: A Photographic History of the Civil War, Vol. 2. Ed. by William C. Davis. 1987. 50.00 o.p. (ISBN 0-316-17664-8). Little.
Touched by Fire: A Photographic Portrait of the Civil War. Ed. by William C. Davis. (Illus.). 1985. 50.00 o.p. (ISBN 0-316-17661-3). Little.
Touched by the Spirit: One Man's Struggle to Understand His Experience of the Holy Spirit. Richard A. Jensen. LC 75-2838. 160p. 1975. pap. 8.95 o.p. (ISBN 0-8066-1484-6, 10-6675, Augsburg). Augsburg Fortress.
Touched with Fire: The Future of the Vietnam Generation. John Wheeler. 272p. 1985. pap. 3.95 o.p. (ISBN 0-380-69886-2, Discus). Avon.
Touches of Sweet Harmony: Pythagorean Cosmology & Renaissance Poetics. S. K. Heninger, Jr. LC 73-78049. (Illus.). 446p. 1974. 29.95 o.p. (ISBN 0-87328-063-6). Huntington Lib.
Touching Closeness. 2nd enl. ed. Carl Thenebe. 1977. 7.00 o.p. (ISBN 0-682-48110-6). Exposition-Phoenix.
Touching for Pleasure: A Guide to Sensual Enhancement. Adele P. Kennedy & Susan Dean. LC 85-62992. (Illus.). 120p. 1986. pap. 14.95 o.p. (ISBN 0-917181-03-4). Chatsworth.
Touchmark. Mildred Lawrence. LC 75-11579. (Illus.). 192p. (gr. 4-7). 1975. 7.50 o.p. (ISBN 0-15-289603-1, HJ). HarBraceJ.
Touchstone: Letters Between Two Women 1953-1964. Patricia F. Lamb & Kathryn J. Hohlwein. (Hall Non-Fiction Ser.). 352p. 1986. pap. 8.95 o.p. (ISBN 0-8398-2912-4). G K Hall.
Touchstones for Prayer. William P. Roberts. 98p. 1983. pap. text ed. 2.95 o.p. (ISBN 0-86716-023-3). St Anthony Mess Pr.
Tough Act to Follow: A Novel. Max Wilk. 1986. 14.45 o.p. (ISBN 0-393-02219-6). Norton.
Tough Calls: An Illustrated Book of Official Baseball Rules. Zach Rebackoff. 160p. 1984. pap. 6.95 o.p. (ISBN 0-380-86777-X, 86777). Avon.
Tough Game. H. W. Kelsey. LC 79-670266. 192p. 1979. 13.50 o.p. (ISBN 0-571-11360-5). Faber & Faber.
Tough Minded Faith for Tender Hearted People. Robert H. Schuller. 1985. 16.95 o.p. (ISBN 0-8161-3806-0, Large Print Bks); pap. 9.95 o.p. (ISBN 0-8161-3815-X). G K Hall.
Tough-Minded Management. Joe D. Batten. 14.95 o.p. (ISBN 0-8144-5477-1). AMACOM.
Tough Teddies & Other Bears. Simon Bond. (Illus.). 64p. 1985. pap. 3.95 o.p. (ISBN 0-517-55832-7, C N Potter Bks.). Crown.
Tough Times Never Last but Tough People Do! Robert H. Schuller. 256p. 1984. pap. 3.95 o.p. (ISBN 0-553-24245-8). Bantam.
Tough Truths for Today's Living. Stuart Briscoe. 178p. 1984. pap. text ed. 5.95 o.p. (ISBN 0-8499-2999-7, 2999-7). Word Bks.
Toughlove Solutions. Phyllis York et al. LC 84-1664. 216p. 1984. 13.95 o.p. (ISBN 0-385-18940-0). Doubleday.
Toughness Characterization & Specifications for HSLA and Structural Steels: Proceedings of the AIME Annual Meeting, Atlanta, 1977. AIME Staff. Ed. by P. L. Mangonon, Jr. (Illus.). 391p. 40.00 o.p. (ISBN 0-89520-352-9); members 26.00 o.p. (ISBN 0-317-34900-7); student members 14.00 o.p. (ISBN 0-317-34901-5). ASM.
Tour De Babil see Power of Babel: A Study of Logophilia.
Tour Eiffel. Roland Barthes. 116p. 1964. 19.95 o.p. (ISBN 0-686-53946-X). French & Eur.
Tour Guide to Old Forts of New Mexico, Arizona, Nevada, Utah, Colorado, Vol. 2. Herbert M. Hart. (Illus.). 65p. (Orig.). 1981. pap. 4.95 o.p. (ISBN 0-87108-581-X). Pruett.
Tour Guide to Old Forts of Texas, Kansas, Nebraska, Oklahoma, Vol. 4. Herbert M. Hart. (Illus.). 65p. (Orig.). 1981. pap. 4.95 o.p. (ISBN 0-87108-583-6). Pruett.
Tour Guide to the Rocky Mountain Wilderness. Raymond Bridge. LC 80-10598. (Illus.). 1980. pap. 5.95 o.p. (ISBN 0-87108-557-7). Pruett.
Tour of Duty. John Dos Passos. LC 73-17919. 336p. 1974. Repr. of 1946 ed. lib. bdg. 90.50x o.p. (ISBN 0-8371-7279-9, AEDOTD). Greenwood.
Touring Book of Britain. British Automobile Association Staff. 320p. (Orig.). 1984. pap. 24.95 o.p. (ISBN 0-86145-193-7, Pub. by Automobile Assn Brit). Salem Hse Pubs.
Touring England. Date not set. (ISBN 0-86145-619-X, Pub. by Auto Assn England). Salem Hse Pubs.
Touring Guide to England. Date not set. (ISBN 0-86145-605-X, Pub. by Auto Assn England). Salem Hse Pubs.
Touring Guide to Ireland. Date not set. (ISBN 0-86145-103-1, Pub. by Auto Assn England). Salem Hse Pubs.
Touring Map of Ireland. (Illus.). Date not set. (ISBN 0-86145-751-X, Pub. by Auto Assn England). Salem Hse Pubs.
Touring Map of Western Europe. (Illus.). Date not set. (ISBN 0-86145-001-9, Pub. by Auto Assn England). Salem Hse Pubs.
Tourism Theory: A Selected Bibliography. Stephen G. Mann. (Public Administration Ser.: P 1835). 51p. 1985. 7.50 o.p. (ISBN 0-89028-685-X). Vance Biblios.
Tourism's Top Twenty. Business Research Division Staff & U. S. Travel Data Center Staff. 109p. 1984. pap. text ed. 25.00 o.s.i. (ISBN 0-89478-108-1). U Co Busn Res Div.
Tourist Business. 4th, rev. ed. Donald E. Lundberg. LC 79-27512. 324p. 1983. 16.95 o.p. (ISBN 0-8436-2181-8); pap. 16.95x o.p. (ISBN 0-8436-2185-0). Van Nos Reinhold.
Tourist in Africa. Evelyn Waugh. 1986. 15.95 o.p. (ISBN 0-316-92651-5); pap. 7.95 o.p. (ISBN 0-316-92650-7). Little.
Tourmaline: A Novel. Randolph Stow. LC 82-50910. 1983. 10.95 o.s.i. (ISBN 0-8008-7797-7). Taplinger.
Tourmalin's Time Cheques. (Greenhill Science Fiction & Fantasy Ser.). 184p. 1987. 15.00 o.p. (ISBN 0-947898-48-4). Kraus Repr.
Tournament Book. 80p. 350.00 o.p. (ISBN 0-8115-0908-7). Kraus Repr.
Tournament Checkers: An Introduction to Pool Checkers. Vladimir Kaplan. LC 78-20697. (Illus.). 1980. 12.95 o.s.i. (ISBN 0-8008-4205-7). Taplinger.
Tournament Chess. Ed. by M. Chandler & A. Miles. (Tournament Chess Ser.: Vol. 5). 176p. 1982. pap. 19.95 o.s.i. (ISBN 0-08-029720-X). Pergamon.
Tournament Chess, Vol. 1. Chandler. Ed. by A. J. Miles. 128p. 1981. pap. 19.95 o.s.i. (ISBN 0-08-026888-9). Pergamon.
Tournament Chess, Vol. 2. Ed. by M. Chandler. (Illus.). 128p. 1982. pap. 19.95 o.s.i. (ISBN 0-08-026891-9). Pergamon.
Tournament Chess, Vol. 3. Ed. by M. Chandler & A. Miles. (Illus.). 170p. 1982. pap. 19.95 o.s.i. (ISBN 0-08-026892-7). Pergamon.
Tournament Chess, Vol. 4. Ed. by M. Chandler & A. Miles. 150p. 1982. pap. 19.95 o.s.i. (ISBN 0-08-026893-5). Pergamon.
Tournament Chess, Vol. 6. Ed. by M. Chandler & A. Miles. 176p. 1983. pap. 19.95 o.s.i. (ISBN 0-08-029721-8). Pergamon.

Tournament Chess, Vol. 7. Ed. by M. Chandler & A. Miles. (Illus.). 143p. 1983. pap. 19.95 o.s.i. (ISBN 0-08-029736-6). Pergamon.
Tournament Chess, Vol. 8. Ed. by M. Chandler & A. Miles. (Illus.). 200p. 1983. pap. 19.95 o.s.i. (ISBN 0-08-029737-4). Pergamon.
Tournament Chess, Vol. 9. Ed. by M. Chandler & A. Miles. (Illus.). 176p. 1983. pap. 19.95 o.s.i. (ISBN 0-08-029742-0, 62). Pergamon.
Tournament Chess, Vol. 10. Ed. by M. Chandler & A. Miles. 166p. 1983. pap. 19.95 o.s.i. (ISBN 0-08-029743-9). Pergamon.
Tournament Chess, Vol. 12. Ed. by M. Chandler. 215p. 1984. pap. 19.95 o.s.i. (ISBN 0-08-029758-7). Pergamon.
Tournament Chess, Vol. 14. Ed. by M. Chandler. 178p. 1984. pap. 28.75 o.s.i. (ISBN 0-08-029760-9). Pergamon.
Tournament Chess, Vol. 15. Ed. by M. Chandler. 188p. 1985. pap. 28.75 o.s.i. (ISBN 0-08-029761-7). Pergamon.
Tournament Chess, Vol. 16. Ed. by M. Chandler. (Illus.). 176p. 1985. pap. 28.75 o.s.i. (ISBN 0-08-029762-5, Pub. by P P L). Pergamon.
Tournament for Terror. H. William & M. Stine. (Wizards, Warriors & You Ser.: No. 10). 1986. pap. 2.50 o.p. (ISBN 0-380-89947-7). Avon.
Tournament of Roses-One Hundredth Anniversary Edition. Joe Hendrickson. (Illus.). 1988. 24.95 o.p. (ISBN 0-89535-215-X). Knapp Pr.
Tournament Tough: A Guide to Junior Championship Tennis. Carlos Goffi. LC 84-19741. (Illus.). 144p. 1985. 13.95 o.p. (ISBN 0-03-071598-9). H Holt & Co.
Tourney Team. C. H. Frick. LC 54-8572. (gr. 7 up). 1954. 5.25 o.p. (ISBN 0-15-289621-X, HJ). HarBraceJ.
Tours by Tape Edinburgh: Your Personal Guide. Date not set. (ISBN 1-850851-06-9). Salem Hse Pubs.
Tours by Tape London: Your Personal Guide. Date not set. (ISBN 1-850851-00-X). Salem Hse Pubs.
Tous les Hommes Sont Mortels: Roman. Simone De Beauvoir. (Coll. Soleil). 1946. 14.50 o.p. (ISBN 0-685-11602-6). Schoenhof.
Tout Compte Fait. Simone De Beauvoir. (Coll. Soleil). 29.75 o.p. (ISBN 0-685-37192-1). Schoenhof.
Tova Difference: Tova Borgnine's Beauty Book. Tova Borgnine & Elaine C. Trebek. (Illus.). 160p. (Orig.). 1984. pap. 9.95 o.p. (ISBN 0-671-50032-5, Fireside). S&S.
Tovar's Classic Beauty Book. Tovar & Lydia P. Encinas. (Illus.). 256p. 1986. 18.95 o.p. (ISBN 0-8092-4867-0). Contemp Bks.
Toward a Coherent U. S. Policy on Strategic Materials. Robert A. Kilmarx. LC 82-74013. (Significant Issues Ser.: Vol. IV, No. 3). 46p. (Orig.). 1982. pap. 6.25 o.p. (ISBN 0-8191-6078-4, CSIS). U Pr of Amer.
Toward a Contemporary Christianity. Brian Wicker. 1967. 21.95 o.p. (ISBN 0-268-00282-7). U of Notre Dame Pr.
Toward a Democracy: A Brief Introduction to American Government. Louis W. Koenig. 1973. pap. text ed. 12.95 o.p. (ISBN 0-15-592183-5, HC). HarBraceJ.
Toward a Healthy Lifestyle: Through Elementary Health Education. John J. Burt et al. 588p. 1980. text ed. (ISBN 0-534-00776-7). Wadsworth Pub.
Toward a Human World Order: Beyond the National Security Straitjacket. Gerald Mische & Patricia Mische. LC 76-41440. 412p. 1977. 9.95 o.p. (ISBN 0-8091-0216-1); pap. 4.95 o.p. (ISBN 0-8091-1977-3). Paulist Pr.
Toward a Jewish Theology of Liberation. Marc H. Ellis. LC 86-23553. 160p. (Orig.). 1987. pap. 9.95 o.p. (ISBN 0-88344-358-9). Orbis Bks.
Toward a Just Correctional System: Experiments in Implementing Democracy in Prisons. Joseph E. Hickey & Peter L. Scharf. LC 78-88112. (Social & Behavioral Science Ser.). 1980. text ed. 26.95x o.p. (ISBN 0-87589-396-1). Jossey-Bass.
Toward a Modern Japanese Theatre: Kishida Kunio. J. Thomas Rimer. LC 72-6521. 428p. 1974. 34.50x o.p. (ISBN 0-691-06249-8). Princeton U Pr.
Toward a New Christianity: Readings in the Death of God Theology. Ed. by Thomas J. Altizer. LC 67-15377. (Orig.). 1967. 6.95 o.p. (ISBN 0-15-190902-4). HarBraceJ.
Toward a New Politics. Ed. by William C. Harper. LC 73-12924. 1973. 29.50x o.p. (ISBN 0-8422-5122-7); pap. text ed. 9.75x o.p. (ISBN 0-8422-0345-1). Irvington.
Toward a New Strategy for Development. Compiled by Rothko. LC 79-9861. 1979. 95.00 o.p. (ISBN 0-08-023913-7); pap. 95.00 o.p. (ISBN 0-08-023912-9). Pergamon.
Toward a One World Jewry: An Essay in Jewish Identity. Ario S. Hyams. 1979. 10.00 o.p. (ISBN 0-682-49503-4). Exposition-Phoenix.
Toward a People's Anthropology. Fei Hsiao Tung. (China Studies). (Illus.). 121p. (Orig.). pap. 6.95 o.p. (ISBN 0-8351-0913-5). China Bks.
Toward a Perspective Realism. Evander B. McGilvary. Ed. by Albert G. Ramsperger. 389p. 1956. 18.95 o.p. (ISBN 0-87548-111-6). Open Court.
Toward a Practical Theology of Aging. K. Brynolf Lyon. LC 85-47720. (Theology & Pastoral Care Ser.). 128p. 1986. pap. 2.95 o.p. (ISBN 0-8006-1735-5, 1-1735, Fortress). Augsburg Fortress.
Toward a Renovated International System see **Trilateral Commission Task Force Reports.**
Toward a Science of Translating. E. A. Nida. 1964. 30.00 o.p. E J Brill USA.
Toward a Self-Managed Life Style. 2nd ed. Robert L. Williams & James D. Long. LC 78-56435. (Illus.). 1979. pap. 12.95 o.p. (ISBN 0-395-26760-9). HM.
Toward a Theory of Economic Growth. Simon Kuznets. 1968. pap. 2.45 o.p. (ISBN 0-393-00429-5, Norton Lib). Norton.
Toward a Theory of Instruction. Jerome Bruner. 1968. pap. 4.95x o.p. (ISBN 0-393-09808-7, NortonC). Norton.
Toward an Evaluation of the Property Tax System in New York State. League of Women Voters of New York State Staff. Ed. by Susan Amlung. (Illus.). 125p. (Orig.). 1979. pap. 4.00 o.p. (ISBN 0-938588-02-8). LWV NYS.
Toward an Urban Strategy. J. Meyer. 1969. pap. text ed. 5.95x o.p. (ISBN 0-8290-1199-4). Irvington.
Toward Effective Instruction in Secondary Social Studies. Ed. by Lee H. Ehman et al. 448p. 1974. text ed. 22.50 o.p. (ISBN 0-395-17625-5). HM.
Toward Equity: An Action Manual for Women in Academe. Karen Bogart. 259p. (Orig.). 1984. pap. 17.00 o.p. (ISBN 0-911696-36-9). Assn Am Coll.
Toward Excellence: A Reader. Vincent Milosevich. 1973. text ed. 8.95 o.p. (ISBN 0-15-592194-0, HC). HarBraceJ.
Toward Independence: An Assessment of Federal Laws & Programs Affecting Persons with Disabilities, with Legislative Recommendations. (Appendix, Topic Papers). 495p. (Orig.). 1986. pap. 23.00 o.p. (ISBN 0-318-21316-8, S/N 052-003-01023-2). USGPO.
Toward Interracial Cooperation. National Interracial Conference Staff. LC 73-97408. 1969. Repr. of 1926 ed. 17.50 o.p. (ISBN 0-8371-2658-4, NAI&). Greenwood.
Toward Love's Horizon: The Loves of Angela Carlyle, Vol. III. Michele DuBarry. 320p. 1981. pap. 2.50 o.p. (ISBN 0-8439-0957-9, Pub. by Leisure Bks CT). Dorchester Pub Co.
Toward New Patterns of Education in India. P. D. Shukla. 1984. text ed. 30.00x o.p. (ISBN 0-86590-276-3, Pub. by Sterling Pubs India). Apt Bks.
Toward Rational Technology in Medicine: Considerations for Health Policy. David Banta et al. (Health Care & Society Ser.: No. 5). 1981. text ed. 28.50 o.p. (ISBN 0-8261-3200-6). Springer Pub.
Toward Rationalizing Allied Weapons Production. Gardiner Tucker. (Atlantic Papers: No. 76/1). 54p. (Orig.). 1976. pap. text ed. 4.75x o.s.i. (ISBN 0-686-83681-2, Pub. by Allanheld). Rowman.
Toward Recovery of the Primordial Tradition: Ancient Insights & Modern Discoveries, Vol. 2. John Rossner. Incl. Bk. 1. From Ancient Magic to Future Technology. LC 79-66892. 15.25 (ISBN 0-8191-0861-8); Bk. 2. Toward a Parapsychology of Religion: from Ancient Religion to Future Science. LC 79-66893. 14.25 (ISBN 0-8191-0862-6). 1979. U Pr of Amer.
Toward Responsible Discipleship. William B. Ward. LC 61-7078. (Orig.). 1961. pap. 2.50 o.p. (ISBN 0-8042-4049-3, John Knox); leader's guide o.p. 1.00 o.p. (ISBN 0-8042-4050-7). Westminster John Knox.
Toward Safer Underground Coal Mines. Commission on Engineering & Technical Systems, National Research Council. 1982. pap. text ed. 10.50x o.p. (ISBN 0-309-03298-9). Natl Acad Pr.
Toward the African Revolution. Frantz Fanon. Tr. by Haakon Chevalier. 1968. pap. 2.25 o.p. (ISBN 0-394-17149-7, B219, BC). Grove.
Toward the Future. Pierre Teilhard De Chardin. Tr. by Rene Hague from Fr. LC 74-23802. (Helen & Kurt Wolff Bk.). 224p. 1975. 6.95 o.p. (ISBN 0-15-190910-5). HarBraceJ.
Toward the Image of Tammuz & Other Essays on Mesopotamian History & Culture. Thorkild Jacobsen. Ed. by William L. Moran. LC 76-95925. (Semitic Ser: No. 21). 1970. 34.50x o.s.i. (ISBN 0-674-89810-9). Harvard U Pr.
Toward the Ph.D for Dogs. Robert J. Martin & Napoleon Chagnon. LC 74-33669. (Illus.). 576p. 1975. 14.95 o.p. (ISBN 0-15-190911-3). HarBraceJ.
Toward the Responsive Organization: The Theory & Practice of Survey Feed. Robert T. Golembiewski & Richard J. Hilles. 354p. 1979. 20.00x o.p. (ISBN 0-89832-001-1); pap. text ed. 17.00 o.p. Pub Horizons.
Toward the Setting of the Sun. Beverly H. Bradley. (Illus.). 1985. 7.95 o.p. (ISBN 0-533-06500-3). Vantage.
Toward the Sunrising: A Story about Preaching. rev ed. W. Glen Harris. 1979. 12.50 o.p. (ISBN 0-682-49227-2, Testament). Exposition-Phoenix.
Toward Theology. Jerry H. Gill. LC 82-45009. 130p. (Orig.). 1982. PLB 25.25 o.p. (ISBN 0-8191-2429-X); pap. text ed. 9.75 o.p. (ISBN 0-8191-2430-3). U Pr of Amer.
Toward Understanding Germany. Robert H. Lowie. (Midway Reprint Ser). xvi, 396p. 1975. pap. text ed. 11.00x o.s.i. (ISBN 0-226-49452-7). U of Chicago Pr.
Towards a Critical Sociology: An Essay on Commonsense & Emancipation. Zygmunt Bauman. (Direct Edition Ser.). 1976. pap. 10.95x o.p. (ISBN 0-7100-8306-8). Routledge Chapman & Hall.
Towards a Cross-National Model for Cooperation in Vocational Education: Implications for Research & Development. Gert Loose. 31p. 1982. 3.25 o.p. (ISBN 0-318-22223-X, OC87). Natl Ctr Res Voc Ed.
Towards a Lasting Settlement. Ed. by Charles R. Buxton. LC 78-147578. (Library of War & Peace; Int'l. Organization, Arbitration & Law). 1972. lib. bdg. 46.00 o.p. (ISBN 0-8240-0343-8). Garland Pub.
Towards a New Iron Age. Marion Campbell. (Illus.). 100p. (Orig.). 1984. pap. 5.95 o.p. (ISBN 0-905209-23-0, Pub. by Victoria & Albert Mus UK). Faber & Faber.
Towards a New Psychology of Women & Men: A Special Issue of Journal of Psychiatric Education. Ed. by Robert Cancro & Zebulen Taintor. 85p. 1984. 9.95 o.p. (ISBN 0-89885-223-4). Human Sci Pr.
Towards a Plan of Actions for Mankind. M. Marois. 558p. 1975. 84.25 o.p. (ISBN 0-444-10722-3, North-Holland). Elsevier.
Towards a Plan of Actions for Mankind, 5 vols. Ed. by Maurice Marois. Incl. Vol. 1. Long Range Mineral Resources & Growth. 1977. 150.00 o.p. (ISBN 0-08-021445-2); Vol. 2. Long Range Energetic Resources & Growth. 1977. 105.00 o.p. (ISBN 0-08-021446-0); Vol. 3. Biological Balance & Thermal Modification. 1977. 150.00 o.p. (ISBN 0-08-021447-9); Vol. 4. Design of Global System Models & Their Limitations. 1977. 160.00 (ISBN 0-08-021448-7); Vol. 5. Conclusions & Perspectives. 1977. 250.00 o.p. (ISBN 0-08-021449-5). 1977. Set. 695.00 o.p. (ISBN 0-08-021850-4). Pergamon.
Towards a Renovated International System. Richard N. Cooper et al. (Triangle Papers: No. 14). 1977. 15.00 o.s.i. (ISBN 0-318-02792-5); pap. 6.00 o.s.i. (ISBN 0-318-02793-3). Trilateral Comm.
Towards a Stable Monetary Policy: Monetarism vs. the Gold Standard. Allan Meltzer & Alan Reynolds. 32p. 1982. pap. 2.00 o.p. (ISBN 0-317-47109-0). Heritage Found.
Towards a Transformation of Philosophy. Karl-Otto Apel. (International Library of Phenomenology & Moral Sciences). 1980. 30.00x o.p. (ISBN 0-7100-0403-6). Routledge Chapman & Hall.
Towards a Visual Culture. Caleb Gattegno. 1971. pap. 1.65 o.p. (ISBN 0-380-01455-6, 11940, Discus). Avon.
Towards Achievement & Acceptance: A Classroom Study of Mildly Intellectually Handicapped Children. Margaret Henry. (Scholar's Library). (Illus.). 359p. 1981. text ed. 42.50x o.p. (ISBN 0-7022-1559-7). U of Queensland Pr.
Towards an Older Australia: Readings in Social Gerontology. Ed. by Anna L. Howe. (Illus.). 356p. 1981. text ed. 27.50x o.p. (ISBN 0-7022-1534-1); pap. text ed. 15.75x o.p. (ISBN 0-7022-1535-X). U of Queensland Pr.
Towards Better Practice. Peter Martin et al. LC 84-14977. (Library of General Practice). (Illus.). 261p. 1985. pap. text ed. 27.65 o.p. (ISBN 0-443-02860-5). Churchill.
Towards Christian Democracy. Stafford Cripps. (ISBN 0-8022-0315-9). Philos Lib.
Towards Global Action for Appropriate Technology: Expert Meeting on International Action for Appropriate Technology, December 5-9 1977, Geneva. Ed. by A. S. Bhalla. LC 78-41191. (Illus.). 240p. 1979. 46.00 o.p. (ISBN 0-08-024305-3); pap. 21.00 o.p. (ISBN 0-08-024277-4). Pergamon.
Towards Industrial Democracy: Europe, Japan & the United States. Ed. by Benjamin C. Roberts. LC 78-71100. (Atlantic Institute for International Affairs Research Ser.: No. 2). 300p. 1979. text ed. 28.50x o.s.i. (ISBN 0-916672-20-4, Pub. by Allanheld). Rowman.
Towards International Government. John A. Hobson. LC 70-147581. (Library of War & Peace; Int'l. Organization, Arbitration & Law). 1972. lib. bdg. 46.00 o.p. (ISBN 0-8240-0345-4). Garland Pub.
Towards Modern Art: Or, King Solomon's Picture Book. Ludwig Goldschieder. LC 52-9478. 1952. Repr. 39.00x o.p. (ISBN 0-403-08924-7). Somerset Pub.
Towards Recurrent & Continuing Education. Ed. by Frank Molyneux. (Radical Forum on Adult Education Ser.). 224p. 1986. 31.00 o.p. (ISBN 0-7099-4646-5, Pub. by Croom Helm UK). Routledge Chapman & Hall.
Towards Team Care. Ed. by J. H. Barber & Charlotte R. Kratz. (Illus.). 176p. 1980. pap. text ed. 14.75 o.p. (ISBN 0-443-02031-0). Churchill.
Towards the Center. Joyce B. Balokovic. 1957. Philos Lib.
Towards the Decolonization of African Literature: African Fiction & Poetry & Their Critics. Chinweizu et al. 320p. 1985. pap. 19.95s o.p. (ISBN 0-7103-0123-5, Kegan Paul). Routledge Chapman & Hall.
Towards the Dynamic Analysis of Spatial Systems. Ed. by R. L. Martin et al. 210p. 1979. 24.50x o.p. (ISBN 0-85086-072-5, NO. 6377, Pub. by Pion England). Routledge Chapman & Hall.
Towards the Elimination of Racism. Ed. by Phyllis A. Katz. 1976. text ed. 34.00 o.p. (ISBN 0-08-018316-6); pap. text ed. 12.75 o.p. (ISBN 0-08-018317-4). Pergamon.
Towards the Life Divine: Sri Aurobindo's Vision. Thomas O'Neil. 1979. 10.50x o.p. (ISBN 0-8364-0546-3). South Asia Bks.
Towards the Mountain. Encore ed. Alan Paton. (Illus.). 1983. 4.95 o.p. (ISBN 0-684-16596-1). Scribner.
Towards the Prevention of Alcohol Problems: Government, Business, & Community Action. Ed. by Dean R. Gerstein. 192p. 1984. pap. text ed. 14.95x o.p. (ISBN 0-309-03485-X). Natl Acad Pr.
Tower Anthology of the San Jose Movement in Fiction, Vol. II. Jon Ilgen et al. Ed. by Merritt Clifton. (Illus.). 1976. pap. 2.50 o.p. (ISBN 0-686-20758-0). Samisdat.
Tower at the Edge of Time. Lin Carter. 1978. pap. 1.50 o.p. (ISBN 0-505-51224-6, Pub. by Tower Bks). Dorchester Pub Co.
Tower of Babel. Andre Parrott. 1956. (ISBN 0-8022-1276-X). Philos Lib.
Tower of David, 1964. Victor E. Reichert. 1964. 4.00 o.p. (ISBN 0-911570-12-8). Vermont Bks.
Tower Room. Dorothy Spicer. 1973. pap. 0.75 o.p. (ISBN 0-380-01589-7, 14506). Avon.
Tower: The Tumultuous History of the Tower of London from 1078. Derek Wilson. Encore ed. 5.95 o.p. (ISBN 0-684-17574-6, ScribT). Scribner.
Towers' International Digital IC Selector. T. D. Towers. 260p. 1983. 19.95x o.p. (ISBN 0-8306-0616-5, 1616). TAB Bks.
Towers of Trebizond. Rose Macaulay. 277p. 1956. 20.00 o.p. (ISBN 0-374-27854-7); pap. 5.95 o.p. (ISBN 0-374-51590-5). FS&G.
Towers to the Sky. James R. Poyner. 128p. 1987. text ed. 12.50 o.p. (ISBN 0-682-40335-0). Exposition-Phoenix.
Town & Country Cat. Lynn Hollyn. LC 82-40389. (Illus.). 144p. 1982. 16.95 o.p. (ISBN 0-89480-214-3, 329). Workman Pub.
Town & Country, City & Region? Raymond Bunker. (Illus.). 164p. 1971. pap. 14.00x o.p. (ISBN 0-522-84012-4, Pub. by Melbourne U Pr). Intl Spec Bk.
Town & Country in Brazil. Marvin Harris. (Illus.). 1971. pap. 2.95x o.p. (ISBN 0-393-00573-9, Norton Lib.). Norton.
Town & Country Matters. John Hollander. LC 72-82864. 60p. 1972. 12.95 o.s.i. (ISBN 0-87923-058-4); pap. 5.95 o.p. (ISBN 0-87923-093-2). Godine.
Town & Dr. Moore. Agatha Young. 1975. pap. 1.50 o.p. (ISBN 0-380-00256-6, 21923). Avon.
Town Down River. Gordon T. Osing. Ed. by Roger R. Easson. LC 84-27700. 112p. 1985. 9.95 o.p. (ISBN 0-918518-36-9, St Luke TN). Peachtree Pubs.
Town Houses of Europe. Horst Buttner & Gunter Meissner. (Illus.). 348p. sewn bdg. 45.00 o.s.i. (ISBN 0-317-54970-7). Apollo.
Town Records of Salem, Massachusetts. Incl. Vol. 2, 1659-1680. 356p. 1913; Vol. 3, 1680-1691. 288p. 1934. o.p.. LC 15-2612. 15.00 ea. o.p. (ISBN 0-88389-040-2). Essex Inst.
Townframe: Environments for Adaptive Housing. Guntis Plesums. LC 77-20679. (Community Development Ser.: Vol. 38). (Illus.). 1982. 44.95 o.p. (ISBN 0-87933-303-0). Van Nos Reinhold.
Townhouses & Condominiums: Residents' Likes & Dislikes. Carl Norcross. LC 73-82886. (Special Report Ser.). (Illus.). 105p. 1973. pap. 16.00 o.p. (ISBN 0-87420-558-1, T02). Urban Land.

Towns for People. M. Posokhin. 1980. 11.50 o.p. (ISBN 0-8285-1927-7, Pub. by Progress Pubs USSR). Imported Pubns.

Toxic Air Contaminants: Health Effects, Monitoring & Control. Air Pollution Control Association Technical Conference, Niagara Falls, N.Y., Oct. 1980. 256p. 1981. 17.00 o.p. (ISBN 0-318-12278-2, VIP-II); members 13.50 o.p. (ISBN 0-318-12279-0). Air & Waste.

Toxic & Hazardous Wastes: Proceedings of the 19th Mid-Atlantic Industrial Waste Conference. Ed. by Jeffrey C. Evans. 729p. 1987. pap. 65.00 o.p. (ISBN 0-317-65574-4). Technomic.

Toxic Constituents in Plant Foodstuffs. I. Liener. (Food Science & Technology Ser.). 1969. 101.00 o.p. (ISBN 0-12-449950-3). Acad Pr.

Toxic Control, Volume IV: Toxic Control in the Eighties. Ed. by Marshall L. Miller. LC 80-80472. (Illus.). 210p. 1980. pap. text ed. 25.00 o.p. (ISBN 0-86587-053-5). Gov Insts.

Toxic Shock Syndrome. National Research Council Staff. 1982. pap. text ed. 10.50x o.p. (ISBN 0-309-03286-5). Natl Acad Pr.

Toxic Substance Sourcebook II. Ed. by Monica Pronin. LC 77-28044. Orig. Title: Toxic Substance Sourcebook Series I. 560p. 1980. 95.00 o.p. (ISBN 0-89947-008-4, EIC Intell). Bowker.

Toxic Substance Sourcebook Series I see Toxic Substance Sourcebook II.

Toxic Substances Control Volume II. Ed. by Marshall L. Miller. LC 78-50807. (Illus.). 256p. 1978. pap. text ed. 25.00 o.p. (ISBN 0-86587-051-9). Gov Insts.

Toxic Substances Control Volume III: Implementing the Regulatory Program. Ed. by Marshall Lee Miller. LC 79-83915. 261p. 1979. pap. text ed. 25.00 o.p. (ISBN 0-86587-052-7). Gov Insts.

Toxic Substances in the Air Environment. Air Pollution Control Association Specialty Conference, Cambridge, MA. 202p. 1977. 10.00 o.p. (ISBN 0-318-12280-4, SP-20); members 8.00 o.p. (ISBN 0-318-12281-2). Air & Waste.

Toxic Substances Laws & Regulations 1977. Ed. by Marshall L. Miller. LC 76-51984. 1977. microfiche 15.00 o.p. (ISBN 0-86587-050-0). Gov Insts.

Toxic Substances Sourcebook: The Professional's Guide to Information Sources, Key Literature, & Laws. Ed. by Steven S. Ross. LC 77-28044. (Series 1). 1978. 95.00 o.p. (ISBN 0-89947-004-1, EIC Intell). Bowker.

Toxic Substances Sourcebook: The Professional's Guide to the Information Sources, Key Literature & Laws of a Critical New Field. Ed. by Steven Ross & Monica Pronin. LC 77-84943. 1978. 95.00 o.p. (ISBN 0-686-05537-3, 5977, EIC Intell). Bowker.

Toxic Susceptibility: Male-Female Differences. Edward J. Calabrese. LC 85-3220. (Environmental Science & Technology Ser.). 336p. 1985. 74.00 o.p. (ISBN 0-471-80903-9). Wiley.

Toxic Tort Litigation. (Litigation & Administrative Practice Course Handbook: Vol. 244). 329p. 1984. 15.00 o.p. (ISBN 0-317-11463-8, H4-4925). PLI.

Toxicity of Pesticides to Fish, Vol. I. Ed. by A. S. Murty. LC 85-4182. 256p. 1986. 99.00 o.p. (ISBN 0-8493-6058-7). CRC Pr.

Toxicity of Plutonium, Americium & Curium. J. C. Nenot & J. W. Stather. (Commission of the European Communities Ser.: EUR 6157). (Illus.). 1979. pap. 65.00 o.p. (ISBN 0-08-023440-2). Pergamon.

Toxicless Diet & Body Purification: The Stay-Ageless Program. 23rd,rev. ed. Paul C. Bragg & Patricia Bragg. LC 84-822373. (Illus.). pap. 3.95 o.p. (ISBN 0-87790-033-7). Health Sci.

Toxicological & Pathological Studies on Psychoactive Drug-Involved Deaths. L. A. Gottschalk & R. H. Cravey. LC 79-56928. 470p. 1980. text ed. 35.00 o.p. (ISBN 0-931890-05-5, Biomed Pubns). Year Bk Med.

Toxicological Aspects of Food Safety: Proceedings of the European Society of Toxicology. Ed. by B. J. Leonard. (Archives of Toxicol, Suppl: Vol. 1). (Illus.). 1978. pap. 51.00 o.p. (ISBN 0-387-08646-3). Springer-Verlag.

Toxicological Evaluation of Some Flavouring Substances & Non-nutritive Sweetening Agents. (Nutrition Meetings Reports: No. 44A). pap. 8.25 o.p. (F1258, FAO). UNIPUB.

Toxicological Evaluation of Some Food Colors, Emulsifiers, Stabilizers, Anti-Caking Agents & Certain Other Substances. (Nutrition Meetings Reports: No. 46). pap. 12.50 o.p. (F1216, FAO). UNIPUB.

Toxicology & Nutrition: Proceedings of the Symposium, Paris, November, 1976. Toxicology & Nutrition Symposium Staff. Ed. by R. Ferrando & R. Truhaut. (World Review of Nutrition & Dietetics Ser.: Vol. 29). (Illus.). 1977. 66.25 o.p. (ISBN 3-8055-2697-0). S Karger.

Toxicology: Biochemistry & Pathology of Mycotoxins. Ed. by Kenji Uraguchi & Mikio Yamazaki. LC 78-8992. 288p. 1978. 59.95x o.p. (ISBN 0-470-26423-3). Halsted Pr.

Toxins: Animal, Plant & Microbial. Ed. by Philip Rosenberg. 1978. 230.00 o.p. (ISBN 0-08-022640-X). Pergamon.

Toy Library: A How-To Handbook. Ed. by Ellen Johnson. 82p. (Orig.). pap. text ed. 14.95x o.p. (ISBN 0-934140-18-9). Toys 'n Things.

Toy Store. Peter Spier. LC 80-1847. (Balloon Bks.). (Illus.). 14p. (ps-k). 1981. 3.95 o.p. (ISBN 0-385-15729-0). Doubleday.

Toymakers Book of Wooden Vehicles. (ISBN 0-671-61043-0). P-H.

Toynbee Hall: The First Hundred Years. Asa Briggs & Anne Macartney. (Illus.). 256p. 1984. 35.00x o.p. (ISBN 0-7102-0283-0). Routledge Chapman & Hall.

Toynbee-Ikeda Dialogue: Man Himself Must Choose. Ed. by Arnold J. Toynbee. Tr. by Daisaku Ikeda & Richard Gage. LC 75-34739. 348p. 1976. 18.25 o.p. (ISBN 0-87011-268-6). Kodansha.

Toyota Celica & Supra 1971-83. LC 80-70267. (Illus.). 224p. pap. 13.50 o.s.i. (ISBN 0-8019-7314-7). Chilton.

Toyota Celica Service Manual: 1978-1983. Bentley, Robert, Inc. LC 82-74333. (Illus.). 600p. (Orig.). 1983. pap. 24.95 o.p. (ISBN 0-8376-0255-6). Bentley.

Toyota Corolla-Carina-Tercel 1970-81. LC 80-70345. (Illus.). 224p. 1980. pap. 11.95 o.p. (ISBN 0-8019-7036-9). Chilton.

Toyota Corolla Tercel Service Manual 1980-1983. Bentley, Robert, Inc. LC 83-70159. (Illus.). 590p. (Orig.). 1984. pap. 24.95 o.p. (ISBN 0-8376-0249-1). Bentley.

Toyota Corolla Tercel: 1980-1982. Bentley, Robert, Inc. (Illus.). 1981. pap. 19.95 o.p. (ISBN 0-8376-0250-5). Bentley.

Toyota Corona, Mark II, Celica, Crown, Stout, Hi-Lux. (A191). Clymer Pub.

Toyota Pick-up Truck & 4-Runner Service Manual: 1978-1987. Bentley, Robert, Inc. 500p. (Orig.). 1987. pap. text ed. 29.95 o.p. (ISBN 0-8376-0253-X). Bentley.

Toyota Service Repair Handbook: Corolla & Carina, 1968-78. 4th ed. Clymer Publications. 1978. pap. 9.95 o.p. (ISBN 0-89287-232-2, A198). Clymer Pub.

Toyota Service-Repair Handbook: Corona, Mark II & Celica, 1970-1978. Ed. by Eric Jorgensen. (Illus.). pap. 10.95 o.p. (ISBN 0-89287-217-9, A192). Clymer Pub.

Toys & Reasons: Stages in the Ritualization of Experience. Erik H. Erikson. 1977. 12.95 o.p. (ISBN 0-393-01123-2). Norton.

Toys & Tales from Grandmother's Attic. Edie Kraska. (gr. 5 up). 1979. 12.95 o.p. (ISBN 0-395-27807-4); pap. 6.95 o.p. (ISBN 0-395-28582-8). HM.

Toys on Wheels. Illus. by Terri Super. (Fast Rolling Bks.). (Illus.). 12p. (ps up). 1986. pap. 5.95 o.p. (ISBN 0-448-09879-2, G&D). Putnam Pub Group.

Toys That Teach Your Child: From Birth to Two. Athina Aston. Ed. by William A. Emerson. LC 84-48038. (Illus.). 128p. 1984. pap. 8.95 o.p. (ISBN 0-88742-015-X). Globe Pequot.

Toys to Make & Ride. C. J. Maginley. LC 77-73059. 1977. 10.00 o.p. (ISBN 0-15-190940-7); pap. 3.95 o.p. (ISBN 0-15-691290-2, Harv). HarBraceJ.

Trabajo y Vida. Alan Garfinkel & Guillermo Latorre. 1983. pap. text ed. 8.25 o.p. (ISBN 0-88377-248-5, 184 PGS.); pap. text ed. 1.95 answer key o.p. (ISBN 0-88377-249-3, 24 PGS.); cassette 12.50 o.p. (ISBN 0-88377-208-6). Newbury Hse.

Trace Analysis of Semiconductor Materials. Ed. by J. P. Cali. 1964. 75.00 o.p. (ISBN 0-08-010031-7). Pergamon.

Trace Atmospheric Constituents: Properties, Transformations & Fates. Stephen E. Schwartz. LC 82-16095. (Advances in Environmental Science & Technology Ser.). 547p. 1983. 85.00 o.p. (ISBN 0-471-87640-2, Pub. by Wiley-Interscience). Wiley.

Trace-Element Content of Soils. Ed. by D. J. Swaine. 157p. 1969. pap. 7.60 o.p. CAB Intl.

Trace Elements. Kathryn L. Knight. 1986. 15.45 o.p. (ISBN 0-393-02333-8). Norton.

Trace Elements & Iron in Human Metabolism. Ananda S. Prasad. LC 78-13446. (Topics In Hematology Ser.). (Illus.). 408p. 1978. 65.00x o.p. (ISBN 0-306-31142-9, Plenum Med Bk). Plenum Pub.

Trace Elements in Agriculture. Vincent Sauchelli. LC 74-81358. 228p. 1969. 18.50 o.p. (ISBN 0-442-15633-2, Pub. by Van Nos Reinhold). Krieger.

Trace Elements in Biochemistry. B. J. Bowen. 1966. 18.00 o.p. (ISBN 0-12-120956-3). Acad Pr.

Trace Metals: Exposure & Health Effects. R. K. Di Ferrante. 1979. pap. 64.00 o.p. (ISBN 0-08-022446-6). Pergamon.

Trace-Organic Sample Handling. Ed. by E. Reid. LC 80-49715. (Methodological Surveys Analysis Ser.: Vol. 10). 383p. 1981. 125.50x o.p. (ISBN 0-470-27071-3). Halsted Pr.

Traceability & Quality Control in the Measurement of Environmental Radioactivity: Seminar Sponsored by the International Committee for Radionuclide Metrology in Braunschweig, June 18-19, 1979. 80p. 1980. pap. 18.25 o.p. (ISBN 0-08-026253-8). Pergamon.

Tracer. Frederick Barthelme. 104p. 1985. 13.70 o.p. (ISBN 0-671-54253-2). S&S.

Tracer: A 6800 Debugging Program. Robert D. Grappel & Jack E. Hemenway. LC 78-7326. 1978. pap. text ed. 11.95 o.p. (ISBN 0-07-024121-X, BYTE Bks). McGraw.

Tracer Methods for in Vitro Kinetics: Theory & Applications. Reginald A. Shipley & Richard E. Clark. 1972. 53.50 o.p. (ISBN 0-12-640250-7). Acad Pr.

Tracer Methods in Hormone Research. E. Gurpide. (Monographs on Endocrinology: Vol. 8). (Illus.). xi, 188p. 1975. 45.00 o.p. (ISBN 0-387-07039-7). Springer-Verlag.

Traces: A Field Guide to the History on Your Doorstep. David Weitzman. (Illus.). 4.95 o.p. (ISBN 0-684-17576-2, ScribT). Scribner.

Traces of Eden: Travels in the Desert Northwest. Mark Klett et al. LC 85-82074. 48p. 1986. 20.00 o.s.i. (ISBN 0-87923-617-5). Godine.

Traces of the Past. encore ed. David Weitzman. (ISBN 0-684-17576-2). Scribner.

Trachaeostomy & Artificial Ventilation in the Treatment of Respiratory Failure. 3rd ed. Ed. by Stanley A. Feldman & Brian E. Crawley. 212p. 1977. pap. 17.50 o.p. (ISBN 0-683-03118-X, WW). Krieger.

Tracing Ancestors with Common Surnames. Arlene H. Eakle. 41p. 1984. pap. 5.00 o.p. (ISBN 0-940764-21-0). Genealog Inst.

Tracing Minnesota's Old Government Roads. Grover Singley. LC 74-4149. (Minnesota Historic Sites Pamphlet Ser.: No. 10). (Illus.). 52p. 1974. pap. 3.95 o.p. (ISBN 0-87351-088-7). Minn Hist.

Tracing the Spirit: Communities, Social Action & Theological Reflection. Ed. by James E. Hug. LC 82-62419. (Woodstock Studies: No. 7). 288p. 1983. pap. 9.95 o.p. (ISBN 0-8091-2529-3). Paulist Pr.

Tracing Your Ancestry: A Step-by-Step Guide to Researching Your Family History. F. Wilbur Helmbold. LC 76-14109. (Illus.). 1976. 9.95 o.p. (ISBN 0-8487-0415-0); logbook o.p. 3.95 o.p. (ISBN 0-8487-0414-2). Oxmoor Hse.

Tracing Your Family Tree. Stella Colwell. LC 84-8084. (Illus.). 112p. (gr. 7 up). 1985. pap. 9.95 o.p. (ISBN 0-571-13590-0). Faber & Faber.

Track & Field. 2nd ed. Ken Foreman. (Physical Education Ser.). 96p. 1983. pap. text ed. write for info. o.p. (ISBN 0-697-07213-4). Wm C Brown.

Track & Field. Jessie Owens & Dick O'Connor. LC 76-11870. (Illus.). 160p. (gr. 7 up). 1976. 7.95 o.p. (ISBN 0-689-10740-4, Atheneum). Macmillan.

Track & Field Athletics: The Records. Peter Matthews. Ed. by Beatrice Frei. (Illus.). 184p. (Orig.). 1986. pap. 12.95 o.p. (ISBN 0-85112-463-1, Pub. by Guinness Superlatives England). Sterling.

Track & Field Coaching. Ralph Steben & Sam Bell. 340p. 1978. text ed. write for info o.p. (ISBN 0-02-416230-2). Macmillan.

Track Management. Andy Bakjian. LC 81-51688. (Illus.). 96p. (Orig.). 1982. pap. 5.00 o.p. (ISBN 0-911521-01-1). Tafnews.

Track of the Snake. Gene Shelton. 1979. pap. 1.75 o.p. (ISBN 0-505-51387-0, Pub. by Tower Bks). Dorchester Pub Co.

Track Racing. Nicole Puleo. LC 72-5419. (Superwheels & Thrill Sports Bks.). (Illus.). 48p. (gr. 3-6). 1974. PLB 9.95 o.p. (ISBN 0-8225-0405-7). Lerner Pubns.

Track Systems & Other Related Railroad Topics. (Transportation Research Record Ser.). 65p. 1977. 4.80 o.p. (ISBN 0-309-02682-2). Transport Res Bd.

Track Train DYNMC & DESGN. Ed. by Gerald J. Moyar & Walter D. Pilkey. LC 78-1678. 484p. 1978. 120.00 o.p. (ISBN 0-08-022153-X). Pergamon.

Trackdown. Arthur Moore. (Orig.). 1980. pap. 1.75 o.p. (ISBN 0-505-51501-6, Pub. by Tower Bks). Dorchester Pub Co.

Tracking. Nancy Steele. 36p. (Orig.). 1976. pap. 5.00 o.p. (ISBN 0-914742-20-5). Copper Canyon.

Tracking Marco Polo. Tim Severin. LC 85-21418. (Illus.). 184p. 1986. 15.95 o.p. (ISBN 0-87226-012-7, Dist. by Har-row). P Bedrick Bks.

Tracking Respondents: A Multi-Method Approach, Vol. II. Vaughn R. Call & Luther B. Otto. LC 79-48034. (Entry into Careers Ser.). 176p. 1982. 25.00x o.p. (ISBN 0-669-03644-7). Lexington Bks.

Tracking Skill & Manual Control. E. Christopher Poulton. 1974. 69.00 o.p. (ISBN 0-12-563550-8). Acad Pr.

Tracking Those Incredible Dinosaurs & the People Who Knew Them. John D. Morris. LC 80-67760. (Illus.). 1980. pap. 5.95 o.p. (ISBN 0-89051-067-9). Master Bks.

Tracks. Elementary Science Study Staff. 1971. tchr's guide 17.24 o.p. (ISBN 0-07-017701-5). McGraw.

Tracks on the Florida Trails. Ned Potter. 128p. 1987. 7.95 o.p. (ISBN 0-8062-2771-0). Carlton.

Tract of Time. Smith Hempstone. 224p. 1985. pap. 2.95 o.p. (ISBN 0-380-69873-0). Avon.

Tractate Baba Kamma. Ed. by I. Epstein. 1964. student's ed. 15.00 o.p. (ISBN 0-900689-67-6). Soncino Pr.

Tractate on the Jews: The Significance of Judaism for the Christian Faith. Franz Mussner. Tr. by Leonard Swidler from Ger. LC 83-5699. 352p. 1983. 9.95 o.p. (ISBN 0-8006-0707-4, 1-707, Fortress). Augsburg Fortress.

Tractatus Logico-Philosophicus. Ludwig Wittgenstein. Tr. by D. F. Pears & B. F. McGuinness. (Inter. Library Philosphy & Scientific Method). 114p. (Ger. & Eng.). 1972. text ed. 27.50x o.p. (ISBN 0-391-00359-3); pap. text ed. 7.95x o.p. (ISBN 0-7100-7923-0). Humanities.

Traction & Orthopaedic Appliances. 2nd ed. J. D. Stewart & J. P. Hallett. LC 74-80738. (Illus.). 316p. 1983. pap. text ed. 36.00 o.p. (ISBN 0-443-02004-3). Churchill.

Traction Made Manageable: A Self Learning Module. Geraldine Carini & Jacqueline J. Birmingham. (Illus.). 1979. text ed. 28.95 o.p. (ISBN 0-07-009841-7). McGraw.

Tractor Pioneer: The Life of Harry Ferguson. Colin Fraser. LC 73-85451. (Illus.). vi, 294p. 1973. 15.00x o.p. (ISBN 0-8214-0134-3). Ohio U Pr.

Tractors & Their Power Units. 3rd ed. John B. Liljedahl et al. 1979. 45.95 o.p. (ISBN 0-87055-472-7). AVI.

Trade. William H. Hallahan. 320p. 1982. pap. 3.95 o.p. (ISBN 0-380-57737-2). Avon.

Trade Adjustment Assistance: New Ideas for an Old Program. LC 87-619836. (OTA-ITA Ser.: No. 346). 75p. 1987. pap. 3.25 o.p. (ISBN 0-317-62908-5, S-N 052-003-01073-9). USGPO.

Trade Agreements Act of 1979: Four Years Later. (Corporate Law & Practice Course Handbook Ser.: Vol. 425). 407p. 1983. 40.00 o.p. (ISBN 0-317-11416-6, B4-6656). PLI.

Trade Among Capitalist Countries. P. Khvoinik. 285p. 1983. 5.95 o.p. (ISBN 0-8285-2509-9, Pub. by Progress Pubs USSR). Imported Pubns.

Trade & Employment in Developing Countries: Synthesis & Conclusions, Vol. 3. Ed. by Anne O. Krueger. LC 80-15826. (National Bureau of Economic Research - Monograph). 232p. 1983. lib. bdg. 25.00x o.s.i. (ISBN 0-226-45494-0). U of Chicago Pr.

Trade & Environment: A Theoretical Enquiry. H. Siebert & J. Eichberger. (Studies in Environmental Science: Vol. 6). 356p. 1980. 89.50 o.p. (ISBN 0-444-41875-X). Elsevier.

Trade & Exchange in Early Mesoamerica. Ed. by Kenneth G. Hirth. LC 83-12483. (Illus.). 345p. 1984. 37.50x o.p. (ISBN 0-8263-0689-6). U of NM Pr.

Trade & Investment Policies in the Americas. Ed. by Stephen E. Guisinger. LC 73-84723. 116p. 1973. 12.50x o.p. (ISBN 0-87074-136-5). SMU Press.

Trade & the Dollar: Coping with Interdependence. Foreign Policy Association Staff. (Headline Ser.: No. 242). (Illus.). 1978. pap. 4.00 o.p. (ISBN 0-87124-052-1). Foreign Policy.

Trade Associations & Professional Bodies of the United Kingdom. 7th ed. P. Millard. 1971. 26.40 o.p. (ISBN 0-08-016596-6). Pergamon.

Trade Associations & Professional Bodies of the United States. 7th ed. P. Millard. 1984. 46.00 o.p. (ISBN 0-08-023024-5). Pergamon.

Trade Associations & Professional Bodies of the United Kingdom. 8th ed. P. Millard. 600p. 1987. 78.00 o.p. (ISBN 0-08-033390-7, PBL). Pergamon.

Trade Financing. Charles J. Gumr. 234p. 1981. 120.00 o.p. (ISBN 0-8002-3402-2). Intl Pubns Serv.

Trade, Growth & Anxiety: New Zealand Beyond the Welfare State. S. Harvey Franklin. (Illus.). 1978. 36.00x o.p. (ISBN 0-456-02320-8, NO. 2830). Routledge Chapman & Hall.

Trade in Agricultural Products: Reports on the Consultation with the European Economic Community, the United States of America & the United Kingdom. (Eng., Fr. & Span.). 1965. pap. 5.50 o.p. (ISBN 0-686-93140-8, G203, GATT). UNIPUB.

Trade in Place of Migration. U. Heimenz & K. W. Schatz. (WEP Study Ser.). x, 118p. 1979. pap. 15.70 o.p. (ISBN 92-2-101865-2, ILO124, ILO). UNIPUB.

Titles

Trade in Services: A Case for Open Markets. Jonathan D. Aaronson & Peter F. Cowhey. 1984. 7.00 o.p. (ISBN 0-8447-3570-1). Am Enterprise.

Trade in Transition: Exports from the Third World, Eighteen Forty to Nineteen Hundred. John R. Hanson. LC 79-6776. (Studies in Social Discontinuity Ser.). 1980. 22.00 o.p. (ISBN 0-12-323450-6). Acad Pr.

Trade of Developing Countries. Incl. Development Plans: Study of the Third Five Year Plan of India. (Fr. & Span.). 1962. pap. 5.00 (ISBN 0-686-93132-7, GATT/1962-3). UNIPUB; Development Plans: Study of the Second Five Year Plan of Pakistan. (Eng., Fr. & Span.). 1962. pap. 5.00 o.p. (ISBN 0-686-93133-5, GATT/1962-7). UNIPUB; Trade in Tropical Products. (Eng. & Span.). 1963. pap. 5.00 (ISBN 0-686-93134-3, G106). UNIPUB; Development Plans Studies: The First Six Year Plan of Nigeria. (Fr.). 1966. pap. 2.00 (ISBN 0-686-93135-1, GATT/1966-5). UNIPUB; Development Plans Studies: The Uganda Development Plan, 1961-66. (Fr.). 1966. pap. 1.50 o.p. (ISBN 0-686-93136-X, GATT/1966-6). UNIPUB. pap. (GATT). UNIPUB.

Trade-Offs: For the Person Who Can't Have Everything. David Hon. LC 80-39625. (Illus.). 163p. 1981. text ed. 15.95 o.p. (ISBN 0-89384-048-3). Univ Assocs.

Trade Patterns in Developing Countries, 1970-1981. Lance Taylor et al. (Working Paper: No. 642). 68p. 1984. 5.00 o.p. (ISBN 0-8213-0362-7, WP 0642). World Bank.

Trade Policies for a Better Future: Proposals for Action. 60p. 1985. pap. 9.50 o.p. (ISBN 9-2870-1016-1, G170 5071, GATT). UNIPUB.

Trade Policy for Developing Countries. Donald B. Keesing. (Working Paper: No. 353). vii, 264p. 1979. 15.00 o.p. (ISBN 0-8213-9263-8, WP-0353). World Bank.

Trade Policy in the 70's: A New Round. G. L. Weil. LC 73-4787. 1969. pap. 10.00 o.p. (ISBN 0-527-02784-7). Kraus Repr.

Trade Policy, Protectionism & the Third World. Michael Davenport. 176p. 1986. 31.00 o.p. (ISBN 0-7099-4516-7, Pub. by Croom Helm Ltd). Routledge Chapman & Hall.

Trade Relations under Flexible Exchange Rates. Richard Blackhurst & Jan Tumlir. (Studies in International Trade: No. 8). 80p. 1981. pap. 10.50 o.p. (ISBN 0-686-69637-9, G143, GATT). UNIPUB.

Trade Secret Litigation: A Course Handbook. Steven J. Stein. 209p. 1985. pap. 15.00 o.p. (G4-3773). PLI.

Trade Shows & Professional Exhibits Directory: Supplement. 2nd ed. Ed. by Robert J. Elster. 300p. 1987. 80.00x o.p. (ISBN 0-8103-2124-6). Gale.

Trade Shows & Professional Exhibits Directory. 2nd ed. Ed. by Robert J. Elster. LC 84-6101. 915p. 1986. 150.00x o.p. (ISBN 0-8103-2113-0). Gale.

Trade, Society & Politics in Bristol: 1500-1640, 2 vols. David H. Sacks. Ed. by Peter Mathias & Stuart Bruchey. LC 84-46011. (British Economic History Ser.). 987p. 1985. lib. bdg. 110.00 o.p. (ISBN 0-8240-6691-X). Garland Pub.

Trade Theory & Policy: Some Topical Issues. Ali El-Agraa. 130p. 1984. 27.00x o.p. (ISBN 0-8448-1473-3, Pub. by Crane Russak & Co). Taylor & Francis.

Trade Union Democracy, Members' Rights & the Law. Patrick Elias & K. D. Ewing. LC 87-7645. (Studies in Labor & Social Law). 1986. 60.00 o.p. (ISBN 0-7201-0729-6). Mansell.

Trade Union Financial Administration. Don H. Taylo. 64p. 1981. 2.85 o.p. (ISBN 92-2-102711-2). Intl Labour Office.

Trade Union Handbook. 3rd ed. Ed. by Arthur Marsh. 430p. 1984. text ed. 59.50 o.p. (ISBN 0-566-02426-8). Gower Pub Co.

Trade Union Rank & File: Trades Councils in Britain, 1900-1940. Alan Clinton. 262p. 1977. 23.50x o.p. (ISBN 0-87471-982-8). Rowman.

Trade Union Rights & Their Relation to Civil Liberties: Proceedings of the International Labour Conference, 54th Session, Geneva, 1970. International Labour Office Staff. 1970. 2.30 o.p. (ISBN 92-2-100070-2). Intl Labour Office.

Trade Union Situation & Industrial Relations in Yugoslavia. 104p. (Orig.). 1985. pap. text ed. 14.00 o.p. (ISBN 92-2-105201-X, IL0539). Intl Labour Office.

Trade Unions & Politics in the 1980's: The 1984 Act & Political Funds. Derek Fatchett. 192p. 1986. 34.50 o.p. (ISBN 0-7099-4903-0, Pub. by Croom Helm UK). Routledge Chapman & Hall.

Trade Unions & the ILO: A Workers' Education Manual. 3rd ed. vii, 96p. 1983. 7.00 o.p. (ISBN 92-2-102003-7). Intl Labour Office.

Trade Unions & the Labour Party. Andrew Taylor. 320p. 1986. 47.50 o.p. (ISBN 0-7099-2471-2, Pub. by Croom Helm Ltd). Routledge Chapman & Hall.

Trade Unions in the Construction Industry. Mary Vance. (Architecture Ser.: Bibliography A-1315). 26p. 1985. pap. 3.75 o.p. (ISBN 0-89028-245-5). Vance Biblios.

Trade Unions: What Are They? T. Van Den Bergh. LC 79-97952. 1970. 70.00 o.p. (ISBN 0-08-006517-1); pap. 70.00 o.p. (ISBN 0-08-006516-3). Pergamon.

Trade: U. S. Policy Since 1945. LC 83-25246. 256p. 1984. pap. 11.95 o.p. (ISBN 0-87187-282-X). Congr Quarterly.

Trade with Manufacturers in Developing Countries: Reinforcing North-South Partnership. Albert Fishlow et al. 1981. Trilateral Comm.

Tradeful Merchants: The Portrayal of the Capitalist in Literature. John McVeagh. 240p. 1981. 32.00x o.p. (ISBN 0-7100-0729-9). Routledge Chapman & Hall.

Trademark Law Handbook 1985-86. United States Trademark Association Staff. (Orig.). 1985. pap. 45.00 o.p. (ISBN 0-87632-523-1). Clark Boardman.

Trademark Litigation: Pragmatic Tactics & Techniques of Winning. Practicing Law Institute Staff & Miles J. Alexander. (Patents, Copyrights, Trademarks, & Literary Property Course Handbook Ser.: No. 173). 368p. 1984. 15.00 o.p. PLI.

Trademarks. Roy Ehrhardt. (Illus.). 1976. Repr. plastic ring bdg. 10.00 o.p. (ISBN 0-913902-06-3). Heart Am Pr.

Trademarks & Logotypes in Japan: Color Edition 2. 330p. 1986. 90.00 o.p. (ISBN 0-8161-8805-X, Pub. by Graphic-Sha Pub Co Ltd Japan). G K Hall.

Trademarks & Symbols of the World. Yasaburo Kuwayama. (Design Sourcebook Ser.). (Illus.). 495p. 1987. 89.95 o.s.i. (ISBN 4-7601-0320-1). Rockport Pubs.

Trademarks in Developing Countries. Ed. by Surendra J. Patel. 122p. 1979. pap. 29.00 o.p. (ISBN 0-08-025223-0). Pergamon.

Tradeoffs: The Executive, Family & Organization. Barrie S. Greiff & Preston K. Munter. 1980. cancelled 9.95 o.p. (ISBN 0-671-22904-4). S&S.

Trader Ike & Our Home in the North. Ira Weisner. 6.00 o.p. (ISBN 0-682-48869-0). Exposition-Phoenix.

Traders. Sonny Kleinfield. LC 83-4383. 176p. 1984. 14.95 o.s.i. (ISBN 0-03-059721-8). H Holt & Co.

Traders. Sonny Kleinfield. LC 83-4383. 216p. 1986. pap. 7.95 o.s.i. (ISBN 0-03-008534-9, Owl Bks). H Holt & Co.

Traders Directory of Foreign Exchange Futures & Options Dealers: 1986. 2nd ed. 778p. 1986. pap. 98.00 o.p. (ISBN 0-8002-4072-3). Intl Pubns Serv.

Traders to the Navajos: The Story of the Wetherills of Kayenta. Frances Gillmor & Louisa W. Wetherill. LC 52-9210. 271p. 1965. pap. 8.95 o.p. (ISBN 0-8263-0040-5). U of NM Pr.

Tradeshow Week Data Book, 1988. Ed. by Bowker, R. R., Staff. 1356p. 1988. pap. 195.00 o.p. (ISBN 0-8352-2460-0). Bowker.

Trading: Inside the World's Leading Stock Exchanges. Susan Goldenberg. LC 85-17570. (Illus.). 352p. 1986. 22.95 o.p. (ISBN 0-15-191005-7). HarBraceJ.

Tradition & Design in Luke's Gospel. John Drury. LC 77-79586. 1977. 7.95 o.p. (ISBN 0-8042-0451-9, John Knox). Westminster John Knox.

Tradition & Dynamism Among Afghan Refugees: A Report on Income-Generating Activities for Afghan Refugees in Pakistan. International Labour Office Staff & UN High Commission for Refugees. xvi, 174p. 1983. pap. 11.40 o.p. (ISBN 92-2-103517-4). Intl Labour Office.

Tradition & Gigli. Edgar F. Herbert-Caesari. 6.95 o.s.i. (ISBN 0-8008-7827-2, Crescendo). Taplinger.

Tradition & Innovation: The Idea of Civilization As Culture & Its Significance. H. T. Wilson. (International Library of Phenomenology & Moral Sciences). 256p. 1984. 35.00x o.p. (ISBN 0-7102-0009-9). Routledge Chapman & Hall.

Tradition & Interpretation in Matthew. Gunther Bornkamm et al. LC 63-10495. 308p. 1963. 13.95 o.s.i. (ISBN 0-664-20453-8, Westminster). Westminster John Knox.

Tradition & Reform in Education. Stephen Tonsor. LC 73-82779. 262p. 1974. 9.95 o.p. (ISBN 0-87548-124-8). Open Court.

Tradition & Renewal: Contemporary Art in the German Democratic Republic. David Elliott. (Illus.). 64p. 1985. pap. 12.50 o.p. (ISBN 0-87663-867-1). Universe.

Tradition & Theology in the Old Testament. Ed. by Douglas A. Knight. LC 76-7872. 352p. 1977. 8.50 o.p. (ISBN 0-8006-0484-9, 1-484, Fortress). Augsburg Fortress.

Tradition, Conflict & Change: Perspectives on the American Revolution. Ed. by Richard E. Brown & Don E. Fehrenbacher. (Studies in Social Discontinuity Ser.). 1977. 19.95 o.p. (ISBN 0-12-137650-8). Acad Pr.

Tradition for Crisis: A Study in Hosea. Walter Brueggemann. LC 68-21008. 164p. 1981. pap. 7.95 o.p. (ISBN 0-8042-0181-1, John Knox). Westminster John Knox.

Tradition of Natural Law: A Philosopher's Reflections. Yves Simon. Ed. by Vukan Kuic. LC 64-24756. xii, 194p. 1965. 20.00 o.p. (ISBN 0-8232-0640-8). Fordham.

Traditional & Modern Medical Systems. Ed. by Ray Elling. (Illus.). 100p. 1981. pap. 18.00 o.p. (ISBN 0-08-028097-8). Pergamon.

Traditional & National Music of Scotland. Francis Collinson. (Illus.). 1972. Repr. of 1966 ed. 25.00 o.p. (ISBN 0-7100-1213-6). Routledge Chapman & Hall.

Traditional Aspects of Hell. James Mew. LC 73-140321. 474p. 1971. Repr. of 1903 ed. 48.00x o.p. (ISBN 0-8103-3693-6). Gale.

Traditional Chinese Festivals. Repr. of 1985 ed. 4.95 o.p. (ISBN 0-8351-1838-X). China Bks.

Traditional Dancing in Scotland. T. M. Flett & J. P. Flett. (Illus.). 313p. 1985. pap. 8.95 o.p. (ISBN 0-7102-0731-X). Routledge Chapman & Hall.

Traditional Health Care Delivery in Contemporary Africa. Ed. by Priscilla Ulin & Marshall Segall. LC 80-27442. (Foreign & Comparative Studies Program, African Ser.: No. 35). 100p. 1980. pap. 8.00x o.p. (ISBN 0-915984-57-1). Syracuse U Foreign Comp.

Traditional Home Plans. 2nd ed. Ed. by Garlinghouse Co. Staff. LC 85-70893. (Illus.). 112p. 1985. pap. 2.95 o.p. (ISBN 0-938708-14-7). L F Garlinghouse Co.

Traditional Home Plans. Ed. by L. F. Garlinghouse Co., Staff. LC 81-86298. (Illus., Orig.). 1982. pap. 2.50 o.s.i. (ISBN 0-938708-02-3). L F Garlinghouse Co.

Traditional Housing in African Cities: A Comparative Study of Houses in Zaria, Ibadan & Marrakech. Freidrich W. Schwerdtfeger. LC 80-41693. 480p. 1982. 115.00x o.p. (ISBN 0-471-27953-6, Pub. by Wiley-Interscience). Wiley.

Traditional Indian Theatre: Multiple Streams. Kapila Vatsyayan. 1982. pap. 10.00x o.p. (ISBN 0-8364-0846-2, Pub. by National Bk). South Asia Bks.

Traditional Islamic Craft in Moroccan Architecture, 2 vols. Andre Paccard. 1980. 495.00x o.p. (ISBN 0-686-69970-X, Pub. by Editions Atelier England). State Mutual Bk.

Traditional Japanese Furniture. Kazuko Koizumi. LC 85-40067. (Illus.). 224p. 1986. 70.00 o.s.i. (ISBN 0-87011-722-X). Kodansha.

Traditional Knitting Patterns from Scandinavia, the British Isles, France, Italy & Other European Countries. James Norbury. (Illus.). 15.75 o.p. (ISBN 0-8446-5071-4). Peter Smith.

Traditional Medicine: Implications of Mental Health, Public Health, Maternal & Child Health & Family Planning. Ira E. Harrison & Sheila Cosminsky. LC 75-24105. (Reference Library of Social Science: Vol. 19). 150p. 1976. lib. bdg. 36.00 o.p. (ISBN 0-8240-9970-2). Garland Pub.

Traditional Music in Modern Java. Judith Becker. LC 80-19180. (Illus.). 1980. text ed. 30.00x o.p. (ISBN 0-8248-0563-1). UH Pr.

Traditional Prayer Book for Sabbath & Festivals. 10.00 o.p. (ISBN 0-317-70172-X). Behrman.

Traditional Recipes of Laos. Phia Sing. (Illus.). 318p. 1981. 20.00x o.p. (ISBN 0-907325-02-5, Pub. by Prospect England); pap. 15.95x o.p. U Pr of Va.

Traditional Values & Contemporary Federation Practices. Bernard Reisman. cancelled o.s.i. Coun Jewish Feds.

Traditions & Revisions: Themes from the History of Sculpture. Gabriel P. Weisberg. LC 75-26708. (Illus.). 162p. 1975. pap. 10.00x o.p. (ISBN 0-910386-23-4, Pub. by Cleveland Mus Art). Ind U Pr.

Traditions & Uniforms of the German Army: 1933-1945, Vol. 2. John R. Angolia & Adolf Schlicht. (Illus.). 448p. 1986. 29.95 o.p. (ISBN 0-912138-34-3). Bender Pub CA.

Trafalgar Square: Emblem of Empire. Rodney Mace. (Illus.). 1976. text ed. 22.50x o.p. (ISBN 0-85315-368-X). Humanities.

Trafalgar True. Stephen Cosgrove. (Serendipity Storybks.). (Illus.). 32p. (gr. k-4). 1980. pap. 1.95 o.s.i. (ISBN 0-8431-0575-5). Price Stern.

Traffic Control & Motorist Information, 6 reports. (Transportation Research Record Ser.). 82p. 1975. 3.60 o.p. (ISBN 0-309-02377-7). Transport Res Bd.

Traffic Control Devices, Geometrics, Visibility, & Route Guidance. (Transportation Research Record Ser.). 121p. 1979. 6.60 o.p. (ISBN 0-309-02992-9). Transport Res Bd.

Traffic Control Devices, Visibility & Geometrics. (Transportation Research Record Ser.). 94p. 1978. 5.40 o.p. (ISBN 0-309-02826-4). Transport Res Bd.

Traffic Control: Signals & Other Devices. (Transportation Research Record Ser.). 57p. 1976. 2.60 o.p. (ISBN 0-309-02567-2). Transport Res Bd.

Traffic Education for Young Pedestrians: A Selection of Papers Adapted from the Proceedings of the 1978 OECD Workshop on Training Objectives for Child Pedestrians. John A. Michon. (Accident Analysis & Prevention Ser.: No. 13). 138p. 1983. pap. 31.00 o.p. (ISBN 0-08-030224-6). Pergamon.

Traffic Equilibrium Methods. Ed. by M. A. Florian. (Lecture Notes in Economics & Mathematical Systems: Vol. 118). 1976. pap. 21.00 o.p. (ISBN 0-387-07620-4). Springer-Verlag.

Traffic Flow Theory & Applications, 10 reports. (Transportation Research Record Ser.). 98p. 1976. 8.00 o.p. (ISBN 0-309-02480-3). Transport Res Bd.

Traffic Flow: Theory & Practice, 4 reports. (Transportation Research Record Ser.). 55p. 1974. 2.40 o.p. (ISBN 0-309-02352-1). Transport Res Bd.

Traffic Law Enforcement: A Guide for Patrolmen. Southwestern Law Enforcement Institute Staff. (Illus.). 116p. 1971. 13.75x o.p. (ISBN 0-398-01816-2). C C Thomas.

Traffic Operations, 5 reports. (Transportation Research Record Ser.). 55p. 1974. 2.40 o.p. (ISBN 0-309-02358-0). Transport Res Bd.

Traffic Planning & Engineering. 2nd, rev. ed. F. D. Hobbs. 1979. 105.00 o.p. (ISBN 0-08-022696-5); pap. 37.00 o.p. (ISBN 0-08-022697-3). Pergamon.

Traffic Records, Accident Analysis & Traffic Law Enforcement. National Research Council (U. S.) Transportation Research Board. LC 83-22086. (Transportation Research Record: No. 910). 1983. 13.00 o.p. (ISBN 0-309-03552-X). Transport Res Bd.

Traffic Records, Law Enforcement, & Motorist-Aid System. (Transportation Research Record Ser.). 54p. 1977. 3.60 o.p. (ISBN 0-309-02672-5). Transport Res Bd.

Traffic-Safety Education of Young Children. T. Rothengatter. 1981. pap. text ed. 28.00 o.p. (ISBN 90-265-0363-6, Pub. by Swets & Zeitlinger Netherlands). CJ Hogrefe Pubs.

Traffic Transit. 8.00 o.p. (ISBN 0-317-65070-X). Am Consul Eng.

Traffic, Transportation & Urban Planning, 2 vols. Ed. by Goodwin, George, Limited Staff. (International Forum Ser.). 1983. Set. 87.95 o.p. (ISBN 0-87933-041-4); Vol. I, 245p. 45.95 o.p. (ISBN 0-87933-402-9); Vol. II, 260p. 45.95 o.p. (ISBN 0-87933-403-7). Van Nos Reinhold.

Traffic World's Question & Answer Book, Vol. 26. Ed. by Colin Barrett. 1977. text ed. 14.00 o.p. (ISBN 0-87408-006-1). Intl Thom Trans Pr.

Traffic World's Question & Answer Book, Vol. 27. Traffic World Editors. 1979. text ed. 16.00 o.p. (ISBN 0-87408-015-0). Intl Thom Trans Pr.

Tragedy & Philosophy. Walter Kaufmann. LC 78-73428. 1979. 40.50x o.p. (ISBN 0-691-07235-3); pap. 12.95x o.p. (ISBN 0-691-02005-1). Princeton U Pr.

Tragedy in the Church. W. Tozer. Ed. by Gerald Smith. 1978. pap. 3.45 o.s.i. (ISBN 0-87509-215-2). Chr Pubns.

Tragedy, Modern Temper & O'Neill. C. Ahuja. 207p. 1984. text ed. 22.50x o.p. (ISBN 0-391-02699-2). Humanities.

Tragedy of a State: A Study of Jacobean Drama. J. W. Lever. (Methuen Library Reprints Ser.). 1980. 45.00x o.p. (ISBN 0-416-30550-4, NO. 2220). Routledge Chapman & Hall.

Tragedy of Antony & Cleopatra see also Antony & Cleopatra.

Tragedy of Capital Tax. Faik Okte. Tr. by Geoffrey Cox from Turkish. 144p. 1987. 39.95 o.p. (ISBN 0-7099-1964-6, Pub. by Croom Helm UK). Routledge Chapman & Hall.

Tragedy of Children under Nazi Rule. Kiryl Sosnowski. LC 81-19506. 1983. Repr. of 1962 ed. 40.00x o.p. (ISBN 0-86527-342-1). Fertig.

Tragedy of Coriolanus see also Coriolanus.

Tragedy of Cymbeline see also Cymbeline.

Tragedy of Europe, Vols. I-V. Francis Neilson. 3503p. 1986. Set. 150.00 o.p. (ISBN 0-317-53294-4). Noontide.

Tragedy of Hamlet, Prince of Denmark see also Hamlet.

Tragedy of Julius Caesar see also Julius Caesar.

Tragedy of King Lear see also King Lear.

Tragedy of Macbeth see also Macbeth.

Tragedy of Nero. Thomas Jones. Ed. by Elliott M. Hill & Stephen Orgel. LC 78-66763. (Renaissance Drama Ser.). 1979. lib. bdg. 40.00 o.p. (ISBN 0-8240-9745-9). Garland Pub.

Tragedy of Othello, the Moor of Venice see also Othello.

Tragedy of Othello: The Moor of Venice. Ed. by Christopher Bentley. 166p. 1983. pap. 9.00x o.p. (ISBN 0-424-00093-8, Pub. by Sydney U Pr). Intl Spec Bk.

Tragedy of the Wahk-Shum. Lucullus McWhorter. 44p. 1968. Repr. 5.50 o.s.i. (ISBN 0-87770-064-8). Ye Galleon.

Tragedy of Troilus & Cressida see also Troilus & Cressida.

Tragic Deception. Hamilton Fish, Sr. 120p. Date not set. 13.00 o.p. (ISBN 0-317-53204-9). Noontide.

Tragic Philosopher. F. A. Lea. (Illus.). 350p. 1957. (ISBN 0-8022-0944-0). Philos Lib.

Tragic Vision of Joyce Carol Oates. Mary K. Grant. LC 77-75617. xiv, 167p. 1978. 15.95 o.p. (ISBN 0-8223-0404-X). Duke.

Tragical Comedy or Comical Tragedy of Punch & Judy. George Cruikshank. (Illus.). 1976. pap. 2.25 o.p. (ISBN 0-7100-8199-5). Routledge Chapman & Hall.

Tragicomedy. David L. Hirst. (Critical Idiom Ser.: No. 43). 120p. 1984. pap. 5.50 o.p. (ISBN 0-416-32770-2, NO. 4152). Routledge Chapman & Hall.

Trail. Date not set. (ISBN 0-8052-0053-3). Random.

Trail. Date not set. pap. (ISBN 0-8052-0416-4). Random.

Trail Cooking. John Weiss. (Illus.). 1982. 16.95 o.p. (ISBN 0-442-29324-0). Van Nos Reinhold.

Trail Led North. Martha F. McKeown. (Illus.). 1960. 10.50 o.p. (ISBN 0-8323-0090-X). Binford-Metropolitan.

Trail of Ashes. Marian Babson. (Nightingale Ser.). 280p. (Orig.). 1985. pap. 9.95 o.p. (ISBN 0-8161-3904-0, Large Print Bks). G K Hall.

Trail of Death. Rose Estes. LC 85-60429. (Find Your Fate Ser.). (Illus.). 128p. (gr. 4-7). 1985. pap. 2.95 o.s.i. (ISBN 0-394-86432-8, BYR). Random.

Trail of Peril. Yvonne Davy. Ed. by Gerald Wheeler. LC 83-17835. (Banner Bks.). (Illus.). 94p. (Orig.). (gr. k up). 1984. pap. 6.95 o.p. (ISBN 0-8280-0223-1). Review & Herald.

Trail Planning & Layout. 76p. 3.50 o.p. (ISBN 0-317-35029-3, B4). Natl Audubon.

Trail Sinister. James Brumbaugh. LC 86-91530. (AD&D Adventure Gamebook Ser.: No. 14). 192p. (Orig.). 1987. pap. 2.95 o.p. (ISBN 0-88038-453-0). TSR Inc.

Trail Through Danger. William O. Steele. LC 65-25307. (Illus.). (gr. 4-6). 1965. 4.95 o.p. (ISBN 0-15-289661-9, HJ). HarBraceJ.

Trail to a Pot of Gold. Sam Mims. (Illus.). 23p. pap. 1.00 o.p. (ISBN 0-911116-46-X). Pelican.

Trailer Life Campground & RV Services Directory. Ed. by Trailer Life Staff. 1400p. 1988. pap. 13.95 o.p. (ISBN 0-934798-16-8). TL Enterprises.

Trailer Life Campground & RV Services Directory: 1989 Edition. 1989. pap. 11.95 o.p. (ISBN 0-934798-19-2). TL Enterprises.

Trailer Life's Guide to Fulltime RVing: Everything You Need to Know to Enjoy the Total Freedom & Adventure of Life on the Road. Trailer Life Editors & Don Wright. (Illus.). 352p. 1981. 12.95 o.p. (ISBN 0-934798-05-2). TL Enterprises.

Trailer Life's Secrets of Successful RVing: Detailed Tips & Hints for Successful RV Trips. John Thompson. (Illus.). 400p. (Orig.). 1981. pap. 12.95 o.p. (ISBN 0-934798-03-6). TL Enterprises.

Trailerable Sailboats. Christopher Caswell. (Illus.). 1982. 19.95 o.p. (ISBN 0-393-03271-X). Norton.

Trailerboating Illustrated. 2nd rev. ed. Patrick M. Royce. LC 81-11398. (Planing Hulls, Trailers, Seamanship Ser.: No. 1). (Illus.). 192p. 1981. pap. 8.95 o.p. (ISBN 0-930030-19-2). Western Marine Ent.

Trailerpark. Russell Banks. LC 81-7662. 288p. 1981. 11.95 o.p. (ISBN 0-395-31547-6). HM.

Trails of the Sawtooth & White Cloud Mountains. new ed. Margaret Fuller. LC 78-68661. (Illus., Orig.). 1979. pap. 8.95 o.p. (ISBN 0-913140-29-5). Signpost Bk Pub.

Train Trips. Rev. ed. William G. Scheller. LC 83-49037. (Illus.). 288p. 1984. pap. 9.95 o.p. (ISBN 0-88742-000-1). Globe Pequot.

Trained Manpower for Agricultural & Rural Development. R. Rowat. (Economic & Social Development Papers: No. 10, suppl.). 26p. 1983. pap. 10.00 o.p. (ISBN 92-5-101387-X, F1963, FAO). UNIPUB.

Trainers' Manual: Staff Training-Consumer Co-Operatives. 98p. 1981. 17.00 o.p. (ISBN 92-2-102226-9). Intl Labour Office.

Training about Girl Scouting. Girl Scouts of the U. S. A. Staff. 72p. 1978. pap. 4.00 o.p. (ISBN 0-88441-431-0, 26-180). Girl Scouts USA.

Training Activities for Teachers in Higher Education, Vol. 2. Ed. by Pat Cryer. 134p. 1985. pap. 56.00 o.p. (ISBN 0-7005-1002-8, Open Univ Pr). Taylor & Francis.

Training & Development Handbook: A Guide to Human Resource Development. 2nd ed. American Society for Training & Development. (Handbook Ser.). (Illus.). 1976. text ed. 67.50 o.p. (ISBN 0-07-013350-6). McGraw.

Training & Development Organizations Directory. 3rd ed. Ed. by Paul Wasserman. 1214p. 1983. 270.00x o.p. (ISBN 0-8103-0432-5). Gale.

Training & Materials Catalog. 186p. 1979. 11.00 o.p. (ISBN 0-317-33103-5, 82275700). Am Petroleum.

Training Dogs: A Manual. Konrad Most. (Popular Dog Ser.). (Illus.). 205p. 1988. 14.95 o.s.i. (ISBN 0-09-161401-5, Pub. by Century Hutchinson). David & Charles.

Training Effective Teachers: A Competency-Based Practicum Model for Teachers of Emotionally Disturbed Children. Betty R. Damren et al. 53p. 1975. pap. text ed. 4.00 o.p. (ISBN 0-89039-134-3). Ann Arbor Pubs.

Training for Agriculture & Rural Development, 1978. (Economic & Social Development Papers: No. 14). 106p. 1979. pap. 14.25 o.p. (ISBN 0-686-59754-0, F1635, FAO). UNIPUB.

Training for Capstan, Turret, & Sequence Controlled Lathe Setters & Operators, 21 vols. Ed. by Engineering Industry Training Board Staff. (Illus.). 1973. Set. 89.95x o.p. (ISBN 0-89563-023-0). Trans-Atl Phila.

Training for Drilling Machine Operators, 17 vols. Ed. by Engineering Industry Training Board Staff. (Illus.). 1978. Set. 69.95x o.p. (ISBN 0-89563-024-9). Trans-Atl Phila.

Training for Fixed Headstock Single Spindle Automatic Lathe Setters & Operators, 30 vols. Ed. by Engineering Industry Training Board Staff. (Illus.). 1978. folder 89.95x o.p. (ISBN 0-85083-425-2). Trans-Atl Phila.

Training for Industrial Site Radiography, 14 vols. Ed. by Engineering Industry Training Board Staff. Incl. Vol. 1. Introduction to Radiography; Vol. 2. Ionizing Radiations; Vol. 4. Image Formation; Vol. 5. Safety; Vol. 6. X-Ray Equipment; Vol. 7. Gamma-Ray Equipment; Vol. 8. Exposure; Vol. 9. Operations; Vol. 10. Pipe-Crawler Equipment. 69.95. (Illus.). 1977. Set. 42.50x o.p. (ISBN 0-89563-025-7). Trans-Atl Phila.

Training for Life: A Practical Guide to Career & Life Planning. Fred J. Hecklinger & Bernadette M. Curtin. 232p. 1984. pap. text ed. 16.95 o.p. (ISBN 0-8403-3309-9, 40330901). Kendall-Hunt.

Training for Manual Metal-Arc Welders, 14 vols. Ed. by Engineering Industry Training Board Staff. Incl. Vol. 1. Metal-Arc Welding; Vol. 2. Welding Electrodes; Vol. 3. Joints & Weld Symbols; Vol. 4. Limiting Distortion; Vol. 5. Basic Welding; Vol. 6. Plate Surfaces; Vol. 7. Fillet Joints; Vol. 8. Single Vee Butt Joints; Vol. 9. Pipe Welding; Vol. 10. Fault Diagnosis; Vol. 11. Branch Connections. 69.95. (Illus.). 1974. Set. 43.95x o.p. (ISBN 0-89563-026-5). Trans-Atl Phila.

Training for Milling Machine Operators & Setters, 22 vols. Ed. by Engineering Industry Training Board Staff. (Illus.). 1977. Set. 69.95x o.p. (ISBN 0-89563-027-3). Trans-Atl Phila.

Training for Multi-Spindle Automatic Lathe Setters & Operators, 31 vols. Ed. by Engineering Industry Training Board Staff. (Illus.). 1979. Set. folder 89.95x o.p. (ISBN 0-85083-463-5). Trans-Atl Phila.

Training for Musicianship. Victoria Glaser. 17.95x o.s.i. (ISBN 0-8008-7829-9, Crescendo). Taplinger.

Training for Negotiating. Bromley Kniveton & Brian Towers. 213p. 1978. text ed. 29.40x o.p. (ISBN 0-220-66347-5, Pub. by Busn Bks England). Gower Pub Co.

Training for Operators of Numerically Controlled Machines. Ed. by Engineering Industry Training Board Staff. Incl. Vol. 1. Introduction to NC Machine Tool; Vol. 2. Rotating Tool; Vol. 3. Rotating Work; Vol. 4. Milling Cutters; Vol. 5. Tape NC Machines; Vol. 6. Automatic Tool & Work Exchanging; Vol. 7. X, Y, & Z Axes; Vol. 8. Positioning of the Tool & Workpiece; Vol. 9. Emergency Stop & Switching Operations; Vol. 10. Operation. 79.95. 1973. Set. 62.50x o.p. (ISBN 0-89563-028-1). Trans-Atl Phila.

Training for Pipe Fitters, 23 vols. Engineering Industry Training Board Staff. 1976. 75.00x o.p. (ISBN 0-89563-031-1). Trans-Atl Phila.

Training for Power Press Setters & Operators, 17 vols. Ed. by Engineering Industry Training Board Staff. (Illus.). 1973. Set. folder 67.50x o.p. (ISBN 0-89563-048-6). Trans-Atl Phila.

Training for Riggers-Erectors, 15 vols. Ed. by Engineering Industry Training Board Staff. (Illus.). 1976. Set. 67.50x o.p. (ISBN 0-89563-030-3). Trans-Atl Phila.

Training for Service Delivery to Minority Clients. Ed. by Emelicia Mizio & Anita J. Delaney. LC 80-234668. 224p. 1980. pap. 13.95 o.p. (ISBN 0-87304-180-1). Family Serv.

Training for Sliding Headstock Single Spindle Automatic Lathe (Swiss Auto) Setters & Operators, 26 vols. Ed. by Engineering Industry Training Board Staff. (Illus.). 1978. Set. folder 79.95x o.p. (ISBN 0-85083-426-0). Trans-Atl Phila.

Training for Sport & Activity: The Physiological Basis of the Conditioning Process. 2nd ed. Wilmore. 1985. 37.95 o.p. (ISBN 0-205-07761-7, 627761). Wm C Brown.

Training in Consultation: Perspectives from Mental Health, Behavioral & Organizational Consultation. Judith L. Alpert & Joel Meyers. (Illus.). 268p. 1983. 26.25x o.p. (ISBN 0-398-04801-0). C C Thomas.

Training in Small Groups: A Study of Five Methods. rev. ed. Ed. by B. Babington Smith. B. A. Farrell. 114p. 1979. 34.00 o.p. (ISBN 0-08-023689-8). Pergamon.

Training Minority Journalists: A Case Study of the San Francisco Examiner Intern Program. Judie Telfer. LC 73-4313. 124p. (Orig.). 1973. pap. 4.00x o.p. (ISBN 0-87772-169-6). UCB IGS.

Training of Prison Governors: Role Ambiguity & Socialization. P. A. Waddington. 177p. 1983. 27.00 o.p. (ISBN 0-7099-2786-X, Pub. by Croom Helm Ltd). Routledge Chapman & Hall.

Training Program Evaluators. Ed. by Lee Sechrest. LC 78-73932. (Program Evaluation Ser.: No. 8). 1980. pap. text ed. 12.95x o.p. (ISBN 0-87589-855-6). Jossey-Bass.

Training the Backwards Child. Herta Loewy. 166p. 1956. (ISBN 0-8022-0991-2). Philos Lib.

Training the Gunfighter. Timothy J. Mullin. (Illus.). 250p. 1981. 24.95 o.p. (ISBN 0-87364-185-X). Paladin Pr.

Training the New Supervisor. James E. Gardner. (Illus.). 1980. 15.95 o.p. (ISBN 0-8144-5564-6). AMACOM.

Training the Reined Horse. Peter Phinny & Jack Brainard. LC 75-38441. (Illus.). 1976. 8.95 o.s.i. (ISBN 0-498-01874-1). A S Barnes.

Training the Roughshooter's Dog. P. R. Moxon. (Popular Dog Ser.). (Illus.). 200p. 1988. 24.95 o.s.i. (ISBN 0-09-144000-9, Pub. by Century Hutchinson). David & Charles.

Training-the-Trainer Resource Book. 1980. pap. 5.00 o.p. (26-181). Girl Scouts USA.

Training Your Donkey. Marjorie Dunkels. pap. (ISBN 0-85131-048-6, NL51, Pub. by J A Allen U K). S R Smith Sporting Bks.

Traite De Dynamique. Jean L. D' Alembert. (Sources of Science Ser). (Fr). 1969. Repr. 38.00 o.p. (ISBN 0-384-00680-9). Johnson Repr.

Traitors. William S. Long. (Australians Ser.: Vol. III). 1984. lib. bdg. 12.95 o.p. (ISBN 0-8398-2826-8, Gregg). G K Hall.

Traitor's Blood. Reginald Hill. LC 86-16443. 256p. 1986. 16.95 o.s.i. (ISBN 0-88150-076-3, Foul Play). Countryman.

Traits of Divine Kingship in Africa. P. Hadfield. LC 78-32120. 1979. Repr. of 1949 ed. lib. bdg. 22.50x o.p. (ISBN 0-8371-5189-9, HDK&, Pub. by Negro U Pr). Greenwood.

Trajan's Parthian War. F. A. Lepper. LC 79-4519. (Illus.). 1979. Repr. of 1948 ed. lib. bdg. 24.75x o.p. (ISBN 0-313-20845-X, LETP). Greenwood.

Trajectories of Artificial Celestial Bodies As Determined from Observations: Proceedings of the COSPAR-IAU-IUTAM Symposium, Paris, 1965. COSPAR-IAU-IUTAM Symposium Staff. Ed. by J. Kovalevsky. (Illus.). 1966. 52.00 o.p. (ISBN 0-387-03681-4). Springer-Verlag.

Trajectories Through Early Christianity. James M. Robinson & Helmut Koester. LC 79-141254. 312p. 1971. pap. 9.95 o.p. (ISBN 0-8006-1362-7, 1-1362, Fortress). Augsburg Fortress.

Tramp & I. Robert T. Thorpe. 1979. 8.00 o.p. (ISBN 0-682-49384-8). Exposition-Phoenix.

Tramping in Europe: A Walking Guide. J. Sydney Jones. 234p. 1984. 14.95 o.p. (ISBN 0-13-926980-0); pap. 7.95 o.p. (ISBN 0-13-926972-X). P-H.

Tramping in New Zealand. Jim DuFresne. (Illus.). 168p. 1989. pap. 6.95 o.p. (ISBN 0-908086-33-4). Lonely Planet.

Trampolining. Jeff T. Hennessy. (Physical Education Activities Ser.). 70p. 1968. pap. text ed. write for info. o.p. (ISBN 0-697-07034-4); tchr's. manual o.p. (ISBN 0-697-07227-4). Wm C Brown.

Trampolining: A Complete Handbook. rev. 2nd ed. Dennis Horne. (Illus.). 224p. 1978. 11.95 o.p. (ISBN 0-571-04868-4); pap. 6.95 o.p. (ISBN 0-571-04945-1). Faber & Faber.

Tramp's Chronicle. Thomas Callaghan. 220p. 1983. 15.95 o.p. (ISBN 0-85362-201-9, Oriel Press). Routledge Chapman & Hall.

Tramps Like Us. Barbara Morgenroth. LC 78-13739. (gr. 6 up). 1979. 6.95 o.p. (ISBN 0-689-30690-3, Atheneum). Macmillan.

Trance in Bali. Jane Belo. LC 77-6361. 1977. Repr. of 1960 ed. lib. bdg. 35.75x o.p. (ISBN 0-8371-9652-3, BETR). Greenwood.

Trancework: An Introduction to Clinical Hypnosis. Michael D. Yapko. LC 84-19758. 350p. 1984. text ed. 38.50x incl. audiocassette o.p. (ISBN 0-8290-1525-6). Irvington.

Tranquilizing of America: Pill-Popping & the American Way of Life. Richard Hughes & Bob Brewin. LC 79-1830. (Illus.). 1979. 11.95 o.p. (ISBN 0-15-191072-3). HarBraceJ.

Trans-Canada Canoe Trail. David Lavender. LC 77-4864. (American Trail Ser.). 1977. text ed. 11.50 o.p. (ISBN 0-07-036678-0). McGraw.

Transactional Analysis & Family Therapy. James Horewitz. LC 79-51923. 1979. 30.00x o.p. (ISBN 0-87668-381-2). Aronson.

Transactional Analysis for Social Workers & Counsellors: An Introduction. Liz Pitman. (Library of Social Work). 172p. (Orig.). 1984. pap. 11.95x o.p. (ISBN 0-7100-9581-3). Routledge Chapman & Hall.

Transactions. Ed. by J. Kozesnik. 1967. 95.00 o.p. (ISBN 0-12-423858-0). Acad Pr.

Transactions, Vol. 92. 1984. lib. bdg. 595.00 o.p. (ISBN 0-89883-591-7, V92). Soc Auto Engineers.

Transactions Nineteen Seventy-Eight. 420p. 1979. 30.00 o.p. (ISBN 0-89520-263-8, 263-8); members o.p. 20.00 o.p. (ISBN 0-317-35850-2); student members o.p. 10.00 o.p. (ISBN 0-317-35851-0). SMM&E Inc.

Transactions of the American Association of Cost Engineers. Ed. by K. K. Humphreys & B. G. McMillan. (Illus.). 334p. 1982. 48.50 o.p. (ISBN 0-930284-15-1); pap. 38.50 o.p. (ISBN 0-930284-14-3). Am Assn Cost Engineers.

Transactions of the American Association of Cost Engineers. Ed. by K. K. Humphreys & T. Novak. (Illus.). 360p. 1983. 48.50x o.p. (ISBN 0-930284-18-6); pap. 38.50x o.p. (ISBN 0-930284-17-8). Am Assn Cost Engineers.

Transactions of the American Association of Cost Engineers, 1980. Ed. by K. K. Humphreys & B. G. McMillan. (Illus.). 429p. 1980. 40.00x o.p. (ISBN 0-930284-07-0); pap. 30.00x o.p. (ISBN 0-930284-08-9). Am Assn Cost Engineers.

Transactions of the American Association of Cost Engineers, 1981. Ed. by K. K. Humphreys & B. G. McMillan. 428p. 1981. 45.00x o.p. (ISBN 0-930284-13-5); pap. 35.00x o.p. (ISBN 0-930284-12-7). Am Assn Cost Engineers.

Transatlantic Dialogue: Selected American Correspondence of Edmund Gosse. Ed. by Paul F. Mattheisen & Michael Millgate. (Illus.). 349p. 1965. 20.00x o.p. (ISBN 0-292-73412-3). U of Tex Pr.

Transcendence Theory & Its Applications. A. Baker & D. W. Masser. 1978. 69.00 o.p. (ISBN 0-12-074350-7). Acad Pr.

Transcendent Meditations. Velma C. Redelfs. 72p. 1988. 7.95 o.p. (ISBN 0-8062-3019-3). Carlton.

Transcribing Speed Studies. Arnold Condon & Alan C. Lloyd. 1973. text ed. 15.56 o.p. (ISBN 0-07-012398-5). McGraw.

Transcript of Ombudsman Workshop: Recent Experience in the United States. Ed. by Stanley V. Anderson & John E. Moore. LC 72-5772. 294p. (Orig., Ombudsman workshop, Honolulu, May 5-7, 1971). 1972. pap. 3.00x o.p. (ISBN 0-87772-154-8). UCB IGS.

Transcript of the Money Market Symposium Relating to Appraisal of Railroad & Utility Properties. Arlo Woolery. (Lincoln Institute Monograph: No. 79-1). 238p. 1979. pap. text ed. 10.00 o.s.i. (ISBN 0-686-28296-5). Lincoln Inst Land.

Transcription of DNA. rev. ed. A. A. Travers. Ed. by J. J. Head. LC 76-29378. (Carolina Biology Readers Ser.: No. 75). (Illus.). 16p. (gr. 10 up). 1978. pap. 1.80 o.p. (ISBN 0-89278-275-7, 45-9675). Carolina Biological.

Transcription Thirty-Six. new ed. Arnold Condon et al. (Illus.). (gr. 11-12). 1976. text ed. 11.68 o.p. (ISBN 0-07-012400-0). McGraw.

Transcripts of Nineteen Eighty Three-Eighty Four: Developments Tapes. 1984. 45.00 o.p. (ISBN 0-88124-129-6). Cal Cont Ed Bar.

Transcripts of Nineteen Eighty-Two Developments Tapes. California Continuing Education of the Bar Staff. LC 77-74476. 245p. 1982. pap. 40.00 o.p. (ISBN 0-88124-091-5). Cal Cont Ed Bar.

Transcripts of 1983 Developments Tapes. LC 77-74476. 248p. 1983. 40.00 o.p. (ISBN 0-88124-116-4). Cal Cont Ed Bar.

Transcultural Nursing: Concepts, Theories & Practices. Madeleine Leininger. LC 77-28250. 532p. 1978. 36.00x o.p. (ISBN 0-471-52608-8, Pub by Wiley Medical). Wiley.

Transcultural Psychiatry. Ed. by John L. Cox. 352p. 1986. 50.00 o.p. (ISBN 0-7099-3428-9, Pub. by Croom Helm Ltd). Routledge Chapman & Hall.

Transfer. Thomas Palmer. LC 82-5518. 416p. 1982. 14.45 o.p. (ISBN 0-89919-130-4). Ticknor & Fields.

Transfer of Care: Psychiatric Deinstitutionalization & Its Aftermath. Phil Brown. 280p. 1984. 22.50x o.p. (ISBN 0-7100-9900-2). Routledge Chapman & Hall.

Transfer of Nuclear Technology. P. J. Howe. 1977. pap. 43.00 o.p. (ISBN 0-08-022132-7). Pergamon.

Titles

Titles

Transfer Processes. 2nd ed. D. K. Edwards et al. LC 78-7883. (Series in Thermal and Fluids Engineering). (Illus.). 1979. text ed. 49.95 o.p. (ISBN 0-07-019041-0). McGraw.

Transfer Theory for Trapped Electromagnetic Energy. 3rd ed. Georges Lucas. LC 84-13106. 104p. 1985. pap. 23.95 o.p. (ISBN 0-471-90573-9). Wiley.

Transferrin Biology. Stuart Kornfeld et al. (Illus.). 220p. 1973. text ed. 29.50x o.p. (ISBN 0-8422-7088-4). Irvington.

Transfiguration of the Commonplace: A Philosophy of Art. Arthur C. Danto. 222p. 1981. text ed. 21.00x o.p. (ISBN 0-674-90345-5). Harvard U Pr.

Transform Coding of Images. R. J. Clarke. (Microelectronics & Signal Processing Ser.). 1985. 59.00 o.p. (ISBN 0-12-175730-7); pap. 49.50 o.p. (ISBN 0-12-175731-5). Acad Pr.

Transform Theory. D. V. Widder. (Pure & Applied Mathematics Ser.: Vol. 42). 1971. 75.50 o.p. (ISBN 0-12-748550-3). Acad Pr.

Transformation el Utilisation des Legumineuses Alimentaires (Application Particuliere aux Pays en Development) A. Siegel & B. Fawcett. 63p. 1978. pap. 6.00 o.p. (ISBN 0-88936-123-1, IDRC-TS1F, IDRC). UNIPUB.

Transformation Groups & Representation Theory. T. Tom Dieck. (Lecture Notes in Mathematics: Vol. 766). 309p. 1979. pap. 21.00 o.p. (ISBN 0-387-09720-1). Springer-Verlag.

Transformation: New York Period see Petersburg & Paris Period.

Transformation of Europe, 1558-1648. Charles Wilson. LC 75-17283. 1976. 45.00x o.p. (ISBN 0-520-03075-3). U of Cal Pr.

Transformation of Nature in Art. Ananda K. Coomaraswamy 11.25 o.p. (ISBN 0-8446-0554-9). Peter Smith.

Transformation of Sin: Studies in Donne, Herbert, Vaughan & Traherne. Patrick Grant. (Illus.). 1974. 11.95x o.p. (ISBN 0-7735-0209-2, McGill Canada). U of Toronto Pr.

Transformation of Tissue Culture Cells by SV - 40 Viruses. Jorgen Fogh et al. LC 72-13562. (Illus.). 220p. 1973. text ed. 28.00x o.p. (ISBN 0-8422-7065-5). Irvington.

Transformation of Wall Street. Joel Seligman. 1982. 27.00 o.p. (ISBN 0-395-31329-5). HM.

Transformation Process in Joyce's Ulysses. Elliott B. Gose, Jr. 1980. 30.00x o.p. (ISBN 0-8020-5492-7). U of Toronto Pr.

Transformational Grammar: A Guide for Teachers. Joseph Aurbach et al. 1969. text ed. 12.95 o.p. (ISBN 0-87789-027-7). ELS Educ Servs.

Transformations. Roger L. Gould. 1978. 9.95 o.p. (ISBN 0-671-22521-9). S&S.

Transformations in Metals. Paul G. Shewmon. (Materials Science & Engineering Ser.). 1969. text ed. 39.00 o.p. (ISBN 0-07-056694-1, C). McGraw.

Transformations in Modern European Drama. Ed. by Ian Donaldson. 240p. 1983. text ed. 28.50x o.p. (ISBN 0-391-02486-8); pap. 10.00x o.p. Humanities.

Transformations in the Facial Region of the Human Embryo. C. Vermeij-Keers. LC 72-95480. (Advances in Anatomy, Embryology, & Cell Biology: Vol. 46, Pt. 5). (Illus.). 1973. pap. 10.70 o.p. (ISBN 0-387-06088-X). Springer-Verlag.

Transformations of Consciousness: Conventional & Contemplative Developmental Approaches. Ken Wilber et al. LC 85-2486. (New Science Library). 325p. (Orig.). 1986. 29.45 o.p. (ISBN 0-394-55537-6); 22.95 o.p. (ISBN 0-394-74202-8). Shambhala Pubns.

Transformations of the Lover, Vol. 7. Adonis. Tr. by Samuel Hazo from Arabic. (International Poetry Ser.). xiv, 95p. 1983. text ed. 18.95x o.p. (ISBN 0-8214-0754-6); pap. 10.95 o.p. (ISBN 0-8214-0755-4). Ohio U Pr.

Transformations of War. Jean L. Colin. LC 77-1125. (West Point Military Library). 1977. Repr. of 1912 ed. lib. bdg. 24.75x o.p. (ISBN 0-8371-9510-1, COTW). Greenwood.

Transformations: The Anthropology of Children's Play. Ed. by Helen B. Schwartzman. LC 78-12577. (Illus.). 398p. 1978. 45.00x o.p. (ISBN 0-306-31128-3, Plenum Pr). Plenum Pub.

Transformed by Thorns. Grant Martin. 156p. 1985. pap. 6.50 o.p. (ISBN 0-89693-397-0). Victor Bks.

Transformed Cell. Ed. by Ivan L. Cameron & Thomas B. Pool. (Cell Biology Ser.). 1981. 77.00 o.p. (ISBN 0-12-157160-2). Acad Pr.

Transformer. 1985. 12.95 o.p. (ISBN 0-8407-2885-9). Nelson.

Transformer & Inductor Design Handbook. C. McLyman. (Electrical Eng. & Electronics Ser.: Vol. 7). 1978. 59.75 o.p. (ISBN 0-8247-6801-9). Dekker.

Transforming Childhood: A Handbook for Personal Growth. Strephon Kaplan-Williams. (Illus.). 226p. 1988. 14.95 o.p. (ISBN 0-317-70102-9). Journey Pr.

Transforming Moment: Understanding Convictional Experiences. James E. Loder. LC 80-8354. 256p. 1981. 15.45 o.p. (ISBN 0-06-065276-4). HarpR.

Transforming Ordinary Income into Capital Gain. Pennsylvania Bar Institute Staff. 43p. 1985. 15.00 o.p. (ISBN 0-318-19076-1, 282). PA Bar Inst.

Transforming the School's Capacity for Problem Solving. Philip J. Runkel et al. LC 79-63379. 1979. 7.95 o.p. (ISBN 0-936276-08-8). Ctr Educ Policy Mgmt.

Transforming Your Office. Leslie Capek. LC 81-68395. (Illus.). 200p. (Orig.). 1981. pap. 6.95 o.p. (ISBN 0-89708-080-7). And Bks.

Transgenerational Family Therapy. Stuart Lieberman. 234p. 1979. 25.00 o.p. (ISBN 0-85664-776-4, Pub. by Croom Helm Ltd). Routledge Chapman & Hall.

Transient Two-Phase Flow: Proceedings of the Specialists Meeting, Toronto, Canada, Aug. 3-4, 1979, 2 vols. Specialists Meeting on Transient Two-Phase Flow Staff. Ed. by S. Banerjee & K. Weaver. (Illus.). 1978. Set. pap. text ed. 139.00 o.p. (ISBN 0-89116-153-8). Hemisphere Pub.

Transistor & Integrated Electronics. 4th ed. Milton S. Kiver. 1972. text ed. 45.95 o.p. (ISBN 0-07-034942-8). McGraw.

Transistor Audio Frequency Amplifiers. J. D. Jones. (Illus.). 100p. 1957. (ISBN 0-8022-0814-2). Philos Lib.

Transistor Circuit Design. Texas Instruments, Inc. Staff. (Illus.). 1963. text ed. 49.00 o.p. (ISBN 0-07-063737-7). McGraw.

Transistor Discontinued Devices. 1987. 70.00 o.p. DATA Busn Pub.

Transistor Replacement & Alternate Source Guide. Ed. by Jim Fitzerald. 200p. 1987. 85.00 o.p. (ISBN 0-317-57582-1). DATA Busn Pub.

Transistor Switching & Sequential Circuits. J. J. Sparkes. 1969. 60.00 o.p. (ISBN 0-08-012982-X); pap. 60.00 o.p. (ISBN 0-08-012981-1). Pergamon.

Transistors. Ed. by E. J. Kendall. LC 70-88307. 1969. text ed. 33.00 o.p. (ISBN 0-08-006511-2); pap. text ed. 12.75 o.p. (ISBN 0-08-006510-4). Pergamon.

Transistors: Fundamentals for the Integrated-Circuit Engineer. R. M. Warner & B. L. Grung. LC 83-10392. 875p. 1983. 69.95 o.p. (ISBN 0-471-09208-8, Pub. by Wiley-Interscience). Krieger.

Transit Development. (Transportation Research Record Ser.). 63p. 1979. 3.40 o.p. (ISBN 0-309-02969-4). Transport Res Bd.

Transit Planning & Operations. (Transportation Research Record Ser.). 63p. 1977. 3.20 o.p. (ISBN 0-309-02650-4). Transport Res Bd.

Transit Point Moscow. Gerald Amster & Bernard Asbell. LC 84-10788. 256p. 1985. 15.95 o.p. (ISBN 0-03-064156-X). H Holt & Co.

Transition from Feudalism to Capitalism. Maurice Dobb et al. 1978. 12.50x o.p. (ISBN 0-902308-51-3, Pub by NLB). Schocken.

Transition from School to Work. Michael A. West & Peggy Newton. 192p. 1982. 25.00 o.p. (ISBN 0-89397-140-5). Nichols Pub.

Transition Metal Chemistry, Vol. 8. Melson. 496p. 85.00 o.p. (ISBN 0-8247-1656-6). Dekker.

Transition Metal Chemistry: A Series of Advances, Vol. 4. Ed. by R. L. Carlin. 1968. 85.00 o.p. (ISBN 0-8247-1079-7). Dekker.

Transition Metal Chemistry: A Series of Advances, Vol. 5. Ed. by Richard L. Carlin. 1969. 85.00 o.p. (ISBN 0-8247-1080-0). Dekker.

Transition Metal Chemistry: A Series of Advances, Vol. 6. Ed. by Richard L. Carlin. LC 65-27431. 1970. 85.00 o.p. (ISBN 0-8247-1081-9). Dekker.

Transition Metal Complexes of Cyclic Polyolefins. G. Deganello. (Organometallic Chemistry Ser.). 1979. 152.00 o.p. (ISBN 0-12-207950-7). Acad Pr.

Transition Metal Intermediates in Organic Synthesis. C. W. Bird. 1967. 69.00 o.p. (ISBN 0-12-099750-9). Acad Pr.

Transition-Metal Organometallic Chemistry: An Introduction. R. B. King. 1969. 59.00 o.p. (ISBN 0-12-408040-5). Acad Pr.

Transition Metals in Homogeneous Catalysis. G. N. Schrauzer. 432p. 1971. 99.75 o.p. (ISBN 0-8247-1608-6). Dekker.

Transition to Socialist Economy. Charles Bettelheim. Ed. by John Mepham. Tr. by Brian Pearce from Fr. (Marxist Theory & Contemporary Capitalism Ser.). 248p. 1975. text ed. 19.00x o.p.; pap. text ed. 12.50x o.p. (ISBN 0-85527-741-6). Humanities.

Transition Toward More Rapid & Labor-Intensive Industrial Development: The Case of the Philippines. Barend A. De Vries. (Working Paper: No. 424). 32p. 1980. pap. 3.50 o.p. (ISBN 0-686-39755-X, WP-0424). World Bank.

Transitional Energy Policy 1980-2030: Alternative Nuclear Technologies. Hugh B. Stewart. (Pergamon Policy Studies on Science & Technology). 266p. 1981. 46.00 o.p. (ISBN 0-08-027183-9); pap. 70.00 o.p. (ISBN 0-08-027182-0). Pergamon.

Transitions: A Photographic Documentary of Squatter Settlements. Edward Popko. LC 77-17777. (Community Development Ser.: Vol. 42). (Illus.). 1982. 41.95 o.p. (ISBN 0-87933-316-2). Van Nos Reinhold.

Transitions: Four Rituals in Eight Cultures. Martha N. Fried & Morton H. Fried. 1980. 14.95 o.p. (ISBN 0-393-01350-2). Norton.

Transkei Region of Southern Africa, 1877-1978: An Annotated Bibliography. Jacqueline A. Kalley. 1980. lib. bdg. 33.50 o.p. (ISBN 0-8161-8297-3, Hall Reference). G K Hall.

Translation from Spanish: An Introductory Course. B. Steel. 1979. pap. 17.50 o.p. (ISBN 84-7143-189-0). E J Brill USA.

Translation of Lao Tzu's "Tao Te Ching" & Wang Pi's "Commentary." Paul J. Lin. (Michigan Monographs in Chinese Studies: No. 30). 232p. (Orig.). 1977. pap. 8.50 o.s.i. (ISBN 0-89264-030-8). U of Mich Ctr Chinese.

Translation of Scientific Russian. V. A. Pertzoff. 1964. text ed. 5.00 o.p. (ISBN 0-682-40068-8, University). Exposition-Phoenix.

Translations of Eastern Poetry & Prose. Tr. by Reynold A. Nicholson. 1969. Repr. of 1922 ed. lib. bdg. 22.50 o.p. (ISBN 0-8371-2301-1, NIEP). Greenwood.

Translations of German Poetry in American Magazines, 1741-1810. Edward Z. Davis. LC 66-27663. 240p. 1966. Repr. of 1905 ed. 35.00x o.p. (ISBN 0-8103-3209-4). Gale.

Transmigration of Bishop Timothy Archer. Philip K. Dick. 1982. 14.95 o.s.i. (ISBN 0-671-44066-7, Timescape). PB.

Transmission. M. A. Clement. 52p. 7.00 o.p. (ISBN 0-317-06288-3). Intertec IL.

Transmission Cost Comparison for Satellite, Fiber Optics & Microwave Radio Community. 225.00 o.p. (ISBN 0-686-32975-9). Info Gatekeepers.

Transmission Lines for Communications. C. W. Davidson. LC 78-4546. 218p. 1982. pap. 24.95x o.p. (ISBN 0-470-27358-5). Halsted Pr.

Transmission of Information by Orthogonal Functions. 2nd ed. H. F. Harmuth. LC 73-166296. (Illus.). 400p. 1972. 24.30 o.p. (ISBN 0-387-05512-6). Springer-Verlag.

Transmission of the Mind Outside the Teaching. Charles Luk. LC 75-15055. 1976. pap. 2.95 o.p. (ISBN 0-394-17888-2, E666, Ever). Grove.

Transnational Corporation & International Trade: Selected Issues. 11.00 o.p. (ISBN 92-1-104232-1, E.85.II.A.4). UN.

Transnational Corporations & International Trade: Selected Issues. United Nations Centre on Transnational Corporations Staff. 93p. 1985. pap. 11.00 o.p. (ISBN 92-1-104232-1, E.85.II.A.4). UN.

Transnational Corporations & Transborder Data Flows: A Technical Paper. 149p. 1982. pap. 12.00 o.p. (ISBN 92-1-104030-2, E.82.II.A.4). UN.

Transnational Corporations & Transborder Data Flows: A Technical Paper. 1982. pap. 12.00 o.p. (ISBN 0-317-66531-6, E.82.II.A.4). UN.

Transnational Corporations, Technology Transfer & Development: A Bibliographic Sourcebook. Tagi Sagafi-nejad & Robert Belfield. LC 80-36887. (Pergamon Policy Studies on International Development). 150p. 1981. 35.00 o.p. (ISBN 0-08-026299-6). Pergamon.

Transnationalism in World Politics & Business. Ed. by Forest L. Grieves. LC 79-1397. (Pergamon Policy Studies). 240p. 1979. 54.00 o.p. (ISBN 0-08-023892-0). Pergamon.

Transneuronal Degeneration in the Pontine Nuclei on the Cat. J. H. Trumpy. LC 78-163744. (Advances in Anatomy, Embryology & Cell Biology: Vol. 44, Pt. 1). (Illus.). 1971. pap. 28.40 o.p. (ISBN 0-387-05424-3). Springer-Verlag.

Transparencies: Philosophical Essays in Honor of J. Ferrater Mora. Ed. by Priscilla Cohn. 235p. 1981. text ed. 17.50x o.p. (ISBN 0-391-02361-6). Humanities.

Transparencies to Accompany Marketing. William G. Zikmund & Michael D'Amico. 152p. 1984. 25.00 o.p. (ISBN 0-471-80314-6). Wiley.

Transparency Acetates to Accompany Engineering Mechanics, Statics & Dynamics, 3rd ed. Russell C. Hibbeler. write for info. o.p.; transparency acetates avail. o.p. (ISBN 0-02-354440-6). Macmillan.

Transparent Eyeball & Other Stories. Dallas Wiebe. (Burning Deck Fiction Ser.). 120p. 1982. pap. 4.00 o.p. (ISBN 0-686-78010-8). Burning Deck.

Transparent Things. Vladimir Nabokov. LC 72-3989. 128p. 1972. text ed. 9.95 o.p. (ISBN 0-07-045734-4). McGraw.

Transparent Watercolor. Edward D. Walker. (Illus.). 176p. 1985. 24.95 o.p. (ISBN 0-89134-163-3). North Light Bks.

Transplants. Cynthia Macdonald. LC 75-30732. (Braziller Series of Poetry). 80p. 1976. 6.95 o.p. (ISBN 0-8076-0809-2); pap. 3.95 o.p. (ISBN 0-8076-0810-6). Braziller.

Transplants in Soil Blocks. Rev. ed. David Tresemer. (Illus.). 32p. 1986. pap. text ed. 3.00 o.p. (ISBN 0-938670-05-0). By Hand & Foot.

Transport & Economy: Turnpike Roads in Eighteenth Century Britain. E. Pawson. 1977. 82.50 o.p. (ISBN 0-12-546950-0). Acad Pr.

Transport & Handling in the Pulp & Paper Industry, Vol. 5. Ed. by John Kalish. LC 74-20162. (Illus.). 160p. 1984. 65.00 o.p. (ISBN 0-87930-158-9). Miller Freeman.

Transport & Handling in the Pulp & Paper Industry, Vol. 3: Proceedings of the International Symposium, 3rd, Vancouver, British Columbia, Canada, Sept., 1978. International Symposium on Transport & Handling in the Pulp & Paper Industry Staff. Ed. by John Kalish. LC 74-20162. (Pulp & Paper Book). (Illus.). 240p. 1979. 37.50 o.p. (ISBN 0-87930-109-0). Miller Freeman.

Transport & Handling in the Pulp & Paper Industry, Vol. 4: Proceedings of the International Symposium, 4th, London, England, Nov., 1980. International Symposium on Transport & Handling in the Pulp & Paper Industry, Staff. Ed. by John E. Kalish. LC 74-20162. (A Pulp & Paper Bk). (Illus.). 208p. 1981. 59.50 o.p. (ISBN 0-87930-127-9). Miller Freeman.

Transport & Handling in the Pulp & Paper Industry, Vol. 6: Proceedings - International Symposium, Lisbon. 180p. 1985. 75.00 o.p. (ISBN 0-87930-169-4). Miller Freeman.

Transport & Regional Development. W. A. Blonk. 352p. 1979. text ed. 47.50x o.p. (ISBN 0-566-00285-X). Gower Pub Co.

Transport & Travel from Nineteen Thirty to the Nineteen Eighty's. Frances Wilkins. (History in Focus Ser.). (Illus.). 72p. (gr. 7-12). 1985. 17.95 o.p. (ISBN 0-7134-4429-0, Pub. by Batsford England). David & Charles.

Transport in Skeletal Muscle. R. A. Sjodin. (Membrane Transport in the Life Sciences Ser.). 174p. 1982. text ed. 40.50 o.p. (ISBN 0-471-05265-5, Pub. by Wiley-Interscience). Krieger.

Transport Mechanisms in Epithelia: Proceedings of the Alfred Benzon Symposium, 5th. Benzon, Alfred, Symposium. Ed. by H. H. Ussing et al. 1973. 65.00 o.p. (ISBN 0-12-709550-0). Acad Pr.

Transport Mechanisms of Tryptophan in Blood Cells, Nerve Cells, & at the Blood-Brain Barrier: Proceedings of the International Symposium, Prilly-Lausanne, July 6-7, 1978. Ed. by P. Baumann. (Journal of Neural Transmission: Suppl. 15). (Illus.). 1979. 64.40 o.p. (ISBN 0-387-81519-8). Springer-Verlag.

Transport Mobility & Deprivation in Inter-Urban Areas. David Banister. 212p. 1980. text ed. 37.95x o.p. (ISBN 0-566-00307-4). Gower Pub Co.

Transport Network Planning. Patrick O'Sullivan et al. 187p. 1979. 28.00 o.p. (ISBN 0-85664-742-X, Pub. by Croom Helm Ltd). Routledge Chapman & Hall.

Transport of Dangerous Goods. 2nd, rev. ed. United Nations Economic & Social Council Staff. LC 82-81841. (Illus.). 462p. 1982. looseleaf 35.00 o.p. (ISBN 0-940394-04-9). INTEREG.

Transport of Ions & Water in Animals. B. L. Gupta et al. 1977. 90.00 o.p. (ISBN 0-12-307650-1). Acad Pr.

Transport Operators Guide to Professional Competence. G. J. Murphy. 314p. 1980. pap. 21.00x o.p. (ISBN 0-09-141591-8, Pub. by Busn Bks England). Gower Pub Co.

Transport Phenomena in Plants. D. A. Baker. (Outline Studies in Biology Ser.). 1978. pap. 8.50 o.p. (ISBN 0-412-15360-2, NO. 6022, Pub. by Chapman & Hall). Routledge Chapman & Hall.

Transport Phenomena Problem Solver. Research & Education Association Staff. LC 84-61816. (Illus.). 864p. 1988. pap. text ed. 28.85 o.p. (ISBN 0-87891-562-1). Res & Educ.

Transport Phenomena: Proceedings of the International School of Statistical Mechanics, Sitges, Barcelona, June, 1974. International School of Statistical Mechanics Staff. Ed. by G. Kirczenow & J. Marro. (Lecture Notes in Physics Ser.: Vol. 31). (Illus.). xiv, 517p. 1974. pap. 25.00 o.p. (ISBN 0-387-06955-0). Springer-Verlag.

Transport Planning: Vision & Practice. John Adams. 288p. (Orig.). 1981. pap. 17.50x o.p. (ISBN 0-7100-0844-9). Routledge Chapman & Hall.

Transport Processes in Solid Electrolytes see Physics of Electrolytes.

Transport Research for Social & Economic Progress: Proceedings of the World Conference, London, 1980, Vol. I. World Conference on Transport Research Staff. Ed. by J. Stuart Yerrell. 712p. 1981. 28.00x o.p. (ISBN 0-566-00443-7, 04708-2, Pub by Gower Pub Co England). Lexington Bks.

Transport Research for Social & Economic Progress: Proceedings of the World Conference, London, 1980, Vol. II. World Conference on Transport Research Staff. Ed. by J. Stuart Yerrell. 736p. 1981. 28.00x o.p. (ISBN 0-566-00444-5, 04709-0, Pub. by Gower Pub Co England). Lexington Bks.

Transport Research for Social & Economic Progress: Proceedings of the World Conference, London, 1980, Vol. III. World Conference on Transport Research Staff. Ed. by J. Stuart Yerrell. 800p. 1981. 28.00x o.p. (ISBN 0-566-00445-3, 04710-4, Pub. by Gower Pub Co England). Lexington Bks.

Transport Research for Social & Economic Progress: Proceedings of the World Conference, London, 1980, Vol. IV. World Conference on Transport Research Staff. Ed. by J. Stuart Yerrell. 536p. 1981. 28.00x o.p. (ISBN 0-566-00446-1, 04711-2, Pub. by Gower Pub Co England). Lexington Bks.

Transport Research for Social & Economic Progress: Proceedings of the World Conference, London, 1980, 4 vols. World Conference on Transport Research Staff. Ed. by J. Stuart Yerrell. 1981. Set. 100.00x o.p. (ISBN 0-686-76673-3, Pub. by Gower Pub Co England). Lexington Bks.

Transport Systems in Nigeria. Ed. by S. A. Olanrewaju & Toyin Falola. (Foreign & Comparative Studies- African Ser.: No. 42). (Orig.). 1986. pap. 14.00x o.p. (ISBN 0-915984-67-9). Syracuse U Foreign Comp.

Transport Technology for Developing Regions: A Study of Road Transportation in Venezuela. Richard M. Soberman. 1967. 25.00x o.p. (ISBN 0-262-19032-X). MIT Pr.

Transportation. Cain. LC 66-28623. (American History & Culture Ser.). (Illus.). (gr. 4 up). 1966. PLB 4.95, 5 or more 3.96 o.p. (ISBN 0-88296-048-2). Gateway Pr MI.

Transportation & Distribution Manager's Guide to Time Sharing. new ed. Malcolm J. Newbourne. Ed. by Kenneth Marshall. LC 79-88410. 1979. 25.00 o.p. (ISBN 0-87408-016-9). Intl Thom Trans Pr.

Transportation & Logistics. rev. ed. Marvin L. Fair & Ernest W. Williams, Jr. 1981. 37.95 o.p. (ISBN 0-256-02308-5). Irwin.

Transportation Costs & Costing, 1917-1973: A Select Annotated Chronological Bibliography. Emanuel B. Ocran, Jr. LC 75-2027. (Reference Library of Social Science: No. 10). 775p. 1975. 103.00 o.p. (ISBN 0-8240-1087-6). Garland Pub.

Transportation Decision-Making: A Guide to Social & Environmental Considerations. (National Cooperative Highway Research Program Report). 135p. 1975. 7.20 o.p. (ISBN 0-309-02331-9). Transport Res Bd.

Transportation Economics & Public Policy: With Urban Extensions. Alan Abouchar. LC 76-51828. 354p. 1977. 29.50 o.p. (ISBN 0-471-02101-6, Pub. by JW). Krieger.

Transportation Energy Conservation & Demand, 6 Reports. (Transportation Research Record Ser.). 68p. 1976. 5.00 o.p. (ISBN 0-309-02471-4). Transport Res Bd.

Transportation Engineering: Planning & Design. Radnor J. Paquette et al. 760p. 32.95x o.p. (ISBN 0-471-06670-2); tchrs.' manual 5.00 o.p. (ISBN 0-471-08440-9). Wiley.

Transportation Environmental & Conservation Concerns: Energy, Noise & Air Quality. (Transportation Research Record Ser.). 76p. 1977. 4.80 o.p. (ISBN 0-317-36108-2). Transport Res Bd.

Transportation Finance & Charges, Programming & Costs. (Transportation Research Record Ser.). 53p. 1978. 3.40 o.p. (ISBN 0-317-36109-0). Transport Res Bd.

Transportation for the Elderly, Handicapped & Disadvantaged: An Annotated Bibliography of Technical Reports. Joseph J. Galin. (Public Administration Ser.: P 1658). 19p. 1985. 3.00 o.p. (ISBN 0-89028-368-0). Vance Biblios.

Transportation for the Elderly, Handicapped & Disadvantaged: A Bibliography of Articles. Joseph J. Galin. (Public Administration Ser.: P 1659). 9p. 1985. 2.00 o.p. (ISBN 0-89028-369-9). Vance Biblios.

Transportation for the Poor, the Elderly & the Disadvantaged, 5 reports. (Transportation Research Record Ser.). 157p. 1974. 2.20 o.p. (ISBN 0-309-02360-2). Transport Res Bd.

Transportation Forecasting & Travel Behavior. (Transportation Research Record Ser.). 211p. 1978. 11.00 o.p. (ISBN 0-309-02813-2). Transport Res Bd.

Transportation Impact of the Canadian Mining Industry. Iain Wallace. 155p. (Orig.). 1977. pap. text ed. 10.50 o.p. (ISBN 0-88757-002-X, Pub. by Ctr Resource Stud Canada). Gower Pub Co.

Transportation Improvements in Madison, Wisconsin: Preliminary Analysis of Pricing Programs for Roads & Parking in Conjunction with Transit Changes. Franklin Spielberg. 65p. 1978. pap. 6.00x o.p. (ISBN 0-87766-234-7, 22400). Urban Inst.

Transportation in Cities. E. O. Pederson. 1981. 19.00 o.p. (ISBN 0-08-024666-4). Pergamon.

Transportation in the World of the Future. rev. ed. Hal Hellman. LC 73-86220. (World of the Future Ser.). (Illus.). 188p. (gr. 7 up). 1974. 6.95 o.p. (ISBN 0-87131-155-0). M Evans.

Transportation Information Sources. Ed. by Kenneth N. Metcalf. LC 65-24657. (Management Information Guide Ser.: No. 8). 308p. 1965. 68.00x o.p. (ISBN 0-8103-0808-8). Gale.

Transportation Investment & Pricing Principles: An Introduction for Engineers & Planners. Martin Wohl & Chris Hendrickson. LC 84-7347. (Construction Management & Engineering Ser.: No. 1-102). 380p. 1984. 49.95 o.p. (ISBN 0-471-87989-4, Pub. by Wiley-Interscience). Wiley.

Transportation Issues: The Disadvantaged, the Elderly & Citizen Involvement. (Transportation Research Record Ser.). 58p. 1976. 2.60 o.p. (ISBN 0-309-02597-4). Transport Res Bd.

Transportation Law. 4th ed. John Guandolo. 1072p. 1984. 58.00 o.p. (ISBN 0-205-11566-7, H1566-2). Allyn.

Transportation Law: Institute 81 (A Practice Primer for the Eighties - 14th Annual) University of Denver, College of Law Staff & Motor Carriers Lawyers Association Staff. 248p. 1981. 25.00 o.p. (ISBN 0-409-20026-3). Butterworth Legal Pubs.

Transportation-Logistics Dictionary 1977. Wallace I. Little. LC 77-79988. text ed. 10.00 o.p. (ISBN 0-87408-009-6). Intl Thom Trans Pr.

Transportation Markings: A Study in Communication. Brian Clearman. LC 80-6184. (Illus.). 489p. (Orig.). 1981. lib. bdg. 30.25 o.p. (ISBN 0-8191-1653-X); pap. text ed. 19.75 o.p. (ISBN 0-8191-1654-8). U Pr of Amer.

Transportation of Hazardous Materials. Office of Technology Assessment Staff. LC 87-13442. 278p. 1987. 22.50 o.p. (ISBN 0-89464-226-X). Krieger.

Transportation Programming & Management: Seven Reports. (Transportation Research Record Ser.). 78p. 1976. 3.60 o.p. (ISBN 0-309-02499-4). Transport Res Bd.

Transportation Programming, Economic Analysis, & Evalution of Energy Constraints. (Transportation Research Record Ser.). 66p. 1976. 3.00 o.p. (ISBN 0-309-02568-0). Transport Res Bd.

Transportation Regulation. 9th ed. Marvin L. Fair & John Guandolo. 496p. 1984. 42.00 o.p. (ISBN 0-205-11565-9, H1565-4). Allyn.

Transportation Requirements for the Handicapped, Elderly & Economically Disadvantaged. (National Cooperative Highway Research Program Synthesis of Highway Practice). 54p. 1976. 4.40 o.p. (ISBN 0-309-02515-X). Transport Res Bd.

Transportation Serving Community Needs, 7 reports. (Transportation Research Record Ser.). 49p. 1974. 2.40 o.p. (ISBN 0-309-02375-0). Transport Res Bd.

Transportation Strategies for the Eighties. Temple, Barker & Sloane, Inc. Staff. 30.00 o.p. (ISBN 0-318-04404-8); member 15.00 o.p. (ISBN 0-318-04405-6). Coun Logistics Mgt.

Transportation Supply Models. Ed. by Michael Florian & Marc Gaudry. 225p. 1981. pap. 34.00 o.p. (ISBN 0-08-026075-6). Pergamon.

Transportation System Analysis. (Transportation Research Record Ser.). 116p. 1978. 6.40 o.p. (ISBN 0-309-02822-1). Transport Res Bd.

Transportation System Analysis & Planning. (Transportation Research Record Ser.). 65p. 1980. 5.20 o.p. (ISBN 0-309-03061-7). Transport Res Bd.

Transportation, Vol. 3 (incl. 1985-1986 Supplements) Ed. by Eleanor C. Goldstein. (Social Issues Resources Ser.). 1987. 45.00 o.p. (ISBN 0-89777-082-X). Soc Issues.

Transporting Epithelia. Michael J. Berridge & James L. Oschman. (Monographs in the Ultrastructure of Cells & Organisms Ser.). 1972. 32.50 o.p. (ISBN 0-12-454135-6). Acad Pr.

Transracial Adoption: A Follow-Up. Rita J. Simon & Howard Altstein. LC 80-8770. 160p. 1981. 28.00x o.p. (ISBN 0-669-04357-5). Lexington Bks.

Transracial Adoption Today: Views of Adoptive Parents & Social Workers. Lucille J. Grow & Deborah Shapiro. LC 75-7553. 91p. 1975. pap. 6.95 o.s.i. (ISBN 0-87868-153-1, 1531). Child Welfare.

Transvestism: A Handbook for Psychologists, Psychiatrists & Counsellors. Harry Brierley. (Illus.). 160p. 1979. 45.00 o.p. (ISBN 0-08-022268-4); pap. 45.00 o.p. (ISBN 0-08-024686-9). Pergamon.

Transylvania: The Roots of Ethnic Conflict. Ed. by John F. Cadzow & Andrew Ludanyi. LC 82-23354. (Illus.). 360p. 1984. 32.50x o.p. (ISBN 0-87338-283-8). Kent St U Pr.

Trap for Perseus. Ludek Pesek. Tr. by Anthea Bell. LC 79-24862. 192p. (YA) (gr. 8 up). 1980. 9.95 o.s.i. (ISBN 0-02-774420-5). Bradbury Pr.

Trap Line. William L. Montalbano & Carl Hiaasen. LC 82-45177. 256p. 1982. 13.95 o.p. (ISBN 0-689-11307-2, Atheneum). Macmillan.

Trapped Charges. Ed. by F. Kieffer. 236p. 1976. pap. 42.00 o.p. (ISBN 0-08-019961-5). Pergamon.

Trapped in the Black Box. R. G. Austin. (Which Way Bks.: No. 12). (Orig.). (gr. 3-6). 1983. pap. 1.95 o.p. (ISBN 0-671-46731-X). Archway.

Trapped on the Golden Flyer. Susan Fleming. LC 77-15941. (Illus.). 126p. 1978. 8.95 o.s.i. (ISBN 0-664-32627-7, Westminster). Westminster John Knox.

Trapper. Thomas York. 496p. 1983. pap. 3.50 o.p. (ISBN 0-380-63156-3, 63156-3). Avon.

Traps & Lures in the Living World. Joan E. Rahn. LC 79-22699. (Illus.). (gr. 4-6). 1980. 8.95 o.p. (ISBN 0-689-30766-7, Atheneum). Macmillan.

Traps to Avoid in Good Administration. Robert E. Bingham. LC 78-67265. 1979. pap. 4.25 o.p. (ISBN 0-8054-2535-7). Broadman.

Traps, Traps. Caryl Churchill. 52p. (Orig.). 1981. pap. 5.95 o.p. (ISBN 0-904383-75-X, NO. 4122). Routledge Chapman & Hall.

Trapunto & Other Forms of Raised Quilting. Mary Morgan & Dee Mosteller. 1981. pap. 3.95 o.p. (ISBN 0-684-16942-8, ScribT). Scribner.

Trapunto Quilting. Mary Morgan & Dee Mosteller. LC 76-26180. (Illus.). 1977. 15.95 o.s.i. (ISBN 0-684-14821-8, ScribT). Scribner.

Trauma Center: Three Days in the Life of an Emergency Room Doctor. Randall S. Sword & Janet Keller. 192p. 1984. 12.95 o.p. (ISBN 0-684-18190-8, ScribT). Scribner.

Trauma of the Chest. Williams & Smith. 273p. 1977. pap. 26.00 o.p. (ISBN 0-7236-0484-3, Pub. by John Wright UK). Butterworth.

Traumatic Dislocation of the Hip. Herman Epstein. LC 79-9482. 336p. (Orig.). 1980. 43.00 o.p. (ISBN 0-683-02906-1, WW). Krieger.

Travail of Nature: The Ambiguous Ecological Promise of Christian Theology. H. Paul Santmire. LC 84-47934. 288p. 1985. 16.95 o.p. (ISBN 0-8006-1806-8, 1-1806, Fortress). Augsburg Fortress.

Travel & Discovery in the Renaissance, 1420-1620. Boies Penrose. LC 55-2546. 1962. pap. text ed. 4.95x o.p. (ISBN 0-689-70153-5, 10, Atheneum). Macmillan.

Travel & Lodging Law: Principles, Statutes & Cases. John R. Goodwin & James M. Rovelstad. 456p. 1984. (ISBN 0-471-84162-5). Wiley.

Travel & Tourism Audiovisual Guide. 2nd ed. Ed. by Jeanne Gay. 1982. pap. write for info. o.p. (ISBN 0-935638-05-9). Travel & Tourism.

Travel & Tourism Bibliography & Resource Guide, 6 vols. 2nd ed. Ed. by Jeanne Gay. (Orig.). 1982. pap. write for info. o.s.i. (ISBN 0-935638-04-0). Travel & Tourism.

Travel & Tourism Marketing Techniques: A Handbook of Travel Agency Advertising & Promotion. Robert T. Reilly. LC 79-92385. (Travel Management Library). 1980. 21.95 o.p. (ISBN 0-916032-08-6). Delmar.

Travel Behavior Analysis, 8 reports. (Transportation Research Record Ser.). 94p. 1974. 4.00 o.p. (ISBN 0-309-02374-2). Transport Res Bd.

Travel Behavior & Values, 6 reports. (Transportation Research Record Ser.). 69p. 1975. 3.20 o.p. (ISBN 0-309-02385-8). Transport Res Bd.

Travel Demand Forecasting, 7 reports. (Transportation Research Record Ser.). 104p. 1974. 4.40 o.p. (ISBN 0-309-02373-4). Transport Res Bd.

Travel Editor's Diary. Leavitt F. Morris. Orig. Title: Editor at Large. 160p. 1981. 12.50 o.p. (ISBN 0-682-49705-3). Exposition-Phoenix.

Travel Estimation Procedures for Quick Response to Urban Policy Issues. (National Cooperative Highway Research Program Report). 70p. 1978. 5.60 o.p. (ISBN 0-309-02774-8). Transport Res Bd.

Travel Games. Louis Phillips & Karen Markoe. (Magic Answer Bks.). (Illus.). 64p. (gr. 3-7). 1984. pap. 2.95 o.s.i. (ISBN 0-671-44922-2). Wanderer Bks.

Travel Guides. 128p. 1984. 4.95 o.p. (ISBN 0-317-07018-5, Berlitz). Macmillan.

Travel Healthy: The Traveler's Complete Medical Kit. Harold M. Silverman. 192p. 1986. pap. 3.50 o.p. (ISBN 0-380-89859-4). Avon.

Travel in Asia: A Guide to Information Sources. Ed. by Neal L. Edgar & Wendy Y. Ma. (Geography & Travel Information Guide Ser.: Vol. 6). 432p. 1983. 68.00x o.p. (ISBN 0-8103-1470-3). Gale.

Travel in Canada: A Guide to Information Sources. Ed. by Nora T. Corley. (Geography & Travel Information Guide Ser.: Vol. 4). 320p. 1982. 68.00x o.p. (ISBN 0-8103-1493-2). Gale.

Travel Industry. Choy Y. Gee & Dexter Choy. (Illus.). 1984. 29.95 o.p. (ISBN 0-87055-441-7). AVI.

Travel Industry Peronnel Directory, 1988. 24th ed. Book Division Staff. 450p. 1988. spiral bound 20.00 o.p. (ISBN 0-87005-667-0). Fairchild.

Travel Library. Rubin. 1987. pap. 22.90 o.p. (ISBN 0-471-62446-2). Wiley.

Travel Photography: Developing a Personal Style. Lisl Dennis. (Illus.). 138p. 1983. pap. text ed. 19.50 o.p. (ISBN 0-240-51765-2). Focal Pr.

Travel Sense: A Guide for Business & Professional Women. Barbara A. Pletcher. 196p. 1980. 9.95 o.p. (ISBN 0-936602-01-5). Kampmann.

Travelaid Guide to Egypt. 192p. 1980. pap. 14.95 o.p. (ISBN 0-902743-14-7, Pub. by Travelaid England). Hippocrene Bks.

Travelers by Night. Vivien Alcock. LC 85-1663. (Illus.). 192p. (gr. 4-6). 1985. pap. 14.95 o.p. (ISBN 0-385-29406-9). Delacorte.

Travelers By Night. Date not set. (ISBN 0-385-29406-9). Delacorte.

Traveler's Guide to Montana. Gary Turbak. LC 83-808928. (Illus.). 256p. (Orig.). 1983. pap. 7.95 o.p. (ISBN 0-934318-14-X). Falcon Pr MT.

Traveling. Nancy King. (Orig.). 1982. pap. 2.00 o.s.i. (ISBN 0-936563-01-X). Signpost.

Traveling a Half-Century: A Selection of Poems. Shirley Robertson. LC 85-51539. 53p. 1985. pap. 6.95x o.p. (ISBN 0-932269-57-5). Wyndham Hall.

Traveling Men of Ballycoo. Eve Bunting. LC 82-15799. (Illus.). 32p. (ps-3). 1983. 12.95 o.s.i. (ISBN 0-15-289792-5, HJ). HarBraceJ.

Traveling Psychoanalyst. new ed. Lawrence J. Friedman. LC 72-180305. (Illus.). 1978. pap. 5.95 o.p. (ISBN 0-8397-8375-2). Eriksson.

Traveling Toward Sunrise see Streams in the Desert.

Traveller in Time. Alison Uttley. (Illus.). 331p. (gr. 3-7). 1981. 9.95 o.p. (ISBN 0-571-06182-6). Faber & Faber.

Traveller in Turkey. Daniel Fearson. 224p. 1987. pap. 12.95 o.p. (ISBN 0-7102-1213-5, Pub. by Routledge UK). Routledge Chapman & Hall.

Traveller to Turkey. Daniel Farson. 224p. 1985. 19.95 o.p. (ISBN 0-7102-0281-4). Routledge Chapman & Hall.

Travellers' Dictionary of Quotation. Compiled by Peter Yapp. 1038p. 1989. pap. 22.50 o.p. (ISBN 0-415-02760-8). Routledge Chapman & Hall.

Travellers' Guide to Elba & the Tuscan Archipelago. Christopher Serpell & Jean Serpell. (Travellers' Guide Ser.). (Illus.). 256p. 1979. 14.95 o.p. (ISBN 0-224-01352-1, Pub. by Jonathan Cape). Salem Hse Pubs.

Traveller's Guide to France. Date not set. (ISBN 0-86145-776-5, Pub. by Auto Assn England). Salem Hse Pubs.

Travellers' Guide to Malta & Gozo. 3rd. ed. Christopher Kininmonth. (Travellers' Guide Ser.). (Illus.). 230p. 1979. pap. 14.95 o.p. (ISBN 0-224-01656-3, Pub. by Jonathan Cape). Salem Hse Pubs.

Traveller's Guide to North Africa. 216p. 1981. pap. 12.95 o.p. (ISBN 0-531-03964-1). Watts.

Traveller's Guide to the Middle East, 1984-85. 248p. 1984. pap. 12.95 o.p. Watts.

Traveller's Guide to West Africa. (Traveller's Guide Ser.). 248p. 1986. 12.95 o.p. (ISBN 0-531-03854-8). Watts.

Travelling. Andrew Taylor. LC 85-26386. 94p. 1987. 12.50 o.p. (ISBN 0-7022-1899-5). U of Queensland Pr.

Travelling Jobs for Women: A Guide to Exciting Career Opportunities. rev. ed. Sylvia B. Coppersmith. LC 73-135315. 48p. 1976. pap. 2.00 o.p. (ISBN 0-87576-037-6). Pilot Bks.

Travelling Soul. Hugh C. Rae. 1978. pap. 1.50 o.p. (ISBN 0-380-01854-3, 36517). Avon.

Travelling Wave Solid State Devices: A Special Issue of International Journal of Electronics, Vol. 58, No. 4. Technische Hochschule, Darmstadt Staff et al. 164p. 1985. pap. 49.00x o.p. (ISBN 0-85066-296-6). Taylor & Francis.

Travels. William Bartram. Ed. by Mark Van Doren. (Illus.). 15.50 o.p. (ISBN 0-8446-1600-1). Peter Smith.

Travels. Jan Morris. LC 76-2531. (Helen & Kurt Wolff Bk.). (Illus.). 160p. 1976. 7.95 o.p. (ISBN 0-15-191075-8). HarBraceJ.

Travels Amongst the Great Andes of the Equator. Edward Whymper. (Illus.). 524p. 1987. Repr. of 1896 ed. 24.95 o.p. (ISBN 0-87905-281-3, Peregrine Smith). Gibbs Smith Pub.

Travels in Arabia Deserta, 2 vols. Charles M. Doughty. Set. 36.00 o.p. (ISBN 0-8446-5750-6); Vol. I. (ISBN 0-8446-5751-4); Vol. II. (ISBN 0-8446-5752-2). Peter Smith.

Travels in Brazil. Henry Koster. Ed. by Harvey C. Gardiner. LC 65-16537. (Latin American Travel Ser.). 216p. 1966. 5.85x o.p. (ISBN 0-8093-0205-5). S Ill U Pr.

Travels in the Interior of Mexico in 1825, 1826, 1827 & 1828: In Baja California & Around the Sea of Cortes. R. W. Hardy. (Beautiful Rio Grande Classics Ser.). 606p. Repr. of 1828 ed. 25.00 o.p. (ISBN 0-87380-146-6). Rio Grande.

Travels of Fa-hsien, 399 to 144 A.D. Or Record of the Buddhistic Kingdoms. Fl. Fa-hsien. Tr. by M. A. Giles & H. A. Giles. LC 81-13362. xx, 96p. 1982. Repr. of 1956 ed. lib. bdg. 35.00x o.p. (ISBN 0-313-23240-7, FATR). Greenwood.

Travels of Lao Can. Liu E. 176p. 1983. pap. 4.95 o.p. (ISBN 0-8351-1075-3). China Bks.

Travels of Soc. (MicroSoc Thinking Games Ser.). (gr. k-8). 1985. 12.50 o.p. (ISBN 0-88671-209-2). Am Guidance.

Travels of the Golden Fish & Other Bilingual Children's Stories. Rafael A. Urena. LC 85-90097. 37p. 1985. 5.95 o.p. (ISBN 0-533-06610-7). Vantage.

Travels to New Guinea. N. Miklouho-Maclay. 519p. 1982. 9.95 o.p. (ISBN 0-8285-2459-9, Pub. by Progress Pubs USSR). Imported Pubns.

Travels with an Angle. Ken Sutton. 1987. 20.00 o.p. (ISBN 0-85115-483-2, Pub. by Boydell & Brewer). Longwood Pub Group.

Travels with Henry. Richard Valeriani. 1979. 12.95 o.p. (ISBN 0-395-27091-X). HM.

Travesties. Tom Stoppard. LC 75-13552. 1975. 6.95 o.p. (ISBN 0-394-49930-1, GP767). Grove.

Traviata. Giuseppes Verdi. (Metropolitan Opera Classics Library). pap. 22.00i o.p. (ISBN 0-316-56842-2); pap. 11.45i o.p. (ISBN 0-316-56843-0). Little.

Treachery at Cimarron. Jim Ross. 320p. 1984. pap. 3.95 o.p. (ISBN 0-8423-7330-6). Tyndale.

Treachery on the Double. H. Eugene Barfield. 1979. 7.00 o.p. (ISBN 0-682-49263-9). Exposition-Phoenix.

Treasure & the Song. Mildred Lawrence. LC 66-10203. (gr. 7 up). 1966. 4.95 o.p. (ISBN 0-15-289950-2, HJ). HarBraceJ.

Treasure from Haunted Pagoda. Eric B. Hare. 1985. pap. 6.50 o.p. Pacific Pr Pub Assn.

Treasure Hunt. Frederick Buechner. LC 77-4743. 1977. 7.95 o.p. (ISBN 0-689-10800-1, Atheneum). Macmillan.

Treasure Hunters Buyers Guide. Ed. by Rosemary Anderson. (Illus.). 128p. (Orig.). 1988. pap. 7.95 o.p. Peoples Pub.

Treasure Island. Robert Louis Stevenson. LC 86-63583. (Illus.). 224p. (gr. 5 up). 1987. 12.95 o.p. (ISBN 0-89577-262-0). Rd Assn.

Treasure of Alpheus Winterborn. John Bellairs. LC 77-88959. (Illus.). (gr. 5-7). 1978. 7.95 o.p. (ISBN 0-15-289936-7, HJ). HarBraceJ.

Treasure of Brewsters Neck or a Busy Little Summer. Walter G. Miller. 1978. 9.00 o.p. (ISBN 0-682-49145-4). Exposition-Phoenix.

Treasure of Green Knowe. Lucy M. Boston. LC 58-8731. (Illus.). (gr. 4-6). 1958. 8.95 o.s.i. (ISBN 0-15-289979-0, HJ). HarBraceJ.

Treasure of Green Knowe. Lucy M. Boston. LC 77-16689. (Illus.). (gr. 4-7). 1978. pap. 1.95 o.p. (ISBN 0-15-691302-X, VoyB). HarBraceJ.

Treasure of Green Knowe see Adventures at Green Knowe.

Treasure of Guatavita: El Tesoro De Guatavita. Adapted by Harriet Rohmer & Jesus G. Rea. LC 76-29081. (Fifth World Tales Ser.). (Illus.). 24p. (gr. k-6). 1976. pap. 5.95 spanish bilingual ed. o.p. (ISBN 0-89239-010-7). Childrens Book Pr.

Treasure of Li-Po. Alice Ritchie. LC 49-10204. (Illus.). (gr. 4-6). 1949. 4.50 o.p. (ISBN 0-15-290158-2, HJ). HarBraceJ.

Treasure of Lost Dragon Castle. Ralph Warner & Toni Ihara. (gr. 3-8). 1975. pap. 3.50 o.p. (ISBN 0-917316-10-X). Nolo Pr.

Treasure of Sainte-Foy. MacDonald Harris. LC 79-23242. 1980. 11.95 o.p. (ISBN 0-689-11025-1, Athenuem). Macmillan.

Treasure of Sao Roque. William Tefler. (Church Historical Society London N. S. Ser.: No. 14). Repr. of 1932 ed. 40.00 o.p. (ISBN 0-8115-3137-6). Kraus Repr.

Treasure of Superstition Mountains. Gary Jennings. (Illus.). 256p. 1974. 7.95 o.p. (ISBN 0-393-08678-X). Norton.

Treasure of Sutton Hoo: Ship Burial for an Anglo-Saxon King. Bernice Grohskopf. LC 74-86555. (Illus.). 1973. pap. text ed. 2.95x o.p. (ISBN 0-689-70362-7, 199, Atheneum). Macmillan.

Treasure of the Atocha. R. Duncan Mathewson, III. LC 85-30978. (Illus.). 192p. 1986. 24.95 o.p. (ISBN 0-86636-044-1, Pub. by Pisces Bks). PBC Intl Inc.

Treasure of Topo-el-Bampo. Scott O'Dell. LC 72-135138. (Illus.). 48p. (gr. k-4). 1973. reinforced bdg. 6.95 o.p. (ISBN 0-395-16962-3). HM.

Treasure of Wonderwhat: A Farstar & Son Novel. Bill Starr. 240p. 1983. pap. 2.50 o.s.i. (ISBN 0-345-30968-5, Del Rey). Ballantine.

Treasure Preserved. David Williams. 224p. 1987. pap. 2.95 o.p. (ISBN 0-380-70256-8). Avon.

Treasure Train. Robert A. McGuire. 224p. (Orig.). 1982. pap. 2.25 o.p. (ISBN 0-8439-1030-5, Pub. by Leisure Bks CT). Dorchester Pub Co.

Treasure-Trove of American Jewish Humor. Henry D. Spalding. LC 75-40192. 429p. 1976. 16.95 o.p. (ISBN 0-8246-0204-8). Jonathan David.

Treasure Trove: The Great Undiscovered Treasures of the World. Tim Haydock. (Illus.). 160p. 1986. pap. 9.95 o.p. (ISBN 0-03-008568-3, Owl Bks). H Holt & Co.

Treasure Wreck: The Fortunes & Fate of the Pirate Ship Whydah. Arthur T. Vanderbilt, II. (Illus.). 160p. 1986. 16.45 o.p. (ISBN 0-395-39975-0). HM.

Treasured Alabama Recipes. rev. & enl. ed. Kathryn T. Windham. LC 67-28975. (Illus.). 1967. 5.95 o.p. (ISBN 0-87397-009-8). Strode.

Treasured Georgia Recipes. Kathryn T. Windham. LC 73-87005. 1973. 4.95 o.p. (ISBN 0-87397-045-4). Strode.

Treasured Tennessee Recipes. Kathryn T. Windham. LC 72-91391. 1972. 5.95 o.p. (ISBN 0-87397-021-7). Strode.

Treasures see Word Studies in the Greek New Testament, for the English Reader.

Treasures from the Kremlin: E. S. Sizov, Chief Curator of the State Museums of the Moscow Kremlin. E. S. Sizov. Tr. by John E. Bowlt. LC 79-1051. (Illus.). 224p. 1979. 9.95 o.p. (ISBN 0-87099-193-0); pap. 29.95 o.p. (ISBN 0-87099-192-2, MPLD2081). Metro Mus Art.

Treasures of Islam. Ed. by Toby Falk. LC 85-50362. (Illus.). 400p. 1985. 45.95 o.p. (ISBN 0-85667-196-7, Pub. by P Wilson Pubs). Sotheby Pubns.

Treasures of Italy. Giuliano Dogo. (Illus.). 1976. 19.85 o.p. (ISBN 0-393-08365-9). Norton.

Treasures of My Heart. Carol R. Bailey. 1985. 5.95 o.p. (ISBN 0-317-28977-2). Vantage.

Treasures of San Marco. Ed. by David Buckton. 1985. 75.00 o.p. (ISBN 0-317-31359-2). Metro Mus Art.

Treasures of the Heras Institute. Kalpana Desai. LC 76-905157. (Illus.). 1976. 20.00x o.p. (ISBN 0-88386-923-3). South Asia Bks.

Treasures of the Holy Land: Ancient Art from the Israel Museum. Curators of the Israel Museum. (Illus.). 280p. 1986. 29.95 o.p. (ISBN 0-87099-471-9, Dist. by Harry N Abrams Inc.); pap. 19.95 o.p. (ISBN 0-87099-470-0, Dist. by Harry N Abrams Inc.). Metro Mus Art.

Treasures of the Holy Land: Ancient Art from the Israel Museum. Curators of the Israel Museum, Jerusalem, Staff. (Illus.). 288p. 1987. 39.50 o.s.i. (ISBN 0-8109-1692-4). Abrams.

Treasures of the Hood Museum of Art, Dartmouth College. Jacquelynn Baas et al. LC 85-14526. (Illus.). 160p. 1985. 35.00 o.p. (ISBN 0-933920-71-7, Dist by Rizzoli); pap. 20.00 museum distribution only o.p. (ISBN 0-933920-72-5). Hudson Hills.

Treasures of the Medranos. Elizabeth H. Atkins. LC 57-8066. (Illus.). (gr. 3-7). 1957. 4.25 o.p. (ISBN 0-395-27666-7, Pub. by Parnassus). HM.

Treasures to See: A Museum Picture-Book. Leonard Weisgard. LC 56-10739. (Illus.). (gr. k-3). 1956. 6.95 o.p. (ISBN 0-15-290337-2, HJ). HarBraceJ.

Treasury Alarm. Jocelyn Davey. 240p. 1982. pap. 2.50 o.p. (ISBN 0-380-58917-6, 58917). Avon.

Treasury Control & Social Administration. Roy M. MacLeod. 62p. 1968. pap. text ed. 5.00x o.p. (ISBN 0-686-70860-1, Pub. by Bedford England). Gower Pub Co.

Treasury of American Poetry: A Collection of the Finest by America's Poets. Intro. by Nancy Sullivan. LC 77-92232. 1978. 21.50 o.p. (ISBN 0-385-12032-X). Doubleday.

Treasury of American Superstitions. Claudia De Lys. LC 79-5441. 320p. 1958. Philos Lib.

Treasury of Animal Stories. Linda Yeatman. Ed. by Kate Klimo. (Illus.). 160p. (gr. k-4). 1982. pap. 7.95 o.s.i. (ISBN 0-671-45632-6, Little Simon). S&S.

Treasury of Art Nouveau Design & Ornament. Carol Belanger Grafton. 1983. 15.75 o.p. (ISBN 0-8446-5949-5). Peter Smith.

Treasury of Birdlore. Ed. by Joseph W. Krutch & Paul S. Eriksson. LC 62-16745. (Illus.). 1977. pap. 7.95 o.p. (ISBN 0-8397-8371-X). Eriksson.

Treasury of Bookplates from the Renaissance to the Present. Ed. by Fridolf Johnson. (Illus.). 14.75 o.p. (ISBN 0-8446-5587-2). Peter Smith.

Treasury of Contemporary Houses. Architectural Record Magazine Editors. (Illus.). 1978. text ed. 52.50 o.p. (ISBN 0-07-002330-1). McGraw.

Treasury of Embroidery Samples. Ondori Publishing Company Staff. LC 80-84416. (Illus.). 96p. 1981. pap. 6.50 o.p. (ISBN 0-87040-496-2). Japan Pubns USA.

Treasury of Epigrams. Samuel Hurwitt. LC 60-15957. 366p. 1961. (ISBN 0-8022-0764-2). Philos Lib.

Treasury of Games & Puzzles. C. Wallace. 256p. 1958. (ISBN 0-8022-1798-2). Philos Lib.

Treasury of Great Poems, 2 vols. rev. ed. Ed. by Louis Untermeyer. Incl. Vol. 1. Chaucer to Burns. 1964. pap. 5.95 o.p. (ISBN 0-671-75020-8); Vol. 2. Wordsworth to Dylan Thomas. 1964. pap. 7.95 o.p. (ISBN 0-671-75021-6). pap. (Fireside). S&S.

Treasury of Knitting Patterns. Barbara G. Walker. LC 67-24064. (Illus.). 1968. 10.00 o.s.i. (ISBN 0-684-10627-2, ScribT). Scribner.

Treasury of Modern Fantasy. Carr & Greenberg. 1983. pap. 8.95 o.p. (ISBN 0-380-77115-2, 77115-2). Avon.

Treasury of Needlecraft Gifts for the New Baby. Jean R. Laury. 1978. pap. 3.95 o.p. (ISBN 0-380-40113-4, 40113). Avon.

Treasury of Needlecraft Gifts for the New Baby. Jean R. Laury. LC 76-12186. (Illus.). 192p. 1976. 12.95 o.s.i. (ISBN 0-8008-7858-2). Taplinger.

Treasury of Needlecrafts. Ed. by Better Homes & Gardens Books Editors. (Illus.). 480p. 1982. 24.95 o.p. (ISBN 0-696-00755-X). BH&G.

Treasury of Parables. Edward J. Bartek. 292p. 1960. (ISBN 0-8022-0070-2). Philos Lib.

Treasury of Parenthood & Its Folklore. Claudia De Lys. 5.00 o.p. (ISBN 0-8315-0016-6). Speller.

Treasury of Philosophy. Dagobert D. Runes. 1308p. (ISBN 0-8022-1452-5). Philos Lib.

Treasury of Plays for Women. Ed. by Frank Shay. LC 79-50030. (One-Act Plays in Reprint Ser.). 1980. 34.50x o.p. (ISBN 0-8486-2054-2). Roth Pub Inc.

Treasury of Superstitions. Claudia De Lys. LC 60-15949. (Illus.). 288p. 1960. (ISBN 0-8022-0374-4). Philos Lib.

Treasury of the Great Children's Book Illustrators. Susan E. Meyer. LC 83-2500. (Illus.). 272p. 1983. 45.00 o.p. (ISBN 0-8109-0782-8). Abrams.

Treasury of Windmill Books. Charles Addams & Jose Aruego. LC 81-48387. (Illus.). 64p. (gr. 3 up). 1982. lib. bdg. 8.79 o.s.i. (ISBN 0-671-44802-1). Messner.

Treasury of Witchcraft. Harry Wedeck. (Illus.). 271p. 1960. (ISBN 0-8022-1840-7). Philos Lib.

Treasury of Woodworking Projects. Ed. by Science & Mechanics Magazine Staff. (Illus.). 224p. 1985. 23.95 o.p. (ISBN 0-668-06325-4). Arco.

Treasury of World Science. Dagobert D. Runes. (Quality Paperback Ser.: No. 108). 978p. (Orig.). 1962. pap. 4.95 o.p. (ISBN 0-8226-0108-7). Littlefield.

Treasury of World Science. Dagobert D. Runes. LC 61-15249. 1978p. 1962. (ISBN 0-8022-1455-X). Philos Lib.

Treaties in Force: A List of Treaties & Other International Agreements of the United States inForce on January 1, 1987. (State Department Publication Ser.: 9433). 360p. 1987. pap. 16.00 o.p. (ISBN 0-318-23532-3, S/N 044-000-02183-8). USGPO.

Treating Martial Arts Injuries. Dennis R. Burke. Ed. by Bill Griffeth. LC 81-81332. (Series 412). 1981. pap. 9.95 o.p. (ISBN 0-89750-075-X). Ohara Pubns.

Treating Mental Illness: Aspects of Modern Therapy. Ed. by Alfred M. Freedman & Harold I. Kaplan. LC 79-178074. (Studies in Human Behavior Ser). 1972. pap. text ed. 4.95x o.p. (ISBN 0-689-70286-8, HB4, Atheneum). Macmillan.

Treating the Mentally Disabled. Ed. by Gary McCuen. (Ideas in Conflict Ser.). (Illus.). 140p. 1988. lib. bdg. 11.95 o.p. (ISBN 0-86596-066-6). GEM McCuen Pubns.

Treatise of Daunces. Bd. with Godly Exhortation by Occasion of the Late Judgement of God at Parris Garden. John Fields. (English Stage Ser.: Vol. 5). 1974. lib. bdg. 61.00 o.p. (ISBN 0-8240-0588-0). Garland Pub.

Treatise of Man. Rene Descartes. Tr. & commentary by Thomas S. Hall. LC 76-173412. (Monographs in the History of Science Ser). (Illus., Fr. & Eng.). 1972. 17.50x o.s.i. (ISBN 0-674-90710-8). Harvard U Pr.

Treatise on Analytical Chemistry, Vol. 7. 2nd ed. I. M. Kolthoff & Philip J. Elving. LC 78-1707. (Treatise on Analytical Chemistry Ser.: Pt. 1). 816p. 1981. 98.95 o.p. (ISBN 0-471-07996-0, Pub. by Wiley-Interscience). Wiley.

Treatise on Ancient Painting. George Turnbull. 248p. Repr. of 1940 ed. cancelled o.s.i. (ISBN 3-7705-0506-9). Adlers Foreign Bks.

Treatise on Angel Magic, Being a Complete Transcription of Ms. Harley 6482 in the British Library. Rudd. Ed. by Adam Mclean. (Magnum Opus Hermetic Sourceworks Ser.: No. 15). (Illus.). 173p. (Orig.). 1987. pap. 18.00 o.p. (ISBN 0-933999-07-0). Phanes Pr.

Treatise on Constitutional Law, 1987: Substance & Procedure, 3 vols. John Nowak & Ronald Rotunda. 292p. 1987. Pocket Parts. write for info. o.p. (ISBN 0-314-42493-8). West Pub.

Treatise on Generating Functions. H. M. Srivastava & H. L. Manocha. LC 83-12913. (Mathematics & Its Applications Ser.: 1-176). 569p. 1984. 95.00x o.p. (ISBN 0-470-20010-3). Halsted Pr.

Treatise on Language. Alexander B. Johnson. Ed. by David Rynin. LC 68-25841. 1969. pap. text ed. 5.00 o.p. (ISBN 0-486-22019-2). Dover.

Treatise on Materials Science & Technology, Vol. 18: Ion Implantation. Ed. by H. Herman. 1980. 89.00 o.p. (ISBN 0-12-341818-6). Acad Pr.

Treatise on Ornithology, 2 vols. in one. Frank M. Chapman. 355p. 1987. 237.55 o.p. (ISBN 0-86650-224-6). Gloucester Art.

Treatise on Political Economy. A. Destutt De Tracy. LC 67-23018. 1970. Repr. of 1817 ed. 45.00x o.s.i. (ISBN 0-678-00656-3). Kelley.

Treatise on Presumptions of Law & Fact, with the Theory & Rules of Presumptive or Circumstantial Proof in Criminal Cases. W. M. Best. 222p. 1981. Repr. of 1845 ed. lib. bdg. 25.00x o.p. (ISBN 0-8377-0319-0). Rothman.

Treatise on Soil Science. K. D. Glinka. 680p. 1963. text ed. 135.00x o.p. (ISBN 0-317-46451-5, Pub. by Keter Pub Jerusalem). Coronet Bks.

Treatise on Solar Energy, Vol. 1: Fundamentals of Solar Energy. H. P. Garg. LC 81-21951. 400p. 1983. 82.95x o.p. (ISBN 0-471-10180-X). Wiley.

Treatise on the Art of Pianoforte Construction. Samuel Wolfenden. 288p. 1984. soft linen-type cover 40.00x o.p. (ISBN 0-905418-09-3, Pub. by Gresham England). State Mutual Bk.

Treatise on the Love of God. Saint Francoise De Sales. Tr. by Henry B. Mackey. LC 71-156190. xiiv, 555p. 1971. Repr. of 1942 ed. lib. bdg. 31.75x o.p. (ISBN 0-8371-6139-8, FRLG). Greenwood.

Treatise on Wood Engraving, Historical & Practical. William A. Chatto. LC 69-16477. (Illus.). 698p. 1969. Repr. of 1861 ed. 65.00x o.p. (ISBN 0-8103-3531-X). Gale.

Treatises & Sermons of Meister Eckhart. Meister Eckhart et al. Tr. by James M. Clark & John V. Skinner. 267p. 1983. Repr. of 1958 ed. lib. bdg. 21.00 o.p. (Octagon). Hippocrene Bks.

Treatment & Management of Urban Solid Waste. David G. Wilson. LC 70-182527. 210p. 1972. pap. 14.95 o.p. (ISBN 0-87762-077-6). Technomic.

Treatment & the Cure. Peter Kocan. LC 85-14818. 1985. 14.95 o.s.i. (ISBN 0-8008-7867-1). Taplinger.

Treatment of Brain Tumors. 1983. 1.50 o.p. (ISBN 0-318-03973-7). Assn Brain Tumor.

Treatment of Burkitt's Tumor: Proceedings. International Union Against Cancer - Chemotherapy Panel. Ed. by J. H. Burchenal & D. P. Burkitt. (U I C C Monograph Ser.: Vol. 8). (Illus.). 1967. 74.40 o.p. (ISBN 0-387-04010-2). Springer-Verlag.

Treatment of Disordered Function from Pain to Sexual Complaints: An Introduction to the Edagawa Method. Lawrence W. Friedmann & Naoyushi Edagawa. (Illus.). 192p. 1981. 20.00x o.p. (ISBN 0-682-49665-0, University). Exposition-Phoenix.

Treatment of Drinking Water for Organic Contaminants: Proceedings of the Second National Conference on Drinking Water, Edmonton, Alberta, Canada, 7-8 April 1986. Ed. by P. M. Huck & P. Toft. (Illus.). 388p. 1987. 92.00 o.p. (ISBN 0-08-031876-2). Pergamon.

Treatment of End Stage Renal Disease in Children. Richard N. Fine & Alan Gruskin. (Illus.). 590p. 1984. write for info. o.p. (ISBN 0-7216-1025-0). Saunders.

Treatment of Malignant Breast Tumors - Indications & Results: A Study Based on 1174 Cases Treated at the Institute Gustave-Roussy Between 1954 & 1962. Pierre Denoix. Tr. by Barbara Crook from Fr. LC 70-117714. (Recent Results in Cancer Research: Vol. 31). (Illus.). 1970. 34.00 o.p. (ISBN 0-387-04996-7). Springer-Verlag.

Treatment of Mycosis with Imidazole Derivatives. W. Raab. (Illus.). 180p. 1980. pap. 17.00 o.p. (ISBN 0-387-09800-3). Springer-Verlag.

Treatment of Partially Edentulous Patients. Louis J. Boucher & Robert P. Renner. LC 81-19016. (Illus.). 352p. 1982. text ed. 43.95 o.p. (ISBN 0-8016-0821-X). Mosby.

Treatment of Phobic & Obsessive Compulsive Disorders. Ed. by John C. Boulougouris & Andreas D. Rabalivas. 1977. 34.00 o.p. (ISBN 0-08-021472-X). Pergamon.
Treatment of Pituitary Adenomas. Ed. by Rudolf Fahlbusch & Klaus Von Werder. LC 77-99148. (Illus.). 458p. 1978. pap. 42.50 o.p. (ISBN 0-88416-236-2). Year Bk Med.
Treatment of Psychotic & Neurologically Impaired Children: A Systems Approach. David M. Brubakken et al. 288p. 1980. 28.95 o.p. (ISBN 0-442-26647-2). Van Nos Reinhold.
Treatment of Sexual Problems in Individuals & Couples Therapy. Ed. by Robert A. Brown & Joan R. Field. 460p. Date not set. 45.00 o.s.i. (ISBN 0-08-035150-6, PBI). Pergamon.
Treatment of Skin Cancer. R. G. Freeman & J. M. Knox. (Recent Results in Cancer Research Ser.: Vol. 11). (Illus.). 1967. 15.00 o.p. (ISBN 0-387-03959-7). Springer-Verlag.
Treatment of the Young Delinquent. J. Arthur Hoyles. 286p. 1953. (ISBN 0-8022-0752-9). Philos Lib.
Treatment or Diagnosis: A Study of Repeat Prescriptions in General Practice. Michael Balint et al. 208p. 1984. pap. text ed. 17.95 o.p. (ISBN 0-422-78770-1, 4004). Routledge Chapman & Hall.
Treatment Planning for External Beam Therapy with Neutrons. Georg Burger. (Illus.). 250p. 1982. 52.00 o.p. (ISBN 0-8067-0271-0). Urban & S.
Treats. Christopher Hampton. 62p. 1976. pap. 4.95 o.p. (ISBN 0-571-10967-5). Faber & Faber.
Treaty Between the U. S. & the Indians of the Willamette Valley. facs. ed. Isaac I. Stevens. 8p. pap. 3.00 o.s.i. (ISBN 0-8466-0112-5, S112). Shorey.
Treaty Between the U. S. & the Nisqually & Other Bands of Indians. facs. ed. Isaac I. Stevens. 8p. pap. 3.00 o.s.i. (ISBN 0-8466-0109-5, S109). Shorey.
Treaty Between the U. S. & the Yakima Nation of Indians. facs. ed. Isaac I. Stevens. 8p. pap. 3.00 o.s.i. (ISBN 0-8466-0110-9, S110). Shorey.
Treaty Ports & China's Modernization: What Went Wrong? Rhoads Murphey. (Michigan Monographs in Chinese Studies: No. 7). 84p. (Orig.). 1970. pap. 6.00 o.s.i. (ISBN 0-89264-007-3). U of Mich Ctr Chinese.
Treaty Veto of the American Senate. Denna F. Fleming. LC 72-147598. (Library of War & Peace; International Law). 1972. lib. bdg. 46.00 o.p. (ISBN 0-8240-0359-4). Garland Pub.
Trebizond: The Last Greek Empire. William Miller. 140p. Repr. of 1926 ed. lib. bdg. 32.50x o.p. (Pub. by AM Hakkert). Coronet Bks.
Tree Burns Green & Other Stories. Dianne S. Peters. 1978. 6.00 o.p. (ISBN 0-682-49193-4). Exposition-Phoenix.
Tree Defects: A Photo Guide. Alex L. Shigo. (Forest Service General Technical Report: NE-82). (Illus.). 168p. 1983. pap. 6.50 o.p. (ISBN 0-318-22464-X, S/N 001-001-00586-0). USGPO.
Tree for Poverty: Somali Poetry & Prose. Margaret Laurence. 146p. 1954. 15.00x o.p. (ISBN 0-7165-1415-X, BBA 02223, Pub. by Cuala Press Ireland). Biblio Dist.
Tree House. Edna P. Weegmann. 1985. 7.95 o.p. (ISBN 0-317-28979-9). Vantage.
Tree House Book. David Stiles. 80p. (gr. 5 up). 1979. pap. 7.95 o.p. (ISBN 0-380-43133-5, 64501-7). Avon.
Tree Is a Tree. King Vidor. Ed. by Bruce S. Kupelnick. LC 76-52132. (Classics of Film Literature Ser.). 1978. lib. bdg. 22.00 o.p. (ISBN 0-8240-2896-1). Garland Pub.
Tree Key. Herbert L. Edlin. (Illus.). 280p. 1985. pap. 10.95 o.s.i. (ISBN 0-684-15890-6, ScribT). Scribner.
Tree Nuts: Production, Processing, Products. 2nd ed. J. G. Woodroof. (Illus.). 1979. 65.95 o.p. (ISBN 0-87055-254-6). AVI.
Tree of Human History. Alan H. Brodrick. 1952. (ISBN 0-8022-0182-2). Philos Lib.
Tree of Liberty. Elizabeth Page. 1939. 10.00 o.p. (ISBN 0-03-029735-4). H Holt & Co.
Tree of Southern Oregon. Art Bernstein. (Illus.). 120p. (Orig.). 1986. pap. 4.95 o.p. (ISBN 0-9617525-0-5). Magnifica Bks.
Tree Pathology. William H. Smith. 1970. 34.50 o.p. (ISBN 0-12-652650-8). Acad Pr.
Tree Physiology & Yield Improvement. Ed. by M. G. Cannell & F. T. Last. 1977. 80.50 o.p. (ISBN 0-12-158750-9). Acad Pr.
Tree That Cried. Doris Schwerin. LC 84-45732. (Illus.). 32p. (ps-2). lib. bdg. 11.45 o.s.i. Caedmon.
Tree Where Man Was Born. Peter Matthiessen. Bd. with African Experience. Eliot Porter. (Illus.). 248p. 1974. pap. 7.45 o.p. (ISBN 0-380-00050-4, 20370). Avon.
Tree You Can Never Climb. Gloria Whiteman. 1985. 12.95 o.p. (ISBN 0-533-06532-1). Vantage.
Treehouse of the Mind. William Swarts, 3rd. 24p. (Orig.). 1981. 2.00 o.p. (ISBN 0-9603840-2-2). Andrew Mtn Pr.
Trees. Martyn Hamer. (Easy Read Fact Bk.). (Illus.). 32p. (gr. 2-4). 1983. PLB 10.90 o.p. (ISBN 0-531-04513-7). Watts.
Trees Alive. Sarah R. Riedman. (Illus.). 128p. (gr. 5 up). 1974. 11.75 o.p. (ISBN 0-688-41574-1); PLB 6.48 o.p. (ISBN 0-688-51574-6). Lothrop.
Trees & Shrubs in the Heart of Dixie, 1961 see **Trees & Shrubs of the Southeast.**
Trees & Shrubs of the Southeast. 3rd, rev. ed. Blanche E. Dean. LC 61-15653. Orig. Title: Trees & Shrubs in the Heart of Dixie, 1961. (Illus.). 270p. 1988. pap. 9.95 o.p. Birm Audubon Soc Pr.
Trees for Southern Landscapes. Bill Adams. LC 76-15457. (Illus.). 96p. (Orig.). 1976. pap. 6.95x o.p. (ISBN 0-88415-881-0, Pub. by Pacesetter Pr). Gulf Pub.
Trees for Town & Country. Peter Bridgeman. LC 79-52380. (Illus.). 1979. 19.95 o.p. (ISBN 0-7153-7841-4). David & Charles.
Trees of Righteousness. Relly J. Parcell. 1984. 12.95 o.p. (ISBN 0-533-05897-X). Vantage.
Trees of the Adirondack High Peak Region. 2nd ed. E. H. Ketchledge. LC 67-28444. (Illus.). pap. 2.95 o.s.i. (ISBN 0-935272-07-0). ADK Mtn Club.
Treffwahrscheinlichkeit und Autokorrelations Funktionen. 2nd, exp. ed. H. Braendli. (Illus.). 154p. (Ger.). 1970. 35.20x o.p. (ISBN 0-8176-0044-2). Birkhauser.
Trekka Round the World. John Guzzwell. (Illus.). 197p. 1980. Repr. 16.95 o.p. (ISBN 0-246-11322-7). Sheridan.
Trekking Across the Mind. James W. Duren. LC 85-50087. 54p. 1985. 5.95 o.p. (ISBN 0-938232-67-3). Winston-Derek.
Trekking in Nepal. Toru Nakano. Tr. by D. T. Ooka from Fr. & Japanese. LC 84-42713. (Illus.). 231p. (Orig.). 1985. pap. 24.95 o.p. (ISBN 0-89346-251-9). Heian Intl.
Trekking in Nepal: A Guide. 4th ed. Stephen Bezruchka. LC 80-72091. (Illus.). 256p. 1981. pap. 8.95 o.p. (ISBN 0-89886-003-2). Mountaineers.
Trekking in the Himalayas. Tomoya Iozawa. Tr. by U. Michiko & David H. Kornhauser. Orig. Title: Himaraya Torekkingu. (Illus.). 208p. 1980. pap. 24.95 o.p. (ISBN 0-89346-212-8). Heian Intl.
Trenchless Construction for Utilities. (Proceedings of NO-DIG Ser.). 330p. 1986. 90.00 o.p. (ISBN 0-905188-07-1, Pub. by T Telford UK). Am Soc Civil Eng.
Trend Analysis of Statistics: Theory & Technique. Max Sasuly. LC 75-136551. 421p. 1973. Repr. of 1934 ed. lib. bdg. 22.50x o.p. (ISBN 0-8371-5476-6, SATA). Greenwood.
Trends & Cycles. John W. Kendrick & Elliott S. Grossman. LC 79-3678. 192p. 1980. text ed. 19.50x o.p. (ISBN 0-8018-2289-0). Johns Hopkins.
Trends in American Publishing. Ed. by Kathryn L. Henderson. (Allerton Park Institute Ser.: No. 14). 105p. 1968. 5.00x o.p. (ISBN 0-87845-009-2). U of Ill Lib Info Sci.
Trends in Autonomic Pharmacology, Vol. 1. Stanley Kalsner. LC 79-17275. (Illus.). 508p. 1979. text ed. 35.00 o.p. (ISBN 0-8067-1001-2). Urban & S.
Trends in Autonomic Pharmacology, Vol. 2. Ed. by Stanley Kalsner. (Illus.). 574p. 1982. text ed. 45.00 o.p. (ISBN 0-8067-1002-0). Urban & S.
Trends in Behavior Therapy. Ed. by Per-Olow Sjoden & Sandra Bates. 1979. 39.95 o.p. (ISBN 0-12-647450-8). Acad Pr.
Trends in Biotechnology & Chemical Patent Law. 230p. 1985. 15.00 o.p. (G4-3772). PLI.
Trends in Computerized Structural Analysis & Synthesis, Vol. 10, No. 1-2. A. K. Noor & H. G. McComb, Jr. 1981. o. p. 83.00 o.p. (ISBN 0-08-023261-2); pap. 91.00 o.p. (ISBN 0-08-028707-7). Pergamon.
Trends in Elementary Particle Theory: Proceedings. Theoretical Physics International Summer Institute, Bonn, 1974. Ed. by H. Rollnick & K. Dietz. LC 75-8826. (Lecture Notes in Physics Ser.: Vol. 37). 480p. 1975. pap. 24.00 o.p. (ISBN 0-387-07160-1). Springer-Verlag.
Trends in Energy Use in Industrial Societies: An Overview. Joy Dunkerley. 149p. 1980. 11.00 o.p. (ISBN 0-317-60268-3). Resources Future.
Trends in Geography: An Introductory Survey. R. V. Cooke & J. H. Johnson. 1969. text ed. 18.00 o.p. (ISBN 0-08-006675-5); pap. text ed. 8.50 o.p. (ISBN 0-08-006674-7). Pergamon.
Trends in International Trade in Manufactured Goods & Structural Change in the Industrial Countries. Bela Balassa & Kenneth Meyers. (Working Paper: No. 611). 44p. 1983. 5.00 o.p. (ISBN 0-8213-0251-5, WP 0611). World Bank.
Trends in International Trade: The Haberler Report. (Eng., Fr. & Span.). pap. 5.50 o.p. (ISBN 0-686-93112-2, G52, GATT). UNIPUB.
Trends in Literature. Joseph T. Shipley. (ISBN 0-8022-1559-9). Philos Lib.
Trends in Management Thinking, 1960-1970. Harold R. Pollard. 331p. 1978. 18.00x o.p. (ISBN 0-87201-880-6). Gulf Pub.
Trends in Medicinal Chemistry: Proceedings of the 9th International Symposium on Medicinal Chemistry. Ed. by E. Mutschler & E. Winterfeldt. 634p. 1987. pap. text ed. 107.00 o.p. (ISBN 0-89573-616-0). VCH Pubs.
Trends in Memory Development. Ed. by Michelene T. Chi. 174p. 1983. pap. 29.50 o.p. (ISBN 3-8055-3661-5). Transaction Pubs.
Trends in Municipal Administration: The Periodical Literature, 1980-1984. Dale E. Casper. (Public Administration Ser.: P 1769). 22p. 1985. 3.00 o.p. (ISBN 0-89028-569-1). Vance Biblios.
Trends in Quantum Electronics. Ed. by A. N. Prokhorov & I. Ursu. viii, 559p. 1986. pap. 53.90 o.p. (ISBN 0-387-17229-7). Springer-Verlag.
Trends in Radiation Dosimetry. Ed. by W. L. McLaughlin. (Illus.). 320p. 1983. pap. 28.00 o.p. (ISBN 0-08-029143-0). Pergamon.
Trends in Radiation Processing: Transactions of the Third International Meeting on Radiation Processing, Held in Tokyo, Japan, October 1980, 3 vols. Ed. by J. Silverman. 1350p. 1982. pap. 155.00 o.p. (ISBN 0-08-026512-X, C145, E110). Pergamon.
Trends in Social Science. Donald P. Ray. LC 61-10611. 176p. 1961. (ISBN 0-8022-1313-8). Philos Lib.
Trends in the Biology of Fermentations for Fuels & Chemicals. Ed. by A. Hollaender et al. LC 81-5928. (Basic Life Sciences Ser.: Vol. 18). 604p. 1981. 95.00x o.p. (ISBN 0-306-40752-3, Plenum Pr). Plenum Pub.
Trends in the Relocation of U.S. Manufacturing. Christina M. Kelton. Ed. by Fred Bateman. LC 83-9117. (Research in Business Economics & Public Policy Ser.: No. 6). 194p. 1983. 42.95 o.p. (ISBN 0-8357-1445-4). UMI Res Pr.
Trends in Urban Firefighting: Periodical Literature, 1980-1984. Dale E. Casper. (Public Administration Ser.: P 1801). 11p. 1985. 2.00 o.p. (ISBN 0-89028-631-0). Vance Biblios.
Trent's Last Case. E. C. Bentley. LC 75-44955. (Crime Fiction Ser). 1976. Repr. of 1912 ed. lib. bdg. 21.00 o.p. (ISBN 0-8240-2353-6). Garland Pub.
Tres Cuentistas Hispanoamericanos. D. A. Yates et al. 1969. pap. text ed. write for info. o.p. (ISBN 0-02-430840-4). Macmillan.
Tres Macho, He Said: Padre Gallegos, New Mexico's First Congressman. Angelico Chavez. 1985. 15.00 o.p. (ISBN 0-88307-669-1). Gannon.
Trespassers. Giles A. Lutz. 1980. pap. 2.50 o.s.i. Ballantine.
Tri-Play Crosswords, No. 1. Len Fellows. Ed. by Henry Hook. (Illus.). 64p. 1984. pap. 6.70 o.p. (ISBN 0-671-50320-0, Fireside). S&S.
Trial. Philip L. Dew. LC 84-12711. 250p. 1984. 8.95 o.p. (ISBN 0-87747-874-0). Deseret Bk.
Trial Advocacy: Expert Witnesses. 1984. (ISBN 0-88129-142-0). Wash Bar CLE.
Trial Advocacy: Passion & Preparation. J. James McKenna. 56p. 1987. 25.00 o.p. PES Inc WI.
Trial & Death of Socrates. Plato. Tr. by John Warrington. 1969. Repr. of 1963 ed. 14.95x o.p. (ISBN 0-460-00457-3, Evman). Biblio Dist.
Trial & Error. D. Michael Tomkins. LC 80-39757. 1981. 9.95 o.p. (ISBN 0-396-07944-X). Dodd.
Trial & Terror. Ed. by Joan Kahn. 1973. 8.95 o.p. (ISBN 0-395-17208-X). HM.
Trial by Death & Fire. D. Carl Anderson. LC 80-14446. (Orion Ser.). 160p. 1980. pap. 3.95 o.p. (ISBN 0-8127-0292-1). Review & Herald.
Trial by Fire: A People's History of the Civil War & Reconstruction. Page Smith. LC 81-18573. 1024p. 1982. text ed. 29.95 o.p. (ISBN 0-07-058571-7). McGraw.
Trial by Fire: The True Story of a Woman's Ordeal at the Hands of Justice. Gerry L. Spence. 416p. 18.95 o.p. (ISBN 0-688-06075-7). Morrow.
Trial by Trial: Destiny of a Believer. Don Stephens. LC 85-80485. 176p. (Orig.). 1985. pap. 6.95 o.p. (ISBN 0-89081-498-8). Harvest Hse.
Trial Court Administrator: A Brochure. National Center for State Courts Staff. 20p. (On loan from NCSC Library). 1978. pap. Natl Ctr St Courts.
Trial Evidence. 157p. 1984. 10.00 o.p. (ISBN 0-318-02448-9). ICLE Georgia.
Trial in Thailand. George K. Tanham. LC 74-75314. 189p. 1974. 19.50x o.p. (ISBN 0-8448-0318-9, Pub. by Crane Russak & Co). Taylor & Francis.
Trial Lawyer & the Federal Rules of Evidence. Ed. by Jeffrey R. White. 630p. 1980. 25.00 o.p. (ISBN 0-941916-03-0). Assn Trial Ed.
Trial Objections. 127p. 1984. 20.00 o.p. (ISBN 0-318-03912-5, 257). PA Bar Inst.
Trial of a Toxic Tort Case. Massachusetts Continuing Legal Education-New England Law Institute, Inc. Staff. LC 84-61754. 486p. write for info. o.p. Mass CLE.
Trial of an Eminent Domain Case. Massachusetts Continuing Legal Education, Inc. Staff. LC 84-61785. 1985. 35.00 o.p. Mass CLE.
Trial of Chaplain Jensen. Andrew Jensen. LC 73-82184. 1974. 7.95 o.p. (ISBN 0-87795-065-2, Arbor Hse). Morrow.
Trial of Faith. R. J. Owen. 1974. 1.60 o.s.i. (ISBN 0-08-017609-7). Pergamon.
Trial of the Assassin Guiteau: Psychiatry & the Law in the Gilded Age. Charles E. Rosenberg. LC 68-16713. 1976. pap. text ed. 10.00x o.s.i. (ISBN 0-226-72717-3, P682, Phoen). U of Chicago Pr.
Trial of the Assassin Guiteau: Psychiatry & the Law in the Gilded Age. Charles E. Rosenberg. LC 68-16712. (Illus.). 1968. lib. bdg. 15.00x o.s.i. (ISBN 0-226-72716-5). U of Chicago Pr.
Trial Skills: Twentieth Annual Practical Skills Series. Massachusetts Continuing Legal Education-New England Law Institute, Inc. Staff. LC 83-63415. write for info. o.p. Mass CLE.
Trial Techniques: A Young Lawyer's Guide to Civil Trial Advocacy. Pennsylvania Bar Institute Staff. 220p. 1988. 55.00 o.p. (ISBN 0-318-19077-X, 428). PA Bar Inst.
Trials & Tribulations. William Kunstler. LC 84-73209. 201p. 1985. 22.50 o.p. (ISBN 0-394-54611-3, E-991, Ever); pap. 7.95 o.p. (ISBN 0-394-62060-7). Grove.
Trials of Counsel: Francis Bacon in 1621. Jonathan Marwil. LC 75-33650. 254p. 1976. text ed. 24.50x o.p. (ISBN 0-8143-1549-6). Wayne St U Pr.
Triangle. Sondra Marshak & Myrna Culbreath. (Orig.). 1983. pap. 2.95 o.p. (ISBN 0-671-49298-5, Timescape). PB.
Triangle. Sondra Marshak & Myrna Culbreath. (Gregg Press Science Fiction - Star Trek Ser.). 192p. 1986. lib. bdg. 11.95x o.p. (ISBN 0-8398-2934-5, Gregg). G K Hall.
Triangle Has Four Sides: True-to-Life Stories Show How Teens Deal with Feelings & Problems. Phyllis R. Naylor. LC 83-72123. 128p. (Orig.). (YA) (gr. 7-10). 1984. pap. 4.50 o.p. (ISBN 0-8066-2067-6, 10-6700, Augsburg). Augsburg Fortress.
Triangle of Love. Colman. 1985. pap. 2.25 o.p. (ISBN 0-671-49631-X). Archway.
Triangles. Paul Vigyikan. 186p. 1978. 8.95 o.p. (ISBN 0-8059-2502-3). Dorrance.
Triangles: A Novel. Ruth Geller. LC 84-15632. (Feminist Ser.). 192p. (Orig.). 1984. 20.95 o.p. (ISBN 0-89594-152-X); pap. 7.95 o.p. (ISBN 0-89594-151-1). Crossing Pr.
Triazoles. K. T. Finley. LC 80-13323. (Chemistry of Heterocyclic Compounds, Series of Monographs: Vol. 39). 349p. 1980. 225.00x o.p. (ISBN 0-471-07827-1). Wiley.
Tribal Eye. David Attenborough. (Illus.). 1977. 14.95 o.p. (ISBN 0-393-04466-1). Norton.
Tribal Living Book: One Hundred Fifty Things to Do & to Make from Traditional Cultures Around the World. David Levinson & David Sherwood. LC 84-80538. (Illus.). 230p. (Orig.). 1984. pap. text ed. 12.95 o.p. (ISBN 0-933472-84-6). Johnson Bks.
Tribesmen & Patriots: Political Culture in a Poly-Ethnic African State. Ndiva Kofele-Kale. LC 80-5734. 375p. 1981. lib. bdg. 31.25 o.p. (ISBN 0-8191-1395-6); pap. text ed. 16.25 o.p. (ISBN 0-8191-1396-4). U Pr of Amer.
Tribology: Friction, Lubrication & Wear. Szeri. 1980. text ed. 55.95 o.p. (ISBN 0-07-062663-4). McGraw.
Triborough Plan. Jose Ramon. 1986. 6.95 o.p. (ISBN 0-533-06589-5). Vantage.
Tribunal Representation. Roger Lawrence. 98p. (Renouf). 1980. pap. text ed. 9.75x o.p. (ISBN 0-7199-1044-7, Pub. by Bedford England). Gower Pub Co.
Tribune of the Slavophiles: Konstantin Aksakov. Edward V. Chmielewski. LC 62-63051. (University of Florida Social Sciences Monographs: No. 12). 1961. pap. 3.50 o.p. (ISBN 0-8130-0047-5). U Presses Fla.
Tributaries. John Bigley. (Illus.). 1977. lib. bdg. 25.00 o.p. (ISBN 0-916908-40-2); pap. 3.50 o.p. (ISBN 0-916908-05-4). Place Herons.
Tributaries of Learning. Jess Shaver. 1977. text ed. 39.50x o.p. (ISBN 0-8422-0553-5); pap. text ed. 9.95x o.p. (ISBN 0-8422-5253-3). Irvington.
Tribute to Freud. H. D., pseud. LC 73-81064. 224p. 1974. 15.00 o.s.i. (ISBN 0-87923-074-6). Godine.
Tribute to Gleason Archer. Ed. by Ronald Youngblood & Walter C. Kaiser, Jr. 1986. text ed. 15.95 o.p. (ISBN 0-8024-8780-7). Moody.

Tribute to Lotte Brand Philip. Barbara Lane. (Illus.). 2267p. 49.50 o.s.i. (ISBN 0-317-65042-4). Abaris Bks.

Trichocystoides. Corps Trichocystoides. Cnidocystes & Colloblastes see Structure & Function in Cilia & Flagella.

Trick of Light. Barbara Corcoran. LC 75-175552. (Illus.). (gr. 5-8). 1972. 4.95 o.p. (ISBN 0-689-30025-5, Atheneum). Macmillan.

Tricks & Games on the Pool Table. Fred Herrmann. LC 67-17985. 1967. lib. bdg. 9.50x o.p. (ISBN 0-88307-551-2). Gannon.

Tricks of the Trade. Toy T. Schofield. 48p. 1987. 7.00 o.p. (ISBN 0-8062-2950-0). Carlton.

Tricks of the Trade for Teachers of Language Arts. Zelia S. Evans. LC 74-84424. 1974. 6.50 o.p. (ISBN 0-682-48070-3, University). Exposition-Phoenix.

Tricyclic Antidepressants. (Landmark Ser.). 1979. 22.50x o.p. (ISBN 0-8422-4114-0). Irvington.

Trident. Joel Hammil. LC 80-70217. 1981. 11.95 o.p. (ISBN 0-87795-306-6, Arbor Hse). Morrow.

Trident Brand. G. Clifton Wisler. 1986. pap. 2.50 o.s.i. (ISBN 0-449-13020-7, GM). Fawcett.

Trig. Robert N. Peck. (Illus.). (gr. 4-6). 1977. 12.95 o.p. (ISBN 0-316-69654-4). Little.

Trig Goes Ape. Robert N. Peck. (Illus.). 96p. (gr. 3-6). 1980. 12.95i o.p. (ISBN 0-316-69657-9). Little.

Trig Sees Red. Robert N. Peck. LC 78-18348. (Illus.). (gr. 3-7). 1978. 12.95 o.p. (ISBN 0-316-69656-0). Little.

Triggering Town: Lectures & Essays on Poetry & Writing. Richard Hugo. 1979. 3.95x o.p. (ISBN 0-393-08839-1). Norton.

Triggers for Six. Nelson Nye. 256p. 1982. pap. 2.50 o.p. (ISBN 0-505-51844-9, Pub. by Tower Bks). Dorchester Pub Co.

Trigonometry. George S. Donovan & Beverly B. Gimmestad. 1980. text ed. write for info. o.p. (ISBN 0-87150-284-4, 2231, Prindle). PWS-Kent Pub.

Trigonometry. 3rd ed. Margaret L. Lial & Charles D. Miller. 1985. text ed. write for info. o.p. (ISBN 0-673-18016-6). Scott F.

Trigonometry for College Students. 3rd ed. Karl J. Smith. LC 83-6336. 350p. 1983. text ed. 24.50 pub net o.p. (ISBN 0-534-02688-5). Brooks-Cole.

Trigonometry with Calculators. Lawrence S. Levy. 330p. 1983. text ed. write for info. o.p. (ISBN 0-02-370450-0). Macmillan.

Trilateral Commission Task Force Reports, Nos. 9-14. Incl. Collaboration with Communist Countries in Managing Global Problems: Am Examination of the Options. Chihiro Hosoya & Henry D. Owen. 1976; Problem of International Confrontations. Egidio Ortona & J. Robert Schaetzel. 1976; Reform of International Institutions. C. Fred Bergsten & Georges Berthoin. 1978; New Regime for the Oceans. Michael Hardy & Ann L. Hollick. 1976; Seeking a New Accommodation in World Commodity Markets. Carl E. Beigie & Wolfgang Hager. 1976; Toward a Renovated International System. Richard N. Cooper & Karl Kaiser. 1977. 30.00 o.s.i. (ISBN 0-318-03634-7). Trilateral Comm.

Trilateral Countries & the Middle East. Joseph J. Sisco & Shlomo Avineri. Trilateral Comm.

Trilateral Countries in the International Economy of the 1980's. Miriam Camps & Ryokichi Hirono. 1982. Trilateral Comm.

Trilateral Relations at the Threshold of the New Decade. Robert R. Bowie et al. Trilateral Comm.

Trilateral Security: Defense & Arms Control Policies in the 1980s. (Triangle Papers: No. 26). 1983. pap. 6.00 o.s.i. Trilateral Comm.

Trilateral-Soviet Relations in Transition. Seweryn Bialer et al. Trilateral Comm.

Trilateral Template. Bernard M. Bane. 6p. 1982. pap. 0.25 o.s.i. (ISBN 0-930924-13-4). BMB Pub Co.

Trilingual Dictionary for Materials & Structures. J. E. Holmstrom et al. 1971. 240.00 o.p. (ISBN 0-08-013370-3). Pergamon.

Trilogy, 3 vols. Klass Schilder. lib. bdg. 47.95 o.p. (ISBN 0-8254-5229-5). Kregel.

Trilogy of Christmas Plays for Children. C. Preston. LC 67-17157. (Illus.). (gr. 5 up). 1967. 5.95 o.p. (ISBN 0-15-290450-6, HJ). HarBraceJ.

Trilogy of Death: Three Complete Novels. P. D. James. 976p. 1984. 19.95 o.s.i. (ISBN 0-684-18243-2). Scribner.

Trimtab Factor: How Business Executives Can Help Solve the Nuclear Weapons Crisis. Harold Willens. LC 83-17202. 180p. 1984. 10.95 o.p. (ISBN 0-688-02661-3). Morrow.

Trio: Portrait of an Intimate Friendship. Aram Saroyan. 1985. 16.45 o.p. (ISBN 0-671-50919-5, Pub. by Linden Pr). S&S.

Triomphe de la Vie. Jean Giono. 296p. 1942. 8.95 o.p. (ISBN 0-686-53993-1). French & Eur.

Trionfo Di Camilla, Regina De 'Volsci. Giovanni Bononcini. Ed. by Howard M. Brown. LC 76-21029. (Italian Opera 1640-1770 Ser.: Vol. 17). 1978. lib. bdg. 77.00 o.p. (ISBN 0-8240-2616-0). Garland Pub.

Tripartite Meeting on Conditions of Work & Employment of Professional Workers: Report: Geneva 22-30 November 1977. 71p. (Eng., Fr. & Span.). 1978. pap. 5.75 o.p. (ISBN 92-2-101936-5, ILO119, ILO). UNIPUB.

Triple Boy. Dale Carlson. LC 76-25501. (gr. 6 up). 1977. 6.95 o.p. (ISBN 0-689-30549-4, Atheneum). Macmillan.

Triple Concordance see Exhaustive Concordance of the Book of Mormon, Doctrine & Covenants & Pearl of Great Peace.

Triple Goddess: An Exploration of the Archetypal Feminine. Adam Mclean. 1987. pap. 15.00 o.p. (ISBN 0-317-57172-9). Phanes Pr.

Triple Indemnity. Judith Richards. LC 82-72060. 1982. 14.95 o.p. (ISBN 0-87795-421-6, Arbor Hse). Morrow.

Triple Struggle: Latin American Peasant Women. Audrey Bronstein. 268p. 1983. 20.00 o.p. (ISBN 0-89608-180-X); pap. 8.50 o.p. (ISBN 0-89608-179-6). South End Pr.

Triple Threat. Helen MacInnes. LC 72-79921. 1973. 8.95 o.s.i. (ISBN 0-15-191155-X). HarBraceJ.

Triples: A New Tennis Game. Geoffrey Godbey et al. (Illus.). 22p. (Orig.). 1980. pap. 2.98x o.p. (ISBN 0-910251-01-0). Venture Pub PA.

Triplet States: No. 3. P. J. Wagner et al. (Topics in Current Chemistry Ser.: Vol 66). 1976. 40.00 o.p. (ISBN 0-387-07655-7). Springer-Verlag.

Triplet States Two. U. P. Wild et al. LC 75-1466. (Topics in Current Chemistry Ser: Vol. 55). (Illus.). 150p. 1975. 36.00 o.p. (ISBN 0-387-07197-0). Springer-Verlag.

Triplets. Barbara Seuling. LC 79-18621. (Illus.). (ps-3). 1980. 7.95 o.p. (ISBN 0-395-29107-0, Clarion). HM.

Tripods Trilogy. 2nd ed. John Christopher. 224p. (YA) (gr. 7 up). 1970. Boxed Set. pap. 11.95 o.s.i. (ISBN 0-02-042571-6, Collier). Macmillan.

Trips with Children in New England. 3rd ed. Harriet Webster. LC 85-50067. (Yankee Magazine Guidebook Ser.). (Illus.). 256p. 1985. pap. 9.95 o.p. (ISBN 0-89909-075-3). Yankee Bks.

Trish for President. Lael Littke. (gr. k up). 1986. pap. 2.50 o.p. (ISBN 0-671-55175-2). Archway.

Tristes Murailles. Dennis Adair & Janet Rosenstock. (Fr.). 1983. pap. 3.50 o.p. (ISBN 0-380-83824-9, 83824-9). Avon.

Tristram Shandy see also Life & Opinions of Tristram Shandy, Gentleman.

Tritium & Its Compounds. E. A. Evans. 441p. 1966. 32.00 o.p. (ISBN 0-442-02339-1, Pub. by Van Nos Reinhold). Krieger.

Tritton's Guide to Better Wine & Beer Making for Beginners. S. M. Tritton. (Illus.). 160p. (Orig.). 1969. pap. 4.50 o.p. (ISBN 0-571-09171-7). Faber & Faber.

Triumph. John Kenneth Galbraith. 1984. pap. 7.95 o.p. (ISBN 0-87795-607-3, Arbor Hse). Morrow.

Triumph. Ernest K. Gann. 408p. 1986. 17.45 o.p. (ISBN 0-671-52829-7). S&S.

Triumph Clear. Lorraine Beim. LC 46-3638. (gr. 7 up). 1966. pap. 0.65 o.p. (ISBN 0-15-691161-2, VoyB). HarBraceJ.

Triumph of Bolshevism: Revolution or Reaction? Stuart R. Tompkins. LC 66-22714. (Illus.). 331p. (Orig.). 1967. 19.50x o.p. (ISBN 0-8061-0727-8); pap. 9.95x o.p. (ISBN 0-8061-1158-5). U of Okla Pr.

Triumph of Culture: Eighteenth Century Perspectives. Paul Fritz & David Williams. LC 80-80055. (McMaster 18th Century Studies). 398p. 1979. lib. bdg. 48.00 o.p. (ISBN 0-8240-4001-5). Garland Pub.

Triumph of Failure, Repr. Of 1899 Ed. Patrick A. Sheehan. Bd. with Flower of Asia. Henry E. Dennehy. Repr. of 1901 ed. LC 75-467. (Victorian Fiction Ser.). 1976. lib. bdg. 73.00 o.p. (ISBN 0-8240-1545-2). Garland Pub.

Triumph of Faith in Habakkuk. Donald E. Gowan. LC 75-32943. (Bible Speaks to Us Today Ser.). 1976. 5.95 o.p. (ISBN 0-8042-0195-1, John Knox). Westminster John Knox.

Triumph of Humanism: A Visual Survey of the Decorative Arts of the Rennaissance. Ed. by Graeme Keith. LC 77-81221. (Illus.). 1977. pap. 3.95 o.p. (ISBN 0-88401-030-9). Fine Arts Mus.

Triumph of Satan. Harry E. Wedeck. 5.95 o.p. (ISBN 0-8216-0159-8, Pub. by Univ Bks). Carol Pub Group.

Triumph of Style: Modes of Non-Fiction. John Knott & Reeve Parker. (Orig.). 1969. pap. 9.50 o.p. (ISBN 0-395-04744-7, 3-30250). HM.

Triumph of Surrender. William M. Fletcher. (Christian Character Library). 190p. 1987. hdbk. 8.95 o.p. (ISBN 0-89109-538-1). NavPress.

Triumph of Time: A Study of the Victorian Concepts of Time, History, Progress & Decadence. Jerome H. Buckley. LC 66-21333. 1966. 15.00x o.s.i. (ISBN 0-674-90960-7, Belknap Pr). Harvard U Pr.

Triumph or Triage? The World Food Problem in Geographical Persective. C. Gregory Knight & R. Paul Wilcox. Ed. by Salvatore J. Natoli. LC 76-29265. (Resource Papers for College Geography Ser.). 1977. pap. text ed. 5.00 o.p. (ISBN 0-89291-115-8). Assn Am Geographers.

Triumph over Temptation. Ward Patterson. (Illus.). 96p. (Orig.). 1984. pap. 2.95 o.p. (ISBN 0-87239-730-0, 39976). Standard Pub.

Triumph over Terror on Flight 847. John Testrake & Dave Wimbish. (Illus.). 1987. 14.95 o.p. (ISBN 0-8007-1527-6). Revell.

Triumph Service-Repair Handbook: TR 7 Series, 1975-1978. Ed. by Eric Jorgensen. (Illus.). pap. 12.95 o.p. (ISBN 0-89287-206-3, A211). Clymer Pub.

Triumph Service-Repair Handbook: TR2-TR6 & GT6, 1954-1976. (Illus.). pap. text ed. 13.95 o.p. (ISBN 0-89287-103-2, A210). Clymer Pub.

Triumph Spitfire Owner's Handbook: 1962-1970. Clymer Publications Staff. (Illus.). 1971. pap. 8.95 o.p. (ISBN 0-89287-254-3, A215). Clymer Pub.

Triumph Tiger Cub & Terrier '52 - '66. Pete Shoemark. (Owners Workshop Manual Ser.). 13.50 o.p. (ISBN 0-85696-414-X, 414). Haynes Pubns.

Triumphs of Temper; a Poem. In Six Cantos see Ode, Inscribed to John Howard.

Triune God. Edmund J. Fortman. (Theological Resources Ser). 1971. 9.95 o.s.i. (ISBN 0-664-20917-3, Westminster). Westminster John Knox.

Triune Identity: God According to the Gospel. Robert W. Jenson. LC 81-43091. 1982. 16.95 o.p. (ISBN 0-8006-0672-8, Fortress). Augsburg Fortress.

Trivial Conquest: The Smart Reference Source for Trivial Pursuit. Lisa Merkin & Eric Frankel. 592p. 1984. pap. 9.95 o.p. (ISBN 0-380-89492-0). Avon.

Trivial Extensions of Abelian Categories: Homological Algebra of Trivial Extensions of Abelian Categories with Applications to Ring Theory. R. M. Fossum et al. (Lecture Notes in Mathematics Ser.: Vol. 456). xi, 122p. (Orig.). 1975. pap. 13.00 o.p. (ISBN 0-387-07159-8). Springer-Verlag.

Trn, Eighth Grade. Date not set. (ISBN 0-07-368269-1). McGraw.

Trn, Fifth Grade. Date not set. (ISBN 0-07-368266-7). McGraw.

Trn, Fourth Grade. Date not set. (ISBN 0-07-368265-9). McGraw.

Trn, Kindergarten. Date not set. (ISBN 0-07-368260-8). McGraw.

Trn, Seventh Grade. Date not set. (ISBN 0-07-368268-3). McGraw.

Trn, Sixth Grade. Date not set. (ISBN 0-07-368267-5). McGraw.

Troika. Clive Egleton. LC 84-45050. 319p. 1984. 14.95 o.s.i. (ISBN 0-689-11479-6, Atheneum). Macmillan.

Troilus & Cressida see also Tragedy of Troilus & Cressida.

Troilus & Criseyde see also Book of Troilus & Criseyde.

Troilus & Criseyde. Geoffrey Chaucer. 1974. 13.95x o.p. (ISBN 0-460-10992-8, Evman). Biblio Dist.

Trois, Six, Neuf. Colette. 1970. 8.95 o.p. (ISBN 0-686-54605-9). French & Eur.

Trojan Gold. Elizabeth Peters. LC 86-26486. 288p. 1987. 15.95 o.p. (ISBN 0-689-11621-7, Atheneum). Macmillan.

Trojans: A Story of Southern California Football. Ken Rappoport. LC 74-81346. (College Sports Ser.). Orig. Title: Southern Cal Football. 1981. 12.95 o.p. (ISBN 0-87397-033-0). Strode.

Tromp-L'oeil Painting: The Illusion of Reality. Skira-Rizzoli Staff & Miriam Milman. LC 82-42851. (Illus.). 130p. 1983. 35.00 o.p. (ISBN 0-8478-0470-4). Rizzoli Intl.

Tron Computer Age Activities. Frank Smith. Ed. by Kate Klimo. (Illus.). 64p. (ps-3). 1982. pap. 1.95 o.s.i. (ISBN 0-671-44551-0). S&S.

Tron Pop-up Book. Intervisual Staff. (Illus.). 16p. (ps-3). 1982. 7.95 o.s.i. (ISBN 0-671-44851-X, Pub. by Simon Says). S&S.

Tron: The Story Book. Larry Weinberg. (Illus.). 64p. (ps-3). 1982. 6.95 o.s.i. (ISBN 0-671-44558-8, Pub. by Simon Says). S&S.

Tropic Gold. Carol Jerina. 320p. (Orig.). pap. 3.95 o.p. (ISBN 0-671-64361-4). Archway.

Tropic of Cancer. Henry Miller. 1961. pap. 4.95 o.s.i. (ISBN 0-394-17760-6, B10, BC). Grove.

Tropic of Cancer. Henry Miller. LC 82-42868. 1983. 7.95 o.p. (ISBN 0-394-60435-0). Modern Lib.

Tropic of Capricorn. Henry Miller. 1962. pap. 4.95 o.s.i. (ISBN 0-394-17295-7, B59, BC). Grove.

Tropica: Color Cyclopedia of Exotic Plants. 2nd ed. Alfred B. Graf. 1981. 115.00 o.s.i. (ISBN 0-684-16771-9, ScribT). Scribner.

Tropical & Geographical Medicine. Ed. by Kenneth S. Warren. Adel A. Mahmoud. (Illus.). 1120p. 1984. text ed. 95.00 o.p. (ISBN 0-07-068327-1). McGraw.

Tropical Baroque: Four Manileno Theatricals. Nick Joaquin. LC 81-12968. (Asian & Pacific Writing Ser.: No. 19). 224p. 1982. text ed. 19.95 o.p. (ISBN 0-7022-1643-7); pap. 9.50 o.p. (ISBN 0-7022-1653-4). U of Queensland Pr.

Tropical Forage Legumes. P. J. Skerman. (Plant Production & Protection Papers: No. 2). 609p. 1977. 40.25 o.p. (ISBN 92-5-100163-4, F1401, FAO). UNIPUB.

Tropical Fruits & Vegetables Cookbook. Emil Kraus & Heinz V. Gaehler. 32p. (Orig.). 1986. pap. 3.00 o.p. (ISBN 0-682-40281-8). Exposition-Phoenix.

Tropical Gardening Along the Gulf Coast. Gerald Arp. LC 78-53815. (Illus.). 96p. (Orig.). 1978. pap. 6.95x o.p. (ISBN 0-88415-883-7, Pub. by Pacesetter Pr). Gulf Pub.

Tropical Gothic. Nick Joaquin. (Asian & Pacific Writing Ser.: No. 2). 284p. 1972. 19.95x o.p. (ISBN 0-7022-0775-6); pap. 9.50 o.p. (ISBN 0-7022-0776-4). U of Queensland Pr.

Tropical Hardwood Trade in the Asia-Pacific Region. Kenji Takeuchi. LC 74-4214. (World Bank Staff Occasional Paper: No. 17). 108p. 1974. pap. 6.50x o.p. (ISBN 0-8018-1627-0). Johns Hopkins.

Tropical Heat. John Lutz. LC 85-27129. 224p. 1986. 14.95 o.p. (ISBN 0-03-006958-0). H Holt & Co.

Tropical Moist Forests. 1982. 5.50 o.p. (ISBN 0-905347-31-5). C I D E.

Tropical Nature: Life & Death in the Rain Forests of Central & South America. Adrian Forsyth & Ken Miyata. (Illus.). 272p. 1984. 17.95 o.s.i. (ISBN 0-684-17964-4, ScribT). Scribner.

Tropical Nursing. A. L. Gregg. (ISBN 0-8022-0626-3). Philos Lib.

Tropical Oysters: Culture & Methods. D. B. Quayle. 80p. (Eng., Fr & Span.). 1980. pap. 6.00 o.p. (ISBN 0-88936-181-9, IDRCTS17, IDRC). UNIPUB.

Tropical Oysters: Culture & Methods. D. B. Quayle. 84p. 1981. pap. 6.00 o.p. (IDRC-TS17, IDRC). UNIPUB.

Tropical Pasture Research: Principles & Methods. Ed. by N. H. Shaw & W. W. Bryan. 454p. 1985. pap. text ed. 34.15 o.p. (ISBN 0-85198-358-8). CAB Intl.

Tropical Tree Crops. Lawrence K. Opeke. 330p. 1982. 67.00 o.p. (ISBN 0-471-10060-9, Pub. by Wiley-Interscience); pap. 29.95x o.p. (ISBN 0-471-10066-8). Wiley.

Tropical Trees: Variation Breeding & Conservation. Ed. by J. Burley & B. T. Styles. 1976. 54.50 o.p. (ISBN 0-12-145150-X). Acad Pr.

Tropics of Fear. Alice W. Hesse. 112p. 1983. 7.00 o.p. (ISBN 0-682-49979-X). Exposition-Phoenix.

Tropospheric Transport of Pollutants & Natural Substances to the Ocean. National Research Council, Ocean Sciences Board Staff. 1978. pap. 13.25 o.p. (ISBN 0-309-02735-7). Natl Acad Pr.

Trotsky. David King et al. (Illus.). 336p. 1986. 39.95 o.p. (ISBN 0-631-14689-X). Basil Blackwell.

Trotsky Bibliography. Wolfgang Lubitz. 458p. 1982. lib. bdg. 50.00 o.p. (ISBN 3-598-10469-3). K G Saur.

Trotsky's Anaylysis of Soviet Bureaucratization: A Critical Essay. David W. Lovell. LC 85-14968. (Flinders Politcal Monographs). 82p. (Orig.). 1985. pap. 11.50 o.p. (ISBN 0-7099-4112-9, Pub. by Croom Helm Ltd). Routledge Chapman & Hall.

Troubadour Songbook. Victor Cockburn & Judith Steinbergh. (Illus.). 68p. (Orig.). (gr. 2-8). 1989. pap. 14.95 o.p. (ISBN 0-944941-02-8). Troubadour Pr.

Troubadour's Romance. Robyn Carr. 288p. 1985. 16.95 o.p. (ISBN 0-316-12976-3). Little.

Trouble after School. Jerrold Beim. LC 57-9738. (Illus.). (gr. 5 up). 1957. 5.50 o.p. (ISBN 0-15-290695-9, HJ). HarBraceJ.

Trouble Brand. Russ Kidd. (Lythway Ser.). 184p. 1988. lib. bdg. 17.50x o.p. (ISBN 0-7451-0685-4, Pub. by Chivers Pr UK). G K Hall.

Trouble-Free Swimming Pools. Dan Ramsey. (Illus.). 176p. (Orig.). 1985. 18.95 o.p. (ISBN 0-8306-0808-7, 1808); pap. 11.60 o.p. (ISBN 0-8306-1808-2, 1808P). TAB Bks.

Trouble in School. Patricia Ross. (YA) (gr. 7 up). 1979. pap. 2.95 o.p. (ISBN 0-380-43703-1, Discus). Avon.

Trouble in Timberline. Max Brand. 347p. 1985. lib. bdg. 13.95 o.p. (ISBN 0-8161-3884-2, Large Print Bks). G K Hall.

Trouble in Tinktonk Land. Mercer Mayer. 32p. (ps). 1985. pap. 4.50 o.p. (ISBN 0-553-15291-2). Bantam.

Trouble on Black Wind Mountain. Xu Li. (Monkey Ser.: No. 4). (Illus.). 54p. (gr. 3 up). 1985. pap. 6.95 o.p. (ISBN 0-8351-1366-3). China Bks.
Trouble on the Blue Fox Island. Dorothy Y. Croman. (Outlands Adventure Ser.). 176p. (gr. 4-7). 1985. 3.50 o.p. (ISBN 0-8423-7345-4). Tyndale.
Trouble on the Massacre. Todhunter Ballard. 160p. 1972. pap. 0.95 o.p. (ISBN 0-380-00042-3, 19364). Avon.
Trouble River. Betsy Byars. (gr. 5-9). 1980. pap. 1.25 o.p. (ISBN 0-380-00345-7, 47001, Camelot). Avon.
Trouble with Ghosts. (Danger Mouse Paperbacks Ser.). 32p. (ps-3). 1986. pap. 3.70i o.p. (ISBN 0-316-14710-9). Little.
Trouble with Mom. Babette Cole. (Illus.). 32p. (gr. k-3). 1984. 12.95 o.p. (ISBN 0-698-20597-9, Coward); pap. 4.95 o.p. Putnam Pub Group.
Trouble with Nowadays: A Curmudgeon Strikes Back. Cleveland Amory. LC 79-52255. 1979. 10.00 o.p. (ISBN 0-87795-238-8, Arbor Hse). Morrow.
Trouble with Thirteen. Betty Miles. 116p. (gr. 3-7). 1980. pap. 2.25 o.p. (ISBN 0-380-51136-3, Camelot). Avon.
Trouble With Thirteen. Betty Miles. 112p. (YA) (gr. 7 up). 1984. pap. 2.50 o.p. (ISBN 0-380-67470-X, Flare). Avon.
Troubled Children-Troubled Parents. Stanley Goldstein. LC 78-12622. 1979. pap. 8.95 o.p. (ISBN 0-689-10936-9, Atheneum). Macmillan.
Troubled Debt Restructuring: An Alternative to Bankruptcy? John G. Hamer. Ed. by Richard Farmer. LC 85-16503. (Research for Business Decisions Ser.: No. 81). 116p. 1985. 39.95 o.p. (ISBN 0-8357-1716-X). UMI Res Pr.
Troubled Family: Sources of Information. Theodore P. Peck. LC 80-29397. 264p. (Orig.). 1982. pap. 19.95x o.p. (ISBN 0-89950-028-5). McFarland & Co.
Troubled Waters of Evolution. 2nd ed. Henry M. Morris. LC 82-15254. (Illus.). 225p. 1975. pap. 6.95 o.p. (ISBN 0-89051-087-3). Master Bks.
Troublemaker. Lynn Hall. (Illus.). 94p. (gr. 3-5). 1976. pap. 1.75 o.p. (ISBN 0-380-00434-8, 52373-6, Camelot). Avon.
Troubleshooters Handbook for Mechanical Systems. Robert H. Emerick. LC 68-28413. (Illus.). 1969. text ed. 59.50 o.p. (ISBN 0-07-019314-2). McGraw.
Troubleshooting & Repairing Personal Computers. Art Margolis. (Illus.). 320p. 1983. 21.95 o.p. (ISBN 0-8306-0139-2); pap. 16.95 o.p. (ISBN 0-8306-1539-3, 1539). TAB Bks.
Troubleshooting & Repairing Satellite TV Systems. Richard Maddox. (Illus.). 400p. 1985. 26.95 o.p. (ISBN 0-8306-0977-6, 1977); pap. 18.60 o.p. (ISBN 0-8306-1977-1). TAB Bks.
Troubleshooting: Basic Writing Skills. 2nd ed. William Herman & Jeffrey M. Young. 1982. pap. text ed. 14.95 o.p. (ISBN 0-03-059118-X). HR&W.
Troubleshooting Old Cars. Ron Bishop. (Illus.). 182p. 1982. 13.95 o.p. (ISBN 0-8306-3075-9); pap. 8.95 o.p. (ISBN 0-8306-2075-3, 2075). TAB Bks.
Troubleshooting with the Oscilloscope. 4th ed. Robert G. Middleton. LC 80-51719. 256p. 1980. 11.95 o.p. (ISBN 0-672-21738-4). Sams.
Troublesome Border. Oscar J. Martinez. LC 87-34294. (PROFMEX Ser.). 177p. 1988. 22.95 o.p. (ISBN 0-8165-1033-4). U of Ariz Pr.
Trouping in the Oregon Country. Alice H. Ernst. LC 74-15552. (Illus.). 197p. 1974. Repr. of 1961 ed. lib. bdg. 35.00x o.p. (ISBN 0-8371-7821-5, EROC). Greenwood.
Trout & Salmon Fishing. Roy Eaton. LC 80-68897. (Illus.). 192p. 1981. 29.95 o.p. (ISBN 0-7153-8117-2). David & Charles.
Trout in the Milk: A Composite Portrait of Richard Hugo. Compiled by Jack Myers. (Illus.). 1982. pap. 6.00 o.s.i. (ISBN 0-917652-12-6). Confluence Pr.
Trout in the Milk: A Composite Portrait of Richard Hugo. (Illus.). 1982. pap. 6.00 o.s.i. (ISBN 0-317-65114-5). Confluence Pr.
Trout the Magnificent. Sheila Turnage. LC 82-15865. (Illus.). 48p. (ps-3). 1984. 12.95 o.p. (ISBN 0-15-290962-1, HJ). HarBraceJ.
Trouveres & Troubadours: A Popular Treatise. Pierre Aubry. Tr. by Claude Aveling. LC 68-59029. Repr. of 1914 ed. 20.00 o.p. (ISBN 0-8154-0265-1). Cooper Sq.
Trove. Peter Smalley. 1978. 8.95 o.p. (ISBN 0-393-08835-9). Norton.
TRS-80 As a Controller. Jerry W. O'Dell. (Illus.). 209p. (Orig.). 1984. spiral binding 12.95 o.p. (ISBN 0-88006-061-1, BK7394). Wayne Green Ent.
TRS-80 BASIC Manual. Lynne Mass & Thomas M. Kemnitz. LC 85-3735. (Kids Working with Computers Ser.). (Illus.). 48p. (gr. 2 up). 1985. lib. bdg. 11.27 o.p. (ISBN 0-516-08431-3). Childrens.
TRS-80 Color Computer Games Master. Brain & Brain. 1985. 14.95 o.p. Sams.
TRS-80 Color LOGO Manual. Lynne Mass & Thomas M. Kemnitz. LC 85-432. (Kids Working with Computers Ser.). (Illus.). 48p. (gr. 2 up). 1985. lib. bdg. 11.27 o.p. (ISBN 0-516-08432-1). Childrens.
TRS-80 for Kids from Eight to Eighty, 2 vols. Michael P. Zabinski. LC 82-61990. 136p. 1982. pap. 10.95 ea. o.p. (22046-6). Vol. 1 (ISBN 0-672-22046-6). Vol. 2 (ISBN 0-672-22070-9). Sams.
TRS-80 Graphics. David A. Kater & Susan Thomas. (Illus.). 256p. 1982. pap. text ed. 15.95 o.p. (ISBN 0-07-033303-3, BYTE Bks). McGraw.
TRS-80 Graphics Handbook. Dennis F. Tanner. 248p. 1984. 31.95 o.p. (ISBN 0-442-28300-8); pap. 21.95 o.p. (ISBN 0-442-28299-0). Van Nos Reinhold.
TRS-80 Model 100: A User's Guide. Joseph Coleman. 288p. (Orig.). 1984. 21.95 o.p. (ISBN 0-8306-0651-3, 1651); pap. 15.15 o.p. (ISBN 0-8306-1651-9). TAB Bks.
TRS-80 Models III & IV: Programming & Applications. Larry J. Goldstein. (Illus.). 320p. 1984. 15.95 o.p. (ISBN 0-89303-903-9). Brady Bks.
TRS-80 Portable Computer Subroutine Cookbook. David D. Busch. (Illus.). 192p. 1984. pap. 12.95 o.p. (ISBN 0-89303-904-7). Brady Bks.
TRS-80 Word Processing with Scripsit. David A. Kater. 176p. 1985. pap. text ed. 21.95 o.p. (ISBN 0-07-033360-2, BYTE Bks). McGraw.
TRS-80 Z80 Assembly Language Library. Craig A. Lindley. (Illus.). 355p. (Orig.). 1983. looseleaf binder 34.97 o.p. (ISBN 0-88006-060-3, BK7395). Wayne Green Ent.
TRS-80 Z80 Assembly Language Library. incl. disks 29.97 o.p. (ISBN 0-317-06047-3). Wayne Green Ent.
Truants. Ron Carlson. 1981. 10.95 o.p. (ISBN 0-393-01383-9). Norton.
Truck. Donald Crews. (Illus.). (gr. k-3). 1981. sound filmstrip incl. 22.95 o.p. (ISBN 0-941078-00-0). Live Oak Media.
Truck. Katherine Dunn. 1974. pap. 1.25 o.p. (ISBN 0-380-01592-7, 19125). Avon.
Truck Ability Work Sheet Pad. 150p. 8.00 o.p. (HS-83). Soc Auto Engineers.
Truck Drivers in America. D. Daryl Wyckoff. LC 78-24793. (Illus.). 176p. 1979. 21.50x o.p. (ISBN 0-669-02818-5). Lexington Bks.
Trucking & Intermodal Freight Issues. LC 84-1956. (Transportation Research Record Ser.: No. 920). 1983. 10.80 o.p. (ISBN 0-309-03608-9). Transport Res Bd.
Trucking Trends. Spence Murray. LC 77-84296. (Pickups & Vans Ser.). (Illus., Orig.). (gr. 9-12). 1977. pap. 3.95 o.p. (ISBN 0-8227-5017-1). Petersen Pub.
Trudeau. George Radwanski. LC 78-67827. 1978. 14.95 o.s.i. (ISBN 0-8008-7897-3). Taplinger.
True Americanism: Green Berets & War Resisters: A Study of Commitment. David M. Mantell. LC 74-2230. 1974. pap. 10.95x o.p. (ISBN 0-8077-2452-1). Tchrs Coll.
True & Fair View in Company Accounts. D. Flint. 1982. pap. 16.95 o.p. (ISBN 0-85258-223-4). Van Nos Reinhold.
True & False Monkey. Ed. by Gao Maingyou. (Monkey Ser.: No. 17). (Illus.). 73p. (gr. 1-4). 1986. pap. 7.95 o.p. (ISBN 0-8351-1731-6). China Bks.
True & Invisible Rosicrucian Order. Paul F. Case. LC 85-3185. (Illus.). 352p. 1985. 22.50 o.p. (ISBN 0-87728-608-6). Weiser.
True BASIC: A Complete Manual. Henry Simpson. (Illus.). 208p. 1985. 22.95 o.p. (ISBN 0-8306-0970-9, 1970); pap. 14.60 o.p. (ISBN 0-8306-1970-4, 1970P). TAB Bks.
True Christian Science. Hani R. Abdu. 64p. 1981. 5.00 o.p. (ISBN 0-682-49632-4). Exposition-Phoenix.
True Confessions of a Sunday School Teacher. Hawley. 1983. 3.95 o.p. (ISBN 0-88207-285-4). Victor Bks.
True Detective. Theodore Weesner. 464p. 1987. 17.45 o.s.i. (ISBN 0-671-40024-X). Summit Bks.
True Devotion. Louis De Montfort. LC 63-12679. 1973. 3.50 o.s.i. (ISBN 0-8198-0517-3); pap. 2.50 o.s.i. Dghtrs St Paul.
True Fellowship. Jerry Bridges. (Christian Character Library). 150p. 1985. handbk. 8.95 o.p. (ISBN 0-89109-521-7). NavPress.
True Francine. Marc Brown. (Snuggle & Read Story Bks.). (Illus.). 32p. (ps-3). 1982. pap. 1.95 o.p. (ISBN 0-380-57083-1, 57083-1, Camelot). Avon.
True History of Joshua Davidson, 1872. Eliza L. Linton. Ed. by Robert L. Wolff. LC 75-1524. (Victorian Fiction Ser.). 1975. lib. bdg. 73.00 o.p. (ISBN 0-8240-1596-7). Garland Pub.
True History of the Captivity & Restoration of Mrs. Mary Rowlandson, Repr. Of 1682 Ed. Bd. with Humiliations Follow'd with Deliverances...with a Narrative, of a Notable Deliverance Lately Received by Some English Captives, from the Hands of Cruel Indians. Cotton Mather. Repr. of 1697 ed. LC 75-7020. (Indian Captivities Ser.: Vol. 1). 1977. lib. bdg. 44.00 o.p. (ISBN 0-8240-1625-4). Garland Pub.
True Intellectual System of the Universe, 2 vols. Ralph Cudworth. Ed. by Rene Wellek. LC 75-11213. (British Philosophers & Theologians of the 17th & 18th Centuries Ser.: Vol. 16). 1978. Repr. of 1678 ed. Set. lib. bdg. 101.00 o.p. (ISBN 0-8240-1767-6). Garland Pub.
True Life. Lewis Foster. LC 77-83656. 96p. (Orig.). 1978. pap. 2.25 o.p. (ISBN 0-87239-192-2, 40047). Standard Pub.
True Life of Sweeney Todd: A Novel in Collage. Cozette De Charmoy. (Paperback Ser.). (Illus.). 1977. pap. 5.95 o.p. (ISBN 0-306-80060-8). Da Capo.
True-Life Treasure Hunts. Judy Donnelly. LC 84-4777. (Step-up Bks.). (Illus.). 72p. (gr. 2-5). 1984. 4.95 o.s.i. (ISBN 0-394-86801-3, Pub. by BYR); lib. bdg. 8.99 o.s.i. (ISBN 0-394-96801-8). Random.
True Love. Herbert Gold. LC 82-72063. 1982. 14.50 o.p. (ISBN 0-87795-425-9, Arbor Hse). Morrow.
True Love: A Novel. Herbert Gold. LC 85-45939. 224p. 1986. pap. 3.95 o.s.i. (ISBN 0-394-62220-0, BC). Grove.
True Love Will Never Die. Frances Ruocco. 36p. 1985. 5.95 o.p. (ISBN 0-533-06242-X). Vantage.
True Prayer: An Invitation to Christian Spirituality. Kenneth Leech. LC 80-8358. 208p. 1981. 12.00 o.p. (ISBN 0-06-065227-6). HarpR.
True Sea: A Novel of the Florida Keys. F. W. Belland. LC 83-18440. 1984. 15.95 o.p. (ISBN 0-03-064014-8, William Abrahams Bk). H Holt & Co.
True Spy Stories. James B. Sweeney. (Triumph Bks.). (Illus.). 96p. (gr. 7 up). 1981. lib. bdg. 11.90 o.p. (ISBN 0-531-04339-8). Watts.
True Stories. Margaret Atwood. 1982. 12.95 o.p. (ISBN 0-671-45271-1); pap. 4.80 o.p. (ISBN 0-671-45971-6). S&S.
True Story of Ah Q. 1969. pap. 2.95 o.p. (ISBN 0-8351-0408-7). China Bks.
True Story of the Notorious Jesse James. Evans Newmans. 1976. 5.00 o.p. (ISBN 0-682-48534-9, Lochinvar). Exposition-Phoenix.
True Surrender & Christian Community of Goods, 1521-1578. Peter Walpot. 1957. pap. 4.00 o.p. (ISBN 0-87486-205-1). Plough.
True Tales of a Soul Traveler. Johnnie McDaniel. 1985. 8.95 o.p. (ISBN 0-533-06175-X). Vantage.
Truebasic: Algebra II. John Kemeny & Tom Kurtz. 1987. Commodore Amiga Version. incl. disk 29.95 o.p. (ISBN 0-471-62834-4); IBM Version. incl. disk 29.95 o.p. (ISBN 0-471-62832-8); Macintosh Version. incl. disk 29.95 o.p. (ISBN 0-471-62833-6). Wiley.
Truebasic: CHIPendale. John Kemeny & Tom Kurtz. 1987. Commodore Amiga Version. incl. disk 29.95 o.p. (ISBN 0-471-62851-4); IBM Version. incl. disk 29.95 o.p. (ISBN 0-471-62853-0); Macintosh Version. incl. disk 29.95 o.p. (ISBN 0-471-62852-2). Wiley.
Truebasic: Discrete Mathematics. John Kemeny & Tom Kurtz. 1987. Commodore Amiga Version. incl. disk 29.95 o.p. (ISBN 0-471-62826-3); IBM Version. incl. disk 29.95 o.p. (ISBN 0-471-62829-8); Macintosh Version. 29.95 o.p. (ISBN 0-471-62827-1). Wiley.
Truebasic: Pre-Calculus. John Kemeny & Tom Kurtz. 1987. Commodore Amiga Version. incl. disk 29.95 o.p. (ISBN 0-471-62841-7); IBM Version. incl. disk 29.95 o.p. (ISBN 0-471-62838-7); Macintosh Version. incl. disk 29.95 o.p. (ISBN 0-471-62839-5). Wiley.
Truebasic: Probability Theory. John Kemeny & Tom Kurtz. 1987. Commodore Amiga Version. incl. disk 29.95 o.p. (ISBN 0-471-62846-8); IBM Version. incl. disk 29.95 o.p. (ISBN 0-471-62828-X); Macintosh Version. incl. disk 29.95 o.p. (ISBN 0-471-62845-X). Wiley.
Truebasic: Trigonometry. John Kemeny & Tom Kurtz. 1987. Commodore Amiga Version. incl. disk 29.95 o.p. (ISBN 0-471-62837-9); IBM Version. incl. disk 29.95 o.p. (ISBN 0-471-62835-2); Macintosh Version. incl. disk 29.95 o.p. (ISBN 0-471-62836-0). Wiley.
Truebasic: TrueSTAT Theory. John Kemeny & Tom Kurtz. 1987. Commodore Amiga Version. incl. disk 59.95 o.p. (ISBN 0-471-62849-2); IBM Version. incl. disk 59.95 o.p. (ISBN 0-471-62847-6); Macintosh Version. incl. disk 59.95 o.p. (ISBN 0-471-62848-4). Wiley.
TruebasicTM: Calculus. John Kemeny & Tom Kurtz. 1987. CommodoreTM Amiga Version. incl. disk 29.95 o.p. (ISBN 0-471-62844-1);, IBM Version. incl. disk 29.95 o.p. (ISBN 0-471-62842-5); Macintosh Version. incl. disk 29.95 o.p. (ISBN 0-471-62843-3). Wiley.
Truffles & Other Chocolate Confections. Pamela Asquith. LC 83-18650. (Illus.). 128p. 1984. 12.95 o.p. (ISBN 0-03-063356-7). H Holt & Co.
Truman Capote. Date not set. (ISBN 0-385-29509-X). Delacorte.
Truman Capote: Dear Heart, Old Buddy. John M. Brinnin. (Illus.). 176p. 1986. pap. 16.95 o.p. (ISBN 0-385-29509-X, Sey Lawr). Delacorte.
Truman Doctrine. Charles M. Dobbs. 1988. price not set o.p. (ISBN 0-89874-988-3). Krieger.
Truman: The Rise to Power. Richard L. Miller. (Illus.). 1985. text ed. 19.95 o.p. (ISBN 0-07-042185-4). McGraw.
Trump: The Building of an Empire. John Dooley. 192p. 1988. pap. 3.50 o.p. (ISBN 1-55547-262-1). Critics Choice Paper.
Trumpet & Trombone. rev. ed. Philip Bate. (Illus.). 1978. 17.95x o.p. (ISBN 0-393-02204-8, NortonC). Norton.
Trumpet Book. Melvin Berger. LC 78-836. (Illus.). (gr. 3-7). 1978. 11.25 o.p. (ISBN 0-688-41832-5); PLB 11.88 o.p. (ISBN 0-688-51832-X). Lothrop.
Trundlewheel. Katrina Van Tassel. (Lamont Hall Chapbook Series for Poetry). 16p. (Orig.). 1981. 1.25 o.p. (ISBN 0-9603840-1-4). Andrew Mtn Pr.
Trust Department Accounting. Bank Administration Institute Staff. 244p. 1976. 36.00 o.p. (ISBN 0-317-33836-6, 108). Bank Admin Inst.
Trust Movement in British Industry: A Study of Business Organization. Henry W. Macrosty. LC 68-16355. 1968. Repr. of 1907 ed. 12.00x o.p. (ISBN 0-87586-007-9). Agathon.
Trustable & Preshus Friends. Ed. by Jane Douglass. LC 77-73048. (Illus.). 1977. 10.00 o.p. (ISBN 0-15-191318-8). HarBraceJ.
Trustees Handbook: A Basic Text on Labor-Management Employee Benefit Plans. 3rd ed. Ed. by Claude L. Kordus. 545p. 1979. pap. text ed. 35.00 o.p. (ISBN 0-89154-113-6). Intl Found Employ.
Trusteeship System of the United Nations. Charmian E. Toussaint. LC 75-27689. 1976. Repr. of 1956 ed. lib. bdg. 25.00x o.p. (ISBN 0-8371-8460-6, TOTS). Greenwood.
Trusteeships: What Are They? 1980. 0.75 o.p. Natl Lawyers Guild.
Trusts. 1977 ed. 1979. 5.00 o.p. (ISBN 0-87526-212-0). Gould.
Truth. Joel S. Goldsmith. 1972. pap. 1.00 o.p. (ISBN 0-87516-141-3). DeVorss.
Truth about AIDS. Fettner. 15.95 o.p. (ISBN 0-8050-0198-0); pap. 8.95 o.p. (ISBN 0-8050-0199-9). H Holt & Co.
Truth about AIDS: Evolution of an Epidemic. Ann G. Fettner & William A. Check. LC 83-22799. 281p. 1984. 15.95 o.p. (ISBN 0-03-069539-2, Owl Bks.); pap. 8.95 o.p. (ISBN 0-8050-0199-9). H Holt & Co.
Truth about Armageddon: What the Bible Says about the End of Times. William S. LaSor. LC 82-47748. 160p. (Orig.). 1982. pap. 6.68i o.p. (ISBN 0-06-064919-4, RD 407). HarpR.
Truth about Cottages. John Woodforde. (Illus.). 1979. pap. 8.95 o.p. (ISBN 0-7100-0165-7). Routledge Chapman & Hall.
Truth about Dragons: An Anti Romance. Hazard Adams. LC 70-134569. 179p. 1971. 6.50 o.p. (ISBN 0-15-191320-X). HarBraceJ.
Truth about Evolution & the Bible. Harriette Curtiss & F. Homer. 1928. 5.50 o.p. (ISBN 0-87516-308-4). DeVorss.
Truth about Kent State. Peter Davies. (Illus.). 241p. 1973. 10.00 o.p. (ISBN 0-374-27938-1). FS&G.
Truth about Kent State. Peter Davies. 1973. pap. 3.50 o.p. (ISBN 0-374-51041-5, Noonday). FS&G.
Truth about Self-Protection: Streetfighting Techniques, Mace, Improvised Weapons & Firearms, Locks, Alarms, & Dogs. M. Ayoob. 1986. lib. bdg. 79.95 o.p. (ISBN 0-8490-3667-4). Gordon Pr.
Truth about the Man Behind the Book That Sparked the War Between the States. Frances Cavanah. LC 75-11566. (Illus.). 188p. (gr. 3-7). 1975. 7.95 o.s.i. (ISBN 0-664-32572-6, Westminster). Westminster John Knox.
Truth about Trusts. John Moody. LC 68-28643. 1970. Repr. of 1904 ed. lib. bdg. 28.75x o.p. (ISBN 0-8371-0572-2, MOTR). Greenwood.
Truth & Dialogue in World Religions: Conflicting Truth Claims. Ed. by John Hick. LC 74-7244. 1974. 5.95 o.s.i. (ISBN 0-664-20713-8, Westminster). Westminster John Knox.
Truth & Meaning. Greenwood. 1957. (ISBN 0-8022-0625-5). Philos Lib.

Titles

Truth & Unity of Man: Letters in Response to a Crisis. M. R. Bawa Muhaiyaddeen. LC 80-18050. 144p. 1980. 10.00 o.p. (ISBN 0-914390-15-5); pap. 3.95 o.s.i. (ISBN 0-914390-14-7). Fellowship Pr PA.

Truth Apparent: Essays on Biblical Preaching. Jay E. Adams. 1982. pap. 4.95 o.p. (ISBN 0-87552-077-4). Presby & Reformed.

Truth for Today. George Merritt. 5.50 o.p. (ISBN 0-89225-202-2). Gospel Advocate.

Truth in Lending Simplification: A Compliance Manual for Creditors & Attorneys on Regulation E. Dennis H. Replansky et al. 329p. 1986. pap. 45.00 o.p. (ISBN 0-941161-08-0). PES Inc WI.

Truth Is Two-Eyed. John A. Robinson. LC 79-25774. 174p. 1980. pap. 6.95 o.s.i. (ISBN 0-664-24316-9, Westminster). Westminster John Knox.

Truth Machine see Heinemann Guided Readers.

Truth Maintenance Systems. David McAllester & Drew McDermott. (Illus.). 75p. 1988. pap. text ed. 12.00 o.p. (ISBN 0-929280-11-3). Amer Artificial.

Truth of a Hopi. 2nd ed. Edmund Nequatewa. LC 73-78419. (Illus.). 137p. 1985. pap. 8.95 o.p. (ISBN 0-87358-386-8). Northland.

Truth of Life. Ambrose G. Beltz. (ISBN 0-8022-0098-2). Philos Lib.

Truth of Poetry: Tensions in Modern Poetry from Baudelaire to the 1960s. Michael Hamburger. LC 72-85012. 1971. pap. 2.95 o.p. (ISBN 0-15-691380-1, HB197, Harv). HarBraceJ.

Truth of Poetry: Tensions in Modern Poetry from Baudelaire to the 1960s. Michael Hamburger. 356p. 1982. Repr. of 1969 ed. 11.95x o.p. (ISBN 0-416-34240-X, NO. 3764). Routledge Chapman & Hall.

Truth of the Gospel: An Exposition of Galatians. Gerhard Ebeling. LC 84-47918. 288p. 1985. 3.95 o.p. (ISBN 0-8006-0728-7, 1-728, Fortress). Augsburg Fortress.

Truth of the Stock Tape. W. D. Gann. (Illus.). 1923. 25.00 o.s.i. (ISBN 0-939093-04-9). Lambert Gann Pub.

Truth Speaks. Richard E. Tottress. 1975. 5.00 o.p. (ISBN 0-682-48160-2). Exposition-Phoenix.

Truth That Killed. Georgi Markov. Tr. by Liliana Brisby. LC 84-20. 304p. 1984. 15.45 o.s.i. (ISBN 0-89919-296-3). Ticknor & Fields.

Truth, the Millennium, & the Battle of Armageddon. Leslie G. Thomas. 1979. pap. 2.50 o.p. (ISBN 0-89225-188-3). Gospel Advocate.

Truth to Life. A. O. Cockshut. LC 74-7460. 224p. 1974. 7.50 o.p. (ISBN 0-15-191322-6). HarBraceJ.

Truth to Life: The Art of Biography in the Nineteenth Century. A. O. Cockshut. LC 75-29326. 1976. pap. 3.95 o.p. (ISBN 0-15-691385-2, Harv). HarBraceJ.

Truth Will Make You Free. Mary L. Eaves. LC 83-90380. 59p. 1985. 7.95 o.p. (ISBN 0-533-05883-X). Vantage.

Truthful Lens. Lucien Goldschmidt & Weston J. Naef. LC 80-66237. (Illus.). 241p. 1980. 125.00x o.p. (ISBN 0-8139-1036-6, Grolier Club). U Pr of Va.

Try Marriage Before Divorce. James Kilgore. 1984. Repr. 5.95 o.p. (ISBN 0-8499-2995-4). Word Bks.

Try This One Strikes Again. Ed. by Cindy S. Hansen. LC 84-81781. (Illus.). 80p. (Orig.). 1984. pap. 5.95 o.p. (ISBN 0-931529-00-X). Group Pub.

Try This One... Too. Ed. by Lee Sparks. LC 82-81331. (Illus.). 80p. (Orig.). 1982. pap. 5.95 o.p. (ISBN 0-936664-05-3). Group Pub.

Try to Remember. Vanessa James. (Nightingale Paperbacks Ser.). 328p. 1987. pap. 10.95 o.p. (ISBN 0-8161-4318-8, Large Print Bks). G K Hall.

Trygve. Trygve Winther. 1979. 12.00 o.p. (ISBN 0-682-49360-0). Exposition-Phoenix.

Trying Freedom: The Case for Liberating Education. Richard Meisler. LC 83-22543. 320p. 1984. 16.95 o.p. (ISBN 0-15-191358-7). HarBraceJ.

Trying Not to Love You. (YA) (gr. 7-9). pap. 2.25 o.p. (ISBN 0-671-54394-6). Archway.

Trying the Toxic Tort Case (3-84) Institute for Continuing Legal Education (New Jersey) Staff. LC 84-150007. (Illus.). ii, 312p. 1985. incl. cassettes 75.00 o.p. NJ Inst CLE.

Ts'ao Chung Weighs an Elephant. Lyndell Ludwig. LC 82-73197. (Illus.). 48p. (Orig.). (ps-1). 1983. pap. 4.95 o.p. (ISBN 0-916870-52-9). Creative Arts Bk.

Tsar Ivan Fourth's Reply to Jan Roktya. Valerie A. Tumins. LC 79-114575. (Slavistic Printings & Reprintings Ser.: No. 84). (Illus.). 1971. text ed. 72.00x o.p. (ISBN 90-2791-764-7). Mouton.

TSCA Inspection Manual Part I. Thomas F. Sullivan. 300p. 1982. pap. text ed. 35.00 o.p. (ISBN 0-686-38763-5). Gov Insts.

TSM in Nineteen Eighty: State of the Art & Future Directions. (Special Report). 70p. 1980. 5.60 o.p. (ISBN 0-309-02996-1). Transport Res Bd.

TTL Data Book, Vol. IV. Texas Instruments Engineering Staff. LC 83-51810. 350p. (Orig.). 1986. pap. text ed. 9.95 o.p. (ISBN 0-89512-154-9, SDZD001B). Tex Instr Inc.

TTL Data Book, Vol. III. Texas Instruments Engineering Staff. LC 83-51810. 800p. (Orig.). 1986. pap. text ed. 12.95 o.p. (ISBN 0-89512-153-0, SDAD001B). Tex Instr Inc.

TTL Data Book, Vol. II. Texas Instruments Engineering Staff. LC 83-51810. 1100p. (Orig.). 1984. pap. text ed. 17.85 o.p. (ISBN 0-89512-096-8, SDLD001). Tex Instr Inc.

Tuba Family. Clifford Bevan. (Illus.). 1978. 27.50 o.s.i. (ISBN 0-684-15477-3, ScribT). Scribner.

Tubulo-Interstitial Nephropathies. Ed. by Ramzi Cotran. (Contemporary Issues in Nephrology Ser.: Vol. 10). (Illus.). 381p. 1982. text ed. 49.50 o.p. (ISBN 0-443-08258-8). Churchill.

Tuckahoe Marble: The Rise & Fall of an Industry in Eastchester, N. Y., 1822-1930. Louis Torres. LC 76-26126. (Illus.). 1976. pap. 6.95 o.p. (ISBN 0-916346-21-8). Harbor Hill Bks.

Tucker's Countryside. George Selden. (Illus.). 167p. (gr. 3-7). 1979. pap. 2.50 o.p. (ISBN 0-380-01584-6, Camelot). Avon.

Tudor Church Music. Ed. by P. C. Buck & E. H. Fellowes. Incl. Vol. 1. John Taverner - Part One; Vol. 2. William Byrd - English Church Music, Part One (ISBN 0-8450-1852-3); Vol. 3. John Tavernen - Part Two; Vol. 4. Orlando Gibbons; Vol. 5. Robert White; Vol. 6. Thomas Tallis; Vol. 7. William Byrd; Vol. 8. Thomas Tomkins; Vol. 9; Vol. 10. Hugh Aston & John Marbeck (ISBN 0-8450-1860-4). 1963. Repr. of 1922 ed. 750.00x set o.p. (ISBN 0-8450-1850-7); 85.00x ea. o.p.; appendix 50.00x o.p. Broude.

Tudor Drama: A History of English National Drama to the Retirement of Shakespeare. C. F. Brooke. xiii, 461p. 1970. Repr. of 1939 ed. 35.00 o.p. (ISBN 0-208-00578-1, Archon). Shoe String.

Tudor Drama & Politics: A Critical Approach to Topical Meaning. David M. Bevington. LC 68-17637. 1968. 27.00x o.s.i. (ISBN 0-674-91230-6). Harvard U Pr.

Tudor Men & Institutions: Studies in English Law & Government. Ed. by Arthur J. Slavin. LC 72-79337. x, 294p. 1972. 32.50 o.p. (ISBN 0-8071-0227-X). La State U Pr.

Tudor Tapestry: Men, Women & Society in Reformation England. Derek Wilson. LC 71-158187. (Illus.). 1972. 29.95x o.p. (ISBN 0-8229-3242-3). U of Pittsburgh Pr.

Tudor Women. Alison Plowden. LC 78-21958. 1979. 10.95 o.p. (ISBN 0-689-10944-X, Atheneum). Macmillan.

Tuesday Club Murders. Agatha Christie. 224p. 1984. pap. 3.50 o.s.i. (ISBN 0-425-08903-7). Berkley Pub.

Tuesday's Child. Nancy Baron. LC 84-2944. 120p. (gr. 4-6). 1984. 10.95 o.s.i. (ISBN 0-689-31042-0, Atheneum Childrens Bks). Macmillan.

Tuffy, the Purple-Footed Duck. Betty Lou Burkart. (ps-1). 1976. 4.00 o.p. (ISBN 0-682-48679-5). Exposition-Phoenix.

Tuition Vouchers: Adam Smith to Ronald Reagan. David W. Kirkpatrick. 1988. 17.95 o.p. (ISBN 0-8022-2550-0). Philos Lib.

Tuk, the Timid: The Story of a Sea Otter. Jean G. Howard. LC 84-50217. (Illus.). 80p. (Orig.). (gr. 3 up). 1984. pap. 10.95 stitched pages o.s.i. (ISBN 0-930954-20-3). Tidal Pr.

Tulitas of Torreon. Tulitas Jamieson. LC 69-20291. 1969. 5.00 o.p. (ISBN 0-87404-014-0). Tex Western.

Tulla's Summer. Rose Lagercrantz. Tr. by George Blecher & Lone Thygesen-Blecher. LC 76-46786. (Illus.). (gr. 3-5). 1977. 6.95 o.p. (ISBN 0-15-291095-6, HJ). HarBraceJ.

Tully Filmus: Selected Drawings. Tully Filmus. LC 70-151314. 96p. 1978. pap. 11.95 o.p. (ISBN 0-8276-0164-6, 424). JPS Phila.

Tully the Tree Kangaroo. Georgeanne Irvine. (Zoo Babies Ser.). (Illus.). 16p. (Orig.). (gr. k-6). 1983. pap. 1.25 o.p. (ISBN 0-8249-8058-1). Ideals.

Tulpa. J. N. Williamson. 1980. pap. 1.95 o.p. (ISBN 0-8439-0799-1, Pub. by Leisure Bks CT). Dorchester Pub Co.

Tulsa Art Deco: An Architectural Era Nineteen Twenty-Five to Nineteen Forty-Two. Junior League of Tulsa, Inc. Staff. 204p. 1980. 40.00 o.p. (ISBN 0-9604368-1-2); pap. 15.95 o.p. (ISBN 0-9604368-2-0). Jr League Tulsa.

Tumble-Down Dick: The Fall of the House of Cromwell. Earl M. Hause. LC 72-81386. 1972. 13.50 o.p. (ISBN 0-682-47514-9, University). Exposition-Phoenix.

Tumbleweed. Janwillem Van De Wetering. 1976. 6.95 o.p. (ISBN 0-395-24352-1). HM.

Tumbleweeds, No. 18. Tom K. Ryan. (Orig.). 1986. pap. 2.25 o.s.i. (ISBN 0-449-12820-2, GM). Fawcett.

Tumbling Book. Jack Wiley. (Illus.). (gr. 7 up). 1978. 8.95 o.p. (ISBN 0-679-20418-0). McKay.

Tumor Associated Antigens & Their Specific Immune Responses. Ed. by F. Spreafico & R. Arnon. (Serono Symposium Ser.). 1979. 76.00 o.p. (ISBN 0-12-658350-1). Acad Pr.

Tumor Immunology. J. Stjernsward et al. (Illus.). 220p. 1972. text ed. 24.50x o.p. (ISBN 0-8422-7060-4). Irvington.

Tumors of the Central Nervous System in Infancy & Childhood. Ed. by D. Voth. (Illus.). 438p. 1982. 44.00 o.p. (ISBN 0-387-11821-7). Springer-Verlag.

Tumulto. Brad Williams. 1974. pap. 1.25 o.p. (ISBN 0-380-01593-5, 18812). Avon.

Tumultuous Years: The Presidency of Harry S. Truman, 1949-1953. Robert J. Donovan. (Illus.). 1982. 19.95 o.p. (ISBN 0-393-01619-6). Norton.

Tune & Repair Your Own Piano. Michael Johnson & Robin Mackworth-Young. LC 78-51046. (Illus.). 82p. 1978. 3.95 o.p. (ISBN 0-15-191383-8). HarBraceJ.

Tune Beyond Us: A Collection of Poetry. Ed. by Myra C. Livingston. LC 68-11502. (gr. 6 up). 1968. 7.50 o.p. (ISBN 0-15-291098-0, HJ). HarBraceJ.

Tune in Tomorrow. Mary Anderson. LC 83-15656. 192p. (gr. 5 up). 1984. 11.95 o.s.i. (ISBN 0-689-31009-9, Atheneum Childrens Bks). Macmillan.

Tuneup & Troubleshooting Illustrated. LC 79-66361. (Illus.). 320p. 1979. 19.95 o.p. (ISBN 0-87851-513-5); pap. 11.50 o.p. (ISBN 0-87851-512-7). Hearst Bks.

T'ung Shu. Tr. by Martin Palmer from Chinese. LC 85-2520. (Illus.). 240p. 1986. pap. 7.95 o.p. (ISBN 0-87773-346-5, 74221-4, Dist. by Random). Shambhala Pubns.

T'ung Shu: The Ancient Chinese Almanac. Ed. & tr. by Martin Palmer. 1986. 7.95 o.p. (ISBN 0-394-74221-4). Shambhala Pubns.

Tungsten-Arc Gas Shielded Welding. Ed. by N. C. Balchin et al. (Engineering Craftsmen Ser.: No. F22). (Illus.). 1977. spiral bdg. 39.95x o.p. (ISBN 0-85083-394-9). Trans-Atl Phila.

Tuniit: First Explorers of the High Arctic. Robert McGhee. (Illus.). 64p. 1981. pap. 4.95 o.p. (ISBN 0-660-50280-1, 56527-0, Pub. by Natl Mus Canada). U of Chicago Pr.

Tuning a Racing Yacht. Mike Fletcher & Bob Ross. (Illus.). 128p. 1974. 8.50 o.p. (ISBN 0-393-03176-4). Norton.

Tuning a Racing Yacht. rev. ed. Mike Fletcher & Bob Ross. (Illus.). 1978. 12.95 o.p. (ISBN 0-393-03218-3). Norton.

Tuning the Green Machine, An Integrated View of Environmental Systems. Institute for Environmental Education Staff & Association of New Jersey Environmental Commissions. LC 77-17902. (Illus.). 320p. 1978. lib. bdg. 12.50 o.p. (ISBN 0-379-00811-4). Oceana.

Tunisia Travel Guide. (Berlitz Travel Guides Ser.). (Illus.). 1982. pap. 4.95 o.p. (ISBN 0-02-969550-3, Berlitz). Macmillan.

Tunisian Ulama 1873-1915: Social Structure & Response to Ideological Currents. Arnold H. Green. (Social, Economic & Political Studies of the Middle East: No. 22). (Illus.). 1978. text ed. 55.00x o.p. (ISBN 90-04-05687-4). Humanities.

Tunku Abdul Rahman. A. M. Healy. LC 82-199789. (Leaders of Asia Ser.). (Illus.). 33p. 1982. 4.95 o.p. (ISBN 0-7022-1790-5). U of Queensland Pr.

Tunnel. Robert Byrne. LC 76-62519. (Illus.). 1977. 8.95 o.p. (ISBN 0-15-191385-4). HarBraceJ.

Tunnel of Hugsy Goode. Eleanor Estes. LC 79-167833. (Illus.). 256p. (gr. 3-7). 1972. 5.95 o.p. (ISBN 0-15-291100-6, HJ). HarBraceJ.

Tunnel to Yesterday. Jerome Beatty, Jr. (Illus.). 160p. (gr. 3-5). 1983. pap. 2.25 o.p. (ISBN 0-380-82537-6, 380-82537-6, Camelot). Avon.

Tunnel War. Joe Poyer. LC 79-63628. 1979. 12.95 o.p. (ISBN 0-689-11009-X, Atheneum). Macmillan.

Tunneling in Solids. C. B. Duke. (Solid State Physics, Suppl. 10). 1969. 90.50 o.p. (ISBN 0-12-607770-3). Acad Pr.

Tunnelling & Negative Resistance Phenomena in P-N Junctions. Dilip K. Roy. 1977. 55.00 o.p. (ISBN 0-08-021044-9). Pergamon.

Tunnelling into Colditz: A Mining Engineer in Captivity. Jim Rogers. (Lythway Ser.). 1987. lib. bdg. 17.50x o.p. (ISBN 0-7451-0594-7, Pub. by Chivers Pr UK). G K Hall.

Tunnelling Research. G. Girnau & A. Haack. 1984. pap. 24.00 o.p. (ISBN 0-08-029952-0). Pergamon.

Tunnels. Gail Gibbons. LC 83-18589. (Illus.). 32p. (ps-3). 1987. pap. 5.95 o.p. (ISBN 0-8234-0670-9). Holiday.

Tunnels: Journey into a Dark Universe. Jon R. Penoi. LC 83-62371. (Illus.). 65p. 1983. pap. 3.50 o.p. (ISBN 0-942316-04-5). Pueblo Pub Pr.

Tunnicliffe's Birds: Measured Drawings by C. N. Tunnicliffe. Ed. by Noel Cusa. LC 84-81060. (Illus.). 1984. 49.95 o.p. (ISBN 0-316-16556-5). Little.

Turbo BASIC Instant Reference. Douglas Hergert. (Prompter Ser.). 393p. (Orig.). 1987. pap. 12.95 o.p. (ISBN 0-89588-485-2). Sybex.

Turbo C Programming for the IBM. Robert Lafore. 600p. 1987. 22.95 o.p. (ISBN 0-672-22614-6). Sams.

Turbo Pascal Compl Ref. (ISBN 0-07-881350-6). McGraw.

Turbo Pascal for BASIC Programmers. Paul Garrison. LC 85-62363. 410p. 1985. pap. 18.95 o.p. (ISBN 0-88022-167-4, 184); disk IBM-PC format 29.95 o.p. (ISBN 0-88022-233-6, 232); CP-M format 29.95 o.p. Que Corp.

Turbo Pascal Library. Douglas S. Stivison. LC 86-60565. 221p. (Orig.). 1986. pap. 14.95 o.p. (ISBN 0-89588-330-9). Sybex.

Turbo Pascal Program Library. Tom Rugg & Phil Feldman. LC 86-60590. 617p. (Orig.). 1986. pap. 19.95 o.p. (ISBN 0-88022-244-1, 35); 29.95 o.p. (ISBN 0-88022-300-6, 264). Que Corp.

Turbo Pascal Programmer's Library. Kris Jamsa & Steven Nameroff. 300p. 1986. pap. text ed. 19.95 o.p. (ISBN 0-07-881238-0). Osborne-Mcgraw.

Turbo Pascal Tips, Tricks and Traps. Tom Rugg & Phil Feldman. LC 86-61149. 490p. 1986. pap. 19.95 o.p. (ISBN 0-88022-266-2, 65). Que Corp.

Turbo Pascal Toolbox. Frank Dutton. 405p. (Orig.). 1988. pap. 18.95 o.p. (ISBN 0-89588-472-0). Sybex.

Turbo Prolog Primer. Dan Shafer. 368p. (Orig.). 1986. pap. 18.95 o.p. (ISBN 0-672-22510-7). Sams.

Turbocharging the Internal Combustion Engine. N. Watson & M. S. Janota. 608p. 1982. 96.50 o.p. (ISBN 0-471-87072-2, Pub. by Wiley-Interscience). Wiley.

Turbott Wolfe. William Plomer. 1987. pap. 8.95 o.p. (ISBN 0-15-691490-5, Harv). HarBraceJ.

Turbulence. 2nd. rev ed. Ed. by P. Bradshaw. (Topics in Applied Physics Ser.: Vol. 12). (Illus.). 1978. pap. 27.00 o.p. (ISBN 0-387-08864-4). Springer-Verlag.

Turbulence & Navier Stokes Equations: Proceedings. Conference Held at the Univ. of Paris-Sud, Orsay, 12-13 June 1975. Ed. by R. M. Temam. (Lecture Notes in Mathematics Ser.: Vol. 565). (Eng. & Fr.). 1977. soft cover 11.00 o.p. (ISBN 0-387-08060-0). Springer-Verlag.

Turbulence: Induced Vibrations & Noise of Structures. 144p. 1983. pap. text ed. 30.00 o.p. (ISBN 0-317-02659-3, H00285). ASME.

Turbulence Phenomena: An Introduction to the Eddy Transfer of Momentum, Mass & Heat, Particularly at Interfaces. J. T. Davies. 1972. 89.00 o.p. (ISBN 0-12-206070-9). Acad Pr.

Turbulence Seminar-Berkeley Nineteen Seventy-Six to Nineteen Seventy-Seven: Organized by A. Chorin, J. Marsden, S. Smale. Ed. by P. Bernard & T. Ratiu. (Lecture Notes in Mathematics: Vol. 615). 1977. pap. text ed. 10.70 o.p. (ISBN 0-387-08445-2). Springer-Verlag.

Turbulent Dream: Passion & Politics in the Poetry of W. B. Yeats. Geoffrey Thurley. LC 83-5728. 235p. 1984. 29.95 o.p. (ISBN 0-7022-1962-2). U of Queensland Pr.

Turbulent History of the North Adriatic Archipelago. Rudy Francin. (Illus.). 304p. 1983. 13.00 o.p. (ISBN 0-682-49977-3). Exposition-Phoenix.

Turf Managers' Handbook. W. H. Daniel & R. P. Freeborg. 424p. pap. 32.00 o.p. Assn Phys Plant Admin.

Turfgrass Pests. Compiled by W. R. Bowen. LC 79-66585. 60p. 1980. pap. 6.00 o.p. (ISBN 0-931876-39-7, 4053). ANR Pubns CA.

Turgenev: The Novelist's Novelist, a Study. Richard Freeborn. 1978. Repr. of 1960 ed. lib. bdg. 24.75x o.p. (ISBN 0-313-20187-0, FRTU). Greenwood.

Turgenev's Letters. Ivan S. Turgenev. Ed. & tr. by A. V. Knowles. 320p. 1983. 30.00 o.p. (ISBN 0-684-17867-2, ScribT). Scribner.

Turkey. (Berlitz Country Guides). (Illus.). 256p. 1988. 4.95 o.p. (ISBN 0-02-969440-X, Berlitz). Macmillan.

Turkey-A Travel Survival Kit. Tom Brosnahan. (Illus.). 328p. (Orig.). 1985. pap. 8.95 o.p. (ISBN 0-908086-45-8). Lonely Planet.

Turkey Beyond the Maeander. George E. Bean. (Illus.). 1980. 20.95 o.p. (ISBN 0-393-01327-8). Norton.

Turkey Hash. Craig Nova. 224p. 1984. pap. 4.50 o.s.i. (ISBN 0-440-38499-0, LE). Dell.

Turkey: Industrialization & Trade Strategy. Bela Balassa et al. 461p. 1983. 20.00 o.p. (ISBN 0-8213-0046-6, BK 0046). World Bank.

Turkey Shoot. Jay H. Potter. (Lythway). 168p. 1988. lib. bdg. 17.50 o.p. (ISBN 0-7451-0638-2, Pub. by Chivers Pr UK). G K Hall.

Turkey Shoot: Tracking the Attica Cover-Up. Malcolm Bell. LC 85-14778. 432p. 1986. 19.50 o.p. (ISBN 0-394-55020-X). Grove.

Turkey's Southern Shore. George E. Bean. (Illus.). 1980. 19.95 o.p. (ISBN 0-393-01326-X). Norton.

Turkish Crossroads. Bernard Newman. 1952. (ISBN 0-8022-1205-0). Philos Lib.

Turkish Folk Music from Asia Minor. Bela Bartok. Ed. by Benjamin Suchoff. LC 75-23186. (Studies in Musicology). 1976. 34.00x o.p. (ISBN 0-691-09120-X). Princeton U Pr.

Turkish Reader. 2nd, rev. ed. P. Wittek. 1956. pap. text ed. 10.00 o.s.i. E J Brill USA.

Turkish Revolution, Nineteen Sixty to Nineteen Sixty-One: Aspects of Military Politics. Walter F. Weiker. LC 79-27852. (Illus.). viii, 172p. 1980. Repr. of 1963 ed. lib. bdg. 22.50x o.p. (ISBN 0-313-22303-3, WETR). Greenwood.

Turkish White. Mel Arrighi. LC 76-54620. 1977. 7.95 o.p. (ISBN 0-15-191390-0). HarBraceJ.

Turn Back the Dawn. Nell Kincaid. (Candlelight Ecstasy Ser.: No. 185). 192p. (Orig.). 1983. pap. 1.95 o.s.i. (ISBN 0-440-19098-3). Dell.

Turn Down an Empty Glass. Frank A. Bartley. 1978. 6.00 o.p. (ISBN 0-682-48918-2). Exposition-Phoenix.

Turn of the Century. Jill Downie. 1982. pap. 3.50 o.p. (ISBN 0-380-80861-7, 80861-7). Avon.

Turn of the Screw. Henry James. 1975. 8.95x o.p. (ISBN 0-460-00912-5, Evman); pap. 1.95x o.p. (ISBN 0-460-01912-0, Evman). Biblio Dist.

Turn of the Years. V. S. Pritchett. 1982. ltd. ed. 17.00 o.p. (ISBN 0-394-52501-9). Random.

Turn on the Dark. Phyllis Martin. (Happy Day Bks.). (Illus.). 24p. (ps-2). 1985. 1.59 o.p. (ISBN 0-87239-881-1, 3681). Standard Pub.

Turn Right at the Fountain. 3rd ed. George Oakes & Alexandra Chapman. 1971. 5.95 o.s.i. (ISBN 0-03-086006-7). H Holt & Co.

Turn Right at the Fountain. 4th, rev. ed. George W. Oakes & Alexandra Chapman. LC 80-17568. (Illus.). 352p. 1981. 16.95 o.p. (ISBN 0-03-047171-0); pap. 9.95 o.p. (ISBN 0-03-059189-9). H Holt & Co.

Turn Toward Life: The Bible & Peacemaking. Jorg Zink. Tr. by Victoria Rhodin from Ger. LC 84-48709. 128p. 1985. pap. 1.00 o.p. (ISBN 0-8006-1829-7, 1-1829, Fortress). Augsburg Fortress.

Turnabout. William Wiesner. LC 72-190380. (Illus.). 40p. (ps-3). 1979. 5.95 o.p. (ISBN 0-395-28832-0, Clarion). HM.

Turnabout Year. Lucy J. Sypher. LC 76-4922. (Illus.). 224p. (gr. 4-6). 1976. 8.50 o.p. (ISBN 0-689-30546-X, Atheneum). Macmillan.

Turnaround: The No-Nonsense Guide to Corporate Renewal. Marvin A. Davis. 1987. 17.95 o.p. (ISBN 0-8092-4780-1). Contemp Bks.

Turner & Beard: American Historical Writing Reconsidered. Lee Benson. LC 79-28641. xiii, 241p. 1980. Repr. of 1960 ed. lib. bdg. 35.00x o.p. (ISBN 0-313-22281-9, BETU). Greenwood.

Turner's Venice. Lindsay Stainton. LC 85-14985. (Illus.). 192p. 1985. 40.00 o.p. (ISBN 0-8076-1134-4). Braziller.

Turner's Wife: A Novel. Norman Garbo. LC 82-14221. 400p. 1983. 15.45 o.p. (ISBN 0-393-01521-1). Norton.

Turnier-Taschenbuch. 4th ed. Alfred Brinkman & Ludwig Rellstab. 1977. pap. 15.00 o.p. (ISBN 0-311-00716-3). De Gruyter.

Turning, Vol. 1. 2nd ed. Ed. by L. Annis et al. (Engineering Craftsmen Ser.: No. H2). (Illus.). 1977. spiral bdg. 37.50x o.p. (ISBN 0-85083-403-1). Trans-Atl Phila.

Turning, Vol. 2. Ed. by S. G. Fletcher et al. (Engineering Craftsmen Ser.: No. H23). 1969. spiral bdg. 37.50x o.p. Trans-Atl Phila.

Turning & Boring: Angles & Applications. Society of Manufacturing Engineers Staff. Ed. by D. Wood. 270p. 1985. 35.00 o.p. (ISBN 0-87263-169-9). SME.

Turning East: The Promise & Peril of the New Orientalism. Harvey Cox. 1979. pap. 7.75 o.p. (ISBN 0-671-24405-1, Touchstone Bks). S&S.

Turning Islands. Paul Wilson. (Orig.). 1976. pap. 1.50 o.p. (ISBN 0-380-00861-0, 31286). Avon.

Turning Point. Naomi J. Karp. LC 76-12987. (gr. 5). 1976. 6.95 o.p. (ISBN 0-15-291238-X, HJ). HarBraceJ.

Turning Point. Michael Tarachow. (Orig.). 1981. pap. 15.00 o.p. (ISBN 0-915316-91-9). Pentagram.

Turning Point: A Program for Women in Transition Participant Packet. Sandra S. Moore. Ed. by Andrea Welborn & Carol Hartman. 142p. (Orig.). 1982. looseleaf 8.00 o.p. (ISBN 0-936352-19-1). U of KS Cont Ed.

Turning Point: A Program for Women in Transition Trainer Manual. Compiled by Sandra S. Moore et al. 238p. (Orig.). 1982. spiral bound 17.50 o.p. (ISBN 0-936352-18-3). U of KS Cont Ed.

Turning Point for Literacy-Adult Education for Development-Spirit & Declaration of Persepolis: Proceedings of the International Symposium for Literacy, Iran, 1975. Ed. by Leon Bataille. LC 76-46206. 1977. 70.00 o.p. (ISBN 0-08-021385-5); pap. 70.00 o.p. (ISBN 0-08-021386-3). Pergamon.

Turning Point II. (Outreach Literature Ser.). 32p. (Orig.). 1986. pap. 0.45 o.p. (ISBN 0-932305-42-3, 612002). Aglow Pubns.

Turning Point in North-South Economic Relations. Richard Gardner et al. (Triangle Papers: No. 3). 1974. pap. 6.00 o.p. Trilateral Comm.

Turning Point of World War II. B. Solovyov. 208p. 1982. 5.95 o.p. (ISBN 0-8285-2432-7, Pub. by Progress Pubs USSR). Imported Pubns.

Turning Point: Science, Society & the Rising Culture. Fritjof Capra. 1982. 17.95 o.p. (ISBN 0-671-24423-X). S&S.

Turning Points. Jim Smoke. 192p. (Orig.). 1985. pap. 5.95 o.p. (ISBN 0-89081-484-8). Harvest Hse.

Turning Points in World History. Geoffrey Barraclough. 1979. 9.95 o.s.i. (ISBN 0-500-25067-7). Thames Hudson.

Turning Your Stress into Strength. Robert H. Schuller. 1979. pap. 1.95 o.s.i. (ISBN 0-449-14262-0, GM). Fawcett.

Turning Your Stress into Strength. Robert H. Schuller. LC 77-88865. 144p. 1978. pap. 4.95 o.p. (ISBN 0-89081-113-X). Harvest Hse.

Turnip: Traditional Folk Tale. 12p. 1982. pap. 1.99 o.p. (Pub. by Progress Pubs USSR). Imported Pubns.

Turquois: A Study in the History, Minerology, Geology, Ethnology, Archaeology, Mythology, Folklore & Technology. Joseph E. Pogue. LC 70-175059. (Beautiful Rio Grande Classics Ser.). 300p. 1983. Repr. of 1914 ed. lib. bdg. 25.00 o.p. (ISBN 0-686-89218-6). Rio Grande.

Turquoise Lament. John D. MacDonald. (Travis McGee Ser.). 256p. 1982. pap. 2.95 o.p. (ISBN 0-449-14200-0, GM). Fawcett.

Turtle. Betty S. Cummings. LC 80-24062. (Illus.). 48p. (ps-5). 1981. PLB 8.95 o.p. (ISBN 0-689-30805-1, Atheneum). Macmillan.

Turtle Beach. Blanche D'Alpuget. 288p. 1983. 14.50 o.p. (ISBN 0-671-49241-1). S&S.

Turtle Throws a Tantrum. Jacquelyn Reinach & Ruth L. Perle. LC 78-54979. (Sweet Pickles Ser.). (Illus.). (gr. k-2). 1978. 2.95 o.p. (ISBN 0-03-042061-X). H Holt & Co.

Turtles. Wilfrid S. Bronson. LC 45-6768. (Illus.). (gr. k-3). 1945. 5.50 o.p. (ISBN 0-15-291411-0, HJ). HarBraceJ.

Turtlesteps: An Introduction to Apple LOGO & Terrapin LOGO. Pamela Sharp. 208p. 1984. 13.95 o.p. (ISBN 0-89303-906-3). Brady Bks.

Tuscany: An Anthology. Compiled by Laura Raison. (Illus.). 262p. 1984. 19.95 o.p. (ISBN 0-87196-858-4). Facts on File.

Tuskegee: Its Story & Its Work. 2nd ed. Max B. Thrasher. LC 73-78587. (Illus.). 1970. Repr. of 1900 ed. 35.00x o.p. (ISBN 0-8371-1422-5, TTU&, Pub. by Negro U Pr). Greenwood.

Tutankhamen: The Untold Story. Thomas Hoving. 384p. 1984. pap. 12.95 o.s.i. (ISBN 0-671-24370-5, Touchstone Bks). S&S.

Tutankhamon: A Novel of Ancient Egypt. Paul Startzman. 1979. 9.00 o.p. (ISBN 0-682-49218-3, Banner). Exposition-Phoenix.

Tutankhamun's Egypt. Cyril Aldred. 1978. pap. 1.49 o.s.i. (ISBN 0-684-15795-0, ScribT); pap. 1.49 encore ed. o.s.i. (ISBN 0-684-16886-3). Scribner.

Tutor. rev., 2nd ed. Ruth J. Colvin & Jane Root. Ed. by V. K. Lawson & Chip Carlin. 103p. 1987. pap. 8.00 o.p. (ISBN 0-317-57700-X). Lit Vol Am.

Tutor! A Handbook for Tutorial Programs. Lillie Pope. 144p. 1976. pap. text ed. 6.95 o.p. (ISBN 0-87594-139-7). Book-Lab.

Tutorial & Selected Papers in Digital Image Processing, Vol. 3. Harry C. Andrews. 748p. 1978. 25.00 o.p. (ISBN 0-317-34769-1). SPIE.

Tutorial for Using the TERAK-RT-11. Robert L. Smith. 136p. 1982. pap. text ed. 10.95 o.p. (ISBN 0-8403-2697-1). Kendall-Hunt.

Tutorial on Models & Metrics for Software Management & Engineering. Victor R. Basili. LC 80-83085. 343p. 1980. 25.00 o.p. (ISBN 0-8186-0310-0, Q310). IEEE Comp Soc.

Tutorial on Software System Design: Description & Analysis. William E. Riddle & Jack C. Wileden. LC 80-83083. (Tutorial Texts Ser.). 242p. 1980. 25.00 o.p. (ISBN 0-8186-0311-9, Q311). IEEE Comp Soc.

Tutorial on Structured Programming: Integrated Practices. Victor R. Basili & F. Terry Baker. LC 80-85248. 290p. 1981. 22.00 o.p. (ISBN 0-8186-0362-3, Q362). IEEE Comp Soc.

Tutorial System & Its Future. W. G. Moore. 1968. 35.00 o.p. (ISBN 0-08-012659-6); pap. text ed. 35.00 o.p. (ISBN 0-08-012658-8). Pergamon.

TV Antennas Signal Distribution Service. (ISBN 0-672-21584-5). Sams.

TV Book. Ed. by Judy Fireman. LC 77-5303. (Illus.). 402p. 1977. 14.95 o.s.i. (ISBN 0-89480-001-9, 149); pap. 7.95 o.p. (ISBN 0-89480-002-7). Workman Pub.

TV Cartoons. 2nd ed. William Armstrong. (Armstrong Cartoon Ser.). (Illus.). 48p. (Orig.). (ps up). 1972. pap. 1.00 o.p. (ISBN 0-913452-31-9). Jesuit Bks.

TV Commercial Film Editing: Professional Motion Picture Pre-& Post-Production Including Animation, Rotoscoping, & Video Tape. Carmine R. De Sarlo. LC 84-43231. 255p. 1985. pap. 29.95x o.p. (ISBN 0-89950-174-5). McFarland & Co.

TV Commercial: How It Is Made. (ISBN 0-671-60793-6). Arco.

TV Commercial Trivia Quiz Book. Bruce Solomon & Michael Uslan. 1984. pap. 5.95 o.p. (ISBN 0-87795-663-4, Arbor Hse). Morrow.

TV Field & Bench Servicer's Handbook. John Spillane. (Illus.). 1979. 9.95 o.p. (ISBN 0-8306-9847-7); pap. 10.60 o.p. (ISBN 0-8306-1082-0, 1082). TAB Bks.

T.V. Hero. (Big Little Bks.: No. 23). (Illus.). 350p. 1984. 6.95 o.p. (ISBN 0-318-02686-4). Bks Nippan.

T.V. Hero, Vol. 2. (Big Little Bks.: No. 42). (Illus.). 350p. 1984. 6.95 o.p. (ISBN 0-318-02694-5). Bks Nippan.

T.V. Hero, Vol. 3. (Big Little Bks.: No. 64). (Illus.). 350p. 1984. 6.95 o.p. (ISBN 0-318-02706-2). Bks Nippan.

Tv in Education & Industry. T. D. Connochie. 1969. 10.00 o.s.i. (ISBN 0-685-12047-3). E J Brill USA.

TV News & the Dominant Culture. John Corry. Ed. by Media Institute Staff. LC 86-60785. (Media in Society Ser.). 54p. (Orig.). 1986. pap. 12.95 o.p. (ISBN 0-937790-34-6). Media Inst.

TV On-Off: Better Family Use of Television. Ellen B. DeFranco. 1980. pap. 9.95 o.p. (ISBN 0-673-16453-5). Scott F.

TV Ritual: Worship at the Video Altar. Gregor T. Goethals. LC 80-66072. (Illus.). 180p. 1982. pap. 12.95x o.p. (ISBN 0-8070-3223-9, BPA3, Pub. by Ariadne Bks). Beacon Pr.

TV Sirens. Michael McWilliams. (Illus.). 256p. 1987. pap. 11.95 o.p. (ISBN 0-399-51292-6, Perigee). Putnam Pub Group.

Twelfth Annual Institute on Securities Regulation. Ed. by Arthur Fleischer, Jr. et al. 611p. 1981. text ed. 30.00 o.p. (ISBN 0-686-76238-X, B2-1280). PLI.

Twelfth Century Renaissance. Christopher Brooke. (History of European Civilization Library). (Illus.). 216p. 1969. pap. text ed. 11.00 net o.p. (ISBN 0-15-592385-4, HC). HarBraceJ.

Twelfth Chapter: Interpretation of God's Mystery. Buster Sigmon. 1977. 6.50 o.p. (ISBN 0-682-48856-9). Exposition-Phoenix.

Twelfth Juror. B. M. Gill. 176p. 1984. 11.95 o.s.i. (ISBN 0-684-18194-0, ScribT). Scribner.

Twelfth Juror. B. M. Gill. 1985. 13.50 o.p. (Large Print Bks). G K Hall.

Twelfth Night. William Shakespeare. Ed. by J. H. Walter. (Players' Shakespeare Ser). (YA) (gr. 9 up). 1959. 3.50 o.p. (ISBN 0-8238-0118-7). Plays.

Twelfth Night: An Annotated Bibliography. Ed. by William L. Godshalk. 1984. lib. bdg. 20.00 o.p. (ISBN 0-8240-9324-0). Garland Pub.

Twelve African Writers. Gerald Moore. LC 80-7988. (Illus.). 328p. 1980. 22.50x o.p. (ISBN 0-253-19619-1). Ind U Pr.

Twelve Caesars. Michael Grant. 1983. 15.95 o.s.i. (ISBN 0-684-14402-6). Scribner.

Twelve Centuries of Bookbindings: Four Hundred to Sixteen Hundred. Paul Needham. LC 79-52345. (Illus.). 368p. 1979. 75.00 o.s.i. (Co-pub by Oxford U Pr); pap. 39.95 o.s.i. (ISBN 0-686-68488-5). Pierpont Morgan.

Twelve Daily Exercises. Gaylord Yost. 1.50 o.p. (ISBN 0-913650-57-9). CPP Belwin.

Twelve Days of Christmas. Harold Belgum. 1974. 2.50 o.p. (ISBN 0-8066-1440-4, 10-6720, Augsburg). Augsburg Fortress.

Twelve Famous Plays of the Restoration & Eighteenth Century, 3 vols. Repr. of 1933 ed. 150.00x o.p. (ISBN 0-403-03071-4). Somerset Pub.

Twelve-Hour BASIC for the IBM PC Compatibles: How to Get the Most from Your Compaq, Corona, Eagle, Columbia, or Other PC Clone. Gary S. Belkin. 288p. 1985. pap. text ed. 12.95 o.p. (ISBN 0-07-004374-4). McGraw.

Twelve Hundred Hostages: A Play in Seven Scenes. Nicholas Wenckheim. Tr. by Sylvia E. Lipp. 1979. 4.00 o.p. (ISBN 0-682-49221-3). Exposition-Phoenix.

Twelve Little Housemates. Karl Von Frisch. Tr. by A. T. Sugar. LC 78-40341. 1979. 21.00 o.p. (ISBN 0-08-021959-4); pap. 9.25 o.p. (ISBN 0-08-021958-6). Pergamon.

Twelve Melodious Studies for Piano, Op. 63. L. Streabbog. Ed. by Hans T. Seifert. (Carl Fischer Music Library: No. 363). 1982. pap. 4.50 o.p. (ISBN 0-8258-0113-3, L363). Fischer Inc NY.

Twelve Million Black Voices: A Folk History of the Negro in the U. S. Richard Wright. LC 69-18562. (American Negro: His History & Literature Ser., No. 2). 1969. Repr. of 1941 ed. 17.00 o.p. (ISBN 0-405-01909-2). Ayer Co Pubs.

Twelve Original Essays on Great American Novels. Ed. by Charles Shapiro. LC 57-13316. (Waynebooks: No. 13). 304p. (Orig.). 1958. pap. text ed. 8.95x o.p. (ISBN 0-8143-1086-9). Wayne St U Pr.

Twelve Photographic Portraits. John H. Griffin. LC 74-134755. (Keepsake Ser.: Vol. 4). (Illus.). 1973. 8.00 o.p. (ISBN 0-87775-036-X); pap. 3.00 o.p. (ISBN 0-87775-077-7). Unicorn Pr.

Twelve Shortcuts to Better Golf. Bob Toski. Ed. by Dick Aultman. (Illus.). 48p. (Orig.). 1974. pap. 3.95 o.p. (ISBN 0-689-10635-1, Atheneum). Macmillan.

Twelve Signs of the Zodiac & Their Irresistible Effect upon the Stock Market. Rudolph H. Worthington. (Illus.). 110p. 1982. 69.85x o.p. (ISBN 0-86654-017-2). Inst Econ Finan.

Twelve Thousand Students & Their English Teachers: Tested Units in Teaching Literature, Language, Composition. Ed. by Commission on English Staff. LC 67-30437. 389p. 1968. pap. 8.50 spiral bdg. o.p. (ISBN 0-87447-097-8, 295725). College Bd.

Twelve Who Prayed: Twentieth Century Models of Prayer. Mark Gibbard. 1977. pap. 3.50 o.p. (ISBN 0-8066-1595-8, Augsburg). Augsburg Fortress.

Twelve Who Survived: An Oral History of the Jews of Lodz, Poland, 1930-1954. Lillian Kranitz-Sanders. 164p. 1983. pap. text ed. 9.95x o.p. Irvington.

Twelve Year Reich. Richard Grunberger. LC 69-16189. (Illus.). 1979. pap. 7.95 o.p. (ISBN 0-03-048226-7). H Holt & Co.

Twentieth AAMI Annual Meeting - Proceedings: Transitions in Health Care Delivery. (Illus.). 110p. 1985. pap. text ed. 6.00 o.p. (ISBN 0-910275-48-3); pap. text ed. 5.00 o.p. Assn Adv Med Instrn.

Twentieth Anniversary of Fluidics Symposium. Ed. by T. M. Drzewiecki & M. E. Franke. 225p. 1980. 30.00 o.p. (ISBN 0-686-69863-0, G00177). ASME.

Twentieth Century American Composers. 2nd ed. Harold Gleason & Warren Becker. LC 80-53732. (Music Literature Outlines: Series IV). 1980. 13.75 o.p. (ISBN 0-89917-266-0, Frangipani Press). TIS Inc.

Twentieth Century American Literature, 1 of 7 vols. Intro. by Warren French. (Great Writers Library). 668p. pap. 14.95 o.p. (ISBN 0-312-34712-X). Academy Chi Pubs.

Twentieth Century American Literature. Ed. by James Vinson. (Great Writer's Library). 668p. (Orig.). 1980. pap. 14.95 o.s.i. (ISBN 0-312-34712-X). St Martin.

Twentieth Century Art. Michael Batterberry. (Discovering Art Ser.). (Illus.). (gr. 5 up). 1969. text ed. 9.95 o.p. (ISBN 0-07-004080-X); pap. (ISBN 0-07-004079-6). McGraw.

Twentieth Century Begins. (Our Nations Heritage Ser.). Date not set. (ISBN 0-07-375405-6). McGraw.

Twentieth Century Biographical Dictionary of Notable Americans, 10 vols. LC 68-19657. 4670p. 1968. Repr. of 1904 ed. Set. 275.00x o.p. (ISBN 0-8103-3162-4). Gale.

Twentieth Century Book. (Our Nations Heritage Ser.). Date not set. (ISBN 0-07-375426-9). McGraw.

Twentieth Century British Jewellery, 1900-1980. Peter Hinks. LC 83-5520. (Illus.). 176p. 1983. 49.95 o.p. (ISBN 0-571-10801-6). Faber & Faber.

Twentieth-Century Capitalist Revolution. Adolf A. Berle. LC 54-11327. 1954. 6.50 o.p. (ISBN 0-15-191703-5). HarBraceJ.

Twentieth Century Decorating Architecture & Gardens. Ed. by House & Garden. LC 80-12593. (Illus.). 320p. 1980. 34.95 o.s.i. (ISBN 0-03-047581-3) (ISBN 0-686-77496-5). H Holt & Co.

Twentieth Century Economic Thought. Glenn E. Hoover. (ISBN 0-8022-0742-1). Philos Lib.

Twentieth Century Education. Ed. by P. F. Valentine. (ISBN 0-8022-1759-1). Philos Lib.

Twentieth Century Engineering. G. Tupholme. Philos Lib.

Twentieth Century English. Ed. by William Knickerbocker. (ISBN 0-8022-0872-X). Philos Lib.

Twentieth Century English Literature: A Soviet View. 477p. 1982. 11.95 o.p. (ISBN 0-8285-2525-0, Pub. by Progress Pubs USSR). Imported Pubns.

Twentieth-Century English Novel. A. F. Cassis. LC 76-24735. (Library of Humanities Reference Bks.: No. 56). 1977. lib. bdg. 55.00 o.p. (ISBN 0-8240-9942-7). Garland Pub.

Twentieth-Century English Poetic Drama: A Reevaluation. K. S. Misra. 376p. 1981. text ed. 30.00x o.p. (ISBN 0-7069-1394-9, Pub. by Vikas India). Advent NY.

Twentieth Century Geography. Griffith Taylor. 1957. (ISBN 0-8022-1699-4). Philos Lib.

Twentieth-Century Harpsichord Music: A Classified Catalog. Frances Bedford & Robert Conant. 1974. pap. 9.50 o.p. (ISBN 0-913574-08-2). Eur-Am Music.

Twentieth Century Hungarian Painting. Z. D. Feher & G. O. Pogany. (Illus.). 1971. 20.00 o.s.i. (ISBN 0-685-25487-9). E J Brill USA.

Twentieth Century Legal Philosophy Series, Vols. 2-7. 1948-1955. Set. 160.00 o.p. (ISBN 0-384-62115-5). Johnson Repr.

Twentieth Century Limited: A History of Recent America, 2 vols. David W. Noble et al. LC 79-90364. 1980. Complete. pap. 25.95 o.p. (ISBN 0-395-28742-1); Vol. I: America Through World War Two. pap. 19.16 o.p. (ISBN 0-395-29271-9); Vol. II: World War Two to the Present. pap. 19.16 o.p. (ISBN 0-395-29272-7); Vol. I & Vol. II packaged together. pap. 30.36 o.p. (ISBN 0-395-32249-9). HM.

Twentieth Century Modern Language Teaching. Maxim Newmark. (ISBN 0-8022-1210-7). Philos Lib.

Twentieth Century Painting. Hugo Munsterberg. 1951. (ISBN 0-8022-1171-2). Philos Lib.

Twentieth Century Philosophy. Runes. (ISBN 0-8022-1456-8). Philos Lib.

Twentieth Century Political Thought. Joseph S. Roucek. (ISBN 0-8022-1397-9). Philos Lib.

Twentieth Century Psychology. P. L. Harriman. (ISBN 0-8022-0683-2). Philos Lib.

Twentieth Century Religious Thought. John Macquarrie. 1983. 19.95 o.p. (ISBN 0-684-17333-6). Scribner.

Twentieth Century Russia. 5th ed. Donald W. Treadgold. 1981. pap. 27.50 o.p. (ISBN 0-395-30758-9). HM.

Twentieth-Century Russian Plays: An Anthology. Ed. & tr. by F. D. Reeve. Orig. Title: Anthology of Russian Plays, Vol. 2. 464p. 1973. pap. 3.95 o.p. (ISBN 0-393-00697-2, Norton Lib.). Norton.

Twentieth-Century Sciences. Ed. by Gerald Holton. 1972. 15.00x o.p. (ISBN 0-393-06384-4). Norton.

Twentieth Century Speech & Voice Correction. Emil Froeschels. (ISBN 0-8022-0552-6). Philos Lib.

Twentieth Century Tenor Banjo Method, Bk. I. Zarh M. Bickford. 1941. 1.25 o.p. (ISBN 0-913650-25-0). CPP Belwin.

Twentieth-Century Warriors: The Development of the Armed Forces of the Major Military Nations in the Twentieth Century. Lord Carver. LC 87-33976. 448p. 1987. 24.95 o.p. (ISBN 1-55584-187-2). Weidenfeld.

Twentieth Publication Design Annual. Society of Publication Designers Staff. (Illus.). 224p. 1968. 39.95 o.p. (ISBN 0-942604-10-5). Madison Square.

Twenty Best Film Plays, 2 vols. John Gassner & Dudley Nichols. LC 76-52104. (Classics of Film Literature Ser.: Vol. 13). 1977. Repr. of 1943 ed. Set. lib. bdg. 69.00 ea. o.p. (ISBN 0-8240-2877-5). Garland Pub.

Twenty Bicycle Tours in & Around New York City. Dan Carlinsky & David Heim. (Bicycle Tours Ser.). 136p. 1984. pap. 6.95 o.p. (ISBN 0-942440-21-8). Backcountry Pubns.

Twenty Bicycle Tours in New Hampshire. Thomas Heavey & Susan Heavey. LC 78-71716. (Twenty Bicycle Tours Ser.). (Illus.). 128p. 1979. pap. 5.95 o.p. (ISBN 0-89725-001-X). Backcountry Pubns.

Twenty Danger Signals. Clyde M. Narramore. 1989. pap. 7.95 o.p. (ISBN 0-89107-507-0, Crossway Bks). Good News.

Twenty Eight More Floral Creations for Cake Decorators. Richard V. Snyder. 1963. pap. 2.50 o.p. (ISBN 0-682-40091-2, Banner). Exposition-Phoenix.

Twenty-Eight Science Fiction Stories. H. G. Wells. 13.25 o.p. (ISBN 0-8446-3152-3). Peter Smith.

Twenty Eighty-Four - the Philosophy of Oneness. Jonathan Gabriel. LC 84-90257. 117p. 1985. 8.95 o.p. (ISBN 0-533-06297-7). Vantage.

Twenty-Elephant Restaurant. Russell Hoban. LC 77-1056. (Illus.). 48p. (gr. k-5). 1978. 9.95 o.s.i. (ISBN 0-689-30593-1, Atheneum Childrens Bk). Macmillan.

Twenty-Fifth Annual Antitrust Law Institute. (Corporate Law & Practice Course Handbook Ser: Vol. 446). 1984. 40.00 o.p. (ISBN 0-685-63706-9, B4-5569). PLI.

Twenty-Five Easy & Progressive Melodic Studies for Piano. J. Concone. Ed. by Maxwell Eckstein. (Carl Fischer Music Library: No. 540). 28p. 1943. pap. 4.75 o.p. (ISBN 0-8258-0139-7, L540). Fischer Inc NY.

Twenty-Five Exciting Computer Games in BASIC for All Ages. David W. Chance. LC 82-19286. (Illus.). 288p. 1983. 21.95 o.p. (ISBN 0-8306-0427-8, 1427P); pap. 12.95 o.p. (ISBN 0-8306-1427-3). TAB Bks.

Twenty-Five German Poets: A Bilingual Collection. Ed. by Walter Kaufmann. 352p. 1976. pap. 3.95x o.p. (ISBN 0-393-00771-5). Norton.

Twenty-Five German Poets: A Bilingual Collection. Ed. & tr. by Walter Kaufmann. 325p. 1975. 8.95x o.p. (ISBN 0-393-04405-X). Norton.

Twenty-Five Graphics Programs in MICROSOFT BASIC. Timothy J. O'Malley. (Illus.). 160p. 1983. 17.95 o.p. (ISBN 0-8306-0133-3, 1533); pap. 11.60 o.p. (ISBN 0-8306-0533-9). TAB Bks.

Twenty-Five Hour Woman. Sybil Stanton. 256p. 1986. 10.95 o.p. (ISBN 0-8007-1487-3). Revell.

Twenty-Five Most Practical Homebuilt Aircraft. Peter M. Bowers. (Illus.). 1978. 8.95 o.p. (ISBN 0-8306-9887-6, 2250H); pap. 5.95 o.p. (ISBN 0-8306-2250-0, 2250). TAB Bks.

Twenty-Five Ski Tours in Maine: From Kittery to Caribou, A Cross-Country Skiers Guide. Karl Beiser. LC 79-64992. (Twenty-Five Ski Tours Ser.). (Illus.). 128p. 1979. pap. 5.95 o.s.i. (ISBN 0-89725-006-0). Backcountry Pubns.

Twenty-Five Year Forecast for Commercial Communications Satellites. 225.00 o.p. (ISBN 0-686-33002-1). Info Gatekeepers.

Twenty-Five Years International Journal of Biometeorology Index. Ed. by H. Schnitzler & H. Lieth. viii, 144p. pap. text ed. 22.50 o.p. (ISBN 90-265-0508-6, Pub. by Swets Pub Serv Holland). Swets North Am.

Twenty-Five Years of Architectural Record Houses. Architectural Record Magazine Editors. Ed. by Herb Smith. (Architectural Record Ser.). (Illus.). 224p. 1981. text ed. 49.95 o.p. (ISBN 0-07-002357-3). McGraw.

Twenty-Five Years of Space Photography. Christopher Knight. LC 85-71321. 1985. cancelled 22.95 o.p. (ISBN 0-393-02280-3); pap. 14.70 o.p. (ISBN 0-393-30291-1). Norton.

Twenty-Four Conversations with Borges: Interviews by Roberto Alifano 1981-1983. Ed. by Roberto Alifano. Tr. by Nicomedes S. Arauz et al. LC 83-49422. (Illus.). 157p. 1984. 17.95 o.p. (ISBN 0-394-53879-X, GP 921). Grove.

Twenty-Four Conversations with Borges: Interviews by Roberto Alifano 1981-1983. Ed. by Roberto Alifano. Tr. by Nicomedes S. Arauz et al. LC 83-49422. (Illus.). 157p. 1984. pap. 8.95 o.p. (ISBN 0-394-62192-1, E940, Ever). Grove.

Twenty-Four Dramatic Cases of the International Academy of Trial Lawyers. Ed. by W. Robert Morgan. LC 74-21445. 1975. 10.00 o.p. (ISBN 0-682-48142-4); pap. 5.00 o.p. (ISBN 0-682-48143-2). Exposition-Phoenix.

Twenty-Four Exercises for Violin, Op. 33. A. Blumenstengel. (Carl Fischer Music Library: No. 621). 1911. pap. 6.50 o.p. (ISBN 0-8258-0082-X, L621). Fischer Inc NY.

Twenty-Four Stories by Premchand. Ed. by Nandini Nopany & P. Lal. (Vikas Library of Modern Moian Writing Ser.: No. 1). 208p. 1981. text ed. 17.95x o.p. (ISBN 0-7069-1199-7, Pub. by Vikas India). Advent NY.

Twenty-Four Tested Ready-to-Run Game Programs in BASIC. Ken Tracton. (Illus.). 1978. 14.95 o.p. (ISBN 0-8306-9876-0); pap. 9.95 o.p. (ISBN 0-8306-1085-5, 1085). TAB Bks.

Twenty-Four Ways to Greater Business Productivity: Master Checklists for Marketing, Advertising, Sales, Distribution & Customer Service. Charles R. MacDonald. LC 81-7096. 446p. 1981. 79.50 o.p. (ISBN 0-87624-203-4, Inst Busn Plan). P-H.

Twenty-Four Women's Programs: Please Pass the Fruit. Jeanette Lockerbie. 96p. (Orig.). 1986. pap. 4.95 o.p. (ISBN 0-87403-226-1, 2979). Standard Pub.

Twenty-Four Worked Engineering Drawing Examples. A. J. Jones & N. Barlow. 1966. pap. text ed. 4.20 o.p. (ISBN 0-08-012080-6). Pergamon.

Twenty-Fourth Annual Advanced Antitrust Seminar: Distribution Problems & Solutions. (Corporate Law & Practice Course Handbook Series 1984-85). 1984. pap. 40.00 o.p. (ISBN 0-685-90319-2, B4-5583). PLI.

Twenty-Fourth Level. Kenneth Benton. 224p. 1986. pap. 2.95 o.p. (ISBN 1-55547-109-9). Critics Choice Paper.

Twenty Greatest Hits: The Beatles. Ed. by Milton Okun. 72p. 1982. pap. 7.95 o.s.i. (ISBN 0-89524-173-0, 1338). Cherry Lane.

Twenty Lectures on Thermodynamics. H. A. Buchdahl. 1975. 35.00 o.p. (ISBN 0-08-018299-2); pap. text ed. 35.00 o.p. (ISBN 0-08-018951-2). Pergamon.

Twenty Most Valuable Books for Speculative Success in the Stock Market with Elucidations Sufficient to Master the Content of Each Single Book. Spencer Fleming. (Illus.). 97p. 1984. pap. 54.75 o.p. (ISBN 0-86654-133-0). Inst Econ Finan.

Twenty-Nine New Floral Creations for Cake Decorators. Richard V. Snyder. 1962. pap. 2.50 o.p. (ISBN 0-682-40092-0, Banner). Exposition-Phoenix.

Twenty-Nine Reasons Not to Go to Law School. Ralph Warner & Toni Ihara. LC 82-99889. 128p. 1984. pap. 6.95 o.p. (ISBN 0-917316-87-8). Nolo Pr.

Twenty-Ninth Estate Planning Institute. 228p. 1984. 12.00 o.p. (ISBN 0-318-02396-2). ICLE Georgia.

Twenty-Ninth Estate Planning Seminar. 1984. (ISBN 0-88129-144-7). Wash Bar CLE.

Twenty-One Keys to a Beautiful Life. Alton E. Carpenter. 1976. 7.50 o.p. (ISBN 0-682-48357-5). Exposition-Phoenix.

Twenty One Kinds of American Folk Art & How to Make Each One. Jean Kinney & Cle Kinney. LC 70-175556. (Illus.). (gr. 4-6). 1972. 6.95 o.p. (ISBN 0-689-30030-1, Atheneum). Macmillan.

Twenty-One Mile Swim. Matt Christopher. LC 79-15197. (gr. 3-7). 1979. 11.95 o.p. (ISBN 0-316-13979-3). Little.

Twenty-One Stories. Date not set. (ISBN 0-8052-3350-4). Random.

Twenty-One Years of World Cup Ski Racing. Serge Lang. (Illus.). 200p. 1987. 19.95 o.p. (ISBN 1-55566-009-6). Johnson Bks.

Twenty Questions for the Writer, a Rhetoric for Readings. 2nd ed. Jacqueline Berke. LC 75-35312. (Illus.). 1976. pap. text ed. 11.95 o.p. (ISBN 0-15-592399-4, HC). HarBraceJ.

Twenty Questions for the Writer: A Rhetoric with Readings. 3rd ed. Jacqueline Berke. 597p. 1981. pap. text ed. 12.00 o.p. (ISBN 0-15-592401-X, HC). HarBraceJ.

Twenty Questions for the Writer: A Rhetoric with Readings. Jacqueline Berke. 528p. 1972. pap. text ed. 11.95 o.p. (ISBN 0-15-592397-8, HC). HarBraceJ.

Twenty-Seven Most Common Mistakes in Advertising. Alec Benn. 1978. 12.95 o.p. (ISBN 0-8144-5478-X). AMACOM.

Twenty-Seven Special Creations for Cake Decorators. Richard V. Snyder. 1955. pap. 2.50 o.p. (ISBN 0-682-40090-4, Banner). Exposition-Phoenix.

Twenty-Seventh Session of the Executive Committee: Abridged Report & Resolutions. (Publications Ser.: No. 417). pap. 25.00 o.p. (W184, WMO). UNIPUB.

Twenty-Six Centuries of Agrarian Reform: A Comparative Analysis. Elias H. Tuma. (Near Eastern Center, UCLA: No. 2). 1965. 34.50x o.p. (ISBN 0-520-01286-0). U of Cal Pr.

Twenty-Six Lessons on the Four Gospels. 2nd ed. Wallace Wartick. (Bible Student Study Guides Ser.). 1977. pap. 9.95 o.p. (ISBN 0-89900-157-2). College Pr Pub.

Twenty-Six Lively Letters-Making an ABC Quiet Book. Barbara Williams & Carol Grundmann. LC 76-133281. 1976. 9.95 o.s.i. (ISBN 0-8008-7918-X). Taplinger.

Twenty Stories of Bible Women. Dixie L. Harris. 1980. 12.50 o.p. (ISBN 0-682-49526-3). Exposition-Phoenix.

Twenty-Third Annual Advanced Antitrust Seminar: Horizontal Problems. (Corporate Law & Practice Course Handbook: Vol. 430). 763p. 1983. 40.00 o.p. (ISBN 0-317-11420-4, B4-6661). PLI.

Twenty Third Annual Tax School: The Tax Reform Act of 1984. 130p. 1984. 30.00 o.p. (ISBN 0-318-03922-2, 270). PA Bar Inst.

Twenty-Third Psalm. Alice J. Davidson. (Alice in Bibleland Ser.). (Illus.). 32p. (ps-3). 1988. 4.95 o.p. (ISBN 0-8378-1840-0). Gibson.

Twenty Third Psalm. Alice J. Davidson. Date not set. Gibson.

Twenty Thousand Words. 7th ed. Louis A. Leslie. LC 77-71178. 1978. text ed. 7.50 o.p. (ISBN 0-07-037392-2); text ed. 7.80 o.p. (ISBN 0-07-037393-0). McGraw.

Twenty-Three Keys to Inner Peace from the 23rd Psalm. Alton E. Carpenter. 1974. 7.50 o.p. (ISBN 0-682-48058-4). Exposition-Phoenix.

Twenty-Three Most Common Mistakes in Public Relations. Alec Benn. 256p. 1982. 17.95 o.p. (ISBN 0-8144-5715-0). AMACOM.

Twenty-Three Varieties of Ethnic Art & How You Can Make Each One. Jean Kinney & Cle Kinney. LC 76-5409. (Illus.). (gr. 4-7). 1976. 8.95 o.p. (ISBN 0-689-30541-9, Atheneum). Macmillan.

Twenty-Twenty Vision. J. Pournelle. pap. 0.95 o.p. (ISBN 0-380-01632-X). Avon.

Twenty-Two Caliber Varmint Rifles. Charles Landis. (Library Classics Ser.). (Illus.). 544p. Repr. of 1947 ed. deluxe ed. cancelled o.s.i. (ISBN 0-935632-60-3). Wolfe Pub Co.

Twenty-Two Days in Mexico. Steve Rogers & Tina Rosa. 1989. pap. 6.95 o.p. (ISBN 0-945465-04-1). John Muir.

Twenty-Two, Twenty-Three. Ellen Raskin. LC 76-5475. (Illus.). 32p. (gr. k-3). 1976. 7.95 o.s.i. (ISBN 0-689-30529-X, Atheneum Childrens Bks). Macmillan.

Twenty Year Phenomenon. Jean Brody & Gail B. Osborne. 1980. 11.95 o.p. (ISBN 0-671-25042-6). S&S.

Twenty Years Indonesian Foreign Policy 1945-1965. Gde Agung Anak. LC 72-93180. 1973. text ed. 46.00x o.p. (ISBN 0-686-22635-6). Mouton.

Twenty Years of Public Housing. Robert M. Fisher. LC 75-29075. (Illus.). 303p. 1975. Repr. of 1959 ed. lib. bdg. 35.00x o.p. (ISBN 0-8371-8411-8, FIPH). Greenwood.

Twice As Fast: Food Processor-Microwave Cooking. Sue Spitler. 192p. 1982. 15.50 o.p. (ISBN 0-8092-5636-3); pap. 9.95 o.p. (ISBN 0-8092-5635-5). Contemp Bks.

Twice Killed. Richard Smitten. 224p. (Orig.). 1987. pap. 3.95 o.p. (ISBN 0-380-75280-8). Avon.

Twice over Lightly. Helen Hayes & Anita Loos. LC 72-75417. 1972. 7.95 o.p. (ISBN 0-15-192150-4). HarBraceJ.

Twice-Told Tales: An Anthology of Short Fiction. Gerard A. Barker. LC 78-69561. 1979. pap. 20.50 o.p. (ISBN 0-395-26635-1). HM.

Twice upon A Time. Avery Hall. (Illus.). 48p. (gr. k up). 1983. lib. bdg. 8.79 o.s.i. (ISBN 0-671-46005-6). Messner.

Twiddle Twins' Haunted House. Howard Goldsmith. LC 85-7794. (Illus.). 40p. (ps-1). PLB 9.45 o.s.i. Caedmon.

Twigs. V. H. Grempel. 1977. 6.00 o.p. (ISBN 0-682-48800-3). Exposition-Phoenix.

Twilight in India. Gervee Baronte. (ISBN 0-8022-0068-0). Philos Lib.

Twilight in South Africa. Henry Gibbs. (ISBN 0-8022-0579-8). Philos Lib.

Twilight Land. H. Pyle. (gr. 4-8). 11.25 o.p. (ISBN 0-8446-2768-2). Peter Smith.

Twilight of British Rail. Michael Bonavia. (Illus.). 176p. 1985. 29.95 o.p. (ISBN 0-7153-8625-5). David & Charles.

Twilight of Empire: Memoirs of Prime Minister Clement Attlee. Francis Williams. LC 78-5918. 1978. Repr. of 1962 ed. lib. bdg. 35.00 o.p. (ISBN 0-313-20450-0, WITE). Greenwood.

Twilight of the Corporate State: How Big Business Hurts the Economy, & What to Do about It. Paul H. Weaver. 224p. 1988. 18.45 o.s.i. (ISBN 0-671-52378-3). S&S.

Twilight of the Gods. Michael Baran. 192p. 1984. 9.00 o.p. (ISBN 0-682-40131-5). Exposition-Phoenix.

Twilight of the Gods: The Music of the Beatles. Wilfrid Mellers. LC 73-3508. (Illus.). 1975. pap. 8.95 o.s.i. (ISBN 0-02-871390-7). Schirmer Bks.

Twilight of the Sea Gods. Thaddeus V. Tuleja. LC 75-32533. (Illus.). 284p. 1976. Repr. of 1958 ed. lib. bdg. 35.00x o.p. (ISBN 0-8371-8367-7, TUTS). Greenwood.

Twilight of Young: The Radical Movements of the 1960's & Their Legacy. Klaus Mehnert. LC 76-58520. 1978. 12.95 o.s.i. (ISBN 0-03-019476-8). H Holt & Co.

Twilight Realm. Christopher Carpenter. LC 85-19259. 237p. (gr. 6 up). 1986. 13.95 o.p. (ISBN 0-448-47771-8, G&D). Putnam Pub Group.

Twilight Waves. Carol Farley. LC 81-1417. 144p. (gr. 4-6). 1981. PLB 8.95 o.p. (ISBN 0-689-30842-6, Atheneum). Macmillan.

Twin Cities Nonprofit Sector in a Time of Government Retrenchment. Barbara Lukerman et al. (Nonprofit Sector Ser.). 87p. 1984. pap. text ed. 12.95x o.p. (ISBN 0-87766-378-5). Urban Inst.

Twin Rivers. Jennie S. Baty. 1980. 12.50 o.p. (ISBN 0-682-49459-3, Lochinvar). Exposition-Phoenix.

Twinkle Twinkle Movie Star. Harry Brundidge. Ed. by Bruce S. Kupelnick. LC 76-52094. (Classics of Film Literature Ser.). 1978. lib. bdg. 22.00 o.p. (ISBN 0-8240-2868-6). Garland Pub.

Twins & Twin Relations. Helen L. Koch. LC 66-20591. (Miway Reprint Ser.). 1977. pap. text ed. 13.00x o.s.i. (ISBN 0-226-44933-5). U of Chicago Pr.

Twins Black & White. R. Travis Osborne. 286p. 1986. 15.00 o.p. (ISBN 0-317-53022-4). Noontide.

Twins: Nature's Amazing Mystery. Kay Cassill. LC 81-69126. (Illus.). 320p. 1982. 14.95 o.p. (ISBN 0-689-11239-4, Atheneum). Macmillan.

Twins: Nature's Amazing Mystery. Kay Cassill. LC 81-69126. 336p. 1984. pap. 7.95 o.p. (ISBN 0-689-70663-4, 305, Atheneum). Macmillan.

Twins: The Story of Twins. Marguerite R. Lerner. LC 61-13577. (Medical Books for Children). (Illus.). (gr. k-6). 1961. PLB 3.95 o.p. (ISBN 0-8225-0009-4). Lerner Pubns.

Twist of Justice-Gripes. Horace Benton. 80p. 1987. 7.95 o.p. (ISBN 0-8062-3068-1). Carlton.

Twisted Sister. (Metal Mania Ser.). (Illus.). 16p. (gr. 4-12). 1985. 3.95 o.p. (ISBN 0-88188-349-2, Robus Books). H Leonard Pub Corp.
Twitchell the Wishful. Marjorie W. Sharmat. LC 80-16845. (Illus.). 40p. (gr. k-3). 1981. reinforced bdg. 9.95 o.p. (ISBN 0-8234-0379-3). Holiday.
Twitchtoe the Beastfinder. William Van Horn. LC 78-3679. (Illus.). (ps-3). 1978. 9.95 o.p. (ISBN 0-689-30670-9, Atheneum). Macmillan.
Two. Sue Porter. (Baby Book Ser.). (Illus.). (ps). 1985. bds. 3.95 o.p. (ISBN 0-911745-99-8, Bedrick Blackie). P Bedrick Bks.
Two Admirals. David McKee. LC 77-5492. (gr. k-3). 1977. 6.95 o.p. (ISBN 0-395-25808-1). HM.
Two Against Cape Horn. Hal Roth. (Illus.). 1978. 18.95 o.p. (ISBN 0-393-03223-X). Norton.
Two Ancient Christologies: A Study in the Christological Thought of the Schools of Alexandria & Antioch in the Early History of Christian Doctrine. Robert V. Sellers. (Church Historical Society London N. S. Ser.: No. 39). Repr. of 1940 ed. 50.00 o.p. (ISBN 0-8115-3162-7). Kraus Repr.
Two & Two Are Four. Carolyn Haywood. LC 40-27326. (Illus.). (gr. 1-5). 1940. 6.50 o.p. (ISBN 0-15-291769-1, HJ). HarBraceJ.
Two Angry Women of Abingdon: A Critical Edition. Henry Porter. Ed. by Marianne B. Evett. LC 79-54336. (Renaissance Drama Ser.). 304p. 1980. lib. bdg. 40.00 o.p. (ISBN 0-8240-4454-1). Garland Pub.
Two Battles of the Little Big Horn. Ed. by John M. Carroll. (Illus.). 1974. 35.00 o.p. (ISBN 0-87140-586-5). Liveright.
Two Blocks from Happiness. Lois Morse. 176p. 1985. pap. 6.95 o.p. (ISBN 0-87239-860-9, 3005). Standard Pub.
Two Burlettas of Kane O'Hara, Midas & the Golden Pippin: An Edition with Commentary. Ed. by Stephen Orgel. (Satire & sense Ser.). 634p. 1987. lib. bdg. 95.00 o.p. (ISBN 0-8240-6023-7). Garland Pub.
Two by O'Hara. John O'Hara. Ed. by Matthew J. Bruccoli. LC 79-1839. 1979. 10.95 o.p. (ISBN 0-15-192224-1). HarBraceJ.
Two by Two. Bo Beskow. 128p. 1981. pap. 2.95 o.p. (ISBN 0-380-55210-8, 55210-8, Bard). Avon.
Two Careers: One Marriage. William M. Jones & Ruth A. Jones. 1980. 12.95 o.p. (ISBN 0-8144-5589-1). AMACOM.
Two Chinese Sex Classics. Howard S. Levy. (Asian Folklore & Social Life Monograph: No. 75). 1976. 17.00x o.p. (ISBN 0-89986-256-X). Oriental Bk Store.
Two Cities. Norman St. John-Stevas. 352p. 1984. 27.50 o.p. (ISBN 0-571-13083-6). Faber & Faber.
Two Crosses: A Passion Play in Three Acts. Hiram Baird. 1979. 5.00 o.p. (ISBN 0-682-49387-2). Exposition-Phoenix.
Two Deaths of Quincas Wateryell. Jorge Amado. 1980. pap. 2.50 o.p. (ISBN 0-380-50047-7, 50047-7, Bard). Avon.
Two Dimensional Anatomy of the Heart: An Atlas for Echocardiographers. David J. Sahn & Fred Anderson. LC 82-7108. 461p. 1982. 52.50 o.p. (ISBN 0-471-08246-5). Wiley.
Two-Dimensional Digital Signal Processing I: Linear Filters. Ed. by T. S. Huang. (Topics in Applied Physics Ser.: Vol. 42). (Illus.). 1981. 53.00 o.p. (ISBN 0-387-10359-7). Springer-Verlag.
Two-Dimensional Digital Signal Processing. Ed. by S. K. Mitra & M. P. Ekstrom. LC 77-25337. (Benchmark Papers in Electrical Engineering & Computer Science: Vol. 20). 400p. 1982. 62.95 o.p. (ISBN 0-87933-320-0). Van Nos Reinhold.
Two-Dimensional Systems, Heterostructures & Superlattices: Proceedings of the International Winterschool Mauterndorf, Austria, Feb. 26-Mar. 2, 1984. Ed. by G. Bauer et al. (Springer Series in Solid-State Sciences: Vol. 53). (Illus.). 290p. 1984. 47.00 o.p. (ISBN 0-387-13584-7). Springer-Verlag.
Two Dogs & Freedom. 1987. pap. 4.95 o.p. (ISBN 0-8050-0637-0). H Holt & Co.
Two Dreams & a Promise. Gladys S. Lewis. LC 83-22436. (gr. 7-10). 1984. pap. 4.25 o.p. (ISBN 0-8054-4611-7, 4246-11). Broadman.
Two Early Political Associations: The Quakers & the Dissenting Deputies in the Age of Sir Robert Walpole. Norman Crowther-Hunt. LC 78-23805. 1979. Repr. of 1961 ed. lib. bdg. 35.00x o.p. (ISBN 0-313-21036-5, HUTW). Greenwood.
Two-Edged Sword: Armed Force in the Modern World, The Reith Lectures 1981. Laurence Martin. 1982. 13.95 o.p. (ISBN 0-393-01655-2). Norton.
Two-Faced Nation. Parker Abell. 1985. 6.95 o.p. (ISBN 0-533-06463-5). Vantage.
Two Faces of Malnutrition. Erik P. Eckholm & Francis Record. LC 76-47787. (Worldwatch Papers). 1976. pap. 4.00 o.p. (ISBN 0-916468-08-9). Worldwatch Inst.
Two for Survival. Arnold Roth. (gr. 7 up). 1979. pap. 1.50 o.p. (ISBN 0-380-44651-0, 56408-4, Flare). Avon.
Two from Galilee. Marjorie Holmes. 224p. 1985. Repr. of 1972 ed. 11.95 o.p. (ISBN 0-8007-1446-6). Revell.
Two from the Dead. Hilary Milton. LC 83-10848. 224p. (gr. 5up). 1983. 6.70 o.p. (ISBN 0-395-34557-X). HM.
Two F's of Modern Living. Franklin Walker. LC 76-56035. 1977. 5.00 o.p. (ISBN 0-682-48723-6). Exposition-Phoenix.
Two Gay Sweatshop Plays. Noel Greig & Drew Griffiths. (Gay Modern Classics Ser.). 142p. (Orig.). 1981. pap. 5.50 o.p. (ISBN 0-907040-06-3, Pub. by GMP England). Alyson Pubns.
Two Gentlemen to See You, Sir: The Autobiography of a Villain. Victor Carasov. LC 76-155091. 1971. 5.50 o.s.i. (ISBN 0-8008-7920-1). Taplinger.
Two German Economies. Herbert Wilkens. 194p. 1981. text ed. 44.50x o.p. (ISBN 0-566-00304-X). Gower Pub Co.
Two Grains of Sand. Sandra Trump. 48p. 1987. 6.95 o.p. (ISBN 0-8062-2982-9). Carlton.
Two Groups of Thessalian Gold. Stella Miller. LC 77-80473. (UC Publications in Classical Studies: Vol. 18). 1979. pap. 23.00x o.p. (ISBN 0-520-09580-4). U of Cal Pr.
Two Hague Conferences & Their Contributions to International Law. William I. Hull. LC 73-147582. (Library of War & Peace; Int'l. Organization, Arbitration & Law). 1972. lib. bdg. 46.00 o.p. (ISBN 0-8240-0346-2). Garland Pub.
Two Hearts Bid. Carol Gaye. (Lythway). 256p. 1988. lib. bdg. 19.50x o.s.i. (ISBN 0-7451-0634-X, Pub. by Chivers Pr UK). G K HAll.
Two Heroines of Plumplington. Anthony Trollope. Ed. by John K. Shannon. (Harting Grange Library). (Illus.). 116p. 1980. lib. bdg. 10.95 o.s.i. (ISBN 0-932282-48-2); pap. 6.95 o.s.i. (ISBN 0-932282-49-0). Caledonia Pr.
Two Homes for Lynn. June Noble. LC 78-14090. (Illus.). (gr. k-3). 1979. 6.95 o.s.i. (ISBN 0-03-046186-3). H Holt & Co.
Two-Horse Cadillac. Zig Ziglar. (Zig Ziglar Ser.: No. 2). 48p. (Orig.). (ps-7). 1987. pap. 2.50 o.p. (ISBN 0-8423-7388-8). Tyndale.
Two Hundred Days of Eight & a Half. Deena Boyer. Ed. by Bruce S. Kupelnick. LC 76-52091. (Classics of Film Literature Ser.). 1978. lib. bdg. 31.00 o.p. (ISBN 0-8240-2867-8). Garland Pub.
Two Hundred Fifty-Five Home Designs for Family Living. Home Planners Editors. 192p. 1985. pap. 3.50 o.p. (ISBN 0-918894-44-1). Home Planners.
Two Hundred Fifty Home Plans for Today's Living. rev. ed. William G. Chirgotis. LC 78-65787. (Illus.). 240p. 1983. pap. 8.95 o.p. (ISBN 0-932944-70-1). Creative Homeowner.
Two Hundred Fifty Years of Afro-American Art: An Annotated Bibliography. Lynn M. Igoe & James Igoe. LC 81-12226. 1266p. 1981. 149.95 o.s.i. (ISBN 0-8352-1376-5). Bowker.
Two Hundred Forty-Four House Plans for Better Living. (Illus.). 192p. 1986. pap. 3.50 o.p. (ISBN 0-918894-56-5). Home Planners.
Two Hundred Good Restaurants: A Guide to Good Eating in the San Francisco Bay Area. Russell Riera. (Creative Arts Communication Bk.). 216p. 1986. pap. 6.95 o.p. (ISBN 0-88739-009-9). Creative Arts Bk.
Two Hundred House Plants in Color. G. Kromdijk. (Illus.). 1972. text ed. 15.95 o.p. (ISBN 0-07-073280-9). McGraw.
Two Hundred One Japanese Verbs Fully Conjugated in All the Forms. Roland A. Lange. LC 76-140634. (Orig.). 1971. pap. text ed. 8.95 o.p. (ISBN 0-8120-0391-8). Barron.
Two Hundred Recipes for the Doufu Devotee. Zhang Desheng. (Illus.). 206p. (Orig.). 1986. pap. 3.95 o.p. (ISBN 0-8351-1807-X). China Bks.
Two Hundred Years of American Art: The Munson-Williams-Proctor Institute. Text by Wayne Craven. 110p. pap. 19.95 o.p. Moyer Bell Limited.
Two Hundred Years of Great American Short Stories. Ed. by Martha Foley. LC 75-1107. 960p. 1975. 14.95 o.p. (ISBN 0-395-20447-X). HM.
Two Hundred Years of Pharmacy in Mississippi. Leslie Campbell. LC 73-86313. 224p. 1974. 2.50x o.p. (ISBN 0-87805-058-2). U Pr of Miss.
Two Hundred Years of the Republic in Retrospect. Ed. by William C. Havard & Joseph L. Bernd. LC 76-45777. 348p. 1976. Repr. 20.00x o.p. (ISBN 0-8139-0690-3). U Pr of Va.
Two If by Sea. Ernest Savage. 224p. 1982. 12.95 o.s.i. (ISBN 0-684-17435-9, ScribT). Scribner.
Two in the City. Robert Kaplow. (gr. 7 up). 1979. 6.95 o.p. (ISBN 0-395-27813-9). HM.
Two Is a Team. Lorraine Beim & Jerrold Beim. LC 45-8600. (Illus.). (gr. k-3). 1945. 8.95 o.p. (ISBN 0-15-291948-1, HJ). HarBraceJ.
Two Is a Team. Lorraine Beim & Jerrold Beim. LC 73-12939. (Illus.). 58p. (gr. k-3). 1974. pap. 1.25 o.p. (ISBN 0-15-692050-6, VoyB). HarBraceJ.
Two Jamaicas. Philip D. Curtin. LC 69-10082. (Illus.). 1970. pap. 3.95x o.p. (ISBN 0-689-70228-0, NL22, Atheneum). Macmillan.
Two Kingdoms. Mark Saxton. 1979. 9.95 o.p. (ISBN 0-395-28152-0). HM.
Two Kingdoms & One World: A Sourcebook in Christian Social Ethics. Ed. by Karl H. Hertz. LC 76-3852. 400p. 1976. pap. 9.50 o.p. (ISBN 0-8066-1538-9, 10-6723, Augsburg). Augsburg Fortress.
Two Kittens Are Born: From Birth to Two Months. Betty Schilling. LC 79-28752. (Illus.). 40p. (gr. 1-3). 1980. 6.95 o.p. (ISBN 0-03-051456-8). H Holt & Co.
Two Little Devils. Robert E. Holt. 1979. 8.95 o.p. (ISBN 0-682-49362-7). Exposition-Phoenix.
Two Little Kittens. Fang Yiqun. (Illus.). 22p. (Orig.). (gr. 2-4). 1982. pap. 2.50 o.p. (ISBN 0-8351-1142-3). China Bks.
Two Magicians. John Langstaff. LC 72-85919. 32p. (ps-3). 1973. 4.95 o.p. (ISBN 0-689-30319-X, Atheneum). Macmillan.
Two Mrs. Grenvilles. Dominick Dunne. (General Ser.). 552p. 1986. lib. bdg. 18.95 o.p. (ISBN 0-8161-4059-6, Large Print Bks). G K Hall.
Two Nations. Richard Gray. LC 73-21175. (Illus.). 373p. 1974. Repr. of 1960 ed. lib. bdg. 22.50x o.p. (ISBN 0-8371-6069-3, GRTN). Greenwood.
Two New Scriptures. pap. 1.00 o.p. (ISBN 0-89036-079-0). Hawkes Pub Inc.
Two Novels by Peter Handke. Peter Handke. 1979. pap. 2.75 o.p. (ISBN 0-380-48033-6, Bard). Avon.
Two of Us: A Novel. Nora Johnson. 288p. 1984. 15.50 o.p. (ISBN 0-671-47302-6). S&S.
Two on an Island. Bianca Bradbury. (Illus.). (gr. 4-6). 1965. 6.95 o.p. (ISBN 0-395-06651-4). HM.
Two on the River. Wil Haygood. (Illus.). 158p. 1986. 29.95 o.p. (ISBN 0-87113-110-2). Atlantic Monthly.
Two Over One Game Force. Max Hardy. LC 84-223762. 146p. 1982. pap. 8.95 o.p. (ISBN 0-939460-26-2). M Hardy.
Two Paychecks: Life in Dual Earner Families. Joan Aldous. (Sage Focus Editions: Vol. 56). (Illus.). 232p. 1982. 35.00 o.p. (ISBN 0-8039-1882-8); pap. 16.95 o.p. (ISBN 0-8039-1883-6). Sage.
Two Persons for One Job. James Hudson. LC 85-91382. 189p. 1986. 11.95 o.p. (ISBN 0-533-06895-9). Vantage.
Two Phase Annular & Dispersed Flow: Proceedings of the International Symposium, University of Pisa, Italy, 24-29 June 1984. Ed. by T. J. Hanratty et al. 200p. 1985. pap. 50.00 o.p. (ISBN 0-08-031653-0, Pub. by Aberdeen Scotland). Pergamon.
Two-Phase Flow & Heat Transfer in the Power & Process Industries. A. E. Bergles et al. (Illus.). 695p. 1981. text ed. 79.50 o.p. (ISBN 0-07-004902-5). McGraw.
Two-Phase Flow & Heat Transfer in the Power & Process Industries. Arthur E. Bergles et al. LC 80-22025. (Illus.). 707p. 1980. text ed. 69.50 o.p. (ISBN 0-89116-197-X). Hemisphere Pub.
Two-Phase Steam Flow in Turbines & Separators. Moore. 399p. 1976. 49.50 o.p. (ISBN 0-89116-499-5). Hemisphere Pub.
Two-Phase Steam Flow in Turbines & Separators: Theory, Instrumentation, Engineering. M. J. Moore & C. H. Sieverding. LC 76-9125. 1976. text ed. 48.00 o.p. (ISBN 0-07-042992-8). McGraw.
Two Plays: Quintus & Lucanus, Andronicus. James Campbell. 64p. 1988. 8.50 o.p. Carlton.
Two Plays: The Palace at 4 A. M., the Folding Green. Howard Moss. LC 80-52196. (Illus.). 120p. 1980. pap. 5.95 o.p. (ISBN 0-935296-12-3). Sheep Meadow.
Two Plays: Uncle Viva & the Lost Equilibrium. Erian L. Hanna. LC 84-90271. 101p. 1985. 7.95 o.p. (ISBN 0-533-06315-9). Vantage.
Two Postwar Recoveries of the German Economy. Horst Mendershausen. LC 73-21101. (Contributions in Economic Analysis Ser.: No. 8). (Illus.). 130p. 1974. Repr. of 1955 ed. lib. bdg. 35.00x o.p. (ISBN 0-8371-6000-6, MEGE). Greenwood.
Two Rats Helping the Kitten. Xiao Ming. (Illus.). 22p. (gr. k-3). 1983. pap. 1.95 o.p. (ISBN 0-8351-1243-8). China Bks.
Two R's: Paragraph to Essay. Shirley Fencl & Susan G. Jager. LC 78-16026. 1979. pap. text ed. write for info. o.p. (ISBN 0-673-15723-7). Scott F.
Two Runaways. Jerry Jenkins. (Bradford Family Adventures Ser.). 128p. (Orig.). (gr. 3-7). 1984. pap. 2.95 o.p. (ISBN 0-87239-792-0, 2942). Standard Pub.
Two Sermons upon S. Judes Epistle. Richard Hooker. LC 70-26033. (English Experience Ser.: No. 195). 56p. 1969. Repr. of 1614 ed. 8.00 o.p. (ISBN 90-221-0195-9). Walter J Johnson.
Two Sewers for a Tennis Court: Or What I Got Out of & Into. Linda M. Desheplo. 1979. 6.00 o.p. (ISBN 0-682-49529-8). Exposition-Phoenix.
Two Short Novels by Henry James see Graded Readers for Students of English As a Second Language.
Two Sides of the Brain. Sid J. Segalowitz. 292p. 1983. 14.95 o.p. (ISBN 0-13-935296-1); pap. 6.95 o.p. (ISBN 0-13-935304-6). P-H.
Two-Six Compounds. B. Ray. LC 72-93126. 1969. 57.00 o.p. (ISBN 0-08-006624-0). Pergamon.
Two Songs This Archangel Sings. George C. Chesbro. LC 86-47668. 320p. 1987. 14.95 o.p. (ISBN 0-689-11659-4, Atheneum). Macmillan.
Two Special Cards. Sonia O. Lisker & Leigh Dean. LC 75-35609. (Illus.). (gr. k-2). 1976. 4.95 o.p. (ISBN 0-15-292222-9, HJ). HarBraceJ.
Two Standards. William F. Barry. Ed. by Robert L. Wolff. LC 75-466. (Victorian Fiction Ser). 1976. Repr. of 1898 ed. lib. bdg. 73.00 o.p. (ISBN 0-8240-1544-4). Garland Pub.
Two-Step: Dancing Toward Intimacy. Eileen McCann. LC 85-14764. (Illus.). 180p. 1985. 17.50 o.p. (ISBN 0-394-55016-1). Grove.
Two Stories for Little Folk: I Love That School Bus & Guess What Flew in the Window. Gertrude B. Bailey. (gr. k-4). 1977. 4.50 o.p. (ISBN 0-682-48684-1). Exposition-Phoenix.
Two Strange Tales. Mircea Eliade. Tr. by William A. Coates from Romanian. LC 86-13026. 130p. 1986. pap. 6.95 o.p. (ISBN 0-87773-386-4). Shambhala Pubns.
Two Strikes, Four Eyes. Ned Delaney. (Illus.). (gr. k-3). 1976. reinforced bdg. 11.45 o.s.i. (ISBN 0-395-24744-6). HM.
Two Studies in Later Roman & Byzantine Administration. Arthur E. Boak. Repr. of 1924 ed. 37.00 o.p. (ISBN 0-384-38814-0). Johnson Repr.
Two Studies on Ming History. Charles O. Hucker. (Michigan Monographs in Chinese Studies: No. 12). (Illus.). 83p. 1971. pap. 6.00 o.s.i. (ISBN 0-89264-012-X). U of Mich Ctr Chinese.
Two Sung Texts on Chinese Painting & the Landscape Styles of the 11th & 12th Centuries. Robert J. Maeda. LC 77-94706. (Outstanding Dissertations in the Fine Arts Ser.). 1978. lib. bdg. 33.00 o.p. (ISBN 0-8240-3238-1). Garland Pub.
Two Symposia: Ethnic Minority Feminism & Two Sides of the Coin. National Association for Women Deans, Administratos & Counselors. 1978. pap. 3.00 o.p. (ISBN 0-686-23415-4). Natl Assn Women.
Two Thousand & Eighty-one: A Hopeful View of the Human Future. Gerard K. O'Neill. 1982. pap. 5.95 o.p. (ISBN 0-671-44751-3). S&S.
Two Thousand Notable Americans. 2nd ed. Ed. by J. M. Evans. LC 83-73395. (Illus.). 500p. 1985. 125.00 o.s.i. (ISBN 0-934544-35-2). Am Biog Inst.
Two Thousand Places to Visit in Great Britain. Date not set. (ISBN 0-86145-635-1, Pub. by Auto Assn England). Salem Hse Pubs.
Two Thousand Years of Calligraphy. Dorothy E. Miner et al. LC 78-20698. (Illus.). 1980. pap. 13.95 o.s.i. (ISBN 0-8008-7919-8, Pentalic). Taplinger.
Two Twelfth Century Texts on Chinese Painting. Robert J. Maeda. (Michigan Monographs in Chinese Studies: No.8). 74p. 1970. pap. 1.50 o.p. (ISBN 0-89264-008-1). U of Mich Ctr Chinese.
Two Tycoons: Charles Clore & Jack Cotton. Charles Gordon. (Illus.). 288p. 1984. 22.95 o.p. (ISBN 0-241-11256-7, Pub. by Hamish Hamilton England). David & Charles.
Two Uncles of Pablo. Harry Behn. LC 59-8949. (gr. 4-6). 1959. 4.95 o.p. (ISBN 0-15-292306-3, HJ). HarBraceJ.
Two Views of American Labor. Frances Perkins & J. Paul St Sure. 1965. 2.00 o.p. (ISBN 0-89215-048-3). U Cal LA Indus Rel.
Two Village Sites in Southwestern Missouri: A Lithic Analysis. F. A. Calabrese et al. Ed. by W. Raymond Wood. LC 72-628906. (Research Ser.: No. 7). (Illus.). 50p. (Orig.). 1969. pap. 2.00 o.s.i. (ISBN 0-943414-09-1). MO Arch Soc.
Two Voices: Writing about Literature. Kenneth M. Symes. LC 75-31015. (Illus.). 320p. 1976. pap. 10.50 o.p. (ISBN 0-395-20607-3). HM.
Two Ways of Caring: A Biblical Design for Balanced Ministry. William E. Hulme. LC 73-78270. 112p. (Orig.). 1973. pap. 3.50 o.p. (ISBN 0-8066-1334-3, 10-6725, Augsburg). Augsburg Fortress.
Two Weeks in Another Town. Irwin Shaw. 1971. pap. 1.25 o.p. (ISBN 0-440-19176-9). Dell.
Two Weeks to Winning Chess. Fred Reinfeld. 1974. pap. 2.95 o.p. (ISBN 0-380-00027-X, 19885). Avon.

Titles

Two Windmills. Maryke Reesink & Georgette Apol. LC 67-6406. (Illus.). (gr. k-3). 1967. 5.25 o.p. (ISBN 0-15-292350-0, HJ). HarBraceJ.

Two Winters & Three Summers. Fyodor Abramov. 1984. 17.95 o.p. (ISBN 0-15-192300-0). HarBraceJ.

Two Words into One Word Puzzle. Edison C. Generoso. 32p. 1986. 5.95 o.p. (ISBN 0-8062-2909-8). Carlton.

Two Worlds & Their Ways. Ivy Compton-Burnett. 1949. 20.95 o.p. (ISBN 0-575-02610-3, Pub by Gollancz England). David & Charles.

Two Worlds of Andrew Wyeth. Thomas Hoving. (Illus.). 1978. 25.00 o.p. (ISBN 0-395-27089-8); pap. 10.95 o.p. (ISBN 0-395-27080-4). HM.

Two Worlds of Coral Harper. Leigh G. Tarlton. LC 82-48758. 160p. (gr. 5 up). 1983. 12.95 o.p. (ISBN 0-15-292371-3, HJ). HarBraceJ.

Two Worlds of Tracy Corbett. Carole G. Page. LC 79-54117. 128p. (YA) (gr. 7-10). 1980. pap. 3.50 o.p. (ISBN 0-8066-1767-5, 10-6727, Augsburg). Augsburg Fortress.

Two Years in the Antarctic. E. W. Walton. (Illus.). 200p. 1955. (ISBN 0-8022-1803-2). Philos Lib.

Two Years in the Melting Pot: China Books & Periodicals. Liu Zongren. LC 84-2090. 208p. 1984. 14.95 o.p. (ISBN 0-8351-1371-X); pap. 8.95 o.p. (ISBN 0-8351-1370-1). China Bks.

Two Year's Journal in New York & Part of Its Territories in America. Charles Wolley. LC 73-5949. (Illus.). 96p. 1973. Repr. of 1902 ed. 7.50 o.p. (ISBN 0-916346-01-3). Harbor Hill Bks.

Tycoons & Locusts: A Regional Look at Hollywood Fiction of the 1930s. Walter Wells. LC 73-4266. (Crosscurrents-Modern Critiques Ser.). 154p. 1973. 6.95x o.p. (ISBN 0-8093-0606-9). S Ill U Pr.

Tyee Cookbook of the University of Washington. Carol James et al. 185p. (Orig.). 1981. pap. 8.95 o.s.i. (ISBN 0-89716-102-5). Peanut Butter.

Tyler-Browns of Brattleboro. Dorothy Sutherland Melville. 1973. 10.00 o.p. (ISBN 0-682-47687-0). Exposition-Phoenix.

Tylers Woman. Linda P. Sandifer. 1985. pap. 3.50 o.p. (ISBN 0-380-89792-X). Avon.

Tyndale Library of Great Biblical Novels, 6 vols. 27.35 o.p. (ISBN 0-8423-7643-7). Tyndale.

Type Identification Chart. Isaac Pitman. 1956. (ISBN 0-8022-1744-3). Philos Lib.

Type One Font of Cap. Date not set. (ISBN 0-07-521240-4). McGraw.

Type Rating (Airplane) Flight Test Guide (AC 61-57A) Federal Aviation Administration. 1975. pap. text ed. 3.00 o.p. (ISBN 0-86677-010-0, Pub. by Cooper Aviation). Aviation.

Type Two Superconductivity. D. Saint-James et al. LC 67-27491. 1969. 80.00 o.p. (ISBN 0-08-012392-9). Pergamon.

Types & Emblems. C. H. Spurgeon. 3.95 o.p. (ISBN 0-686-09088-8). Pilgrim Pubns.

Types from City Streets. facsimile ed. Hatchins Hapgood. 1972. Repr. of 1910 ed. lib. bdg. 29.25 o.p. (ISBN 0-8422-8179-7). Irvington.

Types of Drama: Plays & Essays. 4th ed. Sylvan Barnet et al. 1984. pap. text ed. write for info. o.p. (ISBN 0-673-39192-2). Scott F.

Types of Injuries & Impairments Due to Injuries, United States. John G. Collins. (DHHS Publication PHS Ser.: No. 87-1587). (Illus.). 78p. 1986. pap. 4.00 o.p. (ISBN 0-318-21905-0, S/N 017-022-00982-0). USGPO.

Typewriter Repair Manual. Howard Hutchison. pap. 11.95 o.p. (ISBN 0-8306-1336-6, 1336). TAB Bks.

Typewriter Revolution & Other Poems. D. J. Enright. LC 73-158612. 143p. 1973. 7.95 o.p. (ISBN 0-912050-07-1, Library Pr). Open Court.

Typing for Beginners. Speedwriting Institute Staff. 1976. pap. 4.95 o.p. (ISBN 0-671-18138-6). Monarch Pr.

Typing Made Simple. Nathan Levine. (Made Simple Ser.). 1958. pap. 4.95 o.p. (ISBN 0-385-01224-1). Doubleday.

Typing Power Drills. 2nd ed. Alan C. Lloyd et al. 1965. text ed. 9.60 o.p. (ISBN 0-07-038171-2). McGraw.

Typing Seventy Five: Basic. Ed. by Alan C. Lloyd et al. (Gregg College Typing, Ser. Four). 1979. text ed. 22.80 o.p. (ISBN 0-07-038256-5). McGraw.

Typing the Easy Way. Lieberman & Schimmel. (Easy Way Ser.). 1982. pap. 8.95 o.p. (ISBN 0-8120-2284-X). Barron.

Typographia: Or the Printers Instructor. Thomas F. Adams. LC 78-7449. (Nineteenth Century Bookarts & Printing Ser.). 295p. 1980. lib. bdg. 33.00 o.p. (ISBN 0-8240-3893-2). Garland Pub.

Typographic Samples, Pictures & Polemics. Michael Corris. 1986. 35.00 o.p. (ISBN 0-932526-11-X). Nexus Pr.

Typographical Printing-Surfaces: The Technology & Mechanism of Their Production. Lucien Legros & John C. Grant. Ed. by John Bidwell. LC 78-74403. (Nineteenth-Century Book Arts & Printing History Ser.: Vol. 16). (Illus.). 1980. lib. bdg. 94.00 o.p. (ISBN 0-8240-3890-8). Garland Pub.

Typography Instructor Guide. 1988. 16.00 o.s.i. (ISBN 0-88362-082-0, 0200). Graphic Arts Tech Found.

Typography Seven: The Annual of the Type Directors Club. Designed by Arthur Boden. (Illus.). 384p. 1986. 35.00 o.p. (ISBN 0-8230-5541-8). Watson-Guptill.

Typography Six. Illus. by Olaf Leu. (Illus.). 224p. 1985. 35.00 o.p. (ISBN 0-8230-5540-X). Watson-Guptill.

Typography Three: The Annual of the Type Director's Club. Type Directors Club Staff. (Illus.). 216p. 1982. 29.50 o.p. (ISBN 0-8230-5537-X). Watson-Guptill.

Typology & Early American Literature. Ed. by Sacvan Bercovitch. LC 74-181362. (New England Writers Ser.). 352p. 1971. 20.00x o.p. (ISBN 0-87023-096-4). U of Mass Pr.

Tyranny of the Status Quo. Milton Friedman & Rose Friedman. 192p. 1985. pap. 5.95 o.p. (ISBN 0-380-69878-1). Avon.

Tyranny of Time. Chalinder Allen. (ISBN 0-8022-0021-4). Philos Lib.

Tyranny on Trial: The Evidence at Nuremberg. Whitney R. Harris. LC 54-11298. (Illus.). 648p. 1970. Repr. of 1954 ed. 21.95x o.p. (ISBN 0-87074-073-3). SMU Press.

Tyrant or Father? A Study of Calvin's Doctrine of God. Garret Wilterdink. 185p. (Orig.). 1985. pap. 9.95 o.p. (ISBN 0-932269-19-2). Wyndham Hall.

Tyrants Destroyed & Other Short Stories. Vladimir Nabokov. Tr. by Dmitri Nabokov from Rus. LC 74-19209. 252p. 1975. text ed. 8.95 o.p. (ISBN 0-07-045739-5). McGraw.

Tyrants Destroyed & Other Stories. Vladimir Nabokov. (McGraw-Hill Paperbacks Ser.). 252p. 1981. pap. text ed. 5.95 o.p. (ISBN 0-07-045718-2). McGraw.

Tyrol Travel Guide. Berlitz Editors. 128p. 1984. 4.95 o.p. (ISBN 0-02-969920-7, Berlitz). Macmillan.

Tyrrhenian: A Sea-Guide to Its Coasts & Islands. H. M. Denham. (Illus.). 1976. 19.95 o.p. (ISBN 0-393-03196-9). Norton.

U

U-Boat Peril: An Anti-Submarine Commander's Story. Bob Whinney. (Illus.). 160p. 1987. 24.95 o.p. (ISBN 0-7137-1821-8, Pub. by Blandford Pr England). Sterling.

U-Boat Wars. Edwin P. Hoyt. 1984. 18.95 o.p. (ISBN 0-87795-589-1, Arbor Hse). Morrow.

U-Boats of World War Two, Vol. 1. Robert C. Stern. (Warships Illustrated Ser.: No. 13). (Illus.). 64p. (Orig.). 1988. pap. 9.95 o.p. (ISBN 0-85368-813-3, Pub. by Arms & Armour). Sterling.

U. K. Labor Market Guide. Kenneth Walsh & Richard Pearson. LC 84-13814. (Institute of Manpower Studies: No. 5). 288p. 1984. 32.95x o.p. (ISBN 0-566-00718-5). Gower Pub Co.

U. K. Life Assurance Industry: A Study in Applied Economics. Peter J. Franklin & Caroline Woodhead. (Illus.). 390p. 1980. 80.00 o.p. (ISBN 0-85664-654-7, Pub. by Croom Helm Ltd). Routledge Chapman & Hall.

U. K. Telecommunication Market Opportunities. International Resource Development, Inc. Staff. 186p. 1983. 1650.00x o.p. (ISBN 0-88694-573-9). Intl Res Dev.

U. N. see United Nations.

U. S. see United States.

U. S. A. - France Culture Capsules. J. Dale Miller & Maurice Loiseau. 1977. pap. text ed. 9.00 o.p. (ISBN 0-88377-151-9). Newbury Hse.

U. S. A. - Mexico Culture Capsules. J. Dale Miller & Russell H. Bishop. 1977. pap. text ed. 9.00 o.p. (ISBN 0-88377-150-0). Newbury Hse.

U. S. A. A Picture Book to Remember Her By. (Illus.). 1978. 5.98 o.s.i. (ISBN 0-517-25018-7). Crown.

U. S. A. Country Guide. Berlitz Editors. 256p. 1984. 7.95 o.p. (ISBN 0-02-969900-2, Berlitz). Macmillan.

U. S. A. for Business Travelers 1984. Steve Birnbaum. (Get'em & Go Travel Guide Ser.). 1984. pap. 7.70 o.p. (ISBN 0-395-34834-X). HM.

U. S. A. for Business Travelers, 1985. Steve Birnbaum. (Stephen Birnbaum Travel Guides Ser.). 1984. pap. 7.70 o.p. (ISBN 0-395-36529-5). HM.

U. S. A. for Business Travelers, 1987. Steve Birnbaum. (Illus.). 592p. 1986. pap. 8.70 o.s.i. (ISBN 0-395-42576-X). HM.

U. S. A. Militarism & Economy. R. Faramazyan. 271p. 1974. 4.45 o.p. (ISBN 0-8285-0387-7, Pub. by Progress Pubs USSR). Imported Pubns.

U. S. A. Products Liability Litigation Institute. Mark A. Dombroff. LC 85-139119. (Illus.). Lawyers Co-op.

U. S. A. The Forty-Second Parallel, Nineteen Nineteen, The Big Money. John Dos Passos. (Illus.). 1963. 20.00 o.p. (ISBN 0-395-07627-7). HM.

U. S. A. Today: Tracking Tomorrow's Trends. What We Think about Our Lives & Our Future. Anthony M. Casale. 1986. pap. 8.95 o.p. (ISBN 0-8362-7934-4). Andrews & McMeel.

U. S. A. Today Travel Tips. U. S. A. Today Editors. 160p. (Orig.). 1987. pap. 6.95 o.p. (ISBN 0-8362-9101-8). Andrews & McMeel.

U S A vs. Western Europe. M. K. Bunkina. 197p. 1979. 6.95 o.p. (ISBN 0-8285-1497-6, Pub. by Progress Pubs USSR). Imported Pubns.

U. S.-Mexican Energy Relationships: Realities & Prospects. Ed. by Jerry R. Ladman et al. LC 80-8878. 236p. 1981. 28.50x o.p. (ISBN 0-669-04398-2); pap. 8.00 o.p. (ISBN 0-669-04399-0). Lexington Bks.

U. S.-South Asian Relations, 1947-1982, 3 vols. R. K. Jain. 1400p. 1983. Set. text ed. 150.00x o.p. (ISBN 0-391-02869-3). Vol. 1 (ISBN 0-391-02870-7). Vol. 2 (ISBN 0-391-02871-5). Vol. 3. Humanities.

U. S.-South Korean Alliance. Ed. by Gerald L. Curtis & Sung-Joo Han. LC 82-49205. (Illus.). 256p. 1983. 33.00x o.p. (ISBN 0-669-06438-6). Lexington Bks.

U V Atlas of Organic Compounds, 5 vols. Photoelectric Spectrometry Group, England Staff & Institut fuer Spektrochemie und Angewandte Spektroskopie, Germany Staff. 1966-71. Set. 275.00 o.p. (ISBN 0-306-68300-8, IFI Plenum); 65.00 ea. o.p. Vol. 1 (ISBN 0-306-68301-6). Vol. 2 (ISBN 0-306-68302-4). Vol. 3 (ISBN 0-306-68303-2). Vol. 4 (ISBN 0-306-68304-0). Vol. 5 (ISBN 0-306-68305-9). Plenum Pub.

UAE. Middle East Economic Digest Staff. Ed. by Trevor Mostyn. (MEED Practical Guides Ser.). (Illus.). 324p. (Orig.). 1986. pap. 16.95x o.p. (ISBN 0-946510-03-2). Lynne Rienner.

Uber Deutschland: A Reader on German Affairs. C. H. Moore. 260p. 1972. 19.00 o.p. (ISBN 0-08-016584-2); pap. 9.75 o.p. (ISBN 0-08-016585-0). Pergamon.

Uber Ideenflucht. Ludwig Binswanger. LC 78-66767. (Phenomenology Ser.). 200p. 1980. lib. bdg. 26.00 o.p. (ISBN 0-8240-9568-5). Garland Pub.

Uberlieferungsgeschichtliche Problem des Pentateuch. Rolf Rendtorff. (Beiheft 147 zur Zeitschrift fuer die Alttestamentliche Wissenschaft Ser.). 1977. 54.50 o.p. (ISBN 3-11-006760-9). De Gruyter.

UBIK: The Screenplay. Philip K. Dick. Ed. by Ira M. Thornhill. (Illus.). 160p. 1985. 23.00 o.p. (ISBN 0-911169-06-7); text ed. write for info. o.p. (ISBN 0-911169-07-5). Corroboree Pr.

Ubiquitous Atom. Larry Spruch & Grace M. Spruch. LC 74-507. (Encore Edition). (Illus.). 512p. 1975. 6.95 o.p. (ISBN 0-684-15460-9, ScribT). Scribner.

UBU Repertory Theater Publications, Vols. 1-5. Ubu Repertory Theater Publications Staff. Set. pap. 28.00 o.p. (ISBN 0-913745-13-8). UBU Repertory.

UBU Repertory Theater Publications, Vol. 6-10. Ubu Repertory Theater Publications Staff. Set. pap. 28.00 o.p. (ISBN 0-913745-14-6). UBU Repertory.

UCC State Service, 3 vols. Gould Editorial Staff. 1983. Set. looseleaf 45.00 o.p. Gould.

UCLA Football: Touchdown UCLA. Hendrick Van Leuven. LC 81-85248. (College Sports Ser.). 1982. 12.95 o.p. (ISBN 0-87397-227-9). Strode.

UCSD Pascal Programming. Seymour V. Pollack. 1985. pap. text ed. 21.95x o.p. (ISBN 0-03-069393-4). HR&W.

Udo Fahrt Nach Koln. Peter Lunt. LC 73-20464. (Ger). 1971. pap. 11.60 o.p. (ISBN 0-395-11058-0). HM.

Ueber Mahlerei & Bildhauerarbeit in Rom fur Liebhaber des Schonen in der Kunst, 3 vols. Friedrich W. B. Von Ramdohr. 1080p. Date not set. Repr. of 1787 ed. text ed. 149.04x o.p. (ISBN 0-576-15115-7, Pub. by Gregg Intl Pubs England). Gregg Intl.

Uebungsbuch III see Deutsch X 3.

Uecker. Dieter Honisch. Tr. by Robert E. Wolf. (Illus.). 268p. 1986. 75.00 o.p. (ISBN 0-8109-1707-6). Abrams.

UFO. Rhonda Blumberg. (Illus.). 66p. (gr. 4-7). 1980. pap. 1.95 o.p. (ISBN 0-380-49254-7, 55707-X, Camelot). Avon.

UFO-Dynamics: Psychiatric & Psychic Aspects of the UFO Syndrome, Bk. 1. Berthold E. Schwarz. LC 83-60103. (Illus.). 304p. (Orig.). 1983. pap. 14.95 o.p. (ISBN 0-935834-12-5). Rainbow Books.

UFO-Dynamics: Psychiatric & Psychic Aspects of the UFO Syndrome, Bk. 2. Berthold & Schwarz. (Illus.). 260p. 1983. pap. 14.95 o.p. (ISBN 0-935834-13-3). Rainbow Books.

UFO: Teen Sightings. Walter Oleksy. LC 84-603. (Jem (High Interest-Low Reading Level) Ser.). (Illus.). 64p. (YA) (gr. 7-11). 1984. lib. bdg. 9.29 o.s.i. (ISBN 0-671-44006-3). Messner.

UFOs & Anti-Gravity. Bruce L. Cathie & Peter N. Temm. LC 77-8718. (Illus.). 1971. pap. write for info. o.p. (ISBN 0-89497-011-9). Strawberry Hill.

UFOs-God's Chariots? Flying Saucers in Politics, Science & Religion. Ted Peters. LC 76-44978. 1977. 7.95 o.p. (ISBN 0-8042-2233-9, John Knox). Westminster John Knox.

UFOs-Interplanetary Visitors: A UFO Investigator Reports on the Facts, Fables & Fantasies of the Flying Saucer Conspiracy. Raymond E. Fowler. LC 74-76026. 1974. 8.50 o.p. (ISBN 0-682-47979-9, Banner). Exposition-Phoenix.

UFO's: The Extrauniveral Connection. Roy C. Jarnagin. 1977. 6.50 o.p. (ISBN 0-682-48671-X, Banner). Exposition-Phoenix.

Uganda: Country Economic Memorandum. Mark Baird. v, 161p. 1982. pap. 8.00 o.p. (ISBN 0-8213-0027-X, BK0027). World Bank.

Ugandan: Defiant & Triumphant. Benjamin N. H. Kagwa. (Illus.). 1978. 10.00 o.p. (ISBN 0-682-49032-6). Exposition-Phoenix.

Ugarit. Adrian H. Curtis. (Cities of the Biblical World Ser.). 128p. (Orig.). 1985. pap. 9.95 o.p. (ISBN 0-8028-0166-8). Eerdmans.

Ugglians. L. M. Fallaw. 1957. (ISBN 0-8022-0472-4). Philos Lib.

Ugly Book. Arthur Crowley. (Illus.). (gr. k-3). 1982. PLB 8.95 o.p. (ISBN 0-395-31858-0). HM.

Ugly Duckling. Lorinda B. Cauley. LC 79-12340. (Illus.). 48p. 1979. 11.95 o.s.i. (ISBN 0-15-292435-3, HJ). HarBraceJ.

Ugly Princess. Nancy Luenn. (Illus.). (gr. 3-7). 1981. 9.95 o.p. (ISBN 0-316-53560-5, Joy St Bks). Little.

Uhuru & the Kenya Indians: The Role of a Minority Community in Kenya-1939-1963-Politics. Dana A. Seidenberg. 1983. text ed. 27.50x o.p. (ISBN 0-7069-1959-9, Pub. by Vikas India). Advent NY.

Ukrainian-English, English-Ukrainian Dictionary, 2 vols. Compiled by M. L. Podvesko. (Ukrainian & Eng.). 55.00 set o.p. E J Brill USA.

Ukrainian Political Prisoners in the U. S. S. R. A Directory. Ed. by Marta Harasowska. LC 81-86106. 204p. (Ukrainian.). 1981. 7.25 o.s.i. (ISBN 0-914834-47-9). Smoloskyp.

Ukrainian Priest's Appeals from a Soviet Labor Camp. Ed. by Behdan Yasen. (Documents of Ukrainian Samvydav: No. 3). 1976. 1.00 o.s.i. (ISBN 0-686-58233-0). Smoloskyp.

Ukrainians in Canada & the United States: A Guide to Information Sources. Ed. by Aleksander Sokolyszyn & Vladimir Wertsman. (Ethnic Studies Information Guide Ser.: Vol. 7). 256p. 1981. 68.00x o.p. (ISBN 0-8103-1494-0). Gale.

Ullstein Lexikon der Deutschen Sprache. Rudolf Koester. (Ger.). 1969. 20.00 o.p. (ISBN 3-550-06016-5, M-7672, Pub. by Ullstein Verlag/VVA). French & Eur.

Ullstein Lexikon der Kunst und Architektur. Heiner Knell. (Ger.). 1976. 20.00 o.p. (ISBN 3-550-06013-0, M-7673, Pub. by Ullstein Verlag/VVA). French & Eur.

Ulrich's International Periodicals Directory, 1987-1988, 2 vols. Ed. by Bowker, R. R., Co. Staff. 2500p. 1987. 159.95 o.p. (ISBN 0-8352-2379-5); Microfiche-combined with Irregular Serials & Annuals 650.00 o.p. (ISBN 0-317-58506-1). Bowker.

Ulster & Delaware: Railroad Through the Catskills. Gerald M. Best. LC 70-190176. (Illus.). 208p. 1972. 21.95 o.p. (ISBN 0-87095-041-X). Gldn West Bks.

Ultimate Athlete. George Leonard. 1979. pap. 4.95 o.p. (ISBN 0-380-43067-3, 54098-3). Avon.

Ultimate Baby Catalog. Michelle I. Haber & Barbara Kantrowitz. LC 82-60064. (Illus.). 192p. 1982. pap. 7.95 o.p. (ISBN 0-89480-174-0, 494). Workman Pub.

Ultimate Baseball Book. Daniel Okrent. 1981. 35.00 o.p. (ISBN 0-395-28220-9); pap. 14.95 o.p. (ISBN 0-395-30861-5). HM.

Ultimate Challenge. Barry Pickthall. (Illus.). 1984. 24.50 o.p. (ISBN 0-393-03290-6). Norton.

Ultimate Commune: The Universe & Us. Dana X. Kerola. 1979. 5.50 o.p. (ISBN 0-682-49312-0). Exposition-Phoenix.

Ultimate Country Fake Book Update. (Fake Bks.). 95p. 1985. plastic comb 8.95 o.p. (ISBN 0-88188-389-1, HL00240047). H Leonard Pub Corp.

Ultimate Desires. T. Cooney. 112p. 1958. (ISBN 0-8022-0294-2). Philos Lib.

Ultimate Fat Book. Jim Erskine & Bobbi G. Cooper. (Illus.). 1982. pap. 3.95 o.p. (ISBN 0-03-062086-4, Owl Bks). H Holt & Co.

Ultimate Fishing Book. Lee Eisenberg & Decourcy Taylor. (Illus.). 256p. 1981. 40.00 o.p. (ISBN 0-395-31767-3). HM.

Ultimate Game. Ralph Glendinning. 1981. 13.95 o.p. (ISBN 0-671-42016-X, Wyndham Bks). S&S.

Ultimate Good Luck. Richard Ford. 216p. 1981. 9.95 o.p. (ISBN 0-395-30373-7). HM.

Ultimate Loss: Coping with the Death of a Child. Joan Bordow. 1982. 12.95x o.p. Phoenix Soc.

Ultimate Pipe Book. Richard C. Hacker. LC 84-72427. (Illus.). 305p. 1984. 18.95 o.p. (ISBN 0-931253-00-4). Autumngold Pub.

Ultimate Revolution. Walter Starcke. 155p. 1988. pap. 6.95 o.p. Guadalupe Pr.

Ultimate Tax Book. David Ingram. 192p. (Orig.). 1988. pap. text ed. 12.95 o.p. (ISBN 0-88839-208-7). Hancock House.

Ultimate Worlds. Hugo Gernsback. 1975. pap. 2.25 o.p. (ISBN 0-380-00369-4, 26179). Avon.

Ultimates in the Far East: Travels in the Orient & India. Hudson Strode. LC 75-117576. (Illus.). 1970. 8.95 o.p. (ISBN 0-15-192580-1). HarBraceJ.

Ultra in the West. Ralph Bennett. (Encore Edition). (Illus.). 306p. 1980. encore ed. 6.95 o.p. (ISBN 0-684-17750-1, ScribT). Scribner.

Ultra-Royalism & the French Restoration. Nora E. Hudson. LC 73-670. 209p. 1973. Repr. of 1936 ed. lib. bdg. 17.00x o.p. (ISBN 0-374-94027-4, Octagon). Hippocrene Bks.

Ultracentrifugation in Biochemistry. Howard K. Schachman. 1959. 66.00 o.p. (ISBN 0-12-621050-0). Acad Pr.

Ultracentrifugation of Macromolecules: Modern Topics. J. W. Williams. 1973. 36.50 o.p. (ISBN 0-12-755160-3). Acad Pr.

Ultralight Kit Book. Jack Lambie. LC 84-8884. (Illus.). 252p. (Orig.). 1984. pap. 12.60 o.p. (ISBN 0-8306-2369-8, 2369). TAB Bks.

Ultraman, Vol. 2. (Big Little Bks.: No. 39). (Illus.). 350p. 1984. 6.95 o.p. (ISBN 0-318-02691-0). Bks Nippan.

Ultrashort Light Pulses: Picosecond Techniques & Applications. Ed. by S. L. Shapiro. (Topics in Applied Physics Ser.: Vol. 18). (Illus.). xi, 435p. 1984. 23.30 o.p. (ISBN 0-387-13493-X). Springer-Verlag.

Ultrasonic Examination of the Breast. Ed. by Jack Jellins & Joshiji Kobayashi. 397p. 1984. 35.00 o.p. (ISBN 0-471-90324-8, Dist. by A R Liss). Wiley.

Ultrasonic Fatigue: Proceedings. Champion, Pennsylvania, 1981. Ed. by Joseph M. Wells & Otto Buck. (Illus.). 668p. 60.00 o.p. (ISBN 0-317-36288-7); members 36.00 o.p. (ISBN 0-317-36289-5); students 20.00 o.p. (ISBN 0-317-36290-9). ASM.

Ultrasonic Testing: Non-Conventional Testing Techniques. Ed. by J Szilard. LC 80-41592. 648p. 1982. 141.95 o.p. (ISBN 0-471-27938-2, Pub. by Wiley-Interscience). Wiley.

Ultrasonics in Clinical Diagnosis. 3rd ed. Barry Goldberg & Peter N. Wells. (Illus.). 1983. pap. 46.25 o.p. (ISBN 0-443-02141-4). Churchill.

Ultrasonics in Packaging & Plastics Fabrication. Ralph H. Thomas. 192p. 1983. 28.95 o.p. (ISBN 0-8436-1102-2). Van Nos Reinhold.

Ultrasonics International 87: Conference Proceeding. (Ultrasonics International Ser.). (Illus.). 968p. 1987. 195.00 o.p. (ISBN 0-408-02348-1). Butterworth.

Ultrasonography in Obstetrics & Gynecology. 2nd ed. Peter W. Callen. 512p. (Orig.). 1988. 60.00 o.p. Saunders.

Ultrasonography of Digestive Diseases. 2nd ed. Weill. 1982. 79.00 o.p. (ISBN 0-8016-5376-2). Mosby.

Ultrasound in Clinical Obstetrics. R. G. Law. (Illus.). 148p. 1980. text ed. 31.00 o.p. (ISBN 0-7236-0547-5, Pub. by John Wright UK). Butterworth.

Ultrasound in Gynecology & Obstetrics. N. Hassani. 1978. 49.00 o.p. (ISBN 0-387-90260-0). Springer-Verlag.

Ultrasound in High-Risk Obstetrics. Rudy E. Sabbagha. LC 79-15161. (Illus.). 108p. 1979. text ed. 11.00 o.p. (ISBN 0-8121-0676-8). Lea & Febiger.

Ultrasound in Perinatal Care. Ed. by M. J. Bennett. (Perinatal Practice Ser.). 187p. 1984. 37.00 o.p. (ISBN 0-471-90384-1, Dist. by A R Liss). Wiley.

Ultrasound Interaction in Biology & Medicine. Ed. by R. Millner et al. LC 83-9551. 230p. 1983. 49.50x o.p. (ISBN 0-306-41367-1, Plenum Pr). Plenum Pub.

Ultrastructural Aspects of the Liver & Its Disorders. 2nd ed. Kyuichi Tanikawa. LC 79-84646. (Illus.). 357p. 1979. 62.50 o.p. (ISBN 0-89640-034-4). Igaku-Shoin.

Ultrastructural Pathology of the Adrenal Glands Incushing's Syndrome see Aortic Alterations in Rabbits Following Sheathing with Silastic & Polyethylene Tubes.

Ultrastructure of Bone & Joint Diseases. 2nd ed. Kazushi Hirohata et al. LC 81-80906. (Illus.). 328p. 1981. 60.00 o.p. (ISBN 0-89640-056-5). Igaku-Shoin.

Ultrastructure of Protein Fibers: Proceedings. Ed. by Rubin Borasky. 1963. 36.50 o.p. (ISBN 0-12-117250-3). Acad Pr.

Ultrastructure of the Animal Cell. 2nd ed. L. T. Threadgold. Ed. by G. A. Kerkut. 472p. 1976. 88.00 o.p. (ISBN 0-08-018958-X); pap. 85.00 o.p. (ISBN 0-08-018957-1). Pergamon.

Ultrastructure of the Brain in Hypoxia. N. N. Bogolepov. Tr. by Michael Burov. 208p. 1983. 8.95 o.p. (ISBN 0-8285-2573-0, Pub. by Mir Pubs USSR). Imported Pubns.

Ultrastructure of the Hen Eggshell & Its Physiological Interpretation. (Agricultural Research Reports: No. 158). (Book and Book of Figures). 1971. pap. 24.00 o.p. (ISBN 90-220-0341-8, PDC97, PUDOC). UNIPUB.

Ultrastructure of the Kidney. A. J. Dalton & Francis Haguenau. (Ultrastructure in Biological Systems). 1967. 67.50 o.p. (ISBN 0-12-200956-8). Acad Pr.

Ultrastructure of the Mammalian Heart. Ed. by C. E. Challice & S. Viragh. (Ultrastructure in Biological Systems Series). 1973. 52.50 o.p. (ISBN 0-12-170050-X). Acad Pr.

Ultraviolet Photoelectron Spectroscopy of Gases Absorbed on Metal Surfaces see Photoelectron Spectrometry.

Ultravox: In Their Own Words. 32p. 1985. 5.95 o.s.i. (ISBN 0-7119-0553-3). Cherry Lane.

Ulysses: "Aeolus" "Lestrygonians," & "Scylla & Charybdis" a Facsimile of Page Proofs for Episodes 7-9. James Joyce. Ed. by Michael Groden. LC 77-14621. (James Joyce Archive Ser.). 1978. lib. bdg. 125.00 o.p. (ISBN 0-8240-2817-1). Garland Pub.

Ulysses: "Circe": A Facsimile of Page Proofs for Episode 15. James Joyce. Ed. by Michael Groden. LC 77-14656. (James Joyce Archive Ser.). 1978. lib. bdg. 125.00 o.p. (ISBN 0-8240-2820-1). Garland Pub.

Ulysses: "Circe" & "Eumaeus": A Facsimile of Manuscripts & Typescripts for Episodes 15 (Part II) & 16. James Joyce. Ed. by Michael Groden. LC 77-11971. (James Joyce Archive Ser.). 1978. lib. bdg. 125.00 o.p. (ISBN 0-8240-2825-2). Garland Pub.

Ulysses: "Cyclops" & "Nausicaa", & "Oxen of the Sun": a Facsimile of Page Proofs of Episode 12-14. James Joyce. Ed. by Michael Groden. LC 77-14655. (James Joyce Archive Ser.). 1978. lib. bdg. 125.00 o.p. (ISBN 0-8240-2819-8). Garland Pub.

Ulysses: "Eumaeus," "Ithaca," & "Penelope": A Facsimile of Page Proofs for Chapters 16-18. James Joyce. Ed. by Michael Groden. LC 77-14657. (James Joyce Archive Ser.). 1978. lib. bdg. 125.00 o.p. (ISBN 0-8240-2821-X). Garland Pub.

Ulysses: "Ithaca" & "Penelope." A Facsimile of Manuscripts & Typescripts for Episodes 17 & 18. Ed. by Michael Groden. LC 77-10882. (James Joyce Archive Ser.: Vol. 16). 1978. lib. bdg. 125.00 o.p. (ISBN 0-8240-2826-0). Garland Pub.

Ulysses: "Oxen of the Sun," & "Circe": A Facsimile of Drafts, Manuscripts, & Typescripts 14 & 15 (Part 1) James Joyce. Ed. by Michael Groden. LC 77-22764. (James Joyce Archive Ser.). 1978. lib. bdg. 125.00 o.p. (ISBN 0-8240-2824-4). Garland Pub.

Ulysses: "Sirens," "Cyclops," "Nausicaa," & "Oxen of the Sun." A Facsimile of Placards for Episodes 11-14. Ed. by Michael Groden. LC 78-11931. (James Joyce Archive Ser.: Vol. 19). 1979. lib. bdg. 125.00 o.p. (ISBN 0-8240-2813-9). Garland Pub.

Ulysses: "Telemachus," "Nestor," "Proteus" Calypso" "Lotus Eaters," & "Hades": a Facsimile of Placards for Episodes 1-6. James Joyce. Ed. by Michael Groden. LC 78-16032. (James Joyce Archive Ser.: Vol. 17). 1978. lib. bdg. 125.00 o.p. (ISBN 0-8240-2811-2). Garland Pub.

Ulysses: "Wandering Rocks" & "Sirens" A Facsimile of Page Proofs for Episodes 10-11. James Joyce. Ed. by Michael Groden. LC 77-14654. (James Joyce Archive Ser.). 1978. lib. bdg. 125.00 o.p. (ISBN 0-8240-2818-X). Garland Pub.

Ulysses: "Wandering Rocks," "Sirens," "Cyclops," "Nausicaa": Facsimile of Drafts & Typescripts for Episodes 10-13. Ed. by Michael Groden. LC 77-10196. (James Joyce Archive Ser.). 1978. lib. bdg. 125.00 o.p. (ISBN 0-8240-2823-6). Garland Pub.

Umbrellas, Hats & Wheels. Ann Rand & Jerome Snyder. LC 61-10113. (Illus.). (gr. k-3). 1961. 6.50 o.p. (ISBN 0-15-292485-X, HJ). HarBraceJ.

UN see United Nations.

Unabridged Crossword Puzzle Dictionary. A. F. Sisson. 1964. 10.95 o.p. (ISBN 0-385-02843-1); pap. 12.95 thumb-indexed ed. o.p. (ISBN 0-385-01350-7). Doubleday.

Unabridged Marilyn: Her Life from A to Z. Randall Riese & Neal Hitchens. (Illus.). 608p. 1987. 25.00 o.p. (ISBN 0-86553-176-5). Congdon & Weed.

Unamuno: A Philosophy of Tragedy. Jose Ferrater Mora. Tr. by Philip Silver from Span. LC 81-20162. Orig. Title: Unamuno: Bosquejo De una Filosofia. xx, 136p. 1982. Repr. of 1962 ed. lib. bdg. 35.00x o.p. (ISBN 0-313-23341-1, FMUN). Greenwood.

Unamuno & Spanish Literature. Demetrios Basdekis. LC 68-63733. 101p. 1983. Repr. of 1967 ed. lib. bdg. 19.95x o.p. (ISBN 0-89370-781-3). Borgo Pr.

Unamuno: Bosquejo De una Filosofia see Unamuno: A Philosophy of Tragedy.

Unashamed Accompanist. Gerald Moore. 160p. 1985. 13.95 o.p. (ISBN 0-531-09771-4). Watts.

Unasked Questions: Seven Stories & a Novella. Harry A. Hargrave. 1980. 6.00 o.p. (ISBN 0-682-49254-X). Exposition-Phoenix.

Unbalanced Accounts. Kate Gallison. 1986. 14.95 o.p. (ISBN 0-316-30288-0). Little.

Unbind Your Sons: The Captivity of America in Asia. Alex Campbell. LC 79-114382. (Illus.). 1970. 7.95 o.p. (ISBN 0-87140-500-8); pap. 2.45 o.p. (ISBN 0-87140-027-8). Liveright.

Unbirthday. A. M. Stephenson. 112p. 1982. pap. 1.95 o.p. (ISBN 0-380-79418-7, 60060-9, Flare). Avon.

Unblessed. Berneice Lunday. LC 78-15244. (Orion Ser). 1979. pap. 3.95 o.p. (ISBN 0-8127-0200-X). Review & Herald.

Unblocked Boss: A Guidebook for Managers. Dave Francis & Mike Woodcock. LC 81-51806. 274p. 1981. pap. 12.95 o.p. (ISBN 0-88390-169-2). Univ Assocs.

Unblocked Boss: Activities for Self-Development. Mike Woodcock & Dave Francis. LC 81-51807. 298p. 1981. pap. 12.95 o.p. (ISBN 0-88390-170-6). Univ Assocs.

Unblocking Your Organization. Mike Woodcock & Dave Francis. LC 78-62929. Orig. Title: People at Work. 254p. 1979. pap. 16.50 o.p. (ISBN 0-88390-148-X). Univ Assocs.

Unbought & Unbossed: An Autobiography. Shirley Chisholm. 1970. 5.95 o.p. (ISBN 0-395-10932-9). HM.

Uncensored John Henry Faulk. John H. Faulk. 224p. 1985. 16.95x o.p. (ISBN 0-87719-013-5). Texas Month Pr.

Uncertain Ally. Michael Chichester & John Wilkinson. 264p. 1982. text ed. 38.00x o.p. (ISBN 0-566-00534-4). Gower Pub Co.

Uncertain Chime. Lizabeth Loghry. (Velvet Glove Ser.: No. 17). 192p. 1985. pap. 2.25 o.p. (ISBN 0-380-89669-9). Avon.

Uncertain Glory: Folklore & the American Revolution. Tristram P. Coffin. LC 77-147812. 284p. 1971. 40.00x o.p. (ISBN 0-8103-5040-8). Gale.

Uncertain Heart. Denise Robins. 1977. pap. 1.25 o.p. (ISBN 0-380-00963-3, 32391-5). Avon.

Uncertainty Management in AI Systems. Judea Pearl & Glenn Shafer. (Illus.). 105p. 1988. pap. text ed. 12.00 o.p. (ISBN 0-929280-16-4). Amer Artificial.

UNCITRAL Conciliation Rules. 1.00 o.p. (ISBN 92-1-133245-1, E.81.V.6). UN.

Uncivil Liberties. Calvin Trillin. LC 81-18196. 224p. 1982. 10.45 o.p. (ISBN 0-89919-097-9). Ticknor & Fields.

Uncivil Wars: Ireland Today. Padraig O'Malley. 1983. 19.50 o.p. (ISBN 0-395-34414-X). HM.

Unclassed. George Gissing. 1983. pap. 8.95 o.p. (ISBN 0-686-47743-X, NO. 3879). Routledge Chapman & Hall.

Uncle. Julia Markus. (Literary Fellowship Award Novel Ser.). 1978. 7.95 o.p. (ISBN 0-395-27098-7). HM.

Uncle Bob Talks with My Central Nervous System. Bob DeVine. LC 85-5721. (Designed by God Ser.). (Illus.). 48p. (gr. 4-7). 1985. pap. 4.95 o.p. (ISBN 0-89191-945-7, 59451, Chariot Bks). Cook.

Uncle Bob Talks with My Circulatory System. Bob DeVine. LC 85-6637. (Designed by God Ser.). (Illus.). 48p. (gr. 4-7). 1985. pap. 4.95 o.p. (ISBN 0-89191-943-0, 59436, Chariot Bks). Cook.

Uncle Bob Talks with My Digestive System. Bob DeVine. LC 85-4737. (Designed by God Ser.). (Illus.). 48p. (gr. 4-7). 1985. pap. 4.95 o.p. (ISBN 0-89191-944-9, 59444, Chariot Bks). Cook.

Uncle Bob Talks with My Respiratory System. Bob DeVine. LC 85-3779. (Designed by God Ser.). (Illus.). 48p. (gr. 4-7). 1985. pap. 4.95 o.p. (ISBN 0-89191-941-4, 59410, Chariot Bks). Cook.

Uncle Herschel, Doctor Padilsky, & the Evil Eye: A Novel of Old Brooklyn. I. S. Young. LC 72-91842. 1973. 6.95 o.p. (ISBN 0-15-192690-5). HarBraceJ.

Uncle Hugh: A Fishing Story. Rita G. Gelman & Warner Friedman. LC 78-4918. (Illus.). (gr. k-3). 1978. 6.95 o.p. (ISBN 0-15-292789-1, HJ). HarBraceJ.

Uncle Ike. Linda S. Chandler. LC 80-70520. (gr. 1-6). 1981. 5.95 o.p. (ISBN 0-8054-4264-2, 4242-64). Broadman.

Uncle John's Original Bread Book. 2nd ed. John R. Braue. (Illus.). 1965. 8.50 o.p. (ISBN 0-682-46876-2, Banner). Exposition-Phoenix.

Uncle Josh Stories. Helen C. Noordewier. (Voyager Ser.). 64p. (ps-1). 1983. 12.95 o.p. (ISBN 0-8010-6738-3). Baker Bk.

Uncle New Year. Faridah Fardjam & Meyer Azaad. LC 77-128810. (Illus.). (gr. k-5). 1972. PLB 4.95 o.p. (ISBN 0-87614-014-2). Carolrhoda Bks.

Uncle of Europe: The Social & Diplomatic Life of Edward VII. Gordon Brook-Shepherd. LC 75-29366. (Illus.). 384p. 1976. 12.95 o.p. (ISBN 0-15-192697-2). HarBraceJ.

Uncle Robert's Secret. Wylly F. St. John. 1981. pap. 1.25 o.p. (ISBN 0-380-00909-9, 46326, Camelot). Avon.

Uncle Sam, Super Cop: A Satirical View of American History. Jim Hughes. LC 78-50033. (Illus.). 96p. 1978. pap. 4.95 o.p. (ISBN 0-88208-083-0). Chicago Review.

Uncle Sam's Private, Profitseeking Corporations: Comsat, Fannie Mae, Amtrak, & Conrail. Lloyd D. Musoff. LC 81-48687. 144p. 1982. 23.00x o.p. (ISBN 0-669-05532-8). Lexington Bks.

Uncle Tom's Cabin. Harriet Beecher Stowe. 1976. Repr. of 1909 ed. 14.95x o.p. (ISBN 0-460-00371-2, Evman); pap. 2.95x o.p. (ISBN 0-460-01371-8, Evman). Biblio Dist.

Uncle Traveling Matt's Adventures in Outer Space. Diane D. Hearn. (Fraggle Rock Bks.). (Illus.). (ps-1). 1984. pap. 1.49 o.s.i. (ISBN 0-03-000712-7). H Holt & Co.

Uncle Uriah & Tad. Kimberx Lantry. (Trailblazers Ser.). (gr. 4-8). pap. 1.99 o.p. (ISBN 0-8163-0361-4). Pacific Pr Pub Assn.

Uncle Vanya. Anton Chekhov. Ed. by Jacques Chwat. 1974. pap. 0.75 o.p. (ISBN 0-380-01594-3, 18663, Bard). Avon.

Uncle Wiggily's Happy Days. (Illus.). 48p. (gr. 1-7). 1978. 5.95 o.p. (ISBN 0-448-47625-8, G&D); PLB 5.99 o.p. (ISBN 0-448-13039-4). Putnam Pub Group.

Uncollected Letters. H. P. Lovecraft. Ed. by S. T. Joshi. 56p. (Orig.). 1986. pap. 5.95 o.p. (ISBN 0-940884-06-2). Necronomicon.

Uncollected Letters of James Gates Percival, Poet & Geologist, 1795-1856. James G. Percival. Ed. by Harry R. Warfel. LC 59-62964. (University of Florida Humanities Monographs: No. 1). 1959. pap. 3.50 o.p. (ISBN 0-8130-0186-2). U Presses Fla.

Uncollected Stars. Ed. by P. Anthony et al. 1986. pap. 3.50 o.p. (ISBN 0-380-89596-X). Avon.

Uncomformities in Shakespeare's History Plays. Kristian Smidt. 256p. 1982. text ed. 35.00x o.p. (ISBN 0-391-02488-4). Humanities.

Uncommitted: Alienated Youth in American Society. Kenneth Keniston. LC 65-19062. (Illus.). 1965. 10.75 o.p. (ISBN 0-15-192738-3). HarBraceJ.

Uncommon Clay: The Life & Works of Augustus Saint Gaudens. Burke Wilkinson. LC 85-8480. (Helen & Kurt Wolff Bk.). (Illus.). 400p. 1985. 22.95 o.s.i. (ISBN 0-15-192749-9). HarBraceJ.

Uncommon Entrance. Edward Blishen. 192p. 1983. pap. 9.95 o.p. (ISBN 0-241-10920-5, Pub. by Hamish Hamilton England). David & Charles.

Uncommon Man: The Triumph of Herbert Hoover. Richard N. Smith. (Illus.). 448p. 1988. 22.45 o.p. (ISBN 0-671-46034-X). S&S.

Uncommon Market: Essays in the Economic History of the Atlantic Slave Trade. Ed. by H. A. Gemery & J. S. Hogendorn. LC 79-294. (Studies in Social Discontinuity). 1979. 24.95 o.p. (ISBN 0-12-279850-3). Acad Pr.

Uncommon Therapy: The Psychiatric Techniques of Milton H. Erickson, M. D. Jay Haley. 1977. 10.00x o.p. (ISBN 0-393-01100-3, Norton Lib); pap. 5.95 o.p. (ISBN 0-393-00846-0). Norton.

Uncommon Women & Others. Wendy Wasserstein. 1979. pap. 2.95 o.p. (ISBN 0-380-45997-3, 80580-4, Bard). Avon.

Uncompahgre. Muriel Marshall. LC 80-11666. (Illus.). 210p. (Orig.). 1980. pap. 6.95 o.p. (ISBN 0-87004-282-3). Caxton.

Uncompensated Hospital Care: Rights & Responsibilities. Ed. by Frank A. Sloan et al. LC 85-45045. (Contemporary Medicine & Public Health Ser.). 224p. 1986. text ed. 25.00x o.p. (ISBN 0-8018-2867-8). Johns Hopkins.

Uncompleted Past: Postwar German Novels & the Third Reich. Judith Ryan. LC 83-6744. 184p. 1983. 24.50x o.p. (ISBN 0-8143-1728-6). Wayne St U Pr.

Uncomplicated Christian. LeRoy Dugan. LC 78-66886. 128p. 1978. pap. 2.95 o.p. (ISBN 0-87123-572-2, 200572). Bethany Hse.

Unconditional Democracy: Education & Politics in Occupied Japan, 1945 to 1952. Toshio Nishi. (Publication Ser.: No. 244). 408p. 1982. 19.95x o.p. (ISBN 0-8179-7441-5). Hoover Inst Pr.

Unconditional Surrender: God's Program for Victory. 2nd ed. Gary North. LC 82-84385. 280p. 1983. pap. text ed. 9.95 o.p. (ISBN 0-939404-06-0). Geneva Ministr.

Unconquered Souls: The Resistentialists. C. L. Sulzberger. LC 72-81087. 224p. 1973. 7.95 o.p. (ISBN 0-87951-004-8); 14.95 o.p. Overlook Pr.

Unconscious: A Conceptual Analysis. Alasdair C. MacIntyre. (Studies in Philosophical Psychology). 1976. pap. text ed. 7.95x o.p. (ISBN 0-391-00336-4). Humanities.

Unconscious God. Victor Frankl. 1976. pap. 6.70 o.p. (ISBN 0-671-22426-3, Touchstone Bks). S&S.

Unconventional Approaches to Fusion. Ed. by B. Brunelli & G. G. Leotta. LC 82-3836. (Ettore Majorana International Science Series, Physical Sciences: Vol. 13). 544p. 1982. 95.00x o.p. (ISBN 0-306-41002-8, Plenum Pr). Plenum Pub.

Unconventional Spectroscopy: Proceedings of the SPIE Annual Technical Symposium, 20th, San Diego, 1976. (SPIE Seminar Proceedings: Vol. 082). 84p. 10.00 o.p. (ISBN 0-89252-109-0); members 6.00 o.p. (ISBN 0-317-34772-1). SPIE.

Unconventional Women. Margaret Hess. 1981. pap. 6.50 o.p. (ISBN 0-88207-340-0). Victor Bks.

Uncoupling. Ira Sadoff. 234p. 1982. 12.95 o.p. (ISBN 0-395-32136-0). HM.

Uncovering Bible Times. Merrill T. Gilbertson. LC 68-25799. 1968. pap. 2.50 o.p. (ISBN 0-8066-0830-7, 15-7007, Augsburg). Augsburg Fortress.

UNCTAD & the South-North Dialogue: The First Twenty Years. Ed. by M. Zammit Cutajar. LC 84-6484. 338p. 1985. 47.00 o.p. (ISBN 0-08-028144-3, Pub. by Aberdeen Scotland). Pergamon.

Undaunted. R. Seth. 320p. 1956. (ISBN 0-8022-1535-1). Philos Lib.

Undeclared War Nineteen Forty-Nineteen Forty-One. William L. Langer & S. Everett Gleason. 19.25 o.p. (ISBN 0-8446-1276-6). Peter Smith.

Under a Changing Moon. Margot Benary-Isbert. LC 64-17084. 1964. 5.95 o.p. (ISBN 0-15-292800-6, HJ). HarBraceJ.

Under All is the Land. 127p. members 4.25 o.p. (ISBN 0-318-15197-9, NO. 111-969); 100 or more copies 4.00 ea. o.p. Natl Assoc Realtors.

Under Contract: An Anna Lee Mystery. Liza Cody. 1987. 16.95 o.p. (ISBN 0-684-18780-9). Scribner.

Under Crimson Sails. Lynna Lawton. 352p. 1982. pap. 3.25 o.p. (ISBN 0-505-51852-X, Pub. by Tower Bks). Dorchester Pub Co.

Under His Wings. O. Hallesby. LC 77-84084. 1978. pap. 3.95 o.p. (ISBN 0-8066-1609-1, 10-6790, Augsburg). Augsburg Fortress.

Under Orion. Janice Law. 1978. 7.95 o.p. (ISBN 0-395-26484-7). HM.

Under Scott's Command: Lashly's Antarctic Diaries. Ed. by A. R. Ellis. LC 73-81241. (Illus.). (gr. 10-12). 4.75 o.s.i. (ISBN 0-8008-7936-8). Taplinger.

Under Strange Skies. Harry Simonhoff. 1953. (ISBN 0-8022-1575-0). Philos Lib.

Under Summer Skies. V. Bubnys. 249p. 1979. pap. 5.45 o.p. (ISBN 0-686-91847-9, Pub. by Progress Pubs USSR). Imported Pubns.

Under the Black Flag. Don C. Seitz. LC 78-167167. 354p. 1971. Repr. of 1925 ed. 43.00x o.p. (ISBN 0-8103-3805-X). Gale.

Under the Bridge. Ferris Greenslet. 1943. 3.00 o.p. (ISBN 0-395-07755-9). HM.

Under the Bright Lights. Daniel Woodrell. 1986. 14.95 o.p. (ISBN 0-03-008514-4). H Holt & Co.

Under the Colors. Milovan Djilas. LC 76-134576. 1971. 9.75 o.p. (ISBN 0-15-153470-5). HarBraceJ.

Under the Ether Dome: One Doctor's Apprenticeship at Massachusetts General Hospital. Stephen A. Hoffman. LC 86-17655. 240p. 1987. 18.95 o.p. (ISBN 0-684-18580-6). Scribner.

Under the Goldwood Tree. John Duffy. 64p. 1982. 5.00 o.p. (ISBN 0-682-49869-6). Exposition-Phoenix.

Under the Green Star. Lin Carter. (Hardcover Collections Ser.: Vol. 4). 1988. 19.95x o.p. (ISBN 1-55742-047-5). Starmont Hse.

Under the Northern Lights. Marilyn Cunningham. (Ecstasy Ser.: No. 485). (Orig.). 1987. pap. 2.25 o.p. (ISBN 0-440-16427-3). Dell.

Under the Red Sea Sun. Edward Ellsberg. LC 73-17860. (Illus.). 500p. 1974. Repr. of 1946 ed. lib. bdg. 24.50x o.p. (ISBN 0-8371-7264-0, ELRS). Greenwood.

Under the Roofs of Paris. Henry Miller. LC 84-73204. Orig. Title: Opus Pistorum. 288p. 1985. pap. 3.95 o.s.i. (ISBN 0-394-62030-5, BC). Grove.

Under the Shade of a Coolibah Tree: Australian Studies in Consciousness. Richard A. Hutch & Peter G. Fenner. LC 84-20854. 352p. (Orig.). 1985. lib. bdg. 31.25 o.p. (ISBN 0-8191-4348-0); pap. text ed. 15.50 o.p. (ISBN 0-8191-4349-9). U Pr of Amer.

Under the Streets of Nice. Ken Follett. 1989. pap. 3.95 o.p. (ISBN 0-7701-1043-6). PaperJacks US.

Under the Sunset. Bram Stoker. (Forgotten Fantasy Library: Vol. 17). 1978. pap. 5.95 o.p. (ISBN 0-87877-116-6, F-116). Newcastle Pub.

Underbara Pumpan see Wonderful Pumpkin.

Underconsumption Theories. Michael F. Bleaney. LC 76-26935. 262p. 1977. pap. 3.95 o.p. (ISBN 0-7178-0476-3). Intl Pubs Co.

Undercover Affair. Sydney A. Clary. (Candlelight Supreme Ser.: No. 145). (Orig.). 1986. pap. 3.95 o.p. Dell.

Underdeveloped Areas Within the Common Market. Sergio Barzanti. 1965. 43.50x o.p. (ISBN 0-691-04188-1); pap. 14.50x o.p. (ISBN 0-691-00353-X). Princeton U Pr.

Underdeveloped Capitalism & the General Law of Value. R. Sau. 253p. 1984. text ed. 18.50x o.p. (ISBN 0-391-03097-3). Humanities.

Underdevelopment of African Education: A Black Zimbabwean Perspective. Dickson A. Mungazi. LC 82-13696. (Illus.). 274p. (Orig.). 1982. lib. bdg. 14.00 o.p. (ISBN 0-8191-2669-1); pap. text ed. 14.00 o.p. (ISBN 0-8191-2670-5). U Pr of Amer.

Undergraduate Guides Set, 1989, 2 vols. Date not set. Set. 56.00 o.p. (ISBN 0-87866-809-8); Set. pap. 27.50 o.p. (ISBN 0-87866-808-X). Petersons Guides.

Undergraduate Obstetrics & Gynaecology. Ed. by G. Dixon. (Illus.). 280p. 1980. pap. text ed. 18.50 o.p. (ISBN 0-7236-0564-5, Pub. by John Wright UK). Butterworth.

Undergraduate Woman: Issues in Educational Equity. Ed. by Pamela J. Perun. LC 80-8596. (Illus.). 448p. 1982. 35.00x o.p. (ISBN 0-669-04304-4). Lexington Bks.

Underground Army. Date not set. pap. (ISBN 0-8052-5056-5). Random.

Underground Atlanta. Norman Shavin. (Illus.). 40p. 1979. pap. 3.50 o.p. (ISBN 0-910719-02-0). Capricorn Corp.

Underground Building Design: Commercial & Institutional Structures. Underground Space Center Staff et al. 1983. 29.95 o.p. (ISBN 0-442-28687-2); pap. 21.95 o.p. (ISBN 0-442-28686-4). Van Nos Reinhold.

Underground Coal Gasification. G. H. Lamb. LC 77-77022. (Energy Technology Review Ser.: No. 14). (Illus.). 255p. 1977. 36.00 o.p. (ISBN 0-8155-0670-8). Noyes.

Underground Construction: A Bibliography. Mary Vance. (Architecture Ser.: Bibliography A 1353). 1985. pap. 2.25 o.p. (ISBN 0-89028-323-0). Vance Biblios.

Underground Economy in the United States & Abroad. Ed. by Vito Tanzi. LC 80-8887. 352p. 1982. 35.00x o.p. (ISBN 0-669-04400-8). Lexington Bks.

Underground Electric Haulage. L. Szklarski. 1969. 100.00 o.p. (ISBN 0-08-011663-9). Pergamon.

Underground Manual for Spiritual Survival. Larry Neagle. (Orig.). 1986. pap. 4.95 o.p. (ISBN 0-8024-9052-2). Moody.

Underground Marketplace: A Guide to New England & the Middle Atlantic States. Jonathan Webster & Harriet Webster. LC 80-54401. 176p. 1981. 12.50x o.p. (ISBN 0-87663-348-3); pap. 6.95 o.p. (ISBN 0-87663-555-9). Universe.

Underground Processing of Fuels. 168p. 1963. text ed. 34.00x o.p. (ISBN 0-7065-0217-5, Pub. by Keter Pub Jerusalem). Coronet Bks.

Underground Shopper's Guide to Health & Fitness. Sue Goldstein. 1987. pap. 10.95 o.p. (ISBN 0-449-90228-5, Columbine). Fawcett.

Underground Storage Tank Management: A Practical Guide. 2nd ed. Raymond W. Kane & Albert D. Young, Jr. 312p. 1987. pap. 49.00 o.p. (ISBN 0-86587-726-2). Gov Insts.

Underground Tank Leak Detection Methods: A State-of-the Art Review. Shahzad Niaki & John A. Broscious. (EPA Series 600-2 - 86-001). (Illus.). 129p. 1987. pap. 6.00 o.p. (ISBN 0-318-22589-1, S/N 055-000-00267-3). USGPO.

Undergoround, the Story of a People. Joseph F. Tenenbaum. 1952. (ISBN 0-8022-1704-4). Philos Lib.

Underground Two. Richard Corben et al. (Richard Corben Complete Works Ser.: Vol. 2). (Illus.). 80p. 1986. pap. 10.95 o.p. (ISBN 0-87416-026-X). Catalan Communs.

Undersea Terror: U-Boat Wolf Packs in World War II. Ernest McKay. LC 82-12529. (Illus.). 192p. (YA) (gr. 9 up). 1982. lib. bdg. 9.79 o.p. (ISBN 0-671-44196-5). Messner.

Underside of American History. 3rd ed. Thomas R. Frazier. 1978. 10.95 o.p. (ISBN 0-15-592847-3). HarbraceJ.

Underside of American History, Other Readings. 4th ed. Ed. by Thomas R. Frazier. Incl. Vol. 1. To 1877. 441p. 1982. pap. 10.50 o.p. (ISBN 0-15-592850-3); Vol. 2. Since 1865. 375p. 1982. pap. 10.50 o.p. (ISBN 0-15-592851-1). (Illus., Orig.). 1982. pap. text ed. 12.95 ea. o.p. (HC). HarBraceJ.

Understains: The Sense & Seduction of Advertising. Kathy Myers. (Comedia Ser.). (Illus.). 160p. 1987. pap. 10.00 o.p. M Boyars Pubs.

Understand Accounting-Fast. Robert C. Peterson. (Illus.). 1976. text ed. 26.50 o.p. (ISBN 0-07-049615-3). McGraw.

Understand Employee Regulations. 85p. 1984. 20.00 o.p. (30). Am Consul Eng.

Understanding, Bk. 1. C. Anson Smith. LC 84-90151. 123p. 1985. 10.95 o.p. (ISBN 0-533-06218-7). Vantage.

Understanding a Company's Finances: A Graphic Approach. W. R. Purcell, Jr. (Illus.). 160p. 1981. 10.95 o.p. (ISBN 0-395-30540-3). HM.

Understanding: A Resource Book for Use with Persons Who Have Learning Difficulties, Pt. 2. Ed. by Martha B. Aycock. (Exploring Life Ser.). (Illus.). 128p. (gr. 2-7). 1972. pap. 2.95 pupil packet o.p. (ISBN 0-8042-1196-5, John Knox); tchrs' guide 3.75 o.p. (ISBN 0-8042-1195-7). Westminster John Knox.

Understanding a Woman's Depression. Brenda Poinsett. LC 83-51595. 256p. 1984. pap. 6.95 o.p. (ISBN 0-8423-7764-6). Tyndale.

Understanding Abnormal Behavior. David Sue et al. 1981. text ed. 32.50 o.p. (ISBN 0-395-30752-X). HM.

Understanding Academic Law. Ed. by Walter C. Hobbs. LC 82-82174. (Institutional Advancement: No. 16). 1982. 13.95x o.p. (ISBN 0-87589-900-5). Jossey-Bass.

Understanding Adolescence: Current Developments in Adolescent Psychology. 4th ed. James F. Adams. 512p. 1980. text ed. 34.67 o.s.i. (ISBN 0-205-06931-2, 2469316). Allyn.

Understanding African Poetry: A Study of Ten Poets. Ken Goodwin. 256p. 1982. text ed. 25.00 o.p. (ISBN 0-435-91325-5); pap. text ed. 15.00x o.p. (ISBN 0-435-91326-3). Heinemann Ed.

Understanding Alcohol. Jean Kinney & Gwen Leaton. 268p. 1982. pap. 8.95 o.p. (ISBN 0-8016-2706-0). Mosby.

Understanding Amateur Radio. American Radio Relay League Staff. LC 63-10833. 5.00 o.p. (ISBN 0-87259-603-6). Am Radio.

Understanding American History Through Fiction, 2 vols. Warren A. Beck & Myles L. Clowers. 480p. 1975. Vol. 1: U.S. Colonial to 1877. pap. text ed. 21.95 o.p. (ISBN 0-07-004217-9); Vol. 2: 1865 to Present. pap. text ed. 21.95 o.p. (ISBN 0-07-004218-7). McGraw.

Understanding American Politics Through Fiction. 2nd ed. Myles L. Clowers & Lorin Letendre. 1976. pap. text ed. 21.95 o.p. (ISBN 0-07-011450-1). McGraw.

Understanding America's Industries. Carl Gerbracht & Frank E. Robinson. (gr. 7-9). 1971. text ed. 18.64 o.p. (ISBN 0-87345-499-5). Glencoe.

Understanding & Expressing Convictions Through Paragraph & Essay see From Paragraph to Theme.

Understanding & Flying Ultralights. Frank C. Bailey. (Illus.). 192p. 1986. 29.95x o.p. (ISBN 0-86771-006-3, Pub. by MacD & Co). Trans-Atl Phila.

Understanding & Helping the Schizophrenic: A Guide for Family & Friends. Silvano Arieti. 1981. pap. 9.95 o.s.i. (ISBN 0-671-41252-3, Touchstone Bks). S&S.

Understanding & Living with Brain Damage. Patrick E. Logue. 116p. 1975. spiral bdg. 17.00x o.p. (ISBN 0-398-03420-6). C C Thomas.

Understanding & Managing Organizational Behavior. Alan W. Randolph. 1985. 36.95x o.p. (ISBN 0-256-03231-9). Irwin.

Understanding & Managing Strategic Change. Ansoff. 1982. 47.50 o.p. (ISBN 0-444-86405-9, I-344-82). Elsevier.

Understanding & Programming Computers. Samiha Mourad. 1978. 15.00 o.p. (ISBN 0-682-49033-4, University). Exposition-Phoenix.

Understanding & Programming Microcomputers. Lance Leventhal et al. 114p. 1980. pap. text ed. 10.95 o.p. (ISBN 0-88006-024-7, BK7382). Wayne Green Ent.

Understanding & Promoting the Resources of Aging People: A Guide to Care, Proper Environment & Well-Being. Burgess L. Gordon. 92p. 1981. 5.50 o.p. (ISBN 0-682-49599-9). Exposition-Phoenix.

Understanding & Resolving Grief. Monnette C. Viau. 1985. 7.95 o.p. (ISBN 0-533-06640-9). Vantage.

Understanding & Social Inquiry. Fred R. Dallmayr & Thomas A. McCarthy. LC 76-22404. 1977. text ed. 26.95x o.p. (ISBN 0-268-01912-6). U of Notre Dame Pr.

Understanding & Teaching Emotionally Disturbed Children. new ed. Phyllis L. Newcomer. 456p. 1979. text ed. 33.33 o.s.i. (ISBN 0-205-06843-X, 2468433). Allyn.

Understanding & Teaching the Slower Student. A. Sackmary et al. 1972. pap. text ed. 7.95x o.p. (ISBN 0-8422-0007-X). Irvington.

Understanding & Using dBASE II & dBASE III. Rob Krumm. (Illus.). 448p. 1985. pap. 19.95 o.p. (ISBN 0-89303-917-9). Brady Bks.

Understanding & Using English. 5th ed. Newman P. Birk & Genevieve G Birk. 1972. pap. text ed. write for info. o.p. (ISBN 0-02-310050-8). Macmillan.

Understanding & Using Microcomputers in Business. Steven M. Zimmerman & Leo M. Conrad. LC 85-20293. (Illus.). 339p. 1985. pap. text ed. 31.00 o.p. (ISBN 0-314-93528-2). West Pub.

Understanding Arguments: An Introduction to Informal Logic. 2nd ed. Robert J. Fogelin. 430p. 1982. pap. text ed. 13.50 o.p. (ISBN 0-15-592858-9, HC). HarBraceJ.

Understanding Arguments: An Introduction to Informal Logic. Robert J. Fogelin. 1978. 13.95 o.p. (ISBN 0-15-592860-0). HarbraceJ.

Understanding Artificial Intelligence. Henry C. Mishkoff. Ed. by Jan Stevens & Gerald Luecke. LC 85-51164. (Understanding Ser.). (Illus.). 280p. (Orig.). 1985. pap. 17.95 o.p. (ISBN 0-672-27021-8, LCB8651). Sams.

Understanding Atari ST BASIC Programming. Tim Knight. 315p. (Orig.). 1986. pap. 17.95 o.p. (ISBN 0-89588-344-9). Sybex.

Understanding Automotive Electronics. 2nd. ed. William B. Ribbens & Norman Mansour. LC 84-51470. (Understanding Ser.). (Illus.). 256p. (Orig.). 1984. pap. 17.95 o.p. (ISBN 0-672-27017-X, LCB5771). Sams.

Understanding Automotive Electronics. 2nd ed. William B. Ribbens & Norman P. Mansour. Ed. by Gerald Luecke et al. LC 84-51470. (Understanding Ser.). (Illus.). 288p. 1984. pap. 14.95 o.s.i. (ISBN 0-89512-167-0, LCB8475). Tex Instr Inc.

Understanding Bible Doctrine: Leader's Guide. (Electives Ser.). 1983. pap. 2.50 o.p. (ISBN 0-8024-0308-5). Moody.

Understanding Biblical Symbols. Charles L. Edwards. 96p. 1981. 6.00 o.p. (ISBN 0-682-49704-5). Exposition-Phoenix.

Understanding Book-Collecting. G. Uden. (Understanding Ser.). (Illus.). 280p. 1986. pap. 14.95 o.p. (ISBN 1-85149-028-0). Antique Collect.

Understanding Breast Cancer. Rich & Hager. 448p. 1983. 59.75 o.p. (ISBN 0-8247-7137-0). Dekker.

Understanding Britain: A History of the British People & Their Culture. John Randle. (Illus.). 232p. 1981. 24.95x o.p. (ISBN 0-631-12471-3); pap. 9.95 o.p. (ISBN 0-631-12883-2). Basil Blackwell.

Understanding Broadcasting. 2nd ed. Eugene S. Foster. (Illus.). 544p. 1982. text ed. 24.00 o.p. (ISBN 0-394-35000-6, RanC). Random.

Understanding Business. Nickels. 800p. 1986. text ed. 37.95 o.p. (ISBN 0-8016-3627-2); International student ed. text ed. 15.95 o.p. Mosby.

Understanding Cancer. Mark Renneker & Steven Leib. LC 78-31769. 1979. 19.95 o.p. (ISBN 0-915950-29-4); pap. text ed. 12.95 o.p. (ISBN 0-915950-26-X). Bull Pub.

Understanding Causality. Jean Piaget & R. Garcia. Tr. by Donald Miles & Marguerite Miles. 1977. 10.00x o.p. (ISBN 0-393-01110-0, N858); pap. 2.95 o.p. (ISBN 0-393-00858-4). Norton.

Understanding Children. M. L. Sindwani. 1971. pap. text ed. 4.75x o.p. (ISBN 0-8422-0148-3). Irvington.

Understanding Children: Behavior, Motives, & Thought. Jerome Kagan. 1971. pap. text ed. 10.95 o.p. (ISBN 0-15-592873-2, HC). HarBraceJ.

Understanding Computer Information Networks. Jan Owen. (Handy Guide Ser.). 64p. (Orig.). 1984. pap. 3.50 o.p. (ISBN 0-88284-267-6). Alfred Pub.

Understanding Computer Systems. Harold Lawson. LC 81-17295. (Applications of Computer Science Ser.). 164p. 1982. text ed. 30.00 o.p. (ISBN 0-88175-010-7, Computer Sci Pr); pap. text ed. 30.00 o.p. (ISBN 0-7167-8061-5); exam booklet 30.00 o.p. (ISBN 0-7167-8020-8). W H Freeman.

Understanding Computers & Data Processing: Today & Tomorrow. Charles S. Parker. 1984. text ed. 30.95x o.p. (ISBN 0-03-063424-5). HR&W.

Understanding Computers & Data Processing: Today & Tomorrow with BASIC. Charles S. Parker. LC 83-22724. 630p. 1984. 31.95x o.p. (ISBN 0-03-063427-X). HR&W.

Understanding Computers: Input-Output. 1986. 12.95 o.p. (ISBN 0-8094-5666-4); lib. bdg. write for info. o.p. (ISBN 0-8094-5667-2). Time-Life.

Understanding Computers: Software. 1985. 12.95 o.p. (ISBN 0-8094-5658-3); lib. bdg. 19.94 o.p. (ISBN 0-8094-5659-1). Time-Life.

Understanding Consumer Behavior. rev. ed. Ed. by Martin M. Grossack. (Illus.). 1966. 8.50 o.p. (ISBN 0-8158-0107-6); text ed. 6.00 o.p. (ISBN 0-8158-0146-7). Chris Mass.

Understanding Data Base Management Systems. Joseph A. Vasta. 350p. 1985. pap. (ISBN 0-534-04029-2). Wadsworth Pub.

Understanding Data Communications. G. E. Friend et al. LC 84-50867. (Understanding Ser.). (Illus.). 256p. 1984. pap. text ed. 16.95 o.p. (ISBN 0-672-27019-6, LCB7981). Sams.

Understanding Death & Dying: An Interdisciplinary Approach. 3rd. ed. Ed. by Sandra Galdieri-Wilcox & Marilyn Sutton. 428p. 1984. pap. text ed. 22.95 o.p. (ISBN 0-87484-718-4). Mayfield Pub.

Understanding Deviance & Control: Theory, Research & Social Policy. Craig B. Little. LC 82-61588. 285p. 1983. pap. text ed. 13.50 o.p. (ISBN 0-87581-289-9). Peacock Pubs.

Understanding Divine Healing. Richard M. Sipley. 168p. 1986. pap. 6.95 o.p. (ISBN 0-89693-263-X). Victor Bks.

Understanding Economics. Albert W. Niemi, Jr. 1978. pap. 22.95 o.p. (ISBN 0-395-30683-3). HM.

Understanding Economics Today. Gary M. Walton & Frank C. Wykoff. 1986. pap. 26.95x o.p. (ISBN 0-256-03223-8); study guide 10.50x o.p. (ISBN 0-256-03224-6). Irwin.

Understanding Educational Measurement & Evaluation. Jerry Bergman. 1981. text ed. 29.95 o.p. (ISBN 0-395-30782-1). HM.

Understanding Electricity & Electronics. 4th ed. Peter Buban et al. 1982. text ed. 28.32 o.p. (ISBN 0-07-008678-8). McGraw.

Understanding Electrocardiography: Arrhythmias & the 12 Lead ECG. 4th ed. Mary Conover. (Illus.). 272p. 1984. pap. text ed. 19.95 o.p. (ISBN 0-8016-1123-7). Mosby.

Understanding English. rev. ed. Mary Jane Carrell. 1982. pap. 3.50 o.p. (ISBN 0-88323-182-4, 197). Pendergrass Pub.

Understanding Exceptional Children & Youth. B. Marion Swanson & Diane J. Willis. 1979. text ed. 28.95 o.p. (ISBN 0-395-30754-6); 1.00 o.p. HM.

Understanding FORTH. Joseph Reymann. (Alfred Handy Guide). 47p. 1983. 3.50 o.p. (ISBN 0-88284-237-4). Alfred Pub.

Understanding Futures Markets. Robert W. Kolb. 1985. pap. text ed. write for info. o.p. (ISBN 0-673-15976-0). Scott F.

Understanding Hamlet. P. Winders. 1975. pap. 5.05 o.p. (ISBN 0-08-017777-8). Pergamon.

Understanding History. Bertrand Russell. 1958. (ISBN 0-8022-1412-6). Philos Lib.

Understanding Homosexual Persons: Straight Answers from Gays. Joe Halloran. 1979. 6.00 o.p. (ISBN 0-682-49468-2). Exposition-Phoenix.

Understanding: How It Grows on You & How You Grow on It. Hubert R. Finke. 1977. 0.50 o.p. (ISBN 0-682-48914-X). Exposition-Phoenix.

Understanding Human Behavior. Mary E. Milliken. 224p. 19.95 o.p. (ISBN 0-8273-0338-6); pap. 14.95 o.p.; instr's. guide 8.00 o.p. Delmar.

Understanding Human Behavior. 6th ed. 672p. 1988. text ed. 27.75 o.p. (ISBN 0-03-014229-6). HR&W.

Understanding Human Behavior: An Introduction to Psychology. 5th ed. James V. McConnell. 768p. 1986. text ed. 29.95 o.p. (ISBN 0-03-071096-0). HR&W.

Understanding Human Communication. Ronald B. Adler & George Rodman. 1985. pap. text ed. 17.95 o.p. (ISBN 0-03-059468-5). HR&W.

Understanding Human Motivation: A Cognitive Approach. John Jung. (Illus.). 1978. text ed. write for info. o.p. (ISBN 0-02-361550-8). Macmillan.

Understanding Human Sexuality. Joann S. Delora et al. LC 79-89744. (Illus.). 1980. pap. 21.95 o.p. (ISBN 0-395-28255-1). HM.

Understanding Human Sexuality. 2nd ed. Janet S. Hyde. 640p. 1982. text ed. 30.95 o.p. (ISBN 0-07-031567-1). McGraw.

Understanding HyperCard. Greg Harvey. 581p. (Orig.). 1988. pap. 24.95 o.p. (ISBN 0-89588-506-9). Sybex.

Understanding IC Op-Amps. 2nd ed. Date not set. (ISBN 0-672-21511-X). Sams.

Understanding Islam Through Hadis: Religious Faith or Fanaticism? Ram Swarup. 1983. 13.95 o.p. (ISBN 0-682-49948-X). Exposition-Phoenix.

Understanding Javelin PLUS. John R. Levine et al. 558p. (Orig.). 1987. pap. 19.95 o.p. (ISBN 0-89588-358-9). Sybex.

Understanding Job Satisfaction. Michael M. Gruneberg. LC 78-20782. 170p. 1979. 51.95x o.p. (ISBN 0-470-26610-4). Halsted Pr.

Understanding Judaism. D. L. Davis. (Illus.). 1958. (ISBN 0-8022-0356-6). Philos Lib.

Understanding Loneliness. Edgar N. Jackson. LC 81-43071. 160p. 1981. pap. 7.95 o.p. (ISBN 0-8006-1606-5, 1-1606, Fortress). Augsburg Fortress.

Understanding Loss. Dianna C. Kirkland & Artie M. Morris-Vann. 100p. 1984. pap. 15.00x o.s.i. (ISBN 0-940370-12-3). Aid U Pub.

Understanding Lupus: What It Is, How to Treat It, How to Cope with It. Henrietta Aladjem. (Illus.). 272p. 1985. 15.95 o.s.i. (ISBN 0-684-18348-X, ScribT). Scribner.

Understanding Management Accounting. 2nd ed. T. Walker. 1980. pap. 11.95 o.p. (ISBN 0-85258-226-9). Van Nos Reinhold.

Understanding Management Policy & Making It Work. new ed. Victor Z. Brink. (Illus.). 1978. 19.95 o.p. (ISBN 0-8144-5455-0). AMACOM.

Understanding Management: Study Guide to Management: A Problem-Solving Process. Robert Kreitner & Margaret Sova. LC 79-88719. (Illus.). 1980. pap. 8.95 o.p. (ISBN 0-395-28492-9). HM.

Understanding Maps. J. S. Keates. LC 81-6921. 139p. 1982. pap. 21.95x o.p. (ISBN 0-470-27271-6). Halsted Pr.

Understanding Mass Communication. Melvin L. DeFleur & Everette E. Dennis. LC 80-82762. (Illus.). 528p. 1981. pap. 19.50 o.p. (ISBN 0-395-29722-2). HM.

Understanding Mass Communication. 2nd ed. Melvin L. DeFleur & Everette E. Dennis. LC 84-81983. 608p. 1985. pap. 28.76 o.p. (ISBN 0-395-35929-5). HM.

Understanding Medical Immunology. Evelyne M. Kirkwood & Catriona J. Lewis. LC 82-13444. 128p. 1984. pap. 17.50 o.p. (ISBN 0-471-10529-5, Pub. by Wiley Med). Wiley.

Understanding Medical Statistics. Leonard A. Goldstone. (Illus.). 181p. (Orig.). 1983. pap. 17.50x o.p. (Pub by W Heinemann Med Bks). Sheridan Med Bks.

Understanding Mental Illness: A Layman's Guide. Nancy C. Andreasen. LC 73-88610. 112p. 1974. pap. 4.50 o.p. (ISBN 0-8066-1413-7, 10-6800, Augsburg). Augsburg Fortress.

Understanding Microbes: Laboratory Textbook for Microbiology. William G. Claus. 1988. pap. text ed. (ISBN 0-7167-1809-X). W H Freeman.

Understanding Microprocessors. Don L. Cannon & Gerald Luecke. LC 78-57029. (Understanding Ser.). (Illus.). 288p. (Orig.). 1979. pap. 6.95 o.p. (ISBN 0-89512-021-6, LCB4023). Sams.

Understanding Modern Business Data Processing see Introduction to Data Processing.

Understanding Modern Government: The Rise & Decline of the American Political Economy. Edward S. Greenberg. LC 78-10104. 197p. 1979. pap. text ed. 13.00 o.p. (ISBN 0-02-346640-5). Macmillan.

Understanding Money. Edward Shapiro. (Orig.). 1975. pap. text ed. 8.95 o.p. (ISBN 0-15-592876-7, HC). HarBraceJ.

Understanding Neurologic Disease: A Textbook for Therapists. John H. Warfel & Reinhold E. Schlagenhauff. LC 79-28455. (Illus.). 155p. 1980. 11.95 o.p. (ISBN 0-8067-2131-6). Urban & S.

Understanding Normal & Clinical Nutrition. Eleanor N. Whitney & Corrine Cataldo. (Illus.). 1065p. 1983. text ed. 42.75 o.p. (ISBN 0-314-69685-7). West Pub.

Understanding of Albert Schweitzer. George N. Marshall. LC 65-28763. 188p. 1966. (ISBN 0-8022-1064-3). Philos Lib.

Understanding of Music. 5th ed. Charles R. Hoffer. 1985. text ed. (ISBN 0-534-03939-1). Wadsworth Pub.

Understanding of the Brain. 2nd ed. John C. Eccles. (Illus.). 320p. 1977. text ed. 15.95 o.p. (ISBN 0-07-018865-3). McGraw.

Understanding Organizational Behavior. Stuart M. Klein & Richard R. Ritti. 592p. 1980. text ed. 25.95x o.p. (ISBN 0-534-00755-4, Kent Pub.). PWS-Kent Pub.

Understanding Organizational Behavior. Denis D. Umstot. (Management Ser.). (Illus.). 455p. 1984. text ed. 40.00 o.p. (ISBN 0-314-77850-0). West Pub.

Understanding Our Sexuality. Bryan Strong & Rebecca Reynolds. (Illus.). 530p. 1982. pap. text ed. 29.00 o.p. (ISBN 0-314-63294-8). West Pub.

Understanding Pacemakers. David Sonnenburg & Michael Birnbaum. (Illus.). 192p. 1982. pap. 12.95 o.s.i. (ScribT). Scribner.

Understanding Personal Computers: A Home Study Course. Harry M. Brobst. (Home Study Ser.). 25p. 1982. 28.00 o.p. (ISBN 0-939926-17-2); audio tape incl. o.p. (ISBN 0-939926-16-4). Fruition Pubns.

Understanding Personnel Management. Thomas H. Stone. 600p. 1982. text ed. 33.95x o.p. (ISBN 0-03-045671-1); instr's manual 20.95 o.p. (ISBN 0-03-045676-2). Dryden Pr.

Understanding PostScript Programming. David A. Holzgang. 457p. (Orig.). 1987. pap. 22.95 o.p. (ISBN 0-89588-396-1). Sybex.

Understanding Prayer. Edgar N. Jackson. LC 81-47845. 224p. pap. 6.68i o.p. (ISBN 0-06-064112-6, RD 377). HarpR.

Understanding Process Integration. Institution of Chemical Engineers Staff. 1982. 35.00 o.s.i. (ISBN 0-08-028771-9). Pergamon.

Understanding R: BASE System V. Alan Simpson. 499p. (Orig.). 1986. pap. 21.95 o.p. (ISBN 0-89588-394-5). Sybex.

Understanding R: Base 5000. Alan Simpson. LC 85-62538. 413p. (Orig.). 1985. pap. 19.95 o.p. (ISBN 0-89588-302-3). Sybex.

Understanding Radio Electronics. 4th ed. Milton Kaufman et al. 1972. text ed. 36.95 o.p. (ISBN 0-07-033399-8). McGraw.

Understanding Radioactive Waste. 2nd ed. Raymond L. Murray. Ed. by Judith A. Powell. LC 83-18763. (Illus.). 128p. 1983. pap. 12.50 o.s.i. (ISBN 0-935470-19-0). Battelle.

Understanding Reading. 3rd ed. Frank Smith. 264p. 1982. pap. text ed. 19.95 o.p. (ISBN 0-03-059634-3). HR&W.

Understanding Second & Foreign Language Learning. Ed. by Jack C. Richards. LC 78-24457. 1978. pap. text ed. 15.50 o.p. (ISBN 0-88377-124-1). Newbury Hse.

Understanding Sexual Interaction. 2nd ed. Joann S. Delora et al. (Illus.). 672p. 1981. text ed. 26.95 o.p. (ISBN 0-395-29724-9). HM.

Understanding Social Policy. Michael Hill. 288p. 1983. pap. text ed. 9.95x o.p. (ISBN 0-85520-593-8). Basil Blackwell.

Understanding Standard Costing. T. Walker. 1980. pap. 16.95 o.p. (ISBN 0-85258-185-8). Van Nos Reinhold.

Understanding Statistics. 3rd ed. William Mendenhall & Lyman Ott. LC 79-20914. 1980. text ed. write for info. o.p. (ISBN 0-87150-421-9, Duxbury Pr). PWS-Kent Pub.

Understanding Student & Faculty Life: Using Campus Surveys to Improve Academic Decision Making. Leonard L. Baird & Rodney T. Hartnett. LC 79-24863. (Higher Education Ser.). 1980. text ed. 26.95x o.p. (ISBN 0-87589-443-7). Jossey-Bass.

Understanding Student Learning. Noel Entwhistle & Paul Ramsden. 272p. 1983. 27.50 o.p. (ISBN 0-89397-171-5). Nichols Pub.

Understanding Student-Parent Expectations. National Association of Women Deans & Counselors. 1970. pap. 3.00 o.p. (ISBN 0-686-09573-1). Natl Assn Women.

Understanding the American Experience: Recent Interpretations, 2 vols. James M. Banner, Jr. et al. 1971. Vol 1. 6.95 o.p. (ISBN 0-15-592841-4, HC); Vol 2. 6.95 o.p. (ISBN 0-15-592842-2); pap. text ed. 6.95 ea. o.p. HarBraceJ.

Understanding the Bible. Fred J. Denbeaux. (Layman's Theological Library). 1958. pap. 1.45 o.s.i. (ISBN 0-664-24012-7, Westminster). Westminster John Knox.

Understanding the Books of the New Testament. rev. ed. Ed. by Patrick H. Carmichael. LC 61-9583. 1961. pap. 6.95 o.p. (ISBN 0-8042-3304-7, John Knox). Westminster John Knox.

Understanding the Books of the Old Testament. rev. ed. Ed. by Patrick H. Carmichael. LC 61-9223. 1961. pap. 6.95 o.p. (ISBN 0-8042-3316-0, John Knox). Westminster John Knox.

Understanding the Constitution. 10th ed. J. W. Peltason. LC 84-28982. 368p. 1985. pap. text ed. 17.95 o.p. (ISBN 0-03-071176-2, HoltC). HR&W.

Understanding the Environment. Kenneth E. Watt. 1982. pap. text ed. 34.33 o.s.i. (ISBN 0-205-07265-8, 677265-X); tchr's. ed. avail. o.s.i. (ISBN 0-205-07266-6). Allyn.

Understanding the Heart & Its Disease. J. Ross & R. A. O'Rourke. 1976. 16.95 o.p. (ISBN 0-07-053861-1); pap. text ed. 20.95 o.p. (ISBN 0-07-053862-X). McGraw.

Understanding the Japanese Mind. James C. Moloney. 1954. (ISBN 0-8022-1138-0). Philos Lib.

Understanding the Law of Our Land. Shirley Schwarzrock & C. Gilbert Wrenn. (Coping with Ser.). (Illus.). 51p. (gr. 7-12). 1973. pap. text ed. 3.00 o.p. (ISBN 0-913476-21-8). Am Guidance.

Understanding the Lord's Prayer. Philip B. Harner. LC 75-13035. 144p. 1975. pap. 4.25 o.p. (ISBN 0-8006-1213-2, Fortress). Augsburg Fortress.

Understanding the Microscope. Paul Geisert. (EMI Programmed Biology Ser.). 1967. pap. text ed. 3.00 o.s.i. (ISBN 0-88462-018-2, 3304-18, Ed Methods). Longman Finan.

Understanding the New Telephone Service. Quincy Harris. LC 86-91167. (Illus.). 72p. (Orig.). 1986. pap. text ed. 10.00 o.p. (ISBN 0-682-40299-0). Exposition-Phoenix.

Understanding the New Testament, 10 vols. 1982. Set. pap. 37.50 o.p. (ISBN 0-8054-1346-4). Broadman.

Understanding the New Testament: Acts. Ralph P. Martin. LC 78-9086. 1982. pap. 3.95 o.p. (ISBN 0-8054-1331-6). Broadman.

Understanding the New Testament: Ephesians-2 Thessalonians. W. L. Lane. LC 78-9675. 1982. pap. 3.95 o.p. (ISBN 0-8054-1336-7). Broadman.

Understanding the New Testament: John. R. E. Nixon. LC 78-9114. 1982. pap. 3.95 o.p. (ISBN 0-8054-1330-8). Broadman.

Understanding the New Testament: Luke. E. M. Blaiklock. LC 78-9119. 1982. pap. 3.95 o.p. (ISBN 0-8054-1329-4). Broadman.

Understanding the New Testament: Mark. I. Howard Marshall. LC 78-9118. 1982. pap. 3.95 o.p. (ISBN 0-8054-1328-6). Broadman.

Understanding the New Testament: Matthew. F. F. Bruce. LC 78-9115. 1982. pap. 3.95 o.p. (ISBN 0-8054-1327-8). Broadman.

Understanding the New Testament: Romans. E. M. Blaiklock. LC 78-9794. 1982. pap. 3.95 o.p. (ISBN 0-8054-1332-4). Broadman.

Understanding the New Testament: 1 Corinthians-Galatians. Ralph P. Martin. LC 78-9793. 1982. pap. 3.95 o.p. (ISBN 0-8054-1334-0). Broadman.

Understanding the New Testament: 1 Peter-Revelation. H. L. Ellison. LC 78-9116. 1982. pap. 3.95 o.p. (ISBN 0-8054-1341-3). Broadman.

Understanding the New Testament: 1 Timothy-James. Leon Morris. LC 78-9441. 1982. pap. 3.95 o.p. (ISBN 0-8054-1339-1). Broadman.

Understanding the Nursing Process. 2nd ed. Leslie D. Atkinson & Mary E. Murray. (Illus.). 155p. 1983. pap. text ed. write for info. o.s.i. (ISBN 0-02-304580-9). Macmillan.

Understanding the Old Testament: The Way of Holiness. J. E. Fison. LC 78-21116. 1979. Repr. of 1952 ed. lib. bdg. 35.00x o.p. (ISBN 0-313-20839-5, FIUO). Greenwood.

Understanding the Scriptures. A. Berkeley Mickelsen & Alvera Mickelsen. LC 74-32327. 1977. pap. 3.50 o.p. (ISBN 0-8307-0358-6, 54-021-07). Regal.

Understanding the Soviet Military Threat: How C. I. A. Estimates Went Astray. William T. Lee. 73p. 1977. pap. text ed. 3.95 o.p. (ISBN 0-87855-801-2). Transaction Pubs.

Understanding the Stock Market: A Guide for Young Investors. Janet Low. LC 68-30873. (Illus.). 1968. 10.95 o.p. (ISBN 0-316-53369-6). Little.

Understanding the Teaching of Jesus. David Abernathy & Norman Perrin. 288p. (Orig.). 1983. pap. 13.95 o.p. (ISBN 0-8164-2438-1). HarpR.

Understanding the Twentieth Century: A Course Guide. Open University Staff. (New Viewpoints-Vision Bks.). 1980. pap. 10.95 o.p. (ISBN 0-531-06505-7, EE59). Watts.

Understanding the World of Physics. Frederick J. Bueche. (Illus.). 752p. 1981. text ed. 34.95 o.p. (ISBN 0-07-008863-2). McGraw.

Understanding Three-Dimensional Images: Recognition of Abdominal Anatomy from CAT Scans. Uri Shani. Ed. by Harold Stone. LC 83-15818. (Computer Science: Artificial Intelligence: No. 13). 222p. 1984. 42.95 o.p. (ISBN 0-8357-1521-3). UMI Res Pr.

Understanding U. S. Information Policy, 4 vols. Ed. by Forest W. Horton, Jr. Incl. Vol. I. Resources for the Information Economy. LC 82-81853 (ISBN 0-942774-02-7); Vol. II. Participants in the Information Marketplace. LC 82-81854 (ISBN 0-942774-03-5); Vol. III. Assets of the Information Society. LC 82-81855 (ISBN 0-942774-04-3); Information Policy Primer. LC 82-81852. 25.00 (ISBN 0-942774-01-9). 1982. Set. 99.50 o.p. (ISBN 0-942774-07-8); 49.50 ea. o.p.; any two 74.50 o.p. (ISBN 0-942774-08-6). Info Indus.

Understanding U. S. Information Policy, 1 vol. 49.95 o.p. (ISBN 0-317-44249-X); Vol. I: The Information Policy Primer. 30.00 o.p. Info Indus.

Understanding UNIX: A Conceptual Guide. Paul N. Weinberg & James R. Groff. LC 83-63256. 233p. 1983. pap. 21.95 o.p. (ISBN 0-88022-064-3, 120). Que Corp.

Understanding Wall Street. rev. ed. Jeffrey B. Little & Lucien Rhodes. LC 78-54787. (Illus.). 220p. 1982. pap. 8.95 o.p. (ISBN 0-89709-010-1, 30010). TAB Bks.

Understanding WATFIV. Michel H. Boillot & Carol R. Shingles. (Illus.). 567p. 1980. pap. text ed. 35.25 o.p. (ISBN 0-8299-0232-5). West Pub.

Understanding XENIX: A Conceptual Guide. Paul N. Weinberg & James R. Groff. LC 84-62751. 247p. 1985. pap. 21.95 o.p. (ISBN 0-88022-143-7, 170). Que Corp.

Understanding Yoga. pap. 9.99 o.p. (ISBN 0-85030-480-6, Pub. by Aquarian Pr England). Sterling.

Understanding Your Car. rev. ed. Samuel Beeler. (gr. 10-12). 1967. 13.28 o.p. (ISBN 0-87345-471-5). Glencoe.

Understanding Your Diabetes. A. R. Colwell, Jr. (Illus.). 184p. 1978. spiral bdg. 29.00 o.p. (ISBN 0-398-03682-9). C C Thomas.

Understanding Your Faith: An Introduction to Catholic Christianity for Freshmen. Thomas Zanzig. LC 80-50258. (Illus.). 192p. (gr. 9). 1980. pap. text ed. 7.00x o.p. (ISBN 0-88489-115-1). St Mary's.

Understanding Your Health. Payne & Hahn. 1985. 29.95 o.p. (ISBN 0-8016-3822-4). Mosby.

Understanding Your Pet: The Eckstein Method of Pet Therapy & Behavior Training. Warren Eckstein & Fay Eckstein. LC 85-4754. (Illus.). 246p. 1986. 15.95 o.p. (ISBN 0-03-000699-6). H Holt & Co.

Understanding Your Sexuality. Jane M. Kahan et al. (Illus.). 1980. pap. text ed. 159.00 o.s.i. (ISBN 0-89290-100-4, A793-SATC). Soc for Visual.

Understanding Yourself. Kuthumi et al. Ed. by Mark Prophet & Elizabeth Prophet. LC 79-28089. 182p. 1979. pap. 4.95 o.s.i. (ISBN 0-916766-22-5). Summit Univ.

Understanding Yourself, Society & Marriage. Nehemiah M. Palmer. 288p. 1984. pap. 7.95 o.p. (ISBN 0-912315-82-2). Word Aflame.

Understandings of Man. Perry LeFevre. LC 66-10432. 186p. 1966. pap. 6.95 o.s.i. (ISBN 0-664-24678-8, Westminster). Westminster John Knox.

Understood Betsy. Dorothy C. Fisher. (Illus.). 220p. (gr. 5-9). 1973. pap. 1.50 o.p. (ISBN 0-380-01595-1, 49692-5, Camelot). Avon.

Understudies: Theatre & Sexual Politics. Michelene Wandor. 80p. 1981. pap. 8.95 o.p. (ISBN 0-413-40060-3, NO. 3503). Heinemann Ed.

Undertones of War. Edmund Blunden. LC 66-12379. 1966. pap. 1.85 o.p. (ISBN 0-15-692821-3, Harv). HarBraceJ.

Undertow. Drake Douglas. 400p. (Orig.). 1984. pap. 3.75 o.s.i. (ISBN 0-8439-2121-8, Pub. by Leisure Bks CT). Dorchester Pub Co.

Undertow. Finn Havrevold. Tr. & illus. by Cathy B. Curry. LC 68-12242. (Illus.). (gr. 5-9). 1968. PLB 4.50 o.p. (ISBN 0-689-20585-6, Atheneum). Macmillan.

Underwater Photo-Optical Instrumentation Applications, 1968: Proceedings, Vol. 12. Society of Photo-Optical Instrumentation Engineers Staff. 28.00 o.p. (ISBN 0-89252-015-9). SPIE.

Underwater Photographer's Handbook. Arco.

Underwater Physiology. Ed. by Christian J. Lambertsen. 1971. 39.95 o.p. (ISBN 0-12-434750-9). Acad Pr.

Underwater Sound. V. Albers. 1982. 54.95 o.p. (ISBN 0-87933-006-6). Van Nos Reinhold.

Underwater Technology-Offshore Petroleum: Proceedings of the International Conference, Bergen, Norway, April 14-16 1980. Ed. by L. Atteraas et al. LC 80-40414. 450p. 1980. 105.00 o.p. (ISBN 0-08-026141-8). Pergamon.

Underwater Tour. Margaret Webb. (Illus.). 16p. (gr. 3-5). 1984. 4.95 o.p. (ISBN 0-533-05927-5). Vantage.

Underwater Welding: Proceedings of the Conference, Norway, June 27-28, 1983. Ed. by International Institute of Welding Staff. 350p. 1983. 100.00 o.p. (ISBN 0-08-030537-7). Pergamon.

Underwriting the Physical Risk. Paul S. Entmacher & Edward A. Lew. (FLMI Insurance Education Program Ser.). 1971. pap. 5.00 o.p. (ISBN 0-915322-22-6). LOMA.

Undiscovered Country: In Search of Gurdjieff. Kathryn Hulme. 1972. pap. 4.95 o.p. (ISBN 0-316-38138-1, Pub. by Atlantic Monthly Pr). Little.

Undisputed Andy Capp. Reginald Smythe. 128p. 1980. pap. 1.50 o.s.i. (ISBN 0-449-13668-X, GM). Fawcett.

Undulator Magnets for Synchrotron Radiation & Free Electron Lasers: Symposium in the Adriatico Conference Series, Trieste, Italy, 23-26 June 1987. Ed. by L. Fonda. 280p. 1988. 58.00 o.p. (ISBN 9971-50-709-9, ZB0693PP). World Scientific Pub.

Undying Dedication. R. Vernon Boyd. 1985. pap. 5.95 o.p. (ISBN 0-89225-281-2). Gospel Advocate.

Undying Swan. Moses Altman. Ed. by Ilya A. Mamantov. 252p. (Orig., Rus.). 1976. pap. 4.95x o.p. (ISBN 0-87074-159-4). SMU Press.

Uneeda Review. Louis D. Rubin, Jr. & William Harmon. LC 84-21282. 128p. (Orig.). 1984. pap. 5.95 o.s.i. (ISBN 0-941130-03-7). Lyons & Burford.

Unemployment. Ed. by Bernard Crick. 151p. 1981. pap. 5.95x o.p. (ISBN 0-416-32470-3, NO. 3539). Routledge Chapman & Hall.

Unemployment: Cause & Cure. Patrick Minford et al. 272p. 1983. 45.00x o.p. (ISBN 0-85520-622-5). Basil Blackwell.

Unemployment in France, the Federal Republic of Germany & the Netherlands: A Survey of Trends, Causes & Policy Options. Wouter Van Ginneken & Michel Garzuel. iii, 116p. (Orig.). 1982. pap. 12.25 o.p. (ISBN 92-2-103032-6). Intl Labour Office.

Unemployment, Poverty & Social Policy in Europe. Roger Milton et al. (Occasional Papers on Social Administration: No. 71). 99p. (Orig.). 1983. pap. text ed. 11.25x o.p. (ISBN 0-7199-1110-9, Pub. by Bedford England). Gower Pub Co.

Unemployment, Schooling & Training in Developing Countries: Tanzania, Egypt, the Philippines & Indonesia. Ed. by M. D. Leonor. LC 85-5949. 289p. 1985. 29.00 o.p. (ISBN 0-7099-1329-X, Pub. by Croom Helm Ltd). Routledge Chapman & Hall.

Unemployment, the Regions & Labour Markets: Reactions to Recession. Ed. by Ian Gordon. (London Papers in Regional Science: Vol. 17). 200p. 1987. text ed. 35.00 o.p. (ISBN 0-85086-128-4, Pub. by Pion England). Routledge Chapman & Hall.

Unemployment Theories, Policies & Evidence. Peter Sinclair. 224p. 1985. 34.95x o.p. (ISBN 0-85520-758-2); pap. 14.95x o.p. (ISBN 0-85520-759-0). Basil Blackwell.

Unequal Exchange: A Study of the Imperialism of Trade. Arghiri Emmanuel. Tr. by Brian Pearce from Fr. LC 78-158920. (Illus.). 1972. 16.50 o.p. (ISBN 0-85345-152-4); pap. 6.95 o.p. (ISBN 0-85345-188-5). Monthly Rev.

Unequal Growth: Urban & Regional Employment Change in the U. K. Stephen Fothergill & Graham Gudgin. 210p. 1982. text ed. 25.50x o.p. (ISBN 0-435-84370-2). Gower Pub Co.

UNESCO & World Politics: Engaging in International Relations. James P. Sewell. LC 75-3474. (Center of International Studies). 376p. 1975. 45.00x o.p. (ISBN 0-691-05659-5). Princeton U Pr.

UNESCO on the Eve of Its Fortieth Anniversary. 216p. 1986. pap. text ed. 10.50 o.p. (ISBN 92-3-102399-3, U1492, Pub. by Unesco). UNIPUB.

UNESCO Report of the Director General on the Activities of the Organizations: 1977-1978. 256p. 1980. pap. 10.50 o.p. (ISBN 92-3-101738-1, U967, UNESCO). UNIPUB.

UNESCO Yearbook of Peace Corps, 1981. (ISBN 0-8002-3324-7). Intl Pubns Serv.

Uneven Development in Southern Europe. Ed. by J. Lewis & R. Hudson. 328p. 1985. 65.00 o.p. (ISBN 0-416-32840-7, 9527). Routledge Chapman & Hall.

Uneven Development: Nature, Capital & the Production of Space. Neil Smith. 256p. 1984. 45.00x o.p. (ISBN 0-631-13564-2); pap. 16.95x o.p. (ISBN 0-631-13685-1). Basil Blackwell.

Uneven Score. Carla Neggers. (Velvet Glove Ser.: No. 14). 176p. 1985. pap. 2.25 o.p. (ISBN 0-380-89665-6). Avon.

Unexpected Grandchildren. Jane Flory. LC 77-5085. (Illus.). (gr. k-3). 1977. PLB 6.95 o.p. (ISBN 0-395-25797-2). HM.

Unexpected Hanging & Other Mathematical Diversions. Martin Gardner. 1972. pap. 6.75 o.p. (ISBN 0-671-21425-X, Fireside). S&S.

Unexpected Minority: Handicapped Children in America. John Gliedman & William Roth. LC 79-1823. 1980. 17.95 o.p. (ISBN 0-15-192845-2). HarBraceJ.

Unexpected Peace. Jack Kelly. 240p. 1982. pap. 2.50 o.p. (ISBN 0-505-51849-X, Pub. by Tower Bks). Dorchester Pub Co.

Unexpected Pleasures. Phyllis R. Naylor. 288p. 1986. 17.95 o.p. (ISBN 0-399-13198-1). Putnam Pub Group.

Unexpected Universe. Loren Eiseley. LC 67-20308. 1969. 7.95 o.p. (ISBN 0-15-192851-7). HarBraceJ.

Unexpected Vista: A Physicist's View of Nature. James S. Trefil. LC 82-42654. (Illus.). 256p. 14.95 o.s.i. (ISBN 0-684-17869-9, ScribT). Scribner.

Unfair & Deceptive Acts & Practices: 1982 & 1987 Supplement. LC 82-81234. 108p. 1982. pap. 48.00 o.p. (ISBN 0-943116-01-5). Nat Consumer Law.

Unfair Trade Practices & Intellectual Property. Roger E. Schechter. (Black Letter Ser.). 272p. 1986. pap. text ed. 15.95 o.p. (ISBN 0-314-98619-7). West Pub.

Unfair Trade Practices in a Nutshell. Charles R. McManis. LC 82-13597. (Nutshell Ser.). 444p. 1982. text ed. 10.95 o.p. (ISBN 0-314-68094-2). West Pub.

Unfathomed Mind: A Handbook of Unusual Mental Phenomena. William R. Corliss. LC 81-85081. (Illus.). 760p. 1982. 19.95 o.p. (ISBN 0-915554-08-9). Sourcebook.

Unfinished Heartbeats: Poems. David L. Thompson. 1987. text ed. 8.95 o.p. (ISBN 0-682-40346-6). Exposition-Phoenix.

Unfinished Political Reforms: 1977. Richard S. Childs. 1977. 4.00 o.p. (ISBN 0-682-48923-9, University); pap. 2.00 o.p. (ISBN 0-682-48924-7). Exposition-Phoenix.

Unfinished Portrait. Mary Westmacott. LC 73-184885. 288p. 1981. pap. 6.95 o.p. (ISBN 0-87795-352-X, Arbor Hse). Morrow.

Unfinished Portrait. Mary Westmacott. LC 73-184885. 1972. 6.95 o.p. (ISBN 0-87795-029-6, A4317, Arbor Hse). Morrow.

Unfinished Song: The Life of Victor Jara. Joan Jara. LC 83-24265. (Illus.). 288p. 1984. 15.45 o.p. (ISBN 0-89919-279-3). Ticknor & Fields.

Unfinished Universe. Louise B. Young. 1986. 17.45 o.p. (ISBN 0-671-52376-7). S&S.

Unfinished Universe. Louise B. Young. 240p. 1987. pap. 8.95 o.s.i. (ISBN 0-671-63316-3, Touchstone Bks). S&S.

Unfolding Revelation: The Nature of Doctrinal Development. Jan H. Walgrave. LC 76-102204. (Theological Resources Ser). 430p. 1971. 9.95 o.s.i. (ISBN 0-664-20915-7, Westminster). Westminster John Knox.

Unforbidden Sweets. Jean Anderson. LC 82-72070. (Illus.). 1982. 15.00 o.p. (ISBN 0-87795-433-X, Arbor Hse). Morrow.

Unforbidden Sweets. Jean Anderson. 1983. pap. 6.95 o.p. (ISBN 0-87795-543-3, Arbor Hse). Morrow.

Unforgettable Fire - Awkward Instant. Michael Action, Jr. 32p. 1986. 6.95 o.p. (ISBN 0-8062-2933-0). Carlton.

Unforgettable Hollywood. Nat Dallinger. LC 82-3479. (Illus.). 1982. 20.00 o.p. (ISBN 0-688-01323-6). Morrow.

Unforgettable Hollywood. Nat Dallinger. LC 83-60483. (Illus.). 256p. 1983. pap. 12.95 o.p. (ISBN 0-688-02475-0, Quill NY). Morrow.

Unforgettable Season. G. H. Fleming. LC 80-18299. (Illus.). 336p. 1981. 16.95 o.s.i. (ISBN 0-03-056221-X). H Holt & Co.

Unforgiven. Alan Le May. 304p. 1985. pap. 3.50 o.s.i. (ISBN 0-425-07680-6). Berkley Pub.

Unforgiving. Eva Zumwalt. 336p. (Orig.). 1982. pap. 2.95 o.p. (ISBN 0-505-51804-X, Pub. by Tower Bks). Dorchester Pub Co.

Unfriendly Natives of the Pacific. Glen Wright. Ed. by Carol Murphy. (Illus.). (gr. 3-6). 1981. PLB 6.95 o.p. (ISBN 0-89868-116-2, Read Res); pap. text ed. 4.95 o.p. (ISBN 0-89868-123-5, Read Res). ARO Pub.

Unger's Bible Dictionary. Merrill F. Unger. 1961. 23.95 o.p. (ISBN 0-8024-9035-2). Moody.

Unger's Concise Bible Dictionary. Merrill F. Unger. (Paperback Reference Library). pap. 5.95 o.p. (ISBN 0-8010-9207-8). Baker Bk.

Unglueckselige Atalanta. J. L. Rost. 560p. Repr. of 1717 ed. 60.00 o.p. (ISBN 0-384-52101-0). Johnson Repr.

Unhallowed Ground: A Young Boy's Search for His Father & Brother. Paul Guernsey. Ed. by Maria D. Guarnaschelli. LC 86-8430. 356p. 1986. 16.95 o.p. (ISBN 0-688-06366-7). Morrow.

Unhealed Wounds: France & the Klaus Barbie Affair. Erna Paris. LC 86-218. 256p. 1986. Repr. of 1985 ed. 27.50 o.p. (ISBN 0-394-55390-X). Grove.

Unhurried Chase That Ended at L'Abri. Betty Carlson. LC 83-62688. 158p. 1984. pap. 5.95 o.p. (ISBN 0-89107-304-3). Good News.

UNIA & Black Los Angeles: Ideology & Community in the American Garvey Movement. Emory J. Tolbert. Ed. by Robert A. Hill. LC 80-18054. (Afro-American Culture & Society Monograph: No. 3). (Illus.). 138p. 1980. 13.95x o.p. (ISBN 0-934934-04-5); pap. 8.95x o.s.i. (ISBN 0-934934-05-3). UCLA CAAS.

Unichtozhenie Prioroda Obostrenie Ekologicheskogo Krizisa V SSSR see Destruction of Nature in the Soviet Union.

Unico Camino. Dolores Ibarruri. 586p. (Span.). 1976. 7.95 o.p. (ISBN 0-8285-1446-1, Pub. by Progress Pubs USSR). Imported Pubns.

Unicode, ein Verfahren Zur Optimierung der Begriffiichen Gehirnleistung. David Szekely. (Interdisciplinary Systems Research Ser.: No. 66). 400p. (Ger.). 1980. pap. 51.95x o.p. (ISBN 0-8176-1069-3). Birkhauser.

Unicorn. Dorothea Manusch. 160p. 1984. 8.50 o.p. (ISBN 0-682-40153-6). Exposition-Phoenix.

Unicorn & Dragon. Lynn Abbey. LC 86-90768. (Byron Preiss Bk.). (Illus.). 240p. 1987. pap. 5.95 o.p. (ISBN 0-380-75061-9). Avon.

Unicorn Creed. Elizabeth A. Scarborough. 352p. 1983. pap. 3.50 o.p. (ISBN 0-553-22939-7). Bantam.

Unicorn Journal, Nos. 2-4. Ed. by Teo Savory. (Illus.). 125p. 1972. pap. 3.00 ea. o.p. (ISBN 0-87775-019-X). Unicorn Pr.

Unicorn Journal II: An Illustrated Book with Space for Notes. Illus. by Timothy A. Hildebrandt. (Illus.). 96p. (Orig.). (gr. 5 up). 1985. lib. bdg. 15.90 o.p. (ISBN 0-89471-369-8); pap. 5.95 o.p. (ISBN 0-89471-368-X). Running Pr.

Unicorn Variations. Roger Zelazny. 288p. 1983. 14.50 o.s.i. (ISBN 0-671-49449-X, Timescape). PB.

Unicorns in the Rain. Barbara Cohen. LC 79-22082. 1980. 10.95 o.p. (ISBN 0-689-30735-7, Atheneum). Macmillan.

Unification of Fundamental Particle Interactions II. Ed. by John Ellis & Sergio Ferrara. 530p. 1983. 89.50x o.p. (ISBN 0-306-41166-0, Plenum Pr). Plenum Pub.

Unification of the Fundamental Particle Interactions. Ed. by Sergio Ferrara et al. LC 80-24447. (Ettore Majorana International Science Series, Physical Sciences: Vol. 7). 740p. 1981. 125.00x o.p. (ISBN 0-306-40575-X, Plenum Pr). Plenum Pub.

Unified Directory of Area Codes & Zip Codes, Including Canadian Area Codes, with Population Figures for All Major U. S. & Canadian Cities. LC 83-108785. 192p. (Orig.). 1982. pap. 29.95x o.s.i. (ISBN 0-8486-9999-8, Pub. by Unified Directories). Roth Pub Inc.

Unified Technical Concepts. 2nd, with supplement ed. Center for Occupational Research & Development Staff. (Unified Technical Concepts Ser.). (Illus.). 520p. 1984. pap. text ed. 24.00 o.p. (ISBN 1-55502-161-1). Ctr Res & Dev.

Unified Theories of Elementary Particles: Proceedings. Peter Breitenlohner & Hans-Peter Duerr. (Lecture Notes in Physics: Vol. 160). 217p. 1982. pap. 15.00 o.p. (ISBN 0-387-11560-9). Springer-Verlag.

Unified Theory of Special Functions. Clifford A. Truesdell. (Annals of Math Studies). 1948. 16.00 o.p. (ISBN 0-527-02734-0). Kraus Repr.

Unified Valence Bond Theory of Electronic Structure. N. B. Epictis et al. (Lecture Notes in Chemistry: Vol. 29). 303p. 1982. pap. 23.40 o.p. (ISBN 0-387-11491-2). Springer-Verlag.

Uniform Commercial Code. 2nd ed. James J. White & Robert S. Summers. (Hornbook Ser.). 1250p. 1980. 28.95 o.p. West Pub.

Uniform Commercial Code Reporting: 1965-1983, 42 vols. Ed. by Pike & Fischer Staff. 850.00 o.p. (ISBN 0-317-11803-X); Suppl., 1982. 485.00 o.p.; Suppl., 1983. 545.00 o.p. Callaghan.

Uniform Credit Analysis. 244p. 1982. 78.00 o.s.i. (ISBN 0-318-18146-0); members 55.00 o.s.i. (ISBN 0-318-18147-9). Robt Morris Assocs.

Uniform Product Disclosure for Roll Film Readers: AIIM MS27-1982. Association for Information & Image Management Staff. (Standards & Recommended Practices Ser.). 4p. 1982. pap. 30.00 o.p. (ISBN 0-89258-078-X, MS27). Assn Inform & Image Mgmt.

Uniforms, Badges & Intelligence Data, etc. of the German Force. Ed. by Factus Staff. (War Documents Ser.: No. 24). (Illus.). 64p. 1983. pap. 5.95 o.p. (ISBN 0-86663-993-4). Ide Hse.

Uniforms of the Imperial Russian Army. Boris Mollo. (Illus.). 160p. 1987. pap. 12.95 o.p. (ISBN 0-7137-1939-7, Pub. by Blandford Pr England). Sterling.

Uniforms of the Indo-China & Vietnam Wars. Leroy Thompson. (Illus.). 160p. 1984. 29.95 o.p. (ISBN 0-7137-1264-3, Pub. by Blandford Pr England). Sterling.

Uniforms of the Soldiers of Fortune. Leroy Thompson. (Illus.). 175p. 1985. 14.95 o.p. (ISBN 0-7137-1328-3, Pub. by Blandford Pr England). Sterling.

Uniforms of the World: A Compendium of Army, Navy & Air Force Uniforms, 1700-1937. Richard Knotel et al. (Illus.). 1980. 30.00 o.s.i. (ISBN 0-684-16304-7, ScribT). Scribner.

Unilateral Measurements to Prevent Double Taxation, LXVIb. 550p. 1982. write for info. o.p. (ISBN 90-6544-007-0). Kluwer Academic.

Unilever Overseas: The Anatomy of a Multinational. David K. Fieldhouse. LC 78-20358. (Publications Ser.: No. 205). 1979. 25.00x o.p. (ISBN 0-8179-7051-7). Hoover Inst Pr.

Unio Mystica, 2 vols. 2nd ed. Bhagwan Shree Rajneesh. Ed. by Ma Ananda Vandana. LC 82-245842. (Sufi Ser.). (Illus.). 1980. Vol. I 384p. 17.95 ea. o.p. (ISBN 0-88050-163-4). Vol. II (ISBN 0-88050-164-2). Vol. I. pap. 13.95 ea. o.p. (ISBN 0-88050-663-6). Vol. II 368p 1981 (ISBN 0-88050-664-4). Chidvilas Inc.

Union: A Monthly Record of Moral, Social, & Educational Progress, Nos. 1-10. 1970. Repr. of 1843 ed. lib. bdg. 26.00x o.p. (ISBN 0-8371-9255-2, UN00). Greenwood.

Union & Open-Shop Construction: Compensation, Work Practices, & Labor Markets. Clinton C. Bourdon & Raymond E. Levitt. LC 79-1724. (Illus.). 176p. 1980. 25.50x o.p. (ISBN 0-669-02918-1). Lexington Bks.

Union Club Mysteries. Isaac Asimov. 224p. 1984. pap. 2.95 o.p. (ISBN 0-449-20525-8, Crest). Fawcett.

Union-Free Labor Relations: A Step-by-Step Guide to Staying Union Free. James L. Dougherty. LC 80-11777. 227p. 1980. 3 ring binder 69.00x o.p. (ISBN 0-87201-302-2). Gulf Pub.

Union-Free Supervisor. James L. Dougherty. LC 74-11836. 230p. 1974. 19.00x o.p. (ISBN 0-87201-882-2). Gulf Pub.

Union Government & Organization. Jim Wallihan. 270p. 1983. text ed. 23.00 o.p. (ISBN 0-317-59000-6); pap. text ed. 18.00 o.p. (ISBN 0-317-59001-4). BNA.

Union List of Geologic Field Trip Guidebooks of North America. 4th ed. Ed. by Geoscience Information Society Guidebooks Committee. LC 86-71946. 200p. 1986. pap. 47.50 o.p. (ISBN 0-913312-88-6). Am Geol.

Union Member's Guide to Free Speech. 1980. 0.75 o.p. Natl Lawyers Guild.

Union Member's Right to Vote. 0.75 o.p. Natl Lawyers Guild.

Union of Soviet Socialist Republics see U.S.S.R.

Union Power & New York: Victor Gotbaum & District Council 37. Jewel Bellush & Bernard Bellush. (Illus.). 368p. 1985. pap. 14.95 o.p. (ISBN 0-275-91801-7, B1801). Praeger.

Union Power & the Public Interest. Emerson P. Schmidt. LC 72-95239. (Principles of Freedom Ser.). 204p. 1976. pap. 6.95x o.p. (ISBN 0-916054-88-8, Dist. by Kampmann). Green Hill.

Union Representative's Guide to NLRB RC & CA Cases. Gloria Busman. (Policy & Practice Publication). 163p. 1977. 7.75 o.p. (ISBN 0-89215-089-0). U Cal LA Indus Rel.

Union View of Public Management's Responsibilities in Collective Bargaining see Issues in the Public Employee Relations Library: Series 3.

Unionism & Relative Wages in the United States. H. Gregg Lewis. LC 63-20915. (Midway Reprint Ser.). 1973. pap. text ed. 13.00x o.s.i. (ISBN 0-226-47720-7). U of Chicago Pr.

Unions, Change & Crisis: French & Italian Union Strategy & the Political Economy, 1945-1980. Peter Lange & George Ross. 280p. 1983. text ed. 39.95x o.p. (ISBN 0-04-331088-5). Unwin Hyman.

Unions in Post-Industrial Society. John Schmidman. LC 78-112229. 1979. text ed. 17.95x o.s.i. (ISBN 0-271-00209-3). Pa St U Pr.

Unions: Structure, Development, & Management. Marten Estey. (Orig.). 1967. pap. text ed. 8.95 o.p. (ISBN 0-15-592950-X, HC). HarBraceJ.

Unions: Structure Development, & Management. 2nd ed. Marten Estey. (Orig.). 1976. pap. text ed. 9.95 o.p. (ISBN 0-15-592951-8, HC). HarBraceJ.

Unique Advantages of Being a Mormon. W. Lynn Fluckiger. pap. 3.95 o.p. (ISBN 0-89036-138-X). Hawkes Pub Inc.

Uniquely You. Betty Nethery & Beverly B. Smith. LC 83-51176. (Illus.). 224p. 1984. pap. 9.95 o.p. (ISBN 0-8423-7792-1). Tyndale.

Uniqueness of Pastoral Psycholtherapy. William Kyle. 1985. 10.00x o.p. (ISBN 0-317-62229-3, Guild of Pastoral Psych). State Mutual Bk.

Unit Boxes for Little Kids. Jeri Carroll. (Illus.). 64p. (ps-2). 1984. wkbk 6.95 o.p. (ISBN 0-86653-189-0). Good Apple.

Unit Conversion (Convert) Date not set. 65.00 o.p. Hemisphere Pub.

Unit Dose Primer. Marc Summerfield. 268p. 1983. pap. 25.00 o.p. (ISBN 0-930530-38-1). Am Soc Hosp Pharm.

Unit Processes of Extractive Metallurgy. Robert D. Pehlke. 396p. Date not set. Repr. of 1973 ed. text ed. 37.50 o.p. (ISBN 0-930745-09-4). Williams Bk Co.

Unit Steel Band. John A. Gibbs. 1978. 7.50 o.p. (ISBN 0-682-48775-9). Exposition-Phoenix.

Unitary Calculus for Electronic Orbitals. W. G. Harter & C. W. Patterson. (Lecture Notes in Physics: Vol. 49). 1976. soft cover 13.00 o.p. (ISBN 0-387-07699-9). Springer-Verlag.

Unitary Group Representations. G. W. Mackey. (Mathematics Lecture Note Ser.: No. 55). 1978. 45.95 o.s.i. (ISBN 0-8053-6702-0, Adv Bk Prog MSP); pap. write for info. o.p. (ISBN 0-8053-6703-9, Adv Bk Prog MSP). Addison-Wesley.

UNITAS Twenty-Five: A Silver Anniversary. Ed. by Robert A. Carlisle. (Illus.). 160p. (Span. & Port.). 1985. 23.00 o.p. (ISBN 0-318-11836-X, S/N 008-046-00111-1). USGPO.

United Arab Emirates: A Middle East Economic Digest Guide. Ed. by Trevor Mostyn. 324p. (Orig.). 1982. pap. 15.00 o.p. (ISBN 0-7103-0014-X, Kegan Paul). Routledge Chapman & Hall.

United Arts Fundraising Policybook. American Council for the Arts Staff. 270p. 125.00 o.s.i. (ISBN 0-317-32510-8). Am Council Arts.

United Arts Fundraising: 1985 Campaign Analysis. Ed. by Robert Porter. 95p. 1986. pap. 10.00 o.p. (ISBN 0-915400-52-9). Am Council Arts.

United Arts Fundraising: 1986 Campaign Analysis. Ed. by Robert Porter. 61p. 1987. pap. 20.00 o.p. (ISBN 0-915400-61-8). Am Council Arts.

United in Purpose: A Chronological History of the Ohio AFL-CIO, 1958-1983. Raymond Boryczka. LC 84-622816. (Illus.). 1984. avail. o.p. Ohio Hist Soc.

United Nations & Disarmament, 1970-75. 268p. 1976. 12.00x o.p. (ISBN 0-8002-3323-9). Intl Pubns Serv.

United Nations & World Realities. M. J. Lee. 1965. text ed. 24.00 o.p. (ISBN 0-08-011350-8); pap. text ed. 10.75 o.p. (ISBN 0-08-011349-4). Pergamon.

United Nations Charter & Statute of the International Court of Justice. 87p. 0.75 o.p. (ISBN 0-686-30397-0). WILPF.

United Nations Conference on Prescription (Limitation) in the International Sale of Goods. 31.95 o.p. (ISBN 92-1-133235-4, E.74.V.8). UN.

United Nations Conference on Trade & Development: Proceedings, Vol. III. 329p. 1986. 33.00 o.p. (ISBN 92-1-112192-2, E.83.II.D.8). UN.

United Nations Council on Trade & Development (UNCTAD) Conflict & Compromise. B. Gosovic. 1972. 30.00 o.s.i. (ISBN 9-0286-0091-4). E J Brill USA.

United Nations Disarmament Yearbook, Vol. 5. 493p. 1981. 35.00 o.p. (E.81.IX.3); pap. 28.00 o.p. (81.IX.4). UN.

United Nations Disarmament Yearbook, Vol. 5. United Nations Staff. 481p. 1980. 35.00x o.p. (ISBN 0-8002-2969-X). Intl Pubns Serv.

United Nations Disarmament Yearbook, 1982, Vol. VII. LC 78-641027. 648p. 1984. 35.00 o.p. (ISBN 0-8002-3153-8). Intl Pubns Serv.

United Nations Editorial Manual. 1983. 50.00x o.p. (ISBN 0-8002-3462-6). Intl Pubns Serv.

United Nations: Energy & Raw Materials. pap. 1.00 o.p. (ISBN 92-1-157013-1, E.75.XV.CR/5). UN.

United Nations Giving Countenance to Soviet Strategic Penetrations of Africa. 16p. 1977. stitched 2.50 o.p. (ISBN 90-27-11333-5). Kluwer Academic.

United Nations, Image & Reality. United Nations, Department of Public Information Staff. LC 81-212745. (United Nations, Department of Public Information Ser.). 1983. 0.50 o.p. (DPI/795). UN.

United Nations Political System. D. A. Kay. LC 67-29937. (Illus.). 419p. 1967. text ed. 17.50 o.p. (ISBN 0-471-46110-5, Pub. by Wiley); pap. 9.50 o.p. (ISBN 0-471-46111-3). Krieger.

United Nations Statistical Yearbook. Incl. 1948-1975. pap. 445.00; 1961. pap. 30.00 (E.62.XVII.1); 1962. pap. 30.00 (E.63.XVII.1); 1964. pap. 30.00 (E.65.XVII.1); 1965. pap. 30.00 (E.66.XVII.1); 1966. pap. 25.00 (E.67.XVII.1); 1967. pap. 30.00 (E.68.XVII.1); pap. 30.00 (E.68.XVII.1); 1968. pap. 30.00 (E.69.XVII.1); 1969. pap. 30.00 (E.70.XVII.1); 1971. pap. 25.00 (E.72.XVII.1); 1972. 35.00 (E.73.XVII.1); Supplement. pap. 17.00 (E.74.XVII.2); 1973. pap. 42.00 (E.74.XVII.1); pap. 25.00 (E.74.XVII.1); 1974. pap. 36.00 (E.75.XVII.1); 1975. pap. 50.00 (E.76.XVII.1); pap. 40.00 (E.76.XVII.1); 1976. pap. 50.00 (E.77.XVII.1); pap. 35.00 (E.77.XVII.1); 1977. pap. 50.00 (E.78.XVII.1); Supplement: Methodology & Definitions. pap. 29.00 (E.78.XVII.10); 1978. pap. 50.00 (E.79.XVII.1); 1979-1980. pap. 60.00 (E.81.XVII.1); pap. 52.00 (E.81.XVII.1). UN.

United Nations: The First Ten Years. Ben A. Wortley. LC 74-5776. (Illus.). 206p. 1974. Repr. of 1957 ed. lib. bdg. 22.50x o.p. (ISBN 0-8371-7516-X, WOUN). Greenwood.

United Nations Water Conference: Summary & Main Documents. new ed. Ed. by Asit K. Biswas. LC 77-30461. 1978. 65.00 o.p. (ISBN 0-08-022392-3); 43.00 o.p. (ISBN 0-08-023410-0). Pergamon.

United Nations Yearbook on Human Rights: 1977-1978. 19.00 o.p. (ISBN 92-1-154003-8, E.81.XIV.1). UN.

United Reformed Church. Kenneth Slack. 1978. pap. text ed. 3.15 o.s.i. (ISBN 0-08-021414-2). Pergamon.

United States- Korea Relations. Ed. by Robert A. Scalapino & Han Sung-joo. LC 86-2388. (Research Papers & Policy Studies: No. 19). xii, 226p. (Orig.). 1986. pap. 20.00x o.s.i. (ISBN 0-912966-93-9). IEAS.

U. S. Agricultural Policies: A Market Process Approach. E. C. Pasour. 184p. 1986. pap. 7.95 o.s.i. (ISBN 0-910614-73-3). Foun Econ Ed.

U. S. Air Force. Dodd.

U. S. Air Power in Colour 1. Robbie Shaw. (Illus.). 96p. 1987. 12.95 o.p. (ISBN 0-7106-0431-9). Janes Info Group.

U. S. Airborne Forces of World War Two. Cameron P. Laughlin. (Uniforms Illustrated Ser.: No.18). (Illus.). 72p. 1987. pap. 9.95 o.p. (ISBN 0-85368-737-4, Pub. by Arms & Armour). Sterling.

United States Airborne Forces, 1940-1986. Leroy Thompson. (Illus.). 128p. (Orig.). 1987. pap. 12.95 o.p. (ISBN 0-7137-1921-4, Pub. by Blandford Pr England). Sterling.

U. S. Airfreight Industry. Nawal K. Taneja. LC 78-24840. 272p. 1979. 30.00x o.p. (ISBN 0-669-02853-3). Lexington Bks.

United States & Asia: Changing Attitudes & Policies. William Watts. LC 81-47711. (Illus.). 284p. 1982. 24.00x o.p. (ISBN 0-669-04729-5); pap. 13.00x o.p. (ISBN 0-669-05370-8). Lexington Bks.

U. S. & Canadian Business in South Africa. 180p. 1987. 150.00 o.p. (ISBN 0-931035-21-X). IRRC Inc DC.

United States & Europe: Rivals & Partners. Max Silberschmidt. LC 78-157879. 1972. pap. text ed. 6.95 o.p. (ISBN 0-15-593020-6, HC). HarBraceJ.

United States & International Education. Ed. by Harold G. Shane. (National Society for the Study of Education Yearbooks Ser: No. 68, Pt. 1). 1969. lib. bdg. 7.50x o.s.i. (ISBN 0-226-60094-7). U of Chicago Pr.

U. S. & Israel. Herbert Druks. 1979. pap. 7.95 o.p. (ISBN 0-8315-0147-2). Speller.

United States & Japan. rev. ed. Ed. by Herbert Passin. LC 66-14703. 1975. 3.95 o.p. (ISBN 0-318-23692-3, C-3848); pap. 1.95 o.p. (ISBN 0-318-23693-1, C-3847). Am Assembly.

United States & Latin America. Richard J. Walton. LC 76-171860. 192p. (gr. 6 up). 1979. 5.95 o.p. (ISBN 0-395-28930-0, Clarion). HM.

United States & Malaysia. James W. Gould. LC 76-78518. (American Foreign Policy Library). (Illus.). 1969. 18.50x o.s.i. (ISBN 0-674-92615-3). Harvard U Pr.

U. S. & Mexico. Howard F. Cline. LC 52-12258. 1963. pap. text ed. 4.95x o.p. (ISBN 0-689-70050-4, 40, Atheneum). Macmillan.

U. S. & Mexico. Josefina Z. Vazquez & Lorenzo Meyer. LC 85-1061. (United States in the World: Foreign Perspective Ser.). xiv, 220p. 1985. 29.00x o.s.i. (ISBN 0-226-85023-4). U of Chicago Pr.

United States & the Disruption of the Spanish Empire, 1810-1822. Charles C. Griffin. 1968. lib. bdg. 21.50x o.p. (ISBN 0-374-93287-5, Octagon). Hippocrene Bks.

United States & the Far East. Richard J. Walton. LC 73-14859. 192p. (gr. 6 up). 1979. 6.95 o.p. (ISBN 0-395-28931-9, Clarion). HM.

U. S. & the Independence of Latin America, 1800-1830. Arthur P. Whitaker. 1964. pap. 3.95 o.p. (ISBN 0-393-00271-3, Norton Lib). Norton.

U. S. & the Southern Cone: Argentina, Chile, Uruguay. Ed. by Arthur P. Whitaker. (American Foreign Policy Library). 1977. 29.50x o.s.i. (ISBN 0-674-92841-5). Harvard U Pr.

United States & the World Court. Philip C. Jessup. Incl. What's Wrong with International Law? Wolfgang Friedman; Foreign Policy of a Free Democracy. Philip C. Jessup; Fallacy of a "Preventive" War. Philip C. Jessup; Legal Process & International Order. Hans Kelsen. LC 70-147750. (Library of War & Peace; International Law). 1973. lib. bdg. 46.00 o.p. (ISBN 0-8240-0490-6). Garland Pub.

United States & Vatican Policies, 1914-1918. Dragan Zivojinovic. LC 78-52438. 1978. 22.50x o.p. (ISBN 0-87081-112-6). Univ Pr Colo.

U. S. & West German Housing Markets. Konrad Stahl & Raymond J. Struyk. 154p. 1985. pap. text ed. 21.00 o.p. (ISBN 0-87766-388-2). Urban Inst.

U. S. & Worldwide Travel Accommodations Guide: For 6 to 18 Dollars per Day. 8th ed. Ed. by Mary J. Jensen. 72p. (Orig.). 1988. pap. 11.95 o.p. (ISBN 0-945499-00-0). Campus Travel.

U. S. Arms Exports: Policies & Contractors. Paul L. Ferrari et al. LC 87-80032. 368p. (Orig.). 1987. pap. 60.00 o.p. (ISBN 0-931035-12-0). IRRC Inc DC.

U. S. Army Air Forces in World War II, Vol. 1. Jeffrey Ethell. (Warbirds Illustrated Ser.: No. 38). (Illus.). 72p. (Orig.). 1986. pap. 9.95 o.p. (ISBN 0-85368-722-6, Pub. by Arms & Armour). Sterling.

United States Army Corps of Engineers Officer & Warrant Officer Directory, 1986. 320p. (Orig.). 1986. pap. 15.00 o.p. (S/N 008-022-00229-4). USGPO.

U. S. Army Enlisted Men's Clothing: Quartermaster Supply Catalog QM 3-1. Repr. of 1946 ed. 8.95 o.p. (ISBN 0-938242-03-2). Portrayal.

United States Army in World War 2: War in the Pacific, Leyte, the Return to the Philippines. M. Hamlin Cannon. LC 53-61979. (CMH Publications: Nos. 5-9). (Illus.). 420p. 1954. 15.00 o.p. (ISBN 0-318-22739-8, S/N 008-029-00036-9). USGPO.

United States Army in World War 2: War in the Pacific, Okinawa, the Last Battle. Roy E. Appleman et al. LC 49-45742. (Illus.). 529p. 1948. 22.00 o.p. (ISBN 0-318-22738-X, S/N 008-029-00066-1). USGPO.

United States Army in World War 2: War in the Pacific, Triumph in the Philippines. Robert R. Smith. LC 62-60000. (Illus.). 756p. 1963. 25.00 o.p. (ISBN 0-318-22737-1, S/N 008-029-00033-4). USGPO.

U. S. Army Sniper Training Manual. (Illus.). 196p. 1969. pap. 16.95 o.p. (ISBN 0-87364-120-5). Paladin Pr.

U. S. Army Sniper Training Manual. 1986. lib. bdg. 79.95 o.p. (ISBN 0-8490-3666-6). Gordon Pr.

U. S. Army Uniforms: Europe, Nineteen Forty-Four to Nineteen Forty-Five. C. P. Laughlin & J. P. Langellier. (Uniforms Illustrated Ser.: No. 14). (Illus.). 68p. (Orig.). 1986. pap. 9.95 o.p. (ISBN 0-85368-727-7, Pub. by Arms & Armour). Sterling.

United States Army Weapons Systems, 1986. (Illus.). 165p. 1986. pap. 7.00 o.p. (ISBN 0-318-20379-0, S/N 008-020-01070-7). USGPO.

United States Art Directory & Year-Book. S. R. Koehler. Ed. by H. Barbara Weinberg. Incl. Vol. 1. Guide for Artists, Art Students, Travellers, Etc; Vol. 2. Chronicle of Events in the Art World, & a Guide for All Interested in the Progress of Art in America. LC 75-28874. (Art Experience in Late 19th Century America Ser.: Vol. 10). (Illus.). 1976. Repr. of 1884 ed. lib. bdg. 88.00 o.p. (ISBN 0-8240-2234-3). Garland Pub.

U. S. Battery Industry. Business Communications Staff. 153p. 1987. 1950.00 o.p. (GB-086). BCC.

U. S. Bilateral Assistance in Africa: The Case of Cameroon. Peter Agbor-Tabi. (Illus.). 192p. (Orig.). 1984. lib. bdg. 24.25 o.p. (ISBN 0-8191-3909-2); pap. text ed. 12.25 o.p. (ISBN 0-8191-3910-6). U Pr of Amer.

U. S. Book Publishing Yearbook & Directory 1979-80. Ed. by Terry S. Mollo. (Illus., Orig.). 1979. pap. 35.00x o.p. (ISBN 0-8103-0187-3, Knowledge Industry Publications). Gale.

U. S. Budget in Brief, Fiscal Year 1987. 93p. 1986. pap. 2.00 o.p. (ISBN 0-318-19914-9, S/N 041-001-00301-1). USGPO.

U. S. Business Briefing: BNA International Inc. BNA.

U. S. Business in South Africa: The Economic, Political & Moral Issues. Desaix Myers, III et al. LC 79-3638. 392p. 1980. 25.00X o.p. (ISBN 0-253-11486-1). Ind U Pr.

U. S. Business Support for International Public Service Activities, Pt. 2. James R. Basche. Incl. Support from Foreign Affiliates - Brazil. (No. 616). 25p. 1974. 10.00 (ISBN 0-8237-0057-7); Support from Foreign Affiliates - Argentina. (No. 624). 25p. 1974. 10.00 (ISBN 0-8237-0058-5); Support from Foreign Affiliates - Columbia. (No. 643). 24p. 1974. 20.00 (ISBN 0-8237-0056-9); Support from Foreign Affiliates - Philippines. (No. 657). 24p. 1975. 20.00 (ISBN 0-8237-0076-3); Support from Foreign Affiliates - Mexico. (No. 617). 26p. 1974. 10.00 (ISBN 0-8237-0059-3). (Report Ser.). Conference Bd.

U. S. Civil Aircraft, 6 of 9 vols. Joseph P. Juptner. Incl. ATC 501-600. (Illus.). 1974 (29170); Vol. 7. ATC 601-700. 1978. 19.95 o.p. (ISBN 0-8168-9174-5, 29174); Vol. 8. ATC 801-817 & Series Index. 351p. 1980. 19.95 o.p. (ISBN 0-8168-9178-8, 29178); Vol. 4. ATC 301-400. 1967 (ISBN 0-8168-9162-1); Vol.5. ATC 401-500. 1971 (ISBN 0-8168-9166-4); Vol. 9. ATC 701-800. 240p. 1982. 19.95 (ISBN 0-8168-9182-6, 29182); Vol. 6. ATC 501-600. (Illus.). 1974 (ISBN 0-8168-9170-2). LC 62-15967. 19.95 ea. o.p. (TAB-Aero). TAB Bks.

United States Code: Supplement 3, Vol. 3. 1337p. 1986. Repr. of 1982 ed. 45.00 o.p. (ISBN 0-318-21360-5, S/N 052-001-00260-1). USGPO.

U. S. Commercial Aircraft. Ken Munson. (Illus.). 192p. 1982. 19.95 o.p. (ISBN 0-86720-628-4). Janes Info Group.

U. S. Computer Chess Championship: 1975. David Levy. LC 76-241. 1976. 11.95x o.p. (ISBN 0-914894-00-5, Computer Sci Pr); pap. 6.95x o.p. (ISBN 0-914894-01-3). W H Freeman.

U. S. Congress - Proceedings of Thomas P. O'Neal Jr. Symposium. Ed. by Dennis Hale. 300p. 1981. pap. 10.95 o.p. (ISBN 0-317-69296-8). BU Poli Sci.

United States Constitution. Paul N. McCloskey. (gr. 10-12). 1972. pap. text ed. 12.00 o.s.i. (ISBN 0-8449-0901-7); tchrs' manual 2.00 o.s.i.; test 2.00 o.s.i. Carroll CA.

United States Cotton Industry. Irving R. Starbird et al. (Foreign Agricultural Economic Report: No. 567). (Illus.). 175p. 1987. pap. 3.75 o.p. (ISBN 0-317-62912-3, S-N 001-019-00501-7). USGPO.

United States Court Directory, March 1987. 270p. 1987. pap. 13.00 o.p. (ISBN 0-318-22586-7, S/N 028-004-00067-2). USGPO.

United States Cultural History: A Guide to Information Sources. Ed. by Philip I. Mitterling. LC 79-24061. (American Government & History Information Guide Ser.: Vol. 5). 592p. 1980. 68.00x o.p. (ISBN 0-8103-1369-3). Gale.

U. S. Debate on Industrial Policy: A Bibliography, 1980-1985. Michael Stevenson. (Public Administration Ser.: P 1728). 9p. 1985. 2.00 o.p. (ISBN 0-89028-498-9). Vance Biblios.

U. S. Debt Crisis & World Economy. Angelopoul. 1985. pap. 11.95 o.p. (ISBN 0-275-91667-7, B1667). Praeger.

United States Diplomatic History, Vol. 1. Gerard H. Clarfield. LC 72-5519. 256p. 1973. pap. 11.50 o.p. (ISBN 0-395-14026-9). HM.
United States Diplomatic History: Readings for the Twentieth-Century, Vol. 2. Ed. by Walter V. Scholes. LC 72-6699. 1973. pap. 8.25 o.p. (ISBN 0-395-14057-9, 3-50121). HM.
U. S. Direct Investment Abroad: Nineteen Eighty-Two Benchmark Survey Data. (Illus.). 468p. 1985. pap. 18.00 o.p. (ISBN 0-318-19915-7, S/N 003-010-00161-5). USGPO.
U. S. Economic History. 2nd ed. Albert W. Niemi, Jr. 1980. text ed. 33.95 o.p. (ISBN 0-395-30682-5). HM.
U. S. Economy Demystified: What Their Major Economic Statistics Mean & Their Significance for Business. Albert T. Sommers. LC 84-48451. 160p. 1985. 16.95 o.p. (ISBN 0-669-09427-7); pap. 12.95x o.p. (ISBN 0-669-09821-3). Lexington Bks.
U. S. Eighteen Thirty to Eighteen Fifty. Frederick J. Turner. 1965. pap. 3.95x o.p. (ISBN 0-393-00308-6, Norton Lib). Norton.
U. S. Environmental Protection Agency Guidebook, 1984-1985. Ed. by TFP Sullivan Staff. 280p. 1984. pap. 38.00 o.p. (ISBN 0-86587-070-5). Gov Insts.
U. S. Federal Official Publications: The International Dimension. J. A. Downey. 1978. 93.00 o.p. (ISBN 0-08-021839-3). Pergamon.
U. S. Fighters. Lloyd Jones. LC 75-25246. (Illus.). 1975. 21.60 o.p. (ISBN 0-8168-9201-6, 29201, TAB-Aero). TAB Bks.
U. S. Financing of East-West Trade: The Political Economy of Government Credits & the National Interest. Ed. by Paul Marer. 464p. 1976. pap. 22.50x o.p. (ISBN 0-253-36200-8). Ind U Pr.
U. S. Fleet Carriers of World War II. Richard Humble. (In Action Ser.). (Illus.). 160p. 1986. pap. 14.95 o.p. (ISBN 0-7137-1819-6, Pub. by Blandford Pr England). Sterling.
U. S. Foamed Plastics Markets & Directory 1987. LC 63-59134. 68p. 40.00 o.p. (ISBN 0-87762-457-7). Technomic.
U. S. Force Structure in NATO: An Alternative. Richard D. Lawrence & Jeffrey Record. LC 74-1436. (Studies in Defense Policy). 136p. 1974. pap. 7.95 o.p. (ISBN 0-8157-5171-0). Brookings.
U. S. Foreign Policy & Christian Ethics. John C. Bennett & Harvey Seifert. LC 77-5062. 234p. 1977. 7.95 o.s.i. soft cover (ISBN 0-664-24756-3, Westminster). Westminster John Knox.
U. S. Foreign Policy & the Law of the Sea. Ann L. Hollick. LC 80-8554. 456p. 1981. 42.00x o.p. (ISBN 0-691-09387-3). Princeton U Pr.
United States Foreign Policy & World Order. 3rd ed. James A. Nathan & James K. Oliver. pap. text ed. write for info. o.p. (ISBN 0-673-39465-4). Scott F.
U. S. Foreign Policy: Context, Conduct, Content. Marian D. Irish & Elke Frank. 562p. (Orig.). 1975. pap. text ed. 12.75 o.p. (ISBN 0-15-593822-3, HC). HarBraceJ.
United States Foreign Trade Law. Bruce E. Clubb. 1989. Little.
United States-German Economic Survey 1986. Heinz J. Dielman. 212p. (Ger.). 1986. write for info. o.p. (ISBN 0-86640-024-9). German Am Chamber.
United States-German Economic Yearbook, 1987: Deutsch-Amerikanisches Wirtschaftsjahrbuch, 1987. 13th ed. Ed. by Richard C. Jacob. 225p. (Ger.). 1988. write for info. o.p. (ISBN 0-86640-026-5). German Am Chamber.
United States Global Leadership: The President & Congress. David M. Abshire et al. 96p. 1980. pap. Transaction Pubs.
U. S. Halftracks of World War Two. Steven J. Zaloga. (Tanks Illustrated Ser.: Vol. 15). (Illus.). 64p. (Orig.). 1985. pap. 9.95 o.p. (ISBN 0-85368-697-1, Pub by Arms & Armour). Sterling.
U. S. Health Care System: A Look to the 1990's. Ed. by Eli Ginzberg. (Conservation of Human Resources Ser.: Vol. 26). 160p. 1985. 24.50x o.s.i. (ISBN 0-8476-7468-1, Rowman & Allanheld). Rowman.
U. S. Higher Education: A Guide to Information Sources. Ed. by Franklin Parker & Betty J. Parker. (Education Information Guide Ser.: Vol. 9). 688p. 1980. 68.00x o.p. (ISBN 0-8103-1476-2). Gale.
United States Import Relief Laws: Current Developments in Law & Policy: A Course Handbook. Harvey M. Applebaum & A. Paul Victor. 365p. 1985. pap. 15.00 o.p. (A4-4137). PLI.
United States Imprints on Sub-Saharan Africa: A Guide to Publications Cataloged at the Library of Congress, 1985, Vol. 1. 113p. 1986. pap. 6.00 o.p. (ISBN 0-318-21362-1, S/N 030-000-00175-3). USGPO.
United States in Germany 1944-1955. Harold Zink. LC 74-9321. (Illus.). 374p. 1975. Repr. of 1957 ed. lib. bdg. 23.50x o.p. (ISBN 0-8371-7641-7, ZIUS). Greenwood.
U. S. in the Vietnam War, 1954-1975: A Selected, Annotated Bibliography. Louis A. Peake. LC 84-45409. (WUS-SS Ser.). 600p. 1986. lib. bdg. 70.00 o.p. (ISBN 0-8240-8946-4). Garland Pub.
United States in the World Economy: Selected Papers of C. Fred Bergsten, 1981 to 1982. C. Fred Bergsten. LC 82-49336. 256p. 1983. 26.00x o.p. (ISBN 0-669-06617-6). Lexington Bks.
U. S. Infantry Combat Vehicles Today. Steven J. Zaloga & Michael Green. (Tanks Illustrated Ser.: Vol.13). 1984. pap. 9.95 o.p. (ISBN 0-85368-663-7, Arms & Armour Pr). Sterling.
United States Information Service Libraries. Jodyt Sussman. (Occasional Papers: No. 111). 23p. 1973. pap. 2.00 o.p. (ISBN 0-317-58908-3). U of Ill Lib Info Sci.
U. S. International Trade Laws. Ed. by Alan M. Stowell. 536p. 1986. pap. text ed. 30.00 o.p. (ISBN 0-87179-518-3, 0518). BNA.
U. S. Interventions: A Brief History. Angelo Coleoni. 244p. 1984. text ed. 25.00x o.p. (ISBN 0-86590-312-3, Pub. by Sterling Pubs India). Apt Bks.
U. S. Labor & Employment Laws, 1987 Edition. Ed. by Ruth C. Trussell. 432p. 1987. pap. text ed. 33.00 o.p. (ISBN 0-87179-560-4, 0560). BNA.
U. S. Law of Sovereign Immunity. 1984. 150.00 o.p. (ISBN 0-8002-3170-8). Intl Pubns Serv.
United States Local History Catalog, 2 vols. New York Public Library, Research Libraries Staff. 1115p. 1974. Set. lib. bdg. 200.00 o.p. (ISBN 0-8161-1147-2, Hall Library). G K Hall.
U. S. Lodging Industry. D. Daryl Wyckoff & W. Earl Sasser. LC 78-24716. (Lexington Industry Analysis Casebook Ser.). 336p. 1981. 32.00x o.p. (ISBN 0-669-02819-3). Lexington Bks.
United States: MacKaey Blue Book, 1988, 3 vols. 1988. Set. 125.00 o.p. Manufacturers.
U. S. Marine Corps Story. Abr. ed. J. Robert Moskin. 800p. 1982. pap. text ed. 12.95 o.p. (ISBN 0-07-043454-9). McGraw.
United States Marines in Grenada, 1983. Ronald H. Spector. LC 87-691831. (Illus.). 43p. 1987. pap. 2.25 o.p. (ISBN 0-317-62819-4, S/N 008-055-00170-6). USGPO.
U. S. Marines in World War II. Robert C. Stern. (Uniforms Illustrated Ser.: No. 11). (Illus.). 68p. (Orig.). 1986. pap. 9.95 o.p. (ISBN 0-85368-755-2, Pub. by Arms & Armour). Sterling.
U. S. Medical Directory 1983-84. 6th ed. Ed. by Stanley Alperin. LC 72-92344. 1983. 89.95 o.p. (ISBN 0-916524-20-5). US Direct Serv.
U. S. Medical Licensure Statistics Nineteen Eighty-Five & Licensure Requirements Nineteen Eighty-Six. American Medical Association Staff. 53p. (Orig.). 1987. pap. 32.50 o.p. (ISBN 0-89970-309-7, OP-190/7). AMA.
United States Military Posture for FY 1987. (Illus.). 108p. (Orig.). 1986. pap. 4.00 o.p. (ISBN 0-318-20159-3, S/N 008-004-00023-4). USGPO.
United States Military Posture for FY 1988. (Illus.). 108p. (Orig.). 1987. pap. 5.00 o.p. (ISBN 0-318-22467-4, S/N 008-004-00025-1). USGPO.
United States Minerals Issues--the Seventies, a Review; the Eighties, a Preview: 6th Annual Mineral Economics Symposium, November 12, 1980, Washington DC. Ed. by W. Hibbard. 1981. pap. 33.00 o.p. (ISBN 0-08-027593-1). Pergamon.
U. S. Monetary Policy & European Responses in the 1980's. Kenneth King. (Chatham House Papers in Foreign Policy). 128p. (Orig.). 1982. pap. 10.95x o.p. (ISBN 0-7100-9337-3). Routledge Chapman & Hall.
U. S. Naval & Marine Aircraft Today. Don Linn. (Warbirds Illustrated Ser.: No. 34). (Illus.). 72p. (Orig.). 1985. pap. 9.95 o.p. (ISBN 0-85368-730-7, Pub. by Arms & Armour). Sterling.
U. S. Navy. Dodd.
U. S. Navy Seal Combat Manual. 1986. lib. bdg. 79.95 o.p. (ISBN 0-8490-3559-7). Gordon Pr.
U. S. Newspaper Program: National Union List. 2nd ed. OCLC Online Computer Library Center, Inc. Staff. 1987. pap. 350.00 o.p. (ISBN 0-933418-76-0); microfiche 200.00 o.p. (ISBN 1-55653-023-4). OCLC Online Comp.
United States, Nineteen Eighty. Steve Birnbaum. (Get 'Em & Go Travel Guides Ser.). 1979. 15.00 o.p. (ISBN 0-685-96025-0); pap. 9.95 o.p. (ISBN 0-395-28414-7). HM.
United States, Nineteen Eighty-One. Steve Birnbaum. (Get 'em & Go Travel Guides). 1980. pap. 9.95 o.p. (ISBN 0-395-29753-2). HM.
United States Nineteen Eighty-Seven. Steve Birnbaum. (Illus.). 848p. 1986. pap. 12.70 o.s.i. (ISBN 0-395-42334-1). HM.
United States, Nineteen Eighty-Two. Steve Birnbaum. (Get 'em & Go Travel Guide Ser.). 816p. 1981. pap. 10.95 o.p. (ISBN 0-395-31538-7). HM.
United States, Nineteen Twenty-Nine to Nineteen Forty-Five: Years of Crisis & Change. Richard S. Kirkendall. (Modern America Ser.). (Illus.). 320p. 1974. text ed. 18.95 o.p. (ISBN 0-07-034806-5); pap. text ed. 21.95 o.p. (ISBN 0-07-034805-7). McGraw.
U. S. Nuclear Regulatory Commission. Fred Clement. (Know Your Government Ser.). (Illus.). 112p. (gr. 5 up). 1989. lib. bdg. 14.95 o.p. (ISBN 1-55546-129-8). Chelsea Hse.
United States Paper Money. 5th ed. Chester L. Krause & Robert Lemake. 184p. 18.95 o.s.i. (ISBN 0-87341-090-4). Krause Pubns.
United States Patent System: Legal & Economic Conflicts in AMerican Patent History. Floyd L. Vaughan. LC 72-6846. 355p. 1972. Repr. of 1956 ed. lib. bdg. 35.00x o.p. (ISBN 0-8371-6499-0, VAPS). Greenwood.
U. S. Political Parties in Historial Perspectives: A Checklist, 1980-1984. Dale E. Casper. (Public Administration Ser.: P 1686). 10p. 1985. 2.00 o.p. (ISBN 0-89028-416-4). Vance Biblios.
United States Politics & Elections: A Guide to Information Sources. Ed. by David J. Maurer. LC 78-13669. (American Government & History Information Guide Ser.: Vol. 3). 232p. 1978. 68.00x o.p. (ISBN 0-8103-1367-7). Gale.
U. S. Postal Service: Problems & Prospects. Alva W. Stewart. (Public Administration Ser.: P 1736). 11p. 1985. 2.00 o.p. (ISBN 0-89028-506-3). Vance Biblios.
U. S. Power in a World of Conflict. Ray S. Cline. LC 80-415. (Significant Issues Ser.: Vol. II, No. 7). 54p. (Orig.). 1987. pap. 7.50 o.p. (ISBN 0-8191-6077-6, Pub. by CSIS). U Pr of Amer.
U. S. Press & Iran Foreign Policy & the Journalism of Deference. William A. Dorman & Mansour Farhang. 282p. (Orig.). 1988. pap. 10.95 o.p. (ISBN 0-520-06472-0). U of Cal Pr.
U. S. Prison Library Services & Their Theoretical Bases. (Occasional Papers: No. 110). 21p. 1973. pap. 2.00 o.p. (ISBN 0-317-58905-9). U of Ill Lib Info Sci.
U. S. Productivity Growth: Who Benefited? Lawrence P. Brunner. Ed. by Fred Bateman. LC 83-9108. (Research in Business Economics & Public Policy Ser.: No. 3). 160p. 1983. 42.95 o.p. (ISBN 0-8357-1442-X). UMI Res Pr.
U. S. Rapid Deployment Forces. David Eshel. (Illus.). 208p. 1984. 19.95 o.p. (ISBN 0-668-06211-8, 6211-8). Arco.
United States, Republic of Korea Combined Operations: A Korean Perspective. Taek-Hyung Rhee. (National Security Affairs Monograph). 61p. (Orig.). 1986. pap. 2.00 o.p. (ISBN 0-318-20161-5, S/N 008-020-01074-0). USGPO.
U. S. S. A. S. N. Lewitt. (Young Adult Ser.: Bk. 4). 176p. 1987. pap. 2.95 o.p. (ISBN 0-380-75183-6). Avon.
U. S. S. A. S. C. Sykes. (Young Adult Ser.: Bk. 3). 195p. 1987. pap. 2.95 o.p. (ISBN 0-380-75182-8). Avon.
U. S. S. A. Book 1. Tom DeHaven. LC 86-91605. (Young Adult Ser.: Bk. 1). 185p. 1987. pap. 2.95 o.p. (ISBN 0-380-75180-1, Flare). Avon.
U. S. S. A. Book 1. S. N. Lewitt. LC 86-91605. (Young Adult Ser.: Bk. 2). 176p. 1987. pap. 2.95 o.p. (ISBN 0-380-75181-X, Flare). Avon.
U. S. S. R. & Countries of Africa. E. A. Tarabrin et al. 1980. 8.95 o.p. (ISBN 0-8285-1919-6, Pub. by Progress Pubs USSR). Imported Pubns.
U. S. S. R. & International Copyright Protection. M. Boguslavsky. 303p. 1979. 8.45 o.p. (ISBN 0-8285-1609-X, 133737, Pub. by Progress Pubs USSR). Imported Pubns.
U. S. S. R. & Japan. R. K. Jain. 400p. 1980. text ed. 29.95x o.p. (ISBN 0-391-01898-1). Humanities.
U. S. S. R. Aujourd'hui et Demain. (Collection Marxisme-Leninisme). 270p. (Fr.). 1982. pap. 11.25 o.p. (ISBN 0-828-027060-3). Pergamon.
U. S. S. R.-for Peace Against Aggression Nineteen Thirty-Three to Nineteen Forty-One. I. K. Koblyakov. 244p. 1976. 4.45 o.p. (ISBN 0-8285-0509-8, Pub. by Progress Pubs USSR). Imported Pubns.
U. S. S. R. Geography of the Eleventh Five-Year Plan. Konstantin Spidchenko. 229p. 1984. 6.95 o.p. (ISBN 0-8285-2828-4, Pub. by Progress Pubs USSR). Imported Pubns.
U. S. S. R.-Land of the Russian Bear. Ed. by Natalie Rifkin. LC 78-730222. (National Wildlife Challenge Kit Ser.). (gr. 3-6). 1978. 35.00 o.p. (ISBN 0-912186-26-7). Natl Wildlife.
U. S. S. R. Today. 7th ed. Fred Schulze. Tr. by Current Digest of the Soviet Press Staff. 180p. (Orig.). 1988. pap. 20.00x o.p. (ISBN 0-913601-77-2). Current Digest.
U. S. Senators & Their World. new ed. Donald R. Matthews. 320p. 1973. pap. 3.95 o.p. (ISBN 0-393-00679-4, N679, Norton Lib). Norton.
United States Since Nineteen Forty-Five: The Ordeal of Power. Dewey W. Grantham. (Modern America Ser.). 1976. text ed. 22.95 o.p. (ISBN 0-07-024116-3). McGraw.
U. S. Sky Spies since World War I. Michael O'Leary. (Illus.). 128p. (Orig.). 1986. 24.95 o.p. (ISBN 0-7137-1555-3, Pub. by Blandford Pr England); pap. 12.95 o.p. (ISBN 0-7137-1692-4, Pub. by Blandford Pr England). Sterling.
United States Supreme Court Modifies the Exclusionary Rule: United States v. Leon & Massachusetts v. Sheppard. Robert L. Farb. LC 85-621429. (Administration of Justice Memorandum: No. 84/02). 1984. 2.00 o.p. Institute Government.
U. S. Synchronized Swimming Rulebook, 1985. U. S. Synchronized Swimming Staff. 125p. (Orig.). pap. 5.00 o.p. (ISBN 0-911543-00-7). US Synch Swim.
U. S. Tank Destroyers of World War II. Steven J. Zaloga. (Tanks Illustrated Ser.: No. 19). (Illus.). 64p. (Orig.). 1986. pap. 9.95 o.p. (ISBN 0-85368-770-6, Pub. by Arms & Armour). Sterling.
U. S. Virgin Islands Alive. 2nd ed. Arnold Greenberg & Harriet Greenberg. (Alive Travel Ser.). (Illus.). 250p. pap. 9.95 o.p. (ISBN 0-935572-14-7). Alive Pubns.
U. S. Virgin Islands Alive. Harriet Greenberg. 1983. pap. 5.95 o.p. (ISBN 0-935572-11-2). Alive Pubns.
United States Water Well Industry. 180p. 100.00 o.p. (ISBN 0-318-17407-3). Natl Water Well.
U. S. Week, Vols. 1-2, No. 1. Dodd, William E., Foundation Staff. 1969. Repr. of 1942 ed. lib. bdg. 79.00x o.p. (ISBN 0-8371-9260-9, US00). Greenwood.
United States Women in Aviation, 1930-1939. Claudia M. Oakes. LC 85-600019. (Smithsonian Studies in Air & Space: No. 6). (Illus.). 73p. (Orig.). 1985. pap. 3.50 o.p. (ISBN 0-318-18865-1, S/N 047-002-00028-1). USGPO.
United States: 1830-1850. Frederick J. Turner. (Illus.). 13.25 o.p. (ISBN 0-8446-1454-8). Peter Smith.
United States 1983. Steve Birnbaum. (Get 'em & Go Travel Guide Ser.). 1982. pap. 11.45 o.p. (ISBN 0-395-32875-6). HM.
United States 1984. Steve Birnbaum. 1983. pap. 11.45 o.p. (ISBN 0-395-34631-2). HM.
Unitive Thinking. Tom McArthur. 192p. (Orig.). 1988. pap. 9.99 o.p. (ISBN 0-85030-621-3, Pub. by Aquarian Pr England). Sterling.
Units of Weight & Measure: International (Metric) & U. S. Customary. L. J. Chisholm. LC 74-20726. (Illus.). 256p. 1975. Repr. of 1967 ed. 40.00x o.p. (ISBN 0-8103-4163-8). Gale.
Unity & Nationalism in Europe since 1945. W. Knapp. 1969. text ed. 11.25 o.p. (ISBN 0-08-013440-8); pap. 5.75 o.p. (ISBN 0-08-013439-4). Pergamon.
Unity & Struggle: Speeches & Writings. Amilcar Cabral. LC 79-2337. 298p. 1979. 16.50 o.s.i. (ISBN 0-85345-510-4); pap. 10.00 o.s.i. (ISBN 0-85345-625-9). Monthly Rev.
Unity of Body & Mind. Lother Bickel. 1960. Philos Lib.
Unity of Law & Morality: A Refutation of Legal Positivism. M. J. Detmold. (International Library of Philosophy). 288p. 1984. 25.00x o.p. (ISBN 0-7102-0030-7). Routledge Chapman & Hall.
Unity of One. George L. Pink. 160p. 1982. 8.00 o.p. (ISBN 0-682-49838-6). Exposition-Phoenix.
Unity of Philosophical Experience. Etienne Gilson. 352p. 1982. pap. 15.00 o.p. (ISBN 0-87061-075-9). Chr Classics.
Unity of Religious Ideals. Hazrat Inayat Khan. (Sufi Message of Hazrat Inayat Khan Ser.: Vol. 9). 280p. 1979. 14.95 o.s.i. (ISBN 90-6325-097-5, Pub. by Servire BV Netherlands). Hunter Hse.
Unity of the Fundamental Interactions. Ed. by Antonino Zichichi. (Subnuclear Ser.: Vol. 19). 760p. 1983. 125.00x o.p. (ISBN 0-306-41242-X, Plenum Press). Plenum Pub.
Unity, Solidarity, Internationalism. B. M. Leibzon. 376p. 1981. 5.00 o.p. (ISBN 0-8285-2150-6, Pub. by Progress Pubs USSR). Imported Pubns.
Univalent Functions & Conformal Mapping. James A. Jenkins. (Ergebnisse der Mathematik und Ihrer Grenzgebiete: Vol. 18). (Illus.). 1965. Repr. 33.70 o.p. (ISBN 0-387-03282-7). Springer-Verlag.
Universal Blessings. Leonard Freschner. 1977. 4.00 o.p. (ISBN 0-682-48970-0). Exposition-Phoenix.
Universal Dictionary of Violin & Bow Makers, Vol. 7: Price Guide & Appendix. rev. ed. W. Henley & C. Woodcock. (Illus.). 1976. 40.00 o.p. (ISBN 0-685-12053-8). E J Brill USA.
Universal Energy & Intelligence. O. D. Bluthardt. LC 85-90997. 1985. 12.50 o.p. (ISBN 0-682-40237-0). Exposition-Phoenix.

Universal Machine: Confessions of a Technological Optimist. Pamela McCorduck. 324p. 1986. pap. 7.95 o.p. (ISBN 0-15-692873-6, Harv). HarBraceJ.

Universal Majesty. Milton L. Zeuner. (Illus.). 80p. 1984. 6.00 o.p. (ISBN 0-682-40159-5, Chart). Exposition-Phoenix.

Universal Primary Education in Nigeria: A Study of Kano State. Mark Bray. 272p. (Orig.). 1981. pap. 17.50x o.p. (ISBN 0-7100-0933-X). Routledge Chapman & Hall.

Universals of Second Language Acquisition. Fred Eckman et al. pap. text ed. 17.25 o.p. (ISBN 0-88377-340-6). Newbury Hse.

Universe. Don Dixon. LC 81-1621. (Illus.). 224p. 1981. 34.00 o.p. (ISBN 0-395-31290-6). HM.

Universe Ahead: Stories of the Future. Sylvia L. Engdahl & Rick Roberson. LC 75-8849. 320p. (gr. 7 up). 1975. 8.95 o.p. (ISBN 0-689-30474-9, Atheneum). Macmillan.

Universe & Civilization. V. Sevastyanov. 240p. 1981. pap. 4.00 o.p. (ISBN 0-8285-2009-7, Pub. by Progress Pubs USSR). Imported Pubns.

Universe: From Flat Earth to Quasar. Isaac Asimov. 1977. pap. 3.95 o.p. (ISBN 0-380-01596-X, 62208-4, Discus). Avon.

Universe Next Door: A Complete Guide to Exploring the Skies & Understanding What You See. Terry Holt. LC 85-10751. (Illus.). 416p. 1985. 24.95 o.p. (ISBN 0-684-18358-7, ScribT). Scribner.

Universe Seventeen. Terry Carr. LC 86-29281. (Science Fiction Ser.). 192p. 1987. 12.95 o.s.i. (ISBN 0-385-23853-3). Doubleday.

Universe Sixteen. Terry Carr. LC 86-9000. (Science Fiction Ser.). 192p. 1986. 12.95 o.s.i. (ISBN 0-385-23389-2). Doubleday.

Universities for a Changing World: The Role of the University in the Later Twentieth Century. Ed. by M. D. Stephens & G. W. Roderick. LC 75-6567. 221p. 1975. 21.95x o.p. (ISBN 0-470-82209-0). Halsted Pr.

University & the Public Interest. A. Barlett Giamatti. LC 81-66030. 1981. 12.95 o.p. (ISBN 0-689-11212-2, Atheneum). Macmillan.

University Education & the Labour Market in the Arab Republic of Egypt. B. C. Sanyal. (Illus.). 277p. 1982. 57.00 o.p. (ISBN 0-08-028123-0); pap. 26.00 o.p. (ISBN 0-08-028122-2). Pergamon.

University Education in Botswana. N. O. Setidisho. 1985. 13.95 o.p. (ISBN 0-533-05939-9). Vantage.

University Housing in Canada. John Bland & Norbert Schoenauer. (Illus.). 1966. pap. 6.00 o.p. (ISBN 0-7735-0040-5, McGill Canada). U of Toronto Pr.

University-Industry Research Interactions. Ed. by Herbert I. Fusfeld & Carmela S. Haklisch. (Technology Policy & Economic Growth Ser.). 200p. 1984. 30.00 o.p. (ISBN 0-08-030987-9). Pergamon.

University Jokes Told with Class. S. C. Lee. (Illus.). 202p. (Orig.). 1983. pap. 4.95 o.p. (ISBN 0-87397-223-6). Strode.

University of California Prototype On-Line Catalog: Preliminary Specifications for the Patron Interface. Katharina Klemperer & Michael Berger. (Working Paper: No. 7). 1980. 5.00 o.p. (ISBN 0-686-87248-7). UCDLA.

University of California Union Catalog-Conversion of Catalog Cards to Machine-Readable Form: Phase I-Bibliographic Characteristics of University of California Cataloging. Katharina Klemperer & Bruce D'Ambrosio. (UCULAP PAper: No. 78-1). 1978. pap. 5.00 o.p. (ISBN 0-914602-91-8). UCDLA.

University of California Union Catalog: Conversion of Catalog Cards to Machine-Readable Form, Phase III-Comparison Study of Existing Data Bases for the Use of Retrospective Conversion. Katharina Klemperer & Kitty M. Shih. (Working Paper: No. 6). 1979. 5.00 o.p. (ISBN 0-686-87247-9). UCDLA.

University of California Union Catalog System Design Overview. Michael Berger et al. (Working Paper: No. 5). 1979. 5.00 o.p. (ISBN 0-686-87245-2). UCDLA.

University of Colorado: 1876-1976. Frederick S. Allen et al. LC 76-20623. 322p. 1976. 12.95 o.p. (ISBN 0-15-193000-7). HarBraceJ.

University of Leiden (Athenae Batavae) 1575-1975. Ed. by R. F. Ekkart. (Illus.). 1975. 20.00 o.s.i. (ISBN 0-685-79104-1). E J Brill USA.

University of Massachusetts: A History of One Hundred Years. Harold W. Cary. Date not set. price not set o.p. U of Mass Pr.

University of Nevada: A Centennial History. James W. Hulse. LC 74-2447. (Illus.). xii, 258p. (Orig.). 1974. 8.00 o.p. (ISBN 0-87417-040-0). U of Nev Pr.

University of Oregon Centennial Lectures, 3 vols. B. Jessup et al. 1959. pap. 2.50 boxed o.p. (ISBN 0-87114-008-X). U of Oreg Bks.

University of Papua New Guinea: A Case Study in the Sociology of Higher Education. V. Lynn Meek. LC 81-14727. (Scholars' Library). (Illus.). 263p. 1982. text ed. 37.50x o.p. (ISBN 0-7022-1638-0). U of Queensland Pr.

University of Texas Medical Branch at Galveston: A Seventy-five Year History. Medical Branch of the University of Texas Staff. (Illus.). 457p. 1967. 22.50x o.p. (ISBN 0-292-73697-5). U of Tex Pr.

University of Wisconsin Medical School: A Chronicle, 1848-1948. Paul F. Clark. (Illus.). 286p. 1967. 19.95 o.p. (ISBN 0-299-04350-9). U of Wis Pr.

University Physics. George Arfken. 1984. text ed. 34.00 o.p. (ISBN 0-12-059860-4); student's solution manual 8.00 o.p. (ISBN 0-12-059867-1); study guide 10.00 o.p. (ISBN 0-12-059868-X); instr's. manual 2.00 o.p. (ISBN 0-12-059865-5); transparency masters 50.00 o.p. (ISBN 0-12-059870-1). Acad Pr.

University Physics: International Edition. George Arfken. 1984. 20.00 o.p. (ISBN 0-12-059858-2). Acad Pr.

University Records & Life in the Middle Ages. Tr. by Lynn Thorndike. (Columbia University Records of Civilization Ser.). 476p. 1975. pap. text ed. 6.95x o.p. (ISBN 0-393-09216-X). Norton.

University Student Services. National Association for Women Deans, Administrators & Counselors. 1975. pap. 3.00 o.p. (ISBN 0-686-10455-2). Natl Assn Women.

University: The Anatomy of Academe. Murray G. Ross. 1979. pap. text ed. 4.95 o.p. (ISBN 0-07-053857-3). McGraw.

Universo, Vida, Intelecto. I. S. Shklovski. 383p. (Span.). 1977. 5.95 o.p. (ISBN 0-8285-1700-2, Pub. by Mir Pubs USSR). Imported Pubns.

UNIX, 2 vols. Bell Labs Staff. 1983. Vol. 1, 208 p. pap. 37.45 o.p. (ISBN 0-03-061742-1); Vol. II, 320 p. pap. 37.45 o.p. (ISBN 0-03-061743-X). HR&W.

UNIX--XENIX Text Processing Reference. Specialized Systems Consultants Inc., Staff. 32p. (Orig.). 1986. pap. 6.00 o.s.i. (ISBN 0-916151-15-8). Specialized Sys.

UNIX Command Summary (BSD 4.2) Specialized Systems Consultants, Inc. Staff. 48p. (Orig.). 1984. pap. 6.00 o.s.i. (ISBN 0-916151-05-0). Specialized Sys.

UNIX-Like Shell for MS-DOS. Allen Holub. 30p. 1986. 29.95 o.p. (ISBN 0-934375-11-9). M&T Pub Inc.

UNIX Operating System. Kaare Christian. LC 82-24811. 318p. 1983. 28.95 o.p. (ISBN 0-471-87542-2); pap. 23.95 o.p. (ISBN 0-471-89052-9). Wiley.

UNIX System V Primer. Mitchell Waite et al. LC 84-51098. 432p. 1984. pap. 19.95 o.p. (ISBN 0-672-22404-6). Sams.

UNIX: User's Handbook. Weber Systems, Inc. Staff. 400p. 1985. pap. 16.95 o.p. (ISBN 0-345-32000-X). Ballantine.

Unjust Dismissal & at Will Employment. Joseph Barbash & John D. Feerick. (Litigation & Administrative Practice Course Handbook Ser.). 343p. 1982. pap. 40.00 o.p. (H4-4885). PLI.

Unjust Dismissal Update 1985: How to Evaluate, Litigate, Settle, & Avoid Claims: A Course Handbook. Jerome B. Kauff & Maureen E. McClain. 787p. 1985. pap. 15.00 o.p. (H4-4984). PLI.

Unjust Dismissal, 1983: Litigating, Settling, & Advocating Claims. Joseph Barbash & Jerome Kauff. Ed. by Practising Law Institute Staff. LC 84-101023. (Litigation & Administrative Practice Ser.: No. 240). 560p. 1983. 40.00 o.p. PLI.

Unjust Dismissal 1984: Evaluating, Litigating, Setting, & Avoiding Claims, Vol. 275. Practising Law Institute Staff. 911p. 1984. pap. 40.00 o.p. (ISBN 0-317-27573-9, #H4-4961). PLI.

Unkept Grave of Tom Turbaville. Brad S. Bowden. 256p. 1986. 12.95 o.p. (ISBN 0-8062-3002-9). Carlton.

Unknown California. Jon Eisen et al. Ed. by Dorszynski. 416p. 1985. 17.95 o.p. (ISBN 0-02-535150-8); pap. 10.95 o.p. (ISBN 0-02-048070-9). Macmillan.

Unknown Masterpiece. Honore De Balzac. Tr. by Michael Neff from Fr. LC 82-73423. (Illus.). 72p. (Orig.). 1983. pap. 4.95 o.p. (ISBN 0-916870-55-3, A Donald S. Ellis Book). Creative Arts Bk.

Unknown Orwell. Peter Stansky & William Abrahams. (Illus.). 288p. 1981. pap. 6.95 o.p. (ISBN 0-586-08178-X, Pub. by Granada England). Academy Chi Pubs.

Unknown Paul: Essays on Luke-Acts & Early Christian History. Jacob Jervell. LC 84-24605. 192p. (Orig.). 1984. pap. 12.95 o.p. (ISBN 0-8066-2119-2, 10-6815, Augsburg). Augsburg Fortress.

Unknown Reality: Vol. One of a Seth Book. Jane Roberts. LC 77-1092. 1980. pap. 8.95 o.p. (ISBN 0-13-938779-X). P-H.

Unknown Reality: Vol. 1 of a Seth Book. Jane Roberts. LC 77-1092. 1977. 9.95 o.p. (ISBN 0-13-938704-8); Vol. II. text ed. 10.95 o.p. (ISBN 0-13-938696-3). P-H.

Unknown Sanctuary. Aime Palliere. 1971. 6.95 o.p. (ISBN 0-8197-0271-4). Bloch.

Unknown Virginia Woolf. Roger Poole. 285p. 1982. pap. text ed. 12.50 o.p. (ISBN 0-391-02669-0). Humanities.

Unknown Warrior. James Leasor. 272p. 1981. 10.95 o.p. HM.

Unknown Woman: A Journey to Self-Discovery. Alice Koller. LC 81-47467. 288p. 1982. 14.95 o.p. (ISBN 0-03-059786-2). H Holt & Co.

Unlearning "Indian" Stereotypes. Council on Interracial Books for Children, Inc. Staff. LC 77-88826. 56p. 1977. pap. 4.95 o.s.i. (ISBN 0-930040-36-8). CIBC.

Unleaving. Jill P. Walsh. (YA) (gr. 7 up). 1986. pap. 1.25 o.p. (ISBN 0-380-01785-7, 59360-2, Flare). Avon.

Unless She Burn. Francine Mezo. 176p. 1981. pap. 2.25 o.p. (ISBN 0-380-76968-9, 76968). Avon.

Unless You Die Young. Gladys H. Carroll. 1977. 8.95 o.p. (ISBN 0-393-08776-X). Norton.

Unlimited Power: The New Science of Personal Achievement. Anthony Robbins. 327p. 1986. 17.45 o.s.i. (ISBN 0-671-61088-0). S&S.

Unlocking Doors to Friendship. C. Lynn Fox & Francine L. Weaver. LC 83-60148. (Creative Teaching Ser.). 150p. (Orig.). 1983. pap. 14.95 o.p. (ISBN 0-935266-14-3, BW6614-3). Jalmar Pr.

Unlocking Nontraditional Careers. 1981. Set. 44.00 o.p. (ISBN 0-318-22281-7, RD215); Communication Skills, by Judith A. Sechler. 14.00 o.p. (ISBN 0-318-22282-5, RD215A); Enhancing Placement, by Judith A. Sechler. 20.00 o.p. (ISBN 0-318-22283-3, RD215B); Parent Awareness, by Vivien Canora. 5.10 o.p. (ISBN 0-318-22284-1, RD215C); Recruitment Skills, by Rodney K. Spain. 5.50 o.p. (ISBN 0-318-22285-X, RD215D). Natl Ctr Res Voc Ed.

Unloved: From the Diary of Perla S. Arnost Lustig. 192p. 1985. 14.95 o.p. (ISBN 0-87795-739-8, Arbor Hse). Morrow.

Unlucky Day at Camp How-Ja-Do. Wayne Carley. LC 72-1075. (Garrard Venture Ser.). (Illus.). 64p. (gr. 1-3). 1972. PLB 6.89 o.s.i. (ISBN 0-8116-6955-6). Garrard.

Unmaking of Palestine. Wasif Abboushi. 230p. 1985. lib. bdg. 27.50x o.p. (ISBN 0-906559-20-0). Lynne Rienner.

Unmanifest Destiny. T. D. Allman. LC 84-4224. 480p. 1984. 19.95 o.p. (ISBN 0-385-27464-5, Dial). Doubleday.

Unmarried Woman. Carol Hill. 1978. pap. 1.75 o.p. (ISBN 0-380-01834-9, 36244-9). Avon.

Unmasking Hidden Money: The Periodic Currency Replacement Plan. Julian B. Shealy. 1973. 5.00 o.p. (ISBN 0-682-47632-3). Exposition-Phoenix.

Unmediated Vision. Geoffrey H. Hartman. LC 66-26472. 1966. pap. 1.85 o.p. (ISBN 0-15-692980-5, H053). HarBraceJ.

Unmet Needs & the Delivery of Care. Paul Chapman. 110p. 1979. pap. text ed. 9.75x o.p. (ISBN 0-7199-0962-7, Pub. by Bedford England). Gower Pub Co.

Unnamable. Samuel Beckett. Tr. by Samuel Beckett from Fr. LC 58-10843. 1958. pap. 3.95 o.p. (ISBN 0-394-17030-X, E117, Ever). Grove.

Unnatural Death. Dorothy L. Sayers. 1978. pap. 2.50 o.p. (ISBN 0-380-00794-0, 68353-9). Avon.

Unnatural Lives: Studies in Australian Fiction about the Convicts from James Tucker to Patrick White. Laurie Hergenhan. LC 83-5799. 210p. 1984. text ed. 19.95x o.p. (ISBN 0-7022-1972-X). U of Queensland Pr.

Unnatural Monopolies: The Case for Deregulating Public Utilities. Ed. by Robert W. Poole, Jr. LC 84-40828. 240p. 1985. 29.00x o.p. (ISBN 0-669-10126-5). Lexington Bks.

Unnecessary Woman. Mollie Vesey. (Orig.). 1980. pap. 2.25 o.p. (ISBN 0-505-51503-2, Pub. by Tower Bks). Dorchester Pub Co.

Unobstructed Universe. Stewart E. White. 1988. pap. 7.95 o.p. (ISBN 0-317-61822-9). Ariel OH.

Unofficial Guide to Disneyland. rev. ed. Bob Schlinger. 160p. 1987. pap. 6.95 o.p. (ISBN 0-13-937658-5). P-H.

Unofficial Guide to Walt Disney & Epcot. rev. ed. Bob Sehlinger & John Finley. 204p. 1987. pap. 6.95 o.p. (ISBN 0-13-937666-6). P-H.

Unofficial History. Field-Marshall W. Slim. LC 74-71. (Illus.). 242p. 1974. Repr. of 1962 ed. lib. bdg. 22.50x o.p. (ISBN 0-8371-7363-9, SLUH). Greenwood.

Unopened Letters & a Virgin Page. limited ed. Walter Mitchell. (Illus.). 40p. 1983. 5.50 o.p. (ISBN 0-682-49968-4). Exposition-Phoenix.

Unoriginal Sinner & the Ice-Cream God. John R. Powers. 336p. 1986. pap. 7.95 o.p. (ISBN 0-8092-4992-8). Contemp Bks.

Unpacking a Bundle. Helen Mack. 1977. 6.50 o.p. (ISBN 0-682-48921-2, Banner). Exposition-Phoenix.

Unpaid Work in the Household: A Review of Economic Evaluation Methods. 3rd ed. Luisella Goldschmidt-Clermont. (Women, Work & Development: No. 1). xi, 137p. 1983. 12.25 o.p. (ISBN 92-2-103085-7). Intl Labour Office.

Unperfect Society: Beyond the New Class. Milovan Djilas. Tr. by Dorian Cooke. LC 70-76568. 1969. 9.95 o.p. (ISBN 0-15-193056-2). HarBraceJ.

Unperfect Society: Beyond the New Class. Milovan Djilas. Tr. by Dorian Cooke. LC 70-76568. 267p. 1970. pap. 5.95 o.s.i. (ISBN 0-15-693125-7, Harv). HarBraceJ.

Unplanned Careers: The Working Lives of Middle-Aged Women. Ed. by Lois B. Shaw. LC 82-47925. 160p. 1982. 29.00x o.p. (ISBN 0-669-05701-0). Lexington Bks.

Unpleasantness at the Bellona Club. Dorothy L. Sayers. 1978. pap. 2.50 o.p. (ISBN 0-380-01597-8, 67132-8). Avon.

Unpopular Patient. Felicity Stockwell. 90p. (Orig.). 1984. pap. 10.00 o.p. (ISBN 0-7099-3322-3, Pub. by Croom Helm Ltd). Routledge Chapman & Hall.

Unpublished Letters of H. M. Stanley. Maurice. (Illus.). 190p. 1957. (ISBN 0-8022-1094-5). Philos Lib.

Unpublished Nietzsche Letters. 1959. (ISBN 0-8022-1220-4). Philos Lib.

Unpuzzling Your Past: A Basic Guide to Genealogy. Emily A. Croom. LC 82-24514. (Illus.). 128p. 1983. pap. 7.95 o.p. (ISBN 0-932620-21-3). Betterway Pubns.

Unquiet Death of Julius & Ethel Rosenberg. Alvin H. Goldstein. LC 75-8336. (Illus.). 96p. 1975. 8.95 o.p. (ISBN 0-88208-052-0); pap. 4.95 o.s.i. (ISBN 0-88208-053-9). Chicago Review.

Unquoted Companies, 1986. ITC Information Group Staff. 750p. 1986. 175.00 o.p. (ISBN 0-943818-99-0, Stockton Pr). Groves Dict Music.

Unraveling Zen's Red Thread: Ikkyu's Controversial Way. Jon Carter Covell & Abbot S. Yamada. LC 80-81040. (Illus.). 341p. 1980. 21.50x o.p. (ISBN 0-930878-19-1). Hollym Intl.

Unreached Peoples, Eighty-One. C. Peter Wagner et al. (Orig.). 1981. pap. 8.95 o.p. (ISBN 0-89191-331-9). Cook.

Unreached Peoples '79. C. Peter Wagner & Edward Dayton. 1978. pap. 7.95 o.p. (ISBN 0-89191-146-4). Cook.

Unreached Peoples '80. Edward Dayton & C. Peter Wagner. LC 79-57522. 1980. pap. 8.95 o.p. (ISBN 0-89191-837-X). Cook.

Unreasonable American. Houston Branch & Wendell Smith. Date not set. 9.95 o.p. (ISBN 0-317-63446-1). Acropolis.

Unreformed Local Government System. Bryan Keith-Lucas. 173p. 1980. 27.00 o.p. (ISBN 0-85664-877-9, Pub. by Croom Helm Ltd). Routledge Chapman & Hall.

Unsafe As Houses: A Guide to Home Safety. Nei Ewart. (Illus.). 160p. 1981. 12.50 o.p. (ISBN 0-7137-1090-X, Pub. by Blandford Pr England). Sterling.

Unsafe Sky. William Norris. 224p. 1982. 14.95 o.p. (ISBN 0-393-01596-3). Norton.

Unsaturated Fatty Acids in Atherosclerosis. 2nd ed. J. Enselme. 1969. 39.00 o.p. (ISBN 0-08-013060-7). Pergamon.

Unsettling of America. Wendell Berry. 1978. pap. 5.95 o.p. (ISBN 0-380-40147-9, 64972-1). Avon.

Unshared Care: Parents & Their Disabled Children. Carline Glendinning. (International Library of Social Policy). 370p. (Orig.). 1983. pap. 14.95x o.p. (ISBN 0-7100-9468-X). Routledge Chapman & Hall.

Unsmiling Gun. Cyril Donson. (Lythway Ser.). 1987. lib. bdg. 16.50 o.p. (ISBN 0-7451-0579-3, Pub. by Chivers Pr UK). G K Hall.

Unsolicited Gift. Jacqueline Simms. 160p. 1983. 13.95 o.p. (ISBN 0-15-193079-1). HarBraceJ.

Unspeakable Acts: The True Story of One Community's Nightmare. Jan Hollingsworth. 320p. 1986. 18.95 o.p. (ISBN 0-86553-163-3). Congdon & Weed.

Unspoken Feelings. Barbara Rose. 1985. 5.95 o.p. (ISBN 0-533-06462-7). Vantage.

Unsportsmanlike Conduct. Ed. by Lynette Stokes & Fawn Duchaine. 114p. (Orig.). 1985. pap. 12.95 o.p. (ISBN 0-920792-52-9, Dist. by University Toronto Press). Eden Pr.

Unstable Angina: Recognition & Management. Ed. by Allan G. Adelman & Bernard S. Goldman. LC 80-13211. 358p. 1981. 36.00 o.p. (ISBN 0-88416-271-0). Year Bk Med.

Unsteady Flow in Open Channels, 3 vols. Ed. by K. Mahmood et al. LC 75-9251. 1975. Set. 56.00 o.s.i.; Vol. 1. (ISBN 0-918334-09-8); Vol. 2. (ISBN 0-918334-10-1); Vol. 3. (ISBN 0-918334-11-X). WRP.

Unstill Life. Benedetti. 1969. 6.95 o.p. (ISBN 0-15-292856-1, HJ). HarBraceJ.

Unsuitable Behavior of America Martin. Lillian Pohlmann. 1976. 6.95 o.s.i. (ISBN 0-664-32603-X, Westminster). Westminster John Knox.

Unsung. Martin Buxbaum. Date not set. Vol. I. pap. 2.50 o.p. (ISBN 0-317-63450-X); Vol. II. pap. 2.50 o.p. (ISBN 0-317-63451-8). Acropolis.

Unsung Heroes of Rock 'n' Roll. Nick Tosches. (Illus.). 240p. 1984. 18.95 o.s.i. (ISBN 0-684-18148-7, ScribT); pap. 8.95 o.s.i. (ISBN 0-684-18149-5). Scribner.

Untainted Saint....Ain't. J. Bardarah McCandless. (Illus.). 1984. pap. 3.00 o.s.i. (ISBN 0-936014-06-7). Dawn Valley.

Untangling the Web of Professional Liability. Edward B. Howell & Richard P. Howell. 1976. 20.00 o.p. (ISBN 0-932056-01-6). Design Prof Ins.

Untangling the Web of Professional Liability. 3rd ed. Edward B. Howell & Richard P. Howell. LC 78-104786. 231p. 1980. 20.00 o.p. (ISBN 0-932056-03-2). Design Prof Ins.

Untersuchungen Uber Die Mhd. Johannes Bethmann. 18.00 o.p. (ISBN 0-384-04083-7); pap. 13.00 o.p. (ISBN 0-685-02222-6). Johnson Repr.

Until Love Is Enough. Laura Parker. 208p. 1983. pap. 2.75 o.p. (ISBN 0-380-83865-6, 83865-6). Avon.

Until Summer's End. Valerie Flournoy. LC 86-8808. (Starlight Romance Ser.). 192p. 1986. 12.95 o.p. (ISBN 0-385-23391-4). Doubleday.

Until the Whistle Blows: A Collection of Games, Dances & Activities for Eight to Twelve Year Olds. J. Tillman Hall et al. LC 76-55311. (Illus.). 1977. 15.00x o.p. (ISBN 0-673-16210-9); pap. 15.95 o.p. (ISBN 0-673-16211-7). Scott F.

Until We Reach the Valley. Ann Irwin & Bernice Reida. (Illus.). 173p. (gr. 4-7). 1979. pap. 1.50 o.p. (ISBN 0-380-43398-2, 43398-2, Camelot). Avon.

Untitled Griffen, Thomas, No. 1. Thomas Griffen. 176p. (Orig.). 1987. pap. 2.95 o.p. (Spectra). Bantam.

Unto Death: "Crusade" & "Late Love" Amos Oz. LC 75-16239. (Helen & Kurt Wolff Bk.). (Illus.). 167p. 1975. 6.95 o.p. (ISBN 0-15-193095-3). HarBraceJ.

Unto You & to Your Children. Grace Wiens. (Illus.). 229p. (Orig.). 1976. pap. 5.95 o.p. (ISBN 0-912315-10-5). Word Aflame.

Untold Story of the Computer Revolution: Bits, Bytes, Bauds & Brains. G. Harry Stine. 1984. 15.95 o.p. (ISBN 0-87795-574-3, Arbor Hse). Morrow.

Untold Tale. Erik C. Haugaard. LC 74-135133. (Illus.). (gr. 5 up). 1971. 4.95 o.p. (ISBN 0-395-12366-6). HM.

Untranslatable Riches see Word Studies in the Greek New Testament, for the English Reader.

Untuning of the Sky: Ideas of Music in English Poetry, 1500-1700. John Hollander. (Illus.). 1970. pap. 4.95x o.p. (ISBN 0-393-00551-8, Norton Lib). Norton.

Untying the Knot: A Guide to Civilized Divorce. Janine Bernard & Harold Hackney. 204p. (Orig.). 1983. pap. 7.95 o.s.i. (ISBN 0-86683-800-7). HarpR.

Unusual Seder. Gershon Kranzler. saddle-stitched 5.00 o.p. (ISBN 0-87559-136-1). Shalom.

Unusual Words. Edwin Radford. (ISBN 0-8022-1302-2). Philos Lib.

Unusual World Coins. Colin Bruce. LC 87-81062. (Illus.). 192p. 1987. pap. 14.95 o.s.i. Krause Pubns.

Unveiling. James T. Draper, Jr. LC 83-25229. 1984. pap. 9.95 o.p. (ISBN 0-8054-1504-1). Broadman.

Unvergangliche Geometrie. H. S. Coxeter. (Science & Civilization Ser.: No. 17). (Illus.). 552p. (Ger.). 1963. 53.35x o.p. (ISBN 0-8176-0071-X). Birkhauser.

Unwanted Symbol: American Foreign Policy, the Cold War, & Korea, 1945-1950. Charles M. Dobbs. LC 81-6261. (Illus.). 250p. 1981. 20.00x o.p. (ISBN 0-87338-258-7). Kent St U Pr.

Unwatched Pot. Paula Franklin. LC 75-79991. (Illus.). 144p. 1975. 9.95 o.p. (ISBN 0-916752-00-3). Longman Trade.

Up Against It. Joe Orton. LC 79-52099. 1979. pap. 4.95 o.p. (ISBN 0-394-17475-5, E736, Ever). Grove.

Up Against the Wall. (Illus.). 1982. 1.00 o.p. (ISBN 0-915478-46-3). Galleries Coll.

Up & down & in & Out. Ed. by Porter Productions. (Fold-a-Bks.). (Illus.). 16p. (ps). 1981. 2.95 o.p. (ISBN 0-448-11773-8, G&D). Putnam Pub Group.

Up & down & Roundabout. Kitty Parsons. (Illus.). (gr. 2-4). 1967. 4.00 o.p. (ISBN 0-8233-0080-3). Golden Quill.

Up & Down Catholic Italy. Mary F. Ingoldsby. LC 84-90277. 165p. 1985. 20.95 o.p. (ISBN 0-533-06318-3). Vantage.

Up & down the Yukon. E. H. Wells. 10p. pap. 1.95 o.p. (ISBN 0-685-41846-4, S7). Shorey.

Up & down Vail Mountain. Sherry Oaks & Raymond Gruenfeld. (Illus.). 1978. 8.50x o.s.i. (ISBN 0-89158-137-5). Westview.

Up & down with Elvis Presley. Marge Crumbaker & Gabe Tucker. (Illus.). 320p. 1981. 12.95 o.p. (ISBN 0-399-12571-X, Putnam). Putnam Pub Group.

Up & Running: Adventures of a Software Entrepreneurs. Ed Sherman. 300p. 1984. pap. 15.95 o.p. (ISBN 0-912677-14-7). Tate Pub.

Up for Grabs: Inquiries into Who Wants What. Daniel J. Chasan. LC 77-23881. 134p. 1977. 9.95 o.p. (ISBN 0-914842-18-8); pap. 5.95 o.p. (ISBN 0-914842-17-X). Madrona Pubs.

Up from Dependency: A New National Public Assistance Strategy, Supplement 3, A Self-Help Catalog. 527p. (Orig.). 1986. pap. 30.00 o.p. (ISBN 0-318-22441-0, S/N 040-000-00510-2). USGPO.

Up from Eden. Ed. by Kendra Crossen. Date not set. pap. 14.95 o.p. (ISBN 0-87773-228-0). Shambhala Pubns.

Up in Sister Bay. Charles Ferry. (Illus.). 224p. (gr. 7 up). 1975. 6.95 o.p. (ISBN 0-395-21409-2). HM.

Up in the Clouds, Gentlemen Please. John Mills. LC 80-22002. (Illus.). 320p. 1981. 14.95 o.p. (ISBN 0-89919-024-3). Ticknor & Fields.

Up in the Park: The Diary of the Wife of the American Ambassador to Ireland, 1977-1981. Elizabeth Shannon. LC 82-73037. (Illus.). 384p. 1983. 17.95 o.p. (ISBN 0-689-11364-1, Atheneum). Macmillan.

Up Sixty-Five Years to Larchmont. Francis J. Weber. 30p. 1970. leatherette 10.00 o.p. (ISBN 0-317-11643-6). Dawsons.

Up the down Staircase. Bel Kaufman. 1986. pap. 1.95 o.p. (ISBN 0-380-01598-6, 48421-8). Avon.

Up the EDP Pyramid: The Complete Job Hunting Manual for Computer Professionals. Jack French. LC 81-11605. 200p. (Orig.). 1981. 21.95 o.p. (ISBN 0-471-08925-7, Pub. by John Wiley). Krieger.

Up the I. R. A. Winifred Doyle. (Illus.). 289p. 1983. 15.50 o.p. (ISBN 0-682-49924-2). Exposition-Phoenix.

Up There. Eric Hill. LC 82-60626. (Eric Hill's Baby Bear Bks). (Illus.). 14p. (ps). 1983. pap. 2.50 o.s.i. (ISBN 0-394-85635-X). Random.

Up to Jerusalem. Richard E. Bauerle & Frederick W. Kemper. 1979. pap. 2.75 o.p. (ISBN 0-570-03795-6, 12-2777). Concordia.

Up to My Neck in Haiku. Liberty Campbell. 76p. 1982. 6.00 o.p. (ISBN 0-682-49922-6). Exposition-Phoenix.

Up to No Good. Rosemary Joyce. (Dream Girls Ser.: No.). (YA) (gr. 7 up). 1987. pap. 2.50 o.p. (ISBN 0-671-62115-7). Archway.

Up to Now. Louis B. Lundborg. 1978. 8.95 o.p. (ISBN 0-393-07525-7). Norton.

Up, up, & Away! The Story of Ballooning. Anabel Dean. LC 79-23427. (Illus.). 192p. 1980. 11.95 o.s.i. (ISBN 0-664-32658-7, Westminster). Westminster John Knox.

Up with America see Faith for All Generations.

Up with Creation! Acts, Facts, Impacts, Vol. 3. Duane T. Gish. LC 78-55612. (Illus.). 1978. pap. 6.95 o.p. (ISBN 0-89051-048-2). Master Bks.

Up with Marriage. James L. Mayfield. LC 79-16194. 1979. pap. 6.00 o.p. (ISBN 0-8309-0246-5). Herald Hse.

Up with Worship. Anne Ortlund. LC 82-15063. (Illus.). 128p. (Orig.). 1975. pap. 2.50 o.p. (5417706). Regal.

Up Your Own Organization. rev. ed. Donald Dible. 1985. text ed. 24.95 o.p. (ISBN 0-8359-8087-1, Reston); pap. 23.95 o.p. (ISBN 0-8359-8086-3). P-H.

Up Your Own Organization! A Handbook on How to Start & Finance a New Business. Donald Dible. 1981. pap. 14.95 o.p. (ISBN 0-8359-8088-X, Reston); text ed. 18.00 case o.p. P-H.

Up Your Spirits: Everything You Wanted to Know About Alcohol but Were Not Quite Sober Enough (or Too Scared) to Ask. Jackson A. Smith. LC 78-53837. 1978. 7.95 o.p. (ISBN 0-689-10917-2, Atheneum). Macmillan.

Update Five: Harrison's Principles of Internal Medicine. Ed. by Robert G. Petersdorf et al. (Illus.). 320p. 1984. text ed. 35.00 o.p. (ISBN 0-07-049616-1). McGraw.

Update on Christian Counseling, 2 vols. Jay E. Adams. (Jay Adams Library). 288p. 1986. pap. 9.95 o.p. (ISBN 0-310-51051-1, 12117P). Zondervan.

Update on State & Federal Regulation of Prepaid Legal Services: January Nineteen Eighty-One. 200p. 1981. 75.00 o.p. (ISBN 0-317-40263-3, 3-006); 4 tapes avail. o.p. Am Prepaid.

Update: Report on the Planet Earth. Joel N. Shurkin. (Franklin Institute Bk.). (Illus.). 154p. (gr. 7-10). 1976. 7.95 o.s.i. (ISBN 0-664-32599-8, Westminster). Westminster John Knox.

Update Seven: Harrison's Principles of Internal Medicine. Ed. by Robert G. Petersdorf et al. 320p. 1986. text ed. 37.50 o.p. (ISBN 0-07-049618-8). McGraw.

Updating Your News Service. Ed. by Nancy S. Raley. 194p. 1980. incl. 8 tapes 65.00 o.p. (ISBN 0-89964-166-0). Coun Adv & Supp Ed.

Upgrading the Supervisor's Labor Relations Skill see Issues in the Public Employee Relations Library: Series 2.

Uphill All the Way: A Documentary History of Women in Australia. Compiled by Kay Daniels & Mary Murnane. (Illus.). 335p. 1980. 32.50x o.p. (ISBN 0-7022-1476-0); pap. text ed. 14.95x o.p. (ISBN 0-7022-1345-4). U of Queensland Pr.

Upholstery Repair & Restoration: A Complete Guide to Fabric & Leather Upholstery Repair. Robert J. McDonald. (Illus.). 1978. 12.50 o.s.i. (ISBN 0-684-15335-1, ScribT). Scribner.

Uplands: New Poems. A. R. Ammons. 1970. pap. 2.95 o.p. (ISBN 0-393-04330-4). Norton.

Upon the Shoulders of Giants: The Shaping of the Industrial West. Richard Hardison. (Illus.). 346p. (Orig.). 1985. lib. bdg. 32.75 o.p. (ISBN 0-8191-4516-5); pap. text ed. 15.25 o.p. (ISBN 0-8191-4517-3). U Pr of Amer.

Upon This Rock: The Life of St. Peter. Walter F. Murphy. LC 87-15896. 520p. 1987. 19.95 o.p. (ISBN 0-02-588270-8). Macmillan.

Upper Atmosphere: Meteorology & Physics. Richard A. Craig. (International Geophysics Ser.: Vol. 8). 1965. 52.95 o.p. (ISBN 0-12-194850-1). Acad Pr.

Upper Brainstem in the Human: Its Nuclear Configuration & Vascular Supply. B. Schlesinger. (Illus.). 320p. 1976. 228.00 o.p. (ISBN 0-387-07497-X). Springer-Verlag.

Upper New England. Peter Andrews et al. LC 79-22906. (Country Inns of America Ser.). (Illus.). 96p. (Orig.). 1980. pap. 9.95 o.p. (ISBN 0-03-043711-3). H Holt & Co.

Upper Northern California Counties Public Schools: How Are They Doing? 1985, Vol. 7. Lillian S. Clancy. (California Public Schools Ser.). 325p. (Orig.). 1984. pap. 23.95 o.p. (ISBN 0-939580-25-X). CA Schl Surveys.

Upper Northern California Counties Public Schools, 1988, Vol. 7. Lillian S. Clancy. (California Public Schools: How Are They Doing? Ser.). 400p. (Orig.). 1988. pap. 25.95 o.p. (ISBN 0-939580-51-9). CA Schl Surveys.

Upper Northern California Counties Public Schools, Vol. 7. Lillian S. Clancy. (California Public Schools Ser.: How Are They Doing?). 400p. (Orig.). 1985. pap. 24.95 o.p. (ISBN 0-939580-34-9). CA Schl Surveys.

Upper Northern California Countries Public Schools, 1987, Vol. 7. Lillian S. Clancy. (California Public Schools: How Are They Doing? Ser.). 400p. (Orig.). 1987. pap. 24.95 o.p. (ISBN 0-939580-43-8). CA Schl Surveys.

Upper Room Disciplines, 1986. Ed. by Tom Page. 382p. (Orig.). 1985. pap. 3.95 o.p. (ISBN 0-8358-0507-7). Upper Room.

Upper Room Disciplines 1987. 382p. (Orig.). 1986. pap. 4.50 o.p. (ISBN 0-8358-0531-X). Upper Room.

Upper Room Disciplines, 1988. 382p. (Orig.). 1987. pap. 4.95 o.p. (ISBN 0-8358-0552-2). Upper Room.

Upper Room to Garden Tomb: Messages for Lent & Easter on the Passion Narrative in Mark. Herbert E. Hohenstein. LC 84-21735. 80p. (Orig.). 1984. pap. 4.95 o.p. (ISBN 0-8066-2117-6, 10-6840, Augsburg). Augsburg Fortress.

Uppsala General Catalogue of Twelve Thousand Nine Hundred & Twenty-One Galaxies. Peter Nilson. 456p. (Orig.). 1973. pap. text ed. 85.00x o.p. (ISBN 91-554-0064-7, Pub. by Almqvist & Wiksell). Coronet Bks.

Uprooted. Charles P. May. LC 75-42255. (gr. 6 up). 1976. 7.95 o.s.i. (ISBN 0-664-32591-2, Westminster). Westminster John Knox.

Uprooting & After. Ed. by C. Zwingmann & M. Pfister-Ammende. LC 70-165795. xii, 364p. 1973. 35.00 o.p. (ISBN 0-387-05516-9). Springer-Verlag.

Uprush of Mayhem. Jack S. Scott. LC 81-21298. (Joan Kahn Bk.). 192p. 1982. 10.95 o.p. (ISBN 0-89919-095-2). Ticknor & Fields.

Ups & Downs. Ralph Warner & Toni Ihara. 1974. pap. 3.45 o.p. (ISBN 0-917316-05-3). Nolo Pr.

Ups & Downs of Jorie Jenkins. Betty Bates. (gr. 4-6). 1981. pap. 1.75 o.p. (ISBN 0-671-29950-6). Archway.

Ups & Downs of Marvin. Barbara S. Hazen. LC 76-4471. (Illus.). 40p. (gr. k-2). 1976. 5.95 o.p. (ISBN 0-689-30539-7, Atheneum). Macmillan.

Upset: Australia Wins the America's Cup. Michael Levitt & Barbara Lloyd. LC 83-21910. (Illus.). 240p. (Orig.). 1983. pap. 8.95 o.p. (ISBN 0-89480-674-2, 674). Workman Pub.

Upside-Down Cat. Elizabeth Parsons. LC 80-13507. (Illus.). 48p. (gr. 3-6). 1981. 9.95 o.s.i. (ISBN 0-689-50187-0, M K McElderry). Macmillan.

Upside Down Eddie. Daniel Schantz. (Adventures with Eddie Ser.). 96p. (gr. 4-9). 1985. 2.50 o.p. (ISBN 0-87239-921-4, 2851). Standard Pub.

Upside Down Tree. Hardy Kruger. 320p. 1977. 8.95 o.p. (ISBN 0-8065-0514-1, Pub. by Citadel Pr). Carol Pub Group.

Upstart. Piers P. Read. 352p. 1980. pap. 2.25 o.p. (ISBN 0-380-49023-4, 49023-4). Avon.

Upton Sinclair's: A Monthly Magazine, Nos. 1-10. 1970. Repr. of 1919 ed. lib. bdg. 22.00x o.p. (ISBN 0-8371-9256-0, UM00). Greenwood.

Upton Sinclair's "The Jungle" The Lost First Edition. Upton Sinclair. Ed. & intro. by Gene DeGruson. LC 88-1920. 320p. 1988. 21.95 o.p. (ISBN 0-918518-64-4, St Luke TN). Peachtree Pubs.

Uptown Love. Frances H. Grimes. (Sweet Savage Sophomore Year Ser.: No. 3). 160p. (Orig.). (YA) 1989. pap. 2.95 o.p. (ISBN 1-55802-079-9). Lynx Bks.

Upward Mobility. Catalyst Editors. LC 81-4967. 312p. 1982. 15.95 o.p. (ISBN 0-03-056163-9). H Holt & Co.

Upwelling Ecosystems. Ed. by R. Boje & M. Tomczak. (Illus.). 1978. pap. 34.00 o.p. (ISBN 0-387-08822-9). Springer-Verlag.

Ur 'of the Chaldees' A Revised & Updated Edition of Sir Leonard Woolley's Excavations at Ur by P. R. S. Moorey. Leonard Woolley. 1982. 29.95 o.p. (ISBN 0-8014-1518-7). Cornell U Pr.

Uranium Exploration in Athabaska Basin. Eion M. Cameron. 320p. 1983. pap. text ed. 49.95x o.p. (ISBN 0-660-11508-5, Pub. by Minister Supplies Canada). Gower Pub Co.

Uranium Fuel Supply: Proceedings, American Nuclear Society Executive Conference, Monterey CA, 23-26 January 1977. 456p. 34.00 o.p. (ISBN 0-89448-302-1, 650003). Am Nuclear Soc.

Uranium Nineteen Eighty. Emanuel Gordon. (Technical & Economic Reports: Nuclear Fuel Cycle). 61p. 1981. write for info. o.p. US Coun Energy Awareness.

Uranium, Nonproliferation & Energy Security. Steven J. Warnecke. (Atlantic Papers: No. 37). 121p. 1980. 6.50x o.s.i. (ISBN 0-916672-77-8, Pub. by Allanheld). Rowman.

Uranium Resources - an International Assessment: Proceedings of the American Nuclear Society Topical Symposium, Las Vegas, Sept., 1978. American Nuclear Society Staff. 445p. softcover 29.00 o.p. (ISBN 0-317-33084-5, 700034). Am Nuclear Soc.

Uranus. Marcel Ayme. (Coll. Soleil). 1962. 13.50 o.p. (ISBN 0-685-11611-5). Schoenhof.

Urban Accident Patterns, 5 reports. (Transportation Research Record Ser.). 56p. 1975. 2.60 o.p. (ISBN 0-309-02393-9). Transport Res Bd.

Urban Alternatives: Proceedings of the USERC Environmental Resources & Urban Development Workshop. Ed. by Edward A. Wolff. LC 76-16432. 1976. pap. 20.00 o.p. (ISBN 0-08-021171-2). Pergamon.

Urban America in the Eighties: Perspectives & Prospects. President's Commission for a National Agenda: Panel on Policies & Prospects for Metropolitan & Nonmetropolitan America. Ed. by Donald Hicks. 127p. (Orig.). 1981. pap. 6.95 o.p. (ISBN 0-87855-883-7). Transaction Pubs.

Urban & Regional Economics: A Guide to Information Sources. Ed. by Jean A. Shackelford. LC 74-11556. (Economics Information Guide Ser.: Vol. 14). 190p. 1980. 68.00x o.p. (ISBN 0-8103-1303-0). Gale.

Urban & Regional Transformation of Britain. Ed. by J. B. Goddard & A. G. Champion. 1983. pap. 17.95x o.p. (ISBN 0-416-30900-3, NO. 3924). Routledge Chapman & Hall.

Urban Challenge. Ed. by Larry L. Rose & C. Kirk Hadaway. LC 82-71026. 1982. pap. 5.95 o.p. (ISBN 0-8054-6238-4). Broadman.

Urban Conservation & Historic Buildings. Royal Borough staff. 1987. pap. 49.95 o.p. (ISBN 0-85139-686-0). Van Nos Reinhold.

Urban Dog: How to Understand, Enjoy, & Care for a Dog in the City. Patricia Curtis. 256p. (Orig.). 1986. pap. 8.95 o.p. (ISBN 0-553-34270-3). Bantam.

Urban Economic Development: Suburbanization, Minority Opportunity, & the Condition of the Central City. Bennet Harrison. 1974. lib. bdg. 14.50 o.p. (ISBN 0-87766-098-0); pap. text ed. 8.00 o.p. (ISBN 0-87766-102-2). Urban Inst.

Urban Economics. Werner Z. Hirsch. (Illus.). 496p. 1984. text ed. 24.95 o.p. Macmillan.

Urban Economics. Werner Z. Hirsch. 1983. text ed. write for info. o.p. (ISBN 0-02-354600-X). Macmillan.

Urban Economics. 3rd ed. Edwin S. Mills & Bruce Hamilton. 1984. text ed. write for info. o.p. (ISBN 0-673-15839-X). Scott F.

Urban Economics: Monographs. Mary Vance. (Public Administration Ser.: P 1739). 35p. 1985. 5.25 o.p. (ISBN 0-89028-519-5). Vance Biblios.

Urban Ecosystem: A Holistic Approach. Ed. by F. Stearns & T. Montag. LC 75-1001. (Community Development Ser: Vol. 14). 217p. 1982. 58.95 o.p. (ISBN 0-87933-163-1). Van Nos Reinhold.

Urban Education in Social Perspectives. Albert Lightfoot. 1978. pap. 19.50 o.p. (ISBN 0-395-30660-4). HM.

Urban Experience. Claude S. Fischer. 309p. (Orig.). 1976. pap. text ed. 12.95 o.p. (ISBN 0-15-593497-X, HC). HarBraceJ.

Urban Fields. S. Angel & G. M. Hyman. 180p. 1976. 20.50x o.p. (ISBN 0-85086-052-0, NO. 2948, Pub. by Pion England). Routledge Chapman & Hall.

Urban Finance Policy & Administration: A Guide to Information Sources. Ed. by Jerry McCaffery & John Mikesell. (Urban Studies Information Guide Ser.: Vol. 12). 240p. 1980. 68.00x o.p. (ISBN 0-8103-1464-9). Gale.

Urban Geography. 2nd ed. Ray M. Northam. LC 78-12335. 512p. 1979. 37.50 o.p. (ISBN 0-471-03292-1). Wiley.

Urban Geography: A First Approach. David T. Herbert & Colin J. Thomas. LC 81-16041. 508p. 1982. 73.95 o.p. (ISBN 0-471-10137-0, Pub. by Wiley-Interscience); pap. 37.00 o.p. (ISBN 0-471-10138-9). Wiley.

Urban Growth & Local Taxes in Less Developed Countries. Roy Bahl et al. LC 83-16427. (Papers of the East-West Population Institute: No. 89). vi, 33p. (Orig.). 1983. pap. text ed. 1.25 o.p. (ISBN 0-86638-050-7). EW Ctr HI.

Urban Growth Dynamics: In a Regional Cluster of Cities. Ed. by F. Stuart Chapin, Jr. & Shirley F. Weiss. LC 76-54709. 496p. 1977. Repr. of 1962 ed. 26.50 o.p. (ISBN 0-88275-486-6). Krieger.

Urban Housing--Public & Private: A Guide to Information Sources. Ed. by John E. Rouse, Jr. LC 79-100279. (Urban Studies Information Guide Ser.: Vol. 5). 336p. 1978. 68.00x o.p. (ISBN 0-8103-1398-7). Gale.

Urban Housing Markets: Recent Directions in Research & Policy. Ed. by Larry S. Bourne & John R. Hitchcock. (Orig.). 1979. pap. 17.50x o.p. (ISBN 0-8020-2339-8). U of Toronto Pr.

Urban Housing Policy. William G. Grigsby & Louis Rosenburg. 350p. 1975. 15.00x o.p. (ISBN 0-87855-117-4). Transaction Pubs.

Urban Indicators, Metropolitan Evolution & Public Policy. James W. Hughes. 232p. 1973. pap. (ISBN 0-87855-560-9). Transaction Pubs.

Urban Informal Sector: Critical Perspectives. Ray Bromley. (Illus.). 1979. 53.00 o.p. (ISBN 0-08-024270-7). Pergamon.

Urban Informal Sector in an Urban Economy: A Study in Ahmedabad. T. S. Papola. 156p. 1981. text ed. 15.95x o.p. (ISBN 0-7069-1133-4, Pub by Vikas India). Advent NY.

Urban Informal Sector in Developing Countries: Employment, Poverty & Environment. International Labour Office Staff. Ed. by S. V. Sethuraman. xii, 225p. (Orig.). 1981. 19.95 o.p. (ISBN 92-2-102590-X); pap. 14.25 o.p. (ISBN 92-2-102591-8). Intl Labour Office.

Urban Land Economics. Richard U. Ratcliff. LC 71-135608. (Illus.). 533p. 1972. Repr. of 1949 ed. lib. bdg. 34.25x o.p. (ISBN 0-8371-5195-3, RAUL). Greenwood.

Urban Land Nexus & the State. A. J. Scott. 256p. 1980. 24.00x o.p. (ISBN 0-85086-079-2, NO. 6390, Pub. by Pion England). Routledge Chapman & Hall.

Urban Landscape: Historical Development & Management. Ed. by J. Whitehand. LC 81-68018. (Institute of British Geographer Special Publication: No. 13). 1982. 36.00 o.p. (ISBN 0-12-747020-4). Acad Pr.

Urban Law: A Guide to Information Sources. Ed. by Thomas P. Murphy & Robert D. Kline. (Urban Studies Information Guide: Vol. 11). 352p. 1980. 68.00x o.p. (ISBN 0-8103-1409-6). Gale.

Urban Liberalism & Progressive Reform. John D. Buenker. 1978. pap. 4.95x o.p. (ISBN 0-393-00880-0, N880, Norton Lib). Norton.

Urban Life Styles. Natalie Allon. 250p. 1979. pap. text ed. write for info. o.p. (ISBN 0-697-07558-3). Wm C Brown.

Urban Mass Transportation: A Dozen Years of Federal Policy. George M. Smerk. LC 73-21242. 408p. 1974. 25.00x o.p. (ISBN 0-253-36170-2). Ind U Pr.

Urban Negro Worker in the United States, 1925-1936, 2 Vols. in 1. United States Office of Adviser on Negro Affairs Staff. LC 79-82095. (Illus.). 1938-39. Repr. 28.00 o.p. (ISBN 0-8371-3209-6, UNW&). Greenwood.

Urban Neighborhoods, Networks & Families. Peggy Wireman. LC 80-9016. 224p. 1984. 29.00x o.p. (ISBN 0-669-04503-9). Lexington Bks.

Urban Networks in Ch'ing China & Tokugawa Japan. Gilbert Rozman. LC 72-1986. 400p. 1973. 45.00x o.p. (ISBN 0-691-03082-0). Princeton U Pr.

Urban Open Spaces. Ed. by Lisa Taylor. (Illus.). 128p. 1980. pap. 9.95 o.p. (ISBN 0-8478-0304-X). Rizzoli Intl.

Urban Planning: A Guide to Information Sources. J. Alexander et al. LC 78-13462. (Urban Studies Information Guide Ser.: Vol. 2). 184p. 1979. 68.00x o.p. (ISBN 0-8103-1399-5). Gale.

Urban Planning Analysis: Methods & Models. Donald A. Krueckeberg & Arthur L. Silvers. LC 74-7087. 486p. 1974. (ISBN 0-471-50858-6). Wiley.

Urban Planning in a Capitalist Society. Gwyneth Kirk. 224p. 1980. 27.00 o.p. (ISBN 0-85664-929-5, Pub. by Croom Helm Ltd); pap. 11.95 o.p. (ISBN 0-7099-0302-2). Routledge Chapman & Hall.

Urban Planning in Stockholm: Journal Articles & Monographs Published since 1950. Mary Vance. (Architecture Ser.: A 1425). 10p. 1985. 2.00 o.p. (ISBN 0-89028-475-X). Vance Biblios.

Urban Planning Methods: Research & Policy Analysis. Ian Bracken. LC 81-13013. 420p. 1981. 41.00x o.p. (ISBN 0-416-74860-0, NO. 3564); pap. 17.95x o.p. (ISBN 0-416-74870-8, NO. 3563). Routledge Chapman & Hall.

Urban Policy: A Bibliography of Material Published 1980-1984. Mary Vance. (Public Administration Ser.: P 1730). 19p. 1985. 3.00 o.p. (ISBN 0-89028-500-4). Vance Biblios.

Urban Policy: A Guide to Information Sources. Ed. by Dennis Palumbo & George A. Taylor. LC 78-25957. (Urban Studies Information Guide Ser.: Vol. 6). 216p. 1979. 68.00x o.p. (ISBN 0-8103-1428-2). Gale.

Urban Policy & the Exterior City: Federal, State & Corporate Policies. H. V. Savitch. (Policy Studies). 1979. 95.00 o.p. (ISBN 0-08-023390-2). Pergamon.

Urban Policy Game: A Simulation of Urban Politics. Thomas A. Henderson & John L. Foster. LC 78-17118. 137p. 1978. pap. text ed. write for info. o.p. (ISBN 0-02-353660-8); tchr's. manual avail. o.p. (ISBN 0-02-353690-X). Macmillan.

Urban Problems & Prospects. 2nd ed. Anthony Downs. 1976. pap. 20.95 o.p. (ISBN 0-395-30590-X). HM.

Urban Problems & the Private Sector. Saul Wallen. 14p. 1968. 1.00 o.p. (ISBN 0-89215-053-X). U Cal LA Indus Rel.

Urban Problems in Sociological Perspective. Thomas Shannon. 225p. 1983. pap. text ed. 10.00 o.p. (ISBN 0-394-33423-X, RanC). Random.

Urban Prospect. Lewis Mumford. LC 68-20631. 257p. 1969. pap. 4.95 o.s.i. (ISBN 0-15-693201-6, Harv). HarBraceJ.

Urban Racial Violence, in the Twentieth Century. 2nd ed. Joseph Boskin. 1976. pap. write for info. o.p. (ISBN 0-02-470890-9). Macmillan.

Urban Rail in America: An Exploration of Criteria for Fixed-Guideway Transit. Boris S. Pushkarev et al. LC 81-47293. (Illus.). 320p. 1982. 27.50x o.p. (ISBN 0-253-37555-X). Ind U Pr.

Urban Real Estate Game: Playing Monopoly With Real Money. Joe Feagin. 252p. 1983. 14.95 o.p. (ISBN 0-13-937797-2); pap. 8.95 o.p. (ISBN 0-13-937789-1). P-H.

Urban, Regional, & State Applications: Plus a Special Section on Cadastral Systems, Vol. 3. Laboratory for Computer Graphics & Spatial Analysis, Harvard University Graduate School of Design Staff. (Harvard Library of Computer Graphics, Mapping Collection). (Illus.). 195p. 1979. pap. 15.95 o.p. (ISBN 0-8122-1183-9). U of Pa Pr.

Urban, Regional, & State Government Applications of Computer Mapping: Plus Computer Mapping in Education, Vol. 11. Laboratory for Computer Graphics & Spatial Analysis, Harvard University Graduate School of Design Staff. (Harvard Library of Computer Graphics, Mapping Collection). (Illus.). 232p. 1980. pap. 15.95 o.p. (ISBN 0-8122-1191-X). U of Pa Pr.

Urban Renewal in Liverpool. David M. Muchnick. 120p. 1970. pap. text ed. 6.25x o.p. (ISBN 0-686-70861-X, Pub. by Bedford England). Gower Pub Co.

Urban Retailing System: Location, Cognition & Behaviour. Robert B. Potter. 264p. 1982. text ed. 37.00x o.p. (ISBN 0-566-00458-5). Gower Pub Co.

Urban Service Provision in Australia: Institutional Process & Geographic Outcome. Ed. by Colin Adrian. 208p. 1985. 27.50 o.p. (ISBN 0-949614-04-1, Pub. by Croom Helm Ltd). Routledge Chapman & Hall.

Urban Social Research: Problems & Progress. Ed. by Valdo Pons & Ray Francis. (Sociological Review Monograph: No. 30). 1983. pap. 15.95x o.p. (ISBN 0-7100-9471-X). Routledge Chapman & Hall.

Urban Society. 3rd ed. Jeffrey M. Elliot. LC 82-646006. (Annual Editions Ser.). (Illus.). 256p. 1987. pap. text ed. 9.95x o.p. (ISBN 0-87967-618-3). Dushkin Pub.

Urban Sociology. abr ed. Ed. by Ernest W. Burgess & Donald J. Bogue. 1967. pap. text ed. 3.95x o.s.i. (ISBN 0-226-08056-0, P253, Phoen). U of Chicago Pr.

Urban Sociology. E. W. Butler. (Selected Readings Ser.). 1970. pap. text ed. 9.95x o.p. (ISBN 0-8290-1200-1). Irvington.

Urban Spatial Traffic Patterns. Rodney Vaughan. 318p. 1987. 67.50 o.p. (ISBN 0-85086-122-5, 1162, Pub. by Pion England). Routledge Chapman & Hall.

Urban Stress: Experiments on Noise & Social Stressors. David C. Glass & Jerome E. Singer. LC 78-182640. (Social Psychology Ser.). 1972. 22.00 o.p. (ISBN 0-12-286050-0). Acad Pr.

Urban Structure & Victimization. David L. Decker & David Shichor. LC 79-1865. 128p. 1982. 17.50x o.p. (ISBN 0-669-02951-3). Lexington Bks.

Urban System Operation & Freeways. (Transportation Research Record Ser.). 115p. 1978. 6.40 o.p. (ISBN 0-309-02827-2). Transport Res Bd.

Urban Systems: Contemporary Approaches to Modelling. Ed. by C. S. Bertuglia et al. 688p. 1987. 125.00 o.p. (ISBN 0-7099-3971-X, Pub. by Croom Helm UK). Routledge Chapman & Hall.

Urban Systems Operations. (Transportation Research Record Ser.). 116p. 1979. 6.20 o.p. (ISBN 0-309-02972-4). Transport Res Bd.

Urban Transportation Planning, Evaluation, & Analysis. (Transportation Research Record Ser.). 53p. 1979. 3.40 o.p. (ISBN 0-309-02953-8). Transport Res Bd.

Urban Transportation System: Politics & Policy Innovation. Alan A. Altshuler et al. 1979. text ed. 38.50x o.p. (ISBN 0-262-01055-0); pap. 17.50x o.p. (ISBN 0-262-51023-5). MIT Pr.

Urban Unemployment in Developing Countries: The Nature of the Problem & Proposals for Its Solution. 2nd ed. Paul Bairoch. 1976. 8.75 o.p. (ISBN 92-2-100998-X). Intl Labour Office.

Urban Watershed Management: Flooding & Water Quality. Vanden Bosch et al. Ed. by Philip B. Bedient & Peter G. Rowe. (Rice University Studies: Vol. 65, No. 1). 205p. 1979. pap. 10.00x o.p. (ISBN 0-89263-240-2). Rice Univ.

Urbanisation in the Developing World. David Drakakis-Smith. 272p. 1986. 39.50 o.p. (ISBN 0-7099-0884-9, Pub. by Croom Helm Ltd). Routledge Chapman & Hall.

Urbanization at Teotihuacan, Mexico, Vol. 1, Pts. 1 & 2: The Teotihuacan Map. Ed. by Rene Millon. LC 72-7588. (Illus.). 333p. 1973. 125.00x o.p. (ISBN 0-292-78501-1). U of Tex Pr.

Urbanization, Education, & Marriage Patterns: Four Cases from Asia. Peter C. Smith & Mehtab S. Karim. LC 80-28099. (Papers of the East-West Population Institute: No. 70). vii, 51p. (Orig.). 1980. pap. text ed. 1.50 o.p. (ISBN 0-86638-020-5). EW Ctr HI.

Urbanization: IGU Congress, Moscow, Proceedings, Pt. 3. Ed. by Yuri Medvedkov. 1977. pap. 23.00 o.p. (ISBN 0-08-021324-3). Pergamon.

Urbanization in Australia. C. B. Scheduin & J. W. McCarty. 127p. 1975. pap. 16.00x o.p. (ISBN 0-424-06940-7, Pub. by Sydney U Pr). Intl Spec Bk.

Urbanization in Kenya: A Bottom-Up Approach to Development Planning. R. A. Obudho. LC 82-25099. (Illus.). 426p. (Orig.). 1983. PLB 35.50 o.p. (ISBN 0-8191-3042-7); pap. text ed. 18.75 o.p. (ISBN 0-8191-3043-5). U Pr of Amer.

Urbanization of Modern America: A Brief History. Zane L. Miller. (History of the U. S. Ser.). 241p. 1973. pap. text ed. 9.50 o.p. (ISBN 0-15-593656-5, HC). HarBraceJ.

Urbanization, Water Pollution & Public Policy. George Carey et al. 214p. 1972. pap. (ISBN 0-87855-553-6). Transaction Pubs.

Urdu Manuscripts: A Descriptive Bibliography. Ed. by H. K. Kaul. 1977. 12.50x o.p. (ISBN 0-88386-401-0). South Asia Bks.

Urea Cycle Diseases. Ed. by A. Lowenthal & A. Mori. LC 82-12302. (Advances in Experimental Medicine & Biology Ser.: Vol. 153). 542p. 1982. 85.00x o.p. (ISBN 0-306-41037-0, Plenum Pr). Plenum Pub.

Urgent Copy. Anthony Burgess. LC 69-18477. 1969. 6.95 o.p. (ISBN 0-393-04270-7). Norton.

Urien's Voyage. Andre Gide. Tr. by Wade Baskin. LC 63-19701. 94p. 1964. (ISBN 0-8022-0589-5). Philos Lib.

Urinalysis & Body Fluids. Susan K. Strasinger. LC 84-23824. (Illus.). 217p. 1985. pap. text ed. 26.95 o.p. (ISBN 0-8036-8101-1). Davis Co.

Urinary Cyclic Amp Depressants. (Landmark Ser.). 1979. 24.50x o.p. (ISBN 0-8422-4118-3). Irvington.

Urinary Infections. Bernard Francois & Paul Perrin. 1983. text ed. 79.95 o.p. (ISBN 0-407-00257-X). Butterworth.

Urinary Tract & the Catheter. N. Slade & W. A. Gillespie. 126p. 1985. pap. 32.00 o.p. (ISBN 0-471-90642-5). Wiley.

Urinary Tract Infection: Proceedings of the Symposium, London, England, Sept. 23-24, 1974. Urinary Tract Infection Symposium Staff. Ed. by A. W. Asscher & W. Brumfit. (Journal Kidney International: No. 4). iii, 147p. 1975. pap. 32.00 o.p. (ISBN 0-387-90147-7). Springer-Verlag.

Urine Therapy: Self-Healing Through Intrinsic Medicine. John F. O'Quinn. 40p. 1980. pap. text ed. 6.95 o.s.i. (ISBN 0-9609802-1-0). Life Science.

Urodynamics. Ed. by W. Lutzeyer & H. Melchior. LC 73-81776. (Illus.). 335p. 1973. 82.60 o.p. (ISBN 0-387-06337-4). Springer-Verlag.

Urodynamics: Hydrodynamics of the Ureter & Renal Pelvis. Ed. by Saul Boyarsky. 1971. 101.00 o.p. (ISBN 0-12-121250-5). Acad Pr.

Urological System. 2nd ed. C. A. Charlton. (Penguin Library of Nursing Ser.). (Illus.). 1983. pap. text ed. 15.00 o.p. (ISBN 0-443-02606-8). Churchill.

Urology for Nurses. 3rd ed. Mitchell. 380p. 1980. pap. 16.00 o.p. (ISBN 0-7236-0528-9, Pub. by John Wright UK). Butterworth.

Uroradiology. Sherwood & Talner. (Illus.). 360p. 1980. 88.00 o.p. (ISBN 0-632-00493-2, B-4581-6). Mosby.

Ursula K. LeGuin. Ed. by Joseph D. Olander & Martin H. Greenberg. LC 77-76722. (Writers of the 21st Century Ser.). 1979. 12.95 o.s.i. (ISBN 0-8008-7943-0); pap. 5.95 o.s.i. (ISBN 0-8008-7942-2). Taplinger.

Urticarias. Ed. by R. H. Champion et al. LC 85-374. (Illus.). 237p. 1985. text ed. 49.95 o.p. (ISBN 0-443-03243-2). Churchill.

Uruguay's Tupamaros: The Urban Guerilla. Arturo C. Porzecanski. LC 73-13340. (Special Studies in International Politics & Government). 1973. 34.00x o.p. (ISBN 0-275-28802-1). Irvington.

Usborne Guide to Soccer: Skills, Tricks & Tactics. S. Inglis. (Practical Guides Ser.). (Illus.). 32p. (gr. 6 up). 1981. 7.95 o.p. (ISBN 0-86020-545-2); PLB 12.96 o.p. (ISBN 0-88110-029-3); pap. 4.95 o.p. (ISBN 0-86020-544-4). EDC.

Use & Abuse, Repr. Of 1849 Ed. Felicia Skene. Ed. by Robert L. Wolff. Bd. with Hidden Depths. Repr. of 1866 ed. LC 75-474. (Victorian Fiction Ser.). 1976. lib. bdg. 73.00 o.p. (ISBN 0-8240-1552-5). Garland Pub.

Use & Abuse of Diagnostic Services: The Canadian Experience. Olding C. MacIntosh. 1982. text ed. 19.50 o.p. (ISBN 0-88831-130-3). Eden Pr.

Use & Abuse of History or How the Past Is Taught. Marc Ferro. 256p. 1984. 28.95x o.p. (ISBN 0-7100-9658-5). Routledge Chapman & Hall.

Use & Abuse of Social Science: Behavioral Science & National Policy Making. Ed. by Irving L. Horowitz. 350p. 1971. pap. (ISBN 0-87855-501-3). Transaction Pubs.

Use & Abuse of Social Science: Behavioral Science & National Policy Making. Ed. by Irving L. Horowitz. 350p. 1971. (ISBN 0-87855-001-1). Transaction Pubs.

Use & Abuse of the Bible. Dennis Nineham. LC 76-15690. (Library of Philosophy & Religion Ser.). (Illus.). 295p. 1976. text ed. 28.50x o.p. (ISBN 0-06-495178-2). B&N Imports.

Use & Misuse of Earth's Surface. Ed. by Brian J. Skinner. LC 81-6043. (Earth & Its Inhabitants: Selected Readings from American Scientist Ser.). (Illus.). 216p. (Orig.). 1981. pap. 11.95x o.p. (ISBN 0-913232-95-5). W Kaufmann.

Use & Significance of Pesticides in the Environment. F. L. McEwen & G. R. Stephenson. LC 78-23368. 538p. 1979. 52.50 o.p. (ISBN 0-471-03903-9). Wiley.

Use Even Me. George Barrington. 1983. pap. 10.00 o.p. (ISBN 0-8309-0375-5). Herald Hse.

Use-It-Up Cookbook. Lois Willand. 1979. Encore ed. 3.95 o.p. (ISBN 0-684-17580-0, ScribT). Scribner.

Use of Analog & Digital Computers in Hydrology: Proceedings of the Tucson Symposium, 2 Vols. (Studies & Reports in Hydrology: No. 1). (Illus.). 1969. Set. 22.50 o.p. (ISBN 92-3-000734-X, U711, UNESCO). Vol. 1, 344p. Vol. 2, 411p. UNIPUB.

Use of Antimicrobial Drugs in Office Based Practice: United States, 1980-1981. Gloria J. Gardocki. (Vital & Health Statistics Data from the National Health Survey Series 13: No. 85). 59p. 1986. pap. 3.00 o.p. (S/N 017-022-00955-2). USGPO.

Use of Chemicals in Food Production, Processing, Storage & Distribution. National Research Council, Committee on Food Protection. 40p. 1973. pap. 3.75 o.p. (ISBN 0-309-02136-7). Natl Acad Pr.

Use of Color in Interiors. 2nd ed. Albert O. Halse. (Illus.). 1978. text ed. 56.50 o.p. (ISBN 0-07-025624-1). McGraw.

Use of Computers in Literature Searching & Related Reference Activities in Libraries. Clinic on Library Applications of Data Processing, Proceedings, 1975. Ed. by F. W. Lancaster. LC 76-1790. 1976. 8.00 o.p. (ISBN 0-87845-043-2). U of Ill Lib Info Sci.

Use of Documentary Evidence in the Study of Roman Imperial History. B. W. Jones & R. D. Milns. (Sources in Ancient History Ser.). (Illus.). xvii, 201p. (Orig.). 1984. pap. text ed. 16.95x o.p. (ISBN 0-424-00105-5, Pub. by Sydney U Pr). Intl Spec Bk.

Use of Electronic Information Technologies for Non-School Learning in American Households: Report of Findings from the 1985 Home Information Technology Study (HITS), Contractor Report. John A. Riccobono. 129p. 1986. pap. 7.00 o.p. (ISBN 0-318-21622-1, S/N 065-000-00262-1). USGPO.

Use of Expert Witnesses. Massachusetts Continuing Legal Education-New England Law Institute, Inc. Staff. LC 84-61760. (Illus.). 436p. write for info. o.p. Mass CLE.

Use of FAO Specifications for Plant Protection Products. 2nd, Rev. ed. (Plant Production & Protection Papers: No. 13). 92p. (Eng., Fr. & Span.). 1979. pap. 7.50 o.p. (ISBN 92-5-100704-7, F1597, FAO). UNIPUB.

Use of First & Second Languages in Primary Education: Selected Case Studies. Nadine Dutcher. (World Bank Staff Working Paper: No. 504). iii, 62p. (Eng. & Span.). 1982. pap. 5.00 Eng. Ed. o.p. (ISBN 0-686-39727-4, WP-0504); pap. Span. Ed. avail. o.p. World Bank.

Use of Handbook Tables & Formulas. 22nd ed. John M. Amiss & Franklin D. Jones. Ed. by Henry H. Ryffel. LC 75-10949. (Illus.). 224p. 1984. 9.95x o.p. (ISBN 0-8311-1156-9). Indus Pr.

Use of Human Cells for the Evaluation of Risk from Physical & Chemical Agents. Ed. by Amleto Castellani. LC 83-2429. (NATO ASI Series, Series A, Life Sciences: Vol. 60). 822p. 1983. 129.50x o.p. (ISBN 0-306-41274-8, Plenum Pr). Plenum Pub.

Use of Instructional Materials. Amo DeBernardis. LC 60-11477. (Illus., Orig.). 1960. pap. text ed. 3.95x o.p. (ISBN 0-89197-461-X). Irvington.

Use of Mercury & Alternative Compounds As Seed Dressings: Report of a Joint FAO-WHO Meeting Geneva, March, 1974. (Agricultural Planning Studies: No. 95). 29p. 1974. pap. 5.75 o.p. (ISBN 92-5-101542-2, F489, FAO). UNIPUB.

Use of Microprocessors. M. Aumiaux. Tr. by Annel Hutt. LC 79-42904. (Computing Ser.). 198p. 1980. 54.95 o.p. (ISBN 0-471-27689-8, Pub. by Wiley Interscience). Wiley.

Use of Plants by the Chippewa Indians see How Indians Use Wild Plants for Food, Medicine & Crafts.

Use of Poetry & the Use of Criticism Studies in the Relation of Criticism to Poetry in England. T. S. Eliot. 156p. 1985. pap. 3.95 o.p. (ISBN 0-571-05871-X). Faber & Faber.

Use of Polymers in Highway Concrete. (National Cooperative Highway Research Program Report). 77p. 1978. 5.60 o.p. (ISBN 0-309-02778-0). Transport Res Bd.

Use of Potassium Iodide in Emergency Planning for Nuclear Power Plants: Selected Technical Papers from Radiation Issues. Atomic Industrial Forum Staff. (Technical & Economic Reports: Radiation Protection & Environmental Considerations). 1982. 15.00 o.p. (ISBN 0-318-02243-5). US Coun Energy Awareness.

Use of Radioautography in Investigating Protein Synthesis, Proceedings. International Society for Cell Biology Staff. Ed. by C. P. Leblond & Katherine B. Warren. (Vol. 4). 1966. 74.50 o.p. (ISBN 0-12-611904-X). Acad Pr.

Use of Rhyme in Shakespeare's Plays. Frederic W. Ness. LC 69-12420. (Yale Studies in English Ser.: No. 95). 168p. 1969. Repr. of 1941 ed. 24.00 o.p. (ISBN 0-208-00027-5, Archon). Shoe String.

Use of Slide-Tape Presentations in Academic Libraries. Larry L. Hardesty. 1978. pap. text ed. 8.95x o.p. (ISBN 0-88432-006-5). J Norton Pubs.

Use of Tax Subsidies for Employment: A Report to Congress by the Department of Labor & Treasury. 282p. 1986. pap. 6.50 o.p. (S/N 048-000-00384-2). USGPO.

Use of the Bible in Preaching. Reginald H. Fuller. LC 80-2377. 80p. (Orig.). 1981. pap. 3.95 o.p. (ISBN 0-8006-1447-X, 1-1447, Fortress). Augsburg Fortress.

Use of the Omentum in Plastic Surgery. Ion Kiricuta. (Illus.). 320p. 1981. 83.00 o.p. (ISBN 0-08-026352-6). Pergamon.

Use of the Scanning Electron Microscope. J. W. Hearle et al. 289p. 1972. 56.00 o.p. (ISBN 0-08-016246-0). Pergamon.

Use of Things. Robert M. Shelton. (Illus., Orig.). (gr. 9-12). 1967. pap. 1.25 o.p. (ISBN 0-8042-9341-4, John Knox). Westminster John Knox.

Use of Trusts in Estate Planning 1983. (Tax Law & Estate Planning Course Handbook Ser.). 904p. 1983. 40.00 o.p. (ISBN 0-686-79974-7, D4-5161). PLI.

Use of Waste Materials & Soil Stabilization. (Transportation Research Record Ser.). 69p. 1976. 3.00 o.p. Transport Res Bd.

Use the Right Word. S. I. Hayakawa & Reader's Digest Editors. LC 72-8783. 726p. 1968. 19.95 o.p. (ISBN 0-89577-025-3). RD Assn.

Used Oil: Disposal Options, Management Practices & Potential Liability. John T. Nolan et al. 145p. 1988. pap. text ed. 39.00 o.p. (ISBN 0-86587-744-0). Gov Insts.

Useful Arithmetic, Vol. 2. rev. ed. John D. Wool. 96p. 1981. pap. 3.75 o.p. (ISBN 0-88323-165-4, 253); tchr's. key 1.25 o.p. (ISBN 0-88323-168-9, 254). Pendergrass Pub.

Useful Measurements for Violin Makers: A Reference for Shop Use. Henry A. Strobel. LC 88-90888. (Illus.). 42p. (Orig.). 1988. pap. 10.00 o.p. (ISBN 0-9620673-0-X). H A Strobel.

User & Fabric Filtration Equipment III. Air Pollution Control Association Specialty Conference, Niagara Falls, NY, 1978. 207p. 1978. 11.50 o.p. (ISBN 0-318-12284-7, SP-26); members 9.50 o.p. (ISBN 0-318-12285-5). Air & Waste.

User Friendly Guide to Lap Portables: Featuring TRS Model 100 & Olivetti M-10. S. Redman & M. Standford. 256p. 1985. pap. text ed. 17.95 o.p. (ISBN 0-07-051388-0). McGraw.

User Guide on Process Integration for the Efficient Use of Energy. Institution of Chemical Engineers Staff & B. Linhoff. (Illus.). 252p. 1983. pap. 25.00 o.s.i. (ISBN 0-08-030245-9). Pergamon.

User Guide to the UNIX System. Jean Yates & Rebecca Thomas. 508p. (Orig.). 1982. pap. 18.95 o.p. (ISBN 0-931988-71-3, 71-3). Osborne-McGraw.

User Guide to the Unix Systems. 2nd ed. R. Thomas & J. Yates. 1985. pap. text ed. 18.95 o.p. (ISBN 0-07-931071-0). McGraw.

User Studies. (SPEC Kit & Flyer Ser.: No. 101). 115p. 1984. 20.00 o.p. (ISBN 0-318-03455-7). OMS.

Users Guide for Seeds of Western Trees & Shrubs. William I. Stein & Rodger Danielson. (Forest Service General Technical Report PNW-193). (Illus.). 45p. 1986. pap. 4.25 o.p. (ISBN 0-318-21364-8, S/N 001-000-04465-6). USGPO.

User's Guide for Voice & Data Communications Security Equipment. 75.00 o.p. (ISBN 0-686-32978-3). Info Gatekeepers.

User's Guide to Apple II, II Plus & IIe Computers, Software & Peripherals. Consumer Guide Editors. 1983. spiral bdg. 1.00 o.p. (ISBN 0-517-41678-6). Outlet Bk Co.

User's Guide to dBASE II. James T. Perry. 1984. 15.95 o.p. (ISBN 0-912677-15-5). Tate Pub.

User's Guide to dBASE II. James T. Perry & Robert F. McJunkins. 1985. pap. 15.95 o.p. Tate Pub.

User's Guide to PET-CBM Computers. Jeffrey R. Weber. LC 80-70466. (How to Use Your Personal Computer Ser.). 330p. 1983. pap. 15.95 o.p. (ISBN 0-9604892-8-2). Weber Systems.

User's Guide to Powder Coating. Society of Manufacturing Engineers Staff. 160p. 1985. 22.50 o.p. (ISBN 0-87263-195-8). SME.

User's Guide to Social Work Abstracts. 80p. 1987. 10.95 o.p. (ISBN 0-87101-152-2). Natl Assn Soc Wkrs.

User's Guide to the Federal Building Life-Cycle Cost (FBLCC) Computer Program. Stephen R. Petersen. (National Bureau of Standards Technical Note: No. 1222). 88p. (Orig.). 1986. pap. 4.50 o.p. (ISBN 0-318-22476-3, S/N 003-003-02730-8). USGPO.

User's Handbook of D-A & A-D Converters. Eugene R. Hnatek. LC 75-14341. 472p. 1976. 60.50x o.p. (ISBN 0-471-40109-9, Pub. by Wiley-Interscience). Krieger.

User's Handbook of Semiconductor Memories. Eugene R. Hnatek. LC 77-362. 652p. 1977. 66.50x o.p. (ISBN 0-471-40112-9, Pub. by Wiley-Interscience). Wiley.

User's Handbook to the Atari 400-800. Weber Systems, Inc. Staff. LC 82-51088. (How to Use Your Personal Computer Ser.). 320p. 1983. pap. 13.95 o.p. (ISBN 0-938862-15-4). Weber Systems.

User's Handbook to the IBM Personal Computer. Jeffrey R. Weber. LC 82-71681. (WSI's How to Use Your Personal Computer Ser.). (Illus.). 294p. 1982. pap. 13.95 o.p. (ISBN 0-938862-13-8). Weber Systems.

Uses of a Liberal Education, & Other Talks to Students. Brand Blanshard. 436p. 1973. 17.95 o.p. (ISBN 0-87548-122-1). Open Court.

Uses of Microprocessors. National Computing Centre, Ltd. Staff. Ed. by G. L. Simons. (Illus.). 260p. (Orig.). 1980. pap. 32.50x o.s.i. (ISBN 0-85012-240-6). Intl Pubns Serv.

Uses of Obscurity: The Fiction of Early Modernism. Allon White. 180p. 1981. 30.00x o.p. (ISBN 0-7100-0751-5). Routledge Chapman & Hall.

Uses of Sociology in Education. Ed. by C. Wayne Gordon. LC 6-16938. (National Society for the Study of Education Yearbooks Ser.: No. 73, Pt. 2). xviii, 518p. 1974. lib. bdg. 10.00x o.s.i. (ISBN 0-226-60115-3). U of Chicago Pr.

Usher's Passing. Robert R. McCammon. 416p. 1984. 14.95 o.p. (ISBN 0-03-061833-9). H Holt & Co.

Using Accounting Information: An Introduction. 2nd ed. Paul E. Fertig et al. (Harbrace Business & Economics Ser.). (Illus.). 1971. text ed. 17.95 o.p. (ISBN 0-15-594454-1, HC). HarBraceJ.

Using & Programming the ADAM: Including Ready-To-Run Programs. Timothy O. Knight. (Illus.). 128p. (Orig.). 1984. 14.95 o.p. (ISBN 0-8306-0706-4); pap. 7.70 o.p. (ISBN 0-8306-1706-X, 1706). TAB Bks.

Using & Programming the Apple IIc: Including Ready-to-Run Programs. Tony Fabbri. (Illus.). 256p. 1985. 19.95 o.p. (ISBN 0-8306-0981-4, 1981); pap. 14.60 o.p. (ISBN 0-8306-1981-X). TAB Bks.

Using & Programming the Macintosh, Including 32 Ready-to-Run Programs. Frederick Holtz. (Illus.). 256p. (Orig.). 1986. 16.95 o.p. (ISBN 0-8306-0840-0, 1840); pap. 12.15 o.p. (ISBN 0-8306-1840-6). TAB Bks.

Using & Programming the VIC-20, Including Ready-to-Run Programs. John Herriott. 192p. (Orig.). 1984. 15.95 o.p. (ISBN 0-8306-0702-1, 1702); pap. 9.95 o.p. (ISBN 0-8306-1702-7). TAB Bks.

Using & Understanding Medical Statistics. Ed. by D. E. Matthews & V. Farewell. (Illus.). xii, 200p. 1984. pap. 22.50 o.p. (ISBN 3-8055-3932-0). S Karger.

Using Apple Business Computer. Kenniston Lord, Jr. 1983. 21.95 o.p. (ISBN 0-442-26016-4); pap. 17.95 o.p. (ISBN 0-442-25933-6). Van Nos Reinhold.

Using AppleWorks. Arthur Aron & Elaine Aron. LC 85-60693. 440p. 1985. pap. 16.95 o.p. (ISBN 0-88022-161-5, 181). Que Corp.

Using Applications Software: Tutorials & Activities. Edward G. Martin. 246p. 1986. pap. text ed. 9.95 o.p. (ISBN 0-8273-2723-4); instr's. guide 4.00 o.p. (ISBN 0-8273-2724-2). Delmar.

Using Behavioral Methods in Pastoral Counseling. Howard W. Stone. Ed. by Howard J. Clinebell & Howard E. Stone. LC 79-2287. (Creative Pastoral Care & Counseling Ser.). 96p. 1980. pap. 0.50 o.p. (ISBN 0-8006-0563-2, 1-563, Fortress). Augsburg Fortress.

Using CADKEY. Paul J. Resetarits & Gary R. Bertoline. 320p. 1987. pap. text ed. 35.95 o.p. (ISBN 0-8273-2966-0). Delmar.

Using Children's Books in Social Studies: Early Childhood Through Primary Grades. Joan E. Schreiber. LC 83-63481. (Bulletin Ser.: No. 71). 44p. (Orig.). 1984. pap. text ed. 4.75 o.p. (ISBN 0-87986-047-2, 498-15314). Nat Coun Soc Studies.

Using Communication Support in Projects: The World Bank's Experience. Heli E. Perret. (Working Paper: No. 551). 74p. 1983. 6.95 o.p. (ISBN 0-8213-0119-5, WP 0551). World Bank.

Using Computers in an Information Age. Richard W. Brightman & Jeffrey M. Dimsdale. 672p. 1986. 28.95 o.p. (ISBN 0-8273-2372-7); 10.00 o.p. (ISBN 0-8273-2394-8); study guide 10.95 o.p. (ISBN 0-8273-2369-7); test bank 9.00 o.p. (ISBN 0-8273-2395-6); IBM computerized test bank 89.95 o.p. (ISBN 0-8273-2396-4); Apple computerized test bank 89.95 o.p. (ISBN 0-8273-2722-6). Delmar.

Using Computers in Physics. John R. Merrill. LC 75-25012. (Illus.). 384p. 1976. pap. 9.75 o.p. (ISBN 0-395-21411-4). HM.

Using Computers in the Behavioral Sciences. Paul C. Cozby. 1984. 10.95 o.p. (ISBN 0-87484-714-1). Mayfield Pub.

Using Copyrighted Videocassettes in Classrooms, Libraries, & Training Centers. 2nd ed. J. K. Miller. LC 83-20904. 1987. 19.95 o.p. Copyright Info.

Using Discounted Cash Flow Effectively. Herbert E. Kroeger. LC 84-70259. 250p. 1984. 50.00 o.p. (ISBN 0-87094-553-X). Dow Jones-Irwin.

Using DisplayWrite. Walton Beacham & Deborah Beacham. LC 84-62131. 410p. 1985. 19.95 o.p. (ISBN 0-88022-127-5, 26). Que Corp.

Using Dollars & Sense on the IBM PC. Steve Adams. LC 86-63981. 225p. 1987. pap. 18.95 o.p. (ISBN 0-88022-287-5, 90). Que Corp.

Using Enable. Charles Spezzano. LC 85-623611. 373p. 1985. pap. 19.95 o.p. (ISBN 0-88022-165-8, 186). Que Corp.

Using Evaluation Results: Guidelines & Practice for Using Vocational Evaluation Effectively. Stephen J. Franchak & Michael H. Kean. 86p. 1981. 6.25 o.p. (ISBN 0-318-15584-2, RD212). Natl Ctr Res Voc Ed.

Using Excelerator for System Analysis & Design. Whitten & Bentley. 224p. 1987. pap. text ed. 19.95 o.p. (ISBN 0-8016-5462-9). Mosby.

Using Expert Witnesses. Association of Trial Lawyers of America Education Fund Staff. LC 83-71596. (Illus.). 86p. 1983. write for info. o.p. (ISBN 0-941916-11-1). Assn Trial Ed.

Using Filters. Eastman Kodak Company Staff. LC 81-67034. (Kodak Workshop Ser.). (Illus.). 96p. (Orig.). 1981. pap. 9.95 o.p. (ISBN 0-87985-277-1, KW-13). Eastman Kodak.

Using Groups to Help People. Dorothy Whitaker. (International Library of Group Psychotherapy & Group Process). 436p. 1985. 45.00x o.p. (ISBN 0-7100-9865-0). Routledge Chapman & Hall.

Using Kodak Ektachrome R-3 & R-3000 Chemicals. Ed. by Eastman Kodak Company. (Illus.). 118p. 1985. wkbk. 60.00 o.s.i. (ISBN 0-87985-361-1). Eastman-Kodak.

Using Labor Market Information in Vocational Planning. Harold Starr et al. 105p. 1982. 8.75 o.p. (ISBN 0-318-22230-2, RD228). Natl Ctr Res Voc Ed.

Using Lotus HAL. David Gobel. LC 87-60968. 400p. (Orig.). 1987. pap. 19.95 o.p. (ISBN 0-88022-291-3). Que Corp.

Using Lotus 1-2-3: A Guide for Non-Programmers. Rebecca C. Latif. 1985. pap. text ed. 21.33 o.p. (ISBN 0-8359-8165-7, Reston). P-H.

Using Macintosh BASIC. Richard Norling. 496p. (Orig.). 1985. pap. text ed. 17.95 o.p. (ISBN 0-07-881157-0). Osborne-McGraw.

Using Microcomputers: Applications for Business. Spence & Windsor. 720p. 1986. pap. 31.95 o.p. (ISBN 0-8016-4778-9). Mosby.

Using Microcomputers: Tutorials for dBASE II, WordStar, & 1-2-3. Richard W. Brightman & Jeffrey M. Dimsdale. 320p. 1986. pap. 24.95 o.p. (ISBN 0-8273-2522-3); instr's. guide 8.00 o.p. (ISBN 0-8273-2523-1); instr's. data disk 20.00 o.p. (ISBN 0-8273-2521-5); student data disk 20.00 o.p. (ISBN 0-8273-2520-7). Delmar.

Using Microprocessors & Microcomputers: The 6800 Family. Joseph D. Greenfield & William C. Wray. LC 80-18090. (Electronic Technology Ser.: No. 1-325). 460p. 1981. (ISBN 0-471-02727-8). Wiley.

Using Microsoft Word. Masha Zager & Claire Chase. LC 84-60137. 366p. 1985. pap. 16.95 o.p. (ISBN 0-88022-112-7, 22); IBM PC format software 39.95 o.p. (ISBN 0-88022-151-8, 247). Que Corp.

Using Monitors. Ed. by Jean Robinson & Barbara McVan. LC 80-20948. (Nursing Photobook Ser.). (Illus.). 160p. 1980. text ed. 17.95 o.p. (ISBN 0-916730-26-3). Springhouse Pub.

Using Multi Mate Advantage II Work Book. Ashton-Tate. (Orig.). 1987. pap. text ed. 36.95 o.p. (ISBN 0-912677-95-3). Tate Pub.

Using MultiMate. Kate Barnes. LC 84-60141. 205p. 1985. 18.95 o.p. (ISBN 0-88022-114-3, 216). Que Corp.

Using Our Natural Resources: Nineteen Eighty-Three Yearbook of Agriculture. 611p. 1983. 7.00 o.p. (ISBN 0-318-11838-6, S/N 001-000-04387-1). USGPO.

Using PageMaker on the IBM. Diane Burns & S. Venit. LC 86-63978. 400p. (Orig.). 1987. pap. 24.95 o.p. (ISBN 0-88022-285-9, 89). Que Corp.

Using Paradox. George Chou. (Illus.). 427p. (Orig.). 1986. pap. 19.95 o.p. (ISBN 0-88022-227-1, 191). Que Corp.

Using Paraprofessionals to Deliver Educational Programs. (Program Aid United States Dept of Agriculture Ser.: No. 1379). 66p. 1986. pap. 3.25 o.p. (S/N 001-000-04469-9). USGPO.

Using PC DOS. Chris DeVoney. LC 85-62365. 519p. (Orig.). 1986. pap. 21.95 o.p. (ISBN 0-88022-170-4, 180). Que Corp.

Using Performance Measurement in Local Government: A Guide to Improving Decisions, Performance & Accountability. Paul D. Epstein. (Council on Municipal Performance Ser.). (Illus.). 256p. 1984. 36.95 o.p. (ISBN 0-442-21603-3). Van Nos Reinhold.

Using Photography to Preserve Evidence. Eastman Kodak Company. (Illus.). 49p. 1982. pap. 4.50 o.p. (ISBN 0-87985-166-X, M-2). Eastman Kodak.

Using Problem Solving in Teaching & Training. LeRoy Ford. LC 77-178060. (Multi-Media Teaching & Training Ser.). (Orig.). 1972. pap. 5.50 o.p. (ISBN 0-8054-3415-1). Broadman.

Using Process EM-26. Eastman Kodak Company. (Illus.). 130p. 1981. workbook 45.00 o.p. (ISBN 0-87985-289-5, Z-127). Eastman-Kodak.

Using Professional File on the PC. Linda Rice. (Orig.). 1987. 9.95 o.p. (ISBN 0-942728-36-X). Custom Pub Co.

Using Professional Write on the PC. Linda Rice. (Orig.). 1987. 9.95 o.p. (ISBN 0-942728-35-1). Custom Pub Co.

Using Q&A. David P. Ewing & Bill Langenes. LC 86-61153. 592p. (Orig.). 1986. pap. 19.95 o.p. (ISBN 0-88022-262-X, 61). Que Corp.

Using R: Base: Base 4000. Jonathan Erickson & Nicholas Baran. 256p. (Orig.). 1985. pap. text ed. 18.95 o.p. (ISBN 0-07-881171-6). Osborne McGraw.

Using Rapid File. Edward Jones. (Illus.). 400p. (Orig.). 1987. text ed. 17.95 o.p. (ISBN 0-07-881014-0). Osborne-McGraw.

Using Scripsit. William J. Haga. 1983. PWS-Kent Pub.

Using Scripsit: For TRS-80 Model III & Model I. William James Haga. LC 82-21839. (Illus.). 320p. 1983. pap. (ISBN 0-534-01473-9). PWS-Kent Pub.

Using SI Units (Standard International Metric) in Heating, Air Conditioning, & Refrigeration. W. F. Stoecker. LC 74-26697. (Illus.). 1975. 3.75 o.p. (ISBN 0-912524-12-X). Busn News.

Using Simple Embroidery Stitches. Date not set. (ISBN 0-8052-3934-0). Random.

Using Simulation Games. Pat Baker & Mary R. Marshall. (Youth Work Guide Ser.). (Illus.). 96p. (Orig.). 1973. pap. 7.95 o.p. (ISBN 0-85819-090-7, Pub. by JBCE). Meyer Stone Bks.

Using Space--Today & Tomorrow: Proceedings, Vol. 1. Luigi G. Napolitano & International Astronautical Congress, 28th, Prague, 1977. 1978. 93.00 o.p. (ISBN 0-08-023231-0). Pergamon.

Using Space, Today & Tomorrow, Vol. 2: Communications Satellite Symposium. L. G. Napolitano. 1978. 69.00 o.p. (ISBN 0-08-023232-9). Pergamon.

Using SPRINT: The Professional Word Processor. Kris Jamsa. (Borland-Osborne-McGraw-Hill Business Ser.). 350p. pap. text ed. (ISBN 0-07-881291-7). Osborne-McGraw.

Using Symphony. David Ewing & Geoffrey LeBlond. LC 84-60645. (Symphony Ser.). 655p. 1984. pap. 23.95 o.p. (ISBN 0-88022-124-0, 141). Que Corp.

Using Systematic Observation Techniques in Evaluating Career Education. Ralph J. Kester. 64p. 1979. 4.50 o.p. (ISBN 0-318-15585-0, RD169). Natl Ctr Res Voc Ed.

Using the Apple Computer. Stokes & Lukenbill. 196p. (Orig.). Date not set. lab man. 19.95x o.p. (ISBN 0-88725-047-5). Hunter Textbks.

Using the Case Study in Teaching & Training. LeRoy Ford. LC 71-105324. (Multi-Media Teaching & Training Ser.). (Illus.). 1970. pap. 5.50 o.p. (ISBN 0-8054-3413-5). Broadman.

Using the Commodore 64: A Hand Guide to Getting the Most from the Bestselling Microcomputer. Len Lyons et al. LC 84-2847. 1438p. 1984. pap. 14.95 o.p. (ISBN 0-201-05156-7). Addison-Wesley.

Using the Compaq Portable Computer. Kenniston W. Lord, Jr. 464p. 1984. 25.95 o.p. (ISBN 0-442-25947-6); pap. 19.45 o.p. (ISBN 0-442-25949-2). Van Nos Reinhold.

Using the Eagle PC & 1600 Series. Kenniston W. Lord, Jr. 304p. 1984. 26.95 o.p. (ISBN 0-442-26036-9); pap. 21.95 o.p. (ISBN 0-442-26035-0). Van Nos Reinhold.

Using the IBM-PC: WordStar. C. J. Puotinen. 357p. 1983. pap. 40.95 with diskette o.p. (ISBN 0-03-063981-6); pap. 18.45 o.p. (ISBN 0-03-062857-1). HR&W.

Using the IBM PCjr Personal Computer. Kenniston W. Lord, Jr. 384p. 1984. 27.95 o.p. (ISBN 0-442-25961-1); pap. 19.95 o.p. (ISBN 0-442-25964-6). Van Nos Reinhold.

Using the IBM Personal Computer. Kenniston W. Lord, Jr. LC 82-15999. 336p. 1983. 19.95 o.p. (ISBN 0-442-25815-1); pap. 16.95 o.p. (ISBN 0-442-26078-4). Van Nos Reinhold.

Using the IBM Personal Computer: IBM Easywriter. Ada Finifter. 1984. 17.95 o.p. (ISBN 0-03-063736-8). HR&W.

Using the Kaypro II Personal Computer. Kenniston W. Lord, Jr. LC 84-7402. 272p. 1984. 27.95 o.p. (ISBN 0-442-26038-5); pap. 19.95 o.p. (ISBN 0-442-26037-7). Van Nos Reinhold.

Using the Keypunch & Other Punched Card Equipment. Frederick P. Stutz. 1973. 5.35x o.p. (ISBN 0-916304-07-8). SDSU Press.

Using the Macintosh Toolbox with C. Fred A. Huxham et al. LC 85-63245. 559p. (Orig.). 1985. pap. 24.95 o.p. (ISBN 0-89588-249-3). Sybex.

Using the Mass Media: Communication Problems in American Society. S. Chaffee & M. Petrick. 1975. text ed. 29.95 o.p. (ISBN 0-07-010375-5). McGraw.

Using the Media for Adult Basic Education. Ed. by Anthony Kaye & Keith Harry. (Illus.). 256p. 1982. 28.50 o.p. (ISBN 0-7099-1506-3, Pub. by Croom helm Ltd). Routledge Chapman & Hall.

Using the Microsoft Business BASIC Compiler on the IBM PC. M. L. Lesser. 272p. 1986. pap. text ed. 19.95 o.p. (ISBN 0-07-037299-3, BYTE Bks). McGraw.

Using the Osborne Personal Computer. Kenniston W. Lord, Jr. (Illus.). 336p. 1983. 25.95 o.p. (ISBN 0-442-26010-5); pap. 19.95 o.p. (ISBN 0-442-26054-7). Van Nos Reinhold.

Using the Panel in Teaching & Training. LeRoy Ford. Tr. by Joe McCormick. LC 79-127196. (Multi-Media Teaching & Training Ser.). (Orig.). 1971. pap. 5.50 o.p. (ISBN 0-8054-3414-3). Broadman.

Using the Radio Shack TRS-80 in Your Home. Kenniston W. Lord, Jr. 512p. 1983. 27.95 o.p. (ISBN 0-442-25707-4); pap. 19.95 o.p. (ISBN 0-442-26079-2). Van Nos Reinhold.

Using the TI Professional Personal Computer. Kenniston W. Lord, Jr. 326p. 1984. 27.95 o.p. (ISBN 0-442-25812-7); pap. 19.95 o.p. (ISBN 0-442-25813-5). Van Nos Reinhold.

Using the Timex-Sinclair 1000 & 1500. Ralph M. Coletti. 88p. 1984. pap. 9.95 o.p. (ISBN 0-88006-065-4, BK7397). Wayne Green Ent.

Using the USCD-P System. K. Buckner et al. 1984. pap. text ed. 22.95 o.p. (ISBN 0-8053-1185-8). Benjamin-Cummings.

Using Turbo Pascal. Steve Wood. 350p. (Orig.). 1985. pap. text ed. 19.95 o.p. (ISBN 0-07-881148-1). Osborne-McGraw.

Using Turbo Prolog. Phillip R. Robinson. 300p. (Orig.). 1986. pap. text ed. 19.95 o.p. (ISBN 0-07-881253-4). Osborne-McGraw.

Using Turbo Prolog. Khin Yin. LC 86-62537. 450p. (Orig.). 1987. pap. 19.95 o.p. (ISBN 0-88022-270-0, 69). Que Corp.

Using Turbo Prolog Software. Date not set. (ISBN 0-88022-331-6). Que Corp.

Using Urban Wasteland: A Guide for Community Groups. Susan Lobbenberg. 41p. 1981. pap. 7.50x o.p. (ISBN 0-7199-1049-8, Pub. by Bedford England). Gower Pub Co.

Using Ventura Publisher. Diane Burns & S. Venit. 450p. (Orig.). 1988. pap. 24.95 o.p. (ISBN 0-88022-347-2). Que Corp.

Using WordPerfect. Walton Beacham. 1985. pap. 16.95 o.p. (ISBN 0-88022-132-1). Que Corp.

Using WordPerfect. rev. ed. Walton Beacham & Deborah Beacham. LC 85-63285. 307p. 18.95 o.p. (ISBN 0-88022-239-5, 11). Que Corp.

Using WordStar. Steve Ditlea. LC 86-61806. 350p. (Orig.). 1987. pap. 18.95 o.p. (ISBN 0-88022-267-0, 66). Que Corp.

Using WordStar 2000. Eric Sorensen. LC 85-60686. 233p. 1985. pap. 17.95 o.p. (ISBN 0-88022-148-8, 175). Que Corp.

Using XyWrite III. John Sladek. (Illus.). 300p. (Orig.). 1986. pap. text ed. 17.95 o.p. (ISBN 0-07-881013-2). Osborne-McGraw.

Using 1-2-3. Douglas F. Cobb & Geoffrey LeBlond. (Illus.). 420p. 1983. pap. 21.95 o.p. (ISBN 0-88022-243-3, 24). Que Corp.

USMC Destruction by Demolition, Incendiaries & Sabotage. (Weaponry Ser.). 1986. lib. bdg. 79.95 o.p. (ISBN 0-8490-3851-0). Gordon Pr.

USMC Destruction by Demolition, Incendiaries & Sabotage. lib. bdg. 79.95 o.p. (ISBN 0-8490-3617-8). Gordon Pr.

USSR-FRG Relations: A New Stage. R. Alexeyev. 240p. 1983. pap. 3.95 o.p. (ISBN 0-8285-2599-4, Pub. by Progress Pubs USSR). Imported Pubns.

Usury Laws: 1982 Course Handbook. (Commercial Law & Practice Course Handbook Ser.: 1982-83). 377p. 1982. pap. 35.00 o.p. (ISBN 0-685-07688-1, A4-4037). PLI.

Utah Business & Industry Directory 1987-88. 274p. 1987. pap. 40.00 o.p. (ISBN 0-318-02874-3). Manufacturers.

Utah Civil Procedure, 4 vols. David A. Thomas. 1980. 150.00 o.s.i. (ISBN 0-911712-72-0). BYU Clark Law.

Utah Jazz. Jim Moore. (NBA Today Ser.). (Illus.). 48p. (gr. 4 up). 1984. PLB 10.45 o.p. (ISBN 0-87191-991-5). Creative Ed.

Utah Probate System. H. Reese Hansen & Stanley D. Neeleman. 1977. 60.00 o.s.i. (ISBN 0-686-40389-4). BYU Clark Law.

Utah Rules of Court. Michie Company Editorial Staff. (State Practice Publications Ser.). 550p. 1985. pap. 27.50 o.p. (ISBN 0-87215-854-3). Michie Co.

Utah Women & the Law: A Resource Handbook. Compiled by Utah Governor's Commission on the Status of Women. LC 87-50075. (Bonneville Bks.). 176p. (Orig.). 1987. pap. 1.95 o.p. (ISBN 0-87480-301-2). U of Utah Pr.

Utah's History. Ed. by Richard D. Poll & Thomas G. Alexander. LC 77-20924. (Illus.). 1978. text ed. 17.95x o.p. (ISBN 0-8425-0842-2); pap. 15.95x o.p. (ISBN 0-8425-0838-4). Brigham.

Utamaro: Songs of the Garden. Ed. by Barbara Burn. Tr. by Yasuko Betchaku & Joan B. Mirviss. LC 84-60004. (Illus.). 48p. 16.95 o.p. (ISBN 0-87099-368-2). Metro Mus Art.

Ute War: A History of the White River Massacre. Thomas Dawson & F. J. Skiff. 184p. 1980. pap. 6.95 o.p. (ISBN 0-933472-04-8). Johnson Bks.

Uterine Physiology: Proceedings of the Brook Lodge Workshop. Ed. by Emanual A. Friedman et al. LC 79-332. (Illus.). 156p. 1979. text ed. 21.00 o.p. (ISBN 0-88416-263-X). Year Bk Med.

Utility of Retail Site Selection for the Public Library. William C. Robinson. (Occasional Papers: No. 122). 51p. 1976. pap. 2.00 o.p. (ISBN 0-317-58952-0). U of Ill Lib Info Sci.

Utilization of Alternative Fuels for Transportation, AAS2. Ed. by Martin Newman & Jerry Grey. LC 71-12149. (Illus.). 238p. 1979. 20.00 o.p. (ISBN 0-915928-31-0). AIAA.

Utilization of Geothermal Energy for Electric Power Production & Space Heating. Ed. by E Barbier & M Trindade. (Selected Papers from the UNECE Seminar Held in Florence, Italy 14-17 May 1984). 392p. 1985. pap. 61.00 o.p. (ISBN 0-08-032638-2, Pub. by PPI). Pergamon.

Utilization of Hardwoods Growing on Southern Pines Sites, 3 vols. Peter Koch. LC 83-600592. (Atriculture Handbook). (Illus.). 3710p. 1985. text ed. 75.00 o.p. (ISBN 0-318-20378-2, S/N 001-000-04289-1). USGPO.

Utilization of Krill. G. J. Grantham. (Southern Ocean Fisheries Survey Programmes: GLO-SO-77-3). 67p. (Eng. & Span.). 1977. pap. 7.50 o.p. (ISBN 92-5-100416-1, F1314, FAO). UNIPUB.

Utilization of Mammalian Specific Locus Studies in Hazard Evaluation & Estimation of Genetic Risk. Ed. by Frederick J. De Serres et al. LC 83-11076. (Environmental Science Research: Vol, 28). 352p. 1983. 59.50x o.p. (ISBN 0-306-41380-9, Plenum Pr). Plenum Pub.

Utilization of Short-Stay Hospitals. (Data from the National Health Survey Ser.). 64p. 1986. pap. 3.25 o.p. (ISBN 0-318-20377-4, S/N 017-022-00948-0). USGPO.

Utilization of Short-Stay Hospitals by Diagnosis-Related Groups: United States, 1980-1984. Robert Pokras. (DHHS Publication PHS 86-1748). (Illus.). 49p. 1986. pap. 2.75 o.p. (ISBN 0-318-21375-3, S/N 017-022-00962-5). USGPO.

Utoli Moia Pechali. Lev Kopelev. (Rus.). 1981. 22.00 o.p. (ISBN 0-88233-483-2); pap. 10.00 o.p. (ISBN 0-88233-484-0). Ardis Pubs.

Utopia: Controversy. Ed. by George Kateb. 160p. 1971. 12.95x o.s.i. (ISBN 0-202-24073-8). Lieber-Atherton.

Utopia in Power. Mikhail Heller & Aleksandr Nekrich. 877p. 1986. 24.45 o.s.i. (ISBN 0-671-46242-3). Summit Bks.

Utopia or Oblivion: The Prospects for Mankind. R. Buckminster Fuller. LC 72-81085. 384p. 1973. Repr. of 1969 ed. 11.95 o.s.i. (ISBN 0-87951-003-X). Overlook Pr.

Utopian Vision of D. H. Lawrence. Eugene Goodheart. LC 63-22817. 1963. lib. bdg. 12.00x o.s.i. (ISBN 0-226-30288-1). U of Chicago Pr.

Utopian Vision of Moholy-Nagy. Joseph H. Caton. Ed. by Diane Kirkpatrick. LC 83-18182. (Studies in Photography: No. 5). 200p. 1984. 42.95 o.p. (ISBN 0-8357-1528-0). UMI Res Pr.

Utopias. Ed. by Peter Alexander & Roger Gill. LC 84-1897. 240p. 1985. 19.95 o.p. (ISBN 0-87548-364-X). Open Court.

Utrecht in Drawings-Utrecht Getekend. C. C. Wilmer. (Illus.). 1980. 35.00 o.p. (ISBN 90-247-9023-9). E J Brill USA.

Utter Nonsense. Barney Saltzberg. (Paperbacks Ser.). (Illus.). 80p. (Orig.). 1980. pap. text ed. 3.95 o.p. (ISBN 0-07-054486-7). McGraw.

V

V. A. C. Crispin. 1984. lib. bdg. 13.95 o.p. (ISBN 0-8398-2840-3, Gregg). G K Hall.

V & A Album Four. (Illus.). 400p. (Orig.). 1985. pap. 7.95 o.p. (ISBN 0-948107-16-2, Pub. by Victoria & Albert Mus UK). Faber & Faber.

V & A Album 2. (Illus.). 400p. (Orig.). 1984. pap. 7.95 o.p. (ISBN 0-946345-03-1, Pub. by Victoria & Albert Mus UK). Faber & Faber.

V & A Album 3: Annual. (Illus.). 400p. (Orig.). 1985. pap. 7.95 o.p. (ISBN 0-905209-99-0, Pub. by Victoria & Albert Mus UK). Faber & Faber.

V-Bombers. Bob Downey. (Warbirds Illustrated Ser.: No. 35). (Illus.). 72p. (Orig.). 1985. pap. 9.95 o.p. (ISBN 0-85368-740-4, Pub. by Arms & Armour). Sterling.

V. D. Blues. Educational Broadcasting Corp. Staff. 1973. pap. 0.95 o.p. (ISBN 0-380-01603-6, 15156). Avon.

V: East Coast Crisis. A. C. Crispin & Howard Weinstein. 1984. lib. bdg. 12.95 o.p. (ISBN 0-8398-2841-1, Gregg). G K Hall.

V-Force: The History of Britain's Airborne Deterrent. Andrew Brookes. (Illus.). 173p. 1983. 19.95 o.p. (ISBN 0-86720-639-X). Janes Info Group.

V. S. Naipaul: A Study in Expatriate Sensibility. Sudha Rai. 192p. 1982. text ed. 7.95x o.p. (ISBN 0-391-02696-8). Humanities.

V Was for Victory: Politics & American Culture During World War 2. John M. Blum. LC 75-38730. 384p. 1976. 12.95 o.p. (ISBN 0-15-194080-0). HarBraceJ.

Vacation & Leisure Home Plans. Ed. by Garlinghouse, L. F., Co., Staff. LC 82-84444. (Illus.). 116p. (Orig.). 1983. pap. 2.50 o.p. (ISBN 0-938708-05-8). L F Garlinghouse Co.

Vacation Crafts. Phyllis Meras. 1978. 11.95 o.p. (ISBN 0-395-26309-3); pap. 6.95 o.p. (ISBN 0-395-26498-7). HM.

Vacation Dream Homes. rev. ed. Andy Lang. LC 75-2421. (Illus.). 96p. 1985. pap. 8.95 o.p. Hammond Inc.

Vacation Places Rated. Sylvia McNair. LC 85-73295. (Illus.). 218p. 1986. pap. 12.95 o.p. (ISBN 0-528-88012-8). Rand McNally.

Vacuome Animal see Vacuome de la Cellule Vegetale: Morphologie.

Vacuome de la Cellule Vegetale: Morphologie. P. Dangeard. Bd. with Vacuome Animal. R. Hovasse. (Illus.). 37p; Contractile Vacuoles of Protozoa; Food Vacuoles: Food Vacuoles. J. A. Kitching. (Protoplasmatologia: Vol. 3, Pt. D1, 2, 3a, 3b). (Illus.). iv, 41p. 1956. pap. 57.90 o.p. (ISBN 0-387-80423-4). Springer-Verlag.

Vacuum & Solid State Electronics. D. J. Harris & P. D. Robson. 1963. text ed. 23.00 o.p. (ISBN 0-08-009960-2); pap. text ed. 11.25 o.p. (ISBN 0-08-009959-9). Pergamon.

Vacuum & Thin Film Technology. Ed. by J. Yarwood. 1978. 30.00 o.p. (ISBN 0-08-022112-2). Pergamon.

Vacuum Devices: Proceedings of the Conference, University of Cambridge, 25-27 March 1980. J. Yarwood. 144p. 1981. pap. 26.00 o.p. (ISBN 0-08-027330-0). Pergamon.

Vacuum, Eighty-Four: Technological Aspects of Surface Treatment & Analysis: Proceedings of the Conference Held at the University of York, 1-4 April 1984. Ed. by W. A. Grant. 204p. 1985. pap. 50.00 o.p. (ISBN 0-08-032555-6). Pergamon.

Vacuum Eighty-Two: Proceedings of the Biennial Conference of the Vacuum Group of the Institute of Physics, Chester, 29-31 March 1982. Ed. by W. A. Grant & D. Balfour. 112p. 1983. pap. 31.00 o.p. (ISBN 0-08-029999-7). Pergamon.

Vacuum-Industry-Energy: Proceedings of Second Joint Meeting of the Roland Eotvos Physical Society (Vacuum Physics & Thin Films Section) & the Austrian Vacuum Society, held Niederosterreich, Austria, 27-29 October, 1981. Ed. by R. Dobrozemsky. 128p. 1983. pap. 31.00 o.p. (ISBN 0-08-029993-8). Pergamon.

Vacuum Manual. L. Holland et al. (Illus.). 1974. 55.00x o.p. (ISBN 0-419-10740-1, NO. 6156, Pub. by E & FN Spon). Routledge Chapman & Hall.

Vacuum Sealing Techniques. A. Roth. 1966. 205.00 o.p. (ISBN 0-08-011587-X). Pergamon.

Vacuum Seventy-Eight: Selected Proceedings of the Conference on Medium High & Ultra-High Vacuum Technology, Oxford, England, 1978. Ed. by J. Yarwood. G. S. Grossart. (Illus.). 1979. pap. 32.00 o.p. (ISBN 0-08-024229-4). Pergamon.

Vacuum Technology. Andrew Guthrie. LC 63-20631. 532p. 1963. 61.95 o.p. (ISBN 0-471-33722-6, Pub. by Wiley-Interscience). Wiley.

Vacuum Technology: Selected Proceedings of the 6th Israeli Vacuum Congress, Haifa, Israel, 4-5 April, 1982. Ed. by E. Grunbaum. 64p. 1983. pap. 15.50 o.p. (ISBN 0-08-030567-9). Pergamon.

Vacuum Ultraviolet Radiation Physics: Proceedings of the 4th International Conference. Ed. by E. E. Koch et al. 848p. 1975. 205.00 o.p. (ISBN 0-08-018942-3). Pergamon.

Vadim Shershenevich. Anna Lawton. 1981. 20.00 o.p. (ISBN 0-88233-681-9). Ardis Pubs.

Vagabul & His Shadow. Jean-Claude Marol. (Vagabul Ser.). (Illus.). 32p. (ps up). 1982. PLB 8.95s.p. o.p. (ISBN 0-87191-889-7). Creative Ed.

Vagabul Escapes. Jean-Claude Marol. (Vagabul Ser.). (Illus.). 32p. (ps up). 1982. PLB 8.95s.p. o.p. (ISBN 0-87191-888-9). Creative Ed.

Vagabul in the Clouds. Jean-Claude Marol. (Vagabul Ser.). (Illus.). 32p. (ps up). 1982. PLB 8.95s.p. o.p. (ISBN 0-87191-887-0). Creative Ed.

Vagabul Skis. Jean-Claude Marol. (Vagabul Ser.). (Illus.). 32p. (ps up). 1982. PLB 8.95s.p. o.p. (ISBN 0-87191-886-2). Creative Ed.

Vago. Laurence Gonzales. LC 82-71057. 320p. 1983. 16.95 o.p. (ISBN 0-689-11330-7, Atheneum). Macmillan.

Vagrant Lotus: An Introduction to Buddhist Philosophy. Douglas A. Fox. 224p. 1973. 6.95 o.s.i. (ISBN 0-664-20975-0, Westminster). Westminster John Knox.

Vague Fuids. Edye Falencki & Margrit Newman. Tr. by Nicole Janicaud from Eng. (Illus.). 25p. (Orig., Fr.). 1988. write for info. o.p. Edmar NY.

Vahweh vs. Baal. Norman C. Habel. 128p. 1964. Concordia Schl Grad Studies.

Valamo (Valaam) & Its Message. (Illus.). 287p. Date not set. 50.00 o.p. St Herman AK.

Valdez Marriage. Violet Winspear. (Nightingale Ser.). 1985. pap. 9.95 o.p. (ISBN 0-8161-3856-7, Large Print Bks). G K Hall.

Valedictory. Rooney. 1974. 6.95 o.p. (ISBN 0-15-193349-9). HarBraceJ.

Valency & Molecular Structure. 4th ed. E. Cartnell & G. W. A. Fowles. 1977. 22.95 o.p. (ISBN 0-408-70809-3). Butterworth.

Valency & the English Verb. D. J. Allerton. 1983. 52.00 o.p. (ISBN 0-12-052980-7). Acad Pr.

Valentin Kataev. Robert Russell. (World Authors Ser.). 1981. 16.95 o.p. (ISBN 0-8057-6423-2, Twayne). G K Hall.

Valentin Serov: Paintings, Graphic Works, Stage Designs. Dmitry Sarabyanov & Grigory Arbuzo. LC 80-68475. (Illus.). 328p. 1983. 45.00 o.p. (ISBN 0-8109-1605-3). Abrams.

Valentine Ideals '88. 1988. pap. 3.95 o.p. (ISBN 0-8249-1059-1). Ideals.

Valentine Pontifex. Robert Silverberg. 1983. 15.95 o.p. (ISBN 0-87795-544-1, Arbor Hse); signed limited ed. 35.00 o.p. (ISBN 0-87795-561-1). Morrow.

Valerie. Valerie Chronis. pap. 3.00 o.p. (ISBN 0-938078-11-9). Anhinga Pr.

Valerie Valentine Is Missing. Amelia Walden. LC 76-152337. (gr. 7 up). 1971. 4.75 o.s.i. (ISBN 0-664-32496-7, Westminster). Westminster John Knox.

Valiant Hearts. Donald E. Micue. 192p. 1987. 14.00 o.p. (ISBN 0-8062-3021-5). Carlton.

Valiant Muse: An Anthology of Poems by Poets Killed in the (First) World War. Ed. by Frederic W. Ziv. LC 78-74830. (Granger Poetry Library). 1979. Repr. of 1936 ed. 17.50x o.p. (ISBN 0-89609-150-3). Roth Pub Inc.

Valiant Witness: A Novel of Moroni. Robert Moss. LC 83-81586. 182p. 1983. 8.95 o.p. (ISBN 0-88290-226-1). Horizon-Utah.

Valley & Its Peoples: An Illustrated History of the Lower Merrimack. Paul Hudon. LC 82-50186. (Illus.). 176p. 1988. 22.95 o.p. (ISBN 0-89781-047-3). Windsor Pubns Inc.

Valley Men: A Speculative Account of the Arkansas Expedition of 1807. Donald Jackson. LC 83-4995. (Illus.). 340p. 1983. 16.45 o.p. (ISBN 0-89919-198-3). Ticknor & Fields.

Valley of Darkness: The Japanese People & World War Two. Thomas R. Havens. (Illus.). 1978. 12.95x o.p. (ISBN 0-393-05656-2). Norton.

Valley of Decision. Marcia Davenport. 768p. 1983. pap. 4.50 o.p. (ISBN 0-380-63891-6, 63891-6). Avon.

Valley of the Dry Bones. Rudolphf R. Windsor. LC 83-90249. 162p. 1986. 10.95 o.p. (ISBN 0-317-44672-X). Vantage.

Valley of the Many-Colored Grasses. Ronald Johnson. LC 68-54967. 1969. pap. 1.95 o.p. (ISBN 0-393-04272-3). Norton.

Valley of the Shadow. Brian Garfield. 176p. 1982. pap. 2.25 o.p. (ISBN 0-505-51855-4, Pub. by Tower Bks). Dorchester Pub Co.

Valley of the Shadow. Brian Garfield. 176p. 1983. pap. 1.95 o.p. (ISBN 0-8439-2029-7, Pub. by Leisure Bks CT). Dorchester Pub Co.

Valley of the Shadow. Hanns Lilje. LC 76-55522. 1977. pap. 0.50 o.p. (ISBN 0-8006-1699-5, Fortress). Augsburg Fortress.

Valley of the Vultures. Lawrence J. Joos. LC 82-90303. 299p. 1985. 11.95 o.p. (ISBN 0-533-05399-4). Vantage.

Valley of Vision: Discovering God Around the World. Winifred Walker. LC 80-54377. 64p. (Orig.). 1981. pap. 2.95x o.p. (ISBN 0-8358-0425-9). Upper Room.

Valley of Vye-Vye: A Novel. Rufus M. Reed. 1979. 8.50 o.p. (ISBN 0-682-49483-6). Exposition-Phoenix.

Valley So Low. Manly W. Wellman. LC 87-13694. (Science Fiction Ser.). 192p. 1987. 12.95 o.s.i. (ISBN 0-385-23675-1). Doubleday.

Valois Burgundy. Richard Vaughan. LC 74-34019. (Illus.). ix, 254p. (Orig.). 1975. 25.00 o.p. (ISBN 0-208-01511-6, Archon). Shoe String.

Valuable Property: The Life Story of Michael Todd. Michael Todd, Jr. & Susan M. Todd. (Illus.). 376p. 1983. 16.95 o.p. (ISBN 0-87795-491-7, Arbor Hse). Morrow.

Valuation of a Closely Held Business. Pennsylvania Bar Institute Staff. 96p. 1985. 50.00 o.p. (ISBN 0-318-19078-8, 307). PA Bar Inst.

Valuation of Hotels & Motels. American Institute of Real Estate Appraisers Staff & Stephen Rushmore. 120p. 18.00 o.p. (ISBN 0-318-15198-7, NO. 21-1022). Natl Assoc Realtors.

Value Analysis in Design & Construction. James J. O'Brien. (Modern Structure Ser.). 1976. text ed. 32.50 o.p. (ISBN 0-07-047566-0). McGraw.

Value & Ethics in Organization & Human Systems Development: An Annotated Bibliography. Ed. by Mark S. Frankel. 104p. 1987. pap. 5.00 o.p. AAAS.

Value & Limitations of Various Approaches to the Monitoring of Water Quality for Freshwater Fish. (European Inland Fisheries Advisory Commission (EIFAC): Technical Papers: No. 32). 31p. (Eng. & Fr.). 1978. pap. 7.50 o.p. (ISBN 92-5-100664-4, F1542, FAO). UNIPUB.

Value & Obligation: Systematic Readings in Ethics. Richard B. Brandt. 1961. text ed. 18.95 o.p. (ISBN 0-15-594710-9, HC). HarBraceJ.

Value Areas & Their Development: Theory & Method of Self-Confrontation. Hubert J. Hermans. Tr. by Joseph A. Spiekerman from Dutch. 306p. 1975. text ed. 17.50 o.p. (ISBN 90-265-0225-7, Pub. by Swets & Zeitlinger Netherlands). CJ Hogrefe Pubs.

Value Clarification As Learning Process: A Handbook for Christian Educators. Brian Hall & Maury Smith. LC 73-81108. (Educator Formation Bks.). (Orig.). 1974. pap. 8.95 o.p. (ISBN 0-8091-1797-5). Paulist Pr.

Value Distribution Theory. L. Sario & K. Noshiro. xi, 236p. 1966. 13.50 o.p. (ISBN 0-387-90130-2). Springer-Verlag.

Value Engineering: A Practical Approach for Owners, Designers, & Contractors. Larry Zimmerman & Glen Hart. 272p. 1982. 31.95 o.p. (ISBN 0-442-29587-1). Van Nos Reinhold.

Value Engineering in the Construction Industry. 3rd ed. Alphonse J. Dell'Isola. 376p. 1982. 43.95 o.p. (ISBN 0-442-26202-7). Van Nos Reinhold.

Value, Exploitation & Growth. A. Morishima & G. Catephores. 1978. text ed. 31.95 o.p. (ISBN 0-07-084075-X). McGraw.

Value of Agricultural Land. Colin Clark. (Illus.). 124p. 1973. text ed. 11.75 o.p. (ISBN 0-08-017070-6). Pergamon.

Value: The Representation of Labour in Capitalism. Ed. by Diane Elson. 1980. text ed. 31.25x o.p. (ISBN 0-906336-07-4); pap. text ed. 15.00x o.p. (ISBN 0-906336-08-2). Humanities.

Values & Leisure & Trends in Leisure Services. Academy of Leisure Sciences Staff. (New Directions in Leisure Ser.). 128p. (Orig.). 1983. pap. 9.95x o.p. (ISBN 0-910251-05-3). Venture Pub PA.

Values & Long-Term Care. Ed. by Robert L. Kane & Rosalie A. Kane. LC 81-47581. 320p. 1982. 40.00x o.p. (ISBN 0-669-04685-X). Lexington Bks.

Values & Religion in China Today: A Teaching Workbook & Lesson Series. Mary L. Martin & Donald MacInnis. 141p. (Orig.). 1985. pap. 12.95 o.p. (ISBN 0-88344-527-1). Orbis Bks.

Values, Curriculum & the Elementary School. Alexander Frazier. LC 79-87862. 1980. text ed. 24.76 o.p. (ISBN 0-395-26739-0). HM.

Values, Employment & Status of Professional Women. National Association for Women Deans, Administrators & Counselors Staff. 1977. pap. 3.00 o.p. (ISBN 0-686-21650-4). Natl Assn Women.

Values in Social Policy: Nine Contradictions. Jean Hardy. (Radical Social Policy Ser.). 132p. (Orig.). 1981. pap. 15.95x o.p. (ISBN 0-7100-0782-5). Routledge Chapman & Hall.

Values Tech: A Portable School for Self-Assessment & Self-Enhancement. Don Koberg & Jim Bagnall. LC 75-19488. (Illus.). 242p. 1976. pap. 8.95 o.p. (ISBN 0-913232-23-8); pap. 6.95 o.p. (ISBN 0-913232-24-6). W Kaufmann.

Valuing a Business: The Analysis & Appraisal of Closely Held Companies. Shannon Pratt. LC 80-85475. 424p. 1981. 55.00 o.p. (ISBN 0-87094-205-0). Dow Jones-Irwin.

Valuing Common Stock: The Power of Prudence. George Lasry. 1979. 17.95 o.p. (ISBN 0-8144-5491-7). AMACOM.

Valutare l'Anziano: Manuale de Riferimento dei Mezzi di Studio e di Misura delle Funzioni Mentali, 2 vols. Liliane Israel et al. (Limited Volume Ser.). xxviii, 668p. (Ital.). 1984. bound 249.50 o.p. (ISBN 3-8055-3835-9). S Karger.

Vampire in Europe. Montague Summers. 1961. 7.50 o.p. (ISBN 0-8216-0036-2, Pub. by Univ Bks). Carol Pub Group.

Vampire of Mons. Desmond Stewart. 1977. pap. 1.50 o.p. (ISBN 0-380-01681-8, 33522). Avon.

Vampires. John Rechy. LC 70-155123. 1971. pap. 2.95 o.p. (ISBN 0-394-17817-3, B362, BC). Grove.

Vampires & the Witch. Lee Falk. (Phantom Ser.: No. 12). 1974. pap. 0.95 o.p. (ISBN 0-380-00034-2, 19406). Avon.

Vampires: Two Centuries of Great Vampire Stories. Alan Ryan. LC 86-24238. 576p. 1987. 15.95 o.s.i. (ISBN 0-385-18562-6). Doubleday.

Vampires Unearthed: The Vampire & Dracula Bibliography of Books, Articles, Movies, Records, & Other Material. Martin V. Riccardo. LC 82-49261. (Supernatural Studies). 150p. 1983. lib. bdg. 21.00 o.p. (ISBN 0-8240-9128-0). Garland Pub.

Van Alens: First Family of a Nation's First City. Samuel A. Schreiner, Jr. LC 80-70222. 448p. 1981. 12.95 o.p. (ISBN 0-87795-311-2, Arbor Hse). Morrow.

Van Buren Co., Michigan Platbook of Early 1930's: With Every Name Index. Intro. by Toni Benson. (Illus., Orig.). 1988. pap. 10.00 o.p. F-Ami-Lee.

Van Cortlandt Manor. Joseph T. Butler. LC 77-17531. (Sleepy Hollow Restorations Guidebook). (Illus.). 1978. pap. 1.95 o.p. (ISBN 0-912882-33-6). Sleepy Hollow.

Van der Waals Systems. Ed. by F. L. Boschke. (Topics in Current Chemistry: Vol. 93). (Illus.). 140p. 1981. 42.00 o.p. (ISBN 0-387-10058-X). Springer-Verlag.

Van Dyke & the Mythical City, Hollywood. Robert Cannom. LC 76-52096. (Classics of Film Literature Ser.: Vol. 8). (Illus.). 1977. Repr. of 1948 ed. lib. bdg. 26.00 o.p. (ISBN 0-8240-2870-8). Garland Pub.

Van Gogh. rev. ed. Pierre Cabanne. LC 85-51232. (World of Art Ser.). (Illus.). 288p. 1986. pap. 9.95 o.p. (ISBN 0-500-20092-0). Thames Hudson.

Van Halen. (Metal Mania Ser.). (Illus.). 64p. (gr. 4-12). 1984. 6.95 o.p. (ISBN 0-88188-296-8, Robus Books). H Leonard Pub Corp.

Van Sickle's Modern Airmanship. 5th ed. Ed. by John F. Welch. 878p. 1981. 28.95 o.p. (ISBN 0-442-25793-7). Van Nos Reinhold.

Van Wyck Brooks: A Reference Guide. James R. Vitelli. 1977. lib. bdg. 18.00 o.p. (ISBN 0-8161-7978-6, Hall Reference). G K Hall.

Vancouver Guide Book: The Definitive Guide to Western Canada's Greatest Metropolis. Ginny Evans & Beth Evans. (Illus.). 310p. (Orig.). 1986. pap. 5.95 o.p. (ISBN 0-87701-382-9). Chronicle Bks.

Vancouver Island Railroads. Robert Turner. LC 72-95484. (Illus.). 170p. 21.95 o.p. (ISBN 0-87095-046-0). Gldn West Bks.

Vandalism Control Management in Parks & Recreation. Monty L. Christiansen. (New Directions in Leisure Ser.). (Illus.). 128p. (Orig.). 1983. pap. 9.95 o.p. (ISBN 0-910251-06-1). Venture Pub PA.

Vandalism: The Not-So-Senseless Crime. Arnold Madison. LC 70-125833. 160p. (gr. 6 up). 1979. 8.95 o.p. (ISBN 0-395-28914-9, Clarion). HM.

Vandalism: The Not-So-Senseless Crime. Arnold Madison. 160p. (gr. 6 up). 1981. pap. 3.95 o.p. (ISBN 0-395-30009-6, Clarion). HM.

Vandals of Treason House. Nancy Veglahn. (Illus.). 160p. (gr. 3-6). 1974. 7.95 o.p. (ISBN 0-395-18590-4). HM.

Vanderbilts in My Life. Shirley Burden. LC 81-9012. (Illus.). 144p. 1981. 27.50 o.p. (ISBN 0-89919-049-9). Ticknor & Fields.

Vanessa. Ann Pinchot. LC 76-39717. 1977. 8.95 o.p. (ISBN 0-87795-157-8, Arbor Hse). Morrow.

Vanessa's First Love. Angelo Resciniti. (Impressions Ser.). 96p. (Orig.). (gr. 5-8). 1987. pap. 2.25 o.s.i. (ISBN 0-87406-248-9). Willowisp Pr.

Vangelo Secondo Barabba see Gospel According to Barabbas.

Vanguard: An Anarchist Communist Journal, Vols. 1-4, No. 9. 1970. Repr. of 1939 ed. lib. bdg. 53.00x o.p. (ISBN 0-8371-9257-9, VA00). Greenwood.

Vanguard Management: Redesigning the Corporate Future. James O'Toole. LC 84-24644. (Illus.). 432p. 1985. 19.95 o.s.i. (ISBN 0-385-19842-6). Doubleday.

Vanguard of Nazism: The Free Corps Movement in Postwar Germany, 1918-23. Robert G. Waite. 1969. pap. 4.95 o.p. (ISBN 0-393-00181-4, Norton Lib). Norton.

Vanished Splendor II: A Postcard Album of Oklahoma City. Hal N. Ottaway. LC 82-72945. (Illus.). 88p. 1983. 19.95 o.p. (ISBN 0-910453-01-2). Abalache Bkshop.

Vanished Splendor: Postcard Views of Early Oklahoma City. Hal N. Ottaway & Jim L. Edwards. LC 82-72945. (Illus.). 64p. 1982. 17.95 o.p. (ISBN 0-910453-00-4). Abalache Bkshop.

Vanished World. Anne G. Sneller. LC 64-16923. (Illus.). 1964. 9.95 o.p. (ISBN 0-8156-0037-2). Syracuse U Pr.

Vanishing Breed: Photographs of the Cowboys & the West. William A. Allard. LC 82-60768. 1982. 34.95 o.p. (ISBN 0-8212-1505-1); Deluxe ed. 125.00 o.p. (ISBN 0-8212-1524-8). Little.

Vanishing City. Allen Varney. LC 86-91534. (AD&D Adventure Gamebook Ser.: No. 15). 192p. 1987. pap. 2.95 o.s.i. (ISBN 0-88038-434-4). TSR Inc.

Vanishing Depot. Ranulph Bye. 1984. 35.00 o.p. (ISBN 0-910702-11-X). Bentley PA.

Vanishing Farmland: A Legal Solution for the States. Sarah E. Redfield. 224p. 1984. 30.00x o.p. (ISBN 0-669-08233-3). Lexington Bks.

Vanishing Legion: A History of Mascot Pictures, 1927-1935. Jon Tuska. LC 81-6014. (Illus.). 224p. 1982. lib. bdg. 17.95x o.p. (ISBN 0-89950-030-7). McFarland & Co.

Vanishing Race: Selections from Edward S. Curtis' the North American Indian. Ed. by Mick Gidley. LC 76-23476. (Illus.). 1977. 9.95 o.s.i. (ISBN 0-8008-7945-7). Taplinger.

Vanishing Scarecrow. Phyllis A. Whitney. (Illus.). (gr. 5-9). 1971. 5.50 o.s.i. (ISBN 0-664-32494-0, Westminster). Westminster John Knox.

Vanishing Wilderness. Francesca La Monte & Micaela Welch. (Black & Gold Lib). (Illus.). 1949. 6.95 o.p. (ISBN 0-87140-812-0). Liveright.

Vanity Fair. William Makepeace Thackeray. 1979. Repr. of 1908 ed. 13.95x o.p. (ISBN 0-460-10298-2, Evman); pap. 6.95x o.p. (ISBN 0-460-11298-8, Evman). Biblio Dist.

Vanity Fair. William Makepeace Thackeray. 1950. pap. 3.95x o.s.i. (ISBN 0-394-30933-2, T33, Mod LibC). Modern Lib.

Vanity Fair. rev. ed. William Makepeace Thackeray. Ed. by Harry Shefter et al. (Illus.). (YA) pap. 1.25 o.s.i. (ISBN 0-671-48119-3). WSP.

Vanity Fair's Backgammon to Win. Georges Mabardi & Clare Booth Luce. 1974. 5.95 o.p. (ISBN 0-671-21766-6). S&S.

Vanning Trends. Ed. by Spence Murray. LC 77-84297. (Pickups & Vans Ser.). (Illus., Orig.). 1977. pap. 3.95 o.p. (ISBN 0-8227-5015-5). Petersen Pub.

Vanuatu: Politics, Economics & Ritual in Island Melanesia. Ed. by Michael Allen. LC 81-65767. (Studies in Population). 425p. 1982. 44.00 o.p. (ISBN 0-12-051450-8). Acad Pr.

Vanya. Myrna Grant. 208p. 1976. 3.25 o.p. (ISBN 0-88113-310-8). Edit Betania.

Vanya & the Clay Queen. Gary M. Prince. LC 74-9035. (Illus.). 32p. (gr. 2-5). 1975. PLB 4.95 o.p. (ISBN 0-87614-049-5). Carolrhoda Bks.

Vapor-Liquid Equilibria Using UNIFAC: A Group Contribution Method. Fredenslund et al. 380p. 1977. 129.00 o.p. (ISBN 0-444-41621-8). Elsevier.

Varia. John Ashton. LC 68-9573. (Illus.). 224p. 1968. Repr. of 1894 ed. 35.00x o.p. (ISBN 0-8103-3502-6). Gale.

Variable Impedance Devices. Ed. by M. J. Howes & D. V. Morgan. LC 78-4122. (Solid State Devices & Circuits Ser.). 291p. 1979. 85.00 o.p. (ISBN 0-471-99651-3, Pub. by Wiley-Interscience). Wiley.

Variable Phase Approach to Potential Scattering. F. Calogero. (Mathematics in Science & Engineering Ser.: Vol. 35). 1967. 82.50 o.p. (ISBN 0-12-155550-X). Acad Pr.

Variable Plot Cruising. J. R. Dilworth. 1988. pap. text ed. 6.40x o.p. (ISBN 0-88246-030-7). Oreg St U Bkstrs.

Variable Stars. W. Strohmeier. 287p. 1972. 45.00 o.p. (ISBN 0-08-016675-X). Pergamon.

Variant Spellings in Modern American Dictionaries. rev. ed. Donald W. Emery. LC 73-83843. 130p. (Orig.). 1973. pap. 6.75 o.p. (ISBN 0-8141-5630-4). NCTE.

Variation Method in Quantum Chemistry. Saul T. Epstein. 1974. 101.00 o.p. (ISBN 0-12-240550-1). Acad Pr.

Variational Methods in Nuclear Reactor Physics. Weston M. Stacey, Jr. (Nuclear Science & Technology Ser.). 1974. 67.00 o.p. (ISBN 0-12-662060-1). Acad Pr.

Variational Methods in Theoretical Mechanics. 2nd, rev. ed. J. T. Oden & J. N. Reddy. (Universitext Ser.). 308p. 1982. pap. 23.00 o.p. (ISBN 0-387-11917-5). Springer-Verlag.

Variations & Connections of the Human Thalamus. J. M. Van Buren & R. C. Borke. Incl. Pt. 1. Nuclei & Cerebral Connections of the Human Thalamus; Pt. 2. Variations of the Human Diencephalon. LC 73-174253. (Illus.). 496p. 1972. Set. 231.00 o.p. (ISBN 0-387-05543-6). Springer-Verlag.

Variations in Children's Services among Urban Authorities. Bleddyn Davies. 159p. 1972. pap. text ed. 6.25x o.p. (ISBN 0-7135-1676-3, Pub. by Bedford England). Gower Pub Co.

Variations in Services for the Aged. Bleddyn P. Davies. 164p. 1971. pap. text ed. 6.25x o.p. (ISBN 0-7135-1621-6, Pub. by Bedford England). Gower Pub Co.

Variations of the Human Diencephalon see Variations & Connections of the Human Thalamus.

Variations on the Imperial Theme: Studies in Ceremonial Art & Collecting in the Age of Maximilian II & Rudolf II. Thomas D. Kaufmann. LC 77-94699. (Outstanding Dissertations in the Fine Arts Ser.). 1978. lib. bdg. 29.00x o.p. (ISBN 0-8240-3231-4). Garland Pub.

Variations on Wayne Sleep. Wayne Sleep. (Illus.). 96p. 1983. pap. 12.95 o.p. (ISBN 0-434-70756-2, Pub. by W Heinemann Ltd). David & Charles.

Variations sur les Bucoliques see Bucoliques de Virgile.

Varicella Virus. D. Taylor-Robinson & A. E. Caunt. LC 72-79604. (Virology Monographs: Vol. 12). (Illus.). 88p. 1972. 19.00 o.p. (ISBN 0-387-81065-X). Springer-Verlag.

Varicose Veins. Harold Ellis. LC 82-3975. (Positive Health Guide Ser.). (Illus.). 112p. 1983. pap. 7.95 o.p. (ISBN 0-668-05340-2, 5340). Arco.

Varicose Veins, Related Diseases & Sclerotherapy: A Guide for Practitioners. H. I. Biegeleisen. 255p. 1984. text ed. 35.00 o.s.i. (ISBN 0-920792-18-9). Eden Pr.

Varied Pattern: Studies in the 18th Century. Peter Hughes & David Williams. LC 70-159260. (McMaster 18th Century Studies). 457p. 1979. lib. bdg. 48.00 o.p. (ISBN 0-8240-4000-7). Garland Pub.

Varieties of Jewish Belief. Louis Barish & Rebecca Barish. 1979. Repr. 9.95 o.p. (ISBN 0-8246-0242-0). Jonathan David.

Varieties of Present-Day English. Richard W. Bailey & Jay L. Robinson. (Illus.). 416p. 1973. pap. text ed. write for info. o.p. (ISBN 0-02-305200-7, 30520). Macmillan.

Varieties of Religious Experiences. William James. 1961. pap. 4.95 o.p. (ISBN 0-02-085960-0, Collier). Macmillan.

Variety Film Reviews: 1907-1920, Vol. 1. Ed. by Mike Kaplan. LC 82-15691. (Variety Film Reviews Ser.). 1983. lib. bdg. 165.00 o.p. (ISBN 0-8240-5200-5). Garland Pub.

Variety Film Reviews: 1921-1925, Vo. 2. Ed. by Mike Kaplan. LC 82-15691. (Variety Film Reviews Ser.). 560p. 1983. lib. bdg. 165.00 o.p. (ISBN 0-8240-5201-3). Garland Pub.

Variety Film Reviews: 1926-1929, Vol. 3. Ed. by Mike Kaplan. LC 82-15691. (Variety Film Reviews Ser.). 520p. 1983. lib. bdg. 165.00 o.p. (ISBN 0-8240-5202-1). Garland Pub.

Variety Film Reviews: 1930-1933, Vol. 4. Ed. by Mike Kaplan. LC 82-15691. (Variety Film Reviews Ser.). 592p. 1983. lib. bdg. 165.00 o.p. (ISBN 0-8240-5203-X). Garland Pub.

Variety Film Reviews: 1934-1937, Vol. 5. Ed. by Mike Kaplan. LC 82-15691. (Variety Film Reviews Ser.). 632p. 1983. lib. bdg. 165.00 o.p. (ISBN 0-8240-5204-8). Garland Pub.

Variety Film Reviews: 1938-1942, Vol. 6. Ed. by Mike Kaplan. LC 82-15691. (Variety Film Reviews Ser.). 696p. 1982. lib. bdg. 165.00 o.p. (ISBN 0-8240-5205-6). Garland Pub.

Variety Film Reviews: 1943-1948, Vol. 7. Ed. by Mike Kaplan. LC 82-15691. (Variety Film Reviews Ser.). 1983. lib. bdg. 165.00 o.p. (ISBN 0-8240-5206-4). Garland Pub.

Variety Film Reviews: 1949-1953, Vol. 8. Ed. by Mike Kaplan. LC 82-15691. (Variety Film Reviews Ser.). 664p. 1982. lib. bdg. 165.00 o.p. (ISBN 0-8240-5207-2). Garland Pub.

Variety Film Reviews: 1954-1958, Vol. 9. Ed. by Mike Kaplan. LC 82-15691. (Variety Film Reviews Ser.). 624p. 1983. lib. bdg. 165.00 o.p. (ISBN 0-8240-5208-0). Garland Pub.

Variety Film Reviews: 1959-1963, Vol. 10. Ed. by Mike Kaplan. LC 82-15691. (Variety Film Reviews Ser.). 632p. 1983. lib. bdg. 165.00 o.p. (ISBN 0-8240-5209-9). Garland Pub.

Variety Film Reviews: 1964-1967, Vol. 11. Ed. by Mike Kaplan. LC 82-15691. (Variety Film Reviews Ser.). 592p. 1983. lib. bdg. 165.00 o.p. (ISBN 0-8240-5210-2). Garland Pub.

Variety Film Reviews: 1968-1970, Vol. 12. Ed. by Mike Kaplan. LC 82-15691. (Variety Film Reviews Ser.). 608p. 1983. lib. bdg. 165.00 o.p. (ISBN 0-8240-5211-0). Garland Pub.

Variety Film Reviews: 1971-1974, Vol. 13. Ed. by Mike Kaplan. LC 82-15691. (Variety Film Reviews Ser.). 648p. 1983. lib. bdg. 165.00 o.p. (ISBN 0-8240-5212-9). Garland Pub.

Variety Film Reviews: 1975-1977, Vol. 14. Ed. by Mike Kaplan. LC 82-15691. (Variety Film Reviews Ser.). 560p. 1983. lib. bdg. 165.00 o.p. (ISBN 0-8240-5213-7). Garland Pub.

Variety Film Reviews: 1978-1980, Vol. 15. Ed. by Mike Kaplan. LC 82-15691. (Variety Film Reviews Ser.). 648p. 1983. lib. bdg. 165.00 o.p. (ISBN 0-8240-5214-5). Garland Pub.

Variety Film Reviews: 1983-1984, Vol. 18. Variety Staff. (Variety Film Reviews Ser.). 646p. 1986. lib. bdg. 173.00 o.p. (ISBN 0-8240-5218-8). Garland Pub.

Variety Index Film Reviews, 1907-1980. Mike Kaplan. LC 82-15691. 298p. 1985. 220.00 o.p. (ISBN 0-8240-5215-3). Garland Pub.

Variety: International Motion Picture Marketplace, 1982-1983. Ed. by Mike Kaplan. LC 82-9182. 430p. 1982. 50.00 o.p. (ISBN 0-8240-9378-X). Garland Pub.

Variety: International Show Business Reference. Ed. by Mike Kaplan. LC 81-2329. (Reference Library of the Humanities: Vol. 292). 1135p. 1981. 75.00 o.p. (ISBN 0-8240-9341-0). Garland Pub.

Variety International Showbusiness, 1983. Kaplan. (Variety Bks.). 1983. lib. bdg. 75.00 o.p. (ISBN 0-8240-9089-6). Garland Pub.

Variety's Complete Home Video Directory 1988. 852p. 1988. pap. 129.95 incl. 3 quarterly suppl. o.p. Without adult titles (ISBN 0-8352-2598-4, 0000-1015). With adult titles (ISBN 0-8352-2587-9, 0000-1007). Bowker.

Variety's Who's Who in Show Business. Ed. by Mike Kaplan. 493p. 1983. pap. 15.95 o.p. (ISBN 0-8240-4191-7). Garland Pub.

Varina Howell: Wife of Jefferson Davis. Eron Rowland. 1981. 10.00 o.p. (ISBN 0-88289-283-5). Pelican.

Variorum Civil Disobedience. Henry David Thoreau. Ed. by Walter Harding. 91p. text ed. 24.00x o.p. (ISBN 0-8290-0215-4); pap. text ed. 9.95x o.p. (ISBN 0-8290-0216-2). Irvington.

Variorum Disobedience see Variorum Walden.

Variorum Walden. Henry David Thoreau. Ed. by Walter Harding. 320p. text ed. 29.50x o.p. (ISBN 0-8290-0217-0); pap. text ed. 14.95x o.p. (ISBN 0-8290-0218-9). Irvington.

Variorum Walden. Henry David Thoreau. Ed. by Walter Harding. Bd. with Variorum Disobedience. pap. 1.50 o.s.i. (ISBN 0-671-48507-5). WSP.

Varnell Roberts, Super-Pigeon. Genevieve Gray. 128p. (gr. 5 up). 1975. 5.95 o.p. (ISBN 0-395-21408-4). HM.

Varney's Nurse-Midwifery. Varney. 1987. 44.95 o.p. (ISBN 0-8016-5227-8). Mosby.

Vasari on Technique. Giorgio Vasari. Ed. by B. Baldwin Brown. (Illus.). 16.00 o.p. (ISBN 0-8446-3108-6). Peter Smith.

Vascular & Doppler Ultrasound. Ed. by C. Carl Jaffe. (Clinics in Diagnostic Ultrasound Ser: Vol. 13). (Illus.). 211p. 1984. text ed. 33.00 o.p. (ISBN 0-443-08295-2). Churchill.

Vascular Disease & Aging, 2 vols. Incl. Vol. 1. J. Judson McNamara et al. 194p (ISBN 0-8422-7254-2); Vol. 2. Marjorie Semmens et al. 154p (ISBN 0-8422-7255-0). 1976. text ed. 29.50x ea. o.p. Irvington.

Vascular Disease of the Central Nervous System. 2nd ed. Ross R. W. Russell. (Illus.). 1983. text ed. 98.00 o.p. (ISBN 0-443-02415-4). Churchill.

Vascular Pattern in Embryos with Clefts of Primary & Secondary Palate. E. Frederiks. LC 72-96862. (Advances in Anatomy, Embryology & Cell Biology: Vol. 46, Pt. 6). (Illus.). 60p. 1973. pap. 18.90 o.p. (ISBN 0-387-06128-2). Springer-Verlag.

Vascular Radionuclide Imaging: A Clinical Atlas. Joseph T. Ennis & David J. Dowsett. LC 82-17594. 239p. 1983. 100.00 o.p. (ISBN 0-471-25670-6, Dist. by A R Liss). Wiley.

Vascular Smooth Muscle: Proceedings. International Congress of Physiological Sciences & Annual Meeting of the German Angiological Society, Tuebingen, 1971. Ed. by E. Betz. LC 76-185190. (Illus.). 240p. 1972. pap. 18.90 o.p. (ISBN 0-387-05711-0). Springer-Verlag.

Vascular Surgery. Henry Haimovici. (Illus.). 1976. text ed. 100.00 o.p. (ISBN 0-07-025514-8). McGraw.

Vasculitides. Thomas R. Cupps & Anthony S. Fauci. (Major Problems in Internal Medicine: No.21). 1981. pap. write for info. o.p. (ISBN 0-7216-2794-3). Saunders.

Vasectomy: Current Research in Male Sterilization. Frederick J. Ziegler et al. (Illus.). 220p. 1973. text ed. 32.50x o.p. (ISBN 0-8422-7097-3). Irvington.

Vasidilators in Chronic Heart Failure. Ed. by H. Just & W. D. Bussmann. (Illus.). 233p. 1983. 29.80 o.p. (ISBN 0-387-11616-8). Springer-Verlag.

Vasilisa the Beautiful: Russian Fairy Tales. 213p. 1974. 4.45 o.p. (ISBN 0-8285-1256-6, Pub. by Progress Pubs USSR). Imported Pubns.

Vasko Popa: Selected Poems. Vasko Popa. Tr. by Anne Pennington. LC 78-50706. 1979. 12.50 o.p. (ISBN 0-89255-033-3); pap. 7.95 o.p. (ISBN 0-89255-034-1). Persea Bks.

Vasopressin, I: Chemical & Clinical Aspects. J. D. Glickson et al. 204p. 1974. 24.50x o.p. (ISBN 0-8422-7123-6). Irvington.

Vasopressin, II: Clinical Aspects. C. A. Pissiotis et al. 1973. 24.50x o.p. (ISBN 0-8422-7127-9). Irvington.

Vassouras: A Brazilian Coffee County, 1850-1900. Stanley J. Stein. LC 57-8627. (Studies in American Negro Life). 1970. pap. 5.95x o.p. (ISBN 0-689-70229-9, NL23, Atheneum). Macmillan.

Vast Majority. Michael Harrington. 1978. pap. 8.50 o.p. (ISBN 0-671-24407-8, Touchstone Bks). S&S.

Vatican & Christian Rome. Photos by Mario Carrieri. (Illus.). 522p. 1979. 100.00 o.p. (ISBN 0-89860-025-1). Eastview.

Vatican Art. Karl Ipser. (Illus.). 198p. 1953. (ISBN 0-8022-0779-0). Philos Lib.

Vatican Collections: The Papacy & Art. 1983. 29.95 o.p. (ISBN 0-8109-1710-6). Abrams.

Vatican Connection. Richard Hammer. 352p. 1983. pap. 3.50 o.s.i. (ISBN 0-441-86053-2). Ace Bks.

Vatican Connection: The Astonishing Account of a Billion-Dollar Counterfeit Stock Deal Between the Mafia & the Church. Richard Hammer. LC 82-1044. 1982. 14.95 o.p. (ISBN 0-03-060146-0). H Holt & Co.

Vatican II: Open Questions & New Horizons. Ed. by Gerald M. Fagin. LC 83-82665. (Theology & Life Ser.: Vol. 8). pap. 6.95 o.p. (ISBN 0-89453-366-5). M Glazier.

Vatican Rip. Jonathan Gash. LC 81-14387. (Joan Kahn Bk.). 228p. 1982. 10.95 o.p. (ISBN 0-89919-080-4). Ticknor & Fields.

Vatican Two, A Satanic Victory. James P. McGaughan. 1980. 7.50 o.p. (ISBN 0-682-49470-4). Exposition-Phoenix.

Vatzlav. Slawomir Mrozek. Tr. by Ralph Manheim from Pol. (Illus.). 1970. pap. 1.95 o.s.i. (ISBN 0-394-17290-6, E568, Ever). Grove.

Vaulting: Gymnastics on Horseback. Paki Stedwell. LC 79-11556. (Illus.). 128p. (gr. 7 up). 1980. lib. bdg. 8.79 o.s.i. (ISBN 0-671-34023-9). Messner.

Vazsonyi's Introduction to Data Processing: Study Guide. 3rd ed. Herbert F. Spirer & Marilynn Dueker. 1980. pap. 10.95 o.p. (ISBN 0-256-02381-6). Irwin.

VD: A Doctor's Answers. Suzanne M. Sgroi. LC 73-5245. (gr. 7 up). 1974. 6.50 o.p. (ISBN 0-15-293350-6, HJ). HarBraceJ.

VD: A Guide for Nurses & Counselors. Barbara Morton. (Illus.). 1976. pap. 12.00 o.p. (ISBN 0-316-58530-0). Little.

VEBAs & Fringe Benefits. (Tax Law & Estate Planning Course Handbook: Vol. 203). 905p. 1984. 40.00 o.p. (ISBN 0-317-11446-8, J4-3544). PLI.

Vector Analysis Problem Solver. Research & Education Association Staff. LC 84-61811. (Illus.). 1280p. 1988. pap. text ed. 29.85 o.p. (ISBN 0-87891-554-0). Res & Educ.

Vector & Operator-Valued Measures & Applications. Ed. by Don H. Tucker. 1974. 71.50 o.p. (ISBN 0-12-702450-6). Acad Pr.

Vector Calculus. F. W. Bedford & T. D. Dwivedi. 1970. text ed. 26.00 o.p. (ISBN 0-07-004720-0, C). McGraw.

Vector Control Assittant. (Career Examination Ser.: C-3481). 1988. pap. 16.00 o.p. (ISBN 0-8373-3481-0). Natl Learning.

Vector Measures. N. Dinculeanu. LC 68-6701. 1967. text ed. 36.30 o.p. (ISBN 0-08-012192-6). Pergamon.

Vector Mechanics of Fluids & Magneto-Fluids. Ed. by Salamon Eskinazi. 1967. 63.00 o.p. (ISBN 0-12-242558-8). Acad Pr.

Vectorcardiography. Alberto Benchimol. LC 78-9932. 236p. 1979. Repr. of 1973 ed. lib. bdg. 21.50 o.p. (ISBN 0-88275-762-8). Krieger.

Vectors & Matrices. Pamela Liebeck. 192p. 1971. 37.00 o.p. (ISBN 0-08-015823-4); pap. 17.00 o.p. (ISBN 0-08-015822-6). Pergamon.

Vedanta Dictionary. Ernest Wood. LC 63-18059. 232p. 1964. (ISBN 0-8022-1923-3). Philos Lib.

Vegetable Cookbook. Paul Mayer. Ed. by Jackie Walsh. (Illus.). 192p. 1975. pap. 5.95 o.p. Bristol Pub Ent CA.

Vegetable Crop Diseases. G. R. Dixon. 1981. 37.95 o.p. (ISBN 0-87055-390-9). AVI.

Vegetable Staticks. Stephen Hales. LC 75-101421. 1969. 20.00 o.p. (ISBN 0-685-52454-X). Watson Pub Intl.

Vegetables. Bon Appetit Magazine Editors. LC 83-10088. (Cooking with Bon Appetit Ser.). (Illus.). 144p. 1984. 12.95 o.p. (ISBN 0-89535-119-6). Knapp Pr.

Vegetables in Patches & Pots: A Child's Guide to Organic Vegetable Gardening. Lorelie M. Mintz. LC 76-46998. (Illus.). 128p. (gr. 4 up). 1976. 9.95 o.p. (ISBN 0-374-38091-0). FS&G.

Vegetarian Cooking for Diabetics. Patricia Mozzer. LC 86-72536. (Illus.). 144p. 1987. pap. 9.95 o.p. (ISBN 0-913990-47-7). Book Pub Co.

Vegetarian Gourmet Cookery. Alan Hooker. LC 72-19332. (Illus., Orig.). 1970. pap. 5.95 o.p. (ISBN 0-912238-03-8, One Hund One Prods). Ortho.

Vegetarian Pita Bread Recipes: Delicious Wholefood Meal-In-A-Pocket. Leah Leneman. (Illus.). 112p. (Orig.). 1988. pap. 5.99 o.p. (ISBN 0-7225-1235-X, Pub. by Aquarian Pr England). Sterling.

Vegetarian Primer. Peter Burwash & John Tullius. LC 82-45165. (Illus.). 192p. 1983. 14.95 o.p. (ISBN 0-689-11299-8, Atheneum). Macmillan.

Vegetarian Times Cookbook. Vegetarian Times Editors. 352p. 1984. 18.22 o.p. (ISBN 0-02-621740-6, Collier); pap. 9.95 o.p. (ISBN 0-02-010370-0). Macmillan.

Vegetarian Times Guide to Dining in the U. S. A. Ed. by Kathleen Moore. LC 78-73109. (Illus.). 1980. pap. 8.95 o.p. (ISBN 0-689-10966-0, Atheneum). Macmillan.

Vegetation & the Atmosphere, Vol. 1. Ed. by J. L. Monteith. 1976. 69.00 o.p. (ISBN 0-12-505101-8). Acad Pr.

Vegetation of North Stradbroke Island. H. T. Clifford & R. L. Specht. (Illus.). 1979. pap. 16.50x o.p. (ISBN 0-7022-1267-9). U of Queensland Pr.

Vegetation Surveys of Western Australia: Murchison Memoir No. 6. J. S. Beard. (Vegetation Surveys of W. Australia Ser.). (Illus.). 1977. pap. 12.00x o.p. (ISBN 0-85564-093-6, Pub. by U of W Austral Pr). Intl Spec Bk.

Vegetation Surveys of Western Australia: Swan Memoir No. 7. J. S. Beard. (Illus.). 1977. pap. 20.50x o.p. (ISBN 0-85564-094-4, Pub. by U of W Austral Pr). Intl Spec Bk.

Vegeterian Gourmet Cookery. rev. ed. Alan Hooker. LC 81-22541. (Illus., Orig.). 1982. pap. 6.95 o.p. (ISBN 0-89286-197-5, One Hund One Prods). Ortho.

Vehicle Body Building: Pt. 1. Ed. by B. Coombes et al. (Engineering Craftsmen: Pt. 2). (Illus.). 1968. 49.95x o.p. (ISBN 0-89563-035-4). Trans-Atl Phila.

Vehicle Body Building, Pt. 2, 2 vols. Ed. by B. Coombes. (Engineering Craftsmen: No. E22). (Illus.). 1969. Set. spiral bdg. 82.50x o.p. Trans-Atl Phila.

Vehicle Fitting. Ed. by R. Aylen et al. (Engineering Craftsmen: No. H8). (Illus.). 1978. spiral bdg. 39.95x o.p. (ISBN 0-89563-036-2). Trans-Atl Phila.

Vehicle Painting, Pt. 1. Ed. by F. Brown et al. (Engineering Craftsmen: No. E1). (Illus.). 1968. spiral bdg. 45.00x o.p. Trans-Atl Phila.

Vehicle Painting, Pt. 2. Ed. by F. Brown et al. (Engineering Craftsmen: No. E21). 1970. spiral bdg. 45.00x o.p. Trans-Atl Phila.

Vehicle Structures. Institute of Mechanical Engineers Staff. 1984. 63.00 o.p. (MEP200). Soc Auto Engineers.

Vehicles At War. Denis Bishop & Christopher Ellis. 25.00 o.p. (ISBN 0-8453-1699-0, Cornwall Bks). Assoc Univ Prs.

Veil. George C. Chesbro. 240p. 1987. pap. 3.95 o.p. (ISBN 0-445-40523-6). Mysterious Pr.

Velanidia-The Acorn Tree: The History of a Greek Peasant Family. Harry Bersentes. 1986. 14.95 o.p. (ISBN 0-533-06536-4). Vantage.

Velazquez. Maurice Serullaz. (Library of Great Painters Ser.). 1985. 45.00 o.p. (ISBN 0-8109-1712-2). Abrams.

Velazquez Goya, the Dehumanization of Art & Other Essays. Jose Ortega Y Gasset. Tr. by Alexis Brown. (Illus.). 142p. 1972. 17.50x o.p. (ISBN 0-393-04358-4). Norton.

Velo-News Cyclist's Training Diary. Photos by Robert F. George. (Illus.). 176p. (Orig.). 1982. pap. 6.95 o.p. (ISBN 0-941950-02-6). Vitesse Pr.

Velocette Singles '53 - '70. Jeff Clew. (Owners Workshop Manuals Ser.: No. 186). 1979. 13.50 o.p. (ISBN 0-85696-186-8, Pub. by J H Haynes England). Haynes Pubns.

Velocity of Light. J. M. Sanders. 1965. 23.00 o.p. (ISBN 0-08-011315-X); pap. 10.50 o.p. (ISBN 0-08-011314-1). Pergamon.

Velvet Angel. Jude Deveraux. 1985. lib. bdg. 13.95 o.p. (ISBN 0-8161-3793-5, Large Print Bks). G K Hall.

Velvet Bubble. Alice Winter. 1978. pap. 1.75 o.p. (ISBN 0-505-51325-0, Pub. by Tower Bks). Dorchester Pub Co.

Velvet Covered Brick. Howard Butt. LC 72-11352. 1978. pap. 3.95i o.p. (ISBN 0-06-061259-2, RD 288). HarpR.

Velvet Monkeywrench. rev. ed. John Muir. LC 72-96736. (Illus.). 247p. (Orig.). 1980. pap. 4.50 o.p. (ISBN 0-912528-02-8). John Muir.

Velvet Paws & Whiskers. Jean Chapman. (Teacher Resource Collections Ser.). (Illus.). 168p. (ps-6). 1982. lib. bdg. 19.93 o.p. (ISBN 0-516-08953-6). Childrens.

Velvet Promise. Jude Deveraux. 1984. lib. bdg. 17.95 o.p. (ISBN 0-8161-3783-8, Large Print Bks). G K Hall.

Velvet Song. Jude Deveraux. (General Ser.). 1984. lib. bdg. 13.95 o.p. (ISBN 0-8161-3633-5, Large Print). G K Hall.

Velveteen Rabbit Book & Audiocassette. (Illus.). 1987. 5.98 o.p. (ISBN 0-89471-509-7, Pub. by Courage Bks). Running Pr.

Vendetta. Joel D. Humphreys. 240p. 1983. pap. 2.75 o.p. (ISBN 0-380-63644-1, 63644-1). Avon.

Vendetta for the Saint. Leslie Charteris. (Saint Ser.). 288p. 1979. pap. 1.95 o.p. (ISBN 0-441-86105-9). Ace Bks.

Veneer Craft for Everyone. Harry J. Hobbs. LC 75-45326. (Encore Edition). (Illus.). 1976. 3.95 o.p. (ISBN 0-684-16195-8, ScribT). Scribner.

Veneering Simplified. Harry J. Hobbs. 1981. 11.95 o.s.i. (ISBN 0-684-16763-8, ScribT). Scribner.

Venereological Medicine Pocket Consultant. Willcox & Willcox. (Illus.). 352p. 1982. pap. 19.95 o.p. (ISBN 0-86286-001-6, B-5446-7). Mosby.

Venetian Affair. Helen MacInnes. LC 63-17774. 1963. 8.95 o.s.i. (ISBN 0-15-193501-7). HarBraceJ.

Venetian Empire. Jan Morris. LC 80-14046. (Helen & Kurt Wolff Bk.). (Illus.). 208p. 1980. 19.95 o.p. (ISBN 0-15-193504-1). HarBraceJ.

Venetian Family & Its Fortune, 1500-1900: The Dona & the Conservation of Their Wealth. James C. Davis. LC 74-26309. (Memoirs Ser.: Vol. 106). (Illus.). 1975. 12.00 o.p. (ISBN 0-87169-106-X). Am Philos.

Venetian Mask. Mickey Friedman. 1987. 18.95 o.p. (ISBN 0-684-18783-3). Scribner.

Venetian Vespers. Anthony Hecht. LC 79-52419. 1979. 10.00 o.p. (ISBN 0-689-11015-4, Atheneum); pap. 6.95 o.p. (ISBN 0-689-11019-7). Macmillan.

Venezuela Alive. 3rd ed. Arnold Greenberg & Harriet Greenberg. (Alive Travel Ser.). (Illus.). 250p. pap. 9.95 o.p. (ISBN 0-935572-13-9). Alive Pubns.

Venezuela Alive. Harriet Greenberg & Arnold L. Greenberg. 1974. pap. 2.00 o.p. (ISBN 0-935572-04-X). Alive Pubns.

Venezuela: Oil & Politics. Romulo Betancourt. 1979. 14.95 o.p. (ISBN 0-395-27945-3). HM.

Venezuela, Uncle Sam & OPEC: A Story for All Americans. William H. Gray. 189p. (Orig.). 1982. pap. 7.50 o.p. (ISBN 0-686-94960-9, Pub by O. E. G. Foundation). Exposition-Phoenix.

Venezuelan History: A Comprehensive Bibliography. John V. Lombardi. 1977. lib. bdg. 29.00 o.p. (ISBN 0-8161-7876-3, Hall Reference). G K Hall.

Venezuelan Vernacular. Federico Vegas. (Illus.). 96p. 1985. pap. 25.00 o.p. (ISBN 0-910413-05-3). Princeton Arch.

Vengeance: India after the Assassination of Indira Gandhi. Pranay Gupte. LC 85-7207. 1985. 16.45 o.p. (ISBN 0-393-02230-7). Norton.

Vengeance of the Cat Goddess. Jennifer Stephens. 1973. pap. 0.75 o.p. (ISBN 0-380-01605-2, 15891). Avon.

Vengeance of the God. Lewis Arriola. 206p. 1981. 9.50 o.p. (ISBN 0-682-49687-1). Exposition-Phoenix.

Vengeance of the Lion. Peter Danielson. (Children of the Lion Ser.: Bk. 3). 1985. lib. bdg. 12.95 o.p. (ISBN 0-8398-2871-3, Gregg). G K Hall.

Vengeance Ten. Joe Poyer. LC 80-65990. 1980. 13.95 o.p. (ISBN 0-689-11110-X, Atheneum). Macmillan.

Vengeance: The True Story of an Israeli Counter-Terrorist Team. George Jonas. 376p. 1984. 17.45 o.p. (ISBN 0-671-50611-0). S&S.

Vengeance Trail. Dwight Bruckner. 128p. 1982. pap. 1.75 o.p. (ISBN 0-505-51764-7, Pub. by Tower Bks). Dorchester Pub Co.

Vengeance Valley. Allen Appel. 1979. pap. 1.75 o.p. (ISBN 0-505-51448-6, Pub. by Tower Bks). Dorchester Pub Co.

Vengence Game. Stephen Grave. (Miami Vice Ser.: No. 2). 1985. pap. 2.95 o.p. (ISBN 0-380-89931-0). Avon.

Venice. Alta Macadam. (Blue Guide Ser.). (Illus.). 1982. 24.95 o.p. (ISBN 0-393-01555-6); pap. 13.95 o.p. (ISBN 0-393-30007-2). Norton.

Venice. (Rand McNally Pocket Guides Ser.). (Illus., Orig.). 1987. pap. 5.95 o.p. (ISBN 0-528-84407-5). Rand McNally.

Venice. (Berlitz Deluxe Guides). (Illus.). 336p. 1988. pap. 10.95 o.p. (ISBN 0-02-968230-4, Berlitz). Macmillan.

Venice: A Portable Reader. Ed. by Toby Cole. LC 78-19857. 256p. 1979. 12.00 o.p. (ISBN 0-88208-097-0). Chicago Review.

Venice Train. George Simenon. Tr. by Alastair Hamilton from Fr. LC 74-5759. (Helen & Kurt Wolff Bk.). 168p. 1974. 6.50 o.p. (ISBN 0-15-193506-8). HarBraceJ.

Venison Cookbook: More Than 200 Tested Recipes for Deer, Elk, Moose & Other Game. Jim Zumbo & Lois Zumbo. (Illus.). 208p. 1986. 17.95 o.p. (ISBN 0-13-941519-X). P-H.

Venomous Reptiles. rev. ed. Sherman A. Minton & Madge R. Minton. (Illus.). 320p. 1980. 13.95 o.s.i. (ISBN 0-684-16626-7, ScribT). Scribner.

Venous Thrombosis: Causation & Prediction. Derek Ogston. 1987. write for info. o.p. (ISBN 0-471-91558-0, Dist. by A R Liss). Wiley.

Vent du Changement. Harold Kemp. Tr. by Yves D. Martin. (Illus.). 229p. (Orig., Fr.). 1983. pap. 5.95 o.p. (ISBN 0-914766-97-X). Illum Way Pub.

Ventriloquism: Magic with Your Voice. George Schindler. (Illus.). 1985. pap. 9.95 o.s.i. (ISBN 0-679-21025-3). McKay.

Vents see Oeuvre Poetique.

Ventura County Street Atlas 1985. Thomas Bros. Maps Staff. (Illus.). 96p. pap. 8.95 o.p. (ISBN 0-88130-109-4). Thomas Bros Maps.

Ventura County Street Atlas: 1986. Thomas Bros. Maps Staff. (Illus.). 96p. 1986. pap. 10.95 o.p. (ISBN 0-88130-160-4). Thomas Bros Maps.

Ventura County Street Atlas 1987. Thomas Bros. Maps Staff. (Illus.). 94p. 1987. pap. 12.95 o.p. (ISBN 0-88130-212-0). Thomas Bros Maps.

Ventura County Thomas Guide 1988. Thomas Bros. Maps Staff. (Illus.). 98p. 1988. pap. 12.95 o.p. (ISBN 0-88130-274-0). Thomas Bros Maps.

Ventura-Los Angeles Counties Street Atlas 1985. Thomas Bros. Maps Staff. (Illus.). 384p. pap. 17.50 o.p. (ISBN 0-88130-110-8). Thomas Bros Maps.

Ventura-Los Angeles Counties Street Atlas: 1988. Thomas Bros. Maps Staff. (Illus.). 384p. 1987. pap. 19.95 o.p. Thomas Bros Maps.

Venture to Love. Jocelyn Stirling. LC 87-641. 360p. 1987. 17.95 o.s.i. (ISBN 0-385-23582-8). Doubleday.

Venture to the Interior. Laurens Van der Post. LC 73-13411. 253p. 1974. Repr. of 1951 ed. lib. bdg. 22.50x o.p. (ISBN 0-8371-7058-3, VAVI). Greenwood.

Venture to the Interior. Laurens Van Der Post. LC 79-10524. 253p. 1979. pap. 7.95 o.p. (ISBN 0-15-693529-5, Harv). HarBraceJ.

Venturers: The Hampton, Harrison & Earle Families of Virginia, South Carolina & Texas. Virginia G. Meynard. (Illus.). 1036p. 1981. 42.50 o.s.i. (ISBN 0-89308-241-4, BFH 14). Southern Hist Pr.

Venturi, Rauch & Scott Brown. Venturi, Rauch & Scott Brown Staff. (Architecture Ser.: Bibliography A 840). 63p. 1982. pap. 9.75 o.p. (ISBN 0-88066-250-6). Vance Biblios.

Venus: A Novel Based on the Life of Anais Nin. Darwin Porter. LC 81-70031. 1982. 13.95 o.p. (ISBN 0-87795-366-X, Arbor Hse). Morrow.

Venus International Reference Atmosphere. Ed. by A. J. Kliore et al. (Illus.). 314p. 1986. pap. 52.00 o.p. (ISBN 0-08-034631-6, Pub. by PPL). Pergamon.

Venus, Mars & Satellites of the Outer Planets: Proceedings of Symposium 3 of the COSPAR Twenty-Fifth Plenary Meeting Held in Graz, Austria, 25 June-7 July 1984. Ed. by R. W. Shorthill. (Illus.). 132p. 1985. pap. 54.00 o.p. (ISBN 0-08-033197-1, Pub. by PPL). Pergamon.

Venus Shoe. Carla Neggers. (Velvet Glove Ser.: No. 1). 256p. 1984. pap. 2.25 o.p. (ISBN 0-380-87999-9, 87999-9). Avon.

Verb Handbook. Stuart Reid. 1972. 3.00 o.p. (ISBN 0-682-47465-7). Exposition-Phoenix.

Verb Synonyms & Related Words. Stuart Reid. 1974. 5.00 o.p. (ISBN 0-682-47963-2). Exposition-Phoenix.

Verbal Conditioning & Behavior. J. P. Das. 1970. 40.00 o.p. (ISBN 0-08-012818-1). Pergamon.

Verbal Control with Microcomputers. Mike Rigsby. (Illus.). 312p. (Orig.). 1982. 18.95 o.p. (ISBN 0-8306-2468-6); pap. 11.95 o.p. (ISBN 0-8306-1468-0, 1468). TAB Bks.

Verbal Deficit: A Critique. John C. Gordon. 181p. 1981. 25.00 o.p. (ISBN 0-85664-990-2, Pub. by Croom Helm Ltd). Routledge Chapman & Hall.

Verbal Workbook for the S.A.T. College Entrance Examinations. Gabriel Freedman & M. A. Haller. LC 81-22751. 288p. 1981. pap. 6.00 o.p. (ISBN 0-668-04853-0, 4853). Arco.

Verbatim: A Language Quarterly, 4 vols. Ed. by Laurence Urdang. 1100p. 1982. 24.00x ea. o.p. Vols. 3-4 (ISBN 0-8103-4358-4). Vols. 5-6 (ISBN 0-8103-4359-2). Gale.

Verbes Francais: Formes et Emplois a l'Usage des Etudiants de Langue Etrangere. Anton Andereggen. LC 84-60827. 228p. (Orig., Fr.). 1984. text ed. 22.00 o.p. (ISBN 0-938942-03-4); pap. text ed. 7.50 o.p. Pacific Gallery.

Verbs, Pt. 1. Joan M. Frazer & Cynthia J. Smith. (Shape up Your Language Ser.). 1982. spiral wire 24.95 o.p. (ISBN 0-88450-828-5, 7024-B). Communication Skill.

Verdacht. Friedrich Durrenmatt. Ed. by William Gillis. (gr. 9-12). 1964. pap. 8.25 o.p. (ISBN 0-395-04500-2). HM.

Verdi. Julian Budden. (Master Musicians Ser.). (Illus.). 416p. 1986. 26.95x o.p. (ISBN 0-460-03165-1, Pub. by J M Dent England). Biblio Dist.

Verdi: His Music, Life & Times. Whitney G. Martin. 633p. 1963. lib. bdg. 79.00 o.p. (Pub. by Am Repr Serv). Reprint Servs.

Verdict of Memory. Y. Isayev. 146p. 1981. 6.50 o.p. (ISBN 0-8285-2162-X, Pub. by Progress Pubs USSR). Imported Pubns.

Verdict on the Shroud: Evidence for the Death & Resurrection of Jesus Christ. Kenneth Stevenson & Gary B. Habermas. (Illus.). 220p. 1981. pap. 6.95 o.p. (ISBN 0-89283-174-X). Servant.

Verdict Pending: A Patient Representative's Intervention. Fredonia F. Jacques. LC 83-20896. 237p. (Orig.). 1983. pap. 14.95 o.p. (ISBN 0-912433-00-0). Capistrano Pr.

Verdi's Macbeth: A Source Book. Ed. by David Rosen & Andrew Porter. (Illus.). 700p. 1984. text ed. 39.45 o.p. (ISBN 0-393-95073-5). Norton.

Vergil in Averno. Avram Davidson. LC 86-16622. (Science Fiction Ser.). 192p. 1987. 12.95 o.p. (ISBN 0-385-19707-1). Doubleday.

Vergil Woods. Henry Braun. LC 68-17383. (Orig.). 1968. 4.95 o.p. (ISBN 0-689-10044-2, Atheneum); pap. 2.45 o.p. (ISBN 0-689-10045-0). Macmillan.

Vergilius Romanus. 618p. 2000.00 o.p. (ISBN 0-8115-0910-9). Kraus Repr.

Verification & Validation of Expert Systems. Rolf A. Stachowitz & Chin-Liang Chan. (Illus.). 80p. 1988. pap. text ed. 12.00 o.p. (ISBN 0-929280-20-2). Amer Artificial.

Verification & Validation of Real-Time Software. Ed. by W. J. Quirk. xi, 245p. 1985. 37.00 o.p. (ISBN 0-387-15102-8). Springer-Verlag.

Vermeer. Arthur K. Wheelock, Jr. (Library of Great Painters Ser.). (Illus.). 160p. 1981. 45.00 o.p. (ISBN 0-8109-1730-0). Abrams.

Vermilion. Nathan Aldyne. 1980. pap. 2.25 o.p. (ISBN 0-380-76596-9, 81570-2). Avon.

Vermilion Gate. Lin Yutang. 439p. 1980. 7.95 o.p. (ISBN 0-89955-163-7, Pub. by Mei Ya China); pap. 9.75 o.p. (ISBN 0-89955-192-0, Pub. by Mei Ya China). Intl Spec Bk.

Vermont: A Special World. Ralph Hill et al. (Illus.). 1973. 21.95 o.p. (ISBN 0-395-07794-X). HM.

Vermont: An Explorer's Guide. rev. ed. Christina Tree & Peter Jennison. 320p. 1985. pap. 11.95 o.p. (ISBN 0-88150-048-8). Countryman.

Vermont: An Explorer's Guide. Christina Tree & Peter S. Jennison. 256p. (Orig.). 1983. pap. 10.95 o.p. (ISBN 0-88150-002-X). Countryman.

Vermont: An Illustrated History. John Duffy. LC 85-22621. 264p. 1985. 24.95 o.s.i. (ISBN 0-89781-159-3). Windsor Pubns Inc.

Vermont Business Phone Book, 1987-88. 86p. 1987. pap. 15.00 o.p. (ISBN 0-318-02876-X). Manufacturers.

Vermont Folk-Songs & Ballads. Helen H. Flanders & George Brown. LC 68-20768. iv, 264p. 1968. Repr. of 1931 ed. 40.00x o.p. (ISBN 0-8103-5010-6). Gale.

Vermont Manufacturing Directory 1988. 500p. 1988. pap. 35.00 o.p. Tower Pub Co.

Vermont Neighbors. Walter Hard. LC 60-3953. 122p. 1975. pap. 4.95 o.p. (ISBN 0-911570-14-4). Vermont Bks.

Vermont River. W. D. Wetherell. LC 84-1144. (Illus.). 160p. 1984. 13.95 o.p. (ISBN 0-8329-0365-5, Pub. by Winchester Pr). New Century.

Vermont: Trusts, Vols. 1-2. suppl. 6.00 o.p. (ISBN 0-686-90911-9). Am Law Inst.

Vermonters: Lively Oral Histories from Down Country to the Northeast Kingdom. Ron Strickland. LC 86-14738. (Illus.). 186p. (Orig.). 1986. pap. 12.95 o.p. (ISBN 0-87701-394-2). Chronicle Bks.

Vermont's Anti-Slavery & Underground Railroad Record. Wilbur H. Siebert. 1970. Repr. of 1937 ed. lib. bdg. 22.50 o.p. (ISBN 0-8371-2178-7, SIV). Greenwood.

Vernacular Taxicabs: Jitneys & Gypsies in Urban America. Peter T. Suzuki. (Public Administration Ser.: Bibliography P-1608). 17p. 1985. pap. 2.25 o.p. (ISBN 0-89028-258-7). Vance Biblios.

Veronica: The Autobiography of Veronica Lake. Veronica Lake & Donald Bain. (Illus.). 1971. 6.95 o.p. (ISBN 0-8065-0226-6, Pub. by Citadel Pr). Carol Pub Group.

Veronique. Virginia Coffman. LC 74-18162. 1975. 8.95 o.p. (ISBN 0-87795-107-1, Arbor Hse). Morrow.

Verre en France, d'Emile Galle a Nos Jours. Janine Bloch-Dermant. (Illus.). 312p. (Fr.). 1983. 100.00 o.p. (ISBN 2-85917-029-4, Pub. by Editions de l'Amateur FR). Seven Hills Bk Dists.

Vers de la Mort. Helinandus. 1965. 25.00 o.p. (ISBN 0-384-22210-2); pap. 19.00 o.p. (ISBN 0-384-22200-5). Johnson Repr.

Versailles & After: An Annotated Bibliography of American Diplomatic Relations, 1919-1933. Linda Killen & Richard Lael. LC 82-49115. 500p. 1983. lib. bdg. 66.00 o.p. (ISBN 0-8240-9202-3). Garland Pub.

Versatile Verse for a Rainy Afternoon. Beverly M. Wesp. 48p. 1988. 6.95 o.p. (ISBN 0-8062-3049-5). Carlton.

Verse & Worse. Daniel W. Fry. 1979. 5.00 o.p. (ISBN 0-682-49462-3). Exposition-Phoenix.

Verse & Worse: A Private Collection. Arnold Silcock. 288p. 1958. pap. 4.95 o.p. (ISBN 0-571-05132-4). Faber & Faber.

Verse from Pushkin & Others. Compiled by Oliver Elton. LC 72-114517. 1971. Repr. of 1935 ed. lib. bdg. 35.00x o.p. (ISBN 0-8371-4822-7, EVLP). Greenwood.

Verse from Veola: From Birth Through Pre-Adolescene. Veola J. Blaine. 1983. 5.95 o.p. (ISBN 0-8062-2037-6). Carlton.

Verse Writing in Schools. E. J. Bolton. 1966. 14.50 o.p. (ISBN 0-08-011993-X); pap. 35.00 o.p. (ISBN 0-08-011992-1). Pergamon.

Verses. Jack B. Yeats. 1981. pap. text ed. 6.00x o.p. (ISBN 0-391-01592-3). Humanities.

Versions of Truth: Urdu Short Stories from Pakistan. Ed. by Khalid Hasan. 1983. text ed. 30.00x o.p. (ISBN 0-7069-2128-3, Pub. by Vikas India). Advent NY.

Versuch einer Allegorie, Repr. Of 1766 Ed. J. J. Winckelmann. Bd. with De L'Allegorie. J. J. Winckelmann. Repr. of 1799 ed. LC 75-27890. (Renaissance & the Gods Ser.: Vol. 44). (Illus.). 1976. lib. bdg. 88.00 o.p. (ISBN 0-8240-2093-6). Garland Pub.

Versus: Reflections of a Sociologist. Henry P. Fairchild. (ISBN 0-8022-0469-4). Philos Lib.

Vertebrate Body: Shorter Version. 5th ed. Alfred S. Romer & Thomas S. Parsons. LC 77-11353. (Illus.). 1978. text ed. 34.95 o.p. (ISBN 0-7216-7682-0, CBS C). SCP.

Vertebrate Eye. rev. ed. R. A. Weale. Ed. by J. J. Head. LC 76-29373. (Carolina Biology Readers Ser.: No. 71). (Illus.). 16p. (gr. 10 up). 1978. pap. 1.80 o.p. (ISBN 0-89278-271-4, 45-9671). Carolina Biological.

Vertebrate Lectins: Recent Research. Ed. by Kenneth Olden & James B. Paxent. (Illus.). 288p. 1986. 50.95 o.s.i. (ISBN 0-442-26988-9). Van Nos Reinhold.

Vertebrate Limb Regeneration. Hugh Wallace. LC 80-40963. 276p. 1981. 89.95x o.p. (ISBN 0-471-27877-7, Pub. by Wiley-Interscience). Wiley.

Vertebrate Photoreception. Ed. by H. B. Barlow. LC 76-55064. 1978. 86.00 o.p. (ISBN 0-12-078950-7). Acad Pr.

Vertebrate Regeneration. Ed. by C. S. Thornton & S. C. Bromley. LC 73-13830. (Benchmark Papers in Biological Concepts). 528p. 1982. 68.95 o.p. (ISBN 0-87933-057-0). Van Nos Reinhold.

Vertebrate Social Organization. Ed. by Edwin M. Banks. LC 76-26571. (Benchmark Papers in Animal Behavior: Vol. 8). 1977. 74.00 o.p. (ISBN 0-12-786130-0). Acad Pr.

Vertebrate Visual System. Stephen Polyak. Ed. by Heinrich Kluver. LC 55-5153. (Illus.). 1957. lib. bdg. 100.00x o.s.i. (ISBN 0-226-67494-0). U of Chicago Pr.

Vertebrates of Arizona: With Major Section on Arizona Habitats. Ed. by Charles H. Lowe, Jr. LC 63-11981. 270p. 1964. pap. 8.95x o.p. (ISBN 0-8165-0348-6). U of Ariz Pr.

Vertical Boring. 2nd ed. (Engineering Craftsmen: No. H28/1). (Illus.). 1976. spiral bdg. 37.50x o.p. Trans-Atl Phila.

Vertical Poems. W. S. Merwin & Roberto Juarroz. 1976. 5.00 o.p. (ISBN 0-685-67046-5). Story Line.

Vertical Poetry. Roberto Juarroz. Tr. by W. S. Merwin. (Illus.). 40p. 1977. 5.00 o.p. Kayak.

Vertical Turbulent Buoyant Jets: A Review of Experimental Data. C. J. Chen. (Heat & Mass Transfer Ser.: Vol. 4). (Illus.). 94p. 1979. 35.00 o.p. (ISBN 0-08-024772-5). Pergamon.

Vertigo. M. R. Dix & J. P. Hood. 491p. 1984. 60.00x o.p. (ISBN 0-471-90261-6, Dist. by A R Liss). Wiley.

Verts; or, the Three Creeds, 1876. Charles M. Davies. Ed. by Robert L. Wolff. LC 75-1506. (Victorian Fiction Ser.). 1975. lib. bdg. 66.00 o.p. (ISBN 0-8240-1580-0). Garland Pub.

Very Amateur Guide to Antique Bottle Collecting. Bea Boynton. LC 65-22367. (Illus.). 1967. pap. 1.50 o.p. (ISBN 0-87004-017-0). Caxton.

Very Anxiously Engaged: A Cartoonist's View of Modern Courtship. Val C. Bagley. (Illus.). 96p. (Orig.). 1981. pap. 3.95 o.p. (ISBN 0-88290-157-5, 2042). Horizon Utah.

Very Best Name for Baby. Barbara S. Hazen. 96p. 1986. 7.95 o.p. (ISBN 0-8378-5088-6). Gibson.

Very Best People. Elizabeth Villars. 1985. pap. 3.95 o.s.i. (ISBN 0-671-83232-8). PB.

Very Big Problem of Mr. & Mrs. Bumba. Pearl A. Harwood. LC 73-156354. (Mr. & Mrs. Bumba Bks.). (Illus.). (gr. k-3). 1971. PLB 3.95 o.p. (ISBN 0-8225-0130-9). Lerner Pubns.

Very First Shoe Book. Jeff MacNelly. 1978. pap. 7.95 o.p. (ISBN 0-380-40154-1, 79780-1). Avon.

Very Human President. Jack Valenti. (Illus.). 402p. 1976. 9.95 o.p. (ISBN 0-393-05552-3). Norton.

Very Last Virgin at Hobeck High. Grace Williams. (YA) (gr. 7 up). 1986. pap. 2.50 o.p. (ISBN 0-451-14398-1, Sig Vista). NAL.

Very Much a Lady: The Untold Story of Jean Harris & Dr. Herman Tarnower. Shana Alexander. 1983. 17.00i o.p. (ISBN 0-316-03125-9). Little.

Very Nearest Room. Jane Logan. LC 73-1122. 256p. 1973. 7.95 o.s.i. (ISBN 0-684-13527-2, ScribT). Scribner.

Very Old Money. Stanley Ellin. 1985. 16.95 o.p. (ISBN 0-87795-627-8, Arbor Hse). Morrow.

Very Old Money. Stanley Ellin. 1985. 18.95 o.p. (ISBN 0-8161-3916-4, Large Print Bks). G K Hall.

Very Private Matter of Anorexia Nervosa. Sharon Christian & Margaret Johnson. Ed. by John Sloan. 176p. 1986. pap. 6.95 o.p. (ISBN 0-310-45841-2, 18140P). Zondervan.

Very Special Birthday Present. William Van Horn. LC 81-8053. (Illus.). 32p. (ps-1). 1982. PLB 9.95 o.p. (ISBN 0-689-30895-7, Atheneum). Macmillan.

Very Special Intelligence, No. 9. Patrick Beesly. 304p. 1981. pap. 2.75 o.s.i. (ISBN 0-345-29798-9). Ballantine.

Very Very Slightly Imperfect. Ron Moody. LC 84-26492. 271p. 1985. 16.95 o.p. (ISBN 0-88186-425-0). Parkwest Pubns.

Very Worried Walrus. Richard Hefter. LC 76-43092. (Sweet Pickles Ser.). (Illus.). (gr. k-2). 1977. 2.95 o.p. (ISBN 0-03-018091-0). H Holt & Co.

Very Young Verses. Barbara P. Geismer & Antoinette B. Suter. (Illus.). (gr. 1-3). 1945. 7.95 o.p. (ISBN 0-395-06779-0). HM.

Verzeichnis der Nobelpreistrager 1901-1984. Ed. by Warner Martin. 362p. (Ger.). 1985. lib. bdg. 34.00 o.p. (ISBN 3-598-10578-9). K G Saur.

Verzeichnis der Nobelpreistrager, 1901-1984. Ed. by Werner Martin. 362p. 1985. 34.00 o.p. (ISBN 0-317-70031-6). K G Saur.

Vespa Ciao & Bravo Mopeds '68 on. Pete Shoemark. pap. 13.50 o.p. (ISBN 0-85696-374-7, 374). Haynes Pubns.

Vesper Sparrows. Deborah Digges. LC 85-48124. 80p. 1986. 15.00 o.p. (ISBN 0-689-11767-1, Atheneum); pap. 8.95 o.p. (ISBN 0-689-11768-X, Atheneum). Macmillan.

Vessel of Splendor: A Return to the One. Raymond J. Steiner. 1978. 4.00 o.p. (ISBN 0-682-49214-0). Exposition-Phoenix.

Vessels. Howard Schwartz. LC 76-13960. 1977. 10.00 o.p. (ISBN 0-87775-098-X); pap. 4.00 o.p. (ISBN 0-87775-099-8). Unicorn Pr.

Vest Pocket Spanish Dictionary. rev. ed. Ed. by Ida Hinojo. LC 75-39823. 320p. 1976. pap. 2.95 o.s.i. (ISBN 0-8329-1534-3). New Century.

Vestal Virgin Room. C. W. Smith. LC 84-45036. 256p. 1984. 13.95 o.s.i. (ISBN 0-689-11494-X, Atheneum). Macmillan.

Vestale. Mercadante Saverio. (Italian Opera II Ser.). 225p. 1985. lib. bdg. 85.00 o.p. (ISBN 0-8240-6571-9). Garland Pub.

Vestibular Function on Earth & in Space. J. Stahle. 1970. 80.00 o.p. (ISBN 0-08-015592-8). Pergamon.

Vestibules of Heaven. Mid McKnight. 1982. pap. 3.95 o.p. (ISBN 0-89225-219-7). Gospel Advocate.

Vestiges of a Proud Nation. Raymond J. DeMallie et al. Ed. by Glenn E. Markoe. (Illus.). 176p. 1987. 37.50x o.p. (ISBN 0-934658-02-1); pap. 22.50 o.p. (ISBN 0-934658-01-3). R H Flem Mus.

Vestry Book & Register of St. Peter's Parish, New Kent & James City Counties, Virginia, 1684-1786. C. G. Chamberlayne. xxvi, 840p. 1973. Repr. of 1937 ed. 12.50 o.p. (ISBN 0-88490-037-1). VA State Lib.

Vet Behind the Ears. Christopher Timothy. (Lythway Ser.). 1987. lib. bdg. 16.50x o.p. (ISBN 0-7451-0612-9, Pub. by Chivers Pr UK). G K Hall.

Veterinarian, Doctor for Your Pet. Arline Strong. LC 76-46948. (Illus.). (gr. 2-5). 1977. 7.95 o.p. (ISBN 0-689-30575-3, Atheneum). Macmillan.

Veterinary Annual. 21st ed. C. S. Grunsell & F. W. Hill. (Illus.). 370p. 1981. text ed. 29.50 o.p. (ISBN 0-85608-031-4). Year Bk Med.

Veterinary Contribution to Public Health Practice: Report of a Joint FAO-WHO Expert Committee on Veterinary Public Health, Geneva, 1974. (Agricultural Planning Studies: No. 96). 79p. 1975. pap. 9.50 o.p. (ISBN 92-5-101566-X, F491, FAO). UNIPUB.

Veterinary Critical Care. Ed. by Fred P. Sattler et al. LC 80-27880. (Illus.). 549p. 1981. text ed. 45.00 o.p. (ISBN 0-8121-0702-0). Lea & Febiger.

Veterinary Drug Manufacturing Encyclopedia. Marshall Sittig. LC 81-16815. (Illus.). 507p. 1982. 64.00 o.p. (ISBN 0-8155-0870-0). Noyes.

Veterinary Medical School Admission Requirements in the United States & Canada, 1985-1986. The Association of American Veterinary Medical Colleges. Compiled by Marcia J. Sawyer. 152p. (Orig.). 1985. pap. 8.00 o.p. (ISBN 0-941406-07-5). Betz Pub Co Inc.

Veterinary Medical School Admission Requirements in the United States & Canada, 1986-1987. 2nd ed. Association of American Veterinary Medical Colleges. Compiled by Marcia J. Sawyer. 168p. (Orig.). 1986. pap. 8.00 o.p. (ISBN 0-941406-13-X). Betz Pub Co Inc.

Veterinary Notes for Horse Owners. 15th ed. Horace M. Hayes. Ed. by J. F. Tutt. LC 64-12209. (Illus.). 1964. 19.95 o.p. (ISBN 0-668-00656-0). Arco.

Veterinary Odyssey. Frank H. Manley. (Illus.). 1978. 7.50 o.p. (ISBN 0-682-49115-2). Exposition-Phoenix.

Veterinary Pharmacology & Therapeutics. 5th ed. Nicholas H. Booth & Leslie E. McDonald. (Illus.). 1134p. 1982. text ed. 63.95x o.p. (ISBN 0-8138-1740-4). Iowa St U Pr.

Veterinary Pharmacology & Toxicology. Ruckebusch et al. 1983. 71.95 o.s.i. (ISBN 0-87055-442-5). AVI.

Veterinary Surgeon's Guide for Cat Owners. David Coffey. (Illus.). 216p. 1983. 16.95 o.s.i. (Pub. by Worlds Work). David & Charles.

VHF Antenna Handbook. Alex Barvicks. 94p. 1975-1980. pap. 5.95 o.p. (ISBN 0-88006-014-X, BK 7368). Wayne Green Ent.

VHSIC (Very High Speed Integrated Circuits) Technologies & Tradeoffs. Arpad Barna. LC 81-4356. 114p. 1981. 24.95x o.p. (ISBN 0-471-09463-3, Pub. by Wiley-Interscience). Wiley.

Viable Count: Quantitative & Environmental Aspects. Tsutonu Hattori. write for info. o.p. Sci Tech Pubs.

Viaduct. David Wheldon. LC 83-3832. 157p. 1983. 12.95 o.p. (ISBN 0-8076-1077-1). Braziller.

Vibration Analysis & Control System Dynamic. C. F. Beards. LC 81-6646. (Engineering Science, Civil Engineering Ser.). 169p. 1981. 58.95x o.p. (ISBN 0-470-27255-4). Halsted Pr.

Vibration Syndrome. Ed. by W. Taylor. 1974. 62.50 o.p. (ISBN 0-12-684760-6). Acad Pr.

Vibration White Finger in Industry. Ed. by W. Taylor & P. L. Pelmear. 1975. 39.50 o.p. (ISBN 0-12-684550-6). Acad Pr.

Vibrational Spectroscopy: Modern Trends. Ed. by A. J. Barnes & W. J. Orville-Thomas. 1977. 192.00 o.p. (ISBN 0-444-42001-0). Elsevier.

Vibrational Spectroscopy of Molecular Liquids & Solids. Ed. by S. Bratos & R. M. Pick. LC 80-12174. (NATO ASI Series B, Physics: Vol. 56). 476p. 1980. 79.50x o.p. (ISBN 0-306-40445-1, Plenum Pr). Plenum Pub.

VIC Games for Kids. Clark Kidd & Kathy H. Kidd. Ed. by Compute! Magazine Staff. 220p. (Orig.). (gr. k up). 1983. pap. 12.95 o.p. (ISBN 0-942386-35-3). Compute Pubns.

Vic Merritt: Man of Justice. Jake Cafferty. 208p. 1986. pap. 2.95 o.p. (ISBN 1-55547-126-9). Critics Choice Paper.

VIC-20 User Guide. John Heilborn & Ran Talbott. 388p. (Orig.). 1983. pap. text ed. 2.00 o.p. (ISBN 0-07-047854-6). Osborne-McGraw.

VIC 20 User Guide. (ISBN 0-07-931086-9). McGraw.

Vicar's Daughter. George MacDonald. 216p. 1985. 5.95 o.p. (ISBN 0-89693-330-X). Victor Bks.

Vice & Virtue in Everyday Life. Christina H. Sommers. 653p. 1985. pap. text ed. 15.00 net o.p. (ISBN 0-15-594890-3, HC). HarBraceJ.

Vice Book. Alexander Communications, Inc. Staff. (Illus.). 165p. 1988. pap. 30.00 o.p. (ISBN 0-8230-5804-2). Alexander Comms.

Vice-Consul. Marguerite Duras. (Coll. Soleil). 1966. 12.25 o.p. (ISBN 0-685-11616-6). Schoenhof.

Vice Consul. Date not set. (ISBN 0-394-55898-7). Random.

Vice in a Vicious Society: Crime & Convicts in Mid-Nineteenth Century New South Wales. Michael Sturma. LC 82-8636. (Illus.). 224p. 1983. text ed. 32.50x o.p. (ISBN 0-7022-1911-8). U of Queensland Pr.

Viceroy of Ouidah. Bruce Chatwin. LC 80-17896. 155p. 1980. 11.95 o.s.i. (ISBN 0-671-41253-1). Summit Bks.

Viceroy of Ouidah. Bruce Chatwin. 1982. pap. 4.95 o.s.i. (ISBN 0-671-41254-X). Summit Bks.

Vichy France: Old Guard & New Order, 1940-1944. Robert O. Paxton. 426p. 1975. pap. 5.95 o.p. (ISBN 0-393-00794-4, N794, Norton Lib). Norton.

Vicious Circles. Anthony Stuart. 1979. 8.95 o.p. (ISBN 0-87795-205-1, Arbor Hse). Morrow.

Vicious Circles: The Mafia in the Marketplace. Jonathan Kwitny. 432p. 1981. 14.95 o.p. (ISBN 0-393-01188-7); pap. 6.95 o.p. (ISBN 0-393-00029-X). Norton.

Vicky. Catherine Storr. 160p. (gr. 6-9). 1981. 12.95 o.p. (ISBN 0-571-11762-7). Faber & Faber.

Vico & Marx. Ed. by Giorgio Tagliacozzo. 438p. 1983. text ed. 35.00 o.p. (ISBN 0-391-02629-1). Humanities.

Victim. Saul Bellow. 1984. pap. 1.75 o.p. (ISBN 0-380-00334-1, 36780-7). Avon.

Victim of the Aurora. Thomas Keneally. 1978. 7.95 o.p. (ISBN 0-15-193631-5). HarBraceJ.

Victimes du Devoir. Eugene Ionesco. Ed. by Vera G. Lee. LC 72-4875. (Illus.). 178p. (Orig.). 1972. pap. 7.50 o.p. (ISBN 0-395-12745-9, 3-32658). HM.

Victimization of the Weak: Contemporary Social Reactions. Jacqueline Scherer & Gary Shepherd. (Illus.). 312p. 1982. 37.50 o.p. (ISBN 0-398-04043-5). C C Thomas.

Victims. Dorothy Uhnak. 1986. 17.45 o.p. (ISBN 0-671-45237-1). S&S.

Victims. Colin Vary. (Illus.). 52p. (Orig.). 1976. pap. 5.00x o.p. (ISBN 0-911038-70-1, Inst Hist Rev). Noontide.

Victims & Offenders: Needs & Responsibilities. John Harding. 54p. 1982. pap. 7.25 o.p. (ISBN 0-7199-1083-8, Pub. by Bedford England). Gower Pub Co.

Victims of Crime: A Research Report of Experiencing Victimization. Harris, Louis, & Associates Staff. LC 82-94186. (Reference Library of Social Science). 64p. 1983. lib. bdg. 20.00 o.p. (ISBN 0-8240-9145-0). Garland Pub.

Victims of Groupthink: A Psychological Study of Foreign-Policy Decisions & Fiascoes. Irving Janis. 1972. pap. 11.95 o.p. (ISBN 0-395-14044-7). HM.

Victims of the Creative Spirits. Barbara Hannah. 1985. 10.00x o.p. (ISBN 0-317-62243-9, Guild of Pastoral Psych). State Mutual Bk.

Victims, Offenders, & Alternative Sanctions. Ed. by Joe Hudson & Burt Galaway. LC 80-7578. 224p. 1980. 29.00x o.p. (ISBN 0-669-03758-3). Lexington Bks.

Victor Hugo: Philosophy & Poetry. Henri Peyre. Tr. by Roda P. Roberts from Fr. LC 79-9876. 176p. 1980. 14.00 o.p. (ISBN 0-8173-0017-1). U of Ala Pr.

Victor Mollo's Bridge Club: How to Turn Masterful Plays into Monstrous Points. Victor Mollo. (Illus.). 256p. 1987. pap. 7.95 o.s.i. (ISBN 0-671-64237-5, Fireside). S&S.

Victoria. Knut Hamsun. 1980. pap. 1.75 o.p. (ISBN 0-380-00545-X, 27110, Bard). Avon.

Victoria & Albert. David Duff. LC 72-2203. 1972. 9.95 o.s.i. (ISBN 0-8008-7967-8). Taplinger.

Victoria, Book V: The Story of Canada. Dennis Adair & Janet Rosenstock. 272p. 1983. pap. 3.95 o.p. (ISBN 0-380-85134-2, 85134). Avon.

Victoria Hotel. John Dickson. LC 78-1215. 1979. 10.00 o.p. (ISBN 0-914090-63-1); pap. 5.95 o.p. (ISBN 0-914090-64-X). Chicago Review.

Victorian & Edwardian Photographs. Rev. ed. Margret F. Harker. (Letts Collectors' Guides Ser.). (Illus.). 80p. 1982. 9.95 o.p. (ISBN 0-85097-369-4, Pub by C Letts Bks UK). Seven Hills Bk Dists.

Victorian & Edwardian Theatres: An Architectural & Social Survey. Victor Glasstone. (Illus.). 192p. 1975. 21.00x o.s.i. (ISBN 0-674-93591-8). Harvard U Pr.

Victorian Architecture: Four Studies in Evaluation see Victorian Architecture in England: Four Studies in Evaluation.

Victorian Architecture in England: Four Studies in Evaluation. John Summerson. Orig. Title: Victorian Architecture: Four Studies in Evaluation. (Illus.). 1971. pap. 3.95x o.p. (ISBN 0-393-00577-1, Norton Lib). Norton.

Victorian Book Illustration. Geoffrey Wakeman. LC 72-14042. (Illus.). 182p. 1973. 46.00x o.p. (ISBN 0-8103-2008-8). Gale.

Victorian Childhood. Susan P. Casteras. (Illus.). 64p. 1987. pap. 14.95 o.p. (ISBN 0-8109-2340-8). Abrams.

Victorian Christmas Crafts. (ISBN 0-671-61202-6). P-H.

Victorian Christmas: Eighteen Seventy-Six. Elspeth. 1974. pap. 1.50 o.p. (ISBN 0-87588-106-8, 2323). Hobby Hse.

Victorian Church Art. John Physick. (Illus.). 212p. (Orig.). 1984. pap. 12.95 o.p. (ISBN 0-901486-36-1, Pub. by Victoria & Albert Mus UK). Faber & Faber.

Victorian Church Building & Restoration in Suffolk. Anne Riches. (Illus.). 1982. 27.00 o.p. (ISBN 0-85115-176-0, Pub. by Boydell & Brewer). Longwood Pub Group.

Victorian City: Images & Realities, 2 vols. Ed. by H. J. Dyos & Michael Wolff. (Illus.). 1001p. 1973. Set. 110.00 o.p. (ISBN 0-7100-7384-4); Vol. 1. 60.00 o.p. (ISBN 0-7100-7374-7); Vol. 2. 60.00 o.p. (ISBN 0-7100-7383-6). Routledge Chapman & Hall.

Victorian City-Images & Realities, Vol. 1: Past & Present & Numbers of People. H. J. Dyos & Michael Wolff. (Illus.). 1978. pap. 14.95 o.p. (ISBN 0-7100-8458-7). Routledge Chapman & Hall.

Victorian City-Images & Realities, Vol. 2: Shapes on the Ground & a Change of Accent. Ed. by H. J. Dyos & Michael Wolff. (Illus.). 1978. pap. 14.95 o.p. (ISBN 0-7100-8812-4). Routledge Chapman & Hall.

Victorian Clergy. Alan Haig. 380p. 1984. 33.00 o.p. (ISBN 0-7099-1230-7, Pub. by Croom Helm Ltd). Routledge Chapman & Hall.

Victorian Clerks. Gregory L. Anderson. (Illus.). 1976. lib. bdg. 27.50x o.p. (ISBN 0-678-06794-5). Kelley.

Victorian Cottage Residences. Andrew J. Downing. 1982. 14.50 o.p. (ISBN 0-8446-5883-9). Peter Smith.

Victorian Countryside, 2 vols. Ed. by G. E. Mingay. (Illus.). 1986. Set. pap. 45.00 o.p. (88888). Vol. I, 380 pg (ISBN 0-7102-0884-7). Vol. II, 348 pg (ISBN 0-7102-0886-3). Routledge Chapman & Hall.

Victorian Designs for Needlepoint. Phyllis Kluger. LC 78-2396. (Illus.). 1978. 12.95 o.s.i. (ISBN 0-03-020436-4); pap. 7.95 o.s.i. (ISBN 0-686-66723-9). H Holt & Co.

Victorian Doll Family. rev. ed. Sandy Williams. (Illus.). 32p. 1985. pap. 3.95 o.p. (ISBN 0-87588-241-2, 2327). Hobby Hse.

Victorian Engravings. Hilary Beck. (Illus.). 188p. (Orig.). 1984. pap. 9.95 o.p. (ISBN 0-901486-64-7, Pub. by Victoria & Albert Mus UK). Faber & Faber.

Victorian Experience: The Prose Writers. Intro. by Richard A. Levine. LC 81-22493. x, 239p. 1982. lib. bdg. 22.95x o.p. (ISBN 0-8214-0446-6). Ohio U Pr.

Victorian Florida: America's Last Frontier. Floyd Rinhart & Marion Rinhart. (Illus.). 224p. 1986. 29.95 o.p. (ISBN 0-934601-02-X). Peachtree Pubs.

Victorian Frames, Borders & Cuts from the 1882 Type Catalog of George Bruce's Son & Co. Bruce's Son & Company Staff. 13.25 o.p. (ISBN 0-8446-5468-X). Peter Smith.

Victorian Garden. Tom Carter. (Illus.). 192p. 19.95 o.p. (ISBN 0-317-54976-6). Apollo.

Victorian Gardens: How to Plan, Plant & Enjoy Them. John Highstone. LC 80-8342. (Illus.). 183p. (Orig.). 1982. pap. 9.57i o.p. (ISBN 0-06-250481-9, CN 4004). HarpR.

Victorian Gentlewoman in the Far West: The Reminiscences of Mary Hallock Foote. Mary H. Foote. Ed. by Rodman Paul. LC 72-86535. (Illus.). 416p. 1980. pap. 7.00 o.p. (ISBN 0-87328-057-1). Huntington Lib.

Victorian Ices & Ice Cream: 117 Delicious & Unusual Recipes Updated for the Modern Kitchen. Agnes Marshall. 1985. pap. 9.95 o.p. (ISBN 0-684-18267-X). Scribner.

Victorian Imagination: A Sampler. Ed. by Richard Manton. LC 83-83193. (Victorian Library). 224p. 1984. 17.95 o.p. (ISBN 0-394-53868-4, GP888). Grove.

Victorian Imagination: A Sampler. Ed. by Richard Manton. LC 83-83193. (Victorian Library). 208p. 1985. pap. 3.95 o.s.i. (ISBN 0-394-62074-7, BC). Grove.

Victorian Imperialism. G. C. Eldridge. (Illus.). 1978. text ed. 19.95x o.p. (ISBN 0-391-00823-4); pap. text ed. 10.00x o.p. (ISBN 0-391-00824-2). Humanities.

Victorian in Orbit. Cedric Hardwicke. LC 72-7504. 311p. 1972. Repr. of 1961 ed. lib. bdg. 22.50x o.p. (ISBN 0-8371-6516-4, HAVO). Greenwood.

Victorian Jewellery. rev. ed. Deirdre O'Day. (Letts Collectors' Guides Ser.). (Illus.). 80p. 1982. 9.95 o.p. (ISBN 0-85097-359-7, Pub. by C Letts Bks UK). Seven Hills Bk Dists.

Victorian Knight-Errant: A Study of the Early Literary Career of James Russell Lowell. Leon Howard. LC 72-136072. 1971. Repr. of 1952 ed. lib. bdg. 35.00x o.p. (ISBN 0-8371-5222-4, HOVK). Greenwood.

Victorian Memorial Brasses. David Meara. (Illus.). 224p. 1983. pap. 17.95 o.p. (ISBN 0-7100-9312-8). Routledge Chapman & Hall.

Victorian Modern. Robin Boyd. (ISBN 0-522-84156-2, Pub. by Melbourne U Pr). Intl Spec Bk.

Victorian Myths of the Sea. Cynthia F. Behrman. LC 76-51694. 188p. 1977. 15.95 o.p. (ISBN 0-8214-0351-6). Ohio U Pr.

Victorian Nightmares. Ed. by Hugh Lamb. LC 76-55901. 1977. 8.95 o.s.i. (ISBN 0-8008-7984-8). Taplinger.

Victorian Novel & Social Problems. Kate Flint. (A Volume in the World & Word Ser.). 256p. 1986. 31.00 o.p. (ISBN 0-7099-1023-1, Pub. by Croom Helm UK); pap. 17.00 o.p. (ISBN 0-7099-1093-2, Pub. by Croom Helm UK). Routledge Chapman & Hall.

Victorian Novel: Problems & Portraits of the Child. Basudeo Sharma. 256p. 1982. text ed. 12.50x o.p. (ISBN 0-391-02647-X). Humanities.

Victorian Painters Monograms: A Pocket Identification Guide. Peter Nahum. (Illus.). 225p. 1985. pap. 6.95 o.p. (ISBN 0-572-00973-9, Pub. by W Foulsham & Co. England). Seven Hills Bk Dists.

Victorian People: A Reassessment of Persons & Themes, 1851-67. rev. ed. Asa Briggs. LC 55-7479. (Illus.). 1973. lib. bdg. 25.00x o.s.i. (ISBN 0-226-07487-0). U of Chicago Pr.

Victorian Periodical Press: Samplings & Soundings. Ed. by Joanne Shattock & Michael Wolff. 420p. 1982. 65.00x o.p. (ISBN 0-8020-2463-7). U of Toronto Pr.

Victorian Poet: Poetics & Persona. Joseph Bristow. Ed. by Isobel Armstrong. (World & Word Ser.). 256p. 1987. lib. bdg. 65.00x o.p. (ISBN 0-317-64405-X, Pub. by Croom Helm UK); pap. text ed. 14.95x o.p. (ISBN 0-317-64406-8, Pub. by Croom Helm UK). Routledge Chapman & Hall.

Victorian Poets: A Guide to Research. 2nd ed. Ed. by Frederic E. Faverty. LC 68-15636. 1968. 32.00x o.s.i. (ISBN 0-674-93660-4). Harvard U Pr.

Victorian Popular Fiction, 1860-80. R. C. Terry. 208p. 1983. text ed. 35.00x o.p. (ISBN 0-391-02963-0). Humanities.

Titles

Titles

Victorian Popular Music. Ronald Pearsall. (Illus.). 250p. 1973. 26.00x o.p. (ISBN 0-8103-2002-9). Gale.

Victorian Revival in Interior Design. Jim Kemp. LC 85-2232. (Illus.). 176p. 1985. pap. 24.95 o.s.i. (ISBN 0-671-53061-5). S&S.

Victorian Sage. John Holloway. 1965. pap. 2.95 o.p. (ISBN 0-393-00264-0, Norton Lib). Norton.

Victorian Sheet Music Covers. Ronald Pearsall. LC 72-6422. (Illus.). 116p. 1972. 16.00x o.p. (ISBN 0-8103-2001-0). Gale.

Victorian Shooting Days: East Anglia 1810-1910. Derek Johnson. (Illus.). 112p. 1981. 16.95 o.p. (ISBN 0-85115-156-6, Pub. by Boydell & Brewer). Longwood Pub Group.

Victorian Sketchbook. Ranulph Bye & Margaret B. Richie. (Illus.). 128p. 1980. 35.00 o.p. (ISBN 0-910702-04-7). Bentley PA.

Victorian Staffordshire Figure. Anthony Oliver. (Illus.). 192p. 1980. 75.00 o.p. (ISBN 0-434-54390-X, Pub. by W Heinemann Ltd). David & Charles.

Victorian Studies in Scarlet. Richard D. Altick. LC 70-103962. 1970. 7.95 o.p. (ISBN 0-393-08605-4). Norton.

Victorian Taste: A Study of the Arts & Architecture from 1830 to 1870. John Steegman. 1971. pap. 5.95x o.p. (ISBN 0-262-69028-4). MIT Pr.

Victorian Townscape: The Work of Samuel Smith. Michael Millward & Brian Coe. LC 76-16439. (Illus.). 120p. 1977. 35.00 o.s.i. (ISBN 0-87951-050-1). Overlook Pr.

Victorian Types, Victorian Shadows: Biblical Typology in Victorian Literature, Art & Thought. George P. Landow. 256p. 1980. 27.95x o.p. (ISBN 0-7100-0598-9). Routledge Chapman & Hall.

Victorian Values: Secularism & the Smaller Family. J. A. Banks. 288p. 1981. 26.95x o.p. (ISBN 0-7100-0807-4). Routledge Chapman & Hall.

Victorian Working Women. Michael Hiley. LC 79-92110. (Illus.). 144p. 1980. 18.95 o.s.i. (ISBN 0-87923-324-9). Godine.

Victorian Yearbook, 1983. Intl Pubns Serv.

Victorians. Mary Azrael. LC 81-84759. 76p. (Orig.). 1982. pap. 4.95 o.p. (ISBN 0-87376-039-5). Red Dust.

Victorians & Their Flowers. Nicolette Scourse. (Illus.). 195p. 1984. 22.95 o.p. (ISBN 0-917304-89-6). Timber.

Victorians at Home & Away. Janet Phillips & Peter Phillips. (Illus.). 224p. 1978. 16.00 o.p. (ISBN 0-85664-688-1, Pub. by Croom Helm Ltd). Routledge Chapman & Hall.

Victorians in the Harem: Grove Press Victorian Library. Ed. by Richard Manton. 224p. 1987. pap. 3.95 o.p. (ISBN 0-394-62312-6, BC). Grove.

Victorieux. Jacques Audiberti. 242p. 1947. 9.95 o.p. (ISBN 0-686-54510-9). French & Eur.

Victorine. Maude Hutchins. 191p. 1959. 8.95 o.p. (ISBN 0-8040-0311-4); pap. 4.95 o.p. (ISBN 0-8040-0312-2, 82-72205, Pub by Swallow). Ohio U Pr.

Victorine. Frances P. Keyes. 1974. pap. 1.25 o.p. (ISBN 0-380-00110-1, 20438). Avon.

Victorious Journey: A Physician-Pilot Battles Cancer During a Worldwide Tour. John J. Fisher. (Illus.). 188p. 1983. 11.95 o.p. (ISBN 0-682-49978-1). Exposition-Phoenix.

Victorious Living: A Thought & a Prayer a Day at a Time. Denis Duncan. LC 81-16478. 96p. (Orig.). 1982. pap. 3.95 o.s.i. (ISBN 0-664-24406-8, Westminster). Westminster John Knox.

Victors Divided: America & the Allies in Germany, 1918-1923. Keith L. Nelson. (Illus.). 424p. 1975. 44.00x o.p. (ISBN 0-520-02315-3). U of Cal Pr.

Victors' Justice: The Tokyo War Crimes Trial. Richard H. Minear. LC 74-163211. 248p. 1971. 22.00x o.p. (ISBN 0-691-05645-5). Princeton U Pr.

Victorverehrung Im Christlichen Altertum. Felix Rutten. Repr. of 1936 ed. 15.00 o.p. (ISBN 0-384-52655-1). Johnson Repr.

Victory & Dominion Over Fear. Lester Sumrall. 104p. 1982. pap. 2.75 o.p. (ISBN 0-89274-233-X, HH-233). Harrison Hse.

Victory in the Valleys of Life. Charles L. Allen. 128p. 1984. pap. 2.95 o.p. (ISBN 0-8007-8488-X, Spire Bks). Revell.

Victory: Life Maps. Chuck Swindoll. 64p. 1984. 5.95 o.p. (ISBN 0-8499-0442-0, 0442-0). Word Bks.

Victory over Violence: Jesus & the Revolutionists. Martin Hengel. Tr. by David E. Green from Gr. LC 73-79035. 96p. 1973. pap. 2.50 o.p. (ISBN 0-8006-0167-X, Fortress). Augsburg Fortress.

Vida. Delacorta, pseud. Tr. by Victoria Reiter from Fr. 1985. 12.70 o.s.i. (ISBN 0-671-60424-4). Summit Bks.

Vida De Lenin. Maria Prilezhaeva. 190p. (Span.). 1974. 4.45 o.p. (ISBN 0-8285-1411-9, Pub. by Progress Pubs USSR). Imported Pubns.

Vida De los Novios: The Life of Two Sweethearts. Martin Vinaver. (Illus.). 128p. 4.00 o.p. (ISBN 0-912528-05-2). John Muir.

Vida en Espana. William H. Marshall & Elena L. De Martin. 1977. pap. text ed. 4.75x o.p. (ISBN 0-88334-105-0). Ind Sch Pr.

Vidal in Venice. Gore Vidal. 1985. 22.45 o.s.i. (ISBN 0-671-60691-3). Summit Bks.

Video & Cable Guidelines. 2nd ed. Ed. by Leslie Chamberlin Burk & Roberto Esteves. 461p. 1980. 9.75x o.p. (LITA). ALA.

Video Art. Ira Schneider & Beryl Korot. LC 75-42305. (Illus.). 1976. pap. 9.95 o.p. (ISBN 0-15-193634-X, Harv). HarBraceJ.

Video Blue Book, 1986. 200p. Date not set. 49.50 o.p. (ISBN 0-932089-10-0). Orion Res.

Video Blue Book, 1987. Ed. by Orion Research Corporation Staff. 270p. 1986. 99.50 o.p. (ISBN 0-932089-15-1). Orion Res.

Video Capsule Reviews. Desmond Ryan. 350p. 1985. pap. 7.95 o.p. (ISBN 0-671-49182-2, Pub. by Fireside). S&S.

Video Cassette Recorders: Buying, Using & Maintaining. Bill Pasternak. (Illus.). 156p. (Orig.). 1983. 14.95 o.p. (ISBN 0-8306-0490-1); pap. 8.70 o.p. (ISBN 0-8306-1490-7, 1490P). TAB Bks.

Video Cassettes: Production, Distribution, & Programming for the VCR Marketplace. 494p. 1985. 15.00 o.p. (G4-3774). PLI.

Video Culture: A Critical Investigation. Intro. by John G. Hanhardt. 304p. 1986. 19.95 o.p. (ISBN 0-87905-222-8). Gibbs Smith Pub.

Video Electronics Technology. Dave Ingram. (Illus.). 256p. (Orig.). 1983. 16.95 o.p. (ISBN 0-8306-2474-0); pap. 12.60 o.p. (ISBN 0-8306-1474-5, 1474). TAB Bks.

Video in Higher Education. Ed. by Ortrun Zuber-Skerrit. 250p. 1983. 27.50 o.p. (ISBN 0-89397-165-0). Nichols Pub.

Video Production in Education & Training. Geoff Elliot. LC 84-45558. 150p. 1984. 26.00 o.p. (ISBN 0-7099-0930-6, Pub. by Croom Helm Ltd). Routledge Chapman & Hall.

Video Register & Teleconferencing Resources Directory 1987. Knowledge Industry Publications Staff. 650p. 1986. 74.50 o.p. (ISBN 0-86729-178-8). Knowledge Indus.

Video Register Nineteen Eighty-Five to Nineteen Eighty-Six. Knowledge Industry Publications Staff. 512p. 1985. pap. 59.50 o.p. (ISBN 0-86729-181-8). Knowledge Indus.

Video Tape & Disc Guide to Home Entertainment. 7th ed. National Video Clearinghouse, Inc. Staff. 1000p. (Orig.). 1986. pap. 13.95 o.p. (ISBN 0-935478-31-0). Natl Video.

Video Tape & Disc Guide to Home Entertainment. 6th ed. Ed. by National Video Clearinghouse, Inc. Staff. 826p. 1985. pap. 13.95 o.p. (ISBN 0-935478-28-0). Natl Video.

Video Tape Recorders. 2nd ed. Harry Kybett. LC 78-51582. (Illus.). 400p. 1978. pap. 14.95 o.p. (ISBN 0-672-21521-7). Sams.

Video Techniques in Trial & Pretrial. Practising Law Institute Staff & Fred I. Heller. LC 83-60620. (Litigation & Administrative Practice Ser.). (Illus.). 192p. 1983. 40.00 o.p. PLI.

Video: The Educational Challenge. Robin Moss. 160p. 1983. 25.25 o.p. (ISBN 0-7099-1747-3, Pub. by Croom Helm Ltd). Routledge Chapman & Hall.

Video User's Handbook. 2nd ed. Peter Utz. 500p. 1982. pap. 19.95 o.p. (ISBN 0-86729-036-6). Knowledge Indus.

Videocassette & Videodisc Hardware & Software Markets. International Resource Development, Inc. Staff. 167p. 1983. 1285.00x o.p. (ISBN 0-88694-579-8). Intl Res Dev.

Videolog: Programs for General Interest & Entertainment. Ed. by Lawrence Eidelberg. LC 78-74187. 1979. pap. 20.00 o.p. (ISBN 0-917226-08-9, Video-Forum). J Norton Pubs.

Videolog: Programs for the Health Sciences. Ed. by Lawrence Eidelberg. LC 78-74188. 1979. pap. 35.00 o.p. (ISBN 0-917226-09-7, Video-Forum). J Norton Pubs.

Videotaping Local History. Brad Jolly. LC 82-8730. (Illus.). 140p. 1982. pap. 12.95 o.p. (ISBN 0-910050-57-0). AASLH Pr.

Videotex & the Press. 1983. 30.00 o.p. Learned Info.

Videotex in Europe: Proceedings of Videotex in Europe Conference, Luxembourg, July 1980. 1983. 90.00 o.p. (ISBN 0-317-01040-9). Learned Info.

Videotex: Key to the Information Revolution. (Proceedings of the Online Conference: Held in New York, June 1982). 688p. (Orig.). 1982. pap. text ed. 140.00 o.p. (ISBN 0-903796-88-0, Pub. by Online Conferences England). Gower Pub Co.

Videotex: Papers. Online Conference, Toronto, 1981. 470p. (Orig.). 1981. pap. text ed. 110.25 o.p. (ISBN 0-903796-91-0, Pub. by Online Conferences England). Gower Pub Co.

Vidocq Dossier: The Story of the World's First Detective. Samuel Edwards. 1977. 7.95 o.p. (ISBN 0-395-25176-1). HM.

Vienna Circle. Victor Kraft. 1953. (ISBN 0-8022-0888-6). Philos Lib.

Vienna Girl. Ingeborg Lauterstein. LC 85-18956. 1986. bds. 16.45 o.p. (ISBN 0-393-02264-1). Norton.

Vienna in the Age of Schubert: The Biedermeier Interior, 1815-1848. Intro. by Roy Strong. (Illus.). 112p. (Orig.). 1985. pap. 10.95 o.p. (ISBN 0-904499-07-3, Pub. by Victoria & Albert Mus UK). Faber & Faber.

Vienna in the Biedermeier Era 1815-1848. Ed. by Robert Wassenberger. LC 85-43477. (Illus.). 280p. 1986. 75.00 o.p. (ISBN 0-8478-0715-0). Rizzoli Intl.

Vienna: Introduction & Reminiscence. 3rd, rev. ed. Ernst Hausner. (Illus., Eng., Fr. & Ger.). 1981. 35.00 o.p. E J Brill USA.

Vienna Medical School in the Nineteenth Century. Erna Lesky. 700p. 1975. text ed. 132.00x o.p. (Pub. by Keter Pub Jerusalem). Coronet Bks.

Vietcong Memoir. Truong N. Tang et al. LC 84-25132. (Illus.). 288p. 1985. 17.95 o.p. (ISBN 0-15-193636-6). HarBraceJ.

Vietnam. Mary McCarthy. LC 67-28041. 1967. pap. 0.95 o.p. (ISBN 0-15-193633-1). HarBraceJ.

Vietnam & America: A Documented History. Ed. by Marvin E. Gettleman et al. LC 84-48110. 1985. pap. 14.95 o.p. (ISBN 0-394-62277-4, Ever). Grove.

Vietnam & the Chinese Model: A Comparative Study of Nguyen & Ch'ing Civil Government in the First Half of the Nineteenth Century. Alexander B. Woodside. LC 76-119076. (East Asian Ser: No. 52). (Illus.). xii, 358p. 1971. 27.00x o.p. (ISBN 0-674-93720-1). Harvard U Pr.

Vietnam, Beyond the War. Joseph S. Salzburg. LC 75-10622. 1975. 12.50 o.p. (ISBN 0-682-48258-7, Banner). Exposition-Phoenix.

Vietnam: How We Got in, How to Get Out. David Schoenbrun. LC 68-25589. (Orig.). 1968. pap. 3.25 o.p. (ISBN 0-689-10242-9, Atheneum). Macmillan.

Vietnam on Trial: Westmoreland vs. CBS. Bob Brewin & Sydney Shaw. LC 85-47595. 288p. 1987. 21.95 o.p. (ISBN 0-689-11610-1, Atheneum). Macmillan.

Vietnam Remembered. Richard D. Wandke. 1984. 7.95 o.p. (ISBN 0-533-05868-6). Vantage.

Vietnam: The Battle Comes Home. Gordon Baer & Nancy Howell-Koehler. LC 84-61115. (Illus.). 128p. (Orig.). 1984. pap. 19.95 o.p. (ISBN 0-87100-199-3, 2199). Morgan.

Vietnam: The View from Moscow, Peking, Washington. Daniel S. Papp. LC 80-20117. (Illus.). 263p. 1981. lib. bdg. 19.95x o.p. (ISBN 0-89950-010-2). McFarland & Co.

Vietnam, the War at Home: The Antiwar Movement, 1964-1968. Thomas Powers. 1984. pap. 7.95 o.p. (ISBN 0-8398-2855-1). G K Hall.

Vietnam Trauma in American Foreign Policy 1945-1975. Paul M. Kattenburg. LC 79-66437. 354p. 1980. 19.95 o.p. (ISBN 0-87855-378-9). Transaction Pubs.

Vietnam Veteran - Studies in Post-Traumatic Shock Disorders: A Special Issue of the Journal of Contemporary Psychotherapy. Ed. & intro. by Wilfred Quaytman. 133p. 1987. 24.95 o.p. (ISBN 0-89885-326-5). Human Sci Pr.

Vietnam War Almanac. Harry G. Summers, Jr. (Illus.). 416p. 1987. pap. 12.95 o.p. (ISBN 0-8160-1813-8). Facts on File.

Vietnam War & International Law, 4 vols. Richard A. Falk. Incl. Vol. 1. 1967. 60.50x (ISBN 0-691-09211-7); pap. 18.50x (ISBN 0-691-02751-X); Vol. 2. 1969. 45.00x o.p. (ISBN 0-691-09214-1); pap. 12.50 o.p. (ISBN 0-691-02752-8); Vol. 3. The Widening Context. 1972. 66.00x (ISBN 0-691-09224-9); pap. 20.50x (ISBN 0-691-02753-6); Vol. 4. The Concluding Phase. 1976. 71.00x (ISBN 0-691-09230-3); pap. 29.00x LPE (ISBN 0-691-10041-1). LC 67-31295. pap. Princeton U Pr.

Vietnamese Gulag. Doan Van Toai & David Chanoff. 256p. 1986. 18.45 o.s.i. (ISBN 0-671-60350-7). S&S.

View from a Height. Isaac Asimov. 1983. pap. 1.25 o.p. (ISBN 0-380-00356-2, 45336-3, Discus). Avon.

View from a Long Chair: The Memoirs of Jack Pritchard. Jack Pritchard. (Illus.). 168p. 1984. 25.00x o.p. (ISBN 0-7102-0231-8). Routledge Chapman & Hall.

View from Deacon Hill. Jack S. Scott. LC 80-28532. (Joan Kahn Bk.). 204p. 1981. 9.95 o.p. (ISBN 0-89919-033-2). Ticknor & Fields.

View from Eden: Talks to Students of Orgonomy. Jerome Eden. 1976. 8.00 o.p. (ISBN 0-682-48570-5). Exposition-Phoenix.

View from Lincoln Hill: Men & the Land in a New England Town. Paul Brooks. LC 76-12564. 1976. 8.95 o.p. (ISBN 0-395-24398-X). HM.

View from Pompey's Head. Hamilton Basso. 1985. 6.95 o.p. (ISBN 0-87795-708-8, Arbor Hse). Morrow.

View from the Bench. Red Holzman & Leonard Lewin. (Illus.). 1980. 12.95 o.p. (ISBN 0-393-01351-0). Norton.

View from the Oak. Herbert R. Kohl & Judith Kohl. LC 76-57680. (Illus.). (gr. 10 up). 1977. text ed. 12.95 o.s.i. (ISBN 0-684-15016-6, Pub. by Scribner); pap. 4.95 o.s.i. (ISBN 0-684-15017-4, Pub. by Scribner). Macmillan.

View from the Spire: William Golding's Later Novels. Don Crompton. 208p. 1985. 29.95x o.p. (ISBN 0-631-13826-9). Basil Blackwell.

View from the Stands: Of People, Politics, Military Power & the Arts. John Kenneth Galbraith. 1986. 22.45 o.s.i. (ISBN 0-395-35319-X). HM.

View in Winter: Reflections on Old Age. Ronald Blythe. Ed. by Helen Wolff. LC 79-1813. (Helen & Kurt Wolff Bk.). 1979. 12.95 o.p. (ISBN 0-15-193638-2). HarBraceJ.

View of Dawn in the Tropics. G. Cabrera Infante. Tr. by Suzanne J. Levine from Span. LC 76-5134. 150p. 1981. pap. 6.95 o.p. (ISBN 0-916870-37-5). Creative Arts Bk.

View of Sir Isaac Newton's Philosophy. Henry Pemberton. 1972. Repr. of 1728 ed. 38.00 o.p. (ISBN 0-384-45695-2). Johnson Repr.

View of the Falls: An Illustrated History of Spokane. William Stimson. LC 85-9276. 160p. 1985. 22.95 o.p. (ISBN 0-89781-121-6). Windsor Pubns Inc.

View on Visibility: Regulatory & Scientific. Air Pollution Control Association Specialty Conference, Denver, 1979. 304p. 1980. 12.50 o.p. (ISBN 0-318-12286-3, SP-33); members 10.00 o.p. (ISBN 0-318-12287-1). Air & Waste.

Viewdata in Action: A Comparative Study of Prestel. Rex Winsbury et al. (Illus.). 288p. 1981. text ed. 43.50 o.p. (ISBN 0-07-084548-4). McGraw.

Viewdata '81: Proceedings of the Online Conference, London, 1981. Online Conference Staff. 688p. (Orig.). 1981. pap. text ed. 115.00 o.p. (ISBN 0-903796-85-6, Pub. by Online Conferences England). Online.

Viewpoints on English As a Second Language. Ed. by Burt et al. 1977. text ed. 8.25 o.p. (ISBN 0-88345-298-7, 18476). Prentice ESL.

Views from a French Farmhouse. Julian More & Carey More. LC 85-60192. (Illus.). 142p. 1985. 16.95 o.p. (ISBN 0-03-005007-3). H Holt & Co.

Views from the Hollywood Hills. Julian & Careymore. LC 86-18335. 1987. 19.95 o.p. (ISBN 0-8050-0206-5). H Holt & Co.

Views from the Pews: Christian Beliefs & Attitudes. Ed. by Roger A. Johnson. LC 82-18237. 272p. 1983. pap. 15.95 o.p. (ISBN 0-8006-1695-2, 1-1695, Fortress). Augsburg Fortress.

Views on Science, Technology & Development. Ed. by V. Rabinowitch & E. Rabinowitch. LC 74-32201. 300p. 1975. 75.00 o.p. (ISBN 0-08-018241-0). Pergamon.

Views on the Problems of Regional Planning in an Institutional & Systems Approach. (Working Papers Ser.: No. 78-24). 52p. 1978. pap. 6.00 o.p. (ISBN 0-686-75495-6, CRD065, UNCRD). UNIPUB.

Vigeland: The Sculptor & His Works. Ragna Stang. (Tanum Token Ser.). (Illus.). 190p. 1980. pap. 20.00x o.p. (ISBN 82-518-0152-4, N400). Vanous.

Vigilance: The Problem of Sustained Attention. C. M. Stroh. 1971. 34.00 o.p. (ISBN 0-08-016711-X). Pergamon.

Vigilante. William E. Burrows. LC 76-2725. (Illus.). 320p. 1976. 12.95 o.p. (ISBN 0-15-193655-2). HarBraceJ.

Vigilantism in America. Arnold Madison. LC 72-97771. (gr. 6 up). 1979. 6.95 o.p. (ISBN 0-395-28915-7, Clarion). HM.

Viking Circus Block Books: Circus Parade Zoo-A Book in-a-Box with a Performing Picture, 3 vols. Intervisual Communications. LC 83-80225. (Viking Block Bks.). (Illus.). (gr. 1-5). 1983. Set. 10.95 o.p. (Viking Kestrel). Penguin USA.

Viking Process. Norman Hartley. 1977. pap. 1.95 o.p. (ISBN 0-380-00892-0, 52993-9). Avon.

Viking Settlers in Greenland & Their Descendants During Five Hundred Years. P. Norlund. LC 37-14674. Repr. of 1936 ed. 30.00 o.p. (ISBN 0-527-67600-4). Kraus Repr.

Viking Symbol Mystery. Franklin W. Dixon. (Hardy Boys Ser: Vol. 42). (gr. 5-9). 1963. 4.50 o.p. (ISBN 0-448-08942-4, G&D). Putnam Pub Group.

Viking World. James Graham-Campbell. LC 79-21521. (Illus.). 220p. 1980. 25.00 o.p. (ISBN 0-89919-005-7). Ticknor & Fields.

Vikings. Robert Wernick & Time-Life Books Editors. LC 78-24119. (Seafarers Ser.). 1979. 13.95 o.p. (ISBN 0-8094-2707-9). Time-Life.

Vikings & Their Origins. David Wilson. LC 71-101384. (Illus., Orig.). 1970. pap. text ed. 3.95 o.p. (ISBN 0-07-070679-4). McGraw.

Vilde Affair: Beginnings of the French Resistance. Martin Blumensen. 1977. 10.00 o.p. (ISBN 0-395-25350-0). HM.

Villa Golitsyn. Piers P. Read. 208p. 1983. pap. 3.50 o.p. (ISBN 0-380-61929-6, 61929-6, Bard). Avon.

Villa in the Life of Renaissance Rome. David R. Coffin. LC 78-9049. (Monographs in Art & Archaeology: 43). 1979. 75.50x o.p. (ISBN 0-691-03942-9). Princeton U Pr.

Villa-Lobos Letters. Ed. & tr. by Lisa M. Peppercorn. (Musicians in Letters Ser.: No. 1). (Illus.). 180p. 34.95 o.s.i. (ISBN 0-907689-28-0, Pub. by Toccata Pr UK); pap. 17.95 o.s.i. (ISBN 0-907689-29-9, Pub. by Toccata Pr UK). David & Charles.

Villa of the Ferromonte. Lawrence B. Eisenberg. 1974. 6.95 o.p. (ISBN 0-671-21765-8). S&S.

Village: A History of Germantown, Ohio, 1804-1976. Carl M. Becker. LC 80-16683. (Historical Society of Germantown, Ohio Ser.). (Illus.). xvi, 209p. 1980. 15.00 o.p. (ISBN 0-8214-0550-0). Ohio U Pr.

Village Affairs. Miss Read. 1978. 7.95 o.p. (ISBN 0-395-26482-0). HM.

Village Centenary. Miss Read. 240p. 1981. 10.95 o.p. (ISBN 0-395-31262-0). HM.

Village Children. E. Smith. 180p. 1982. 4.95 o.p. (ISBN 0-8285-2422-X, Pub. by Progress Pubs USSR). Imported Pubns.

Village Detective. V. Lipatov. 419p. 1970. pap. 4.45 o.p. (ISBN 0-8285-1008-3, Pub. by Progress Pubs USSR). Imported Pubns.

Village India: Studies in the Little Community. Ed. by McKim Marriott. LC 55-9326. 1969. pap. text ed. 3.45x o.s.i. (ISBN 0-226-50644-4, P328, Phoen). U of Chicago Pr.

Village Japan. Richard K. Beardsley et al. LC 58-13802. (Illus.). xvi, 498p. 1969. 20.00x o.s.i. (ISBN 0-226-03997-8, P327); pap. 3.95 o.s.i. (ISBN 0-226-03998-6, 327, Phoenix). U of Chicago Pr.

Village Level Integrated Population Education: A Case Study of Bangladesh. Muhiuddin Haider. LC 81-43722. (Illus.). 184p. (Orig.). text ed. 29.25 o.p. (ISBN 0-8191-2489-3); pap. text ed. 12.50 o.p. (ISBN 0-8191-2490-7). U Pr of Amer.

Village Life & Labour. Ed. by Raphael Samuel. (History Workshop Ser.). (Illus.). 300p. 1983. pap. 10.95 o.p. (ISBN 0-7100-7500-6). Routledge Chapman & Hall.

Village Life in China. Samuel S. Kung & Jeanne L. Kung. 96p. 1981. pap. text ed. 6.50x o.p. (ISBN 0-917974-62-X). Waveland Pr.

Village Life under the Soviets. Karl Borders. 200p. 1986. pap. text ed. 8.95x o.p. (ISBN 0-8290-2020-9). Irvington.

Village of Stepanchikovo. Fyodor Dostoyevsky. Tr. by Ignat Avsey from Rus. 1983. 22.50 o.p. (ISBN 0-946162-06-9); pap. 12.95 o.p. (ISBN 0-946162-07-7). Dufour.

Village Song & Culture. M. Pickering. 192p. 1981. 27.50 o.p. (ISBN 0-7099-0059-7, Pub. by Croom Helm Ltd). Routledge Chapman & Hall.

Village Studies: Data Analysis & Bibliography: Africa, Middle East & North Africa, Asia (Excluding India), Pacific Islands, Latin America, West Indies & the Caribbean, 1950-1975, Vol. 2. Compiled by Mick Moore & John Connell. 346p. 1978. pap. text ed. 43.00x o.p. (ISBN 0-7201-0797-0). Mansell.

Villagers & Strangers: An English Proletarian Village over Four Centuries. Patricia H. Fleming. 168p. 1979. 18.95x o.p. (ISBN 0-87073-818-6); pap. 9.95x o.p. (ISBN 0-87073-819-4). Schenkman Bks Inc.

Villas & Cottages: A Series of Designs Prepared for Execution in the United States. 2nd ed. Calvert Vaux. (Illus.). 1970. pap. 6.50 o.p. (ISBN 0-486-22009-5). Dover.

Villas of Tuscany. Harold Acton. (Illus.). 1985. 45.00f o.s.i. (ISBN 0-500-24085-X). Thames Hudson.

Ville. (ISBN 0-8052-0876-3). Random.

Ville Dont le Prince Est un Enfant. Henry de Montherlant. (Folio 293). 1973. 4.50 o.p. (ISBN 0-686-55536-8). Schoenhof.

Villiane Petite Sorciere: The Horrible Impossible Bad Witch Child. Barbara Williams. (Illus.). 32p. (Fr.). (ps-3). 1983. pap. 2.25 o.p. (ISBN 0-380-85100-8, Camelot). Avon.

Vilna Goan Views Life. 1982. 4.00 o.p. (ISBN 0-686-76275-4). Feldheim.

Vince Lombardi. Dave Klein. (Illus.). 192p. pap. 10.95 o.p. (ISBN 0-317-61837-7). Lion Bks.

Vince Lombardi Story. Dave Klein. LC 74-170971. (Illus.). 192p. (YA) 1971. 10.95 o.p.; lib. bdg. 10.95 o.p. (ISBN 0-87460-257-2). Lion Bks.

Vincent Van Gogh: Vision & Reality. Ingo F. Walther. (Illus.). 96p. (Orig.). 1987. pap. 7.95 o.p. (ISBN 3-8228-0041-4). Parkwest Pubns.

Vindication of the Rights of Woman. Mary Wollstonecraft. Ed. by Carol H. Poston. (Critical Edition Ser). 1976. 10.00 o.p. (ISBN 0-393-04427-0); pap. text ed. 7.95x o.p. (ISBN 0-393-09213-5). Norton.

Vindication of the Rights of Woman. Mary Wollstonecraft. Ed. by Charles W. Hagelman, Jr. 1967. pap. 3.95 o.p. (ISBN 0-393-00373-6, Norton Lib). Norton.

Vindication of William Prynne see Mr. William Prynn-His Defence of Stage-Plays: Retraction of a Former Book of His Called 'Histrio-Mastix'.

Vintage Guitar. Mac Yasuda. (Illus.). 75p. 1982. text ed. 22.00 o.p. (ISBN 4-401-62031-3, Pub. by Shinko Music Japan). Bold Strummer Ltd.

Vinte Contos Brasileiros. R. Anthony Castagnaro. 218p. 1980. pap. text ed. 8.95 o.s.i. (ISBN 0-87840-079-6). Georgetown U Pr.

Vinyl Cations. Peter J. Stang et al. LC 79-21330. 1979. 89.00 o.p. (ISBN 0-12-663780-6). Acad Pr.

Vinyl-Chloride Mutagenesis. (Landmark Ser.). 1979. 22.50x o.p. (ISBN 0-8422-4120-5). Irvington.

Vinyl Polymerization. Ed. by G. E. Ham. (Kinetics & Mechanisms of Polymerization Ser.: Vol. 1, Pts. 1 & 2). 992p. Pt. 1, 1967. 115.00 o.p. (ISBN 0-8247-1292-7); Pt. 2, 1969. 110.00 o.p. (ISBN 0-8247-1294-3). Dekker.

Violence: A Guide for the Caring Professions. R. Glynn Owens & J. Barrie Ashcroft. LC 84-23865. 198p. 1985. 26.00 o.p. (ISBN 0-7099-1931-X, Pub. by Croom Helm Ltd); pap. 13.95 o.p. (ISBN 0-7099-1938-7). Routledge Chapman & Hall.

Violence Against Women: An Annotated Bibliography. Carolyn F. Wilson. xiii, 111p. 1981. lib. bdg. 25.00 o.s.i. (ISBN 0-8161-8497-6, Hall Reference). G K Hall.

Violence & Responsibility. John Harris. 1980. 20.00x o.p. (ISBN 0-7100-0448-6). Routledge Chapman & Hall.

Violence in America. Stephen Goode. LC 83-25033. 192p. (YA) (gr. 7-12). 1984. lib. bdg. 9.79 o.p. (ISBN 0-671-45810-8). Messner.

Violence in Intimate Relationships. Ed. by Gordon W. Russell. 320p. Date not set. 40.00 o.s.i. (ISBN 0-88-035143-3, PBI). Pergamon.

Violence in Lincoln County, 1869-1881: A New Mexico Item. William A. Keleher. LC 82-1984. (Illus.). 416p. 1982. 22.50 o.p. (ISBN 0-8263-0620-9, V-2); pap. 12.95 o.p. (ISBN 0-8263-0616-0). U of NM Pr.

Violence in Northern Ireland: Understanding Prostestant Perspectives. John F. Galliher & Jerry L. DeGregory. 208p. 1985. 36.50 o.p. (ISBN 0-8419-1027-8). Holmes & Meier.

Violence in the Communications Industry, 7 vols. Ed. by Canadian Royal Commission. 1977. Set. pap. text ed. 85.00x o.p. (ISBN 0-685-87415-X). Gower Pub Co.

Violence in the Family: An Annotated Bibliography. Elizabeth Kemmer. LC 83-48198. (Reference Library of Social Science: Vol. 182). 192p. 1984. lib. bdg. 24.50 o.p. (ISBN 0-8240-9090-X). Garland Pub.

Violence of Pity in Euripides' Medea. Pietro Pucci. LC 79-52501. (Cornell Studies in Classical Philology: Vol. XLI). (Illus.). 208p. 1980. 22.50x o.p. (ISBN 0-8014-1190-4). Cornell U Pr.

Violence, the Ku Klux Klan, & the Struggle for Equality. 72p. 1981. 4.95 o.p. (ISBN 0-8106-1419-7). NEA.

Violence Within. 2nd ed. Paul Tournier. LC 78-3139. 208p. 1982. pap. 6.95 o.p. (ISBN 0-06-068295-7, RD376). HarpR.

Violent Bear It Away see Wise Blood.

Violent Land. Jorge Amado. 1979. pap. 2.75 o.p. (ISBN 0-380-47696-7, 47696-7, Bard). Avon.

Violent Men. 2nd ed. Hans Toch. 292p. 1969. 15.95x o.p. (ISBN 0-87073-887-9); pap. text ed. 8.95 o.p. (ISBN 0-685-99685-9). Schenkman Bks Inc.

Violent Sundays. Bob Chandler. (Orig.). 1984. pap. 8.70 o.p. (ISBN 0-671-47460-X, Fireside). S&S.

Violent Weather: Hurricanes, Tornadoes & Storms. Stan Gibilisco. LC 84-8873. (Illus.). 176p. (Orig.). 1984. pap. text ed. 13.60 o.p. (ISBN 0-8306-1805-8, 1805). TAB Bks.

Violet Apple & the Witch. David Lindsay. Ed. & intro. by J. B. Pick. LC 75-18962. 300p. 1977. 15.00 o.p. (ISBN 0-914090-12-7); pap. 4.95 o.p. (ISBN 0-914090-13-5). Chicago Review.

Violet Soup: Common Edible Plants of the Rockies. Daniel Beshoar. (Illus.). 70p. 1982. 8.00 o.p. (ISBN 0-86541-009-7); pap. avail. o.p. Filter.

Violets. Roy E. Coombs. 142p. 1985. 12.95 o.p. (Croom Helm). Intl Spec Bk.

Violets Grow in Secret Places. Marilyn C. Donahue. (Pennypinchers Ser.). 128p. (gr. 5-9). 1984. pap. 2.95 o.p. (ISBN 0-89191-885-X, 58859). Cook.

Violets: The History & Cultivation of Scented Violets. Roy E. Coombs. (Illus.). 144p. 1981. 17.00 o.p. (Pub. by Croom Helm Ltd). Routledge Chapman & Hall.

Violin & Keyboard: The Duo Repertoire, 2 vols. Abram Loft. Incl. Vol. 1. From the Seventeenth Century to Mozart. 1973. Vol. 1. 20.00 o.p. (ISBN 0-670-74701-7); Vol. 2. From Beethoven to the Present. 1973. Vol. 2. 20.00 o.p. (ISBN 0-670-74702-5). LC 72-93279. (Illus.). 832p. 1973. Set. 40.00 o.p. (ISBN 0-670-74700-9, Grossman). Penguin USA.

Violin & the Viola. Sheila M. Nelson. (Illus.). 277p. 1972. 12.50x o.p. (ISBN 0-393-02092-4). Norton.

Violin Identification & Price Guide, Bk. 1. Roy Ehrhardt. (Illus.). 1977. Repr. plastic ring bd. 25.00 o.p. (ISBN 0-913902-22-5). Heart Am Pr.

Violin Makers of the Guarneri Family, 1626-1762. Alfred Hill et al. (Illus.). Repr. 55.00 o.p. (ISBN 0-87556-125-X). Saifer.

Violin: Six Lessons with Yehudi Menuhin. Yehudi Menuhin. (Illus.). 1981. pap. 8.95 o.p. (ISBN 0-393-00080-X). Norton.

Viper. Raymond Thorp. 192p. (ISBN 0-8022-1721-4). Philos Lib.

Viral Equation of State. E. A. Mason & T. H. Spurling. LC 69-17903. 1970. 80.00 o.p. (ISBN 0-08-013292-8); pap. text ed. 80.00 o.p. (ISBN 0-08-018988-1). Pergamon.

Viral Immunodiagnosis. Ed. by Edouard Kurstak & Richard Morisset. 1974. 56.00 o.p. (ISBN 0-12-429750-1). Acad Pr.

Viral Immunology & Immunopathology. Ed. by Abner L. Notkins. 1975. 65.50 o.p. (ISBN 0-12-522050-2). Acad Pr.

Viral Infections of Humans: Epidemiology & Control. 2nd ed. Ed. by Alfred S. Evans. LC 82-1984. 758p. 1982. 69.50x o.p. (ISBN 0-306-40676-4, Plenum Med Bk). Plenum Pub.

Viral Infections of Humans: Epidemiology & Control. 2nd ed. Ed. by Alfred S. Evans. LC 84-1984. 758p. 1984. pap. 27.50x o.p. (ISBN 0-306-41635-2, Plenum Med Bk). Plenum Pub.

Viral Transformation & Endogenour Viruses. Ed. by Albert S. Kaplan. 1974. 41.50 o.p. (ISBN 0-12-397060-1). Acad Pr.

Virgil Thomson Reader. Virgil Thomson. 576p. 1981. 25.00 o.p. (ISBN 0-395-31330-9). HM.

Virgin. Geoffrey Ashe. 272p. 1988. pap. 12.95 o.p. (ISBN 1-85063-100-X). Routledge Chapman & Hall.

Virgin. James Patterson. 1980. text ed. 10.95 o.p. (ISBN 0-07-048820-7). McGraw.

Virgin Guide to London. Ed. by Mark Williams. 1986. pap. 7.95 o.p. (ISBN 0-394-74421-7). Pantheon.

Virgin Islands National Park. updated ed. Ruth Radlauer. LC 80-22457. (Parks for People Ser.). (Illus.). 48p. (gr. 3 up). 1981. PLB 13.27 o.p. (ISBN 0-516-07741-4). Childrens.

Virgin Luck. Laurence W. Meynell. 1964. 8.95 o.p. (ISBN 0-671-79020-X). S&S.

Virgin Mary in Evangelical Perspective. Heiko A. Oberman. LC 70-157546. (Facet Bks.). 38p. (Orig.). 1971. pap. 0.50 o.p. (ISBN 0-8006-3067-X, 1-3067, Fortress). Augsburg Fortress.

Virgin Soil. Ivan S. Turgenev. Tr. by Constance Garnett from Rus. LC 77-78078. 1977. pap. 3.95 o.p. (ISBN 0-394-17015-6, E699, Ever). Grove.

Virgin Soil Upturned, 2 vols. M. Sholokhov. 806p. 1979. 10.20 o.p. (ISBN 0-8285-1619-7, Pub. by Progress Pubs USSR). Imported Pubns.

Virginia: Agency. 8.50 o.p. (ISBN 0-686-90912-7). Am Law Inst.

Virginia & the English Commercial System, 1689-1773: Studies in the Development & Fluctuations of a Colonial Economy under Imperial Control. John M. Hemphill, II. Ed. by Stuart Bruchey. LC 84-45424. (American Economic History Ser.). 351p. 1985. lib. bdg. 46.00 o.p. (ISBN 0-8240-6669-3). Garland Pub.

Virginia City. Hank Mitchum. (Nightingale Paperbacks Ser.). 288p. 1987. pap. 11.95 o.p. (ISBN 0-8161-4325-0, Large Print Bks). G K Hall.

Virginia: Conflict of Laws. 8.50 o.p. (ISBN 0-686-90916-X). Am Law Inst.

Virginia Country Civil War, Vol. III. Robert Krick et al. Ed. by Garrison Ellis. 80p. 1985. pap. 4.95 o.p. (ISBN 0-9610772-4-7). Country Pub Inc.

Virginia Country's Civil War Quarterly, Vol. VIII. Ed. by Kent Brown et al. (Illus.). 80p. 1987. pap. 4.95 o.p. (ISBN 0-9610772-9-8). Country Pub Inc.

Virginia Goverment & Politics: Readings & Comments. Ed. by Morris R. Thomas & Larry Sabato. 231p. 1984. 13.50 o.p. (ISBN 0-318-04158-8). U Va Ctr Pub Serv.

Virginia Local History: A Bibliography. xxxvi, 46p. 1976. pap. 2.00 o.p. (ISBN 0-88490-026-6). VA State Lib.

Virginia Property & Casualty. 1982. write for info. o.p. Merritt Co.

Virginia Rules Annotated. Michie Company Editorial Staff. 470p. 1979. pap. 25.00 o.p. (ISBN 0-87215-317-7). Michie Co.

Virginia Rules Annotated: 1985 Edition. Michie Company Editorial Staff. 1146p. 1985. 30.00 o.p. (ISBN 0-87215-954-X). Michie Co.

Virginia Supreme Court: An Institutional & Political Analysis. Thomas R. Morris. cancelled o.s.i. U VA Ctr Pub Serv.

Virginia Tech Symposium on Applied Behavioral Science, Vol. I. Ed. by Joseph A. Sgro. LC 80-8614. 320p. 1981. 35.00x o.p. (ISBN 0-669-04332-X). Lexington Bks.

Virginia: Torts. 8.50 o.p. (ISBN 0-686-90918-6). Am Law Inst.

Virginia Woolf. Quentin Bell. LC 72-79926. (Illus.). 544p. 1972. 12.50 o.p. (ISBN 0-15-193765-6). HarBraceJ.

Virginia Woolf. Susan R. Gorsky. (English Authors Ser.). 176p. 1982. 13.50 o.p. (ISBN 0-8057-6712-6, Twayne); pap. 5.95 o.p. (ISBN 0-8057-6890-4). G K Hall.

Virginia Woolf. Winifred Holtby. 206p. 1978. lib. bdg. 11.95 o.p. (ISBN 0-915864-90-8); pap. 1.00 o.s.i. (ISBN 0-915864-89-4). Academy Chi Pubs.

Virginia Woolf: A Commentary. Bernard Blackstone. LC 49-9253. 256p. 1972. pap. 2.45 o.p. (ISBN 0-15-693570-8, Harv). HarBraceJ.

Virginia Woolf & Bloomsbury: A Centenary Celebration. Ed. by Jane Marcus. LC 85-45296. 320p. 1985. 24.95x o.p. (ISBN 0-253-36261-X). Ind U Pr.

Virginia Woolf & Her Works. Jean Guiguet. Tr. by Jean Stewart. 1976. pap. 4.95 o.p. (ISBN 0-15-693630-5, Harv). HarBraceJ.

Virginia Woolf & Her World. John Lehmann. 127p. 1976. 12.95 o.p. (ISBN 0-15-193771-0). HarBraceJ.

Virginia Woolf's Vision of Life & Her Search for Significant Form: A Study in the Shaping Vision. Vijay Kapur. 195p. 1980. text ed. 17.50 o.p. (ISBN 0-391-01753-5). Humanities.

Virginian. Owen Wister. LC 88-60581. (Illus.). 368p. 1988. 13.95 o.p. (ISBN 0-89577-305-8). RD Assn.

Virginia's Eastern Shore: A History of Northampton & Accomack Counties, 2 vols. Ralph T. Whitelaw. (Illus.). 48.00 o.p. (ISBN 0-8446-1478-5). Peter Smith.

Virginity. Otto Nemecek. (Illus.). 144p. 1958. (ISBN 0-8022-1189-5). Philos Lib.

Virginius Affair. Richard H. Bradford. LC 20-520000. 1980. 19.50x o.p. (ISBN 0-87081-080-4). Univ Pr Colo.

Virility Factor. Robert Merle. LC 76-58513. 320p. 1977. text ed. 9.95 o.p. (ISBN 0-07-041496-3). McGraw.

Viroids & Viroid Diseases. T. O. Diener. LC 78-21681. 270p. 1979. 37.50 o.p. (ISBN 0-471-03504-1, JW). Krieger.

Virology of Flowering Plants. W. A. Stevens. (Tertiary Level Biology Ser.). 1982. 39.95x o.p. (ISBN 0-412-00061-X, NO. 5011, Pub. by Chapman & Hall); pap. 19.95 o.p. (ISBN 0-412-00071-7, NO. 5012). Routledge Chapman & Hall.

Virtual Memory Management. Richard W. Carr. Ed. by Harold Stone. LC 84-140. (Computer Science: Systems Programming: No. 20). 186p. 1984. 42.95 o.p. (ISBN 0-8357-1533-7). UMI Res Pr.

Virtual Work in Structural Analysis. Glyn A. Davies. LC 81-15926. 325p. 1982. 79.95x o.p. (ISBN 0-471-10112-5). Wiley.

Virtue of Philosophy: An Interpretation of Plato's "Charmides" Drew A. Hyland. LC 81-38355. xii, 156p. 1981. text ed. 22.95x o.p. (ISBN 0-8214-0588-8). Ohio U Pr.

Virus Directed Host Response. Morris Pollard. (Perspectives in Virology: Vol. 5). 1967. 61.50 o.p. (ISBN 0-12-560550-1). Acad Pr.

Virus Diseases in Man, Plant, & Animal. G. Seiffert. 1952. (ISBN 0-8022-1533-5). Philos Lib.

Virus Inclusions in Insect Cells see Multiplication of Viruses.

Virus Inclusions in Plant Cells see Multiplication of Viruses.

Virus-Induced Immunopathology. Ed. by Morris Pollard. (Perspectives in Virology: Vol. 6). 1969. 57.50 o.p. (ISBN 0-12-560556-0). Acad Pr.

Virus Receptors, Part 1: Bacterial Viruses see Queues: Receptors & Recognition Series B.

Virus Receptors, Part 2: Animal Viruses see Queues: Receptors & Recognition Series B.

Virus Structure. Robert W. Horne. 1974. 33.00 o.p. (ISBN 0-12-355750-X). Acad Pr.

Virus Transformed Cell Membranes. Ed. by Claude Nicolau. 1979. 72.50 o.p. (ISBN 0-12-518650-9). Acad Pr.

Virus Tumorigenesis & Immunogenesis. Ed. by W. S. Ceglowski & Herman Friedman. 1973. 60.50 o.p. (ISBN 0-12-165050-2). Acad Pr.

Viruses. rev. ed. F. Kingsley Sanders. Ed. by J. J. Head. LC 77-94289. (Carolina Biology Readers Ser.). (Illus.). 32p. (gr. 10 up). 1981. pap. 2.10 o.p. (ISBN 0-89278-264-1, 45-9664). Carolina Biological.

Viruses & Environment. Edouard Kurstak & Karl Maramorosch. 1979. 29.95 o.p. (ISBN 0-12-429766-8). Acad Pr.

Viruses & Immunity: Toward Understanding Viral Immunology & Immunopathology. Claude Koprowski & Hilary Koprowski. 1975. 35.00 o.p. (ISBN 0-12-420350-7). Acad Pr.
Viruses & the Environment. J. I. Cooper & F. O. MacCallum. (Illus.). 190p. 1984. 32.00x o.p. (ISBN 0-412-22870-X, NO. 6437); pap. 15.95x o.p. (ISBN 0-412-22880-7, NO. 6869). Routledge Chapman & Hall.
Viruses, Evolution & Cancer. Ed. by Edouard Kurstak & Karl Maramorosch. 1974. 104.00 o.p. (ISBN 0-12-429760-9). Acad Pr.
Viruses of Potatoes & Seed-Potato Production. Ed. by De Bokx. 232p. 1971. 17.50 o.p. (ISBN 90-220-0358-2, PDC100, PUDOC). UNIPUB.
Viscoelasticity. 2nd ed. W. Fluegge. (Illus.). 200p. 1975. 22.00 o.p. (ISBN 0-387-07344-2). Springer-Verlag.
Viscosity of Protoplasm. L. V. Heilbrunn. (Protoplasmatologia: Vol. 2, Pt. C1). (Illus.). 1958. pap. 32.50 o.p. (ISBN 0-387-80485-4). Springer-Verlag.
Viscous Flow Theory: Laminar Flow, Vol. 1. Pai. LC 56-11758. 400p. 1965. 23.50 o.p. (ISBN 0-442-06417-9, Pub. by Van Nos Reinhold). Krieger.
Visibility: Effects of Vehicle & Lighting Characteristics, 6 Reports. (Transportation Research Record Ser.). 69p. 1974. 3.40 o.p. Transport Res Bd.
Visible & Invisible Group: Two Perspectives on Group Psychotherapy & Group Process. Yvonne Agazarian & Richard Peters. (Illus.). 304p. 1981. 29.95x o.p. (ISBN 0-7100-0692-6). Routledge Chapman & Hall.
Visible Words: The Interpretation & Practice of Christian Sacraments. Robert W. Jenson. LC 77-78631. 224p. 1978. 10.95 o.p. (ISBN 0-8006-0507-1, 1-507, Fortress). Augsburg Fortress.
VisiCalc Disk Guide. David A. Wilson. (DiskGuides Ser.). 14p. (Orig.). 1983. pap. text ed. 4.00 o.p. (ISBN 0-07-931098-2). Osborne-McGraw.
VisiCalc for Apple II, II Plus, & IIe. John Craver. LC 83-82398. (Illus.). 192p. 1983. 17.95 o.p. (ISBN 0-89586-274-3). Price Stern.
VisiCalc for Scientists & Engineering. Stanley R. Trost & Charles Pomernacki. LC 83-60045. (Illus.). 203p. 1983. pap. 15.95 o.p. (ISBN 0-89588-096-2). SYBEX.
VisiCalc Home & Office Companion. David M. Castlewitz & Lawrence Chisausky. 1982. pap. text ed. 4.00 o.p. (ISBN 0-07-931050-8). McGraw.
VisiCalc Made Simple. Thomas M. O'Donovan. LC 84-3680. 151p. 1984. 23.95 o.p. (ISBN 0-471-90457-0). Wiley.
VisiCalc Program Made Easy. David M. Castlewitz. 160p. (Orig.). 1983. pap. text ed. 14.95 o.p. (ISBN 0-07-931089-3, 89-3). Osborne-McGraw.
Vision. Ken Carey. Ed. by Jim Gross. 110p. 1986. pap. 6.95 o.p. (ISBN 0-913299-30-8, Dist. by NAL). Stillpoint.
Vision. David Wilkerson. 144p. 1974. pap. 3.50 o.p. (ISBN 0-8007-8150-3, Spire Bks). Revell.
Vision & Strategy for Church Growth. 2nd ed. Waldo J. Werning. 1983. pap. 4.50 o.p. (ISBN 0-8010-9658-8). Baker Bk.
Vision & Virtue: Essays in Christian Ethical Reflection. Stanley Hauerwas. LC 80-54877. 264p. 1981. text ed. 9.95 o.p. (ISBN 0-268-01921-5); pap. text ed. 9.95x o.p. (ISBN 0-268-01922-3, NDP 270). U of Notre Dame Pr.
Vision & Visual Perception. Ed. by Clarence H. Graham. LC 65-12711. 637p. 1965. 95.95x o.p. (ISBN 0-471-32170-2). Wiley.
Vision from God. Fred Parsons. 1978. 4.00 o.p. (ISBN 0-682-49022-9). Exposition-Phoenix.
Vision in Fishes-New Approaches in Research. Ed. by M. A. Ali. LC 75-8570. (Nato ASI Series A, Life Sciences: Vol. 1). 850p. 1975. 89.50x o.p. (ISBN 0-306-35601-5, Plenum Pr). Plenum Pub.
Vision of an Artist & Writer. James J. Davidson. (Illus.). 1981. 6.95 o.p. (ISBN 0-533-04806-0). Vantage.
Vision of Cosmic Order in the Vedas. Jeanine Miller. 320p. 1985. 39.95x o.p. (ISBN 0-7102-0369-1). Routledge Chapman & Hall.
Vision of Doom. Mary Kirchoff. LC 86-90005. (Endless Quest Bks.: No. 35). 160p. (Orig.). (gr. 3-8). 1986. pap. 2.25 o.p. (ISBN 0-88038-307-0). TSR Inc.
Vision of Hope: The Churches & Change in Latin America. Ed. by Trevor Beeson & Jenny Pearce. LC 83-48927. 288p. 1984. pap. 6.95 o.p. (ISBN 0-8006-1758-4, 1-1758, Fortress). Augsburg Fortress.
Vision of Landscape in Renaissance Italy. Richard A. Turner. LC 66-11977. (Illus.). 336p. 1974. 46.00x o.p. (ISBN 0-691-03849-X, 319); pap. 8.50x o.p. (ISBN 0-691-00307-6, 319). Princeton U Pr.
Vision of Matthew: Christ, Church & Morality in the First Gospel. John P. Meier. LC 78-70820. 1979. pap. 8.95 o.p. (ISBN 0-8091-2171-9). Paulist Pr.
Visionaries & Their Apocalypses. Ed. by Paul D. Hanson. LC 83-5488. (Issues in Religion & Theology Ser.). 176p. 1983. pap. 2.50 o.p. (ISBN 0-8006-1765-7, 1-1765, Fortress). Augsburg Fortress.
Visionary Apparatus: Michael Snow & Juan Geuer. Dana Friis-Hansen & Jeanne Randolph. LC 86-62271. (Illus.). 52p. (Orig.). 1986. pap. 5.00 o.p. (ISBN 0-938437-15-1). MIT List Visual Arts.
Visiones de Hoy. Robert B. Brown & Barry J. Luby. 228p. 1971. pap. text ed. 9.95 o.p. (ISBN 0-15-594930-6, HC). HarBraceJ.
Visions & Business: Support & Tools for the Entrepreneur see Empowering Vision: For Your Service Business.
Visions & Revisions--a Guide for Creative Writing. Lyn Walker. 200p. (Orig.). 1981. pap. text ed. 12.95x o.p. (ISBN 0-917962-72-9). T H Peek.
Visions & Voices. Jonathan Cott. LC 87-6750. 216p. 1987. pap. 17.95 o.p. (ISBN 0-385-24144-5, Dolp). Doubleday.
Visions from the Ramble. John Hollander. LC 65-15913. (Orig.). 1965. 4.50 o.p. (ISBN 0-689-10128-7, Atheneum). Macmillan.
Visions in Depth. Gary Wayne Plourde, Sr. 1977. 4.00 o.p. (ISBN 0-682-48795-3). Exposition-Phoenix.
Visions of America: How We Saw the 1984 Election. William A. Henry, III. LC 85-47631. 288p. 1985. 17.95 o.p. (ISBN 0-87113-012-2). Atlantic Monthly.
Visions of Christ: A Posthumous Cycle of Poems. Rainer M. Rilke. Ed. by Siegfried Mandel. Tr. by Aaron Kramer from Ger. LC 67-23560. (Illus.). 1967. 19.50x o.p. (ISBN 0-87081-021-9). Univ Pr Colo.
Visions of Culture: Voltaire, Guizot, Burckhardt, Lamprecht, Huizinga, Ortega Y Gasset. Karl J. Weintraub. LC 66-13893. 1969. pap. text ed. 2.95x o.s.i. (ISBN 0-226-89089-9, P340, Phoen). U of Chicago Pr.
Visions of Faith: An Anthology of Reflections. Reverend William G. Sykes. 544p. 1986. 19.95 o.s.i. (ISBN 0-920792-25-1). Eden Pr.
Visions of Hope: Apocalyptic Themes from Biblical Times. David Sneen. LC 77-84098. 1978. pap. 3.95 o.p. (ISBN 0-8066-1624-5, 10-6850, Augsburg). Augsburg Fortress.
Visions of James Thomson ("B.V.") An Exploration. Gurdit Singh. (English Language & Literature Ser.: No. 6). 185p. 1980. text ed. 12.50x o.p. (ISBN 0-391-02522-8). Humanities.
Visions of the Past. Christopher Taylor & Richard Muir. (Illus.). 352p. 1983. 24.95x o.p. (ISBN 0-460-04556-3, Pub. by J M Dent England). Biblio Dist.
Visions of Victory: Selected Vietnamese Communist Military Writings, 1964-1968. Patrick J. McGarvey. LC 69-18374. (Publications Ser.: No. 81). 1969. 10.95x o.p. (ISBN 0-8179-1811-6); pap. 6.95 o.p. (ISBN 0-8179-1812-4). Hoover Inst Pr.
Visions of Yesterday. James E. Toal. 32p. 1988. 7.50 o.p. (ISBN 0-8062-3062-2). Carlton.
Visit. Friedrich Durrenmatt. Tr. by Patrick Bowles from Ger. 1962. pap. 4.95 o.p. (ISBN 0-394-17239-6, E344, Ever). Grove.
Visit from St. Alphabet. Dave Morice. LC 80-24865. (Illus.). 20p. (Orig.). (gr. 3 up). 1980. pap. 5.00 o.p. (ISBN 0-915124-47-5, Pub. by Toothpaste). Coffee Hse.
Visit to the Vatican for Young People. Donald Wuerl & Michael Wilson. (Illus.). (gr. 3-7). 1980. 3.50 o.s.i. (ISBN 0-8198-8002-7). Dghtrs St Paul.
Visitants. Randolph Stow. 192p. 1987. pap. 7.95 o.s.i. (ISBN 0-8008-8017-X). Taplinger.
Visitants: A Novel. Randolph Stow. LC 80-53710. 192p. 1981. 12.95 o.s.i. (ISBN 0-8008-8018-8). Taplinger.
Visitations. Mitch Sisskind. Ed. by Laurance Wieder. LC 84-71460. 96p. 1984. 10.95 o.p. (ISBN 0-918305-02-0). Brightwaters.
Visitations of Churches Belonging to St. Paul's Cathedral in 1297 & 1458. London - St. Paul's Cathedral Staff. Repr. of 1895 ed. 27.00 o.p. (ISBN 0-384-33490-3). Johnson Repr.
Visiting & Reliving the Lands of the Bible. David J. Miller. 1976. 6.00 o.p. (ISBN 0-682-48418-0). Exposition-Phoenix.
Visiting Boise: A Personal Guide. Dwight W. Jensen. LC 80-27098. (Illus.). 145p. 1981. pap. 7.95 o.p. (ISBN 0-87004-290-4). Caxton.
Visiting Cards of Painters. F. C. Schang. (Illus.). 115p. 1983. pap. 15.00 o.s.i. (ISBN 0-8390-0332-3). Abner Schram Ltd.
Visiting Hours. 2.00 o.p. (ISBN 0-936672-49-8). Aerial Photo.
Visitor. Jack Hayford. 128p. 1986. pap. 4.95 o.p. (ISBN 0-8423-7802-2). Tyndale.
Visitors. Clifford D. Simak. 1980. pap. 2.95 o.p. (ISBN 0-345-28387-2, Del Rey). Ballantine.
Vistas in Astronomy, Vol. 23 Complete. P. Beer & A. Beer. 1980. 140.00 o.p. (ISBN 0-08-026046-2). Pergamon.
Vistas in Astronomy, Vol. 25. Ed. by P. Beer & K. Pounds. (Illus.). 436p. 1984. 160.00 o.p. (ISBN 0-08-031042-7). Pergamon.
Vistas in Astronomy, Vol. 26. Ed. by P. Beer. (Illus.). 426p. 1985. 180.00 o.p. (ISBN 0-08-032314-6). Pergamon.
Vistas in Astronomy, Vol. 27. Ed. by P. Beer et al. (Illus.). 486p. 1986. 162.00 o.p. (ISBN 0-08-033235-8, C150, Pub. by PPL). Pergamon.
Vistas in Astronomy, Vol. 28. Ed. by P. Beer et al. (Illus.). 650p. 1986. 162.00 o.p. (ISBN 0-08-034129-2, Pub. by PPL). Pergamon.
Vistas in Astronomy, Supplement: Far Infrared Astronomy. Ed. by Michael Rowan-Robinson. 352p. 1976. 90.00 o.p. (ISBN 0-08-020513-5). Pergamon.
Vistas in Physical Reality. Ed. by Ervin Laszlo & Emily B. Sellon. LC 75-34356. (Illus.). 228p. 1976. 45.00x o.p. (ISBN 0-306-30884-3, Plenum Pr). Plenum Pub.
Visual & Spatial Structure of Landscapes. Tadahiko Higuchi. Tr. by Charles Terry from Japanese. (Illus.). 218p. 1983. 27.50x o.p. (ISBN 0-262-08120-2). MIT Pr.
Visual & Transfer Skill Mastery, 2 levels. Kitty Wehrli. (Michigan Arithmetic Program Ser.). 1976. wkbk. 8.50 ea. o.p.; Level 1. (ISBN 0-89039-948-4); Level 2. 8.50 o.p. (ISBN 0-89039-850-X). Ann Arbor Pubs.
Visual Arabic Grammar-Lexicon. E. J. Tubbs. 1972. pap. 20.00 o.s.i. (ISBN 0-685-47305-8). E J Brill USA.
Visual Art in the Life of the Church: Encouraging Creative Worship & Witness in the Congregation. Richard R. Caemmerer, Jr. LC 83-70504. 96p. (Orig.). 1983. pap. 12.95 o.p. (ISBN 0-8066-2010-2, 10-6855, Augsburg). Augsburg Fortress.
Visual Art, Mathematics & Computers: Selections from the Journal Leonardo. Ed. by Frank J. Malina. 1979. 100.00 o.p. (ISBN 0-08-021854-7). Pergamon.
Visual Blight in America. P. Lewis et al. LC 73-88850. (CCG Resource Papers Ser.: No. 23). (Illus.). 1973. pap. text ed. 5.00 o.p. (ISBN 0-89291-070-4). Assn Am Geographers.
Visual Concepts for Photographers. Leslie Stroebel et al. (Illus.). 350p. 1980. 22.95 o.p. (ISBN 0-240-51025-9). Focal Pr.
Visual Data. Roger E. Kranich & Jerry L. Messec. 84p. 1979. pap. 3.75 o.p. (ISBN 0-88323-153-0, 243); answer key 1.25 o.p. (ISBN 0-88323-157-3, 250). Pendergrass Pub.
Visual Dimension: Aspects of Jewish Art. Ed. by Clare Moore. (Publications of the Oxford Centre for Postgraduate Hebrew Study Ser.: Vol. 5). (Illus.). 320p. 1987. text ed. 40.00x o.s.i. (ISBN 0-86598-081-0, Rowman & Littlefield). Rowman.
Visual Disability in the Elderly. Tim Cullinan. 128p. (Orig.). 1986. pap. 13.50 o.p. (ISBN 0-7099-3409-2, Pub. by Croom Helm Ltd). Routledge Chapman & Hall.
Visual Display Terminals: A Manual Covering Ergonomics, Workplace Design, Health & Safety, Task Organization. A. Cakir et al. LC 80-40070. 307p. 1980. 88.95x o.p. (ISBN 0-471-27793-2, Pub. by Wiley-Interscience). Wiley.
Visual History of Costume: The Eighteenth Century. Aileen Ribeiro. LC 83-14120. (Illus.). 144p. 1983. text ed. 19.95x o.s.i. (ISBN 0-89676-077-4). Drama Bk.
Visual History of Costume: The Nineteenth Century. Vanda Foster. LC 83-14120. (Visual History of Costume Ser.). (Illus.). 152p. 1984. text ed. 19.95x o.s.i. (ISBN 0-89676-079-0). Drama Bk.
Visual in Metaphysical Poetry. Mary Sloane. 1980. text ed. 15.00x o.p. (ISBN 0-391-00890-0). Humanities.
Visual Information Processing: Proceedings of the Carnegie Symposium on Cognition, 8th, Annual. Carnegie Symposium on Cognition Staff. Ed. by William G. Chase. 1973. 54.50 o.p. (ISBN 0-12-170150-6). Acad Pr.
Visual Literacy Connections to Thinking, Reading & Writing. photocopy ed. Richard Sinatra. (Illus.). 326p. 1986. 40.75 o.p. (ISBN 0-398-05192-5). C C Thomas.
Visual Notes for Architects & Designers. Crowe & Laseau. 1983. 26.95 o.s.i. (ISBN 0-442-29335-6). Van Nos Reinhold.
Visual Prosthesis: The Interdisciplinary Dialogue, Proceedings. Ed. by T. Sterling et al. LC 74-137600. (ACM Monograph Ser). 1971. 88.00 o.p. (ISBN 0-12-666150-2). Acad Pr.
Visual Solutions: Activities, Experiments, & Projects for Solving Art & Design Problems. Robin Landa. (ISBN 0-13-942434-2). S&S.
Visual Tracking. R. Robert Geake & Donald E. Smith. (Michigan Tracking Program Ser.). 1975. pap. 3.95x o.p. (ISBN 0-914004-43-3). Ulrich.
Visually Handicapped Children & Young People. Elizabeth K. Chapman. (Special Needs in Education Ser.). 1978. 16.95x o.p. (ISBN 0-7100-8878-7). Routledge Chapman & Hall.
Vita. Daniel Gillis. LC 79-52906. 111p. 1979. pap. 5.00 o.p. (ISBN 0-87867-072-6). Ramparts.
Vita Nuova. Dante Alighieri. Ed. by J. Chelsey Mathews. Tr. by R. W. Emerson. 1960. 15.00 o.p. (ISBN 0-384-10795-8). Johnson Repr.
Vita: The Life of Vita Sackville-West. Victoria Glendinning. LC 83-47961. (Illus.). 426p. 1983. 17.45 o.s.i. (ISBN 0-394-52023-8). Knopf.
Vital Approach. 2nd ed. Donald Mattam. 1973. 21.00 o.p. (ISBN 0-08-017700-X); pap. 9.25 o.p. (ISBN 0-08-017701-8). Pergamon.
Vital Church Management. Philip M. Larson, Jr. LC 76-12394. 1977. 3.99 o.p. (ISBN 0-8042-1883-8, John Knox). Westminster John Knox.
Vital Karate. Masutatsu Oyama. LC 67-19867. (Illus.). pap. 6.25 o.p. (ISBN 0-87040-143-2). Japan Pubns USA.
Vital Lies, Simple Truths: The Psychology of Self-Deception & Shared Illusions. Daniel Goleman. 1985. 17.45 o.p. (ISBN 0-671-45058-1). S&S.
Vital National Seminar: The Role of the Supreme Court in American Political Life. Richard Funston. LC 78-51944. 226p. 1978. pap. text ed. 11.95 o.p. (ISBN 0-87484-409-6). Mayfield Pub.
Vital Probe: My Life As a Brain Surgeon. I. S. Cooper. (Illus.). 1981. 15.95 o.p. (ISBN 0-393-01469-X). Norton.
Vital Signs. Michael Weiner. LC 82-84738. (Illus.). 128p. (Orig.). 1983. pap. 8.95 o.p. (ISBN 0-932238-20-3, Pub. by Avant Bks). Slawson Comm.
Vital Statistics of the United States, 1980, Vol. 2. (Mortality Ser.: Pt. A). 588p. 1985. 26.00 o.p. (ISBN 0-318-18868-6, S/N 017-022-00874-2). USGPO.
Vital Statistics of the United States 1982: Vol. 1, Natality. (DHHS Publication PHS 87-1100). 426p. 1987. 29.00 o.p. (ISBN 0-318-22578-6, S/N 017-022-00984-6). USGPO.
Vitality of Old Testament Traditions. Walter Brueggemann & Hans W. Wolff. LC 74-7830. 157p. (Orig.). 1974. pap. 4.95 o.p. (ISBN 0-8042-0111-0, John Knox). Westminster John Knox.
Vitamin Assay: Tested Methods. 2nd ed. Rolf Strohecker & Heinz M. Henning. LC 65-22514. (Illus.). 360p. 1972. 33.60x o.p. (ISBN 3-527-25280-0). VCH Pubs.
Vitamin C in Health & Disease. T. K. Basu & C. J. Schorah. (Illus., Orig.). 1982. 24.95 o.p. (ISBN 0-87055-406-9). AVI.
Vitamin C in the Animal Cell see Ascorbinsaeure in der Pflanzenzelle.
Vitamin C: Its Molecular Biology & Medical Potential. S. Lewin. 1976. 61.00 o.p. (ISBN 0-12-446350-9). Acad Pr.
Vitamin Co-Factors of Enzyme Systems. F. A. Robinson. 1966. 220.00 o.p. (ISBN 0-08-011319-2). Pergamon.
Vitamin D. Ed. by D. E. Lawson. 1978. 117.00 o.p. (ISBN 0-12-439850-2). Acad Pr.
Vitamin D: The Calcium Homeostatic Hormone. Anthony W. Norman. (Basic & Applied Science of Nutrition Ser.). 1979. 83.00 o.p. (ISBN 0-12-521050-7). Acad Pr.
Vitamin E: Key to Youthful Longevity. Raymond F. Bock. LC 74-34509. 1975. 4.00 o.p. (ISBN 0-682-48204-8, Banner). Exposition-Phoenix.
Viva Juarez! A Biography. Charles A. Smart. LC 74-24588. (Illus.). 444p. 1975. Repr. of 1963 ed. lib. bdg. 28.25x o.p. (ISBN 0-8371-6145-2, SMVJ). Greenwood.
Viva Knievel. John Stanley. 1977. pap. 1.50 o.p. (ISBN 0-380-01738-5, 34421). Avon.
Viva la Muerte. Fernando Arrabal. 111p. 1971. 10.95 o.p. (ISBN 0-686-54478-1). French & Eur.
Vivaldi. Michael Talbot. (Master Musicians Ser.). (Illus.). 275p. 1978. 17.95x o.p. (ISBN 0-460-03164-3, Pub. by J. M. Dent England). Biblio Dist.
Vivaldi: Genius of the Baroque. Marc Pincherle. 1962. pap. 4.95 o.p. (ISBN 0-393-00168-7, Norton Lib). Norton.
Vivan los Artesanos! Ed. by Patricia B. Altman. LC 80-84338. (Illus.). 48p. 1980. 6.95 o.s.i. (ISBN 0-317-68016-1). Mingei Intl Mus.
Vivien: The Life of Vivien Leigh. Alexander Walker. LC 87-20966. (Illus.). 352p. 1987. 18.95 o.s.i. (ISBN 1-55584-080-9). Weidenfeld.
Viviendo Sobrio. 126p. (Span.). 1981. pap. 1.15 o.p. (ISBN 0-916856-08-9). AAWS.
Vivir Hoy. Ed. by Gloria Duran & Manuel Duran. (Span.). 1973. pap. text ed. 9.95 o.p. (ISBN 0-15-594947-0, HC). HarBraceJ.
Vixen's Kiss. Jackie Black. (Candlelight Ecstasy Ser.: No. 510). (Orig.). 1987. pap. 2.25 o.p. (ISBN 0-440-19342-7). Dell.
Vizzini: The Secret Lives of Americas' Most Successful Undercover Agent. Sal Vizzini et al. LC 77-184886. 1972. 8.95 o.p. (ISBN 0-87795-050-4, Arbor Hse). Morrow.

VLA Guide to Copyright Series, Nos. 1-3. Timothy S. Jensen. 1987. 5.95 ea. o.p. VLA Guide to Copyright for the Performing Arts, 40pp (ISBN 0-917103-07-6, 8001). VLA Guide to Copyright for Musicians & Composers, 40pp (ISBN 0-917103-08-4, 8002). VLA Guide to Copyright for Visual Arts, 32pp (ISBN 0-917103-09-2, 8003). Vol Lawyers Arts.

Vladimir Mayakovsky: Innovator. A. Metchenko et al. 312p. 1977. 5.45 o.p. (ISBN 0-8285-1094-6, Pub. by Progress Pubs USSR). Imported Pubns.

VLSI--the Coming Revolution in Applications & Design. Rex Rice. LC 79-93146. (Tutorial Texts Ser.). 315p. 1980. 30.00 o.p. (ISBN 0-8186-0288-0, Q288). IEEE Comp Soc.

VLSI Eighty-One: Very Large Scale Integration. Ed. by John Gray. LC 81-68035. 1981. 50.50 o.p. (ISBN 0-12-296860-3). Acad Pr.

VLSI Systems & Computations. Ed. by H. T. Kung et al. (Digital Systems Design Ser.). 415p. 1981. text ed. 39.95 o.p. (ISBN 0-914894-35-8, Computer Sci Pr). W H Freeman.

VNR Concise Encyclopedia of Mathematics. Ed. by W. Gellert et al. (Illus.). 816p. 1977. 31.95 o.s.i. (ISBN 0-442-22646-2). Van Nos Reinhold.

VNR Investor's Dictionary. David M. Brownstone & Irene M. Franck. 320p. 1980. 21.95 o.p. (ISBN 0-442-21578-9). Van Nos Reinhold.

VNR Manual of Rendering with Pen & Ink. 2nd ed. Robert Gill. 1984. pap. 22.95 o.p. (ISBN 0-442-22824-4). Van Nos Reinhold.

Vocabula Amatoria: French-English Dictionary of Erotica. Ed. by John S. Farmer. 1965. 10.00 o.p. (ISBN 0-8216-0160-1, Pub. by Univ Bks). Carol Pub Group.

Vocabulaire Forestier Francais, Allemand, Danois. C. Jacobi. 207p. (Fr., Ger. & Danish.). 1907. pap. 12.50 o.p. (ISBN 0-686-56985-7, M-6322). French & Eur.

Vocabulaire Technique Des Assurances: Anglais-Francais, Francais-Anglais. J. Lesobre & H. Sommer. 255p. (Eng. & Fr.). 1972. 27.50 o.p. (ISBN 0-686-57013-8, M-6354). French & Eur.

Vocabulari Catala-Castella. 3rd ed. Eduard Artells. 465p. (Catalan & Span.). 1961. 5.25 o.p. (ISBN 84-7226-345-2, S-50354). French & Eur.

Vocabulario Chatino de Tataltepec. Leslie Pride & Kitty Pride. (Vocabularios Indigenas Ser.: No. 15). 103p. (Span.). 1970. pap. 0.00 o.s.i. (ISBN 0-88312-655-9); microfiche (2) 4.00 o.p. (ISBN 0-88312-377-7). Summer Inst Ling.

Vocabulario Del Espanol Hablado. Luis Marquez Villegas. 128p. (Span.). 1975. pap. 5.95 o.p. (ISBN 84-7143-048-7, S-50027). French & Eur.

Vocabulario Electronico Internacional. 318p. (Span.). 1975. 14.95 o.p. (ISBN 84-237-0148-4, S-50247). French & Eur.

Vocabularium Nocentium Florae. 4th ed. R. Kwizda. (Lat.). 1963. pap. 23.50 o.p. (ISBN 0-387-80646-6). Springer-Verlag.

Vocabulary for Annie Brigitte Gilles Tardos. Jackson MacLow. 1980. ltd. signed ed. 50.00 o.s.i. (ISBN 0-930794-73-7). Station Hill Pr.

Vocabulary for Fiber Optics & Lightwave Communications. 40.00 o.p. (ISBN 0-686-32964-3). Info Gatekeepers.

Vocabulary One Thousand. Morton J. Cronin. (Orig., Prog. Bk.). 1969. pap. text ed. 8.95 o.p. (ISBN 0-15-594985-3, HC). HarBraceJ.

Vocabulary: The Words Used to Express Ideas & Feelings. Joan Roloff-Stoddard et al. 1981. pap. text ed. write for info. o.p. (ISBN 0-02-477440-5). Macmillan.

Vocal Sight Reading Tests for Treble Voices. Stuart Wade. pap. 1.50 o.s.i. (ISBN 0-8008-8021-8, Crescendo). Taplinger.

Vocal Songs in the Plays of Shakespeare: A Critical History. Peter J. Seng. 314p. Repr. of 1967 ed. lib. bdg. 39.00 o.p. (Pub. by Am Repr Serv). Reprint Servs.

Vocal Truth: Some of the Things I Teach. E. Herbert-Caesari. 1979. 6.95 o.s.i. (ISBN 0-8008-8027-7, Crescendo). Taplinger.

Vocation of Man. Johann G. Fichte. Tr. by William Smith from Ger. 190p. 1965. 12.95 o.p. (ISBN 0-87548-074-8); pap. 5.95 o.p. (ISBN 0-87548-075-6). Open Court.

Vocation of the Theologian. Ed. by Theodore W. Jennings, Jr. LC 84-48722. 160p. 1985. pap. 1.00 o.p. (ISBN 0-8006-1838-6, 1-1838, Fortress). Augsburg Fortress.

Vocational Development. National Association for Women Deans, Administrators & Counselors. 1974. pap. 3.00 o.p. (ISBN 0-686-09582-0). Natl Assn Women.

Vocational Education. Ed. by Melvin L. Barlow. (National Society for the Study of Education Yearbooks Ser: No. 64, Pt. 1). 1965. lib. bdg. 7.50x o.s.i. (ISBN 0-226-60077-7). U of Chicago Pr.

Vocational Education: A Look into the Future. Richard Ruff & Bruce Shylo. 78p. 1981. 5.50 o.p. (ISBN 0-318-15588-5, RD207). Natl Ctr Res Voc Ed.

Vocational Education & Economic Development. National Center for Research in Vocational Education Staff. 44p. 1984. 4.95 o.p. (ISBN 0-318-22231-0, BB73). Natl Ctr Res Voc Ed.

Vocational Education Evaluation: Problems, Alternatives, Recommendations. William W. Stevenson. 61p. 1979. 4.50 o.p. (ISBN 0-318-15590-7, RD182). Natl Ctr Res Voc Ed.

Vocational Education for a Changing Society. Harry Knutton. 19p. 1982. 2.20 o.p. (ISBN 0-318-22237-X, OC81). Natl Ctr Res Voc Ed.

Vocational Education for Gifted & Talented Students. Bruce G. Milne. 52p. 1982. 4.95 o.p. (ISBN 0-318-22238-8, IN236). Natl Ctr Res Voc Ed.

Vocational Education for High Technology. ERIC Clearinghouse on Adult, Career, & Vocational Education Staff. 69p. 1983. 4.95 o.p. (ISBN 0-318-22239-6, BB68). Natl Ctr Res Voc Ed.

Vocational Education for Migrant Youth. J. Steven Picou. 29p. 1982. 3.75 o.p. (ISBN 0-318-22241-8, IN238). Natl Ctr Res Voc Ed.

Vocational Education in Corrections. Sherman R. Day & Mel R. McCane. 37p. 1982. 4.25 o.p. (ISBN 0-318-22243-4, IN237). Natl Ctr Res voc Ed.

Vocational Education: Teaching the Handicapped in Regular Classes. Ed. by Robert A. Weisgerber. LC 78-68174. 96p. 1978. pap. text ed. 4.25 o.p. (ISBN 0-86586-093-9). Coun Exc Child.

Vocational Evaluation & Work Adjustment Bulletin, Special Edition: Final Report. Vocational Evaluation & Work Adjustment Association Staff. Ed. by Julien M. Nadolsky. (Illus.). 165p. (Orig.). 1975. pap. 4.75x o.s.i. (ISBN 0-916671-13-5). Material Dev.

Vocational Guidance & Human Development. Edwin L. Herr. 576p. 1974. text ed. 18.50 o.p. (ISBN 0-395-17437-6). HM.

Vocational Training of Seafarers: Proceedings of the International Labour Conference, 55th Session, 1970. International Labour Office Staff. 1970. 1.50 o.p. Intl Labour Office.

Vocations for Boys. rev. ed. Harry D. Kitson & Edgar M. Stover. LC 55-8677. (gr. 7 up). 1955. 5.95 o.p. (ISBN 0-15-293917-2, HJ). HarBraceJ.

Vocations for Girls. rev. ed. Mary R. Lingenfelter & Harry D. Kitson. LC 39-22231. (gr. 7 up). 1951. 5.95 o.p. (ISBN 0-15-294096-0, HJ). HarBraceJ.

Voelkerrecht in programmierter Form mit Vertiefungshinweisen. I. Von Muench. (Illus.). 445p. 1971. 22.50 o.p. (ISBN 3-11-002162-5). De Gruyter.

Vogue Complete Beauty. LC 82-11740. (Illus.). 224p. 1982. 12.98 o.p. (ISBN 0-517-54875-5, Harmony). Crown.

Vogue Dictionary of Knitting Stitches. Anne Matthews. LC 84-61901. (Illus.). 192p. 1985. pap. 17.95 o.p. (ISBN 0-688-04687-8). Morrow.

Vogue Modern Style: How to Achieve It. Charlotte Du Cann. (Illus.). 208p. 1988. 34.95 o.p. (ISBN 0-7126-1802-3, Pub. by Century Hutchinson); pap. 19.95 o.p. (ISBN 0-7126-1807-4, Pub. by Century Hutchinson). David & Charles.

Vogue Poster Book: A Collection of Magazine Covers from Vogue (1911-1927) Intro. by Diana Vreeland. (Illus.). 48p. 1975. 15.00 o.p. (ISBN 0-517-52007-9, Harmony); pap. 8.95 o.p. (ISBN 0-517-52044-3). Crown.

Voice. Walter De la Mare. LC 86-16640. 32p. (gr. 1-4). 1987. pap. 12.95 o.p. (ISBN 0-385-29532-4). Delacorte.

Voice. Date not set. (ISBN 0-385-29532-4). Delacorte.

Voice at the Back Door. Elizabeth Spencer. 336p. 1986. pap. 4.50 o.p. (ISBN 0-380-70104-9). Avon.

Voice Crying in the Wilderness: Essays on the Problem of Science & World Affairs. Bernard T. Feld. (Illus.). 1980. 46.00 o.p. (ISBN 0-08-023106-3); pap. 17.50 o.p. (ISBN 0-08-026065-9). Pergamon.

Voice Development Hints see Your Voice: Methods for Strengthening & Developing the Voice.

Voice Disorders & Their Management. Ed. by Margaret Fawcus. 304p. (Orig.). 1986. pap. 24.00 o.p. (ISBN 0-7099-1070-3, Pub. by Croom Helm Ltd). Routledge Chapman & Hall.

Voice for All Children: Report of an Independent Committee of Injury. Injury Committee. 54p. (Orig.). 1982. pap. text ed. 6.95x o.p. (ISBN 0-7199-1090-0, Pub. by Bedford England). Gower Pub Co.

Voice from Colorado's Past for the Present: Selected Writings of George Norlin. George Norlin. Ed. by Ralph Ellsworth. LC 85-72909. 1986. 15.00x o.p. (ISBN 0-87081-157-6). Univ Pr Colo.

Voice from Germany: Speeches by Richard von Weizsacker. Richard Von Weizsacker. Tr. by Karin Von Abrams from Ger. LC 86-11177. 120p. 1987. 12.95 o.p. (ISBN 1-55584-016-7). Weidenfeld.

Voice from Harper's Ferry. Osborne P. Anderson. Ed. by Vince Copeland. 102p. 1974. pap. 2.00 o.p. (ISBN 0-89567-048-8). World View Forum.

Voice in the Dark. Claire Lorrimer. 256p. 1988. 18.95 o.p. (ISBN 0-7126-0949-0, Pub. by Century Hutchinson). David & Charles.

Voice in the Mountain. Peter Davison. LC 77-76552. 1977. pap. 4.95 o.p. (ISBN 0-689-10812-5, Atheneum). Macmillan.

Voice in the Night. Velda Johnston. 1985. 13.95 o.p. (ISBN 0-8161-3786-2, Large Print Bks). G K Hall.

Voice Manual. George A. Brouillet. LC 74-14145. 1974. pap. 2.00 o.s.i. (ISBN 0-8008-8024-2, Crescendo). Taplinger.

Voice of Music. Robina B. Willson. LC 77-3225. (Illus.). 224p. (gr. 7 up). 1977. 8.95 o.p. (ISBN 0-689-50096-3, Atheneum). Macmillan.

Voice of Prose: Early Prose & Autobiography. Boris Pasternak. Ed. & intro. by Christopher Barnes. 272p. 1986. 19.95 o.s.i. (ISBN 0-394-55604-6, Ever); pap. 9.95 o.s.i. (ISBN 0-394-62285-5). Grove.

Voice of the Angel. Jonathan Gabriel. 1984. 7.95 o.p. (ISBN 0-533-05978-X). Vantage.

Voice of the Clown. Brenda B. Canary. 288p. 1982. pap. 2.95 o.p. (ISBN 0-380-79624-4, 79624-4). Avon.

Voice of the Dolphins. Leo Szilard. 1961. pap. 1.95 o.p. (ISBN 0-671-79261-X, Touchstone Bks). S&S.

Voice of the Herald. A. Bels. 368p. 1980. 8.45 o.p. (ISBN 0-8285-1879-3, Pub. by Progress Pubs USSR). Imported Pubns.

Voice of the Masters: Writing & Authority in Modern Latin American Literature. Roberto Gonzalez-Echevarria. (Latin American Monographs: No. 64). 207p. 1985. text ed. 20.00x o.p. (ISBN 0-292-78716-2). U of Tex Pr.

Voice of the Negro Magazine, 4 vols, No. 10. 1970. Repr. of 1907 ed. 210.00x o.p. (ISBN 0-8371-9123-8, VON&). Greenwood.

Voice of the People. Ed. by Sylvester J. Hemleben. 175p. 1971. pap. text ed. 7.95x o.p. (ISBN 0-8290-1092-0). Irvington.

Voice of the Steppe. I. Kramov. 478p. 1981. 9.60 o.p. (ISBN 0-8285-2056-9, Pub. by Progress Pubs USSR). Imported Pubns.

Voice of the Visitor. Larry Slonaker. 240p. 1986. pap. 3.50 o.p. (ISBN 0-380-75112-7). Avon.

Voice of Warning. Parley P. Pratt. 1974. pap. 3.50 o.p. (ISBN 0-89036-044-8). Hawkes Pub Inc.

Voice Without Passport. Abdullah Al-Udhari. 1974. sewn in wrappers 1.25 o.p. (ISBN 0-685-78970-5, Pub. by Menard Pr). Small Pr Dist.

Voices Against Tyranny: Writings of the Spanish Civil War. Ed. by John Miller. (Signature Editions Ser.). 200p. 1986. 15.95 o.p. (ISBN 0-684-18697-7); pap. 7.95 o.p. (ISBN 0-684-18698-5). Scribner.

Voices & Choices. Donald Deffner. 1984. pap. 2.08 o.p. (ISBN 0-570-03939-8, 12-2874). Concordia.

Voices & Words of Women & Men. Ed. by Cheris Kramarae. 195p. 1981. 46.00 o.p. (ISBN 0-08-026106-X). Pergamon.

Voices Behind the Wall: Ninety Prison Stories. John P. Farrell. LC 86-3019. 128p. 1986. 13.95 o.p. (ISBN 0-8050-0052-6). H Holt & Co.

Voices Eighteen Seventy to Nineteen Fourteen. Peter Vansittart. 1986. pap. 4.95 o.p. (ISBN 0-380-69857-9, Discus). Avon.

Voices from the Deep. Prem Kirpal. 96p. 1987. pap. text ed. 7.95x o.p. (ISBN 0-7069-3288-9, Pub. by Vikas India). Advent NY.

Voices from the Great War. Peter Vansittart. 320p. 1985. pap. 4.95 o.p. (ISBN 0-380-69856-0, Discus). Avon.

Voices from the Hills: Selected Readings from Southern Appalachia. Ed. by Robert J. Higgs & Ambrose N. Manning. LC 75-4949. 520p. (Orig.). 1975. 14.50 o.s.i. (ISBN 0-8044-2383-0); pap. 14.95 o.s.i. (ISBN 0-8044-6271-2). Ungar.

Voices from the Islands. Gordon Keith. LC 81-69091. (Illus.). 1982. pap. 9.95 o.p. (ISBN 0-8323-0405-0). Binford-Metropolitan.

Voices from the Rapids: An Underwater Search for Fur Trade Artifacts, 1960-73. Robert C. Wheeler et al. LC 75-1194. (Minnesota Historical Archaeology Ser.). (Illus.). 115p. 1975. pap. 6.95 o.p. (ISBN 0-87351-086-0). Minn Hist.

Voices from Three-Mile Island: The People Speak Out. Robert Leppzer. LC 80-20933. (Illus.). 86p. 1980. 16.95 o.p. (ISBN 0-89594-041-8); pap. 5.95 o.p. (ISBN 0-89594-042-6). Crossing Pr.

Voices from Yiddish. Date not set. (ISBN 0-8052-0495-4). Random.

Voices in a Haunted Room. Philippa Carr, pseud. 1984. lib. bdg. 16.95 o.p. (ISBN 0-8161-3780-3, Large Print Bks). G K Hall.

Voices in an Empty Room. Francis King. 320p. 1984. 15.45i o.p. (ISBN 0-316-49348-1). Little.

Voices in Exile: The Decembrist Memoirs. Glynn R. Barratt. (Illus.). 408p. 1974. 18.50x o.p. (ISBN 0-7735-0183-5, McGill Canada). U of Toronto Pr.

Voices in Summer. Rosamunde Pilcher. (Nightingale Large Print Bk.). 1985. pap. text ed. 11.95 o.p. (ISBN 0-8161-3792-7, Large Print Bks). G K Hall.

Voices of American Fundamentalism: Seven Biographical Studies. C. Allyn Russell. LC 76-5886. 1976. 15.00 o.s.i. (ISBN 0-664-20814-2, Westminster). Westminster John Knox.

Voices of Authority. Nicholas Lash. LC 76-29603. viii, 119p. 1976. pap. 3.95x o.p. (ISBN 0-915762-03-X). Patmos Pr.

Voices of Baseball: Quotations on the Summer Game. Bob Chieger. LC 82-73027. 288p. (Orig.). 1983. pap. 8.95 o.p. (ISBN 0-689-70646-4, Atheneum). Macmillan.

Voices of French Pacifism. Incl. La Paix et l'Enseignement Pacifiste, Lecons Professees a l'Ecole des Hautes Etudes Sociales. Estournelles De Constant et al; International Peace: Speeches. Estournelles De Constant et al; Le Mensonge du Pacifisme. Ferdinand Brunetiere; A Propos du Pacifisme. Frederic Passy et al. LC 71-147705. (Library of War & Peace; Problems of the Organized Peace Movement: Selected Documents). 1973. lib. bdg. 46.00 o.p. (ISBN 0-8240-0239-3). Garland Pub.

Voices of German Pacifism. Incl. Das Personliche Wirken und Werben. Arthur Muller; German Pacifism During the War. Caroline E. Playne; Die Fuhrer der Deutschen Friedensbewegung, 1890-1923. Hans Wehberg; Hans Wehberg Als Pazifist in Weltkrieg. Hans Wehberg. LC 71-147710. (Library of War & Peace; Problems of the Organized Peace Movement: Selected Documents). 1973. lib. bdg. 46.00 o.p. (ISBN 0-8240-0241-5). Garland Pub.

Voices of Great Black Baseball Leagues. John Holway. (Illus.). 363p. 1985. pap. 10.95 o.p. (ISBN 0-396-08512-1). Dodd.

Voices of Survival in the Nuclear Age. Ed. by Dennis Paulson. (Illus.). 288p. (Orig.). 1986. pap. 8.95 o.p. (ISBN 0-88496-249-0). Capra Pr.

Voices of the Civil Rights Movement: Black American Freedom Songs, 1960-66. (Smithsonian Collection of Recordings Ser.). incl. 3-LP boxed set 19.95 o.p. (ISBN 0-252-01009-4). U of Ill Pr.

Voices of the Dead: A Novel. Autran Dourado. Tr. by John M. Parker from Port. LC 81-4470. Orig. Title: Opera Dos Mortos. 248p. 1981. 10.95 o.s.i. (ISBN 0-8008-8030-7). Taplinger.

Voices of the Passion: Meditations for Lent & Easter. rev. ed. O. P. Kretzmann & A. C. Oldsen. LC 77-84080. 1977. pap. 3.50 o.p. (ISBN 0-8066-1605-9, 10-6860, Augsburg). Augsburg Fortress.

Voices of the Rainbow. Frwd. by Kenneth Rosen. LC 80-52071. 232p. 1980. pap. 4.95 o.p. (ISBN 0-394-17747-9). Seaver Bks.

Voidism. Edward Echols. 1981. pap. 3.00 o.p. (ISBN 0-682-49813-0). Exposition-Phoenix.

Voies du Salut. Pierre Boulle. 256p. 1958. 9.95 o.p. (ISBN 0-686-54117-0). French & Eur.

Vol De Nuit. Antoine De Saint-Exupery. (Coll. Soleil). 1953. 13.50 o.p. (ISBN 0-685-11624-7). Schoenhof.

Volcanic Land Forms & Surface Features: A Photographic Atlas & Glossary. Ed. by J. Green & N. M. Short. LC 70-144791. (Illus.). 1971. 72.50 o.p. (ISBN 0-387-05328-X). Springer-Verlag.

Volcanoes & the Earth's Interior: Readings from Scientific American. Scientific American Editors. LC 81-15092. (Illus.). 141p. 1982. text ed. 21.95 o.p. (ISBN 0-7167-1383-7); pap. text ed. 12.95 o.p. (ISBN 0-7167-1384-5). W H Freeman.

Volcanoes: Nature's Fireworks. Hershell H. Nixon & Joan L. Nixon. LC 77-16873. (Illus.). (gr. 2-5). 1978. 8.95 o.p. (ISBN 0-396-07559-2). Dodd.

Volcanoes of the World: A Regional Gazetteer & Chronology of Volcanism During the Last 10,000 Years. Tom Simkin et al. LC 81-6594. 240p. 1982. 31.95 o.p. (ISBN 0-87933-408-8). Van Nos Reinhold.

Volcker: Portrait of the Money Man. William R. Neikirk. (Illus.). 224p. 1987. 18.95 o.p. (ISBN 0-86553-178-1). Congdon & Weed.

Voleur d'Enfants. Jules Supervielle. 214p. 1949. 5.95 o.p. (ISBN 0-686-55107-9). Schoenhof.

Volkisch Ideology & the Roots of Nazism: The Early Writings of Arthur Moeller van den Bruck. Paul H. Silfen. LC 73-86549. 1973. 5.00 o.p. (ISBN 0-682-47786-9, University). Exposition-Phoenix.

Volkswagen Fox Official Factory Repair Manual: 1987-1988. Volkswagen United States Inc. (Orig.). 1987. pap. 29.95 o.p. (ISBN 0-8376-0360-9). Bentley.

Volkswagen, GTI, Golf, & Jetta Official Factory Repair Manual: 1985, 1986 & 1987 Gasoline, Diesel & Turbo Diesel Including Golf, GT, Jetta, GLI, & 16V Models. Volkswagen United States, Inc. (Orig.). 1987. pap. (ISBN 0-8376-0337-4). Bentley.

Volkswagen GTI, Golf, Jetta Official Factory Repair Manual including GLI, Gasoline, Diesel & Turbo Diesel Models: 1985. Volkswagen of America, Inc. (Illus.). 1985. pap. 39.95 o.p. (ISBN 0-8376-0185-1). Bentley.

Volkswagen GTI Golf Jetta Official Service Manual: 1985-1988. Robert Bentley, Inc. 416p. (Orig.). 1987. pap. 39.95 o.p. (ISBN 0-8376-0190-8). Bentley.

Volkswagen GTI Official Service Manual: 1985-1987. Bentley, Robert, Inc. 416p. (Orig.). 1987. pap. price not set o.p. (ISBN 0-8376-0204-1). Bentley.

Volkswagen Jetta Official Service Manual: 1985-1987. Bentley, Robert, Inc. 416p. (Orig.). 1987. pap. price not set o.p. (ISBN 0-8376-0186-X). Bentley.

Volkswagen Performance Tuning: 1200-2000cc Air-Cooled Engines, All Years. 2nd ed. Ed. by Jeff Robinson. (Illus.). pap. text ed. 12.95 o.p. (ISBN 0-89287-223-3, A128). Clymer Pub.

Volkswagen Quantum Official Factory Repair Manual: 1982-1985, Including Gasoline & Turbo Diesel. Volkswagen of America, Inc. (Illus.). 1985. pap. 49.95 o.p. (ISBN 0-8376-0355-2). Bentley.

Volkswagen Service--Repair Handbook: Dasher, 1974-1980. Ed. by Jeff Robinson. (Illus.). pap. 11.95 o.p. (ISBN 0-89287-154-7, A121). Clymer Pub.

Volkswagen Service--Repair Handbook: Rabbit, Scirocco-1975-1981. Ed. by Jeff Robinson. (Illus.). 1978. pap. 11.95 o.p. (ISBN 0-89287-157-1, A122). Clymer Pub.

Volkswagen Service-Repair Handbook: Type 3, 1962-1973. Ed. by Jeff Robinson. (Illus.). pap. text ed. 12.95 o.p. (ISBN 0-89287-039-7, A120). Clymer Pub.

Volkswagen Vanagon Official Factory Repair Manual: 1980-1987. Volkswagen United States Inc. 1040p. (Orig.). 1987. pap. 59.95 o.p. (ISBN 0-8376-0359-5). Bentley.

Volleyball. Dewey Schurman. LC 74-77622. (Illus.). 160p. 1974. 7.95 o.p. (ISBN 0-689-10632-7, Atheneum). Macmillan.

Volleyball Guide 1987. 1987. 5.95 o.p. (ISBN 0-88314-371-2). AAHPERD.

Volleyball Rules 1987. 1987. pap. 1.95 o.p. (ISBN 0-88314-372-0). AAHPERD.

Volney et L'Amerique D'appres Des Documents Inedits et Sa Correspondance Avec Jefferson. G. Chinard. 1973. Repr. of 1923 ed. 19.00 o.p. (ISBN 0-384-08797-3). Johnson Repr.

Vologeso Re De Parti. Rinaldo DiCapua. Ed. by Howard M. Brown. LC 76-20970. (Italian Opera, 1640-1770 Ser.: Vol. 38). (Libretto by G. E. Luccarelli). 1978. lib. bdg. 77.00 o.p. (ISBN 0-8240-2641-1). Garland Pub.

Volpone. Ben Jonson. (Royal Shakespeare Company Playtext Ser.). 48p. 1983. pap. 4.95 o.p. (ISBN 0-413-53350-6, NO. 3900). Heinemann Ed.

Voltaire. Wayne Andrews. LC 80-29565. (Illus.). 1981. 7.95 o.s.i. (ISBN 0-8112-0800-1); pap. 6.95 o.s.i. (ISBN 0-8112-0802-8, NDP519). New Directions.

Voltaire. 3rd ed. Theodore Besterman. (Illus.). 1977. lib. bdg. 33.00x o.s.i. (ISBN 0-226-04430-0). U of Chicago Pr.

Voltaire: A Biography. Haydn Mason. LC 80-8868. (Illus.). 224p. 1981. 22.50x o.p. (ISBN 0-8018-2611-X). Johns Hopkins.

Voltaire & Sensibility. R. S. Ridgway. 312p. 1973. 12.50x o.p. (ISBN 0-7735-0130-4, McGill Canada). U of Toronto Pr.

Voltaire, Non-Conformist. Rebecca H. Gross. LC 65-14264. (ISBN 0-8022-0637-9). Philos Lib.

Voltaire Smile & Other Stories. Ron Harvie. 196p. (Orig.). 1982. pap. 6.95 o.s.i. (ISBN 0-9604724-1-X). Gay Pr NY.

Voltaire's Politics: The Poet As Realist. 2nd ed. Peter Gay. Date not set. 40.00 o.p.; pap. 15.95 o.p. Yale U Pr.

Volterra & Weiner Theories of Nonlinear Systems. Martin Schetzen. LC 79-13421. 531p. 1980. 55.50x o.p. (ISBN 0-471-04455-5). Wiley.

Voltmeier: Or, the Mountain Men. William G. Simms. Ed. by John C. Guilds. LC 68-9190. (Centennial Edition of the Writings of William Gilmore Simms: Vol. 1). (Illus.). xxxii, 448p. 1969. 35.95x o.p. (ISBN 0-87249-140-4). U of SC Pr.

Volume Feeding Menu Selector. Alta Atkinson. Ed. by Eulalia Blair. LC 78-145861. 185p. 1983. 21.95 o.p. (ISBN 0-8436-0528-6). Van Nos Reinhold.

Volume the First. Date not set. (ISBN 0-8052-3937-5). Random.

Voluntarism & Social Work Practice: A Growing Collaboration. Ed. by Florence S. Schwartz. LC 83-21749. 248p. (Orig.). 1984. lib. bdg. 39.50 o.p. (ISBN 0-8191-3677-8); pap. text ed. 23.25 o.p. (ISBN 0-8191-3678-6). U Pr of Amer.

Voluntarism at the Crossroads. Gordon Manser & Rosemary H. Cass. LC 75-27967. 262p. 1976. 13.95 o.p. (ISBN 0-87304-140-2). Family Serv.

Voluntary Action in a Changing World. F. J. Gladstone. 137p. 1979. pap. text ed. 9.75x o.p. (ISBN 0-7199-1033-1, Pub. by Bedford England). Gower Pub Co.

Voluntary & Statutory Collaboration. Diana Leat & Gerry Smolka. 216p. 1981. pap. text ed. 24.50 o.p. (ISBN 0-7199-1054-4, Pub. by Bedford England). Gower Pub Co.

Voluntary Associations & Nordic Party Systems. Victor A. Pestoff. LC 79-67048. 210p. 24.95 o.p. (ISBN 0-87855-354-1). Transaction Pubs.

Voluntary Organizations. 191p. 1980. pap. text ed. 9.75x o.p. (ISBN 0-686-78518-5, Pub. by Bedford England). Gower Pub Co.

Voluntary Organizations: An NCVO Directory 1983-84. 192p. 1983. pap. text ed. 12.25x o.p. (ISBN 0-7199-1061-7, Pub. by Bedford England). Gower Pub Co.

Voluntary Retail Identification Standard Specification. members 16.00 o.p. (ISBN 0-87102-082-3). Natl Ret Merch.

Voluntary Servitude: Whites in the Negro Movement. Charles J. Levy. LC 68-19311. (Orig.). 1968. pap. text ed. 5.95x o.p. (ISBN 0-89197-467-9). Irvington.

Voluntary Simplicity: Toward a Way of Life That Is Outwardly Simple, Inwardly Rich. Duane Elgin. LC 81-643. (Illus.). 312p. 1981. 10.95 o.p. (ISBN 0-688-03647-3). Morrow.

Volunteer: A Photo Novel. Anne Turyn. (Illus.). 32p. (Orig.). 1982. pap. 5.50 o.p. (ISBN 0-939784-04-1). CEPA Gall.

Volunteer Force: A Social & Political History, 1859-1908. Hugh Cunningham. LC 75-22126. (Illus.). 168p. 1975. 22.00 o.p. (ISBN 0-208-01569-8, Archon). Shoe String.

Volunteer Portfolio. 1982. pap. 1.50 o.p. (ISBN 0-88441-448-5, 26-182). Girl Scouts USA.

Volunteer Resource Book. 64p. 1982. pap. 6.50 o.p. (ISBN 0-88441-447-7, 26-183). Girl Scouts USA.

Volunteer Vacations. Bill McMillon. LC 87-6624. (Illus.). 260p. (Orig.). 1987. pap. 11.95 o.p. (ISBN 1-55652-002-6). Chicago Review.

Volunteerism in the Eighties: Fundamental Issues in Voluntary Action. Ed. by John D. Harman. LC 81-40622. (Illus.). 292p. (Orig.). 1982. lib. bdg. 32.00 o.p. (ISBN 0-8191-2398-6); pap. text ed. 14.00 o.p. (ISBN 0-8191-2399-4). U Pr of Amer.

Volunteers in Social Services: Consumer Assessment of Nursing Homes. E. C. Durman & Burton Dunlop. 183p. 1979. pap. text ed. 7.00x o.p. (ISBN 0-87766-261-4). Urban Inst.

Volunteers in the School Media Center. Linda L. Bennett. 256p. 1984. lib. bdg. 23.50 o.p. (ISBN 0-87287-351-X). Libs Unl.

Volvo Nineteen Seventy to Nineteen Eighty-One. LC 80-66512. (Illus.). 288p. 1981. 12.50 o.p. (ISBN 0-8019-7040-7). Chilton.

Volvo Service-Repair Handbook: 122s Series & P 1800, All Years. Clymer Publications Staff. (Illus.). pap. text ed. 11.95 o.p. (ISBN 0-89287-066-4, A220). Clymer Pub.

Volvo Service Repair Handbook: 140 Series, 1967-1974. Ed. by Jeff Robisnon. (Illus.). pap. 12.95 o.p. (ISBN 0-89287-227-6, A222). Clymer Pub.

Von Percy Zum Wunderhorn: Beitraege Zur Geschichte der Wolksliedforschung in Deutschland. Heinrich Lohre. (Ger.). 18.00 o.p. (ISBN 0-384-33415-6); pap. 13.00 o.p. (ISBN 0-685-02192-0). Johnson Repr.

Vonda Rosegood. Richard Dohrman. 1973. pap. 1.25 o.p. (ISBN 0-380-01606-0, 16584). Avon.

Voodoo! Bill Pronzini. LC 79-56021. 1980. 10.95 o.p. (ISBN 0-87795-262-0, Arbor Hse). Morrow.

Voodoo & the Art of Haiti. S. Williams. (Illus.). 1969. pap. 10.00 o.p. (ISBN 0-685-58549-2). E J Brill USA.

Voodoo Science, Twisted Consumerism. Peter Harnik & Michael F. Jacobson. 67p. (Orig.). 1982. pap. 4.00 o.p. (ISBN 0-89329-095-5). Ctr Sci Public.

Vor. James Blish. 1958. pap. 1.95 o.p. (ISBN 0-380-44966-8, 44966-8). Avon.

Vorlesungen Uber Funktionalgleichungen und Ihre Anwendungen. J. Aczel. (Mathematische Reihe Ser.: No. 25). (Illus.). 331p. (Ger.). 1961. 44.95x o.p. (ISBN 0-8176-0002-7). Birkhauser.

Vortex. David Heller. 1979. pap. 1.95 o.p. (ISBN 0-380-42762-1, 42762). Avon.

Vortex Universe. Mario Priletta. 1985. 10.00 o.p. (ISBN 0-533-06555-0). Vantage.

Voter Information & Education Programs 1: Designing Effective Voter Information Programs. Ed. by William C. Kimberling. (Illus.). 64p. (Orig.). 1986. pap. 3.75 o.p. (ISBN 0-318-20376-6, S/N 052-006-00036-8). USGPO.

Voting Patterns in the United States: Recent Writings, 1980-1984. Dale E. Casper. (Public Administration Ser.: P 1716). 9p. 1985. 2.00 o.p. (ISBN 0-89028-466-0). Vance Biblios.

Vouivre. Marcel Ayme. (Illus.). deluxe ed. 61.25 o.p. (ISBN 0-685-37184-0). French & Eur.

Vous les Entendez? Nathalie Sarraute. (Coll. le Chemin Ser.). 8.95 o.p. (ISBN 0-685-36550-6). Schoenhof.

Vox--Diccionario Fundamental de la Lengua Espanola. 604p. (Span.). 1975. leatherette 10.50 o.p. (ISBN 84-7153-229-8, S-26961). French & Eur.

Vox Feminae: Studies in Medieval Woman's Songs. Ed. by John F. Plummer. LC 81-3981. (Studies in Medieval Culture XV). viii, 223p. (Orig.). 1981. pap. 10.95x o.s.i. (ISBN 0-918720-12-5). Medieval Inst.

Vox Pop: Last Days of the Roman Republic. John Arden. LC 83-8423. 352p. 1983. Repr. of 1982 ed. 14.95 o.p. (ISBN 0-15-182629-3). HarBraceJ.

Voyage. Adele Geras. LC 82-13760. 192p. (gr. 7 up). 1983. 12.95 o.s.i. (ISBN 0-689-30955-4, Atheneum Childrens Bks). Macmillan.

Voyage a la Louisiane, et Sur le Continent De L'amerique Septentrionale Fait Dans les Annees Seventeen Ninety-Four to Seventeen Ninety-Eight. Baudry Des Lozieres & Louis Narcisse. (Illus.). 382p. 1968. Repr. of 1802 ed. 25.00 o.p. (ISBN 0-8398-0156-4). Parnassus Imprints.

Voyage & Other Versions of Poems by Baudelaire. Robert Lowell. (Illus.). 60p. 1968. 15.00 o.p. (ISBN 0-374-28540-3). FS&G.

Voyage of Re-Discovery: The Veneration of St. Vincent. Anne F. Francis. 1978. 15.00 o.p. (ISBN 0-682-48429-6, University). Exposition-Phoenix.

Voyage of Sea Lion. Will Corry. (Illus.). 1978. 8.95 o.p. (ISBN 0-393-03207-8). Norton.

Voyage of the "Dawn Treader" C. S. Lewis. (Chronicles of Narnia Ser.: Vol. 3). 284p. (gr. 4-8). 1986. lib. bdg. 13.95x o.p. (ISBN 0-8161-4091-X, Large Print Bks.). G K Hall.

Voyage of the Javelin. Stephen W. Meader. 1959. 3.50 o.p. (ISBN 0-15-294454-0, HJ). HarBraceJ.

Voyage of the Jolly Boat. Margret Rettich. Tr. by Olive Jones from Ger. (Illus.). 32p. (gr. k-4). 1981. 9.95 o.p. (ISBN 0-416-30791-4, NO. 0227). Routledge Chapman & Hall.

Voyage of the "Pourquoi Pas?" in the Antarctic: The Journal of the Second French South Polar Expedition, 1908-1910. Jean Charcot. LC 77-20265. (Illus.). vi, 315p. 1978. Repr. of 1911 ed. 35.00 o.p. (ISBN 0-208-01644-9, Archon). Shoe String.

Voyage of the Secret Duchess. Florence Hurd. (Orig.). 1975. pap. 0.95 o.p. (ISBN 0-380-00353-8, 24554). Avon.

Voyage of the Starfire to Atlantis. Edwin Mumford. 1973. 4.00 o.p. (ISBN 0-682-47692-7). Exposition-Phoenix.

Voyage of the Stella. R. D. Lawrence. LC 81-6901. (Illus.). 276p. 1982. 15.45 o.p. (ISBN 0-03-058901-0). H Holt & Co.

Voyage Round My Father. John Mortimer. 186p. 1984. pap. 5.95 o.p. (ISBN 0-14-007268-3). Penguin.

Voyage Through Childhood to the Adult World. E. A. Frommer. 1969. text ed. 29.00 o.p. (ISBN 0-08-006496-5); pap. 11.50 o.p. (ISBN 0-08-006495-7). Pergamon.

Voyage Through Interplanetary Space. Harold C. Watkins. LC 84-80073. (Illus.). 1984. pap. 3.95 o.p. (Inst Creation). Master Bks.

Voyage to Greenland: A Personal Initiation into Anthropology. Frederica De Laguna. (Illus.). 1977. 9.95 o.p. (ISBN 0-393-06413-1). Norton.

Voyage to the South Seas. William Bligh. 1980. 29.00 o.p. (ISBN 0-09-135440-4, NO. 0219, Pub. by Hutchinson England). Routledge Chapman & Hall.

Voyager. Gerald Kingsland. 192p. 1987. 29.95 o.p. (ISBN 0-450-40656-3, Pub. by Hodder & Stoughton UK). David & Charles.

Voyager: A Life of Hart Crane. John Unterecker. LC 69-11575. (Illus.). 832p. 1969. 15.00 o.p. (ISBN 0-374-28568-3). FS&G.

Voyager: The Story of a Space Mission. Margaret Poynter & Arthur L. Lane. LC 80-18723. (Illus.). 160p. (gr. 5-9). 1981. 12.95 o.s.i. (ISBN 0-689-30827-2, Atheneum Childrens Bks). Macmillan.

Voyages & Discoveries of the Companions of Columbus. Washington Irving. Ed. by James W. Tuttleton. (Twayne Critical Editions Ser.: Vol. 12). 624p. 1987. lib. bdg. 65.00x o.s.i. (ISBN 0-8057-8517-5, Twayne). G K Hall.

Voyages Down & Other Poems. Charles Philbrick. LC 67-19205. 84p. 1967. 9.95 o.p. (ISBN 0-15-194070-3). HarBraceJ.

Voyages of Samuel De Champlain, Sixteen Four to Sixteen Eighteen. Ed. by W. L. Grant. (Original Narratives). 374p. 1967. Repr. of 1907 ed. 21.50x o.p. (ISBN 0-06-480330-9). B&N Imports.

Voyages of the Steamboat Yellowstone. Donald Jackson. (Illus.). 192p. 1985. 16.45 o.p. (ISBN 0-89919-306-4). Ticknor & Fields.

Voyageur Solitaire Est Un Diable. Henry De Montherlant. 1961. pap. 10.95 o.p. (ISBN 0-685-11627-1). Schoenhof.

Voyageur Solitaire est un Diable. Henry De Montherlant. (Illus.). deluxe ed. 341.25 o.p. (ISBN 0-685-36999-4). Schoenhof.

Voyageur Solitaire est un Diable. Henry de Montherlant. 212p. (Soleil). 1961. 9.95 o.p. (ISBN 0-686-55537-6). Schoenhof.

Voyaging Stars. David Lewis. (Illus.). 1978. 10.95 o.p. (ISBN 0-393-03226-4). Norton.

Voyaging under Power. Robert P. Beebe. LC 74-21847. (Illus.). 272p. 1975. 9.95 o.p. (ISBN 0-915160-18-8). Seven Seas.

Voyeur. Alain Robbe-Grillet. Tr. by Richard Howard from Fr. (Orig.). 1958. pap. 6.95 o.p. (ISBN 0-394-17117-9, B133, BC). Grove.

Vulture. Sidney Simon. (Illus.). 72p. 1977. pap. 3.95 o.p. (ISBN 0-317-60035-4). Tabor Pub.

Vuta Kamba: The Development of Trade Unions in Tanganyika. William H. Friedland. LC 74-81689. (Publications Ser.: No. 84). 1969. 11.95x o.p. (ISBN 0-8179-1841-8); pap. 7.95x o.p. (ISBN 0-8179-1842-6). Hoover Inst Pr.

VW Bodywork: Beetles, Transporter, Squareback, & Fastback. (Illus.). pap. 13.95 o.p. (ISBN 0-89287-228-4, A109). Clymer Pub.

VW Rabbit Tune-up & Repair. Ed. by Spence Murray. LC 79-53095. (Tune-up & Repair Ser.). (Illus.). 1979. pap. 4.95 o.p. (ISBN 0-8227-5045-7). Petersen Pub.

Vybor V Adu: Zhizneutverzhdenie solzhenitsynskikh geroev. Rita Brackman. LC 83-26381. 144p. (Rus.). 1984. pap. 7.50 o.p. (ISBN 0-938920-20-0). Hermitage.

W

W. B. Yeats & the Craft of Verse. Malati Ramratnam. (Illus.). 146p. (Orig.). 1986. lib. bdg. 26.25 o.p. (ISBN 0-8191-5017-7); pap. text ed. 10.00 o.p. (ISBN 0-8191-5018-5). U Pr of Amer.

W. B. Yeats As Literary Critic. V. V. Jain. 322p. 1980. text ed. 12.75x o.p. (ISBN 0-391-02527-9). Humanities.

W. B. Yeats: Man & Poet. A. Norman Jeffares. 365p. 1949. 22.50 o.p. (ISBN 0-7100-1607-7). Routledge Chapman & Hall.

W. E. B. Dubois on Sociology & the Black Community. W. E. B. Dubois. Ed. by Dan S. Green & Edwin D. Driver. LC 78-770. 1980. pap. text ed. 5.50x o.s.i. (ISBN 0-226-16760-7, 866, Phoen). U of Chicago Pr.

W. Eugene Smith: His Photographs & Notes. LC 70-99254. (Illus.). 144p. pap. 22.50 o.p. (ISBN 0-912334-09-6). Aperture.

W. H. Auden: The Life of a Poet. Charles Osborne. LC 79-1840. (Illus.). 1979. 17.95 o.p. (ISBN 0-15-194286-2). HarBraceJ.

W. H. Hudson: A Biography. Ruth Tomalin. 321p. 1982. 29.95 o.p. (ISBN 0-571-10599-8). Faber & Faber.

W. I. Thomas on Social Organization & Social Personality. William I. Thomas. Ed. by Morris Janowitz. LC 66-23701. (Heritage of Sociology Ser). 1966. pap. text ed. 3.95 o.s.i. (ISBN 0-226-39315-1, P242, Phoen). U of Chicago Pr.

W. Robertson Smith & the Sociological Study of Religion. T. O. Beidelman. LC 73-87311. 1974. lib. bdg. 1.95x o.s.i. (ISBN 0-226-04160-3, P618, Phoen). U of Chicago Pr.

W. S. Gilbert, His Life & Letters. Sidney Dark & Rowland Grey. LC 71-164210. 282p. 1971. Repr. of 1923 ed. 40.00x o.p. (ISBN 0-8103-3789-4). Gale.

W. Somerset Maugham & His World. Frederick Raphael. LC 76-19742. (Encore Edition Ser.). (Illus.). 1977. 3.95 o.p. (ISBN 0-684-16552-X, ScribT). Scribner.

Wabash Factor. E. V. Cunningham. LC 86-14339. 421p. 1986. 14.95 o.p. (ISBN 0-89621-736-1). Thorndike Pr.

Wacky World of Alvin Fernald. Clifford B. Hicks. LC 81-5099. (Illus.). 144p. (gr. 4-6). 1981. 9.95 o.p. (ISBN 0-03-057783-7). H Holt & Co.

Waddell System of Nutritional Analysis. J. P. Waddell. 176p. 1987. 9.95 o.p. (ISBN 0-8062-3010-X). Carlton.

Wage & Salary Program Based on Position Evaluation for Administrative & Supervisory Staff. Rhone. 1980. 8.95 o.p. (ISBN 0-910170-15-0). Assn Sch Busn.

Wage Determination & Comparable Worth for Librarians: A Checklist of Materials. Lorna Peterson. (Public Administration Ser.: Bibliography P 1635). 1985. pap. 2.25 o.p. (ISBN 0-89028-305-2). Vance Biblios.

Wage Determination: Market or Power Forces? Ed. by Richard Perlman. LC 76-56370. (Illus.). 1977. Repr. of 1964 ed. lib. bdg. 22.50x o.p. (ISBN 0-8371-9423-7, PEWD). Greenwood.
Wage-Hour & Employment Practices Manual for the Multihousing Industry. Harry Weisbrod et al. Ed. by Peggy J. Schleker. LC 78-70825. 210p. 1979. 25.95 o.p. (ISBN 0-912104-36-8, 807). Inst Real Estate.
Wage, Labour & Capital. Karl Marx. 1978. pap. 1.95 o.p. (ISBN 0-8351-0547-4). China Bks.
Wage Restraint & the Control of Inflation: An International Survey. Ed. by Beth Wilson. 208p. 1986. 40.00 o.p. (ISBN 0-7099-3929-9, Pub. by Croom Helm UK). Routledge Chapman & Hall.
Wage Restraint by Consensus: Britain's Search for an Income Policy Agreement, 1965-1979. Warren H. Fishbein. 300p. 1984. 35.00x o.p. (ISBN 0-7102-0074-9). Routledge Chapman & Hall.
Wages: A Bibliography of Statistical Sources. Marian Dworaczek. (Public Administration Ser.: Bibliography P 1631). 1985. pap. 4.50 o.p. (ISBN 0-89028-301-X). Vance Biblios.
Wages, Price & Profit. Karl Marx. 1965. pap. 1.95 o.p. (ISBN 0-8351-0422-2). China Bks.
Waggleby of Fraggle Rock. Stephanie Calmenson. LC 84-16599. (Illus.). (ps-2). 1985. 5.95 o.s.i. (ISBN 0-03-003259-8). H Holt & Co.
Waging Industrial Peace in Nigeria. Akanimo J. Etukudo. 1977. 8.00 o.p. (ISBN 0-682-48850-X, University). Exposition-Phoenix.
Wagner. rev. ed. Robert L. Jacobs. (Master Musicians Ser.: No. M150). (Illus.). 1977. pap. 7.95 o.p. (ISBN 0-8226-0724-7). Littlefield.
Wagner. rev. ed. Robert L. Jacobs. (Master Musicians Ser.). (Illus.). 288p. 1974. 13.50x o.p. (ISBN 0-460-03153-8, Pub. by J. M. Dent England). Biblio Dist.
Wagner. Walter J. Turner. LC 78-12226. (Illus.). 1979. Repr. of 1948 ed. lib. bdg. 35.00x o.p. (ISBN 0-313-21084-5, TUWG). Greenwood.
Wagner: A Biography, with a Survey of Books, Editions, & Recordings. Robert Anderson. LC 80-374. (Concertgoers Companion Ser.). 154p. 1980. 19.50 o.p. (ISBN 0-208-01677-5, Linnet). Shoe String.
Wagner-Artaud: A Play of 19th & 20th Century Critical Fictions. Samuel R. Delany. 80p. (Orig.). 1988. pap. 12.00 signed & numbered ed. o.p. (ISBN 0-945195-00-1); pap. 7.00 o.p. (ISBN 0-945195-01-X). Ansatz Pr.
Wagner at Bayreuth. Geoffrey Skelton. LC 66-20191. (Illus.). 1966. 6.50 o.p. (ISBN 0-8076-0381-3). Braziller.
Wagon Man. Arthur Crowley. (Illus.). (gr. k-3). 1981. PLB 8.95 o.p. (ISBN 0-395-30346-X). HM.
Wait Don't Pull That Plug: The Story of Timmy. Zerah A. Campbell. 96p. 1979. 5.00 o.p. (ISBN 0-682-49278-7). Exposition-Phoenix.
Wait for the Dawn. Martha Albrand. 1973. pap. 0.95 o.p. (ISBN 0-380-01607-9, 14696). Avon.
Wait until Dark. Ronald L. Morris. 1980. 17.95 o.p. (ISBN 0-87972-149-9). Bowling Green Univ.
Waiter & Waitress Training Manual. 2nd ed. Sondra Dahmer & Kurt Kahl. LC 73-83574. 112p. 1983. pap. 15.95 o.p. (ISBN 0-8436-2251-2). Van Nos Reinhold.
Waiting & Loving: Thoughts Occasioned by the Illness & the Death of a Parent. Martha H. Hickman. LC 83-51399. 160p. (Orig.). 1984. pap. 5.95 o.p. (ISBN 0-8358-0483-6). Upper Room.
Waiting for Cordelia. Herbert Gold. LC 76-29231. 1977. 8.95 o.p. (ISBN 0-87795-154-3, Arbor Hse). Morrow.
Waiting for Death: The Philosophical Significance of Beckett's En Attendant Godot. Ramona Cormier & Janis L. Pallister. LC 76-10218. (Studies in Humanities: No. 19). 176p. 1979. 14.25 o.p. (ISBN 0-8173-7605-4). U of Ala Pr.
Waiting for Godot. Samuel Beckett. Tr. by Samuel Beckett from Fr. 1970. 10.00 o.p. (ISBN 0-394-47529-1, GP640). Grove.
Waiting for Godot. Samuel Beckett. Tr. by Samuel Beckett from Fr. 1954. pap. 4.50 o.p. (ISBN 0-394-17204-3, E33, Ever). Grove.
Waiting for My Life: Poems. Linda Pastan. 1981. 14.95 o.p. (ISBN 0-393-01441-X); pap. 4.95 o.p. (ISBN 0-393-00049-4). Norton.
Waiting for Sheila. John Braine. LC 79-24757. 1977. 9.95 o.p. (ISBN 0-416-00571-3, NO. 0183). Routledge Chapman & Hall.
Waiting for Surabiel. Raja Proctor. (Asian & Pacific Writing Ser.). 238p. 1981. text ed. 18.00 o.p. (ISBN 0-7022-1566-X); pap. 12.50 o.p. (ISBN 0-7022-1567-8). U of Queensland Pr.
Waiting for the End of the World. Madison S. Bell. LC 85-2743. 1985. 16.45 o.p. (ISBN 0-89919-377-3). Ticknor & Fields.
Waiting for the King of Spain. Diane Wakoski. LC 76-44512. 158p. (Orig.). 1980. 17.50 o.p. (ISBN 0-87685-294-0); pap. 6.00 o.p. (ISBN 0-87685-293-2). Black Sparrow.
Waiting for the Rain. Charles Mungoshi. (African Writers Ser.). 1975. pap. text ed. 7.00 o.p. (ISBN 0-435-90170-2). Heinemann Ed.
Waiting Room Cartoons. 2nd ed. William Armstrong. (Armstrong Cartoon Ser.). (Illus.). 48p. (ps up). 1971. pap. 1.00 o.p. (ISBN 0-913452-10-6). Jesuit Bks.
Waiting: The Hope & Frustrations of a Childless Couple. Joan Y. McGowan. 1983. 10.95 o.p. (ISBN 0-533-05705-1). Vantage.
Waiting Works. Joanna Stewart. 1979. pap. 5.00 o.p. (ISBN 0-682-49414-3). Exposition-Phoenix.
Wake Kitten. Emanuel Schongut. Ed. by Kate Klimo. (Kitten Board Bks.). (Illus.). 14p. 1983. 3.80 o.s.i. (ISBN 0-671-46383-7, Little Simon). S&S.
Wake-up America. Robert L. Preston. 128p. 1972. pap. 3.95 o.p. (ISBN 0-89036-027-8). Hawkes Pub Inc.
Wake up, Poor American People. Mae Wilson. 48p. 1985. pap. 5.00 o.p. (ISBN 0-682-40227-3). Exposition-Phoenix.
Wake up, World-We're People Too. Edward J. Kerneckel, Jr. 53p. 1985. 7.95 o.p. (ISBN 0-533-06255-1). Vantage.
Wakefield's Course. Mazo De La Roche. (Jalna Ser.). 1977. pap. 1.95 o.s.i. (ISBN 0-449-23431-2, Crest). Fawcett.
Waking Slow. Michael Mewshaw. 1976. pap. 1.75 o.p. (ISBN 0-380-00804-1, 30791). Avon.
Waking Up. Charles T. Tart. LC 86-11844. (New Science Library). 300p. 1986. 17.45 o.p. (ISBN 0-87773-374-0). Shambhala Pubns.
Walden. Henry David Thoreau. Ed. by Dudley C. Lunt. (Masterworks of Literature Ser). (Illus.). 1951. pap. 3.95x o.p. (ISBN 0-8084-0312-5, M8). New Coll U Pr.
Walden. Henry David Thoreau. (Classics Ser.). 1966. dust jacket 12.95 o.p. (ISBN 0-88088-994-2). Peter Pauper.
Walden: A Writer's Edition. Henry David Thoreau. Ed. by Larzer Ziff. (Orig.). 1961. pap. text ed. 5.25 o.p. (ISBN 0-03-010845-4). H Holt & Co.
Walden by Henry David Thoreau. 48p. (Orig.). 1988. pap. 9.95 o.p. (ISBN 1-55651-952-4); cassette o.p. (ISBN 1-55651-953-2). Cram Cassettes.
Walden: Down the River with Henry Thoreau. Henry David Thoreau. 352p. 1981. pap. 5.95 o.p. (ISBN 0-87905-093-4, Peregrine Smith). Gibbs Smith Pub.
Waldensians. rev. ed. Giorgio Tourn et al. 350p. 1989. pap. 18.95 o.p. (ISBN 88-7016-089-0). Friendship Pr.
Wales Bed & Breakfast. Date not set. (ISBN 1-85013-027-2). Salem Hse Pubs.
Wales Road Atlas. (Illus.). Date not set. (ISBN 0-86145-626-2, Pub. by Auto Assn England). Salem Hse Pubs.
Wales: The Shaping of a Nation. David Thomas & Prys Morgan. (Illus.). 256p. 1984. 35.95 o.p. (ISBN 0-7153-8418-X). David & Charles.
Wales Tourist Map. rev. ed. pap. 2.95 o.p. (ISBN 1-85013-003-5, Pub. by Automobile Assn Brit). Salem Hse Pubs.
Wales' Work. Robert Walshe. 1986. 16.45 o.p. (ISBN 0-89919-430-3). Ticknor & Fields.
Walk a Rocky Road. Mildred Lawrence. LC 73-161387. 187p. (gr. 7 up). 1971. 6.50 o.p. (ISBN 0-15-294505-9, HJ). HarBraceJ.
Walk in Dread: Twelve Classic Eerie Tales. Ed. by Dorothy Tomlinson. LC 72-2204. 285p. 1972. 6.95 o.s.i. (ISBN 0-8008-8037-4). Taplinger.
Walk in Love. Raymond Roseliep. (W.N.J. Ser: No. 5). 1976. 6.00 o.p. (ISBN 1-55780-054-5). Juniper Pr WI.
Walk in My Moccasins. large type ed. Mary P. Warren. (Illus.). (gr. 4-6). 1966. 4.75 o.s.i. (ISBN 0-664-32373-1, Westminster). Westminster John Knox.
Walk in the Spring Rain. Rachel Maddux. 1978. pap. 1.50 o.p. (ISBN 0-380-01833-0, 36236). Avon.
Walk in the Sun & Other Stories. Norman D. Hunter. 1977. 4.00 o.p. (ISBN 0-682-48626-4). Exposition-Phoenix.
Walk in Wolf Wood. Mary Stewart. 192p. 1984. pap. 3.50 o.p. (ISBN 0-449-20678-5, Crest). Fawcett.
Walk in Wolf Wood. rev. ed. Mary Stewart. LC 80-13010. (Illus.). 160p. (gr. 5up). 1984. 10.25 o.p. (ISBN 0-688-03679-1). Morrow.
Walk Me to the Distance. Percival Everett. LC 84-8845. 240p. 1985. 14.45 o.p. (ISBN 0-89919-321-8). Ticknor & Fields.
Walk My Way. Paige Dixon. LC 79-23291. 156p. (gr. 6-9). 1980. 7.95 o.s.i. (ISBN 0-689-30738-1, Atheneum Childrens Bk). Macmillan.
Walk on the West Side: California on the Brink. Herbert Gold. LC 80-70216. 208p. 1981. 12.95 o.p. (ISBN 0-87795-305-8, Arbor Hse); pap. 5.95 o.p. (ISBN 0-87795-322-8). Morrow.
Walk Out of the World. Ruth Nichols. LC 69-13777. (Illus.). (gr. 4-6). 1969. 6.95 o.p. (ISBN 0-15-294514-8, HJ). HarBraceJ.
Walk the Dark Streets: A Sam Birge Mystery. William Krasner. 1985. pap. 3.95 o.p. (ISBN 0-684-18361-7, Collier). Macmillan.
Walk the Dinosaur Trial. Barbara Sauer. LC 81-68314. 1981. pap. 3.95x o.p. (ISBN 0-89051-078-4); tchr's guide 2.95x o.p. (ISBN 0-686-33035-8). Master Bks.
Walk the Distant Hills: The Story of Longri Ao. Richard G. Beers. (Bold Believers Ser.). 1969. pap. 0.95 o.p. (ISBN 0-377-84171-4). Friendship Pr.
Walk the High Horizon. Jane W. Murray. LC 74-6309. (gr. 7 up). 1974. 5.50 o.s.i. (ISBN 0-664-32551-3, Westminster). Westminster John Knox.
Walk Through Britain. John Hillaby. 1978. 7.95 o.p. (ISBN 0-395-07796-6); pap. 4.95 o.p. (ISBN 0-395-25016-1). HM.
Walk Through the Shire: Wherein We Discover Some Rare Drawings of Hobbit Life. Michael Green. LC 80-52955. (Illus., Orig.). 1980. lib. bdg. 12.90 o.p. (ISBN 0-89471-114-8); pap. 5.95 o.p. (ISBN 0-89471-115-6). Running Pr.
Walk Toward Peace. Johanna Schaefer. 1977. 4.50 o.p. (ISBN 0-682-48798-8). Exposition-Phoenix.
Walk with the Beast. Ed. by Charles M. Collins. 1969. pap. 1.25 o.p. (ISBN 0-380-00506-9, 26476). Avon.
Walkabout. James V. Marshall. 1978. pap. 1.50 o.s.i. (ISBN 0-505-51319-6, Pub. by Tower Bks). Dorchester Pub Co.
Walker in Jerusalem. Samuel Heilman. 380p. 1986. 18.45 o.s.i. (ISBN 0-671-54433-0). Summit Bks.
Walker in the City. Alfred Kazin. LC 53-18408. 1968. Repr. of 1951 ed. 11.95 o.p. (ISBN 0-15-194186-6). HarBraceJ.
Walker Percy: Art & Ethics. Ed. by Jac L. Tharpe. LC 80-12227. (Southern Quarterly Ser.). 168p. 1980. 10.00x o.p. (ISBN 0-87805-119-8); pap. 5.00 o.p. (ISBN 0-87805-120-1). U Pr of Miss.
Walker's Manual Incorporated. 78th, annual ed. National Standards Association Staff. LC 10-19951. 1950p. 1986. 345.00 o.p. (ISBN 0-916234-11-8). Cambridge MD.
Walker's Manual of Western Corporations, 2 vols. 74th annual ed. Walker's Manual Incorporated Staff. LC 10-19951. 1700p. 1982. (ISBN 0-916234-07-X). Cambridge MD.
Walker's Manual of Western Corporations, 2 vols. 75th annual ed. Walker's Manual Incorporated Staff. LC 10-19951. 1850p. 1983. Set. 260.00 o.p. (ISBN 0-916234-08-8). Cambridge MD.
Walker's Manual of Western Corporations, 2 vols. 76th annual ed. Walker's Manual Incorporated Staff. LC 10-19951. 1850p. 1984. Set. 295.00 o.p. (ISBN 0-916234-09-6). Cambridge MD.
Walker's Manual of Western Corporations, 2 vols. 77th annual ed. Walker's Manual Incorporated Staff. LC 10-19951. 1950p. 1985. 335.00 o.p. (ISBN 0-916234-10-X). Cambridge MD.
Walker's Remodeling Estimator's Reference Book. Harry Hardenbrook. (Illus.). 325p. 1982. 9.95 o.s.i. (ScribT). Scribner.
Walkies. Barbara Woodhouse. (Illus.). 32p. 1983. 7.95 o.s.i. (ISBN 0-671-46892-8). Summit Bks.
Walking a Thin Line. I. S. Grant. LC 84-91453. 139p. 1985. 10.95 o.p. (ISBN 0-533-06524-0). Vantage.
Walking after Midnight. Maureen McCoy. LC 85-9506. 223p. 1985. 14.70 o.s.i. (ISBN 0-671-55423-9, Poseidon). PB.
Walking Drum. Louis L'Amour. (General Ser.). 1984. lib. bdg. 16.95 o.p. (ISBN 0-8161-3735-8, Large Print Bks); pap. 10.95 o.s.i. (ISBN 0-8161-3737-4). G K Hall.
Walking from Inn to Inn: The San Francisco Bay Area. Jacqueline Kudler & Arlene Stark. LC 85-45697. (Illus.). 288p. 1986. pap. 8.95 o.p. (ISBN 0-88742-068-0). Globe Pequot.
Walking Home. Carol M. Storrer & Vicki Hesterman. LC 82-72636. 160p. (Orig.). 1983. pap. 6.95 o.p. (ISBN 0-8066-1942-2, 10-6922, Augsburg). Augsburg Fortress.
Walking in Wisdom: A Woman's Workshop on Ecclesiastes. Barbara Bush. (Woman's Workshop Ser.). 128p. (Orig.). 1982. pap. 2.95 o.p. (ISBN 0-310-43041-0, 12014P). Zondervan.
Walking into the Morning. Margaret Walpole. 48p. 1986. pap. 7.95 o.s.i. (ISBN 0-8378-5093-2). Gibson.
Walking on Air. Pierre Delattre. 1980. 10.95 o.p. (ISBN 0-395-29118-6); pap. 4.95 o.p. (ISBN 0-395-29119-4). HM.
Walking, Talking Words. Ivan Sherman. LC 80-13760. (Illus.). 32p. (gr. k-3). 1980. 7.95 o.p. (ISBN 0-15-294511-3, HJ). HarBraceJ.
Walking the Dartmoor Waterways. Eric Hemery. (Illus.). 128p. 1986. 14.95 o.p. (ISBN 0-7153-8627-1). David & Charles.
Walking Though Northern England. Charlie Emett & Mick Hutton. (Illus.). 192p. 1982. 16.95 o.p. (ISBN 0-7153-8285-3). David & Charles.
Walking Through Israel. Daniel Gavron. 448p. 1980. 12.95 o.p. (ISBN 0-395-27777-9). HM.
Walking Through the Dark. Phyllis R. Naylor. LC 75-23039. 224p. (gr. 5-9). 1976. 6.95 o.s.i. (ISBN 0-689-30509-5, Atheneum Childrens Bks). Macmillan.
Walking Through the Lake District. Michael Dunn. (Illus.). 224p. 1984. 18.95 o.p. (ISBN 0-7153-8443-0). David & Charles.
Walking Through the Mist of Life. Arthur L. Conway. LC 82-61883. 56p. 1983. pap. 4.95 o.p. (ISBN 0-938232-18-5). Winston-Derek.
Walking Through Tigerland. Barry Oakley. 154p. 1978. 17.50x o.p. (ISBN 0-7022-1099-4); pap. 7.95 o.p. (ISBN 0-7022-1105-2). U of Queensland Pr.
Walking to Sleep: New Poems & Translations. Richard Wilbur. LC 69-20054. 1969. 4.95 o.p. (ISBN 0-15-194188-2). HarBraceJ.
Walking to Sleep: New Poems & Translations. Richard Wilbur. LC 69-20054. 81p. 1971. pap. 4.95 o.s.i. (ISBN 0-15-694185-6, Harv). HarBraceJ.
Walking with a Camera in Herries Lakeland. Trevor Haywood. (Illus.). 128p. 1987. 19.95 o.p. (ISBN 0-86343-023-6, Pub. by Fountain Pr UK). Seven Hills Bk Dists.
Walking with Jesus. V. Gilbert Beers & Ronald A. Beers. (Illus.). 192p. (gr. 1-6). 1984. 14.95 o.p. (ISBN 0-89840-069-4). Heres Life.
Walks in the Catskills. John Bennet & Seth Masia. LC 74-81304. (Illus.). 204p. 1974. pap. 7.95 o.p. (ISBN 0-914788-00-0). Globe Pequot.
Walks of Jesus. Bessie Lewis. 1976. 1.25 o.p. (ISBN 0-8042-3598-8, John Knox). Westminster John Knox.
Wall Charts: Overview of Corporate Planning Process & Unique Elements of Corporate Planning. (Illus.). 1978. pap. 2.00 o.p. (ISBN 0-88441-434-5, 26-162). Girl Scouts USA.
Wall Jumper. Peter Schneider. Tr. by Leigh Hafrey. LC 83-47749. 140p. 1983. 11.45 o.p. (ISBN 0-394-52928-6). Pantheon.
Wall of Eyes. Margaret Millar. 1974. pap. 0.95 o.p. (ISBN 0-380-00067-9, 19927). Avon.
Wall of the Pacific. Jean-Francois Lyotard. Tr. by Cecile Lindsay from Fr. (Illus.). 95p. 1989. 15.95 o.p. (ISBN 0-932499-64-3). Lapis Pr.
Wall of the Plague. Andre Brink. LC 84-16325. 447p. 1985. 17.45 o.s.i. (ISBN 0-671-54189-7). Summit Bks.
Wall People: In Search of a Home. Joseph Di Certo. LC 84-21535. (Illus.). 168p. (gr. 3 up). 1985. 11.95 o.s.i. (ISBN 0-689-31090-0, Atheneum Childrens Bks). Macmillan.
Wall Reader. (Arlen House - Maxwell House Winners Ser.). 112p. pap. 4.95 o.p. (ISBN 0-905223-10-1, Dist. by Scribner). M Boyars Pubs.
Wall Street Gurus: How You Can Profit from Investment Newsletters. Peter Brimelow. LC 85-28153. 256p. 1986. 19.95 o.p. (ISBN 0-394-54202-9). Random.
Wall Street Journal on Management: The Best of the Manager's Journal. Ed. by David Asman & Adam Meyerson. 200p. 1985. 19.95 o.p. (ISBN 0-87094-685-4). Dow Jones-Irwin.
Wall Street Journal on Marketing. Ronald Alsop & Bill Abrams. 250p. 1986. 19.95 o.p. (ISBN 0-87094-896-2). Dow Jones-Irwin.
Wall Street Ventures & Adventures Through Forty Years. Richard D. Wyckoff. LC 68-28651. (Illus.). 1969. Repr. of 1930 ed. lib. bdg. 22.50x o.p. (ISBN 0-8371-0767-9, WYWS). Greenwood.
Wall Writing. Paul Auster. 1976. signed ed. 10.00 o.p. (ISBN 0-685-79213-7); pap. 3.00 o.p. (ISBN 0-685-79214-5). Figures.
Wallace-Homestead Price Guide to American Country Antiques. Don Raycraft & Carol Raycraft. pap. (ISBN 0-87069-406-5). Wallace-Homestead.
Wallace-Homestead Price Guide to American Country Antiques. 6th ed. Don Raycraft & Carol Raycraft. LC 86-640023. (Illus.). 1987. pap. 11.95 o.p. (ISBN 0-87069-477-4). Wallace-Homestead.
Wallace-Homestead Price Guide to Antiques & Pattern Glass. 10th ed. Ed. by Robert W. Miller. 672p. pap. 11.95 o.p. (ISBN 0-87069-386-7). Wallace-Homestead.
Wallace-Homestead Price Guide to Dolls, 1982-1983 Prices. Robert W. Miller. pap. 10.95 o.p. (ISBN 0-87069-410-3). Wallace-Homestead.
Wallace-Homestead Price Guide to Dolls: 1984-1985 Prices. Robert W. Miller. 216p. 1984. pap. 12.95 o.p. (ISBN 0-87069-394-8). Wallace-Homestead.
Walled Gardens: Their Planting & Design. Diana Saville. (Illus.). 168p. 1982. 24.95 o.p. (ISBN 0-7134-1494-4, Pub. by Batsford England). David & Charles.
Wallenberg. Kati Morton. 1985. pap. 3.95 o.s.i. (ISBN 0-345-30364-4). Ballantine.
Wallis & Edward: Letters 1931-1937. Ed. by Michael Block. (Large Print Bks). (Illus.). 531p. 1987. lib. bdg. 20.95 o.p. (ISBN 0-8161-4237-8, Large Print Bks). G K Hall.

Wallpaper: A History. Francoise Teynac et al. (Illus.). 249p. 35.00 o.p. (ISBN 0-317-55069-1). Apollo.

Walls of Windy Troy: A Biography of Heinrich Schliemann. Marjorie Braymer. LC 60-6207. (gr. 7 up). 1966. pap. 1.45 o.p. (ISBN 0-15-694201-1, VoyB). HarBraceJ.

Wallstein: Edition Critique. Benjamin Constant & Jean Rene Derre. 264p. 1965. 19.95 o.p. (ISBN 0-686-54616-4). French & Eur.

Wally's Stories. Vivian G. Paley. LC 80-21882. 208p. 1981. text ed. 16.00x o.p. (ISBN 0-674-94592-1). Harvard U Pr.

Wally's Walk. Carol Leith. (Ringling Bros. & Barnum & Bailey Circus Bks.). (Illus.). 16p. (ps-k). 1986. 6.70 o.p. (ISBN 0-316-52036-5). Little.

Walnut Grove. Jane G. Rushing. 1979. pap. 1.95 o.p. (ISBN 0-380-44164-0, 44164). Avon.

Walsh Functions & Their Applications. K. G. Beauchamp. (Techniques of Physics Ser.). 1976. 39.50 o.p. (ISBN 0-12-084050-2). Acad Pr.

Walt Disney: A Guide to References & Resources. Gartley Lynn & Elizabeth Leebron. 1979. lib. bdg. 34.50 o.p. (ISBN 0-8161-8004-0, Hall Reference). G K Hall.

Walt Disney World. Steve Birnbaum. 1981. pap. 4.95 o.p. (ISBN 0-395-31792-4). HM.

Walt Disney World Nineteen Eighty-Seven. Steve Birnbaum. (Illus.). 192p. 1986. pap. 8.95 o.s.i. (ISBN 0-395-42719-3). HM.

Walt Disney World, 1983. rev. ed. Steve Birnbaum. 1982. pap. 4.95 o.p. (ISBN 0-395-32952-3). HM.

Walt Disney World 1984. Steve Birnbaum. 1983. pap. 6.95 o.p. (ISBN 0-395-34891-9). HM.

Walt Disney World, 1985. Steve Birnbaum. (Stephen Birnbaum Travel Guide Ser.). (Orig.). 1984. pap. 6.95 o.p. HM.

Walt Disney's Donald Duck: Fifty Years of Happy Frustration. Walt Disney Productions. LC 84-80405. (Illus.). 96p. 1984. 14.95 o.p. (ISBN 0-89586-333-2). Price Stern.

Walt Disney's EPCOT: Creating the New World of Tomorrow. Richard R. Beard. (Illus.). 240p. 1982. 35.00 o.s.i. (ISBN 0-8109-0819-0). Abrams.

Walt Disney's The Penguin That Hated the Cold. Barbara Brenner. (Disney's Wonderful World of Reading Ser.: No. 7). (Illus.). (ps-3). 1973. 4.95 o.p. (ISBN 0-394-82628-0, BYR); lib. bdg. 4.99 o.p. (ISBN 0-394-92628-5). Random.

Walt Whitman: The Critical Heritage. Ed. by Milton Hindus. 1971. 29.95x o.p. (ISBN 0-7100-7087-X). Routledge Chapman & Hall.

Walt Whitman: Thinker & Artist. Arthur E. Briggs. 1952. (ISBN 0-8022-0175-X). Philos Lib.

Walt Whitman's Concept of the American Common Man. Leadie N. Clark. 192p. 1955. (ISBN 0-8022-0255-1). Philos Lib.

Walt Whitman's Poetry: A Psychological Journey. Edwin H. Miller. LC 69-19259. (Orig.). (YA) (gr. 9 up). 1968. pap. 5.75 o.p. (ISBN 0-395-04895-8, 3-37620, RivSL). HM.

Walter Benjamin. J. Roberts. (Contemporary Social Theory (Theoretical Traditions in Social Science) Ser.). 250p. 1982. pap. text ed. 13.00x o.p. (ISBN 0-391-02796-4). Humanities.

Walter Burley Griffin, Marion Mahoney Griffin: Architectural Drawings in the Burnham Library of Architecture. John Zukowsky. (Illus.). 16p. (Orig.). 1981. pap. 4.00 o.p. (ISBN 0-86559-047-8). Art Inst Chi.

Walter Gaudnek Retrospective. Montgomery Museum of Fine Arts Staff. Intro. by Henry F. Robert, Jr. LC 77-94108. (Illus.). 1977. pap. 6.50 o.p. (ISBN 0-89280-008-9). Montgomery Mus.

Walter Pater. Arthur C. Benson. LC 67-23876. (Library of Lives & Letters: British Writers Ser.). 240p. 1968. Repr. of 1906 ed. 30.00x o.p. (ISBN 0-8103-3054-7). Gale.

Walter Reed: A Biography. William B. Bean. LC 81-16123. (Illus.). 1982. 16.95x o.p. (ISBN 0-8139-0913-9). U Pr of Va.

Walton War & Tales of the Great Smoky Mts. Cal Carpenter. 96p. 1980. pap. 5.95 o.p. (ISBN 0-932298-03-6). Tri-State Pr Corp.

W.A.M.T. Jo Schaper. 1979. pap. 1.00 o.p. (ISBN 0-686-25263-2). Samisdat.

Wand. Allan W. Eckert. (Illus.). 256p. (gr. 3-7). 1985. 14.45i o.p. (ISBN 0-316-20882-5). Little.

Wanderer: A Reissue with a New Introduction & Illustrations. Sterling Hayden. (Illus.). 1977. 10.95 o.p. (ISBN 0-393-07521-4). Norton.

Wanderer on My Native Shore. George Reiger. 1983. 14.50 o.p. (ISBN 0-671-25423-5). S&S.

Wanderers. Richard Price. 1979. pap. 1.75 o.p. (ISBN 0-380-00242-6, 44545-X). Avon.

Wanderers. Richard Price. 1974. 5.95 o.p. (ISBN 0-395-18477-0). HM.

Wanderer's Guide to New Mexico: Route 66 Revisted. (Wanderer's Guide Ser.: Vol. 2). (Illus.). 120p. (Orig.). 1986. pap. 6.95 o.p. (ISBN 0-317-64259-6). Nakii Ent.

Wandering in the Wilderness: Christians & the New Culture. Robert Benne. LC 72-80401. 160p. (Orig.). 1972. pap. 0.50x o.p. (ISBN 0-8006-0117-3, 1-117, Fortress). Augsburg Fortress.

Wandering Jew. Stefan Heym. LC 83-4374. 324p. 1984. 14.95 o.p. (ISBN 0-03-064153-5, Owl Bks.). H Holt & Co.

Wandering Jew. Stefan Heym. LC 83-4374. 300p. (Ger.). 1985. pap. 6.95 o.p. (ISBN 0-394-62088-7, Ever). Grove.

Wandering People of God: An Investigation of the Letter to the Hebrews. Ernst Kasemann. Tr. by Roy A. Harrisville. LC 84-20523. 272p. (Orig.). 1984. 22.95 o.p. (ISBN 0-8066-2121-4, 10-6940, Augsburg). Augsburg Fortress.

Wandering Saints of the Early Middle Ages. Eleanor Duckett. 1964. pap. 3.45x o.p. (ISBN 0-393-00266-7, Norton Lib). Norton.

Wandering Sea Gull. Brone Martin. Tr. by Jonas Zdanys from Lithuanian. 1979. 9.50 o.p. (ISBN 0-682-49436-4). Exposition-Phoenix.

Wandering Taoist. Ming-Dao Deng. LC 82-48925. (Illus.). 224p. 1983. 14.37i o.p. (ISBN 0-06-250225-5). HarpR.

Wandering Thoughts. Thomas Smyth. 1979. 5.00 o.p. (ISBN 0-682-49385-6). Exposition-Phoenix.

Wandering Thoughts Again Wander. Thomas Smyth. 80p. 1983. 6.50 o.p. (ISBN 0-682-40124-2). Exposition-Phoenix.

Wandering Thoughts Doze. Thomas Smyth. 1985. 6.50 o.p. (ISBN 0-682-40240-0). Exposition-Phoenix.

Wandering Thoughts Sleep. Thomas Smyth. LC 86-91196. 80p. 1986. text ed. 8.50 o.p. (ISBN 0-682-40300-8). Exposition-Phoenix.

Wandering Thoughts Still Come. Thomas Smyth. 80p. 1983. 6.50 o.p. (ISBN 0-682-49943-9). Exposition-Phoenix.

Wandering Unicorn: A Novel. Manuel M. Lanez. Tr. by Mary Fitton from Span. LC 82-19598. 1983. 16.95 o.s.i. (ISBN 0-8008-8041-2). Taplinger.

Wanderings. Chaim Potok. 576p. 1982. pap. 3.95 o.p. (ISBN 0-449-24270-6, Crest). Fawcett.

Wanderings in South America, the Northwest of the United States, & the Antilles in the Years Eighteen Twelve, Eighteen Sixteen, Eighteen Twenty, & Eighteen Twenty-Four. Charles Waterton. 341p. 1968. Repr. of 1828 ed. 25.00 o.p. (ISBN 0-8398-2157-3). Parnassus Imprints.

Wanderings of a Spiritualist. Arthur Conan Doyle. 320p. 1988. pap. 9.95 o.p. (ISBN 0-317-66791-2). Ronin Pub.

Wanderings of an Elephant Hunter. W. Bell. (Illus.). 187p. 35.00 o.p. Saifer.

Wanderlust. Date not set. (ISBN 0-385-29463-8). Delacorte.

Wandor's Journey. Roland Green. pap. 0.95 o.p. (ISBN 0-380-00328-7, 45641-9). Avon.

Wandor's Ride. Roland Green. 1976. pap. 0.95 o.p. (ISBN 0-380-00575-1, 45658-3). Avon.

Wanted! A Horse! Babbis Friis. Tr. by Lise S. McKinnon from Norwegian. LC 72-153952. 192p. 1972. 5.95 o.p. (ISBN 0-15-294750-7, HJ). HarBraceJ.

Wanton. Rosemary Rogers. 505p. 1986. lib. bdg. 18.95 o.p. (ISBN 0-8161-4009-X, Large Print Bks). G K Hall.

Wanton Chase. Peter Quennell. LC 80-66007. 1980. 9.95 o.p. (ISBN 0-689-11081-2, Atheneum). Macmillan.

War. Gwynne Dyer. 272p. 1985. pap. text ed. (ISBN 0-534-10518-1). Wadsworth Pub.

War: A Concise History, 1939-1945. Louis L. Snyder. 1966. 17.50 o.p. (ISBN 0-671-79652-6). S&S.

War Against Poetry. Russell Fraser. LC 71-113001. 1970. 28.00x o.p. (ISBN 0-691-06190-4). Princeton U Pr.

War Against the Chtorr: Vol. 1-A Matter for Men. David Gerrold. 1983. 16.50 o.s.i. (ISBN 0-671-46493-0, Timescape); 6.75 o.s.i. (ISBN 0-671-46494-9, Timescape). PB.

War Against the Jew. D. D. Runes. LC 67-13371. 218p. 1968. (ISBN 0-8022-1457-6). Philos Lib.

War Against the Jews 1933-1945. Lucy S. Dawidowicz. LC 74-15470. (Illus.). 480p. 1975. 15.00 o.p. (ISBN 0-03-013661-X). H Holt & Co.

War All the Time. Charles Bukowski. 1984. signed cloth 25.00 o.p. (ISBN 0-87685-639-3). Black Sparrow.

War & Breed. David S. Jordan. 70p. 1986. pap. 3.50 o.p. (ISBN 0-317-53021-6). Noontide.

War & Christian Ethics. Arthur F. Holmes. LC 75-14602. pap. 13.95 o.p. (ISBN 0-8010-4170-8). Baker Bk.

War & Government in the Middle Ages: Essays in Honour of J. O. Prestwich. Ed. by John Gillingham & J. C. Holt. LC 84-423. (Illus.). 210p. 1984. 45.00x o.p. (ISBN 0-389-20475-7, 08037). B&N Imports.

War & Its Alleged Benefits. Jacques Novicow. LC 75-147482. (Library of War & Peace; the Character & Causes of War). 1972. lib. bdg. 46.00 o.p. (ISBN 0-8240-0274-1). Garland Pub.

War & Military Courts: Judicial Interpretation of Its Meaning. Dorothy Schaffter. 184p. 1980. 20.00 o.p. (ISBN 0-682-49570-0, University). Exposition-Phoenix.

War & Moral Discourse. Ralph B. Potter. LC 69-18111. (Orig.). 1969. pap. 3.95 o.p. (ISBN 0-8042-0863-8, John Knox). Westminster John Knox.

War & Other Measures. Gary Geddes. (House of Anansi Poetry Ser.: No. 35). 78p. (Orig.). 1976. pap. 4.95 o.p. (ISBN 0-88784-036-1, Pub. by Hse Anansi Pr Canada). U of Toronto Pr.

War & Peace. Leo Tolstoy. 1973. pap. 3.95 o.p. (ISBN 0-380-01608-7, 18143). Avon.

War & Peace in Jalemo: The Management of Conflict in Highland New Guinea. Klaus-Friedrich Koch. LC 73-92579. 288p. 1974. text ed. 17.50x o.s.i. (ISBN 0-674-94590-5). Harvard U Pr.

War & the Christian. Charles E. Raven. LC 75-147675. (Library of War & Peace; Relig. & Ethical Positions on War). 1972. lib. bdg. 46.00 o.p. (ISBN 0-8240-0432-9). Garland Pub.

War & the Workers. Norman Angell. LC 74-147518. (Library of War & Peace; Labor, Socialism & War). 1973. lib. bdg. 46.00 o.p. (ISBN 0-8240-0455-8). Garland Pub.

War & Weapons. National Army Museum, London Staff. (Modern Knowledge Library). (Illus.). 48p. (gr. 5 up). 1982. PLB 11.40 o.p. (ISBN 0-531-09059-0). Watts.

War at Sea: Nineteen Thirty-Nine to Nineteen Forty-Five. John Hamilton. (Illus.). 272p. 1986. 49.95 o.p. (ISBN 0-7137-1660-6, Pub. by Blandford Pr England); deluxe ed. 350.00 o.p. (ISBN 0-7137-1739-4). Sterling.

War Between Russia & China. Harrison E. Salisbury. (Illus.). 1969. 4.95 o.p. (ISBN 0-393-05394-6). Norton.

War Between the Generals: Inside the Allied High Command. David Irving. LC 80-68916. (Illus.). 456p. 1983. 17.95 o.p.; pap. 14.95 o.p. (ISBN 0-312-92921-8). Congdon & Weed.

War Books: A Study of Historical Criticism. Jean N. Cru. Ed. by Stanley J. Pincetl & Ernest Marchand. 1976. pap. 5.00x o.p. (ISBN 0-916304-22-1). SDSU Press.

War Diaries of Jean-Paul Sartre: November 1939 to March 1940. Jean-Paul Sartre. LC 84-18947. 1985. 10.95 o.s.i. (ISBN 0-394-53813-7). Pantheon.

War Eagle: A Story of Auburn Football. Rev. & enl. ed. Clyde Bolton. LC 73-83502. (College Sports Ser.). 1979. 9.95 o.p. (ISBN 0-87397-023-3). Strode.

War for the Union: The Improvised War, 1861-1862 see Ordeal of the Union.

War for the Union: The Organized War to Victory, 1864-1865 see Ordeal of the Union.

War for the Union: The Organized War, 1863-1864 see Ordeal of the Union.

War for the Union: War Becomes Revolution, 1862-1863 see Ordeal of the Union.

War Games. James P. Sloan. 192p. 1976. pap. 3.50 o.p. (ISBN 0-380-01609-5, 67835). Avon.

War Hound & the World's Pain. Michael Moorcock. 1981. 12.95 o.s.i. (ISBN 0-671-43708-9, Timescape). PB.

War in Algeria. Jules Roy. Ed. by Richard Howard. LC 75-11429. (Fr.). 128p. 1975. Repr. of 1961 ed. lib. bdg. 22.50x o.p. (ISBN 0-8371-8184-4, ROWA). Greenwood.

War in Southwest Virginia 1861-65. 5th ed. Gary C. Walker. Date not set. 24.95 o.p. (ISBN 0-317-67961-9). A & W Enterprises.

War in the Ancient World: A Social History. Yvon Garlan. Ed. by M. I. Finley. Tr. by Janet Lloyd. (Ancient Culture & Society Ser.). (Illus.). 200p. 1976. 7.95x o.p. (ISBN 0-393-05566-3). Norton.

War in the Crimea. Edward B. Hamley. 1971. Repr. of 1891 ed. lib. bdg. 35.00x o.p. (ISBN 0-8371-5009-4, HAWA). Greenwood.

War in the Far East. Fiona Reynolds. 80p. (Orig.). 1983. pap. text ed. 6.50x o.p. (ISBN 0-435-31882-9). Heinemann Ed.

War in Uganda: The Legacy of Idi Amin. Tony Avirgan & Martha Honey. LC 82-12123. 260p. 1982. 16.95 o.s.i. (ISBN 0-88208-136-5); pap. 9.95 o.s.i. (ISBN 0-88208-137-3). Chicago Review.

War Is Heaven. D. Keith Mano. 1981. pap. 0.95 o.p. (ISBN 0-380-01460-2, 06957). Avon.

War Lords. Sima Qian. Tr. by William Dolby & John Scott. 168p. 1974. 12.95 o.p. (ISBN 0-900025-08-5); pap. 10.95 o.p. (ISBN 0-900025-09-3). Dufour.

War Lords. A. J. Taylor. LC 77-13962. 1978. 10.00 o.p. (ISBN 0-689-10840-0, Atheneum). Macmillan.

War Machine: The Case Against the Arms Race. James A. Joyce. 240p. 1982. pap. 3.95 o.p. (ISBN 0-380-59915-5, 59915-5, Discus). Avon.

War Magician. David Fisher. 256p. 1983. 16.95 o.p. (ISBN 0-698-11140-0, Coward). Putnam Pub Group.

War Medicine. Winfield S. Pugh. (ISBN 0-8022-2019-3). Philos Lib.

War Myth in U. S. History see Propaganda & Myth in Time of War.

War of Dreams. Angela Carter. LC 74-1157. 288p. 1974. 6.95 o.p. (ISBN 0-15-144375-0). HarBraceJ.

War of Illusions: German Policies, 1911-1914. Fritz Fischer. Tr. by Marion Jackson from Ger. 578p. 1975. 9.95x o.p. (ISBN 0-393-09161-9). Norton.

War of Powers: In the Shadow of Omizatrim, Bk. 5. Robert E. Vardeman & Victor Milan. 224p. 1981. pap. 2.50 o.p. (ISBN 0-87216-999-5, Playboy). Putnam Pub Group.

War of the Classes. Jack London. (Illus.). 278p. 1982. pap. 6.95 o.s.i. (ISBN 0-932458-11-4). Star Rover.

War of the Gods: The Social Code in Indo-European Mythology. Jarich G. Oosten. (International Library of Anthropology). 240p. 1985. 32.50x o.p. (ISBN 0-7102-0289-X). Routledge Chapman & Hall.

War on Want. Ed. by G. Evans. 1962. pap. 40.00 o.p. (ISBN 0-08-009667-0). Pergamon.

War over the Family: Capturing the Middle Ground. Brigitte Berger & Peter L. Berger. LC 82-45237. 264p. 1984. 14.95 o.p. (ISBN 0-385-18001-2, Anchor Pr); pap. 7.95 o.p. (ISBN 0-385-18006-3, Anchor Pr). Doubleday.

War Party. William O. Steele. LC 78-52815. (gr. k-3). 1978. 4.95 o.p. (ISBN 0-15-294789-2, HJ). HarBraceJ.

War Party. William O. Steele. LC 78-52815. (Let Me Read Ser.). (Illus.). (gr. k-4). 1978. pap. 1.95 o.p. (ISBN 0-15-694697-1, VoyB). HarBraceJ.

War, Peace, & the Future. Ellen Key. LC 78-147728. (Library of War & Peace; the Character & Causes of War). 1973. lib. bdg. 46.00 o.p. (ISBN 0-8240-0507-4). Garland Pub.

War Poetry: An Anthology. Ed. by D. L. Jones. 1968. 4.15 o.p. (ISBN 0-08-012621-9); pap. text ed. 2.48 o.p. (ISBN 0-08-012622-7). Pergamon.

War Powers Resolution: Balance of War Powers in the Eighties. Robert Clark et al. LC 85-600614. (National War College Strategic Study). 91p. (Orig.). 1985. pap. 2.75 o.p. (ISBN 0-318-20164-X, S/N 008-020-01049-9). USGPO.

War Propoganda & the United States. James Wechsler & Harold Lavine. LC 72-147476. (Library of War & Peace; the Character & Causes of War). 1972. lib. bdg. 46.00 o.p. (ISBN 0-8240-0268-7). Garland Pub.

War Report: D-Day to VE-Day. Compiled by Desmond Hawkins. 368p. 1986. pap. 7.95 o.p. (ISBN 0-563-20421-4, Pub. by BBC). Parkwest Pubns.

War Secrets in the Ether, 2 vols. Wilhelm F. Flicke. LC 77-88801. (Cryptographic Ser.). 1977. Vol. 1. 18.80 o.p. (ISBN 0-89412-021-2); Vol. 2. 18.80 o.p. (ISBN 0-89412-023-9). Aegean Park Pr.

War the Infantry Knew, 1914-1919: A Chronicle of Service in France & Belgium. J. C. Dunn. (Illus.). 704p. 1987. 29.95 o.p. (ISBN 0-7106-0485-8). Janes Info Group.

War Toys. Hampton Howard. 272p. 1984. pap. 3.50 o.p. (ISBN 0-380-65557-8, 65557). Avon.

War Train. Brown Meggs. LC 79-55612. 1981. 13.95 o.p. (ISBN 0-689-11052-9, Atheneum). Macmillan.

War-Wasted Asia: Letters, 1945-46. Otis Cary et al. LC 75-11395. (Illus.). 322p. 16.95x o.p. (ISBN 0-87011-257-0). Kodansha.

War Within & Without: Diaries & Letters 1939-1944. Anne M. Lindbergh. 464p. 1981. pap. 3.95 o.s.i. (ISBN 0-425-05084-X). Berkley Pub.

Warday: And the Journey Onward. Whitley Strieber & James W. Kunetka. LC 83-18678. 1984. 15.95 o.p. (ISBN 0-03-070731-5). H Holt & Co.

Warehousing -- A Guide for Both Users & Operators. new ed. Kenneth B. Ackerman. LC 76-10120. 1977. text ed. 18.50 o.p. (ISBN 0-87408-013-4). Intl Thom Trans Pr.

Warfare by Land & Sea. Eugene S. McCartney. LC 63-10284. (Our Debt to Greece & Rome Ser). (Illus.). Repr. of 1930 ed. 17.50x o.p. (ISBN 0-8154-0149-3). Cooper Sq.

Warlock. Oakley Hall. LC 79-25080. viii, 471p. 1980. 32.50x o.p. (ISBN 0-8032-2311-0); pap. 8.95 o.p. (ISBN 0-8032-7206-5, BB 737, Bison). U of Nebr Pr.

Warlock Enraged. Christopher Stasheff. 256p. 1986. pap. 2.95 o.s.i. (ISBN 0-441-87340-5, Pub. by Charter Bks). Ace Bks.

Warlock in Spite of Himself. Christopher Stasheff. Ed. by Lester Del Ray. LC 75-433. (Library of Science Fiction). 1975. lib. bdg. 21.00 o.p. (ISBN 0-8240-1436-7). Garland Pub.

Warlock Is Missing. Christopher Stasheff. (Warlock Ser.: Vol. 7). 208p. 1986. pap. 3.50 o.s.i. (ISBN 0-441-84826-5, Pub. by Ace Science Fiction). Ace Bks.

Warlock of the Witch World. Andre Norton. (Witch World Ser.: No. 5). 1986. pap. 3.50 o.s.i. (ISBN 0-441-87316-2, Pub. by Ace Science Fiction). Ace Bks.

Warlock Unlocked. Christopher Stasheff. 288p. 1986. pap. 3.50 o.s.i. (ISBN 0-441-87330-8, Pub. by Charter Bks). Ace Bks.

Warlock's Book. Peter Haining. (Illus.). 1971. 6.00 o.p. (ISBN 0-8216-0161-X, Pub. by Univ Bks). Carol Pub Group.

Warlord. Malcolm Bosse. LC 82-19696. 717p. 1983. 17.25 o.p. (ISBN 0-671-44332-1). S&S.

Warlord: Yen Hsi-Shan in Shansi Province, 1911-1949. Donald G. Gillin. 1966. 40.00x o.p. (ISBN 0-691-03067-7). Princeton U Pr.

Warlords, 2 bks. David Cook. LC 86-90221. (One-On-One Adventure Gamebook: No. 7). (Orig.). 1986. pap. 5.95 o.p. (ISBN 0-88038-, 304-6). TSR Inc.

Warm Air Heating. D. Kut. LC 71-122009. 1975. 61.00 o.p. (ISBN 0-08-015853-6); pap. 71.00 o.p. (ISBN 0-08-019006-5). Pergamon.

Warm As Wool, Cool As Cotton: The Story of Natural Fibers & Fabrics & How to Work with Them. Carter Houck. LC 74-18089. (Illus.). 96p. (gr. 3-6). 1979. 6.95 o.p. (ISBN 0-395-28861-4, Clarion). HM.

Warm-Soft Village: Chinese Essays on Love. Tr. by Howard S. Levy. (Illus.). 1964. 10.00x o.p. (ISBN 0-686-00727-1). Oriental Bk Store.

Warm Tones & Tiny Miracles, Vol. I. Don J. Black. LC 78-186682. 136p. (Orig.). 1972. pap. 4.50 o.p. (ISBN 0-8425-1409-0, 8782). Pubs Bk Sales.

Warm up for Little League Baseball. Morris Shirts. LC 70-151708. (Illus.). 176p. (gr. 2 up). 1976. 8.95 o.p. (ISBN 0-8069-4044-1); PLB 10.99 o.p. (ISBN 0-8069-4045-X). Sterling.

Warm up for Little League Baseball. Morris A. Shirts. (Illus.). 208p. (gr. 3 up). 1984. pap. 2.25 o.p. (ISBN 0-671-47198-8). Archway.

Warman's Americana & Collectibles. Ed. by Harry L. Rinker. (Warman's Price Key Ser.). (Illus.). 576p. 1984. pap. 12.95 o.p. (ISBN 0-911594-04-3). Warman.

Warman's Americana & Collectibles. 2nd ed. Ed. by Harry L. Rinker. LC 84-643834. (Warman's Price Key Ser.). (Illus.). 592p. (Orig.). 1985. pap. 12.95 o.p. (ISBN 0-911594-07-8). Warman.

Warman's Antiques & Their Prices. 17th ed. Ed. by Harry L. Rinker. LC 79-4331. (Illus.). 712p. 1983. pap. 10.95 o.p. (ISBN 0-911594-03-5). Warman.

Warman's Antiques & Their Prices. 18th ed. Ed. by Harry L. Rinker. (Illus.). 736p. 1984. pap. 10.95 o.p. (ISBN 0-911594-05-1). Warman.

Warman's Antiques & Their Prices. 19th ed. Ed. by Harry L. Rinker. LC 82-643542. (Illus.). 700p. 1985. pap. 10.95 o.p. (ISBN 0-911594-06-X). Warman.

Warman's Antiques & Their Prices. 20th ed. Ed. by Harry L. Rinker. LC 82-643542. (Illus.). 736p. 1986. pap. 10.95 o.p. (ISBN 0-911594-09-4). Warman.

Warman's Antiques & Their Prices. 21st ed. Ed. by Harry L. Rinker. LC 82-643542. (Illus.). 720p. 1987. pap. 11.95 o.p. (ISBN 0-911594-10-8). Warman.

Warming Up. Dan Zadra. (Sports Instruction Ser.). (Illus.). 32p. (gr. 4 up). PLB 8.95 o.p. (ISBN 0-317-31108-5). Creative Ed.

Warning: Accident at Three Mile Island. Mike Gray & Ira Rosen. (Illus.). 1982. 14.95 o.p. (ISBN 0-393-01522-X). Norton.

Warning & Response. Julian Critchley. LC 78-8810. 144p. 1978. 19.50x o.p. (ISBN 0-8448-1362-1, Pub. by Crane Russak & Co). Taylor & Francis.

Warp & Weft: A Dictionary of Textile Terms. Dorothy K. Burnham. (Illus.). 240p. 1982. 35.00 o.p. (ISBN 0-684-17332-8, ScribT). Scribner.

Warpaint. Les Wayne. 208p. (Orig.). 1982. pap. 2.25 o.s.i. (ISBN 0-8439-1042-9, Pub. by Leisure Bks CT). Dorchester Pub Co.

Warplanes of the World, Nineteen Eighteen to Nineteen Thirty-Nine. Michael J. Taylor. 1981. encore ed. 5.95 o.p. (ISBN 0-684-16984-3, ScribT). Scribner.

Warranties & the Practitioner. Douglas J. Whaley. 271p. 1981. text ed. 40.00 o.p. (ISBN 0-686-76239-8, A1-1284). PLI.

Warranties in the Sale of Business Equipment & Consumer Products. (Nineteen Eighty-Two to Nineteen Eighty-Three Commercial Law & Practice Course Handbook Ser.). 686p. 1982. pap. text ed. 35.00 o.p. (ISBN 0-686-69173-3). PLI.

Warranties in the Sale of Business Equipment & Consumer Products 1985: Vol. 346. 382p. 1985. pap. 15.00 o.p. (ISBN 0-317-27436-8, #A4-4113). PLI.

Warrants for Highway Lighting. (National Cooperative Highway Research Project Report). 117p. 1974. 6.40 o.p. (ISBN 0-309-02303-3). Transport Res Bd.

Warren's Heaton Pamphlet Edition, New York SCPA-EPTL, Anatomical Gifts Act (Public Health Law) As Ammended Through the July 2, 1982 Recess of the Regular Legislative Session of 1982. Oscar Waren & Willis E. Heaton. Ed. by New York State Staff & Matthew Bender Publishers Staff. LC 83-179315. Date not set. price not set o.p. Bender.

Warrick. Marilyn Harris. LC 82-46011. 456p. 1985. 16.95 o.p. (ISBN 0-385-18815-3). Doubleday.

Warrior & the Priest: Woodrow Wilson & Theodore Roosevelt. John M. Cooper. (Illus.). 448p. 1983. 25.00 o.p. (ISBN 0-674-94750-9, Belknap). Harvard U Pr.

Warrior Koans: Early Zen in Japan. Trevor Leggett. 256p. 1985. pap. 8.95 o.p. (Ark Paperbks). Routledge Chapman & Hall.

Warrior Who Carried Life. Ryman. 1987. pap. 2.95 o.p. (ISBN 0-553-26344-7, Spectra). Bantam.

Warrior Who Walked Home: A Young Man Learns to Conquer Himself. Pavel Mikoloski. (Orig.). 1989. pap. cancelled o.s.i. (ISBN 0-945127-05-7). Upword Pr.

Warrior Women of Weymouth: Wizards, Warriors & You Ser, No. 18. Barbara Siegel & Scott Siegel. 112p. 1986. pap. 2.95 o.p. (ISBN 0-380-75047-3). Avon.

Warriors. Joaquim Jaquiera & Manuel B. Mansa. Tr. by Jan Feidel. (Illus.). 1972. 8.50 o.p. (ISBN 0-685-83016-0, Pub. by Mushinsha Bks); pap. 3.95 o.p. (ISBN 0-685-83017-9). Small Pr Dist.

Warriors & Worthies. Helmut Nickel. LC 69-18965. (Illus.). (gr. 7 up). 1969. PLB 10.00 o.p. (ISBN 0-689-30009-3, Atheneum). Macmillan.

Warriors for Jerusalem: The Six Days That Changed the Middle East. Donald Neff. 384p. 1984. 17.45 o.p. (ISBN 0-671-45485-4, Linden Pr). S&S.

Warriors of the Political Arena: The Presidential Election of 1984. John Forest. 1986. 14.95 o.p. (ISBN 0-317-39353-7). Vantage.

Warriors Without Weapons: A Study of the Society & Personality Development of the Pine Ridge Sioux. Gordon Macgregor et al. (Midway Reprint Ser.). (Illus.). 228p. 1975. pap. text ed. 9.00x o.s.i. (ISBN 0-226-50034-9). U of Chicago Pr.

War's Heretics: A Plan for the Conscientious Objector see Is Conscience a Crime?.

Wars in Vietnam, Cambodia & Laos, 1945-1982: A Bibliographic Guide. Richard D. Burns & Milton Leitenberg. LC 80-13246. (War-Peace Bibliography Ser.: No. 18). 290p. 1984. 58.50 o.p. (ISBN 0-87436-310-1). ABC-Clio.

War's Long Shadow: China, Russia, Britain, America. Bradley F. Smith. 304p. 1986. 18.45 o.p. (ISBN 0-671-52434-8). S&S.

Wars of the Roses: Lancastrians & Yorkists. Davis R. Cook. (Seminar Studies in History). (Illus.). 1984. pap. 7.25 o.p. (ISBN 0-582-35384-X). Longman.

Wars of Truth: Studies in the Decay of Christian Humanism in the Earlier 17th Century. Herschel Baker. 11.75 o.p. (ISBN 0-8446-0472-0). Peter Smith.

Warsaw Fall Seminars in Mathematical Economics 1975. Ed. by M. Wycech-Los et al. (Lecture Notes in Economics & Mathematical Systems Ser.: Vol. 133). 1976. pap. 13.00 o.p. (ISBN 0-387-07871-1). Springer-Verlag.

Warsaw Pact: Arms, Doctrine & Strategy. Institute of Foreign Policy Analysis Staff. Ed. by William J. Lewis. (Illus.). 512p. 1983. text ed. 37.00 o.p. (ISBN 0-07-031746-1). McGraw.

Warship, Vol. VI. Ed. by John Roberts. LC 78-55455. (Illus.). 288p. 1983. 24.95 o.p. (ISBN 0-87021-981-2). Naval Inst Pr.

Warships Associated with World War 2 in the Pacific. Harry A. Butowsky. (National Historic Landmark Theme Study). (Illus.). 756p. (Orig.). 1985. pap. 22.00 o.p. (ISBN 0-318-18869-4, S/N 024-005-00961-2). USGPO.

Warships of the Royal Navy. rev. ed. John E. Moore. (Illus.). 128p. 1981. 19.50 o.p. (ISBN 0-86720-566-0). Janes Info Group.

Warships of the Soviet Navy. John E. Moore. (Illus.). 224p. 9.95 o.p. (ISBN 0-86720-567-9). Janes Info Group.

Warships of the U. S. Navy. Samuel L. Morrison & John S. Rowe. 1983. 9.95 o.p. (ISBN 0-86720-667-5). Janes Info Group.

Warships of the World. Antony Preston. (Illus.). 224p. 1981. 16.95 o.p. (ISBN 0-86720-580-6). Janes Info Group.

Wartime. Milovan Djilas. Tr. by Michael B. Petrovich. LC 76-55148. 1977. 14.95 o.p. (ISBN 0-15-194609-4). HarBraceJ.

Wartime English. R. W. Zandvoort. LC 74-5556. 254p. 1974. Repr. of 1957 ed. lib. bdg. 24.75x o.p. (ISBN 0-8371-7509-7, ZAWE). Greenwood.

Wartime Origins of the Berlin Dilemma. Daniel J. Nelson. 256p. 1978. 19.95 o.p. (ISBN 0-8173-4727-5). U of Ala Pr.

Warton on Pope see Popeiana.

Was It Murder (Centralia Massacre) William C. Smith. 48p. pap. 3.95 o.s.i. (ISBN 0-8466-0127-3, S127). Shorey.

Was Jesus a Revolutionist? Martin Hengel. Ed. by John Reumann. Tr. by William Klassen from Ger. LC 77-157545. (Facet Bks.). 64p. (Orig.). 1971. pap. 1.50 o.p. (ISBN 0-8006-3066-1, 1-3066, Fortress). Augsburg Fortress.

Was Orwell Right? A Constitutional Perspective on Criminal Procedure. 272p. 1978. 15.00 o.p. (ISBN 0-88129-124-2). Wash Bar CLE.

Was That a Real Poem & Other Essays. Robert Creeley. Ed. by Donald Allen. LC 78-16254. (Writing: 39). 150p. 1979. 12.00 o.p. (ISBN 0-87704-041-9); pap. 5.00 o.p. (ISBN 0-87704-042-7). Four Seasons Foun.

Wasatch Trails. Betty Bottcher & Mel Davis. (Illus.). 77p. 1973. pap. 2.00 o.p. (ISBN 0-915272-00-8). Wasatch Pubs.

Wasatch Trails, Vol. 2. Daniel Geery. (Illus., Orig.). 1977. pap. 2.50 o.p. (ISBN 0-915272-10-5). Wasatch Pubs.

Wash & Gouache. Marjorie B. Cohn. 1977. 8.25 o.p. (ISBN 0-318-18702-7). Am Inst Conser Hist.

Washday. Susan Merrill. LC 77-12621. (Illus.). 32p. (ps-4). 1979. 6.95 o.p. (ISBN 0-395-28817-7, Clarion). HM.

Washington. Joan S. Mann. LC 73-79764. (This Beautiful World Ser: Vol. 47). (Illus.). 134p. (Orig.). 1982. pap. 5.25 o.p. (ISBN 0-87011-211-2). Kodansha.

Washington & Two Marches. Samuel F. Yette & Frederick W. Yette. Date not set. pap. 16.95 o.p. (ISBN 0-317-63427-5). Acropolis.

Washington Bullets. Jim Moore. LC 83-73294. (NBA Today Ser.). (Illus.). 48p. (gr. 4 up). 1984. PLB 10.45 o.p. (ISBN 0-87191-992-3). Creative Ed.

Washington: City of Scandals. Donald Lambro. 352p. 1984. 17.95 o.p. (ISBN 0-316-51288-5). Little.

Washington Commercial Law Deskbook. Washington State Bar Association, Continuing Legal Education Committee. LC 82-61858. 1982. Wash Bar CLE.

Washington Community: 1800-1828. James S. Young. LC 66-14080. (Illus.). 1968. pap. 6.95 o.p. (ISBN 0-15-694825-7, Harv). HarBraceJ.

Washington: Conflict of Laws. 8.50 o.p. (ISBN 0-686-90921-6). Am Law Inst.

Washington Contra la Habana. E. Grinevich & B. Gvozdariov. 304p. 1985. pap. 1.95 o.p. (ISBN 0-8285-3359-8, Pub. by Progress Pubs. USSR). Imported Pubns.

Washington, D. C. Richard S. Wurman. (Access Guidebooks). (Illus.). 168p. 1984. pap. 9.95 o.p. Access Pr.

Washington, D. C.-Access. (Access Guides Ser.). pap. 9.95 o.p. (ISBN 0-671-60339-6). S&S.

Washington, D. C. in Your Pocket. 3rd ed. Griffiths. 160p. 1985. pap. 2.95 o.p. (ISBN 0-8120-2837-6). Barron.

Washington, D. C. on Thirty-Five Dollars a Day, 1984-85. (Dollar a Day Guides). 286p. 1984. 8.95 o.p. (ISBN 0-671-46799-9). Prentice Hall Pr.

Washington, D. C. to Washington Square. John Brademas. LC 86-11112. 272p. 1986. 18.95 o.s.i. (ISBN 1-55584-015-9). Weidenfeld.

Washington: Eine Den Besucher Faszinierende Stadt (A Guide to Washington in German) D. C. Institute for Careers in Tourism. (Ger.). Date not set. pap. 4.95 o.p. (ISBN 0-317-63453-4). Acropolis.

Washington II. Photos by Ray Atkeson. LC 70-81401. (Belding Imprint Ser.). (Illus.). 128p. (Text by Archie Satterfield). 1973. 32.50 o.s.i. (ISBN 0-912856-12-2). Gr Arts Ctr Pub.

Washington Information Directory, 1984-85. Congressional Quarterly, Inc. Staff. LC 75-646321. 902p. 1984. 35.95 o.p. (ISBN 0-87187-295-1). Congr Quarterly.

Washington Information Directory, 1985-86. Congressional Quarterly, Inc. Staff. LC 75-646321. 900p. 1985. 39.95 o.p. (ISBN 0-87187-340-0). Congr Quarterly.

Washington Information Directory 1986-87. Congressional Quarterly, Inc. Staff. 967p. 1986. 49.95 o.p. (ISBN 0-87187-370-2). Congr Quarterly.

Washington Information Directory 1987-88. Congressional Quarterly, Inc. Staff. 1024p. 1987. 49.95 o.p. (ISBN 0-87187-420-2). Congr Quarterly.

Washington Irving: A Reference Guide. Haskell S. Springer. 1976. lib. bdg. 29.00 o.p. (ISBN 0-8161-1101-4, Hall Reference). G K Hall.

Washington Irving: A Tribute. Ed. by Andrew B. Myers. LC 77-189961. (Illus.). 86p. 1972. 3.95 o.p. (ISBN 0-912882-04-2); pap. 2.95 o.s.i. (ISBN 0-912882-05-0). Sleepy Hollow.

Washington Lobby. 4th ed. Congressional Quarterly, Inc. Staff. LC 82-12525. 179p. 1982. pap. 11.95 o.p. (ISBN 0-87187-240-4). Congr Quarterly.

Washington Magnificent Wilderness. John Fielder. LC 86-50063. (Illus.). 112p. 1986. 19.95 o.s.i. (ISBN 0-942394-21-6). Westcliffe Pubs Inc.

Washington Motor Vehicle Accident Insurance Deskbook. 1989. looseleaf 80.00 o.p. (ISBN 0-88129-222-2). Wash Bar CLE.

Washington Plenary Meeting of the Trilateral Commission. Trilateral Comm.

Washington Post: The First Hundred Years. Chalmers M. Roberts. 1977. 15.95 o.p. (ISBN 0-395-25854-5). HM.

Washington: Property, Vols. 1-2. Set. 8.50 o.p. (ISBN 0-686-90923-2). Am Law Inst.

Washington Real Estate Review Questions. National Real Estate Institute Staff. 225p. (Orig.). 1982. pap. 19.95x wkbk. o.p. (ISBN 0-915799-01-4). Natl Real Estate Inst.

Washington Redskins. Julian May. (NFL Today Ser.). (Illus.). (gr. 3-6). 1977. PLB 10.45 o.p. (ISBN 0-87191-597-9); pap. 4.25 o.p. (ISBN 0-686-67472-3). Creative Ed.

Washington Representatives, 1987. Ed. by Arthur C. Close & John P. Gregg. LC 76-21152. 650p. 1987. pap. 50.00 o.p. (ISBN 0-910416-65-6). Columbia Bks.

Washington Representatives 1988. 12th ed. Intro. by Arthur C. Close & Gregory Bologna. LC 76-21152. 685p. 1988. pap. 50.00 o.p. (ISBN 0-910416-72-9). Columbia Bks.

Washington Shores. Photos by David Muench. LC 80-85369. (Illus.). 128p. (Text by Spencer Gill). 1981. 28.50 o.s.i. (ISBN 0-912856-68-8). Gr Arts Ctr Pub.

Washington Square Poems: Bicentennial Edition. George H. McCullough. 1975. 4.00 o.p. (ISBN 0-682-48207-2). Exposition-Phoenix.

Washington Wilderness: The Unfinished Work. Harvey Manning & Pat O'Hara. (Illus.). 120p. 1985. pap. 20.00 o.p. (ISBN 0-89886-116-0). Mountaineers.

Wassim-Countersimulation Von Wasserversorgung Ung Abwasserentsorgung in Verdichtungsraeumen. G. Morlock-Rahn. (Interdisciplinary Systems Research Ser.: No. 71). 259p. (Ger.). 1979. pap. 34.95x o.p. (ISBN 0-8176-1113-4). Birkhauser.

Waste Discharge into the Marine Environment: Principles & Guidelines for a Mediterranean Action Plan. World Health Organization. LC 82-3806. (Illus.). 436p. 1982. 105.00 o.p. (ISBN 0-08-026194-9, G135, G145). Pergamon.

Waste Land: Facsimile & Transcript. facsimile ed. T. S. Eliot. Ed. by Valerie Eliot. LC 73-12627. 184p. 1974. pap. 9.95 o.s.i. (ISBN 0-15-694870-2, Harv). HarBraceJ.

Waste Management Eighty: American Nuclear Society, Symposium on Waste Management, Tuscon Az. March 10-14, 1980 see Waste Management Seventy-Five: Proceedings.

Waste Management Eighty - Four: Proceedings see Waste Management Seventy-Five: Proceedings.

Waste Management Eighty - One: Proceedings see Waste Management Seventy-Five: Proceedings.

Waste Management Eighty - Three see Waste Management Seventy-Five: Proceedings.

Waste Management Eighty - Two: Proceedings see Waste Management Seventy-Five: Proceedings.

Waste Management in Colleges & Universities. 115p. 5.00 o.p. (ISBN 0-913359-07-6); members 3.50 o.p. (ISBN 0-317-33670-3). Assn Phys Plant Admin.

Waste Management Seventy-Five: Proceedings. Incl. Waste Management Seventy-Nine: Proceedings. 662p. 1979. 23.00 (ISBN 0-317-36773-0, 700033); Waste Management Eighty: American Nuclear Society, Symposium on Waste Management, Tuscon Az. March 10-14, 1980, 2 Vols. 754p. 1980. pap. 32.00 (ISBN 0-317-36774-9, 700046); Waste Management Eighty - One: Proceedings. 1228p. 1981. 34.00 (ISBN 0-317-36775-7, 700057); Waste Management Eighty - Two: Proceedings, 3 Vols. 1688p. 1982. 51.00 set (ISBN 0-317-36776-5, 700072); Waste Management Eighty - Three. 946p. 1983. 40.00 (ISBN 0-317-36777-3, 700084); Waste Management Eighty - Four: Proceedings, 2 Vols. 1282p. 1984. 48.00 set (ISBN 0-317-36778-1, 700091). 275p. 1975. 8.50 o.p. (ISBN 0-317-36772-2, 700012). Am Nuclear Soc.

Waste Management Seventy-Nine: Proceedings see Waste Management Seventy-Five: Proceedings.

Waste Management '75: Proceedings. American Nuclear Society, Symposium on Waste Management, Tucson, March 24-26, 1975. 275p. pap. 10.00 o.p. (ISBN 0-317-33024-1, 700012). Am Nuclear Soc.

Waste Management '79: Proceedings. American Nuclear Society. Symposium on Waste Management, Tuscon, February 26-March 1, 1979. 662p. softcover 26.00 o.p. (ISBN 0-317-33025-X, 700033). Am Nuclear Soc.

Waste of Money. Raymond C. Crippen. LC 76-8794. 1977. 19.95 o.s.i. (ISBN 0-87949-079-9). Ashley Bks.

Waste Recovery by Micro-Organisms. 1978. pap. 13.25 o.p. (ISBN 0-685-65236-X, UM36, UNESCO). UNIPUB.

Waste Treatment & Disposal Aspects: Combustion & Air Pollution Control Processes. Air Pollution Control Associaton Specialty Conference. 216p. 1981. 15.00 o.p. (ISBN 0-318-12288-X, SP-42); members 12.00 o.p. (ISBN 0-318-12289-8). Air & Waste.

Wastes in the Ocean, Vol. 4: Energy Wastes in the Ocean. Iver W. Duedall. Ed. by Bostwick H. Ketchum et al. LC 84-22071. (Environmental Science & Technology Ser.). 818p. 1985. 100.00 o.p. (ISBN 0-471-89332-3). Wiley.

Wastewater Treatment & Disposal. Arceivala. (Pollution Engineering & Technology Ser.: Vol. 15). 920p. 1981. 115.00 o.p. (ISBN 0-8247-6973-2). Dekker.

Watch Out for the Chicken Feet in Your Soup. Tomie De Paola. LC 74-8201. (Illus.). (ps-3). 1985. 12.95 o.s.i. (ISBN 0-13-945782-8, Pub. by Treehouse); pap. 5.95 o.s.i. (ISBN 0-13-945766-6). P-H.

Watch Out for the Foreign Guests! China Encounters the West. Orville Schell. 1981. pap. 3.95 o.p. (ISBN 0-394-74899-9). Pantheon.

Watch Out for These Three Leavers. William McGrath. pap. 1.25 o.p. (ISBN 0-686-32336-X). Rod & Staff.

Watchdog. Faith Sullivan. 1982. text ed. 11.95 o.p. (ISBN 0-07-062355-4). Mcgraw.

Watcher. Charles Maclean. 350p. 1983. 14.50 o.p. (ISBN 0-671-25531-2). S&S.

Watcher Bee. Mary Melwood. (Illus.). 272p. (gr. 9 up). 1983. 9.95 o.p. (ISBN 0-233-97432-6). Andre Deutsch.

Watchers. Jane L. Curry. LC 75-8582. (Illus.). 240p. (gr. 5-9). 1975. 6.95 o.p. (ISBN 0-689-50030-0, Atheneum). Macmillan.

Watching Birds: An Introduction to Ornithology. Roger F. Pasquier. 1977. 11.95 o.p. (ISBN 0-395-25343-8). HM.

Watching Sea Birds. Richard Perry. LC 75-904. (Illus.). 240p. 1975. 10.95 o.s.i. (ISBN 0-8008-8047-1). Taplinger.

Watching Television. Ed. by Todd Gitlin. LC 86-42640. 256p. 1986. 19.45 o.p. (ISBN 0-394-54496-X); pap. 9.95 o.p. (ISBN 0-394-74651-1). Pantheon.

Watching the New Baby. Joan Samson. LC 73-84833. (Illus.). 80p. (gr. 3-6). 1974. 7.95 o.p. (ISBN 0-689-30119-7, Atheneum). Macmillan.

Watching Through Tall Windows. Dilorio. 144p. 1982. 7.50 o.p. (ISBN 0-682-49841-6, Banner). Exposition-Phoenix.

Watching TV: Four Decades of American Television. H. Castleman & W. J. Podrazik. 320p. 1982. text ed. 22.95 o.p. (ISBN 0-07-010268-6); pap. text ed. 14.95 o.p. (ISBN 0-07-010269-4). McGraw.

Watchmen of Eternity: Blake's Debt to Jacob Boehme. Bryan Aubrey. (Illus.). 208p. (Orig.). 1986. PLB 28.50 o.p. (ISBN 0-8191-5220-X); pap. text ed. 14.00 o.p. (ISBN 0-8191-5221-8). U Pr of Amer.

Watchwords of Liberty: A Pageant of American Quotations. rev. ed. Robert Lawson. (Illus.). (gr. 4-6). 1957. 10.95 o.p. (ISBN 0-316-51742-9). Little.

Water. Cyril S. Fox. 1952. (ISBN 0-8022-0524-0). Philos Lib.

Water, 2 Vols. (Class B, Class C). 1984. Class B. 126P. loose-leaf ed. 10.00 o.p. (ISBN 0-318-15039-5); Class C. 118P. loose-leaf ed. 6.00 o.p. (ISBN 0-318-15040-9). NARUC.

Water Allocation in California: Legal Rights & Reform Needs. Harrison C. Dunning. LC 82-6110. (IGS Research Papers). 62p. 1982. pap. 4.50x o.p. (ISBN 0-87772-288-9). UCB IGS.

Water & Aqueous Solutions: Introduction to a Molecular Theory. Arieh Ben-Naim. LC 74-7325. (Illus.). 474p. 1974. 75.00x o.p. (ISBN 0-306-30774-X, Plenum Pr). Plenum Pub.

Water & Baptismal Fonts Through the Ages: A Bibliography of Scholarship Dealing with Stylistic, Design, & Iconographic Aspects. Carole Cable. (Architecture Ser.: A 1484). 8p. 1985. 2.00 o.p. (ISBN 0-89028-614-0). Vance Biblios.

Water & Energy Development in an Arid Environment: The Colorado River Basin. G. V. Skogerboe. 1982. pap. 63.00 flexi-cover o.p. (ISBN 0-08-028752-2). Pergamon.

Water & Its Impurities. 2nd ed. Thomas Camp & Robert L. Meserve. LC 74-7012. (Illus.). 384p. 1982. 55.95 o.p. (ISBN 0-87933-112-7). Van Nos Reinhold.

Water & Landscape. Landscape Architecture Magazine Editors. (Illus.). 1979. text ed. 34.95 o.p. (ISBN 0-07-036190-8). McGraw.

Water & Life. Lorus Milne & Margery Milne. LC 64-14923. (Illus.). 1964. pap. 3.25 o.p. (ISBN 0-689-70334-1, 193, Atheneum). Macmillan.

Water & Plant Life: Problems & Modern Approaches. Ed. by O. L. Lange et al. LC 76-42191. (Ecological Studies: Vol. 19). 1977. 63.00 o.p. (ISBN 0-387-07838-X). Springer-Verlag.

Water & Society, Conflicts in Development: Water Conflicts & Research Priorities, Part 2. (Water Development, Supply & Management Ser.: Vol. 8). (Illus.). 260p. 1980. 63.00 o.p. (ISBN 0-08-023422-4). Pergamon.

Water & the West: The Colorado River Compact & the Politics of Water in the American West. Norris Hundley, Jr. LC 73-93054. (Illus.). 432p. 1975. 42.00x o.p. (ISBN 0-520-02700-0). U of Cal Pr.

Water As a Factor in Energy Resources Development. (Water Resources Ser.: No. 60). 77p. 1986. 9.50 o.p. (ISBN 92-1-119280-3, E.85.II.F.7). UN.

Water at the Surface of the Earth: An Introduction to Ecosystem Hydrodynamics. D. H. Miller. 1977. 82.00 o.p. (ISBN 0-12-496750-7). Acad Pr.

Water Chlorination: Environmental Impact & Health Effects, 2 vols. Ed. by Robert L. Jolley et al. LC 77-92588. (Illus.). 1200p. 1980. 65.00 o.p. (ISBN 0-250-40342-0). Butterworth.

Water Chlorination: Environmental Impact & Health Effects, Vol. 1. Ed. by Robert L. Jolley. LC 77-92588. 1978. 34.95 o.p. (ISBN 0-250-40200-9). Butterworth.

Water Chlorination: Environmental Impact & Health Effects, Vol. 2. Ed. by Robert L. Jolley et al. LC 77-92588. 1978. 34.95 o.p. (ISBN 0-250-40201-7). Butterworth.

Water Dancer. Jennifer Levin. 361p. 1982. 15.50 o.s.i. (ISBN 0-671-44764-5, Poseidon). PB.

Water, Earth & Man. Ed. by Richard J. Chorley. 1969. 66.00x o.p. (ISBN 0-416-12030-X, NO. 2138). Routledge Chapman & Hall.

Water Engine & Mr. Happiness. David Mamet. LC 78-3118. 1978. 10.00 o.s.i. (ISBN 0-394-50120-9, GP811); pap. 7.95 o.p. (ISBN 0-394-17043-1). Grove.

Water for the Thousand Millions, Vol. 4. Ed. by Arnold Pacey. LC 77-23127. 1977. pap. 8.00 o.p. (ISBN 0-08-021805-9). Pergamon.

Water Gardens. Gordon T. Ledbetter. (Illus.). 1980. 13.95 o.p. (ISBN 0-393-01332-4). Norton.

Water Horse. Genevieve Scott. 1973. pap. 0.75 o.p. (ISBN 0-380-01611-7, 16659). Avon.

Water, Human Values & the Eighties. Ed. by M. L. De Wayne. 100p. 1981. pap. 16.75 o.p. (ISBN 0-08-028098-6). Pergamon.

Water in Landscape Architecture. Craig Campbell. 128p. 1982. pap. 9.95 o.p. (ISBN 0-442-21589-4). Van Nos Reinhold.

Water in the Basement. Alfred Gingold. 1988. pap. 5.95 o.p. Workman Pub.

Water Is Wide. Pat Conroy. 1979. pap. 3.50 o.p. (ISBN 0-380-46037-8, 67124-7). Avon.

Water Is Wide. Pat Conroy. LC 70-177537. 1976. 9.95 o.p. (ISBN 0-395-13644-X). HM.

Water Law. William Goldfarb. LC 84-9597. 300p. 1984. text ed. 39.95 o.p. (ISBN 0-250-40627-6). Butterworth.

Water Laws in Moslem Countries, Vol. 1. D. A. Caponera. (Irrigation & Drainage Papers: No. 20-1). 229p. 1973. pap. 15.75 o.p. (ISBN 92-5-100013-1, F989, FAO). UNIPUB.

Water Lilies & Dragonflies. Relly J. Parcell. LC 84-90299. 78p. 1985. 7.95 o.p. (ISBN 0-533-06341-8). Vantage.

Water Management & Environment in Latin America: Analysis & Case Studies of Water Management, Including New Approaches Through Simulation Modelling & the Environmental Consequences of Past & Potential Trends in Water Use. United Nations Economic Commission for Latin America. (Environmental Sciences & Applications Ser.: Vol. 12). 1979. 105.00 o.p. (ISBN 0-08-023580-8); pap. 36.00 o.p. (ISBN 0-08-024457-2). Pergamon.

Water Management for Arid Lands: Proceedings. Training Workshop on Water Management for Arid Regions, Ministry of Irrigation, Government of Egypt, in Cooperation with the United Nations Environment Programme, Cairo, Egypt. Ed. by M. A. Samaha et al. LC 79-40504. (Water Development, Supply & Management Ser.: Vol. 13). (Illus.). 280p. 1980. 65.00 o.p. (ISBN 0-08-022431-8). Pergamon.

Water Management Organization in China. Ed. by James E. Nickum. LC 80-5458. 288p. 1981. 35.00 o.p. (ISBN 0-87332-140-5). M E Sharpe.

Water Music. Bianca Vanorden. LC 58-10887. 1958. 3.95 o.p. (ISBN 0-15-195015-6). HarBraceJ.

Water of Life: A Treatise on Urine Therapy. 2nd ed. John W. Armstrong. 136p. 1957. pap. text ed. 11.95 o.p. (ISBN 0-88697-016-4). Life Science.

Water Plants in the Aquarium. Ines Scheurmann. 1987. pap. 3.95 o.p. (ISBN 0-08-120392-6). Pergamon.

Water Pollution. Julian McCaull & Janice Crossland. Ed. by Barry Commoner. 224p. (Orig.). 1974. pap. text ed. 9.95 o.p. (ISBN 0-15-595125-4, HC). HarBraceJ.

Water Pollution: A Guide to Information Sources. Ed. by Allen W. Knight & Mary Ann Simmons. LC 73-17537. (Man & the Environment Information Guide Ser.: Vol. 9). 288p. 1980. 68.00x o.p. (ISBN 0-8103-1346-4). Gale.

Water Pollution Control in Developing Countries. E. A. Ouano et al. 1978. 230.00 o.p. (ISBN 0-08-023567-0). Pergamon.

Water Pollution: Disposal & Reuse, Vol. 2. J. E. Zajic. 272p. 1971. 75.00 o.p. (ISBN 0-8247-1816-X). Dekker.

Water Pollution Research: Proceedings of the Second International Conference. 2nd ed. Ed. by O. Jaag et al. 1966. Set. 270.00 o.p. (ISBN 0-08-011438-5). Pergamon.

Water Purification in the EEC. Water Research Enter. LC 77-5475. 1977. pap. 115.00 o.p. (ISBN 0-08-021225-5). Pergamon.

Water Quality & Treatment. Ed. by R. Urbistondo & L. R. Bays. 76p. 1985. 24.00 o.p. (ISBN 0-08-031432-5). Pergamon.

Water Quality, Conduits & Geometrics: Four Reports. (Transportation Research Record Ser.). 51p. 1975. 4.00 o.p. (ISBN 0-309-02463-3). Transport Res Bd.

Water Quality: Management & Pollution Control Problems. S. H. Jenkins. 1973. 90.00 o.p. (ISBN 0-08-017006-4). Pergamon.

Water Research Topics, Vol. 1. Ed. by I. M. Lamont. LC 81-4192. (Water Research Topics Ser.). 263p. 1981. 79.95x o.p. (ISBN 0-470-27212-0). Halsted Pr.

Water Resource Investment & the Public Interest: An Analysis of Federal Expenditures in Ten Southern States. Robert Haveman. LC 65-18545. 1965. 11.95x o.p. (ISBN 0-8265-1077-9). Vanderbilt U Pr.

Water Resources in the Southern Rockies & High Plains: Forest Recreation Use and Aquatic Life. Loren D. Potter & James R. Gosz. LC 83-16833. (Illus.). 347p. 1984. 29.95x o.p. (ISBN 0-8263-0692-6). U of NM Pr.

Water Row Review. Ed. by Jeffrey Weinberg. 58p. 1987. pap. 10.00 o.p. (ISBN 0-317-61714-1). Water Row Pr.

Water, Sanitation, Health - For All? 1981. 5.50 o.p. (ISBN 0-905347-27-7). C I D E.

Water Supplies for Fire Protection. 3rd ed. International Fire Service Training Association Staff. Ed. by Jerry Laughlin & Connie E. Williams. LC 78-58881. (Illus.). 147p. 1978. pap. text ed. 11.00 o.p. (ISBN 0-87939-029-8). Fire Protect Pubns.

Water Supply: Second Atlantic Workshop: Prooceedings of the Specialised Workshop of the ISWA Held in Nice, France, 3-7 March 1984. Ed. by R. Urbistondo & L. R. Bays. 176p. 1985. pap. 73.00 o.p. (ISBN 0-08-034131-4, Pub. by PPL). Pergamon.

Water Supply: The Decade-Half Way: Part of the Proceedings of the Regional Conference of the IWSA Held in Conjunction with the 3rd Congress of the UADE in Libreville, Gabon, 10-15 June, 1985. Ed. by G. Dassonville. 372p. 1986. pap. 66.00 o.p. (ISBN 0-08-034142-X, Pub. by PPL). Pergamon.

Water, the Life Sustaining Resource. Robert Gardner. LC 82-2231. 192p. (gr. 7 up). 1982. lib. bdg. 9.79 o.p. (ISBN 0-671-43655-4). Messner.

Water Trails West. Western Writers of America. 1979. pap. 3.50 o.p. (ISBN 0-380-47688-6, Discus). Avon.

Water Use Efficiency & Competition Between Arid Zone Annuals, Especially the Grasses Phalaris Minor & Hordeum Murinum. H. Lof. (Agricultural Research Reports: No. 853). 1977. pap. 20.00 o.p. (ISBN 90-220-0605-0, PDC101, PUDOC). UNIPUB.

Water Vapour Line Parameters from Microwave to Medium Infrared: An Atlas of H2 to the Sixteenth, O; H2 to the Seventeenth, O; H2 to the Eighteenth, O; Line Positions & Intensities Between O & 4350 Cm to the -1. J. M. Flaud & C. Camy-Peyret. (International Tables of Constants Ser.: Vol. 19). xvi, 259p. 1981. 100.00 o.p. (ISBN 0-08-026181-7). Pergamon.

Water Waves. N. F. Barber & G. Ghey. (Wykeham Science Ser.: No. 5). 152p. 1969. 18.00x o.p. (ISBN 0-8448-1107-6, Pub. by Crane Russak & Co). Taylor & Francis.

Watercolorist's Guide to Painting Water. Illus. by Ferdinand Petrie. (Illus.). 144p. 1985. 27.50 o.p. (ISBN 0-8230-5693-7). Watson-Guptill.

Watercress File. Andrew Gilchrist. 176p. 1986. pap. 2.95 o.p. (ISBN 0-317-66396-8). Critics Choice Paper.

Waterflooding. (SPE Reprint Ser.). 291p. 1973. 18.50x o.p. (ISBN 0-317-32939-1, 30502). Soc Petrol Engineers.

Waterfowl: Ducks, Geese & Swans of the World. Frank S. Todd. LC 79-63521. (Illus.). 1979. 45.00 o.p. (ISBN 0-15-004036-9). HarBraceJ.

Waterfowl Studies. Bruce Burk. LC 82-62596. 1976. 24.95 o.s.i. (ISBN 0-8329-1807-5, Pub. by Winchester Pr). New Century.

Watergate: A Crisis for the World: A Survey of British & French Press Reaction Toward an American Political Crisis. LC 79-40708. (Illus.). 260p. 1980. 53.00 o.p. (ISBN 0-08-020582-8). Pergamon.

Waterland. Graham Swift. LC 83-21248. 1984. 15.50 o.s.i. (ISBN 0-671-49863-0, Poseidon). PB.

Waterlilies. Philip Swindells. (Illus.). 159p. 1983. 17.95 o.p. (ISBN 0-917304-52-7). Timber.

Waterloo Directory of Victorian Periodicals. Ed. by Michael Wolff et al. 1203p. 1981. 285.00 o.p. (ISBN 0-08-026079-9). Pergamon.

Waterman. Doug Hornig. 352p. 1987. 16.95 o.p. (ISBN 0-89296-256-9). Mysterious Pr.

Watershed Forest Influences in the Tropics & Subtropics: A Selected, Annotated Bibliography. Julia Williams & Lawrence S. Hamilton. xiii, 217p. (Orig.). 1982. pap. text ed. 3.00 o.p. (ISBN 0-86638-036-1). EW Ctr HI.

Waterways: Poetry in the Mainstream, 1987 Index. Ed. by Barbara Fisher & Richard Spiegal. (Illus.). 16p. (Orig.). 1987. pap. 5.00 o.p. (ISBN 0-317-67338-6). Ten Penny.

Watson's Apology. Beryl Bainbridge. 222p. 1985. text ed. 14.95 o.p. (ISBN 0-07-003254-8). McGraw.

Watsonville: Memories That Linger, Vol. 2. Betty Lewis. LC 76-41500. (Illus.). 154p. 1980. 11.95 o.p. (ISBN 0-934136-08-4, Valley Calif). Western Tanager.

Watteau & the North Studies in the Dutch & Flemish Baroque Influence on French Rocco Painting. Oliver Banks. LC 76-23602. (Outstanding Dissertations in the Fine Arts Ser.). 1977. lib. bdg. 76.00 o.p. (ISBN 0-8240-2676-4). Garland Pub.

Watteau's Drawings: Their Use & Significance. Martin Eidelberg. LC 76-23616. (Outstanding Dissertations in the Fine Arts - 18th Century). (Illus.). 1977. Repr. of 1965 ed. lib. bdg. 68.00 o.p. (ISBN 0-8240-2687-X). Garland Pub.

Watty Piper's Trucks. (Platt & Munk Cricket Bks.). (Illus.). 24p. (ps-3). 1978. pap. 2.50 o.p. (ISBN 0-448-46526-4, G&D); PLB 3.59 o.p. (ISBN 0-448-13068-8). Putnam Pub Group.

Wave Mechanics. G. Ludwig. 1968. 36.00 o.p. (ISBN 0-08-012302-3); pap. 60.00 o.p. (ISBN 0-08-012303-1). Pergamon.

Wave of Destiny. Martha Melahn. 320p. 1981. pap. 2.75 o.p. (ISBN 0-380-79152-8, 79152). Avon.

Wave Propagation & Underwater Acoustics. Ed. by J. Keller & J. Papadakis. (Lecture Notes in Physics Ser: Vol. 70). 1977. pap. 18.00 o.p. (ISBN 0-387-08527-0). Springer-Verlag.

Wave Propagation in Dissipative Material: A Reprint of Five Memoirs. B. D. Coleman et al. 1965. 11.80 o.p. (ISBN 0-387-03424-2). Springer-Verlag.

Wave Scattering from Statistically Rough Surfaces. F. G. Bass & M. Fuchs. LC 77-23113. 1979. 135.00 o.p. (ISBN 0-08-019896-1). Pergamon.

Waveform Quantization & Coding. Ed. by N. S. Jayant. LC 75-44651. 624p. cancelled o.s.i. (ISBN 0-87942-073-1, PC00687). Inst Electrical.

Waveguide Tapers, Transitions & Couplers. Hans-Georg Unger. Ed. by Frank Sporleder. (IEE Electromagnetic Waves Ser.: No. 6). (Illus.). 320p. 1979. casebound 58.00 o.s.i. (ISBN 0-906048-16-8, EW006). Inst Elect Eng.

Wavelength Standards in the Infrared. K. N. Rao. 1966. 63.50 o.p. (ISBN 0-12-580650-7). Acad Pr.

Waverley. Walter Scott. 1976. 12.50x o.p. (ISBN 0-460-00075-6, Evman); pap. 5.95x o.p. (ISBN 0-460-01075-1, Evman). Biblio Dist.

Waverly Dictionary. 2nd ed. May Rogers. LC 66-27850. 358p. 1967. Repr. of 1885 ed. 37.00x o.p. (ISBN 0-8103-3222-1). Gale.

Waves & Tides. R. C. Russell & D. H. MacMillan. (Illus.). 348p. 1953. (ISBN 0-8022-1421-5). Philos Lib.

Waves of Change. 2nd ed. Charles P. Lecht. 1979. pap. text ed. 12.95 o.p. (ISBN 0-07-036967-4). McGraw.

Waves on Water of Variable Depth. Ed. by D. G. Provis. (Lecture Notes in Physics: Vol. 64). 1977. 18.00 o.p. (ISBN 0-387-08253-0). Springer-Verlag.

Wax Portraits & Silhouettes. Ethel S. Bolton. LC 71-164115. 90p. 1974. Repr. of 1914 ed. 40.00x o.p. (ISBN 0-8103-3168-3). Gale.

Way. Josemaria Escriva de Balaguer. Orig. Title: Camino. 1979. pap. 4.95 o.p. (ISBN 0-933932-01-4). Scepter Pubs.

Way & Its Power: A Study of the Tao Te Ching & Its Place in Chinese Thought. Arthur Waley. 1958. pap. 9.95 o.s.i. (ISBN 0-394-17207-8, E84, Ever). Grove.

Way down & Out: The Occult in Symbolist Literature. John Senior. LC 68-23326. (Illus.). 1968. Repr. of 1959 ed. lib. bdg. 22.50x o.p. (ISBN 0-8371-0218-9, SESL). Greenwood.

Way down East, or Portraitures of Yankee Life. Seba Smith. 1986. pap. text ed. 6.95x o.p. (ISBN 0-8290-1952-9). Irvington.

Way down South, up North. E. Frederic Morrow. LC 72-13451. 1973. 6.95 o.p. (ISBN 0-8298-0246-0). Pilgrim NY.

Way Grampa Tells Stories. Bob Loos. (Illus.). 32p. (ps-2). 1982. 5.75 o.p. Exposition-Phoenix.

Way Home. Joan Phipson. LC 73-75440. (gr. 5-9). 1973. 5.50 o.p. (ISBN 0-689-30322-X, Atheneum). Macmillan.

Way Home. Raymond Rawson. LC 84-90242. 113p. 1985. 10.95 o.p. (ISBN 0-533-06294-2). Vantage.

Way Howe to Lymne: Tudor Miniatures Observed. Jim Murrell. (Illus.). 120p. 23.95 o.p. (ISBN 0-905209-39-7, Pub. by Victoria & Albert Mus UK). Faber & Faber.

Way in the Desert. Doug Sewell. 48p. 1985. 4.95 o.p. (ISBN 0-8407-5458-2). Paperback Ser. Nelson.

Way It Is. Ed. by John Holland. LC 69-11495. (Curriculum Related Bks.). (Illus.). (gr. 7 up). 1969. 6.75 o.p. (ISBN 0-15-294830-9, HJ). HarBraceJ.

Way It Was-Eighteen Seventy-Six. Suzanne Hilton. LC 74-20665. (Illus.). 224p. (gr. 6 up). 1975. 6.95 o.s.i. (ISBN 0-664-32558-0, Westminster). Westminster John Knox.

Way It Was in Bible Times. Merrill T. Gilbertson. LC 59-10759. (Illus.). 1959. pap. 7.95 o.p. (ISBN 0-8066-1442-0, 10-7000, Augsburg). Augsburg Fortress.

Way Men Love: A Study into the Emotional Subconscious. Arthur H. McNary. (Illus.). cancelled o.s.i. (ISBN 0-89920-001-X). Am Inst Psych.

Way of All Flesh see also Ernest Pontifex.

Way of All Flesh Tones: A History of Color Motion Picture Processes, 1895-1929. Robert A. Nowotny. Ed. by Garth S. Jowett. LC 81-48351. (Dissertations on Film Ser.). 359p. 1983. lib. bdg. 55.00 o.p. (ISBN 0-8240-5109-2). Garland Pub.

Way of All the Earth. Anna Akhmatova. Tr. by D. M. Thomas from Rus. LC 79-1953. 96p. 1980. 11.95x o.p. (ISBN 0-8214-0429-6); pap. 6.95 o.p. (ISBN 0-8214-0430-X). Ohio U Pr.

Way of Being. Carl R. Rogers. 288p. 1980. 12.95 o.p. (ISBN 0-395-29915-2). HM.

Way of Dharma. Paul Twitchell. 1970. pap. 3.95 o.p. (ISBN 0-914766-18-X). Illum Way Pub.

Way of Knowing. William P. Montague. 1962. Repr. of 1978 ed. text ed. 19.95x o.p. (ISBN 0-391-00568-5). Humanities.

Way of Life: King, Householder, Renouncer; Essays in Honour of Louis Dumont. T. N. Madan. 400p. 1982. text ed. 45.00x o.p. (ISBN 0-7069-1843-6, Pub. by Vikas India). Advent NY.

Way of Life, Like Any Other. Darcy O'Brien. 1978. 7.95 o.p. (ISBN 0-393-08798-0). Norton.

Way of Love, a Way of Life: A Young Person's Introduction to What It Means to Be Gay. Frances Hanckel & John Cunningham. LC 79-2424. (Illus.). (YA) (gr. 9-12). 1979. 11.25 o.p. (ISBN 0-688-41907-0); PLB 11.88 o.p. (ISBN 0-688-51907-5). Lothrop.

Way of Non-Attachment. Dhiravamsa. pap. 8.99 o.p. (ISBN 0-85500-210-7, Pub. by Turnstone Pr England). Sterling.

Way of Passion. Elizabeth Lee. 320p. 1981. pap. 2.75 o.p. (ISBN 0-380-78287-1, 78287). Avon.

Way of Salvation N. T. 1982. pap. 3.95 o.s.i. (ISBN 0-89225-220-0). Gospel Advocate.

Way of Seeing: A Critical Study of James Agee. Alfred T. Barson. LC 75-181365. 232p. 1971. 17.50x o.p. (ISBN 0-87023-094-8). U of Mass Pr.

Way of Splendor: Jewish Mysticism & Modern Psychology. Edward Hoffman. LC 81-50967. (Illus.). 250p. 1981. 15.00 o.s.i. (ISBN 0-87773-209-4, 74885-9); 10.95 o.s.i. (ISBN 0-87773-210-8). Shambhala Pubns.

Way of the Ascetics: The Ancient Tradition of Discipline & Inner Growth. Tito Colliander. LC 61-7341. 128p. 1982. 7.64i o.p. (ISBN 0-06-061526-5). HarpR.

Way of the Brush: Painting Techniques of China & Japan. Fritz Van Briessen. LC 62-14119. (Illus.). 1962. 47.50 o.p. (ISBN 0-8048-0625-X). C E Tuttle.

Way of the Bull. Leo F. Buscaglia. 192p. 1984. pap. 3.50 o.p. (ISBN 0-449-20820-6, Crest). Fawcett.

Way of the Hunters: An Illustrated Commentary & Prehistoric Record. Raoul M. Dixon. (Illus.). 256p. 1987. 14.95 o.p. (ISBN 0-8062-2864-4). Carlton.

Way of the Peaceful Warrior: A Basically True Story. Dan Millman. LC 79-66725. 210p. 1980. 8.95 o.p. (ISBN 0-87477-121-8). J P Tarcher.

Way of the Sword: The Tengu-geijutsu-ron of Chozan Shissai. Reinhard Kammer. Tr. by Betty J. Fitzgerald from Japanese. 144p. 1986. pap. 5.95 o.p. (ISBN 1-85063-043-7). Routledge Chapman & Hall.

Way of the White Clouds. Bhagwan Shree Rajneesh. (Illus.). 1979. pap. 9.95 o.s.i. (ISBN 0-394-17089-X, E729, Ever). Grove.

Way of the Yacht. Alan Hollingsworth. (Illus.). 136p. 1974. 10.00 o.p. (ISBN 0-393-03181-0). Norton.

Way of Transformation: Daily Life As Spiritual Exercise. Karlfried G. Durckheim. 1988. pap. 10.95 o.p. Unwin Hyman.

Way of Words: An Informal Logic. Ronald Munson. LC 75-31028. (Illus.). 448p. 1976. text ed. 26.95 o.p. (ISBN 0-395-20625-1). HM.

Way Prayer Works: A Space Age View of the Timeless Substance of the Lord's Prayer. Roy H. Murray. 1977. 5.00 o.p. (ISBN 0-682-48830-5). Exposition-Phoenix.

Way Society Develops. E. Plimak & A. Volodin. 143p. 1983. pap. 1.45 o.p. (ISBN 0-8285-2734-2, Pub. by Progress Pubs USSR). Imported Pubns.

Way the World Works: How Economics Fail & Succeed. rev. ed. Jude Wanniski. 1983. pap. 9.95 o.p. (ISBN 0-671-43862-X, Touchstone Bks). S&S.

Way Things Work: An Encyclopedia of Modern Technology, Vol. 1. (gr. 7 up). 1967. 19.25 o.p. (ISBN 0-671-22621-5). S&S.

Way Things Work: An Encyclopedia of Modern Technology, Vol. 2. 1971. 19.25 o.p. (ISBN 0-671-21086-6). S&S.

Way Things Work: Book of the Body. 1979. 18.95 o.p. (ISBN 0-671-22454-9). S&S.

Way to Christ: Spiritual Exercises. Pope John Paul II. LC 83-48426. 160p. 1984. 10.53i o.p. (ISBN 0-06-064204-1). HarpR.

Way to Go Home. Eric Pendry. 1978. 8.95 o.p. (ISBN 0-393-08834-0). Norton.

Way to God. D. L. Moody. pap. 3.95 o.p. (ISBN 0-8024-9231-2). Moody.

Way to God. Maxwell Silver. (ISBN 0-8022-1569-6). Philos Lib.

Way to Natural Beauty. Cheryl Tiegs. (Illus.). 288p. 1983. pap. 9.50 o.p. (ISBN 0-671-47245-3, Fireside). S&S.

Way to Nicea: The Dialectical Development of Trinitarian Theology. Bernard Lonergan. LC 76-20792. 176p. 1977. 9.50 o.s.i. (ISBN 0-664-21340-5, Westminster). Westminster John Knox.

Way to St. Ives. Sonia Gernes. 288p. 1982. 13.95 o.s.i. (ISBN 0-684-17492-8, ScribT). Scribner.

Way to the Old Sailor's Home. Thomas Baird. 1978. pap. 1.75 o.p. (ISBN 0-380-39008-6, 39008). Avon.

Way to Worship, Vol. I. Marjory Alexander. (Illus.). 22p. (gr. k-4). cancelled o.s.i. CEF Press.

Way Ward Pokey. Ann Bischoff. 40p. 1986. 5.75 o.p. (ISBN 0-8062-2843-1). Carlton.

Way We Were. Arthur Laurents. 1973. pap. 1.25 o.p. (ISBN 0-380-01613-3, 15289). Avon.

Way West. Alfred B. Guthrie, Jr. 352p. (gr. 8 up). 1984. pap. 3.95 o.p. (ISBN 0-553-24785-9). Bantam.

Waymakers: Eyewitnesses to the Christ. M. Pamela Smith, Sr. LC 82-71664. (Illus.). 80p. (Orig.). 1982. pap. 4.95 o.p. (ISBN 0-87793-254-9). Ave Maria.

Wayne Gretzky. Gelfand. (Sports Superstars Ser.). (Illus.). 32p. (gr. 4 up). 1985. PLB 8.95 o.p. (ISBN 0-317-31206-5). Creative Ed.

Wayne Gretzky. Rothaus et al. (Sports Superstars Ser.). (Illus.). 32p. Date not set. PLB 8.95 o.p. Creative Ed.

Wayne Gretzky: Portrait of a Hockey Player. Craig T. Wolff. (Illus.). 80p. (gr. 3-7). 1983. pap. 1.95 o.p. (ISBN 0-380-82420-5, 82420-5, Camelot). Avon.

Waynesburg College Story, 1849-1974. William H. Dusenberry. LC 74-27386. (Illus.). 489p. 1975. 12.50x o.p. (ISBN 0-87338-173-4). Kent St U Pr.

Waynflete Lectures on Physics: Selected Topics in Contemporary Physics & Astrophysics. V. L. Ginzburg & P. N. Lebedev. Tr. by D. ter Haar. LC 82-24619. (International Series in Natural Philosophy: Vol. 106). (Illus.). 133p. 1983. 34.00 o.p. (ISBN 0-08-029147-3). Pergamon.

Ways & Means of Statistics. Leonard J. Tashman & Kathleen R. Lamborn. 527p. 1979. text ed. 24.00 o.p. (ISBN 0-15-595132-7, HC). HarBraceJ.

Ways & Means of Using Birds in Combating Noxious Insects. Ed. by L. P. Poznanin. 138p. 1956. text ed. 26.50x o.p. (ISBN 0-317-46490-6, Pub. by Keter Pub Jerusalem). Coronet Bks.

Ways & Teachings of the Church. Lefferd M. Haughwout. (Orig.). 3.50 o.p. (ISBN 0-8192-1041-2). Morehouse Pub.

Ways of Darkness. Joseph Hayes. LC 84-29497. 1985. 16.95 o.p. (ISBN 0-688-04289-9). Morrow.

Ways of Escape. Graham Greene. 1981. 13.95 o.p. (ISBN 0-671-41219-1). S&S.

Ways of Exchange: The Enga Tee of Papua New Guinea. D. K. Feil. LC 83-23414. (Illus.). 269p. 1985. text ed. 37.50x o.p. (ISBN 0-7022-1994-0). U Of Queensland Pr.

Ways of Health: Holistic Approaches to Ancient & Contemporary Medicine. David S. Sobel. 1979. 14.95 o.p. (ISBN 0-15-195308-2). HarBraceJ.

Ways of Health: Holistic Approaches to Ancient & Contemporary Medicine. Ed. by David S. Sobel. LC 78-14081. 1979. pap. 8.95 o.p. (ISBN 0-15-694992-X, Harv). HarBraceJ.

Ways of Living. Joan Solomon. (Science in a Social Context Ser.). 1986. pap. text ed. 6.95x o.p. (ISBN 0-631-91960-0). Basil Blackwell.

Ways of Loving. Brendan Gill. 1976. pap. 1.75 o.p. (ISBN 0-380-00582-4, 27326). Avon.

Ways of Loving. Brendan Gill. 1974. 7.95 o.p. (ISBN 0-15-195312-0). HarBraceJ.

Ways of Teaching. Dorothy B. Fritz. 1965. pap. 2.25 o.s.i. (ISBN 0-664-24659-1, Westminster). Westminster John Knox.

Ways of the Hour. facsimile ed. James Fenimore Cooper. 512p. Repr. of 1850 ed. 44.00 o.p. (ISBN 0-8290-1953-7). Irvington.

Ways to Poetry. Stanley A. Clayes & John Gerrietts. 400p. 1975. pap. text ed. 9.95 o.p. (ISBN 0-15-595137-8, HC). HarBraceJ.

Ways to Self Rule: Beyond Marxism & Anarchism. George Fischer. 1978. 7.50 o.p. (ISBN 0-682-49132-2, University). Exposition-Phoenix.

Ways to Teach Children. Iris V. Cully. LC 66-24201. 1966. 1.00x o.p. (ISBN 0-8006-0076-2, Fortress). Augsburg Fortress.

Ways to the Center: An Introduction to World Religions. 2nd ed. Denise L. Carmody & John T. Carmody. 416p. 1984. text ed. (ISBN 0-534-03121-8). Wadsworth Pub.

Wayside Blossoms. Emma C. Brannon. 77p. 1979. 5.00 o.p. (ISBN 0-682-49390-2). Exposition-Phoenix.

Wayside Poems. Joseph R. Garcia. 96p. 1982. pap. 5.00 o.p. (ISBN 0-682-49908-0). Exposition-Phoenix.

Wayward Head & Heart. Claude P. Crebillon. Tr. by Barbara Bray. LC 78-16439. 1978. Repr. of 1963 ed. lib. bdg. 35.00x o.p. (ISBN 0-313-20578-7, CRWH). Greenwood.

Wayward Splendor. Jerry W. Butler. 1987. 10.00 o.p. (ISBN 0-533-06927-0). Vantage.

WCBS Smokers' Clinic Book. Art Athens. LC 79-22546. (Illus.). 224p. 1979. 10.95 o.p. (ISBN 0-03-044116-1); pap. 4.95 o.p. (ISBN 0-03-044111-0). H Holt & Co.

We All Come from Puerto Rico Too. Julia Singer. LC 76-46600. (Illus.). (gr. 4-6). 1977. 6.95 o.p. (ISBN 0-689-30573-7, Atheneum). Macmillan.

We All Come from Someplace: Children of Puerto Rico. Julia Singer. LC 75-46577. (Illus.). 96p. (gr. 4-6). 1976. 6.95 o.p. (ISBN 0-689-30531-1, Atheneum). Macmillan.

We Americans, Vol. I. 2nd ed. Leonard Pitt. 448p. 1983. pap. text ed. 21.95 o.p. (ISBN 0-8403-3027-8). Kendall-Hunt.

We Americans, Vol. II. 2nd ed. Leonard Pitt. 608p. 1983. pap. text ed. 20.95 o.p. (ISBN 0-8403-3028-6). Kendall-Hunt.

We Are Having a Baby. Vicki Holland. (Illus.). (gr. k-1). 1972. 8.95 o.s.i. (ISBN 0-684-12809-8, Pub. by Scribner); pap. 5.95 o.s.i. (ISBN 0-684-16012-9, SL 835, Pub. by Scribner). Macmillan.

We Are Immortal. A. C. Ferber. 1975. 7.00 o.p. (ISBN 0-682-48288-9, Testament). Exposition-Phoenix.

We Are One Another. Arthur Guirdham. 227p. 1985. pap. 9.95 o.p. (ISBN 0-85500-166-6). Newcastle Pub.

We Are One Another: A Record of Group Reincarnation. Arthur Guirdham. LC 86-33425. 227p. 1986. Repr. of 1974 ed. lib. bdg. 19.95x o.p. (ISBN 0-8095-7034-3). Borgo Pr.

We Are One in the Spirit: How to Receive & Use the Holy Spirit's Gifts. Omar Stuenkel. LC 78-66949. 1979. pap. 2.95 o.p. (ISBN 0-8066-1693-8, 10-7010, Augsburg). Augsburg Fortress.

We Are the Children. Judith M. Spiegelman & UNICEF Staff. Ed. by Jennifer Weis. (Illus.). 224p. 1986. 29.95 o.p. (ISBN 0-87113-105-6). Atlantic Monthly.

We Are the Fallen Angels. Alice W. Edminster. 1979. 5.00 o.p. (ISBN 0-682-49441-0). Exposition-Phoenix.

We Are the Targets: Environmental Impacts. Harold McKenna, Jr. (Student Scientist Ser.). (Illus.). 115p. (gr. 7-12). 1980. PLB 10.97 o.p. (ISBN 0-8239-0474-1). Rosen Group.

We Are the World: The Photos, Music, & Inside Story of One of the Most Historic Events in American Popular Music. (Illus.). 1985. pap. 5.95 o.p. (ISBN 0-399-51172-5, Perigee). Putnam Pub Group.

We Are Your Sisters: Black Women in the Nineteenth Century. Dorothy Sterling. LC 83-42684. (Illus.). 416p. 1984. 22.00 o.p. (ISBN 0-393-01728-1). Norton.

We Are Your Sons: The Legacy of Ethel & Julius Rosenberg. Michael Meeropol & Robert Meeropol. LC 75-2197. 416p. 1975. 10.00 o.p. (ISBN 0-395-20552-2). HM.

We Ate Gooseberries: Growing up on a Minnesota Farm During the Depression. Vernon J. Schaefer. 1974. 8.50 o.p. (ISBN 0-682-47836-9). Exposition-Phoenix.

We Bake Cookies. Faith Carlson. (Illus.). 28p. (Orig.). (ps-2). 1987. pap. 5.00 o.p. (ISBN 0-932591-06-X). Baggeboda Pr.

We Believe in Creation. Charles Ryrie. 62p. 1976. pap. 0.50 o.p. (ISBN 0-937396-54-0). Walterick Pubs.

We Call Ourselves Disciples. 2nd ed. Kenneth L. Teegarden. LC 82-24455. 116p. 1983. pap. 5.95 o.p. (ISBN 0-8272-4215-8). CBP.

We Came to Help. Monika Schwinn & Bernhard Diehl. LC 76-13882. (Helen & Kurt Wolff Bk.). (Illus.). 1976. 8.95 o.p. (ISBN 0-15-195595-6). HarBraceJ.

We Can Make It...Together. Joseph A. Jordan. (Illus.). 64p. 1984. 5.50 o.p. (ISBN 0-682-40157-9). Exposition-Phoenix.

We Can Make It...Together. Joseph A. Jordan. (Illus.). 112p. 1985. Repr. of 1984 ed. 5.50 o.p. Exposition-Phoenix.

We Can Speak for Ourselves. Paul Williams & Bonnie Schoultz. LC 83-49409. (Illus.). 264p. 1984. 17.50x o.p. (ISBN 0-253-36365-9); pap. 8.95x o.p. (ISBN 0-253-28915-7). Ind U Pr.

We Can't All Be Heroes: A History of the Separate Infantry Regiments in World War II. Melvin Curtis Walthall. 1975. 7.50 o.p. (ISBN 0-682-48209-9). Exposition-Phoenix.

We Can't All Be Heroes, You Know. Linda Anderson. LC 84-16359. 208p. 1985. 14.45 o.p. (ISBN 0-89919-333-1). Ticknor & Fields.

We Can't Pay? We Won't Pay! Dario Fo. 72p. (Orig.). 1981. pap. 4.95 o.p. (ISBN 0-86104-204-2). Routledge Chapman & Hall.

We Choose Peace. V. Fedosov & A. Fyodorov. 200p. 1985. pap. 1.95 o.p. (ISBN 0-8285-3092-0, Pub. by Progress Pubs USSR). Imported Pubns.

We Christians & Jews. Paul J. Kirsch. LC 74-26332. 160p. 1975. pap. 0.50 o.p. (ISBN 0-8006-1094-6, Fortress). Augsburg Fortress.

We Crown Them All: An Illustrated History of Danbury. William Devlin. (Illus.). 144p. 1984. 22.95 o.s.i. (ISBN 0-89781-092-9). Windsor Pubns Inc.

We Don't Know How: An Independent Audit of What They Call Success in Foreign Assistance. William Paddock & Elizabeth Paddock. 1973. pap. 8.95x o.p. (ISBN 0-8138-1755-2). Iowa St U Pr.

We Gather Together: The Church Worships God. John S. Groenfeldt. (Orig.). 1971. pap. 1.65 o.p. (ISBN 0-8042-9060-1, John Knox). Westminster John Knox.

We Go Shopping: A First-Look-It-Up Book. (Learning Curves Bks.). (Illus.). 12p. (ps-1). 1987. pap. 5.95 o.p. (ISBN 0-553-18357-5). Bantam.

We Got This New Baby at Our House: How a Child Feels When a Brother or Sister Is Born. Janet Sinberg. (Illus.). 49p. 1980. pap. 3.95 o.p. (ISBN 0-380-76083-5, 76083-5). Avon.

We-Gyet Wanders On. (Illus.). 74p. 14.95 o.s.i. (ISBN 0-919654-99-1). Hancock House.

We Had a Shore Fast Line. Mervin E. Borgnis. (Illus.). 246p. 1979. 20.00 o.p. (ISBN 0-682-49411-9). Exposition-Phoenix.

We Have Eaten the Forest: The Story of a Montagnard Village in the Central Highlands of Vietnam. Georges Condominas. Tr. by Adrienne Foulke from Fr. (Illus.). 448p. 1977. 17.50 o.p. (ISBN 0-686-63835-2); pap. 10.95 o.p. (ISBN 0-8090-1386-X). Hill & Wang.

We Have Met the Enemy: The Life of Commodore Oliver Hazard Perry. Richard Dillon. LC 77-17039. 1978. text ed. 12.95 o.p. (ISBN 0-07-016981-0). McGraw.

We Have to Get Rid of These Puppies! Marilyn D. Anderson. (Treetop Tales Ser.). (Illus.). 96p. (gr. 3-5). 1986. 1.95 o.s.i. (ISBN 0-87406-150-4). Willowisp Pr.

We Have Tomorrow. Arna Bontemps. (gr. 9 up). 1945. 6.95 o.p. (ISBN 0-395-06646-8). HM.

We Left Jehovah's Witnesses. Edmond C. Gruss. pap. 5.95 o.p. (ISBN 0-8010-3696-8). Baker Bk.

We Loved While We Died. Annette Dominic. 64p. 1985. 7.50 o.p. (ISBN 0-682-40279-6). Exposition-Phoenix.

We Make Freedom: Women in South Africa Speak. Beata Lipman. 232p. (Orig.). 1984. pap. 9.95 o.p. (ISBN 0-86358-034-3, Pandora Pr). Routledge Chapman & Hall.

We Make Our Own Music. Carola Grindea. 64p. 1982. pap. 4.95 o.s.i. (ISBN 0-8008-8115-X, Crescendo). Taplinger.

We Must March, My Darlings. Diana Trilling. 315p. 1978. pap. 3.95 o.s.i. (ISBN 0-15-695706-X). HarBraceJ.

We of the Never-Never & the Little Black Princess. Aeneas Gunn. 256p. 1984. pap. 3.95 o.p. (ISBN 0-380-87791-0, Discus). Avon.

We Persuade Men. V. P. Black. Ed. by J. D. Thomas. LC 72-87861. (Twentieth Century Sermons Ser). 1969. 9.95 o.p. (ISBN 0-89112-302-4). Abilene Christ U.

We Rode the Wind: Recollections of 19th-Century Tribal Life. Ed. by Jane B. Katz. LC 74-11909. (Voices of the American Indian Ser.). (Illus.). 112p. (gr. 7 up). 1975. PLB 8.95 o.p. (ISBN 0-8225-0639-4). Lerner Pubns.

We Saw Stars. Stan Musial & Jack Buck. LC 76-27220. 1976. pap. 3.95 o.p. (ISBN 0-8272-4211-5). CBP.

We Shall Be All: A History of the Industrial Workers of the World. Melvyn Dubofsky. LC 87-16725. 1988. 39.95 o.p. (ISBN 0-252-01408-1). U of Ill Pr.

We Shall Not Sleep. Clyde O. Jackson. (Illus.). 1985. 8.00 o.p. (ISBN 0-682-40219-2). Exposition-Phoenix.

We Share New Life (Baptism Program) Brian A. Haggerty et al. Reflections & Activities for Families. 2.95 o.p. (ISBN 0-8091-9183-0); Activities for Children. 2.75 o.p. (ISBN 0-8091-9182-2); director's manual 7.95 o.p. (ISBN 0-8091-9181-4); celebrations bk. 4.95 o.p. (ISBN 0-8091-9184-9). Paulist Pr.

We Sing Your Praise, O Lord: Dramas & Meditations on Six Favorite Hymns. W. A. Poovey. LC 80-67792. 128p. 1980. pap. 4.50 o.p. (ISBN 0-8066-1853-1, 10-7022, Augsburg); pap. 1.95 o.p. (ISBN 0-8066-1854-X, 10-7023). Augsburg Fortress.

We Speak for Ourselves: Experiences in Homosexual Counselling. Jack Babuscio. LC 77-78623. 160p. 1977. pap. 1.50 o.p. (ISBN 0-8006-1264-7, 1-1264, Fortress). Augsburg Fortress.

We Survived: Fourteen Histories of the Hidden & Hunted of Nazi Germany. 3rd ed. Eric H. Boehm. 320p. 1985. lib. bdg. 21.00 o.p. (ISBN 0-87436-429-9). ABC-Clio.

We the Creators of Heavens & Earths. Frank R. Wallace. 1987. 17.50 o.p. (ISBN 0-911752-51-X). I & O Pub.

We the People. Richard Halverson. LC 87-4808. 128p. 1987. 15.95 o.s.i. (ISBN 0-8307-1220-8, 5111709). Regal.

We the People. Forrest McDonald. LC 58-14905. (Midway Reprint Ser). xii, 436p. 1976. pap. text ed. 14.00x o.s.i. (ISBN 0-226-55721-9). U of Chicago Pr.

We the People: Congressional Power. Robert Liston. 160p. (gr. 9-12). 1975. text ed. 7.95 o.p. (ISBN 0-07-038067-8). McGraw.

We, the Teachers. Terry Herndon. 192p. 1983. 7.95 o.p. (ISBN 0-8106-1427-8). NEA.

We, the Teachers: Terry Herndon on Education & Democracy. Terry Herndon. LC 83-8597. 192p. 1983. 13.95 o.p. (ISBN 0-932020-20-8); pap. 7.95 o.p. (ISBN 0-932020-21-6). Seven Locks Pr.

We, the Victors. Curtis B. Pepper. LC 83-18481. 312p. 1984. 17.95 o.p. (ISBN 0-385-19122-7). Doubleday.

We Think the World of You. J. R. Ackerley. LC 61-13183. 190p. 1981. pap. 5.95 o.p. (ISBN 0-916870-36-7). Creative Arts Bk.

We Thought We Could Do Anything: Hollywood's Glamorous Days - Behind the Scenes. Henry Ephron. 1977. 8.95 o.p. (ISBN 0-393-07510-9). Norton.

We Touch the Sky. Rod McKuen. 1979. 8.95 o.p. (ISBN 0-671-24828-6); deluxe ed. 15.00 o.p. S&S.

We: Understanding the Psychology of Romantic Love. Robert A. Johnson. LC 83-47725. 144p. 1983. 10.45 o.p. (ISBN 0-06-250435-5). HarpR.

We Walked Very Warily: A History of Women at McGill. Margaret Gillett. (Illus.). 496p. 1981. 18.95 o.p. (ISBN 0-920792-08-1). Eden Pr.

We Were Dreamers. James Lehrer. LC 75-14679. 256p. 1975. 7.95 o.p. (ISBN 0-689-10693-9, Atheneum). Macmillan.

Weak Interaction of Elementary Particles. L. B. Okun. 1965. 80.00 o.p. (ISBN 0-08-011122-X); pap. 80.00 o.p. (ISBN 0-08-013702-4). Pergamon.

Weak Interactions & High Energy Neutrino Physics. Ed. by T. D. Lee. (Italian Physical Society Ser.: Course 32). 1966. 75.00 o.p. (ISBN 0-12-368832-9). Acad Pr.

Weak Interactions & Higher Symmetries: Proceedings. International University Courses on Nuclear Physics, 3rd, Schladming, Austria, 1964. Ed. by P. Urban. (Illus.). 1965. 67.90 o.p. (ISBN 0-387-80746-2). Springer-Verlag.

Wealth & Inequality in Britain. W. D. Rubinstein. (Historical Handbooks Ser.). 1986. pap. 9.95 o.p. (ISBN 0-571-13924-8). Faber & Faber.

Wealth & Poverty. George Gilder. 1987. 13.95 o.p. (ISBN 0-907675-01-8, Pub. by Buchan & Enright England). Seven Hills Bk Dists.

Wealth of Experience: The Lives of Older Women. Susan Hemmings. 192p. (Orig.). 1985. pap. 8.95 o.p. (ISBN 0-86358-031-9). Routledge Chapman & Hall.

Wealth of Self & Wealth of Nations: Self Axis of the Great Ascent. Philip McShane. LC 74-34517. 1975. 8.00 o.p. (ISBN 0-682-48205-6, University). Exposition-Phoenix.

Wealth of the Mind. Wissman. LC 70-137788. 72p. 1971. (ISBN 0-8022-2047-9). Philos Lib.

Wealth Report Two. Ed. by Frank Field. (Inequality in Society Ser.). 200p. (Orig.). 1983. pap. 15.95x o.p. (ISBN 0-7100-9452-3). Routledge Chapman & Hall.

Wealth Transfer of Inflation: How to Compute It, Account for It, & Profit from It. H. Morris Hansen. LC 81-6250. 250p. 1981. 49.50 o.p. (ISBN 0-87624-014-7, Inst Busn Plan). P-H.

Wealth, Walk & Warfare of the Christian. Ruth Paxson. 224p. 1939. 11.95 o.p. (ISBN 0-8007-0340-5). Revell.

Weapon Systems, Nineteen Eighty-Five. (Illus.). 159p. 1985. pap. 8.00 o.p. (ISBN 0-318-11842-4, S/N 008-020-01024-3). USGPO.

Weaponless Defense: A Law Enforcement Guide to Non-Violent Control. Jack Hibbard & Bryan A. Fried. (Illus.). 184p. 1980. spiral bdg. 19.25x o.p. (ISBN 0-398-03936-4). C C Thomas.

Weapons & Armor: A Pictorial Archive of Woodcuts & Engravings. Harold H. Hart. 1983. 14.50 o.p. (ISBN 0-8446-5937-1). Peter Smith.

Weapons & Tactics of the Soviet Army. David C. Isby. (Illus.). 320p. 1981. 34.95 o.p. (ISBN 0-86720-568-7). Janes Info Group.

Weapons & Warfare in Ancient Times. Rivka Gonen. LC 72-10802. (Archaeology Ser.). (Illus.). (gr. 5 up). 1976. PLB 7.95 o.p. (ISBN 0-8225-0832-X). Lerner Pubns.

Weapons of War: Present & Future Weapons, Systems & Strategies. Christy Campbell. LC 83-71621. (Illus.). 304p. 1983. 19.95x o.p. (ISBN 0-911745-13-0). P Bedrick Bks.

Wear of Materials. Ed. by W. A. Glaeser et al. Incl. Wear of Materials, 1979. Ed. by K. C. et al. Ludema. 685p. 1979. 60.00 (H00143); Wear of Materials. Ed. by K. C. Ludema. 1983. pap. text ed. 85.00 (H00254). 585p. 1977. pap. text ed. 50.00 o.p. (ISBN 0-685-81976-0, H00100). ASME.

Wear of Materials see Wear of Materials.

Wear of Materials, 1979 see Wear of Materials.

Wear of Metals. A. D. Sarkar. 1976. 36.00 o.p. (ISBN 0-08-019738-8); pap. 15.25 o.p. (ISBN 0-08-019737-X). Pergamon.

Wearing the Grey: Being Personal Portraits, Scenes & Adventures of the War. John E. Cooke. LC 59-13533. (Indiana University Civil War Centennial Ser.). (Illus.). 1968. Repr. of 1959 ed. 36.00 o.p. (ISBN 0-527-19270-8). Kraus Repr.

Weather. Jan Pienkowski. Ed. by Kate Klimo. (Concept Bks.). (Illus.). 32p. (ps-k). 1983. 4.80 o.s.i. (ISBN 0-671-46245-8, Little Simon). S&S.

Weather Almanac. Ed. by Frank E. Bair & James Ruffner. 1979. pap. 7.95 o.p. (ISBN 0-380-43000-2, 52654-9). Avon.

Weather & Bird Behaviour. Norman Elkins. (Illus.). 320p. 1983. 37.50 o.p. (ISBN 0-85661-035-6, Pub. by T & A D Poyser England). Buteo.

Weather & Climate on Planets. K. Y. Kondratyev & G. E. Hunt. (Illus.). 750p. 1981. 140.00 o.p. (ISBN 0-08-026493-X). Pergamon.

Weather & Flight: An Introduction to Meteorology for Pilots. Ron R. Dickson. 186p. 1982. 16.95 o.p. (ISBN 0-13-947119-7); pap. 7.95 o.p. (ISBN 0-13-947101-4). P-H.

Weather & Us, Bk. 1. Eileen L. Corcoran. (Science Ser.). 1967. pap. 2.25x o.p. (ISBN 0-88323-078-X, 175). Pendergrass Pub.

Weather & Us, Bk. 2. Eileen L. Corcoran. (Science Ser.). 1967. pap. 1.50x o.p. (ISBN 0-88323-079-8, 176). Pendergrass Pub.

Weather Book. Ralph Hardy et al. LC 81-84683. (Illus.). 224p. 1982. 24.95 o.p. (ISBN 0-316-34623-3). Little.

Weather Data Handbook. Ecodyne Corporation Staff. 320p. 1980. text ed. 42.50 o.p. (ISBN 0-07-018960-9). McGraw.

Weather for Outdoorsmen. Walter Dabberdt. (Illus.). 224p. 1981. Encore ed. 4.95 o.p. (ISBN 0-684-16865-0, ScribT). Scribner.

Weather Routing of Ships. R. Motte. 1972. 15.00 o.p. (ISBN 0-540-00382-4). E J Brill USA.

Weather Satellites, Stereoscopy & Sounding: Proceedings of the Topical Meeting of the COSPAR Interdisciplinary Scientific Commission A (Meetings A3 & A4) of the COSPAR 24th Plenary Meeting held in Ottawa, Canada, 16 May-2 June, 1982, Vol. 2/6. Ed. by H. Yates & A. F. Hasler. (Illus.). 190p. 1983. pap. 50.00 o.p. (ISBN 0-08-030428-1). Pergamon.

Weather Works. M. Wilks. 1983. 12.95 o.p. (ISBN 0-03-059591-6). H Holt & Co.

Weather Works. Mike Wilks. LC 82-23306. (Illus.). 32p. (gr. k-2). 1982. 24.95 o.s.i. (ISBN 0-03-062421-5). H Holt & Co.

Weathered Texture Workshop. Richard Bolton. (Illus.). 144p. 1984. 27.50 o.p. (ISBN 0-8230-5697-X). Watson-Guptill.

Weatherman. Ed. by Harold Jacobs. LC 75-132205. (Illus.). 519p. (Orig.). 1971. o. p. 20.00 o.p. (ISBN 0-87867-001-7); pap. 4.95 o.p. (ISBN 0-671-20725-3). Ramparts.

Weathermonger. Date not set. (ISBN 0-385-29450-6). Delacorte.

Weave of Women. E. M. Broner. LC 77-13609. 1978. 8.95 o.p. (ISBN 0-03-018461-4). H Holt & Co.

Weavers & War: A True Story. Richard E. Early. (Illus.). 196p. 1984. 19.95x o.p. (ISBN 0-7102-0186-9). Routledge Chapman & Hall.

Weaver's Craft. L. E. Simpson & M. Weir. (Illus.). 222p. 1984. 20.95 o.s.i. (ISBN 0-85219-130-8, Pub. by Batsford England). David & Charles.

Weaving: A Handbook of Fiber Arts. 2nd ed. Shirley E. Held. LC 77-24219. (Illus.). 384p. 1978. 21.95 o.p. (ISBN 0-03-042821-1, HoltC); pap. 31.95 o.p. (ISBN 0-03-022691-0). H Holt & Co.

Weaving the Sheets: Poems. Judith Root. (Illus.). 1985. 15.00 o.p. (ISBN 0-317-40765-1). Abattoir.

Weaving with Foot-Power Looms. Edward F. Worst. (Illus.). 14.75 o.p. (ISBN 0-8446-5101-X). Peter Smith.

Web. Andrew Harvey. 1987. 16.45 o.s.i. (ISBN 0-395-42921-8). HM.

Web of Angels. John M. Ford. (Orig.). 1980. pap. 2.25 o.s.i. (ISBN 0-671-82947-5, Timescape). PB.

Web of Darkness. Marion Zimmer Bradley. LC 80-22995. 1983. pap. 6.95 o.p. (ISBN 0-89865-032-1, Starblaze). Donning Co.

Web of Light. Marion Zimmer Bradley. LC 82-23456. (Illus., Orig.). 1982. pap. 6.95 o.p. (ISBN 0-89865-162-X, Starblaze). Donning Co.

Web of Space-Time: A Step by Step Exploration of Relativity. Mitch Struble. (Franklin Institute Bk). (Illus.). (gr. 7-10). 1973. 5.95 o.s.i. (ISBN 0-664-32527-0, Westminster); pap. 3.95 o.s.i. (ISBN 0-664-34005-9, Westminster). Westminster John Knox.

Web of the Romulans. M. S. Murdock. (Star Trek Ser.). 224p. 1984. lib. bdg. 10.95 o.p. (ISBN 0-8398-2833-0, Gregg). G K Hall.

Web of Urban Housing. Frank de Leeuw et al. 231p. 1975. 16.95x o.p. (ISBN 0-87766-151-0, 12900); pap. 6.95x o.p. (ISBN 0-87766-150-2, 12700). Urban Inst.

Web of Victory: Grant at Vicksburg. Earl S. Miers. LC 78-1838. (Illus.). 1978. Repr. of 1955 ed. lib. bdg. 25.75 o.p. (ISBN 0-313-20354-7, MIWV). Greenwood.

Web of Violence: A Study of Violence in the Family. Jean Renvoizie. 1978. 19.95x o.p. (ISBN 0-7100-8804-3). Routledge Chapman & Hall.

Web Offset Press Operating. 2 ed. David B. Crouse et al. LC 83-83335. (Illus.). 304p. 1984. 50.00 o.p. (ISBN 0-88362-066-9, 1516). Graphic Arts Tech Found.

Web She Weaves: An Anthology of Mystery & Suspense Stories by Women. Ed. by Marcia Muller & Bill Pronzini. 1985. pap. 9.95 o.p. (ISBN 0-688-04831-5, Quill). Morrow.

Webs of Everywhere. John Brunner. 192p. 1982. pap. 2.25 o.s.i. (ISBN 0-345-30680-5, Del Rey). Ballantine.

Webs of Power: International Cartels & the World Economy. Kurt R. Mirow & Harry Maurer. 525p. 1982. 15.95 o.p. (ISBN 0-395-30536-5). HM.

Webster Illustrated Contemporary Dictionary. 1122p. 1987. (ISBN 0-89434-081-6). Ferguson.

Webster's Dictionary: English-Tagalog, Tagalog-English Dictionary. 455p. 4.50x o.p. (ISBN 968-432-111-2). Colton Bk.

Webster's New World Dictionary. 2nd college ed. 1983. leatherkraft bdg. 17.95 o.p. (ISBN 0-671-47035-3). S&S.

Webster's New World Dictionary. 1987. 16.95 o.p. (ISBN 0-671-41809-2). S&S.

Webster's New World Dictionary: Second College Edition. 1728p. plain-edged 15.95 o.p. (ISBN 0-671-41807-6). S&S.

Webster's New World Thesaurus: LeatherKraft Gift Edition. 688p. 1984. 15.95 o.p. (ISBN 0-671-53095-X). S&S.

Webster's Super New School & Office Dictionary. 1981. pap. 2.95 o.p. (ISBN 0-449-23249-2, Crest). Fawcett.

Wedded or Wedlocked? Peter M. Kalellis. LC 78-73624. (Illus., Orig.). 1979. pap. 2.75 o.p. (ISBN 0-8189-1157-3, 157, Pub. by Alba Bks). Alba.

Wedding Bells. Dunbar H. Ogden. (Orig.). 1945. pap. 3.25 o.p. (ISBN 0-8042-1884-6, John Knox). Westminster John Knox.

Wedding Birds. Jutta Ash. (Joy Street Bk.). (Illus.). (ps-3). 1987. 12.95 o.s.i. (ISBN 0-316-05386-4). Little.

Wedding Day. Joan Solomon. (Illus.). (ps-3). 1981. 9.95 o.p. (ISBN 0-241-10552-8, Pub. by Hamish Hamilton England). David & Charles.

Wedding Day in Literature & Art: A Collection of the Best Descriptions of Wedding from the Works of the World's Leading Novelists & Poets. Charles F. Carter. LC 74-86598. 318p. 1969. Repr. of 1900 ed. 30.00x o.p. (ISBN 0-8103-0154-7). Gale.

Wedding Procession of the Rag Doll & the Broom Handle & Who Was in It. Carl Sandburg. LC 67-10211. (Illus.). (gr. k-3). 1967. 10.95 o.p. (ISBN 0-15-294930-5, HJ). HarBraceJ.

Wedding Resource Directory. M. Susan Portz. 104p. (Orig.). 1987. pap. 7.95 o.p. (ISBN 0-9617718-0-1). Bascom Pr.

Wedding Resource Directory: An Annual Directory of Wedding Services in the Denver-Boulder Area. 2nd ed. M. Susan Portz. (Illus.). 104p. 1988. pap. 7.95 o.p. (ISBN 0-9617718-1-X). Bascom Pr.

Wedding Treasure. David Williams. 224p. 1987. pap. 2.95 o.p. (ISBN 0-380-70258-4). Avon.

Wedlocked. Joyce Sparling 256p. 1984. 15.95 o.p. (ISBN 0-396-08357-9). Dodd.

Wednesday's Children. Leontine Young. LC 63-23464. 1971. pap. text ed. 4.95 o.p. (ISBN 0-07-072559-4). McGraw.

Wee Peter Puffin. 3rd ed. Jane Weinberger. LC 84-51988. (Illus.). 40p. (gr. k-8). 1984. 9.95 o.p. (ISBN 0-932433-03-0). Windswept Hse.

Wee Sing & Play. Pamela Beall & Susan Nipp. (Illus.). 64p. (Orig.). 1981. pap. 2.25 o.p. (ISBN 0-8431-0391-4). Price Stern.

Wee Sing Silly Songs. Pamela Beall. (Illus.). 64p. (Orig.). 1982. pap. 2.25 o.p. (ISBN 0-8431-0310-8). Price Stern.

Weed-Crop Ecology: Principles in Weed Management. R. J. Aldrich. text ed. (ISBN 0-534-02833-0). PWS-Kent Pub.

Weed for Burning. Conrad Detrez. Tr. by Lydia Davis. LC 83-22844. 256p. 1984. 13.95 o.p. (ISBN 0-15-195596-4). HarbraceJ.

Weed King & Other Stories. Jack Conroy. LC 85-5438. 312p. 1985. 17.95 o.p. (ISBN 0-88208-185-3); pap. 9.95 o.p. (ISBN 0-88208-186-1). Chicago Review.

Weeding Library Collections II. 2nd, rev. ed. Stanley J. Slote. LC 81-20724. 198p. 1982. text ed. 23.50 o.p. (ISBN 0-87287-283-1). Libs Unl.

Weeding of Covent Garden & the Sparagus Garden. Richard Brome. Ed. by Donald S. McClure & Stephen Orgel. LC 79-54351. (Renaissance Drama Second Ser.). 438p. 1980. lib. bdg. 61.00 o.p. (ISBN 0-8240-4468-1). Garland Pub.

Weedy Rough. Douglas C. Jones. LC 80-28297. 352p. 1981. 13.95 o.s.i. (ISBN 0-03-050931-9). H Holt & Co.

Weegee's New York: Photographs, Nineteen Thirty-Five to Nineteen Sixty. (Illus.). 334p. 1984. 60.00 o.s.i. (ISBN 0-394-53875-7). Grove.

Week As Andrea Benstock. Jill Emerson. LC 74-18161. 1975. 7.95 o.p. (ISBN 0-87795-100-4, Arbor Hse). Morrow.

Weekday Early Education: Art Idea Book. Patricia Elkins. LC 77-87252. (Illus.). 1978. spiral bdg 8.50 o.p. (ISBN 0-8054-4919-1, 4249-19). Broadman.

Weekend Adventures for City-Weary People: Overnight Trips in Northern California. rev. ed. Carole T. Meyers. LC 83-26139. (Weekend Adventures for City-Weary People in the U. S. A. Ser.). (Illus.). 1984. pap. 11.95 o.p. (ISBN 0-917120-07-8). Carousel Pr.

Weekend Escapes: Southeast. Ed. by Mike Michaelson. (Illus.). 352p. 1986. pap. 6.95 o.p. (ISBN 0-528-84091-6). Rand McNally.

Weekend Escapes: Southeast Texas. Ed. by Mike Michaelson. (Illus.). 351p. 1986. pap. 6.95 o.p. (ISBN 0-528-84093-2). Rand McNally.

Weekend Escapes: Southern California. Ed. by Mike Michaelson. (Illus.). 352p. 1986. pap. 6.95 o.p. (ISBN 0-528-84095-9). Rand McNally.

Weekend Getaway Guide: Chicago. 3rd ed. Mike Michaelson. LC 79-88688. (Illus.). 1984. pap. 5.95 o.p. (ISBN 0-528-84752-X). Rand McNally.

Weekend in Dinlock. Clancy Sigal. 1976. pap. 1.65 o.p. (ISBN 0-380-01463-7, 12229, Bard). Avon.

Weekend Projects for the Radio Amateur, Vol. 1. Ed. by Marian S. Anderson. LC 79-89723. 61p. 1979. pap. 3.00 o.p. (ISBN 0-87259-816-0). Am Radio.

Weekend Real Estate Investor: The New Low-Risk Team Approach That Transforms Everyday Opportunities into Big Profits. Weston P. Hatfield. 1978. text ed. 9.95 o.p. (ISBN 0-07-027023-6). McGraw.

Weekend Visit. LC 84-73542. 1985. pap. 5.95 o.s.i. (ISBN 0-394-62014-3, E-986, Ever). Grove.

Weekender's Guide to the Four Seasons. Robert Shosteck. 490p. 1984. pap. 8.95 o.p. (ISBN 0-88289-451-X). Pelican.

Weekly Compact Sets. K. Floret. (Lecture Notes in Mathematics Ser.: Vol. 801). 123p. 1980. pap. 13.00 o.p. (ISBN 0-387-09991-3). Springer-Verlag.

Weep & Know Why. Elisabeth Ogilvie. 1976. pap. 1.75 o.p. (ISBN 0-380-00621-9, 29009). Avon.

Weep Not for Anger: A Novel of a Slavic-American Family in New England. J. G. Lohsen. 1979. 8.50 o.p. (ISBN 0-682-49219-1). Exposition-Phoenix.

Weep Not for Me. John V. Taylor. LC 86-71639. 64p. 1987. pap. 3.95 o.p. (ISBN 0-89622-313-2). Twenty-Third.

Weeping in Ramah. J. R. Lucas. LC 85-70477. 250p. (Orig.). 1985. pap. 7.95 o.p. (ISBN 0-89107-357-4, Crossway Bks). Good News.

WEESKA Patenets. Konold et al. (What Every Engineer Should Know Ser.). 200p. 1988. 39.75 o.p. (ISBN 0-8247-8010-8). Dekker.

Weg Zum Lesen. 2nd ed. Van Horn Vail & Kimberly Sparks. 254p. 1974. 12.00 o.p. (ISBN 0-15-595152-1, HC). HarBraceJ.

Weighing an Elephant. 1981. pap. 3.95 o.p. (ISBN 0-8351-0893-7). China Bks.

Weight Training & Conditioning for Basketball. Robert V. Wilcox. LC 86-71206. (Illus.). 88p. (Orig.). (YA) (gr. 10 up). 1986. pap. 8.00 o.p. (ISBN 1-55618-006-3). Brunswick Pub.

Weight Training for Baseball. Robert V. Wilcox. LC 87-72624. (Illus.). 120p. (Orig.). 1987. pap. 8.00 o.p. (ISBN 1-55618-029-2). Brunswick Pub.

Weight Training for Football. Robert V. Wilcox. LC 86-70138. (Illus.). 98p. (Orig.). (YA) (gr. 10-12). 1986. pap. 8.00 o.p. (ISBN 0-931494-88-5). Brunswick Pub.

Weight Training for the Young Athlete. Frederick C. Hatfield. LC 79-55614. (Illus.). 120p. (gr. 5 up). 1982. 9.95 o.p. (ISBN 0-689-11041-3, Atheneum); pap. 6.95 o.p. (ISBN 0-689-70632-4, 285). Macmillan.

Weight Training for Young Athletes. Franco Columbu et al. 1979. 9.95 o.p. (ISBN 0-8092-7479-5); pap. 6.95 o.p. (ISBN 0-8092-7478-7). Contemp Bks.

Weight Training in Athletics. Rev. ed. Jim Murray & Peter Karpovich. (Illus.). 216p. 1983. 12.95 o.p. (ISBN 0-13-947978-3); text ed. 12.95 o.p. (ISBN 0-13-948018-8); pap. 7.95 o.p. (ISBN 0-13-948000-5). P-H.

Weight Training in Sports: A Bibliography with Special Reference to Body-Building & Olympic Power Lifting. Donald D. Macchia. LC 83-48256. 108p. 1984. lib. bdg. 18.00 o.p. (ISBN 0-8240-9103-5). Garland Pub.

Weights & Measures. J. T. Graham. (Shire Album Ser.: No. 44). (Illus.). 32p. (Orig.). 1983. pap. 2.95 o.p. (ISBN 0-85263-479-X, Pub. by Shire Pubns England). Seven Hills Bk Dists.

Weil's Representation & the Spectrum of the Metaplectic Group. S. S. Gelbart. (Lecture Notes in Mathematics: Vol. 530). 1976. soft cover 13.00 o.p. (ISBN 0-387-07799-5). Springer-Verlag.

Weimar Republic: A Historical Bibliography. LC 83-21522. (Research Guides Ser.: No. 9). 285p. 1984. lib. bdg. 34.00 o.p. (ISBN 0-87436-378-0). ABC-Clio.

Weird & Wonderful Science Facts. Magnus Pyke. LC 83-24288. (Illus.). 128p. (gr. 5 up). 1984. 10.95 o.p. (ISBN 0-8069-4688-1); PLB 12.49 o.p. (ISBN 0-8069-4689-X). Sterling.

Weirdstone of Brinsingamen. Alan Garner. 1981. pap. 1.95 o.s.i. (ISBN 0-345-29043-7, Del Rey). Ballantine.

Welcome! Thomas Shapcott. LC 83-5857. 95p. 1984. 15.95 o.p. (ISBN 0-7022-1922-3); pap. 7.95 o.p. (ISBN 0-7022-1932-0). U of Queensland Pr.

Welcome Baby: Patchwork & Applique Projects for Infants & Toddlers. Betsy Potter & Jill Jarnow. (Illus.). 160p. 1986. 19.95 o.p. (ISBN 0-684-18397-8). Scribner.

Welcome Home, Charlie. Louise Kantenwein. (Illus.). 64p. (gr. 2 up). 1981. 5.00 o.p. (ISBN 0-682-49681-2). Exposition-Phoenix.

Welcome the Stranger. Carol Greene. (Illus.). (gr. k-4). 1984. 5.57 o.p. (ISBN 0-570-04105-8, 561497). Concordia.

Welcome to Flying: A Primer for Pilots. Don Dwiggins. (Illus.). 224p. (Orig.). 1984. pap. 13.60 o.p. (ISBN 0-8306-2362-0, 2362P). TAB Bks.

Welcome to Hard Times. E. L. Doctorow. 224p. 1976. pap. 2.95 o.s.i. (ISBN 0-553-14189-9, 14189-9). Bantam.

Welcome to Paradise. Rose A. Forrest. (Illus.). 96p. 1981. pap. 1.95 o.p. (ISBN 0-380-76901-8, 76901). Avon.

Welcome to the Monkey House. Kurt Vonnegut, Jr. 302p. 1970. pap. 9.95 o.p. (ISBN 0-385-29127-2, Delta). Dell.

Welcome to the Monkey House. Date not set. pap. (ISBN 0-385-29127-2). Delacorte.

Welcome to the Stork Club. Mearle L. Allen. LC 79-5424. 300p. 1980. 14.95 o.s.i. (ISBN 0-498-02395-8). A S Barnes.

Welcoming Silence. D. Scott Rogo. 7.95 o.p. (ISBN 0-8216-0206-3, Pub. by Univ Bks). Carol Pub Group.

Welcoming Your Second Baby. Vicki Lansky. 1984. pap. 2.95 o.p. (ISBN 0-553-34071-9). Bantam.

Welding & Brazing Qualifications. (Boiler & Pressure Vessel Code Ser.: Sec. 9). 1980. 60.00 o.p. (ISBN 0-685-76828-7, P00090); pap. 185.00 loose-leaf o.p. (ISBN 0-685-76829-5, V00090). ASME.

Welding & Cutting Safety. Resource Systems International Staff. 1982. pap. text ed. 15.00 o.p. (ISBN 0-686-32085-9, Reston). P-H.

Welding & Welding Technology. Richard L. Little. 1973. text ed. 43.95 o.p. (ISBN 0-07-038095-3). McGraw.

Welding: Blueprint Reading. Resource Systems International Staff. 1982. pap. text ed. 15.00 o.p. (ISBN 0-8359-8617-9, Reston). P-H.

Welding: Design, Testing, & Inspection. Resource Systems International Staff. 1982. pap. text ed. 15.00 o.p. (ISBN 0-8359-8618-7, Reston). P-H.

Welding in Energy-Related Projects: Proceedings of the International Conference on Welding in Energy-Related Projects; Toronto, Canada, September 20-21, 1983. Ed. by Welding Institute of Canada. (Illus.). 502p. 1984. 130.00x o.p. (ISBN 0-08-025412-8). Pergamon.

Welding: Performance Qualifications. Resource Systems International Staff. 1982. pap. text ed. 15.00 o.p. (ISBN 0-8359-8620-9, Reston). P-H.

Welding: Principles & Applications. Larry Jeffus & Harold Johnson. LC 83-71046. 1984. text ed. 29.95 o.p. (ISBN 0-8273-1806-5). Delmar.

Welding: Principles & Practice. Henry Horwitz. LC 77-76341. (Illus.). 1979. text ed. 30.50 o.p. (ISBN 0-395-24473-0). HM.

Welfare: A Handbook for Friend & Foe. Timothy J. Sampson. LC 72-8551. 1972. pap. 5.95 o.p. (ISBN 0-8298-0255-X). Pilgrim NY.

Welfare Analysis of Policies Affecting Prices & Products. Robert D. Willig. LC 78-75051. (Outstanding Dissertations in Economics). 1980. lib. bdg. 24.00 o.p. (ISBN 0-8240-4129-1). Garland Pub.

Welfare, Capitalism & After. Date not set. (ISBN 0-8052-3868-9). Random.

Welfare Economics & Peak Load Pricing: A Theoretical Application to Municipal Water Utility Practices. Robert Lee Greene. LC 75-631068. (University of Florida Social Sciences Monographs: No. 42). (Illus.). 1970. pap. 3.50 o.p. (ISBN 0-8130-0309-1). U Presses Fla.

Welfare Economics & Subsidy Programs. Milton Z. Kafoglis. LC 62-62830. (University of Florida Social Sciences Monographs: No. 11). 1961. pap. 3.50 o.p. (ISBN 0-8130-0125-0). U Presses Fla.

Welfare Economics: Introduction & Development of Basic Concepts. Yew-Kwang Ng. LC 79-22797. 332p. 1980. text ed. 36.95x o.p. (ISBN 0-470-26886-7). Halsted Pr.

Welfare Mother. Susan Sheehan. LC 76-13439. 1976. 8.95 o.p. (ISBN 0-395-24505-2). HM.

Welfare Mothers Speak Out: We Ain't Gonna Shuffle Anymore. Milwaukee County Welfare Rights Organization. (Illus.). 192p. 1972. pap. 2.95 o.p. (ISBN 0-393-01073-2). Norton.

Welfare of Nations. Michele Fiore. 1955. (ISBN 0-8022-0502-X). Philos Lib.

Welfare of the Poor. Mary B. Sanger. LC 79-20923. 1979. 26.50 o.p. (ISBN 0-12-618650-2). Acad Pr.

Welfare on Skid Row. Beatrice Garrett. 1974. 6.00 o.p. (ISBN 0-682-47611-0). Exposition-Phoenix.

Welfare, Power, & Juvenile Justice: The Social Control of Delinquent Youth. Robert Harris & David Webb. LC 86-23148. (ISBN 0-422-60460-7, Tavistock Pubns). Routledge Chapman & Hall.

Welfare Rights-the Local Authorities Role. Anne Howard. 52p. 1978. pap. text ed. 4.50x o.p. (ISBN 0-7199-0946-5, Pub. by Bedford England). Gower Pub Co.

Welfare State & Canadian Federalism. Keith G. Banting. 216p. 1982. 22.50x o.p. (ISBN 0-7735-0380-3, McGill Canada); pap. 12.95c o.p. (ISBN 0-7735-0384-6, McGill Canada). U of Toronto Pr.

Well. Jack Cady. LC 80-67623. 1980. 11.95 o.p. (ISBN 0-87795-287-6, Arbor Hse). Morrow.

Well. Jack Cady. 208p. 1982. pap. 2.50 o.p. (ISBN 0-380-57901-4, 57901). Avon.

Well. Gene Kemp. (Illus.). 90p. (gr. 4-8). 1984. 11.95 o.p. (ISBN 0-571-13284-7). Faber & Faber.

Well Adult, Vol. 1. Angelina Frantz. (RN Nursing Assessment Ser.). 152p. 1982. pap. 15.95 o.p. (ISBN 0-87489-281-3). Med Economics.

Well-Being Guide to Health Spas in North America. Melissa Schnirring. LC 82-45311. 160p. 1982. pap. 6.95 o.p. (ISBN 0-689-11195-9, Atheneum). Macmillan.

Well-Bound Words: A Rhetoric. John J. Ruszkiewicz. 1981. text ed. write for info. o.p. (ISBN 0-673-15355-X). Scott F.

Well, Dearie! The Letters of Edward Burra. Edward Burra. Ed. by William Chappell. (Illus.). 224p. (Orig.). 1986. 29.95 o.p. (ISBN 0-918825-35-0, Dist. by Kampmann & Co.). Moyer Bell Limited.

Well Family: A Developmental Approach to Assessment. Judith H. Kandzari & Joan R. Howard. 15.00 o.p. (ISBN 0-316-48269-2). Little.

Well Family Book. Charles T. Kuntzleman. 256p. 1985. 13.95 o.p. (ISBN 0-89840-092-9). Heres Life.

We'll Have a Friend for Lunch. Jane Flory. LC 73-18452. (Illus.). 32p. (gr. k-3). 1974. 6.95 o.p. (ISBN 0-395-18448-7). HM.

We'll Laugh about This... Someday. Ann Combs. LC 83-45067. 320p. 1983. 14.95 o.s.i. (ISBN 0-689-11393-5, Atheneum). Macmillan.

Well-Mannered Balloon. Nancy Willard. LC 75-29158. (Illus.). 32p. (gr. k-3). 1976. 5.50 o.s.i. (ISBN 0-15-294985-2, HJ). HarBraceJ.

Well Met by Witchlight. Nina Beachcroft. LC 73-75430. (gr. 3-7). 1973. PLB 5.95 o.p. (ISBN 0-689-30414-5, Atheneum). Macmillan.

Well of the Unicorn. George U Fletcher. Ed. by Lester Del Ray. LC 75-405. (Library of Science Fiction). 1975. lib. bdg. 21.00 o.p. (ISBN 0-8240-1410-3). Garland Pub.

Well-Seasoned Marriage. Nina S. Fields. 174p. 1986. 18.95 o.p. (ISBN 0-89876-114-X). Gardner Pr.

Well-Tempered Clavier by Johann Sebastian Bach. Hermann Keller. Tr. by Leigh Gerdine. 1977. 18.50 o.p. (ISBN 0-393-02187-4). Norton.

Well-Tempered Lyre: Songs & Verse of the Temperance Movement. George W. Ewing. LC 77-8523. (No. 5). (Illus.). 308p. 1977. 15.00x o.p. (ISBN 0-87074-000-8). SMU Press.

Well-Wishers. Edward Eager. LC 60-6209. (Illus.). (gr. 3-7). 1960. 5.50 o.p. (ISBN 0-15-294991-7, HJ). HarBraceJ.

Wellington Commander: The Iron Duke's Generalship. Paddy Griffith et al. 224p. 1986. 45.00 o.p. (ISBN 0-907319-08-4). Faber & Faber.

Wellington: Mainstay of Bomber Command. Peter G. Cooksley. (Illus.). 176p. 1987. pap. 19.95 o.p. (ISBN 0-85059-851-6, Pub. by PSL P Stephens England). Sterling.

Wellington's Army, Eighteen Hundred Nine to Eighteen Fourteen. Charles Oman. 395p. 1986. 25.00 o.p. (ISBN 0-947898-41-7). Kraus Repr.

Wellness R.S.V.P. Robert F. Valois et al. 1986. 9.95 o.p. (ISBN 0-8053-2297-3). Benjamin-Cummings.

Wells & Water Supply. John Vince. (Shire Album: No. 36). (Illus.). 32p. (Orig.). pap. 2.95 o.p. (ISBN 0-85263-441-2, Pub. by Shire Pubns England). Seven Hills Bk Dists.

Wellspring. Janice H. Giles. LC 75-15989. 272p. 1975. 8.95 o.p. (ISBN 0-395-20731-2). HM.

Wellspring. Edward Hawkins. 1978. text ed. 9.95 o.p. (ISBN 0-07-027295-6). McGraw.

Wellsprings of Democracy. John M. Brewer. 1952. (ISBN 0-8022-0172-5). Philos Lib.

Welsh Corgi. Margaret A. Cole. (Bartholomew Pet Care Ser.). (Illus.). 96p. (Orig.). 1981. pap. text ed. 5.00x o.p. (ISBN 0-7028-8490-1, Pub. by J Bartholomew & Sons). Kathleen Rais.

Welsh Dylan. John Ackerman. (Illus.). 143p. 1982. pap. 6.95 o.p. (ISBN 0-586-08350-2, Pub. by Granada England). Academy Chi Pubs.

Welsh in Their History. Gwyn A. Williams. (Illus.). 218p. 1982. 26.00 o.p. (ISBN 0-7099-2739-8, Pub. by Croom Helm Ltd); pap. 11.95 o.p. (ISBN 0-7099-3651-6). Routledge Chapman & Hall.

Welsh People: Chapters on Their Origin, History, Laws, Language, Literature & Characteristics. 4th ed. John Rhys & David B. Jones. 1969. Repr. of 1906 ed. lib. bdg. 35.00x o.p. (ISBN 0-8371-1960-X, RHWP). Greenwood.

Welsh Proverbs with English Translations. Henry H. Vaughan. LC 68-17945. 386p. (Eng. & Welsh.). 1969. Repr. of 1889 ed. 43.00x o.p. (ISBN 0-8103-3205-1). Gale.

Welty's Book of Procedures for Meetings, Boards, Committees & Officers. Joe Welty. 1982. 9.95 o.p. (ISBN 0-89803-086-2, Dist. by Kampmann). Green Hill.

Wembley & the Soggy Map. Louise Gikow. LC 85-18959. (Illus.). 32p. (ps-2). 1986. 4.95 o.s.i. (ISBN 0-03-007242-5). H Holt & Co.

Wembley Fraggle & the Magic Stone. Louise Gikow. LC 86-4638. (Fraggle Rock Bks.). (Illus.). 32p. (gr. k-3). 1986. 4.95 o.s.i. (ISBN 0-8050-0069-0). H Holt & Co.

Wembley's Egg. Laura Phillips. LC 84-15851. (Illus.). 48p. (gr. 1-4). 1985. 7.95 o.s.i. (ISBN 0-03-003262-8). H Holt & Co.

Wendell & Ann Phillips: The Community of Reform 1840-1880. Irving H. Bartlett. (Illus.). 1981. 17.95 o.p. (ISBN 0-393-01426-6). Norton.

Wendell Phillips, Brahmin Radical. Irving H. Bartlett. LC 73-11849. 438p. 1973. Repr. of 1961 ed. lib. bdg. 22.50x o.p. (ISBN 0-8371-7071-0, BAWP). Greenwood.

Wendy Dilemma: When Women Stop Mothering Their Men. Dan Kiley. LC 84-12325. 256p. 1984. 15.95 o.p. (ISBN 0-87795-625-1, Arbor Hse). Morrow.

Wendy Ramshaw. Shirley Bury. (Illus.). 60p. (Orig.). 1984. pap. 9.95 o.p. (ISBN 0-905209-27-3, Pub. by Victoria & Albert Mus UK). Faber & Faber.

Wer ist das? 144p. pap. 2.50 o.p. (ISBN 3-581-66118-7). Langenscheidt.

Were Ancient Heresies Disguised Social Movements? A. H. Jones. Ed. by Clarence L. Lee. LC 66-11534. (Facet Bks.). 1966. pap. 0.50 o.p. (ISBN 0-8006-3023-8, 1-3023, Fortress). Augsburg Fortress.

We're Still Here: The Rise, Fall & Resurrection of the South Bronx. Jill Jonnes. Ed. by Peter Davison. LC 85-47632. (Illus.). 1986. 19.95 o.p. (ISBN 0-87113-020-3). Atlantic Monthly.

Were Those the Days? H. C. Barnard. 1970. 17.25 o.p. (ISBN 0-08-007107-4). Pergamon.

Were We Controlled. 4.95 o.p. (ISBN 0-8216-0175-X, Pub. by Univ Bks). Carol Pub Group.

Were You There. rev. ed. Tom Houston. Ed. by Kathi Mills. LC 86-29801. Orig. Title: Characters Around the Cross. 175p. (Orig.). 1987. 11.95 o.s.i. (ISBN 0-8307-1230-5, 5111739). Regal.

Werefox. Elizabeth Coatsworth. LC 74-20675. Orig. Title: Pure Magic. (Illus.). 80p. (gr. 3-6). 1975. pap. 1.25 o.s.i. (ISBN 0-02-042760-3, Collier). Macmillan.

Wereling. David Robbins. 336p. 1983. pap. 3.50 o.p. (ISBN 0-8439-2032-7, Pub. by Leisure Bks CT). Dorchester Pub Co.

Werewolf. Richard Corben. (Illus.). 76p. 1985. 12.95 o.p. (ISBN 0-87416-007-3). Catalan Communs.

Werewolf! Bill Pronzini. 1979. 12.95 o.p. (ISBN 0-87795-210-8, Arbor Hse). Morrow.

Werewolf. Montague Summers. 1966. 10.00 o.p. (ISBN 0-8216-0040-0, Pub. by Univ Bks). Carol Pub Group.

Werewolf Family. Jack Gantos. (Illus.). (gr. k-3). 1980. PLB 8.95 o.p. (ISBN 0-395-28760-X). HM.

Werther see Sorrows of Young Werther.

West. rev. ed. Jerry E. Jennings. LC 78-54256. (United States Ser.). (Illus.). (gr. 5 up). 1979. text ed. 9.93 o.p. (ISBN 0-88296-077-6); tchr's. annotated ed. 13.68 o.p. (ISBN 0-88296-347-3). Gateway Pr MI.

West African Narrow Strip Weaving. Venice Lamb & Alastair Lamb. Ed. by Patricia Fiske. (Illus.). 48p. 1975. pap. 6.00 o.p. (ISBN 0-685-56285-9). Textile Mus.

West American Cenozoic Echinoidea. Ulysses S. Grant, IV & L. G. Hertlein. 1967. Repr. of 1938 ed. 23.00 o.p. (ISBN 0-384-09680-8). Johnson Repr.

West & Southwest Wind Atlas. De Harpporte. 1983. 24.95 o.p. (ISBN 0-442-21823-0). Van Nos Reinhold.

West Bank Story. Rafik Halibi. Tr. by Ina Friedman from Hebrew. LC 81-47900. 312p. 1982. 12.95 o.p. (ISBN 0-15-195741-X). HarBraceJ.

West by East: The American West in the Gilded Age. Gene M. Gressley. (Charles Redd Monographs in Western History: No. 1). 54p. 1972. pap. 2.50 o.p. (ISBN 0-941214-30-3, Dist. by Signature Bks). C Redd Ctr.

West Coast Bed & Breakfast Guide: California-Oregon-Washington. Courtia Worth & Terry Berger. 1986. pap. 12.95 o.p. (ISBN 0-671-62946-8). P-H.

West Country Historic Houses & Their Families, Vol. 2: Dorset, Wiltshire & N. Somerset. Eric R. Delderfield. 16.95 o.p. (ISBN 0-7153-4910-4). David & Charles.

West Federal Taxation: Comprehensive Volume, 1988. William H. Hoffman, Jr. 1100p. 1987. text ed. 51.00 o.p. (ISBN 0-314-34511-6). West Pub.

West from Abilene. Al Cody. (Gunsmoke Western Ser.). 176p. 1988. text ed. 12.95x o.p. (ISBN 0-85997-852-4, Pub. by Firecrest Pub Ltd). Prescott Pr NH.

Titles

West German Politics. Geoffrey K. Roberts. LC 77-185875. 206p. 1972. 10.95 o.s.i. (ISBN 0-8008-8151-6); pap. 5.95 o.s.i. (ISBN 0-8008-8152-4). Taplinger.

West Germany: A European & Global Power. Wilfied L. Kohl & Giorgio Basevi. (Illus.). 240p. 1980. 22.00x o.p. (ISBN 0-669-03162-3). Lexington Bks.

West Highland Railway. John Thomas. (Illus.). 198p. 1984. 24.95 o.p. (ISBN 0-946537-14-3). David & Charles.

West Highland White Terrier. 2nd ed. Barbara Hands. (Pet Care Ser.). (Illus.). 95p. (Orig.). 1984. pap. 5.00 o.p. (ISBN 0-7028-1074-6, Pub. by J Bartholomew & Son). Kathleen Rais.

West Indian Literature. Ed. by Bruce King. LC 79-1255. 247p. 1980. 23.00 o.p. (ISBN 0-208-01814-X, Archon). Shoe String.

West Indian Slavery: Selected Pamphlets. LC 75-100310. 1816-27. Repr. 35.00x o.p. (ISBN 0-8371-2954-0, WEI&, Pub. by Negro U Pr). Greenwood.

West Indian Stories. Ed. by Andrew Salkey. 224p. (Orig.). 1968. pap. 4.95 o.p. (ISBN 0-571-08630-6). Faber & Faber.

West Indies: Their Social & Religious Condition. Edward B. Underhill. LC 73-107525. 1971. Repr. of 1862 ed. lib. bdg. 24.75x o.p. (ISBN 0-8371-3772-1, UWI&). Greenwood.

West of Eden. Harry Harrison. LC 84-6306. 496p. 1984. 15.95 o.p. (ISBN 0-553-05065-6). Bantam.

West of Ireland. Sean Jennett. (Illus.). 1980. 14.95 o.p. (ISBN 0-393-01338-3). Norton.

West of Omaha. Les Wayne. (Orig.). 1981. pap. 1.75 o.p. (ISBN 0-8439-0925-0, Pub. by Leisure Bks CT). Dorchester Pub Co.

West of Wichita: Settling the High Plains of Kansas, 1865-1890. Craig Miner. (Illus.). 312p. pap. 9.95 o.p. (ISBN 0-7006-0364-6). U Pr of KS.

West of Wichita: Settling the High Plains of Kansas, 1865-1890. Craig Miner. LC 85-26013. (Illus.). viii, 304p. 1988. pap. 9.95 o.p. (ISBN 0-317-67991-0). U Pr of KS.

West Point Fitness & Diet Book. James L. Anderson & Martin Cohen. 1978. pap. 3.95 o.p. (ISBN 0-380-01894-2, 37242-8). Avon.

West Point Fitness & Diet Book. James L. Anderson & Martin Cohen. 256p. 1981. pap. 2.95 o.p. (ISBN 0-380-54205-6, 54205-6). Avon.

West to Eden. Gloria Goldreich. 384p. 1987. 18.95 o.p. (ISBN 0-02-544400-X). Macmillan.

West Virginia: Agency. 8.50 o.p. (ISBN 0-686-90438-9). Am Law Inst.

West Virginia Business Directory, 1988-89. American Directory Publishing Co., Inc. Staff. 500p. (Orig.). 1988. pap. 100.00 o.p. (ISBN 0-944316-32-8). Amer Directory.

West Virginia: Conflict of Laws. 8.50 o.p. (ISBN 0-686-90927-5). Am Law Inst.

West Virginia: Contracts. 8.50 o.p. (ISBN 0-686-90442-7). AM Law Inst.

West Virginia History: Bibliography & Guide to Studies. Harold M. Forbes. 359p. 1981. 9.00 o.p. (ISBN 0-937058-03-3). West Va U Pr.

West Virginia Practice Handbook. 2nd ed. Ed. by Duke N. Stern & Karen G. Sampson. 1058p. 1977. 60.00 o.p. (ISBN 0-87215-195-6). Michie Co.

West Virginia Rules Annotated. Michie Company Editorial Staff. 996p. 1986. 35.00x o.p. (ISBN 0-87215-968-X). Michie Co.

West Virginian's View of Musical Life Yesterday & Today with Successful Techniques for Teaching Band Instruments. Randolph E. Spencer. 208p. 1982. 12.00 o.p. (ISBN 0-682-49854-8). Exposition-Phoenix.

West Wandering Wind. Carl W. Breihan & W. R. Garwood. LC 85-24605. (Double D Western Ser.). 192p. 1986. 12.95 o.p. (ISBN 0-385-23504-6). Doubleday.

West Wind: The Life Story of Joseph Reddeford Walker. Douglas S. Watson. LC 81-50578. (Illus.). 1984. 32.50 o.p. (ISBN 0-930704-09-6). Sagebrush Pr.

West Wind Wild. Carolyn Vaughter. 416p. (Orig.). 1981. pap. 2.95 o.p. (ISBN 0-380-78691-5, 78691). Avon.

Westchester County, a Pictorial History. Susan C. Swanson & Elizabeth G. Fuller. LC 81-3133. (Illus.). 1981. 25.00 o.p. (ISBN 0-915585-01-4). Harbor Hill Bks.

Westering Man: The Life of Joseph Walker. Bil Gilbert. LC 82-69128. 352p. 1983. 17.95 o.p. (ISBN 0-689-11241-6, Atheneum). Macmillan.

Western Alliance: European American Relations since 1945. Alfred Grosser. 416p. 1980. 19.50 o.p. (ISBN 0-8264-0004-3). Continuum.

Western American Writing: Tradition & Promise. Jay Gurian. LC 74-82195. 1975. lib. bdg. 25.00 o.p. (ISBN 0-912112-04-2). Everett-Edwards.

Western Australia: A History from Its Discovery to the Inauguration of the Commonwealth. J. S. Battye. LC 79-670401. 1979. 35.00x o.p. (ISBN 0-85564-136-3, Pub. by U of W Austral Pr). Intl Spec Bk.

Western Campgrounds & Trailer Parks see Campground & Trailer Park Guide: U. S. Canada - Mexico.

Western Civilization, Vol. 1. William Hughes. LC 82-645823. (Annual Editions Ser.). (Illus.). 224p. 1987. pap. text ed. 9.95 o.p. (ISBN 0-87967-678-7). Dushkin Pub.

Western Civilization, Vol. 2. 4th ed. William Hughes. (Annual Editions Ser.). (Illus.). 224p. 1987. pap. text ed. 9.95 o.p. (ISBN 0-87967-679-5). Dushkin Pub.

Western Civilization: A Concise History, 1 vol. ed. Marvin Perry et al. LC 80-82843. (Illus.). 704p. 1981. pap. 28.50 o.p. (ISBN 0-395-29313-8). HM.

Western Civilizations. 8th ed. Edward M. Burns. (Illus.). 990p. 1973. text ed. 14.95x o.p. (ISBN 0-393-09343-3); Vol. 1. pap. text ed. 9.95 o.p. (ISBN 0-393-09351-4); Vol. 2. pap. text ed. 9.95 o.p. (ISBN 0-393-09364-6). Norton.

Western Coast. Paula Fox. 1973. pap. 1.50 o.p. (ISBN 0-380-01614-1, 17897). Avon.

Western Europe after Hitler. B. J. Elliot. (Modern Times Ser.). (Illus.). 162p. (Orig.). (gr. 9-12). 1968. pap. text ed. 4.95 o.p. (ISBN 0-582-20436-4). Longman.

Western Europe Today. V. N. Shenayev. 478p. 1980. 11.00 o.p. (ISBN 0-8285-2001-1, Pub. by Progress Pubs USSR). Imported Pubns.

Western Films: An Annotated Critical Bibliography. John Nachbar. LC 75-6696. (Reference Library of Humanities: Vol. 17). 110p. 1975. lib. bdg. 25.00 o.p. (ISBN 0-8240-1086-8). Garland Pub.

Western Garden Book. (Illus.). 512p. 1979. pap. 14.95 o.p. Sunset-Lane.

Western Greek Land: Use & City-Planning in the Archaic Period. Guy P. Metraux. LC 77-94709. (Outstanding Dissertations in the Fine Arts Ser.). 1978. lib. bdg. 25.00 o.p. (ISBN 0-8240-3241-1). Garland Pub.

Western Hemisphere Idea: Its Rise & Decline. Ed. by Arthur P. Whitaker. (Paperback Ser.). 204p. 1965. pap. 5.95x o.p. (ISBN 0-8014-9001-4). Cornell U Pr.

Western Iowa Prehistory. Facsimile ed. Duane Anderson. (Illus.). 86p. 1975. 6.95x o.p. (ISBN 0-8138-2223-8). Iowa St U Pr.

Western Lawmen. Frank Surge. LC 68-30568. (Pull Ahead Bks.). (Illus.). 64p. (gr. 5-10). 1969. PLB 5.95 o.p. (ISBN 0-8225-0451-0). Lerner Pubns.

Western Literature: Themes & Writers. 2nd ed. G. Robert Carlsen et al. (Themes & Writers Ser.). (Illus.). 768p. (gr. 12). 1972. text ed. 25.72 o.p. (ISBN 0-07-009906-5). McGraw.

Western Mandala: A Survey of the Mandala in the Western Esoteric Tradition. Adam McClean. (Illus.). 1987. pap. 15.00 o.p. (ISBN 0-317-57173-7). Phanes Pr.

Western Masters. Jean Stern. LC 81-83939. (Illus.). 124p. 1981. lib. bdg. 21.00 o.p. (ISBN 0-8227-8040-2, Dist. by DeRu's Fine Art). Petersen Pub.

Western Motel. Polly Gross. LC 84-45621. 288p. 1985. 16.95 o.p. (ISBN 0-689-11552-0, Atheneum). Macmillan.

Western Painting Illustrated: Giotto to Cezanne. Ed. by John Canaday. (Illus.). 1972. pap. 3.50 o.p. (ISBN 0-393-00667-0, Norton Lib). Norton.

Western Philosophy: An Introduction. R. J. Hollingdale. LC 79-63624. 158p. 1983. pap. 5.95 o.s.i. (ISBN 0-8008-8130-3). Taplinger.

Western Policies on East-West Trade. Stephen Woolcock. (Chatham House Papers: No. 15). 96p. (Orig.). 1982. pap. 10.95x o.p. (ISBN 0-7100-9314-4). Routledge Chapman & Hall.

Western Pulp Hero. Compiled by Nick Carr. (Popular Culture Studies: No. 3). 1988. 21.95 o.p.; pap. 11.95 o.p. Starmont Hse.

Western Sahara, 5 vols. International Court of Justice Staff. (Pleadings, Oral Arguments & Documents Ser.). 1982. Set. 20.00 o.p. UN.

Western Sahara: A Comprehensive Bibliography. Lynn F. Sipe. LC 82-49258. (Reference Library of Social Science). 500p. 1984. lib. bdg. 54.00 o.p. (ISBN 0-8240-9125-6). Garland Pub.

Western Scar: The Theme of the Been-to in West African Literature. William Lawson. LC 82-6372. x, 151p. 1982. lib. bdg. 18.95x o.p. (ISBN 0-8214-0649-3); pap. text ed. 11.95 o.p. (ISBN 0-8214-0695-7). Ohio U Pr.

Western States Life & Health. 1984. write for info. o.p. (ISBN 0-930868-30-7). Merritt Co.

Western States Property & Casualty. 1987. write for info. o.p. (ISBN 0-930868-31-5). Merritt Co.

Western Story: Fact, Fiction & Myth. Philip Durham & Everett L. Jones. 384p. (Orig.). 1975. pap. text ed. 8.95 o.p. (ISBN 0-15-595316-8, HC). HarBraceJ.

Western Strategic Interests in Saudi Arabia. Anthony Cordesman. 320p. 1986. 52.50 o.p. (ISBN 0-7099-4823-9, Pub. by Croom Helm UK). Routledge Chapman & Hall.

Western Tradition to Sixteen Sixty. T. Katsaros et al. 1972. pap. text ed. 3.50x o.p. (ISBN 0-8422-0240-4). Irvington.

Western Way: A Practical Guide to the Western Mystery Tradition. Caitlin Matthews & John Matthews. (Hermetic Tradition Ser.: Vol. II). 261p. 1986. pap. 11.95 o.p. (ISBN 1-85063-017-8). Routledge Chapman & Hall.

Western Way: A Practical Guide to the Western Mystery Tradition. Caitlin Matthews & John Matthews. 160p. (Orig.). 1985. pap. 8.95 o.p. (ISBN 1-85063-012-7, Ark Paperbks). Routledge Chapman & Hall.

Western Window in the Arab World. Leon B. Blair. (Illus.). 342p. 1970. 17.50x o.p. (ISBN 0-292-70083-0). U of Tex Pr.

Westerns: A Picture Quiz Book. John Cocchi. (Film Ser.). (Illus.). 128p. (Orig.). 1976. pap. 3.95 o.p. (ISBN 0-486-23288-3). Dover.

Westmacott-Christie Reader: Six Novels by Agatha Christie Writing under the Name Mary Westmacott. Agatha Christie, pseud. 1983. 25.00 o.p. (ISBN 0-87795-494-1, Arbor Hse). Morrow.

Westminister Confession for Today. George S. Hendry. LC 60-6283. 1980. pap. 3.13 o.p. (ISBN 0-8042-0756-9, John Knox). Westminster John Knox.

Westminster Confession of Faith. G. I. Williamson. pap. 6.95 o.p. (ISBN 0-8010-9591-3). Baker Bk.

Westminster Dictionary of Christian Education. Ed. by Kendig B. Cully. 1963. 6.00 o.s.i. (ISBN 0-664-20448-1, Westminster). Westminster John Knox.

Westminster Historical Atlas to the Bible. rev. ed. Ed. by G. Ernest Wright & Floyd V. Filson. LC 56-9123. 130p. 1956. 18.95 o.s.i. (ISBN 0-664-20535-6, Westminster). Westminster John Knox.

West's Comprehensive Cosmetology Outline. Linnea M. Lindquist. 361p. 1982. pap. text ed. 26.75 o.p. (ISBN 0-314-68253-8). West Pub.

West's Federal Court of Appeals Manual: 1986 Pocket Part. David G. Knibb. (Handbook Ser.). 350p. 1986. (ISBN 0-314-29529-1). West Pub.

West's Review Covering Multistate Subjects. Jerome A. Barron et al. LC 79-24976. 448p. 1979. pap. text ed. 23.95 o.p. (ISBN 0-8299-2081-1). West Pub.

Westside Lanes: A Sole-Proprietorship Service Business for Chapters 1-10 see College Accounting Fundamentals.

Westward Adventure: The True Stories of Six Pioneers. William O. Steele. LC 62-9479. (Illus.). (gr. 4-6). 1962. 5.95 o.p. (ISBN 0-15-294999-2, HJ). HarBraceJ.

Westward Enterprise: English Activites in Ireland, the Atlantic & America 1480-1650. Ed. by K. R. Andrews et al. LC 79-13801. 326p. 1979. 27.50x o.p. (ISBN 0-8143-1647-6). Wayne St U Pr.

Westward the Monitors Roar see Fight or Die.

Westward: The Romance of the American Frontier. E. Douglas Branch. LC 76-92485. 626p. Repr. of 1930 ed. 28.50x o.p. (ISBN 0-8154-0311-9). Cooper Sq.

Westwood Clay National. Keramos Staff. LC 79-93100. 1980. pap. 5.00 o.p. (ISBN 0-935066-08-X). Keramos Bks.

Wet Paint. Gwynn Popovac. 1986. 19.45 o.s.i. (ISBN 0-395-38222-X). HM.

Wetland Drainage in Europe. 1984. 7.50 o.p. (ISBN 0-905347-52-8). C I D E.

Wetlands Regulations. Massachusetts Continuing Legal Education, Inc. Staff. 1983. Mass CLE.

Wetlands: Their Use & Regulation. (Office of Technology Assessment 0 206 Ser.). 215p. (Orig.). 1984. pap. 8.00 o.p. (ISBN 0-318-11843-2, S/N 052-003-00944-7). USGPO.

Wetlands Utilization for Management of Community Wastewater: Concepts & Operations in Michigan. David E. Hammer & Robert H. Kadlec. (Illus.). 28p. 1980. 12.00 o.p. (ISBN 0-938654-28-4). Indus Dev Inst Sci.

Wetting, Spreading & Adhesion. Ed. by J. F. Padday. 1978. 120.00 o.p. (ISBN 0-12-544350-1). Acad Pr.

We've got the Power: Witches among Us. Lady Foxglove. LC 81-11098. (Jem Bks.). (Illus.). 64p. (Teens reading on a 2-3rd grade level). (gr. 2-3). 1981. lib. bdg. 9.29 o.s.i. (ISBN 0-671-43604-X). Messner.

WGT Surprises for PR. Date not set. (ISBN 0-07-017585-3). McGraw.

Whack Your Porcupine & Other Drawings. B. Kliban. LC 76-52861. (Illus.). 160p. 1977. pap. 3.95 o.p. (ISBN 0-911104-92-5). Workman Pub.

Whale: Going...Going...Gone? Marion Phillips. 1988. 6.50 o.p. (ISBN 0-682-48892-5, 200658). Exposition-Phoenix.

Whale of a Rescue. Eleanor Hudson. Ed. by Jane Gerver. LC 82-61014. (Sea World Mini-Storybooks). (Illus.). 32p. (gr. 1-5). 1983. pap. 1.25 o.p. (ISBN 0-394-85642-2). Random.

Whaler Round the Horn. Stephen W. Meader. LC 50-9530. (Illus.). (gr. 7 up). 1950. 5.95 o.p. (ISBN 0-15-295170-9, HJ). HarBraceJ.

Whalers. A. B. Whipple & Time-Life Books Editors. (Seafarers). (Illus.). 1979. 13.95 o.p. (ISBN 0-8094-2670-6). Time-Life.

Whalers & Whaling: The Story of the Whaling Ships up to the Present Day. E. Keble Chatterton. LC 79-178626. (Illus.). 248p. 1975. Repr. of 1925 ed. 40.00x o.p. (ISBN 0-8103-4028-3). Gale.

Whales, Dolphins, & Porpoises. Ronald M. Lockley. LC 79-88317. (Illus.). 1979. 18.95 o.p. (ISBN 0-393-01283-2). Norton.

Whales, Dolphins, & Porpoises. Ed. by Kenneth S. Norris. (Library Reprint Ser.: No.73). 1978. 70.00x o.p. (ISBN 0-520-03283-7). U of Cal Pr.

Whales, Dolphins, & Porpoises of the World. Mary L. Baker. LC 86-2010. (Illus.). 224p. 1987. 35.00 o.s.i. (ISBN 0-385-15366-X). Doubleday.

Whalesong. Robert Siegel. LC 81-66610. 144p. 1981. 9.95 o.p. (ISBN 0-89107-219-5, Crossway Bks). Good News.

Whaling for Glory. Sharon S. Shebar. LC 78-18247. (Illus.). 96p. (gr. 4-6). 1978. lib. bdg. 8.29 o.s.i. (ISBN 0-671-32917-0). Messner.

Wham! Philip Kamin. (Illus.). 32p. 1985. pap. 4.95 o.p. (ISBN 0-318-04249-5, Pub. by Robus Bks). H Leonard Pub Corp.

Wharton Annual: 1984. Wharton School Staff. 185p. 1984. Vol. 8. pap. 30.00 o.p. (ISBN 0-08-030929-1). Pergamon.

What a Beautiful Sunday! Jorge Semprun. Tr. by Alan Sheridan from Fr. LC 82-47662. (Helen & Kurt Wolff Bk.). 444p. 1982. 14.95 o.p. (ISBN 0-15-195857-2). HarBraceJ.

What a Good Lunch! Shigeo Watanabe. LC 79-19535. (I Can Do It All by Myself Bks.). (Illus.). 28p. (ps). 1980. 6.95 o.p. (Philomel); PLB 6.99 o.p. (ISBN 0-399-61181-9). Putnam Pub Group.

What a Wonderful Bird the Frog Are: An Assortment of Humorous Poetry-Verse. Ed. by Myra C. Livingston. LC 72-88171. (gr. 5 up). 1973. 5.25 o.p. (ISBN 0-15-295400-7, HJ). HarBraceJ.

What about Baptism? Larry Christenson. 24p. (Orig.). 1986. pap. 1.50 o.p. (ISBN 0-8066-2257-1, 23-3009, Augsburg). Augsburg Fortress.

What Agitates the Mind of the East. M. I. Siddiqui. 1981. 1.25 o.p. (ISBN 0-686-97862-5). Kazi Pubns.

What America Means to Me. Lucius Brown. 1978. 4.00 o.p. (ISBN 0-682-49173-X, Testament). Exposition-Phoenix.

What America Stands for. Ed. by Stephen D. Kertesz & M. A. Fitzsimons. (International Studies). 238p. 1959. 19.95 o.p. (ISBN 0-268-00298-3). U of Notre Dame Pr.

What Americans Should Do about Crime. L. Harold DeWolf. LC 75-36728. (Illus.). 160p. (Orig.). 1976. pap. 4.95i o.p. (ISBN 0-06-061912-0, RD138). HarpR.

What Are Human Rights? Maurice Cranston. LC 73-4849. 1978. pap. 4.95 o.s.i. (ISBN 0-8008-8149-4). Taplinger.

What Are Street Games? Anthony Ravielli. LC 80-22657. 1981. 9.95 o.p. (ISBN 0-689-30838-8, Atheneum). Macmillan.

What Are the Theologians Saying. Monika Hellwig. (Orig.). 1970. pap. 2.95 o.s.i. (ISBN 0-8278-9051-6, Pub. by Pflaum Pr). Pflaum Pr.

What Are We Going To Do With All These Rotting Fish? & Seven Other Short Plays for Church & Community. Ed. by Norman C. Habel. LC 79-119766. (Open Bks). (Illus.). 160p. (Orig.). 1970. pap. 3.25 o.p. (ISBN 0-8006-0147-5, 1-147, Fortress). Augsburg Fortress.

What Are You? Imelda O. Shanklin. 1929. 6.95 o.p. (ISBN 0-87159-171-5). Unity School.

What Are You Going to Do about Life? Henry Miller. 1986. 42.50 o.p. (ISBN 0-317-55075-6). Bern Porter.

What Are You up to, William Thomas? Suzanne Newton. LC 77-23460. (gr. 6-9). 1977. 7.95 o.s.i. (ISBN 0-664-32618-8, Westminster). Westminster John Knox.

What Auditors Should Know about Data Processing. Donald L. Dawley. Ed. by Richard N. Farmer. LC 83-17879. (Research for Business Decisions Ser.: No. 63). 250p. 1983. 44.95 o.p. (ISBN 0-8357-1483-7). UMI Res Pr.

What Became of Jane Austen? And Other Questions. Kingsley Amis. LC 74-153678. 1971. 6.50 o.p. (ISBN 0-15-195860-2). HarBraceJ.

What Beckoning Ghost? Kenneth Lillington. 128p. (YA) (gr. 7 up). 1983. 10.95 o.p. (ISBN 0-571-11959-X). Faber & Faber.

What Belongs: A Book-in-a-Book. (Learning Curves Bks.). (Illus.). 10p. (ps-1). 1987. pap. 5.95 o.p. (ISBN 0-553-18356-7). Bantam.

What Bloody Man Is That? Simon Brett. 196p. 1987. 14.95 o.p. (ISBN 0-684-18824-4). Scribner.

What Bothers Us About Grownups. Ed. by Russel Hamilton & Stephanie Greene. 1973. pap. 1.25 o.p. (ISBN 0-380-01615-X, 15008). Avon.

What Business Can Get from the Government. N. H. Mager & S. K. Mager. LC 81-24210. 657p. 1982. 75.00 o.p. (ISBN 0-932648-21-5). Boardroom.

What Can Children Learn in Geography? A Review of Research. Marion J. Rice & Russell L. Cobb. 130p. 1979. 9.95 o.p. (ISBN 0-89994-235-0). Soc Sci Ed.

What Can I Do About the Part of Me I Don't Like? David Belgum. LC 73-88609. 96p. (Orig.). 1974. pap. 4.50 o.p. (ISBN 0-8066-1412-9, 10-7025, Augsburg). Augsburg Fortress.

What Can I Do for Christ? Clementine Lenta. 5.50 o.p. (ISBN 0-910984-17-4). Montfort Pubns.

What Can I Grow in the Shade? Suzanne W. Pierot. (Illus.). 1977. 10.95 o.p. (ISBN 0-87140-627-6). Liveright.

What Can I Say to a Friend with Cancer. Randy Becton. 160p. pap. cancelled o.s.i. (ISBN 0-89225-320-7). Gospel Advocate.

What Can We Share? A Lutheran-Episcopal Resource & Study Guide. Ed. by William Norgren et al. (Lutheran-Episcopal Dialogue Ser.). 88p. (Orig.). 1985. pap. 2.00 o.p. (ISBN 0-88028-047-6). Forward Movement.

What Can You Do? Bill Gillham. LC 85-28137. (Look & Talk Bks.). (Illus.). 24p. (ps-1). 1986. 5.95 o.p. (ISBN 0-399-21324-4, Putnam). Putnam Pub Group.

What Child Is This? Martha Marshall. LC 82-7239. (Illus.). (gr. 1-2). 1982. lib. bdg. 6.95 o.p. (ISBN 0-89693-204-4). Dandelion Hse.

What Child Is This? Readings & Prayers for Advent-Christmas. Samuel H. Miller. LC 82-5084. (Illus.). 64p. (Orig.). 1982. pap. 0.95 o.p. (ISBN 0-8006-1638-3, 1-1638, Fortress). Augsburg Fortress.

What Christians Stand For in the Secular World. William Temple. Ed. by Franklin Sherman. LC 65-21081. (Facet Bks.). (Orig.). 1965. pap. 0.50 o.p. (ISBN 0-8006-3021-1, 1-3021, Fortress). Augsburg Fortress.

What Color Is Caesar. Maxine Kumin. (Illus.). (ps-3). 1978. text ed. 8.95 o.p. (ISBN 0-07-035638-6). McGraw.

What Color Is Love? Joan W. Anglund. LC 66-13795. (Illus.). (ps-6). 1966. 3.95 o.s.i. (ISBN 0-15-295260-8, HJ). HarBraceJ.

What Color Is Your God? Black Consciousness & the Christian Faith. Christopher Salley & Ronald Behm. LC 81-6758. 132p. (Orig.). 1981. pap. 4.50 o.p. (ISBN 0-87784-791-6). Inter-Varsity.

What Color Is Your Parachute? 2nd, rev. & enl. ed. Richard N. Bolles. LC 81-50471. 384p. 1984. 15.95 o.p. (ISBN 0-89815-144-9); pap. 8.95 o.p. (ISBN 0-89815-143-0). Ten Speed Pr.

What Color Is Your Parachute. Richard N Bolles. 1984. pap. 8.95 o.p. (ISBN 0-89815-120-1). Ten Speed Pr.

What Color Is Your Parachute, 1986: 1986. Richard N. Bolles. LC 81-50471. (Illus.). 416p. 1986. 15.95 o.p. (ISBN 0-89815-158-9); pap. 8.95 o.p. (ISBN 0-89815-157-0). Ten Speed Pr.

What Color Is Your Parachute? 1987. updated ed. Richard N. Bolles. LC 84-649334. (Illus.). 416p. 1987. 16.95 o.p.; pap. 8.95 o.p. (ISBN 0-89815-176-7). Ten Speed Pr.

What Computers Can Do. 2nd ed. Donald D. Spencer. (Illus.). 368p. 1984. pap. 12.95 o.s.i. (ISBN 0-684-18037-5, ScribT). Scribner.

What Constitutes Authentic Christianity? N. F. Grundtvig. Ed. & tr. by Ernest D. Nielsen. LC 84-48728. 128p. 1985. pap. 6.95 o.p. (ISBN 0-8006-1844-0, 1-1844, Fortress). Augsburg Fortress.

What Did God Make? Marilyn McAuley. (Peek & Find Bks.). (Illus.). 28p. (ps). 1984. bds. 3.95 o.p. (ISBN 0-89191-878-7, 58784). Cook.

What Did I Do Wrong? Mothers, Children, Guilt. Lynn Caine. 1985. 15.95 o.p. (ISBN 0-87795-623-5, Arbor Hse). Morrow.

What Did Jesus Do. William A. Poovey. LC 69-14180. 1969. pap. 4.50 o.p. (ISBN 0-8066-0901-X, 10-7042, Augsburg). Augsburg Fortress.

What Did Jesus Say about That? Stanley C. Baldwin. 224p. 1984. pap. 2.95 missal size o.p. (ISBN 0-89693-312-1). Victor Bks.

What Did Luther Understand by Religion? Karl Holl. Ed. by James L. Adams & Walter F. Bense. Tr. by Fred W. Meuser & Walter R. Wietzke. LC 76-62611. 128p. 1977. pap. 1.95 o.p. (ISBN 0-8006-1260-4, 1-1260, Fortress). Augsburg Fortress.

What Do Catholics Believe about Mary? Alan Schreck. 20p. (Orig.). 1983. pap. 0.50 o.p. (ISBN 0-89283-252-5). Servant.

What Do Doozers Do? Michaela Muntean. LC 83-22709. (Illus.). (gr. k-2). 1984. 5.95 o.s.i. (ISBN 0-03-071091-X); pap. 1.95 o.s.i. (ISBN 0-03-071888-0). H Holt & Co.

What Do I Have to Do---Break My Neck? Erling Wold & Marge Wold. LC 73-88604. 112p. (Orig.). 1974. pap. 4.50 o.p. (ISBN 0-8066-1407-2, 10-7045, Augsburg). Augsburg Fortress.

What Do I Hear? Harriet Ziefert. (Illus.). 24p. (gr. 5 up). 1988. pap. 3.95 o.p. (ISBN 0-553-05452-X). Bantam.

What Do I See? Harriet Ziefert. (Illus.). 24p. (Orig.). (gr. 5 up). 1988. pap. 3.95 o.p. (ISBN 0-553-05456-2). Bantam.

What Do I Smell? Harriet Ziefert. (Illus.). 24p. (Orig.). (gr. 5 up). 1988. pap. 3.95 o.p. (ISBN 0-553-05457-0). Bantam.

What Do I Taste? Harriet Ziefert. (Illus.). 24p. (gr. 5 up). 1988. pap. 3.95 o.p. (ISBN 0-553-05453-8). Bantam.

What Do I Touch? Harriet Ziefert. (Illus.). 24p. (Orig.). (gr. 5 up). 1988. pap. 3.95 o.p. (ISBN 0-553-05454-6). Bantam.

What Do These Things Mean? Lucy Pennell. (Illus., Orig.). (gr. 1-3). 1969. pap. 2.95 o.p. (ISBN 0-8042-9730-4, John Knox). Westminster John Knox.

What Do You Do with a...? Jan Demers. LC 85-51099. (Predictable Read Together Bks.). (Illus.). 24p. (gr. k-4). 1985. 7.95 o.s.i. (ISBN 0-87406-034-6). Willowisp Pr.

What Do You Do with a...? Jan Demers. (Predictable Reading Bks). (Illus.). 32p. (gr. k-2). 1985. 1.95 o.s.i. (ISBN 0-87406-010-9). Willowisp Pr.

What Do You Hear from Walden Pond? Jack Douglas. 1974. pap. 0.95 o.p. (ISBN 0-380-00053-9, 19950). Avon.

What Do You Mean by "Average"? Means, Medians, & Modes. Elizabeth James & Carol Barkin. LC 78-7227. (Illus.). (gr. 3-8). 1978. 10.25 o.p. (ISBN 0-688-41854-6); PLB 10.88 o.p. (ISBN 0-688-51854-0). Lothrop.

What Do You Mean by That? W. G. Ryckman. LC 80-66024. 229p. 1980. 19.95 o.p. (ISBN 0-87094-218-2). Dow Jones-Irwin.

What Do You Really Want for Your Children? Wayne W. Dyer. LC 85-10652. 396p. 1985. 17.95 o.p. (ISBN 0-688-04527-8). Morrow.

What Do You See? An Optical Illusion Study. Theoni Pappas. (Illus.). 160p. 1985. pap. 24.95 with slides o.p. (ISBN 0-933174-34-9). Wide World-Tetra.

What Do You Think, Vol. 4. (Vegetable Puppets Ser.). (Illus.). 10p. (ps). 1979. 2.50 o.p. (ISBN 0-89346-119-9, Pub. by Froebel-Kan Japan). Heian Intl.

What Does Childhood Taste Like? Mental Workouts That Will Stretch, Bend, & Energize the Way You Think, Respond, Dream, & Create. Jack Maguire. LC 86-12238. 224p. (Orig.). 1986. pap. 9.95 o.p. (ISBN 0-688-06344-6, Quill). Morrow.

What Does God Do All Day? Joseph R. Swain. 1977. 7.00 o.p. (ISBN 0-682-48919-0, Testament). Exposition-Phoenix.

What Does God Require in Race Relations? Marion A. Boggs. (Orig.). (gr. 10-12). 1964. pap. 1.25 o.p. (ISBN 0-8042-9311-2, John Knox). Westminster John Knox.

What Does It Mean to Believe in Jesus. Lois B. Sovenson. (Cornerstone Ser.). 32p. 1981. pap. 2.00 o.p. (ISBN 0-930756-64-9, 533004). Aglow Pubns.

What Does the Old Testament Say About God? new ed. Claus Westerman. Ed. by F. W. Golka. LC 78-52448. 1979. 8.95 o.p. (ISBN 0-8042-0190-0, John Knox). Westminster John Knox.

What Does This Mean? Luther's Catechisms Today. Ed. by Phillip E. Pederson. LC 79-50082. 1979. pap. 8.95 o.p. (ISBN 0-8066-1723-3, 10-7047, Augsburg). Augsburg Fortress.

What Dread Hand. Sarah Kemp. LC 86-16488. (Crime Club Ser.). 192p. 1987. 12.95 o.s.i. (ISBN 0-385-19459-5). Doubleday.

What Dread Hand? Sarah Kemp. (Lythway). 280p. 1988. lib. bdg. 19.50 o.s.i. (ISBN 0-7451-0665-X, Pub. by Chivers Pr UK). G K HAll.

What Every Child Would Like His Parents to Know to Help Him with the Emotional Problems of Everyday Life. Lee Salk. 224p. 1984. pap. 8.70 o.p. (ISBN 0-671-49219-5, Fireside). S&S.

What Every Christian Should Know about God: A Study Manual. Rick Yohn. LC 76-20396. 80p. 1976. 3.95 o.p. (ISBN 0-89081-054-0). Harvest Hse.

What Every Engineer Should Know about Inventing. William H. Middendorf. 149p. 12.75 o.s.i. (ISBN 0-318-16906-1). Mindsight Pub.

What Every Lawyer Needs to Know about Bankruptcy. Pennsylvania Bar Institute Staff. 1985. 50.00 o.p. (ISBN 0-318-19079-6, 325). PA Bar Inst.

What Every Manager Needs to Know about Marketing & the Law. Robert J. Posch. 1984. pap. text ed. 18.95 o.p. (ISBN 0-07-050567-5). McGraw.

What Every Potential Homeowner Should Know about Construction, Vol. I, General Construction: Residential Construction Information & Details That Every Potential Homeowner Should Be Familiar With. Douglas E. Hedlund. (Illus.). 176p. (Orig.). 1988. pap. write for info. o.p. Condata Co.

What Every Supervisor Should Know: The Basics of Supervisory Management. 4th ed. Lester R. Bittel. LC 79-16387. 1980. 27.50x o.p. (ISBN 0-07-005573-4); text ed. 27.65x o.p. (ISBN 0-07-005561-0). McGraw.

What Every Trucking Executive Needs to Know about Tax Reform. American Trucking Associations, Inc. Staff & Arthur Andersen & Co. 40p. 1986. pap. text ed. 15.00 o.p. (ISBN 0-88711-074-6). Am Trucking Assns.

What Every Woman Ought to Know about Love & Marriage. Joyce Brothers. 335p. 1984. 15.45 o.p. (ISBN 0-671-44159-0). S&S.

What Every Woman Should Know about Men. Joyce Brothers. 1982. 14.50 o.p. (ISBN 0-671-25020-5). S&S.

What Every Writer Should Know about Publishing His Own Book. 21st ed. Edward Uhlan et al. 1976. pap. 3.00 o.p. (ISBN 0-682-48674-4, Banner). Exposition-Phoenix.

What Everyone Should Know about Death. Augustus De Gregory. (Library of the Phenomena of the Mind). (Illus.). 147p. 1982. 47.85 o.p. (ISBN 0-89266-344-8). Am Classical Coll Pr.

What Everyone Should Know about Judaism. Morton W. Applebaum. 112p. 1959. (ISBN 0-8022-0036-2). Philos Lib.

What Faith Has Meant to Me. Ed. by Claude A. Frazier. 1974. pap. 4.95 o.s.i. (ISBN 0-664-24825-X, Westminster). Westminster John Knox.

What Fires Kindle Genius? A. F. Scott. LC 81-90430. 97p. 8.95 o.p. (ISBN 0-533-05188-6). Vantage.

What? Four Little Surprises! Esther Lee Millett. (ps-2). 1977. 4.00 o.p. (ISBN 0-682-48727-9). Exposition-Phoenix.

What God Can Do. Mabel N. McCaw. LC 81-70865. (gr. k-2). 1982. 5.95 o.p. (ISBN 0-8054-4290-1, 4242-90). Broadman.

What God Has Joined. Elisabeth Elliot. 32p. 1983. Repr. 1.50 o.p. (ISBN 0-89107-276-4). Good News.

What Goes Around Comes Around. Angela Peabody-DeShield. 1980. 6.00 o.p. (ISBN 0-682-49568-9). Exposition-Phoenix.

What Good Is Your Religion Doing You? Margaret W. Peters. 72p. 1987. 6.95 o.p. (ISBN 0-8062-2830-X). Carlton.

What Happened in Salem? 2nd ed. David Levin. Incl. Mirror for Witches. Esther Forbes. pap.; Young Goodman Brown. Nathaniel Hawthorne. pap. (HC). 238p. (Orig.). 1960. pap. text ed. 7.95 o.p. (ISBN 0-15-595598-5, HC). HarBraceJ.

What Happened Next? Nine Messages on Some of Jesus' Great Acts & Stories. George W. Hoyer. LC 87-30814. 112p. (Orig.). 1987. pap. 5.95 o.p. (ISBN 0-8066-2299-7, 10-7049, Augsburg). Augsburg Fortress.

What Happened to the Donkey After Christmas? Joseph R. LoBianco. (Illus.). (gr. k-5). 1979. 4.00 o.p. (ISBN 0-682-49212-4). Exposition-Phoenix.

What Happens in Public Relations. Ed. by Gerald J. Voros & Paul Alvarez. 224p. 1981. 17.95 o.p. (ISBN 0-8144-5652-9). AMACOM.

What Happens in Therapy. Sara Gilbert. LC 82-15233. 144p. (gr. 6 up). 1982. PLB 11.88 o.p. (ISBN 0-688-01456-9); pap. 6.50 o.p. (ISBN 0-688-01459-3). Lothrop.

What Happens in Therapy. Betrand Slaff. (gr. 7 up). 1982. pap. 6.50 o.p.; PLB 11.88 o.p. Morrow.

What Happens When God Answers. Evelyn Christenson. 160p. 1986. 9.95 o.p. (ISBN 0-8499-0569-9). Word Bks.

What Happens When We Sleep? Patricia M. Eldred. (Creative's Questions & Answers Ser.). (Illus.). 32p. (ps-4). 1981. PLB 8.95 o.p. (ISBN 0-87191-752-1). Creative Ed.

What Husbands Expect of Wives. Brent A. Barlow. LC 83-70707. 160p. 1983. 8.95 o.p. (ISBN 0-87747-971-2). Deseret Bk.

What I Did Last Summer. Glory St. John. LC 78-5678. (Illus.). (gr. 4-6). 1978. 9.95 o.p. (ISBN 0-689-30666-0, Atheneum). Macmillan.

What I Know So Far. Gordon Lish. LC 83-12980. 1984. 14.95 o.p. (ISBN 0-03-070609-2). H Holt & Co.

What I Know So Far: Short Stories. Gordon Lish. (Signature Editions Ser.). 176p. 1986. pap. 4.95 o.p. (ISBN 0-684-18644-6). Scribner.

What I Wish I'd Learned in Seminary. John Guest. 192p. 1987. 9.95 o.p. (ISBN 0-8499-0518-4). Word Bks.

What If They Knew. Patricia Hermes. LC 79-90033. (gr. 4-6). 1980. 10.95 o.p. (ISBN 0-15-295317-5, HJ). HarBraceJ.

What Is a Case? Wing. (Illus.). 268p. 1981. 48.00 o.p. (ISBN 0-86286-003-2, B-5603-6). Mosby.

What Is a Gospel? The Genre of the Canonical Gospels. Charles H. Talbert. LC 77-78645. 168p. 1977. 5.00 o.p. (ISBN 0-8006-0512-8, 1-512, Fortress). Augsburg Fortress.

What Is a Jew. rev. ed. Morris N. Kertzer. LC 73-77280. 217p. 1973. Repr. of 1953 ed. 8.95x o.p. (ISBN 0-8197-0299-4). Bloch.

What Is a Wife Worth? A Leading Expert Places a High Dollar Value on Homemaking. Michael H. Minton & Jean L. Block. 292p. 1984. pap. text ed. 6.95 o.p. (ISBN 0-07-042414-4). McGraw.

What Is Bowling? Anthony Ravielli. LC 75-13572. (Illus.). 32p. (gr. 8-12). 1975. 6.95 o.p. (ISBN 0-689-30492-7, Atheneum). Macmillan.

What Is Contemplation? Thomas Merton. 1978. pap. 4.95 o.p. Templegate.

What Is Creation Science. Henry M. Morris. LC 82-70114. (Illus.). 1982. pap. 10.95 o.p. (ISBN 0-89051-081-4). Master Bks.

What is Creative Thinking? Catharine Patrick. 224p. 1955. (ISBN 0-8022-1288-3). Philos Lib.

What Is "Democratic Socialism"? Ed. by P. Fedoseyev. 143p. 1980. pap. 3.50 o.p. (ISBN 0-8285-2051-8, Pub. by Progress Pubs USSR). Imported Pubns.

What Is Faith? Kathy England. (Illus.). 27p. (gr. 1-5). 1981. pap. 4.95 o.p. (ISBN 0-87747-876-7). Deseret Bk.

What Is Golf? Anthony Ravielli. LC 75-38342. (gr. 4-8). 1976. 6.95 o.p. (ISBN 0-689-30518-4, Atheneum). Macmillan.

What Is Good Teaching. Philadelphia School Study Council Group C Staff. 1962. pap. 1.25x o.p. (ISBN 0-8134-0074-0, 74). Inter Print Pubs.

What is Literature? Jean-Paul Sartre. LC 62-17831. 1949. (ISBN 0-8022-1492-4). Philos Lib.

What Is Living & What Is Dead in the Philosophy of Hegel. Benedetto Croce. LC 83-48504. (Philosophy of Hegel Ser.). 245p. 1984. lib. bdg. 30.00 o.p. (ISBN 0-8240-5627-2). Garland Pub.

What Is Loving? Mabel McCaw. (Plastic Book Ser.). (Illus.). 12p. (ps). 1987. 1.10 o.p. (ISBN 0-8378-4408-8). Gibson.

What Is Man? Eric S. Dillett. 80p. 1985. 6.50 o.p. (ISBN 0-682-40254-0). Exposition-Phoenix.

What Is Man? B. L. Smith. 1977. 4.00 o.p. (ISBN 0-682-48831-3). Exposition-Phoenix.

What Is Man: Contemporary Anthropology in Theological Perepective. Wolfhart Pannenberg. Tr. by Duane A. Priebe from Ger. LC 74-101429. 168p. 1972. pap. 3.75 o.p. (ISBN 0-8006-1252-3, 1-1252, Fortress). Augsburg Fortress.

What Is New Testament Theology? The Rise of Criticism & the Problem of a Theology of the New Testament. Hendrikus Boers. Ed. by Dan O. Via, Jr. LC 79-7372. (Guides to Biblical Scholarship: New Testament Ser.). 96p. 1979. pap. 4.50 o.p. (ISBN 0-8006-0466-0, 1-466, Fortress). Augsburg Fortress.

What Is Pure French; see Preliminary Announcement.

What Is Romanticism? Henri Peyre. Tr. by Roda P. Roberts from Fr. LC 75-42374. 1977. 15.50 o.p. (ISBN 0-8173-7003-X). U of Ala Pr.

What Is Soviet Power? Vladimir I. Lenin. 65p. 1969. 2.95 o.p. (ISBN 0-8285-0178-5, Pub. by Progress Pubs USSR). Imported Pubns.

What Is Structural Exegesis? Daniel Patte. Ed. by Dan O. Via, Jr. LC 75-36454. (Guides to Biblical Scholarship: New Testament Ser.). 96p. (Orig.). 1976. pap. 4.50 o.p. (ISBN 0-8006-0462-8, 1-462, Fortress). Augsburg Fortress.

What Is Symbolism? Henri Peyre. Tr. by Emmett Parker from Fr. LC 79-4686. 224p. 1980. 16.50 o.p. (ISBN 0-8173-7004-8). U of Ala Pr.

What Is Tennis? Anthony Ravielli. LC 77-1062. (gr. 4-8). 1977. 6.95 o.p. (Atheneum). Macmillan.

What Is the Conscious Process? Da Free John. LC 83-73637. 1983. pap. 8.95 o.s.i. (ISBN 0-913922-82-X). Dawn Horse Pr.

What Is Theatre. Eric Bentley. LC 68-56839. (Orig.). 1968. pap. 4.95 o.p. (ISBN 0-689-70012-1, Atheneum, 131). Macmillan.

What Is This For. Lawrence Henry. Ed. by Kate Klimo. (Learn with E.T. Ser.). (Illus.). 24p. 1983. pap. 1.90 o.s.i. (ISBN 0-671-46444-2, Little). S&S.

What Is Thought? James H. Stirling. LC 83-48631. (Philosophy of Hegel Ser.). 432p. 1984. lib. bdg. 50.00 o.p. (ISBN 0-8240-5638-8). Garland Pub.

What Is to Be Done? Lenin. 253p. 1973. 5.95 o.p. (ISBN 0-8351-0567-9); pap. 3.95 o.p. (ISBN 0-8351-0426-5). China Bks.

What Is to Be Done with Our Criminals? A Letter to the Right Honorable the Lord Mayor. Charles Pearson. LC 83-49228. (Crime & Punishment in England 1850-1922 Ser.). 134p. 1984. lib. bdg. 33.00 o.p. Garland Pub.

What Is Value? Everett W. Hall. (International Library of Psychology, Philosophy & Scientific Method). 1961. Repr. of 1952 ed. text ed. 15.00x o.p. (ISBN 0-391-00452-2). Humanities.

What Is Wrong with the Truth? Helen W. Crounse, pseud. 1971. 14.95x o.p. (ISBN 0-8084-0357-5). New Coll U Pr.

What Is Your Name: A Popular Account of the Meaning & Derivations of Christian Names. Sophy Moody. LC 73-5523. 324p. 1975. Repr. of 1863 ed. 45.00x o.p. (ISBN 0-8103-4250-2). Gale.

What Kids Need Most in a Dad. Tim Hansel. LC 83-22902. 192p. 1984. 10.95 o.p. (ISBN 0-8007-1390-7). Revell.

What Kind of a Dog Is That? Nina Leen. (Illus.). 1979. 9.95 o.p. (ISBN 0-393-01206-9); pap. 4.95 o.p. (ISBN 0-393-00934-3). Norton.

What Makes the Crops Rejoice: An Introduction to Gardening. Robert Howard & Eric Skjei. 1986. 16.95 o.p. (ISBN 0-316-37474-1). Little.

What Makes You Think We Read the Bills? H. L. Richardson. LC 78-66391. 1978. 7.95 o.p. (ISBN 0-916054-78-0, Dist. by Kampmann). Green Hill.

What Management Should Know about Industrial Advertising. Emil Hofsoos. LC 70-114692. 122p. 1970. 14.00x o.p. (ISBN 0-87201-386-3). Gulf Pub.

What Manner of Beast. Donald Finkel. LC 81-66012. 1981. 12.95 o.p. (ISBN 0-689-11226-2, Atheneum); pap. 7.95 o.p. (ISBN 0-689-11225-4). Macmillan.

What Men Don't Tell Women. Roy Blount, Jr. 160p. 1984. 14.95 o.p. (ISBN 0-316-10002-1). Little.

What Next in Mission? Paul A. Hopkins. LC 77-21776. 122p. 1977. pap. 3.95 o.s.i. (ISBN 0-664-24143-3, Westminster). Westminster John Knox.

What on Earth Is God Doing? Satan's Conflict with God: Study Guide. Renald E. Showers. 48p. 1983. pap. 3.50 o.p. (ISBN 0-87213-785-6). Loizeaux.

What Price Economic Growth? Ed. by Klaus E. Knorr. William J Baumol. LC 77-781. (Illus.). 1977. Repr. of 1961 ed. lib. bdg. 35.00x o.p. (ISBN 0-8371-9356-7, KNWP). Greenwood.

What Real Socialism Means to the People. R. Belousov. 261p. 1982. pap. 2.95 o.p. (ISBN 0-8285-2300-2, Pub. by Progress Pubs USSR). Imported Pubns.

What Religion Is. Bernard Bosanquet. LC 78-12709. 1979. Repr. of 1920 ed. lib. bdg. 35.00x o.p. (ISBN 0-313-21202-3, BOWR). Greenwood.

What Rough Beast? Sydney Labour History Group Staff. 276p. 1983. text ed. 29.50X o.p. (ISBN 0-86861-332-0). Unwin Hyman.

What Schools Can Do. Joseph Featherstone. 1976. 8.95 o.p. (ISBN 0-87140-619-5). Liveright.

What Shall I Do with This? Margaret Hutchings. (gr. 4-7). 1965. 3.95 o.s.i. (ISBN 0-8008-8231-8). Taplinger.

What Shall We Draw? Adrian Hill. (Illus.). 80p. (Orig.). 1986. pap. 7.95 o.p. (ISBN 0-7137-1829-3, Pub. by Blandford Pr England). Sterling.

What Shall We Name the Baby. Ed. by Winthrop Ames. (Illus.). 1959. pap. 5.95 o.s.i. (ISBN 0-671-81210-6, Fireside). S&S.

What Shall We Tell the Kids? Bennett Olshaker. LC 71-169923. 1971. 6.95 o.p. (ISBN 0-87795-022-9, Arbor Hse). Morrow.

What Shall We Tell the Kids? Bennett Olshaker. 1982. pap. 6.95 o.p. (ISBN 0-87795-407-0, Arbor Hse). Morrow.

What Shall We Wear to This Party? The Man in the Gray Flannel Suit Twenty Years Before & after. Sloan Wilson. LC 75-11152. 1976. 12.95 o.p. (ISBN 0-87795-119-5, Arbor Hse). Morrow.

What Should a Hippo Wear? Jane Sutton. (gr. k-3). 1979. PLB 6.95 o.p. (ISBN 0-395-27800-7). HM.

What Should You Do When...? Amy C. Bahr. LC 85-80574. (It's OK to Say No Picture Bks.). (Illus.). 32p. (ps-2). 1986. 4.95 o.p. (ISBN 0-448-15327-0, G&D). Putnam Pub Group.

What Students Know & Can Do: Profiles of Three Age Groups. National Assessment of Educational Progress Staff. (Across Learning Areas). 126p. 1977. 4.65 o.p. (ISBN 0-318-14005-5, ED-135-846, Natl Assessment Ed Progress). Ed Comm States.

What Susan Wanted. Sally Scott. LC 56-5235. (Illus.). (gr. 1-4). 1956. 3.95 o.p. (ISBN 0-15-295528-3, HJ). HarBraceJ.

What Teenagers Want to Know. Shideler Harpe & Wesley W. Hall. (Illus.). 1986. pap. 2.99 o.p. (ISBN 0-910304-11-4). Budlong.

What the Bible Can Mean for You. Reginald W. Deitz. LC 62-8206. 1962. bds. 0.50 o.p. (ISBN 0-8006-2011-9, Fortress). Augsburg Fortress.

What the Bible Says about End Time. 3rd ed. Russell Boatman. LC 79-56542. (What the Bible Says Ser.). 1980. 13.95 o.p. (ISBN 0-89900-075-4). College Pr Pub.

What the Bible Says about God the Ruler. Jack Cottrell. (What the Bible Says about Ser.). 465p. 13.95 o.p. (ISBN 0-89900-087-8). College Pr Pub.

What the Bible Says about the Church. Russell Boatman. (What the Bible Says Ser.). text ed. 13.95 o.p. (ISBN 0-89900-098-3). College Pr Pub.

What the Bible Says about the Great Tribulation. William Kimball. LC 83-71918. (What the Bible Says Ser.). (Illus.). 291p. 1983. 13.95 o.p. (ISBN 0-89900-093-2). College Pr pub.

What the Bible Says about the Promised Messiah. James E. Smith. (What the Bible Says Ser.). 530p. 1984. 13.95 o.p. (ISBN 0-89900-095-9). College Pr Pub.

What the Bible Says about the Unfolded Plan of God. Don Hunt. LC 81-82988. (What the Bible Says Ser.). 500p. 1981. 13.95 o.p. (ISBN 0-89900-084-3). College Pr Pub.

What the Bible Says about Worship. Lynn Hieronymus. (What the Bible Says Ser.). 300p. 1984. 13.95 o.p. (ISBN 0-89900-097-5). College Pr Pub.

What the Bible Tells Us: A Series for Young Children. Illus. by Kees De Kort. Incl. Jesus Is Born (ISBN 0-8066-1576-1, 10-3520); Jesus at the Wedding (ISBN 0-8066-1577-X, 10-3490); The Good Samaritan (ISBN 0-8066-1578-8, 10-2815); Jesus Is Alive (ISBN 0-8066-1579-6, 10-3518). (Illus.). (gr. 1-4). 1977. pap. 2.95 ea. o.p. (Augsburg). Augsburg Fortress.

What the Bible Tells Us: A Series for Young Children. Incl. Jesus Heals a Blind Man (ISBN 0-8066-1684-9, 10-3514); Jesus Heals a Sick Man (ISBN 0-8066-1685-7, 10-3515); Jesus & the Storm (ISBN 0-8066-1683-0, 10-3485); Zacchaeus (ISBN 0-8066-1699-7, 10-7550). (Second Ser.). (Illus.). (gr. 1-4). 1979. pap. 2.95 ea. o.p. (Augsburg). Augsburg Fortress.

What the Bible Tells Us: Third Series, 4 bks. Illus. by Kees De Kort. Incl. Baby Called John. 28p (ISBN 0-8066-1770-5, 10-0538); Jesus & a Little Girl. 28p (ISBN 0-8066-1771-3, 10-3479); Son Who Left Home. 28p (ISBN 0-8066-1773-X, 10-5852); Jesus Goes Away. 28p (ISBN 0-8066-1774-8, 10-3510). (gr. 1-4). 1980. pap. 2.95 ea. o.p. (Augsburg). Augsburg Fortress.

What the Buddha Taught. rev. ed. Walpola Rahula. (Illus.). 168p. 1974. pap. 8.95 o.p. (ISBN 0-394-17827-0, E641, Ever). Grove.

What the New Bankruptcy Legislation Means to You, 2 vols. 463p. 1984. 30.00 o.p. (ISBN 0-318-03918-4, 266). PA Bar Inst.

What the Printer Should Know about Paper. William H. Bureau. LC 81-86238. 320p. 1982. 40.00 o.p. (ISBN 0-88362-013-8, 1308). Graphic Arts Tech Found.

What the Woman Lived: Selected Letters of Louise Bogan, 1920-1970. Ed. by Ruth Limmer. LC 73-9737. 1973. 14.50 o.p. (ISBN 0-15-195878-5). HarBraceJ.

What, Then, Is a Human Beinge...? National Association for Women Deans, Administrators & Counselors. 1973. pap. 3.00 o.p. (ISBN 0-686-09580-4). Natl Assn Women.

What Then Is Man? 355p. 1958. Concordia Schl Grad Studies.

What, Then, Is Man? A Symposium. 356p. 1971. 5.00 o.p. (12-2361). Concordia.

What Thou Lovest Well, Remains American: Poems. Richard Hugo. 71p. 1975. 7.95 o.p. (ISBN 0-393-04410-6); pap. 3.95 o.p. (ISBN 0-393-04417-3). Norton.

What Time Is It? David Willoughby. Ed. by Arthur L. Clanton. 1976. pap. 3.95 o.p. (ISBN 0-912315-49-0). Word Aflame.

What Time Is It, Nana? Beverly Andrews. 136p. 1982. 7.50 o.p. (ISBN 0-682-49795-9). Exposition-Phoenix.

What to Believe? The Questions of Christian Faith. Carl E. Krieg. LC 74-80415. 128p. (Orig.). 1974. pap. 1.00 o.p. (ISBN 0-8006-1085-7, 1-1085, Fortress). Augsburg Fortress.

What to Do about Bill? Rev. ed. Gayl G. Hermann et al. 1982. pap. text ed. 9.95 o.p. (ISBN 0-88450-824-2, 2041-B). Communication Skill.

What to Do about Performance Appraisal. rev. ed. Marion S. Kellogg. LC 75-8604. 224p. 1975. 14.95 o.p. (ISBN 0-8144-5389-9). AMACOM.

What to Do Before the Books Arrive. Jean D. Maculaitis & Mona Scheraga. (Illus.). 173p. 1981. pap. text ed. 8.95x o.p. (ISBN 0-88084-008-0). Alemany Pr.

What to Do on Thursday. Jay E. Adams. 1982. pap. 3.95 o.p. (ISBN 0-87552-074-X). Presby & Reformed.

What to Do on Thursday: A Layman's Guide to the Practical Use of the Scriptures. Jay E. Adams. 144p. 1982. pap. 3.95 o.p. (ISBN 0-8010-0188-9). Baker Bk.

What to Do till Jesus Comes. Knofel Staton. LC 81-14594. 112p. 1983. pap. 2.25 o.p. (ISBN 0-87239-481-6, 41016). Standard Pub.

What To Do When You Think You Can't Have a Baby. Karol White. 1982. pap. 6.95 o.p. (ISBN 0-03-061659-X, Owl Bks). H Holt & Co.

What to Do When You're Depressed: A Christian Psychoanalyst Helps You Understand & Overcome Your Depression. George A. Benson. LC 75-22712. 144p. 1975. pap. 5.95 o.p. (ISBN 0-8066-1519-2, 10-7052, Augsburg). Augsburg Fortress.

What to Expect If You Are...The Pregnant Father. David F. Raine. 1978. 6.50 o.p. (ISBN 0-682-49269-8). Exposition-Phoenix.

What to Know about the Treatment of Cancer: Clear, Sensible Answers to the Questions Asked by Cancer Patients, Their Families & Friends from a Concerned Physicians & Specialist in the Day-to-Day Treatment of Cancer. Vincent Anku. LC 84-20148. (Illus.). 152p. (Orig.). 1984. pap. 7.95 o.s.i. (ISBN 0-88089-002-9). Madrona Pubs.

What to Listen for in Music. rev. ed. Aaron Copland. (Illus.). 1957. text ed. 16.95 o.p. (ISBN 0-07-013089-2). McGraw.

What to Memorize. pap. 0.40x o.p. (ISBN 0-8192-4020-6). Morehouse Pub.

What to Name the Cat. Thelma Kandel. 1983. pap. 4.95 o.p. (ISBN 0-671-46000-5, Linden Pr). S&S.

What to Read in Microcomputing. Ed. by C. Saiady & A. V. Stokes. 112p. (Orig.). 1982. pap. text ed. 23.50x o.p. (ISBN 0-566-03403-4). Gower Pub Co.

What to Remember to Be Happy. John Da Free. (Illus.). pap. 5.95 o.s.i. (ISBN 0-913922-36-6). Dawn Horse Pr.

What to Say to Clara. Barney Saltzberg. LC 83-15567. (Illus.). 32p. (gr. k up). 1984. 9.95 o.s.i. (ISBN 0-689-31041-2, Atheneum Childrens Bks). Macmillan.

What to Tell Your Child about Sex. rev. ed. CSAAT. 1974. 5.70 o.p. (ISBN 0-87183-241-0). Jewish Bd Family.

What Today's Youth is Reading & Why. Ed. by John T. Corrigan. (CLA Studies in Librarianship). 46p. 1981. 5.00 o.p. (ISBN 0-87507-047-7). Cath Lib Assn.

What Type Stripe? David N. Bruskin. (Story Bus Subseries: City Bus). (Illus.). 10p. (ps-2). 1988. bds. 14.95 o.p. (ISBN 1-55929-011-0). Bound Fun Inc.

What Was Literature? Leslie A. Fiedler. 1982. 14.50 o.p. (ISBN 0-671-24983-5). S&S.

What Was Literature? Class Culture & Society. Leslie A. Fiedler. 258p. 1984. pap. 6.75 o.p. (ISBN 0-671-24984-3, Touchstone). S&S.

What We Know about Heaven. James E. Nelson. 80p. 1987. pap. 2.95 o.p. (ISBN 0-8423-7921-5). Tyndale.

What Went Right, What Went Wrong? Truman Dollar. 1988. write for info. o.p. Victor Bks.

What Will Be Has Always Been: The Words of Louis I. Kahn. Richard S. Wurman. (Illus.). 384p. 1986. 45.00 o.p. (ISBN 0-915461-11-0); pap. 30.00 o.p. (ISBN 0-915461-12-9). Access Pr.

What Will the Neighbors Say? Facing the Fear of Disapproval. Patricia H. Berne & Louis M. Savary. LC 82-14076. 176p. 1982. 10.95 o.p. (ISBN 0-8264-0196-1). Continuum.

What Wives Expect of Husbands. Brent A. Barlow. LC 82-70919. 164p. 1982. 9.95 o.p. (ISBN 0-87747-911-9). Deseret Bk.

What Works When Life Doesn't. rev. ed. Stuart Briscoe. 176p. 1984. pap. 2.95 o.p. (ISBN 0-89693-709-7). Victor Bks.

What You Can Do to Prevent Cancer. Oliver Alabaster. 1985. 17.45 o.p. (ISBN 0-671-49537-2). S&S.

What You Do If... Jane B. Moncure. LC 85-10418. (Illus.). 32p. (ps-k). 1985. PLB 4.95 o.p. (ISBN 0-89693-227-3). Dandelion Hse.

What You Need to Know about Planned Parenthood: What Is It? How Does It Affect You & Your Children? What Can You Do about It? JoAnn Gasper. 150p. (Orig.). 1989. pap. 6.95 o.p. (ISBN 0-89283-620-2). Servant.

What You Need to Know When You Buy a Franchise (Plus a Listing of the World's Leading Franchising Companies) 264p. 1987. 4.95 o.p. (ISBN 0-317-66127-2). Intl Franchise Assn.

What You Should Know About Drugs. Charles Gorodetzky & Samuel T. Christian. LC 74-128366. (Illus.). (gr. 4 up). 1970. 5.95 o.p. (ISBN 0-15-295510-0, HJ). HarBraceJ.

What You Should Know about Marriage, Divorce, Annulment, Separation & Community Property in Louisiana. R. Lee Eddy, III. LC 73-91094. 1974. 10.00 o.p. (ISBN 0-682-47861-X); pap. 6.00 o.p. (ISBN 0-682-47862-8). Exposition-Phoenix.

What You Should Know about the American Flag. Earl P. Williams, Jr. LC 87-61317. (Illus.). 75p. 1987. pap. 5.95 o.p. (ISBN 0-917882-25-3); pap. 5.95 o.p. (ISBN 0-317-59836-8). MD Hist Pr.

What You Should Know If You're Accused of a Crime. Joyce B. David. 32p. (Orig.). 1986. pap. 4.00 o.p. (ISBN 0-9617121-0-4). Balaban Pub.

What You Should Know to Make Money from Your Investments. Robert M. Sutton. 1979. 10.00 o.p. (ISBN 0-682-49206-X, Banner). Exposition-Phoenix.

What Your Handwriting Reveals. Margaret Gullan-Whur. pap. 8.99 o.p. (ISBN 0-85030-378-8, Pub. by Aquarian Pr England). Sterling.

What Your Patients Should Know about DRG's & the Prospective Payment System. LC 84-110279. 24p. 1984. pap. 1.50 o.p. (ISBN 0-89970-264-3, OP-336). AMA.

Whatcom Seascapes: The Influence of the Sea on Whatcom County. Whatcom Museum of History & Art Staff. LC 77-140515. (Whatcom Museum Ser.). (Illus.). 80p. 1970. pap. 5.00 o.p. (ISBN 0-295-95578-3). U of Wash Pr.

Whatever Became of Salvation? James Bullock. LC 78-71049. 1979. 8.95 o.p. (ISBN 0-8042-1468-9, John Knox). Westminster John Knox.

Whatever Became of....? The Best & Newest of the Lamparaki Profiles of Personalities. Richard Lamparski. (Eighth Ser.). (Illus.). 320p. 1982. 17.95 o.p. (ISBN 0-517-54346-X); pap. 9.95 o.p. (ISBN 0-517-54855-0). Crown.

Whatever Book, 2 bks. (gr. 3-7). 1981. Bk. 1. pap. 2.95 o.s.i. (ISBN 0-671-43051-3); Bk. 2. pap. (ISBN 0-671-43052-1). Wanderer Bks.

Whatever Happened to Beverly Bigler's Birthday. Barbara Williams. LC 78-20575. (Let Me Read Ser.). (gr. 1-5). 1979. 6.95 o.p. (ISBN 0-15-295286-1, HJ). HarBraceJ.

Whatever Happened to Beverly Bigler's Birthday. Barbara Williams. LC 78-20575. (Let Me Read Ser.). (Illus.). (gr. 1-5). 1979. pap. 1.95 o.p. (ISBN 0-15-696083-4, VoyB). HarBraceJ.

Whatever Happened to the Dinosaurs? William Jaber. LC 78-15939. (Illus.). 160p. (gr. 7 up). 1978. lib. bdg. 8.79 o.s.i. (ISBN 0-671-32872-7). Messner.

Whatever It Is, I'm Against It. Ed. by Nat Shapiro. 1984. 17.45 o.p. (ISBN 0-671-49748-0); pap. 8.95 o.p. (ISBN 0-671-50837-7). S&S.

Whatever You Do: An Essay in Christian Ethics. James H. Burtness. LC 67-25372. (Tower Books Ser). 1967. pap. 2.95 o.p. (ISBN 0-8066-9356-8, 10-7055, Augsburg). Augsburg Fortress.

What's a Body to Do? A Handbook About Health. Ruth S. Odor. LC 80-17584. (Living the Good Life Ser.). (Illus.). 112p. (Orig.). (gr. 1-6). 1980. pap. 5.95 o.p. (ISBN 0-89565-176-9). Childs World.

What's A Fraggle? Louise Gikow. (Illus.). 32p. (gr. k-2). 1984. 5.70 o.s.i. (ISBN 0-03-071086-3); pap. 1.95 o.s.i. (ISBN 0-03-071889-9). H Holt & Co.

What's a Mom to Do? Julie Hagstorm. (Orig.). 1985. pap. 6.95 o.p. (ISBN 0-671-49707-3, Fireside). S&S.

What's Ahead for the Economy. Louis Rukeyser. 1985. pap. 8.95 o.p. (ISBN 0-671-55790-4, Touchstone Bks.). S&S.

What's Ahead for the Economy: The Challenge & the Chance. Louis Rukeyser. 256p. 1983. 15.50 o.p. (ISBN 0-671-44996-6). S&S.

What's Ahead?... the U. S. Economy. Edward Boorstein. LC 84-15867. 240p. 1984. 10.00 o.p.; pap. 5.95 o.p. (ISBN 0-7178-0614-6). Intl Pubs Co.

What's Behind That Tree? Leslie Williams. LC 84-11052. (Illus.). 24p. (ps-3). 1984. 12.95 o.p. (ISBN 0-911745-64-5, Bedrick Blackie). P Bedrick Bks.

What's Cooking Down in Maine. William C. Roux. 1964. pap. 4.50 o.p. (ISBN 0-89272-007-7). Down East.

What's Cooking on Cape Cod. Anita Buddington & Marion Vuilleumier. (Illus.). 228p. (Orig.). 1983. pap. 7.95 o.p. (ISBN 0-88492-043-7). W S Sullwold.

What's Eating You? Elizabeth Keyes & Paul K. Chivington. (Illus.). 1978. pap. 4.50 o.p. (ISBN 0-87516-263-0). DeVorss.

What's for Dinner in the Northwest? Maryana Vollstedt. (Illus.). 144p. (Orig.). 1982. pap. 5.95 o.p. (ISBN 0-910983-14-3). Cookbook Fact.

What's for Lunch: Animal Feeding at the Zoo. Sally Tongren. LC 81-80981. (Illus.). 128p. (Orig.). 1981. 12.95 o.p. (ISBN 0-939456-00-1); pap. 8.95 o.p. (ISBN 0-939456-01-X). Galison.

What's Happening to American English? A. M. Tibbetts & Charlene Tibbetts. LC 78-10349. 1979. 8.95 o.s.i. (ISBN 0-684-15982-1, ScribT). Scribner.

"What's Happening to My Body?" Book for Boys: A Growing-up Guide for Parents & Sons. Lynda Madaras & Dane Saavedra. LC 84-16667. (Illus.). 240p. (gr. 4 up). 1984. 14.95 o.p. (ISBN 0-937858-39-0); pap. 9.95 o.p. (ISBN 0-937858-40-4). Newmarket.

What's Happening to My Body? Book for Girls: A Growing-up Guide for Parents & Daughters. Lynda Madaras & Area Madaras. LC 83-8202. (Illus.). 208p. (gr. 4 up). 1983. 14.95 o.p. (ISBN 0-937858-25-0); pap. 9.95 o.p. (ISBN 0-937858-21-8). Newmarket.

What's in a Name? C. Stella Davies & John Levitt. 112p. (Orig.). 1981. pap. 5.95 o.p. (ISBN 0-7100-0685-3). Routledge Chapman & Hall.

What's in a Name: Famous Brand Names. Oren Arnold. LC 79-15555. 128p. (gr. 7 up). 1979. lib. bdg. 8.79 o.s.i. (ISBN 0-671-32932-4). Messner.

What's in an Egg? Joan Budai. LC 80-80559. 1980. pap. 4.95 o.p. (ISBN 0-89051-061-X). Master Bks.

What's Inside of Animals. Herbert S. Zim. (Illus.). (gr. 11 up). 1953. PLB 11.88 o.p. (ISBN 0-688-26518-9). Morrow.

What's It Worth? A Guide to Current Personal Injury Awards & Settlements. Robert Harley et al. LC 85-23093. (Kluwer Damages Library). 753p. 1985. text ed. 75.00 o.p. (ISBN 0-930273-53-2). Michie Co.

What's Missing: A Book-in-a-Book. (Learning Curves Bks.). (Illus.). 28p. (ps-1). 1987. pap. 5.95 o.p. (ISBN 0-553-18355-9). Bantam.

What's Next. Neil F. Moore. 1977. 5.50 o.p. (ISBN 0-682-48819-4). Exposition-Phoenix.

What's Psychotherapy...& Who Needs It? Herbert L. Collier. 1976. pap. 5.95 o.p. (ISBN 0-89019-056-9). Norwalk Pr.

What's Right? Eugene H. Baker. LC 81-16999. (Successful Living Ser.). (Illus.). 112p. (gr. 2-6). 1981. lib. bdg. 8.95 o.p. (ISBN 0-89565-208-0). Routledge Chapman & Hall.

What's Right: A Handbook about Values. Eugene Baker. LC 80-17552. (Living the Good Life Ser.). (Illus.). 112p. (Orig.). (gr. 1-6). 1980. pap. 5.95 o.p. (ISBN 0-89565-175-0). Childs World.

What's Skin For? Pat Blakely. (Creative Question & Answer Library). (Illus.). 32p. (ps-4). 1981. PLB 8.95 o.p. (ISBN 0-87191-745-9). Creative Ed.

What's Skin For? Claypool et al. (Little Question Bks.). (Illus.). 32p. Date not set. PLB 8.95 o.p. Creative Ed.

What's That You Said. Ann E. Weiss. LC 79-3767. (Let Me Read Ser.). (Illus.). 48p. (gr. k-3). 1980. 6.95 o.p. (ISBN 0-15-295525-9, HJ). HarBraceJ.

What's That You Said? How Words Change. Ann E. Weiss. LC 79-3765. (Let-Me-Read Ser.). (Illus.). 48p. (ps-3). 1980. pap. 2.25 o.p. (ISBN 0-15-696119-9, VoyB). HarBraceJ.

What's the Difference? How Men & Women Compare. Jane B. Stump. LC 85-502. 247p. 1986. pap. 7.95 o.p. (ISBN 0-688-06263-6, Quill). Morrow.

What's the Difference: How Men & Women Compare. Jane B. Stumpp. LC 84-20569. 252p. 1985. 12.95 o.p. (ISBN 0-688-04192-2). Morrow.

What's the Fair Ward? Psychiatric Humor. Edwin Mumford. (Illus.). 1979. pap. 3.00 o.p. (ISBN 0-682-49422-4). Exposition-Phoenix.

What's the Funny Ward? Or My Last Ten Years with Snooksie the Guinea Pig. Edwin Mumford. (Illus.). 1979. pap. 4.00 o.p. (ISBN 0-682-49522-0). Exposition-Phoenix.

What's the Good Ward? Caustic Cartoons. Edwin Mumford. (Illus.). 1974. pap. 2.50 o.p. (ISBN 0-682-48017-7). Exposition-Phoenix.

What's the Matter with Christy? Ruth Allen. LC 82-8036. 110p. (Orig.). 1982. pap. 3.95 o.p. (ISBN 0-87123-629-X, 210629). Bethany Hse.

What's the Matter with the Dobsons. Hila Colman. (gr. 5-7). 1982. pap. 1.95 o.p. (ISBN 0-671-43143-9). Archway.

What's to Eat? & Other Questions Kids Ask about Food: Yearbook of Agriculture, 1979. LC 79-600189. 142p. (gr. 3-8). 1979. 8.50 o.p. (ISBN 0-318-11844-0, S/N 001-000-04041-3). USGPO.

What's up Duck? Mike Thaler. (Illus.). 128p. (gr. 3-7). 1981. pap. 1.95 o.p. (ISBN 0-380-53363-4, 53363-4, Camelot). Avon.

What's What in Sports: The Visual Glossary of the Sports World. Ed. by David Fisher & Reginald Bragonier, Jr. LC 84-9082. (Illus.). 256p. 1984. 19.95 o.p. (ISBN 0-8437-3528-7); lexotone 14.95 o.p. (ISBN 0-8437-3529-5). Hammond Inc.

What's Where: The Official Guide to College Majors. Joyce S. Mitchell. (YA) (gr. 10-12). 1979. pap. 3.95 o.p. (ISBN 0-380-45559-5). Avon.

What's Wildlife Worth? 1982. 5.50 o.p. (ISBN 0-905347-35-8). C I D E.

What's Wrong, Who's Right in Central America: A Citizen's Guide. Richard Nuccio & Kelly A. McBride. LC 85-31093. 160p. 1986. 15.95 o.p. (ISBN 0-8160-1374-8). Facts on File.

What's Wrong with Daddy? Alida E. Young. 176p. (gr. 5-8). 1986. 2.25 o.s.i. (ISBN 0-87406-066-4). Willowisp Pr.

What's Wrong with My Child? R. Gattozi. 384p. 1986. text ed. 19.95 o.p. (ISBN 0-07-038781-8). McGraw.

What's Wrong with My Plant? Chuck Crandall. 128p. 1980. pap. 2.50 o.p. (ISBN 0-380-45468-8, 45468). Avon.

What's Wrong with the Law? Ed. by Michael Zander. 136p. 1970. 5.00 o.p. (ISBN 0-7735-0086-3, McGill Canada). U of Toronto Pr.

What's Your Game Plan? Creating Business Strategies That Work. Milton Lauenstein. 1985. 19.95 o.p. (ISBN 0-87094-593-9). Dow Jones-Irwin.

Wheat & Chaff. Mitterand. (ISBN 0-8050-0185-9). Seaver Bks.

Wheat & the Chaff, 2 pts. in 1. Francois Mitterand. Tr. by Richard Woodward & Concilia Hayter. 1982. 16.95 o.p. Seaver Bks.

Wheat Flour Messiah: Eric Jansson of Bishop Hill. Paul Elmen. LC 76-28380. (Illus.). 239p. 1976. 8.95x o.p. (ISBN 0-8093-0787-1). S Ill U Pr.

Wheat Flour Messiah: Eric Jansson of Bishop Hill. Paul Elmen. LC 76-28380. 222p. 1976. 7.95 o.p. (ISBN 0-318-16626-7). Swedish-Am.

Wheatgrass Juice-Gift of Nature. rev. ed. Ed. by Betsy Russell-Manning. 1986. pap. 2.95 o.p. (ISBN 0-930165-06-3). Greensward Pr.

Wheatheart Chronicles, 4 bks. Set. 17.95 o.p. (ISBN 0-89693-700-3). Victor Bks.

Wheel & the Cross: A Christian Response to the Technological Revolution. Waldo Beach. pap. 5.95 o.p. (ISBN 0-8042-0866-2, John Knox). Westminster John Knox.

Wheel, Camel, Fish & Plow: Yoga for You. Rachel Carr. (Illus.). (gr. 5 up). 1981. 9.95 o.s.i. (ISBN 0-13-956045-9). P-H.

Wheel of Fortune. Willard Anderson. 1985. 11.95 o.p. (ISBN 0-317-28984-5). Vantage.

Wheel of Fortune. Susan Howatch. 1184p. 1984. 19.45 o.p. (ISBN 0-671-49989-0). S&S.

Wheel of Truth: An Ancestral Saga. Gertrude S. Lowry. (Illus.). 1977. 15.00 o.p. (ISBN 0-682-48886-0, University). Exposition-Phoenix.

Wheel Within the Wheel. Richard G. Hutcheson, Jr. LC 79-11481. 1979. 6.00 o.p. (ISBN 0-8042-1886-2, John Knox). Westminster John Knox.

Wheelchair Summer see Summer Dreams.

Wheeler's Last Raid. Lewis A. Lawson. (Illus.). 497p. 1986. 25.00 o.p. (ISBN 0-317-37934-8). Penkevill.

Wheeling & Dealing: Confessions of a Capitol Hill Operator. Bobby Baker & Larry L. King. (Illus.). 304p. 1980. pap. 5.95 o.p. (ISBN 0-393-00972-6). Norton.

Wheeling & Dealing: Confessions of a Capitol Hill Operator. Bobby Baker & Larry L. King. (Illus.). 1978. 14.95 o.p. (ISBN 0-393-07523-0). Norton.

Wheels. Arthur Hailey. LC 77-152790. 1971. 12.95 o.s.i. (ISBN 0-385-02829-6). Doubleday.

Wheels on the Mountains. James E. Craft. (Illus.). 1969. 8.00 o.p. (ISBN 0-87012-072-7). McClain.

Wheels Teacher's Guide. Stephen Steurer. (Wheels Ser.). 64p. 1980. 2.65 o.p. (ISBN 0-317-35489-2). New Readers.

Wheels Workbook. Stephen Steurer. (Wheels Ser.). 64p. 1980. 2.50 o.p. (ISBN 0-317-35490-6). New Readers.

When a Caring Family Faces Crises. Charles W. Stewart. LC 80-69089. (When Bks.). (Illus.). 96p. (Orig.). pap. 2.45 o.p. (ISBN 0-87029-169-6, 20264-8). Abbey.

When a Christian Sins. John R. Rice. 1954. pap. 3.95 o.p. (ISBN 0-8024-9434-X). Moody.

When a Family Loses a Loved One. Paul F. Wilczak. LC 81-68846. (WHEN Bk. Ser.). 96p. (Orig.). 1981. pap. 2.45 o.p. (ISBN 0-87029-179-3, 20272-1). Abbey.

When a Jew & Christian Marry. Samuel Sandmel. LC 77-78639. 128p. (Orig.). 1977. pap. 3.25 o.p. (ISBN 0-8006-1311-2, 1-1311, Fortress). Augsburg Fortress.

When a Man Loves a Woman: How to Love a Woman of the Eighties. Claude M. Steiner. LC 85-71164. 256p. 1986. 19.50 o.s.i. (ISBN 0-394-54945-7). Grove.

When a Member of the Family Needs Counseling. John A. Larsen. LC 79-51274. (When Bk.). (Illus.). 1979. pap. 2.45 o.p. (ISBN 0-87029-147-5, 20234-1). Abbey.

When a Parent Imposes Limits: Discipline, Authority, & Freedom in Today's Family. Beth Michel. LC 81-68517. (WHEN Bk.). 96p. (Orig.). 1981. pap. 2.45 o.p. (ISBN 0-87029-178-5, 20269-7). Abbey.

When a Parent Is Mentally Ill: What to Say to Your Child. Helene S. Arnstein. 36p. 1974. pap. 1.50 o.p. (ISBN 0-686-12282-8). Jewish Bd Family.

When a Pastor Search Committee Comes... or Doesn't. J. William Harbin. LC 85-13541. 1985. pap. 4.95 o.p. (ISBN 0-8054-2545-4). Broadman.

When a Story Would Help: An Approach to Creative Parenting. Lucie W. Barber. LC 80-70550. (When Bk.). (Illus.). 88p. (Orig.). 1981. pap. 2.45 o.p. (ISBN 0-87029-173-4, 20267-1). Abbey.

When Adam Clarke Preached, People Listened. Wesley Tracy. 238p. (Orig.). 1981. pap. 4.95 o.p. (ISBN 0-8341-0714-7). Beacon Hill.

When All You've Ever Wanted Isn't Enough. Harold S. Kushner. 1986. 16.45 o.s.i. (ISBN 0-671-54342-3). Summit Bks.

When Bad Things Happen to Good People. Harold S. Kushner. (General Ser.). 1982. lib. bdg. 13.95 o.p. (ISBN 0-8161-3465-0, Large Print Bks). G K Hall.

When Batistine Made Bread. Treska Lindsey. LC 84-42988. (Illus.). 48p. (gr. k-3). 1985. 9.95 o.s.i. (ISBN 0-02-759120-4). Macmillan.

When Cancer Comes. Clarence McConkey. LC 74-1330. 128p. 1974. pap. 2.95 o.s.i. (ISBN 0-664-24987-6, Westminster). Westminster John Knox.

When Cancer Strikes. P-H.

When Children Think: Using Journals to Encourage Creative Thinking. Gabriel Jacobs. LC 71-78837. 1970. pap. text ed. 4.95x o.p. (ISBN 0-8077-1558-1). Tchrs Coll.

When Couples Part: How the Legal System Can Work for You. Lawrence E. Kahn. 192p. 1981. 10.95 o.p. (ISBN 0-531-09944-X). Watts.

When Daddy Was a Little Boy. A. Raskin. 120p. 1976. 4.45 o.p. (ISBN 0-8285-1262-0, Pub. by Progress Pubs USSR). Imported Pubns.

When Dana Was the Sun: A Story of Personal Journalism. Charles J. Rosebault. 1970. Repr. of 1931 ed. lib. bdg. 35.00x o.p. (ISBN 0-8371-4009-9, RODS). Greenwood.

When Death Draws Near: Meditations for All Who Walk in the Valley of the Shadow. Philip W. Williams. LC 78-66945. 1979. pap. 3.95 o.p. (ISBN 0-8066-1694-6, 10-7067, Augsburg). Augsburg Fortress.

When Divorce Ends Your Marriage...It Hurts. Amy R. Mumford. (Accent Expressions Ser.). (Illus.). 24p. (Orig.). 1982. 4.95 o.p. (ISBN 0-89636-099-7). Accent Bks.

When Doctors Love. Ursula Bloom. (Lythway Ser.). 1987. lib. bdg. 16.95x o.p. (ISBN 0-7451-0575-0, Pub. by Chivers Pr UK). G K Hall.

When Dragons Dance. Elliot Tokson. 416p. (Orig.). 1982. pap. 3.25 o.p. (ISBN 0-380-79145-5, 79145). Avon.

When Food Is a Four Letter Word: Programs for Recovery from Anorexia, Bulimia, Bulimarexia, Obesity, & Other Appetite Disorders. Paul Haskew & Cynthia Adams. 200p. 1984. 14.95 o.p. (ISBN 0-13-956111-0); pap. 6.95 o.p. (ISBN 0-13-956103-X). P-H.

When Freedom Came: A Novel. (Vikas Library of Modern Indian Writing: No. 13). 1982. text ed. 20.00x o.p. (ISBN 0-7069-1333-7, Pub. by Vikas India). Advent NY.

When French Women Cook: A Gastronomic Memoir. Madeleine Kamman. LC 76-11582. 1976. 13.95 o.p. (ISBN 0-689-10747-1, Atheneum). Macmillan.

When Fresno Rode the Rails. Edward Hamm, Jr. Ed. by Mac Sebree. (Special Ser.: No. 73). (Illus.). 1979. pap. 12.95 o.p. (ISBN 0-916374-37-8). Interurban.

When God Is at Home with Your Family. David M. Thomas. LC 78-73019. (When Bk.). (Illus.). 1978. pap. 2.45 o.p. (ISBN 0-87029-146-7, 20231-7). Abbey.

When God Speaks. Philip A. Quanbeck. LC 68-13428. (Tower Books No. 9). (Orig.). 1968. pap. 1.50 o.p. (ISBN 0-8066-9358-4, 10-7057, Augsburg). Augsburg Fortress.

When Governments Become Land Developers: Notes on the Public-Sector Experience in the Netherlands & California. George Lefcoe. (Lincoln Institute Monograph: No. 78-3). 1978. pap. 5.00 o.p. (ISBN 0-686-12251-8). Lincoln Inst Land.

When I Go Visiting. Anne Rockwell & Harlow Rockwell. LC 83-17586. (Illus.). 24p. (ps-k). 1984. 8.95 o.s.i. (ISBN 0-02-777740-5). MacMillan.

When I Grow Up. Harry Bornstein. (Signed English Ser.). 46p. 1974. pap. 5.95 o.p. (ISBN 0-913580-35-X, Clerc Bks). Gallaudet Univ Pr.

When I Was Old. Georges Simenon. LC 70-153690. (Helen & Kurt Wolff Bk.). (Illus.). 343p. 1971. 8.50 o.p. (ISBN 0-15-195950-1). HarBraceJ.

When I Whistle. Shusaku Endo. Tr. by Van C. Gessel from Japanese. LC 79-13183. 1979. 8.95 o.s.i. (ISBN 0-8008-8243-1). Taplinger.

When in Doubt, Hug 'em: How to Develop a Caring Church. Cecil B. Murphey. LC 77-15751. 1978. 5.95 o.p. (ISBN 0-8042-1890-0, John Knox). Westminster John Knox.

When It Hits the Fan: Managing the Nine Crises of Business. Gerald C. Meyers & John Holusha. 1986. 17.45 o.s.i. (ISBN 0-395-41171-8). HM.

When Its Time to Talk about Sex. Gordon J. Lester. LC 81-65691. (When Bk.). 96p. (Orig.). 1981. pap. 2.45 o.p. (ISBN 0-87029-176-9, 20268-9). Abbey.

When It's Your Turn to Decide. David Belgum. LC 77-84091. 1978. pap. 3.50 o.p. (ISBN 0-8066-1616-4, 10-7066, Augsburg). Augsburg Fortress.

When Jesus Comes Again: What the Bible Says. Rolf E. Asseng. LC 83-72118. 96p. (Orig.). 1984. pap. 4.95 o.p. (ISBN 0-8066-2062-5, 10-7070, Augsburg). Augsburg Fortress.

When Jesus Was a Baby see Bible Pop-O-Rama Books.

When Jesus Was a Little Boy. 32p. 1981. pap. 2.95 o.p. (ISBN 0-8249-8009-3). Ideals.

When Jesus Was Four-or Maybe Five. Mary D. Bangham. (Illus., Orig.). (ps). 1968. pap. 4.95 o.p. (ISBN 0-8066-0824-2, 10-7058, Augsburg). Augsburg Fortress.

When Jew & Christian Meet. LaVonne Althouse. (Illus.). 1966. pap. 1.50 o.p. (ISBN 0-377-36221-2). Friendship Pr.

When Junior Highs Invade Your Home. Cliff Schimmels. 160p. (Orig.). 1984. pap. 4.95 o.p. (ISBN 0-8007-5144-2, Power Bks). Revell.

When LaGuardia Was Mayor: New York's Legendary Years. August Heckscher & Phyllis Robinson. (Illus.). 1978. 17.50 o.p. (ISBN 0-393-07534-6). Norton.

When Leisure Is the Lord's. Thomas L. Jones. (Orig.). (gr. 9-12). 1964. pap. 1.25 o.p. (ISBN 0-8042-9316-3, John Knox). Westminster John Knox.

When Love Becomes Anger. Kathy C. Miller. 144p. (Orig.). 1985. pap. 5.95 o.p. (ISBN 0-317-13928-2). Heres Life.

When Love Remains. Victoria Pade. (Avon Romance Ser.). 384p. (Orig.). 1983. pap. 2.95 o.p. (ISBN 0-380-82610-0, 82610-0). Avon.

When Love Unites the Church. Richard M. Lawless. LC 81-72000. (When Bks.). 88p. (Orig.). 1982. pap. 2.45 o.p. (ISBN 0-87029-181-5, 20273-9). Abbey.

When Mama Was a Little Girl: Memories of a Georgia Childhood. Eleanor D. Clark. (Illus.). 77p. 1980. 6.00 o.p. (ISBN 0-682-49663-4). Exposition-Phoenix.

When Marriage Ends. Russell J. Becker. Ed. by Willam E. Julme. LC 74-152366. (Pocket Counsel Bks). 64p. (Orig.). 1971. pap. 1.75 o.p. (ISBN 0-8006-1102-0, 1-1102, Fortress). Augsburg Fortress.

When Marriage Ends: A Study in Status Passage. Nicky Hart. 277p. 1976. pap. 12.95x o.p. (ISBN 0-422-74690-8, NO. 6371, Pub. by Tavistock England). Routledge Chapman & Hall.

When Mother Got the Flu. Beverly Keller. (Illus.). 64p. (gr. 1-4). 1984. PLB 6.99 o.p. (ISBN 0-698-30743-7, Coward). Putnam Pub Group.

When Negroes March. Herbert Garfinkel. LC 69-15522. (Studies in American Negro Life Ser). 1969. pap. 3.25x o.s.i. (ISBN 0-689-70078-4, NL13, Atheneum). Macmillan.

When Next We Love. Heather X. Graham. (Candlelight Ecstasy Ser.: No. 117). (Orig.). 1983. pap. 1.95 o.s.i. (ISBN 0-440-19588-8). Dell.

When Night the Moon Awakes. Kenneth M. Kelly. LC 85-91002. 48p. 1985. 6.00 o.p. (ISBN 0-682-40232-X). Exposition-Phoenix.

When Nomads Settle: Processes of Sedentarization As Adaptation & Response. Ed. by Philip C. Salzman. 192p. 1980. 24.95x o.p. (ISBN 0-03-052501-2). Bergin & Garvey.

When Opposites Attract. John M. Drescher. LC 79-53272. (When Bks.). (Illus., Orig.). 1979. pap. 2.45 o.p. (ISBN 0-87029-153-X, 20239-0). Abbey.

When Pregnancy Fails: Families Coping with Miscarriage, Stillbirth, & Infant Death. Susan O. Borg & Judith Lasker. LC 80-28898. 224p. 1981. 14.95x o.p. (ISBN 0-8070-3226-3); pap. 8.95 o.p. (ISBN 0-8070-3227-1, BP613). Beacon Pr.

When Pregnancy Is a Problem. Regis Walling. LC 79-51280. (When Book Ser.). (Illus.). 1980. pap. 2.45 o.p. (ISBN 0-87029-152-1, 20235-8). Abbey.

When Reason Fails: Vol. I, Church Slavonic-South Slavic-West Slavic. Myron S. Augsburger. (Yale Russian & East European Publications). 112p. 1985. pap. 4.95 o.p. (ISBN 0-936586-03-6). Tyndale.

When Religion Gets Sick. Wayne E. Oates. LC 76-114727. 196p. 1970. pap. 4.95 o.s.i. (ISBN 0-664-24891-8, Westminster). Westminster John Knox.

When Rich Men Die. Harold Adams. LC 86-24148. 240p. 1987. 16.95 o.s.i. (ISBN 0-385-24005-8). Doubleday.

When Rock Was Young: A Nostalgic Review of the Top Forty Era. Bruce Pollock. LC 80-23460. (Illus.). 224p. 1981. 13.95 o.s.i. (ISBN 0-03-049836-8, Owl Bks); pap. 6.95 o.s.i. (ISBN 0-03-049841-4). H Holt & Co.

When Rocks Dance. Elizabeth Nunez-Harrell. 1986. 17.95 o.p. (ISBN 0-399-13209-0). Putnam Pub Group.

When Russia Was in America: The Alaska Boundary Treaty Negotiations, 1824-25. M. Huculak. (Illus.). 1971. 17.50 o.s.i. E J Brill USA.

When School Districts Bargain see Issues in the Public Employee Relations Library: Series 1.

When Schools Are Desegregated: Problems & Possibilities for Students, Educators, Parents & the Community. Ed. by Murray L. Wax. LC 79-66449. 300p. 19.95 o.p. (ISBN 0-87855-376-2). Transaction Pubs.
When Science Fails. John H. Tiner. (Direction Bks). 1974. pap. 3.95 o.p. (ISBN 0-8010-8823-2). Baker Bk.
When Shlemiel Went to Warsaw & Other Stories. Isaac Bashevis Singer. 1979. pap. 1.25 o.p. (ISBN 0-440-49306-4, YB). Dell.
When Someone You Love Is Dying. Norma S. Upson. 192p. 1986. pap. 6.95 o.p. (ISBN 0-671-61079-1, Fireside). S&S.
When the City Stopped. Joan Phipson. LC 78-6930. 180p. (gr. 7-9). 1978. 8.95 o.p. (ISBN 0-689-50121-8, Atheneum). Macmillan.
When the Coast Was Wild & Lonely: Early Settlers of The Sur. Rosalind S. Wall. (Illus.). 190p. 1987. pap. 9.95 o.p. (ISBN 0-940168-03-0). Boxwood.
When the Cold Came & Other Stories see Night of the Sphinx & Other Stories.
When the Comforter Came. Albert B. Simpson. pap. 2.95 o.p. (ISBN 0-87509-042-7). Chr Pubns.
When the Flowers Die (Remember Me) Ernestine N. Adams. 1978. 9.00 o.p. (ISBN 0-682-49095-4). Exposition-Phoenix.
When the Ku Klux Rode. Eyre Damer. LC 70-106882. 1972. Repr. of 1912 ed. lib. bdg. 22.50x o.p. (ISBN 0-8371-3278-9, DAK&). Greenwood.
When the Man You Love Is an Alcoholic. Jean Klewin & Thomas Klewin. LC 79-51276. (When Bks). (Illus.). 1979. pap. 2.45 o.p. (ISBN 0-87029-149-1, 20232-5). Abbey.
When the Music Mattered: Rock in the 1960s. Bruce Pollack. LC 83-10853. (Illus.). 214p. 1983. 15.95 o.s.i. (ISBN 0-03-060426-5); pap. 9.95 o.s.i. (ISBN 0-03-060421-4). H Holt & Co.
When the People Say No. James E. Dittes. LC 78-15879. (Orig.). 1979. pap. 6.68 o.p. (ISBN 0-06-061923-6, RD 228). HarpR.
When the Road Bends: A Book about the Pain & Joy Of Passage. Karl A. Olsson. LC 78-66948. 1979. 8.95 o.p. (ISBN 0-8066-1695-4, 10-7073, Augsburg); pap. 5.95 o.p. (ISBN 0-8066-1674-1, 10-7074). Augsburg Fortress.
When the Road Gets Rough. Edward Hindson & Walter Byrd. 160p. 1986. 9.95 o.p. (ISBN 0-8007-1495-4). Revell.
When the Sacred Gin Mill Closes. Lawrence Block. 1986. 15.95 o.p. (ISBN 0-87795-774-6). Morrow.
When the Spotlight Fades. Susan Marie. LC 87-9014. (Starlight Romance Ser.). 192p. 1987. 12.95 o.s.i. (ISBN 0-385-24335-9). Doubleday.
When the Tide Goes Far Out. Lorus Milne & Margery Milne. (Illus.). (gr. 4-8). 1970. PLB 4.25 o.p. (ISBN 0-689-20606-2, Atheneum). Macmillan.
When the Time Had Fully Come: Christmas Service for Church Schools. Sharon Lee. 32p. (Orig.). 1984. pap. 0.90 ea. o.p. (ISBN 0-8066-2101-X, 23-3010, Augsburg). Augsburg Fortress.
When the Wind Blows. Cyril Hare. LC 75-44980. (Crime Fiction Ser). 1976. Repr. of 1949 ed. lib. bdg. 21.00 o.p. (ISBN 0-8240-2373-0). Garland Pub.
When the Wind Blows. Date not set. (ISBN 0-8052-3829-8). Random.
When the Woman You Love Is an Alcoholic. Joan Curlee-Salisbury. LC 78-73017. (When Bk). (Illus.). 1978. pap. 2.45 o.p. (ISBN 0-87029-143-2, 20229-1). Abbey.
When They Ask for Bread: Pastoral Care & Counseling. G. F. Bennett. LC 77-15743. 1978. 8.95 o.p. (ISBN 0-8042-1159-0, John Knox). Westminster John Knox.
When to Sell Stocks Portfolio Liquidation: The Key to Superior Performance Without Stock Selection. Eric S. Emory. 1978. 10.00 o.p. (ISBN 0-682-49019-9, Banner). Exposition-Phoenix.
When TV Is a Member of the Family. Edward N. McNulty. LC 79-55860. (When Bk). 96p. (Orig.). 1981. pap. 2.45 o.p. (ISBN 0-87029-160-2, 20266-3). Abbey.
When Two or More Are Gathered Together. Neal Slavin. 133p. 1976. 25.00 o.p. (ISBN 0-374-28908-5); pap. 10.95 o.p. (ISBN 0-374-51410-0). FS&G.
When We Teach Juniors. Jane B. Harris. 1957. pap. 1.00 o.s.i. (ISBN 0-664-24214-6, Westminster). Westminster John Knox.
When William Fourth Was King. John Ashton. LC 67-23943. (Social History Reference Ser.). 372p. 1968. Repr. of 1896 ed. 35.00x o.p. (ISBN 0-8103-3255-8). Gale.
When You Are Alone It Keeps You Capone: An Approach to Creative Writing with Children. Myra C. Livingston. LC 73-80758. 256p. 1973. 7.95 o.p. (ISBN 0-689-10579-7, Atheneum). Macmillan.
When You Are Concerned with Homosexuality. Alfred Messer. LC 79-55861. (When Books). (Orig.). 1980. pap. 2.45 o.p. (ISBN 0-87029-161-0, 20262-2). Abbey.
When You Can't Find Time for Each Other. Wayne E. Oates. LC 81-71999. (WHEN Bks). 96p. (Orig.). 1982. pap. 2.45 o.p. (ISBN 0-87029-182-3, 20274-7). Abbey.
When You Can't Pay Your Taxes! How to Deal with the IRS. Robert S. Schriebman. 200p. 1986. pap. 14.95 o.p. (ISBN 0-87094-752-4); 19.95 o.p. (ISBN 0-87094-906-3). Dow Jones-Irwin.
When You Feel Like a Failure... Gene Getz. LC 77-99282. 1978. pap. 5.95 o.s.i. (ISBN 0-8307-0631-3, 54-096-08); study guide only o.p. 1.39 o.s.i. (ISBN 0-8307-0649-6, 6101402). Regal.
When You Feel Like a Failure. Margaret Parker. (Study & Grow Electives). 64p. 1985. pap. 3.95 leader's guide o.s.i. (ISBN 0-8307-1036-1, 6102073). Regal.
When You Feel Like Screaming: Help for Frustrated Mothers. Pat Holt & Grace Ketterman. 112p. (Orig.). 1988. pap. 6.95 o.p. Shaw Pubs.
When You Fight the Tiger. Joan Hewett. (Illus.). 96p. (gr. 5 up). 1984. 14.95 o.p. (ISBN 0-316-35956-4). Little.
When You Go to Tonga. Edward Tremblay. (Illus.). 1954. 3.25 o.p. (ISBN 0-8198-0173-9). Dghtrs St Paul.
When You Graduate. Charles L. Allen & Mouzon Biggs. 64p. 1972. 7.95 o.p. (ISBN 0-8007-0527-0). Revell.
When You Need a Special Sermon Series. 1981. pap. 5.95 o.p. (ISBN 0-570-03836-7, 12-2801). Concordia.
When You Receive a Child. Judy B. Hull. LC 79-55859. (When Books). (Illus., Orig.). 1980. pap. 2.45 o.p. (ISBN 0-87029-159-9, 20261-4). Abbey.
When You Think You're in Love. Sandra Drescher & John Drescher. LC 81-65208. (When Bks.). 96p. 1981. pap. 2.45 o.p. (ISBN 0-87029-174-2, 20270-5). Abbey.
When You Went Away. Gladys W. DuRapau. LC 84-90174. (Illus.). 51p. 1985. 5.95 o.p. (ISBN 0-533-06232-2). Vantage.
When Your Child Becomes Your Friend. Marion Duckworth. LC 81-71998. (When Bk.). 96p. (Orig.). 1982. pap. 2.45 o.p. (ISBN 0-87029-183-1, 20275-4). Abbey.
When Your Child Hurts. Charlotte Adelsperger. LC 81-68639. 112p. 1985. pap. 5.95 o.p. (ISBN 0-8066-2161-3, 10-7088, Augsburg). Augsburg Fortress.
When Your Child Is Hyperactive. Kenneth Heiting. LC 78-73015. (When Bk). (Illus., Orig.). 1978. pap. 2.45 o.p. (ISBN 0-87029-142-4, 20227-5). Abbey.
When Your Child Is Overweight. Leslie-Jane Maynard. LC 79-55863. (When Books). (Illus.). 96p. (Orig.). 1980. pap. 2.45 o.p. (ISBN 0-87029-162-9, 20263-0). Abbey.
When Your Child Learns to Choose. Andrew D. Thompson. LC 78-73018. (When Bk). (Illus.). 1978. pap. 2.45 o.p. (ISBN 0-87029-145-9, 20228-3). Abbey.
When Your Child Needs a Hug. Larry Losoncy. LC 78-73016. (When Bk). (Illus.). 1978. pap. 2.45 o.p. (ISBN 0-87029-141-6, 20226-7). Abbey.
When Your Marriage Goes Stale. James Kenny & Mary Kenny. LC 79-51277. (When Bks). (Illus.). 1979. pap. 2.45 o.p. (ISBN 0-87029-150-5, 20236-6). Abbey.
When Your Son or Daughter Plans for the Future. Thomas D. Bachhuber. LC 78-73014. (When Bk). (Illus.). 1978. pap. 2.45 o.p. (ISBN 0-87029-144-0, 20230-9). Abbey.
When Your Teenager Stops Going to Church. James Di Giacomo. LC 80-65401. (When Books). (Illus.). 96p. (Orig.). 1980. pap. 2.45 o.p. (ISBN 0-87029-165-3, 20260-6). Abbey.
When Your Wife Wants to Work. Mary Shivanandan. LC 79-51278. (When Bks). (Illus.). 1980. pap. 2.45 o.p. (ISBN 0-87029-151-3, 20237-4). Abbey.
When You're Divorced & Catholic. James J. Young. LC 80-69090. (When Bk). 96p. 1980. pap. 2.45 o.p. (ISBN 0-87029-172-6, 20265-5). Abbey.
When You're in You're Out. Mollie Thompson. LC 86-10977. (Illus.). 192p. (Orig.). 1986. pap. 5.95 o.p. (ISBN 0-932581-50-1). Word Aflame.
When You're Married. William B. Ward. (Orig.). 1947. pap. 1.95 o.p. (ISBN 0-8042-2604-0, John Knox). Westminster John Knox.
Whence the Threat to Peace. 4rd ed. U. S. S. R. Ministry of Defense Staff. 100p. 1984. pap. 2.95 o.p. (ISBN 0-8285-9137-7, Pub. by Military Pubs USSR). Imported Pubns.
Where Are All the Kittens? Jennifer Perryman. LC 83-63492. (Cuddle Shape Bks.). (Illus.). 14p. (ps-1). 1984. bds. 3.95 o.s.i. (ISBN 0-394-86793-9, Pub. by BYR). Random.
Where Are the Jobs. Erdlen. 1982. 12.95 o.p. (ISBN 0-15-195964-1). HarBraceJ.
Where Are The Jobs. Erdlen. 1982. pap. 6.95 o.p. (ISBN 0-15-600030-X). HarBraceJ.
Where Are We Running? June Strong. LC 78-26271. (Orion Ser.). 1979. pap. 3.95 o.p. (ISBN 0-8127-0207-7). Review & Herald.
Where Are You, Angela Von Hauptmann, Now That I Need You? Barbara Williams. LC 79-1069. (gr. 5-9). 1979. 7.95 o.p. (ISBN 0-03-050606-9). H Holt & Co.
Where Are You, Cow Patty? Elizabeth-Ann Sachs. LC 84-2950. 156p. (gr. 5-8). 1984. 10.95 o.s.i. (ISBN 0-689-31057-9, Atheneum Childrens Bks). Macmillan.
Where Are You God from 9 to 5. Nancy Barcus. (Illus.). 160p. 1987. 8.95 o.p. (ISBN 0-8007-1518-7). Revell.
Where Are You Going? A Guide to the Spiritual Journey. Ed. by Swami Muktananda. LC 81-52192. 168p. (Orig.). 1981. pap. 7.50 o.s.i. (ISBN 0-914602-75-6). SYDA Found.
Where Are You Now, Bo Diddley? The Artists Who Made Us Rock & Where They Are Now. Edward Kiersh. LC 86-31092. (Illus.). 400p. 1986. 9.95 o.p. (ISBN 0-385-19448-X, Dolp). Doubleday.
Where Atlantans Dine. Ed. by Barbara Robinson. LC 86-21519. 80p. 1986. 3.95 o.p. (ISBN 0-932419-03-8). Susan Hunter.
Where Did You Go? Out - What Did You Do? Nothing. Robert P. Smith. (Illus.). 1957. Repr. of 1958 ed. 3.95 o.p. (ISBN 0-393-07328-9). Norton.
Where Do Babies Come from? & How to Keep Them There! What a Teenager Should Know about Sex, Love, Marriage & Birth Control. LeMon Clark. 1978. 8.50 o.p. (ISBN 0-682-49100-4, Banner). Exposition-Phoenix.
Where Do You Look? Whom Do You Ask? How Do You Know? An Information Resource for Child Advocates. Janet L. Shur et al. LC 80-66458. 128p. (Orig.). 1980. pap. 5.50 o.p. (ISBN 0-938008-13-7). Children's Defense.
Where Does My Cat Sleep? Norma Simon. Ed. by Kathy Tucker. LC 82-10872. (Just For Fun Bks.). (Illus.). 32p. (ps-3). 1982. PLB 10.25 o.p. (ISBN 0-8075-8926-8). A Whitman.
Where Does Your Money Go? Donald L. Blair. LC 76-56034. 1977. 4.50 o.p. (ISBN 0-682-48754-6). Exposition-Phoenix.
Where Eagles Dare. Alistair MacLean. 1984. pap. 3.50 o.p. (ISBN 0-449-20707-2, Crest). Fawcett.
Where Faith & Economics Meet: A Christian Critique. David M. Beckmann. LC 80-67796. 160p. (Orig.). 1981. pap. 7.95 o.p. (ISBN 0-8066-1858-2, 10-7068, Augsburg). Augsburg Fortress.
Where Have All Our People Gone? New Choices for Old Churches. Carl S. Dudley. LC 79-525. (Illus.). 1979. pap. 6.95 o.p. (ISBN 0-8298-0359-9). Pilgrim NY.
Where Have All the Voters Gone? The Fracturing of America's Political Parties. Everett C. Ladd, Jr. (Illus.). 1978. 7.95x o.p. (ISBN 0-393-05691-0); pap. 4.95x o.p. (ISBN 0-393-09011-6). Norton.
Where Human Rights Are Real. G. Morris. 176p. 1980. 6.45 o.p. (ISBN 0-8285-1861-0, Pub. by Progress Pubs USSR). Imported Pubns.
Where in the World Do You Live? Al Hine & John Alcorn. LC 62-7728. (Illus.). 40p. (gr. 1-3). 1962. 4.50 o.p. (ISBN 0-15-295605-0, HJ). HarBraceJ.
Where Is Bobby Now? Marvin Moore. (Flame Ser.). 1976. pap. 1.25 o.p. (ISBN 0-8127-0106-2). Review & Herald.
Where Is Bone? Palmer & Weinert. (Illus.). 1980. pap. 1.50 o.p. (ISBN 0-380-75242-5, 75242-5, Camelot). Avon.
Where Is God? Three Church Dramas. Barbara H. Dudley. LC 72-90268. 1973. pap. 1.95 o.p. (ISBN 0-8066-1316-5, 10-7065, Augsburg). Augsburg Fortress.
Where Is My Heart? Amelia Walden. LC 60-5205. (gr. 9 up). 1960. 4.95 o.s.i. (ISBN 0-664-32228-X, Westminster). Westminster John Knox.
Where is the Afikomen? Judye Groner & Madeline Wikler. LC 85-80781. (Illus.). 12p. (ps). 1985. bds. 4.95 o.p. (ISBN 0-930494-52-0). Kar Ben.
Where Is the Lost Ark? Doug Wead. LC 82-71755. 122p. (Orig.). 1982. pap. 2.95 o.p. (ISBN 0-87123-628-1, 200628). Bethany Hse.
Where Is the Wilderness? Pat Bridges. (Illus.). 28p. (Orig.). 1984. pap. 4.00 o.p. (ISBN 0-916897-00-1); ltd. ed. 10.00 o.p. (ISBN 0-916897-01-X). Andrew Mtn Pr.
Where Medicine Fails. rev. 2nd. ed. Ed. by Anselm L. Strauss. LC 72-87665. (Society Bks). 1973. pap. text ed. 3.95x o.p. (ISBN 0-87855-540-4); 9.95 o.p. (ISBN 0-87855-047-X). Transaction Pubs.
Where Medicine Fails. 3rd ed. Ed. by Anselm L. Strauss. LC 78-62893. 296p. 1979. pap. 4.95x o.p. (ISBN 0-87855-676-1). Transaction Pubs.
Where Mountains Meet the Sea: An Illustrated History of Puget Sound. James R. Warren. (Illus.). 288p. 1986. 24.95 o.p. (ISBN 0-89781-175-5). Windsor Pubns Inc.
Where Rivers Meet: An Illustrated History of Ottawa. Courtney C. Bond. LC 84-19571. (Illus.). 192p. 1984. 24.95 o.s.i. (ISBN 0-89781-111-9). Windsor Pubns Inc.
Where the Chill Came From: Cree Windigo Tales & Journeys. Tr. by Howard Norman. LC 81-81506. 144p. 1982. 17.50 o.s.i. (ISBN 0-86547-047-2); pap. 9.00 o.s.i. (ISBN 0-86547-048-0). N Point Pr.
Where the Dai People Live. Ed. by An Chunyang & Liu Bohua. (Illus.). 117p. (Orig.). 1985. pap. 19.95 o.p. (ISBN 0-8351-1187-3). China Bks.
Where the Jackals Howl & Other Stories. Amos Oz. Tr. by Nicholas De Lange & Philip Simpson. LC 80-8754. (Helen & Kurt Wolff Bk.). 228p. 1981. 12.95 o.p. (ISBN 0-15-196038-0). HarBraceJ.
Where the Jobs Are: Communications. Maynard Hicks. 1977. 8.00 o.p. (ISBN 0-682-48949-2). Exposition-Phoenix.
Where the Law Ends, the Social Control of Corporate Behavior. Christopher Stone. 16.00 o.p. (ISBN 0-8446-5863-4). Peter Smith.
Where the Rainbow Ends. Christopher Hudson. LC 86-26624. 320p. 1987. 17.95 o.p. (ISBN 0-689-11917-8, Atheneum). Macmillan.
Where the Road Ends. Ella T. Ellis. LC 73-84824. 208p. (gr. 5-9). 1974. 5.95 o.p. (ISBN 0-689-30134-0, Atheneum). Macmillan.
Where the Sky Began: Land of the Tallgrass Prairie. John Madson. (Illus.). 295p. 1982. 13.95 o.p. (ISBN 0-395-25718-2). HM.
Where the Spirit Leads: Seventeen American Denominations Today. Ed. by Martin E. Marty. LC 80-82197. 208p. (Orig.). 1980. pap. 2.10 o.p. (ISBN 0-8042-0868-9, John Knox). Westminster John Knox.
Where the Truth Lies. Helen Cannon. 1981. pap. 2.50 o.p. (ISBN 0-380-78709-1, 78709). Avon.
Where the World Is: Teaching Basic Skills Outdoors. John Dacey. (Illus.). 192p. 1981. pap. 12.95 o.p. (ISBN 0-673-16458-6). Scott F.
Where There's a Will: Nero Wolfe. Rex Stout. 1941. pap. 1.50 o.p. (ISBN 0-380-01620-6, 39529). Avon.
Where There's Smoke... How to Protect Yourself, Your Family, Your Property, Your Environment from Fire. Robin F. Pendergrast. LC 81-69076. (Illus.). 144p. 1982. 9.95 o.p. (ISBN 0-916752-50-X). Longman Trade.
Where They Lived in London: A Guide to Famous Doorsteps. Maurice Rickards. LC 72-145542. (Illus.). 112p. 1972. 7.95 o.s.i. (ISBN 0-8008-8245-8). Taplinger.
Where to Find the Oregon in Oregon 1988-89. rev. ed. Bridget B. McCarthy. (Illus.). 128p. 1988. pap. 6.95 o.p. (ISBN 0-9616696-2-4). B B McCarthy.
Where to Go in Britain. Date not set. (ISBN 0-86145-455-3, Pub. by Auto Assn England). Salem Hse Pubs.
Where to Go in Greece. 2nd, rev. ed. Trevor Webster. (Illus.). 130p. 1987. pap. 8.95 o.s.i. (ISBN 0-87052-355-4). Hippocrene Bks.
Where to Go in the West of Ireland. Hugh Oram. (Illus.). 70p. (Orig.). 1984. pap. 5.95 o.p. (ISBN 0-86281-135-X, Pub. by Appletree Pr). Irish Bks Media.
Where to Go with Your Troubles. William F. Burton. 80p. 1969. pap. 1.00 o.p. (ISBN 0-88243-627-9, 02-0627). Gospel Pub.
Where to Live for Your Health. Norman Carlisle & Madelyn Carlisle. LC 79-2760. (Illus.). 224p. 1980. 10.95 o.p. (ISBN 0-15-196061-5). HarBraceJ.
Where to Put Your Money. Cloverdale Press Staff & Peter Passell. 64p. 1984. pap. 3.95 o.p. (ISBN 0-446-37954-9). Warner Bks.
Where to Retire on a Small Income. 24th, rev. ed. Norman D. Ford. (Illus.). 327p. 1985. pap. text ed. 6.95 o.p. (ISBN 0-686-46668-3). Allsport Pub.
Where to Start: An Annotated Career-Planning Bibliography 1983-85. 4th ed. Madeline T. Rockcastle. 206p. (Orig.). 1983. pap. 11.95 o.p. (ISBN 0-87866-260-X). Petersons Guides.
Where to Start: Essential Resource Guide for Career Planning & Job Hunting, 1987-1989. 6th ed. 296p. (Orig.). 1987. pap. 14.95 o.s.i. (ISBN 0-87866-597-8). Petersons Guides.
Where to Stay in London. Date not set. Salem Hse Pubs.
Where to Stay in Northern Ireland. Date not set. Salem Hse Pubs.
Where to Stay U. S. A. Council on International Educational Exchange Staff. 492p. 1986. pap. 9.95 o.p. (ISBN 0-671-55632-0). S&S.
Where to Stay U. S. A., 1984-85. Council on International Educational Exchange Staff & Marjorie A. Cohen. 448p. 1984. 8.95 o.p. (ISBN 0-671-47604-1). Prentice Hall Pr.
Where to Watch Birds in Europe. John Gooders. LC 77-84451. (Illus.). 1978. 10.95 o.s.i. (ISBN 0-8008-8246-6). Taplinger.
Where Was Everyone When Sabrina Screamed? Amelia Walden. LC 72-13458. 160p. (gr. 7 up). 1973. 4.95 o.s.i. (ISBN 0-664-32525-4, Westminster). Westminster John Knox.

Where You'll Find Me: And Other Stories. Ann Beattie. 1986. 14.70 o.p. (ISBN 0-671-62220-X, Linden Pr). S&S.
Where's Jim Now. Bianca Bradbury. (gr. 5-9). 1978. 7.95 o.p. (ISBN 0-395-27160-6). HM.
Where's Waldo Now? Martin Handford. 1988. 10.45 o.p. Little.
Wherever We Step the Land Is Mined. Natalie Scott. 240p. 1980. 8.95 o.p. (ISBN 0-531-09939-3). Watts.
Whetstone. John Knoepfle. LC 81-670240. 1972. 1.00 o.p. (ISBN 0-933532-29-6). BkMk.
Whey Cookery (Treats Made with Milk Sugar) Forman & Weeks. (Illus.). pap. 2.95 o.p. (ISBN 0-89036-064-2). Hawkes Pub Inc.
Which Jesus? John W. Bowman. LC 74-100953. 1970. pap. 3.75 o.s.i. (ISBN 0-664-24879-9, Westminster). Westminster John Knox.
Which Way Are You Headed? Brenda Sears. 32p. 1986. 4.95 o.p. (ISBN 0-8062-2065-1). Carlton.
Which Way Courage. Eiveen Weiman. LC 80-36725. 144p. (gr. 4-8). 1981. PLB 8.95 o.p. (ISBN 0-689-30835-3, Atheneum). Macmillan.
Which Way Out of the Men's Room? Gordon Johnston. LC 76-63542. 1979. 14.95 o.p. (ISBN 0-498-02409-1). A S Barnes.
Which Way the Wind. Hans Herlin. 240p. 1980. pap. 2.25 o.p. (ISBN 0-380-48306-8, 48306). Avon.
Which Way the Wind Blows: Part II of Valley of Many Winds. Mario Edlosi. 1978. 7.50 o.p. (ISBN 0-682-49073-3). Exposition-Phoenix.
Which Way, Young Americans. E. Madison George. LC 62-8187. (Orig.). 1962. pap. 2.00 o.p. (ISBN 0-87004-051-0). Caxton.
While My Guitar Gently Weeps: A Novel. Paul Breeze. LC 80-22065. 222p. 1981. 9.95 o.s.i. (ISBN 0-8008-8247-4). Taplinger.
Whilst Thy Tower Crumbles. Opal A. Doubleday. 8.95 o.p. (ISBN 0-533-05965-8). Vantage.
Whimsey Anthology. Carolyn Wells. LC 73-5528. xiv, 236p. 1976. Repr. of 1963 ed. 35.00x o.p. (ISBN 0-8103-4115-8). Gale.
Whip. Catherine Cookson. (Illus.). 384p. 1982. 14.50 o.s.i. (ISBN 0-671-43272-9). Summit Bks.
Whipping Star. Frank Herbert. 1980. pap. 14.50 o.p. (ISBN 0-8398-2648-6, Gregg). G K Hall.
Whirligigs: Design & Construction. Anders S. Lunde. LC 85-73429. 80p. 1985. pap. 6.95 o.p. (ISBN 0-8019-7709-6). Chilton.
Whirlpool. George Gissing. Ed. by Patrick Parrinder. 496p. (Orig.). 1985. pap. 7.95 o.p. (ISBN 0-416-01081-4, NO. 9281). Routledge Chapman & Hall.
Whirlwind. Stephen Clissold. (ISBN 0-8022-0266-7). Philos Lib.
Whirlwind Courtship. Jayne Taylor. (Orig.). 1980. pap. 1.75 o.p. (ISBN 0-8439-8012-5). Dorchester Pub Co.
Whiskers the Rabbit. Rebecca Anders. Tr. by Dyan Hammarberg from Fr. LC 76-1236. (Animal Friends Bks). (Illus.). 24p. (Eng.). (gr. k-4). 1976. PLB 5.95 o.p. (ISBN 0-87614-070-3). Carolrhoda Bks.
Whisper. Gina Wilson. LC 83-25298. 160p. (gr. 6 up). 1984. 11.95 o.p. (ISBN 0-571-11930-1). Faber & Faber.
Whisper & the Secret of Dark Hollow. Christopher Brown. (Whisper the Winged Unicorn Ser.). (Illus.). 24p. (gr. 3-7). 1985. pap. 1.95 o.p. (ISBN 0-89954-289-1). Antioch Pub Co.
Whisper My Name. Fern Michaels. (Nightingale Paperbacks Ser.). 1984. pap. 9.95 o.p. (ISBN 0-8161-3738-2, Large Print Bks). G K Hall.
Whisper on the Wind. Nell Kincaid. (Candlelight Ecstasy Supreme Ser.: No. 7). (Orig.). 1983. pap. 2.50 o.s.i. (ISBN 0-440-19519-5). Dell.
Whispering Gate. Mary Wibberley. (Nightingale Paperbacks). 1985. pap. 9.95 o.p. (ISBN 0-8161-3871-0, Large Print Bks). G K Hall.
Whispering Statue. Carolyn Keene. LC 72-106316. (Nancy Drew Ser.: Vol. 14). (Illus.). (gr. 4-7). 1937. 4.50 o.p. (ISBN 0-448-09514-9, G&D); PLB 3.29 o.p. Putnam Pub Group.
Whispering Voices. Doris Stokes. (Lythway Ser.). 1987. lib. bdg. 17.50x o.p. (ISBN 0-7451-0595-5, Pub. by Chivers Pr UK). G K Hall.
Whispering Wind. Marion H. Freeman. 96p. 1982. 6.00 o.p. (ISBN 0-682-49880-7). Exposition-Phoenix.
Whisperings in the Silence. Zella Townsend. 1972. pap. 2.00 o.p. (ISBN 0-87516-121-9). DeVorss.
Whisper's Mysterious Adventure. Jeff Simons. (Whisper the Winged Unicorn Ser.). (Illus.). 24p. (gr. 2-6). 1984. pap. 1.95 o.p. (ISBN 0-89954-280-8). Antioch Pub Co.
Whispers of Living Memories: Poetry & Prose. Bienvenido Emata, Sr. (Illus.). 1980. 5.00 o.p. (ISBN 0-682-49410-0). Exposition-Phoenix.
Whispers on the Wind. Richard Heasler. 1979. 4.00 o.p. (ISBN 0-936204-07-9). Jelm Mtn.
Whispers VI. Ed. by Stuart D. Schiff. (Science Fiction Ser.). 192p. 1987. 12.95 o.s.i. (ISBN 0-385-19927-9). Doubleday.
Whistler in the Dark. John Malcolm. (Lythway Ser.). 272p. 1988. lib. bdg. 19.50 o.p. (ISBN 0-7451-0651-X, Pub. by Chivers Pr UK). G K Hall.
Whistler in the Dark: A Tim Simpson Mystery. John Malcolm. 160p. 1987. 14.95 o.p. (ISBN 0-684-18701-9). Scribner.
Whistler Lithographs. Mervyn Levy. (Illus.). 1975. 40.00 o.s.i. (ISBN 0-915346-36-2). A Wofsy Fine Arts.
Whistles & Strings. Elementary Science Study Staff. 1971. tchr's. guide 17.32 o.p. (ISBN 0-07-017728-7). McGraw.
Whistles Blow No More: Railroad Logging in the Sierra Nevada, 1874-1942. Hank Johnston. Ed. by Mac Sebree. (Trans Anglo Bks.: No. 267). (Illus.). 160p. 1984. 25.95 o.p. (ISBN 0-87046-067-6, Pub. by Trans-Anglo). Interurban.
Whistling Boy. Ruth M. Arthur. LC 69-13531. (Illus.). (gr. 5-9). 1969. PLB 5.95 o.p. (ISBN 0-689-20614-3, Atheneum). Macmillan.
Whitaker's Almanack, 1983. 115th ed. (Illus.). 1220p. 46.00x o.p. (ISBN 0-8103-0671-9). Gale.
Whitaker's Children's Books in Print, 1987. Ed. by Whitaker, J. & Sons Ltd. 750p. 1987. 75.00 o.p. (ISBN 0-85021-173-5, Pub. by J Whitaker UK). Bowker.
Whitaker's Religious Books in Print, 1987. Ed. by Whitaker, J. & Sons Ltd. 700p. 1987. 89.00 o.p. (ISBN 0-85021-176-X, Pub. by J Whitaker UK). Bowker.
White Archer: An Eskimo Legend. James Houston. LC 79-14458. (Illus.). (gr. 4-7). 1979. pap. 2.25 o.p. (ISBN 0-15-696224-1, VoyB). HarBraceJ.
White Archer: An Eskimo Legend. James Houston. LC 67-17154. (Illus.). 96p. (gr. 3-7). 1967. 6.95 o.p. (ISBN 0-15-295851-7, HJ). HarBraceJ.
White-Boned Demon: A Biography of Madame Mao Zedong. Ross Terrill. Ed. by Pat Golbitz. LC 83-13316. (Illus.). 576p. 1984. 18.95 o.p. (ISBN 0-688-02461-0). Morrow.
White Canada Forever: Popular Attitudes & Public Policy toward Orientals in British Columbia. W. Peter Ward. 207p. 1978. 15.00x o.p. (ISBN 0-7735-0318-8, McGill Canada); pap. 6.50 o.p. (ISBN 0-7735-0319-6, McGill Canada). U of Toronto Pr.
White Caps: Nurse's Training Fifty Years Ago. Mabel R. Kyle. 1978. 8.50 o.p. (ISBN 0-682-48974-3). Exposition-Phoenix.
White Collar & Economic Crime: Multidisciplinary & Cross-National Perspectives. Peter M. Wickman & Timothy E. Dailey. LC 81-47561. 304p. 1981. 33.00x o.p. (ISBN 0-669-04665-5). Lexington Bks.
White Collar & Professional Stress. Ed. by C. L. Cooper & J. Marshall. LC 79-41779. (Studies in Occupational Stress). 257p. 1980. 73.95x o.p. (ISBN 0-471-27760-6, Pub. by Wiley-Interscience). Wiley.
White Collar Crime. August Bequai. LC 77-11242. (Illus.). 1978. 18.95 o.p. (ISBN 0-669-01900-3); pap. 17.00x o.p. (ISBN 0-669-05907-2). Lexington Bks.
White Collar Criminal Practice 1985, Vol. 137. Practising Law Institute Staff. 331p. 1985. pap. 40.00 o.p. (ISBN 0-317-27654-9, C4-4169). PLI.
White Collar Unemployment: Impact & Stress. Stephen Fineman. (Wiley Series Organizational Change & Development). 154p. 1983. 51.95x o.p. (ISBN 0-471-10490-6, Pub. by Wiley-Interscience). Wiley.
White Collar Workers, Trade Unions & Class. Peter Armstrong et al. 224p. 1986. 34.50 o.p. (ISBN 0-7099-0571-8, Pub. by Croom Helm Ltd). Routledge Chapman & Hall.
White Coolies. Betty Jeffrey. 1956. (ISBN 0-8022-0798-7). Philos Lib.
White Dawn: An Eskimo Saga. James Houston. LC 72-134575. 1971. 8.50 o.p. (ISBN 0-15-196115-8, HJ). HarBraceJ.
White Embroidery Story: Candlewicking. Etsuko Inoue. (Illus.). 74p. (Orig.). 1986. pap. 7.50 o.p. (ISBN 0-87040-704-X). Japan Pubns USA.
White Fang. Jack London. (Dent's Illustrated Children's Classics Ser.). (Illus.). 238p. (gr. 4 up). 1975. Repr. of 1967 ed. 11.00x o.p. (ISBN 0-460-05073-7, BKA 01609, Pub. by J M Dent England). Biblio Dist.
White Fang see Call of the Wild.
White Fire. Robert E. Vardeman. (Jade Demons Ser.: No. 4). 199p. 1986. pap. 2.95 o.p. (ISBN 0-380-89801-2). Avon.
White Forest Battle. Harold Calin. 1979. pap. 1.75 o.s.i. (ISBN 0-8439-0624-3, Pub. by Leisure Bks CT). Dorchester Pub Co.
White Fury. Dulci Nemec. 150p. (Orig.). 1988. pap. 3.98 o.p. (ISBN 0-9618998-4-0). Nemec Pub.
White Gold: The Story of African Ivory. Derek Wilson & Peter Ayerst. LC 76-363. (Illus.). (YA) (gr. 10 up). 1976. 9.95 o.s.i. (ISBN 0-8008-8251-2). Taplinger.
White Gold Wielder. Stephen R. Donaldson. (Second Chronicles of Thomas Covenant Ser.: Bk. 3). 480p. 1983. 14.95 o.p. (ISBN 0-345-30307-5, Del Rey). Ballantine.
White Haired Girl. He & Ying. 1987. 4.95 o.p. (ISBN 0-8351-1562-3). China Bks.
White Horse Inn. Georges Simenon. Tr. by Norman Denny. LC 79-3363. (Helen & Kurt Wolff Bk.). 144p. 1980. 7.95 o.p. (ISBN 0-15-196240-5). HarBraceJ.
White House Fever. Robert Bendiner. LC 60-5437. (Illus.). 1960. 3.75 o.p. (ISBN 0-15-196257-X). HarBraceJ.
White House Ghosts. Hans Holzer. Orig. Title: Spirits (1976), Ghosts (1971) 1979. pap. 1.75 o.p. (ISBN 0-8439-0692-8, Pub. by Leisure Bks CT). Dorchester Pub Co.
White Island. Nina Lansdale. LC 74-18157. 1975. 8.95 o.p. (ISBN 0-87795-104-7, Arbor Hse). Morrow.
White Kikuyu. Anne Malatesta & Ronald Friedland. LC 77-78765. (Illus.). (gr. 6 up). 1978. text ed. 9.95 o.p. (ISBN 0-07-039750-3). McGraw.
White Lantern. Evan S. Connell. 1981. pap. 5.95 o.s.i. (ISBN 0-03-059154-6). H Holt & Co.
White Lies. Trevor Shearston. 206p. 1986. (ISBN 0-7022-1898-7). U of Queensland Pr.
White Light. Patricia Volk. LC 87-17122. 256p. 1987. 18.95 o.p. (ISBN 0-689-11868-6, Atheneum). Macmillan.
White Mandarin. Dan Sherman. LC 81-66957. 352p. 1982. 15.25 o.p. (ISBN 0-87795-325-2, Arbor Hse). Morrow.
White Mandarin. Dan Sherman. 1984. pap. 3.50 o.s.i. (ISBN 0-345-30895-6). Ballantine.
White Man's Saga. Eric Linklater. 1983. 30.00x o.p. (ISBN 0-317-20377-0, Pub. by Macdonald Pub UK). State Mutual Bk.
White Minority: Pioneers for Racial Equality. Richard Stiller. LC 77-76442. (Illus.). 120p. (gr. 7-9). 1977. 6.95 o.p. (ISBN 0-15-295877-0, HJ). HarBraceJ.
White Notebook. Andre Gide. 1965. pap. 1.25 o.p. (ISBN 0-8065-0029-8, 185, Pub. by Citadel Pr). Carol Pub Group.
White Paper on International Trade: Japan 1980. 32nd ed. Ed. by Japan External Trade Organization (JETRO) Staff. LC 52-36099. (Illus.). 299p. (Orig.). 1981. pap. 72.00x o.s.i. (ISBN 0-8002-2912-6). Intl Pubns Serv.
White Paper on NLRB. 4.00 o.p. Natl Lawyers Guild.
White Papers of Japan, 1978-79: Annual Abstract of Official Reports & Statistics of the Japanese Government, Tokyo. Ed. by Japan Institute of International Affairs Staff. LC 72-620531. (Illus.). 228p. (Orig.). 1980. pap. 40.00x o.s.i. (ISBN 0-8002-2734-4). Intl Pubns Serv.
White Papers of Japan, 1979-80: Annual Abstract of Official Reports & Statistics of the Japanese Government, Tokyo. Ed. by Japan Institute of International Affairs Staff. LC 72-620531. (Illus.). 220p. (Orig.). 1981. pap. 40.00x o.s.i. (ISBN 0-8002-2911-8). Intl Pubns Serv.
White Papers of Japan, 1980-81: Annual Abstract of Official Reports & Statistics of the Japanese Government, Tokyo. Japan Institute of International Affairs Staff. LC 72-620531. (Illus.). 232p. 1982. pap. 40.00x o.s.i. (ISBN 0-8002-3058-2). Intl Pubns Ser.
White, Red, & Black: The Seventeenth-Century Virginian. Wesley F. Craven. 1977. pap. 2.95x o.p. (ISBN 0-393-00857-6, N857, Norton Lib). Norton.
White River, Brown Water: A Record-Making Kayak Journey Down the Amazon. Alan Holman. (Illus.). 192p. 1985. 13.95 o.p. (ISBN 0-89886-113-6). Mountaineers.
White Road: A Russian Odyssey 1919-1923. Olga Ilyin. LC 83-26692. 336p. 1984. 17.95 o.p. (ISBN 0-03-000078-5). H Holt & Co.
White Sand, Wild Sea. Diana Blayne. (Candlelight Ecstasy Ser.: No. 138). (Orig.). 1983. pap. 1.95 o.p. (ISBN 0-440-19627-2). Dell.
White Seal. Rudyard Kipling. (Illus.). (ps-3). 1982. PLB 13.27 o.p. (ISBN 0-516-09224-3). Childrens.
White Seal. Rudyard Kipling. Ed. by Chuck Jones. (Illus.). 48p. (gr. k-6). 1982. 4.95 o.p. (ISBN 0-8249-8042-5). Ideals.
White Seal. Rudyard Kipling. 1985. 5.95 o.p. (ISBN 0-8249-8118-9). Ideals.
White Silk Dress. Peter Simonds. (Illus.). 304p. 1985. 13.00 o.p. (ISBN 0-682-40163-3). Exposition-Phoenix.
White Slave. Fanny Howe. 324p. 1980. pap. 4.95 o.p. (ISBN 0-380-45591-9, 45591-9). Avon.
White Sox: A Pictorial History. Richard Whittingham. (Illus.). 1983. 15.95 o.p. (ISBN 0-8092-5769-6); pap. 7.95 o.p. (ISBN 0-8092-5768-8). Contemp Bks.
White Sparrow. Roy Brown. LC 74-19352. 160p. (gr. 6 up). 1979. 6.95 o.p. (ISBN 0-395-28897-5, Clarion). HM.
White Town Drowsing: Journeys to Hannibal. Ron Powers. LC 86-17472. 320p. 1986. 17.95 o.p. (ISBN 0-87113-103-X). Atlantic Monthly.
White Use of Blacks in America. Dan Lacy. LC 77-175286. 1972. 7.95 o.p. (ISBN 0-689-10476-6, Atheneum). Macmillan.
White Work Embroidery 1987. Barbara Dawson. (Illus.). 240p. 1987. 42.50 o.p. (ISBN 0-317-61729-X). Branford.
Whitehall Madness. Richard Lamb. 1987. 26.95 o.p. (ISBN 0-907675-47-6, Pub. by Buchan & Enright England). Seven Hills Bk Dists.
Whitehall: Tragedy & Farce. Clive Ponting. 190p. 1987. 24.95 o.p. (ISBN 0-241-11835-2, Pub. by Hamish Hamilton England). David & Charles.
Whitehead's Philosophy of Organism. Dorothy M. Emmet. LC 81-4141. (Illus.). xliii, 291p. 1981. Repr. of 1966 ed. lib. bdg. 35.00x o.p. (ISBN 0-313-23070-6, EMWP). Greenwood.
Whitehead's Philosophy of Science. Robert M. Palter. LC 60-7241. (Illus.). 1960. lib. bdg. 16.00x o.s.i. (ISBN 0-226-64523-1). U of Chicago Pr.
Whiteoak Brothers. Mazo De La Roche. (Jaina Ser.). 1978. pap. 1.75 o.s.i. (ISBN 0-449-23643-9, Crest). Fawcett.
Whiteoak Harvest. Mazo De La Roche. (Jaina Ser.). 1978. pap. 1.75 o.s.i. (ISBN 0-449-23521-1, Crest). Fawcett.
Whiteoak Heritage. Mazo De La Roche. 1979. pap. 1.95 o.s.i. (ISBN 0-449-22214-4, Crest). Fawcett.
Whitetail Hunting. Jim Dawson. LC 82-5661. (Illus.). 224p. 14.95 o.p. (ISBN 0-8117-1872-7). Stackpole.
Whitewater. Paul Horgan. LC 76-122830. 337p. (YA) (gr. 8 up). 1970. 6.95 o.p. (ISBN 0-374-28970-0). FS&G.
Whitey & the Colt-Killers. Glen Rounds. (Illus.). 88p. (gr. 3-7). 1982. pap. 1.95 o.p. (ISBN 0-380-57158-7, 57158-7, Camelot). Avon.
Whitey Takes a Trip. Glen Rounds. (Illus.). 88p. (gr. 3-7). 1982. pap. 1.95 o.p. (ISBN 0-380-57133-1, 57133-1, Camelot). Avon.
Whitey's First Roundup. Glen Rounds. (Illus.). 88p. (gr. 3-7). 1982. pap. 1.95 o.p. (ISBN 0-380-57141-2, 57141-2, Camelot). Avon.
Whitey's New Saddle. Glen Rounds. (Illus.). 88p. (gr. 3-7). 1982. pap. 1.95 o.p. (ISBN 0-380-57125-0, 57125-0, Camelot). Avon.
Whither Europe - Union or Partnership? M. J. Bonn. 1952. (ISBN 0-8022-0152-0). Philos Lib.
Whither Mankind. Ed. by Charles A. Beard. LC 78-109708. 408p. 1973. Repr. of 1934 ed. lib. bdg. 35.00x o.p. (ISBN 0-8371-4199-0, BEWM). Greenwood.
Whither the Wind Bloweth. Elaine L. Schulte. 1982. pap. 2.25 o.p. (ISBN 0-380-79384-9, 79384-9, Flare). Avon.
Whitman at Auction: 1899-1972. Ed. by Gloria A. Francis & Artem Lozynsky. LC 77-16647. (Authors at Auction Ser.). (Illus.). 504p. 1978. 44.00x o.p. (ISBN 0-8103-0921-1, Bruccoli Clark). Gale.
Whitman: Explorations in Form. Howard J. Waskow. LC 66-13892. 1966. lib. bdg. 17.50x o.s.i. (ISBN 0-226-87414-1). U of Chicago Pr.
Whitman Massacre. facs. ed. Matilda S. Delaney. 46p. pap. 3.95 o.s.i. (ISBN 0-8466-0130-3, S130). Shorey.
Whitney's Star Finder: Revised for 1982 Through 1985. Charles A. Whitney. LC 81-47523. 128p. 1981. pap. 10.95 o.p. (ISBN 0-394-74953-7). Knopf.
Whittlin' Bill's Folk Characters. Bill Higginbotham. LC 84-16349. (Illus.). 128p. (gr. 10). 1985. pap. 7.95 o.p. (ISBN 0-8069-7994-1). Sterling.
Whittling & Woodcarving. Elmer J. Tangerman. lib. bdg. 13.50x o.p. (ISBN 0-88307-262-9). Gannon.
Whiz Kids: Success at an Early Age. Marilyn Machlowitz. 256p. 1985. 15.95 o.p. (ISBN 0-87795-637-5, Arbor Hse). Morrow.
Who Am I? Asks the Alcoholic: A Study Based on Concepts a Recovering Alcoholic Heard, Heeded & Now Teaches. Ivan Lackey. LC 74-34514. 1975. 10.00 o.p. (ISBN 0-682-48199-8, Banner). Exposition-Phoenix.
Who & What & Where in the Bible. Donald M. McFarlan. LC 74-3709. (Illus.). 216p. (Orig.). 1974. pap. 4.50 o.p. (ISBN 0-8042-0001-7, John Knox). Westminster John Knox.
Who Are We Americans? Josephine McConnell. 80p. 1986. 9.95 o.p. (ISBN 0-8062-2865-2). Carlton.
Who Are You, Lord? Gertrude Priester. (Illus., Orig.). (gr. 1-6). 1969. pap. 2.95 o.p. (ISBN 0-8042-9702-9, John Knox). Westminster John Knox.
Who Are You Monsieur Gurdjieff? Rene Zuber. Tr. by Jenny Koralek. 80p. 1980. pap. 4.95 o.p. (ISBN 0-7100-0674-8). Routledge Chapman & Hall.

Who Bears the Tax Burden? Joseph A. Pechman & Benjamin A. Okner. LC 74-280. (Studies of Government Finance). 119p. 1974. 26.95 o.p. (ISBN 0-8157-6968-7); pap. 9.95 o.p. (ISBN 0-8157-6967-9). Brookings.

Who Becomes a Bishop? A Study of Priests Who Become Bishops in the Episcopal Church (1960 to 1980) John H. Morgan. 65p. (Orig.). 1985. pap. 9.95x o.p. (ISBN 0-932269-28-1). Wyndham Hall.

Who Blowed up the Church House? & Other Ozark Folk Tales. Ed. by Vance Randolph. LC 75-31424. (Illus.). 232p. 1975. Repr. of 1952 ed. lib. bdg. 22.50x o.p. (ISBN 0-8371-8497-5, RACH). Greenwood.

Who Can Be Educated? Milton Schwebel. 1968. pap. 3.45 o.s.i. (ISBN 0-394-17274-4, E494, Ever). Grove.

Who Controls Me? A Psychotheological Reflection. Thomas A. Kane. LC 74-22261. 1974. 4.50 o.p. (ISBN 0-682-48186-6). Exposition-Phoenix.

Who Dares to Preach? The Challenge of Biblical Preaching. Wallace E. Fisher. LC 79-54112. 200p. (Orig.). 1979. pap. 7.50 o.p. (ISBN 0-8066-1769-1, 10-7076, Augsburg). Augsburg Fortress.

Who Dares Wins. Ed. by Rory McGrath & Denise O'Donoghue. LC 85-20434. (Orig.). 1986. pap. 9.95 o.p. (ISBN 0-571-13774-1). Faber & Faber.

Who Distributes What & Where: An International Directory of Publishers, Imprints, Agents, & Distributors. 3rd ed. Ed. by Bowker, R. R., Staff. 445p. 1983. pap. 65.00 o.p. (ISBN 0-8352-1455-9). Bowker.

Who Do You Say That I Am? Joseph E. Monti. LC 83-82023. (Orig.). 1984. pap. 4.95 o.p. (ISBN 0-8091-2598-6). Paulist Pr.

Who Do You Think You Are? Digging for Your Family Roots. Suzanne Hilton. LC 75-40274. (A Junior Literary Guild Selection). (Illus.). 190p. (gr. 7 up). 1976. 9.95 o.s.i. (ISBN 0-664-32587-4, Westminster). Westminster John Knox.

Who Done It? Alice Laurance & Isaac Asimov. 1980. 9.95 o.p. (ISBN 0-395-29166-6). HM.

Who Goes Home? John R. Butler. 75p. 1970. pap. text ed. 5.00x o.p. (ISBN 0-7135-1593-7, Pub. by Bedford England). Gower Pub Co.

Who Goes There: The Search for Intelligent Life in the Universe. Edward Edelson. (Illus.). 228p. 1980. pap. text ed. 4.95 o.p. (ISBN 0-07-018986-2). McGraw.

Who in Their Own Words. Compiled by Steve Clarke. (Illus.). 1982. pap. 6.95 o.p. (ISBN 0-399-41006-6, Perigee). Putnam Pub Group.

Who Invented It & What Makes It Work. (Illus.). 48p. (gr. 1-7). 1978. 5.95 o.p. (ISBN 0-448-47612-6, G&D); PLB 5.99 o.p. (ISBN 0-448-13037-8). Putnam Pub Group.

Who Is Carla Hart? Joanna Barnes. LC 72-82170. 1973. 6.95 o.p. (ISBN 0-87795-039-3, Arbor Hse). Morrow.

Who Is For Life? Francis A. Schaffer et al. LC 83-62685. 64p. 1984. pap. 2.95 o.p. (ISBN 0-89107-305-1, Crossway Bks). Good News.

Who Is Jesus? A Woman's Workshop on Mark. Carolyn Nystrom. (Woman's Workshop Ser.). 144p. 1987. pap. 4.95 o.p. (ISBN 0-310-42001-6, 11289P). Zondervan.

Who Is Sylvia? Lucy Freeman. LC 78-57327. 1979. 9.95 o.p. (ISBN 0-87795-197-7, Arbor Hse). Morrow.

Who Is the Antichrist? John L. Benson. LC 78-2426. 1978. pap. 2.50 o.p. (ISBN 0-87227-058-0). Reg Baptist.

Who Is the River. Paul Zalis. LC 85-47638. 336p. 1986. 17.95 o.p. (ISBN 0-689-11594-6, Atheneum). Macmillan.

Who Is Tracking the Terrorists? W. Raymond Wannall. Ed. by Hale, Nathan, Institute Staff. (Orig.). 1984. pap. text ed. 3.00 o.p. (ISBN 0-935067-02-7). Nathan Hale Inst.

Who Kidnapped Princess Saralinda. Megan Stine & H. William Stine. (Wizards, Warriors & You Ser.: Bk. 3). 112p. (Orig.). (gr. 4 up). 1984. pap. 2.25 o.p. (ISBN 0-380-89268-5). Avon.

Who Killed Joe McCarthy? William B. Ewald, Jr. 1984. 17.25 o.p. (ISBN 0-671-44946-X). S&S.

Who Killed the Red Baron? P. J. Carisella & James Ryan. 1979. pap. 2.75 o.p. (ISBN 0-380-47514-6, 47514-6). Avon.

Who Knows: A Guide to Washington Experts. 8th ed. Washington Researchers, Limited Staff. (Business Research Ser.: Vol. 5). 425p. (Orig.). 1986. pap. 125.00 o.p. (ISBN 0-934940-32-0). Wash Res Pub.

Who Knows: A Guide to Washington Experts. 9th ed. Washington Researchers Publishing Staff. (Business Research Ser.: Vol. 5). Orig. Title: Researcher's Guide to Washington Experts. (Orig.). 1988. pap. 125.00 o.p. (ISBN 0-934940-55-X). Wash Res Pub.

Who Knows about Foreign Industries & Markets: Country Experts in the Federal Government. 9th ed. Washington Researchers Publishing Staff. (Briefcase Ser.). 1987. pap. 50.00 o.p. (ISBN 0-934940-57-6). Wash Res Pub.

Who Knows about Foreign Industries & Markets. VIII ed. Washington Researchers Staff. (Briefcase Ser.: Vol. 3). 70p. 1986. pap. 50.00 o.p. (ISBN 0-934940-34-7). Wash Res Pub.

Who Knows about Foreign Industries & Markets. 10th ed. (Briefcase Ser.: Bk. 3). 1988. pap. 50.00 o.p. (ISBN 0-934940-65-7). Wash Res Pub.

Who Knows about Industries & Markets: Industry Analysts in the Federal Government. 9th ed. Washington Researchers Publishing Staff. (Briefcase Ser.). 1987. pap. 50.00 o.p. (ISBN 0-934940-58-4). Wash Res Pub.

Who Knows about Industries & Markets. 10th ed. Washington Researchers Publishing Staff. (Briefcase Ser.: Bk. 4). 1988. pap. 50.00 o.p. (ISBN 0-934940-66-5). Wash Res Pub.

Who Knows about Industries & Markets. VIII ed. Washington Researchers Staff. (Briefcase Ser.: Vol. 4). 54p. (Orig.). 1986. pap. 50.00 o.p. (ISBN 0-934940-33-9). Wash Res Pub.

Who Laughs Last. Rosalind E. Dickenson. 64p. 1982. 5.00 o.p. (ISBN 0-682-49847-5). Exposition-Phoenix.

Who Let Muddy Boots into the White House. Robert Quackenbush. (Illus.). 40p. 1986. 11.95 o.s.i. (ISBN 0-13-958257-6). P-H.

Who Lies Inside. Timothy Ireland. 127p. (Orig.). 1984. pap. 6.50 o.p. (ISBN 0-907040-30-6, Pub. by GMP England). Alyson Pubns.

Who Likes the Sun. Beatrice S. De Regniers & Leona Pierce. LC 61-6112. (Illus.). 32p. (gr. k-3). 1961. 3.95 o.p. (ISBN 0-15-296065-1, HJ). HarBraceJ.

Who Me? A Missionary? Daniel W. Bacon. 1985. pap. 1.25 o.p. (ISBN 9971-972-32-8). Gower Pub Co.

Who Needs a Bear? Barbara Dillon. LC 80-26530. (Illus.). 64p. (gr. k-3). 1981. 10.25 o.p.; PLB 10.88 o.p. (ISBN 0-688-00446-6). Morrow.

Who Needs Her? Lorraine Hare. LC 82-13899. (Illus.). 32p. (gr. 2-5). 1983. 9.95 o.s.i. (ISBN 0-689-50268-0, M K McElderry). Macmillan.

Who Needs Me. Florence P. Heide. LC 71-159011. (ps-2). 1971. 5.50 o.p. (ISBN 0-8066-1134-0, 10-7075, Augsburg). Augsburg Fortress.

Who Needs Midlife at Your Age? A Survival Guide for Men over 30. Jack Roberts & Dick Gunther. 128p. (Orig.). 1983. pap. 4.95 o.p. (ISBN 0-380-84103-7, 84103). Avon.

Who Offers Part-Time Degree Programs? A National Survey of Postsecondary Institutions Offering Daytime, Evening, Weekend, Summer & External Degree Programs - 1981 Edition. Ed. by Patricia Consolloy. LC 81-8665. 350p. 1981. pap. 6.95 o.p. (ISBN 0-87866-121-2). Petersons Guides.

Who Owns America? Edmund B. Bolles. (Illus.). 288p. 1984. pap. 8.95 o.p. (ISBN 0-87131-450-9). M Evans.

Who Owns Appalachia? Landownership & Its Impact. Appalachian Land Ownership Task Force Staff. LC 82-40173. (Illus.). 272p. 1983. 25.00x o.p. (ISBN 0-8131-1476-4). U Pr of Ky.

Who Owns the Moon? Sonia Levitin. LC 73-77124. (Illus.). (ps-3). 1973. 6.95 o.p. (ISBN 0-395-27657-8, Pub. by Parnassus); PLB 5.38 o.p. (ISBN 0-87466-005-X). HM.

Who Owns the Moon? Sonia Levitin. (Illus.). (gr. k-3). 1973. Repr. PLB 6.95 o.p. (ISBN 0-395-27656-X). HM.

Who Owns Whom: Australasia & the Far East, 1986. 1400p. 1986. 245.00 o.p. (ISBN 0-8002-4066-9). Intl Pubns Serv.

Who Owns Whom: Continental Europe, 1986, 2 vols. 1986. 290.00 o.p. (ISBN 0-8002-4065-0). Intl Pubns Serv.

Who Owns Whom: North America, 1985. 17th ed. 1985. 240.00 o.p. (ISBN 0-8002-3950-4). Intl Pubns Serv.

Who Owns Whom: North America, 1986. 1640p. 1986. 295.00 o.p. (ISBN 0-8002-4049-9). Intl Pubns Serv.

Who Played in Movies. Date not set. (ISBN 0-8052-3766-6); (ISBN 0-8052-0676-0). Random.

Who Puts the Water in the Taps? 1983. 5.50 o.p. (ISBN 0-905347-47-1). C I D E.

Who Really Starves? Women & World Hunger. Lisa Leghorn & Mary Roodkowsky. (Orig.). 1977. pap. 1.25 o.p. (ISBN 0-377-00066-3). Friendship Pr.

Who Rides in the Dark? Stephen W. Meader. LC 37-27469. (Illus.). (gr. 7 up). 1966. pap. 0.75 o.p. (ISBN 0-15-696315-9, VoyB). HarBraceJ.

Who Rules the Joint? A Study of the Changing Political Culture of Maximum-Security Prisons in America. Charles Stasny & Gabrielle Tyrnauer. LC 78-14157. 256p. 1982. 30.00x o.p. (ISBN 0-669-02661-1). Lexington Bks.

Who Runs Congress? 4th ed. Mark Green & Michael Waldman. (Orig.). 1984. pap. 3.95 o.p. (ISBN 0-440-19676-0). Dell.

Who Runs the City. (Platt & Munk Pandabacks Ser.). (Illus.). 24p. (ps-3). 1978. pap. 4.99 o.p. (ISBN 0-448-13136-6, G&D). Putnam Pub Group.

Who Said There's No Man on the Moon? A Story of Jules Verne. Robert Quackenbush. LC 84-22314. (Illus.). 40p. (gr. 2-6). 1985. 10.95 o.s.i. (ISBN 0-13-958430-7). P-H.

Who Says It Can't Be Done? Marie Weiss. 1979. 9.95 o.p. (ISBN 0-682-49286-8). Exposition-Phoenix.

Who Says You Can't Find Good Help Anymore? Kathleen Koszyk. 1986. 8.95 o.p. (ISBN 0-533-06766-9). Vantage.

Who Shall Be the Sun?: Poems Based on the Lore, Legends, & Myths of Northwest Coast & Plateau Indians. David Wagoner. LC 78-1836. (Midland Bks.: No. 271). (Illus.). 144p. 1978. 9.95x o.p. (ISBN 0-253-36527-9); pap. 4.95x o.p. (ISBN 0-253-20271-X). Ind U Pr.

Who Should Elect the President. League of Women Voters of the United States Staff. LC 70-91300. 158p. 1969. pap. 0.50 o.p. (ISBN 0-89959-047-0, 345). LWV US.

Who Should Play God? Jeremy Rifkin & Ted Howard. 272p. 1977. pap. 2.75 o.p. (ISBN 0-440-39504-6); tchr's. guide by Jeremy Rifkin & Ted Howard 0.50 o.p. Dell.

Who Should Survive the Purge in American Education & Why. Daniel T. Grant. (Illus.). 1978. 7.50 o.p. (ISBN 0-682-48659-0). Exposition-Phoenix.

Who Stole Alligator's Shoe? Jacquelyn Reinach. LC 77-7251. (Sweet Pickles Ser.). (gr. k-2). 1977. 2.95 o.p. (ISBN 0-03-021431-9). H Holt & Co.

Who Switched Price Tags? How to Make Life Better in Your Work, Family & Church. Tony Campolo. 224p. 1986. 11.95 o.p. (ISBN 0-8499-0491-9). Word Bks.

Who Threw That Pie? The Birth of Movie Comedy. Robert Quackenbush. Ed. by Kathy Pacini. LC 78-27047. (Illus.). (gr. 3 up). 1979. PLB 10.25 o.p. (ISBN 0-8075-9058-4). A Whitman.

Who to Trust with Your Money. John Barnes. LC 85-11566. 1985. 16.95 o.p. (ISBN 0-688-04715-7). Morrow.

Who Wakes the Groundhog? Ronald Rood. (Illus.). 192p. 1973. 6.95 o.p. (ISBN 0-393-08524-4). Norton.

Who Walks with Me: A Novel. (Vikas Library of Modern Indian Writing: No. 21). 1982. text ed. 20.00x o.p. (ISBN 0-7069-1613-1, Pub. by Vikas India). Advent NY.

Who Was Kit Marlow? The Story of the Poet & Playwright. Della Hilton. LC 76-53911. (Illus.). 1977. 8.50 o.s.i. (ISBN 0-8008-8291-1). Taplinger.

Who Was Who in Journalism: Nineteen Twenty-Five to Nineteen Twenty-Eight. LC 78-13580. (Composite Biographical Dictionary Ser.: No. 4). 672p. 1978. 98.00x o.p. (ISBN 0-8103-0401-5). Gale.

Who, What, When, Where Bible Busy Book. William Coleman. 32p. (gr. 2-8). 1984. pap. 2.50 o.p. (ISBN 0-89191-853-1). Cook.

Who, What, When, Where Book about the Bible. William Coleman. (Illus.). (gr. 1-5). 1980. 11.95 o.p. (ISBN 0-89191-291-6). Cook.

Who Will Be My Teacher? The Christian Way to Stronger Schools. Marti W. Garlett. 256p. 1985. 12.95 o.p. (ISBN 0-8499-0471-4, 0471-4). Word Bks.

Who Will Study Justice. John W. Brabner-Smith. (Focus I Ser.). 16p. (Orig.). 1986. pap. text ed. 5.00 o.s.i. (ISBN 0-944561-13-6). Chr Legal.

Who Will Take Our Children? The Story of the Evacuation of Britain 1939-1945. Carlton Jackson. (Illus.). 224p. 1985. 17.95 o.p. (ISBN 0-413-58130-6, 9526). Heinemann Ed.

Who Writes What - 1988 Edition. Ed. by Price Gaines. 291p. 1988. plastic spiral 17.25 o.p. (ISBN 0-87218-058-1). Natl Underwriter.

Who Writes What, 1987. Ed. by Price Gaines. 315p. 1987. 16.25 o.p. (ISBN 0-87218-053-0). Natl Underwriter.

Who Wrote the Book of Love? Thomas Farber. 1977. 6.95 o.p. (ISBN 0-393-08799-9). Norton.

Who Ya Gonna Call?-Ghostbusters! Christopher Brown. (Ghostbusters Collector Sticker Bks.). (Illus.). 24p. (gr. 3-7). 1985. pap. 1.95 o.p. (ISBN 0-89954-391-X). Antioch Pub Co.

Whoever Said Life Is Fair? Sara K. Cohen. 1980. 7.95 o.s.i. (ISBN 0-684-16449-3). Scribner.

Whole Armor & the Secret Ladder. Wilson Harris. 260p. 1973. pap. 5.95 o.p. (ISBN 0-571-10231-X). Faber & Faber.

Whole Birth Catalog: A Sourcebook for Choices in Childbirth. Ed. by Janet I. Ashford. LC 83-838. (Illus.). 300p. (Orig.). 1983. 16.95. o.p. (ISBN 0-89594-108-2); pap. 16.95 o.p. (ISBN 0-89594-107-4). Crossing Pr.

Whole Counsel of God. Carl E. Braaten. LC 73-88345. 176p. 1974. 0.50 o.p. (ISBN 0-8006-0277-3, Fortress). Augsburg Fortress.

Whole Craft of Number. Douglas Campbell. 1976. write for info. o.p. (ISBN 0-87150-206-2, PWS 1691, Prindle). PWS-Kent Pub.

Whole Earth Access Mail Order Catalog. rev. ed. LC 84-51170. (Illus.). 480p. 1985. pap. 14.95 o.p. (ISBN 0-89815-132-5). Ten Speed Pr.

Whole Earth Atlas: New Census Edition. Ed. by Martin A. Bacheller. LC 82-83211. (Illus.). 256p. 1986. pap. 8.95 o.p. (ISBN 0-8437-2499-4). Hammond Inc.

Whole Earth Cookbook. Sharon Cadwallader & Judi Ohr. 1975. 7.95 o.p. (ISBN 0-395-13642-3); pap. 4.95 o.p. (ISBN 0-395-21983-3). HM.

Whole Earth Cookbook 2. Sharon Cadwallader. LC 75-23317. 1975. 7.95 o.p. (ISBN 0-395-21984-1, Co-Pub. by San Francisco Bk. Co.). HM.

Whole Earth Software Catalog. Stewart Brand. LC 84-15096. 208p. 1984. pap. 17.50 o.p. (ISBN 0-385-19166-9, Quantum Pr). Doubleday.

Whole Golf Catalog. Ed. by Larry Sheehan. LC 78-20351. (Illus.). 1979. pap. 14.95 o.p. (ISBN 0-689-10979-2, Atheneum). Macmillan.

Whole Heart Book. James J. Nora. LC 80-387. 352p. 1980. 17.95 o.s.i. (ISBN 0-03-048251-8); pap. 9.95 o.s.i. (ISBN 0-03-048246-1). H Holt & Co.

Whole House Catalog. Rev ed. Consumer Guide Editors. 384p. 1981. pap. 9.95 o.s.i. (ISBN 0-671-43640-6, Fireside). S&S.

Whole Learning Catalog. Ed. by Bruce Raskin. LC 76-29238. (Learning Ideabooks Ser.). 1976. pap. 15.95 o.p. (ISBN 0-8224-1913-0). D S Lake Pubs.

Whole Ocean Catalog. Ed. by Craig Lockwood. 272p. 1987. pap. 7.95 o.p. (ISBN 0-89586-599-8). Price Stern.

Whole Sewing Catalog. Rev ed. Consumer Guide Editors. 256p. 1982. pap. 11.95 o.p. (ISBN 0-671-45189-8, Fireside). S&S.

Whole Synthesizer Catalogue. Ed. by Tom Darter. (Keyboard Synthesizer Library). (Illus.). 160p. (Orig.). 1985. pap. 12.95 o.p. (ISBN 0-88188-396-4, HL00183895, Pub. by GPI Pubns). H Leonard Pub Corp.

Whole Truth Home Computer Handbook. Charles Platt. 208p. 1984. pap. 5.95 o.p. (ISBN 0-380-86736-2, 86736). Avon.

Whole Wheat Harvest-Recipes for Unground Wheat. Michael Collings & Judith Collings. pap. 2.95 o.p. (ISBN 0-89036-143-6). Hawkes Pub Inc.

Whole Word Catalogue. Teachers & Writers Collaborative Staff. 72p. 1972. 7.75 o.p. (ISBN 0-317-35352-7, 57092); members 4.75 o.p. (ISBN 0-317-35353-5). NCTE.

Whole Word Catalogue 2. Ed. by Bill Zavatsky & Ron Padgett. LC 76-56387. (Orig.). 1977. pap. 14.95 o.p. (ISBN 0-07-063239-1). Tchrs & Writers Coll.

Whole World Cookbook. One Hundred & One Productions Editors. (Illus.). 512p. 1983. pap. 14.95 o.p. (ISBN 0-684-17891-5, ScribT). Scribner.

Whole World Knows. Bob Barrall. (Illus.). 158p. 1981. 7.95 o.p. (ISBN 0-682-49773-8). Exposition-Phoenix.

Wholesale Prices & Price Index Numbers in North China: 1913-1929. Nankai University Committee on Social & Economic Research. Ed. by Ramon Myers. LC 80-8822. (China During the Interrgnum 1911-1949, the Economy & Society Ser.). 145p. 1982. lib. bdg. 24.00 o.p. (ISBN 0-8240-4677-3). Garland Pub.

Wholistic Health & Living Yoga. Malcolm Strutt. LC 77-85790. (Illus.). 320p. (Orig.). 1978. pap. 9.95 o.p. (ISBN 0-916438-08-2). Univ of Trees.

Whom God Chooses: The Child in the Church. rev. ed. Ralph R. Sundquist, Jr. 94p. 1973. pap. 1.65 o.s.i. (ISBN 0-664-71004-2, Westminster). Westminster John Knox.

Whom God Hath Joined. rev. ed. David R. Mace. LC 73-8871. 96p. 1984. pap. 6.95 o.s.i. (ISBN 0-664-24510-2, Westminster). Westminster John Knox.

Whom Shall I Marry? Dorothy Voshell. 1979. pap. 4.50 o.p. (ISBN 0-87552-509-1). Presby & Reformed.

Whom the Gods Love: A Lyrical Drama in Three Acts. David Hess. LC 76-44184. 1977. 4.00 o.p. (ISBN 0-682-48680-9, University). Exposition-Phoenix.

Whoppers. Nancy S. Hopper. (YA) (gr. 7-9). pap. 2.50 o.p. (ISBN 0-671-55420-4). Archway.

Whore of Babylon. Marianne G. Riely. LC 79-54330. (Renaissance Drama Ser.). 294p. 1980. lib. bdg. 40.00 o.p. (ISBN 0-8240-4476-2). Garland Pub.

Who's a Horn? What's an Antler? Crafts of Bone & Horn. Janet P. D'Amato. LC 82-2286. 96p. (gr. 4 up). 1982. lib. bdg. 9.29 o.s.i. (ISBN 0-671-41975-7). Messner.

Who's Afraid of Sixth Grade? Janet A. Bloss. 128p. (gr. 5-8). 1985. 2.50 o.s.i. (ISBN 0-317-61033-3). Willowisp Pr.

Who's Afraid of the Dark? Morse Hamilton. 32p. (gr. 3-7). 1983. pap. 2.25 o.p. (ISBN 0-380-82883-9, 82883-9, Camelot). Avon.

Who's Nobody in America. Derek Evans & David Fulwiler. LC 81-47457. 132p. (Orig.). 1981. pap. 4.95 o.p. (ISBN 0-03-059327-1). HR&W.

Who's Number One. Joe White. 144p. 1986. pap. 4.95 o.p. (ISBN 0-8423-8215-1). Tyndale.

Who's on First? Ed. by Richard J. Anobile. (Illus.). 256p. 1974. pap. 4.45 o.p. (ISBN 0-380-01622-2, 19323). Avon.

Who's on First. William F. Buckley, Jr. LC 79-55374. 1980. 13.95 o.p. (ISBN 0-385-14681-7). Doubleday.

Who's Poisoning America: Corporate Polluters & Their Victims in the Chemical Age. Ed. by Ralph Nader et al. LC 80-29608. 320p. 1981. 12.95 o.s.i. (ISBN 0-87156-276-6). Sierra.

Who's Running Your Life? Erling Wold & Marge Wold. LC 76-3863. 128p. (Orig.). 1976. pap. 4.50 o.p. (ISBN 0-8066-1540-0, 10-7100, Augsburg). Augsburg Fortress.

Who's Running Your Life: A Look at Young People's Rights. Jules Archer. (Illus.). (YA) (gr. 7 up). 1979. 7.95 o.p. (ISBN 0-15-296058-9, HJ). HarBraceJ.

Who's Sick. W. B. Park. LC 83-8429. (Illus.). 32p. (gr. k-3). 1983. 9.70 o.s.i. (ISBN 0-395-33229-X). HM.

Who's Teaching? Who's Learning? Active Learning in Elementary Schools. Dale Brubaker. LC 77-20894. 1979. pap. 12.95 o.p. (ISBN 0-673-16152-8). Scott F.

Who's That Girl with the Gun? Story of Annie Oakley. Robert Quackenbush. LC 87-11545. (Illus.). 40p. 1988. 11.95 o.s.i. (ISBN 0-13-957671-1). P-H.

Who's the Boss? Love, Authority & Parenting. Gerald E. Nelson & Richard W. Lewak. LC 85-8184. Orig. Title: One-Minute Scolding. (Illus.). 164p. 1985. pap. 6.95 o.p. (ISBN 0-87773-342-2, 74223-0). Shambhala Pubns.

Who's the Boss? Love, Authority, & Parenting. Gerald E. Nelson & Richard W. Lewak. pap. 6.95 o.p. (ISBN 0-394-74223-0). Shambhala Pubns.

Who's Who among American High School Students, 1985-1986, 10 vols. 20th ed. LC 68-43796. 1986. 10-vol. set 28.50 ea. o.p. (ISBN 0-930315-12-X). Vol. 1 (ISBN 0-930315-13-8). Vol. 2 (ISBN 0-930315-14-6). Vol. 3 (ISBN 0-930315-15-4). Vol. 4 (ISBN 0-930315-16-2). Vol. 5 (ISBN 0-930315-17-0). Vol. 6 (ISBN 0-930315-18-9). Vol. 7 (ISBN 0-930315-19-7). Vol.8,9 & 10 (ISBN 0-930315-20-0). Educ Comm.

Who's Who among American High School Students, 1986-87, 12 vols. 21st ed. Incl. Vol. 1 (ISBN 0-930315-28-6); Vol. 2 (ISBN 0-930315-29-4); Vol. 3 (ISBN 0-930315-30-8); Vol. 4 (ISBN 0-930315-31-6); Vol. 5 (ISBN 0-930315-32-4); Vol. 6 (ISBN 0-930315-33-2); Vol. 7 (ISBN 0-930315-34-0); Vol. 8 (ISBN 0-930315-35-9); Vol. 9 (ISBN 0-930315-36-7); Vol. 10 (ISBN 0-930315-37-5); Vol. 11 (ISBN 0-930315-41-3); Vol. 12 (ISBN 0-930315-42-1). LC 68-43796. 1986. Set. write for info. o.p. (ISBN 0-930315-27-8); 28.50 ea. o.p. Educ Comm.

Who's Who among Living Authors of Older Nations. LC 28-28492. 488p. 1966. Repr. of 1931 ed. 47.00x o.p. (ISBN 0-8103-3022-9). Gale.

Who's Who in America: Professional Geographic Index. 43rd ed. 520p. 1984. 72.00x o.s.i. (ISBN 0-8379-1503-1). Marquis.

Who's Who in America, 1984-1985, 2 vols. 43rd ed. LC 84-16934. 1984. 250.00 o.s.i. (ISBN 0-8379-0143-X, 030293). Marquis.

Who's Who in America: 1986-1987. 44th, rev. ed. 3900p. 1986. 250.00 o.s.i. (ISBN 0-8379-0144-8). Marquis.

Who's Who in American Art. 17th ed. Ed. by Bowker, R. R., Staff. 1200p. 1986. lib. bdg. 94.50 o.p. (ISBN 0-8352-2220-9). Bowker.

Who's Who in American Art. 16th ed. Ed. by Jaques Cattell Press Staff. 1200p. 1984. 85.00 o.p. (ISBN 0-8352-1878-3). Bowker.

Who's Who in American Politics. 10th ed. Compiled by Jaques Cattell Press Staff. 1800p. 1985. 125.00 o.p. (ISBN 0-8352-2075-3). Bowker.

Who's Who in Art. 22nd ed. 600p. 1986. 90.00x o.p. (ISBN 0-8103-0533-X, Pub. by Art Trade Pr). Gale.

Who's Who in Australia, 1985. 25th ed. 1985. 95.00 o.p. (ISBN 0-8002-3977-6). Intl Pubns Serv.

Who's Who in Austria. cancelled o.s.i. (ISBN 3-921-22044-0). Adlers Foreign Bks.

Who's Who in Aviation. LC 73-88547. 311p. 1974. 105.00 o.p. (ISBN 0-08-018205-4). Pergamon.

Who's Who in Banking in Europe, 1984-85. 3rd ed. 1984. 225.00 o.p. (ISBN 0-8002-3832-X). Intl Pubns Serv.

Who's Who in D. H. Lawrence. Graham Holderness. LC 75-34782. (Who's Who in Literature Ser.). 128p. 1976. 8.95 o.s.i. (ISBN 0-8008-8272-5). Taplinger.

Who's Who in Ferrous Products Including: Steel Wire & Steel Products: Directory of Names, Titles, Addresses, Telephone, Fax & Telex Numbers. Richard J. Callahan. Ed. by Eugene S. Reed & Amy G. Staniszewski. 300p. (Orig.). 1988. pap. write for info. o.p. Hungerford & Holland.

Who's Who in Finance & Industry: 1985-1986. 24th ed. LC 70-616550. 1985. 165.00 o.s.i. (ISBN 0-8379-0324-6, 30358). Marquis.

Who's Who in Frontier Science & Technology. 1st. ed. LC 82-82015. 846p. 1984. 99.50 o.s.i. (ISBN 0-8379-5701-X, 030290). Marquis.

Who's Who in Frontier Science & Technology. 2nd, rev. ed. 800p. 1985. 99.50x o.p. (ISBN 0-8379-5702-8). Marquis.

Who's Who in Genealogy. Ed. by Mary K. Meyer & P. William Filby. LC 81-69203. 1982. 70.00x o.p. (ISBN 0-8103-1630-7). Gale.

Who's Who in George Eliot. Phyllis Hartnoll. LC 76-39621. (Who's Who in Literature Ser.). 1977. 9.50 o.s.i. (ISBN 0-8008-8273-3). Taplinger.

Who's Who in Germany, 2 vols. deluxe ed. cancelled o.s.i. (ISBN 3-921220-47-5). Adlers Foreign Bks.

Who's Who in Health Care. 2nd ed. Ed. by Elliot A. Sainer. LC 77-79993. 612p. 1982. text ed. 79.95 o.p. (ISBN 0-89443-092-0). Aspen Pub.

Who's Who in Henry James. Glenda Leeming. LC 75-34783. (Who's Who in Literature Ser.). 224p. 1976. 7.95 o.s.i. (ISBN 0-8008-8268-7). Taplinger.

Who's Who in Horror & Fantasy Fiction. Mike Ashley. LC 77-4608. 1978. pap. 4.95 o.s.i. (ISBN 0-8008-8278-4). Taplinger.

Who's Who in Insurance. Ed. by R. Wilmot. 303p. 1975. 26.00x o.p. (ISBN 0-86010-023-5). Graham & Trotman.

Who's Who in International Banking: 1986/87. 3rd ed. 1986. 150.00 o.p. (ISBN 0-8002-4110-X). Intl Pubns Serv.

Who's Who in Israel & Jewish Personalities from All over the World, 1985-86. 20th ed. Ed. by I. Ben. (Who's Who in Israel Ser.). 1985. 100.00x o.p. E J Brill USA.

Who's Who in Jane Austen & the Brontes. Glenda Leeming. LC 73-17674. (Who's Who in Literature Ser.). 192p. 1974. 6.95 o.s.i. (ISBN 0-8008-8267-9). Taplinger.

Who's Who in Lebanon, 1986-87. 9th ed. Charles Gedeon. 667p. 1986. lib. bdg. 95.00 o.p. (ISBN 2-903188-04-1, Pub. by Publitec Publications & the Middle East Commercial Information Center). ABC-Clio.

Who's Who in Malaysia & Singapore, 1983. 15th ed. 144.00 o.p. (ISBN 0-317-12279-7). Intl Pubns Serv.

Who's Who in Medicine: Austria, Germany, Switzerland, 2 vols. 5th ed. LC 78-641400. 1505p. 1983. (WWIR 101). Intl Pubns Serv.

Who's Who in Microcomputing. Datapro Research Corporation Staff. 1983. pap. text ed. 42.95 o.p. (ISBN 0-07-015405-8, Pub. by Datapro). McGraw.

Who's Who in Nonferrous Products Including: Copper Bare & Insulated, Aluminum Bare & Insulated, Magnet Wire, Fiber Optics: Directory of Names, Titles, Addresses, Telephone, Fax & Telex Numbers. Richard J. Callahan. Ed. by Eugene S. Reed & Amy G. Staniszewski. 350p. (Orig.). 1988. pap. write for info. o.p. Hungerford & Holland.

Who's Who in Philosophy. D. D. Runes. 1943. 14.95 o.p. (ISBN 0-8022-1460-6). Philos Lib.

Who's Who in Prepaid Legal Services: 1987 Membership Directory. 83p. 1986. 15.00 o.p. Am Prepaid.

Who's Who in Rock. Michael Bane. (Illus.). 260p. 1982. pap. 10.95 o.p. (ISBN 0-89696-184-2, Everest House Book). Dodd.

Who's Who in Rock Video. MTV Staff. 1984. pap. 13.95 o.p. (ISBN 0-688-04042-X, Quill NY). Morrow.

Who's Who in Science Fiction. Brian Ash. LC 76-11667. 1978. pap. 4.95 o.s.i. (ISBN 0-8008-8279-2). Taplinger.

Who's Who in Science in Europe, 3 vols. 4th ed. 2500p. 1984. 500.00 o.p. (ISBN 0-582-90109-X). Intl Pubns Serv.

Who's Who in Shakespeare. Robin May. LC 73-5334. (Who's Who in Literature Ser). 190p. 1973. 6.50 o.s.i. (ISBN 0-8008-8269-5). Taplinger.

Who's Who in Shaw. Phyllis Hartnoll. LC 74-21719. (Who's Who in Literature Ser.). 256p. 1975. 8.95 o.s.i. (ISBN 0-8008-8270-9). Taplinger.

Who's Who in Sherlock Holmes. Scott R. Bullard & Michael Collins. LC 79-66638. 1980. 14.95 o.s.i. (ISBN 0-8008-8281-4); pap. 7.95 o.s.i. (ISBN 0-8008-8282-2). Taplinger.

Who's Who in Soviet Cinema. G. Dulmatovskaya & I. Shilova. 685p. 1982. 12.50 o.p. (ISBN 0-8285-1553-0, Pub. by Progress Pubs USSR). Imported Pubns.

Who's Who in Special Libraries, 1987-88. Special Libraries Association Staff. 296p. pap. 25.00 o.p. (ISBN 0-87111-331-7). SLA.

Who's Who in Technology: Austria, Germany, Switzerland. 2nd ed. 1984. 240.00 o.p. (ISBN 0-8002-3837-0). Intl Pubns Serv.

Who's Who in Technology Today, 5 vols. 4th ed. Incl. Vol. 1. Electronics & Computer Science. 95.00 (ISBN 0-943692-09-1); Vol. 2. Physics & Optics. 95.00 (ISBN 0-943692-10-5); Vol. 3. Chemistry & Biotechnology. (ISBN 0-943692-11-3); Vol. 4. Mechanical, Civil, Energy, & Earth Science. 95.00 (ISBN 0-943692-12-1); Vol. 5. The Expertise Index to Who's Who in Technology Today. Set. 95.00 (ISBN 0-943692-13-X). Set. 450.00 o.p. (ISBN 0-943692-15-6). Res Pubns CT.

Who's Who in the Arab World, 1986-1987. 8th ed. Charles Gedeon. 1432p. 1986. lib. bdg. 155.00 o.p. (ISBN 2-903188-03-3, Pub. by Publitec-Butterworth & the Middle East Commercial Information Center). ABC-Clio.

Who's Who in the Arab World 1986-1987. 8th ed. 1432p. 1986. 155.00 o.p. (ISBN 2-90318-803-3). ABC-Clio.

Who's Who in the Arts & Literature, 3 Vols. in 4 Pts. 3rd ed. Ed. by Karl Strute & Dr. Theodor Doelken. Incl. Vol 1, Pt. 1. The Fine Arts (A-O) UNIPUB; Vol. 1, Pt. 2. The Fine Arts (P-Z) UNIPUB; Vol. 2. Applied Arts and Music. UNIPUB; Vol. 3. Literature. UNIPUB. 2915p. 1983. Set 160.00 o.p. (ISBN 3-921220-50-5, WWIR100, WWIR). UNIPUB.

Who's Who in the Commonwealth. 3rd ed. 1985. (ISBN 0-8002-3891-5). Intl Pubns Serv.

Who's Who in the East, 1985-1986. 20th ed. 828p. 1984. 165.00 o.s.i. (ISBN 0-8379-0620-2, 030366). Marquis.

Who's Who in the South & Southwest, 1984-1985. 19th ed. LC 50-58231. 928p. 1984. 165.00 o.s.i. (ISBN 0-8379-0819-1, 030292). Marquis.

Who's Who in the Theatre, 2 vols. 17th ed. Ed. by Ian Herbert. 768p. 1981. Set. 120.00x o.p. (ISBN 0-8103-0234-9). Gale.

Who's Who in the World, 1984-1985. 7th ed. LC 79-139215. 1110p. 1984. 199.00 o.s.i. (ISBN 0-8379-1107-9, 030337). Marquis.

Who's Who in Thomas Hardy. Glenda Leeming. LC 74-24527. (Who's Who in Literature Ser). 144p. 1975. 8.95 o.s.i. (ISBN 0-8008-8271-7). Taplinger.

Who's Who in Venture Capital. 2nd ed. A. David Silver. LC 85-31502. 548p. 1986. 79.95 o.p. (ISBN 0-471-01172-X). Wiley.

Who's Who of Horrors. David J. Hogan. LC 79-17606. 1980. 14.95 o.s.i. (ISBN 0-498-02591-8). A S Barnes.

Who's Who of Jazz: Storyville to Swing Street. John Chilton. 419p. Repr. of 1972 ed. lib. bdg. 59.00 o.p. (Pub. by Am Repr Serv). Reprint Servs.

Who's Who on TV Soaps, Mini Serials Movies & Lots More. Doris F. Plott. 112p. 1986. 8.95 o.p. (ISBN 0-8062-2971-3). Carlton.

Whose Body? Dorothy L. Sayers. 1978. pap. 2.50 o.p. (ISBN 0-380-00897-1, 69781-5). Avon.

Whose FBI? Ed. by Richard O. Wright. LC 74-60. 405p. 1974. 9.95 o.p. (ISBN 0-87548-148-5). Open Court.

Whose Land? A Glimpse into the Middle East. John Peddie. LC 84-90106. 86p. 1985. 7.95 o.p. (ISBN 0-533-06180-6). Vantage.

Whose Life Is It Anyway? Brian Clark. 160p. 1980. pap. 2.95 o.p. (ISBN 0-380-52407-4, 64808-3, Bard). Avon.

Whose Music? A Sociology of Musical Language. John Shepherd et al. 300p. 1980. 19.95 o.p. (ISBN 0-87855-384-3); pap. text ed. 7.95 o.p. Transaction Pubs.

Whose Side Are You On? Emily Moore. 128p. (gr. 3-7). 1987. 11.95 o.p. (ISBN 0-374-38409-6). FS&G.

Why, Vols. 1-2, No. 7. 1970. Repr. of 1914 ed. lib. bdg. 30.00x o.p. (ISBN 0-8371-9259-5, WH00). Greenwood.

Why A B M? Policy Issues in the Missile Defense Controversy. Ed. by J. J. Holst & W. Schneider, Jr. 1969. 85.00 o.p. (ISBN 0-08-015625-8). Pergamon.

Why a Christian Leader May Fall. Clyde M. Narramore. 128p. 1988. pap. 5.95 o.p. (ISBN 0-89107-504-6, Crossway Bks). Good News.

Why a Duck? Ed. by Richard J. Anobile. (Illus.). 288p. 1974. pap. 5.95 large-format o.p. (ISBN 0-380-00452-6, 40774-4). Avon.

Why Am I Crying? Martha Maughon. 1983. pap. 6.95 o.p. (ISBN 0-310-37671-8, 11221P). Zondervan.

Why Am I Shy? Turning Shyness into Confidence. Norman B. Rohrer & S. Philip Sutherland. LC 78-52182. 1978. pap. 6.95 o.p. (ISBN 0-8066-1656-3, 10-7130, Augsburg). Augsburg Fortress.

Why Am I So Miserable If These Are the Best Years of My Life? Andrea B. Eagan. (YA) (gr. 7 up). 1979. pap. 2.50 o.p. (ISBN 0-380-46136-6, 60134-6, Flare). Avon.

Why America Will Survive: Some Thoughts on the Survival of Civilizations. William A. O'Toole. 1979. 7.50 o.p. (ISBN 0-682-49243-4). Exposition-Phoenix.

Why Are the British Bad at Manufacturing? Karel Williams & Dennis Thomas. 160p. 1983. pap. 15.95x o.p. (ISBN 0-7100-9561-9). Routledge Chapman & Hall.

Why Are Your Papers in Order? Cartoons for 1984. Ed. by Sam Gross. 192p. 1983. pap. 4.95 o.p. (ISBN 0-380-85035-4, 85035). Avon.

Why Buildings Stand Up: The Strength of Architecture. Mario Salvadori. (Illus.). 1980. 15.95 o.p. (ISBN 0-393-01401-0). Norton.

Why Can't He Be Mine? Alison Strickland. 96p. (gr. 4-8). 1983. 1.95 o.s.i. (ISBN 0-87406-182-2). Willowisp Pr.

Why Capitalism Means War. Henry N. Brailsford. LC 70-147494. (Library of War & Peace; the Political Economy of War). 1972. lib. bdg. 46.00 o.p. (ISBN 0-8240-0287-3). Garland Pub.

Why Children? Ed. by Stephanie Dowrick & Sibyl Grundberg. LC 80-84688. 1981. 12.95 o.p. (ISBN 0-15-196324-X). HarBraceJ.

Why Children Misbehave: A Guide To Positive Parenting. Bruce S. Narramore. 248p. 1987. pap. 7.95 o.p. (ISBN 0-310-30501-2, 11247P). Zondervan.

Why? Children's Questions: What They Mean & How to Answer Them. Ruth Formanek & Anita Gurian. 1980. 8.95 o.p. (ISBN 0-395-29190-9). HM.

Why David Can. Loyd Littlepage. (Illus.). 16p. (ps-3). 1977. 3.50 o.p. (ISBN 0-911336-67-2). Sci of Mind.

Why Denominationalism? Murry M. Campbell. LC 84-90492. 140p. 1985. 10.00 o.p. (ISBN 0-533-06376-0). Vantage.

Why Didn't He Tell Me? Annette V. Dominic. 28p. 1985. 6.95 o.p. (ISBN 0-533-06329-9). Vantage.

Why Do Christians Break Down? William A. Miller. LC 73-78260. 1973. pap. 7.95 o.p. (ISBN 0-8066-1325-4, 10-7140, Augsburg). Augsburg Fortress.

Why Do Some People Get Fat? Jane Claypool. (Creative's Little Question Books). (Illus.). 32p. (ps-4). 1982. PLB 8.95 o.p. (ISBN 0-87191-898-6). Creative Ed.

Why Do Some Urban Schools Succeed? The Phi Delta Kappa Study of Exceptional Urban Elementary Schools. LC 80-81869. 225p. 1980. pap. 7.00 o.p. (ISBN 0-87367-773-0). Phi Delta Kappa.

Why Do We Age? Hilton Hotema. 65p. 1959. pap. text ed. 7.95 o.s.i. (ISBN 0-88697-018-0). Life Science.

Why Do We Eat? Pamela Espeland. (Creative's Questions & Answers Library). (Illus.). 32p. (ps-4). 1981. PLB 8.95 o.p. (ISBN 0-87191-747-5). Creative Ed.

Why Do We Have Earthquakes? Norita D. Larson. (Creative's Little Question Bks.). (Illus.). 32p. (ps-4). 1982. PLB 8.95 o.p. (ISBN 0-87191-879-X). Creative Ed.

Why Do We Have Hair? Pat Blakely. (Creative's Little Question Bks.). (Illus.). 32p. (ps-4). 1982. PLB 8.95 o.p. (ISBN 0-87191-881-1). Creative Ed.

Why Do We Have Skeletons? Pat Blakely. (Creative Questions & Answers Ser.). (Illus.). 32p. (ps-4). 1982. PLB 7.95 o.p. (ISBN 0-87191-750-5). Creative Ed.

Why Do We Laugh? A. A. Redpath. (Creative's Questions & Answers Ser.). (Illus.). 32p. (ps-4). 1981. PLB 8.95s.p. o.p. (ISBN 0-87191-751-3). Creative Ed.

Why Do We Not See Little People, Miss Wintergreen? see Magga Birds of Ranatan.

Why Does Evil Exist? A Philosophical Study of the Contemporary Presentation of the Question. Colm Connellan. LC 74-76020. 1974. 10.00 o.p. (ISBN 0-682-47940-3). Exposition-Phoenix.

Why Doesn't God Do Something? Phoebe Cranor. LC 78-118. 144p. (YA) (gr. 7-12). 1978. pap. 3.95 o.p. (ISBN 0-87123-605-2, 200605). Bethany Hse.

Why Glass Breaks, Rubber Bends, & Glue Sticks: How Everyday Materials Work. Malcolm E. Weiss. LC 77-76443. (Illus.). 74p. (gr. 5 up). 1977. 6.95 o.p. (ISBN 0-15-296290-5, HJ). HarBraceJ.

Why Gold? The One Sure Cure for Inflation & Economic Tyranny. Leslie Snyder. LC 73-92853. 1974. 6.00 o.p. (ISBN 0-682-47884-9, University). Exposition-Phoenix.

Why Has Development Neglected Rural Women? A Review of the South Asian Literature. Nici Nelson. LC 79-40235. (Women in Development Ser.: Vol. 1). (Illus.). 1979. 35.00 o.p. (ISBN 0-08-023377-5); pap. 35.00 o.p. (ISBN 0-08-023376-7). Pergamon.

Why I Am a Christian. O. Hallesby. LC 77-73797. 1977. pap. 3.95 o.p. (ISBN 0-8066-1571-0, 10-7156, Augsburg). Augsburg Fortress.

Why I Believe in the Baptism with the Holy Spirit. Stanford E. Linzey. 12p. 1962. pap. 0.75 o.p. (ISBN 0-88243-764-X, 02-0764). Gospel Pub.

Why I Cannot Take a Lover. Grace Cavalieri. (Ser. One). 1975. pap. 2.00 o.p. (ISBN 0-931846-01-3). Wash Writers Pub.

Why Ireland Starved: A Quantitative & Analytical History of the Irish Economy, 1800-1850. Joel Mokyr. (Illus.). 360p. 1983. text ed. 44.95x o.p. (ISBN 0-04-941010-5). Unwin Hyman.

Why Kill Arthur Potter? Ray Harrison. 160p. 1984. 11.95 o.s.i. (ISBN 0-684-18131-2, ScribT). Scribner.

Why Managers Fail. John J. McCarthy. 1978. text ed. 10.95 o.p. (ISBN 0-07-044316-5); pap. text ed. 7.95 o.p. (ISBN 0-07-044315-7). McGraw.

Why Me? Piggie Fields. 1979. 4.50 o.p. (ISBN 0-682-49259-0). Exposition-Phoenix.

Why Me, Lord? Paul W. Powell. 120p. 1981. pap. 4.95 o.p. (ISBN 0-89693-007-6). Victor Bks.

Why Me, Lord? Meaning & Comfort in Times of Trouble. Carl W. Berner. LC 73-78267. 112p. (Orig.). 1973. pap. 5.95 o.p. (ISBN 0-8066-1331-9, 10-7172, Augsburg). Augsburg Fortress.

Why Nations Realign: Foreign Policy Restructuring in the Post War World. K. J. Holsti et al. 240p. 1982. text ed. 29.95x o.p. (ISBN 0-04-351062-0). Unwin Hyman.

Why Not Stay for Breakfast? Penny Dann. (Illus.). 58p. 1988. 8.95 o.p. (ISBN 0-241-11926-X, Pub. by Hamish Hamilton). David & Charles.

Why Not the Best? Jimmy Carter. pap. 1.95 o.p. (ISBN 0-8054-5564-7). Broadman.

Why, O Lord? Psalms & Sermons from Namibia. Zephania Kameeta. LC 86-45211. 80p. 1987. pap. 3.95 o.p. (ISBN 0-8006-1923-4, 1-1923, Fortress). Augsburg Fortress.

Why Our Schools Have Failed Us. Albert Brill. 1978. 4.00 o.p. (ISBN 0-682-49106-3). Exposition-Phoenix.

Why People Buy: Motivation Research & Its Successful Application. Louis Cheskin. 1959. 6.95x o.p. (ISBN 0-87140-962-3). Liveright.

Why Read Aloud to Children? Julie M. Chan. (Micromonograph Ser.). 12p. 1974. pap. 1.50 o.p. (ISBN 0-87207-877-9). Intl Reading.

Why Should I? Pamela R. Venti. LC 83-7360. (Illus.). 32p. (gr. 1-2). 1983. PLB 4.95 o.p. (ISBN 0-89693-213-3). Dandelion Hse.

Why Should I Hire You? How to Get the Job You Really Want! Melvin R. Thompson. LC 75-822. (Illus.). 1977. pap. 3.95 o.p. (ISBN 0-15-696400-7, Harv). HarBraceJ.

Why So Few? Women Academics in Australian Universities. Bettina Cass et al. 253p. (Orig.). 1983. pap. 14.95x o.p. (ISBN 0-424-00095-4, Pub. by Sydney U Pr). Intl Spec Bk.

Why Some Positive Thinkers Get Powerful Results. Norman Vincent Peale. LC 86-5145. 224p. 1986. 15.95 o.p. (ISBN 0-8407-9053-8). Oliver-Nelson.

Why Stocks Go up (& Down) A Guide to Sound Investing. William H. Pike. LC 82-71875. 298p. 1983. 19.95 o.p. (ISBN 0-87094-314-6). Dow Jones-Irwin.

Why Teachers Organized. Wayne J. Urban. LC 82-11160. 203p. 1982. 22.50x o.p. (ISBN 0-8143-1714-6). Wayne St U Pr.

Why the Courts Don't Work. Richard Neely. 1983. text ed. 15.95 o.p. (ISBN 0-07-046152-X); pap. text ed. 7.95 o.p. (ISBN 0-07-046151-1). McGraw.

Why the Jackal Won't Speak to the Hedgehog. Harold Berson. LC 69-13439. (Illus.). 32p. (ps-3). 1979. 6.95 o.p. (ISBN 0-395-28768-5, Clarion). HM.

Why the Jews? The Reason for Anti-Semitism. Dennis Prager & Joseph Telushkin. 224p. 1983. 15.45 o.s.i. (ISBN 0-671-45270-3). S&S.

Why the Sky Is Far Away. Mary-Joan Gerson. LC 73-17343. (gr. k-3). 1974. 8.95 o.p. (ISBN 0-15-296310-3, HJ). HarBraceJ.

Why the Sun & the Moon Live in the Sky. Elphinstone Dayrell. (Illus.). (gr. k-3). 1977. 3.75 o.p. (ISBN 0-395-06741-3); pap. 1.95 o.p. (ISBN 0-395-25381-0, Sandpiper). HM.

Why the United States Purchased Alaska. Peter P. Sgroi. (Illus.). 64p. 1970. U of Alaska Pr.

Why the Wilderness Is Called Adirondack: The Earliest Account of Founding of the MacIntyre Mine. Henry Dornburgh. LC 79-25055. 1980. pap. 3.95 o.p. (ISBN 0-916346-39-0). Harbor Hill Bks.

Why There Aren't Witches & Other Tales. V. P. Fieg. (Illus.). (gr. 4-7). 1980. 5.95 o.p. (ISBN 0-395-28758-8). HM.

Why They Call It Politics: A Guide to America's Government. 3rd ed. Robert Sherrill. 382p. 1979. pap. text ed. 10.95 o.p. (ISBN 0-15-596002-4, HC). HarBraceJ.

Why They Call It Politics: A Guide to America's Government. 2nd ed. Robert Sherrill. (Illus.). 320p. (Orig.). 1974. pap. text ed. 9.95 o.p. (ISBN 0-15-596001-6, HC). HarBraceJ.

Why Things Are. Neil Ardley. (Illus.). 128p. 1984. lib. bdg. 11.79 o.p. (ISBN 0-671-49993-9). Messner.

Why Tomorrow? Li Shufen. (Illus.). 49p. (Orig.). (gr. 3-5). 1983. pap. 3.95 o.p. (ISBN 0-8351-1094-X). China Bks.

Why Tragedy Happens to Christians. Charles Capps. 187p. (Orig.). 1980. pap. 3.75 o.p. (ISBN 0-89274-175-9, HH-175). Harrison Hse.

Why Universal Life. 2nd ed. Thomas F. Eason & David L. Manzler. LC 82-63204. (Illus.). 352p. 1983. pap. 14.95 o.p. (ISBN 0-87218-028-X). Natl Underwriter.

Why Vegan. Kath Clements. (Illus.). 96p. (Orig.). 1986. pap. 5.50 o.p. (ISBN 0-946097-18-6, Pub. by GMP England). Alyson Pubns.

Why War? Frederick Howe. LC 70-147497. (Library of War & Peace; the Political Economy of War). 1972. lib. bdg. 46.00 o.p. (ISBN 0-8240-0291-1). Garland Pub.

Why Waste Your Illness: Let God Use It for Growth. Mildred Tengbom. LC 83-72113. 144p. (Orig.). 1984. pap. 6.95 o.p. (ISBN 0-8066-2057-9, 10-7182, Augsburg). Augsburg Fortress.

Why We Do Not Speak in Tongues. Don R. Pegram. 1982. pap. 1.25 o.p. (ISBN 0-89265-086-9). Randall Hse.

Why We Do What We Do: A Look at Psychology. Elizabeth Hall. LC 73-7902. (Illus.). 256p. (gr. 5 up). 1973. 6.95 o.p. (ISBN 0-395-17516-X). HM.

Why We Were in Vietnam. Norman Podorhetz. 250p. 1983. pap. 8.95 o.p. (ISBN 0-671-47061-2, Touchstone). S&S.

Why Wembley Fraggle Couldn't Sleep. H. B. Gilmour. LC 84-19286. (Illus.). 32p. (gr. k-2). 1985. 4.95 o.s.i. (ISBN 0-03-004557-6). H Holt & Co.

Why Were We Born? Eric S. Dillett. 1980. 6.00 o.p. (ISBN 0-682-49534-4). Exposition-Phoenix.

Why Winners Win! John Torquato. 256p. 1983. 15.95 o.p. (ISBN 0-8144-5770-3). AMACOM.

Why Women Choose the Wrong Men. Sidney Lecker. 1985. 14.95 o.p. (ISBN 0-87795-675-8, Arbor Hse). Morrow.

Why Won't My Teeter-Totter? Vicki Freeman & Suzy Adams. (Illus.). 48p. (YA) (gr. 9 up). 1972. 2.50 o.p. (ISBN 0-8065-0269-X, Pub. by Citadel Pr). Carol Pub Group.

Why World Evangelism. David Howard. pap. 0.75 o.p. (ISBN 0-87784-141-1). Inter-Varsity.

Why You Should Invest in Bank Stocks Now. Spencer Fleming. (Illus.). 117p. 1989. 57.75 o.p. Inst Econ Finan.

Why Your House May Endanger Your Health. Alfred Zamm. 1980. 12.95 o.p. (ISBN 0-671-24128-1). S&S.

Whys & Wherefores of Littabelle Lee. Vera Cleaver & Bill Cleaver. LC 72-86929. 160p. (gr. 7 up). 1973. 6.95 o.p. (ISBN 0-689-30080-8, Atheneum). Macmillan.

Wichita County Beginnings. Louise Kelly. 39.95 o.p. (ISBN 0-89015-347-7). Eakin Pr.

Wichita Grammar. David S. Rood. LC 75-25122. (American Indian Linguistics Ser.). 1977. lib. bdg. 51.00 o.p. (ISBN 0-8240-1972-5). Garland Pub.

Wicked Enchantment. Margot Benary-Isbert. LC 55-8671. (Illus.). (gr. 5 up). 1955. 5.50 o.p. (ISBN 0-15-296423-1, HJ). HarBraceJ.

Wicked Godmother. Marion Chesney. (Nightingale Ser.). 260p. 1988. pap. 12.95x o.p. (ISBN 0-8161-4400-1). G K Hall.

Wicked Marquis. Marnie Ellingson. 192p. 1983. pap. 2.50 o.p. (ISBN 0-380-65821-6, 65821). Avon.

Wicked Stepmother. Axel Young. 256p. 1983. pap. 3.50 o.p. (ISBN 0-380-84210-6, 84228-9). Avon.

Wicked Witch of Troll Cave. Don A. Torgersen. LC 80-12043. (Troll Stories Ser.). (Illus.). 32p. (gr. k-4). 1980. PLB 9.95 o.p. (ISBN 0-516-03672-6); pap. 3.50 o.p. (ISBN 0-516-43672-4). Childrens.

Wicked Wizard & the Wicked Witch. Seymour Leichman. LC 72-76365. (Illus.). 32p. (gr. k-3). 1972. 6.50 o.p. (ISBN 0-15-296455-X, HJ). HarBraceJ.

Wide Angle Photography. Kalton C. Lahue. LC 77-74100. (Photography How-to Ser.). (Illus.). 1977. pap. 3.95 o.p. (ISBN 0-8227-4014-1). Petersen Pub.

Wide Awake: And Other Poems. Myra C. Livingston. LC 59-5629. (Illus.). 48p. (gr. 1-4). 1959. 3.95 o.p. (ISBN 0-15-296602-1, HJ). HarBraceJ.

Wide Net & Other Stories. Eudora Welty. LC 44-1666. 1943. 9.95 o.s.i. (ISBN 0-15-196395-9). HarBraceJ.

Wide, Wide World. Susan Warner. LC 72-78850. 1851. Repr. 69.00x o.p. (ISBN 0-403-01989-3). Somerset Pub.

Wide World of Aaron Burr. Helen Orlob. (gr. 5-9). 1968. 4.95 o.s.i. (ISBN 0-664-32416-9, Westminster). Westminster John Knox.

Wide World of Arbitration: An Anthology. Ed. by Charlotte Gold & Susan Mackenzie. 236p. 15.00 o.p. (ISBN 0-943001-22-6). Am Arbitration.

Wideacre. Philippa Gregory. 464p. 1987. 18.45 o.s.i. (ISBN 0-671-63462-3). S&S.

Widening Horizons. Zdenek Kopal. LC 73-99307. (Illus.). (gr. 9 up). 6.95 o.s.i. (ISBN 0-8008-8320-9). Taplinger.

Widening Sphere: Changing Roles of Victorian Women. Ed. by Martha Vicinus. LC 76-26433. (Midland Bks.: No. 245). (Illus.). 352p. 1977. 20.00x o.p. (ISBN 0-253-36540-6); pap. 7.95x o.p. (ISBN 0-253-20245-0). Ind U Pr.

Wider Arc: Poems. Melville Cane. LC 47-4510. 9.95 o.p. (ISBN 0-15-196533-1). HarBraceJ.

Wider Circle. Roger Hutson & Patsy Hutson. 112p. 1985. pap. 3.95 o.p. (ISBN 0-310-29421-5, 6895P). Zondervan.

Wider Horizons. Dorothy Martin. (Peggy Ser.: No. 7). (gr. 7). 1985. pap. 3.50 o.p. (ISBN 0-8024-8307-0). Moody.

Widerspruch und Hoffnung Des Daseins see Human Existence: Contradiction & Hope.

Widow Julia. Margaret F. Csovanyos. 1978. pap. 5.50 o.p. (ISBN 0-682-49083-0). Exposition-Phoenix.

Widower. Georges Simenon. Tr. by Robert Baldick from Fr. LC 81-48256. 1982. 10.95 o.p. (ISBN 0-15-196644-3). HarBraceJ.

Widow's Guide. Date not set. (ISBN 0-8052-3769-0). Random.

Wie Geht's: An Introductory German Course. 2nd ed. Dieter Sevin et al. 478p. 1984. text ed. 31.95 o.p. (ISBN 0-03-063972-7). HR&W.

Wieland und Bodmer. Fritz Budde. 1910. 27.00 o.p. (ISBN 0-384-06206-7); pap. 22.00 o.p. (ISBN 0-384-06205-9). Johnson Repr.

Wieland Wagner: The Positive Sceptic. Geoffrey Skelton. 222p. Repr. of 1971 ed. lib. bdg. 39.00 o.p. (Pub. by Am Repr Serv). Reprint Servs.

Wielding a Red Sword. Piers Anthony. (Incarnations of Immortality Ser.: Bk. 4). 1986. 16.45 o.p. (ISBN 0-345-32220-7, Del Rey). Ballantine.

Wife. Bharati Mukherjee. LC 75-2120. 224p. 1975. 7.95 o.p. (ISBN 0-395-20439-9). HM.

Wife of Bath. Vera Chapman. 1978. pap. 1.75 o.p. (ISBN 0-380-38976-2, 38976). Avon.

Wife Savers III. Ed. by Joan Sobczak. LC 82-62679. 64p. 1982. pap. 3.95 o.s.i. (ISBN 0-89821-047-X). Reiman Assocs.

Wife to Mr. Milton. Robert Graves. 1979. Repr. of 1944 ed. lib. bdg. 26.00x o.p. (ISBN 0-374-93240-9, Octagon). Hippocrene Bks.

Wigger. William Goldman. LC 74-4497. (gr. 2-5). 1974. 4.75 o.p. (ISBN 0-15-296784-2, HJ). HarBraceJ.

Wigmore on Evidence: Indexes, Vol. X. Dorothy Thomas. LC 84-939. write for info. o.p. Little.

Wigmore on Evidence: 1984 Supplement. Walter A. Reiser, Jr. LC 61-10756. 644p. 1984. 65.00 o.p. (ISBN 0-316-73967-7). Little.

Wikchamni Grammar. Geoffrey Gamble. LC 77-8566. (UC Publications in Linguistics: Vol. 89). 1979. pap. 19.95x o.p. (ISBN 0-520-09589-8). U of Cal Pr.

Wilbur & Orville: The Otter Twins. (Zoo Babies Ser.). 16p. (gr. k-6). 1982. pap. 1.25 o.p. (ISBN 0-8249-8034-4). Ideals.

Wilbur the Hat. Hendrik W. Van Loon. 1925. 3.50 o.p. (ISBN 0-87140-824-4). Liveright.

Wild. Bob Graham. LC 86-22219. (Illus.). 32p. (ps-3). 1987. 12.95 o.p. (ISBN 0-87226-139-5). P Bedrick Bks.

Wild about Harry. Paul Pickering. LC 85-47611. 224p. 1985. 13.95 o.p. (ISBN 0-689-11622-5, Atheneum). Macmillan.

Wild Angel. Elizabeth C. Spykman. 1957. 3.95 o.p. (ISBN 0-15-296960-8, HJ). HarBraceJ.

Wild Animal Trainer in America. Joanne Joys. LC 82-436. (Illus.). 200p. 1982. 39.95 o.p. (ISBN 0-87108-621-2). Pruett.

Wild Animals, Vol. 7. (Happy Animals Ser.). (Illus.). 10p. (ps). 1979. 2.50 o.p. (ISBN 0-89346-113-X, Pub. by Froebel-Kan Japan). Heian Intl.

Wild Animals, Gentle Women. Margery Facklam. LC 77-88961. (Illus.). (gr. 7 up). 1978. 5.95 o.p. (ISBN 0-15-296987-X, HJ). HarBraceJ.

Wild Animals I Have Known. (Classics Illus. Ser.). (Illus.). pap. 0.59 o.p. (ISBN 0-685-74101-X, 152). Guild Bks.

Wild Animals of Africa. Klaus Paysan. LC 70-102894. (Nature & Man Ser.). (Illus.). (gr. 5-12). 1971. PLB 9.95 o.p. (ISBN 0-8225-0563-0). Lerner Pubns.

Wild Animals of North America. LC 79-18452. 14.95 o.p. (ISBN 0-87044-294-5); deluxe ed. 26.90 in deluxe slipcase with Our Continent o.p. (ISBN 0-686-66211-3). Natl Geog.

Wild Babies: A Canyon Sketchbook. Irene Brady. (Illus.). (gr. 1-12). 1979. 8.95 o.p. (ISBN 0-395-27464-8). HM.

Wild Bananas. Sandra Thompson. Ed. by Joyce Johnson. LC 85-47788. 248p. 1985. 15.95 o.p. (ISBN 0-87113-032-7). Atlantic Monthly.

Wild Bill Hiccup's Riddle Book. Ann Bishop. Ed. by Caroline Rubin. LC 75-33161. (Riddle Bks.). (Illus.). (gr. 1-4). 1975. PLB 7.75 o.p. (ISBN 0-8075-9097-5). A Whitman.

Wild Bird's Nest: Poems from the Irish. Frank O'Connor. 56p. 1971. Repr. of 1932 ed. 15.00x o.p. (ISBN 0-7165-1374-9, BBA 02075, Pub. by Cuala Press Ireland). Biblio Dist.

Wild Birds of the Americas. Terence Shortt. 1977. 14.95 o.p. (ISBN 0-395-25786-7). HM.

Wild Cat. Robert N. Peck. (Illus.). (gr. 6-12). 1977. pap. 0.95 o.p. (ISBN 0-380-01728-8, 34173, Camelot). Avon.

Wild Coffee & Tea Substitutes of Canada. Nancy J. Turner & Adam F. Szczawinski. (Illus.). 1978. pap. 12.95 o.p. (ISBN 0-660-00090-3, 56558-0, Pub. by Natl Mus Canada). U of Chicago Pr.

Wild Duck. Henrik Ibsen. 1965. pap. 0.95 o.p. (ISBN 0-380-01624-9, 23093, Bard). Avon.

Wild Flavor. Marilyn Kluger. LC 84-2760. 288p. 1984. 8.95 o.p. (ISBN 0-87477-338-5). J P Tarcher.

Wild Flowers of California. Mary E. Parsons. (Illus.). 423p. Repr. of 1897 ed. 10.00 o.p. (ISBN 0-940228-06-8). Calif Acad Sci.

Wild Flowers of California. Mary E. Parsons. Ed. by Roxana S. Ferris. (Illus.). 1966. pap. 6.95 o.p. (ISBN 0-486-21678-0). Dover.

Wild Flowers of the Northeastern States. New York Botanical Garden Staff. (Illus.). 1978. text ed. 24.95 o.p. (ISBN 0-07-046371-9, P&RB). McGraw.

Wild Flowers of Wilson's Promontory National Park. J. Ros Garnet. (Illus.). 1979. 7.95 o.p. (ISBN 0-85091-111-7, Pub. by Lothian). Intl Spec Bk.

Wild Food Plants of Indiana & Adjacent States. Alan McPherson & Sue McPherson. LC 76-48528. (Illus.). 192p. 1977. 12.50x o.p. (ISBN 0-253-19039-8); pap. 4.95 o.p. (ISBN 0-253-28925-4). Ind U Pr.

Wild Fowl Decoys. Joel Barber. (Illus.). 15.25 o.p. (ISBN 0-8446-1590-0). Peter Smith.

Wild Game & Fish Cookbook. Jim Bryant. (Illus.). 224p. 1984. 15.45i o.p. (ISBN 0-316-11327-1, 113271). Little.

Wild Goats of Ein Gedi. Herbert Weiner. LC 61-12601. (Temple Bks). 1970. pap. 2.95 o.p. (ISBN 0-689-70235-3, T-16, Atheneum). Macmillan.

Wild-Goose Chase: A Modern Critical Edition with Commentary and Notes Based on the 1652 Folio. John Fletcher. Ed. by Rota H. Lister & Stephen Orgel. LC 79-54349. (Renaissance Drama Second Ser.). 200p. 1980. lib. bdg. 26.00 o.p. (ISBN 0-8240-4466-5). Garland Pub.

Wild Habitats. Aleta Karstad. (Illus.). 1979. 2.95 o.p. (ISBN 0-684-16236-9, ScribT); encore ed. 2.95 o.p. (ISBN 0-684-17582-7). Scribner.

Wild Hamster. Alain Vaes. (Illus.). (ps-3). 1985. 14.95 o.p. (ISBN 0-316-89504-0). Little.

Wild Hearts. Virginia Henley. (Avon Romance Ser.). 448p. 1985. pap. 3.50 o.p. (ISBN 0-380-89536-6). Avon.

Wild Honey. 6.95 o.p. (ISBN 0-317-31488-2, 9045). Routledge Chapman & Hall.

Wild Hop Leaf. Y. Avedeyenko. 372p. 1979. pap. 6.45 o.p. (ISBN 0-8285-0944-1, Pub. by Progress Pubs USSR). Imported Pubns.

Wild in the World. John Donovan. (gr. 7 up). 1983. pap. 0.95 o.p. (ISBN 0-380-01625-7, 29264). Avon.

Wild Irish Girl. Lady Morgan. (Mothers of the Novel Reprints Ser.). 288p. 1986. pap. 7.95 o.p. (ISBN 0-86358-097-1, 80971). Routledge Chapman & Hall.

Wild Jack. John Christopher. LC 74-6428. 160p. (gr. 5-9). 1974. 9.95 o.s.i. (ISBN 0-02-718300-9, 71830). Macmillan.

Wild Land, Wild Love. Mallory Burgess. 368p. (Orig.). 1986. pap. 3.95 o.p. (ISBN 0-380-75167-4). Avon.

Wild Life in Alaska. Lawrence S. Telford. 1980. 7.50 o.p. (ISBN 0-682-49581-6). Exposition-Phoenix.

Wild Nights. Emma Tennant. LC 79-3365. 132p. 1980. 7.95 o.p. (ISBN 0-15-196725-3). HarBraceJ.

Wild Northern Scenes or Sporting Adventures with Rifle & the Rod. Samuel H. Hammond. LC 79-15834. (Illus.). 1979. Repr. of 1857 ed. 12.50 o.p. (ISBN 0-916346-33-1). Harbor Hill Bks.

Wild Notes from the Lyre of a Native Minstrel. Charles Thompson. (Australian Literary Reprints Ser). 88p. 1974. Repr. 21.00x o.p. (ISBN 0-424-06560-6, Pub. by Sydney U Pr). Intl Spec Bk.

Wild Orphan Babies: Mammals & Birds Caring for Them & Setting Them Free. 2nd ed. William J. Weber. LC 78-4352. (Illus.). 160p. (gr. 5 up). 1978. 9.95 o.s.i. (ISBN 0-03-044976-6); pap. 5.95 o.s.i. (ISBN 0-03-056821-8). H Holt & Co.

Wild Orphan Friends. William J. Weber. LC 76-11738. (Illus.). 160p. (gr. 5 up). 1976. pap. 3.95 o.s.i. (ISBN 0-03-056822-6). H Holt & Co.

Wild Plants of the San Juan Islands. Scott Atkinson & Fred Sharpe. (Illus.). 176p. (Orig.). 1985. pap. 9.95 o.s.i. (ISBN 0-89886-104-7). Mountaineers.

Wild Plants You Can Eat. Darrell D. Young. LC 83-9344. 96p. 1983. lib. bdg. 9.79 o.s.i. (ISBN 0-671-42407-6). Messner.

Wild Rose. Rene J. Garrord. (Avon Romance Ser.). 1985. pap. 3.50 o.p. (ISBN 0-380-89784-9). Avon.
Wild Roses. Julia Grice. 1980. pap. 2.95 o.p. (ISBN 0-380-75069-4, 78022-4). Avon.
Wild Spenders. Diana Davenport. 272p. 1985. pap. 3.95 o.p. (ISBN 0-380-69894-3). Avon.
Wild Style: The Next Wave. Cyn Zarco & Robert Hofler. 1985. pap. 7.95 o.p. (ISBN 0-671-55470-0, Pub. by Fireside). S&S.
Wild Swan. Celeste De Blasis. LC 83-46001. 592p. 1984. 16.95 o.p. (ISBN 0-553-05059-1). Bantam.
Wild Sweet Witch. Araby Scott. 336p. 1981. pap. 2.95 o.p. (ISBN 0-380-77339-2, 77339-2). Avon.
Wild Thyme, Winter Lightning: The Symbolic Novels of L. P. Hartley. Anne Mulkeen. LC 73-18047. 210p. 1974. text ed. 22.50x o.p. (ISBN 0-8143-1494-5). Wayne St U Pr.
Wild Tribes of the Soudan. Frank L. James. LC 73-94481. Repr. of 1883 ed. 35.00x o.p. (ISBN 0-8371-2366-6, JAT&). Greenwood.
Wild Turkey Management: Current Problems & Programs. Ed. by Glen C. Sanderson & Helen C. Schultz. LC 72-87838. (Illus.). 366p. 1973. text ed. 37.00x o.p. (ISBN 0-8262-0133-4). U of Mo Pr.
Wild Vines. Beverly C. Warren. LC 86-1068. (Starlight Romance Ser.). 192p. 1986. 12.95 o.p. (ISBN 0-385-23564-X). Doubleday.
Wild West: A History of the Wild West Shows. Don Russell. LC 77-102755. (Illus.). 150p. 1970. 9.95 o.p. (ISBN 0-88360-017-X, Dist. by Univ. of Texas Pr). Amon Carter.
Wild West Riddles & Jokes. Joseph Rosenbloom. LC 85-2632. (Illus.). 128p. (gr. 3). 1985. 10.95 o.p. (ISBN 0-8069-4704-7); lib. bdg. 12.49 o.p. (ISBN 0-8069-4705-5); pap. 3.50 o.p. (ISBN 0-8069-7996-8). Sterling.
Wildcats: Kentucky Football. Russ Rice. LC 75-26071. (College Sports Ser.). 1980. 11.95 o.p. (ISBN 0-87397-075-6). Strode.
Wildcatter: A Portrait of Robert O. Anderson. Kenneth Harris. LC 87-8183. (Illus.). 224p. 1987. 18.95 o.s.i. (ISBN 1-55584-048-5). Weidenfeld.
Wildering. Claire Lorrimer. 320p. 1983. pap. 3.95 o.s.i. (ISBN 0-345-30917-0). Ballantine.
Wilderness above the Sound: The Story of Mount Rainer National Park. Arthur Martinson. LC 85-63418. (Western Horizons Bk.). (Illus.). 96p. (Orig.). 1986. pap. 11.95 o.p. (ISBN 0-87358-398-1). Northland.
Wilderness Britain. Anthony Burton. (Illus.). 196p. 1988. pap. 14.95 o.s.i. (ISBN 0-233-98162-4, Pub. by A Deutsch England). David & Charles.
Wilderness Cabin. rev. ed. Calvin Rutstrum. 192p. 1972. pap. 4.95 o.p. (ISBN 0-02-098500-2, Collier). Macmillan.
Wilderness Called Peace. Edmund Keeley. 1985. 16.45 o.p. (ISBN 0-671-47416-2). S&S.
Wilderness Colors of Tao-Chi. Marilyn Fu & Wen Fong. (Illus.). 48p. 1973. 14.95 o.p. (ISBN 0-87099-078-0). Metro Mus Art.
Wilderness Cookbook. Berndt Berglund & Clare Bolsby. LC 72-12158. 192p. 1973. 4.95 o.p. (ISBN 0-684-17082-5, ScribT); pap. 3.95 o.p. (ISBN 0-684-14715-7, ScribT). Scribner.
Wilderness Essays. John Muir. Ed. by Frank Buske. (Literature of the American Wilderness Ser.). 288p. 1980. pap. 4.95 o.p. (ISBN 0-87905-072-1, Peregrine Smith). Gibbs Smith Pub.
Wilderness Handbook. Paul Petzoldt. LC 74-2058. (Illus.). 286p. 1974. 10.95 o.p. (ISBN 0-393-08691-7). Norton.
Wilderness Handbook. Paul Petzoldt. (Illus.). 1977. pap. 6.95 o.p. (ISBN 0-393-08778-6). Norton.
Wilderness Has Ears. Alice Wellman. LC 75-10130. 160p. (gr. 5 up). 1975. 6.95 o.p. (ISBN 0-15-297285-4, HJ). HarBraceJ.
Wilderness Journey. William O. Steele. LC 55-9006. (Illus.). (gr. 4-6). 1953. 6.75 o.p. (ISBN 0-15-297318-4, HJ). HarBraceJ.
Wilderness Medicine. William W. Forgey. LC 79-89027. (Illus.). 1979. pap. 7.95 o.p. (ISBN 0-934802-02-5). ICS Bks.
Wilderness Milepost 1987. Alaska Northwest Publishing Staff. (Illus.). 1987. pap. 14.95 o.p. (ISBN 0-88240-286-2). Alaska Northwest.
Wilderness of Vines. Hal Bennett. (Library of Contemporary Literature). 350p. pap. 7.95 cancelled o.s.i. (ISBN 0-88258-153-8). Howard U Pr.
Wilderness Plots: Tales about the Settlement of the American Land. Scott R. Sanders. LC 83-7988. (Illus.). 128p. 1983. 9.95 o.p. (ISBN 0-688-02147-6). Morrow.
Wilderness Protection: A Bibliographic Review. Alva W. Stewart. (Public Administration Ser.: Bibliography P 1642). 1985. pap. 2.00 o.p. (ISBN 0-89028-332-X). Vance Biblios.
Wilderness Survival. Bernard Shanks. LC 80-17508. (Illus.). 224p. 1980. text ed. 15.00x o.p. (ISBN 0-87663-343-2); pap. 6.95x o.p. (ISBN 0-87663-998-8); pap. 19.95 o.p. Universe.
Wilderness Tattoo: A Narrative of Juan Ortiz. William O. Steele. LC 77-167838. (Illus.). (gr. 5-9). 1972. 5.95 o.p. (ISBN 0-15-297325-7, HJ). HarBraceJ.
Wilderness, the Discovery of a Continent of Wonder. Rutherford Platt. LC 72-9919. (Illus.). 310p. 1973. Repr. of 1961 ed. lib. bdg. 22.50x o.p. (ISBN 0-8371-6608-X, PLWI). Greenwood.
Wilderness Trek. Zane Grey. 256p. 1988. pap. 2.95 o.s.i. (ISBN 0-671-60501-1). PB.
Wilderness Waterways: A Guide to Information Sources. Ed. by Ronald Ziegler. LC 78-10410. (Sports, Games, & Pastimes Information Guide Ser.: Vol. 1). 328p. 1979. 68.00x o.p. (ISBN 0-8103-1434-7). Gale.
Wildfire. Richard M. Stern. 1986. 15.45 o.p. (ISBN 0-393-02258-7). Norton.
Wildfire Trace. Cathy G. Thacker. (Velvet Glove Ser.: No. 5). 192p. (Orig.). 1984. pap. 2.25 o.p. (ISBN 0-380-88260-4). Avon.
Wildfires, Bk. 4: The Story of Canada. Dennis Adair & Janet Rosenstock. 336p. 1983. pap. 3.95 o.p. (ISBN 0-380-82313-6, 82313-6). Avon.
Wildflowers Along Forest & Mesa Trails. Nelson T. Bernard. LC 83-23344. (Coyote Bk. Ser.). (Illus.). 191p. 1984. pap. 9.95 o.p. (ISBN 0-8263-0730-2). U of NM Pr.
Wildflowers & the Stories Behind Their Names. Phyllis S. Busch. LC 73-1351. (Illus.). (gr. 3up). 1977. 10.00 o.s.i. (ISBN 0-684-14820-X, Pub. by Scribner). Macmillan.
Wildlands & Woodlots: The Story of New England's Forests. Lloyd C. Irland. LC 81-69943. (Futures of New England Ser.). (Illus.). 233p. 1985. pap. 10.95 o.p. U Pr of New Eng.
Wildlife. Date not set. (ISBN 0-385-29560-X). Delacorte.
Wildlife: Activity Book. K. D. McKowen. (Illus.). 32p. (gr. 2-6). 1985. pap. 1.25 o.p. (ISBN 0-913635-00-6). Aspen Prods.
Wildlife & Plants of the Southern Rocky Mountains. Charles Yocom et al. (American Wildlife Region Ser.: Vol. 7). (Illus.). 138p. (gr. 4 up). 1969. 11.95 o.p. (ISBN 0-911010-13-0); pap. 5.95 o.p. (ISBN 0-911010-12-2). Naturegraph.
Wildlife Community: From the Tundra to the Tropics in North America. Clarence J. Hylander. (Illus.). (gr. 7 up). 1966. 8.95 o.p. (ISBN 0-395-06839-8). HM.
Wildlife Ecology & Management. William L. Robinson & Eric G. Bolen. 608p. 1984. text ed. write for info. o.p. (ISBN 0-02-402250-0). Macmillan.
Wildlife Family Album. David F. Robinson. Ed. by Alma D. MacConomy & Barbara Peters. LC 81-81904. (Illus.). 208p. 1981. 16.95 o.p. Natl Wildlife.
Wildlife Habitat Improvement. 96p. 3.00 o.p. (ISBN 0-317-35030-7, B5). Natl Audubon.
Wildlife in Tanzanian Settlement Policy: The Case of the Selous. Gordon Matzke. LC 77-18175. (Foreign & Comparative Studies Program, Africa Ser.: No. 28). 122p. 1977. pap. 7.00x o.p. (ISBN 0-915984-50-4). Syracuse U Foreign Comp.
Wildlife of China. Ed. by Tang Guang You & Li Wei. (Illus.). 134p. 1986. text ed. 39.95 o.p. (ISBN 0-8351-1785-5). China Bks.
Wildlife of Eastern Australia. Stanley Breeden & Kay Breeden. (Illus.). 260p. 1974. 12.95 o.s.i. (ISBN 0-8008-8332-2). Taplinger.
Wildlife of the Mountains. Edward R. Ricciuti. (Wildlife Habitat Ser.). (Illus.). 1979. 19.95 o.p. (ISBN 0-8109-1757-2). Abrams.
Wildlife of the Oceans. Albert C. Jensen. (Wldlife Habitat Ser.). (Illus.). 1979. 19.95 o.p. (ISBN 0-8109-1758-0). Abrams.
Wildlife of the Polar Regions. G. Carleton Ray & M. G. McCormick-Ray. (Wildlife Habitat Ser.). (Illus.). 232p. 1981. 19.95 o.p. (ISBN 0-8109-1768-8). Abrams.
Wildlife of the Prairies & Plains. Kai Curry-Lindahl. LC 80-27927. (Wildlife Habitat Ser.). (Illus.). 232p. 1981. 19.95 o.p. (ISBN 0-8109-1766-1). Abrams.
Wildlife Resources & Economic Development. S. K. Eltringham. LC 83-21661. 325p. 1984. 68.95 o.p. (ISBN 0-471-90213-6). Wiley.
Wiley Medical Dictionary. deluxe ed. 1988. write for info. o.p. (ISBN 0-471-85765-3). Churchill.
Wiley Reader: Designs for Writing. brief ed. Caroline D. Eckhardt & David H. Stewart. LC 78-15326. 1979. pap. 13.20x o.p. (ISBN 0-673-15669-9). Scott F.
Wilfred Owen, 1893-1918: A Bibliography. William White. LC 66-28409. (Serif Ser.: No. 1). 1967. 10.00x o.p. (ISBN 0-87338-017-7). Kent St U Pr.
Wilfred's Hospital Ship: Wilfred Grenfell. Dolores Ready. LC 77-86603. (Stories About Christian Heroes Ser.). (Illus.). (gr. 1-5). 1977. pap. 1.95 o.p. (ISBN 0-03-041651-5). HarpR.
Wilhelm Reich: The Evolution of His Work. David Boadella. 400p. (Orig.). 1986. pap. 9.95 o.p. (ISBN 1-85063-034-8). Routledge Chapman & Hall.
Wilhelm Schmidt & the Origin of the Idea of God. Ernest Brandewie. 352p. (Orig.). 1983. lib. bdg. 31.50 o.p. (ISBN 0-8191-3363-9); pap. text ed. 16.50 o.p. (ISBN 0-8191-3364-7). U Pr of Amer.
Wilhelmstrasse: A Study of German Diplomats under the Nazi Regime. Paul Seabury. LC 76-2403. (Illus.). 217p. 1976. Repr. of 1954 ed. lib. bdg. 22.50x o.p. (ISBN 0-8371-8790-7, SEWI). Greenwood.
Wilkes-Barre & Hazelton RY. E. J. Quinby. LC 72-87786. 1972. pap. 3.95 o.p. (ISBN 0-911868-01-1). Carstens Pubns.
Wilkie Collins. Norman Page. (Critical Heritage Ser.). 304p. 1985. pap. 15.00 o.p. (ISBN 0-7102-0589-9). Routledge Chapman & Hall.
Will It Freeze? Joan Hood. (Illus.). 192p. 1982. 4.95 o.s.i. (ISBN 0-684-17495-2, ScribT). Scribner.
Will My Dog Go to Heaven? Heidi Zink & Jorg Zink. Tr. by William Oyler. LC 72-90267. 1973. pap. 5.95 o.p. (ISBN 0-8066-1315-7, 10-7197, Augsburg). Augsburg Fortress.
Will She Be Right? The Future of Australia. Herman Kahn & Thomas Pepper. (Illus.). 199p. 1981. text ed. 25.00 o.p. (ISBN 0-7022-1568-6); pap. 9.95 o.p. (ISBN 0-7022-1569-4). U of Queensland Pr.
Will the Real Renie Lake Please Stand up. Barbara Morgenroth. LC 80-21904. 168p. (gr. 6 up). 1981. PLB 9.95 o.p. (ISBN 0-689-30820-5, Atheneum). Macmillan.
Will the Real Teacher Please Stand Up? 2nd ed. Mary Greer & Bonnie Rubenstein. 1977. pap. 12.95 o.p. (ISBN 0-673-16153-6). Scott F.
Will the Real Winner Please Stand Up. Dallas Groten. 160p. 1985. pap. 4.95 o.p. (ISBN 0-87123-819-5, 210819). Bethany Hse.
Will the Real You Please Remain Standing! John A. Lynn. 204p. 1981. pap. 2.95 o.p. (ISBN 0-910068-38-0). Am Christian.
Will the Real You Please Stand Up! John A. Lynn. 113p. 1980. pap. 2.95 o.p. (ISBN 0-910068-28-3). Am Christian.
Will There Be Enough Food? LC 81-600143. (Yearbook of Agriculture, 1981). (Illus.). 344p. 1981. 7.00 o.p. (ISBN 0-318-22478-X, S/N 001-000-04257-2). USGPO.
Will They Love Me When I Leave? A Weekend Father's Struggle to Stay Close to His Kids. C. W. Smith. 224p. 1987. 17.95 o.p. (ISBN 0-399-13249-X, Putnam). Putnam Pub Group.
Will to Live. Hugh Franks. 1979. 15.00x o.p. (ISBN 0-7100-0181-9). Routledge Chapman & Hall.
Will to Live-Will to Die: Ethics & the Search for a Good Death. Kenneth L. Vaux. LC 78-52188. 1978. 8.95 o.p. (ISBN 0-8066-1659-8, 10-7200, Augsburg). Augsburg Fortress.
Will You Count the Stars Without Me? Jane B. Zalben. LC 78-16069. (Illus.). 32p. (ps-3). 1979. 10.95 o.p. (ISBN 0-374-38433-9). FS&G.
Willaby. Rachel Isadora. LC 77-4469. (Illus.). 32p. (gr. k-3). 1977. 9.95 o.s.i. (ISBN 0-02-747460-7). Macmillan.
Willem de Kooning: Drawings-Paintings-Sculpture, A Whitney Museum Book. Paul Cummings et al. (Illus.). 1983. 44.50 o.p. (ISBN 0-393-01840-7). Norton.
Willem De Kooning: The First Twenty-Six Years in New York. Sally Yard. Ed. by S. J. Freedberg. (Outstanding Dissertations in the Fine Arts Ser.). (Illus.). 510p. 1985. Repr. of 1980 ed. 40.00 o.p. (ISBN 0-8240-6872-6). Garland Pub.
Willem De Kooning: The North Atlantic Light. Carter Ratcliff. (Illus.). 128p. (Eng. & Dutch.). 1988. pap. 15.00 o.p. (ISBN 0-918825-90-3). Moyer Bell Limited.
Willful Misconduct: The Story of the Crash of Pan American Flight 806 & of What Happened Afterward. William Norris. LC 82-14381. 320p. 1984. 17.45 o.p. (ISBN 0-393-01796-6). Norton.
William & His Kitten. Marjorie Flack. (gr. k-3). reinforced bdg. 5.95 o.p. (ISBN 0-395-20212-4). HM.
William & John Linnell: 18th Century London Furniture Makers, 2 vols. Helena Hayward & Pat Kirkham. (Illus.). Set. 75.00 o.p. (ISBN 0-317-54993-6). Vol. 1, 260 pgs. Vol. 2, 170 pgs. Apollo.
William & Mary: A Story. Penelope Farmer. LC 74-76272. (gr. 5-9). 1974. 5.95 o.p. (ISBN 0-689-50005-X, Atheneum). Macmillan.
William Balston, Paper Maker, 1759-1849. Thomas Balston. Ed. by John Bidwell. LC 78-74387. (Nineteenth-Century Book Arts & Printing History Ser.: Vol. 2). (Illus.). 1979. lib. bdg. 26.00 o.p. (ISBN 0-8240-3876-2). Garland Pub.
William Barclay: The Authorized Biography. Clive Rawlins. 704p. 1984. 29.95 o.p. (ISBN 0-8028-3598-8). Eerdmans.
William Bartram: Botanical & Zoological Drawings, 1756-88. Joseph Ewan. LC 68-8640. (Memoirs Ser.: Vol. 74). (Illus.). 1968. 50.00 o.p. (ISBN 0-87169-074-8). Am Philos.
William Blake. Basil De Selincourt. LC 72-162018. (Illus.). 1972. Repr. of 1909 ed. 28.50x o.p. (ISBN 0-8154-0389-5). Cooper Sq.
William Blake. Jack Lindsay. 1978. 27.50x o.p. (ISBN 0-09-462080-6, Pub. by Constable Pubs UK). Trans-Atl-Phila.
William Blake: America; a Prophecy. Intro. by G. E. Bentley, Jr. LC 73-93217. 1974. 35.00 o.p. (ISBN 0-913130-03-6, St Luke TN). Peachtree Pubs.
William Blake: Book Illustrator, Vol. I. Roger R. Easson & Robert N. Essick. LC 72-82993. 1972. pap. 20.00 o.p. (ISBN 0-913130-01-X, St Luke TN). Peachtree Pubs.
William Blake: Book Illustrator, Vol. II. Roger R. Easson & Robert N. Essick. 1979. 125.00 o.p. (ISBN 0-913130-07-9, St Luke TN); pap. 45.00 o.p. (ISBN 0-913130-08-7). Peachtree Pubs.
William Blake: Europe, a Prophecy. G. E. Bentley. LC 73-93218. 1976. ltd. ed. 60.00 o.p. (ISBN 0-913130-30-3, St Luke TN). Peachtree Pubs.
William Caxton & Charles Knight. Intro. by Kenneth Day. (Illus.). 240p. pap. 8.95 o.p. (ISBN 0-913720-06-2, Sandstone). Beil.
William Cobbett & the Politics of Earth. Gerald Duff. (Salzburg Studies in English Literature, Romantic Reassessment: No. 24). 143p. 1972. pap. text ed. 25.00x o.p. (ISBN 0-391-01366-1). Humanities.
William Cooper's - A Catalogue of Chymicall Books, 1673-88: A Verified Version. Stanton J. Linden. LC 86-27165. (Garland Reference Library of the Humanities). 1987. lib. bdg. 37.00 o.p. (ISBN 0-8240-8557-4). Garland Pub.
William Cullen Bryant. John Bigelow. LC 79-78114. (Library of Lives & Letters Ser.). 366p. 1970. Repr. of 1890 ed. 34.00x o.p. (ISBN 0-8103-3369-4). Gale.
William Cullen Bryant. Chas Brown. LC 79-143949. (Illus.). 1971. 12.50 o.s.i. (ISBN 0-684-12370-3, ScribT). Scribner.
William E. Borah & American Foreign Policy. Robert J. Maddox. LC 74-86429. xxi, 272p. 1969. 32.50 o.p. (ISBN 0-8071-0907-X). La State U Pr.
William Eggleston's Guide, with an Essay by John Szarkowski. John Szarkowski. 1976. 22.95 o.p. (ISBN 0-262-05018-8). MIT Pr.
William Ellery Channing: An Intellectual Portrait. David P. Edgell. LC 83-18491. xv, 264p. 1983. Repr. of 1955 ed. lib. bdg. 35.00x o.p. (ISBN 0-313-24253-4, EWEC). Greenwood.
William Faulkner. Frederick J. Hoffman. (United States Authors Ser.). 1966. lib. bdg. 16.95 o.s.i. (ISBN 0-8057-0244-X, Twayne). G K Hall.
William Faulkner. rev. ed. Frederick J. Hoffman. (United States Authors Ser.). 1985. pap. 6.95 o.s.i. (ISBN 0-8057-7444-0, Twayne). G K Hall.
William Faulkner, Letters & Fictions. James G. Watson. 232p. 1987. text ed. 25.00 o.p. (ISBN 0-292-76503-7). U of Tex Pr.
William Faulkner: Research Opportunities & Dissertation Abstracts. Tetsumaro Hayashi. LC 82-15236. 336p. 1982. lib. bdg. 35.00x o.p. (ISBN 0-89950-048-X). McFarland & Co.
William Faulkner: The Critical Heritage. Ed. by John Bassett. (Critical Heritage Ser.). 1975. 36.00x o.p. (ISBN 0-7100-8124-3). Routledge Chapman & Hall.
William Faulkner: The Yoknapatawpha Fiction. Ed. by A. Robert Lee. LC 84-6274. (Critical Studies). 224p. 1986. 28.50x o.p. (ISBN 0-389-20489-7, BNB-08051). B&N Imports.
William Faulkner: Three Decades of Criticism. Frederick J. Hoffman & Olga W. Vickery. LC 60-11481. 1963. pap. 5.25 o.p. (ISBN 0-15-696755-3, Harv). HarBraceJ.
William Faulkner's Light in August: A Critical Casebook. Francois Pitavy. LC 81-48416. 300p. 1982. lib. bdg. 48.00 o.p. (ISBN 0-8240-9385-2). Garland Pub.
William Gilmore Simms: A Reference Guide. Keen Butterworth & James E. Kibler, Jr. 1980. lib. bdg. 31.50 o.s.i. (ISBN 0-8161-1059-X, Hall Reference). G K Hall.
William Golding: A Critical Study. 2nd ed. Mark Kinkead-Weeks & Ian Gregor. 282p. 1984. pap. 7.95 o.p. (ISBN 0-571-13259-6). Faber & Faber.
William Grant Still & the Fusion of Cultures in American Music. William G. Still. Ed. by Robert B. Haas. LC 72-5955. 200p. 1975. 14.00 o.p. (ISBN 0-87685-149-9); pap. 7.50 o.p. (ISBN 0-87685-247-9). Black Sparrow.
William H. Jackson. Beaumont Newhall & Diana E. Edkins. LC 73-89076. (Illus.). 158p. 15.95 o.p. (ISBN 0-88360-039-0, Dist. by Univ. of Texas Pr). Amon Carter.
William Harvey: His Life & Times; His Discoveries; His Methods. Louis Chauvois. 1957. (ISBN 0-8022-0235-7). Philos Lib.
William Hazlitt. Augustine Birrell. LC 70-98817. Repr. of 1902 ed. lib. bdg. 35.00x o.p. (ISBN 0-8371-2848-X, BIWH). Greenwood.

Titles

William Hickling Prescott: A Biography. C. Harvey Gardiner. (Illus.). 388p. 1969. 20.00x o.p. (ISBN 0-292-70005-9). U of Tex Pr.
William Jay & the Constitutional Movement for the Abolition of Slavery. Bayard Tuckerman. LC 69-19000. (Illus.). 1969. Repr. of 1893 ed. 35.00x o.p. (ISBN 0-8371-4592-9, TUJ&). Greenwood.
William Jennings Bryan: Missionary Isolationist. Kendrick A. Clements. LC 82-8342. (Illus.). 232p. 1983. text ed. 23.95x o.p. (ISBN 0-87049-364-7). U of Tenn Pr.
William Klein: Photographs. William Klein. Ed. by John Heilpern. (Monograph). (Illus.). 192p. 1981. 50.00 o.p. (ISBN 0-89381-049-5); 400.00 o.p. (ISBN 0-89381-053-3). Aperture.
William Law: Christian Perfection. Rev. ed. William Law. 96p. 1986. pap. 4.95 o.p. (ISBN 0-8423-0259-X). Tyndale.
William Morgan: Bibliography & Building List. Edward H. Teague. (Architecture Ser.: A 1436). 6p. 1985. 2.00 o.p. (ISBN 0-89028-486-5). Vance Biblios.
William Morris. Richard Tames. (Shire Lifelines Ser.: No. 3). (Illus.). 48p. pap. 4.95 o.p. (ISBN 0-85263-142-1, Pub. by Shire Pubns England). Seven Hills Bk Dists.
William Morris: A Reference Guide. Gary L. Aho. (Reference Guides to Literature Ser.). 420p. 1985. lib. bdg. 53.00 o.s.i. (ISBN 0-8161-8449-6). G K Hall.
William Morris: His Life & Work. Jack Lindsay. LC 79-13075. (Illus.). 1979. 14.95 o.s.i. (ISBN 0-8008-8339-X). Taplinger.
William Morris: The Critical Heritage. Ed. by Peter Faulkner. (Critical Heritage Ser.). 1984. pap. 15.00 o.p. (ISBN 0-7102-0393-4). Routledge Chapman & Hall.
William O. Douglas: A Biography. Edwin P. Hoyt. LC 78-19868. (Illus.). 1979. 8.95 o.p. (ISBN 0-8397-8598-4). Eriksson.
William O'Brien & the Course of Irish Politics, 1881-1918. Joseph V. O'Brien. LC 74-22970. 350p. 1976. 38.50x o.p. (ISBN 0-520-02886-4). U of Cal Pr.
William Oughtred: A Great Seventeenth-Century Teacher of Mathematics. Florian Cajori. 106p. 1916. 6.95 o.p. (ISBN 0-87548-174-4). Open Court.
William S. Burroughs: An Annotated Bibliography of His Works & Criticism. Michael B. Goodman. LC 75-23007. (Reference Library of the Humanities: Vol. 24). 100p. 1975. lib. bdg. 25.00 o.p. (ISBN 0-8240-9989-3). Garland Pub.
William Saroyan. Howard R. Floan. (U. S. Authors Ser.: No. 100). 1978. lib. bdg. 15.95 o.p. (ISBN 0-8057-0652-6, Twayne). G K Hall.
William Saroyan. Aram Saroyan. (Illus.). 224p. 1983. 16.95 o.p. (ISBN 0-15-196762-8). HarBraceJ.
William Saroyan. Aram Saroyan. LC 83-21313. (Illus.). 224p. 1983. pap. 8.95 o.p. (ISBN 0-15-696780-4, Harv). HarBraceJ.
William Strickland. Lamia Doumato. (Architecture Ser.: A 1513). 8p. 1985. 2.00 o.p. (ISBN 0-89028-663-9). Vance Biblios.
William the Silent: William of Nassau, Prince of Orange, 1533-1584. Cicely V. Wedgwood. (Illus.). 1968. pap. 3.95x o.p. (ISBN 0-393-00185-7, Norton Lib). Norton.
William Wordsworth: A Biography. Hunter Davies. LC 80-66004. (Illus.). 1980. 17.95 o.s.i. (ISBN 0-689-11087-1, Atheneum). Macmillan.
William Wordsworth: The Poetry of Grandeur & of Tenderness. David Pirie. 320p. 1982. 35.00x o.p. (ISBN 0-416-31300-0, NO. 3651). Routledge Chapman & Hall.
William Wycherley: A Biography. B. Eugene McCarthy. LC 79-9210. (Illus.). xii, 255p. 1980. 20.95x o.p. (ISBN 0-8214-0410-5). Ohio U Pr.
Williams Family of Painters. Jan Reynolds. (Illus.). 331p. 1977. 44.50 o.p. (ISBN 0-902028-41-3). Antique Collect.
Williamsburg. 1982. 17.50 o.p. (ISBN 0-686-76279-7). Feldheim.
Williamsburg Collection of Antique Furnishing. Colonial Williamsburg Foundation Staff. LC 73-86811. 1974. 11.95 o.p. (ISBN 0-03-089492-1). H Holt & Co.
Williamsburg Trilogy. Daniel Fuchs. pap. 5.45 o.p. (ISBN 0-380-01468-8, 13672). Avon.
Williamsport: Frontier Village to Regional Center. Robert H. Larson et al. LC 84-21930. (Illus.). 208p. 1984. 22.95 o.p. (ISBN 0-89781-110-0). Windsor Pubns Inc.
Willie & Phil. Joyce Thompson. 1980. pap. 1.95 o.p. (ISBN 0-380-75804-0, 75804). Avon.
Willie de Wit: Lord of the Ring. Michael Beaudin. 304p. 1984. pap. 3.25 o.p. (ISBN 0-380-89485-8). Avon.
Willie Geary "Bunk" Johnson: The New Iberia Years. Austin M. Sonnier, Jr. LC 76-16330. 1977. pap. 5.00 o.s.i. (ISBN 0-8008-1122-4, Crescendo). Taplinger.
Willie in the Big World: An Adventure with Numbers. Sven Nordqvist. LC 85-15307. (Illus.). 32p. (ps-3). 1986. 11.75 o.p. (ISBN 0-688-06142-7); lib. bdg. 11.88 o.p. (ISBN 0-688-06143-5). Morrow.
Willie Visits Tulip Time. Lory Bertsch. (Illus.). 40p. (gr. k up). 1983. 4.50 o.p. (ISBN 0-682-49980-3). Exposition-Phoenix.
Willingly. Tess Gallagher. LC 83-82867. 96p. 1984. 12.00 o.p. (ISBN 0-915308-45-2); pap. 6.00 o.p. (ISBN 0-915308-46-0). Graywolf.
Willmaker. 2nd ed. Legisoft Staff. LC 84-63151. (Illus.). 202p. (Orig.). 1986. pap. 49.95 incl. diskette o.p. (ISBN 0-87337-026-0). Nolo Pr.
Willow Whip. Irene B. Brown. LC 79-11725. (gr. 4-6). 1979. 10.95 o.p. (ISBN 0-689-30703-9, Atheneum). Macmillan.
Willow's End. Dale R. Todd. LC 84-91321. 144p. 1985. 10.95 o.p. (ISBN 0-533-06414-7). Vantage.
Wills & Intestacies. J. Comyn & R. Johnson. LC 78-92109. 1970. text ed. 18.00 o.p. (ISBN 0-08-006691-7); pap. text ed. 8.50 o.p. (ISBN 0-08-006690-9). Pergamon.
Willy Remembers. Irvin Faust. LC 79-157508. 1971. 6.95 o.p. (Arbor Hse). Morrow.
Willys Dream Kit. Jan Novak. LC 84-25321. 320p. 1985. 19.95 o.p. (ISBN 0-15-196766-0). HarBraceJ.
Wilshire's, Vols. 1-17, No. 13. 1970. Repr. of 1915 ed. lib. bdg. 715.00x o.p. (ISBN 0-8371-9261-7, WI00). Greenwood.
Wilson Era: Years of Peace, 1910-1917. Josephus Daniels. LC 74-9269. (Illus.). 615p. 1974. Repr. of 1944 ed. lib. bdg. 37.00x o.p. (ISBN 0-8371-7634-4, DAYP). Greenwood.
Wilson Era: Years of War & After, 1917-1923. Josephus Daniels. LC 74-9271. (Illus.). 654p. 1974. Repr. of 1946 ed. lib. bdg. 34.00x o.p. (ISBN 0-8371-7635-2, DAYW). Greenwood.
Wilson: The Road to the White House. Arthur S. Link. 1947. 50.50x o.p. (ISBN 0-691-04577-1); pap. 13.95x o.p. (ISBN 0-691-00557-5). Princeton U Pr.
Wilson: The Struggle for Neutrality, 1914-1915. Arthur S. Link. 1960. 52.50x o.p. (ISBN 0-691-04579-8). Princeton U Pr.
Wilson's Disease. I. Herbert Scheinberg & Irmin Sternlieb. (Major Problems in Internal Medicine Ser.: Vol. 23). (Illus.). 192p. 1984. (ISBN 0-7216-7953-6). Saunders.
Wilton Gardens: New & Rare Inventions of Water-Works. Isaac Caus. Ed. by John D. Hunt. LC 79-57005. (English Landscape Garden Ser.). (Illus.). 91p. 1982. lib. bdg. 19.00 o.p. (ISBN 0-8240-0178-8). Garland Pub.
Wily Witch & Other Fairy Tales & Fables. Godfried Bomans. Tr. by Patricia Crampton from Dutch. LC 76-54196. (Illus.). 208p. (gr. 3 up). 1977. 9.95 o.p. (ISBN 0-916144-09-7). Stemmer Hse.
Wimsey Family. C. W. Scott-Giles. 1979. pap. 3.95 o.p. (ISBN 0-380-46417-9, 46417-9). Avon.
Win More Sailboat Races. C. Stanley Ogilvy. (Illus.). 1976. 8.95 o.p. (ISBN 0-393-03191-8). Norton.
Win or Lose? What You Should Know About the ERA. Collis H. White. 1976. 7.50 o.p. (ISBN 0-682-48596-9). Exposition-Phoenix.
Win-Win: Approaches to Conflict Resolution at Home, in Business, Between Groups & Across Cultures. Arnold Gerstein & James Reagan. (Illus.). 128p. 1986. 14.95 o.p. (ISBN 0-87905-215-5). Gibbs Smith Pub.
Winchester Press Fish Finding Guide. rev. ed. Leonard M. Wright. LC 77-79048. (Illus.). 128p. 1983. pap. 6.95 o.p. (ISBN 0-8329-0338-8). Lyons & Burford.
Winchester Story. Barry Shurlock. (Illus.). 96p. 1987. 9.95 o.p. (ISBN 0-903852-91-8, Pub. by Milestone Pubns UK). Seven Hills Bk Dists.
Wind. Dorothy Scarborough. (Barker Texas History Center Ser.: No. 4). 357p. 1979. 14.95 o.p. (ISBN 0-292-79012-0); pap. (ISBN 0-292-79013-9). U of Tex Pr.
Wind & Sand: The Story of the Wright Brothers at Kitty Hawk. Ed. by Lynanne Wescott & Paula Degen. (Illus.). 192p. 1988. pap. 19.95 o.p. (ISBN 0-8109-2385-8). Abrams.
Wind Around the Moon. Marcia L. Masters. (Living Poets Ser.: No. 35). 80p. 1986. pap. 5.00 o.p. (ISBN 0-934218-35-8). Dragons Teeth.
Wind Atlas. 1984. Set. 84.95 o.p. (ISBN 0-442-21879-6). Van Nos Reinhold.
Wind Energy. L. Jarass et al. (Illus.). 209p. 1981. 48.00 o.p. (ISBN 0-387-10362-7). Springer-Verlag.
Wind Energy Abstracts, 1983, Pt. I. Farrell S. Seiler. LC 84-51152. (Wind Energy Abstract Ser.: one of four vol. set). 100p. 1984. pap. 72.50 o.s.i. (ISBN 0-88016-016-0). Windbks.
Wind Energy Abstracts, 1983, Pt. II. Ed. by Farrell S. Seiler. LC 84-51152. (Wind Energy Abstract Ser.: one of four vol. set). 100p. 1984. pap. 72.50 o.s.i. (ISBN 0-88016-017-9). Windbks.
Wind Energy Abstracts: 1984, 3 vols, Pt. II. Farrell S. Seiler. LC 84-51152. 100p. 1986. pap. 72.50 o.s.i. (ISBN 0-88016-062-4). WindBks.
Wind Energy Abstracts, 1984, Pt. I. Ed. by Farrell S. Seiler. LC 84-51152. (Wind Energy Abstracts Ser.: one of four vol. set). 100p. 1984. pap. 72.50 o.s.i. (ISBN 0-88016-027-6). Windbks.
Wind Energy Abstracts: 1985, 2 vols. Farrell S. Seiler. LC 84-51152. 100p. 1986. Pt. 1. pap. 72.50 o.s.i. (ISBN 0-88016-063-2); Pt. 2. pap. 72.50 o.s.i. (ISBN 0-88016-064-0). WindBks.
Wind Energy & Small Power Production. R. Lornell & D. A. Schaller. (Small Power Production & Wind Energy Ser.). 65p. 1984. pap. 25.00 o.p. (ISBN 0-88016-032-2). Windbks.
Wind Energy in Rural United States. Ed. by National Rural Electric Cooperative Association Staff. 320p. 1984. pap. 40.00 o.s.i. (ISBN 0-88016-030-6). Windbks.
Wind Energy Systems Performance & Size Estimating. Roger L. Moment. (Illus.). 63p. 1984. pap. 19.00 o.s.i. (ISBN 0-88016-044-6). Windbks.
Wind Engineering: Proceedings of the 5th International Conference, Colorado State University, July 8-14, 1979, 2 vols. Ed. by J. E. Cermak. LC 80-40753. (Illus.). 1400p. 1980. Set. 315.00 o.p. (ISBN 0-08-024745-8). Pergamon.
Wind Forces in Engineering. 2nd ed. P. Sachs. 1972. 55.00 o.p. (ISBN 0-08-016607-5). Pergamon.
Wind Forces in Engineering. 2nd ed. P. Sachs. 1978. 89.00 o.p. (ISBN 0-08-021299-9). Pergamon.
Wind Forces on Structures. Task Committee on Wind Forces. 76p. 1961. 4.00 o.p. (ISBN 0-317-59770-1). Am Soc Civil Eng.
Wind from America, Vol. 2. Claude Manceron. LC 78-54928. (French Revolution Ser.: Vol. 2). (Illus.). 1978. 17.95 o.p. (ISBN 0-394-49883-6). Knopf.
Wind from an Enemy Sky: A Novel. D'Arcy McNickle. LC 76-50450. (Native American Ser.). 272p. 1982. pap. 3.12i o.p. (ISBN 0-06-451051-4, P 5003). HarpR.
Wind from Hastings. Morgan Llywelyn. 1978. 8.95 o.p. (ISBN 0-395-26474-X). HM.
Wind in the Rose Bush & Other Stories of the Supernatural. Mary E. Wilkins Freeman. 1986. pap. text ed. 12.95x o.p. (ISBN 0-8290-1956-1). Irvington.
Wind in the Willows: A Musical Adaptation. Don Trifiletti. LC 76-27775. 1977. 10.00 o.p. (ISBN 0-682-48648-5, Banner). Exposition-Phoenix.
Wind in the Willows Pop-up-Book. Kenneth Grahame. LC 83-80060. (Illus.). 12p. (gr. k-4). 1983. 11.95 o.p. (ISBN 0-03-063862-3). H Holt & Co.
Wind in the Willows: The Open Road. Kenneth Grahame. (Illus.). 48p. (ps-3). 1986. pap. 9.95 o.s.i. (ISBN 0-671-61095-3, Little Simon). S&S.
Wind Is Round. Ed. by Sara Hannum & John T. Chase. LC 79-115083. (Illus.). (gr. 6 up). 1970. PLB 4.75 o.p. (ISBN 0-689-20594-5, Atheneum). Macmillan.
Wind Loading on Buildings. Argus J. Macdonald. LC 75-11988. 219p. 1975. 44.95x o.p. (ISBN 0-470-55976-4). Halsted Pr.
Wind on the Prairies: How the West Was Really Won. Helen P. French. (Illus.). 240p. 1982. 10.50 o.p. (Lochnivar). Exposition-Phoenix.
Wind Power Potential: A Prospector's Handbook of Remote Sensing Techniques. J. E. Wade et al. 329p. (Orig.). 1984. pap. text ed. 65.00 o.s.i. (ISBN 0-88016-034-9). Windbks.
Wind Power Prospecting: A Guide to Biological Indicators. J. E. Wade & E. W. Hewson. 110p. 1984. pap. 21.50 o.s.i. (ISBN 0-88016-018-7). Windbks.
Wind River. Gary McCarthy. 480p. (Orig.). 1984. pap. 3.95 o.s.i. (ISBN 0-345-30431-4). Ballantine.
Wind, Sand & Stars. Antoine de Saint-Exupery. Tr. by Lewis Galantiere. LC 65-35872. (Illus.). 1949. 12.95 o.s.i. (ISBN 0-15-197085-8). HarBraceJ.
Wind Song. Carl Sandburg. LC 60-10248. (Illus.). (gr. 5 up). 1960. 5.95 o.p. (ISBN 0-15-297497-0, HJ). HarBraceJ.
Wind Song. Carl Sandburg. LC 60-10248. (Illus.). (gr. 5 up). 1965. pap. 1.50 o.p. (ISBN 0-15-697096-1, VoyB). HarBraceJ.
Wind That Swept Mexico: The History of the Mexican Revolution of 1910-1942. Anita Brenner & George R. Leighton. (Texas Pan American Ser.). (Illus.). 320p. 1971. pap. 24.95 o.p. (ISBN 0-292-70106-3). U of Tex Pr.
Wind the Clock by Bittersweet. Bill Pauly. 32p. 1977. 10.00 o.p. (ISBN 0-913719-03-X); pap. 3.50 o.p. (ISBN 0-913719-02-1). High-Coo Pr.
Wind Thief. Judith Barrett. LC 76-40407. (Illus.). (ps-2). 1977. 7.95 o.p. (ISBN 0-689-30564-8, Atheneum). Macmillan.
Wind Turbine Arrays & Power Systems Operation. R. A. Schlueter et al. 1984. pap. 49.50 o.s.i. (ISBN 0-88016-020-9). Windbks.
Wind Turbine Technology: Horizontal Axis Megawatt Wind Energy Systems. Ed. by David Spera. (Illus.). 450p. 1984. pap. 85.00 o.s.i. (ISBN 0-88016-043-8). Windbks.
Wind Turbine Technology: Vertical Axis Wind Energy Systems. (Illus.). 1984. pap. 65.00 o.s.i. (ISBN 0-88016-007-1). Windbks.
Wind Whales of Ishmael. Philip Jose Farmer. 160p. 1981. pap. 1.95 o.s.i. (ISBN 0-441-89240-X). Ace Bks.
Wind Will Not Subside: Years in Revolutionary China,1964-1969. David Milton & Nancy D. Milton. LC 75-10370. 1976. pap. 7.95 o.p. (ISBN 0-394-70936-5). Pantheon.
Wind Workshop V: Biennial Wind Energy Conference & Workshop, 1981, 3 Vols. (Illus.). 1500p. 1984. Set. pap. 155.00 o.s.i. (ISBN 0-88016-036-5). Windbks.
Wind Workshop V: Biennial Wind Energy Conference & Workshop, 1981, Vol. 1. (Illus.). 550p. 1984. pap. 55.00 o.s.i. (ISBN 0-88016-037-3). Windbks.
Wind Workshop V: Biennial Wind Energy Conference & Workshop, 1981, Vol. 2. (Illus.). 730p. 1984. pap. 73.00 o.s.i. (ISBN 0-88016-038-1). Windbks.
Wind Workshop V: Biennial Wind Energy Conference & Workshop, 1981, Vol. 3. (Illus.). 330p. 1984. pap. 33.00 o.s.i. (ISBN 0-88016-039-X). Windbks.
Wind Workshop VI: Biennial Wind Energy Conference & Workshop, 1983. (Illus.). 900p. 1984. Set. pap. 175.00 o.s.i. (ISBN 0-88016-040-3). Windbks.
Wind Workshop VII: Biennial Wind Energy Conferences & Workshop, 1985. 1986. pap. 95.00 o.s.i. (ISBN 0-88016-059-4). Windbks.
Windigo: An Anthology of Fact & Fantastic Fiction. John R. Colombo. (Illus.). vii, 208p. 1982. 17.95 o.p. (ISBN 0-88833-097-9, Pub. by West Prod CN). U of Nebr Pr.
Winding Quest. Alan T. Dale. (Illus.). 432p. (Orig.). 1973. pap. 9.95 o.p. (ISBN 0-8192-1150-8). Morehouse Pub.
Winding Stair. Douglas C. Jones. LC 79-4195. 288p. 1979. pap. 5.95 o.s.i. (ISBN 0-03-000098-X). H Holt & Co.
Windmills. Frank Brangwyn & Hayter Preston. LC 70-176821. (Illus.). 160p. 1975. Repr. of 1923 ed. 43.00x o.p. (ISBN 0-8103-4077-1). Gale.
Windmills & Windpumps. Ed. by Farrell S. Seiler. LC 84-51179. (Wind Energy Systems Ser.: Vol. 3 (of 4 vol. set)). (Illus.). 400p. 1987. pap. 125.00 o.s.i. (ISBN 0-88016-024-1). Windbks.
Window Goes On. Patricia A. Rousseau. 40p. 1987. 6.50 o.p. (ISBN 0-8062-2901-2). Carlton.
Window in the Sky. A. T. Lawton. 1979. 28.00 o.p. (ISBN 0-08-024663-X). Pergamon.
Window into a Nest. Geraldine L. Flanagan & Sean Morris. LC 75-17028. (Illus.). 96p. (gr. 7 up). 1976. 10.95 o.p. (ISBN 0-395-21895-0). HM.
Window over the Sink. Peg Bracken. 256p. 1982. pap. 3.50 o.p. (ISBN 0-380-58149-3). Avon.
Window over the Sink: A Mainly Affectionate Memoir. Peg Bracken. LC 80-8739. 240p. 1981. 10.95 o.p. (ISBN 0-15-196986-8). HarBraceJ.
Windowless View. Neal Stanford. (Illus.). 96p. 1985. 10.00 o.p. (ISBN 0-682-40278-8). Exposition-Phoenix.
Windowlight: A Woman's Journal from the Edge of America. Ann Nietzke. LC 81-12206. 224p. (Orig.). 1982. pap. 8.95 o.p. (ISBN 0-88496-173-7). Capra Pr.
Windows. James T. Bagby. (Illus.). 80p. 1987. pap. 6.95 o.p. (ISBN 0-89505-451-5). Tabor Pub.
Windows. David Miller. LC 73-83377. (Illus.). 144p. (Orig.). 1973. pap. 6.00 o.p. (ISBN 0-912528-06-0). John Muir.
Window's Guide to Living Alone. Judith Fabisch. 128p. 1983. pap. 6.95 o.p. (ISBN 0-310-43481-5, 11168P). Zondervan.
Windows of the Mind. Howard A. Johnson. 1978. 5.00 o.p. (ISBN 0-682-49204-3). Exposition-Phoenix.
Windows on California. David C. King et al. LC 77-91596. (Illus., Gr. 4). 1978. pap. 7.16 o.p. (ISBN 0-395-26276-3). HM.
Windows on Japan. Frank L. Ryan & James I. Clark. LC 78-60692. (Social Studies Readers Ser.). (Illus., Gr. 4-6). 1979. pap. 5.64 o.p. (ISBN 0-395-27183-5). HM.
Windows on the Parables. rev. ed. Warren W. Wiersbe. 160p. 1984. pap. 2.95 o.p. (ISBN 0-89693-710-0). Victor Bks.
Windows on the U. S. A. 1000 Word Level. R. Decker. Incl. Windows on the U. S. A. 1500 Word Level. 1983. (ISBN 0-07-016293-X); Windows on the U. S. A. 500 Word Level. R. Decker. 1983. text ed. 2.60 (ISBN 0-07-016290-5); Windows on the U. S. A. 750 Word Level. 1983. text ed. 2.60 (ISBN 0-07-016291-3). 1983. McGraw.

Windows on the U. S. A. 1500 Word Level see Windows on the U. S. A. 1000 Word Level.
Windows on the U. S. A. 500 Word Level see Windows on the U. S. A. 1000 Word Level.
Windows on the U. S. A. 750 Word Level see Windows on the U. S. A. 1000 Word Level.
Windows on the World: Complete Wine Course. Kevin Zraly. LC 84-26851. (Illus.). 192p. 1985. 18.95 o.p. (ISBN 0-8069-5582-1). Sterling.
Windows on the World Complete Wine Course. rev. ed. Kevin Zraly. LC 84-26851. (Illus.). 192p. 1987. 19.95 o.p. (ISBN 0-8069-6642-4). Sterling.
Windows: The Official Guide to Microsoft's Operating Environment. Nancy Andrews. 320p. 1986. pap. 17.95 o.p. (ISBN 0-914845-70-5). Microsoft.
Windows to Our Children. Violet Oaklander. LC 78-10387. 1978. 10.00 o.p. (ISBN 0-911226-16-8); pap. 6.50 o.p. (ISBN 0-911226-17-6). Real People.
Windrose. Brewster Ghiselin. (University of Utah Press Poetry Ser.). 252p. 1980. 19.95 o.p. (ISBN 0-87480-167-2). U of Utah Pr.
Winds' Child. Mark Taylor. LC 72-86952. (Illus.). 48p. (gr. k-3). 1973. 4.95 o.p. (ISBN 0-689-30121-9, Atheneum). Macmillan.
Winds in the Cornfields of Early Pueblo County. Arla Aschermann. (Illus.). 52p. 1982. pap. 3.50 o.p. (ISBN 0-915617-04-8). Pueblo Co Hist Soc.
Winds in the Woods: The Story of John Muir. John Stewart. LC 74-20708. (Illus.). (gr. 5 up). 1975. 7.95 o.s.i. (ISBN 0-664-32556-4, Westminster). Westminster John Knox.
Winds Obey Him! Rochelle N. Barsuhn. LC 83-7344. (Illus.). 32p. (gr. 3-4). 1983. PLB 4.95 o.p. (ISBN 0-89693-216-8). Dandelion Hse.
Winds of Change. Marie Nowinson. 1979. 2.95 o.p. (ISBN 0-345-31188-4); pap. 2.25 o.p. (ISBN 0-345-27587-X). Ballantine.
Winds of Darkover. Marion Zimmer Bradley. (Darkover Ser.). 1979. lib. bdg. 9.95 o.p. (ISBN 0-8398-2511-0, Gregg). G K Hall.
Winds of Destiny. Pat Dalton. LC 85-27577. (Starlight Romance Ser.). 192p. 1986. 12.95 o.p. (ISBN 0-385-23268-3). Doubleday.
Winds of Enchantment. Jan McGowan. 352p. (Orig.). pap. 3.95 o.p. (ISBN 0-671-63407-0). Archway.
Winds of Terror. Patricia Hagan. 144p. 1976. pap. 2.50 o.p. (ISBN 0-380-00460-7, 85266). Avon.
Winds of Time. Chad Oliver. 1975. pap. 2.25 o.p. (ISBN 0-380-00318-X, 23887-X). Avon.
Winds over Lake Huron: Chronicles in the Life of a Great Lakes Mariner. Robert A. Sinclair. 1977. 7.50 o.p. (ISBN 0-682-48709-0). Exposition-Phoenix.
Windswept. Ann F. Barron. 464p. 1985. pap. 3.95 o.p. (ISBN 0-380-89589-7). Avon.
Windy Landowner's Guide to Wind Farm Development. Donald Bain et al. LC 84-51114. 175p. 1984. pap. 29.95 o.s.i. (ISBN 0-88016-035-7). Windbks.
Wine. rev. ed. Hugh Johnson. 288p. 1975. 18.45 o.p. (ISBN 0-671-21997-9). S&S.
Wine & Beermaking at Home. Kenneth Hill. LC 75-40968. (Illus.). 116p. 1976. 11.95 o.p. (ISBN 0-87523-185-3). Emerson.
Wine & Food Society Menu Book: Recipes for Celebration. Alice W. Salmon & Hugo Dunn-Meynell. (Illus.). 256p. 1984. 27.95 o.s.i. (ISBN 0-442-28051-3). Van Nos Reinhold.
Wine & the Artist: One Hundred & Four Prints & Drawings from the Christian Brothers Collection at the Wine Museum of San Francisco. Ed. by Wine Museum of San Francisco Staff. LC 77-93393. (Pictorial Archive Ser.). 1979. pap. 6.95 o.p. (ISBN 0-486-23759-1). Dover.
Wine & the Music. David A. Kaufelt. 1982. pap. 3.95 o.p. (ISBN 0-440-19376-1). Dell.
Wine Bibber's Bible. rev., 2nd ed. James N. Pratt. LC 80-24680. (Illus.). 192p. 1981. pap. 6.95 o.p. (ISBN 0-89286-182-7, One Hund One Prods). Ortho.
Wine Bibber's Bible. rev. ed. James N. Pratt & Jacques De Caso. LC 79-177349. (Illus.). 1975. pap. 4.95 o.p. (ISBN 0-912238-71-2, One Hund One Prods). Ortho.
Wine Country: California. Sunset Magazine & Books Editors. LC 82-81743. (Illus.). 160p. 1982. pap. 7.95 o.p. (ISBN 0-376-06945-7, Sunset Bks.). Sunset-Lane.
Wine Handbook. Serena Sutcliffe. 240p. 1982. pap. 14.50 o.s.i. (ISBN 0-671-45537-0, Fireside). S&S.
Wine in the Chalice. Peter Lappin. (Orig.). 1972. pap. 3.25 o.p. (ISBN 0-89944-031-2). Don Bosco Multimedia.
Wine Lover's Guide to France. Michael Busselle. 1986. 24.95 o.p. (ISBN 0-316-11839-7). Little.
Wine Lover's Quiz Book: Challenging Questions & Answers for Wine Buffs & Bluffers. Peter Adams. 144p. 1987. pap. 9.95 o.p. (ISBN 0-89586-633-1). Price Stern.
Wine of Violence. James Morrow. LC 81-1153. 324p. 1981. 13.95 o.p. (ISBN 0-03-059051-5). H Holt & Co.
Wine Spectator Guide to Selected Wines, 1985. Ed. by Marvin Shanken. 96p. 1985. pap. 3.95 o.p. (ISBN 0-671-54247-8, Pub. by Fireside). S&S.
Wine Spectator Wine Maps: The Complete Guide to Wineries, Restaurants & Lodging in California Wine Country. rev. & exp. ed. Marvin R. Shanken. (Illus.). 46p. 1984. pap. 3.00 o.p. (ISBN 0-918076-26-9). M Shanken Comm.
Wine Spectator Wine Maps: The Complete Guide to Wineries, Restaurants & Lodging in California Wine Country, 1985. rev. ed. Marvin R. Shanken. (Illus.). 110p. 1985. pap. text ed. 5.20 o.p. (ISBN 0-918076-36-6). M Shanken Comm.
Wine Spectator Wine Maps, 1986: The Complete Guide to Wineries, Restaurants & Lodging in California Wine Country. 3rd, rev. ed. Marvin R. Shanken. (Illus.). 1986. pap. text ed. 5.20 o.p. (ISBN 0-918076-39-0). M Shanken Comm.
Wine with Food: A Guide to Entertaining Through the Seasons. Barbara Ensrud. (Illus.). 224p. 1984. 18.95 o.p. (ISBN 0-312-92026-1). Congdon & Weed.
Winemaking in California. Ruth Teiser & Catherine Harroun. 1982. text ed. 24.95 o.p. (ISBN 0-07-063401-7). McGraw.
Wines & Wineries of New South Wales. James Halliday. 165p. 1981. text ed. 14.50x o.p. (ISBN 0-7022-1570-8). U of Queensland Pr.
Wines & Wineries of South Australia. James Halliday. (Illus.). 144p. 1981. text ed. 14.50 boards o.p. (ISBN 0-7022-1571-6). U of Queensland Pr.
Wines & Wineries of Victoria. James Halliday. (Illus.). 152p. 1982. bds. 14.50 o.p. (ISBN 0-7022-1740-9). U of Queensland Pr.
Wines & Wineries of Western Australia. James Halliday. (Illus.). 119p. 1983. text ed. 14.50x o.p. (ISBN 0-7022-1673-9). U of Queensland Pr.
Wines of America. 3rd, rev. ed. Leon D. Adams. 640p. 1985. text ed. 22.95 o.p. (ISBN 0-07-000319-X). McGraw.
Wines of California, the Pacific Northwest & New York: First Classification of the Wineries & Vineyards. Roy A. De Groot. LC 82-10638. 448p. 1982. 19.25 o.p. (ISBN 0-671-40049-5). Summit Bks.
Wines of Pentagoet. John Gould. 1986. 14.45 o.p. (ISBN 0-393-02303-6). Norton.
Wines of Spain. Jan Read. (Books on Wine). (Illus.). 272p. 1983. 12.95 o.p. (ISBN 0-571-11937-9); pap. 6.95 o.p. (ISBN 0-571-11938-7). Faber & Faber.
Wines of the United States & Canada. John J. Baxevanis. 208p. 1988. 24.95 o.s.i. (ISBN 0-8476-7431-2). Rowman.
Winesburg, Ohio. Sherwood Anderson. pap. 3.95 o.p. (ISBN 0-14-000609-5). Penguin.
Wing Chun Kung Fu: An Effective & Logical Approach to Self Defense. Karen Armstrong & Sifu Jim Fung. 119p. (Orig.). 1985. pap. 8.95 o.p. (ISBN 0-86568-071-X, 542, Pub. by Dragon Bks Ltd). Unique Pubns.
Wing Theory in Supersonic Flow. E. Carafoli. 1969. 150.00 o.p. (ISBN 0-08-012330-9). Pergamon.
Wingarden. Elsie Lee. LC 71-16744. 1971. 5.95 o.p. (ISBN 0-87795-019-9, Arbor Hse). Morrow.
Winged Stallion: Fighting & Training with the First Airborne. Michael Packe. (Illus.). 256p. 1988. 24.95 o.p. (ISBN 0-7137-2037-9, Pub. by Blandford Pr England). Sterling.
Winged Watchman. Hilda Van Stockum. LC 62-16280. (Illus.). 228p. (gr. 4 up). 1963. 6.95 o.p. (ISBN 0-374-38448-7); pap. 3.45 o.p. (ISBN 0-374-48405-8). FS&G.
Wingless Victory. Laszlo Tarnoi. (Illus.). 352p. 1982. 15.00 o.p. (ISBN 0-682-49846-7, Banner). Exposition-Phoenix.
Wingmen. Ensan Case. 1979. pap. 2.50 o.p. (ISBN 0-380-47647-9, 47647-9). Avon.
Wings. Neal Travis. 336p. 1985. pap. 3.95 o.p. (ISBN 0-380-89802-0). Avon.
Wings in Your Future: Aviation for Young People. rev. ed. Leo Schneider & Maurice U. Ames. LC 55-5966. (Illus.). (gr. 7 up). 1960. 4.95 o.p. (ISBN 0-15-297855-0, HJ). HarBraceJ.
Wings of Adrian. Jan Seabaugh. 224p. 1986. pap. 5.95 o.p. (ISBN 0-310-47341-1, 15580P). Zondervan.
Wings of Anger. Alfred V. Beaumont. LC 84-90259. 163p. 1985. 10.95 o.p. (ISBN 0-533-06298-5). Vantage.
Wings of Darkness. Ellen Milburn. (Inflation Fighter Ser.). 192p. 1982. pap. (ISBN 0-8439-1121-2, Pub. by Leisure Bks CT). Dorchester Pub Co.
Wings of Eagles Feet of Clay. Leonard Garrett. 48p. 1987. 6.95 o.p. (ISBN 0-8062-2829-6). Carlton.
Wings of Faith. H. V. Martin. 1951. (ISBN 0-8022-1070-8). Philos Lib.
Wings of Man: The Legend of Captain H.T. Dick Merrill. Jack L. King. (Illus.). 416p. 1981. 5.95x o.p. (ISBN 0-911721-91-6). Aviation.
Wings of the Navy. Eric Brown. Ed. by William Green. (Illus.). 192p. 1980. 19.95 o.p. (ISBN 0-86720-579-2). Janes Info Group.
Wings of the Wind. Ronald Hardy. 416p. 1987. 19.95 o.p. (ISBN 0-399-12986-3, Putnam). Putnam Pub Group.
Wings on the Cross. P. Hamilton Pollock. 1978. 8.50 o.p. (ISBN 0-682-48999-9). Exposition-Phoenix.
Wings: The Early Years of Aviation. Richard Rosenblum. LC 79-26363. (Illus.). 64p. (gr. 3-7). 1980. 8.95 o.s.i. (ISBN 0-02-777380-9, Four Winds). Macmillan.
Wingshooter's Autumn. Willow Creek Press Editors. (Illus.). 256p. 1986. 65.00x o.s.i. (ISBN 0-932558-31-3). Willow Creek Pr.
Winnemah Spirit. Carolyn Lane. LC 74-30158. (Illus.). 128p. (gr. 2-5). 1975. 5.95 o.p. (ISBN 0-395-20490-9). HM.
Winner Names the Age: A Collection of Writings. Lillian Smith. Ed. by Michelle Cliff. 224p. 1978. 10.95 o.p. (ISBN 0-393-08826-X). Norton.
Winner Take All! John Gollehon. 176p. 1986. 6.95 o.p. (ISBN 0-914839-09-8). Gollehon Pr.
Winners & Losers. Sydney J. Harris. LC 73-78534. (Illus.). 1973. pap. 4.95 o.p. (ISBN 0-913592-21-8). Tabor Pub.
Winners & Losers: Battles, Retreats, Gains, Losses & Ruins from the Vietnam War. Jules Archer. 422p. 1978. pap. 4.95 o.p. (ISBN 0-15-697212-3). HarBraceJ.
Winners: Eight Special Young People. Dorothy S. Siegel. LC 77-27985. 192p. (gr. 7 up). 1978. lib. bdg. 9.79 o.s.i. (ISBN 0-671-32861-1). Messner.
Winner's Guide to Casino Gambling. Edwin Silberstang. LC 79-19848. 320p. 1980. 12.95 o.s.i. (ISBN 0-03-053481-X). H Holt & Co.
Winners in Gymnastics. Frank Litsky. (Illus.). 48p. (gr. 6 up). 1979. pap. 1.25 o.p. (ISBN 0-380-43299-4, 43299-4, Camelot). Avon.
Winners Never Quit: Athletes Who Beat the Odds. Nathan Aaseng. LC 80-12305. (Sports Heroes Library). (Illus.). (gr. 4 up). 1980. PLB 7.95 o.p. (ISBN 0-8225-1060-X). Lerner Pubns.
Winners on the Tennis Court. William G. Glickman. 48p. (gr. 6 up). 1979. pap. 1.25 o.p. (ISBN 0-380-43307-9, 43307-9, Camelot). Avon.
Winners: Part II of Joyce Haber's the Users. Dominick Dunne. 1982. 14.50 o.p. (ISBN 0-671-24978-9). S&S.
Winners! Super-Champions of Ice Hockey. Ross R. Olney. (Illus.). 128p. (gr. 6 up). 1982. 11.00 o.p. (ISBN 0-89919-109-6, Clarion); pap. 4.80 o.p. (ISBN 0-89919-134-7). HM.
Winners: The Successful Strategies Entrepreneurs Use to Build New Businesses. Carter Henderson. LC 85-5511. 256p. 1987. 15.95 o.p. (ISBN 0-03-001887-0); pap. 7.95 o.p. H Holt & Co.
Winners Without Races. Robert Killian. 256p. 1986. 12.95 o.p. (ISBN 0-8062-2925-X). Carlton.
Winnin' Times: The Rise & Rise of the Los Angeles Lakers. Scott Ostler & Steve Springer. (Illus.). 320p. 1986. 17.95 o.p. (ISBN 0-02-594080-5). Macmillan.
Winning at Weight Loss. Craig Stratton. 150p. 1983. 19.95 o.p. (ISBN 0-943154-01-4). Longman Trade.
Winning at Zoning. Dudley Hinds & Neil Carn. (Illus.). 1979. text ed. 24.50 o.p. (ISBN 0-07-028937-9). McGraw.
Winning by Letting Go: Control Without Compulsion, Surrender Without Defeat. Elizabeth Brenner. LC 84-25152. 240p. 1985. 14.95 o.p. (ISBN 0-15-197130-7). HarBraceJ.
Winning by Negotiation. Tessa A. Warshaw. LC 80-14535. 264p. 1980. text ed. 10.95 o.p. (ISBN 0-07-000780-2). McGraw.
Winning by Telephone: Telephone Effectiveness for the Business Man & Consumer. Gary S. Goodman. 144p. 1982. 14.95 o.p. (ISBN 0-13-960971-7); pap. 5.95 o.p. (ISBN 0-13-960963-6). P-H.
Winning Collection Strategies. C. Connie Firm. 1988. manual 15.00 o.p. (00375-1). PES Inc WI.
Winning Combination. Julie Anthony & Nick Bollettieri. (Illus.). 272p. 1982. pap. 6.95 o.p. (ISBN 0-684-17637-8, ScribT); 4.95 o.p. (ISBN 0-684-17583-5). Scribner.
Winning Combination. Nick Bolliettieri & Julie Anthony. (Illus.). 224p. 1980. 4.95 o.s.i. (ISBN 0-684-16710-7, ScribT). Scribner.
Winning Combinations for Junior High-Middle School Student Councils. 1975. pap. 5.00 o.p. (ISBN 0-88210-063-7). Natl Assn Principals.
Winning Croquet: From Backyard to Greensward. Jack R. Osborn & Jesse Kornbluth. 1983. pap. 9.50 o.p. (ISBN 0-671-47276-3). S&S.
Winning Edge: A Foreman's Guide to Supervision. Hal Wallace & Dave Heberle. 192p. 1983. pap. 14.95 o.p. (ISBN 0-8436-0821-8). Van Nos Reinhold.
Winning for Peace: The Great Victory - Its World Impact. B. N. Ponomarov. 136p. 1985. pap. 1.95 o.p. (Pub. by Progress Pubs USSR). Imported Pubns.
Winning Golf the Professional Way. Bob Zender & Charles Cleveland. (Illus.). 224p. 1985. 15.95 o.p. (ISBN 0-396-08368-4). Dodd.
Winning Hand. Tom Cutter. (Tracker Ser.). 176p. 1983. pap. 2.25 o.p. (ISBN 0-380-83899-0, 83899-0). Avon.
Winning Hitter: How to Play Championship Baseball. Charley Lau & Alfred Glossbrenner. (Illus.). 192p. 1984. 14.95 o.p. (ISBN 0-688-03391-1, Hearst Bks). Morrow.
Winning Ideas in the Social Studies. Steven L. Jantzen. LC 77-9530. (Illus.). 1977. pap. text ed. 5.95x o.p. (ISBN 0-8077-2541-2). Tchrs Coll.
Winning Image. James Gray, Jr. 192p. 1982. 13.95 o.p. (ISBN 0-8144-5667-7). AMACOM.
Winning in the Futures Market. George Angell. LC 86-6280. (Illus.). 336p. 1987. pap. 19.95 o.p. (ISBN 0-385-19949-X). Doubleday.
Winning Money for College: The High School Student's Guide to Scholarship Contests. Alan Deutschman. LC 83-22151. 219p. (Orig.). 1984. pap. 7.95 o.p. (ISBN 0-87866-261-8). Petersons Guides.
Winning Negotiations Strategies for Bankers. 147p. 1987. 54.00 o.p. (ISBN 0-317-66461-1, 645). Bank Admin Inst.
Winning NLRB Elections: Management's Strategy & Preventive Programs. 2nd ed. Robert Lewis & William A. Krupman. 499p. 1979. text ed. 40.00 o.p. (ISBN 0-685-92237-5, HI-2949). PLI.
Winning Soccer. Al Miller & Norm Wingert. (Illus.). 149p. 1975. 8.95 o.p. (ISBN 0-8092-8308-5); pap. 6.95 o.p. (ISBN 0-8092-8307-7). Contemp Bks.
Winning Softball. Joan Joyce & John Anquillare. (Illus.). 1975. 8.95 o.p. (ISBN 0-8092-8430-8); pap. 6.95 o.p. (ISBN 0-8092-8429-4). Contemp. Bks.
Winning Support for Parks & Recreation. National Park Service Staff. (New Directions in Leisure Ser.). 136p. (Orig.). 1983. pap. 9.95 o.p. (ISBN 0-910251-04-5). Venture Pub PA.
Winning Techniques for Athletic Fund Raising. Ed. by Particia L. Alberger. 97p. 1981. 14.50 o.p. (ISBN 0-89964-188-1). Coun Adv & Supp Ed.
Winning the Diet Wars. Meridee Merzer. LC 79-2765. 1980. 9.95 o.p. (ISBN 0-15-196378-9). HarBraceJ.
Winning the Game. Pauline Reich. LC 87-82858. 216p. cancelled o.s.i. (ISBN 0-87011-859-5). Kodansha.
Winning the High Technology Sales Game. James T. Healy. 373p. 1985. 30.95 o.p. (ISBN 0-317-39391-X). Robot Inst Am.
Winning: The Psychology of Competition. Stuart Walker. (Illus.). 1980. 11.95 o.p. (ISBN 0-393-03255-8). Norton.
Winning: The Psychology of Successful Investing. Srully Blotnick. 1978. text ed. 34.50 o.p. (ISBN 0-07-006119-X). McGraw.
Winning the Second American Revolution, Plus Winning your Personal Battle For Financial Success. Donald L. Krumm. (Illus.). 331p. (Orig.). 1985. pap. text ed. 14.95x o.p. (ISBN 0-917209-00-1). Am Liberty.
Winning Through Intimidation. Robert J. Ringer. 1981. pap. 2.95 o.p. (ISBN 0-449-23589-0, Crest). Fawcett.
Winning Walk. H. Edwin Young. LC 82-70048. 1982. pap. 5.95 o.p. (ISBN 0-8054-5191-9). Broadman.
Winning Ways: A Management Performance Game. Ray Bard & Larry Davis. LC 79-20395. 1979. vinyl binder 104.50 o.p. (ISBN 0-89384-043-2). Univ Assocs.
Winning with Christ. Rick Arndt. 1982. pap. 1.75 o.p. (ISBN 0-570-03627-5, 39-1073). Concordia.
Winning with Words, 2 vols. Ed. by World Book, Inc. Staff. LC 84-51396. (Illus.). 704p. (gr. 7-12). 1984. text ed. write for info o.p. (ISBN 0-7166-3171-7). World Bk.
Winning Words: Devotions for Athletes. Curtis French. LC 77-75467. 1983. pap. 5.95 o.p. (ISBN 0-8499-2805-2). Word Bks.
Winslow the Hamster. Rebecca Anders. Tr. by Dyan Hammarberg from Fr. LC 76-40966. (Animal Friends Books). (Illus.). (gr. k-4). 1977. PLB 5.95 o.p. (ISBN 0-87614-078-9). Carolrhoda Bks.
Winston Churchill: A Political Biography. V. Trukhanovsky. 390p. 1978. 9.45 o.p. (ISBN 0-8285-9151-2, Pub. by Progress Pubs USSR). Imported Pubns.
Winston Churchill's Afternoon Nap: A Wide-Awake Inquiry into the Human Nature of Time. Jeremy Campbell. 432p. 1987. 18.45 o.p. (ISBN 0-671-47547-9). S&S.

Winston S. Churchill: Companion Vol. III, 2 parts. Martin Gilbert. 1973. 78.00 o.p. (ISBN 0-395-16974-7); Pt. 1: July 1914-April 1915. 39.00 o.p. (ISBN 0-395-14754-9); Pt. 2: May 1915-December 1916. 39.00 o.p. (ISBN 0-395-14755-7). HM.

Winston S. Churchill: Companion Vol. V, Part One, The Exchequer Years 1922-1929. Martin Gilbert. 1981. 95.00 o.s.i. (ISBN 0-395-27778-7). HM.

Winston S. Churchill: Finest Hour, Nineteen Thirty-Nine to Nineteen Forty-One, Vol. 6. Martin Gilbert. LC 66-12065. (Illus.). 1308p. 1983. 39.00 o.s.i. (ISBN 0-395-34402-6). HM.

Winston S. Churchill: Vol. V: Pt. 3, The Coming of War 1936-1939. Martin Gilbert. 1983. 94.00 o.p. (ISBN 0-395-33076-9). HM.

Winston S. Churchill, 1916-1922, Vol 4. Martin Gilbert. LC 66-12065. (Stricken World Ser.). 992p. 1975. 39.00 o.p. (ISBN 0-395-20436-4). HM.

Winter. C. S. Vendrell & J. M. Parramon. (Exploring the Seasons Ser.). (Illus.). 32p. (ps-3). 1981. 11.93 o.p. (ISBN 0-516-02384-5). Childrens.

Winter Brothers: A Season at the Edge of America. Ivan Doig. LC 80-7933. (Illus.). 252p. 1980. 10.95 o.p. (ISBN 0-15-197186-2). HarBraceJ.

Winter Camp Kid & Will. Dusty Richards. 172p. 7.00 o.p. Intl Univ Pr.

Winter Count. Barry H. Lopez. (Illus.). 96p. 1981. encore ed. 2.95 o.p. (ISBN 0-684-16817-0, ScribT). Scribner.

Winter Danger. William O. Steele. LC 54-5157. (Illus.). (gr. 4-6). 1954. 6.75 o.p. (ISBN 0-15-298034-2, HJ). HarBraceJ.

Winter Dream. Shirley Schoonover. 240p. 1980. pap. 2.25 o.p. (ISBN 0-380-75671-4, 75671). Avon.

Winter Dreams: An American in Moscow. Jay Martin. 1979. 10.95 o.p. (ISBN 0-395-27589-X). HM.

Winter Festivals. Contributors to Family Festivals Magazine Staff. LC 86-60893. 123p. (Orig.). 1986. pap. 7.95 o.p. (ISBN 0-89390-077-X). Resource Pubns.

Winter Flame. Katherine Myers. 336p. 1984. pap. 2.95 o.p. (ISBN 0-380-87148-3, 87148). Avon.

Winter Fun. Fern Hollow. (Fern Hollow Pop-Up Bks.). (Illus.). (ps-1). 1985. 2.98 o.p. (ISBN 0-517-48291-6). Outlet Bk Co.

Winter Fun. Pete Kersten & Rick Kersten. (Kersten Brothers' Critter Tales Stick'n Play Bks.). 16p. (gr. 1-3). 1986. 6.95 o.p. (ISBN 0-316-49004-0). Little.

Winter Hearts. Marjorie Burrows & Avan Ramancese. (Avon Romance Ser.). 432p. 1985. pap. 3.50 o.p. (ISBN 0-380-89513-7). Avon.

Winter Hiking & Camping. rev. ed. John A. Danielsen. (Illus.). 220p. 1986. pap. 8.95 o.p. (ISBN 0-935272-37-2). ADK Mtn Club.

Winter Hunger. Cliff Schimmels. 180p. 1985. pap. 4.95 o.p. (ISBN 0-89693-333-4). Victor Bks.

Winter in Eden. Harry Harrison. (Spectra Ser.: Vol. 2). 416p. (Orig.). 1986. pap. 18.95 o.p. (ISBN 0-553-05163-6, Spectra). Bantam.

Winter in Jerusalem. Blanche D'Alpuget. LC 86-1758. 270p. 1986. 16.45 o.p. (ISBN 0-671-49808-8). S&S.

Winter in the Enchanted Forest. (Enchanted Forest Ser.). (Illus.). (ps-1). 1985. 2.98 o.s.i. (ISBN 0-517-46982-0). Outlet Bk Co.

Winter in Wartime. Jan Terlouw. LC 75-41345. 144p. (gr. 7-12). 1976. lib. bdg. 7.95 o.p. (ISBN 0-07-063504-8). McGraw.

Winter of the Fisher. Cameron Langford. LC 77-139382. 1971. 5.95 o.p. (ISBN 0-393-08638-0). Norton.

Winter of the Salamander: The Keeper of Importance. Ray Young Bear. LC 79-4719. (Harper & Row Native American Publishing Program Ser.). 1980. 8.95i o.p. (ISBN 0-06-452750-6); pap. 3.95i o.p. (ISBN 0-06-452751-4). HarpR.

Winter on Her Own. Elizabeth J. Howard. LC 68-16625. (gr. 7 up). 1968. 11.75 o.p. (ISBN 0-688-21710-9). Morrow.

Winter Quarters. Conrey Bryson. LC 86-2146. (Illus.). 191p. 1986. 9.95 o.p. (ISBN 0-87579-011-9). Deseret Bk.

Winter Signs. Melissa Goldsmith. 1985. 5.95 o.p. (ISBN 0-533-06606-9). Vantage.

Winter Simulation Conference Proceedings, (Atlanta) Arne Thesen. 963p. Date not set. 75.00 o.p. (ISBN 0-911801-32-4). Soc Computer Sim.

Winter Simulation Conference Proceedings. Incl. Arlington, 2 vols. Stephen Roberts. 1983. 48.00 ea.; 1982. Harold Highland. 650p. 1982. 48.00 (ISBN 0-317-31363-0); Orlando, 2 vols. Oren. 1980p. 75.00. Soc Computer Sim.

Winter Song. Dorothy Oxley. LC 84-71419. 144p. (gr. 6-10). 1984. pap. 3.95 o.p. (ISBN 0-89107-320-5, Crossway Bks). Good News.

Winter Thunder. Mari Sandoz. LC 54-9400. 64p. (gr. 5-9). 1954. 5.75 o.s.i. (ISBN 0-664-30053-7, Westminster). Westminster John Knox.

Winter Wheat. Mildred Walker. LC 44-40006. 1966. pap. 3.95 o.p. (ISBN 0-15-697225-5, Harv). HarBraceJ.

Winter Wife. Jessica Auerbach. LC 83-5079. 204p. 1983. 13.45 o.p. (ISBN 0-89919-194-0). Ticknor & Fields.

Winter Wife. Anne E. Crompton. (Illus.). 48p. (gr. 1-3). 1975. 12.45i o.p. (ISBN 0-316-16143-8, Pub. by Atlantic Monthly Pr). Little.

Winter Wren. Brock Cole. (Illus.). 32p. (gr. 1 up). 1988. pap. 4.95 o.p. (ISBN 0-374-48408-2, Sunburst). FS&G.

Wintergreen: Rambles in a Ravaged Land. Robert M. Pyle. 320p. 1987. 19.95 o.p. (ISBN 0-684-18321-8). Scribner.

Wintering. Joan Williams. LC 78-134571. 1971. 7.50 o.p. (ISBN 0-15-125225-4). HarBraceJ.

Winter's Coming. Eve Bunting. LC 76-28321. (Illus.). (gr. 1-3). 1977. 4.95 o.p. (ISBN 0-15-298036-9, HJ). HarBraceJ.

Winter's Coming. Eve Bunting. LC 76-28321. (Let Me Read Ser.). (Illus.). 32p. (ps-3). 1977. pap. 1.65 o.p. (ISBN 0-15-298037-7, VoyB). HarBraceJ.

Winter's Daughter. Charles Whitmore. 224p. 1986. pap. 3.50 o.p. (ISBN 0-380-70117-0). Avon.

Winter's Daughter: The Saying of Signe Ragnhilds-Datter, A Novel. Charles Whittmore. 1984. 14.70 o.s.i. (ISBN 0-671-49984-X). S&S.

Winter's Journey. David Updike. LC 85-9334. (Illus.). 40p. (gr. 1-4). 1985. 12.95 o.s.i. (ISBN 0-13-961566-0). P-H.

Winterthur Portfolio, No. 2. Ed. by Milo M. Naeve. (Winterthur Bk.). (Illus.). 1978. lib. bdg. 15.00x o.s.i. (ISBN 0-226-92126-3). U of Chicago Pr.

Wintertime in Fraggle Rock. Lauren Attinello. (Illus.). 48p. (gr. k-1). 1985. 0.99 o.s.i. (ISBN 0-03-005633-0). H Holt & Co.

Winthrop Covenant. Louis Auchincloss. LC 75-33042. 1976. 8.95 o.p. (ISBN 0-395-24081-6). HM.

Winthrop Woman. Anya Seton. 1958. 10.00 o.p. (ISBN 0-395-08176-9). HM.

Wintu Grammar. Harvey Pitkin. LC 84-16268. (Publications in Linguistics: Vol. 94). 322p. 1985. 25.00x o.p. U of Cal Pr.

Wired: The Short Life & Fast Times of John Belushi. Bob Woodward. LC 84-5334. (Illus.). 461p. 1984. 17.45 o.p. (ISBN 0-671-47320-4). S&S.

Wireline Logging Tool Catalog. LC 83-82854. 176p. 1984. 40.00x o.p. (ISBN 0-87201-907-1). Gulf Pub.

Wisconsin. Photos by Tom Algire. LC 80-85370. (Illus.). 128p. (Text by Justin Isherwood). 1981. 28.50 o.s.i. (ISBN 0-912856-67-X). Gr Arts Ctr Pub.

Wisconsin. new ed. Ed. by Jill W. Dean. LC 78-15753. (Illus.). 1978. 24.50 o.p. (ISBN 0-915024-17-9). WI Trails.

Wisconsin Biennial, 1982. Jane Livingston. 36p. 1982. pap. 3.95 o.p. (ISBN 0-913883-02-6). Madison Art.

Wisconsin Biennial, 1984. George Neubert. (Illus.). 36p. (Orig.). 1985. 4.95 o.p. (ISBN 0-913883-12-3). Madison Art.

Wisconsin Bike Trips: Twenty Tours for Young & Old. Philip Van Valkenberg. LC 74-77230. (Illus.). 52p. (Orig.). 1974. pap. 5.95 o.p. (ISBN 0-915024-01-2). WI Trails.

Wisconsin Business Directory, 1987-88. rev. ed. American Directory Publishing Co., Inc. Staff. 1550p. 1987. pap. 95.00 o.s.i. (ISBN 0-944316-13-1). Amer Directory.

Wisconsin Chippewa Myths & Tales & Their Relation to Chippewa Life. Victor Barnouw. LC 76-53647. 304p. 1977. 25.00x o.p. (ISBN 0-299-07310-6); pap. (ISBN 0-299-07314-9). U of Wis Pr.

Wisconsin: Conflict of Laws. 8.50 o.p. (ISBN 0-686-90972-0). Am Law Inst.

Wisconsin: Contracts. 8.50 o.p. (ISBN 0-686-90448-6). Am Law Inst.

Wisconsin Country Cookbook & Journal. Edward H. Heth. LC 78-21695. Orig. Title: Wonderful World of Cooking. (Illus.). 1979. pap. 5.95 o.p. (ISBN 0-915024-20-9). WI Trails.

Wisconsin Death Trip. Michael Lesy. LC 72-12383. 1983. pap. 12.95 o.p. (ISBN 0-394-72139-X). Pantheon.

Wisconsin Garden Guide. rev. & enl. ed. Jerry A. Minnich. LC 82-3388. (Illus.). 321p. 1982. pap. 9.95 o.p. (ISBN 0-88361-086-8). Stanton & Lee.

Wisconsin Lore. Robert E. Gard & L. G. Sorden. LC 62-12168. 335p. 1971. 9.95 o.p. (ISBN 0-88361-083-3). Stanton & Lee.

Wisconsin Manufacturers Register, 1988. 568p. 1987. 87.00 o.p. (ISBN 0-318-02840-9). Manufacturers.

Wisconsin Misdemeanors & Moving Traffic Violations. Ed. by Vicky H. Speck. 1984. looseleaf 95.00 o.p. (ISBN 0-86678-257-5). Butterworth MN.

Wisconsin Services Directory: 1988. 500p. 1988. 87.00 o.p. (ISBN 0-318-23577-3). Manufacturers.

Wisconsin Supplement for Modern Real Estate Practice. 3rd ed. Lawrence Sager. LC 83-24442. 124p. 1984. pap. text ed. 9.95 o.p. (ISBN 0-88462-500-1, 1510-36, Real Estate Ed.). Longman Finan.

Wisconsin Supplement for Modern Real Estate Practice. 1986. 21.95 o.p. (ISBN 0-88462-586-9, 1510-36, Pub. by Longman Fin Serv Pub). Longman Finan.

Wisconsin: Trusts. 8.50 o.p. (ISBN 0-686-90975-5). Am Law Inst.

Wisconsin Women: A Gifted Heritage. Rev. ed. AAUW, Wisconsin State Division Staff. Ed. by Anne Short et al. (Illus.). 328p. 1982. 14.95 o.p. (ISBN 0-910122-63-6). Amherst Pr.

Wisconsin Writers. William A. Titus. LC 77-145704. 446p. 1974. Repr. of 1930 ed. 48.00x o.p. (ISBN 0-8103-3658-8). Gale.

Wisden Cricketers' Almanack 1985. Ed. by John Woodcock. (Illus.). 1316p. 1985. 29.95 o.p. (ISBN 0-947766-00-6, Pub. by Gollancz England); pap. 22.95 o.p. (ISBN 0-947766-01-4). David & Charles.

Wisden Cricketers' Almanack 1986. Ed. by John Woodcock. (Illus.). 1280p. 1986. 34.95 o.p. (ISBN 0-947766-04-9, Pub. by Gollancz England); pap. 34.95 o.p. (ISBN 0-947766-05-7, Pub. by Gollencz England). David & Charles.

Wisdom: A Manifesto. Jacques Maritain et al. 1965. pap. 1.00x o.p. (ISBN 0-87343-015-8). Magi Bks.

Wisdom & Education. Douglas E. Lawson. LC 61-11660. 168p. 1961. 4.95x o.p. (ISBN 0-8093-0048-6). S Ill U Pr.

Wisdom from the East: Meditations, Reflections, Proverbs & Chants. Ellen K. Hua. LC 73-21886. (Illus.). 128p. (Orig.). 1974. pap. 3.00 o.p. (ISBN 0-87407-202-6, FP2). Thor.

Wisdom from Women in the Bible. Edith Deen. LC 77-20460. 1978. 9.95i o.p. (ISBN 0-06-061851-5). HarpR.

Wisdom in the Old Testament Traditions. Donn F. Morgan. LC 80-84653. 180p. 1982. 17.50 o.s.i. (ISBN 0-8042-0188-9, John Knox); pap. 9.50 o.s.i. (ISBN 0-8042-0189-7). Westminster John Knox.

Wisdom, Madness & Folly: The Making of a Psychiatrist, 1927-1957. R. D. Laing. (Illus.). 160p. 1985. text ed. 14.95 o.p. (ISBN 0-07-035849-4). McGraw.

Wisdom of Confucius. Confucius. 1965. 5.95 o.p. (ISBN 0-88088-100-3). Peter Pauper.

Wisdom of God Manifested in the Works of the Creation. John Ray. LC 75-11250. (British Philosophers & Theologians in the 17th & 18th Century Ser.). 247p. 1979. lib. bdg. 51.00 o.p. (ISBN 0-8240-1801-X). Garland Pub.

Wisdom of Laotse. Iverson L. Harris. 36p. 1972. pap. 0.75 o.p. (ISBN 0-913004-05-7). Point Loma Pub.

Wisdom of Pierre Charron: An Original & Orthodox Code of Morality. Jean D. Charron. LC 78-12595. (Illus.). 1979. Repr. of 1961 ed. lib. bdg. 35.00x o.p. (ISBN 0-313-21064-0, CHWO). Greenwood.

Wisdom of the Body. Walter B. Cannon. 1963. pap. 6.95x o.p. (ISBN 0-393-00205-5, Norton Lib). Norton.

Wisdom of the Fool: Stories & Poems. Scott T. Eastham. ii, 135p. (Orig.). 1985. pap. 6.95 o.p. (ISBN 0-932269-15-X). Wyndham Hall.

Wisdom of the Forest: Selections from the Hindu Upanishads. Tr. & intro. by Geoffrey Parrinder. LC 75-42114. (Wisdom Bks). 96p. 1976. 6.50 o.p. (ISBN 0-8112-0606-8); pap. 1.95 o.p. (ISBN 0-8112-0607-6, NDP414). New Directions.

Wisdom of the Land. Solon Robinson. (Illus.). 1977. pap. 7.95 o.p. (ISBN 0-89328-012-7). Lorenz Corp.

Wisdom of the Sands, 2 vols. Bhagwan Shree Rajneesh. Ed. by Ma Yoga Sudha. LC 80-903299. (Sufi Ser.). (Illus., Orig.). 1980. Vol. I, 380 pgs. 19.95 ea. o.p. (ISBN 0-88050-174-X). Vol. II, 404 pgs. 1980 (ISBN 0-88050-175-8). Vol.1 386p 1980. pap. 15.95 ea. o.p. (ISBN 0-88050-674-1). Chidvilas Inc.

Wisdom of the Sands. Bhagwan Shree Rajneesh & Ma Yoga Sudha. LC 80-903299. (Sufi Ser.: Vol. II). 412p. (Orig.). 1980. pap. 15.95 o.p. (ISBN 0-88050-675-X). Chidvilas Inc.

Wisdom of the Talmud. Ben Z. Bokser. 1951. (ISBN 0-8022-0150-4). Philos Lib.

Wisdom of the Torah. D. D. Runes. 1956. (ISBN 0-8022-1459-2). Philos Lib.

Wise Blood. Flannery O'Connor. Bd. with Violent Bear It Away; Everything That Rises Must Converge. 1983. pap. 3.50 o.p. (ISBN 0-451-51770-9, Sig Classic). NAL.

Wise Men: Architects of the American Century. Walter Isaacson & Evan Thomas. 816p. 1986. 22.45 o.p. (ISBN 0-671-50465-7). S&S.

Wise Wound: Myths, Realities, & Meanings of Menstruation. rev. ed. Penelope Shuttle & Peter Redgrove. 368p. 1988. pap. 9.95 o.p. (ISBN 0-8021-3128-X). Grove.

Wiseguy: The Rise & Fall of a Mobster. Nicholas Pileggi. LC 85-22047. 256p. 1986. 17.45 o.p. (ISBN 0-671-44734-3). S&S.

Wish Again, Big Bear. Richard J. Margolis. LC 75-160070. (Illus.). 40p. (gr. k-3). 1974. pap. 0.95 o.s.i. (ISBN 0-02-044480-X, Collier). Macmillan.

Wish for Little Sister. Jacqueline Ayer. LC 60-7032. (Illus.). (gr. k-3). 1960. 6.50 o.p. (ISBN 0-15-298213-2, HJ). HarBraceJ.

Wish You Were Here. Pasadena Art Alliance Staff. 1979. pap. 5.95 o.p. (ISBN 0-937042-02-1). Pasadena Art.

Wishes & Dreams. Pete Kersten & Rick Kersten. (Kersten Brothers' Critter Tales Sturdi-Flap Bks.). 12p. (ps-3). 1986. 4.95 o.p. (ISBN 0-316-49000-8). Little.

Wishful Thinking. Howard Blum. LC 84-45609. 256p. 1985. 16.95 o.p. (ISBN 0-689-11543-1, Atheneum). Macmillan.

Wishing Bottle. Sheila Dolan. (gr. 1-4). 1979. 7.95 o.p. (ISBN 0-395-28479-1). HM.

Wisps of Wit & Wisdom, or Knowledge in a Nutshell. Albert P. Southwick. LC 68-30582. 296p. 1968. Repr. of 1892 ed. 35.00x o.p. (ISBN 0-8103-3095-4). Gale.

Wisteria Cottage. Robert M. Coates. 1985. 5.95 o.p. (ISBN 0-87795-710-X, Arbor Hse). Morrow.

Wit & Humor from Old Cathay. Tr. by Jon Kowallis from Chinese. 211p. (Orig.). 1986. pap. 4.95 o.p. (ISBN 0-8351-1333-7). China Bks.

Wit & Humour from Ancient China: One Hundred Cartoons by Ding Cong. Ding Cong. Tr. by Ma Mingtong from Chinese. (Illus.). 219p. (YA) (gr. 9 up). 1986. pap. 9.95 o.p. (ISBN 0-8351-1656-5). China Bks.

Wit & Whimsy of Washington Irving. Washington Irving. Ed. by Bruce D. MacPhail. LC 79-2567. (Illus.). 64p. 1979. 2.95 o.s.i. (ISBN 0-912882-37-9). Sleepy Hollow.

Wit & Wisdom of Anon: Humor, Vol. 1. Marjorie C. Mahoney. LC 83-7650. (Illus.). 96p. 1983. 5.95 o.p. (ISBN 0-932620-25-6). Betterway Pubns.

Wit & Wisdom of Wall Street. Bill Adler & Bill Adler, Jr. LC 83-70857. 87p. (Orig.). 1984. pap. 10.95 o.p. (ISBN 0-87094-575-0). Dow Jones-Irwin.

Wit & Wisdom of Yogi Berra. Phil Pepe. 1977. pap. 1.50 o.s.i. (ISBN 0-505-51141-X, Pub. by Tower Bks). Dorchester Pub Co.

Wit, Wisdom & Foibles of the Great. Charles A. Shriner. LC 68-30617. 704p. 1969. Repr. of 1918 ed. 46.00x o.p. (ISBN 0-8103-3297-3). Gale.

Witch Diggers. West. 191. 5.75 o.p. (ISBN 0-15-197637-6). HarBraceJ.

Witch Family. Eleanor Estes. LC 60-11250. (Illus.). (gr. 3-7). 1960. 11.95 o.p. (ISBN 0-15-298571-9, HJ). HarBraceJ.

Witch Herself. Phyllis R. Naylor. LC 78-5437. (Illus.). 176p. (gr. 3-7). 1978. 7.95 o.s.i. (ISBN 0-689-30664-4, Atheneum Childrens Bk). Macmillan.

Witch of Edmonton by Thomas Dekker: A Critical Edition. Ed. by Etta S. Onat & Stephen Orgel. LC 79-54355. (Renaissance Drama Second Ser.). 400p. 1980. lib. bdg. 53.00 o.p. (ISBN 0-8240-4472-X). Garland Pub.

Witch of the Cumberlands. Mary Jo Stephens. LC 73-22062. (Illus.). 240p. (gr. 4-9). 1974. 8.95 o.p. (ISBN 0-395-18509-2). HM.

Witch Queen of Mongo. Alex Raymond. (Flash Gordon Ser.: No. 5). 1974. pap. 0.95 o.p. (ISBN 0-380-00180-2, 21378). Avon.

Witch Tree Symbol. rev. ed. Carolyn Keene. LC 75-1580. (Nancy Drew Ser.: Vol. 33). (Illus.). 196p. (gr. 4-7). 1975. 4.50 o.p. (ISBN 0-448-09533-5, G&D); PLB 3.29 o.p. (ISBN 0-448-19533-X). Putnam Pub Group.

Witch Water. Phyllis R. Naylor. LC 77-1057. (Illus.). 192p. (gr. 4-7). 1977. 9.95 o.s.i. (ISBN 0-689-30595-8, Atheneum). Macmillan.

Witch Who Became Someone Else. Anne C. Masland. (Illus.). 32p. (gr. k up). 1983. 6.95 o.p. (ISBN 0-682-40133-1). Exposition-Phoenix.

Witch Who Saved Halloween. Marian T. Place. (Illus.). (gr. 2-5). 1978. pap. 2.50 o.p. (ISBN 0-380-00097-0, Camelot). Avon.

Witch World. Andre Norton. 288p. 1986. pap. 3.50 o.s.i. (ISBN 0-441-89708-8, Pub. by Ace Science Fiction). Ace Bks.

Witchcraft. L. Mair. (Orig.). 1969. pap. text ed. 3.95 o.p. (ISBN 0-07-039723-6). McGraw.

Witchcraft & the Nature of Man. Mark Graubard. 326p. (Orig.). 1985. 30.00 o.p. (ISBN 0-8191-4313-8); pap. text ed. 15.50 o.p. (ISBN 0-8191-4314-6). U Pr of Amer.

Witchcraft in Old & New England. George L. Kittredge. LC 58-12929. 1972. pap. text ed. 4.75x o.p. (ISBN 0-689-70292-2, 186, Atheneum). Macmillan.

Witches & Warlocks. Philip W. Sergeant. LC 72-164055. (Illus.). 324p. 1975. Repr. of 1936 ed. 34.00x o.p. (ISBN 0-8103-3979-X). Gale.

Witches' Children. Patricia Clapp. LC 81-13678. 160p. (gr. 6 up). 1982. 11.75 o.p. (ISBN 0-688-00890-9). Lothrop.

Witches of Eastwick. John Updike. LC 83-49048. 336p. 1984. 15.45 o.p. (ISBN 0-394-53760-2); ltd. ed. 65.00 o.p. (ISBN 0-394-53765-3). Knopf.
Witching. Colin John. 336p. (Orig.). 1982. pap. 3.25 o.p. (ISBN 0-505-51806-6, Pub. by Tower Bks). Dorchester Pub Co.
Witch's Dream. Florinda Donner. 280p. 1985. 16.45 o.p. (ISBN 0-671-55198-1). S&S.
Witch's Egg. Madeleine Edmondson. LC 72-97769. (Illus.). 48p. (ps-3). 1979. 5.95 o.p. (ISBN 0-395-28790-1, Clarion). HM.
Witch's Garden. Miriam Young. LC 72-85922. 160p. (gr. 5-9). 1973. 6.95 o.p. (ISBN 0-689-30323-8, Athenuum). Macmillan.
Witch's Guide to Gardening. Dorothy Jacob. (Illus.). 1965. 4.95 o.s.i. (ISBN 0-8008-8400-0). Taplinger.
Witch's Omen. Carolyn Keene. LC 78-57929. (Dana Girls Ser.: No. 17). (Illus.). (gr. 2-6). 1978. 2.95 o.p. (ISBN 0-448-09097-X, G&D). Putnam Pub Group.
Witchwood. Tim Lukeman. 192p. 1984. 13.50 o.s.i. (ISBN 0-671-47549-5, Timescape). PB.
With a Tangled Skein. Piers Anthony. LC 85-6179. (Incarnations of Immortality Ser.: Bk. 3). 1985. 14.45 o.s.i. (ISBN 0-345-31884-6, Del Rey). Ballantine.
With Aesop along the Black Border. Ambrose E. Gonzales. LC 73-97424. Repr. of 1924 ed. 35.00x o.p. (ISBN 0-8371-2732-7, GOW&). Greenwood.
With All My Heart. Jennifer K. Adams. Ed. by Mary Wallace. (Illus.). 104p. 1984. pap. 4.95 o.p. (ISBN 0-912315-78-4). Word Aflame.
With an Oriental Flavor. Maxine Fritz. 46p. 1976. pap. 1.50 spiral binding o.p. (ISBN 0-8341-0402-4). Beacon Hill.
With Blood in Their Eyes. Steven G. Lawrence. 1978. pap. 1.25 o.p. (ISBN 0-8439-0572-7, Pub. by Leisure Bks CT). Dorchester Pub Co.
With Cat's Eyes You'll Never Be Afraid of the Dark. Joanna Stubbs. (Illus.). 32p. (gr. k-2). 1983. 9.95 o.p. (ISBN 0-233-97485-7). Andre Deutsch.
With Chennault in China: A Flying Tiger's Diary. Robert M. Smith & Philip D. Smith. (Illus.). 160p. (Orig.). 1984. pap. 12.15 o.p. (ISBN 0-8306-2336-1, 2336). TAB Bks.
With Custer in Seventy-Four: James Calhoun's Diary of the Black Hills Expedition. Ed. by Lawrence A. Frost. LC 79-13132. (Illus.). 1979. 12.95 o.p. (ISBN 0-8425-1620-4). Brigham.
With Enough Shovels: Reagan, Bush, & Nuclear War. Robert Scheer. 304p. 1983. 14.95 o.p. (ISBN 0-394-41482-9, Vin); pap. 4.95 o.p. (ISBN 0-394-72203-5). Random.
With Friends Like These... Alan D. Foster. 256p. 1983. pap. 2.75 o.p. (ISBN 0-345-31189-2, Del Rey). Ballantine.
With Friends Possessed. Holmes Alexander. LC 75-92683. 1970. 5.95 o.p. (ISBN 0-87004-196-7). Caxton.
With Friends Possessed: A Life of Edward FitzGerald. Robert B. Martin. LC 84-45627. (Illus.). 320p. 1985. 17.95 o.p. (ISBN 0-689-11557-1, Atheneum). Macmillan.
With Head & Heart: The Story of Howard Thurman. Howard Thurman. LC 79-1848. (Illus.). 1979. 10.00 o.s.i. (ISBN 0-15-142164-1). HarBraceJ.
With Hearts Courageous. Edna Kenton. (Black & Gold Lib). (Illus.). 1948. 6.95 o.p. (ISBN 0-87140-910-0). Liveright.
With Hemingway: A Year in Key West & Cuba. Arnold Samuelson. 216p. 1985. pap. 7.95 o.p. (ISBN 0-03-005617-9). H Holt & Co.
With His Hand in Yours. Phyllis Hobe. (Illus.). 48p. 1985. 6.95 o.p. (ISBN 0-8378-5074-6). Gibson.
With Hitler in New York. Richard A. Grayson. LC 78-20695. 1979. 7.95 o.s.i. (ISBN 0-8008-8406-X). Taplinger.
With Ignorance. C. K. Williams. 1977. pap. 4.95 o.p. (ISBN 0-395-25339-X). HM.
With MacArthur in Japan. William J. Sebald & Russell Brines. (Illus.). 1965. 6.95 o.p. (ISBN 0-393-07401-3). Norton.
With Magical Horses to Ride. Winifred Morris. LC 84-21633. 156p. (gr. 4-8). 1985. 11.95 o.s.i. (ISBN 0-689-31108-7, Atheneum Childrens Bks). Macmillan.
With My Face to the Rising Sun. Robert M. Screen. LC 77-76441. (Illus.). 106p. (gr. 5-9). 1977. 6.95 o.p. (ISBN 0-15-298780-0, HJ). HarBraceJ.
With One Sky above Us: Life on an American Indian Reservation at the Turn of the Century. M. Gidley. LC 84-22088. (Illus.). 160p. (Orig.). pap. 9.95 o.p. (ISBN 0-295-96164-3). U of Wash Pr.
With Only One Ear. 41p. 1977. 1.00 o.p. (ISBN 0-914389-17-3). Common Cause.
With Open Eyes: Conversations with Matthieu Galey. Marguerite Yourcenar. Tr. by Arthur Goldhammer. LC 84-45074. 291p. 1984. 19.95 o.p. (ISBN 0-8070-6354-1). Beacon Pr.
With Open Eyes: Conversations with Matthieu Galey. Marguerite Yourcenar. Tr. by Arthur Goldhammer from Fr. LC 85-45074. 291p. 1986. pap. 10.95 o.p. (ISBN 0-8070-6355-X, BP707). Beacon Pr.
With Pen of Truth: A Reading of Walden. Raymond P. Tripp. 1972. pap. 10.00 o.p. (ISBN 0-9502699-0-5). Soc New Lang Study.
With Respect to Readers: Dimensions of Literary Response. Walter J. Slatoff. LC 77-123995. 224p. 1970. 22.50x o.p. (ISBN 0-8014-0580-7). Cornell U Pr.
With Silk Wings: Asian American Women at Work. Elaine Kim. (Illus.). 150p. 1983. pap. 10.95 o.p. (ISBN 0-936434-06-6). SF Study Ctr.
With the Contras: A Reporter in the Wilds of Nicaragua. Christopher Dickey. 1986. 18.45 o.s.i. (ISBN 0-671-53298-7). S&S.
With Their Ears Pricked Forward, Tales of Mules I've Known. Joshua A. Lee. 138p. 10.00 o.p. (ISBN 0-318-12513-7). Am Donkey.
With Two Wheels & a Camera. Bert Kopperl. 1979. 12.50 o.p. (ISBN 0-682-49352-X, Banner). Exposition-Phoenix.
With Wings As Eagles. William B. Oglesby, Jr. (Illus., Orig.). 1967. pap. 3.45 o.p. (ISBN 0-8042-9623-5, John Knox). Westminster John Knox.
Within-&-Without Wears His Coat Wrong-Side-Out. 16p. 1975. pap. 0.99 o.p. (ISBN 0-8285-1274-4, Pub. by Progress Pubs USSR). Imported Pubns.
Within the Whirlwind. Eugenia S. Ginzburg. Tr. by Ian Boland. LC 80-8748. (Helen & Kurt Wolff Bk.). 448p. 1981. 17.50 o.p. (ISBN 0-15-197517-5). HarBraceJ.
Within This Wilderness. Feenie Ziner. 240p. 1981. pap. 3.95 o.p. (ISBN 0-393-00041-9). Norton.
Without a Man in the House. Wilma Burton. LC 78-68403. pap. 5.95 o.p. (ISBN 0-89107-158-X). Good News.
Without a Thorn: A Guide to Rose Gardening in the Pacific Northwest. Stuart Mechlin & Ellen Bonanno. LC 78-13890. (Illus.). 108p. (Orig.). 1978. pap. 7.50 o.p. (ISBN 0-917304-37-3). Timber.
Without a Trace: A Fresh Investigation of Eight Lost Ships & Their Fates. John Harris. LC 80-20934. (Illus.). 1981. 14.95 o.p. (ISBN 0-689-11120-7, Atheneum). Macmillan.
Without Bombast & Blunders: An Executive's Guide to Effective Writing. Frances D. Naczi. LC 80-17857. 1980. pap. 5.95 o.s.i. (ISBN 0-87863-007-4, 2425-02, Farnsworth Pub Co). Longman Finan.
Without Help or Hindrance: Religious Identity in American Culture. Eldon G. Ernst. LC 76-27742. 1977. pap. 6.95 o.s.i. (ISBN 0-664-24128-X, Westminster). Westminster John Knox.
Without Noise of Arms. Walter Briggs. LC 75-11163. (Illus.). 222p. 1976. pap. 19.95 o.p. (ISBN 0-87358-418-X, Entrada Bks). Northland.
Without Orders. Martha Albrand. 1972. pap. 0.75 o.p. (ISBN 0-380-01472-6, 04465). Avon.
Without Precedent. John G. Adams. 1983. 17.00 o.p. (ISBN 0-393-01616-1). Norton.
Without Precedent: The Story of the Death of McCarthyism. John G. Adams. 288p. 1985. pap. 6.70 o.p. (ISBN 0-393-30230-X). Norton.
Without Rhetoric: An Architectural Aesthetic 1955-1972. Alison Smithson & Peter Smithson. 1974. 17.50x o.p. (ISBN 0-262-19119-9). MIT Pr.
Witness the Power of Woman. Olive K. Gilliam. 6.95 o.p. (ISBN 0-533-04372-7). Vantage.
Witness to History. Charles E. Bohlen. (Illus.). 1973. pap. 6.95x o.p. (ISBN 0-393-09287-9, 9287). Norton.
Witness to the Truth: Christ & His Interpreters. rev. ed. Edith Hamilton. 1962. pap. 4.95 o.p. (ISBN 0-393-00113-X, Norton Lib). Norton.
Witness to the World: The Christian Mission in Theological Perspective. David J. Bosch. LC 79-91241. (New Foundations Theological Library). 285p. (Series editors Peter Toon & Ralph Martin). 1980. 12.95 o.p. (ISBN 0-8042-3706-9, 3706-9, John Knox). Westminster John Knox.
Witnesses. Marcy Heidish. 1980. 10.95 o.p. (ISBN 0-395-29196-8). HM.
Wit's End: Days & Nights of the Algonquin Round Table. James R. Gaines. LC 77-73050. (Illus.). 1977. 12.95 o.p. (ISBN 0-15-197521-3). HarBraceJ.
Wit's End: Days & Nights of the Algonquin Round Table. James R. Gaines. LC 79-10464. (Illus.). 1979. pap. 6.95 o.p. (ISBN 0-15-697651-X, Harv). HarBraceJ.
Witt: A Book of Poems. Patti Smith. 1973. pap. 4.95 o.p. (ISBN 0-910664-33-1). Gotham.
Wittenberg, Revisited: A Polymorphous Critique of Religion & Theology. Howard P. Kainz. LC 81-40729. 236p. (Orig.). 1982. 29.00 o.p. (ISBN 0-8191-1949-0); pap. text ed. 13.25 o.p. (ISBN 0-8191-1950-4). U Pr of Amer.
Wittgenstein. William H. Bruening. 1977. pap. text ed. 12.00 o.p. (ISBN 0-8191-0289-X). U Pr of Amer.
Wittgenstein: A Critique. J. N. Findlay. (International Library of Philosophy). 240p. 1985. 29.95x o.p. (ISBN 0-7102-0330-6). Routledge Chapman & Hall.
Wittgenstein: A Life, Young Ludwig, 1889-1921. Brian McGuinness. (Illus.). Date not set. 22.50 o.p. (ISBN 0-520-06496-8). U of Cal Pr.
Wittgenstein & Knowledge: The Importance of "On Certainty" Thomas Morawetz. LC 79-13039. 1980. pap. text ed. 7.95x o.p. (ISBN 0-391-01034-4). Humanities.
Wittgenstein & Political Philosophy: A Re-Examination of the Foundation of Social Science. John W. Danford. LC 78-6716. 1978. lib. bdg. 20.00x o.s.i. (ISBN 0-226-13593-4). U of Chicago Pr.
Wittgenstein & Political Philosophy: A Re-Examination of the Foundations of Social Science. John W. Danford. LC 78-6716. xiv, 166p. 1981. pap. text ed. 6.95x o.s.i. (ISBN 0-226-13594-2). U of Chicago Pr.
Wittgenstein Bibliography. Compiled by V. A. Shanker & S. G. Shanker. (Critical Assessment & Bibliography Ser.). 352p. 1986. 69.00 o.p. (Pub. by Croom Helm UK). Routledge Chapman & Hall.
Wittgenstein: Language & World. John V. Canfield. Date not set. price not set o.p. U of Mass Pr.
Wittgenstein on Meaning. Colin McGinn. 160p. 1985. 65.00x o.p. (ISBN 0-631-13764-5). Basil Blackwell.
Wittgenstein, Skepticism & Political Participation: An Essay in the Epistemology of Democratic Theory. Aryeh Botwinick. 52p. (Orig.). 1985. pap. text ed. 6.00 o.p. (ISBN 0-8191-4816-4). U Pr of Amer.
Wittgenstein, the Early Philosophy: An Exposition of the Tractatus. Henry L. Finch. LC 73-135985. 1982. text ed. 19.95x o.p. (ISBN 0-391-00123-X). Humanities.
Wittgenstein-the Later Philosophy: An Exposition of the Philosophical Investigations. Henry L. Finch. LC 76-46421. 1977. text ed. 17.50x o.p. (ISBN 0-391-00680-0). Humanities.
Wittgenstein: To Follow a Rule. Ed. by Steven H. Holtzman & Christopher M. Leich. (International Library of Philosophy). 250p. 1981. 30.00x o.p. (ISBN 0-7100-0760-4). Routledge Chapman & Hall.
Wittgenstein's Lectures, Cambridge 1932-1935. Ludwig Wittgenstein. Ed. by Margaret Macdonald & Alice Ambrose. LC 81-19818. (Phoenix Ser.). xii, 226p. 1982. pap. text ed. 6.95 o.s.i. (ISBN 0-226-90439-3). U of Chicago Pr.
Wives & Lovers. Margaret Millar. 1974. pap. 1.25 o.p. (ISBN 0-380-00080-6, 19976). Avon.
Wives & Mistresses. Suzanne Morris. LC 85-25235. 584p. 1986. 18.95 o.s.i. (ISBN 0-385-19099-9). Doubleday.
Wives of the Presidents. Arden D. Melick. Ed. by Ernest Dupuy. LC 77-141. (Hammond Profile Ser.). (Illus.). 96p. (gr. 7 up). 1985. 8.95 o.p. (ISBN 0-8437-3813-8). Hammond Inc.
Wives of the Presidents. 2nd ed. Arden D. Melick. Ed. by Ernest Dupuy. LC 77-141. (Profile Ser.). (Illus.). 96p. (gr. 7 up). 1989. 10.95 o.p. Hammond Inc.
Wives' Tales. Pasadena Art Alliance Staff. 1982. pap. 5.95 o.p. (ISBN 0-937042-05-6). Pasadena Art.
Wizard Children of Finn. Mary Tannen. 216p. (YA) (gr. 3-7). 1983. pap. 1.95 o.p. (ISBN 0-380-57661-9, 65607-8, Camelot). Avon.
Wizard in the Well. Harry Behn. LC 56-5232. (Illus.). (gr. k-3). 1956. 4.95 o.p. (ISBN 0-15-298929-3, HJ). HarBraceJ.
Wizard of Odd. Lou Buchanan. (Danger Mouse Picture Bks.). (Illus.). 32p. (gr. k-3). 1986. 7.95 o.p. (ISBN 0-316-75724-1). Little.
Wizard of Oz. L. Frank Baum. (Children's Classics Ser.). 32p. (gr. k-3). 1988. 5.95 o.p. (ISBN 0-8249-8264-9). Ideals.
Wizard of the Winds. Ward T. Van Orman & Robert. Hull. (Illus.). 1978. 12.00 o.p. (ISBN 0-87839-032-4). North Star.
Wizards of Armageddon. Fred Kaplan. 464p. 1984. pap. 10.95 o.s.i. (ISBN 0-671-52822-X, Touchstone Bks). S&S.
Wizards of Armageddon: Strategists of the Nuclear Age. Fred Kaplan. 1983. 18.25 o.p. (ISBN 0-671-42444-0). S&S.
Wodehouse at War. Iain Sproat. LC 81-84189. 176p. 1981. 9.95 o.p. (ISBN 0-89919-098-7). Ticknor & Fields.
Wodehouse Bestiary. P. G. Wodehouse. Ed. by D. R. Bensen. 276p. 1985. 16.45 o.p. (ISBN 0-89919-396-X). Ticknor & Fields.
Wodehouse on Crime. P. G. Wodehouse. Ed. by D. R. Bensen. LC 81-5697. (Joan Kahn Bk.). 300p. 1981. 12.95 o.p. (ISBN 0-89919-044-8). Ticknor & Fields.
Woe to Live On. Daniel Woodrell. LC 86-22953. 1987. 16.95 o.s.i. (ISBN 0-8050-0283-9). H Holt & Co.
Woerterbuch der Deutschen Aussprache. 2nd ed. Hans Krech. 549p. (Ger.). 1967. 19.95 o.p. (ISBN 0-686-56643-2, M-7033). French & Eur.
Woerterbuch der Voelkerkunde. Walter Hirschberg. (Ger.). 1965. 17.50 o.p. (ISBN 3-520-20501-7, M-6945). French & Eur.
Wok Cook Book. Sunset Magazine & Books Editors. LC 78-53676. (Illus.). 80p. 1978. pap. 5.95 o.p. (ISBN 0-376-02963-3, Sunset Bks.). Sunset-Lane.
Wokosani Road: A Novel of Indian Love in the Southwest. John Mockingbird. 1963. 20.00 o.p. (Lochinvar). Exposition-Phoenix.
Wole Soyinka. James Gibbs. LC 85-80890. 170p. 1986. 27.50 o.p. (ISBN 0-394-55137-0). Grove.
Wole Soyinka. James Gibbs. LC 85-80890. 170p. 1986. pap. 11.95 o.p. (ISBN 0-394-62111-5, Ever). Grove.
Wolf & the Seven Little Kids. Felix Hoffman. LC 59-16357. (Illus.). 32p. (ps-3). 1959. 6.95 o.p. (ISBN 0-15-299108-5, HJ). HarBraceJ.
Wolf Bell. Shirley R. Murphy. LC 78-10415. 1979. 8.95 o.p. (ISBN 0-689-30692-X, Atheneum). Macmillan.
Wolf Bell. Shirley R. Murphy. 176p. 1980. pap. 2.25 o.p. (ISBN 0-380-50666-1, 62216-5, Flare). Avon.
Wolf-Children & Feral Man. Joseph A. Singh & Robert M. Zingg. LC 66-23445. (Illus.). xli, 379p. 1966. Repr. of 1942 ed. 32.50 o.p. (ISBN 0-208-00599-4, Archon). Shoe String.
Wolf Country. Will Brennan. (Lythway Ser.). 168p. 1988. lib. bdg. 17.50x o.p. (ISBN 0-7451-0712-5, Pub. by Chivers Pr UK). G K Hall.
Wolf King. Ann Turnbull. LC 75-25513. 144p. (gr. 6 up). 1979. 5.95 o.p. (ISBN 0-395-28927-0, Clarion). HM.
Wolf Not Native France. Guy B. Wiser. 1978. 8.95 o.p. (ISBN 0-15-198023-3). HarBraceJ.
Wolf Run: A Caribou Eskimo Tale. James Houston. LC 78-140778. (Illus.). (gr. 2-5). 1971. 5.75 o.p. (ISBN 0-15-299104-2, HJ). HarBraceJ.
Wolf Strikes. John S. Morgan. 288p. (Orig.). 1981. pap. 2.25 o.p. (ISBN 0-505-51733-7, Pub. by Tower Bks). Dorchester Pub Co.
Wolf Tracks. David Case. (Orig.). 1980. pap. 1.95 o.p. (ISBN 0-505-51485-0, Pub. by Tower Bks). Dorchester Pub Co.
Wolf! Wolf! Elizabeth Rose & Gerald Rose. (Illus.). 32p. (Orig.). (ps-k). 1984. pap. 5.95 o.p. (ISBN 0-571-13375-4). Faber & Faber.
Wolfbane. Craig Thomas. 1978. 8.95 o.s.i. (ISBN 0-03-022466-7). H Holt & Co.
Wolfe Archipelago. Gene Wolfe. LC 83-60768. (Illus.). 135p. 1983. 15.95 o.p. (ISBN 0-917488-13-X); 30.00 o.p. (ISBN 0-917488-14-8). Mark Ziesing.
Wolfgang Amadeus Mozart. Dyneley Hussey. LC 70-104288. (Illus.). 1971. Repr. of 1928 ed. lib. bdg. 35.00x o.p. (ISBN 0-8371-3957-0, HUWM). Greenwood.
Wolfgang Puck's Modern French Cooking. Wolfgang Puck. (Illus.). 352p. 1981. 19.45 o.p. (ISBN 0-395-31328-7). HM.
Wolfhart Pannenberg & Religious Philosophy. David McKenzie. LC 80-8171. 169p. 1980. lib. bdg. 25.00 o.p. (ISBN 0-8191-1314-X); pap. text ed. 12.00 o.p. (ISBN 0-8191-1315-8). U Pr of Amer.
Wolfman of Beacon Hill. Kathleen Kilgore. LC 82-47910. 192p. (gr. 7 up). 1982. 13.45i o.p. (ISBN 0-316-49306-6). Little.
Wolftrap. Eric Bercovici. LC 78-21598. 1979. 7.95 o.p. (ISBN 0-689-10949-0, Atheneum). Macmillan.
Wolftrap. Nelson Nye. (Nightingale Ser.). 210p. 1988. pap. 12.95 o.p. (ISBN 0-8161-4424-9, Large Print Bks). G K Hall.
Wolftrap. Nelson Nye. 1989. pap. 3.50 o.p. (ISBN 0-7701-0865-2). PaperJacks US.
Wolverine. Jack Slade. (Lassiter Ser.). 1978. pap. 1.50 o.p. (ISBN 0-505-51225-4, Pub. by Tower Bks). Dorchester Pub Co.
Wolves of Minong: Their Vital Role in a Wild Community. Durwood Allen. (Illus.). 1979. 17.50 o.p. (ISBN 0-395-27626-8). HM.
Wolves of Paris. Daniel P. Mannix. 1979. pap. 1.95 o.p. (ISBN 0-380-47555-3, 47555). Avon.
Woman. Edward Boubat. LC 72-86679. (Illus.). 143p. 1973. 15.00 o.s.i. (ISBN 0-8076-0664-2). Braziller.
Woman Activist Guide for Women Candidates. rev. ed. Flora Crater. 1978. pap. 1.00 o.p. (ISBN 0-917560-11-6). Woman Activist.
Woman Activist Guide to Lobbying, 1977. rev. ed. Flora Crater. 1977. pap. 1.00 o.p. (ISBN 0-917560-08-6). Woman Activist.
Woman Activists. Anne W. Garland. Date not set. price not set o.p. Feminist Pr.
Woman at Apocalypse. Frederick W. Ayer. 1981. pap. 5.00 o.p. (ISBN 0-682-49809-2). Exposition-Phoenix.

Titles

Titles

Woman Between. Jaroldeen Edwards. 1980. pap. 2.25 o.p. (ISBN 0-380-75846-6, 75846-6). Avon.
Woman Called En. Tomie O'Hara. 160p. 1986. 17.50 o.p. (ISBN 0-86358-079-3, Pandora Pr); pap. 6.95 o.p. (ISBN 0-86358-082-3). Routledge Chapman & Hall.
Woman-Doctor: The Education of Jane Patterson, M.D. Jane Patterson & Lynda Madaras. 224p. 1983. pap. 3.95 o.p. (ISBN 0-380-83063-9, 83063-9). Avon.
Woman in a Man-Made World. 2nd ed. Nona Y. Glazer & Helen Y. Waehrer. 1977. pap. 19.95 o.p. (ISBN 0-395-30607-8). HM.
Woman in a World of Men: An Autobiography of a Farmer's Daughter. Mary L. Little. LC 85-90285. 49p. 1986. 7.95 o.p. (ISBN 0-533-06782-0). Vantage.
Woman in Athletic Administration. Jackie Lapin & Bonnie L. Parkhouse. 1980. text ed. write for info. o.p. (ISBN 0-673-16213-3). Scott F.
Woman in the Eighteenth Century & Other Essays. Paul Fritz & Richard Morton. (McMaster Eighteenth Century Studies). 386p. 1979. lib. bdg. 43.00 o.p. (ISBN 0-686-88536-8). Garland Pub.
Woman in the House. William E. Barrett. 224p. 1972. pap. 0.95 o.p. (ISBN 0-380-01473-4, 07260). Avon.
Woman in the Modern World: Six Hundred & Thirty-Seven Pronouncements from Leo Thirteenth to Pius Twelfth. Ed. by Monks of Solesmes Staff. 4.00 o.s.i. (ISBN 0-8198-0178-X). Dghtrs St Paul.
Woman in the Wraparound Skirt. Anna E. Anderson. 152p. 1979. 7.50 o.p. (ISBN 0-682-49450-X). Exposition-Phoenix.
Woman in the Year Two Thousand. Ed. by Maggie Trip. LC 74-80707. 1981. pap. 6.00 o.p. (ISBN 0-87795-091-1, Arbor Hse). Morrow.
Woman in White. Wilkie Collins. 1982. pap. 4.75x o.p. (ISBN 0-460-01464-1, Evman). Biblio Dist.
Woman in White. Wilkie Collins. Ed. by Kathleen Tillotson. LC 72-5304. 1969. pap. 3.95 o.p. (ISBN 0-395-05211-4, B116, RivEd). HM.
Woman in White: T. V. Edition. Wilkie Collins. Ed. by Julian Symons. 1982. pap. 3.95 o.p. (ISBN 0-14-005980-6). Penguin.
Woman Like That. Susan Shreve. LC 76-50602. 1977. 8.95 o.p. (ISBN 0-689-10776-5, Atheneum). Macmillan.
Woman Named Solitude. Andre Schwarz-Bart. Tr. by Ralph Manheim from Fr. LC 84-70645. 190p. 1985. pap. 7.95 o.p. (ISBN 0-916870-87-1, A Donald S. Ellis Book). Creative Arts Bk.
Woman: New Dimensions. Ed. by Walter J. Burghardt. LC 76-50965. 1977. pap. 5.95 o.p. (ISBN 0-8091-2011-9). Paulist Pr.
Woman of Andros. Thornton Wilder. 1975. pap. 1.65 o.p. (ISBN 0-380-00308-2, 49460-4, Bard). Avon.
Woman of Justice. Georgia DiDonato. 1981. pap. 2.50 o.p. (ISBN 0-380-55798-3, 55798). Avon.
Woman of Justice. Georgia DiDonato. (General Ser.). 1980. lib. bdg. 15.95 o.p. (ISBN 0-8161-3132-5, Large Print GBks). G K Hall.
Woman of the Maya. Stella G. Zarate. 1978. 7.50 o.p. (ISBN 0-682-49053-9). Exposition-Phoenix.
Woman on Her Own. Jean R. Jones. Ed. by Jim Beasley. (Orig.). 1988. pap. 9.50 o.p. (ISBN 0-936204-60-5). Jelm Mtn.
Woman on the American Frontier. William W. Fowler. LC 73-12867. 532p. 1974. Repr. of 1878 ed. 56.00x o.p. (ISBN 0-8103-3702-9). Gale.
Woman Question: Selections from the Writings of Karl Marx, Frederick Engels, V. I. Lenin, Joseph Stalin. rev. ed. Karl Marx et al. 96p. 1970. pap. 1.25 o.p. (ISBN 0-7178-0256-6). Intl Pubs Co.
Woman Said Yes: Encounters with Life & Death. Jessamyn West. LC 75-40368. 180p. 1976. 7.95 o.p. (ISBN 0-15-198400-X). HarBraceJ.
Woman, Society & Change. Evelyne Sullerot. Tr. by Margaret S. Archer from Fr. LC 78-90234. (Illus., Orig.). 1971. 4.95 o.p. (ISBN 0-07-062336-8); pap. text ed. 3.95 o.p. (ISBN 0-07-062335-X). McGraw.
Woman True TG. Date not set. (ISBN 0-07-020438-1). McGraw.
Woman Unliberated: Difficulties & Limitations in Changing Self. C. M. Hall. LC 78-21874. 170p. 1979. pap. 26.95 o.p. (ISBN 0-89116-097-3). Hemisphere Pub.
Woman Vanishes. Caroline Crane. 215p. 1984. 12.95 o.p. (ISBN 0-396-08310-2). Dodd.
Woman Vanishes. Caroline Crane. (Nightingale Ser.). 288p. 1988. pap. 15.95 o.p. (ISBN 0-8161-4478-8). G K Hall.
Woman Versus Woman: The Extra Marital Affair. Shirley Eskapa. 212p. 1984. 13.95 o.p. (ISBN 0-531-09845-1). Watts.
Woman Wants God. Mary L. Lacy. 1959. pap. 1.25 o.p. (ISBN 0-8042-3596-1, John Knox). Westminster John Knox.
Woman Who Disappeared see Heinemann Guided Readers.
Woman Who Escaped from Shame. Toby Olson. LC 85-18389. 352p. 1986. 16.45 o.s.i. (ISBN 0-394-54715-2). Random.
Woman Who Has Sprouted Wings: Poems by Contemporary Latin American Women Poets. 2nd ed. Ed. by Mary Crow. Tr. by John Felstiner & Donald Walsh. LC 84-5672. 1984. pap. 13.95 o.s.i. (ISBN 0-935480-14-5). Lat Am Lit Rev Pr.
Woman Who Lived in a Prologue. Nina Schneider. 1980. 13.95 o.p. (ISBN 0-395-28211-X). HM.
Woman Who Murdered Black Satin: The Bermondsey Horror. Albert Borowitz. LC 80-39756. (Illus.). 347p. 1981. 21.50 o.p. (ISBN 0-8142-0320-5). Ohio St U Pr.
Woman Who Works, the Parent Who Cares: A Revolutionary Program for Raising Your Child. Sirgay Sanger & John Kelly. 1987. 17.95 o.p. (ISBN 0-316-77049-3). Little.
Woman, Work & Property in North-West India. Ursula Sharma. 1980. 25.00x o.p. (ISBN 0-422-77120-1, NO.2018, Pub. by Tavistock); pap. 13.95 o.p. (ISBN 0-422-78640-3, NO. 3926). Routledge Chapman & Hall.
Womanchange! Louise McCants. 160p. 1986. text ed. 12.50 o.p. (ISBN 0-682-40293-1). Exposition-Phoenix.
Womanlist. Marjorie P. Weiser & Jean S. Arbeiter. LC 80-65983. (Illus.). 512p. 1981. 19.95 o.p. (ISBN 0-689-11083-9, Atheneum); pap. 10.95 o.p. (ISBN 0-689-11113-4). Macmillan.
Womanpower & Health Care. Marlene Grissum & Carol Spengler. LC 75-41571. 1976. pap. 14.00 o.p. (ISBN 0-316-32895-2). Little.
Woman's Being, Woman's Place: Female Identity & Vocation in American History. Ed. by Mary Kelley. 386p. 1979. 23.50 o.p. (ISBN 0-8161-8324-4). G K Hall.
Woman's Book of Non-trivial Trivia. Barbara Wachman. LC 85-62497. (Illus.). 195p. 1986. pap. 8.95 o.p. (ISBN 0-933341-15-6). Quinlan Pr.
Woman's Choice: Living Through Your Problems. Eugenia Price. 192p. 1983. pap. 6.95 o.p. (ISBN 0-310-31381-3, 16217P). Zondervan.
Woman's Choice: New Options in the Treatment of Breast Cancer. Mary Spletter. LC 81-66192. 192p. 1981. 14.50x o.p. (ISBN 0-8070-3258-1); pap. 9.95 o.p. (ISBN 0-8070-2153-9, BP 661). Beacon Pr.
Woman's Choices: The Relief Society Legacy Lectures. LC 83-25517. 196p. 1984. 7.95 o.p. (ISBN 0-87747-999-2). Deseret Bk.
Woman's Creation. Elizabeth Fisher. 504p. 1980. pap. text ed. 6.95 o.p. (ISBN 0-07-021105-1). McGraw.
Woman's Day Book of Calligraphy. Janice Bandyk-Glander & Dennis Droge. 96p. 1982. pap. 7.95 o.p. (ISBN 0-671-25019-1, Fireside). S&S.
Woman's Day Book of Calligraphy. Dennis Droge & Glander-Bandyk. 1980. 12.95 o.p. (ISBN 0-671-25018-3, 25018). S&S.
Woman's Day Book of Great Sandwiches. Diane Harris. LC 81-20021. (Illus.). 170p. 1982. 16.95 o.p. (ISBN 0-03-061539-9, Owl Bks.); pap. 9.95 o.p. (ISBN 0-03-058967-3, Owl Bks). H Holt & Co.
Woman's Day Book of Soft Toys & Dolls. Joan Russell. (Illus.). 256p. 1975. 12.50 o.p. (ISBN 0-671-22085-3). S&S.
Woman's Day Book of Thin Italian Cooking. Carol Truax. 1978. 9.95 o.p. (ISBN 0-395-26313-1). HM.
Woman's Day Book of Weekend Crafts: More Than 100 Quick-to-Finish Projects. Woman's Day Editors. LC 77-15496. 1978. 11.95 o.p. (ISBN 0-395-26284-4). HM.
Woman's Day Guide to Organizing Your Life. Diane Harris. 1985. pap. 8.95 o.p. (ISBN 0-03-063931-X, Owl Bks). H Holt & Co.
Woman's Day Low-Calorie Dessert Cookbook. Carol Cutler. 1980. 9.95 o.p. (ISBN 0-395-28947-5). HM.
Woman's Decision: Breast Care, Treatment & Reconstruction. Karen Berger & John Bostwick, III. 288p. 1984. cloth 14.95 o.p. (ISBN 0-8016-0598-9). Mosby.
Woman's Engagement Journal 1989. (Illus.). 112p. 1988. 9.95 o.p. (ISBN 0-89471-622-0). Running Pr.
Woman's Guide to a Safe Abortion. Maria Corsaro & Carole Korzeniowsky. LC 82-15652. (Illus.). 200p. 1983. 12.95 o.p. (ISBN 0-03-060603-9); pap. 6.95 o.p. (ISBN 0-03-060602-0). H Holt & Co.
Woman's Guide to Selling Residential Real Estate Successfully. Carolyn Janik. 288p. 1982. 11.95 o.p. (ISBN 0-89696-131-1, Everest House Book). Dodd.
Woman's Guide to Starting a Business. rev. ed. Claudia Jessup & Genie Chipps. 288p. 1980. 12.95 o.p. (ISBN 0-03-047131-1); pap. 6.95 o.p. (ISBN 0-03-047126-5). H Holt & Co.
Woman's Guide to Staying Safe. Cheryl Reimold. LC 84-62845. 138p. Date not set. pap. (ISBN 0-671-55620-7). Monarch Pr.
Woman's Legal Guide to Separation & Divorce in All 50 States. Norma Harwood. 304p. 1985. 22.50 o.p. (ISBN 0-684-18136-3); pap. 11.95 o.p. (ISBN 0-684-18146-0). Scribner.
Woman's Ministry: Mary Collson's Search for Reform as a Unitarian Minister, Hull House Social Worker, & a Christian Science Practioner. Cynthia G. Tucker. (American Civilization Ser.). 222p. 1984. 27.95 o.p. (ISBN 0-87722-338-6). Temple U Pr.
Woman's Path to Godliness. Martha Reapsome. LC 86-18214. 176p. 1986. 10.95 o.p. (ISBN 0-8407-9067-8). Oliver-Nelson.
Woman's Place: An Oral History of Working Class Women, 1890-1940. Elizabeth Roberts. 272p. 1984. 24.95x o.p. (ISBN 0-631-13572-3). Basil Blackwell.
Woman's Place: An Oral History of Working-Class Women 1890-1940. Elizabeth Roberts. 256p. 1986. pap. text ed. 15.95x o.p. (ISBN 0-631-14754-3). Basil Blackwell.
Woman's Place Nineteen Ten to Nineteen Seventy-Five. Ruth Adam. (Illus.). 1977. 8.95 o.p. (ISBN 0-393-05622-8). Norton.
Woman's Place: Women & Politics in Australia. Marian Sawer & Marian Sims. 240p. 1984. text ed. 34.95x o.p. (ISBN 0-86861-400-9); pap. text ed. 14.95x o.p. (ISBN 0-86861-408-4). Unwin Hyman.
Woman's Selling Game: How to Sell Yourself & Anything Else. Carole Hyatt. LC 79-11166. 252p. 1979. 8.95 o.p. (ISBN 0-87131-289-1). M Evans.
Woman's Voices in American Poetry: "The Beauty of Inflections or the Beauty of Innuendoes. Ed. by Susan Van Dyne. 54p. 1981. pap. 3.50 o.p. (ISBN 0-87391-024-9). Smith Coll.
Woman's Way: The Memoirs of Flora Solomon. Flora Solomon & Barry Litvinoff. 240p. 1984. 16.45 o.p. (ISBN 0-671-46002-1). S&S.
Woman's Who's Who of America: A Biographical Dictionary of Contemporary Women of the United States & Canada, 1914-1915. LC 74-6280. 946p. 1976. Repr. of 1914 ed. 95.00x o.p. (ISBN 0-8103-4018-6). Gale.
Womans Workshop on Proverbs. Diane Bloem. 1978. leader's manual 5.95 o.p. (ISBN 0-310-21371-1, 10684P); student manual 4.50 o.p. (ISBN 0-310-21361-4, 10683P). Zondervan.
Woman's Worth: Sexual Economics & the World of Women. Lisa Leghorn & Katherine Parker. 352p. 1981. 22.95x o.p. (ISBN 0-7100-0836-8); pap. 10.50 o.p. (ISBN 0-7100-0855-4). Routledge Chapman & Hall.
Women: A Bibliography of Bibliographies. Patricia K. Ballou. 1980. lib. bdg. 22.00 o.s.i. (ISBN 0-8161-8292-2, Hall Reference). G K Hall.
Women: A Book for Men. Ed. by James Wagenvoord. 1979. pap. 7.95 o.p. (ISBN 0-380-42994-2, 76018). Avon.
Women: A Feminist Perspective. 3rd ed. Jo Freeman. (Orig.). 1984. pap. text ed. 19.95 o.p. (ISBN 0-87484-568-8). Mayfield Pub.
Women & Achievement: Social & Motivational Analyses. Ed. by M. S. Mednick et al. LC 75-22047. 447p. 1975. 37.50x o.p. (ISBN 0-470-59025-4); pap. 11.95x o.p. (ISBN 0-470-99150-X). Halsted Pr.
Women & American Trade Unions. 2nd ed. James J. Kenneally. 256p. 1981. pap. 8.95 o.p. (ISBN 0-920792-10-3). Eden Pr.
Women & Analysis: Dialogues on Psychoamalytic Views of Femininity. Ed. by Jean Strouse. (Non-Fiction Ser.). 375p. 1985. pap. 8.95 o.p. (ISBN 0-8398-2878-0, Gregg). G K Hall.
Women & Children First: Home Link- A Neighborhood Education Project. Susan Bell et al. LC 84-6561. (Bernard van Leer Foundation International Series on Education). (Illus.). 213p. (Orig.). 1984. pap. text ed. 10.00 o.p. (ISBN 0-931114-26-8). High-Scope.
Women & Crime in America. Lee H. Bowker. 1981. pap. text ed. write for info. o.p. (ISBN 0-02-476830-8). Macmillan.
Women & Development: Perspectives from South & Southeast Asia. Ed. by Rounaq Jahan & Hanna Papanek. 1980. pap. 14.00x o.p. (ISBN 0-8364-0596-X, Pub. by Bangladesh Inst Law India). South Asia Bks.
Women & Economics: A Study of the Economic Relation Between Men & Women As a Factor in Social Evolution. Charlotte P. Gilman. Ed. by Carl N. Degler. 18.50 o.p. (ISBN 0-8446-2130-7). Peter Smith.
Women & Fatigue: Effective Solutions to This Very Real Problem. Holly Atkinson. (Illus.). 320p. 1986. 17.95 o.p. (ISBN 0-399-13050-0). Putnam Pub Group.
Women & Friendship. Joel D. Block & Diane Greenberg. 304p. 1985. 17.95 o.p. (ISBN 0-531-09707-2). Watts.
Women & Friendship: Modern Responses to Changing Roles. Jan Yager. 200p. Date not set. 18.95x o.s.i. (ISBN 0-8476-7400-2, Rowman & Littlefield). Rowman.
Women & Global Corporations: Work, Roles, & Resistance. 90p. 1979. pap. 4.50 o.p. (ISBN 0-686-95358-4). Am Fr Serv Comm.
Women & Madness. Phyllis Chesler. 1976. pap. 4.95 o.p. (ISBN 0-380-01627-3, 65672-8, Discus). Avon.
Women & Men Speaking. Cheris Kramarae. 216p. (Orig.). 1980. pap. text ed. 15.00 o.p. (ISBN 0-88377-179-9). Newbury Hse.
Women & Men Together: An Anthology of Short Fiction. Dawson Gaillard & John Mosier. (Illus., LC 77-078566). 1978. pap. 17.50 o.p. (ISBN 0-395-25032-3). HM.
Women & Public Policies. Joyce Gelb & Marian L. Palley. LC 82-400. 208p. 1982. 21.00 o.p. (ISBN 0-691-07639-1); pap. 7.50 o.p. (ISBN 0-691-02209-7). Princeton U Pr.
Women & Russia: Feminist Writings from the Soviet Union. Ed. by Tatyana Mamonova. LC 82-73963. 224p. 1984. 23.95x o.p. (ISBN 0-8070-6708-3); pap. 10.95x o.p. (ISBN 0-8070-6709-1, BP 670). Beacon Pr.
Women & Self Esteem: Understanding & Improving the Way We Think & Feel About Ourselves. Linda T. Sanford & Mary E. Donovan. LC 82-45269. 480p. 1984. 17.95 o.p. (ISBN 0-385-17310-5, Anchor Pr). Doubleday.
Women & Sport: From Myth to Reality. Ed. by Carole A. Oglesby. LC 77-19255. (Illus.). 256p. 1978. pap. 11.00 o.p. (ISBN 0-8121-0618-0). Lea & Febiger.
Women & the Ancestors: Black Carib Kinship & Ritual. Virginia Kerns. LC 82-2601. (Illus.). 246p. 1983. 14.95 o.p. (ISBN 0-252-00982-7). U of Ill Pr.
Women & the Law in Washington State. Ed. by Northwest Women's Law Center Staff. 128p. 1982. pap. 5.95 o.p. (ISBN 0-914842-84-6). Madrona Pubs.
Women & the Making of the Working Class: Lyon 1830-1870. Laura S. Strumingher. LC 78-74841. 1979. 14.95 o.p. (ISBN 0-88831-027-7). Eden Pr.
Women & the Subsistence Sector: Economic Participation & Household Decisionmaking in Nepal. Meena Acharya & Lynn Bennett. (Working Paper: No. 526). 160p. 1983. 8.00 o.p. (ISBN 0-8213-0024-5, WP 0526). World Bank.
Women & the Warlords. Hugh Cook. LC 87-73288. (Chronicles of an Age of Darkness Ser.: Vol. 3). 275p. 1988. 19.95 o.p. (ISBN 0-86140-265-0, Pub. by Colin Smythe Ltd Britain). Dufour.
Women & the Word: Sermons. Ed. by Helen G. Crotwell. LC 77-78627. 144p. (Orig.). 1978. pap. 0.50 o.p. (ISBN 0-8006-1318-X, 1-1318, Fortress). Augsburg Fortress.
Women & the World of Work. Ed. by Anne Hoiberg. (NATO Conference Series III, Human Factors: Vol. 18). 404p. 1982. 65.00x o.p. (ISBN 0-306-41009-5, Plenum Pr). Plenum Pub.
Women & Urban Society: A Guide to Information Sources. Ed. by Hasia R. Diner. LC 78-13109. (Urban Studies Information Guide Ser.: Vol. 7). 152p. 1979. 68.00x o.p. (ISBN 0-8103-1425-8). Gale.
Women & Violence. Miriam F. Hirsch. 416p. 1980. 24.95 o.p. (ISBN 0-442-26148-9). Van Nos Reinhold.
Women & Writing. Michele Barrett. 1980. 8.95 o.p. (ISBN 0-15-193775-3). HarBraceJ.
Women Are Wonderful. Charles Allen. 192p. 1987. 11.95 o.p. (ISBN 0-8499-0610-5). Word Bks.
Women As They Age: Challenge, Opportunity, & Triumph. Intros. by J. Dianne Garner & Susan O. Mercer. (Journal of Women & Aging Ser.: Vol. 1, Nos. 1/2). (Illus.). 412p. pap. text ed. cancelled o.s.i. (ISBN 0-918393-62-0). Harrington Pk.
Women at the Pump. Knut Hamsun. Tr. by Oliver Stallybrass & Gunnvor Stallybrass. LC 78-5342. 356p. 1978. 10.95 o.p. (ISBN 0-374-29280-9); pap. 4.95 o.p. (ISBN 0-374-51503-4). FS&G.
Women at Work. Sylvia Senter et al. 304p. 1983. pap. 6.95 o.p. (ISBN 0-399-50701-9, Perigee). Putnam Pub Group.
Women at Work: Annotated Bibliography. Mei L. Bickner & Marlene Shaughnessey. 420p. 1977. Vol. II. 12.00 o.p. (ISBN 0-89215-064-5). U Cal LA Indus Rel.
Women Beware Women & Pity in History. Howard Barker. LC 87-4477. 128p. (Orig.). 1988. pap. 9.95 o.p. (ISBN 0-7145-4134-6). Riverrun NY.
Women: Beyond Equal Rights. Dee Jepsen. 1986. pap. 7.95 o.p. (ISBN 0-8499-3051-0). Word Bks.
Women Coming of Age. Jane Fonda & Mignon McCarthy. (Illus.). 444p. 1984. 20.95 o.s.i. (ISBN 0-671-46997-5). S&S.
Women Composers: A Checklist of Works for the Solo Voice. Miriam Stewart-Green. 1980. lib. bdg. 52.00 o.p. (ISBN 0-8161-8498-4, Hall Reference). G K Hall.
Women Confined. Date not set. (ISBN 0-8052-3743-7). Random.

Women, Crime, & Criminology: A Feminist Critique. Carol Smart. 1976. 18.95x o.p. (ISBN 0-7100-8449-8). Routledge Chapman & Hall.

Women, Crime, & Society: A Critique of Theoretical Criminology. Eileen B. Leonard. LC 81-8148. (Illus.). 256p. (Orig.). 1982. text ed. 18.00 o.p. (ISBN 0-582-28288-8); pap. text ed. 16.95 o.p. (ISBN 0-582-28289-6). Longman.

Women, Divorce, & Money. Mary Rogers. 1982. pap. text ed. 4.95 o.p. (ISBN 0-07-053497-7). McGraw.

Women Exploited: The Other Victims of Abortion. Paula A. Ervin. LC 85-71563. 160p. (Orig.). 1985. pap. 6.95 o.p. (ISBN 0-87973-847-2, 847). Our Sunday Visitor.

Women Facing Divorce. Becoming One Inc. Staff. 1986. 9.95 o.p. (ISBN 0-932419-04-6); cassette incl. o.p. Susan Hunter.

Women, Family, & Ritual in Renaissance Italy. Christiane Klapisch-Zuber. Tr. by Lydia G. Cochrane from Fr. LC 84-28061. (Illus.). xvi, 338p. 1985. 27.50x o.s.i. (ISBN 0-226-43925-9). U of Chicago Pr.

Women From Birth to Death: The Female Life Cycle in Britain 1830-1914. Ed. by P. Jalland & J. Hooper. LC 85-27070. 348p. 1986. text ed. 37.50x o.p. (ISBN 0-391-03382-4). Humanities.

Women, Health & Healing. 12.95 o.p. (ISBN 0-317-31490-4, 9329). Routledge Chapman & Hall.

Women, Health & Healing: Toward a New Perspective. Ed. by Ellen Lewin. Virginia Olesen. (Contemporary Issues in Health, Medicine, & Social Policy). 300p. (Orig.). 1985. 33.00x o.p. (9263, Pub. by Tavistock England); pap. 12.95 o.p. (ISBN 0-422-78030-8, 9264). Routledge Chapman & Hall.

Women Helping Women: A State by State Directory of Services. Women's Action Alliance Staff. 208p. 1981. 4.75x o.p. (ISBN 0-9605828-0-0). Women's Action.

Women, Heroes, & a Frog. Nina Leen. LC 71-116125. (Illus.). 1970. pap. 7.95 o.p. (ISBN 0-393-08624-0). Norton.

Women in a Changing World. Uta West. (McGraw Hill Paperbacks). (Orig.). 1975. pap. text ed. 3.95 o.p. (ISBN 0-07-069465-6). McGraw.

Women in a Hungry World. pap. 5.50 o.p. (ISBN 0-686-95402-5). Am Fr Serv Comm.

Women in a Strange Land: A Search for a New Image. Ed. by Clare B. Fischer et al. LC 74-26326. 144p. 1975. pap. 3.95 o.p. (ISBN 0-8006-1204-3, Fortress). Augsburg Fortress.

Women in Academe. Ed. by R. L. Dudovitz. 118p. 1984. 19.25 o.p. (ISBN 0-08-030819-8, 26/13). Pergamon.

Women in American Life. Anne F. Scott. LC 71-125122. (Life in America Ser). (Illus.). (gr. 7-12). 1970. 5.56 o.p. (ISBN 0-395-03156-7); pap. 6.08 o.p. (ISBN 0-395-03155-9). HM.

Women in Banking: A Bibliography. Marian Dworaczek. (Public Administration Ser.: Bibliography P 1634). 1985. pap. 2.00 o.p. (ISBN 0-89028-304-4). Vance Biblios.

Women in Changing Japan. Ed. by Joyce Lebra et al. LC 75-33663. 1976. pap. 10.95 o.p. (ISBN 0-8047-0971-8). Stanford U Pr.

Women in China. Hasna J. Moudud. (Illus.). 120p. 1980. text ed. 15.00x o.p. (ISBN 0-7069-1084-2, Pub. by Vikas India). Advent NY.

Women in China: Bibliography of Available English Language Materials. Ed. by Lucie Cheng et al. LC 84-81228. (China Research Monograph (Special) Ser.). 100p. (Orig.). 1984. pap. 12.00x o.p. (ISBN 0-912966-72-6). IEAS.

Women in Defense Work During World War II: An Analysis of the Labor Problem & Women's Rights. Chester W. Gregory, II. LC 78-152123. 1974. 9.00 o.p. (ISBN 0-682-47234-4, University). Exposition-Phoenix.

Women in Distance Education: International Perspectives. Ed. by Karlene Faith. (Radical Forum on Education Ser.). 400p. 1988. lib. bdg. 55.00 o.p. (ISBN 0-415-00566-3). Routledge Chapman & Hall.

Women in Federal Employment Programs. Lorraine A. Underwood. 53p. 1979. pap. text ed. 6.50 o.p. (ISBN 0-87766-242-8, 24400). Urban Inst.

Women in Futures Research. Ed. by Margrit Eichler & Hilda Scott. (Women's Studies Quarterly: Vol. 4, No. 1). (Illus.). 124p. 1982. 21.00 o.p. (ISBN 0-08-028100-1). Pergamon.

Women in India & Nepal. Michael Allen & Sal Mokherjee. 1982. pap. 24.00x o.p. (ISBN 0-908070-07-1, Pub. by Australia Nat Univ). South Asia Bks.

Women in India's Freedom Struggle. Manmohan Kaur. 1985. text ed. 35.00x o.p. (ISBN 0-86590-617-3, Pub. by Sterling Pubs India). Apt Bks.

Women in Law: Explorations in Law, Family & Sexuality. Ed. by Julia Brophy & Carol Smart. 192p. 1985. 26.95x o.p. (ISBN 0-7102-0607-0); pap. 12.95 o.p. (ISBN 0-7102-0259-8). Routledge Chapman & Hall.

Women in Love. D. H. Lawrence. LC 37-27406. 1937. 6.95 o.s.i. (ISBN 0-394-60442-3). Modern Lib.

Women in Migration. (IMR Special Issues Ser.). pap. 14.95 o.p. (A4). Ctr Migration.

Women in Ministry. L. E. Maxwell. 156p. 1987. pap. 6.95 o.p. (ISBN 0-89693-337-7). Victor Bks.

Women in Modern America: A Brief History. Lois W. Banner. (Harbrace History of the United States Ser.). 276p. (Orig.). 1974. pap. text ed. 11.95 o.p. (ISBN 0-15-596193-4, HC). HarBraceJ.

Women in Parliament Nineteen Eighteen to Nineteen Seventy. Beverly P. Stobaugh. 1978. 9.00 o.p. (ISBN 0-682-49056-3, University). Exposition-Phoenix.

Women in Revolutionary Paris, 1789-1795. Ed. by Darline G. Levy et al. LC 79-4102. 326p. 1979. text ed. 25.00 o.s.i. (ISBN 0-252-00409-4); pap. 9.95 o.s.i. (ISBN 0-252-00855-3). U of Ill Pr.

Women in Science: Portraits from a World in Transition. Vivian Gornick. 177p. 1983. 15.45 o.p. (ISBN 0-671-41738-X). S&S.

Women in Southeast Asia: A Bibliography. Kok S. Fan. 1982. lib. bdg. 57.50 o.p. (ISBN 0-8161-8407-0, Hall Reference). G K Hall.

Women in Sports: Records, Stars, Feats, & Facts. Louis Phillips & Karen Markoe. LC 79-87527. (Illus.). 192p. 1979. 2.95 o.p. (ISBN 0-15-299186-7, HJ). HarBraceJ.

Women in the Armed Forces. M. C. Devilbiss. LC 84-48010. 100p. 1986. lib. bdg. 15.00 o.p. (ISBN 0-8240-8911-1). Garland Pub.

Women in the Kibbutz. Lionel Tiger & Joseph Shepher. LC 76-13603. (Illus.). 1976. pap. 4.45 o.p. (ISBN 0-15-698300-1, Harv). HarBraceJ.

Women in the New Eden. Anne Voth. LC 82-24793. (Illus.). 224p. (Orig.). 1983. lib. bdg. 28.50 o.p. (ISBN 0-8191-2917-8); pap. text ed. 13.25 o.p. (ISBN 0-8191-2918-6). U Pr of Amer.

Women in the Wind. Margaret Ritter. 685p. 1985. 18.45 o.p. (ISBN 0-671-54327-X). S&S.

Women in World Trends: Facts & Trends. John McHale & Magda C. McHale. 63p. 1975. pap. text ed. 5.95x o.p. (ISBN 0-87855-726-1). Transaction Pubs.

Women Like Us: A Milestone Study Drawn from Women of the Harvard Business School Class of '75. Liz R. Gallese. LC 84-19095. 288p. 1985. 15.95 o.p. (ISBN 0-688-02176-X). Morrow.

Women Making It. Ruth Halcomb. LC 79-51129. 1979. 13.95 o.p. (ISBN 0-689-10995-4, Atheneum). Macmillan.

Women, Media, Crisis: Femininity & Disorder. Michele Mattelart. (Comedia Ser.). 128p. (Orig.). 1987. pap. 7.50 o.p. (ISBN 0-906890-96-9). M Boyars Pubs.

Women, Men, & the Division of Labor. Kathleen Newland. LC 80-51662. (Worldwatch Papers). 1980. pap. 4.00 o.p. (ISBN 0-916468-36-4). Worldwatch Inst.

Women of Asia: Yesterday & Today. Soon Man Rhim. 140p. (Orig.). 1982. pap. 7.95 o.p. (ISBN 0-377-00134-1). Friendship Pr.

Women of Cuba. Inger Holt-Seeland. LC 82-2889. (Illus.). 128p. 1982. 14.95 o.p. (ISBN 0-88208-142-X); pap. 7.95 o.p. (ISBN 0-88208-143-8). Chicago Review.

Women of Forty. M. E. Landau. 50p. 1957. (ISBN 0-8022-0913-0). Philos Lib.

Women of Ideas: And What Men Have Done to Them. Dale Spender. 800p. (Orig.). 1984. pap. 9.95 o.p. (ISBN 0-7448-0003-X, Ark Paperbks). Routledge Chapman & Hall.

Women of Iron & Velvet: French Women Writers After George Sand. Margaret Crosland. LC 75-8202. 192p. 1976. 10.95 o.s.i. (ISBN 0-8008-8436-1). Taplinger.

Women of Power: The Life & Times of Catherine de Medici. Mark Strage. LC 75-35771. (Helen Kurt Wolff Bk.). (Illus.). 416p. 1976. 12.95 o.p. (ISBN 0-15-198370-4). HarBraceJ.

Women of South Asia: A Guide to Resources. Carol Sakala. 1980. lib. bdg. 18.00 o.p. (ISBN 0-686-92573-4). French & Eur.

Women of the Mayflower & Women of Plymouth Colony. Ethel J. Noyes. LC 73-12780. 197p. Repr. of 1921 ed. 36.00x o.p. (ISBN 0-8103-3668-5). Gale.

Women of the Plains. Kate Sullivan. 1977. pap. 1.75 o.p. (ISBN 0-8439-0434-8, LB434, Pub. by Leisure Bks CT). Dorchester Pub Co.

Women of the Reformation: From Spain to Scandinavia. Roland H. Bainton. LC 76-27089. 1977. 9.95 o.p. (ISBN 0-8066-1568-0, 10-7245, Augsburg). Augsburg Fortress.

Women of the Reformation: In Germany & Italy. Roland H. Bainton. LC 70-135235. 1971. 11.95 o.p. (ISBN 0-8066-1116-2, 10-7240, Augsburg). Augsburg Fortress.

Women of the Soviet Union. Barbara Clements & Colette Shulman. 160p. 1987. 12.95 o.p. (ISBN 0-88738-707-1). Transaction Pubs.

Women of the Twenties. George H. Douglas. LC 86-1848. (Illus.). 230p. 1986. 16.95 o.s.i. (ISBN 0-933071-06-X). Saybrook Pub Co.

Women of the World: A Chartbook for Developing Regions. (Women in Development Ser.: No. 5). (Illus.). 72p. 1985. pap. 2.75 o.p. (ISBN 0-318-18873-2, S/N 003-024-06202-0). USGPO.

Women of Valor. Samuel Kostman. (MS Ser.). (YA) (gr. 7-12). 1978. PLB 8.97 o.p. (ISBN 0-8239-0425-3). Rosen Group.

Women of Value, Men of Renown: New Perspectives in Trobriand Exchange. Annette B. Weiner. (Illus.). 321p. 1976. pap. 20.00x o.p. (ISBN 0-292-79004-X). U of Tex Pr.

Women of Wisdom. Tsultrim Allione. (Illus.). 224p. (Orig.). 1985. pap. 12.95 o.p. (ISBN 0-7102-0240-7). Routledge Chapman & Hall.

Women of Wisdom. Tsultrim Allione. (Illus.). 320p. 1986. pap. 11.95 o.p. (ISBN 1-85063-044-5). Routledge Chapman & Hall.

Women on the Line. Ruth Cavendish. 166p. 1982. pap. 12.50x o.p. (ISBN 0-7100-0987-9). Routledge Chapman & Hall.

Women on the Porch. Caroline Gordon. LC 78-164524. 1972. Repr. of 1944 ed. 19.50x o.p. (ISBN 0-8154-0393-3). Cooper Sq.

Women Out of Bondage & in Love. Beatrice B. Kennedy. 1978. 4.00 o.p. (ISBN 0-682-49152-7). Exposition-Phoenix.

Women Physicians of the World: Autobiographies of Medical Pioneers. Leone M. Hellstedt. (Illus.). 1978. text ed. 37.50 o.p. (ISBN 0-07-027954-3). McGraw.

Women Pioneers of Science. rev. ed. Louis Haber. LC 79-87517. (gr. 5-9). 1979. 12.95 o.p. (ISBN 0-15-299202-2, HJ). HarBraceJ.

Women Poets of the World. Joanna Bankier & Deirdre Lashgari. 416p. 1983. pap. text ed. write for info. o.p. (ISBN 0-02-305720-3). Macmillan.

Women: Portraits. James B. Hall et al. (Patterns in Literary Art Ser.). 1976. text ed. 13.80 o.p. (ISBN 0-07-025575-X). McGraw.

Women, Power & Policy. Ellen Boneparth. (Pergamon Policy Studies on Social Policy). 300p. 1982. text ed. 47.00 o.p. (ISBN 0-08-028048-X); pap. 13.25 o.p. (ISBN 0-08-028047-1). Pergamon.

Women Public Opinion, & Politics: The Changing Political Attitudes of American Women. Keith Poole & L. Harmon Zeigler. LC 84-7155. 208p. 1984. text ed. 25.00 o.p. (ISBN 0-582-28274-8); pap. text ed. 13.95 o.p. (ISBN 0-582-28273-X). Longman.

Women Recounted: Narrative Thinking & the God of Israel. James G. Williams. (Bible & Literature Ser.: No. 6). 128p. pap. 10.95x o.s.i. (Pub. by Almond Pr England). Eisenbrauns.

Women-Search for Utopia. Date not set. (ISBN 0-8052-3900-6). Random.

Women See Men. I. Kalmus & R. Ripp. 1977. text ed. 12.95 o.p. (ISBN 0-07-033248-7). McGraw.

Women, Sexuality & Social Control. Carol Smart & Barry Smart. (Orig.). 1978. pap. 8.95x o.p. (ISBN 0-7100-8723-3). Routledge Chapman & Hall.

Women, Technology & Innovation. Ed. by Joan Rothschild. (Journal of Women's Studies International Quarterly 4(Si)). 88p. 1982. 23.00 o.p. (ISBN 0-08-028943-6). Pergamon.

Women under Attack: Victories, Backlash & the Fight for Reproductive Freedom. CARASA Collective Staff. Ed. by Sue Davis. 80p. (Orig.). 1988. pap. 5.00 o.p. (ISBN 0-89608-356-X). South End Pr.

Women under the Knife. Herbert Keyser. LC 83-61171. 160p. 1984. 9.95 o.p. (ISBN 0-89313-036-2). G F Stickley Co.

Women, Vol. 3 (incl. 1984-1987 Supplements, Vol. 3. Ed. by Eleanor C. Goldstein. (Social Issues Resources Ser.). 1988. 60.00 o.p. (ISBN 0-89777-076-5). Soc Issues.

Women, War, & Work: The Impact of World War I on Women in the United States. Maurine W. Greenwald. LC 80-540. (Contributions in Women's Studies: No. 12). (Illus.). xxvii, 309p. 1982. pap. 12.95 o.p. (ISBN 0-313-23606-2, GWWPB). Greenwood.

Women Who Made the West. Western Writers of America Staff. 1981. pap. 2.95 o.p. (ISBN 0-380-56507-2, 56507-2, Discus). Avon.

Women Who Made the West. Western Writers of America Staff. LC 79-8442. (Illus.). 1980. 11.95 o.p. (ISBN 0-385-15801-7). Doubleday.

Women Who Marry Houses: Panic & Protest in Agoraphobia. Robert Seidenberg & Karen DeCrow. LC 82-14934. 204p. 1983. text ed. 15.95 o.p. (ISBN 0-07-016284-0); pap. text ed. 7.95 o.p. (ISBN 0-07-016283-2). McGraw.

Women Who Want to Be Boss: Business Revelations & Success Strategies from America's Top Female Executives. Marlene Jensen. LC 86-16707. 192p. 1987. 15.95 o.p. (ISBN 0-385-23375-2). Doubleday.

Women Who Went Away. Firth Haring. LC 80-28832. 228p. 1981. 12.95 o.p. (ISBN 0-03-059514-2). H Holt & Co.

Women, Work, & Health: Challenge to Corporate Policy. Ed. by D. C. Walsh & R. H. Egdahl. (Springer Series on Industry & Health: Vol. 8). 259p. 1980. pap. 12.00 o.p. (ISBN 0-387-90478-6). Springer-Verlag.

Women Workers in the Japanese Cotton Mills: 1880-1920. Yasue A. Kidd. LC 78-108068. (East Asia Papers: No. 20). 81p. 1978. 3.00 o.p. (ISBN 0-939657-20-1). Cornell East Asia Pgm.

Women Working: Prostitution Now. Eileen McLeod. (Illus.). 180p. 1982. pap. 15.00 o.p. (ISBN 0-7099-1717-1, Pub. by Croom Helm Ltd). Routledge Chapman & Hall.

Women Working: Theories & Facts in Perspective. 2nd ed. Ed. by Ann H. Stromberg & Shirley Harkess. 448p. 1987. pap. 21.95 o.p. (ISBN 0-87484-744-3, Dist. by Kampmann). Mayfield Pub.

Women Working Together for Personal, Economic & Community Development. Suzanne Kindervatter. LC 83-61079. (Illus.). 103p. (Orig.). 1983. pap. text ed. 10.00 o.p. (ISBN 0-912917-01-6). OEF Intl.

Womenfolks: Growing up down South. Shirley Abbott. LC 82-16880. 224p. 1983. 13.45 o.p. (ISBN 0-89919-156-8). Ticknor & Fields.

Women's Activism & Social Change: Rochester, New York, 1822-1872. Nancy A. Wewitt. LC 83-45940. 288p. 1988. pap. 9.95x o.p. (ISBN 0-8014-9509-1). Cornell U Pr.

Women's & Men's Wars. Ed. by J. Stiehm. 90p. 1983. 18.75 o.p. (ISBN 0-08-027949-X). Pergamon.

Women's Annual, No. 1: 1980--The Year in Review. Ed. by Barbara Haber. 343p. 1981. 39.00 o.p. (ISBN 0-8161-8530-1, Hall Reference). G K Hall.

Women's Annual, No. 2: 1981--The Year in Review. Ed. by Barbara Haber. 344p. 1982. lib. bdg. 39.00 o.p. (ISBN 0-8161-8614-6, Hall Reference). G K Hall.

Women's Basketball. 2nd ed. Mildred J. Barnes. (Illus.). 1980. text ed. write for info. o.p. (ISBN 0-205-06604-6, 6266045). Allyn.

Women's Changing Role. Rev. ed. Ed. by Mark A. Siegel & Nancy R. Siegel. (Information Aids Ser.). 96p. 1986. pap. text ed. 15.95 o.p. (ISBN 0-936474-58-0). Info Plus TX.

Women's Changing Role. (Information Aids Ser.). 96p. 1986. pap. 14.95 o.p. Info Plus TX.

Women's Coats, Suits, Rainwear & Furs. Fairchild Market Research Division Staff. (Fairchild Fact Files Ser.). (Illus.). 55p. 1985. pap. 17.50 o.p. (ISBN 0-87005-523-2). Fairchild.

Women's Drug Store. Harold M. Silverman. (Orig.). 1985. pap. 9.95 o.p. (ISBN 0-440-59648-3, Dell Trade Pbks). Dell.

Women's Imprisonment: The Meanings of Women's Imprisonment in Scotland. Pat Carlen. 192p. (Orig.). 1983. pap. 10.50x o.p. (ISBN 0-7100-9441-8). Routledge Chapman & Hall.

Women's Inner Fashions: Nightwear, Daywear, & Loungewear. Fairchild Market Research Division Staff. (Fairchild Fact Files Ser.). (Illus.). 55p. 1985. pap. 17.50 o.p. (ISBN 0-87005-520-8). Fairchild.

Women's Lacrosse for Coaches & Players. Agnes B. Kurtz. LC 77-85214. (Illus.). 1979. pap. text ed. 8.95 o.p. (ISBN 0-9601420-1-0). ABK Pubns.

Women's Liberation & Literature. Elaine Showalter. 1971. pap. text ed. 8.00 o.p. (ISBN 0-15-596195-0, HC). HarBraceJ.

Women's Liberation & the Dialectics of Revolution Reaching for the Future: A 35-Year Collection of Essays - Historic, Philosophic, Global. R. Dunayevskaya. 302p. 1985. text ed. 39.95x o.p. (ISBN 0-391-03318-2); pap. text ed. 15.95 o.p. (ISBN 0-391-03349-2). Humanities.

Women's Liberation in China. Claudie Broyelle. Tr. by Michele Cohen & Gary Herman. LC 76-4524. (Marxist Theory & Contemporary Capitalism Ser.). 1977. text ed. 22.50x o.p. (ISBN 0-391-00587-1). Humanities.

Women's Liberation Movement: Europe & North America. Ed. by J. Bradshaw. 100p. 1982. 23.00 o.p. (ISBN 0-08-028932-0). Pergamon.

Women's Networks. Carol Kleinman. 1981. pap. 2.95 o.s.i. (ISBN 0-345-29355-X). Ballantine.

Women's Pictures: Feminism & Cinema. Annette Kuhn. 200p. (Orig.). 1982. pap. 10.50 o.p. (ISBN 0-7100-9044-7). Routledge Chapman & Hall.

Women's Rights Movement in Iran: Mutiny, Appeasement, & Repression from 1900 to Khomeini. Eliz Sanasarian. 190p. 1982. pap. 15.95 o.p. (ISBN 0-275-91587-5, B1587). Praeger.

Women's Rites: Essays in the Erotic Imagination. Jeanne De Berg. Tr. by Anselm Hollo from Fr. LC 86-45524. 128p. 1987. 15.95 o.s.i. (ISBN 0-8021-0048-1). Grove.

Women's Roles: A Cross-Cultural Perspective. Eileen Newmark. 128p. 1981. pap. 10.25 o.p. (ISBN 0-08-026073-X). Pergamon.

Women's Roles & Population Trends in the Third World. Ed. by Richard Anker et al. 288p. 1982. 33.50 o.p. (ISBN 0-7099-0508-4, Pub. by Croom Helm Ltd). Routledge Chapman & Hall.

Women's Room. Marilyn French. LC 77-24918. 1977. 12.95 o.s.i. (ISBN 0-671-40010-X). Summit Bks.

Women's Silence, Men's Violence: Sexual Assault in England, 1770-1845. Anna Clark. 192p. pap. 12.95 o.p. (ISBN 0-7102-0971-1, 09711, Pub. by Routledge UK). Routledge Chapman & Hall.

Women's Studies. James E. Davis & Hazel R. Davis. 108p. 1981. 6.25 o.p. (ISBN 0-8141-5811-0). NCTE.

Women's Studies: A Recommended Core Bibliography. Esther Stineman & Catherine Loeb. LC 79-13679. 670p. 1979. lib. bdg. 45.00x o.p. (ISBN 0-87287-196-7). Libs Unl.

Women's Vote: Beyond the Nineteenth Amendment. League of Women Voters Education Fund. (Illus.). 1983. pap. 1.75 o.p. (425). Scott F.

Women's Welfare-Women's Rights. Ed. by Jane Lewis. (Illus.). 240p. 1982. 29.25 o.p. (ISBN 0-7099-1610-8, Pub. by Croom Helm); pap. 13.50 o.p. (ISBN 0-7099-4100-5). Routledge Chapman & Hall.

Women's Wiles. Michele Slung. LC 79-1835. 1979. 9.95 o.p. (ISBN 0-15-198421-2). HarBraceJ.

Women's World Handbook. Dorothy VanderKaay. LC 74-79541. 1983. 3.95 o.p. (ISBN 0-87227-063-7); pap. 2.25 o.p. (ISBN 0-87227-048-3). Reg Baptist.

Wonder-Book. Nathaniel Hawthorne. Bd. with Tanglewood Tales. (gr. 9 up). 9.95 o.p. (ISBN 0-395-07079-1). HM.

Wonder Book of Trains. (gr. k-3). 1980. 0.79 o.p. (ISBN 0-8431-4158-1). Wonder.

Wonder-Filled. Mary Fearon & Mary J. Tully. 1983. pap. 4.00 o.p. (ISBN 0-697-01853-9); tchr's. manual 6.00 o.p. (ISBN 0-697-01854-7); parent book 3.75 o.p. (ISBN 0-697-01855-5). Wm C Brown.

Wonder O' the Wind. W. Phillip Keller. 1982. 9.95 o.p. (ISBN 0-8499-0337-8). Word Bks.

Wonder of His Love. Palmer T. Ellard. 26p. 1985. 5.95 o.p. (ISBN 0-533-06379-5). Vantage.

Wonder of the Real: A Sketch in Basic Philosophy. rev., enlarged ed. Francis J. Klauder. LC 72-94706. (Illus.). 116p. 1973. 9.95 o.p. (ISBN 0-8158-0300-1). Chris Mass.

Wonder of Words: An Introduction to Language for Every Man. Isaac Goldberg. LC 74-164294. 502p. 1971. Repr. of 1938 ed. 48.00x o.p. (ISBN 0-8103-3777-0). Gale.

Wonder World of Ants. Wilfrid S. Bronson. LC 37-27454. (Illus.). (gr. 3-7). 1937. 5.25 o.p. (ISBN 0-15-299287-1, HJ). HarBraceJ.

Wonderful Pumpkin. Lennart Hellsing. LC 75-24223. Orig. Title: Underbara Pumpan. (Illus.). (ps-3). 1975. 5.95 o.p. (ISBN 0-689-50056-4, Atheneum). Macmillan.

Wonderful Shrinking Shirt. Leone C. Anderson. Ed. by Ann Fay. LC 83-1297. (Just for Fun Bks.). (Illus.). (gr. k-2). 1983. PLB 10.75 o.p. (ISBN 0-8075-9171-8). A Whitman.

Wonderful Surprise. Martha Marshall. LC 83-7343. (Illus.). 32p. (gr. 1-2). 1983. PLB 4.95 o.p. (ISBN 0-89693-214-1). Dandelion Hse.

Wonderful Ways with Food. Margaret D. Murphy. Ed. by Marilyn G. Kostick. LC 82-71811. (Illus.). 144p. 1982. 10.95 o.p. (ISBN 0-916752-58-5); pap. 5.95 o.p. (ISBN 0-916752-60-7). Longman Trade.

Wonderful World of Coca-Cola. Norman Shavin & Martin Shartar. (Illus.). 68p. 1987. pap. 4.95 o.s.i. (ISBN 0-910719-01-2). Spanish edition (ISBN 0-910719-20-9). Capricorn Corp.

Wonderful World of Cooking see Wisconsin Country Cookbook & Journal.

Wonderful World of Ginkel Bugs. Helen Lowry. 32p. 1987. 6.50 o.p. (ISBN 0-8062-2928-4). Carlton.

Wonderful World of Mammals: Adventuring with Stamps. Roger Caras. LC 73-5235. (Illus.). (gr. 4-6). 1973. 6.95 o.p. (ISBN 0-15-299300-2, HJ). HarBraceJ.

Wonderful World of Oprah. J. Dooley. 128p. (Orig.). 1988. pap. 2.95 o.p. (ISBN 1-55547-238-9). Critics Choice Paper.

Wonderful World of Professional Golf. Mark H. McCormack. LC 68-13716. (Illus.). 1973. 20.00 o.p. (ISBN 0-689-10550-9, Atheneum). Macmillan.

Wondering. James Campbell et al. (Themepaks Ser.). (gr. 1-6). 1976. 4.95 o.p. (ISBN 0-8042-1461-1, John Knox). Westminster John Knox.

Wonderous Power, Wonderous Love. 250p. 1983. 8.95 o.p. (ISBN 0-89066-048-4); pap. 5.95 o.p. (ISBN 0-89066-052-2). World Wide Pubs.

Wonders Around the Sun. Mary G. Bonner. (Illus.). (gr. 4-7). PLB 6.19 o.p. (ISBN 0-8313-0010-8). Lantern.

Wonders from the Heavens. Ruth Starr. 1977. 7.00 o.p. (ISBN 0-682-48828-3). Exposition-Phoenix.

Wonders of Cattle. Vincent Scuro. LC 80-1019. (Wonders Ser.). (Illus.). 80p. (gr. 4 up). 1980. PLB 9.95 o.p. (ISBN 0-396-07892-3). Dodd.

Wonders of Inventions. Mary G. Bonner. (Illus.). (gr. 4-9). 1961. PLB 6.19 o.p. (ISBN 0-8313-0007-8). Lantern.

Wonders of Italy. 16th rev. ed. Ed. by J. Fattorusso. (Illus.). 1974. 60.00 o.s.i. (ISBN 0-685-12054-6). E J Brill USA.

Wonders of Mules. Lavine & Scuro. (Illus.). 64p. 8.00 o.p. (ISBN 0-318-01794-6). Am Donkey.

Wonders of Seeds. Alfred Stefferud. LC 56-6921. (gr. 5 up). 1956. 4.95 o.p. (ISBN 0-15-299466-1, HJ). HarBraceJ.

Wonders: Writings & Drawings for the Child in Us All. Ed. by Jonathan Cott & Mary Gimbel. LC 80-17146. (Rolling Stone Press Bk.). (Illus.). 1980. 17.95 o.s.i. (ISBN 0-671-40053-3). Summit Bks.

Wondrous Apple. L. Kuzmin. 87p. 1985. 6.95 o.p. (ISBN 0-8285-3199-4, Pub. by Raduga Pubs USSR). Imported Pubns.

Wood Adhesives: Chemistry & Technology, Vol. 2. Pizzi. 424p. 1989. 125.00 o.p. Dekker.

Wood As a Raw Material. G. Tsoumis. 1968. text ed. 19.00 o. p. o.p. (ISBN 0-08-012378-3). Pergamon.

Wood As an Industrial Arts Material. Wayne K. Murphey & Richard Jorgensen. 1974. 31.00 o.p. (ISBN 0-08-017906-1); pap. 17.00 o.p. (ISBN 0-08-017907-X). Pergamon.

Wood Carvers of Cordova, New Mexico: Social Dimensions of an Artistic "Revival" Charles L. Briggs. LC 79-20883. 272p. 1980. 26.95x o.p. (ISBN 0-87049-275-6). U of Tenn Pr.

Wood Carving. George Jack. 1978. pap. 9.95 o.s.i. (ISBN 0-8008-8462-0, Pentalic). Taplinger.

Wood Finishing. J. W. Collier. 1967. 65.00 o.p. (ISBN 0-08-011242-0). Pergamon.

Wood Finishing & Refinishing. Alan Hall & James Heard. LC 81-4708. (Illus.). 216p. 1982. 16.95 o.p. (ISBN 0-03-018856-3, Owl Bks); pap. 9.95 o.p. (ISBN 0-03-018861-X). H Holt & Co.

Wood-Frame Housed Construction. L. O. Anderson. (Agriculture Handbook Ser.: 73). (Illus.). 275p. 1975. pap. 7.50 o.p. (ISBN 0-318-23854-3). USGPO.

Wood Heat Safety. Jay W. Shelton. LC 79-17951. (Illus.). 165p. 1979. pap. 9.95 o.s.i. (ISBN 0-88266-160-4, Garden Way Pub). Storey Comm Inc.

Wood Materials & Processes. John L. Feirer. (Illus.). 592p. 1976. encore ed 13.75 o.p. (ISBN 0-684-17585-1, ScribT). Scribner.

Wood Notes: A Companion & Guide for Birdwatchers. Richard H. Wood. (Illus.). 192p. 1984. 15.95 o.p. (ISBN 0-13-962580-1); pap. 6.95 o.p. (ISBN 0-13-962572-0). P-H.

Wood Polishing & Finishing Techniques. Aidan Walker. 1986. 9.95 o.p. (ISBN 0-316-91847-4). Little.

Wood Warblers' World. Hal H. Harrison. (Illus.). 288p. 1984. 19.45 o.p. (ISBN 0-671-47798-6). S&S.

Wood Warbler's World. Hal H. Harrison. 1986. pap. 10.95 o.p. (ISBN 0-671-62098-3, Fireside). S&S.

Woodall's Campground Directory, 1983: North American. pap. 13.50 o.p. (ISBN 0-671-45921-X). Woodall.

Woodall's Campground Directory, 1983: Western Edition. pap. 8.25 o.p. (ISBN 0-671-45923-6). Woodall.

Woodall's Eastern Campground Directory. 1984 ed. 900p. 1984. pap. 7.95 o.p. (ISBN 0-671-49463-5). S&S.

Woodall's Eastern Campground Directory 1985. 1000p. 1985. pap. 8.95 o.p. (ISBN 0-671-54217-6). Woodall.

Woodall's Eastern Campground Directory, 1986. 1000p. 1986. pap. 7.95 o.s.i. (ISBN 0-671-60646-8). Woodall.

Woodall's Eastern Campground Directory, 1988. 1100p. 1988. pap. 8.95 o.p. (ISBN 0-671-64735-0). Woodall.

Woodall's Eastern Tent Camping Guide 1988. 300p. 1988. pap. 7.95 o.p. (ISBN 0-671-65919-7). Woodall.

Woodall's North American Campground Directory. 1984 ed. 1000p. 1984. pap. 12.95 o.s.i. (ISBN 0-671-49461-9). S&S.

Woodall's North American Campground Directory 1985. 1500p. 1985. pap. 12.95 o.p. (ISBN 0-671-54218-4). Woodall.

Woodall's North American Campground Directory, 1986. 1500p. 1986. pap. 12.95 o.s.i. (ISBN 0-671-60645-X). Woodall.

Woodall's North American Campground Directory, 1988. 1700p. 1988. pap. 13.95 o.p. (ISBN 0-671-64736-9). Woodall.

Woodall's Tenting Directory, 1985: Central Edition. 1985. pap. 6.95 o.p. (ISBN 0-671-55515-4). Woodall.

Woodall's Tenting Directory, 1985: Western Edition. 1985. pap. 6.95 o.p. (ISBN 0-671-55516-2). Woodall.

Woodall's Tenting Directory, 1986: Eastern Edn. Ed. by Woodall's Staff. 1986. pap. 6.95 o.s.i. (ISBN 0-671-61288-3). Woodall.

Woodall's Western Campground Directory. 1984 ed. 500p. 1984. pap. 7.95 o.p. (ISBN 0-671-49462-7). S&S.

Woodall's Western Campground Directory, 1986. 500p. 1986. pap. 7.95 o.s.i. (ISBN 0-671-60647-6). Woodall.

Woodall's Western Campground Directory, 1988. 600p. 1988. pap. 8.95 o.p. (ISBN 0-671-64737-7). Woodall.

Woodall's Western Campground Directory: 1985 Edition. 500p. 1985. pap. 8.95 o.p. (ISBN 0-671-54216-8). S&S.

Woodcarving, with Projects. Jack Wiley. (Illus.). 354p. (Orig.). 1984. 16.95 o.p. (ISBN 0-8306-0639-4, 1639); pap. 11.15 o.p. (ISBN 0-8306-1639-X). TAB Bks.

Wooden Man. Max Bolliger. LC 74-1141. (Illus.). 24p. (ps-3). 1979. pap. 6.95 o.p. (ISBN 0-395-28769-3, Clarion). HM.

Wooden People. Myra Paperny. (Illus.). (gr. 7-12). 1976. 8.95 o.p. (ISBN 0-316-69040-6). Little.

Wooden Ship. Jan Adkins. (Illus.). (gr. 5 up). 1978. 6.95 o.p. (ISBN 0-395-26449-9). HM.

Wooden Toys & Games. Ralph F. Parkison. LC 83-70775. (Illus.). 224p. (Orig.). 1984. pap. 10.95 o.p. (ISBN 0-8019-7295-7). Chilton.

Woodframe Furniture Restoration. Alan Smith. 1986. 9.95 o.p. (ISBN 0-316-80172-0). Little.

Woodland Conservation & Management. George Peterken. 350p. 1981. 55.00x o.p. (ISBN 0-412-12820-9, NO. 6405, Pub. by Chapman & Hall England). Routledge Chapman & Hall.

Woodland Crossings. Stephen Krensky. LC 77-21244. (Illus.). (gr. 1-4). 1978. 5.95 o.p. (ISBN 0-689-30630-X, Atheneum). Macmillan.

Woodland Walks in Britain. Gerald Wilkinson. (Illus.). 320p. 1985. 19.95 o.p. (ISBN 0-03-005853-8). H Holt & Co.

Woodpile Mouse & Other Stories. Duane J. Parks. 32p. (ps-5). 1986. 5.75 o.p. (ISBN 0-8062-2774-5). Carlton.

Woodrow Wilson: A Great Life in Brief. John A. Garraty. LC 76-54860. 1977. Repr. of 1956 ed. lib. bdg. 22.50x o.p. (ISBN 0-8371-9371-0, GAWW). Greenwood.

Woodrow Wilson: Life & Letters, 8 vols. Ray S. Baker. LC 68-8332. (Illus.). 1971. Repr. of 1939 ed. Set. lib. bdg. 222.00x o.p. (ISBN 0-8371-0010-0, BAWW); Vol. 1. lib. bdg. (ISBN 0-8371-1789-5, BAWA); Vol. 2. lib. bdg. (ISBN 0-8371-0866-7, BAWB); Vol. 3. lib. bdg. (ISBN 0-8371-0867-5, BAWC); Vol. 4. lib. bdg. (ISBN 0-8371-0868-3, BAWD); Vol. 5. lib. bdg. (ISBN 0-8371-0869-1, BAWE); Vol. 6. lib. bdg. (ISBN 0-8371-0870-5, BAWF); Vol. 7. lib. bdg. (ISBN 0-8371-0871-3, BAWG); Vol. 8. lib. bdg. (ISBN 0-8371-0872-1, BAWH). Greenwood.

Woods Hole Cantata: Essays on Science & Society. Gerald Weissmann. 256p. 1985. 14.95 o.p. (ISBN 0-396-08618-7). Dodd.

Woods Words. Walter F. McCulloch. 219p. 1958. pap. 19.95 o.p. (Pub. by Oregon Historical Society & Champorg Press). Miller Freeman.

Woodsmoke. Susan Sibley. 1979. pap. 1.95 o.p. (ISBN 0-380-45435-1). Avon.

Woodstock Art Heritage. Ed. by The Woodstock Artists Association Staff. 1988. pap. 24.95 o.p. (ISBN 0-317-67053-0). Overlook Pr.

Woodturner's Handbook. Frank W. Coggins. (Illus.). 224p. 21.95 o.p. (ISBN 0-8306-0769-2, 1769); pap. 12.60 o.p. (ISBN 0-8306-1769-8, 1769P). TAB Bks.

Woodturning Handbook: With Projects. Lewis H. Hodges. (Illus.). 240p. (Orig.). 1984. 21.95 o.p. (ISBN 0-8306-0655-6); pap. 14.15 o.p. (ISBN 0-8306-1655-1, 1655). TAB Bks.

Woodturning in Pictures. Bruce Boulter. (Illus.). 144p. 1983. pap. 12.95 o.p. (ISBN 0-8069-7742-6). Sterling.

Woodwind Instruments & Their History. rev. ed. Anthony Baines. (Illus.). 1963. 11.95x o.p. (ISBN 0-393-09723-4, NortonC). Norton.

Woodwork - for Student, Apprentice & Handyman. Frank Wilkins. 373p. 1986. 23.95 o.p. (ISBN 0-7233-0644-3, Pub. by Whitcoulls NZ). Intl Spec Bk.

Woodworker's Handbook: A Complete Course for Craftsmen, Do-It-Yourselfers & Hobbyists. London College of Furniture Staff & Victor Hutchins. (Illus.). 216p. 1984. 27.95 o.p. (ISBN 0-668-06162-6, 6162-6). Arco.

Woodworker's Reference Guide & Sourcebook. John L. Feirer. (Illus.). 384p. 1983. 35.00 o.s.i. (ISBN 0-684-17859-1, ScribT). Scribner.

Woodworking Projects I. 2nd ed. Sunset Editors. LC 75-6222. (Illus.). 96p. 1975. pap. 5.95 o.s.i. (ISBN 0-376-04885-9, Sunset Bks.). Sunset-Lane.

Woof! Danae Dobson. 1985. pap. 3.95 o.p. (ISBN 0-8499-3024-3, 3024-3). Word Bks.

Wool Growth. Michael L. Ryder & Stuart K. Stephenson. LC 66-16694. (Illus.). 1968. 104.00 o.p. (ISBN 0-12-605150-X). Acad Pr.

Woolcraft Book: Spinning, Dyeing, & Weaving. Constance Jackson & Judith Plowman. (Illus.). 192p. 1982. 24.95 o.s.i. (ISBN 0-684-17419-7, ScribT). Scribner.

Wooster of the Middle West, Vol. 1. Lucy L. Notestein. LC 38-718. 345p. 1971. Repr. of 1937 ed. 15.00x o.p. (ISBN 0-87338-111-4). Kent St U Pr.

Wooster of the Middle West, Vol. 2. Lucy L. Notestein. LC 38-718. 444p. 1971. 15.00x o.p. (ISBN 0-87338-104-1). Kent St U Pr.

Worcester Blue & White Porcelain, 1751-1790. Lawrence Branyan et al. (Illus.). 367p. 1981. 105.00 o.p. (ISBN 0-09-144060-2, Pub. by Barrie & Jenkins England). Seven Hills Bk Dists.

Worcester Porcelain: From the Klepser Collection. Simon Spero. (Illus.). 256p. 1985. 48.00 o.s.i. (ISBN 0-8390-0342-0). Abner Schram Ltd.

Word. John C. Souter. 96p. 1985. 4.95 o.p. (ISBN 0-8423-8394-8). Tyndale.

Word Accomplished. A. B. Christopher. (ISBN 0-8022-0246-2). Philos Lib.

Word Alchemy. Lenore Kandel. 1970. pap. 2.45 o.p. (ISBN 0-394-17303-1, E439, Ever). Grove.

Word & Faith. Gerhard Ebling. 444p. pap. 15.75 o.p. (ISBN 0-317-31483-1, 30-1803-259, Fortress). Augsburg Fortress.

Word Association. Phebe Cramer. LC 68-14652. 1968. 27.50 o.p. (ISBN 0-12-196450-7). Acad Pr.

Word Bible Handbook. Lawrence O. Richards. 1982. 10.95 o.p. (ISBN 0-8499-0279-7). Word Bks.

Word Book. American Heritage Dictionary Editors. LC 76-698. 1976. 3.95 o.p. (ISBN 0-395-24521-4). HM.

Word Directory: Spelling-Division. Adele Christoffers. 1957. 5.50 o.p. (ISBN 0-682-40023-8). Exposition-Phoenix.

Word Discoveries see Diagnostic Prescriptive Reading Program.

Word for Word. Andrew A. Rooney. 288p. 1986. 16.95 o.p. (ISBN 0-399-13200-7, Perigee Bks). Putnam Pub Group.

Word for Word: A Comparative Guide to Word Processing Software. Janet Crider. 250p. (Orig.). 1984. pap. text ed. 16.95 o.p. (ISBN 0-07-881154-6). Osborne-McGraw.

Word for Word: The Rewriting of Fiction. Wallace Hildick. 1966. pap. 2.95x o.p. (ISBN 0-393-09674-2, NortonC). Norton.

Word Game: Improving Communications. Edgar Dale. LC 75-19957. (Fastback Ser.: No. 60). (Orig.). 1975. pap. 0.90 o.p. (ISBN 0-87367-060-4). Phi Delta Kappa.

Word Gifts: Keys to Charismatic Power. Fred Lilly. 100p. (Orig.). 1984. pap. 2.95 o.p. (ISBN 0-89283-182-0). Servant.

Word Grammar. Richard Hudson. 300p. 1984. 49.95x o.p. (ISBN 0-631-13186-8). Basil Blackwell.

Word in Action: The Acts of the Apostles for Our Time. Ross Mackenzie. LC 72-6968. 128p. (Orig.). 1973. pap. 3.25 o.p. (ISBN 0-8042-9088-1, John Knox). Westminster John Knox.

Word in Season: Essays in Honour of William McKane. James D. Martin & Phillip R. Davies. (JSOT Supplement Ser.: No. 42). 225p. pap. text ed. 15.95x o.s.i. (Pub. by JSOT Pr England). Eisenbrauns.

Word-Information Processing: Applications, Skills & Procedures. L. Joyce Arntson. LC 82-18009. 434p. 1983. 21.50 o.p. (ISBN 0-534-01345-7). PWS-Kent Pub.

Word Made Flesh: The Meaning of the Christmas Season. Pope John Paul II. LC 84-47738. 144p. 1985. 11.49 o.s.i. (ISBN 0-06-064203-3). HarpR.

Word Made Fresh, Vol. 1: Genesis - Kings. Andrew Edington. LC 75-13457. 249p. (Orig.). 1975. pap. 4.95 o.p. (ISBN 0-8042-0075-0, John Knox). Westminster John Knox.

Word Made Fresh, Vol. 2: Chronicles - Malachi. Andrew Edington. LC 75-+011. 294p. (Orig.). 1975. pap. 4.95 o.p. (ISBN 0-8042-0076-9, John Knox). Westminster John Knox.

Word Made Fresh, Vol. 3: New Testament. Andrew Edington. LC 75-13457. 1976. pap. 5.95 o.p. (ISBN 0-8042-0077-7, John Knox). Westminster John Knox.

Word Meanings in the New Testament: Hebrews-Revelation, Vol. 6. Ralph Earle. 174p. 1984. 9.95 o.p. (ISBN 0-8341-0943-3). Beacon Hill.

Word Meanings in the New Testament, Vol. 3: Romans. Ralph Earle. 264p. 1974. 9.95 o.p. (ISBN 0-8341-0512-8). Beacon Hill.

Word Meanings in the New Testament, Vol. 1: Matthew, Mark, Luke. Ralph Earle. 285p. 1980. 9.95 o.p. (ISBN 0-8341-0683-3). Beacon Hill.

Word Meanings in the New Testament, Vol. 5: Philemon-Philippians. Ralph Earle. 1977. 9.95 o.p. (ISBN 0-8341-0493-8). Beacon Hill.

Word Meanings in the New Testament: 1 & 2 Corinthians, Ephesians, Vol. 4. Ralph Earle. 350p. 1979. 9.95 o.p. (ISBN 0-8341-0567-5). Beacon Hill.

Word, Object, & Conceptual Development. Jeremy M. Anglin. (Illus.). 1977. 14.95x o.p. (ISBN 0-393-01132-1). Norton.

Word of God: A Guide to English Versions of the Bible. Lloyd R. Bailey. LC 81-85335. 228p. 1982. 4.75 o.p. (ISBN 0-8042-0079-3, John Knox). Westminster John Knox.

Word of God in Words: Reading & Preaching the Gospels. Bernard B. Scott. LC 85-5227. (Fortress Resources for Preaching). 96p. 1985. pap. 1.95 o.p. (ISBN 0-8006-1142-X, 1-1142, Fortress). Augsburg Fortress.

Word of God, Word of Earth. Davie Napier. LC 75-45312. 120p. 1976. 5.95 o.p. (ISBN 0-8298-0304-1); pap. 3.25 o.p. (ISBN 0-8298-0307-6). Pilgrim NY.

Word of Honor. Nelson DeMille. (Special Editions Ser.). 930p. 1986. lib. bdg. 21.95 o.p. (ISBN 0-8161-4082-0, Large Print Bks); pap. 13.95 o.p. (ISBN 0-8161-4083-9, Large Print Bks.). G K Hall.

Word or Two with You. Eve Merriam. LC 81-1282. (Illus.). 40p. (gr. 4 up). 1981. 9.95 o.s.i. (ISBN 0-689-30862-0, Atheneum Childrens Bks). Macmillan.

Word Parents Handbook. Lawrence O. Richards. 1983. 9.95 o.p. (ISBN 0-8499-0328-9). Word Bks.

Word: People Participating in Preaching. Martin E. Marty. LC 83-16611. 112p. 1984. pap. 3.95 o.p. (ISBN 0-8006-1778-9, 1-1778, Fortress). Augsburg Fortress.

Word Pictures. Josephine K. Chastain. 108p. 1983. 7.00 o.p. (ISBN 0-682-49950-1). Exposition-Phoenix.

Word Power: A Short Guide to Vocabulary & Spelling. rev. ed. Byron H. Gibson. 1975. pap. 4.00 o.p. (ISBN 0-912112-22-0). Everett-Edwards.

Word Processing. Thomas J. Anderson & W. Trotter. LC 73-94097. (Illus.). 192p. 1974. 23.95 o.p. (ISBN 0-8144-5356-2); user's manual 9.95 o.p. AMACOM.

Word Processing: A Systems Approach to the Office. Helen M. McCabe & Estelle L. Popham. (Illus.). 180p. (Orig.). 1977. pap. text ed. 12.00 net o.p. (ISBN 0-15-596666-9, HC). HarBraceJ.

Word Processing: An Up-to-Date Assessment. Ed. by Online Conferences Ltd. 1978. pap. text ed. 53.00x o.p. (ISBN 0-903796-46-5, Pub. by Online Conference England). Gower Pub Co.

Word Processing & Beyond: The Introductory Computer Book. Fred Stern. LC 83-62394. (Illus.). 221p. 1983. pap. 9.95 o.p. (ISBN 0-912528-32-X). John Muir.

Word Processing Buyer's Guide. Arthur Naiman. LC 82-17898. (Illus.). 304p. 1983. pap. text ed. 19.95 o.p. (ISBN 0-07-045869-3, BYTE Bks). McGraw.

Word Processing: Current Practices & Future Developments. 327p. (Orig.). 1980. pap. text ed. 88.00x o.p. (ISBN 0-903796-55-4, Pub. by Online Conferences England). Gower Pub Co.

Word Processing Equipment Survey. Derek Skelcher. 222p. (Orig.). 1980. pap. 137.50 o.p. (ISBN 0-903796-56-2, Pub. by Online Conferences England). Gower Pub Co.

Word Processing for Executives & Professionals. Timothy R. Foster. 160p. 1983. 25.95 o.p. (ISBN 0-442-22717-5). Van Nos Reinhold.

Word Processing for Solicitors. Kevin Townsend & Kate Taphouse. 186p. 1983. text ed. 37.00 o.p. (ISBN 0-566-03450-6). Gower Pub Co.

Word Processing for the IBM PC & PCjr & Compatible Computers. Carol B. Matthews & Martin S. Matthews. (Illus.). 428p. 1985. pap. text ed. 20.95 o.p. (ISBN 0-07-040952-8, Byte Bks). McGraw.

Word Processing Handbook. Katherine Aschner. pap. 8.95 o.s.i. (ISBN 0-88908-913-2, 9530). TAB Bks.

Word Processing Handbook: A Step-by-Step Guide to Automating the Office. Katherine Aschner. 200p. 1983. pap. 24.95 o.p. (ISBN 0-442-21076-0). Van Nos Reinhold.

Word Processing Handbook: Wang OIS 142 System. Jacklyn M. Williford. LC 83-16683. 116p. 1984. pap. 14.95 o.p. (ISBN 0-471-88258-5, 1-999). Wiley.

Word Processing in the Transitional Office. Joseph L Kish, Jr. (Illus.). 208p. 1985. 31.95 o.p. (ISBN 0-442-24713-3). Van Nos Reinhold.

Word Processing Made Simple. Ronald W. Hadley et al. 512p. 1984. spiral bound 40.00x o.p. (ISBN 0-669-07410-1). Lexington Bks.

Word Processing Mastery for Everyone: Typewriter Drills for Learning Keyboarding. Sheryl L. Lindsell. LC 83-9947. 128p. 1984. spiral bdg. 8.95 o.p. (ISBN 0-668-05752-1); lib. bdg. 12.95 o.p. (ISBN 0-668-06035-2). Arco.

Word Processing on the IBM Personal Computer. Danny Goodman. LC 83-50376. 464p. 1983. pap. 19.95 o.p. (ISBN 0-672-22081-4, 22081). Sams.

Word Processing: Selection, Implementation & Usage into the 80's. 358p. 1981. pap. text ed. 98.00x o.p. (ISBN 0-903796-76-7, Pub. by Online Conferences England). Gower Pub Co.

Word Processing: Selection, Implementation & Uses. Ed. by Online Conference, Ltd. 1979. text ed. 63.50x o.p. (ISBN 0-903796-32-5, Pub. by Online Conference England). Gower Pub Co.

Word Processing Simplified & Self-Taught. Joseph Coleman. LC 82-24501. (Simplified & Self-Taught Ser.). (Illus.). 128p. 1983. lib. bdg. 11.95 o.p. (ISBN 0-668-05599-5); pap. 4.95 o.p. (ISBN 0-668-05601-0). Arco.

Word Processing Software for the IBM PC. P. B. Seybold & R. T. Marshak. (Illus.). 201p. 1985. pap. text ed. 16.95 o.p. (ISBN 0-07-056322-5, Byte Bks). McGraw.

Word Processing Users' Manual. Thomas J. Anderson & William R. Trotter. LC 73-94097. 1976. pap. 12.95 o.p. (ISBN 0-8144-5424-0). AMACOM.

Word Processing with the IBM PC. Jeremy Hewes & Bill Grout. LC 85-12381. (IBM Personal Computer Ser.: 1-646). 178p. 1985. pap. 16.95 o.p. (ISBN 0-471-88663-7). Wiley.

Word Processing with Your ADAM. Barbara Spear. (Illus.). 160p. (Orig.). 1984. 15.95 o.p. (ISBN 0-8306-0766-8); pap. 8.95 o.p. (ISBN 0-8306-1766-3, 1766). TAB Bks.

Word Processor Buyer's Survival Manual. Ralph Roberts. (Illus.). 320p. (Orig.). 1984. 18.95 o.p. (ISBN 0-8306-0642-4); pap. 10.60 o.p. (ISBN 0-8306-1642-X, 1642). TAB Bks.

Word Shadows of the Great: The Lure of Autograph Collecting. Thomas F. Madigan. LC 70-145705. (Illus.). 318p. 1971. Repr. of 1930 ed. 43.00x o.p. (ISBN 0-8103-3378-3). Gale.

Word Studies in the Greek New Testament, for the English Reader, 16 bks. Kenneth S. Wuest. Incl. Bk. 1. Golden Nuggets. pap. 4.95 o.p. (ISBN 0-8028-1242-2); Bk. 2. Bypaths. pap. 3.95 o.p. (ISBN 0-8028-1318-6); Bk. 3. Treasures. pap. 3.95 o.p. (ISBN 0-8028-1243-0); Bk. 4. Untranslatable Riches. pap. 4.95 o.p. (ISBN 0-8028-1241-4); Bk. 5. Studies in Vocabulary. pap. 3.95 o.p. (ISBN 0-8028-1240-6); Bk. 6. Great Truths to Live by. pap. 4.95 o.p. (ISBN 0-8028-1246-5); Bk. 7. Mark. pap. 5.95 o.p. (ISBN 0-8028-1230-9); Bk. 8. Romans. pap. 9.95 (ISBN 0-8028-1231-7); Bk. 9. Galatians. pap. 4.95 o.p. (ISBN 0-8028-1232-5); Bk. 10. Ephesians & Colossians. pap. 6.95 o.p. (ISBN 0-8028-1233-3); Bk. 11. Philippians. pap. 5.95 o.p. (ISBN 0-8028-1234-1); Bk. 12. Pastoral Epistles. pap. 6.95 (ISBN 0-8028-1236-8); Bk. 13. Hebrews. pap. 6.95 (ISBN 0-8028-1235-X); Bk. 14. First Peter. pap. 5.95 o. p. (ISBN 0-8028-1237-6); Bk. 15. In These Last Days. pap. 4.95 o.p.. (ISBN 0-8028-1238-4); Bk. 16. Prophetic Light in the Present Darkness. pap. 2.95 o.p. (ISBN 0-8028-1239-2). Set. pap. 85.20 o.p. (ISBN 0-8028-1248-1); Current 4 vols. 79.95 o.p. (ISBN 0-8028-2280-0). Eerdmans.

Word Studies in the New Testament, 2 Vols. Marvin Vincent. 1957. 49.95 o.p. (ISBN 0-8028-8083-5). Eerdmans.

Word System. Happy Caldwell. 60p. 1981. pap. 1.50 o.p. (ISBN 0-89274-176-7). Harrison Hse.

Word to the Wise. Alison C. Herzig & Jane L. Mali. (Illus.). (gr. 3-7). 1978. 12.45 o.p. (ISBN 0-316-35898-3). Little.

Word Ways. Joan McNichols & Gerri Purkiss. (Math Is Everywhere Ser.). (Illus., Orig.). (gr. 1-9). 1974. pap. 6.50 o.p. (ISBN 0-918932-44-0). Activity Resources.

Wordless Book Visualized. Ruth Overholtzer. (Illus.). 42p. (gr. k-4). pap. text ed. cancelled o.s.i. CEF Press.

Wordless Workshop. Ed. by Harry Walton. LC 66-12947. (Illus.). (gr. 8 up). pap. 0.95 o.s.i. (ISBN 0-8008-8500-7). Taplinger.

Wordly Wise. Imogene Forte. (Skills Stretchers Ser.). (Illus.). 32p. (gr. 2-5). 1981. pap. 3.95 o.p. (ISBN 0-86530-034-8, IP348). Incentive Pubns.

WordPerfect Book (Covering Versions 4.0 & 4.1) Leo J. Scanlon. (Illus.). 256p. 1986. 24.95 o.p. (ISBN 0-8306-0857-5); pap. 16.95 o.p. (ISBN 0-8306-2757-X, NO. 2757). TAB Bks.

WordPerfect Tips & Tricks. Alan R. Neibauer. 441p. (Orig.). 1986. pap. 18.95 o.p. (ISBN 0-89588-360-0). Sybex.

WordPerfect Tips & Tricks. 2nd ed. Alan R. Neibauer. 488p. 1987. pap. 19.95 o.p. (ISBN 0-89588-489-5). Sybex.

WordPerfect Tips, Tricks & Traps. Charles O. Stewart, III & Daniel J. Rosenbaum. LC 86-63837. 400p. 1987. pap. 19.95 o.p. (ISBN 0-88022-313-8, 84). Que Corp.

WordPerfect 4.2 Macros. Donna Mosich. (Illus.). 300p. 1988. pap. 18.60 o.p. (ISBN 0-8306-9324-6, 3024). TAB Bks.

Words. Leo Lionni. LC 84-10082. (To Talk About Ser.). (Illus.). 12p. (ps). 1985. 3.95 o.s.i. (ISBN 0-394-87004-2, Pant Bks Young). Pantheon.

Words. Ed. by Mark Soppeland. LC 80-24846. (Illus.). 152p. (Orig.). 1980. pap. 6.95 o.p. (ISBN 0-913232-60-2). W Kaufmann.

Words about Words: A Dictionary of 2000 Words - Old, New, & Surprising - for the Styles, Devices, Defects & Oddities of the Craft of Prose Writing. David Grambs. 432p. 1984. text ed. 17.95 o.p. (ISBN 0-07-024048-5). McGraw.

Words about Words: Nonconventional Methods of Handling Chemical Information. Donald L. Dorward. (Occasional Papers: No. 76). 11p. 1965. pap. 1.00 o.p. (ISBN 0-317-58858-3). U of Ill Lib Info Sci.

Words & Faces. Hiram C. Haydn. LC 74-7184. 352p. 1974. 8.95 o.p. (ISBN 0-15-198460-3). HarBraceJ.

Words & Idioms. Logan P. Smith. LC 77-148923. 314p. 1971. Repr. of 1925 ed. 46.00x o.p. (ISBN 0-8103-3651-0). Gale.

Words & Places, or Etymological Illustrations of History, Ethnology, & Geography. 4th ed. Isaac Taylor. 470p. 1968. Repr. of 1909 ed. 37.00x o.p. (ISBN 0-8103-3240-X). Gale.

Words & Sounds Ahoy. Dianne S. Barad. 137p. (gr. 1-8). 1983. pap. text ed. 18.95 spiral bdg. o.p. (ISBN 0-88450-875-7, 4692-B). Communication Skill.

Words & Their Use. Stephen Ullmann. 1951. (ISBN 0-8022-1746-X). Philos Lib.

Words & Wonders: A Collection of Proverbs, Poems & Song Lyrics. Arthur C. Ford. 96p. 1984. 6.50 o.p. (ISBN 0-682-40187-0). Exposition-Phoenix.

Words at Work. 2nd ed. Joseph Bellafiore. (gr. 10-12). 1968. pap. text ed. 8.25 o.p. (ISBN 0-87720-320-2). AMSCO Sch.

Word's Body: An Incarnational Aesthetic of Interpretation. Alla Bozarth-Campbell. LC 79-111. 189p. 1980. 18.75 o.p. (ISBN 0-8173-0009-0). U of Ala Pr.

Words, Conversation & Poetry: From the Musical, "Omar, Man of Fire" Omar Maximillian. 64p. (Orig.). 1983. pap. 5.50 o.p. (ISBN 0-682-40120-X). Exposition-Phoenix.

Words, Facts & Phrases: A Dictionary of Curious, Quaint, & Out-of-the-Way Matters. Eliezer E. Edwards. LC 68-21768. 640p. 1968. Repr. of 1881 ed. 42.00x o.p. (ISBN 0-8103-3087-3). Gale.

Words for Dr. Y: Uncollected Poems of Anne Sexton with Three Stories. Ed. by Linda G. Sexton. 1978. 8.95 o.p. (ISBN 0-395-27081-2); pap. 3.95 o.p. (ISBN 0-395-27268-8). HM.

Words for Telemarketing. 19.95 o.p. (ISBN 0-317-59300-5, Asher-Gallant). Caddylak Systs.

Words for Work: Writing Fundamentals for Vocational-Technical Students. Alec Ross. (Illus., Orig.). 1970. pap. 11.95 o.p. (ISBN 0-395-05333-1). HM.

Words for Your Wedding, the Wedding Service Book. David L. Glusker & Peter L. Misner. LC 83-80796. 186p. (Orig.). 1983. pap. 0.00 o.p.; looseleaf 14.95 o.p. (ISBN 0-912769-01-7). L Tapley.

Words: Form & Function. Pauline Smolin & Philip T. Clayton. 1980. pap. text ed. 11.00 o.p. (ISBN 0-669-02573-9). Heath.

Words from My Mind. Linda William. 1985. 6.95 o.p. (ISBN 0-533-06507-0). Vantage.

Words from the Exodus. Isaac Asimov. (Illus.). (gr. 7 up). 1963. 7.95 o.p. (ISBN 0-395-06570-4). HM.

Words from Within. Marty Irwin. LC 85-4103. 62p. 1985. pap. 5.95 o.p. (ISBN 0-938232-94-0, Dist. by Baker & Taylor Co.). Winston-Derek.

Words in Action: A Rhetoric Reader. Martin Steinmann, Jr. (Illus.). 424p. 1979. pap. text ed. 11.95 o.p. (ISBN 0-15-596700-2, HC). HarBraceJ.

Words Like Arrows. Date not set. (ISBN 0-8052-3918-9). Random.

Words Like Fire: Discourses on Jesus. Bhagwan S. Rajneesh. LC 80-8343. 288p. (Orig.). 1981. pap. 7.64i o.p. (ISBN 0-06-066787-7, RD 347). HarpR.

Words of a Woman Who Breathes Fire. Kitty Tsui. LC 83-60254. 80p. 1983. pap. 5.95 o.p. (ISBN 0-933216-06-8). Spinsters Aunt Lute.

Words of Faith. Francois Mauriac. 1955. (ISBN 0-8022-1093-7). Philos Lib.

Words of Faith: A Devotional Dictionary. Charles S. Mueller. 160p. (Orig.). 1985. pap. 6.50 o.p. (ISBN 0-570-03968-1, 12-3003). Concordia.

Words of Science. Isaac Asimov. (Illus.). 288p. (gr. 7 up). 1959. 10.95 o.p. (ISBN 0-395-06571-2). HM.

Words of Wisdom in Counted Cross-Stitch. Bonnie Woods. LC 81-12529. 35p. 1981. pap. 3.95 o.p. (ISBN 0-87747-887-2). Deseret Bk.

Words on Cassette 1987. Ed. by Bowker, R. R., Staff. 1486p. 1987. 85.00 o.p. (ISBN 0-8352-2383-3). Bowker.

Words on Tape 1987-1988: An International Guide to the Audio Cassette Market. 1987. pap. 29.95 o.p. (ISBN 0-88736-222-2). Meckler Corp.

Words to Read. Watson. (Picture Word Bks.). (gr. k-2). 1980. PLB 10.95 o.p. (ISBN 0-86020-394-8, Usborne-Hayes). EDC.

Words with a Flair. Murray Bromberg & Julius Liebb. LC 78-17661. 1979. pap. 7.95 o.p. (ISBN 0-8120-0979-7). Barron.

Words, Words, Words. C. M. Matthews. 1980. 12.95 o.s.i. (ISBN 0-684-16405-1, ScribT). Scribner.

Words, Words, Words, Words. (Platt & Munk Cricket Bks.). (Illus.). 24p. (ps-1). 1978. 2.50 o.p. (ISBN 0-448-46518-3, G&D); PLB 3.59 o.p. (ISBN 0-448-13061-0). Putnam Pub Group.

WordStar Customizing Guide 3.3: Modifications That Improve Your Productivity. Stuart E. Bonney. (Power User Ser.). 185p. (Orig.). 1986. pap. 24.95 o.p. (ISBN 0-915381-81-8). Wordware Pub.

WordStar for the IBM PC: A Self-Guided Tutorial. Edwin W. Meyer & Molly Oldfield. LC 83-21375. (Illus.). 384p. 1984. pap. 15.95 o.p. (ISBN 0-89303-956-X). Brady Bks.

WordStar Handbook. Dennis P. Curtin. (Illus.). 160p. (Orig.). 1983. pap. 16.50 o.s.i. (ISBN 0-930764-64-1). Weber Systems.

WordStar Made Easy: A Self-Pacing Manual. Pamela A. Patey. 100p. (Orig.). 1983. 10.95 o.p. (ISBN 0-942728-10-6). Custom Pub Co.

WordStar Tips & Traps. Dick Andersen et al. 239p. (Orig.). 1986. pap. 17.95 o.p. (ISBN 0-89588-261-2). Sybex.

Wordsworth. Illus. by Patricia Machin. (Pocket Poets Ser.). (Illus.). 52p. 1985. 4.95 o.p. (ISBN 0-86350-045-5). Salem Hse Pubs.

Wordsworth. William Wordsworth. (Plain Texts of the Poets Ser.). 1968. pap. 2.50x o.p. (ISBN 0-7022-0629-6). U of Queensland Pr.

Wordy Gurdy, No. 1. United Features Syndicate Staff. 160p. (Orig.). 1982. pap. 1.95 o.s.i. (ISBN 0-441-90895-0). Ace Bks.

Work After Work. Judy Kirby. 156p. 1986. pap. 6.95 o.p. (ISBN 0-907621-27-9, Pub. by Quiller Pr England). Intl Spec Bk.

Work Analysis & Design for Hotels, Restaurants & Institutions. 2nd ed. Edward A. Kazarian. (Illus.). 1979. 29.95 o.p. (ISBN 0-87055-317-8). AVI.

Work & Madness: The Rise of Community Psychiatry. 2nd, rev. ed. Diana Ralph. 1988. 35.95 o.p. (ISBN 0-921689-25-X, Dist. by U of Toronto Pr); pap. 16.95 o.p. (ISBN 0-921689-24-1, Dist. by U of Toronto Pr). Black Rose Bks.

Work & Marriage: The Two-Profession Couple. Roslyn K. Malmaud. Ed. by Peter Nathan. LC 84-104. (Research in Clinical Psychology Ser.: No. 10). 300p. 1984. 42.95 o.p. (ISBN 0-8357-1543-4). UMI Res Pr.

Work & Organizational Behavior. William W. Rambo. 1982. text ed. 37.95 o.p. (ISBN 0-03-056133-7). HR&W.

Work & Play in Fern Hollow. (Fern Hollow Board Bks.). (Illus.). (ps). 1985. bds. 1.49 o.s.i. (ISBN 0-517-45848-9). Outlet Bk Co.

Work & Retirement: Policy Issues. Ed. by Pauline K. Ragan. LC 79-91688. 178p. 1980. pap. 9.00x o.p. (ISBN 0-88474-094-3, 05747-9). Lexington Bks.

Work & the Helpless Self: The Social Organization of a Nursing Home. Jackie L. Howsden. LC 81-40132. (Illus.). 176p. (Orig.). 1982. lib. bdg. 26.75 o.p. (ISBN 0-8191-1750-1); pap. text ed. 11.50 o.p. (ISBN 0-8191-1751-X). U Pr of Amer.

Work As Praise. Ed. by George W. Forell & William H. Lazareth. LC 78-54549. (Justice Bks.). 64p. (Orig.). 1979. pap. 0.95 o.p. (ISBN 0-8006-1555-7, 1-1555, Fortress). Augsburg Fortress.

Work Experience in Secondary Schools. Ed. by John Eggleston. (Routledge Education Bks.). 192p. 1983. 21.50x o.p. (ISBN 0-7100-9219-9). Routledge Chapman & Hall.

Work for Everyone. Helen Prevo. 1971. pap. 2.50x o.p. (ISBN 0-88323-085-2, 189). Pendergrass Pub.

Work Hardening in Tension & Fatigue: Proceedings of the TMS-AIME Fall Meeting, Cincinnati, 1975. TMS Staff & AIME Staff. Ed. by Anthony W. Thompson. LC 77-76058. (Illus.). 259p. 1977. pap. 17.50 o.p. (ISBN 0-317-32945-6). Minerals Metals.

Work Hazards & Industrial Conflict. Carl Gersuny. LC 80-51506. (Illus.). 178p. 1981. 20.00x o.p. (ISBN 0-87451-189-5). U Pr of New Eng.

Work of Craft. Carla Needleman. 160p. 1981. pap. 2.95 o.p. (ISBN 0-380-55871-8, 55871-8, Discus). Avon.

Work of Craft. Carla Needleman. 160p. 1987. pap. 8.95 o.p. (ISBN 1-85063-061-5, 30615, Ark Paperbks). Routledge Chapman & Hall.

Work on Women: A Guide to Literature. Mary Evans & David Morgan. viii, 84p. 1979. 10.95x o.p. (ISBN 0-422-77130-9, NO. 2852, Pub. by Tavistock England); pap. 6.95x o.p. (ISBN 0-422-77140-6, NO. 2853). Routledge Chapman & Hall.

Work Organization Research: American & European Perspectives. Anant R. Negandhi & Bernhard Wilpert. LC 77-13350. 350p. 1978. 17.50x o.p. (ISBN 0-87338-207-2, Pub. by Comparative Adm. Research Institute). Kent St U Pr.

Work, Organizations, & Technological Change. Ed. by Gerhard O. Mensch & Richard J. Niehaus. LC 82-3751. (NATO Conference Series II, Systems Science: Vol. 11). 424p. 1982. 69.50x o.p. (ISBN 0-306-40993-3, Plenum Pr). Plenum Pub.

Work, Play, & Worship in a Leisure-Oriented Society. Gordon Dahl. LC 72-78566. 128p. 1972. pap. 3.50 o.p. (ISBN 0-8066-1233-9, 10-7290, Augsburg). Augsburg Fortress.

Work Simplification. Gerald Nadler. 1957. text ed. 41.50 o.p. (ISBN 0-07-045767-0). McGraw.

Work-Stress Connection: How to Cope with Job Burnout. Robert L. Veninga & James P. Spradley. 348p. 1981. 16.95 o.p. (ISBN 0-316-80747-8). Little.

Work Transformed: Automation & Labor in the Computer Age. Harley Shaiken. 288p. 1985. 17.95 o.p. (ISBN 0-03-042681-2). H Holt & Co.

Work, Women, & the Labour Market. Ed. by Jackie West. 192p. 1982. pap. 11.50x o.p. (ISBN 0-7100-0970-4). Routledge Chapman & Hall.

Work, Women & the Stuggle for Self-Sufficiency: The Win Experience. Aliki Coudroglou. LC 82-13679. 214p. 1982. lib. bdg. 29.75 o.p. (ISBN 0-8191-2654-3); pap. text ed. 13.25 o.p. (ISBN 0-8191-2655-1). U Pr of Amer.

Work Your Way Around the World. Susan Griffith. LC 83-12437. (Illus.). 292p. (Orig.). 1983. pap. 10.95 o.p. (ISBN 0-89879-125-1). Writers Digest.

Work Your Way Around the World. 2nd ed. Susan Griffith. (Illus.). 320p. 1987. pap. 10.95 o.p. (ISBN 0-907638-72-4, Pub. by Vacation-Work England). Writers Digest.

Workbench Treasury of Chair Projects. Workbench Magazine Staff. LC 81-86464. (Illus.). 56p. 1982. pap. 4.95 o.p. (ISBN 0-86675-004-5, 45). Mod Handcraft.

Workbench Treasury of Occasional & End Table Projects. Workbench Magazine Staff. LC 82-18769. (Illus.). 56p. (Orig.). 1983. pap. 4.95 o.p. (ISBN 0-86675-006-1, 61). Mod Handcraft.

Workbook for Emergency Care in the Streets. 2nd ed. James C. McClintock & Nancy L. Caroline. 1983. pap. text ed. 13.50 o.p. (ISBN 0-316-55434-0). Little.

Workbook for Mass Communication & Society. 3rd ed. Val E. Limburg. 160p. 1986. pap. text ed. 13.50 o.p. (ISBN 0-8403-4034-6). Kendall-Hunt.

Workbook for Papier-Mache Dolls & Furniture. Marie L. Sitton. (Illus.). 34p. 1984. pap. 3.95 o.p. (ISBN 0-87588-211-0, 2643). Hobby Hse.

Workbook for Planning Christian Education. Kenneth D. Blazier. 48p. 1983. pap. 3.95 o.p. (ISBN 0-8170-0996-5). Judson.

Workbook for Speech Fundamentals. David H. Dobkins & Richard Kneller. 128p. 1980. pap. text ed. 8.95 o.p. (ISBN 0-8403-2257-7). Kendall-Hunt.

Workbook in Clinical Electrocardiography: Two Hundred Problems for Self-Assessment. Hyman M. Chernoff. 162p. 1972. pap. 18.50 o.p. (ISBN 0-686-65358-0). Krieger.

Workbook in Creative Photography. Josepha Haveman. 1976. 5.95 o.p. (ISBN 0-87100-048-2). Morgan.

Workbook in General Anthropology. Jack A. Lucas & Michael A. Park. 1979. pap. text ed. 10.95 o.p. (ISBN 0-8403-1950-9, 40195001). Kendall-Hunt.

Workbook in Introductory Economics. 3rd ed. Ed. by C. D. Harbury. (Illus.). 176p. 1982. pap. text ed. 9.25 o.p. (ISBN 0-08-027442-0). Pergamon.

Workbook in Second Language Acquisition. Larry Selinker & Susan Gass. 192p. 1984. wkbk. 10.95 o.p. (ISBN 0-88377-435-6). Newbury Hse.

Workbook in Second Language Aquisition. Larry Selinker & Susan Gass. 118p. 1984. tchr's. ed. 4.50 o.p. (ISBN 0-88377-293-0). Newbury Hse.

Workbook of Basic Writing Skills. Cora L. Robey et al. 297p. 1979. pap. 8.95 o.p. (ISBN 0-15-596715-0, HC). HarBraceJ.

Workbook of Current English. 3rd ed. William E. Mahaney. 1985. write for info. o.p. (ISBN 0-673-15959-0). Scott F.

Workbook of Solutions & Dosages of Drugs, Including Arithmetic. 12th ed. Thora Vervoren & Joan Oppeneer. (Illus.). 215p. 1983. pap. text ed. 17.95 o.p. (ISBN 0-8016-5228-6). Mosby.

Workbook on the Four Gospels. Richard C. Mills. (Illus.). 128p. (Orig.). (gr. 6 up). 1948. pap. 3.95 o.p. (ISBN 0-87239-327-5, 3347). Standard Pub.

Workbook TE Basic Goals. Date not set. (ISBN 0-07-033924-4). McGraw.

Worked Examples in Basic Electronics. P. W. Crane. 1967. 75.00 o.p. (ISBN 0-08-012217-5); pap. 75.00 o.p. (ISBN 0-08-012216-7). Pergamon.

Worked Examples in Construction Management. Frank Harris & Ronald McCaffer. 171p. 1978. pap. text ed. 15.00x o.p. (ISBN 0-258-97091-X, Pub. by Granada England). Gower Pub Co.

Worked Examples in Electrical Machines & Drives. J. Hindmarsh. (Applied Electricity & Electronics Ser.). (Illus.). 150p. 1981. text ed. 28.00 o.p. (ISBN 0-08-026131-0); pap. text ed. 19.25 o.p. (ISBN 0-08-026130-2). Pergamon.

Worked Examples in Quantity Surveying Measurement. P. Goodacre. (Illus.). 175p. 1982. pap. 25.00 o.p. (ISBN 0-419-12340-7, NO. 6727, E & FN Spon). Routledge Chapman & Hall.

Worked Examples in Turbomachinery: Fluid Mechanics & Thermodynamics. S. L. Dixon. LC 75-9757. 116p. 1975. text ed. 24.00 o.p. (ISBN 0-08-019797-3); pap. text ed. 11.00 o.p. (ISBN 0-08-019700-0). Pergamon.

Worked Problems in Heat, Thermodynamics & Kinetic Theory. L. Pincherle. 1966. 40.00 o.p. (ISBN 0-08-012016-4); pap. 40.00 o.p. (ISBN 0-08-012015-6). Pergamon.

Worker Productivity: A Challenge for Voc Ed. Gary E. Clayton. 30p. 1982. 3.75 o.p. (ISBN 0-318-22249-3, IN235). Natl Ctr Res Voc Ed.

Workers & Commissars: Trade Union Policy in the People's Republic of China. Merton D. Fletcher. (Illus.). vi, 148p. 1974. (ISBN 0-914584-06-5, BW6615-1). WWUCEAS.

Workers & Workplaces in Revolutionary China. Ed. by Stephen Andors. Tr. by Jay Mathews et al. LC 76-53710. (China Book Project Ser.). 440p. 1977. 40.00 o.p. (ISBN 0-87332-094-8). M E Sharpe.

Workers Co-Operatives: Jobs & Dreams. Jenny Thornley. 1981. text ed. 45.00x o.p. (ISBN 0-435-83890-3). Gower Pub Co.

Workers' Compensation. 184p. 1982. 7.00 o.p. (ISBN 0-318-02487-X). ICLE Georgia.

Workers' Compensation. 312p. 1983. 7.50 o.p. (ISBN 0-318-02489-6). ICLE Georgia.

Workers' Compensation. 398p. 1984. 17.50 o.p. (ISBN 0-318-02490-X). ICLE Georgia.

Workers' Compensation Law Institute. 204p. 1982. 8.00 o.p. (ISBN 0-318-02488-8). ICLE Georgia.

Workers' Compensation Law Institute. 75p. 1983. 7.00 o.p. (ISBN 0-318-02491-8). ICLE Georgia.

Workers' Compensation Law of Ohio. 2nd ed. James L. Young. 395p. 1972. Suppl. 1984. 47.50 o.p. Anderson Pub Co.

Workers' Compensation Update. 310p. 1984. 25.00 o.p. (ISBN 0-88129-123-4). Wash Bar CLE.

Workers' Cooperatives: Potential & Problems. Mary Linehan & Vincent Tucker. Ed. by Bank of Ireland Centre for Co-op Studies Staff. 256p. 1983. 6.00 o.s.i. (ISBN 0-318-17943-1, W08A). NASCO.

Worker's Council (Third International, Nos. 1-10. 1968. Repr. of 1921 ed. 17.75x o.p. (ISBN 0-8371-9254-4, WC00). Greenwood.

Workers' Education for International Understanding. (Education Studies & Documents: No. 8). pap. 16.00 o.p. (UNESCO). UNIPUB.

Workers in Bondage: The Origins & Bases of Unfree Labour in Queensland 1824-1916. Kay Saunders. LC 81-11386. (Scholar's Library). (Illus.). 213p. 1982. text ed. 37.50x o.p. (ISBN 0-7022-1283-0). U of Queensland Pr.

Workers in Society. T. Timofeyev. 320p. 1981. 8.00 o.p. (ISBN 0-8285-2050-X, Pub. by Progress Pubs USSR). Imported Pubns.

Workers in the Dawn. George Gissing. Ed. by Pierre Coustillas. 920p. (Orig.). 1985. pap. 8.95 o.p. (ISBN 0-416-01101-2, NO. 9283). Routledge Chapman & Hall.

Workers in the Industrial Revolution: Recent Studies of Labor in the United States & Europe. Ed. by Peter N. Stearns & Daniel J. Walkowitz. LC 73-85101. (Social History Ser.). 442p. 1974. 14.95 o.p. (ISBN 0-87855-081-X); pap. 6.95 o.p. (ISBN 0-87855-577-3). Transaction Pubs.

Workers in World News. B. Moore. 1969. pap. 35.00 o.p. (ISBN 0-08-013423-8). Pergamon.

Workers' Participation in an Internationalized Economy. Ed. by Bernhard Wilpert et al. LC 78-1388. 300p. 1978. 17.50x o.p. (ISBN 0-87338-214-5). Kent St U Pr.

Workers' Participation in Industry. rev ed. Michael Poole. 1978. pap. 7.95x o.p. (ISBN 0-7100-8824-8). Routledge Chapman & Hall.

Workers' Self-Management & Participation National Reports, Vol. I: Bangladesh, Malta, Peru, Yugoslavia. Ed. by Jorge Avendano et al. xxiv, 455p. (Orig.). 1980. 20.00x o.p. (ISBN 92-9038-012-8, Pub. by Intl Ctr Pub Yugoslavia). Kumarian Pr.

Working. Graeme Salaman. (Key Ideas Ser.). 128p. 1986. 19.95 o.p. (ISBN 0-85312-881-2, 9893, Pub. by Tavistock England); pap. 7.50 o.p. (ISBN 0-85312-920-7, 9877, Pub. by Tavistock England). Routledge Chapman & Hall.

Working. Studs Terkel. 800p. 1976. pap. 3.50 o.p. (ISBN 0-380-00259-0, 58842-0). Avon.

Working. Studs Terkel. LC 73-18037. 1974. 21.45 o.p. (ISBN 0-394-47884-3). Pantheon.

Working Approach to Chemistry. Wendy W. Sonntag. 1979. 15.95 o.p. (ISBN 0-8403-2048-5). Kendall-Hunt.

Working at Home: Is It for You? William Atkinson. LC 85-70192. 1985. 10.95 o.p. (ISBN 0-87094-630-7). Dow Jones-Irwin.

Working Bibliography of American Doctoral Dissertations in Children's & Adolsecents' Literature, 1930-1971. W. Bernard Lukenbill. (Occasional Papers: NO. 103). 55p. 1972. pap. 2.00 o.p. (ISBN 0-317-58884-2). U of Ill Lib Info Sci.

Working Bibliography on Norwegian Vernacular Architecture. William H. Tishler. (Architecture Ser.: A 1465). 7p. 1985. 2.00 o.p. (ISBN 0-89028-555-1). Vance Biblios.

Working Class & Its Allies. L. Moskvin. 1980. 8.45 o.p. (ISBN 0-8285-1850-5, Pub. by Progress Pubs USSR). Imported Pubns.

Working Class & Trade Unions in the U. S. S. R. The Period of Developed Socialism. E. Vittenberg. 316p. 1985. pap. 3.95 o.p. (ISBN 0-8285-2971-X, Pub. by Progress Pubs USSR). Imported Pubns.

Working Class in England, 1875-1914. Ed. by John Benson. LC 84-17672. 214p. 1984. 27.50 o.p. (ISBN 0-7099-0692-7, Pub. by Croom Helm Ltd). Routledge Chapman & Hall.

Working Class in Welfare Capitalism: Work, Unions & Politics in Sweden. Walter Korpi. (International Library of Sociology). 472p. 1981. pap. 18.50x o.p. (ISBN 0-7100-0683-7). Routledge Chapman & Hall.

Working Class: The Leading Force of the World Revolutionary Process. V. V. Zagladin. 190p. 1976. pap. 2.95 o.p. (ISBN 0-8285-0414-8, Pub. by Progress Pubs USSR). Imported Pubns.

Working Classes in Victorian Fiction. P. J. Keating. (Illus.). 1979. pap. 10.95x o.p. (ISBN 0-7100-0196-7). Routledge Chapman & Hall.

Working Clock-Timer. Joel Moskowitz. (Paper Machine Ser.: Vol. 1). 1985. 7.95 o.p. (ISBN 0-671-55183-3). S&S.

Working Cowboys. Douglas K. Hall. LC 84-6630. 118p. 1984. 23.45 o.p. (ISBN 0-03-070417-0, Owl Bks); pap. 12.45 o.p. (ISBN 0-03-070418-9). H Holt & Co.

Working Decoy Plans: Kit I. Charles F. Murphy. (Illus.). 1984. boxed kit & book 24.95 o.p. (ISBN 0-8329-0359-0, Pub. by Winchester Pr). New Century.

Working Decoy Plans: Kit II. Charles F. Murphy. (Illus.). 1986. boxed kit & instr's. bk. 24.95 o.p. (ISBN 0-8329-0405-8, Pub. by Winchester Pr). New Century.

Working Detroit: The Making of a Union Town. Steve Babson. LC 84-11019. (Illus.). 256p. 1984. 19.95 o.p. (ISBN 0-915361-01-9, Dist. by Watts). Adama Pubs Inc.

Working Drawing Handbook. 2nd ed. Robert C. McHugh. (Illus.). 1982. 27.95 o.p. (ISBN 0-442-25648-5); pap. 17.95 o.p. (ISBN 0-442-26326-0). Van Nos Reinhold.

Working for Life: Careers in Biology. Thomas A. Easton. 118p. 1984. 12.95 o.p. Learned Info.

Working Free: Practical Alternatives to the Nine to Five Job. John Applegath. 192p. 1982. 13.95 o.p. (ISBN 0-8144-5658-8); pap. 6.95 o.p. AMACOM.

Working Friendship: The Correspondence between Richard Strauss & Hugo Von Hofmannsthal. Richard Strauss. 558p. Repr. of 1961 ed. lib. bdg. 69.00 o.p. (Pub. by Am Repr Serv). Reprint Servs.

Working Group Meeting on Energy Planning: Proceedings, 5th Session. National Resources Committee. (Energy Resources Development Ser.: No. 20). 151p. 1980. pap. 12.00 o.p. (ISBN 92-1-119180-7, E.79.11.F.11). UN.

Working Group Meeting on Environmental Managementin Mineral Resource Development: Proceedings. (Mineral Resources Development Ser.: No. 49). 141p. 1983. pap. 12.00 o.p. (ISBN 92-1-119187-4, E.82.11.F.9). UN.

Working in Space, AAS5. Ed. by George V. Butler et al. LC 81-20528. (Illus.). 138p. 1981. 20.00 o.p. (ISBN 0-915928-57-4). AIAA.

Working in Teams: A Practical Manual for Improving Work Groups. James H. Shonk. 128p. 1982. 14.95 o.p. (ISBN 0-8144-5718-5). AMACOM.

Working in the Redwood in California. Moe E. Waltenspiel. 79p. 1984. 8.50 o.p. (ISBN 0-533-05837-6). Vantage.

Working Lives: The "Southern Exposure" History of Labor in the South. Ed. by Marc S. Miller. (Illus.). 1980. 17.95 o.p. (ISBN 0-394-50912-9); pap. 7.95 o.p. (ISBN 0-394-73965-5). Pantheon.

Working Man: A Weekly Record of Social & Industrial Progress Ser. 1: Nos. 1-26, Ser. 2: Nos. 1-25. 1971. Repr. of 1866 ed. lib. bdg. 150.00x o.p. (ISBN 0-8371-9264-1, WM00). Greenwood.

Working on It. Joan F. Oppenheimer. LC 79-3763. (gr. 7 up). 1980. 7.95 o.p. (ISBN 0-15-299629-X, HJ). HarBraceJ.

Working on Working. WGBH Educational Foundation, Office of Radio & Television for Learning Staff. 84p. 1979. 5.50 o.p. (ISBN 0-318-15602-4, SN24). Natl Ctr Res Voc Ed.

Working Order. Eric Batstone. 376p. 1985. 39.95x o.p. (ISBN 0-631-13751-3). Basil Blackwell.

Working Out: The Total Shape-Up Guide for Men. Charles Hix. LC 82-19208. (Illus.). 224p. 1983. 17.45 o.p. (ISBN 0-671-45793-4). S&S.

Working Out with AutoCAD. Martha Lubow. LC 86-61227. (Illus.). 360p. 1987. pap. 29.95 o.p. (ISBN 0-934035-10-5); Support Disk 14.95 o.p. (ISBN 0-934035-42-3). New Riders Pub.

Working Out with AutoCAD Curriculum Training Guide. New Riders Publishing Staff. 59p. 1987. pap. 9.95 o.p. (ISBN 0-934035-11-3). New Riders Pub.

Working out Without Weights: A Gymnast's Fitness Program You Can Do at Home Without Special Equipment. Chuck Gaylord. LC 84-29606. (Illus.). 1985. 17.95 o.p. (ISBN 0-688-04811-0). Morrow.

Working Papers from Project SPAN. Project SPAN Staff. LC 82-10510. (Project SPAN Reports Ser.). 160p. (Orig.). 1982. pap. 15.95 o.p. (ISBN 0-89994-275-X). Soc Sci Ed.

Working Parent Dilemma: How to Balance the Responsibilities of Children & Careers. Earl A. Grollman & Gerri L. Sweder. LC 85-47941. 244p. 1986. 15.95 o.p. (ISBN 0-8070-2702-2). Beacon Pr.

Working Photographer: The Complete Manual for the Money-Making Professional. Marija Bryant & Tod Bryant. 128p. 1985. pap. 7.95 o.p. (ISBN 0-380-89526-9). Avon.

Working Posture: Case Studies in Ergonomic Practice, Vol. 3. Ed. by John Wilson. 140p. 1986. pap. (ISBN 0-85066-342-3). Taylor & Francis.

Working Terrier. D. Brian Plummer. (Illus.). 226p. 1978. 24.00 o.p. (ISBN 0-85115-099-3, Pub. by Boydell & Brewer). Longwood Pub Group.

Working Through Conflict. Joseph P. Folger & Marshall S. Poole. 1984. pap. text ed. write for info. o.p. (ISBN 0-673-15836-5). Scott F.

Working Toward a Fairer Civil Justice System. 15.00 o.p. Insur Info.

Working with Animal Supplies & Services. Roy Dillon. Ed. by Jasper S. Lee. (Career Preparation for Agriculture-Agribusiness Ser.). (Illus.). 1980. text ed. 19.96 o.p. (ISBN 0-07-016951-9). McGraw.

Working with Aspects of Language. 2nd ed. Mansoor Alyeshmerni & Paul Taubr. 1975. pap. text ed. 6.50 o.p. (ISBN 0-15-503869-9, HC). HarBraceJ.

Working with Aspects of Language. Mansoor Alyeshmerni & Paul Taubr. 1970. pap. text ed. 6.95 o.p. (ISBN 0-15-503866-4, HC). HarBraceJ.

Working with Children & the Liturgy. Paul Larose. LC 81-14984. (Illus.). 95p. 1982. pap. 2.95 o.p. (ISBN 0-8189-0428-3). Alba.

Working with Computers: A Guide to Jobs & Careers. 3rd ed. National Computing Centre, Ltd. Staff. (Illus.). 75p. (Orig.). 1982. pap. 8.50x o.s.i. (ISBN 0-85012-359-3). Intl Pubns Serv.

Working with NEPA: Environmental Impact Analysis for the Resource Manager. Ed. by Peter E. Black & Lee P. Herrington. LC 74-23639. 145p. 1974. pap. text ed. 4.75x o.p. (ISBN 0-8422-0483-0). Irvington.

Working with Orthopedic Patients. Ed. by Jean Robinson & Barbara McVan. LC 82-2979. (Nursing Photobook Ser.). (Illus.). 160p. 17.95 o.p. (ISBN 0-916730-44-1). Springhouse Pub.

Working with People: A Selected Social Casework Bibliography. 2nd ed. Compiled by Marion S. Blank. LC 81-43789. 126p. 1982. 8.95 o.p. (ISBN 0-87304-193-3). Family Serv.

Working with Structuralism: Essays & Reviews on Nineteenth & Twentieth Century Literature. David Lodge. 224p. 1986. pap. 5.95 o.p. (ISBN 0-7448-0043-9). Routledge Chapman & Hall.

Working with the Atom: Careers for You. (Public Affairs & Information Program: General). 41p. 1982. pap. 1.75 o.p. (ISBN 0-318-02236-2). US Coun Energy Awareness.
Working with the Computer. Gilbert Mansell. 156p. 1971. pap. 13.00 o.p. (ISBN 0-08-016014-X). Pergamon.
Working with the Dreaming Body. Arnold Mindell. 128p. 1985. 19.95x o.p. (ISBN 0-7102-0609-7); pap. 8.95 o.p. (ISBN 0-7102-0465-5). Routledge Chapman & Hall.
Working with the Pregnant Teenager: A Guide for Nutrition Educators. Nancy Crane. (Illus.). 36p. 1981. pap. 2.00 o.p. (ISBN 0-318-22483-6, S/N 001-000-04402-8). USGPO.
Working with the Study of Economics: Principles, Concepts & Applications. Turley Mings. 152p. 1983. pap. 5.20 o.p. (ISBN 0-87967-324-9). Dushkin Pub.
Working with the Wool: How to Weave a Navajo Rug. Noel Bennett. Bd. with Designing with the Wool. slipcased 14.95 o.s.i. (ISBN 0-87358-422-8). Northland.
Working with under Fives. David Wood et al. LC 80-27714. (Oxford Preschool Research Project Ser.: Vol. 5). 256p. 1980. pap. 10.00 o.p. (ISBN 0-931114-13-6). High-Scope.
Working with Volunteers. (Leadership Pamphlet Ser.: No. 10). 1956. 1.40 o.p. (ISBN 0-88379-022-X). A A A C E.
Working with Watercolour. Leslie Worth. (Leisure Arts Ser.: Bk. 2). (Illus.). 32p. 1984. pap. 2.95 o.p. (ISBN 0-317-04199-1, Pub. by North Light). Writers Digest.
Working with Wood. Herbert Horowitz. (Illus.). 1970. pap. text ed. 2.95 o.p. (ISBN 0-88323-084-4, 181). Pendergrass Pub.
Working with Words: Careers for Writers. Ed. by Margaret Harmon. LC 76-57192. 154p. (gr. 7 up). 1977. 7.95 o.s.i. (ISBN 0-664-32610-2, Westminster). Westminster John Knox.
Working with Youth. Ray Willey. 144p. 1982. 10.95 o.p. (ISBN 0-88207-199-8). Victor Bks.
Working Woman. Joanne Wallace. (Illus.). 192p. (Orig.). 1985. pap. 12.95 o.p. (ISBN 0-8007-1455-5). Revell.
Working Woman Report: Succeeding in Business in the Eighties. Gay Bryant & Working Woman Editors. 355p. 1984. 16.45 o.p. (ISBN 0-671-47454-5). S&S.
Working Woman's Success Book. Ed. by Working Woman Magazine Staff. 224p. (Orig.). 1981. pap. 8.95 o.s.i. (ISBN 0-441-90901-9). Ace Bks.
Working Women & Divorce: An Account of Evidence Given on Behalf of the Women's Co-operative Guild Before the Royal Commission on Divorce, London, 1911. Women's Co-operative Guild & Anna Martin. Bd. with Married Working Woman: A Study, London, 1911. 1980. lib. bdg. 15.00 o.p. (ISBN 0-8240-0128-1). Garland Pub.
Working Women & the Law. W. B. Creighton. (Studies in Labour & Social Law: Vol. 3). 304p. 1979. 35.00x o.p. (ISBN 0-7201-0552-8). Mansell.
Working Your Way to the Bottom: The Feminization of Poverty. Hilda Scott. 180p. 1985. pap. 8.95 o.p. (ISBN 0-86358-011-4, Pandora Pr). Routledge Chapman & Hall.
Workingman's Paradise. John Miller. Ed. by Michael Wilding. 272p. 1980. 3.00x o.p. (ISBN 0-424-00057-1, Pub. by Sydney U Pr Australia). Intl Spec Bk.
Workingmen of Waltham: Mobility in American Urban Industrial Development, 1850-1890. Howard M. Gitelman. LC 74-6822. (Illus.). 208p. 1974. 24.50x o.p. (ISBN 0-8018-1570-3). Johns Hopkins.
Workings of Old Testament Narrative. Peter D. Miscall. LC 82-48570. (Semeia Studies). 160p. 1983. pap. 8.95 o.p. (ISBN 0-8006-1512-3, Fortress). Augsburg Fortress.
Worklife Estimates: Effects of Race & Education. Shirley J. Smith. (Labor Statistics Bureau Bulletin: No. 2254). 33p. (Orig.). 1986. pap. 1.75 o.p. (ISBN 0-318-20165-8, S/N 029-001-02889-0). USGPO.
Workmen's Compensation in Maryland. 2nd ed. Maurice J. Pressman. 785p. 1977. with 1980 suppl. 50.00x o.p. (ISBN 0-87215-196-4); 1980 suppl. only 15.00x o.p. (ISBN 0-87215-435-1). Michie Co.
Workplace Democracy. Daniel Zwerdling. 188p. 1978. 9.95 o.p. (ISBN 0-318-15078-6, Pub. by Harper & Row). NASCO.
Workplace Industrial Relations in Britain. W. W. Daniel & Neil Millward. (Policy Studies Institute Ser.). xx, 333p. 1983. text ed. 38.50x o.p. (ISBN 0-566-05152-4); pap. text ed. 21.00x o.p. (ISBN 0-435-83191-7). Gower Pub Co.
Works. Aristophanes. Incl. Vol. I. Acharnians, Clouds, Knights, Wasps (ISBN 0-674-99197-4); Vol. II. Peace, Birds, Frogs (ISBN 0-674-99198-2); Vol. III. Lysistrata, Thesmophoriazusae, Ecclesiazusae, Plutus (ISBN 0-674-99199-0). (Loeb Classical Library: No. 178-180). 14.50x ea. o.p. Harvard U Pr.
Works, 14 Vols. Francis Bacon. Ed. by J. Spedding et al. Set. cancelled o.s.i. (ISBN 3-7728-0023-8). Adlers Foreign Bks.
Works, 12 vols. Edmund Burke. Repr. of 1899 ed. 895.00x o.p. (ISBN 0-403-04342-5). Somerset Pub.
Works, 4 vols. Samuel Clarke. LC 75-11207. (British Philosophers & Theologians of the 17th & 18th Century Ser.: Vol. 12). 3274p. 1976. Repr. of 1742 ed. Set. lib. bdg. 204.00 o.p. (ISBN 0-8240-1762-5). Garland Pub.
Works. Randy McClave. 1987. 5.95 o.p. (ISBN 0-8062-2421-5). Carlton.
Works, 8 vols. Margaret Sanger. Incl. Vol. 1. Margaret Sanger, an Autobiography. Intro. by A. Guttmacher. 1938. 130.00 o.p. (ISBN 0-08-018730-7); Vol. 2. Happiness in Marriage. 1969. 34.00 o.p. (ISBN 0-08-018731-5); Vol. 3. Motherhood in Bondage: Motherhood in Bondage. 1928. 120.00 o.p. (ISBN 0-08-018732-3); Vol. 4. My Fight for Birth Control. 1931. 33.00 o.p. (ISBN 0-08-018733-1); Vol. 5. The New Motherhood. 1922. 34.00 o.p. (ISBN 0-08-018734-X); Vol. 6. Pivot of Civilization. 1922. 75.00 o.p. (ISBN 0-08-018735-8); Vol. 7. What Every Boy & Girl Should Know. 1969. 27.00 o.p. (ISBN 0-08-018736-6); Vol. 8. Woman & the New Race. 1920. 34.00 o.p. (ISBN 0-08-018737-4). 1976. Repr. 215.00 set o.p. (ISBN 0-08-020244-6). Pergamon.
Works, 4 vols. Benjamin Whichcote. LC 75-11265. (British Philosophers & Theologians of the 17th & 18th Centuries: Vol. 64). 1977. Repr. of 1751 ed. lib. bdg. 204.00 ea. o.p. (ISBN 0-8240-1814-1). Garland Pub.
Works & Wonders. Ed. by Unity School of Christianity Staff. LC 78-68931. 1979. 5.95 o.p. (ISBN 0-87159-175-8). Unity School.
Work's Indiana Practice with Forms, 1971-1981, 7 vols. Arch N. Bobbitt & Frederic C. Sipe. Set. 315.00 o.p.; Suppl. 1985. 75.00 o.p. Anderson Pub Co.
Works of Allan Ramsay, 3 vols. Allan Ramsay. Incl. Vols 1 & 2. Ed. by Burns Martin & John W. Oliver; Vol. 3. Ed. by Alexander M. Kinghorn & Alexander Law. 1961. Repr. of 1951 ed. Set. 92.00 o.p. (ISBN 0-384-49543-5). Johnson Repr.
Works of Art from the Collection of Paul J. Sachs see Exhibition Catalogues from the Fogg Art Museum.
Works of Charles Darwin: The Structure & Distribution of Coral Reefs, Vol. VII. 3rd ed. Ed. by Paul H. Barrett & R. B. Freeman. (Illus.). 256p. 1987. 75.00 o.s.i. (ISBN 0-8147-1792-6). NYU Pr.
Works of Charles T. Griffes: A Descriptive Catalogue. Donna K. Anderson. Ed. by George Buelow. LC 83-4983. (Studies in Musicology: No. 68). 588p. 1983. 64.95 o.p. (ISBN 0-8357-1419-5). UMI Res Pr.
Works of English Poets, from Chaucer to Cowper, 21 Vols. Alexander Chalmers. Repr. of 1810 ed. Set. cancelled o.s.i. (ISBN 3-487-02603-1). Adlers Foreign Bks.
Works of Geoffrey Chaucer. 2nd ed. Geoffrey Chaucer. Ed. by F. N. Robinson. (New Cambridge Editions). xliv, 1002p. 1972. text ed. 40.76 o.p. (ISBN 0-395-05568-7). HM.
Works of Girolamo Savoldo: The 1955 Dissertation, with a Review of Research, 1955-1985. Creighton E. Gibert. Ed. by S. J. Freedberg. (Outstanding Dissertations in Fine Arts Ser.). (Illus.). 690p. 1985. Repr. of 1955 ed. 70.00 o.p. (ISBN 0-8240-6856-4). Garland Pub.
Works of John Day. John Day. Ed. by A. H. Bullen. 35.00x o.p. (ISBN 0-87556-044-X). Saifer.
Works of Man. Lisle M. Phillipps. 1952. (ISBN 0-8022-1967-5). Philos Lib.
Works of Ralph Vaughan Williams. Michael Kennedy. 776p. Repr. of 1964 ed. lib. bdg. 89.00 o.p. (Pub. by Am Repr Serv). Reprint Servs.
Works of Sir David Lindsay of the Mount, 1490-1555, 4 vols. Ed. by Douglas Hamer. 1931-1936. 150.00 o.p. (ISBN 0-384-32819-9). Johnson Repr.
Works of Tennyson, 9 vols. Alfred Tennyson. Ed. by Hallam Tennyson. Incl. Vol. 1. lib. bdg. 32.50 o.s.i. (ISBN 0-8371-4571-6, TEWL); Vol. 2. lib. bdg. 18.75 o.s.i. (ISBN 0-8371-4572-4, TEWM); Vol. 3. lib. bdg. 18.75 o.s.i. (ISBN 0-8371-4573-2, TEWN); Vol. 4. lib. bdg. 22.50 o.s.i. (ISBN 0-8371-4574-0, TEWP); Vol. 5. lib. bdg. 19.75 (ISBN 0-8371-4575-9, TEWQ); Vol. 6. lib. bdg. 18.75 o.s.i. (ISBN 0-8371-4576-7, TEWR); Vol. 7. lib. bdg. 19.75 o.s.i. (ISBN 0-8371-4577-5, TEWS); Vol. 8. lib. bdg. 18.75 o.s.i. (ISBN 0-8371-4578-3, TEWT); Vol. 9. lib. bdg. 19.75 o.s.i. (ISBN 0-8371-4579-1, TEWU). (Illus.). 1970. Repr. Set. lib. bdg. 148.50x o.p. (ISBN 0-8371-4570-8, TEWK). Greenwood.
Works of Zbigniew Kazimierz Brzezinski. Christine E. Thompson. (Public Administration Ser.: P 1666). 7p. 1985. 2.00 o.p. (ISBN 0-89028-376-1). Vance Biblios.
Works on Facility Management: A Bibliography. John B. Evans. (Architecture Ser.: A 1414). 13p. 1985. 2.00 o.p. (ISBN 0-89028-444-X). Vance Biblios.
Works, Political, Metaphysical, Chronological, 6 Vols. James Steuart. LC 66-21694. 1967. Repr. of 1805 ed. 175.00x set o.p. (ISBN 0-678-00226-6). Kelley.
Works with English Texts. Ed. by Warburton. (Johann Christian Bach Ser.). 1985. lib. bdg. 75.00 o.p. (ISBN 0-8240-6074-1). Garland Pub.
Workshoes for Christ. A. D. Wright. 1979. pap. 3.75 o.p. (ISBN 0-89225-185-9). Gospel Advocate.
Workshop Book of Knitting. Ursula Von Wartburg. LC 71-157313. (Illus.). 160p. (gr. 3 up). 1973. 9.95 o.p. (ISBN 0-689-20696-8, Atheneum); pap. 4.95 o.p. (ISBN 0-689-70564-6). Macmillan.
Workshop Calculations. G. S. Sethi & K. C. Kakkar. 150p. 1982. text ed. 2.00 o.p. (ISBN 0-07-451903-4). McGraw.
Workshop for Automated Photogrammetry & Cartography of Highways & Transport Systems. American Society of Photogrammetry Staff. 138p. 1981. 14.00 o.p. (ISBN 0-937294-33-0); pap. 9.00 members o.p. ASP & RS.
Workshop on Cellular & Molecular Toxicology. Don W. Fawcett & James W. Newburne. LC 79-26853. 300p. 1980. 22.00 o.p. (ISBN 0-683-06996-9). Krieger.
Workshop on Interactive Computing, CAD-CAM, Electrical Engineering Education, 2nd, 1983: Proceedings. LC 83-82758. 163p. 30.00 o.p.; pap. 30.00 o.p. (ISBN 0-8186-0521-9). IEEE Comp Soc.
Workshop on Public Accounting & Auditing: Report-UN Headquarters March 2-10, 1981. United Nations, Department of Technical Cooperation for Development Staff. iii, 23p. 1981. write for info. o.p. UN.
Workshop on Radiotheraphy for Lung Cancer: King's College, Cambridge, England, June 26-30, 1984, Cancer Treatment Symposia. Norman M. Bleehen. (Illus.). 150p. (Orig.). 1985. pap. 8.50 o.p. (ISBN 0-318-18874-0, S/N 017-042-00183-8). USGPO.
Workshop Processes, Practices & Materials. Bruce J. Black. (Illus.). 282p. 1979. pap. 22.50x o.p. (ISBN 0-7131-3409-7). Trans-Atl Phila.
Workshop Technology, Pt. 1. 5th ed. W. A. Chapman. (Illus.). 1976. pap. 24.00x o.p. (ISBN 0-7131-3269-8). Trans-Atl Phila.
Workshop Technology, Pt. 2. 4th ed. W. A. Chapman. (Illus.). 1972. 24.00x o.p. (ISBN 0-7131-3272-8). Trans-Atl Phila.
Workshop Technology, Part 3. 3rd ed. W. A. Chapman. (Illus.). 675p. 1975. pap. 33.50x o.p. (ISBN 0-7131-3351-1). Trans-Atl Phila.
Workshop Wage Determination. S. W. Lerner et al. 1969. pap. 75.00 o.p. (ISBN 0-08-006578-3). Pergamon.
World According to Robo the Robot. Jones. 1985. 12.95 o.p. (ISBN 0-8104-6331-8). Sams.
World Accumulation, Fourteen Ninety-Two to Seventeen Eighty-Nine. Andre G. Frank. LC 77-91746. 1980. pap. 5.95 o.p. (ISBN 0-85345-493-0). Monthly Rev.
World Accumulation, 1492-1789. Andre G. Frank. LC 77-91746. 303p. 1978. 16.50 o.p. (ISBN 0-85345-442-6). Monthly Rev.
World After Oil: The Shifting Axis of Power & Wealth. Bruce Nussbaum. 1984. pap. 7.70 o.p. (ISBN 0-671-50597-1, Touchstone Bks.). S&S.
World Airline Fleets, 1987-88. Ed. by Gunter G. Endres. (Illus.). 322p. 1987. pap. 24.00 o.p. Aviation.
World Almanac & Book of Facts 1985. Ed. by Hana U. Lane. 928p. 1984. 12.95 o.p. (ISBN 0-345-31880-3); pap. 4.95 o.p. Pharos Bks NY.
World Almanac & Book of Facts, 1986. Newspaper Enterprise Association Editors. LC 84-3781. (Illus.). 928p. 1985. 12.95 o.s.i. (ISBN 0-385-23292-6). Doubleday.
World Almanac Book of Facts 1983. Newspaper Enterprise Association Staff. LC 4-3781. (Illus.). 976p. 1982. 10.95 o.p. (ISBN 0-385-18348-8). Doubleday.
World Almanac Book of World War II. Ed. by Peter Young. 624p. 1981. pap. 10.95 o.p. (ISBN 0-345-29775-X). Pharos Bks NY.
World Almanac Crossword Puzzle Book, Bk. 1. 1986. pap. 2.95 o.s.i. (ISBN 0-345-33314-4). Ballantine.
World Almanac Guide to Natural Foods. Shirley Ross. 256p. (Orig.). 1985. pap. 8.95 o.p. (ISBN 0-345-32628-8). Pharos Bks NY.
World Almanac of the American West. Ed. by John S. Bowman. 1986. 29.45 o.s.i. (ISBN 0-345-33720-4). Ballantine.
World Almanac of Who's Who of Film. Tom Aylesworth & John Bowman. LC 87-50075. 448p. 1987. 24.95 o.p. (ISBN 0-317-61976-4, World Almanac). Pharos Bks NY.
World & I: Memoirs of a Nobody. Jay Stauter. 96p. 1982. 6.00 o.p. (ISBN 0-682-49794-0). Exposition-Phoenix.
World & Us. Don Clark. 160p. (Orig.). 1985. pap. 6.95 o.s.i. (ISBN 0-934318-76-X). Falcon Pr Mt.
World & Warren's Cartoons. Walter Consuelo Langsam. LC 76-44926. 1977. 12.50 o.p. (ISBN 0-682-48703-1, Banner). Exposition-Phoenix.
World Apart: The Journal of a Gulag Survivor. Gustav Herling. Tr. by Andrzej Ciozkosz from Pol. 288p. 1986. 16.95 o.p. (ISBN 0-87795-821-1). Morrow.
World Armaments & Disarmament: SIPRI Yearbook 1976. Stockholm International Peace Research Institute (SIPRI) Staff. LC 76-15848. 1976. 45.00 o.p. (ISBN 0-262-19149-0). MIT Pr.
World Around Us: A Book of Readings. Rodger H. Charlier & John J. Karpeck. 253p. 1970. pap. text ed. 8.95x o.p. (ISBN 0-8290-1087-4). Irvington.
World As I See It. Albert Einstein. 1958. (ISBN 0-8022-0440-6). Philos Lib.
World Atlas of Agriculture: Europe, U. S. S. R., Asia Minor; South & East Asia, Oceania; the Americas; & Africa, 5 Vols. Instituto Geografico de Agostini Staff. LC 73-78857. (Illus.). 2248p. (Atlas, Vols. 1 & 3 published 1972; Vol. 2 1974; Vol. 4 August 1975). 1975. Set. 795.00 o.p. (ISBN 0-685-52999-1, IGA100, FAO). UNIPUB.
World Atlas of Architecture. (Illus.). 408p. 75.00 o.p. (ISBN 0-317-54967-7). Apollo.
World Atlas of Military History: 1860-1945. Arthur Banks. LC 73-90857. (Illus.). 200p. 1978. 22.50 o.p. (ISBN 0-88254-454-3). Hippocrene Bks.
World Atlas of Military History 1861-1945. Arthur Banks. (Quality Paperbacks Ser.). (Illus.). 180p. 1988. pap. 12.95 o.p. (ISBN 0-306-80332-1). Da Capo.
World Atlas of Revolution. Andrew Wheatcroft. LC 83-675888. (Illus.). 208p. 1983. 19.95 o.p. (ISBN 0-671-46286-5); pap. 10.95 o.p. (ISBN 0-671-47207-0). S&S.
World Bayonets: Eighteen Hundred to Present. Anthony Carter. (Illus.). 72p. 1987. 14.95 o.p. (ISBN 0-85368-855-9, Pub. by Arms & Armour). Sterling.
World Beyond. Ruth Montgomery. 176p. 1982. pap. 2.75 o.p. (ISBN 0-449-24085-1, Crest). Fawcett.
World Book Atlas. Ed. by Edward B. Espenshade & Joel L. Morrison. LC 84-61526. (Illus.). 448p. (gr. 8-12). 1985. lib. bdg. write for info. o.p. (ISBN 0-7166-3173-3). World Bk.
World Book Atlas of the United States & Canada. Ed. by World Book, Inc. Staff. LC 84-52718. (Illus.). 448p. (gr. 6-12). 1985. lib. bdg. write for info. o.p. (ISBN 0-7166-3179-2). World Bk.
World Book Desk Reference Set. rev. ed. Ed. by World Book, Inc. Staff. LC 85-50384. (Illus.). 1985. PLB write for info. o.p. (ISBN 0-7166-3180-6). World Bk.
World Book Desk Reference Set. World Book Staff. Incl. Grammar & Style Guide. LC 83-60800 (ISBN 0-7166-3167-9); Instant Facts. LC 83-60801 (ISBN 0-7166-3168-7); Book of Nations. LC 83-60799 (ISBN 0-7166-3166-0); Tables & Formulas. LC 83-60798 (ISBN 0-7166-3165-2). (Illus.). 928p. (YA) (gr. 4 up). 1983. lib. bdg. (ISBN 0-7166-3164-4). World Bk.
World Book Dictionary, 2 vols. Ed. by Clarence L. Barnhart & Robert K. Barnhart. LC 86-71197. (Illus.). 2554p. (gr. 4-12). 1987. (ISBN 0-7166-0287-3). World Bk.
World Book Dictionary: 1988, 2 vols. Ed. by Clarence L. Barnhart & Robert K. Barnhart. LC 87-50782. (Illus.). 2554p. 1988. lib. bdg. (ISBN 0-7166-0288-1). World Bk.
World Book Encyclopedia: 1988 Edition, 22 vols. Ed. by World Book Editors. LC 87-50087. (Illus.). 14000p. 1987. PLB (ISBN 0-7166-0088-9). World Bk.
World Book Encyclopedia: 1988 Edition, 22 vols. Ed. by World Book, Inc. Staff. LC 87-51239. 1988. PLB (ISBN 0-7166-0089-7). World Bk.
World Book Health & Medical Annual. Ed. by World Book Staff. (Illus.). (gr. 6-12). 1986. (ISBN 0-7166-1187-2). World Bk.
World Book Health & Medical Annual. Ed. by World Book Staff. LC 87-648075. (Illus.). 1987. lib. bdg. (ISBN 0-7166-1188-0). World Bk.
World Book Illustrated Home Medical Encyclopedia, 4 vols. Ed. by World Book, Inc. Staff. LC 79-56907. (Illus.). 1038p. 1980. write for info. o.p. (ISBN 0-7166-2060-X). World Bk.
World Book of America's Presidents, 2 vols. rev. ed. Ed. by World Book, Inc. Staff. LC 87-51146. (Illus.). 448p. (YA) (gr. 4 up). 1988. Set. PLB (ISBN 0-7166-3196-2). World Bk.
World Book Student Handbook: Information Finder, Vol. 2. rev. ed. Ed. by World Book, Inc. Staff. LC 81-51365. (Illus.). 432p. (gr. 7-12). 1981. PLB write for info. o.p. (ISBN 0-7166-3122-9). World Bk.

World Book Student Handbook: Student Guide, Vol. I. rev. ed. Ed. by World Book, Inc. Staff. LC 81-51365. (Illus.). 304p. (gr. 7-12). 1981. PLB write for info. o.p. (ISBN 0-7166-3121-0). World Bk.

World Book Year Book. Ed. by World Book, Inc. Staff. LC 62-4818. (Illus.). 608p. (gr. 6-12). 1985. PLB write for info. o.p. (ISBN 0-7166-0485-X). World Bk.

World Book Year Book. Ed. by World Book, Inc. Staff. LC 62-4818. (Illus.). 608p. 1986. lib. bdg. write for info. o.p. (ISBN 0-7166-0486-8). World Bk.

World Book Year, 1987. Ed. by World Book Staff. LC 62-4818. (Illus.). (gr. 6-12). 1987. (ISBN 0-7166-0487-6). World Bk.

World Business Travel Guide. Uniglobe Travel International Incorporated Staff. (Illus.). 400p. (Orig.). 1987. pap. 9.95 o.p. (ISBN 0-920197-39-6, Pub. by Summerhill CN). Sterling.

World Calendar: Addresses & Occasional Papers Chronologically Arranged on the Progress of Calendar Reform Since 1930. Elisabeth Achelis. LC 73-102214. 194p. Repr. of 1937 ed. 40.00x o.p. (ISBN 0-8103-3784-3). Gale.

World Capitalist Economy. V. V. Rymalov. 327p. 1982. 8.95 o.p. (ISBN 0-8285-2404-1, Pub. by Progress Pubs USSR). Imported Pubns.

World Car Catalogue see World Cars, 1972.

World Cars, 1972. Compiled by Automobile Club of Italy Staff. Orig. Title: World Car Catalogue. (Illus.). 440p. 1972. 85.00 o.p. (ISBN 0-910714-04-5). Herald Bks.

World Cars 1973. Ed. by Automobile Club of Italy Staff. LC 73-3055. (Illus.). 440p. 1973. 75.00 o.p. (ISBN 0-910714-05-3). Herald Bks.

World Cars, 1975. annual Ed. by Automobile Club of Italy Staff. LC 74-643381. (Illus.). 440p. 1975. 95.00 o.p. (ISBN 0-910714-07-X). Herald Bks.

World Cars 1977. Ed. by Automobile Club of Italy Staff. LC 7-643381. (Illus.). 1977. 45.00 o.p. (ISBN 0-910714-09-6). Herald Bks.

World Cars 1981. Ed. by Automobile Club of Italy Staff. LC 74-643381. (Illus.). 1981. 75.00 o.p. (ISBN 0-910714-13-4). Herald Bks.

World Cars, 1983. Automobile Club of Italy Staff. LC 74-643381. (Illus.). 440p. 1983. 41.75 o.p. (ISBN 0-910714-15-0). Herald Bks.

World Cars, 1984. Automobile Club of Italy Staff. LC 74-643381. (Illus.). 440p. 1984. 45.95 o.p. (ISBN 0-910714-16-9). Herald Bks.

World Catastrophe: Behold He Cometh. Rhodalee M Hailey. 128p. 1986. 7.75 o.p. (ISBN 0-8062-2704-4). Carlton.

World Citizen Curriculum - Teacher Resource Guide. Kirk Bergstrom. (Illus.). 395p. (YA) (gr. 7-12). 1985. pap. 29.95 o.p. (ISBN 0-943804-57-4). U of Denver Teach.

World Citizen Curriculum Student Resource Book. Kirk Bergstrom. (Illus.). 39p. (gr. 7-12). 1984. pap. 29.95 o.p. (ISBN 0-943804-58-2). U of Denver Teach.

World Civilization since Seventeen Seventy. Margaret L. Inglehart. 232p. 1983. pap. text ed. 19.95 o.p. (ISBN 0-8403-3088-X). Kendall-Hunt.

World Civilizations, 2 vols. 5th ed. Edward M. Burns & Philip L. Ralph. (Illus.). 1974. 19.95x o.p. (ISBN 0-393-09276-3); Vol. 1. pap. text ed. 13.95x o.p. (ISBN 0-393-09266-6); Vol. 2. pap. text ed. 13.95x o.p. (ISBN 0-393-09272-0). Norton.

World Class Championship Crosswords. Will Shortz. 96p. 1982. pap. 6.95 o.s.i. (ISBN 0-671-44319-4, Fireside). S&S.

World-Class Executive: How to Do Business Like a Pro Anywhere on the Globe. Neil Chesanow. LC 84-43106. 320p. 1985. 16.95 o.p. (ISBN 0-89256-258-7). Rawson Assocs.

World Collectors Annuary, 35 vols. A. M. Van Voorthuijsen. write for info. vols. 1-34, 1946-1982 o.p.; vol. 35, 1983-84 125.00 o.p. (ISBN 90-70139-13-8). E J Brill USA.

World Collectors Annuary, 1983-84, Vol. XXXV. Ed. by M. E. Van Eijk Van Voorthuijsen. 1985. 125.00x o.p. (ISBN 0-317-40189-0). E J Brill USA.

World Collectors Index, 1946-1972, with Supplements 1978-81: An Alphabetical Index to Volumes 1-33 of World Collectors Annuary. J. J. Van Voorthuijsen. 1976. 60.00 o.p. (ISBN 90-70139-01-4). E J Brill USA.

World Communist Movement. Ed. by V. V. Zagladin. 485p. 1973. 4.95 o.p. (ISBN 0-8285-0415-6, Pub. by Progress Pubs USSR). Imported Pubns.

World Conference on Cultural Policies: Final Report-Mexico City, July 26-August 6,1982. UNESCO Staff. xxxix, 197p. 1982. write for info. o.p. (UNESCO). UNIPUB.

World Constitutions. Vishnoo Bhagwan & Vidya Bhushan. 727p. 1984. text ed. 15.95x o.p. (ISBN 0-86590-314-X, Pub. by Sterling Pubs India). Apt Bks.

World Debt Tables, 1986-87. 538p. 1987. 125.00 o.p. (ISBN 0-8213-0888-2, BK0888). World Bank.

World Defense Forces: A Compendium of Current Military Information for All Countries of the World. Ed. by Barbara H. Pope. 137p. 1987. lib. bdg. 24.50 o.p. (ISBN 0-87436-486-8). ABC-Clio.

World Demand for Raw Materials in 1985-2000. Mining Informational Services Staff. LC 78-10538. 1980. text ed. 25.50 o.p. (ISBN 0-07-039789-9). McGraw.

World Demilitarized. Yoshikazu Sakamoto & Richard A. Falk. 1980. pap. 2.00 o.p. Transaction Pubs.

World Design Sources Directory 1980: An ICOGRADA ICSID Publication. Ed. by Centre De Creation Industrielle, Paris, France Staff. LC 79-41455. 192p. 1980. 46.00 o.p. (ISBN 0-08-025676-7). Pergamon.

World Directory of Mathematicians 1986. 7th ed. Ed. by International Mathematical Union Staff. 976p. 30.00 o.p. (WRLDIR/8). Am Math.

World Directory of Pharmaceutical Manufacturers. 6th ed. 1985. 340.00 o.p. (ISBN 0-8002-3890-7). Intl Pubns Serv.

World Directory of Stockshot & Film Production Libraries. J. Chittock. 1969. 40.00 o.p. (ISBN 0-08-013246-4). Pergamon.

World Economic Data: A Compendium of Current Economic Information for All Countries of the World. Ed. by Cecelia A. Albert. (Illus.). 231p. 1987. lib. bdg. 28.50 o.p. (ISBN 0-87436-485-X). ABC-Clio.

World Economic Survey. Incl. 1967, 2 Pts. Set. 6.00 (ISBN 0-686-93626-4, UN68/2C1CL); Set. pap. 3.50 (ISBN 0-686-99152-4, UN68/2C2); 1968, 2 Pts. pap. 3.00 (ISBN 0-686-93628-0, UN69/2C/6); 1969-1970: The Developing Countries in the 1960s. 1970. pap. 5.50 (ISBN 0-686-93629-9, UN71/2C1); 1971: Current Economic Developments. pap. 3.50 (ISBN 0-686-93630-2, UN72/2C/2); 1972: Current Economic Developments. pap. 4.00 (ISBN 0-686-93631-0, UN73/2C/1); 1973, 2 Pts. Pt. 1: Population & Developments. pap. 8.50 (ISBN 0-686-93632-9, UN74/2C/1); Pt. 2: Current Economic Developments. pap. 9.50 (ISBN 0-686-99153-2, UN74/2C2); 1974, 2 Pts. Pt. 1: Mid-Term Review. pap. 11.00 (ISBN 0-686-93634-5, UN75/2C1); Pt. 2: Current Economic Developments. pap. 9.50 (ISBN 0-686-99154-0, UN75/2C3); 1975: Fluctuation & Development in the World Economy, 2 Pts. pap. 13.00 (ISBN 0-686-93636-1, UN76/2C1); Supplement. pap. 19.00 (ISBN 0-686-99155-9, UN77/2C2); 1976: Current Trends in the World Economy, 2 Pts. pap. 9.50 (ISBN 0-686-93638-8, UN77/2C1); Supplement. pap. 13.00 (ISBN 0-686-99156-7, UN78/2C2); 1977. pap. 13.00 (ISBN 0-686-93640-X, UN78/2C1); 1978: Current Trends in the World Economy. pap. 10.00 (ISBN 0-686-93641-8, UN80/2C1); Supplement to World Economic Survey, 1978: The Expansion of Exports from Developing Countries & Policies of Structural Adjustment in Developed Countries. 69p. 1980. pap. 7.00 (ISBN 0-686-93642-6, UN81/2C1); 1979-1980: Current Trends in the World Economy. pap. 10.00 (ISBN 0-686-93643-4, UN80/2C2). UN.

World Economic Survey, 1980-1981. United Nations Staff. LC 48-1401. (Illus.). 85p. (Orig.). 1981. pap. 8.00x o.p. (E.81.11.C.2). UN.

World Economic Survey, 1981-82. Ed. by United Nations. LC 48-1401. (Illus.). 105p. (Orig.). 1982. pap. 9.00x o.p. (ISBN 0-8002-1110-3, E.82.11.C.1). UN.

World Economic Survey 1984: Current Trends in the World Economy. United Nations Publications Staff. 1984. pap. 12.00 o.p. (ISBN 92-1-109043-1, E.84.II.C.1). UN.

World Economic Survey, 1985: Current Trends & Policies in the World Economy. 115p. 1985. 14.50 o.p. (ISBN 92-1-109107-1, E.85.II.C.1). UN.

World Electric Locomotives. Ken Harris. (Illus.). 160p. 1981. 17.95 o.p. (ISBN 0-86720-569-5). Janes Info Group.

World Electronic Warfare Aircraft. Martin Streetly. 1983. 17.95 o.p. (ISBN 0-86720-665-9). Janes Info Group.

World Employment Programme: Proceedings of the International Labour Conference, 56th Session. 2nd ed. International Labour Office Staff. (Employment Prospects for the 1970's Employment Policies in Developing Countries; International Action & the Role of the ILO). 1973. 3.00 o.p. (ISBN 92-2-100137-7). Intl Labour Office.

World Employment Programme: Proceedings of the International Labour Conference, 53rd Session, 1969. 2nd ed. International Labour Office Staff. 1970. 3.00 o.p. (ISBN 92-2-100136-9). Intl Labour Office.

World Encyclopedia of Aero Engines. Bill Gunston. (Illus.). 192p. 1987. 24.95 o.p. (ISBN 0-85059-717-X, Pub. by PSL P Stephens England). Sterling.

World Encyclopedia of Model Soldiers. John G. Garrett. (Illus.). 218p. 75.00 o.p. (ISBN 0-317-55110-8). Apollo.

World Energy Directory. 2nd ed. Ed. by J. A. Bauly & C. B. Bauly. 600p. 1985. 230.00x o.p. (ISBN 0-582-90026-3, Pub. by Longman). Gale.

World Energy Supplies: 1964-1978. Incl. 1950-1974. pap. 45.00 (E.76.XVII.5); 1965-1968. (Eng. & Fr.). pap. 3.00; 1966-1969. (Eng. & Fr.). pap. 3.00; 1968-1971. pap. 9.00 (E.73.XVII.10); 1969-1972. pap. 9.00 (E.74.XVII.7); 1970-1973. pap. 12.00 (E.75.XVII.13); 1971-1975. pap. 17.00 (E.77.XVII.4); 1972-1976. pap. 17.00 (E.78.XVII.17); 1973-1978. pap. 20.00 (E.79.XVII.13). UN.

World Energy: The Facts & the Future. 2nd ed. Ed. by Euromonitor Publications, Ltd. Staff. (Illus.). 304p. 45.00x o.p. (ISBN 0-8160-1615-1). Facts on File.

World Factbook, Nineteen Eighty-Six. 304p. 1986. pap. 19.00 o.p. (ISBN 0-318-21327-3, S/N 041-015-00163-9). USGPO.

World Factbook: 1987. (Illus.). 300p. 1987. pap. 19.00 o.p. (041-015-00166-3). USGPO.

World Facts in Brief. (Illus.). 272p. 1985. 19.95 o.p. (ISBN 0-528-83188-7); pap. 9.95 o.p. (ISBN 0-528-83189-5). Rand McNally.

World Fighters, Nineteen Forty-Five to Nineteen Eighty-Five. Michael J. Taylor. (Warbirds Illustrated Ser.: No. 28). 1984. pap. 9.95 o.p. (ISBN 0-85368-668-8, Arms & Armour Pr). Sterling.

World Food Problem: Consensus & Conflict. Ed. by Radha Sinha & Gordon Drabek. 1978. pap. 26.00 o.p. (ISBN 0-08-024318-5). Pergamon.

World Forest Biomass & Primary Production Data. Ed. by M. G. Cannell. 1982. 76.00 o.p. (ISBN 0-12-158780-0). Acad Pr.

World Full of Strangers. Cynthia Freeman. LC 74-18154. 1975. 8.95 o.p. (ISBN 0-87795-102-0, Arbor Hse). Morrow.

World Guide to Abbreviations of Associations & Institutions, 1972. (ISBN 3-7940-1398-0). Intl Pubns Serv.

World Guide to Abbreviations of Organizations. 7th ed. Ed. by F. A. Buttress. 750p. 1984. 115.00x o.p. (ISBN 0-8103-2049-5, Pub. by Grand River). Gale.

World Guide to Abbreviations of Organizations, 1974. (ISBN 0-8103-2015-0). Intl Pubns Serv.

World Guide to Battery Powered Road Transportation. Jeffrey M. Christian & Gary G. Reibsamen. (Illus.). 352p. 1980. text ed. 61.50 o.p. (ISBN 0-07-010790-4). McGraw.

World Guide to Beer. Ed. by Michael Jackson. (Illus.). 255p. 1984. Repr. of 1977 ed. 14.98 o.p. (ISBN 0-89471-292-6, Pub. by Courage Bks). Running Pr.

World Guide to House Plants: Origins, Care, & Cultivation. Ed. by Anthony Huxley. (Illus.). 224p. 1984. 19.95 o.p. (ISBN 0-684-18164-9, ScribT). Scribner.

World Guide to Libraries. 8th ed. Ed. by Helga Legenfelder et al. (Handbook of International Documentation & Information Ser.). 1340p. 1987. lib. bdg. 220.00 o.p. (ISBN 3-598-20536-8). K G Saur.

World Guide to Whales, Dolphins & Porpoises. Donald S. Heintzelman. LC 80-20823. 176p. 1981. pap. 12.95 o.p. (ISBN 0-8329-3230-2, Pub. by Winchester Pr). New Century.

World History of the Dance. Kurt Sachs. Tr. by Bessie Schonberg. 1963. 15.00x o.p. (ISBN 0-393-02205-6). Norton.

World History of the Dance. Kurt Sachs. (Illus.). 1963. pap. 8.95 o.p. (ISBN 0-393-00209-8, Norton Lib). Norton.

World History Syllabus: Ancient & Medieval Times, Vol. I. William H. Maehl. 180p. (Orig.). 1980. pap. text ed. 7.95x o.p. (ISBN 0-89459-111-8). Hunter Textbks.

World History Syllabus: Early Modern Times, Vol. II. William H. Maehl. 133p. (Orig.). 1980. pap. text ed. 6.95x o.p. (ISBN 0-89459-107-X). Hunter Textbks.

World History Syllabus: Modern Times, Vol. III. William H. Maehl. 247p. (Orig.). 1980. pap. text ed. 8.95x o.p. (ISBN 0-89459-082-0). Hunter Textbks.

World Hotel Directory. Ed. by Financial Times Staff. 1986. 95.00 o.p. (ISBN 0-912289-65-1); Standing Order. 85.50 o.p. St James Pr.

World Hunger: Twelve Myths. Frances M. Lappe & Joseph Collins. (Food First Ser.). 192p. pap. 8.95 o.p. (ISBN 0-394-62297-9, Ever). Grove.

World Hydrocarbon Markets-Current Status, Projected Prospects & Future Trends: Proceedings of the International Workshop, Mexico City, April 1982. World Hydrocarbon Markets Staff & M. S. Wionczek. (Illus.). 225p. 1982. 48.00 o.p. (ISBN 0-08-029962-8). Pergamon.

World I Knew: What Was So Good about the Good Old Days? Jay Stauter. 55p. 1983. 5.50 o.p. (ISBN 0-682-49919-6). Exposition-Phoenix.

World I Love to See. Ulrike Welsch. 1977. pap. 6.95 o.p. (ISBN 0-395-25400-0). HM.

World in a Drop of Water. Alvin Silverstein & Virginia Silverstein. LC 69-13524. (Illus.). (gr. 3-7). 1969. 4.95 o.p. (ISBN 0-689-20632-1, Atheneum). Macmillan.

World in Crisis. 4th ed. Frederick H. Hartmann. Ed. by James J. Carroll. 519p. 1973. pap. text ed. write for info. o.p. (ISBN 0-02-351380-2). Macmillan.

World in Crisis? Geographical Perspectives. Ed. by R. J. Johnston & P. J. Taylor. 304p. 1986. text ed. 55.00x o.p. (ISBN 0-631-13466-2); pap. text ed. 15.95x o.p. (ISBN 0-631-13524-3). Basil Blackwell.

World in Depression Nineteen Twenty-Nine to Nineteen Thirty-Nine: History of the World Economy in the Twentieth Century, Vol. 4. Charles P. Kindleberger. LC 72-97743. (Library Reprint Ser: No. 64). 1975. pap. 10.95 o.p. (ISBN 0-520-02514-8). U of Cal Pr.

World in Figures. 3rd ed. 294p. 1981. 72.00x o.p. (ISBN 0-85058-046-3, Pub. by Economist). Gale.

World in the Evening. Christopher Isherwood. 1979. pap. 2.50 o.p. (ISBN 0-380-01857-8, 36541-3, Bard). Avon.

World in Transition: Challenges to Human Rights, Development & World Order. Ed. by Henry H. Han. LC 79-66422. 1979. pap. text ed. 22.50 o.p. (ISBN 0-8191-0824-3). U Pr of Amer.

World Insurance. Ed. by Financial Times Staff. 1986. 95.00 o.p. (ISBN 0-912289-64-3); Standing Order. 55.50 o.p. St James Pr.

World Is My Eggshell. Date not set. (ISBN 0-385-29432-8). Delacorte.

World Is Round. Gertrude Stein. (Illus.). 96p. (gr. 3-5). 1973. pap. 0.95 o.p. (ISBN 0-380-01475-0, 08169, Camelot). Avon.

World Issues in the Problems of Schizophrenic Psychoses. Ed. by Tetsuo Fukuda & Hisatoshi Mitsuda. LC 79-88950. 196p. 1979. 24.50 o.p. (ISBN 0-89640-035-2). Igaku-Shoin.

World Leaders: Heads of Government in the Postwar Period. Jean Blondel. LC 79-63826. (Political Executives in Comparative Perspective: a Cross-National Empirical Study: Vol. 1). 282p. 1980. 28.00 o.p. (ISBN 0-8039-9830-9); pap. 12.50 o.p. (ISBN 0-8039-9831-7). Sage.

World Leaders I Have Known. Jerome Davis. (Orig.). pap. 1.75 o.p. (ISBN 0-8065-0019-0, 149, Pub. by Citadel Pr). Carol Pub Group.

World List of Universities. 16th ed. Compiled by International Association of Universities Staff. 618p. (Eng. & Fr.). 1985. 70.00x o.p. (ISBN 0-943818-16-8, Stockton Pr). Groves Dict Music.

World Market Today. D. Kostyukhin. 320p. 1979. pap. 4.95 o.p. (ISBN 0-8285-0390-7, Pub. by Progress Pubs USSR). Imported Pubns.

World Masterpieces, 2 vols. rev. ed. Ed. by Maynard Mack et al. (Orig.). 1965. Vol. 1. text ed. 9.95x o.p. (ISBN 0-393-09624-6); Vol. 2. text ed. 9.45x o.p. (ISBN 0-393-09661-0); Vol. 1. pap. 8.25x o.p. (ISBN 0-393-09659-9); Vol. 2. pap. 7.75x o.p. (ISBN 0-393-09547-9). Norton.

World Masterpieces, 2 vols. 3rd ed. Ed. by Maynard Mack et al. 1973. Vol. 1. 13.95 o.p. (ISBN 0-393-09421-9); Vol. 2. 13.95 o.p. (ISBN 0-393-09658-0); Vol. 1. pap. 10.95 o.p. (ISBN 0-393-09616-5); Vol. 2. pap. 10.95 o.p. (ISBN 0-393-09717-X). Norton.

World Masterpieces Continental Comp. abr. 3rd ed. Ed. by Maynard Mack et al. 2250p. 1974. pap. text ed. 16.95x o.p. (ISBN 0-393-09316-6). Norton.

World Masterpieces, Continental Edition, 2 vols. 3rd ed. Ed. by Maynard Mack et al. 1974. pap. Vol. 1. pap. 10.95 o.p. (ISBN 0-393-09319-0); Vol. 2. pap. 10.95 o.p. (ISBN 0-393-09313-1). Norton.

World Masterpieces, Continental Edition, 2 Vols. enl. ed. Ed. by Maynard Mack et al. (Orig.). 1966. Vol. 1. 8.45x o.p. (ISBN 0-393-09507-X, NortonC); Vol. 1. pap. 6.95x o.p. (ISBN 0-393-09678-5); Vol. 2. pap. 7.45x o.p. (ISBN 0-393-09517-7). Norton.

World Measurement Guide. 4th ed. 240p. 1980. 72.00x o.p. (ISBN 0-85058-045-5, Pub. by Economist). Gale.

World Military Aircraft Since Nineteen Forty-Five. Robert Jackson. (Illus.). 1980. 4.50 o.s.i. (ISBN 0-684-16265-2, ScribT); encore ed. 4.50 o.s.i. (ISBN 0-684-17236-4). Scribner.

World Military Expenditures & Arms Transfers, 1986: Arms Control & Disarmament Agency Publication 127, No.17. 1987. pap. 8.00 o.p. (ISBN 0-318-23536-6, 002-000-00092-0). USGPO.

World Money & Securities Markets. 450p. 1984. pap. 120.00 o.p. (ISBN 0-8002-4071-5). Intl Pubns Serv.

World Natural Gas-Two Thousand. 232p. 1978. 180.00 o.p. (ISBN 0-686-76143-X). Barrows Co.

World Nuclear Directory. 7th ed. C. W. Wilson. 100p. 1985. 220.00x o.p. (ISBN 0-582-90025-5, Pub. by Longman). Gale.

World Nuclear Energy International Conference: Proceedings. 266p. 44.00 o.p. (ISBN 0-317-33042-X, 140001). Am Nuclear Soc.

World Nutritional Determinants. Ed. by Geoffrey H. Bourne. 237p. 1985. 118.75 o.p. (ISBN 3-8055-3948-7). Transaction Pubs.

World of a Thousand Colors. Robert Silverberg. LC 82-72055. 1982. 14.95 o.p. (ISBN 0-87795-417-8, Arbor Hse); pap. 6.95 o.p. (ISBN 0-87795-493-3). Morrow.

World of Allah. David D. Duncan. 1982. 39.00 o.p. (ISBN 0-395-32504-8). HM.

World of Amphibians & Reptiles. Milli U. Tanara. Tr. by Simon Pleasance. LC 79-1441. (Abbeville Press Encyclopedia of Natural Science). (Illus.). 256p. 1979. 13.95 o.p. (ISBN 0-89659-037-2); pap. 7.95 o.p. (ISBN 0-89659-031-3). Abbeville Pr.

World of Ballet. Robin May. Ed. by Wendy Barish. 96p. (gr. 3-7). 1984. 10.75 o.s.i. (ISBN 0-671-50072-4). Wanderer Bks.

World of Bees. Gilbert Nixon. (Illus.). 224p. 1955. (ISBN 0-8022-1223-9). Philos Lib.

World of Biology. 2nd ed. P. William Davis & E. P. Solomon. 1979. text ed. 34.95 o.p. (ISBN 0-07-015552-6). McGraw.

World of Bionics. Alvin Silverstein & Virginia B. Silverstein. (Illus.). (gr. 5 up). 1979. 8.95 o.p. (ISBN 0-416-30221-1, NO. 0140). Routledge Chapman & Hall.

World of Birds. Gianfranco Bologna. Tr. by Simon Pleasance. LC 79-1190. (Abbeville Press Encyclopedia of Natural Science). (Illus.). 256p. 1979. 13.95 o.p. (ISBN 0-89659-034-8); pap. 7.95 o.p. (ISBN 0-89659-028-3). Abbeville Pr.

World of Bob Timberlake. Bob Timberlake. LC 79-88457. (Illus.). 1979. 50.00 o.p. (ISBN 0-8487-0500-9). Oxmoor Hse.

World of Business Game. Harold K. Wilson & Ronald D. Hickman. 89p. 1983. pap. (ISBN 0-471-89731-0). Wiley.

World of Col. John W. Thomason, USMC. Martha A. Turner. 400p. 1984. 19.95 o.p. (ISBN 0-89015-439-2). Eakin Pr.

World of Defoe. Peter Earle. LC 76-40310. 1977. 12.50 o.p. (ISBN 0-689-10772-2, Atheneum). Macmillan.

World of Difference. Heather McHugh. 1981. 9.95 o.p. (ISBN 0-395-30231-5); pap. 5.95 o.p. (ISBN 0-395-30232-3). HM.

World of Dinosaurs. Richard Moody. LC 77-73208. (Illus.). (gr. 4-8). 1977. 3.95 o.p. (ISBN 0-448-14342-9, G&D); PLB 3.99 o.p. (ISBN 0-448-13438-1). Putnam Pub Group.

World of Don Camillo. Giovanni Guareschi. 576p. 1982. 20.95 o.p. (ISBN 0-575-02933-1, Pub. by Gollancz England). David & Charles.

World of Drafting. Stan Ross. (gr. 7-9). 1971. text ed. 18.64 o.p. (ISBN 0-87345-078-7). Glencoe.

World of Dreams. Henri Bergson. 64p. 1958. (ISBN 0-8022-0109-1). Philos Lib.

World of Electronics, 4 Bks. Griffin & Beale. (Electronic World Ser.). (gr. 4-8). 12.95 o.p. (ISBN 0-86020-643-2). EDC.

World of Embroidery. Mary Gostelow. LC 74-25172. (Encore Edition). 1975. 9.95 o.p. (ISBN 0-684-15250-9, ScribT). Scribner.

World of Eric Lim. C. Ray Wylie. (Illus.). 128p. 1987. 8.95 o.p. (ISBN 0-682-40356-3). Exposition-Phoenix.

World of Europe to Eighteen Fifteen, Vol. 2. DeLamar Jensen et al. LC 78-67276. 1979. pap. text ed. 12.95x o.s.i. (ISBN 0-88273-331-1). Forum Pr IL.

World of Farley Mowat: A Selection from His Works. Farley Mowat. Ed. by Peter Davison. 320p. 1980. 16.95 o.p. (ISBN 0-316-58689-7). Little.

World of Fish. Franco De Carli. Tr. by Jean Richardson. LC 79-1436. (Abbeville Press Encyclopedia of Natural Science). (Illus.). 1979. 13.95 o.p. (ISBN 0-89659-035-6); pap. 7.95 o.p. (ISBN 0-89659-029-1). Abbeville Pr.

World of Golf: The Best of Peter Dobereiner. Peter Dobereiner. LC 80-66010. 1981. 14.95 o.p. (ISBN 0-689-11094-4, Atheneum). Macmillan.

World of Goods: Towards an Anthropology of Consumption. Mary Douglas & Baron Isherwood. 1982. pap. 4.95 o.p. (ISBN 0-393-30022-6). Norton.

World of Gymnastics. Peter Tatlow et al. LC 78-5389. (Illus.). 1978. 13.95 o.p. (ISBN 0-689-10899-0, Atheneum). Macmillan.

World of HO Scale, 1988: A Walthers Catalog & Reference Manual. (Illus.). 720p. 1987. pap. 13.98 o.p. (913-634). W K Walthers.

World of Horseback Riding. Neal Shapiro & Steve Lehrman. LC 76-13244. 1976. 6.95 o.p. (ISBN 0-689-10752-8, Atheneum). Macmillan.

World of Horses. Jan Burgess. Ed. by Wendy Barish. (Illus.). 96p. (gr. 3 up). 1984. 9.95 o.s.i. (ISBN 0-671-52528-X). Wanderer Bks.

World of Hurt: A Novel. Bo Hathaway. LC 80-18147. 272p. 1981. 11.95 o.s.i. (ISBN 0-8008-8586-4). Taplinger.

World of Inflation. Geoffrey Maynard & W. Van Ryckeghem. LC 75-26030. 272p. 1975. text ed. 27.50x o.p. (ISBN 0-06-494673-8). B&N Imports.

World of Insects. Adriano Zanetti. Tr. by Catherine Atthill. LC 79-1424. (Abbeville Press Encyclopedia of Natural Science). (Illus.). 256p. 1979. 13.95 o.p. (ISBN 0-89659-036-4); pap. 7.95 o.p. (ISBN 0-89659-030-5). Abbeville Pr.

World of Jan Saudek. Jan Saudek. LC 82-73758. (Illus.). 144p. 1983. 35.00 o.p. (ISBN 0-89381-116-5). Aperture.

World of Japanese Ceramics. Herbert H. Sanders & Kenkichi Tomimoto. LC 67-16771. (Illus.). 267p. 1983. pap. 18.95 o.s.i. (ISBN 0-87011-557-X). Kodansha.

World of John Cleaveland: Family & Community in Eighteenth-Century New England. Christopher M. Jedrey. (Illus.). 1979. 15.95x o.p. (ISBN 0-393-01270-0). Norton.

World of Late Antiquity: 150-750. Peter Brown. (History of European Civilization Library). (Illus.). 1971. pap. text ed. 8.00 o.p. (ISBN 0-15-597633-8, HC). HarBraceJ.

World of Learning 1987. 37th ed. 1896p. 1987. 190.00x o.p. (ISBN 0-946653-28-3, Pub. by Europa England). Gale.

World of Learning, 1988. 38th ed. LC 47-30172. 1925p. 1988. 220.00x o.p. (Pub. by Europa England). Gale.

World of Manufacturing. (gr. 7-9). text ed. 19.28 o.p. (ISBN 0-87345-550-9); tchr's. guide 34.64 o.p. (ISBN 0-87345-552-5); lab. manual 7.96 o.p. (ISBN 0-87345-551-7); game 16.50 o.p. (ISBN 0-686-31680-0); filmstrip set 425.00 o.p. (ISBN 0-686-31681-9); transparency set 450.00 o.p. (ISBN 0-686-31682-7). Glencoe.

World of Marcel Proust. Germaine Bree. LC 66-5642. 1966. pap. 5.75 o.p. (ISBN 0-395-04229-1, 3-05950, RivSL). HM.

World of Mr. Mulliner. P. G. Wodehouse. 1979. pap. 5.95 o.p. (ISBN 0-380-43141-6, 43141). Avon.

World of Moses. Paul F. Bork. LC 78-5022. (Horizon Ser.). 1978. pap. 5.95 o.p. (ISBN 0-8127-0166-6). Review & Herald.

World of N & Z, 1988: A Walthers Catalog & Reference Manual. (Illus.). 368p. 1987. pap. 9.98 o.p. (ISBN 0-941952-22-3, 913-628). W K Walthers.

World of Our Fathers. Irving Howe. LC 76-53818. 1977. pap. 6.95 o.p. (ISBN 0-671-22755-6, Touchstone). S&S.

World of Philip Potter. William H. Gentz. 1974. pap. 2.95 o.p. (ISBN 0-377-00006-X). Friendship Pr.

World of Placido Domingo. Daniel Snowman. (Illus.). 320p. 1985. text ed. 15.95 o.p. (ISBN 0-07-059527-5). McGraw.

World of Professional Golf Annual, 1974. annual Mark H. McCormack. LC 68-13716. (Illus.). 576p. 1974. 14.95 o.p. (ISBN 0-689-10623-8, Atheneum). Macmillan.

World of Professional Golf Annual, 1975. Mark H. McCormack. (Illus.). 1975. 14.95 o.p. (ISBN 0-689-10670-X, Atheneum). Macmillan.

World of Professional Golf: Golf Annual 1972. Mark H. McCormack. (Illus.). 486p. 1972. 12.95 o.p. (ISBN 0-689-10461-8, Atheneum). Macmillan.

World of Professional Golf: Golf Annual 1973. Mark H. McCormack. LC 72-190399. (Illus.). 500p. 1973. 12.95 o.p. (ISBN 0-689-10551-7, Atheneum). Macmillan.

World of Professional Golf: Golf Annual 1976. Mark H. McCormack. 1976. 15.95 o.p. (ISBN 0-689-10762-5, Atheneum). Macmillan.

World of Professional Golf: Golf Annual 1977. Mark H. McCormack. LC 68-13716. 1977. 15.95 o.p. (ISBN 0-689-10831-1, Atheneum). Macmillan.

World of Quino. Quino. 72p. 1986. 8.95 o.p. H Holt & Co.

World of Sail & Power Nineteen Seventy-Eight to Nineteen Seventy-Nine. Ed. by Frank Page. (Illus.). 1979. 32.50 o.p. (ISBN 0-393-03240-X). Norton.

World of Salads. Rosalie Swedlin. LC 80-18134. 1981. 17.95 o.p. (ISBN 0-03-053391-0, Owl Bks.); pap. 9.95 o.p. (ISBN 0-03-059191-0). H Holt & Co.

World of Shakespeare. Alan Dent. LC 78-20691. 1979. pap. 7.95 o.s.i. (ISBN 0-8008-8597-X). Taplinger.

World of Sports Statistics. Arthur Friedman. Ed. by Joel C. Cohen. LC 77-76799. (Illus.). 1978. 10.95 o.p. (ISBN 0-689-10821-4, Atheneum). Macmillan.

World of Terrariums. Charles L. Wilson. LC 74-30396. (Illus.). 1975. 14.95 o.p. (ISBN 0-8246-0194-7). Jonathan David.

World of the Buddha: An Introduction to Buddhist Literature. Lucien Stryk. 1982. pap. 9.95 o.s.i. (ISBN 0-394-17974-9, E803, Ever). Grove.

World of the California Gray Whale. Tom Miller. (Illus.). 1975. pap. 4.00x o.p. (ISBN 0-914622-02-1). Baja Trail.

World of the Contemporary Counselor. C. Gilbert Wrenn. LC 72-4800. 368p. (Orig.). 1973. pap. 18.95 o.p. (ISBN 0-395-13901-5). HM.

World of the Diamond. Isaac G. Pollak. LC 74-80687. 1975. 10.00 o.p. (ISBN 0-682-48006-1, Banner). Exposition-Phoenix.

World of the Italian Renaissance. E. R. Chamberlin. (Illus.). 176p. 1982. 25.00 o.p. (ISBN 0-04-900035-7). Unwin Hyman.

World of the Italian Renaissance. E. R. Chamberlin. (Illus.). 311p. 1983. pap. text ed. 10.95x o.p. (ISBN 0-04-900036-5). Unwin Hyman.

World of the Jaguar. Richard Perry. LC 78-117933. (Illus.). (gr. 10 up). 6.50 o.s.i. (ISBN 0-8008-8590-2). Taplinger.

World of the Japanese Garden: From Chinese Origins to Modern Landscape Art. Loraine Kuck. (Illus.). 416p. 37.50 o.s.i. (ISBN 0-317-54974-X). Apollo.

World of the Restaurateur. H. Berberoglu. 256p. 1980. pap. 16.50 o.p. (ISBN 0-318-22871-8). Kendall Hunt.

World of the Spirit. Xavier & Viera. LC 65-27462. 118p. 1966. (ISBN 0-8022-1778-8). Philos Lib.

World of the Virtuoso. Marc Pincherle. (Illus.). 1963. 7.95x o.p. (ISBN 0-393-02115-7). Norton.

World of Time Inc. Nineteen Sixty to Nineteen Eighty. Curtis Prendergast & Geoffrey Colvin. (Illus.). 704p. 1986. 25.00 o.p. (ISBN 0-689-11315-3, Atheneum). Macmillan.

World of Vegetable Cookery. Rev. ed. Alex D. Hawkes. 288p. 1984. 24.45 o.p. (ISBN 0-671-54187-0). S&S.

World of Vegetable Cookery. Alex D. Hawkes. 1986. pap. 12.95 o.p. (ISBN 0-671-62101-7, Fireside). S&S.

World of Venice. rev. ed. James Morris. LC 73-18461. (Helen & Kurt Wolff Bk.). (Illus.). 1974. 8.95 o.p. (ISBN 0-15-199086-7). HarBraceJ.

World of Venice. rev. ed. James Morris. LC 73-18461. (Illus.). 328p. 1974. pap. 3.95 o.p. (ISBN 0-15-698355-9, Harv). HarBraceJ.

World of Voltaire. (Illus.). 72p. 1969. 1.50 o.p. (ISBN 0-318-18406-0). Michigan Mus.

World of Walther Nernst: The Rise & Fall of German Science, 1864-1941. K. Mendelssohn. LC 73-7605. 1973. 19.95x o.p. (ISBN 0-8229-1109-4). U of Pittsburgh Pr.

World of Wok Cookery. Gail Piazza. LC 82-71462. (Illus.). 144p. 1982. pap. 5.95 o.p. (ISBN 0-916752-59-3). Longman Trade.

World of Words. Israel Rosenberg. 224p. 1973. 8.95 o.p. (ISBN 0-8022-2101-7). Philos Lib.

World of Words: The Personalities of Language. rev., updated ed. Gary Jennings. LC 84-45030. 282p. 1984. 16.95 o.p. (ISBN 0-689-11518-0, Atheneum); pap. 10.95 o.p. (ISBN 0-689-70678-2, 318, Atheneum). Macmillan.

World of Workers. rev. ed. Ira M. Bank. 80p. (gr. 2-3). 1981. pap. 2.75 o.p. (ISBN 0-912578-13-0). Chron Guide.

World Order & Local Disorder: The United Nations & Internal Conflicts. L. B. Miller. (Center of International Studies Ser.). 1967. 26.00x o.p. (ISBN 0-691-05637-4). Princeton U Pr.

World Palaeontological Collections. R. J. Cleevely. 450p. 1982. 100.00x o.p. (ISBN 0-7201-1655-4). Mansell.

World Peace. H. Pearl. 1959. (ISBN 0-8022-1293-X). Philos Lib.

World Politics & the Arab-Israeli Conflict. Ed. by Robert O. Freedman. (Pergamon Policy Studies). 1979. 56.00 o.p. (ISBN 0-08-023380-5). Pergamon.

World Politics since Nineteen Forty-Five. 4th ed. Peter Calvocoressi. LC 81-6055. 516p. 1982. pap. 14.95x o.p. (ISBN 0-582-29586-6); pap. 19.95 5th ed o.p. (ISBN 0-582-29713-3). Longman.

World Politics 1988-89. 9th, rev. ed. Ed. by Suzanne Ogden. LC 80-643193. (Annual Editions Ser.). (Illus.). 288p. 1988. pap. text ed. 9.95 o.p. (ISBN 0-87967-734-1). Dushkin Pub.

World Population Profile, 1985. (WP-85 Ser.). (Illus.). 59p. (Orig.). 1986. pap. 4.25 o.p. (ISBN 0-318-21814-3, 003-024-06218-6). USGPO.

World Population Projections 1984: Short & Long Term Estimates by Age & Sex with Related Demographic Statistics. My T. Vu. 480p. 35.00 o.p. (ISBN 0-8213-0431-3, BK 0431). World Bank.

World Population Trends & Policies: 1981 Monitoring Report. United Nations, Department of International Economic & Social Affairs Staff. LC 83-172048. 1983. Vol. I. 27.00 o.p. (E.82.XIII.2); Vol. II. 21.00 o.p. (ISBN 92-1-151084-8, E.82.XIII.3). UN.

World Power. (Our Nations Heritage Ser.). Date not set. (ISBN 0-07-375425-0). McGraw.

World Power or Decline: The Controversy Over Germany's Aims in the First World War. Fritz Fischer. Tr. by Lancelot L. Farrar et al from Ger. 131p. 1974. pap. 3.95x o.p. (ISBN 0-393-09413-8). Norton.

World Radio & TV Handbook, 1984. J. M. Frost. 600p. 1984. pap. 17.50 o.p. (ISBN 0-8230-5912-X, Billboard Bks). Watson-Guptill.

World Radio & TV Handbook, 1985. J. M. Frost. 600p. 1985. pap. 19.95 o.p. (ISBN 0-8230-5914-6). Watson-Guptill.

World Radio & TV Handbook, 1986. J. M. Frost. 600p. 1986. pap. 19.95 o.p. (ISBN 0-8230-5916-2, Billboard Bks); 119.70 o.p. (ISBN 0-8230-5917-0). Watson-Guptill.

World Radio TV Handbook, 1987. J. M. Frost. 600p. 1987. pap. 19.95 o.p. (ISBN 0-8230-5918-9, Billboard Bks). Watson-Guptill.

World Repeater Atlas. Intro. by Chris Brown. 274p. 1980. pap. 2.00 o.p. (ISBN 0-88006-005-0, BK 7315). Wayne Green Ent.

World Revolutionary Process. V. Pavlenko. 174p. 1983. pap. 1.45 o.p. (ISBN 0-8285-2402-5, Pub. by Progress Pubs USSR). Imported Pubns.

World Rule of Law: Prospects & Problems. Ann Van Wynen Thomas & A. J. Thomas, Jr. LC 74-13554. 106p. 1975. 6.95x o.p. (ISBN 0-87074-144-6, Pub. by Time-Life). SMU Press.

World Series. John R. Tunis. LC 41-13402. (Illus.). 1949. 4.95 o.p. (ISBN 0-15-299645-1, HJ). HarBraceJ.

World Series Records 1903-1983. 480p. 1984. pap. 11.50 o.p. (ISBN 0-89204-147-1). Sporting News.

World Situation. Paul Tillich. Ed. by Franklin Sherman. LC 65-12765. (Facet Bks.). 51p. 1965. pap. 1.00 o.p. (ISBN 0-8006-3017-3, 1-3017, Fortress). Augsburg Fortress.

World Steel in the 1980's: A Case for Survival. William T. Hogan. LC 75-41587. 288p. 1982. 29.00x o.p. (ISBN 0-669-00465-0). Lexington Bks.

World Still to Win: The Reconstruction of the Post-War Working Class. Trevor Blackwell & Jeremy Seabrook. LC 85-20574. 176p. (Orig.). 1986. pap. 10.95 o.p. (ISBN 0-571-13701-6). Faber & Faber.

World Supply & Demand Picture for Canned Small Pelagic Fish. B. V. Lanier. (Fisheries Technical Papers: No. 220). 123p. 1981. pap. 7.50 o.p. (ISBN 92-5-101143-5, F2264, FAO). UNIPUB.

World Survey, Nos. 1-7. 1968. Repr. of 1942 ed. lib. bdg. 20.00x o.p. (ISBN 0-8371-9265-X, WS00). Greenwood.

World Survey of Drug & Narcotic Control: A Medical Subject Analysis & Research Index with Bibliography. Clarence A. Levy. LC 83-71739. 140p. 1985. 34.50 o.p. (ISBN 0-88164-014-X); pap. 26.50 o.p. (ISBN 0-88164-015-8). ABBE Pubs Assn.

World Symposium on Warm-Water Pond Fish Culture: Proceedings, Rome, 1966, 2 Vols. (Fisheries Reports: No. 44, Vols. 3-4). 1967-68. Vol. 3, 426p. pap. 27.50 o.p. (ISBN 0-686-92950-0, F1395, FAO); Vol. 4, 495p. pap. 27.55 o.p. (ISBN 0-686-98807-8, F1664). UNIPUB.

World Systems of Traditional Resources Management. Ed. by Gary A. Klee. LC 80-17711. (Scripta Ser. in Geography). 290p. 1980. 49.95x o.p. (ISBN 0-470-27008-X). Halsted Pr.

World Tales. Idries Shaw. LC 79-1734. (Illus.). 1979. 19.95 o.p. (ISBN 0-15-199434-X). HarBraceJ.

World Tanks & Reconnaissance Vehicles since 1945. Noel Ayliffe-Jones. (Illus.). 144p. 1984. 19.95 o.p. (ISBN 0-88254-978-2). Hippocrene Bks.

World That Perished. John C. Whitcomb. pap. 5.95 o.p. (ISBN 0-8010-9537-9). Baker Bk.

World Trade & Prospects for Ordinary Wine. (Trade Intelligence Paper). 1966. pap. 5.00 o.p. (ISBN 0-686-93118-1, G113, GATT). UNIPUB.

World Trade at a Crossroads. League of Women Voters Education Fund Staff. 8p. 1982. 1.25 o.p. (ISBN 0-89959-332-1, 643). LWV US.

World Trademarks & Logotypes: A Collection of Symbols & Their Applications. Ed. by Takenbou Igarashi. (Reference Books - Graphic Arts). 368p. 1986. 95.00x o.p. (ISBN 0-8161-8808-4, Pub. by Graphic-Sha Pub Co Ltd Japan). G K Hall.

World Truck Handbook. Nick Georgano. (Jane's Handbooks). (Illus.). 335p. 1983. pap. 14.95 o.p. (ISBN 0-86720-657-8). Janes Info Group.

World Truck Handbook. 2nd ed. Nick Georgano. 336p. pap. 16.95 o.p. (ISBN 0-7106-0366-5). Janes Info Group.

World Truth Bible. Benjamin Cordell. 219p. 1981. 12.50 o.p. (ISBN 0-682-49758-4). Exposition-Phoenix.

World Turned Upside Down. Marcia Sewall. (Illus.). 32p. (ps-3). 1986. lib. bdg. 13.95 o.p. (ISBN 0-316-78182-7, Joy St Bks). Little.

Titles

Titles

World Uranium Geology & Resource Potential. Joint Steering Group on Uranium Resources of the OECD Nuclear Energy Agency & the International Atomic Energy Agency Staff. LC 80-81724. (Illus.). 524p. 1980. pap. 50.00 o.p. (ISBN 0-87930-085-X). Miller Freeman.

World Urbanization, Nineteen Fifty to Nineteen Eighty. Davis. LC 76-4570. (Population Monograph Ser.: No. 4 & 9). 1976. Repr. of 1972 ed. lib. bdg. 62.50 o.p. (ISBN 0-8371-8828-8, DAWU). Greenwood.

World View 1982: An Economic & Geopolitical Yearbook. Rev. ed. Pluto-Maspero Project Staff. Tr. by Patrick Camiller. (Illus.). 313p. (Orig.). 1982. pap. 10.00 o.p. (ISBN 0-89608-148-6). South End Pr.

World War II: Decisive Battles of the Soviet Army. V. Larionov et al. 527p. 1985. 10.95 o.p. (ISBN 0-8285-2955-8, Pub. by Progress Pubs USSR). Imported Pubns.

World War II: Myths & Realities. O. Rzheshevsky. 279p. 1985. 10.95 o.p. (ISBN 0-8285-2991-4, Pub. by Progress Pubs USSR). Imported Pubns.

World War III. John Stanley. 1976. pap. 1.95 o.p. (ISBN 0-380-00487-9, 26872). Avon.

World Water Supply: Proceedings of the Fourteenth World Congress of the International Water Supply Association held in Zurich, Switzerland, 6-10 September, 1982. Ed. by R. Urbistondo & E. Trueb. (Illus.). 604p. 1983. pap. 145.00 o.p. (ISBN 0-08-030463-X). Pergamon.

World Weather Extremes. Pauline Riordan. (Illus.). 84p. 1985. pap. 4.50 o.p. (ISBN 0-318-22482-8, S/N 008-022-00230-8). USGPO.

World Who's Who of Women. 5th ed. Ed. by Ernest Kay. (Illus.). 1167p. 1980. 65.00x o.p. (ISBN 0-900332-54-9, BMA 03163). Biblio Dist.

World Who's Who of Women, Vol. VI. (Illus.). 904p. 1982. text ed. 85.00x o.p. (ISBN 0-900332-59-X, BMA 04745). Biblio Dist.

World Who's Who of Women, 1982. 6th ed. 850p. 138.00 o.p. (ISBN 0-900332-59-X). Intl Pubns Serv.

World-Wide Directory of Manufacturers of Vacuum Plant, Components & Associated Equipment. Ed. by B. Halliday. 80p. 1986. pap. 16.50 o.p. (ISBN 0-08-033426-1, Pub. by PPL). Pergamon.

World-Wide French Dictionary. Ed. by Robert Switzer. (Fr.). 1981. pap. 2.95 o.p. (ISBN 0-449-30849-9, Prem). Fawcett.

World-Wide Spanish Dictionary. Ed. by Emilio LeFort. (Span.). 1981. pap. 2.95 o.p. (ISBN 0-449-30851-0, Prem). Fawcett.

World Wired Up: Unscrambling the New Communications Puzzle. Brian Murphy. (Comedia Ser.). 192p. 1983. 15.00 o.p. (ISBN 0-906890-25-X, Dist. by Scribner); pap. 6.95 o.p. (ISBN 0-906890-24-1). M Boyars Pubs.

World Within Walls: Japanese Literature of the Pre-Modern Era 1600-1867. Donald Keene. LC 78-66793. 1979. pap. 9.50 o.p. (ISBN 0-394-17074-1, E723, Ever). Grove.

World Without End, Amen. Jimmy Breslin. 1976. pap. 1.75 o.p. (ISBN 0-380-01628-1, 19042). Avon.

World Wreckers. Marion Zimmer Bradley. 1979. lib. bdg. 11.50 o.p. (ISBN 0-8398-2515-3, Gregg). G K Hall.

World Youth & the Family. Joseph A. Cussen. 1984. pap. 6.95 o.s.i. (ISBN 0-941850-14-5). Liturgical Pubns.

Worldly Christians: A Call to Faith, Prayer & Action. Jerry Folk. LC 82-72652. 144p. 1983. pap. 6.95 o.p. (ISBN 0-8066-1959-7, 10-7343, Augsburg). Augsburg Fortress.

Worldly Theologians: The Persistence of Religion in Nineteenth Century American Thought. Michael D. Clark. LC 80-5840. 328p. (Orig.). 1982. lib. bdg. 30.75 o.p. (ISBN 0-8191-1778-1); pap. text ed. 15.25 o.p. (ISBN 0-8191-1779-X). U Pr of Amer.

Worlds Apart. Robert Oliver. 1985. 8.95 o.p. (ISBN 0-533-06564-X). Vantage.

World's Best Business Hotels. Ed. by William Davis. 1985. 65.00 o.p. (ISBN 0-912289-54-6). St James Pr.

World's Best Fishing Holes: Over Seventy Great Destinations Where the Joy of Fishing Is Worth a Special Trip. E. L. Rogers. (Illus.). 256p. 1986. 16.95 o.p. (ISBN 0-13-968892-7). P-H.

World's Best Food: For Health & Long Life. Michael Bateman et al. (Illus.). 256p. 1981. 19.95 o.p. (ISBN 0-395-30529-2). HM.

World's Best Short Stories. Ed. by Reader's Digest Editors. LC 87-12823. 480p. 1987. 17.97 o.p. (ISBN 0-89577-272-8). RD Assn.

World's Congress Addresses. Charles C. Bonney. 88p. 1900. pap. 6.95 o.p. (ISBN 0-912050-48-9). Open Court.

World's End & Other Stories. Paul Theroux. 1980. 9.95 o.p. (ISBN 0-395-29453-3). HM.

World's Fair. E. L. Doctorow. (Large print Books). 476p. 1986. lib. bdg. 19.95 o.p. (ISBN 0-8161-4085-5, Large Print Bks). G K Hall.

World's Fair of Eighteen Fifty-Five: Modern Art in Paris 1855-1900. Ed. by Theodore Reff. 694p. 1981. lib. bdg. 53.00 o.p. (ISBN 0-8240-4701-X). Garland Pub.

World's Fair of Eighteen Sixty-Seven. Ed. by Theodore Reff. (Modern Art in Paris 1855 to 1900). 224p. 1981. lib. bdg. 53.00 o.p. (ISBN 0-8240-4702-8). Garland Pub.

World's First Female Flattery Book. Hal Lowe. 83p. 1983. 10.00 o.p. (ISBN 0-86516-027-9). Bolchazy-Carducci.

World's Great Love: The Prayer of the Rosary. Fulton J. Sheen. (Illus.). 1978. pap. 4.95 o.p. (ISBN 0-8164-2182-X). HarpR.

World's Greatest Freak Show. Ellen Raskin. (Illus.). (gr. k-3). 1971. 4.95 o.p. (ISBN 0-689-20640-2, Atheneum). Macmillan.

World's Greatest Guitar Book. Ed. by Milton Okun & Dan Fox. (Red Edition Ser.). 288p. 1980. pap. 9.95 o.s.i. (ISBN 0-89524-104-8). Cherry Lane.

World's Greatest Guitar Book: Blue Edition. Ed. by Milton Okun. (Illus.). 288p. (Orig.). 1977. pap. 9.95 o.s.i. (ISBN 0-89524-107-2). Cherry Lane.

World's Greatest Leaders: The Akens Book of Supernatural Records. David S. Akens. LC 80-52087. 1980. pap. 4.95 o.p. (ISBN 0-87397-181-7). Strode.

World's Greatest Monster. (Big Little Bks.: No. 122). (Illus.). 350p. 1984. 6.95 o.p. (ISBN 0-318-02730-5). Bks Nippan.

World's Greatest Quotations. Ed. by Max L. Forman. 1969. 18.95 o.p. (ISBN 0-682-46844-4). Exposition-Phoenix.

World's Greatest Stamp Collectors. Stanley M. Bierman. LC 80-70957. (Illus.). 320p. 1981. 17.95 o.p. (ISBN 0-8119-0347-8). Fell.

Worlds into Words: Understanding Modern Poems. Diane Middlebrook. 1980. pap. 3.95 o.p. (ISBN 0-393-00960-2). Norton.

World's Living Religions. Archie J. Bahm. (Arcturus Books Paperbacks). 384p. 1971. pap. 13.95x o.p. (ISBN 0-8093-0529-1). S Ill U Pr.

World's Money. Michael Moffitt. 320p. 1983. 15.50 o.p. (ISBN 0-671-44682-7). S&S.

World's Money: International Banking from Bretton Woods to the Brink of Insolvency. Michael Moffitt. 1984. pap. 6.70 o.p. (ISBN 0-671-50596-3, Touchstone Bks). S&S.

Worlds of Existentialism. Ed. by Maurice Friedman. 1973. pap. text ed. 13.50x o.s.i. (ISBN 0-226-26348-7, P560, Phoen). U of Chicago Pr.

Worlds of Fritz Leiber. Fritz Leiber. 1979. lib. bdg. 15.95 o.p. (ISBN 0-8398-2477-7, Gregg). G K Hall.

Worlds of Jazz. Andre Hodeir. Tr. by Noel Burch from Fr. 1972. pap. 5.95 o.p. (ISBN 0-394-17770-3, E572, Ever). Grove.

Worlds of Music. Cecil Smith. LC 73-7312. 328p. 1973. Repr. of 1952 ed. lib. bdg. 35.00x o.p. (ISBN 0-8371-6925-9, SMWM). Greenwood.

Worlds of Robert E. Sherwood: Mirror to His Times, Eighteen Ninety-Six to Nineteen Thirty-Nine. John M. Brown. LC 78-27835. (Illus.). 1979. Repr. of 1962 ed. lib. bdg. 37.50x o.p. (ISBN 0-313-20937-5, BRWO). Greenwood.

Worlds of Washington Irving, 1783-1859: An Anthology Exhibition from the Collections of The New York Public Library. Ed. by Andrew B. Myers. LC 74-76746. (Illus.). 144p. 1974. 8.95 o.s.i. (ISBN 0-912882-10-7); pap. 5.50 o.p. (ISBN 0-912882-11-5). Sleepy Hollow.

World's Refugees: A Test of Humanity. Gil Loescher & Ann D. Loescher. LC 82-47936. (Illus.). 160p. (gr. 7 up). 1982. 13.95 o.p. (ISBN 0-15-299650-8, HJ). HarBraceJ.

World's Religious Traditions. Ed. by Frank Whaling. 320p. 1984. 22.95 o.p. (ISBN 0-567-09353-0, Pub. by T & T Clark UK). Bks Intl VA.

World's Shells. S. Peter Dance. LC 76-16581. (Illus.). 1976. text ed. 12.95 o.p. (ISBN 0-07-015291-8). McGraw.

Worlds to Explore: Brownie & Junior Leaders' Guide. Girl Scouts of the U. S. A. Staff. (Illus.). 112p. 1981. pap. 2.75 o.p. (ISBN 0-88441-318-7, 20-702). Girl Scouts USA.

Worlds to Explore Handbook for Brownie & Junior Girl Scouts. Girl Scouts of the U. S. A. Staff. (Illus.). 392p. (gr. 1-6). 1977. pap. text ed. 4.00 o.p. (ISBN 0-88441-316-0, 20-700). Girl Scouts USA.

World's Tragedy. Aleister Crowley. Ed. by Israel Regardie. 160p. 1985. pap. 8.95 o.s.i. (ISBN 0-941404-18-8). Falcon Pr Az.

World's Whales: The First Complete Illustrated Guide. Stanley Minasian et al. LC 84-14142. (Illus.). 224p. 1984. 27.50 o.p. (ISBN 0-89599-014-8, Dist. by Norton). Smithsonian Bks.

Worlds Within Worlds: An Introduction to Biology. Thomas C. Emmel. (Illus.). 1977. text ed. 20.95 o.p. (ISBN 0-15-597672-9, HC). HarBraceJ.

Worldviews: Crosscultural Explorations in Human Beliefs. Ninian Smart. (Illus.). 224p. 1983. 13.95 o.s.i. (ISBN 0-684-17811-7, ScribT). Scribner.

Worldwide Directory of Mineral Industries Education & Research. Ed. by H. Wohlbier et al. LC 68-9304. 1968. 37.50x o.p. (ISBN 0-87201-912-8). Gulf Pub.

Worldwide Encyclopedia of Study & Learning Opportunities Abroad. J. M. De La Croix & Carole Copeland. (Illus.). 136p. 1987. pap. 30.00 o.p. (ISBN 0-939893-07-X). Elite Assocs.

Worldwide Guide to Equivalent Irons & Steels. 1979. 120.00 o.p. (ISBN 0-87170-088-3). ASM.

Worldwide Guide to Equivalent Nonferrous Metals & Alloys. 1980. 120.00 o.p. (ISBN 0-87170-101-4). ASM.

Worldwide Problems of Nutrition. J. C. Somogyi et al. 94p. 1983. pap. 45.00x o.p. Transaction Pubs.

Worldwide Robotics Survey & Directory 1981. 40p. 1981. pap. 28.00 o.p. (ISBN 0-318-01087-9, RIA(02)). Robot Inst Am.

Worldwide Robotics Survey & Directory 1982. 40p. 1982. pap. 15.00 o.p.; Set. pap. 20.00 1981 & 1982 o.p. (ISBN 0-318-01089-5, RIA(03A)). Robot Inst Am.

Worldwide Robotics Survey & Directory. 3rd ed. 79p. 1985. pap. 41.00 o.p. (ISBN 0-317-39394-4). Robot Inst Am.

Worldwide What & Where. Ralph DeSola. 1977. pap. 5.95 o.p. (ISBN 0-380-01721-0, 34074). Avon.

Worm for Dinner. Ned Delaney. LC 76-62504. (gr. k-3). 1977. reinforced bdg. 6.95 o.p. (ISBN 0-395-25153-2). HM.

Worm of Consciousness & Other Essays. Nicola Chiaromonte. LC 75-31868. 120p. 1976. 10.00 o.p. (ISBN 0-15-199440-4). HarBraceJ.

Worm of Consciousness & Other Essays. Nicola Chiaromonte. Ed. by J. Ferrone & D. Willen. LC 76-29695. 270p. 1977. pap. 3.95 o.p. (ISBN 0-15-698370-2, Harv). HarBraceJ.

Worm Story. Robert Tallon. LC 77-10709. (ps-3). 1978. reinforced edition 6.95 o.p. (ISBN 0-03-021536-6). H Holt & Co.

Worried Money: A Guide to Swiss Banking. Frank Wayne. LC 81-20213. 1982. pap. 4.50 o.p. (ISBN 0-86663-891-1). Ide Hse.

Worry & Wonder of Being Human. Albert C. Winn. (Illus., Orig.). 1967. pap. 3.45 o.p. (ISBN 0-8042-9270-1, John Knox). Westminster John Knox.

Worry Free Worry. Ben Leach. (Uplook Ser.). 32p. 1982. pap. 0.99 o.p. (ISBN 0-8163-0516-1). Pacific Pr Pub Assn.

Worry Pill & Other Stories Based on Proverbs. (gr. 2-6). cancelled o.s.i. (ISBN 0-318-21964-6, 2850001). CEF Press.

Worship. Siudy. 1980. 6.15 o.p. (ISBN 0-8298-0393-9). Pilgrim NY.

Worship & Ethics: A Study in Rabbinic Judaism. Max Kadushin. LC 63-10586. 350p. 1975. pap. 8.95x o.p. (ISBN 0-8197-0011-8). Bloch.

Worship: Good News in Action. Ed. by Mandus A. Egge. LC 73-88598. 144p. (Orig.). 1974. pap. 3.50 o.p. (ISBN 0-8066-1402-1, 10-7350, Augsburg). Augsburg Fortress.

Worship in Our Family. Paul Henshaw & Harold Weemhoff. LC 81-52045. 84p. 1981. pap. 4.95x o.p. (ISBN 0-8358-0421-6). Upper Room.

Worship Is a Verb. Robert E. Webber. 224p. 1985. 12.95 o.p. (ISBN 0-8499-0371-8, 0371-8). Word Bks.

Worship Is All of Life. Robert A. Morey. LC 83-73375. (Illus.). 115p. (Orig.). 1984. pap. 5.45 o.p. (ISBN 0-87509-336-1). Chr Pubns.

Worship Leader's Guide. Shari Iverson. (Illus.). 40p. 1986. pap. 4.50 o.p. (ISBN 0-914936-97-2). Bible Temple.

Worship of the Early Church. Ferdinand Hahn. Ed. by John Reumann. Tr. by David E. Green from Ger. LC 72-87063. 144p. 1973. pap. 4.95 o.p. (ISBN 0-8006-0127-0, 1-127, Fortress). Augsburg Fortress.

Worship the Night. Mary Vigilante. 288p. (Orig.). 1982. pap. 2.95 o.p. (ISBN 0-505-51781-7, Pub. by Tower Bks). Dorchester Pub Co.

Worshipful Preaching. Gerard S. Sloyan. LC 83-48911. (Fortress Resources for Preaching Ser.). 80p. 1984. pap. 0.95 o.p. (ISBN 0-8006-1781-9, 1-1781, Fortress). Augsburg Fortress.

Worst of the Wretched Mess News. Milford S. Poltroon. LC 85-3116. 96p. 1985. pap. 4.98 o.p. (ISBN 0-8329-0369-8, Pub. by Winchester Pr). New Century.

Worst Peanuts in Town. Illus. by Mary B. Schwark. (Zig Ziglar Ser.). 48p. 1988. pap. 2.50 o.p. (ISBN 0-8423-8849-4). Tyndale.

Worst Street in North London: A Social History of Campbell, Bunk, Islington, Between the Wars. Jerry White. (History Workshop Ser). 228p. 1986. 19.95 o.p. (ISBN 0-7102-0700-X). Routledge Chapman & Hall.

Worth His Weight in Gold. Molly Katz. (Ecstasy Ser.: No. 480). (Orig.). 1987. pap. 2.25 o.p. (ISBN 0-440-19792-9). Dell.

Worthington Botts & the Steam Machine. Betty Baker. LC 80-24627. (Ready-to-Read Ser.). (Illus.). 56p. (gr. 1-4). 1981. PLB 7.95 o.s.i. (ISBN 0-02-708190-7). Macmillan.

Worthy Matron's Year Book. 1985. Repr. s.p. hardcover, looseleaf 12.00 o.p. (ISBN 0-88053-333-1). Macoy Pub.

Wortkritik und Sprachbereicherung in Adelungs Worterbuch. Max Muller. 18.00 o.p. (ISBN 0-384-40410-3); pap. 13.00 o.p. (ISBN 0-685-13640-X). Johnson Repr.

Would-Be Saint. Robin Jenkins. LC 79-9653. 207p. 1980. 9.95 o.s.i. (ISBN 0-8008-8710-7). Taplinger.

Would You Let Your Daughter? Norman Parkinson. LC 85-80753. (Illus.). 128p. 1985. 35.00 o.p. (ISBN 0-394-55086-2). Grove.

Would You Rather Be a Tiger? Robyn Supraner. LC 72-7962. (Illus.). 32p. (gr. k-3). 1973. reinforced bdg. 3.95 o.p. (ISBN 0-395-15495-2). HM.

Wound Repair. 2nd ed. Erle E. Peacock & Walton Van Winkle. LC 16-8584. (Illus.). 1976. text ed. 130.00 o.p. (ISBN 0-7216-7124-1); text ed. 130.00 o.p.; text ed. 260.00 o.p. Saunders.

Wounded Cormorant & Other Stories. Liam O'Flaherty. 256p. 1973. pap. 5.95 o.p. (ISBN 0-393-00704-9, Norton Lib). Norton.

Wounded Knee: An Indian History of the American West. Dee Brown. Ed. by Amy Ehrlich. LC 73-17400. (Illus.). 224p. (gr. 6 up). 1974. reinforced bdg. 6.95 o.s.i. (ISBN 0-03-091559-7). H Holt & Co.

Wounded Land: Book One of the Second Chronicles of Thomas Covenant. Stephen R. Donaldson. 512p. 1981. 12.95 o.p. (ISBN 0-345-28647-2). Ballantine.

Wounded Sky. Diane Duane. (Gregg Press Science Fiction - Star Trek Ser.). 256p. 1986. lib. bdg. 11.95x o.p. (ISBN 0-8398-2933-7, Gregg). G K Hall.

Woven Nights & Days: The Like & the Unlike. David Hess. 1979. 5.00 o.p. (ISBN 0-682-49366-X). Exposition-Phoenix.

Wow God. Sr. Francis Clare. LC 75-32009. 192p. 1975. 5.95 o.p. (ISBN 0-89221-006-0); pap. 2.95 o.p. (ISBN 0-89221-057-5). New Leaf.

Wow! You Can Fly! R. G. Austin. (Which Way Secret Door Bks.: No. 1). (Illus.). (gr. 1-3). 1983. pap. 1.95 o.p. (ISBN 0-671-46979-7). Archway.

WOZ: The Prodigal Son of Silicon Valley. Doug Garr. 160p. (Orig.). 1984. pap. 2.75 o.p. (ISBN 0-380-88484-4). Avon.

WQ-Ten Electro Acupuncture Machine. Jake Fratkin. Ed. by Robert L. Felt. 48p. (Orig.). pap. 7.95 o.p. (ISBN 0-912111-03-8). Paradigm Pubns.

Wrack & Other Stories. Siegfried Lenz. Ed. by C. A. Russ. 168p. (Orig.). 1967. pap. text ed. 5.50x o.p. (ISBN 0-435-38536-4). Heinemann Ed.

Wreck Diving: A Guide for Sport Divers. Dick Geyer. LC 82-10575. (New Century Aquatics Ser.). (Illus.). 1982. pap. 8.95 o.p. (ISBN 0-8329-0131-8). New Century.

Wrecker. Robert Louis Stevenson & Lloyd Osbourne. (Illus.). 448p. 1982. pap. 6.95 o.p. (ISBN 0-486-24367-2). Dover.

Wren: His Life & Times. John Lindsey. 1952. (ISBN 0-8022-0979-3). Philos Lib.

Wrestlin Jacob: A Portrait of Religion in the Old South. Erskine Clark. LC 78-52453. 1979. pap. 3.95 o.s.i. (ISBN 0-8042-1089-6, John Knox). Westminster John Knox.

Wrestling Superstars II. Daniel Cohen & Susan Cohen. (gr. 4 up). pap. 2.50 o.p. (ISBN 0-671-63224-8). Archway.

Wrestling with God: Messages for Lent & Easter on the Life of Jacob. Vernon R. Schreiber. LC 78-66939. 1979. pap. 3.50 o.p. (ISBN 0-8066-1696-2, 10-7360, Augsburg). Augsburg Fortress.

Wriggles: The Little Wishing Pig. Pauline Watson. LC 78-5855. (Illus.). (gr. k-3). 1979. 7.95 o.p. (ISBN 0-395-28828-2, Clarion). HM.

Wright Morris: A Reader. Wright Morris. 688p. 1974. pap. 4.45 o.p. (ISBN 0-380-01519-6, 18119). Avon.

Write & Get Paid for It. Terry Prone. (Arlen House Ser.). 144p. pap. 5.95 o.p. (ISBN 0-905223-15-2, Dist. by Scribner). M Boyars Pubs.

Write On: Teaching Written Communication. Ohio Department of Education Staff. 88p. 1980. 6.00 o.s.i. (ISBN 0-8141-5863-3). NCTE.

Write Right! Jan Venolia. LC 82-80234. 128p. 6.95 o.p. (ISBN 0-89815-062-0); pap. 4.95 o.p. (ISBN 0-89815-061-2); spiral bdg. 5.95 o.p. (ISBN 0-89815-063-9). Ten Speed Pr.

Write to Learn. Donald M. Murray. 1984. pap. text ed. 14.95 o.p. (ISBN 0-03-061996-3). HR&W.

Write What You Mean: A Handbook of Business Communication. new ed. Allen Weiss. LC 77-11954. 1977. 9.95 o.p. (ISBN 0-8144-5453-4). AMACOM.

Write What You Mean: A Handbook of Business Communications. Allen Weiss. LC 77-11954. 192p. 1981. pap. 5.95 o.p. (ISBN 0-8144-7544-2). AMACOM.

Writer & Society: Heinrich Mann & Literary Politics in 1890-1940. David Gross. LC 79-11707. 1980. text ed. 17.50x o.p. (ISBN 0-391-00972-9). Humanities.

Writer & the Past: Proceedings of the Indiana State University, Department of Foreign Languages, Literature Circle Symposium, 1980. Indiana State University, Department of Foreign Languages, Literature Circle Symposium Staff & Donald L. Jennermann. 1981. 5.00 o.p. (ISBN 0-940100-00-2). Ind St Univ.

Writer As Celebrity: Intimate Interviews. Maralyn L. Polak. 24p. 1986. pap. 9.95 o.p. (ISBN 0-87131-477-0). M Evans.

Writer in Our World: A Triquarterly Symposium. Ed. by Reginald Gibbons. LC 86-3317. 296p. 1986. 17.95 o.p. (ISBN 0-87113-107-2); pap. 8.95 o.p. (ISBN 0-87113-119-6). Atlantic Monthly.

Writer on Her Work. Ed. by Janet Sternburg. 1980. 14.95 o.p. (ISBN 0-393-01361-8). Norton.

Writer Teaches Writing. Donald M. Murray. LC 68-6986. (Illus.). 1968. pap. 18.50 o.p. (ISBN 0-395-04989-X). HM.

Writers & Politics: A Partisan Review Reader. Ed. by Edith Kurzweil & William Phillips. 352p. 1983. pap. 11.95 o.p. (ISBN 0-7100-9316-0). Routledge Chapman & Hall.

Writers & Their Background: Alexander Pope. Ed. by Peter Dixon. LC 72-85534. (Writers & Their Background Ser.). xx, 324p. 1972. 20.00x o.p. (ISBN 0-8214-0113-0); pap. 10.00x o.p. (ISBN 0-8214-0114-9, 82-81172). Ohio U Pr.

Writers & Their Background: Alfred Tennyson. Ed. by David J. Palmer. LC 72-95818. (Writers & Their Background Ser.). xvi, 279p. 1973. 18.00x o.p. (ISBN 0-8214-0116-5); pap. 9.00x o.p. (ISBN 0-8214-0117-3). Ohio U Pr.

Writers & Their Background: John Dryden. Ed. by Earl Miner. LC 72-95818. (Writers & Their Background Ser.). xxvi, 363p. 1972. 20.00x o.p. (ISBN 0-8214-0119-X); pap. 10.00x o.p. (ISBN 0-8214-0120-3). Ohio U Pr.

Writers & Their Background: Samuel Taylor Coleridge. Ed. by R. L. Brett. LC 72-85533. (Writers & Their Background Ser.). xvii, 296p. 1972. 20.00x o.p. (ISBN 0-8214-0109-2); pap. 10.00x o.p. (ISBN 0-8214-0110-6). Ohio U Pr.

Writer's Art. James J. Kilpatrick, Jr. 256p. 1984. 14.95 o.p. (ISBN 0-8362-7919-0). Andrews & McMeel.

Writer's Art, A Collection of Short Stories. Wallace E. Stegner. LC 74-148645. 358p. 1972. Repr. of 1950 ed. lib. bdg. 22.50x o.p. (ISBN 0-8371-6009-X, STWA). Greenwood.

Writer's Block: The Cognitive Dimension. Mike Rose. 132p. 1984. 10.95 o.p. (ISBN 0-317-37083-9). NCTE.

Writer's Choices. Leonora Woodman & Thomas P. Adler. 1985. text ed. write for info. o.p. (ISBN 0-673-15584-6). Scott F.

Writer's Control of Tone. Edward M. White. 1970. pap. text ed. 4.95x o.p. (ISBN 0-393-09894-X, NortonC). Norton.

Writer's Craft: A Process Reader. Sheena Gillespie et al. 1986. pap. text ed. write for info. o.p. (ISBN 0-673-18173-1). Scott F.

Writer's Cue. Stuart Reid. 1973. 5.50 o.p. (ISBN 0-682-47694-3). Exposition-Phoenix.

Writers Directory, 1986-88. 1986. 85.00 o.p. (ISBN 0-912289-28-7); standing order 75.00 o.p. St James Pr.

Writers, Editors, & Moneymen: An Introduction to the Realities of Book Publishing. Clarkson N. Potter. 400p. 1988. 19.95 o.p. (ISBN 0-02-925391-8). Free Pr.

Writers for Young Adults: Biographies Master Index. 2nd ed. Ed. by Adele Sarkissian. (Biographical Index Ser.: Vol. 6). 416p. 1984. 92.00x o.p. (ISBN 0-8103-1473-8). Gale.

Writer's Handbook. Janice L. Gorn. 128p. 1984. pap. 5.95 o.p. (ISBN 0-671-50424-X). Monarch Pr.

Writer's Handbook, 1988. Ed. by Sylvia K. Burack. LC 36-28596. 800p. 1988. 26.95 o.p. (ISBN 0-87116-151-6). Writer.

Writers in Love: Katherine Mansfield, George Eliot, Colette & the Men They Lived With. Mary K. Benet. LC 84-9079. 273p. 1984. pap. 7.95 o.p. (ISBN 0-8398-2854-3, Gregg). G K Hall.

Writers in Politics. Ngugi. (Studies in African Literature). 1981. text ed. 25.00 o.p. (ISBN 0-435-91751-X); pap. text ed. 13.50x o.p. (ISBN 0-435-91752-8). Heinemann Ed.

Writers in Revolt: The Anvil Anthology, 1933-1940. Ed. by Jack Conroy & Curt Johnson. LC 73-81748. 256p. 1973. osi 8.95 o.p. (ISBN 0-88208-025-3); pap. 4.95 o.p. (ISBN 0-88208-026-1). Chicago Review.

Writers in Russia: 1917-1978. Max Hayward. Ed. by Patricia Blake. Leonard Schapiro. LC 82-47671. (Helen & Kurt Wolff Bk.). 352p. 1983. 22.95 o.p. (ISBN 0-15-183278-1). HarBraceJ.

Writers Inspirational Market News. Thomas A Noton. 1987p. pap. 3.00 o.p. (ISBN 0-317-65885-9). Dobbs Pubns.

Writer's Manual & Workbook. enl. ed. Paul P. Kies et al. 1936. text ed. 19.95x o.p. (ISBN 0-89197-475-X). Irvington.

Writer's Market, 1983. Ed. by P. J. Schemenaur. 936p. 1982. 18.95 o.p. (ISBN 0-89879-083-2). Writers Digest.

Writer's Market, 1984. Ed. by Bernadine Clark. 960p. 1983. 18.95 o.p. (ISBN 0-89879-120-0). Writers Digest.

Writer's Market, 1985. Paula Deimling. 1056p. 1984. 19.95 o.p. (ISBN 0-89879-151-0). Writers Digest.

Writer's Market '86. Ed. by Paula Deimling. 1056p. 1985. 19.95 o.p. (ISBN 0-89879-198-7, 2709). Writers Digest.

Writer's Market '87. Ed. by Becky Williams. 1056p. 1986. 21.95 o.p. (ISBN 0-89879-243-6). Writers Digest.

Writer's Market 88. Glenda T. Neff. 1080p. 1987. 21.95 o.p. (ISBN 0-89879-273-8). Writers Digest.

Writers of Colonial New England. Trentwell M. White & Paul W. Elhmann. LC 70-16525. 186p. 1971. Repr. of 1929 ed. 40.00x o.p. (ISBN 0-8103-3742-8). Gale.

Writer's Quotation Book. Ed. by James Charlton. 1980. 10.95 o.p. (ISBN 0-916366-08-1). Pushcart Pr.

Writer's Reader. 4th ed. Donald Hall & D. L. Emblen. 1985. pap. text ed. write for info. o.p. (ISBN 0-673-39217-1); tchr's. ed. avail. o.p. Scott F.

Writer's Roundtable. Ed. by Helen R. Hull & Michael Drury. LC 73-138116. 201p. 1971. Repr. of 1959 ed. lib. bdg. 35.00x o.p. (ISBN 0-8371-5692-0, HUWR). Greenwood.

Writer's Workshop: A Self-Paced Program for Composition Mastery. 3rd ed. Robert M. Frew et al. 282p. 1984. pap. 15.95x wkbk. o.p. (ISBN 0-917962-52-4). T H Peek.

Writing. Gregory Cowan & Elizabeth Cowan. 1980. text ed. write for info. o.p. (ISBN 0-673-15665-6). Scott F.

Writing: A College Rhetoric. Laurie G. Kirszner & Stephen R. Mandell. 1984. text ed. 21.95 o.p. (ISBN 0-03-059151-1). HR&W.

Writing: A College Rhetoric, Brief Edition. Laurie G. Kirszner & Stephen R. Mandell. 448p. 1985. pap. text ed. 16.95 o.p. (ISBN 0-03-001417-4). HR&W.

Writing-A College Workbook: Ancillary for Writing a College Handbook. James A. Heffernan & John E. Lincoln. 300p. 1982. pap. 9.95x o.p. (ISBN 0-393-95177-4). Norton.

Writing a Practical Guide. Joseph P. Dagher. LC 74-11784. (Illus.). 1976. pap. 21.96 o.p. (ISBN 0-395-18621-8). HM.

Writing: A Preparation for College Composition. 2nd ed. Robert C. Slack & Beekman W. Cottrell. 1978. pap. text ed. write for info. o.p. (ISBN 0-02-478250-5). Macmillan.

Writing a Thesis: A Guide to Long Essays & Dissertations. George Watson. 120p. (Orig.). 1987. pap. text ed. 9.95 o.p. (ISBN 0-582-49465-6). Longman.

Writing about Literature & Film. Margaret B. Bryan & Boyd H. Davis. 192p. 1975. pap. text ed. 7.25 o.p. (ISBN 0-15-597854-3, HC). HarBraceJ.

Writing: Analysis & Application. Robert F. Willson, Jr. 1980. pap. text ed. (ISBN 0-02-428120-4). Macmillan.

Writing & Communication in Business. 3rd ed. J. Harold Janis. (Illus.). 500p. 1978. text ed. write for info. o.p. (ISBN 0-02-360300-3, 36030). Macmillan.

Writing & Difference. Jacques Derrida. Tr. by Alan Bass from Fr. LC 77-25933. 1978. lib. bdg. 25.00x o.s.i. (ISBN 0-226-14328-7). U of Chicago Pr.

Writing & Reading Across the Curriculum. 2nd ed. Laurence Behrens & Leonard Rosen. 1985. write for info. o.p. (ISBN 0-673-39196-5). Scott F.

Writing & Reporting Broadcast News. E. Joseph Broussard & Jack F. Holgate. 1982. text ed. write for info. o.p. (ISBN 0-02-315270-2). Macmillan.

Writing & Rewriting. 2nd ed. Janet Mayes. 1981. pap. text ed. (ISBN 0-02-378200-5). Macmillan.

Writing & Selling Science Fiction. Ed. by Science Fiction Writers of America Staff. LC 76-25893. 191p. 1982. pap. 7.95 o.p. (ISBN 0-89879-079-4). Writers Digest.

Writing & the Writer. Frank Smith. 1982. pap. text ed. 17.95 o.p. (ISBN 0-03-058837-5). HR&W.

Writing Antiques. George Mell. (Shire Album Ser.: No. 54). (Illus.). 32p. (Orig.). 1983. pap. 2.95 o.p. (ISBN 0-85263-519-2, 3380309, Pub. by Shire Pubns England). Seven Hills Bk Dists.

Writing Away. Imogene Forte. (Skills Stretchers Ser.). (Illus.). 32p. (gr. 2-5). 1981. pap. 3.95 o.p. (ISBN 0-86530-033-X, IP 33-X). Incentive Pubns.

Writing Better Letters, Reports, & Memos. (AMA Reprint Collections Ser.). 1976. 7.50 o.p. (ISBN 0-8144-6949-3). AMACOM.

Writing Business Programs in C Language. Martin Franz & Phillip I. Good. LC 84-45695. 190p. (Orig.). 1985. pap. 16.95 o.p. (ISBN 0-8019-7611-1). Chilton.

Writing by Design. Walter E. Klarner et al. LC 76-14652. (Illus.). 1977. pap. 17.95 o.p. (ISBN 0-395-24428-5). HM.

Writing Commitment. Michael E. Adelstein & Jean G. Pival. 1976. text ed. 11.95 o.p. (ISBN 0-15-597855-1, HC). HarBraceJ.

Writing Commitment. 2nd ed. Michael E. Adelstein & Jean G. Pival. 536p. 1980. text ed. 15.95 o.p. (ISBN 0-15-597851-9, HC). HarBraceJ.

Writing Commitment. 3rd ed. Michael E. Adelstein & Jean G. Pival. 536p. 1984. text ed. 15.00 net o.p. (ISBN 0-15-597833-0, HC). HarBraceJ.

Writing: Discovering Form & Meaning. Charles W. Bridges & Ronald F. Lunsford. 399p. 1984. text ed. (ISBN 0-534-02998-1). Wadsworth Pub.

Writing Dynamics: A Guidebook for Communications in the Office of the 80's. Nancy B. Finn. 176p. 1983. 18.95 o.p. (ISBN 0-8436-0868-4). Van Nos Reinhold.

Writing Effective Reports on Police Investigations: Concepts, Procedures, Samples. Robert C. Levie & Lou E. Ballard. 1978. text ed. 32.67 o.s.i. (ISBN 0-205-06098-6, 826098-2). Allyn.

Writing English As a Second Language. Mary R. Smalley. 1982. text ed. write for info. o.p. (ISBN 0-02-411800-1). Macmillan.

Writing Essays about Literature: A Guide & Style Sheet. Kelly Griffith, Jr. 195p. 1982. pap. text ed. 8.00 o.p. (ISBN 0-15-597860-8, HC). HarBraceJ.

Writing Exercise Set. National Assessment of Educational Progress Staff. (Exercises or Items). 245p. 1976. 17.60 o.p. (ISBN 0-318-14006-3, 05-W-25). Ed Comm States.

Writing Experience. 2nd ed. Carol Schoen et al. 1982. pap. text ed. (ISBN 0-673-39298-8). Scott F.

Writing for a Reason. William H. Barnwell. LC 82-83174. 432p. 1983. pap. 18.95 o.p. (ISBN 0-395-32597-8). HM.

Writing for Action: A Guide for the Health Care Professional. Earl N. Harbert & John L. DiGaetani. LC 83-73710. 225p. 1984. 22.50 o.p. (ISBN 0-87094-478-9), Dow Jones-Irwin.

Writing for Children & Teenagers. Lee Wyndham & Arnold Madison. LC 79-24459. 268p. (Orig.). 1985. pap. 10.95 o.p. (ISBN 0-89879-177-4). Writers Digest.

Writing for College: A Practical Approach. Robert E. Yarber. 1985. pap. text ed. (ISBN 0-673-16639-2). Scott F.

Writing for Communication in Science & Medicine, or Out of Your Mind with Comprehensive Assurance. Barbara S. Lynch & Charles F. Chapman. 336p. 1980. 26.95 o.p. (ISBN 0-442-24959-4). Van Nos Reinhold.

Writing for Decision Makers. Marya Holcombe & Judith Stein. LC 80-24900. 260p. 1981. 19.95 o.p. (ISBN 0-534-97980-7, Lifetime Learn). Van Nos Reinhold.

Writing for Results: In Business, Government, the Sciences & the Professions. 2nd ed. David W. Ewing. 464p. 1985. pap. 14.95 o.p. (ISBN 0-471-82590-5). Wiley.

Writing for Technicians. 2nd, rev. ed. Marva T. Barnett. LC 80-69550. (Technical Communications Ser.). 358p. 1982. pap. text ed. 17.95 o.p. (ISBN 0-8273-1867-7); 5.25 o.s.i. instr's. guide (ISBN 0-8273-1868-5). Delmar.

Writing for the Joy of It. Leonard L. Knott. LC 83-1329. 240p. 1983. 11.95 o.p. (ISBN 0-89879-106-5). Writers Digest.

Writing for the Soaps. Jean Rouverol. LC 84-17410. 232p. 1984. 14.95 o.p. (ISBN 0-89879-146-4). Writers Digest.

Writing for Theological Education by Extension. Lois McKinney. 64p. (Prog. Bk.). 1975. 1.95x o.p. (ISBN 0-87808-905-5). William Carey Lib.

Writing from Experience. William Nichols. (Orig.). 1975. pap. text ed. 8.00 o.p. (ISBN 0-15-597861-6, HC). HarBraceJ.

Writing Fundamentals. David A. McMurrey & M. S. Campman. 448p. 1983. pap. text ed. write for info. o.p. (ISBN 0-02-379670-7). Macmillan.

Writing in a State of Siege. Andre Brink. 1986. pap. 8.95 o.s.i. (ISBN 0-671-62289-7). Summit Bks.

Writing in Context. Mary E. Capek. LC 75-44874. (Illus.). 256p. 1976. pap. text ed. 1.00 o.p. (ISBN 0-15-597897-7, HC). HarBraceJ.

Writing in General & the Short Story in Particular. Rust Hills. LC 77-21224. 1979. 10.95 o.p. (ISBN 0-395-25715-8). HM.

Writing in Style. Washington Post Writers Group. 1975. pap. 9.95 o.p. (ISBN 0-395-24018-2). HM.

Writing in the Content Areas: Research Implications. Joanne M. Yates. (What Research Says to the Teacher Ser.). 32p. 1983. 2.95 o.p. (ISBN 0-8106-1060-4). NEA.

Writing in the Sand. Carsten Johnsen & Sylvi Johnsen. LC 83-90928. 56p. 1985. 6.95 o.p. (ISBN 0-533-05940-2). Vantage.

Writing Instruction for Verbally Talented Youth: The Johns Hopkins Model. Ben Reynolds et al. LC 84-270. 228p. 1984. 28.95 o.p. (ISBN 0-89443-585-X). Aspen Pub.

Writing Instructional Objectives & Activities for the Modern Curriculum. Earl J. Ogletree & Maxine Hawkins. LC 73-1017. 72p. 1973. pap. text ed. 4.95x o.p. (ISBN 0-8422-0278-1). Irvington.

Writing Local History: A Practical Guide. David Dymond. 91p. 1981. pap. 8.00x o.p. (ISBN 0-7199-1048-X, Pub. by Bedford England). Gower Pub Co.

Writing Medical Papers: A Practical Guide. J. Calnan & A. Barabas. (Illus.). 1977. pap. 8.50 o.p. (ISBN 0-433-05005-5). E J Brill USA.

Writing of History in the Soviet Union. Anatole G. Mazour. LC 76-99084. (Publications Ser.: No. 87). 1971. 19.50x o.p. (ISBN 0-8179-1871-X). Hoover Inst Pr.

Writing of One Novel. Irving Wallace. 1968. 4.95 o.p. (ISBN 0-671-20116-6, Fireside); pap. 1.95 o.p. (ISBN 0-671-20345-2). S&S.

Writing on the Wall & Other Literary Essays. Mary McCarthy. LC 70-100498. Orig. Title: Hanging by a Thread & Other Literary Essays. 1970. 6.75 o.s.i. (ISBN 0-15-199711-X). HarBraceJ.

Writing Out Loud: A Self-Help Guide to Clear Business Writing. John L. DiGaetani & Earl N. Harbert. LC 82-73623. 190p. 1983. 14.95 o.p. (ISBN 0-87094-374-X). Dow Jones-Irwin.

Writing Process. 2nd ed. John M. Lannon. 1986. pap. text ed. write for info. o.p. (ISBN 0-673-39275-9). Scott F.

Writing Prose That Makes a Difference, & the Grammar Minimum. Oxford S. Stroud. LC 79-84651. 1979. pap. text ed. 8.00 o.p. (ISBN 0-8191-0740-9). U Pr of Amer.

Writing Research Papers: A Norton Guide. Melissa Walker. 1984. pap. text ed. 6.95x o.p. (ISBN 0-393-95347-5). Norton.

Writing Research Papers Across the Curriculum. Susan M. Hubbuch. 256p. 1985. pap. text ed. 7.95 o.p. (ISBN 0-03-063193-9, HoltC). HR&W.

Writing Science News for the Mass Media. 2nd ed. David W. Burkett. LC 72-84334. 223p. 1973. 15.00x o.p. (ISBN 0-87201-924-1). Gulf Pub.

Writing Secret Codes & Sending Hidden Messages. Gyles Brandreth. LC 83-24230. (Illus.). (YA) (gr. 7 up). 1986. pap. 3.95 o.p. (ISBN 0-8069-6306-9); 8.95 o.p. (ISBN 0-8069-4690-3); RLE o.p. 10.99 o.p. (ISBN 0-8069-4691-1). Sterling.

Writing Seminars in the Content Area: In Search of Hemingway, Salinger, & Steinbeck. Brooke Workman. 321p. 1983. pap. 15.25 o.p. (ISBN 0-8141-5886-2). NCTE.

Writing Study Guides. Anita Morris. (Orig.). 1984. pap. text ed. 8.95x o.p. (ISBN 0-86184-127-1). Trans Atl Phila.

Writing Term Papers: The Research Paper - the Critical Paper. 2nd ed. Hulon Willis. 154p. (Orig.). 1983. pap. text ed. 7.50 o.p. (ISBN 0-15-598283-4, HC). HarBraceJ.

Writing Term Papers: The Research Paper-the Critical Paper. Hulon Willis. 1977. 6.95 o.p. (ISBN 0-15-598281-8). HarbraceJ.

Writing the Absence of the Father: Undoing Oedipal Structures in the Contemporary American Novel. Francesco A. Ancona. 172p. (Orig.). 1986. lib. bdg. 26.00 o.p. (ISBN 0-8191-5097-5); pap. text ed. 12.25 o.p. (ISBN 0-8191-5098-3). U Pr of Amer.

Writing the Business & Technical Report. William J. Gallagher. LC 80-19781. 120p. 1983. pap. 15.95 o.p. (ISBN 0-8436-0796-3). Van Nos Reinhold.

Writing: The Business Letter. Albert G. Craz & Edward P. Mavragis. (Writing Ser.). 68p. 1981. wkbk. 3.95 o.p. (ISBN 0-9602800-1-4). Comp Pr.

Writing the Expository Essay. Jane Kahan & Marie K. Stone. LC 78-730063. (Illus.). 1977. pap. text ed. 159.00 o.s.i. (ISBN 0-89290-123-3, A322). Soc for Visual.

Writing: The Personal Voice. Jill W. Cohn. 214p. (Orig.). 1975. pap. text ed. 8.75 o.p. (ISBN 0-15-597787-3, HC). HarBraceJ.

Writing the Research Paper: A Handbook. Anthony C. Winkler & Jo Ray McCuen. 276p. 1979. pap. text ed. 7.95 o.p. (ISBN 0-15-598290-7, HC). HarBraceJ.

Writing to the Point: Six Basic Steps. William J. Kerrigan. 1974. pap. text ed. 8.95 o.p. (ISBN 0-15-598310-5, HC). HarBraceJ.

Writing to the Point: Six Basic Steps. 3rd ed. William J. Kerrigan. 172p. 1983. pap. text ed. 10.50 o.p. (ISBN 0-15-598312-1, HC). HarBraceJ.

Writing to the Point: Six Basic Steps. William J. Kerrigan. 1979. 9.95 o.p. (ISBN 0-15-598311-3). HarbraceJ.

Writing Tom Sawyer: The Adventures of a Classic. Charles A. Norton. LC 82-17164. 168p. 1983. lib. bdg. 18.95x o.p. (ISBN 0-89950-067-6). McFarland & Co.

Writing Well. 5th ed. Donald Hall. 1985. pap. text ed. write for info. o.p. (ISBN 0-673-39216-3); avail.tchr's.manual o.p. Scott F.

Writing with a Purpose. short, 6th ed. James M. McCrimmon. LC 76-47875. 1977. text ed. 9.95 o.p. (ISBN 0-395-25004-8). HM.

Writing with a Purpose. 6th ed. James M. McCrimmon. 1976. text ed. 14.95 o.p. (ISBN 0-395-19235-8); text ed. 10.95 o.p. HM.

Writing with a Purpose. 7th ed. James M. McCrimmon et al. LC 79-88599. 1980. text ed. 17.95 o.p. (ISBN 0-395-28253-5). HM.

Writing with a Purpose: Short Edition. 7th ed. James M. McCrimmon et al. LC 79-90088. 1980. pap. 17.95 o.p. (ISBN 0-395-28939-4). HM.

Writing with a Voice: A Rhetoric Handbook. Diana Hacker & Betty Renshaw. 1985. pap. text ed. write for info. o.p. (ISBN 0-673-39215-5); tchr's. ed. avail. o.p. Scott F.

Writing with Confidence. 2nd ed. Alan Meyers. 1984. pap. text ed. write for info. spiral bdg. o.p. (ISBN 0-673-15878-0). Scott F.

Writing Women. Date not set. (ISBN 0-8052-3869-7). Random.

Writing Your College Application & Essay. Max Holmes. 96p. (Orig.). 1984. pap. 5.95 o.p. (ISBN 0-671-52453-4). Monarch Pr.

Writing Your College Application Essay. Sarah M. McGinty. 1987. pap. 9.95 o.p. (ISBN 0-317-64588-9). College Bd.

Writings & Speeches of Professor D. R. Gadgil on Planning & Development: 1967-71. D. R. Gadgil. Ed. by A. R. Kamat. LC 75-901569. 1974. 10.00x o.p. (ISBN 0-88386-567-X). South Asia Bks.

Writings in the Dust. Carl E. Price. 112p. (Orig.). 1984. pap. 4.75 o.p. (ISBN 0-8358-0474-7). Upper Room.

Writings of Charles Jencks, Apostle, by Post-Modernism. Carole Cable. (Architecture Ser.: A 1455). 9p. 1985. 2.00 o.p. (ISBN 0-89028-545-4). Vance Biblios.

Writings of President Frederick M. Smith, Vol. 1. Ed. by Norman D. Ruoff. LC 78-6428. 1978. pap. 10.00 o.p. (ISBN 0-8309-0215-5). Herald Hse.

Writings of President Frederick M. Smith, Vol. 2. Ed. by Norman D. Ruoff. LC 78-6428. 1979. pap. 10.00 o.p. (ISBN 0-8309-0239-2). Herald Hse.

Writings of President Frederick M. Smith, Vol. III: The Zionic Enterprise. Ed. by Norman D. Ruoff. 1981. pap. 10.00 o.p. (ISBN 0-8309-0300-3). Herald Hse.

Written for Children: An Outline of English-Language Children's Literature. John R. Townsend. (Illus.). 1974. pap. 8.00 o.p. (ISBN 0-87675-278-4). Horn Bk.

Written in Blood: The Story of the Haitian People 1492-1971. Robert D. Heinl, Jr. & Nancy G. Heinl. 1978. 21.95 o.p. (ISBN 0-395-26305-0). HM.

Written in the Book of Life. P. Mirny. 327p. 1982. 8.95 o.p. (ISBN 0-8285-2454-8, Pub. by Progress Pubs USSR). Imported Pubns.

Written Language Instruction: Theory & Remediation. Trisha Phelps-Gunn & Diana Phelps-Terasaki. LC 81-10824. 290p. 1982. text ed. 34.50 o.p. (ISBN 0-89443-360-1). Aspen Pub.

Written Letters: Twenty-Nine Alphabets for Calligraphers. rev. ed. Jacqueline Svaren. LC 81-86266. (Illus.). 64p. 1982. pap. 14.95 o.s.i. (ISBN 0-8008-8734-4, Pentalic). Taplinger.

Written out of History: Our Jewish Foremothers. 2nd, rev. ed. Sondra Henry & Emily Taitz. LC 82-74284. (Illus.). 300p. 1983. 12.00 o.p. (ISBN 0-930395-03-4); pap. 9.00 o.p. (ISBN 0-9602036-8-0). Biblio NY.

Wrong Diagnosis-Wrong Treatment: An Alcoholics Plight. Joseph Beasley. 1987. 12.95 o.p. (ISBN 0-917634-29-2). Creative Infomatics.

Wrong Kind of Girl. Francine Pascal. (Sweet Valley High Ser.: No. 10). (gr. 7 up). 1984. pap. 2.75 o.p. (ISBN 0-553-26620-9). Bantam.

Wrong Side of the Tracks. Charles M. Haar & Daniel W. Fessler. 1986. 18.45 o.p. (ISBN 0-671-60187-3). S&S.

Wrongful Death Litigation. LC 83-71583. (Civil Practice Ser.: No. 5). 147p. (Orig.). 1983. pap. 30.00 o.p. (ISBN 0-941916-10-3). Assn Trial Ed.

Wujing Well. 1981. 1.95 o.p. (ISBN 0-8351-0938-0). China Bks.

Wuthering Heights. Emily Bronte. LC 82-62131. (Illus.). 303p. 1982. 12.95 o.p. (ISBN 0-89577-159-4). RD Assn.

Wuthering Heights. Emily Bronte. 48p. (Orig.). 1988. pap. 9.95 o.s.i. (ISBN 1-55651-950-8); cassette o.s.i. (ISBN 1-55651-951-6). Cram Cassettes.

Wuthering Heights. Emily Bronte. (Movieworld (easy reading edition) Ser.). (Illus.). 32p. (Orig.). (gr. 7-12). 1985. pap. text ed. 5.95 o.p. (ISBN 0-582-33098-X). Longman.

Wuzzles Book of Go-Togethers. Don E. Plumme. LC 85-61160. (Chunky Bks.). (Illus.). 28p. (ps). 1986. 2.95 o.s.i. (ISBN 0-394-87848-5). Random.

Wuzzles' Fair. Barbara George. LC 85-18357. (Illus.). 32p. (ps-3). 1986. 3.95 o.s.i. (ISBN 0-394-87912-0). Random.

Wuzzle's Wishing Flower. Ali Reich. LC 85-60207. (Illus.). 14p. (gr. 2-4). 1985. 4.95 o.s.i. (ISBN 0-394-87501-X, BYR). Random.

WW II: Luftwaffe Combat Planes & Aces. Joe Christy. pap. 6.95 o.p. (ISBN 0-8306-2275-6, 2275). TAB Bks.

WW II: Marine Fighting Squadron Nine (VF-9M) Jess C. Barrow. pap. 7.95 o.p. (ISBN 0-8306-2289-6, 2289). TAB Bks.

WWII: Flying the B-26 Marauder over Europe. Carl H. Moore. (Illus.). 176p. 1982. pap. 7.95 o.p. (ISBN 0-8306-2311-6, 2311). TAB Bks.

Wyatt: The Critical Heritage. Ed. by Patricia Thomson. (Critical Heritage Ser.). 196p. 1974. 29.95x o.p. (ISBN 0-7100-7907-9). Routledge Chapman & Hall.

Wycliffe & the Winsor Blue. W. J. Burley. LC 87-8823. (Crime Club Ser.). 192p. 1987. 12.95 o.s.i. (ISBN 0-385-24311-1). Doubleday.

Wyeth at Kuerners. Betsy J. Wyeth. 1977. 75.00 o.p. (ISBN 0-395-21990-6). HM.

Wymore Story. 2nd ed. Richard C. Kistler. Ed. by James J. Reisdorff. (Illus.). 64p. 1984. pap. 9.00 o.p. (ISBN 0-9609568-3-2). South Platte.

Wyndham Lewis: A Descriptive Bibliography. Omar Pound & Philip Grover. LC 78-315951. (Illus.). 198p. 1978. 25.00 o.p. (ISBN 0-208-01725-9, Archon). Shoe String.

Wyoma. Lynn G. Temple. 1978. 6.00 o.p. (ISBN 0-682-49004-0). Exposition-Phoenix.

Wyoming Frontier Cooking. American Cancer Society Staff. 136p. 1981. pap. 6.00 o.p. (ISBN 0-686-31488-3). Am Cancer WY.

Wyoming in Profile. Jean Mead. LC 82-12230. (Illus.). 250p. 1982. 16.95 o.p. (ISBN 0-87108-600-X); pap. 7.95 o.p. (ISBN 0-87108-601-8). Pruett.

Wyoming Scientist: Horses to Spaceships. Emerson M. Pugh & Ruth Edgin. 1979. 15.00 o.p. (ISBN 0-682-49392-9). Exposition-Phoenix.

Wyoming: Trusts. 8.50 o.p. (ISBN 0-686-90977-1). Am Law Inst.

Wyoming: Wild & Wooly. William F. Bragg. LC 83-9603. (Illus.). 168p. 1983. 14.95 o.p. (ISBN 0-87108-628-X); pap. 7.95 o.p. (ISBN 0-87108-631-X). Pruett.

Wyoming's People. 2nd ed. Clarice Whittenburg & Carol Stinneford. 213p. 1978. pap. 7.95x o.p. (ISBN 0-933472-12-9); 5.00 o.p. (ISBN 0-933472-37-4). Johnson Bks.

X

X-Craft Raid. Thomas Gallagher. LC 74-15386. 170p. 1971. 6.75 o.p. (ISBN 0-15-199726-8). HarBraceJ.

X-Ray Diffraction Topography. B. K. Tanner. LC 75-45196. 1976. 50.00 o.p. (ISBN 0-08-019692-6). Pergamon.

X-Ray Information Book: A Consumers' Guide to Avoiding Unnecessary Medical & Dental X-Rays. Public Citizen Health Research Group Staff & Priscilla W. Laws. 154p. 1983. 14.50 o.p. (ISBN 0-374-29342-2); pap. 5.95 o.p. (ISBN 0-374-51730-4). FS&G.

X-Ray Measurements in the Auroral Zone from July to October 1964. G. Kremser et al. (Illus.). 1965. pap. 10.70 o.p. (ISBN 0-387-03365-3). Springer-Verlag.

X-Ray Photoelectron Spectroscopy. T. A. Carlson. LC 77-28499. (Benchmark Papers in Physical Chemistry & Chemical Physics: Vol. 2). 341p. 1982. 57.95 o.p. (ISBN 0-87933-325-1). Van Nos Reinhold.

X-Ray Photoelectron Spectroscopy: Application to Metals & Alloys see Photoelectron Spectrometry.

X-Raying the Pharaohs. James E. Harris & Kent R. Weeks. LC 72-1180. (Encore Edition). (Illus.). 265p. 1973. pap. 2.95 o.p. (ISBN 0-684-16899-5, ScribT). Scribner.

X Stands for Unknown. Isaac Asimov. 224p. 1985. pap. 3.95 o.p. (ISBN 0-380-69847-1, Discus). Avon.

Xala. Sembene Ousmane. Tr. by Clive Wake from Fr. LC 75-41811. (Illus.). 112p. 1976. pap. 10.00 o.p. (ISBN 0-88208-067-9); pap. text ed. 6.95 o.p. Chicago Review.

Xenakis. Nouritza Matossian. (Illus.). 272p. 1986. 19.95 o.s.i. (ISBN 0-8008-4050-X). Taplinger.

Xenophon's Socratic Discourse. Leo Strauss. LC 71-38122. 201p. 1973. 17.50x o.p. (ISBN 0-8014-0712-5); pap. 8.95x o.p. (ISBN 0-8014-9133-9). Cornell U Pr.

Xerus Won't Allow It. Jacquelyn Reinach. Ed. by Ruth L. Perle. LC 78-54979. (Sweet Pickles Ser.). (Illus.). (gr. k-2). 1978. 2.95 o.p. (ISBN 0-03-042076-8). H Holt & Co.

Xi'an Tourist Map. (Illus.). 2p. 1983. pap. 2.95 o.p. (ISBN 0-8351-1204-7). China Bks.

Xiao Ming & Katie Visit the Zoo. 1981. 1.95 o.p. (ISBN 0-8351-0775-2). China Bks.

Xiaoying's Cartoons for Children. Le Xiaoying. (Illus.). 18p. (Orig.). (ps-6). 1987. pap. 1.95 o.p. (ISBN 0-8351-1572-0). China Bks.

XII Programming Manuals: Volumes 1 & 2 Sold As Set. Adrian Nye. 700p. 1987. pap. text ed. 60.00 o.p. (ISBN 0-937175-25-0). O'Reilly & Assocs.

Xochipala: The Beginnings of Olmec Art. Carlo T. E. Gay. LC 70-187566. (Publications of the Princeton Univ. Art Museum). (Illus.). 64p. 1972. 21.00x o.p. (ISBN 0-691-03880-5); pap. 3.95 o.p. (ISBN 0-691-03877-5). Princeton U Pr.

Xu Beihong: Life of a Master Painter. Liao Jingwen. Tr. by Zhang Peiji from Chinese. (Illus.). 365p. (Orig.). 1987. pap. 8.95 o.p. (ISBN 0-8351-1551-8). China Bks.

XyWrite Made Easier: Revised & Expanded to Include Version XyWrite III Plus. David Rothman. (Illus.). 352p. (Orig.). 1987. 27.95 o.p. (ISBN 0-8306-1220-3); pap. 21.95 o.p. (ISBN 0-8306-2820-7). TAB Bks.

XYY Man. Kenneth Royce. 192p. 1973. pap. 0.75 o.p. (ISBN 0-380-01629-X, 14258). Avon.

Y

Ya Lo Leo. Programa de Proyecto Frontera Staff. Ed. by Nathan Quinones. LC 76-2731. (Illus.). 1976. pap. text ed. 2.95 o.p. (ISBN 0-8120-0677-1). Barron.

Yakety-Yak-Yak Yak. Richard Hefter & Jacquelyn Reinach. LC 77-7250. (Sweet Pickles Ser.). (gr. k-2). 1977. 2.95 o.p. (ISBN 0-03-021436-X). HR&W.

Yakov Sverdlov. K. Sverdlova. 135p. 1981. 5.00 o.p. (ISBN 0-8285-2016-X, Pub. by Progress Pubs USSR). Imported Pubns.

Yakutia: Before Its Incorporation into the Russian State. A. P. Okladnikov. Ed. by Henry N. Michael. (Anthropology of the North Ser). 529p. 1970. 25.00x o.p. (ISBN 0-7735-9068-4, McGill Canada). U of Toronto Pr.

Yalkut Eliezer. Eliezer Z. Soffer. (Hebrew.). 32.00 o.p. (ISBN 0-87559-080-2). Shalom.

Yalta Myths: An Issue in U. S. Politics, 1945-1955. Athan Theoharis. LC 70-105269. 280p. 1970. 28.00x o.p. (ISBN 0-8262-0088-5). U of Mo Pr.

Yalu Flows see Grass Roof.

Yamagata. Austin Jaynes. (Illus.). 144p. 1986. 50.00 o.p. (ISBN 0-88363-386-8). H L Levin.

Yamaha Revised & Updated. Ted Macauley. (Illus.). 283p. 16.95 o.p. (ISBN 0-85429-419-8, BL419). Haynes Pubns.

Yamaha RS100 & 125 Singles '74-'79. Pete Shoemark. pap. 13.50 o.p. (ISBN 0-85696-331-3, 331). Haynes Pubns.

Yamaha Seca 750. (M391). Clymer Pub.

Yamaha Service-Repair Handbook: 90-200cc Twins, 1966-1977. Ed. by Eric Jorgensen. (Illus.). pap. 11.95 o.p. (ISBN 0-89287-179-2, M400). Clymer Pub.

Yamaha Snowmobiles: Nineteen Seventy-Five to Nineteen Eighty Service, Repair & Maintenance. Ed. by Eric Jorgensen. (Illus.). 180p. (Orig.). 1980. pap. text ed. 8.95 o.p. (ISBN 0-89287-323-X, X954). Clymer Pub.

Yamaha: TX500 & XS500 Twins, 1973-1978--Service, Repair, Performance. Ed. by Eric Jorgensen. (Illus.). pap. 10.95 o.p. (ISBN 0-89287-241-1, M406). Clymer Pub.

Yamaha XS1100 Fours: 1978-1981 Service-Repair-Performance. Ed Scott. (Illus., Orig.). pap. text ed. 17.95 o.s.i. (ISBN 0-89287-309-4, M411). Clymer Pub.

Yamaha: XS360 & XS-400 Twins, 1976-81, Service, Repair, Maintenance. Ed. by Eric Jorgensen. (Illus.). pap. 11.95 o.p. (ISBN 0-89287-170-9, M402). Clymer Pub.

Yamaha 200 Twins '71 - '79. Mark Reynolds & P. Shoemark. (Owners Workshop Manuals Ser.: No. 156). 1974. 13.50 o.p. (ISBN 0-85696-156-6, Pub. by J H Haynes England). Haynes Pubns.

Yamaha 250 & 350 Twins '70 - '79. Jeff Clew. (Owners Workshop Manuals Ser.: No. 040). 1980. 13.50 o.p. (ISBN 0-85696-505-7, Pub. by J H Haynes England). Haynes Pubns.

Yamaha: 250-400cc Piston Port Singles, 1968-76, Service, Repair, Performance. 3rd ed. Clymer Publications Staff. (Illus.). pap. 13.95 o.s.i. (ISBN 0-89287-276-4, M415). Clymer Pub.

Yamaha: 250-400cc, 1965-1979 - Service, Repair, Performance. 3rd ed. Clymer Publications Staff. (Illus.). pap. 13.95 o.s.i. (ISBN 0-89287-283-7, M401). Clymer Pub.

Yamaha: 50-100cc Rotary Valve Singles, 1963-1976--Service, Repair, Maintenance. 3rd ed. Ed. by Eric Jorgensen. (Illus.). pap. 11.95 o.p. (ISBN 0-89287-220-9, M389). Clymer Pub.

Yan'an Women & the Communist Party. Patricia Stranahan. (China Research Monographs: No. 26). 130p. (Orig.). 1984. pap. 12.00x o.p. (ISBN 0-912966-66-1). IEAS.

Yankee among the Nullifiers: An Autobiography. Asa Greene. 143p. 1986. pap. text ed. 5.95x o.p. (ISBN 0-8290-1961-8). Irvington.

Yankee & the Belle. Catherine Creel. 1979. pap. 2.25 o.p. (ISBN 0-505-51432-X, Pub. by Tower Bks). Dorchester Pub Co.

Yankee & the Belle. Catherine Creel. 320p. 1984. pap. 3.25 o.p. (ISBN 0-8439-2102-1, Pub. by Leisure Bks CT). Dorchester Pub Co.

Yankee Blitzkrieg: Wilson's Raid Through Alabama & Georgia. James P Jones. LC 74-15206. 270p. 1976. pap. 20.00x o.p. (ISBN 0-8203-0370-4). U of Ga Pr.

Yankee Bookseller. Charles E. Goodspeed. LC 73-15401. (Illus.). 325p. 1974. Repr. of 1937 ed. lib. bdg. 24.75x o.p. (ISBN 0-8371-7173-3, GOYB). Greenwood.

Yankee Communes: Another American Way. Flo Morse. LC 73-157875. (Curriculum Related Bks.). (Illus.). 179p. (gr. 7 up). 1971. 5.95 o.p. (ISBN 0-15-299710-5, HJ). HarBraceJ.

Yankee Diplomacy: U. S. Intervention in Argentina. Oscar E. Smith, Jr. LC 79-25196. (Arnold Foundation Studies: Vol, III, New Ser.). 196p. 1980. Repr. of 1953 ed. lib. bdg. 35.00x o.p. (ISBN 0-313-22124-3, SMYD). Greenwood.

Yankee Doodle Cousins. Anne Malcolmson. (Illus.). (gr. 4-8). 7.95 o.p. (ISBN 0-395-06896-7). HM.

Yankee Doodle-Doo: A Collection of Songs of the Early American Stage. Grenville Vernon. LC 73-78662. 172p. 1972. Repr. of 1927 ed. 43.00x o.p. (ISBN 0-8103-3872-6). Gale.

Yankee Dreamers & Doers. Ellsworth S. Grant. (Illus.). 269p. 1974. 9.95x o.p. (ISBN 0-686-26751-6). Conn Hist Soc.

Yankee Eloquence in the Middle West: The Ohio Lyceum, 1850-1870. Carl D. Mead. LC 77-5130. 1977. Repr. of 1951 ed. lib. bdg. 25.00x o.p. (ISBN 0-8371-9323-0, MEYE). Greenwood.

Yankee Ghosts. Hans Holzer. Ed. by Jennifer Adams. LC 86-80336. 208p. 1986. Repr. of 1966 ed. 12.95 o.p. (ISBN 0-89909-102-4). Yankee Bks.

Yankee in Mexican California, Abel Stearns, 1798-1948. Doris M. Wright. (Wallace Hebberd Editions). 1977. 12.50 o.p. (ISBN 0-686-74504-3). Dawsons.

Yankee in Mexican California: Abel Stearns, 1798-1848. Doris M. Wright. x, 177p. 1977. 12.50 o.p. (ISBN 0-317-11664-9). Dawsons.

Yankee Lover. John L. Reynolds. 1980. 7.95 o.p. (ISBN 0-682-49508-5). Exposition-Phoenix.

Yankee Magazine's Great New England Recipes: And the Cooks Who Made Them Famous. Ed. by Sandra Taylor. LC 82-51210. (Illus.). 320p. 1983. 15.95 o.p. (ISBN 0-911658-36-X). Yankee Bks.

Yankee Magazine's Home Fix-It Book. Earl Proulx. Ed. by Lila Walz. LC 81-52931. (Illus.). 64p. (Orig.). 1982. pap. 3.95 o.p. (ISBN 0-911658-33-5). Yankee Bks.

Yankee Magazine's Street Maps of Boston. 32p. 1984. pap. 5.95 o.p. (ISBN 0-911658-11-4). Yankee Bks.

Yankee Magazine's Travel Guide to New England & Its Neighbors. 1988. 3.95 o.p. (ISBN 0-317-67754-3). Yankee Bks.

Yankee Missionaries in the South: The Penn School Experiment. Elizabeth Jacoway. LC 79-21024. xviii, 306p. 1980. text ed. 32.50 o.p. (ISBN 0-8071-0571-6). La State U Pr.

Yankee Reformers in the Urban Age: Social Reform in Boston, 1880-1900. Arthur Mann. (Midway Reprint Ser). 328p. 1974. pap. text ed. 10.00x o.s.i. (ISBN 0-226-50336-4). U of Chicago Pr.

Yankee Stranger. Ed Figueroa & Dorothy Harshman. (Illus.). 231p. 1982. 11.00 o.p. (ISBN 0-682-49902-1). Exposition-Phoenix.

Yankee Teacher. Kurt F. Leidecker. (ISBN 0-8022-0957-2). Philos Lib.

Yankee Verse by Nathan Marshall Southwick (1872-1963) The Wit & Wisdom of a New England Philosopher. Compiled by Lawrence Southwick. 1979. 10.00 o.p. (ISBN 0-682-49205-1). Exposition-Phoenix.

Yankee Way with Wood. Phyllis Meras. LC 75-14221. 1975. 14.95 o.p. (ISBN 0-395-20423-2). HM.

Yankee's Book of Whatsits. Ed. by Clarissa M. Silitch. LC 75-17109. (Illus.). 64p. (Orig.). 1975. pap. 4.95 o.p. (ISBN 0-911658-67-X). Yankee Bks.

Yankees under Sail. Ed. by Richard Heckman. LC 68-31685. (Illus.). 254p. 1983. pap. 18.95 o.p. (ISBN 0-911658-58-0). Yankee Bks.

Yaqui Myths & Legends. Ruth W. Giddings. LC 60-63129. (Illus.). 180p. 1968. pap. 6.50 o.p. (ISBN 0-8165-0467-9). U of Ariz Pr.

Yardbird Lives! Ed. by Ishmael Reed & Al Young. LC 77-18321. 1978. pap. 5.95 o.p. (ISBN 0-394-17041-5, E710, Ever). Grove.

Yardbird Suite: A Compendium of the Music & Life of Charlie Parker. Lawrence O. Koch. (Illus.). 300p. 1983. write for info. o.p. Bowling Green Univ.

Yarn Art Projects. Jean Lyon. (Illus.). 64p. (gr. 3-9). 1985. wkbk. 6.95 o.p. (ISBN 0-86653-325-7). Good Apple.

Yarn: The Things It Makes & How to Make Them. Carolyn Meyer. LC 72-76367. (Illus.). 128p. (gr. 5 up). 1972. 5.95 o.p. (ISBN 0-15-299713-X, HJ). HarBraceJ.

Yarns of Wisconsin. Ed. by Sue McCoy & Jill Dean. LC 76-25119. (Illus., Orig.). 1978. pap. 7.95 o.p. (ISBN 0-915024-08-X). WI Trails.

Yasmina's Daughter. Corinne Childs. 1981. pap. 2.50 o.p. (ISBN 0-8439-0838-6, Pub. by Leisure Bks CT). Dorchester Pub Co.

Yazoo: Law & Politics in the New Republic, Case of Fletcher V. Peck. C. Peter Magrath. 1967. pap. 2.95 o.p. (ISBN 0-393-00418-X, Norton Lib). Norton.

Ye Are Gods. Annalee Skarin. (ISBN 0-8022-1583-1). Philos Lib.

Ye Olden Time: English Customs in the Middle Ages. Emily S. Holt. LC 72-164343. 226p. 1971. Repr. of 1884 ed. 35.00x o.p. (ISBN 0-8103-3798-3). Gale.

Ye Shall Be Comforted. William F. Rogers. 1975. pap. 1.95 o.s.i. (ISBN 0-664-24776-8, Westminster). Westminster John Knox.

Yea, Wildcats. John R. Tunis. LC 44-8408. (gr. 7 up). 1944. 4.95 o.p. (ISBN 0-15-299716-4, HJ). HarBraceJ.

Yeah, But. Fanny Howe. 128p. (YA) (gr. 7 up). 1982. pap. 1.95 o.p. (ISBN 0-380-79186-2, 79186-2, Flare). Avon.

Year Ahead: 1985. Naisbitt Group Staff & John Naisbitt. 64p. 1985. pap. 6.95 o.p. AMACOM.

Year-Around Conditioning for Part-Time Golfers. Keith Jennison & William A. Pratt. LC 78-53836. (Illus.). 1979. 9.95 o.p. (ISBN 0-689-10875-3, Atheneum). Macmillan.

Year Book of Anesthesia, 1980. Ed. by James E. Eckenhoff et al. 400p. 1980. 42.95 o.p. (ISBN 0-8151-3040-6). Year Bk Med.

Year Book of Social Policy in Britain, 1984-1985. Ed. by Maria Brenton & Catherine Jones. 256p. 1985. 42.50x o.p. (ISBN 0-7102-0603-8). Routledge Chapman & Hall.

Year Boston Won the Pennant. John F. Noonan. 1970. pap. 2.45 o.p. (ISBN 0-394-17380-5, E530, Ever). Grove.

Year in Benares. Eleanor Edgerton. (Orig.). 1981. pap. 12.50x o.p. (ISBN 0-8364-0697-4, Pub. by Priyamvada India). South Asia Bks.

Year in the Beeyard. Roger A. Morse. (Illus.). 192p. 1983. 14.95 o.p. (ISBN 0-684-17876-1, ScribT). Scribner.

Year in the Life of Rosie Bernard. rev. ed. Barbara Brenner. (Illus.). 184p. (gr. 3-7). 1979. pap. 1.25 o.p. (ISBN 0-380-01630-3, 43380-X, Camelot). Avon.

Year King. Penelope Farmer. LC 77-3165. 228p. (gr. 9 up). 1977. 6.95 o.p. (ISBN 0-689-50090-4, Atheneum). Macmillan.

Year of Decision. Bernard De Voto. 1950. 7.95 o.p. (ISBN 0-395-07611-0). HM.

Year of Decision, 1788: Virginia's Ratification of the United States Constitution. cancelled o.s.i. U Va Ctr Pub Serv.

Year of Protest, 1956. Ed. by Hugh McLean & Walter N. Vickery. LC 74-8359. 269p. 1974. Repr. of 1961 ed. lib. bdg. 29.75x o.p. (ISBN 0-8371-7575-5, MCYP). Greenwood.

Year of Small Shadow. Evelyn S. Lampman. LC 73-152694. 190p. (gr. 5-7). 1971. 5.95 o.p. (ISBN 0-15-299815-2, HJ). HarBraceJ.

Year of Snow Accumulation at Plateau Station; Thermal Properties & Heat Transfer Processes of Low-Temperature Snow; Radiative Heat Transfer; Process in Snow & Ice; Papers 1, 2, 3 & 4: Meteorological Studies at Plateau Station, Antarctica. Paul Dalrymple et al. Ed. by Joost A. Businger. (Antarctic Research Ser.: Vol. 25). (Illus.). 1977. pap. 13.50 o.p. Am Geophysical.

Year of Sweet Senior Insanity. Sonia Levitin. LC 81-8081. 204p. (gr. 7 up). 1982. 10.95 o.s.i. (ISBN 0-689-30883-3, Atheneum Childrens Bks). Macmillan.

Year of the Angler. rev. ed. Steve Raymond. LC 73-78825. (Illus.). 216p. 1983. pap. 19.95 o.p. (ISBN 0-8329-0319-1, Pub. by Winchester Pr). New Century.

Year of the Bloody Sevens. William O. Steele. LC 63-16036. (Illus.). (gr. 4-6). 1963. 6.75 o.p. (ISBN 0-15-299800-4, HJ). HarBraceJ.

Year of the Cougar. Jesse Bier. LC 75-43776. 288p. 1976. 8.95 o.p. (ISBN 0-15-199736-5). HarBraceJ.

Year of the Greylag Goose. Konrad Lorenz. Ed. by Helen Wolff. Tr. by Robert Martin. LC 79-1834. (Helen & Kurt Wolff Bk.). 1979. 25.00 o.p. (ISBN 0-15-199737-3). HarBraceJ.

Year of the Gun. Michael Mewshaw. LC 83-45511. 288p. 1984. 14.95 o.s.i. (ISBN 0-689-11433-8, Atheneum). Macmillan.

Year of the Handicapped. J. C. Poole. 118p. 1983. 8.00 o.p. (ISBN 0-682-49990-0). Exposition-Phoenix.

Year of the Intern. Robin Cook. LC 72-75414. 1972. 6.75 o.p. (ISBN 0-15-199740-3). HarBraceJ.

Year of the Lord: A. D. 1844. Charles W. Meister. LC 82-23976. 264p. 1983. lib. bdg. 18.95x o.p. (ISBN 0-89950-037-4). McFarland & Co.

Year of the Mongoose. William Hogan. LC 81-66022. 1981. 12.95 o.p. (ISBN 0-689-11209-2, Atheneum). Macmillan.

Year of the Raccoon. Lee Kingman. (Illus.). (gr. 6-8). 1966. 8.95 o.p. (ISBN 0-395-06865-7). HM.

Year of the Trout. Steve Raymond. LC 85-6155. (Illus.). 208p. 1985. 19.95 o.p. (ISBN 0-8329-0384-1, Pub. by Winchester Pr). New Century.

Year of Three Kings: 1483. Giles St. Aubyn. LC 83-45083. (Illus.). 296p. 1983. 13.95 o.s.i. (ISBN 0-689-11409-5, Atheneum). Macmillan.

Year of Victory. Ivan Konev. Tr. by David Mishne. (Illus.). 248p. 1984. 7.95 o.p. (ISBN 0-8285-2826-8, Pub. by Progress Pubs USSR). Imported Pubns.

Year the Dreams Came Back. Anita M. Feagles. LC 76-4469. 176p. (gr. 5-8). 1976. 7.95 o.p. (ISBN 0-689-30538-9, Atheneum). Macmillan.

Year the Lights Came On. Terry Kay. LC 76-15170. 1976. 8.95 o.p. (ISBN 0-395-24403-X). HM.

Year the World Was Out of Step with Jancy Fried. Jean Fiedler. LC 81-47530. 156p. 1981. 9.95 o.p. (ISBN 0-15-299818-7, HJ). HarBraceJ.

Year They Sold Wall Street: The Inside Story of the Shearson-American Express Merger, and How it Changed Wall Street Forever. Timothy Carrington. (Illus.). 235p. 1985. 16.45 o.p. (ISBN 0-395-34394-1); pap. 7.95 o.p. HM.

Yearbook. Lutheran Church of America. pap. 4.00 o.p. (ISBN 0-685-93022-X, 50-180, Fortress). Augsburg Fortress.

Yearbook. David Marlow. LC 76-39716. 1977. 8.95 o.p. (ISBN 0-87795-156-X, Arbor Hse). Morrow.

Yearbook National Accounts Statistics, 1980, 3 vols. United Nations Staff. Set. 125.00 o.p. (E.82.XVII.6). UN.

Yearbook of Air & Space Law, 1965. Ed. by Rene H. Mankiewicz. 1967. 27.50x o.p. (ISBN 0-7735-0037-5, McGill Canada). U of Toronto Pr.

Yearbook of Air & Space Law, 1966. Ed. by Rene H. Mankiewicz. 1968. 27.50x o.p. (ISBN 0-7735-0052-9, McGill Canada). U of Toronto Pr.

Yearbook of Air & Space Law, 1967. Ed. by Rene H. Mankiewicz. 536p. 1971. 27.50x o.p. (ISBN 0-7735-0064-2, McGill Canada). U of Toronto Pr.

Yearbook of American Labor. Colston Warne. (ISBN 0-8022-1810-5). Philos Lib.

Yearbook of Astronomy, 1970. rev. ed. Ed. by Patrick Moore. (Illus.). 1970. 4.95 o.p. (ISBN 0-393-06375-5). Norton.

Yearbook of Astronomy, 1975. Ed. by Patrick Moore. (Illus.). 1975. 8.95 o.p. (ISBN 0-393-06401-8). Norton.

Yearbook of Astronomy, 1976. Ed. by Patrick Moore. (Yearbook of Astronomy Ser.). (Illus.). 215p. 1976. 9.95 o.p. (ISBN 0-393-06404-2). Norton.

Yearbook of Astronomy 1977. Ed. by Patrick Moore. (Illus.). 1977. 9.95 o.p. (ISBN 0-393-06412-3). Norton.

Yearbook of Astronomy, 1978. Ed. by Patrick Moore. (Yearbook of Astronomy Ser.). (Illus.). 1978. 10.95 o.p. (ISBN 0-393-06430-1). Norton.

Yearbook of Astronomy, 1980. Ed. by Patrick Moore. (Illus.). 1980. 12.95 o.p. (ISBN 0-393-01318-9). Norton.

Yearbook of Astronomy, 1981. Ed. by Patrick Moore. (Illus.). 1981. 14.95 o.p. (ISBN 0-393-01415-0). Norton.

Yearbook of Astronomy, 1982. Ed. by Patrick Moore. (Illus.). 1982. 15.95 o.p. (ISBN 0-393-01492-4). Norton.

Yearbook of Astronomy, 1983. Ed. by Patrick Moore. (Illus.). 1983. 15.95 o.p. (ISBN 0-393-01700-1). Norton.

Yearbook of Astronomy, 1984. Ed. by Patrick Moore. (Illus.). 1983. pap. 9.70 o.p. (ISBN 0-393-30147-8). Norton.

Yearbook of Astronomy, 1986. 1985. 15.45 o.p. (ISBN 0-393-30254-7). Norton.

Yearbook of Astronomy, 1987. Ed. by Patrick Moore. 1986. 16.45 o.p. (ISBN 0-393-02391-5). Norton.

Yearbook of Construction Statistics, 1973-1980. 221p. 1983. 25.00 o.p. (E.82.XVII.15). UN.

Yearbook of Human Rights, 1979. 330p. 39.00 o.p. (ISBN 92-1-154051-8, E.85.XIV.7). UN.

Yearbook of Industrial Statistics. Incl. Vol. 1. General Industrial Statistics, 1974 (E.76.XVII.3); Vol. 2. Commodity Production Data, 1965-1974 (E.76.XVII.4); Vol. 1. General Industrial Statistics, 1975. pap. 35.00 (E.77.XVII.7); Vol. 2. Commodity Production Data, 1966-1975. pap. 35.00 (E.77.XVII.8); Vol. 1. General Statistics, 1976. pap. 35.00 (UN78/17/3); Vol. 2. Commodity Production Data, 1967-1976. pap. 35.00 (E.78.XVII.4); Vol. 1. General Industrial Statistics, 1977. 639p. 1979. pap. 35.00 (E.79.XVII.9); Vol. 2. Commodity Production Data, 1968-1977. 750p. 1979. pap. 35.00 (E.79.XVII.10); Vol. 1. General Industrial Statistics, 1978. 645p. 1980. pap. 35.00 (E.80.XVII.9); Vol. 1. General Industrial Statistics, 1979, 2 Vols. 605p. 1982. pap. 45.00; Vol. 1. General Industrial Statistics, 1980, 2 Vols. 612p. 1983. pap. 45.00 (E.82.XVII.11); Vol. 2. Commodity Production Data, 1971-80, 2 Vols. 750p. 1983. pap. 45.00 (E.82.XVII.12). UN.

Yearbook of Industrial Statistics, 1979: Vol. 1-General Industrial Statistics. 13th ed. United Nations Staff. LC 76-646970. (Illus.). 603p. 1981. 45.00x o.s.i. (ISBN 0-8002-1140-5). Intl Pubns Serv.

Yearbook of Industrial Statistics, 1978. Vol. I. 1979, 45.00 o.p.; Vol. II. 45.00 o.p. (E.81.XVII.9). UN.

Yearbook of Industrial Statistics 1981. 14th ed. United Nations. Incl. Vol. I-General Industry Statistics, 1971-80. 613p. 45.00x (ISBN 92-1-161098-2, E.83.XVII.5); Vol. II-Commodity Production Data, 1971-1980. 750p. 45.00x (ISBN 92-1-161099-0, E.83.XVII.6). LC 76-646970. (Illus.). 1983. UN.

Yearbook of International Insurance. 88th ed. Assecuranz & Compass. 1751p. 1983. 305.00x o.p. (ISBN 0-8002-3334-4). Intl Pubns Serv.

Yearbook of International Organizations 1986-87, 3 vols. Ed. by Union of International Associations, Brussels Editors. 4200p. (Eng. & Fr.). 1986. Set. lib. bdg. 555.00 o.p. (ISBN 3-598-21869-9). K G Saur.

Yearbook of International Organizations, 1987-88: Global Networks: Classified Directory by Subject & Region (Subject Volume, Vol. 3. 5th ed. Ed. by Union of International Organizations Staff. 1450p. 1987. 215.00 o.p. (ISBN 3-598-21876-1). K G Saur.

Yearbook of International Organizations, 1987-88: International Organization Participation: Country Directory of Secretariats & Membership (Geographic Volume, Vol. 2. Ed. by Union of International Organizations Staff. 1450p. (Eng. & Fr.). 1987. 250.00 o.p. (ISBN 3-598-21875-3). K G Saur.

Yearbook of International Organizations, 1987-88: Organizations Descriptions & Index, Vol. 1. 24th ed. Ed. by Union of International Organizations Staff. 1650p. (Fr. & Eng.). 1987. 250.00 o.p. (ISBN 3-598-21874-5). K G Saur.

Yearbook of International Organizations 1986-87, Vol. 2: International Organization Participation Country Directory of Secretariats & Membership (Geographic Volume) 4th ed. Union of International Associations, Brussels Editors. 1500p. 1986. lib. bdg. 225.00 o.p. (ISBN 3-598-21871-0). K G Saur.

Yearbook of International Organizations 1986-87, Vol. 3: Global Networks Classified Directory by Subject & Region. 4th ed. Union of International Associations, Brussels Editors. 1464p. (Eng. & Fr.). 1986. lib. bdg. 180.00 o.p. (ISBN 3-598-21872-9). K G Saur.

Yearbook of International Trade Statistics-Annuaire Statistique du Commerce International, 1980: Vol. 1-Trade by Country; Vol. 2-Trade by Commodity, 2 vols. 29th ed. United Nations Staff. LC 51-8987. (Illus.). 2525p. (Eng. & Fr.). 1981. Set. 75.00x o.s.i. (ISBN 0-8002-1118-9). Intl Pubns Serv.

Yearbook of International Trade Statistics. Incl. 1950-1975; 1967. 1967. pap. 22.00 (E.69.XVII.2); Trade by Country, Vol. 1. 1976. Trade by commodity-Commodity Matrix Tables, Vol. 2. 60.00 set (E.77.XVII.14); 1980, 2 Vols. 1290p. 1981. pap. 75.00 (ISBN 0-686-96519-1, E.81.XVII.13); Vols. 1 & 2. 1982. (Fr. & Eng.). 1985. Set. 80.00 (E.84.XVII.6). UN.

Yearbook of International Trade Statistics: 1979, 2 Vols. 28th ed. 1979. pap. 70.00 set o.p. (E.80.XVII.5). UN.

Yearbook of International Trade Statistics 1981: Includes Vol. 1 - Trade by Commodity & Vol. 2 - Matrix Tables, 2 Vols. 1983. Set. text ed. 75.00 o.p. (ISBN 92-1-061002-4, E.82.XVII.7). UN.

Yearbook of International Trade Statistics 1982: Volume I: Trade by Country & Volume II: Trade by Commodity. 2534p. 1985. Set. 80.00 o.p. (E.84.XVII.6). UN.

Yearbook of Labor Statistics 1980. 40th ed. International Labor Office, Geneva Staff. (Illus.). 690p. 1980. 67.50x o.p. (ISBN 92-2-002526-4). Intl Pubns Serv.

Yearbook of Labor Statistics, 1982. 42nd ed. Ed. by International Labour Organisation (ILO) Staff. LC 36-130. (Illus.). 760p. 1983. 75.00x o.s.i. (ISBN 92-2-003262-7). Intl Pubns Serv.

Yearbook of Labor Statistics, 1983. 43rd ed. 847p. 1984. 80.00x o.p. (ISBN 92-20-03589-8). Intl Pubns Serv.

Yearbook of Labor Statistics, 1986. 91.00 o.p. (ISBN 0-8002-4111-8). Intl Pubns Serv.

Yearbook of Landscape Architecture: Historic Preservation. Richard L. Austin et al. 1983. 36.95 o.p. (ISBN 0-442-20885-5). Van Nos Reinhold.

Yearbook of National Accounts Statistics, 1981, 2 vols. 25th ed. United Nations Staff. LC 58-3718. (Illus.). 2337p. 1983. Set. 125.00x o.s.i. (ISBN 0-8002-1124-3). Intl Pubns Serv.

Yearbook of National Accounts Statistics, 1981, 3 vols. 125.00 o.p. (ISBN 92-1-161061-3, E.83.XVII.3). UN.

Yearbook of National Accounts Statistics, 19 Vols. Incl. 1964. pap. 22.00 o.p.; 1967. pap. 22.00 o.p.; 1968, 2 Vols. pap. 22.00 o.p.; 1970, 2 Vols. 1983. Set. pap. 34.00 (UN72/17/3); Vol. 2. 1971, 3 Vols. 761p. Set. pap. 43.00 (UN73/17/3); 1972, 3 Vols. 2139p. 1979. Set. pap. 50.00 (UN74/17/3); 1973, 3 Vols. Set. pap. 55.00 (UN75/17/2); 1974, 3 Vols. Set. pap. 70.00 (UN75/17/5); 1975, 3 Vols. Set. pap. 70.00 (UN76/17/2, UN); 1976, 2 Vols. Set. pap. 60.00 (UN77/17/2, UN); Vol. 1. 1977, 2 Vols. 1969p. 1983. Set. pap. 70.00 (UN78/17/2); 1981, 2 Vols. 2036p. 1983. Set. pap. 125.00 (UN83/17/3, UN); 1957-1975 Microfiche. pap. 430.00. UN.

Yearbook of National Accounts Statistics, Vol. 1. pap. 22.00 o.p. (E.70.XVII.2). UN.

Yearbook of Obstetrics & Gynecology, 1985. Pitkin. 1985. 42.95 o.p. (ISBN 0-8151-6694-X). Year Bk Med.

Yearbook of Psychiatry & Applied Mental Health, 1985. Freedman. 1985. 42.95 o.p. (ISBN 0-8151-6027-5). Year Bk Med.

Yearbook of Science & Technology, 1986. McGraw-Hill Editors. 528p. 1986. text ed. 55.00 o.p. (ISBN 0-07-046181-3). McGraw.

Yearbook of Social Policy in Britain 1980-1981. Ed. by Catherine Jones & June Stevenson. 239p. 1982. 35.00x o.p. (ISBN 0-7100-9083-8). Routledge Chapman & Hall.

Yearbook of Social Policy in Britain 1982. June Stevenson & Catherine Jones. 260p. 1983. 32.50x o.p. (ISBN 0-7100-9537-6). Routledge Chapman & Hall.

Yearbook of Social Policy, 1983. Catherine Jones & June Stevenson. 260p. 1984. 33.95x o.p. (ISBN 0-7102-0275-X). Routledge Chapman & Hall.

Yearbook of Symbolic Anthropology. Ed. by Erik Schwimmer. 1978. 22.35x o.p. (ISBN 0-7735-0500-8, McGill Canada). U of Toronto Pr.

Yearbook of the International Law Commission 1984, Pt. I. 356p. 1985. 35.00 o.p. (ISBN 92-1-133336-9, UN85). UNIPUB.

Titles

Yearbook of the International Law Commission: 1964, 1978-84. Incl. 1964, 2 Vols. Vol. 1. pap. 7.00 o.p. (ISBN 0-686-93768-6, UN65/5/1); Vol. 2. pap. 7.00 o.p. (ISBN 0-686-99168-0, UN65/5/2); 1967, 2 Vols. Vol. 1. pap. 7.00 o.p. (ISBN 0-686-93770-8, UN68/5/1); Vol. 2. pap. 7.00 o.p. (ISBN 0-686-99169-9, UN68/5/2); 1968, 2 Vols. Vol. 1. pap. 7.00 o.p. (ISBN 0-686-93772-4, UN69/5/3); Vol. 2. pap. 7.00 o.p. (ISBN 0-686-99170-2, UN69/5/4); 1969, 2 Vols. Vol. 1. pap. 7.00 o.p. (ISBN 0-686-93774-0, UN70/5/7); Vol. 2. pap. 7.00 o.p. (ISBN 0-686-99171-0, UN70/5/8); 1970, 2 Vols. Vol. 1. pap. 7.00 o.p. (ISBN 0-686-93776-7, UN71/5/6); Vol. 2. pap. 8.50 o.p. (ISBN 0-686-99172-9, UN71/5/7); 1971, Vol. 2, 2 Pts. Pt. 1. pap. 11.00 o.p. (ISBN 0-686-93778-3, UN72/5/6); Pt. 2. pap. 8.50 o.p. (ISBN 0-686-99173-7, UN72/5/6); 1972, Vol. 2. pap. 14.50 o.p. (ISBN 0-686-93780-5, UN73/5/5); 1973, Vol. 1. pap. 9.50 o.p. (ISBN 0-686-93781-3, UN74/5/4); 1975, 2 Vols. pap. 14.50 o.p. (ISBN 0-686-93782-1, UN76/5/3); pap. 11.00 o.p. (UN76/5/4); 1976, 2 Vols. Vol. 1. pap. 16.00 o.p. (UN77/5/4); Vol. 2. pap. 13.00 o.p. (ISBN 0-686-93783-X, UN77/5/5); 1977, 2 Vols. Vol. 1. pap. 19.00 o.p. (ISBN 0-686-93785-6, UN78/5/1); Vol. 2, Pt. 1. pap. 12.00 o.p. (ISBN 0-686-99175-3, UN78/5/2). Vol. 2, Pt. 2 (UN78/5/2); 1978, 2 Vols. Vol. 1. pap. 19.00 o.p. (ISBN 0-686-93787-2, UN79/5/5); Vol. 2, Pt. 1. pap. 18.00 o.p. (ISBN 0-686-99176-1, UN79/5/6-1); Vol. 2, Pt. 2. pap. 13.00 o.p. (ISBN 0-686-99177-X, UN79/5/6-2); Vol. 1. 1979. 247p. 1980. pap. 17.00; Vol. 2, Pt.1. 1979: Documents of the 31st Session Excluding the Report of the Commission to the General Assembly. pap. 18.00 (UN80/5/5P1); Vol. 2, Pt. 2. 1979. pap. 16.00 (E.80.V.5/P.2); Vol. 1. 1981. 297p. 1984. pap. 20.00 (E.82.V.5.3). UN.

Yearbook of the United Nations, Vol. 31. Ed. by United Nations Staff. LC 47-7191. (Illus.). 1120p. 1980. 50.00x o.p. (ISBN 0-8002-1127-8). Intl Pubns Serv.

Yearbook of the United Nations, Vol. 33. United Nations Staff. LC 47-7191. 1294p. 1982. 72.00x o.p. UN.

Yearbook of the United Nations, Vol. 32: Nineteen Seventy-Eight. United Nations Staff. LC 47-7191. 1294p. 1981. 60.00x o.p. (ISBN 0-8002-2883-9). UN.

Yearbook of the United Nations: 1978 & Beyond. Incl. Vol. 32. 1978. 1312p. 60.00 (UN80/1/1). UNIPUB; Vol. 33. 1979. 1450p. 1980. 72.00 (ISBN 0-686-43291-6). UNIPUB. UN). UNIPUB.

Yearbook on Human Rights: 1960-78, 12 Vols. Incl. 1960. 15.00 (E.63XIV.1); 1961. 15.00 (E.64.XIV.1); 1962. 15.00 (E.65.XIV.1); 1963. 15.00 o.p. (UN66/14/1); 1964. 15.00 (E.67.XIV.1); 1965. 15.00 o.p. (UN68/14/1); 1966. 15.00 (E.69.XIV.1); 1967. pap. 15.00 (E.70.XIV.1); 1968. pap. 15.00 o.p. (UN71/14/1); 1972. pap. 30.00 (E.75.XIV.1); 1973-1974. pap. 15.00 o.p. (UN76/14/1PA); 1977-1978. pap. 19.00 (E.81.XIV.1). UN.

Yearbook on International Communist Affairs, 1969. Ed. by Richard V. Allen. LC 67-31024. (Publications Ser.: No. 92). 1970. 25.00x o.p. (ISBN 0-8179-1921-X). Hoover Inst Pr.

Yearbook on International Communist Affairs: 1975. Ed. by Richard F. Starr. 25.00 o.p. Hoover Inst Pr.

Yearbook: Untold Stories. Bill Wolfe & Janita Wolfe. LC 83-60667. (Illus.). 80p. (Orig.). 1983. pap. 5.95 o.s.i. (ISBN 0-936664-10-X). Group Pub.

Yearling. Marjorie K. Rawlings. 428p. 1982. rack size 4.95 o.p. (ISBN 0-684-17617-3, ScribT); 9.95 o.p. (ISBN 0-684-71878-2). Scribner.

Yearly Planning Guide for the Church Usher. Thomas L. Clark. 1986. pap. 3.95 o.p. (ISBN 0-8054-9407-3). Broadman.

Years & Me. George Collier. LC 85-90847. 144p. (Orig.). 1985. pap. 6.95 o.s.i. (ISBN 0-934318-61-1). Falcon Pr MT.

Years Before School: Guiding Preschool Children. 3rd ed. Vivian E. Todd & H. Heffernan. 1977. text ed. write for info. o.p. (ISBN 0-02-420880-9). Macmillan.

Years of Darkness, Days of Glory. Larry Richards. LC 76-6582. (Bible Alive Ser). (Illus.). 1977. pap. text ed. 2.95 o.p. (ISBN 0-912692-97-9); tchr's. ed. o.p. 3.95 o.p. (ISBN 0-912692-96-0). Cook.

Years of Protest: A Collection of American Writings of the 1930's. Ed. by Jack Salzman & Barry Wallenstein. LC 67-13489. (Illus., Orig.). 1967. pap. write for info. o.p. (ISBN 0-02-405380-5). Macmillan.

Years of the City. Fred Pohl. 1984. 15.45 o.s.i. (ISBN 0-671-49940-8). S&S.

Years of the Week. Patricia Cockburn. (Comedia Ser.). 288p. (Orig.). 1987. pap. 12.00 o.p. (ISBN 0-906890-84-5). M Boyars Pubs.

Year's Residence in the United States of America. William Cobbett. LC 64-14796. (Centaur Classics Ser.). 338p. 1964. 19.50x o.p. (ISBN 0-8093-0149-0). S Ill U Pr.

Year's Scholarship in Science Fiction & Fantasy, 1976-1979. Marshall B. Tymn & Roger C. Schlobin. LC 82-16190. (Serif Series of Bibliographies & Checklists: Vol. 40). 251p. 1983. 22.50x o.p. (ISBN 0-87338-257-9). Kent St U Pr.

Year's Scholarship in Science Fiction, Fantasy, & Horror Literature, 1982. Marshall Tymn. 100p. 1985. pap. 9.50x o.p. (ISBN 0-87338-302-8). Kent St U Pr.

Years That Were Fat: The Last of Old China. George N. Kates. 1967. 16.50 o.p. (ISBN 0-262-11063-6). MIT Pr.

Year's Work in English Studies. Incl. Vol. 43, 1962. 1964. lib. bdg. 6.50x (ISBN 0-686-51444-0); Vol. 44, 1963. 1965. lib. bdg. 15.00x (ISBN 0-686-51445-9); Vol. 45, 1964. 1966. lib. bdg. 15.00x; Vol. 48, 1967. 1969. lib. bdg. 1.00; Vol. 49, 1968. 1970. bds. 15.00x (ISBN 0-7195-2189-0); Vol. 50, 1969. Jubilee Volume. 1971. lib. bdg. 15.00x (ISBN 0-391-00213-9); Vol. 51, 1970. 1972. lib. bdg. 15.00x (ISBN 0-7195-2845-3); Vol. 52, 1971. 1973. lib. bdg. 15.00x; Vol. 53, 1972. 1974. lib. bdg. 15.00x (ISBN 0-391-00363-1); Vol. 54, 1973. 1975. lib. bdg. 17.50x (ISBN 0-391-00606-1); Vol. 55, 1975. Ed. by J. Redmond. 1974. text ed. 22.50x (ISBN 0-391-00648-7); Vol. 56, 1975. 1977. text ed. 31.25x (ISBN 0-391-00748-3). Humanities.

Year's Work in English Studies: Vol. 57, 1976. Ed. by J. Redmond et al. 1979. text ed. 38.50x o.p. (ISBN 0-391-00917-6). Humanities.

Yearwood. Hazel. 1987. pap. 3.95 o.p. (ISBN 0-553-26681-0, Spectra). Bantam.

Yeats & Eliot: Perspectives on India. R. Shah. 188p. 1983. text ed. 19.95x o.p. (ISBN 0-391-02932-0). Humanities.

Yeats the Initiate: Essays on Certain Themes in the Work of William Butler Yeats. Kathleen Raine. (Illus.). 456p. 1986. 30.00 o.p. (ISBN 0-8076-1073-9). Braziller.

Yeats's Epitaph: A Key to Symbolic Unity in His Life & Work. James L. Allen. LC 80-5848. 282p. (Orig.). 1982. lib. bdg. 32.00 o.p. (ISBN 0-8191-2592-X); pap. text ed. 14.00 o.p. (ISBN 0-8191-2593-8). U Pr of Amer.

Yeats's Golden Dawn. George M. Harper. (Illus.). 332p. (Orig.). 1987. pap. 14.95 o.p. (ISBN 0-85030-607-8, Pub. by Aquarian Pr). Sterling.

Yedo. Lynn Guest. 292p. 1986. pap. 3.95 o.p. (ISBN 0-931773-73-3). Critics Choice Paper.

Yellow Book: A Parent's Guide to Teacher-Tested Educational Software. National Education Association Computer Services Staff. 120p. 1984. pap. 12.95 o.p. (ISBN 0-8240-8900-6); lib. bdg. 18.95 o.p. (ISBN 0-8240-6999-4). Garland Pub.

Yellow Dog. Gary Lawless. 1986. pap. 3.00 o.p. (ISBN 0-942396-40-5). Blackberry ME.

Yellow-Dog Contract. Ross Thomas. 1983. pap. 1.75 o.p. (ISBN 0-380-01828-4, 36186). Avon.

Yellow Earth, Green Jade: Constants in Chinese Political Mores. Simon De Beaufort. LC 78-56502. (Studies in International Affairs: No. 41). (gr. 10 up). 1979. text ed. 8.95x o.p. (ISBN 0-87674-044-1); pap. text ed. 3.95x o.p. (ISBN 0-87674-043-3). U Pr of Amer.

Yellow Lola. Edward Dorn. LC 80-68260. 132p. 1981. 20.00 o.p. (ISBN 0-932274-14-5); pap. 6.00 o.p. (ISBN 0-932274-13-7). Cadmus Eds.

Yellow Pages. John Linssen. LC 78-73873. 1980. 9.95 o.p. (ISBN 0-87795-226-4, Arbor Hse). Morrow.

Yellow Pages for Students & Teachers. Imogene Forte & Joy Mackenzie. LC 79-93126. 96p. (gr. 2-6). 1980. pap. text ed. 7.95 o.p. (ISBN 0-913916-88-9, IP 88-9). Incentive Pubns.

Yellow River: A Five Thousand Year Journey Through China. Kevin Sinclair. (Illus.). 206p. 1987. 35.00 o.p. (ISBN 0-89535-192-7). Knapp Pr.

Yellow Robe Monster. Ed. by Zhang Wen. (Monkey Ser.: No. 8). (Illus.). 74p. (gr. 4 up). 1985. pap. 7.95 o.p. (ISBN 0-8351-1368-X). China Bks.

Yellow Thread Cat. Mary A. Tien. LC 84-4793. (Illus.). 20p. (Orig.). (gr. 1-6). 1984. pap. 3.25 o.p. (ISBN 0-9603840-8-1). Andrew Mtn Pr.

Yellowlegs. John Janovy, Jr. 1981. pap. 5.95 o.p. (ISBN 0-395-31539-5). HM.

Yellowstone: A Wilderness Beseiged. Richard A. Bartlett. LC 85-988. 437p. 1985. 24.95 o.p. (ISBN 0-8165-0890-9). U of Ariz Pr.

Yellowstone National Park. John Muir. Ed. by William R. Jones. (Illus.). 1978. pap. 3.95 o.p. (ISBN 0-89646-043-6). Outbooks.

Yellowstone National Park: Guide & Reference Book. Cliff McAdams. LC 80-28129. (Illus.). 1981. 4.50 o.p. (ISBN 0-87108-571-2). Pruett.

Yellowstone: The First National Park. Ruth Kirk. LC 74-76273. (Illus.). 112p. (gr. 5 up). 1974. 6.25 o.p. (ISBN 0-689-50006-8, Atheneum). Macmillan.

Yemenite Girl. Curt Leviant. 1978. pap. 1.95 o.p. (ISBN 0-380-41293-4). Avon.

Yer Dailege! Kuna Women's Art. Mari L. Salvador. (Illus.). 103p. (Orig.). 1978. pap. 10.95 o.p. (ISBN 0-8263-0539-3, Pub. by Maxwell Mus Anthropology). U of NM Pr.

Yersinia, Pasteurella & Francisella: Proceedings of the International Symposium, Malmoe, April, 1972. International Symposium on Yersinia, Pasteurella & Francisella Staff. Ed. by Winblad. (Contributions to Microbiology & Immunology Ser.: Vol. 2). 1973. 50.00 o.p. (ISBN 3-8055-1636-3). S Karger.

Yes, Dog, That's Right! Warren Eckstein & Fay Eckstein. LC 79-54766. (Illus.). 1980. 2.98 o.p. (ISBN 0-931866-03-0). Alpine Pubns.

Yes My Son, There Is a God! Don J. Black. 36p. (Orig.). (YA) (gr. 11 up). 1978. pap. 2.00 o.p. (ISBN 0-942241-24-X, 8815). Pubs Bk Sales.

Yes or No? Straight Answers to Tough Questions about Christianity. Peter Kreeft. 168p. (Orig.). 1984. 5.95 o.p. (ISBN 0-89283-217-7). Servant.

Yes, Today's Mortgages Make Home Buying Easier, 25 vols. National Association of Home Builders Staff. 12p. 1986. pap. 15.50 o.p. (ISBN 0-86718-254-7). Nat Assn H Build.

Yes You Can Teach. Florence Nelson. LC 77-73639. (Illus.). 56p. 1977. pap. 5.00 spiral o.s.i. (ISBN 0-918328-00-4). Carma.

Yesterday & Today: A Dictionary of Recent American History. Stanley Hochman. LC 79-12265. (Illus.). 407p. 1979. text ed. 43.50 o.p. (ISBN 0-07-029103-9). McGraw.

Yesterday & Tomorrow: Roots of the National Revolution. 96p. 1986. pap. 6.50 o.p. (ISBN 0-317-53270-7). Noontide.

Yesterday... Came Suddenly: The Definitive History of the Beatles. Bob Cepican & Waleed Ali. (Illus.). 320p. (Orig.). 1984. pap. 12.95 o.p. (ISBN 0-87795-620-0, Arbor Hse). Morrow.

Yesterday or Tomorrow? Aspects of the Work of Robert A. Heinlein. Ed. by R. Reginald & George Slusser. (Studies in Literary Criticism: Vol. 5). 1988. 19.95x o.p. (ISBN 0-916732-76-2); pap. 9.95x o.p. (ISBN 0-916732-75-4). Starmont Hse.

Yesterday-the Beatles 1963-1965. Robert Freeman. (Illus.). 96p. 1983. 10.95 o.s.i. (ISBN 0-03-064033-4, Owl Bks); pap. 6.95 o.s.i. (ISBN 0-03-000094-7). H Holt & Co.

Yesterday, Today & Tomorrow. Elizabeth M. Trotter. 1980. 5.00 o.p. (ISBN 0-682-49478-X). Exposition-Phoenix.

Yesterday, Today, & What Next? Reflections on History & Hope. Roland H. Bainton. LC 78-52204. 1978. pap. 7.50 o.p. (ISBN 0-8066-1670-9, 10-7400, Augsburg). Augsburg Fortress.

Yesterday's Cake. Eddie White. 1985. 15.95 o.p. (ISBN 0-533-06428-7). Vantage.

Yesterday's Daughter. Helen F. Daringer. LC 48-6025. (Illus.). (gr. 7 up). 1964. 4.95 o.p. (ISBN 0-15-299821-7, HJ). HarBraceJ.

Yesterday's Music. Megan Hughes. 288p. 1984. pap. 2.95 o.p. (ISBN 0-8439-2085-8, Pub. by Leisure Bks CT). Dorchester Pub Co.

Yesterday's News. R. B. Walker. 256p. 1980. 33.00x o.p. (ISBN -0424-00079-2, Pub. by Sydney U Pr Australia). Intl Spec Bk.

Yesterdays: Popular Song in America. Charles Hamm. (Illus.). 1979. 11.95x o.p. (ISBN 0-393-01257-3). Norton.

Yesterday's Son. A. C. Crispin. (Star Trek Ser.). 1984. lib. bdg. 10.95 o.p. (ISBN 0-8398-2830-6, Gregg). G K Hall.

Yesterday's Trains. Patrick C. Dorin. LC 81-3696. (Superwheels & Thrill Sports Bks.). (Illus.). (gr. 4-9). 1981. PLB 9.95 o.p. (ISBN 0-8225-0439-1, ASTERISKS). Lerner Pubns.

•**Yet More Wandering Thoughts.** Thomas Smyth. 80p. 1982. 6.00 o.p. (ISBN 0-682-49884-X). Exposition-Phoenix.

Yet Not I. David Campbell. 88p. (Orig.). 1978. pap. 1.95 o.p. (ISBN 0-912315-39-3). Word Aflame.

Yet to Be Served: Special Issue of Exceptional Children. Ed. by M. Angele Thomas. 96p. 1979. pap. 5.00 o.p. (ISBN 0-86586-095-5). Coun Exc Child.

Yet Will I Trust Him. Rob Burkhart. LC 79-91705. (Study & Grow Electives). 64p. 1985. pap. 3.95 o.s.i. (ISBN 0-8307-1016-7, 6102002). Regal.

Yetta the Trickster. Andrea Zimmerman. LC 78-6164. (Illus.). 48p. (gr. 1-4). 1979. 6.95 o.p. (ISBN 0-395-28836-3, Clarion). HM.

Yevgeniy Shvarts: Three Plays. Ed. by Avril Pyman. 288p. 1972. pap. 70.00 o.p. (ISBN 0-08-016294-0). Pergamon.

Yevgeny Yevtushenko: Bilingual Edition. Ed. by H. Marshall. 1967. text ed. 14.75 o.p. (ISBN 0-08-012464-X). Pergamon.

YHWH: Tetragrammaton. Henry Little. LC 84-90091. 177p. 1985. 12.95 o.p. (ISBN 0-533-06173-3). Vantage.

Yiddish Linguistics: A Classified Bilingual Index of Yiddish Serials & Collections, 1913-1958. David M. Bunis. 1984. lib. bdg. 25.00 o.p. (ISBN 0-8240-9758-0). Garland Pub.

Yiddish Linguistics: A Multilingual Bibliography, 1959-1973. Joan G. Bratkowsky. 1984. lib. bdg. 50.00 o.p. (ISBN 0-8240-9804-8). Garland Pub.

Yiddish Stories Old & New. Ed. by Irving Howe & Eliezer Greenberg. (YA) (gr. 7 up). 1977. pap. 2.50 o.p. (ISBN 0-380-00887-4, 47803, Bard). Avon.

Yidish Launiversitah: Hebrew Edition of "College Yiddish" Uriel Weinreich. Tr. by S. Bahat & M. Goldwasser. (Illus.). 1977. pap. text ed. write for info. o.p. (ISBN 0-914512-35-8). Yivo Inst.

Yidn in England; Studies & Materials, 1880-1940. (Bibliotek Fun Yivo). 302p. (Yiddish.). 1966. 10.00 o.p. (ISBN 0-914512-14-5, HE66-1946). Yivo Inst.

Yield Table for Wrap-Around Mortgage No. 707. rev. ed. 27.50 o.p. (ISBN 0-685-59991-4). Finan Pub.

Yin Sun & the Lucky Dragon. Mabel Watts. 1969. 3.75 o.s.i. (ISBN 0-664-32434-7, Westminster). Westminster John Knox.

Yindala: An Original Australian Story. Barbara McNab. 42p. (gr. 3-5). 1986. 4.95 o.p. (ISBN 0-533-06398-1). Vantage.

Ylide Chemistry. A. William Johnson. (Organic Chemistry Ser.: Vol. 7). 1966. 75.00 o.p. (ISBN 0-12-386450-X). Acad Pr.

YMCA Camping Centennial: No. 3, Promotion. YMCA of the U. S. A. Staff. 1983. 4.95x o.s.i. (ISBN 0-931250-69-2). Human Kinetics.

YMCA Camping Centennial Series. YMCA of the U. S. A. Staff. 1984. 3-ring notebook 12.50x o.p. (ISBN 0-931250-81-1, Pub. by YMCA USA). Human Kinetics.

YMCA Cardiac Therapy Participant's Handbook. YMCA of the U. S. A. Staff. 40p. 1979. pap. 3.00x o.p. (ISBN 0-88035-066-0, Pub. by YMCA USA). Human Kinetics.

YMCA Competitive Swimming & Diving Coaches Manual. Ed. by John M. Ferrell et al. 1981. 3 ring binder 18.00x o.p. (ISBN 0-88035-028-8, Pub. by YMCA USA). Human Kinetics.

YMCA Directory, 1985. YMCA of the U. S. A. Staff. 1985. pap. text ed. 20.00x o.p. (ISBN 0-87322-001-3). Human Kinetics.

YMCArdiac Therapy. Gary Fry & Kathy Berra. (Illus.). 400p. 1981. text ed. 10.00x o.p. (ISBN 0-88035-000-8, YMCA USA). Human Kinetics.

Ynamine: A Versatile Tool in Organic Synthesis. Ed. by Jacqueline Ficini. 38p. 1976. pap. 15.50 o.p. (ISBN 0-08-020466-X). Pergamon.

Yobgorgle: Mystery Monster of Lake Ontario. Daniel M. Pinkwater. LC 79-11364. 156p. (gr. 3-6). 1979. 8.95 o.p. (ISBN 0-395-28970-X, Clarion). HM.

Yoga & Beyond. Date not set. pap. (ISBN 0-8052-0541-1). Random.

Yoga Cookbook. E. Thompson. 160p. 1959. (ISBN 0-8022-1713-3). Philos Lib.

Yoga Dictionary. Ernest Wood. 224p. 1956. (ISBN 0-8022-1924-1). Philos Lib.

Yoga for All Ages. Rachel Carr. (Illus.). 160p. 1975. pap. 8.50 o.p. (ISBN 0-671-22151-5, Fireside). S&S.

Yoga for Your Children. Date not set. (ISBN 0-8052-0630-2). Random.

Yoga of Light: The Classic Esoteric Handbook of Kundalini Yoga. Rieker Hans-Ulrich. Tr. by Elsy Becherer. LC 79-167868. (Illus.). 1974. pap. 7.95 o.s.i. (ISBN 0-913922-07-2). Dawn Horse Pr.

Yoga Way to Figure & Facial Beauty. Richard Hittleman. 1971. pap. 1.50 o.p. (ISBN 0-380-00896-3, 23770). Avon.

Yojokun: Japanese Secret of Good Health. Ekiken Kaibara. 1974. 9.95 o.p. (ISBN 0-89346-101-6); pap. 2.95 o.p. (ISBN 0-89346-047-8). Heian Intl.

Yoke Made Easy. Alfred Doerffler. LC 75-2344. 128p. 1974. pap. 5.95 o.p. (ISBN 0-570-03027-7, 6-1155). Concordia.

Yoko Ono. Jerry Hopkins. (Illus.). 320p. 1987. 17.95 o.p. (ISBN 0-02-553950-7). Macmillan.

Yokuts Language of California. Stanley S. Newman. pap. 19.00 o.p. (ISBN 0-384-41210-6). Johnson Repr.

Yon Mountain: A Doctor of Faith Walks with God. Alta W. Eitel. LC 85-90286. 101p. 1986. 10.95 o.p. (ISBN 0-533-06783-9). Vantage.

Yonnondio. Tillie Olsen. 16.25 o.p. Peter Smith.

Yorck & the Era of Prussian Reform. Peter Paret. 1966. 45.00x o.p. (ISBN 0-691-05163-1). Princeton U Pr.

York Ballad Operas & Yorkshiremen. Ed. by Walter H. Rubsamen. (Ballad Opera Ser.). 1975. lib. bdg. 61.00 o.p. (ISBN 0-8240-0926-6). Garland Pub.

Yorkist Age: Daily Life During the Wars of the Roses. Paul M. Kendall. 1970. pap. 7.95x o.p. (ISBN 0-393-00558-5, Norton Lib). Norton.

Yorkshire Terrier: Origin, History & Complete Care. Aileen M. Martello. LC 74-146912. (Illus.). 1971. 10.00 o.p. (ISBN 0-682-47245-X, Banner). Exposition-Phoenix.

Yoruba Sculpture in Los Angeles Collections. Frwd. by Danuta Batorska. (Illus.). 40p. 1969. 1.00 o.p. (ISBN 0-915478-17-X). Galleries Coll.

Yosemite: Its Discovery, Its Wonders & Its People. Margaret Sanborn. LC 81-40237. (Illus.). 288p. 1981. 17.00 o.p. (ISBN 0-394-51794-6). Random.

Yosemite: The Story Behind the Scenery. rev. ed. William R. Jones. LC 80-82917. (Illus.). 48p. 1980. 8.95 o.p. (ISBN 0-916122-33-6); pap. 4.50 o.p. (ISBN 0-916122-08-5). KC Pubns.

Yoshitoshi-the Splendid Decadent: The Last Master of Ukiyo-e. Shinichi Segi. Tr. by Alfred Birnbaum. LC 84-48700. (Illus.). 128p. 1985. 49.50 o.s.i. (ISBN 0-87011-712-2). Kodansha.

Yost Violin Method, Vol. I. Gaylord Yost. 1946. 1.75 o.p. (ISBN 0-913650-22-6). CPP Belwin.

You. Joseph Frank. (Illus.). 281p. 1972. pap. text ed. 9.95 o.p. (ISBN 0-15-598420-9, HC). HarBraceJ.

You Always Communicate Something. Shirley Schwarzrock & C. Gilbert Wrenn. (Coping with Ser.). (Illus.). 58p. (gr. 7-12). 1973. pap. text ed. 3.00 o.p. (ISBN 0-913476-20-X). Am Guidance.

You & Aunt Arie: A Guide to Cultural Journalism. Pamela Wood. (Illus.). 220p. 6.95 o.p. (ISBN 0-318-14395-X). Inst Dev & Econ.

You & I. Leonard Nimoy. 1973. pap. 1.50 o.p. (ISBN 0-380-00846-7, 17616). Avon.

You & I Have Simply Got to Stop Meeting This Way. R. Dunsing. 1981. pap. 5.95 o.p. (ISBN 0-317-31403-3). AMACOM.

You & I Have Simply Got to Stop Meeting This Way. Richard J. Dunsing. LC 78-2516. (Illus.). 176p. 1981. 5.95 o.p. (ISBN 0-8144-7558-2). AMACOM.

You & Me. Deanna Boden. (Illus.). (ps-3). 1979. pap. 3.95 o.p. (ISBN 0-87516-290-8). DeVorss.

You & Me. Tessa Colina. Ed. by Jane Buerger. (Illus.). 112p. (gr. k-4). 1980. 5.95 o.p. (ISBN 0-89565-179-3, 4936). Standard Pub.

You & Me: A Handbook about Needs. Jane B. Moncure & Tessa Colina. LC 80-17679. (Living the Good Life Ser.). (Illus.). 112p. (Orig.). (gr. 1-6). 1980. pap. 5.95 o.p. (ISBN 0-89565-179-3). Childs World.

You & Me, Baby. 2nd ed. Susan Regnier. LC 83-23826. (Illus.). 192p. 1984. pap. 9.95 o.p. (ISBN 0-671-54495-0). Meadowbrook.

You & Others: An Introduction to Interpersonal Communication. Donald L. MacRae et al. (Illus.). 1976. text ed. 25.95 o.p. (ISBN 0-07-082256-5). McGraw.

You & the Alcoholic in Your Home. Duane Mehl. LC 78-66947. 1979. pap. 6.95 o.p. (ISBN 0-8066-1697-0, 10-7408, Augsburg). Augsburg Fortress.

You & the Armed Forces: Career & Educational Opportunities for a Secure Future. Texe Marrs. LC 82-16386. 176p. 1983. lib. bdg. 12.95 o.p. (ISBN 0-668-05685-1); pap. 7.95 o.p. (ISBN 0-668-05693-2). Arco.

You & the Law. Jules Archer. LC 78-52812. 1978. 7.95 o.p. (ISBN 0-15-299852-7, HJ). HarBraceJ.

You & the Psychic Within. Joseph L. D'Albert & Richard A. Herbert. 1977. 6.00 o.p. (ISBN 0-682-48879-8). Exposition-Phoenix.

You & the Senior Boom: New Challenges & Opportunities for All. Louise M. Odell & Charles E. Odell. (Illus.). 1980. 12.50 o.p. (ISBN 0-682-49492-5, Banner). Exposition-Phoenix.

You & Your Aging Parent: The Modern Family's Guide to Emotional, Physical & Financial Problems. Barbara Silverstone & Helen K. Hyman. 1982. 16.00 o.p. (ISBN 0-394-52169-2); pap. 8.95 o.p. (ISBN 0-394-74948-0). Pantheon.

You & Your Body. Aaron E. Klein. (Illus.). (gr. 3-5). 1980. pap. 1.50 o.p. (ISBN 0-671-29899-2). Archway.

You & Your Cells. Leo Schneider. LC 64-71496. (Illus.). (gr. 7 up). 1964. 5.95 o.p. (ISBN 0-15-299840-3, HJ). HarBraceJ.

You & Your Community in the World. Chadwick F. Alger & David G. Hoovler. (CISE Learning Packages in International Studies). 172p. 1978. pap. text ed. 4.00x o.p. (ISBN 0-317-34814-0). LRIS.

You & Your Eyes. 2nd rev. ed. Lawrence Lewison. 1978. 10.00 o.p. (ISBN 0-682-48926-3). Exposition-Phoenix.

You & Your Heart. Paul Kezdi. LC 76-53757. (Illus.). 1977. 9.95 o.p. (ISBN 0-689-10743-9, Atheneum); pap. 4.95 o.p. (ISBN 0-689-70575-1, 243). Macmillan.

You & Your National Government. League of Women Voters Education Fund Staff. (Illus.). 32p. 1977. pap. 1.00 o.p. (ISBN 0-89959-027-6, 273); pap. 3.75, 5 copies, 12.50 25 copies o.p. (ISBN 0-686-77308-X). LWV US.

You & Your Network. Fred Smith. 1984. 9.95 o.p. (ISBN 0-8499-0373-4). Word Bks.

You & Your Pet: Aquarium Pets. Phil Steinberg. LC 78-54359. (You & Your Pet Bks.). (Illus.). (gr. 4 up). 1978. PLB 5.95 o.p. (ISBN 0-8225-1255-6). Lerner Pubns.

You & Your Pet: Birds. Phil Steinberg. LC 78-54352. (You & Your Pet Bks.). (Illus.). (gr. 4 up). 1978. PLB 5.95 o.p. (ISBN 0-8225-1251-3). Lerner Pubns.

You & Your Poodle. Mollie Skelton. 7.95 o.p. (ISBN 0-87666-362-5, PS-641). TFH Pubns.

You & Your Senses. Leo Schneider. LC 56-5875. (gr. 5 up). 1956. 6.50 o.p. (ISBN 0-15-299857-8, HJ). HarBraceJ.

You & Your Will: The Planning & Management of Your Estate. Paul P. Ashley. (Illus.). 252p. (Orig.). 1975. text ed. 19.95 o.p. (ISBN 0-07-002407-3). McGraw.

You Are a Computer: Cybernetics in Everyday Life. V. H. Brix. (gr. 9 up). 1970. 9.95 o.p. (ISBN 0-87523-169-1). Emerson.

You Are All Sanpaku. George Oshawa. 4.95 o.p. (ISBN 0-8216-0164-4, Pub. by Univ Bks). Carol Pub Group.

You Are Always Your Own Experience! 4th ed. Tom Johnson. 269p. 1982. pap. 7.95 o.p. (ISBN 0-941992-01-2). Los Arboles Pub.

You Are Here - Boston Celebrations: Environmental Art. (Illus.). 91p. 1976. pap. 5.00 o.s.i. (ISBN 0-317-19049-0). ICA Inc.

You Are My Beloved Sermon Book. Frederick Kemper & George M. Bass. 1980. pap. 7.50 o.p. (ISBN 0-570-03821-9, 12-2761). Concordia.

You Are Not the Target. Laura Huxley. 289p. 1963. 8.95 o.p. (ISBN 0-374-29380-5). FS&G.

You Are Special. (Four Very Special Gift Bks.). 48p. 1985. 2.25 o.p. (ISBN 0-8407-6678-5). Nelson.

You Are What You Choose. Maralene Wesner & E. Miles. LC 84-3110. (Orig.). 1984. pap. 4.95 o.p. (ISBN 0-8054-5247-8). Broadman.

You Be the Judge. Don Stewart. 96p. (Orig.). 1983. 2.95 o.p. (ISBN 0-89840-055-4). Heres Life.

You Bring the Confetti. Luci Swindoll. 160p. 1986. 9.95 o.p. (ISBN 0-8499-0527-3). Word Bks.

You Can Be a Great Parent. Charlie W. Shedd. LC 76-128353. 1982. pap. 2.25 o.p. (ISBN 0-8499-4166-0, 98070). Word Bks.

You Can Be a Soulwinner. Norvel Hayes. 150p. (Orig.). 1983. pap. 4.95 o.p. (ISBN 0-89274-269-0). Harrison Hse.

You Can Be a Writer: A Career & Leisure Guide. Clifford L. Alderman. LC 80-28306. 160p. (gr. 7 up). 1981. lib. bdg. 9.79 o.s.i. (ISBN 0-671-34047-6). Messner.

You Can Become Whole Again: A Guide to Healing for Christians in Grief. Jolonda Miller. LC 80-84652. 1981. pap. 6.50 o.s.i. (ISBN 0-8042-1156-6, John Knox). Westminster John Knox.

You Can Build a Successful Team or Department. (You Can Bks.). (Orig.). 1984. pap. 14.95 o.p. (ISBN 0-87280-100-4, Asher-Gallant). Caddylak Systs.

You Can Conquer Depression. J. E. Adams. pap. 1.25 o.p. (ISBN 0-8010-0094-7). Baker Bk.

You Can Control Your Class: A Practical Guide to Classroom Management. Abel Gudmundson et al. 1979. pap. text ed. 3.50 o.p. (ISBN 0-89039-236-6). Ann Arbor Pubs.

You Can Correct a Problem Employee. LC 84-17487. (You Can Bks.). (Orig.). 1984. pap. 14.95 o.p. (ISBN 0-87280-110-1, Asher-Gallant). Caddylak Systs.

You Can Do It! Kids Diet. Dee Matthews et al. LC 84-8944. 272p. (gr. 4 up). 1985. 14.95 o.p. (ISBN 0-8050-0620-6). H Holt & Co.

You Can Draw. Kenneth Jameson. LC 79-92494. (Start to Paint Ser.). (Illus.). 1980. pap. 3.95 o.s.i. (ISBN 0-8008-8755-7, Pentalic). Taplinger.

You Can Enjoy Your Aging Parents. LC 12-2797. 1.75 o.p. Concordia.

You Can Find a Good Mate. Richard D. Dobbins. pap. 0.75 o.p. (ISBN 0-8010-2913-9). Baker Bk.

You Can Find Anyone: A Missing Persons Search Manual. E. Ferraro. 1986. lib. bdg. 79.95 o.p. (ISBN 0-8490-3721-2). Gordon Pr.

You Can Find Comfort. Chevis Horne. pap. 0.75 o.p. (ISBN 0-8010-4245-3). Baker Bk.

You Can Fool All of the People All of the Time. Art Buchwald. (Large Print Books). (Illus.). 572p. 1986. lib. bdg. 18.95 o.p. (ISBN 0-8161-4102-9, Large Print Bks); pap. 11.95 o.p. (ISBN 0-8161-4103-7). G K Hall.

You Can Get Anything You Want: But You Have to Do More Than Ask. Roger Dawson. 1987. 17.45 o.p. (ISBN 0-671-63512-3). S&S.

You Can Have a Happy Marriage. Cyril J. Barber & Aldyth A. Barber. LC 83-25542. 192p. (Orig.). 1984. pap. 6.95 o.p. (ISBN 0-8254-2248-5). Kregel.

You Can Have a Near-Perfect Memory. Mort Herold. (Illus.). 272p. 1983. pap. 8.95 o.p. (ISBN 0-8092-5942-7). Contemp Bks.

You Can Heal Your Life. Louise L. Hay. 224p. (Orig.). 1984. lib. bdg. 10.00 o.p. (ISBN 0-317-52419-4); pap. 10.00 o.p. (ISBN 0-937611-01-8). Hay House.

You Can Help Make It Happen. Wilfred Bockelman. LC 72-135217. (Orig.). 1971. pap. 3.50 o.p. (ISBN 0-8066-1104-9, Augsburg, 10-7410). Augsburg Fortress.

You Can Hire the Perfect Employee. (You Can Bks.). (Orig.). 1984. pap. 14.95 o.s.i. (ISBN 0-87280-099-7, Asher-Gallant). Caddylak Systs.

You Can Know It's True Love. John M. Drescher. pap. 1.25 o.p. (ISBN 0-8010-2932-5). Baker Bk.

You Can Make a Difference: American Mother of the Year Shares the Secret of Dynamic Christian Living. Ruth Y. Nelson. LC 74-77678. 112p. (Orig.). 1974. pap. 3.95 o.p. (ISBN 0-8066-1429-3, 10-7412, Augsburg). Augsburg Fortress.

You Can Manage a Project for Success. LC 84-17443. (You Can Bks.). (Orig.). 1984. pap. 14.95 o.s.i. (ISBN 0-87280-105-5, Asher-Gallant). Caddylak Systs.

You Can Organize a Successful Meeting Large or Small. (You Can Bks.). (Orig.). 1983. pap. 14.95 o.s.i. (ISBN 0-87280-098-9, Asher-Gallant). Caddylak Systs.

You Can Overcome Fear. J. E. Adams. pap. 1.25 o.p. (ISBN 0-8010-0093-9). Baker Bk.

You Can Plan a Good Marriage. John M. Drescher. pap. 1.25 o.p. (ISBN 0-8010-2907-4). Baker Bk.

You Can Profit from the New Tax Law. Joseph L. Wiltsee & Donna Sammons. 1982. pap. text ed. 5.95 o.p. (ISBN 0-07-070963-7). McGraw.

You Can Save Your Breast: One Woman's Experience With Radiation Therapy. Larry Althouse & Valere Althouse. LC 81-18721. 192p. 1982. 12.95 o.p. (ISBN 0-393-01507-6). Norton.

You Can Save Your Breast: One Woman's Experience with Radiation Therapy. Larry Althouse & Valere Althouse. 192p. 1984. pap. 5.70 o.p. (ISBN 0-393-30161-3). Norton.

You Can Sell Anything by Telephone. Gary S. Goodman. 144p. 1984. 14.95 o.p. (ISBN 0-13-976770-3); pap. 6.95 o.p. (ISBN 0-13-976762-2). P-H.

You Can Still Own a Home: A Strategy for Stretching Your Housing Dollar. Cathy McNellis & Bob McNellis. 1978. 7.00 o.p. (ISBN 0-682-49030-X). Exposition-Phoenix.

You Can Stop. Jacquelyn Rogers. 1978. 9.95 o.p. (ISBN 0-671-22587-1). S&S.

You Can Succeed by Managing Upward. LC 84-17505. (You Can Bks.). (Orig.). 1984. pap. 14.95 o.p. (ISBN 0-87280-097-0, Asher-Gallant). Caddylak Systs.

You Can Teach Children Successfully. Twila Sias. (Training Successful Teachers Ser.). 48p. (Orig.). 1984. pap. 2.95 o.p. (ISBN 0-87239-806-4, 3206). Standard Pub.

You Can Teach Preschoolers Successfully. Betty Aldridge. (Training Successful Teachers Ser.). 48p. (Orig.). 1984. pap. 2.95 o.p. (ISBN 0-87239-805-6, 3205). Standard Pub.

You Can Tell the World: New Directions for Christian Writers. Sherwood E. Wirt & Ruth McKinney. LC 75-2834. 128p. (Orig.). 1975. pap. 3.50 o.p. (ISBN 0-8066-1479-X, 10-7413, Augsburg). Augsburg Fortress.

You Can Train Your Cat. Jo Loeb & Paul Loeb. 1979. pap. 8.95 o.p. (ISBN 0-671-25147-3, Fireside). S&S.

You Can Win. Roger Campbell. 132p. 1985. pap. 5.50 o.p. (ISBN 0-89693-317-2). Victor Bks.

You Can Win at Office Politics: Techniques, Tips, & Step-by-Step Plans for Coming out Ahead. Robert Bell. 272p. 1985. pap. 7.95 o.p. (ISBN 0-03-005863-5). H Holt & Co.

You Can Work Your Own Miracles. Napoleon Hill. 1982. pap. 2.95 o.p. (ISBN 0-449-14167-5, GM). Fawcett.

You Can Write a Winning Report. (You Can Bks.). (Orig.). 1984. pap. 14.95 o.s.i. (ISBN 0-87280-102-0, Asher-Gallant). Caddylak Systs.

You Can Write! Practical Writing Skills for Hawaii. Victor C. Pellegrino. LC 81-71307. (Illus.). 296p. 1982. text ed. 12.95 o.p. (ISBN 0-935848-05-3); pap. text ed. 9.95 o.p. (ISBN 0-935848-04-5); wkbk, Feb. 1985 4.95 o.p. (ISBN 0-935848-28-2); Tchr's manual 3.00 o.p. Bess Pr.

You Can't Borrow from Tomorrow. Betty Carmichael. 1984. 8.95 o.p. (ISBN 0-8062-2410-X). Carlton.

You Can't Fly Home Again. Ron Rendleman. LC 79-89581. 1980. pap. 2.95 o.p. (ISBN 0-89221-066-4). New Leaf.

You Can't Get Lost in Capetown. Zoe Wicomb. LC 86-42977. 176p. 1987. 10.95 o.p. (ISBN 0-394-56030-2). Pantheon.

You Can't Get There from Here. Mary Anderson. LC 81-10813. 216p. (gr. 7 up). 1982. PLB 10.95 o.p. (ISBN 0-689-30903-1, Atheneum). Macmillan.

You Can't Keep a Good Woman Down: Stories. Alice Walker. LC 80-8761. 180p. 1981. 10.95 o.s.i. (ISBN 0-15-199754-3). HarBraceJ.

You Can't Make It by Bus. James L. Summers. (gr. 7 up). 1969. 3.95 o.s.i. (ISBN 0-664-32450-9, Westminster). Westminster John Knox.

You Can't Take It with You: Plan Your Estate Now. Edward L. Jenkins. LC 84-90179. 172p. 1985. 12.95 o.p. (ISBN 0-533-06226-8). Vantage.

You Can't Take Twenty Dogs on a Date. Betty Cavanna. LC 77-432. 180p. (gr. 5-9). 1977. 8.95 o.s.i. (ISBN 0-664-32613-7, Westminster). Westminster John Knox.

You Come Too. Robert Frost. (gr. 4 up). 9.95 o.p. (ISBN 0-03-089530-8); pap. 3.95 o.p. H Holt & Co.

You Count-You Really Do! William A. Miller. LC 76-27078. 1977. pap. 6.95 o.p. (ISBN 0-8066-1569-9, 10-7420, Augsburg). Augsburg Fortress.

You Don't Have to Ache: Orthotherapy. Arthur A. Michelle. LC 73-150795. 224p. 1983. pap. 5.95 o.p. (ISBN 0-87131-411-8). M Evans.

You Have a Point There: A New & Complete Guide to Punctuation. Eric Partridge. (Orig.). 1978. pap. 7.95 o.p. (ISBN 0-7100-8753-5). Routledge Chapman & Hall.

You Have a Right: A Guide for Minors. Leland S. Englebardt. LC 79-4678. (gr. 6 up). 1979. 11.75 o.p. (ISBN 0-688-41893-7); PLB 11.88 o.p. (ISBN 0-688-51893-1). Lothrop.

You Know When You're over Fifty When... Herbert I. Kavet. (Illus.). 96p. (Orig.). 1984. pap. 3.95 o.p. (ISBN 0-8092-5342-9). Contemp Bks.

You Know When You're over Forty When... Herbert I. Kavet. (Illus.). 96p. 1984. pap. 3.95 o.p. (ISBN 0-8092-5363-1). Contemp Bks.

You Make the Difference: Cadette & Senior Girl Scout Leaders' Guide. Girl Scouts of the U. S. A. Staff. 40p. (Orig.). 1980. pap. text ed. 3.00 o.p. (ISBN 0-88441-330-6, 20-705). Girl Scouts USA.

You Make the Difference: The Handbook for Cadette & Senior Girl Scouts. Girl Scouts of the U. S. A. Staff. (Illus.). 72p. (Orig.). (YA) (gr. 7-12). 1980. pap. text ed. 3.75 o.p. (ISBN 0-88441-329-2, 20-704). Girl Scouts USA.

You Must Die Before You Live. Mel Hawkins. (Illus.). 64p. 1982. 5.00 o.p. (ISBN 0-682-49796-7). Exposition-Phoenix.

You Must Remember This: Popular Songwriters, 1900-1980. Mark White. 320p. 1985. 14.95 o.p. (ISBN 0-684-18433-8, ScribT). Scribner.

You Only Have One Life--Give It Your Best Shot: Five Steps to Health, Wealth, Happiness. Richard S. Clarke. 1979. 8.99 o.p. (ISBN 0-682-49280-9, Banner). Exposition-Phoenix.

You: Prayer for Beginners & Those Who Have Forgotten How. Mark Link. LC 76-41584. 1976. pap. 4.95 o.p. (ISBN 0-913592-78-1). Tabor Pub.

You, Still, Can Become a Millionaire by 1984! Investments Perspectives Through the Mid-1980s & Applicable Investment Strategy. Andrew Willman. (Illus.). 1980. pap. 5.95 o.p. (ISBN 0-686-77448-5). Exposition-Phoenix.

You, Still, Can Become a Millionaire by 1984: Investment Perspectives Through the Mid-1980's & Applicable Investment Strategy. Andrew Willman. 1979. 10.00 o.p. (ISBN 0-682-49203-5, Banner). Exposition-Phoenix.

You Think You Got Troubles. Janice Potulny. (Illus.). 64p. (ps-2). 1984. 5.50 o.p. (ISBN 0-682-40189-7). Exposition-Phoenix.

You Thought I Would Never Leave You. Victoria Freeman. (Illus.). 64p. 1973. 4.00 o.p. (ISBN 0-8065-0366-1, Pub. by Citadel Pr). Carol Pub Group.

You, Too, Can Golf in the Eighties: An Effective Strategy for Reducing Strokes. Dick Carr. 1977. 5.00 o.p. (ISBN 0-682-48664-7, Banner). Exposition-Phoenix.

You, Too, Can Stop Drinking. G. Z. Patten. LC 76-57471. (Illus.). 1977. 10.00 o.p. (ISBN 0-682-48733-3). Exposition-Phoenix.

You-Two. Jean Ure. LC 84-8947. (Illus.). (gr. 4-7). 1984. 10.25 o.p. (ISBN 0-688-03857-3, Morrow Junior Books). Morrow.

You Were Saying, Andy Capp. Reginald Smythe. 128p. 1980. pap. 1.50 o.s.i. (ISBN 0-449-14346-5, GM). Fawcett.

You Will Never Be the Same. Cordwainer Smith. Ed. by Lester Del Ray. LC 75-429. (Library of Science Fiction). 1975. lib. bdg. 21.00 o.p. (ISBN 0-8240-1429-4). Garland Pub.

You Win Some, You Lose Some. Date not set. (ISBN 0-385-29434-4). Delacorte.

You, Your Stars & Your Partner. Diana Hunt. LC 79-107016. 1970. 6.95 o.s.i. (ISBN 0-8008-8763-8). Taplinger.

You'd Better Not Tell. Curt Schleier. LC 78-20921. 94p. 1979. 7.50 o.s.i. (ISBN 0-664-32646-3, Westminster). Westminster John Knox.

You'll Need a Guardian Angel. Alec Thackeray. 1980. 11.95 o.p. (ISBN 0-393-01274-3). Norton.

You'll Never Come Back. Elizabeth W. Freeman. LC 79-66735. 1979. pap. write for info. o.p. (ISBN 0-87930-124-4). Miller Freeman.

Young Adult Book Review Index, 1988. Ed. by Barbara Beach. cancelled o.s.i. (ISBN 0-8103-4374-6). Gale.

Young Adult Catalog of the Boston Public Library, 2 vols. Boston Public Library Staff. 1112p. 1972. Set. lib. bdg. 200.00 o.p. (ISBN 0-8161-1028-X, Hall Library). G K Hall.

Young America: A Folk-Art History. Jean Lipman & Elizabeth V. Warren. LC 86-10248. (Illus.). 200p. 1986. 45.00 o.p. (ISBN 0-933920-75-X, Dist. by Rizzoli); pap. 25.00 museum distribution only o.p. (ISBN 0-933920-76-8). Hudson Hills.

Young American's Dictionary. Johnson. (ISBN 0-8022-0808-8). Philos Lib.

Young & Famous: Hollywood's Newest Superstars. Daniel Cohen & Susan Cohen. (gr. 4 up). 1987. pap. 2.50 o.p. (ISBN 0-671-63493-3). Archway.

Young Bess. Irwin. 1966. pap. 0.75 o.p. (ISBN 0-15-699824-6, VoyB). HarBraceJ.

Young Black Adults: Liberation & Family Attitudes. George B. Thomas. 1974. pap. 1.95 o.p. (ISBN 0-377-00002-7). Friendship Pr.

Young Children & Their Environments... A Readings Book Approach. Norma Fulbright et al. 150p. 1975. pap. text ed. 6.95x o.p. (ISBN 0-8290-1389-X). Irvington.

Young Children in Hospital. 2nd ed. James Robertson. 1970. pap. 12.95 o.p. (ISBN 0-422-75060-3, NO. 2410, Pub. by Tavistock England). Routledge Chapman & Hall.

Young Defector. Robert A. Karlowich. LC 82-60641. (Illus.). 80p. (gr. 4-6). 1983. lib. bdg. 9.29 o.s.i. (ISBN 0-671-45202-9). Messner.

Young Disciples. Joyce M. Smith. 50p. (gr. 7-11). 1983. pap. 2.95 o.p. (ISBN 0-8423-8599-1). Tyndale.

Young Doctors in Love. Michael Elias & Michael Eustis. 168p. 1982. pap. 2.75 o.p. (ISBN 0-380-80671-1, 80671-1). Avon.

Young Emma. W. H. Davies. LC 80-70274. 158p. 1981. 9.95 o.p. (ISBN 0-8076-1009-7). Braziller.

Young Filmmakers. Rodger Larson & Ellen Meade. (gr. 7-12). 1980. pap. 0.95 o.p. (ISBN 0-380-01479-3, 08250). Avon.

Young Freud: The Origins of Psychoanalysis in Late Nineteenth-Century Viennese Culture. Billa Zanuso. 192p. 1986. 29.95x o.p. (ISBN 0-631-13749-1). Basil Blackwell.

Young Gemini. Alec McCowen. LC 79-1991. 1979. 7.95 o.p. (ISBN 0-689-11004-9, Atheneum). Macmillan.

Young George Du Maurier: A Selection of His Letters, 1860-67. George L. Du Maurier. Ed. by Daphne Du Maurier. LC 73-97329. Repr. of 1951 ed. lib. bdg. 35.00x o.p. (ISBN 0-8371-2830-7, DUDU). Greenwood.

Young Grizzly. Paige Dixon. LC 73-84827. (Illus.). 112p. (gr. 4-6). 1974. 6.95 o.p. (ISBN 0-689-30137-5, Atheneum). Macmillan.

Young Hart. William H. Harding. LC 82-15493. 356p. 1983. 16.95 o.p. (ISBN 0-03-062754-0). H Holt & Co.

Young Hearts Crying. Richard Yates. 362p. 1986. pap. 8.95 o.p. (ISBN 0-385-29441-7, Pub. by Delta). Dell.

Young Hearts Crying. Date not set. pap. (ISBN 0-385-29441-7). Delacorte.

Young Hemingway. Michael Reynolds. 281p. 1986. 34.95x o.p. (ISBN 0-631-14786-1). Basil Blackwell.

Young John Dewey: An Essay in American Intellectual History. Neil Coughlan. LC 74-33519. 200p. 1975. lib. bdg. 13.00x o.s.i. (ISBN 0-226-11604-2). U of Chicago Pr.

Young John Kennedy. Gene Schoor. LC 63-9092. (Illus.). (gr. 7 up). 1963. 6.95 o.p. (ISBN 0-15-299876-4, HJ). HarBraceJ.

Young Landlords. Walter D. Meyers. 1980. pap. 1.95 o.p. (ISBN 0-380-52191-1, 67561-7, Flare). Avon.

Young Man in Paris: 1927-1932. John Weld. (Illus.). 208p. 1985. 14.95 o.p. (ISBN 0-89733-111-7). Academy Chi Pubs.

Young Man in Search of Love. Isaac Bashevis Singer. LC 77-2538. (Windfall Bks.). (Illus.). 1978. 6.95 o.p. (ISBN 0-385-12357-4); limited ed. 50.00 o.p. (ISBN 0-385-13492-4). Doubleday.

Young Mother's Book of Ideas. Marjorie Palmer & Ethel Bowman. 1979. gift boxed 5.95 o.p. (ISBN 0-8423-8601-7). Tyndale.

Young Nathan. Marion M. Brown. (Illus.). (gr. 5-9). 1949. 4.75 o.s.i. (ISBN 0-664-32050-3, Westminster). Westminster John Knox.

Young People's Bible Dictionary. Barbara Smith. 1965. 5.00 o.s.i. (ISBN 0-664-20537-2, Westminster). Westminster John Knox.

Young People's Hebrew History. Louis Wallis. 128p. 1953. (ISBN 0-8022-1800-8). Philos Lib.

Young People's Job Finding Guide: Job Power. Bernard Haldane. LC 82-3934. 1982. 10.95 o.p.; pap. 4.95 o.p. (ISBN 0-87491-609-7). Acropolis.

Young People's Science Encyclopedia, 20 Vols. rev. ed. National College of Education Staff. LC 67-17925. (Illus.). (gr. 3-9). 1979. Set. PLB 265.35 o.p. (ISBN 0-516-00100-0). Childrens.

Young Person's Book of Catholic Signs & Symbols. Catholic Heritage Press Staff & Francis Tiso. LC 81-43459. 128p. 1982. pap. 3.50 o.p. (ISBN 0-385-17951-0, Im). Doubleday.

Young Person's Guide to European Arms & Armor in the Metropolitan Museum of Art. Edith Watts. Ed. by Rosanne Wasserman. (Illus.). 40p. (Orig.). (gr. 7-8). 1982. pap. 1.95 o.p. (ISBN 0-87099-282-1). Metro Mus Art.

Young Photographer's Handbook. George Haines. LC 83-19656. (Illus.). 224p. (YA) (gr. 7 up). 1984. 9.95 o.p. (ISBN 0-668-06048-4). Arco.

Young Playwrights Festival Collection. Dramatists Guild Foundation Editors. 256p. 1983. pap. 3.95 o.p. (ISBN 0-380-83642-4, 83642-4, Bard). Avon.

Young Programs for Older Workers: Case Studies in Progressive Personnel Policies. Beverly Jacobson. (Van Nostrand Reinhold Work in America Institute Series). 224p. 1980. 21.95 o.p. (ISBN 0-442-25405-9). Van Nos Reinhold.

Young Radicals: Notes on Committed Youth. Kenneth Keniston. LC 68-23578. 1968. 6.95 o.p. (ISBN 0-15-165432-8). HarBraceJ.

Young Radicals: Notes on Committed Youth. Kenneth Keniston. LC 68-23578. 1968. pap. 2.45 o.p. (ISBN 0-15-665508-X, Harv). HarBraceJ.

Young Renny. Mazo De La Roche. 1976. pap. 1.50 o.p. (ISBN 0-449-22842-8, Q2842, Crest). Fawcett.

Young Rider's Companion. George Wheatley. LC 81-27509. (Books for Adult & Young Adults). (Illus.). 120p. (gr. 4 up). 1981. PLB 15.95 o.p. (ISBN 0-8225-0767-6, AACR1). Lerner Pubns.

Young Swimmer. Bill Libby. LC 82-17289. (Illus.). 160p. (gr. 4 up). 1983. 10.25 o.p. (ISBN 0-688-01992-7). Lothrop.

Young Tycoons. Gloria D. Miklowitz & Madelein Yates. LC 80-8803. (Illus.). 128p. (gr. 7 up). 1981. 9.95 o.p. (ISBN 0-15-299879-9, HJ). HarBraceJ.

Young Voter's Manual: A Topical Dictionary of American Government & Politics. Leon W. Blevins. (Quality Paperback: No. 260). 366p. (Orig.). 1975. pap. 9.50 o.p. (ISBN 0-8226-0260-1). Littlefield.

Young Wife's Tale. Renee Shann. (Lythway). 1988. lib. bdg. 19.50 o.p. (ISBN 0-7451-0670-6, Pub. by Chivers Pr UK). G K HAll.

Young Witness: Evangelism to & by Children & Youth. Jane Hagstrom. 56p. (Orig.). 1986. pap. 4.95 o.p. (ISBN 0-8066-2233-4, 23-3036, Augsburg). Augsburg Fortress.

Young Woman's Guide to Sex. Jacqueline Voss & Jay Gale. LC 86-4786. (Illus.). 256p. 1987. 16.95 o.s.i. (ISBN 0-8050-0082-8). H Holt & Co.

Young Wrestler. Thompson Clayton. LC 77-1208. (Illus.). 125p. 1977. pap. 4.95 o.s.i. (ISBN 0-87095-064-9, Athletic). Gldn West Bks.

Young Writer at Work. Jessie Rehder. 286p. 1962. text ed. write for info. o.p. (ISBN 0-02-399200-X). Macmillan.

Younger Brothers. Carl W. Breihan. 1961. 12.50 o.p. (ISBN 0-686-67701-3). Exposition-Phoenix.

Younger Skin: How to Get It, How to Keep It. Jonathan Zizmor & Sharon Sabin. 128p. 1983. 9.95 o.p. (ISBN 0-03-061577-1). H Holt & Co.

Young's Analytical Concordance to the Bible. rev. ed. Robert Young. LC 82-14203. 1982. 22.95 o.p. (ISBN 0-8407-4971-6); indexed 26.95 o.p. (ISBN 0-8407-4972-4). Nelson.

Young's Learning Medical Terminology Step by Step: Textbook & Workbook. 5th ed. Miriam G. Austrin. LC 82-14110. (Illus.). 400p. 1983. pap. 19.95 o.p. (ISBN 0-8016-5662-1). Mosby.

Your Adolescent: An Owner's Manual. Carol Rinzler. LC 81-66000. 1981. 8.95 o.p. (ISBN 0-689-11137-1, Atheneum). Macmillan.

Your Ant Is a Which: Fun with Homophones. Bernice K. Hunt. LC 75-37582. (Let Me Read Ser.). (Illus.). 32p. (gr. 1-5). 1976. 4.95 o.p. (ISBN 0-15-299880-2, HJ). HarBraceJ.

Your Ant Is a Which: Fun with Homophones. Bernice K. Hunt. LC 75-37582. (Let Me Read Ser.). (Illus.). (gr. 1-5). 1976. pap. 1.65 o.p. (ISBN 0-15-299881-0, VoyB). HarBraceJ.

Your Basic Love Story. Jack Blumner. (Illus.). 1984. pap. 4.95 o.p. (ISBN 0-03-069581-3). H Holt & Co.

Your Body - Biofeedback at Its Best. Beata Jencks. LC 77-24618. (Illus.). 304p. 1978. 24.95x o.s.i. (ISBN 0-88229-351-6); pap. 12.95x o.s.i. (ISBN 0-88229-508-X). Nelson-Hall.

Your Body Is Trying to Tell You Something: How to Understand Its Signals & Respond to Its Needs. Richard Stiller. LC 79-87529. (gr. 7 up). 1979. 7.95 o.p. (ISBN 0-15-299894-2, HJ). HarBraceJ.

Your Body, Your Baby, Your Life. Angela Phillips. (Illus.). 192p. (Orig.). 1983. pap. 5.95 o.p. (ISBN 0-86358-006-8, Pandora Pr). Routledge Chapman & Hall.

Your Book of Knitted Toys. Brenda Morton. LC 72-11090. 1973. 5.95 o.s.i. (ISBN 0-8008-8757-3). Taplinger.

Your Book of Music. Michael Short & Imogen Holst. LC 82-9377. (Your Book of... Ser.). (Illus.). 96p. (gr. 3-6). 1983. 11.95 o.p. (ISBN 0-571-18031-0). Faber & Faber.

Your Book of Patchwork. Priscilla Lobley. LC 74-6048. 6.50 o.s.i. (ISBN 0-8008-8760-3). Taplinger.

Your Burro Is No Jackass. Jim Aylward. LC 81-4603. (Illus.). 64p. (gr. 4-7). 1981. 7.95 o.p. (ISBN 0-03-059527-4). H Holt & Co.

Your Burro is No Jackass: And over 100 Other Things No One Ever Told You. Jim Aylward. (Illus.). 64p. (gr. 3-7). 1983. pap. 2.25 o.p. (ISBN 0-380-63453-8, 63453-8, Camelot). Avon.

Your Business & the Law: A Guide for Minnesota Business Owners. Jonathan Adams. LC 85-227944. xiv, 234p. 1985. 45.00 o.p. Butterworth MN.

Your Career: Choices, Chances, Changes. David C. Borchard et al. 304p. 1984. pap. text ed. 16.95 o.p. (ISBN 0-8403-3343-9, 40334301). Kendall-Hunt.

Your Career in Harness Racing. Steve Lehrman. LC 75-38343. (YA) (gr. 9 up). 1976. 6.95 o.p. (ISBN 0-689-10714-5, Atheneum). Macmillan.

Your Career in Travel & Tourism. rev. ed. Laurence Stevens. LC 83-60852. 1981. pap. 7.50 o.p. (ISBN 0-916032-02-7). Delmar.

Your Career in Travel & Tourism. Rev. ed. Laurence Stevens. LC 83-60852. (Illus.). 190p. 1983. softcover 10.00 o.p. (ISBN 0-916032-19-1). Delmar.

Your Children, Their Teeth & Their Health. A. M. Pratt. LC 74-76035. 1974. 5.00 o.p. (ISBN 0-682-47959-4, Banner). Exposition-Phoenix.

Your Child's Dreams. Patricia Garfield. LC 84-91042. 356p. (Orig.). 1984. pap. 3.95 o.s.i. (ISBN 0-345-31047-0). Ballantine.

Your Child's First Journey: A Guide to Prepared Birth from Pregnancy to Parenthood. Childbirth Education Association of Jacksonville, Fla., Inc. Staff & Ginny Brinkley. (Avery's Childbirth Education Ser.). (Illus.). 256p. (Orig.). 1982. pap. 9.95 o.p. (ISBN 0-89529-150-9). Avery Pub.

Your Child's Reading & What You Can Do about It. Harold Newman. 1973. pap. 6.95 o.p. (ISBN 0-8422-0341-9). Irvington.

Your Child's Vision: The Complete Guide to Growth & Development. Richard S. Kavner. LC 85-1859. (Illus.). 320p. 1986. 16.45 o.p. (ISBN 0-671-55449-2, Fireside); pap. 8.95 o.p. (ISBN 0-671-46176-1, Fireside). S&S.

Your Chinese Horoscope. Hans Wilhelm. 208p. 1980. pap. 4.95 o.p. (ISBN 0-380-75275-1, 75275-1). Avon.

Your Chinese Horoscope for Nineteen Eighty-Nine. Neil Somerville. (Illus.). 144p. (Orig.). 1988. pap. 4.99 o.p. (ISBN 0-85030-649-3, Pub. by Aquarian Pr England). Sterling.

Your Choice: A Young Woman's Guide to Making Decisions about Unmarried Pregnancy. Caryl Hansen. 176p. (Orig.). 1980. pap. 2.25 o.p. (ISBN 0-380-75853-9, Flare). Avon.

Your Church: A Dynamic Community. Arleon L. Kelley. LC 81-23159. (Illus.). 120p. (Orig.). 1982. pap. 7.95 o.s.i. (ISBN 0-664-24411-4, Westminster). Westminster John Knox.

Your Church Has a Fantastic Future! A Possibility Thinker's Guide to a Successful Church. rev. ed. Robert H. Schuller. LC 86-11906. (Illus.). 336p. 1986. 14.95 o.s.i. (ISBN 0-8307-1180-5, 5111659). Regal.

Your Commodore 64. (ISBN 0-07-881114-7). McGraw.

Your Complete Wedding Planner. Marjabelle Y. Stewart. (Illus.). 1980. gift edition 13.95 o.s.i. (ISBN 0-679-50744-2). McKay.

Your Directory to Profitable Prospecting. 3.50 o.p. (ISBN 0-686-31045-4, 29022). Rough Notes.

Your Dog: Companion & Helper. Milo D. Pearsall & Margaret E. Pearsall. LC 80-14115. (Illus.). 160p. 1980. 9.98 o.p. (ISBN 0-931866-07-3). Alpine Pubns.

Your Down's Syndrome Child: Everything Today's Parents Need to Know about Raising Their Special Child. Eunice McClurg. LC 85-31098. 288p. 1986. 15.95 o.p. (ISBN 0-385-23023-0). Doubleday.

Your Faith & You. James Finley & Michael Pennock. LC 78-53834. (Illus.). 272p. (gr. 11-12). 1978. pap. text ed. 4.95 o.p. (ISBN 0-87793-153-4); tchr's manual 2.75 o.p. (ISBN 0-87793-154-2). Ave Maria.

Your Faith Can Heal You. Norvel Hayes. 80p. 1983. pap. 2.50 o.p. (ISBN 0-89274-273-9). Harrison Hse.

Your Family. rev. & expanded ed. John MacArthur, Jr. (Moody Press Electives Ser.). 1983. pap. 3.95 o.p. (ISBN 0-8024-0257-7). Moody.

Your Family & Its Money. Helen M. Thal. (gr. 9-12). 1973. text ed. 17.76 o.p. (ISBN 0-395-14225-3). HM.

Your Family Records. 2nd ed. Carol Pladsen & Denis Clifford. LC 84-60121. 215p. 1986. pap. 14.95 o.p. (ISBN 0-87337-036-8). Nolo Pr.

Your Favorite Recipes. Theodora FitzGibbon. 186p. (Orig.). 1985. pap. 5.95 o.p. (ISBN 0-7171-1420-1, Pub. by Gill & MacMillan). Seven Hills Bk Dists.

Your First Apple II Program. Rodnay Zaks. LC 83-50717. (Illus.). 182p. 1983. pap. 10.95 o.p. (ISBN 0-89588-136-5). SYBEX.

Your First Atari Program. Rodnay Zaks. LC 83-51191. (Illus.). 182p. 1984. pap. 10.95 o.p. (ISBN 0-89588-130-6). SYBEX.

Your First BASIC Program. Rodnay Zaks. LC 83-60488. (Illus.). 182p. 1983. pap. 14.95 o.p. (ISBN 0-89588-092-X). SYBEX.

Your First Computer. Rodnay Zaks. 8.95 o.p. (ISBN 0-317-06040-6). Wayne Green Ent.

Your First Computer: A Guide to Business & Personal Computing. 2nd ed. Rodnay Zaks. LC 80-51036. (Illus.). 258p. 1980. pap. 7.95 o.p. (ISBN 0-89588-045-8). SYBEX.

Your First Pet: & How to Take Care of It. Carla Stevens. LC 74-2267. (Ready-to-Read Ser.). 128p. (gr. 1-4). 1974. 8.95 o.s.i. (ISBN 0-02-788200-4). Macmillan.

Your First Resume. Ronald W. Fry. 192p. (Orig.). 1988. 9.95 o.p. (ISBN 0-317-66752-1). Career Pr Inc.

Your Florida Garden. 5th ed. John V. Watkins & Herbert S. Wolfe. LC 68-23403. 382p. 1968. 9.95 o.p. (ISBN 0-8130-0233-8). U Presses Fla.

Your Future: A Guide for the Handicapped Teenager. rev. ed. S. Norman Feingold & Norma Miller. (gr. 7-12). 1986. 9.97 o.p. (ISBN 0-8239-0424-5). Rosen Group.

Your Future As a Secretary. Rev. ed. Nell B. Noyes. LC 73-88829. (Careers in Depth Ser.). (Illus.). (gr. 7 up). 1979. PLB 10.97 o.p. (ISBN 0-8239-0483-0). Rosen Group.

Your Future As a Shorthand Reporter. Edward Van Allen. LC 69-13005. (Careers in Depth Ser.). (gr. 7 up). 1977. PLB 9.97 o.p. (ISBN 0-8239-0401-6). Rosen Group.

Your Future As a Working Woman. Rev. ed. Gloria S. Pearlstein. (Careers in Depth Ser.). (Illus.). 144p. (gr. 7-12). 1981. PLB 9.97 o.p. (ISBN 0-8239-0307-9). Rosen Group.

Your Future As a Writer. Rick Mitz. (Careers in Depth Ser.). (Illus.). 128p. 1981. lib. bdg. 9.97 o.p. (ISBN 0-8239-0516-0). Rosen Group.

Your Future As an Airline Steward-Stewardess. Lyman K. Randall. 1979. 9.97 o.p. Rosen Group.

Your Future Career in the American Government. Rick Mitz. (gr. 7-12). 1978. PLB 9.97 o.p. (ISBN 0-8239-0452-0). Rosen Group.

Your Future in a Dental Hygiene Career. 2nd rev. ed. Barbara E. Paige. LC 69-14464. (Careers in Depth Ser.). (Illus.). (gr. 9 up). 1980. PLB 9.97 o.p. (ISBN 0-8239-0434-2). Rosen Group.

Your Future in a Mental Health Career. Fenton Keyes. (Careers in Depth Ser.). (Illus.). 180p. (gr. 7-12). 1981. PLB 9.97 o.p. (ISBN 0-8239-0362-1). Rosen Group.

Your Future in a Public Relations Career. rev. ed. Edward L. Bernays. (Careers in Depth Ser.). 1983. PLB 9.97 o.p. (ISBN 0-8239-0443-1). Rosen Group.

Your Future in Agribusiness. Chester Hutchison. (Careers in Depth Ser.). (Illus.). (gr. 7-12). 1977. PLB 9.97 o.p. (ISBN 0-8239-0394-X). Rosen Group.

Your Future in Architecture. Richard Roth. LC 60-11116. (Careers in Depth Ser.). (gr. 7-12). 1979. PLB 9.97 o.p. Rosen Group.

Your Future in Aviation Careers in the Air. rev. ed. Kimball Scribner. (Careers in Depth Ser.). (Illus.). (gr. 7-12). 1982. PLB 9.97 o.p. (ISBN 0-8239-0490-3). Rosen Group.

Your Future in Aviation Careers on the Ground. rev. ed. Kimball Scribner. (Careers in Depth Ser.). (Illus.). (gr. 7-12). 1983. PLB 9.97 o.p. (ISBN 0-8239-0491-1). Rosen Group.

Your Future in Big Business. Charles Heath. (Careers in Depth Ser.). 120p. 1980. lib. bdg. 9.97 o.p. (ISBN 0-8239-0498-9). Rosen Group.

Your Future in Broadcasting. Rev. ed. John R. Rider. LC 70-146047. (Careers in Depth Ser.). (Illus.). (gr. 7 up). 1979. PLB 9.97 o.p. (ISBN 0-8239-0454-7). Rosen Group.

Your Future in Foreign Service Careers. James P. Duncan, Jr. (Careers in Depth Ser.). (gr. 7-12). 1979. PLB 9.97 o.p. (ISBN 0-8239-0460-1). Rosen Group.

Your Future in Insurance Careers. Barry Bloomgarden. (Careers in Depth Ser.). (gr. 7-12). 1978. PLB 9.97 o.p. (ISBN 0-8239-0455-5). Rosen Group.

Your Future in Medical Assisting. rev. ed. Norma B. Chernok. 1982. 9.97 o.p. (ISBN 0-8239-0359-1). Rosen Group.

Your Future in Medical Illustrating: Art & Photography. Julia Nakamura & Massy Nakamura. LC 78-140096. (Careers in Depth Ser.). (Illus.). (gr. 7 up). 1971. PLB 9.97 o.p. (ISBN 0-8239-0236-6). Rosen Group.

Your Future in Museums. William Burns. LC 67-15470. (Careers in Depth Ser.). (gr. 7-12). 1974. PLB 9.97 o.p. (ISBN 0-8239-0053-3). Rosen Group.

Your Future in New Optometric Careers. James R. Gregg. (Careers in Depth Ser.). (gr. 7 up). 1978. PLB 9.97 o.p. (ISBN 0-8239-0449-0). Rosen Group.

Your Future in the Beauty Business. Rev. ed. Fashion Group Inc., Friends & Staff. Ed. by Christine Le Vathes. LC 68-31559. (Careers in Depth Ser.). (Illus.). (gr. 9 up). 1979. PLB 9.97 o.p. (ISBN 0-8239-0482-2). Rosen Group.

Your Future in the New World of American Fashion. Ed. by Christine LeVathes. Fashion Group Members Staff. (Careers in Depth Ser.). (gr. 7-12). 1979. PLB 10.97 o.p. (ISBN 0-8239-0458-X). Rosen Group.

Your Future in the Nursery Industry. Rev. ed. John J. Pinney. LC 67-10084. (Careers in Depth Ser). (Illus.). 144p. (gr. 7 up). 1982. PLB 9.97 o.p. (ISBN 0-8239-0331-1). Rosen Group.

Your Future in the Performing Arts. Glenn Loney & Laurence Epstein. (Careers in Depth Ser.). (Illus.). 1980. lib. bdg. 9.97 o.p. (ISBN 0-8239-0511-X). Rosen Group.

Your Future in the Science of Oceanography. Jonathan S. Wood. (Careers in Depth Ser.). (Illus.). (gr. 7-12). 1979. lib. bdg. 9.97 o.p. (ISBN 0-8239-0438-5). Rosen Group.

Your Future in Veterinary Medicine. rev. ed. Wayne H. Riser. LC 77-105442. (Careers in Depth Ser.). (gr. 7 up). 1982. PLB 9.97 o.p. (ISBN 0-8239-0400-8). Rosen Group.

Your Future in Word Processing. rev. ed. Phyllis Peck & Gilbert Konkel. (Careers in Depth Ser.). (Illus.). 140p. (gr. 7-12). 1985. lib. bdg. 9.97 o.p. (ISBN 0-8239-0532-2). Rosen Group.

Your God-Given Potential. Winifred W. Hausmann. LC 77-80458. 1978. 5.95 o.p. (ISBN 0-87159-182-0). Unity School.

Your Guide to Care of the Heart. Albert Goldin. LC 83-61170. 128p. 1985. 10.95 o.p. (ISBN 0-89313-035-4). G F Stickley Co.

Your Guide to Home Storage. Alan Briscoe. 21p. 1974. pap. 1.95 o.p. (ISBN 0-88290-041-2). Horizon Utah.

Your Guide to IRAs & Fourteen Other Retirement Plans. Harry J. Lister. 224p. 1985. pap. 15.95 o.p. (ISBN 0-673-15995-7). Scott F.

Your Guide to the Seventh Edition of James M. McCrimmon's: Writing with a Purpose. Sharon McConnell & Jolyne Daughtry. (Orig.). 1980. pap. text ed. 20.95 o.p. (ISBN 0-8403-2706-4, 40270601). Kendall-Hunt.

Your Hand in Mine. Sam Cornish. LC 74-103833. (Curriculum Related Bks.). (Illus.). (gr. 2-4). 1970. 5.50 o.p. (ISBN 0-15-299916-7, HJ). HarBraceJ.

Your Handbook for Healing. Craig Carter. 64p. 1981. pap. 6.95 o.p. (ISBN 0-911336-86-9). Sci of Mind.

Your Health & You: How Awareness, Attitudes, & Faith Contribute to a Healthy Life. Edgar N. Jackson. LC 86-22226. (Augsburg Religion & Medicine). 112p. (Orig.). 1986. pap. 6.95 o.p. (ISBN 0-8066-2221-0, 10-7426, Augsburg). Augsburg Fortress.

Your Health & Your Hair. 13th, rev. ed. Paul C. Bragg & Patricia Bragg. LC 84-82235. pap. 4.95 o.p. (ISBN 0-87790-034-5). Health Sci.

Your Health Is What You Make It: A Guide for Diet, Vitamin Supplementation, Cholesterol Control, Exercise, Mental Health, and Longevity. C. W. Whitmoyer, Sr. 1972. 10.00 o.p. (ISBN 0-682-47522-X, Banner). Exposition-Phoenix.

Your Healthy Heart: The Family Guide to Staying Healthy & Living Longer. Christiaan Barnard & Peter Evens. (Illus.). 224p. 1986. text ed. 18.95 o.p. (ISBN 0-07-003729-9). McGraw.

Your Home Is Money: Managing Your Home for Profit. Consumer Guide Editors. 1978. pap. text ed. 6.95 o.p. (ISBN 0-07-018997-8). McGraw.

Your Hope of Glory. Elizabeth S. Turner. 1959. 6.95 o.p. (ISBN 0-87159-183-9). Unity School.

Your Incredible Cat: Understanding the Secret Powers of Your Pet. David Greene. LC 85-27375. (Illus.). 216p. 1986. 12.95 o.s.i. (ISBN 0-385-23436-8). Doubleday.

Your Inner Child of the Past. W. Hugh Missildine. 1971. 13.95 o.p. (ISBN 0-671-21147-1). S&S.

Your Job in the Computer Age: The Complete Guide to the Computer Skills You Will Need to Get the Job You Want. Joyce S. Mitchell. LC 45-437. 192p. 1984. 14.95 o.s.i. (ISBN 0-684-18100-2, ScribT); pap. 8.95 o.s.i. (ISBN 0-684-18099-5). Scribner.

Your Kingdom Come: Bible Studies for the Church Year Based on the Wcc Mission & Evangelism Theme, Melbourne 1980. (Orig.). 1980. pap. 2.25 o.p. (ISBN 0-377-00093-0). Friendship Pr.

Your Manners Are Showing: A Handbook about Etiquette. Eugene H. Baker. LC 80-17617. (Living the Good Life Ser.). (Illus.). 112p. (gr. 1-6). 1980. pap. 5.95 o.p. (ISBN 0-89565-178-5). Childs World.

Your Marriage Has Real Possibilities. Cyril J. Barber & Aldyth A. Barber. LC 83-25537. 168p. (Orig.). 1984. pap. text ed. 6.95 o.p. (ISBN 0-8254-2249-3). Kregel.

Your Medicine Chest: A Consumer's Guide to the Effects of Prescription & Non Prescription Drugs. Wayne O. Evans & Johnathan O. Cole. LC 78-7497. 1978. pap. 5.95 o.p. (ISBN 0-316-25823-7). Little.

Your Money & Your Life. C. Hardy. 1983. pap. 9.95 o.p. (ISBN 0-317-31404-1). AMACOM.

Your Money & Your Life: How to Plan Your Long-Range Financial Security. C. Colburn Hardy. (Illus.). 1979. 15.95 o.p. (ISBN 0-8144-5529-8). AMACOM.

Your Money & Your Life: Planning Your Financial Future. 2nd ed. C. Colburn Hardy. 352p. 1982. 19.95 o.p. (ISBN 0-8144-5574-3). AMACOM.

Your Moves to Make see Fashion Your Figure: The Ten-Minutes-A-Day Program for Fitness.

Your Mule Is Crowing. Callie B. Young. 112p. 1988. 8.95 o.p. (ISBN 0-8062-3034-7). Carlton.

Your Name Company: Accounting Practice Set for the Computer. Thomas W. Charles & Frederic M. Stiner, Jr. 130p. 1985. pap. 17.50 o.p. (ISBN 0-534-04506-5). PWS-Kent Pub.

Your Natural Gifts: How to Recognize & Develop Them for Success & Self-Fulfillment. Margaret E. Broadley. LC 77-23379. (Illus.). 1977. pap. 6.95 o.p. (ISBN 0-914440-19-5). EPM Pubns.

Your New Home & How to Take Care of It, 10 vols. rev. ed. (Illus.). 64p. 1988. pap. 20.00 o.p. (ISBN 0-86718-318-7). Nat Assn H Build.

Your New Life in the United States, in Chinese. Language & Orientation Resource Center Staff. 215p. (Orig., Chinese.). 1981. pap. 9.95x o.p. (ISBN 0-15-599117-5). Ctr Appl Ling.

Your New Life in the United States, in Hmong. Language & Orientation Resource Center Staff. 215p. 1981. pap. 9.95x o.p. (ISBN 0-15-599118-3). Ctr Appl Ling.

Your New Life in the United States, in Khmer. Language & Orientation Resource Center Staff. 215p. (Khmer.). 1981. pap. 9.95x o.p. (ISBN 0-15-599120-5). Ctr Appl Ling.

Your New Life in the United States, in Lao. Language & Orientation Resource Center Staff & Center for Applied Linguistics Staff. 215p. (Orig., Laotian.). 1981. pap. 9.95x o.p. (ISBN 0-15-599127-2). Ctr Appl Ling.

Your New Life in the United States, in Vietnamese. Language & Orientation Resource Center Staff. 215p. (Orig., Vietnamese.). 1981. pap. 9.95 o.p. (ISBN 0-15-599129-9). Ctr Appl Ling.

Your Nineteen Eighty-Seven to Eighty-Eight Guide to Social Security Benefits. Leona R. Rubin. 208p. 1986. 16.95x o.p. (ISBN 0-8160-1567-8); pap. 9.95x o.p. (ISBN 0-8160-1568-6). Facts on File.

Your Own Financial Aid Factory: The Guide to Locating College Money. 3rd ed. Robert Leider. LC 80-11185. (Illus.). 190p. (Orig.). 1982. pap. 6.95 o.s.i. (ISBN 0-917760-29-8). Octameron Assocs.

Your Own Financial Aid Factory: The Guide to Locating College Money. Robert Leider. LC 80-11185. 212p. 1983. pap. 6.95 o.p. (ISBN 0-87866-259-6). Petersons Guides.

Your Own Pigs You May Not Eat. Paula G. Rubel & Abraham Rosman. LC 78-7544. (Illus.). 1978. lib. bdg. 30.00x o.s.i. (ISBN 0-226-73082-4). U of Chicago Pr.

Your Pastor's Problems: A Guide for Ministers & Laymen. William E. Hulme. LC 66-12249. 1967. pap. 4.95 o.p. (ISBN 0-8066-0717-3, 10-7480, Augsburg). Augsburg Fortress.

Your Paths in Ink: Graphoanalysis & the Personality. Johanna L. Wyland. (Illus.). 86p. 1980. 6.95 o.p. (ISBN 0-682-49604-9). Exposition-Phoenix.

Your Pension Rights at Divorce: What Women Need to Know. Women's Legal Defense Fund Staff. 21p. 1983. 3.00 o.p. (ISBN 0-317-67863-9). Women's Legal Defense.

Your People Are Your Business: A Manager's Manual for Making Millions in Merchandising. Melvin S. Landow. LC 73-78868. 1973. 10.00 o.p. (ISBN 0-682-47729-X, Banner). Exposition-Phoenix.

Your Perfect Right: A Guide to Assertive Living. 4th ed. Robert E. Alberti & Michael L. Emmons. LC 81-20265. 224p. 1982. 8.95 o.p. (ISBN 0-915166-06-2); pap. 6.95 o.p. (ISBN 0-915166-05-4). Impact Pubs Cal.

Your Personal Colors & Numbers. Louise L. Hay. LC 86-82079. 56p. 1986. pap. 3.95 o.p. (ISBN 0-937611-16-6). Hay House.

Your Personality & How to Live with It. Gregory G. Young. LC 78-55423. 1978. 9.95 o.p. (ISBN 0-689-10918-0, Atheneum). Macmillan.

Your Potential Under God: Resources for Growth. William E. Hulme. LC 77-84092. 1978. 9.50 o.p. (ISBN 0-8066-1617-2, 10-7485, Augsburg); pap. 5.50 o.p. (ISBN 0-8066-1618-0, 10-7484). Augsburg Fortress.

Your Power of Encouragement. 2nd ed. Jeanne Doering. (Moody Press Electives Ser.). (Orig.). 1985. pap. text ed. 3.95 o.p. (ISBN 0-8024-0687-4); leader's guide 2.50 o.p. (ISBN 0-8024-0688-2). Moody.

Your Prayers & Mine. Elizabeth Yates. (Illus.). (gr. 7-9). 1954. 3.95 o.p. (ISBN 0-395-07212-3). HM.

Your Real Medicare Handbook. Jeffrey Spitzer-Resnick. (Illus.). 91p. (Orig.). 1987. pap. 8.00 o.p. (ISBN 0-932622-10-0). Ctr Public Rep.

Your Research Dollar. Arlene H. Eakle. 24p. 1973. pap. 4.00 o.p. (ISBN 0-940764-06-7). Genealog Inst.

Your Resume: Key to a Better Job. Leonard Corwen. (Orig.). 1977. pap. 4.00 o.p. (ISBN 0-668-03733-4). Arco.

Your Retirement. P-H.

Your Rights to Privacy. Trudy Hayden & Jack Novik. (ACLU Handbook Ser.). 1980. pap. 2.50 o.p. (ISBN 0-380-75895-4, 75895-4). Avon.

Your Roles As a Medical Assistant. Clyde Hardy & Nancy Martin. 1974. casebound 19.95 o.p. (ISBN 0-87489-044-6). Med Economics.

Your Secret Servant: Fix & Freeze Hors D'oeuvre for Easy Entertaining. Ann Reed & Marilyn Pfaltz. 1970. pap. 2.95 o.p. (ISBN 0-684-13222-2, SL411, ScribT). Scribner.

Your Seven Year Old. Date not set. (ISBN 0-385-29382-8). Delacorte.

Your Sexual Bill of Rights: An Analysis of the Harmful Effects of Sexual Prohibitions. Leonard V. Ramer. LC 72-94861. 1973. 5.00 o.p. (ISBN 0-682-47607-2); pap. 2.50 o.p. (ISBN 0-682-48766-X). Exposition-Phoenix.

Your Spiritual Gifts Can Help Your Church Grow. Jim Larson & Joanne Feldmeth. 64p. 1985. pap. 3.95 o.s.i. (ISBN 0-8307-1008-6, 6101951). Regal.

Your Team of Tigers: Getting Good People & Keeping Them. Craig S. Rice. 288p. 1982. 15.95 o.p. (ISBN 0-8144-5605-7). AMACOM.

Your Telephone: Operation, Selection & Installation. Martin Clifford. LC 83-50377. 336p. 1983. pap. 13.95 o.p. (ISBN 0-672-22065-2, 22065). Sams.

Your Turn. N. Durova. 221p. 1980. 7.45 o.p. (ISBN 0-8285-1857-2, Pub. by Progress Pubs USSR). Imported Pubns.

Your Turn, Mr. Moto. John P. Marquand. 288p. 1985. pap. 3.95 o.p. (ISBN 0-316-54697-6). Little.

Your Vital Papers Logbook. AARP's Worker Equity Dept. 32p. 1985. pap. 4.95 o.p. (ISBN 0-673-24833-X). Am Assn Retire.

Your Voice: Methods for Strengthening & Developing the Voice. Eugene Feuchtinger. Orig. Title: Voice Development Hints. 6.95 o.p. (ISBN 0-911012-28-1). Nelson-Hall.

Your Wealth in God's World. John J. Davis. LC 83-19286. 144p. 1984. pap. 4.95 o.p. (ISBN 0-87552-219-X). Presby & Reformed.

Your Wealth in God's World: Does the Bible Support the Free Market? John J. Davis. 134p. Date not set. pap. 4.95 o.p. (ISBN 0-8010-2965-1). Baker Bk.

Your Window Greenhouse. Leigh Seddon. (Illus.). 32p. 1986. pap. 4.95 o.p. (ISBN 0-88266-343-7, Garden Way Pub). Storey Comm Inc.

You're a Right Hero, Andy Capp. Reginald Smythe. (Andy Capp Ser.). (Illus.). 1978. pap. 1.25 o.s.i. (ISBN 0-449-13561-6, P3561, GM). Fawcett.

You're All Heart, Andy Capp. Reginald Smythe. 128p. (Orig.). 1984. pap. 2.25 o.s.i. (ISBN 0-449-12654-4, GM). Fawcett.

You're Dumber in the Summer: And Over 100 Other Things No One Ever Told You. Jim Aylward. (Illus.). 64p. (gr. 3-7). 1983. pap. 2.25 o.p. (ISBN 0-380-57935-9, 57935-9, Camelot). Avon.

You're Next. Joseph Drust. 1979. 5.00 o.p. (ISBN 0-682-49377-5). Exposition-Phoenix.

You're Only Old Once: Devotions in Large Print. large type ed. Catharine Brandt. LC 76-27085. 1977. pap. 6.95 o.p. (ISBN 0-8066-1570-2, 10-7495, Augsburg). Augsburg Fortress.

You're Our Child: A Social-Psychological Approach to Adoption. Jerome Smith & Franklin I. Miroff. LC 80-5957. 110p. (Orig.). 1981. lib. bdg. 24.25 o.p. (ISBN 0-8191-1416-2); pap. text ed. 9.00 o.p. (ISBN 0-8191-1417-0). U Pr of Amer.

You're Smarter Than You Think: At Least 500 Fun Ways to Expand Your Intelligence. Linda P. Moore. (Illus.). 254p. 1985. pap. 9.95 o.s.i. (ISBN 0-03-063858-5, Owl Bks). H Holt & Co.

You're the Boss, Andy Capp. Reginald Smythe. (Andy Capp Cartoons Ser.). 128p. 1982. pap. 1.75 o.s.i. (ISBN 0-449-13631-0, GM). Fawcett.

Your're Really a Model Now! Marcie Anderson. 96p. (gr. 5-8). 1985. 2.25 o.s.i. (ISBN 0-87406-042-7). Willowisp Pr.

Yours by Choice: A Guide for Adoptive Parents. rev ed. Jane Rowe. 1982. pap. 7.95 o.p. (ISBN 0-7100-9035-8). Routledge Chapman & Hall.

Yours Truly, King Arthur: How Medieval People Wrote... & How You Can, Too. Marc Drogin. LC 79-66643. 1982. 10.95 o.s.i. (ISBN 0-8008-8765-4, Pentalic). Taplinger.

Yours with Love, Kate. Miriam E. Mason. (Illus.). (gr. 7 up). 1952. 6.95 o.p. (ISBN 0-395-06901-7). HM.

Yourself Ten Years from Now: A Career Planning Guide. David Klein & Marymae E. Klein. LC 77-76438. (Illus.). 152p. (gr. 7 up). 1977. 7.95 o.p. (ISBN 0-15-299940-X, HJ). HarBraceJ.

Youth. Ed. by Robert J. Havighurst & Philip H. Dreyer. LC 6-16938. (National Society for the Study of Education Yearbook Ser: No. 74, Pt. 1). xiv, 464p. 1975. lib. bdg. 11.00x o.s.i. (ISBN 0-226-60116-1). U of Chicago Pr.

Youth & Alcoholic Beverages. John S. Lyles. (Illus., Orig.). (gr. 8-11). 1967. pap. 1.25 o.p. (ISBN 0-8042-9376-7, John Knox). Westminster John Knox.

Youth & Dissent. Kenneth Keniston. LC 71-160404. 403p. 1971. 9.95 o.p. (ISBN 0-15-199890-6). HarBraceJ.

Youth & Dissent: The Rise of a New Opposition. Kenneth Keniston. LC 71-160404. 1972. pap. 2.95 o.p. (ISBN 0-15-699954-4, Harv). HarBraceJ.

Youth & Justice: Young Offenders in Ireland. Geoffrey Cooke et al. (Turoe Press Ser.). 230p. pap. 15.00 o.p. (ISBN 0-905223-24-1, Dist. by Scribner). M Boyars Pubs.

Youth & Leisure. Kenneth Roberts. (Leisure & Recreation Ser.: No. 3). 240p. 1983. text ed. 34.95x o.p. (ISBN 0-04-301165-9). Unwin Hyman.

Youth & Values: Getting Self Together. Carl A. Elder. LC 76-58063. 1978. 7.50 o.p. (ISBN 0-8054-5326-1, 4253-26). Broadman.

Youth Employment & Public Policy. Ed. by Bernard E. Anderson & Isabel V. Sawhill. LC 79-27022. 1980. 11.95 o.p. (ISBN 0-13-982413-8); pap. 5.95 o.p. (ISBN 0-13-982405-7). Am Assembly.

Youth Employment Series, 4 bks. YMCA of the U. S. A. Staff & Anthony L. Monaco, Jr. 1980. pap. text ed. 8.00x o.s.i. (ISBN 0-88035-038-5). Human Kinetics.

Youth: Expectations & Transitions. Millicent E. Poole. 300p. 1983. pap. 20.00x o.p. (ISBN 0-7100-9283-0). Routledge Chapman & Hall.

Youth Gangs. Edward F. Dolan, Jr. & Shan Finney. 144p. (gr. 7 up). 1984. lib. bdg. 9.79 o.p. (ISBN 0-671-46524-4). Messner.

Youth Group How-To Book. Ed. by Lee Sparks. LC 81-81966. (Illus.). 224p. (Orig.). 1981. pap. 14.95 o.p. (ISBN 0-936664-03-7). Group Pub.

Youth Group Travel Directory. Ed. by Lee Sparks. LC 81-64228. 174p. (Orig.). 1983. pap. 7.95 o.p. (ISBN 0-936664-09-6). Group Pub.

Youth Group Travel Directory: 1981-82 Edition. Ed. by Thom Schultz. 112p. (Orig.). 1981. pap. 7.95 o.p. (ISBN 0-936664-02-9). Group Pub.

Youth in American Life. L. Bressler & M. Bressler. (Life in America Ser). 1972. pap. 5.52 o.p. (ISBN 0-395-03137-0, 2-33200). HM.

Youth Participation in Documenting CETA Youth Employment Programs. Bruce Dollar & Peter Kleinbard. 62p. 1981. pap. 5.00 o.p. (ISBN 0-912041-10-2). Natl Comm Res Youth.

Youth Restored. Mikhail Zoshchenko. Tr. by Joel Stern. 210p. 1984. 20.00 o.p. (ISBN 0-88233-629-0). Ardis Pubs.

Youth: The Law, Rights, Privileges & Obligations. Irving J. Sloan. (Legal Almanac Ser.: No. 46). 120p. 1970. (ISBN 0-379-11073-3). Oceana.

Youth Training & the Search for Work: A Study of Young People in Crisis. Ed. by Denis Gleeson. (Routledge Education Bks.). 200p. (Orig.). 1983. pap. 19.95x o.p. (ISBN 0-7100-9513-9). Routledge Chapman & Hall.

Youth Unemployment. Michael D. Jackson. LC 84-29332. 180p. 1985. 29.00 o.p. (ISBN 0-7099-1453-9, Pub. by Croom Helm Ltd). Routledge Chapman & Hall.

Youth Unemployment & State Intervention. Teresa L. Rees & Paul Atkinson. 160p. 1983. pap. 12.50x o.p. (ISBN 0-7100-9263-6). Routledge Chapman & Hall.

Youth Unrest. Ed. by S. Giora Shoham. 1976. 12.95 o.p. (ISBN 0-87855-274-X). Transaction Pubs.

Youth, Vol 3 (Incl. 1986-1987 Supplements) Ed. by Eleanor C. Goldstein. 1987. 15.00 o.p. (ISBN 0-89777-086-2). Soc Issues.

Youth WAV Curriculum, Vol. 1. Spencer Nordyke & Cyndy Nordyke. 105p. (Orig.). 1984. wkbk. 40.00 o.s.i. (ISBN 0-914307-20-7). R Tilton Ministries.

Youth, World, & Church. Sara Little. LC 68-11684. (Orig.). 1968. pap. 3.45 o.p. (ISBN 0-8042-1478-6, John Knox). Westminster John Knox.

Youth's a Stuff Will Not Endure. Paul Grabill. 1978. pap. 1.75 o.p. (ISBN 0-380-01938-8, 37879). Avon.

You've Got It Made: Make-Ahead Meals for the Family & for Cooperative Dinner Parties. Marian Burros. LC 84-60444. 352p. 1984. 13.95 o.p. (ISBN 0-688-03187-0). Morrow.

Y's Way to Physical Fitness. Rev. ed. Ed. by Lawrence Golding et al. (Illus.). 172p. 1982. text ed. 26.95x o.p. (ISBN 0-88035-002-4, YMCA USA). Human Kinetics.

Ysopet-Avionnet: The Latin & French Texts. Aesopus. Ed. by Kenneth McKenzie & William A. Oldfather. 22.00 o.p. (ISBN 0-384-36680-5). Johnson Repr.

Yuganta: The End of an Epoch. Iravati Karve. 1974. lib. bdg. 4.50x o.p. (ISBN 0-8364-0482-3). South Asia Bks.

Yugoslav Economic System: The First Labor-Managed Economy in the Making. Branko Horvat. LC 75-46111. 296p. 1976. o.p 22.50 o.p. (ISBN 0-87332-074-3); pap. 17.95 o.p. (ISBN 0-87332-175-8). M E Sharpe.

Yugoslavia: Republics & Provinces. Ed. by K. Rakic. (Illus.). 1979. 10.00 o.p. E J Brill USA.

Yugoslavic Dictionary, 2 Vols. M Benson. 1980p. (Serbian, Croatian & Eng.). 65.00x ea. o.p. (Y786); Vol. 1, Serbocroation-English. 65.50x o.p. (ISBN 0-89918-786-2, Y787). Vol. 2, English-Serbocroation (ISBN 0-89918-787-0). Vanous.

Yugoslavic Pocket Dictionary: Croatian-English. R. Flipovic et al. 468p. 1979. 20.00x o.p. Vanous.

Yugoslavs. Z. Kostelski. 1952. (ISBN 0-8022-0886-X). Philos Lib.

Yukiho. MacDonald Harris. 1979. pap. 2.25 o.p. (ISBN 0-380-42895-4, 42895). Avon.

Yukon -- Exploration & Geology, 1982. 257p. 1984. pap. text ed. 10.00x o.p. (ISBN 0-660-11450-X, Pub. by Canadian Govt Pub Ctr). Gower Pub Co.

Yukpa Cultivation System: A Study of Shifting Cultivation in Columbia & Venezuela. Kenneth Ruddle. (UC Publications in Ibero-Americana: Vol. 52). 1975. pap. 24.00x o.p. (ISBN 0-520-09497-2). U of Cal Pr.

Yup the Organization. James Wavada. 224p. 1986. 15.95 o.p. (ISBN 0-531-15503-X). Watts.

Yuri Bondarev, Yuri Bondarev on Craftmanship. Yu Idashkin & Yu Bondarev. 285p. 1985. 7.95 o.p. (ISBN 0-8285-2821-7, Pub. by Raduga Pubs USSR). Imported Pubns.

Yuri Gagarin: First Man in Space. Mitchell R. Sharpe. LC 74-75841. (Heroes of Space Ser.). (Illus.). (gr. 7 up). 1969. 4.95 o.p. (ISBN 0-87397-203-1). Strode.

Yury Olesha: The Complete Short Stories & the Three Fat Men. Yury Olesha. Tr. by Aimee Fisher from Rus. 1979. 17.50 o.p. (ISBN 0-88233-213-9); pap. 7.00 o.p. (ISBN 0-88233-214-7). Ardis Pubs.

Yves Brayer. Jean Giono. (Coll. Art Moderne). deluxe ed. 55.25 o.p. (ISBN 0-685-34175-5). French & Eur.

Yves Klein. Pierre Restany. (Illus.). 1982. 75.00 o.p. (ISBN 0-8109-1205-8). Abrams.

Yves Saint Laurent Exhibition Checklist. Ed. by Barbara Burn. Jean R. Dreusedow. 24p. 1984. pap. 1.25 o.p. (ISBN 0-317-05156-3). Metro Mus Art.

Z

Z Is for Zombie. Theodore Roscoe. (Facsimile Fiction Ser.: Vol. 2). 1988. 17.95x o.p. (ISBN 1-55742-043-2); pap. 8.95x o.p. (ISBN 1-55742-042-4). Starmont Hse.

Z-Papers. Geoffrey S. Simmons. LC 74-31429. 1976. 7.95 o.p. (ISBN 0-87795-108-X, Arbor Hse). Morrow.

Z-80 Microprocessor Advanced Interfacing. Date not set. (ISBN 0-672-22003-2). Sams.

Z-8000 Assembly Language Programming. Lance A. Leventhal et al. 928p. (Orig.). 1980. pap. text ed. 19.95 o.p. (ISBN 0-07-931036-2). Osborne-McGraw.

Zabern Nineteen Hundred Thirteen: Consensus Politics in Imperial Germany. David Schoenbaum. 208p. 1982. text ed. 29.95x o.p. (ISBN 0-04-943025-4). Unwin Hyman.

Zachary Goes to the Zoo. Jill Krementz. LC 86-60109. (Tough Enough Bks.). (Illus.). 24p. (ps-1). 1986. 3.95 o.s.i. (ISBN 0-394-88236-9, BYR). Random.

Zagat 1987 Chicago Restaurant Survey. Eugene H. Zagat, Jr. & Nina S. Zagat. Ed. by Carolyn McGuire. (Orig.). 1987. pap. 8.95 o.p. (ISBN 0-9612574-7-4). Zagat.

Zagat 1987 Los Angeles Restaurant Survey. Eugene H. Zagat, Jr. & Nina S. Zagat. Ed. by Merrill Shindler & Karen Berk. 125p. (Orig.). 1986. pap. 8.95 o.p. (ISBN 0-9612574-6-6). Zagat.

Zagat 1987 New York City Restaurant Survey. Eugene H. Zagat, Jr. & Nina S. Zagat. 144p. (Orig.). 1986. pap. 8.95 o.p. (ISBN 0-9612574-4-X). Zagat.

Zagat 1987 San Francisco Restaurant Survey. Eugene H. Zagat, Jr. & Nina S. Zagat. Ed. by Anthony D. Blue & Edwin J. Schwartz. (Orig.). 1987. pap. 8.95 o.p. (ISBN 0-9612574-8-2). Zagat.

Zagat 1987 Washington D.C. Restaurant Survey. Eugene H. Zagat, Jr. & Nina S. Zagat. Ed. by Olga Boikess. 91p. (Orig.). 1986. pap. 8.95 o.p. (ISBN 0-9612574-5-8). Zagat.

Zaibatsu. John Brown. 320p. 1985. pap. 3.50 o.p. (ISBN 0-380-89516-1). Avon.

Zaibatsu Dissolution in Japan. T. A. Bisson. LC 76-5412. 314p. 1976. Repr. of 1954 ed. lib. bdg. 22.50x o.p. (ISBN 0-8371-8816-4, BIZD). Greenwood.

Zaire: Current Economic Situation & Constraints. Bension Varon. v, 191p. 1980. pap. 10.00 o.p. (ISBN 0-686-36127-X, BK9128). World Bank.

Zamani Goes to Market. Muriel L. Feelings. LC 70-97032. (Illus.). 48p. (ps-3). 1979. 6.95 o.p. (ISBN 0-395-28791-X, Clarion). HM.

Zambia: A Country Study. 3rd ed. Ed. by Irving Kaplan. LC 79-21324. (Area Handbook Ser.: DA Pam 550-75). (Illus.). 308p. 1979. 11.00 o.p. (ISBN 0-318-21901-8, S/N 008-020-00814-1). USGPO.

Zane Grey's Arizona. Candace Kant. (Illus.). 225p. pap. 11.95 o.p. (ISBN 0-87358-424-4). Northland.

Zane Grey's Arizona Ames: Gun Trouble in Tonto Basin. Romer Z. Grey. (Orig.). 1980. pap. 1.95 o.p. (ISBN 0-505-51479-6, Pub. by Tower Bks). Dorchester Pub Co.

Zane Grey's Arizona Ames: King of the Outlaw Horde. Romer Z. Grey. (Orig.). 1980. pap. 1.95 o.p. (ISBN 0-505-51509-1, Pub. by Tower Bks). Dorchester Pub Co.

Zane Grey's Buck Duane: King of the Range. Romer Z. Grey. (Orig.). 1980. pap. 1.95 o.p. (ISBN 0-505-51499-0, Pub. by Tower Bks). Dorchester Pub Co.

Zane Grey's Buck Duane: The Rider of Distant Trails. Romer Z. Grey. 1980. pap. 1.95 o.p. (ISBN 0-505-51469-9, Pub. by Tower Bks). Dorchester Pub Co.

Zane Grey's Greatest Western Stories. Zane Grey. Ed. by Loren Grey. 1978. pap. 1.50 o.p. (ISBN 0-505-51273-4, Pub. by Tower Bks). Dorchester Pub Co.

Zane Grey's Laramie Nelson: The Lawless Land. Romer Z. Grey. (Zane Grey Westerns). 288p. 1984. pap. 2.75 o.s.i. (ISBN 0-8439-2116-1, Pub. by Leisure Bks CT). Dorchester Pub Co.

Zane Grey's Laramie Nelson: The Other Side of the Canyon. Romer Z. Grey. 1980. pap. 1.95 o.p. (ISBN 0-505-51489-3, Pub. by Tower Bks). Dorchester Pub Co.

Zane Grey's Laramie Nelson: The Other Side of the Canyon. Romer Z. Grey. (Gunsmoke Western Ser.). 176p. 1988. text ed. 12.95x o.p. (ISBN 0-85997-854-0, Pub. by Firecrest Pub Ltd). Prescott Pr NH.

Zane Grey's Nevada Jim Lacy: Beyond the Mogollon Rim. Romer Z. Grey. (Orig.). 1980. pap. 1.95 o.p. (ISBN 0-505-51529-6, Pub. by Tower Bks). Dorchester Pub Co.

Zane Grey's Yaqui: Siege at Forlorn River. Romer Z. Grey. (Orig.). 1980. pap. 1.95 o.p. (ISBN 0-505-51519-9, Pub. by Tower Bks). Dorchester Pub Co.

Zane Nutrition: Sensible Way of Eating. Frank C. Zane & Christine Zane. 1986. 16.45 o.p. (ISBN 0-671-47326-3). S&S.

Zane Way to a Beautiful Body Through Weight Training for Men & Women. Frank Zane & Christine Zane. (Illus.). 1979. 15.95 o.p. (ISBN 0-671-24367-5). S&S.

Zanuck: The Rise & Fall of Hollywood's Last Tycoon. Leonard Mosley. (Illus.). 512p. 1984. 19.45i o.p. (ISBN 0-316-58538-6). Little.

Zap! The Rise & Fall of Atari. Scott Cohen. 192p. 1984. text ed. 14.95 o.p. (ISBN 0-07-011543-5). McGraw.

Zapping of America: Microwaves, Their Deadly Risk & the Cover-up. Paul Brodeur. (Illus.). 1977. 14.95 o.p. (ISBN 0-393-06427-1); pap. write for info. o.p. (ISBN 0-393-00931-9). Norton.

Zarco. Ignacio M. Altamirano. Ed. by Raymond L. Grismer & Miguel Ruelas. 1933. 3.95x o.p. (ISBN 0-393-09442-1, NortonC). Norton.

Zarine. Ulric Devore. 1954. (ISBN 0-8022-0386-8). Philos Lib.

Zay Jeffries. W. D. Magerman. 1973. 8.00 o.p. (ISBN 0-686-95225-1). ASM.

Zaza's Seventh Husband & Some Others. J. Leonard Douglas. 1978. 5.50 o.p. (ISBN 0-682-49011-3). Exposition-Phoenix.

Zazie dans le Metro. Raymond Queneau. (Coll. Soleil). 1959. 25.00 o.p. (ISBN 0-685-11633-6). Schoenhof.

ZBC of Ezra Pound. Christine Brooke-Rose. LC 75-138284. 1971. 21.00x o.p. (ISBN 0-520-01848-6); pap. 10.50x o.p. (ISBN 0-520-03041-9). U of Cal Pr.

Zeal for Zen. Norimoto Iino. LC 66-26968. 96p. 1967. (ISBN 0-8022-0772-3). Philos Lib.

Zeal of His House. Eldon Weisheit. LC 73-76988. 1973. 3.50 o.p. (ISBN 0-570-03516-3, 14-2020). Concordia.

Zealots & Rebels: A History of the Communist Party of Czechoslovakia. Zdenek L. Suda. (Publication Ser.: No. 234). 426p. (Orig.). 1980. pap. 8.95x o.p. (ISBN 0-8179-7342-7). Hoover Inst Pr.

Zealots of Masada: Story of a Dig. Moshe Pearlman. LC 67-23691. (Illus.). (gr. 7 up). 1967. pap. 2.45 o.s.i. (ISBN 0-684-71867-7, ScribT). Scribner.

Zed. Rosemary Harris. 192p. (YA) (gr. 7 up). 1984. 12.95 o.p. (ISBN 0-571-11947-6). Faber & Faber.

Zeffirelli: An Autobiography. Franco Zeffirelli. (Illus.). 376p. 1986. 19.95 o.s.i. (ISBN 1-55584-022-1). Weidenfeld.

Zeiss Ikon Cameras, 1926-1939. D. B. Tubbs. (Illus.). 144p. 1980. 22.95 o.p. (ISBN 0-906447-21-6, Pub. by Hove Foto Bks). Seven Hills Bk Dists.

Zelda. Nancy Milford. 1976. pap. 1.95 o.p. (ISBN 0-380-00784-3, 40014). Avon.

Zelda the Zebra. (Zoo Babies Ser.). 16p. (gr. k-6). 1982. pap. 1.25 o.p. (ISBN 0-8249-8035-2). Ideals.

Zen & Christian: The Journey Between. John Eusden. 224p. 1981. 10.95 o.p. (ISBN 0-8245-0099-7). Crossroad NY.

Zen & Now: The Baby Boomers Guide to Middle Life. Mark Breslin et al. 1985. 5.95 o.p. (ISBN 0-87795-715-0, Arbor Hse). Morrow.

Zen & the Art of Calligraphy. Omori Sogen & Terayama Katsujo. Tr. by John Stevens from Japanese. (Illus.). 128p. (Orig.). 1983. pap. 13.95 o.p. (ISBN 0-7100-9284-9). Routledge Chapman & Hall.

Zen & the Bible: A Priest's Experience. J. K. Kadowaki. (Orig.). 1980. pap. 8.95 o.p. (ISBN 0-7100-0402-8). Routledge Chapman & Hall.

Zen & the Mind: A Scientific Approach to Zen Practice. Tomio Hirai. (Illus., Orig.). 1978. 10.50 o.p. (ISBN 0-87040-391-5). Japan Pubns USA.

Zen & the Taming of the Bull: Towards the Definition of Buddhist Thought. Walpola Rahula. 1978. text ed. 17.50x o.p. (ISBN 0-900406-69-0). Humanities.

Zen Buddhism: Selected Writings of D. T. Suzuki. Daisetz T. Suzuki. 1956. pap. 5.50 o.p. (ISBN 0-385-09300-4, A90, Anch). Doubleday.

Zen Catholicism: A Suggestion. Dom A. Graham. LC 63-10596. 1967. pap. 2.95 o.p. (ISBN 0-15-699960-9, HB118, Harv). HarBraceJ.

Zen Dawn. Tr. by Jonathan C. Cleary from Chinese. LC 85-27904. 135p. (Orig.). 1986. pap. 8.95 o.p. (ISBN 0-87773-359-7, 74388-1). Shambhala Pubns.

Zen Effects: The Life of Alan Watts. Monica Furlong. 1986. 17.45 o.s.i. (ISBN 0-395-35344-0). HM.

Zen Expressionists: Paintings of the Japanese Counterculture 1600-1800. Peter Drucker. 28p. 1982. 2.00 o.p. (ISBN 0-915478-41-2). Galleries Coll.

Zen in the Art of J. D. Salinger. Gerald Rosen. LC 77-72494. (Modern Authors Monograph Ser.: No. 3). 40p. 1977. pap. 3.50 o.p. (ISBN 0-916870-06-5). Creative Arts Bk.

Zen in the Art of Painting. Helmut Brinker. 192p. 1988. pap. 14.95 o.p. (ISBN 1-85063-058-5, Arkana). Routledge Chapman & Hall.

Zen Meditation & Psychotherapy. Tomio Hirai. LC 85-81591. (Illus.). 160p. (Orig.). 1986. pap. 11.95 o.p. (ISBN 0-87040-666-3). Japan Pubns USA.

Zen of Cubing: In Search of the Seventh Side. Jack Feder & Kathryn W. Merrick. LC 82-72610. (Illus.). 120p. (Orig.). 1982. pap. 4.95 o.p. (ISBN 0-89708-103-X). And Bks.

Zen Poems of Ryokan. Tr. by Nobuyuki Yuasa from Japanese. LC 80-8585. (Princeton Library of Asian Translations). (Illus.). 196p. 1981. 28.00x o.p. (ISBN 0-691-06466-0). Princeton U Pr.

Zen Teaching of Huang Po: On the Transmission of the Mind. Huang Po. Tr. by John Blofeld. 1959. pap. 9.95 o.p. (ISBN 0-394-17217-5, E171, Ever). Grove.

Zen Teaching of Rinzai (Rinzai Roku) Tr. by Irmgard Schloegl from Chinese. LC 75-40262. 104p. 1976. pap. 3.50 o.p. (ISBN 0-87773-087-3). Shambhala Pubns.

Zen Yoga Therapy. Masahiro Oki. LC 79-1060. (Illus.). 1979. pap. 12.50 o.p. (ISBN 0-87040-459-8). Japan Pubns USA.

Zen: Zest, Zip Zap & Zing. Bhagwan Shree Rajneesh. Ed. by Ma Prem Asha. LC 83-183222. (Question & Answer Ser.). (Illus.). 472p. (Orig.). 1981. 23.95 o.p. (ISBN 0-88050-192-8); pap. 19.95 468p 1981 o.p. (ISBN 0-88050-692-X). Chidvilas Inc.

Zeppelin. Ronald Florence. LC 81-66959. 416p. 1982. 14.95 o.p. (ISBN 0-87795-327-9, Arbor Hse). Morrow.

Zero! Martin Caidin. 1979. pap. 2.25 o.s.i. (ISBN 0-345-28305-8). Ballantine.

Zero. Ignacio De Loyola Brandao. Tr. by Ellen Watson. 272p. 1983. pap. 4.50 o.p. (ISBN 0-380-84533-4, 84533, Bard). Avon.

Zero-Base Budgeting Comes of Age. Logan Cheek. (Illus.). 1979. pap. 8.95 o.p. (ISBN 0-8144-7516-7). AMACOM.

Zero Based Budgeting for Libraries & Information Centers: A Continuing Education Manual. Benjamin F. Speller, Jr. (gr. 4-8). 1979. 8.00 o.p. (ISBN 0-931510-03-1). Hi Willow.

Zero Coupons: How to Make a Fortune & Secure Your Financial Future with Zero Coupon Bonds. Michael Rago & Joann Bach. 144p. 1986. 17.95 o.p. (ISBN 0-8092-4977-4). Contemp Bks.

Zero Is Something. Marnie Luce. LC 68-28034. (Math Concept Bks.). (Illus.). (gr. 3-6). 1969. PLB 3.95 o.p. (ISBN 0-8225-0571-1). Lerner Pubns.

Zero People. Ed. by Jeffrey Hensley. 310p. 1983. pap. 7.95 o.p. (ISBN 0-89283-126-X). Servant.

Zero-Sum Solution: Building a World Class American Economy. Lester Thurow. 1985. 18.45 o.s.i. (ISBN 0-671-55232-5). S&S.

Zerovalent Compounds of Metals. Li Malatesta & S. Cenini. 1975. 54.50 o.p. (ISBN 0-12-466350-8). Acad Pr.

Zeta-Functions of Simple Algebras. R. Godement & H. Jacquet. LC 72-76391. (Lecture Notes in Mathematics: Vol. 260). 197p. 1972. pap. 10.00 o.p. (ISBN 0-387-05797-8). Springer-Verlag.

Zhen Zhen's Dream. Mei Ying. (Illus.). 45p. (Orig.). (ps-4). 1982. pap. 2.95 o.p. (ISBN 0-686-81669-2). China Bks.

Zhou Enlai. Merrilyn Fitzpatrick. (Leaders of Asia Ser.). 1984. pap. 4.95 o.p. (ISBN 0-7022-1884-7). U of Queensland Pr.

Zhou Enlai: A Profile. Percy J. Fang & Lucy G. Fang. (Illus.). 238p. 1986. pap. 9.95 o.p. (ISBN 0-8351-1712-X). China Bks.

Zhurbins. V. Kochetov. 461p. 1980. 11.25 o.p. (ISBN 0-8285-1928-5, Pub. by Progress Pubs USSR). Imported Pubns.

Ziggurat. Robert Katz. 1977. 7.95 o.p. (ISBN 0-395-25352-7). HM.

Ziggy in the Rough. Tom Wilson. 104p. (Orig.). 1985. pap. 5.95 o.p. (ISBN 0-8362-2076-5). Andrews & McMeel.

Zinc Enzymes, Vol. 5. Thomas G. Spiro. LC 88-8295. (Metal Ions in Biology Ser.: No. 1-457). 376p. 1983. 104.00 o.p. (ISBN 0-471-89081-2, Pub. by Wiley). Krieger.

Zingo Complete. Date not set. (ISBN 0-07-376776-X). McGraw.

Zingo Marker PK 500. Date not set. (ISBN 0-07-373312-1). McGraw.

Zingo Math Box Body. Date not set. (ISBN 0-07-376793-X). McGraw.

Zingo Math 1 Bx Lbl. Date not set. (ISBN 0-07-376785-9). McGraw.

Zingo Math 1 Rec Sh. Date not set. (ISBN 0-07-376796-4). McGraw.

Zingo Math 1 Record. Date not set. (ISBN 0-07-376777-8). McGraw.

Zingo Math 2 Bx Lbl. Date not set. (ISBN 0-07-376786-7). McGraw.

Zingo Math 2 Mre Ad. Date not set. (ISBN 0-07-376769-7). McGraw.

Zingo Math 2 Rec Sh. Date not set. (ISBN 0-07-376797-2). McGraw.

Zingo Math 2 Record. Date not set. (ISBN 0-07-376778-6). McGraw.

Zingo Math 2 Tea Sh. Date not set. (ISBN 0-07-376805-7). McGraw.

Zingo Math 2-25 CDS. Date not set. (ISBN 0-07-376760-3). McGraw.

Zingo Math 2-25 CDS. Date not set. (ISBN 0-07-376761-1). McGraw.

Zingo Math 3 Box Lbl. Date not set. (ISBN 0-07-376787-5). McGraw.

Zingo Math 3 Rec Sh. Date not set. (ISBN 0-07-376798-0). McGraw.

Zingo Math 3 Record. Date not set. (ISBN 0-07-376779-4). McGraw.

Zingo Math 3 Sub. Date not set. (ISBN 0-07-376770-0). McGraw.

Zingo Math 3 Tea Sh. Date not set. (ISBN 0-07-376806-5). McGraw.

Zingo Math 3-25 CDS. Date not set. (ISBN 0-07-376762-X). McGraw.

Zingo Math 4 Box Lbl. Date not set. (ISBN 0-07-376788-3). McGraw.
Zingo Math 4 Mre Sb. Date not set. (ISBN 0-07-376771-9). McGraw.
Zingo Math 4 Rec Sh. Date not set. (ISBN 0-07-376799-9). McGraw.
Zingo Math 4 Record. Date not set. (ISBN 0-07-376780-8). McGraw.
Zingo Math 4 Tea Sh. Date not set. (ISBN 0-07-376807-3). McGraw.
Zingo Math 4-25 CDS. Date not set. (ISBN 0-07-376763-8). McGraw.
Zingo Math 5 Box Lbl. Date not set. (ISBN 0-07-376789-1). McGraw.
Zingo Math 5 Mult. Date not set. (ISBN 0-07-376772-7). McGraw.
Zingo Math 5 Rec Sh. Date not set. (ISBN 0-07-376800-6). McGraw.
Zingo Math 5 Record. Date not set. (ISBN 0-07-376781-6). McGraw.
Zingo Math 5 Tea Sh. Date not set. (ISBN 0-07-376808-1). McGraw.
Zingo Math 5-25 CDS. Date not set. (ISBN 0-07-376764-6). McGraw.
Zingo Math 6 Box Lbl. Date not set. (ISBN 0-07-376790-5). McGraw.
Zingo Math 6 Mre Ml. Date not set. (ISBN 0-07-376773-5). McGraw.
Zingo Math 6 Rec Sh. Date not set. (ISBN 0-07-376801-4). McGraw.
Zingo Math 6 Record. Date not set. (ISBN 0-07-376782-4). McGraw.
Zingo Math 6 Tea Sh. Date not set. (ISBN 0-07-376809-X). McGraw.
Zingo Math 6-25 CDS. Date not set. (ISBN 0-07-376765-4). McGraw.
Zingo Math 7 Box Lbl. Date not set. (ISBN 0-07-376791-3). McGraw.
Zingo Math 7 Div. Date not set. (ISBN 0-07-376774-3). McGraw.
Zingo Math 7 Rec Sh. Date not set. (ISBN 0-07-376802-2). McGraw.
Zingo Math 7 Record. Date not set. (ISBN 0-07-376783-2). McGraw.
Zingo Math 7 Tea Sh. Date not set. (ISBN 0-07-376810-3). McGraw.
Zingo Math 7-25 CDS. Date not set. (ISBN 0-07-376766-2). McGraw.
Zingo Math 8 Box Lbl. Date not set. (ISBN 0-07-376792-1). McGraw.
Zingo Math 8 Mre Div. Date not set. (ISBN 0-07-376775-1). McGraw.
Zingo Math 8 Rec Sh. Date not set. (ISBN 0-07-376803-0). McGraw.
Zingo Math 8 Record. Date not set. (ISBN 0-07-376784-0). McGraw.
Zingo Math 8 Tea Sh. Date not set. (ISBN 0-07-376811-1). McGraw.
Zingo Math 8-25 CDS. Date not set. (ISBN 0-07-376767-0). McGraw.
Zingo Reading Box. Date not set. (ISBN 0-07-373317-2). McGraw.
Zingo Reading Compl. Date not set. (ISBN 0-07-373304-0). McGraw.
Zingo Reading 1 Bg Cons. Date not set. (ISBN 0-07-373303-2). McGraw.
Zingo Reading 1 Cons CD. Date not set. McGraw.
Zingo Reading 1 Cons RC. Date not set. (ISBN 0-07-373308-3). McGraw.
Zingo Reading 1 Rec Sh. Date not set. (ISBN 0-07-373321-0). McGraw.
Zingo Reading 1 Tea Sh. Date not set. (ISBN 0-07-373325-3). McGraw.
Zingo Reading 2 Cons CD. Date not set. (ISBN 0-07-373300-8). McGraw.
Zingo Reading 2 Cons RG. Date not set. (ISBN 0-07-373309-1). McGraw.
Zingo Reading 2 Rec Sh. Date not set. (ISBN 0-07-373322-9). McGraw.
Zingo Reading 2 Tea Sh. Date not set. (ISBN 0-07-373326-1). McGraw.
Zingo Reading 3 Cont CD. Date not set. (ISBN 0-07-373301-6). McGraw.
Zingo Reading 3 Cont RC. Date not set. (ISBN 0-07-373310-5). McGraw.
Zingo Reading 3 Contrac. Date not set. (ISBN 0-07-373306-7). McGraw.
Zingo Reading 3 Rec Sh. Date not set. (ISBN 0-07-373323-7). McGraw.
Zingo Reading 3 Tea Sh. Date not set. (ISBN 0-07-373327-X). McGraw.
Zingo Reading 4 Rec Sh. Date not set. (ISBN 0-07-373324-5). McGraw.
Zingo Reading 4 Tea Sh. Date not set. (ISBN 0-07-373328-8). McGraw.
Zingo Reading 4 Word Bld. Date not set. (ISBN 0-07-373307-5). McGraw.
Zingo Reading 4 Word CD. Date not set. (ISBN 0-07-373302-4). McGraw.
Zingo Reading 4 Word RC. Date not set. (ISBN 0-07-373311-3). McGraw.
Zingo Tdg 2 Cons BL. Date not set. (ISBN 0-07-373305-9). McGraw.
Zingo 1 Add Tea Sh. Date not set. (ISBN 0-07-376804-9). McGraw.
Zingo 1 Cons Bx LB. Date not set. (ISBN 0-07-373313-X). McGraw.
Zingo 2 Cons Bln Bx. Date not set. (ISBN 0-07-373314-8). McGraw.
Zingo 3 Cont Bx. Date not set. (ISBN 0-07-373315-6). McGraw.
Zingo 4 Word Box. Date not set. (ISBN 0-07-373316-4). McGraw.
Zinsser Microbiology. 18th ed. Ed. by Wolfgang Joklik. (Illus.). 1328p. 1984. 65.00 o.p. (ISBN 0-8385-9978-8). Appleton & Lange.
Zion, the City of the Great King: A Theological Symbol of the Jerusalem Cult. Ben C. Ollenburger. (JSOT Supplement Ser.: No. 41). 240p. pap. text ed. 13.50x o.s.i. (Pub. by JSOT Pr England). Eisenbrauns.
Zionism: Enemy of Peace & Social Progress. (Miscellany of Papers under the General Editorship of Lionel Dadiani). 160p. 1981. 7.50x o.p. (ISBN 0-317-53802-0, Pub. by Collets (UK)). State Mutual Bk.
Zionism: Enemy of Peace & Social Progress Issues, No. 2. Tr. by Francis Longman from Rus. 168p. 1983. 13.75x o.p. (ISBN 0-317-53828-4, Pub. by Collets (UK)). State Mutual Bk.
Zionism: Enemy of Peace & Social Progress Issue, No. 3. Tr. by Barry Jones from Rus. 220p. 1984. 13.75x o.p. (ISBN 0-317-53829-2, Pub. by Collets (UK)). State Mutual Bk.
Zionism, Imperialism, & Racism. Ed. by Abdul W. Kayyali. 304p. 1979. 32.00 o.p. (ISBN 0-85664-761-6, Pub. by Croom Helm Ltd). Routledge Chapman & Hall.
Zionism in the Age of the Dictators. Lenni Brenner. LC 82-23369. 300p. 1983. 16.95o.p. (ISBN 0-88208-163-2); pap. 9.95 o.p. (ISBN 0-88208-164-0). Chicago Review.
Zionist Anthology. Yoram Beck & David Zohar. LC 76-24526. (Orig.). 1979. pap. 5.95x o.p. (ISBN 0-87855-632-X). Transaction Pubs.
Zip Goes Zebra. Richard Hefter. LC 76-44019. (Sweet Pickles Ser.). (Illus.). (gr. k-2). 1977. 2.95 o.p. (ISBN 0-03-018081-3). HR&W.
Zippers. Ed. by Playgirl Editors. (Illus.). 80p. (Orig.). 1983. pap. 7.75 o.p. (ISBN 0-671-47692-0, Fireside). S&S.
Zirconium: Metallurgy of Zirconium. (Atomic Energy Review Ser.: Supplement). 1971. 32.00 o.p. (ISBN 92-0-159071-7, IAER/571, IAEA). UNIPUB.
Zit Wars: The Battle for Great Skin. Robert Stone & Webster Stone. 1986. pap. 5.95 o.p. (ISBN 0-87795-794-0). Morrow.
Zoar Blue. Janet Hickman. LC 78-3828. 156p. (gr. 6 up). 1978. 9.95 o.s.i. (ISBN 0-02-743740-X). Macmillan.
Zodiac Poems. Robin K. Willoughby. 1978. 1.00 o.p. (ISBN 0-934834-19-9). White Pine.
Zoe's Zodiac. Mary Jo Stephens. (gr. 3-7). 1974. 8.95 o.p. (ISBN 0-395-12760-2). HM.
Zoe's Zodiac. Mary Jo Stephens. (Illus.). 192p. (gr. 3-7). 1974. pap. 0.95 o.p. (ISBN 0-395-18561-0, Sandpiper). HM.
Zola. Philip Walker. 288p. 1985. 32.50x o.p. (ISBN 0-7102-0518-X). Routledge Chapman & Hall.
Zola Dictionary. J. G. Patterson. LC 68-27179. 272p. 1969. Repr. of 1912 ed. 34.00x o.p. (ISBN 0-8103-3173-X). Gale.
Zoltan Szabo Paints Landscapes: Advanced Techniques in Watercolor. Zoltan Szabo. (Illus.). 176p. 1977. 29.95 o.p. (ISBN 0-8230-5980-4). Watson-Guptill.
Zondervan Nineteen Eighty-Seven Pastor's Annual: A Planned Preaching Program for the Year. T. T. Crabtree. (Pastor's Annual Ser.). 384p. 1986. 12.95 o.p. (ISBN 0-310-22701-1, 11384P). Zondervan.
Zone of Fire. Conrad Detrez. Tr. by Lydia Davis. LC 86-4289. 320p. 1986. 17.95 o.p. (ISBN 0-15-199989-9). HarBraceJ.
Zone of Silence. Gerry Hunt. 232p. 1986. pap. 3.95 o.p. (ISBN 0-380-89806-3). Avon.
Zone System: Testing Procedures for All Formats. Thomas L. McCartney. (Illus.). 96p. (Orig.). 1987. pap. 14.95 o.p. (ISBN 0-87100-251-5, 2251). Morgan.
Zoning & Development Rights: A Bibliography. Mary E. Huls. LC 85-233574. (Public Administration Series-Bibliography). 6p. 1985. 2.00 o.p. (ISBN 0-89028-564-0, P1764). Vance Biblios.
Zoning & Housing Costs: The Impact of the Land-Use Controls on Housing Price. Lynne B. Sagalyn & George Sternlieb. 132p. 1973. pap. 8.00 o.p. Transaction Pubs.
Zoning & Property Rights. Robert H. Nelson. 1977. 18.50x o.p. (ISBN 0-262-14028-4); pap. 10.95x o.p. (ISBN 0-262-64019-8). MIT Pr.
Zoning & Zoning Law: A Revision of A-481. Mary Vance. (Architecture Ser.: a 1507). 45p. 1985. 6.75 o.p. (ISBN 0-89028-657-4). Vance Biblios.
Zoning at Sixty: Mediating Public & Private Rights. Ed. by Charles M. Haar & Jerold S. Kayden. LC 88-71466. (Illus.). 400p. (Orig.). Date not set. lib. bdg. (ISBN 0-918286-57-3); pap. Planners Pr.
Zoo: Animals, People, Places. Bernard Livingston. LC 74-80706. (Illus.). 1974. 8.95 o.p. (ISBN 0-87795-087-3, Arbor Hse). Morrow.
Zoo Conspiracy. Betty Levin. (Illus.). (gr. 3-7). 1979. pap. 1.50 o.p. (ISBN 0-380-43265-X, 43265, Camelot). Avon.
Zoo in Your Room. Roger Caras. LC 74-24322. (Illus.). 96p. (gr. 7 up). 1975. 5.95 o.p. (ISBN 0-15-299968-X, HJ). HarBraceJ.
Zoo Lady: Belle Benchley & the San Diego Zoo. Margaret Poynter. LC 79-13700. (Illus.). 80p. (gr. 6 up). 1980. PLB 7.95 o.p. (ISBN 0-87518-181-3). Dillon.
Zoo That Never Was. R. D. Lawrence. LC 80-18956. (Illus.). 304p. 1981. 13.95 o.p. (ISBN 0-03-056811-0). H Holt & Co.
Zoo Two Thousand: A Look Beyond the Bars. Jeremy Cherfas. (Illus.). 244p. 1987. 22.95 o.p. (ISBN 0-563-20281-5, Pub. by BBC). Parkwest Pubns.
Zoo Two Thousand: Twelve Stories of Science Fiction & Fantasy Beasts. Jane H. Yolen. LC 72-97773. (gr. 6 up). 1979. 7.95 o.p. (ISBN 0-395-28934-3, Clarion). HM.
Zoogeography & Diversity in Plankton. Ed. by S. Van der Spoel & A. C. Pierrot-Bults. LC 79-9494. 410p. 1979. 101.95x o.p. (ISBN 0-470-26798-4). Halsted Pr.
Zoology for Everybody. Eugen Kolisko. (Illus.). 1986. Vol. 7, Insects. pap. 6.50 o.p. (ISBN 0-906492-47-5, Pub. by Kolisko Archives); pap. 4.95 o.p. (ISBN 0-317-56619-9). St George Bk Serv.
Zoology for Everybody, Vol. 8: Amphibians & Reptiles. Eugen Kolisko. (Illus.). 1986. pap. 6.50 o.p. (ISBN 0-906492-48-3, Pub. by Kolisko Archives). St George Bk Serv.
Zoology in Postage Stamps. W. Dennis Way & O. D. Standen. 1952. (ISBN 0-8022-1822-9). Philos Lib.
Zoology Lab Manual. Judy A. Stamps et al. 280p. 1981. pap. text ed. 17.50 o.p. (ISBN 0-8403-2506-1). Kendall-Hunt.
Zoom. Mary Chiamos et al. (Illus., Orig.). (gr. k-3). 1973. pap. 7.95 o.p. (ISBN 0-918932-46-7). Activity Resources.
Zooming in: Photographic Discoveries Under the Microscope. Barbara J. Wolberg. LC 73-18631. 64p. (gr. 5-8). 1974. 7.75 o.p. (ISBN 0-15-299970-1, HJ). HarBraceJ.
Zoot-Suit Riots: The Psychology of Symbolic Annihilation. Mauricio Mazon. (Mexican American Monograph: No. 8). (Illus.). 179p. 1984. 14.95 o.p. (ISBN 0-292-79801-6). U of Tex Pr.
Zora & the Hibernauts. Fernando Fernandez. (Illus.). 112p. (Orig.). 1984. pap. 11.95 o.p. (ISBN 0-87416-001-4). Catalan Communs.
Zora Neale Hurston: A Reference Guide. Adele S. Newson. (Reference Guides to Literature). 110p. 1987. lib. bdg. 28.00x o.s.i. (ISBN 0-8161-8902-1, Hall Reference). G K Hall.
Zora Neale Hurston & Jessie Redmond Fauset: Glistening Reflections from a Bygone Day. Schavi M. Diara. 64p. 1984. 5.50 o.p. (ISBN 0-682-40136-6). Exposition-Phoenix.
Zucchini Cookbook. Paula Simmons. 1977. pap. 6.95 o.p. (ISBN 0-914718-10-X). Pacific Search.
Zucchini Plague: And Other Tales of Suburbia. William Geist. 288p. 1987. pap. 7.95 o.s.i. (ISBN 0-671-63434-8, Fireside). S&S.
Zucker und Zuckeraustauschstoffe: Proceedings of the Symposium, Muenchen, 1974. Symposium, Muenchen Staff. Ed. by N. Zoellner & P. Heuckenkamp. (Journal: Nutrition & Metabolism: Vol. 18, Suppl. 1). (Illus.). 200p. 1975. 31.50 o.p. (ISBN 3-8055-2173-1). S Karger.
Zunis of Cibola. C. Gregory Crampton. LC 77-72586. (Illus.). 1978. 19.95 o.p. (ISBN 0-87480-120-6). U of Utah Pr.
Zurueck ins Morgen. Karl Farkas. 1946. 3.00 o.p. (ISBN 0-685-57211-0). M S Rosenberg.
Zvezdopad. Leonid Rzhevsky. LC 84-635. 267p. (Rus.). 1984. pap. text ed. 12.00 o.s.i. (ISBN 0-938920-47-2). Hermitage.
Zweiwertige und Mehrwertige Logik: Ein Beitrag Zur Geschichte und Einheit der Logik. Peter Rutz. (Analytica). 108p. 1973. lib. bdg. 40.00x o.p. (ISBN 3-88405-039-7). Philosophia Pr.
Zwingli: A Reformed Theologian. Jaques Courvoisier. (Orig.). 1963. pap. 3.95 o.p. (ISBN 0-8042-1092-6, John Knox). Westminster John Knox.
Zwingli the Reformer. Oskar Farner. 1952. Philos Lib.
ZX81-TS1000 Home Computer Book. D. C. Foyt. 1983. pap. text ed. 4.00 o.p. (ISBN 0-07-881106-6). McGraw.
Zytologie und Mikrobiologie der Vagina. 3rd ed. J. D. Schnell. (Illus.). 92p. 1980. 32.75 o.p. (ISBN 3-8055-1428-X). S Karger.
ZZ Top. Philip Kamin. (Robus Bks.). (Illus.). 32p. (Orig.). (gr. 3 up). 1986. pap. 4.95 o.p. (ISBN 0-88188-419-7, HL00183950). H Leonard Pub Corp.
Z80 Microcomputer Handbook. William Barden, Jr. LC 77-93166. 304p. 1978. pap. 13.95 o.p. (ISBN 0-672-21500-4, 21500). Sams.

BOOKS IN PRINT
1989-90
VOLUME 7
O.P.-O.S.I.
AUTHORS

Authors

A

A L A see American Library Association.
A. R. E. New York Members Staff. Economic Healing.
AA Board of Regents Staff. Certified Internal Auditor Examination, May 1980: Questions & Suggested Solutions.
AAAS Staff, ed. AAAS Handbook Nineteen Eighty-Eight to Eighty-Nine: Officers, Organization, Activities.
--AAAS Handbook Nineteen Eighty-Seven to Eighty-Eight: Officers, Organization, Activities.
AACD Library Staff, ed. Counseling Children & Adolescents.
--Counseling Practices & Programs K-12.
--Counseling the Aging.
--Counseling the Handicapped.
--Counselor Preparation & Supervision.
AAG Consulting Services Panel Staff. Suggestions for Self-Evaluation of Geography Programs with Self-Study Data Forms.
Aaker, David A. Developing Business Strategies.
--Strategic Market Management.
Aaker, David A. & Myers, John G. Advertising Management.
Aakre, Nancy, ed. see Moss, Gillian.
Aaltio, M-H. Finnish for Foreigners: Pt 2, Lessons 26 to 40.
Aaltio, M. J. Finnish for Foreigners, Pt. 1: Lessons 1-25.
Aalto, Alvar. Alvar Aalto Furniture. Pallasmaa, Juhani, ed.
AAMI Staff. Annual Meeting Proceedings, 1986 New Directions - Advancement Through Knowledge.
--Association for the Advancement of Medical Instrumentation 22nd Annual Meeting: Proceedings (1987)
Aarflot, Andreas. Hans Nielsen Hauge: His Life & Message.
Aarle, Thomas Van. Don't Put Your Cart Before the Race Horse.
Aaron, Benjamin. The Strike: A Current Assessment.
Aaron, Benjamin, jt. auth. see American Arbitration Association Staff.
Aaron, Benjamin, et al, eds. Public-Sector Bargaining.
Aaron, Chester. An American Ghost.
--Better Than Laughter.
--Hello to Bodega.
--Spill.
Aaron, David. State Scarlet.
Aaron, Henry. Street Furniture.
Aaron, James. The Gay Trivia Quiz Book.
Aaron, Jan. India on Fifteen & Twenty-Five Dollars a Day.
Aaron, Richard I. Bankruptcy Law Handbook.
Aaron, Sam, intro. by. Florence Fabricant's Pleasures of the Table: Innovative Menus for Entertaining, Easily Prepared Recipes, & the Wines to Serve Them with.
Aaron, Shirley L. & Scales, Pat R., eds. School Library Media Annual 1984.
Aaronovitch, S. & Smith, R. The Political Economy of British Capitalism: A Marxist Analysis.
Aarons, Edward S. Assignment--Moon Girl.
Aarons, Trudy & Koelsch, Francine. One Hundred One Language Arts Activities.
--One Hundred One Math Activities.
--One Hundred One Reading Activities.
--One Hundred One Science Activities.
Aaronson, David E. Maryland Criminal Jury Instructions & Commentary.
Aaronson, H. I., ed. see TMS-AIME Fall Meeting, Niagara Falls,1976.
Aaronson, Hubert I. & Laughlin, David E., eds. International Conference on Solid-Solid Phase Transformations: Proceedings, Pittsburgh, 1981.
Aaronson, Jonathan D. & Cowhey, Peter F. Trade in Services: A Case for Open Markets.
AARP's Worker Equity Dept. Your Vital Papers Logbook.
Aart, Dick Van Der see Van Der Aart, Dick.
Aaseng, Nathan. Baseball's Hottest Hitters.
--Batting Ninth for the Braves.
--Winners Never Quit: Athletes Who Beat the Odds.
Aaseng, Rolf. God Is Great, God Is Good: Devotions for Families.
Aaseng, Rolf E. Come, Lord Jesus.
--Jesus Loves Me, This I Know: Devotions for Families with Young Children.
--Sacred Sixty-Six.
Aasheim, Ashley. The Apostate.
AAUW, Wisconsin State Division Staff. Wisconsin Women: A Gifted Heritage. Short, Anne, et al, eds.
Aavani, Gholam R., tr. see Nasr, Seyyed H.
ABA, Committee to Study Foreign Investment in U.S., Corporation, Banking & Business Law Section. High Interest-Easy Reading: For Junior & Senior High School Students. Agee, Hugh, ed.
Abadie, Ann J., jt. ed. see Fowler, Doreen.
Abadie, Ann J., jt. ed. see Harrington, Evans.
Abadie, J., ed. Integer & Non-Linear Programming.
Abadie, M. J., jt. auth. see Raphael, Sally J.
Abagnale, Frank W., Jr. Catch Me If You Can.
Abalos, David T. Latinos in the United States: The Sacred & the Political.
Abasiekong, Edet M. Integrated Rural Development in the Third World: Its Concepts, Problems & Prospects.
Abayakoon, Cyrus. Astro-Palmistry.
Abbensetts, Michael. Sweet Talk.
Abbey, Dawn, ed. see Sutphen, Dick.
Abbey, Edward. Black Sun.
--The Brave Cowboy.
--Fire on the Mountain.
--One Life at a Time, Please.
Abbey, Edward & Muench, David. Desert Images: An American Landscape.
Abbey, F., jt. auth. see Thomas, A. F.
Abbey, James R., jt. auth. see Astroff, Milton T.
Abbey, Lynn. Unicorn & Dragon.
Abbey, Merrill R. Communication in Pulpit & Parish.
--Communication in Pulpit & Parish.
Abbey, Merrill R. & Edwards, O. C. Epiphany.
Abbey, S. Goldsmith's & Silversmith's Handbook.
Abbot, David W. & Rogowsky, Edward T. Political Parties.
Abbot, Thomas K., tr. see Kant, Immanuel.
Abbot, W. Practical Geometry & Engineering Graphics.
Abbot Herman, jt. auth. see Rose, Seraphim.
Abbott, Abbe, jt. auth. see Green, Paul.
Abbott, Ann A. Professional Choices: Values at Work.
--Professional Values.
Abbott, Berenice. New York in the Thirties.
Abbott, Carl. Portland: Gateway to the Northwest.
Abbott, Craig S., jt. auth. see Williams, William P.
Abbott, Dorothy. Nothing's Changed: Diary of a Mastectomy.
Abbott, Frank F. Roman Politics.
Abbott, George, jt. auth. see University of Glasgow Staff.
Abbott, George C. International Indebtedness & the Developing Countries.
Abbott, Graham & Little, Geoffrey, eds. The Respectable Sydney Merchant: A. B. Spark of Tempe.
Abbott, J. Student Life in a Class Society.
Abbott, J. C. Marketing Problems & Improvement Programs.
Abbott, John. The Keys of Power: A Study of Indian Ritual & Belief.
Abbott, John, jt. auth. see Prillaman, Douglas.
Abbott, Katherine M. Old Paths & Legends of New England: Saunterings over Historic Roads with Glimpses of Picturesque Fields & Old Homesteads in Massachusetts, Rhode Island & New Hampshire.
--Old Paths & Legends of the New England Border: Connecticut, Deerfield, Berkshire.
Abbott, Morris W. Cog Railway to Pike's Peak.
Abbott, Sandra. Castle of Evil.
Abbott, Sheldon L. Automotive Brakes: Text-Lab Manual.
--Automotive Transmissions.
Abbott, Shirley. Womenfolks: Growing up down South.
Abbott, W. Technical Drawing.
Abbott, Ward. North.
Abbotts, John, jt. auth. see Nader, Ralph.
Abboushi, Wasif. The Unmaking of Palestine.
Abdallah, Wagdy M. Internal Accountability: An International Emphasis. Farmer, Richard, ed.
Abdel-Fadil, Mahmoud. Informal Sector Employment in Egypt: Employment Opportunities & Equity in Egypt. International Labour Office, ed.
Abdu, Hani R. Christian Psychology.
--The True Christian Science.
Abdul-Baki, Houda S. A Select Annotated Bibliography on Women & the Ethnic Minorities of Color in Social Work Education.
Abdulbhan, P., jt. ed. see Tabucanon, M. T.
Abdul Huq, A. M. & Aman, Mohammed M. Librarianship & the Third World.
Abdul-Karim, Aliyah. Power Skills in Reading.
Abdul-Rauf, Muhammed. Marriage in Islam: A Manual.
Abe, Kobo. Inter Ice Age Four. Saunders, E. Dale, tr. from Japanese.
Abeel, Erica. Last Romance.
Abegglen, James, jt. auth. see Warner, W. Lloyd.
Abehsera, Michel. Cooking for Life.
Abel, Alison M. Make Hay While the Sun Shines.
Abel, Dorothy. The Tender Melody.
Abel, E. L. Marihuana: The First Twelve Thousand Years.
Abel, E. W., jt. auth. see Rochow, E. G.
Abel, Lionel. The Intellectual Follies: A Memoir of the Literary Venture in New York & Paris.
--The Intellectual Follies: A Memoir of the Literary Venture in New York & Paris.
Abel, Robert. The Progress of a Fire.
Abel, Sally. How to Become a U. S. Citizen.
Abel, Sally A. How to Become a United States Citizen: Como Hacerse Ciudadano de Los Estados Unidos. Oberti, Martha, tr.
Abela, Joseph S. Felix Culpa.
Abelard, Felix. My Wife, the Condesa.
Abelard, Max. Night of the Ninja.
Abell, George. Exploration of the Universe.
--Realm of the Universe.
Abell, George O. Exploration of the Universe.
Abell, George O. & Singer, Barry, eds. Science and the Paranormal.
Abell, Parker. Pandora's Box.
--A Two-Faced Nation.
Abell, Ron. Tap City.
Abella, Alex. The Total Banana.
Abelman, Paul. Beyond Nakedness.
--Shoestring.
Abelmann, Henry W. Cancer As I See It.
Abeloe, William N. To the Top of the Mountain: The Life of Father Umberto Olivieri, "Padre of the Otomis"
Abelow, Dan. Total Sex.
Abels, Linda F. Mosby's Manual of Critical Care: Practices & Procedures, 1979.
Abel-Smith, Brian. British Doctors at Home & Abroad.
--The Poor & the Poorest.
Abelson. If I Were King of the Universe.
Abelson, Hal. TI LOGO.
Abelson, Herbert, jt. auth. see Karlins, Marvin.
Abelson, Philip H., ed. Food: Politics, Economics, Nutrition & Research.
Aben, Hillar. Integrated Photoelasticity.

Aber, Ita. The Art of Judaic Needlework: Traditional & Contemporary Designs.
Aberbach, Alan D. The Ideas of Richard Wagner: An Examination & Analysis of His Major Aesthetic, Political, Economic, Social, & Religious Thoughts.
Abercrombie, M. L. Aims & Techniques of Group Teaching.
Abercrombie, Nicholas & Urry, John. Capital, Labour & the Middle Classes.
Abernathy, David & Perrin, Norman. Understanding the Teaching of Jesus.
Abernathy, M. Glenn. Civil Liberties under the Constitution.
Abernethy, Rose & Lynn, Diana. Never Look Back.
Abert, James G., ed. Resource Recovery Guide.
Aberth, Oliver. Computable Analysis.
Abeshouse, Matthew & Abeshouse, Tevin. Music Video Trivia.
Abeshouse, Tevin, jt. auth. see Abeshouse, Matthew.
Abeson, Marion & Bailey, Charity. Playtime with Music.
Abeysekera, Dayalal. Regional Patterns of Intercensal & Lifetime Migration in Sri Lanka.
Abhedananda, Swami. How to Be a Yogi.
Abidi, A. H. China, Iran & the Persian Gulf.
Abikoff, W. The Real Analytic Theory of Teichmueller Space.
Abilene Christian University Lectureship Staff. Crowning Fifty Years. Thomas, J. D., ed.
Abio, Rufus O. Angels of Double Faces.
Abir, David, ed. Contributions to Mechanics.
Ablon, jt. auth. see Olsen.
Ablon, L. J., et al. Module IA: Practical Mathematics (Decimals, Ratios, Proportions, & Per Cent)
Ablon, Leon, et al. Series in Mathematics Modules.
--The Steps in Mathematics Modules I-V.
Ablon, Leon J., ed. see Siner, Helen B.
Abodaher, David J. Great Moments in Sports Car Racing.
Abouchar, Alan. Transportation Economics & Public Policy: With Urban Extensions.
Aboucher, Alan. Economic Evaluation of Soviet Socialism.
Abou-Sabe, Morad, ed. Microbial Genetics.
Abraham. Radioassay Systems in Clinical Endocrinology.
Abraham, Fern-Rae. Tin Craft of the Southwest: A Workbook.
Abraham, Gerald, ed. see Calvocoressi, M. D.
Abraham, Gerald E. The Music of Schubert.
Abraham, M. Francis. Perspectives on Modernization: Toward a General Theory of Third World Development.
Abraham, Paul & Mackey, Joan. Contact U. S. A. An ESL Reading & Vocabulary Textbook.
Abraham, Williard. Living with Preschoolers.
Abrahams, J. R. & Pridham, G. J. Semiconductor Circuits: Theory, Design & Experiment.
Abrahams, K., et al, eds. Nuclear Structure.
--Symmetries in Nuclear Structure.
Abrahams, Peter. This Island Now.
Abrahams, William. Prize Stories 1986: The O. Henry Awards.
Abrahams, William, jt. auth. see Stansky, Peter.
Abrahams, William, ed. Prize Stories 1986: The O. Henry Awards.
Abrahams-Curiel, Diana, tr. see Linssen, Robert.
Abrahamsen, David. The Mind of the Accused: A Psychiatrist in the Courtroom.
Abrahamsen, M. A. Cooperative Business Enterprise.
Abrahamson, Bergljot. Ninety Dollar Circle Tour: The Value of Traveling.
--Scandinavia Revisited: A Norwegian-American Tours Her Homeland.
Abrahamson, E. M. & Pezet, A. W. Body, Mind & Sugar.
--Body, Mind & Sugar.
Abrahamson, Edwin & Ostroy, Sanford E., eds. Molecular Processes in Vision.
Abrahamson, I. A., Jr. Know Your Eyes.
Abrahms, Eliot R., jt. auth. see Ellis, Albert.
Abrahms, Sally. Children in the Crossfire: The Tragedy of Parental Kidnapping.
--Children in the Crossfire: The Tragedy of Parental Kidnapping.
Abram, Morris B. The Day Is Short: An Autobiography.
Abramov, Fyodor. Two Winters & Three Summers.
Abramovitch, R. A., ed. Chemistry of Heterocyclic Compounds.
Abrams, Alan E., ed. Journalist Biographies Master Index.
--Media Personnel Directory.
Abrams, Bill, jt. auth. see Alsop, Ronald.
Abrams, Connie. God Is in the Night.
Abrams, J. D. Duke-Elder's Practice of Refraction.
Abrams, Joy, et al. Look Good - Feel Good Through Yoga.
Abrams, Karin von see Von Weizsacker, Richard.
Abrams, Kathleen & Abrams, Lawrence. Logging & Lumbering.
Abrams, Kathleen S. Career Prep: Electronics Servicing.
Abrams, Lawrence, jt. auth. see Abrams, Kathleen.
Abrams, Linsey. Double Vision.
Abrams, M. H., et al, eds. The Norton Anthology of English Literature.
--The Norton Anthology of English Literature.
Abrams, Philip. Origins of British Sociology: Eighteen Thirty-Four to Nineteen Fourteen: An Essay with Selected Papers.
Abrams, Richard. F 4-U Corsair at War.
Abrams, Richard I. & Hutchinson, Warner. An Illustrated Life of Jesus: From The National Gallery of Art Collection.
Abramson, Alan J., jt. auth. see Salamon, Lester M.
Abramson, David H., jt. auth. see Sagerman, Robert H.
Abramson, David I., ed. Blood Vessels & Lymphatics.
--Circulation in the Extremities.
Abramson, Paul, et al. Change & Continuity in the 1984 Elections.
Abrash, Henry & Hardcastle, Kenneth. Chemistry.
Abrashkin, Raymond, jt. auth. see Williams, Jay.
Abrecht, Paul, ed. Faith & Science in an Unjust World, Vol. 2: Reports & Recommendations.
--Faith, Science, & the Future.
Abrecht, Paul, jt. ed. see Francis, John.
Abreu, Manuel. Llegaron los Hippies.
Abreu, Rosendo, jt. auth. see Lanzano, Susan.
Abriel, Battalion Chief Warren W. Thirty Years of Smoke, Heat & Hell.
Abrikosov, A. A., et al. Quantum Field Theoretical Methods in Statistical Physics.
Abroms, Gene M. & Greenfield, Norman S., eds. New Hospital Psychiatry: Proceedings of a Conference.
Abruzzo, James. Jobs in Arts & Media Management: What They Are & How to Get One.
Abse, Dannie, ed. Modern European Verse.
Abshire, David M., et al. United States Global Leadership: The President & Congress.
Abt, Clark C. Strategy for Terminating a Nuclear War.
Abt, Lawrence, jt. auth. see Stuart, Irving.
Abt, Lawrence E. & Stuart, Irving R. Social Psychology & Discretionary Law.
Abt, Lawrence E., jt. auth. see Rosner, Stanley.
Abu Jaber, Kamel S. Arab Ba'th Socialist Party History, Ideology, & Organization.
Aby, Carroll D. & Vaughn, Donald E., Jr. Financial Management Classics.
Academic Library Statistics Task Force Staff. One Hundred Libraries Statistical Survey, 1984.
Academy of Criminal Justice Sciences Staff, jt. auth. see Hochstedler, Ellen.
Academy of Criminal Justice Sciences Staff & Decker, Scott H. Juvenile Justice Policy: Analyzing Trends & Outcomes.
Academy of Korean Studies, Wilson Center Staff. Reflections on a Century of United States-Korean Relations.
Academy of Leisure Sciences Staff. Values & Leisure & Trends in Leisure Services.
Academy of Natural Sciences of Philadelphia Staff, ed. Catalog of the Library of the Academy of Natural Sciences of Philadelphia.
Academy of Traditional Chinese Medicine, Shanghai Staff. An Outline of Chinese Acupuncture.
Acers, Thomas E. Congenital Abnormalities of the Optic Nerve & Related Forebrain.
Aceves, Joseph B. & King, H. Gill. Introduction to Anthropology.
Achad, Frater. Melchizedek Truth Principles.
Acharya, K. R., et al. Pre-University Chemistry.
Acharya, Meena & Bennett, Lynn. Women & the Subsistence Sector: Economic Participation & Household Decisionmaking in Nepal.
Acharya, Shankar N. Incentives for Resource Allocation: A Case Study of Sudan.
Achebe, Chinua. Things Fall Apart. Dabey, John, ed.
Achelis, Elisabeth. World Calendar: Addresses & Occasional Papers Chronologically Arranged on the Progress of Calendar Reform Since 1930.
Achen, Sven T. Symbols Around Us.
Achenbach, J. D. A Theory of Elasticity with Microstructure for Directionally Reinforced Composites.
Acheson, Dean. Struggle for a Free Europe.
--This Vast External Realm.
Achong, B. G., jt. ed. see Epstein, M. A.
Achtemeier, Elizabeth. The Community & Message of Isaiah Fifty Six-Sixty Six: A Theological Commentary.
--Deuteronomy, Jeremiah. McCurley, Foster R., ed.
--Old Testament & the Proclamation of the Gospel.
--The Old Testament & the Proclamation of the Gospel.
Achtemeier, Elizabeth, jt. auth. see Achtemeier, Paul J.
Achtemeier, Elizabeth, ed. see Carlston, Charles.
Achtemeier, Elizabeth, ed. see Clifford, Richard J. & Rockwell, Hays H.
Achtemeier, Elizabeth, ed. see Fiorenza, Elisabeth S. & Holmes, Urban T.
Achtemeier, Elizabeth, ed. see Fuller, Reginald H.
Achtemeier, Elizabeth, et al, eds. see Achtemeier, Paul J. & Mebust, J. Leland.
Achtemeier, Elizabeth, et al, eds. see Borsch, Frederick H. & Napier, Davie.
Achtemeier, Elizabeth, et al, eds. see Burgess, Joseph A. & Winn, Albert C.
Achtemeier, Elizabeth, et al, eds. see Edwards, O. C., Jr. & Taylor, Gardner C.
Achtemeier, Elizabeth, et al, eds. see Fuller, Reginald H.
Achtemeier, Elizabeth, et al, eds. see Furnish, Victor P. & Thulin, Richard L.
Achtemeier, Elizabeth, et al, eds. see Harrisville, Roy A. & Hackett, Charles D.
Achtemeier, Elizabeth, et al, eds. see Jeske, Richard L. & Barr, Browne.
Achtemeier, Elizabeth, et al, eds. see Juel, Donald H. & Buttrick, David.
Achtemeier, Elizabeth, et al, eds. see Kee, Howard C. & Gomes, Peter J.
Achtemeier, Elizabeth, et al, eds. see Kingsbury, Jack D. & Pennington, Chester.
Achtemeier, Elizabeth, et al, eds. see Krentz, Edgar & Vogel, Arthur A.
Achtemeier, Elizabeth, et al, eds. see Micks, Marianne H. & Ridenhour, Thomas E.
Achtemeier, Elizabeth, et al, eds. see Minear, Paul S. & Adams, Harry B.
Achtemeier, Elizabeth, et al, eds. see Nieting, Lorenz.
Achtemeier, Elizabeth, et al, eds. see Pervo, Richard I. & Carl, William J., III.
Achtemeier, Elizabeth, et al, eds. see Reid, Richard & Crum, Milton, Jr.
Achtemeier, Elizabeth, et al, eds. see Saunders, Ernest W. & Craddock, Fred B.
Achtemeier, Elizabeth, et al, eds. see Thulin, Richard L.
Achtemeier, Elizabeth, et al, eds. see Tiede, David L. & Kavanagh, Aidan.
Achtemeier, Elizabeth, et al, eds. see Trotti, John B.
Achtemeier, Elizabeth R., jt. auth. see Achtemeier, Paul J.
Achtemeier, Paul J. Pentecost Three.
Achtemeier, Paul J. & Achtemeier, Elizabeth R. Epiphany.
Achtemeier, Paul J. & Achtemeier, Elizabeth. The Old Testament Roots of Our Faith.
Achtemeier, Paul J. & Mebust, J. Leland. Advent-Christmas. Achtemeier, Elizabeth, et al, eds.
Achtemeier, Paul J., tr. see Marxsen, Willi.
Achterberg, Jeanne. Imagery in Healing: Shamanism & Modern Medicine.
Achterberg, Jeanne & Lawlis, Frank. Bridges of the Bodymind.
Achtert, Walter S., jt. auth. see Gibaldi, Joseph.
Achtmeier, Paul J., et al see Shelp, Earl E. & Sunderland, Ronald H.
Ackart, Robert. A Celebration of Vegetables: Menus for Festive Meat-Free Dining.
--The Frugal Fish Cookbook: 300 Delicious Recipes for All Seasons.
--Souffles, Mousses, Jellies & Creams.
--Spirited Cooking: An Introduction to Wines in the Kitchen.
Acker, Arnold. How to Do Practical Construction Cost Estimates. Howell, J. N., ed.
Acker, David D. History of the Defense Systems Management College: Center of Excellence in Acquistion Management Education & Research. Clark, Catherine M., ed.
Acker, Kathy. Blood & Guts in High School.
--Blood & Guts in High School.
--Don Quixote.
--Don Quixote.
--Empire of the Senseless.
--Great Expectations.
Acker, Robert F., et al, eds. Proceedings of the Third International Congress on Marine Corrosion & Fouling.
Ackerley, J. R. We Think the World of You.
Ackerman. Chinese Art.
Ackerman, Allan D., et al. In the Bank...or up the Chimney? A Dollars & Cents Guide to Energy-Saving Home Improvements.
Ackerman, Charles. Mastering MultiMate Advantage.
Ackerman, Diane. On Extended Wings.
Ackerman, Eugene, et al. Simulation of Infectious Disease Epidemics.
Ackerman, Forrest J, jt. auth. see Strickland, A. W.
Ackerman, Forrest J., jt. auth. see Strickland, A. W.
Ackerman, Gretchen P., jt. auth. see Ackerman, Robert W.
Ackerman, James S., et al. Teaching the Old Testament in English Classes.
Ackerman, John. Welsh Dylan.
Ackerman, Karen. Flannery Row.
Ackerman, Kenneth B. Practical Handbook of Warehousing.
--Warehousing -- A Guide for Both Users & Operators.
Ackerman, Robert K. South Carolina Colonial Land Policies.
Ackerman, Robert W. & Ackerman, Gretchen P. Sir Frederic Madden: A Bibliography & Biographical Sketch.
Ackerman, Winona B. & Lohnes, Paul R. Research Methods for Nurses.
Ackermann, L. V., jt. auth. see Hamperl, H.
Ackermann, Philip G., jt. auth. see Bauer, John D.
Ackermann, Philip G., jt. auth. see Remson, Susan T.
Ackermann, Philip G., jt. auth. see Toro, Gelson.
Ackland, Donald, et al. Broadman Comments, July-September 1988.
Ackland, Donald F. Broadman Comments.
--Broadman Comments, 1987-88.
Ackland, Donald F., et al. Broadman Comments, April-June 1988.
--Broadman Comments, April-June, 1989.
--Broadman Comments, January-March 1988.
--Broadman Comments, January-March 1989.
--Broadman Comments, October-December 1988.
Ackland, Valentine. For Sylvia: An Honest Account.
Ackroyd, Joyce, tr. see Hakuseki, Arai.
Ackroyd, Peter. T. S. Eliot: A Life.
--T. S. Eliot: A Life.
Ackroyd, Ted J., ed. Health & Medical Economics: A Guide to Information Sources.
Acland, Robert D. Microsurgery Practice Manual.
Acocella, Bart, et al. The All-Time All-Star Baseball Book.
Acocella, Nick & Dewey, Donald. All-Stars: All Star Baseball Book.
Acock, Malcolm. Informal Logic Examples & Exercises.
Acquaviva, Francis A. & Malone, Robert A. The Power of Positive Persuasion: A Professional's Guide to Communications.
ACSM-ASP Fall Convention Staff. Technical Papers: Proceedings of the ACSM-ASP Fall Convention, September 1982.
Actemeier, Elizabeth, et al, eds. see Brown, Schuyler & Saliers, Don E.
Action, Michael, Jr. The Unforgettable Fire - Awkward Instant.
Acton, Alfred, ed. & tr. see Swedenborg, Emanuel.
Acton, Alfred, tr. & pref. by see Swedenborg, Emanuel.
Acton, David, jt. auth. see Loring, John.
Acton, Harold. Nancy Mitford: A Memoir.
--Villas of Tuscany.
Acton, Lord see Acton, John E.
Acton, Ronald T. Immunobiological & Immunochemical Studies of the Oyster, Crassptrea Virginica.
Acton, Ronald T., et al. Invertebrate Immune Defense Mechanisms.
Acupuncture Research Institute Staff. Acupuncture Made Easy.
Acyutananda, Swami, ed. Songs of the Vaisnava Acaryas.
Aczel, J. Vorlesungen Uber Funktionalgleichungen und Ihre Anwendungen.
Ada, G. L., jt. auth. see Nossal, G. J.
Adachi, Fumie, tr. & illus. see Matsuya Piece-Goods Store Staff.
Adachi, Sakyo, tr. see Webber, Bert.
Adair, Aileen. The Moon is Full.
Adair, Dennis. Thundergate, Book III: The Story of Canada.
Adair, Dennis & Rosenstock, Janet. Bitter Shield: Book II - The Story of Canada.
--Kanata: The Story of Canada.
--Les Portes du Tonnere.
--Tristes Murailles.
--Victoria, Book V: The Story of Canada.
--Wildfires, Bk. 4: The Story of Canada.
Adair, Douglass. Fame & the Founding Fathers. Colbourn, H. Trevor, ed. & intro. by.
Adair, Gilbert, tr. see Ciment, Michel.
Adair, James R., jt. auth. see Jorden, Paul J.
Adair, Robert. Concepts in Physics.
Adam, G., ed. see Deutsche Gesellschaft Fur Biophysik, Annual Meeting, Konstanz, October 1979.
Adam, G., et al, eds. Brain & Behaviour: Proceedings of the 28th International Congress of Physiological Sciences, Budapest, 1980.
Adam, J. H. Longman Concise Dictionary of Business English.
Adam, J. H., ed. Longman Dictionary of Business English.
Adam, Ruth. Woman's Place Nineteen Ten to Nineteen Seventy-Five.
Adam, Ruth, jt. auth. see Muggeridge, Kitty.
Adam, Ruth C. Living with Mysterious Epilepsy: My 48-Year Victory Over Fear. Alvarez, Walter C., ed.
Adam, Yehudi. Mature Judaism: A Programmatic Outline.

Authors

Adamiak, John M. Deterioration of the English Language.
Adamic, K. J., jt. ed. see Herak, J. N.
Adams, jt. auth. see Ferguson.
Adams, Abigail. Letters.
Adams, Alice. Beautiful Girl.
--Return Trips.
Adams, Alicen. Changing Stations.
Adams, Anthony & Jones, Esmor. English Teaching: Programs & Policies.
Adams, Barbara, et al. Gypsies & Government Policy in England.
Adams, Bert N. The Family: A Sociological Interpretation.
Adams, Bill. Trees for Southern Landscapes.
Adams, C., jt. ed. see Ferguson, R.
Adams, C. G., jt. ed. see Hedley, R. H.
Adams, C. J., jt. auth. see Downs, A. J.
Adams, C. K. A Beginner's Guide to Computers & Microprocessors--with Projects.
Adams, C. R., tr. see Falbe, J.
Adams, Carol, jt. ed. see Ferguson, Rosemary.
Adams, Caroline, et al. Laboratory Manual for Principles of Biology.
Adams, Catherine F. Nutritive Value of American Foods in Common Units.
Adams, Catherine G. & Macione, Alberta. Handbook of Psychatric & Mental Health Nursing.
Adams, Charles F. Richard Henry Dana.
Adams, Clinton. American Lithographers, 1900-1960: The Artists & Their Printers.
Adams, Cynthia, jt. auth. see Haskew, Paul.
Adams, D., et al, eds. Electronic Equipment Wiring & Assembling: Part One.
--Electronic Inspection & Test.
Adams, D. R., et al, eds. Static Electrical Equipment Testing.
Adams, Dennis M., ed. Computers & Teacher Training: A Practical Guide.
Adams, Edgar H. The Julius Guttag Collection of Latin American Coins.
Adams, Edgar H., jt. auth. see Rozel, Nicholas J.
Adams, Edith. My Little Pony & The New Friends.
Adams, Edward L., Jr. Career Advancement Guide.
Adams, Elizabeth, jt. auth. see Haggar, Reginald.
Adams, Ernestine N. When the Flowers Die (Remember Me)
Adams, Evangeline. Astrology for Everyone.
Adams, F. & Dams, R. Applied Gamma-Ray Spectrometry.
Adams, Frank. AMI-Rowe Jukeboxes Nineteen Twenty-Nine to Nineteen Eighty-Eight.
Adams, Frank, ed. see Seeburg Company Staff.
Adams, George. How to Photograph a Woman.
--The Lemniscatory Ruled Surface in Space & Counterspace. Eberhart, Stephen, tr. from Ger. & Eng.
Adams, George & Whicher, Olive. The Plant Between Sun & Earth.
Adams, George L., et al. Boies's Fundamentals of Otolaryngology: A Textbook of Ear, Nose & Throat Diseases.
Adams, George R., jt. auth. see Nichols, Roger I.
Adams, Gleason R., jt. tr. see Latortue, Regine.
Adams, Gordon. The Politics of Defense Contracting: The Iron Triangle.
Adams, H. Greg. Effective Supervisory Safety Salesmanship.
Adams, Harold. Can Supernutrition Make the Difference?
--When Rich Men Die.
Adams, Harry. ProSet Eighty-One.
Adams, Harry & Simpson, R. W. Propjet 1989.
Adams, Harry B. Propjet 1988.
Adams, Harry B., jt. auth. see Minear, Paul S.
Adams, Hazard. The Academic Tribes.
--Joyce Cary's Trilogies: Pursuit of the Particular Real.
--Truth about Dragons: An Anti Romance.
Adams, Henry E. & Boardman, William K. Advances in Experimental Clinical Psychology.
Adams, Herbert B. & Wood, Henry. Columbus & His Discovery of America.
Adams, Herbert F., jt. auth. see Cooke, Nelson M.
Adams, I. H. Agrarian Landscape Terms: A Glossary for Historical Geography Ser.
Adams, Ian. S, Portrait of a Spy.
Adams, Ian H. The Making of Urban Scotland.
Adams, J. E. You Can Conquer Depression.
--You Can Overcome Fear.
Adams, J. M. Optical Measurements in the Printing Industry.
Adams, J. Michael & Faux, David D. Printing Technology.
Adams, J. T. New England in the Republic.
Adams, James. The Financing of Terror.
Adams, James E. Electrical Principles & Practices.
Adams, James F. Understanding Adolescence: Current Developments in Adolescent Psychology.
Adams, James L. Conceptual Blockbusting: A Guide to Better Ideas.
--The Prophethood of All Believers. Beach, George K., ed.
Adams, James L., ed. see Holl, Karl.
Adams, James M. Data Processing: An Introduction.
Adams, James R. Secrets of the Tax Revolt.
Adams, James T. Provincial Society, Sixteen Ninety to Seventeen Sixty-Three.
Adams, Jane. Seattle Green.
Adams, Jay E. Counseling & the Five Points of Calvinism.
--Four Weeks with God & Your Neighbor.
--Grist from Adams' Mill.
--Journal of Pastoral Practice.
--Journal of Pastoral Practice.
--Journal of Pastoral Practice.
--Journal of Pastoral Practice.
--Journal of Pastoral Practice.
--Journal of Pastoral Practice.
--Journal of Pastoral Practice.
--Language of Counseling.
--Language of Counseling.
--Ready to Restore.
--Truth Apparent: Essays on Biblical Preaching.
--Update on Christian Counseling.
--What to Do on Thursday.
--What to Do on Thursday: A Layman's Guide to the Practical Use of the Scriptures.
Adams, Jay E., ed. Journal of Pastoral Practice.
Adams, Jennifer, ed. see Holzer, Hans.
Adams, Jennifer A. The Solar Church. Hoffman, Douglas R., ed.
Adams, Jennifer K. With All My Heart. Wallace, Mary, ed.
Adams, Joey. Roast of the Town.
Adams, John. Beekeeping: The Gentle Craft.
--Cases & Materials on Sale of Goods.
--Correspondence of John Adams & Thomas Jefferson.
--Transport Planning: Vision & Practice.
Adams, John A. & Lowder, Wayne M., eds. Natural Radiation Environment.
Adams, John C. Outline of Fractures.
Adams, John D. Introduction to TRS-80 Data Files.
Adams, John F. Beekeeping.
Adams, John G. Without Precedent.
--Without Precedent: The Story of the Death of McCarthyism.
Adams, Jonathan. Your Business & the Law: A Guide for Minnesota Business Owners.
Adams, Julian. The Student Journalist & Mass Communication.
Adams, Kathleen & MacNeilage, Linda. Assertiveness at Work: How to Increase Your Personal Power on the Job.
Adams, Kay Angana & Walker, Jerry. Improving the Accountability of Career Education Programs: Evaluation Guidelines & Checklists.
Adams, Leigh & Madara, Lynda. Great Expectations.
Adams, Lela C. Marriages of Patrick County, Virginia, 1791-1850.
Adams, Leon D. The Wines of America.
Adams, M. J. An Introduction to Optical Waveguides.
Adams, M. L., Jr., ed. Rotor Dynamical Instability.
Adams, Mildred, tr. see Ortega y Gasset, Jose.
Adams, Norman & Singer, Joe. Drawing Animals.
Adams, Oscar F. Dictionary of American Authors.
Adams, Patsy. Ceramica Culina.
Adams, Peter. The Wine Lover's Quiz Book: Challenging Questions & Answers for Wine Buffs & Bluffers.
Adams, Priscilla B. Thinking on Paper.
Adams, R. L. & Burdon, R. H. Biochemistry of Nucleic Acids.
Adams, R. W., et al. Field Guide to the Geology of San Salvador. Gerace, D. T., ed.
Adams, Raymond D. & Lyon, G. Neurology of Hereditary Metabolic Diseases of Children.
Adams, Raymond D., jt. auth. see Isselbacher, Kurt J.
Adams, Richard N. Crucifixion by Power: Essays on Guatemalan National Social Structure, 1944-1966.
Adams, Richard N., jt. ed. see Fogelson, Raymond D.
Adams, Richard P. Faulkner: Myth & Motion.
Adams, Robert. Abysmal Gloom.
--Denver: A Photographic Survey of the Metropolitan Area.
Adams, Robert, ed. The New Times Network: Groups & Centres for Personal Growth.
Adams, Robert L., & Associates Staff. The Pennsylvania Job Bank: A Comprehensive Guide to Major Local Employers.
Adams, Robert Lang, & Associates Staff & Michael J. The National Job Bank: A Comprehensive Guide to Major Employers in the Nation's Key Job Markets.
Adams, Robert Lang, & Associates Staff. The Northern California Job Bank: A Comprehensive Guide to Major Local Employers.
Adams, Robert Lang, & Associates Staff & Michael, J. The Southwest Job Bank: A Comprehensive Guide to Major Local Employers.
Adams, Robert Lang, & Associates Staff. The Texas Job Bank: A Comprehensive Guide to Major Local Employers. Noble, John H., ed.
Adams, Robert M. Proteus: His Lies, His Truth.
--The Roman Stamp: Frame & Facade in Some Forms of Neo-Classicism.
Adams, Robert W., jt. auth. see Kotecha, Ken C.
Adams, Roe R., III, jt. auth. see Consumer Guide Editors.
Adams, Ronald C., et al. Games, Sports & Exercises for the Physically Handicapped.
Adams, Ruth & Murray, Frank. Improving Your Health with Vitamin A.
Adams, Samuel H. The Erie Canal.
Adams, Samuel H., jt. auth. see Penman, Kenneth A.
Adams, Scott. Information for Science & Technology: The International Scene.
Adams, Sexton & Fyffe, Don. Corporate Promotables.
Adams, Sexton & Griffin, Adelaide. Modern Personnel Management.
Adams, Steve. Using Dollars & Sense on the IBM PC.
Adams, Suzy, jt. auth. see Freeman, Vicki.
Adams, Swain. Blood River Gold.
Adams, T. W. AKEL: The Communist Party of Cyprus.
Adams, Thomas B. A New Nation.
Adams, Thomas F. Typographia: Or the Printers Instructor.
Adams, Vicki, ed. see Woodsmall, Annabel W., et al.
Adams, W. Lindsay & Borza, Eugene N., eds. Philip II: Alexander the Great & the Macedonian Heritage.
Adams, W. M. Nature's Place: Conservation Sites & Countryside Change.
Adams, W. Peter, ed. see International Geographical Congress Staff.
Adams, W. Royce & Brody, Jane. Reading Beyond Words.
Adams, W. Royce, jt. auth. see Frakes, G. E.
Adams, Walter & Brock, James. The Bigness Complex: Industry, Labor, & Government in the American Economy.
Adams, Walter J., Jr. Second Chance.
Adams, William, ed. see Momaday, N. Scott.
Adams, William, et al, eds. Afro-American Literature: Fiction.
--Afro-American Literature: Nonfiction.
--Afro-American Literature: Poetry.
Adams, William D., ed. English Epigrams.
Adams, William J. Finite Mathematics: For Business & Social Science.
Adams, William L. A Melodrame Entitled "Treason, Stratagems, & Spoils" Belknap, George N., ed.
Adamson, Arthur. A Textbook of Physical Chemistry.
Adamson, Douglas. Charles Bear & the Mystery of the Forest.
Adamson, Joy. Forever Free.
--Friends from the Forest.
--Living Free.
--Peoples of Kenya.
--Pippa's Challenge.
--Queen of Shaba: The Story of an African Leopard.
--The Searching Spirit: Joy Adamson's Autobiography.
--Spotted Sphinx.
Adamsons, K., ed. see International Symposium on Diagnosis & Treatment of Disorders Affecting the Intrauterine Patient, Dorado, Puerto Rico, 1967.
Adar, et al. The IBM Personal Computer: What You Should Know.
Adasch, N., et al. Topological Vector Spaces: The Theory Without Convexity Conditions.
Adatto, I. J., jt. auth. see Snider, Arthur J.
Adcock, Don & Segal, Marilyn. From One to Two Years.
--Making Friends: Ways of Encouraging Social Development in Young Children.
Adcock, Don, jt. auth. see Segal, Marilyn.
Adcock, Thomas L. Precinct Nineteen.
Addams, Charles. Creature Comforts.
Addams, Charles & Aruego, Jose. A Treasury of Windmill Books.
Addams, Jane, et al. Child, the Clinic, & the Court.
Addicott, James, jt. ed. see English, John A.
Addinall, Eric & Ellington, Henry. Nuclear Power in Perspective.
Addington, A. C. The Royal House of Stuart: The Descendants of King James VI of Scotland, James I of England.
Addink, A. D. & Spronk, N., eds. Exogenous & Endogenous Influences on Metabolic & Neural Control, Vol. 1: Invited Lectures: Proceedings of the Third Congress of the European Society for Comparative Physiology & Biochemistry, August 31-September 3, 1981, Noorwijkerhout Netherlands.
--Exogenous & Endogenous Influences on Metabolic & Neural Control, Vol. 2: Abstracts: Proceedings ot the Third Congress of the European Society for Comparative Physiology & Biochemistry, August 31-September 3, 1981, Noorwijkerhout, Netherlands.
Addison, Daniel D. Lucy Larcom: Life, Letters & Diary.
Addison, Joseph. Letters.
Addison, William G. The Renewed Church of the United Brethren, 1722-1930.
Addlestone, David F., et al. The Rights of Veterans.
Addy, John & Reeves, Marjorie. A Coal & Iron Community in the Industrial Revolution.
Adebonojo, Festus, et al. How Baby Grows.
Adedoyin, Kunle. The Rape of Manhood: A Plan.
Adegbite, Edeward. Black Enterprise with the Third World.
Adelberg, Roy P. Now Hear This!
Adelberg, Tina Z., jt. ed. see Shelly, Maynard W.
Adelman, Allan G. & Goldman, Bernard S., eds. Unstable Angina: Recognition & Management.
Adelman, Bob, jt. auth. see Off the Wall Street Journal, Inc. Staff.
Adelman, Clem, jt. auth. see Walker, Robert.
Adelman, Clifford, ed. see Hantle, Terry W. & Harris, John.
Adelman, Paul. Gladstone, Disraeli & Later Victorian Politics, 2E.
Adelman, Sherri, ed. see Gibson, Litzkah R.
Adelman, William. Pilsen & the West Side.
Adelsperger, Charlotte. When Your Child Hurts.
Adelstein, Michael E. & Pival, Jean G. The Writing Commitment.
--The Writing Commitment.
--The Writing Commitment.
Aderholt, Alice B., ed. Index to the United States Patent Classification.
--Index to the United States Patent Classification, December 1987.
Aderman, Ralph M., jt. auth. see Kerr, Elizabeth M.
Aderman, Ralph M., et al, eds. Letters: Volume II, 1823-1838.
Adey, R. A. & Brebbia, C. A. Basic Computational Techniques for Engineers.
Adie, Ian W. Oil, Politics, & Seapower: The Indian Ocean Vortex.
Adiyodi, K. G., jt. auth. see Bell, W. J.
Adjali, Mia. Of Life & Hope: Toward Effective Witness in Human Rights.
Adke, S. R. & Manjunath, Shri S. An Introduction to Finite Markov Processes: Continuous Time Finite Markow Processes.
Adkins, A. W. Moral Values & Political Behavior in Ancient Greece.
--Moral Values & Political Behaviour in Ancient Greece.
Adkins, J. S., jt. auth. see Bodwell, C. E.
Adkins, Jan. Art & Ingenuity of the Woodstove.
--Wooden Ship.
Adler. The Itinerary of Benjamin of Tudela. Adler, Marcus N., tr.
Adler, A. Education of the Individual.
Adler, Alexandra. Guiding Human Misfits.
Adler, Alfred. Case of Mrs. A: The Diagnosis of a Life-Style. Shulman, Bernard, ed.
--Cooperation Between the Sexes: Writings on Women, Love, Marriage & Its Disorders.
--Souvenirs Fresh & Rancid.
--Souvenirs Fresh & Rancid.
Adler, Allan, ed. Litigation Under the Federal Freedom of Informaton Act & Privacy Act: 1987.
Adler, Bill. Baseball Wit.
--The Cosby Wit: His Life & Humor.
--The Lottery Book: For People Who Play to Win.
--Ronnie & Nancy.
Adler, Bill & Adler, Bill, Jr. The Wit & Wisdom of Wall Street.
Adler, Bill & Slavitt, David R. Agent.
Adler, Bill, compiled by. Kids' Letters to President Reagan.
Adler, Bill, ed. Please Save My World: Children Speak Out Against Nuclear War.
Adler, C. S. The Evidence That Wasn't There.
--Shadows on Little Reef Bay.
Adler, Claire F. Modern Geometry.
Adler, Elizabeth. Leonie.
Adler, France-Michele. Sportsfashion.
Adler, Franx, et al. The Home of the Learned Man: A Symposium on the Immigrant Scholar in America. Kosa, John, ed.
Adler, Freda & Simon, Rita J. The Criminology of Deviant Women.
Adler, Freda, jt. auth. see Mueller, Gerhard.
Adler, Gerhard. Consciousness & Cure.
Adler, Irving. Readings in Mathematics.
Adler, James R., jt. auth. see Delaney, Patrick R.
Adler, Kathleen & Garb, Tamar. Berthe Morisot.
Adler, Larry. Heroes of Soccer.
--It Ain't Necessarily So: An Autobiography.
Adler, Laurie, jt. ed. see Ensign, Marie S.
Adler, Laurie N., jt. auth. see Ensign, Marie.
Adler, Laurie N., jt. ed. see Ensign, Marie S.
Adler, Marcus N., tr. see Adler.

Adler, Marvin S. & McCarroll, Jesse C. Elementary Teachers' Music Almanack: Timely Lesson Plans for Every Day of the School Year.
Adler, Max K. Modern Market Research.
Adler, Mortimer J., jt. auth. see Michael, Jerome.
Adler, Norman T., et al. Mating Reflexes.
Adler, Paul. Saucer Hill.
Adler, Peter. Momentum: A Theory of Social Action.
Adler, R. Introduction to General Relativity.
Adler, Ronald B. Confidence in Communication: A Guide to Assertive & Social Skills.
Adler, Ronald B. & Rodman, George. Understanding Human Communication.
Adler, Thomas P., jt. auth. see Woodman, Leonora.
Adler, Warren. American Quartet: A Novel about the Mortal Link between Four Marked Presidents of the United States.
--American Sextet.
--American Sextet.
Adler-Nissen, J. & Eggum, B. O., eds. Biochemical Aspects of New Protein Food.
Adlington, tr. see Apuleius, Lucius.
Administrative Agencies Staff. Ohio Monthly Record.
Administrative Conference of the U. S. Staff. Federal Administrative Procedure Sourcebook: Statutes & Related Materials.
Admiral Lord Mountevans. Arctic Solitudes.
Adnan, Etel. Sitt Marie-Rose. Kleege, Georgina, tr. from Fr.
Adoff, Arnold. Big Sister Tells Me That I'm Black.
Adoko, Akena. From Obote to Obote.
Adolfson, John A. & Berghage, Thomas E. Perception & Performance Underwater.
Adolph, E. F. Origins of Physiological Regulations.
Adolph, Harold & Bourne, David L. Stop Making Yourself Sick.
Adolph, L. & Lorenz, Rita. Diagnostico Enzimatico en las Enfermedades de Corazon, Higado y Pancreas.
Adonis. Transformations of the Lover. Hazo, Samuel, tr. from Arabic.
Adorno, Rolena. Guaman Poma: Writing & Resistance in Colonial Peru.
Adorno, T. W. Aesthetic Theory. Lenhardt, G., tr. from Ger.
Adorno, T. W., et al. Authoritarian Personality.
Adorno, Theodor W. The Jargon of Authenticity. Tarnowski, Knut & Will, Frederick, trs.
Adriaansens, Hans P. Talcott Parsons & the Conceptual Dilemma.
Adrian, Charles R. & Press, Charles. Governing Urban America.
Adrian, Colin, ed. Urban Service Provision in Australia: Institutional Process & Geographic Outcome.
Adrian, Dennis. Robert Barnes, Nineteen Fifty-Six to Nineteen Eighty-Four: A Survey. Myers, Trent, ed.
Adrian, Dennis & Myers, Trent. Chicago: Some Other Traditions.
Adrian, Mary. Firehouse Mystery.
Adrian, R. H. The Nerve Impulse. Head, J. J., ed.
Adrian, R. H., ed. Reviews of Physiology, Biochemistry, & Pharmacology.
Adrian, R. H., et al, eds. Reviews of Physiology.
--Reviews of Physiology, Biochemistry & Pharmacology.
--Reviews of Physiology, Biochemistry & Pharmacology.
--Reviews of Physiology, Biochemistry & Pharmacology.
Adshead, Gladys L. & Duff, Annis. Inheritance of Poetry.
Adshead, S. D., et al, eds. see Liverpool Town Planning & Housing Exhibition Staff.
Adulbhan, P. & Tabucanon, M. T., eds. Decision Models for Industrial Systems Engineers & Managers.
Adult Education Association Staff. Administration of Continuing Education.
--The Guidance Function & Counseling Roles in an Adult Education Program.
Advanced Learning, Inc. Auto Body Repair for the Do-It-Yourselfer.
--Can-Do Tune-up: Pinto & Vega Cars, 1971-74.
Advanced Sales Reference Service Department Staff. Social Security Manual.
Advanced Sales Reference Service Department Editorial Staff. Social Security Manual.
Advanced Sales Reference Service Dept. Staff. Tax Facts on Investments.
--Tax Facts on Life Insurance.
Advanced Sales Reference Service Department Staff. Tax Facts on Life Insurance.
Advani, L. T. Horsepower Tables for Agitator Impellers.
Advani, Rukun. E. M. Forster As Critic.
Advincular, A. J. Guide to Close Combat for Infantry Soldier.
Advisory Committee. The Community of Women & Men in the Church: A Study Program.
AE. By Still Waters.
Aebi, Hans-J., jt. auth. see Spiegel, Rene.
Aedric. Swordwield.
Aegerter, Ernest E. & Kilpatrick, John A., Jr. Orthopedic Diseases: Physiology, Pathology, Radiology.
Aero Publishers, Inc., Aeronautical Staff, et al. Boeing P12, F4B.
--Curtiss P-40.
Aero Publishers, Inc., Aeronautical Staff. Kamikaze.
--Republic P-47.
--Supermarine Spitfire.
Aero Staff. Federal Aviation Regulations for Pilots, (FAR) Gentle, Ernest J., ed.
Aerobic Gram-Negative Bronchopneumonias Symposium Staff. Aerobic Gram-Negative Bronchopneumonias: Proceedings of the Symposium, Brussels, Sept. 22, 1978. Thys, J., et al, eds.
Aeronautical Research Institute of Sweden Staff, ed. see Muller, B.
Aers, David. Chaucer, Langland & the Creative Imagination.
Aers, David, et al. Romanticism & Ideology.
Aeschliman, Bonnie. Step by Step Microwave Cooking for Boys & Girls.
--Step-by-Step Microwave Cooking for Boys & Girls.
Aesop. Aesop's Fables.
Aesopus. Ysopet-Avionnet: The Latin & French Texts. McKenzie, Kenneth & Oldfather, William A., eds.
AFA Staff. Mundane Data Nineteen Eighty-Four.
Afanasiev, V. Fundamentos del Comunismos Cientifico.
Afanasyev, Alexander, compiled by. Russian Folk Tales. Chandler, Robert, tr. from Rus.
Afanasyev, V. Social Information & Regulation of Social Development.
Afansyev, V. Fundamentals of Scientific Communism.
Affabee, Eric. Attack on the King.
--Dragon Queen's Revenge.
--The Siege of the Dragonriders.
Affron, Charles. Stage for Poets: Studies in the Theatre of Hugo & Musset.
Afgan, N., ed. see Heat & Mass Transfer in Buildings Summer Seminar Staff.
Afgan, N. H. & Schlunder, E. U. Heat Exchangers: Design & Theory.
Afghan, B. K. & Mackay, D., eds. Hydrocarbons & Halogenated Hydrocarbons in the Aquatic Environment.
Afifi, A. A. & Azen, S. P. Statistical Analysis: A Computer Oriented Approach.
Africa, Thomas W. Ancient World.
African-American Materials Project Staff, compiled by. Newspapers & Periodicals by & about Black People: Southeastern Library Holdings.
African Association for Public Administration & Management Staff. The Ecology of Public Administration & Management in Africa.
African Association of Public Administration & Management Staff. Public Enterprises & Privatization in Africa.
Aftenposten. Facts about Norway. Royal Ministry of Foreign Affairs Staff, ed.
Aftenposten, A., ed. Norway: Facts About.
Afzelius, B., ed. The Functional Anatomy of the Spermatazoan.
Aganbegyan, A. G. Regional Studies for Planning & Projection: The Siberian Experience.
Agard, Frederick B. & Di Pietro, Robert J. The Sounds of English & Italian.
Agardy, Franklin J. How to Read Faster & Better.
Agarwal, G. S. Quantum-Statistical Theories of Spontaneous Emission & Their Relation to Other Approaches.
Agarwal, N. K. Management of Working Capital.
Agarwal, V. P., ed. see All India Symposium Staff.
Agassi, Joseph. Faraday As a Natural Philosopher.
Agazarian, Yvonne & Peters, Richard. The Visible & Invisible Group: Two Perspectives on Group Psychotherapy & Group Process.
Agbor-Tabi, Peter. U. S. Bilateral Assistance in Africa: The Case of Cameroon.
Age Discrimination Workshop Staff, et al. Age Discrimination Workshop Nineteen Eighty-Five: State & Federal Litigation.
Agee, Hugh, ed. see ABA, Committee to Study Foreign Investment in U.S., Corporation, Banking & Business Law Section.
Agee, James & Evans, Walker. Let Us Now Praise Famous Men.
Agee, Jon. Ludlow Laughs.
Agee, William C. & Morrin, Peter. The Advent of Modernism: Post-Impressionism & North American Art 1900-1918.
Agel, Jerome. Sports at Random: Q & A.
Agel, Jerome & Boe, Eugene. Deliverance in Shanghai.
Agel, Jerome B. American at Random: Q. & A.
--Beyond Trivia: Expanded Answers to America's Most Loved Trivia Game.
Ageloff. Primer on SQL.
Ageloff, Roy & Mojena, Richard. Applied Structured WATFIV.
Ager, Stanley & St Aubyn, Fiona. The Butler's Guide: To Clothes Care, Managing the Table, Running the Home & Other Graces.
Aggarwal, M. R. Regional Economic Cooperation in South Asia.
Aggarwal, Narindar K. Bibliography of Studies in Hindi Language & Linguistics.
Aggeler, Geoffrey. Anthony Burgess: The Artist As Novelist.
Agius, Pauline. British Furniture: 1880-1915.
--China Teapots. Riley, Noel, ed.
Agle, Nan H. Maple Street.
Aglietta, Michel. A Theory of Capitalist Regulation: The U. S. Experience.
Aglow Editors. Come Celebrate: A Daily Devotional.
Aglow Staff. Aglow in the Kitchen.
Agnew, H. Wayne, jt. auth. see Breithaupt, Sandra.
Agnoli, A., ed. see Round Table Conference, Rome, Oct. 30-31, 1974.
Agnon, S. Y. The Bridal Canopy. Lask, I. M., tr. from Hebrew.
--A Guest for the Night. Louvish, Misha, tr. from Hebrew.
Agoston, Tom. Blunder! How U. S. Gave Away Nazi Supersecrets.
Agran, Larry. Cancer Connection: And What We Can Do About It.
Agranoff, B. W., et al. Progress in Molecular & Subcellular Biology. Hahn, F. E., et al, eds.
Agrawal, A. N. Indian Economy: Problems of Development & Planning.
Agrawal, D. P. The Archaeology of India.
Agrawal, H. N. A Portrait of Nationalised Banks.
Agrawal, Surendra P., jt. auth. see Hallbauer, Rosalie C.
Agrawala, P. K. Goddesses in Ancient India.
Agria, John J. College Housing: A Critique of the Federal College Housing Loan Program.
Agricultural Division Of Imperial Chemical Industries Limited. Catalyst Handbook.
Agricultural Sector Symposium Staff. Increasing Agricultural Productivity: Proceedings of the Agricultural Sector Symposium, 3rd. Davis, Ted J., ed.
Agriculture Panel of the Intermediate Technology Development Group (London), compiled by. Land Clearance: Alternative Techniques for Removing Trees & Bushes.
Agrimson, J. Elmo, ed. Gifts of the Spirit & the Body of Christ: Perspectives on the Charismatic Movement.
Agrios, George N. Plant Pathology.
--Plant Pathology.
Agrippa, Henry C. The Philosophy of Natural Magic.
Agris, Paul F., ed. Biomolecular Structure & Function.
Aguera, Helen & Diaz, Modesto. Lecturas Basicas: A Cultural Reader.
Aguila, Richard. The Iroquois Restoration: Iroquois Diplomacy on the Colonial Frontier, 1701-1754.
Aguilera-Malta, Demetrio. Seven Serpents & Seven Moons. Rabassa, Gregory, tr.
Agus, Jacob B. Jewish Identity in an Age of Ideologies.
Ahier, John & Flude, Michael, eds. Contemporary Education Policy.
Ahkmatova, A. Soviet Russian Poetry of the Nineteen Fifties to Nineteen Seventies.
Ahl, David. David Ahl's BASIC Computer Adventures: Ten Treks & Travels Through Time & Space.
Ahlback, Tore, ed. Saami Religion: Scripta Instituti Donneriani Aboensis XII.
Ahlbrandt, Roger S. A New Public Policy for Neighborhood Preservation.
Ahlfors, Lars V., et al, eds. Contributions to Analysis: A Collection of Papers Dedicated to Lipman Bers.
Ahlin, et al. Maxillofacial Orthopaedics: Clinical Approach for the Growing Child.
Ahlstrand, Alan. Datsun F10 & 310: 1976-1981 Shop Manual.
--Datsun 4-Wheel Drive Pickups: 1980-1983 Shop Manual. Wauson, Sydnie A., ed.
--MGA-MGB All Models: 1956-1980 Service, Repair Handbook. Robinson, Jeff, ed.
Ahlstrom, Goran. Engineers & Industrial Growth: Higher Technical Education & the Engineering Profession During the 19th & Early 20th Centuries: France, Germany, Sweden & England.
Ahluwalia, H. P. The Hermit Kingdom: Ladakh.
Ahluwalia, Isher J. Behavior of Prices & Output in India.
Ahmad, Alia. Agricultural Stagnation under Population Pressure: The Case of Bangladesh.
Ahmad, F., et al, eds. Differentiation & Development: Miami Winter Symposia.
Ahmad, Iqbal, ed. see AIME Staff.
Ahmad, Muzaffer. The Role of the Public Sector in Developing Countries: Bangladesh.
Ahmanson, John. Secret History: An Eyewitness Expose of the Rise of Mormonism. Archer, Gleason L., tr. from Danish.
Ahmed, A. S. Millenium & Charisma among Pathans: A Critical Essay in Social Anthroplogy.
Ahmed, N. & Rao, K. R. Orthogonal Transforms for Digital Signal Processing.
Ahmed, Osman S. The Potential Effects of Income Redistribution on Selected Growth Constraints: A Case Study of Kenya.
Ahmed, Paul I., jt. ed. see Plog, Stanley C.
Ahmed, Sadiq. Shadow Prices for Economic Appraisal of Projects: An Application to Thailand.
Aho, Gary L. William Morris: A Reference Guide.
Aho, Jennifer J. & Petras, John W. Learning About Sex: A Guide for Children & Their Parents.
Ahr, Albert H. Democracy at Its Best: America's Hope - the People's Branch of Government.
Ahrens, C. Donald. Meteorology Today.
Ahrens, Donald L., et al. Concrete & Concrete Masonry.
Ahrens, L., jt. auth. see Schlesselman, R.
Ahrens, L. H. Ionization Potentials: Some Variations, Implications & Applications.
--Origin & Distribution of the Elements: First & Second Symposium.
--Physics & Chemistry of the Earth.
Ahrland, S; see Dunitz, J. D., et al.
Ahrland, S., et al. The Chemistry of the Actinides.
Ahuja, C. Tragedy, Modern Temper & O'Neill.
Ahuja, Narendra & Schachter, Bruce J. Pattern Models.
Ahumada, Rodolfo. A History of Western Ontology from Thales to Heidegger.
Ai. Cruelty.
--Killing Floor.
Aichele, Douglas B. & Olson, Melfried. Geometric Selections for Elementary & Middle School Teachers.
Aichele, Douglas B. & Reys, Robert E. Readings in Secondary School Mathematics.
Aichele, George, Jr. The Limits of Story.
Aicken, Frederick. The Nature of Science.
Aiello, Greg, jt. auth. see Perkins, Steve.
Aifantis, E. C. & Davison, L., eds. Media with Microstructures & Wave Propagation: Proceedings of the Conference, Houghton, MI, January 1983.
Aigler, Ralph W., et al. Cases on Property.
Aigner, Kurt W. Allistar: Journey Through a Mind.
Aigner, M. Combinatorial Theory.
Aijmer, Goran. Economic Man in Sha Tin: Vegetable Gardeners in a Hong Kong Valley.
Aikawa, Masamichi & Sterling, Charles R. Intracellular Parasitic Protozoa.
Aiken, Conrad. Great Circle.
Aiken, Joyce. The Portable Needlepoint Boutique.
Aiken, Joyce & Laury, Jean Ray. The Total Tote Bag Book: Designer Totes to Craft & Carry.
Aiken, Joyce, jt. auth. see Laury, Jean R.
Aiken, Lewis R. Later Life.
Aiken, Miles & Rowe, Peter. American Football: The Records.
Aiken, S. R. & Leigh, C. H. Development & Environment in Peninsular Malaysia.
Aikman, David. Pacific Rim: Area of Change, Area of Opportunity.
Aikman, Ralph & Schwartz, Rachel. Life Cycle Cost Analysis Handbook.
AIME Annual Meeting Staff. Structure & Properties of Dual-Phase Steels: Proceedings of the AIME Annual Meeting, New Orleans, 1979. Kot, R. A. & Morris, J. W., eds.
AIME Staff. Advanced Fibers & Composites for Elevated Temperatures: Proceedings of the AIME Annual Meeting, New Orleans, 1979. Ahmad, Iqbal & Norton, Bryan, eds.
--Microbiological Effects on Metallurgical Processes: Proceedings of the AIME Annual Meeting, 114th, New York, February, 1985. Haas, L. A. & Clum, J. A., eds.
--Theory of Alloy Phase Formation: Proceedings of the AIME Annual Meeting, New Orleans, 1979. Bennett, L. H., ed.
--Toughness Characterization & Specifications for HSLA and Structural Steels: Proceedings of the AIME Annual Meeting, Atlanta, 1977. Mangonon, P. L., Jr., ed.
AIME Staff, jt. auth. see TMS Staff.
Ainslie, Tom. Ainslie's Complete Guide to Thoroughbred Racing.
--Ainslie's Complete Guide to Thoroughbred Racing.
--Ainslie's New Complete Guide to Harness Racing.
Ainsworth, Charles H., ed. Selected Readings for Introductory Anthropology.
--Selected Readings for Introductory Sociology.
--Selected Readings for Marriage & the Family.
Ainsworth, Stanley. Stuttering: What It Is & What to Do About It.
Ainsworth, W. A. Mechanisms of Speech Recognitions.
Ainsztein, R., tr. see Simonov, Konstantin M.
Ai Qing. Selected Poems of Ai Qing. Eyoang, Eugene C., et al, eds.

Air Conditioning & Refrigeration Institute Staff. Refrigeration & Air Conditioning.
Air Pollution Control Association. Air Pollution Meteorology.
--Control of Air Emissions from Coke Plants: Proceedings of the Air Pollution Control Association, Technical Conference, Pittsburgh, PA, 1979.
--Electrostatic Precipitation of Fly Ash.
--Recognition of Air Pollution Injury to Vegetation: A Pictorial Atlas.
Air Pollution Control Association Government Affairs Seminar, 8th Washington, D.C. 1980. Summary of the Eighth APCA Government Affairs Seminar.
Air Pollution Control Association Government Affairs Seminar, 7th, Washington, D.C., 1979. Summary of the Seventh APCA Government Affairs Seminar.
Air Pollution Control Association Specialty Conference. Air Pollution Control in the Iron & Steel Industry: Proceedings, San Francisco, Ca., Jan 1981.
--Dispersion Modeling from Complex Sources: Proceedings, St. Louis, Mo., April 1981.
--Economic Incentives for Clean Air: Proceedings, San Francisco, Ca., Jan, 1981.
--Waste Treatment & Disposal Aspects: Combustion & Air Pollution Control Processes.
Air Pollution Control Association Specialty Conference, Anaheim, CA, 1978. Emission Factors & Inventories.
Air Pollution Control Association Specialty Conference, Minneapolis, 1978. Handbook of Methodology for the Assessment of Air Pollution Effects on Vegetation.
Air Pollution Control Association Specialty Conference, New York, 1977. Hydrocarbon Control Feasibility: Its Impact on Air Quality.
Air Pollution Control Association Specialty Conference, Pittsburgh, PA, 1980. Operation & Maintenance of Gas Cleaning Equipment.
Air Pollution Control Association Specialty Conference, Houston, 1979. Ozone Oxidants: Interactions with the Total Environment II.
Air Pollution Control Association Specialty Conference. The Proposed SOx & Particulate Standard: Proceedings, Atlanta, Ga.
Air Pollution Control Association Specialty Conference, New Orleans, 1979. Quality Assurance in Air Pollution Measurement.
Air Pollution Control Association Specialty Conference, Danvers, MA & Seattle, WA, 1980. Technical Basis for a Size-Specific Particulate Standard.
Air Pollution Control Association Specialty Conference, Cambridge, MA. Toxic Substances in the Air Environment.
Air Pollution Control Association Specialty Conference, Niagara Falls, NY, 1978. The User & Fabric Filtration Equipment III.
Air Pollution Control Association Specialty Conference, Denver, 1979. View on Visibility: Regulatory & Scientific.
Air Pollution Control Association Technical Conference, Niagara Falls, N.Y., Oct. 1980. Toxic Air Contaminants: Health Effects, Monitoring & Control.
Aird, Catherine. Dead Liberty.
--Slight Mourning.
Airey, Dennis D. Basic Mathematics.
Airey, Stephen, et al. Messer Rondo & Other Stories by Gay Men.
Airey, T., et al, eds. Aircraft Erecting.
Airguide Publications Staff. Flight Guide Airport & Frequency Manual, Vol. 2: Eastern & Central States. Navarre, Monte, ed.
Aisenberg, Alan C. Glycolysis & Respiration of Tumors.
Aiserman, Mark A., et al. Logic, Automata & Algorithms.
AISLIN Staff & Sarrazin, Johan. Tootle.
Aitchison, Ian J. & Paton, J. E., eds. Progress in Nuclear Physics, Vol. 13: Rudolf Peierls & Theoretical Physics - Proceedings of the Peierls Symposium.
Aitchison, Jean. The Articulate Mammal: An Introduction to Psycholinguistics.
Aitken, C., ed. Psychosomatics & Pleasure: Proceedings of the Twenty-Third Annual Conference of the Society for Psychosomatic Research Held at the Royal College of Physicians, London, 19-20 November 1979.
Aitken, D. J., ed. see International Association of Universities Staff.
Aitken, F. C. & Wilson, W. K., eds. Rabbit Feeding for Meat & Fur.
Aitken, G. W., ed. Optical Engineering for Cold Environments.
Aitken, Gloria S., ed. see Stone, Hannah & Stone, Abraham.
Aitken, Hugh G., ed. Conference on the State & Economic Growth, New York, 1956.
Aitken-Swan, Jean. Fertility Control & the Medical Profession.
Aitkin, Don, ed. Surveys of Australian Political Science.
Aitkin, Lindsay, jt. ed. see Syka, Josef.
Aitmatov, C. Tales of the Mountains & the Steppes.
Aitmatov, Chinghiz. The Scaffold. Ward, Natasha, tr. from Rus.
Aitmatov, Chingiz & Mukhamedzhanov, Kaltai. The Ascent of Mount Fuji.
Aivanhov, Omraam M. Know Thyself: Jnani Yoga.
Aiyer, Arjun, et al. Bibliographic Specifications for Display: University of California Union Catalog.
Aizcorbe, Roberto. Argentina, the Peronist Myth: An Essay on the Cultural Decay in Argentina After the Second World War.
Ajaya, Swami, ed. Psychology East & West.
Akagha, Fidelis S. Strategies for Economic Development in Africa: Theory & Policies.
Akana, Akaiko, tr. see Kaaiakamanu, D. M. & Akina, J. K.
Akcasu, Ziya, et al. Mathematical Methods in Nuclear Reactor Dynamics.
Akens, David S. World's Greatest Leaders: The Akens Book of Supernatural Records.
Akenson, Donald H. Between Two Revolutions: Islandmagee County Antrim, Seventeen Ninety-Eight to Nineteen Twenty.
--A Protestant in Purgatory: Richard Whately, Archbishop of Dublin.
Aker, Sharon Z. Microsoft BASIC Programming for the Mac.
Akert, K., ed. Biological Order & Brain Organization: Selected Works of W. R. Hess.
Akeson, A. & Ehrenburg, A. Structure & Function of Oxidation Reduction Enzymes.
Akhadov, Ya Y. Dielectric Properties of Binary Solutions: A Data Handbook.
Akhmanova, O. S., et al. Exact Methods in Linguistic Research. Haynes, David G. & Mohr, Dolores V., trs.
Akhmatova, Anna. Requiem & Poem Without a Hero. Thomas, D. M., tr. from Rus.
--Way of All the Earth. Thomas, D. M., tr. from Rus.
Akimov, Yu K. Scintillation Counters in High Energy Physics.
Akimushkin, I. Adonde? y Como?
--Rare Animals.
Akin, Herbert L. Clergy Compensation & Financial Planning Workbook.
Akin, J. E. & Gray, W. H., eds. Computer Technology in Fusion Energy Research: PVP-PB-31.
Akina, J. K., jt. auth. see Kaaiakamanu, D. M.
Akiyama, Terukazu, et al. Arts of China, Vol. 1: Neolithic Cultures to the T'ang Dynasty.
Akmajian, Adrian. Aspects of the Grammar of Focus in English. Hankamer, Jorge, ed.
Akrasanee, Narongchai, ed. ASEAN-Japan Relations: Trade & Development.
Akrigg, George P. Jacobean Pageant: The Court of King James First.
Akroyd, Robert. A Guide to Contracting for the Sale of Goods.
Aksenov, Vasily. Pravo na Ostrov.
Aksyonov, Vasily, et al, eds. Metropol: A Literary Almanac.
Aksyonov, Vassily. The Island of Crimea. Heim, Michael H., tr.
Akutagawa, Ryunosuke. Exotic Japanese Stories.
--Japanese Short Stories. Kojima, Takashi, tr.
Akyuz, O., jt. auth. see Odabasi, Halis.
Al Fateh Staff & IFAC Staff. Automatic Control in Desalination & the Oil Industry, Appropriate Applications: Proceedings of the Al Fateh-IFAC Workshop, 1st, Tripoli, Libya, May 1980. El Hares, H. & Dali, T., eds.
ALA see American Library Association.
Alabaster, Oliver. The Power of Prevention: Reduce Your Risk of Cancer Through Diet & Nutrition.
--What You Can Do to Prevent Cancer.
Al-Abdul-Razzak, Fatimah H. Marine Resources of Kuwait: Their Role in the Development of Non-Oil Resources.
Aladjem, Henrietta. Understanding Lupus: What It Is, How to Treat It, How to Cope with It.
Alan, Ray. The Beirut Pipeline.
Alan Sloan, Inc., jt. auth. see Sea World Press Staff.
Aland, Barbara, jt. auth. see Aland, Kurt.
Aland, Kurt. Four Reformers: Luther, Melanchthon, Zwingli, Calvin. Schaaf, James L., tr.
Aland, Kurt & Aland, Barbara. The Text of the New Testament: An Introduction to the Critical Editions & to the Theory & Practice of Modern Textual Criticism.
Al-Asfour, Taiba A. Changing Sea-Level along the North Coast of Kuwait Bay.
Alaska Geographic Staff, ed. The Aleutians.
Alaska Northwest Books Staff. Alaska Almanac 1989: Facts about Alaska.
Alaska Northwest Publishing Staff, ed. The Alaska Almanac, 1986.
Alaska Northwest Publishing Staff. Alaska Milepost 1987.
--The Alaska Wilderness Milepost 1988.
--The Milepost.
Alaska Northwest Publishing Staff, ed. Northwest Mileposts, 1986.
Alaska Northwest Publishing Staff. Wilderness Milepost 1987.
Alaszewski, Andy. Institutional Care & the Mentally Handicapped: The Mental Handicap Hospital.
Alaszewski, Andy, jt. auth. see Ayer, Sam.
Alaszewski, Andy, jt. auth. see Haywood, Stuart.
Alatis, James E., et al, eds. Georgetown University Round Table on Language & Linguistics: Applied Linguistics & the Preparation of Second Language Teachers- Toward a Rationale.
Alauddin, Mohammad & Faruqee, Rashid. Population & Family Planning in Bangladesh: A Study of the Research.
Alavi, Hamza, et al. Capitalism & Colonial Production: Essays on the Rise of Capitalism in Asia.
Alavi, Y. & Lick, D. R., eds. Theory & Applications of Graphs: Proceedings, Michigan, May 11-15, 1976.
Alavi, Y., et al, eds. see Conference on Graph Theory Staff.
Alawar, Mohamed A. A Concise Bibliography of Northern Chad & Fezzan in Southern Libya.
Alaxander, Frank, ed. see Levin, Beatrice.
Al Bahanna, H. M. The Arabian Gulf States: Their Legal & Political Status.
Albaiges, J., jt. auth. see International Congress on Analytical Techniques in Environmental Chemistry Staff.
Albaiges, J., ed. see International Congress on Analytical Techniques in Environmental Chemistry Staff.
Albanese, Catherine L. King Crockett: Nature & Civility on the American Frontier.
Albanese, Jay S. Organized Crime in America.
Albanese, Joseph & Bond, Thomas. Drug Interactions: Basic Principles & Clinical Problems.
Albanese, Robert. Managing: Toward Accountability for Performance.
Albanese, Rosetta T. One Thousand One Temple Avenue.
Albano, Peter. Second Voyage of Seventh Carrier.
Albanse, Robert & Van Fleet, David D. Organizational Behavior: A Managerial Viewpoint.
Albany, Eric A., ed. see Nuffield Foundation Staff.
Al-Bashir, Faisal Safooq. A Structural Econometric Model of the Saudi Arabian Economy: Nineteen Sixty to Nineteen Seventy.
Albaugh, Dan & Lemke, Bob. Sports Collectors' Digest Baseball Cards Price Guide.
--Sports Collectors Digest Baseball Price Card Guide.
Albee, Edward. All Over.
--Box. Bd. with Quotations from Chairman Mao Tse-Tung. Macmillan.
--Delicate Balance.
--The Plays, Vol. 4: Everything in the Garden, Malcolm, the Ballad of the Sad Cafe.
Albee, Edward A. Everything in the Garden.
--Malcolm.
--Seascape.
--Tiny Alice.
Albee, Edward A. & McCullers, Carson. The Ballad of the Sad Cafe.
Alben, Alex. Our Man in Mongoa.
Alberger, Particia L., ed. Winning Techniques for Athletic Fund Raising.
Alberger, Patricia, jt. ed. see Carter, Virginia L.
Alberger, Patricia L., jt. ed. see Smith, Virginia C.
Alberione, James. A Month with St. Paul.
--The Spirit in My Life.
Alberman, E. D. & Peckham, C. A., eds. Childhood Epidemiology.
Alberni, Arturo. Eternal Duality.
Alberry, Nicholas, ed. How to Save the World: A Fourth World Guide to the Politics of Scale.
Albers, V. Underwater Sound.
Albert, Cecelia A., ed. World Economic Data: A Compendium of Current Economic Information for All Countries of the World.
Albert, Ethel M., jt. ed. see Vogt, Evon Z.
Albert, Harold. Shape Up.
Albert, Helen M. Serving Successful Salads: A Merchandising Cookbook.
Albert, Martin L., jt. auth. see Obler, Loraine K.
Albert, Marvin. The Medusa Complex.
Albert, Marvin H. The Gargoyle Conspiracy.
--Operation Lila.
Albert, Rosamond T. Sonata.
Albert, Roy E. Thorium: Its Industrial Hygiene Aspects.
Alberti, Barbara. Delirium. Venuti, Lawrence, tr. from Ital.
Alberti, K. G., jt. ed. see Karran, S. J.
Alberti, K. H., jt. ed. see Marks, V.
Alberti, Leon B. De Re Aedificatoria.
Alberti, Robert E. & Emmons, Michael L. Your Perfect Right: A Guide to Assertive Living.
Alberts, Bruce & Fox, C. Fred, eds. Mechanistic Studies of DNA Replication & Genetic Recombination.
Alberts, Robert C. Benjamin West: A Biography.
Alberty, Robert A. Physical Chemistry.
Albery, Nobuko. The House of Kanze.
Albeverio, S. A. & Hoegh-Krohn, R. J. Mathematical Theory of Feynman Path Integrals.
Albin, Francis M. Consumer Economics & Personal Money Management.
Albin, Len. Secrets of the Video Game Superstars.
Albinski, Henry S. Australian Policies & Attitudes Toward China.
Albohm, Marjorie J. Management of Sports Injuries for Women.
Albon, jt. auth. see Bennett.
Albrand, Martha. Endure No Longer.
--None Shall Know.
--The Obsession of Emmet Booth.
--Remembered Anger.
--Wait for the Dawn.
--Without Orders.
Albrecht, Bob, et al. How to Play with Your Timex Sinclair 1000.
--Atari BASIC.
Albrecht, Gary L. & Higgins, Paul C. Health, Illness & Medicine: A Reader in Medical Sociology.
Albrecht, Karl. Learn to Improve Your Thinking Skills.
--Organization Development: A Total Systems Approach to Positive Change in Any Business Organization.
Albrecht, P., jt. ed. see Birch, C.
Albrecht-Carrie, Rene. Europe after Eighteen Fifteen.
--France, Europe & the Two World Wars.
Albright, David E., ed. Communism in Africa.
Albright, John & Schaeffer, Elizabeth. AutoCAD Standards for Architects & Engineers.
Albright, Verne. Horseback Across Three Americas.
Albritton, Claude C. Philosophy of Geohistory.
Albuquerque, E. X. & Eldefrawi, A. T., eds. Myasthenia Gravis.
Alburey, Pat. Harrods Book of Cakes & Desserts.
Alburger, Mary A. Scottish Fiddlers & Their Music.
Alcalay, Ammiel, tr. see Kis, Danilo.
Alcalay, Klara, tr. see Kis, Danilo.
Alcamo, Yana I. Dimensions Interwoven.
Alcega, Juan de see De Alcega, Juan.
Alcock, John. Animal Behavior: An Evolutionary Approach.
Alcock, Randal H. Botanical Names for English Readers.
Alcock, Roy. The Feedback Loop.
Alcock, Vivien. The Cuckoo Sister.
--Travelers by Night.
Alcorn, Alfred. The Pull of the Earth.
Alcorn, John, jt. auth. see Hine, Al.
Alcorn, John, jt. auth. see Joslin, Sesyle.
Alcorn, Maria D. Elasticidades Poeticas.
Alcorn, Pat. Success & Survival in the Family Owned Business.
Alcorn, Wallace. Momentum.
--Teacher's Guide to Elijah: Prophet of God.
Alcott, Louisa May. Hospital Sketches.
--Jo's Boys.
--Little Women.
--Old-Fashioned Girl.
Alcover, Madeleine, et al. Studies in French.
Alda, Alan, jt. auth. see Alda, Arlene.
Alda, Arlene. Matthew & His Dad.
--Sonya's Mommy Works. Klimo, Kate, ed.
Alda, Arlene & Alda, Alan. The Last Days of Mash.
Aldcroft, Derek, jt. auth. see Freeman, Michael.
Alden, Peter & Gooders, John. Finding Birds Around the World.
Alden, Raymond M. A Shakespeare Handbook.
Alden, Robert L. Proverbs: A Commentary on an Ancient Book of Timeless Advice.
Alden, Ruth. Guide to Private Schools of the Northeast.
Alder, Jim. Guide to Services Selection in Low Rise Buildings.
Alder, Kurt & Winther, Aage, eds. Coulomb Excitation: A Collection of Reprints.
Alderfer, Clayton, jt. ed. see Cooper, Cary L.
Alder-Karlsson, G. The Political Economy of East-West-South Cooperation.
Alderman, Clifford L. You Can Be a Writer: A Career & Leisure Guide.
Alderman, Geoffrey. British Elections.
Alderman, John. Imagine Me.
Alderson, Brian, compiled by. Cakes & Custards: Children's Rhymes.
Alderson, Brian, tr. see Andersen, Hans Christian & Grandfather Drewsen.
Alderson, Michael. International Mortality Statistics.
--An Introduction to Epidemiology.
Alderson, P. G., jt. auth. see Withers, Lyndsey A.
Aldgate, Anthony & Richards, Jeffrey. Britain Can Take It: The British Cinema in the Second World War.
Al-Din, Shaykh M. The Rising of al-Husayn: Its Impact on the Consciousness of Muslim Society. Howard, I. K., tr.
Aldington, Richard, tr. see De Laclos, Choderlos.
Aldis, Dorothy. Nothing Is Impossible: The Story of Beatrix Potter.

Aldiss, Brian. Enemies of the System.
--Neanderthal Planet.
--Starship.
Aldiss, Brian, ed. Galactic Empires.
--Galactic Empires.
Aldiss, Brian W. Helliconia Summer.
--Helliconia Winter.
--Seasons in Flight.
Aldous, Joan. Two Paychecks: Life in Dual Earner Families.
Aldred, Cyril. Tutankhamun's Egypt.
Aldrich, R. J. Weed-Crop Ecology: Principles in Weed Management.
Aldrich, Richard. An Introduction to the History of Education.
Aldrich, Winifred. Metric Pattern Cutting: For Menswear Including Unisex Casual Clothes.
Aldridge, Alan, ed. Beatles Illustrated Lyrics.
--Beatles Illustrated Lyrics.
Aldridge, Betty. You Can Teach Preschoolers Successfully.
Aldridge, John W. After the Lost Generation.
Aldridge, Josephine H. Best of Friends.
--Penny & a Periwinkle.
Aldridge, Meryl. British New Towns: A Programme Without a Policy.
Aldridge, Robert C. The Counterforce Syndrome: A Guide to United States Nuclear Weapons & Strategic Doctrine.
Aldskogius, H. Indirect & Direct Wallerian Degeneration in the Intramedullary Root Fibers of the Hypoglossal Nerve: An Electron Microscopal Study in the Kitten.
Aldwell, Edward & Schachter, Carl. Harmony & Voice Leading.
--Harmony & Voice Leading.
Aldyne, Nathan. Vermilion.
Alechinsky, Pierre. Pierre Alechinsky; les Estampes, 1946-1972.
Alefeld, G. & Crigorieff, R. D., eds. Fundamentals of Numerical Computation: International Conference.
Alefeld, G. & Voelkl, J., eds. Hydrogen in Metals I: Basic Properties.
Alegret Sanroma, Salvador. Doccionari De L'utillatage Quimic.
Alegria, Fernando. Instructions for Undressing the Human Race.
Alegria, Ricardo E., ed. Three Wishes: A Collection of Puerto Rican Folktales. Culbert, Elizabeth, tr.
Aleixandre, Vicente. A Bird of Paper: Poems of Vicente Aleixandre. Barnstone, Willis & Garrison, David, trs. from Span.
Aleksander, I., ed. Artificial Vision for Robots.
Aleksander, Igor. The Human Machine: A View of Intelligent Mechanisms.
Aleksander, Igor, ed. Computing Techingues for Robots.
Aleksandrov, I. V. Theory of Nuclear Magnetic Resonance.
Alekseeva, G. V. Professor Dowell's Head.
Alembert, Jean L. D' see D' Alembert, Jean L.
Aler, Jan, ed. Proceedings of the Fifth International Congress of Aesthetics.
Alerich, Walter. Electric Motor Control.
--Electric Motor Control.
Alert, Daniel M., jt. auth. see Scheie, Harold G.
Alesen, Lewis A. Mental Robots.
--Physician's Responsibility As a Leader.
Aleshin, V. G., jt. auth. see Nemoshkalenko, V. V.
Alesi, Gladys & Pantell, Dora. Family Life in the U. S. A.
Alessandra, Anthony J., jt. auth. see Hunsacker, Philip.
Alessio, jt. auth. see Bilas.
Aletrino, L. Six World Religions. Foran, Mary, tr.
Aleveyev, M. Cherry Pool.
Alex, Ben, jt. auth. see Alex, Marlee.
Alex, Marlee & Alex, Ben. I Love You.
--A Parent's Journey into Magic Moments in the Kingdom of Kids.
Alexander, Anne. Connie.
Alexander, Bruce, ed. Crafts & Craftsmen.
Alexander, C. H. & Beach, T. J. Learn Chess: A New Way for All.
Alexander Communications, Inc. Staff. The Vice Book.
Alexander, David M. The Chocolate Spy.
Alexander, David P. & Perlick, Walter W. Introduction to Business: Workbook.
Alexander, Dorothy L. Effective Compensatory Eduction Sourcebook, Vol. 3: Project Profiles.
Alexander, F. Matthias. The Resurrection of the Body. Maisel, Edward, ed.
Alexander, Frank. How to Make Your Own Trail Wines.
--I'm in Love with a Mannequin.
Alexander, Franz. Fundamentals of Psychoanalysis.
--Psychoanalysis & Psychotherapy.
--Psychosomatic Medicine.
Alexander, Guy B. Chromatography: An Adventure in Graduate School.
Alexander, H. G. Leibniz-Clarke Correspondence.
Alexander Hamilton Institute,Inc. Financial Sourcebook.
Alexander, Herbert E. Financing Politics, Money, Elections & Political Reform.
Alexander, Holmes. With Friends Possessed.
Alexander, J., et al. Urban Planning: A Guide to Information Sources.
Alexander, J. Estill & Filler, Ronald C. Attitudes & Reading.
Alexander, J. P., et al. Odd Order Group Actions & Witt Classification of Innerproducts.
Alexander, James I. Blue Coats-Black Skin: The Black Experience in New York City Police Department Since 1891.
Alexander, Jann, jt. auth. see Babb, Drew.
Alexander, John W. & Gibson, L. Economic Geography.
Alexander, Lamar. Steps along the Way: A Governor's Scrapbook.
Alexander, Laurence, ed. Downtown Planning & Development Annual, 1977.
Alexander, Laurence A., ed. Downtown Mall Annual & Urban Design Report.
--Promoting Effectively for Downtown Business: Dynamic New Case Studies.
--Strategies for Stopping Shopping Centers: A Guidebook on Minimizing Excessive Shopping Center Growth.
Alexander, Lester, ed. Beyond Words.
Alexander, Lewis M. Marine Regionalism in the Southeast Asian Seas.
Alexander, Lloyd. Time Cat.
Alexander, Lynne. Safe Houses.
Alexander, Margaret F. Learning to Nurse: Integrating Theory & Practice.
Alexander, Marjory. The Way to Worship.
Alexander, Mary J. Designing Interior Environment.
Alexander, Matilda. Judges.
Alexander, Michael & Anand, Shushila. Queen Victoria's Maharajah: Duleep Singh, 1838-1893.
Alexander, Michael, ed. Old English Literature.
Alexander, Mike, jt. auth. see Boag, David.
Alexander, Miles J., jt. auth. see Practicing Law Institute Staff.
Alexander, Nancy. Father of Texas Geology: Robert T. Hill.
Alexander, Nancy J., jt. auth. see Parakkal, P. F.
Alexander, P., jt. auth. see Bacq, Z. M.
Alexander, Pat, ed. The Lion Encyclopedia of the Bible.
Alexander, Patricia & Muia, Joseph. Gifted Education: A Comprehensive Roadmap.
Alexander, Patsy R. Textile Products: Selection, Use & Care.
Alexander, Paul. Sri Lankan Fishermen: Rural Capitalism & Peasant Society.
Alexander, Peter. Introductions to Shakespeare.
Alexander, Peter & Gill, Roger, eds. Utopias.
Alexander, R. & Steinbach, A. Faith & Love.
Alexander, R. McNeill. Locomotion of Animals.
Alexander, Robert J. Communist Party of Venezuela.
Alexander, Roy. Mehdi: Nothing Is Impossible.
Alexander, Roy, jt. auth. see Newman, James A.
Alexander, Shana. Dangerous Games.
--Nutcracker: Money, Madness, Murder-A Family Album.
--Nutcracker: Money, Madness, Murder, A Family Album.
--Very Much a Lady: The Untold Story of Jean Harris & Dr. Herman Tarnower.
Alexander, Sue. Dear Phoebe.
--Small Plays for You & a Friend.
Alexander, Thomas G., jt. auth. see Arrington, Leonard J.
Alexander, Thomas G., ed. Soul Butter & Hog Wash & Other Essays on the American West.
Alexander, Thomas G., jt. ed. see Poll, Richard D.
Alexander, Virginia & Elliott, Colleen M. Pendleton District & Anderson County, S. C. Wills, Estates & Legal Records, 1793 to 1857.
Alexander, W. Film on the Left: American Documentary Film from 1931 to 1942.
Alexander, W. C. Short Synopsis of the Most Essential Points in Hawaiian Grammar.
Alexander, William T. History of the Colored Race in America, Containing Also Their Ancient & Modern Life in Africa, the Origin & Development of Slavery, the Civil War.
Alexander, Yonah, jt. auth. see Kilmarx, Robert A.
Alexander, Yonah & Finger, Seymour M., eds. Terrorism: Interdisciplinary Perspectives.
Alexander, Yonah, jt. ed. see Rapoport, David C.
Alexander, Zane. Till Death Do Us Part or Something Else Comes up.
Alexandrov, Victor. Khrushchev of the Ukraine.
Alexeyev, M. Men at War.
Alexeyev, R. USSR-FRG Relations: A New Stage.
Alexeyev, S. Stories about Magnitka. Belskaya, Natalia, tr.
Alexis Pub. Staff. Extraordinaire: Little Tidbits.
Al-Farsy, Fouad. Saudi Arabia: A Case Study in Development.
Alfers, et al. America's Second Century: Topical Readings, 1865-Present.
Alfert, M., et al, eds. see Branton, D. & Deamer, D. W.
Alfert, M., et al, eds. see Satir, P.
Alfian. Political Science in Indonesia.
Alfidi, jt. auth. see Haaga.
Alfidi, Ralph J., jt. ed. see Haaga, John R.
Alfonsi, Ferdinando P. & Alfonsi, Sandra R. An Annotated Bibliography of Moravia Criticism in Italy & the English-Speaking World.
Alfonsi, Sandra R., jt. auth. see Alfonsi, Ferdinando P.
Alford, Henry. The New Testament for English Readers.
Alford, John M. Children of the Dawn.
Alford, Roger C. The NSC800 Microprocessor Cookbook.
Alford, Terry. Prince among Slaves. Okrent, Daniel, ed.
Alfred, Richard L., ed. Institutional Impacts on Campus, Community, & Business Constituencies.
Algar, Ayla E. The Complete Book of Turkish Cooking.
Algebraic Topology Symposium Staff. Proceedings. Hilton, P. J., ed.
Algee, Isabelle R. Moorings - Past & Present.
Algeo, John. Problems in the Origins & Development of the English Language.
Algeo, John, jt. auth. see Pyles, Thomas.
Alger, Chadwick F. & Hoovler, David G. You & Your Community in the World.
Algermissen, Jo A. Pure Mischief.
Algier, Ann S. & Algier, Keith W., eds. Improving Reading & Study Skills.
Algier, Keith W., jt. ed. see Algier, Ann S.
Algire, Tom, photos by. Wisconsin.
Algo Publishing Staff. C Language Statement-to-Statement Dictionary.
--Intermediate Transfer Methods for Eliminating goto's from C Language Programs.
Algosaibi, Ghazi A. Arabian Essays.
--Arabian Essays.
Algozin, Bruce. Claw of the Dragon.
--Danger, Second-Hand.
Algozzine, Bob, et al. Childhood Behavior Disorders: Applied Research & Educational Practice.
Algren, Nelson. Chicago: City on the Make.
--The Devil's Stocking: A Last Interview by W. J. Weatherby.
Al-Hibri, A., ed. Hypatia.
ALI-ABA, Committee on Continuing Professional Education, jt. auth. see Computer Law Institute Staff.
ALI-ABA Committee on Continuing Professional Education & American Bar Association Committee on Continuing Professional Education. New Pension Legislation: ALI-ABA Video Law Review Study Materials.
ALI-ABA Committee on Continuing Professional Education. Planning Techniques in Divorce Transactions under the Tax Reform Act of 1984: Video Law Review Study Materials.
--Retirement Planning for Small Business & Professionals Entering the Top-Heavy & Parity Age: ALI-ABA Video Law Review Study Materials.
Ali, Agha S. Bone-Sculpture.
Ali, M. A., ed. Vision in Fishes-New Approaches in Research.
Ali, Majid, jt. ed. see Tracht, Myron E.
Ali, S. V., tr. from Arabic. The Holy Qur'an.
Ali, Waleed, jt. auth. see Cepican, Bob.
Aliaga, Barbara. Learn to Type Fast.
--Start & Run a Profitable Home Typing Business.
Aliano, Richard A. American Defense Policy from Eisenhower to Kennedy: The Politics of Changing Military Requirements, 1957-1961.
Aliber, Robert Z., ed. National Monetary Policies & the International Financial System.
Aliboni, Roberto, et al. Egypt's Economic Potential.
Alifano, Roberto, ed. Twenty-Four Conversations with Borges: Interviews by Roberto Alifano 1981-1983. Arauz, Nicomedes S., et al, trs.
--Twenty-Four Conversations with Borges: Interviews by Roberto Alifano 1981-1983. Arauz, Nicomedes S., et al, trs.
Alighieri, Dante. The New Life.
Aliki. Hush Little Baby.
--The Many Lives of Benjamin Franklin.
Alikonis, Justin J. Candy Technology.
Alinder, James. The Contact Print, Nineteen Forty-Six to Nineteen Eighty-Two.
Alinder, James, ed. Nine Critics - Nine Photographs.
Alisin, V. V., jt. auth. see Kragelsky, I. V.
Alison, A. England in Eighteen Fifteen & Eighteen Forty-Five.
Al-Jundi, Sef. A Long May; I Have Come a Long Way; I Have a Long Way to Go.
Alkemade, Cornelis T. & Herrmann, Roland. Fundamentals of Analytical Flame Spectroscopy.
Alkire, Leland G., Jr., ed. New Periodical Title Abbreviations.
--Periodical Title Abbreviations: By Abbreviation.
--Periodical Title Abbreviations: By Title.
All India Symposium Staff. Advancement of Ecology: Proceedings of the All India Symposium, Muzaffarnagar, Dec. 1976. Agarwal, V. P. & Sharma, V. K., eds.
Alla, M. Ata. Arab Sruggle for Economic Independence.
Allaback, Steven. Alexander Solzhenitsyn.
Allain, Marie-Francoise. The Other Man: Conversations with Graham Greene. Waldman, Guido, tr.
Allal, M. & Chuta, E. Cottage Industries & Handicrafts: Some Guidelines for Employment Promotion.
Allan, Elizabeth, ed. see International Association of Business Communicators Staff.
Allan, John. Mysteries.
Allan, Leslie, et al. Promised Lands 1: Subdivisions in Deserts & Mountains.
Allan, Mabel E. The Night Wind.
--Romansgrove.
Allan, Margaret. Teaching English with Video.
Allan, Mea. Darwin & His Flowers: The Key to Natural Selection.
Allan, Stella. No Marks for Trying.
Allan, W. B. Fibre Optics: Theory & Practice.
Alland, Alexander, Jr. To Be Human: An Introduction to Cultural Anthropology.
Allanson, Patrick R. Doctor at Sea.
Allard, G. F., et al, eds. High Speed Can Manufacture.
Allard, Harry. There's a Party at Mona's Tonight.
Allard, S. Metals: Thermal & Mechanical Data.
Allard, William A. Vanishing Breed: Photographs of the Cowboys & the West.
Allbeck, Willard D. Studies in the Lutheran Confessions.
Allbeury, Ted. The Alpha List.
Allbuery, Ted. Children of Tender Years.
Allchin, Bridget, et al, eds. The Prehistory & Palaeogeography of the Great Indian Desert.
Allcock, H. R. Heteroatom Ring Systems & Polymers.
Alldis, James. Animals As Friends: A Head Keeper Remembers London Zoo.
Allegretto, Michael. Death on the Rocks: A Jacob Lomax Mystery.
Allem, ed. see De Musset, Alfred.
Alleman, Herbert C., ed. New Testament Commentary: A General Introduction to & a Commentary on the Books of the New Testament.
Allen, jt. auth. see Clark.
Allen, A. The Story of Archaeology.
Allen, Arthur. Art of Preaching.
Allen, Bob. George Jones: The Saga of an American Singer.
Allen, Carol & Lustig, Herbert. Tea with Demons.
Allen, Cecil J. Modern Railways: Their Engineering, Equipment & Operation.
Allen, Chalinder. The Tyranny of Time.
Allen, Charles. A Mountain in Tibet: The Search for Mount Kailas & the Sources of the Great Rivers of Asia.
--My Lord & My God.
--Plain Tales from the Raj.
--Women Are Wonderful.
Allen, Charles L. Victory in the Valleys of Life.
Allen, Charles L. & Biggs, Mouzon. When You Graduate.
Allen, Charlotte V. Daddy's Girl.
--Destinies.
--Illusions.
--Memories.
--Pieces of Dreams.
--Time Steps.
Allen, D. J. & Imrie, P. R. Discovering the North Downs Way.
Allen, David. English Teaching Since 1965: How Much Growth?
Allen, Dick. Science Fiction: The Future.
Allen, Dick & Allen, Lori. Looking Ahead: The Vision of Science Fiction.
Allen, Diogenes. Between Two Worlds: A Guide for Those Beginning to Be Religious.
--Finding Our Father.
Allen, Donald & Butterick, George F. The Postmoderns: New American Poetry Revised.
Allen, Donald, ed. see Creeley, Robert.
Allen, Donald M. & Butterick, George F., eds. The Postmoderns: The New American Poetry Revised.
Allen, Durwood. Wolves of Minong: Their Vital Role in a Wild Community.
Allen, E. L. Christian Humanism: A Guide to the Thought of Jacques Maritain.
--Christianity & Society: A Guide to the Thoufht of Reinhold Hiebuhr.
--Great Religious Thinkers.
--Great Religious Thinkers: Creation & Grace - A Guide to the Thought of Emil Brunner.
--Great Religious Thinkers: The Self & Its Hazards - A Guide to the Thought of Karl Jaspers.
--Great Religious Thinkers: The Sovereignty of God & the Word of God - A Guide to the Thought of Karl Barth.
Allen, Edward D. & Valette, Rebecca M. Modern Language Classroom Techniques: A Handbook.
Allen, Edward D., et al. Habla Espanol: Essentials.
--Habla Espanol? An Introductory Course.
Allen, Edward Van see Van Allen, Edward.

Authors

Allen, Eliot D. & Colbrunn, Ethel B. A Short Guide to Writing a Critical Review.
--A Short Guide to Writing a Research Paper: Manuscript Form & Documentation.
--Student Writer's Guide.
Allen, Elizabeth. Misty Isles-Here, There, Nowhere Land.
Allen, Elizabeth, ed. see Noland, Ronald G., et al.
Allen, Frederick S., et al. The University of Colorado: 1876-1976.
Allen, G., et al, eds. Laboratory Techniques in Biochemistry & Molecular Biology: Vol. 9, Sequencing of Proteins & Peptides.
Allen, G. C. Japan As a Market & Source of Supply.
Allen, G. Freeman. Railways the World Over.
Allen, G. R. A Field Guide to Inland Fishes of Western Australia.
Allen, Gary. None Dare Call it Conspiracy.
Allen, Geoffrey F., ed. Jane's World Railways, 1983-1984.
--Jane's World Railways 1984-85.
--Jane's World Railways, 1985-1986.
--Jane's World Railways 1986-87.
Allen, Gerald, jt. auth. see Moore, Charles.
Allen, Gerald D., et al, eds. Dental Analgesia.
Allen, Gerald R. Damselfishes.
Allen, Gertrude E. Everyday Insects.
--Everyday Turtles, Toads, & Their Kin.
--Everyday Wildflowers.
Allen, Grant. The British Barbarians. Fletcher, Ian & Stokes, John, eds.
Allen, H. C. & Thompson, Roger, eds. Contrast & Connection: Bicentennial Essays in Anglo-American History.
Allen, H. G. Analysis & Design of Structural Sandwich Panels.
Allen, H. G. & Bulson, P. S. Background to Buckling.
Allen, H. Warner. Romance of Wine.
Allen, Harold B. Linguistic Atlas of the Upper Midwest.
--The Linguistic Atlas of the Upper Midwest.
--The Linguistic Atlas of the Upper Midwest.
--The Linguistic Atlas of the Upper Midwest.
Allen, Henry. Fool's Mercy.
Allen, Hervey. Anthony Adverse.
Allen, Horace T., Jr. A Handbook for the Lectionary.
Allen, Ida B. Best Loved Recipes of the American People.
Allen, Ira. Natural & Political History of the State of Vermont.
Allen, J., et al, eds. Grinding.
Allen, J. F. Super-Fluid Helium.
Allen, Jack & Moristo, Dennis. An Introduction to the BIA Affairs.
Allen, James. As a Man Thinketh.
--Out from the Heart.
Allen, James E. The Negro in New York.
Allen, James F. & Webber, Bonnie L. Natural Language: Beyond Single Sentence Systems.
Allen, James L. The Choir Invisible.
--Yeats's Epitaph: A Key to Symbolic Unity in His Life & Work.
Allen, James T. First Year of Greek.
Allen, Jana & Gin, Margaret. Innards & Other Variety Meats.
Allen, Jelisaveta S., ed. Dumbarton Oaks Bibliographies Based on "Byzantinische Zeitschrift"
--Dumbarton Oaks Bibliographies Based on "Byzantinische Zeitschrift" Literature on Byzantine Art 1892-1967, Vol. 2, by Categories.
Allen, Jerry. The Adventures of Mark Twain.
Allen, John. Annual Editions: Environment, 1985-86.
--Masters of British Drama.
--Masters of European Drama.
--The Nineteen Eighty-Eight Summer Theater Guide, from an Actor's Viewpoint.
Allen, John & Nelson, Mark. Space Biospheres.
Allen, John, ed. Environment 1988-89.
Allen, John E. Aerodynamics: The Science of Fluid in Motion.
Allen, John R., et al. Thinking about TLC LOGO.
Allen, Joseph P. & Martin, Russell. Entering Space: An Astronaut's Odyssey.
Allen, June, tr. see Garin, Eugenio.
Allen, K. Eileen & Goetz, Elizabeth M. Early Childhood Education: Special Problems, Special Solutions.
Allen, K. Eileen, jt. ed. see Goetz, Elizabeth M.
Allen, Keith, jt. ed. see Stavrakas, Nick.
Allen, L. Essentials of Lasers.
Allen, L. E. Great Religious Thinkers: Freedom in God.
Allen, Lori, jt. auth. see Allen, Dick.
Allen, Louis A. Management Profession.
Allen, M. W. & Noffsinger, Ella M. A Revision of the Marine Nematodes of the Superfamily Draconematoidea Filipjev, 1918 (Nematoda: Draconematina)
Allen, Marjorie N. One, Two, Three---Ah-Choo!
Allen, Mark. Chrysalis: A Journey into the New Spiritual America.
--Seeds to the Wind: Poems, Songs, Meditations.
Allen, Marshall B., Jr., ed. see Pituitary Symposium Staff.
Allen, Martin. Particular Friendships.
--Red Saturday.
Allen, Mary B., ed. Comparative Biochemistry of Photoreactive Systems.
Allen, Maury, jt. auth. see Pinella, Lou.
Allen, Mearle L. Welcome to the Stork Club.
Allen, Michael & Mokherjee, Sal. Women in India & Nepal.
Allen, Michael, ed. Vanuatu: Politics, Economics & Ritual in Island Melanesia.
Allen, Michael G. & McEwin, Kenneth. Middle Level Social Studies: From Theory to Practice.
Allen, Morse S., jt. auth. see Hughes, Arthur H.
Allen, Nancy. Film Study Collections: A Guide to Their Development & Use.
Allen, Norman. New Century Vest-Pocket: Webster Dictionary.
Allen, Oliver E., jt. auth. see Crocket, James U.
Allen, Opal S. Narcissa Whitman.
Allen, P. Sales & Sales Management.
Allen, P. C. & MacLeod, A. B. Rails in the Isle of Wight.
Allen, P. David & Watson, Dorothy J., eds. Findings of Research in Miscue Analysis: Classroom Implications.
Allen, Pat, ed. see Levine, Mark L.
Allen, Patricia, ed. see Scavo, Janet.
Allen, Paul M., intro. by see Steiner, Rudolf, et al.
Allen, Paula G. The Sacred Hoop: Recovering the Feminine in American Indian Traditions.
Allen, Peter, ed. The Office Supply Industry.
Allen, R. Colour Chemistry.
Allen, R. Earl. Let It Begin in Me.
Allen, Randy L. Bottom Line Issues in Retailing.
Allen, Richard C., jt. auth. see Shampine, Lawrence F.
Allen, Richard E., tr. see Konrad, George.
Allen, Richard E., tr. see Konrad, George & Szelenyi, Ivan.
Allen, Richard S. Old North Country Bridges: Upstate New York.
Allen, Richard V., ed. Yearbook on International Communist Affairs, 1969.
Allen, Roach V. Language Experiences in Communication.
Allen, Robert. How to Save the World.
Allen, Robert D. & Kamiya, Noburo, eds. Primitive Motile Systems in Cell Biology.
Allen, Robert G. Creating Wealth.
--Nothing Down.
Allen, Rodger van see Van Allen, Rodger.
Allen, Rodney F. Energy Education: Goals & Practices.
Allen, Rosemary & Purkis, Andrew. Health in the Round: Voluntary Action & Antenatal Services.
Allen, Ross. How to Keep Snakes in Captivity.
Allen, Rowena, tr. & illus. see Fisher, Robert.
Allen, Ruth. What's the Matter with Christy?
Allen, T. O. & Roberts, Alan P. Production Operations.
Allen, Thomas, jt. auth. see Polmar, Norman.
Allen, Thomas B., jt. auth. see Polmar, Norman.
Allen, Thomas B., et al. America's Wildlife Sampler.
--Earth's Amazing Animals. Parker, Cecilia I., ed.
Allen, Tony J. Computer Courses for Adults: Anxious Human Meets Computer (A Resource Book for Instructors)
Allen, Vernon L., ed. Children As Teachers: Theory & Research on Tutoring.
Allen, Walter. As I Walked Down New Grub Street.
Allen, Walter C., ed. Serial Publications in Large Libraries.
Allen, Walter P. A Cultural Checklist: A Technique for Selecting Reading Materials for Foreign Students.
Allen, William. The Fire in the Birdbath & Other Disturbances.
Allen, William D., et al. Africa & South America.
Allen-Browne, Patricia, ed. see Long, Leslie, et al.
Allende, Isabel. La Casa de los Espiritus.
Allendoerfer, Carl B., et al. Elementary Functions.
Allentuck, Andrew J. & Bivens, Gordon E. Consumer Choice: The Economics of Personal Living.
Aller, Catherine. The Challenge of Pierre Teilhard de Chardin.
Allerton, D. J. Valency & the English Verb.
Alles, jt. auth. see Rubinson.
Alles, Wesley F., jt. auth. see Eddy, James M.
Alley, Rewi. Peking Opera.
Alley, Ronald, compiled by. Catalogue of the Tate Gallery's Collection of Modern Art Other Than Works by British Artists.
Allfrey, V. G., et al, eds. Organization & Expression of Chromosomes.
Allgeier, Albert, jt. auth. see Allgeier, Elizabeth.
Allgeier, Elizabeth & Allgeier, Albert. Sexual Interactions.
Allgoewer, M. The Dynamic Compression Plate (DCP)
Allgower, M. & Perren, S. M. Internal Fixation: Basic Principles, Modern Means, Biomechanics.
Alliance Against Sexual Coersion Staff. Fighting Sexual Harassment: An Advocacy Handbook.
Alliance of Guardian Angels, Inc. Staff & Sliwa, Curtis. Street-Smart: The Guardian Angel Guide to Safe Living.
Allibone, S. Austin. Critical Dictionary of English Literature & British & American Authors.
Allibone, Samuel A. Prose Quotations from Socrates to Macauley.
Allibone, T. E. The Royal Society & Its Dining Clubs.
Allinger, Norman, et al. Topics in Stereochemistry.
Allinson, Francis G. Lucian, Satirist & Artist.
Allio, Robert J., jt. auth. see Pennington, Malcom W.
Allione, Tsultrim. Women of Wisdom.
--Women of Wisdom.
Alliot, Maurice. Le Culte d'Horus a Edfou: Au Temps des Ptolemees.
Allis, Oswald T. The Five Books of Moses.
--Prophecy & the Church.
Allison, A. F. & Goldsmith, V. F. Titles of English Books & of Foreign Books Printed in England: An Alphabetical Finding-List by Title of Books Published Under the Author's Name, Pseudonym, or Initials, 1475-1640.
--Titles of English Books & of Foreign Books Printed in England: An Alphabetical Finding-List by Title of Books Published Under the Author's Name, Pseudonym, or, Initials, Volume Two, 1641-1700.
Allison, Anne M. Factors Affecting Administration in United States Academic Libraries During the Period 1971-1975.
Allison, C. Fitzsimons & Kelber, Werner H. Epiphany.
Allison, Dale C., Jr. The End of the Ages Has Come: An Early Interpretation of the Passion & Resurrection of Jesus.
Allison, F. C., jt. auth. see Klaften, E. B.
Allison, Henry E. Kant's Transcendental Idealism: An Interpretation & Defense.
Allison, Ira S. & Palmer, Donald F. Geology: The Science of a Changing Earth.
Allison, James P., jt. ed. see Tom, Baldwin H.
Allison, Joseph D., ed. see Massey, James E.
Allison, Margaret. Indicators of Suicide & Depression Among Drug Abusers: 1979-1981.
Allison, Sonia. The Book of Microwave Cookery.
--Making Gifts with Food.
Allison, Thomas. English Religious Life in the Eighth Century.
Allison-Booth, William. Devil's Island: Revelations of the French Penal Settlements in Guiana.
Alliss, Peter. The Supreme Champions.
Allman, Margaret see Chuan, Helen.
Allman, T. D. Unmanifest Destiny.
Allon, Natalie. Urban Life Styles.
Allon, Yigal. My Father's House. Ben-Yosef, Reuven, tr. from Hebrew.
Alloway, David N., jt. ed. see Cordasco, Francesco.
Alloway, Thomas, ed. Communication & Affect-a Comparative Approach.
Allphin, McKay. Eternal Grit: Up-to-Heaven Insights & Down-to-Earth Wisdom.
Allport, Gordon W. Personality & Social Encounter: Selected Essays.
Allport, Susan. Explorers of the Black Box: The Search for the Cellular Basis of Memory.
Allsen, Philip E. Conditioning & Physical Fitness: Current Answers to Relevant Questions.
Allsen, Philip E. & Witbeck, Pete. Racquetball.
Allsop, Bruce. A History of Renaissance Architecture.
Allsopp, Bruce. A Modern Theory of Architechture.
--A Modern Theory of Architecture.
--Social Responsibility & the Responsible Society.
Allswang, John M. Macintosh: The Definitive User's Guide.
Alltounian, Howard S. & Moore, Marcia. Journeys into the Bright World: A Personal Account of the Ketamine Experience.
Allured, Michael, ed. see MC Publishing Company Staff.
Allwood, Martin S. & Wilhelmsen, Inga. Basic Swedish Word List.
Almaini, A. E. Electronic Logic Systems.
Al-Majilisi, Muhammad B. The Life & Religion of Muhammad. Merrick, James, tr.
Almansi, Guido & Henderson, Simon. Harold Pinter.
Almasi, George S. & Gottlieb, Allan. Highly Parallel Processing.
Almeder, Robert, ed. Praxis & Reason: Studies in the Philosophy of Nicholas Rescher.
Almon, Muriel, tr. see Ludwig, Otto.
Almond, Gabriel A. & Powell, G. Bingham, Jr. Comparative Politics: System, Process, & Policy.
Almond Growers Exchange Staff & Schmidt, Michelle. The New Almond Cookery.
Almond, T., tr. see Bartknecht, W.
Al-Moosa, Abdulrasool & McLachlan, Keith. Immigrant Labour in Kuwait.
Almroth, B., jt. auth. see Brush, Don O.
Al-Muminin, Amir. Supplications (Du'a) Chittick, William C., tr. from Arabic & Eng.
Al-Muzaffar, Muhammed R. The Faith of Shi'a Islam.
Almy, Millie. Early Childhood Education at Work.
Alo, R. A., et al, eds. TOPO 72: General Topology & Its Applications.
Aloi, G. Hotel-Motel (Architecture)
--Restaurants (Architecture)
--Stairs.
Aloi, R. Fifty Villas of Our Time.
--Museums: Architecture, Technics.
--Theatres & Auditoriums Architecture.
Aloi, R. & Bassi, C. Hospitals (Architecture)
Al-Otaiba, M. S. OPEC & the Petroleum Industry.
Al-Otaiba, Mana S. Essays on Petroleum.
--The Petroleum Concession Agreements of the United Arab Emirates: Adu Dhabi 1939-1981.
Al-Otaiba, Mana Saeed. Petroleum & the Economy of the United Arab Emirates.
Alotta, Robert I. Number Two: A Look at the Vice Presidency.
Alovert, Nina. Baryshnikov in Russia. Huntoon, Irene, tr. from Rus.
Alpatov, Mikhail. Russian Impact on Art.
Alpaugh, Patricia & Haney, Margaret. Counseling the Older Adult: A Training Manual.
Alper, Lynne & Holmberg, Meg. Parents, Kids & the Commodore 64.
Alperin, Stanley, ed. Directory of Medical Schools Worldwide.
--The Federal Hospital Phone Book: 1983-84.
--Hospital Phone Book 1987-88 Edition.
--U. S. Medical Directory 1983-84.
Alpers, David H., et al. Manual of Nutritional Therapeutics.
Alpert. Motor Vehicle No-Fault Law: Florida.
Alpert, George. The Queens.
Alpert, Judith L. & Meyers, Joel. Training in Consultation: Perspectives from Mental Health, Behavioral & Organizational Consultation.
Alpert, Norman. Cardiac Hypertrophy.
Alpert, Stuart W., jt. auth. see Taylor, Delores A.
Alpha Pyramis Research Division Staff. Catering Services: Creative Suggestion Pages.
Alsberg, P. In Quest of Man.
Alschuler, Alfred S. School Discipline: A Socially Literate Solution.
Alsop, Joseph W. From the Silent Earth: A Report of the Greek Bronze Age.
Alsop, Ronald & Abrams, Bill. The Wall Street Journal on Marketing.
Alsop, Stewart & Branden, Thomas. Sub Rosa: The O.S.S. & American Espionage.
Alsop, Susan M. The Congress Dances.
--Lady Sackville: A Biography.
Alspach, JoAnn G. Educational Process in Critical Care Nursing.
Alston, Edith & Cutler, David. Emergency Room: Confessions of an E. R. Doctor.
Alston, Frank M., et al. Contracting with the Federal Government.
Alston, Lee J. & Bruchey, Stuart, eds. Costs of Contracting & the Decline of Tenancy in the South, 1930-1960.
Alston, Philip, ed. see Vasek, Karel.
Alston, William P. Religious Belief & Philosophical Thought.
Alston, Y. R., jt. auth. see Coombs, J.
Alt, David & Hyndman, Donald. Rocks, Ice, & Water.
Alt, Edith, jt. auth. see Alt, Herschel.
Alt, Franz L. Electronic Digital Computers: Their Uses in Science & Engineering.
Alt, Herschel & Alt, Edith. Russia's Children.
Altabe. Temas y Dialogos.
Altabe, David F. Temas y Diálogos.
Al-Tajir, Mahdi A. Bahrain Nineteen Twenty to Nineteen Forty-Five: Britain, the Shaikh & the Administration.
Altamirano, Ignacio M. El Zarco. Grismer, Raymond L. & Ruelas, Miguel, eds.
Altasen, J., et al. Immortality.
Altbach, Philip G. Comparative Higher Education: Research Trends & Bibliography.
Altbach, Philip G. & Laufer, Robert, eds. Students Protest.
Altbach, Phillip G., et al. Comparative Education.
Altemeyer, A., jt. auth. see Bucksch, H.
Altenbernd, Lynn & Lewis, Leslie L. Handbook for the Study of Drama.
--Handbook for the Study of Poetry.
Alter, G., tr. see Ulehla, Ivan, et al.
Alter, Ida. How to Retain & Regain Your Health & Your Youth.
Alter, JoAnne. A Part-Time Career for Full-Time You.
Alter, Judy. Mattie.
Alter, M., jt. auth. see Schaumann, B.
Alter, Solomon. Solomon's Words of Wisdom.
Alter, Stephen. Silk & Steel.

Alterman, Hyman. Counting People: The Census in History.
Alterman, Ira. Do Diapers Give You Leprosy? What Every Parent Should Know about Bringing Up Babies.
--Sex Manual for People over Thirty.
Alternative Museum Staff. Adrian Piper: Reflections, 1967-1987.
--The Art of Appropriation.
--Dennis Adams: Building Against Image 1979-1987.
--Irving Norman: The Human Condition Paintings, 1965-1985.
--Rita Myers: Rift-Rise, Video Installation.
Alth, Charlotte, jt. auth. see Alth, Max.
Alth, Max & Alth, Charlotte. Disastrous Hurricanes & Tornadoes.
Althaus, Catherine & French-Hodges, Peter F. Cook Now, Dine Later.
Althoff, Victoria. Summer Break.
Althos, Anthony G., jt. auth. see Pascale, Richard T.
Althouse, Andrew & Turnquist, C. H. Modern Refrigeration & Air Conditioning.
Althouse, Larry & Althouse, Valere. You Can Save Your Breast: One Woman's Experience With Radiation Therapy.
--You Can Save Your Breast: One Woman's Experience with Radiation Therapy.
Althouse, LaVonne. When Jew & Christian Meet.
Althouse, Valere, jt. auth. see Althouse, Larry.
Altick, Richard D. Art of Literary Research.
--To Be in England.
--Victorian Studies in Scarlet.
Altimiras, J. Sailing Knots. Willis, Tom, tr.
Altimonte, Paul, jt. auth. see Labuz, Ronald A.
Altizer, Thomas J., ed. Toward a New Christianity: Readings in the Death of God Theology.
Altizer, Thomas J., jt. ed. see Griffin, David R.
Altman, Dennis. Homosexual: Oppression & Liberation.
--The Homosexualization of America.
Altman, Edward & Subrahmanyam, Marti G. Recent Advances in Corporate Finance.
Altman, Edward I. & Subrahmanyam, Marti G. Recent Advances in Corporate Finance.
Altman, Edward I., ed. Financial Handbook.
Altman, Ida & Lockhart, James, eds. Provinces of Early Mexico: Variants of Spanish American Regional Evolution.
Altman, Irwin & Wohlwill, J. F., eds. Human Behavior & Environment.
--Human Behavior & Environment, Vol. 2.
--Human Behavior & Environment, Vol. 3: Children & the Environment.
Altman, Kurt I. Radiation Biochemistry. Incl. Vol. 1. Cells. Okada, Shigefumi; Vol. 2. Tissues & Body Fluids. Altman, Kurt I. & Gerber, Georg B.. Acad Pr.
Altman, Louis. Callmann Unfair Competition, Trademarks & Monopolies: 1933-1984. Callmann, Rudolf, ed.
Altman, Moses. The Undying Swan. Mamantov, Ilya A., ed.
Altman, Nathaniel, jt. auth. see Rosa, Jose A.
Altman, Patricia B., ed. Vivan los Artesanos!
Altman, Steven & Hodgetts, Richard M. Readings in Organizational Behavior.
Altman, Stuart & Sapolsky, Harvey M., eds. Federal Health Programs: Improving the Health-Care System?
Altman, Stuart H., et al. Ambulatory Care: Problems of Cost & Access.
Altmann, et al, eds. Current Topics in Pathology.
Altmann, A. & Kleiman, S. Introduction to Grothendieck Duality Theory.
Altmann, A., ed. see Israeli, Isaac.
Altmann, S. L. Band Theory of Metals.
Altomara, Rita E. Hollywood on the Palisades: A Filmography of Silent Feaures Made in Fort Lee, New Jersey 1903-1927.
Altschul, Annie T., ed. Psychiatric Nursing.
Altshul, Selig, jt. auth. see Bender, Marylin.
Altshuler, Alan A., et al. The Urban Transportation System: Politics & Policy Innovation.
Altshuler, David, ed. see Zamir, Yaron.
Altshuler, G. see Huth, F., et al.
Altshuller, Marc, intro. by. Izbrannye Rasskazy Shestidesyatykh.
Altstein, Howard, jt. auth. see Simon, Rita J.
Al-Udhari, Abdullah. Voice Without Passport.
Al-Udhari, Abdullah, tr. Fireflies in the Dark.
--A Mirror for Autumn.
Aluko, T. M. One Man, One Matchet.
Aluri, Rao & Robinson, Judith. A Guide to U. S. Government Scientific & Technical Resources.
Alurista. Spik in Glyph?
Alvarado, Manuel & Stewart, John. Made for Television: Euston Films Limited.
Alvarez, A. The Biggest Game in Town.
Alvarez, Joseph A. From Reconstruction to Revolution: The Blacks' Struggle for Equality.
Alvarez, Julia. Homecoming. Pack, Robert, ed.
Alvarez, L. W., ed. Strong Interactions.
Alvarez, Paul, jt. ed. see Voros, Gerald J.
Alvarez, Walter C., ed. see Adam, Ruth C.
Alvarez-Gaume, L., et al, eds. Superstrings 1987: Proceedings of the Trieste Spring School on Superstrings, 1987.
Alvera. The Tiny Little Tow Truck.
Alverson, Lyle T. How to Write Puts & Calls.
Alves, Dora. Anti-Nuclear Attitudes in New Zealand & Australia.
Alves, Maria H. State & Opposition in Military Brazil.
Alves, Michael J., jt. ed. see Cassidy, Daniel J.
Alves, Rubem. I Believe in the Resurrection of the Body. McCoy, L. M., tr. from Ger. & Port.
Alvim, Paulo De T. see De T. Alvim, Paulo.
Al-Wahhab, Muhammad I. Kitab Al Tawhid.
Alward, Ron & Shapiro, Andy. Low-Cost Passive Solar Greenhouses: A Design & Construction Guide.
Alwin, Robert H. & Hackworth, Robert D. Algebra Programmed.
--Algebra Programmed, Pt. 1.
Alwin, Robert H., et al. Algebra Programmed.
Alwine, Nevin S., ed. Readings for Foundations of Education.
Alyeshmerni, Mansoor & Taubr, Paul. Working with Aspects of Language.
--Working with Aspects of Language.
Alzofon, David. Mastering Guitar.
Amabile, Teresa M & Stubbs, Margaret L., eds. Psychological Research in the Classroom: Issues for Educators & Researchers.
Amadi, Elechi. Ethics in Nigerian Culture.
--Sunset in Biafra.
Amado, Jorge. Dona Flor & Her Two Husbands.
--Sea of Death. Rabassa, Gregory, tr. from Port.
--The Two Deaths of Quincas Wateryell.
--The Violent Land.
Amai, Robert L., jt. auth. see Clark, Ronald D.
Amalrik, Andrei. Involuntary Journey to Siberia, Russian Edition.
Aman, Mohammed M. Arab Periodicals & Serials: A Classified Directory.
Aman, Mohammed M., jt. auth. see Abdul Huq, A. M.
Amann, Barbara, jt. auth. see Amann, Dick.
Amann, Dick & Amann, Barbara. Caribbean Trip Planner: A New Looseleaf Guide to the Caribbean.
Amanne, E. Dictionnaire de Theologie Catholique.
Amara, Roy C. & Lipinski, Andrew J. Business Planning for an Uncertain Future: Scenarios & Strategies.
Amaral, Anthony. Movie Horses: The Fascinating Techniques of Training.
Amari, S. Differential-Geometrical Methods in Statistics.
Amary, Issam B. Effective Meal Planning & Food Preparation for the Mentally Retarded-Developmentally Disabled: Comprehensive & Innovative Teaching Methods.
Amateur Hockey Association of the U. S. Staff. Hockey Coaching.
Amato, Matthew F., Jr. Jersey City: A City in Socio-Economic & Political Change.
Amato, Pete. Our Grandmothers' Cures & Remedies.
Amatora, Sr. Mary. The Queen's Heart of Gold: The Complete Story of Our Lady of Beauraing.
--The Queen's Portrait: The Story of Guadalupe.
--El Retrato de la Reina: La Historia de Nuestra Senora de Guadalupe.
Amavis, R. & Commission of the European Communities, eds. Principles & Methods for Determining Ecological Criteria on Hydrobiocenoses.
Amavis, R., et al, eds. Hardness of Drinking Water & Public Health: Proceedings.
Amazing Life Games Staff. Good Cents.
--Good Cents: Every Kid's Guide to Making Money.
Ambachtsheer, Keith P. Pension Funds & the Bottom Line: Managing the Corporate Pension Fund as a Financial Business.
Ambler, Eric. The Levanter.
Ambler, John S., et al. Papers in Political Science.
Ambrester, Marcus L., jt. auth. see Strause, Glynis H.
Ambron, Sueann R. & Salkind, Neil J. Child Development.
Ambrose, Alice, ed. see Wittgenstein, Ludwig.
Ambrose, Anthony, ed. see Centre for Advanced Study in the Developmental Sciences.
Ambrose, E. J. & Roe, F. J. The Biology of Cancer.
Ambrose, Peter. The Quiet Revolution.
Ambrose, Stephen E. Eisenhower, Vol. I: Soldier, General of the Army, President-Elect 1890-1952.
--Eisenhower, Vol. 2: The President.
--Pegasus Bridge: June 6, 1944.
Ambrose, William G. College Algebra.
Ambrosi, Antonio. Mas Alla de los Paralelos.
Ambrosius, Saint Opera.
Ambrus, Victor G. Brave Soldier Janosh.
--Seven Skinny Goats.
--Three Poor Tailors.
AMC Maine Mountain Guide Book Committee. AMC Guide to Mount Desert Island & Acadia National Park.
--AMC Maine Mountain Guide.
AMC River Guide Committee. AMC River Guide I: Vol. 1: Maine. Schweiker, Roioli, ed.
Amdrup, E., jt. ed. see Rehfeld, J. F.
Amdur, Neil, jt. auth. see Evert-Lloyd, Chris.
Ameen, Mark, et al. Three New York Poets.
Ameiss, Albert P. & Kargas, Nicholas A. Accountant's Desk Handbook.
Amen, Carol. Teetering on the Tightrope.
Amendola, Sal. Perspective for the Artist.
Amenkhienan, Felix E. Accounting in Developing Countries: A Framework for Standard Setting. Farmer, Richard N., ed.
America Bar Association Section of Family Law. American Bar Association Section of Family Law 1987 Annual Meeting Compendium.
America, R. & Anderson, B. Moving Ahead: Black Managers in American Business.
American Academy of Facial Plastic & Reconstructive Surgery Staff. Plastic & Reconstructive Surgery of the Face & Neck.
American Academy of Orthopaedic Surgeons Staff. Atlas of Orthotics: Biomechanical Principles & Application.
--Instructional Course Lectures.
--Symposium on the Foot & Ankle. Kiene, Richard H. & Johnson, Kenneth A., eds.
--Symposium on the Foot & Leg in Running Sports.
American Academy of Orthopedic Surgeons Staff. Symposium on Idiopathic Low Back Pain. White, Agustus A. & Gordon, Stephen L., eds.
American Academy of Pediatrics, Committee on Fetus & Newborn. Guidelines for Perinatal Care.
American Academy of Political And Social Science Staff. Negro's Progress in Fifty Years.
American Academy of Political & Social Science, Philadelphia Staff. Prisons in Transformation: Proceedings. Sellin, Thorsten, ed.
American Alliance for Health Physical Education Recreation, & Dance Staff. Dance Therapy.
American Alliance for Health, Physical Education, Recreation & Dance Staff. Encyclopedia of Physical Education, Fitness, & Sports: Training, Environment, Nutrition & Fitness.
--Shaping the Body Politic.
American Antiquarian Society Staff. Catalogue of the Manuscript Collections of the American Antiquarian Society.
American Arbitration Association Staff. Arbitration & the Law, 1983. Miller, Linda, ed.
--Arbitration & the Law, 1985. Miller, Linda & Doyle, Margaret, eds.
American Arbitration Association Staff & Colosi, Thomas R. Dispute Resolution Training: The State of the Art. Gold, Charlotte & Lyons, Ruth, eds.
American Arbitration Association Staff & Aaron, Benjamin. The Future of Labor Arbitration in America.
American Arbitration Association Staff. Impact of the Media on Collective Bargaining. Miller, Linda, ed.
American Arbitration Association Staff & McCarthy, Jane E. Negotiating Settlements: A Guide to Environmental Mediation.
American Arbitration Association Staff. Survey of International Arbitration Sites.
American Association for the Advancement of Science, Public Sector Staff, ed. Research & Development in FY Nineteen Eighty-Six: Colloquium Proceedings.
American Association of Critical Care Nurses Staff. Critical Care Nursing of the Multi-Injured Patient. Mann, James K. & Oakes, Annalee R, eds.
American Association of Individual Investors Staff. Individual Investor's Guide to No-Load Mutual Funds.
--Individual Investor's Microcomputer Resource Guide.
American Association of Motor Vehicle Administrators, & American Trucking Association, State Laws. International Registration Plan.
American Association of School Librarians Staff. Certification Model for Professional School Media Personnel.
American Association of Vocational Instructional Materials Staff. Home Electrical Wiring & Maintenance Made Easy.
--Planning & Building Fences & Gates.
American Bar Association Committee on Continuing Professional Education, jt. auth. see ALI-ABA Committee on Continuing Professional Education.
American Camping Association Publications Committee, ed. Guide to a Counselor-in-Training Program.
--Sing.
American Cancer Society Staff. Wyoming Frontier Cooking.
American Ceramic Society, Inc. Staff. Cements Research Progress 1975. Young, J. Francis, ed.
American Chemical Society Staff. Biogenesis of Plant Cell Wall Polysaccharides: Proceedings of the American Chemical Society, 164th National Meeting. Loewus, Frank, ed.
American College of Emergency Physicians Staff. Emergency Medicine: A Comprehensive Study Guide. Krome, Ronald L. & Rothstein, Robert J., eds.
American College Testing Program Staff. College Planning-Search Book.
--College Planning Search Book.
American Congress on Surveying & Mapping & American Society for Photogrammetry & Remote Sensing Staff. Cartography & Education, Vol. I: ASPRS-ACSM Annual Convention Technical Papers.
--Surveying Instrumentation, & the Global Positioning System, Vol. II: ASPRS-ACSM Annual Convention, Washington, DC.
American Consulting Engineers Council Staff. ACEC Membership Directory, 1984-85.
--Guidelines for Ad Hoc Collaboration Agreements Between Consulting Firms.
American Contract Bridge League Staff, jt. auth. see Grant, Audrey.
American Correctional Association Staff. Community Corrections.
--Correctional Law: An Updated Bibliography of Selected Books & Articles.
--Correctional Management.
--Corrections & Public Awareness.
American Correctional Association Staff & Hippchen, Leonard J. Handbook on Correctional Classification: Programming for Treatment & Reintegration.
American Correctional Association Staff. Model Correctional Rules & Regulations.
American Council for the Arts Staff. United Arts Fundraising Policybook.
American Demographics Magazine Staff, ed. State Demographics: Population Profiles of the 50 States.
American Diabetes Association Staff & American Dietetic Association Staff. The American Diabetes Association & the American Dietetic Association Family Cookbook.
--American Dietetic Association Family Cookbook.
American Dietetic Association Staff, jt. auth. see American Diabetes Association Staff.
American Directory Publishing Co., Inc. Staff. Alabama Business Directory, 1988-89.
American Directory Publishing Co., Inc. Chicago Area Business Directory, 1987-88.
American Directory Publishing Co., Inc. Staff. Colorado Business Directory, 1987-88.
American Directory Publishing Co., Inc. Downstate Illinois Business Directory, 1987-88.
American Directory Publishing Co., Inc. Staff. Illinois Business Directory, 1987-88.
--Indiana Business Directory, 1987-88.
--Iowa Business Directory, 1987-88.
--Kansas Business Directory, 1987-88.
--Kansas Business Directory, 1988-89.
--Kentucky Business Directory, 1987-88.
--Louisiana Business Directory,1988-1989.
--Minnesota Business Directory, 1987-88.
--Missouri Business Directory, 1988.
--Oklahoma Business Directory, 1987-88.
--Tennessee Business Directory, 1987-88.
--West Virginia Business Directory, 1988-89.
--Wisconsin Business Directory, 1987-88.
American Ethnological Society Staff & Bennett, John W. The New Ethnicity, Perspectives from Ethnology: Proceedings.
American Fabrics Magazine Staff, ed. Encyclopedia of Textiles.
American Fisheries Society Fish Health Section Staff. Procedures for the Detection & Identification of Certain Fish Pathogens. McDaniel, D. W., ed.
American Football Coaches Association Staff, compiled by. Football Coaching.
American Forestry Association Staff & Wildlife Society Staff. Choices in Silviculture for American Forests.
American Friends Service Committee. A Compassionate Peace: A Future for the Middle East.
--Struggle for Justice: A Report on Crime & Punishment in America.
American Geographical Society Library, New York Staff, ed. Research Catalogue of the American Geographical Society: First Supplement. Incl. Pt. 1. Regional Catalogue; Pt. 2. Topical Catalogue. G K Hall.
American Geographical Society Staff. Index to Maps in Books & Periodicals, Third Supplement.
American Geological Institute Staff. Deep Sea Drilling Project, Legs 1-25.
--Deep Sea Drilling Project, Legs 26-44.
--Deep Sea Drilling Project, Legs 45-62.
--Directory of the Geologic Division, U. S. Geological Survey.
American Health Magazine Editors, et al. The Relaxed Body Book: A High-Energy Anti-Tension Program. Coleman, Daniel, ed.

Authors

American Heritage Dictionary Editors. America in Time.
--Concise American Heritage Dictionary.
--Exercises to Accompany American Heritage Dictionary.
--The Word Book.
American Heritage Editors & Catton, Bruce. The American Heritage Picture History of the Civil War.
American Heritage Magazine Staff, jt. auth. see UPI Staff.
American Heritage Staff, ed. A Sense of History: The Best Writing from the Pages of American Heritage.
American Home Editors. The American Home All-Purpose Cookbook.
--American Home Garden Book & Plant Encyclopedia.
American Honey Institute Staff, ed. Old Favorite Honey Recipes.
American Horticultural Society Staff. North American Horticulture.
American Hospital Association Clearinghouse for Hospital Management Engineering Staff, ed. Computer-Assisted Medical Record Systems: An Examination of Case Studies.
American Hospital Association Clearinghouse for Hospital Management Engineering Staff. In-House Training Programs on Quantitative Techniques: A Collection of Case Studies.
--Nurse Staffing Based on Patient Classification: An Examination of Case Studies.
American Hospital Association, Society for Hospital Social Work Directors. Cost Accountability for Hospital Social Work.
American Hospital Association Staff. Catalog of the Library of the American Hospital Association, Asa S. Bacon Memorial Chicago Library.
--Health Management Briefing: Consumer Satisfaction with Health Care Services.
--Health Management Briefing: Hospital-Physician Joint Ventures.
--Health Management Briefing: Selective Contracting for Medicaid.
American Institute Architects Staff, et al. Architectural Graphic Standards.
American Institute of Architects Central Arizona Chapter Staff. A Guide to the Architecture of Metro Phoenix.
American Institute of Architects Staff. The Architect's Guide to Facility Programming.
American Institute of Architects Staff & Griffin, C. W. Manual of Built-up Roof Systems.
American Institute of Certified Public Accountants, Federal Taxation Division Staff. Alternatives to the Present Tax System for Increasing Saving & Investment.
American Institute of Certified Public Accountants. Continuing Professional Education Division Staff & McKeen, Gregory B. S Corporations.
American Institute of Real Estate Appraisers Staff & Rushmore, Stephen. The Valuation of Hotels & Motels.
American Institutes for Research Staff. Resource Directory: Organization & Publications That Promote Sex Equity in Postsecondary Education.
American Instructors of the Deaf Staff. Focus on Infusion: Proceedings of the American Instructor's of the Deaf, 50th Biennial Meeting, Rochester, NY, June 1981. Solano, Frances, et al, eds.
American Investor Information Services Staff, ed. Investor's Guide to High Technology Corporations, 1983-84.
American Kennel Club. The Complete Dog Book: The Official Publication of the American Kennel Club.
American Kennel Club Staff. The American Kennel Club, 1884-1984: A Source Book. O'Neill, Charles A., ed.
American Law Institute-American Bar Association Committee for Continuing Professional Education, jt. auth. see National Trust for Historic Preservation in the United States.
American Law Institute-American Bar Association Committee for Continuing Professional Education, jt. auth. see Massachusetts Continuing Legal Education Inc.
American Law Institute-American Bar Association Committee on Continuing Professional Education, jt. auth. see University of Colorado, Boulder School of Law Staff.
American Law Institute-American Bar Association Committee on Continuing Professional Education, jt. auth. see Massachusetts Continuing Legal Education-New England Law Institute, Inc. Staff.
American Law Institute-American Bar Association Committee on Continuing Professional Education, jt. auth. see University of Akron, School of Law Staff.
American Law Institute-American Bar Association Committee on Continuing Professional Education, jt. auth. see Massachusetts Continuing Legal Education-New England Law Institute, Inc. Staff.
American Law Institute-American Bar Association Committee on Continuing Professional Education. Employment Discrimination & Civil Rights in the Federal Courts: ALI-ABA Course of Study Materials.
American Law Institute-American Bar Association Committee for Continuing Professional Education. Representing the Growing Technology Company.
American Law Institute Staff. Federal Income Tax Project.
American Law Institute Staff, jt. auth. see Shepard's Citation, Inc. Staff.
American Library Association, Library Administration Division, Buildings & Equipment Section, Buildings for College & University Libraries Committee. Running Out of Space: What Are the Alternatives?
American Library Association, Office for Intellectual Freedom Staff. Censorship Litigation & the Schools.
American Library Association, Resources & Technical Division, Bookdealer-Library Relations Committee. Guidelines for Handling Library Orders for Serials & Periodicals.
American Library Association, Social Responsibilities Round Table Staff, ed. Alternatives in Print, 77-78.
American Library Association Staff. ALA Handbook of Organization & Membership Directory, 1987-1988.
--ALA Handbook of Organization, 1987-1988.
American Library Association Task Force on Alternatives in Print of the Social Responsibilities Round Table Staff. Alternatives in Print: An International Catalog of Books, Pamphlets, Periodicals & Audiovisual Materials.
American Machinist Magazine Staff. Metalcutting: Today's Techniques for Engineers & Shop Personnel.
--Metalforming: Modern Machines, Methods & Tooling for Engineers & Operating Personnel.
--Practical Ideas for Metalworking Operations, Tooling & Maintenance.
American Mathematical Society Staff. A Crash Course on Kleinian Groups: Proceedings of the American Mathematical Society, Special Session, San Francisco, Jan., 1974. Bers, L. & Kra, I., eds.
American Medical Association. American Medical Directory.
--American Medical Directory: Update to the 27th Edition.
American Medical Association & American Medical Association. AMA Drug Evaluations.
American Medical Association, Division of Library & Archival Services Staff. Index to Medical Socioeconomic Literature, 1962-1970.
American Medical Association Staff. Alcohol & Pregnancy: Why They Don't Mix.
--Allied Health Education Directory.
--CPT-Dermatogolgy, Plastic & Reconstructive Surgery.
--CPT-General Surgery.
--CPT-Gynecology, Obstetrics & Urology.
--CPT-Head & Neck Surgery, Otorhinolaryngology & Opthalmology.
--CPT-Hospital Outpatient Surgery.
--CPT-Medical Specialties.
--CPT-Neurological & Orthopaedic Surgery.
--CPT-Pathology & Laboratory.
--CPT, Radiology, Nineteen Eighty-Eight.
--CPT 1988: Physician's Current Procedural Terminology.
--Digest of Official Actions, Nineteen Eighty-Five to Nineteen Eighty-Six.
--Fee-For-Services Medicine: The Overlooked Alternative.
--Guides to the Evaluation of Permanent Impairment.
--The Illness Called Alcoholism.
--Medical Information Sources: A Referral Directory.
--Physician Characteristics & Distribution in the U. S.
--U. S. Medical Licensure Statistics Nineteen Eighty-Five & Licensure Requirements Nineteen Eighty-Six.
American Medical Association, Subcommittee on Classification of Sports in Injuries, et al, eds. Standard Nomenclature of Athletic Injuries.
American Museum of Natural History Staff & Perkins, John. To the Ends of the Earth: Four Expeditions to the Arctic, the Congo, the Gobi, & Siberia.
American National Standards Committee, X3, Information Processing System. American National Dictionary for Information Systems.
American National Standards committee 239 on LIbrary Work & Information Scienes. American National Standard for Basic Criteria for Indexes.
American National Standards Institute Staff. Conveyor Terms & Definitions.
American Nuclear Society Staff. American Nuclear Society Transactions: Proceedings of the Transfer of Nuclear Energy Iran Conference.
--Nuclear News: Buyers Guide, 1985.
--Nuclear News: Buyers Guide, 1986.
--Uranium Resources - an International Assessment: Proceedings of the American Nuclear Society Topical Symposium, Las Vegas, Sept., 1978.
American Nuclear Society Staff Executive Conference. Pan American Nuclear Technology Exchange: PRoceedings of the American Nuclear Society, Executive Conference.
American Nuclear Society, Symposium on Waste Management, Tucson, March 24-26, 1975. Waste Management '75: Proceedings.
American Nuclear Society. Symposium on Waste Management, Tuscon, February 26-March 1, 1979. Waste Management '79: Proceedings.
American Philosophical Society. Catalogue of Instruments & Models. Multhauf, Robert P., ed.
American Philosophical Society Staff. Catalogue of Portraits & Other Works of Art.
American Physiological Society & American Society of Zoologists, Joint Symposium. Nitrogen Metabolism & the Environment. Campbell, J. W. & Goldstein, L., eds.
American Presbyterian Mission Staff. The Isle of Palms: Sketches of Hainan.
American Psychiatric Association Conference Staff. The Chronic Mental Patient: Problems, Solutions, & Recommendations for a Public Policy, Report of the American Psychiatric Association Conference, January 1979. Talbot, John A., ed.
American Psychiatric Association Staff. Continuing Medical Education Syllabus.
--Quick Reference to the Biographical Directory.
--Tardive Dyskinesia, Task Force Report Eighteen.
American Psychological Association Staff. Casebook on Ethics in Research with Human Participants.
American Psychological Association Staff, ed. Graduate Study in Psychology & Associated Fields, 1986 Edition with 1987 Addendum.
American Radio Relay League. The ARRL Antenna Anthology.
American Radio Relay League Inc., Staff. The Beginner's Guide to Amateur Radio.
American Radio Relay League Staff. FM & Repeaters for the Radio Amateur.
--Hints & Kinks.
--Understanding Amateur Radio.
American School of Classical Studies at Athens Staff. Catalogue of the Gennadius Library. American School of Classical Studies at Athens, Second Supplement.
American Showcase Staff. American Illustration Showcase.
American Showcase Staff, Inc. Staff, compiled by. Corporate Showcase Five: Illustration, Photography & Graphic Design.
American Society for Hospital Engineering of the American Hospital Association Staff. Hospital Engineering Handbook.
American Society for Information & Science Staff, ed. see Knowledge Industry Publications Staff.
American Society for Information & Science Staff, jt. ed. see Knowledge Industry Publications Staff.
American Society for Legal History Staff. Essays in Jurisprudence in Honor of Roscoe Pound. Newman, Ralph A., ed.
American Society for Microbiology, Education & Training Board Staff. Directory of Colleges & Universities Granting Degrees in Microbiology, 1980.
--Highlights in Microbiology Nineteen Seventy-Nine to Eighty.
American Society for Photogrammetry & Remote Sensing Staff, jt. auth. see American Congress on Surveying & Mapping.
American Society for Training & Development. Training & Development Handbook: A Guide to Human Resource Development.
American Society of Association Executives Staff. Association Executive Compensation Study 1987.
--Blue Chip Salary Study, 1988.
--How to Conduct Association Surveys.
--The Personal Equation.
American Society of Civil Engineers Staff, compiled by. Consulting Engineering: A Guide for the Engagement of Engineering Services.
--Consulting Engineering: A Guide to the Engagement of Engineering Services.
--Consumptive Use of Water & Irrigation Water Requirements.
--Earth Reinforcement.
--Economical Construction of Concrete Dams.
American Society of Civil Engineers Staff & Steyert, Richard D., eds. The Economics of High-Rise Apartment Buildings of Alternate Design Configuration.
American Society of Civil Engineers Staff, compiled by. Ethics, Professionalism, & Maintaining Competence.
--Ground Water Management.
--Inspection, Maintenance & Rehabilitation of Old Dams.
--Metal Bridges.
American Society of Criminology Staff & Waldo, Gordon P. Career Criminals.
American Society of Hospital Pharmacists. Clinical Pharmacy Sourcebook: Key Articles from the American Journal of Hospital Pharmacy.
--Sourcebook on Clinical Pharmacy.
American Society of Mechanical Engineers Staff. ASME Handbook: Engineering Tables.
American Society of Photogrammetry Staff. Eighth Biennial Workshop on Color Aerial Photography in the Plant Sciences & Related Fields.
--Proceedings: Second Technology Exchange Week in Panama.
--Workshop for Automated Photogrammetry & Cartography of Highways & Transport Systems.
American Spiritualist Assembly Staff, ed. see Rizer, Arden, Jr.
American Trucking Association Satistical Analysis Department. Executive & Ownership Report.
American Trucking Association, State Laws, jt. auth. see American Association of Motor Vehicle Administrators,.
American Trucking Associations. Survey of Information Systems Interests Report July 1987.
American Trucking Associations, Inc. Staff & Arthur Andersen & Co. What Every Trucking Executive Needs to Know about Tax Reform.
American Trucking Associations, Management Systems Department. ATA-MSC Software Directory: American Trucking Associations Management Systems Committee July 1987.
American Type Founders Co. Staff. Specimens of Type, Brass Rulers & Dashes, Ornaments & Borders, Society Emblems, Check Lines, Cuts, Initials & Other Productions of the American Type Founders Co. Bidwell, John, ed.
American Workers Party Staff. Labor Age. Incl. Greenwood.
American Youth Hostels Staff. Hosteling, U. S. A. The Official American Youth Hostels Handbook.
Americanists Staff. Acculturation in the Americas: Proceedings of the International Congress of Americanists, 29th. Tax, Sol, ed.
Amerine, M. A. & Ough, C. S. Methods for Analysis of Musts & Wines.
Amerio, L., jt. auth. see Prouse, G.
Amerman, Lockhart. Cape Cod Casket.
Amerongen, Jerry van see Van Amerongen, Jerry.
Amery & Hindley. Letters, Numbers, & Colors.
Ames, F. Kashmir Shawl.
Ames, H. B. City Below the Hill.
Ames, Herman V. The Proposed Amendments to the Constitution of the United States: During the First Century of Its History.
Ames, Kenneth L. Beyond Necessity: Art in the Folk Tradition.
Ames, Lois, jt. ed. see Sexton, Linda G.
Ames, Mary E. Outcome Uncertain: Science & the Political Process.
Ames, Maurice U., jt. auth. see Schneider, Leo.
Ames, Mildred. Anna to the Infinite Power.
Ames, W. F., ed. Nonlinear Partial Differential Equations: A Symposium on Methods of Solution.
--Nonlinear Partial Differential Equations in Engineering.
Ames, Winthrop, ed. What Shall We Name the Baby.
Ames-Lewis, Francis. The Library & Manuscripts of Piero Di Cosimo De'Medici.
Ames-Lewis, Francis & Wright, Joanne. Drawing in the Italian Renaissance Workshop.
Ami Press Staff. The Message of Marienfried: According to Our Lady's Apparitions in 1946.
Amidei, Rosemary E., compiled by. Environment: The Human Impact, Selections from the Science Teacher.
Amin, Ash & Goddard, John. Technological Change, Industrial Restructuring & Regional Development.
Amin, Mohamed, et al. Defenders of Pakistan.
Amin, Samir. Class & Nation, Historically & in the Current Crisis.
Aminoff, David, ed. Blood & Tissue Antigens: A Symposium Volume.
Amiri, Imanu see Harrison, Paul C.
Amis, Edward S. Solvent Effects on Reaction Rates & Mechanisms.
Amis, Edward S. & Hinton, James F. Solvent Effects on Chemical Phenomena.
Amis, Kingsley. Ending Up.
--Green Man.
--I Like It Here.
--I Want It Now.
--My Enemy's Enemy.
--New Maps of Hell.

--One Fat Englishman.
--What Became of Jane Austen? And Other Questions.
Amishai-Maisels, Ziva. Gauguin's Religious Themes. Freedberg, S. J., ed.
Amiss, John M. & Jones, Franklin D. The Use of Handbook Tables & Formulas. Ryffel, Henry H., ed.
Amlaner, C. & Macdonald, D., eds. A Handbook on Biotelemetry & Radio Tracking: International Conference: Biotelemetry & Radio Tracking in Biology & Medicine, Oxford, 20-22 March 1979.
Amling, Frederick. Investments.
--Principles of Investment.
Amlund, Curtis A. New Perspectives on the Presidency.
Amlung, Susan, ed. see League of Women Voters of New York State Staff.
Amman, Jost. Kunstbuchlin: Two Hundred & Ninety-Three Renaissance Woodcuts for Artists & Illustrators.
Ammerman, David L., jt. ed. see Tate, Thad W.
Ammons, A. R. A Coast of Trees.
--Diversifications: Poems.
--Sphere: The Form of a Motion.
--Tape for the Turn of the Year.
--Uplands: New Poems.
Amodeo, John & Amodeo, Kris. Being Intimate: A Guide to Successful Relationships.
Amodeo, Kris, jt. auth. see Amodeo, John.
Amon, Aline. The Earth Is Sore: Native Americans on Nature.
--Orangutan: Endangered Ape.
--Reading, Writing, Chattering Chimps.
--Road Runners & Other Cuckoos.
Amon Carter Museum Staff. Amon Carter Museum: Nineteen Sixty-One to Nineteen Seventy-Seven.
Amon Carter Museum Staff & Palmquist, Peter E. Carleton E. Watkins: Photographer of the American West.
Amoore, John E. Molecular Basis of Odor.
Amoore, Susannah, et al. Poetry Introduction.
Amory, Cleveland. The Trouble with Nowadays: A Curmudgeon Strikes Back.
Amory, Mark, ed. see Waugh, Evelyn.
Amos & Birkinshaw. Television Engineering.
Amos, Bernard, ed. Progress in Immunology.
Amos, D. Fish Handling & Preservation at Sea: A Fisherman's Guide to Various Methods of Handling & Preserving Fish on Board Fishing Vessels.
Amos, D. Bernard, et al, eds. Immune Mechanisms & Disease.
Amos, John W., II. Palestinian Resistance: Organization of a Nationalist Movement.
Amos, Martha T. Fanny the Soccer Star.
Amoss, Berthe. The Chalk Cross.
Amowitz, Georgette W. And after the Journey.
Amr, et al. Energy Systems in the United States.
Amrine, Harold T. & Ritchey, John A. Manufacturing Organization & Management.
Amstead, B. H., et al. Manufacturing Processes.
Amster, Gerald & Asbell, Bernard. Transit Point Moscow.
Amstrong, Tilly. Pretty Penny.
Amstutz, Arnold E. Computer Simulation of Competitive Market Response.
Amstutz, Eveline. Caterina.
Amstutz, G. Glossary of Mining Geology.
Amstutz, G. C., ed. Spilites & Spilitic Rocks.
Amstutz, H. E., ed. Bovine Medicine & Surgery.
Amstutz, H. E., et al, eds. Equine Medicine & Surgery.
Amtmann, E. Mechanical Stress, Functional Adaptation & the Variation Structure of the Human Femur Diaphysis.
Amundsen, Roald. To the North Magnetic Pole & Through the Northwest Passage.
Amur, G. S., et al, eds. Essays on Comparative Literature & Linguistics.
Amuzegar, Jahangir & Fekrat, M. Ali. Iran: Economic Development Under Dualistic Conditions.
Anacker. Efficiency & Limits of Radiologic Examination of the Pancreas.
Anafulu, Joseph C. The Ibo-Speaking Peoples of Southern Nigeria: A Selected Annotated List of Writings, 1627 to 1970.
Anagnostopoulos, Athan, tr. see Nephele, Maria.
Anagnostopoulos, Athan, tr. see Terzakis, Angelos.
Anak, Gde Agung. Twenty Years Indonesian Foreign Policy 1945-1965.
Anand, Mulk R. Between Tears & Laughter.
Anand, Mulk R., ed. Kama Sutra of Vatsyayana.
Anand, R. P., ed. Asian States & the Development of International Law.
Anand, Shushila, jt. auth. see Alexander, Michael.
Anand, Valerie. The Disputed Crown.
Ananda Marga Editors. Ananda Marga: Serving the People of North America.
Anania, Michael. Red Menace.
Ananichev, K. Environment: International Aspects.
Ananoff, Alexandre. Boucher's Complete Paintings.
Ananthakrishnan, R., et al. Human Biochemical Genetics.
Ananyi, Chris. Phoenix Ascent.
Anapol'skaya, L. E. Environmental Factors in the Heating of Buildings.
Anastas, Robert & Lulow, Kalia. The Contract for Life.
Anastasas, Florence H. And They Called Him Amos: The Story of John Amos Comenius-a Woodcut in Words.
--Belshazzar: Prince of Babylon.
--The Legend of Good Women: Written in Praise of Women Faithful in Love by Geoffrey Chaucer.
Anastasi, Anne. Differential Psychology.
Anastasi, T. Speaking of Selling.
Anastasi, Thomas E., Jr. Listen! Techniques for Improving Communication Skills.
Anastasia, Salvatore & Willig, Paul M. Structure of Factors.
Anastasio, Dina. Romper Room Book of ABC's.
--Romper Room Book of One, Two, Threes.
--Romper Room Book of Shapes.
Anastasoff, Christ. The Bulgarians: From Their Arrival in the Balkans to Modern Times--Thirteen Centuries of History.
Anastos, Peter, jt. auth. see Baryshnikov, Mikhail.
Anckarsvard, Karin. Aunt Vinnie's Invasion.
--Doctor's Boy. MacMillan, Annabelle, tr.
--Madcap Mystery. MacMillan, Annabelle, tr.
--Madcap Mystery. MacMillan, Annabelle, tr. from Swedish.
--Mysterious Schoolmaster. MacMillan, Annabelle, tr.
--Mysterious Schoolmaster. MacMillan, Annabelle, tr.
--Robber Ghost. MacMillan, Annabelle, tr.
--Robber Ghost. MacMillan, Annabelle, tr.
Ancona, Antoinette. St. Jude & "His People"
Ancona, Francesco A. Writing the Absence of the Father: Undoing Oedipal Structures in the Contemporary American Novel.
Ander, Sel. Call Me Maria.
Ander, Tjeerd van see Van Andel, Tjeerd.
Ander Egg, Ezequiel. Diccionario del Trabajo Social.
Anderegg, G., ed. see International Union of Pure & Applied Chemistry Staff.
Andereggen, Anton. Verbes Francais: Formes et Emplois a l'Usage des Etudiants de Langue Etrangere.
Anders, see Lype, E. J., pseud.
Anders, Rebecca. Careers in a Library.
--A Look at Alcoholism.
--A Look at Death.
--Whiskers the Rabbit. Hammarberg, Dyan, tr. from Fr.
--Winslow the Hamster. Hammarberg, Dyan, tr. from Fr.
Anders, W. An Army in Exile: The Story of the Second Polish Corps.
Andersen, A. C., et al. Dogs & Other Large Mammals in Aging Research.
Andersen, Carl E. Andersen on Financial Planning: How to Increase & Preserve Your Money No Matter How Much You Make.
--Andersen on Mutual Funds: The Investor's Game Plan for Building Personal Wealth.
Andersen, Christopher, jt. auth. see Myers, Albert.
Andersen, Christopher P., jt. auth. see Myers, Albert.
Andersen, Dick. Data Sharing with 1-2-3 & Symphony; Including MainFrame Links.
--Jazz Tips & Traps.
--Symphony Encore: Program Notes.
Andersen, Dick & Cobb, Douglas. One-Two-Three Tips, Tricks, & Traps.
Andersen, Dick & McBeen, Janet. Andersen's Symphony Tips & Tricks.
Andersen, Dick, et al. WordStar Tips & Traps.
Andersen, Hans Christian. Andersen's Fairy Tales.
--Emperor's New Clothes.
--The Emperor's New Clothes.
--Favorite Tales of Hans Andersen. James, M. R., tr. from Danish.
--Hans Andersen's Fairy Tales. Lewis, Naomi, ed.
--It's Perfectly True: And Other Stories. Leyssac, Paul, tr.
--The Nightingale.
--Snow Queen.
--Steadfast Tin Soldier.
--The Steadfast Tin Soldier.
--Swineherd.
Andersen, Hans Christian & Grandfather Drewsen. Christine's Picture Book. Alderson, Brian, tr.
Andersen, Hans Christian see Andersen, Hans Christian.
Andersen, Hans Christian, jt. auth. see Brown, Marcia.
Andersen, Juel. Curry Primer: A Grammar of Spice Cookery.
--Juel Andersen's Sesame Primer.
--Tofu Primer: A Beginner's Book of Bean Cake Cookery.
Andersen, Juel, jt. auth. see Clute, Robin.
Andersen, Juel, jt. auth. see Ford, Richard.
Andersen, Kurt. The Real Thing.
Andersen, R. & Barlag, R. They Were There.
Andersen, Richard. Positive Power of Christian Partnership.
Andersen, Sigrid, jt. auth. see Clute, Robin.
Anderson, A. E. School Dictionary.
Anderson, A. W. Plants of the Bible.
Anderson, Alan R. & Belnap, Nuel D., Jr. Entailment: The Logic of Relevance & Necessity.
Anderson, Ann K. My Favorite Verse.
Anderson, Anna E. Pain: The Essence of a Mental Illness.
--Woman in the Wraparound Skirt.
Anderson, Arthur J. Rules of the Aztec Language: Classical Nahuatl Grammar.
Anderson, B. & Shapiro, P. Emergency Childbirth Handbook.
Anderson, B., jt. auth. see America, R.
Anderson, B. D., jt. auth. see Clements, D. J.
Anderson, B. D. & Ljung, L., eds. Adaptive Control.
Anderson, B. L. & Latham, A. J., eds. The Market in History.
Anderson, Barbara & Shapiro, Pamela J. Obstetrics for the Nurse.
Anderson, Barbara G. The Aging Game: Success, Sanity & Sex after Sixty.
--The Aging Game: Success, Sanity & Sex After Sixty.
Anderson, Barry F. Cognitive Psychology: The Study of Knowing, Learning & Thinking.
Anderson, Bernard E. & Sawhill, Isabel V., eds. Youth Employment & Public Policy.
Anderson, Bernhard W. The Eighth Century Prophets: Amos, Hosea, Isaiah, Micah. McCurley, Foster R., ed.
Anderson, Bernhard W., ed. see Herberg, Will.
Anderson, Beverly, jt. auth. see McConnell, Adeline P.
Anderson, Bruce & Hoare, John. Clay Statements: Australian Contemporary Ceramics.
Anderson, Bruce, compiled by. Passive Solar Design Handbook.
Anderson, Bruce N. Solar Energy: Fundamentals in Building Design.
Anderson, Burton. Burton Anderson's Guide to Italian Wines.
--The Simon & Schuster Pocket Guide to Italian Wines.
Anderson, Carl R. Management: Skills, Functions & Organization Performance.
--Management: Skills, Functions & Organization Performance.
Anderson, Carl R., jt. auth. see Paine, Frank T.
Anderson, Chaney & Pierce, R. C., Jr. Elementary Calculus for Business, Economics & Social Sciences.
Anderson, Charles S. Faith & Freedom: The Christian Faith According to the Lutheran Confessions.
--Reformation, Then & Now.
Anderson, Charles S., ed. see Bender, Harold S.
Anderson, Charles S., ed. see Hagglund, Bengt.
Anderson, Charles S., ed. see Kirchner, Hubert.
Anderson, Charles S., ed. see McNally, Robert E.
Anderson, Charles S., ed. see Prenter, Regin.
Anderson, Chris. Style As Argument: Contemporary American Nonfiction.
Anderson, Christian & Hawes, J. L. Basic Experimental Chemistry: A Laboratory Manual for Beginning Students.
Anderson, Christopher, jt. auth. see Myers, Albert.
Anderson, Clarence W. Blaze & the Gray Spotted Pony.
--Blaze & the Indian Cave.
--Blaze & the Mountain Lion.
Anderson, D., et al, eds. Pipe & Tube Fabrication.
Anderson, D. A., et al. Computational Fluid Mechanics & Heat Transfer.
Anderson, D. Carl. Trial by Death & Fire.
Anderson, D. Chris & Borkowski, John G. Experimental Psychology: Research Tactics & Their Applications.
Anderson, D. Chris, jt. auth. see Borkowski, John G.
Anderson, D. L. Embryology & Phylogeny in Annelids & Arthropods.
Anderson, Dave, jt. auth. see Iooss, Walter, Jr.
Anderson, David. The Piano Makers.
Anderson, David R., et al. An Introduction to Management Science: Quantitative Approaches to Decision Making.
Anderson, Decima M. Computer Programming: FORTRAN IV.
Anderson, Dennis & Leiserson, Mark. Rural Enterprise & Nonfarm Employment.
Anderson, Dick & McBean, Janet. MultiMate Tips & Techniques.
Anderson, Dick, jt. auth. see Buoniconti, Nick.
Anderson, Don. Public & Private Education: The Australian Dimension.
Anderson, Donna K. The Works of Charles T. Griffes: A Descriptive Catalogue. Buelow, George, ed.
Anderson, Douglas A. New Approaches to Family Pastoral Care.
Anderson, Douglas R. Testing the Field of Vision.
Anderson, Duane. Western Iowa Prehistory.
Anderson, E. P., et al. Projecting a Picture of Home Economics: Public Relations in Secondary Programs.
Anderson, Eben M. Key of the Keelson.
--There's the Sea.
Anderson, Edgar. Plants, Man & Life.
Anderson, Edward. Thieves Like Us.
--Thieves Like Us.
Anderson, Eleanor C., illus. Gifts for Alcestis.
Anderson, Elizabeth M. Disabled Schoolchild: A Study of Integration in Primary Schools.
Anderson, Elizabeth M. & Clarke, Lynda. Disability in Adolescence.
Anderson, Eugene & Anderson, Marja L. Mountain & Water: Essays on the Cultural Ecology of South Coastal China.
Anderson, Eugene N. Social & Political Conflict in Prussia, 1858-1864.
Anderson, Everett, et al. The Meiotic Process, I: Pairing, Recombination & Chromosome Movements.
Anderson, Frank R. Loss-Free Benchmark Investing.
Anderson, Fred, jt. auth. see Sahn, David J.
Anderson, G. Lester, ed. Educating for the Professions.
Anderson, Gerald & Stransky, Thomas, eds. Mission Trends: Faith Meets Faith.
Anderson, Gordon J. How to Compete Successfully in Real Estate Investing: A Guide to Exploring & Understanding the Factors That Affect Values.
Anderson, Gregory L. Victorian Clerks.
Anderson, H. George, tr. see Thielicke, Helmut.
Anderson, Henry R. & Raiborn, Mitchell H. Basic Cost Accounting Concepts.
Anderson, Herbert. The Family & Pastoral Care: Theology & Pastoral Care.
Anderson, Hershel M., jt. auth. see Sommerfeld, Ray M.
Anderson, Howard R., ed. see Kublin, Hyman.
Anderson, Howard R., jt. ed. see Wade, Richard C.
Anderson, I. G., ed. Directory of European Associations: National Industrial, Trade & Professional Associations.
--Directory of European Associations: National Learned, Scientific & Technical Societies.
Anderson, Irvine H. The Standard-Vacuum Oil Company & United States East Asian Policy, 1933-1941.
Anderson, J., ed. Chemisorption & Reactions on Metallic Films.
Anderson, J. C., jt. ed. see Chapman, Brian N.
Anderson, J. D., et al, eds. Nuclear Isospin.
Anderson, J. E., tr. see Bloch, Marc.
Anderson, J. J., ed. Parturient Hypocalcemia.
Anderson, J. R. Structure of Metallic Catalysts.
Anderson, J. S., jt. auth. see Fothergill, R.
Anderson, Jack A. & Little, J. Wesley. Change & Innovation in Education.
Anderson, James. The Affair of the Blood-Stained Egg Cosy.
--Hooray for Homicide.
--Lovers & Other Killers.
--The Murder of Sherlock Holmes.
Anderson, James A., jt. auth. see Ploghoft, Milton E.
Anderson, James E. Cases in Public Policy-Making.
--Public Policy-Making.
Anderson, James F., ed. Contemporary Economic Issues & Answers.
Anderson, James L. & Cohen, Martin. The West Point Fitness & Diet Book.
--The West Point Fitness & Diet Book.
Anderson, James V., jt. auth. see Schenk, Fredrick J.
Anderson, Jean. Food Is More Than Cooking: A Basic Guide for Young Cooks.
--The Haunting of America: Ghost Stories from Our Past.
--Jean Anderson's Processor Cooking.
--Unforbidden Sweets.
--Unforbidden Sweets.
Anderson, Jean & Kimball, Yeffe. The Art of American Indian Cooking.
Anderson, Jennifer. The Thinking Woman's Beauty Book.
Anderson, Jervis. A. Philip Randolph: A Biographical Portrait.
Anderson, Jim. How to Live Tax-Free & Rent-Free Now & into the 1990's.
--How to Live Tax-Free-Legally & Rent-Free-Now & Into the 1990's.
Anderson, Joan W. The Best of Both Worlds: A Guide to Home-Based Careers.
Anderson, Jock. A Dynamic Simulation Model of the World Jute Economy.
Anderson, John. Education & Inquiry. Phillips, D. Z., ed.
--Mackinaws Down the Missouri. Barrett, Glenn, ed.
Anderson, John & Hevenor, Hilary. Burning Down the House: MOVE & the Tragedy of Philadelphia.

Authors

Anderson, John B. The American Economy We Need: But Won't Get from the Republicans or the Democrats.
Anderson, John D., Jr. Introduction to Flight: Its Engineering & History.
Anderson, John M., ed. see Calhoun, John C.
Anderson, John R. The Architecture of Cognition.
Anderson, Jon. In Sepia.
Anderson, Joy. Pai-Pai Pig.
Anderson, Karen & Milliren, Alan. Structured Experiences for Integration of Handicapped Children.
Anderson, Karen & Robinson, Jo. Full House: The Story of the Anderson Quintuplets.
Anderson, Kathryn H., ed. see Warlick, Jennifer L., et al.
Anderson, Kenneth. Orphan Drugs: Your Complete Guide to Effective, Proven Medications Available Outside the U. S. - & How to Get Them.
Anderson, Kenneth, ed. The Accredited Resident Manager Profile, 1984.
--Computer Applications in Property Management Accounting.
--Expense Analysis: Condominiums, Cooperatives, & Planned Unit Developments.
--Expense Analysis: Condominiums, Cooperatives, & Planned Unit Developments.
--Income-Expense Analysis: Apartments.
--Income-Expense Analysis: Apartments.
--Income-Expense Analysis: Apartments Condominums & Cooperatives, 1977.
--Income-Expense Analysis: Suburban Office Buildings, 1977.
--Income-Expense Analysis: Suburban Office Buildings.
--Income-Expense Analysis: Suburban Office Buildings.
Anderson, Kenneth & Ruiz, Stacey, eds. Expense Analysis: Condominiums, Cooperatives & Planned Unit Developments, 1984.
--Income-Expense Analysis: Apartments, 1984.
--Income-Expense Analysis: Office Buildings (Downtown & Suburban), 1984.
Anderson, Kenneth N. Eagle Claw Fish Cookbook.
Anderson, Kenneth R. & Ruiz, Stacey L., eds. Expense Analysis: Condominiums, Cooperatives, & Planned Unit Developments.
--Expense Analysis: Condominiums, Cooperatives, & Planned Unit Developments, 1983 Edition.
--Income-Expense Analysis: Apartments.
--Income-Expense Analysis: Apartments, 1983.
--Income-Expense Analysis: Office Buildings.
--Income-Expense Analysis: Office Buildings, 1983 Edition.
Anderson, Kenneth R., ed. see Institute of Real Estate Management Staff.
Anderson, L. O. Wood-Frame Housed Construction.
Anderson, Larry, jt. auth. see Hansen, George.
Anderson, Lee F., et al. Legislative Roll-Call Analysis.
Anderson, Leith. Making Happiness Happen.
Anderson, Leone C. My Friend Next Door.
--Surprise at Muddy Creek.
--The Wonderful Shrinking Shirt. Fay, Ann, ed.
Anderson, Linda. We Can't All Be Heroes, You Know.
Anderson, Lindsay. Making a Film.
Anderson, Lorraine. Jeanne & the Men in Her Life.
Anderson, Lynne. Exploring Careers in Library Science. Rosen, R., ed.
Anderson, M. Government in France: An Introduction to the Executive Power.
Anderson, M. A., jt. ed. see Mular, A. L.
Anderson, M. S. Geography of Living Things.
Anderson, Mabel, et al. That All Children May Learn We Must Learn: Looking Forward to Teaching.
Anderson, Mabry I. Low & Slow: An Insider's History of Agricultural Aviation.
Anderson, Madelyn K., ed. see Burns, Sheila L.
Anderson, Madelyn K., ed. see Herda, D. J.
Anderson, Marcie. Nothing to Cheer About.
--Your're Really a Model Now!
Anderson, Margaret. Momentos Felices Con Dios.
Anderson, Margaret J. I Want the Truth.
Anderson, Margaret M. Insect Friends & Enemies.
Anderson, Marian S., ed. Weekend Projects for the Radio Amateur.
Anderson, Marilyn D. Barkley Come Home.
--The Bridesmaid Wears Track Shoes.
--The Horse That Came to Breakfast.
--Maggie's Wish.
--We Have to Get Rid of These Puppies!
Anderson, Marja L., jt. auth. see Anderson, Eugene.
Anderson, Mary. F T C Superstar.
--F.T.C. & Company.
--I'm Nobody! Who Are You?
--Just the Two of Them.
--Matilda Investigates.
--The Menopause.
--That's Not My Style.
--Tune in Tomorrow.
--You Can't Get There from Here.
Anderson, Mary E. Lovers Guide to Palmistry.
Anderson, Maxwell. Four Verse Plays. Incl. High Tor; Winterset; Elizabeth the Queen; Mary of Scotland. HarBraceJ.
Anderson, N. & Waller, P. J., eds. The Epidemiology & Control of Gastrointestinal Parasites of Cattle in Australia.
Anderson, N., et al, eds. General Practice in Australia.
Anderson, Nancy D., ed. French Mathematical Seminars.
Anderson, Nels. The Right to Work.
Anderson, Osborne P. A Voice from Harper's Ferry. Copeland, Vince, ed.
Anderson, Paul. Mercenaries of Tomorrow.
--Terrorists of Tomorrow.
Anderson, Paul R. & Fisch, Max H. Philosophy in America from Puritans to James.
Anderson, Paul Z. The High Crusade.
Anderson, Pauline & Burkard, Martha. The Dental Assistant.
Anderson, Pauline C. The Dental Assistant.
Anderson, Penny S. The Sound of the Bell.
Anderson, Poul. Ensign Flandry.
--The Night Face & Other Stories.
Anderson Publishers Staff. Ohio Criminal Code: Handbook for Law Enforcement Officers 1987.
Anderson, R. C. & Frankis, G. G. A History of Royal Blue Express Services.
Anderson, R. C., ed. CIH Keys to the Nematode Parasites of Vertebrates, No. 5: Keys to Genera of the Superfamily Metastrongyloidea.
Anderson, R. C. & Bain, O., eds. CIH Keys to the Nematode Parasites of Vertebrates, No. 9: Keys to Genera of the Superfamilies Rhabditoidea, Dioctophymatoidea, Trichinelloidea & Muspiceoidea.
Anderson, R. C., et al, eds. CIH Keys to the Nematode Parasites of Vertebrates.
Anderson, R. S., ed. Nutrition & Behavior in Dogs & Cats: Proceedings of the First Nordic Symposium on Small Animal Veterinary Medicine, Oslo, Norway, September 15-18, 1982.
Anderson, R. T., et al. Large Rotating Machine Winding.
Anderson, R. T., et al, eds. Electrical Fitting.
--Rotating Electrical Equipment Winding & Building.
Anderson, Ralph E. Bank Security.
Anderson, Ray S. On Being Human: Essays in Theological Anthropology.
Anderson, Reed. Federico Garcia Lorca.
--Federico Garcia Lorca.
Anderson, Richard E. & Kasl, Elizabeth. The Costs of Financing of Adult Education & Training.
Anderson, Richard V., jt. auth. see Jahn, Larry A.
Anderson, Robert. Wagner: A Biography, with a Survey of Books, Editions, & Recordings.
Anderson, Robert, jt. auth. see Cartwright, Ann.
Anderson, Robert, jt. auth. see Haast, William E.
Anderson, Robert A. Cooks & Bakers.
Anderson, Robert D. Avoiding Malpractice for the California Nurse.
--Legal Boundaries of California Nursing Practice.
Anderson, Robert H., jt. auth. see Goodlad, John I.
Anderson, Robert H. & Shane, Harold G., eds. As the Twig Is Bent: Readings in Early Childhood Education.
Anderson, Robert H. & Shinebourne, Elliot A., eds. Paediatric Cardiology Vol. 1, 1977.
Anderson, Robert S. Gun Digest Hunting Annual 1984.
--Metallic Cartridge Reloading.
Anderson, Robert S., ed. Gun Digest Hunting Annual 1985.
--Gun Digest Hunting Annual 1986.
--Gun Digest Hunting Annual, 1988.
Anderson, Ronald H. Selecting & Developing Media for Instruction.
Anderson, Rosemary, ed. Treasure Hunters Buyers Guide.
Anderson, Russell E. Biological Paths to Energy Self-Reliance.
Anderson, Ruth, jt. auth. see Woolsey, Raymond H.
Anderson, Scarvia B. & Coburn, Louisa V., eds. Academic Testing & the Consumer.
Anderson, Sherwood. Beyond Desire.
--Buck Fever Papers. Taylor, Welford D., ed.
--Dark Laughter.
--Kit Brandon.
--Sherwood Anderson's Notebook 1926.
--Winesburg, Ohio.
Anderson, Stanley V. & Moore, John E., eds. Transcript of Ombudsman Workshop: Recent Experience in the United States.
Anderson, Stephen R. The Organization of Phonology.
Anderson, Theodore W. & Sclove, Stanley L. An Introduction to the Statistical Analysis of Data.
--Introductory Statistical Analysis.
Anderson, Thomas C. The Foundation & Structure of Sartrean Ethics.
Anderson, Thomas J. & Trotter, W. Word Processing.
Anderson, Thomas J. & Trotter, William R. Word Processing Users' Manual.
Anderson, Thomas P. Politics in Central America: Guatemala, El Salvador, Honduras, & Nicaragua. Wesson, Robert, ed.
Anderson, Urton & Holman, Richard. Quality Assurance for Internal Auditing.
Anderson, W. & Fuller, K. R. Ring & Categories of Modules.
Anderson, W. L. Railroad Track Briefs for the Plant Engineer.
Anderson, W. L. & Stageberg, Norman C., eds. Introductory Readings on Language.
Anderson, W. P., ed. Ion Transport in Plants.
Anderson, Walter. A Place of Power: The American Episode in Human Evolution.
Anderson, Walter T. Rethinking Liberalism.
Anderson, Willard. Wheel of Fortune.
Anderson, William. Laura Ingalls Wilder: Pioneer & Author.
Anderson, William H. Financing Modern Government.
Anderson, William J. & Spiers, Richard P. The Architecture of Ancient Rome: An Account of Its Historic Development.
Andersson, Christiane & Talbot, Charles. From a Mighty Fortress: Prints, Drawings, & Books in the Age of Luther, 1483-1546.
Andersson, Theodore & Boyer, Mildred. Bilingual Schooling in the United States.
Anderton, Johana G. More Twentieth Century Dolls.
--More Twentieth Century Dolls: A-H.
Ando, T., et al. Protamines: Isolation, Characterization, Structure & Function.
Andoh, Elizabeth. An American Taste of Japan.
Andors, Stephen, ed. Workers & Workplaces in Revolutionary China. Mathews, Jay, et al, trs.
Andrade, Kerry M. & Ontiveros, Suzanne R., eds. Organizational Behavior: Contemporary Viewpoints.
Andrade, Sally J., ed. Latino Families in the United States: A Resourcebook for Family Life Education.
Andre, Sam, jt. auth. see Fleisher, Nat.
Andrea, Alfred J. & Schmokel, Wolfe W. The Living Past: Western Historiographical Traditions.
Andreae, Bernard. Odysseus: Archaeology of the European Image of Man. Shabhazi, Shapur, tr. from Ger.
Andreae, John H. Thinking with the Teachable Machine.
Andreasen, M. Myrup, et al. Design for Assembly.
Andreasen, Nancy C. Understanding Mental Illness: A Layman's Guide.
Andreassi, Michael W. & MacRae, C. Duncan. Homeowner Income Tax Provisions & Metropolitan Housing Markets: A Simulation Study.
Andrecht, Venus C. The Outrageous Herb Lady: How to Make a Mint in Selling & Multi-Level Marketing. McWhorter, Margaret L., ed.
Andree, Josephine P., ed. Lines from the O. U. Mathematics Letter. Incl. Vol. 1. Number Extensions; Vol. 2. Theory of Games; Vol. 3. Geometric Extensions. NCTM.
Andrejko, jt. auth. see Wright.
Andreoli, Kathleen G., et al. Comprehensive Cardiac Care: A Text for Nurses, Physicians & Other Health Practitioners.
Andreoli, M., jt. ed. see Cassano, C.
Andreoli, Thomas E., et al, eds. Membrane Physiology.
Andreopoulos. Aging of America & the Role of the Academic Health Center.
Andresen, A. F. & Maeland, A., eds. Hydrides for Energy Storage: Proceedings of an International Symposium Held in Norway, Aug. 1977.
Andresen, William, et al. Laboratory Inquiries into Concepts of Biology.
Andreski, Stanislav. Military Organization & Society.
Andreu, Helene C. Jazz Dance: An Adult Beginner's Guide.
Andrews, Albert H., Jr. & Polanyi, Thomas. Microscopic & Endoscopic Surgery with the Carbon Dioxide Laser.
Andrews, Barbara. Escape from the Storm.
Andrews, Bart. I Love Lucy Book.
Andrews, Beverly. What Time Is It, Nana?
Andrews, Charles H. The Perplexing History of the European Empires.
Andrews, Charles M. Colonial Period of American History: The Settlements.
Andrews, Clarence A. Technical & Business Writing.
Andrews, Colman. Best Restaurants Los Angeles.
--Best Restaurants, Los Angeles.
Andrews, Denison. Hammock: How to Make Your Own & Lie in It.
Andrews, Edward D. & Andrews, Faith. Religion in Wood: A Book of Shaker Furniture.
Andrews, Faith, jt. auth. see Andrews, Edward D.
Andrews, Frank M., ed. Scientific Productivity: The Effectiveness of Research Groups in Six Countries.
Andrews, Glenn. Mood Food: A Galaxy of Feasts to Calm You down; Cheer You up; Warm Your Cockles, Excite Your Palate, Comfort, Soothe, & Delight You.
Andrews, Harry C. Computer Techniques in Image Processing.
--Tutorial & Selected Papers in Digital Image Processing.
Andrews, Herbert K. The Technique of Byrd's Vocal Polyphony.
Andrews, Ian. Pompeii.
Andrews, Isabelle. No-Fault Divorce, an Expose.
Andrews, J. Glacial Isostasy.
Andrews, J., ed. see International Association of Gerontology Staff.
Andrews, James E. & Burgess, Joseph A. An Invitation to Action: The Lutheran-Reformed Dialogue, Ser. III, 1981-1983; A Study of Ministry, Sacraments & Recognition.
Andrews, James R. The Practice of Rhetorical Criticism.
Andrews, John. The Price Guide to Antique Furniture.
--The Price Guide to Victorian, Edwardian & 1920's Furniture.
Andrews, John M., et al, eds. Amyotrophic Lateral Sclerosis: Recent Research Trends.
Andrews, John R., illus. The Ghost of Amador.
Andrews, K. R., et al, eds. Westward Enterprise: English Activites in Ireland, the Atlantic & America 1480-1650.
Andrews, Kenneth R. The Concept of Corporate Strategy.
Andrews, Lisa. Building Cost Manual 1988.
Andrews, Lisa, ed. Building Cost Manual, 1988.
Andrews, Lucilla. After a Famous Victory.
--The Phoenix Syndrome.
--The Phoenix Syndrome.
Andrews, Lynn V. Medicine Woman.
Andrews, M. C., ed. Port Dues, Charges & Accommodation Throughout the World.
Andrews, Mark. Body Rub.
--Bomb Squad.
--Satan's Manor.
Andrews, May. The Grass Is Green Again.
Andrews, Nancy. Command Performance: Microsoft Word.
--Microsoft File: Organizing Your Business on the Apple Macintosh.
--Windows: The Official Guide to Microsoft's Operating Environment.
Andrews, Peter, jt. auth. see Busk, Fred.
Andrews, Peter, ed. Classic Country Inns of America.
--Country Inns of America. Incl. Vol. I. New England & the Maritimes; Vol. II. The Mid Atlantic & the South; Vol. III. The Pacific Coast & the Southwest. H Holt & Co.
--Country Inns of California.
Andrews, Peter, et al. California.
--Upper New England.
Andrews, Ronald, jt. auth. see Frith, James.
Andrews, Sandy & Pine, Nicholas. The Price Guide to Crested China, 1985.
Andrews, Spike. C.A.T. No. 1: Tower of Blood.
Andrews, Stephanie. Fearless Love.
Andrews, Theodora, et al. Bibliography on Herbs, Herbal Remedies, Natural Foods, & Unconventional Treatment.
Andrews, V. C. Dark Angel.
--Heaven.
--Heaven.
--My Sweet Audrina.
Andrews, Wayne. Voltaire.
Andrews, William. At the Sign of the Barber's Pole.
Andreyev, A., et al. The Komsomol: Question & Answers.
Andreyev, I. The Noncapitalist Way.
Andreyev, Y. Soviet Russian Literature: Selected Reading.
Andrien, Kenneth J. Crisis & Decline: The Viceroyalty of Peru in the Seventeenth Century.
Andriole, Stephen J., jt. ed. see Paschall, Lee M.
Androgeus, John C., ed. The Lost Gospel of the Ages: Key to Immortality & Companion to the Holy Bible.
Andronov, Alexander, et al. Theory of Oscillators.
Andronow, A. A., et al. Qualitative Theory of Dynamic Systems of Second Order.
Andruk, Susie & O'Connor, David. Redundancies, Again!
Andrus, Hyrum L. Joseph Smith & World Government.
Andrus, Lisa F. Measure & Design in American Painting, 1760-1860.
Andrykovitch, George, jt. auth. see Stanley, Melissa.
Andrzejewski, Jerzy. The Inquisitors. Syrop, Konrad, tr. from Polish.
Anell, Lars & Nygren, Birgitta. The Developing Countries & the World Economic Order.
Anfinsen, C. B., ed. Aspects of Protein Biosynthesis.
Anfinsen, C. B. & Schechter, Alan N., eds. Current Topics in Biochemistry.

Anfinsen, C. B., et al. Current Topics in Biochemistry: National Institute of Health Lectures in Biomedical Sciences.
Anfinsen, C. B., et al, eds. Current Research in Oncology.
Angadi, Patricia. The Highly Flavoured Ladies.
Angas, George F. Savage Life & Scenes in Australia & New Zealand: Being an Artist's Impressions of Countries & People at the Antipodes.
Angel, Allen R. Algebra: An Elementary Approach.
Angel, Heather. Nature Photography-Its Art & Technique.
Angel, Juvenal L. & Dixson, Robert J. Metodo Directo de Conversacion en Espanol.
--Tests & Drills in Spanish Grammar.
Angel, M. V. Progress in Oceanography.
Angel, M. V. & O'Brien, J. Progress in Oceanography.
Angel, M. V. & O'Brien, J., eds. Progress in Oceanography.
Angel, M. V. & O'Brien, J. J., eds. Progress in Oceanography.
--Progress in Oceanography.
Angel, Marc D. The Jews of Rhodes: The History of a Sephardic Community.
Angel, Marie. The Art of Calligraphy: A Practical Guide.
Angel, S. & Hyman, G. M. Urban Fields.
Angele, H. Four-Language Technical Dictionary of Chromatography: English, German, French, Russian.
Angeles, Peter A. Possible Dream: Toward Understanding the Black Experience.
Angeles de, la Rosa see De La Rosa, Angeles & Fernandez, C. Gandia.
Angeli, Arthur C. De see De Angeli, Arthur C. & De Angeli, Marguerite.
Angeli, Marguerite De see De Angeli, Arthur C. & De Angeli, Marguerite.
Angeli, Marguerite De see De Angeli, Marguerite.
Angelici, Robert J. Synthesis & Technique in Inorganic Chemistry.
Angelini, Anthony, et al. International Lending, Risk & the Euromarkets.
Angell, Barbara. Games & Puzzles.
Angell, C. Roy. God's Gold Mines.
Angell, Ellen. The Layman's Handbook of Interior Design.
Angell, George. Agricultural Options: Trading Puts & Calls in the New Grain & Livestock Futures Market.
--Winning in the Futures Market.
Angell, Judie. Ronnie & Rosey.
Angell, Norman. War & the Workers.
Angell, Roger. Late Innings: A New Baseball Companion.
Angell, Roger, Jr., jt. auth. see Iooss, Walter.
Angelo, Ivan. Celebration. Colchie, Thomas, tr.
Angelo, Ray. Botanical Index to the Journal of Henry David Thoreau.
Angeloni, Elvio. Annual Editions: Anthropology, 1985-86.
--Anthropology, 1988-89.
Angelopoul. U. S. Debt Crisis & World Economy.
Angelucci, Enzo. Airplanes: From the Dawn of Light to the Present Day.
Anghelov, S. Socialist Internationalism: Theory & Practice of International Relations of a New Type.
Angier, Bradford. Feasting Free on Wild Edibles.
Angier, Bradford & Corcoran, Barbara. Ask for Love & They Give You Rice Pudding.
Angino, E. D. & Long, D. T., eds. Geochemistry of Bismuth.
Angira, Jared. Silent Voices.
Angle, Robert O. Handbook of Probate Law.
Angleitner, A., et al, eds. Personality Psychology in Europe: Current Trends & Controversies.
Anglin, Donald L., jt. auth. see Crouse, William H.
Anglin, Douglas G., jt. auth. see Shaw, Timothy M.
Anglin, Jeremy M. Word, Object, & Conceptual Development.
Anglo, Sydney, ed. The Damned Art.
Anglund, Joan W. A Is for Always: An ABC Book.
--Un Ami, C'est Quelqu'un Qui T'Aime.
--Amor Est Sensus Quidam Peculiaris. Lyne, G. M., tr.
--Brave Cowboy.
--Childhood Is a Time of Innocence.
--A Child's Book of Old Nursery Rhymes.
--Cowboy & His Friend.
--Cowboy & His Friend.
--The Cowboy's Christmas.
--Cowboy's Secret Life.
--Cup of Sun: A Book of Poems.
--A Friend Is Someone Who Likes You.
--A Gift of Love.
--Goodbye, Yesterday.
--Joan Walsh Anglund Sampler.
--Love Is a Special Way of Feeling.
--Pocketful of Proverbs.
--What Color Is Love?
Anglund, Joan W. & Walsh, Joan. Packet of Pictures.
--Slice of Snow: A Book of Poems.
Angolia, John R. On the Field of Honor: A History of the Knight's Cross Bearers.
Angolia, John R. & Schlicht, Adolf. Traditions & Uniforms of the German Army: 1933-1945.
Angus, Fay. How to Do Everything Right & Live to Regret It: Confessions of a Harried Housewife.
Angus, Ian, jt. ed. see Orwell, George.
Angus, Ian, ed. see Orwell, George.
Angus, Margaret. Kingston General Hospital: A Social & Institutional History.
Angus, Samuel. Mystery Religions.
Angus, T. C. The Control of Indoor Climate.
Anheuser-Busch Brewing Company Staff. Budweiser Cookbook.
Animal Medical Center Editors & Kay, William J. The Complete Book of Cat Health.
Animal Orientation Symposium Staff. Proceedings of the Animal Orientation Symposium, Garmisch, Partenkirchen, 1962. Autrum, H., et al, eds.
Anisman, H. & Bignami, G., eds. Psychopharmacology of Aversively Motivated Behavior.
Anjaria, D. C. From Existence to Life.
Ank, John A., jt. auth. see Breyer, Donald E.
Ankel-Simons, Friderun. A Survey of Living Primates & Their Anatomy.
Ankenbruck, John. The Fort Wayne Story: A Pictorial History.
Anker, Richard, et al, eds. Women's Roles & Population Trends in the Third World.
Ankerst, Jaro, et al. Cell Surface Alteration As a Result of a Malignant Transformation.
Anku, Vincent. What to Know about the Treatment of Cancer: Clear, Sensible Answers to the Questions Asked by Cancer Patients, Their Families & Friends from a Concerned Physicians & Specialist in the Day-to-Day Treatment of Cancer.
Ann, Lee Soo, ed. Economic Relations Between West Asia & Southeast Asia.
Annechild, Annette. Getting into Your Wok with Annette Annechild.
Annett, Cora. Dog Who Thought He Was a Boy.
Annis, L., et al, eds. Turning.
Annis, Linda F. The Child Before Birth.
Annis, Sheldon. God & Production in a Guatemalan Town.
Annixter, Jane & Annixter, Paul. The Last Monster.
Annixter, Paul, jt. auth. see Annixter, Jane.
Anno, Mitsumasa. Anno's Britain.
Annual Conference for Psychosomatic Research Staff. The Psychosomatic Approach to Prevention of Disease: Proceedings of the 20th Annual Conference for Psychosomatic Research, London, Nov. 15-16, 1976. Carruthers, M. & Priest, R., eds.
Annual Hormone Research Symposium Staff. Hormone Research I: Proceedings of the Annual Symposium, 1st, 1974. Norvell, M. & Shellenberger, T., eds.
--Hormone Research II: Proceedings of the Annual Symposium, 2nd, 1975. Norvell, M. J. & Shellenberger, T. E., eds.
--Hormone Research III: Proceedings of the Annual Symposium, 3rd, 1976. Norvell, M. J. & Shellenberger, T. E., eds.
Annual Meeting of the American Society of Psychopathology, 4th, Belmont, Mass., October 1969. Conscious & Unconscious Expressive Art: Theories, Methodology & Pathographies - Proceedings of the. Jakab, Irene, ed.
Annual Meeting of the Deutsche Gesellschaft Fuer Neurochirurgie Staff, et al. Brain Hypoxia Pain: Proceedings of the Annual Meeting, Heidelberg, May 1-3, 1975. Penzholz, H. & Brock, M., eds.
Annual Meeting of the Materials Research Society Staff. Ion Implantation Metallurgy: Proceedings of the Annual Meeting of the Materials Research Society, Cambridge, 1979. Preece, Carolyn M. & Hirvonen, J. K., eds.
Annual Meeting on Brain Edema Staff. Brain Edema, Pathophysiology & Therapy, Cerebello Pontine Angle Tumors, Diagnosis & Surgery: Proceedings of the Annual Meeting, 24th, 1973. Schuermann, et al, eds.
Annual Office of Children's Service Staff. Children's Books, 1985.
--Children's Books, 1987.
Annual Office of Children's Services Staff. Children's Books, 1986.
Annual Research Conference Staff. The City & the World of Work-A Critical Examination of Life in Los Angeles & Urban America in the Mid-Sixties: Proceedings of the Annual Research Conference, 9th, UCLA, 1966.
--The Generation Gap: Implications for Labor-Management Relations: Proceedings of the Annual Research Conference, 13th, UCLA, 1970.
--National Incomes Policy & Manpower Problems: Proceedings of the Annual Research Conference, 14th, UCLA, 1972.
--Problems in Contract Negotiation & Problems & Goals in Manpower Policy: Proceedings. Annual Research Conference, 11th & 12th, UCLA, 1968-1969.
--Research Conference on Labor Relations: Proceedings, Annual Research Conference, 8th, UCLA, 1965.
Anobile, Richard J. The Book of Fame.
--Hooray for Captain Spaulding.
Anobile, Richard J., ed. Alien: The Movie Novel.
--Casablanca.
--A Flask of Fields.
--Frankenstein.
--The Maltese Falcon.
--Ninotchka.
--Psycho.
--Stagecoach.
--Who's on First?
--Why a Duck?
Anokhin, Peter K. Biology & Neurophysiology of the Conditioned Reflex & Its Role in Adaptive Behavior. Corson, Samuel A., tr.
Anouilh, Jean. Jean Anouilh: Five Plays. Incl. Ardele; Time Remembered; Mademoiselle Colombe; Restless Heart; Lark. Hill & Wang.
Anozie, Sunday O. Structural Models & African Poetics: Towards a Pragmatic View of Literature.
Anquillare, John, jt. auth. see Joyce, Joan.
Ansal, Kusum. Sing Me No Songs: A Novel.
Ansel, Howard C. Introduction to Pharmaceutical Dosage Forms.
Ansell, Jack. Dynasty of Air.
--Giants.
--Gospel.
--Jelly.
--The Shermans of Mannerville.
--Summer.
Anselm, A. Introduction to Semiconductor Theory.
Anshen, Ruth N. Biography of an Idea.
Anshen, Ruth N., ed. see Tillich, Paul.
Ansky, S. The Dybbuk: A Play.
Ansley, Norman. Quick Reference Guide to Polygraph Admissibility, Licensing Laws & Limiting Laws.
--Quick Reference Guide to Polygraphy Admissibility, Licensing Laws & Limiting Laws.
Ansoff. Understanding & Managing Strategic Change.
Anson, E. How to Prepare & Write Your Employee Handbook.
Anson, Edward M. A Civilization Primer.
Anson, Robert S. Best Intentions: The Education & Killing of Edmund Perry.
--Exile: The Unquiet Oblivion of Richard M. Nixon.
Anson, W. S. Mottoes & Badges of Families, Regiments, Schools, Colleges, States, Towns, Livery Companies, Societies, Etc.
Anstall, Harold B. & Urie, Paul M. A Manual of Hemotherapy.
Ansteinsson, J. Norwegian Technical Dictionary: English-Norwegian Oil Supplement.
Ansteinsson, J., ed. Norwegian Technical Dictionary: Norwegian-English.
Antal, Frederick. Florentine Painting & Its Social Background.
Anthony. Management Accounting.
Anthony, Arthur B. Economic & Social Problems of the Machine Age.
Anthony, Catherine P. & Thibodeau, Gary A. Anatomy & Physiology Laboratory Manual.
--Basic Concepts in Anatomy & Physiology: A Programmed Presentation.
--Structure & Function of the Body.
--Textbook of Anatomy & Physiology.
Anthony, David, et al. Man & Animals: Living, Working & Changing Together.
Anthony, E. J. Three Clinical Faces of Childhood. Gilpin, D. C., ed.
Anthony, E. James, ed. Explorations in Child Psychiatry.
Anthony, Evelyn. A Place to Hide.
Anthony, J. J. J.'s Bluff: Or the Theory of Business Relativity.
Anthony, James R. French Baroque Music.
--French Baroque Music.
--French Baroque Music: From Beaujoyeulx to Rameau.
--Michel-Richard Delalande's "De Profundis" Grand Motet for Soloists, Chorus, Woodwinds, Strings, & Continuo.
Anthony, John W., et al. The Mineralogy of Arizona.
Anthony, Julie & Bollettieri, Nick. A Winning Combination.
Anthony, Julie, jt. auth. see Bolliettier, Nick.
Anthony, P., et al, eds. Uncollected Stars.
Anthony, Peter. The Foundation of Management.
Anthony, Piers. Bio of a Space Tyrant: Mercenary.
--Bio of a Space Tyrant: Politician.
--Bio of a Space Tyrant: Refugee.
--Macroscope.
--On a Pale Horse.
--Out of Phaze.
--Phthor.
--Wielding a Red Sword.
--With a Tangled Skein.
Anthony, Raymond G., jt. auth. see Holland, Charles D.
Anthony, Robert & Young, David. Management Control in Nonprofit Organizations.
Anthony, Robert, et al. Management Control Systems.
Anthony, Robert N. Tell It Like It Was: A Conceptual Framework for Financial Accounting.
Anthony, Robert N. & Reece, James S. Accounting Principles.
--Accounting: Text & Cases.
Anthony, Sally, jt. ed. see McCabe, Robert.
Anthony, William P. Managing Incompetency.
Anthraquinone Symposium Staff. Natural Anthraquinone Drugs: Proceedings of the Anthraquinone Symposium, Buergenstock-Luzern, September 1978. Fairbairn, J. W., ed.
Antinucci, F., jt. auth. see Parisi, D.
Antl, Boris. Currency Risk.
Antl, Boris, jt. ed. see Ensor, Richard.
Antoine, Jean-Pierre & Tirapegui, Enrique, eds. Functional Integration: Theory & Applications.
Antoine, Robert, tr. see Kalidasa.
Anton, Hector R., et al. Contemporary Issues in Cost & Managerial Accounting: A Discipline in Transition.
Anton, Howard. Elementary Linear Algebra.
Anton, Howard & Kolman, Bernard. Applied Finite Mathematics with Calculus.
Anton, John P., jt. ed. see Walton, Craig.
Antonacci, Robert J. Soccer for Young Champions.
Antonacci, Robert J. & Barr, Jene. Football for Young Champions.
Anton-Guirgis, Hoda, jt. auth. see Lynch, Henry T.
Antonia, Fraser. Oxford Blood: A Jemima Shore Mystery.
Antoniades, Anthony C. Introduction to Environmental Design.
Antoniak, Pete. Power User's Guide to 1-2-3.
Antoniak, Peter, jt. auth. see Tymes, Elna.
Antonick, Michael. Illustrated Corvette Buyer's Guide.
Antoniou, J. Environmental Management: Planning for Traffic.
Antrim, Harry T. T. S. Eliot's Concept of Language: A Study of its Development.
Antrobus, John. Ronnie & the Great Knitted Robbery.
--Ronnie & the Haunted Rolls Royce.
Antrobus, Molly. District Nursing: The Nurse, the Patients & the Work.
Antropov, L. Theoretical Electrochemistry.
Antzak, R. Denny Davis & the Drooping Ears.
Anurag, Ma Yoga, ed. see Rajneesh, Bhagwan Shree.
Anwar, Khaidir. Indonesian: The Development & Use of a National Language.
Anyanwu, K. C. The African Experience in the American Marketplace: A Comparative Study of Cultural Philosophy.
Anzieu, Didier. The Group & the Unconscious. Kiborne, Benjamin, tr. from Fr.
Aoki, Katsutada, jt. auth. see Shimizu, Akinao.
Aoki, Masanao. Optimization of Stochastic Systems.
Aoki, Michiko Y. Ancient Myths & Early History of Japan.
Aoyagi, Akiko, jt. auth. see Shurtleff, William.
Aoyagi, Akiko, jt. ed. see Shurtleff, William.
APA Commission on Psychiatric Therapies. The Psychosocial Therapies. Karasu, Toksoz B., ed.
APA Staff, ed. Journals in Psychology: A Resource Listing for Authors.
Apalin, G. & Mityayev, U. Militarism in Peking's Policies.
Apartment Life Editors, ed. The New Apartment Book.
Apblett, William R., Jr., ed. Shell & Tube Heat Exchangers.
Apel, Karl-Otto. Towards a Transformation of Philosophy.
Apelian, D. & Brody, H., eds. Modeling of Casting & Welding Processes: Proceedings, Rindge, New Hampshire, 1980.
Apelian, D., jt. ed. see Szekely, J.
Apelman, Maja, tr. see Brecht, Bertolt.
Apelt, Otto. Platonis Sophista: Recentsuit, Prolegomenis et Commentariis Instruxit. Taran, Leonardo, ed.
Aperyan, V. A. Manpower Resources & Population under Socialism.
Apfel, Necia H. It's All Relative: Einstein's Theory of Relativity.
Apgar, Kathryn & Riley, Donald P. Life Education in the Workplace: How to Design, Lead & Market Employee Seminars.
Apker, Wesley L. Reflections with Dream Songs & Other Tales.
Aplan, F. F. & Pernichele, A. D., eds. Solution Mining Symposium.
Apol, Georgette, jt. auth. see Fennema, Ilona.
Apol, Georgette, jt. auth. see Reesink, Maryke.
Apollinaire, Guillaume. Alcools.
--Le Bestiaire.
--Le Bestiaire ou Cortege d'Orphee. Shakely, Lauren, tr. from Fr.

Authors

--Le Flaneur des Deux Rives.
--Oeuvres Completes. Decaudin, ed.
--Les Onze Mille Virges. Rootes, Nina, tr. from Fr.
--Poesies Libres.
--Tendre comme le Souvenir.
Aponte, Barbara B. Alfonso Reyes & Spain: His Dialogue with Unamuno, Valle-Inclan, Ortega y Gasset, Jimenez, & Gomez de la Serna.
Apostol, T. M. Modular Functions & Dirichlet Series in Number Theory. Gehring, F. W. & Moore, C. C., eds.
Apostolakis, G., et al, eds. Synthesis & Analysis Methods for Safety & Reliability Studies.
Apostoliti, Carmelina. The Love Story of Lisa & Snowball, Two Beloved Pets.
App, Austin J. The Six Million Swindle.
--The Sudeten-German Tragedy.
Appalachian Land Ownership Task Force Staff. Who Owns Appalachia? Landownership & Its Impact.
Appalachian Mountain Club. Maine Mountain Guide.
--River Guide Two: Central & Southern New England.
Appel, Alfred, Jr., ed. & intro. by see Nabokov, Vladimir.
Appel, Allen. Vengeance Valley.
Appel, Ellen, jt. auth. see Swit, Loretta.
Appel, Martin, jt. auth. see Seaver, Tom.
Appel, Willa. Cults in America: Programmed for Paradise.
Appelbaum, Richard P. Theories of Social Change.
Appelbaum, Stanley, ed. Scenes from the Nineteenth-Century Stage in Advertising Woodcuts.
Appelbaum, Stanley, tr. see Brahms, Johannes.
Appelbaum, Stephen, ed. The Anatomy of Change: The Menninger Foundation Report on Testing the Effects of Psychotherapy.
Appelfeld, Aharon. The Age of Wonders. Bilu, Dalya, tr. from Hebrew.
--Badenheim Nineteen Thirty-Nine.
--To the Land of the Cattails.
Appelqvist, L. A. & Ohlson, R., eds. Rapeseed.
Appenzeller, Otto & Atkinson, Ruth A., eds. Sports Medicine: Fitness, Training, Injuries.
Appert, Robert. New Century World Wide German Dictionary.
Appiah-Kubi, Kofi & Torres, Sergio, eds. African Theology En Route: Papers from the Pan-African Conference of Third World Theologians, December 17-23, 1977, Accra, Ghana.
Apple, J. Lawrence & Smith, Ray F., eds. Integrated Pest Management.
Apple, Michael W. Teachers & Texts.
Apple, Michael W., ed. Cultural & Economic Reproduction in Education.
Apple, R. W., Jr. Apple's Europe: An Uncommon Guidebook.
Applebaum, Eileen, et al, eds. Readings in Economics.
Applebaum, Harvey M. & Victor, A. Paul. United States Import Relief Laws: Current Developments in Law & Policy: A Course Handbook.
Applebaum, Morton W. What Everyone Should Know about Judaism.
Applebaum, Stan & Cox, Victoria. Going My Way?
--Going My Way?
Applebaum, Stanley, ed. Show Songs from the Black Crook to the Red Mill: Original Sheet Music for 60 Songs from 50 Shows, 1866-1906.
Applebaum, Stanley & Camner, James, eds. Stars of the American Musical Theater in Historic Photographs.
Applebee, Arthur N. The Child's Concept of Story: Ages Two to Seventeen.
Applebee, Roger K., jt. auth. see Squire, James R.
Appleby, David P. The Music of Brazil.
Appleby, Harrison, jt. auth. see Donovan, Michael.
Applegate & Waldhart. Communication One Hundred One Course Manual.
Applegate, Frank G. Indian Stories from the Pueblos: Tales of New Mexico & Arizona.
Applegate, Howard G. & Bath, C. Richard, eds. Air Pollution along the United States-Mexico Border.
Applegath, John. Working Free: Practical Alternatives to the Nine to Five Job.
Appleman, John A. How to Increase Your Money-Making Power in the 80's.
Appleman, Milo D. Epitaph for Planet Earth: How to Survive the Approaching End of the Human Species.
Appleman, Philip. Open Doorways.
Appleman, Philip, ed. Darwin.
Appleman, Roy E., ed. Abraham Lincoln: From His Own Words & Contemporary Accounts.
Appleman, Roy E., et al. United States Army in World War 2: War in the Pacific, Okinawa, the Last Battle.
Appleman, Solomon. The Jewish Woman in Judaism: The Significance of Women's Status in Religious Culture.
Appleton, George. Daily Prayer & Praise.
--Prayers from a Troubled Heart.
--The Quiet Heart: Prayers & Meditations for Each Day of the Year.
Appleton, Jon H. & Perera, Ronald C., eds. The Development & Practice of Electronic Music.
Appleton, Nicholas & Benevento, Nicole. Cultural Pluralism in Education: Theoretical Foundations, IE.
Appleton, William S. It Takes More Than Excellence.
Appley, Lawrence A. & Irons, Keith L. Manager Manpower Planning: A Professional Management System.
Appley, M. H. Adaptation-Level Theory: A Symposium.
Apps. Forty Educational Games for the BBC Micro.
Apps, Jerold W. Barns of Wisconsin.
--How to Improve Adult Education in Your Church.
--Ideas for Better Church Meetings.
Aprieto, Virginia L. Fishery Management & Extended Maritime Jurisdiction: The Philippine Tuna Fishery Situation.
April, Ernest W., jt. auth. see PreTest Service Inc.
Aprison, M. H., jt. ed. see Haber, Bernard.
Apte, Robert Z. Halfway Houses.
Apte, Stuart C. Stu Apte's Fishing in the Florida Keys & Flamingo.
Apter, David. Politics of Modernization.
Apter, David E. Introduction to Political Analysis.
Apter, T. E. Fantasy Literature: An Approach to Reality.
Aptheker, Herbert. The Negro People in America.
Aptheker, Herbert, ed. Nat Turner's Slave Rebellion: Together with the Full Text of the So-Called "Confessions" of Nat Turner Made in Prison in 1831.
Aptheker, Herbert, ed. see Du Bois, W. E. B.
Apthorp, Stephen P. Alcohol & Substance Abuse.
Apuleius, Lucius. Golden Asse. Adlington, tr.
Aqua, E. N. & Whitman, C. I., eds. Modern Developments in Powder Metallurgy. Incl. Vol. 15. Principles & Processes; Vol. 16. Ferrous & Nonferrous Materials; Vol. 17. Special Materials. Am Powder Metal.
AQUA Group Staff. Contract Administration for Architects & Quantity Surveyors.
--Pre-Contract Practice for Architects & Quality Surveyors.
--Tenders & Contracts for Building.
Aqua, Ronald. Local Institutions & Rural Development in South Korea.
Aquila, Mirella. Selected Poems.
Aquilano, Nicholas J., jt. auth. see Chase, Richard B.
Aquilon, Jeff & Aquilon, Nancy D. One on One: Exercising Together, the Sensual Way to Superbly Conditioned Bodies.
Aquilon, Nancy D., jt. auth. see Aquilon, Jeff.
Aquino, John. Fantasy in Literature.
--Film in the Language Arts Classes.
--Science Fiction As Literature.
Aquistapace, Jean-Noel. Diccionario de la Politica.
Arab World & Iran Business Guides. The Arab World & Iran in Trade with the U. S. A., U. K., EEC, Comecon, Japan & the Third World: 1978.
--Corporate & Personal Taxation in the Arab World: 1978.
--Economic Development Projects in the Arab World & Iran: 1978.
--Foreign Investment Regulations & Labour Employment Conditions in the Arab World.
--Oil Pricing, the Oil Weapon & the Arms Race in the Middle East.
Arab World Business Guides Staff. Nineteen Eighty Businessman's Guide to the Arab World & Iran: 1980.
Arad, Miriam, tr. see Megged, Aharon.
Arad, Miriam, tr. see Ron-Feder, Galila.
Arad, Uzi B., et al. Sharing Global Resources.
Aragno, Anna. The Story of Felicity.
Aragon, George A., jt. auth. see Viscione, Jerry A.
Arakawa & Gins, Madeline H. Arakawa: The Mechanism of Meaning.
Araki, James T. The Ballad-Drama of Medieval Japan.
Aram, John D. Dilemmas of Administrative Behavior.
Arana, Victoria, tr. see Arciniegas, German.
Arana Soto, Salvador. Diccionario de Temas Regionalistas En la Poesia Puertorriquena.
Aranson, Peter H. American Government: Strategy & Choice.
Aranyi, Laszlo & Goldman, Larry L. Design of Long-Term Care Facilities.
Araoz, Daniel L. & Bleck, Robert T. Hypnosex: Sexual Joy Through Self-Hypnosis.
Araoz, Daniel L. & Bleck, Robert T. Hypnosex: Sexual Joy Through Self-Hypnosis.
Arasteh, A. R. Anxious Search: The Way to Universal Self.
--Creativity in the Life Cycle. Incl. Vol. 1. An Annotated Bibliography; Vol. 2. An Interpretative Account of Creativity in Childhood, Adolescence & Adulthood. E J Brill USA.
--Education & Social Awakening in Iran, 1850-1968.
--Faces of Persian Youth: A Sociological Study.
--Man & Society in Iran.
--Rumi the Persian.
--Teaching Through Research.
Arasteh, A. Reza. Growth to Selfhood: The Sufi Contribution to Islam.
Arato, Andrew, tr. see Konrad, George & Szelenyi, Ivan.
Arauz, Nicomedes S., et al, trs. see Alifano, Roberto.
Arbaugh, George B., jt. auth. see Arbaugh, George E.
Arbaugh, George E. & Arbaugh, George B. Kierkegaard's Authorship: A Guide to the Writings of Kierkegaard.
Arbeit, Eleanor W. Mrs. Cat Hides Something.
Arbeiter, Jean, ed. see Lewis, Howard R. & Lewis, Martha E.
Arbeiter, Jean S., jt. auth. see Weiser, Marjorie P.
Arbel, Avner. How to Beat the Market with High-Performance Generic Stocks: Your Broker Won't Tell You about.
Arber, Edward, ed. see Latimer, Hugh.
Arber, W., et al, eds. Current Topics in Microbiology & Immunology.
Arberry, A. J., tr. see Attar, Farid.
Arbib, Michael. Computers & the Cybernetic Society.
Arbib, Michael A. Algebraic Theory of Machines, Languages & Semigroups.
Arbib, Michael A., jt. auth. see Padulo, Louis.
Arbib, Robert & Soper, Tony. Hungry Bird Book: How to Make Your Garden Their Haven on Earth.
Arbib, Robert S., Jr. Enjoying Birds Around New York City.
Arbit, Naomi & Turner, June. Pies & Pastries.
Arbiter, N., jt. ed. see Somasundaran, P.
Arblaster, Anthony. The Rise & Decline of Western Liberalism.
Arblay, Frances B. Fanny Burney & Her Friends: Select Passages from Her Diary & Other Writings.
Arble, Mead. The Long Tunnel.
Arbogast, Karen K. Exchange Lists & Diet Patterns.
Arbona, Fred L., Jr. Mayflies, the Angler, & the Trout.
Arbor, Jane. Roman Summer.
Arbore, Lily. Princess & the Unicorn.
Arbuckle, J. Gorden & Frick, G. William. Environmental Law Handbook.
Arbuckle, J. Gordon, et al. Environmental Law Handbook.
--Emergency Planning & Community Right-to-Know Act Handbook.
Arbuckle, Wendell S. Ice Cream.
Arbuzo, Grigory, jt. auth. see Sarabyanov, Dmitry.
Arcaro, A., et al. Selected Readings for Casework Supervisors in Public Agencies.
Arceivala. Wastewater Treatment & Disposal.
Arceneaux, Marc, illus. The Little Big Rig.
--The Little Cement Mixer.
--The Little Fire Engine.
--The Little Garbage Truck.
Arch, John C. Income Tax Guide for Teachers: NEA Federal.
Archaeological Textiles Staff. Irene Emery Roundtable on Museum Textiles: 1974 Proceedings. Fiske, Patricia, ed.
Archambeault, James, photos by. Kentucky.
Archbishop Bergan Mercy Hospital Staff. Comprehensive Cardiac Rehabilitation Program.
Archdiocese of Newark, Office of Pastoral Renewal Staff. Renew, Parish Book.
Archdiocese of San Francisco. Great Misconceptions: People with Disabilities.
Archer. Bacterial Transformation.
Archer, Dane. How to Expand Your S. I. Q. (Social Intelligence Quotient)
Archer, Gleason L., tr. see Ahmanson, John.
Archer, J. & Birke, L. Exploration in Humans & Animals.
Archer, Jeffrey. First among Equals.
--First among Equals.
--Kane & Abel.
--A Matter of Honor.
--A Matter of Honor.
--The Prodigal Daughter.
Archer, Jerome W. & Schwartz, A. Reader for Writers.
Archer, Jules. Epidemic! The Story of the Disease Detectives.
--Legacy of the Desert: Understanding the Arabs.
--Who's Running Your Life: A Look at Young People's Rights.
--Winners & Losers: Battles, Retreats, Gains, Losses & Ruins from the Vietnam War.
--You & the Law.
Archer, M. & Dakin, C. Introductory Business Management Simulation: Guide for Participants.
Archer, Margaret S., tr. see Sullerot, Evelyne.
Archer, R. W. A Bibliography on Land Pooling - Readjustment - Redistribution for Planned Urban Development in Asian-Pacific Countries.
--Land Pooling by Local Government for Planned Urban Development in Perth.
Archer-Lofton, Eleanor. The Shenanigans of Mr. B.
Archimedes. Geometrical Solutions Derived from Mechanics. Heiberg, J. L., tr.
Architectural Record Magazine Editors. Apartments, Townhouses & Condominiums.
--Building for the Arts.
--Contextual Architecture: Responding to Existing Styles. Ray, Keith, ed.
--Engineering for Architecture. Fischer, Robert E., ed.
--Hospitals & Health Care Facilities.
--Institutional Buildings: Architecture of the Controlled Environment.
--More Houses Architects Design for Themselves.
--New Life for Old Buildings.
--Places for People: Hotel, Restaurants, Bars, Clubs, Community Recreation Facilities Camps, Parks, Plazas, Playgrounds.
--Public, Municipal & Community Buildings.
--Record Houses of 1971.
--Record Houses, 1981.
Architectural Record Magazine Editors & Wagner, Walter F., Jr. Record Houses, 1985.
Architectural Record Magazine Editors. Record Interiors, 1981.
--Record Interiors, 1982.
--Record Interiors, 1983.
--Record Interiors, 1984.
--Religious Buildings.
--A Treasury of Contemporary Houses.
--Twenty-Five Years of Architectural Record Houses. Smith, Herb, ed.
Architectural Record Magazine Staff. Records Interiors, 1987.
ARCIC II Staff. Salvation & the Church.
Arciniegas, Gabriela, tr. see Arciniegas, German.
Arciniegas, German. America in Europe: A History of the New World in Reverse. Arciniegas, Gabriela & Arana, Victoria, trs.
Arco Editiorial Board. Arithmetic Simplified & Self-Taught.
Arco Editorial Board. College Level Examinations in Mathematics: Algebra, Algebra-Trigonometry, Trigonometry.
--Court Officer.
--Graduate Management Admission Test.
--Post Office Clerk-Carrier.
--Supervising Clerk-Stenographer.
Arcos, Joseph C., et al. Chemical Induction of Cancer. Incl. Vol. 1; Vol. 2A; Vol. 2B. Acad Pr.
Ard, Ben N., Jr. Living Without Guilt & or Blame: Conscience, Superego & Psychotherapy.
--Sexual Dysfunction.
Ardagh, John. Guide to the South of France.
Ardell, Donald & Tager, Mark J. Planning for Wellness: A Guidebook for Achieving Optimal Health.
Arden, Cathy. My Sister's Picture.
Arden, John. Vox Pop: Last Days of the Roman Republic.
Arden, John & D'Arcy, Margaretta. The Hero Rises up.
Arden, John, jt. auth. see D'Arcy, Margaretta.
Arden, Kelvin J. & Whalen, William J. Effective Publications for Colleges & Universities.
Arden, Leon. One Fine Day.
Ardener, Shirley, ed. Defining Females: The Nature of Women in Society.
--Perceiving Women.
Ardener, Shirley, jt. ed. see Callan, Hilary.
Arditti, Rita, et al, eds. Test-Tube Women: What Future for Motherhood? Klein, Renate D. & Minden, Shelley.
Ardizzone, G. D., jt. auth. see Zeisler, R.
Ardley, Neil. How Things Work.
--Why Things Are.
Ardman, Harvey. Endgame.
--Normandie: Her Life & Times.
Ardoin, John. The Callas Legacy.
--The Callas Legacy: A Biography of a Career.
Ardrey, Robert. African Genesis.
--The Hunting Hypothesis: A Personal Conclusion Concerning the Evolutionary Nature of Man.
--The Territorial Imperative: A Personal Inquiry into the Animal Origins of Property & Nations.
Arecchi, F. T. & Aussenegg, F. R. Current Trends in Optics.
Areeda, Phillip E. & Hovenkamp, Herbert. Antitrust Law: Nineteen Eighty-Six Supplement.

Areen, Judith. Family Law, Cases & Materials on: 1983 Supplement.
Arem. Gems & Jewelry.
Arem, Joel E. Color Encyclopedia of Gemstones.
Aremu, Odaleye, jt. auth. see Stevick, E. W.
Arena, James W., jt. auth. see Hardin, James W.
Arenas, Bibi Armas De see Armas de Arenas, Bibi.
Arends, Mark. Product Rendering with Markers.
Arendsen, Carl. Business Mathematics.
Arendt, Hannah. Men in Dark Times.
--Origins of Totalitarianism.
--Rahel Varnhagen: The Life of a Jewish Woman. Winston, Richard & Winston, Clara, trs. from Ger.
Arendt, Hannah, ed. see Jaspers, Karl.
Arenhovel, H. & Drechsel, D., eds. Nuclear Physics with Electromagnetic Interactions: Proceedings, International Conference, Mainz, Germany, June 1979.
Arens, Moshe, et al. Middle East Opportunities.
Arens, William F., jt. auth. see Bovee, Courtland L.
Ares, Jacques d' Encyclopedia de l'Esoterisme.
--Encyclopedie De l'Esoterisme1risme, 2: Religions Non Chretiennes. Jacques D'ares.
Areskoug, S., et al, eds. Off-Road Transportation & Soil-Working: Means to Promote Development & Operations.
Arfken, George. University Physics.
--University Physics: International Edition.
Argall, George O., Jr., ed. see International Tailing Symposium Staff.
Argall, George O., Jr., ed. see International Mine Drainage Symposium Staff.
Argall, George O., Jr., ed. see International Coal Exploration Symposium Staff.
Argall, George O., Jr., ed. see International Symposium on the Transportation & Handling of Minerals Staff.
Argea, Angelo & Edmondson, Jolee. The Bear & I: The Story of the World's Most Famous Caddie.
Argens, Jean Baptiste De Boyer see Baptiste De Boyer Argens, Jean.
Argers, Helen. A Lady of Independence.
Argoff, Allen. The Social Studies Student Investigates Money.
Arguelles, Jose. Earth Ascending: An Illustrated Treatise on the Law Governing Whole Systems.
Argy, Victor & Nevile, John, eds. Inflation & Unemployment: Theory, Experience & Policy-Making.
Argyle, Michael. Bodily Communication.
--The Scientific Study of Social Behavior.
Argyle, Michael & Beit-Hallahmi, Benjamin. Social Psychology of Religion.
Argyris, Chris. Behind the Front Page: Organizational Self-Renewal in Metropolition Newspapers.
Arian, Asher. The Elections in Israel: Nineteen Seventy-Seven.
Arias, Esther & Arias, Mortimer. Cry of My People.
Arias, Mortimer, jt. auth. see Arias, Esther.
Arico, Diane, ed. see Dolan, Edward F., Jr.
Arico, Diane, ed. see Milton, Hilary.
Aridas, Christopher. Soundings: A Thematic Guide for Daily Scripture Prayer.
Arieti, et al. Love Can Be Found.
Arieti, Silvano. Understanding & Helping the Schizophrenic: A Guide for Family & Friends.
Ariew, Roger, ed. see Duhem, Pierre.
Arima, Masataka, et al, eds. The Developing Brain & its Disorders.
Ariman, T., ed. Earthquake Behavior & Safety of Oil & Gas Storage Facilities, Buried Pipelines & Equipment.
Ariman, T., jt. ed. see Shibata, H.
Aris, Pepita. The Sauce Book.
Aris, Stephen. Going Bust: Inside the British Bankruptcy Business.
Aristophanes. Works. Incl. Vol. I. Acharnians, Clouds, Knights, Wasps; Vol. II. Peace, Birds, Frogs; Vol. III. Lysistrata, Thesmophoriazusae, Ecclesiazusae, Plutus. Harvard U Pr.
Aristophanes see Weiss, Samuel A.
Aristotelian Society for the Systematic Study of Philosophy Staff. Mind, Matter & Purpose: Proceedings, Supplementary Vol. 8.
Aristotle. Aristotle's Physics. Hope, Richard, tr.
--Ethics. Warrington, John, tr.
--Politics & the Athenian Constitution. Warrington, John, tr.
Ariyama, Joe, et al. Radiology in Disorders of the Liver, Biliary Tract & Pancreas.
Ariza, A. K. & Ariza, I. F., eds. Lauro Olmo: La Camisa.
Ariza, I. F., jt. ed. see Ariza, A. K.
Arizona State University Library Staff. Solar Energy Index.
--Solar Energy Index: Supplement I.
Arjona, Doris K. & Helman, Edith F., eds. Cuentos Contemporaneos.
Arkava, Morton L. Beginning Social Work Research.
Arkell, David. Looking for Laforgue: An Informal Biography of Jules Laforgue.
Arkharov, A. Theory & Design of Cryogenic Systems.
Arkin, Frieda. More Kitchen Wisdom.
Arkin, H. & Arkin, R. Statistical Sampling Software for Auditing & Accounting.
Arkin, R., jt. auth. see Arkin, H.
Arkin, William, jt. auth. see Pringle, Peter.
Arkush, Michael. An Oral History of an American High School.
Arledge, Byron W. Laugh with Your Teenager.
Armas, Frederick de see De Armas, Frederick, et al.
Armas de Arenas, Bibi. Luces y Sombras de un Destierro.
Armbrust, Steven & Deringer, Janice L. Dynamics of Symphony Macros.
Armbruster, Greg, jt. ed. see Dorter, Tom.
Armbruster, Wally. Noodles du Jour.
Arme, C., et al. Studies in Parasitology in Memory of Clark P. Read. Byram, J. E. & Stewart, George, eds.
Armelagos, George, jt. auth. see Farb, Peter.
Armen, Harry, ed. Applications of Numerical Methods to Forming Processes: AMD. Jones, R. F., Jr.
Armendares, S. & Lisker, R. Human Genetics.
Armenian, Haroutune K., jt. ed. see Bryce, Jennifer W.
Armentani, Andy & Donatelli, Gary. The Monday Night Football Cookbook & Restaurant Guide.
Armfield, W. A., Jr. The Energy Investment Game: How to Play It & Win with Oil & Gas.
Armintrout, W. C. Mean Streets.
Armitage, Ronda. Lighthouse Keeper's Lunch.
Armor, David J., jt. auth. see Polich, J. Michael.
Armor, Murray. The Home Plans Book.
Armorer, Harry. Africa & Her Children: An Introduction to the Origin of Civilization.
Armour, David A., ed. see Dunnigan, Brian L.
Armour, David A., ed. see Widder, Keith R.
Armour, Richard. American Lit Relit.
--Classics Reclassified.
--English Lit Relit.
--Golf Is a Four-Letter Word: The Intimate Confessions of a Hooked Slicer.
--It All Started with Marx.
--Punctured Poems.
--Short History of Sex.
Armour, Richard & Galdone, P. Insects All Around Us.
Arms, Karen & Camp, Pamela S. Biology.
Arms, Suzanne. Immaculate Deception: A New Look at Childbirth in America.
Armson, K. A. Forest Soils: Properties & Processes.
Armstrong, Adam E. In the Last Analysis.
Armstrong, Ann. Breath of Life.
Armstrong, Aubry & Mozine, Stane, eds. Managing Training & Training Managers in Public Enterprises in Developing Countries.
Armstrong, B. H. & Nicholls, R. W. Emission, Absorption & Transfer of Radiation in Heated Atmospheres.
Armstrong, David M. Perception & the Physical World.
Armstrong, Eric & Lucas, Rosemary. Improving Industrial Relations: The Advisory Role of ACAS.
Armstrong, Eunice, jt. auth. see Baker, Allen.
Armstrong, Frederick. The Forest City: An Illustrated History of London, Canada. Mosher, Jerry, ed.
Armstrong, Harry G. The Emerging Death Mystique: The Challenge & the Promise.
Armstrong, Isobel, ed. see Bristow, Joseph.
Armstrong, James A. From the Underside: Evangelism from a Third World Vantage Point.
Armstrong, John A. The European Administrative Elite.
Armstrong, John W. The Water of Life: A Treatise on Urine Therapy.
Armstrong, Karen & Sifu Jim Fung. Wing Chun Kung Fu: An Effective & Logical Approach to Self Defense.
Armstrong, L. The Home Front: Notes from the Family War Zone.
Armstrong, Larry. Disaster & Deliverance.
Armstrong, Louis. Kiss Daddy Goodnight Ten Years Later.
Armstrong, Louise. Arthur Gets What He Spills.
--How to Turn Lemons into Money.
--How to Turn Lemons into Money.
--How to Turn up into Down into Up: A Child's Guide to Inflation, Depression, & Economic Recovery.
--How to Turn War into Peace: A Child's Guide to Conflict Resolution.
--How to Turn War into Peace: A Child's Guide to Conflict Resolution.
--Kiss Daddy Goodnight.
Armstrong, Margaret E., et al. McGraw-Hill's Handbook of Clinical Nursing.
Armstrong, Mary A. The Rumrunner & Other Stories.
Armstrong, Michael. How to Be a Better Manager.
Armstrong, Nancy. Fans.
Armstrong, Nell & Wakat, Diane. The Energetic Diabetic: A Personal Fitness Guide.
Armstrong, Patrick. Discovering Geology.
Armstrong, Patrick H. Discovering Ecology.
Armstrong, Peter, et al. White Collar Workers, Trade Unions & Class.
Armstrong, R. Personal Income Tax Practice Set.
--Personal Income Tax Practice Set: 1983 Edition.
Armstrong, R. D., ed. Solid Ionic & Ionic-Electronic Conductors.
Armstrong, R. D., ed. see International Meeting on Solid Electrolytes Staff.
Armstrong, R. F., tr. see Gruber, U. F.
Armstrong, Robert P. The Affecting Presence: An Essay in Humanistic Anthropology.
Armstrong, Russ, jt. auth. see Hemingway, Joan.
Armstrong, Stephen. The Clay Courts of Norwich.
Armstrong, Terrence, et al. The Circumpolar North: A Political & Economic Geography of the Arctic & Sub-Artic.
Armstrong, William. The Angels Must Have Smiled.
--Clerical Cartoons.
--Family Fun Cartoons.
--Hospital Humor Cartoons.
--Senior Citizens' Cartoons.
--Tavern Cartoons.
--TV Cartoons.
--Waiting Room Cartoons.
Armstrong, William C. Pioneer Families of Northwestern New Jersey.
Armstrong, William M. E. L. Godkin & American Foreign Policy: 1865-1900.
Armstrong, Wm. Las Aventuras De Pepito. Igartua, Arturo & Armstrong, Wm., trs.
--Benedictine Cartoons.
--Ecclesiastical Cartoons.
--Franciscan Cartoons.
--I Ate the Whole Thing.
--Prayer-Poems.
--Summer Cabin Cartoons.
Armstrong, Wm., tr. see Armstrong, Wm.
Armytage, W. H. & Peel, John, eds. Perimeter of Social Repair.
Arn, E. A. Group Technology: An Integrated Planning & Implementation Concept for Small & Medium Batch Production.
Arnason, H. H. History of Modern Art: Painting, Sculpture, & Architecture.
Arnaud, J. A. Beam & Fiber Optics.
Arndt, Christian O., ed. Community Education.
Arndt, Diether. Manganese Compounds As Oxidizing Agents in Organic Chemistry. Lee, Donald G., ed. Claff, Chester, Jr., tr. from Ger.
Arndt, K. A., et al, eds. Cutaneous Laser Therapy: Principles & Methods.
Arndt, Karl J. The Annotated & Enlarged Edition of Ernst Steiger's Precentennial Bibliography, "The Periodical Literature of the United States of America"
Arndt, Paul. Gesellschaftliche Verhaltnisse der Ngadha.
Arndt, Rick. Winning with Christ.
Arneil, Gavin C., jt. auth. see Forfar, John O.
Arneson, D. J. Friend Indeed.
--Sometimes in the Dead of Night. Schneider, Meg, ed.
Arneson, D. J. & Brett, Bernard. Sometimes in the Dead of Night.
Arnett, John A. Bibliopegia; or, the Art of Bookbinding in All Its Branches. Bidwell, John, ed.
Arnett, Ross H., Jr. Checklist of the Beetles of North & Central America & the West Indies: The Rove Beetles & Related Groups.
--Checklist of the Beetles of North & Central America & the West Indies: Ground Beetles, Water Beetles, & Related Groups.
--Checklist of the Beetles of North & Central America & the West Indies: The Scarab Beetles, Buprestid Beetles, & Related Groups.
--Checklist of the Beetles of North & Central America & the West Indies: The Click Beetles, Fireflies, Checkered Beetles, & Related Groups.
--Checklist of the Beetles of North & Central America & the West Indies: The Ladybird Beetles & Related Group.
--Checklist of the Beetles of North & Central America & the West Indies: The Darkling Beetles, Strepsiptera, & Related Groups.
--Checklist of the Beetles of North & Central America & the West Indies: The Fungus Weevils, Bark Beetles, Weevils & Related Groups.
--Checklist of the Beetles of North & Central America & the West Indies: Introduction.
--Checklist of the Beetles of North & Central America & the West Indies, Vol. 10: Bibliography.
--Entomological Information Storage & Retrieval.
Arnett, Ross H., Jr., jt. auth. see Wilcox, John A.
Arnett, Ross H., Jr., et al. Checklist of the Beetles of North & Central America & the West Indies.
Arnett, W. David, jt. ed. see Schramm, David N.
Arnheim, Daniel D. Modern Principles of Athletic Training.
Arnikar, H. J. Essentials of Nuclear Chemistry.
Arnljot, Harald A., et al, eds. Oral Health Care Systems.
Arnobius, Afer. Adversus Nationes Libri Seven.
Arnof, Dorothy, jt. auth. see Davis, Bertha.
Arnold. The Historic Hotels of London.
--Selected Poems & Prose.
Arnold, Armin. D. H. Lawrence & America.
Arnold, Bob. Back Road Caller.
Arnold, Caroline. Animals That Migrate.
Arnold, Carolyn. Charts & Graphs: Fun, Facts & Activities.
Arnold, Charles B., et al. Advances in Disease Prevention.
Arnold, D. M., et al, eds. Abelian Group Theory: Proceedings of the 2nd New Mexico State University Bicentennial Conference on Abelian Group, Held at Las Cruces, New Mexico, Dec. 9-12 1976.
Arnold, David. The Age of Discovery: 1400-1600.
Arnold, David & PC World Editors. Getting Started with PC's & Compatibles.
Arnold, David E. & Cortesi, David. Hey Junior! Using IBM's Home Computer.
Arnold, Denis & Fortune, Nigel, eds. Beethoven Reader.
--Monteverdi Companion.
Arnold, Dovie & Posey, Kayte Lee. Do It Yourself.
Arnold, Eberhard. God's Revolution: The Witness of Eberhard Arnold. Hutterian Society of Brothers Staff & Yoder, John H., eds.
--Salt & Light: Talks & Writings of the Sermon on the Mount.
--Salt & Light: Talks & Writings on the Sermon on the Mount.
Arnold, Edmund C. Student Journalist & Editing the Yearbook.
Arnold, Edwin. Light of Asia.
--The Light of Asia or, the Great Renunciation (Mahabhinishkramana) Being the Life & Teaching of Gautama, Prince of India, Founder of Buddhism.
Arnold, Edwin, tr. The Light of Asia & the Indian Song of Songs: Gita Govinda.
--The Song Celestial or Bhaggvad-Gita: From the Mahabharata, Being a Discourse Between Arjuna, Prince of India, & the Supreme Being under the Form of Krishna.
Arnold, Elliot. The Commandos.
Arnold, Emily. A Craving.
Arnold, Emmy. Torches Together: The Beginning & Early Years of the Bruderhof Communities.
Arnold, Eric H. & Loeb, Jeffrey. Lights Out! Kids Talk about Summer Camp.
Arnold, G. Economic Co-operation in the Commonwealth.
Arnold, Guy. Aid in Africa.
Arnold, Henri & Lee, Bob. Jumble Book.
Arnold, James. All Drawn by Horses.
Arnold, Jim, jt. auth. see Leben, Joe.
Arnold, John D. The Art of Decision-Making: Seven Steps to Achieving More Effective Results.
--Make up Your Mind! The Seven Building Blocks to Better Decisions.
Arnold, Joseph & Schank, Kenneth, eds. Exploratory Electricity.
Arnold, Joseph L. Maryland: Old Line to New Prosperity.
Arnold, Julean & Myers, Ramon H. Commerical Handbook of China.
Arnold, Oren. Aim for a Job in Cattle Ranching.
--Guide Yourself Through Old Age.
--Junior Saints: The Rich Rare Humor of Kids in Church.
--What's in a Name: Famous Brand Names.
Arnold, Richard. Better Sport Skating.
Arnold, Susan. Eggshells to Objects: A New Approach to Eggcraft.
Arnold, Thomas W. Painting in Islam.
Arnold, Thurman. Fair Fights & Foul: A Dissenting Lawyer's Autobiography.
Arnold, Tom & Vaden, Frank S. Invention Protection for Practicing Engineers.
Arnold, Wendy. The Historic Country Hotels of England: A Select Guide.
--The Historic Hotels of London.
Arnold, Willard B. Essays on Honesty, Morality, & Competition.
Arnold, William. The Compaq Portable Computer: Use, Applications & BASIC.
--Frances Farmer: Shadowland.
Arnold, William & Brungardt, Terrence. Juvenile Misconduct & Delinquency.
Arnold, William D. Oakfield; Or, Fellowship in the East, 1854. Wolff, Robert L., ed.
Arnon, R., jt. ed. see Spreafico, F.
Arnosky, Jim. Mouse Numbers & Letters.
--Mouse Writing.
Arnot, William. The Parables of Our Lord.
Arnott, Anna L. People Speak.
Arnould, E. J., ed. see Henry Duke of Lancaster.
Arnout, Susan. The Frozen Lady.
Arnow, Murray. The Apple CP-M Book.
Arnstein, Helene S. When a Parent Is Mentally Ill: What to Say to Your Child.

Authors

Arnstein, Walter L. A History of England, Vol. IV: Britain Yesterday & Today 1830 to Present.
Arntson, L. Joyce. Word-Information Processing: Applications, Skills & Procedures.
Aroen. For I Am! The Reaching.
Aron, Arthur & Aron, Elaine. Using AppleWorks.
Aron, Elaine, jt. auth. see Aron, Arthur.
Aron, John, jt. auth. see Lindsay, Leslie.
Aron, Raymond. In Defense of Decadent Europe.
--Opium of the Intellectuals.
Aron, Raymond & Heckscher, August. Diversity of Worlds.
Aronfsky, J. S., jt. auth. see Greynolds, Elbert B.
Aronoff, Craig & Baskin, Otis W. Interpersonal Communication in Organizations.
Aronowitz, Stanley. The Crisis in Historical Materialism: Class, Politics & Culture in Marxist Theory.
--False Promises: The Shaping of American Working-Class Consciousness.
Aronson, Elliot, et al. The Jigsaw Classroom.
Aronson, Geoffrey. Creating Facts: Israel, Palestinians & the West Bank.
Aronson, Howard I. Georgian: A Reading Grammar.
Aronson, S. M. & Volk, B. W., eds. Cerebral Sphingolipidoses: A Symposium on Tay-Sach's Disease & Allied Disorders.
--Inborn Disorders of Sphingolipid Metabolism.
Aronson, Steven M., jt. auth. see Robins, Natalie.
Aronson, Theo. Royal Family: Years of Transition.
Aronson, Virginia. A Practical Guide to Optimal Nutrition: Nutri-Plan.
Arora, Jasbir S., jt. auth. see Haug, Edward J.
Arora, M. N. A Textbook of Cost Accountancy.
Arosio, G. Enciclopedia de la Construccion.
Arp, Gerald. Tropical Gardening Along the Gulf Coast.
Arp, Thomas R., jt. auth. see Perrine, Laurence.
Arpin, Gary Q. John Berryman: A Reference Guide.
Arr, Marjory. Tiny Tales from Happywood.
Arrabal, Fernando. L' Architecte et l'Empereur d'Assyrie.
--Burial of the Sardine. Bowles, Patrick, tr. from Fr.
--Ceremonie Pour une Chevre Sur un Nuage.
--The Compass Stone. Hurley, Andrew, tr. from Span.
--Fetes et Rites De la Confusion.
--Guernica.
--Lettre Aux Communistes Espagnols.
--Le New York d'Arrabal.
--La Panique: Inedit.
--Sur Fischer: Initiation Aux Echecs.
--Viva la Muerte.
Arrabel, F. La Torre: Herida Por el Rayo.
Arras, John & Hunt, Robert. Ethical Issues in Modern Medicine.
Arrasjid, Dorine, jt. auth. see Arrasjid, Harun.
Arrasjid, Harun & Arrasjid, Dorine. Media: A Pocket Guide.
Arrick, Fran. Chernowitz!
Arrighi, Mel. Delphine.
--On Tour.
--Turkish White.
Arrigo, Joseph A. & Batt, Cara M. Plantations: Forty-Four of Louisiana's Most Beautiful Antebellum Plantation Houses.
Arrington, Fred. History of Dickens County: Ranches & Rolling Plains.
Arrington, Leonard J. & Alexander, Thomas G. A Dependent Commonwealth: Utah's Economy from Statehood to the Great Depression. May, Dean, intro. by.
Arrington, Leonard J. & Bitton, Davis. Saints Without Halos: The Human Side of Mormon History.
Arrington, Leonard J. & Hansen, Gary B. The Richest Hole on Earth: A History of the Bingham Copper Mine.
Arriola, Lewis. Vengeance of the God.
Arrow Pub Staff, ed. Arrow Street Guide of Berkshire County.
Arrow Pub. Staff, ed. Arrow Street Guide of Cleveland.
Arrow Pub Staff, ed. Arrow Street Guide of the North Shore.
--Arrow Zip Code Directory.
ARS Enterprises Editors. Directory of Radio Collectors & Suppliers: Including Phonograph & TV Collectors.
Arsan, Emmanuelle. Emmanuelle One. Bair, Lowell, tr. from Fr.
--Emmanuelle Two. Hollo, Anselm, tr. from Fr.
Arsdale, Steven van see Sisk, Jonathan & Van Arsdale, Steven.
Arstila, A. U., jt. ed. see Trump, Benjamin F.
Arstila, Antti U., jt. ed. see Trump, Benjamin F.
Art & Architecture Book Guide Editors. Art & Architecture Book Guide: 1974.
Art Directors Club of Los Angeles. ADLA 2.
Art Flicks Editors. Art Flicks New Streamside Guide to Naturals & Them Imitations.
Art Institute of Chicago, Ryerson Library Editors. Index to Art Periodicals.
Art Institute of Chicago, Ryerson Library Staff. Index to Art Periodicals, 1st Supplement.
Artaud, Antonin. Oeuvres Completes: Avec: Le Momo, Cigit, La Culture Indienne, Lettre a Peter Watson.
--Oeuvres Completes: Avec: Van Gogh, Pour en Finir avec le Jugement de Dieu, Le Theatre de la Cruante.
--Oeuvres Completes: Supplement Au Tome 1.
--Oeuvres Completes: Suppots et Supplications.
--Oeuvres Completes: Suppots et Supplications.
--Selected Writings of Artaud. Sontag, Susan, ed. Weaver, Helen, tr. from Fr.
--Les Tarahumaras.
--Theater & Its Double. Richards, Mary C., tr. from Fr.
Artells, Eduard. Vocabulari Catala-Castella.
Arter, Elisabeth. The Salad Garden.
Arterburn, Stephen, jt. auth. see Timmons, Tim.
Arthos, John. Shakespeare's Use of Dream & Vision.
Arthur Andersen & Co., jt. auth. see American Trucking Associations, Inc. Staff.
Arthur, Bradford. Teaching English to Speakers of English.
Arthur, Budd, jt. auth. see Arthur, Burt.
Arthur, Burt & Arthur, Budd. Canavan's Trail.
--Ride a Crooked Trail.
--The Saga of Denny McCune.
--Three Guns North.
Arthur D. Little, Inc. Nuclear Environment Information-Resources & Action Plans: AIF-NESP-001.
Arthur, Elizabeth. Binding Spell.
Arthur, John P. History of Watauga County, North Carolina.
Arthur, Robert M. Application of On-Line Analytical Instrumentation to Process Control.
--Procedures & Practices in Activated Sludge Process Control.
Arthur, Ruth M. After Candlemas.
--Miss Ghost.
--An Old Magic.
--On the Wasteland.
--Portrait of Margarita.
--The Whistling Boy.
Arthur, Thomas, jt. auth. see Garrett, Ray.
Artin, E. Geometric Algebra.
Artis, Michael J. & Nobay, A. R., eds. Contemporary Economic Analysis: Papers Presented at the Conference of the Association of University Teachers of Economics April 1977.
Artis, Vicki K. Pajama Walking.
Artiss, Kenneth. The Brain: In Wisdom, Loving & Hating.
Artman, John. Good Apple & Grammar Fun.
--Slanguage II.
Artobolevsky, I. Mechanisms in Modern Engineering Design.
--Mechanisms in Modern Engineering Design.
Artobolevsky, I. I. Mechanisms in Modern Engineering Design.
Artsibasov, A. In Disregard for the Law. Kuleshov, Vadim, tr.
Artsimovich, L. A Physicist's ABC on Plasma.
Aruego, Jose, jt. auth. see Addams, Charles.
Arum, Nancy. Ice Cream & Ices. Stein, Margery, ed.
Arvine, Kazlitt. Cyclopedia of Anecdotes of Literature.
Arvy, L. Histoenzymology of the Endocrine Gland.
Arya, A. S. Protection of Educational Buildings Against Earthquakes.
Arzooni, O. G. The Israeli Film: Social & Cultural Influences 1912-1973. Jowett, Garth S., ed.
Asaf'ev, Boris V. Russian Music from the Beginning.
Asakawa, K. The Russo-Japanese Conflict: Its Causes & Issues.
Asakura, Sho, jt. auth. see Oosawa, Fumio.
Asamani, J. O. Index Africanus.
Asano, Takashi. Artificial Recharge of Groundwater.
Asanuma, Hiroshi, ed. & pref. by. Intergration in the Nervous System.
Asanuma, T. Flow Visualization.
Asbell, Bernard, jt. auth. see Amster, Gerald.
Asberg, M. & Stern, W. T., eds. Linnaeus's Oland & Gotland Journey, 1741: Casebound Edition of Biological Journal of the Linnean Society, Vol. 5, No's 1 & 2.
Asbjornsen, P. C. The Squire's Bride: A Norwegian Folk Tale.
Asboe-Hansen. Connective Tissue in Health & Disease.
Asbraf, Mary. Political Verse & Song from Britain & Ireland.
Ascani, Sparky. Ransomed Heart.
Asch, Frank. Bear Shadow.
--Bear's Bargain.
--Happy Birthday, Moon.
--Happy Birthday, Moon.
--Just Like Daddy.
--Just Like Daddy.
--Mooncake.
--Mooncake.
--Moongame.
--Moongame.
--Skyfire.
Asch, Sholem. East River.
Asche, F. Marion & Vogler, Daniel E. Assessing Employer Satisfaction with Vocational Education Graduates.
Aschermann, Arla. Winds in the Cornfields of Early Pueblo County.
Ascherson, Neal, et al. The Nazi Legacy: Klaus Barbie & the International Fascist Connection.
Aschinger, G. A. Stabilitatsaussagen uber Klassen Von Matrizen mit Verschwindenden Zeilensummen.
Aschner, Katherine. The Word Processing Handbook.
--The Word Processing Handbook: A Step-by-Step Guide to Automating the Office.
Aschwanden, Maria. Congratulations, America.
Asgar Ali Engineer. Islamic State.
Ash, Brian. Faces of the Future: The Lessons of Science Fiction.
--Who's Who in Science Fiction.
Ash, Jutta. Wedding Birds.
Ash, Major M., Jr. & Ramfjord, Sigurd P. An Introduction to Functional Occlusion.
Ash, Milton. Optimal Shutdown Control of Nuclear Reactors.
Ash, Milton S. Nuclear Reactor Kinetics.
Ash, Norma C. Sheza Joy.
Ash, Raymond H., jt. auth. see Deshpande, Pradeep B.
Ash, Russell. The Pig Book.
Asha, Ma Prem, ed. see Rajneesh, Bhagwan Shree.
Ashbee, K. H., jt. auth. see Smallman, R. E.
Ashbery, John, et al, trs. see Jacob, Max.
Ashbrook, Marguerite L., jt. auth. see Sumption, Lois L.
Ashby, Gene, ed. see Micronesian Community College Students Staff.
Ashby, Lloyd W. Effective School Board Member.
Ashby, Lynn. As I Was Saying. Lubeck, Scott, ed.
--As Your Acknowledged Leader: The Best of Lynn Ashby. Rodriguez, Barbara, ed.
Ashby, M. F. & Brown, L. M., eds. Perspectives in Creep Fracture.
Ashby, Thomas. The Roman Campagna in Classical Times.
Ashby, Yvonne. The Monster Alphabet Book.
Ashcraft, Keith W., jt. auth. see Holder, Thomas M.
Ashcroft, J. Barrie, jt. auth. see Owens, R. Glynn.
Ashcroft-Nowicki, Dolores. First Steps in Ritual: Safe, Effective Techniques for Experiencing the Inner Worlds.
Ashdown, Inez. Stories of Old Lahaina.
Ashe, Arthur. Getting Started in Tennis. Robinson, Louie, ed.
Ashe, Geoffrey. Kings & Queens of Early Britain.
--The Virgin.
Ashe, Geoffrey, jt. auth. see Debretts Peerage Editors.
Ashe, Marjorie D. The Princess & the Enchanted Wood & Other Fairy Tales.
Asheim, Ivar, ed. Christ & Humanity.
Asheim, Lester, ed. Forum on the Public Library Inquiry.
Asher, Marty. Shelter.
Asher, R. E., tr. see Pillai, Thakazhi S.
Ashford, Douglas E. British Dogmatism & French Pragmatism: Central-Local Policy Making in the Welfare State.
Ashford, F. C. Designing for Industry.
Ashford, Janet I., ed. Birth Stories: The Experience Remembered.
--The Whole Birth Catalog: A Sourcebook for Choices in Childbirth.
Ashford, Mark. Psychic Adventure on Wall Street: Or, You Can Win the Wall Street Game!
Ashford, Ray. Loving Ourselves.
--Take It Easy.
Ashkenazy, Vladimir, jt. auth. see Parrott, Jasper.
Ashley, et al. Cobol Self Teaching.
Ashley, Alma. Love's Raging Torment.
Ashley, Bernard. Dodgem.
--High Pavement Blues.
Ashley, David J. Evan's Histological Appearances of Tumours.
Ashley, Faye. Adam's Daughter.
Ashley, George. The Punctured Thumb: Cactus & Other Succulents.
Ashley, Laura. Laura Ashley: Home Furnishings.
--Laura Ashley Home Furnishings Catalog: 1985.
Ashley, Lawrence M. & Chiasson, Robert B. Laboratory Anatomy of the Shark.
Ashley, Leonard R., ed. Nineteenth-Century British Drama: An Anthology of Representative Plays.
Ashley, Maurice. England in the Seventeenth Century.
Ashley, Michael & Jeeves, Terry. The Complete Index to Astounding-Analog.
Ashley, Mike. Who's Who in Horror & Fantasy Fiction.
Ashley, Paul P. Oh Promise Me But Put It in Writing: Living Together Agreements Without, Before, During & After Marriage.
--You & Your Will: The Planning & Management of Your Estate.
Ashley, Richard K. Political Economy of War & Peace.
Ashley, Ruth & Fernandez, Judi N. Structured COBOL Library.
Ashley, Ruth, jt. auth. see Tabler, Donna.
Ashley, Sally. Connecting: A Handbook for Housewives Returning to Paid Work.
Ashley, William L., jt. auth. see Selz, Nina.
Ashley, William L., et al. Adaptation to Work: An Exploration of Processes & Outcomes.
Ashley Montagu. Growing Young.
--The Reproductive Development of the Female: A Study in the Comparative Physiology of the Adolescent Organism.
Ashley Montagu & Matson, Floyd. The Dehumanization of Man.
--The Human Connection.
--The Human Connection.
Ashley-Montagu & Matson, Floyd. The Human Connection.
Ashmore, Harry. Hearts & Minds: The Anatomy of Racism from Roosevelt to Reagan.
Ashmore, Nancy V. Greenville: Woven from the Past. Mosher, Jerry, ed.
Ashmun, Margaret E. Singing Swan: An Account of Anna Seward & Her Acquaintance with Doctor Johnson, Boswell & Others of Their Time.
Ashour, S. Sequencing Theory.
Ashton, Ann. If Love Comes.
--Right Time to Love.
--Right Time to Love.
Ashton, D. L., jt. auth. see McPherson, E.
Ashton, Debra. The Complete Guide to Planned Giving: Everything You Need to Know to Compete for Major Gifts in the 1980's.
Ashton, E. B., tr. see Jaspers, Karl.
Ashton, E. O. Swahili Grammar.
Ashton, Geoffrey. Giselle.
--Petrushka.
Ashton, Jean. Harriet Beecher Stowe: A Reference Guide.
Ashton, John. Adventures & Discourses of Captain John Smith.
--Century of Ballads.
--Curious Creatures in Zoology.
--Dawn of the Nineteenth Century in England.
--Fleet: Its River, Prison, & Marriages.
--Gossip in the First Decade of Victoria's Reign.
--History of English Lotteries.
--History of Gambling in England.
--Humour, Wit & Satire of the Seventeenth Century.
--Modern Street Ballads.
--Old Times.
--Social England under the Regency.
--Varia.
--When William Fourth Was King.
Ashton, John, jt. auth. see Mew, James.
Ashton, Patricia M. E., et al. Teacher Education in the Classroom: Initial & In-Service.
Ashton, Robert. The English Civil War: Conservatism & Revolution, 1603-1649.
Ashton, Robert J. The Bottle Collector's Price List: For Embossed, Ink & Pontil-Scarred Bottles.
Ashton-Tate. Using Multi Mate Advantage II Work Book.
Ashton-Tate, ed. see Forefront Corporation Staff.
Ashton-Tate Staff. Ashton-Tate Developer's Registry.
Ashton-Tate Staff, jt. auth. see Enabling Technology Staff.
Ashton-Tate Staff, ed. see Expert Systems Staff.
Ashton, Thomas S. An Economic History of England: The Eighteenth Century.
Ashton-Warner, Sylvia. Spinster.
Ashvagosha. Awakening of Faith. Walton, Alan H., ed. Richard, Timothy, tr.
Ashwal, Stephen, jt. auth. see Swaiman, Kenneth F.
Ashwin, Clive. History of Graphic Design & Communications: A Sourcebook.
Ashworth, G. J., jt. auth. see Burtenshaw, D.
Ashworth, Georgina & Bonnerjea, Lucy. The Invisible Decade: U. K. Women in the United Nations Decade 1976-1985.
Ashworth, J. M. Cell Differentiation.
Ashworth, M. F. Analytical Methods for Organic Cyano Groups.
Ashworth, M. R. Analytical Methods for Glycerol.
--The Determination of Sulphur-Containing Groups.
Ashworth, Mae H. Six Times True.
Asian Cultural Centre for Unesco, compiled by. More Festivals in Asia.
Asian Programme of Educational Innovation for Development. Social Change & New Profiles of Educational Personnel: National Studies: India, Nepal, Philippines, Republic of Korea.
Asian Studies Center. Briefing Book: President Reagan's Trip to Asia.
Asimov, Isaac. Adding a Dimension.
--Asimov on Science Fiction.
--Best Mysteries of Isaac Asimov.
--Best Science Fiction of Issac Asimov.
--The Birth of the United States, 1763-1816.

--Change! Seventy-One Glimpses of the Future.
--A Choice of Catastrophes.
--A Choice of Catastrophes.
--Constantinople: The Forgotten Empire.
--Counting the Eons.
--Dark Ages.
--Easy Introduction to the Slide Rule.
--Egyptians.
--Enciclopedia Biografica De Ciencia y Tecnologia.
--Eyes on the Universe: A History of the Telescope.
--Foundation Trilogy.
--From Earth to Heaven.
--Futuredays: A Nineteenth-Century Vision of the Year 2000.
--The Gods Themselves.
--The Golden Door: The United States from 1865 to 1918.
--Great Ideas of Science.
--How Did We Find Out about Antarctica?
--How Did We Find Out about Atoms?
--How Did We Find Out about Comets?
--How Did We Find Out about Dinosaurs?
--How Did We Find Out about Earthquakes?
--How Did We Find Out about Energy?
--How Did We Find Out about Germs?
--How did We Find Out about Life in the Deep Sea?
--How Did We Find Out about Our Human Roots?
--How Did We Find Out about Outer Space?
--How Did We Find Out about Solar Power?
--Human Body.
--Human Brain.
--I, Robot.
--In Joy Still Felt: Autobiography of Isaac Asimov 1954-1978.
--In Memory Yet Green: The Autobiography of Isaac Asimov, 1920-1954.
--Isaac Asimov's Fantasy. McCarthy, Shawna, ed.
--Isaac Asimov's Near Futures & Far.
--The Key Word & Other Mysteries.
--The Kite That Won the Revolution.
--Land of Canaan.
--Life & Energy.
--Machines That Think.
--More Words of Science.
--Near East: 10,000 Years of History.
--The Neutrino.
--Of Time, Space, & Other Things.
--Opus Two Hundred.
--Our Federal Union: The United States from 1816-1865.
--Please Explain.
--Quick & Easy Math.
--Realm of Algebra.
--Realm of Measure.
--The Road to Infinity.
--Robots & Empire.
--Roman Empire.
--Roman Republic.
--The Shaping of France.
--The Shaping of North America: From Earliest Times to 1763.
--The Sun Shines Bright.
--The Union Club Mysteries.
--The Universe: From Flat Earth to Quasar.
--View from a Height.
--Words from the Exodus.
--Words of Science.
--X Stands for Unknown.
Asimov, Isaac, jt. auth. see Laurance, Alice.
Asimov, Isaac & Greenberg, Martin H., eds. The Last Man on Earth.
--Miniature Mysteries: One Hundred Malicious Little Mystery Stories.
--Science Fiction A to Z.
Asimov, Isaac & Laurance, Alice, eds. Speculations.
Asimov, Isaac, et al, eds. Science Fictional Solar System.
--Microcosmic Tales: One Hundred Wondrous Science Fiction Short-Short Stories.
--One Hundred Great Science Fiction Short Short Stories.
--Machines That Think: The Best Science Fiction Stories about Robots & Computers.
Asinger, H. Mono-Olefins: Chemistry & Technology.
Asinof, Eliot. Bleeding Between the Lines.
ASJA Publications Committee. American Society of Journalists & Authors, 1984: A Listing of Professional Free-Lance Writers.
Askeland, J. Norwegian Painting: A Survey.
Askenasy, Hans. Are We All Nazis?
Asker, jt. auth. see Hauglid.
Askew, A. J., et al, eds. Logistics & Benefits of Using Mathematical Models of Hydrologic & Water Resource Systems: Selected Papers from an International Symposium, IIASA Laxenburg, Austria.
Askew, Thomas A., Jr. & Spellman, Peter W. The Churches & the American Experience.
Askey, Donald E., et al. Nordic Area Studies in North America: A Survey & Directory of the Human & Material Resources.
Aslett, Don A. Is There Life after Housework?
Asman, David & Meyerson, Adam, eds. The Wall Street Journal on Management: The Best of the Manager's Journal.
Aspin, Isabel S., ed. Anglo-Norman Political Songs.
Aspinall, D., jt. ed. see Paleg, L. G.
Aspinall, David, jt. auth. see Dagless, Erik L.
Aspinall, David & Dagless, Erik, eds. Introduction to Microprocessors.
Aspinwall, Dorothy, tr. see Aspinwall, Dorothy B. & Reda, Jacques.
Aspinwall, Dorothy B. & Reda, Jacques. Recitatif. Aspinwall, Dorothy, tr.
Aspinwall, Jack. Hit Me Again: More after Dinner Stories from the Houses of Parliament.
Aspinwall, Margaret, ed. see Mathews, Zena P.
Asprey, Robert B. Frederick the Great: The Magnificent Enigma.
Asquith, Pamela. Truffles & Other Chocolate Confections.
Asquith, Pamella. Pamella Z. Asquith's Ultimate Chocolate Cake Book.
Asquith, Pamella Z. Pamella Asquith's Ultimate Chocolate Cake Book.
Asquith, R. S., ed. Chemistry of Natural Protein Fibers.
Asquith, Stewart, jt. auth. see Clark, Chris L.
Asquith, Stuart. Military Modelling Guide to Wargaming.
Assael, Henry. Consumer Behavior & Marketing Action.
Assaf, Karen & Assaf, Said. Handbook of Mathematical Calculations for Science Students & Researchers.
Assaf, Said, jt. auth. see Assaf, Karen.
Assali, N. S. Biology of Gestation.
Assali, Nicholas S. A Doctor's Life.
Assarsson-Rizzi, Kerstin & Bohrn, Harold. Gunnar Myrdal: A Bibliography, 1919-1981.
Asscher, A. W. & Brumfitt, W. Microbial Disease in Nephrology.
Asscher, A. W., ed. see Urinary Tract Infection Symposium Staff.
Assecuranz & Compass. Yearbook of International Insurance.
Asselain, Jean-Charles. Planning & Profit in Socialist Economies.
Asselin, E. Donald. Portuguese-American Cookbook.
Assembly of Behavioral & Social Sciences. Deterrence & Incapacitation: Estimating the Effects of Criminal Sanctions on Crime Rates.
Assembly of Life Sciences, National Research Council. Alternatives to the Current Use of Nitrite in Foods.
--Ecological Aspects of Development in the Humid Tropics.
Asseng, Rolf E. When Jesus Comes Again: What the Bible Says.
Assimil. Assimil Language Courses: English for Children - Assimil Junior.
Assis, Machado De see De Assis, Machado.
Assmann, E. Principles of Forest Yield Study.
Associated Features Inc. Editors. Home Run: Baseball's Greatest Hits & Hitters. Hollander, Zander, ed.
--The Masked Marvels: Baseball's Great Catchers.
Associated Press. The Associated Press Stylebook.
Associated Press & Currier, Chet. The Investor's Encyclopedia.
Associated Press, jt. auth. see Goldstein, Norm.
Associated Press Editors. One Day in Our World.
Associated Press Staff & Goldstein, Norm. Frank Sinatra: Ol' Blue Eyes.
Associated Press Staff, jt. auth. see Currier, Chet.
Association For Asian Studies, ed. Cumulative Bibliography of Asian Studies, 1941-1965, Subject Bibliography.
Association for Asian Studies Editors. Cumulative Bibliography of Asian Studies, 1941-1965, Author Bibliography.
Association for Information & Image Management Staff. Document Mark (BLIP) Used in Image Mark Retrieval Systems: ANSI-AIIM MS8-1979.
--An Introduction to Micrographics. Meyer, Ellen T., ed.
Association for Information & Image Management. Practice for Operational Procedures: Inspection & Quality Control of First-Generation Silver-Gelatin Microfilm of Documents (ANSI-AIIM MS23-1983)
--Practice for Uniform Product Disclosure for Unitized Microform Readers (Microfiche, Jackets & Image Cards) ANSI/AIIM MS22-1979.
Association for Information & Image Management Staff. Uniform Product Disclosure for Roll Film Readers: AIIM MS27-1982.
Association of American Geographers. Field Trip Guide, 1984.
Association of American Veterinary Medical Colleges. Veterinary Medical School Admission Requirements in the United States & Canada, 1985-1986. Sawyer, Marcia J., compiled by.
--Veterinary Medical School Admission Requirements in the United States & Canada, 1986-1987. Sawyer, Marcia J., compiled by.
Association of Educational Data Systems. Capitol-izing on Computers in Education: Proceedings. Martin, C. Dianne, ed.
Association of New Jersey Environmental Commissions, jt. auth. see Institute for Environmental Education Staff.
Association of Research Libraries, Office of Management Studies. Annual Report, 1981.
--Annual Report, 1982.
Association of Specialized & Cooperative Library Agencies, Headquaters Staff, compiled by. Directory: State Library Agencies, Consultants, & Adminstrative Staff 1985.
Association of the Bar of the City of New York Staff & Medina, H. R. Freedom of the Press & Fair Trial: Final Report with Recommendations.
Association of Theatrical Artists & Craftspeople Staff. The New York Theatrical Sourcebook 1988.
Association of Trial Lawyers of America. Education Fund Staff. Medical Negligence & Hospital Liability.
Association of Trial Lawyers of America Education Fund Staff. Using Expert Witnesses.
Astafiev, V. Horse with the Pink Mane.
Astaire, Fred. Steps in Time.
--Steps in Time.
Astbury. Introduction to Electrical Applied Physics.
Aste, H., jt. auth. see Cheli, R.
Asthana, Rama K. Henry James: A Study in the Aesthetics of the Novel.
Asthma & Allergy Foundation of America Staff, jt. ed. see Norback, Craig T.
Astin, Alexander W. & Scherrei, Rita A. Maximizing Leadership Effectiveness: Impact of Administrative Style on Faculty & Students.
Astley, Thea. The Acolyte.
--An Item from the Late News.
Aston, Athina. How to Play with Your Baby.
--Toys That Teach Your Child: From Birth to Two. Emerson, William A., ed.
Aston, Hugh see Buck, P. C. & Fellowes, E. H.
Aston, Margaret. The Fifteenth Century: The Prospect of Europe.
Aston, Michael. Interpreting the Landscape: Landscape Archaeology.
Aston, Paul, tr. see Konrad, George.
Aston, Trevor, ed. Crisis in Europe, Fifteen Sixty to Sixteen Sixty: Essays from "Past & Present"
Astor, Brooke. The Last Blossom on the Plum Tree.
Astrachan, Anthony. How Men Feel: Their Response to Women's Demands for Independence, Equality & Power.
Astroff, Milton T. & Abbey, James R. Convention Sales & Services.
Astrom, Paul, jt. auth. see Gullberg, Elsa.
Astuni, Maria R. A Guide to the Archives.
Asturias, Miguel A. Mulata.
Aszkenas, Kathy R., ed. see Carter, Paul V.
Atal, C. K., et al, eds. see Survey & Cultivation of Edible Mushrooms in India, National Symposium Staff.
Atamian, Sarkis. Armenian Community.
Atanassova, T., et al. Bulgarian-English Dictionary.
AT&T Computer Information Systems, Inc. Staff. AT&T Computer Software Guide.
Atassi, M. Z., ed. Immunobiology of Proteins & Peptides II.
Atcheson, Jean, ed. see Johner, Martin & Goldberg, Gary.
Atcheson, Jean, ed. see Sass, Lorna J.
Atcheson, Jean, ed. see Sax, Richard.
Atcheson, Jean, ed. see Taylor, Suzanne.
Atcheson, Mack & Mills, John. ECONOCALC (TM) Project & Venture Economics & Analysis.
Atcheson, Richard, ed. see Dupree, Nathalie.
Atcheson, Richard, ed. see Middione, Carlo.
Atcheson, Richard, ed. see Urvater, Michele.
Atchison, Evelyn, jt. auth. see Glass, Marion.
Atchison, Thomas J. & Hill, Winston W. Management Today: Managing Work in Organizations.
Athanasoulis, Christos A., et al. Interventional Radiology.
Athanassova, T. & Roussev, M. Bulgarian-English, English-Bulgarian Dictionary (1973-1975)
Athayde, Roberto. Miss Margarida's Way.
Athearn, Furden. How to Divorce Your Wife.
--How to Divorce Your Wife.
Athearn, Robert G. The Mythic West in Twentieth-Century America.
Athenaeum of Philadelphia Staff. Catalog of Architectural Drawings: The Athenaeum of Philadelphia.
Athens, Art. The WCBS Smokers' Clinic Book.
Atherton, Alexine L., ed. International Organizations: A Guide to Information Sources.
Atherton, Henry V. & Newlander, John A. Chemistry & Testing of Dairy Products.
Atherton, J. C. & Mumphrey, Anthony. Essential Aspects of Career Planning & Development.
Atherton, W., et al. Power Plant Fitting & Testing.
Athey, Thomas H. & Zmud, Robert W. Introduction to Computers & Information Systems Without Basic.
--Introduction to Computers & Information Systems with BASIC.
Athey, Thomas H., et al. Computers & End-User Software: With BASIC.
--Computers & End User Software Without Basic.
Athill, Diana. After a Funeral.
Athreya, Balu H. Clinical Methods in Pediatric Diagnosis.
Atil, Esin, et al. Islamic Metalwork in the Freer Gallery of Art.
Atiya, Aziz S. The Crusade: Historiography & Bibliography.
Atiyah, P. S. Accidents, Compensation & the Law.
Atkeson, Ray, photos by. The Oregon Coast.
--Oregon II.
--Portrait of California.
--Portrait of Washington.
--Washington II.
Atkin, Jane. A Fragile Deception.
--Knights of Illusions.
Atkin, M. J., ed. ICCH Commodities & Financial Futures Yearbook, 1983-84.
Atkin, William W. Architectural Presentation Techniques.
Atkins, A. G., et al. History of GWR Goods Wagons.
Atkins, Dale V. Sisters.
Atkins, E. Wulstan. The Elgar-Atkins Friendship.
Atkins, Elizabeth H. Treasures of the Medranos.
Atkins, G. L. Multicompartment Models for Biological Systems.
Atkins, Hazel. The Receptionist.
Atkins, John. Six Novelists Look at Society.
Atkins, M. H. & Lowe, J. F. Case Studies in Pollution Control in the Textile Dyeing & Finishing Industries: A Study in Non-Technical Language of Essential Information on the Economics of Control, the Problems & Their Solutions.
--Economics of Pollution Control in the Non-Ferrous Metals Industry.
Atkins, Michael D. Insects in Perspectives.
Atkins, Robert C., ed. Peritonial Dialysis.
Atkins, Stuart, ed. Age of Goethe: An Anthology of German Literature 1749-1832.
Atkinson, Alta. Volume Feeding Menu Selector. Blair, Eulalia, ed.
Atkinson, C. T., jt. auth. see Johnson, Arthur H.
Atkinson, Carroll. The Show Must Go On -- Even for Children.
Atkinson, Christine. Making Sense of Piaget: The Philosophical Roots.
Atkinson, Clifford W. A Lay Ministers Guide to the Book of Common Prayer.
Atkinson, David. Hotel & Catering French: A New Approach for Advanced Students & Practitioners.
--Menu French.
Atkinson, G. Origin & Chemistry of Petroleum: Proceedings of the Third Annual Karcher Symposium, Oklahoma, 1979. Zuckerman, J. J., ed.
Atkinson, Holly. Women & Fatigue: Effective Solutions to This Very Real Problem.
Atkinson, Hugh. The Rainbow Below. Oswald, Kent, ed.
Atkinson, Hugh C., ed. Theodore Dreiser: A Checklist.
Atkinson, J. Baines. The Beauty of Holiness.
Atkinson, J. Maxwell. Order in Court: The Organization of Verbal Interaction in Judicial Settings.
Atkinson, James. An Account of the State of Agriculture & Grazing in New South Wales.
Atkinson, James, ed. Luther: Early Theological Works.
Atkinson, Leslie D. & Murray, Mary E. Understanding the Nursing Process.
Atkinson, Lloyd C. Economics: The Science of Choice.
Atkinson, Margaret E., ed. see Tieck, Ludwig & Brentano.
Atkinson, Paul. The Clinical Experience.
Atkinson, Paul, jt. auth. see Rees, Teresa L.
Atkinson, R. S., et al. A Synopsis of Anaesthesia.
Atkinson, Rhonda H. & Longman, Debbie. Reading Enhancement & Development.
Atkinson, Rita L., et al. Introduction to Psychology.
--Introduction to Psychology.
Atkinson, Ruth A., jt. ed. see Appenzeller, Otto.
Atkinson, Sallyanne. Around Brisbane: Including Gold Coast, Sunshine Coast & Toowoomba.
--Brisbane Guide.
Atkinson, Scott & Sharpe, Fred. Wild Plants of the San Juan Islands.

Atkinson, William. Working at Home: Is It for You?
Atlantic Council's Special Committee on Intergovernmental Organization & Reorganization. Beyond Diplomacy.
Atlas, James. Delmore Schwartz: The Life of an American Poet.
--The Great Pretender.
Atlas, Ronald M. Microbiology: Fundamentals & Applications.
Atlas, Ronald M. & Brown, Alfred E. Experimental Microbiology.
Atluri, S. N., jt. ed. see Perrone, N.
Atluri, Satya & Perrone, Nicholas, eds. Computer Methods for Nonlinear Solids & Structural Mechanics.
Atomic Industrial Forum Staff. Industry's Role in Development of Fusion Power: Set of Papers.
--An Overview of Decommissioning Nuclear Power Plants.
--Positive Experiences in Constructing & Operating Nuclear Power Plants Worldwide.
--Radiation Education Notebook.
--Radiation Issues for the Nuclear Industry: Set of Papers from AIF Conference on Radiation.
--Use of Potassium Iodide in Emergency Planning for Nuclear Power Plants: Selected Technical Papers from Radiation Issues.
Atomic Industries Forum, Inc., Nuclear Energy Services Division Staff. An Engineering Evaluation of Nuclear Power Reactor Decommissioning Alternatives (AIF-NESP-009).
Atre, Shaku. Database Management Systems for the Eighties.
Atre, Shakuntala. Data Base: Structured Techniques for Design, Performance & Management: With Case Studies.
Atreya, S. K. & Caldwell, J. J., eds. Planetary Aeronomy & Astronomy.
Atta, Robert E. Van see Van Atta, Robert E.
Atta, Winfred Van see Van Atta, Winfred.
Attar, Farid. Muslim Saints & Mystics: Episodes from the Tadhkirat Al-Auliya (Memorial of the Saints) Arberry, A. J., tr. from Persian.
Attar, Farid Ud-Din. The Conference of the Birds: A Sufi Fable. Nott, C. S., tr.
Attardi, Guiseppe, et al. Animal Ribosomes: Experimental Studies of the Last Five Years.
Atteberry, William L., et al. Real Estate Law.
Attenborough, David. The Tribal Eye.
Atteraas, L., et al, eds. Underwater Technology-Offshore Petroleum: Proceedings of the International Conference, Bergen, Norway, April 14-16 1980.
Atterbury, Paul. English Rivers & Canals.
Atthill, Catherine, tr. see Zanetti, Adriano.
Attia, Zizo. A Flower Veils the Sun.
Attikiouzel, J. Pascal for Electronic Engineers.
Attikioyzel. Pascal for Electrical Engineers.
Attinelli, E. J. A Bibliography of American Numismatic Auction Catalogues, 1828-1875.
Attinello, Lauren. Wintertime in Fraggle Rock.
Attinello, Lauren, illus. Baby Piggy's Purse.
Attinger, E. O., ed. Global Systems Dynamics.
Attiret, Jean D. & Shenstone, William. A Particular Account of the Emperor of China's Gardens Near Peking with Unconnected Thoughts on Gardening & Other Items: An Essay on Design in Gardening. Hunt, John D., ed.
Attiyeh & Lumsden. The American Economics Series.
Attman, Arthur. American Bullion in the European World Trade 1600-1800.
--The Bullion Flow Between Europe & the East, 1000-1750.
Attner, Raymond F., jt. auth. see Plunkett, Warren R.
Attoe, Wayne. Architecture & Critical Imagination.
Attwood, C., ed. Practical Tables, Vol. 3: Six-Figure Trigonometrical Functions of Angles in Degrees & Minutes.
Attwood, John. A Roof over My Head.
Attwood, William. Making It Through Middle Age: Notes While in Transit.
Attwood, William, tr. see Vadim, Roger.
Atwan, Robert, jt. auth. see McQuade, Donald.
Atwan, Robert & Forer, Bruce, eds. Bedside Hollywood.
Atwater, Constance. Tap Dancing: Techniques, Routines, Terminology.
Atwater, H. A. Introduction to General Relativity.
Atwater, W. Eastwood. Adolescence.
Atwood, Ann. Haiku: The Mood of the Earth.
Atwood, Evangeline. Frontier Politics: Alaska's James Wickersham.
Atwood, Margaret. Bluebeard's Egg & Other Stories.
--Dancing Girls: And Other Stories.
--Dancing Girls & Other Stories.
--Lady Oracle.
--Life Before Man.
--Life Before Man.
--True Stories.
Aubin, Jean-Pierre. Applied Abstract Analysis.
--Applied Functional Analysis.
Aubrey, Bryan. Watchmen of Eternity: Blake's Debt to Jacob Boehme.
Aubrey, John. Brief Lives.
Aubrey, John, jt. auth. see Washburn, W-Ilcomb E.
Aubrey, Paul & Chiltern, Crispin, eds. Nineteen-Eighty-Four in 1984: Autonomy, Control & Communication.
Aubrey, Roger F. Career Development Needs of Thirteen-Year Olds.
Aubrey, Wilson, jt. auth. see Stacey, Nicholas A.
Aubry, Pierre. Trouveres & Troubadours: A Popular Treatise. Aveling, Claude, tr.
Auburn, Mark & Burkman, Katherine. Drama Through Performance.
Auchincloss, Louis. The Country Cousin.
--The Dark Lady.
--Diary of a Yuppie.
--Embezzler.
--Embezzler.
--Honorable Men.
--I Come As a Thief.
--Life, Law & Letters: Essays & Sketches.
--The Partners.
--Pioneers & Caretakers: A Study of Nine American Women Novelists.
--Powers of Attorney.
--Rector of Justin.
--The Rector of Justin.
--Romantic Egoists.
--Skinny Island: More Tales of Manhattan.
--The Winthrop Covenant.
Auchmuty, James A., Jr. Brothers of the Bible.
Auckett, Amelia D. Baby Massage: Parent-Child Bonding Through Touching.
Audah, Abdul Q. Al-Islam bain Jahl 'Abna'ihi wa Ajz Ulama'ihi.
Auden, W. H. Secondary Worlds.
Audi of America Inc. Audi 4000S, 4000CS & Coupe GT Offical Factory Repair Manual: 1984-1987.
Audiberti, Jacques. L' Abhumanisme.
--Ange Aux Entrailles.
--Coeur a Cuivre.
--La Hobereaute.
--Monorail.
--L' Opera du Monde.
--L' Ouvre-Boite: Colloque Abhumaniste.
--Theatre.
--Le Victorieux.
Audretsch, David B. The Effectiveness of Antitrust Policy Towards Horizontal Mergers. Bateman, Fred, ed.
Audubon, John J. The Eighteen Twenty-Six Journal of John James Audubon. Ford, Alice, ed.
Audubon, John J., illus. The Audubon Notebook.
Aue, Maximilian A. E., tr. see Wittgenstein, Ludwig.
Auer, John J. An Introduction to Research in Speech.
Auer, L. The Pathogenesis of Hypertensive Encephalography.
Auer, Leopold, ed. see Corelli, A.
Auerbach & Geehr. Management of Wilderness & Environmental Emergencies.
Auerbach, Charlotte. Mutation Research: Problems, Results & Perspectives.
--Notes for Introductory Courses in Genetics.
Auerbach, Doris. Sam Shepard, Arthur Kopit, & the Off-Broadway Theater.
Auerbach, Elias. Moses. Lehman, Israel O. & Barclay, Robert A., trs. from Ger.
Auerbach, Jessica. Winter Wife.
Auerbach, Leo. The Babylonian Talmud.
Auerbach, Nina. Ellen Terry: Player in Her Time.
Auerbach, Paul S. & Geehr, Edward C., eds. Management of Wilderness & Environmental Emergencies.
Auerbach, Robert D. Financial Markets & Institutions.
Auerbach, William. Last of the Panzers: German Tanks 1944-1945.
Aufiero, Lawrence J., jt. auth. see Fuori.
Aufmann, Richard N. & Barker, Vernon C. Arithmetic: An Applied Approach.
--Basic College Mathematics: An Applied Approach.
--Intermediate Algebra: An Applied Approach.
--Introductory Algebra: An Applied Approach.
Aufmann, Richard N., jt. auth. see Barker, Vernon C.
Augarten, Stan. Bit by Bit: An Illustrated History of Computers.
--State of the Art: A Photographic History of the Integrated Circuit.
Augelli, John P. Caribbean Lands.
Augelli, John P., ed. American Neighbors.
--American Neighbors.
Augenstein, Moshe & Tenenbaum, Aaron M. Data Structures Using Pascal.
Auger, G. Hooper's Voluntary Liquidation.
Auger, Pierre. Current Trends in Scientific Research.
Augsburger, David. Cherishable: Love & Marriage.
--The Freedom of Forgiveness.
--Sustaining Love: Healing & Growth in the Passages of Marriage. Roe, Earl, ed.
Augsburger, David W. Anger & Assertiveness in Pastoral Care. Clinebell, Howard J. & Stone, Howard W., eds.
Augsburger, Myron S. When Reason Fails: Vol. I, Church Slavonic-South Slavic-West Slavic.
Augur, Helen. The Book of Fairs.
August, J. Thomas, ed. Biological Response Mediators & Modulators (Symposium)
August, Tony, jt. auth. see Lownds, Camille.
Augustin, John S. The Indian Family in Transition.
Augustine, Lloyd, jt. auth. see Gabler, MaryJean.
Augustinus, Aurelius. De Perfectione Ivstitiae Hominis, De Gestis Pelagii, De Gratia Christi et De Peccato Originali Liber Duo.
--De Utilitate Credendi. Bd. with De Duabus Animabus; Contra Fortunatem; Contra Adimantum. Johnson Repr.
Augustinus, Saint Aurelius. Retractationum Libri Duo.
Auken, Robert C. Van see Van Auken, Robert C.
Aukerman, Louise R., jt. auth. see Aukerman, Robert C.
Aukerman, Robert C. Basil Reader Approach to Reading.
Aukerman, Robert C. & Aukerman, Louise R. How Do I Teach Reading?
Aulen, Gustaf. The Faith of the Christian Church. Wahlstrom, Eric H., tr. from Swedish.
--Jesus in Contemporary Historical Research. Hjelm, Ingalill H., tr. from Swedish.
Aulen, Gustaf E. Reformation & Catholicity. Wahlstrom, Eric H., tr. from Swedish.
Auletta, Ken. Greed & Glory on Wall Street: The Fall of House of Lehman.
Aulock, Wilhelm H. Von see Von Aulock, Wilhelm H.
Ault, Norman, ed. Elizabethan Lyrics from the Original Texts.
Ault, Orvill E. The Castles in Spain.
Aultman, Dick, jt. auth. see Trevino, Lee.
Aultman, Dick, ed. see Toski, Bob.
Aumiaux, M. The Use of Microprocessors. Hutt, Annel, tr.
Aumont, Jean-Pierre. Sun & Shadow.
Aune, David E. Jesus & the Synoptic Gospels: A Bibliographic Study Guide. Branson, Mark L., ed.
--Prophecy in Early Christianity & the Ancient Mediterranean World.
Aung San Suu Kyi. Aung San.
Auping, Michael. Jess: Pasteups Nineteen Fifty-One to Nineteen Eighty-Three.
Aurbach, Joseph, et al. Transformational Grammar: A Guide for Teachers.
Aurigemma, Ann & Bohny, Barbara. Dosage Calculation: Method & Workbook.
Aurobindo, Sri. Sri Aurobindo on the Tantra. Pandit, Sri M. P., compiled by.
Ausberger, Carolyn & Martin, Margaret J. Learning to Talk Is Child's Play.
Ausdle, Stephen Van see Van Ausdle, Stephen.
Ausdle, Steven Van see Van Ausdle, Steven.
Ausebel, J. & Biswas, A. K. Climatic Constraints & Human Activities.
Auslander, D. M., ed. Case Studies in Computer Control.
Auslander, David & Sagues, Paul. Microprocessors for Measurement & Control.
Auslender, A., et al, eds. Optimization & Optimal Control: Proceedings.
Aussenegg, F. R., jt. auth. see Arecchi, F. T.
Austen, Jane. The Jane Austen Library Vol. I: Lady Susan. Chapman, R. W., ed.
--Mansfield Park.
--Pride & Prejudice.
--Pride & Prejudice.
Austen, Jane, et al. Sanditon.
Austen, W. Gerald, jt. auth. see Behrendt, Douglas M.
Auster, Paul. Wall Writing.
Auster, Paul, ed. & tr. see Joubert, Joseph.
Auster, Rolf. Depreciation Desk Book.
--Option Writing & Hedging Strategies: With Special Chapters on the Chicago Board Options Exchange, Convertible Strategies, Warrant Strategies.
--Tax Tested Strategies in Securities & Options Investments.
Austgen, Robert J. Natural Motivation in the Pauline Epistles.
Austin, Allan D. African Muslims in Antebellum America: A Sourcebook.
Austin, Bill. How to Get What You Pray For.
Austin, C. The Cow & the Coronary: Diary of Discovery, Nineteen Forty-Eight to Nineteen Seventy-Eight.
Austin, Dee. Promise Forever.
--Reckless Heart.
Austin, Douglas V., et al. Modern Banking: A Practical Guide to Managing Deregulated Financial Institutions.
Austin, E. L. Earth's Greatest Day.
Austin, G. R. Early Childhood Education: An International Perspective.
Austin, Gregory A., et al. Drug Use & Abuse: A Guide to Research Findings.
Austin, Harold S. Bread & Water: Welfare & Prison Affluence.
Austin, Jacqueline & Isern, Margarita S. Technical Mathematics.
Austin, Karl L., tr. see Dexeus, Santiago, Jr., et al.
Austin, L. G., et al. Process Engineering of Size Reduction: Ball Milling.
Austin, Larry & Clark, Thomas. Learning to Compose.
Austin, Larry M. & Burns, James R. Management Science.
Austin, Larry M., jt. auth. see Burns, James R.
Austin, Martha & Lynch, Regina. Saad Ahaah Sinil: Dual Language.
Austin, Mary S. Philip Freneau, the Poet of the Revolution. Vreeland, Helen K., ed.
Austin, Melanie, jt. auth. see Rodabaugh, Barbara J.
Austin, P. B. Life & Songs of Carl Michael Bellman.
Austin, Phil. Capturing Mood in Watercolor.
Austin, R. G. The Black Box.
--Creatures of the Dark.
--Happy Birthday to You.
--Islands of Terror.
--The Secret Life of Toys.
--The Shadow Stealers.
--Ten-Ton Monster.
--Trapped in the Black Box.
--Wow! You Can Fly!
Austin, Richard. Report Graphics: Writing the Design Report.
Austin, Richard L., et al. Yearbook of Landscape Architecture: Historic Preservation.
Austin, William M. Job Outlook in Brief.
Austin-Lett, Genelle & Sprague, Janet. Talk to Yourself: Experiencing Intrapersonal Communication.
Austrian Academy of Sciences Symposium Staff. Synchronization of EEG Activity in Epilepsies: Proceedings of the Austrian Academy of Sciences Symposium, Vienna, 1971. Petsche, H. & Brazier, Mary A., eds.
Austrian Society for Electron Microscopy Staff. Principles of Neurotransmission: Proceedings of the International Symposium of the Austrian Society for Electron Microscopy, Vienna, Nov. 30, 1973. Stockinger, L., ed.
Austrin, Miriam G. Young's Learning Medical Terminology Step by Step: Textbook & Workbook.
Austwick, Brian, jt. auth. see Austwick, Jill.
Austwick, Jill & Austwick, Brian. Decorated Tile: An Illustrated History of English Tile-Making & Design.
Ausubel, Frederick, et al, eds. Current Protocols in Molecular Biology.
Ausubel, Herman. In Hard Times: Reformers among the Late Victorians.
Ausubel, Nathan. Pictorial History of the Jewish People.
Auth, Joanne B. Deskbook of Math Formulas & Tables.
Auth, Tony. Behind the Lines: Cartoons.
Author's Guild Inc. Staff. Creation & Annihilation Operators.
Automatic Demonstrations Symposium Staff. Proceedings of the Automatic Demonstration Symposium, Versaille, 1968. Laudet, M., et al, eds.
Automation Technology Symposium Staff. Automation Technology for Management & Productivity Advancements Through CAD-CAM & Engineering Data Handling: Proceedings of the Automation Technology Symposium, 3rd, Monterey, Calif, Sept. 1981. Wang, Peter C., ed.
Automobile Association of England. Book of British Towns.
--Book of the Car.
--Hand-Picked Tours of Britain.
Automobile Association of England Staff. Illustrated Guide to Britain.
--New Book of the Road.
Automobile Association Staff. AA Touring Map of Western Europe.
Automobile Club of Italy Staff. World Cars, 1983.
--World Cars, 1984.
Automobile Club of Italy Staff, compiled by. World Cars, 1972.
Automobile Club of Italy Staff, ed. World Cars 1973.
--World Cars, 1975.
--World Cars 1977.
--World Cars 1981.
Automobile Quarterly Staff. Mercedes-Benz: A Century of Invention.
Autrum, H., et al, eds. see Animal Orientation Symposium Staff.
Autrup, Herman N., jt. ed. see Harris, Curtis C.
Autry, William O., Jr. & Hinshaw, Jane S. A Cultural Resource Reconnaissance of the Tennessee National Wildlife Refuge with Archaeological Survey of Selected Areas.
Autumn, Violeta. A Russian Jew Cooks in Peru.
Auxter, David & Pyfer, Jean. Principles & Methods of Adapted Physical Education & Recreation.
Au-Yang, M. K., ed. Flow-Induced Vibration of Power Plant Components.

Au-Yang, M. K. & Brown, S. J., Jr., eds. Fluid-Structure Interaction Phenomena in Pressure Vessel & Piping Systems, Series PVP-PB-026.
Au-Yang, M. K. & Moody, F. J., eds. Interactive-Fluid-Structural Dynamic Problems in Power Engineering.
Au-Yang, M. K., et al, eds. Dynamics of Fluid-Structure Systems in the Energy Industry.
Avalos, B. & Haddad, W. Resena de la Investigacion sobre Efectividad de los Maestros en Africa, America Latina, Filipinas, India, Malasia, Medio Oriente y Tailandia: Sintesis de Resultados.
Avanesov, G. Principles of Criminology.
Avanesov, R. I. Modern Russian Stress.
Avant, Gayle. American Government.
Avant, William E. The Story of How the Easter Bunny Got His Wife.
Avato, Rose M., jt. ed. see Foy, Felician A.
Avedeyenko, Y. Wild Hop Leaf.
Avedon, Luciana & Molli, Jeanne. Luciana Avedon's Body Book.
Aveling, Claude, tr. see Aubry, Pierre.
Aveling, Edward, tr. see Engels, Frederick.
Avellani, Pamela B., jt. auth. see Vandergoot, David.
Aven, Del. Anna's Tree Swing.
Avenarius, Ferdinand. Das Bild Als Naar.
Avendano, Jorge, et al, eds. Workers' Self-Management & Participation National Reports, Vol. I: Bangladesh, Malta, Peru, Yugoslavia.
Aveni, Anthony F., ed. Native American Astronomy.
Averbakh, Y. Chess Endings: Essential Knowledge.
Averitt, Max W. Boatwatch.
Avers, Charlotte. Genetics, Revised Edition.
Avery, C. The New Century Handbook of Leaders of the Classical World.
Avery, Clarence G., jt. auth. see Istvan, Donald F.
Avery, Curtis E. & Johannis, Theodore B., Jr. Love & Marriage: A Guide for Young People.
Avery, David R., jt. auth. see McDonald, Ralph E.
Avery, Emmett L., ed. see Congreve, William.
Avery, H. E. & Shaw, D. J. Basic Physical Chemistry Calculations.
Avery, Mary E. & Litwack, Georgia. Born Early: The Story of a Premature Baby.
Avery Memorial Library, Columbia University. Avery Index to Architectural Periodicals: 1987.
Avery, Virginia. Big Book of Applique.
--Quilts to Wear.
Avestruz, Fred S. Risk & Technology Choice in Developing Countries: The Case of Philippine Sugar Factories.
Aviado, D. M., jt. auth. see Salem, H.
Aviation Book Company, ed. see Federal Aviation Administration Staff.
Aviation Maintenance Publishers Staff. Pilot Logbook.
Aviation Supplies & Academics. Flight Instructor Test Book.
Aviation Supplies & Academics Staff. Aim, 1988.
--Aviation Mechanic Airframe Test Guide.
--FAR, 1988.
Aviel, S. David, jt. auth. see Duncan, Doris G.
Avila, jt. auth. see Combs, Arthur W.
Avineri, Shlomo, jt. auth. see Sisco, Joseph J.
Avioli, Louis V. & Krane, Stephen M., eds. Metabolic Bone Disease.
Avirgan, Tony & Honey, Martha. War in Uganda: The Legacy of Idi Amin.
Avis, F. C. Bookman's Concise Dictionary.
--Boxing Dictionary.
--Printers Arithmetic.
Avis, Paul. The Foundations of Modern Historical Thought: From Machiavelli to Vico.
Avis, Paul D. The Church in the Theology of the Reformers. Toon, Peter & Martin, Ralph, eds.
Avitable, Gunhild G. Cloisonne & Champleve, Fourteen Hundred to Nineteen Hundred.
Avi-Yonah, M., et al, eds. see Jones, Arnold H.
Avi-Yonah, Michael. The Art of Mosaics.
--Search for the Past: An Introduction to Archaeology.
Avogaro, P., jt. ed. see Galli, C.
Avon Products. Looking Good, Feeling Beautiful.
Avrett, Roz. My Turn.
--Seventy-Second & Rodeo.
Avsey, Ignat, tr. see Dostoyevsky, Fyodor.
Avtgis, Alexander W., jt. auth. see Villanucci, Robert S.
Avyzius, J. The Lost Home.
Aw, S. E. Chemical Evolution.
Awad, A. G., et al. Evaluation of Quality of Care in Psychiatry: Proceedings of a Symposium Held at the Queen St. Mental Health Centre, Toronto, Canada, June 22, 1979.
Awad, Mubarak, jt. auth. see Kennedy, Scott.
Awashti, D. D. Catalogue of the Lichens from India, Nepal, Pakistan & Ceylon.
Awasthi, Rajendra. The Red Soil.
Awdry, Philip & Nicholls, C. S. Cataract.
Awh, Robert Y. Microeconomics: Theory & Applications.
Axe, John. Collectible Sonja Henie.
--Tammy & Dolls You Love to Dress.
Axe, John & Mandeville, Glenn A. Celebrity Doll Price Guide & Annual.
Axelrad, D. R., ed. see CISM (International Center for Mechanical Sciences), Department of Mechanics of Solids Staff.
Axelrod, A. Reanimacion Sin Sensaciones.
Axelrod, Alan, ed. The Colonial Revival in America.
Axelrod, Herbert, jt. auth. see Emmens, Clifford W.
Axelrod, Regina. Conflict Between Energy & Urban Environment: Consolidated Edison Versus the City of New York.
Axinn, Donald E. Against Gravity: Poems.
--Against Gravity: Poems Nineteen Eighty-Two to Nineteen Eighty-Five.
--The Hawk's Dream & Other Poems.
Axline, Virginia M. Dibs: In Search of Self.
Axline, W. Andrew. Caribbean Integration: The Politics of Regional Negotiations.
Axnick, Karen & Yarbrough, Mary. Infection Control: An Integrated Approach.
Axsom, Richard H. Parade: Cubism As Theater.
Axtell, James. The School Upon a Hill: Education & Society in Colonial New England.
Axton, Richard. European Drama of the Early Middle Ages.
Ayal, Eliezer B., ed. Micro Aspects of Development.
Ayala, Francisco. El Rapto. Boring, Phyllis Z., ed.
Ayala, Mitzi. The Farmer's Cookbook: A Collection of Favorite Recipes, Economical Meal Planning Methods & Other Tips & Pointers from America's Farm Kitchens.
Ayandele, Emmanuel A. Missionary Impact on Modern Nigeria, 1842-1914.
Ayckbourn, Alan. The Norman Conquests: Table Manners, Living Together, Round & Round the Garden.
--Three Plays: Absurd Person Singular, Absent Friends, & Bedroom Farce.
Aycock, Martha B., ed. Understanding: A Resource Book for Use with Persons Who Have Learning Difficulties.
Aydon, Cyril. How to Finance Your Company.
Ayensu, Edward S., et al. Our Green & Living World: The Wisdom to Save It. Goodwin, Joseph, ed.
Ayer, A. J. Part of My Life: The Memoirs of a Philosopher.
Ayer, Eleanor, jt. ed. see Jene-Hagan Bookcorp Staff.
Ayer, Frederick W. Woman at Apocalypse.
Ayer, Jacqueline. Nu Dang & His Kite.
--Wish for Little Sister.
Ayer, Jacqueline, ed. & illus. see Grimm, Jacob & Grimm, Wilhelm K.
Ayer, Sam & Alaszewski, Andy. Community Care & the Mentally Handicapped: Services for Mothers & Their Mentally Handicapped Children.
Ayer, W. R., ed. Some Social Aspects of Dentistry.
Ayers, John. Japanese Ceramics.
Ayers, John, jt. auth. see Howard, David S.
Ayers, Ruby M. Starless Night.
Ayerst, David. Garvin of the OBSERVER.
Ayerst, Peter, jt. auth. see Wilson, Derek.
Aykroyd, Peter. Modern Gymnastics: Skills & Techniques.
Aylen, R., et al. Heavy Vehicle Fitting.
Aylen, R., et al, eds. Light Vehicle Fitting.
--Vehicle Fitting.
Aylesworth, Jim. Hush Up!
--Mary's Mirror.
--Tonight's the Night. Fay, Ann, ed.
Aylesworth, Thomas G. Science Looks at Mysterious Monsters.
--The Story of Dragons & Other Monsters.
--The Story of Werewolves.
Aylesworth, Tom & Bowman, John. The World Almanac of Who's Who of Film.
Aylett, B. J. Organometallic Compounds, Vol. 1, Pt. 2: Groups IV & V.
Ayliffe, G. A. & Taylor, L. J. Hospital-Acquired Infection: Principles & Prevention.
Ayliffe-Jones, Noel. World Tanks & Reconnaissance Vehicles since 1945.
Aylward, Jim. Your Burro Is No Jackass.
--Your Burro is No Jackass: And over 100 Other Things No One Ever Told You.
--You're Dumber in the Summer: And Over 100 Other Things No One Ever Told You.
Aylwin, Susan. Structure in Thought & Feeling.
Ayme, Marcel. La Belle Image.
--Le Boeuf Clandestin.
--Brulebois.
--Le Chemin des Ecoliers.
--The Green Mare. Denny, Norman, tr.
--Jambees.
--Jument Verte.
--La Jument Verte.
--La Mouche Bleue.
--Les Oiseaux de Lune.
--Le Passe-Muraille.
--Uranus.
--La Vouivre.
Aynesworth, Hugh, jt. auth. see Michaud, Stephen G.
Ayoob, M. The Truth about Self-Protection: Streetfighting Techniques, Mace, Improvised Weapons & Firearms, Locks, Alarms, & Dogs.
Ayres, A. Jean. Interpreting the Southern California Sensory Integration Tests.
Ayres, John C. & Kirschman, John C., eds. Impact of Toxiology on Food Processing.
Ayres, Ruby M. Life Steps In.
Ayscough, Florence & Lowell, Amy, trs. from Chinese. Fir-Flower Tablets.
Azaad, Meyer, jt. auth. see Fardjam, Faridah.
Azad, Hardam S. Industrial Wastewater Management Handbook.
Azar, Edward E. & Burton, John W., eds. International Conflict Resolution: Theory & Practice.
Azar, J. J. Matrix Structural Analysis.
Azarov, Y. Book about Bringing Up Children.
Azbel, David. Chemical & Process Equipment Design: Vessel Design & Selection.
Azbel, David S., jt. ed. see Cheremisinoff, Nicholas P.
Azbel, Mark Y. Refusenik: Trapped in the Soviet Union. Forbes, Grace P., ed.
Azen, S. P., jt. auth. see Afifi, A. A.
Azevedo, Carlos de see De Azevedo, Carlos.
Azevedo, Ross. Labor Economics: A Guide to Information Sources.
Aziz, A. K., ed. The Mathematical Foundations of the Finite Element Method with Applications to Partial Differential Equations.
Aziz, A. K., et al, eds. Control Theory of Systems Governed by Partial Differential Equations.
Aziz, Harry. Police Procedures & Defense Tactics Training Manual. Halet, Sydney S., ed.
Aziza, C. & Olivieri, C. Dictionnaire des Types et Charateres Litteraires.
Azrael, Mary. Victorians.
Azzolina, David S. Tale Type & Motif Indexes: An Annotated Bibliography.
Azzone, G. F., ed. Mechanisms in Bioenergetics.
Azzone, G. F., ed. see Biochemistry & Biophysics of Mitochondrial Membranes Symposium Staff.

B

Baader, Juan. The Sailing Yacht. Moore, Inge, tr.
Baar, James & Howard, William E. Polaris! The Concept & Creation of a New & Mighty Weapon.
Baar, James A. Great Free Enterprise Gambit.
Baark, Erik. Context of National Information Systems in Developing Countries: India & China in a Comparative Perspective.
Baartz, A. P., tr. see Hahn, W.
Baas, Jacquelynn, et al. Treasures of the Hood Museum of Art, Dartmouth College.
Baba, Meher. The Narrow Lane. Le Page, William, ed.
Baba, Meher, et al. Meher Baba Journal. Patterson, Elizabeth, ed.
--Meher Baba Journal. Patterson, Elizabeth C., ed.
--Meher Baba Journal. Patterson, Elizabeth C., ed.
--Meher Baba Journal. Patterson, Elizabeth C., ed.
--Meher Baba Journal. Patterson, Elizabeth C., ed.
Babad, Elisha Y. & Birnbaum, Max. The Social Self: Group Influences on Personal Identity.
Babalova, L. L. & Iyevleva, Z. N. Russian for Everybody: Introductory Lessons.
Babb, Drew & Alexander, Jann. The No Book.
Babb, Harold, jt. auth. see Taylor, Vic.
Babb, Hugh W., tr. see Lenin, V. I., et al.
Babb, Hugh W., tr. see Petrazhitskii, Lev I.
Babb, Janice B. & Dordick, B. F., eds. Real Estate Information Sources.
Babbage, Ross. Rethinking Australia's Defence.
Babbie, Earl. The Practice of Social Research.
Babbitt, Natalie. Goody Hall.
--Knee-Knock Rise.
--The Search for Delicious.
Babcock, Dennis & Boyd, Preston. Careers in the Theater.
Babcock, Dorothy E. & Keepers, Terry D. Raising Kids O. K.
Babcock, Nicolas. Billy's Army.
Babel, Issac. Benya Krik, the Gangster & Other Stories. Yarmolinsky, Avraham, ed.
Babic, S. Serbo-Croat for Foreigners.
--Serbo-Croatian Reading Passages, with Comments, Exercises, Vocabulary.
Babic, Slauna. Serbo-Croatian for Foreigners.
Babin, David E. Celebration of Life: Our Changing Liturgy.
--Doing the Eucharist: A Guide to Trial Use.
--Introduction to the Liturgy of the Lord's Supper.
Babin, E., jt. auth. see Wackenheim, A.
Babington, K. G. The Kremlin Cat & the Bomb.
Babister, A. W. Aircraft Stability & Control.
Babor, Daryl, jt. auth. see Marten, Gerald G.
Babrius, Valerius. Aesop's Fables. Hull, Denison B., tr. from Gr.
Babson, Marian. Murder on a Mystery Tour.
--A Trail of Ashes.
Babson, Marion. Death in Fashion.
Babson, Steve. Working Detroit: The Making of a Union Town.
Babuscio, Jack. We Speak for Ourselves: Experiences in Homosexual Counselling.
Baca. Los Angeles in Your Pocket.
Baca, Leonard M. & Cervantes, Hermes. The Bilingual Special Education Interface.
Baca, Murtha, tr. see Pignatti, Terisio.
Baccetti, Baccio, ed. Comparative Spermatology.
Bacchylides. Bacchylides: Complete Poems. Fagles, Robert, tr.
Bach, C. Microeconomics: Analysis & Applications.
Bach, Fritz H., ed. Clinical Immunobiology.
Bach, Fritz H. & Good, Robert A., eds. Clinical Immunobiology.
Bach, Fritz H., et al, eds. see ICN-UCLA Symposia Staff.
Bach, George L. Economics: An Introduction to Analysis & Policy.
--Macroeconomics: Analysis & Applications.
Bach, Hans. Jean Pauls Hesperus.
Bach, J. S. Fifteen Three-Part Inventions for Piano. Czerny, Carl, ed.
Bach, Joann, jt. auth. see Rago, Michael.
Bach, Kent & Harnish, Robert M. Linguistic Communication & Speech Acts.
Bach, Michael K., ed. Immediate Hypersensitivity: Modern Concepts & Developments.
Bach, Othello. Lilly, Willy & the Mail-Order Witch.
Bach, Steven. Final Cut: Dreams & Disasters in the Making of Heaven's Gate.
Bach, W., et al, eds. Renewable Energy Prospects: Proceedings of the Conference on Non-Fossil Fuel & Non-Nuclear Fuel Energy Strategies, Honolulu, USS, January 1979.
Bacharach, A. L., jt. ed. see Laurence, D. R.
Bacharach, Alfred L., jt. ed. see Gray, Charles H.
Bacharach, S. L., et al. Electricity & Electronic Fundamentals.
Bachardy, Don, jt. auth. see Isherwood, Christopher.
Bache, William B. Measure for Measure As Dialectical Art.
Bachelard, Gaston. The New Scientific Spirit. Goldhammer, Arthur, tr. from Fr.
Bachelard, H. S. Brain Biochemistry.
Bachelder, Louise, ed. The Gift of Music.
Bachelin, Anita. Mask of Death.
Bacheller, Martin A., ed. Medallion World Atlas: New Census Edition.
--The Whole Earth Atlas: New Census Edition.
Bachhuber, Thomas D. When Your Son or Daughter Plans for the Future.
Bachhuber, Thomas D. & Harwood, Richard K. Directions: A Guide to Career Planning.
Bachl, Norbort, et al. Current Topics in Sports Medicine.
Bachman, George K. Pipefitters & Plumbers Vest Pocket Reference Book.
Bachman, John W. Faith That Makes a Difference.
--Media-Wasteland Or Wonderland: Opportunities & Dangers for Christians in the Electronic Age.
Bachman, Richard. Thinner.
Bachman, Van Cleaf. Peltries or Plantations: The Economic Policies of the Dutch West India Company in New Netherland, 1623-1639.
Bachmann, E. Theodore, tr. see Froer, Hans.
Bachmann, P. A., ed. New Developments in Diagnostic Virology.
Bachmeyer, jt. auth. see Hauenstein.
Bachrach, A. G., ed. see Huygens, L., et al.
Bachrach, A. G., tr. see Huygens, L., et al.
Bachrach, A. L. & Pearce, J. R., eds. The Musical Companion.
Bachrach, Uriel. Function of Naturally Occuring Polyamines.
Bach-Y-Rita, P., jt. ed. see Lennerstrand, G.
Bach-Y-Rita, Paul & Collins, C. C., eds. Brain Mechanisms in Sensory Substitution.
Bacigalupo, Leonard. The Franciscans & Italian Immigration in America.
Bacila, Metry, et al, eds. Biochemistry & Genetics of Yeasts: Pure & Applied Aspects.
Back, Kate, jt. auth. see Back, Ken.
Back, Ken & Back, Kate. Assertiveness at Work: A Practical Guide to Handling Awkward Situations.
Back, M. & Laidler, K. J., eds. Selected Readings in Chemical Kinetics.
Back, Philippa, jt. auth. see Loewenfeld, Claire.
Back, W., jt. ed. see Freeze, R. A.
Back, William R. & Freeze, Allan, eds. Chemical Hydrogeology.
Backe, Torild, et al. Concise Swedish-English Glossary of Legal Terms.
Backer, Dorothy. The Parma Legacy.
Backer, John H. The Decision to Divide Germany: American Foreign Policy in Transition.
Backer, Thomas E. Strategic Planning for Workplace Drug Abuse Programs.

Authors

Backhouse, D., et al. Illustrated Dictionary of Photography.
Backhouse, Janet. The Lindisfarne Gospels.
Backhouse, Janet, et al see Kren, Thomas.
Backhouse, Roger. The History of Modern Economic Analysis.
Backhuys, W. Land & Fresh Water Molluscs of the Azores.
Backman, Milton V., Jr. Christian Churches of America.
Backmund, Herbert, jt. auth. see Decker, Kurt.
Backpacker Magazine Staff, ed. see Bunnelle, Hasse R.
Backscheider, P. R., ed. see Boaden, James.
Backscheider, P. R., ed. see Johnson, Samuel.
Backscheider, P. R., jt. ed. see Kenny, Shirley S.
Backscheider, P. R., ed. see Pix, Mary & Trotter, Catherine.
Backscheider, Paula R. & Nussbaum, Felicity A. Annotated Bibliography of Twentieth Century Critical Studies of Women & Literature, 1660-1800.
Backscheider, Paula R., ed. see Dennis, John.
Backscheider, Paula R., ed. see Gildon, Charles.
Backscheider, Paula R., ed. see Hoole, John.
Backscheider, Paula R., ed. see Inchbald, Elizabeth.
Backscheider, Paula R., ed. see Jephson, Robert.
Backscheider, Paula R., ed. see Murphy, Arthur.
Backscheider, Paula R., ed. see Thomson, James.
Backstrand, G. Resources, Society & Future.
Backus, Jean L., ed. Letters from Amelia: An Intimate Portrait of Amelia Earhart.
Backus, John. The Acoustical Foundations of Music.
Backus, Richard H., jt. auth. see Lineweaver, Thomas H., III.
Bacon, C. Paediatric Emergencies.
Bacon, Daniel W. Who Me? A Missionary?
Bacon, E. M. Principles of Wheel Alignment Service: A Text-Workbook.
Bacon, Francis. Works. Spedding, J., et al, eds.
Bacon, James. Hollywood Is a Four Letter Town.
Bacon, Paul, jt. auth. see Schneider, Steven J.
Bacon, Richard M. The Forgotten Art of Building & Using a Brick Bake Oven.
--The Forgotten Arts.
Bacon, Walter M., Jr., ed. Behind Closed Doors: Secret Papers on the Failure of Romanian-Soviet Negotiations 1931-1932.
Bacq, Z. M. Chemical Transmission of Nerve Impulses: A Historical Sketch.
Bacq, Z. M. & Alexander, P. Fundamentals of Radiobiology.
Bacq, Z. M., et al, eds. Fundamentals of Biochemical Pharmacology.
Badawy, A. A., ed. Biomedical Aspects of Drug Dependence: International Biomedical Research Symposium on Drug Dependence, Tangier, Morocco, 11-15 October 1982.
Badcock, C. R. The Psychoanalysis of Culture.
Badcock, Francis J. The History of the Creeds.
Baddeley, Hiram. Radiological Investigation: A Guide to the Use of Medical Imaging in Clinical Practice.
Baden, John A., jt. auth. see Stroup, Richard L.
Baden-Fuller, A. J. Engineering Field Theory.
--Engineering Field Theory: Text & Examples.
Badenhuizen, N. P. Chemistry & Biology of the Starch Granule.
Baden-Powell, Heather. Baden Powell: A Family Album.
Bader, William & Burt, Daniel S. Miller Analogies Test.
Baderschneider, Earl R. & Miller, Paul F., eds. Labor Arbitration in Health Care.
Badger, D. D. & Bogardus, James. Origins of Cast Iron Architecture in America.
Badger, Daniel D. Badger's Illustrated Catalogue of Cast-Iron Architecture.
Badi, Joseph, ed. Fundamental Laws of the State of Israel.
Badura-Skoda, Eva. Interpreting Mozart on the Keyboard.
Badzinski, Stanley. Carpentry in Commercial Construction.
Bae, Yoong. Paper UFO's.
Baechner, Thomas S. Norman Rockwell Treasury.
Baeck, Leo. Judaism & Christianity: Essays. Kaufmann, Walter, tr.
Baeder, John. Diners.
--Gas, Food, & Lodging.
Baeft, A. & Jeanmart, L., eds. Clinical Computer Tomography Head & Trunk.
Baehler, James R. Book of Perks.
Baehr, Consuelo S. Report from the Heart.
Baehr, H. D., et al, eds. Power Engineering & Technology: Energy Efficient Use of Working Fluids, Alternative Processes, Heat Pumps& Organic Rankine Cycle.
Bae Hrens, Aemilius. Poetae Latini Minores, Leipzig, 1879-1883. Commager, Steele, ed.
Baen, James P., ed. see Bradley, Marion Zimmer.
Baer, Charles J. & Ottaway, John R. Electrical & Electronics Drawing.
Baer, Donald M., jt. auth. see Bijou, Sidney W.
Baer, Gordon & Howell-Koehler, Nancy. Vietnam: The Battle Comes Home.
Baer, J. A. & Lowenhaupt, Cecile K. Dining In - St. Louis.
Baer, Jean. The Self-Chosen: "Our Crowd" Is Dead--Long Live "Our Crowd"
--The Self-Chosen: Our Crowd Is Dead-Long Live Our Crowd!
Baer, Judy. Moonglow.
Baer, Katie. Government by the People.
Baer, Michael, ed. Theory of Chemical Reaction Dynamics.
Baer, Reinhold. Linear Algebra & Projective Geometry.
Baer, Werner & Samuelson, Larry. Latin America in the Post-Import Substitution Era.
Baeriswyl, D. & Bishop, A. Solitons & Polarons in Solid State Physics.
Baernreither, Joseph M. English Associations of Working Men. Taylor, A., tr.
Baeslack, W. A. & Hasson, D. F., eds. Advances in Titanium Welding.
Baetjer, Katharine. European Paintings in the Metropolitan Museum of Art, by Artists Born in or Before 1865: A Summary Catalogue. Shultz, Ellen, ed.
Baeumer, Max L., jt. ed. see Fink, Karl J.
Baeyens, Dennis A. Experimental Physiology.
Bagby, James T. Windows.
Bagby, Joseph R. Real Estate Financing Desk Book.
--Real Estate Financing Desk Book.
Bagchi, P. C. India & China.
Bagchi, T. P. & Templeton, J. G. Numerical Methods in Markov Chains & Bulk Queues.
Bagdikian, Ben H. The Information Machines: Their Impact on Man & the Media.
Bage, Robert. Barham Downs. Paulson, Ronald, ed.
--James Wallace. Paulson, Ronald, ed.
Bage, Robert & Paulson, Ronald. Man As He Is.
Baggett, Glick. Dollhouse Kit & Dining Room Accessories.
--Dollhouse Lamps & Chandeliers.
Bagherzadeh, Firouz, et al. Iran Bastan Museum, Teheran.
Baglee & Morlee. More Street Jewellery.
Bagley, Desmond. Bahama Crisis.
Bagley, Edward B., jt. ed. see Peleg, Micha.
Bagley, F. R., ed. & tr. see Bamdad, Badr ol-Moluk.
Bagley, J. A. & Finley, P. J., eds. Progress in Aerospace Sciences.
Bagley, J. J. Historical Interpretation. Incl. Vol. 1. Sources of English Medieval History, 1066-1540; Vol. 2. Sources of English History, 1540 to Present Day. St Martin.
Bagley, Joyce M. Share My Thoughts, Pretty Please.
Bagley, Val. C. Newlywed Nonsense a Cartoonist's View of the First Year of Marriage.
Bagley, Val C. Very Anxiously Engaged: A Cartoonist's View of Modern Courtship.
Bagnall, Jim, jt. auth. see Koberg, Don.
Bagnato, Stephen J. & Neisworth, John T. Linking Developmental Assessment & Curricula: Prescriptions for Early Intervention.
Bagshaw, Malcolm A. Cancer of the Prostate.
Bahadur, Lal. Indian Freedom Movement & Thought, 1919-1929. Johari, J. C., ed.
Bahar, Mehrdad. Bastoor.
Bahat, S., tr. see Weinreich, Uriel.
Baha'u'llah. Tablets of Baha'u'llah Revealed after the Kitab-i-Aqdas. Effendi, Shoghi & Taherzadeh, Habib, trs.
Bahl, I. J. & Bhartia, P. Microstrip Antennas.
Bahl, Roy, et al. Urban Growth & Local Taxes in Less Developed Countries.
Bahm, Archie J. World's Living Religions.
Bahnsen, Greg L. Homosexuality: A Biblical Perspective.
--Theonomy in Christian Ethics.
Bahr, Amy C. Sometimes It's OK to Tell Secrets.
--What Should You Do When...?
Bahr, Gunter F., jt. auth. see Wied, George.
Bahr, Howard M., et al. Life in Large Families: Views of Mormon Women.
Bahrang, Samuel. Little Black Fish.
Baid, Lloyd. Managing Performance.
Baigell, Matthew. Albert Bierstadt.
Baikov, V. & Sigalov, E. Reinforced Concrete Structures.
Baikova, I. Museums in & Around Moscow.
Bailar, John C., Jr., et al. Chemistry.
Bailes, Frederick. The Secret of Healing.
Bailes, Jack C. Management Budgeting for CETA.
Bailey, A. E., ed. Microwave Measurements.
Bailey, A. J. Support for School Management.
Bailey, Andrew D., jt. auth. see Miller, Martin A.
Bailey, Anne M., ed. The Asiatic Mode of Production: Science & Politics.
Bailey, Anthony. Rembrandt's House.
Bailey, Brian. The English Village Green.
Bailey, Carol R. Treasures of My Heart.
Bailey, Charity, jt. auth. see Abeson, Marion.
Bailey, Christina A., jt. auth. see Bailey, Philip S.
Bailey, D. K. & MacDonald, R., eds. The Evolution of the Crystalline Rocks.
Bailey, D. W. British Military Longarms Eighteen Fifteen to Eighteen Sixty-Five.
Bailey, Dan A., jt. auth. see Knepper, William E.
Bailey, David & Harrison, Martin. Shots of Style: Great Fashion Photographs Chosen by David Bailey.
Bailey, Dudley, ed. Introductory Language Essays.
Bailey, E. Discovering Music with Young Children.
Bailey, Edward P., Jr. The Practical Writer: From Paragraph to Theme.
Bailey, F. L. & Greenya, John. For the Defense.
Bailey, Frank C. Understanding & Flying Ultralights.
Bailey, Geoffrey. Maverick: Succeeding As a Freelance Entrepreneur.
Bailey, George. Armageddon in Prime Time.
--Germans: The Biography of an Obsession.
Bailey, George, ed. Kontinent Four: Contemporary Russian Writers.
Bailey, George G. The Patch Unit.
Bailey, George L., ed. Hemodialysis: Principles & Practice.
Bailey, Gertrude B. If Words Could Set Us Free.
--Two Stories for Little Folk: I Love That School Bus & Guess What Flew in the Window.
Bailey, Guy. Bienvenue Chez Nous-Welcome to Our Town.
Bailey, Helen M., et al. The Latin Americans: Past & Present.
Bailey, Henry J., III. Oregon Uniform Commercial Code.
--Oregon Uniform Commercial Code.
--Secured Transactions in a Nutshell.
Bailey, Jack S. Inside a Mormon Mission.
Bailey, James. Energy Systems: An Analysis for Engineers & Policy Makers.
Bailey, James, jt. auth. see Broyles, Frank.
Bailey, Janet. Keeping Food Fresh.
Bailey, John A. & Deverall, Brian J. The Dynamics of Host Defence.
Bailey, Joyce & Dash, Michael. Picture the People of the Caribbean.
Bailey, Joyce W., et al, eds. Handbook of Latin American Art, Bibliographic Compilation: General References & Art of the 19th & 20th Centuries, North America.
Bailey, Larry J. & Stadt, Ronald W. Career Education: New Approaches to Human Development.
Bailey, Leo L. A Step-by-Step Guide to Landscaping & Gardening.
Bailey, Leslie E., jt. ed. see Shibata, Shoji.
Bailey, Lloyd R. The Word of God: A Guide to English Versions of the Bible.
Bailey, Lloyd R., Sr. Biblical Perspectives on Death. Brueggemann, Walter & Donahue, John R., eds.
Bailey, Michael T. Fight That Ticket in Oregon.
Bailey, N. Louise, et al. Biographical Directory of the South Carolina Senate.
Bailey, Norman T. Mathematics, Statistics & Systems for Health.
Bailey, Philip S. & Bailey, Christina A. Organic Chemistry: A Brief Survey of Concepts & Applications.
Bailey, R., jt. auth. see Foren, R.
Bailey, Richard. Marketing Life & Health Insurance: Student Guide.
Bailey, Richard W. & Robinson, Jay L. Varieties of Present-Day English.
Bailey, Ross R., ed. Single Dose Treatment of Urinary Tract Infection.
Bailey, S. D., ed. Parliamentary Government in the Commonwealth.
Bailey, Samuel. Critical Dissertation on the Nature, Measure & Causes of Value.
Bailey, Thomas C. Descendants of Star.
Bailey, Vicki, jt. ed. see Huisingh, Donald.
Bailey, William A., et al. Bill Bailey Came Home.
Bailey, William J. & Tsuruta, Teiji, eds. Contemporary Topics in Polymer Science.
Baillie, A. & Gilbert, R. J., eds. Automation, Mechanization & Data Handling in Microbiology.
Baillie, Colin. Elizabeth Vige Le Brun.
Baillie, G. H. Clocks & Watches, 1344 to 1800.
Baillie, J. B., tr. see Hegel, Georg W.
Baillie, James B. The Origin & Significance of Hegel's Logic.
Baillie, Kate & Salmon, Tim. The Rough Guide to Paris.
Baillie, Kate, et al. The Rough Guide to France.
Baillie, Thomas W., jt. ed. see De Boer, Jan.
Baily, P. J. Purchasing & Supply Management.
Bailyn, Bernard. The Origins of American Politics.
Bailyn, Bernard & Garrett, Jane N., eds. Pamphlets of the American Revolution, 1750-1776: Vol. 1, 1750-1765.
Bailyn, Bernard, et al. The Great Republic: A History of the American People.
Bain, A. G. & Bonnington, S. T. Hydraulic Transport of Solids by Pipelines.
Bain, Carl, et al. Norton Introduction to Literature: Combined Shorter Ed.
Bain, Carl E., et al, eds. The Norton Introduction to Literature.
--The Norton Introduction to Literature.
Bain, Chester A. The Far East. Bain, June W., ed.
Bain, D. Heavy Current Fluidics.
Bain, David H. Aftershocks: A Tale of Two Victims.
Bain, Donald, jt. auth. see Lake, Veronica.
Bain, Donald, et al. Windy Landowner's Guide to Wind Farm Development.
Bain, E C. Pioneering in Steel Research.
Bain, George. The Methods of Construction of Celtic Art.
Bain, June W., ed. see Bain, Chester A.
Bain, O., jt. ed. see Anderson, R. C.
Bain, Robert N., ed. Cossack Fairy Tales & Folk-Tales.
Bain, Simon. Railroaded! The Battle for Woodhead Pass.
Bainbridge, Beryl. English Journey: Or, The Road to Milton Keynes.
--Sweet William.
--Watson's Apology.
Bainbridge, E. Gordon. The Old Rhinebeck Aerodrome.
Baine, Sean. Community Action & Local Government.
Baines, Anthony. Brass Instruments: Their History & Development.
--Woodwind Instruments & Their History.
Baines, Barbara J. The Lust Motif in the Plays of Thomas Middleton.
Baines, Gwendolyn L. People in the Web of Life.
Baines, John M. Revolution in Peru: Mariategui & the Myth.
Bainton, Roland. The Martin Luther Easter Book.
Bainton, Roland H. Concerning Heretics.
--Women of the Reformation: From Spain to Scandinavia.
--Women of the Reformation: In Germany & Italy.
--Yesterday, Today, & What Next? Reflections on History & Hope.
Bainum, P. M., jt. ed. see Stoewer, H.
Bair, Dierdre. Samuel Beckett.
--Samuel Beckett: A Biography.
Bair, Frank. Countries of the World & Their Leaders Yearbook: 1987.
Bair, Frank E., ed. Countries of the World & Their Leaders Yearbook 1986.
--Countries of the World & their Leaders Yearbook, 1987: Supplement.
--Countries of the World & Their Leaders Yearbook, 1988: Supplement.
--International Marketing Handbook, Nineteen Eighty-Five.
--International Marketing Handbook Supplement.
Bair, Frank E & Ruffner, James, eds. The Weather Almanac.
Bair, Fred, jt. auth. see Norris, James E.
Bair, Lowell, tr. see Arsan, Emmanuelle.
Bair, Lowell, tr. see Delacorta.
Baird. Introduction to Decision Analysis.
--Power of Positive Self Image.
Baird, A. Craig, et al. Essentials of General Speech Communication.
Baird, Chuck, et al. Encyclopedia for the TRS-80. Putnam, Katherine & Comiskey, Kate, eds.
Baird, David C. Experimentation: An Introduction to Measurement Theory & Experiment Design.
Baird, Hiram. Two Crosses: A Passion Play in Three Acts.
Baird, J. A., jt. auth. see Ozelton, E. C.
Baird, J. Arthur, ed. see Tyson, Joseph B. & Longstaff, Thomas R. W.
Baird, J. C. Psychophysical Analysis of Visual Space.
Baird, John D., ed. Editing Texts of the Romantic Period.
Baird, Joseph A., Jr., et al. Sacred Places of San Francisco.
Baird, Leonard L. & Hartnett, Rodney T. Understanding Student & Faculty Life: Using Campus Surveys to Improve Academic Decision Making.
Baird, Mark. Uganda: Country Economic Memorandum.
Baird, Martha & Reiss, Ellen, eds. The Press Boycott of Aesthetic Realism: Documentation.
Baird, Robert D. Category Formation & the History of Religions.
Baird, Robert D., ed. Religion in Modern India.
Baird, Thomas. The Way to the Old Sailor's Home.
Bairnsfather, Bruce. Best Fragments from France. Holt, Valmai & Holt, Tonie, eds.
Bairoch, Paul. Urban Unemployment in Developing Countries: The Nature of the Problem & Proposals for Its Solution.
Bajaj & Singh. Cost-Effective Energy Management.
Bajaj, K. K., et al, eds. Spectroscopy of Shallow Centers in Semiconductors: Selected Proceedings of the International Conference, 1st, Berkeley, CA, Aug. 2-3, 1984.
Bajcar, A. Poland: A Tourist Guide.
Bajema, Carl J., ed. Artificial Selection & Development of Evolutionary Theory.
--Eugenics: Then & Now.
Bajpai, A. C., et al. Numerical Methods for Engineers & Scientists.

Bajpai, U. S., ed. Non-Alignment: Perspective & Prospects.
Bajura, R. A., ed. Polyphase Flow & Transport Technology.
Bajusz, E., ed. Physiology & Pathology of Adaptation Mechanisms: Neural-Neuroendocrine-Hormonal.
Bak, Janos, ed. see Szabo, Ervin.
Bakan, David. Disease, Pain & Sacrifice: Toward a Psychology of Suffering.
--Duality of Human Existence: Isolation & Communion in Western Man.
Bakay, Louis, et al. Head Injury.
Bakeer. Jewish Mystical Tradition.
Bakeless, John. Signers of the Declaration.
Baker, A. & Masser, D. W. Transcendence Theory & Its Applications.
Baker, A. D. & Betteridge, D. Photoelectron Spectroscopy: Chemical & Analytical Aspects.
Baker, A. J. Finite Element Computational Fluid Mechanics.
Baker, A. W. Death Is a Good Solution: The Convict Experience in Early Australia.
Baker, Adelaide N. Return to Arcady.
Baker, Alan. Benjamin's Book.
Baker, Allen & Armstrong, Eunice. Poultry & Egg Statistics, 1960-85.
Baker, Allen & Hamrick, Kathy. Conceptual Programming Using BASIC.
Baker, Archibald G., ed. Short History of Christianity.
Baker, Arthur. Calligraphic Alphabets.
--The Calligraphic Art of Arthur Baker.
Baker, Bernard S., ed. Hydrocarbon Fuel Cell Technology: A Symposium.
Baker, Betty. And Me, Coyote!
--Seven Spells to Farewell.
--Worthington Botts & the Steam Machine.
Baker, Bobby & King, Larry L. Wheeling & Dealing: Confessions of a Capitol Hill Operator.
--Wheeling & Dealing: Confessions of a Capitol Hill Operator.
Baker, Bruce L., et al. As Close As Possible.
Baker, C., et al, eds. Aluminium-Lithium Alloys III.
Baker, C. B. see Hopkin, John A., et al.
Baker, C. C., jt. auth. see Oram, R. B.
Baker, C. Richard & Hayes, Rick S. Accounting, Finance, & Taxation: A Basic Guide for Small Business.
Baker, C. Richard, jt. auth. see Hayes, Rick S.
Baker, Carlos. Ernest Hemingway: A Life Story.
Baker, Carroll. Baby Doll.
--Baby Doll: An Autobiography.
Baker, Catherine J., ed. see Schweiker, Roioli.
Baker, Charlotte. Cockleburr Quarters.
Baker, Christopher. The Crabtree & Evelyn Cookbook.
Baker, Clyde. Modern Gunsmithing.
Baker, Cozy. Through the Kaleidoscope.
Baker, D. A. Transport Phenomena in Plants.
Baker, David. How to Play Bebop, Vol. 1: The Bebop Scales & Other Scales in Common Use.
--Jazz Improvisation: A Comprehensive Method of Study for All Players.
--Strategic Defense Initiative.
Baker, David & Baker, Jeanne. Jazz Quiz Book. Baker, Lida, ed.
Baker, David R., jt. auth. see Canan, Michael J.
Baker, Donald G. & Sheldon, Charles H. Postwar America: The Search for Identity.
Baker, Donald G., ed. Race, Ethnicity & Power: A Comparative Study.
Baker, Dorothy, ed. see Masters, Roy.
Baker, E. Solaraust Microcomputer Solar Analysis Package.
Baker, E. W., ed. Organic Geochemistry Two: A Selection of Papers from the Second Australian Geochemistry Conference, University of Melbourne, 28-29 May 1984.
Baker, Elizabeth. Printers & Technology.
--Tammy Camps in the Rocky Mountains.
Baker, Elliott. Klynts Law.
Baker, Eugene. What's Right: A Handbook about Values.
Baker, Eugene H. What's Right?
--Your Manners Are Showing: A Handbook about Etiquette.
Baker, F. Terry, jt. auth. see Basili, Victor R.
Baker, Fay. My Darling Darling Doctors.
Baker, Frank H., ed. Dairy Science Handbook: International Stockmen's School Handbooks.
--International Stockman's School Handbooks, 1984. Incl. Vol. 20. Beef Cattle Science Handbook; Vol. 16. Dairy Science Handbook; Vol. iv. Sheep & Goat Handbook. Westview.
Baker, Fred. Ptolia.
Baker, George A., Jr. & Gammel, John L., eds. Pade Approximant in Theoretical Physics.
Baker, George T., jt. ed. see Rockstein, Morris.
Baker, H. F. Introduction to Plane Geometry.
Baker, Herschel. The Wars of Truth: Studies in the Decay of Christian Humanism in the Earlier 17th Century.
Baker, Herschel, ed. Later Renaissance in England: Nondramatic Verse & Prose, 1600-1660.
Baker, Howard. Howard Baker's Washington.
--Ode to the Sea & Other Poems.
Baker, J. A., tr. see Von Campenhausen, Hans.
Baker, J. Newton. Law of Disputed & Forged Documents.
Baker, J. R. Cytological Technique.
Baker, James. Eric Hoffer.
Baker, James, jt. auth. see Kearny, Mary Ann.
Baker, James T. A Southern Baptist in the White House.
Baker, Jan. The Church of England.
Baker, Jane & Ostmann, Barbara G., eds. Food Editors' Favorites Cookbook.
--Food Editors' Hometown Favorites Cookbook: American Regional & Local Specialties.
Baker, Jeanne, jt. auth. see Baker, David.
Baker, Jenny. The Student's Cookbook.
Baker, John, jt. ed. see Taylor, Angela.
Baker, John A., tr. Gospel Message & Hellenistic Culture.
Baker, Keith A., ed. Bilingual Education: A Reappraisal of Federal Policy. Kenter, Adriana A.
Baker, Keith M. Condorcet: From Natural Philosophy to Social Mathematics.
Baker, Kenneth W. Alone in the Valley.
Baker, Kyle. The Cowboy Wally Show.
Baker, Laura N. The Friendly Beasts.
Baker, Lida, ed. see Baker, David & Baker, Jeanne.
Baker, Liva. Miranda: Crime, Law & Politics.
--Miranda: The Crime, the Law, the Politics.
Baker, M. C., jt. auth. see Winn, Charles S.
Baker, Margaret. Discovering the Folklore of Plants.
Baker, Mark. Cops: Their Lives in Their Own Words.
Baker, Mary L. Whales, Dolphins, & Porpoises of the World.
Baker, Muriel L., ed. Scribner Book of Embroidery Designs.
Baker, Nina B. Nickels & Dimes: The Story of F. W. Woolworth.
Baker, P. F. & Reute, H. Calcium Movement in Excitable Cells.
Baker, Pat & Marshall, Mary R. Using Simulation Games.
Baker, Paul. Contemporary Christian Music: Where It Came from, Where It Is, Where It Is Going.
Baker, R. Jerry, jt. auth. see Kuehne, Robert S.
Baker, R. Lisle, jt. auth. see Schnidman, Frank.
Baker, R. M., ed. see International Astronautical Congress, 12th, Washington, 1961.
Baker, Ray S. Woodrow Wilson: Life & Letters.
Baker, Richard D. Judicial Review in Mexico: A Study of the Amparo Suit.
Baker, Richard H. DBASE III PLUS: Advanced Applications for Non-Programmers.
--Scuttle the Computer Pirates: Software Protection Schemes.
Baker, Robert T. Baker's Ohio School Law Guide 1981-1986.
Baker, Robert W. Commodore 64 Programmer's Library.
Baker, Roger D., et al. Human Infection with Fungi, Actinomycetes & Algae.
Baker, Samm S. & Schur, Sylvia. Delicious Quick-Trim Diet.
Baker, Samm S., jt. auth. see Bellak, Leopold.
Baker, Samm S., jt. auth. see Stillman, Irwin M.
Baker, Samuel W. The Nile Tributaries of Abyssinia, & the Sword Hunters of the Hamran Arabs. Bd. with Sword Hunters of the Hamran Arabs. Johnson Repr.
Baker, Scott, jt. auth. see Reinhart, Ken.
Baker, Sharon. Quarreling, They Met the Dragon.
Baker, Stephen. Systematic Approach to Advertising Creativity.
Baker, Susan P., et al. The Injury Fact Book.
Baker, Tammy & Dudley, Cliff. I Gotta Be Me!
Baker, Theodore. On the Music of the North American Indians (1976) Harrison, Frank, ed.
Baker, Vaughan B., jt. ed. see Conrad, Glenn R.
Baker, W. M. Bell's Acrostic Dictionary.
Baker, Wesley C. More Than a Man Can Take: A Study of Job.
Baker, Will. Chip.
Baker, William. George Eliot-George Henry Lewes Library: An Annotated Bibliography of Their Books at Dr. William's Library.
Baker, William S. Bibliotheca Washingtoniana.
Baker, Wilma Sinclar LeVan. The Silk Pictures of Thomas Stevens.
Baker-Carr, Janet. Evening at Symphony.
Baker-Cohen, K. F. Comparative Enzyme Histochemical Observations on Submammalian Brains. Incl. Pt. 1: Striatal Structures in Reptiles & Birds; Pt. 2: Basal Structures of the Brainstem in Reptiles & Birds. Springer-Verlag.
Bakerman & De Marr. Adol Feminists Portraits.
Baker of Windrush, Lord. Enterprise Versus Bureaucracy: The Development of Structural Air-Raid Precautions During the 2nd World War.
Bakewell, Caroline, et al. The Nineteen Eighty-Two Amendments to the Voting Rights Act.
Bakewell, K. G., ed. Management Principles & Practice: A Guide to Information Sources.
Bakewell, Peter. Miners of the Red Mountain: Indian Labor in Potosi, 1545-1650.
Bakhtiar, Laleh. Sufi: Expressions of the Mystic Quest.
Bakhtin, V., ed. Selected Poems: Alexander Prokofiev.
Bakjian, Andy. Track Management.
Bakke, Gary L. Microcomputers in a Law Office.
Bakker, Elna. An Island Called California: An Ecological Introduction to Its Natural Communities.
Bakker, Jim. Survival-Unite to Live.
Bakker, Jim & Bakker, Tammy. Run to the Roar.
Bakker, Tammy, jt. auth. see Bakker, Jim.
Baklanoff, Eric N., ed. Mediterranean Europe & the Common Market: Studies of Economic Growth & Integration.
Bako, Elemer. Guide to Hungarian Studies.
Bakos, Susan C. This Wasn't Supposed to Happen: Single Women over Thirty Talk Frankly about Their Lives.
Bakr, As-Sayyid. Studies in Arabic Philology.
Bakst, Leon. The Decorative Art of Leon Bakst. Melvill, Harry, tr.
Bakunin, M. A. Bakunin's Writings.
Bal, Sant S. George Orwell: The Ethical Imagination.
Balaban, A. T. Chemical Applications of Graph Theory.
Balaban, John. Coming down Again.
Balaban, Miriam. Biological Foundations & Human Nature.
Balaban, Miriam, jt. ed. see Oplatka, Avraham.
Balachandran, M., ed. Regional Statistics: A Guide to Information Sources.
Balachandran, Sarojini. Employee Communication: A Bibliography.
Balachandran, Sarojini, ed. New Product Planning.
Balaguer, Josemaria Escriva de see Escriva de Balaguer, Josemaria.
Balahura, Robert. Test Bank to Accompany General Chemistry. LW, LC & GLH, eds.
Balakian, Peter & Smith, Bruce. Invisible Estate.
Balakrishna, A. V., ed. Control Theory & the Calculus of Variations.
Balakrishna, A. V. & Neustadt, Lucien W., eds. Computing Methods in Optimization Problems: Proceedings.
--Mathematical Theory of Control: Proceedings.
Balakrishna, A. V., et al, eds. see Optimization Symposium Staff.
Balakrishnan, A. V. Introduction to Optimization Theory in a Hilbert Space.
--Stochastic Differential Systems One Filtering & Control: A Function Space Approach.
Balakrishnan, A. V. & Neustadt, L. W., eds. Techniques of Optimization.
Balakrishnan, A. V., ed. see Egardt, B.
Balakrishnan, A. V., ed. see International Conference on Computing Methods in Optimization Problems - 2nd San Remo, Italy - 1968.
Balakrishnan, T. R., et al. Fertility & Family Planning in a Canadian Metropolis.
Balam, Pablo, ed. see Luxton, Richard.
Balas, Robert S. Qu'est-ce Qui Se Passe? Conversation-Revision de Grammaire.
Balaskas, Arthur S. & Stirk, John L. Soft Exercise.
Balaskas, Janet. Active Birth.
Balassa, Bela. The Newly Industrialized Countries in the World Economy.
--The Process of Industrial Development & Alternative Development Strategies.
--Thailand: Industrial Development Strategy in Thailand.
Balassa, Bela & Meyers, Kenneth. Trends in International Trade in Manufactured Goods & Structural Change in the Industrial Countries.
Balassa, Bela, ed. Changing Patterns in Foreign Trade & Payments.
Balassa, Bela, et al. Turkey: Industrialization & Trade Strategy.
Balay, Maurice. Lexique Informatique.
Balbo, P. J., jt. auth. see Bourgeron, J. P.
Balch, Emily G., ed. Occupied Haiti: Being the Report of a Committee of Six Disinterested Americans Representing Organizations Exclusively American.
Balchin, N. C., ed. Manual Metal-Arc Welding.
Balchin, N. C., et al, eds. Metal-Arc Gas Shielded Welding.
--Oxy-Acetylene Welding.
--Tungsten-Arc Gas Shielded Welding.
Balcomb, Mary. Nicolai Fechin.
Bald, S. Novelists & Political Consciousness: Literary Expression of Indian Nationalism 1919-1947.
Balderston, Frederick E., et al. Proposition Thirteen, Property Transfers, & the Real Estate Markets.
Baldick, Robert, tr. see Simenon, Georges.
Baldini, Umberto. Primavera: The Restoration of Botticelli's Masterpiece.
Baldridge, C. Le Roy, jt. auth. see Bankhage, Hilman R.
Baldry, George. The Rabbitskin Cap. Haggard, Lilias R., ed.
Balducci, Carolyn. A Self-Made Woman: Biography of Nobel-Prize-Winner Grazia Deledda.
Baldwin, B. Studies on Greek & Roman History & Literature.
Baldwin, Bettye, jt. auth. see Gabriel, Joyce.
Baldwin, Carol, jt. ed. see Wright, Jonathan V.
Baldwin, Christine, jt. auth. see Brown, Judith N.
Baldwin, Claudia. Nigerian Literature: A Bibliography of Criticism, 1952-1976.
Baldwin, Deirdra & Davis, Gene. Inside Outside.
Baldwin, Deirdra B. Gathering Time.
Baldwin, Ed. Makin' Things for Kids.
Baldwin, Ed & Baldwin, Stevie. Building Birdhouses & Bird-Feeders: Attract Birds to Your Backyard with Birdhouses & Feeders You've Built Yourself.
Baldwin, Faith. Thursday's Child.
Baldwin, Fred D., et al. Conflicting Interests: Corporate-Governance Controversies.
Baldwin, J. Norman. Differences & Similarities Between the Public & Private Sectors: A Bibliography.
Baldwin, James. The Evidence of Things Not Seen.
--Notes of a Native Son.
Baldwin, Marshall W. The Mediaeval Church.
Baldwin, Michael, ed. King Horn: Poems Written at Montolieu in Old Languedoc, 1969-1981.
Baldwin, R. W., ed. Secondary Spread of Cancer.
Baldwin, Robert E. & Sapir, Andre, eds. European-United States Trade Relations.
Baldwin, Roger & Paris, Ruth. The Book of Similes.
Baldwin, Roger see Thomas, Norman.
Baldwin, Roger, ed. see Kropotkin, Peter.
Baldwin, Sally. The Costs of Caring: Families with Disabled Children.
Baldwin, Scott, et al. Preparation of a Product Liability Case: 1986 (March) Supplement.
Baldwin, Stanley C. What Did Jesus Say about That?
Baldwin, Stanley C., jt. auth. see Mallory, James D.
Baldwin, Stevie, jt. auth. see Baldwin, Ed.
Baldwin, Thomas F. & McVoy, D. Stevens. Cable Communication.
Baldwin, William P. Day Trips Out of Charleston - A Guide to Low Country Adventures.
Baldyga, Jerzy A., tr. see Strzelecki, Z.
Balescu, R., et al. Lectures in Statistical Physics.
Balet, J. M. Rembrandt & Spinoza.
Baley, James A. & Matthews, David L. Law & Liability in Athletics, Physical Education, & Recreation.
Balfour, D., jt. ed. see Grant, W. A.
Balfour, I. B., ed. see De Bary, Anton.
Balgopal, Pallassana R. & Vassil, Thomas V. Groups in Social Work: An Ecological Approach.
Balin, Bobbi. Miss Raggedy Taggedy.
Balin, George. Afrika Korps.
--D-Day Tank Battles: Beachhead to Breakout.
Balin, H. & Glasser, S., eds. Reproductive Biology.
Balint, Michael. Primary Love & Psycho-Analytic Technique. Jones, Ernest, ed.
--Problems of Human Pleasure & Behavior.
Balint, Michael, et al. Treatment or Diagnosis: A Study of Repeat Prescriptions in General Practice.
Balis, Andrea & Reiser, Robert. P. J.
Balk, P., ed. The Si-Sio2 System.
Balk, P. & Folberth, O. G., eds. Solid State Devices, 1985.
Balkan, Eric. The Directory of Software Publishers: How & Where to Sell Your Program.
Balkin, Alfred B. & Taylor, Jack A. Involvement with Music: Essential Skills & Concepts.
Balkin, Richard. How to Understand & Negotiate a Book Contract or Magazine Agreement.
Balkuv-Ulutin, S., ed. see Gaffney, P. J.
Ball, A. The Price Guide to Pot-Lids & Other Underglaze Multicolour Prints on Ware.
Ball, A. Gordon, ed. Size, Structure, & Future of Farms. Heady, Earl O.
Ball, Barbara. Coffee Talk: Sharing Christ Through Friendly Gatherings.
Ball, C. J. Introduction to the Theory of Diffraction.
Ball, Derek S. An Introduction to Real Analysis.
Ball, Donald A., et al. International Business.
Ball, Eve. Indeh: An Apache Odyssey.
Ball, George W. The Past Has Another Pattern: Memoirs.
Ball, Gordon, ed. & intro. by see Ginsberg, Allen.
Ball, Howard. Courts & Politics: The Federal Judicial System.
Ball, J. & DeTar, C., eds. Proceedings of the Salt Lake City Meeting: Third Regular Meeting of the Division of Particles & Fields of the American Physical Society, Salt Lake City, Utah 14-17 January 1987.
Ball, Jerry, jt. auth. see Mick, Colin K.
Ball, John. Cheif Tallon & the S.O.R.
Ball, John N., jt. auth. see Pearson, Ronald.
Ball, Joyce, ed. Foreign Statistical Documents: A Bibliography of General, International Trade & Agricultural Statistics, Including Holdings of the Stanford University Libraries.

Authors

Ball, Larry A. Those Incomparable Bonanzas,1944-1972.
Ball, M., jt. auth. see Mattar, E. P.
Ball, M. Margaret. NATO & the European Union Movement.
Ball, Michael. Housing Policy & Economic Power: The Political Economy of Owner Occupation.
Ball, Michael, et al, eds. Land Rent, Housing & Urban Planning: A European Perspective.
Ball, Samuel. An Account of the Cultivation & Manufacture of Tea in China.
Ball, Stephen J. The Micro-Politics of the School Towards a Theory of School Organization.
Ball, Terence, ed. Political Theory & Praxis: New Perspectives.
Ballam, John D. Shadows & the Crosses.
Ballanoff, Paul A., ed. Genetics & Social Structure: Mathematical Structuralism in Population Genetics & Social Theory.
Ballantine, Jeanne A. Schools & Society: A Reader in Education & Sociology.
Ballantine, Jeanne H., jt. auth. see Cargan, Leonard.
Ballantine, Richard. Richard's Bicycle Book.
Ballantyne. Forensic Toxicology.
Ballantyne & Groves. Synopsis of Otolaryngology.
Ballantyne & Morrison. The Ear.
Ballantyne, Alexander, tr. see Tardy.
Ballantyne, Duncan. Cooperative Programs for Transition from School to Work.
Ballantyne, John. Deafness.
Ballard, A. B. One More Day's Journey: The Story of a Family & a People.
Ballard, Edward G. Art & Analysis: An Essay Toward Theory in Aesthetics.
Ballard, F., et al, eds. Press Toolmaking.
Ballard, George A. The Influence of the Sea on the Political History of Japan.
Ballard, J., jt. ed. see Hunt, G. E.
Ballard, J. A., ed. Policy-Making in a New State: Papua New Guinea 1972-77.
Ballard, J. G. Empire of the Sun.
Ballard, Joseph, et al, eds. Special Education in America: Its Legal & Governmental Foundations.
Ballard, Lou E., jt. auth. see Levie, Robert C.
Ballard, Riley R. He Is Here.
Ballard, Thomas. Knowin' All Them Things That Ain't So: Managing Today's Public Library.
Ballard, Todhunter. Fight or Die.
--Trouble on the Massacre.
Ballardo, Victoria M. Count Me among the Living: The Story of My Wheelchair Liberation.
Ballast, David K. The Architect's Handbook.
Ballenger, Marcus, et al. Primary School Potpourri. Cohen, Monroe D., ed.
Ballenger, Nicole. Government Intervention in Agriculture: Measurement, Evaluation, & Implications for Trade Negotiations.
Ballentine, Rebecca, compiled by. Publications of the Institute of Government: Cumulative Supplement, 1963-1979.
Ballentyne, D. W. & Lovett, D. R. Dictionary of Named Effects & Laws in Chemistry, Physics & Mathematics.
Ballentyne, D. W. & Walker, L. E. Diccionario de Leyes y Efectos Cientificos En Quimica-Fisica Matematicas.
Baller, Eleazar, ed. Communism & Cultural Heritage.
Baller, Warren B. Bed-Wetting: Origins & Treatment.
Balliett, Whitney. Such Sweet Thunder: Forty-Nine Pieces on Jazz.
Balling, L. Christian. Mallory's Gambit.
Ballingall, James. A Taste of China.
Ballinger, Bill S. The Corsican.
Ballio, Giulio & Mazzolani, Federico. Theory & Design of Steel Structures.
Ballman, Fred C. An Officer Pay Plan.
Ballonoff, P. A., jt. ed. see Weiss, K. M.
Ballou, John D., ed. see Real Estate Education Company Staff.
Ballou, Patricia K. Women: A Bibliography of Bibliographies.
Ballou, Robert O., et al, eds. The Bible of the World.
Ballou, Ronald H. Basic Business Logistics.
Ballou, Stephen V. Model for Theses & Research Papers.
Ballou, Stephen V., jt. auth. see Campbell, William G.
Bally, G. Von see Von Bally, G.
Balma, Phillip & Fitler, William. Programmer's Guide to GEM.
Balogh, Andras & Imam, Zafar. A Political History of National Liberation Movement in Asia & Africa, 1914-1985.
Balogh, Thomas. Fact & Fancy in International Economic Relations: An Essay on International Monetary Reform.
Balokovic, Joyce B. Towards the Center.
BALPA Medical Study Group Staff. Fit to Fly: A Medical Handbook for Pilots.
Balsama, George D. The Politics of National Despair: French Royalism in the Post-Reformation Era.
Balsan, Francois. Capricorn Road.
Balson, Diane. Nothing but the Best.
Balston, Thomas. James Whatman, Father & Son. Bidwell, John, ed.
--William Balston, Paper Maker, 1759-1849. Bidwell, John, ed.
Balsys, Algis & De Cock-Morgan, Liliane. Morgan & Morgan Darkroom Book.
Baltes, Paul B. & Schaie, K. Warner, eds. Life Span Developmental Psychology: Personality & Socialization.
Balthasas, Hans von see Von Balthasar, Hans U.
Baltus, R. K. Personal Psychology for Life & Work.
Baltz, Howard B. Fundamentals of Inferential Statistics for Business Analysis.
Baltzell, D. Catherine & Dentler, Robert A. Selecting American School Principals: A Sourcebook for Educators.
Balukas, Jean. Pocket Billiards. Cohen, Joel H., ed.
Baluses, Jane E. Legal Aspects of the Hospital's Role in Obtaining Organs for Transplantation.
Baly, Denis & Rhodes, Royal W. The Faith of Christians.
Balzac, Honore de see De Balzac, Honore.
Balzac, Honore De see De Balzac, Honore.
Balzac, Honore de see De Balzac, Honore.
Balzac, Honore De see De Balzac, Honore.
Balzac, Honore de see De Balzac, Honore.
Balzac, Honore De see De Balzac, Honore.
Balzac, Honore De see De Balzac, Honore.
Balzac, Honore de see De Balzac, Honore.
Balzac, Honore de see De Balzac, Honore.
Balzac, Honore de see De Balzac, Honore & Meininger, Anne-Marie.
Balzac, Honore de see De Balzac, Honore & Richard, Marie Helene.
Balzac, Honore de see De Balzac, Honore & Pierrot, Roger.
Bamberger, Bernard J. The Search for Jewish Theology.
--Story of Judaism.
Bamberger, Michael & Gonzalez-Polio, Edgardo. Evaluation of Sites & Services Projects: The Evidence from El Salvador.
Bamberger, Michael & Sanyal, Bishwapriya. Evaluation of Sites & Sevices Projects: The Experience from Lusaka, Zambia.
Bambrey, Thomas E., jt. auth. see Lewis, Ann C.
Bambrough, Renford. Reason, Truth & God.
Bamdad, Badr ol-Moluk. From Darkness into Light: Women's Emancipation in Iran. Bagley, F. R., ed. & tr.
Bame, E. Allen & Cummings, Paul. Exploring Technology.
Bamford, James. The Puzzle Palace: A Report on America's Most Secret Agency.
Banac, Ivo & Bushkovitch, Paul, eds. The Nobility in Russia & Eastern Europe.
--The Nobility in Russia & Eastern Europe.
Banard, Robert. A Little Local Murder.
Banasinski, Antoni, ed. see Lange, Oskar.
Banathy, B. H., ed. Evolutionary Visions of the Future.
Bancroft & Chein-Pai Han. Statistical Theory & Inference in Research.
Bancroft, Anne. Origins of the Sacred.
Bancroft, Caroline. Denver's Lively Past.
Bancroft, George. History of the Formation of the Constitution of the United States of America.
Bancroft, John. Human Sexuality & Its Problems.
Bancroft, John D. & Chalk, Brian T. Self-Assessment in Histological Techniques.
Bancroft Library University of California, Berkeley Editors. The Bancroft Library, University of California, Berkeley: Catalog of Printed Books, Third Supplement.
Bancroft Library, University of California, Berkeley Editors. Index to Printed Maps.
Bancroft-Hunt, Norman & Werner, Forman. The Indians of the Great Plains.
Bander, Edward J. Change of Name & Law of Names.
Bander, Edward J., jt. auth. see Marke, Julius J.
Banderbyll, H. R. Cosmic Symphony.
Bandi, Hans-Georg. Eskimo Prehistory.
Bandler, L. S., ed. Education for Clinical Social Work Practice: Continuity & Change.
Bandura, Albert. Aggression: A Social Learning Analysis.
Bandy, Melanie. Mind Forg'd Manacles: Evil in the Poetry of Blake & Shelley.
Bandyk-Glander, Janice & Droge, Dennis. Woman's Day Book of Calligraphy.
Bandyopadhyay, Bimal. Metal Sculptures of Eastern India.
Bandyopadhyaya, Kalyani. Burma & Indonesia: Comparative Study of Political Economy & Foreign Policy.
Bane, Berard M. Is President John F. Kennedy Alive... & Well?
Bane, Bernard M. Breaking Through.
--Is President John F. Kennedy Alive... & Well?
--On the Socio-Political Fault Line.
--The Trilateral Template.
Bane, John, Jr., jt. auth. see Macdonald, Michael C.
Bane, Michael. Who's Who in Rock.
Bane, S., et al. Advanced Pipework.
Banerjee, A. C. English Law in India.
Banerjee, J. India in Soviet Global Strategy.
Banerjee, K. India & Britain, 1947-1968.
Banerjee, Maria N. Terminal Paradox: The Novels of Milan Kundera.
Banerjee, N. V. Buddhism & Marxism: A Study in Humanism.
Banerjee, P. K. & Butterfield, R. Boundary Element Methods in Engineering Science.
Banerjee, Projesh. Indian Ballet Dancing.
Banerjee, S., ed. see Specialists Meeting on Transient Two-Phase Flow Staff.
Banerji, P. Aesthetics of Indian Folk Dance.
Banerji, R. B., ed. see Systems Symposium - 4th - Case Western Reserve University, Institute of Technology.
Banerji, S., jt. ed. see Krauss, G.
Banerji, S. K., ed. see TMS-AIME Fall Meeting Symposium Staff.
Banes, Sally. Terpsichore in Sneakers: Post-Modern Dance.
Bang, N. U., ed. Thrombosis & Bleeding Disorders: Theory & Methods.
Bangert, Ethel. Child of the Wind.
Bangert, Jeff, jt. auth. see Diedrich, William M.
Bangert, William V. A History of the Society of Jesus.
Bangham, Mary D. When Jesus Was Four-or Maybe Five.
Bangor Public Library Editors, ed. Bibliography of the State of Maine.
Banin, A., ed. see Soil Chemistry, Soil Fertility & Soil Clay Mineralogy Commissions of the International Society of Soil Science, 13-18 July 1976, Jerusalem.
Banis, Carolyn S., jt. auth. see Shipley, Kenneth G.
Banis, V. J. San Antone.
Banis, William J., jt. auth. see Krannich, Ronald L.
Banister, David. Transport Mobility & Deprivation in Inter-Urban Areas.
Banister, Judith. The Population of Vietnam.
Banister, Judith & Thapa, Shyam. The Population Dynamics of Nepal.
Banister, Manly. Bookbinding As a Handcraft.
Bank, A. V. Byzantine Art.
Bank Administration Institute. Bank Records: A Guide to Management & Retention.
--Loss Prevention for Smaller Banks.
Bank Administration Institute Staff. An Audit Guide for the Community Bank.
--Trust Department Accounting.
Bank, Dena C. How Things Get Done: The Nitty-Gritty of Parliamentary Procedure.
Bank, H., et al, eds. Patent Information & Documentation in Western Europe.
Bank, Ira M. Community Careering Gamebook.
--Community Careering Guidebook.
--Curriculum Careering Gamebook.
--Curriculum Careering Guidebook.
--World of Workers.
Bank of Ireland Centre for Co-op Studies Staff, ed. see Linehan, Mary & Tucker, Vincent.
Bank Street College of Education Staff & Brenner, Barbara. Love & Discipline.
Banker, John, et al. Bahnar Dictionary.
Banker, John C. Personal Finances for Ministers.
Bankes, James L. Clinical Ophthalmology: A Text & Colour Atlas.
Bankhage, Hilman R. & Baldridge, C. Le Roy. I Was There! with the Yanks in France.
Bankier, Joanna & Lashgari, Deirdre. Women Poets of the World.
Bankoff, George. Plastic Repair of Benito Urinary Defects.
Bankoff, S. G., jt. ed. see Chen, J. C.
Bankoff, S. G., jt. ed. see Jones, O. C., Jr.
Bankowski, Zenon, jt. ed. see Mungham, Geoff.
Banks, Arthur. A World Atlas of Military History: 1860-1945.
--A World Atlas of Military History 1861-1945.
Banks, Arthur S. Cross-National Data Analysis.
Banks, Arthur S., ed. Political Handbook of the World: 1981.
Banks, Arthur S., et al. Economic Handbook of the World: 1981.
Banks, Bruce & Kenny, Dick. Looking at Sails.
Banks, Bunny. Damn Yankee.
Banks, Carolyn. Patchwork.
Banks, Edwin M., ed. Vertebrate Social Organization.
Banks, F. R. The Penguin Guide to London.
Banks, Ferdinand E. The Political Economy of Coal.
--The Political Economy of Oil.
Banks, J. A. Victorian Values: Secularism & the Smaller Family.
Banks, J. Houston, jt. auth. see Sobel, Max A.
Banks, James. Multiethnic Education: Theory & Practice.
Banks, James A. Teaching the Black Experience: Methods & Materials.
Banks, Jerry & Hohenstein, Charles L., Jr. Procurement & Inventory Ordering Tables.
Banks, Lenore, ed. see League of Women Voters of New York State Staff.
Banks, Oliver. Watteau & the North Studies in the Dutch & Flemish Baroque Influence on French Rocco Painting.
Banks, P. Killey's Fractures of the Middle Third of the Facial Skeleton.
Banks, Pam. Denver Nuggets.
--Philadelphia Seventy-Sixers.
Banks, R. E., ed. Preparation, Properties & Industrial Applications of Organoflourine Compounds.
Banks, Russell. The Book of Jamaica.
--Family Life.
--Hamilton Stark.
--Trailerpark.
Banks, Sam W. & Laufman, Harold. Atlas of Surgical Exposures of the Extremities.
Banks, Syd. Second Chance.
Banks, William K., ed. see Lanzano, Susan & Abreu, Rosendo.
Bankson, Nicholas W., jt. auth. see Bernthal, John E.
Bannasch, P. Cytoplasm of Hepatocytes During Carcinogenesis: Electron & Lightmicroscopial Investigations of the Nitrosomorphiline-Intoxicated Rat Liver.
Bannatyne, Jack. The Mountain Eagles.
Banner, Hubert S. Calamities of the World.
Banner, James M., Jr., et al. Understanding the American Experience: Recent Interpretations.
Banner, Lois W. Women in Modern America: A Brief History.
Banning, Robert. Hello Star: The One Minute Word Star Word Processing Manual.
Bannister, D., jt. auth. see Fransella, F.
Bannister, D., ed. Perspectives in Personal Construct Theory.
Bannister, D., jt. ed. see Stringer, P.
Bannister, Don & Fransella, Fay. Inquiring Man.
Bannister, Helen H. A Coat of Blue & a Coat of Gray.
Bannister, J. V., ed. see European Molecular Biology International Workshop, Fifth, Marine Biological Laboratory of the University of Malta, Malta, August 2-4, 1976.
Bannister, Jo. Mason Codex.
--Mosaic.
Bannister, Robert C. American Values in Transition: A Reader.
Bannon, Laura. Make Room for Rags.
--Red Mittens.
Banov, A. Paints & Coating Handbook.
Bansal. Active Carbons. Donnet, Stoeckl, ed.
Bansal, H. L. & Bansal, R. S. Magnetic Cure for Common Diseases.
Bansal, R. S., jt. auth. see Bansal, H. L.
Banta, David, et al. Toward Rational Technology in Medicine: Considerations for Health Policy.
Banta, Martha. Failure & Success in America: A Literary Debate.
Banthin, Joanna, jt. auth. see Stelzer, Leigh.
Banting, Keith G. The Welfare State & Canadian Federalism.
Bants, William J., jt. auth. see Krannich, Ronald L.
Banville, Aurelian. European Independence & the Approaching Third World Conflagration.
Banville, John. Birchwood.
--Doctor Copernicus.
Banwart, George J. Basic Food Microbiology.
Banwart, George J., ed. Basic Food Microbiology.
Banz, Hans. Building Construction Details: Practical Drawings.
Bapat. Shanty Town City: The Case of Poona.
Baptiste De Boyer Argens, Jean. Chinese Letters, Seventeen Forty-One.
Bara, Louis. Science de la Paix.
Barabas, A., jt. auth. see Calnan, J.
Barabash, Y. Aesthetics & Poetics.
Baraclay, William. God's Young Church.
Barad, Dianne S. All the Games Kids Like.
--Speech News.
--Words & Sounds Ahoy.
Barak, M. & Swift-Hook, D. T., eds. Energy Options.
Barak, Ronald S. Foreign Investment in U. S. Real Estate.
Baral, Jaya K. The Pentagon & the Making of U. S. Foreign Policy: A Case Study of Vietnam 1960-1968.
Baram, R., et al, eds. see Midwest Autumn Immunology Conference Staff.
Baram, Robert. Illustrated Poems for Children.
Baran, Michael. Atlantis Reconsidered: A New Look at the Ancient Deluge Legends & an Analysis of Mysterious Modern Phenomena.
--Insights into Prehistory.
--Twilight of the Gods.
Baran, Nicholas, jt. auth. see Erickson, Jonathan.
Baranov, Alvin. How to Evict a Tenant.
Baranov, Alvin B. How to Evict a Tenant.
Baranyay, E. P. Mentally Handicapped Adolescent: The Slough Project of the National Society for Mentally Handicapped Children.
Baras, Edward. Osborne, McGraw-Hill Guide to Using Lotus 1-2-3.
Baras, Edward M. The Jazz Book: A Complete Tutorial.
Barasch, Marc I. The Little Black Book of Atomic War.
Barasch, Stephen B. Recreational Planning for New Communities.

Authors

Barash, David P. & Lipton, Judith E. Stop Nuclear War! A Handbook.
Barash, Samuel T. Encyclopedia of Real Estate Appraising Forms & Model Reports.
Barash, Samuel T., ed. Complete Guide to Appraising Condominiums & Cooperatives.
Barb, S., ed. see Dyson, Stephen L.
Barbacetto, Gianni. Design Interface: How Man & Machine Communicate: Olivetti Design Research.
Barbach, Lonnie, jt. auth. see Levine, Linda.
Barbach, Lonnie G. Erotic Interludes: Tales Told by Women.
--Pleasures: Women Write Erotica.
Barbaer, Lynda G. & Warren, Elizabeth V. Personality Decorating.
Barbalet, J. M. Marx's Construction of Social Theory.
Barban, Arnold M., jt. auth. see Dunn, S. Watson.
Barbash, Joseph & Feerick, John D. Unjust Dismissal & at Will Employment.
Barbash, Joseph & Kauff, Jerome. Unjust Dismissal, 1983: Litigating, Settling, & Advocating Claims. Practising Law Institute Staff, ed.
Barbash, Joseph, jt. auth. see Practising Law Institute Staff.
Barbashov, B. M. & Nesterenko, V. V. Introduction to the Relativistic String Theory. Dumbrajs, T. Y., tr.
Barbasso, Salvatore & Impagliazzo, John. Precalculus: A Functional Approach with Applications.
Barbe, Dominique. A Theology of Conflict: & Other Writings on Nonviolence.
Barbeau, Marius. All Hands Aboard Scrimshawing.
--Modern Growth of the Totem Pole on the Northwest Coast.
Barbely, A A. Pharmacological Modifications of Evolked Brain Potentials.
Barber, Aldyth A., jt. auth. see Barber, Cyril J.
Barber, Alfred W. Experimenter's Guide to Solid State Electronics Projects.
Barber, C. L., et al. Contributions to English Syntax & Philology.
Barber, C. R. Life Journeys.
Barber, Chris. More Mysterious Wales.
Barber, Cyril J. Nehemiah & the Dynamics of Effective Leadership: Study Guide.
Barber, Cyril J. & Barber, Aldyth A. You Can Have a Happy Marriage.
--Your Marriage Has Real Possibilities.
Barber, David, jt. auth. see Berwin, Derek.
Barber, Henry. British Family Names.
Barber, Hugh R., jt. ed. see Van Nagell, John R., Jr.
Barber, Iyonne C. The Psychic Reality of Dreams.
Barber, J. H., ed. General Practice Medicine.
Barber, J. H. & Kratz, Charlotte R., eds. Towards Team Care.
Barber, James D., ed. Choosing the President.
Barber, Joel. Wild Fowl Decoys.
Barber, Linda L. & Lampert, Junko. The Tofu Gourmet.
Barber, Lucie W. When a Story Would Help: An Approach to Creative Parenting.
Barber, N. F. & Ghey, G. Water Waves.
Barber, Natalie. Dr. & Mrs. Fix-It: The Story of Frank & Bessie Beck.
Barber, Noel. A Farewell to France.
Barber, P. W. & Hill, S. C. Computational Light Scattering.
Barber, Paul J. & Legge, David. Perception & Information.
Barber, Paul J., jt. auth. see Legge, David.
Barber, Peggy, ed. Sixty-Eight Great Ideas: The Library Awareness Handbook.
Barber, Richard. A Strong Land & a Sturdy England in the Middle Ages.
Barber, Richard, ed. Arthurian Literature IV.
Barber, Sandra & Mihankhah, Kianpour. Learning by Doing BASIC.
Barber, Theodore X. Pitfalls in Human Research: Ten Pivotal Points.
Barber, W. H., et al, eds. see Besterman, Theodore.
Barbernitz, Patricia. RCIA Team Manual: How to Implement the Rite of Christian Initiation of Adults in Your Parish.
Barbier, E., ed. The Application of Nuclear Techniques in Geothermal Investigations.
--The Application of Nuclear Techniques to Geothermal Studies: Proceedings.
--Cerro Prieto Geothermal Field: Proceedings of the First Symposium Held at San Diego, California, Sept. 1978.
--Cerro Prieto Geothermal Field: Proceedings of the Second Symposium, 17-19 October 1979, Mexicali, Mexico-Selected Papers.
Barbier, E & Trindade, M, eds. Utilization of Geothermal Energy for Electric Power Production & Space Heating.
Barbieri, Edward J., ed. see PreTest Service, Inc. Staff, et al.
Barbosa, Manuel P. Growth, Migration & the Balance of Payments in a Small Open Economy: Portugal.
Barbour, Beverly. Cooking with Spirits.
--The Low Salt Diet & Recipe Book.
Barbour, Ian G., et al, eds. Finite Resources & the Human Future: Population-Food-Energy.
Barbour, James M. The Church Music of William Billings.
Barchas, Jack. Serotonin & Behavior. Usdin, Earl, ed.
Barchilon, John. The Crown Prince: A Novel.
Barck, Oscar T. & Blake, Nelson M. Since Nineteen Hundred: A History of the United States in Our Times.
Barckhausen. Montesquieu Ses Idees et Ses Oeuvres d'apres les Papiers de La Brede.
Barclay & Kernahan. Plastic Surgery.
Barclay, C. N. The New Warfare.
Barclay, George W. Techniques of Population Analysis.
Barclay, Harold. People Without Government: An Anthropology of Anarchism.
Barclay, Morgan J. & Strong, Jean W. The Samuel Milton Jones Papers: An Inventory to the Microfilm Edition.
Barclay, Robert A., tr. see Auerbach, Elias.
Barclay, William. Fishers of Men.
--God's Young Church.
--Guide to Daily Prayer.
--Jesus of Nazareth.
--King & the Kingdom.
--The Life of Jesus for Everyman.
--Marching On: Daily Readings for Younger People. Duncan, Denis, ed.
--Marching Orders: Daily Readings for Younger People.
--Men & Affairs. Rawlins, C. L., ed.
--The New Testament: A New Translation.
--The Old Law & the New Law.
--Prayers for Help & Healing.
Barcus, Nancy. Where Are You God from 9 to 5.
Bard, Rachel. Country Inns of the Far West: Pacific NW.
Bard, Rachel & Kellogg, Caroline. Squash.
Bard, Ray & Davis, Larry. Winning Ways: A Management Performance Game.
Bardell, P. R. Magnetic Materials in Industry.
Barden, William, Jr. IBM-PC Programs.
--Z80 Microcomputer Handbook.
Bardens, Dennis. Portrait of a Statesman.
Bardes, B A., jt. auth. see Dubnick, M. J.
Bardes, Barbara A., et al. American Government & Politics Today: Essentials.
Bardi, Edward J., jt. auth. see Coyle, John J.
Bardige, Betty, ed. see Segal, Marilyn.
Bardill, Donald R., jt. auth. see Mueller, Charles S.
Bardin, C. Wayne, jt. ed. see Krieger, Dorothy T.
Bardon, Franz. The Key to the True Quabbalah. Dimai, Peter A., tr. from Ger.
Bardsley, Barney. Flowers in Hell: An Investigation into Women & Crime.
Bardsley, W., et al, eds. Crystal Growth: A Tutorial Approach.
Bardwell, Edward C. New Profits: Business Interruption Insurance.
Bardwell, George, jt. auth. see Seligson, Harry.
Bardwick, Judith. In Transition: How Feminism, Sexual Liberation, & the Search for Self-Fulfillment Have Altered America.
Bare, Harold R. One-Room Rural Schools: The Building Blocks for Today's Schools.
Barea, Arturo. Lorca: The Poet & His People.
Barenie, James, jt. ed. see Ripa, Louis.
Barents, Els. Jeff Wall: Transparencies.
Bares, Jiri, et al. Collection of Problems in Physical Chemistry.
Baressi, Barry J., ed. Ocular Assessment.
Barfield, A. Owen. Abecedarium Philosophicum.
Barfield, H. Eugene. Treachery on the Double.
Barfield, Owen. Saving the Appearances: A Study in Idolatry.
Barfoot, Joan. Dancing in the Dark.
Barford, Carol. Let Me Hear the Music.
Barghoorn, Frederick C. Soviet Foreign Propaganda.
Bargmann, V., ed. Group Representations in Mathematics & Physics: Battelle Seattle 1969 Rencontres.
Bargmann, W., ed. see International Symposium on Neurosecretion, Kiel, 1969.
Bargmann, Wolfgang, ed. see Tillmann, Bernhard.
Bargo, Michael. Monster Trucks: Car Crushers & Crowd Pleasers.
Barham, Jerry N. & Thomas, William L. Anatomical Kinesiology: A Programmed Text.
Barham, Peter. Schizophrenia & Human Value: Chronic Schizophrenia, Science & Society.
Barice, E. Joan & Jonah, Kathleen. The Palm Beach Long-Life Diet.
Barich, Madeline C. Confetti.
Barilleaux, Rene P. Sculptors on Paper: New York.
Barin, I. & Knacke, O. Thermochemical Properties of Inorganic Substances.
Barin, I., et al. Thermochemical Properties of Inorganic Substances: Supplement.
Baring, Maurice. Flying Corpse Headquarters 1914-18.
Baring-Gould, Sabine. Book of Nursery Songs & Rhymes.
--Cliff Castles & Cave Dwellings of Europe.
--Early Reminiscences, 1834-1864.
--Freaks of Fanaticism & Other Strange Events.
--Old English Home & Its Dependencies.
--Strange Survivals, Some Chapters in the History of Man.
Barish, Jonas A. Ben Jonson & the Language of Prose Comedy.
Barish, Louis & Barish, Rebecca. Varieties of Jewish Belief.
Barish, Rebecca, jt. auth. see Barish, Louis.
Barish, Wendy, ed. see Burgess, Jan.
Barish, Wendy, ed. see Carroll, Lewis.
Barish, Wendy, ed. see Cohen, Daniel.
Barish, Wendy, ed. see Daly, Kathleen N.
Barish, Wendy, ed. see Darden, Ellington.
Barish, Wendy, ed. see May, Robin.
Barish, Wendy, ed. see Rotsler, William.
Barish, Wendy, ed. see Saunders, Rubie.
Barish, Wendy, ed. see Seaver, Tom & Appel, Martin.
Barish, Wendy, ed. see Spyri, Johanna.
Barish, Wendy, ed. see Taylor, L. B., Jr.
Barish, Wendy, ed. see Twain, Mark.
Barisse, Rita, tr. see Pagnol, Marcel.
Baritz, Loren. Backfire: A History of How American Culture Led Us into Vietnam & Made Us Fight the Way We Did.
Bark, L. S. & Bark, S. M. Thermometric Titrimetry.
Bark, S. M., jt. auth. see Bark, L. S.
Barkas, J. L. The Help Book.
--Single in America.
Barkdull, Tom. Lonesome Walls: An Odyssey Through Ghost Towns of the Old West.
Barke, Harvey E., jt. auth. see Pyenson, Louis L.
Barkely, William D., jt. auth. see Martin, Alexander C.
Barker, A. L. A Heavy Feather.
Barker, A. N. & Gould, G. W., eds. Spore Research 1971.
Barker, A. N., et al, eds. Spore Research.
--Spore Research.
Barker, Anthony. Public Participation in Britain.
Barker, Brian. The Symbols of Sovereignty.
Barker, Clive. Books of Blood.
--Damnation Game.
--In the Flesh.
--The Inhuman Condition.
--Inhuman Condition.
Barker, Eugene C. Life of Stephen F. Austin, Founder of Texas, 1793-1836: A Chapter in the Westward Movement of the Anglo-American People.
Barker, George. Anno Domini.
Barker, Gerard A. Twice-Told Tales: An Anthology of Short Fiction.
Barker, Harold R. History of the Rhode Island Combat Units in the Civil War, 1861-1865.
Barker, Howard. Women Beware Women & Pity in History.
Barker, J. & Smith, T., eds. The Role of Peptides in Neuronal Function.
Barker, Jack, et al. Arithmetic.
--Intermediate Algebra.
Barker, Kenneth. Seven Dramatic Moments in the Life of Christ: Plays for Church Events.
Barker, Larry L. Communication.
--Communication in the Classroom.
Barker, Lewis M. The Psychobiology of Human Food Selection.
Barker, M. A., et al. A Reader of Modern Urdu Poetry.
Barker, Michael J. Directory for the Environment: Organisations in Britain & Ireland, 1984-85.
Barker, Paul, ed. The Other Britain: A New Society Collection.
Barker, Peter, ed. see Einstein Centennial Celebration Staff.
Barker, Philip, et al. The Residential Psychiatric Treatment of Children.
Barker, Philip J. Behaviour Therapy Nursing.
--Patient Assessment in Psychiatric Nursing.
Barker, Ralph. Blockade Busters.
Barker, Raymond C., jt. auth. see Holmes, Ernest.
Barker, Rodney. Political Ideas in Modern Britain.
Barker, Roger G. & Schoggen, Phil. Qualities of Community Life: Measurement of Environment & Behavior in an American & an English Town.
Barker, Roger G., et al. Adjustment to Physical Handicap & Illness.
Barker, Ruth B. He Took Me to Heaven.
Barker, Stephen F. Elements of Logic.
Barker, Sue. Playing Tennis.
Barker, V. A., ed. Sparse Matrix Techniques.
Barker, Vernon C. & Aufmann, Richard N. Essential Mathematics with Applications.
Barker, Vernon C., jt. auth. see Aufmann, Richard N.
Barker, Wayne G. Cryptanalysis of an Enciphered Code Problem: Where an "Additive" Method of Encipherement Has Been Used.
Barker, Wayne G., ed. The History of Codes & Ciphers in the United States During World War I.
--History of Codes & Ciphers in the United States Prior to World War I.
Barker, Wiley F., jt. auth. see Gaspar, Max R.
Barker, Will. Fresh Water Friends & Foes.
Barker, William P. A Savior for All Seasons.
Barkin & Rosen. Emergency Pediatrics.
Barkin, Carol & James, Elizabeth. Helpful Hints for Your Pregnancy. Paton, Kathi, ed.
Barkin, Carol, jt. auth. see James, Elizabeth.
Barkin, Kenneth. Controversy over German Industrialization, 1890-1902.
Barkley, John & Rosenthal, Lynne S. Issues in the Management of Microcomputer Systems.
Barkley, Katherine T. The Ambulance: The Story of Emergency Transportation of Sick & Wounded Through the Centuries.
Barkley, Paul W. Economics: The Way We Choose.
--An Introduction to Macroeconomics.
--An Introduction to Microeconomics.
Barkley, Paul W. & Seckler, David. Economic Growth & Environmental Decay: The Solution Becomes the Problem.
Barkley, Richard A. Oceanographic Atlas of the Pacific Ocean.
Barkman, Alma. Days Remembered.
Barkow, Al. Golf's Golden Grind: The History of the Tour.
Barks, Carl. Donald Duck.
Barks, Carl, frwd. by. Huey, Dewey, & Louie.
Barksdale, Lilburn S. Building Self-Esteem.
Barksdale, William C., jt. auth. see Wood, Oliver G., Jr.
Barkuizen, B. The Succulents of Southern Africa.
Barkus, Philip. How to Prepare for the Postal Clerk Carrier Examination.
Barlag, R., jt. auth. see Andersen, R.
Barlett, Donald L. & Steele, James B. Forevermore: Nuclear Waste in America.
Barlett, Michael & Gillen, Bob, eds. The Tennis Book.
Barlett, Peggy F. Agricultural Choice & Change: Decision Making in a Costa Rican Community.
Barley, Nigel. Ceremony: An Anthropologist's Misadventures in the African Bush.
Barlin, G. B. The Pyrazines.
Barlow, Anna M; see Corrigan, Robert W.
Barlow, Brent A. What Husbands Expect of Wives.
--What Wives Expect of Husbands.
Barlow, D. W., et al, eds. Grinding.
Barlow, David H., jt. auth. see Hersen, Michel.
Barlow, Fred. Mental Prodigies.
Barlow, H. B., ed. Vertebrate Photoreception.
Barlow, Joseph W. Basic Oral Spanish.
Barlow, Judith, ed. Plays by American Women: The Early Years.
Barlow, Melvin L., ed. Vocational Education.
Barlow, N., jt. auth. see Jones, A. J.
Barlow, Nora, ed. see Darwin, Charles.
Barlow, Ronald S. How to Be Successful in the Antique Business.
--How to Be Successful in the Antique Business.
Barlow, T. Ed. Congregational House Churches.
Barlow, T. Edward. Living Saints Witness at Work.
Barlowe, Raleigh. Land Resource Economics: The Economics of Real Estate.
Barlowe, Wayne D. Expedition.
Barmash, Isadore. Always Live Better Than Your Clients.
--Net Net.
Barme, Geremie, jt. auth. see Lee, Bennett.
Barme, Geremie, tr. see Yang Jiang.
Barna, Arpad. High Speed Pulse & Digital Techniques.
--VHSIC (Very High Speed Integrated Circuits) Technologies & Tradeoffs.
Barna, Frances, ed. Artists of the Book, Nineteen Eighty-Eight: A Facet of Modernism.
Barnabas, Bentley. Beatitudes for the Balmy: And Other Poems.
Barnao, Jack. Hammerlocke.
Barnard & Skillicorn. FORTRAN 77 for Engineers & Scientists.
Barnard, Alan & Good, Anthony. Research Practices in the Study of Kinship.
Barnard, C. J., ed. Producers & Scroungers Strategics of Exploitation & Parasitism.
Barnard, C. O. The Native Egyptians: The Historical Essence of an Outstanding Early Culture.
Barnard, Carolyn & Potter, Loren D. New Mexico Grasses: A Vegetative Key.
Barnard, Christiaan. Good Life Good Death: A Doctor's Case for Euthanasia & Suicide.
Barnard, Christiaan & Evans, Peter. Christiaan Barnard's Program for Living with Arthritis.
Barnard, Christiaan & Evens, Peter. Your Healthy Heart: The Family Guide to Staying Healthy & Living Longer.
Barnard, D. S. Fifty Daily Telegraph Brain-Twisters.
Barnard, David T. & Skillcorn, David B. Pascal for Engineers.
Barnard, H. C. Were Those the Days?
Barnard, Mary. Mythmakers.
Barnard, Philip. Don't Tickle the Elephant Tree: Sensitive Plants.

Authors

Barnard, Robert. The Case of the Missing Bronte: A Perry Trethowan Mystery.
--The Cherry Blossom Corpse.
--Corpse in a Gilded Cage.
--Death & the Princess.
--Death by Sheer Torture.
--Fete Fatale.
--A Little Local Murder.
--Out of the Blackout.
--Political Suicide.
--School for Murder.
Barndt, Joseph R. Liberating Our White Ghetto.
Barndt, Joseph R., jt. auth. see Smith, Louis A.
Barnea, Aharon, jt. auth. see Barnea, Amalia.
Barnea, Amalia & Barnea, Aharon. Bridging the Gap. Chava, Amir, tr. from Hebrew.
Barner-Barry, Carol, jt. auth. see Barry, Donald.
Barnes. Art in Painting.
Barnes, A. J. & Orville-Thomas, W. J., eds. Vibrational Spectroscopy: Modern Trends.
Barnes, Albert. The Atonement.
Barnes, Barry. Interests & the Growth of Knowledge.
Barnes, C. D. & Eltherington, L. G. Drug Dosage in Laboratory Animals: A Handbook.
Barnes, C. G., jt. ed. see Lehner, T.
Barnes, Charles D., jt. ed. see Hughes, Maysie J.
Barnes, Charles W. Earth, Time & Life: An Introduction to Geology.
Barnes, Christopher, ed. & intro. by see Pasternak, Boris.
Barnes, Clive. Inside American Ballet Theatre.
Barnes, D. & Bliss, P. Biological Control of Nitrogen in Wastewater Treatment.
Barnes, D. & Wilson, F. The Design & Operation of Small Sewage Works.
Barnes, D. W. & Mack, J. M. An Algebraic Introduction to Mathematical Logic.
Barnes, David H., jt. auth. see Morrison, Clinton D.
Barnes, Donald G. George Third & William Pitt, 1783-1806.
Barnes, Douglas. Practical Curriculum Study.
Barnes, E. B., jt. ed. see Dougherty, David M.
Barnes, F. A. Canyon Country Camping.
Barnes, Frances J., ed. Love: From Black Women to Black Men.
Barnes, Frances Johnson, ed. Love: From Black Men to Black Women.
Barnes, Frank C. Cartridges of the World.
Barnes, George W. How to Make Bamboo Fly Rods.
Barnes, Harry E. American Way of Life: An Introduction to the Study of Contemporary Society.
Barnes, Harry E., ed. Introduction to the History of Sociology.
Barnes, Hatry E. Historical Sociology.
Barnes, Hazel E. An Existentialist Ethics.
Barnes, Jack. Social Care Research.
Barnes, Joanna. The Deceivers.
--Pastora.
--Pastora.
--Silverwood.
--Silverwood.
--Who Is Carla Hart?
Barnes, John. The Man Who Pulled Down the Sky.
--Who to Trust with Your Money.
Barnes, Josephine. Care of the Expectant Mother.
Barnes, Kate. Using MultiMate.
Barnes, Lan. Introducing dBASE III.
Barnes, Leroy. Annual Editions: Social Problems, 1985-86.
Barnes, LeRoy W., ed. Social Problems 1988-89.
Barnes, Lucinda & Glenn, Constance W. Eric Fischl Scenes Before the Eye: The Evolution of Year of the Drowned Dog & Floating Islands. Bledsoe, Jane K., ed.
Barnes, Marjorie H. Midwest Meets Mideast.
Barnes, Martin. Civil Engineering Standard Method of Measurement: Examples.
--Examples of the CESMM.
Barnes, Michael F. Measurement & Modelling Methods for Computer Systems Performance Studies.
Barnes, Mike, jt. auth. see Mills, Desmond.
Barnes, Mildred, jt. ed. see Barnes, Virgil.
Barnes, Mildred J. Women's Basketball.
Barnes, Mildred J. & Kentwell, Richard G. Field Hockey: The Coach & the Player.
Barnes, R. H., ed. see Kohler, Josef.
Barnes, R. J., jt. ed. see Johnson, T. B.
Barnes, R. M. Plasma Spectrochemistry: Proceeding of the 1984 Winter Conference on Plasma Spectrochemistry, San Diego, Jan. 2-6, 1984.
Barnes, R. M., ed. Plasma Spectrochemistry: Proceedings of the Winter Conference, Orlando, Florida, January 4-9, 1982.
Barnes, R. S. A Synoptic Classification of Living Organisms.
Barnes, R. S. & Hughes, R. N. An Introduction to Marine Ecology.
Barnes, Ramon M., ed. Emission Spectroscopy.
Barnes, Robert D. Invertebrate Zoology.
Barnes, Robert D. & Pickering, James D., eds. Nature vs. Nurture: Gettysburg College Senior Scholars' Seminar 1983-1984.
Barnes, Robert L. Invertebrate Zoology.
Barnes, Robert M. Making High Profits in Uncertain Times: Successful Investing in Inflation & Depression.
Barnes, Thomas. Origin & Destiny of the Earth's Magnetic Field.
Barnes, Thomas G. Physics of the Future.
Barnes, Virgil & Barnes, Mildred, eds. Tektites.
Barnes-Murphy, Rowan. Old MacDonald Had a Farm.
Barness, Lewis A., et al, eds. Nutrition & Medical Practice.
Barnet, G., et al, eds. Mechanical Fitting.
Barnet, Richard J. The Alliance: America, Europe, Japan-Makers of the Post-War World.
--The Alliance: America, Europe, Japan-Makers of the Postwar World.
--Economy of Death.
--The Giants: Russia & America.
--The Lean Years: Politics in the Age of Scarcity.
Barnet, Richard J., jt. ed. see Falk, Richard J.
Barnet, Sylvan. A Short Guide to Writing about Art.
Barnet, Sylvan & Stubbs, Marcia. Barnet & Stubbs's: Practical Guide to Writings with Additional Readings.
Barnet, Sylvan, jt. ed. see Stubbs, Marcia.
Barnet, Sylvan, et al. An Introduction to Literature: Fiction, Poetry, Drama.
--Types of Drama: Plays & Essays.
Barnet, Sylvan, et al, eds. Literature for Composition: Essays, Fiction, Poetry, & Drama.
Barnett & Morley. Clinical Diagnostic Ultrasound.
Barnett, A., jt. auth. see Helbling, Robert E.
Barnett, Carne S. & Young, Sharon. Teaching Kids Math: Problem-Solving Activities to Help Young Children Learn & Enjoy Mathematics.
Barnett, Coleman. An Introduction to Structured Programming Using BASIC.
Barnett, Gene & Chang, C. Nora, eds. Pharmacokinetics & Pharmacodynamics of Psychoactive Drugs.
Barnett, H. J., jt. ed. see Handa, Hajime.
Barnett, Madlyn. The Strategic Planning Process: 1986 Small Cities Goodall Award Winning Program.
Barnett, Marva A., jt. auth. see Valdman, Albert.
Barnett, Marva T. Writing for Technicians.
Barnett, Paul, tr. see Vassal, Jacques.
Barnett, R., jt. auth. see Baruch, G.
Barnett, Raymond A. College Algebra.
--College Algebra.
Barnett, Regina R. Let Out the Sunshine.
Barnett, Rosalind, jt. auth. see Rivers, Caryl.
Barnett, Vivian E., jt. auth. see Swendsen, Louise A.
Barney, Garold D. Mormons, Indians & the Ghost Dance Religion of 1890.
Barney, George C. Intelligent Instrumentation: Microprocessor Applications in Measurement & Control.
Barnhard, Robert. The Cherry Blossom Corpse.
Barnhart, Clarence L., ed. Scott, Foresman Advanced Dictionary.
Barnhart, Clarence L. & Barnhart, Robert K., eds. The World Book Dictionary.
--The World Book Dictionary: 1988.
Barnhart, Ed, ed. Physicians' Desk Reference, 1988.
Barnhart, Jefferson C. Principles of the In-Finite Philosophy.
Barnhart, Robert K., jt. ed. see Barnhart, Clarence L.
Barnick, Bernard C. Penn's Woods: A Love Story.
Barnidge, Thomas & Grow, Douglas. The Jim Hart Story.
Barnidge, Tom, ed. Best Sports Stories, 1987.
Barnitt, Rosemary E., jt. auth. see Partridge, Cecily J.
Barnouw, Victor. Anthropology: A General Introduction.
--Wisconsin Chippewa Myths & Tales & Their Relation to Chippewa Life.
Barnow, Benjaming. Basic Roof Framing.
Barnstone, Willis, tr. from Gr. Greek Lyric Poetry.
Barnstone, Willis, tr. see Aleixandre, Vicente.
Barnum, H. L. The Spy Unmasked: Or, the Memoirs of Enoch Crosby, Alias Harvey Birch, the Hero of James Fenimore Cooper's "the Spy"
Barnwell, William H. Writing for a Reason.
Barolini, Helen. Love in the Middle Ages: A Novel. Golbitz, Pat, ed.
Baron, Bonnie D., ed. see Roche, Ruth.
Baron, G. Society, Schools & Progress in England.
Baron, Gayle & Chapin, Kim. The Beauty of Running.
Baron, Marvin J., jt. auth. see Smith, Eugene H.
Baron, N. S. Language & Historical Change.
Baron, Nancy. Tuesday's Child.
Baron, Robert A. & Byrne, Donn. Exploring Social Psychology.
Baron, Robert J. & Shapiro, Linda G. Data Structures & Their Implementation.
--Data Structures & Their Implementation.
Baron, Sylvia, jt. auth. see Hicks, Bruce.
Baron, W. M. Organization in Plants.
Barondes, Samuel H., ed. see International Society for Cell Biology Staff.
Barondess-MacLean, Barbara. One Life Is Not Enough.
Barone, Dennis. Forms - Froms.
Baroni, Daniele & D'Auria, Antonio. Kolo Moser.
Baronov, I., et al. Mathematics for Pre-College Students.
Baronte, Gervee. Twilight in India.
Baroschini, Peter. Holding out for the Moon.
Barr, Ann & Levy, Paul. The Official Foodie Handbook.
Barr, Avron & Barr, Dina. Introduction to AI & Expert Systems.
Barr, Beverly. I'd Like to See Less of You.
Barr, Browne, jt. auth. see Jeske, Richard L.
Barr, David L. & Piediscalzi, Nicholas, eds. The Bible in American Education.
Barr, Dina, jt. auth. see Barr, Avron.
Barr, Donald. Arithmetic for Billy Goats.
Barr, Howard N. Fifty Best of Baltimore & Ohio Railroad.
Barr, J., et al, eds. Instrument Fitting.
Barr, James. Fundamentalism.
Barr, Jene, jt. auth. see Antonacci, Robert J.
Barr, John. The Officina Bodoni.
Barr, John R; see O'Neal, William B.
Barr, Larry, ed. Library Education: 2000 A.D. & After.
Barr, Linda. The After School Secret.
--Nothing Hurts but My Heart.
Barr, M., ed. see Midwest Category Seminar, 3rd.
Barr, M., et al. Exact Categories & Categories of Sheaves.
Barr, N. A., jt. auth. see Prest, A. R.
Barr, Rebecca & Dreeben, Robert. How Schools Work.
Barr, Robert see Lodge, James P., Jr.
Barr, William, tr. see Starokadomskiy, L. M.
Barra, Allen, jt. auth. see Ignatin, George.
Barracato, John & Michelmore, Peter. Arson!
Barraclaugh, Geoffrey, ed. see Chesneaux, Jean.
Barraclough, Geoffrey. The Turning Points in World History.
Barraclough, Geoffrey, ed. The Times Atlas of World History.
Barraclough, Geoffrey, ed. see Bautier, Robert-Henri.
Barraclough, Geoffrey, ed. see Littman, Robert J.
Barraclough, June. The Heart of The Rose.
Barraclough, Norman. Preology: The Scientific Study of the Planning of Human Development.
Barrall, Bob. The Whole World Knows.
Barranger, John A. & Brady, Roscoe O., eds. Molecular Basis of Lysosomal Storage Disorders.
Barranger, M. S. & Dodson, Daniel B. Generations: An Introduction to Drama.
Barras, Diane M., jt. auth. see Corbo, Margaret E.
Barras, Diane M., jt. auth. see Corbo, Margarete S.
Barrass, Robert. Students Must Write: A Guide to Better Writing in Course Work & Examinations.
Barratt, Glynn. The Rebel on the Bridge: A Life of the Decembrist Baron Andrey Rozen, 1800-84.
Barratt, Glynn R. Voices in Exile: The Decembrist Memoirs.
Barratt, M. B. & Mahowald, M. E., eds. Geometric Applications of Homotopy Theory I: Proceedings, Evanston, March 21-26, 1977.
--Geometric Applications of Homotopy Theory II: Proceedings, Evanston, March 21-26, 1977.
Barratt-Boyes, Brian G., jt. auth. see Kirklin, John W.
Barrell, Jospeh. A Philisophical Study of the Human Mind.
Barrese, Pauline. Home Style Italian Cookery.
Barret, Stephen, jt. auth. see Reynolds, Linda.
Barrett, Andrea. The Diabetic's Brand-Name Food Exchange Handbook: Food Exchanges for Over 3,000 Supermarket, Grocery Store & Fast-Food Products.
Barrett, Bernard M., ed. Manual of Patient Care in Plastic Surgery.
Barrett, C. K. The Gospel of John & Judaism. Smith, D. M., tr.
--Reading Through Romans.
--The Signs of an Apostle. Reumann, John, ed.
Barrett, Charles S., et al, eds. Advances in X-Ray Analysis.
Barrett, Charles S., jt. ed. see Russ, John C.
Barrett, Colin, ed. Traffic World's Question & Answer Book.
Barrett, D., ed. see Gordon, Douglas H.
Barrett, E. C. Climatology from Satellites.
Barrett, Florence E. A Pocket in a Petticoat: Memoirs.
Barrett, Frank & Barrett, Lynn. How to Watch a Football Game.
Barrett, G. Vincent & Blair, John P. How to Conduct & Analyze Real Estate Market & Feasibility Studies.
Barrett, Glenn, ed. see Anderson, John.
Barrett, James. Not an Average Guy.
Barrett, James T. Basic Immunology & Its Medical Application.
--Textbook of Immunology: An Introduction to Immunochemistry & Immunobiology.
Barrett, Jane, et al, eds. South African Women Speak.
Barrett, John. The Easter Bear.
--The Great Bear Scare.
Barrett, Judith. An Apple a Day.
--Peter's Pocket.
--The Wind Thief.
Barrett, Junelle P., et al. Teaching Global Awareness: An Approach for Grades 1-6.
Barrett, Leonard E. The Rastafarians: Sounds of Cultural Dissonance.
Barrett, Lynn, jt. auth. see Barrett, Frank.
Barrett, Marvin, ed. Broadcast Journalism.
Barrett, Michele. Women & Writing.
Barrett, Neal, Jr. Through Darkest America.
Barrett, Paul H. & Freeman, R. B., eds. The Works of Charles Darwin: The Structure & Distribution of Coral Reefs.
Barrett, Richard H., jt. auth. see Hanson, Marvin L.
Barrett, Samuel A. Ancient Aztalan.
Barrett, Stephen, jt. auth. see Cornacchia, Harold J.
Barrett, Susan & Fudge, Colin, eds. Policy & Action: Essays on the Implementation of Public Policy.
Barrett, Theodosia. Russell County.
Barrett, Thomas & Morrissey, Robert, Jr. Marathon Runners.
Barrett, W. J. Thirty-Five mm Microfilming for Drawing Offices.
Barrett, William E. Death of the Soul.
--To the Last Man.
--A Woman in the House.
Barrette, Pierre. Microcomputers in K-Twelve Education: Second Annual Conference Proceedings.
Barrette, Pierre, ed. Microcomputers in K-Twelve Education, First Annual Conference Proceedings.
Barrie, James M. Peter Pan.
--Peter Pan: Or the Boy Who Would Not Grow Up.
--Plays of J. M. Barrie.
Barrientos, Lawless J. Maryland Business Kit for Starting & Existing Businesses.
--New Jersey Business Kit for Starting & Existing Businesses.
--New York Business Kit for Starting & Existing Business.
Barrier, Gerard, jt. auth. see Musset, Alfred de.
Barrier, Smith. On Tobacco Road: Basketball in North Carolina.
Barringer, Felicity. Flight from Sorrow: The Life & Death of Tamara Wall.
Barrington, George. Use Even Me.
Barris, R. & Kielhofner, G. Psychosocial Occupational Therapy: Practice in a Pluralistic Arena.
Barro, Robert. Macroeconomics.
Barroll, Clare. The Shadow Man.
Barroll, J. Leeds. Artificial Persons: The Formation of Character in the Tragedies of Shakespeare.
Barron. Economics: An Application of Logic.
Barron & Lynch. Economics Two.
Barron, Ann F. Proud Glory.
--Windswept.
Barron, Anne D., jt. auth. see Daniels, Diane.
Barron, C. H. Numerical Control for Machine Tools.
Barron, Frank X. Artists in the Making.
Barron, Howard H. Orson Hyde: Missionary, Apostle, Colonizer.
Barron, Howard H., ed. Of Everlasting Value.
--Of Everlasting Value.
Barron, Hugh see Hirschfeld, Burt, pseud.
Barron, J. Operative Plastic & Reconstructive Surgery. Saad, M. N., ed.
Barron, J. & Saad, M. N. Operative Plastic & Reconstructive Surgery.
Barron, Jerome & Dienes, Thomas. Constitutional Law.
Barron, Jerome A., et al. West's Review Covering Multistate Subjects.
Barron, Norman. Pig Farmer's Vet Book.
Barron, Robert, jt. auth. see Fisk, Jim.
Barron's College Division Staff, ed. Barron's Compact Guide to Colleges.
--Barron's Guide to the Best, Most Popular, & Most Exciting Colleges.
--Barron's Guide to the Most Prestigious Colleges.
Barron's Educational Series, Inc. College Division Staff. Barron's Profiles of American Colleges: Descriptions of the Colleges.
Barron's Educational Series, Inc., College Division Staff. Barrons Profiles of American Colleges: The Northeast.
Barrons, Keith C. Are Pesticides Really Necessary?
Barros-Neto, Jose. College Algebra with Applications.
Barrow, Christopher J., jt. auth. see Saha, Suranjit K.

Authors

Barrow, Connye M. Job Placement: Programs for the Future.
Barrow, Isaac. The Geometrical Lectures. Child, J. M., ed.
Barrow, Jess C. WW II: Marine Fighting Squadron Nine (VF-9M)
Barrow, Sir John. Mutiny of the Bounty. Kennedy, Gavin, ed.
Barrow, Logie. Independent Spirits: Spiritualism & English Plebians 1850-1910.
Barrow, Lu Ann, jt. auth. see Huffman, Carolyn.
Barrow, R. St., jt. auth. see Woods, R. G.
Barrow, Robin. Radical Education: A Critique of Preschooling & Deschooling.
Barrows, Anita, tr. see Benmussa, Simone.
Barrows, David P. Berbers & Blacks: Impressions of Morocco, Timbuktu & the Western Sudan.
Barrs, Jerram, jt. auth. see Macaulay, Ranald.
Barry, B. Austin. Construction Measurements.
Barry, Brett De see Nee, Victor G. & De Barry, Brett.
Barry, Brian. Sociologists, Economists & Democracy.
Barry, Donald & Barner-Barry, Carol. Contemporary Soviet Politics: An Introduction.
Barry, James C., ed. Preaching in Today's World.
Barry, John W. & Henry, Porter J. Effective Sales Incentive Compensation.
Barry, Katharina, jt. auth. see Joslin, Sesyle.
Barry, Peter J. see Hopkin, John A., et al.
Barry, R. Basic Business English.
--Construction of Buildings.
--The Construction of Buildings: Foundations, Walls, Floors & Roofs. Incl. Vol. I; Vol. II; Vol. III; Vol. IV; Vol. V. Gower Pub Co.
Barry, R. D., jt. ed. see Mahy, B. W.
Barry, R. G. & Perry, A. H. Synoptic Climatology: Methods & Applications.
Barry, Roger G. & Chorley, R. J. Atmosphere, Weather & Climate.
Barry, Roger G., jt. auth. see Ives, Jack D.
Barry, Sheila A. Super-Colossal Book of Puzzles, Tricks & Games.
Barry, Stephen P. Royal Service.
Barry, T. B. The Archaeology of Medieval Ireland.
Barry, Tom & Preusch, Deb. The Central America Fact Book.
--The Central America Fact Book.
Barry, Tom, et al. Dollars & Dictators: A Guide to Central America.
--Other Side of Paradise: Foreign Control in the Caribbean.
Barry, Vincent. Applying Ethics: A Text with Readings.
--Moral Issues in Business.
Barry, William F. The Two Standards. Wolff, Robert L., ed.
Barrymaine, Norman. Time Bomb: A Veteran Journalist Assesses Today's China from the Inside.
Barsh, Carol. The Olive Schreiner Reader: Writings on Women & South Africa.
Barshay, Robert H. Philip Wylie: The Man & His Work.
Barsic, S., ed. Quasi One-Dimensional Conductors Two.
Barsis, Max. The Common Man Through the Centuries: A Book of Costume Drawings.
Barskaya, Anna, compiled by. Monet.
Barson, Alfred T. A Way of Seeing: A Critical Study of James Agee.
Barson, John. La Grammaire a l'Oeuvre.
Barson, John M., jt. auth. see Rolfe, Stanley T.
Barsoum, R. S., ed. Simplified Methods in Pressure Vessel Analysis, PVP-PB-029.
Barston, R. P. & Birnie, Patricia, eds. The Maritime Dimension.
Barstow, Mrs. Montagu see Orczy, Baroness.
Barstow, Mrs. Montagu see Orczy, Emmuska.
Barsuhn, Rochelle. Sometimes I Feel.
Barsuhn, Rochelle N. The Winds Obey Him!
Bart, Peter. Thy Kingdom Come.
Bart, Sheldon. Ruby Sweetwater & the Ringo Kid.
Bart, William M. & Wong, Martin R., eds. Psychology of School Learning. Incl. Vol. 1. Environmentalism; Vol. 2. Nativism & Interactionism. Irvington.
Bar-Tal, Daniel & Saxe, Leonard. Social Psychology of Education: Theory & Research.
Bartalini. Opera Psychotherapy.
Bartch, Marian, et al. The First & Last Gravelsburg Spelling Bee.
Bartch, Marian R. & Mallett, Jerry J. Poor Old Ernie.
Bartch-Mallett. Good Old Ernie.
Bartee, Thomas C. Introduction to Computer Science.
Bartek, Edward J. Treasury of Parables.
Bartel, Richard D., ed. & intro. by. The Challenge of Economics: Readings from "Challenge" the Magazine of Economic Affairs.
Bartell, Linda L. Brianna.
Bartenbach, Jean. Rockhound Trails.
Bartenev, G. M. & Zuyev, Yu. S. Strength & Failure of Visco-Elastic Materials.
Barter, E. G. Relativity & Reality.
Barth, Christina. Bodywork: Look Good - Keep Fit - Feel Great.
Barth, Fredrik. Features of Person & Society in Swat-Collected Essays on Pathans: Selected Essays of Frederik Barth.
--Selected Essays of Fredrik Barth: Process & Form in Social Life.
Barth, Jack, jt. auth. see Kessler, Stephen.
Barth, Karl. Against the Stream.
--Dogmatics in Outline.
--How I Changed My Mind.
--The Only Way.
Barth, Karl & Thurneysen, Eduard. Revolutionary Theology in the Making: Barth-Thurneysen Correspondence 1914-1925. Smart, J. D., tr.
Barth, Markus. Jesus the Jew. Prussner, Frederick, tr. from Ger.
--The People of God.
Barthel, Joan. A Death in California.
Barthelme, Donald. Paradise.
--Snow White.
Barthelme, Frederick. Moon Deluxe.
--Second Marriage.
--Tracer.
Barthes, Roland. Et la Chine?
--New Critical Essays. Howard, Richard, tr. from Fr.
--La Tour Eiffel.
Barthes, Roland, et al. Ecrire Pour Quoi? Pour Qui.
--Analyse Structurale et Exegese Biblique.
Bartho & Pike. Factory Electrification.
Barthold, Walter. Attorney's Guide to Effective Discovery Techniques.
Bartholomae, David, jt. ed. see Petrosky, Anthony.
Bartholomaeus, Anglicus. Medieval Lore. Steele, R., ed.
Bartholomew, Alexander. Conservatories, Greenhouses & Garden Rooms.
Bartholomew, Barbara. The Great Gradepoint Mystery.
Bartholomew, David J. Mathematical Methods in Social Science.
Bartholomew, Doris. A Manual for Practical Grammars.
Bartholomew, Mel. Cash from Square Foot Gardening.
Bartholomew, Paul J. Shadows of Turning.
Bartholomew's Cartographic Staff, illus. Bartholomew World Atlas.
Bartimo, Jim. Managing Your Money with Managing Your Money.
Bartke, Wolfgang. Oil in the People's Republic of China: Industry Structure, Production, Exports.
Bartknecht, W. Explosions: Course, Prevention, Protection. Burg, H. & Almond, T., trs. from Ger.
Bartlett, Albert B. Improve Your Health & Save Money at the Same Time.
Bartlett, David F., ed. The Metric Debate.
Bartlett, David L. The Shape of Scriptural Authority.
Bartlett, David L., jt. auth. see Orr, Dick.
Bartlett, E. G. Basic Karate.
Bartlett, Elizabeth. Memory Is No Stranger.
Bartlett, Irving H. Daniel Webster.
--Wendell & Ann Phillips: The Community of Reform 1840-1880.
--Wendell Phillips, Brahmin Radical.
Bartlett, Jennifer. History of the Universe.
Bartlett, John. Familiar Quotations.
Bartlett, John A. Jericho. Davies, Graham I., ed.
Bartlett, John R. Literature of the Rebellion.
Bartlett, Kim. Buying Time: An Established Business Fights for Survival.
--The Finest Kind: The Fisherman of Gloucester.
--Gulf Star Forty-Five.
Bartlett, Laile. PSI Trek.
Bartlett, Lee. Karl Shapiro: A Descriptive Bibliography.
Bartlett, Lynn M. Promise Me Love.
Bartlett, M. S. Probability, Statistics & Time: A Collection of Essays.
--Statistical Analysis of Spatial Pattern.
--Stochastic Population Models in Ecology & Epidemology.
Bartlett, Mable M. The Flood of Thirty-Seven.
Bartlett, Michael. The Golf Book.
Bartlett, Michael & Fishman, Joanne A. The Sailing Book.
Bartlett, Nigel, jt. auth. see Lane, Maggie.
Bartlett, Richard A. Yellowstone: A Wilderness Beseiged.
Bartlett, Roger W. Power Base Attribution & the Perceived Legitimacy of Managerial Accounting. Farmer, Richard N., ed.
Bartlett, Roland W. Modern Private Enterprise: Is It Successful.
--Success of Modern Private Enterprise.
Bartlett, Truman H. The Art Life of William Rimmer: Sculptor, Painter, & Physician.
Bartlett, William W. To Fathoms in Hell & Back.
Bartley, Frank A. Turn Down an Empty Glass.
Bartman, J. Werner Illus. by see Homan, Beulah.
Bartman, William J., jt. auth. see Downes, Robert C.
Bartok, B. & Suchoff, B. Rumanian Music: 1967-1975.
Bartok, Bela. Bela Bartok Letters.
--Turkish Folk Music from Asia Minor. Suchoff, Benjamin, ed.
Bartok, Bela & Suchoff, Benjamin. Rumanian Folk Music. Teodorescu, E. C., et al, trs. from Rumanian. Incl. Vol. 1. Instrumental Melodies; Vol. 2. Vocal Melodies; Vol. 3. Texts; Vol. 4. Carols & Christmas Songs (Colinde; Vol. 5. Maramures County. E J Brill USA.
Bartol, Curt R. Criminal Behavior: A Psychosocial Approach.
Bartoli, Cecilia & Swenson, Pina. Basic Conversational Italian.
Bartoli, Jennifer. In a Meadow, Two Hares Hide. Pacini, Kathy, ed.
Bartolo, Baldassare Di see Di Bartolo, Baldassare.
Barton, et al, eds. see Deslongchamps, Pierre.
Barton, et al, eds. see Paquette, Leo A.
Barton, A. D. Anatomy of Accounting.
Barton, A. F., ed. see Burton, A. S.
Barton, Amsel. Chummy Chipmunk's First Family.
Barton, Byron. Elephant.
Barton, D. H., ed. see Jung, M.
Barton, David K. Radar System Analysis.
Barton, David K., ed. Radars: Radar Clutter.
--Radars: The Radar Equation.
Barton, Derek, ed. see Ovchinniko, Yu A. & Ivanov, V. T.
Barton, Derek, et al. Tetrahedron Reports on Organic Chemistry.
Barton, Donald F. Their Blood Runneth Orange: Inside Clemson Football.
Barton, Frederick. Courting Pandemonium.
Barton, Fredrick. El Cholo Feeling Passes.
Barton, G. Introduction to Advanced Field Theory.
Barton, George A. Religions of the World.
Barton, H. Arnold. Letters from the Promised Land: Swedes in America 1840-1914.
Barton, H. Arnold, ed. Letters from the Promised Land: Swedes in America, 1840-1914.
Barton, Len & Walker, Stephen, eds. Education & Social Change.
--Gender, Class & Education.
--Race, Class & Education.
Barton, Len, ed. see Shears, Barbara & Wood, Susan.
Barton, P. K. Building Services Integration.
Barton, Peggy Ann. Step-by-Step Sugar Artistry.
Barton, Roger E., jt. auth. see Richardson, Richard E.
Barton, Roy F. Ifugao Law.
Barton, S. W., jt. auth. see Kurland, Michael.
Barton, Taylor J. The Illustrated Jazz Book.
Barton, William A., jt. auth. see Marcus, Eric H.
Barton, William E. Safed the Sage.
Bartos, J. & Pesez, M. Colormetric & Fluorimetric Analysis of Steroids.
Bartos, V., jt. ed. see Malek, P.
Bartram, Gerry, ed. see Zanzucchi, Anne M.
Bartram, William. Travels. Van Doren, Mark, ed.
Bartson, Lester, ed. see Hammond, Mason.
Bart-Williams, P. J. Evolution & the Word of God.
Baruch, Dorothy W. New Ways in Discipline.
Baruch, G. & Barnett, R. Lifeprints: New Patterns of Love & Work for Today's Women.
Barut, A. O. & Brittin, Wesley E., eds. Lectures in Theoretical Physics, Vol. 14A: Topics in Strong Interactions.
Barut, Asim O. & Brittin, W., eds. Lectures in Theoretical Physics, Vol. 14 B: Mathematical Methods in Theoretical Physics.
Barut, Asim O. & Brittin, Wesley E., eds. Lectures in Theoretical Physics Vol. 13: Desitter & Conformal Groups & Their Applications.
Barvicks, Alex. VHF Antenna Handbook.
Barwell, F. T. Automation & Control in Transport.
Barwick, James. The Kremlin Contract.
Barwise, Jon & Perry, John. Situations & Attitudes.
Bary, Anton De see De Bary, Anton.
Bar-Yosef, Rivkah, jt. auth. see Eisenstadt, Samuel N.
Baryshnikov, Mikhail & Anastos, Peter. The Swan Prince.
Barz, W., et al, eds. Plant Tissue Culture & Its Bio-Technical Application: Proceedings.
Barzanti, Sergio. Underdeveloped Areas Within the Common Market.
Barzum, Jacques, ed. see Crispin, Edmund.
Barzun, J., ed. see Cross, Amanda.
Barzun, J., ed. see Francis, Dick.
Barzun, J., ed. see Hillerman, Tony.
Barzun, J., ed. see James, P. D.
Barzun, J., ed. see MacDonald, John D.
Barzun, J., ed. see Peters, Ellis.
Barzun, J., ed. see Rendell, Ruth.
Barzun, Jacques. Berlioz & the Romantic Century.
--Clio & the Doctors: History, Psycho-History, Quanto History.
--Music in American Life.
--On Writing, Editing, & Publishing: Essays Explicative & Hortatory.
Barzun, Jacques & Graff, Henry F. The Modern Researcher.
Barzun, Jacques, ed. & tr. see Berlioz, Hector.
Barzun, Jacques, ed. see MacDonald, Ross.
Basa, Eniko M. Sandor Petofi.
Basabe, Fernando M. Japanese Youth Confronts Religion: A Sociological Survey.
--Religious Attitudes of Japanese Men.
Basar, T. Dynamic Modelling & Control of National Economies, 1983: Proceedings of the IFAC-IFORS Symposium, 4th, Washington, DC, June 1983. Pau, F. L., ed.
Basche, James R. U. S. Business Support for International Public Service Activities, Pt. 2. Incl. Support from Foreign Affiliates - Brazil; Support from Foreign Affiliates - Argentina; Support from Foreign Affiliates - Columbia; Support from Foreign Affiliates - Philippines; Support from Foreign Affiliates - Mexico. Conference Bd.
Bascio, Patrick. Building a Just Society.
Basdekis, Demetrios. Unamuno & Spanish Literature.
Basdevant, J. L. & Gastmans, R., eds. Fundamental Interactions: Cargese 1981.
Base, Ron. Matinee Idol.
Baselt, R., ed. Advances in Analytical Toxicology.
Baselt, Randall C. Analytical Procedures for Therapeutic Drug Monitoring & Emergency Toxicology.
--Biological Monitoring Methods for Industrial Chemicals.
--Disposition of Toxic Drugs & Chemicals in Man.
--Disposition of Toxic Drugs & Chemicals in Man: Centrally-Acting Drugs.
--Disposition of Toxic Drugs & Chemicals in Man: Peripherally-Acting Drugs & Common Toxic Chemicals.
Baselt, Randall C., jt. ed. see Cravey, Robert H.
Baserga, Renato, ed. Cell Cycle & Cancer.
--Multiplication & Division in Mammalian Cells.
Basetto, A., et al, eds. see International University Courses on Nuclear Physics Staff.
Basevi, Giorgio, jt. auth. see Kohl, Wilfied L.
Basgoz, Ilhan & Wilson, H. E. Educational Problems in Turkey, 1920-1940.
Bash, Ewald. Legends from the Future.
Bash, Lee, jt. auth. see Kuzmich, John, Jr.
Basham, Don. Spiritual Power.
Bashevis Singer, Isaac see Singer, Isaac Bashevis & Burgin, Richard.
Bashinsky, Sloan. Kill All the Lawyers? A User Friendly Guide to Working with a Lawyer.
--Selling Your Home Sweet Home.
Bashshur, Rashid L., et al. Telemedicine: Explorations in the Use of Telecommunications in Health Care.
Basic Environmental Problems of Man in Space II, International Symposium Staff & Klein, K. E. Proceedings: Proceedings of the Basic Environmental Problems of Man in Space II, International Symposium, 6th, Bonn, Germany, November 3-6, 1980. Hordinsky, J. R., ed.
Basil, Douglas & Cook, Curtis W. The Management of Change.
Basile, Frank. Professional Multihousing Management.
Basile, G., ed. see CISM (International Center for Mechanical Sciences), Department of Automation & Information Staff.
Basile, Giovanni. Pentamerone.
Basili, Victor R. Tutorial on Models & Metrics for Software Management & Engineering.
Basili, Victor R. & Baker, F. Terry. Tutorial on Structured Programming: Integrated Practices.
Baskett, Edward. Entrapped.
Baskett, T. F. Essential Management of Obstetric Emergencies.
Baskin, Cathryn, ed. see Sturmer, Marie.
Baskin, John. In Praise of Practical Fertilizer: Thoughts from Near New Burlington.
--New Burlington: The Life & Death of an American Village.
Baskin, Leonard. Baskin: Sculpture, Drawings, Prints.
--Figures of Dead Men.
Baskin, Otis W., jt. auth. see Aronoff, Craig.
Baskin, Wade. Classics in Education.
--Dictionary of Satanism.
Baskin, Wade & Powers, Pat. Sex Education: Issues & Directives.
Baskin, Wade & Powers, G. Pat, eds. New Outlooks in Psychology.
Baskin, Wade, tr. see Gide, Andre.
Baskin, Wade, tr. see Kraepelin, Emil.
Baskov, Alexand. Izvenite za Vnimanie: Collection of Poems & Stories.
Baslow, Morris H. Marine Pharmacology.
Basmanov, M. The Revolutionary Vanguard: Battle of Ideologies.
Bass, Alan, tr. see Derrida, Jacques.
Bass, Arnold M. & Broida, H. P., eds. Formation & Trapping of Free Radicals.
Bass, Donna, et al. The Tale of the Dark Crystal.
Bass, Ellen, jt. ed. see Howe, Florence.

Bass, F. G. & Fuchs, M. Wave Scattering from Statistically Rough Surfaces.
Bass, George M., jt. auth. see Kemper, Frederick.
Bass, H., ed. Algebraic K-Theory 3: Hermitian K-Theory & Geometric Applications.
Bass, Hyman, et al, eds. Contributions to Algebra: A Collection of Papers Dedicated to Ellis Kolchin.
Bass, Jean. Exercises in Mathematics. Scripta Technica, tr.
Bass, R. M. Credit Management: How to Manage Credit Effectively.
Bass, William M. Human Osteology: A Laboratory & Field Manual of the Human Skeleton. Evans, David R., ed.
Bassage, Harold. Time for Choice.
Bassali, Maurice. Medicine for the Soul.
Bassan, Fernande, et al. An Annotated Bibliography of French Language & Literature.
Bassani, F. & Parravicini, Pastori. Electron States & Optical Transitions in Solids.
Bassani, Giorgio. Behind the Door.
--Five Stories of Ferrara.
--The Heron.
--The Smell of Hay.
Bassano, Sharron & Christison, Mary A. Drawing Out: Second Language Acquisition Through Student-Created Images. Olsen, Roger E., ed.
Bassett, Frank E., jt. auth. see Noel, John V., Jr.
Bassett, Jack. Shooting Trail.
Bassett, John, ed. William Faulkner: The Critical Heritage.
Bassett, John S. Expansion & Reform Eighteen Eighty Nine to Nineteen Twenty-Six.
--Federalist System: Seventeen Eighty-Nine to Eighteen Hundred & One.
Bassett, John S., ed. Southern Plantation Overseer As Revealed in His Letters.
Bassett, Marion. A New Sex Ethics & Marriage Structure.
Bassett, Randall K., jt. auth. see Burns, Paul C.
Bassey, M. School Science for Tomorrow's Citizens.
Bassi, C., jt. auth. see Aloi, R.
Bassingthwaighte, Brian see Bruton, Sheila.
Bassiouni, M. C., ed. International Extradition: U. S. Law & Practice, Releases 1 & 2.
Bassis, Michael S., et al. Social Problems. Merton, Robert K., ed.
Bassnett-McGuire, Susan. Luigi Pirandello.
Basso, Dave, ed. Mark Twain in the Virginia Evening Bulletin & Gold Hill Daily News.
--Nevada's Public Museums: A Guide.
Basso, Dave, ed. see Taylor, Alexander S.
Basso, Hamilton. The View from Pompey's Head.
Bassow, H. Construction & Use of Atomic & Molecular Models.
Basten, Fred E. Glorious Technicolor: The Movies' Magic Rainbow.
Bastenie, Paul A. & Ermans, A. M. Thyroiditis & Thyroid Function: Clinical, Morphological, & Physiopathological Studies.
Bastiat, Frederic. Paix et Liberte, ou le Budget Republicain. Bd. with On the Causes of War, & the Means of Reducing Their Number. Laveleye, Emile L. Garland Pub.
Bastin, Harold. Plants Without Flowers.
Basu, C. R. Central Banking in a Planned Economy: The Indian Experiment.
Basu, Durga D. Introduction to the Constitution of India.
Basu, P., ed. Circulating Fluidized Bed Technology: Proceedings of the First International Conference on Circulating Fluidized Beds, Halifax, Canada, 18-20 November 1985.
Basu, Shankar. Culture & Civilization of the U. S. S. R.
Basu, T. K. & Schorah, C. J. Vitamin C in Health & Disease.
Bat, Alfred De see De Bat, Alfred.
Bata, L., ed. Advances in Liquid Crystal Research & Applications: Proceedings of the Third Liquid Crystal Conference of the Socialist Countries, Budapest, 27-31 August 1979.
Bataille, Leon, ed. A Turning Point for Literacy-Adult Education for Development-Spirit & Declaration of Persepolis: Proceedings of the International Symposium for Literacy, Iran, 1975.
Bataillon, Lionel, jt. auth. see Febvre, Lucien.
Batangtaris, Daim. Hand Dynamics.
Batchelor, John. Ainu Life & Lore: Echoes of a Departing Race.
Batchelor, John C. American Falls.
Batchelor, Julie F. Communication: From Cave Writing to Television.
Batchelor, Julie F. & De Lys, Claudia. Superstitious? Here's Why!
--Superstitious? Here's Why!
Batchelor, Laurie J., jt. auth. see Phelps, L. Allen.
Batchelor, Stephen. Alone with Others. Rosset, Hannelore, ed.
Batchelor, Walter D. Gateway to Survival Is Storage.
Bate, Philip. Flute.
--The Flute.
--The Oboe.
--The Oboe.
--Trumpet & Trombone.
Bate, R. R., et al. Fundamentals of Astrodynamics.
Bate, R. T., jt. auth. see Carter, D. L.
Bate, W. Jackson. The Burden of the Past & the English Poet.
Bateman, Barry L. & Pitts, Gerald N. JCL in a System-370 Environment.
Bateman, David N., jt. auth. see Sigband, Norman B.
Bateman, Donald & Zidonis, Frank. Effect of a Study of Transformational Grammar on the Writing of Ninth & Tenth Graders.
Bateman, F., jt. auth. see Soal, Samuel G.
Bateman, Fred, ed. see Audretsch, David B.
Bateman, Fred, ed. see Brunner, Lawrence P.
Bateman, Fred, ed. see Harris, Barry C.
Bateman, Fred, ed. see Kang Rae Cho.
Bateman, Fred, ed. see Kelton, Christina M.
Bateman, Fred, ed. see Maskus, Keith E.
Bateman, Fred, ed. see Scahill, Edward M.
Bateman, Fred, ed. see Switzer, Lorne.
Bateman, Fred, ed. see White, Alice P.
Bateman, Fred, ed. see Williams, Donald R.
Bateman, Fred, ed. see Williams, Mansfield W.
Bateman, Fred, ed. see Wolff, Nancy.
Bateman, Michael, et al. The World's Best Food: For Health & Long Life.
Bateman, Selby & Noel, Lee, Jr. Compute's Atari ST Artist.
Bater, James H. St. Petersburg, Industrialization & Change.
Bates. Commercial Language Systems.
--Input-Output.
--Removable Partial Denture Construction.
Bates, Alan P. & Julian, Joseph. Sociology: Understanding Social Behavior.
Bates, Albert C. The Charter of Connecticut: A Study.
Bates, Albert D. Retailing & Its Environment.
Bates, Betty. Bugs in Your Ears.
--Call Me Friday the Thirteenth.
--Herbert & Hortense. Tucker, Kathleen, ed.
--Love Is Like Peanuts.
--Love Is Like Peanuts.
--My Mom, the Money Nut.
--That's What T. J. Says.
--The Ups & Downs of Jorie Jenkins.
Bates, E. Language & Context: The Acquisition of Pragmatics.
Bates, G. L., jt. auth. see Gill, F. W.
Bates, H. E. My Uncle Silas.
--Poacher.
Bates, I. P. & Burnet, N. G., eds. Drug Transport Across the Blood-Brain Barrier.
Bates, J. D., jt. auth. see Jeffries, J. R.
Bates, John R., jt. auth. see O'Steen, Van.
Bates, Margaret. Talking About Cakes with an Irish & Scottish Accent.
Bates, Paul A., ed. Faust: Sources, Works, Criticism.
Bates, Ralph K. Looking at Christmas from the Inside.
Bates, Robert L. & Jackson, Julie. Our Modern Stone Age.
Bates, Robert L. & Jackson, Julia A., eds. Glossary of Geology.
Bates, Sandra, jt. ed. see Sjoden, Per-Olow.
Bates, Shirley. Popular Pottery.
Bates, Stephen, jt. auth. see Diamond, Edwin.
Bates, Steven L. & Orr, Sidney D. Concordance to the Poems of Ben Jonson.
Bates, Timothy & Bradford, William. Financing Black Economic Development.
Bates, William & Fortino, Andres. DBASE III Plus & Total Area Network: A Managers Guide.
Bateson, Gregory, jt. auth. see Ruesch, Jurgen.
Batey, P. W. Theory & Method in Urban & Regional Analysis.
Batey, P. W., jt. ed. see Massey, Doreen B.
Bath, C. Richard, jt. ed. see Applegate, Howard G.
Batham, M. J. Guide to Travel Agency Accounting.
Bathe, K. J., ed. Nonlinear Finite Element Analysis & Adina: Proceedings of the 3rd Adina Conference, Massachussetts, U. S. A., 10-12 June 1981.
Batherman, Muriel. Before Columbus.
Bathory, Peter D. Political Theory As Public Confession.
Batino. Nitrogen & Air: Gas Solubilities.
Batiste, Angel D., intro. by. Africa South of the Sahara: Index to Periodical Literature, Third Supplement.
Batley, Richard, jt. auth. see Edwards, John.
Batman, Richard. American Ecclesiastes.
Batman, Stephen. The Golden Booke of the Leaden Gods. Bd. with The Third Part of the Countess of Pembroke's Yvychurch. Fraunce, Abraham; The Fountaine of Ancient Fiction. Lynche, Richard. Garland Pub.
Bator, J. W. International Airline Phrase Book.
Bator, Paul, et al. A Constitutional Convention: How Well Would It Work?
Bator, Paul M. The International Trade in Art.
Batorska, Danuta, frwd. by. Yoruba Sculpture in Los Angeles Collections.
Batra, Gretchen, jt. ed. see Markson, Elizabeth.
Batra, Lekh R., ed. Insect-Fungus Symbiosis: Nutrition, Mutualism & Commensalism.
Batra, Ravi. Prout: The Alternative to Capitalism & Marxism.
Batschelet, Ralph J. The Flick & I.
Batson, C. Daniel, et al. Commitment Without Ideology.
Batstone, Eric. Working Order,
Batt, Cara M., jt. auth. see Arrigo, Joseph A.
Battaglia, Aurelius, illus. Seasons.
Battaglia, Bruno & Beardmore, John A., eds. Marine Organisms: Genetics, Ecology, & Evolution.
Battat, Joseph Y. Management in Post-Mao China: An Insider's View. Farmer, Richard, ed.
Battelle Memorial Institute Conference Staff. Category Theory, Homology Theory & Their Applications, 2: Proceedings of the Batelle Memorial Institute Conference, Seattle, 1968. Hilton, Peter J., ed.
Battelle Seattle Research Center Symposium Staff. Molecular Orbital Studies in Chemical Pharmacology: Proceedings of the Batelle Seattle Research Center Symposium, 1969. Kier, Lemont B., ed.
Battelle Summer Institute, Seattle, Jul. 3-28, 1972. Nonlinear Problems in the Physical Sciences & Biology: Proceedings. Stakgold, I., et al, eds.
Batten, A. H. Binary & Multiple Systems of Stars.
Batten, J. W. & Gibson, J. Sullivan. Soils, Their Nature, Classes, Distribution, Uses, & Care.
Batten, Jack. The Complete Jogger.
Batten, Joe D. Tough-Minded Management.
Batten, Robert W. & Hider, George M. Group Life & Health Insurance.
Batterberry, Michael. Twentieth Century Art.
Battersby, H. Prevost. Man Outside Himself: The Facts of Astral Projection.
Battershill, Norman. Draw Landscapes.
--Draw Trees.
Battie, David & Turner, Michael. The Price Guide to Nineteenth & Twentieth Century British Pottery.
Battin, Margaret P. & Maris, Ronald, eds. Suicide & Ethics.
Battino. Oxygen & Ozone: Gas Solubilities.
Battiscombe, Georgina, intro. by see Queen Alexandra.
Battista, O. A. Research for Profit.
Battista, O. A., ed. Business-One Thousand Directory, 1984.
Battiste see Jackson, et al.
Battistella, B. Little White Hood.
Battisti, Eugenio. Cimabue.
Battle, Carl W. Legal-Wise: Self-Help Legal Forms Guide.
Battles, Ford L., ed. see Calvin, John.
Batty, J. Accounting for Research & Development.
--Advanced Cost Accountancy.
--The Board & the Presentation of Financial Information to Management.
Batty, J., et al. Industrial Administration & Management.
Batty, J. W. Textile Auxiliaries.
Battye, J. S. Western Australia: A History from Its Discovery to the Inauguration of the Commonwealth.
Baty. English for Business.
Baty, Jennie S. Twin Rivers.
Baty, Wayne M., jt. auth. see Himstreet, William C.
Bauchum, Rosalind G. The Black Business & Professional Woman: Selected References of Achievement (A Tribute to the 50th Year of the National Association of Negro Business & Professional Women's Clubs, Inc.)
--Needs Assessment Methodologies in the Development of Impact Statements.
Baucom, John Q. Fatal Choice: The Teenage Suicide Crisis.
Baudelaire, Charles. Ecrits sur l'Art.
--La Fanfarlo: Bilingual Edition. Boyd, Greg, tr.
--Journaux Intimes.
--Lettres Inedites aux Siens.
--Oeuvres Completes.
Bauder, Donald C. Captain Money & the Golden Girl.
--Captain Money & the Golden Girl: The J. David Affair.
Baudet, Henri & Van Der Meulen, Henk, eds. Consumer Behaviour & Economic Growth in the Modern Economy.
Baudin, Robert. Confessions of a Promiscuous Counterfeiter.
Baudler, P. G. Directory of American Business in Germany.
Baudouy, Michel-Aime. More Than Courage. Ponsot, Marie, tr.
--Old One-Toe. Ponsot, Marie, tr.
Bauer, Bertrand, jt. auth. see Chou, Ya-Lun.
Bauer, Camille. France Actuelle.
Bauer, Carol & Ritt, Lawrence, eds. Free & Ennobled: Source Readings in the Development of Victorian Feminism.
Bauer, D. J. Chemotherapy of Virus Diseases.
Bauer, Douglas. Prairie City, Iowa: Three Seasons at Home.
Bauer, F., et al. A Computational Method in Plasma Physics.
--Supercritical Wing Sections: A Handbook.
--Supercritical Wing Sections III.
--A Theory of Supercritical Wing Sections, with Computer Programs & Examples.
Bauer, F. L., et al, eds. see Rutishauser, H.
Bauer, Frederic M., jt. auth. see Forgione, Albert G.
Bauer, G., et al, eds. Two-Dimensional Systems, Heterostructures & Superlattices: Proceedings of the International Winterschool Mauterndorf, Austria, Feb. 26-Mar. 2, 1984.
Bauer, Hanskurt. Color Atlas of Colposcopy.
Bauer, Jeffrey C., jt. auth. see Snyder, Thomas L.
Bauer, John D. & Ackermann, Philip G. Clinical Laboratory Methods.
Bauer, K. & Haller, G. Organometallic Compounds-Models of Synthesis, Physical Constants & Chemical Reactions, Vol. 1: Compounds of Transition Metals. Dub, M., ed.
Bauer, Marion D. Foster Child.
--Tangled Butterfly.
Bauer, P. T. Dissent on Development: Studies & Debates in Development Economics.
Bauer, Robert. The New Catalogue of Historical Records: 1898 to 1908-09.
Bauer, Roger. Coping with Stress.
Bauer, S. J. Physics of Planetary Ionospheres.
Bauer, W., ed. Lecture Notes in Computer Science, Vol. 1: Proceedings of the Gesellschaft fuer Informatik Symposium, 3 Jahrestagung, Hamburg, 1973.
Bauer, Walter. Orthodoxy & Heresy in Earliest Christianity. Kraft, Robert A. & Krodel, Gerhard, eds.
Bauer, Wolfgang. Change & Other Plays.
--China & the Search for Happiness: Recurring Themes in Four Thousand Years of Chinese Cultural History. Shaw, Michael, tr. from Ger.
Bauerle, Richard E. & Kemper, Frederick W. Up to Jerusalem.
Baues, H. J. Obstruction Theory on the Homotopy Classification of Maps.
Baugh, A., et al, eds. Mechanical Maintenance.
Baughan, E. C; see Dunitz, J. D., et al.
Baughan, Peter E. A Regional History of the Railways of Great Britain: North & Mid Wales.
Baugher, Joseph F. On Civilized Stars: The Search for Intelligent Life in Outer Space.
Baughman, James P., et al. Environmental Analysis for Management.
Baughman, Linda, ed. see Cobb, Douglas, et al.
Baughman, Linda, ed. see Cobb, Steven S., et al.
Baughn, William H. & Walker, Charls E., eds. The Banker's Handbook.
Bauly, C. B., jt. ed. see Bauly, J. A.
Bauly, J. A. & Bauly, C. B., eds. World Energy Directory.
Baum & Roman, I. Modern Aspects of Medicine.
Baum, Alan. Montesquieu & Social Theory.
Baum, Gregory. Constitution on the Church: De Ecclesia.
Baum, Gunter. Basic Values on Single Span Beams: Tables for Calculating Continuous Beams & Frame Constructions, Including Prestressed Beams.
Baum, H. & Gergely, J., eds. Molecular Aspects of Medicine.
--Molecular Aspects of Medicine.
--Molecular Aspects of Medicine.
--Molecular Aspects of Medicine: Vol. 1, Complete.
Baum, H., et al, eds. Molecular Aspects of Medicine.
--Molecular Aspects of Medicine.
Baum, Harold, jt. auth. see Green, David E.
Baum, L. Frank. American Fairy Tales.
--Dorothy & the Wizard in Oz.
--The Life & Adventures of Santa Claus.
--The Marvelous Land of Oz.
--The Wizard of Oz.
Baum, Lawrence. The Supreme Court.
Baum, Lloyd & McCoy, Richard B. Advanced Restorative Dentistry.
Baum, M. & Kay, R., eds. Clinical Trails in Early Breast Cancer.
Baum, Robert J. Ethical Arguments for Analysis.
--Ethical Arguments for Analysis: Brief Edition.
Baum, S. J., et al, eds. Experimental Hematology Today, 1985.
Baum, Stuart J. & Scaife, Charles W. Chemistry: A Life Science Approach.
Baum, Thomas. Hugo the Hippo.
Baum, Warren C. Partners Against Hunger: The Consultative Group on International Agricultural Research.
Bauman, Edward W. An Introduction to the New Testament.
--An Introduction to the New Testament.
Bauman, Robert. The Gentleman from Maryland: The Conscience of a Gay Conservative.
Bauman, Wes, et al. Country Kitchen Cookbook.
Bauman, Zygmunt. Memories of Class.

--Towards a Critical Sociology: An Essay on Commonsense & Emancipation.
Baumann, Duane D. & Dworkin, Daniel M., eds. Planning for Water Reuse.
Baumann, Elwood D. Rip-Roaring Races & Rallies.
Baumann, P., ed. Transport Mechanisms of Tryptophan in Blood Cells, Nerve Cells, & at the Blood-Brain Barrier: Proceedings of the International Symposium, Prilly-Lausanne, July 6-7, 1978.
Baumann, Roland M., ed. Dissertations on Pennsylvania History, 1886-1976: A Bibliography.
Baumback, Clifford M. & Mancuso, Joseph R. Entrepreneurship & Venture Management: Text & Readings.
Baumeister, Theodore. Marks' Standard Handbook for Mechanical Engineers.
Baumel, Philip, jt. auth. see Semat, Henry.
Baumert, L. Cyclic Difference Sets.
Baumgaertner, John H. Meet the Twelve.
Baumgartner, Diane. Melissa.
Baumol, William G. & Bowen, William G. Performing Arts: The Economic Dilemma.
Baumol, William J. Economic Dynamics.
Baumol, William J. & Blinder, Alan S. Economics: Principles & Policy.
--Economics: Principles & Policy.
--Macroeconomics.
--Microeconomics.
Baumol, William J. & Panzar, John C. Contestable Markets & the Theory of Industry Structure.
Baumol, William J see Knorr, Klaus E.
Baunach, Phyllis J. Mothers in Prison.
Baur, John I. & Wootten, Richard. The Early Works of Charles E. Burchfield, 1915-1921. Roberts, Norma, ed.
Baur, R. Morphometry of the Placental Exchange Area.
Baus, Herb. Best Restaurants, Orange County.
--Best Restaurants Orange County.
--Best Restaurants Orange County.
Bausell, R. Barker, et al. The Bausell Home Learning Guide: Teach Your Child to Write.
--The Bausell Home Learning Guide: Teach Your Child Math.
Bautier, Robert-Henri. The Economic Development of Medieval Europe. Barraclough, Geoffrey, ed.
Bautista, jt. auth. see Enriquez.
Bautista, Romeo M. Exchange Rate Adjustment under Generalized Currency Floating: Comparative Analysis among Developing Countries.
Bautista, Veltisezar B. The Book of U. S. Postal Exams: How to Score 95-100 & Get a 20,000 a Year Job.
Bavasi, Buzzie & Strege, John. Off the Record.
Bavetta, Lucien A., jt. ed. see Slavkin, Harold C.
Baviello, Mary A. & Bowie, Alexandra. The Scrubber Strategy: The How & Why of Flue Gas Desulfurization.
Bavier, Robert N., Jr. The New Yacht Racing Rules, 1973-1976.
--New Yacht, Rules-Racing.
Bavinck, Herman. Our Reasonable Faith: A Survey of Christian Doctrine. Zylstra, Henry, tr.
Bavinck, J. H. Introduction to the Science of Missions.
Bawa Muhaiyaddeen, M. R. The Truth & Unity of Man: Letters in Response to a Crisis.
Bawcutt, P., jt. ed. see Riddy, F.
Bawden, C. R. Shamans, Lamas & Evangelicals: The English Missionaries in Siberia.
Bawden, Nina. Carrie's War.
--Carrie's War: T.V. Ed.
--Devil by the Sea.
--Squib.
Bax, Clifford. Letters & Poems of Mary Stuart.
Bax, Clifford, ed. Florence Farr, Bernard Shaw & W. B. Yeats.
Bax, D. Hieronymous Bosch: His Picture-Writing Deciphered. Bax-Botha, M. A, tr. from Dutch.
Baxa, Donald E. & Petska, Darrell E. Noise Control in Internal Combustion Engines.
Baxandall, Lee, ed. Marxism & Aesthetics: A Selective Annotated Bibliography.
Bax-Botha, M. A, tr. see Bax, D.
Baxevanis, John J. The Wines of the United States & Canada.
Baxter, Brian. Alienation & Authenticity.
Baxter, Carol. Business Report Writing.
Baxter, David, intro. by. Texas Wildlife: Photographs from Texas Parks & Wildlife Magazine.
Baxter, Elmar, jt. auth. see Miller, Tom.
Baxter, Gordon. How to Fly.
--Jenny 'n Dad.
Baxter, J. Sidlow. Majesty! The God You Should Know.
--The Master Theme of the Bible, Pt. I: The Doctrine of the Lamb.
Baxter, John. The Bidders.
--The Hollywood Exiles.
--Macintosh Desktop Design: Second in a Series on Macintosh Desktop Publishing.
--Macintosh Desktop Typography: First in a Series on Macintosh Desktop Publishing.
--Science Fiction in the Cinema.
Baxter, Nancy N., ed. Hoosier Farmboy in Lincoln's Army.
Baxter, Paul R., jt. auth. see Drummond, Lewis A.
Baxter, R. & Williams, I. Population Forecasting & Uncertainty at the National & Local Scale.
Baxter, R. E. & Phillips, C. Ports, Inland Waterways & Civil Aviation. Maunder, W. F., ed.
Baxter, Robert T. Play, Plays, Play: Seven One-Act Plays for Stage & Screen.
Baxter, W. Depreciating Assets.
Bay, Austin. The Coyote Cried Twice.
Bay, Austin, jt. auth. see Dunnigan, James F.
Bayer, Barry D. & Sobel, Joseph J. Dynamics of VisiCalc.
Bayer Symposium, 4th. Psychic Dependence: Definition, Assessment in Animals & Man, Theoretical and Clinical Implications. Hoffmeister, F. & Goldberg, L., eds.
Bayer Symposium, 5th - Proteinase Conference, 2nd, Cologne, Germany, 1973. Proteinase Inhibitors: Proceedings. Fritz, H., et al, eds.
Bayer, William. Pattern Crimes.
--Switch.
--Switch.
Bayes De Luna, A. J., ed. see International Symposium on Diagnosis & Treatment of Cardiac Arrhythmias Staff.
Bayh, Marvella & Kotz, Mary L. Marvella: A Personal Journey.
--Marvella: A Personal Journey.
Bayles, Michael D. Principles of Legislation: The Uses of Political Authority.
Bayless. Current Therapy in Gastroenterology & Liver Disease 1984-1985.
Bayless, Raymond. Apparitions & Survival of Death.
--Experiences of a Physical Researcher.
--The Other Side of Death.
Bayley, Ada E. Donovan, a Novel, 1882. Wolff, Robert L., ed.
Bayley, C. C. Mercenaries for the Crimea: The German, Swiss, & Italian Legions in British Service, 1854-1856.
Bayley, Gordon. Local Government: Is It Manageable?
Bayley, J. I. & Kessel, L. Shoulder Surgery.
Bayley, James R. A Brief Sketch of the Early History of the Catholic Church on the Island of New York.
Bayley, John. The Order of Battle at Trafalgar & Other Essays.
Bayley, John B., ed. see Letarouilly, Paul.
Bayley, Nicola, illus. One Old Oxford Ox.
Bayley, Peter & Coleman, Dorothy G., eds. The Equilibrium of Wit: Essays for Odette de Mourgues.
Baylin, Frank & Gale, Brent. The Home Satellite TV Installation & Troubleshooting Manual.
--The Home Satellite TV Installation & Troubleshooting Manual.
--Ku-Band Satellite TV: Theory, Installation & Repair.
--Satellite & Cable TV: Scrambling & Descrambling.
Baylin, Frank & Toner, Amy. Satellites Today: The Complete Guide to Satellite Television.
Baylis, Fred S. Rhyme & Reason.
Baylis, J. A., ed. Safety of Computer Control Systems, 1983: Achieving Safe Real Time Computer Systems, Proceedings of the Third IFAC-IFIP Workshop, SAFECOMP 'Eighty-Three, Cambridge, U. K., September 20-22, 1983.
Baylis, Maggie. House Plants for the Purple Thumb.
Bayliss, Major, et al, trs. see Larsen, Jens P.
Baylor, J. & Moore, James. People & Ideas: A Rhetoric Reader.
Baylor, Robert A. Detail & Pattern: Essays for Composition.
Baym, Nina. The Scarlet Letter: A Reading.
Bayne, B. L., ed. Cellular Toxicology & Marine Pollution.
Bayne, E. A. Four Ways of Politics: State & Nation in Italy, Somalia, Israel, Iran.
Bayne, James W., jt. auth. see Konzo, Seichi.
Bayne, Neil. Inoculate!
Bayne, Stephen. Now Is the Accepted Time. Woodhams, Wilbur, ed.
Baynes, Ken. Art in Society.
Bayo, J. W., tr. see Gottinger, W.
Bayrd, Edwin. The Thin Game: Dieting Scams & Dieting Sense.
Bayrd, Ned & Quilter, Chris. Food for Champions: How to Eat to Win.
Bayros, Franz von see Von Bayros, Franz.
Bays, L. R., jt. ed. see Urbistondo, R.
Baytop, Turhan, jt. auth. see Mathew, Brian.
Bazant, Vladimir, et al, eds. Handbook of Organosilicon Compounds: Advances Since 1961.
Bazaraa, M. S. & Shetty, C. M. Foundations of Optimization.
Bazerman, Charles. The Informed Writer.
Bazerman, Charles, jt. auth. see Wiener, Harvey.
Bazerman, Charles, jt. auth. see Wiener, Harvey S.
Bazin, Andre. French Cinema of the Occupation & Resistance: The Birth of a Critical Esthetic. Hochman, Stanley, tr.
--Jean Renoir.
Bazin, Germain. The Baroque: Principles, Styles, Modes, Themes.
--Mont-Saint-Michel.
Bazzi, Maria. Enciclopedia De las Tecnicas Pictoricas.
BB. Recollections of a Longshore Gunner.
Beach, Barbara. MS & Us.
Beach, Barbara, ed. Book Review Index, 1987: Periodical Issues.
--Young Adult Book Review Index, 1988.
Beach, Barbara & Tarbert, Gary C., eds. Children's Book Review Index Cumulation 1985.
Beach, Barbara, jt. ed. see Tarbert, Gary C.
Beach, Dale S. Managing People at Work: Readings in Personnel.
Beach, Don M. Reaching Teenagers: Learning Centers for the Secondary Classroom.
Beach, E. F. Economic Models: An Exposition.
Beach, Edward L. Cold Is the Sea.
Beach, Edward L., jt. auth. see Noel, John V., Jr.
Beach, George K., ed. see Adams, James L.
Beach, Joseph W. American Fiction, Nineteen Twenty to Nineteen Forty.
Beach, Lynn. Attack of the Insecticons.
--The Haunted Castle of Ravencurse.
--Invaders from Dark Land.
Beach, Mark. Editing Your Newsletter: A Guide to Writing, Design & Production.
--Editing Your Newsletter: How to Produce an Effective Publication using Traditional Tool & Computers.
Beach, T. J., jt. auth. see Alexander, C. H.
Beach, Waldo. Christian Life.
--Wheel & the Cross: A Christian Response to the Technological Revolution.
Beacham, Deborah, jt. auth. see Beacham, Walton.
Beacham, Walton. Using WordPerfect.
Beacham, Walton & Beacham, Deborah. Using DisplayWrite.
--Using WordPerfect.
Beachcroft, Nina. Well Met by Witchlight.
Beacon Bible Commentary Staff. Galatians-Philemon.
--Genesis-Deuteronomy.
--Hebrews-Revelation.
--Hosea-Malachi.
--Isaiah-Daniel.
--Job-Song of Solomon.
--John: Acts.
--Joshua-Esther.
--Matthew-Luke.
--Romans, II-Corinthians.
Beacon Bible Expositions Staff. Acts.
--Corinthians.
--Galatians-Ephesians.
--Hebrews, James, I-II Peter.
--John.
--John, Jude, Revelation.
--Luke.
--Mark.
--Matthew.
--Philippians, Colossians, Philemon.
--Romans.
Beacon Bible ExpositionsStaff. Thessalonians, Titus.
Beaconsfield, P. Placenta - a Neglected Experimental Animal.
Beaconsfield, R. & Birdwood, G., eds. Placenta: The Largest Human Biopsy.
Beadle, Muriel. The Cat: History, Biology & Behavior.
Beadle, Patricia. Investing in the Eighties: What to Buy & When.
Beadles, William T., jt. auth. see Greider, Janice E.
Beadnell, Charles M. Encyclopaedic Dictionary of Science & War.
Beagle, Peter S. The Folk of the Air.
Beahrs, Virginia O. The Fire & the Glory: Lafayette & America's Fight for Freedom.
Beakley, George C. Computer-Aided Processes In Instruction & Research.
Beakley, George C. & Lovell, Robert E. Computation, Calculators & Computers: Tools of Engineering Problem Solving-Including FORTRAN.
Beakley, George C., et al. Engineering: An Introduction to a Creative Profession Instructor's Manual.
Beal, Edwin F., jt. auth. see Begin, Jame P.
Beal, Merrill D. Grand Canyon: The Story Behind the Scenery.
Beal, Peter W; see O'Neal, William B.
Beal, Raymond H., et al. Subterranean Termites: Their Prevention & Control in Buildings.
Beale, jt. auth. see Griffin.
Beale, Edgar. Sturt: The Chipped Idol.
Beall, Carl M. The Thunderbird Song.
Beall, Chandler B. La Fortune du Tasse en France.
Beall, Christine. Masonry Design & Detailing: For Architects, Engineers & Builders.
Beall, Julianne, et al, eds. see Dewey, Melvil.
Beall, Karen F., ed. Cries & Itinerant Trades: A Bibliography.
Beall, Pamela. Wee Sing Silly Songs.
Beall, Pamela & Nipp, Susan. Wee Sing & Play.
Beals, Carleton. Porfirio Diaz, Dictator of Mexico.
Beam, Emmett. The Illustrated C Programming Book.
Beam, Jacob D. Multiple Exposure: An American Ambassador's Unique Perspective on East-West Issues.
Beam, Lura, jt. auth. see Dickinson, Robert L.
Beaman, Joyce P. Broken Acres.
Beamish, F. E. & Van Loon, J. C. Recent Advances in the Analytical Chemistry of the Noble Metals.
Beams, Floyd A. Advanced Accounting.
Bean, A. R. & Simons, R. H. Lighting Fittings, Performance & Design.
Bean, G. P., jt. auth. see Jones, R. A.
Bean, George E. Aegean Turkey.
--Turkey Beyond the Maeander.
--Turkey's Southern Shore.
Bean, George L. Lycian Turkey: An Archaeological Guide.
Bean, H. S., et al. Advances in Pharmaceutical Sciences.
Bean, Henry. False Match.
Bean, Jacob. Seventeenth Century Italian Drawings in the Metropolitan Museum of Art.
Bean, Philip. Punishment: A Philosophical & Criminological Inquiry.
Bean, Philip & MacPherson, Stewart, eds. Approaches to Welfare.
Bean, Philip & Whynes, David, eds. Barbara Wooton: Social Science & Public Policy.
Bean, Phillip, et al, eds. In Defense of Welfare.
Bean, Reynold & Clemes, Harris. Elementary Principal's Handbook: New Approaches to Administrative Action.
Bean, William B. Walter Reed: A Biography.
Beane, Leona. The Essentials of Corporation Law.
Bear, D., ed. Telecommunication Traffic Engineering.
Bear, Greg. Blood Music.
--Corona.
--The Infinity Concerto.
--Sleepside Story.
Bear, H. S. Lectures on Gleason Parts.
Bear, John. How to Get the Degree You Want: Bear's Guide to Non-Traditional College Degrees.
Bear, Ruedi. Pianta Su: Ski Like the Best.
Bearchell, Charles A. Retailing: A Professional Approach.
Beard, Adelia, jt. auth. see Beard, Lina.
Beard, Charles A. The Republic: Conversations on Fundamentals.
Beard, Charles A., ed. Whither Mankind.
Beard, Charles R. Lucks & Talismans: A Chapter of Popular Superstition.
Beard, Daniel C. Shelters, Shacks, & Shanties.
Beard, E., et al. Risk Theory: The Stochastic Basis of Insurance.
Beard, Geoffrey, ed. see Gilbert, Christopher.
Beard, Henry & McKie, Roy. Growing Ups & Downs.
Beard, Henry, ed. Miss Piggy's Treasury of Art Masterpieces: From the Kermitage Collection.
Beard, J. S. Vegetation Surveys of Western Australia: Murchison Memoir No. 6.
--Vegetation Surveys of Western Australia: Swan Memoir No. 7.
Beard, James. How to Eat & Drink Your Way Through a French or Italian Menu.
Beard, James, et al. The International Cook's Catalogue.
Beard, James A. Fowl & Game Bird Cookery.
--James Beard: The Fireside Cookbook.
--Menus for Entertaining.
Beard, Lina & Beard, Adelia. American Girls Handy Book.
Beard, Peter, ed. Longing for Darkness: Kamante's Tales from Out of Africa.
Beard, Richard R. Walt Disney's EPCOT: Creating the New World of Tomorrow.
Beard, Ruth M. An Outline of Piaget's Developmental Psychology.
Beard, Ruth M. & Bligh, Donald. Research into Teaching Methods in Higher-Education.
Bearden, Donna. Monica the Computer Mouse.
Beardmore, John A., jt. ed. see Battaglia, Bruno.
Beardon, A. F. Complex Analysis: The Argument Principle in Analysis & Topology.
Beards, C. F. Vibration Analysis & Control System Dynamic.
Beardshaw, John. Economics: A Student's Guide.
Beardslee, William A. Literary Criticism of the New Testament. Via, Dan O., Jr., ed.
Beardslee, William A., ed. see Calloud, Jean.
Beardslee, William A., ed. see Funk, Robert W.
Beardslee, William A., ed. see Polzin, Robert M.
Beardslee, William A., ed. see Pregeant, Russell.
Beardslee, William A., ed. see Tannehill, Robert C.

Beardslee, William E., et al, eds. see Crossan, John D.
Beardsley, Aubrey. Later Work of Aubrey Beardsley.
Beardsley, Edward H. The Rise of the American Chemistry Profession, 1850-1900.
Beardsley, Elizabeth L., jt. auth. see Beardsley, Monroe C.
Beardsley, Monroe C. Aesthetics: Problems in the Philosophy of Criticism.
Beardsley, Monroe C. & Beardsley, Elizabeth L. Invitation to Philosophical Thinking.
Beardsley, Richard K., et al. Village Japan.
Beardsley, Theodore S., Jr. Hispano-Classical Translations: Printed Between 1482 & 1699. Koren, J., ed.
Bearman, Graham. The French Revolution.
Beasley, James, ed. see Bonar, John A.
Beasley, Jim, ed. see Jones, Jean R.
Beasley, Joseph. Wrong Diagnosis-Wrong Treatment: An Alcoholics Plight.
Beason, Robert G. Hanging On.
Beater, Jack. Electric Motor Test & Repair.
Beath, O. A., jt. auth. see Rosenfeld, Irene.
Beath, Warren N. The Death of James Dean.
Beatles. Beatlemania: Nineteen Sixty-Seven to Nineteen Seventy.
--Beatlemania: Nineteen Sixty-Three to Nineteen Sixty-Six.
Beaton, J. R., et al, eds. Horizontal Boring.
Beaton, P., tr. see Frankl, Ludwig A.
Beaton, Patrick W., ed. Municipal Needs, Services & Financing: Readings on Municipal Expenditures.
Beaton, William R., et al. Real Estate.
Beatrice. It Can Happen to You.
Beattie, Ann. Spectacles.
--Where You'll Find Me: And Other Stories.
Beattie, D. H. & Somerville, W. M. Ship's Gear: A Review of Deck Machinery.
Beattie, James. Elements of Moral Science. Wellek, Rene, ed.
--Essay on Truth.
Beattie, Susan. Alfred Stevens, 1817-1875.
Beatts, Anne & Head, John, eds. Saturday Night Live.
Beatty, Grace J., jt. auth. see Gardner, David C.
Beatty, Hetty B. Blitz.
Beatty, Jerome, Jr. Maria Looney & the Cosmic Circus.
--Maria Looney & the Remarkable Robot.
--Maria Looney on the Red Planet.
--Matthew Looney. Incl. Matthew Looney & the Space Pirates; Matthew Looney in the Outback. Beatty, Jerome, Jr; Matthew Looney's Invasion of the Earth. Beatty, Jerome, Jr; Matthew Looney's Voyage to the Earth. Avon.
--The Tunnel to Yesterday.
Beatty, John L., jt. auth. see Johnson, Oliver A.
Beatty, John R. Planning for the Mobilization of the Nation's Medical Resources.
Beatty, Michael & Nulte, James. Guide to Art Museums: Midwest Edition.
Beatty, Patricia. Jonathan Down under.
--Melinda Takes a Hand.
Beatty, R. W., jt. auth. see Kerns, D. M.
Beatty, William E. Mathematical Relationships in Business & Economics.
Beaty, David. Strange Encounters: Mysteries of the Air.
Beaty, H. Wayne, jt. auth. see Fink, Donald G.
Beaty, Jerome, ed. Norton Introduction to Literature: Fiction.
Beauchamp, Edward. An American Teacher in Early Meiji Japan.
Beauchamp, K. G. Walsh Functions & Their Applications.
Beauchamp, Kenneth P., jt. auth. see McDorman, Ted L.
Beauchamp, Tom L. & Walters, LeRoy, eds. Contemporary Issues in Bioethics.
Beauchamp, William M. Aboriginal Place Names of New York.
Beauchemin, Yves. The Alley Cat. Fischman, Sheila, tr.
Beauchene, Roy E., et al. Enzyme Activities & Aging.
Beauclair, Inez de see De Beauclair, Inez.
Beauclerk, Helen, tr. see Colette.
Beaud, Michel. A History of Capitalism, 1500-1980. Dickman, Tom & Lefebvre, Anny, trs. from Fr.
Beaudin, Michael. Willie de Wit: Lord of the Ring.
Beaudoin, Cathleen C., jt. auth. see Whitehouse, Robert A.
Beaufort, Simon de see De Beaufort, Simon.
Beaugrande, R. de. Factors in a Theory of Poetic Translating.
Beaujean, ed. see Littre.
Beaujean, Marion, ed. Metropolitan Libraries on Their Way into the 80's.
Beaujean, Von Marion Herausgegeben see Beaujean, Marion.
Beaulieu, Harry J. & Buchan, Roy M. Quantitative Industrial Hygiene.
Beaumarchais, Pierre-Augustin. Barber of Seville. Ellis, Brobury P., ed. & tr.
Beaumarchais, Pierre de. Theatre Complet: Paris, Eighteen Sixty-Nine to Eighteen Seventy-One.
Beaumarchais, Pierre de & Rat, Maurice. Theatre: Avec: Le Barbier de Seville, Le Marriage de Figaro, La Mere Coupable.
Beaumont, Alfred V. Wings of Anger.
Beaumont, Cyril W. The Mysterious Toyshop.
Beaumont, G. P. Probability & Random Variables.
Beaumont, John R. & Keys, Paul. Future Cities: Spatial Analysis of Energy Issues.
Beaumont, John R. & Williams, Stephen W. Project Work in the Geography Curriculum: An Advanced Level Primer.
Beaumont, P. B. Safety at Work & the Unions.
Beauregard, J. Histoire de France illustree.
Beauregard, Raymond A. & Fraleigh, John B. A First Course in Linear Algebra.
Beausay, William J., ed. Outlines & Readings in Educational Tests & Measurements.
Beautement, Margaret. Approaches to Modern Embroidery.
Beauvais, Robert. The Half Jew. Salemson, Harold J., tr. from Fr.
Beauvoir, Simone de. L' Existentialisme et la Sagesse Des Nations.
--La Longue Marche: Essai Sur la Chine.
Beauvoir, Simone De see De Beauvoir, Simone.
Beauvoir, Simone de see De Beauvoir, Simone.
Beauvoir, Simone De see De Beauvoir, Simone.
Beaver, Allan. Mind Your Own Travel Business: A Manual of Retail Travel Practice.
Beaver, Bonnie. Comparative Anatomy of Domestic Animals: A Guide.
Beaver, Bruce. Headlands.
Beaver, Harold, ed. see Melville, Herman.
Beaver, Marion L. Human Service Practice with the Elderly.
Beaver, Marion L. & Miller, Don. Clinical Social Work Practice with the Elderly: Primary, Secondary, & Tertiary Intervention.
Beaver, Paul. The British Aircraft Carrier.
--British Naval Air Power: Nineteen Forty-Five to the Present.
--NATO Navies of the 1980s.
Beaver, Robert J. & Mendenhall, William. Programmed Study Guide for Introduction to Probability & Statistics.
Beaver, Roy C. Bessemer & Lake Erie Railroad, 1869-1969.
Beavers, Myrtle, jt. auth. see Goggans, Janice W.
Beaverton School District Staff, jt. auth. see Lewis & Clark College Staff.
Beazley, Charles R. Dawn of Modern Geography.
Beazley, J. M. & Lobb, M. O. Aspects of Care in Labour.
Beazley, Richard M. Library Statistics of Colleges & Universities, 1976 Institutional Data (Libgis II, Hegis XI)
Bebb, Philip N., ed. see Verkamp, Bernard J.
Bebek, Borna. The Third City: Philosophy at War with Positivism.
Bebey, Francis. Agatha Moudio's Son. Hutchinson, Joyce A., tr. from Fr.
--The Ashanti Doll. Hutchinson, Joyce, tr.
Beccar-Varela, Adele, jt. auth. see Lappe, Frances M.
Becherer, Elsy, tr. see Hans-Ulrich, Rieker.
Bechtel, Robert B. Enclosing Behavior.
Bechtle, Thomas C. & Riley, Mary F. Dissertations in Philosophy Accepted in American Universities, 1861-1975.
Beck, A., ed. see International Conference on Probability in Banach Spaces Staff.
Beck, A., et al. Continuous Flows in the Plane.
Beck, A. H. Handbook of Vacuum Physics.
Beck, Aaron T. Diagnosis & Management of Depression.
Beck, Alan & Katcher, Aaron. Between Pets & People: The Importance of Animal Companionship.
Beck, Brenda E. Perspectives on a Regional Culture: Essays About the Coimbatore Area of South India.
--The Three Twins: The Telling of a South Indian Folk Epic.
Beck, Brian E. Reading the New Testament for Today: An Introduction to the Study of the New Testament.
Beck, Carl, et al. Comparative Communist Political Leadership.
Beck, Cornelia M. & Rawlins, Ruth Parmelee. Mental Health - Psychiatric Nursing: A Holistic Life-Cycle Approach.
Beck, Donald R. Basic Hospital Financial Management.
Beck, Doris. The Adventures of Sidney & Fred Or When Two Bears Go to Play.
Beck, Dorothy F. Marriage & the Family Under Challenge: An Outline of Issues, Trends, & Alternatives.
Beck, Dorothy F. & Jones, Mary Ann. How to Conduct a Client Follow-up Study.
--Progress on Family Problems: A Nationwide Study of Clients' & Counselors' Views on Family Agency Services.
Beck, Ernest W. & Monsen, Harry. Mosby's Atlas of Functional Human Anatomy.
Beck, Evelyn T., ed. Nice Jewish Girls: A Lesbian Anthology.
Beck, F. B, ed. Sinkholes - Their Geology, Engineering & Environmental Impact: First Multidisciplinary Conference on Sinkholes, Orlando, Florida, 15-17 October 1984.
Beck, Felix & Lloyd, John B., eds. The Cell in Medical Science.
Beck, Hilary. Victorian Engravings.
Beck, Hubert F. & Otterstad, Robert L. Into the Wilderness: Dialogue Meditations on the Temptations of Jesus.
Beck, J. Walter & Davies, John E. Medical Parasitology.
Beck, James C. The Potentially Violent Patient & the Tarasoff Decision in Psychiatric Practice.
Beck, John & Cox, Charles, eds. Advances in Management Education.
Beck, Lester F. Human Growth: The Story of How Life Begins & Goes On.
Beck, Lewis W., ed. Kant Studies Today.
Beck, Lewis W., ed. see Fischer, Kuno.
Beck, Lewis W., ed. see Prichard, H. A.
Beck, Lewis W., ed. see Schilpp, Paul A.
Beck, Lewis W., ed. see Seth, Andrew.
Beck, Lewis W., ed. see Vaihinger, Hans.
Beck, Lewis W., ed. see Ward, James.
Beck, Lewis W., tr. see Kant, Immanuel.
Beck, Madeline H. & Williamson, Lamar, Jr. Mastering New Testament Facts. Incl. Bk. 1. Introduction & Synoptic Gospels; Bk. 2. The Fourth Gospel & Acts; Bk. 3. Pauline Letters; Bk. 4. The General Letters & Revelation. Westminster John Knox.
--Mastering Old Testament Facts. Incl. Bk. 1. Introduction on-Deut; Bk. 2. Joshua-Esther. Westminster John Knox.
--Mastering Old Testament Facts, Bk. 4: Isaiah-Malachi.
Beck, Madeline H., jt. auth. see Overholser, Grace M.
Beck, May R. Ghosts of Old Mobile.
--Great Grandpapa Billie.
Beck, Nita K. Five Feet to the Line.
Beck, Pamela & Massman, Patti. Fling.
Beck, R. E. & Kolman, B. Computers in Nonassociative Rings & Algebras.
Beck, R. H., et al. Introductory Soil Science: A Laboratory Manual.
Beck, Robert. Naked Soul of Iceberg Slim.
Beck, Robert C. Applying Psychology: Understanding People.
Beck, Roger. Microeconomic Analysis of Issues in Business, Government & Society.
Beck, S. William. Gloves: Their Annals & Associations.
Beck, Simone & James, Michael. New Menus from Simca's Cuisine.
--New Menus from Simca's Cuisine.
Beck, Toni & Swank, Patsy. Fashion Your Figure: The Ten-Minutes-A-Day Program for Fitness.
Beck, Walter G. Beitrage Zur Kulturgeschichte der Afrikanischen Feldarbeit.
Beck, Warren A. & Clowers, Myles L. Understanding American History Through Fiction.
Beck, William S. Human Design: Molecular, Cellular & Systematic Physiology.
Beck, William S., jt. auth. see Simpson, George G.
Beck, Yoram & Zohar, David. A Zionist Anthology.
Becke, Louis. South Sea Supercargo. Day, A. Grove, ed.
Becker, Alida, ed. The Tolkien Scrapbook.
Becker, Anne, ed. see Yueh, Jean.
Becker, Anton E., jt. auth. see Gussenhoven, Elma J.
Becker, Arthur H. Guilt: Curse or Blessing.
Becker, Bruce. Backgammon for Blood.
Becker, Carl M. The Village: A History of Germantown, Ohio, 1804-1976.
Becker, D. E., ed. Recommendations for the Presentation of Infrared Absorption Spectra in Data Collections-A: Condensed Phases.
Becker, E. B., jt. auth. see Oden, J. T.
Becker, E. Lovell see Zabriskie, John B., et al.
Becker, Ernest. Denial of Death.
Becker, Ernest I., tr. see Lefevre, M. J.
Becker, Frederick F., ed. The Liver: Normal & Abnormal Functions.
Becker, G. & Theden, G., eds. Annual Report on Wood Protection, 1953-1954.
--Annual Report on Wood Protection, 1957-1958.
Becker, Gail L. Heart Smart: A Plan for Low-Cholesterol Living.
Becker, George J., ed. Documents of Modern Literary Realism.
Becker, H. A. Dimensionless Parameters: Theory & Methodology.
Becker, H. A. & Dueuzeide, H. Educational Research in Europe: A New Look at the Relationship Between School Education & Work: Second All-European Conference for Directors of Educational Research Institutions, Madrid, Sept. 11-13, 1979. Carelli, M. Dino, compiled by.
Becker, Joachim. Messianic Expectation in the Old Testament. Green, David E., tr. from Ger.
Becker, Judith. Traditional Music in Modern Java.
Becker, Jurek. Jacob the Liar. Kornfeld, Melvin, tr.
--Sleepless Days. Vennewitz, Leila, tr. Wolff, Helen, ed.
Becker, Kenneth L. & Gazdar, Adi. The Endocrine Lung in Health & Disease.
Becker, Laurence A., jt. auth. see Tuttle, Frederick B., Jr.
Becker, Lawrence C. Property Rights: Philosophic Foundations.
Becker, Marvin B. Florence in Transition. Incl. Vol. 1. The Decline of the Commune; Vol. 2. Studies in the Rise of the Territorial State. Johns Hopkins.
Becker, Muriel R. Clifford D. Simak: A Primary & Secondary Bibliography.
Becker, Peter E., et al, eds. see Tsuboi, T.
Becker, Peter W. & Jensen, Finn. Design of Systems & Circuits for Maximum Reliability or Maximum Production Yield.
Becker, R. Theory of Heat. Leibfried, G., tr.
Becker, Ralph S. & Wentworth, Wayne. General Chemistry.
Becker, Ralph S. & Wentworth, Wayne E. General Chemistry.
Becker, Robert O. & Marino, Andrew A. Electromagnetism & Life.
Becker, Russell J. When Marriage Ends. Julme, Willam E., ed.
Becker, Stephen, tr. see Malraux, Andre.
Becker, Walter. Tables of Ordinary & Extraordinary Refractive Indices, Group Refractive Indices & - H-Sub-Ox - F Curves for Standard Ionospheric Layer Models.
Becker, Warren, jt. auth. see Gleason, Harold.
Becker, William E. Marketing Checklist for the Development of a Single-Family Residential Community.
Beckerman, Bernard, ed. see Binnie, Eric.
Beckerman, Jay, jt. auth. see Rosner, Bernard.
Beckett. East Midlands from AD 1000: A Regional History of England.
Beckett, Derrick. Stephensons' Britain.
Beckett, James, ed. The Official Price Guide to Football Cards, 1988.
--The Official Price Guide to Football Cards, 1987.
Beckett, R. B., ed. Further Documents & Correspondence of John Constable R. A.
Beckett, Samuel. Collected Poems in English & French.
--The Collected Shorter Plays of Samuel Beckett.
--The Collected Works of Samuel Beckett.
--Company.
--Disjecta. Cohn, Ruby, ed.
--Endgame. Beckett, Samuel, tr. from Fr.
--Ends & Odds: Dramatic Pieces.
--First Love & Other Shorts. Beckett, Samuel, tr. from Fr.
--Fizzles.
--Happy Days.
--Happy Days.
--How It Is. Beckett, Samuel, tr. from Fr.
--Ill Seen Ill Said.
--Immobile.
--The Lost Ones.
--Malone Dies.
--Mercier & Camier.
--Molloy. Beckett, Samuel & Bowles, Patrick, trs. from Fr.
--More Pricks Than Kicks.
--Murphy.
--Ohio Impromptu, Catastrophe, & What Where: Three Plays.
--Poems in English.
--Proust.
--Rockaby & Other Works.
--Stories & Texts for Nothing.
--The Unnamable. Beckett, Samuel, tr. from Fr.
--Waiting for Godot. Beckett, Samuel, tr. from Fr.
--Waiting for Godot. Beckett, Samuel, tr. from Fr.
Beckett, Samuel see Weiss, Samuel A.
Beckett, Samuel, et al, trs. see Bosquet, Alain.
Beckett, Sarah. Herbs for Prostate & Bladder Troubles.
--Herbs for Rheumatism & Arthritis.
Beckey, Fred. Cascade Alpine Guide: Climbing & High Routes-Stevens Pass to Rainy Pass.
--Mountains of North America.
Beckey, H. D. Field Ionization & Field Desorption Mass Spectroscopy.
--Principles of Field Ionization & Field Desorption Mass Spectrometry.
Beckford, James A. Cult Controversies: The Societal Response to the New Religious Movements.
--Religious Organization: A Trend Report & Bibliography Prepared for the International Sociological Association Under the Auspices of the International Committee for Social Science Documentation.
Beckford, William. Modern Novel Writing, or the Elegant Enthusiast: And Interesting Emotions of Arabella Bloomville, a Rhapsodical Romance, Interspersed with Poetry, by the Right Hon. Lady Harriet Marlow.

--Recollections of an Excursion to the Monasteries of Alcobaca & Batalha.
Beckhand, Richard, jt. auth. see Schmidt, Warren H.
Beckhard, R. & Harris, R. T. Organizational Transitions: Managing Complex Change.
Beckhardt, Robin, ed. see Hillman, Libby.
Beckman, Gunnel. The Girl Without a Name. Parker, Anne, tr. from Swedish.
Beckman, Patti. Spotlight to Fame.
Beckmann, Charles R., jt. auth. see Ellis, Jeffery W.
Beckmann, Charles R., jt. auth. see Ellis, Jeffrey W.
Beckmann, David M. Where Faith & Economics Meet: A Christian Critique.
Beckmann, David M. & Donnelly, Elizabeth A. The Overseas List: Opportunities for Living & Working in Developing Countries.
Beckmann, M., ed. Scientific Papers of Tjalling Koopmans.
Beckner, William, et al, eds. Conference on Harmonic Analysis in Honor of Antoni Zygmund.
Beckwith, Burham P. Religion, Philosophy, & Science.
Beckwith, Burnham P. The Case for Liberal Socialism.
--Liberal Socialism: The Pure Welfare Economics of a Liberal Socialist Economy.
--Next Five Hundred Years.
Beckwith, Burnham Putnam. Religion, Philosophy & Science.
Beckwith, Charlie A. & Knox, Donald. Delta Force.
Beckwith, Glenwood J. How to Make Your Backyard More Interesting Than TV.
Becoming One Inc. Staff. Women Facing Divorce.
Becton, Randy. What Can I Say to a Friend with Cancer.
Becvar, J., ed. Mathematical Foundations of Computer Science 1979: Proceedings, 8th Symposium, Olomouc, Czechoslovakia, September 3-7, 1979.
Bedarida, Francois. A Social History of England, Eighteen Fifty-One to Nineteen Eighty-Six. Forster, A. S., tr.
--A Social History of England, Eighteen Fifty-One to Nineteen Seventy-Five.
Bedau, Hugo A. Justice & Equality.
Beddie, James S., jt. ed. see Sontag, Raymond J.
Beddoe, Deirdre. Discovering Women's History: A Practical Handbook.
Bedeian, Arthur G. Management.
Bedeian, Arthur G. & Glueck, William F. Management.
Bedell, Eugene F. The Computer Solution: Strategies for Success in the Information Age.
Bederka, John, jt. ed. see Khan, M. A.
Bedford. Atlas of Canine Surgical Techniques.
Bedford, A. Goff. The Life & Times of a Killer.
Bedford, Arthur. The Evil & Danger of Stage Plays.
Bedford, F. W. & Dwivedi, T. D. Vector Calculus.
Bedford, Frances & Conant, Robert. Twentieth-Century Harpsichord Music: A Classified Catalog.
Bedford, Henry, et al. The Americans: A Brief History.
--The Americans: A Brief History.
--The Americans: A Brief History.
Bedford, Henry F. & Colbourn, Trevor. The Americans: A Brief History.
Bedford, Herbert. Robert Schumann, His Life & His Work.
Bedford, John R. Graphic Engineering Geometry.
Bedford, Michael J., jt. ed. see Fawcett, Don W.
Bedford, Sybille. Sudden View: A Traveller's Tale from Mexico.
Bedichek, Wendell M. & Tannahill, Neal. Public Policy in Texas.
Bedichek, Wendell M., jt. auth. see Tannahill, Neal.
Bedient, P. E., jt. auth. see Rainville, E. D.
Bedient, Philip B., ed. see Bosch, Vanden, et al.
Bedlington, Stanley S. Malaysia & Singapore: The Building of New States. Kahin, G. M., ed.
Bednarek, A. R. & Cesari, L., eds. Dynamical Systems.
Bedrosian, S. D. & Porter, W. A., eds. Recent Trends in Systems Theory.
Bedwell, Stephen. Fort Rock Basin: Prehistory & Environment.
Bedwinek, Anne P. Supplemental Audio Cassettes: For Adults with Neurogenic Communicative Disorders.
Beebe, Brooke, et al. Nutrition & Good Health.
Beebe, Joyce. Joy of Canvas Painting.
Beebe, Robert P. Voyaging under Power.
Beech, G., ed. Computer Assisted Learning in Science Education.
Beech, H. R. & Fransella, F. Research & Experiment in Stuttering.
Beechcroft, William. Image of Evil.
Beecher, Marguerite, jt. auth. see Beecher, Willard.
Beecher, Willard & Beecher, Marguerite. The Sin of Obedience.
Beeching, Jack. The Chinese Opium Wars.
Beeck, Frans J. van see Van Beeck, Frans J.
Beecroft, Glynis. Casting Techniques.
Beeghley, Leonard, jt. auth. see Turner, Jonathan E.
Beehler, Rodger. Moral Life.
Beek, Steve van see Van Beek, Steve.
Beekman, Daniel. The Mechanical Baby: A Popular History of Writings on the Theory & Practice of Child Care.
Beekman, Robert, et al. Barron's How to Prepare for the Certified Public Accountant Examination.
Beeks, Graydon. Hosea Globe & the Fantastical Peg-Legged Chu.
Beeler, Myrton F., jt. ed. see Freeman, James A.
Beeler, Raymond, ed. The Princeton Journal: Thematic Studies in Architecture.
Beeler, Samuel. Understanding Your Car.
Beeley, H. Industrial Management Services.
Beenhakker, Arie. A System for Development Planning & Budgeting.
Beenhakker, H. L. & Lago, A. M. Economic Appraisal of Rural Roads: Simplified Operational Procedures for Screening & Appraisal.
Beer, A., jt. auth. see Beer, P.
Beer, Arthur, ed. see Jordan, Pascual.
Beer, Edith L. Monarch's Dictionary of Investment Terms.
Beer, Frances F., tr. see Le Gentil, Pierre.
Beer, G. R. De see De Beer, G. R.
Beer, George L. Old Colonial System.
Beer, John, ed. Coleridge's Variety: Bicentenary Studies.
Beer, Martin. Programming Microcomputers with Pascal.
Beer, P. & Beer, A. Vistas in Astronomy.
Beer, P., ed. Vistas in Astronomy.
Beer, P. & Pounds, K., eds. Vistas in Astronomy.
Beer, P., et al, eds. Vistas in Astronomy.
--Vistas in Astronomy.
--Longitude Zero Eighteen Eighty-Four to Nineteen Eighty-Four: Proceedings of an International Symposium held at the National Maritime Museum, Greenwich, London, 9-13 July 1984 to Mark the Centenary of the Adoption of the Greenwich Meridian.
Beer, Stafford. The Heart of Enterprise.
Beer, T. & Kucherawy, M. D. The Aerospace Environment.
Beer, William R. Househusbands: Men & Housework in American Families.
Beerbower, J. R. Field Guide to Fossils.
Beers, Henry A. History of English Romanticism in the Eighteenth Century.
Beers, Henry S., Jr. Computer Leasing.
Beers, James, jt. ed. see Henderson, Edmund.
Beers, Joan. Campus Vacations Directory.
Beers, P. & Murdin, P., eds. The Observatories of the Canaries: On the Occasion of Their Inauguration, June 28-29, 1985.
Beers, Richard G. Walk the Distant Hills: The Story of Longri Ao.
Beers, Ronald A., jt. auth. see Beers, V. Gilbert.
Beers, V. Gilbert & Beers, Ronald A. Bible Stories to Live By.
--Walking with Jesus.
Beery, W. T., ed. see International Clean Air Congress, 2nd.
Beesley, Patrick. Room Forty: British Naval Intelligence 1914-1918.
Beesly, Patrick. Very Special Intelligence.
Beeson, Glen, jt. auth. see Slesinger, Reuben.
Beeson, Irene, jt. auth. see Hirst, David.
Beeson, John F. Deep Pools.
Beeson, Nora S., ed. Henry E. Sigerist: Autobiographical Writings.
Beeson, Trevor. Discretion & Valour: Religious Conditions in Russia & Eastern Europe.
Beeson, Trevor & Pearce, Jenny, eds. A Vision of Hope: The Churches & Change in Latin America.
Beeston, D. T. Statistical Methods for Building Price Data.
Beet, E. A. Mathematical Astronomy for Amateurs.
Beethoven, Ludwig Van. Complete String Quartets & Grosse Fuge: From the Breitkopf & Hartel Complete Works Edition.
--Eighth & Ninth Symphonies in Full Orchestral Score.
--First, Second & Third Symphonies in Full Orchestral Score.
--Fourth & Fifth Symphonies in Full Orchestral Score.
--New Beethoven Letters.
--Six Great Overtures in Full Score.
--Sixth & Seventh Symphonies in Full Orchestral Score.
Beets, Richard Van Der see Bowen, James K. & Van Der Beets, Richard.
Beevor, Antony. The Spanish Civil War.
Befu, Harumi, jt. auth. see Mannari, Hiroshi.
Begg, Ean. The Cult of the Black Virgin.
Begg, P. R. & Kesling, Peter C. Orthodontic Theory & Technique.
Begg, R. W., ed. see Canadian Cancer Conference Staff.
Beggs, Donald L. & Lewis, Ernest L. Measurement & Evaluation in the Schools.
Begin, Jame P. & Beal, Edwin F. The Practice of Collective Bargaining.
Beglan, Peter, tr. see Vadim, Roger.
Beglo, Jo N. Thomas H. Mawson, 1861-1933: A Selected Bibliography.
Begne, Leopold P. Essentials of Syntactic Design.
Begner, Edith. Accident of Birth.
--A Dark & Lonely Hiding Place.
--Golden Opportunity.
--Just off Fifth.
--Red in the Morning.
--Son & Heir.
Bego, Mark. Cher.
Begon, Michael & Mortimer, Martin. Population Ecology: A Unified Study of Animals & Plants.
Begoun, Paula. The Best Places to Kiss in the Northwest.
--Blue Eye Shadow Should Be Illegal: A Beautifully Different Makeup Manual.
Begtrup, Holger Foreword by see Hoffmann, Robert G.
Beguelin, Richard H. The Secrets of Syndication: How to Make Money Using Other People's Money.
Behan, Brendan. Brendan Behan's New York.
Behan, P. O. & Currie, S. Clinical Neuroimmunology.
Behar, R. N. Bucket, or, Murder Near Birmingham Cathedral.
Behasa, S., jt. auth. see Creekmore, W.
Behbehani, H. S. China's Foreign Policy in the Arab World 1955-75.
Behler, Ernst, et al. Studies in German in Memory of Robert L. Kahn. Eichner, Hans & Kahn, Lisa, eds.
Behling, John H. Research Methods: Statistical Concepts & Research Practicum.
Behling, Robert. Computers & Information Processing: An Introduction.
Behlmer, Rudy, ed. Memo from: David O. Selznick.
Behm, Karen, jt. auth. see Halasz, Ida.
Behm, Ronald, jt. auth. see Salley, Christopher.
Behme, R., et al. Biology of Nematodes: Current Studies.
Behn, Harry. Crickets & Bullfrogs & Whispers of Thunder: Poems & Pictures by Harry Behn. Hopkins, Lee B., ed.
--Golden Hive.
--Little Hill.
--Two Uncles of Pablo.
--Wizard in the Well.
Behn, Harry, tr. Cricket Songs: Japanese Haiku.
--More Cricket Songs: Japanese Haiku.
Behn, Noel. Seven Silent Men.
Behn, Wolfgang, jt. ed. see Pearson, J. D.
Behnke, Frances L. The Natural History of Termites.
Behnke, John A., et al, eds. The Biology of Aging.
Behnke, W. B., Jr., et al. Clinch River: The Case for Completion.
Behr, Joyce. Picture Puzzle Riddle Book.
Behrend, Hilde. Problems of Labour & Inflation.
Behrendt, Douglas M. & Austen, W. Gerald. Patient Care in Cardiac Surgery.
Behrenfeld, William H. Accounting Desk Book.
--Estate Planning Desk Book.
--Estate Planning Desk Book.
Behrens, C. B. The Ancien Regime.
Behrens, David W. Pacific Coast Nudibranchs.
--Pacific Coast Nudibranchs: A Guide to the Opisthobranchs of the Northeastern Pacific.
Behrens, Frank. Dante's Infernal Guide to Your School.
Behrens, Laurence & Rosen, Leonard. Writing & Reading Across the Curriculum.
Behrens, Michael. The Devil & the Deep Blue Sea.
Behrens, Robert H., jt. auth. see Frey, Thomas L.
Behringer, Marjorie P. Techniques & Materials in Biology.
Behrman, Carol H. Miss Dr. Lucy. Wheeler, Gerald, ed.
--The Remarkable Writing Machine.
Behrman, Cynthia F. Victorian Myths of the Sea.
Behrman, Daniel. Solar Energy: The Awakening Science.
Behrman, Harold, jt. ed. see Jaffe, Bernard.
Behrmann, Michael M. & Lahm, Liz, eds. National Conference on the Use of Microcomputers in Special Education, Proceedings, Hartford, CT, March 10-12, 1983.
Beichner, Paul E. Petri Riage Biblia Versificato: Petri Rigue Biblia Versificato, a Verse Commentary on the Bible.
Beidelman, T. O. W. Robertson Smith & the Sociological Study of Religion.
Beidelman, William. Story of the Pennsylvania Germans: Embracing an Account of Their Origin, Their History, Their Dialect.
Beigie, Carl E., et al. Seeking a New Accommodation in World Commodity Markets.
Beiglbeeck, W., et al, eds. Feynman Path Integrals: Proceedings, International Colloquium, Marseilles May 1978.
Beiglboeck, W., et al, eds. Group Theoretical Methods in Physics.
Beihl, Bessie. Blessed Are Your Eyes.
Beijing Administration of Gardens & Parks Staff, ed. Gardens & Scenic Spots of Beijing.
Beijing Institute of Foreign Trade Staff, jt. ed. see Beijing Language Institute.
Beijing Language Institute & Beijing Institute of Foreign Trade Staff, eds. Business Chinese 500.
Beijing Language Institute Staff. An Everyday Chinese-English Dictionary.
Beijing Language Institute Staff, ed. Readings From Chinese Writers: Nineteen Nineteen to Nineteen Forty-Nine.
--Readings From Chinese Writers Series: Nineteen Nineteen to Nineteen Forty-Nine.
Beilby, M. H. Economics & Operational Research.
Beilenson, John, ed. Prayers for Inner Strength: In Times of Bereavement: A Book-Greeting Card.
Beilke, Patricia F., jt. auth. see Carroll, Frances Laverne.
Beilock, Richard P., ed. see Boulding, Kenneth E.
Beim, George. Principles of Modern Soccer.
Beim, Jerrold. Trouble after School.
Beim, Jerrold, jt. auth. see Beim, Lorraine.
Beim, Lorraine. Carol's Side of the Street.
--Triumph Clear.
Beim, Lorraine & Beim, Jerrold. Little Igloo.
--Two Is a Team.
--Two Is a Team.
Beimer, Martin E. In Celebration of Louisville. Stull, Karl, ed.
Bein, Alex. Theodore Herzl: A Biography of the Founder of Modern Zionism. Samuel, Maurice, tr. from Ger.
Bein, Vic. Mountain Skiing.
Beinhart, Larry. No One Rides for Free.
Beiser, Arthur, jt. auth. see Krauskopf, Konrad B.
Beiser, Karl. Twenty-Five Ski Tours in Maine: From Kittery to Caribou, A Cross-Country Skiers Guide.
Beisner, E. Calvin. Prosperity & Poverty: The Compassionate Use of Resources in a World of Sacrity.
Beit-Hallahmi, Benjamin, jt. auth. see Argyle, Michael.
Beitler, Arline. Adventures of a Cheap Antiquer.
Beizer, Boris. Micro-Analysis of Computer System Performance.
Beker, J. C., jt. auth. see Hageman, Howard G.
Bekkum, O. Van see Van Bekkum, O. & De Vries, H.
Bel, Rene. Un Complot Contre la Vie.
Bela Balassa & Associates. Development Strategies in Semi-Industrial Economies.
Belair, Robert R. Data Quality of Criminal History Records.
Belben, Howard. The Mission of Jesus.
Belch & Belch. Advertising & Promotion: Management & Strategy.
Belch, Jean, ed. Contemporary Games: A Directory & Bibliography Describing Play Situations or Simulations, Vol. 1: Directory.
--Contemporary Games: A Directory & Bibliography Describing Play Situations or Simulations, Vol. 2.
Belcher, C. Francis. Logging Railroads of the White Mountains.
Belcher, David W. Compensation Administration.
Belcher, Finley E. & Stickney, Clyde P. Business Combinations & Consolidated Financial Statements.
Belcher, Harold H. Subnuclear Resonance Science Unification Key: Old Data-New Concepts.
Belcher, R., ed. Instrumental Organic Elemental Analysis.
Belden, Henry M., ed. Ballads & Songs Collected by the Missouri Folk-Lore Society.
Belevitskaia-Khalizaieja, V. S. Exercises in Russian Syntax: The Compound & Complex Sentence.
Belfield, Robert, jt. auth. see Sagafi-nejad, Tagi.
Belfiglio. Best of Italian Cooking, Texas Style: Cav Valentine.
Belfiglio, Cavaliere V. The Italian Experience in Texas.
Belfiglio, Valentine J. American Foreign Policy.
Belfort, Sophie. The Lace Curtain Murders: A Romance.
Belforte, David, jt. auth. see Levitt, Morris.
Belforte, David A., ed. Industrial Laser Materials Processing Bibliography.
Belforte, G., ed. see CISM (International Center for Mechanical Sciences) Staff.
Bel Geddes, Norman. Horizons.
Belgrado, Fernando D., ed. Songs of the Synagogue of Florence. Incl. Vol. 1. The Three Festivals; Vol. 2. The High Holy Days. Hermon.
Belgum, David. Religion & Personality in the Spiral of Life.
--What Can I Do About the Part of Me I Don't Like?
--When It's Your Turn to Decide.

Belgum, Harold. Twelve Days of Christmas.
Belinfante, F. J. Measurements of Time Reversal in Objective Quantum Theory.
--Survey of Hidden Variables Theories.
Belitt, Ben. The Double Witness: Poems, Nineteen Seventy to Nineteen Seventy-Six.
Belitt, Ben, ed. & tr. see Neruda, Pablo.
Belitt, Ben, ed. & intro. by see Neruda, Pablo.
Belitt, Ben, tr. see Neruda, Pablo.
Belkaoui, Ahmed. Accounting Theory.
--Cost Accounting: A Multidimensional Emphasis.
Belker, L. The First Time Manager.
Belker, Loren B. The First Time Manager.
Belkin, Gary S. Contemporary Psychotherapies.
--Introduction to Counseling.
--Twelve-Hour BASIC for the IBM PC Compatibles: How to Get the Most from Your Compaq, Corona, Eagle, Columbia, or Other PC Clone.
Belkin, Gary S. & Goodman, N. Marriage, Family & Intimate Relationships.
Belkin, Gary S. & Skydell, Ruth H. Foundations of Psychology.
Belkin, John N. Fundamentals of Entomology.
Belkin, Samuel. Essays in Traditional Jewish Thought.
--In His Image: The Jewish Philosophy of Man As Expressed in Rabbinic Tradition.
Belknap, George N. The Blue Ribbon University.
--Henry Villard & the University of Oregon.
--Oregon Imprints 1845-1870.
Belknap, George N., ed. see Adams, William L.
Belknap, Waldron P., Jr. American Colonial Painting: Materials for a History. Sellers, Charles C., ed.
Bell, A. G. The Machine Plays Chess.
Bell, A. J. & Bell, E. Q. Adam User's Guide.
Bell, A. T. & Bonet, C., eds. Plasma Chemistry: Font Romeu & Rome, 1975.
Bell, Adrian. The Green Bond.
Bell, Anne O., ed. & pref. by see Woolf, Virginia.
Bell, Anne O., ed. see Woolf, Virginia.
Bell, Anthea, tr. see Fahrmann, Willi.
Bell, Anthea, tr. see Koenig, Alma J.
Bell, Anthea, tr. see Nostlinger, Christine.
Bell, Anthea, tr. see Pesek, Ludek.
Bell, Arthur H., jt. auth. see Sigband, Norman B.
Bell, Bob. Gun Digest Book of Scopes & Mounts: Scopes & Mounts.
Bell, C. F. Syntheses & Physical Studies of Inorganic Compounds.
Bell, Charles H. The History of Exeter, N.H.
Bell, Charlotte R. Federal Historic Preservation Case Law: A Special Report.
Bell, Clair H., ed. see Fabrizius, Peter.
Bell, Colin & Encel, Sol, eds. Inside the Whale: Ten Personal Accounts of Social Research.
Bell, Dana. A-10 Thunderbolt II.
Bell, Daniel. Marxian Socialism in the U. S.
Bell, Darlene, jt. auth. see Bell, Foster.
Bell, David, jt. ed. see Manor, Oded.
Bell, David S., ed. The Conservative Government: 1979-1984.
--Labour into the Eighties.
Bell, Donald. Being a Man: The Paradox of Masculinity.
Bell, Doug. Cast Iron Wonder: Chevrolet's Fabulous Six, 1929-1953. Clymer Publications, ed.
--Early Chevrolet History: 1912-1945. Clymer Publications, ed.
Bell, E. C. & Whitehead, R. W. Basic Electrical Engineering & Instrumentation for Engineers.
Bell, E. Q., jt. auth. see Bell, A. J.
Bell, Eric T. Men of Mathematics.
Bell, Eric T. see Taine, John, pseud.
Bell, Foster & Bell, Darlene. Queener: The Man Behind the Preaching.
Bell, Frank. Patient Lifting Devices in Hospitals.
Bell, Gordon M., ed. Light Metals 1981: Proceedings. AIME Annual Meeting, Chicago, 1981.
Bell, H. F. Talks on Religion.
Bell, H. F. & MacFarland, C. S. Religion Through the Ages.
Bell, H. Idris. Cults & Creeds in Graeco-Roman Egypt.
Bell, Henry H. Obeah: Witchcraft in the West Indies.
Bell, Hermon F. Current Problems in Religion.
Bell, Hugh S. How to Succeed in Life Insurance Selling.
Bell, Ian F. Critic As Scientist: The Modernist Poetics of Ezra Pound.
Bell, Irene W., jt. auth. see Wieckert, Jeanne E.
Bell, Irving. Christmas in Old New England.
Bell, J., et al, eds. General Welding & Cutting.
Bell, James F. Physics of Large Deformation of Crystalline Solids.
Bell, Jeanenne. Answers to Questions About Old Jewelry (1840-1950)
Bell, Jerry. Howard Hughes.
Bell, Jess G., jt. auth. see Stone, Wilfred.
Bell, John B., ed. Purdue Thirty-Ninth Industrial Waste Conference.
Bell, John M., ed. Purdue Thirty-Eighth Industrial Waste Conference: Proceedings.
Bell, Johnny F., jt. auth. see Thompson, Charles L.
Bell, Jonathan W. The Prairie Dancers: A Novel.
Bell, L. F., jt. auth. see Grant, Eugene L.
Bell Labs Staff. UNIX.
Bell, Louis. The Telescope.
Bell, Madison S. Straight Cut.
--Waiting for the End of the World.
Bell, Malcolm. The Turkey Shoot: Tracking the Attica Cover-Up.
Bell, Marion V. & Swidan, Eleanor A. Reference Books: A Brief Guide.
Bell, Martin L. Marketing: Concepts & Strategy.
Bell, Marvin. Escape into You.
--These Green-Going-to-Yellow.
Bell, Mary W. Terra & the Tornado.
Bell, Michael. The Salesman in the Field: Conditions of Work & Employment of Commercial Travellers & Representatives. International Labour Office, Geneva Staff, ed.
Bell, Michael E. & Lande, Paul S., eds. Regional Dimensions of Industrial Policy.
Bell, Mimi. Offbeat Oregon: A Connoisseur's Collection of Travel Discovery in Oregon.
Bell, P. Multiple Choice Questions in Medicine for the MRCP Examination, Part I.
Bell, P. B. & Staines, P. J. Reasoning & Argument in Psychology.
Bell, Quentin. Virginia Woolf.
Bell, R. C. Board & Table Game Antiques.
--Discovering Backgammon.
--Discovering Chess.
Bell, Rivian & Koenig, Teresa. Careers at a Movie Studio.
Bell, Robert. Having It Your Way: The Strategy of Settling Everyday Conflicts.
--You Can Win at Office Politics: Techniques, Tips, & Step-by-Step Plans for Coming out Ahead.
Bell, Robert & Coplans, John. Decisions, Decisions: Game Theory & You.
Bell, Robert, ed. Early Ballads, Illustrative of History, Traditions, & Customs.
Bell, Robert E. Dictionary of Classical Mythology.
Bell, Robert W. & Lockerbie, D. Bruce. The Best Way to Plan Your Day.
Bell, Rose S. Beyond the Strawberry Patch. Graves, Helen, ed.
Bell, S. Peter. Biographical Index of British Engineers in the 19th Century.
Bell, Sam, jt. auth. see Steben, Ralph.
Bell, Steven C., jt. auth. see Fragomen, Austin T.
Bell, Steven C., jt. auth. see Fragomen, Austin T., Jr.
Bell, Susan, et al. Women & Children First: Home Link- A Neighborhood Education Project.
Bell, T. The Fossil Malacostracous Crustacea.
Bell, W. Wanderings of an Elephant Hunter.
Bell, W. J. & Adiyodi, K. G. American Cockroach.
Bell, Wendell, jt. auth. see Shevky, Eshref.
Bell, William E. & McCormick, William F. Increased Intracranial Pressure in Children.
--Neurologic Infections in Children.
Bell, William H., et al. Surgical Correction of Dentofacial Deformities.
Bell, William T. & Carde, Ring T., eds. Chemical Ecology of Insects.
Bellace, Janice, jt. auth. see Dunfee, Thomas W.
Bellace, Janice R. The Landrum-Griffin Act: Twenty Years of Federal Protection of Union Members' Rights.
Bellack, Alan S., jt. ed. see Hersen, Michel.
Bellack, Alison, jt. auth. see Oliphant, David.
Bellafiore, Joseph. Words at Work.
Bellah, Robert N. Beyond Belief: Essays on Religion in a Post-Traditional World.
Bellairs, John. The Treasure of Alpheus Winterborn.
Bellak, Leopold. Porcupine Dilemma.
Bellak, Leopold & Baker, Samm S. Reading Faces.
Bellamy, D. J., jt. auth. see Moore, P. D.
Bellamy, David. The Mouse Book: The Story of Apodemus, a Longtailed Field Mouse.
Belland, F. W. The True Sea: A Novel of the Florida Keys.
Bellavance, Russell C., ed. see Institute for Paralegal Training Staff.
Belle, Barbara. Pixel Pixie's Birthday Party.
Belle, Marion. In the Shadow of the Sun.
Bellegarde-Smith, P. In the Shadow of Powers: Dantes Bellegarde in Haitian Social Thought.
Bellen, A. Mathematische Auswahl-Funktionen und Gesellschaftliche Entscheidungen.
Beller, Alan L., jt. auth. see Practising Law Institute Staff.
Beller, F. K., et al. Gynecology: A Textbook for Students.
Beller, Fritz & MacGillivray, Ian, eds. Hypertensive Disorders in Pregnancy.
Belles, Donald W. Fire Hazard Analysis from Plastic Insulation in Exterior Walls of Buildings.
Bellhouse, G. T. Immortal Longings.
Belli, Frederick, jt. auth. see Moss, Howard.
Belli, Melvin. The Belli Files.
Belli, Melvin M., Sr. & Carlova, John. Belli for Your Malpractice Defense.
Bellina, J. H., ed. Gynecologic Laser Surgery.
Bellinger, W. H. Psalmody & Prophecy.
Bellini, Gianpaolo, jt. ed. see Trower, W. Peter.
Bellini, Lisa, jt. auth. see Perry, Susan M.
Belliston, Larry & Hanks, Kurt. Extra Cash for Kids.
Belliveau, Jim & Belliveau, Mary. Riches under Your Roof: How to Make Your Home Worth Thousands More.
Belliveau, Mary, jt. auth. see Belliveau, Jim.
Bellman, R. Dynamic Programming-Code.
Bellman, Richard E. Adaptive Control Processes: A Guided Tour.
Bellman, Richard E. & Dreyfus, S. Applied Dynamic Programming.
Bello, Ignacio & Britton, Jack. Beginning Algebra.
Belloli, Jay & Jacob, Mary J., eds. Kick Out the Jams: Detroit's Cass Corridor 1963-1977.
Belloli, Robert C. Contemporary Physical Science: Our Impact on Our World.
Bellon, Errol M. Radiologic Interpretation of ERCP: A Clinical Atlas.
Bellow, A. & Kolzow, D., eds. Measure Theory: Proceedings of the Conference Held at Oberwolfach, 15-21 June, 1975.
Bellow, Saul. The Adventures of Augie March.
--Dangling Man.
--Henderson: The Rain King.
--Henderson the Rain King.
--The Victim.
Bellush, Bernard, jt. auth. see Bellush, Jewel.
Bellush, Jewel & Bellush, Bernard. Union Power & New York: Victor Gotbaum & District Council 37.
Belmar, Terri. Brezhia.
Belmonte, Mimi. The Diabetic Child & Young Adult.
Belnap, Nuel D., Jr., jt. auth. see Anderson, Alan R.
Belo, Jane. Trance in Bali.
Beloff, Hala. Getting into Life.
Belok, Michael V. Forming the American Minds: Early School Books & Their Compilers (1783-1837)
Belote, Julianne. Guide to Recommended Country Inns of the West Coast, (California, Oregon, Washington)
Belousov, R. What Real Socialism Means to the People.
Beloussov, V. V. Continental Endogenous Regimes.
Belov, A. F., jt. ed. see Williams, J. C.
Belov, N. V., jt. auth. see Shubnikov, A. V.
Belov, V. Morning Rendezvous.
Belove, Charles. A First Circuits Course for Engineering Technology.
Belove, Charles & Drossman, Melvyn. Systems & Circuits for Electrical Engineering Technology.
Bels, A. Voice of the Herald.
Belshaw, Michael. Economics of Underdeveloped Countries.
Belsinger, Susan & Dille, Carolyn. Cooking With Herbs.
Belskaya, Natalia, tr. see Alexeyev, S.
Belsky, Dick. One for the Money.
Belsky, Marvin S. & Gross, Leonard. How to Choose & Use Your Doctor.
--How to Choose Your Doctor.
Belstead, John S., jt. auth. see Thomas, Meirion.
Belt, E. R. Complete Electrical Estimating Course.
Belt, Guy Chester. Love's Answer from Eternity.
Belth, Joseph M. Participating Life Insurance Sold by Stock Companies.
Belth, Nathan C. A Promise to Keep: A Narrative of the American Encounter with Anti-Semitism.
Belton, Don. Almost Midnight: The Story of a Powerful, Black Religious Leader Told by the Women Who Loved Him.
Beltsville Symposia in Agricultural Research Staff, ed. Animal Reproduction.
Beltz, Ambrose G. Truth of Life.
Belveal, L. Dee. Charting Commodity Market Price Behavior.
Belyayev, N. M. Problems in the Strength of Materials.
Belz, Herman. Emancipation & Equal Rights: Politics & Constitutionalism in the Civil War Era.
Bembe, John P., jt. auth. see Darey-Bembe, Francoise.
Bemis, Samuel F. John Quincy Adams & the Foundations of American Foreign Policy.
--Latin American Policy of the U. S.
Bemis, Virginia. Energy Guide: A Directory of Information Resources.
Ben, I., ed. Who's Who in Israel & Jewish Personalities from All over the World, 1985-86.
Benacerraf, Baruj, jt. ed. see Katz, David.
Benagh, Jim, jt. ed. see Boehm, David.
Benagh, Jim, et al. Monday Morning Quarterback.
Ben-Ami, Aharon. Social Change in a Hostile Environment: The Crusaders' Kingdom of Jerusalem.
Benary-Isbert, Margot. Ark.
--The Ark. Winston, Clara & Winston, Richard, trs. from Ger.
--Blue Mystery.
--Blue Mystery.
--Castle on the Border.
--Long Way Home.
--Under a Changing Moon.
--Wicked Enchantment.
Benassi, Victor, jt. auth. see Houston, John P.
Bence, Evelyn. Following Jesus: A Woman's Workshop on Luke.
--Growing.
--Leaving Home.
--The Promise.
Benchimol, Alberto. Vectorcardiography.
Benchley, Nathaniel. Sweet Anarchy.
Benchley, Peter. Q Clearance.
Bender & Gaston. A Concordance to Conrad's the Arrow of Gold.
Bender, A. E. & Brookes, L. J., eds. Body Weight Control: The Physiology, Clinical Treatment & Prevention of Obesity.
Bender, A. E., et al, eds. Evaluation of Novel Protein Products.
Bender, Arnold & Nash, Tony. Pocket Encyclopedia of Calories & Nutrition.
Bender, Averam B. Apache Indians. Horr, David A., ed.
--The March of Empire: Frontier Defense in the Southwest, 1848-1860.
Bender, David L., ed. The American Military: Opposing Viewpoints.
--The Arms Race: Opposing Viewpoints.
Bender, Filmore E., et al. Statistical Methods for Food & Agriculture.
Bender, Harold S. Anabaptists & Religious Liberty in the Sixteenth Century. Anderson, Charles S., ed.
Bender, Jay, jt. auth. see Ferguson, Albert B.
Bender, Lloyd D., jt. auth. see Knutson, Marlys.
Bender, M. P. Community Psychology.
Bender, Marilyn J. & Webb, Paul A. Archaeological Investigations at the Roos Site, St. Clair County, Illinois.
Bender, Marylin & Altshul, Selig. Chosen Instrument: The Triumph & Tragedy of Pan Am & Its Founder, Juan Trippe.
Bender, Myron L. & Brubacher, Lewis J. Catalysis.
Bender, Paul S. Resource Management: An Alternative View of the Management Process.
Bender, Richard N. A Philosophy of Life.
Bender, Stephen O., et al. Issues in Income Distribution. Soligo, Ronald & Von der Mehden, Fred R., eds.
Bender, Todd K. Concordance to Conrad's Secret Agent.
--Concordances to Conrad's Tales of Unrest, Tales of Hearsay.
--Concordances to Conrad's the Shadow Line & Youth.
Bender, Todd K., jt. auth. see Briggum, Sue M.
Bender, Todd K., jt. auth. see Sabol, C. Ruth.
Bender, Todd K., et al. A Concordance to Conrad's Lord Jim.
--Concordance to Conrad's Victory.
Bender, William. The Scale Coordinate & Its Geometry: The Quantization of Riemannian Geometry.
Bender's Editorial Staff & Reiss, Peter. Doctor's Tax Manual.
Bendersky, David, et al. Resource Recovery Processing Equipment.
Bendick, Jeanne. Super People: Will They Replace Us?
Bendick, Jeanne & Bendick, Robert. The Consumer's Catalog of Economy & Ecology.
Bendick, Jeanne & Levin, Marcia. Mathematics Illustrated Dictionary: Facts, Figures & People, Including the New Math.
Bendick, Marc, Jr., jt. auth. see Campbell, Toby H.
Bendick, Marc, Jr., jt. ed. see Struyk, Raymond J.
Bendick, Robert, jt. auth. see Bendick, Jeanne.
Bendiner, Robert. White House Fever.
Bending, C. W. Communication & the Schools.
Bendix, G. Press Point Therapy.
Bendix, Reinhard, jt. auth. see Lipset, Seymour M.
Bendor-Samuel, David. Hierarchical Structures in Guajajara.
Bendz, G. & Lindqvist, I., eds. Biochemistry of Silicon & Related Problems.
Benecke, Gerhard. Maximillian I, Fourteen Fifty-Nine to Fifteen Nineteen.
Benedek, G., jt. ed. see Obal, F.
Benedek, W., jt. ed. see Ginther, K.
Benedetti. Unstill Life.
Benedetti, Robert L. The Actor at Work.
Benedetto, J. Harmonic Analysis on Totally Disconnected Sets.
Benedict. The Computer Connection.
Benedict, Barbara. Lovestorm.
Benedict, Brad. Fame II.
Benedict, Don. Born Again Radical.
Benedict, Lynn. The Fatal Flower.
Benedict, Madeline. Sudden Door.

Authors

Benedict, Michael L. A Compromise of Principle: Congressional Republicans & Reconstruction 1863-1869.
Benedict, Miriam. To Seek Where Shadows Are.
Benedict, Robert P. Fundamentals of Gas Dynamics.
Benedictus, David. The Antique Collector's Guide.
Benedikt, Michael, ed. The Poetry of Surrealism: An Anthology.
Benefield, Larry D., jt. auth. see Randall, Clifford W.
Benegar, John, jt. auth. see Johnson, Jacquelyn.
Beneich, Denis, jt. auth. see Breton, Thierry.
Benenson, F. C. Probability, Objectivity & Evidence.
Benes, Edward. Memoirs: From Munich to New War & New Victory. Lias, Geoffrey, tr.
Benesovsky, F., ed. see Plansec Seminar De Re Metallica, Reutte, 4th, 1961.
Benesovsky, F., ed. see Plansee Seminar De Re Metallica, Reutte, 4th, 1961.
Benesovsky, F., ed. see Plansee Seminar De Re Metallica - 3rd - Reutte - 1958.
Benesovsky, F., ed. see Plansee Seminar De Re Metallica-5th-Reutte-1964.
Benesovsky, F., ed. see Plansee Seminar De Re Metallica - 6th - Reutte-1968.
Benest, E. E. Inland Waterways of the Netherlands.
Benet, Mary K. Writers in Love: Katherine Mansfield, George Eliot, Colette & the Men They Lived With.
Benet, Stephen V. The Devil & Daniel Webster & Other Stories.
Benevento, Nicole, jt. auth. see Appleton, Nicholas.
Benevolo, Leonardo. The Architecture of the Renaissance. Landry, Judith, tr.
Benezra, Neal, jt. auth. see Speyer, A. James.
Benezra, Neal D. The Murals & Sculpture of Josef Albers. Freedberg, S. J., ed.
Benford, Gregory. Across the Sea of Suns.
--Against Infinity.
--Of Space-Time & the River.
Benge, Eugene J. Elements of Modern Management.
Benham, Harvey. The Salvagers.
Benham, Hervey. The Codbangers.
--The Stowboaters.
Benham, P. P. Elementary Mechanics of Solids.
Benice, Daniel D. Mathematics: Ideas & Applications.
Beniere, F. & Catlow, C. R., eds. Mass Transport in Solids.
Benirschke, K., jt. auth. see Hsu, T. C.
Benirschke, K. & Hsu, T. C., eds. Chromosome Atlas: Fish, Amphibians, Reptiles & Birds.
Benirschke, K., ed. see International Conference on Comparative Mammalian Cytogenetics Staff.
Benirschke, K., et al, eds. Pathology of Laboratory Animals.
--Chromosome Atlas: Fish, Amphibians, Reptiles, & Birds.
Benis, Martin, jt. auth. see Carmichael, Douglas R.
Benjamin, Alan. One Thousand Monsters.
--One Thousand Space Monsters--(Have Landed)
Benjamin, Alfred D. The Helping Interview.
Benjamin, Allen & Co. Staff & Green, William Brothers Staff. Eighteen Ninety-Seven Watches.
Benjamin, Carol L. Dog Training for Kids.
Benjamin, James J. & Kratchman, Stanley H. Practice Problems in Intermediate I Accounting (Val's Videoland)
Benjamin, James J., et al. Financial Accounting.
--Principles of Accounting.
Benjamin, Janice Y., jt. auth. see Vinitsky, Barbara B.
Benjamin, Ludy T., Jr. & Warwick, Robert J. Introduction to Psychology: Selected Readings.
Benjamin, Paul. Squeeze Play.
Benjamin, S. G. Art in America: A Critical & Historical Sketch. Weinberg, H. Barbara, ed.
--Our American Artists: With Portraits, Studios & Engravings of Paintings. Bd. with Second Series. Painters, Sculptors, Illustrators, Engravers & Architects. Garland Pub.
Benjamin, Thomas E., et al. Music for Analysis: Examples from the Common Practice Period & the Twentieth Century.
--Techniques & Materials of Tonal Music: With an Introduction to Twentieth-Century Techniques.
Benjamin, Walter. Reflections: Essays, Aphorisms, Autobiography Writings. Jephcott, Edmond, tr.
Benjamin, William P. Plastic Tooling: Techniques & Applications.
Benjaminson, Peter. Death in the Afternoon: America's Newspaper Giants Struggle for Survival.
--The Story of Motown.
Ben-Menachem, Yoram. Angiography in Trauma: A Work Atlas.
Ben-Moring, Alvin L. Balthazar, the Black & Shining Prince.
--Quadrus & Goliath.
Benmussa, Simone. Benmussa Directs: Portrait of Dora by Helene Cixous & the Singular Life of Albert Nobbs by Simone Benmussa. Barrows, Anita & Wright, Barbara, trs. from Fr.
Benn, Alec. The Twenty-Seven Most Common Mistakes in Advertising.
--The Twenty-Three Most Common Mistakes in Public Relations.
Benn, Douglas R. Love-God's Greatest Gift.
Benn, S. I. & Mortimore, G. W., eds. Rationality & the Social Sciences: Contributions to the Philosophy & Methodology of the Social Sciences.
Benn, Timothy. The Almost Compleat Angler.
Ben-Naim, Arieh. Water & Aqueous Solutions: Introduction to a Molecular Theory.
Benne, Bart. The Illustrated PC-FOCUS Book.
Benne, Robert. The Ethic of Democratic Capitalism: A Moral Reassessment.
--Wandering in the Wilderness: Christians & the New Culture.
Benne, Robert & Hefner, Philip. Defining America: A Christian Critique of the American Dream.
Bennet, John & Masia, Seth. Walks in the Catskills.
Bennet, Lowitz Barry B., jt. auth. see Casciato, Dennis A.
Bennett & Albon. Chemosurgery.
Bennett & Nelson. Mathematics: An Informal Approach.
Bennett, A. E. & Siy, L. Blueprint Reading for Welders.
Bennett, A. LeRoy. International Organizations: Principles & Issues.
Bennett, Addison C. Improving Management Performance in Health Care Institutions: A Total Systems Approach.
Bennett, Bob. The T.F.H. Book of Pet Rabbits.
Bennett, Cleaves M. & Cameron, Charles. Control Your Blood Pressure Without Drugs.
Bennett, D. Machine Embroidery with Style.
Bennett, David, et al. The Politics of Uncertainty: Regulating Recombinant DNA Research in Britain.
Bennett, David H. Cardiac Arrhythmias: Practical Notes on Interpretation & Treatment.
Bennett, Dominique, et al. Horizons: An Introduction to French Language & Culture.
Bennett, Douglas. Collecting Irish Silver.
Bennett, Dudley. Successful Team Building Through TA.
--TA & the Manager.
--TA & the Manager.
Bennett, E. W. Structural Concrete Elements.
Bennett, Edward L., jt. ed. see Rosenzweig, Mark R.
Bennett, Emerson. Forest Rose: A Tale of the Frontier. Facs. of 1885 Ed.
Bennett, Frank M. Steam Navy of the United States.
Bennett, G. F. When They Ask for Bread: Pastoral Care & Counseling.
Bennett, George F. The Perenning Apprentice.
Bennett, Gordon C. God Is My Fuehrer.
--Happy Tales, Fables & Plays.
--Readers Theatre Comes to Church.
Bennett, H. & Reed, R. A. Chemical Methods of Silicate Analysis: A Handbook.
Bennett, Hal. A Wilderness of Vines.
Bennett, Harold & Bennett, Judy. Cambridge Glass Book.
Bennett, Henry S. Six Medieval Men & Women.
Bennett, Jack W., jt. auth. see Strange, Marliss G.
Bennett, James O. Much Loved Books.
Bennett, Jane G., et al. Complete German Shepherd Dog.
Bennett, Jay. The Killing Tree.
--The Pigeon.
--The Pigeon.
--Slowly, Slowly I Raise the Gun.
Bennett, John C. The Radical Imperative: From Theology to Social Ethics.
Bennett, John C. & Seifert, Harvey. U. S. Foreign Policy & Christian Ethics.
Bennett, John E., ed. Building Voluntary Support for the Two-Year College.
Bennett, John W. The Ecological Transition.
--Northern Plainsmen: Adaptive Strategy & Agrarian Life.
Bennett, John W., jt. auth. see American Ethnological Society Staff.
Bennett, Judy, jt. auth. see Bennett, Harold.
Bennett, L. H., ed. see AIME Staff.
Bennett, Leonard E. Million-Dollar Foxhole: The Story of the Richey Family.
Bennett, Linda L. Volunteers in the School Media Center.
Bennett, Luella. Scarie Dearie.
Bennett, Lynn, jt. auth. see Acharya, Meena.
Bennett, M. D., et al, eds. Chromosomes Today.
Bennett, M. J., ed. Ultrasound in Perinatal Care.
Bennett, Marian. Helping.
--House Full of Prayers.
--I Learn to Pray.
--Loving.
--My Bible Book.
--My Friend Jesus.
--Obeying.
--Sharing.
Bennett, Michael E., et al. Elementary Algebra.
Bennett, Noel. Working with the Wool: How to Weave a Navajo Rug. Bd. with Designing with the Wool. Northland.
Bennett, Norman R. A History of the Arab State of Zanzibar.
Bennett, Paula. My Life a Loaded Gun: Female Creativity & Feminist Poetics.
Bennett, Philip M. Construction Detail Banking: Systematic Storage & Retrieval.
Bennett, R. J. The Finance of Cities in West Germany.
--Spatial Time Series Analysis-Forecasting-Control.
Bennett, R. J., ed. European Progress in Spatial Analysis.
Bennett, Ralph. Ultra in the West.
Bennett, Rebecca. Jesus Grows Up.
Bennett, Richard R., ed. Police at Work: Policy Issues & Analysis.
Bennett, Robert. God's Work of Liberation: A Journey Through the Old Testament with the Liberation Heroes of Israel.
--Raising Rabbits the Modern Way.
Bennett, Robert A. & Edwards, O. C. The Bible for Today's Church.
Bennett, Robert J., jt. ed. see Wrigley, Neil.
Bennett, Ruth, ed. Aging, Isolation & Resocialization.
Bennett, Thomas J. Goodwill Ambassador.
Bennett, Thomas L., ed. Perception: An Adaptive Process.
Bennett, Tom. Six Seventeen Squadron: The Dambusters at War.
Bennett, William H. Catholic Footsteps in Old New York: A Chronicle of Catholicity in the City of New York from 1524 to 1808.
Bennett-Sandler, Georgette, et al. Law Enforcement & Criminal Justice: An Introduction.
Benneward, Patrice, ed. From Outrage to Action: The Story of the National Audubon Society.
Benninghoven, A., et al, eds. see International Conference on Secondary Ion Mass Spectrometry Staff.
Bennis, Warren G., et al, eds. Leadership & Motivation: Essays of Douglas McGregor.
Bennison, R. L. The Impact of Town Centre Shopping Schemes in Britain: Their Impact on Traditional Retail Environments.
Bennitt, Roger. Borrowing Money: A Reference Book of Math, Strategies & Information.
Benoit, Philip & Hausman, Carl. Do Your Own Public Relations.
Benoit, Raymond. Single Nature's Double Name: The Collectedness of the Conflicting in British & American Romanticism.
Benoit de Saint-More. Roman de Troie.
Benowicz, Robert J. Drugs, Diet & You.
Bensasson, R. V. & Truscott, T. G. Flash Photolysis & Pulse Radiolysis: Contributions to the Chemistry of Biology & Medicine.
Bensch, D. E., jt. auth. see Burke, J. L.
Bense, Walter F, ed. see Holl, Karl.
Bense, Walter F., ed. see Holl, Karl.
Bensen, D. R., ed. see Wodehouse, P. G.
Bensinger, Charles. The Home Video Handbook.
Benskina, Orelia. To Whom It May Concern or Hello, Someone's Darling.
Benskina, Princess Orelia. I Have Loved You Already.
--I Thank You, Father: Peace-It's Wonderful.
Benson, A. C. The Memoirs of Arthur Hamilton B. A.
Benson, Arthur C. Walter Pater.
Benson, Bob. He Speaks Softly.
Benson, Brian J. & Dillard, Mabel M. Jean Toomer.
Benson, Carl & O'Neal, Robert, eds. Essays for Exposition.
Benson, Charles S. The Economics of Public Education.
Benson, Christopher. Careers in Agriculture.
--Careers in Animal Care.
--Careers in Auto Sales & Service.
--Careers in Conservation.
--Careers in Education.
--Careers with the City.
Benson, Dennis, jt. auth. see Benson, Marilyn.
Benson, Dennis C. The Bible Creative: John.
Benson, Dennis C. & Benson, Marilyn J. Promises to Keep: A Workbook of Experiences for Covenant Living.
Benson, Denzel E., ed. Readings in Deviant Behavior.
Benson, E. F. Queen Lucia.
Benson, E. S. & Strandjord, P. E., eds. Multiple Laboratory Screening.
Benson, Ellen. Philip's Little Sister.
Benson, Eugene. J. M. Synge.
Benson, F. A. Electric Circuit Problems with Solutions: SI-Version.
--Problems in Electronics with Solutions.
Benson, George, jt. auth. see Sachs, William S.
Benson, George A. What to Do When You're Depressed: A Christian Psychoanalyst Helps You Understand & Overcome Your Depression.
Benson, George C. & McClleland, Harold F. Consolidated Grants: A Means of Maintaining Fiscal Responsibility.
Benson, Herbert. The Mind-Body Effect.
Benson, J. L. Horse, Bird, & Man: The Origins of Greek Painting.
Benson, Jackson J., ed. The Short Stories of Ernest Hemingway: Critical Essays.
Benson, Jeffrey & Mackenzie, Alastair. Sauternes: A Study of the Great Sweet Wines of Bordeaux.
Benson, John, ed. The Working Class in England, 1875-1914.
Benson, John H. & Carey, A. G. Elements of Lettering.
Benson, John L. Who Is the Antichrist?
Benson, Lee. Turner & Beard: American Historical Writing Reconsidered.
Benson, Leslie. Proletarians & Parties: Five Essays in Social Class.
Benson, M. Yugoslavic Dictionary.
Benson, Marilyn & Benson, Dennis. The Hard Times Catalog for Youth Ministry.
Benson, Marilyn J., jt. auth. see Benson, Dennis C.
Benson, Morton. Serbo-Croatian, English: English-Serbo Croatian Dictionary.
Benson, Peter L., et al. Religion on Capitol Hill: Myths & Realities.
Benson, Ragnar. Eating Cheap.
--Ragnar's Tall Tales.
Benson, Ramsey J. & Rochester, Jack B. The Adam's Companion.
Benson, Raymond. The James Bond Bedside Companion.
Benson, Renate. German Expressionist Drama: Ernst Toller & Georg Kaiser.
--German Expressionist Drama: Ernst Toller & Georg Kaiser.
Benson, Robert E. Natural Trigonometric Functions.
Benson, Robert H. The Friendship of Christ.
Benson, Robert L. & Constable, Giles, eds. Renaissance & Renewal in the Twelfth Century.
--Renaissance & Renewal in the Twelfth Century.
Benson, Rowland S. Advanced Engineering Thermodynamics.
Benson, Rowland S. & Whitehouse, N. D. Internal Combustion Engines.
Benson, Tedd & Gruber, James. Building the Timber Frame House.
Benson, Toni, intro. by. Van Buren Co., Michigan Platbook of Early 1930's: With Every Name Index.
Benson, Warren E., Jr., ed. Car Buyer's Illustrated Fact & Figure Book 1981.
Benson, William H. & Jacoby, Oswald. New Recreations with Magic Squares.
Bensoussan, A. Stochastic Control by Functional Analysis Methods.
Bensoussan, A. & Lions, J. L., eds. Analysis & Optimization of Systems: Proceedings.
--Analysis & Optimization of Systems: Proceedings of the Sixth International Conference on Analysis & Optimization of Systems, Nice, June 19-22, 1983.
--New Trends in Systems Analysis: International Symposium, Versailles, France, Dec. 13-17, 1976.
Bensoussan, A., ed. see International Symposium on Control Theory, Numerical Methods & Computer Systems Modelling, June, 1974.
Benstock, Bernard, jt. ed. see Staley, Thomas F.
Benston, George, ed. Financial Services: Changing Institutions & Government Policy.
Bent, Robert J. & Sethares, George C. BASIC: An Introduction to Computer Programming with the Apple.
--Business BASIC.
Bente, Elizabeth H. The Farm Plan.
Benteen, John. Gunbelt.
Bentham, Jeremy & Hart, H. L. Introduction to the Principles of Morals & Legislation.
Benthem, Johan van see Van Benthem, Johan.
Bentley, jt. auth. see Whitten.
Bentley, Arthur F. Process of Government.
--Relativity in Man & Society.
Bentley, Barbara. Mistress Nancy.
--Mistress Nancy.
Bentley, Beth. Country of Resemblances.
--Phone Calls from the Dead.
Bentley, Christopher, ed. The Tragedy of Othello: The Moor of Venice.
Bentley, E. C. Trent's Last Case.
Bentley, Eric. Bernard Shaw.
--Brecht Commentaries.
--The Brecht Commentaries.
--In Search of Theatre.
--The Playwright As Thinker.
--Theatre of Commitment.
--What Is Theatre.
Bentley, Eric, ed. The Classic Theatre: Six French Plays. Incl. Misanthrope. Moliere; Cid. Corneille, Pierre; Phaedra. Racine, Jean; Turcaret. Le Sage, Alain R; False Confessions. Marivaux, Pierre C; Marriage of Figaro. De Beaumarchais, Pierre A. Doubleday.
Bentley, Eric, tr. see Brecht, Bertolt.

Authors

Bentley, G. E. William Blake: Europe, a Prophecy.
Bentley, G. E., Jr. A Bibliography of George Cumberland (1754-1848)
Bentley, G. E., Jr., intro. by. William Blake: America; a Prophecy.
Bentley, Howard B., ed. Building Construction Information Sources.
Bentley, James, retold by. The Children's Bible.
Bentley, John. Historical View of Hindu Astronomy.
Bentley, Nelson B. Iron Man of the Hoh.
Bentley, Peter J. Endocrines & Osmoregulation: A Comparative Account of the Regulation of Water & Salt in Vertebrates.
Bentley, R. Molecular Asymmetry in Biology.
Bentley, Richard. Eight Boyle Lectures on Atheism. Wellek, Rene, ed.
Bentley, Robert, Inc. Toyota Celica Service Manual: 1978-1983.
--Toyota Corolla Tercel Service Manual 1980-1983.
--Toyota Corolla Tercel: 1980-1982.
--Toyota Pick-up Truck & 4-Runner Service Manual: 1978-1987.
--Volkswagen GTI Official Service Manual: 1985-1987.
--Volkswagen Jetta Official Service Manual: 1985-1987.
Bentley, Stacey & Hatfield, Fred. Toning Your Body: A Bodybuilding Program for Women.
Bentley, Trevor J. Making Computers Work.
--Practical Cost Reduction.
Bentley, Ursula. Private Accounts.
Bentley, Virginia W. Bentley Farm Cook Book.
--Let Herbs Do It.
Bentley, William. Record of the Parish List of Deaths, 1785-1819.
Bently, G. E., Jr., ed. Editing Eighteenth-Century Novels.
Benton. Door Ajar.
Benton, Allen H. & Werner, William E., Jr. Manual of Field Biology & Ecology.
Benton, Angelo Ames. The Church Cyclopaedia: A Dictionary of Church Doctrine, History, Organization & Ritual, & Containing Original Articles on Special Topics, Written Expressly for This Work by Bishops, Presbyters, & Laymen.
Benton, Bill, et al. Social Services: Federal Legislation vs. State Implemention.
Benton, E. V., et al, eds. Nuclear Track Registration: Proceedings of the Pacific Northwest Conference, 5th, Hanford Engineering Development Laboratory, Westinghouse Hanford Company, Richland, WA, July 28-29, 1982.
Benton, Fred W., jt. auth. see Osborn, Robert.
Benton, Horace. A Twist of Justice-Gripes.
Benton, John. Candi.
Benton, Kenneth. Twenty-Fourth Level.
Benton, Ted. Philosophical Foundations of the Three Sociologies.
Benton, Wilbourn E. & Grimm, Georg, eds. Nuremberg: German Views of the War Trials.
Benton, Will. Buffalo Butte.
--Horsethief.
Benward, Bruce & Jackson, Barbara G. Practical Beginning Theory.
Beny, Roloff, jt. auth. see Stassinopoulos, Arianna.
Beny, Roloff, photos by. The Romance of Architecture.
Benyahia, Hadj. Education & Technological Innovations: Academic Performance & Economical Advantages.
Ben-Yehuda, Nachman. Deviance & Moral Boundaries: Witchcraft, the Occult, Science Fiction, Deviant Sciences & Scientists.
Benyo, Richard & Provost, Rhonda. Feeling Fit in Your Forty's: How to Get the Most from the Best Years of Your Life.
Ben-Yosef, Reuven, tr. see Allon, Yigal.
Benziger, Theodore H., ed. Temperature. Incl. Pt. 1. Arts & Concept; Pt. 2. Thermal Homeostasis. Acad Pr.
Benzon, Alfred, Symposium. Role of Nucleotides for the Function & Conformation of Enzymes: Proceedings of the Alfred Benzon Symposium, 1st. Kalckar, H. M., et al, eds.
--Transport Mechanisms in Epithelia: Proceedings of the Alfred Benzon Symposium, 5th. Ussing, H. H., et al, eds.
Benzon, Alfred, Symposium, et al. Ion Homeostasis of the Brain: Proceedings of The Alfred Benzon Symposium, 3rd, Copenhagen & Lund, 1970. Siesjo, B. K. & Sorensen, S. C., eds.
Benzoni, Juliette. Belle Catherine.
--Catherine, Royal Mistress.
--Catherine's Quest.
--Catherine's Time for Love.
Bequai, August. White Collar Crime.
Beranbaum, Rose L. Romantic & Classic Cakes. Sparks, Jennifer, ed.
Beranek, B. A., ed. Annuale Mediaevale.
Beranek, B. A. & Petik, H., eds. Annuale Mediaevale.
Berberick, Nancy. Jewels of Elvish.
Berberoglu, H. The World of the Restaurateur.
Berchen, Ursula, jt. auth. see Berchen, William.
Berchen, William. Maine.
Berchen, William & Berchen, Ursula. Aspects of Boston.
Berchtold, W., tr. see Hopper, A. G.
Bercken, J. H. Van Den see Van Den Bercken, J. H., et al.
Bercovici, Eric. So Little Cause for Caroline.
--Wolftrap.
Bercovici, Konrad. The Story of the Gypsies.
Bercovitch, Sacvan, ed. Typology & Early American Literature.
Bercusson, Brian. Fair Wages Resolutions.
Bercy, Drovin De see De Bercy, Drouin.
Berdiaer, Nicolaii. The Realm of Spirit & the Realm of Caesar. Luurie, Donald A., tr. from Rus.
Berdie, Mitchell, jt. auth. see Muldoon, Joseph A.
Berdyaev, Nicholas. Christianity & Anti-Semitism.
Bereano, Philip L. Technology As a Social & Political Phenomenon.
Beregi, E., et al, eds. Pulmonary Pathology & Aging.
Berelson, Bernard & Steiner, Gary A. Human Behavior: An Inventory of Scientific Findings Shorter Ed.
Berenblum, I. Cancer Research Today.
Berendt, Joachim. The Jazz Book: From New Orleans to Rock & Free Jazz. Morgenstern, Dan, ed. & tr. from Ger.
Berendt, Joachim-Ernst. Jazz: A Photo History.
Berens, H., jt. auth. see Butzer, P. L.
Berenson, Bernard G., jt. auth. see Carkhuff, Robert R.
Berenson, Bernhard. Aesthetics & History.
--Alberto Sani: An Artist Out of His Time.
Berenstain, Janice, jt. auth. see Berenstain, Stan.
Berenstain, Michael. Peat Moss & Ivy & the Birthday Present.
Berenstain, Stan & Berenstain, Janice. The Berenstain Bears & the Messy Room.
--Berenstain Bears Forget Their Manners.
--The Berenstains' Baby Book.
--How to Teach Your Children about Sex.
--Stan & Jan Berenstain's It's All in the Family.
Berentes, Drew. MacPascal Programming.
Bereny, Justin A., ed. Industrial Robots: A Survey of Domestic & Foreign Patents (1969-1983), Vol. 6 (Robotics & Artificial Intelligence Applications Series.
Beres, Louis R. People, States, & World Order.
Beresford, Maurice. The Lost Villages of England.
Beresford, T. P., jt. ed. see Hall, R. C.
Beresford, W. A. Chondroid Bone, Secondary Cartilage & Metaplasia.
Beresiner, Yasha. British County Maps: A Reference & Price Guide.
Berez, Natalie R. One World under God.
Berezin, Nancy. After a Loss in Pregnancy: Help for Families Affected by a Miscarriage, a Still Birth, or a Newborn's Death.
Berg, Barbara J. The Crisis of the Working Mother: Resolving the Conflict Between Family & Work.
Berg, C. Circumpolar Problems: Habitat, Economy & Social Relations in the Arctic.
Berg, David N. & Smith, Kennwyn K. Exploring Clinical Methods for Social Research.
Berg, George G. & Maillie, H. David, eds. Measurement of Risks.
Berg, Ian, jt. ed. see Hersov, Lionel.
Berg, J. Gary. Managing Compensation: Developing & Administering the Total Compensation Program.
Berg, J. M. Genetic Counseling in Relation to Mental Retardation.
Berg, J. M., et al. The DeLange Syndrome.
Berg, Jean De see De Berg, Jean.
Berg, Jean H. I Cry When the Sun Goes Down: The Story of Herman Wrice.
--Moses: Leader & Lawgiver.
--There's Nothing to Do, So Let Me Be You.
Berg, Jeanne de see De Berg, Jeanne.
Berg, John, ed. The Soviet Submarine Fleet: A Photographic Survey.
Berg, Kare, ed. Genetic Damage in Man Caused by Environmental Agents.
Berg, Lasse & Berg, Lisa. Face to Face: Fascism & Revolution in India. Kurtin, Norman, tr. from Swedish.
Berg, Leila. Look at Kids.
Berg, Lisa, jt. auth. see Berg, Lasse.
Berg, Lucian, jt. auth. see Berg, Sally.
Berg, Norman A. General Management.
Berg, Per-Olof. Emotional Structures in Organisations: A Study of the Process of Change.
Berg, Sally & Berg, Lucian. New Food for All Palates.
Berg, Sanford V. Innovative Electric Rates: Issues in Cost-Benefit Analysis.
Berg, Sheila R., ed. Microbiology for Medical Technologists: PreTest Self-Assessment & Review.
Berg, Stephen, ed. Singular Voices: American Poetry Today.
Berg, Thomas. Aim for a Job in Welding.
Bergen, Candice. Knock Wood.
--Knock Wood.
Berger. Taming of the Shrew.
Berger, Alan S. Longitudinal Studies on the Class of 1961: The Graduate Science Students.
Berger, Arthur. Aaron Copland.
Berger, Arthur A. Signs in Contemporary Culture.
Berger, Arthur V. Aaron Copland.
Berger, Brigitte & Berger, Peter L. War over the Family: Capturing the Middle Ground.
Berger, Brigitte & Callahan, Sidney, eds. Child Care & Mediating Structures.
Berger, Donald, jt. auth. see Pimsleur, Paul.
Berger, Elmer. Memoirs of an Anti-Zionist Jew.
Berger, Gary S., et al, eds. Second Trimester Abortion: Perspectives after a Decade of Experience.
Berger, Gilda. All in the Family: Animal Species Around the World.
--PMS: An Infobook for Teenage Women, Their Friends & Families.
Berger, Gilda & Berger, Melvin. Bizarre Murders.
Berger, Jordan C. & Brody, Marvin D. Professional's Guide to the Estate Tax Audit.
Berger, Joseph, ed. see Milinaire, Caterine.
Berger, Karen & Bostwick, John, III. A Woman's Decision: Breast Care, Treatment & Reconstruction.
Berger, Linda. Guide to Dining on the Outer Banks of North Carolina: 1985-86 Edition.
Berger, Martin. Engels, Armies & Revolution: The Revolutionary Tactics of Classical Marxism.
Berger, Melvin. Computer Talk.
--Data Processing.
--Disastrous Volcanoes.
--The Photo Dictionary of Football.
--The Trumpet Book.
Berger, Melvin, jt. auth. see Berger, Gilda.
Berger, Michael. Self-Assessment in Radiology 2: Gastro-Intestinal Radiology.
Berger, Michael, jt. auth. see Klemperer, Katharina.
Berger, Michael, et al. Hockey Scouting Report, Nineteen Eighty-Six to Nineteen Eighty-Seven.
--University of California Union Catalog System Design Overview.
Berger, Mike. Bittersweet: True Stories of Decisions That Shaped Eternal Paths.
Berger, Mike, jt. auth. see Radke, Barbara.
Berger, Nomi. Love's Proud Masquerade.
Berger, Pamela C. The Insignia of the Notitia Dignitatum: A Contribution to the Study of Late Antique Illustrated Manuscripts.
Berger, Peter L., jt. auth. see Berger, Brigitte.
Berger, Phil. The State-of-the-Art Robot Catalog: Robots for Fun, Show, Personal & Home Use & Industry.
Berger, Rene & Eby, Lloyd, eds. Art & Technology.
Berger, Renee A., jt. auth. see Fosler, Scott.
Berger, S., et al. Berger Building Cost File 1987.
--Berger Building Cost File 1988.
Berger, Stuart M. Divorce Without Victims: Helping Children Through Divorce with a Minimum of Pain & Trauma.
--Dr. Berger's Immune Power Diet.
Berger, T. & Davisson, L. D. Advances in Source Coding: Courses & Lectures.
Berger, Terry. Friends.
Berger, Terry, jt. auth. see Worth, Courtia.
Berger, Terry, ed. Black Fairy Tales.
Berger, Thomas. Little Big Man.
--Nowhere.
--Nowhere.
Bergerhoff, Walther. Atlas of Normal Radiographs of the Skull.
Bergeron, David M. English Civic Pageantry, 1558-1642.
--Shakespeare's Romances & the Royal Family.
Bergeron, Thomas R., et al. Head & Neck Imaging: Excluding the Brain.
Bergerud, Marly & Gonzalez, Jean. Slide Presentation & Script for Word Information Processing.
Berges, Marshall. The Life & Times of Los Angeles: A Newspaper, a Family & a City.
Berges, Ruth. The Collector's Cabinet.
Bergesen, Albert, ed. Studies of the Modern World System.
Bergethon, Bjorner, jt. auth. see Nye, Robert E.
Bergevin, Paul & McKinley, John. Participation Training for Adult Education.
Bergfield, Philip B. Principles of Real Estate Law.
Bergh, T. Van Den see Van Den Bergh, T.
Berghage, Thomas E., jt. auth. see Adolfson, John A.
Berghauser, Tom W., jt. auth. see Schlieve, Paul.
Bergholtz, Richard C., ed. Drawn & Quartered: The Best Political Cartoons of Paul Conrad.
Bergier, Jacques, jt. auth. see Pauwels, Louis.
Bergin, Edward J. & Grandon, Ronald E. The American Survival Guide: How to Survive in Your Toxic Environment.
Bergland, Glen D. & Gordon, Ronald D. Software Design Strategies.
Bergler, Edmund. Divorce Won't Help.
--Parents Not Guilty of Their Children's Neuroses.
--Principles of Self Damage.
--Tensions Can Be Reduced to Nuisances.
Bergles, A. E., et al. Two-Phase Flow & Heat Transfer in the Power & Process Industries.
Bergles, Arthur E., et al. Two-Phase Flow & Heat Transfer in the Power & Process Industries.
Berglund, Berndt & Bolsby, Clare. Wilderness Cookbook.
Berglund, Berndt & Bolsby, Clare E. The Complete Outdoorsman's Guide to Edible Wild Plants.
Berglund, J. F. & Hoffmann, K. H. Compact Semitopological Semigroups & Weakly Almost Periodic Functions.
Bergman, E., jt. ed. see Pullman, B.
Bergman, E. D. & Pullman, Bernard, eds. Conformation of Biological Molecules & Polymers.
Bergman, Floyd. Occupation: English Teacher.
--Reading: Who? What? When? Where? Why? How?
Bergman, Ingmar. Four Screenplays of Ingmar Bergman.
Bergman, Jerry. Understanding Educational Measurement & Evaluation.
Bergman, M., ed. Subsurface Space--Environment Protection, Low Cost Storage, Energy Savings: Proceedings of the International Symposium, Stockholm, Sweden, June 23-27, 1980.
Bergman, Magnus, ed. Rockstore Seventy-Seven: Proceedings of the First International Symposium on Storage in Excavated Rock Caverns, Stockholm, Sweden, Sept. 5-8 1977.
Bergman, Mary. Survival Family.
Bergman, Stefan. Integral Operators in the Theory of Linear Partial Differential Equations.
Bergmann, E. D. & Pullman, B., eds. Aromaticity, Pseudoaromaticity, Antiaromaticity.
--Physiochemical Mechanisms of Carcinogenesis: Proceedings.
Bergmann, E. D., ed. see Jerusalem Symposia on Quantum Chemistry & Biochemistry Staff.
Bergmann, Frithjof. On Being Free.
Bergmann, Lothar. Der Begehungsort Im Internationalen Strafrecht Deutschlands, Englands und der Vereinigten Staaten Von Amerika.
Bergmann, Peter G. & De Sabbath, Venzo, eds. Cosmology & Gravitation: Spin, Torsion, Rotation, & Supergravity.
Bergmann, Wolfgang, ed. see Borchard, Franz.
Bergquist, Charles W. Coffee & Conflict in Colombia, 1886-1910.
Bergsma, Jurrit & Thomasma, David. Health Care: Its Psychosocial Dimensions.
Bergson, Abram. The Economics of Soviet Planning.
--Essays in Normative Economics.
Bergson, Henri. Creative Mind.
--Le Rire.
--Risa.
--The World of Dreams.
Bergson, Phillip. Holland.
Bergsten, C. Fred. The United States in the World Economy: Selected Papers of C. Fred Bergsten, 1981 to 1982.
Bergsten, C. Fred, et al. American Multinationals & American Interests.
--The Reform of International Institutions.
Bergsten, Staffan. Mary Poppins & Myth.
Bergstrom, Kirk. World Citizen Curriculum - Teacher Resource Guide.
--World Citizen Curriculum Student Resource Book.
Bergstrom, Lars. The Alternatives & Consequences of Actions: An Essay on Certain Fundamental Notions in Teleological Ethics.
Bergstrom, Peter V. Markets & Merchants: Economic Diversification in Colonial Virginia, 1700-1775. Bruchey, Stuart, ed.
Berjonneau, Gerald & Sonnery, Jean-Louis, eds. Rediscovered Masterpieces of Mesoamerica: Mexico-Guatemala-Honduras.
Berk, Emanuel. Downtown Improvement Manual.
--Downtown Improvement Manual.
Berk, Karen, ed. see Zagat, Eugene H., Jr. & Zagat, Nina S.
Berk, Richard A., et al, eds. A Measure of Justice: An Empirical Study of Changes in the California Penal Code, 1955-1971.
Berk, Robert N. & Clemett, Arthur R. Radiology of the Gallbladder & Bile Ducts.
Berk, Robert N., et al. Radiology of the Gallbladder & Bile Ducts: Diagnosis & Intervention.
Berk, Ronald A., ed. A Guide to Criterion-Referenced Test Construction.
Berke, Jacqueline. Twenty Questions for the Writer, a Rhetoric for Readings.
--Twenty Questions for the Writer: A Rhetoric with Readings.
--Twenty Questions for the Writer: A Rhetoric with Readings.
Berkeley, Arthur E., jt. auth. see Colosi, Thomas R.

Authors

Berkeley, Edmund, Jr., ed. Autographs & Manuscripts: A Collector's Manual.

Berkeley Holistic Health Center. Holistic Health Handbook.

Berkeley Holistic Health Center Staff, compiled by. The Holistic Health Handbook: A Tool for Attaining Wholeness of Body, Mind & Spirit.

Berkeley, Maud. Maud: The Illustrated Diary of a Victorian Woman.

Berkeley, R. C. & Ellwood, D. C., eds. Microbial Polysaccharides & Polysaccharases.

Berkeley, Sara. Penn.

Berkey, Dennis D. Calculus.

Berkey, Robert F. & Edwards, Sarah A., eds. Christological Perspectives.

Berki, R. N. Insight & Vision: The Problem of Communism in Marx's Thought.

Berki, S. E. & Heston, Alan W., eds. Nation's Health: Some Issues.

Berkley, George. The Democratic Policeman.

--The No-Drug Approach to Lowering Your Blood Pressure.

Berkman, Harold W. & Vernan, Ivan R. Contemporary Perspectives in International Business.

Berkman, Joyce. Olive Schreiner: Feminism on the Frontier.

Berko, Roy M. & Wolvin, Andrew D. Communicating: A Social & Career Focus.

Berkovits, Elieser. Judaism: Fossil or Ferment?

Berkovitz, L. D. Optimal Control Theory.

Berkovsky, Boris, ed. see International Advanced Course & Workshop on Thermomechanics of Magnetic Fluids Participants.

Berkow, Ira. Beyond the Dream.

Berkow, Robert. The Merck Manual of Diagnosis & Therapy.

Berkow, Robert, ed. The Merck Manual: General Medicine.

--The Merck Manual: Obstetrics, Gynecology, Pediatrics, Genetics.

Berkowitz. Marketing: International Edition.

Berkowitz, et al. Marketing.

--Marketing.

Berkowitz, A. E. & Kneller, E., eds. Magnetism & Metallurgy.

Berkowitz, B. J., jt. ed. see Fiore, N. F.

Berkowitz, Bernard, jt. auth. see Newman, Mildred.

Berkowitz, David S. & Thorne, Samuel E., eds. George Meriton. Sir Henry Spelman. Anon. Charles Fearne.

Berkowitz, Eric W., jt. auth. see Hillestad, Steven G.

Berkowitz, Gerald, jt. auth. see Neimark, Paul.

Berkowitz, Gerald, ed. see Garrick, David.

Berkowitz, Gerald M. New Broadways: Theatre Across America 1950-1980.

Berkowitz, Joseph & Groeneveld, Karl-Ontjes, eds. Molecular Ions: Geometric & Electronic Structures.

Berkowitz, Leonard. Advances in Experimental Social Psychology.

Berkowitz, Leonard, ed. Cognitive Theories in Social Psychology: Papers from Advances in Experimental Social Psychology.

Berkowitz, Monroe & Hill, M. Anne, eds. Disability & the Labor Market: Economic Problems, Policies & Programs.

Berkowitz, Sol, et al. A New Approach to Sight Singing.

Berkson, Isaac B. Ethics, Politics, & Education.

Berkstresser, Gordon A., III. Textile Marketing Management.

Berlak, Ann & Berlak, Harold. Dilemmas of Schooling.

Berlak, Harold, jt. auth. see Berlak, Ann.

Berle, Adolf A. Power.

--Power Without Property: A New Development in American Political Economy.

--Twentieth-Century Capitalist Revolution.

Berle, Adolf A. & Means, Gardiner C. The Modern Corporation & Private Property.

Berle, Beatrice B. & Jacobs, Travis B. Navigating the Rapids, Nineteen Eighteen to Nineteen Seventy-One.

Berleant-Schiller, Riva & Shanklin, Eugenia, eds. The Keeping of Animals: Adaptation & Social Relations in Livestock Producing Communities.

Berlin, Helene, ed. see Klock, P. Joseph.

Berlin, Howard M. The Dow Jones-Irwin Guide to Buying & Selling Treasury Securities.

Berlin, Isaiah. The Hedgehog & the Fox.

Berlin, K. D., jt. ed. see McEwen, W. E.

Berlin, Normand. Eugene O'Neill.

Berlin, Richard, et al, eds. Molecular Basis of Biological Degradative Processes.

Berlin, Susan T., jt. auth. see Paulin, Mary Ann.

Berliner, Arthur K. Psychoanalysis & Society: The Social Thought of Sigmund Freud.

Berliner, David C., jt. auth. see Gage, Nathaniel L.

Berliner, Don. Managing Your Hard Disk.

Berliner, Hans, ed. Computer Game Playing.

Berliner, Herman & Salvatore, Dominick. Economics.

Berliner, Thomas H., ed. see Stultz, Russell A.

Berliner, Thomas H., III & Kathman, Clemens A. The Illustrated TK! Solver Book.

Berlinsky, Ellen B. & Biller, Henry B. Parental Death & Psychological Development.

Berlioz, Hector. Evenings with the Orchestra. Barzun, Jacques, ed. & tr. from Fr.

--Evenings with the Orchestra.

--Memoirs of Hector Berlioz. Cairns, David, tr. from Fr.

Berlitz, Charles. Charles Berlitz's World of Strange Phenomena.

--The Mystery of Atlantis.

Berlitz, Charles, jt. auth. see Moore, William.

Berlitz Editors. Algrave Travel.

--Amsterdam Travel Guide.

--Barcelona Travel Guide.

--Berlin Travel Guide.

--Berlitz Arabic for Travellers.

--Berlitz Chinese for Travellers.

--Berlitz European Menu for Travellers.

--Berlitz French for Your Trip.

--Berlitz German for Your Trip.

--Berlitz Greek for Your Trip.

--Berlitz Italian for Your Trip.

--Berlitz Latin-American Spanish for Your Trip.

--Berlitz Spanish for Your Trip.

--Berlitz Travel Guide: London.

--Berlitz Travel Guide: Paris.

--Berlitz Travel Guide: Rome.

--Berlitz Travel Guide: Southern Caribbean.

--Berlitz Travel Guide to Corfu.

--Berlitz Travel Guide to Costa Brava.

--Berlitz Travel Guide to Costa Dorada & Barcelona.

--Berlitz Travel Guide to Crete.

--Berlitz Travel Guide to Istria.

--Berlitz Travel Guide to Moscow.

--Berlitz Travel Guide to Venice.

--Berlitz Travel Guide: Virgin Islands.

--Berlitz Travel Kits: China.

--Berlitz Travel Kits: France.

--Berlitz Travel Kits: Great Britain.

--Berlitz Travel Kits: Hong Kong.

--Berlitz Travel Kits: Italy.

--Berlitz Travel Kits: Japan.

--Berlitz Travel Kits: Mexico.

--Berlitz Travel Kits: Singapore.

--Berlitz Travel Kits: Spain.

--Berlitz Travel Kits: Switzerland.

--Berlitz Travel Kits: Thailand.

--Brussels Travel Guide.

--Canary Islands Travel Guide.

--China Country Guide.

--Dutch-English Dictionary.

--English (British) for Spanish Travellers.

--Florence Travel Guide.

--French for Spanish Travellers.

--French Speaking Switzerland Travel Guide.

--Greek Islands Travel Guide.

--Ibiza & Formentera Travel Guide.

--Istria Croatian Coast Travel Guide.

--Italian Travel Guide.

--Jamaica Travel Guide.

--Latin American Spanish for Travellers.

--Madrid Travel Guide.

--Majorca Travel Guide.

--Oslo Travel Guide.

--Oxford & Stratford Travel Guide.

--Rhine Valley Travel Guide.

--Rhodes Travel Guide.

--Salonica Travel Guide.

--Split & Dalmatia.

--Sri Lanka Travel Guide.

--Switzerland Country Travel Guide.

--Switzerland French Speaking Travel Guide.

--Switzerland Travel Guide.

--Tyrol Travel Guide.

--U. S. A. Country Guide.

Berlitz Staff. Moscow Travel Guide.

Berlo, David K. The Process of Communication: An Introduction to Theory & Practice.

Berlo, Janet C. The Art of Pre-Hispanic MesoAmerica: An Annotated Bibliography.

Berloquin, Pierre. The Garden of the Sphinx: One Hundred Fifty Challenging & Instructive Puzzles.

Berlow, Peter. Introduction to Chemistry of Life.

Berlye, Milton K. Encyclopedia of Working with Glass.

Berlyn, David. Exploring Careers in Cable-TV.

Berlyne, D. E. & Madsen, K. B. Pleasure, Reward, Preference: Their Nature, Determinants, & Role in Behavior (Based Upon a Symposium Held at the Klarskovgaard Training Institute, Near Korsor, Denmark, June, 1972)

Berman, A. Cones, Matrices & Mathematical Programming.

Berman, Abraham & Plemmons, Robert J. Non-Negative Matrices in the Mathematical Sciences.

Berman, Barry, jt. auth. see Evans.

Berman, Barry, jt. auth. see Rachman, David J.

Berman, David R. American Government, Politics & Policymaking.

Berman, Dorothy M., jt. auth. see Matthews, Joseph L.

Berman, Elaine R., jt. ed. see Michaelson, I. C.

Berman, Eleanor. The Palm-Aire Spa's Seven-Day Plan to Change Your Life: A Diet, Fitness & Beauty Program.

--Thomas Jefferson among the Arts.

Berman, Elizabeth. Mathematics Revealed.

Berman, Greta. The Lost Years: Mural Painting in New York City Under the Works Progress Administration's Federal Art Project 1935-1943.

Berman, Harold J. Religion & Law: The First Amendment in Historical Perspective.

Berman, I. & Schroeder, J. W., eds. Explosive Welding, Forming, Plugging, & Compaction.

Berman, Jonathan. Rachel's Walk.

Berman, Larry. Planning a Tragedy: The Americanization of the War in Vietnam.

Berman, Lee & Leonard, Ken. The BASIC Explorer for the Commodore 64.

Berman, Marshall. All That Is Solid Melts into Air.

--All That Is Solid Melts into Air: The Experience of Modernity.

--Politics of Authenticity: Radical Individualism & the Emergence of Modern Society.

Berman, Russell, tr. see Leonhard, Karl.

Berman, Steve. The Six Demons of Love: A Book about Men & Love.

Berman, W. W., ed. see Row, T. S.

Bermant, Chaim. Belshazzar: A Cat's Story for Humans.

Bermel, Albert. Farce.

--Farce: From Aristophanes to Woody Allen.

Bermingham, Alan, et al. The Small TV Studio: Equipment & Facilities.

Bermudes, Robert W. Conquering Cancer.

Berna, Kurt. Christ Did Not Perish on the Cross: Christ's Body Buried Alive.

Bernal, Guillermo & Sorensen, James L. A Family Life Yours: Breaking the Patterns of Drug Abuse.

Bernanos, Georges. Le Chemin de la Croix des Ames.

--Dialogue Des Carmelites.

--Les Enfants Humilies Journal (1939-1940)

Bernard, H. Russell. Human Way: Readings in Anthropology.

Bernard, H. Russell & Pelto, Pertti J. Technology & Social Change.

Bernard, J. R. A Short Guide to Traditional Grammar.

Bernard, James E., ed. An Overview of Simulation in Highway Transportation.

Bernard, Janine & Hackney, Harold. Untying the Knot: A Guide to Civilized Divorce.

Bernard, Josef. The Dow Jones-Irwin Guide to Laptop Computers.

Bernard, Michael M., ed. Annotated Bibliography on Taxation As an Instrument of Land Planning Policy.

Bernard, Nelson T. Wildflowers Along Forest & Mesa Trails.

Bernard, Nora. Hollywood's Irish Rose.

Bernard, Otis. Put a Little Starch in Your Faith.

Bernard, P. & Ratiu, T., eds. Turbulence Seminar-Berkeley Nineteen Seventy-Six to Nineteen Seventy-Seven: Organized by A. Chorin, J. Marsden, S. Smale.

Bernard, Paul P. Jesuits & Jacobins: Enlightenment & Enlightened Despotism in Austria.

Bernard, Raymond. The Danger We All Face: Suppressed Truth about Radiation.

--Hollow Earth.

--Nutritional Methods of Blood Regeneration.

--Nutritional Sex Control & Rejuvenation.

--Secret of Rejuvenation: Professor Brown Squad's Great Discovery of the Fountain of Youth.

Bernard, Robert. A Catholic Education.

Bernard, Theos. Hindu Philosophy.

Bernardo, Aldo S. Petrarch, Scipio & the "Africa" The Birth of Humanism's Dream.

Bernasconi, J. & Schneider, Toni, eds. Physics in One Dimension: Proceedings.

Bernasconi, Melvin. Opinions.

Bernays, Edward L. Crystallizing Public Opinion.

--Your Future in a Public Relations Career.

Bernbach, Linda. Food Service Supervisor-School Lunch Manager.

Bernbeck, Rupprecht & Sinios, Alexander. Neuro-Orthopedic Screening in Infancy: Schedules, Examination & Findings.

Bernd, Edward I. Business Opportunities Brokerage: Strategies & Techniques for Real Estate Professionals.

Bernd, Joseph L., jt. ed. see Havard, William C.

Berndt, Catherine, jt. auth. see Berndt, Ronald.

Berndt, Ronald & Berndt, Catherine. First Australians.

Berndt, Ronald M. Djanggawul.

--Love Songs of Arnhem Land.

Berne & Levy. Physiology.

Berne, Eric. Layman's Guide to Psychiatry & Psychoanalysis.

Berne, Patricia H. & Savary, Louis M. What Will the Neighbors Say? Facing the Fear of Disapproval.

Berne, Patricia H., jt. auth. see Savary, Louis M.

Berne, Richard R., jt. auth. see Lancaster, Anita S.

Berne, Robert M. & Levy, Matthew N., eds. Physiology.

Bernen, Robert. Tales from the Blue Stacks.

Bernen, Robert, jt. auth. see Bernen, Satia.

Bernen, Satia & Bernen, Robert. A Guide to Myth & Religion in European Painting 1270-1700.

Berner, Carl W. Teardrops to Diamonds: How God's Love Turns Sorrow into Joy.

--Why Me, Lord? Meaning & Comfort in Times of Trouble.

Berner, R. Thomas. Editing.

--Language Skills for Journalists.

Bernet, Michael M., tr. see Chouraqui, Andre N.

Berney, Arthur L., et al. Legal Problems of the Poor: Cases & Materials.

Berney, Paul R. & Gartska, Stanley J. Accounting: Concepts & Applications.

Berney, Paul R., et al. Financial Accounting & Reporting.

Bernhard, S., ed. Patterns of Change in Earth Evolution: Report of the Dahlem Workshop on Patterns of Change in Earth Evolution, Berlin, 1983, May 1-6.

Bernhard, Thomas. Correction.

Bernhard, Winfred E., jt. ed. see Emerson, Everett.

Bernhardsen, Christian. Fight in the Mountains. Sinding, Franey, tr.

Bernhardt, Kenneth L. & Kinnear, Thomas C. Cases in Marketing Management.

--Cases in Marketing Management.

Bernheim, Evelyne, jt. auth. see Bernheim, Marc.

Bernheim, Marc & Bernheim, Evelyne. African Success Story: The Ivory Coast.

--The Drums Speak: The Story of Kofi, a Boy of West Africa.

--From Bush to City: A Look at the New Africa.

--In Africa.

Bernick, E. Lee. Legislative Decision-Making & the Politics of Tax Reform: The Oklahoma Senate.

--Legislative Voting Patterns & Partisan Cohesion in a One-Party Dominant Legislature.

Bernier, Donald R., et al. Nuclear Medicine: Technology & Techniques.

Bernikow, Louise. Abel.

Berning, Randall K., jt. auth. see Snyder, Thomas L.

Bernkopf, Michael. Mathematics: An Appreciation.

Bernsohn, Joseph & Grossman, Herbert J., eds. Lipid Storage Diseases: Enzymatic Defects & Clinical Implications.

Bernstein, jt. auth. see Woodward, Bob.

Bernstein, Art. Tree of Southern Oregon.

Bernstein, Basil. Class, Codes & Control, Vol. 3: Towards a Theory of Educational Transmissions.

Bernstein, Burton. Plane Crazy: A Celebration of Flying.

--Thurber: A Biography.

Bernstein, Carl, jt. auth. see Woodward, Bob.

Bernstein, Carol, jt. auth. see Bertherat, Therese.

Bernstein, Douglas A. & Nietzel, Michael T. Introduction to Clinical Psychology.

Bernstein, Eckhard. German Humanism.

Bernstein, I. M. & Thompson, Anthony W., eds. Hydrogen Effects in Metals: Proceedings of a Meeting held at Moran, Wyoming, 1980.

Bernstein, I. M., jt. ed. see Thompson, Anthony W.

Bernstein, Irving. A Caring Society: The New Deal, the Worker & the Great Depression.

--The Lean Years: A History of the American Worker 1920-1933.

Bernstein, Jacob. How to Profit from Seasonal Commodity Spreads: A Complete Guide.

Bernstein, Jerrold G. Handbook of Drug Therapy in Psychiatry.

Bernstein, Joanne E. Dmitry: A Young Soviet Immigrant.

--Loss & How to Cope with It.

Bernstein, Kenneth. Music Lover's Europe: A Guidebook & Companion.

Bernstein, Leonard. Joy of Music.

Bernstein, Levitt & Richardson, Anthony. Specification Clauses for Rehabilitation & Conversion Work.

Bernstein, M. D., jt. ed. see Singh, A.

Bernstein, Marcelle. The Russian Bride.

Bernstein, Margery & Kobrin, Janet. The Summermaker: An Ojibway Indian Myth.

Bernstein, Marver H. Politics of Israel: The First Decade of Statehood.

Bernstein, Mary. Auditory & Reading Comprehension Exercises in French.

Bernstein, Norman R. Emotional Care of the Facially Burned & Disfigured Patients.

Bernstein, Paula R. Family Ties, Corporate Bonds: How We Act Out Family Roles in the Office.

Bernstein, Peretz. Jew - Hate as a Sociological Problem.

Bernstein, Philip A., et al. Distributed Data Base Management.

Bernstein, Richard. Megastar.

Bernstein, Richard J. The Restructuring of Social & Political Theory.

Bernstein, Ronald A. Successful Direct Selling: How to Plan, Launch, Promote, & Maintain a Profitable Direct Selling Company.

Bernstein, Samuel J. & Mellon, W. Giles. Selected Readings in Quantitative Urban Analysis.

Bernstein, Samuel J., ed. Computers in Public Administration: An International Perspective.

Bernstein, Seymour & Solomon, S., eds. Chemical & Biological Aspects of Steroid Conjugation.

Bernstein, Seymour, et al. Physical Properties of Steroid Conjugates.

Bernthal, John E. & Bankson, Nicholas W. Articulation Disorders.

Bernthal, Louann. Parent & Child in the Christian Kitchen.

Bernussou, J. Point Mapping Stability.

Berolzheimer, Ruth, ed. The American Woman's Cookbook.

--Culinary Arts Institute Encyclopedic Cookbook.

Beron, Alberto, et al. Guia de Studios Essential Arithmetic: Spanish Study Guide for Essential Arithmetic.

Beroza, Morton, ed. Chemicals Controlling Insect Behavior.

Beroza, Morton, ed. see Chemistry & Action of Insect Juvenile Hormones Symposium Staff.

Berquist, Goodwin F. & Bowers, Paul C., Jr. The New Eden: James Kilbourne & the Development of Ohio.

Berra, Kathy, jt. auth. see Fry, Gary.

Berres, Michael S. & Knoblock, Peter. Program Models for Mainstreaming: Intergrating Students with Moderate to Severe Disabilities.

Berri, L. Y., ed. Planning a Socialist Economy.

Berridge, David. Children's Homes.

Berridge, Michael J. & Oschman, James L. Transporting Epithelia.

Berrie, W. W. A Theology of Generosity: Principles & Practice of Giving Based on Bible Teaching.

Berriedale-Johnson, Michelle. Food Repair Handbook: Culinary First-Aid Manual.

Berrin, Elliott R. Investigative Photography.

Berrington, Hugh B. Backbench Opinion in the House of Commons, 1945-1955.

Berrisford, Judith. Backyards & Tiny Gardens.

Berry, A. J., ed. see European Symposium on Marine Biology, 12th.

Berry, Ana M. Animals in Art.

Berry, Brewton & Tischler, Henry L. Race & Ethnic Relations.

Berry, Brian J. & Conkling, Edgar C. Geography of Economic Systems.

Berry, Charles N. & Hovde, Christian A. Human Anatomy Atlas.

Berry, Faith, ed. see Hughes, Langston.

Berry, Francis. Poets' Grammar: Person, Time, & Mood in Poetry.

Berry, Henry. Semper Fi Mac: Living Memories of the U. S. Marines in World War II.

Berry, Herbert. Assembly Language for IBM Compatible Processors: A Systematic Approach.

Berry, I. William. Dollarwise Guide to Skiing U. S. A. East.

Berry, J. W. & Dasen, P. R. Culture & Cognition: Readings in Cross-Cultural Psychology.

Berry, J. W., ed. see International Conference of Selected Papers Staff.

Berry, Jeffrey M. The Interest Group Society.

Berry, Jo. Growing, Sharing, Serving.

Berry, Joan P. Faith in the Center Ring: An Elephantine Question.

Berry, John & Waite Group. Inside the Amiga with C.

Berry, Lloyd E., intro. by. Geneva Bible: A Facsimile of the Fifteen-Sixty Edition.

Berry, M. The Political Economy of Australian Urbanization.

Berry, M., jt. auth. see Mott, Nevill.

Berry, Michael V. Diffraction of Light by Ultrasound.

Berry, Paul. The Essential Self: An Introduction to Literature.

--Operating the IBM-PC Networks.

Berry, Peggy. The Corporate Couple: Living the Corporate Game.

Berry, R. How to Write a Research Paper.

Berry, R. Albert, et al, eds. Politics of Compromise: Coalition Government in Colombia.

Berry, R. E. & Meekings, B. A. A Book on C.

Berry, R. J. Inheritance & Natural History.

Berry, R. J., jt. ed. see Bonner, W. N.

Berry, Ralph. The Shakespearean Metaphor: Studies in Language & Form.

Berry, Richard W., jt. auth. see Tver, David F.

Berry, Roger W. Creative Writing: A Review of the Study at the College Level.

Berry, Roland. Mechanical Giants.

Berry, Roland & Moses, Frank. Amazing Trains of the World.

Berry, Timothy. Business Planning with IBM Personal Decision Software.

Berry, Turner W. & Johnson, A. F. Catalogue of Specimens of Printing Types by English & Scottish Printers & Founders 1665-1830.

Berry, Wendell. Clearing.

--The Collected Poems of Wendell Berry, 1957-1982.

--The Memory of Old Jack.

--Openings.

--The Unsettling of America.

Berry, William, jt. auth. see Gray, Jane.

Berryman, John. His Toy, His Dream, His Rest.

--A Homage to Mistress Bradstreet & Other Poems.

--Short Poems.

Bers, L., ed. see American Mathematical Society Staff.

Bersentes, Harry. Velanidia-The Acorn Tree: The History of a Greek Peasant Family.

Bershadsky, Luba & Millington, Ada. I Know His Touch.

Berson, Harold. Larbi & Leila: A Tale of Two Mice.

--The Thief Who Hugged a Moonbeam.

--Why the Jackal Won't Speak to the Hedgehog.

Berta, I., jt. auth. see Horvath, T.

Bertalanffy, Ludwig Von see Von Bertalanffy, Ludwig.

Bertazzoni, Umberto & Bollum, Fred J., eds. Terminal Transferase In Immunobiology & Leukemia.

Bertelli, A., ed. Future Trends in Chemotheraphy: Proceedings of the International Symposium, Tirrenia, May 6-7, 1974.

Bertelli, A., et al, eds. New Anti-Inflammatory & Antirheumatic Drugs: Proceedings of an International Symposium.

Bertherat, Therese & Bernstein, Carol. The Body Has Its Reasons.

Berthoff, Warner. Example of Melville.

Berthold & Schwarz. UFO-Dynamics: Psychiatric & Psychic Aspects of the UFO Syndrome.

Berthoud, Roger. Graham Sutherland: A Biography.

Berti, F. & Folco, G., eds. Leukotrienes & Prostacyclin.

Berti, Luciano. Raphael.

Berti, Luciano, intro. by. The Official Catalogue of the Uffizi.

Bertin, Celia. Marie Bonaparte: A Life.

Bertin, John J. Engineering Fluid Mechanics.

Bertin, John J. & Smith, Michael L. Aerodynamics for Engineers.

Bertinchamps, A. J., et al, eds. Effects of Ionizing Radiation on DNA: Physical, Chemical & Biological Aspects.

Bertini, I., et al, eds. Advances in Solution Chemistry.

Bertman, Stephen, ed. The Conflict of Generations in Ancient Greece & Rome.

Bertoline, Gary R., jt. auth. see Resetarits, Paul J.

Berton, Peter & Wu, Eugene. Contemporary China: A Research Guide.

Berton, Pierre. The Dionne Years: A Thirties Melodrama.

Bertram, Gordon W. Consolidated Bargaining in California Construction: An Appraisal of Twenty-Five Years' Experience.

Bertrand, A. Indoor Plants & How to Grow Them.

--Succulent Plants.

Bertrand, A. R., jt. auth. see Kohnke, Helmut.

Bertrand, John. Born to Win: A Life-Long Struggle to Capture the America's Cup.

Bertsch, Gary K. East-West Strategic Trade, COCOM & the Atlantic Alliance.

--Policy Making in Communist Party States.

Bertsch, Lory. Willie Visits Tulip Time.

Bertuglia, C. S., et al, eds. Urban Systems: Contemporary Approaches to Modelling.

Berube, Francoise D. & Berube, John-Paul. Sacrament of Peace.

Berube, John-Paul, jt. auth. see Berube, Francoise D.

Berven, Ken. Blest Be the Tie That Frees.

Berwick, Robert C. & Weinberg, Amy S. The Grammatical Basis of Linguistic Performance: Language Use & Acquisition.

--The Grammatical Basis of Linguistic Performance: Language Use & Acquisition.

Berwin, Derek & Barber, David. Creative Techniques in Underwater Photography.

Berzins, Gunars. Born in Sorrow: An Essay Concerning Human Nature.

Berzonsky. Adolescent Development.

Bes, J. Chartering & Shipping Terms: Time-Sheet Supplements.

Besancon. Soviet Syndrome.

Besant, Walter. In Deacon's Orders, 1895. Wolff, Robert L., ed. Bd. with Red Pottage, 1899. Cholmondely, Mary. Garland Pub.

Beschloss, Michael R. Kennedy & Roosevelt: The Uneasy Alliance.

--Kennedy & Roosevelt: The Uneasy Alliance.

Besemeres, John. Socialist Population Politics: The Political Implications of Demographic Trends in the U. S. S. R. & Eastern Europe.

Beshlyage, V., et al. Do You Know How the Sun Laughs?

Beshoar, Daniel. Violet Soup: Common Edible Plants of the Rockies.

Beskow, A. Look at Norway.

Beskow, Bo. Two by Two.

Beskow, Elsa. Children of the Forest.

--Peter in Blueberry Land.

Beskow, Per. Strange Tales About Jesus: A Survey of Unfamiliar Gospels.

Bessel, Richard & Feuchtwanger, E. J., eds. Social Change & Political Development in Weimar Germany.

Besser, G. M., jt. ed. see Martini, Luciano.

Bessis, M. Corpuscles: Atlas of Red Blood Cell Shapes.

Besson, Patrick. Dara.

Bessonette, Colin. Back Roads & City Streets: Weekend Getaways in & Around Georgia.

Best, A. M., Staff. Best's Five Year Historical Exhibits.

--Best's Flit Compend.

Best, David. Philosophy & Human Movement.

Best, E. A. Following Jesus: Discipleship in the Gospel of Mark.

Best, Ernest. From Text to Sermon: Responsible Use of the New Testament in Preaching.

Best, Gerald M. Iron Horses to Promontory Railroad: Central Pacific-Union Pacific.

--Promontory's Locomotives.

--Railroads of Hawaii.

--The Ulster & Delaware: Railroad Through the Catskills.

Best, Harry. The Soviet State & Its Inception.

Best, Hugh. Debrett's Texas Peerage.

Best Report Editors. The New Book of Bests: A Guide to the Best Things Life Has to Offer.

Best, Steven L. Housing Rehabilitation: An Updated Bibliography.

Best, W. M. A Treatise on Presumptions of Law & Fact, with the Theory & Rules of Presumptive or Circumstantial Proof in Criminal Cases.

Bester, John, tr. see Hasegawa, Nyozekan.

Bester, John, tr. see Kato, Shuichi.

Bester, John, tr. see Mishima, Yukio.

Bester, John, tr. see Suzuki, Juzo & Oka, Isaburo.

Besterman, Theodore. The Age of the Enlightenment: Studies Presented to Theodore Besterman. Barber, W. H., et al, eds.

--The Beginning of Systematic Bibliography.

--Voltaire.

Besterman, Theodore, ed. see Crawley, Ernest.

Bestgen, Barbara J. & Reys, Robert E. Films in the Mathematics Classroom.

Bestic, Alan, jt. auth. see Vrba, Rudolf.

Bestmann, H. & Zimmermann, R. Chemistry of Organophosphorous Compounds, 2.

Beta. Enchanted Closet.

Betancourt, Jeanne. Dear Diary.

Betancourt, John G. Starskimmer.

Betancourt, Philip. Cooking Vessels from Minoan Kommos: A Preliminary Report.

Betancourt, Romulo. Venezuela: Oil & Politics.

Betchaku, Teiichi, et al. Biology of Turbellaria: Experimental Advances, II.

Betchaku, Yasuko, tr. see Burn, Barbara.

Beth Israel Hospital Staff & Friedman, Emanuel A. Gynecologic Decision Making.

--Obstetrical Decision Making.

Bethancourt, T. Ernesto. Doris Fein: Dead Heat at Long Beach.

--Doris Fein: Quartz Boyar.

--Instruments of Darkness.

--The Tomorrow Connection.

Bethe, Hans A. & Jackiw, Roman W. Intermediate Quantum Mechanics.

Bethe, Hans A. & Salpeter, E. E. Quantum Mechanics of One & Two Electron Atoms.

Bethe, Monica, tr. see Nishikawa, Kyotaro.

Bethea, Robert M. Air Pollution Control Technology.

Bethell, Donald & Gold, V. Carbonium Ions, an Introduction.

Bethell, E., et al, eds. Electrical Assembly & Wiring.

Bethell, Jean. Playmates.

Bethell, Nicholas, tr. see Solzhenitsyn, Alexander.

Bethge, Eberhard & Bethge, Renate, eds. Last Letters of Resistance: Farewells from the Bonhoeffer Family. Slabaugh, Dennis, tr.

Bethge, K., ed. Experimental Methods in Heavy Ion Physics.

Bethge, Renate, jt. ed. see Bethge, Eberhard.

Bethke, Frederick J. Three Victorian Travel Writers: An Annotated Bibliography of Criticism on Mrs. Frances Milton Trollope, Samuel Butler, & Robert Louis Stevenson.

Bethmann, Johannes. Untersuchungen Uber Die Mhd.

Bethune, J. Essentials of Drafting.

Betjeman, John. A Life in Pictures. Hiller, Bevis, compiled by.

Betson, Carol L. Managing the Medical Enterprise: A Study of Physician Managers. Farmer, Richard, ed.

Bett, Henry. Nicholas of Cusa.

Bett, W. R. The Infirmaties of Genius.

Bettelheim, Bruno. Children of the Dream.

--Informed Heart.

--Love Is Not Enough.

Bettelheim, Bruno, commentary by see Carotenuto, Aldo.

Bettelheim, Charles. The Transition to Socialist Economy. Mepham, John, ed. Pearce, Brian, tr. from Fr.

Bettelheim, Frederick A. & March, Jerry. Introduction to General, Organic & Biochemistry.

Better Homes & Gardens Books Editors, ed. Treasury of Needlecrafts.

Better Homes & Gardens Editors. Baby Book.

--Best Recipes Yearbook 1987.

--Better Homes & Gardens Baby Book.

--Better Homes & Gardens Best-Recipes Yearbook: 1985.

--Better Homes & Gardens Crockery Cooker Cook Book.

--Better Homes & Gardens Easy Bazaar Crafts.

--Better Homes & Gardens Low-Salt Cooking.

--Better Homes & Gardens Microwave Cook Book.

--Better Homes & Gardens, 1984: Best-Recipes Yearbook.

--Easy Bazaar Crafts.

--Toaster Oven Cook Book.

Betteridge, D., jt. auth. see Baker, A. D.

Betteridge, Terry. An Algebraic Analysis of Storage Fragmentation. Stone, Harold, ed.

Betterley, Melvin L. Sheet Metal Drafting.

Betterton, Don. How to Pay for College 1987-88.

--How to Pay for College 1988-89.

Bettey, J. Church & Parish: A Guide for Local Historians.

Bettger, Frank. How I Raised Myself from Failure to Success in Selling.

--How I Raised Myself from Failure to Success in Selling.

Betti, Claudia W. & Sale, Teel. Drawing: A Contemporary Approach.

Bettis, D. G., ed. see Conference on Numerical Solution of Ordinary Differential Equations.

Bettis, Mervin, jt. auth. see Hoerner, Thomas.

Bettoja, Jo & Cornetto, Anna M. Italian Cooking in the Grand Tradition.

Betts, C. W. & Crane, Stephen W., eds. Manual of Small Animal Surgical Therapeutics.

Betts, Jim, jt. auth. see Heimbold, Noreen.

Betts, Leonard C. Garden Pools.

Betts, Robert B. Christians in the Arab East.

Betz, Carl, text by. Postwar Paintings from Brandeis University.

Betz, E., ed. see International Congress of Physiological Sciences & Annual Meeting of the German Angiological Society, Tuebingen, 1971.

Betz, Hans D. Essays on the Sermon on the Mount.

Betzler, M., jt. ed. see Herfarth, C.

Beuchat, Henri, jt. auth. see Mauss, Marcel.

Beucler, Andre. Last of the Bohemians: Twenty Years with Leon-Paul Fargue. Sainsbury, Geoffrey, tr.

Beuhrig, E. Perversity of Politics.

Beukenkamp, Cornelius. Fortunate Strangers.

Beurdeley, Michel. Giuseppe Castiglione: A Jesuit Painter at the Court of the Chinese Emperors.

Beus, A. A. Geochemistry of the Lithosphere.

Beus, J. G. De see De Beus, J. G.

Beusterien, Pat, ed. Summer Employment Directory of the U. S., 1988.

Beutler, Ernest. Hemolytic Anemia in Disorders of Red Cell Metabolism.

Bevan, Clifford. The Tuba Family.

Bevan, D. & Hagenmuller, P. Non-Stoichiometric Compounds: Tungsten Bronzes; Vanadium Bronzes; & Related Compounds.

Bevan, Gwyn, et al. Health Care Priorities & Management.

Bevan, James. The Family First Aid & Medical Guide.

Bevan, P. Gilroy. Reconstructive Procedures in Surgery.

Bevan, Vaughan. The Development of British Immigration Law.

Bevans, Charles F. Ideas for the Thoughtful Teacher: Bicentennial Edition.

Bevans, Jerry T., ed. Thermal Design Principles of Spacecraft & Entry Bodies.

--Thermal Design Principles, PAAS21.

--Thermophysics: Applications to Thermal Design of Spacecraft, PAAS23.

Bever, David L. Safety: A Personal Focus.

Bever, M. B. & Henstock, M. E., eds. Recycling: Opportunities & Constraints: Proceedings of the Conference Co-Sponsored by the Federation of Materials Science & the U. S. Bureau of Mines, Washington, D. C., U. S. A., 17-19 July 1984.

Bever, M. B., jt. ed. see Henstock, M.

Bever, Thomas G. & Terrace, Herbert S., eds. Human Behavior: Prediction & Control in Modern Society.

Beveridge, D. L., jt. auth. see Pople, J. A.

Beveridge, Phyllis, jt. auth. see Corbett, Nancy A.

Beveridge, W. I. Art of Scientific Investigation.

Bevington, David M. Tudor Drama & Politics: A Critical Approach to Topical Meaning.

Bevington, Helen. Along Came the Witch: A Journal of the 1960's.

--Beautiful Lofty People.

Bevis, Donald J. & Perry, Raymond E. Accounting for Income Taxes: An Interpretation of APB Opinion No. 11.

Bevis, Em O. Curriculum Building in Nursing.
Bevlin, Marjorie E. Design Through Discovery.
Bewersdorff, A., ed. Materials Science in Space.
--Materials Science in Space: Proceedings of the Topical Meeting of the COSPAR Interdisciplinary Scientific Commission G (Meeting G1) of the COSPAR Twenty-Fifth Plenary Meeting Held in Graz, Austria, 25th June - 7th July 1984.
Bewes, Richard, jt. auth. see Hicks, Robert.
Bewes, Richard, ed. John Wesley's England: A Nineteenth Century Pictorial History Based on an 18th Century Journal.
Bewick, Michael W., ed. Handbook of Organic Waste Conversion.
Bewick, Thomas. Eighteen Hundred Woodcuts by Thomas Bewick & His School. Cirker, Blanche, ed.
Bewley, Marius. Masks & Mirrors: Essays in Criticism.
Bexley, James B. Banking Management.
Beyer, Admiral Raymond H. Compiled by see Dickert, Rev. Roy E.
Beyer, Andrew. My Fifty Thousand Dollar Year at the Races.
--My Fifty Thousand Dollar Year at the Races.
--Picking Winners: A Horse Players Guide.
Beyer, Beverly. Passport to Europe's Small Hotels & Inns.
Beyer, Edward. Ibsen: The Man & His Work.
Beyer, Maximilian. Christ.
Beyer, Werner W. Keats & the Daemon King.
Beyer, William H., ed. Standard Mathematical Tables.
Beyerlin, Walter, ed. Near Eastern Religious Texts Relating to the Old Testament. Bowden, John, tr.
Beyers, Coralie M. Man Meets Grizzly: Encounters in the Wild from Lewis & Clark to Modern Times. Young, F. M., ed.
Beyers, Marjorie, et al. The Clinical Practice of Medical-Surgical Nursing.
Beyle, Henri see Stendhal, pseud.
Beyle, Marie H. see Stendhal.
Beymer, Robert. The Boundary Waters Canoe Area: The Western Region.
Beynon, Granville, ed. Solar-Terrestrial Physics: Proceedings of an International Symposium, Innsbruck, Austria, 1978.
Bezella, Winfred A., jt. auth. see Ott, Karl O.
Beznoska, Dennis, et al. HDE Manual of Fine Restaurant Service.
Bezruchka, Stephen. Trekking in Nepal: A Guide.
Bhaerman, Robert D. Career Education: Collaboration with the Private Sector.
Bhagavantam, S. & Venkatarayudu, T. Theory of Groups & Its Application to Physical Problems.
Bhagwan, Vishnoo & Bhushan, Vidya. World Constitutions.
Bhagwati, Jagdish. Economics of Underdeveloped Countries.
Bhagwati, Jagdish, ed. The Brain Drain & Income Taxation.
Bhaktivedanta, Swami A. C. Krsna: The Supreme Personality of Godhead.
--Srimad Bhagavatam: Eighth Canto.
--Srimad Bhagavatam: Fifth Canto.
--Srimad Bhagavatam: First Canto.
--Srimad Bhagavatam: Fourth Canto.
--Srimad Bhagavatam: Second Canto.
--Srimad Bhagavatam: Seventh Canto.
--Srimad Bhagavatam: Sixth Canto.
--Srimad Bhagavatam: Third Canto.
Bhaktivedanta, Swami Prabhupada A. C. Srimad-Bhagavatam: Tenth Canto.
--Srimad-Bhagavatam: Tenth Canto.
--Srimad-Bhagavatam: Tenth Canto.
Bhaktivedanta Swami. Light of the Bhagavat.
--Srimad Bhagavatam: 11th Canto, Vol. 5.
--Srimad Bhagavatam: 12th Canto, Vol. 2.
Bhaktivedanta Swami & Das Goswami, Hridayananda. Srimad Bhagavatam: 12th Canto, Vol. 1.
Bhaktivendanta, Swami A. C. Srimad Bhagavatam: Ninth Canto.
Bhalla, A. S., ed. Towards Global Action for Appropriate Technology: Expert Meeting on International Action for Appropriate Technology, December 5-9 1977, Geneva.
Bhallas, A., ed. see International Labour Office Staff.
Bhamre, Suresh T. Hatha Yoga for Kids: A Guidebook for Parents & Children.
Bhappu, R. B. & Mular, A. L., eds. Mineral Processing Plant Design.
Bhappu, Roshan B., jt. ed. see Mular, Andrew L.
Bhar, Tarak N. & McMahon, Edward J. Control of Electrostatic Discharge.
Bharath, A. V. The Black Princess & Other Stories.
Bharatha, S., jt. auth. see Truesdell, C.
Bharati, Agahananda. The Ochre Robe: An Autobiography.
Bharati, Saroja, et al. Cardiac Surgery & the Conduction System.
Bhardraithe, T. De see De Bhardraithe, T.
Bhardwaj, Raman. The Dilemma of the Horn of Africa.
Bharti, Ma Satya. Death Comes Dancing: Celebrating Life with Bhagwan Shree Rajneesh.
--Drunk on the Divine: An Account of Life in Ashram of Bhagwan.
Bhartia, P., jt. auth. see Bahl, I. J.
Bhasin, Kul, jt. ed. see Frey, Jeffrey.
Bhat, Rajendra R. Managing the Demand for Fashion Items. Farmer, Richard, ed.
Bhatia, B., et al, eds. Selected Topics in Environmental Biology.
Bhatia, H. L. Centre-State Financial Relations in India.
--Public Finance.
Bhatia, H. S. Martial Law: Theory & Practice.
Bhatia, H. S., ed. International Law & Practice in Ancient India.
Bhatia, N. P. & Szegoe, G. P. Dynamical Systems: Stability Theory & Applications.
--Stability Theory of Dynamical Systems.
Bhatia, O. K. & Bhatia, Vijay. Business Statistics.
Bhatia, Vijay, jt. auth. see Bhatia, O. K.
Bhatt, H. G., et al. Management of Toxic & Hazardous Wastes.
Bhatt, S. Aviation, Environment & World Order.
Bhatt, Vinayak V. & Roe, Alan R. Capital Market Imperfections & Economic Development.
Bhattacharjee, G. P. Southeast Asia Politics: Malayasia & Indonesia.
Bhattacharjee, J. B. Cachar under British Rule in North East India.
Bhattacharji, Sukumari. The Indian Theogony: Comparative Study of Indian Mythology from the Vedas to the Puranas.
Bhattacharya, Bhabani. He Who Rides a Tiger.
--Music for Mohini.
Bhattacharya, Bhabani, ed. Contemporary Indian Short Stories.
Bhattacharya, Deben, tr. & intro. by. Songs of the Bards of Bengal.
Bhattacharya, Krishna. An Intensive Course in Bengali.
Bhattacharya, Mohinimohana. Platonic Ideas in Spenser.
Bhattacharya, P. B., et al. First Course in Linear Algebra.
Bhattacharya, Sauripad. Pursuit of National Interest Through Neutralism: India's Foreign Policy in the Nehru Era.
Bhattacharyya, Buddhadeva. Satyagrahas in Bengal, Nineteen Twenty-One to Nineteen Thirty-Nine.
Bhattacharyya, M. N. Comparison of Box-Jenkins & Bonn Monetary Prediction Performance.
Bhushan, Vidya, jt. auth. see Bhagwan, Vishnoo.
Bialer, Seweryn, et al. Trilateral-Soviet Relations in Transition.
Bialk, Eliza. The Horse Called Pete.
Bialosky, Alan, jt. auth. see Bialosky, Peggy.
Bialosky, Peggy & Bialosky, Alan. The Teddy Bear Catalog.
--The Teddy Bear Catalog.
Bianchi, G., jt. ed. see Morecki, A.
Bianchi, Raymond, jt. auth. see Lyle, Carl.
Bianchi, Suzanne M. & Spain, Daphne. American Women: Three Decades of Change.
Bianchina, Paul. Illustrated Dictionary of Building Materials & Techniques.
Bianchine, Joseph, jt. ed. see Yetiv, Jack.
Bianco, Bob. The Guitar in Fourths Based upon a Uniform System of Tuning & Fingering.
Bianco, Enzo. Don Bosco's Lay Religious: Essays on the Salesian Brother. Swain, Peter, tr.
--Don Bosco's Lay Religious: Profiles in Courage. Swain, Peter, tr.
Bibb, Henry. Narrative of the Life & Adventures of Henry Bibb, an American Slave.
Bibb, John, jt. auth. see Graham, Lou.
Bibeault, Donald. Corporate Turnaround: How Managers Turn Losers into Winners.
Bibiena, Guiseppe G. Architectural & Perspective Designs.
Bibliographic Guide Editors. Bibliographic Guide to Art & Architecture: 1975.
--Bibliographic Guide to Art & Architecture: 1981.
--Bibliographic Guide to Art & Architecture: 1978.
--Bibliographic Guide to Art & Architecture: 1980.
--Bibliographic Guide to Art & Architecture: 1976.
--Bibliographic Guide to Art & Architecture: 1982.
--Bibliographic Guide to Black Studies: 1977.
--Bibliographic Guide to Black Studies: 1978.
--Bibliographic Guide to Black Studies: 1981.
--Bibliographic Guide to Black Studies: 1980.
--Bibliographic Guide to Black Studies: 1982.
--Bibliographic Guide to Black Studies, 1984.
--Bibliographic Guide to Business & Economics: 1979.
--Bibliographic Guide to Business & Economics: 1978.
--Bibliographic Guide to Business & Economics: 1981.
--Bibliographic Guide to Business & Economics: 1975.
--Bibliographic Guide to Business & Economics: 1976.
--Bibliographic Guide to Business & Economics: 1977.
--Bibliographic Guide to Business & Economics: 1980.
--Bibliographic Guide to Business & Economics: 1982.
--Bibliographic Guide to Conference Publications: 1979.
--Bibliographic Guide to Conference Publications: 1978.
--Bibliographic Guide to Conference Publications: 1981.
--Bibliographic Guide to Conference Publications: 1975.
--Bibliographic Guide to Conference Publications: 1976.
--Bibliographic Guide to Conference Publications: 1980.
--Bibliographic Guide to Conference Publications: 1982.
--Bibliographic Guide to Dance: 1975.
--Bibliographic Guide to Dance: 1979.
--Bibliographic Guide to Dance: 1980.
--Bibliographic Guide to Dance: 1981.
--Bibliographic Guide to Education: 1979.
--Bibliographic Guide to Education: 1980.
--Bibliographic Guide to Education: 1981.
--Bibliographic Guide to Education: 1982.
--Bibliographic Guide to Education: 1983.
--Bibliographic Guide to Government Publications - U. S. 1980.
--Bibliographic Guide to Government Publications - U. S. 1976.
--Bibliographic Guide to Government Publications - U. S. 1981.
--Bibliographic Guide to Government Publications - U. S. 1975.
--Bibliographic Guide to Government Publications - U. S. 1979.
--Bibliographic Guide to Government Publications - U. S. 1978.
--Bibliographic Guide to Government Publications - U. S. 1977.
--Bibliographic Guide to Government Publications-Foreign: 1976.
--Bibliographic Guide to Government Publications-Foreign: 1980.
--Bibliographic Guide to Government Publications-Foreign: 1981.
--Bibliographic Guide to Government Publications-Foreign: 1978.
--Bibliographic Guide to Government Publications-Foreign: 1979.
--Bibliographic Guide to Government Publications-Foreign: 1977.
--Bibliographic Guide to Government Publications-Foreign: 1982.
--Bibliographic Guide to Government Publications-U.S. 1982.
--Bibliographic Guide to Latin American Studies: 1981.
--Bibliographic Guide to Latin American Studies: 1979.
--Bibliographic Guide to Latin American Studies: 1980.
--Bibliographic Guide to Latin American Studies: 1982.
--Bibliographic Guide to Latin American Studies: 1983.
--Bibliographic Guide to Law: 1977.
--Bibliographic Guide to Law: 1978.
--Bibliographic Guide to Law: 1979.
--Bibliographic Guide to Law: 1980.
--Bibliographic Guide to Law: 1981.
--Bibliographic Guide to Law: 1982.
--Bibliographic Guide to Law, 1983.
--Bibliographic Guide to Maps & Atlases: 1981.
--Bibliographic Guide to Maps & Atlases: 1980.
--Bibliographic Guide to Maps & Atlases: 1982.
--Bibliographic Guide to Music: 1980.
--Bibliographic Guide to Music: 1981.
--Bibliographic Guide to Music: 1982.
--Bibliographic Guide to North American History: 1980.
--Bibliographic Guide to North American History: 1978.
--Bibliographic Guide to North American History: 1979.
--Bibliographic Guide to North American History: 1982.
--Bibliographic Guide to Psychology: 1975.
--Bibliographic Guide to Psychology: 1976.
--Bibliographic Guide to Psychology: 1977.
--Bibliographic Guide to Psychology: 1978.
--Bibliographic Guide to Psychology: 1979.
--Bibliographic Guide to Psychology: 1980.
--Bibliographic Guide to Psychology: 1981.
--Bibliographic Guide to Psychology: 1982.
--Bibliographic Guide to Psychology: 1984.
--Bibliographic Guide to Soviet & East European Studies: 1981.
--Bibliographic Guide to Soviet & East European Studies: 1980.
--Bibliographic Guide to Soviet & East European Studies: 1982.
--Bibliographic Guide to Technology: 1976.
--Bibliographic Guide to Technology: 1978.
--Bibliographic Guide to Technology: 1979.
--Bibliographic Guide to Technology: 1980.
--Bibliographic Guide to Technology: 1981.
--Bibliographic Guide to Technology: 1982.
--Bibliographic Guide to Theatre Arts: 1976.
--Bibliographic Guide to Theatre Arts: 1980.
--Bibliographic Guide to Theatre Arts: 1981.
--Bibliographic Guide to Theatre Arts: 1982.
Bibliographic Research Library Staff. Academic Architecture & the Work of Paul Schweikher: A Selected Bibliography.
--Architecture in the American Southwest & the Work of John Gaw Meem: A Selected Bibliography.
--The Architecture of Johnson-Burgee: A Selected Bibliography.
--Cave Architecture in History: A Selected Bibliography.
--Henry Austin & the Italian Villa Style in American Architecture: A Selected Bibliography.
--Hotel Architecture & the Work of Morris Lapidus: A Selected Bibliography.
--John Webb & Seventeenth Century English Architecture: A Selected Bibliography.
--Joseph Urban & American Theater Architecture: A Selected Bibliography.
--New York City Architecture & the Empire State Building: A Selected Bibliography.
--Orson Squire Fowler & the Octagon House: A Selected Bibliography.
--Terrace & Row Houses in Architectural Design: A Selected Bibliography.
Bibliographic Society of Northern Illinois Staff. Index to Reviews of Bibliographical Publications, 1978. Oggel, Terry, ed.
Bibliotheque Imperiale Publique de St. Petersbourg Staff. Catalogue de la Section des Russica: Ecrits Sur la Russie en Langues Etrangere.
Bibo, Istvan. The Paralysis of International Institutions & the Remedies: A Study of Self-Determination, Concord among the Major Powers & Political Arbitration.
Bic, Lubomir. MICOS: A Microprogrammable Computer Simulator.
Bicher, Haim I. & Bruley, Duane F., eds. Oxygen Transport to Tissue IV.
Bichler, Joyce. DES Daughter: The Joyce Bichler Story.
Bichteler, K. Integration Theory: With Special Attention to Vector Measures.
Bick, T. A. Introduction to Abstract Mathematics.
Bickel, Lennard. Mawson's Will.
Bickel, Lother. Unity of Body & Mind.
Bickel, Margot & Steigert, Hermann. Harvest the Day. Frost, Gerhard E., ed.
Bickerstaff, Issac. The Plays of Isaac Bickerstaff. Tasch, Peter A., ed.
Bickersteth, J. Burgon. The Land of Open Doors: Being Letters from Western Canada, 1911-1913.
Bickerton, Derek. Roots of Language.
Bickerton, L. M. An Illustrated Guide to Eigtheenth Century English Drinking Glasses.
Bickford, Zarh M. Twentieth Century Tenor Banjo Method.
Bicknell, A. J. Bicknell's Victorian Buildings: Floor Plans & Elevations for 45 Houses & Other Structures.
Bicknell, J. & McQuiston, L., eds. Design for Need.
Bickner, Mei L. & Shaughnessey, Marlene. Women at Work: Annotated Bibliography.
Bicudo, Carlos M. Contribution to the Knowledge of the Desmids of the State of Sao Paulo.
Bidault, M. L'Abbe, jt. auth. see Tardy.
Biddle, Gordon. Great Railway Stations of Britain.
Biddle, Marcia M. Contributions of Women: Labor.
Biddle, Richard E. Discrimination: What Does It Mean?
Biddle, Wayne. Coming to Terms: From Alpha to X-Ray, a Lexicon for the Science-Watcher.
Biddlecombe, Terry. Tales of Racing & Chasing.
Biddulph, M. W., jt. ed. see Henstock, M. E.
Biddulph, Michael W. The Golf Shot.
Bideleux, Robert. Communism & Development.
Bidwell, John. The Size of the Sheet in America: Paper-Moulds Manufactured by N & D Sellers of Philadelphia.
Bidwell, John, ed. see American Type Founders Co. Staff.
Bidwell, John, ed. see Arnett, John A.
Bidwell, John, ed. see Balston, Thomas.
Bidwell, John, ed. see Brightly, Charles.
Bidwell, John, ed. see Hoe, R., & Co.
Bidwell, John, ed. see Legros, Lucien & Grant, John C.
Bidwell, John, ed. see Munsell, Joel.
Bidwell, John, ed. see Nicholson, James B.
Bidwell, John, jt. ed. see Ringwalt, J. Luther.
Bidwell, John, ed. see Thompson, John S.
Bidwell, R. L., jt. ed. see Serjeant, R. B.
Bie, Oskar. Schubert, the Man.
Bie, S. W., ed. see ISSS Working Group Staff.
Bieber, Margaret. History of the Greek & Roman Theater.

Authors

Biechler, Sydney S. The Behavior of Matter: Laboratory Experiments in Introductory Chemistry.

Biedenharn, L. C., et al. Algebra of Representations of Some Finite Groups.

Biederman-Thorson, M. A., tr. see Nachtigall, W.

Biederwolf, William E. The Second Coming Bible Commentary.

Biegeleisen, H. I. Varicose Veins, Related Diseases & Sclerotherapy: A Guide for Practitioners.

Biehler, Fred. Aviation Maintenance Law.

Biehler, Robert F. Child Development: An Introduction.

--Child Development: An Introduction.

--Psychology Applied to Teaching.

Biehler, Robert F. & Snowran, Jack. Psychology Applied to Teaching.

Biehler, Robert F., ed. Psychology Applied to Teaching: Selected Readings.

Bielawski, Larry & Parks, A. Franklin. Organizational Writing.

Bielenberg, Christabel. Ride Out the Dark: The Experiences of an Englishwoman in Wartime Germany.

Bieler, Henry G. Food Is Your Best Medicine.

Bielski, Benon H. & Gebicki, Janusz M. Atlas of Electron Spin Resonance Spectra.

Bielstein, R. M. The Practical Approach to Industrial Relations for Line Supervisors.

Biely, Andrei. St. Petersburg. Cournos, John, tr. from Rus. & intro. by.

Biely, Andrey. Silver Dove. Reavey, George, tr. from Rus.

Biemel, Walter. Martin Heidegger: An Illustrated Study. Mehta, J. L., tr.

Bienefeld, Manfred A. & Godfrey, E. Martin, eds. The Struggle for Development: National Strategies in an International Context.

Bienen, Henry. Nigeria: Absorbing the Oil Wealth.

Bier, Jesse. The Rise & Fall of American Humor.

--Year of the Cougar.

Bierberbach, L. Theorie der Geometrishen Konstruktionen.

Bierch, J. R., jt. auth. see Ranke, M. B.

Bierlein, Lawrence W. Red Book on Transportation of Hazardous Materials.

Bierman, et al. Practical Oscilloscope Handbook.

Bierman, Harold, Jr. & Drebin, Allan R. Financial Accounting: An Introduction.

Bierman, John. Odyssey.

Bierman, Stanley M. The World's Greatest Stamp Collectors.

Biersted, Sonja. A Humanistic View of Religion.

Biesanz, Richard, et al. The Costa Ricans.

Biezais, Haralds, ed. Religious Symbols & Their Functions.

Bigart, Robert, ed. Environmental Pollution in Montana.

Bigelow, John. William Cullen Bryant.

Bigelow, Lyn. God's Message to Me.

Biggers, Don H. German Pioneers in Texas.

Biggers, Earl D. The Black Camel.

--Charlie Chan Carries On.

Biggers, W. Watts, jt. auth. see Goodman, Joseph I.

Biggerstaff, Ray. Public Health Administration: An Instrument for Evaluation.

Biggle, Lloyd, Jr. All the Colors of Darkness.

--Interface for Murder.

Biggs, Don. How to Avoid Lawyers: A Step by Step Guide to Being Your Own Lawyer in Almost Every Situation.

--Pressure Cooker.

Biggs, Donald A., jt. ed. see Giroux, Roy F.

Biggs, Mouzon, jt. auth. see Allen, Charles L.

Biggs, Rosa F. A Tender Reflection.

Biggs, W. D. The Mechanical Behaviour of Engineering Materials.

Bigley, John. Tributaries.

Bigmore, F. C. A Bibliography of Printing.

Bignami, G., jt. ed. see Anisman, H.

Bignell, James & Donovan, Robert. Digital Electronics.

Bigoness. International Human Resource Management.

Bigsby, Christopher W. Joe Orton.

Bihalji-Merin, Oto. Caprichos: Their Hidden Truth. Woods, John E., tr.

--Goya Then & Now: Paintings, Portraits, & Frescoes. Woods, John E., tr.

Bihun, Yaroslav, ed. Boomerang: The Works of Valentyn Moroz.

Bijou, Sidney W. & Baer, Donald M. Behavior Analysis of Child Development.

Bijou, Sidney W. & Ribes-Inesta, Emilio, eds. Behavior Modification: Issues & Extensions.

Bikerman, J. J. Foams.

--Physical Surfaces.

Bikkenin, N. B. Socialist Ideology.

Biko, Stephen. Steve Biko: I Write What I Like. Stubbs, Adrian, ed.

Bilainkin, George. Tito.

Bilas & Alessio. The Essentials of Macroeconomic Analysis.

Bilbo, Theodore G. Take Your Choice-Separation or Mongrelization.

Bilek, Arthur J., et al. Legal Aspects of Private Security.

Bilenky, S. M. Introduction to Feynman Diagrams.

--Introduction to the Physics of Electroweak Interactions.

Biles, William E. & Swain, James J. Optimization & Industrial Experimentation.

Biles, William E., jt. auth. see Gajda, Walter J., Jr.

Bilgin, Bahir. The Roles of Women & Community Development.

Bilgrami, K. S. & Misra, R. S., eds. Advancing Frontiers of Mycology & Plant Pathology: Prof. K. S. Bhargava Commemoration Volume.

Bilgrami, K. S., et al. Fundamentals of Botany.

Bilhartz, Terry O., ed. Francis Asbury's America: An Album of Early American Methodism.

Bilheimer, Robert S. A Spirituality for the Long Haul: Biblical Risk & Moral Stand.

Bilheimer, Robert S., ed. Faith & Ferment: An Interdisciplinary Study of Christian Beliefs & Practices.

Bilibin, I. The Frog Princess.

Bill, E. G., compiled by. The Queen Anne Churches: A Catalogue of the Papers in Lambeth Palace Library of the Commission for Building Fifty New Churches in London & Westminster, 1711-1759.

Bill, J. Brent. Stay Tuned: A Guide to Selective Viewing.

Bill, Shirley, jt. ed. see Gottschalk, Louis.

Billcliffe, Roger. Mackintosh Textile Designs.

Biller, Henry & Solomon, Richard. Child Maltreatment & Paternal Deprivation: A Manifesto for Research, Prevention, & Treatment.

Biller, Henry B., jt. auth. see Berlinsky, Ellen B.

Billheimer, Paul E. Destined for the Cross.

Billick, David J. Jose de Espronceda: An Annotated Bibliography, 1834 to 1978.

Billig, M. Social Psychology & Intergroup Relations.

Billigheimer, C. E., tr. see Polya, G. & Szego, G.

Billings, Diane M. & Stokes, Lillian G. Medical-Surgical Nursing: Common Health Problems of Adults & Children Across the Life Span.

Billings, Donald E. Guide to the Solar Corona.

Billings, Richard N., jt. auth. see Donnelly, Honoria M.

Billings, Richard N., jt. auth. see Schirra, Walter M.

Billingsley, Andrew & Giovannoni, Jeanne M. Children of the Storm: Black Children & American Child Welfare.

Billingsley, Patrick. Statistical Inference for Markov Processes.

Billington, Douglas S., ed. Physics of Solids: Radiation Damage in Solids.

Billington, E. W. & Tate, A. The Physics of Deformation & Flow.

Billington, M. S. Building Physics: Heat.

Billington, Michael. Alan Ayckbourn.

--Alan Ayckbourn.

Billington, Monroe L. American South: A Brief History.

Billington, Rachel. Occasion of Sin.

--Occasion of Sin.

Billington, Ray A. American History after Eighteen Sixty-Five.

--Guide to American History Manuscript Collections in Libraries of the United States.

Billis, David, et al. Organising Social Services Departments.

Billnitzer, Harold. Chances in a Mixed Marriage.

Billowitz, JoAnn, ed. see Family Circle Editors.

Bills, Robert E. A System for Assessing Affectivity.

Bills, Steven H. Lillian Hellman: An Annotated Bibliography.

Billstein, R., et al. A Problem Solving Approach to Mathematics for Elementary School Teachers.

Billy, Christopher, ed. Business & Management Jobs 1985.

--Engineering, Science, & Computer Jobs 1985.

Billy, George J., et al. Sources of Information in Transportation: Part 3, Shipping.

Bilodeau, Edward A., ed. Acquisition of Skill.

Bilstein, Roger E. Flight in America, Nineteen Hundred to Nineteen Eighty-Three: From the Wrights to the Astronauts.

Bilton, Jan. The International Dinner Party Cookbook.

Bilu, Dalya, tr. see Appelfeld, Aharon.

Bilu, Dalya, tr. see Shahar, David.

Bimler, Richard W. Grand Opening.

Binchy, Maeve. London Transports.

Binchy, William. Is Divorce the Answer? An Examination of No-Fault Divorce Against the Background of the Irish Debate.

Bindeman, Steven L. Heidegger & Wittgenstein: The Poetics of Silence.

Binder, A. W. Biblical Chants.

Binder, George A., et al. Computed Tomography of the Brain in Axial, Coronal, & Sagittal Planes.

Binder, Henry, ed. see Crane, Stephen.

Binder, Leonard. The Ideological Revolution in the Middle East.

Binder, R., jt. auth. see Novak, J.

Binder, V., et al. Modern Therapies.

Binder, Z., ed. see IFAC Symposium Staff.

Bindon, Kathleen R. Inventories & Foreign Currency Translation Requirements. Farmer, Richard N., ed.

Bindra, Jasjit S. Prostaglandin Synthesis.

Biner, Pierre. The Living Theatre.

Bines, Hazel. Redefining Remedial Education: Policies & Practice in Secondary Schools.

Binford, Jesse S., Jr. Foundations of Chemistry.

Binford, Lewis R. Bones: Ancient Men & Modern Myths.

--In Pursuit of the Past: Decoding the Archaeological Record.

--Nunamuit Ethnoarchaeology.

Bing, David, ed. The Chemistry & Physiology of the Human Plasma Proteins: Proceedings of a Conference Sponsored by the Center for Blood Research, Boston, 1978.

Bing, Gordon. Corporate Divestment.

Bing, Samuel. Artistic America, Tiffany Glass & Art Nouveau.

Bing, V. & Braet Von Uberfeldt, J. Regional Costumes of the Netherlands.

Bingaman, Joseph W. Latin America: A Survey of Holdings at the Hoover Institution on War, Revolution & Peace.

Binger, Carl. Thomas Jefferson: A Well-Tempered Mind.

Bingham, Edwin R. Charles F. Lummis: Editor of the Southwest.

Bingham, Hiram. A Residence of Twenty-One Years in the Sandwich Islands: A Civil, Religious & Political History.

Bingham, Howard R. Living with Teens: A Parent's Handbook.

Bingham, Joan & Riccio, Dolores. The Smart Shopper's Guide to Food Buying & Preparation.

--The Smart Shopper's Guide to Food Buying & Preparation.

Bingham, Madelene. The Great Lover: Herbert Beerbohm Tree.

Bingham, R. C. & Von Schleyer, P. R. Chemistry of Adamantanes: Recent Developments in the Chemistry of Adamantane & Related Polycyclic Hydrocarbons.

Bingham, Richard D. Reapportionment of the Oklahoma House of Representatives: Politics & Process.

Bingham, Robert E. Traps to Avoid in Good Administration.

Bingley, Clive. The Business of Book Publishing.

Bingwen, Liu, tr. see Shoubao, Huang.

Binh, Vu T., ed. Surface Mobilities on Solid Materials: Fundamental Concepts & Applications.

Binhammer, Robert T., jt. auth. see Crafts, Roger C.

Binkley, Luther J. Contemporary Ethical Theories.

Binnie, Carl A. Communication Training Through Amplification: Audiologic Management of Adults.

Binnie, Eric. The Theatrical Designs of Charles Ricketts. Beckerman, Bernard, ed.

Binns, Bronwyn & Jones, Ian. Against the Wind: Screenplay.

Binns, David & Mars, Gerald. Castlemilk: Family, Community & Unemployment.

Binns, K. J. & Lawrenson, P. J. Analysis & Computation of Electric & Magnetic Field Problems.

Binns, Richard. France a la Carte.

--French Leave.

--French Leave.

--Hidden France.

--Richard Binns' Best of Britain.

Binns, Ronald. Malcolm Lowry.

Bin-Nun, Aaron. The Language of Faith.

Binswanger, Barbara & Ryan, Betsy. Live in Child Care: Complete Guide.

Binswanger, Ludwig. Uber Ideenflucht.

Binyon, J. Physiology of Echinoderms.

Binyon, Lawrence. Engraved Designs of William Blake.

Biochemical Society Symposium, 27th. Metabolic Roles of Citrate: Proceedings. Goodwin, T. W., ed.

Biochemical Society Symposium, 28th. Porphyrins & Related Compounds: Proceedings. Goodwin, T. W., ed.

Biochemical Society Symposium, 29th. Natural Substances Formed Biologically from Mevalonic Acid: Proceedings. Goodwin, T. W., ed.

Biochemical Society Symposium, 30th. British Biochemistry: Past & Present. Goodwin, T. W., ed.

Biochemical Society Symposium, 31st. Chemical Reactivity & Biological Role of Functional Groups in Enzymes: Proceedings. Smellie, R. M., ed.

Biochemical Society Symposium, 34th. Biological Hydroxylation Mechanisms: Proceedings. Boyd, G. S. & Smellie, R. M., eds.

Biochemistry & Biophysics of Mitochondrial Membranes Symposium Staff. Biochemistry & Biophysics of Mitochondrial Membranes: Proceedings. Azzone, G. F., ed.

Biochemistry & Physiology of Visual Pigments Symposium Staff. Proceedings of the Biochemistry & Physiology of Visual Pigments Symposium, Bochum University, Germany, 1972. Langer, H., ed.

Biometerological Congress Staff. Biometeorology Seven: Proceedings, of the International Biometerological Congress 8th, Sept.9-15, 1979. Zemel, Z. & Hyslop, N., eds.

Bion, M. Construction & Principle Use of Mathematical Instruments, 1758. Stone, Edmund, tr. from Lat.

Biorci, Giuseppe, ed. Network & Switching Theory.

Bioy Casares, Adolfo. The Invention of Morel & Other Stories.

Biram, John G., ed. see Levy, Jean-Philippe.

Birch & Brooks. The Hand.

Birch, jt. auth. see Mauch.

Birch, B. J., ed. see International Summer School for Theoretical Physics Staff.

Birch, Bruce C. & Rasmussen, Larry L. Bible & Ethics in the Christian Life.

Birch, C. & Albrecht, P., eds. Genetics & the Quality of Life.

Birch, C. Allan, et al. The House Physician's Handbook.

Birch, Cyril, ed. & intro. by. Studies in Chinese Literary Genres.

Birch, Derek W. & Cuthbert, Robert E. Costing Open Learning in Further Education.

Birch, Gordon G., et al. Food Science.

Birch, Herbert G. & Gussow, Joan D. Disadvantaged Children: Health, Nutrition, & School Failure.

Birch, J. R., ed. Fourier Transform Spectroscopy: Proceedings of the International Conference, Durham, U. K., 19-22 September, 1983.

Birch, Jack, jt. auth. see Sellin, Don.

Birch, Richard. The Family Financial Planning Book.

Birch, William G. A Guide to Pregnancy & Childbirth.

Birch, William G. & Meilach, Dona Z. Doctor Discusses Pregnancy.

Birchal, Harold F. Modern Surveying.

Bircheat, Linda. On Love & Life.

Bircher, Dr. Ralph Foreword by see Wong, Hon Sun.

Birchon, D. Dictionary of Metallurgy.

Bird. Golden Chersonese.

Bird, C. W. Transition Metal Intermediates in Organic Synthesis.

Bird, Caroline. Enterprising Women: Their Contribution to the American Economy, 1776-1976.

Bird, Gail B., jt. auth. see Verrall, Harold E.

Bird, Isabella. Golden Chersonese.

Bird, Malcolm. The Sticky Child.

Bird, R. B. & Shetter, W. Z. Dutch: Een Goed Begin, a Contemporary Dutch Reader.

Bird, Sarah. Alamo House: Women Without Men, Men Without Brains.

--Do Evil Cheerfully.

Bird, Stuart L. Converting to Timex-Sinclair BASIC.

Birdsall, Charles K. & Bridges, William B. Electron Dynamics of Diode Regions.

Birdsall, Derek, jt. auth. see Cipolla, Carlo M.

Birdsall, Nancy. Child Schooling & the Measurement of Living Standards.

Birdsell, J. B. Human Evolution.

Birdwell, Cleo. Amazons.

Birdwood, G., jt. ed. see Beaconsfield, R.

Birdwood, G. F., et al, eds. Parkinson's Disease: A New Approach to Treatment.

Birdwood, Lord. Khaki & Gown.

Birk, Genevieve B., jt. auth. see Birk, Newman P.

Birk, Genevieve G, jt. auth. see Birk, Newman P.

Birk, Newman P. & Birk, Genevieve B. Practice for Understanding & Using English: Eighty Exercises Workbook.

Birk, Newman P. & Birk, Genevieve G. Understanding & Using English.

Birke, G., et al, eds. Physiology & Pathophysiology of Plasma Protein Metabolism.

Birke, L., jt. auth. see Archer, J.

Birkelbach, Aubrey W. A Sampler of New England Land Use.

Birkelbach, Aubrey W., Jr. & Wassall, Gregory H. The Case Against the Sale of Development Rights of Connecticut's Agricultural Land.

Birkey, Verna & Turnquist, Jeanette. A Mother's Problem Solver.

Birkhaeuser, H., et al, eds. Advances in Tuberculosis Research.

Birkhauser, Kaspar. Light from the Darkness: Paintings by Peter Birkhauser. Wertenschlag, Eva, ed.

Birkinshaw, jt. auth. see Amos.

Birkner, Rudolf. Normal Radiologic Patterns & Variances of the Human Skeleton: An X-Ray Atlas of Adults & Children.

Birkofer, L. Organic Chemistry: Syntheses & Reactivity.

Birks, H. J. & West, R. G., eds. Quaternary Plant Ecology: Fourteenth Symposium of the British Ecological Society, University of Cambridge, 28-30 March 1972.
Birks, J. B. & Birks, J. B., eds. Proceedings of the Rutherford Jubilee International Conference-Manchester, 1962.
Birks, L. S. Electron Probe Microanalysis.
Birley, Sue. New Enterprises: A Start-up Case Book.
Birmingham Historical Society Staff & Blake, Thomas H. Birmingham Since 1885.
Birmingham, Jacqueline J. The Problem-Oriented Record: A Self-Learning Module.
Birmingham, Jacqueline J., jt. auth. see Carini, Geraldine.
Birmingham, Joan. The Christmas Creatures.
Birmingham, Richard. Boat Building Techniques Illustrated.
Birmingham Shakespeare Library Staff, compiled by. Shakespeare Bibliography: The Catalogue of the Birmingham Shakespeare Library.
Birmingham, Stephen. The Auerbach Will.
--The LeBaron Secret.
--Life at the Dakota: New York's Most Unusual Address.
Birnbaum, Alfred, tr. see Segi, Shinichi.
Birnbaum, Henrik. Lord Novgorod the Great Essays in the History & Culture of a Medieval City State, Pt. 1: The Historical Background.
Birnbaum, Hubert C. Amphoto Guide to Cameras.
Birnbaum, Jacob S. The Musculoskeletal Manual.
Birnbaum, Martin. Last Romantic.
Birnbaum, Max, jt. auth. see Babad, Elisha Y.
Birnbaum, Michael, jt. auth. see Sonnenburg, David.
Birnbaum, Philip. The Birnbaum Haggadah.
Birnbaum, Philip, ed. The New Treasury of Judaism.
Birnbaum, Steve. Birnbaum's Canada, 1986.
--Birnbaum's Caribbean, 1986.
--Birnbaum's Disneyland, 1986.
--Birnbaum's Europe for Business Travelers, 1986.
--Birnbaum's Europe, 1986.
--Birnbaum's France, 1986.
--Birnbaum's Great Britain & Ireland 1986.
--Birnbaum's Hawaii, 1986.
--Birnbaum's Mexico, 1986.
--Birnbaum's South America, 1986.
--Birnbaum's United States, 1986.
--Canada, Nineteen Eighty.
--Canada, Nineteen Eighty-One.
--Canada Nineteen Eighty-Seven.
--Canada, Nineteen Eighty-Two.
--Canada 1983.
--Canada 1984.
--Canada, 1985.
--The Caribbean, Bermuda & the Bahamas, Nineteen Eighty-Two.
--The Caribbean, Bermuda, & the Bahamas, 1980.
--The Caribbean, Bermuda, & the Bahamas 1981.
--The Caribbean, Bermuda & the Bahamas 1983.
--Caribbean, Bermuda, & the Bahamas 1987.
--Disneyland Nineteen Eighty-Seven.
--Disneyland 1983.
--Disneyland 1984.
--Disneyland, 1985.
--Europe for Business Travelers, 1985.
--Europe for Business Travelers: 1987.
--Europe, Nineteen Eight-Two.
--Europe, Nineteen Eighty.
--Europe, Nineteen Eighty-One.
--Europe, 1984.
--Europe, 1985.
--Europe: 1987.
--France Nineteen Eighty-Seven.
--France, 1985.
--Great Britain & Ireland Nineteen Eighty-Two.
--Great Britain & Ireland Nineteen Eighty-Seven.
--Great Britain & Ireland 1983.
--Great Britain & Ireland 1984.
--Great Britain, 1985.
--Hawaii Nineteen Eighty-Seven.
--Hawaii 1983.
--Hawaii 1984.
--Hawaii, 1985.
--Houghton Mifflin Travel Guides, Vol. 1: The United States.
--Houghton Mifflin Travel Guides, Vol. 2: Mexico.
--Houghton Mifflin Travel Guides, Vol. 3: The Caribbean.
--Italy Nineteen Eighty-Seven.
--Mexico, Nineteen Eighty.
--Mexico Nineteen Eighty-Seven.
--Mexico, Nineteen Eighty-Two.
--Mexico, 1981.
--Mexico 1983.
--Mexico 1984.
--Mexico, 1985.
--South America, Nineteen Eighty-One.
--South America, Nineteen Eighty-Two.
--South America, 1980.
--South America 1983.
--South America 1984.
--South America, 1985.
--South America, 1987.
--Steve Birnbaum Brings You the Best of Walt Disney World.
--U. S. A. for Business Travelers 1984.
--U. S. A. for Business Travelers, 1985.
--U. S. A. for Business Travelers, 1987.
--United States, Nineteen Eighty.
--United States, Nineteen Eighty-One.
--United States Nineteen Eighty-Seven.
--United States, Nineteen Eighty-Two.
--United States 1983.
--United States 1984.
--Walt Disney World.
--Walt Disney World Nineteen Eighty-Seven.
--Walt Disney World, 1983.
--Walt Disney World 1984.
--Walt Disney World, 1985.
Birnbaumer, L., jt. ed. see O'Malley, B. W.
Birnbaumer, Lutz, jt. ed. see O'Malley, B. W.
Birney, Alice L. Satiric Catharsis in Shakespeare: A Theory of Dramatic Structure.
Birnie, Patricia, jt. ed. see Barston, R. P.
Biro, Charlotte S. Flavors of Hungary.
Biro, Gyuri, jt. auth. see Hoffman, Peggy.
Biro, Lajos & Wimperis, Arthur. The Private Life of Henry VIII. Kupelnick, Bruce S., ed.
Biro, Val. Gumdrop & the Secret Switches.
--Gumdrop Finds a Friend.
--Gumdrop Finds a Ghost.
--Gumdrop Gets His Wings.
--Gumdrop Has a Birthday.
Biro, Z., et al, eds. Homeostasis in Injury & Shock: Proceedings of a Satellite Symposium of the 28th International Congress of Physiological Sciences, Budapest, Hungary, 1980.
Biros, Florence K., ed. see Reid, Thomas F., et al.
Birrell. Logan Turner's Diseases of the Nose, Throat & Ear.
Birrell, Anne, tr. New Songs from a Jade Terrace: An Anthology of Early Chinese Love Poetry.
Birrell, Augustine. William Hazlitt.
Birrell, J. F. Paediatric Otolaryngology.
Birren, Faber. Light, Color, & Environment.
--Principles of Color: A Review of Past Traditions & Modern Theories.
Birren, James E., et al. Developmental Psychology: A Life-Span Approach.
Birsner, E. P. How to Improve Customer Service.
Birtles, Philip. Mosquito.
--Planemakers: DeHavilland.
BIS-PEDDER Associates, Ltd. Staff. Computing Marketplace: A Directory of Computing Services & Software Supplies for Word Processors, Micros, Minis, & Mainframes.
Bisagno, John. God Is.
--Positive Obedience: The Christian's Response to the Ten Commandments.
Bisagno, John R. Life Without Compromise.
Bisby, J. R., et al, eds. Electrical Fitting.
Bischel, Jon E. & Feinschreiber, Robert. Fundamentals of International Taxation.
Bischof, Eunice S., jt. auth. see Bischof, George P.
Bischof, George P. Atoms at Work.
Bischof, George P. & Bischof, Eunice S. Sun, Earth, & Man.
Bischoff, jt. auth. see Woodard.
Bischoff, Ann. Way Ward Pokey.
Bischoff, David. Manhattan Project.
Bisco, Jim. A Greater Look at Greater Buffalo.
Bish, Tommy L. Home Gunsmithing Digest.
Bishop, A., jt. auth. see Baeriswyl, D.
Bishop, A. A., jt. ed. see Corradini, M. L.
Bishop, Ann. Merry-Go-Riddle.
--Wild Bill Hiccup's Riddle Book. Rubin, Caroline, ed.
Bishop, Audrey & Bishop, Owen. Take off with the Electron & BBC Micro.
Bishop, Audrey, jt. auth. see Bishop, Owen.
Bishop, Bernice P., Museum Editors. Dictionary Catalog of the Library of the Bernice P. Bishop Museum.
Bishop, Beverly. Basic Neurophysiology.
Bishop, Chara, jt. auth. see Mroczkowski, George.
Bishop, Claire H. Here Is France.
--Martin De Porres, Hero.
--Martin De Porres, Hero.
Bishop, David. Subject Area Reading in the Middle School.
Bishop, Denis & Ellis, Christopher. Vehicles At War.
Bishop, Elizabeth. The Complete Poems: 1927-1979.
Bishop, George, jt. auth. see Linkletter, Art.
Bishop Graphics, Inc. Staff. The Design & Drafting of Printed Circuits.
Bishop, Hillman, jt. auth. see Hendel, Samuel.
Bishop, Joseph M. Applied Oceanography.
Bishop, Joseph P. The Eye of the Storm.
Bishop, Lee. Gunblaze.
Bishop, Michael. Ancient of Days.
Bishop, Mike. Dodge Plymouth Tune-up Maintenance: Vans & Pickups, 1965-1978. Jorgensen, Eric, ed.
--Ford Tune-up & Maintenance: Vans & Pickups, 1969-1978. Jorgensen, Eric, ed.
--Kawasaki Snowmobiles Nineteen Seventy-Six to Nineteen Eighty: Service, Repair, Maintenance. Jorgensen, Eric, ed.
Bishop, Morris. Middle Ages.
--A Survey of French Literature.
Bishop, Nancy, jt. auth. see Camden, Thomas M.
Bishop, Olga B. Canadian Official Publications.
Bishop, Owen & Bishop, Audrey. BBC Micro Wargaming.
--Practical Programs for the BBC Micro.
Bishop, Owen, jt. auth. see Bishop, Audrey.
Bishop, Richard B. Practical Polymerization for Polystyrene.
Bishop, Richard L. & Crittenden, R. J. Geometry of Manifolds.
Bishop, Robert. The American Chair: Three Centuries of Style.
Bishop, Ron. Basic Microprocessors & Sixty-Eight Hundred.
--Troubleshooting Old Cars.
Bishop, Russell H., jt. auth. see Miller, J. Dale.
Bishop, Sheila. Penelope Devereux.
Bismarck, Otto von. Gesammelte Werke: Nineteen Twenty-Four to Nineteen Thirty-Five.
Bisnow, Mark. Diary of a Dark Horse: The 1980 Anderson Presidential Campaign.
Bisplinghoff, Gretchen, jt. auth. see Wexman, Virginia W.
Bisschop, W. R. The Saar Controversy.
Bisselle, Walter C., jt. auth. see Sanders, Irwin T.
Bisseret, Noelle. Education, Class Language & Ideology.
Bissett, D. E., et al, eds. The Printing Ink Manual. Leach, R. H. & Williams, C. H.
Bisson, T. A. Zaibatsu Dissolution in Japan.
Bisson, Thomas N, ed. Medieval Representative Institutions: Their Origins & Nature.
Biswas. Terracotta Art Manual of Bengal.
Biswas, A. K., jt. auth. see Ausebel, J.
Biswas, A. K., jt. ed. see Golubev, G. N.
Biswas, Asit K., ed. The Ozone Layer: Synthesis of Papers Based on the UNEP Meeting on the Ozone Layer, Washington DC, March 1977.
--Systems Approach to Water Management.
--United Nations Water Conference: Summary & Main Documents.
Biswas, D. C. Shakespeare in His Own Time.
Bito, L. & Davson, H., eds. The Ocular & Cerebrospinal Fluids: Experimental Eye Research Supplement.
Bitsadze, A. V. & Kalinichenko, D. F. A Collection of Problems on the Equations of Mathematical Physics.
Bittar, E. E. & Bittar, N., eds. Biological Basis of Medicine.
Bittar, N., jt. ed. see Bittar, E. E.
Bittel, Lester R. Business in Action: An Introduction to Business.
--Encyclopedia of Professional Management.
--What Every Supervisor Should Know: The Basics of Supervisory Management.
Bitter, Gary. Microcomputer Applications for Calculus.
Bitter, Gary G. & Gore, Kay. The Best of Educational Software for the Commodore 64.
Bitter, Gary G., jt. ed. see Craighead, Donna.
Bitter, Gary G. & Geer, Charles. Materials for Metric Instruction.
Bitting, K. Gastronomic Bibliography.
Bittinger, Marvin L., et al. Mathematics for Consumer Survival.
Bittman, Sam. Out of Control.
Bittman, Sam & Zalk, Sue R. Expectant Fathers.
Bittner, John R. Fundamentals of Communication.
--Mass Communication: An Introduction.
--Mass Communication: An Introduction.
Bittner, Vernon J. Make Your Illness Count: A Hospital Chaplain Shows How God's Healing Power Can Be Released in Your Life.
Bitton, Davis, jt. auth. see Arrington, Leonard J.
Biumo, Panza di see Di Biumo, Panza.
Bivens, Gordon E., jt. auth. see Allentuck, Andrew J.
Bixley, William. The Guilty & the Innocent.
Bizzi, E., ed. see International Congress on Physiological Sciences Staff.
Bjerke, L. & Soraas, H., eds. Norwegian Dictionary: English-Norwegian.
Bjorge, James R. Forty Ways to Fortify Your Faith.
--Forty Ways to Say Thank You, Lord.
--Lord of the Mountain: Messages for Lent & Easter.
--The Love Road to Calvary: Sermons for Lent & Easter on 1 Corinthians 13.
Bjork, Gordon C. Stagnation & Growth in the American Economy, 1784-1792. Bruchey, Stuart, ed.
Bjork, Russell, jt. auth. see Townsley, David.
Bjorkhagen, I. Modern Swedish Grammar.
Bjorkland, Gary, jt. auth. see Sparks, Ken.
Bjorn, L. O. Light & Life.
Bjorn, Thyra F. Once upon a Christmas Time.
Bjorneboe, Jens. Moment of Freedom.
Bjorset, Brynjolf. Man & This Mysterious Universe.
Bjurstedt, H., ed. see International Symposium On Basic Environmental Problems Of Man In Space - 2nd - Paris - 1965.
Bjurstedt, H., ed. see International Symposium On Basic Environmental Problems Of Man In Space - 1st - Paris - 1962.
Blaauw, Adriaan & Schmidt, Maarten, eds. Galactic Structure.
Blachere, Regis & Chouemi, Moustafa. Dictionnaire Arabe-Francais-Anglais, 2.
Black. Cost Accounting.
Black, Betty, jt. auth. see Green, Karen.
Black, Bruce J. Manufacturing Technology for Level-2 Technicians.
--Manufacturing Technology for Level-3 Technicians.
--Workshop Processes, Practices & Materials.
Black, Campbell. Letters from the Dead.
Black, Carol M., jt. ed. see Jayson, Malcolm I.
Black, Charles L., Jr. Capital Punishment: The Inevitability of Caprice & Mistake.
Black, Clementina. Married Women's Work: Being the Report of an Inquiry Undertaken by the Women's Industrial Council.
Black, Cyril E., et al. Neutralization & World Politics.
Black, David. Medicine Man: A Young Doctor on the Brink of the Twenty-First Century.
--Minds.
--Murder at the Met.
--Murder at the Met.
--The Plague Years: A Chronicle of Aids, Epidemic of Our Times.
Black, Don J. Students, My Friends: A Personal Journal of Experiences with Young People.
--Through Clouds & Sunshine.
--Warm Tones & Tiny Miracles.
--Yes My Son, There Is a God!
Black, Donald. The Manners & Customs of the Police.
Black, Elinor G. From Adam's Rib to Women's Lib & Other Ventures.
Black, Eugene R. Diplomacy of Economic Development.
Black, F. O., et al. Congenital Deafness: A New Approach to Early Detection of Deafness Through a High Risk Register.
Black, George F. Gypsy Bibliography.
Black, Harold. Manual of Horsemanship.
Black, Harry & Broadfoot, Patricia. Keeping Track of Teaching: Assessment in the Modern Classroom.
Black, Homer A. & Edwards, James D., eds. The Managerial & Cost Accountant's Handbook.
Black, Hugh C., et al. The Great Educators: Readings for Leaders in Education.
Black, J. Anderson & Garland, Madge. A History of Fashion.
Black, J. Thomas & Morina, Michael. Downtown Office Growth & the Role of Public Transit.
Black, J. Thomas, et al. Mixed-Use Development Projects in North America: Project Profiles.
Black, Jackie. Dark Paradise.
--The Vixen's Kiss.
Black, James M. The Basics of Supervisory Management: Mastering the Art of Effective Supervision.
Black, Jay & Whitney, Frederick C. Introduction to Mass Communication.
Black, Jeanette. Silent Tears.
Black, Jeremy. The British & the Grand Tour.
--The English Press in the Eighteenth Century.
Black, Jim & Bowl, Ric. Social Work in Context.
Black, John. The Economists of Modern Britain: An Introduction to Macroeconomics.
Black, John G. & Stanley, Delmar S. Practical Accounting.
Black, John W. & Moore, Wilbur E. Speech: Code, Meaning, & Communication.
Black, Kenneth, jt. auth. see Huebner, S. S.
Black, Kenneth, Jr. & Huebner, S. S. Life Insurance.
Black, Kenneth, Jr. & Skipper, Harold, Jr. Life Insurance.
Black, Leyardia, jt. auth. see Wescott, Patsy.
Black, Linda. Pediatric Policy & Procedure Manual.
Black, Lionel. Death by Hoax.
--The Eve of the Wedding.
--The Penny Murders.
Black, Max. Models & Metaphors: Studies in Language & Philosophy.
Black, Max, ed. Philosophical Analysis: A Collection of Essays.
Black, Naomi. Seashore Entertaining.
Black, Naomi, jt. auth. see Smith, Mark.
Black, P. Strength of Materials.
Black, Perry, ed. Physiological Correlates of Emotion: Based Upon a Symposium.
Black, Peter E., ed. Readings in Soil & Water Conservation.
Black, Peter E. & Herrington, Lee P., eds. Working with NEPA: Environmental Impact Analysis for the Resource Manager.
Black, R. & Boden, P., eds. Alkaline Ring Complexes in Africa: Proceedings of the International Conference Held in Zaria, Nigeria, Dec. 6-10, 1983.
Black, Ronald E., jt. ed. see Schultz, Julius.

Black, Stanley, et al. Foundations of Financial Management: First Canadian Edition.
Black, Theodore M. Straight Talk About American Education.
Black, Thomas K. The Biological & Social Analysis of a Mississippian Cemetery from Southeast Missouri: The Turner Site 23b21a.
Black, Tyrone & Daniel, Donnie L. Money & Banking: Contemporary Policies, Practices & Issues.
Black, V. P. We Persuade Men. Thomas, J. D., ed.
Blackaby, Suzy, ed. see Knight, Diane.
Blackadar, Thomas. The Apple IIc: A Practical Guide.
Blackadder, D. A. & Nedderman, R. M. Handbook of Unit Operations.
Blackbeard, Bill, ed. see Caniff, Milton.
Blackburn. Enzyme Structure & Function.
Blackburn, Bill & Blackburn, Deana. Stress Point in Marriage.
Blackburn, Deana, jt. auth. see Blackburn, Bill.
Blackburn, Gary M., jt. auth. see Bullock, Lyndal M.
Blackburn, Graham. Illustrated Basic Carpentry.
Blackburn, Henry. Randolph Caldecott.
Blackburn, Jack. The Rodda Act--One Year Later.
Blackburn, Laurence H. God Wants You to Be Well.
Blackburn, Paul. Early Selected Y Mas: Collected Poems, 1949-1966. Kelly, Robert, ed.
Blackburn, Paul, tr. see Cortazar, Julio.
Blacker, Frank & Shimmin, Sylvia. Applying Psychology in Organizations.
Blackett, D. W. Elementary Topology: A Combinatorial & Algebraic Approach.
Blackey, Robert. Revolutions & Revolutionists: A Comprehensive Guide to the Literature.
Blackham, H. J. Education for Personal Autonomy.
Blackhurst. Body, Mind, & Creativity.
Blackhurst, Richard & Tumlir, Jan. Trade Relations under Flexible Exchange Rates.
Blackie, Bruce L. Gods of Goodness: The Sophisticated Idolatry of the Main Line Churches.
Blackith, R. E. & Reyment, R. A. Multivariate Morphometrics.
Blackith, R. E., tr. see Gabe, M.
Blackledge, Ethel. An Hour Is Forever.
Blacklock, Craig, jt. auth. see Link, Mike.
Blackman, D. E. & Sanger, D. J., eds. Contemporary Research in Behavioral Pharmacology.
Blackman, John L. Presidential Seizure in Labor Disputes.
Blackman, L. C. Modern Aspects of Graphite Technology.
Blackman, Richard. Follow the Leaders.
Blackmore, Howard L. English Pistols.
Blackmore, Susan J. Beyond the Body.
Blackmur, Richard P. Eleven Essays in the European Novel.
Blackshaw, Kenneth, jt. auth. see Severinghaus, Sheldon.
Blackstock, Nelson, et al. Cointelpro: The FBI's Secret War on Political Freedom. Perkus, Cathy, ed.
Blackstone, Bernard. Virginia Woolf: A Commentary.
Blackstone, Tessa. Education & Day Care for Young Children in Need: The American Experience.
--Education & Day Care for Young Children in Need: The American Experience.
Blackstone, Tessa, jt. auth. see Williams, Gareth.
Blackwell, Albert L., tr. see Wohlfarth, Hannsdieter.
Blackwell, Alice S., tr. Some Spanish-American Poets.
Blackwell, Gordon W. The Selected Addresses of Gordon W. Blackwell, President of Florida State University, Sept. 16, 1960 to Jan. 31, 1965.
Blackwell, John. The Passion As Story: The Plot of Mark.
Blackwell, John, jt. auth. see Walton, Alan G.
Blackwell, Muriel F. The Keeping Shelf.
Blackwell, Roger D., jt. auth. see Engel, James F.
Blackwell, Thomas. Letters Concerning Mythology.
Blackwell, Trevor & Seabrook, Jeremy. A World Still to Win: The Reconstruction of the Post-War Working Class.
Blackwell, William. Geometry in Architecture.
Blackwood, Brian, jt. auth. see Blackwood, George.
Blackwood, Brian D. & Blackwood, George H. Applesoft Language.
--Disks, Files, & Printers for the Apple II.
Blackwood, Cheryl P. & Slattery, Kathryn. A Bright-Shining Place.
Blackwood, George & Blackwood, Brian. Applesoft for the Apple IIe.
Blackwood, George H., jt. auth. see Blackwood, Brian D.
Blackwood, James R. House on College Avenue: The Comptons at Wooster, 1891-1913.
Blades, James. Orchestral Percussion Technique.
Blades, Joan. Mediate Your Divorce: A Guide to Cooperative Custody, Property & Support Agreements.
Blades, William. Books in Chains & Other Bibliographical Papers.
Blaffer, Sarah C. The Black-Man of Zinacantan: A Central American Legend.
Blaguy, John. The Foundation of Moral Goodness. Wellek, Rene, ed.
Blaikie, William G. Heroes of Israel.
--Public Ministry of Christ.
Blaiklock, E. M. The Bible & I.
--Blaiklock's Handbook to the Bible.
--Understanding the New Testament: Luke.
--Understanding the New Testament: Romans.
Blain, Beryl B., et al. Skills Development in Reading, Writing & Quantatitive. Braestrup, Angelica & Hassan, Aftab, eds.
Blain, Virginia, ed. see Surtees, R. S.
Blaine, Veola J. Verse from Veola: From Birth Through Pre-Adolescene.
Blaine, Vera & Clark, Scott. Progression.
Blair, Alan, tr. see Josephson, Lennart.
Blair, Arthur W. & Burton, William H. Growth & Development of the Preadolescent.
Blair, Carole L. & Salerno, Elizabeth M. The Expanding Family: Childbearing.
Blair, Charles & Sherrill, John. The Man Who Could Do No Wrong.
Blair, Clay. Beyond Courage.
--The Forgotten War: America in Korea 1950-1953.
Blair, Cynthia. Just Married.
Blair, D. E. Contact Manifold in Riemannian Geometry.
Blair, Donald L. Where Does Your Money Go?
Blair, Dorothy. A History of Glass in Japan.
--A History of Glass in Japan.
Blair, Edward. Leadville: Colorado's Magic City.
Blair, Eulalia, ed. see Atkinson, Alta.
Blair, Eulalia C. Casseroles & Vegetables for Foodservice Menu Planning.
--Garnishes, Relishes & Sauces for Foodservice Menu Planning.
--Luncheon & Supper Dishes for Foodservice Menu Planning.
--Meat & Poultry Entrees for Foodservice Menu Planning.
Blair, F. Michael. A Spinal Specialist's Guide to Exercise, Fitness & Health.
Blair, George S. Government at the Grass-Roots.
Blair, Ian. Investigating Rape: A New Approach for Police.
Blair, J. A., jt. auth. see Johnson, R. H.
Blair, J. Allen. Job: Living Patiently.
--John: Living Eternally.
Blair, John M. Economic Concentration: Structure, Behavior & Public Policy.
Blair, John P., jt. auth. see Barrett, G. Vincent.
Blair, Karin. Meaning in Star Trek.
Blair, Katherine D. Four Villages-Architecture in Nepal: Studies of Village Life.
Blair, Leon B. Western Window in the Arab World.
Blair, Louis H., et al. Monitoring the Impacts of Prison & Parole Services: An Initial Examination.
Blair, Lowell, tr. see Halter, Marek.
Blair, Margot C. & Ryan, Cathleen. Banners & Flags: How to Sew a Celebration.
Blair, Sam, jt. auth. see Trevino, Lee.
Blair, Timothy R., jt. auth. see Rupley, William H.
Blaisdell, Donald C. Technology-the Key to Better Environment: Values, Profits, & Growth in Post Industrial Society.
Blaisdell, Harold F. The Art of Fishing with Worms & Other Live Bait.
Blaise, W. Liffick, ed. The Byte Book of Pascal.
Blake, Clarence N. & Martin, Donald F. Quiz Book on Black America.
Blake, David H., et al. Social Auditing: Evaluating the Impact of Corporate Programs.
Blake, E. Jamaica: Beautiful Jamaica.
--Jamaica: Beautiful Jamaica.
Blake, Faye S. Shaping Your Child into an Athlete.
Blake, Gary, jt. auth. see McGaw, Charles J.
Blake, Gerald, ed. Maritime Boundaries & Ocean Resources.
Blake, Herman, jt. auth. see Newton, Huey P.
Blake, Ian F. & Mullin, Ronald C. An Introduction to the Mathematical Theory of Coding.
Blake, Ian F., jt. auth. see Walker, B. J.
Blake, Ian F., ed. Algebraic Coding Theory: History & Development.
Blake, Jennifer. Fierce Eden.
Blake, Marion E. Ancient Roman Construction in Italy from the Prehistoric Period to Augustus.
Blake, Mindy. The Golf Swing of the Future.
--Golf: The Technique Barrier.
Blake, Nelson M., jt. auth. see Barck, Oscar T.
Blake, Nigel & Pole, Kay, eds. Dangers of Deterrence: Philosophers on Nuclear Strategy.
--Objections to Nuclear Defence: Philosophers on Deterrence.
Blake, Noel S., jt. auth. see Gyll, Catherine.
Blake, Patricia, ed. see Hayward, Max.
Blake, Peter. God's Own Junkyard.
Blake, Quentin & Yeoman, John. The Improbable Book of Records.
Blake, Robert R. & Mouton, Jane S. Diary of an OD Man.
--Making Experience Work: The Grid Approach to Critique.
Blake, Robert R., et al. Managing Intergroup Conflict in Industry.
Blake School Parent Association Cookbook Staff. The Educated Palate. Nordstrom, Lois, ed.
Blake, Thomas H. Birmingham since Eighteen Eighty-Five.
Blake, Thomas H., jt. auth. see Birmingham Historical Society Staff.
Blake, Wendon. Creative Color for the Oil Painter.
--Landscape Drawing.
--Landscapes in Watercolor.
Blake, William. Blake: Selected Poems & Letters. Bronowski, J., ed.
--The Book of Urizen.
--Drawings of William Blake: Ninety-two Pencil Studies. Keynes, Geoffrey, intro. by.
--Milton: A Poem.
--Songs of Innocence & of Experience.
Blakeborough, Richard. Legends of Highwaymen & Others.
Blakebrough, N., ed. Biochemical & Biological Engineering Science.
Blakely, Caroline. Occupations One.
Blakely, Jack. Introduction to the Properties of Crystal Surfaces.
Blakely, Pat. How Do We Smell?
--What's Skin For?
--Why Do We Have Hair?
--Why Do We Have Skeletons?
Blakemore, John, jt. auth. see Bondurant, Bob.
Blakeney, Michael. Australia & the Jewish Refugees, 1933-48.
Blaker, Alfred A. Photography: Art & Technique.
--Photography: Art & Technique.
Blaker, Karen. Intimate Secrets: Which to Keep & Which to Tell.
Blakeslee, Alton, et al. More FYI: Further Tips for Healthful Living. Brandt, Nat, ed.
Blakeslee, Thomas R. The Right Brain: A New Understanding of the Unconscious Mind & Its Creative Powers.
Blakey & Hutton. Engineering Mathematics.
Blamires, Harry. The Bloomsday Book: A Guide Through Joyce's Ulysses.
--On Christian Truth.
Blamires, Harry, ed. A Guide to Twentieth-Century Literature in English.
Blamires, Harry, et al. Chosen Vessels: Portraits of Ten Outstanding Christian Men. Turner, Charles, ed.
Blanch, Lesley. Pierre Loti: The Legendary Romantic.
Blanch, Stuart Y. The Burning Bush.
Blanchard, Charles A. Getting Things from God.
Blanchard, Homer D., ed. Organs of Our Time.
Blanchard, Homer D., tr. see Klais, Hans G.
Blanchard, Homer D., tr. see Lindow, Ch. W.
Blanchard, Kenneth H., jt. auth. see Hersey, Paul.
Blanchard, Marjorie. The Sprouter's Cookbook: For Fast Kitchen Crops.
Blanchard, Nina. How to Break into Motion Pictures, Television Commercials & Modeling.
Blanchard, Paul. Southern Italy.
--Southern Italy: From Rome to Calabria.
Blanchard, Robert G. The First Editions of John Buchan: A Collector's Bibliography.
Blanchfield, William C. & Oser, Jacob. Economics: Reality Through Theory.
Blanchfield, William C., jt. auth. see Oser, Jacob.
Blanco, Ralph F. Prescriptions for Children with Learning & Adjustment Problems.
Blanco, Richard L. Rommel the Desert Warrior: The Afrika Korps in World War II.
Bland, Brian F. Crop Production: Cereals & Legumes.
Bland, C. C., tr. see De Nogent, Guibert.
Bland, Jeffrey. Nutraerobics.
--Nutraerobics: The Complete Individualized Nutrition & Fitness Program for Life after 30.
Bland, John & Schoenauer, Norbert. University Housing in Canada.
Blandford, Percy W. Building Better Beds.
--Fifty-Eight Home Shelving & Storage Projects.
--Fifty-Three Space-Saving Built-In Furniture Projects.
--Master Handbook of Woodworking Techniques.
--One Hundred Eleven & Garden Projects-from Boxes & Bins to Tables & Tools.
--Practical Knots & Ropework.
Blanding, Don. Paradise Loot.
Blanding, Warren. Blanding's Practical Physical Distribution.
Blandino, Betty. Coiled Pottery: Traditional & Contemporary Ways.
Blandino, Giovanni. Theories on the Nature of Life.
Blane, Linda. Development of Psycho-Motor Competence: Selected Readings.
Blane, William N. Excursion Through the United States & Canada During the Years 1822-1823.
Blaney, D., jt. auth. see May, Ernest.
Blank. Chest Radiographic Analysis.
Blank, Chotsie. California Artists Cookbook.
Blank, H., jt. ed. see Muller, W.
Blank, Helen & Wilkins, Amy. State Child Care Fact Book 1986. Children's Defense Fund Staff, ed.
Blank, Joan C., jt. ed. see Kimmel, Karen S.
Blank, Joani. Good Vibrations: The Complete Guide to Vibrators.
Blank, Marion S., compiled by. Working with People: A Selected Social Casework Bibliography.
Blank, Robert H. Regional Diversity of Political Values: Idaho Political Culture.
Blank, Sheldon H. Prophetic Faith in Isaiah.
Blank, Steven. Practical Business Research Methods.
Blanken, M. C. Force of Order & Methods... An American View into the Dutch Directed Society.
Blankenagel, John C., ed. see Pascal, Blaise.
Blankenbaker, E. Keith. Modern Plumbing.
Blankenburg, Peter von. Agricultural Extension Systems in Some African & Asian Countries.
Blankenship, A. B., jt. auth. see Breen, George E.
Blankenship, A. Wade. Earning, Saving, Investing... & Planning.
Blankenship, Martha L. & Moer Chen, Barbara D. Home Economics Education.
Blankenship, Russell. American Literature As an Expression of the National Mind.
Blankenship, William. Blood Stripe.
Blankenship, William D. Brotherly Love.
Blankenstein, M. Van & Welbergen, U. R. The Development of the Infant: The First Year of Life in Photographs.
Blankfort, Michael. An Exceptional Man.
Blanpain, Jan, et al. National Health Insurance & Health Resources: The European Experience.
Blanpain, Roger, ed. Employee Participation at the Level of the Enterprise: Labour Relations at the European Level & in Different Countries.
--Guaranteed Income Funds: Labour Relations at the European Level.
Blanshard, Brand. Nature of Thought.
--The Uses of a Liberal Education, & Other Talks to Students.
Blansitt, Edward L., Jr., ed. see Linguistic Association of Canada & the U. S. Staff.
Blanton, Cherie. A Little Fur in the Meringue Never Really Hurts the Filling.
Blanton, Linda L. Elementary Composition Practice.
--Elementary Composition Practice Book 1.
Blanton, Mary T. God Made It All!
--Knock on a Door.
Blaquiere, A., et al. Quantitative & Qualitative Games.
Blaquiere, A., et al, eds. Dynamical Systems & Microphysics.
Blaquiere, Austin. Nonlinear System Analysis.
Blaquriere, Austin & Leitmann, George, eds. Dynamical Systems & Microphysics.
Blase, M., et al. Readings in International & Agricultural Economic Development.
Blasecki. Mechanisms of Immunity to Virus-Induced Tumors.
Blaser, A., ed. Data Base Techniques for Pictorial Applications.
Blaser, A., ed. see IBM Informatik Symposium Staff.
Blaser, Werner. Architecture Nineteen Seventy to Nineteen Eighty in Switzerland.
Blaser, Werner, ed. Myron Goldsmith: Concepts & Buildings.
Blashfield, Jean. The Ghost Tower.
Blashfield, Jean & Ward, James M. Faeriemound of Dragonkind.
--Gnomes--One Hundred, Dragons--Zero.
Blasis, Carlo. The Code of Terpsichore.
Blasis, Celeste de see De Blasis, Celeste.
Blasius, W. Problems of Life Research.
Blassingame, John W. & Henderson, Mae G. Antislavery Newspapers & Periodicals: Annotated Index of Letters, 1817 - 1871, Vol. III: 1836-1854.
Blate. The Natural Healer's Acupressure Handbook.
Blate, Michael. The Natural Healer's Acupressure Handbook: G-Jo Fingertip Technique.
--The Tao of Health: The Way of Total Well-Being.
Blatner, Barbara Ann. The Pope in Space.
Blatner, Howard A. Acting-In: Practical Applications of Psychodramatic Methods.
Blatt, Art. Gun Digest Book of Trap & Skeet Shooting.
Blatt, J. & Weisskopf, V. F. Theoretical Nuclear Physics.
Blatter, Dorothy. Cap & Candle.
Blattner, John. Growing in the Fruit of the Spirit.
Blattner, John W., et al. Encyclopedia for the TRS-80. Putnam, Katherine & Comiskey, Kate, eds.
Blatty, William P. The Exorcist.

--Legion.
Blau, Clare, ed. see Worrell, Estelle A.
Blau, Diane S., jt. auth. see Kottler, Jeffrey A.
Blau, Gary. Human Resource Accounting.
Blau, Peter M. Exchange & Power in Social Life.
Blau, Rosalie, et al. Activities for School-Age Child Care.
Blauberg, I. V., et al. Systems Theory: Philosophical & Methodological Problems.
Blaug, Mark. Education & the Employment Problem in Developing Countries.
Blaustein, Albert P., ed. Fundamental Legal Documents of Communist China.
Blaustein, Bernard D., ed. Chemical Reactions in Electrical Discharges.
Blaustein, Saul J. & Craig, Isabel. An International Review of Unemployment Insurance Schemes.
Blaxter, J. H. The Early Life History of Fish.
Blaxter, K. L., ed. see Symposium on Energy Metabolism, Troon Scotland, 3d, 1964.
Blayne, Diana. Dark Surrender.
--A Loving Arrangement.
--Night of the Unicorn.
--White Sand, Wild Sea.
Blazac, Honore de see De Balzac, Honore.
Blaze-Gosden, Tony. Drug Abuse: The Truth about Today's Drug Scene.
Blazer, Dan G., jt. ed. see Busse, Ewald W.
Blazer, Howard A. Angels, Their Origin, Nature, Mission & Destiny.
Blazier, Kenneth D. Workbook for Planning Christian Education.
Blazier, William H. Lights! Action! Camera! Learn!
Blazquez, Jose M. Diccionario De las Religiones Prerromanas De Hispania.
Bleach, Mervyn. CZ125, 175, & 175 Trail '69 - '76.
--Garelli Mopeds '72 to '78.
--Honda C50, C70 & C90 '72 - '81.
--Honda Owner's Workshop Manual: XR75 Dirt Bikes '72 - '78.
Bleaney, Michael F. Underconsumption Theories.
Blecher, George, tr. see Jersild, P. C.
Blecher, George, tr. see Lagercrantz, Rose.
Blecher, Lone T., tr. see Jersild, P. C.
Blecher, Melvin, ed. Methods in Receptor Research.
Blechman, Fred. Sanyo MBC 550-555 Beginners & Intermediate Guide.
Blechman, Fred, et al. Encyclopedia for the TRS-80. Putnam, Katherine & Comiskey, Kate, eds.
Blechman, Mark, jt. auth. see Fox, Donna R.
Blechschmidt, E. The Beginnings of Human Life. Transemantics, Inc., tr. from Ger.
Bleck, Robert T., jt. auth. see Araoz, Daniel L.
Blecke, Curtis J. & Gotthilf, Daniel L. Financial Analysis for Decision Making.
Bledsoe, Jane K., ed. see Barnes, Lucinda & Glenn, Constance W.
Bledsoe, Jerry. Carolina Curiosities: Jerry Bledsoe's Outlandish Guide to the Dadblamest Things to See & Do in North Carolina.
Bledsoe, Thomas. Meanwhile Back at the Henhouse: A Novel.
Bleehen, Norman M. Workshop on Radiotheraphy for Lung Cancer: King's College, Cambridge, England, June 26-30, 1984, Cancer Treatment Symposia.
Bleek, Robert T., jt. auth. see Araoz, Daniel L.
Blegvad, Erik, jt. auth. see Blegvad, Lenore.
Blegvad, Erik, jt. auth. see Livingston, Myra C.
Blegvad, Erik, illus. Burnie's Hill: A Traditional Rhyme.
Blegvad, Lenore. Moon-Watch Summer.
Blegvad, Lenore & Blegvad, Erik. Great Hamster Hunt.
--Mister Jensen & Cat.
--One Is for the Sun.
Blegvad, Lenore, ed. Hark! Hark! the Dogs Do Bark: And Other Rhymes About Dogs.
--The Parrot in the Garret & Other Rhymes about Dwellings.
Bleher, Petra, tr. see Nicolai, Jurgen.
Blehl, Vincent & Connolly, Francis X., eds. Newman's Apologia: A Classic Reconsidered.
Bleiberg, Aaron H. & Leubling, Harry. Parents Guide to Cleft Palate Habilitation: The Team Approach.
Bleiberg, German. Diccionario de Historia de Espana.
Bleicher, M. N., tr. see Bronshtein, I. N. & Semendyayev, K. A.
Bleifeld, Maurice. Biology, Including Modern Biology in Review.
--How to Prepare for the College Board Achievement Test - Biology.
Bleifeld, Maurice, ed. see Edwards, Gabrielle & Cimmino, Marion.
Bleikasten, Andre. Faulkner's As I Lay Dying. Little, Roger, tr.
Bleiler, E. F., ed. see Dunsany, Lord.
Bleiler, E. F., ed. see Woelcken, Fritz.
Bleiler, Ellen H., tr. see Donizetti, Gaetano.
Bleiler, Ellen H., tr. & see Mozart, Wolfgang A.
Bleiler, Everett F. Essential Japanese Grammar.
Blelloch, A., ed. Measurements of the Impacts of Materials Substitution: A Case Study in the Automobile Industry.
Blensly, Douglas L. & Plank, Tom M. Accounting Desk Book.
Blerkom, Jonathan Van & Motta, Pietro. The Cellular Basis of Mammalian Reproduction.
Bles, W. & Brandt, T., eds. Disorders of Posture & Gait.
Bleuler, K. & Reetz, A., eds. Differential Geometrical Methods in Mathematical Physics.
Bleuler, K., et al, eds. Differential Geometrical Methods in Mathematical Physics II: Proceedings, University of Bonn, July 13-16, 1977.
Blevins, Dorothy. The Diabetic & Health Care.
Blevins, Leon W. The Young Voter's Manual: A Topical Dictionary of American Government & Politics.
Blewitt, Mary. Celestial Navigation.
Blexrud, Jan. A Toast to Sober Spirits & Joyous Juices: A Collection of Non-Alcoholic Beverage Recipes.
Bley, Nancy S. & Thornton, Carol A. Teaching Mathematics to the Learning Disabled.
Blickenstaff, R. T., jt. auth. see Hadd, H. E.
Bliek, Ruth de, jt. auth. see Pena, Alberto.
Bliemetzrieder, Franz P. Literarische Polemik zu Beginn des grossen Abendlaendischen Schismas.
Bligh, Donald, jt. auth. see Beard, Ruth M.
Bligh, Donald, ed. Professionalism & Flexibility in Learning: SRHE Leverhulme VI.
Bligh, William. A Voyage to the South Seas.
Blight, John. Holiday Sea Sonnets.
Blij, Harm J. De see De Blij, Harm J. & Muller, Peter O.
Blikle, A., ed. see Mathematical Foundations of Computer Science Symposium Staff.
Blinder, Alan S., jt. auth. see Baumol, William J.
Blinder, Alan S. & Friedman, Philip, eds. Natural Resources, Uncertainty, & General Equilibrium System Memory: Essays in Honor of Rafael Lusky.
Blinder, S. M. Foundations of Quantum Dynamics.
Blinn, James D., ed. Cost-of-Risk Survey 1985. Levin, Michael R.
Blish, James. And All the Stars a Stage.
--Black Easter.
--Cities in Flight.
--Titan's Daughter.
--Vor.
Blish, James & Lawrence, J. A. Star Trek.
Blishen, Edward. Uncommon Entrance.
Bliss, Anne. North American Dye Plants.
Bliss, Beatrice L. Reluctant Pioneer: Mary Vowell Adams.
Bliss, Corinne D. The Same River Twice.
Bliss, Edwin C. Doing It Now: A Twelve-Step Program for Curing Procrastination & Achieving Your Goals.
--Getting Things Done.
--Getting Things Done: The ABC's of Time Management.
Bliss, Joan, et al. Qualitative Data Analysis for Educational Research: A Guide to Uses of Systemic Networks.
Bliss, Michael. The Discovery of Insulin.
Bliss, P., jt. auth. see Barnes, D.
Bliss, Richard. Origins: Two Models. Gish, Duane T. & Moore, John N., eds.
Blissett, William. Editing Illustrated Books: Papers Given at the Fifteenth Annual Conference on Editorial Problems, University of Toronto, 2-3 November 1979.
Blissmer, Robert H., et al. Microsoft Works Short BASIC Combo 88-89.
Blitt, Casey D., ed. Monitoring in Anesthesia & Critical Care Medicine.
Blitzer, Barbara. Nothing but the Best for Baby.
Bliven, Bruce, Jr. From Pearl Harbor to Okinawa.
Bloch, ed. Journal of Jewish Bibliography.
Bloch, Alfred, ed. The Real Poland: An Anthology of National Self-Perception.
Bloch, C., ed. Many-Body Description of Nuclear Structure & Reactions.
Bloch, Dorothy. So the Witch Won't Eat Me: Fantasy & the Child's Fear of Infanticide.
Bloch, Ernest. Inside Investment Banking.
Bloch, Lucienne S. Finders Keepers.
Bloch, Marc. Memoirs of War, 1914-15. Fink, Carole, tr. from Fr.
--The Royal Touch: Sacred Monarchy & Scrofula in England & France. Anderson, J. E., tr.
Bloch, Maurice, ed. Political Language & Oratory in Traditional Society.
Bloch, Michael. Operation Willi: The Nazi Plot to Capture the Duke of Windsor.
Bloch, Norman J. & Michaels, John G. Linear Algebra.
Bloch, Penelope, jt. auth. see Harris, Ron.
Bloch, R. Howard. Moses in the Promised Land.
Bloch, Ricard I., jt. auth. see Zack, Arnold M.
Bloch, Robert. Cold Chills.
--Out of My Head. Mann, Jim, ed.
Bloch-Dermant, Janine. Le Verre en France, d'Emile Galle a Nos Jours.
Block, Barry H. Foot Talk: A Complete Guide to the Good Health & Care of the Feet.
Block, Dennis J., et al, eds. The Corporate Counsellor's Desk Book.
Block, Eric, ed. Reactions of Organosulfur Compounds.
Block, Herbert. Herblock Special Report.
--Herblock Through the Looking Glass.
Block, J. Bradford. The Signs & Symptoms of Chemical Exposure.
Block, Jean L., jt. auth. see Minton, Michael H.
Block, Jerome B., ed. Oncology.
Block, Joel D. & Greenberg, Diane. Women & Friendship.
Block, Julian. Julian Block's Guide to Year-Round Tax Savings, 1984.
--Julian Block's Guide to Year-Round Tax Savings, 1985.
Block, Lawrence. A.K.A. Chip Harrison.
--Ariel.
--The Burglar Who Painted Like Mondrian.
--Eight Million Ways to Die.
--In the Midst of Death.
--Like a Lamb to Slaughter.
--Sometimes They Bite.
--A Stab in the Dark.
--Telling Lies for Fun & Profit: A Manual for Fiction Writers.
--Time to Murder & Create.
--When the Sacred Gin Mill Closes.
Block, Michael, ed. Wallis & Edward: Letters 1931-1937.
Block, Richard A., ed. Operator of Uninspected Towing Vessels (200-Tons-200-Miles)
Block, Richard A., et al, eds. Limited Master, Mate & Operator License Study Course.
Block, Stanley B. & Hirt, Geoffrey A. Foundations of Financial Management.
Block, Thomas H. Orbit.
Blockcolsky, V. D., et al. Peel & Put Complete Program for Speech & Language Development.
Blockcolsky, Valeda & Frazer, Joan M. Star Trails: Reproducible Carryover Worksheets for R, S, L, TH, SH, CH.
Blockley, D. I. The Nature of Structure-Design & Safety.
Blockley, John. Creative Watercolour Techniques.
Blocksma, Dewey, jt. auth. see Blocksma, Mary.
Blocksma, Mary & Blocksma, Dewey. Easy-to-Make Water Toys That Really Work.
Blocksom, Claudia. It's Your World.
Bloedow, Edmund F. Alcibiades Reexamined.
Bloem, Diane. A Womans Workshop on Proverbs.
Bloesch, Donald G. Battle for the Trinity: The Debate over Inclusive God-Language.
--The Struggle of Prayer.
Blofeld, John, tr. see Huang Po.
Blois, M. S., ed. Symposium on Free Radicals in Biological Systems.
Blok, C. & Jezewski, W. Dictionnaire Illustre de l'Automobile "Kluwer," en 6 Langues.
Blom, Eric. Everyman's Dictionary of Music.
Blomberg, Belinda. Mobility & Sedentism: The Navajo of Black Mesa Arizona.
Blomberg, Craig, jt. auth. see Wenham, David.
Blommers, Paul J. & Forsyth, Robert A. Elementary Statistical Methods in Psychology & Education.
Blondel, Jean. World Leaders: Heads of Government in the Postwar Period.
Blonder, Ellen, illus. Parade Pony.
Blonk, W. A. Transport & Regional Development.
Blonsky, Richard & Givens, Mary J. The Exercise Program.
Blood, F. R., ed. Essays in Toxicology. Incl. Vol. 1; Vol. 2; Vol. 3. Hayes, Wayland J., Jr; Vol. 4; Vol. 5; Vol. 6; Vol. 7. Acad Pr.
Blood-Horse, Inc. Staff, ed. Auctions of 1981.
--A Guide to Equine Facilities & Services: The List, 1987.
--Principal Winners Abroad of 1979.
--Principal Winners Abroad of 1980.
--Sires of Runners of 1979.
--Stakes Winners of 1981.
Blood-Horse Staff. The Fifth Breeders' Cup: Annual Supplement to Blood-Horse.
Blood Horse Staff. The Third Breeders' Cup: Annual Supplement.
Blood Horse Staff, ed. Stallion Register, 1981.
Blood-Horse Staff, ed. Stallion Register, 1983: Annual Supplement to the Blood-Horse.
Bloodstein, Oliver. Speech Pathology: An Introduction.
Bloodworth, Dennis. The Messiah & the Mandarins.
Bloom, Barry R. & David, John R., eds. In Vitro Methods in Cell-Mediated & Tumor Immunity.
Bloom, Barry R. & Glade, Philip R., eds. In Vitro Methods in Cell-Mediated Immunity.
Bloom, C. O. & Kazarinoff, N. D. Short Wave Radiation Problems in Homogeneous Media: Asymptotic Solutions.
Bloom, Celia. Seventy Years & Never a Dull Moment.
Bloom, Edward A., et al, eds. The Order of Poetry: An Introduction.
Bloom, Freddy. Our Deaf Children: Into the 80's.
Bloom, Gilbert D., jt. auth. see Newton, Grant W.
Bloom, Harold. The Flight to Lucifer: A Gnostic Fantasy.
--Ringers in the Tower.
Bloom, Herschel M. & Mills, David W. Partnership Taxation: An Advanced Tax Program, 1985.
Bloom, J. Harvey. Folk-Lore, Old Customs & Superstitions in Shakespeare Land.
Bloom, Kathryn, et al. An Arts in Education Source Book: A View from the JDR 3rd Fund.
Bloom, Lawrence, et al, eds. Facilitating Communication Change: An Interpersonal Approach to Therapy & Counseling.
Bloom, Lynn Z. The Easy Connection.
Bloom, M. H., ed. see Computers in Aerodynamics Symposium Staff.
Bloom, Marc. The Marathon: What It Takes to Go the Distance.
Bloom, Marc, jt. auth. see Shorter, Frank.
Bloom, Martin. The Paradox of Helping: Introduction to the Philosophy of Scientific Practice.
Bloom, Mortimer, jt. auth. see Booth, Verne H.
Bloom, S. R., ed. Gut Hormones. Polack, J. M.
Bloom, Stanley. Beneath the Fur.
Bloom, Ursula. When Doctors Love.
Bloom, Ursula see Burns, Sheila, pseud.
Bloom, Ursula see Essex, Mary, pseud.
Bloomenthal, Harold S. Securities Law Handbook, 1985.
Bloomer, M. & Shaw, K. E. Challenge of Education Change: The Content & Organization of Schooling.
Bloomfield, Arthur. The Changing Climate.
Bloomfield, B. C., ed. Middle East Studies & Libraries: A Felicitation Volume for J. D. Pearson.
Bloomfield, Dennis A., jt. auth. see Simon, Hansjorg.
Bloomfield, Jay A., ed. Lakes of New York State, Vol. 3: Ecology of the Lakes of East-Central New York.
Bloomfield, Leonard. Linguistic Aspects of Science.
Bloomfield, Molly M. Chemistry & the Living Organism.
Bloomgarden, Barry. Your Future in Insurance Careers.
Bloomingdale, L., ed. Attention Deficit Disorders: Diagnostic, Cognitive & Therapeutic Understanding.
Bloor, C. H. Pathology.
Bloor, David. Knowledge & Social Imagery.
Bloss, F. D. Crystallography & Crystal Chemistry.
--Introduction to the Methods of Optical Crystallography.
Bloss, Janet A. New Girl.
--Who's Afraid of Sixth Grade?
Blotnick, Srully. Winning: The Psychology of Successful Investing.
Blough, H. A. & Tiffany, J. M. Cell Membranes & Viral Envelopes.
Blough, H. A. & Tiffany, J. M., eds. Cell Membranes & Viral Envelopes.
Blount, Charles. Miscellaneous Works.
Blount, Roy, Jr. What Men Don't Tell Women.
Blowers, Margaret G. & Sims, Roberta S. How to Read an ECG.
Bluck, R. S. Plato's Phaedo.
Bludau, August. Die Pilgerreise der Aetheria.
Bludau, Lea V. Mosaics from Memories.
Blue, Allan G. Pictorial History of the B24 Liberator Bomber.
Blue, Anthony D., ed. see Zagat, Eugene H., Jr. & Zagat, Nina S.
Blue, Martha, jt. auth. see Davidson, Marion.
Blue, Rose. Cold Rain on the Water.
--My Mother the Witch.
Bluestein, Bill & Bluestein, Enid. Mom, How Come I'm Not Thin?
Bluestein, Enid, jt. auth. see Bluestein, Bill.
Bluglass, Robert. A Guide to the Mental Health Act, 1983.
Bluhm, Donna L. Teaching the Retarded Visually Handicapped: Indeed They Are Children.
Blum, A & McHugh, P. Self-Reflection in the Arts & Sciences.
Blum, Alexander. Russian Dialogues.
Blum, Andre. The Origins of Printing & Engraving. Lydenberg, H. M., tr. from Fr.
Blum, Deborah. Bad Karma: A True Story of Obsession, & Murder.
Blum, Eva M. & Blum, Richard H. Alcoholism: Modern Psychological Approaches to Treatment.
Blum, Fred. Music Monographs in Series: A Bibliography of Numbered Monograph Series in the Field of Music Current Since 1945.
Blum, Howard. Wishful Thinking.
Blum, James D. & Goldstein, Mark S. Business Law: Selected Questions & Unofficial Answers Indexed to Content Specification Outline.
Blum, Jerome. Our Forgotten Past: Seven Centuries of Life on the Land.
Blum, John M. The Progressive Presidents: Theodore Roosevelt, Woodrow Wilson, Franklin D. Roosevelt, Lyndon B. Johnson.
--Republican Roosevelt.
--V Was for Victory: Politics & American Culture During World War 2.

Authors

Blum, John M., et al. The National Experience.
--The National Experience: A History of the United States.
--The National Experience: A History of the United States.
--The National Experience: A History of the United States.
Blum, K., ed. Alcohol & Opiates: Neurochemical & Behavioral Mechanisms.
Blum, Paul Von see Von Blum, Paul.
Blum, Richard H., jt. auth. see Blum, Eva M.
Blum, Richard H., et al. Society & Drugs, Social & Cultural Observations. Incl. Vol. 2. Students & Drugs, College & High School Observations. Jossey-Bass.
Blum, Robert. Drawing the Line: The Origin of the American Containment Policy in South Asia.
Blum, Robert S. The Girl from the Emeraline Island.
Blum, William & Hogaboom, George B. Principles of Electroplating & Electroforming.
Bluman, G. W. & Cole, J. D. Similarity Methods for Differential Equations.
Blumberg, Abraham S., jt. auth. see Niederhoffer, Arthur.
Blumberg, Abraham S., ed. Law & Order: The Scales of Justice.
Blumberg, Leda. The Horselover's Handbook: An Introduction to Owning, Caring for, & Riding Horses.
Blumberg, Morris B. Passion in China.
Blumberg, Rhoda L. & Dwarkai, Leela. India's Educated Women.
Blumberg, Rhonda. Sharks.
--UFO.
Blume, C. & Jakob, W. PASRO Pascal for Robots.
Blume, Friedrich, et al. Protestant Church Music.
Blume, Howard. The Backyard Birder's Journal.
Blume, Philip & Freier, Esther, eds. Enzymology in the Practice of Laboratory Medicine.
Blume, Stuart S. Perspectives In the Sociology of Science.
Blumensen, Martin. The Vilde Affair: Beginnings of the French Resistance.
Blumenson, Martin. Anzio: The Gamble That Failed.
Blumenstengel, A. Twenty-Four Exercises for Violin, Op. 33.
Blumenthal, Arthur. Giulio Parigi's Stage Designs: Florence & the Early Baroque Spectacle. Freedberg, S. J., ed.
Blumenthal, H. T., ed. see International Association of Gerontology Staff.
Blumenthal, Henry. France & the United States: Their Diplomatic Relations, 1789-1914.
Blumenthal, John. The Case of the Hardboiled Dicks: A Novel.
Blumenthal, Joseph C. English 2200: A Programed Course in Grammar & Usage.
--English 2600: A Programed Course in Grammar & Usage.
--English 3200: A Programed Course in Grammar & Usage.
Blumenthal, Lassor A. Successful Business Writing: How to Write Successful Letters, Proposals, Resumes, & Speeches.
Blumenthal, Paul Illus. by see Burkart, Betty Lou.
Blumenthal, Robert M. Markov Processes & Potential Theory.
Blumenthal, Sidney. The Permanent Campaign.
--The Permanent Campaign: Inside the World of Elite Political Operatives.
Blumenthal, Vera De see De Blumenthal, Vera.
Blumfield, H. H., et al. TM: Discovering Inner Energy & Overcoming Stress.
Blumgart, L., jt. auth. see Kennedy, A. C.
Blumgart, L. H., ed. The Biliary Tract.
Blumhardt, Doreen & Brake, Brian. Craft New Zealand: The Art of the Craftsman.
Blumner, Jack. Your Basic Love Story.
Blunck, Jurgen. Mars & Its Satellites: A Detailed Commentary on the Nomenclature.
--Mars & Its Satellites: A Detailed Commentary on the Nomenclature.
Blundell, John. Physiological Psychology.
Blundell, T. L., jt. auth. see Noble, D.
Blundell, T. L., jt. ed. see Noble, D.
Blunden, Edmund. Undertones of War.
Blunden, John & Curry, Nigel, eds. The Changing Countryside.
Blunt, Anthony & Lockspeiser, Edward. French Art & Music since Fifteen Hundred.
Blunt, Jerry. Composite Art of Acting.
Blunt, John H. Dictionary of Sects, Heresies, Ecclesiastical Parties & Schools of Religious Thought.
Blunt, M. H. The Blood of Sheep: Composition & Function.
Blust, Robert A. The Proto-Oceanic Palatals.
Bluth, Brad & Bluth, Toby. Siegfried's Silent Night.
Bluth Brothers Staff. A Day for Knights.
--Somebody's Hero.
Bluth, Toby. The Buddies Tenderfoot.
--Cinderella.
--Little Luv Angel.
--Mark Twain's Tom Sawyer.
Bluth, Toby, jt. auth. see Bluth, Brad.
Bluth, Toby, illus. & retold by. Babes in Toyland.
Bluthardt, O. D. Universal Energy & Intelligence.
Bly. Complete Consultants Library.
Bly, John. The Confident Collector: How to Recognize an Authentic Antique.
Bly, Robert. The Man in the Black Coat Turns.
--Out of the Rolling Ocean & Other Love Poems.
Bly, Stephen. Quality Living in a Complicated Age.
Blyakhman, L. & Shkaratan, O. Man at Work.
Blye, Irwin & Friedberg, Ardy. Secrets of a Private Eye: Or, How to Be Your Own Private Investigator.
Blyth, Alan. Opera on Record.
Blythe, Ronald. Characters & Their Landscapes.
--The View in Winter: Reflections on Old Age. Wolff, Helen, ed.
Blyton, Enid. A Cat in Fairyland & Other Tales.
--The Enchanted Sea & Other Tales.
--Five Go Adventuring Again.
--Five on a Treasure Island.
--The Goblin Aeroplane: And Other Tales.
--A Puppy in Wonderland: And Other Tales.
BNA Editorial Staff. Law Officer's Pocket Manual, 1987-88.
BNA Environment & Safety Services Staff. Air Water Pollution Control.
BNA Library Staff & King, Kamla J., eds. BNA's Directory of State Courts, Judges & Clerks: A State-by-State Listing.
BNA's Environment & Safety Services Staff. Loss Prevention & Control.
Boa, Elizabeth & Reid, J. H. Critical Strategies: German Fiction in the Twentieth Century.
Boa, Kenneth, jt. auth. see Livgren, Kerry.
Boadella, David. Wilhelm Reich: The Evolution of His Work.
Boaden, James. The Plays of James Boaden. Backscheider, P. R. & Cohan, Steven, eds.
Boag, David & Alexander, Mike. The Atlantic Puffin.
Boak, Arthur E. Two Studies in Later Roman & Byzantine Administration.
Boak, Gerald. The Prediction Book of Taromancy.
Boakes, R. A. & Halliday, M. S. Inhibition & Learning.
Boal, D. H. & Kamal, A. N., eds. Particles & Fields 1.
Boal, David H. & Woloshyn, Richard M., eds. Short-Distance Phenomena in Nuclear Physics.
Boalt, G., et al, eds. Communication & Communication Barriers in Sociology.
Boamah-Wiafe, Daniel. Africa Today: Its Peoples & Comtempory Cultures.
Boar, Bernard H. Application Prototyping: A Project Management Perspective.
Boardman, A. D. Physics Programs. Incl. Applied Physics; Magnetism; Optics; Solid State Physics. Wiley.
Boardman, Charles. An Artistic & Romantic Chronicle of the New England Seacoast.
Boardman, David. Graphicacy & Geography Teaching.
Boardman, Elliot B. see Hill, Richard F., et al.
Boardman, Helen E, et al. The Neglected Battered Child Syndrome: Role Reversal in Parents.
Boardman, J. M. & Vogt, R. M. Homotopy Invariant Algebraic Structures on Topological Spaces.
Boardman, William K., jt. auth. see Adams, Henry E.
Boardroom's Experts & Editors. The Boss's Encyclopedia.
--Business Confidential.
--Consumers Confidential.
--Health & Wellness Confidential.
Boas, Franz. Chinook Indian Language.
--A Franz Boas Reader: Shaping of American Anthropology, 1883-1911. Stocking, George W., ed.
--Introduction to Handbook of American Indian Languages. Holder, Preston, ed. Bd. with Indian Linguistic Families of America North of Mexico. Powell, J. W. U of Nebr Pr.
--Introduction to the Handbook of American Indian Languages.
--Race, Language & Culture.
Boas, Frederick S. An Introduction to Eighteenth Century Drama, 1700-1780.
--An Introduction to Tudor Drama.
--Thomas Heywood.
Boas, Frederick S., ed. Songs & Lyrics from the English Masques & Light Operas.
Boas, George. The Inquiring Mind: An Introduction to Epistemology.
Boas, George, jt. auth. see Lovejoy, Arthur O.
Boas, Maurits. It Did Happen.
Boas, Maurits I. Preludes.
Boase, Paul H., jt. auth. see Eisenson, Jon.
Boase, Paul H., jt. auth. see Whitman, Richard F.
Boat, Jaydee. Dining In - Denver.
Boateng, Yaw M. The Return.
Boatman, Russell. What the Bible Says about End Time.
--What the Bible Says about the Church.
Boatner, Mark M., III. The Civil War Dictionary.
Boatner, Maxine & Gates, John E. A Dictionary of American Idioms. Makkai, Adam, ed.
Boatner, Patricia. All Our Tomorrows.
Boatwright, Howard. Introduction to the Theory of Music.
Boatwright, Victor T., jt. ed. see Sheets, Herman E.
Boba, A. Essays on Future Trends in Anaesthesia.
Bobak, Irene, jt. auth. see Jensen, Margaret.
Bobak, Irene M. & Jensen, Margaret D. Essentials of Maternity Nursing.
--A Modular Study Guide to Maternity Care.
Bobak, Irene M., jt. auth. see Jensen, Margaret D.
Bobart, Henry H. Basketwork Through the Ages.
Bobath, B. Abnormal Postural Reflex Activity Caused by Brain Lesions.
Bobbi. Feelings from Within.
Bobbitt, Arch N. & Sipe, Frederic C. Work's Indiana Practice with Forms, 1971-1981.
Bobgan, Deidre. Lord of the Dance: The Beauty of the Disciplined Life.
Bobik, Joseph, ed. Nature of Philosophical Inquiry.
Bobker, Lee R. Elements of Film.
--Making Movies: From Script to Screen.
Bobrow, Daniel & Kiczales, Gregor. Programming with the Common Lisp Object System.
Bobrow, Edwin E. & Bobrow, Mark D. Marketing Handbook.
Bobrow, Edwin E. & Wizenberg, Larry, eds. Sales Manager's Handbook.
Bobrow, Jerry. Barron's How to Prepare for the Civil Service Examinations.
--How to Prepare for the Law School Admission Test (LSAT)
Bobrow, Mark D., jt. auth. see Bobrow, Edwin E.
Bocage, Ducarmel. The General Economic Theory of Francois Perroux.
Boccaccio, G. Chamber of Love.
Boccaccio, Giovanni. The Corbaccio. Cassell, Anthony K., ed. & tr. from Ital.
--Decameron.
--Filostrato of Giovanni Boccaccio. Griffin, Nathaniel E. & Myrick, Arthur B., trs.
Bocchi, Achille. Symbolicarum Quaestionum de Universo Genere. Orgel, Stephen, ed.
Bochkarev, Y. Soviet Russian Stories of the 1960's & 1970's.
Bochkov, A. E. & Zaikov, G. E. Chemistry of the O-Glycosidic Bond: Formation & Cleavage.
Bochkova, O. P. & Shreyder, E. Y. Spectroscopic Analysis of Gaseous Mixtures.
Bochmann, G. V. Architecture of Distributed Computer Systems.
Bochner, Salomon. Role of Mathematics in the Rise of Science.
Bock, Audie. Japanese Film Directors.
Bock, Darrell L. Proclamation from Prophecy & Pattern: Lucan Old Testament Christiology.
Bock, Fred G., et al. Carcinogenesis: Recent Investigations.
Bock, Hal. Save: Hockey's Brave Goalies.
Bock, P. Approaches to Earth Survey Problems Through the Use of Space Techniques.
Bock, Paul. In Search of a Responsible World Society: The Social Teachings of the World Council of Churches.
Bock, R. Darrell, jt. auth. see Mislevy, Robert.
Bock, Raymond F. Vitamin E: Key to Youthful Longevity.
Bock, Richard. Camper Cookery.
--The Galley Guide to Fine Food.
Bockelman, A. E. Practical Guide for Altar Guilds.
Bockelman, Wilfred. Money---Guilt or Excitement?
--You Can Help Make It Happen.
Bockelman, Wilfred, ed. Tapestry.
Bocker, Peter. ISDN: Concepts, Methods, & Systems.
Bockett, J. C., et al. Belfast: The Making of the City.
Bockhoff, K. H., ed. see Central Bureau for Nuclear Measurements Staff.
Bockmon, Guy A. & Starr, William J. Scored for Listening: A Guide to Music.
Bockris, J. O. Energy: The Solar Hydrogen Alternative.
Bockris, J. O. M. & Khan, S. U. Quantum Electrochemistry.
Bockris, John O. Energy Options: Real Economics & the Solar-Hydrogen System.
Bodanis, David. The Secret House: Twenty-Four Hours in the Strange & Unexpected World in Which We Spend Our Nights & Days.
Bodansky, Oscar. Biochemistry of Human Cancer.
Bodanza, Mary F. Clinical & Laboratory Procedures in the Physician's Office.
Bodde, Derk. Festivals in Classical China: New Year & Other Annual Observations During the Han Dynasty 206 B. C. - A. D. 220.
Boddington, M. J., et al, eds. Chlorinated Dioxins & Related Compounds 1984: Proceedings of the Fourth International Conference held at Ottawa, Canada October 16-18 1984.
Boddy, David, jt. auth. see Buchanan, David A.
Bode, Carl. Maryland.
Bode, Ch., jt. ed. see Martini, G. A.
Bodecker, N. M. It's Raining Said John Twaining: Danish Nursery Rhymes.
--Let's Marry Said the Cherry: & Other Nonsense Poems.
--The Lost String Quartet.
--The Mushroom Center Disaster.
Boden, Arthur, designed by. Typography Seven: The Annual of the Type Directors Club.
Boden, Deanna. You & Me.
Boden, P., jt. ed. see Black, R.
Boden, Robin, jt. auth. see MacLeod, Hilary.
Bodenheimer, Edgar, et al. The Anglo-American Legal System, Readings & Cases in Itroduction to.
Bodett, Tom. As Far As You Can Go Without a Passport: The View from the End of the Road.
Bodey & Rodriquez. Hospital Associated Infections in the Compromised Host.
Bodey, Hugh. Immigrants & Emigrants.
Bodger, Joan. Clever-Lazy: The Girl Who Invented Herself.
Bodger, Joan & Thurman, Mark. Belinda's Ball.
Bodie & Kane. Investments.
Bodie, Idella. South Carolina Women: They Dared to Lead.
Bodie, Idella F. A Hunt for Life's Extras, the Story of Archibald Rutledge.
Bodin, Frederik D. The Freelance Photographer's Handbook.
Bodin, Jean. Method for Easy Comprehension of History. Reynolds, Beatrice, tr.
Bodker, Cecil. The Leopard. Poulsen, Gunnar, tr. from Danish.
Bodkin, Cora, et al. Crafts for Your Leisure Years.
Bodnar, Edward W. & Mitchell, Charles. Cyriacus of Ancona's Journeys in the Propontis & the Northern Aegean: 1444-1445.
Bodner, Richard A. Secrets of Smart Airline Travelers.
Bodo, Ferenc J. A Drive Across Africa.
Bodo, John R. A Gallery of New Testament Rogues: From Herod to Satan.
Bodo, Peter & Hishey, David. Pele's New World.
Bodoni, Giambattista. Manuale Typografia.
Bodurtha, Frank T. Industrial Explosion Prevention & Protection.
Bodwell, C. E. & Adkins, J. S. Protein Quality in Humans: Assessment & in Vitro Estimation.
Body, R., jt. auth. see Evans, D.
Bodyazhina, V. I. Textbook of Obstetrics.
Boe, Eugene, jt. auth. see Agel, Jerome.
Boecker, Hans J. Law & the Administration of Justice in the Old Testament & Ancient East. Moiser, Jeremy, tr.
Boeckh, J. Anthony & Coghlan, Richard T., eds. The Stock Market & Inflation.
Boeckmann, J., tr. see Schill, Gottfried.
Boeckx, R., jt. ed. see Moyer, T.
Boeckx, Roger L., jt. auth. see Hicks, Jocelyn M.
Boehm, A. The Rigged Hiblert Space & Quantum Mechanics: Lectures in Mathematical Physics at the University of Texas at Austin.
Boehm, A., ed. see Drechsler, W. & Mayer, M. E.
Boehm, Barbara D., tr. see Grodecki, Louis & Brisac, Catherine.
Boehm, Bruce & Winn, Janet. Connecticut Low.
Boehm, C., ed. Calculus & Computer Science Theory: Proceedings of the Symposium in Rome, March 25-27, 1975.
Boehm, David & Benagh, Jim, eds. Guinness Sports Record Book 1987-1988.
Boehm, David A., ed. Daring Rascals: True Tales of the Outrageous.
--Guinness Sports Record Book 1988-89.
Boehm, David A., jt. ed. see Russel, Alan.
Boehm, Eric H. We Survived: Fourteen Histories of the Hidden & Hunted of Nazi Germany.
Boehm, Klaus, jt. auth. see Sharmon, Fay.
Boehm, Laszlo. Modern Music Notation.
Boehm, N. see Huth, F., et al.
Boehme, S., et al, eds. Astronomy & Astrophysics Abstracts, Vol. 13: Literature 1975, Pt. 1.
--Astronomy & Astrophysics Abstracts, Vol. 18: Literature 1976, Pt. 2.
--Astronomy & Astrophysics Abstracts, Vol. 19: Literature 1977, Pt. 1.
--Astronomy & Astrophysics Abstracts, Vol. 20: Literature 1977, Pt. 2.
Boehmer, Raquel. A Foraging Vacation: Edibles from Maine's Sea & Shore.
Boehne, Patricia J. J. V. Foix.
Boeing Computer Service Co. Staff & Lines, M. Vardell. Minicomputer Systems.
Boen, James R. & Zahn, Douglas A. The Human Side of Statistical Consulting.

Boening, John, ed. & intro. by. The Reception of Classical German Literature in England, 1760-1860: A Documentary History from Contemporary Periodicals. Incl. Vol. 1. General Introduction & Reviews from 1760 to 1813; Vol. 2. Reviews from 1813 to 1835; Vol. 3. Reviews from 1835 to 1860; Vol. 4. Authors from Bodmer to Klopstock; Vol. 5. Authors from Lavater to Novalis; Vol. 6. The Reception of Early German Romantics: Richter, the Brothers Schlegel, Tieck & Hoffmann; Vol. 7. General Critical Articles on Goethe & Reviews Which Discuss Goethe & Schiller Together, Arranged in Order of Appearance; Vol. 8. Reviews of Werther, Goethe's Early Works, His Poems & Faust; Vol. 9. The Works of Goethe's Midcareer, Wilhelm Meister & Such Works As Dichtung und Wahrheit, Etc; Vol. 10. The English Reception of Specific Works of Schiller, from the Early Plays to the Historical Works. Garland Pub.
Boeninger, Hildegard R. & Pietschmann, D., eds. Ich Lausche Dem Leben.
Boenisch, Edmond W., Jr., jt. auth. see Haney, C. Michele.
Boer, C. H. De see Harrison, R. G. & DeBoer, C. H.
Boer, Jan De see De Boer, Jan & Baillie, Thomas W.
Boer, K. W., ed. Sharing the Sun. Incl. Vol. 1. International & U. S. Programs Solar Flux; Vol. 2. Solar Collectors; Vol. 3. Solar Heating & Cooling Buildings; Vol. 4. Solar System, Simulation, Design; Vol. 5. Solar Thermal & Ocean Thermal; Vol. 6. Photovoltaics & Materials; Vol. 7. Agriculture, Biomass, Wind, New Developments; Vol. 8. Storage, Water Heater, Data Communication, Education; Vol. 9. Socio - Economics & Cultural; Vol. 10. Business & Commercial Implications. Pergamon.
Boerhaave Course, Univ of Leiden, Netherlands, 1969. Physiology & Pathology in the Perinatal Period: Proceedings. Gevers, R. H. & Ruys, J. H., eds.
Boeri, David. People of the Ice Whale: Eskimos, White Men & the Whale.
Boericke & Shapiro. The Craftsman Builder.
Boerner, David. Sentencing in Washington.
Boers, Hendrikus. What Is New Testament Theology? The Rise of Criticism & the Problem of a Theology of the New Testament. Via, Dan O., Jr., ed.
Boeschen, John. The Build-a-Bed Book.
Boesky, Ivan F. Merger Mania: Arbitrage-Wall Street's Best-Kept Money-Making Secret. Madrick, Jeffrey, ed.
Boesler, K. A. Geography & Capital.
Boethal, D. J. & Eikenbary, R. D., eds. Pest Management Programs for Deciduous Tree Fruits & Nuts.
Boettcher, Barry, ed. Immunological Influence on Human Fertility.
Boettcher, Henry J. Three Philosophies of Education.
Boettcher, Robert & Freedman, Gordon L. Gifts of Deceit: Sun Myung Moon, Tongsun Park & the Korean Scandal.
Boettiger, John R. A Love in Shadow.
Boffi, S. & Passatore, G., eds. Nuclear Optical Model Potential.
Bogachinskaya, Inna. Stichija: Poems.
Bogard, Travis & Bryer, Jackson R., eds. The Selected Letters of Eugene O'Neill.
Bogardus, James, jt. auth. see Badger, D. D.
Bogart, Karen. Toward Equity: An Action Manual for Women in Academe.
Bogart, Kenneth P. The Functions of Algebra & Trigonometry.
Bogart, Louis. The Teachers.
Bogart, Shirley. The New Jewish Homemaker: A Treasury of Tips, Crafts, Foods & Stories.
Bogason, S. O. English-Icelandic Dictionary.
Bogdandy, L. V. & Engell, H. J. Reduction of Iron Ores: Scientific Basis & Technology.
Bogdankevich, O. V. & Nikolayev, F. A. Methods in Bremsstrahlung Research.
Bogdanovich, Peter. Pieces of Time: Peter Bogdanovich on the Movies.
Bogelsack, G., et al, eds. Terminology for the Theory of Machines & Mechanisms.
Bogen, M. Arthur. Barely Undercover.
--Double Dealing.
--Mind Games.
Boger, Ann C. & DeOreo, Joellen K. Sacred India: Hinduism, Buddhism, Jainism.
Boger, H. Batterson, jt. auth. see Boger, Louise A.
Boger, Louise. Dictionary of World Pottery & Porcelain.
Boger, Louise A. & Boger, H. Batterson. Dictionary of Antiques & the Decorative Arts.
Boggess, Louis. How to Write Short Stories that Sell.
Boggs, Edward. Stop Smoking Activity Book.
Boggs, Marion A. What Does God Require in Race Relations?
Boggs, Robert F. Shark Man: Master Hunter of the Deep.
Boggs, Robert G. Elementary Structural Analysis.
Boggs, Vernon, et al, eds. The Apple Sliced: Studies of New York City.
Bogin, Meg. The Path to Pain Control.
Bogle, Kate C., jt. auth. see Cutler, Katherine N.
Bogle, Michael. Textile Dyes, Finishes & Auxiliaries.
Bognar, Botond. Contemporary Japanese Architecture: Its Development & Challenge.
Bogner, Norman. Arena.
--California Dreamers.
Bogner, R. E. & Constantinides, A. G., eds. Introduction to Digital Filtering.
Bogolepov, Alexander. Church Reforms in Russia, 1905-1918.
--Orthodox Hymns of Christmas, Easter, & Holy Week.
Bogolepov, N. N. Ultrastructure of the Brain in Hypoxia. Burov, Michael, tr.
Bogomolny, Robert L., ed. Human Experimentation.
Bogomolov, A. S., jt. auth. see Oizerman, T. I.
Bogoslovski, V., jt. auth. see Solodovnikov, V.
Bograd, Larry. Lost in the Store.
Bogue, Donald J., jt. ed. see Burgess, Ernest W.
Bogue, Robert H. The Dawn of Christianity.
Bogus, Ronald, jt. ed. see Landau, Sidney I.
Boguslavsky, M. U. S. S. R. & International Copyright Protection.
Bohannan, Harry M. see Morris, Alvin L.
Bohannan, Jean E., ed. Claude Hanna Retraces Memory's Road.
Bohannan, P. All the Happy Families: Exploring the Varieties of Family Life.
Bohannan, Paul, ed. African Homicide & Suicide.
Bohannon, Richard, et al. Food for Life: The Cancer Prevention Cookbook.
Bohi, Charles, jt. auth. see Grant, H. Roger.
Bohigas Rosell, Mauricio. Diccionario Ingles-Espanol, Spanish-English.
Bohleber, Larry W. Foreword by see Hanson, Anne M.
Bohlen, Charles E. Witness to History.
Bohlen, E. Crop Pests in Tanzania & Their Control.
Bohlke, Laurie. Eating for Two.
Bohlmann, F., et al. Naturally Occurring Acetylenes.
Bohm, G. J., et al, eds. Components & Structural Dynamics.
Bohn, Henry G. A Dictionary with Description & Prices of the Famous Bernal Collection of Pottery, Porcelain & Other Works of Art As It Was Disposed at the End of the Last Century.
Bohn, Henry G., ed. Hand-book of Games.
--Polyglot of Foreign Proverbs - with English Translations.
Bohn, Ralph C., jt. auth. see Silvius, G. Harold.
Bohner, H. O., ed. Light Metal, 1985.
Bohny, Barbara, jt. auth. see Aurigemma, Ann.
Bohoun, C., ed. Neuroblastomas: Biochemical Studies.
Bohr, Peter. The Money-Wise Guide to Sports Cars.
Bohr, Peter, ed. Road & Track's Used Car Classics.
Bohrn, Harold, jt. auth. see Assarsson-Rizzi, Kerstin.
Bohrnstedt, George W. & Knoke, David. Statistics for Social Data Analysis.
Bohrnstedt, George W., jt. ed. see Borgatta, Edgar F.
Bohua, Liu, jt. ed. see Chunyang, An.
Bohuslov, Ronald L. Basic Mathematics for Technical Occupations.
Boice, James M. Genesis.
--Genesis: An Expositional Commentary.
--Genesis: An Expositional Commentary, Vol. 3, Genesis Thirty-Seven thru Fifty Twenty-Six.
--The Minor Prophets: An Expositional Commentary (Hosea-Jonah)
--The Minor Prophets: An Expositional Commentary (Micah-Malachi)
Boice, John D. Multiple Primary Cancers in Connecticut & Denmark.
Boikess, Olga, ed. see Zagat, Eugene H., Jr. & Zagat, Nina S.
Boillot, Michel H. & Shingles, Carol R. Understanding WATFIV.
Boissard, Janine. A New Woman.
--A Time to Choose. Feeney, Mary, tr.
Boissier, J. R., et al, eds. International Congress of Pharmacology, 7th, Paris, 1978: Abstracts.
Boitani, Piero. Chaucer & the Imaginary World of Fame.
Boje, R. & Tomczak, M., eds. Upwelling Ecosystems.
Bojrab, M. Joseph, ed. Pathophysiology in Small Animal Surgery.
Bok, Hannes, jt. auth. see Merritt, Abraham.
Bokenkotter, Thomas, tr. Essential Catholicism.
Bokor, H. S. Hungarian Perspectives on Questions of International Law.
Bokser, Ben Z. From the World of the Cabbalah.
--The Legacy of Maimonides.
--The Wisdom of the Talmud.
Bol, L. J. Adriaen Coorte: A Unique Late Seventeenth Century Dutch Still-Life Painter.
Boland, Bridget & Boland, Maureen. Old Wives' Lore for Gardeners.
Boland, Ian, tr. see Ginzburg, Eugenia S.
Boland, James F. Nuclear Reactor Instrumentation (In-Core)
Boland, Maureen, jt. auth. see Boland, Bridget.
Boland, Peter. New Healthcare Market: A Guide to PPOs for Purchasers, Payors & Providers.
Boland, Yvonne. National Student Register, 1973.
Bolay, Karl H. I Seek an Island.
Bolc, L., ed. Natural Language Communication with Computers.
Bold, Alan. The Ballad.
--Hugh MacDiarmid: The Terrible Crystal.
--MacDiarmid: The Terrible Crystal.
Bold, Alan, ed. The Quest for Le Carre.
Bolden, John H. Developing a Competency-Based Instructional Supervisory System: A School Management Development Program.
Bolden, Theodore E., et al. Dental Hygiene Examination Review.
Boldman, Craig, jt. auth. see Erskine, Jim.
Boldt, Christine, ed. AIS New Car Cost Guide 1985.
Boleat, Mark. National Housing Finance Systems: A Comparative Study.
Boleat, Mark & Coles, Adrian. The Mortgage Market: Theory & Practice of Housing Finance.
Bolen, Eric G., jt. auth. see Robinson, William L.
Bolen, Jean S. Goddesses in Everywoman: A New Psychology of Women.
Bolen, William H. Contemporary Retailing.
Boles, H. Leo. Eldership of the Churches of Christ.
--The Holy Spirit.
--Questions & Answers: Sermon Outlines & Bible Study Notes.
Boles, Harold W., et al. Multidisciplinary Readings in Educational Leadership.
Boles, Paul D. Night Watch.
Boley, Bruno A. Crossfire in Professional Education.
Bolger, Philip C. Thirty-Odd Boats.
Bolin, B., et al, eds. The Global Carbon Cycle.
Bolin, T. D., jt. auth. see Davis, A. E.
Bolinger, Dwight. Aspects of Language.
--Aspects of Language.
Bolis, L., et al, eds. see Symposium on Biophysics & Physiology of Biological Transport, Frascati, 1965.
Bolitho, A. R. & Sandler, P. L. Learn English for Science.
--Study English for Science.
Bolitho, A. R., jt. auth. see Nogas, G. D.
Bolitho, Harold. Meiji Japan.
Bolitho, Hector & Mulgan, John. The Emigrants: Early Travellers to the Antipodes.
Boll, Heinrich. Abenteuer Eines Brotbeutels und Andere Geschichten. Plant, Richard, ed.
--Billiards at Half-Past Nine.
--The Bread of Those Early Years. Vennewitz, Leila, tr. from Ger.
--The Clown.
--Group Portrait with Lady. Vennewitz, Leila, tr. from Ger.
--The Lost Honor of Katharina Blum.
--Missing Persons. Vennewitz, Leila, tr. from German.
Boll, John J. Introduction to Cataloging, Vol. 2: Entry Headings with Emphasis on Cataloging Process & Personal Names.
Bolle, H. J., jt. ed. see Ohring, G.
Boller, Henry A. Among the Indians: Four Years on the Upper Missouri, 1858-1862. Quaife, Milo M., ed.
Boller, Paul F., Jr. George Washington & Religion.
--Quotemanship: The Use & Abuse of Quotations for Polemical & Other Purposes.
Bolles, Edmund B. Who Owns America?
Bolles, Richard N. What Color Is Your Parachute?
--What Color Is Your Parachute.
--What Color Is Your Parachute, 1986: 1986.
--What Color Is Your Parachute? 1987.
Bollet, A. J., ed. see PreTest Service, Inc. Staff.
Bollettieri, Nick & McDermott, Barry. Nick Bollettieri's Junior Tennis.
Bollettieri, Nick, jt. auth. see Anthony, Julie.
Bolliettier, Nick & Anthony, Julie. A Winning Combination.
Bolliger, Max. The Bridge Across.
--Fireflies. Hoover, Rosenna, tr.
--The Wooden Man.
Bolliger, Max & Lenica, Jan. The Magic Bird.
Bolling, Christine H. Colombia: An Export Market Profile.
Bollinger, L. L. & Tully, J. R. Personal Aircraft Business at Airports.
Bollinger, L. L., et al. Terminal Airport Financing & Management.
Bollum, Fred J., jt. ed. see Bertazzoni, Umberto.
Bolocan, David. JAZZ!
--Lotus 1-2-3 Simplified.
Bologh, Roslyn W. Dialectical Phenomenology: Marx's Method.
Bologna, Ferdinando, 1st. I Pittori Ala Corte Angionina Di Napoli, 1266-1414. Briganti, Giuliano, ed.
Bologna, Gianfranco. The World of Birds. Pleasance, Simon, tr.
Bologna, Gregory, jt. ed. see Close, Arthur C.
Bolotin, Norm. Klondike Lost: A Decade of Photographs by Kinsey & Kinsey.
Bolsby, Clare, jt. auth. see Berglund, Berndt.
Bolsby, Clare E., jt. auth. see Berglund, Berndt.
Bolshakov, V. This Whole Human Rights Business.
Bolsterli, Margaret J. The Early Community at Bedford Park: The Pursuit of "Corporate Happiness" in the First Garden Suburb.
Bolte, Charles, ed. Portrait of a Woman Down East: Selected Writings of Mary Bolte.
Bolten, Steven E. Managerial Finance: Principles & Practice.
Bolton, Angela. The Maturing Sun: An Army Nurse in India, 1942-45.
Bolton, B. Electromagnetism & Its Applications.
Bolton, Charlotte. No More Dead Horses.
Bolton, Clyde. Alabama Football: The Crimson Tide.
--The Crimson Tide: Alabama Football.
--War Eagle: A Story of Auburn Football.
Bolton, E. J. Verse Writing in Schools.
Bolton, Ethel S. Wax Portraits & Silhouettes.
Bolton, Evelyn. Ride When You're Ready.
Bolton, H. Philip. Dickens Dramatized.
Bolton, Henry C. Counting-Out Rhymes of Children.
Bolton, James. Ancient Crete & Mycenae. Reeves, Marjorie, ed.
Bolton, Melvin. The Softener.
Bolton, Muriel R. The Golden Porcupine.
Bolton, P. M. Civil Rights.
Bolton, Ralph. Systems Contracting.
Bolton, Richard. Painting Weathered Textures in Watercolor.
--Weathered Texture Workshop.
Bolton, Robert H. People Skills: How to Assert Yourself, Listen to Others & Resolve Conflicts.
Bolton, Urgil, ed. see Minnesota Trade Office Staff.
Bolton, W. F. A Short History of Literary English.
Bolton, W. F., ed. see Jonson, Ben.
Boltz, David F. & Howell, James A. Colorimetric Determination of Nonmetals.
Boltzmann Equation Symposium Staff. The Boltzmann Equation (Theory & Applications) Proceedings of the Symposium, Vienna, 1972. Cohen, E. G. & Thirring, W., eds.
Bolwell, Christine. Directory of Educational Software in Nursing, 1987.
Bolwig, Tom G., ed. Aspects of Epilepsy & Psychiatry. Trimble, Michael R.
Bomans, Godfried. The Wily Witch & Other Fairy Tales & Fables. Crampton, Patricia, tr. from Dutch.
Bombal, Maria L. New Islands & Other Stories. Cunningham, Richard, tr. from Span.
Bombaugh, Charles C. Gleanings for the Curious from the Harvest Fields of Literature: A Melange of Excerpta.
Bombeck, Erma. Aunt Erma's Cope Book.
--If Life Is a Bowl of Cherries, What Am I Doing in the Pits?
--If Life Is a Bowl of Cherries-What Am I Doing in the Pits?
--Motherhood: The Second Oldest Profession.
Bombeck, Erma & Keane, Bil. Just Wait till You Have Children of Your Own!
Bombelles, Joseph T. Economic Development of Communist Yugoslavia, 1947-1964.
Bombin-Bombin, Luis M. Seed Legislation.
Bomely, Steven. Glory to God: A Candlelight Service for Christmas.
Bomgren, Marilyn J. Godparents, Why?
Bomze, Howard. Programming Digital's Personal Computer: BASIC.
Bon Appetit, ed. Beef, Veal, Lamb & Pork.
Bon Appetit Magazine Editors. Appetizers.
--Beef, Veal, Lamb & Pork.
--The Best of Bon Appetit.
--The Best of Bon Appetit.
--The Best of Bon Appetit.
--Bon Appetit Too Busy to Cook?
--Breads: Breads.
--Breakfast & Brunches.
--Buffets.
--Cakes.
--Cooking with Bon Appetit: American Regional Favorites.
--Cooking with Bon Appetit: Make-Ahead Meals.
--Easy Entrees.
--French Country Favorites.
--Gifts from the Kitchen.
--Italian Favorites.
--Light Desserts.
--New York's Master Chefs. Sax, Richard, ed.
--One-Dish Meals.
--Oriental Favorites.
--Pasta & Pizza.
--Picnics & Barbecues.
--Pies & Tarts.
--Poultry.
--Seafood.
--Soups & Salads.
--Special Occasion Desserts.
--Vegetables.
Bona, Constantin. Idiotypes & Lymphocytes.

Bonadonna, G., jt. ed. see Veronesi, U.
Bonadonna, Gianni, ed. Breast Cancer: Diagnosis & Treatment.
Bonafoux, Pascal. The Impressionists: Portraits & Confidences.
--Rembrandt Self-Portraits.
Bonanno, Ellen, jt. auth. see Mechlin, Stuart.
Bonanno, Joseph & Lalli, Sergeo. A Man of Honor: The Autobiography of Joseph Bonanno.
Bonansea, B. M. Man & His Approach to God in John Duns Scotus.
Bonansea, Bernardino M. Tommaso Campanella: Renaissance Pioneer of Modern Thought.
Bonar, John A. Goliaths of the World. Beasley, James, ed.
Bonar, Lore S., et al. Say It in Another Language: Phrases in Spanish, French, Japanese, Swahili, & German.
Bonavia, Michael. Twilight of British Rail.
Bonavia, Michael R. British Rail: The First Twenty-Five Years.
Boncer, Lois. Aardvark to Zebra.
Bond, Ann S. Saturdays in the City.
Bond, Courtney C. Where Rivers Meet: An Illustrated History of Ottawa.
Bond, David & McDonald, Rod. Educational Development Through Consultancy.
Bond, Edward. The Pope's Wedding.
--Summer.
Bond, Gary. Inside the Apple IIGS.
Bond, Harold L. The Literary Art of Edward Gibbon.
Bond, Harold Lewis. An Encyclopedia of Antiques.
Bond, Horace M. Negro Education in Alabama: A Study in Cotton & Steel.
Bond, J. Mark. The Gold Seekers.
Bond, Michael. Paddington & the Knickerbocker Rainbow.
Bond, Michael R. Pain-Its Nature, Analysis, & Treatment.
Bond, P. S., jt. auth. see Garber, Max B.
Bond, R. L., ed. Porous Carbon Solids.
Bond, Richmond P. Queen Anne's American Kings.
Bond, Richmond P., jt. auth. see Weed, Katherine K.
Bond, Robert E. The Source Book of Franchise Opportunities.
Bond, Robert J. & Bowman, Arthur G. California Real Estate Practice.
Bond, Robert J., jt. auth. see Bowman, Arthur G.
Bond, Simon. Have a Nice Day: Over 30 Pop-ups for "Adults"
--Tough Teddies & Other Bears.
Bond, Thomas, jt. auth. see Albanese, Joseph.
Bond, Victor P., et al, eds. Mammalian Radiation Lethality: A Disturbance in Cellular Kinetics.
Bondanella, Julia, tr. see Rousseau, Jean-Jacques.
Bondarev, Yu, jt. auth. see Idashkin, Yu.
Bonderoff, Jason. Barbara Walters: Today's Woman.
--Soap Opera Babylon.
Bonderunt, Bill, ed. see Sayers, Gayle & Griese, Bob.
Bonds, Parris A. Blue Moon.
Bonds, Ray, ed. A Illustrated Guide to the Soviet Ground Forces.
--An Illustrated Guide to World War II Tanks & Fighting Vehicles.
Bondurant, Bill, ed. see Buoniconti, Nick & Anderson, Dick.
Bondurant, Bob & Blakemore, John. Bob Bondurant on High Performance Driving.
Bondurant, Joan V. Conquest of Violence: The Gandhian Philosophy of Conflict.
Bone, Drummond. Byron.
Bone, Larry E., ed. Library School Teaching Methods: Courses in the Selection of Adult Materials.
Bone, Robert W. The Maverick Guide to Australia, 1983.
--Maverick Guide to Australia: 1984-1985.
--Maverick Guide to Australia, 1986-87.
--The Maverick Guide to Hawaii: 1983.
--Maverick Guide to Hawaii, 1985.
--Maverick Guide to Hawaii, 1986.
--The Maverick Guide to Hawaii, 1987.
--The Maverick Guide to New Zealand, 1983.
--Maverick Guide to New Zealand, 1985-1986.
Bone, Roger C., ed. Pulmonary Disease Reviews.
Bonebreak, Robert L. Practical Techniques of Electronic Circuit Design.
Boneff, N., ed. see International Astronautical Congress, 13th, Varna, 1962.
Bonello, Frank J., jt. auth. see Swartz, Thomas R.
Boneparth, Ellen. Women, Power & Policy.
Bonet, C., jt. ed. see Bell, A. T.
Boney, Mary L. God Calls.
Bonfanti, Joe. Italian Jokes.
Bonfils, S., jt. ed. see Lewin, M.
Bonforte, John. Philosophy of Epictetus.
Bongard-Levin, G. M. Mauryan India.
Bongartz, Roy. Dollarwise Guide to the Southwest.
Bonge, Dusti. Dusti Bonge: The Life of an Artist. Longnecker, Nancy, ed.
Bongertz, Roy. Frommer's Dollarwise Guide to the Southwest.
Bongiovanni, Gail. Manual of Clinical Gastroenterology.
Bonham, Frank. Premonitions.
Bonhoeffer, Dietrich. Fiction from Prison: Gathering up the Past. Green, Clifford, tr. from Ger.
--Prayers from Prison. Hampe, Johann C., tr. from Ger.
Bonhomme, Denise see Quebedeau, Denise B., pseud.
Boni, Sylvain. The Self & the Other in the Ontologies of Sartre & Buber.
Boniface. The Letters of St. Boniface. Emerton, Ephraim, tr. from Lat.
Bonifazi, Conrad. A Theology of Things.
Bonin, Edmond, ed. see St. Cyprian of Carthage.
Bonington, Chris. Kongur: China's Elusive Summit.
Bonington, Chris & Clarke, Charles. Everest: The Unclimbed Ridge.
Bonino, Jose M. Room to Be People: An Interpretation of the Message of the Bible for Today's World. Leach, Vickie, tr. from Span.
Bonivento, C., ed. Going...Teach.
Bonn, George S., ed. Information Resources in the Environmental Sciences.
Bonn, George S. & Faibisoff, Sylvia G., eds. Changing Times: Changing Libraries.
Bonn, M. J. Whither Europe - Union or Partnership?
Bonnefoy, Claude, et al. Dictionnaire de Litterature Francais Contemporaine.
Bonnel, Peter & Sedwick, Frank. Conversation in French: Points of Departure.
Bonnell, Peter & Sedwick, Frank. Conversation in German: Points of Departure.
Bonner, James & Varner, Joseph, eds. Plant Biochemistry.
Bonner, John T. Cells & Societies.
--Morphogenesis: An Essay on Development.
Bonner, Mary G. Wonders Around the Sun.
--Wonders of Inventions.
Bonner, Miller, jt. auth. see Nelson, Mark.
Bonner, W. N. & Berry, R. J., eds. Ecology in the Antarctic.
Bonnerjea, Lucy, jt. auth. see Ashworth, Georgina.
Bonney, Charles C. World's Congress Addresses.
Bonney, Stuart E. The WordStar Customizing Guide 3.3: Modifications That Improve Your Productivity.
Bonnici, Virginia. Conversations.
Bonnifield, Paul. The Dust Bowl: Men, Dirt, & Depression.
Bonnington, S. T., jt. auth. see Bain, A. G.
Bonno, John A. & Fields, Kent T. Introduction to COBOL.
Bonnot, Bernard R. Pope John Twenty-Third: A Clever, Pastoral Leader.
Bonoma & Hall. Marketing Management: Text & Cases.
Bonoma, Thomas V. & Zaltman, Gerald. Psychology for Management.
Bonomi, Patricia U., ed. Party & Political Opposition in Revolutionary America.
Bononcini, Giovanni. Il Trionfo Di Camilla, Regina De 'Volsci. Brown, Howard M., ed.
Bonotto, S., jt. ed. see Brachet, Jean.
Bonotto, Silvano, et al, eds. Biology & Radiobiology of Anucleate Systems.
Bonpensiere. New Pathways to Piano Technique.
Bonsal, Philip W. Cuba, Castro, & the United States.
Bonsdorff, Bertel Von see Von Bonsdorff, Bertel.
Bonsignore, Giovanni, jt. ed. see Cumming, Gordon.
Bonsignore, John J., et al. Before the Law: An Introduction to the Legal Process.
Bontemps, Arna. We Have Tomorrow.
Bontemps, Arna & Conroy, Jack. Fast Sooner Hound.
Bontly, Thomas. Celestial Chess.
Bonventre, Peter, jt. auth. see Cosell, Howard.
Bonventure, Peter, jt. auth. see Cosell, Howard.
Bonvenure, Peter, jt. auth. see Cosell, Howard.
Bonwick, G. J. Seamanship Handbook for Basic Studies.
Bonynge, David B. Commodore Sixty-Four, MicroMasion: Using Your Computer to Have a Safer, More Convenient Home.
--IBM-PC, MicroMasion: Using Your Computer to Have a Safer, More Convenient Home.
Booch, Grady. Software Engineering with Ada.
Boocock, Sarane S. Introduction to the Sociology of Learning.
--Sociology of Education: An Introduction.
Boodhoo, Ken I., ed. Eric Williams: The Man & the Leader.
Boodin, John E. Religion of Tomorrow.
Booher & Thibodeau. Athletic Injury Assessment.
Booher, Dianna. Letter Perfect: A Handbook of Model Letters for Managers & Executives.
Booij, H. L. & Bungenberg De Jong, H. G. Biocolloids & Their Interactions with Special Reference to Coacervates & Related Systems.
Book Division Staff. The Travel Industry Peronnel Directory, 1988.
Booker, Frank. The Great Western Railway: A New History.
Booker, Marjorie M. To Hell with Male Chauvinism!
Booker, Richard. Blow the Trumpet in Zion.
--Radical Christian Living.
Books on Tape, Inc. Staff, ed. Books on Tape Catalog, 1988.
Boole, George. Investigation of the Laws of Thought.
--The Mathematical Analysis of Logic.
Boom, Corrie Ten. Amazing Love.
--In My Father's House.
--Not I, But Christ.
--Prison Letters.
--A Prisoner & Yet.
--This Day Is the Lord's.
Boon. Computer Design.
--Management Information Systems.
Boon, Emilie. Peterkin Meets a Star.
--Peterkin's Very Own Garden.
Boon, Jean P. & Yip, Sidney. Molecular Hydrodynamics.
Boone, jt. auth. see Cosenza.
Boone, Edna, jt. auth. see Boone, Tom.
Boone, J. Allen. The Language of Silence.
Boone, James C. Remington No. Two: Good Day for a Hangin'
--Remington, No. 3: Showdown at Comanche Butte.
--Remington, No. 4: Lawman's Justice.
--Remington, No. 5: Wyoming Blood Trail.
--Remington, No. 9: The Lawless Clan.
Boone, Louis E. Classic in Consumer Behavior.
Boone, Louis E. & Johnson, James C. Marketing Channels.
Boone, Louis E. & Kurtz, David L. Contemporary Business.
--Contemporary Marketing.
Boone, Louis E., jt. auth. see Kurtz, David L.
Boone, Louis E., et al. The Sales Management Game.
Boone, Tom & Boone, Edna. Prayer & Action.
Boor, W. De see De Boor, W. & Grossarth-Maticek, R.
Boorman, John T., jt. auth. see Havrilesky, Thomas M.
Boorsch, Suzanne, et al. Giorgio Ghisi: The Engravings.
Boorstein, Edward. Economic Transformation of Cuba.
--What's Ahead?... the U. S. Economy.
Boorstin, Daniel J. Genius of American Politics, Nineteen Fifty-eight.
--Mysterious Science of the Law.
Boose, John & Gaines, Brian R. Knowledge Acquisition for Knowledge-Based Systems.
Booss, C. & Horowitz, P., eds. Jack London Series II.
Booth, Alan & Pack, Melvyn. Employment, Capital & Economic Policy: Great Britain 1918-1939.
Booth, Bradford A., ed. see Stevenson, Robert Louis.
Booth, C. Fusarium: A Laboratory Guide to the Indentification of the Major Species.
Booth, Charles. The Aged Poor in England & Wales.
Booth, Edwin. Leadville.
--Rebel's Return.
Booth, Elizabeth M., jt. auth. see Dickerson, John W.
Booth, George. Pussycats Need Love, Too.
--Rehearsal's Off!
--Think Good Thoughts about a Pussycat.
Booth, George, jt. auth. see Morgan, Henry.
Booth, George C. The Food & Drink of Mexico.
Booth, Howard J. Edwin Diller Starbuck: Pioneer in the Psychology of Religion.
Booth, John, jt. ed. see Funke, Lewis.
Booth, Julianne. Bible Verses to Remember.
Booth, L. Venchael, ed. Crowned with Glory & Honor: The Life of Rev. Lacey Kirk Williams.
Booth, Larry, jt. auth. see Weinstein, Robert A.
Booth, Martin. Hiroshima Joe.
Booth, Nicholas H. & McDonald, Leslie E. Veterinary Pharmacology & Therapeutics.
Booth, Norman. Industrial Gases.
Booth, S., et al, eds. Inspection & Measurement.
Booth, Sally S. Seeds of Anger: Revolts in America, 1670-1771.
Booth, Stanley. Elvis Presley's Graceland.
--Sir Alfred Munnings Eighteen Seventy-Eight to Nineteen Fifty-nine.
--Sir Alfred Munnings 1878-1959: An Appreciation of the Artist & a Selection of His Paintings.
Booth, Tony. Growing up in Society.
Booth, Tony & Statham, June, eds. The Nature of Special Education: People, Places & Change.
Booth, Verne H. & Bloom, Mortimer. Physical Science: A Study of Matter & Energy.
Booth, W. Edwin. The Colorado Gun.
Boothby, Guy. Enter Dr. Nikola!
Boothby, William M. An Introduction to Differentiable Manifolds & Riemannian Geometry.
Booth-Clibborn, Edward, ed. American Photography Three.
--European Illustration: The Twelfth Annual.
--European Illustration, 1983.
--European Photography, 1983-84.
Boothe, Norris, jt. auth. see CEP Staff.
Boothroyd. Fundamentals of Metal Machining & Machine Tools.
Boozer, LuZanne. Heritage of Buddha.
Boquist, jt. auth. see Engler.
Boraks, Jagna, tr. see Busza, Andrzej.
Borasky, Rubin, ed. Ultrastructure of Protein Fibers: Proceedings.
Borba, Michele, jt. auth. see Ungaro, Dan.
Borbely, A. & Valatx, J., eds. Sleep Mechanisms.
Borchard, David C., et al. Your Career: Choices, Chances, Changes.
Borchard, Edwin M., jt. auth. see Lage, William.
Borchard, Franz. The Adrenergic Nerves of the Normal & Atrophied Heart. Bergmann, Wolfgang & Doerr, Wilhelm, eds. Hirsch, H. J., tr. from Ger.
Borchardt, Ann, tr. see Wiesel, Elie.
Borchardt, Anne, tr. see Wiesel, Elie.
Borchardt, D. H. Australian Bibliography: A Guide to Printed Sources of Information.
--How to Find Out in Philosophy & Psychology.
Borchardt, L. M. God's Children Praying.
--Jesus Prays.
--The Lord's Prayer.
Borchers, jt. auth. see Oppenheimer, S. L.
Borchert, John R., et al. Legacy of Minneapolis: Preservation Amid Change.
Borchgrave, Arnaud de see Moss, Robert & De Borchgrave, Arnaud.
Bord, Colin, jt. auth. see Bord, Janet.
Bord, Janet & Bord, Colin. Earth Rites: Fertility Practices in Pre-Industrial Britain.
--A Guide to Ancient Sites in Britain.
--Mysterious Britain.
Bordelon, Abbe L. A History of the Ridiculous Extravagancies of Monsieur Oufle Occasion'd by His Reading Books Treating of Magick, the Black-Art Demoniacks... & Other Superstitious Practices.
Borden, Thomas A., jt. ed. see Crawford, E. David.
Borders, Karl. Village Life under the Soviets.
Bordes, Francois. Old Stone Age.
Bordow, Joan. The Ultimate Loss: Coping with the Death of a Child.
Borea, Phyllis. Seymour, a Gibbon: About Apes & Other Animals & How You Can Help to Keep Them Alive.
Boren, James H. The Bureaucratic Zoo: The Search for the Ultimate Mumble.
Borenstein, Audrey. Older Women in Twentieth Century America: A Selected Annotated Bibliography.
--Redeeming the Sin: Social Science & Literature.
Boretz, Benjamin & Cone, Edward T., eds. Perspectives on American Composers.
--Perspectives on Contemporary Music Theory.
--Perspectives on Notation & Performance.
--Perspectives on Schoenberg & Stravinsky.
Borevich, Z. I. & Shafarevich, I. R. Number Theory.
Borg, Seth A. & Rosenthal, Susan. Handbook of Cancer Diagnosis & Staging: A Clinical Atlas.
Borg, Susan O. & Lasker, Judith. When Pregnancy Fails: Families Coping with Miscarriage, Stillbirth, & Infant Death.
Borg, Walter S. & Gall, Meredith D. Educational Research.
Borgatta, Edgar F. & Bohrnstedt, George W., eds. Sociological Methodology 1970.
Borgen, Joe, jt. auth. see Davis, Dwight.
Borges, Jorge L. Ficciones. Kerrigan, Anthony, ed. & intro. by.
--A Personal Anthology. Kerrigan, Anthony, ed. & frwd. by.
Borgese, Elizabeth, tr. see Falassi, Alessandro & Catoni, Guiliano.
Borgin, Karl & Corbett, Kathleen. The Destruction of a Continent: Africa & International Aid.
Borgman, Albert. Technology & the Character of Contemporary Life: A Philosophical Inquiry.
Borgman, Jim. The Great Communicator.
Borgnine, Tova & Trebek, Elaine C. The Tova Difference: Tova Borgnine's Beauty Book.
Borgnis, Mervin E. We Had a Shore Fast Line.
Borgstedt, H. V., ed. Material Behavior & Physical Chemistry in Liquid Metal Systems.
Borgstrom, Bengt-Erik. The Patron & the Panca.
Borich, Michael. A Different Kind of Love.
--A Different Kind of Love.
Borick, Paul M., ed. Chemical Sterilization.
Boring, Edwin G. Sensation & Perception in the History of Experimental Psychology.
Boring, Phyllis Z., jt. auth. see Castells, Matilde O.
Boring, Phyllis Z., ed. see Ayala, Francisco.
Boris, Robert, jt. auth. see Hannibal, Edward.
Boris, Shelley, jt. ed. see Harrison, Jamie.
Borish, Elaine. Literary Lodgings.
Borisov, et al. Diccionario de Economia Politica.
--Diccionario de Economia Politica.
Borisov, P. Can Man Change the Climate?
Borisovich, Yu., et al. Introduction to Topology.

Authors

Bork, A., ed. Computer Assisted Learning in Physics Education.
Bork, Paul F. The World of Moses.
Borka, H., jt. ed. see Slamecka, V.
Borkat, Roberta F., ed. see Cumberland, Richard.
Borke, R. C., jt. auth. see Van Buren, J. M.
Borkowski, John G. & Anderson, D. Chris. Experimental Psychology: Tactics of Behavioral Research.
Borkowski, John G., jt. auth. see Anderson, D. Chris.
Borkowski, L., jt. auth. see Slupecki, J.
Borland, Barbara D. This Is the Way My Garden Grows: And Comes Into My Kitchen.
Borland, D. W., et al, eds. Physics of Materials.
Borland, Georgia O. Light upon the Path: Poems & Prose & Points.
Borland, Hal. Hal Borland's Book of Days.
--Hal Borland's Twelve Moons of the Year.
--High, Wide & Lonesome: Growing up on the Colorado Frontier.
--The History of Wildlife in America. Bourne, Russell & MacConomy, Alma D., eds.
Borman, J. B. & Gotsman, M. S., eds. Rheumatic Valvular Disease in Children.
Bormann, Ernest. Communication Theory.
Bormann, Ernest G. & Bormann, Nancy. Effective Committees & Groups in the Church.
Bormann, Nancy, jt. auth. see Bormann, Ernest G.
Born, David O., jt. auth. see Pozoz, Robert S.
Born, Gustav R., et al, eds. Factors In Formation & Regression of the Atherosclerotic Plaque.
Born, Roscoe C. The Suspended Sentence: A Guide for Writers.
Born, Wolfgang. American Landscape Painting: An Interpretation.
Borneman, Walter & Lampert, Lyndon J. Climbing Guide to Colorado's Fourteeners.
Borning, Bernard C. The Political & Social Thought of Charles A. Beard.
Bornkamm, Gunther. The New Testament: A Guide to Its Writings. Fuller, Reginald H. & Fuller, Ilse, trs. from Ger.
Bornkamm, Gunther, et al. Tradition & Interpretation in Matthew.
Bornstein, Harry. Sand, Sea, Shells & Sky.
--When I Grow Up.
Bornstein, Morris, ed. Comparative Economic Systems: Models & Cases.
Bornstein, Ruth. The Dancing Man.
--The Dream of the Little Elephant.
--Jim.
Borodin, A., jt. auth. see Gotlieb, C. C.
Boross, L., jt. auth. see Kremmer, T.
Borovik, G., jt. auth. see Ignatiev, O.
Borovsky, Natasha. A Daughter of the Nobility.
Borow, Henry, et al. Career Guidance for a New Age.
Borowitz, Albert. A Gallery of Sinister Perspectives: Ten Crimes & a Scandal.
--The Woman Who Murdered Black Satin: The Bermondsey Horror.
Borowitz, Eugene B. A New Jewish Theology in the Making.
Borowski, J. F. A Comparison of the Reading Interests of Kankakee Senior High School Students with Those Revealed in Nationwide Surveys.
Borowski, M. & Murch, M. Marital Violence: The Community Responses.
Borras, Maria L. Picabia.
Borrisavlietvitch, M. Golden Number.
Borrutto, Franco, et al, eds. Fetal Ultrasonography: The Secret Prenatal Life.
Borsch, Frederick H. God's Parable.
--Pentecost One.
--Son of Man in Myth & History.
Borsch, Frederick H. & Napier, Davie. Advent-Christmas. Achtemeier, Elizabeth, et al, eds.
Borsheim, Roger M. Earth Watch.
Borsi, Franco. The Monumental Era: European Architecture & Design 1929-1939. Marwood, Pamela, tr.
Borst, Diane, jt. ed. see Montana, Patrick H.
Borst, Karen G., jt. ed. see Ford, Patrick K.
Borstein, Susan B. Parents of Newborns.
Borsy, Z., jt. ed. see Kadar, L.
Borten, Helen. Jungle.
Borthwick, J. S. The Down East Murders.
Borthwick, Meredith. Keshub Chunder Sen: A Search for Cultural Synthesis in India.
Bortz, John, jt. auth. see Mader, Chris.
Borus, Michael E. Measuring the Impact of Employment Related Social Programs: A Primer on the Evaluation of Employment & Training, Vocational Education, Vocational Rehabilitation, Other Job Oriented Programs.
--Tomorrow's Workers.
Boryczka, Raymond. United in Purpose: A Chronological History of the Ohio AFL-CIO, 1958-1983.
Borza, Eugene N., jt. ed. see Adams, W. Lindsay.
Borzaga, Reynold. In Pursuit of Religion.
Bos, D., et al, eds. Entrepreneurship.
Bosanquet, B. Meeting of Extremes in Contemporary Philosophy.
Bosanquet, Bernard. Essentials of Logic: Being Ten Lectures on Judgment & Inference.
--What Religion Is.
Bosanquet, Nicholas, jt. ed. see Townsend, Peter.
Bosch, David J. Witness to the World: The Christian Mission in Theological Perspective.
Bosch, Juan. Hostos el Sembrador.
Bosch, Paul. The Paschal Cycle.
Bosch, Vanden, et al. Urban Watershed Management: Flooding & Water Quality. Bedient, Philip B. & Rowe, Peter G., eds.
Bosche, Susanne. Jenny Lives with Eric & Martin.
Boschke, F. & Leary, O. All-Valence Electrons S. C. F. Calculations.
Boschke, F., ed. Carbohydrate Chemistry.
--Cosmochemistry.
--Dynamic Chemistry.
--Dynamic Stereochemistry.
--Inorganic & Analytical Chemistry.
--Molecular Orbitals.
--N M R Spectroscopy of Annulenes.
--New Concepts One.
--New Methods in Chemistry.
--New Results in Boron Chemistry.
--Photochemistry.
--Photochemistry.
--Preparative Organic Chemistry.
--Reactive Intermediates.
--Stereo & Theoretical Chemistry.
--Stereochemistry One: In Memory of van't Hoff.
--Stereochemistry Two: In Memory of van't Hoff.
Boschke, F., ed. see Fluck, E., et al.
Boschke, F., ed. see Kompa, K. L.
Boschke, F., et al, eds. Inorganic & Analytical Chemistry.
--Nuclear Quadrupole Resonance. Boschke, F.
--Structure & Transformations of Organic Molecules.
Boschke, F. L., ed. Aspects of Molybdenum & Related Chemistry.
--Biochemistry.
--Biochemistry I.
--Bonding & Structure.
--Instrumental Inorganic Chemistry.
--Large Amplitude Motion in Molecules One.
--Micelles.
--Organic Chemistry.
--Syntheses of Natural Products.
--Van der Waals Systems.
Boschke, G., et al. PI Complexes of Transition Metals.
Boschmann, Roger. Hong Kong by Night.
Boschot, ed. see Gautier, Theophile.
Bosco, James J. & Robin, Stanley S. The Hyperactive Child & Stimulant Drugs.
Boscovich, Roger J. Theory of Natural Philosophy.
Bosisio, Gina B., jt. auth. see Cretti, Luciano.
Boskin, Joseph. Urban Racial Violence, in the Twentieth Century.
Boskin, Michael J. Too Many Promises: The Uncertain Future of Social Security.
Boskind-White, Marlene & White, William C., Jr. Bulimarexia: The Binge-Purge Cycle.
Bosler, Nan. Australian Patchwork & Applique.
Bosley, Judith, ed. The Big Fat Red Juicy Apple Cook Book.
Bosmajian, Haig. Principles & Practice of Freedom of Speech.
Bosquet, Alain. Selected Poems. Beckett, Samuel, et al, trs. from Fr. & Eng.
Bosqui & Co. Staff. Grapes & Grapevines of California.
Boss, Benjamin, et al, eds. see Carnegie Institution of Washington, Department of Meridian Astronomy Staff.
Boss, Bert G. Tall Are the Hills.
Boss, Jim. Ambush at Vermejo.
Boss, Medard. The Analysis of Dreams.
Bossa, Francesco, et al, eds. Structure & Function Relationships in Biochemical Systems.
Bosse, Malcolm. Fire in Heaven: A Novel.
--The Warlord.
Bosse, Raymond & Rose, Charles L. Smoking & Aging.
Bosselman, Fred, et al. The Permit Explosion: Coordination of the Proliferation.
Bostetter, Edward E. Romantic Ventriloquists: Wordsworth, Coleridge, Keats, Shelley, Byron.
Bostick, W. H., et al, eds. Energy Storage, Compression, & Switching.
Boston Athenaeum. Journal of the Proceedings of the Society which Conducts the Monthly Anthology & Boston Review: Oct. 3, 1805 to July 2, 1811.
Boston Athenaeum Staff. Index of Obituaries in Boston Newspapers, 1704-1800.
Boston, L. M. The Fossil Snake.
--The Guardians of the House.
--Perverse & Foolish.
--The Stones of Green Knowe.
Boston, Lucy M. Adventures at Green Knowe. Incl. The Children of Green Knowe; Treasure of Green Knowe; The River at Green Knowe; Stranger at Green Knowe; An Enemy at Green Knowe. HarBraceJ.
--Children of Green Knowe.
--The Children of Green Knowe.
--An Enemy at Green Knowe.
--Nothing Said.
--River at Green Knowe.
--River at Green Knowe.
--Strongholds.
--Treasure of Green Knowe.
--The Treasure of Green Knowe.
Boston Medical Library Staff, jt. auth. see Harvard Medical Library Staff.
Boston, Pamela, jt. ed. see Moller, Aage R.
Boston Public Library Staff. Canadian Manuscripts in the Boston Public Library: A Descriptive Catalog.
--Catalog of the Defoe Collection in the Boston Public Library.
--Catalogue of the Spanish Library, & of the Portuguese Books Bequeathed by George Ticknor to the Boston Public Library.
--Dictionary Catalog of the Music Collection, Boston Public Library.
--Manuscripts of the American Revolution in the Boston Public Library: A Descriptive Catalog.
--Young Adult Catalog of the Boston Public Library.
Boston Symphony Orchestra Staff. The Boston Symphony Cookbook.
Boston University Libraries Staff. Catalog of African Government Documents.
--List of French Doctoral Dissertations on Africa, 1884-1961.
Boston Urban Gardeners. A Handbook of Community Gardening. Naimark, Susan, ed.
Bostwick, Burdette. One Hundred Eleven Proven Techniques & Strategies for Getting the Job Interview.
Bostwick, Burdette E., ed. Resume Writing: A Comprehensive How-to-Do-It Guide.
Bostwick, Dora M. Down to the Bay.
Bostwick, Henry A. Genealogy of the Bostwick Family in America.
Bostwick, John, III, jt. auth. see Berger, Karen.
Boswall, Jeffery. Birds for All Seasons.
Boswell, David M., ed. The Handicapped Person in the Community. Wingrove, Janet M.
Boswell, James. Boswell in Extremes: 1776-1778. Weis, Charles M. & Pottle, Frederick A., eds.
--Letters.
Boswell, John, jt. auth. see Fitzgerald, Jim.
Boswell, Kathryn, jt. auth. see O'Connor, Francine.
Boswick, John A., Jr., ed. Current Concepts in Hand Surgery.
Bosworth. Montgomery Clift.
Bosworth, Bruce. Codes, Ciphers, & Computers: An Introduction to Information Security.
Bosworth, Frank. Bear-Claw Range.
--Rawhide.
Bosworth, J. A. Neknus & Other Poems.
Bosworth, Sheila. Almost Innocent.
Botein, Michael & Rice, David, eds. Network Television & the Public Interest: A Preliminary Inquiry.
Botermans, Jack, jt. auth. see Van Delft, Pieter.
Botfield, Beriah. Notes on the Cathedral Libraries of England.
Bothma, Guido H. Madhres...or Survival.
Bothmer, Dietrich von see Von Bothmer, Dietrich.
Bothmer, Dietrich Von see Von Bothmer, Dietrich & Mertens, Joan R.
Bothmer, Gerry, tr. see Hansson, Carola, et al.
Bothmer, Gerry, tr. see Lindgren, Astrid.
Bothwell, Jean. African Herdboy: A Story of the Masai.
--Dancing Princess.
--Defiant Bride.
--Promise of the Rose.
Bothwell, Lin K. The Art of Leadership: Skill-Building Techniques That Produce Results.
Botkin, Benjamin A. New York City Folklore: Legends, Tall Tales, Anecdotes, Stories, Sagas, Heroes & Characters, Customs, Traditions & Sayings.
Botsford, Keith, jt. auth. see Jones, Alan.
Botsford, Shirley. Between Thimbles & Thumb.
Bott, M. H. Interior of the Earth: Its Structure, Constitution & Evolution.
Bott, R., et al. Lectures on Algebraic & Differential Topology: Delivered at the II. ELAM.
Bottcher, Betty & Davis, Mel. Wasatch Trails.
Bottema, O. & Roth, B. Theoretical Kinematics.
Botterill, J. S. Fluid-Bed Heat Transfer: Gas-Fluidized Bed Behavior & Its Influence on Bed Thermal Properties.
Botting, Douglas, jt. auth. see Sayer, Ian.
Bottner, Barbara. Myra.
Bottom, Norman R. & Kostanoski, John. Security & Loss Control.
Bottomley, A. Keith. Prison Before Trial.
Bottomley, Frank. The Castle Explorer's Guide to England, Scotland, & Wales.
Bottomley, Gill, jt. ed. see Burns, Ailsa.
Bottomley, Tom, jt. auth. see Whiting, John.
Bottomley, Trevor. An Introduction to Co-Operatives.
Bottomore, Tom, ed. Karl Marx.
--Readings from the Frankfurt School.
Bottomore, Tom, tr. see Hilferding, Rudolf.
Bottoms, Lawrence. Ecclesiastes Speaks to Us Today.
Bottrall, Anthony F. Comparative Study of the Management & Organization of Irrigation Projects.
Botvinnik, M. M. Computers, Chess & Long-Range Planning. Brown, A., tr.
Botwin, Carol. Is There Sex after Marriage?
Botwinick, Aryeh. Hobbes & Modernity: Five Exercises in Political Philosophical Exegesis.
--Wittgenstein, Skepticism & Political Participation: An Essay in the Epistemology of Democratic Theory.
Boubat, Edward. Woman.
Bouchard, Donald F. Milton: A Structural Reading.
Bouchard, Donald F., ed. & tr. see Foucault, Michel.
Bouchard, M. Angeline, tr. see Simonet, Andre.
Bouchard, Ronald A., et al, eds. Interview Guide for Supervisors.
Bouchard, Rosemary & Owens, Norma F. Nursing Care of the Cancer Patient.
Bouchard, Sharon, jt. auth. see Fruehling, Rosemary T.
Boucher, Bernard. The Megawind Cancellation.
Boucher, Louis J. & Renner, Robert P. Treatment of Partially Edentulous Patients.
Bouchier, David. Radical Citizenship: The New American Activism.
Bouchier, Ian A., ed. Recent Advances in Gastroenterology.
Boucourechliev, Andre. Schumann. Boyars, Arthur, tr.
Boudaille, George, jt. auth. see Dominguin, Luis M.
Boudarel, R., et al. Dynamic Programming & Its Applications to Optimal Control.
Boudhiba, Abdelwahab. La Sociologie Du Developpement Africain: Tendances Actuelles De la Recherche et Bibliographie.
Boudin, Louis B. Socialism & War.
Boudon, Philippe. Lived-In Architecture: Le Corbusier's Pessac Revisited. Onn, Gerald, tr.
Boudon, Raymond. The Logic of Social Action: An Introduction to Sociological Analysis. Silverman, David, tr. from Fr.
Boufjaily, Vance. The End of My Life.
Boughey, Arthur S. Ecology of Populations.
--Man & the Environment.
Boughton, Brian. Reinforced Concrete Detailer's Manual.
--Reinforced Concrete Detailer's Manual.
Boughton, Brian W. Building & Civil Engineering Construction.
Bougis, P., ed. Marine Plankton Ecology.
Bouis, Antonina W., tr. see Volkov, Solomon.
Boulaich, Abdeslam, et al. Five Eyes. Bowles, Paul, ed.
Boulden, James. I Am All.
Boulder Conference on High Energy Physics Staff. Proceedings. Mahanthappa, K. T., et al, eds.
Bouldin, Richard. Calculus with Applications to Business, Economics & Social Science.
--Mathematics with Applications to Business, Economics & Social Sciences.
Boulding, Elise, jt. auth. see Boulding, Kenneth E.
Boulding, Kenneth E. Beasts, Ballads, & Bouldingisms. Beilock, Richard P., ed.
--Collected Papers of Kenneth E. Boulding, Vol. 3: Political Economy. Singell, Larry D., ed.
--Collected Papers of Kenneth E. Boulding, Vol. 4: Toward a General Social Science. Singell, Larry D., ed.
--Collected Papers of Kenneth E. Boulding, Vol. 5: International Systems. Singell, Larry D., ed.
--Sonnets from the Interior Life & Other Autobiographical Verse.
Boulding, Kenneth E. & Boulding, Elise. Introduction to the Global Society: Interdisciplinary Perspectives.
Boulez, Pierre. Notes of an Apprenticeship.
Boulgarides, James & Fischer, Mary. Are You in the Right Job?
Boulle, Pierre. Le Bourreau.
--La Face.
--Le Jardin De Kanashima.
--Le Jeux de l'Esprit.
--Le Sacrilege Malais.
--Les Voies du Salut.
Boulougouris, John C. & Rabalivas, Andreas D., eds. The Treatment of Phobic & Obsessive Compulsive Disorders.
Boult, Adrian C. My Own Trumpet: The Memoirs of Sir Adrian Boult.
Boulter, Bruce. Woodturning in Pictures.
Boulton, A. J., jt. ed. see Katritzky, A. R.
Boulton, Majorie. The Anatomy of Poetry.
Boulton, Mary G. On Being a Mother.
Bouma, Arnold H., ed. Shell Dredging & Its Influence on Gulf Coast Environments.
Bouma, J. J., jt. ed. see Tromp, S. W.
Bouma, J. L. Beyond Vengeance.
--Burning Valley.
Bouman, Herbert J., tr. see Von Loewenich, Walter.

Authors

Boumans, P. W. Atomic Absorption Spectroscopy-Past, Present & Future: To Commemorate the 25th Anniversary of Alan Walsh's Landmark Paper in Spectrochimica Acta.
Boumans, P. W., ed. Analytical Spectroscopy: A Polychrome Branch of Science: Proceedings of the Twenty-third Colloquim International, including the 10th International Conference on Atomic Spectroscopy, Amsterdam, 26 June-1 July 1983.
--Atomic Absorption Spectroscopy: Past, Present & Future, Pt. 2: To Commemorate the 25th Anniversary of Alan Walsh's Landmark Paper in Spectrochimica Acta.
--Plasma Spectrochemistry 3: Proceedings of the 1985 European Winter Conference on Plasma Spectrochemistry, 7-11 January 1985, Leysin, Switzerland.
Boumans, P. W., et al, eds. A Profile of Current Developments in Atomic Spectroscopy: Dedicated to Kurt Laqua on the Occasion of His 65th Birthday.
Bound, Charles. Incantations.
Bouquet, Alan C. Religious Experience: Its Nature, Types, & Validity.
Bouquet, Frank L. Computer Technology: Simplified.
--The Do-it-Yourself Mutual Fund Book.
--Introduction to Materials Engineering.
Bouquet, Frank L., ed. & illus. Great Sermons.
Bourdette, Robert E. Richard Bentley: A Descriptive, Annotated Bibiography.
Bourdon, Clinton C. & Levitt, Raymond E. Union & Open-Shop Construction: Compensation, Work Practices, & Labor Markets.
Bourgaut, P. C., jt. auth. see Ciancio, S. G.
Bourgeois, Andre, et al. Studies in French Literature.
Bourgeron, J. P. & Balbo, P. J. Nude Nineteen Twenty-Five.
Bourgeron, J. P., ed. Nude Nineteen Hundred.
Bourgoignie, jt. auth. see Fontaine.
Bourjaily, Vance. Confessions of a Spent Youth.
--The Great Fake Book.
Bourke, Myles M. Job.
Bourne, A., jt. ed. see Steele, F.
Bourne, David L., jt. auth. see Adolph, Harold.
Bourne, Edward G., jt. ed. see Olson, Julius E.
Bourne, Frank C., abridged by see Gibbon, Edward.
Bourne, G. H. & Danielli, J. F. International Review of Cytology Supplement.
Bourne, G. H; see Metzner, H.
Bourne, G. H., ed. Chimpanzee: A Series of Volumes on the Chimpanzee. Incl. Vol. 1. Anatomy, Behavior, & Diseases of Chimpanzees; Vol. 2. Physiology, Behavior, Serology, & Diseases of Chimpanzees; Vol. 3. Immunology, Infections, Hormones, Anatomy, & Behavior; Vol. 4. Behavior, Growth, & Pathology of Chimpanzees; Vol. 5. Histology, Reproduction, & Restraint; Vol. 6. Anatomy & Pathology with General Subject Index & Condensed Bibliographic Index. S Karger.
Bourne, Geoffrey. Division of Labor in Cells.
Bourne, Geoffrey, ed. The Biochemistry & Physiology of Bone.
Bourne, Geoffrey H. The Structure & Function of Muscle.
Bourne, Geoffrey H., ed. Human & National Nutrition.
--Non-Human Primates & Medical Research.
--Nutritional Considerations in a Changing World.
--World Nutritional Determinants.
Bourne, Geoffrey H., jt. ed. see Sandler, Maurice.
Bourne, Geoggrey H. & Danielli, James F., eds. International Review of Cytology.
Bourne, Gordon. Baby's First Year.
Bourne, Joanna W. Her Ladyship's Companion.
Bourne, Larry S. Geography of Housing.
Bourne, Larry S. & Hitchcock, John R., eds. Urban Housing Markets: Recent Directions in Research & Policy.
Bourne, Miriam A. First Family: George Washington & His Intimate Relations.
--The Ladies of Castine.
Bourne, P. G., ed. Psychology & Physiology of Stress.
Bourne, Peter G., ed. Addiction.
Bourne, Russell, ed. see Borland, Hal.
Bournonville, August. My Theatre Life. McAndrew, Patricia, tr.
Bouros, Michael P. Getting into VSAM: An Introduction & Technical Reference.
Bourque, Daniel P. Report to Congress & the Secretary by the Task Force on Long-Term Health Care Policies.
Boussard, Jacques. Civilization of Charlemagne.
Boussel, Patrice, et al. History of Pharmacy & the Pharmaceutical Industry.
Boussinot, R. L' Encyclopedie du Cinema: A-H.
--L' Encyclopedie du Cinema: I-Z.
Bouteille, Daniel. Fluid Logic Controls & Industrial Automation.
Bouterin, Antoine & Crossman, Elizabeth. Cooking with Antoine at Le Perigord.
Bouwens, A. J. Digital Instrumentation.
Bova, Ben. Amazing Laser.
--Assured Survival: How to Stop the Nuclear Arms Race.
--The High Road.
--Notes to a Science Fiction Writer.
--Science--Who Needs It?
--Starflight & Other Improbabilities.
Bova, Ben, ed. The Science Fiction Hall of Fame.
--The Science Fiction Hall of Fame.
Bove, Alexander A. Joint Property.
Bove, Alfred A., jt. ed. see Santamore, William P.
Bovee, Courtland L. Better Business Writing for Bigger Profits.
--Business Writing Workshop.
Bovee, Courtland L. & Arens, William F. Contemporary Advertising.
Bovey, Frank A. High Resolution NMR of Macromolecules.
--Nuclear Magnetic Resonance Spectroscopy.
--Polymer Conformation & Configuration.
Bovis, H. Eugene. Jerusalem Question: 1917-1968.
Bow & Arrow Magazine Staff & Lewis, Jack, eds. Archery Equipment Illustrated.
Bowden, Brad S. The Unkept Grave of Tom Turbaville.
Bowden, Charles. Killing the Hidden Waters.
Bowden, Charles M., et al, eds. Optical Bistability One.
Bowden, Douglas M. Aging in Nonhuman Primates.
Bowden, John & Richmond, James, eds. A Reader in Contemporary Theology.
Bowden, John, tr. see Beyerlin, Walter.
Bowden, John, tr. see Busch, Eberhard.
Bowden, John, tr. see Cullmann, Oscar.
Bowden, John, tr. see Dumas, Andre.
Bowden, John, tr. see Grollenberg, Lucas.
Bowden, John, tr. see Hengel, Martin.
Bowden, John, tr. see Herrmann, Siegfried.
Bowden, John, tr. see Jagersma, Henk.
Bowden, John, tr. see Reventlow, Henning G.
Bowden, John, tr. see Schmithals, Walter.
Bowden, John, tr. see Theissen, Gerd.
Bowden, Ken, jt. auth. see Nicklaus, Jack.
Bowden, Malcolm. Rise of the Evolution Fraud.
Bowditch, James L., jt. auth. see Buono, Anthony F.
Bowdler, G. W. Measurements in High-Voltage Test Circuits.
Bowdon, Boyce A. Empowered: Living Experience of Talking with God.
Bowdon, Susan J., jt. auth. see Munger, Evelyn M.
Bowe, Forrest & Daniels, Mary F., eds. French Literature in Early American Translation: A Bibliographical Survey of Books & Pamphlets Printed in the United States from 1668 Through 1820.
Bowe, Frank G. Personal Computers & Special Needs.
Bowen, A. & Vagner, R., eds. Passive & Low Energy Alternatives I: The First International PLEA Conference, Bermuda, September 13-15, 1982.
Bowen, Alice. Intimate Persuasion.
Bowen, B. J. Trace Elements in Biochemistry.
Bowen, D. Q., ed. Quaternary Science Reviews.
--Quaternary Science Reviews.
--Quternary Science Reviews.
Bowen, Elbert R., et al. Communicative Reading.
Bowen, Elizabeth. Death of the Heart.
--The Heat of the Day.
--Seven Winters.
Bowen, Francis. The Principles of Political Economy, Applied to the Condition, the Resources, & the Institutions of the American People.
Bowen, Frank M. & Lee, Eugene C. Limiting State Spending: The Legislature or the Electorate.
Bowen, Ian. Acceptable Inequalities.
Bowen, J. Donald, jt. auth. see Marquez, Ely.
Bowen, James K. & Van Der Beets, Richard, eds. American Short Fiction: Readings & Criticism.
Bowen, John. The McGuffin.
--These Primal Years.
Bowen, K. C., ed. Management Science in Defence.
Bowen, R. N. Exploration of Time.
Bowen, Ray P. The Dramatic Construction of Balzac's Novels.
Bowen, Rich & Fay, Dick. Hot Dog Chicago: A Native's Dining Guide.
Bowen, Robert T., jt. auth. see Manjone, Joseph A.
Bowen, Tang, jt. ed. see Stockwell, Foster.
Bowen, W. R., compiled by. Turfgrass Pests.
Bowen, William G., jt. auth. see Baumol, William G.
Bowen, William, Jr. Globalism: America's Demise.
Bower, Blair T., jt. auth. see Brady, Gordon L.
Bower, Eli M., jt. auth. see Shears, Loyda M.
Bower, Fay L. Process of Planning Nursing Care: A Theoretical Model.
Bower, George. The Jordons.
Bower, John. In Search of the Past: An Introduction to Archaelogy.
Bower, Sharon A. Painless Public Speaking.
Bower, Virginia & Thorp, Robert L. Spirit & Ritual: The Morse Collection of Ancient Chinese Art.
Bowerman, Guy E., Jr. The Compensations of War: The Diary of an Ambulance Driver during the Great War. Carnes, Mark C., ed.
Bowerman, William J. Coaching Track & Field.
Bowerman, William J. & Harris, W. E. Jogging.
Bowers, Arden C. & Thompson, June M. Clinical Manual of Health Assessment.
Bowers, Carolyn. Taxing Insurers: The Revolution Ahead. Hadley, Richard D., ed.
Bowers, Cathy, jt. auth. see Newman, Anne.
Bowers, Fredson, ed. see Nabokov, Vladimir.
Bowers, J. K. & Cheshire, P. C. Agriculture, the Countryside & Land Use: An Economic Critique.
Bowers, Mary B., ed. Stories About Birds & Bird Watchers: From Bird Watcher's Digest.
Bowers, Paul C., Jr., jt. auth. see Berquist, Goodwin F.
Bowers, Peter M. Antique Plane Guide.
--A Complete Guide to Aviation Photography.
--Guide to Homebuilts.
--The Twenty-Five Most Practical Homebuilt Aircraft.
Bowers, Q. David & Martin, Mary L. The Postcards of Alphonse Mucha.
Bowers, Mrs. R. L., ed. Early Settlers of Terry County.
Bowers, Richard A. Optical-Electronic Publishing Directory, 1986.
--Optical Publishing Directory.
Bowers, Tom. Maxwell.
Bowersox, Donald J., et al. Introduction to Transportation.
Bowes, Frederick P. The Culture of Early Charleston.
Bowhill, S. A., ed. Review Papers: International Solar-Terrestrial Physics Symposium, Sao-Paolo, June, 1974.
Bowick, Chris & Kearney, Tim. Introduction to Satellite TV.
Bowie, Alexandra, jt. auth. see Baviello, Mary A.
Bowie, Donald. Cable Harbor.
Bowie, J. see Walters, Richard F., et al.
Bowie, Norman E., ed. Ethical Issues in Government.
Bowie, Robert R., et al. Trilateral Relations at the Threshold of the New Decade.
Bowie, Theodore & Thimme, Diether, eds. The Carrey Drawings of the Parthenon Sculptures.
Bowker, Lee H. Women & Crime in America.
Bowker, R. R., Co. Staff, ed. American Book Trade Directory, 1987-1988.
--American Library Directory, 1987-1988.
--Books in Print Supplement, 1987-88.
--Books in Print 1987-88.
--The Software Encyclopedia, 1988.
--Ulrich's International Periodicals Directory, 1987-1988.
Bowker, R. R., Staff, ed. American Art Directory.
--Books Out of Print, 1983-87.
--Bowker's Law Books & Serials in Print, 1988.
--Children's Books in Print, 1987-88.
--The Complete Directory of Large Print Books & Serials, 1988.
--Directory of American Research & Technology, 1988.
--El-Hi Textbooks & Serials in Print, 1988.
--Irregular Serials & Annuals, 1987.
--Literary Market Place, 1988.
--Medical & Health Care Books & Serials in Print, 1988.
--Paperbound Books in Print-Spring, 1988.
--Scientific & Technical Books & Serials in Print, 1988.
--Subject Guide to Books in Print, 1987-88.
--Subject Guide to Children's Books in Print, 1987-88.
--Tradeshow Week Data Book, 1988.
--Who Distributes What & Where: An International Directory of Publishers, Imprints, Agents, & Distributors.
--Who's Who in American Art.
--Words on Cassette 1987.
Bowker, Richard. Marlborough Street.
Bowl, Ric, jt. auth. see Black, Jim.
Bowle, John. Man Through the Ages.
Bowler, M. G. Gravitation & Relativity.
--Nuclear Physics.
Bowler, Peter J. Evolution: The History of an Idea.
Bowles, Ella S. About Antiques.
Bowles, Eric. One Doubles Enough.
Bowles, G. Strategies for Women's Studies in the Eighties.
Bowles, Joseph E. Engineering Properties of Soils & Their Measurements.
--Physical & Geotechnical Properties of Soils.
Bowles, Patrick, tr. see Arrabal, Fernando.
Bowles, Patrick, tr. see Beckett, Samuel.
Bowles, Patrick, tr. see Durrenmatt, Friedrich.
Bowles, Paul. Next to Nothing: Collected Poems 1926-1977.
Bowles, Paul, ed. see Boulaich, Abdeslam, et al.
Bowles, Paul, tr. She Woke Me Up So I Killed Her.
Bowles, Stephen E. Sidney Lumet: A Guide to References & Resources.
Bowley, Agatha. Guiding the Normal Child.
Bowling, Ann. Delegation in General Practice: A Study of Doctors & Nurses.
Bowling, W. Kerby & Loving, Waldon. Management Fumbles & Union Recoveries.
Bowlt, John E., intro. by. Russian Theater & Costume Designs from the Fine Arts Museums of San Francisco.
Bowlt, John E., tr. see Krasovskaya, Vera.
Bowlt, John E., tr. see Sizov, E. S.
Bowman. Dictionary of Pharmacology.
Bowman & McQueen. Corporations Formation with Forms: Missouri.
Bowman, Arthur G. & Bond, Robert J. California Real Estate Principles.
Bowman, Arthur G., jt. auth. see Bond, Robert J.
Bowman, Arthur G., jt. auth. see Ogden, Melvin B.
Bowman, Clell Edgar. The Bereaved Husband.
--Crossexion.
--Human Equation.
--Saturday's Child.
Bowman, Ethel, jt. auth. see Palmer, Marjorie.
Bowman, George M. How to Be an Effective Bible Teacher.
Bowman, Joel P. & Branchaw, Bernadine P. Business Report Writing.
Bowman, John, jt. auth. see Aylesworth, Tom.
Bowman, John S., ed. The World Almanac of the American West.
Bowman, John W. Which Jesus?
Bowman, Kathleen. New Women in Art & Dance.
Bowman, Leona, ed. The Indespensable Shopping Guide. Jenkins, Jo-An. McColl, Patricia, ed.
Bowman, Locke E., Jr. Straight Talk About Teaching in Today's Church.
--Teaching Today: The Church's First Ministry.
Bowman, M. J. & Esaias, W. E., eds. Oceanic Fronts in Coastal Processes: Proceedings of a Workshop Held at the Marine Science Research Center, May 25-27, 1977.
Bowman, Michael P. Nursing Management & Education: A Conceptual Approach.
Bowman, Richard E., jt. auth. see Kircher, John F.
Bowman, Robert. Basic Financial Accounting.
Bowman, Rufus D. Church of the Brethren & the War, 1788-1914.
Bowman, Russell. From Chicago. Pace Gallery Publications Staff, ed.
--Philip Pearlstein: The Complete Paintings.
Bowman, Stephen. Morning Ran Red.
Bowman, Thomas H., Jr., ed. see Real Estate Education Company Staff.
Bowman, W. C., ed. Pharmacology & Therapeutics.
--Pharmacology & Therapeutics.
Bowman, William R. Limiting Conventional Forces in Europe: An Alternative to the Mutual & Balanced Force Reduction Negotiations.
Bown, Colin & Mooney, Peter. Cold War to Detente.
Bowring, Dave. Largemouth, Smallmouth & Close Kin.
Bowron, P. & Stephenson, F. W. Active Filters for Communication & Instrumentation.
Bowser, Eileen, ed. Biograph Bulletins: 1908-1912.
Bowyer, Jack. History of Building.
Bowyer, Kevin W. & Tomboulian, Sherryl J. Pascal for the IBM-PC: Turbo Pascal, PC-DOS Pascal, & UCSD p-System Pascal.
Bowyer, R. The Lowenfeld World Technique: Studies in Personality.
Box, George E. George E. P. Box: The Selected Works. Tiao, George C., ed.
Box, JoAnn. Naughty Jokes Rated "R"
Boxall, V. E. Drawing & Materials.
Boxer, Arabella. Fashionable First Courses.
Boxer, Charles R. The Church Militant & Iberian Expansion: 1440-1770.
Boxill, Edith H. Music Therapy for the Developmentally Disabled.
Boy Scouts of America. Canoeing.
--Cub Scout Family Book.
--Handbook for Skippers.
Boyajian, Ned R., jt. auth. see Collins, Henry H.
Boyan, Lee. Successful Cold Call Selling.
Boyang, Zuo, tr. see Stockwell, Foster & Bowen, Tang.
Boyars, Arthur, tr. see Boucourechliev, Andre.
Boyars, Carl & Klager, Karl, eds. Propellants Manufacture, Hazards, & Testing.
Boyarsky, Saul, ed. Urodynamics: Hydrodynamics of the Ureter & Renal Pelvis.
Boyarsky, Saul & Polakoski, Kenneth, eds. Goals in Male Reproductive Research: Proceedings of Conference on Future Goals in Reproductive Medicine & Surgery, 20 September, 1979, Bethesda, Md.
Boyce, Benjamin. Benevolent Man: A Life of Ralph Allen of Bath.
Boyce, D. E., et al. Optimal Subset Selection: Multiple Regression, Interdependence & Optimal Network Algorithms.

Boyce, Jefferson C. Microprocessor & Microcomputer Basics.
Boyce, Ronald R. The Bases of Economic Geography.
--Geographic Perspectives on Global Problems: An Introduction to Geography.
Boyce, William E. & DiPrima, Richard C. Introduction to Differential Equations.
Boycott, Rosie. Batty, Bloomers & Boycott: A Little Etymology of Eponymous Words.
Boyd & Walker. Marketing Management.
Boyd, A. An Atlas of World Affairs.
Boyd, A., jt. auth. see Kimber, Richard T.
Boyd, A. W., ed. Radiation Chemistry in Nuclear Reactor Technology.
Boyd, Elizabeth F. Bloomsbury Heritage: Their Mothers & Their Aunts.
Boyd, Ernest, ed. see De Balzac, Honore.
Boyd, Frank M. Ages & Dispensations.
Boyd, G. S., ed. see Biochemical Society Symposium, 34th.
Boyd, Gavin, jt. ed. see Feld, Werner.
Boyd, Greg, tr. see Baudelaire, Charles.
Boyd, Harper W., jt. auth. see Britt, Stewart H.
Boyd, Harper W., Jr. & Massy, William F. Marketing Management.
Boyd, Harper W., Jr., et al. Marketing Research: Text & Cases.
Boyd, John, compiled by. Tools for Agriculture: A Buyer's Guide to Low-Cost Agricultural Implements.
Boyd, John, et al. Counselor Supervision: Approaches, Preparation, Practices.
Boyd, Julianne, jt. auth. see Silver, Joan M.
Boyd, Laura M. Majistyka: A Case of Mental Rape.
Boyd, Margaret A. The Sew & Save Source Book: Your Guide to Supplies for Creative Sewing.
Boyd, Martin. Nuns in Jeopardy.
Boyd, Pauline, jt. auth. see Boyd, Selma.
Boyd, Preston, jt. auth. see Babcock, Dennis.
Boyd, R. Vernon. Undying Dedication.
Boyd, Robert D. As the Lord Revealed It to Me.
Boyd, Robert F. General Microbiology.
Boyd, Robin. Victorian Modern.
Boyd, Selma & Boyd, Pauline. Footprints in the Refrigerator.
Boyd, Shylah. American Made.
Boyd, Sterling. The Adam Style In America. Freedberg, S. J., ed.
Boyd, Sterling M; see O'Neal, William B.
Boyd, Susan, et al, eds. Groundwater: A Community Action Guide.
--Drinking Water: A Community Issue.
Boyd, William. School Ties: Two Screenplays. Guarnaschelli, Maria D., ed.
Boyd, William L., jt. ed. see Immegart, Glenn L.
Boyda, Ellen K. Respiratory Problems.
Boyd-Barrett, Oliver. The International News Agencies.
Boyd-Barrett, Oliver & Braham, Peter, eds. Media, Knowledge & Power.
Boyden, A. A. Perspectives in Zoology.
Boyden, Donald P., jt. ed. see Gill, Kay.
Boydston, Jo Ann, ed. Guide to the Works of John Dewey.
Boyer, Carl, III, jt. auth. see Jacobus, Donald L.
Boyer, Carl, 3rd. Ancestral Lines Revised.
Boyer, David L., et al, eds. The Philosopher's Annual, 1978.
Boyer, Deena. The Two Hundred Days of Eight & a Half. Kupelnick, Bruce S., ed.
Boyer, G. G. Morgette in the Yukon.
--Morgette on the Barbary Coast.
Boyer, Harriet, jt. ed. see Cabrera, Vicente.
Boyer, Mildred, jt. auth. see Andersson, Theodore.
Boyer, Patricia A., jt. auth. see Gibson, Charles H.
Boyer, R. E. Field Guide to Rock Weathering.
Boyer, Richard & Savageau, David. Places Rated Almanac: Your Guide to Finding the Best Places to Live in America.
--Rand McNally Retirement Places Rated.
Boyer, Rick. The Penny Ferry.
Boyer, Robert H. & Zahorski, Kenneth J. Fantasists on Fantasy.
Boyer, Walter E., et al. Songs along the Mahantonga: Pennsylvania Dutch Folksongs.
Boyer Argens, Jean Baptiste De see Baptiste De Boyer Argens, Jean.
Boyers, Judith T., ed. Pensions in Perspective: A Guide to Qualified Retirement Plans.
Boyers, Peggy, jt. ed. see Boyers, Robert.
Boyers, Robert & Boyers, Peggy, eds. The Salmagundi Reader.
Boyes, Lindy. Pilot's Weather Guide.
Boykin, James H. Inter-Ethnic Death Rate Differential in Florida.
Boyko, P. America Latina: Expansion del Imperialismo y Crisis de la Via Capitalista de Desarrollo.
Boylan, Brian. Benedict Arnold: The Dark Eagle.
Boylan, Carle. Last Resorts: A Novel.
Boylan, Claire. Holy Pictures.
Boyle, Andrew. The Fourth Man.
Boyle, D. J. A Student's Guide to Piaget.
Boyle, Denis & Braddick, Bill. The Challenge of Change: Developing Business Leaders for the 1980s.
Boyle, Donzella C. Quest of a Hemisphere.
Boyle, Robert H. & Ciampi, Elgin. Bass.
Boyle, Veronica. A Mind of Her Own.
Boyles, C. Allan. Acoustic Waveguides: Applications to Oceanic Science.
Boyles, Marcia V., et al. The Health Professions.
Boyles, Margaret. The Margaret Boyles Book of Needle Art.
--Margaret Boyles' Designs for Babies.
--Margaret Boyles' Designs for Babies.
Boyles-Martin, Susan & Koek, Karin, eds. Encyclopedia of Associations: Index.
--Encyclopedia of Associations, Vol. 3: New Associations & Projects.
Boylestad, Robert L. & Nashelsky, Louis. Electricity, Electronics, & Electromagnetics: Principles & Applications.
--Electronic Devices & Circuit Theory.
Boynton, Alton L. & McKeehan, Wallace L., eds. Ions, Cell Proliferation & Cancer.
Boynton, Bea. That Hilarious First Year.
--A Very Amateur Guide to Antique Bottle Collecting.
Boynton, Edward C., ed. see United States Army, Continental Army Staff.
Boynton, G. R. & Kim, Chong Lim. Legislative Systems in Developing Countries.
Boynton, Robert. Human Color Vision.
Boynton, Rose W., et al. Manual of Ambulatory Pediatrics.
--Manual of Ambulatory Pediatrics.
Boynton, Sandra. If at First...
Boytinck, Paul. C. P. Snow: A Reference Guide.
Bozarth-Campbell, Alla. Life Is Goodbye-Life Is Hello: Grieving Well Through All Kinds of Loss.
--The Word's Body: An Incarnational Aesthetic of Interpretation.
Bozell, Patricia, jt. auth. see Whelan, James R.
Bozhilov, Bozhidar. American Pages. Bozhilova, Cornelia, tr.
Bozhilova, Cornelia, tr. see Bozhilov, Bozhidar.
Bozzoli, Belinda. The Political Nature of a Ruling Class Capital & Ideology in South Africa, 1890-1933.
Braaten, Carl E. Eschatology & Ethics: Essays on the Theology & Ethics of the Kingdom of God.
--The Flaming Center: A Theology of the Christian Mission.
--New Directions in Theology Today.
--Stewards of the Mysteries: Sermons for Festivals & Special Occasions.
--The Whole Counsel of God.
Braaten, Carl E. & Braaten, LaVonne. The Living Temple: A Practical Theology of the Body & the Foods of the Earth.
Braaten, Carl E., ed. The New Church Debate: Issues Facing American Lutheranism.
Braaten, Carl E., tr. see Kahler, Martin.
Braaten, LaVonne, jt. auth. see Braaten, Carl E.
Brabander, M. De see De Brabander, M., et al.
Brabazon, Francis. Four & Twenty Blackbirds.
--The Silent Word.
Brabazon, James. Dorothy L. Sayers.
--Dorothy L. Sayers: A Biography.
Brabb, George J. Computers & Information Systems.
--Computers & Information Systems in Business.
Brabbs, Derry. English Country Pubs.
Brabec, Barbara. Homemade Money: The Definitive Guide to Success in a Home Business.
--Homemade Money: The Definitive Guide to Success in a Homebased Business.
Brabner-Smith, John W. Who Will Study Justice.
Brace. Between Wind & Water.
Brace, Gerald W. Between Wind & Water.
--Days That Were.
Bracewell, R. N. The Fourier Transform & Its Applications.
Bracey, Doris C. The Tale of Two Towns.
Bracey, H. E. People & the Countryside.
Bracey, Hyler J., et al. Basic Management: An Experience Based Approach.
Bracher, Marjory L. Love Is No Luxury.
Brachet, J. Introduction to Molecular Embryology.
Brachet, Jean & Bonotto, S., eds. Biology of Acetabularia: Proceedings.
Bracken. Animal Crackers.
Bracken, Carolyn, illus. The Baby Bear.
Bracken, Carolyn & Barbaresi, Nina, illus. Farmhouse.
Bracken, Dorothy K. & Redway, Maurine W. Early Texas Homes.
Bracken, Ian. Urban Planning Methods: Research & Policy Analysis.
Bracken, Peg. The I Hate to Cook Almanack: A Book of Days.
--A Window over the Sink.
--A Window over the Sink: A Mainly Affectionate Memoir.
Bracken, Susan. Canadian Almanac & Directory 1982.
Bracken, Susan, ed. Canadian Almanac & Directory 1985.
Brackenbury, Mark. Normandy & Channel Islands Pilot: Calais to St. Malo.
Brackenbury, Rosalind. Sense & Sensuality.
Brackett, Leigh. Eric John Stark: Outlaw of Mars.
Brackin, Ivan L. & Fitzgerald, William. Darts.
Brackman, Rita. Vybor V Adu: Zhizneutverzhdenie solzhenitsynskikh geroev.
Bradbury, Bianca. Boy on the Run.
--I'm Vinny, I'm Me.
--In Her Father's Footsteps.
--Loner.
--Mutt.
--Mutt.
--My Pretty Girl.
--Those Traver Kids.
--Two on an Island.
--Where's Jim Now.
Bradbury, D. E., jt. ed. see Thrower, Norman J.
Bradbury, E. M. & Javaherian, K., eds. The Organization & Expression of the Eukaryotic Genome.
Bradbury, Frederick. Bradbury's Book of Hallmarks.
--Bradbury's Book of Hallmarks.
--History of Old Sheffield Plate.
Bradbury, Jim. Shakespeare & His Theatre. Reeves, Marjorie, ed.
Bradbury, Katherine, et al. Futures for a Declining City: Simulations for the Cleveland Area.
Bradbury, Malcolm. Saul Bellow.
Bradbury, Malcolm & Temperley, Howard, eds. Introduction to American Studies.
Bradbury, Parnell. Mechanics of Healing: Spinology.
Bradbury, Ray. The Complete Poems of Ray Bradbury.
--Fahrenheit Four Fifty-One.
--Fahrenheit Four Fifty-One.
--Machineries of Joy.
--Something Wicked This Way Comes.
Bradbury, S. The Microscope.
--The Microscope Past & Present.
Braddick, Bill, jt. auth. see Boyle, Denis.
Braddock, David. Opening Closed Doors: The Deinstitutionalization of Disabled Individuals.
Braddon, Russell. The Finalists.
--The Naked Island.
Braddy, Haldeen. Three Dimensional Poe.
Brademas, John. Washington, D. C. to Washington Square.
Braden, Charles S. Christian Science Today: Power, Policy, Practice.
Bradford. Great Siege.
--Nelson Essential Hero.
Bradford, Barbara Taylor. Designs for Casual Living.
--Hold the Dream.
--How to Solve Your Decorating Problems.
--Luxury Designs for Apartment Living.
--Making Space Grow.
Bradford, Charles E. The God Between. Coffen, Richard W., ed.
Bradford, Ernie. The Story of the Mary Rose.
Bradford, Ernle. Cleopatra.
--Four Centuries of European Jewelry.
Bradford, H. F., ed. Neurotransmitter Interaction & Compartmentation.
Bradford, H. F. & Marsden, C. D., eds. Biochemistry & Neurology.
Bradford, Kirk A. Existentialism & Casework.
Bradford, Larry J., ed. Physiological Measures of the Audiovestibular System.
Bradford, Leland P. Preparing for Retirement: A Program for Survival - A Participant's Workbook.
--Preparing for Retirement: A Program for Survival - A Trainer's Kit.
Bradford, Michael. Counter-Coup.
Bradford, Ned & Bradford, Pam. Boston's Locke-Ober Cafe.
Bradford, Pam, jt. auth. see Bradford, Ned.
Bradford, Richard H. The Virginius Affair.
Bradford, W. Murray. Business Tax Deduction Master Guide: Strategies for Business & Professional People.
Bradford, W. Murray & Davis, Glenn B. Business Tax Deduction Master Guide.
--J. K. Lasser's Business Tax Deduction Master Guide 1988.
Bradford, William & Winslow, Edward. Mourt's Relation.
Bradford, William, jt. auth. see Bates, Timothy.
Bradlee, Benjamin C. Conversations with Kennedy.
Bradley. Applied Market & Social Research.
Bradley, Anthony, ed. Contemporary Irish Poetry: An Anthology.
Bradley, B. J., ed. see Ferreira, T. Gomes & Proddow, Mary P.
Bradley, Bert. Fundamentals of Speech Communication: The Credibility of Ideas.
Bradley, Beverly H. Toward the Setting of the Sun.
Bradley, Bill. The Last of the Great Stations. Walker, Jim, ed.
Bradley, Bill, jt. auth. see Farewell, R. C.
Bradley, Bill, ed. see Middleton, William D.
Bradley, Charles W. Manager's Guide to Small Computers.
Bradley, David, jt. auth. see Jones, Dewitt.
Bradley, E. R. Selected Readings in Modern World History.
Bradley, Edward S., jt. auth. see Teweles, Richard J.
Bradley, Francis S., ed. see United States Children's Bureau Staff.
Bradley, Ian, ed. & intro. by. The Annotated Gilbert & Sullivan.
Bradley, James. Introduction to Data-Base Management in Business.
Bradley, Jessica, ed. see Fry, Philip.
Bradley, Julia C. Microsoft BASIC Using Modular Structure.
Bradley, Lavinia. Inkle Weaving: A Comprehensive Manual.
Bradley, Marion Zimmer. The Brass Dragon.
--The City of Sorcery.
--The Colors of Space. Stine, Hank, ed.
--Darkover Landfall.
--The Door Through Space. Baen, James P., ed.
--Drums of Darkness (Leo)
--Endless Universe.
--The Forbidden Tower.
--The Heritage of Hastur.
--The House Between the Worlds.
--Mists of Avalon.
--The Planet Savers.
--The Planet Savers. Bd. with The Sword of Aldones. Ace Bks.
--The Ruins of Isis. Freas, Polly & Freas, Kelly, eds.
--The Shattered Chain.
--Star of Danger.
--Stormqueen!
--The Sword of Aldones.
--The Web of Darkness.
--Web of Light.
--The Winds of Darkover.
--The World Wreckers.
Bradley, P. B. & Costa, E., eds. Studies of Narcotic Drugs: 26th International Congress of Physiological Sciences, New Delhi, October 1974.
Bradley, Rodger. GWR Two Cylinder 4-6-0s & 2-6-9s.
Bradley, Ronald J., jt. ed. see Smythies, John R.
Bradley, Sculley, et al, eds. see Crane, Stephen.
Bradley, Sculley, et al, eds. see Hawthorne, Nathaniel.
Bradley, Sculley, et al, eds. see Whitman, Walt.
Bradley, Ute. Applied Market & Social Research.
Bradley, W. B., et al, eds. Emerging Energy Technologies: 1978.
Bradman, Tony. John Lennon.
Bradon, Russel, et al. River Journeys.
Bradshaw, Annette & Franson, Gwyn. Forever Families.
Bradshaw, Buck. The Tomahawk.
Bradshaw, Gillian. Hawk of May.
--In Winter's Shadow.
--Kingdom of Summer.
Bradshaw, J., ed. The Women's Liberation Movement: Europe & North America.
Bradshaw, Jonathan & Harris, Toby, eds. Energy & Social Policy.
Bradshaw, L. Jack. Introduction to Molecular Biological Techniques.
Bradshaw, P., ed. Turbulence.
Bradshaw, Reagan, jt. auth. see Smith, Griffin, Jr.
Bradsher, Frances. The Preacher Had Ten Kids.
Bradstreet, Valerie. The Fortune Wheel.
--The Ivory Fan.
Bradt, George N., jt. auth. see Bradt, Hilary J.
Bradt, Hilary. Backpacker's Africa.
Bradt, Hilary & Pilkington, John. Backpacking & Trekking in Chile & Argentina.
Bradt, Hilary J. & Bradt, George N. Backpacking in North America: The Great Outdoors.
Bradway, Lauren. Children with Special Needs in the Classroom.
Brady, C., et al, eds. Industrial-Commercial Refrigeration Maintenance.
Brady, Donald. Logic of the Scientific Method.
Brady, Donald, ed. Philosophy in the Flesh: A Reader.
Brady, Frank, ed. see Wels, Byron G.
Brady, G. S. & Clauser, Henry. Materials Handbook.
Brady, Gerald P., jt. auth. see Thompson, George C.
Brady, Gordon L. & Bower, Blair T. Air Quality Management: Qualifying Benefits.
Brady, Irene. Beaver Year.
--A Mouse Named Mus.
--Owlet the Great Horned Owl.
--Wild Babies: A Canyon Sketchbook.
Brady, J. M. The Theory of Computer Science: A Programming Approach.
Brady, James E. & Holum, John R. Fundamentals of Chemistry.
Brady, James E. & Humiston, Gerard E. General Chemistry: Principles & Structure.
Brady, John. The Craft of the Screenwriter.
Brady, Joseph V., jt. auth. see Meyer, Eugene.
Brady, Katherine. Father's Days.
Brady, Kathleen. Inside Out.
Brady, L. W., et al. Ovarian Tumors.
Brady, Maureen. Give Me Your Good Ear.

Authors

Brady, Maxine. Bloomingdales.
Brady, Maxine, jt. auth. see Hasegawa, Goro.
Brady, Michael. The Complete Ski Cross-Country.
Brady, Roscoe O., jt. ed. see Barranger, John A.
Brady, Terence & Jones, Evan. The Fight Against Slavery.
Brady, Upton, ed. see Chase, Alston.
Brady, Upton, ed. see Household, Geoffrey.
Brady, Upton, ed. see Morley, John D.
Brady, Upton, ed. see Searle, Ronald.
Brady, Upton B., ed. see Madden, Deirdre.
Braemer, Alice & Hayford, Dolores. Cultism to Charisma: My Seven Years with Jeane Dixon.
Braendli, H. Treffwahrscheinlichkeit und Autokorrelations Funktionen.
Braestrup, Angelica, ed. see Blain, Beryl B., et al.
Braet Von Uberfeldt, J., jt. auth. see Bing, V.
Bragard, Roger. Musical Instruments in Art & History.
Bragdon, Allen D., ed. Basic Car Care Illustrated.
Bragdon, Claude. The Beautiful Necessity.
Bragdon, Clifford R., ed. Noise Pollution: A Guide to Information Sources.
Bragdon, H. D. Counseling the College Student.
Bragg, Bill. Enemy in Sight.
--Enemy in Sight.
Bragg, John E. In Search of Truth.
Bragg, Linda B. Rainbow Roun' Mah Shoulder.
Bragg, Melvyn. Josh Lawton.
--Land of the Lakes.
--The Maid of Buttermere.
Bragg, Miriam C. The Incredible Miles & Other Poems.
Bragg, Patricia. Nature's Healing System for Better Eyesight.
Bragg, Patricia, jt. auth. see Bragg, Paul C.
Bragg, Paul C. & Bragg, Patricia. Bragg Apple Cider Vinegar System.
--Bragg Vegetarian Gourmet Recipes.
--Building Powerful Nerve Force.
--Building Strong Feet.
--Fitness Program with Spine Motion.
--How to Keep the Heart Healthy Fit.
--Miracle of Fasting: For Physical, Mental & Spiritual Prjuvenation.
--Natural Way to Reduce.
--New Science of Health.
--Shocking Truth about Water.
--Toxicless Diet & Body Purification: The Stay-Ageless Program.
--Your Health & Your Hair.
Bragg, W. F. Buckskin Rider.
--Legacy of a Gunfighter.
Bragg, William F. Wyoming: Wild & Wooly.
Bragger, Jeanette D. & Shupp, Robert P. Chere Francoise: Revision de la Grammaire Francaise.
Bragger, Jeannette & Shupp, Robert P. First-Year French: Debuts Culturels.
Bragonier, Reginald, Jr., jt. ed. see Fisher, David.
Braham, Peter, jt. ed. see Boyd-Barrett, Oliver.
Braham, Randolph L., ed. Documents on Major European Governments.
Brahms, Johannes. Complete Piano Works for Four Hands. Mandyczewski, Eusebius, ed.
--Complete Songs for Solos Voice & Piano. Mandyczewski, Eusebius, ed. Appelbaum, Stanley, tr. from Ger.
--Johannnes Brahms & Theodor Billroth: Letters From a Musical Friendship.
Braibanti, Ralph J., ed. Political & Administrative Development.
Braiker, Harriet B., ed. see Polich, J. Michael & Armor, David J.
Brailsford, Henry N. Why Capitalism Means War.
Brain & Brain. TRS-80 Color Computer Games Master.
Brain & Carbone. Current Therapy In Hematology-Oncology 1985-1986.
Brain Edema Symposium Staff. Proceedings of the Brain Edema Symposium, Vienna, 1965. Klatzo, I. & Seitelberger, F., eds.
Brain, Paul F., ed. Alcohol & Aggression.
Brain, Robert, tr. see Simenon, Georges.
Brainard, Jack, jt. auth. see Phinny, Peter.
Brainard, John B. Control of Migraine.
Braine, John. Waiting for Sheila.
Braitenberg, Valentino, jt. auth. see Kemali, Milena.
Braithwaite, George, tr. see Takekoshi, Yosaburo.
Braithwaite, Henry W. The Conductor's Art.
Braithwaite, John. Corporate Crime in the Pharmaceutical Industry.
--Prisons, Education & Work: Towards a National Employment Strategy for Prisoners.
Braithwaite, Julia & Gorder, Christine. In the States: Wisconsin, Arizona, New York.
Braithwaite, Rick. The Dictionary of Soccer.
Braithwrite, Catherine, ed. see Pearson, Kevin.
Braitsch, O. Salt Deposits, Their Origin & Composition. Burek, P. J. & Nairn, A. E., trs. from Ger.
Brake, Brian, jt. auth. see Blumhardt, Doreen.
Brake, Mike. The Sociology of Youth Culture & Youth Subcultures.
Brakel, Willem, jt. auth. see De Vries, Barend A.
Bramah, Ernest. The Celestial Omnibus: Collected Tales of Kai Lung.
Brambilla, Robert. Learning from Atlanta.
Bramble, Donna L. & Davis, Dwight F. Evaluations of Social Service Programs: An Annotated & Unannotated Bibliography.
Brame, Edward & Graselli, Jeanette. Infrared & Raman Spectroscopy.
Bramer, Mary. This Is My Story, This Is My Song.
Bramer, T. C., et al. Basic Vibration Control.
Bramfitt, B. L. & Magonon, P. L., eds. Metallurgy of Continuous Annealed Sheet Steel.
Bramfitt, B. L., jt. ed. see Mangonon, P. L., Jr.
Bramfitt, Bruce L., jt. ed. see Kot, Richard A.
Bramly, Serge. Macumba: The Teachings of Maria-Jose, Mother of the Gods.
Brammer, William. The Gay Place.
Bramnick, Lea & Simon, Anita. The Parents' Solution Book.
--The Parents' Solution Book: Your Child from Five to Twelve.
Brams, Jane M. Golden Ingots.
Brams, Steven J., jt. ed. see C Q Press Staff.
Bramsen, Michele B. A Portrait of Elie Halevy.
Bramson, M. A. Infrared Radiation: A Handbook for Applications.
Bramson, Morris, jt. auth. see Selub, Morton.
Bramson, Morris, jt. auth. see Solomon, Lawrence.
Bramson, Robert M. & Bramson, Susan. Stressless Home: A Step-by-Step Guide to Turning Your Home into the Haven You Deserve.
Bramson, Robert M., jt. auth. see Harrison, Allen F.
Bramson, Robert N. Coping with Difficult People.
Bramson, Susan, jt. auth. see Bramson, Robert M.
Branca, Margherita, et al. Immune Complexes & Their Role in the Pathogenesis of Various Diseases.
Brancato, Gilda & Polebaum, Elliot E. The Rights of Police Officers.
Brancato, Robin. Blinded by the Light.
Brancazio, Peter J. Sportscience: Physical Laws & Optimum Performance.
Branch, Alan E. Elements of Export Marketing & Management.
--Elements of Export Practice.
Branch, Anna H. Shoes That Danced & Other Poems.
Branch, E. Douglas. Westward: The Romance of the American Frontier.
Branch, Houston & Smith, Wendell. The Unreasonable American.
Branch, Tom. The Photographer's Build-It-Yourself Book.
Branch, Watson G., ed. Melville: The Critical Heritage.
Branchaw, Bernadine P., jt. auth. see Bowman, Joel P.
Brand, Carl F. The British Labour Party: A Short History.
Brand, Eugene. Rite Thing.
Brand, Eugene L. Baptism: A Pastoral Perspective.
Brand, Janet & Tolins, Stephen. The Nursing Student's Guide to Surgery.
Brand, Jeanne L., jt. auth. see Mora, George.
Brand, John. Observations on the Popular Antiquities of Great Britain: Chiefly Illustrating the Origin of Our Vulgar & Provincial Customs, Ceremonies & Superstitions.
Brand, Katarzyna Mroczkowska see Kapuscinski, Ryszard.
Brand, Larry. Birthpyre.
Brand, Max. The Bandit of the Black Hills.
--The Gentle Desperado.
--Mighty Lobo.
--The Rangeland Avenger.
--Rawhide Justice.
--Three on the Trail.
--Trouble in Timberline.
Brand, Mildred. Candy & Candy Molding.
--Candy Cookbook. Kuse, James A., ed.
--Easy Cake Decorating.
Brand, Stewart. Whole Earth Software Catalog.
Brand, Stewart, ed. Next Whole Earth Catalog.
Brand, William R., tr. see Kapuscinski, Ryszard.
Brand, William R., tr. see Micewski, Andrzej.
Brandao, Ignacio D. And Still the Earth.
Brandao, Ignacio De Loyola see De Loyola Brandao, Ignacio.
Brandejs, Jan F., jt. ed. see Day, Stacey B.
Brandel, Marc. A Life of Her Own.
--Murder in the Family.
Brandel, R. Music of Central Africa: An Ethnomusicological Study.
Branden, Barbara. The Passion of Ayn Rand.
Branden, Thomas, jt. auth. see Alsop, Stewart.
Brandes, David, ed. Male Accessory Sex Organs: Structure & Function in Mammals.
Brandes, G. Impressions of Russia.
Brandes, Stanley H. Migration, Kinship & Community: Tradition & Transition in a Spanish Village.
Brandeth, Gielgud. John Gielgud: A Celebration.
Brandewie, Ernest. Wilhelm Schmidt & the Origin of the Idea of God.
Brandis, Henry, Jr. Brandis on North Carolina Evidence: With 1986 Supplement.
Brandner, Gary. The Howling III.
Brandom, Robert, jt. auth. see Rescher, Nicholas.
Brandon, Brumsic, Jr. Luther's Got Class.
--Outta Sight, Luther.
Brandon, Dick H. Data Processing Cost Reduction & Control.
--Management Standards for Data Processing.
Brandon, Dick H., et al. Data Processing Contracts: Structure, Contents, & Negotiations.
Brandon, JoAnna. Never Give In.
Brandon, Peter S., jt. auth. see Ferry, Douglas J.
Brandon, Peter S. & Powell, James A, eds. Quality & Proflt in Building Design.
Brandon, William. The American Heritage Book of Indians. Josephy, Alvin M., Jr., ed.
--The Men & the Mountain: Fremont's Fourth Expedition.
Brandon-Cox, Hugh. Summer of a Million Wings: Arctic Quest for the Sea-Eagle.
Brandow, Karen, jt. auth. see Vocations for Social Change Staff.
Brandreth, Gyles. Amazing Facts about Prehistoric Animals.
--The Book of Solo Games.
--Discovering Pantomime.
--A Guide to Playing the Scrabble Brand Crossword Game: How to Improve Your Skills & Strategies.
--The Scrabble Brand Puzzle Book.
--Writing Secret Codes & Sending Hidden Messages.
Brandt, A. Von see Von Brandt, A.
Brandt, Catharine. Flowers for the Living.
--God Bless Grandparents.
--Praise God for This New Day: Second Thoughts for Busy Women.
--Still Time to Pray.
--Still Time to Sing: Prayers & Praise for Late in Life.
--You're Only Old Once: Devotions in Large Print.
Brandt, Conrad. Stalin's Failure in China, 1924-1927.
Brandt, David. Don't Stop Now, You're Killing Me: The Sadomasochism Game in Everyday Life & How Not to Play It.
--Is That All There Is? Overcoming Disappointment in an Age of Diminished Expectations.
Brandt, Edith, jt. auth. see Brandt, Leslie.
Brandt, Henry R. The Struggle for Inner Peace.
Brandt, Herman F. Psychology of Seeing.
Brandt, Leslie & Brandt, Edith. Growing Together: Prayers for Married People.
Brandt, N. B. & Chudinov, S. M. Electronic Structure of Metals.
Brandt, Nat, ed. see Blakeslee, Alton, et al.
Brandt, Paul see Licht, Hans, pseud.
Brandt, Rhonda, jt. auth. see Reece, Barry L.
Brandt, Rhonda O., jt. auth. see Reece, Barry L.
Brandt, Richard B. Value & Obligation: Systematic Readings in Ethics.
Brandt, Sue R. Facts about the Fifty States.
Brandt, Susan, jt. auth. see Cantacuzino, Sherban.
Brandt, T., jt. ed. see Bles, W.
Brandwein, Paul F. Memorandum: On Renewing Schooling & Education. Jovanovich, William, intro. by.
Brandwein, Paul F. & Ruchlis, Hy. Invitations to Investigate: An Introduction to Scientific Exploration.
Brandwein, Paul F., ed. see Reed, W. Maxwell.
Brandwein, Paul F., ed. see Reed, W. Maxwell & Bronson, Wilfrid S.
Brangwyn, Frank & Preston, Hayter. Windmills.
Branham, V. C. & Kutash, S. B. Encyclopedia of Criminology.
Brann, Donald R. How to Build Outdoor Furniture.
--How to Build Workbenches.
--How to Modernize a Basement.
Brannan, Sherry. The Human Track.
Brannen, Julia & Collard, Jean. Marriages in Trouble: The Process of Seeking Help.
Brannon. Cincinnati Reds.
--Cleveland Indians.
--Los Angeles Dodgers.
--San Francisco Giants.
Brannon, Emma C. Wayside Blossoms.
Brannon, Evelyn, ed. see Larsen, Judith L. & Gull, Carol W.
Brannon, Joan G. Misdemeanors with Punishments Not Exceeding a Fine of Fifty Dollars or Imprisonment of Thirty Days.
--North Carolina Manual for Magistrates.
Brannon, Joan G. & Farb, Robert L., eds. Arrest Warrant Forms, March 1982: Replacement Pages for the Second Edition.
Branover, H. Magnetohydrodynamic Flows in Ducts.
Branscum, Robbie. Me & Jim Luke.
--Toby Alone.
--Toby & Johnny Joe.
Bransford, Kent. The No-Nonsense Guide to Get You into Medical School.
Branson, Greg. It's All Due to Leprechauns.
Branson, Mark L., ed. see Aune, David E.
Branson, Mark L., ed. see Goldingay, John.
Bransonnard, Robert W. The Political Disintegration of Europe & the Cultural Collapse of the Human Race.
Branton, D. & Deamer, D. W. Membrane Structure. Alfert, M., et al, eds.
Branton, P. E., et al. Polyoma Virus: Current Research.
Branyan, Lawrence, et al. Worcester Blue & White Porcelain, 1751-1790.
Branyon, Alexandra, jt. auth. see Lee, Karen.
Braodbent, Donald, jt. ed. see Pribram, Karl.
Brasch, Wayne E. Real Estate By the Numbers.
Braselle, Keefe. Cannibals.
Brasher, Ruth E. & Garrison, Carolyn L. Modern Household Equipment.
Brasnett, Clive. English for Engineers.
--English for Medical Students.
Brasol, Boris, tr. see Dostoyevsky, Fyodor.
Brasseaux, Carl A., ed. see De Villiers du Terrage, Marc.
Brasselle, Keefe. The Barracudas.
Brasseur De Bourbourg, E. Ch. Histoire de Canada, de Son Eglise et De Ses Missions.
Brassley, Paul. Agricultural Economy of Northumberland & Durham in the Period 1640-1750.
Braswell, David, jt. auth. see Logan, Gerald E.
Brateau, Paul, jt. auth. see Tardy.
Brater, Craig. Drug Use in Renal Disease.
Brathwaite, Cyril A. Therapies, Myths & Cosmic Powers.
Bratko, I. & Stele, F. Slovenia: A Portrait.
Bratkowsky, Joan G. Yiddish Linguistics: A Multilingual Bibliography, 1959-1973.
Bratos, S. & Pick, R. M., eds. Vibrational Spectroscopy of Molecular Liquids & Solids.
Bratt, James D. Dutch Calvinism in Modern America: A History of a Conservative Subculture.
Brattgard, Helge. God's Stewards.
Bratton, J. S. The Impact of Victorian Children's Fiction.
Braue, John R. Uncle John's Original Bread Book.
Brauer, Jerald C. Images of Religion in America. Wolf, Richard C., ed.
Brauer, Jerald C., ed. Religion & the American Revolution.
Brauer, W. Net Theory & Applications Proceedings.
Braum, Helga. The Survival of Helga Braun: A Memoir.
Brauman, J. I., jt. auth. see Streitwieser, A., Jr.
Braun, A. C. & Stonier, T. Morphology & Physiology of Plant Tumors.
Braun, David P. & Griffin, James B. Contribution Eight in Research Reports in Archaeology: The Snyders Mound & Five Other Mound Groups in Calhoun County, Illinois.
Braun, Edward L. Digital Computer Design: Its Logic, Circuitry, & Synthesis.
Braun, Hans-Gert, et al, eds. The European Economy in the Nineteen Eighties: Proceedings.
Braun, Henry. Vergil Woods.
Braun, Herbert. Jesus of Nazareth: The Man & His Time. Kalin, Everett R., tr. from Ger.
Braun, Hugh. Elements of English Architecture.
Braun, J. P., jt. auth. see Wackenheim, A.
Braun, Katherine M. Saga of the Bluebird.
Braun, Phyllis C., ed. Biology, 1988-89.
Braun, Robert D. & Walters, Fred H. Applications of Chemical Analysis: Lab Manual.
Braun, Robert J. Teachers & Power.
Braun, Simon, jt. auth. see Sheldon, Huntington.
Braun, Tamara. Hapana Mbale.
Braun, Thomas. On Stage with Flip Wilson.
Braun, Thomas, ed. see Rosenthal-Schneider, Ilse.
Braun, W., jt. ed. see Landy, Maurice.
Braun, W., ed. see Symposium of the Institute of Microbiology, Rutgers University, 1967.
Braun, W., et al, eds. see Cyclic AMP, Cell Growth, & the Immune Response Symposium Staff.
Braund, H. E., ed. Calling to Mind: An Account of the First Hundred Years of Steel Brothers & Company Ltd.
Brauns, Dorothy A., jt. auth. see Brauns, Friedrich E.
Brauns, Friedrich E. & Brauns, Dorothy A. Chemistry of Lignin: Supplementary Volume Covering Literature for 1949-58.
Braunstein, Herbert. Outlines of General & Systemic Pathology.
Braunstein, Michael. House Fever: Buying, Selling, Remodeling, Decorating & Agonizing over Your Home.
Braunwald. Heart Disease.
Brauza, Irene. Let's Discuss.
Brav, Stanley R. Marriage & the Jewish Tradition.
Bravard, Robert S., jt. auth. see Peplow, Michael W.

Authors

Braver, John M., jt. auth. see Jones, Bronwyn.
Braverman, Avishay, et al. Reducing Input Subsidies to Livestock Producers in Cyprus: An Economic Analysis.
Braverman, H. Precalculus Mathematics: Algebra, Trigonometry & Analytical Geometry.
Braverman, Jack R., ed. see Educational Research Council of America Staff.
Braverman, Jordan. A Consumer's Book of Health: Advice on Stretching Your Health Care Dollar.
Brawley, Edward A. & Schnidler, Ruben. Community & Social Service Education in the Community College: Issues & Characteristics.
Brawley, Ernest. The Alamo Tree.
--The Rap.
--Selena.
Brawner, C. O., pref. by. Gold Mining 87: Proceedings of the First International Conference on Gold Mining.
Brawner, C. O., ed. see International Mine Drainage Symposium Staff.
Brawner, C. O., ed. see International Symposium on Stability in Coal Mining Staff.
Brawner, C. O., jt. ed. see Szwilski, A. B.
Bray, Alan. Homosexuality in Renaissance England.
Bray, Barbara, tr. see Chandernagor, Francoise.
Bray, Barbara, tr. see Crebillon, Claude P.
Bray, Barbara, tr. see Duras, Marguerite.
Bray, Barbara, tr. see Nadeau, Maurice.
Bray, Barbara, tr. see Trefusis, Violet.
Bray, Bonita. Afghans: Traditional & Modern.
Bray, Francesca. The Rice Economies: Technology & Development in Asian Societies.
Bray, Frank, jt. auth. see Cottrell, Alvin J.
Bray, George A. Recent Advances in Obesity Research.
Bray, Gerald L. Holiness & the Will of God: Perspectives on the Theology of Tertullian.
Bray, H. G. & White, K. Kinetics & Thermodynamics in Biochemistry.
Bray, Mark. Educational Planning in a Decentralized System: The Papua New Guinean Experience.
--Universal Primary Education in Nigeria: A Study of Kano State.
Bray, Natalie. Dress Fitting.
--Dress Fitting: Basic Principles & Practice.
--Dress Pattern Designing: The Basic Principles of the Cut & Fit.
--More Dress Pattern Designing.
Bray, Robert T. European Trade Goods from the Utz Site & the Search for Fort Orleans.
Braybrooke, Neville, ed. The Ackerley Letters.
Braymer, Marjorie. Walls of Windy Troy: A Biography of Heinrich Schliemann.
Brayton, R., jt. auth. see Spence, R.
Brayton, R. K., et al. Modern Network Theory: An Introduction. Moschytz, G. S. & Neirynck, J., eds.
Brazelton, T. Berry. Infants & Mothers.
Brazier, L. R., et al, eds. Die & Mould Making.
Brazier, Mary, jt. auth. see Cooper, Edwin.
Brazier, Mary, jt. ed. see Sigman, David S.
Brazier, Mary A., ed. see Austrian Academy of Sciences Symposium Staff.
Brazier, Mary A., jt. ed. see Buchwald, Nathaniel A.
Brazini, Luigi. The Europeans.
Breach, N., jt. auth. see Fishman, William J.
Breakwell, Glynis M. The Quiet Rebel: How to Survive As a Woman & Businessperson.
Brealy, Richard, jt. auth. see Lorie, James.
Brearley, Joan McD. This Is the Irish Setter.
Brearley, P., et al. Admission to Residential Care.
Brearley, Paul C. & Hall, M. R. P. Risk & Aging.
Breasted, Charles. Pioneer to the Past: The Story of James Henry Breasted, Archaeologist.
Brebbia, C. A. Progress in Boundary Element Methods.
Brebbia, C. A., jt. auth. see Adey, R. A.
Brebbia, C. A., ed. Applied Numerical Modeling: Proceedings of the First International Conference, Held at the University of Southampton, 11-15 July, 1977.
Brebbia, C. A., jt. ed. see Keramidas, George A.
Brebbia, Carlos A. The Boundary Element Method for Engineers.
Breccia, A. & Cavalleri, B., eds. Nitroimidazoles: Chemistry, Pharmacology & Clinical Application.
Breccia, A., et al, eds. Advanced Topics on Radiosensitizers of Hypoxic Cells.
Brecher, Michael. Israel, the Korean War & China.
Brechner, Irv, jt. auth. see Schwartz, Lester.
Brecht, Arnold. Political Education of Arnold Brecht: An Autobiography: 1884-1970.
Brecht, Bertolt. Bertolt Brecht: Poems - 1913-1956. Willett, John & Manheim, Ralph, eds.
--Caucasian Chalk Circle. Bentley, Eric & Apelman, Maja, trs. from Ger.
--The Mother.
--Mother Courage & Her Children. Bentley, Eric, tr. from Ger.
--Selected Poems. Hays, H. R., tr.
Brecht, Bertolt see Weiss, Samuel A.
Breck, Allan D. & Yourgrau, Wolfgang, eds. Biology, History & Natural Philosophy.
Breckenridge, Karl. I Hear You're in Real Estate!
Breckenridge, Roger A., ed. Remote Sensing of Earth from Space: Role of "Smart Sensors", PAAS67.
Breckenridge, Walter J. Reptiles & Amphibians of Minnesota.
Breckon, Don. The Railway Paintings of Don Breckon.
--Railway Paintings of Don Breckon.
Breckon, Garry L., tr. see De Muralt, Andre.
Brede, H. D. & Stevens, E. A. Regulatory Control & Standardization of Allergenic Extracts.
Bredenforder, Elisabeth. Die Texte der Handel-Oratorien.
Bredes, Don. Hard Feelings.
--Muldoon.
Bredow, Miriam. Handbook for the Medical Secretary.
Bree, Germaine. Marcel Proust & Deliverance from Time. Richards, R. J. & Truitt, A. D., trs. from Fr.
--World of Marcel Proust.
Bree, Germaine & Guiton, Margaret. The French Novel from Gide to Camus.
Bree, Germaine, ed. see Robbe-Grillet, Alain.
Bree, Loris, ed. State By State Guide to Budget Motels: 1985-1986 Edition.
Bree, Loris G., ed. State by State Guide to Budget Motels: 1984-85.
--State by State Guide to Budget Motels: Spring 1987 to Spring 1988.
Breeden, Kay, jt. auth. see Breeden, Stanley.
Breeden, Stanley & Breeden, Kay. Wildlife of Eastern Australia.
Breen, Dana. The Birth of a First Child: Towards an Understanding of Femininity.
Breen, George E. & Blankenship, A. B. Do-It-Yourself Marketing Research.
Breen, T. H. The Character of the Good Ruler: Puritan Political Ideas in New England, 1630-1730.
Breese, S., Jr., jt. ed. see Zacharia, Theodore P.
Breeze, Katie. Nekkid Cowboy.
Breeze, Paul. While My Guitar Gently Weeps: A Novel.
Breffny, Brian de see De Breffny, Brian.
Breffny, Brian De see De Breffny, Brian.
Breffny, Brian de see De Breffny, Brian & Mott, George.
Breheny, M. & Hooper, A., eds. Rationality in Planning: Critical Essays on the Role of Rationality in Urban & Regional Planning.
Breheret, Yves, jt. auth. see Mabire, Jean.
Brehm, Henry P., jt. auth. see Coe, Rodney M.
Brehrens, Dietlinde, jt. auth. see Pack, Janet.
Breihan, Carl W. Younger Brothers.
Breihan, Carl W. & Garwood, W. R. West Wandering Wind.
Breiman, Leo. Probability & Stochastic Processes, with a View Toward Applications.
Breimer, D. D. & Speiser, P., eds. Topics in Pharmaceutical Sciences II: Proceedings of the 43rd International Congress of the F.I.P., Montreux, Switzerland September 5-9,1983.
Breit, et al. Readings in Microeconomics.
Breit, William & Elzinga, Kenneth G. The Antitrust Casebook.
Breitenkamp, Edward C., tr. see Seele, Hermann.
Breitenlohner, Peter & Duerr, Hans-Peter. Unified Theories of Elementary Particles: Proceedings.
Breiter, M. W. Electrochemical Processes in Fuel Cells.
Breithardt, Gunter & Loogen, Franz, eds. New Aspects in the Medical Treatment of Tachyarrhythmias: Role of Amiodarone.
Breithaupt, Herman A. How We Started Students on Successful Foodservice Careers.
Breithaupt, Sandra & Agnew, H. Wayne. The Dallas Doctors' Diet: A Revolutionary Way to Eat Yourself Thin.
Breitkopf, Herman L., jt. auth. see New Jersey Institute for Continuing Legal Education Staff.
Breitman, Richard, jt. auth. see Laqueur, Walter.
Brejcha, Mathias F. & Samuels, Clifford L. Automotive Chassis & Accessory Circuits.
Brekhman, I. I. Man & Biologically Active Substances: Introduction to the Pharmacology of Health.
Brekhman, I. I. & Nesterenko, I. F. Brown Sugar & Health.
Brekke, Milo L., et al. Ten Faces of Ministry: Perspectives on Pastoral & Congregational Effectiveness Based on Survey of 5000 Lutherans.
Bremer, Hans J., et al. Disturbances of Amino Acid Metabolism: Clinical Chemistry & Diagnosis.
Bremer, Kathy A., ed. see U.S.S. Will Rogers Wive's Staff.
Bremer, Stuart A. Simulated Worlds: A Computer Model of National Decision-Making.
Bremer-Kamp, Cherie. Living on the Edge: The Winter Ascent of Kanchenjunga.
Bremmer, Jan. The Early Greek Concept of the Soul.
Bremner, Joseph & Miller, Peggy. A Guide to Database Distribution: Legal Aspects & Model Contracts.
Bremner, Robert H. American Philanthropy.
Bremner, Robert H., et al, eds. Children & Youth in America: A Documentary History.
Brems, Marianne. Swim for Fitness.
Bremser, W., et al. Carbon-13 NMR Spectral Data: A Living COM-Microfiche Collection of Reference Material.
Bren, Frank. Poland.
Brena, Steven F. Chronic Pain.
Brenauer, K., et al. Theoretical Inorganic Chemistry: No. 2.
Brendel, Alfred. Musical Thoughts & Afterthoughts.
Brenden, B. B., jt. auth. see Hildebrand, B. P.
Brendon, Piers. Eminent Edwardians.
--The Life & Death of the Press Barons.
Brengelmann, J. C. Effect of Repeated Electroshock on Learning in Depressives.
Brengle, Kenneth G. Principles & Practices of Dryland Farming.
Brenkert, George G. Marx's Ethics of Freedom.
Brenman-Gibson, Margaret. Clifford Odets: American Playwright.
Brennan, Alice. Sleep Well, Christine.
--Thirty Days Hath July.
Brennan, Anthony. Shakespeare's Dramatic Structures.
Brennan, Dan. One of Our Bombers Is Missing.
Brennan, Fanny, tr. see Guerard, Michel.
Brennan, Frank. Too Much Order with Too Little Law.
Brennan, J. H. Dark Moon.
Brennan, Jennifer. The Original Thai Cookbook.
Brennan, Lawrence, et al. Resumes for Better Jobs.
Brennan, Mary E. Managing Corporate Benefit Plans 1983.
Brennan, Mary E., ed. Benefits Processing Institute Proceedings. December 8-11, 1982, Orlando, Florida.
--Canadian Conference: Proceedings 13th Annual, Oct. 4-8, 1980.
--Canadian Conference: Proceedings, 15th Annual, 1982.
--Canadian Conference, 14th Annual Nov. 23-27, 1981 Proceedings.
--Canadian Employee Benefit Plans, 1983.
--Claims Processing for Benefit Plans, 1983.
--Containing Corporate Health Care Costs, 1983.
--E D P Institute, Las Vegas, Oct. 12-15, 1980: Proceedings.
--International Benefits Seminar Proceedings, Oct. 21-24, 1981, Montreal.
--Public Employee Benefit Plans, 1983.
--Public Employees Conference, Dec. 7-10, 1980, Monterey, CA: Proceedings. Incl. Public Employees Conference Proceedings, December 5-8, 1982, Orlando, Florida. Brennan, Mary E., ed; Public Employees Conference Proceedings, Nov. 11-14, 1981, Williamsburg. Brennan, Mary E., ed. Intl Found Employ.
--Shedding Light on Benefits Issues: Educational Conference Proceedings 1984 Annual.
Brennan, Michael J., et al, eds. Breast Cancer: New Concepts in Etiology & Control.
Brennan, Wilfred K. Changing Special Education.
Brennan, Will. Cowman's Vengeance.
--Wolf Country.
Brenner, Anita & Leighton, George R. The Wind That Swept Mexico: The History of the Mexican Revolution of 1910-1942.
Brenner, Barbara. Walt Disney's The Penguin That Hated the Cold.
--A Year in the Life of Rosie Bernard.
Brenner, Barbara, jt. auth. see Bank Street College of Education Staff.
Brenner, David. Nobody Ever Sees You Eat Tuna Fish.
--Revenge Is the Best Exercise.
--Soft Pretzels with Mustard.
Brenner, Egon & Javid, M. Analysis of Electric Circuits.
Brenner, Elizabeth. Winning by Letting Go: Control Without Compulsion, Surrender Without Defeat.
Brenner, Lenni. Zionism in the Age of the Dictators.
Brenner, Menachem. Option Pricing: Theory & Applications.
Brenner, N., ed. International Gas Chromatography Symposium, Third.
Brenner, Paul F., jt. ed. see Mishell, Daniel R.
Brenner, Robert M. Elements of Biology.
Brenner, Vladimir. Count Witte: Scenes from His Life & Times, 1902-1915.
Brent, Madeleine. Golden Urchin.
--A Heritage of Shadows.
--Stormswift.
Brent, Peter. Charles Darwin: A Man of Enlarged Curiosity.
Brent, R. L. The Exchange.
Brentano, jt. auth. see Tieck, Ludwig.
Brenton, Howard. Sore Throats & Sonnets of Love & Opposition.
Brenton, Maria & Jones, Catherine, eds. The Year Book of Social Policy in Britain, 1984-1985.
Breo, Dennis L. Extraordinary Care.
Breo, Dennis L., jt. auth. see Keane, Noel P.
Brescia, Frank & Mehlman, Stanley. Chemistry: A Modern Introduction.
Brescia, Frank, et al. Fundamentals of Chemistry: A Modern Introduction.
Bresinsky, A. & Huber, J. Schluessel Fuer Die Ggattung Hygrophorus Nach Exsikkatenmerkmalen.
Breslauer, Sandra J., et al. Document Organization, Management & Production.
Bresler, David E. & Trubo, Richard. Free Yourself from Pain.
--Free Yourself from Pain.
Bresler, Fenton. Beastly Law.
Bresler, S. E. Introduction to Molecular Biology.
Breslin, Jimmy. World Without End, Amen.
Breslin, Mark, et al. Zen & Now: The Baby Boomers Guide to Middle Life.
Bresnan, Joan W. Theory of Complementation in English Syntax. Hankamer, Jorge, ed.
Bress, Helene. The Craft of Macrame.
--Inkle Weaving.
--The Macrame Book.
Bress, Steve. Commodore 64 Assembly Language Arcade Game Programming.
Bressler, L. & Bressler, M. Youth in American Life.
Bressler, M., jt. auth. see Bressler, L.
Bressler, M. H., et al. Criteria for Nuclear Safety Related Piping & Component Support Snubbers.
Brestoff, Nelson. How to Borrow Money Below Prime.
Brestoff, Nelson E. How to Write Off Your Down Payment.
Bretano, Franz. Philosophical Investigations on Space, Time & Continuum. Smith, Barry, tr. from Ger.
Breternitz, David A., jt. ed. see Smith, Watson.
Breton, Andre. La Cle des Champs.
--Fata Morgana. Mills, Clark, tr.
--Poemes.
Breton, Andre, et al. The Surrealists Look at Art. Hulten, Pontus, ed.
Breton, Denise. This Lie Called Evil.
Breton, Raymond, et al. Cultural Boundaries & the Cohesion of Canada.
Breton, Thierry & Beneich, Denis. Softwar. Howson, Mark, tr.
Bretschneider, Charles L. Topics in Ocean Engineering. Incl. Vol. 1; Vol. 2; Vol. 3. Gulf Pub.
Bretsznajder, S. Prediction of Transport & Other Physical Properties of Fluids.
Brett, Bernard. Ghosts.
Brett, Bernard, jt. auth. see Arneson, D. J.
Brett, George. Psychology, Ancient & Modern.
Brett, R. L., ed. Writers & Their Background: Samuel Taylor Coleridge.
Brett, Richard M. The Country Journal Woodlot Primer: The Right Way to Manage Your Woodland.
Brett, Simon. An Amateur Corpse.
--Dead Giveaway.
--Dead Giveaway.
--Dead Romantic.
--Dead Romantic.
--Murder in the Title: A Charles Paris Mystery.
--Murder Unprompted: A Charles Paris Mystery.
--A Nice Class of Corpse.
--Not Dead, Only Resting.
--Not Dead, Only Resting: A Charles Paris Mystery.
--Situation Tragedy.
--What Bloody Man Is That?
Brett, William & Sentlowitz, Michael. Elementary Algebra by Example.
Brett-Billowitz, JoAnn, ed. see Family Circle Editors.
Brett-Billowitz, JoAnn, ed. see Family Circle Staff.
Brettel, Richard R. The Art of the Edge: European Frames 1300-1900.
Brettell, Richard R. & McCullagh, Suzanne F. Degas: In the Art Institute of Chicago.
Breuer, Karin. Mac Harshberger: Art Deco Americain.
Breuer, Salomon. Chochmo U'Mussar.
Brewer, D. S., ed. see Chaucer, Geoffrey.
Brewer, David Illus. by see Bevans, Charles F.
Brewer, Derek & Jeffares, A. Norman, eds. English Gothic Literature.
Brewer, E. Cobham. Historical Note-Book.
Brewer, Earl J. Juvenile Rheumatoid Arthritis.
Brewer, Gail S. Nine Months, Nine Lessons.
Brewer, Gail S., ed. Pregnancy after Thirty Workbook: A Program for Safe Childbearing-No Matter What Your Age.
Brewer, J. W., ed. see Conference on Commutative Algebra.
Brewer, James, et al. Power Selling.
Brewer, John D. Mosley's Men: The British Union of Fascists in the West Midlands.
Brewer, John M. Wellsprings of Democracy.
Brewer, K. R. & Hanif, M. Sampling with Unequal Probabilities.

Authors

Brewer, Mary, jt. ed. see Scott, Thomas.
Brewer, Norma B. Tailoring Vocational Education to Adult Needs.
Brewer, R. G., et al, eds. NC-CNC Machining II.
Brewin, Bob & Shaw, Sydney. Vietnam on Trial: Westmoreland vs. CBS.
Brewin, Bob, jt. auth. see Hughes, Richard.
Brewitt-Taylor, C. H., tr. see Lo, Kuan-Chung.
Brewster, David. Northwest Best Places.
Brewster, David C., jt. auth. see Hallett, John W., Jr.
Brewster, Melvin & Hoyem, George A. Remington Bullet Knives.
Brey, J. & Jones, R. B., eds. Critical Phenomena.
Brey, Rita J. Du see DuBrey, Rita J.
Brey, Ron & Grigsby, Charles. Telecourse Student Survey, 1984.
Breyer, Donald E. & Ank, John A. Design of Wood Structures.
Breyfogle, Newell D. The Common Sense Medical Guide & Outdoor Reference.
Brez, E. M. Those Dark Eyes.
Brezhnev, L. Memorias.
Brezhnev, Leonid I. Peace, Detente, & Soviet-American Relations: A Collection of Public Statements by Leonid Brezhnev.
Brezik, Victor B., ed. One Hundred Years of Thomism: Aeterni Patris & Afterwards - A Symposium.
Breznitz, Shlomo. Stress in Israel.
Brians, Pearl. Adventist Evangelist's Diary.
--During My Conversion.
--Letters from SDA Pastors to Pearl.
--My Appetite Control.
--Overweight Ladies.
--Prayer Meeting at Our House.
Bricault, G. & Carr, J., eds. Sunday Telegraph Business Finance Directory 1985-86: The Guide to Sources of Corporate Finance in Britain.
Brichta, A. & Sharp, P. E. From Project to Production.
Brickell, Christopher. Step-by-Step Guide to Pruning.
Bricker, Clark E. College Chemistry: A Laboratory Manual.
--Foundations of Chemistry: A Laboratory Manual.
Bricker, Dianne D., jt. ed. see Schiefelbusch, Richard L.
Bricker, Neal S. & Kirschenbaum, Michael A., eds. The Kidney: Diagnosis & Management.
Bricker, Victoria R. & Spores, Ronald, eds. Supplement to the Handbook of Middle American Indians, Vol. 4: Ethnohistory.
Brickhill, Paul. Great Escape.
--Reach for the Sky.
Bricklin, Mark. The Natural Healing Annual for 1987.
--Natural Healing Cookbook.
--The Practical Encyclopedia of Natural Healing.
Brickman, Richard, jt. auth. see Irwin, Robert.
Brickner, Dave, et al. Annotated BASIC: A New Technique for Neophytes. McCarthy, Nan & Crocker, Chris, eds.
Bricose, Jill. Here Am I; Send Aaron!
Bridbury, A. R. England & the Salt Trade in the Later Middle Ages.
Bridenbaugh, Carl. Fat Mutton & Liberty of Conscience.
Bridenthal, Renate & Koonz, Claudia. Becoming Visible: Women in European History.
Bride's Magazine Editors. The New Bride's Book of Etiquette. Conde Nast, ed.
Bride's Magazine Editors & Calderone, Mary. Questions & Answers about Love & Sex.
Bridge, John & Dodds, J. C. Planning & the Growth of the Firm.
Bridge, Raymond. America's Backpacking Book.
--The Complete Canoeist's Guide.
--The Complete Guide to Kayaking.
--New Complete Snow Camper's Guide.
--The Runner's Book.
--Tour Guide to the Rocky Mountain Wilderness.
Bridgeman, Bruce & Bridgeman, Dinae, eds. Readings on Fundamental Issues on Learning & Memory.
Bridgeman, Dinae, jt. ed. see Bridgeman, Bruce.
Bridgeman, P. W. The Nature of Some of Our Physical Concepts.
Bridgeman, Peter. Trees for Town & Country.
Bridges, B. A. & Harnden, D. G., eds. Ataxia Telangiectasia: A Cellular & Molecular Link Between Cancer, Neuropathology & Immune Deficiency.
Bridges, Brian, ed. see Harris, Stuart.
Bridges, Charles W. & Lunsford, Ronald F. Writing: Discovering Form & Meaning.
Bridges, Derek. Flower Arranger's Bible.
Bridges, George W. Annals of Jamaica.
Bridges, J. W. & Chasseaud, L. F. Progress in Drug Metabolism.
Bridges, Jacqueline K. Sackcloth & Ashes.
Bridges, Jerry. The Practice of Godliness.
--The Pursuit of Holiness.
--True Fellowship.
Bridges, Kent W. see Mueller-Dombois, Dieter.
Bridges, Pat. Where Is the Wilderness?
Bridges, Robert, et al. Preliminary Announcement. Commager, Steele, ed. Incl. On English Homophones; A Few Practical Suggestions; The Pronunciation of English Words; The Englishing of French Words; On Hyphens & Shall & Will, Should & Would; English Influence on the French Vocabulary; What Is Pure French; The Language of Anatomy; On Grammatical Inversion. Garland Pub.
--The Society's Work. Commager, Steele, ed. Incl. The Nature of Human Speech; English Handwriting; Notes on Relative Clauses; On Some Disputed Points in English Grammar; English Vowel Sounds; The Study of American English; English Handwriting; Shakespeare's English; American Pronunciation. Garland Pub.
Bridges, Ronald F. First Love.
Bridges, William B., jt. auth. see Birdsall, Charles K.
Bridgewater, A. & Lidgren, H. Household Waste Management in Europe.
Bridgman, Elizabeth. All the Little Bunnies.
Bridgman, Jon & Clarke, David E. German Africa: A Select Annotated Bibliography.
Bridgman, P. W. The Nature of Thermodynamics.
--Reflections of a Physicist.
--The Thermodynamics of Electrical Phenomena in Metals & a Condensed Collection of Thermodynamic Formulas.
Bridgwater, A. V. & Lidgren, K. Energy in Packaging & Waste.
Bridgwater, J., ed. Developments in Chemical Engineering: A Festschrift for P. V. Danckwerts.
Bridwell, Norman. Clifford at the Circus.
--Clifford Takes a Trip.
--Clifford the Big Red Dog.
--Clifford, the Small Red Puppy.
--Clifford Va de Viaje. Palacios, Argentina, tr. from Span.
--Clifford's Tricks.
Bridwell, Raymond. Hydroponic Gardening: The Magic of Hydroponics for the Home Gardener.
Bridwell, Ric. Manchu Delta.
Brieger, E. M. Structure & Ultrastructure of Microorganisms.
Brieger, Gert H., ed. Reading from the Literature.
Brier, jt. auth. see Rhine.
Brierley, David. Blood Group O.
--Shooting Star.
Brierley, Harry. Transvestism: A Handbook for Psychologists, Psychiatrists & Counsellors.
Brierley, Louise. King Lion & His Cooks.
Brierly, David. Cold War.
--Skorpion's Death: A Novel.
Briessen, Fritz Van see Van Briessen, Fritz.
Briffault, Herma, tr. see Colette.
Briffault, Herma, tr. see Moliere.
Briffault, Robert. The Mothers. Taylor, Gordon R., ed. & intro. by.
Briganti, Giuliano, ed. see Bologna, Ferdinando, 1st.
Brigden, Roy. Agricultural Hand Tools.
Briggs, A. D., tr. see Medvedev, Roy A.
Briggs, Anna & Oliver, Judith, eds. Caring: Experiences of Looking after Severely Disabled Relatives.
Briggs, Arthur E. Walt Whitman: Thinker & Artist.
Briggs, Asa. The Collected Essays of Asa Briggs.
--The Power of Steam: An Illustrated History of the World's Steam Age.
--Victorian People: A Reassessment of Persons & Themes, 1851-67.
Briggs, Asa & Macartney, Anne. Toynbee Hall: The First Hundred Years.
Briggs, Carl & Trudell, Clyde F. Quarterdeck & Saddlehorn: The Story of Edward F. Beale, 1822-1893.
Briggs, Charles L. The Wood Carvers of Cordova, New Mexico: Social Dimensions of an Artistic "Revival"
Briggs, Dinus M., jt. auth. see Briggs, Hilton M.
Briggs, Geoffrey, ed. Civic & Corporate Heraldry: A Dictionary of Impersonal Arms of England, Wales, & Northern Ireland.
Briggs, Hilton M. & Briggs, Dinus M. Modern Breeds of Livestock.
Briggs, John. The Collector's Beethoven.
Briggs, Katherine M. A Dictionary of British Folk-Tales.
--Fairies in Tradition & Literature.
--Personnel of Fairyland: A Short Account of the Fairy People of Great Britain for Those Who Tell Stories to Children.
Briggs, Philip J., ed. Politics in America: Readings & Documents.
Briggs, Raymond. Jim & the Beanstalk.
--The Tin-Pot Foreign General & the Old Iron Woman.
Briggs, S. R. & Elliott, J. H. Six Hundred Bible Gems & Outlines.
Briggs, T., et al, eds. Mechanical Fitting.
Briggs, Walter. Without Noise of Arms.
Briggs, Wm. & Co.Staff. Designs & Patterns for Embroiderers & Craftsmen: 512 Motifs from the Wm. Briggs & Co. "Album of Transfer Patterns" Nichols, Marion, ed.
Briggum, Sue M. & Bender, Todd K. A Concordance to Conrad's "Almayer's Folly"
Brigham, Eugene F. Financial Management: Theory & Practice.
--Fundamentals of Financial Management.
Brigham, Eugene F. & Gapenski, Louis J. Intermediate Financial Management.
Brigham, Eugene F., jt. auth. see Weston, J. Fred.
Brigham, Eugene F., et al. Cases in Managerial Finance.
Brigham, Harold W. I Have Seen the Stars.
Brigham, John. Civil Liberties & American Democracy.
Brigham, Thomas A., jt. ed. see Catania, A. Charles.
Brigham Young University Press Staff, ed. How to Involve Parents in Early Childhood Education.
Bright, Bill. The Holy Spirit: The Key to Supernatural Living.
Bright, Deborah. Creative Relaxation: Turning Your Stress into Positive Energy.
Bright, F. T., et al, eds. Jig Boring.
Bright, Freda. Futures.
--Infidelities.
Bright, J. Diaries of John Bright. Walling, R., ed.
Bright, James R. Automation & Management.
Bright, John & McGregor, Gordon. Teaching English As a Second Language.
Bright, Robert. Georgie's Christmas Carol.
--My Red Umbrella.
Bright, Susan. Julia. Lomax, Joseph F. & Whitebird, J., eds.
Bright, Thomas & Pequegnat, Linda, eds. Biota of the West Flower Garden Bank.
Brightfield, Myron F. Issue in Literary Criticism.
Brightfield, Richard. The Phantom Submarine.
Brightly, Charles. The Method of Founding Stereotype As Practised by Charles Brightly. Bidwell, John, ed.
Brightly, S. G. Setting Out: A Guide for Site Engineers.
Brightman, Alan. Like Me.
Brightman, Richard W. & Dimsdale, Jeffrey M. Software Tools for the IBM PC.
--Using Computers in an Information Age.
--Using Microcomputers: Tutorials for dBASE II, WordStar, & 1-2-3.
Brightman, Robert. Fix It.
--One-Hundred One Practical Uses for Propane Torches.
Brighton, Catherine. My Hands, My World.
Brigley, Catherine M. Pediatrics for the Practical Nurse.
Brigstocke, T. D., jt. auth. see Wilson, P. N.
Brihaye, J., ed. Neurosurgery, 6th European Congress: Organized by the European Association of Neurosurgical Societies of Paris, July 15-20, 1979.
Briles, Judith. Money Phases.
--Money Phases: The Six Financial Stages of a Woman's Life.
Briley, John. Gandhi: Screenplay for the Film by Richard Attenborough.
Briley, M., et al, eds. New Concepts in Alzheimer's Disease.
Brill, A., et al, eds. Advances in Medical Imaging & Related Dosimetry: International School of Radiation Damage Protection & Anomalies.
Brill, Albert. Why Our Schools Have Failed Us.
Brill, Henry, jt. auth. see Mule, S. J.
Brill, John. The Chance of Character of Human Existence.
Brillat-Savarin, Jean. The Physiology of Taste. Fisher, M. F., tr.
Brillat-Savarin, Jean A. Physiology of Taste: Meditations on Transcendental Gastronomy.
Brilliant, Alan. Journeyman.
Brilliant, R. The Arch of Septimius Severus in the Roman Forum.
Brillinger, Peter C., jt. auth. see Cohen, Doron J.
Brillouin, Leon. Relativity Reexamined.
Brim, Orville G., Jr. & Wheeler, Stanton. Socialization after Childhood: Two Essays.
Brimelow, Peter. The Wall Street Gurus: How You Can Profit from Investment Newsletters.
Brimer, John. Growing Herbs in Pots.
Brin, Ruth F. David & Goliath.
Brinch-Hanson, P. Architecture of Concurrent Programs.
Brinckloe, William D. & Coughlin, Mary T. Managing Organizations.
Brinckmeyer, Edward, ed. Mitternachzeitung Fuer Gebildete Stand.
Brindze, Ruth. Hurricanes: Monster Storms from the Sea.
--Investing Money: The Facts about Stocks & Bonds.
--Look How Many People Wear Glasses: The Magic of Lenses.
--Rise & Fall of the Seas: The Story of the Tides.
Brine, Jenny, et al, eds. Home School & Leisure in the Soviet Union.
Brines, Russell, jt. auth. see Sebald, William J.
Bring, Mitchell & Wayembergh, Josse. Design & Meaning in Japanese Gardens.
Bringsvaard, T. Phantoms & Fairies.
Bringuier, Jean-Claude. Conversations with Jean Piaget. Gulati, Basia, tr.
Brink, A. W., ed. The Life of the Reverend Mr. George Trosse.
Brink, Andre. Ambassador.
--The Wall of the Plague.
--Writing in a State of Siege.
Brink, Carol R. Baby Island.
Brink, Jeanie R., ed. Female Scholars: A Tradition of Learned Women Before 1800.
Brink, Joseph, jt. auth. see Shreve, R. Norris.
Brink, Pamela J. & Wood, Marilynn T. Basic Steps in Planning Nursing Research.
Brink, Randall. The Flight School Handbook.
--Restoring & Flying a Sport Plane on a Budget.
Brink, Victor Z. Understanding Management Policy & Making It Work.
Brinker, Helmut. Zen in the Art of Painting.
Brinkerhoff, David B. & White, Lynn K. Sociology.
Brinkhorst, L. J. & Schermers, H. G. Supplement to Judicial Remedies in the European Communities.
Brinkley, Christie. Christie Brinkley's Outdoor Fitness & Beauty Book.
Brinkley, F. Samurai, the Invincible Warriors. Lucas, Charles, ed.
Brinkley, Ginny, jt. auth. see Childbirth Education Association of Jacksonville, Fla., Inc. Staff.
Brinkley, Roberta F., ed. English Poetry of the Seventeenth Century.
Brinkman, Alfred & Rellstab, Ludwig. Turnier-Taschenbuch.
Brinkman, Ronald. Programming in Structured BASIC.
Brinkmann, William & Ditewig, William. Leading Our Children to God.
Brinkworth, Malcolm. Tomorrow's World: Energy.
Brinn, Ruth E. & Saypol, Judyth R. Let's Have a Party: 101 Mix & Match a Party Ideas for the Jewish Holidays.
Brinnin, John M. Truman Capote: Dear Heart, Old Buddy.
Brino, Giovanni. Carlo Mollino.
Brinson, Winifred. Deafness in the Adult: What a Hearing Loss Means & What Can Be Done to Help.
Brinster, Ralph L., et al. Recent Studies on Preimplantation Mammalian Embryos In Vitro.
Brinton, Anna C. Maphaeus Vegius & His Thirteenth Book of the "Aeneid" Commager, Steele, ed.
Brinton, Crane. Lives of Talleyrand.
Brinton, Crane & Christopher, John B. A History of Civilization: 1648 to the Present.
Brinton, Crane, et al. History of Civilization: Vol. 1, Prehistory to 1715.
--A History of Civilization: Prehistory to 1715.
Brinton, Daniel G. The Myths of the New World: A Treatise on the Symbolism & Mythology of the Red Race in America.
--Religions of Primitive Peoples.
Brisac, Catherine, jt. auth. see Grodecki, Louis.
Brisbane, Robert H. Black Activism.
Brisbin, James S., ed. Belden, the White Chief: Or, Twelve Years among the Wild Indians of the Plains from the Diaries & Manuscripts of George P. Belden.
Brisby, Liliana, tr. see Markov, Georgi.
Brisco, Jill. Caleb's Colt.
Briscoe, Alan. Cooking with Wild Plants: How to Recognize & Prepare Edible Wilderness Plants of the Rocky Mountains.
--Your Guide to Home Storage.
Briscoe, D. Stuart. Patterns for Power.
Briscoe, Eugenia R. City by the Sea: A History of Corpus Christi, Texas, 1519-1875.
Briscoe, Jill. Harrow Sparrow.
--Prime Rib & Apple.
Briscoe, Jill & Golz, Judy. Space to Breathe, Room to Grow: The Hows & Whys of Loving, Intimate Relationships.
Briscoe, Jill, jt. auth. see Briscoe, Stuart.
Briscoe, Laurel A. Lectura y Lengua: Curso Intermedio.
Briscoe, Stuart. Tough Truths for Today's Living.
--What Works When Life Doesn't.
Briscoe, Stuart & Briscoe, Jill. Our Favorite Verse.
Briskin, Jacqueline. Dreams Are Not Enough.
--Dreams Are Not Enough.
--Everything & More.
--Paloverde.
--Too Much Too Soon.
Brisley, Chester L., ed. Fixed Interval Work Sampling.
Brislin, Richard W. & Segall, Marshall H. Cross-Cultural Research: The Role of Culture in Understanding Human Behavior.
Brissett, Dennis & Edgley, Charles. Life As Theater: A Dramaturgical Sourcebook.
Brister, C. W. Take Care.
Bristol, Claude. The Magic of Believing.

Bristol, James. Nonviolence: Not First for Export.
Bristol, Lee H. The Big Picnic & Other Meals in the New Testament.
Bristol, Marc. Homegrown Music.
Bristol, Michael D. Carnival & Theatre: Plebian Culture & the Structure of Authority in Renaissance England.
Bristow, Joseph. The Victorian Poet: Poetics & Persona. Armstrong, Isobel, ed.
Bristow, Linda. Bed & Breakfast: California.
Bristow, Linda K. Bed & Breakfast - California: A Selective Guide.
--Bread & Breakfast.
Bristow, M. R., jt. ed. see Cross, D. T.
Britchky, Seymour. The Restaurants of New York: 1985 Edition.
British Automobile Association Staff. Discover France: A Travellers' Guide.
--Guesthouses, Farmhouses & Inns in Britain.
--Lake District: Ordnance Survey Leisure Guide.
--The Touring Book of Britain.
British Columbia, Ministry of Education Staff. Handwriting Resource Book: Grades 1-7.
British Combinatorial Conference Staff. Combinatorial Surveys: Proceedings of British Combinatorial Conference, Sixth. Cameron, Peter, ed.
British Council Staff, ed. English As an International Language.
British Family Research Committee. Families in Britain.
British Film Inst. Staff. First Supplement of the Catalogue of the Book Library of the British Film Institute.
British Film Institute, London Staff. Catalogue of the Book Library of the British Film Institute.
British Horse Society & Pony Club Staff. The Instructors' Handbook.
--The Manual of Horsemanship.
--Mounted Games & Gymkhanas.
British Hotels, Restaurants, & Caterers Association. Hotels & Restaurants in Britain 1983.
British Hotels, Restaurants & Caterers Association Staff. Hotels & Restaurants of Britain, 1988.
British Leyland Motors. The Land Rover Series III Parts Catalogue.
British Medical Association. Smoking & Health: A Report of the British Medical Association Professional Division.
British Medical Association's Board of Science & Education Staff. The Medical Effects of Nuclear War.
British Museum (Natural History) Nature Stored, Nature Studied: Collections, Conservation & Allied Research at the British Museum (Natural History)
British Occupational Hygiene Society. Hygiene Standards of Chrysotile Asbestos Dust.
British Tourist Authority Staff. A Second Touring Guide to Britain.
Brito, Dagobert & Intriligator, Michael D., eds. Strategies for Managing Nuclear Proliferation: Economic & Political Issues.
Britt, Albert, jt. auth. see Richberg, Donald R.
Britt, Kenneth W. Handbook of Pulp & Paper Technology.
Britt, Nellie. His Promises.
Britt, Stewart H. & Boyd, Harper W. Marketing Management & Administrative Action.
Brittan, Arthur & Maynard, Mary. Sexism, Racism & Oppression.
Brittan, Gordon G., Jr., jt. auth. see Lambert, Karel.
Brittan, Samuel. Steering the Economy: The British Experiment.
Britten, F. W. Britten's Old Clocks & Watches & Their Makers.
Brittin, Burdick H. International Law for Seagoing Officers.
Brittin, W., jt. ed. see Barut, Asim O.
Brittin, Wesley E. & Odabasi, Halis, eds. Topics in Modern Physics: Tribute to E. U. Condon.
Brittin, Wesley E., jt. ed. see Barut, A. O.
Brittin, Wesley E., jt. ed. see Barut, Asim O.
Britton, D. K. Cereals in the United Kingdom.
Britton, Dana. Survive, Thrive & Be Happy - While You Work: A Manual for Working Women.
Britton, Dorothy. The Japanese Crane: Bird of Happiness.
Britton, G., ed. see International Symposium on Carotenoids Staff.
Britton, Jack, jt. auth. see Bello, Ignacio.
Britton, James A., Jr. & Kerwood, Lewis O., eds. Financing Income-Producing Real Estate.
Britton, Lewis W. Spreadsheet Books for Specialists.
Britton, Raymond L. The Arbitration Guide.
Britton, Susan M. & Looney, Jackie N. Floral Patterns for Stencilling.
Britvec, S. J. The Stability of Elastic Systems.
Britz, B. Digital Simulation in Electrochemistry.
Brix, V. H. You Are a Computer: Cybernetics in Everyday Life.
Broad, Charles D. Scientific Thought.
Broad, William & Wade, Nicholas. Betrayers of the Truth.
Broad, William J. Star Warriors.
--Star Warriors: A Penetrating Look into the Lives of the Young Scientists Behind Our Space Age Weaponry.
Broadbent, Geoffrey. Design in Architecture & the Human Sciences.
Broadbent, Geoffrey, et al, eds. Meaning & Behaviour in the Built Environment.
Broadbent, Michael. Michael Broadbent's Complete Guide to Wine Tasting & Wine Cellars.
--Michael Broadbent's Pocket Guide to Wine Tasting.
Broadbent, Stephen R., ed. Jane's Avionics 1986-87.
Broadfoot, Patricia. Assessment, Schools & Society.
Broadfoot, Patricia, jt. auth. see Black, Harry.
Broadhurst, P. L., ed. Drugs & the Inheritance of Behavior: A Survey of Comparative Psychopharmacogenetics.
Broadley, Margaret E. Your Natural Gifts: How to Recognize & Develop Them for Success & Self-Fulfillment.
Broadwell. Supervisory Library.
Broadwell, Bruce, jt. auth. see Edwards, Perry.
Broady, Maurice. Planning for People.
--Tomorrow's Community-the Development of Neighborhood Organisations.
Broat, I. G. The Entrepreneur.
--The Master Mechanic.
Broat, T. G. The Junketeers.
Broberg, G., ed. Linnaeus: Progress & Prospects in Linnaean Research.
Brobreck, Stephen, jt. auth. see Hoffman, Naphtali.
Brobst, Harry M. Understanding Personal Computers: A Home Study Course.
Brocardo, G. Minerals & Gemstones: An Identification Guide.
Brock, Alice M. My Life As a Restaurant.
Brock, B. B. A Global Approch to Geology: The Background of a Mineral Exploration Strategy Based on Significant Form in the Patterning of the Earth's Crust.
Brock, Betty. The Shades.
Brock, Horace R., jt. auth. see Klingstedt, John P.
Brock, James, jt. auth. see Adams, Walter.
Brock, Jonathan. Managing People in Public Agencies: Personnel & Labor Relations.
Brock, Karen L. Autumn Grasses & Water: Motifs in Japanese Art.
Brock, Katherine M., jt. auth. see Brock, Thomas D.
Brock, M., ed. see Annual Meeting of the Deutsche Gesellschaft Fuer Neurochirurgie Staff, et al.
Brock, M., et al, eds. Cerebral Blood Flow: Clinical & Experimental Results.
Brock, Robert C. The Commands of Christ for Christian Living: An Exposition of the Bible's Second Set of Commandments.
Brock, Stanley E. Jungle Cowboy.
--More about Leemo.
Brock, T. E., ed. see International Conference on Industrial Robot Technology Staff & International Symposium on Industrial Robots, 6th, Univ. Nottingham, Eng., Mar. 1976.
Brock, Thomas D. & Brock, Katherine M. Basic Microbiology with Applications.
Brock, Thomas D., et al. Biology of Microorganisms.
Brock, W. R. Character of American History.
Brockbank, Bernard P. Commandments & Promises of God.
Brockdorff, E. Von see Prinzhorn, H.
Brockett, O. & Findlay, R. Century of Innovation: A History of European & American Theatre & Drama, 1870-1970.
Brockett, Oscar, ed. see Rokem, Freddie.
Brockett, Oscar G. The Essential Theatre.
Brockett, William A. & Keker, John W. Effective Direct & Cross-Examination.
Brockhurst, Robert J., et al, eds. Controversy in Ophthalmology.
Brockington, Dave, jt. auth. see White, Roger.
Brockington, R. Financial Accounting.
Brocklehurst, J. C., jt. auth. see Kamal, Asif.
Brockman, Bennett see Butler, Francelia, et al.
Brockman, C. Frank & Merriam, Lawrence C., Jr. Recreational Use of Wild Lands.
Brockman, Norbert. Ordained to Service: A Theology of the Permanent Diaconate.
Brockmann, Ellen-Mary. Teaching Handicapped Students in the Mathematics Classroom.
Brod. Der Meister.
Brod, Alice F. Estate Planning: Complete Guide & Workbook.
Brod, Max. Der Master.
Brod, Richard I. & Neel, Jasper P., eds. Profession '78.
Broda, E. Evolution of Bioenergetic Processes.
Brodal, A., et al, eds. see Phillips, I. R.
Broder, Bill, jt. auth. see Broder, Gloria K.
Broder, Gloria K. & Broder, Bill. Remember This Time.
Broder, Nathan. Great Operas of Mozart.
--Samuel Barber.
Broder, Nathan, ed. The Great Operas of Mozart.
Broderick, Carlfred B. Marriage & the Family.
Broderick, Damien. Black Grail.
Brodeur, Paul. The Zapping of America: Microwaves, Their Deadly Risk & the Cover-up.
Brodie, B. B., et al, eds. see International Workshop on Ergot Alkaloids Staff.
Brodie, Fawn. Thaddeus Stevens, Scourge of the South.
Brodie, Fawn M. Devil Drives: A Life of Sir Richard Burton.
--Thomas Jefferson: An Intimate History.
Brodie, Iain. Ferrets & Ferreting.
Brodie, Leo, jt. auth. see Forth, Inc. Staff.
Brodie, Martin J. & Harrison, P. Ian, eds. Practical Prescribing.
Brodin, Dorothy, jt. auth. see Brodin, Pierre.
Brodin, Pierre & Brodin, Dorothy. Presence Contemporaines: Auteurs Franeais du Vingtieme Siecle.
Brodine, Virginia. Air Pollution. Commoner, Barry, ed.
--Radioactive Contamination. Commoner, Barry, ed.
Brodrick, Alan H. Danger Spot of Europe.
--The Tree of Human History.
Brodskaya, Minna, tr. see Kamshilov, M. M.
Brodskaya, N. Henri Rousseau.
Brodsky, Archie, jt. auth. see Peele, Stanton.
Brodsky, Beverley, adapted by. & illus. The Story of Job.
Brodsky, Gary. The Art of Getting Even.
--The Contemporary Devil's Dictionary.
Brodsky, Joseph. Konets Prekrasnoi Epokhi.
--The Nobel Lecture: Bilingual Edition. Rubin, Barry, tr.
--Rimskie Elegii.
Brodsky, Stanley L., jt. ed. see Fischer, Constance T.
Brodtkorb, Reidar. Gold Coin. Kingsland, L. W., tr.
Brody, A., jt. ed. see Carter, A.
Brody, Alvan & Brody, Betty. The Legal Rights of Nonsmokers.
Brody, Betty, jt. auth. see Brody, Alvan.
Brody, Eugene B. Minority Group Adolescents in the United States.
Brody, H., jt. ed. see Apelian, D.
Brody, Harry. As Once to Birth I went New I Am Taken Back.
Brody, Harvey. The Book of Low Fire Ceramics.
Brody, Jane, jt. auth. see Adams, W. Royce.
Brody, Jean. A Coven of Women.
Brody, Jean & Osborne, Gail B. The Twenty Year Phenomenon.
Brody, Joel, tr. see Lubich, Gino & Lazzarin, Piero.
Brody, Lora A. Growing up on the Chocolate Diet: A Memoir with Recipes.
--Growing up on the Chocolate Diet: A Memoir with Recipes.
Brody, Marcia, et al. Bioenergetics & Metabolism of Green Algae.
Brody, Marvin D., jt. auth. see Berger, Jordan C.
Brody, Nathan. Personality: Research & Theory.
Brody, Steve. How to Break Ninety Before You Reach It.
Broeg, R. & Ewbank, Weeb. Football Greats.
Broeg, Robert. The Pilot Light & the Gas House Gang.
Broekel, Ray. The Great American Candy Bar Book.
--The Mystery of the Funny Money.
--The President Jackson Case.
--The Shoelace Solution.
Broening, Angela M., ed. English Language Arts in the Secondary School.
Broer, Marion R. & Zernicke, Ronald F. Efficiency of Human Movement.
Brogan, Francis. Estate Planning for Owners of Closely-Held Corporations.
Brogan, Patrick & Zarca, Albert. Deadly Business: Sam Cummings, Interarms, & the Arms Trade.
Broger, Achim. Francie's Paper Puppy.
Broglie, Marie-Blanche De see De Broglie, Marie-Blanche & Zukas, Harriet.
Broglio, John, tr. see Volguine, Alexandre.
Brohi, A. K. Testament of Faith.
Broida, H. P., jt. ed. see Bass, Arnold M.
Broida, Peter B. Guide to Federal Labor Relations Authority Law & Practice.
--Guide to Merit Systems Protection Board Law & Practice.
Broido, Lucy, jt. auth. see Cheret, Jules.
Bro. Ignatius. In God We Trust: Creation's Mysteries Revealed.
Brokamp, Marilyn. Prayer Times for Intermediate Grades.
Brokamp, Sr. Marilyn, jt. auth. see Brokamp, Sr. Marlene.
Brokamp, Sr. Marlene & Brokamp, Sr. Marilyn. Eucharist: God's Gift of Love.
Brokensha, D. & Crowder, M. Africa in the Wider World.
Brokering, Herbert. In a Promise.
Brokering, Herbert F. In Due Season.
--Surprise Me, Jesus.
Brokering, Lois. Rainbow Bags: Instructions for Making Six Colorful Bags of Soft Toys.
Brokhoff, Barbara. Bitter-Sweet Recollections.
Brolin, S. E., ed. Structure & Metabolism of the Pancreatic Islets.
Broman, Betty L. The Early Years in Childhood Education.
--The Early Years in Childhood Education.
Broman, Betty L., jt. auth. see Burns, Paul C.
Bromberg, J. Philip. Clean Air Act Handbook.
Bromberg, Liebb. Six Hundred & One Words You Need to Know for the SAT.
Bromberg, Murray & Gordon, Melvin. Eleven Hundred Words You Need to Know.
Bromberg, Murray & Liebb, Julius. Words with a Flair.
Bromberg, Murray, et al. Five Hundred & Four Absolutely Essential Words.
--Five Hundred Four Absolutely Essential Words.
Bromberg, Walter. Crime & the Mind, an Outline of Psychiatric Criminology.
Brombert, Victor. Novels of Flaubert: A Study of Themes & Techniques.
Brome, Richard. A Mad Couple Well Match'd. Spove, Steen H. & Orgel, Stephen, eds.
--The Weeding of Covent Garden & the Sparagus Garden. McClure, Donald S. & Orgel, Stephen, eds.
Brome, Vincent. Ernest Jones: A Biography.
--Jung: Man & Myth.
--Six Studies in Quarrelling.
Bromfield, Ken. Old Bores Almanack, Nineteen Eighty-Six AD.
Bromfield, Louis. The Farm.
Bromige, Iris. The Changing Tide.
Bromiley, Geoffrey W. Children of Promise: The Case for Baptizing Infants.
--God & Marriage.
Bromley, D. Allan & Hughes, V. W., eds. Facets of Physics.
Bromley, D. B., ed. Gerontology: Social & Behavioural Perspectives.
Bromley, David G. & Shupe, Anson D., Jr. Moonies in America: Cult, Church, & Crusade.
Bromley, Ray. The Urban Informal Sector: Critical Perspectives.
Bromley, Ray & Gerry, Chris, eds. Casual Work & Poverty in Third World Cities.
Bromley, S. C., jt. ed. see Thornton, C. S.
Brommer, ed. Lexique Anglais-Francais des Termes Appartenant Aux Techniques En Usage a I.G.N.
Brommer, Gerald. Drawing: Ideas, Materials, Techniques. Horn, George F., ed.
Brommer, Gerald F. Discovering Art History.
Bromwich, Geoffrey. Insuring Business Risks in Canada: How to Get the Most for Your Money.
Brondum, Jack, tr. see Scherfig, Hans.
Broner, E. M. A Weave of Women.
Bronfenbrenner, Martin, et al. Economics. Incl. Macroeconomics; Microeconomics. HM.
Bronfman, Sam. San Francisco Celebrity Chef. Hosner, Sheila, ed.
Bronk, Detlev W., ed. see Rockefeller University Staff, et al.
Bronner, Edwin. The Encyclopedia of the American Theatre.
Bronner, Felix & Peterlik, Meindrad, eds. Calcium & Phosphate Transport Across Biomembranes.
Bronner, Rolf. Decision Making under Time Pressure: An Experimental Study of Stress Behavior in Business Management.
Bronner, Stephen & Kellner, Douglas, eds. Passion & Rebellion: The Expressionist Heritage.
Bronowski, J. The Identity of Man.
Bronowski, J., ed. see Blake, William.
Bronshtein, I. N. & Semendyayev, K. A. A Guide-Book to Mathematics. Jaworowsky, J. & Bleicher, M. N., trs. from Rus.
Bronson, Dorrance C. Concepts of Actuarial Soundness in Pension Plans.
Bronson, J. & Bronson, R. Early American Weaving & Dyeing: The Domestic Manufacturer's Assistant & Family Directory in the Arts of Weaving & Dyeing.
Bronson, R., jt. auth. see Bronson, J.
Bronson, Walter C., ed. English Poems: The Elizabethan Age & the Puritan Period (1550-1660)
--English Poems: Vol. 3-Restoration & Eighteenth Century.
Bronson, Wilfrid S. Beetles.
--Cats.
--Coyotes.
--Dogs: Best Breeds for Young People.
--Freedom & Plenty: Ours to Save.
--Goats.
--Grasshopper Book.
--Horns & Antlers.
--Turtles.
--Wonder World of Ants.
Bronson, Wilfrid S., jt. auth. see Reed, W. Maxwell.
Bronsted, H. V. Atomic Age & Our Biological Future.

Authors

Bronstein, Alvin J. Representing Prisoners: A Course Handbook.
Bronstein, Alvin J. & Hirschkop, Philip J. Prisoners Rights Nineteen Seventy-Nine.
Bronstein, Audrey. The Triple Struggle: Latin American Peasant Women.
Bronstein, Daniel J., et al. Basic Problems of Philosophy.
Bronte, Charlotte. Jane Eyre.
--Jane Eyre.
--Jane Eyre. Dunn, Richard J., ed.
Bronte, Emily. Wuthering Heights.
--Wuthering Heights.
--Wuthering Heights.
Bronte, Stephen. Japanese Finance.
Bronwell, Arthur B. Science & Technology in the World of the Future.
Brook, Barry S., et al, eds. Perspectives in Musicology.
Brook, Charles G. All About Adolescence.
Brook, George L. History of the English Language.
Brook, Stephen. Honkytonk Gelato: Travels through Texas.
--New York Days, New York Nights.
Brooke, C. F. The Tudor Drama: A History of English National Drama to the Retirement of Shakespeare.
Brooke, C. N., tr. see Knowles, David.
Brooke, Christopher. The Twelfth Century Renaissance.
Brooke, D. The Railway Navvy.
Brooke, Dinah. Death Games.
Brooke, Fulke G. Poems & Dramas of Fulke Greville First Lord Brooke.
Brooke, George J. Exegesis at Qumran: Four Q Florilegium in Its Jewish Context.
Brooke, I. English Costume in the Age of Elizabeth.
--English Costume of the Later Middle Ages.
--English Costume of the Seventeenth Century.
Brooke, Michael Z. & Remmers, H. Lee. International Management & Business Policy.
Brooke, Nicholas. Shakespeare's Early Tragedies.
Brooke, Roger. Santa's Christmas Journey.
Brooke, Rosalind. Law, Justice & Social Policy.
Brooke, Tal. Avatar of Night: The Hidden Side of Sai Baba.
Brooke-Little, J. P. An Heraldic Alphabet.
Brookeman, Christopher. American Culture & Society since the Nineteen Thirties.
Brooker, Belinda. Blue Wren.
Brooker, Donald B., et al. Drying Cereal Grains.
Brooke-Rose, Christine. A ZBC of Ezra Pound.
Brookes, A. M. Advanced Electric Circuits.
--Basic Electric Circuits.
--Basic Instrumentation for Engineers & Physicists.
Brookes, Andrew. V-Force: The History of Britain's Airborne Deterrent.
Brookes, Edgar H. & Macaulay, J. B. Civil Liberty in South Africa.
Brookes, John. A Place in the Country.
--Room Outside.
--Timetable Planning.
Brookes, L. G. & Motamen, H. The Economics of Nuclear Energy.
Brookes, L. J., jt. ed. see Bender, A. E.
Brookes, Michael C. & German, Katherine L. Meeting the Challenges: Developing Faculty Careers. Fife, Jonathan D., ed. & frwd. by.
Brookes, Owen. Deadly Communion.
--Forget Me Knots.
--The Gatherer.
Brooke-Shepherd, Gordon. Royal Sunset: The European Dynasties & the Great War.
Brookesmith, F. I Remember Tall Ships.
Brookfield, Harold. Interdependent Development.
Brookings, jt. auth. see Institute for Research on Public Policy, Canada.
Brookins, Dana. Rico's Cat.
Brooklyn Museum, ed. Carl Larsson.
Brookman Stamp Co., ed. Price Guide of United States, Canada & United Nations: 1988 Edition.
--Price Guide of United States Stamps: 1988 Edition.
Brookner, Anita. The Debut.
--Family & Friends.
--Family & Friends.
Brooks. Heat Treatment of Ferrous Alloys.
Brooks, jt. auth. see Birch.
Brooks, Alfred M. Architecture.
Brooks, B. David, jt. auth. see Goble, Frank.
Brooks, C. E. Climate in Every Day Life.
Brooks, Charles E. The Henry's Fork.
--Larger Trout for the Western Fly Fisherman.
--Nymph Fishing for Larger Trout.
Brooks, Cleanth & Warren, Robert Penn. Fundamentals of Good Writing.
--Modern Rhetoric.
Brooks, Courtaney. Plays & Puppets et Cetera.
Brooks, Daniel R. & Wiley, E. O. Evolution As Entropy: Toward a Unified Theory of Biology.
Brooks, Daniel R., et al. Principles & Methods of Phylogenetic Systematics: A Cladistics Workbook.
Brooks, Daniel T. Computer Law Institue 1985.
--Computer Law Institute 1983-84.
Brooks, David & Mallick, Netar. Renal Medicine & Urology: Library of General Practice.
Brooks, David K., Jr., jt. ed. see McFadden, John.
Brooks, Earl & Odiorne, George S. Managing by Negotiations.
Brooks, Glenn E., jt. auth. see Rourke, Francis E.
Brooks, Hugh. Encyclopedia of Building & Construction Terms.
Brooks, J. & Shaw, G. Origin & Development of Living Systems.
Brooks, Janice Y. Seventrees.
Brooks, John. Once in Golconda: A True Dream of Wall Street, 1920-1938.
Brooks, John, ed. South American Handbook, 1984.
--The South American Handbook, 1988.
Brooks, Juanita. John Doyle Lee: Zealot, Pioneer Builder, Scapegoat.
Brooks, Lisa. Thomas B. Turtle.
Brooks, Lucy. The Nurse Assistant.
Brooks, Martin. The Dream Weaver.
Brooks, Marvin B. & Brooks, Sally W. Lifelong Lover.
--Lifelong Sexual Vigor: How to Avoid & Overcome Impotence.
Brooks, Maurice G. Appalachians.
Brooks, Nelson. Language & Language Learning: Theory & Practice.
Brooks, Noel. Scriptural Holiness.
Brooks, Pat & Garvan, Fran J. Country Inns of New England.
Brooks, Patricia. Best Restaurants New England.
--Best Restaurants Southern New England.
Brooks, Paul. The House of Life: Rachel Carson at Work.
--The View from Lincoln Hill: Men & the Land in a New England Town.
Brooks, Philip C. Research in Archives: The Use of Unpublished Primary Sources.
Brooks, R. M., ed. see Several Complex Variables Symposium Staff.
Brooks, R. R. Biological Methods of Prospecting for Minerals.
Brooks, Sally W., jt. auth. see Brooks, Marvin B.
Brooks, Simon & Cuthertson, Keith. The Exchange Rate Enviroment.
Brooks, Stewart M. Nurse's Drug Reference.
Brooks, Thomas R. Clint: Biography of a Labor Intellectual Clinton S. Golden.
--The Road to Dignity.
Brooks, Van Wyck. The Flowering of New England, 1815-1865.
Brooks, William D. & Friedrich, Gustav W. Teaching Speech Communication in the Secondary School.
Brooks, William D., jt. auth. see Emmert, Philip.
Brook-Sheperd, Gordon. Uncle of Europe: The Social & Diplomatic Life of Edward VII.
Brook-Shepherd, Gordon. The Storm Petrels.
--The Storm Petrels: The Flight of the First Soviet Defectors.
Broom, Robert. Finding the Missing Link.
Broome, H. B. Gunfighters.
Brooner, E. G. & Wells, Phil. Computer Communication Techniques.
Brooten, Dorothy, jt. auth. see Downs, Florence.
Brophy, Brigid. Palace Without Chairs.
Brophy, James & Paolucci, Henry, eds. The Achievement of Galileo.
Brophy, James J. Basic Electronics for Scientists.
Brophy, Jere E., jt. auth. see Good, Thomas L.
Brophy, Julia & Smart, Carol, eds. Women in Law: Explorations in Law, Family & Sexuality.
Brosche, P. & Suendermann, J., eds. Tidal Friction & the Earth's Rotation.
Broscious, John A., jt. auth. see Niaki, Shahzad.
Brose, Olive J. Frederick Denison Maurice: Rebellious Conformist, 1805-1872.
Brosman, Catharine S., et al. Studies in French in Honor of Andre Bourgeois.
Brosman, Catherine S. Jean-Paul Sartre.
Brosnahan. Frommer's Guide to Montreal & Quebec City.
Brosnahan, Tom. Frommer's Guide to Cancun, Cozumel, & the Yucatan.
--Frommer's Guide to Mexico City & Acapulco.
--Frommer's Mexico on Twenty Dollars a Day: Including a Special Section on Guatemala.
--Mexico on Twenty Dollars a Day.
--Turkey-A Travel Survival Kit.
Bross, Irwin D. Scientific Strategies in Human Affairs: To Tell the Truth.
Brosset, Raymond & Fondaneche, Pierre. Dictionnaire Memento D'electronique.
Broster, W. H. & Swan, Henry. Feeding Strategy for the High Yielding Dairy Cow.
Broszat, Martin, jt. auth. see Krausnick, Helmut.
Brother Andrew, et al. God's Smuggler.
Brother Lawrence. God-Illuminated Cook: The Practice of the Presence of God.
Brothers, A. J., ed. & tr. Terence: The Self-Tormentor (Heaton Timoroumenos).
Brothers, Connie, ed. The Iowa Writers' Workshop Cookbook.
Brothers, J., ed. Readings in the Sociology of Religion.
Brothers, Joyce. The Brothers System for Liberated Love & Marriage.
--How to Get Everything You Want Out of Life.
--What Every Woman Ought to Know about Love & Marriage.
--What Every Woman Should Know about Men.
Brotherston, G., ed. Spanish American Modernista Poets.
Brotherston, Gordon. Image of the New World: The American Continent Portrayed in Native Texts.
--Image of the New World: The American Continent Portrayed in Native Texts.
Brotherton, Germaine. Rush & Leafcraft.
Brotherton, Jack. The Annals of Stanislaus County.
Brothwell, C., et al, eds. Maintenance of Numerically Controlled Machine Tools.
Brothwell, Don R. Digging Up Bones: The Excavation, Treatment & Study of Human Skeletal Remains.
Brouch, Virginia M., ed. Microcomputers in Art Education.
Broudy, Harry S. The Real World of the Public Schools.
Brough, James. Margaret: The Tragic Princess.
Brough, R. Clayton. His Servants Speak: Statements by Latter-day Saint Leaders on Contemporary Topics.
--The Lost Tribes: History Doctrine, Prophecies & Theories About Israel's Lost Ten Tribes.
Brough, Walter & Sutton, Michael. Explosion: The Day Texas City Died.
Broughel, Barbara, jt. auth. see Conrad, Tony.
Brouillet, George A. Voice Manual.
Brouk, B. Plants Consumed by Man.
Brouker, Jose de see Camara, Dom H.
Broumas, Olga. Soie Sauvage.
Broun, G. B., et al, eds. Enzyme Engineering.
Broun, Kenneth S. & Meisenholder, Robert. Evidence Problems.
Broussard, E. Joseph & Holgate, Jack F. Writing & Reporting Broadcast News.
Broussine, Michael & Guerrier, Yvonne. Surviving As a Middle Manager.
Brow, Thea J. The Secret Cross of Lorraine.
Browder, Robert P. The Origins of Soviet-American Diplomacy.
Browder, Sue. The American Biking Atlas & Touring Guide.
Brower, David, ed. see Jeffers, Robinson.
Brower, David J., jt. auth. see Godschalk, David R.
Brower, David J, jt. auth. see Godschalk, David R.
Brower, Margaret & Brower, Scott. How You Can Go from Broke to Broker in Real Estate.
Brower, Millicent & Koshkin, Naomi. One Hundred Luscious Diet Drinks.
Brower, Scott, jt. auth. see Brower, Margaret.
Brower, Walter A., jt. auth. see Lee, D. E.
Brown. Barron's How to Prepare for the New Medical College Admission Test (MCAT)
--Someone Special, Just Like You.
Brown, ed. see Townsley, David & Bjork, Russell.
Brown, A. Great Ideas in Communications.
Brown, A., tr. see Botvinnik, M. M.
Brown, A. Theordore & Dorsett, Lyle W. K.C. A History of Kansas City, Missouri.
Brown, Aggrey, jt. ed. see Stone, Carl.
Brown, Alan, tr. see Kattan, Naim.
Brown, Alan G., jt. ed. see Hillis, W. Edward.
Brown, Alan W. The Metaphysical Society: Victorian Minds in Crisis, 1869-1880.
Brown, Alexander C. Life with Grover.
Brown, Alexis, tr. see Ortega Y Gasset, Jose.
Brown, Alfred E., jt. auth. see Atlas, Ronald M.
Brown, Alpha. One Hundred & One Practical Activities for Use in Classes of Pupils Who Are Retarded.
Brown, Andrew. A New Companion to Greek Tragedy.
Brown, Ann A., jt. auth. see Towle, Laird.
Brown, Annice H. Thank You, Lord, for Little Things.
Brown, Arthur M. & Stubbs, Donald W., eds. Medical Physiology.
Brown, B. Images of Family Life in Magazine Advertising: 1920-1978.
Brown, B. Baldwin, ed. see Vasari, Giorgio.
Brown, Barbara. Between Health & Illness: New Notions on Stress & the Nature of Well Being.
Brown, Barbara, jt. auth. see Hawkins, David.
Brown, Barbara, jt. ed. see Rose, James M.
Brown, Beverly S. Erica the Ecologist.
Brown, Bill, jt. auth. see Sullivan, William C.
Brown, Bruce. Browns Index to Photocomposition Typography.
--Marx, Freud, & the Critique of Everyday Life: Toward a Permanent Cultural Revolution.
--Mountain in the Clouds: A Search for the Wild Salmon.
--Mountain in the Clouds: A Search for the Wild Salmon.
Brown, Bryan. The Alfred Hitchcock Movie Quiz Book.
Brown, C. R. Joseph Rusling Meeker: Images of the Mississippi.
Brown, C. Reynolds. Clara Weaver Parrish.
Brown, Calvin, et al, eds. Masterworks of World Literature. Incl. Vol. 1. Homer to Cervantes; Vol. II. Shakespeare to Sartre. Irvington.
Brown, Catherine R., et al. Building for the Arts: A Guidebook for the Planning & Design of Cultural Facilities.
Brown, Charles H. News Editing & Display.
Brown, Charles T. The Art of Rock & Roll.
Brown, Chas. William Cullen Bryant.
Brown, Chris, intro. by. World Repeater Atlas.
Brown, Christopher. Ghostbusters Training Manual.
--Images of a Golden Past: Dutch Genre Painting of the 17th Century.
--Whisper & the Secret of Dark Hollow.
--Who Ya Gonna Call?-Ghostbusters!
Brown, Christopher C. Daddy's Gonna Buy Me a Diamond Ring.
Brown, Christopher K., jt. auth. see Gruner, Mark.
Brown, Clara D. & Smith, Lynn S. Serials: Past, Present & Future.
Brown, Clare, jt. auth. see Brown, Karen.
Brown, Clarence & Merwin, W. S., trs. from Rus. Selected Poems of Osip Mandelstam.
Brown, Colin B. Manual of Renal Disease.
Brown, Craig & Cunliffe, Lesley. The Book of Royal Lists.
Brown, Cynthia L., et al. High School & Beyond Student Financial Assistance: Student Loans.
Brown, D., jt. auth. see Clark, R.
Brown, D. K. An Introduction to the Finite Element Method Using BASIC Programs.
Brown, D. S. W., et al. The Geological Evolution of Australia & New Zealand.
Brown, David. Draw Birds.
--Draw Horses.
--The Landlord's Law Book - Evictions: California.
--Planter; or, Thirteen Years in the South.
Brown, David, ed. Bible Wisdom for Modern Living: Arranged by Subject.
Brown, David E. North Carolina: New Directions for an Old Lane: An Illustrated History of Tar Heel Enterprise.
Brown, Dee. A Conspiracy of Knaves.
--Killdeer Mountain.
--Lonesome Whistle.
--Wounded Knee: An Indian History of the American West. Ehrlich, Amy, ed.
Brown, Deena, ed. American Yoga.
Brown, Delwin. To Set at Liberty: Christian Faith & Human Freedom.
Brown, Diane, ed. see Que Corporation.
Brown, Diane, ed. see Southern, Karen.
Brown, Donald R., jt. auth. see Harvey, Donald F.
Brown, Dorothy S. Handle with Care: A Question of Alzheimer's.
Brown, E. D., jt. auth. see Schwarzenberger, Georg.
Brown, E. H. & Waters, R. S., eds. Progress in Geomorphology: Papers in Honour of David L. Linton.
Brown, E. T., ed. Rock Characterization, Testing & Monitoring: ISRM Suggested Methods.
Brown, E. T., jt. ed. see Jenkins, J. P.
Brown, Edward E. Tassajara Bread Book.
--Tassajara Bread Book.
--Tassajara Cooking.
--Tassajara Cooking: A Vegetarian Cooking Book.
Brown, Elizabeth M., et al, eds. Pilgrims & Their Times.
Brown, Eric. Wings of the Navy. Green, William, ed.
Brown, F., et al, eds. Vehicle Painting.
--Vehicle Painting.
Brown, Francis J. One America: The History, Contributions, & Present Problems of Our Racial & National Minorities.
Brown, Fred L. Combat Ready, Bk. 1: The Victor.
Brown, Frederic. The Deep End.
--The Fabulous Clipjoint.
Brown, Fredric. The Office.
Brown, G. R., jt. ed. see Michaels, Rhoda M.
Brown, G. Thompson. Christianity in the People's Republic of China.
Brown, Gabrielle. The New Celibacy.
--The New Celibacy: Why More Men & Women Are Abstaining from Sex & Enjoying It.
Brown, Gary D. System-370 Job Control Language.
Brown, George, jt. auth. see Flanders, Helen H.
Brown, George D. & Ladd, George T. Excursions in Historical Geology: A Modular Approach.
--Excursions in Historical Geology: A Modular Approach, Units 1-12.
Brown, George E. The Pruning of Trees, Shrubs & Conifers.
Brown, Gilbert, jt. auth. see Gotsch, Carl.
Brown, H. C., ed. The Nonclassical Ion Problem.
Brown, H. D. Biochemical Microcalorimetry.
Brown, H. James, jt. ed. see Roberts, Neal A.
Brown, Hamish. The Great Walking Adventure.
--Hamish's Groats End Walk: One Man & His Dog on a Hill Route Through Britain & Ireland.
Brown, Harold, et al. Security in the 1980's.

Brown, Harold I. Perception, Theory & Commitment: The New Philosophy of Science.
Brown, Harry D. Chemistry of the Cell Interface.
Brown, Harry J. & Williams, Frederick D., eds. Diary of James A. Garfield: Vol. I, 1848-1871, Vol. II, 1872-1874.
Brown, Harry M. Business Report Writing.
Brown, Harry M. & Reid, Karen K. Business Writing & Communication.
Brown, Helen G. Having It All: Love Success Sex-Money.
Brown, Helen Gurley. Helen Gurley Brown's Outrageous Opinions.
Brown, Henry P. & Hopkins, Sheila V. Perspectives of Wages & Prices.
Brown, Herbert C. Explorations in the Nonclassical Ion Area.
Brown, Herbert P. & Schanzer, Stephan N. Female Sterilization.
Brown, Howard. Familiar Faces, Hidden Lives: The Story of Homosexual Men in America Today.
Brown, Howard M. Music in the French Secular Theater 1400-1550.
Brown, Howard M. & Lascelle, Joan. Musical Iconography: A Manual for Cataloguing Musical Subjects in Western Art Before 1800.
Brown, Howard M., jt. auth. see Handel, George F.
Brown, Howard M., ed. see Bononcini, Giovanni.
Brown, Howard M., ed. see Caldara, Antonio.
Brown, Howard M., ed. see Cavalli, Francesco.
Brown, Howard M., ed. see Cesti, Antonio.
Brown, Howard M., ed. see DiCapua, Rinaldo.
Brown, Howard M., ed. see Fux, Johann J.
Brown, Howard M., ed. see Galuppi, Baldassare.
Brown, Howard M., ed. see Legrenzi, Giovanni.
Brown, Howard M., ed. see Pasquini, Bernardo.
Brown, Howard M., ed. see Piccinni, Niccolo.
Brown, Howard M., ed. see Rossi, Luigi.
Brown, Howard M., ed. see Scarlatti, Alessandro.
Brown, Howard M., ed. see Stradella, Alessandro.
Brown, Howard M., ed. see Traetta, Tommaso.
Brown, Howard M., ed. see Vivaldi, Antonio.
Brown, Huntington. Rabelais in English Literature.
Brown, Irene B. Willow Whip.
Brown, Irving H. Gypsy Fires in America.
Brown, Ivor. No Idle Words, & Having the Last Word.
Brown, J., et al, eds. An Arctic Ecosystem: The Coastal Tundra at Barrow, Alaska.
Brown, J. A. Psychiatry for Every Man.
--The Social Psychology of Industry: Human Relations in the Factory.
Brown, J. Douglas. The Human Nature of Organizations.
Brown, J. H. Advances in Biomedical Engineering.
Brown, J. H., ed. Advances in Biomedical Engineering.
--Advances in Biomedical Engineering.
Brown, J. H. & Dickson, James F., eds. Advances in Biomedical Engineering.
Brown, J. H. U. & Gann, Donald, eds. Engineering Principles in Physiology.
Brown, Jack H., ed. Physiology of Man in Space: Proceedings.
Brown, James. Hot Wire.
Brown, James & Tucker, Bruce. James Brown: The Godfather of Soul.
Brown, James, et al. The Relationship of the Library to Instructional Systems. Corrigan, John T., ed.
Brown, James H. & Gibson, Arthur C. Biogeography.
Brown, James I. Reading Power.
Brown, James R. & Butwill, N. Religion, Society, & the Homosexual.
Brown, James R. & Woodruff, A. M., eds. Land for the Cities of Asia.
Brown, James T. Harvest of the Sun: An Illustrated History of Riverside County.
Brown, James W., jt. auth. see Churchill, Ruel V.
Brown, Jan, jt. auth. see Dragonwagon, Crescent.
Brown, Jane. Lanning Roper & His Gardens.
Brown, Jared. The Fabulous Lunts: A Biography of Alfred Lunt & Lynn Fontanne.
Brown, Jeffrey. Secret Ingredients: Inactive Ingredients in Drugs.
Brown, Jennifer S., jt. ed. see Peterson, Jacqueline.
Brown, Jim. The Case for the Cruising Trimaran.
Brown, Joan W. Never Alone.
--Penross Manor.
Brown, John. First Peter.
--John Bunyan, (1628-1688) His Life, Times & Work. Harrison, Frank M., ed.
--Zaibatsu.
Brown, John, jt. auth. see Clarke, R. H.
Brown, John, jt. auth. see Moore, Colin.
Brown, John, jt. auth. see Jones, Kathleen.
Brown, John E. Responsible Before God.
Brown, John H., ed. see De Haan, Stefan.
Brown, John M. The Worlds of Robert E. Sherwood: Mirror to His Times, Eighteen Ninety-Six to Nineteen Thirty-Nine.
Brown, John P. & York, Richard L. Covenant of Peace: A Liberation Prayer Book.
Brown, John R. Shakespeare's Othello: The Harbrace Theater Edition.
Brown, John T. Among the Bantu Nomads.
Brown, Jonathan, jt. auth. see Enggass, Robert.
Brown, Judith N. & Baldwin, Christine. A Second Start: A Widow's Guide to Financial Survival at a Time of Emotional Crisis.
Brown, June, jt. auth. see Brown, Karen.
Brown, June H., et al. Child, Family, Neighborhood: A Master Plan for Social Service Delivery.
Brown, K. D., ed. The First Labour Party Nineteen Six to Nineteen Fourteen.
Brown, Karen. English, Welsh & Scottish Country Inns & Castle Hotels.
--French Country Inns & Chateau Hotels.
--French Country Inns & Chateaux.
Brown, Karen & Brown, Clare. Italian Country Inns & Villas.
--Swiss Country Inns & Chalets.
Brown, Karen & Brown, June. English, Welsh & Scottish Country Inns.
--English, Welsh, Scottish Country Inns.
Brown, Karen A. French Country Inns & Chateau Hotels.
Brown, Kent, et al, eds. Virginia Country's Civil War Quarterly.
Brown, L. B. Psychology in Contemporary China.
Brown, L. M. Aims of Education.
Brown, L. M., jt. ed. see Ashby, M. F.
Brown, Larry W. Images That Last.
Brown, Lawrence A. Innovation Diffusion: A New Perspective.
Brown, Lennox see Harrison, Paul C.
Brown, Les. Television: The Business Behind the Box.
--Television: The Business Behind the Box.
Brown, Leslie K. The Registry of California Wineries.
Brown, Lester, et al. Running on Empty: The Future of the Automobile in An Oil-Short World.
Brown, Lester R., jt. auth. see Eckholm, Erik.
Brown, Lester R., et al. The Future of the Automobile in an Oil-Short World.
Brown, Lillie V. Gleanings along Life's Way.
Brown, Lisa & Panter, Gideon. The Pregnancy Diary.
Brown, Luanne, jt. auth. see Rachid, Sidna.
Brown, Lucius. What America Means to Me.
Brown, Lyle C., jt. auth. see Jones, Eugene W.
Brown, M. B., jt. ed. see Dixon, W. J.
Brown, M. H. Brown's Lawsuit Cookbook: How to Sue & Win.
Brown, Malcolm. The Politics of Irish Literature: From Thomas Davis to W. B. Yeats.
Brown, Malcolm & Seaton, Shirley. Christmas Truce (The Western Front December 1914)
Brown, Malcolm, ed. see Orlova, Alexandra.
Brown, Marc. Arthur's Eyes.
--Arthur's Nose.
--Arthur's Valentine.
--The True Francine.
Brown, Marcia. Bun: A Tale from Russia.
--Listen to a Shape.
--The Three Billy Goats Gruff.
Brown, Marcia & Andersen, Hans Christian. The Snow Queen.
Brown, Marcia & Perrault, Charles. Cinderella.
Brown, Marcia, ed. & illus. Three Billy Goats Gruff.
Brown, Marice C. Amen, Brother Ben: A Mississippi Collection of Children's Rhymes.
Brown, Marie S. & Murphy, Mary A. Ambulatory Pediatrics for Nurses.
Brown, Marilyn R. Gypsies & Other Bohemians: The Myth of the Artist in Nineteenth-Century France. Foster, Stephen, ed.
Brown, Marion M. Marnie.
--Young Nathan.
Brown, Martin. A Maine Deeper In: Washington & Aroostook Counties.
Brown, Martin P. Jr., ed. Compendium of Communication & Broadcast Satellites 1958-1980.
Brown, Mary. Playing the Jack.
Brown, Maurice J. E. Schubert Songs, by Maurice J. E. Brown.
Brown, Mervyn. Madagascar Rediscovered: A History from Early Times to Independence.
Brown, Meta & Mulholland, Joyce. Basic Drug Calculations.
Brown, Michael. Marked to Die.
Brown, Mik & Offerman, Lynn. Little Simon Jokes & Riddles.
Brown, Millie. Low-Stress Fitness: The-Low Stress Way to Get in Shape.
Brown, Muriel, ed. The Structure of Disadvantage.
Brown, Murray, et al, eds. Regional National Econometric Modeling with an Application to the Italian Economy.
Brown, Nettie. Albert C-One-Thirty & the Blue Angels' A-4 Skyhawk Jets.
Brown, Neville, et al. Nuclear First Use.
Brown, Nina W., jt. ed. see Grob, Paul.
Brown, Norman O. Life Against Death: The Psychoanalytical Meaning of History.
Brown, P. J. Macroprocessors & Techniques for Portable Software.
Brown, Paul & Clary, Jack. P. B. The Paul Brown Story.
Brown, Paul B., jt. auth. see Smith, Geoffrey.
Brown, Paul L., jt. auth. see Presbie, Robert J.
Brown, Pauline. Embroidery: A Complete Course in Embroidery Design & Technique.
Brown, Peter. The World of Late Antiquity: 150-750.
Brown, Peter & Gaines, Steven. The Love You Make: An Insider's Story of the Beatles.
Brown, Peter G. & MacLean, Douglas, eds. Human Rights & U. S. Foreign Policy: Principles & Applications.
Brown, Peter L. Megaliths & Masterminds.
--Megaliths, Myths & Men: An Introduction to Astro-Archaeology.
Brown, Phil. The Transfer of Care: Psychiatric Deinstitutionalization & Its Aftermath.
Brown, R. & Campbell, G. A. How to Find Out about the Chemical Industry.
Brown, R. Don & Daigneault, Ernest A. Pharmacology of Hearing: Experimental & Clinical Bases.
Brown, R. G. The Male Nurse.
Brown, R. L. Design & Manufacture of Plastic Parts.
Brown, Raymond. Slillful Hands.
Brown, Raymond D. Forty-Four Terrific Woodworking Plans & Projects.
--How To Do Your Own Professional Picture Framing.
Brown, Raymond E. Semitic Background of the Term, Mystery in the New Testament. Reumann, John, ed.
Brown, Raymond E., et al. Peter in the New Testament.
Brown, Raymond E., et al, eds. Mary in the New Testament: A Collaborative Assessment by Protestant & Roman Catholic Scholars.
Brown, Reuben R. Love Divine.
Brown, Richard, ed. Daily Bread Nineteen Eighty-Eight.
Brown, Richard E. & Fehrenbacher, Don E., eds. Tradition, Conflict & Change: Perspectives on the American Revolution.
Brown, Robert. Student Developement in Tomorrow's Higher Education.
Brown, Robert A. & Field, Joan R., eds. Treatment of Sexual Problems in Individuals & Couples Therapy.
Brown, Robert B. Guide to Life Insurance.
Brown, Robert B. & Luby, Barry J. Visiones de Hoy.
Brown, Robert E. Charles Beard & the Constitution.
--Joetta Community Library: A Simulation Exercise in Library Administration.
Brown, Robert H. Farm Electrification.
Brown, Robert H. & Wishard, Roy H. Biology Lab Text.
Brown, Robert M. Brother, Which Drummer.
--Gustavo Gutierrez.
--Pseudonyms of God.
--Religion & Violence: A Primer for White Americans.
Brown, Robert M., ed. The Hereticus Papers.
Brown, Robert W., et al. Africa & International Crises.
Brown, Robin. The Lure of the Dolphin.
Brown, Rosellen. Cora Fry.
Brown, Roy. The Cage.
--Escape the River.
--Find Debbie!
--No Through Road.
--Suicide Course.
--The Swing of the Gate.
--The White Sparrow.
Brown, Rudd. A Killing in Real Estate. Chirich, Nancy, ed.
Brown, Ruth S. Someday You Will Understand.
Brown, S. J., Jr., jt. ed. see Au-Yang, M. K.
Brown, S. S. Topics in Child Psychology.
Brown, Sam E. Activities for Teaching Metrics in Kindergarden.
Brown, Schuyler & Saliers, Don E. Pentecost Three. Actemeier, Elizabeth, et al, eds.
Brown, Sheldon S. Learning Psychology by Doing.
Brown, Spencer H. Foreword by see Chavis, Grace L.
Brown, Stanley. Men from under the Sky: The Arrival of Westerners in Fiji.
Brown, Stanley C. God's Plan for Marriage.
Brown, Stanley H., jt. auth. see Girard, Joe.
Brown, Stanley J., jt. auth. see Practising Law Institute Staff.
Brown, Stephen. Heirs with the Prince.
Brown, Stephen G. & DiSaisa, Philip J. Cancer of the Cervix.
Brown, Sterling. Negro Poetry & Drama & the Negro in American Fiction.
Brown, Steven S. The Cellular Telephone Directory: How to Use Your Cellular Telephone Throughout the U. S. & Canada.
Brown, Stuart. A Man Named Tony.
Brown, Susan J. Robber Rocks: Letters & Memories of Hart Crane, 1923-1932.
Brown, Suzanne, ed. see Korenblit, Joan & Janger, Kathie.
Brown, Suzanne S., jt. auth. see Neal, James M.
Brown, Theodore L. & LeMay, H. Eugene. Chemistry: The Central Science.
--Chemistry: The Central Science, Qualitative Inorganic Analysis.
Brown, Theodore L. & LeMay, H. Eugene, Jr. Chemistry: The Central Science.
--Chemistry: The Central Science.
Brown, Thomas. Observations on the Nature & Tendency of the Doctrine of Mr. Hume Concerning the Relation of Cause & Effect.
Brown, Thomas L. Site Engineering for Developers & Builders.
Brown, Thomas S. & Wallace, Patricia. Physiological Psychology.
Brown, Timothy B. Alien Realms: Eight Excursions Beyond Human Space.
Brown, Timothy G., jt. auth. see Media Institute Staff.
Brown University, Department of Art Staff. Portrait Bust, Renaissance to Enlightenment.
Brown University Staff. Dictionary Catalogue of the Harris Collection of American Poetry & Plays, Brown University.
Brown, Valerie P. Seven Shades.
Brown, Virginia. Defy the Thunder.
--Storm of Passion.
Brown, Virginia P. The Gold Disc of Coosa.
Brown, W. C., et al. Bosporus Bridge.
Brown, W. Elgar. Hydraulics for Operators.
Brown, Walter C. Blueprint Reading for Industry.
Brown, William E. & Sacks, Richard S. Review Manual for Operators.
Brown, William G. The Dynamo & the Tree: My Twins & I Journeying in a Technate in the Year of 1981.
Brown, William H. Brother Sunshine-Father Rain.
--Introduction to Organic & Biochemistry.
Brown, William H. & Tawes, Roy L. Review Questions in General Vascular Surgery.
Brown, William S., jt. auth. see Parker, William S.
Brown, Willis M. How I Got Faith.
Brown, Wilton J. Do Russian People Stand for War.
Browne. Basic Facts of Fractures.
Browne, Anita, ed. Homespun.
Browne, Anthony. Bear Hunt.
Browne, Arthur, et al. I, Koch: A Decidedly Unauthorized Biography of the Mayor of New York City.
Browne, Corinne. Casualty: A Memoir of Love & War.
Browne, D. J. Economics for 'A' Level.
Browne, Dan. Alternative Home Heating.
--The Housebuilding Book.
Browne, Dik. Best of Hagar the Horrible.
Browne, George E. I Saw It in the Mirror by the Moonbeam.
Browne, Gerald A. Eleven Harrowhouse.
--Green Ice.
--Hazard.
--Nineteen Purchase Street.
--Slide.
--Stone Five Eighty-Eight.
--Stone Five Eighty-Eight.
Browne, Harry. How I Found Freedom in an Unfree World.
Browne, J. C., et al. Antenatal Care.
Browne, J. S. Basic Theory of Structures.
Browne, Jerry. Playwright's Theatre: The English Stage Company of the Royal Court.
Browne, John R. Apache Country.
Browne, Kathryn W., jt. auth. see Gordon, Ann.
Browne, L. B., ed. Experimental Analysis of Insect Behavior.
Browne, Merle L. Arousers.
Browne, Muriel. Exalt His Name: A Christmas Program.
Browne, Peter. Things Divine & Supernatural Conceived by Analogy with Things Natural & Human. Wellek, Rene, ed.
Browne, Robert E. The Ministry of the Word.
Browne, Thomas. Prose of Sir Thomas Browne. Endicott, Norman J., ed.
--Selected Writings of Sir Thomas Browne. Keynes, Geoffrey, ed.
Browne, Wolfen. Hitler's Son.
Brownell, Blaine A. & Stickle, Warren E., eds. Bosses & Reformers: Urban Politics in America, 1880-1920.
Brownell, David. Hemmings' Vintage Auto Almanac.
Brownell, Emery A. Legal Aid in the United States: A Study of the Availability of Lawyers' Services for Persons Unable to Pay Fees.
Brownfield, Charles A. Brain Benders: A Study of the Effects of Isolation.
--Humanizing College Learning: A Taste of Hemlock.
Brownhill, R. J. Education & the Nature of Knowledge.
Brownhill, Robert & Smart, Patricia. Political Education.
Browning, Al. Bowl, Bama, Bowl.
Browning, Dixie. Renegade Player.

Browning, Don S. Religious Thought & the Modern Psychologies: A Critical Conversation in the Theology of Culture.
Browning, Edgar K. & Browning, Jacqueline M. Microeconomic Theory & Applications.
Browning, Elizabeth Barrett. Elizabeth Barrett Browning's Letters to Mrs. David Ogilvy. Heydon, Peter N. & Kelley, Philip, eds.
--Sonnets from the Portuguese.
--Sonnets from the Portuguese.
Browning, J. D. Biography in the Eighteenth Century: Publications of the McMaster University Association for 18th Century Studies.
Browning, Jacqueline M., jt. auth. see Browning, Edgar K.
Browning, John & Morton, Richard. Religion in the Eighteenth Century.
Browning, John, ed. Education in the Eighteenth Century.
Browning, John D. Satire in the Eighteenth Century.
Browning, Phillip & Carter, Jeri. Computer Technology for the Handicapped in Special Education & Rehabilitation: A Resource Guide.
Browning, Robert. Browning: Plain Texts of the Poets.
--Byzantine Empire.
--Dramatic Idyls.
--Men & Women & Other Poems. Harper, J. W., ed.
Browning, Robert M., ed. Freude Am Lesen: A German Reader.
Browning, Stella. Butter in the Buttercups.
Browning, Vivienne. My Browning Family Album. Coley, Betty A., ed.
Brownjohn, J. Maxwell, tr. see Gregor-Dellin, Martin.
Brownjohn, J. Maxwell, tr. see Hecht, Ingeborg.
Brownjohn, J. Maxwell, tr. see Herlin, Hans.
Brownlee, Claudia J. Colonel Joe, the Last of the Rough Riders: Recollections of a Centenarian.
Brownlie, William D. Life Insurance: Its Rate of Return.
Brownlow, Leroy. For Love's Sake.
--God's Plan for Financial Success.
Brownmiller, Susan. Femininity.
Brownstein & Weiner. Barron's How to Prepare for the Graduate Record Examination (GRE)
--Barron's How to Prepare for the Preliminary Scholastic Aptitude Test - National Merit Scholarship Q Test (PSAT - NMSQT)
Brownstein, Bill, et al, eds. The Great Canadian Character Anthology.
Brownstein, Karen. In a Certain Light.
Brownstein, Michael. Country Cousins.
Brownstein, Michael, ed. see Jacob, Max.
Brownstein, R., jt. auth. see Moos, R. H.
Brownstein, Robert, jt. auth. see Moos, Rudolf.
Brownstein, Ronald & Easton, Nina. Reagan's Ruling Class: Portraits of the President's Top 100 Officials.
Brownstein, Samuel C. & Weiner, Mitchel. Barron's How to Prepare for College Entrance Examinations (SAT)
--Barron's Vocabulary Builder: A Systematic Plan for Building a Vocabulary, Testing Progress & Applying Knowledge.
--Basic Tips on the SAT.
--Compact Guide to Colleges.
Brownstein, Samuel C., et al. How to Prepare for the SAT College Entrance Examinations.
Brownstone, David M. Moneywise! Financial Survival on the Road to Riches.
Brownstone, David M. & Franck, Irene M. Dictionary of Publishing.
--The VNR Investor's Dictionary.
Brownwell, Carlton. Criminal Procedure in New York, 1971-1982, Part Two: Criminal Evidence.
Browse, Phillip M. Step-by-Step Guide to Plant Propagation.
Broyard, Anatole. Men, Women & Other Anticlimaxes.
Broyelle, Claudie. Women's Liberation in China. Cohen, Michele & Herman, Gary, trs. from Fr.
Broyles, Frank & Bailey, James. Hog Wild: The Autobiography of Frank Broyles.
Broyles, Susan G., et al. Education Directory: Colleges & Universities, 1985-86.
Brubacher, John S. Philosophies of Education.
Brubacher, Lewis J., jt. auth. see Bender, Myron L.
Brubaker, Dale. Who's Teaching? Who's Learning? Active Learning in Elementary Schools.
Brubaker, Darrel J., jt. ed. see Sider, Ronald J.
Brubaker, Sterling. In Command of Tomorrow: Resource and Environmental Strategies for Americans.
Brubakken, David M., et al. Treatment of Psychotic & Neurologically Impaired Children: A Systems Approach.
Bruccoli, Matthew J. James Gould Cozzens: A Life Apart.
--The Price Was High: The Last Uncollected Stories of F. Scott Fitzgerald.
--Ross MacDonald.
--Some Sort of Epic Grandeur: The Life of F. Scott Fitzgerald.
Bruccoli, Matthew J. & Layman, Richard, eds. A Matter of Crime: New Stories from the Masters of Mystery & Suspense.
Bruccoli, Matthew J., jt. ed. see Clark, C. E., Jr.
Bruccoli, Matthew J., ed. see Fitzgerald, F. Scott.
Bruccoli, Matthew J., ed. see O'Hara, John.
Bruccoli, Matthew J., et al, eds. Conversations with Jazz Musicians.
Bruce, A. D. & Cowley, R. A. Structural Phase Transitions.
Bruce, A. M. Sewage Sludge Stabilization & Disinfection.
Bruce, A. P. Annotated Bibliography of the British Army, Sixteen Sixty to Nineteen Fourteen.
Bruce, Colin. Social Cost-Benefit Analysis: A Guide for Country & Project Economists to the Derivation & Application of Economic & Social Accounting Prices.
--Unusual World Coins.
Bruce, Colin, ed. Collecting World Coins: A Century of Monetary Issues.
Bruce, Colin, ed. see Pick, Albert.
Bruce, Colin R., II & Rhodes, Nicholas. The Standard Guide to South Asian Coins & Paper Money Since 1556, A. D.
Bruce, Debra. Pure Daughter.
Bruce, F. F. The Epistles of John.
--Philippians: A Good News Commentary.
--Second Thoughts on the Dead Sea Scrolls.
--Understanding the New Testament: Matthew.
Bruce, Harry J. Distribution & Transportation Handbook.
Bruce, J. M. The Bristol Fighter.
--Britain's First Warplanes.
--Sopwith Fighters.
Bruce, Jeffrey & Cohen, Sherry S. About Face: An Hour a Week to Radiant Skin & Flawless Make-Up.
Bruce, Jo Anne Czecowski. Privacy & Confidentiality of Health Care Information.
Bruce, John. Airscream.
Bruce, Jon W., et al. Modern Property Law, Cases & Materials.
Bruce, Lennart. Letter of Credit.
--Observations.
Bruce, Leo. Case for Sergeant Beef.
Bruce, Marjory. The Book of Craftsmen: The Story of Man's Handiwork Through the Ages.
Bruce, Sheilah. The Radish Day Jubilee.
Bruce, T., jt. auth. see Collins, T.
Bruce, V. Awakening the Slower Mind.
Bruce-Briggs, B., ed. The New Class?
Bruce-Novoa. Chicano Authors: Inquiry by Interview.
--Chicano Poetry: A Response to Chaos.
Bruce's Son & Company Staff. Victorian Frames, Borders & Cuts from the 1882 Type Catalog of George Bruce's Son & Co.
Bruchey, Stuart, jt. ed. see Alston, Lee J.
Bruchey, Stuart, ed. see Bergstrom, Peter V.
Bruchey, Stuart, ed. see Bjork, Gordon C.
Bruchey, Stuart, ed. see Hemphill, John M., II.
Bruchey, Stuart, ed. see Johnston, Valerie J.
Bruchey, Stuart, ed. see McGuire, Robert A.
Bruchey, Stuart, ed. see Menard, Russell R.
Bruchey, Stuart, ed. see Nuxoll, Elizabeth M.
Bruchey, Stuart, ed. see Sacks, David H.
Bruchey, Stuart, ed. see Shepherd, James F.
Bruchey, Stuart, ed. see Wettereau, James O.
Bruck, Axel. Close-up Photography in Practice.
Bruck, Mary T. Night Sky.
Bruck, R. H. Survey of Binary Systems.
Brucke, Craig, contrib. by. Craig Brucke's Great American Authors Series - Ernest Hemingway Set.
Brucke, Craig, ed. Craig Brucke's Great American Humorists Series - Mark Twain Individual.
Brucker, Jerry. Horsethief Canyon.
Bruckmann, G., ed. Contributions to the Von Neumann Growth Model.
--Input-Output Approaches in Global Modeling: Proceedings of the Fifth IIASA Symposium on Global Modeling, Sept. 26-29,1977.
Bruckner, Christine. Flight of Cranes. Hein, Ruth, tr. from Ger.
Bruckner, Dwight. The Vengeance Trail.
Bruder, J. Simon. Archaeological Investigations at the Hedgepeth Hills Petroglyph Site.
Brudney, jt. auth. see Meier.
Brudney, Jeffrey L. & England, Robert E. Citizen-Based Indicators of Community Service Performance: The Case of Norman, Oklahoma.
Brudney, Victor & Chirelstein, Marvin A. Corporate Finance, Cases & Materials: 1984 Supplement.
Brudno, Barbara E. Income Redistribution Theories & Programs: Cases, Commentary & Analyses.
Brudno, Ezra. Guide for the Misguided.
Brueckner, Keith A., ed. Advances in Theoretical Physics.
Brueckner, Leo J. Educational Diagnosis: Nat'l Society for the Study of Education 34th Yearbook.
Brueggeman, Walter, ed. see Westermann, Claus.
Brueggemann, Walter. Advent-Christmas: Series B.
--In Man We Trust: The Neglected Side of Biblical Faith.
--Tradition for Crisis: A Study in Hosea.
Brueggemann, Walter & Wolff, Hans W. The Vitality of Old Testament Traditions.
Brueggemann, Walter, ed. see Bailey, Lloyd R., Sr.
Brueggemann, Walter, ed. see Hamerton-Kelly, Robert.
Brueggemann, Walter, ed. see Harrington, Daniel J.
Brueggemann, Walter, ed. see Johnson, Luke T.
Brueggemann, Walter, ed. see Patrick, Dale.
Brueggemann, Walter, ed. see Zimmerli, Walther.
Bruegmann, Robert. Benicia: Portrait of an Early California Town.
Bruell, Steven C., jt. auth. see Schneider, G. Michael.
Bruemmer, Fred, et al. The Arctic World. Taylor, William E., Jr., ed.
Bruening, Andrew C. Journal of Voyage to Australia.
Bruening, William H. Wittgenstein.
Brues, Alice M. People & Races.
Brugel, Werner. Nuclear Magnetic Resonance Spectra & Chemical Structure.
Bruggen, Peter & O'Brian, Charles. Surviving Adolescence: A Handbook for Adolescents & Their Parents.
Brugger, Bill & Hannan, Kate. Modernisation & Revolution.
Brugmann, Mary C. Events Which Have Occured since I Met Senator Richard B. Russell.
Bruhn, W. & Tilke, M. A Pictorial History of Costume.
Brul, Caroline Van Den see Van Den Brul, Caroline & Spindler, Susan.
Bruland, Esther B. & Mott, Stephen C. A Passion for Jesus: A Passion for Justice.
Brule, Marcel, tr. see Fisher, David & Bragonier, Reginald, Jr.
Bruley, Duane F., jt. ed. see Bicher, Haim I.
Brumbaugh, James. Trail Sinister.
Brumbaugh, Robert S. Ancient Greek Gadgets & Machines.
--Plato's Mathematical Imagination: The Mathematical Passages in the Dialogues & Their Interpretation.
Brumbaugh, Robert S. & Lawrence, Nathaniel. Philosophical Themes in Modern Education.
Brumbaugh, Thoburn T. My Marks & Scars I Carry: The Story of Ernst Kisch.
Brumfit, C. J. & Roberts, J. T. An Introduction to Language & Language Teaching.
Brumfit, C. J., ed. Language Teaching Projects for the Third World.
--Teaching Literature Overseas: Language-Based Approaches.
Brumfit, W., ed. see Urinary Tract Infection Symposium Staff.
Brumfitt, Shelagh. Counseling.
Brumfitt, W., jt. auth. see Asscher, A. W.
Brun, Henry J. The Social Scientist Investigates Women of the Ancient World.
--Social Studies Student Investigates the Retreat from Imperialism.
Brun, Kim, ed. see Federico, Pat A., et al.
Brun, L., jt. ed. see Mandel, J.
Brun, P. & Waegell, B. Reactivite des hypobromites.
Brundage, Burr C. The Fifth Sun: Aztec Gods, Aztec World.
--A Rain of Darts: The Mexica Aztecs.
Brundidge, Harry. Twinkle Twinkle Movie Star. Kupelnick, Bruce S., ed.
Brundle, F., jt. auth. see Choong, E.
Brundy, Clyde M. Call up the Morning.
--Grasslands.
--High Empire.
Brune, J. A., ed. see Wood, Manfri F.
Brunelle, Harvey R. Ascension.
Brunelli, B. & Leotta, G. G., eds. Unconventional Approaches to Fusion.
Bruner, Edward M., ed. Text, Play, & Story, 1983: The Construction & Reconstruction of Self & Society.
Bruner, Frederick D. & Hordern, William E. The Holy Spirit-Shy Member of the Trinity.
Bruner, Jerome. Toward a Theory of Instruction.
Bruner, Jerome S. The Relevance of Education.
Bruner, William T. Children of the Devil.
Brunet, David P. Fumbling for Words.
Brunetti, Frank L. & Yellin, Stanley J. Business Acquisitions: Tax & Legal Guide.
Brungardt, Terrence, jt. auth. see Arnold, William.
Brunhammer, Yvonne, et al. Art Nouveau Belgium-France.
Brunhoff, Jean De see De Brunhoff, Jean.
Brunhoff, Laurent de. Bonhomme et la Grosse Bete qui avait des Escailles sur le Dos.
Bruni, J. Edward, jt. auth. see Montemurro, Donald G.
Bruni, V., et al, eds. Pediatric & Adolescent Gynecology.
Bruning, Nancy. The Beach Book.
Brunius, Teddy. Theory & Taste: Four Studies in Aesthetics.
Brunk, Thomas W. Leonard B. Willeke: Excellence in Architecture & Design.
Brunkow, Robert de V., ed. Religion & Society in North America: An Annotated Bibliography.
Brunner & Gravas. Clinical Hypertension & Hypotension.
Brunner, Calvin R. Incineration Systems: Selection & Design.
--Incineration Systems Seminar Notebook.
Brunner, Calvin R., jt. auth. see Schwarz, Stephen C.
Brunner, Emil. Scandal of Christianity: The Gospel as Stumbling Block to Modern Man.
Brunner, John. The Webs of Everywhere.
Brunner, K. W. & Nagel, G. A., eds. Internistische Krebstherapie.
Brunner, Lawrence P. U. S. Productivity Growth: Who Benefited? Bateman, Fred, ed.
Brunner, Marguerite. Gold Mine of Money-Making Ideas.
Brunner, Nancy A. Orthopedic Nursing: A Programmed Approach.
Brunner, S., et al, eds. Early Detection of Breast Cancer.
Brunner, Thomas W., et al. The Legal Assistant's Handbook.
Brunning, Bob. Blues: The British Connection.
Bruno, Bryan. How to Get What You Want in Your Life Today.
Bruno, Joseph. Baseball's Golden Dozen.
Bruno, Joseph A., Jr. & Lotz, Agnes M. Members Directory, 1986.
Bruno, Michael S., jt. auth. see DePasquale, Nicholas P.
Bruno, Susan & Quaresima, Donna. Insiders' Guide to Williamsburg, Virginia.
Bruno, Vincent J., ed. The Parthenon.
Brunor, Martin A. Arts & Crafts of the Austral Islands: A Special Exhibition, 17 December 1968 to 30 April 1969.
Bruns, Bill, jt. auth. see Sorenson, Jacki.
Bruns, Bill, jt. auth. see Wulff, Kurt.
Brunschwig, Henri. Enlightenment & Romanticism in Eighteenth-Century Prussia. Jellinek, Frank, tr. from Fr.
Brunsden, D. Slopes: Form & Process.
Brunsden, Denys, jt. auth. see Thornes, John.
Brunsdon, Charlotte & Morley, David. Everyday Television: Nationwide.
Brunskill, R. W. Illustrated Handbook of Vernacular Architecture.
Brunson, George S. Intelligent Investing: Profit-Making Moves in the Stock Market.
Brunswick, Ann F. Evaluation of College of the Air Course, "The American Economy," on the Basis of a National Survey of High School Social Studies Teachers.
Brunton, David W., ed. Index to the Contemporary Scene.
--Index to the Contemporary Scene.
Brunton, Mary. Discipline.
--Self Control.
Brunton, Virginia H. A Brevity, a Brilliance & Other Poems.
Brunvand, Jan H. The Mexican Pet: More "New" Urban Legends & Some Old Favorites.
--Study of American Folklore: An Introduction.
--Study of American Folklore: An Introduction.
Brus, Wlodzimierz. Socialist Ownership & Political Systems under Socialism.
Brusch, Clayton. Of Human Condition.
Brush, Don O. & Almroth, B. Buckling of Bars, Plates, Shells.
Brush, F. Robert, ed. Aversive Conditioning & Learning.
Brush, Stephanie. Men: An Owner's Manual.
Brush, Stephen B. Mountain, Field, & Family: The Economy & Human Ecology of an Andean Valley.
Brush, Stephen G., ed. see International Working Seminar on the Role of the History of Physics in Physics Education Staff.
Brusha, O. F. This Is It, Our Bountiful America.
Brushwood, Carolyn, tr. see Galindo, Sergio.
Brushwood, John, tr. see Galindo, Sergio.
Brusick, David. Principles of Genetic Toxicology.
Bruskin, David N. Cat at Bat.
--A Cat Out of Water.
--Hippo's Tips on Hips.
--Hortense Is a Star.
--Melvin Is a Big Cheese.
--The Mouse Will Play.
--Susy in a Movie?
--Susy's Free Shopping Spree.
--Too Many Mice!
--What Type Stripe?
Bruss, Robert. Smart Investers Guide to Real Estate.
--Smart Investors Guide to Real Estate.
Brussell, Eugene E. Dictionary of Quotable Definitions.
Brusselmans, C., ed. Jesus Loves Children.
Brutents, K. National Liberation Revolutions Today.
--Newly-Free Countries in the Seventies.
Bruton, Eric. The Longcase Clock.
Bruton, J. G. Ejercicios de espanol.

Authors

Bruton, Ronald W. An Ounce of Prevention Plus a Pound of Cure: Tests & Techniques for Aiding Individual Readers.
Bruton, Sheila, ed. Indaba: Let's Talk. Bassingthwaighte, Brian & Hooper, Janet. Eugard, Athol, ed.
Brutten, Milton, et al. Something's Wrong with My Child: A Parents' Book About Children with Learning Disabilities.
--Something's Wrong with My Child: A Parent's Handbook about Children with Learning Disabilities.
Bruyere, Toni M. & Robey, Sidney J. For Gourmets with Ulcers.
Bruylants, A., ed. Synthetic Organic Chemistry-1: Proceedings of the First International Conference, Louvain, Belgium, 1974.
Bry, Adelaide. EST.
Bryan, Ashley. I Greet the Dawn: Poem of Paul Laurence Dunbar.
Bryan, Bill, jt. auth. see Dean, James.
Bryan, C. D. National Air & Space Museum.
Bryan, Charles V. The Child That Nobody Wanted.
Bryan, G. McLeod. Naude: Prophet to South Africa.
Bryan, J., III. Merry Gentlemen (& One Lady)
Bryan, John. This Soldier Still at War.
Bryan, John & Castle, Coralie. Edible Ornamental Garden.
Bryan, John E. Small World Vegetable Gardening.
Bryan, Lana K., jt. auth. see Whitsitt, Robert E., II.
Bryan, Malcolm A. Dominoes: Sixty-Seven Games & Tricks.
Bryan, Margaret B. & Davis, Boyd H. Writing about Literature & Film.
Bryan, Paul. Programming Your Apple II Computer.
Bryan, Robert A., et al, eds. All These to Teach: Essays in Honor of C. A. Robertson.
Bryan, W. W., jt. ed. see Shaw, N. H.
Bryan, William B, et al. Software Configuration Management.
Bryans, J. T., ed. see International Conference on Equine Infectious Diseases Staff.
Bryant, Al. Day by Day with C. H. Spurgeon.
Bryant, Al. Time out.
Bryant, Al, ed. New Every Morning: Three Hundred Sixty-Six Daily Meditations from Your Favorite Christian Writers.
Bryant, Betty. Leaning into the Wind: The Wilderness of Widowhood.
Bryant, Beverley & Williams, Jean. Portraits in Roses: One Hundred Nine Years of Kentucky Derby Winners.
Bryant, Christopher. The River Within: The Search for God in Depth.
Bryant, Claire. The Adventures of Binkie, Dog Extraordinaire.
Bryant, D. & Niehaus, R., eds. Manpower Planning & Organization Design.
Bryant, Donald C. Rhetorical Dimensions in Criticism.
Bryant, Donald C., ed. Rhetoric & Poetic.
Bryant, Gay & Working Woman Editors. The Working Woman Report: Succeeding in Business in the Eighties.
Bryant, Ina. Foot Reflexology.
Bryant, Jim. The Wild Game & Fish Cookbook.
Bryant, John & Lacher, Chris. College Math.
Bryant, Marija & Bryant, Tod. The Working Photographer: The Complete Manual for the Money-Making Professional.
Bryant, Marjorie. Recall the Poppies.
Bryant, Mark. Riddles: Ancient & Modern.
Bryant, Neville J. Review Manual for Immunohematology.
Bryant, Nigel, tr. see De Troyes, Chretien.
Bryant, Peter S. & Johnson, Jane A., eds. Advancing the Two-Year College.
Bryant, Spurgeon Q., Sr. Ole Nell, Mama, & Me.
Bryant, Steven & Saltz, Daniel. Precalculus & Mathematics: Algebra & Trigonometry.
Bryant, Steven, jt. ed. see Chapman, Gary.
Bryant, T. H. E. & Lovell, J. MCQs in Radiological Physics.
Bryant, Tod, jt. auth. see Bryant, Marija.
Bryant, Willis R. Mortgage Lending: Fundamentals & Practices.
Bryce, Charles F., ed. Biochemical Education.
Bryce, James. Study of American History.
Bryce, Jennifer W. & Armenian, Haroutune K., eds. In Wartime: The State of Children in Lebanon.
Bryce-Laporte, Roy S., ed. Sourcebook on New Immigration.
Bryce-Smith, D. & Gilbert, A. The Organic Photochemistry of Benzene-I.
Bryden, Bill see Goldoni, Carolo.
Bryditzki, Victor V. The Selling of Jesus.
Brydson, J. A., jt. ed. see Whelan, A.
Brye, David L., ed. European Immigration & Ethnicity in the United States & Canada: A Historical Bibliography.
Bryen, Diane N. Inquiries into Child Language.
Bryer, Jackson R., ed. Sixteen Modern American Authors: A Survey of Research & Criticism.
Bryer, Jackson R., jt. ed. see Bogard, Travis.
Bryer, Jackson R., ed. see Fitzgerald, F. Scott.
Bryl, Y. First Snow.
Brymer, Robert A. Introduction to Hotel & Restaurant Management: A Book of Readings.
Bryne, P. & Cadman, B. D. Risk: Uncertainty & Decision Making in Property Management.
Bryne, Richard. The Complete Art of Breaking. Lee, Mike, ed.
Bryson, Conrey. Winter Quarters.
Bryson, Harold T. The Reality of Hell & the Goodness of God.
Bryson, Maurice C. & Heiny, Robert L. Basic Inferential Statistics.
Bryson, Norman, jt. ed. see Kappeler, Susanne.
Bryson, Vernon & Vogel, Henry J., eds. Evolving Genes & Proteins: A Symposium.
Brzin, M., et al, eds. Synaptic Constituents in Health & Disease: Proceedings of the Third Meeting of the European Society for Neurochemistry, Bled, August 31st-Sept, 5th, 1980.
Buban, Peter, et al. Understanding Electricity & Electronics.
Bubb, Diana I. Neurologic Problems.
Bube, Richard H. Electrons in Solids: An Introductory Survey.
Bubenik, Vit. The Phonological Interpretation of Ancient Greek: A Pandialectal Analysis.
Buber, Martin. Hasidism.
--I & Thou.
Bubis, Gerald B. & Wasserman, Harry. Synagogue Havurot: A Comparative Study.
Bubnys, V. Under Summer Skies.
Bucco, Martin. Critical Essays on Sinclair Lewis.
Bucer, Martin. Instruction in Christian Love.
Buchan, David. Scottish Tradition: A Collection of Scottish Folklore.
Buchan, David, ed. A Book of Scottish Ballads.
Buchan, James. A Parish of Rich Women.
Buchan, John. History of the Great War.
Buchan, Roy M., jt. auth. see Beaulieu, Harry J.
Buchan, Stuart. All Our Yesterdays.
--Malibu Summer.
Buchanan. The Secret of the Unknown Powers.
Buchanan, C. D. Spelling.
Buchanan, David A. & Boddy, David. Organizations in the Computer Age.
Buchanan, Jack. Exodus from Hell.
Buchanan, James W., et al. Dogs & Other Large Mammals in Aging Research.
Buchanan, Jim. Canadian Indian Policy: A Bibliography Supplement.
--Fair Housing & Families: Discrimination Against Children.
--Government Regulation of Private Schools: A Bibliography.
--A Guide to Materials about Public Aid to Religious Schools.
--Reverse Discrimination: A Resource Guide.
--Timesharing: Concept, Reality & Regulation.
Buchanan, Lou. The Wizard of Odd.
Buchanan, O. Lexton, Jr. Limits: A Transition to Calculus. Meder, Albert E., Jr., ed.
Buchanan, R. A. Technology & Social Progress.
Buchanan, Robert. The New Abelard: A Romance. Wolff, Robert L., ed.
Buchanan, Scott. Essays in Politics.
Buchanan, William J. Present Danger.
Buchanan-Brown, John. Phiz!: Illustrator of Dickens' World.
Buchdahl, G. Fine Structure History of Science: Lessons for Methodology.
Buchdahl, G., ed. Changing Views About the Principles of Scientific Theory Evaluation.
Buchdahl, H. A. Twenty Lectures on Thermodynamics.
Buchenholz, Gretchen & Nursery School Staff. Merricat's Castle Nursery School Games for Pre-Schoolers. Sies, Leora M., ed.
Bucher, Charles A. & Koenig, Constance R. Methods & Materials for Secondary School Physical Education.
Bucher, Charles A. & Prentice, William E. Fitness for College & Life.
Bucher, Charles A., jt. auth. see Wilson, Eugene S.
Bucher, Charles A. & Thaxton, Nolan A., eds. Physical Education for Children: Movement Foundations & Experiences.
Bucher, Glenn R., ed. Straight-White-Male.
Bucher, Glenn R. & Hill, Patricia R., eds. Confusion & Hope: Clergy, Laity, & the Church in Transition.
Bucher, J. Frank. The Third Pagoda & Other Legends of China.
Bucher, Nancy, et al, eds. Cell Division & Aging.
Buchhave, P., et al, eds. see LDA-Symposium Staff.
Buchholtz, Barbara & Gilberg, Laura S. Needlepoint Designs from Amish Quilts.
Buchholz, Rogene A. Business Environment & Public Policy: Implications for Management.
--Business Environment & Public Policy: Implications for Management & Strategy Formulation.
Buchholz, Suzanne. The Middle-Earth Quiz Book.
Buchholz, William J., ed. Communication Training & Consulting in Business, Industry, & Government.
Buchler, Justus. Charles Peirce's Empiricism.
Buchner, Georg. Georg Buchner: The Complete Collected Works. Schmidt, Henry J., ed.
Buchner, T., et al, eds. Acute Leukemias.
Buchsbaum, Herbert, jt. auth. see Lifshitz, Samuel.
Buchtal, Hugo. The Miniatures of the Paris Psalter: A Study in Middle Byzantine Painting.
Buchtal, Hugo & Kurz, Otto. Hand List of Illuminated Oriental Christian Manuscripts.
Buchtel, Henry A. The Conceptual Nervous System.
Buchter, H. H. Industrial Sealing Technology.
Buchwald, Art. Irving's Delight.
--You Can Fool All of the People All of the Time.
Buchwald, Emilie. Floramel & Esteban.
--Gildaen: The Heroic Adventures of a Most Unusual Rabbit.
Buchwald, Nathaniel A. & Brazier, Mary A., eds. Brain Mechanisms in Mental Retardation: Based upon a Symposium.
Buck, Alan. Little Giant: The Life of I. K. Brunel, A Novel.
Buck, C. H. Problems of Product Design & Development.
Buck, Carl D. Dictionary of Selected Synonyms in the Principal Indo-European Languages.
Buck, Ellen, jt. auth. see Buck, R. Creighton.
Buck, Jack, jt. auth. see Musial, Stan.
Buck, Joan J. Daughter of the Swan.
--The Only Place To Be.
Buck, John L. Chinese Farm Economy. Myers, Ramon H., ed.
Buck, Otto & Wolf, Stanley M., eds. Nondestructive Evaluation: Microstructural Characterization & Reliability Strategies Proceedings. Fall Meeting, Pittsburgh, 1980.
Buck, Otto, et al, eds. Electron & Positron Spectroscopies in Material Science & Engineering.
Buck, Otto, jt. ed. see Wells, Joseph M.
Buck, P. C., ed. John Taverner: Part 1.
--John Taverner: Part 2.
--Orlando Gibbons.
Buck, P. C. & Fellowes, E. H., eds. Tudor Church Music. Incl. Vol. 1. John Taverner - Part One; Vol. 2. William Byrd - English Church Music, Part One; Vol. 3. John Tavernen - Part Two; Vol. 4. Orlando Gibbons; Vol. 5. Robert White; Vol. 6. Tallis, Thomas; Vol. 7. Byrd, William; Vol. 8. Thomas Tomkins; Vol. 9; Vol. 10. Aston, Hugh & Marbeck, John.. Broude.
Buck, P. C., ed. see Byrd, William, et al.
Buck, P. C., ed. see Tallis, Thomas, et al.
Buck, P. C., ed. see Tomkins, Thomas.
Buck, P. C., et al, eds. Robert White.
Buck, Philip W. & Travis, Martin B., Jr., eds. Control of Foreign Relations in Modern Nations.
Buck, R. Creighton & Buck, Ellen. An Introduction to Differential Equations.
Buck, R. Creighton & Willcox, Alfred B. Calculus of Several Variables.
Buck, Ray. Danny White: The Kicking Quarterback.
--Gary Carter; The Kid.
Buckby, R. J., jt. auth. see Johnson, R. P.
Buckett, M. Introduction to Farm Organization & Managements.
Buckhingham, James S. Slave States of America.
Buckingham, A. D., et al, eds. Organic Liquids: Structure, Dynamics & Chemical Properties.
Buckingham, H. & Price, E. M. Principles of Electrical Measurements.
Buckingham, Jamie. Parable of Jesus.
Buckingham, Robert W. A Special Kind of Love: Care for the Dying Child.
Buckland, Charles E. Dictionary of Indian Biography.
Buckland, Michael K. Book Availability & the Library User.
--Library Services in Theory & Context.
Buckland, R. A. Broadcasting by Satellite.
Buckle, Henry T. On Scotland & the Scotch Intellect. Hanham, H. J. & Clive, John, eds.
Buckle, Mary, jt. auth. see Day, Lewis F.
Buckle, Richard. Buckle at the Ballet: Selected Ballet Writings.
--Diaghilev.
--In the Wake of Diaghilev.
Buckley, D. H. Surface Effects in Adhesion, Friction, Wear & Lubrication.
Buckley, Earle A. How to Write Better Business Letters.
Buckley, Francis J. Reconciling.
Buckley, Gary J., jt. auth. see Mansfield, Don L.
Buckley, Jerome H. Tennyson: The Growth of a Poet.
--Triumph of Time: A Study of the Victorian Concepts of Time, History, Progress & Decadence.
Buckley, John J., jt. auth. see Mulliken, Ruth K.
Buckley, Marie. Breaking into Prison: A Citizen Guide to Volunteer Action.
Buckley, Michael & Samagalski, Alan. China-A Travel Survival Kit.
Buckley, Peter, jt. auth. see Mack, Walter S.
Buckley, Peter J. & Enderwick, Peter. The Industrial Relations Practices of Foreign-Owned Firms in Britain.
Buckley, Peter J., et al. Direct Investment in the United Kingdom by Smaller European Firms.
Buckley, Richard. The Foolish Tortoise.
--The Greedy Python.
Buckley, Walter, ed. Modern Systems Research for the Behavioral Scientist: A Sourcebook.
Buckley, William F., Jr. Overdrive: A Personal Documentary.
--Right Reason.
--See You Later, Alligator.
--The Temptation of Wilfred Malachey.
--Who's on First.
Buckmann, Carol I., jt. auth. see Siegel, Mayer.
Bucknall, Benjamin, tr. see Viollet-Le-Duc, Eugene E.
Bucknell, P. Misuse of Drugs & the Law.
Bucknell, P. & Ghodse, H. Misuse of Drugs - Supplement 1.
Buckner, K., et al. Using the USCD-P System.
Bucksch, H. & Altemeyer, A. Dictionnaire des Canalisations a Grande Distance: Anglais-Francais-Allemand.
Bucksch, Herbert. Getriebe-Worterbuch.
Buckton, David, ed. The Treasures of San Marco.
Buckwalter, Jane, jt. auth. see Sears, Cecil.
Buckwell, Allan, et al. The Costs of the Common Agricultural Policy.
Budai, Joan. What's in an Egg?
Budak, Aram. Circuit Theory Fundamentals & Applications.
Buday, George. The History of the Christmas Card.
Budberg, Moura, tr. see Simenon, Georges.
Budd, Art. The Kook Book.
Budd, Lillian. April Harvest.
--April Snow.
--Land of Strangers.
Budd, Millie. The Light Company.
Budd, Richard W. & Ruben, Brent D., eds. Beyond Media: New Approaches to Mass Communications.
Budde, Fritz. Wieland und Bodmer.
Budde, James F. Measuring Performance in Human Service Systems: Planning, Organization & Control.
Budden, Julian. Verdi.
Buddhananda, tr. see Ramprasad.
Buddhist Text Translation Society Staff, tr. see Tripitaka Master Hua.
Buddhist Text Translation Society, tr. see Master Hua, Tripitaka.
Buddhist Text Translation Society, tr. see Master Hua, Triptaka.
Buddhist Text Translation Society, tr. see Tripitaka Master Hua.
Buddington, Anita & Vuilleumier, Marion. What's Cooking on Cape Cod.
Budge, E. A. The Book of the Dead.
--The Book of the Dead: An English Translation of the Chapters, Hymns, Etc., of the Theban Recension.
Budge, E. A., intro. by. The Book of the Dead.
Budge, E. Wallis. Amulets & Superstitions.
--Divine Origin of the Craft of the Herbalist.
--Egyptian Magic.
--Egyptian Religion.
--Egyptian Religion.
--Egyptian Religion.
Budge, Ernest A. Nile--Notes for Travellers in Egypt & the Egyptian Sudan: Notes for Travellers in Egypt & the Egyptian Sudan.
Budge, Wallis. Egyptian Magic.
Budge, Wallis E., ed. Book of the Dead: Egyptian Literature.
Budke, George H. & Christie, J. Elmer, eds. Old Nyack: The Finest Written Historical Sketch of Old Nyack Village.
Budke, Wesley, compiled by. Directory of Vocational Education Personnel (1985-1986)
Budovsky, E. I., jt. ed. see Kochetkov, N. K.
Budrys, Algis. Rogue Moon.
Budy, A. M., jt. auth. see McLean, F. C.
Budzik, Richard S. Short Course in Sheet Metal Shop Theory: Including 25 Practical Projects.
Bueche, Frederick J. Understanding the World of Physics.
Buecher, T., ed. see Gesellschaft Fuer Biologische Chemie, 20th Colloquium, Mossbach-Baden, 1969.
Buechner, Frederick. Entrance to Porlock.
--Godric.
--Lion Country.
--Love Feast.
--Open Heart.
--Treasure Hunt.
Buel, Richard, Jr. Securing the Revolution: Ideology in American Politics, 1789-1815.
Buell, Victor P., et al, eds. Handbook of Modern Marketing.
Buelow, George, ed. see Anderson, Donna K.
Buelow, George, ed. see Schulenberg, David.
Buelow, George J., ed. see Hancock, Virginia.
Buende, R., et al. MHD Power Generation: Selected Problems of Combustion MHD Generation. Raeder, J., ed.
Buenker, John D. Urban Liberalism & Progressive Reform.

Authors

Buenker, John D. & Burckel, Nicholas C. Immigration & Ethnicity: A Guide to Information Sources.
Buenning, Erwin. Physiological Clock: Circadian Rhythms & Biological Chronometry.
Buerger, Jane & Davis, Jennie. Helping Is.
Buerger, Jane, ed. see Colina, Tessa.
Buerger, Jane, ed. see Odor, Ruth.
Buerki, F. A. Stagecraft for Nonprofessionals.
Buerki, K., et al see Huth, F., et al.
Buero Vallejo, Antonio. En la Ardiente Oscuridad. Wofsy, Samuel A., ed.
Buescher, E. Stephen, jt. auth. see Hughes, Walter T.
Buettner, Stewart. American Art Theory, 1945-1970. Kuspit, Donald, ed.
Buff, Conrad, jt. auth. see Buff, Mary.
Buff, Iva M. A Thematic Catalog of the Sacred Works of Giacomo Carissimi.
Buff, Mary & Buff, Conrad. Apple & the Arrow.
--The Apple & the Arrow.
--Hah-Nee.
--Magic Maize.
Buff, Sheila, jt. auth. see Olstein, Judi.
Buffa, Elwood S. Meeting the Competitive Challenge: Manufacturing Strategy for U. S. Companies.
--Meeting the Competitive Challenge: Manufacturing Strategies for U. S. Companies.
Buffaloe, Neal D. & Ferguson, Dale V. Microbiology.
Buffinger, Hazel. Bible Questions Answered.
Bufford, Rodger K. The Human Reflex: Behavioral Psychology in Biblical Perspective.
Buffum, Richard D. The Brema Brasses.
Buford, Thomas O. Personal Philosophy: The Art of Living.
Buford, Thomas O., ed. Essays on Other Minds.
Bufton, Nigel, ed. Exploring Mathematics with Microcomputers.
Bugaev, Boris N. Lug Zelenyi: Kniga Statei.
Bugeja, P. Maltese-English, English-Maltese Dictionary.
Bugelski, B. R. Some Practical Laws of Learning.
Bugg, J. L., Jr. & Stewart, P. C. Jacksonian Democracy.
Bugge, Lawrence J., et al. Complying with Consumer Credit: A Creditor's Guide.
Buggie, Frederick D. New Product Development Strategies.
Bugliarello, George & Doner, Dean B., eds. The History & Philosophy of Technology.
Bugliarello, George & Simon, H. A., eds. Technology, the University, & the Community.
Bugliarello, George, et al. The Impact of Noise Pollution: A Socio-Technological Introduction.
Bugliosi, Vincent & Gentry, Curt. Helter Skelter: The True Story of the Manson Murders.
Bugrov, Y. S. & Nikolsky, S. M. Fundamentals of Linear Algebra & Analytical Geometry. Levant, Leonid, tr.
Bugrov, Ya S. & Nikolsky, S. M. Differential & Integral Calculus.
Bugsby, W. New Perspectives in Behavior: A Book of Readings.
Buhagiar, Marion, ed. The Great Book of Inside Knowledge.
Buheiry, Marwan R. The Formation & Perception of the Modern Arab World: Studies by Marwan R. Buheiry. Conrad, Lawrence I., et al, eds.
Buhlmann, Walbert. Courage, Church! Essays in Ecclesial Spirituality. Smith, Mary, tr. from Ital.
Buikema, Arthur L., Jr., jt. auth. see Cairns, John, Jr.
Building Research Advisory Board. Criteria for Underground Heat Distribution Systems.
Building Research Advisory Board Staff. An Exploratory Study on Responsibility, Liability & Accountability for Risks in Construction.
Buisseret, David. Historic Architecture of the Caribbean.
Buitenen, J. A. van see Dimmitt, Cornelia.
Buitenhuis, Peter. Grasping Imagination: The American Writings of Henry James.
Buitrago, Ann & Immerman, Leon A. Are You Now or Have You Ever Been in the FBI Files? How to Secure & Interpret Your FBI Files.
Bukharin, Nikolai, jt. auth. see Luxemburg, Rosa.
Bukist, Melvin J. Sandman's Dust.
Bukofzer, Manfred F. Studies in Medieval & Renaissance Music.
Bukowski, Charles. War All the Time.
Bulani, W., jt. auth. see Dumas, T.
Bulatao, Rodolfo A. & Fawcett, James T. Influences on Childbearing Intentions Across the Fertility Career: Demographic & Socioeconomic Factors & the Value of Children. Ward, Sandra E., ed.
Bulatao, Rodolfo A. & Lee, Ronald D. Determinants of Fertility in Developing Countries.
Bulbrook, R. D., jt. ed. see Hayward, J. L.
Bulgakov, Mikhail. Heart of a Dog. Ginsburg, Mirra, tr. from Rus.
--Heart of a Dog. Ginsburg, Mirra, tr.
--Master & Margarita. Ginsburg, Mirra, tr. from Rus.
Bulgakov, Sergius. A Bulgakov Anthology: From Marxism to Christian Orthodoxy. Zernov, Nicolas & Pain, James, eds.
Bulhof, Francis, ed. Nijhoff, Van Ostaijen, "De Stijl" Modernism in the Netherlands & Belgium in the First Quarter of the 20th Century.- Six Essays (1976)
Bulka, Reuven P. & Spero, Moshe H. A Psychology-Judaism Reader.
Bulkin, Rena. Frommer's Guide to Washington D. C.
Bull, Donald, et al. American Breweries.
Bull, Ethel F. The Spirit of the Santee.
Bull, G. M., ed. Real Time Programming, 1983: Proceedings of the IFAC-IFIP Workshop, 12th, Hertford, U. K., March 1983.
Bull, Geoffrey. I Am a Fish.
--I Am a Sparrow.
--I Hid in the Reeds.
Bull, Hedley, ed. see Wight, Martin.
Bull, Henric. Cruise of the Antarctic.
Bull, Inez. Cross Fork Tales: True Stories from the Pennsylvania Black Forest & Ole Bull's Lost Colony.
--Ole Bull Returns to Pennsylvania: The Biography of a Norwegian Violin Virtuoso & Pioneer in the Keystone State.
--Ole Bull's Activities in the United States Between 1843 & 1880.
--Retarded Child.
Bull, James. Evolution of Sex Determining Mechanisms.
Bull, John. New British Political Dramatists.
--New British Political Dramatists.
Bull, Malcolm. The Pick Operating System.
Bull, Molly N. The Rogue's Daughter.
Bull, Norman. Parables of Jesus.
Bull, Norman J. Stories Jesus Told.
Bull, Ray, jt. auth. see Clifford, Brian.
Bullard, Helen. My People in Wood.
Bullard, Oral, ed. see Lowe, Don & Lowe, Roberta.
Bullard, Scott R. & Collins, Michael. Who's Who in Sherlock Holmes.
Bullard, Scott R., ed. Library Acquisitions Special Reports.
Bulle, Florence. God Wants You Rich: And Other Enticing Doctrines.
Bullen, A. H., ed. see Day, John.
Bullen, Anne. Showing Ponies.
Bullen, K. E. The Earth's Density.
Bullen, Ripley P. The Terra Ceia Site, Manatee County, Florida.
Buller, H. & Hoggart, K. Nondecision-Making & Community Power: Residential Development Control in Rural Areas.
Buller, Henry, jt. auth. see Hoggart, Keith.
Bulletin of the Atomic Scientists Staff, ed. The Final Epidemic: Physicians & Scientists on Nuclear War.
Bullinger, Ethelbert W. Commentary on Revelation.
Bullis, Douglas. California Fashion Designers: Art & Style.
Bulloch, Anthony W., et al, eds. see Green, Peter.
Bullock, A. L., ed. see Oxford University, British Commonwealth Group Staff.
Bullock, Alan. The Humanist Tradition in the West.
Bullock, Barbara, et al, eds. Pathophysiology: Adaptations & Alterations in Function.
Bullock, C. Hassell. Introduction to Old Testament Poetic Books.
Bullock, Charles S., jt. auth. see Rodgers, Harrell R.
Bullock, Clarence C. Bullock: The Autobiography of an Artist.
Bullock, Clifton. The Master Plan.
Bullock, Henry A. History of Negro Education in the South: From 1619 to the Present.
Bullock, James. Whatever Became of Salvation?
Bullock, John, jt. auth. see Owen, Robert.
Bullock, Lyndal M. & Blackburn, Gary M. A Modular Learning Approach to Accompany Educational Aspects of Behavioral Problems in Children & Youth.
Bullock, Micheal, tr. see Busza, Andrzej.
Bullock, Orin M., Jr. The Restoration Manual: An Illustrated Guide to the Preservation & Restoration of Old Buildings.
Bullock, Spencer M. & Hosie, Kenneth. Learning to Care: The Training of Staff for Residential Social Work with Young People.
Bullock-Davies, Constance. English Pronunciation from the Fifteenth to the Eighteenth Century: A Handbook to the Study of Historical Grammar.
Bullough, Vern L., ed. The Scientific Revolution.
Bullough, Vern L., et al. An Annotated Bibliography of Homosexuality.
Bullough, William S. The Dynamic Body Tissues.
Bulmer, Kenneth. City Under the Sea.
Bulmer, Martin, ed. Mining & Social Change: Durham County in the Twentieth Century.
Bulmer, Simon & Wessels, Wolfgang. The European Council: Decision-Making in European Politics.
Bu'Lock, J. D., et al. Bioactive Microbial Products: Search & Discovery.
Bulow, Von Hans see Cramer, J. B.
Bulson, P. S., jt. auth. see Allen, H. G.
Bultena, Louis. Deviant Behavior in Sweden.
Bultmann, Rudolf. The Second Letter to the Corinthians. Harrisville, Roy A., tr.
Bulwer-Lytton, Edward G. The Coming Race.
--Money: Royal Shakespeare Company.
Bump, Jerome. Gerard Manley Hopkins.
Bumpus, John S. Dictionary of Ecclesiastical Terms: Being a History & Explanation of Certain Terms Used in Architecture, Ecclesiology, Liturgiology, Music, Ritual, Cathedral, Constitution, Etc.
Bunbury, E. H. A History of Ancient Geography: Among the Greeks & Romans from the Earliest Ages till the Fall of the Roman Empire.
Bunch, Bryan. Mathematical Fallacies & Paradoxes.
Bunch, Charlotte & Pollack, Sandra, eds. Learning Our Way: Essays in Feminist Education.
Bunch, Gay. Crossword Puzzles for Texas: The Land & Its People.
Bunche, Ralph J. The Political Status of the Negro in the Age of F. D. R. Grantham, Dewey W., ed.
Buncke & Furnas. Symposium on Frontiers in Reconstructive Microsurgery.
Bundesen, Lynne, ed. Dear Miss Liberty.
Bundgaard, Hans, et al. Drug Design & Adverse Reactions.
Bundschuh, Rick. Glow in the Dark.
Bundy, A., ed. Catalogue of Artificial Intelligence Tools.
Bundy, Carol, jt. ed. see Zell, Hans.
Bundy, McGeorge. Strength of Government.
Bundy, William, ed. America & the World, 1983.
Bundy, William P., ed. America & the World, 1978.
--America & the World, 1979.
--America & the World, 1981.
Bundy, William P., jt. ed. see Foreign Affairs Staff.
Bungay, Henry R. Energy, the Biomass Options.
Bunge, Frederica M. & Cooke, Melinda W., eds. Oceania: A Regional Study.
Bunge, Frederica M. & Shinn, Rinn-Sup, eds. China: A Country Study.
Bunge, M. Foundations of Physics.
Bungenberg De Jong, H. G., jt. auth. see Booij, H. L.
Bunger, Robert L. Islamization among the Upper Pokomo.
Buni, Andrew & Rogers, Alan. Boston: City on a Hill.
Bunich, P. C. & Kharchev, K. Ocean & Its Resources.
Bunis, David M. Yiddish Linguistics: A Classified Bilingual Index of Yiddish Serials & Collections, 1913-1958.
Bunker, Dusty. Dream Cycles.
Bunker, Raymond. Town & Country, City & Region?
Bunkina, M. Current Problems of Contemporary Capitalism.
Bunkina, M. K. U S A vs. Western Europe.
Bunn, James H. The Dimensionality of Signs, Tools & Models: An Introduction.
Bunn, John W. Art of Officiating Sports.
Bunnell, F., tr. see Ziswiler, V.
Bunnell, P., tr. see Ziswiler, V.
Bunnell, Peter, intro. by. Barbara Morgan.
Bunnelle, Hasse. Food for Knapsackers & Other Trail Travellers.
Bunnelle, Hasse R. Movable Feasts: The Backpacker Magazine Cookbook. Backpacker Magazine Staff, ed.
Bunsell, A. R., et al, eds. Advances in Composite Materials: Proceedings of the Third International Conference on Composite Materials, Paris, France, 26-29 August, 1980.
Bunte, Hermann & Langhans, Peter, eds. A Century of Ulcer Surgery: Medical & Surgical Therapy Today.
Buntenkoetter, S., jt. auth. see Kaemmerer, K.
Bunting, Eve. The Big Cheese.
--The Big Red Barn.
--Clancy's Coat.
--Demetrius & the Golden Goblet.
--Goose Dinner.
--Goose Dinner.
--The Great White Shark.
--Monkey in the Middle.
--The Sea World Book of Sharks.
--The Spook Birds. Tucker, Kathleen, ed.
--The Traveling Men of Ballycoo.
--Winter's Coming.
--Winter's Coming.
Bunting, G. R. & Lee, M. J. Evolution of the United Nations.
Bunting, William H. Portrait of a Port: Boston, 1852-1914.
Bunyan. Computer Systems Measurement.
--Data Base Systems.
Bunyan, John. The Family Pilgrim's Progress. Watson, Jean, retold by.
--The Holy War.
--The Pilgrim's Progress.
--The Pilgrim's Progress. Helms, Hal M., ed.
Bunyan, John & Parkhurst, Louis G., Jr. John Bunyan: Pilgrim's Prayer Book.
Bunye, Maria V. & Yap, Elsa P. Cebuano Grammar Notes. McKaughan, Howard P., ed.
Bunzel, John H. New Force on the Left: Tom Hayden & the Campaign Against Corporate America.
Bunzel, Ruth L., jt. ed. see Mead, Margaret.
Buonanno, C. Beyond the Flag.
Buonarroti, Michelangelo see Michelangelo.
Buonarroti, Philippe. History of Babeuf's Conspiracy for Equality. O'Brien, Bronterre, tr.
Buonassisi, Vincenzo. Pizza.
Buoniconti, Nick & Anderson, Dick. Defensive Football. Bondurant, Bill, ed.
Buonicore, Anthony J., jt. ed. see Theodore, Louis.
Buono, Anthony F. & Bowditch, James L. The Human Side of Mergers & Acquisitions: Managing Collisions Between People, Cultures, & Organizations.
Buono, Franco Silvestro. Into the Beyond: A Dramatic Romance in Four Acts.
Burack, A. S., ed. One Hundred Plays for Children.
Burack, Elmer H. & Torda, Florence. The Manager's Guide to Change.
Burack, Elmer H. & Negandhi, Anant, eds. Organization Design: Theoretical Perspectives & Empirical Findings.
Burack, Sylvia K., ed. The Writer's Handbook, 1988.
Burago, Alla, jt. ed. see Raffel, Burton.
Burak, John. There Goes My Aching Back.
Burbach, Hal. Especially for Him: A Beginner's Cookbook for Men.
Burbach, Roger & Flynn, Patricia. Agribusiness in the Americas: The Political Economy of Corporate Agriculture.
Burbank, Nelson L. & Romney, Arnold B. House Construction Details.
Burbank, Rex. Thornton Wilder.
Burbank, Rex J. Sherwood Anderson.
Burbidge, G. & Hewitt, A., eds. Telescopes for the Nineteen Eighties.
Burbidge, J. W. On Hegel's Logic: Fragments of a Commentary.
Burch, jt. auth. see Street.
Burch, Beverly, jt. auth. see Esau, Truman.
Burch, Brian. Still under the Thumb.
Burch, James. Lubyanka.
Burch, Kathleen. Indicia...A Romance.
Burch, Martin & Wood, Bruce. Public Policy in Britain.
Burch, Noel, tr. see Hodeir, Andre.
Burch, Pat. Rokudan: A Tale of Love in Six Movements.
Burch, Robert M. Colour Printing & Colour Printers.
Burchard, Marshall & Burchard, S. H. Sports Star: Tom Seaver.
--Sports Star: Tom Seaver.
Burchard, S. H. Sports Star: Bob Griese.
--Sports Star: Bob Griese.
--Sports Star: Brad Park.
--Sports Star: Brad Park.
--Sports Star: Chris Evert Lloyd.
--Sports Star: Chris Evert Lloyd.
--Sports Star: Dorothy Hamill.
--Sports Star: Earl Campbell.
--Sports Star: Earl Campbell.
--Sports Star: Elvin Hayes.
--Sports Star: Elvin Hayes.
--Sports Star: Fernando Valenzuela.
--Sports Star: Franco Harris.
--Sports Star: Franco Harris.
--Sports Star: George Brett.
--Sports Star: George Brett.
--Sports Star: Herschel Walker.
--Sports Star: Herschel Walker.
--Sports Star: Jim "Catfish" Hunter.
--Sports Star: Jim "Catfish" Hunter.
--Sports Star: John McEnroe.
--Sports Star: John McEnroe.
--Sports Star: Larry Bird.
--Sports Star: Larry Bird.
--Sports Star: Mark "The Bird" Fidrych.
--Sports Star: Mark "The Bird" Fidrych.
--Sports Star: "Mean" Joe Greene.
--Sports Star: "Mean" Joe Greene.
--Sports Star: Nadia Comaneci.
--Sports Star: Nadia Comaneci.
--Sports Star: Pele.
--Sports Star: Pele.
--Sports Star: Reggie Jackson.
--Sports Star: Reggie Jackson.
--Sports Star: Sugar Ray Leonard.
--Sports Star: Sugar Ray Leonard.
--Sports Star: The Book of Baseball Greats.
--Sports Star: The Book of Baseball Greats.
--Sports Star: Tommy John.
--Sports Star: Tommy John.
--Sports Star: Tony Dorsett.
--Sports Star: Tony Dorsett.
--Sports Star: Tracy Austin.
--Sports Star: Tracy Austin.
--Sports Star: Walt Frazier.

--Sports Star: Walt Frazier.
--Sports Star: Wayne Gretzky.
--Sports Star: Wayne Gretzky.
Burchard, S. H., jt. auth. see Burchard, Marshall.
Burchell, Robert. Planned Unit Development: New Communities American Style.
Burchell, Robert W. Frontiers of Planned Unit Development.
Burchell, Robert W. & Listokin, David. Cities under Stress.
Burchenal, J. H., ed. see International Union Against Cancer - Chemotherapy Panel.
Burchette, Dorothy. More Needlework Blocking & Finishing.
--Needlework Blocking & Finishing.
--Needlework: Blocking & Finishing.
Burck, H. D., et al. Counseling & Accountability: Methods & Critique.
Burckel, Nicholas C., jt. auth. see Buenker, John D.
Burckhalter, David. The Seris.
Burckhardt, Carl J. Richelieu & His Age.
Burckhardt, J. L., tr. from Arabic. Arabic Proverbs: Or the Manners & Customs of the Modern Egyptian, Illustrated from Their Proverbial Sayings Current at Cairo.
Burd, Shirley, ed. see Tennessee Nurses' Association Staff.
Burda, Edward. Consumer Finance.
Burden, Richard J., et al. Numerical Analysis.
Burden, Shirley. The Vanderbilts in My Life.
Burden, Tom & Campbell, Mike. Capitalism & Public Policy in the U. K.: A Marxist Approach.
Burden, Tom & Chapman, Reg. Business in Society: Consensus & Conflict.
Burdette, Kay. Fabric Painting in Tole.
Burdette, W. J., ed. Invertebrate Endocrinology & Hormonal Heterophyllly.
Burdick, Charles B. Ralph Lutz & the Hoover Institution.
Burdick, Charles B. & Lutz, Ralph H., eds. The Political Institutions of the German Revolution, 1918-1919.
Burdick, Charles B., jt. ed. see Detwiler, Donald S.
Burdick, John & Weiser, Peter B. ProDOS Quick & Simple: For the Apple II Family.
Burdick, Loraine. The Shirley Temple Scrapbook.
Burdick, Neal S. & Goodwin, Tony, eds. Guide to Adirondack Trails: High Peaks Region.
Burdick, Neal S., ed. see Haberl, Art.
Burdick, Neal S., ed. see O'Shea, Peter V.
Burdick, Neal S., ed. see Tisdale, Betsy.
Burdick, Neal S., ed. see Wadsworth, Bruce.
Burdon, R. H., jt. auth. see Adams, R. L.
Bureau of Census Staff, ed. Congressional District Data Book, 98th Congress.
Bureau of Government Research Staff, ed. State Debt & Public Liability in Oklahoma.
Bureau, William H. What the Printer Should Know about Paper.
Burek, P. J., tr. see Braitsch, O.
Buren, J. M. Van see Van Buren, J. M. & Borke, R. C.
Buren, Martin Van see Van Buren, Martin.
Bures, Jan, et al. The Mechanism & Application of Leao's Spreading Depression of Electroencephalographic Activity.
Burfeindt-Moral & Zacher, H. H. Satz-Lexikon des Englischen Geschaeftsbriefes.
Burford, Anne M. & Greenya, John. Are You Tough Enough? An Insider's View of Washington Power Politics.
Burg, David, tr. see Solzhenitsyn, Alexander.
Burg, H., tr. see Bartknecht, W.
Burge, David L. The Official Transcript of the Perfect Pitch Workshop.
--The Official Transcript of the Perfect Pitch Master Class.
Burge, William. Commentaries on the Law of Suretyship, & the Rights & Obligations of Parties Thereto. Helmholz, R. H. & Reams, Bernard D., Jr., eds.
Burger, Alfred. Drugs & People: Medications, Their History & Origins, & the Way They Act.
Burger, Chester. The Chief Executive: Realities of Corporate Leadership.
Burger, Denis R., jt. ed. see Kirkpatrick, Charles H.
Burger, E., ed. Technical Reference Dictionary.
Burger, Georg. Treatment Planning for External Beam Therapy with Neutrons.
Burger, Isabel B. Creative Drama in Religious Education.
Burger, K. Organic Reagents in Metal Analysis.
Burger, M. A., jt. auth. see Harmon, R. B.
Burger, Neal R., jt. auth. see Simpson, George E.
Burger, Pixie & Percivall, Julie. Taking Off.
Burger, Pixie, jt. auth. see Percival, Julia.
Burger, Rex. Colorado Trivia.
Burger, Robert J. Siblings.
Burger, Thomas. Max Weber's Theory of Concept Formation: History, Laws, & Ideal Types.
Burges, A. & Cregg, J. S., eds. Soil Mechanics & Foundation Engineering: Proceedings of the 4th Regional Conference for Africa, Cape Town, 1967.
Burgess, Alan. The Small Woman: The Story of Gladys Aylward of China.
Burgess, Anthony. Beard's Roman Women.
--But Do Blondes Prefer Gentlemen?
--Clockwork Orange.
--Devil of a State.
--Earthly Powers.
--The End of the World News.
--Enderby's Dark Lady: Or, No End to Enderby.
--Flame into Being: The Life & Work of D. H. Lawrence.
--Joysprick: An Introduction to the Language of James Joyce.
--The Kingdom of the Wicked.
--Little Wilson & Big God: The Autobiography.
--Man of Nazareth.
--Napoleon Symphony.
--Nineteen Eighty-Five.
--Ninety-Nine Novels: The Best in English since 1939.
--On Going to Bed.
--This Man & Music.
--Urgent Copy.
Burgess, C. & Knowles, A. Standards in Absorption Spectrometry.
Burgess, C., jt. ed. see Knowles, A.
Burgess, C. R. Meteorology for Seamen.
Burgess, Carol, compiled by. County Salaries in North Carolina.
Burgess, Charles. In Care & into Work.
Burgess, Claudia. Cooking with Country.
Burgess, Eric. Celestial BASIC: Astronomy On Your Computer.
Burgess, Ernest W., jt. auth. see Park, Robert W.
Burgess, Ernest W. & Bogue, Donald J., eds. Urban Sociology.
Burgess, Gelett. The Purple Cow.
Burgess, Harold D. Sixty Years at the Bar: Anecdotes of a Corporation Lawyer.
Burgess, James. The Chronology of Modern India for Four Hundred Years From the Close of the Fifteenth Century, A.D. 1494-1894.
Burgess, Jan. The World of Horses. Barish, Wendy, ed.
Burgess, Joseph A. & Winn, Albert C. Epiphany. Achtemeier, Elizabeth, et al, eds.
Burgess, Joseph A., jt. auth. see Andrews, James E.
Burgess, Joseph A., ed. The Role of the Augsburg Confession: Catholic & Lutheran Views.
Burgess, Mallory. Passion Rose.
--Wild Land, Wild Love.
Burgess, N. How to Find Out in Banking & Investment.
Burgess, Philip M. & Harf, James E. Global Analysis: A Data Scheme & Deck for Univariate & Bivariate Analysis.
Burgess, R. A. The Construction Industry Handbook.
Burgess, R. E., ed. Fluctuation Phenomena in Solids.
Burgess, R. L. & Sharpe, S. M., eds. Forest Island Dynamics in Man-Dominated Landscapes.
Burgess, Robert G. Experiencing Comprehensive Education: A Study of Bishop McGregor School.
Burgess, Robert H. Sea, Sails & Shipwreck: The Career of the Four Masted Schooner Purnell T. White.
Burgess, Robert L. & Huston, Ted L., eds. Social Exchange in Developing Relationships.
Burgess, Thornton W. Favorite Tales by Thornton Burgess.
--Old Mother West Wind.
Burgess, W. Randolph. Interpretations of Federal Reserve Policy in the Speeches of Benjamin Strong, Governor of the Federal Reserve Bank of New York.
Burgess, Warren E. Butterflyfishes of the World.
Burgess, Yvonne. Life to Live: A Novel.
--The Strike.
Burghardt, E., et al. Cervical Pathology & Colopscopy.
Burghardt, Erich. Early Histological Diagnosis of Cervical Cancer.
Burghardt, Walter J. Lovely in Eyes Not His: Homilies for an Imaging of Christ.
Burghardt, Walter J., ed. Religious Freedom, Nineteen Sixty-Five to Nineteen Seventy-Five: A Symposium on a Historic Document.
--Woman: New Dimensions.
Burghelea, D. & Lashof, R. Groups of Automarphisms of Manifolds.
Burghes, David N. & Downs, A. M. Modern Introduction to Classical Mechanics & Control.
Burgin, Richard, jt. auth. see Singer, Isaac Bashevis.
Burgmann, Verity. In Our Time: Socialism & the Rise of Labor, 1885-1905.
Burgner, Goldene F. Greene County Marriages, 1783 to 1868.
--North Carolina Land Grants in Tennessee, 1778 to 1791.
Burgoin, Gillian. Guide to the Weimaraner.
Burgoyne, Jacqueline & Clark, David. Making a Go of It: A Study of Stepfamilies in Sheffield.
Burhans, Robert D. The First Special Service Force: A War History of the North Americans 1942-1944.
Burhard, Rachel C. Green Figs & Tender Grapes.
Burhenne, H. Joachim & Li, David K. Radiology: Focus on Clinical Diagnosis.
Burhop, E. H., ed. High Energy Physics.
Burian, Barbara & Fink, Stuart. Business Data Processing.
Burington, Richard S. & May, Donald C., Jr. Handbook of Probability & Statistics with Tables.
Burk, Bruce. Game Bird Carving.
--Waterfowl Studies.
Burk, C. A. & Drake, C. L., eds. The Geology of Continental Margins.
Burk, John, jt. auth. see Holland, Marjorie.
Burk, John N., ed. see Hale, Philip.
Burk, Leslie Chamberlin & Esteves, Roberto, eds. Video & Cable Guidelines.
Burk, Tom. Do It in the Dark.
Burkan, Bruce T., jt. auth. see Keyes, Ken, Jr.
Burkan, Peggy D. Guiding Yourself into a Spiritual Reality: A Workbook.
Burkard, Martha, jt. auth. see Anderson, Pauline.
Burkard, Michael. Fictions from the Self: Poems.
Burkart, Betty Lou. Elmer, the Bucket-Mouthed Pelican.
--Tuffy, the Purple-Footed Duck.
Burke, A., et al. The Search for a New Europe, 1919-1971.
Burke, Alan D. Driven to Murder. Curtis, C. Michael, ed.
Burke, Anna M. The Plain Brown Wrapper Book of Computers.
Burke, Bill. I Want to Take Picture.
Burke, Carol, ed. Plain Talk.
Burke, Cornelius G. The Collector's Haydn.
Burke, D. Barlow, Jr. Law of Real Estate Brokers: 1985 Supplement.
Burke, Daniel. Notes on Literary Stucture.
Burke, Dennis R. Treating Martial Arts Injuries. Griffeth, Bill, ed.
Burke, Ed, et al. Inside the Cyclist. Velo-News, ed.
--Inside the Cyclist. Velo-News Staff, ed.
Burke, Edmund. Works.
Burke, Edmund & Mansfield, Harvey C., Jr., eds. Selected Letters of Edmund Burke.
Burke, Edmund R. Science of Cycling.
Burke, Fred. Africa: Regional Study.
Burke, Fred, tr. see Buronson & Hara, Tetsuo.
Burke, Fred, tr. see Hara, Buronson & Hara, Tetsuo.
Burke, Helen N. Foods from the Founding Fathers: Recipes from Five Colonial Seaports.
Burke, Herman E. Pro Football: NFL Facts & Statistics.
Burke, J., et al. The Past in Perspective.
Burke, J. E. Progress in Ceramic Science.
Burke, J. L. & Bensch, D. E. Mount Pleasant & the Early Quakers of Ohio.
Burke, J. Terence, et al. Ohio Supplement for Modern Real Estate Practice.
Burke, James D. Jan Both: Paintings, Drawings & Prints.
Burke, James L. The Convict.
--Gathering of Horsemen.
--The Neon Rain.
Burke, John. Bible Sharing: How to Grow in the Mystery of Christ.
--Gospel Power: Toward the Revitalization of Preaching.
--Life in the Castle in Medieval England.
--Musical Landscapes.
--Roman England.
Burke, John F. Surgical Physiology.
Burke, John F. & Hildick-Smith, Gavin Y. The Infection-Prone Hospital Patient.
Burke, John J. & Weiss, Volker, eds. Advances in Metal Processing.
--Fatigue: Environment & Temperature Effects.
--Surface Treatments for Improved Performance & Properties.
Burke, Marjorie. Origin of History as Metaphysics.
Burke, Martyn. The Commissar's Report.
Burke, Mary J., et al. Sources of Information in Transportation: Part 1, General Transportation.
Burke, Michael. Outrageous Good Fortune.
Burke, Michael E. The Royal College of San Carlos: Surgery & Spanish Medical Reform in the Late Eighteenth Century.
Burke, P. G. Potential Scattering in Atomic Physics.
Burke, Patrick T. The Reluctant Vision: An Essay in the Philosophy of Religion.
Burke, Robert E., ed. see Patenaude, Lionel V.
Burke, Ronald S. Administrative Skills for the Manager.
Burke, Ronald S. & Kramer, Arthur D. Microcomputer Courseware for Technical Mathematics (Apple II & TRS-80) User's Manual.
Burke, Shirley R. The Composition & Function of Body Fluids.
Burke, Thomas. The History of the Ford Rotunda 1934-1962-Dearborn's Pride of the Past.
Burke, William J. Literature of Slang.
Burke, William P. The Irish Priests in Penal Times.
Burkert, Walter. Lore & Science in Ancient Pythagoreanism. Minar, Edwin L., Jr., tr. from Ger.
Burkett, David W. Writing Science News for the Mass Media.
Burkett, J., ed. Directory of Scientific Directories: A World Guide to Scientific Directories Including Medicine, Agriculture, Engineering, Manufacturing, & Industrial Directories.
Burkett, Larry & Proctor, William. How to Prosper in the Underground Economy.
Burkhalter, A. Louis. Ancient & Oriental Music (by) Romain Goldron.
Burkhalter, Pamela K. & Donley, Diana, eds. Dynamics of Oncology Nursing.
Burkhard, Arthur, tr. see Grillparzer, F.
Burkhard, R. E. & Derigs, U. Assignment & Matching Problems: Solution Methods with FORTRAN-Programs.
Burkhardt, Frederick, et al, eds. see James, William.
Burkhart, Charles. Anthology for Musical Analysis.
Burkhart, Rob. I Hate Witnessing Leader's Guide.
--Yet Will I Trust Him.
Burkholder, Lloyd K., Sr. Process & Industrial Pipe Estimating.
Burkholder, Ruth C. & Goddard, Carrie L. Exploring Korea.
Burkholtz, Herbert & Irving, Clifford. The Sleeping Spy.
Burkholz, Herbert. The Sensitives.
--The Snow Gods.
Burki, N. K. Pulmonary Diseases.
Burkin, A. R., ed. Topics in Non-Ferrous Extractive Metallurgy.
Burkitt, D. P., ed. see International Union Against Cancer - Chemotherapy Panel.
Burkitt, Miles. Old Stone Age.
Burkman, Katherine, jt. auth. see Auburn, Mark.
Burkman, Katherine H. Literature Through Performance: "Shakespeare's Mirror" & "A Canterbury Caper"
Burks, Ardath. The Modernizers: Overseas Students, Foreign Employees, & Meiji Japan.
Burks, Arthur W. Chance, Cause, Reason: An Inquiry into the Nature of Scientific Evidence.
Burks, Mary P. Requirements for Certification of Teachers, Counselors, Librarians, Administrators: For Elementary Schools, Secondary Schools & Junior Colleges.
--Requirements for Certification of Teachers, Counselors, Librarians, Adminstrators: For Elementary Schools, Secondary Schools & Junior Colleges.
--Requirements for Certification of Teachers, Counselors, Librarians, Administrators: For Elementary Schools, Secondary Schools....(Etc)
Burl, Aubrey. Rings of Stone: The Prehistoric Stone Circles of Britain & Ireland.
Burland, C. A., jt. auth. see Hooper, J. T.
Burlatsky, F. Mao-Tse-Tung: An Ideological & Psychological Portrait.
Burleigh, R. Carbon-Fourteen Dating.
Burley, J. & Styles, B. T., eds. Tropical Trees: Variation Breeding & Conservation.
Burley, T. & Tregear, P. African Development & Europe.
Burley, W. J. Wycliffe & the Winsor Blue.
Burling, Robbins. Sounding Right.
Burlingame, Hardin J. Leaves from Conjurors' Scrap Books, or, Modern Magicians & Their Works.
Burlingame, Roger. Inventors Behind the Inventor.
--Of Making Many Books.
Burlingham, Dorothy. Psychoanalytic Studies of the Sighted & the Blind.
Burman, Ben L. Blow a Bugle at Catfish Bend.
--Blow a Wild Bugle for Catfish Bend.
--Children of Noah.
--Generals Wear Cork Hats: An Amazing Adventure That Made World History.
--High Treason at Catfish Bend.
--High Water at Catfish Bend.
Burman, Ben. L. High Water at Catfish Bend.
Burman, Ben L. Look Down That Winding River: An Informal Profile of the Mississippi.
--The Owl Hoots Twice at Catfish Bend.
--Seven Stars for Catfish Bend.
--Sign of the Praying Tiger.
--The Strange Invasion of Catfish Bend.
--Street of the Laughing Camel.
--Three from Catfish Bend. Incl. High Water at Catfish Bend; Seven Stars for Catfish Bend; The Owl Hoots Twice at Catfish Bend. Taplinger.
Burman, Bina R. Religion & Politics in Tibet.
Burman, C. R. How to Find Out in Chemistry.
Burman, Edward. The Inquisition: The Hammer of Heresy.
Burn, Barbara, ed. Utamaro: Songs of the Garden. Betchaku, Yasuko & Mirviss, Joan B., trs. from Japanese.

Authors

--Yves Saint Laurent Exhibition Checklist. Dreusedow, Jean R.
Burn, William L. Age of Equipoise.
Burnand, Tony. Dictionnaire de la Chasse.
Burnard, Francis C. My Time & What I've Done with It: An Autobiography, Compiled from the Diary, Notes & Personal Recollections of Cecil Colvin, 1874.
Burne, Kevin G., et al. Functional English for Writers.
Burner, David. Herbert Hoover: A Public Life.
--The Politics of Provincialism: The Democratic Party in Transition, 1918-1932.
Burner, David, et al. Test Bank for an American Portrait.
Burnes, R. H. Handbook of R. H. Burnes' Cetacean Dissections.
Burness, Tad. American Car Spotter's Guide 1940-1965.
--The Auto Album.
--Monstrous American Car Spotter's Guide 1920-1980.
Burness, Ted. Ford Spotter's Guide: 1920-1980.
Burnet, Alastair. The Book of the Royal Wedding.
--In Person: The Prince & Princess of Wales.
Burnet, Frank M. Integrity of the Body.
Burnet, Jean. Next-Year Country: A Study of Rural Social Organization in Alberta.
Burnet, N. G., jt. ed. see Bates, I. P.
Burnet, Thomas. Sacred Theory of the Earth.
Burnett, Alan D. & Taylor, Peter J., eds. Political Studies from Spatial Perspectives: Anglo-American Essays on Political Geography.
Burnett, Allison L., ed. Biology of Hydra.
Burnett, D., jt. auth. see ICLG Conference, 1977.
Burnett, David, jt. ed. see Foley, Martha.
Burnett, Edmund C. The Continental Congress.
Burnett, Frances H. That Lass O'Lowries.
Burnett, John. Plenty & Want: A Social History of Diet in England from 1815 to the Present Day.
--A Social History of Housing, Eighteen Fifteen to Nineteen Eighty-Five.
--A Social History of Housing Eighteen Fifteen to Nineteen Seventy.
Burnett, John J. Promotion Management: A Strategic Approach.
Burnett, W. R. High Sierra.
Burney, Charles. An Eighteenth-Century Musical Tour in Central Europe & the Netherlands.
--An Eighteenth-Century Musical Tour in France & Italy.
--A General History of Music, From the Earliest Ages to the Present Period (1789)
Burnford, J. F., jt. auth. see Chennault, Joann.
Burnham. Frommer's Amsterdam & Holland.
Burnham, Charles R., jt. auth. see Phillips, Ronald L.
Burnham, Dorothy K. Warp & Weft: A Dictionary of Textile Terms.
Burnham, Frank. Cleared to Land.
Burnham, James. The Managerial Revolution.
Burnham, John C. Paths into American Culture: Psychology, Medicine, & Morals.
Burnham, Phillip & Lederer, Richard. Theme & Paragraph.
Burnham, Walter D. Critical Elections & the Mainsprings of American Politics.
Burnham, Walter D., jt. auth. see Kleppner, Paul.
Burningham, John. John Burningham's Number Play Series: A Great New Concept in Teaching Math! Incl. Pigs Plus: Learning Addition; Ride Off: Learning Subtraction; Read One: Numbers as Words; Five Down: Numbers as Signs; Count Up: Learning Sets; Just Cats: Learning Groups. Penguin USA.
Burnley, Ian & Forrest, James, eds. Living in Cities: Urbanism & Society in Metropolitan Australia.
Burns, Ailsa & Bottomley, Gill, eds. The Family in the Modern World.
Burns, C. L. Elvis Aaron Presley.
Burns, D. T. & Townshend, A. Inorganic Reaction Chemistry: Reactions of the Elements & Their Compounds. Carter, A. H., ed.
Burns, D. T., et al. Inorganic Reaction Chemistry: Systematic Chemical Separation.
Burns, David & Mars, Gerald. Castlemilk: Family, Community & Unemployment.
Burns, David C., jt. auth. see Holmes, Arthur W.
Burns, Diane & Venit, S. Using PageMaker on the IBM.
--Using Ventura Publisher.
Burns, Diane, jt. auth. see Venit, Sharyn.
Burns, E. Bradford. A History of Brazil.
Burns, Edward, ed. see Stein, Gertrude.
Burns, Edward M. Western Civilizations.
Burns, Edward M. & Ralph, Philip L. World Civilizations.
Burns, Eveline M. Social Welfare in the Nineteen Eighties & Beyond.
Burns, George. Dear George: Advice & Answers from America's Leading Expert on Everything from A to B.
--Dear George: Advice & Answers from America's Leading Expert on Everything from A to B.
--Dr. Burns' Prescription for Happiness.
--How to Live to Be One Hundred - or More: The Ultimate Diet, Sex & Exercise Book.
Burns, George W. Plant Kingdom.
Burns, Gerald. Introduction to Group Theory with Applications.
Burns, Henry. Corrections: Organization & Administration.
Burns, J., et al, eds. The Food Industry: Economics & Policies.
Burns, J. Patout, ed. see Helgeland, John & Daly, Robert J.
Burns, James M. Edward Kennedy & the Camelot Legacy.
--The Power to Lead: The Crisis of the American Presidency.
--Presidental Government: The Crucible of Leadership.
--Roosevelt: The Lion & the Fox.
--Roosevelt: The Lion & the Fox. Bd. with Roosevelt: The Soldier of Freedom. HarBraceJ.
--Roosevelt: The Soldier of Freedom.
Burns, James M., et al. Government by the People. Incl. National, State, Local; Basic; National. P-H.
--Government by the People: Basic.
--Government by the People: Basic.
--Government by the People: National.
--Government by the People: National, State & Local.
--Government by the People: National, State, Local.
Burns, James R. & Austin, Larry M. Management Science Models & the Microcomputer.
Burns, James R., jt. auth. see Austin, Larry M.
Burns, John H. The Gallery.
Burns, LaMont. Down Home Southern Cooking.
Burns, Linda A. & Mancino, Douglas M. Joint Ventures Between Hospitals & Physicians: A Competitive Strategy for the Healthcare Marketplace.
Burns, Marilyn. The Hink Pink Book.
Burns, Nancy. Nursing & Cancer.
Burns, Norman T. Christian Mortalism from Tyndale to Milton.
Burns, Paul C. & Bassett, Randall K. Language Arts Activities for Elementary Schools.
Burns, Paul C. & Broman, Betty L. The Language Arts in Childhood Education.
Burns, Paul C. & Roe, Betty D. Informal Reading Assessment.
--Teaching Reading in Today's Elementary Schools.
Burns, R. M., ed. One Country or Two?
Burns, Richard C., jt. auth. see Cohen, Stephen.
Burns, Richard D. & Leitenberg, Milton. The Wars in Vietnam, Cambodia & Laos, 1945-1982: A Bibliographic Guide.
Burns, Robert D. & Stiles, Karl A. Laboratory Explorations in General Zoology.
Burns, Robert E. The Shape & Form of Puget Sound.
Burns, Robert W., Jr. & Hasty, Ronald W. A Survey of User Attitudes Toward Selected Services Offered by the Colorado State University Libraries.
Burns, Ruby. Josephine Clardy Fox.
Burns, Shannon, et al. An Annotated Bibliography of Texts on Writing Skills: Grammar, Composition, Rhetoric, Technical Writing.
Burns, Sheila, pseud. Bridal Sweet.
Burns, Sheila L. Cancer: Understanding & Fighting It. Anderson, Madelyn K., ed.
Burns, Shelia L. Allergies & You.
Burns, T. J. & Hendrickson, Harvey S. The Accounting Sampler.
Burns, Tom & Stalker, G. M. Management of Innovation.
Burns, William. Your Future in Museums.
Burnside, C. D. Electromagnetic Distance Measurement: Aspects of Modern Land Surveying.
Burnside, Irene M. Psychosocial Nursing Care of the Aged.
Burny, F., et al, eds. Electrical Stimulation of Bone Growth & Repair.
Buronson & Hara, Tetsuo. Fist of the North Star. Horibuchi, Seiji, ed. Fujii, Satoru & Burke, Fred, trs.
--Fist of the North Star. Horibuchi, Seiji, ed. Fujii, Satoru & Burke, Fred, trs.
--Fist of the North Star. Horibuchi, Seiji, ed. Fujii, Satoru & Burke, Fred, trs.
--Fist of the North Star. Horibuchi, Seiji, ed. Fujii, Satoru & Burke, Fred, trs.
Burov, Michael, tr. see Bogolepov, N. N.
Burr, Allston, ed. Sir Walter Scott, an Index, Placing the Short Poems in His Novels & His Long Poems & Dramas.
Burr, Samuel E., Jr. Colonel Aaron Burr, the American Phoenix.
Burra, Edward. Well, Dearie! The Letters of Edward Burra. Chappell, William, ed.
Burrage, Henry S., ed. Early English & French Voyages, Fifteen Thirty-Four to Sixteen Eight, Chiefly from Hakluyt.
Burr Carter, Jane. Greek Ivory-Carving in the Orientalizing & Archaic Periods. Freedberg, S. J., ed.
Burrell, Berkeley G., jt. auth. see Seder, John.
Burrell, David B. Knowing the Unknowable God: Ibn-Sina, Maimonides, Aquinas.
Burrell, Jill & Burrell, Maurice. Arctic Mission.
Burrell, Joseph T. Clouds over Israel.
Burrell, Lenette O. & Burrell, Zeb L., Jr. Critical Care.
Burrell, M. C. & Wright, J. S. Today's Sects.
Burrell, Maurice, jt. auth. see Burrell, Jill.
Burrell, Maurice C. The Challenge of the Cults.
Burrell, O. K. Gold in the Woodpile: An Informal History of Banking in Oregon.
Burrell, R. M. & Cottrell, Alvin J. Politics, Oil & the Western Mediterranean.
Burrell, W. Teacher Education at Salve Regina College.
Burrell, Zeb L., Jr., jt. auth. see Burrell, Lenette O.
Burridge, Kenelm O. Encountering Aborigines, a Case Study: Anthropology & the Australian Aboriginal.
Burrill, Harry & Crist, Raymond F. Report on Trade Conditions in China.
Burrington, Gillian. How to Find Out about Statistics.
--How to Find Out about the Social Sciences.
Burris, Joanna. Basic Mathematics: An Individualized Approach.
Burron, Arnold H. Discipline That Can't Fail.
Burros, Marian. Keep It Simple.
--Pure & Simple.
--You've Got It Made: Make-Ahead Meals for the Family & for Cooperative Dinner Parties.
Burroughs. The Adding Machine.
Burroughs, Barkham. Barkham Burroughs' Encyclopaedia of Astounding Facts & Useful Information 1889-1986 Date Book. Burroughs, Miggs, ed.
Burroughs, Edgar Rice. John Carter of Mars.
--Lad & the Lion.
Burroughs, Jean M. Children of Destiny.
Burroughs, Miggs, ed. see Burroughs, Barkham.
Burroughs, William S. Cities of the Red Night.
--The Job: Interviews by Daniel Odier.
--The Last Words of Dutch Schultz.
--Naked Lunch.
--The Place of Dead Roads.
--Soft Machine.
--The Third Mind.
--Ticket That Exploded.
--The Ticket That Exploded.
Burrow. Science & Man's Behavior.
Burrow, Martha G. Developing Women Managers: What Needs to Be Done?
Burrowes, Sharon & Burrowes, Ted. Improving CAI in BASIC.
Burrowes, Ted, jt. auth. see Burrowes, Sharon.
Burrows, Edwin G. Hawaiian Americans: An Account of the Mingling of Japanese, Chinese, Polynesian, & American Cultures.
Burrows, Graham D. & Norman, Trevor R., eds. Psychotropic Drugs: Plasma Concentration & Clinical Response.
Burrows, Marjorie & Ramancese, Avan. The Winter Hearts.
Burrows, Stephen G. God's Daughter in Nassau.
--Responsible Parenting among Men & Nations: A Challenge for Uncle Sam & the World.
Burrows, Stephen G. E. That's the Lawyer.
Burrows, William E. Richthofen: A True History of the Red Baron.
--Vigilante.
Burrows, William R. & Hedrick, Hannah H., eds. Allied Health Education Directory.
Bursch, J. H., jt. ed. see Heintzen, Paul H.
Bursell, F. Introduction to Insect Physiology.
Bursian, Konrad. Geschichte der Classischen Philologie in Deutschland Von Den Anfangen Bis Zur Gegenwart.
Bursk, Edward C. & Grayser, Stephen A. Advanced Cases in Marketing Management.
Bursky, Dave. The S-One Hundred Bus Handbook.
Burson, Nancy, et al. Composites: Computer-Generated Portraits.
Burst, Jess, jt. auth. see Segal, Hillel.
Burstein. The Get Well Hotel.
Burstein, Chaya. The Jewish Kids Catalog.
--Rifka Bangs the Teakettle.
Burstein, Chaya M. Joseph & Anna's Time Capsule: A Legacy of Old Jewish Prague.
Burstein, Joel V. State of New York Law Revision Committee Reports, 1954-1956.
Burstein, John. Slim Goodbody: The Inside Story.
--Slim Goodbody's Healthy Days Diary: Activity Book.
Burstein, Leigh, jt. ed. see Roberts, Karlene H.
Burstein, Nancy. The Executive Body: A Complete Guide to Fitness & Stress Management for the Working Woman.
--Soft Aerobics: The New Low-Impact Workout for Injury Free Exercise.
Burstinger, Irving. Run Your Own Retail Store: From Raising the Money to Counting the Profits.
--Small Business Handbook: Comprehensive Guide to Starting & Running Your Own Business.
Burt, et al, eds. Viewpoints on English As a Second Language.
Burt, Daniel S., jt. auth. see Bader, William.
Burt, Deanne Davila. Sorry So Sloppy: A Teacher's Portfolio.
Burt, John J. & Meeks, Linda B. Education for Sexuality: Concepts & Programs for Teaching.
Burt, John J., et al. Toward a Healthy Lifestyle: Through Elementary Health Education.
Burt, Marina K. & Kiparsky, Carol. The Gooficon: A Repair Manual for English.
Burt, R. A. British Cruisers in World War One.
--British Destroyers in World War II.
Burt, R. A., jt. auth. see Trotter, W. P.
Burt, Rob. Surf City-Drag City.
Burtchaell, James, ed. Abortion Parley.
Burtchaell, James T., et al. Marriage among Christians: A Curious Tradition.
Burtenshaw, D. & Ashworth, G. J. The City in West Europe.
Burthogge, Richard. The Philosophical Writings of Richard Burthogge. Landes, Margaret W., ed.
Burtle, James L., jt. auth. see Rolfe, Sidney E.
Burtness, James. Shaping the Future: The Ethics of Dietrich Bonhoeffer.
Burtness, James H. Whatever You Do: An Essay in Christian Ethics.
Burton. Introducing Microcom.
Burton, A. S. Alcohols with Water. Barton, A. F., ed.
Burton, Anthony. Embrace of the Butcher.
--Wilderness Britain.
Burton, Arthur. Interpersonal Psychotherapy.
Burton, Betty. Jude.
Burton, Bob. Top Secret: A Clandestine Operator's Glossary of Terms.
Burton, Deirdre. Dialogue & Discourse: A Socio-Linguistic Approach to Modern Drama Dialogue & Naturally-Occurring Conversation.
--Dialogue & Discourse: A Sociolinguistic Approach to Modern Drama, Dialogue, & Naturally Occuring Conversation.
Burton, Dolores M. Shakespeare's Grammatical Style: A Computer-Assisted Analysis of "Richard II" & "Antony & Cleopatra"
Burton, Dwight L., et al. Teaching English Today.
Burton, E. Milby. Charleston Furniture, Seventeen Hundred to Eighteen Twenty-Five.
Burton, Elsie C. The New Physical Education for Elementary School Children.
Burton, Ernest J. The British Theatre: It's Repertory & Practice, 1100-1900 A.D.
Burton, Gabrielle. Heartbreak Hotel: A Novel.
--I'm Running Away from Home, but I'm Not Allowed to Cross the Street.
Burton, John, et al. Britain Between East & West: A Concerned Independence.
Burton, John A. Gold Mining in the American West.
Burton, John C. A Revised Financial Reporting Model for Municipalities.
Burton, John F. Interstate Variations in Employers' Cost of Workmen's Compensation: Effect on Plant Location Exemplified in Michigan.
Burton, John W., jt. ed. see Azar, Edward E.
Burton, Lindy, ed. Care of the Child Facing Death.
Burton, Mary E., ed. see Wordsworth, Mary.
Burton, Maurice. The Sixth Sense of Animals.
Burton, Nelson, Jr. Bowling. Levine, Jerry, ed.
Burton, Philip E. A Dictionary of Word Processing & Printers.
Burton, Rebecca. The Loving Season.
Burton, Robert A., et al. Key Issues in Health.
Burton, Robert E. Democrats of Oregon: The Pattern of Minority Politics, 1900-1956.
Burton, Sarah K. & Short, Douglas D. Sixth International Conference on Computers & the Humanities.
Burton, T. A., ed. Mathematical Biology-a Conference on Theoretical Aspects of Molecular Science: Proceedings of a Conference Held at Southern Illinois University at Carbondale, May 27-28, 1980.
Burton, Ursula & Dolley, Janice. Christian Evolution.
Burton, Virginia L. Life Story.
--Maybelle, the Cable Car.
Burton, W. R. & Hasslam, C. J. Nuclear Power, Pollution, & Politics.
Burton, William F. Where to Go with Your Troubles.
Burton, William H., jt. auth. see Blair, Arthur W.
Burton, Wilma. Sidewalk Psalms... & Some from Country Lanes.
--Without a Man in the House.
Burtt, J. Douglas. Senseless.
Buru, Mukhtar, et al. Planning & Development in Modern Libya.
Burum, Linda. The Junk Food Alternative.
Burwash, Peter & Tullius, John. Vegetarian Primer.

Authors

Burwell, Robert L., Jr. Manual of Symbols & Terminology for Physicochemical Quantities & Units: Part 2 - Heterogeneous Catalysis.
Bury, J. B., et al. Hellenistic Age.
Bury, Shirley. Wendy Ramshaw.
Burzynski, Norbert J. see Melnick, Michael.
Busby, Robert C., jt. auth. see Kolman, Bernard.
Busby, Trent. Be Good to Your Body.
Buscaglia, Leo F. Living, Loving & Learning.
--The Way of the Bull.
Busch & Wilkie Brothers Foundation Staff. Fundamentals of Dimensional Metrology.
Busch, Arthur W. Aerobic Biological Treatment of Waste Waters.
Busch, Betty J. The Simple Joys of Womanhood.
Busch, Briton C. Hardinge of Penshurst: A Study in the Old Diplomacy.
Busch, David. Teach Your TRS-80 to Program Itself.
Busch, David D. Apple Soft Subroutine Cookbook.
--Blast off with BASIC Games for Your Commodore 64.
--Inside Secrets of Wordstar 2000 & 2000 Plus.
--Secrets of MacWrite, MacPaint, & MacDraw.
--TRS-80 Portable Computer Subroutine Cookbook.
Busch, Eberhard. Karl Barth: His Life from Letters & Autobiographical Texts. Bowden, John, tr. from Ger.
Busch, Frederick. Rounds.
Busch, G. & Schade, D. Lectures on Solid State Physics.
Busch, Gunter, ed. see Modersohn-Becker, Paula.
Busch, Harris. Histones & Other Nuclear Proteins.
--The Molecular Biology of Cancer.
Busch, Harris & Smetana, Karel, eds. Nucleolus.
Busch, Harris, et al, eds. Effects of Drugs on the Cell Nucleus: Bristol-Meyers Cancer Symposia.
Busch, Kenneth W., jt. auth. see Kenner, Charles T.
Busch, Phyllis S. Wildflowers & the Stories Behind Their Names.
Busche, Don & Locke, Flora M. College Mathematics for Business & Workbook to Accompany: College Mathematics Ser.
Buschman, Al see Kalil, Ford.
Buser, Robert L., jt. auth. see Gholson, Ronald E.
Busev, A. I., et al. Chemistry: Definitions, Notions, Terminology.
Bush, Barbara. Walking in Wisdom: A Woman's Workshop on Ecclesiastes.
Bush, Bernard J., ed. Coping: Issues of Emotional Living in an Age of Stress for Clergy & Religious.
Bush, Catharine S. Communicards.
--Communicards II: Synonyms & Concepts Set.
--Language Remediation & Expansion: One Hundred Skill-Building Reference Lists.
--Teachers' Treasury of Useful Lists & Facts.
Bush, Douglas. Mythology & the Renaissance Tradition in English Poetry.
Bush, Duncan. SALT.
Bush, George. Notes on Leviticus.
Bush, Gregory. Campaign Speeches of American Presidential Candidates, 1948-1984.
Bush, I. E., et al. The Chromatography of Steroids.
Bush, Lewis. Japan Dictionary.
Bush, Marcella. The Community of God.
Bush, Richard C. The Politics of Cotton Textiles in Kuomintang China, 1927-1937: China During the Interregnum 1911-1949, the Economy & Society. Myers, Ramon H., ed.
Bush, Russ & Nettles, Tom. Baptists & the Bible.
Bush, Virginia. The Colossal Sculpture of the Cinquecento.
Bush-Brown, Albert & Grube, Oswald W. Skidmore, Owings & Merrill: Architecture & Urbanism 1973-1983.
Bushe-Fox, Joscelyn P. Fourth Report on the Excavation of the Roman Fort at Richborough, Kent.
Bushell, Chris & Stonham, Peter, eds. Jane's Urban Transport Systems, 1986.
Bushell, Garry, et al. Ozzy Osbourne: Diary of a Madman.
Bushell, Peter. London's Secret History.
Bushey, Jerry. The Barge Book.
Bushkovitch, Paul, jt. ed. see Banac, Ivo.
Bushman, J. A., jt. ed. see Payne, J. P.
Bushman, Richard L. Joseph Smith & the Beginning of Mormonism.
Bushman, Richard L., ed. The Great Awakening: Documents on the Revival of Religion, 1740-1745.
--The Great Awakening: Documents on the Revival of Religion, 1740-1745.
Bushnaq, Inea, tr. see Jiryis, Sabri.
Bushong, Stewart C. Radiologic Science for Technologists: Physics, Biology, & Protection.
Bushrui, S., ed. Essays & Studies, 1982.
Busi, Aldo. The Ordinary Life of a Temporary Pantyhose Salesman. Rosenthal, Raymond, tr.
Business Communications Staff. Advanced Composites.
--Artificial Intelligence.
--Barrier Coextruded Plastic Systems: Markets, Developments, Technologies.
--Biocompatible Products for Humans.
--Biopolymers.
--Biotechnology in Food.
--Chemicals for the Military.
--Commercial Opportunities in Electrochemistry.
--Dairy Industry & Dairy Packaging.
--Drug Delivery Systems.
--Emerging Local Area Network Business.
--The Expanding Plastic Bag Market.
--Futures for Natural Non-Chemical Pest Control.
--Growth Opportunities in Wire, Cable & Fiber Optics: G-070.
--High Tech Filtration.
--Industrial Organic Coatings: Update.
--Inorganic Polymers.
--Large Food & Selected Non-Food Containers.
--Laser Industry.
--Material Requirements for Fiber Optics.
--Material Requirements for Fiber Optics.
--Medical Diagnostic Kits & Products.
--Printed Circuit Board Industry: A Strategic Analysis.
--Rapidly-Solidified Amorphous Materials.
--Restaurant & Institutional Food Service Industry.
--Specialty & Hi Performance Fiber: Update.
--Substrates & Supports for Separations & Immobilizations.
--Technology for Management of Hazardous Waste.
--The U. S. Battery Industry.
Business Research Division Staff & U. S. Travel Data Center Staff. Tourism's Top Twenty.
Business Week Magazine Staff. The Decline of U. S. Power & What We Can Do about It.
--The Reindustrialization of America.
Businger, Joost A., ed. see Dalrymple, Paul, et al.
Busk, Fred & Andrews, Peter. Country Inns of America: Pacific Northwest.
Buske, Frank, ed. see Muir, John.
Buske, Terry & Weschcke, Carl L., eds. Llewellyn's Moon Sign Book, 1984.
Buske, Terry, ed. see Llewellyn Publications Staff.
Buskin, John & Gingold, Alfred. Dr. Booboo's Baby & Child Repair.
Buskirk, Bruce, jt. auth. see Buskirk, Richard H.
Buskirk, Phyllis, jt. auth. see Ford, Katherine.
Buskirk, Richard H. & Buskirk, Bruce. Retailing.
Busman, Gloria. Union Representative's Guide to NLRB RC & CA Cases.
Busoni, Ferruccio. Essence of Music & Other Papers.
Busrewil, M. T., jt. ed. see Salem, M. J.
Buss, Allan R. A Dialectical Psychology.
Buss, Allan R., ed. Psychology in Social Context.
Buss, C. A. China: The People's Republic of China & Richard Nixon.
Buss, Martin J., et al, eds. Encounter with the Text: Form & History in the Hebrew Bible.
Bussabarger, Robert F. & Robins, Betty D. Everyday Art of India.
Bussard, Paul. How to Get Ready to Sleep, How to Get Ready for Surgery, & How to Get Ready to Die: A Thanatology.
Busse, Ewald W. & Blazer, Dan G., eds. Handbook of Geriatric Psychiatry.
Bussell, Harold. Lord, I Can Resist Anything but Temptation.
Busselle, Michael. The Manual of Male Photography.
--The Wine Lover's Guide to France.
Busselle, Michelle. Beyond Glamour: A Guide to Nude Photography.
Bussink, Willem & Davies, David. Poverty & the Development of Human Resources: Regional Perspective.
Bussmann, W. D., jt. ed. see Just, H.
Bustad, Leo K. Animals, Aging, & the Aged.
Bustanoby, Andre. Being a Success at Who You Are.
--Eight Keys to Communicate Better.
Bustanoby, Andre & Bustanoby, Fay. Just Talk to Me: Talking & Listening for a Happier Marriage.
Bustanoby, Fay, jt. auth. see Bustanoby, Andre.
Busteed, H. E. Echoes from Old Calcutta.
Busto, M. Pequeno Diccionario Tecnologico: Farmacia, Quimica, Fisica, Medicina y Ciencias Naturales.
Buswell, G., tr. see Marxsen, Willi.
Buswell, Guy T. Teaching of Arithmetic.
Buswell, J. Oliver, Jr. The Philosophies of F. R. Tenant & John Dewey.
Busza, Andrzej. Astrologer in the Underground. Boraks, Jagna & Bullock, Micheal, trs. from Pol. & Eng.
Butah, Jon, jt. auth. see Grant, Charles W.
Butcher, D. G. & Parnell, A. C. Smoke Control in Fire Safety Design.
Butcher, E. G. & Parnell, A. C. Designing for Fire Safety.
Butcher, F., et al, eds. Electrical Maintenance & Installation: Part One.
Butcher, Grace. Before I Go Out on the Road.
Butcher, James N., jt. auth. see Coleman, James C.
Butcher, Julia. The Sheep & the Rowan Tree.
Butcher, Larry L., ed. Cholinergic-Monoaminergic Interactions in the Brain.
Butcher, Phillip A., ed. see Wiener, Harvey S.
Butcher, Samuel S. & Charlson, Robert J. Introduction to Air Chemistry.
Butel-Dumont, Georges M. Histoire et Commerce des Colonies Angloises Dans L'amerique Septentrionale, (Londres, 1755)
Buten, Howard. Burt. Marks, Bobbi, ed.
Butenko, A. P. Consolidation of the Socialist Countries' Unity.
Butigan, Ken, jt. ed. see Joranson, Philip N.
Butler & Rosenthal. Behavior & Rehabilitation.
Butler, Alan, ed. Aging: Recent Advances & Creative Responses.
Butler, Barbara M. The Evolution of the Black Nurse Midwife.
Butler, C. S. Test the Spirits.
Butler, C. V. Domestic Service.
Butler, Charles. Principles of Musik, in Singing & Setting.
Butler, Chester. Our Legacy from Ma & Pa.
Butler, David. The Fall of Saigon: Scenes from the Sudden End of a Long War.
--The Men Who Mastered Time.
Butler, Diane. Futurework.
Butler, Dorothy. Babies Need Books.
--Babies Need Books: How Books Can Help Your Child Become a Happy & Involved Human Being.
Butler, E. M. Heinrich Heine: A Biography.
Butler, E. W. Urban Sociology.
Butler, Eliza M. Heinrich Heine: A Biography.
Butler, Eugenia, et al. Correct Writing, Form Two.
--An Auto-Instructional Text in Correct Writing.
Butler, F. Donald. The Plymouth & De Soto Story. Dammann, George H., ed.
Butler, Francelia, et al, eds. Children's Literature. Brockman, Bennett & Sheidley, William E. Incl. Vol. 1; Vol. 2; Vol. 3; Vol. 4; Vol. 5; Vol. 6. Temple U Pr.
Butler, Francine. Biofeedback: A Survey of the Literature.
Butler, George & Gaines, Charles. Charles Atlas Yours in Perfect Manhood.
Butler, George, jt. auth. see Gaines, Charles.
Butler, George V., et al, eds. Working in Space, AAS5.
Butler, Ivan. Choosing a Play for Your Amateur Group.
Butler, Jan, tr. see Kuzmenko, Yuri.
Butler, Jerry. Swift to Hear, Slow to Speak.
Butler, Jerry W. Wayward Splendor.
Butler, John R. Who Goes Home?
Butler, Johnnella E. Black Studies: Pedagogy & Revolution; A Study of Afro-American Studies & the Liberal Arts Tradition through the Discipline of Afro-American Literature.
Butler, Joseph T. Van Cortlandt Manor.
Butler, Katherine G. & Wallach, Geraldine P. Language Disorders & Learning Disabilities, Topics in Language Disorders.
Butler, Lucy. Diana: The Fairy Tale Princess.
Butler, M. C. Esperanto-English.
Butler, Marian, ed. Canadian Books in Print 1987.
Butler, Mary M. Hrotsvitha: The Theatricality of Her Lays.
Butler, Octavia E. Patternmaster.
Butler, Orton C. An Introductory Soils Laboratory Handbook.
Butler, R. & Rosenthal, G. Behaviour & Rehabilitation.
Butler, Robert N. & Lewis, Myrna I. Aging & Mental Health.
Butler, Ron. Best of the West: The Texas Monthly Guidebook. Rodriquez, Barbara, ed.
Butler, Ruth M. Social Functioning Framework: An Approach to the Human Behavior & Social Environment Sequence.
Butler, Samuel. Characters & Passages from Notebooks.
--The Fair Haven: A Work in Defence of the Miraculous Element in Our Lord's Ministry Upon Earth. Wolff, Robert L., ed.
Butler, T. G., jt. ed. see Kana, D. D.
Butler, William, et al. Methods & Techniques of Business Forecasting.
Butlin, J., jt. auth. see Lidgren, K.
Butlin, L., et al, eds. Numerically Controlled or Special Purpose Machining I.
Butlin, Martin & Joll, Evelyn. The Paintings of J. M. W. Turner.
Butlin, R. A., jt. ed. see Dodgshon, R. A.
Butlin, S. Foundations of the Australian Monetary System, 1788-1851.
Butnarescu, Glenda F. & Tillotson, Delight M. Maternity Nursing: Theory to Practice.
Butor, Michel. La Banlieue de Paris a l'Aurore, Mouvement Brownien.
--Bryen en Temps Conjuges.
--Carte Commentee.
--Une Chanson Pour Don Juan.
--Description de San Marco.
--Dialogue avec Trente Trais Variations de Ludwig van Beethoven sur une Valse de Diabelli.
--Entretiens avec Georges Charbonnier.
--Essais sur le Roman.
--Essais sur les Essais.
--Essais sur les Modernes.
--Le Genie du Lieu, II.
--Herold.
--Matiere des Reves.
--Mobile.
--L' Oeil Ces Sangasses.
--Les Petits Miroirs.
--Portraits de L'artiste en Jeune Singe.
--Repertoire: Essais Critiques.
--Reseau Aerien.
--Les Sept Femmes de Gilbert le Mauvais.
--Six-Million Huit-Cent Dix Mille Litres D'eau Par Seconde.
Butowsky, Harry A. Warships Associated with World War 2 in the Pacific.
Butrym, Zofia. Medical Social Work in Action.
Butrym, Zofia & Horder, John. Health, Doctors, & Social Workers.
Butsch, Charlotte. Electronic Calculator: Student Guide.
--The Printing Calculator: Student Guide.
Butt, Howard. The Velvet Covered Brick.
Butt, John & Tillotson, Kathleen. Dickens at Work.
Butt, John E., jt. auth. see Dyson, Henry V.
Butterfield, B. G. & Meylan, B. Three-Dimensional Structure of Wood.
Butterfield, Lyman H., et al, eds. Diary of Charles Francis Adams: January 1820-September 1829.
--Adams Family Correspondence: December 1761-March 1778.
--The Diary & Autobiography of John Adams.
--Legal Papers of John Adams.
Butterfield, R., jt. auth. see Banerjee, P. K.
Butterfiled, Jan, ed. see Selz, Peter.
Butterick, George, ed. Charles Olson: Man & Poet.
Butterick, George F., jt. auth. see Allen, Donald.
Butterick, George F., jt. ed. see Allen, Donald M.
Butters, N. Selected Readings in Neuropsychology.
Butters, Roger. First Person Singular: A Review of the Life & Work of Mr. Sherlock Holmes, the Worlds First Consulting Detective.
Butterworth, Bill. My Kids are My Best Teachers.
Butterworth, Bill & Nix, John. Farm Mechanization for Profit.
Butterworth, C. E., Jr., jt. auth. see Weinsier, Roland L.
Butterworth, Charles A. & Skidmore, David. Caring for the Mentally Ill in the Community.
Butterworth Company of Cape Cod, Inc. Staff. Cape Cod & Islands Atlas & Guide Book.
Butterworth Editorial Staff. Dunnell Minnesota Digest.
Butterworth, F. Edward. Roots of the Reorganization: French Polynesia.
--Secrets of the Mighty Sioux.
--Sword of Laban.
Butterworth, John. Debt Collection Letters in Ten Languages.
Butterworth, Keen & Kibler, James E., Jr. William Gilmore Simms: A Reference Guide.
Butterworth, Michael. The Five Million Dollar Prince.
Butterworth, Vida. The Girls in White.
Butterworth, William E. Leroy & the Old Man.
--A Member of the Family.
Buttinger, Joseph. Manko of Mankoland. Incl. Vol. 1. The Adventures of Young & Impressionable Manko As He Meets His Jungle Friends; Vol. 2. Further Adventures of Manko-Delights & Frights; Vol. 3. Manko Goes to New York & Becomes Famous. Exposition-Phoenix.
Buttner, Horst & Meissner, Gunter. Town Houses of Europe.
Buttner, Marguerite E. Search for Neotiques - Values to Shape the Future.
Button, John. Making Love Work.
Buttress, F. A., ed. World Guide to Abbreviations of Organizations.
Buttrey, T. V. & Hubbard, Clyde. Guide Book of Mexican Coins Eighteen Twenty-Two to date.
--A Guide Book of Mexican Coins, 1822 to Date.
Buttrick, David. Epiphany.
Buttrick, David, jt. auth. see Juel, Donald H.
Buttrick, George A. Prayer in Life: Life in Prayer.
Butts, D. P. A Summary of Research in Science Education 1979.
Butts, M., ed. see Linker, Robert.
Butturff, Diane & Coffman, Mary E. French: Language & Life Styles.
Butwill, N., jt. auth. see Brown, James R.
Butzer, P. L. & Berens, H. Semi-Groups of Operators & Approximation.
Buurman, Peter, ed. Podzols: Temperate Regions.
Buxbaum, Martin. The Unsung.
Buxbaum, Susan K., jt. auth. see Gelman, Rita G.

Authors

Buxton, Barry. The Sustainable Society: Implications for Limited Growth.
Buxton, Charles R., ed. Towards a Lasting Settlement.
Buxton, Frank & Owen, Bill. The Big Broadcast 1920-1950.
Buxton, I. L., et al. Cargo Access Equipment for Merchant Ships.
Buyers, Rebecca. The Marvelous Macadamia Nut.
Buytendijk, F. J. Prologomena to an Anthropological Physiology.
Buzacott, J. A., et al, eds. Scale in Production Systems: Based on an IIASA Workshop June 26-29, 1979.
Buzan, Barbara, ed. see Foundation Center Staff.
Buzby, Walter J. & Paine, David. Hotel & Motel Security Management.
Buzuev, V. & Gorodnov, V. Que es el Marxismo-Leninismo?
Buzzacott & Wymore. Bi-Sexual Man or Evolution of the Sexes.
Buzzacott, Francis H. The Mystery of the Sexes.
Buzzard, Lynn & Ericcson, Samuel. The Battle for Religious Liberty.
Buzzard, Lynn R. Lawyers' Quest III: Vocation, Work & Calling.
Buzzard, Lynn R. & Eck, Laurence. Tell It to the Church.
Byars, Betsy. After the Goat Man.
--Betsy Byars Boxed Set.
--The Eighteenth Emergency.
--The Midnight Fox.
--Rama, the Gypsy Cat.
--The Summer of the Swans.
--Trouble River.
Byars, Lloyd L., jt. auth. see Rue, Leslie W.
Byars, Lloyd L., et al. Readings & Cases in Personnel Management.
Byatt, Antonia. Still Life.
Bycott, James F. & Gladding, Nicholas C. Superfund Environmental Liability Update.
Bye, Ranulph. Vanishing Depot.
Bye, Ranulph & Richie, Margaret B. Victorian Sketchbook.
Byer, Trevor A., jt. auth. see Fallen-Bailey, Darrel G.
Byerke & Sorass, eds. English-Norwegian Dictionary: Norweigian Dictionary.
Byerly, Greg. Online Searching: A Dictionary & Bibliographic Guide.
Byerly, Greg & Rubin, Rick. Pornography: The Conflict over Sexually Explicit Materials in the United States. An Annotated Bibliography.
Byers, Carolyn. Mary Andrews: Companion of Sorrow. Wheeler, Gerald, ed.
Byers, Edward E. Ten Thousand Medical Words.
Byers, Edward E., ed. see Rosenberg, R. Robert, et al.
Byers, John R., Jr. & Owen, James J. A Concordance to the Five Novels of Nathaniel Hawthorne.
Byers, R. A. The DBASE II for Every Business.
--The DBASE III for Every Business.
--The dBASE III for Every Business.
--Everyman's Data Base Primer Featuring dBASE III Plus.
--Everyman's Database Primer Featuring dBASE III.
--Introduction to UNIX System V.
Byers, Robert A. The DBASE III for Every Business.
--Everyman's Database Primer: Featuring dBASE III.
Byfield, Brian & Orpin, Alan. Every Great Chess Player Was Once a Beginner.
Byington, Steven, tr. see Stirner, Max.
Bykov, O. Creating a Climate of Confidence.
Bykov, Vasil. His Battalion & Live until Dawn: Contemporary Russian Writing. Woodhouse, Jennifer & Woodhouse, Robert, trs.
Bylander, Tom, jt. auth. see Chandrasekaran, B.
Bylinsky, Gene. Mood Control.
Bynon, James, ed. see Colloquium of Linguistics Association of Great Britain, Historical Section, University of London Staff.
Bynon, Theodora, ed. see Colloquium of Linguistics Association of Great Britain, Historical Section, University of London Staff.
Bynum, Curtis. Marriage Bonds of Tryon & Lincoln Counties, North Carolina.
Byram, J. E., ed. see Arme, C., et al.
Byram, Michael, jt. ed. see Goodings, Richard.
Byrd & Horton. Keeping Your Balance.
Byrd, Anne. Omelettes & Souffles. Rich, Irene, ed.
Byrd, Cecil K. The Pacific Northwest, 1542-1846.
Byrd, D. H. I'm an Endangered Species: The Autobiography of a Free Enterpriser.
Byrd, Elizabeth. The Famished Land.
--Rest Without Peace.
--The Search for Maggie Hare.
Byrd, Harold E. The Black Experience in Big Business.
Byrd, Jay. Huey Lewis & the News.
--Ratt.
Byrd, P. F. & Friedman, M. D. Handbook of Elliptic Integrals for Engineers & Scientists.
Byrd, Richard E. Discovery: The Story of the Second Byrd Antarctic Expedition.
--A Guide to Personal Risk Taking.
Byrd, Walter, jt. auth. see Hindson, Edward.
Byrd, William see Buck, P. C. & Fellowes, E. H.
Byrd, William, et al. Gradualia. Buck, P. C., ed.
--The Fitzwilliam Virginal Book. Maitland, J. A. & Squire, W. B., eds.
Byrde, R. J. & Willetts, H. J. Brown Rot Fungi of Fruit: Their Biology & Control.
Byrde, R. J., ed. see Long Ashton Research Station Symposium Staff.
Byrivers, Patricia. Goodbye to Arthritis.
Byrkit. Elements of Business Statistics.
Byrn, Anne. Dining in Atlanta. Hosner, Shiela, ed.
Byrne, Catherine A., jt. ed. see Singler, Robert E.
Byrne, Donn, jt. auth. see Baron, Robert A.
Byrne, Dymphna. Israel & the Holy Land.
Byrne, Jim. The One Dollar League.
Byrne, John. Cuttin' a Rug.
--The Slab Boys.
Byrne, John see Milne, John.
Byrne, John & Rich, Daniel, eds. Technology & Energy Choice.
Byrne, John E., intro. by. Codification of Presidential Proclamations & Executive Orders, Jan. 20, 1961-Jan. 20, 1985.
Byrne, Julia. Curiosities of the Search-Room.
Byrne, Miles. Memoirs of Miles Byrne.
Byrne, Robert. Byrne's Standard Book of Pool & Billiards.
--The Dam.
--The Other Six Hundred Thirty-Seven Best Things Anybody Ever Said.
--Skyscraper.
--The Tunnel.
Byrne, Robert & Skelton, Teressa. Cat Scan: Three Thousand Years of the Best Things Ever Said about Cats.
Byrnes, Edward T., jt. auth. see Dunn, Charles W.
Byrns, Ralph T. & Stone, Gerald W. Economics.
Byrns, Ralph T. & Stone, Gerald W. Jr. Macroeconomics.
Byrns, Ralph T. & Stone, Gerald W., Jr. Microeconomics.
Byron, Gilbert. The Lord's Oysters.
Byron, Leo C. From Tourist to Hostage: A Traveler's Tale of Terrorism. Ziegenfuss, James T., Jr., ed.
Byron, Lord see Byron, George G.
Byrt, W. J. The Australian Company: Studies in Strategy & Structure.
Bysiewicz, Shirley R. Monarch's Dictionary of Legal Terms.
Bywater, Ingram. Aristotle on the Art of Poetry.
Bywater, R. Hardware-Software Design of Digital Systems.
Bywater, William G., Jr. Clive Bell's Eye.
Byzova, N. L. Investigation of the Bottom Three Hundred Meter Layer of the Atmosphere.
Bzoch, Kenneth. Communicative Disorders Related to Cleft Lip & Palate.

C

C. A. S. D. S. Study Group on Mechanisms of Language Development, London, 1968. Language Acquisition: Models & Methods. Huxley, Renira & Ingram, Elisabeth, eds.
C & MA Home Department Board Staff. The Pastor's Handbook.
C Q Press Staff & Brams, Steven J. Rational Politics: Decisions, Games & Strategies.
C. Q. Press Staff & Conway, M. Margaret. Political Participation in the U. S.
Cabaj, Janice. The Elvis Image.
Caballero, Jane A. & Whordley, Derek. Children Around the World.
Caballero, Justo. Guia-Diccionario del Quijote.
Cabaniss, Allen, ed. Son of Charlemagne: A Contemporary Life of Louis the Pious.
Cabanne, Pierre. Van Gogh.
Cabannes, H., ed. Pade Approximants Methods & Its Applications to Mechanics.
Cabannes, H., ed. see International Conference on Numerical Methods in Fluid Mechanics, 3rd.
Cabannes, H., et al, eds. Sixth International Conference on Numerical Methods in Fluid Dynamics: Proceedings of the Conference, Tbilisi, (U. S. S. R.) June 21-24, 1978.
Cabannes, Henri. Theoretical Magnetofluid-Dynamics.
Cabat, Louis, et al. Barron's How to Prepare for the College Board Achievement Tests - French.
Cabeceiras, James. The Multimedia Library: Materials Selection & Use.
Cabestrero, Teofilo, ed. Faith: Conversations with Contemporary Theologians. Walsh, Donald D., tr. from Span.
Cable, Carole. The Architect & the Computer - Design, Office Automation, & Building Management: A Bibliography of Recent Periodical Literature.
--The Architecture & Writings of Diana Agrest & Mario Gandelsonas.
--The Architecture of Houston, Texas: A Bibliography of Articles, 1978 to 1983, An Update to Architecture Ser: Bibliography A-2.
--Atomic Bomb Shelters & Blast-Resistant Building: A Selective Bibliography of Periodical Literature.
--A Bibliography of Writings by & about Sir Reginald Theodore Bloomfield, 1856 to 1942.
--Children's Spaces: A Bibliography of Recent Periodical Literature Dealing with Environments for the Child.
--The Contemporary Pied-a-Terre: A Bibliography of Recent Periodical Literature.
--Giorgio Vasari, Architect: A Selected Bibliography of Books & Articles.
--The Gothic Cathedral in France & England: Style, Form, & Sources.
--Italian New Wave Design - Memphis & the Recent Work of Ettore Sottsass, Jr. A Bibliography.
--A Listing of Cartoons on Architectural Subjects Within Selected Anthologies, Including Brief Descriptions with Subject & Building Type Indexing.
--Periodical Scholarship on Islamic Architecture Published 1973-1983: A Bibliography.
--The Publications of William Pain, 1730 to 1790: Architect & Carpenter.
--Showroom Design in the United States: A Bibliography of Articles, 1978-1983.
--Water & Baptismal Fonts Through the Ages: A Bibliography of Scholarship Dealing with Stylistic, Design, & Iconographic Aspects.
--The Writings of Charles Jencks, Apostle, by Post-Modernism.
Cable, Carole A. Ove Arup; Ove Arup & Partners, Architects; & Arup Associates: A Bibliography of Articles.
Cable, Mary. Lost New Orleans.
Cable, Vincent. Economics & the Politics of Protection: Some Case Studies of Industries.
Cable-Alexander, June, et al. Giving A Children's Party: Planning, Ideas, Food & Games For One to Ten Year Olds.
Cabot, Cain. Assault on Fellawi.
Cabot, Thomas D. Beggar on Horseback: The Autobiography of Thomas D. Cabot.
Cabral, Amilcar. Unity & Struggle: Speeches & Writings.
Cabral, Olga. In the Empire of Ice.
Cabrera, James C., jt. auth. see Morin, William J.
Cabrera, Vicente & Boyer, Harriet, eds. Critical Views on Vicente Aleixandre's Poetry.
Cabrera, Y. Arturo & Perea, Jose A. Community College Conflict: Chicano Under Fire.
Cabrera Infante, G. View of Dawn in the Tropics. Levine, Suzanne J., tr. from Span.
Cabriel, Marcel. Philosophy of Existence.
Cacciari, E., et al, eds. Obesity in Childhood.
Caceres, C. A., ed. Biomedical Telemetry.
--Clinical Electrocardiography & Computers: A Symposium Vol.
Cachiaras, Dot. God Created Me Too!
Cadawallader, Sylvanus. Three Years with Grant: As Recalled by War Correspondent Sylvanus Cadwallader. Thomas, Benjamin P., ed.
Cadbury, Henry J., ed. see Fox, George.
Caddell, Foster. Keys to Successful Color.
Caddell, Robert M. Deformation & Fracture of Solids.
Caddy, Eileen. The Spirit of Findhorn.
Cadell, Elizabeth. The Empty Nest: A Novel of Intrigue & Romance. Williams, Jennifer, ed.
Cadez, Mary J., jt. auth. see Striefel, Sebastian.
Cadfryn-Roberts, John, ed. Old London.
Cadiou, Yves L. & Szecske, Tibor. French Foreign Legion: Nineteen-Forty to the Present.
Cadman, B. D., jt. auth. see Bryne, P.
Cadogan, George, et al. Cadogan's Crimea.
Cadoux, T., pref. by. The Sorrowful & Immaculate Heart of Mary: Message of Berthe Petit, Franciscan Tertiary (1870-1943)
Cadrain, Linda A., adapted by. The Diary of Anne Frank.
Caduto, Michael J. Pond & Brook: A Guide to Nature Study in Freshwater Environments.
Cadwallader, Sharon. Cooking Adventures for Kids.
--Whole Earth Cookbook 2.
Cadwallader, Sharon & Ohr, Judi. Whole Earth Cookbook.
Cady, Dale R. Pilot's Bahamas Aviation Guide.
Cady, Howard, ed. see Hough, Richard.
Cady, Jack. The Jonah Watch.
--The Jonah Watch: A True-Life Ghost Story in the Form of a Novel.
--McDowell's Ghost.
--The Man Who Could Make Things Vanish.
--The Well.
--The Well.
Cadzow, John F. & Ludanyi, Andrew, eds. Transylvania: The Roots of Ethnic Conflict.
Caemmerer, Richard R., Jr. Visual Art in the Life of the Church: Encouraging Creative Worship & Witness in the Congregation.
Caes, Charles. Stock Market Arithmetic: A Primer for New Investors.
Caesar, Julius. The Battle for Gaul. Wiseman, Anne & Wiseman, Peter, trs. from Lat.
Cafarelli, Eugene J. Developing New Products & Repositing Mature Brands: A Risk-Reduction System That Produces Investment Alternatives.
Cafferty. A Complete Defence to 1P-K4: A Study of Petroff's Defence.
Cafferty, Jake. Vic Merritt: Man of Justice.
Cage, John M., jt. auth. see Oliver, Bernard M.
Cage, R. A., ed. The Scots Abroad: Labour, Capital, Enterprise, 1750-1914.
Caggiano, Biba. Northern Italian Cooking.
Caggiano, Philip, adapted by. The Ring: Four Plays for Children.
Cagle, Charles V. Adhesive Bonding: Techniques & Applications.
Cagle, Eldon B. Quadrangle: The History of Fort Sam Houston.
Cagle, James V. The Story of Santa Claus, Junior.
Cagle, Paul R., Jr. & Wallace, Mary H. The Curtain of Time.
Cagnac, B. & Pebay-Peyroula, J. C. Modern Atomic Physics: Quantum Theory & Its Application.
Cagnacci-Schwicker, Angelo. Dictionnaire International de Metallurgie, Mineralogie, Geologie et Industries Extractives.
Cahan, et al. Interventional Neuroradiology.
Cahill, Bob, jt. auth. see Stephenson, John G.
Cahill, Donald R. & Orland, Matthew J. Atlas of Human Cross-Sectional Anatomy.
Cahill, Lawrence B. Environmental Audits.
Cahill, Lawrence B., et al, eds. Environmental Audits.
Cahill, Lisa S. Between the Sexes.
Cahill, Susan & Cahill, Thomas. A Literary Guide to Ireland.
Cahill, Thomas, jt. auth. see Cahill, Susan.
Cahn, Cynthia. The Day the Sun Split.
Cahn, Rolf. Self-Defense for Gentle People.
Cahn, Sammy. I Should Care: The Sammy Cahn Story.
--The Songwriter's Rhyming Dictionary.
Cahn, William. Lawrence Nineteen Twelve: The Bread & Roses Strike.
Cahoon, Margaret C., ed. Cancer Nursing.
Caianiello, E. R., ed. Automata Theory.
--Lectures on Field Theory & the Many-Body Problem.
--The Many-Body Problem.
Caiati, Carl. Advanced Airbrushing Techniques Made Simple.
--Airbrushing.
--Basic Body Repair & Refinishing for the Weekend Mechanic.
Caiati, Carl, rev. by see Girdler, Allan.
Caiden, Gerald E. & Siedentopf, Heinrich. Strategies for Administrative Reform.
Caidin, Martin. Cyborg.
--Cyborg Four.
--Fork-Tailed Devil: The P-38.
--High Crystal.
--Operation Nuke.
--A Torch to the Enemy.
--Zero!
Caidin, Martin, jt. auth. see Combs, Harry B.
Caille, J. M. & Salomon, G., eds. Computerized Tomography: Proceedings.
Cailliet, Emile, ed. see Pascal, Blaise.
Cailliet, Rene. Low Back Pain Syndrome.
--Soft Tissue Pain & Disability.
Cailliet, Rene & Gross, Leonard. Rejuvenation Strategy: A Medically Approved Fitness Program to Remove the Effects of Aging.
Caillois, Roger. Jeux et Sports.
Caillou, Alan. Assault on Kolchak.
--Diamonds Wild.
Caillou, Allan. The League of Hawks.
Caimite. Don't Get Hit by a Cocoanut.
Cain. Transportation.
Cain, H. W. & Hunt, R. L. Principles of Chemistry Laboratory: Manual for CH 111A & 112A.
Cain, James M. The Baby in the Icebox: And Other Short Fiction. Hoopes, Roy, ed.
--Cloud Nine.
--Double Indemnity.
--Money & the Woman: The Embezzler.
--Past All Dishonour.
Cain, Louis & Uselding, Paul, eds. Business Enterprise & Economic Change: Essays in Honor of H. F. Williamson.
Caine, Lynn. What Did I Do Wrong? Mothers, Children, Guilt.
Caine, Tom, et al. Personal Styles in Neurosis: Implications for Small Group Psychotherapy & Behavior Therapy.
Caird, Edward. Critical Philosophy of Immanuel Kant.
--Evolution of Theology in the Greek Philosophers.
Caird, G. B. Saint Luke.
Caird, Mona. The Daughters of Danaus.

Cairncross, Alec & Eichengreen, Barry. Sterling in Decline.

Cairncross, Frances, ed. Changing Perceptions in Economic Policy: Essays in Honour of the Seventieth Birthday of Sir Alec Cairneross.

Cairnes, John E. Examination into the Principles of Currency Involved in the Bank Charter Act of 1844.

Cairnie, A. B., ed. Stems Cells: Renewing Cell Population.

Cairns, Alison. Strained Relations.

Cairns, David. The Image of God in Man.

Cairns, David, tr. see Berlioz, Hector.

Cairns, J., Jr. Biological Monitoring in Water Pollution.

Cairns, John. Stressed Ecosystems.

Cairns, John, Jr. & Buikema, Arthur L., Jr. Restoration of Habitats Impacted by Oil Spills.

Cairns, L. C., jt. auth. see Turney, C.

Cairns, L. G., jt. auth. see Turney, C.

Cairns, S. S., ed. Differential & Combinatorial Topology: A Symposium in Honor of Marston Morse.

Cairns, Trevor, ed. Europe & the World.

Caitlin, Thomas & Tremlett, George. Caitlin: Life with Dylan Thomas.

Caiwei, Ouyang, tr. see Qifeng, Fu.

Caiwei, Ouyang, tr. see Zhiyan, Li & Wen, Cheng.

Cajal, Santiago Ramon Y see Ramon Y Cajal, Santiago.

Cajori, Florian. History of Mathematical Notations. Incl. Vol. 1. Notations in Elementary Mathematics; Vol. 2. Notations Mainly in Higher Mathematics. Open Court.

--William Oughtred: A Great Seventeenth-Century Teacher of Mathematics.

Cakir, A., et al. Visual Display Terminals: A Manual Covering Ergonomics, Workplace Design, Health & Safety, Task Organization.

Calabrese, Edward & Dorsey, Michael. Healthy Living in an Unhealthy World.

--Healthy Living in an Unhealthy World: What You Can Do Now to Reduce the Risks of Cancer & Other Environmentally Induced Diseases for Yourself & Your Family.

Calabrese, Edward J. Toxic Susceptibility: Male-Female Differences.

Calabrese, F. A., et al. Two Village Sites in Southwestern Missouri: A Lithic Analysis. Wood, W. Raymond, ed.

Calaby, J. H., jt. auth. see Mulvaney, D. J.

Calais, Aloy J. Consumer Legislation in France.

Calandra, Denis. New German Dramatists.

--New German Dramatists.

CALC Staff. Living for Justice: A Study Guide to Hunger for Justice: the Politics of Food & Faith.

Caldara, Antonio. Olimpiade. Brown, Howard M., ed.

Caldecott, Moyra. Etheldreda.

--The Lily & the Bull.

Calder, Angus, et al, eds. Summer Fires: New Poetry of Africa.

Calder, G. The Principles & Techniques of Engineering Estimating.

Calder, Isabel M. The New Haven Colony.

Calder, Jenni. There Must Be a Lone Ranger: The American West in Film & in Reality.

--There Must Be a Lone Ranger: The American West in Myth & Reality.

Calder, Julian & Garrett, John. The Thirty-Five MM Photographer's Handbook.

Calder, Julian, et al. The Thirty-Five Millimeter Photographer's Handbook.

Calder, Nigel. The English Channel.

--Technopolis.

Calder, Ritchie. How Long Have We Got?

Calderon de la Barca, Pedro. The Mayor of Zalamea: Or the Best Garroting Ever Done.

--The Surgeon of His Honour. Campbell, Roy, tr. from Span.

Calderone, Mary, jt. auth. see Bride's Magazine Editors.

Caldirola, P., ed. Ergodic Theories.

Caldwell, Brice & Caldwell, Craig, eds. Basic Bodywork & Painting.

Caldwell, Craig, jt. ed. see Caldwell, Brice.

Caldwell, Dan, ed. Soviet International Behavior & U. S. Policy Options.

Caldwell, David, ed. Scottish Weapons & Fortifications, 1100-1800.

Caldwell, Erskine. Deep South: Memory & Observation.

Caldwell, Gaylon L. & Lawrence, Robert. American Government Today.

Caldwell, Geoffery, et al, eds. Gambling in Australia.

Caldwell, Happy. The Word System.

Caldwell, J. The Book of Ultimates.

Caldwell, J. J., jt. ed. see Atreya, S. K.

Caldwell, Joseph. The Deer at the River.

--In Such Dark Places.

--In Such Dark Places.

Caldwell, Louis. The Adventure of Becoming One.

Caldwell, Louis O. Good Morning, Lord: Devotions for College Students.

--Good Morning, Lord: Meditations for Modern Marrieds.

Caldwell, Pablo. Diccionario de Modismos Ingleses.

Caldwell, Peter. Draw Boats & Harbours.

Caldwell, R. L., jt. ed. see Lidicker, W. Z., Jr.

Caldwell, Stanley, jt. ed. see MacGibbon, James.

Caldwell, Taylor. Answer As a Man.

--Answer As a Man.

--Great Lion of God.

--A Pillar of Iron.

Caldwell, Taylor & Stearn, Jess. I, Judas.

Caleel, Richard & Littell, John. Surgeon: The Making of an Inner-City Doctor.

Caley, Ray L. The Ragged Statue & Other Stories.

Calfa, Ambroise. Dictionnaire Armenien-Francais.

Calfee, Robert C. & Drum, Priscilla A., eds. Teaching Reading in Compensatory Classes.

Calhoon, Robert M. The Loyalists in Revolutionary America 1760-1781.

Calhoun, David, jt. ed. see Core, Lucy.

Calhoun, James & Kempe, Helen. Louisiana Almanac 1979-80.

Calhoun, James & Kempe, Helen, eds. Louisiana Almanac, 1975-76 Ed.

Calhoun, James, jt. ed. see Calhoun, Nancy.

Calhoun, John C. Calhoun: Basic Documents. Anderson, John M., ed.

Calhoun, Mary. Horse Comes First.

Calhoun, Nancy & Calhoun, James, eds. Pelican Guide to Plantation Homes of Louisiana.

Calhoun, Richard J., ed. James Dickey: The Expansive Imagination.

Calhoun, Robert M. Revolutionary America: An Interpretive Overview.

Cali, J. P., ed. Physicochemical Measurements: Catalogue of Reference Materials from National Laboratories.

--Trace Analysis of Semiconductor Materials.

Cali, Vincent M. The New Lower-Cost Way to End Gum Trouble Without Surgery.

Caliendo, Mary A. Nutrition & Preventative Health Care.

Califano, Joseph A., Jr. Governing America.

California Coastal Commission. The California Coastal Access Guide.

California Continuing Eduacation of the Bar Staff & Hargrove, John O. Business Buy-out Agreements.

California Continuing Education of the Bar Staff & Karplus, Curtis M. Advising California Partnerships.

California Continuing Education of the Bar Staff & Sigman, Harry C. Attorney's Handbook on Division Nine.

California Continuing Education of the Bar Staff, et al. California Civil Discovery Practice.

California Continuing Education of the Bar Staff. California Civil Writs.

--California Mechanics' Liens & Other Remedies.

California Continuing Education of the Bar Staff, et al. California Misdemeanor Procedure Benchbook, Revised.

California Continuing Education of the Bar Staff & Hargrove, John O. California Taxes.

California Continuing Education of the Bar Staff. Estate Planning for the General Practitioner.

--Estate Planning: 1980.

California Continuing Education of the Bar Staff, et al. Speedy Trial: Practice & Procedure.

California Continuing Education of the Bar Staff. Transcripts of Nineteen Eighty-Two Developments Tapes.

California Critic Editors, ed. Best Restaurants of Los Angeles & Southern California.

--Best Restaurants of San Francisco & Northern California.

California Magazine Staff & Hayes, Harold, eds. The Best of California: Some People, Places & Institutions of the Most Exciting State in the Nation, as Featured in California Magazine, 1976-1986.

California Policy Seminar Staff & Musgrave, Peggy B. States under Stress: A Report on the Finances of Massachusetts, Michigan, Texas, & California: California Policy Seminar Conference Report.

California Restaurant Association Staff. Cuisine of California.

California State Library Staff. Catalog of California State Grants Assistance, 1987.

California State Library Sutro Branch San Francisco. Catalogue of Mexican Pamphlets in the Sutro Collection 1623-1888. Radin, P. & Gans, A. I., eds.

California State Water Resources Control Board Staff, et al. Health Aspects of Wastewater Recharge: A State-of-the-Art Review.

California University Committee on International Relations. The Southwest Pacific & the War.

Calin, Andrei & Fries, James F. Ankylosing Spondylitis.

Calin, Harold. White Forest Battle.

Calingaert, Efrem F. & Serwer, Jacquelyn D. Pasta & Rice Italian Style.

Calingaert, Peter. Assemblers, Compilers, & Program Translation.

Calisher, Hortense. Age.

--Collected Stories of Hortense Calisher.

--Eagle Eye.

--Herself.

--On Keeping Women.

--Queenie.

--Saratoga Hot.

--Standard Dreaming.

Calisher, Hortense & Ravenel, Shannon, eds. The Best American Short Stories, 1981.

Calixte, Demosthenes P. Haiti: The Calvary of a Soldier.

Calk, James P. The Geometry of the Stars.

Calkin, Ruth H. Letters to a Young Bride.

--Love Is So Much More, Lord.

Calkins, Earnest E. Louder Please: The Autobiography of a Deaf Man.

Calkins, Fay. The CIO & the Democratic Party.

Calkins, Frank. Riley's Last Hunt.

Call, Steven T. & Holahan, William L. Microeconomics.

Call, Vaughn R. & Otto, Luther B. Tracking Respondents: A Multi-Method Approach.

Calladine, G. R. Engineering Plasticity.

Callaghan & Company Publisher's Staff. Callaghan's Wisconsin Digest: 1950.

Callaghan & Company Staff, ed. see Henderson, James M.

Callaghan, John. British Trotskyism: Theory & Practice.

Callaghan, Thomas. The Tramp's Chronicle.

Callahan, Daniel. Setting Limits: Medical Goals in an Aging Society.

Callahan, Dorothy, jt. auth. see Payne, Alma.

Callahan, James J., Jr. & Wallack, Stanley S., eds. Reforming the Long-Term-Care System: Financial & Organizational Options.

Callahan, James M. Diplomatic History of the Southern Confederacy.

Callahan, P. J. How to Serve on a Jury.

Callahan, Philip S. Birds & How They Function.

Callahan, Richard J. Who's Who in Ferrous Products Including: Steel Wire & Steel Products: Directory of Names, Titles, Addresses, Telephone, Fax & Telex Numbers. Reed, Eugene S. & Staniszewski, Amy G., eds.

--Who's Who in Nonferrous Products Including: Copper Bare & Insulated, Aluminum Bare & Insulated, Magnet Wire, Fiber Optics: Directory of Names, Titles, Addresses, Telephone, Fax & Telex Numbers. Reed, Eugene S. & Staniszewski, Amy G., eds.

Callahan, Roger. Five Minute Phobia Cure.

Callahan, Sidney, jt. ed. see Berger, Brigitte.

Callahan, Steven. Adrift.

Callan, Eileen T. Hardy Race of Men: America's Early Indians.

Callan, Hilary & Ardener, Shirley, eds. The Incorporated Wife.

Callan, Victor & Noller, Patricia. Marriage & the Family.

Callaway, Enoch, jt. ed. see Lehmann, Dietrich.

Callaway, Henry. Nursery Tales, Traditions, & Histories of the Zulus: In their Own Words, with a Translation.

Callaway, Joseph. Electron Energy Bands in Solids.

Callaway, Kathy. Heart of the Garfish.

Callebaut, M., et al. Meiosis: Current Research.

Callen, Peter W. Ultrasonography in Obstetrics & Gynecology.

Callis, Robert, et al, eds. Ethical Standards Casebook.

Callmann, Rudolf, ed. see Altman, Louis.

Calloud, Jean. Structural Analysis of Narrative. Beardslee, William A., ed. Patte, Daniel, tr. from Fr.

Callow, Patricia, et al. Ten Black People Who Helped to Build America.

Callow, Simon. Being an Actor.

Calloway, Jo. Mirrors of Love.

Calloway, Stephen. English Prints for the Collector.

Calloway, Sue D. Nursing & the Law.

Calmenson, Stephanie. Waggleby of Fraggle Rock.

Calmenson, Stephanie, ed. Never Take a Pig to Lunch.

Calmer, Ned. Bay of Lions.

Calmus, Thomas W., jt. auth. see Sampson, Roy J.

Calnan, J. One Way to do Research: The A-Z for Those Who Must.

Calnan, J. & Barabas, A. Writing Medical Papers: A Practical Guide.

Calo, J. M. & Henley, E. J., eds. Stagewise & Mass Transfer Operations.

Calogero, F. Variable Phase Approach to Potential Scattering.

Calow, Peter, jt. ed. see Townsend, Colin R.

Calter, Paul. Problem Solving with Computers.

Calvacorlessi, Peter. Top Secret Ultra.

Calvert, E., et al, eds. Injection Moulding.

Calvert, Judith, jt. ed. see Jerse, Dorothy W.

Calvert, P., jt. auth. see Dieppe, P.

Calvert, Thomas B. The Illustrated Q & A.

Calvez, Jean-Yves. Politics & Society in the Third World. OConnell, Matthew J., tr. from Fr.

Calvin, John. Institution of the Christian Religion Embracing Almost the Whole Sum of Piety, & Whatever Is Necessary to Know the Doctrine of Salvation. Battles, Ford L., ed.

--John Calvin's Treatises Against the Anabaptists & Against the Libertines. Farley, Benjamin W., tr.

Calvino, Italo. The Castle of Crossed Destinies.

--Difficult Loves. Weaver, William, et al, trs.

--If on a Winter's Night a Traveler. Weaver, William, tr. from Ital.

--Marcovaldo or The Seasons in the City: 01027514x. Weaver, William, tr. from Ital.

--Saul Steinberg: Still Life & Architecture.

Calvocoressi, M. D. Mussorgsky. Abraham, Gerald, ed.

--Mussorgsky.

--The Principles & Methods of Musical Criticism.

--A Survey of Russian Music.

Calvocoressi, Michel D. Modest Mussorgsky.

Calvocoressi, Peter. World Politics since Nineteen Forty-Five.

Calvo-Sotelo, Joaquin. La Herencia. Klein, Richard B., ed.

Camara, Dom H. A Thousand Reasons for Living. De Brouker, Jose, ed. Neame, Alan, tr. from Fr.

Camara, Sory. Gens De la Parole: Essai Sur la Condition et le Role Des Griots Dans la Societe Malinke.

Camaro Editors. California Gallery Guide.

--Hidden Corners of California.

Camatini, Marina, ed. Myriapod Biology.

Cambel, A. B., ed. Energy Devices & Processes: Proceedings of a Workshop on the Second Law of Thermodynamics, Held at the George Washington University, Wash. D. C., 14-16 Aug. 1979.

Cambel, A. B, et al, eds. The Solar Energy-Utility Interface.

Cambel, Ali B., et al. Real Gases.

Cambitoglou, Alexander. Studies in Honour of Arthur Dale Trendal.

Cambra, Ronald E., jt. auth. see Klopf, Donald W.

Cambridge Communication, Ltd. Staff. Anatomy & Physiology: A Self Instructional Course.

Cambridge Consultants Training Ltd. Programmed Introduction to Critical Path Methods.

Cambridge, Joan. Clarise Cumberbatch Want to Go Home.

Cambridge Summer School in Mathematical Logic Staff. Proceedings of the Cambridge Summer School in Mathematical Logic, 1971. Mathias, A. R. & Rogers, H., eds.

Cambridge Women's Peace Collective Staff, ed. My Country Is the Whole World: An Anthology of Women's Work on Peace & War.

Camden, Archie. Blow by Blow: The Memories of a Musical Rogue & Vagabond.

Camden Society, Royal Historical Society Staff, ed. The Rule of Walter De Wenlok, Abbot of Westminster.

Camden Society Staff. Camden Society Publications: Series 1.

Camden, Thomas M. & Bishop, Nancy. How to Get a Job in Dallas, Fort Worth: The Insider's Guide.

--How to Get a Job in Dallas-Ft. Worth: The Insider's Guide.

Camden, Thomas M. & Fleming-Holland, Susan. How to Get a Job in New York: The Insider's Guide.

Camden, William. Britannia.

Camellion, Richard. Behavior Modification.

Cameron & Scaletta. Business Law: Legal Environment, Transaction & Regulation.

Cameron, A. G., jt. ed. see Jastrow, R.

Cameron, A. G., jt. ed. see Ponnamperuma, Cyril.

Cameron, A. J. Mathematical Enterprises for Schools.

Cameron, Allan. The Science of Food & Cooking.

Cameron, Angus, jt. ed. see Frank, Roberta.

Cameron, Ann. The Journey.

Cameron, Barry, ed. Carboniferous Basins of Southeastern New England.

Cameron, Bruce F., ed. see Miami Winter Symposium Staff.

Cameron, Charles, jt. auth. see Bennett, Cleaves M.

Cameron, David K. The Ballad & the Plough.

--The Cornkister Days.

Cameron, E. Hyaluronidase & Cancer.

Cameron, Eion M. Uranium Exploration in Athabaska Basin.

Cameron, Eleanor. The Court of the Stone Children.

Cameron, Elizabeth. Big Book of Real Trucks.

Cameron, George G., ed. see Chiera, Edward.

Cameron, Ian. The Mountains at the Bottom of the World.

--Mountains of the Gods.

Cameron, Ivan L. & Jeter, James R., Jr., eds. Acidic Proteins of the Nucleus.

Cameron, Ivan L. & Padilla, George M., eds. Cell Synchrony: Studies in Biosynthetic Regulation.

--Developmental Aspects of the Cell Cycle.

Cameron, Ivan L. & Pool, Thomas B., eds. The Transformed Cell.

Cameron, Ivan L. & Thrasher, Jack D., eds. Cellular & Molecular Renewal in the Mammalian Body.
Cameron, J. & Dodd, W. A. Society, Schools & Progress in Tanzania.
Cameron, James. The Making of Israel.
--Point of Departure.
Cameron, James B., et al. Advanced Accounting: Theory & Practice.
Cameron, James R. Frederic William Maitland & the History of English Law.
Cameron, John. If Mice Could Fly.
--JSP & JSD: The Jackson Approach to Software Development.
Cameron, John & Hurst, Paul, eds. International Handbook of Education Systems: Sub-Saharan Africa - North Africa & the Middle East.
Cameron, John L. Current Surgical Therapy 1984-1985.
Cameron, Kenneth see Corrigan, Robert W.
Cameron, Kenneth N. Marx & Engels Today: A Modern Dialogue on Philosophy & History.
Cameron, Lou. The Hot Car.
Cameron, Meg. Savage Spirit.
Cameron, Nigel. The Face of China As Seen by Photographers or Travelers: 1860-1912.
Cameron, Norman. Personality Development & Psychopathology: A Dynamic Approach.
Cameron, Peter, ed. see British Combinatorial Conference Staff.
Cameron, Richard M. The Rise of Methodism: A Source Book.
Cameron, Robert. Above Los Angeles.
--Above San Francisco.
Cameron, William E. Great Dramas of the Bible.
Camiller, Patrick, tr. see Pluto-Maspero Project Staff.
Camillus, John C. Budgeting for Profit.
--Budgeting for Profit: How to Exploit the Potential of Your Business.
Camm, A. John, jt. ed. see Martin, Anthony.
Camm, F. J. Math Tables & Formulae.
Cammett, John, tr. see Hobsbawm, Eric.
Cammock, Ruth. Primary Health Care Buildings.
Camner, James, jt. ed. see Applebaum, Stanley.
Camougis, G. Environmental Biology for Engineers: A Guide to Environmental Assessment.
Camp, Catherine C. De see De Camp, L. Sprague & De Camp, Catherine C.
Camp, Deborah. Blazing Embers.
Camp, Jeffery. The Drawing Book.
Camp, John. Magic, Myth & Medicine.
Camp, L. Sprague De see De Camp, L. Sprague & De Camp, Catherine C.
Camp, L. Sprague De see De Camp, L. Sprague & Pratt, Fletcher.
Camp, Pamela S., jt. auth. see Arms, Karen.
Camp, R. L. Papal Ideology of Social Reform: A Study in Historical Development, 1878-1967.
Camp, Thomas & Meserve, Robert L. Water & Its Impurities.
Camp, Wesley D., tr. see Egret, Jean.
Campagna, Anthony S. Macroeconomics: Theory & Policy.
Campbell, jt. auth. see Ellis.
Campbell, jt. auth. see Tulley.
Campbell, Ada M. & Penfield, Marjorie. Experimental Study of Food.
Campbell, Alastair V. Moral Dilemmas in Medicine.
--Professionalism & Pastoral Care.
--Rediscovering Pastoral Care.
Campbell, Alastair W. Professional Care: Its Meaning & Practice.
Campbell, Alex. Unbind Your Sons: The Captivity of America in Asia.
Campbell, Alexander & Haff, Gerry. Live with Jesus.
Campbell, Alistair. Island to Island.
Campbell, Arthur, Inc. Staff. How to Make Your Own Liqueurs.
Campbell, Barbara, jt. ed. see Swansea, Charleen.
Campbell, Bernard G. Humankind Emerging.
Campbell, Bruce A. The American Electorate.
Campbell, Charles S., Jr. Anglo-American Understanding: Eighteen Ninety-Eight to Nineteen Hundred Three.
Campbell, Christy. Weapons of War: Present & Future Weapons, Systems & Strategies.
Campbell, Craig. Water in Landscape Architecture.
Campbell, D. B. The Old Testament for Modern Readers.
Campbell, David. The Eternal Sonship: A Refutation According to Adam Clarke.
--Yet Not I.
Campbell, Diana. The Good Mixer Cookbook.
Campbell, Donald & Spence, Alastair A. Norris & Campbell's Anaesthetics, Resuscitation, & Intensive Care.
Campbell, Donald K. Nehemiah: Man in Charge.
Campbell, Donald T., jt. auth. see Webb, Eugene J.
Campbell, Douglas. The Whole Craft of Number.
Campbell, Dowling. The Intimate Grand: Inside Arizona's Grand Canyon.
Campbell, Dugald. In the Heart of Bantuland.
Campbell, E. L. The Science of Law According to the American Theory of Government.
Campbell, Eugene E., jt. auth. see Gowans, Fred R.
Campbell, F. & Singer, G. Stress, Drugs & Health - Recent Brain-Behavior Research.
Campbell, F. Gregory. Confrontation in Central Europe: Weimar Germany & Czechoslovakia.
Campbell, Frank & Sinaer, George. Brain & Behaviour: Psychobiology of Everyday Life.
Campbell, G. A., jt. auth. see Brown, R.
Campbell, G. D. Oral Hypoglycaemic Agents.
Campbell, George. A Dissertation on Miracles, Containing an Examination of the Principles Advanced by David Hume, Esq. in an Essay on Miracles.
Campbell, H. J. Correlative Physiology of the Nervous System.
Campbell, Harry H. The Early History of Motley County.
Campbell, Helen. Darkness & Daylight: Or, Lights & Shadows of New York Life: A Pictorial Record of Personal Experiences by Day & Night in the Great Metropolis with Hundreds of Thrilling Anecdotes & Incidents.
Campbell, Hilbert H. James Thomson: An Annotated Bibliography of Selected Writings & the Important Criticism.
Campbell, Howard E. Concepts of Algebra & Trigonometry.
--Concepts of College Algebra.
--Concepts of Trigonometry.
Campbell, J. D., ed. see CISM (International Center for Mechanical Sciences), Dept. for Mechanics of Deformable Bodies, 1970.
Campbell, J. F. Leabhar Na Feinne.
Campbell, J. W., ed. Comparative Biochemistry of Nitrogen Metabolism.
Campbell, J. W., ed. see American Physiological Society & American Society of Zoologists, Joint Symposium.
Campbell, James. Two Plays: Quintus & Lucanus, Andronicus.
Campbell, James, ed. Scottish Short Stories.
Campbell, James, et al. Masterpak.
--Remembering.
--Sensing.
--Wondering.
--Belonging.
Campbell, James, et al, eds. Beginnings & Endings.
Campbell, James M. Pressure!
Campbell, Jeremy. Grammatical Man: Information, Entropy, Language, & Life.
--Winston Churchill's Afternoon Nap: A Wide-Awake Inquiry into the Human Nature of Time.
Campbell, John. Speak Softly of Christmas.
Campbell, John A. Obstetrical Diagnosis by Radiographic, Ultrasonic & Nuclear Methods.
Campbell, John C., et al. Energy: A Strategy for International Action.
--Energy: The Imperative of a Trilateral Approach.
Campbell, John D., jt. auth. see Leinbaugh, Harold P.
Campbell, John F. Popular Tales of the West Highlands.
Campbell, John G. Superstitions of the Highlands & Islands of Scotland.
Campbell, John R. & Lasley, John F. The Science of Animals That Serve Mankind.
Campbell, Joseph. Flight of the Wild Gander.
Campbell, Katherine, ed. see Montgomery Museum of Fine Arts Staff.
Campbell, Leslie. Two Hundred Years of Pharmacy in Mississippi.
Campbell, Liberty. Up to My Neck in Haiku.
Campbell, M. J., ed. Technology & the Rural Community: The Social Impact.
Campbell, Marion. Towards a New Iron Age.
Campbell, Mike. Capitalism in the U. K. A Perspective from Marxist Political Economy.
Campbell, Mike, jt. auth. see Burden, Tom.
Campbell, Murry M. Why Denominationalism?
Campbell, Oscar J. English Poetry of the Nineteenth Century.
Campbell, P. N. The Structure & Function of Animal Cell Components.
Campbell, Pamela, jt. auth. see Patton, Annie.
Campbell, Patrick. Patrick Campbell's Travels.
Campbell, Paul B., et al. High School Vocational Graduates: Which Doors Are Open?
Campbell, Penelope. Maryland in Africa: The Maryland State Colonization Society, 1831-1857.
Campbell, Peter, jt. auth. see McMahon, Edwin.
Campbell, Peter N. Techniques in Protein Biosynthesis.
Campbell, R. D. & Jones, J. The Microlight Flying Manual.
Campbell, R. K. Parables in Matthew's Gospel: Matthew 13.
Campbell, R. M., jt. auth. see IFAC Symposium Staff.
Campbell, R. W. & Murray, A., eds. Dynamic Electrocardiography.
Campbell, R. Wright. Fat Tuesday.
--Malloy's Subway.
Campbell, Ramsey. Cold Print.
--Scared Stiff: Tales of Sex & Death.
Campbell, Robert. The Chasm.
--Fisherman's Guide: A Systems Approach to Creativity & Organization.
Campbell, Robert E. & Shaltry, Paul, eds. Perpectives on Adult Career Development & Guidance.
Campbell, Robert W. Soviet-Type Economies: Performance & Evolution.
Campbell, Roger. You Can Win.
Campbell, Roger, jt. auth. see Porter, Greg.
Campbell, Ron. Bovine Excrement.
Campbell, Ross & Gray, Randall. How to Keep Going When the Storms Keep Coming.
Campbell, Roy, tr. see Calderon de la Barca, Pedro.
Campbell, Roy J. Janey.
--Peggy.
Campbell, Russell. Cinema Strikes Back: Radical Filmmaking in the United States, 1930-1942. Kirkpatrick, Diane, ed.
Campbell, Russell, compiled by. Photographic Theory for the Motion Picture Cameraman.
Campbell, Russell N. & Lindfors, Judith W. Insights into English Structure: A Programmed Course.
Campbell, Steuart. The Loch Ness Monster: The Evidence.
Campbell, Toby H. & Bendick, Marc, Jr. A Public Assistance Data Book.
Campbell, Tony. Early Maps.
Campbell, Will D. Race & the Renewal of the Church.
Campbell, William A. In Rem Foreclosures: The U. S. Supreme Court Imposes Additional Notice Requirements.
--North Carolina Guidebook for Registers of Deeds.
Campbell, William A., ed. Guidebook for North Carolina Registers of Deeds.
Campbell, William G. & Ballou, Stephen V. Form & Style: Theses, Reports, Term Papers.
Campbell, William G., et al. Form & Style: Theses, Reports, Term Papers.
Campbell, Zerah A. Wait Don't Pull That Plug: The Story of Timmy.
Campbell-Allen, D., jt. auth. see Davis, E. H.
Campbell-Harding, Valerie. Flowers & Plants in Embroidery.
Campbells Soup Company Staff. Creative Cooking with Soup Cookbook.
--Campbell's Microwave Cookbook.
Campbell-Thrane, Lucille, compiled by. Equity in Vocational Education: A Futures Agenda.
Campen, Joseph A. Van see Sholiton, Robert D. & Van Campen, Joseph A.
Campen, Shirley Van see Van Campen, Shirley.
Campenhausen, Hans von see Von Campenhausen, Hans.
Campenhausen, Hans Von see Von Campenhausen, Hans & Chadwick, Henry.
Campion, Nicholas. The Practical Astrologer.
--The Practical Astrologer.
Campion, Polly, jt. auth. see Kent, Louise A.
Campling, Elizabeth. How & Why: The Russian Revolution.
Campling, Jo, ed. Image of Ourselves: Women with Disabilities Talking.
Campman, M. S., jt. auth. see McMurrey, David A.
Campo-Flores, Filemon, jt. auth. see Chang, Y. N.
Campolo, Anthony. Partly Right.
Campolo, Tony. Who Switched Price Tags? How to Make Life Better in Your Work, Family & Church.
Campos, Deoclecio R. De see De Campos, Deoclecio R.
Campos, Joseph J., jt. auth. see Lamb, Michael E.
Campos-De Metro, Joseph. The Slugger Heart & Other Stories.
Camps, Miriam & Gwin, Catherine. Collective Management: The Reform of Global Economic Organizations.
Camps, Miriam & Hirono, Ryokichi. The Trilateral Countries in the International Economy of the 1980's.
Camus, Albert. Etat De Siege.
--L' Ete: Essai.
--Homme Revolte: Essai.
--Le Malentendu. Bd. with Caligula. Schoenhof.
--Notebooks: Nineteen Forty-Two to Nineteen Fifty-One.
--Notebooks: 1935-1942.
--Peste.
--Possedees: Theatre.
--Requiem Pour une Nonne: Theatre.
Camus, Raoul F. Military Music of the American Revolution.
Camuse, Ruth, ed. Fourth Annual Microcomputers in Education Conference: Literacy Plus.
Camuti, Louis J. All My Patients Are under the Bed.
Camy-Peyret, C., jt. auth. see Flaud, J. M.
Canaan, Lionel A. The Doctor's Quartet & More.
--Odds & Ends.
--Stories for the Sophisticated.
Canaday, John. Baroque Painters.
--Late Gothic to Renaissance Painters.
--Neoclassic to Post-Impressionist Painters.
Canaday, John, ed. Western Painting Illustrated: Giotto to Cezanne.
Canaday, Ouida. Georgia Sketch Book.
Canadian Association of Oilwell Drilling Contractors Staff. Drilling Rig Task Details & Performance Standards.
Canadian Cancer Conference Staff. Proceedings. Begg, R. W., ed. Incl. Vol. 1. 1st Conference, 1954; Vol. 2. 2nd Conference, 1956; Vol. 3. 3rd Conference, 1958; Vol. 4. 4th Conference, 1960; Vol. 5. 5th Conference, 1962. Acad Pr.
Canadian Reliability Engineers Staff. Reliability Engineering Nineteen Seventy-Eight: Proceedings of the SRE Reliability Symposium, Ottawa, Ontario, Canada, October, 1978.
--Reliability Engineering, 1975.
Canadian Reliabilty Engineers Staff. Reliability Engineering 1980: Proceedings of the 1980 Canadian SRE Reliability Symposium, Ottawa, Ontario, Canada May 15-16 1980.
Canadian Royal Commission, ed. Violence in the Communications Industry.
Canady, John. The New York Times Guide to Dining Out in N. Y.
Canan, Michael J. Qualified Retirement & Other Employee Benefit Plans, 1988.
Canan, Michael J. & Baker, David R. Qualified Retirement Plans.
Canary, Brenda B. Home to the Mountain.
--The Voice of the Clown.
Canavan, Jean. The Shadow of the Flame.
Canavan, P. Joseph. Rhetoric & Literature.
Canby, William C., Jr. American Indian Law.
Cancro, Robert & Dean, Stanley R., eds. Research in the Schizophrenic Disorder, Vol. 1 & Vol. 2: The Stanley R. Dean Award Lectures.
Cancro, Robert & Taintor, Zebulen, eds. Towards a New Psychology of Women & Men: A Special Issue of Journal of Psychiatric Education.
Candlin, C. N., jt. ed. see Riley, Philip.
Candullo, C. System Developments Standards.
Candy, David J. Biological Functions of Carbohydrates.
Cane, Melville. And Pastures New: A Collection of Poems.
--Bullet-Hunting, & Other New Poems.
--Eloquent April: New Poems & Prose.
--The First Firefly: New Poems & Prose.
--Snow Toward Evening: Poems.
--So That It Flower: A Gathering of Poems.
--To Build a Fire: Recent Poems & a Prose Piece.
--A Wider Arc: Poems.
Canestano, James C. Real Estate Financial Feasibility Analysis Handbook & Workbook.
Canfield, Cass. The Iron Will of Jefferson Davis.
--Outrageous Fortunes: The Story of the Medici, the Rothschilds, & J. Pierpont Morgan.
Canfield, Dorothy. Harvest of Stories: From a Half Century of Writing.
Canfield, John V. Wittgenstein: Language & World.
Canham, Marsha. China Rose.
Caniff, Milton. Terry & the Pirates (1935-1936) Blackbeard, Bill, ed.
--Terry & the Pirates (1936-1937) Blackbeard, Bill, ed.
--Terry & the Pirates (1938-1939) Blackbeard, Bill, ed.
--Terry & the Pirates (1939-1940) Blackbeard, Bill, ed.
Canino, Robert. The Divorcee's Kitchen Give You Servings from One to Six.
Canjar, Lawrence & Manning, Francis. Thermodynamic Properties & Reduced Correlations for Gases.
Cann, Kevin. David Bowie.
Cannegieter, C. A. The Human Aspects of Economics: A Human Treatise of Unemployment, Inflation & World Poverty.
Cannell, Charles F., jt. auth. see Kahn, Robert L.
Cannell, Charles F., et al. Experiments in Interviewing Techniques: Field Experiments in Health Reporting, 1971-1977.
Cannell, M. G., ed. World Forest Biomass & Primary Production Data.
Cannell, M. G. & Last, F. T., eds. Tree Physiology & Yield Improvement.
Canney, Maurice A. Encyclopaedia of Religions.
Cannin, Hugh. The Opera Gazetteer.
Canning, E. V. & Wright, C. A., eds. Behavioural Aspects of Parasite Transmission.
Canning, George. The Occasional Horseman.
Canning House Library Editors, ed. Catalogues of the Canning House Library: Author & Subject Catalogues. Incl. Pt. 1. Hispanic Catalogues. Canning House Library Editors; Pt. 2. Luso-Brazilian Catalogues. Canning House Library Editors. G K Hall.
Canning, John, ed. One Hundred Great Kings, Queens & Rulers of the World.
Canning, Victor. Table Number Seven.
Cannom, Robert. Van Dyke & the Mythical City, Hollywood.
Cannon, Don L. & Luecke, Gerald. Understanding Microprocessors.

Authors

Cannon, Donald Q., jt. auth. see Cook, Lyndon W.
Cannon, Donald W., jt. auth. see Cook, Lyndon W.
Cannon, Garland. An Integrated Transformational Grammar of the English Language.
Cannon, Geoffrey & Einzig, Hetty. Dieting Makes You Fat: A Guide to Energy, Food, Fitness & Health.
Cannon, Hal, intro. by see Kiskaddon, Bruce.
Cannon, Helen. A Better Place I Know.
--Seasons Change.
--Where the Truth Lies.
Cannon, James S. Converting New York State Utilities to Coal: A Study of the Costs & Environmental Impacts of Conversion.
Cannon, M. Hamlin. United States Army in World War 2: War in the Pacific, Leyte, the Return to the Philippines.
Cannon, M. Samuel, jt. auth. see Sucheston, Martha E.
Cannon, Minuha. Sweets Without Guilt.
Cannon, P. F. & Minter, D. W. The Rhytismataceae of the Indian Subcontinent.
Cannon, Peter. The Chronology Out of Time: Dates in the Fiction of H. P. Lovecraft.
Cannon, Ralph S. Adam, Where Art Thou.
Cannon, Ray & Williams, Gareth. Calculus for Management, Social & Life Sciences.
Cannon, Taffy. Convictions: A Novel of the Sixties. Lister, Laurie, ed.
Cannon, Walter B. Wisdom of the Body.
Cannon, William A. & Fox, Fred K. Studebaker: The Complete Story.
Cannon, William R. A Disciple's Profile of Jesus.
--The Gospel of Matthew.
Cannon-Alfred, C., jt. auth. see Tyrone, Alfred J.
Cannon-Brookes, Peter. Ivor Roberts-Jones.
Canobbio, E., ed. Heating in Toroidal Plasmas II: Proceedings of the 2nd Joint Grenoble-Varenna International Symposium.
Canon, Jack. An Angel for Paradise.
Canonico & Margison, G. P., eds. Carcinogenesis.
Canovan, Margaret. G. K. Chesterton: Radical Populist.
--The Political Thought of Hannah Arendt.
--Populism.
Canright, D. M. Seventh-Day Adventism in a Nutshell.
--Seventh-Day Adventism Renounced.
Cantacuzino, Sherban. Architecture in Continuity: Building in the Islamic World Today.
Cantacuzino, Sherban & Brandt, Susan. Saving Old Buildings.
Cantelo, William W. & Webb, Raymond E. Insects & Diseases of Vegetables in the Home Garden.
Canter, David. Fires & Human Behaviour.
Canter, Lee & Canter, Marlene. Assertive Discipline: Competency-Based Resource Materials & Guidelines.
Canter, Marlene, jt. auth. see Canter, Lee.
Cantin, Marc & Seelig, Mildred S., eds. Magnesium in Health & Disease.
Canton, H. J., et al, eds. New Scientific Aspect.
Cantoni, Louise. St. Germaine.
Cantor, Arthur, jt. auth. see Little, Stuart W.
Cantor, Fitzgerald Collection, Inc. Staff. Rodin & Balzac: Bronzes from the Cantor, Fitzerald Collection, Inc.
Cantor, G. & Franklin, R. The Ten Best Ways to Save Taxes.
Cantor, Georg. Contributions to the Founding of the Theory of Transfinite Numbers. Jourdain, P. E., tr.
Cantor, Jay. The Space Between: Literature & Politics.
Cantor, Leonard & Roberts, I. F. Further Education Today.
Cantor, Milton & Laurie, Bruce, eds. Class, Sex, & the Woman Worker.
Cantor, Milton, jt. ed. see Quint, Howard H.
Cantor, Norman F. Church, Kingship & Lay Investiture in England, 1089-1135.
--Perspectives on the European Past: Conversations with Historians.
Cantow, H. J., ed. see Casale, A., et al.
Cantow, H. J., ed. see Henrici-Olive, G., et al.
Cantow, M. J., ed. Polymer Fractionation.
Cantrell, James C. Geometric Topology.
Cantril, Albert H., et al, eds. Polling on the Issues. Germond, Jack & Grespi, Irving.
Cantu, Robert C., ed. Health Maintenance Through Physical Conditioning.
Cantuti, V., ed. Air Pollution: Proceedings, International Symposium on the Chemical Aspects of Air Pollution, Held in Cortina D'ampezzo, Italy, 9-10 July, 1969.
Cantwell, Denton. Once upon an Earth.
Cantwell, George, ed. Insect Diseases.
Cantwell, James M. Highway Number One: A Vietnamese Odyssey in Verse.
Canudo, Eugene R. Marriage, Divorce & Adoption: New York.
--New York Corporations.
Canuto, V., jt. auth. see Gordon, C. W.
Canzano, Dorthea & Canzano, Phyllis. A Practical Guide to Multi-Level Modular ESL.
Canzano, Phyllis, jt. auth. see Canzano, Dorthea.
Cao-Pinna, Vera & Shatalin, Stanislav S. Consumption Patterns in Eastern & Western Europe.
Cap, Ferdinand, tr. see Karpman, V. I.
Capablanca, Jose R. Chess Fundamentals.
--Primer of Chess.
Capaldi, N., jt. ed. see Norton, D. F.
Capaldi, Roderick A., ed. Membrane Proteins & Their Interaction with Lipids.
Capdevila Font, Juan. Diccionario Actualizado de la Lengua Espanola.
--Diccionario Actualizado De Sinonimos y Contrarios De la Lengua Espanola.
--Diccionario de Citas.
--Diccionario Enciclopedico Distein 2.
--Diccionario Escolar De Sinonimos y Contrarios De la Lengua Espanola.
--Diccionario Ideologico Manual de la Lengua Espanola.
--Diccionario Practico Escolar de la Lengua Espanola.
--Diccionario Simultaneo en 6 Idiomas.
Capdevilla Font, Juan. Diccionario Basico Escolar de la Lengua Espanola.
--Diccionario Simultaneo en 21 Idiomas.
Capek, Leslie. Transforming Your Office.
Capek, Mary E. Writing in Context.
Capel, Lee M., tr. see Kierkegaard, Soren.
Capell, A. A Survey of New Guinea Languages.
Capell, Elizabeth A. Constitutional Officers, Agencies, Boards & Commissions in California State Government: 1849-1975.
Capelle, J. Tomorrow's Education: The French Experience.
Capers, Gerald M. The Mississippi River: Before & after Mark Twain.
Caperton, Alastair M., jt. auth. see Paynter, Raymond A., Jr.
Capes, Edward C., et al, eds. Coal Processing.
Capetti, Giselda, ed. Cronistoria.
Capie, Forrest. Depression & Protectionism: Britain Between the Wars.
Capitaine, Jean L. & Charton, Balthazar. Le Affiche De Cinema.
Caplan, David, ed. Biological Studies of Mental Processes.
Caplan, Paula, jt. auth. see Kinsbourne, Marcel.
Caplen, R. H. A Practical Approach to Quality Control.
Caplin, Lee E., ed. The Business of Art.
--The Business of Art.
Caplow. Managing an Organization.
Capobianco, M., et al, eds. see New York City Graph Theory Conference Staff.
Capon. Food for Thought.
Capon, Robert F. Capon on Cooking.
Caponera, D. A. Water Laws in Moslem Countries.
Capote, Truman. Selected Writings of Truman Capote.
Capozzi, Angelo. Change of Face: What You Should Know if You Choose Cosmetic Surgery.
Cappel, Constance. Hemingway in Michigan.
Cappel, R. The S.W.A.T Team Manual.
Cappellanus, George. Latin Can Be Fun. Needham, Peter, tr.
Cappellari, Marjorie, jt. ed. see Walsh, Don.
Cappellini, V. & Marconi, R., eds. Advances in Image Processing & Pattern Recognition.
Capper, John, et al. Chesapeake Waters: Pollution, Public Health, & Public Opinion, 1607-1972.
Capper, P. L. & Cassie, W. F. Mechanics of Engineering Soils: SI Version.
Capper, P. L., et al. Problems in Engineering Soils.
Cappiello, Rose. Oh Lucky Country. Rando, Gaetano, tr. from Ital.
Capps, Charles. Dynamics of Faith & Confession.
--Kicking over Sacred Cows.
--Paul's Thorn in the Flesh.
--Why Tragedy Happens to Christians.
Capps, Donald. Biblical Approaches to Pastoral Counseling.
--Life Cycle Theory & Pastoral Care.
--Pastoral Care: A Thematic Approach.
--Pastoral Care & Hermeneutics.
Capps, Jack L. Emily Dickinson's Reading, 1836-1886.
Capps, Walter H. Hope Against Hope: From Moltmann to Merton in One Theological Decade.
Cappuccilli, Edmund, et al. Synthetic Organic Chemicals: United States Production & Sales, 1984.
Cappuccinelli, P. Motility of Living Cells.
Capra, Fritjof. The Turning Point: Science, Society & the Rising Culture.
Capri, Anton Z. & Kamal, Abdul N., eds. Particles & Fields 2.
Caprino, Luciano, ed. Platelet Aggregation & Drugs.
Caprio, Frank B., jt. auth. see Caprio, Frank S.
Caprio, Frank S. Add Life to Your Years.
--Female Homosexuality: A Psychodynamic Study of Lesbianism.
--Power of Sex.
Caprio, Frank S. & Caprio, Frank B. Parents & Teenagers.
Capurro, L. R. & Reid, Joseph L., eds. Contributions on the Physical Oceanography of the Gulf of Mexico.
Capusan, I., et al. Systemic Sclerosis: Current Research.
Caputi, Anthony. Buffo: The Genius of Vulgar Comedy.
Caputo, M., jt. ed. see Coulomb, J.
Caputo, Philip. Del Corso's Gallery.
--A Rumor of War.
Capuzzi, Frank, tr. see Heidegger, Martin.
CARA Staff. Hi There! What Is Your Name?
Carafoli, E. Wing Theory in Supersonic Flow.
Caraganis, Lynn. Garish Days.
Caraion, Ion. Ion Caraion: Poems. Dorian, Marguerite & Urdang, Elliott B., trs. from Romanian.
Carano, Paul & Sanchez, Pedro C. A Complete History of Guam.
Caras, Roger. The Forest.
--Going to the Zoo with Roger Caras.
--Mara Simba: The African Lion.
--Mysteries of Nature: Explained & Unexplained.
--The Roger Caras Dog Book.
--The Wonderful World of Mammals: Adventuring with Stamps.
--A Zoo in Your Room.
Caras, Roger & Graham, Pamela C. Dogs: Records, Stars, Feats, & Facts.
Caras, Roger A. A Celebration of Cats.
--Dangerous to Man.
Caras, Steven. Peter Martins: Prince of the Dance.
CARASA Collective Staff. Women under Attack: Victories, Backlash & the Fight for Reproductive Freedom. Davis, Sue, ed.
Carasov, Victor. Two Gentlemen to See You, Sir: The Autobiography of a Villain.
Carbaugh, Robert J. International Economics.
Carberry, M., et al. Foundations of Computer Science.
Carberry, Patrick R. CAD-CAM with Personal Computers.
Carbo, Norman. Cabal.
Carbone, jt. auth. see Brain.
Carbonell, Jaime, jt. auth. see Langley, Pat.
Carchedi, Guglielmo. Problems in Class Analysis.
Card, Emily. Staying Solvent: A Comprehensive Guide to Equal Credit for Women.
Card, James. Clark Gable: Legends.
Carde, Ring T., jt. ed. see Bell, William T.
Cardella, Carol A. Builders Guide to Merchandising.
--Salespersons Guide to Merchandising.
Cardenal, Ernesto. Flights of Victory: Songs in Celebration of the Nicaraguan Revolution. Zimmerman, Marc, ed. & tr.
--Love.
Cardiff, Gladys. To Frighten a Storm.
Cardinale, H. E. Orders of Knighthood, Awards & the Holy See: A Historical Juridical & Practical Compendium.
Cardon, A. & Fransen, L. Dynamic Semiconductor RAM Structures.
Cardona, Rodolfo, ed. Novelistas Espanoles de Hoy.
Cardoso, Bill. The Maltese Sangweech & Other Heroes.
Cardoza, Anne & Vlk, Suzee J. High-Paying Jobs in Six Months or Less.
--Robotics.
Cardozo, Manoel D. The Portuguese in America, 590 BC-1974: A Chronology & Fact Book.
Cardus, Neville. Neville Cardus: Autobiography.
Cardwell, Jerry D. Mass Media Christianity: Televangelism & the Great Commission.
--Social Psychology: A Symbolic Interaction Perspective.
Cardwell, Thomas A. Command Structure for Theater Warfare: The Quest for Unity of Command.
Carelli, M. Dino, compiled by see Becker, H. A. & Dueuzeide, H.
Carelse, Xavier. Making Science Laboratory Equipment: A Manual for Students & Teachers in Developing Countries.
Carenza, L. & Zichella, L., eds. Emotion & Reproduction.
Carenza, L., ed. see International Congress of Psychosomatic Obstetrics & Gynecology Staff.
Carenza, L., et al, eds. Clinical Psychoneuroendocrinology in Reproduction.
Careri, G., ed. Liquid Helium.
Carew, Jan. Children of the Sun.
--The Third Gift.
Carew, Jocelyn. Crown of Passion.
--Follow the Shadows.
--The Golden Sovereigns.
--Pavilion of Passion.
Carey, A. G., jt. auth. see Benson, John H.
Carey, David. Story of the Motor Car.
Carey, Diane. Final Frontier.
Carey, Ernestine G., jt. auth. see Gilbreth, Frank B., Jr.
Carey, Frances & Griffiths, Antong. The Print in Germany.
Carey, George, et al. Urbanization, Water Pollution & Public Policy.
Carey, Helen & Greenberg, Judith E. How to Read a Newspaper.
Carey, Helen, jt. auth. see Greenberg, Judith E.
Carey, Henry. The Plays of Henry Carey. Macey, Samuel C., ed.
Carey, Henry C. Credit System in France, Great Britain & the United States.
Carey, James C. Peru & the United States, 1900-1962.
Carey, John, ed. see Thomas, Aaron J. & Thomas, Ann.
Carey, John L. The Rise of the Accounting Profession.
Carey, Karen L. The Last Voyage of Odysseus: A Novel.
Carey, Katherine & Perkins, Alice, eds. Shock.
Carey, Katherine W. & McVan, Barbara, eds. Pain.
Carey, Ken. Notes to My Children: A Simplified Metaphysics.
--Vision. Gross, Jim, ed.
Carey, Lou. Measuring & Evaluating School Learning.
Carey, Mary, jt. auth. see McCormick, Harry.
Carey, Mary K. How Long Must I Hide.
Carey, Matthew. Essays on Political Economy.
Carey, Neil G. Guide to the Queen Charlotte Islands.
Carey, Roy & Isaac, E. D. Mag..tic Domains & Techniques for Their Observation.
Carey Jones, N. S. The Pattern of a Dependent Economy: The National Income of British Honduras.
Careymore, jt. auth. see Julian.
Cargan, Leonard & Ballantine, Jeanne H. Sociological Footprints: Introductory Readings in Sociology.
Cargas, Harry. I Lay Down My Life.
Cargas, Harry J. & Corrigan, John T. The Holocaust: An Annotated Bibliography.
Cargas, Harry J., ed. Responses to Elie Wiesel.
Cargher, John. How to Enjoy Opera Without Really Trying.
Cargill, Burton F., jt. auth. see O'Brien, Michael.
Cargill, Thomas F. & Garcia, Gillian G. Financial Reform in the 1980s.
Carillo, Charles. Shepherd Avenue. Kroupa, Melanie & Meeker, Amy, eds.
Carillo, Mary. Rick Elstein's Tennis Kinetics with Martina Navratilova.
Carillon, Annie & Goutel, Beatrice de. Dictionnaire du Scrabble.
Carini, Geraldine & Birmingham, Jacqueline J. Traction Made Manageable: A Self Learning Module.
Carini, Louis. The Theory of Symbolic Transformations: A Humanistic Scientific Psychology.
Carino, Benjamin V. Filipinos on Oahu, Hawaii.
Carisella, P. J. & Ryan, James. Who Killed the Red Baron?
Carkhuff, Robert R. & Berenson, Bernard G. Beyond Counseling & Therapy.
Carl, Angela. Child Abuse: What You Can Do about It.
Carl, Angela R. A Matter of Choice.
Carl, Linda. The Alumni College Movement.
Carl, William J., II. Preaching Christian Doctrine.
Carl, William J., III, jt. auth. see Pervo, Richard I.
Carl, William J., III, jt. auth. see Vawter, Bruce.
Carlbom, Ingrid. High-Performance Graphics System Architecture: A Methodology for Design & Evaluation. Stone, Harold S., ed.
Carle, Eric. One, Two, Three to the Zoo.
Carlen, Pat. Women's Imprisonment: The Meanings of Women's Imprisonment in Scotland.
Carleton, R. O., jt. auth. see Jaffe, A.
Carleton, William. The Black Prophet.
--Stories from Carleton.
Carley, Larry W. Chrysler K-Cars, (1981-1984) Do-It-Yourself Car Care.
--How to Make Your Own Alcohol Fuels.
--The Mechanics Guide to Front Wheel Drive.
--Propane Conversion of Cars, Trucks & RVs.
Carley, Lionel & Threlfall, Robert. Delius.
Carley, Wayne. Unlucky Day at Camp How-Ja-Do.
Carli, Franco De see De Carli, Franco.
Carlile, Clancy. Spore Seven.
Carlile, M., ed. Primitive Sensory & Communication Systems, Taxes & Tropisms of Microorganisms & Cells.
Carlin, Chip, ed. see Colvin, Ruth J. & Root, Jane.
Carlin, R. L. & Van Duyneveldt, A. J. Magnetic Properties of Transition Metal Compounds.
Carlin, R. L., ed. Transition Metal Chemistry: A Series of Advances.
Carlin, Richard L., ed. Transition Metal Chemistry: A Series of Advances.
--Transition Metal Chemistry: A Series of Advances.
Carliner, David. The Rights of Aliens.
Carling, T. E. Complete Book of Drink.
Carlinsky, Dan & Heim, David. Twenty Bicycle Tours in & Around New York City.

Authors

Carlisle, Elliott. Dialogues on "MAC" Management Organization.
Carlisle, Madelyn, jt. auth. see Carlisle, Norman.
Carlisle, Norman & Carlisle, Madelyn. Where to Live for Your Health.
Carlisle, Olga. Island in Time: A Memoir of Childhood.
Carlisle, Olga A., tr. see Pasternak, Boris.
Carlisle, Robert A., ed. UNITAS Twenty-Five: A Silver Anniversary.
Carlo, Andrea De see De Carlo, Andrea.
Carlos. Albear: The Dog Who Could Talk.
Carlova, John, jt. auth. see Belli, Melvin M., Sr.
Carlova, John, jt. auth. see Horsley, Jack E.
Carlozzi, Annette. Fifty Texas Artists: A Critical Selection of Painters & Sculptors Working in Texas.
Carlozzi, Carl G. Confirmation: A Workbook.
Carlozzo, Ann-Therese, ed. see Farmworker Justice Fund Staff & Wilk, Valerie A.
Carlsen. Encounters Training.
--Insights Training.
Carlsen, Clarence J., tr. see Hallesby, O.
Carlsen, G. Robert, et al. Western Literature: Themes & Writers.
Carlsen, G. Robert, et al, eds. Encounters: Themes in Literature. Tovatt, Anthony.
Carlsen, John. Economic & Social Transformation in Rural Kenya.
Carlsen, Martin, et al. Student Workbook for Introduction to the Administration of Justice.
Carlsen, Ruth C. Half-Past Tomorrow.
Carlson, Betty. The Unhurried Chase That Ended at L'Abri.
Carlson, Betty, jt. auth. see Smith, Jane S.
Carlson, Bruce M., ed. & intro. by see Sidorova, Vera F.
Carlson, Carole C., jt. auth. see Ross, Skip.
Carlson, Claire L. & Swisher, James H., eds. Innovative Approaches to Mined Land Reclamation.
Carlson, Dale. Baby Needs Shoes.
--Boys Have Feelings Too.
--The Human Apes.
--The Secret of the Invisible City.
--Triple Boy.
Carlson, David B. & Heinberg, John D. How Housing Allowances Work: Integrated Findings to Date from the Experimental Housing Allowance Program.
Carlson, Edgar M. The Classic Christian Faith.
--The Future of Church-Related Higher Education.
Carlson, Edgar M., tr. see Wingren, Gustaf.
Carlson, Edward H. Kids & the IBM PC & PCjr. Compute! Publications, Inc. Staff, ed.
Carlson, Faith. We Bake Cookies.
Carlson, G. E., jt. auth. see Putnam, R.
Carlson, Gene P., ed. see IFSTA Committee.
Carlson, George. Crossword Adventures.
Carlson, Greg N. Reference to Kinds in English. Hankamer, Jorge, ed.
Carlson, Jean. The Cup.
Carlson, Kurt. One American Must Die: A Hostage's Personal Account of the Hijacking of Flight 847.
Carlson, Lars A., et al, eds. see International Conference on Atherosclerosis, Milan Staff.
Carlson, Marvin. The Italian Stage: From Goldoni to D'Annunzio.
Carlson, Natalie S. Alphonse, That Bearded One.
--The Ghost in the Lagoon.
Carlson, Neal. To Die is Gain.
Carlson, Oliver. Brisbane: A Candid Biography.
Carlson, P. M. Audition for Murder.
--Murder Is Pathological.
Carlson, Paul R. O Christian! O Jew!
Carlson, Per & Trower, W. Peter, eds. Physics in Collision: High-Energy ee-ep-pp Interactions.
Carlson, Peter. Roughneck: The Life & Times of Big Bill Haywood.
--Roughneck: The Life & Times of Big Bill Haywood.
Carlson, R. A. David, the Chosen King: A Traditio-Historical Approach to the 2nd Book of Samuel.
Carlson, Ray, jt. auth. see Millkie, Ron.
Carlson, Richard E. Meterology Manual & Lecture Guide.
Carlson, Richard O. Orderly Career Opportunities.
Carlson, Rodger D. The Economics for the Profitable Mining & Marketing of Gold, Silver, Copper, Lead & Zinc Ores.
Carlson, Ron. Betrayed by F. Scott Fitzgerald.
--Truants.
Carlson, Ruth K. Speaking Aids Through the Grades.
Carlson, Sevinc. Malaysia: Search for National Unity & Economic Growth.
Carlson, Stephen P., jt. auth. see Schneider, Fred W.
Carlson, T. A. X-Ray Photoelectron Spectroscopy.
Carlson, Thorsten R. Administrators & Reading.
Carlson, Vada & Witherspoon, Gary. Black Mountain Boy.
--Grandfather Stories.
Carlson, William, jt. auth. see Rio, Michel.
Carlsson, A., et al, eds. Current Topics in Extrapyramidal Disorders.
Carlsson, J., ed. Mechanical Behaviour of Materials: Proceedings of the Fourth International Conference on Mechanical Behaviour of Materials, Stockholm, Sweden, August 15-19, 1983.
Carlston, Charles. Epiphany. Achtemeier, Elizabeth, ed.
Carlston, Charles E. The Parables of the Triple Tradition.
Carlton, Jay. The Economical Economy.
--Neurology of Mentality.
Carlucci, Rocco, jt. auth. see Gargiulo, Albert F.
Carlut, Charles. A Concordance to Flaubert's Bouvard et Pecuchet.
--A Concordance to Flaubert's "Madame Bovary"
Carlut, Charles & Meiden, Walter. French for Oral Written Review.
Carlut, Charles, et al. A Concordance to Flaubert's L'Education Sentimentale.
--A Concordance to Flaubert's La Tentation de Saint Antoine.
--A Concordance to Flaubert's Salammbo.
--A Concordance to Flaubert's Trois Contes.
Carlyle, Thomas. The Letters of Thomas Carlyle to His Brother Alexander, with Related Family Letters. Marrs, Edwin W., Jr., ed.
Carmack, Robert & Cofacci, Gino. Desserts with Spirit!
Carmack, Robert M. Quichean Civilization: The Ethnohistoric, Ethnographic & Archaelogical Sources.
Carman, Bliss & Hovey, Richard. Songs from Vagabondia.
Carman, Bliss, compiled by. Canadian Poetry in English.
Carman, John S. Obstacles to Mineral Development: A Pragmatic View. Varon, Benison, ed.
Carman, Marilyn J., jt. auth. see Carman, Robert A.
Carman, Oneal. God Is Alive & Well.
Carman, Robert A. & Carman, Marilyn J. Quick Arithmetic.
Carman, Robert A. & Saunders, Hal M. Modern Technical Mathematics with Calculus.
Carmell, Pamela, tr. see Juarroz, Roberto.
Carmen, Ira H. Power & Balance: An Introduction to American Constitutional Government.
Carmen, Rolando Del see Del Carmen, Rolando.
Carmi, A., ed. Euthanasia.
Carmi, S., jt. ed. see Peterson, F.
Carmichael, Alasdair. Kintyre.
Carmichael, Amy W. If.
Carmichael, Betty. You Can't Borrow from Tomorrow.
Carmichael, Calum M. The Laws of Deuteronomy.
Carmichael, Carrie. Non-Sexist Childraising.
Carmichael, D. G. Structural Modeling & Optimization.
Carmichael, Douglas. Pendragon.
Carmichael, Douglas R. & Benis, Martin. Auditing Standards & Procedures Manual 1986-87.
Carmichael, Lucianne B. McDonogh Fifteen: Becoming a School.
Carmichael, Mary C. Oh, Boy! Joy Roy!
Carmichael, Patrick H., ed. Understanding the Books of the New Testament.
--Understanding the Books of the Old Testament.
Carmines, Edward G., jt. auth. see Zeller, Richard A.
Carmo, M. Do, ed. Geometry & Topology.
Carmody, Denise L. & Carmody, John T. Becoming One Flesh.
--Christianity: An Introduction.
--Christianity: An Introduction.
--Ways to the Center: An Introduction to World Religions.
Carmody, Denise L., jt. auth. see Carmody, John T.
Carmody, John. Maturing a Christian Conscience.
--The Quiet Imperative: Meditations on Justice & Peace Based on Readings from the New Testament.
--Theology for the Nineteen-Eighties.
Carmody, John T. & Carmody, Denise L. Contemporary Catholic Theology: An Introduction.
Carmody, John T., jt. auth. see Carmody, Denise L.
Carmona, J., et al, eds. Non-Commutative Harmonic Analysis.
Carn, Neil, jt. auth. see Hinds, Dudley.
Carnap, Rudolf. Meaning & Necessity: A Study in Semantics & Modal Logic.
Carnegie Council on Children Staff, jt. auth. see Keniston, Kenneth.
Carnegie Council on Policy Studies in Higher Education Staff. Giving Youth a Better Chance: Options for Education, Work, & Service.
Carnegie Council Staff & DeLone, Richard. Small Futures: Children, Inequality & the Limits of Liberal Reform.
Carnegie, Dale. How Enjoy Your Life & Your Job.
--How to Enjoy Your Life & Your Job.
--How to Stop Worrying & Start Living.
--How to Stop Worrying & Start Living.
--How to Stop Worrying & Start Living.
--How to Win Friends & Influence People.
Carnegie Institute, Museum of Art Staff. Carnegie Treasures Cookbook.
Carnegie Institution of Washington, Department of Meridian Astronomy Staff. General Catalogue of Thirty Three Thousand Three Hundred Forty-Two Stars for the Epoch 1950. Boss, Benjamin, et al, eds.
Carnegie Institution of Washington Staff. Papers Concerning the Palaeontology of the Pleistocene of California & the Tertiary of Oregon.
Carnegie Symposium on Cognition Staff. Visual Information Processing: Proceedings of the Carnegie Symposium on Cognition, 8th, Annual. Chase, William G., ed.
Carnell, Edward J. A Philosophy of the Christian Religion.
Carnes, Mark C., ed. see Bowerman, Guy E., Jr.
Carnes, Patrick J. Sexual Addiction.
Carnes, William T. Effective Meetings for Busy People: Let's Decide It & Go Home.
--Effective Meetings for Busy People: Let's Decide It & Go Home.
Carnevale, Anthony P. The Real Supply-Side Economics.
Carnevale, Nino, jt. auth. see Wapnick, Simon.
Carney, Charles P. New Hope for Your Marriage.
Carney, Clarke G. & McMahon, Sarah L., eds. Exploring Contemporary Male-Female Roles: A Facilitator's Guide.
Carney, David E. Government & Economy in British West Africa.
Carney, Glandion. Creative Urban Youth Ministries.
Carney, James D. & Scheer, Richard K. Fundamentals of Logic.
Carney, Louis P. Probation & Parole: Legal & Social Dimensions.
Carney, Magdalene M., ed. Issues, Perspectives, & Definitions: Selected Readings.
Carney, Rena B. Happy Day Ranch.
Carney, Thomas P. Instant Evolution: We'd Better Get Good at It.
Carniero, Robert L., ed. see Spencer, Herbert.
Carnine, Douglas, jt. auth. see Engelmann, Siegfried.
Carnoy, Martin. Education & Employment: A Critical Appraisal.
Caro, Robert A., et al. Extraordinary Lives. Zinsser, William, intro. by.
Carola, Robert, et al. Human Anatomy & Physiology.
Carolan, Milou, jt. auth. see Ulrich, Christine.
Caroli, Betty B. Italian Repatriation from the United States, 1900-1914.
Caroline, Nancy L., jt. auth. see McClintock, James C.
Caron, Fabien, ed. see Universite Laval, Centre d'Etudes Nordiques, Quebec Staff.
Carone, Pasquale A., et al, eds. Mental Health Needs of Workers & Management: Expectations & Reality.
Caroselli, Remus F. Mystery at Long Crescent Marsh.
Carosso, Vincent P. More Than a Century of Investment Banking: The Didder, Peabody & Co. Story.
Carotenuto, Aldo. A Secret Symmetry: Sabina Spielrein Between Jung & Freud. Bettelheim, Bruno, commentary by. Pomerans, Arno, et al, trs.
Carpenter, Alton E. The Infinite Thought Projections of Jesus.
--Twenty-One Keys to a Beautiful Life.
--Twenty-Three Keys to Inner Peace from the 23rd Psalm.
Carpenter, Cal. The Walton War & Tales of the Great Smoky Mts.
Carpenter, Christopher. The Twilight Realm.
Carpenter, Edward. Iolaus: An Anthology of Friendship.
Carpenter, Frederic I. American Literature & the Dream.
Carpenter, H. J. Popular Christianity & the Early Theologians. Lee, Clarence L., ed.
Carpenter, Humphrey. Inklings: C. S. Lewis & His Friends.
--The Inklings: C. S. Lewis, J. R. R. Tolkien & Their Friends.
--Secret Gardens: A Study of the Golden Age of Children's Literature.
--Tolkien: A Biography.
Carpenter, Humphrey & Tolkien, Christopher, eds. The Letters of J. R. R. Tolkien.
Carpenter, Kenneth, ed. Pellagra.
Carpenter, Kevin. Penny Dreadfuls & Comics: English Periodicals for Children from Victorian Times to the Present Day.
Carpenter, Mark, ed. see Culver, Robert D.
Carpenter, Mimi G. The Cross-Eyed Cat.
Carpenter, Philip L. Immunology & Serology.
Carpenter, R. H. Movements of the Eyes.
Carpenter, William. Political Letters & Pamphlets by William Carpenter.
Carpentier, Alejo. The Lost Steps.
Carpentier, Hortense, tr. see Valenzuela, Luisa.
Carper, L. Dean. GIB.
Carpi, Amilcare, ed. The Pharmacology of Cerebral Circulation.
Carpineto, Jane. Husband Hunting: How to Win at the Mating Game.
Carpino, Pasquale. Recipes from Pasquale's Kitchen.
Carr & Greenberg. Treasury of Modern Fantasy.
Carr, D. J. & Carr, S. G., eds. People & Plants in Australia.
--Plants & Man in Australia.
Carr, D. J., ed. see International Conference on Plant Growth Substances Staff.
Carr, Dick. You, Too, Can Golf in the Eighties: An Effective Strategy for Reducing Strokes.
Carr, Donald E. Energy & the Earth Machine.
Carr, Edward H. The Romantic Exiles.
Carr, Gerald F., jt. ed. see Rauch, Irmengard.
Carr, Ian. Miles Davis: A Biography.
--Miles Davis: A Critical Biography.
Carr, J., ed. Major Companies of the Far East 1986: East Asia-Peoples' Republic of China, Hong Kong, Japan, Republic of Korea, Taiwan.
--Major Companies of the Far East 1986: South East Asia-Brunei, Indonesia, Malaysia, The Philippines, Singapore, Thailand.
Carr, J., jt. ed. see Bricault, G.
Carr, J. G., et al, eds. see Long Ashton Symposium - Fourth, University of Bristol, September, 1974.
Carr, James G., ed. Criminal Law Review 1986.
Carr, Janet & Shepherd, Roberta. Early Care of the Stroke Patient: A Positive Approach.
Carr, Janet see Yule, William.
Carr, Janet H. & Shepherd, Roberta B. Early Care of the Stroke Patient: A Positive Approach.
Carr, Jayge. Rabelasian Reprise.
Carr, Jean. Another Story: Women & the Falklands War.
Carr, John, jt. ed. see Corneli, James.
Carr, John D. Till Death Do Us Part.
Carr, John Dickson. Panic in Box C.
Carr, John F., jt. ed. see Pournelle, Jerry.
Carr, Joseph J. CMOS, TTL: A User's Guide With Projects.
--IC Timer Handbook with One Hundred Projects & Experiments.
--Interfacing Your Microcomputer to Virtually Anything.
Carr, Joseph J., jt. auth. see Swearer, Harvey F.
Carr, Micheline, jt. auth. see Crouch, James.
Carr, Nick, compiled by. The Western Pulp Hero.
Carr, P. Personal Computing for Professionals in Government & Business.
Carr, P. J., et al. Community Psychiatric Nursing.
Carr, Pat & Tracey, Steve. Mindstretchers: Level 2. Incl. Star Gazing; Who Done It; Great Explorations; Enchantments. D S Lake Pubs.
Carr, Philippa. Midsummer's Eve.
Carr, Philippa, pseud. Voices in a Haunted Room.
Carr, Rachel. Wheel, Camel, Fish & Plow: Yoga for You.
--Yoga for All Ages.
Carr, Reg. Anarchism in France: The Case of Octave Mirbeau.
Carr, Richard, jt. auth. see Sutton, Ann.
Carr, Richard W. Virtual Memory Management. Stone, Harold, ed.
Carr, Robyn. The Braeswood Tapestry.
--By Right of Arms.
--The Troubadour's Romance.
Carr, Roy & Murray, Charles S. David Bowie: An Illustrated Record.
Carr, S. G., jt. ed. see Carr, D. J.
Carr, Sandy. The Simon & Schuster Pocket Guide to Cheese.
Carr, Stephen L. The Historical Guide to Utah Ghost Towns.
Carr, T. R. & Colston, Stephanie. State & Urban Policy Analysis: An Annotated Bibliography.
Carr, T. R., et al. Quantitative Research in Public Administration & Policy Analysis: A Methodologically Annotated Bibliography.
Carr, Terry. Best SF of the Year.
--Universe Seventeen.
--Universe Sixteen.
Carr, William N. & Mize, Jack P. MOS-LSI Design & Application.
Carra, Lawrence, jt. auth. see Dean, Alexander.
Carraher, Charles E. & Sheats, John, eds. Organometallic Polymers.
Carraher, Charles E., Jr. & Sperling, L. H., eds. Polymer Applications of Renewable-Resource Materials.
Carran, Archie B. Genic Psychology: Method & Theory.
Carranza, et al. Scanning Electron Microscope: Atlas of Periodontal Biology & Pathology.
Carranza, Fermin A. Glickman's Clinical Periodontology: Prevention, Diagnosis & Treatment of Periodontal Disease in the Practice of General Dentistry.
Carrasco Martinez, Castulo. Diccionario de Medicina, Farmacia Veterinaria y Quimica.
Carre, John Le see Le Carre, John.

Carrell, jt. auth. see Dean.
Carrell, Mary Jane. Understanding English.
Carrera, Liane. Anna Held & Flo Ziegfeld.
Carreras, J., et al. Shear Zones in Rocks: Papers Presented at the International Conference Held at the University of Barcelona, May 1979.
Carr-Gregg, Charlotte. Kicking the Habit: Four Australian Therapeutic Communities.
Carr-Hill, Roy & Stern, Nicholas. Crime, the Police & Criminal Statistics: An Analysis of Official Statistics for England & Wales Using Economic Methods.
Carrier, George F. Partial Differential Equations.
Carrier, Karen B., ed. see Sturm, Dorothy.
Carrier, Robert. Menu Planner.
--Robert Carrier's Menu Planner.
--A Taste of Morocco: A Culinary Journey.
Carriere, Anne-Marie. Le Dictionnaire des Hommes.
Carriere, Dean & Day, Fraser. Solar Houses for a Cold Climate.
Carrieri, Mario, photos by. The Vatican & Christian Rome.
Carrigan, Ana. Salvador Witness: The Life & Calling of Jean Donovan.
Carrigan, Richard A. & Trower, W. Peter, eds. Magnetic Monopoles.
Carrighar, Sally. The Glass Dove.
--Home to the Wilderness.
Carriker, S. David. Railroading in the Carolina Sandhills: "The Hoffman & Troy Railroad" & "Sandhill Shays"
Carrillo, Santiago. Eurocommunism & the State. Green, Nan & Elliott, A. M., trs.
Carrington. Computers for Spectroscopists.
Carrington, Alan. Microwave Spectroscopy of Free Radicals.
Carrington, Elsie R., jt. auth. see Willson, J. Robert.
Carrington, Frank & Lyle, Joseph L., Jr. Christian Burial: A Case of Murder & the Perversion of Justice.
Carrington, Joanna. Landscape Painting for Beginners.
Carrington, Paul D., et al. Justice on Appeal.
Carrington, Timothy. The Year They Sold Wall Street: The Inside Story of the Shearson-American Express Merger, and How it Changed Wall Street Forever.
Carrington, Ulrich S. The Making of an American: An Adaptation of Memorable Tales by Charles Sealsfield.
Carrion, Arturo M., et al. Puerto Rico: A Political & Cultural Odyssey.
Carris, Joan D. The Revolt of Ten-X.
Carris, Joan D. & Crystal, Michael R. SAT Success: Peterson's Study Guide to English & Math Skills for College Entrance Examinations: SAT, ACT and PSAT.
Carritt, Edgar F. The Theory of Morals.
Carroll, Archie B., jt. auth. see Huseman, Richard C.
Carroll, Archie B., jt. auth. see Watson, Hugh H.
Carroll, Archie B., jt. auth. see Watson, Hugh J.
Carroll, Archie B., jt. ed. see Watson, Hugh J.
Carroll, B. J. General English Tests Elementary One Pack.
--General English Tests Instruction Booklet.
Carroll, Bill. Chevrolet Performance Guide.
Carroll, David. The Magic Makers.
--The Matinee Idols.
Carroll, David & Saxe, Barry. Natural Magic.
Carroll, David, jt. auth. see Simenauer, Jacqueline.
Carroll, Dewey E., ed. see Clinic on Library Applications of Data Processing Staff.
Carroll, Diahann & Firestone, Ross. Diahann.
Carroll, Donald. The Best Excuse.
Carroll, E. Malcolm. Germany & the Great Powers, 1866-1914: A Study in Public Opinion & Foreign Policy.
Carroll, Eugene A. The Drawings of Rosso Fiorentino.
Carroll, Faye. South West Africa & the United Nations.
Carroll, Frances L. Promises: A Guide to Christian Commitment.
--Temptation: How Christians Can Deal with It.
Carroll, Frances Laverne & Beilke, Patricia F. Guidelines for the Planning & Organization of School Library Media Centres.
Carroll, Gladys H. As the Earth Turns.
--Dunnybrook.
--Unless You Die Young.
Carroll, Jackson & Wilson, Robert. Too Many Pastors? The State of the Clergy Job Market.
Carroll, James. Family Trade.
--Prince of Peace.
Carroll, James J., ed. see Hartmann, Frederick H.
Carroll, James L., ed. Contemporary School Psychology: Readings from Psychology in the Schools.
Carroll, Jean G. Patient Care Audit Criteria: Standards for Hospital Quality Assurance.
--Restructuring Hospital Quality Assurance: The New Guide for Health Care Providers.
Carroll, Jeffrey. Climbing to the Sun.
Carroll, Jeri. Unit Boxes for Little Kids.
Carroll, Joellyn. A Flight of Splendor.
Carroll, John. Guilt: The Grey Eminence behind Character, History & Culture.
--Sceptical Sociology.
Carroll, John, Jr. Solutions for the Major Problems That Face America Today & Beyond.
Carroll, John M. Data Base & Computer Systems Security. Curtice, Robert M., ed.
Carroll, John M., ed. The Benteen-Gold Letters on Custer & His Last Battle.
--The Black Military Experience in the American West.
--Black Military Experience in the American West.
--The Two Battles of the Little Big Horn.
Carroll, Jon & Lorant, Terry. The Pickle Family Circus: The Romance & History of America's One-Ring Traveling Circus.
Carroll, Lewis. Alice in Wonderland: Through the Looking Glass.
--Alice's Adventures in Wonderland. Bd. with Through the Looking Glass. G K Hall.
--Alice's Adventures in Wonderland.
--Alice's Adventures in Wonderland.
--Alice's Adventures in Wonderland & Through the Looking Glass. Barish, Wendy, ed.
--Alice's Adventures in Wonderland (Pennyroyal-California Edition)
--Alice's Adventures Under Ground.
--Anderson's Alice: Walter Anderson Illustrates Alice's Adventures in Wonderland by Lewis Carroll.
--Humorous Verse of Lewis Carroll.
--Journeys in Wonderland.
--Nursery Alice.
--The Rectory Umbrella & Mischmasch.
--Through the Looking-Glass: And What Alice Found There.
Carroll, Mitchell B. Global Perspectives of an International Tax Lawyer.
--A Ring of Jingles.
Carroll, Peter N. It Seemed Like Nothing Happened: The Tragedy & Promise in America of the 1970s.
--It Seemed Like Nothing Happened: The Tragedy & Promise of America in the 1970s.
Carroll, R. W. & Showalter, R. E. Singular & Degenerate Cauchy Problems.
Carroll, Rosalynn. Enchanted Encore.
Carroll, Stephen J., Jr. & Paine, Frank T. Management Process: Cases & Readings.
Carroll, Vern, ed. Adoption in Eastern Oceania.
--Pacific Atoll Populations.
Carroll, W. E., jt. auth. see Krider, J. L.
Carron, Albert V. Social Psychology of Sport: An Experiential Approach.
Carron, Harold & McLaughlin, Robert E. Management of Low Back Pain.
Carrow, Milton M., jt. ed. see Nyhart, J. D.
Carr-Saunders, Sir Alexander M. New Universities Overseas.
Carruth, Gorton, jt. ed. see Pulliam, Tom.
Carruthers, Ian, ed. Social & Economic Perspectives on Irrigation.
Carruthers, M., ed. see Annual Conference for Psychosomatic Research Staff.
Carse, James P. & Dallery, Arlene B., eds. Death & Society: A Book of Readings & Sources.
Carsley, Anne. This Triumphant Fire.
Carson, Anne. Eros the Bittersweet: An Essay.
Carson, Bryan. A Dream of Naked Women.
Carson, Carol S. GNP: An Overview of Source Data & Estimating Methods.
Carson, D. A., ed. Biblical Interpretation & the Church: The Problem of Contextualization.
--The Church in the Bible & the World: An International Study.
Carson, Gerald. The Dentist & the Empress: The Adventures of Dr. Tom Evans in Gaslight Paris.
--The Golden Egg: The Personal Income Tax, Where It Came from, How It Grew.
Carson, Hampton L. see Mueller-Dombois, Dieter.
Carson, John H. Design of Microprocessor Systems.
Carson, John H., jt. auth. see Liebowitz, Burt H.
Carson, Jonathan E. Making College Pay: How to Earn Money While You're Still in School.
Carson, Linwood. The Avenging Angels.
Carson, M. A. The Mechanics of Erosion.
Carson, Neil. Arthur Miller.
Carson, Rachael L. Silent Spring.
Carson, Rachel. Edge of the Sea.
Carson, Rachel L. Silent Spring.
Carson, Russell M. Peaks & People of the Adirondacks.
Carson, S. McB, ed. Environmental Education-Principles & Practice.
Carson, T. R. & Roberts, M. J., eds. Atoms & Molecules in Astrophysics.
Carstens, Harold H., ed. Circus Trains & Modelling.
Carstensen, Russell V. EMI Control in Boats & Ships. White, Donald R., ed.
Carswell, Catherine. Life of Robert Burns.
Cartari, Vincenzo. Le Imagini...Degli Dei.
Carter, jt. auth. see Kricka.
Carter, A. & Brody, A., eds. Contributions to Input-Output Analysis.
Carter, A. H., ed. see Burns, D. T. & Townshend, A.
Carter, Alice C. Neutrality or Commitment: The Evolution of Dutch Foreign Policy, 1667-1795.
Carter, Angela. Moonshadow.
--The Passion of New Eve.
--The War of Dreams.
Carter, Anthony. World Bayonets: Eighteen Hundred to Present.
Carter, Ashley. Miz Lucretia of Falconhurst.
Carter, Barbara L. The Copts in Egyptian Politics 1918 - 1952.
Carter, Bernard A., Jr. Carter, Williams, Boyle, Smith & Mulvihill Families.
Carter, Bruce. Buzzbugs.
Carter, Charles F. The Wedding Day in Literature & Art: A Collection of the Best Descriptions of Wedding from the Works of the World's Leading Novelists & Poets.
Carter, Codell K. A Contemporary Introduction to Logic with Applications.
Carter, Craig. How to Use the Power of Mind in Everyday Life.
--Your Handbook for Healing.
Carter, D. L. & Bate, R. T. Physics of Semimetals & Narrow-Gap Semiconductors.
Carter, Dorothy S. The Enchanted Orchard.
Carter, Dorothy S., ed. Greedy Mariani: And Other Folktales of the Antilles.
Carter, E. A. & Seaquist, V. G. Extreme Weather History & Climate Atlas from Alabama.
Carter, E. F. Dictionary of Inventions & Discoveries.
Carter, Elizabeth, jt. ed. see Gilreath, James.
Carter, Elizabeth A. & McGoldrick, Monica, eds. The Family Life Cycle: A Framework for Family Therapy.
Carter, Giles F. Principles of Physical & Chemical Metallurgy.
Carter, Gwendolen M. Government of France.
--Government of the Soviet Union.
--Government of the United Kingdom.
Carter, Gwendolen M. & Morgan, E. Philip, eds. From the Frontline: Speeches of Sir Seretse Khama.
Carter, Gwendolen M. & O'Meara, Patrick, eds. Southern Africa: The Continuing Crisis.
Carter, Gwendolen M. & Paden, Ann, eds. Expanding Horizons in African Studies: Program of African Studies, Northwestern University, Proceedings of the Twentieth Anniversary Conference, 1968.
Carter, Hodding. First Person Rural.
Carter, Hodding, ed. Louisiana Almanac 1968.
--Louisiana Almanac, 1969.
Carter, J. P., ed. La Famine en Afrique: Rapports de Conference d'un Groupe de Travail sur la Famine en Afrique a Kinshasha au Zaire en janvier 1980.
Carter, James E. Help for the Evangelistic Preacher.
Carter, Jane Burr see Burr Carter, Jane.
Carter, Jeri, jt. auth. see Browning, Phillip.
Carter, Jesse B. Religious Life of Ancient Rome.
Carter, Jimmy. Why Not the Best?
Carter, John M., intro. by. Magazine Publishing Career Directory 1986: 24 Top Industry Leaders.
Carter, Juanita E. & Young, Darroch F. Electronic Calculators: A Mastery Approach Year.
Carter, L. J., ed. Communication Satellites.
Carter, Lamore J., jt. auth. see Cheers, Arlynne Lake.
Carter, Lanie. Congratulations! You're Going to Be a Grandmother.
Carter, Lief H. Reason in Law.
Carter, Lin. Horror Wears Blue.
--The Tower at the Edge of Time.
--Under the Green Star.
Carter, Loretta M. & Yaman, Peter. Dental Instruments.
Carter, M. Geotechnical Engineering Handbook.
Carter, M. P. Education, Employment & Leisure.
Carter, Nick. Blood of the Falcon.
Carter, Paul. Backstage Handbook: An Illustrated Almanac of Technical Information.
Carter, Paul A. Idea of Progress in Recent American Protestant Thought, 1930-1960. Wolf, Richard C., ed.
Carter, Paul V. Styles. Aszkenas, Kathy R., ed.
Carter, R. Capitalism: Class Conflict & the New Middle Class.
Carter, Robert. Sail Far Away: Reflections on Life Afloat.
--The Sugar Factory.
Carter, Robert M., ed. Communication in Organizations: An Annotated Bibliography & Sourcebook.
Carter, Roger. Business Administration: A Textbook for the Computer Age.
Carter, Ronald, ed. Linguistics & the Teacher.
Carter, Rosalynn. First Lady from Plains.
Carter, Stephen, et al. Chemotherapy of Cancer.
Carter, Stephen K., et al, eds. Bleomycin: Current Status & New Developments.
Carter, Tom. The Victorian Garden.
Carter, Vertie Lee. How to Get a Career Job.
Carter, Virginia B. I'm Going to Be a Missionary.
Carter, Virginia L. & Alberger, Patricia, eds. Building Your Alumni Program.
Carter, W. A., ed. Selective Inhibitors of Viral Functions.
Carter, W. D. & Engman, E. T., eds. Remote Sensing from Satellites: Proceedings of Workshops I & IX of the COSPAR Interdisciplinary Scientific Commission A (Meetings A2) of the COSPAR 25th Plenary Meeting Held in Graz, Austria 25 June - 7 July 1974.
Carter, Walter, jt. auth. see Widner, Ellis.
Carter, William C. & Vines, Robert F., eds. A Concordance to the Oeuvres Completes of Arthur Rimbaud.
Carter, Wilmoth A. The New Negro of the South.
Carter, Winifred. Dr. Johnson's "Dear Mistress"
Cartier, Francis A. The Language of the Air Force in English.
Cartier, R. Colposcopie Pratique.
Cartland, Barbara. Danger by the Nile.
Cartledge, Gwendolyn & Milburn, JoAnne F., eds. Teaching Social Skills to Children.
Cartledge, Paul. Sparta & Lakonia: A Regional History Thirteen Hundred to Three Sixty-Two B.C.
Cartnal, Alan. California Crazy.
Cartnell, E. & Fowles, G. W. A. Valency & Molecular Structure.
Cartographic Editors of Gousha, ed. City Map Library.
--State Map Library.
Carton & Dimon. Discovering BASIC with Wozzy: For the Apple II Plus, IIe, & IIc.
Cartoon Archetypical Slogan Theatre Staff. Confessions of a Socialist.
Cartwright, Ann. The Dignity of Labour? A Study of Childbearing & Induction.
Cartwright, Ann & Anderson, Robert. General Practice Revisited: A Second Study of Patients & Their Doctors.
Cartwright, Ann & Cartwright, Reg. Norah's Ark.
Cartwright, Carol A. & Cartwright, G. Phillip. Developing Observation Skills.
Cartwright, D. E., tr. see Marchuk, G. I. & Kagan, B. A.
Cartwright, Desmond S. Introduction to Personality.
Cartwright, G. Phillip, jt. auth. see Cartwright, Carol A.
Cartwright, G. Phillip, et al. Educating Special Learners.
Cartwright, Gary. Blood Will Tell.
Cartwright, John, ed. see Hay, Gilbert.
Cartwright, Reg, jt. auth. see Cartwright, Ann.
Carty, Jay. Counterattack: Taking Back Ground Lost to Sin.
Carty, Sally C. How to Make Braided Rugs.
Caruana, Russell A. A Guide to Organizing a Health Care Fiscal Services Division with Job Descriptions for Key Functions.
Carus, Julius V. Geschichte der Zoologie Bis Auf Johann Mueller und Charles Darwin.
Caruso, Peter. Destination.
Carus-Wilson, Eleanora M., ed. Essays in Economic History. Incl. Vol. 1; Vol. 2; Vol. 3. St Martin.
Carvalho-Neto, Paulo de see De Carvalho-Neto, Paulo.
Carver, D. Keith. Beginning BASIC.
--Beginning Structured COBOL.
--Beginning Structured COBOL 2D.
--Structured COBOL for Microcomputers.
Carver, Jean T. The Extracurricular Homemaker.
Carver, Joyce S. Johnny Lincoln & His Three Dogs.
Carver, Judith, jt. ed. see Carver, Richard.
Carver, Larry, ed. see Kelly, Hugh.
Carver, Lord. Twentieth-Century Warriors: The Development of the Armed Forces of the Major Military Nations in the Twentieth Century.
Carver, Raymond. If It Please You.
Carver, Raymond & Ravenel, Shannon, eds. The Best American Short Stories 1986.
Carver, Richard & Carver, Judith, eds. One Day U. S. A. A Self Portrait of America's Cities.
Carver, Robert C. & Thiess, Susan. The Creator's World.
Carver, Tina K. & Fotinos, S. Douglas. A Conversation Book: English in Everyday Life.
--A Conversation Book: English in Everyday Life.
Carwell, L'Ann. Baby's First Book about Creation.
Carwin, Merle A. Supervised Occupational Experience Manual.
Cary, Diana S. Hollywood's Children: An Inside Account of the Child Star Era.
Cary, Harold W. The University of Massachusetts: A History of One Hundred Years.
Cary, Max. A History of the Greek World: 323-146 B.C.
Cary, Otis, et al. War-Wasted Asia: Letters, 1945-46.

Cary, William L. & Eisenberg, Melvin. Corporations, Cases & Materials on: 1986 Supplement.
Carylye, J. A., ed. see Irving, David.
Carynnyk, Marco, tr. see Osadchy, Mykhaylo.
Casa, Frank P. En Busca de Espana.
Casada, James A. Dr. David Livingstone & Henry Morton Stanley: An Annotated Bibliography with Commentary.
Casale, A., et al. Advances in Polymer Science: Polymerization. Cantow, H. J., ed.
Casale, Anthony M. U. S. A. Today: Tracking Tomorrow's Trends. What We Think about Our Lives & Our Future.
Casals, Felipe G. The Syncretic Society. Meyer, Alfred G., ed. Daniels, Guy, tr. from Fr.
Casals, Pablo. Conversations with Casals.
Casanova, Giacomo. History of My Life.
--History of My Life.
--History of My Life. Trask, Willard R., tr.
--History of My Life. Trask, Willard R., tr.
--History of My Life. Trask, Willard R., tr.
--History of My Life. Trask, Willard R., tr.
Casanova, Olivier & Casanova, Patrice. Short Cuts: Styling & Caring for Short Hair.
Casanova, Pablo G., ed. La Sociologie Du Developpement Latino-Americain: Tendances Actuelles De la Recherche et Bibliographie. Incl. Pt. 1. Etudes Generales; Pt. 2. Etudes Sectorielles. Mouton.
Casanova, Patrice, jt. auth. see Casanova, Olivier.
Casanova, Patrice, jt. auth. see Geutary, Helene.
Casares, Adolfo Bioy see Bioy Casares, Adolfo.
Casarett, George W., jt. auth. see Rubin, Phillip.
Casarie, W. A., jt. ed. see Van Zeist, W.
Casasent, David. Digital Electronics.
Casata, Mary A. Cher.
Casavant, Helen. Christmas by Mail: A Series of Letters.
Casciato, Dennis A. & Bennet, Lowitz Barry B. Manual of Bedside Oncology.
Casclato, Arthur D. & West, James L., III, eds. Critical Essays on William Styron.
Cascone, Annette, jt. auth. see Cascone, Gina.
Cascone, Gina & Cascone, Annette. Jump off the Cliff Notes: A Parody.
Casdorph, Paul D. Republicans, Negroes, & Progressives in the South, Nineteen Twelve to Nineteen Sixteen.
Case, C. M. South Asian History, Seventeen Fifty to Nineteen Fifty: A Guide to Periodicals, Dissertations & Newspapers.
Case, Christine & Johnson, Ted. Laboratory Experiments in Microbiology: Brief Edition.
Case, David. Wolf Tracks.
Case, Ensan. Wingmen.
Case, James L. Clinical Management of Voice Disorders.
Case, James L., jt. auth. see Mowrer, Donald E.
Case, Lloyd A. Laboratory Physics.
Case, Lynn M. French Opinion on War & Diplomacy During the Second Empire.
Case, Paul F. The True & Invisible Rosicrucian Order.
Case, Peg. Death Blade.
Case, Richard T., et al. The Money Diet: Biblical Prescriptions for Financial Success.
Casebier, Allan. Film Appreciation.
Casement, Richard. Man Suddenly Sees to the Edge of the Universe.
Caserta, John G. The Golden Guitar & Other Poems.
Casewit, Curtis. Quit Smoking: Forty Major Techniques to Help You Stop Smoking. Werkman, Sidney L., intro. by.
Casewit, Curtis W. Foreign Jobs: The Most Popular Countries.
--The Saga of the Mountain Soldiers: The Story of the Tenth Mountain Division.
Casey, jt. auth. see Paris.
Casey, Clifford B. Sul Ross State University: The Cultural Center of Trans-Pecos Texas 1917-1975.
Casey, Douglas R. Strategic Investing: How to Profit from the Coming Inflationary Depression.
Casey, John. An American Romance.
--Testimony & Demeanor: Stories.
Casey, Robert L. Journey to the High Southwest: A Traveler's Guide.
--Journey to the High Southwest: A Traveler's Guide.
Casey, Todd. Dinobots Strike Back.
--Dinobots Strike Back.
Cash, Alan. Daily Telegram Quick Crosswords.
Cash, J. & Hopkinson, J. British Freshwater Rhizopoda & Heliozoa.
Cash, James I., Jr., et al. Corporate Information Systems Management: Text & Cases.
Cash, John D., ed. Progress in Transfusion Medicine.
Cash, June C. From the Heart.
Cash, Phyllis. How to Prepare for the Miller Analogies Test (MAT)
--How to Write a Research Paper.
Cash, Richard, et al, eds. Child Health & Survival: The UNICEF GOBI-FFF Program.
Cash, William B., Jr., jt. auth. see Stewart, Charles J.
Cashel Diocesan Library, County Tipperary, Republic of Ireland Staff. Catalogue of the Cashel Diocesan Library.
Cashell, G. T. & Durran, I. M. Handbook of Orthoptic Principles.
Cashin, James A. Handbook for Auditors.
Cashin, James A. & Lerner, Joel J. Schaum's Outline of Accounting I.
Cashion, Barbara G., jt. auth. see Eshleman, J. Ross.
Cashion, Jerry. Guide to North Carolina Historical Highway Markers.
Cashman, Richard & McKernan, Michael, eds. Sport in History.
Cashman, Victoria S. & Fetter, Theodore J. State Courts: Options for the Future.
Cashmore, Ernest. Black Sportsmen.
--Rastaman: The Rastafarian Movement in England.
Casida, John E., ed. Pyrethrum: The Natural Insecticide.
Casida, John E., jt. ed. see Pallos, Ferenc M.
Casier, Edgar. Faune Ichthyologique Du London Clay: Text & Atlas.
Caskey, C. Thomas & Robbins, D. Christopher, eds. Somatic Cell Genetics.
Casler, Lawrence. NRJD on Three Eighty-Seven Glizzits a Day.
Casner, A. James. Estate Planning: 1986 Supplement.
Caso, Jacques De see Pratt, James N. & De Caso, Jacques.
Casorti. The Technic of the Bow Op. 50 for Violin.
Caspari, E. W. & Ravin, A. W., eds. Genetic Organization.
Caspary, Vera. Laura.
--Laura.
Casper, Dale E. The Administrative History of the Federal Government: Recent Journal Articles, 1980-1982.
--City Profiles in Periodical Literature: A Checklist, 1974-1984.
--Community Development - Planning & Action: Recent Writings, 1980-1984.
--The Community Experiences of Immigrant Minorities: A Selected Bibliography.
--Eminent Domain, Taking for the Public Good: A Review of Legal Articles, 1980-1985.
--The English Urban Environment: Recent Writings, 1980-1983.
--Equal Opportunity in the Workplace: A Checklist, 1980-1983.
--Housing & Community Development: Recent Writings, 1980-1983.
--Laboring Class Movements in the United States: Historical Perspectives.
--Legal Aspects of Zoning Practices: A Checklist, 1980-1984.
--The Literature of Unemployment: A Checklist, 1980-1984.
--Local Government & Public Employees: Journal Articles, 1974-1984.
--Media & the Formation of Public Opinion: A Checklist, 1975-1984.
--Municipal Budget & Accounting Systems: A Review of the Periodical Literature, 1980 - 1984.
--Municipal Disaster Preparedness: A List of Periodical Literature, 1980-1984.
--Municipal Renewal - Central Business Districts: A Checklist, 1974-1984.
--The Nation's Response to Its Environment at Risk: Historical Perspectives, 1974-1984.
--Parent-Child Relationship in the Law: Recent Actions & Cases, 1980-1985.
--Public Pressures & the Practice of U. S. Foreign Policy: A Checklist, 1979 to 1983.
--Spatial Distribution of Urban Populations: A Bibliography.
--Trends in Municipal Administration: The Periodical Literature, 1980-1984.
--Trends in Urban Firefighting: Periodical Literature, 1980-1984.
--U. S. Political Parties in Historial Perspectives: A Checklist, 1980-1984.
--Voting Patterns in the United States: Recent Writings, 1980-1984.
Casper, Georgia Moats & Doden, Imogene Moats. I Would Do It Again.
Casper, Leonard. A Lion Unannounced: Twelve Stories & a Fable.
Caspers, H., jt. auth. see Speckman, E. J.
Caspersson, Torbjorn & Zech, Lore, eds. Chromosome Identification.
Cass, Angelica W. Letters for Everyday Use.
Cass, Bettina, et al. Why So Few? Women Academics in Australian Universities.
Cass, David & Shell, Karl, eds. The Hamiltonian Approach to Dynamic Economics.
Cass, Joan E. The Role of the Teacher in the Nursery School.
Cass, Robbie. High Jinks Down under: It Happened One Night at Mulubat.
Cass, Rosemary H., jt. auth. see Manser, Gordon.
Cassano, C. & Andreoli, M., eds. Current Topics in Thyroid Research.
Cassee, E. & Reuland, R., eds. The Management of Hospitality.
Cassel, Don. EasyWriter Simplified for the IBM Personal Computer.
Cassell, Anthony K., ed. & tr. see Boccaccio, Giovanni.
Cassell, Carol. Swept Away: Why Women Fear their Own Sexuality.
--Swept Away: Why Women Fear Their Own Sexuality.
Cassell, Christine. Teaching Poor Readers in the Secondary School.
Cassell, Dana K. Making Money with Your Home Computer.
Cassell, Eric J. The Healer's Art.
Cassell, Phyllis, jt. ed. see McCoy, Vivian.
Cassells, Cyrus. The Mud Actor.
Cassells Editors. Cassell's New Compact French Dictionary: French-English, English-French.
--Cassell's New Compact German Dictionary.
--Cassell's New Compact Latin Dictionary.
--Cassell's New Compact Spanish Dictionary: Spanish-English, English-Spanish.
Casselman, P. H. Cooperative Movement & Some of Its Problems.
--Labor Dictionary.
Cassels, J. W. Introduction to the Geometry of Numbers.
Cassels, J. W. & Frohlich, A., eds. Algebraic Number Theory.
Casserly, J. Langmead. Death of Man.
Casserly, John J. The Ford White House: The Diary of a Speechwriter.
Cassetty, Judith. Standards for Child-Support Payments: Intra-Family Transfers.
Cassetty, Judith, ed. The Parental Child-Support Obligation: Research, Practice, & Social Policy.
Cassidy. Textbook of Pediatric Rheumatology.
Cassidy, Daniel J. & Alves, Michael J., eds. The Scholarship Book: The Complete Guide to Private Sector Scholarships, Grants, & Loans for Undergraduates.
Cassidy, Diane. Circus Animals.
--Circus People.
Cassidy, James T., ed. Textbook of Pediatric Rheumatology.
Cassidy, John. The Aerobie Book.
--The Boomerang Book.
--Pumping Plastic: The Jump Rope Fitness Plan.
Cassidy, John & Rimbeaux, B. C. Juggling for the Complete Klutz.
Cassidy, Jude, jt. ed. see Spears, Ross.
Cassidy, Laurence L. Existence & Presence: The Dialectics of Divinity.
Cassidy, Robert. The Livable Cities: A Grass-Roots Guide to Rebuilding Urban America.
Cassidy, William L. Political Kidnapping.
Cassie, W. F., jt. auth. see Capper, P. L.
Cassill, Kay. Twins: Nature's Amazing Mystery.
--Twins: Nature's Amazing Mystery.
Cassill, R. V. After Goliath.
--Flame.
--Labors of Love.
Cassill, R. V., ed. The Norton Anthology of Short Fiction.
--The Norton Anthology of Short Fiction.
Cassimati, Nina. Guide to East Africa: Kenya, Tanzania & Seychells.
Cassina, Edward B. & Cassina, Shirley E. Dicky: A True Story of a California Valley Quail.
Cassina, Shirley E., jt. auth. see Cassina, Edward B.
Cassinis, R., ed. The Solution of the Inverse Problem in Geophysical Interpretation.
Cassiodorus Senator. Introduction to Divine & Human Readings. Jones, Leslie W., tr.
Cassis, A. F. The Twentieth-Century English Novel.
Cassity, Joan. Now & Again.
Casson, M. Introduction to Mathematical Economics.
Casson, Ronald W. Language, Culture & Cognition: Readings in Cognitive Anthropology.
Cassorla, Albert. The Skateboarder's Bible: Technique, Equipment, Stunts, Terms, Etc.
Cassou, Jean. Jenkins.
Castagnaro, R. Anthony. Vinte Contos Brasileiros.
Castaldo, George, ed. see Doane, Jim.
Castaneda, Carlos. The Eagle's Gift.
--The Fire from Within.
--Journey to Ixtlan.
--The Second Ring of Power.
--Tales of Power.
--The Teachings of Don Juan.
Castanza, Philip. Films of Jeannette MacDonald & Nelson Eddy.
Castell, Alburey. An Introduction to Modern Philosophy: Examining the Human Condition.
Castell, C. P., et al. British Mesozoic Fossils.
Castellani, Amleto, ed. The Use of Human Cells for the Evaluation of Risk from Physical & Chemical Agents.
Castellani, L., et al. Supergravity Theory: A Geometric Perspective.
Castellanos Alentorn, Prado, jt. auth. see Guisset Poch, Consuelo.
Castelli, Louis & Cleeland, Caryn L. David Lean: A Guide to References & Resources.
Castello, Jorge, tr. see Valenzuela, Luisa.
Castellon, Rolando, ed. see Lobos, Amilcar & Mellot, Leland.
Castells, Manuel. The Economic Crisis & American Society.
Castells, Matilde O. & Boring, Phyllis Z. Lengua y Lectura: Un Repaso y una Continuacion.
Castellucci, Nicholas T. Seafood Creations by an Italian Gourmet.
Castelo Matran, Julio. Diccionario Basico De Seguros.
Castelot, Andre. King of Rome.
Casteras, Susan P. Victorian Childhood.
Casteret, N. Descent of Pierre-Saint-Martin.
Castiglia, Julie. Jill the Pill.
Castiglione, Baldassare. The Book of the Courtier. Hoby, Thomas, tr.
Castillo-Feliu, Guillermo I. & Mullen, Edward J. Lecturas Basicas: A Literary Reader.
--Lecturas Basicas Literaturas: A Literary Reader.
Castle, Alfred, jt. auth. see Gin, Margaret.
Castle, Coralie. The Hors d'Oeuvre Book.
--Leftovers.
--Soup.
Castle, Coralie & Gin, Margaret. Country Cookery of Many Lands.
Castle, Coralie & Killeen, Jacqueline. Country Inns Cookery: The Best of American Regional Cooking.
Castle, Coralie & Lawrence, Barbara. Hors d'oeuvre, Etc.
Castle, Coralie & Newton, Astrid. The Art of Cooking for Two.
Castle, Coralie, jt. auth. see Bryan, John.
Castle, Irene. Castles in the Air.
Castle, Jayne. The Gentle Pirate.
--Right of Possession.
Castle, Mary. Hospital Infection Control: Principles & Practices.
Castle, Raymond N., ed. Condensed Pyridazines Including Cinnolines & Phthaiazines.
--Pyridazines.
Castle, Sue. Nutrition for Your Child's Most Important Years: Birth to Age Three. Paton, Kathi, ed.
Castle, Tony. Celebrations for the Family.
Castle, Tony, ed. The Light of Christ: Meditations for Every Day of the Year.
Castleman, Barry. Asbestos: Medical & Legal Aspects.
Castleman, Craig. Getting Up: Subway Graffiti in New York.
Castleman, Deke, ed. see Stanley, David.
Castleman, H. & Podrazik, W. J. Watching TV: Four Decades of American Television.
Castleman, Michael. Crime Free.
--Crime Free.
Castleman, Riva. American Impressions: Prints since Pollock.
Castleman, William J. Beauty & the Mission of the Teacher.
Castleton, Virginia. Handbook of Natural Beauty.
Castlewitz, David M. The VisiCalc Program Made Easy.
Castlewitz, David M. & Chisausky, Lawrence. VisiCalc Home & Office Companion.
Casto, James E. Huntington: An Illustrated History.
Castoriadis, Cornelius. Redefining Revolution.
Castro, Americo. Iberoamerica.
Castro, Fidel. The Cuban Revolution, National Liberation & the Soviet Union: Two Speeches by Fidel Castro.
Castro, L. Advanced Programmer's Guide Featuring dBASE III Plus.
Castro, L. & Rettig, T. Advanced Programmer's Guide Featuring dBASE III & dBASE II.
Castro, Luis, et al. Advanced System Analysis & Design for dBASE II & dBASE III.
Castro, Michael. Interpreting the Indian: Twentieth-Century Poets & the Native American.
Castroleal, jt. auth. see Suarez.
Castroleal, Alicia. Aprende en Espanol y en Ingles: Level One-Reader A.
--Aprende en Espanol y en Ingles: Level One-Reader B.
Castroleal, Alicia & Suarez, Diamantina V. Aprende en Espanol y en Ingles: Level 1-Reader A.
Castronovo, David. Edmund Wilson.
Casty, Alan. Building Writing Skills: A Programmed Approach to Sentences & Paragraphs.
--Development of the Film: An Interpretive History.
Caswell, Christopher. Trailerable Sailboats.
Caswell, Christopher & Ullman, David. Championship Dinghy Sailing.
Casy, A. F., ed. PMR Spectroscopy in Medicinal & Biological Chemistry.
Cataldo, Corrine, jt. auth. see Whitney, Eleanor N.
Cataldo, John. Pen Calligraphy.
Catalyst Editors. Upward Mobility.
Catalyst Staff. Making the Most of Your First Job.
Catalytic, Inc. Staff. Study of the Effects of Reduced Occupational Radiation Exposure Limits on the Nuclear Power Industry (AIF-NESP-017)

Catania, A. Charles & Brigham, Thomas A., eds. Handbook of Applied Behavior Analysis: Social & Instructional Processes.
Catanzaro, Angela. Mama Mia Italian Cookbook.
Catchpole, Clive. Owls.
Cate, Curtis. George Sand: A Biography.
Cate, Curtis, jt. auth. see Goldovsky, Boris.
Cate, Phillip D., jt. auth. see Schimmel, Herbert D.
Cate, Rikki. A Cat's Tale.
Cate, Ten A. Richard see Ten Cate, A. Richard.
Catephores, G., jt. auth. see Morishima, A.
Cater, DouglasS & Lee, Philip R., eds. Politics of Health.
Cater, John C. Electronically Speaking: Computer Speech Generation.
Cater, John P. Electronically Hearing Computer Speech Recognition.
Cath, Stanley, et al. Father & Child: Developmental & Clinical Perspectives.
Cathcart, Charles D. Money, Credit & Economic Activity.
Cathcart, E., tr. see Savigny, Friedrich K.
Cathcart, Helen. Prince Charles: The Making of a Prince.
Cathcart, Robert S., et al. Small Group Communication: A Reader.
Cather, Willa. April Twilights (Nineteen Hundred Three) Slote, Bernice, ed.
--My Antonia.
Catherall, Ed. Investigating Graphs.
Catherine, Renee. The King & Queen...a Fairy Tale.
Cathie, Bruce L. & Temm, Peter N. UFOs & Anti-Gravity.
Catholic Church-Sacred Congregation of Divine Worship Staff. Celebrating the Saints. International Committee on English in the Liturgy, Confraternity of Christian Doctrine for the New American Bible, tr. from Lat.
Catholic Heritage Press Staff & Tiso, Francis. A Young Person's Book of Catholic Signs & Symbols.
Catholic University of America, Washington, D. C. Staff. Catalog of the Oliveira Lima Library.
Cathon, Laura E., et al, eds. Stories to Tell to Children: A Selected List.
Catlett, Robert H. Readings in Animal Energetics.
Catlin, Daniel, Jr. Liberal Education at Yale: The Yale College Course of Study 1945-1978.
Catling, D. M. & Graywon, J. Identification of Vegetable Fibers.
Catlow, C. R. & Mackrodt, W. C., eds. Computer Simulation of Solids.
Catlow, C. R., jt. ed. see Beniere, F.
Cato, Ingemar, jt. auth. see Olausson, Eric.
Cato, Nancy. Forefathers.
Caton, Joseph H. The Utopian Vision of Moholy-Nagy. Kirkpatrick, Diane, ed.
Caton, R. L., et al, eds. Rotating Electrical Equipment Testing.
Catoni, Guiliano, jt. auth. see Falassi, Alessandro.
Catovsky, Daniel. The Leukemic Cell.
Catsimpoolas, Nicholas, ed. Isoelectric Focusing.
--Methods of Protein Separation.
--Methods of Protein Separation.
Catsimpoolas, Nicholas & Drysdale, James, eds. Biological & Biomedical Applications of Isoelectric Focusing.
Catt, K. J. An ABC of Endocrinology.
Cattaneo, Anne, tr. see Strauss, Botho.
Cattaneo, Frank. Shop Made Easy.
Cattell, Nancy G. & Sharp, Shirley I. College & Career: Adjusting to College & Selecting an Occupation.
Cattell, Raymond B., ed. The Scientific Use of Factor Analysis in Behavioral & Life Sciences.
Catterall, R. D., ed. Sexually Transmitted Diseases.
Cattermole, Peter J., jt. auth. see Moore, Patrick.
Cattier, Michel. The Life & Work of Wilhelm Reich.
Catton, Bruce. American Heritage Short History of the Civil War.
--Civil War.
--Coming Fury.
--Michigan.
Catton, Bruce & Catton, William B. The Bold & Magnificent Dream: America's Founding Years, 1492-1815.
Catton, Bruce, jt. auth. see American Heritage Editors.
Catton, I. & Torrance, K. E., eds. Natural Convection in Enclosures: HTD.
Catton, W. T. Physical Methods in Physiology.
Catton, William B., jt. auth. see Catton, Bruce.
Cattonar, Nell A., tr. see Vidali, Vittorio.
Catullus. The Poems of Catullus. Gregory, Horace, ed. & tr.
Caudill, Paul R. First Corinthians: A Translation with Notes.
Caudwell, Christopher. Illusion & Reality.
Caufield, Page, jt. ed. see Jacobson, Alex.
Caughey, Winslow, ed. Clinical & Biochemical Aspects of Hemoglobin Abnormalities.
Caughey, Winslow S., ed. Biochemical & Clinical Aspects of Oxygen.
Caughill, Rita E. The Dying Patient: A Supportive Approach.
Caughley, Graeme. The Deer Wars: The Story of Deer in New Zealand.
Cauley, Lorinda B. The Goose & the Golden Coins.
--The New House.
--The New House.
--The Ugly Duckling.
Cauley, Lorinda B., jt. auth. see Hancock, Sibyl.
Cauley, Lorinda B., ed. The Goose & the Golden Coins.
Caulfield, Don & Caulfield, Joan. The Incredible Detectives.
Caulfield, Joan, jt. auth. see Caulfield, Don.
Caulfield, Sophia F. House Mottoes & Inscriptions.
Cauman, Samuel, jt. auth. see Janson, H. W.
Caunt, A. E., jt. auth. see Taylor-Robinson, D.
Cauper, Eunice. The Story of the Pilgrims & Their Indian Friends: A Thanksgiving Story for Children.
Caus, Isaac. Wilton Gardens: New & Rare Inventions of Water-Works. Hunt, John D., ed.
Caussade, Jean-Pierre de see De Caussade, Jean-Pierre.
Caute, David. The Fellow-Travellers: Intellectual Friends of Communism.
Cauthen, Kenneth. The Ethics of Enjoyment: The Christian's Pursuit of Happiness.
Cauthen, Kenneth, ed. see Mathews, Shailer.
Cautley, H. Munro. Norfolk Churches.
--Suffolk Churches.
Cauweberghe, Marc Van see Ohsawa, George.
Cava, Esther Laden. Parents Guide to Successful Child Rearing: How to Say No Without Guilt.
Cava, Michael P. & Mitchell, M. J. Cyclobutadiene & Related Compounds.
Cava, Olha della see Della Cava, Olha.
Cavafy, C. P. Complete Poems of Cavafy. Dalven, Rae, tr.
Cavaiani, Mabel. New Diabetic Cookbook.
Cavalieri, Grace. Why I Cannot Take a Lover.
Cavalleri, B., jt. ed. see Breccia, A.
Cavalli, Francesco. Gli Amori d'Apollo e di Dafne. Brown, Howard M., ed.
--Scipione Africano. Brown, Howard M., ed.
Cavalli-Sforza, L. L. Elements of Human Genetics.
Cavallito, C. J., ed. Structure-Activity Relationships & Theory.
Cavan, Ruth S. & Das, Man S., eds. Communes: Historical & Contemporary.
Cavanagh, Darol M., jt. auth. see Fielding, Anthony J.
Cavanah, Frances. The Truth about the Man Behind the Book That Sparked the War Between the States.
Cavanah, Frances, ed. Favorite Christmas Stories.
Cavanaugh, J. J. The Lawyer in Society.
Cavanaugh, Joseph H. Evidence for Our Faith.
Cavanaugh, Merry. Preschool & Daycare Book.
Cavanna, Betty. Black Spaniel Mystery.
--Catchpenny Street.
--A Girl Can Dream.
--Going on Sixteen.
--Lasso Your Heart.
--Love, Laurie.
--Paintbox Summer.
--Spring Comes Riding.
--Spurs for Suzanna.
--You Can't Take Twenty Dogs on a Date.
Cavanna, Betty A. Touch of Magic.
Cavarnos, Constantine. Modern Orthodox Saints: Vol. 6-St. Arsenios of Paros.
--Modern Orthodox Saints: Vol. 7-St. Nectarios of Aegina.
Cave, Alfred A. Jacksonian Democracy & the Historians.
Cave, Martin, et al, eds. New Trends in Soviet Economics. Cave, Martin, tr. from Rus.
Cave, Peter L., compiled by. Five Hundred Games.
Cave, Richard, ed. see Moore, George.
Cave, Sydney. The Christian Way.
Cave, William, jt. auth. see Chesler, Mark A.
Cavender, Nancy M. & Weiss, Leonard A. Thinking in Sentences: A Guide to Clear Writing.
Cavendish, Butch. How to Cheat on College Exams & Get Away with It.
Cavendish, Richard. A History of Magic.
Cavendish, Ruth. Women on the Line.
Cavendish, Thomas. The Last Voyage of Thomas Cavendish, 1591-1592. Quinn, David B., ed.
Cavert, C. Edward. Keep It Running.
Cavert, C. Edward, et al. Keep It Running: A Study Guide.
Caves, Richard E. American Industry: Structure, Conduct, Performance.
Caves, Richard E., et al. Britain's Economic Prospects.
Cavett, Dick & Porterfield, Christopher. Eye on Cavett.
Cavier, R., ed. Chemotherapy of Helminthiasis.
Cavin, Ruth. One Pinch of Sunshine, One-Half Cup of Rain.
Cavitch, David. My Soul & I: The Inner Life of Walt Whitman.
Cavoto, Nino, tr. see Grillo, Salvatore.
Cawelti, John G. Apostles of the Self-Made Man.
--Six-Gun Mystique.
Cawley, A. C., ed. Everyman.
Cawley, J. C., et al, eds. Hairy Cell Leukaemia.
Cawley, James, jt. auth. see Cawley, Margaret.
Cawley, John F., ed. Developmental Teaching of Mathematics for the Learning Disabled.
--Practical Mathematics Appraisal of the Learning Disabled.
--Secondary School Mathematics for the Learning Disabled.
Cawley, John F., et al, eds. Cognitive Strategies & Mathematics for the Learning Disabled.
Cawley, Margaret & Cawley, James. Exploring the Little Rivers of New Jersey.
Cawley, Robert & Yost, George. Studies in Sir Thomas Browne.
Cawood, Diana. Assertiveness for Managers.
Caws, Peter. Sartre.
Cawson, Broderick A., jt. auth. see McCracken, Alexander W.
Cawson, R. A. Essentials of Dental Surgery & Pathology.
Cawson, R. A., jt. auth. see Scully, C.
Cawson, Roderick A. & McCracken, Alexander W. Pathologic Mechanisms & Human Disease.
Cayce, H. L. Gifts of Healing.
Cayford, John E. Fort Knox-Fortress in Maine.
Cayrord, John E. Penobscot Expedition.
Cayton, Horace R., jt. auth. see Drake, St. Clair.
Cazaud, R. Fatigue of Metals.
Cazort, Mary & Johnson, Catherine. Bolognese Drawings in North American Collections 1500-1800.
Cazort, Mimi, intro. by see Jackson, H. A.
Cazzaroli, Gianni. Enciclopedia Del Mar y De la Navegacion Deportiva.
CBD Research Staff. Current British Directories.
CBEMA, Inc. Staff. Computer & Business Equipment Market Book.
CBS, Inc. Staff & Fury, Kathleen. Dear Sixty Minutes.
CDF Staff. Day Care: Investing in Ohio's Children.
Cea, J. & Murthy, M. K. Lectures on Optimization: Theory & Algorithms.
Ceausescu, E. Sterospecific Polymerization of Isoprene.
Cebeci. Momentum Transfer in Boundary Layers.
Cebrian, Juan L. Red Doll. Silver, Philip W., tr.
Cebula, Richard J. Geographic Living-Cost Differentials.
Cebulash, Mel. I'm an Expert: Motivating Independent Study Projects for Grades 4-6.
Ceccarelli, B., ed. see International Symposium on Cell Biology & Cytopharmacology Staff.
Cecchettini, Philip A. CLEP Resource Manual: Introduction to Sociology.
--CLEP Resource Manual: Introduction to Business Management.
--CLEP Resourse Manual: Introduction to General Psychology.
Cecchini, Tina. Enciclopedia Practica de Floricultura y Jardineria.
Ceccio, Cathy M., jt. auth. see Ceccio, Joseph F.
Ceccio, Joseph F. & Ceccio, Cathy M. Effective Communication in Nursing: Theory & Practice.
Cech, E. Point Sets.
Cech, Joseph J., jt. auth. see Moyle, Peter B.
Cecil, David. Max: A Biography of Max Beerbohm.
--Melbourne.
Cecil, Mirabel. Cora the Crow, a Spring Story.
--Ruby the Donkey: A Winter Story.
--Spiky the Hedgehog.
Cecil, Paula B. Office Automation: Concepts & Application.
Cedering-Fox, Siv. The Blue Horse & Other Night Poems.
Cedoline, Anthony J. Job Burnout in Public Education: Symptoms, Causes, & Survival Skills.
Ceen, Allan. The Quartiere de Banchi: Urban Planning in Rome in the First Half of the Cinquecento. Freedberg, S. J., ed.
Ceglowski, W. S. & Friedman, Herman, eds. Virus Tumorigenesis & Immunogenesis.
Ceidigh, P. O., jt. ed. see Keegan, B. F.
Cela, Camilo J. Family of Pascual Duarte.
--The Hive.
Celada, Franco, et al, eds. Protein Conformation As an Immunological Signal.
Celan, Paul. Paul Celan: Poems. Hamburger, Michael, tr. from Ger.
Cela Trulock, Camilo J. Diccionario Secreto.
Celebrity Kitchens Staff. The Art of Budget Cooking: The Minute Rice Cookbook.
Celestin, Martial. New Concepts of Life After Death.
Celine, Louis-Ferdinand D. Entratiens avec le Professeur Y.
--Oeuvres.
--Progres.
Celis, J. E. & Smith, J. D., eds. Nonsense Mutations & RNA Suppressors.
Cell, C. P., ed. Revolution at Work: Mass Campaigns in China.
Cell in Mitosis Symposium Staff. Proceedings of the Cell in Mitosis Symposium. Levine, Lawrence, ed.
Cellard, Maurice. My Violin.
Celms, Theodor. Der Phanomenologische Idealismus Husserls. Natanson, ed.
Cenini, S., jt. auth. see Malatesta, Li.
Cennini, C. D'Andrea. The Craftsman's Handbook. Thompson, D. V., Jr., tr.
Centeno-Beltran, Violeta. Look-I'm Flat Again.
Center for Advanced Computation Staff. Energy Flow Through the United States Economy: A Wall Chart.
Center for Applied Linguistics Staff, jt. auth. see Language & Orientation Resource Center Staff.
Center for Applied Linguistics, Washington, D. C. Staff. Dictionary Catalog of the Library of the Center for Applied Linguistics, Washington, D. C.
Center for Business Information Staff, ed. Appropriate Technology Organizations: A Worldwide Directory.
Center for Criminal Justice Case Western Reserve University. Ohio Criminal Justice, 1987.
Center for Equal Education Staff. Covering the Desegregation Story.
Center for Futures Research, ed. see O'Toole, James.
Center for International & Strategic Affairs, Univ. of California, Los Angeles Staff & Spiegel, Steven, eds. The Middle East & the Western Alliance.
Center for Learning Staff. Experiencing Shakespeare I.
Center for Occupational Research & Development Staff. Application Modules.
--Metrology.
--Unified Technical Concepts.
Center for Research in Ambulatory Health Care Administration Staff, ed. see Schafer, Eldon L., et al.
Center for Research in Ambulatory Health Care Administration. Manual on Insurance.
Center for Research in Cognition & Effect Staff. Adaptive Functions of Imagery: Proceedings of the Center for Research in Cognition & Effect, 3rd, Conference, New York City, 1971. Segal, Sydney J., ed.
Center for South & Southeast Asia Studies Staff. Berkeley Working Papers on South & Southeast Asia: Vol. 1, 1975-1976.
Center for Strategic & International Studies, Georgetown University Staff. Future of Business - Annual Review 1980-81: Practical Issues. Slappey, G. Sterling, ed.
Center for the Study of Services Staff. The Complete Guide to Lower Phone Costs.
Center for the Study of Services Staff & Krughoff, Robert. The IRA Book: The Complete Guide to IRA's & Retirement Planning.
Center for the Study of Social Policy-SRI International Staff & Markley, O. W., eds. Changing Images of Man.
Centlivre, Susanna. The Plays of Susanna Centlivre. Frushell, Richard C., ed.
Centlivre, Susannah. A Bold Stroke for a Wife. Stathas, Thalia, ed.
Central Bureau for Nuclear Measurements Staff. Neutron Data of Structural Materials for Fast Reactors: Proceedings of the Specialists Meeting of the Central Bureau for Nuclear Measurements, Geel, Belgium, Dec. 5-8, 1977. Bockhoff, K. H., ed.
Central Intelligence Agency Staff. The Freedom Fighter's Manual.
Central State University Ohio Editors. Index to Periodical Articles by & about Negroes, Decennial Cumulation, 1950-1959.
--Index to Periodical Articles by & About Negroes, 1977.
Central State University Staff & Hallie Q. Brown Memorial Library Staff, eds. Index to Black Periodicals: 1984.
Centre De Creation Industrielle, Paris, France Staff, ed. World Design Sources Directory 1980: An ICOGRADA ICSID Publication.
Centre de Mathematique Sociale Ecole des Hautes Etudes En Sciences Sociales Staff. Combinatorics Graphs & Algebra.
Centre for Advanced Study in the Developmental Sciences Study Group Staff. The Origins of Human Social Relations: Proceedings. Schaffer, H. R., ed.
Centre for Advanced Study in the Developmental Sciences. Stimulation in Early Infancy: Proceedings. Ambrose, Anthony, ed.
Centre for Research in Mathematics, University of Montreal Symposium Staff. Applications of Number Theory to Numerical Analysis: Proceedings of the Centre for Research in Mathematics, University of Montreal Symposium, Sept. 1971. Zaremba, S. K., ed.
Centre for Scientific Culture Ettore Majorana, International School of Electron Microscopy Staff. Electron Microscopy in Material Science. Valdre, U., ed.

Centro Internacional de Agricultura Tropical Staff. Potential for Field Beans-Phaseolus Vulgaris L.-In West & North Africa.
CEP Staff & Boothe, Norris. Cleaning Up: The Cost of Refinery Pollution Control. Haley, Mary J., ed.
CEP Staff & Simich, Tina L. Shortchanged Update: Minorities & Women in Banking. Schwartz, Wendy C., ed.
Cepican, Bob & Ali, Waleed. Yesterday... Came Suddenly: The Definitive History of the Beatles.
Cerami, Charles A. More Profits, Less Risk: Your New Financial Strategy.
Cerling, Charles. Freedom from Bad Habits.
Cermak, J. E., ed. Wind Engineering: Proceedings of the 5th International Conference, Colorado State University, July 8-14, 1979.
Cermak, Laird S. Improving Your Memory.
Cerminara, Gina Foreword by see James, Paul.
Cernea, Michael M. Measuring Project Impact: Monitoring & Evaluation in the PIDER Rural Development Project - Mexico.
Cerney, Joseph, ed. Nuclear Spectroscopy & Reactions.
Cernuschi, Alberto C. Theory of Autodeism.
Cerny, Philip G. & Schain, Martin A., eds. French Politics & Public Policy.
Cerquiglini, S., et al, eds. see International Seminar on Biomechanics Staff.
Cerreto, Frank. Power Skills in Mathematics II.
Cerutti, Edwina. Mystic with the Healing Hands: The Life of Olga Worrall.
--Olga Worrall: Mystic with the Healing Hands.
Cervantes, Hermes, jt. auth. see Baca, Leonard M.
Cervantes, Miguel de see De Cervantes, Miguel.
Cervantes, Miguel De see De Cervantes Saavedra, Miguel.
Cervantes de Saavedra, Miguel. The Adventures of Don Quixote. Jones, Olive, ed. Cohen, J. M., tr. from Span.
Cervantes-Saavedra, Miguel De. Miguel De Cervantes-Saavedra: Two Cervantes Short Novels: El Curioso Impertinente & El Celoso Extremeno. Pierce, F. F., ed.
Cervin, Russell A. Mission in Ferment.
Cervos-Navarro, J., et al, eds. see International Symposium, Berlin, Sep, 1973.
Cesaire, Aime & Picasso, Pablo. Lost Body.
Cesaire, Aime see Harrison, Paul C.
Cesari, L. Asymptotic Behavior & Stability Problems in Ordinary Differential Equations.
Cesari, L., jt. ed. see Bednarek, A. R.
Cesari, Lamberto & Kannan, Rangacesari, eds. Nonlinear Analysis: A Collection of Papers in Honor or Eric Rothe.
Cesari, Lamberto, et al. Dynamical Systems: An International Symposium.
Cesari, Lamberto, et al, eds. Dynamical Systems: An International Symposium.
Cescinsky, H. Gentle Art of Faking Furniture.
Ceserani, Gian P. Christopher Columbus.
Cespedes, Alba de. Remorse. Weaver, William, tr. from Ital.
Cess, R. D., jt. auth. see Sparrow, E. M.
Cessario, Romanus. Christian Satisfaction in Aquinas: Towards a Personalist Understanding.
Cesti, Antonio. L' Argia. Brown, Howard M., ed.
Cetron, Marvin, et al. Schools of the Future: Education into the Twenty-First Century.
Cha, Young K. Northeast Asian Security: A Korean Perspective.
Chabaud, A. G., ed. CIH Keys to the Nematode Parasites of Vertebrates, No. 6: Keys to Genera of the Superfamilies Cosmocercoidea, Seuratoidea, Heterakoidea & Subuluroidea.
Chabersky, Stephen G., jt. auth. see Krasner, Michael A.
Chabner, Bruce A. Pharmacologic Principles of Cancer Treatment.
Chabod, Federico. A History of Italian Fascism. Grindrod, Muriel, tr. from Ital.
Chabot, Brain F. & Mooney, Hal. A, eds. Physiological Ecology of North American Plant Communities.
Chabot, Leon, jt. auth. see Mallow, Alex.
Chace, Fenner A., Jr., jt. ed. see Pequegnat, Willis E.
Chace, William & Collier, Peter, eds. Justice Denied: The Black Man in White America.
Chackett, K. Radionuclide Technology.
Chadan, K. & Sabatier, P. C. Inverse Problems in Quantum Scattering Theory.
Chadderdon, H. Determining Effectiveness of Teaching Home Economics.
Chadwick, George. A Systems View of Planning: Towards a Theory of the Urban & Regional Planning Process.
Chadwick, Henry, jt. auth. see Von Campenhausen, Hans.
Chadwick, Henry, jt. ed. see Oulton, J. E.
Chadwick, Janet B. The Country Journal Woodburner's Cookbook.
Chadwick, John & Chadwick, Suzanne. The Chadwick System: Discovering the Perfect Hairstyle for You.
Chadwick, John W. Computing for Executives.
Chadwick, Joselyn. Evil Is the Night.
Chadwick, Lee. Cuba Today.
Chadwick, M. J. & Goodman, G. T. The Ecology of Resource Degradation & Renewal.
Chadwick, M. J. & Kristoferson, L. A., eds. Renewable Energy Technologies.
Chadwick, M. J. & Lindman, N., eds. Environmental Implications of Expanded Coal Utilization.
Chadwick, O., jt. ed. see Nuttall, Geoffrey F.
Chadwick, Owen, ed. The Mind of the Oxford Movement.
Chadwick, Suzanne, jt. auth. see Chadwick, John.
Chadwick-Jones, J. K. Social Exchange Theory: Structure & Influence in Social Psychology.
Chadzynski, Martin & Lakland, Carli. The Runaway!
Chaet. The Art of Drawing.
Chafe, Wallace L. Meaning & the Structure of Language.
Chafee, Zechariah, Jr., ed. Documents on Fundamental Human Rights, the Anglo-American Tradition.
Chafets, Ze'ev. Israel: Heroes & Hustlers, Hard Hats & Holy Men.
Chafetz, Morris E. The Alcoholic Patient: Diagnosis & Management.
Chafetz, Morris E., et al, eds. Frontiers of Alcoholism.
Chaffee, S. & Petrick, M. Using the Mass Media: Communication Problems in American Society.
Chaffin, Kenneth L. The Reluctant Witness.
Chafin, Kenneth L. & Ogilvie, Lloyd J. The Communicator's Commentary: Corinthians First; Second.
Chagall, David. The New Kingmakers.
Chagnon, Napoleon, jt. auth. see Martin, Robert J.
Chahal, Pritpal, jt. auth. see Stevenson, John C.
Chaigne, Louis. Paul Claudel: The Man & the Mystic.
Chaika, Elaine. Language: The Social Mirror.
Chaiken, Irwin M., et al. Affinity Chromatography & Biological Recognition (Symposium)
Chaillu, Paul B. Du see Du Chaillu, Paul.
Chaillu, Paul Du see Du Chaillu, Paul.
Chaison, Gary N. & Rose, Joseph B., eds. Readings in Canadian Industrial Relations.
Chaisson, Eric. Cosmic Dawn: The Origins of Matter & Life.
Chaitow, Leon. Candida Albicans: Could Yeast Be Your Problem?
Chajes. Student's Guide Through the Talmud.
Chakerian, Don, et al. Geometry: A Guided Inquiry.
Chakoo, B. L. Aldous Huxley & Eastern Wisdom.
Chakrabart, C. L., ed. Progress in Analytical Atomic Spectroscopy.
Chakrabarti, C. L. Progress in Analytical Atomic Spectroscopy.
Chakrabarti, C. L., ed. Progress in Analytical Atomic Spectroscopy.
--Progress in Analytical Atomic Spectroscopy.
--Progress in Analytical Atomic Spectroscopy.
--Progress in Analytical Atomic Spectroscopy. Sturgeon, R. E.
Chakrabarti, C. L. & Sturgeon, R. E., eds. Progress in Analytical Atomic Spectroscopy.
Chakrabarti, Jayanta. Techniques in Indian Mural Painting.
Chakraberti, Kanchan. Society, Religion & Art of the Kushana India: A Historico-Symbiosis.
Chakraborty, R., jt. ed. see Schull, W. J.
Chakravarti, Aravinda. Human Population Genetics.
Chalfont, Alan. Star Wars: Suicide or Survival?
Chalfont, Alun. Montgomery of Alamein.
Chalk, Brian T., jt. auth. see Bancroft, John D.
Chalk, William, jt. auth. see Levens, Alexander.
Chalker, Jack. The Devil's Voyage.
Chalklin, C. W. The Provincial Towns of Georgian England: A Study of the Building Process, 1740-1820.
Chall, Jeanne. Reading 1967-1977: A Decade of Change & Promise.
Challener, Richard D., ed. The Legislative Origins of American Foreign Policy. Incl. Vol. 1. Proceedings, April 7, 1913 to March 7, 1923; Vol. 2. Proceedings, December 3, 1923 to March 3, 1933; Vol. 3. Legislative Origins of the Truman Doctrine, March to April, 1947; Vol. 4. Foreign Relief Aid, 1947; Vol. 5. Foreign Relief Assistance Act of 1948. Garland Pub.
--Reviews of the World Situation: 1949-50.
Challice, C. E. & Viragh, S., eds. Ultrastructure of the Mammalian Heart.
Challinor, John, jt. auth. see Platt, John.
Chalmers, Alexander. The Works of English Poets, from Chaucer to Cowper.
Chalmers, B., ed. Progress in Materials Science.
Chalmers, R. A. Microprocessors in Analytical Chemistry.
Chalmers, R. A., ed. Gains & Losses: Errors in Trace Analysis.
--Talanta-Scandinavian Honour Issue: Special Issue of Talanta.
Chalmers Hunt, B. L., jt. auth. see Haynes, J. H.
Chalpin, Lila. A New Look at Microwave Cooking.
Chamala, Shankarish, jt. ed. see Crouch, Bruce R.
Chambadal, Lucien. Diccionario de las Matematicas Modernas.
Chamberlain, Barbara. Ride the West Wind.
Chamberlain, Craig. All about the Commodore 64.
--All about the Commodore 64. Compute! Publications, Inc. Staff, ed.
Chamberlain, Ellsworth T. Lost Frontier.
Chamberlain, Geoffrey & Lumley, Judith. Prepregnancy Care: A Manual for Practice.
Chamberlain, Joseph. A Political Memoir, 1880-1892. Howard, C. H., ed.
Chamberlain, Joseph W. Theory of Planetary Atmospheres: An Introduction to Their Physics & Chemistry.
Chamberlain, Lesley. Food & Cooking of Russia.
Chamberlain, Margaret, illus. Sing a Song of Sixpence.
Chamberlain, Mary. Fenwomen: A Portrait of Women in an English Village.
Chamberlain, Narcissa. The Omelette Book.
Chamberlain, Narcisse, tr. see Guerard, Michel.
Chamberlain, Neil W. & Kuhn, J. W. Collective Bargaining.
Chamberlain, Neil W., et al. The Labor Sector.
Chamberlain, Nugent F. The Practice of NMR Spectroscopy: With Spectra-Structure Correlations for Hydrogen-One.
Chamberlain, Robert S. Conquest & Colonization of Honduras, 1502-1550.
Chamberlain, Samuel. Small House in the Sun.
Chamberlain, Trevor, jt. auth. see Ranson, Ron.
Chamberlain, V. B., 3rd, jt. ed. see Rogers, Robert S.
Chamberlain, Walter. Manual of Woodcut Printmaking.
--The Thames & Hudson Manual of Wood Engraving.
Chamberlain, William J. Fighting for Peace: The War Resistance Movement.
Chamberlayne, C. G. The Vestry Book & Register of St. Peter's Parish, New Kent & James City Counties, Virginia, 1684-1786.
Chamberlin, C. J. & Chamberlin, D. J. Colour: Its Measurement, Computation & Application.
Chamberlin, D. J., jt. auth. see Chamberlin, C. J.
Chamberlin, E. R. The World of the Italian Renaissance.
--The World of the Italian Renaissance.
Chamberlin, Hal. Musical Applications of Microprocessors.
Chamberlin, J. Gordon. The Educating Act: A Phenomenological View.
Chamberlin, Roy B. & Feldman, Herman. Dartmouth Bible.
Chamberlin, Roy B. & Feldman, Herman, eds. Dartmouth Bible.
Chamberlin, T. L. Selling & Today's Consumer: Buying? Selling? Then Do It Right!
Chamberlin, William H. Soviet Planned Economic Order.
Chambers. Imperial Age of Venice.
Chambers, jt. auth. see Mactaggart.
Chambers, C. M., jt. ed. see Chambers, P. L.
Chambers, Carl D. & Heckman, Richard D. Employee Drug Abuse: A Manager's Guide for Action.
Chambers, Claire. The Siecus Circle.
Chambers, Colin. Other Spaces: New Theatre & the Royal Shakespeare Company.
Chambers, Constance. The Book of English Desserts.
Chambers, D. S. The Imperial Age of Venice: 1380-1580.
Chambers, Eric. Reproduction Photography for Lithography.
Chambers, Erve. Applied Anthropology: A Practical Guide.
Chambers, Frank P. History of Taste: An Account of the Revolutions of Art Criticism & Theory in Europe.
Chambers, James. The Devil's Horsemen.
--The Devil's Horsemen: The Mongol Invasion of Europe.
Chambers, John M., et al. Graphical Methods for Data Analysis.
Chambers, John W. Footlight Summer.
Chambers, Kenneth. Mammals, Amphibians, & Reptiles of the Northeastern United States.
Chambers, Melvin T. Born Out of Season.
--A Dog Named Sam.
Chambers, Mortimer, ed. Fall of Rome: Can It Be Explained?
Chambers, Oswald. Daily Thoughts for Disciples.
--Studies in the Sermon on the Mount.
Chambers, P. L. & Chambers, C. M., eds. New Toxicology for Old, A Critique of Accepted Requirements & Methodology: Proceedings.
Chambers, P. L. & Guenze, P., eds. Mechanism of Toxic Action on Some Target Organs.
Chambers, Patricia. River Runner's Recipes.
Chambers, Richard L., jt. ed. see Polk, William R.
Chambers, Robert. Popular Rhymes of Scotland.
Chambers, Sue. Rachz: The True Story of a Fox.
Chamblain De Marivaux, Pierre C. De see De Chamblain De Marivaux, Pierre C.
Chambliss, J. E. Life & Labors of David Livingstone.
Chambliss, Rollin. Meaning for Man.
Chambre, Tim, jt. auth. see Hounsome, Terry.
Chambrun, Rene De see De Chambrun, Rene.
Chamelin, Neil C. & Truzzi, Marcello, eds. Criminal Law for Police Officers.
Chametzky, Jules. From the Ghetto: The Fiction of Abraham Cahan.
Chamowicz, Marc C. Cafe du Reve.
Champa, Kermit S. Mondrian Studies.
Champeney, D. C. Fourier Transforms & Their Physical Applications.
Champion, A. G., jt. ed. see Goddard, J. B.
Champion, Anthony G., jt. ed. see Davies, Ross L.
Champion, David. The Basic of Bead Stringing.
Champion, Dean. Basic Statistics for Social Research.
Champion, John M. & James, John H. Critical Incidents in Management.
Champion, K. S. W., jt. auth. see Schmidtke, G.
Champion, R. H., et al, eds. The Urticarias.
Champion, Sara. Dictionary of Terms & Techniques in Archaeology.
Champlin, Connie. Puppetry & Creative Dramatics in Storytelling. Schwalb, Ann W., ed.
Champlin, Joseph M. Together in Peace: Priest's Edition.
Champlin, Kathy, ed. see Kelley, Clarence.
Chan. Disorders of Renal-Electrolytes & Mineral Metabolism.
Chan, Chin-Liang, jt. auth. see Stachowitz, Rolf A.
Chan, James C., ed. Hypertension, Steroid & Mineral Metabolsim: Festschrift to Frederic C. Bartter.
Chan, Julie M. Why Read Aloud to Children?
Chan, Lily. Struggle of a Hong Kong Girl.
Chan, Pedro. Ear Acupressure.
--Finger Acupressure.
Chan, T. S. Distribution Channel Strategy for Export Marketing: The Case of Hong Kong Firms. Farmer, Richard N., ed.
Chan, W. Y., et al. Oxytocin: Current Research.
Chanan, Michael, tr. see Mattelart, Armand.
Chance, Britton, ed. Energy-Linked Functions of Mitochondria.
--Rapid Mixing & Sampling Techniques in Biochemistry.
Chance, Britton, et al, eds. Control of Energy Metabolism.
--Hemes & Hemoproteins.
--Probes of Structure & Function of Macromolecules & Membranes.
Chance, David. Thirty Computer Programs for the Homeowner, in BASIC.
Chance, David W. Computer Graphics with Twenty-Nine Ready-to-Run Programs.
--Twenty-Five Exciting Computer Games in BASIC for All Ages.
Chance, John N. Spy on Spider.
Chance, Sparky. From Puppets to Eternity.
Chancellor, John. Charles Darwin.
Chancellor, Robin, tr. see Dutourd, Jean.
Chances, Ellen B. Conformity's Children: An Approach to the Superfluous Man in Russian Literature.
Chand, Meira. The Bonsai Tree.
--The Gossamer Fly.
--Last Quadrant.
Chandernagor, Francoise. The King's Way: The Life of Madame de Maintenon. Bray, Barbara, tr.
Chandler. Tournament Chess. Miles, A. J., ed.
Chandler, A. C. Making Waves.
Chandler, Arthur B. Old Tales of San Francisco.
Chandler, Bob. Violent Sundays.
Chandler, C., ed. see Durey, Peter.
Chandler, Daniel, ed. Exploring English with Microcomputers.
Chandler, David. Kelly.
--The Masters Connection.
--The Middleman.
Chandler, David L. & Eisen, Johnathan. Overcoming Clumsiness: Physical Dexterity for People Who Thought It Was Impossible.
Chandler, Edna W. Five Cent, Five Cent (Liberia)
Chandler, George. Libraries in the East: An International & Comparative Study.
Chandler, J. A. Public Policy for Local Government.
Chandler, John & Cockle, Paul. Techniques of Scenario Planning.
Chandler, Linda S. Uncle Ike.
Chandler, M., ed. Tournament Chess.
--Tournament Chess.
--Tournament Chess.
--Tournament Chess.
--Tournament Chess.
Chandler, M. & Miles, A., eds. Tournament Chess.
--Tournament Chess.
--Tournament Chess.
--Tournament Chess.
--Tournament Chess.
--Tournament Chess.
--Tournament Chess.

Authors

--Tournament Chess.
Chandler, Marjorie O., jt. ed. see Stern, Joyce D.
Chandler, Melbourne C. Of Garry Owen in Glory: The History of the Seventh U. S. Cavalry Regiment.
Chandler, Peter. Bucks.
Chandler, Raymond. The Big Sleep.
--Killer in the Rain.
--The Lady in the Lake.
--The Long Goodbye.
--Midnight Raymond Chandler.
--Raymond Chandler Speaking. Gardiner, Dorothy & Walker, Katherine S., eds.
Chandler, Robert, tr. The Magic Ring & Other Russian Folktales.
Chandler, Robert, tr. see Afanasyev, Alexander.
Chandler, Tertius. Godly Kings & Early Ethics.
--Progress: Social Progress from Mercury to Kennedy.
--Remote Kingdoms.
Chandor, Anthony. Diccionario de Computadores.
Chandra, Bipan, ed. The Indian Left: Critical Appraisals.
Chandra, Prakash. International Law.
--International Relations.
Chandra, R. K., ed. Progress in Food & Nutrition Science.
Chandrasekaran, B. & Bylander, Tom. Task-Specific Problem Solving Architectures.
Chandrasekharan, K. R. Bhabani Bhattacharya.
Chaneles, Sol. Three Children of the Holocaust.
Chaney, Margaret S. & Ross, Margaret L. Nutrition.
Chaney, Margaret S., et al. Nutrition.
Chang, C. Nora, jt. ed. see Barnett, Gene.
Chang, Hao. Liang Ch'i-Ch'ao & Intellectual Transition in China, 1890-1907.
Chang, Hsin-Pao. Commissioner Lin & the Opium War.
Chang, Paul K. Control of Flow Separation: Energy Conservation, Operational Efficiency & Safety.
Chang, Rodney. Mental Evolution & Art.
Chang, S. K. & Fu, K. S., eds. Pictorial Information Systems.
Chang, Sherwood, jt. auth. see Wood, John A.
Chang, Sonia. Echocardiography: Techniques & Interpretation.
Chang, T. M., ed. Biomedical Applications of Immobilized Enzymes & Proteins. Incl. Vol. 1; Vol. 2. Plenum Pub.
Chang, T. M., ed. see Meeting on Hemoperfusion, Kidney & Liver Supports & Detoxification Staff.
Chang, T. Y. & Krempl, F., eds. Inelastic Behavior of Pressure Vessel & Piping Components, PVP-PB-028.
Chang, Y. A. & Smith, J. F. Calculation of Phase Diagrams & Thermochemistry of Alloy Phases.
Chang, Y. A., ed. see TMS Staff & AIME Staff.
Chang, Y. N. & Campo-Flores, Filemon. Business Policy & Strategy.
--Business Policy & Strategy: Text & Cases.
Chang Chung-Yuan, ed. The Original Teachings of Ch'an Buddhism.
Chaning-Pearce, Melville. The Conflict of Values.
Channan, Krishan K. The Lure of Politics.
Channel, Kimberley, jt. auth. see Horine, Billie.
Channels, Vera & Vestermark, Mary. Freedom Is an Inside Job.
Channels, Vera G. Experiences in Interpersonal Relationships.
Channing, Alissa. Royal Blood.
Channing, Cornelia C. & Segal, Sheldon J., eds. Intraovarian Control Mechanisms.
Channing, William E. Discourses on War.
Channon, Derek F. & Jalland, Michael. Multinational Strategic Planning.
Channon, Robert. On the Place of the Progressive Palatalization of Velars in the Relative Chronology of Slavic.
Chanoff, David & Van Toai, Doan. Portrait of the Enemy.
Chanoff, David, jt. auth. see Diem, Bui.
Chanoff, David, jt. auth. see Van Toai, Doan.
Chan-Palay, V., jt. auth. see Palay, S. L.
Chansler, Robert J., Jr. Efficient Use of Systems with Many Processors. Stone, Harold, ed.
Chant, Joy. The Grey Mane of Morning.
Chant, Peter D., et al. Griffin, Williams, & Larson's Advanced Accounting. Canadian Edition.
Chantico Press Staff. CASE: The Potential & the Pitfalls.
Chantico-QED Staff. Telecommunications Planning.
Chantiles, Vilma L. The New York Ethnic Food Market Guide & Cookbook.
Chantler, Eric N. & Elder, James B., eds. Mucus In Health & Disease II.
Chantry, G. W. Submillimetre Spectroscopy.
Chanute, Octave. Progress in Flying Machines.
Chao, L. Statistics: Methods & Analyses.
Chao Kuo-Chun. Agrarian Policy of the Chinese Communist Party, Nineteen Twenty-One to Nineteen Fifty-Nine.
Chapchal, George, ed. Arthrodesis in the Restoration of Working Ability.
--Injuries of the Ligaments & Their Repair: Hand-Knee-Foot.
--Pseudarthroses & Their Treatment.
Chapel, Charles E. The Gun Collector's Handbook of Values.
Chapin & Hassett. Credit & Collection Principles & Practice.
Chapin, Brenda. Guide to the Recommended Country Inns of the Mid-Atlantic States & Chesapeake Region, (Delaware, Maryland, New Jersey, New York, Pennsylvania, Virginia, Washington, D. C. and West Virginia)
Chapin, F. Stuart, Jr. & Weiss, Shirley F., eds. Urban Growth Dynamics: In a Regional Cluster of Cities.
Chapin, Kim, jt. auth. see Baron, Gayle.
Chapin, Ned. Three-Sixty-Three-Seventy Programming in Assembly Language.
Chapin, Robert Maps by see Chandler, Tertius.
Chaplin, H., ed. The Organization of the Library Profession.
Chaplin, Jack W. Metal Manufacturing Technology.
Chaplin, Ralph. Centralia Conspiracy.
Chapman, jt. auth. see Watson, T. J.
Chapman, et al. Introduction & Methodology to the Study of Police Assaults in the South Central United States.
Chapman, Alexandra, jt. auth. see Oakes, George.
Chapman, Alexandra, jt. auth. see Oakes, George W.
Chapman, Annie B., jt. auth. see Hart, Albert B.
Chapman, Antony J. & Foot, Hugh C. It's a Funny Thing Humour: The International Conference on Humor & Laughter.
Chapman, Antony J., jt. ed. see McGhee, Paul E.
Chapman, Antony J., et al, eds. Pedestrian Accidents.
Chapman, Brian N. & Anderson, J. C., eds. Science & Technology of Surface Coatings.
Chapman, C. Keeler & Traister, John E. Homes for the Nineteen-Eighties: An Energy & Construction Design Aid.
Chapman, Carl H., ed. see Hamilton, Henry, et al.
Chapman, Carl H., ed. see Hamilton, Henry W. & Willoughby, Charles C.
Chapman, Carolyn K. Inspirational Poems to Touch the Heart.
Chapman, Charles F. & Maloney, Elbert S. Chapman's Piloting, Seamanship & Small Boat Handling.
Chapman, Charles F., jt. auth. see Lynch, Barbara S.
Chapman, Clark R. Inner Planets.
--Planets of Rock & Ice: From Mercury to the Moons of Saturn.
Chapman, D. J., jt. auth. see Chapman, V. J.
Chapman, David J., jt. ed. see Ragan, Mark A.
Chapman, David W., ed. Improving College Information for Prospective Students.
Chapman, Dennis & Magnus, P. D. Introduction to Practical High Resolution Nuclear Magnetic Resonance Spectroscopy.
Chapman, Elizabeth K. Visually Handicapped Children & Young People.
Chapman, Elwood N. Comfort Zones: A Practical Guide for Retirement Planning.
Chapman, Emalee. Fifteen-Minute Meals: Fresh, Fantastic & Nutritious Recipes.
Chapman, F. S., jt. auth. see Holland, F. A.
Chapman, Frank M. A Treatise on Ornithology.
Chapman, Gary. Now That You Are Single Again.
Chapman, Gary & Bryant, Steven, eds. Melodic Index to Haydn's Instrumental Music: A Thematic Locator for the Hoboken Thematisch-Bibliographisches Werkverzeichnis.
Chapman, Gaynor, illus. Aesop's Fables.
Chapman, George. The Plays of George Chapman: The Comedies. Holaday, Alan, ed.
Chapman, George see Harrier, Richard C.
Chapman, George, et al. Bussy d'Ambois. Evans, Maurice, ed.
Chapman, J. Dudley. Feminine Mind & Body.
Chapman, Jean. Moon Eyes. Lacis, Astra, tr.
--Velvet Paws & Whiskers.
Chapman, Jefferson. The Icehouse Bottom Site.
Chapman, John. Adult English Two.
Chapman, John S. The Atypical Mycobacteria & Human Mycobacteriosis.
Chapman, L. R. The Process of Learning Mathematics.
Chapman, Laura. A Change of Heart.
Chapman, Malcolm. The Gaelic Vision in Scottish Culture.
Chapman, Murray, jt. ed. see Prothero, Mansell.
Chapman, N. B. & Shorter, J., eds. Advances in Linear Free-Energy Relationships.
Chapman, Orville L., ed. Organic Syntheses.
Chapman, Paul. Unmet Needs & the Delivery of Care.
Chapman, Peter, jt. auth. see Martin, Margaret J.
Chapman, R. W., ed. see Austen, Jane.
Chapman, Reg, jt. auth. see Burden, Tom.
Chapman, Richard A. Leadership in the British Civil Service.
Chapman, Richard N. Contours of Public Policy, Nineteen Thirty-Nine to Nineteen Forty-Five. Freidel, Frank, ed.
Chapman, Robert. Pilot Fatigue: A Deadly Coverup.
Chapman, Robert D. Crimson Web of Terror.
Chapman, Roger. No Time on Our Side.
Chapman, Samuel. The Postage Stamps of Mexico, 1856-1868.
Chapman, Simon. Great Expectorations: Advertising & the Tobacco Industry.
Chapman, Tom. Heaven on the Halfshell: Edible Treasures from the Sea.
Chapman, V. J. Coastal Vegetation.
Chapman, V. J. & Chapman, D. J. Seaweeds & Their Uses.
Chapman, V. J., ed. The Marine Algae of New Zealand: Phaeophyceae.
Chapman, Vera. Blaedud the Birdman.
--The Green Knight.
--King Arthur's Daughter.
--The King's Damsel.
--The Wife of Bath.
Chapman, W. A. Workshop Technology.
--Workshop Technology.
--Workshop Technology.
Chapnick, Howard, ed. see Thoreau, Henry David.
Chapnick, Howard, ed. see Whitman, Walt.
Chapouton, Anne-Marie. Billy the Brave.
Chappel, Bernice M. Independent Language Arts Activities: Seatwork for the Primary Grades.
Chappel, James. The Potter's Complete Book of Clay & Glazes.
Chappell, Clovis G. The Best of C. G. Chappell.
Chappell, J. B. The Energetics of Mitochondria. Head, J. J., ed.
Chappell, V. C., ed. Hume: A Collection of Critical Essays.
Chappell, Warren, ed. The Nutcracker: Based on the Alexandre Dumas pere Version of the Story by E. T. A. Hoffmann.
--Sleeping Beauty.
Chappell, Willard & Peterson, Kathy. Molybdenum in the Environment, Vol. 2: The Geochemistry, Cycling, & Industrial Uses of Molybdenum.
Chappell, William, ed. see Burra, Edward.
Chappell, Williard R. & Paterson, Kathy K. Molybdenum in the Environment, Vol. 1: The Biology of Molybdenum.
Chappelle, Joseph. The Owl That Could Not Fly.
Chappelle, Joseph N. The Return of Otis.
Chapuisat, X., et al, eds. Theory.
Chaput, Donald. Francois X. Aubry.
Chaput, Linda, ed. see Teyler.
Char, Rene. Les Matinaux: Avec: La Parole en Archipel.
--Le Monde de l'Art n'est pas le Morde du Pardon.
Charcot, Jean. The Voyage of the "Pourquoi Pas?" in the Antarctic: The Journal of the Second French South Polar Expedition, 1908-1910.
Chard, Chester S. Northeast Asia in Prehistory.
Chardenon, Ludo. In Praise of Wild Herbs: Remedies & Recipies From Old Provence. Kinnell, Susan & Frederick, John, trs. from Fr.
Chardin, Pierre Teilhard De see Teilhard De Chardin, Pierre.
Charell, Ralph. How to Get the Upper Hand.
--Satisfaction Guaranteed: The Ultimate Guide to Consumer Self-Defense.
Charernbhak, Wichit. Chicago School Architects & Their Critics. Foster, Stephen, ed.
Charitonuk, Katherine E. Book of Prayers.
Charlebois, Robert, et al. Saints for Kids by Kids.
Charles, C. M. Building Classroom Discipline: From Models to Practice.
Charles, David. Self-Assessment of Current Knowledge in Obstetrics & Gynecology.
Charles, K. J. Total Development: Essays Toward an Integration of Marxian & Gandhian Perspectives.
Charles, R. H., ed. & The Book of Enoch: Or One Enoch.
Charles, R. H., ed. The Book of the Secrets of Enoch.
Charles, Rodger. Social Teaching of Vatican II: Its Origin & Development. Catholic Social Ethics-an Historical & Comparative Study.
Charles, Scott. All about Geneva.
Charles, Steven. Academy of Terror.
--The Enemy Within.
--The Last Alien.
Charles, Thomas W. & Stiner, Frederic M., Jr. Your Name Company: Accounting Practice Set for the Computer.
Charleston, Robert J., jt. auth. see Scheurleer, Lunsingh.
Charleston, Robert J., ed. see Liverani, Giuseppe.
Charleston, Robert J., ed. see Reinheckel, Gunter.
Charlesworth, A. S. & Fletcher, J. R. Systematic Analog Computer Programming.
Charlesworth, Edward A. & Nathan, Ronald G. Stress Management: A Comprehensive Guide to Wellness.
Charlesworth, M. P., tr. see Parvan, Vasile.
Charlet, James D., et al. North Carolina: Our People, Places & Past.
Charley, Julian. Fifty Key Words: The Bible.
Charlier, Rodger H. & Karpeck, John J. The World Around Us: A Book of Readings.
Charlier, Roger H. Tidal Energy.
Charlip, Remy. I Love You.
Charlot, G. & Tremillon, B. Chemical Reactions in Solvents & Melts.
Charlot, G., et al, eds. Selected Constants: Oxidation & Reduction Potentials of Inorganic Substances in Aqueous Solutions.
Charlotte-Georgi & Fate, Terry. Fund-Raising, Grants, & Foundations: A Comprehensive Bibliography.
Charlson, Robert J., jt. auth. see Butcher, Samuel S.
Charlton, C. A. The Urological System.
Charlton, D. G., jt. ed. see Potts, D. C.
Charlton, James. Surface Chic.
Charlton, James, ed. The Writer's Quotation Book.
Charlton, Peter. John Stainer.
Charlton, T. M. Model Analysis of Plane Structures.
Charmatz, Jan P. & Daggett, Harriet S., eds. Comparative Studies in Community Property Law.
Charmley, John, ed. see Shuckburgh, Evelyn.
Charmoy, Cozette De. The True Life of Sweeney Todd: A Novel in Collage.
Charney, Betty J., jt. auth. see Charnley, Nathaniel.
Charney, Maurice. Joe Orton.
--Joe Orton.
--Joe Orton.
--Sexual Fiction.
Charney, Ted. Student Chemist Explores Organic Compounds.
Charnley, Nathaniel & Charney, Betty J. Martha Ann & the Mother Store.
Charnock, Richard S. Ludus Patronymicus: Or, the Etymology of Curious Surnames.
Charon, Jean. Cosmology: Theories of the Universe. Moore, Patrick, tr. from Fr.
Charpen. Football Fantasy 1988.
Charpentier, Cliff. Fantasy Football Digest, 1988.
Charques, R. D., tr. see Fadieev, Aleksandr A.
Charriere, George. Scythian Art.
Charriere, Henri. Papillon.
Charron, Jean D. The Wisdom of Pierre Charron: An Original & Orthodox Code of Morality.
Charroux, Robert. The Mysteries of the Andes.
Charsky, Jennie, pseud. Persons Lowly Born.
Charteris, Leslie. Alias the Saint.
--Angels of Doom.
--The Avenging Saint.
--Call for the Saint.
--Catch the Saint.
--Enter the Saint.
--Featuring the Saint.
--Follow the Saint.
--The Last Hero.
--The Misfortunes of Mr. Teal.
--Prelude for War.
--The Saint Abroad.
--The Saint & Mr. Teal.
--The Saint & the Happy Highwayman.
--The Saint & the Hapsburg Necklace.
--The Saint & the People Importers.
--The Saint & the Sizzling Saboteur.
--The Saint Errant.
--The Saint Goes on.
--The Saint Goes West.
--The Saint in Action.
--The Saint Intervenes.
--The Saint Meets the Tiger.
--The Saint on the Spanish Main.
--The Saint Overboard.
--The Saint Returns.
--The Saint Steps in.
--The Saint to the Rescue.
--The Saint vs. Scotland Yard.
--Saint's Getaway.
--Thanks to the Saint.
--Vendetta for the Saint.
Charton, Balthazar, jt. auth. see Capitaine, Jean L.
Charton, Nancy, ed. The Ciskei: Economics & Politics of Dependence in a South African Homeland.
Chartrand, Gary. Graphs As Mathematical Models.
Chartrand, R. L. Information Technology Serving Society.
Chartrand, Robert L., ed. Computers in the Service of Society.
Chartres, John, et al. Northern Ireland Scrapbook.
Charyn, Jerome. Blue Eyes.
--The Catfish Man: A Conjured Life.
--Darlin' Bill.
--The Education of Patrick Silver.
--The Education of Patrick Silver.
--The Franklin Scare.
--Marilyn the Wild.
--Metropolis: New York As Myth, Marketplace, & Magical Land.
--Panna Maria: Which in English Means "Virgin Mary"

--Pinocchio's Nose.
--Pinocchio's Nose.
--Secret Isaac.
--The Seventh Babe.
Chasan, Daniel J. Up for Grabs: Inquiries into Who Wants What.
Chase, Agnes, ed. see Smithsonian Institution, Washington, D. C. Staff.
Chase, Alston. Playing God in Yellowstone: The Destruction of America's First National Park. Brady, Upton, ed.
Chase, Carroll. The Three-Cent Stamp of the United States, 1851-1857 Issue.
Chase, Claire, jt. auth. see Zager, Masha.
Chase, Deborah. Dying at Home with Hospice.
Chase, Edward L. Big Book of Horses.
Chase, Elaine R. Best Laid Plans.
--Dare the Devil.
--Double Occupancy.
Chase, Elizabeth, ed. Pioneer Churches of Florida.
Chase, Glen. Cherry Delight up Your Ante.
Chase, Harold, et al, eds. Biographical Dictionary of the Federal Judiciary.
Chase, Harold W., ed. see Corwin, Edward S.
Chase, Helen M., jt. auth. see Chase, William D.
Chase, Janet. Daughters of Change: Growing up Female in America.
Chase, John. Louisiana Purchase: America's Best Buy.
Chase, John T., jt. ed. see Hannum, Sara.
Chase, Leslie, jt. ed. see Rosenau, Fred S.
Chase, Leslie R. & Henderson, Faye, eds. Information Sources, 1985.
Chase, Leslie R. & Landers, Robert, eds. Strategic Marketing: Techniques, Technologies & Realities in the Electronic Information Marketplace.
Chase, Leslie R. & Tuttle, Patti, eds. Information Sources, 1986.
Chase, Leslie R., jt. ed. see Rosenau, Fred S.
Chase, Marian T, jt. auth. see Chase, Stuart.
Chase, Mary E. Journey to Boston.
Chase, Mildred L. Housekeeping Management for Health Care Facilities.
Chase, Richard, ed. Melville: A Collection of Critical Essays.
Chase, Richard B. & Aquilano, Nicholas J. Production & Operations Management: A Life Cycle Approach.
Chase, Robert A. Atlas of Hand Surgery.
Chase, Sarah L. Open House Cookbook.
Chase, Stuart & Chase, Marian T. Power of Words.
Chase, U. & Sweedler, M. E. Hopf Algebras & Galois Theory Two.
Chase, Virginia. Speaking of Maine: A Selection from the Writings of Virginia Chase. Shea, Margaret, ed.
Chase, William D. & Chase, Helen M. Chase's Annual Events: Special Days, Weeks & Months in 1985.
--Chase's Annual Events: Special Days, Weeks & Months in 1986.
--Chase's Annual Events: Special Days, Weeks & Months in 1987.
Chase, William G., ed. see Carnegie Symposium on Cognition Staff.
Chasin, Mark. Assembly Language: Programming for the Atari Computer.
Chassan, J. B. Research Design in Clinical Psychology & Psychiatry.
Chasseaud, L. F., jt. auth. see Bridges, J. W.
Chastain, James G., tr. see Stadelmann, Rudolph.
Chastain, Josephine K. Word Pictures.
Chastain, Kenneth. Developing Second Language Skills: Theory to Practice.
--Spanish Grammar in Review: Patterns for Communication.
Chastain, Madye L. Bright Days.
--Emmy Keeps a Promise.
--Emmy Keeps a Promise.
--Magic Island.
--Plippen's Palace.
Chastain, Thomas. Nightscape.
Chasteen, Joseph E. Essentials of Clinical Dental Assisting.
Chastel, Andre & Grayson, Cecil. The Renaissance: Essays in Interpretation.
Chateaubriand, Rene de. Lettres a Madame Recamier.
--Lettres et Manuscrits (Illustre) Nombres Lettres Inedites de Chateaubriand a Benjamin Constant, a Armand Carrel, au Sculpteur Emoyne.
--Oeuvres Completes: Paris, 1826-1831.
Chatelet, Albert. Impressionist Painting.
Chatelet, Francois, et al. La Revolution Sans Modele.
Chaterjee, S. S. Principles & Practice of Management.
Chatfield, Charles. Devere Allen & a Radical Approach to War.
--Kirby Page & the Social Gospel: Pacifist & Socialist Aspects.
Chatfield, Charles, jt. auth. see Gara, Larra.
Chatfield, Charles, ed. see Cook, Blanche.
Chatham, Larry. Banjo's Brand.
Chattarji, Dipankar. The Theory of Auger Transitions.
Chatterjee, Enakshi, tr. see Gangopadhyay, Sunil.
Chatterjee, Margaret. Gandhi's Religious Thought.
Chatterjee, Vera. All This Is Ended: The Life & Times of Her Highness Begum Sumroo.
Chatterji, M., ed. Space Location & Regional Development.
Chatterji, M. & Rompuy, P. Van, eds. Energy, Regional Science & Public Policy.
--Environment Regional Science & Interregional Modeling.
Chatterji, Manas, et al, eds. Spatial, Environmental, & Resource Policy in the Developing Countries.
Chatterji, Ruby. Existentialism in American Literature.
Chatterton, E. Keble. Whalers & Whaling: The Story of the Whaling Ships up to the Present Day.
Chatterton, Wayne. Irvin S. Cobb.
Chatterton, William A. Consumer & Small Business Bankruptcy: A Complete Working Guide.
Chatto, William A. Treatise on Wood Engraving, Historical & Practical.
Chattopadhyaya, Debiprasad. Marxism & Indology.
Chatty, Dawn. From Camel to Truck: The Bedouin in the Modern World.
Chatwin, Bruce. In Patagonia.
--The Viceroy of Ouidah.
--The Viceroy of Ouidah.
Chatwin, Bruce & Theroux, Paul. Patagonia Revisited.
Chau, W. C., et al, trs. see Yunlu, Ke, et al.
Chaucer, Geoffrey. The Canterbury Tales.
--The Complete Poetry & Prose of Geoffrey Chaucer. Fisher, John H., ed.
--The Parlement of Foulys. Brewer, D. S., ed.
--Troilus & Criseyde.
--Works of Geoffrey Chaucer. Robinson, F. N., ed.
Chaudhri, D. P. & Dasgupta, Ajit K. Agriculture & the Development Process: A Study of Punjab.
Chaudhuri, Haridas. Philosophy of Meditation.
Chaudier, Louann, ed. Leading Consultants in Technology 1983.
Chaudler, Christine. Every Man's Book of Superstitions.
Chauhan, Eklavya, jt. auth. see Desh Bandhu.
Chauhan, Ela, jt. auth. see Harris, Helen.
Chauhan, Manhar, illus. Let's Pretend with the Muppet Babies.
--Muppet Babies Take a Bath.
Chauhan, P. P. Sonnets of Wordsworth: A Critical Study.
Chauliaguet, Charles, et al. Solar Energy in Buildings.
Chauncey, George A. Decisions! Decisions!
Chauvois, Louis. William Harvey: His Life & Times; His Discoveries; His Methods.
Chava, Amir, tr. see Barnea, Amalia & Barnea, Aharon.
Chavez, Angelico. New Mexico Triptych.
--Tres Macho, He Said: Padre Gallegos, New Mexico's First Congressman.
Chavis, Grace L. Reflections on Africa.
Chavkin, Samuel. Murder of Chile.
Chayefsky. Television Plays.
Chayes. International Legal Process (1968)
Chaykin C. P. A. Review Staff & Lakin, Leonard. Business Law.
Chaykin, Sterling. Biochemistry Laboratory Techniques.
Chaze, Elliott. Goodbye, Goliath.
--Mr. Yesterday.
Chazel, Francois, et al, eds. L' Analyse des Processus Sociaux.
Chazov, E., et al, eds. Advances in Myocardiology.
--Advances in Myocardiology.
Chazov, E. I., ed. Cardiology in the U. S. S. R.
Chazov, Eugene I., ed. Myocardial Infraction.
Cheadle, Russell F., jt. auth. see Leventhal, Ruth.
Cheatham, Carole B. Cost Management for Profit Centers.
Cheatham, K. Follis. The Best Way Out.
--Bring Home the Ghost.
--Life on a Cool Plastic Ice Floe.
--Spotted Flower & the Ponokomita.
Cheatum, Billye A., jt. auth. see Ebert, Frances H.
Check, William A., jt. auth. see Fettner, Ann G.
Checkland, S. G., jt. ed. see Slaven, A.
Chee, Stephen. Local Institutions & Rural Development in Malaysia.
--Rural Local Government & Rural Development in Malaysia.
Cheek, Logan. Zero-Base Budgeting Comes of Age.
Cheeke, Peter R. & Shull, L. R. Natural Toxicants in Feeds & Poisonous Plants.
Cheers, Arlynne Lake & Carter, Lamore J. Teaching & Learning in the Model Classroom: The Conditions, Relationships & Instructional Specifics.
Cheeseman, Kenneth W. Fort Pendleton's Finest: Love Among the Ruins.
Cheeseman, Peter, ed. Fight for Shelton Bar.
Cheesman, Paul R. Early America & the Polynesians.
Cheesman, Paul R., ed. see Porter, Larry.
Cheesman, Willard. Kansas Night Wind.
Chee Soo. Taoist Ways of Healing: The Chinese Art of Pa Chin Hsien.
Cheever, Susan. The Cage.
Che Guevara see also Guevara, Ernesto.
Chein-Pai Han, jt. auth. see Bancroft.
Chekhov, Anton. Best Plays. Young, Stark, tr.
--Cherry Orchard.
--Oeuvres: Recits (1887-1892)
--Oeuvres: Recits (1892-1903)
--The Sea Gull. Popkin, Henry, ed. Jellicoe, Ann, tr.
--Three Sisters.
--Uncle Vanya. Chwat, Jacques, ed.
Chekhov, Anton see Weiss, Samuel A.
Chekki, Danesh A. The Social System & Culture of Modern India: A Research Bibliography.
Cheli, R. & Aste, H. Duodenitis.
Chelin, Jean. The Hands of Fate.
Chelkowski, Peter J. Mirror of the Invisible World: Tales from the Khamseh of Nizami.
Chellis, Marcia. Living with the Kennedys: The Joan Kennedy Story.
--Living with the Kennedys: The Joan Kennedy Story.
Chellis, Robert D., et al, eds. Congregate Housing for Older People: A Solution for the 1980's.
Chelmo, Harriet. It's Fun to Bake & Decorate.
Chemiakin, Mihail. Petersburg & Paris Period. Incl. Vol. II. Transformation: New York Period. Riverrun NY.
Chemical & Pharmaceutical Press Staff. Crop Protection Chemicals Reference.
Chemical Engineering Magazine Editors, jt. auth. see Matley, Jay.
Chemical Engineering Magazine Editors. Calculator Programs for Chemical Engineers.
--Chemical Engineering Guide to Corrosion in the Process Industries.
--Modern Cost Engineering Methods & Data.
--Physical Properties.
Chemical Engineering Magazine Editors & Kraus, Milton N. Pneumatic Conveying of Bulk Materials.
Chemical Engineering Magazine Editors. Process Energy Conservation: Methods & Technology.
--Process Piping Systems. Deutsch, David J., ed.
--Safe & Efficient Plant Operation & Maintenance.
--Selecting Materials for Process Equipment.
--Separation Techniques I: Liquid-Liquid Systems.
--Separation Techniques II: Gas-Liquid-Solid Systems.
--Skills Vital to Successful Managers.
--Solids Handling. McNaughton, Kenneth J., ed.
--Synfuels Engineering.
Chemistry & Action of Insect Juvenile Hormones Symposium Staff. Insect Juvenile Hormones: Chemistry & Action, Proceedings of the Symposium, Washington, D.C., 1971. Menn, Julius J. & Beroza, Morton, eds.
Chemsak, John A. & Linsley, E. G. Checklist of the Beetles of North & Central America & the West Indies: The Longhorned Beetles.
Chen. Active Network & Feedback Amplifier Theory.
Chen, C. H. Nonlinear Maxium Entropy Spectral Analysis Methods for Signal Recognition.
Chen, C. H., ed. Issues in Acoustics Signal-Image Processing & Recognition.
--Pattern Recognition & Artificial Intelligence: Proceedings of a Joint Workshop held at Hyannis, Mass., June 1976.
Chen, C. J. Vertical Turbulent Buoyant Jets: A Review of Experimental Data.
Chen, Donna H. Compensation for Librarians: A Checklist of Materials.
Chen, Han-Seng A. Industrial Capital & Chinese Peasants: A Study of the Livelihood of Chinese Tobacco Cultivators. Myers, Ramon H., ed.
Chen, J. C. & Bankoff, S. G., eds. Nonequilibrium Interfacial Transport Processes.
Chen, Jerome. State Economic Policies of the Ch'ing Government: 1840-1895.
Chen, K. C. & McGarrah, Robert E. Productivity Management: Test & Cases.
Chen, Kan, ed. Technology & Social Institutions.
Ch'en, Kung-Po. Communist Movement in China.
Chen, P. Problems Among Nations.
Chen, P., ed. see CISM (International Center for Mechanical Sciences), Department for Mechanics of Rigid Bodies Staff.
Chen, P. P., ed. Entity-Relationship Approach to Information Modeling & Analysis: Proceedings of the Second International Conference on Entity-Relationship Approach, Washington, D. C., Oct. 12-14, 1981.
Chen, P. Y., ed. Flow-Induced Vibration Design Guidelines.
Chen, Peter P., jt. auth. see Chu, Wesley W.
Chen, R. F. & Edelhoch, H., eds. Biochemical Fluorescence: Concepts.
Chen, Richard. Paper Folding Magic.
Chen, S. S. & Paidoussis, M. P., eds. Flow-Induced Vibration of Circular Cylindrical Structures 1982.
Chen, Stephen. Missouri in the Federal System.
Chen, Susan W., tr. see Feng Jicai.
Chen, T. T., ed. Research in Protozoology.
Chen, Wai-Fah & Saleeb, Atef F. Constitutive Equations for Engineering Materials: Elasticity & Modeling.
Chen, Yung-Ping. Background Paper on Income for the Nineteen Seventy-One White House Conference on Aging.
Chen, Yung-Ping see Yung-Ping Chen & Rohrlich, George F.
Chenault, Libby. Battlelines: World War I Posters from the Bowman Gray Collection.
Chenault, Steve. Re'lize Whut Ahm Talkin' 'Bout.
Chenault, V. Michele. Clinical Chemistry Lab Manual for the Medical Technology Student.
Chenel, Laura & Siegfried, Linda. American Cheese.
Chenery, Hollis. Industrialization & Growth - The Experience of Large Countries.
Chenetier, Marc. Richard Brautigan.
Chenevert, Melodie. STAT: Special Techiques in Assertiveness Training for Women in the Health Professions.
Cheney, Glenn A. Mineral Resources.
Cheney, Liana. The Paintings of the Casa Vasari. Freedberg, S. J., ed.
Cheney, Sheldon. Expressionism in Art.
Cheney, T. A. Land of the Hibernating Rivers: Life in the Arctic.
Cheney, William. H. Dickon Arkwright's Digest of a Journey Lately Undergone.
Chenfeld, Mimi B. Teaching Language Arts Creatively.
Cheng, Chung-ying, ed. Philosophical Aspects of the Mind-Body Problem.
Cheng, H. S., jt. ed. see Rohde, S. M.
Cheng, Hou-Tien. The Chinese New Year.
Cheng, Lucie, et al, eds. Women in China: Bibliography of Available English Language Materials.
Cheng, Philip C. Accounting & Fianancing for Motor Carriers.
Cheng, T. O., ed. The International Textbook of Cardiology.
Cheng, Thomas, ed. Current Topics in Comparative Pathobiology.
Cheng, Thomas C. General Parasitology.
Cheng, Thomas C., ed. Molluscicides in Schistosomiasis Control.
Cheng'en, Wu. Journey to the West. Jenner, W. J. F., tr. from Chinese.
Cheng Wang. The Kuomintang: A Sociological Study of Demoralization. Myers, Ramon H., ed.
Ch'en Kou-chun. Studies on the Society of Aborigines in Kweichow, China.
Chen Li-Fu. Philosophy of Life.
Chennault, Joann & Burnford, J. F. Human Services Professional Development: Future Directions.
Chenoweth, Clyde G. Our Tragic Inflation Orgy & What to Do About It: An Introduction to the Fascinating Economics of Tomorrow.
Chenoweth, D., jt. ed. see Henderson, L. W.
Chenoweth, Harry H., jt. auth. see Jensen, Alfred E.
Chenoweth, J. M. & Impagliazzo, M., eds. Fouling in Heat Exchange Equipment.
Chenowith, Bob. Army Gunships in Vietnam.
Chen-Tau, Wu. Studies on the Tea in Modern Taiwan.
Chen Wai-Kai. Active Network Feedback Amplifier Theory.
--Theory & Design of Broadband Matching Networks.
Cheradame, H., jt. auth. see Gandini, A.
Cheraskin, E., Jr. & Ringsdorf, W. M., Jr. New Hope for Incurable Diseases.
Cheraskin, Emanuel. Psychodietetics.
Cheremisinoff. Encyclopedia of Engineering Materials, Pt. A: Polymer Science & Tech, Vol. 3: Properties & Processing Operations.
Cheremisinoff, Nicholas P. & Azbel, David S., eds. Liquid Filtration.
Cheremisinoff, Nicholas P. & Gupta, Ramesh, eds. Handbook of Fluids in Motion.
Cheremisinoff, Paul N. & Young, Richard A. Pollution Engineering Practice Handbook.
Cheremisnoff. Encyclopedia of Engineering Materials.
--Encyclopedia of Engineering Materials.
Cheret, Jules & Broido, Lucy. The Posters of Jules Cheret.
Cherfas, Jeremy. Zoo Two Thousand: A Look Beyond the Bars.
Cherin, Robin, jt. auth. see Garcia, Richard.
Cherington, P. W. Airline Price Policy: A Study of Airline Passenger Fares.
Cherlin, G. Model Theoretic Algebra Selected Topics.
Cherna, Ilene, ed. see Milward, John.
Chernenko, Konstantin. Selected Speeches & Writings.

Chernetsov, V. N. & Moszynska, W. I. Prehistory of Western Siberia. Michael, Henry N., ed.
Chernev, Irving. Most Instructive Games of Chess Ever Played.
Cherniack. Current Therapy in Respiratory Disease, 1986-87.
Cherniack, Reuben M. Current Therapy in Respiratory Medicine 1984-1985.
Cherniak, Laurence. The Great Books of Hashish.
Chernicoff. Mac Revealed: Programming with the Macintosh Toolbox.
Chernicoff, Stephen. Macintosh Revealed, Vol. I: Unlocking the Toolbox.
--Macintosh Revealed, Vol. II: Programming with the Toolbox.
Chernicott. Macintosh Revealed: Programming with the Macintosh Toolbox.
Chernik, Barbara E. Introduction to Library Services for Library Technicians.
Chernikov, G. The Crisis of Capitalism & the Condition of the Working People.
Chernin, Kim. In My Mother's House.
Cherniss, Harold. The Riddle of the Early Academy.
Chernoff, Hyman M. Workbook in Clinical Electrocardiography: Two Hundred Problems for Self-Assessment.
Chernoff, John M. African Rhythm & African Sensibility.
Chernoff, P. R. & Marsden, J. E. Properties of Infinite Dimensional Hamiltonian Systems.
Chernogorova, V. Enigmas del Micromundo.
Chernok, Norma B. Your Future in Medical Assisting.
Chernow, Burt. The Drawings of Milton Avery.
--Gabor Peterdi: Paintings.
Cherns, Albert, intro. by see Shoham, S. Giora.
Cherns, J. J. Official Publishing, an Overview: An International Survey & Review of the Role, Organization & Principles of Official Publishing.
Chernukhin, A. E. English-Russian Polytechnical Dictionary.
Chernyi, G. G. Introduction to Hypersonic Flow. Probstein, Ronald F., ed.
Cherrholmes. Dis Others Picpkt G1.
Cherrington, jt. auth. see Jensen.
Cherrington, B. E. Gaseous Electronics & Gas Lasers.
Cherrington, David J., jt. auth. see Jensen, Ronald.
Cherry, Colin. The Age of Access: Information Technology & Social Revolution. Edmondson, William, ed.
Cherry, Conrad. Nature & Religious Imagination: From Edwards to Bushnell.
Cherry, Don & Fischler, Stan. Grapes: A Vintage View of Hockey.
Cherry, Joetta & Tomlin, Gwynne. Disco Dancing.
Cherry, Kelly. Augusta Played.
--In the Wink of an Eye.
--The Lost Traveller's Dream.
Cherry, Kenneth F. Plating Waste Treatment.
Cherry, R. C., et al, eds. Materials of Construction of Fluid Machinery & Their Relationship to Design & Performance.
Cherry, Raymond. General Leathercraft.
--General Plastics: Projects & Procedures.
Cherry, Richard L., et al. The Essay: Structure & Purpose.
Cherry, Richard L., et al, eds. A Return to Vision. Conley, Robert J. & Hirsch, Bernard A.
Chertijin, V., et al. America Latina: Nacionalismo, Democracia y Revolucion.
Chertok, L., ed. see International Brain Research Organization.
Chertok, Semen. Poslednyaya lyubov' Maykovskogo.
Chesanow, Neil. The World-Class Executive: How to Do Business Like a Pro Anywhere on the Globe.
Chesbro, George C. Two Songs This Archangel Sings.
--Veil.
Cheshire, M. V. Nature & Origin of Carbohydrates in Soils.
Cheshire, Maxine & Greenya, John. Maxine Cheshire, Reporter.
Cheshire, P. C., jt. auth. see Bowers, J. K.
Cheskin, Louis. Basis for Marketing Decisions Through Controlled Motivation Research.
--Color for Profit.
--Why People Buy: Motivation Research & Its Successful Application.
Chesler, Bernice. Bed & Breakfast in New England.
--Bed & Breakfast in the Mid-Atlantic States.
--Bed & Breakfast in the Northeast: From Maine to Washington, D. C., 300 Selected B&B's.
Chesler, Mark A. & Cave, William. A Sociology of Education.
Chesler, Mark A., et al. Making Desegregation Work.
Chesler, Phyllis. Mothers on Trial: The Battle for Children & Custody.
--Women & Madness.
Cheslow, Melvyn. A Road Pricing & Transit Improvement Program in Berkeley, California: A Preliminary Analysis.
Chesneau, Roger, ed. Scale Models in Plastic.
Chesneaux, Jean. Peasant Revolts in China 1840-1949. Barraclaugh, Geoffrey, ed. Curwen, C. A., tr. from Fr.
Chesney. A Radiographer's Handbook of Hospital Practice.
Chesney & Chesney. Care of the Patient in Diagnostic Radiography.
Chesney, Francis R. Expedition for the Survey of the Rivers Euphrates - Tigris, Carried Out by Order of the British Government in the Years 1835-1837. Incl. Geographical & Historical Notices of the Regions Situated Between the Rivers Nile & Indus; Vol. 1; Vol. 2. Greenwood.
Chesney, Marion. Daphne.
--Deirdre & Desire.
--Diana the Huntress.
--The French Affair.
--Milady in Love.
--Minerva.
--The Miser of Mayfair.
--Plain Jane.
--The Wicked Godmother.
Chesney, Marion, ed. Diana the Huntress.
Chesnoff, Richard Z. The Philippines.
Chesnutt, David R., ed. The Papers of Henry Laurens.
Chess, V., jt. auth. see Goldberg, S. J.
Chess, Victoria. Catcards for Christmas.
--Poor Esme.
Chesseman, G. W. & Cookson, R. F., eds. Condensed Pyrazines.
Chesser. Live & Let Live.
Chesser, Eustace. Cruelty to Children.
Chester, Andrew, tr. see Schweizer, Edward.
Chester, Carol. Going Alone: Woman's Guide to Travel Know How.
Chester, Carole. Amsterdam.
--California & the Golden West.
--Florida.
--Germany.
--New York.
Chester, David. The Olympic Games.
Chester, Deborah. Heart's Desire.
Chester, Michael. Robots: Facts Behind the Fiction.
Chester, R. & Peel, J., eds. Equalities & Inequalities in Family Life.
Chester, R., jt. ed. see Roberts, D. F.
Chesterton, G. K. The Autobiography of G. K. Chesterton.
--Napoleon of Notting Hill.
--Orthodoxy.
--The Scandal of Father Brown.
Chestnut, H., et al, eds. Supplemental Ways for Improving International Stability: Proceedings of the IFAC Workshop, Laxenburg, Austria, 13-15, September, 1983.
Cheston, Stephen T. & Loeffke, Bernard, eds. Aspects of Soviet Policy Toward Latin America.
Chetham, Charles. The Role of Vincent Van Gogh's Copies in the Development of His Art.
Chetin, Helen. Cat.
--How Far Is Berkeley?
Chetta, Holly. Poems Toward the Twenty-First Century.
Chetwin, Grace. On All Hallows' Eve.
Chetwynd, Jane & Hartnett, Oonagh, eds. The Sex-Role System: Psychological & Sociological Perspectives.
Cheung, William. Kung Fu Butterfly Swords. Lee, Mike, ed.
Cheung, Y. K. Finite Strip Method in Structural Analysis. Neal, B. G., ed.
Cheuse, Alan. Fall Out of Heaven: An Autobiographical Journey.
--The Grandmothers' Club.
Chevalier, Christa. Spence Makes Circles. Tucker, Kathy, ed.
Chevalier, Haakon, tr. see Fanon, Frantz.
Chevalier, Michel. On the Probable Fall in the Value of Gold. Cobden, Richard, ed.
Chevalley, C., ed. Methode et Philosophie en Physique Fondamentale Aujourd'Hui.
Chevalley, Claude. Fundamental Concepts of Algebra.
Cheville, N. F. Cytopathology in Viral Diseases. Melnick, J. L., ed.
Cheviot, Andrew, ed. Proverbs, Proverbial Expressions, & Popular Rhymes of Scotland.
Chevrier, Jean-Francois, jt. auth. see Hers, Francois.
Chew, Al H., et al. Technical Mathematics.
Chew, Peter. Inner World of the Middle-Aged Man.
Chew, Samuel C. Crescent & the Rose: Islam & England During the Renaissance.
Chew Kang, Lee. Orchids.
Chewoweth, J., ed. Flow Induced Heat Exchanger Tube Vibration-1980.
Cheymol, J. Neuromuscular Blocking & Stimulating Agents.
Cheyney, Edward P. A History of England from the Defeat of the Armada to the Death of Elizabeth.
Chi, Michelene T., ed. Trends in Memory Development.
Chia, L. S., jt. auth. see MacAndrews, C.
Chiamos, Mary, et al. Zoom.
Chianese, Robert L. Peaceable Kingdoms: An Anthology of Utopian Writings.
Chiang, C. Nora & Lee, Charles C., eds. Prenatal Drug Exposure: Kinetics & Dynamics.
Chiang, Hai D., jt. ed. see Ooi, Jin-Bee.
Chiang Yee. Silent Traveller in Paris.
--The Silent Traveller in Japan.
Chiarappa, L., ed. Crop Loss Assessment Methods.
--Crop Loss Assessment Methods: Complete Work Manual.
Chiari, Joseph. Contemporary French Poetry.
Chiaromonte, Nicola. The Worm of Consciousness & Other Essays.
--The Worm of Consciousness & Other Essays. Ferrone, J. & Willen, D., eds.
Chiasson, Robert B. Laboratory Anatomy of the White Rat.
Chiasson, Robert B., jt. auth. see Ashley, Lawrence M.
Chiazze, Leonard, Jr. & Lundin, Frank E., eds. Methods & Issues in Occupational & Environmental Epidemiology.
Chiba, Milan. Noonblaze.
Chibata, Ichiro & Fukui, Saburo, eds. Enzyme Engineering.
Chibbett, David G., tr. see Doppo, Kunikida.
Chibnall, Bernard. Teaching for Effective Study. Hills, P. J., ed.
Chibnall, Marjorie. Anglo-Norman England Ten Sixty-Six to Eleven Sixty-Six.
Chicago Cutlery Staff. Cooking with Style.
Chichester, Michael & Wilkinson, John. The Uncertain Ally.
Chicken, J. C. Nuclear Power Hazard Control Policy.
Chicken, John C. Hazard Control Policy in Britain.
Chidamian, Claude. The Book of Cacti & Other Succulents.
Chiddick, D. & Spedding, A., eds. Land Management: New Directions.
Chief Dan George & Hirnschall, Helmut. My Heart Soars.
Chieger, Bob. Voices of Baseball: Quotations on the Summer Game.
Chien, Chao C. Advanced Business BASIC for Microcomputers.
--Introduction to the Microcomputer & Its Applications: PC-DOS, Wordstar, Lotus, 1-2-3 & dBASE.
Chiera, Edward. They Wrote on Clay: The Babylonian Tablets Speak Today. Cameron, George G., ed.
Chigier, N. A. Progress in Energy & Combustion Science.
Chigier, N. A., ed. Energy & Combustion Science: Selected Papers from Progress in Energy & Combustion Science.
--Progress in Energy & Combustion Science.
--Progress in Energy & Combustion Science.
--Progress in Energy & Combustion Science.
--Progress in Energy & Combustion Science.
--Progress in Energy & Combustion Science.
--Progress in Energy & Combustion Science.
Chihal, Jane. Premenstrual Syndrome.
Chihara, D. Borobudur: The Buddhist Monument of Java.
Chih-Mai, Ch'En. Chinese Calligraphers & Their Art.
Chikazumi, S., jt. ed. see Miura, N.
Chilcote, Ronald H. Revolution & Structural Change in Latin America.
Chilcote, Ronald H., compiled by. Emerging Nationalism in Portuguese Africa: A Bibliography of Documentary Ephemera Through 1965.
--Emerging Nationalism in Portuguese Africa: Documents.
Chilcote, Russell Q. Sharad: Camel Driver for the Kings.
Child, Arodel & Johnson, Lynn. A Research Project on Workfare.
Child, Frank S. Colonial Parson of New England.
Child, Harold, ed. see Hudson, Derek.
Child, Heather. Calligraphy Today.
Child, J. M., ed. see Barrow, Isaac.
Child Welfare League of America, Committee on Standards. Child Welfare League of America Standards for Services to Unmarried Parents.
Childbirth Education Association of Greater Philadelphia, Inc. Staff. Counseling the Nursing Mother.
Childbirth Education Association of Jacksonville, Fla., Inc. Staff & Brinkley, Ginny. Your Child's First Journey: A Guide to Prepared Birth from Pregnancy to Parenthood.
Children's Defense Fund Staff. Children & the Federal Budget.
--Children in Adult Jails.
--Children Out of School in America.
--Children Without Health Care.
--Children Without Homes: An Examination of Public Responsibility to Children in Out-of-Home Care.
--A Children's Defense Budget FY 1988: An Analysis of Our Nation's Investment in Children.
--A Corporate Reader: Work & Family Life in the 1980's.
--For the Welfare of Children.
--How to Help Handicapped Children Get an Education: A Success Story.
Children's Defense Fund Staff, ed. see Blank, Helen & Wilkins, Amy.
Children's Defense Fund Staff, et al. In Celebration of Children: An Interfaith Religious Action Kit.
--School Suspensions: Are They Helping Children?
Children's Hospital & Medical Center Staff, Seattle, Washington. Nursing Care Plans for the Pediatric Patient.
Children's Television Workshop Staff & Stein, Sara B. Learn at Home the Sesame Street Way.
Childress, Alice. A Hero Ain't Nothin' but a Sandwich.
--A Short Walk.
Childress, David H. A Hitchhiker's Guide to Africa & Arabia.
Childs, Brevard S. Biblical Theology in Crisis.
--Old Testament Books for Pastor and Teacher.
Childs, Christopher, ed. see Thoreau, Henry David.
Childs, Corinne. Yasmina's Daughter.
Childs, David. Britain since Nineteen Forty-Five: A Political History.
Childs, Harwood L. Reference Guide to the Study of Public Opinion.
Childs, James M., Jr. Christian Anthropology & Ethics.
Childs, Marjorie. Fabric of the ERA: Congressional Intent.
Childs, Marquis. Mighty Mississippi: Biography of a River.
Childs, Richard S. Unfinished Political Reforms: 1977.
Chiles, Fran. Parties, Parties.
Chiles, L. B., et al, eds. Lift (Elevator) Erection.
--Lift (Elevator) Practice.
--Lift (Elevator) Servicing & Maintenance.
Chiles, Webb. The Open Boat - Across the Pacific.
Chileshe, Jonathan H. Third World Countries & Development Options: Zambia.
Chilivumbo, Alifeyo. Migration & Uneven Rural Development in Africa: The Case of Zambia.
Chiltern, Crispin, jt. ed. see Aubrey, Paul.
Chilton. Chilton's Easy Car Care.
--Chilton's Ford-Mercury FWD 1981 - 1985.
Chilton Automotives Editorial Staff. AMC, Nineteen Seventy Five to Nineteen Eighty-Two.
--Buick Century-Regal 1975-85.
--Buick-Olds-Pontiac Full-Size, 1975-87.
--Buick-Olds-Pontiac 1975-85.
--Cadillac Nineteen Sixty-Seven to Nineteen Eighty Four: RTUG.
--Chevette T-1000 1976-84.
--Chevrolet GMC Pick-Ups 1970-84: Repair & Tune-up Guide - Includes Suburban.
--Chevrolet-GMC Vans 1967-84: Repair & Tune-up Guide.
--Chevy S-10 Blazer, S-15 Jimmy 1982-85.
--Chevy S-10, GMC S15 Pick up 1982-85.
--Chilton's Auto Repair Manual (CARM) 1980-87.
--Chilton's Auto Repair Manual 1977-84.
--Chilton's Auto Repair Manual 1979-86.
--Chilton's Auto Service Manual Nineteen Eighty-Four to Nineteen Eighty-Eight: Motor-Age Professional Mechanics Edition.
--Chilton's Easy Car Care.
--Chilton's Ford Vans 1961 - 1986.
--Chilton's Guide to Small Engine Repair: Up to Twenty Horse Power.
--Chilton's Guide to Small Engine Repair Up to 6HP: Includes Honda, Tanaka, John Deere.
--Chilton's Guide to Small Engine Repair 6-20HP: Includes Honda, John Deere.
--Chilton's Import Auto Repair Manual 1977-84.
--Chilton's Import Car Repair Manual 1979-86.
--Chilton's Import Car Repair Manual: 1980-87.
--Chilton's Import Car Repair Manual 1985.
--Chilton's Labor Guide & Parts Manual 1979-85.
--Chilton's Motor Professional Automotive Service Manual 1981.
--Chilton's Repair & Tune-Up Guide: Chevrolet-GMC S-10, S-15 1982-83.
--Chilton's Repair & Tune-Up Guide: Corvette 1963-84.
--Chilton's Repair & Tune-up Guide: Ford Bronco 1966-83.
--Chilton's Repair & Tune-up Guide for Datsun Z & ZX 1970-1984.
--Chilton's Repair & Tune-up Guide for Mazda 1971-1984: RTUG.
--Chilton's Repair & Tune-up Guide for Opel, 1964-1970.
--Chilton's Repair & Tune-up Guide for VW Front Wheel Drive 1974-85.
--Chilton's Repair & Tune-up Guide: Toyota Truck 1970-83.

Authors

--Chilton's Small Engines: Repair & Tune-up Guide.
--Chilton's Toyota Trucks 1970-86.
--Chilton's Toyota 1966 - 1970.
--Chilton's Truck & Van Manual 1973-1980: Gasoline & Diesel Engines.
--Chilton's Truck & Van Repair Manual 1977-84.
--Chrysler K-Car & E-Car 1981-1985.
--Datsun 1200, 210 & Nissan Sentra 1973-84: RTUG.
--Datsun 200 SX, 510, 610, 710, 810, 1973-84: RTUG.
--Dodge - Plymouth Vans 1967-84: RTUG.
--Dodge Colt & Challenger Nineteen Seventy-one to Nineteen Eighty-One.
--Dodge-Plymouth Vans, Nineteen Sixty-Seven to Nineteen Eighty-Two.
--Dodge Trucks Nineteen Sixty-Seven through Eighty-Four: RTUG - Includes Pick-Ups, Ramcharger, Trailduster.
--Escort & Lynx, 1981 to 1982.
--Ford Bronco, Nineteen Sixty-Six to Nineteen Eighty-One.
--Ford Pick-Ups 1965-84: RTUG.
--GM A-Body, 1982-85.
--Honda 1973-84: RTUG.
--Chilton's Repair & Tune-up Guide for Datsun Nissan Pick-ups 1970-84.
--Omni-Horizon 1978-1984: Repair & Tune-up Guide.
--Subaru 1970-84: RTUG.
Chilton, Bruce D. The Glory of Israel: The Theology & Provenience of the Isaiah Targum.
Chilton, C. H., jt. auth. see Perry, Robert H.
Chilton, John. Who's Who of Jazz: Storyville to Swing Street.
Chilton, Richard L. The Great American Baseball Lineup Quiz Book.
Chilton Staff. Chilton's Tune-up Emission Diagnosis & Service Manual, 1988: Motor Age Professional Mechanic's Edition.
Chilton, Stuart, ed. Selected Readings in Education Adminstration.
Chilton's Automotives Editorial Staff. Chevy S-Ten--S-Fifteen Blazer, 1982 to 1987.
--Chilton's Guide To Electronic Engine Controls 1978-87.
Chilver, J. W. The Human Aspects of Management: A Case Study Approach.
China International Famine Relief Commission. Herr Raiffeisen among Chinese Farmers.
China International Travel Service Staff, ed. Official Guidebook to China.
China Pictorial Staff, ed. China in Pictures.
China Pictorial, "The People's Republic of China" Editors. Chinese Cuisine: From the Master Chefs of China.
Chinal, J. Design Methods for Digital Systems. Preston, A., tr. from Fr.
Chinard, G. Volney et L'Amerique D'appres Des Documents Inedits et Sa Correspondance Avec Jefferson.
Chin-Chiu, Lee. Essential Biology.
Chinery, Michael. A Field Guide to the Insects of Britain & Northern Europe.
Chinese Academy of Science Staff, jt. auth. see Institute of National Science Staff.
Chinese Academy of Sciences Staff. Issues in Cognition: Proceedings of a Joint Conference in Psychology. National Academy of Sciences Staff, ed.
Ching, Frank. Architectural Graphics.
Chinitz, Benjamin, ed. City & Suburb.
Chin-Li, C. Memory of a Girlhood in China. Israel, Abby, tr. from Fr.
Chinmoy, Sri. The Jewel of Humility.
--Something, Somehow, Somewhere, Someday.
--Sri Chinmoy Speaks. Incl. Pt. 1; Pt. 2; Pt. 3; Pt. 4; Pt. 5; Pt. 6; Pt. 7; Pt. 8; Pt. 9; Pt. 10. Aum Pubns.
Chinnery, John D. & Mingqui, Cui. Corresponding English & Chinese Proverbs & Phrases.
Chinweizu, et al. Towards the Decolonization of African Literature: African Fiction & Poetry & Their Critics.
Chipeta, Chinyamata. Indigenous Economics: A Cultural Approach.
Chipman, George, jt. auth. see Chipman, Jeane.
Chipman, Jeane & Chipman, George. Games! Games! Games!
Chipman, John S., et al, eds. Preferences, Utility, & Demand: A Minnesota Symposium.
Chipps, Genie, jt. auth. see Jessup, Claudia.
Chiquita Banana Cookbook Staff. The Chiquita Banana Cookbook.
Chirelstein, Marvin A. Federal Income Taxation: A Law Student Guide to the Leading Cases & Concepts.
Chirelstein, Marvin A., jt. auth. see Brudney, Victor.
Chirgotis, William G. Two Hundred Fifty Home Plans for Today's Living.
Chirich, Nancy. Life with Wine: A Self-Portrait of the Wine Business in the Napa & Sonoma Valleys Plus 100 Recipes That Go with the Product. Stengel, Gretchen, ed.
Chirich, Nancy, ed. see Brown, Rudd.
Chirico, Peter. Infallibility: The Crossroads of Doctrine.
Chirlan, Barbara. The Tenderfoot's Guide to Word Processing.
Chirls, Richard, jt. auth. see Klaiman, Henry S.
Chirot, Daniel. Social Change in the Twentieth-Century.
Chirot, Daniel, ed. Social Changes in a Peripheral Society: The Creation of a Balkan Colony.
Chisausky, Lawrence, jt. auth. see Castlewitz, David M.
Chisholm, Anthony H. & Tyers, Rodney, eds. Food Security in Asia & the Pacific Rim: Perspectives & Policy Issues.
Chisholm, Clarence E. & Stewart, Alva W. Regulatory Reform since Nineteen Seventy-Seven: A Bibliographic Overview.
Chisholm, E. Operas of Leos Janacek.
Chisholm, Emily, tr. see Thurian, Max.
Chisholm, J., jt. auth. see Enoeda, K.
Chisholm, L. J. Units of Weight & Measure: International (Metric) & U. S. Customary.
Chisholm, Shirley. Unbought & Unbossed: An Autobiography.
Chisolm, J. J. & O'Hara, D. M. Lead Absorption in Children: Management, Clinical & Environmental Aspects.
Chissell, Joan. Clara Schumann: A Dedicated Spirit; A Study of Her Life & Work.
Chissick, S. S., jt. auth. see Michaels, L.
Chiswick, Malcolm L. Neonatal Medicine.
Chitham, Robert. Measured Drawings for Architects.
Chitnis, Anand C. The Scottish Enlightenment & Early Victorian English Society.
Chittenden, Hiram M. American Fur Trade in the Far West.
Chittick, Donald E. The Controversy: Roots of the Creation-Evolution Conflict.
Chittick, William C., ed. see Tabataba'I, Allamah.
Chittick, William C., tr. see Al-Muminin, Amir.
Chittock, J. World Directory of Stockshot & Film Production Libraries.
Chittum, Ida. The Cat's Pajamas.
Chiu, Tony. Making the Best Deal: Your Car.
--Making the Best Deal: Your Health & Wealth.
--Making the Best Deal: Your Home.
Chiumello, Giuseppe & Laron, Z., eds. Recent Progress in Pediatric Endocrinology.
Chiurdoglu, G., ed. Conformational Analysis: Proceedings of an International Symposium, Brussels, 1969.
--Conformational Analysis: Scope & Present Limitations.
Chivington, Paul K., jt. auth. see Keyes, Elizabeth.
Chizhikov, T. & Shchastlivyi, J. Tellurium & Tellurides.
Chizhikov, V. & Shchastlivyi, T. Selenium & Selenides.
Chlapowski, F., jt. auth. see PreTest Service, Inc.
Chmielewski, Edward V. Tribune of the Slavophiles: Konstantin Aksakov.
Chmura, Louis J., jt. auth. see Ledgard, Henry F.
Chmura, Louis J., Jr., jt. auth. see Ledgard, Henry F.
Cho, Chin-Kuei. An Introduction to Software Quality Control.
Cho, Gene J. Melodic, Dyadic & Harmonic Singing: Graded Exercises.
--Melody Harmonization at the Keyboard.
Cho, Paul Y. & Manzano, R. Whitney. Prayer: Key to Revival.
Choate, Curt & Haynes, J. H. Honda Hawk 400 Twins '78-'81.
Choate, Judith. Gourmet Preserves: Sweet or Savory, Spread, Sauce or Condiment, a Complete Guide to Delicious & Unique Preserving.
Choate, Pat, jt. auth. see Schwartz, Gail G.
Choate, Robert, jt. auth. see Rossi, Nick.
Choate, Robert A. & Francis, William H. Patent Law, Cases & Materials Also Including Trade Secrets - Copyrights - Trademaks.
Choate, Robert A., ed. Documentary Report of the Tanglewood Symposium.
Choco, John & Choco, Ronalyn. Britain & Ireland on Your Own.
Choco, Ronalyn, jt. auth. see Choco, John.
Chodorow, Stanley. The Other Side of Western Civilization-Readings in Everyday Life: The Ancient World to the Reformation.
Chodos, A., et al, eds. Lewes Workshop on Solutions in Nuclear & Elementary Particle Physics: Proceedings, Delaware University, June 1984.
Choh Hao Li, ed. Hormonal Proteins & Peptides: Gonadotropic Hormones.
--Hormonal Proteins & Peptides: Prolactin.
Choi, C. Y. Chinese Migration & Settlement in Australia.
Choi, Sunu. National Museum of Korea, Seoul.
Choi, Woonsang. Fall of the Hermit Kingdom.
Choisy, Maryse. Psychoanalysis of the Prostitute.
--Sigmund Freud: A New Appraisal.
Cholmondely, Mary see Besant, Walter.
Chomiak, Martha & Rosenthal, Bernice. A Revolution of the Spirit: Crisis of Value in Russia, Eighteen-Ninety to Nineteen-Eighteen. Schwarz, Marian, tr.
Chomsky, Noam. Essays on Form & Interpretation.
--Language & Mind.
Chong, Key R. Americans & Chinese Reform & Revolution, 1898-1922: The Role of Private Citizens in Diplomacy.
Chonko & Enis. Sales Management.
Chonko, jt. auth. see Enis.
Choong, E. & Brundle, F. Book of Badminton.
Choppin. Evaluation in Education: An Experiment in Rural Primary Schools in Malaysia.
Choppin, B. & Postlethwaite, N., eds. Evaluation in Education: Vol. 1, International Progress.
Choppin, B. H., ed. Evaluation in Education.
Choppin, B. H. & Postlethwaite, T. N., eds. Evaluation in Education.
--Evaluation in Education.
--Evaluation in Education: Four Complete.
Choppin, G. & Ryberg, J., eds. Nuclear Chemistry: Theory & Applications.
Chopra, H. S., jt. ed. see Lall, K. B.
Chopra, M. G. & Kumar, Ram. FORTRAN IV Programming.
Chopra, Maharaj K. India & the Indian Ocean: New Horizons.
Chopra, Ravi, jt. auth. see Morehouse, Ward.
Chopra, S. R., ed. Early Man in North-West India.
Chorafas, Dimitris N. Handbook of Data Communication & Computer Networks.
--Personal Computers & Data Communications.
Chorafas, Dimitrius N. Control Systems Functions & Programming Approaches.
Chorao, Kay. Ida Makes a Movie.
--Magic Eye for Ida.
--Molly's Lies.
--Molly's Moe.
Chorley, R. J. & Haggett, P. Socio-Economic Models in Geography.
Chorley, R. J., jt. auth. see Barry, Roger G.
Chorley, R. J., et al. History of the Study of Landforms; or, the Development of Geomorphology, Vol. 2: The Life & Work of William Morris Davis.
Chorley, Richard J., ed. Integrated Models in Geography. Haggett, Peter.
--Introduction to Physical Hydrology.
--Water, Earth & Man.
Chorley, Richard J. & Haggett, Peter, eds. Models in Geography.
Chou, George. Using Paradox.
Chou, Marylin & Harmon, David P., Jr. Critical Food Issues of the Nineteen Eighties.
Chou, Ya-Lun & Bauer, Bertrand. Modern Business Statistics.
Choudhary, B. The Elements of Complex Analysis.
Choudhary, G. & Keith, L. H., eds. Chlorinated Dioxins & Dibenzofurans in the Total Environment.
Choudhury, Rabindra N., tr. see Tagore, Rabindranath.
Chouemi, Moustafa, jt. auth. see Blachere, Regis.
Chouraqui, Andre N. Between East & West: A History of the Jews of North Africa. Bernet, Michael M., tr. from Fr.
Chou Shu-Jen. Ah Q & Others: Selected Stories of Lusin. Wang, Chi-Chen, tr. from Chinese.
Chow, W. F. Principles of Tunnel Diode Circuits.
Chow, William. Cost Reduction in Product Design.
Choy, Dexter, jt. auth. see Gee, Choy Y.
Choy, Penelope. Basic Grammar & Usage.
--Basic Grammar & Usage.
Chretien, J. & Marsac, J., eds. Sarcoidosis & Other Granulomatous Disorders: International Conference, 9th, Paris, 31 August - 4 September 1981.
Chrimes, K. M. Ancient Sparta.
Chrisholm, Clarence E. & Toomer, Clarence. Health Care Construction: A Bibliography.
Christ, Adolph E. & Flomenhaft, Kalman, eds. Psychosocial Family Interventions In Chronic Pediatric Illness.
Christal, M. A Journey Thru Earlyland.
Christan, J. W., et al, eds. Progress in Materials Science.
Christenberry, William. Southern Photographs.
Christenbury, Leila, ed. Developing Lifelong Readers.
Christensen, Bernhard M. The Inward Pilgrimage: Spiritual Classics from Augustine to Bonhoeffer.
Christensen, Erwin. Early American Woodcarving.
Christensen, Gary L. Cable Television, 1985: Retrospective & Perspective.
Christensen, James J., et al. Handbook of Proton Ionization Heats.
Christensen, James R. Field Guide to the Butterflies of the Pacific Northwest.
Christensen, Jo I. Teach Yourself Needlepoint.
Christensen, Joe J. To Grow in Spirit.
Christensen, Mark. Mortal Belladaywic.
Christensen, Paul. Charles Olson: Call Him Ishmael.
Christensen, Ronald. Data Distributions.
Christensen, Terry, et al. The California Connection: Politics in the Golden State.
Christenson, Evelyn. What Happens When God Answers.
Christenson, Larry. Family Pocket Promise Book.
--Hacia Donde Va la Familia?
--Larry Christenson's Financial Record System for Families & Individuals.
--What about Baptism?
Christenson, Reo M. Heresies Right & Left: Some Political Assumptions Reexamined.
Christgau, Robert. Christgau's Record Guide: Rock Albums of the Seventies.
Christian, jt. auth. see Desai.
Christian, Bud. Nicknames in Sports: A Quiz Book.
Christian Character Library Staff & Rinehart, Stacy P. Living in Light of Eternity.
Christian, Esther. Family Enrichment: A Manual for Promoting Family Togetherness. Sorenson, Don L., ed.
Christian, J. W. & Haasen, P., eds. Progress in Materials Science.
--Progress in Materials Science.
Christian, J. W., et al. Progress in Materials Science.
Christian, J. W., et al, eds. Materials Science Progress: Anniversary Vol. - Progress in Materials Science.
--Progress in Material Science.
--Progress in Materials Science.
Christian, Jeffrey M. & Reibsamen, Gary G. World Guide to Battery Powered Road Transportation.
Christian, Kaare. The UNIX Operating System.
Christian Legal Society. The Equal Access Act: Implications for Secondary School Policies.
Christian, Mary B. April Fool.
--Christmas Reflections.
--Grandfathers: God's Gift to Children.
--Grandmothers: God's Gift to Children.
--The Lucky Man.
--Sebastian (SuperSleuth) & the Santa Claus Caper.
Christian, Portia, ed. Agricultural Enterprises Management in an Urban-Industrial Society: A Guide to Information Sources.
Christian, R., jt. auth. see Wiener, R.
Christian, S. D. & Zuckerman, J. J. Energy & the Chemical Sciences.
Christian, Samuel T., jt. auth. see Gorodetzky, Charles.
Christian, Sharon & Johnson, Margaret. The Very Private Matter of Anorexia Nervosa. Sloan, John, ed.
Christian, W., jt. auth. see Tsuboi, T.
Christian, William A., Jr. Person & God in a Spanish Valley.
Christiani, Leon. Evidence of Satan in the Modern World.
Christiansen, J. R., et al. Disaster Preparedness: A Family Protection Handbook.
Christiansen, Monty L. Vandalism Control Management in Parks & Recreation.
Christiansen, R. Regional History of the Railways of Great Britain, Vol. 13: Thames & Severn.
Christiansen, Rex. Forgotten Railways: West Midlands.
Christie, A. B. Infectious Diseases: Epidemiology & Clinical Practice.
Christie, Agatha. Agatha Christie: An Autobiography.
--Appointment with Death.
--Cards on the Table.
--Crooked House.
--Elephants Can Remember.
--Gaints' Bread.
--Partners in Crime.
--Thirteen Clues for Miss Marple.
--The Tuesday Club Murders.
Christie, Agatha, pseud. The Westmacott-Christie Reader: Six Novels by Agatha Christie Writing under the Name Mary Westmacott.
Christie, Agatha see Westmacott, Mary, pseud.
Christie, Agatha, et al. The Scoop. Bd. with Behind the Screen. Ace Bks.
Christie, Ian, ed. Powell, Pressburger & Others.
Christie, Ian R. & Labaree, Benjamin W. Empire Or Independence, 1760-1776: A British-American Dialogue.
Christie, J. Elmer, jt. ed. see Budke, George H.
Christie, Les. Dating & Waiting: A Christian View of Love, Sex, & Dating.
--Getting a Grip on Time Management.
Christie, Linda G. Managing Today & Tomorrow with On-Line Information.
Christie, Linda Gail, jt. auth. see Perloe, Mark.
Christie, Richard & Jahoda, Marie, eds. Studies in the Scope & Method of "The Authoritarian Personality"
Christina, Frank & Christina, Teresa. Billy Jack.
Christina, Teresa, jt. auth. see Christina, Frank.
Christison, Mary A., jt. auth. see Bassano, Sharron.
Christ-Janer, Albert. Eliel Saarinen: Finnish-American Architect & Educator.
--Eliel Saarinen: Finnish-American Architect & Educator.
Christman, Elizabeth. A Broken Family.
Christman, Henry M., ed. Indira Gandhi Speaks on Democracy, Socialism & Third World Non-Alignment.
Christmas, Joyce. Dark Tide.

Christmas, Rachel J. & Christmas, Walter. Fielding's Bermuda & the Bahamas.
--Fielding's Bermuda & the Bahamas, 1985.
--Fielding's Bermuda & the Bahamas, 1986.
--Fielding's Bermuda & the Bahamas, 1987.
--Fielding's Bermuda & the Bahamas, 1988.
Christmas, Walter, jt. auth. see Christmas, Rachel J.
Christodolou, Anastasios & Craig, Tom, eds. Commonwealth Universities Yearbook 1986.
Christofalo, Vincent J., jt. ed. see Rothblat, George H.
Christoffers, Adele. A Word Directory: Spelling-Division.
Christoph, H. J. Diseases of Dogs.
Christophe, Henri. Henri Christophe & Thomas Clarkson, a Correspondence. Griggs, Earl L. & Praton, Clifford H., eds.
Christopher. Scott.
Christopher, A. B. The Word Accomplished.
Christopher, A. J. Colonial Africa.
Christopher, Beth. Love for the Taking.
Christopher, Constance. Dead Man's Flower.
Christopher, F. J. & Christopher, Rosemary B. Craftsman Manual Set.
Christopher, John. No Blade of Grass.
--The Tripods Trilogy.
--Wild Jack.
Christopher, John B., jt. auth. see Brinton, Crane.
Christopher, Kenneth. Damien & the Island of Sickness: A Story About Damien.
Christopher, Matt. Earthquake.
--Jackrabbit Goalie.
--Power Play.
--The Twenty-One Mile Swim.
Christopher, Paula. The Dreaming Pool.
Christopher, Robert. The Japanese Mind: The Goliath Explained.
Christopher, Rosemary B., jt. auth. see Christopher, F. J.
Christopher Street Magazine Editors. And God Bless Uncle Harry & His Roommate Jack Who We Are Not Supposed to Talk About.
Christophers, Richard A. George Abbot, Archbishop of Canterbury, 1562-1633: A Bibliography.
Christopherson, W. M., jt. auth. see Riotton, G.
Christopherson, William, jt. auth. see Riotton, C.
Christophorou, Loucas G., ed. Gaseous Dielectrics II: Proceedings of the Second International Symposium on Gaseous Dielectrics, Knoxville, Tenn., U. S. A., March 9-13, 1980.
Christy, Joe. Engines for Homebuilt Aircraft & Ultralights.
--High Adventure: The First Seventy-Five Years of Civil Aviation.
--Maintaining & Overhauling Lycoming Engines.
--WW II: Luftwaffe Combat Planes & Aces.
Christy, Joe, jt. auth. see Ethell, Jeff.
Chritton, Michael, photos by. Cyclist's Training Diary.
Chronicle Guidance Publications, Inc., Research Staff. Chronicle Agricultural Occupations Guidebook.
--Chronicle Business Occupations Guidebook.
--Chronicle Health Occupations Guidebook.
--Chronicle Home Economics Occupations Guidebook.
--Chronicle Industrial Technology Occupations Guidebook.
Chronicle Guidance Publications Staff. Occupational Profiles.
Chronis, Valerie. Valerie.
Chu, Benjamin. Laser Light Scattering.
Chu, Charles. A Sketch of Chinese Geography (in Characters)
Chu, David S., ed. Sociology & Society in Contemporary China, 1979-1983: A Special Issue of Chinese Sociology & Anthrology.
Chu, Grace S. June.
Chu, Grace Z. The Pleasures of Chinese Cooking.
Chu, W. K., jt. auth. see Sherrill, W. A.
Chu, Wesley W. & Chen, Peter P. Centralized & Distributed Data Base Systems.
Chuan, Helen, ed. Medical-Surgical Nursing: Pretest Self-Assessment & Review. Allman, Margaret.
Chuan, Victor L. California Debt Collection Manual.
Chubin, Barry. The Feet of a Snake.
Chudacoff, Howard P. The Evolution of American Urban Society.
Chudinov, S. M., jt. auth. see Brandt, N. B.
Chudoba, Bohdan. Spain & the Empire: 1519-1643.
Chudodeyev, Y. V., et al. Soviet Volunteers in China, Nineteen Twenty-Five to Nineteen Forty-Five.
Chudy, Harry T. The Complete Guide to Automotive Refinishing.
Chugh, Y. P., intro. by. State-of-the-Art of Ground Control in Longwall Mining & Mining Subsidence.
Chugh, Yoginder P., ed. Ground Control in Room & Pillar Mining.
Chuilleanain, Eilean N., ed. & intro. by see Riain, Noirin N., et al.
Chukofky, Kornei. The Silver Crest: My Russian Boyhood. Stillman, Beatrice, tr. from Rus.
Chun, Patrick. Cardiopulmonary Technology Examination Review Book.
Chun, Patrick K. Cardiovascular Diseases.
Chung, Chin O. Pyongyang Between Peking & Moscow: North Korea's Involvement in the Sino-Soviet Dispute, 1958-1975.
Chung, Chin S. & Steinhoff, Patricia G. The Effects of Induced Abortion on Subsequent Reproductive Function & Pregnancy Outcome: Hawaii.
Chung, Chong-Wha, ed. Modern Far Eastern Stories.
Chung, Edward K. Electrocardiography: Practical Applications with Vectorial Principles.
Chung, K. L. & Williams, Ruth. An Introduction to Stochastic Integration.
Chung, P. M., et al. Electric Probes in Stationary & Flowing Plasmas: Theory & Application.
Chung, Stanley M., ed. Hip Disorders in Infants & Children.
Chun-shu Chang. Premodern China: A Bibliographical Introduction.
Chunyang, An & Bohua, Liu, eds. Where the Dai People Live.
Church, Albert M., ed. Non-Renewable Resource Taxation in the Western States.
Church, Alonzo. Calculi of Lambda Conversion.
Church, Austin H. Centrifugal Pumps & Blowers.
Church, Benjamin. The History of King Philip's War.
Church, Charles F. Easy Going: A Comprehensive Guide to Sauk & Columbia Counties.
Church, D. C. & Pond, W. G. Basic Animal Nutrition & Feeding.
Church, Gale E. Angel of the East & a Winter's Day.
Church, Julie A. Joy in a Woolly Coat.
Church, Leslie. Early Methodist People.
Church, Olive. Office Dynamics Company: An Office Services & Temporary Help Agency Practice Set.
Church, Randolph W. Appellate Litigation: A Virginia Law Practice System.
Church, Virginia, jt. auth. see Wiselogle, Anndy.
Church, W. H. Gods in the Making: And Other Writings.
Church, William F. Richelieu & Reason of State.
Churchill, Caryl. Traps, Traps.
Churchill, Colin & Westlake, Ray. British Army Collar Badges - 1881 to Present.
Churchill, Gilbert A. Marketing Research.
Churchill, Larry R. Rationing Health Care in America: Perceptions & Principles of Justice.
Churchill, Peter. Riding from A to Z: A Practical Manual of Horsemanship.
Churchill, R. C. Bibliography of Dickensian Criticism, Eighteen Thirty-Six to Nineteen Seventy-Four.
Churchill, Richard E. The Six-Million-Dollar Cucumber.
Churchill, Ruel V. & Brown, James W. Complex Variables & Applications.
Churchill, Winston S. Great Contemporaries.
--The Island Race.
--Liberalism & the Social Problem.
--The Second World War: Chartwell Edition.
Churchward, L. G. Australia & America: 1788-1972.
Churgin, Bathia. Giovanni Battista Sammartini's "Sonate a tre Stromenti:" Six Notturnos for String Trio, Op. 7.
Chusid, Martin. A Catalogue of Verdi's Operas.
Chuta, E., jt. auth. see Allal, M.
Chute, Carolyn. The Beans of Egypt Maine.
Chute, Patricia. Castine.
Ch'u T'ung-tsu. Local Government in China under the Ch'ing.
Chwast, Seymour. Sweetheart & Others.
Chwast, Seymour, jt. ed. see Heller, Steven.
Chwat, Jacques, ed. see Chekhov, Anton.
Chwat, Jacques, ed. see Gorky, Maxim.
Chwat, Jacques, ed. see Marlowe, Christopher.
Chwat, Jacques, ed. see Strindberg, August.
Cialdini, Robert B. Influence.
--Influence: How & Why People Agree to Do Things.
Ciampi, C. & Martino, A. A. Artificial Intelligence & Legal Information.
Ciampi, Elgin, jt. auth. see Boyle, Robert H.
Ciancio, S. G. & Bourgaut, P. C. Clinical Pharmacology for Dental Professionals.
Ciarcia, Steve. Steve Ciarcia's Ask Byte.
Ciardi, John. I Met a Man.
Ciarlet, P. G. The Finite Element Method for Elliptic Problems.
Ciba. Research & Medical Practice: Their Interaction.
CIBA Foundation. Extrasensory Perception. Woltenholme, G. E. & Emiller, Elaine C., eds.
Ciba Foundation Staff. Development of Mammalian Absorptive Processes.
--Major Mental Handicap: Methods & Costs of Prevention.
--Outcome of Severe Damage to the Central Nervous System.
--Polypeptide Hormones: Molecular & Cellular Aspects.
CIBA Foundation Symposium. Development of the Autonomic Nervous System: Symposium No. 83.
--Tinnitus - Symposium No. 85.
Cibber, Colley. The Plays of Colley Cibber. Hayley, Rodney, ed.
Cibber, Susanna, jt. auth. see Cibber, Tehophilus.
Cibber, Tehophilus & Cibber, Susanna. The Plays of Tehophilus & Susanna Cibber. Mann, David, ed.
Cicciarella, Gloria. Mama's Italian Cooking.
Cicco, Philip Di see Krutza, William J. & Dicicco, Philip P.
Cicero, Marcus T. Letters of Cicero: A Selection in Translation. Wilkinson, L. P., ed. & tr.
Cichy, F. C. & Schenck, H. V. Corrosion of Steel & Aluminum Scuba Tanks.
Cicourel, A., jt. ed. see Knorr-Cetina, K.
Cicourel, A. V. Theory & Method in a Study of Argentine Fertility.
Cicourel, Aaron V., et al. Language Use & School Performance.
Cid Campeador. Poem of the Cid. Huntington, Archer M., tr.
Cienkus, Robert, jt. auth. see Manoni, Mary H.
Cierjacks, S., ed. Neutron Sources: For Applied & Pure Nuclear Research.
Ciesla, Betty, et al, eds. see Pottiglio, Denise H. & Powers, Lawerence W.
Ciesla, William M., intro. by. Color Aerial Photography in the Pl Sc & Related Fields: Seventh Biennial Workshop.
Cieslik, Jurgen & Cieslik, Marianne. Lehmann Toys.
Cieslik, Marianne, jt. auth. see Cieslik, Jurgen.
Cigan, T. S., ed. see World Symposium at the AIME Annual Meeting Staff.
Cigler, Allan & Loomis, Burdett. Interest Group Politics.
Cihak, R. Ontogenesis of the Skeleton & the Intrinsic Muscles of the Human Hand & Foot.
Cikovsky, Nicolai, Jr. The Life & Work of George Inness.
Cilliers, J. K. Counter-Insurgency in Rhodesia.
Cilmore, William J. Psychohistorical Inquiry: A Comprehensive Bibliography.
Ciment, Jill. Small Claims.
Ciment, Michel. Conversations with Losey.
--Kubrick. Adair, Gilbert, tr. from Fr.
Cimino, Louis. Apple Dining & Entertainment Club. Dozier, Marc & Ryan, Michael, eds.
Cimmino, Marion, jt. auth. see Edwards, Gabrielle.
Cincinnatus. Self-Destruction: The Disintegration & Decay of the U. S. Army During the Vietnam Era.
CineBooks Staff. Foreign Films.
--Horror Films.
Cinnamon, Kenneth M., jt. auth. see Morris, Kenneth T.
Cinnamon, Pamela A. & Swanson, Marilyn A. Everything about Exchange Values for Foods.
--Everything You Always Wanted to Know about Exchange Values for Foods.
Cinquin, Emmanuelle. To Share with God's Poor: Sister among the Outcasts.
Cintron, Ralph. Maria, Maria, Look!
Cioni, Ray & Cioni, Sally. The Droodles Storybook of Proverbs.
Cioni, Sally, jt. auth. see Cioni, Ray.
Cioppa, Anne L., jt. ed. see McIntire, Sue N.
Cioran, E. M. Drawn & Quartered. Howard, Richard, tr. from Fr.
Ciozkosz, Andrzej, tr. see Herling, Gustav.
Cipolla, Carlo M. Before the Industrial Revolution: European Society & Economy, 1000-1700.
Cipolla, Carlo M. & Birdsall, Derek. The Technology of Man: A Visual History.
Cipolla, Carlo M., ed. The Fontana Economic History of Europe: The Middle Ages.
--The Fontana Economic History of Europe: The Twentieth Century.
Ciranna, Alfonso. Giorgio De Chirico's Graphic Work.
Circe, Dai. Astrology: Trash & Treasure.
Cirillo, Dennis P. & Rubenstein, Mark. The Complete Book of Cosmetic Facial Surgery: A Step-by-Step Guide to the Physical & Psychological Process.
Cirillo, Dennis P., jt. auth. see Rubinstein, Mark.
Cirker, Blanche, ed. see Bewick, Thomas.
Cirker, Blanche, jt. ed. see Cirker, Hayward.
Cirker, Hayward & Cirker, Blanche, eds. The Golden Age of the Poster.
Cisin, Fred & Parvin, Jack. How to Keep Your Honda Car Alive: A Manual of Step by Step Procedures for the Compleat Idiot.
CISM (International Center for Mechanical Sciences), Department of Automation & Inforamation Staff. Algebraic Methods in Pattern Recognition: Proceedings of the CISM, Department of Automation & Information, Academy of Sciences, Warsaw, 1971. Kulikowsky, J., ed.
CISM (International Center for Mechanical Sciences), Department of Automation & Information Staff. Coding for Markov Sources: Proceedings of the CISM, Department of Automation & Information University of Trieste, 1971. Longo, G., ed.
CISM (International Center for Mechanical Sciences) Deartment of Automation & Information Staff. Combinatorial Search Problems. Katona, G., ed.
CISM (International Center for Mechanical Sciences), Department of Automation & Information Staff. Controlled & Conditioned Invariance: Proceedings of the CISM, Department of Automation & Information, University of Geneva, 1971. Basile, G., ed.
CISM (International Center for Mechanical Sciences) Dept. of Automation & Information, 1973. Cooperative & Non-Cooperative Many Players Differential Games. Lietmann, G., ed.
CISM (International Center for Mechanical Sciences), Department for Mechanics of Deformable Bodies Staff. Creep Transition in Cylinders. Seth, B. R., ed.
CISM (International Center for Mechanical Sciences), Dept. for Mechanics of Deformable Bodies, 1970. Dynamic Plasticity of Metals. Campbell, J. D., ed.
CISM (International Center for Mechanical Sciences), Department of Experimental Methods in Mechanics Staff. Dynamic Positioning of Vessels at Sea: Proceedings of the CISM, Department of Experimental Methods in Mechanics, 1971. Pinkster, J., ed.
CISM (International Center for Mechanical Sciences), Department of Mechanics of Solids Staff. Entropy, Absolute Temperature & Coldness in Thermodynamics Boundary Conditions in Porous Material: Proceedings of CISM, Department of Mechanics of Solids, 1971. Muller, I., ed.
--Field Equations for Thermoelastic Bodies with Uniform Symmetry - Acceleration Waves in Thermoelastic Bodies. Wang, C. C., ed.
CISM (International Center for Mechanical Sciences), Department of Hydro & Gasdynamics Staff. Fluid Dynamics of Jet Amplifiers: Proceedings of CISM, Department of Hydro Gasdynamics, Technical Univ. of Turin, 1970. Romiti, A., ed.
CISM (International Center for Mechanical Sciences) Staff. Fluidic Applications. Belforte, G., ed.
--Foundations of the Mathematical Theory of Structures. Oliveira, E. De Arantes, ed.
CISM (International Center for Mechanical Sciences), Department for General Mechanics Staff. The General & Restricted Problems of Three Bodies: Proceedings of the CISM, Department for General Mechanics, 1973. Szebehely, V., ed.
CISM (International Center for Mechanical Sciences), Department of Automation & Information Staff. General Theory of Noiseless Channels: Proceedings of the CISM, Department of Automation & Information, 1970. Katona, G., ed.
CISM (International Center for Mechanical Sciences) Staff. Gyrodynamics. Magnus, K., ed.
CISM (International Center for Mechanical Sciences), Dept. of Automation & Information, Cambridge, 1970. Information Theory & Reliable Communication. Gallager, R., ed.
CISM (International Center for Mechanical Sciences) Staff. Laser Cinematography of Explosions. Oppenheim, A. K. & Kamel, M. M., eds.
--Lectures on Radiating Gasdynamics: General Equations & Boundary Conditions. Ferrari, C., ed.
CISM (International Center for Mechanical Sciences), Department of Mechanics of Solids Staff. Magneto-Thermoelasticity: Proceedings of CISM, Department of Mechanics of Solids, Vienna, 1972. Parkus, H., ed.
CISM (International Center for Mechanical Sciences), Department of Automation & Information Staff. Mathematical Structure of Finite Random Cybernetic Systems. Quiasu, S., ed.
CISM (International Center for Mechanical Sciences), Department of Mechanics of Solids Staff. Matrix Analysis of Discrete Elastic Systems: Proceedings of CISM, Department of Mechanics of Solids, 1972. Kardestuncer, H., ed.
CISM (International Center for Mechanical Sciences, Department of Mechanics of Solids Staff. Micropolar Elasticity: Proceedings of CISM, Department of Mechanics of Solids, 1972. Olszak, W. & Nowacki, W., eds.
CISM (International Center for Mechanical Sciences), Dept. for Mechanics of Deformable Bodies, 1969. Mixed Boundary Value Problems of Plane Anisotropic Bodies.
CISM (International Center for Mechanical Sciences Staff. Nonlinear Thermoelasticity. Stojanovic, R., ed.

Authors

CISM (International Center for Mechanical Sciences) Staff. Polarization Gradient in Elastic Dielectric. Mindlin, R. D., ed.
CISM (International Center for Mechanical Sciences), Department of Automation & Information Staff. Quantitative-Qualitative Measure of Information. Longo, G., ed.
CISM (International Center for Mechanical Sciences), Department for Mechanics of Defamable Bodies Staff. Radiation Damage: Proceedings of CISM, Department for Mechanics of Defamable Bodies, Univ. of Vienna, 1970. Schmid, E. & Lintner, K., eds. Incl. Behavior of Insonated Metals. Springer-Verlag.
CISM (International Center for Mechanical Sciences), Department of Mechanics of Solids Staff. Random Theory of Deformation of Structured Media: Thermodynamics of Deformation in Structured Media. Axelrad, D. R. & Provan, J. W., eds.
CISM (International Center for Mechanical Sciences), Department for Mechanics for Deformable Bodies Staff. Recent Developments in the Theory of Polar Continua: Proceedings of CISM, Department for Mechanics of Deformable Bodies, Univ. of Belgarde, 1970.
CISM (International Center for Mechanical Sciences), Department for General Mechanics Staff. Rotational Dynamics of Orbiting Gyrostats: Proceedings of CISM, Department for General Mechanics, Dubrovnik, 1971. Roberson, R., et al, eds.
CISM (International Center for Mechanical Sciences), Department of Automation & Information Staff. Selected Topics in Information Theory: Proceedings of CISM, Department of Hydro & Gas Dynamics, 1970. Longo, G., ed.
--Source Coding Theory. Longo, G., ed.
CISM (International Center for Mechanical Sciences), Department for General Mechanics Staff. Special Problems in Gyrodynamics: Proceedings of CISM, Department for Genaeral Mechanics, 1970. Muller, P. C., ed.
CISM (International Center for Mechanical Sciences) Staff. Structural Dynamics Heat Conduction. De Veubeke, B. F., et al, eds.
CISM (International Center for Mechanical Sciences), Department of Automation & Information Staff. Theory of Bilinear Dynamical Systems: Proceedings of CISM, Department of Automation & Information, 1972. Isidori, A., et al, eds.
CISM (International Center for Mechanical Sciences), Department for Mechanics of Deformable Bodies Staff. Theory of Couple-Stresses in Bodies with Constrained Rotations: Proceedings of CISM, Department for MEchanics of Deformable Bodies, 1970. Sokolowski, M., ed.
CISM (International Center for Mechanical Sciences), Department for Mechanics of Rigid Bodies Staff. Thermodynamic Effects in Wave Propogation. Chen, P., ed.
CISM (International Center for Mechanical Sciences), Department of Mechanics of Solids Staff. Thermodynamics in Contemporary Dynamics. Glansdorff, P., ed.
--Thermodynamics of Materials with Memory. Coleman, B. D., ed.
Cissell, Helen, et al. Mathematics of Finance.
Cissell, Robert, et al. Mathematics of Finance.
Cissley, Charles H. Management Science in Life Companies.
--Systems & Data Processing in Insurance Companies: Student Guide.
Citizens Research & Investigation Committee Staff & Tackwood, Louis. The Glass House Tapes. Freed, Donald, ed.
Citizen's Scholarship Foundation of America Staff, ed. see Johnson, Marlys C. & Thompson, Linda J.
Citizen's Scholarship Foundation of America Staff, ed. see Thompson, Linda J. & Johnson, Marlys C.
Ciucci, Giorgio, et al. The American City: From the Civil War to the New Deal. La Penta, Barbara L., tr. from Ital.
Civen, Janice D. Illuminations.
Clabby, J. History of the Royal Army Veterinary Corps. 1919-1961.
Claes, Frans M. A Bibliography of Netherlandic Dictionaries: Dutch-Flemish.
Claeson, Eva, tr. see Ekstrom, Margareta.
Claff, Chester, Jr., tr. see Arndt, Diether.
Clague, Ewan. Statistics & Economic Policy.
Claiborn, William, jt. ed. see Evans, Dorothy.
Claiborne, Craig. Craig Claiborne's Gourmet Diet.
--A Feast Made for Laughter.
Claiborne, Craig & Franey, Pierre. Cooking with Craig Claiborne & Pierre Franey.
Claiborne, Robert. Saying What You Mean: A Commonsense Guide to American Usage.
Clain. Demonstrations of Physical Signs on Clinical Surgery.
Clain-Stefanelli. Charter For Progress.
Clair, Andree. Bemba: An African Adventure. Ponsot, Marie, tr.
Clair, Bernard & Daniele, Anthony. Consultation with a Divorce Lawyer: Everything You Must Know to Protect Your Rights.
Clair, Bernard E. & Daniele, R. Anthony. Love Pact: A Layman's Complete Guide to Legal Living Together Agreements.
Clair, Colin. Dictionnaire des Herbes et des Epices.
Clair, David st. see St. Clair, David.
Claire, Anne. Andro, Star of Bethlehem. Mahany, Patricia, ed.
Claire, Evelyn. Presciption for Love.
Claire, Hilary, jt. auth. see Salmon, Phillida.
Clairmont, George B. & Sokoloff, Kiril. Street Smart Investing: A Price-Value Approach to Stock Market Profits.
Clairmont, Ingrid & Clairmont, Leonard. Blood in the Furrows: A Historical Novel.
Clairmont, Leonard, jt. auth. see Clairmont, Ingrid.
Clance, Pauline R. The Impostor Phenomenon: Overcoming the Fear That Haunts Your Success.
Clanchy, M. T. From Memory to Written Record in England, 1066-1307.
Clancy, Ambrose & Donahoe, Peter M. The Night Line.
Clancy, Gwendolyn. Quote: Because I Must.
Clancy, John. John Clancy's Christmas Cookbook.
Clancy, Lillian S. Alameda County Public Schools: How Are They Doing? (1984)
--Bay Area Counties Public Schools: How Are They Doing? 1985.
--Bay Area Counties Public Schools, 1986.
--Bay Area Counties Public Schools, 1987.
--Bay Area Counties Public Schools, 1988.
--Bay Area Public Schools: How Are They Doing? (1984)
--Central California Counties Public Schools, 1986.
--Central California Counties Public Schools, 1987.
--Central California Counties Public School, 1988.
--Central California Counties Public Schools: How Are They Doing? 1985.
--Contra Costa Country Public Schools, 1986.
--Contra Costa County Public Schools: How Are They Doing?
--Contra Costa County Public Schools: How Are They Doing? (1984)
--Contra Costa County Public Schools: How Are They Doing? 1985.
--Los Angeles County Public Schools: How Are They Doing? (1984)
--Los Angeles County Public Schools: How Are They Doing? 1985.
--Los Angeles County Public Schools, 1986.
--Los Angeles County Public Schools, 1987.
--Los Angeles County Public Schools, 1988.
--North Central California Counties Public Schools, 1986.
--North Central California Counties Public Schools, 1987.
--North Central California Counties Public Schools, 1988.
--Northern California Public Schools: How Are They Doing? (1984)
--Northern Central California Counties Public Schools: How Are They Doing? 1985.
--Orange County Public Schools: How Are They Doing? (1984)
--Sacramento, El Dorado, Placer & Yolo Counties Public Schools: How Are They Doing? (1984)
--San Bernardino County Public Schools: How Are They Doing? (1984)
--San Diego County Public Schools: How Are They Doing? (1984)
--San Francisco & North Bay Counties Public Schools: How Are They Doing? (1984)
--San Mateo, Santa Clara & Santa Cruz Counties Public Schools: How Are They Doing? (1984)
--Santa Barbara & Ventura Counties Public Schools: How Are They Doing? (1984)
--South Central California Counties Public Schools: How Are They Doing? 1985.
--South Central California Counties Public Schools, 1986.
--South Central California Counties Public Schools, 1987.
--South Central California Counties Public Schools, 1988.
--Southern California Counties Public Schools, 1986.
--Southern California Counties Public Schools, 1987.
--Southern California Counties Public Schools, 1988.
--Southern California Counties Public Schools: How Are They Doing?
--Southern California Public Schools: How Are They Doing? (1984)
--The Top One Hundred: How Are They Doing? 1985.
--The Top One Hundred, 1986.
--The Top One Hundred, 1987.
--The Top One-Hundred, 1988.
--Upper Northern California Counties Public Schools: How Are They Doing? 1985.
--Upper Northern California Counties Public Schools, 1988.
--Upper Northern California Counties Public Schools.
--Upper Northern California Countries Public Schools, 1987.
Clancy, Michael, jt. auth. see Cooper, Doug.
Clancy, Thomas H. An Introduction to Jesuit Life: The Constitutions & History Through 435 Years. Ganss, George E., ed.
Clancy, Tom. Patriot Games.
Clanton, Arthur L., ed. see Willoughby, David.
Clanton, Bruce. Family Adventures.
--In Season & Out.
Clanton, Charles, ed. see Thompson, Mollie.
Clapesattle, Helen. Dr. Webb of Colorado Springs.
Clapham, John. Dvorak.
Clapin, Sylvia. New Dictionary of Americanisms.
Clapp, Andrew D., ed. Merger Yearbook.
Clapp, Joy & Stevens, Paul C. Geography of Colorado.
Clapp, Patricia. Witches' Children.
Clapperton, Chalmers, ed. Scotland: A New Study.
Clapperton, R. H. The Papermaking Machine.
Clar, E. Polycyclic Hydrocarbons.
Clar, Lawrence M. & Hart, James A. Mathematics for the Technologies.
Clarac see Proust, Marcel.
Clare, Anthony. Lovelaw: Love, Sex, & Marriage Around the World.
Clare, Frederick. They Blew Our Weather.
Clareman, Neil. Easy Favors.
Claremon, Neil. Borderland.
Clarfield, Gerard H. United States Diplomatic History.
Claridge, Gordon S., et al. Personality Differences & Biological Variations: A Study of Twins.
Clark. Social Therapy in Psychiatry.
Clark & Allen. Occupational Therapy for Children.
Clark, A. F. & Reed, R. P., eds. Advances in Cryogenic Engineering.
Clark, A. F., jt. ed. see Reed, R. P.
Clark, Admont G. They Built Clipper Ships in Their Back Yard.
Clark, Ailsa M. & Rowe, Francis W. Monographs of the Shallow-Water Indo-West Pacific Echinoderms.
Clark, Al. The Film Yearbook 1983.
--The Film Yearbook, 1985.
Clark, Alfred. The Chemisorptive Bond: Basic Concepts.
Clark, Andrew H. Acadia: The Geography of Early Nova Scotia to 1760.
Clark, Anna. Women's Silence, Men's Violence: Sexual Assault in England, 1770-1845.
Clark, Anna K., jt. ed. see Murray, Janet H.
Clark, Bernadine, ed. Writer's Market, 1984.
Clark, Beverly L. Lewis Carroll. Schlobin, Roger C., ed.
Clark, Bill. Professional Cleaning & Building Maintenance: How to Organize a Money Saving Service Business or a Department for Floor & Building Cleaning.
Clark, Brian. Whose Life Is It Anyway?
Clark, Bruce. Deathstalk.
--Tales of Maritime Maine: The Vanished Years of the Maine Coast Brought to Life in Three Absorbing Tales. Mason, Jill, ed.
Clark, Bryant R. Rains in Meadow Valley.
Clark, Buddy & Davis, Craig. Alone, Unarmed, but Safe! An Illustrated Guide to Judo Defense.
Clark, C. E. Frazer, Jr., ed. Hawthorne at Auction 1894-1971.
Clark, C. E., Jr. & Bruccoli, Matthew J., eds. Pages: The World of Books, Writers & Writing.
Clark, Carol. Thomas Moran: Watercolors of the American West.
Clark, Carol, ed. Charles M. Russell.
Clark, Catherine M., ed. see Acker, David D.
Clark, Champ. Flood.
Clark, Charles & Parker, David. Do-It-Yourself Marketing for Small-Volume Builders: How to Beat the Competition on a Shoestring.
Clark, Charles W. River of Tears.
Clark, Chris L. & Asquith, Stewart. Social Work & Social Philosophy: A Guide for Practice.
Clark, Colin. Value of Agricultural Land.
Clark, Cumberland. Shakespeare & the Supernatural.
Clark, D. H. & Stephenson, F. R., eds. Historical Supernovae.
Clark, David, jt. auth. see Burgoyne, Jacqueline.
Clark, David G. & Hutchinson, Earl R., eds. Mass Media & the Law.
Clark, David H. How Secondary School Graduates Perform in the Labor Market: A Study of Indonesia.
--Superstars: How Stellar Explosions Shape the Destiny of Our Universes.
Clark, David L., et al. Stratigraphy & Glacial-Marine Sediments of the Amerasian Basin, Central Arctic Ocean.
Clark, Don. The World & Us.
Clark, Dorothy J. Terre Haute: Wabash River City.
Clark, Douglas L. Starting a Successful Business on the West Coast.
Clark, Duvie. The Peculiar Truth.
Clark, Edith. My Mother Who Fathered Me: A Study of the Family in the Selected Communities in Jamaica.
Clark, Eleanor. Plate Collecting: A Guide to a Fascinating Hobby.
--Rome & a Villa.
Clark, Eleanor D. When Mama Was a Little Girl: Memories of a Georgia Childhood.
Clark, Ellery H., Jr. Boston Red Sox: Seventy-Fifth Anniversary History, 1901-1975.
--Red Sox Fever.
--Red Sox Forever.
Clark, Emily. Ingenue among the Lions: The Letters of Emily Clark to Joseph Hergesheimer. Langford, Gerald, ed.
Clark, Eric. China Run.
--Send in the Lions.
--The Sleeper.
Clark, Ernest. Fatal Run.
Clark, Erskine. Wrestlin Jacob: A Portrait of Religion in the Old South.
Clark, Ewen M. & Forbes, J. A. Evaluating Primary Care: Some Experiments in Quality Measurement in an Academic Unit of Primary Medical Care.
Clark, Frank P. Special Effects in Motion Picture: Some Methods for Producing Mechanical Special Effects.
Clark, Frank P., ed. Technologies in the Laboratory Handling of Motion Picture & Other Long Films.
Clark, Frederick R., jt. auth. see Nosow, Sigmund.
Clark, Garth. Michael Cardew.
Clark, George N. The Seventeenth Century.
Clark, Gertrude M. Teacher, Twist Your Head Around!
Clark, Glenn. Holy Spirit.
--How to Find Health Through Prayer.
--I Will Lift up Mine Eyes.
Clark, Glenn T., jt. auth. see Solberg, William K.
Clark, Grahame. The Identity of Man.
Clark, H. A First Course in Quantum Mechanics.
Clark, Harold B. & Spencer, M. Callaghan's Michigan Civil Practice Forms: 1968-1983.
Clark, J., et al. Thin Seam Coal Mining Technology.
Clark, J. B., jt. ed. see Comins, N. R.
Clark, J. G. Prehistoric Europe.
Clark, J. H. Aeroplanes & Aero-Engines.
Clark, J. R. Essentials of Economics: Instructor's Manual & Test Bank.
Clark, James I., jt. auth. see Ryan, Frank L.
Clark, James L. & Clark, Lyn R. How Four: A Handbook for Office Workers.
--How Three: A Handbook for Office Workers.
--How Two: Handbook for Office Workers.
Clark, James M., tr. see Eckhart, Meister, et al.
Clark, James T. A Book of Life.
Clark, John B. Essentials of Economic Theory.
Clark, John D. The Prehistory of Africa.
Clark, John G. The Grain Trade in the Old Northwest.
--Mesolithic Settlement of Northern Europe.
Clark, John G. & Yanick, Paul, Jr. Tinnitus & Its Management: A Clinical Text for Audiologists.
Clark, John R. The Beaches of Maui County.
Clark, John W., jt. auth. see Partridge, Eric.
Clark, Jon & Hoffer, Jeffrey A. Physical Data Base Record Design.
Clark, June & Henderson, Jill, eds. Community Health.
Clark, K. S. Nobby Clark's Auckland.
Clark, Kent, jt. auth. see Not-Twain, Mark.
Clark, L. R., et al. The Ecology of Insect Populations in Theory & Practice.
Clark, Lawrence. Sayula Popoluca Texts.
Clark, Leadie N. Walt Whitman's Concept of the American Common Man.
Clark, LeMon. Where Do Babies Come from? & How to Keep Them There! What a Teenager Should Know about Sex, Love, Marriage & Birth Control.
Clark, Leonard H. & Klein, Raymond L. The American Secondary School Curriculum.
Clark, Linda. Handbook of Natural Remedies for Common Ailments.
Clark, Lyn R., jt. auth. see Clark, James L.
Clark, M. Douglas. Managing the Troubled Employee.
--Risk Control for Churches.
Clark, M. Douglas & Germain, George L. Supervisory Safety Promotion.
Clark, M. J. Politics & the Media: Film & Television for the Political Scientist & Historian.
Clark, Malcolm, Jr. The Eden Seekers: The Settlement of Oregon, 1818-1862.
Clark, Marden. Morgan Triumphs.
Clark, Margaret G. Barney & the UFO.
Clark, Martire & Bartolomeo, Inc. Staff. Relating to Readers in the 'Eighties.
Clark, Mary E. Contemporary Biology.
Clark, Mary H. Stillwatch.

Authors

Clark, Mavis T. If the Earth Falls In.
Clark, Michael. Jacques Lacan: An Annotated Bibliography.
Clark, Michael D. Worldly Theologians: The Persistence of Religion in Nineteenth Century American Thought.
Clark, N. F., et al, eds. Electronic Equipment Wiring & Assembling: Part Two.
Clark, Paul F. University of Wisconsin Medical School: A Chronicle, 1848-1948.
Clark, Philip M. New Approaches to the Measurement of Public Library Use by Individual Patrons.
Clark, R. & Brown, D. The Chemistry of Vanadium, Niobium & Tantalum.
Clark, R., et al. The Chemistry of Titanium, Zirconium & Hafnium.
Clark, R. J. & Hester, R. E., eds. Advances in Infrared & Raman Spectroscopy.
Clark, R. Lee & Cumley, Russell W. The Book of Health.
Clark, Ramsey, jt. auth. see Ervin, Sam J., Jr.
Clark, Richard E., jt. auth. see Shipley, Reginald A.
Clark, Robert, et al. War Powers Resolution: Balance of War Powers in the Eighties.
Clark, Roger A., jt. auth. see Practising Law Institute Staff.
Clark, Ronald. Bertrand Russell & His World.
--Sir Edward Appleton, C.B.E., K.C.B., F.R.S.
Clark, Ronald D. & Amai, Robert L. Chemistry: The Science & the Scene.
Clark, Ruth. Strangers & Sojourners at Port Royal.
Clark, S. K. & Dodge, R. N. A Handbook for the Rolling Resistance of Pneumatic Tires.
Clark, Samuel. Social Origins of the Irish Land War.
Clark, Scott, jt. auth. see Blaine, Vera.
Clark, Steven. Fight Against Time.
Clark, T. & Rees, J. Practical Management of Asthma.
Clark, Thomas, jt. auth. see Austin, Larry.
Clark, Thomas L. A Yearly Planning Guide for the Church Usher.
Clark, Thomas L., et al. Needed Research in American English.
Clark, Tim W. & Stromberg, Mark S. Mammals in Wyoming. Collins, Joseph T., ed.
Clark, Tom. The Exile of Celine.
--Jack Kerouac.
--Jack Kerouac.
--Short Guide to the High Plains.
Clark, Tom C., jt. auth. see U. S. Department of Justice Staff.
Clark, Velma B. Quest for Freedom.
Clark, William Andrews, Memorial Library, Los Angeles Staff. Dictionary Catalog of William Andrews Clark Memorial Library.
Clark, William D. Death Valley: The Story Behind the Scenery.
Clark, William J. Great American Sculptures.
Clark, William R. & Golstein, Pierre, eds. Mechanisms of Cell-Mediated Cytotoxicity.
Clarke, A. B. & Clarke, A. B., eds. Mathematical Methods in Queueing Theory: Proceedings.
Clarke, Anna. Soon She Must Die.
Clarke, Arthur C. Arthur C. Clarke's July 20, 2019: Life in the 21st Century.
--The Deep Range.
--Earthlight.
--Expedition to Earth.
--The Fountains of Paradise.
--Imperial Earth.
--The Lion of Comarre. Bd. with Against the Fall of Night. HarBraceJ.
--Nine Billion Names of God.
--The Other Side of the Sky.
--Prelude to Mars.
--Prelude to Space.
--Reach for Tomorrow.
--Rendezvous with Rama.
--Tales from the White Hart.
--Tales of Ten Worlds.
Clarke, Arthur C. & Proctor, George, eds. The Science Fiction Hall of Fame, Vol. 3: The Nebula Winners.
Clarke, Athur C. Profiles of the Future: An Inquiry into the Limits of the Possible.
Clarke, B. M., jt. auth. see Crocetti, Gino.
Clarke, Bill. Building, Owning & Flying a Composite Homebuilt.
Clarke, Brian. Architectural Stained Glass.
Clarke, C. Elementary General Relativity.
Clarke, C. P. Every Man's Book of Saints.
Clarke, Carl D. Metal Casting of Sculpture & Ornament.
--Molding & Casting: Its Technique & Application.
Clarke, Charles, jt. auth. see Bonington, Chris.
Clarke, Clorinda. The American Revolution, Seventeen Seventy-Five to Seventeen Eighty-Three. Reeves, Marjorie, ed.
Clarke, D. & Grainger, J. F. Polarized Light & Optical Measurements.
Clarke, D. A. A London Bibliography of Social Sciences, Ninth Supplement: 1974.
--London Bibliography of Social Sciences, Tenth Supplement: 1975, Vol. 33.
--A London Bibliography of the Social Sciences: Eleventh Supplement, 1976.
--A London Bibliography of the Social Sciences: Eighth Supplement, 1972-1973, Vols. 29-31.
Clarke, D. A., ed. London Bibliography of the Social Sciences: Fourteenth Supplement, 1979, Vol. 37.
--A London Bibliography of the Social Sciences, Twelfth Supplement, 1977.
--London Bibliography of the Social Sciences: Thirteenth Supplement, 1978, Vol. 36.
Clarke, D. S., Jr. Practical Inferences.
Clarke, David D. & Crossland, Jill. Action Systems: An Introduction to the Analysis of Complex Behavior.
Clarke, David E., jt. auth. see Bridgman, Jon.
Clarke, Doug, ed. see Ring, Leonard.
Clarke, Frank, tr. see Kasemann, Ernst.
Clarke, Frank, tr. see Van Oyen, Hendrik.
Clarke, Frank H. & Henkel, James G., eds. Molecular Graphics on the Apple Microcomputer.
Clarke, Frank H., jt. ed. see Henkel, James G.
Clarke, Gerald E. Airling.... & Other Poems.
Clarke, H. Harrison. Application of Measurement to Health & Physical Education.
Clarke, James, jt. auth. see Coulson, David.
Clarke, James M. The Life & Adventures of John Muir.
--The Life & Adventures of John Muir.
Clarke, Janet K. Chasing Fame.
Clarke, Jennifer. In Our Grandmothers' Footsteps: A Walking Tour of London.
Clarke, John J. A History of Local Government of the United Kingdom.
Clarke, Liam. Domiciliary Services for the Elderly.
Clarke, Loyal & Davidson, Robert L. Manual for Process Engineering Calculations.
Clarke, Lynda, jt. auth. see Anderson, Elizabeth M.
Clarke, M. R., ed. see International Conference on Advances in Computer Chess Staff.
Clarke, Magnus. The Nuclear Destruction of Britain.
Clarke, Mary W. John Chisum: Jinglebob King of the Pecus.
Clarke, Michael & Mowlam, Marjorie, eds. Debate on Disarmament.
Clarke, Patti. Creative Jewelry.
Clarke, Peter B. Black Paradise: The Rastafarian Movement.
Clarke, R. H. & Brown, John. Diffraction Theory & Antennas.
Clarke, R. J. Process Engineering in the Food Industry.
--Transform Coding of Images.
Clarke, Richard S. You Only Have One Life--Give It Your Best Shot: Five Steps to Health, Wealth, Happiness.
Clarke, Robert. Less Than Human.
Clarke, Robin. Building for Self-Sufficiency.
Clarke, Samuel. The Works.
Clarke, Stephen. The Lord Peter Wimsey Companion.
Clarke, Steve, compiled by. The Who in Their Own Words.
Clarke, Stevens H. Law of Probation & Parole in North Carolina.
Clarke, Stevens H. & Rubinsky, Elizabeth W. North Carolina's Fair Sentencing Act: Explanation, Text, & Felony Classification Table.
Clarke, Stevens H., et al. North Carolina Crimes: A Guidebook for Law Enforcement Officers.
--The Effectiveness of Bail Systems: An Analysis of Failure to Appear in Court & Rearrest while on Bail.
Clarke, Thomas A., et al. Biology of Plankton.
Clarke, Thomas E., ed. Above Every Name: The Lordship of Christ & Social Systems.
Clarke, Thurston, jt. auth. see Werbell, Frederick E.
Clarke, W. J., et al, eds. Myeloproliferative Disorders of Animals & Man: Proceedings.
Clarke, W. M. How the City Works: An Introduction to Its Financial Markets.
--Private Enterprise in Developing Countries.
Clarke, W. M., ed. How the City Works: The Professions.
Clarke, W. N. An Outline of Christian Theology.
Clarkson, George. The Mysticism of William Law.
Claro, Joe. Family Ties: Alex Gets the Business.
Clarricoats, P. J., ed. Optical-Fibre Waveguides.
Clary, Jack. The Captains.
Clary, Jack, jt. auth. see Brown, Paul.
Clary, John J., et al, eds. Formaldehyde: Toxicology-Epidemiology-Mechanisms.
Clary, Sydney A. Undercover Affair.
Clary, Wayne. OS Debugging for the COBOL Programmer.
CLASS Cooperative Library for Systems & Services Staff. The CLASS Directory of Inter Library Loan Policies.
Classen, M., jt. ed. see Demling, L.
Classical & Quantum Mechanical Aspects of Heavy Ion Collisions Symposium Staff. Proceedings of the Classical & Quantum Mechanical Aspects of Heavy Ion Collisions Symposium, Max Planck Institut Fuer, Kernphysik, Heidelberg, Oct. 2-5, 1974. Harney, H. L., et al, eds.
Claude, Inis L., Jr. Power & International Relations.
Claudel, Paul. Essence of the Bible.
--The Eye Listens.
--Otage: Theatre.
--Pain Dur: Theatre.
Claudin, Anatole. Histoire de l'Imprimerie en France au XVe et au XVIe Siecle.
Claudin, Fernando. The Communist Movement: From Comintern to Cominform. Pearce, Brian, tr. from Fr.
Claudy, Nicholas H., ed. Directory of Geoscience Departments.
--Directory of Geoscience Departments.
Claus, Bernie. Fire & Spirit.
Claus, R., et al. Light Scattering by Phonon Polaritons.
Claus, William G. Understanding Microbes: Laboratory Textbook for Microbiology.
Clausen, Andy. Austin, Texas.
Clauser, Henry, jt. auth. see Brady, G. S.
Clavell, James. Shogun.
--Tai-Pan.
Clawson, Cynthia. My Favorite Verse.
Clawson, Marion. The Land System of the United States: An Introduction to the History & Practice of Land Use & Land Tenure.
Clawson, Virginia. The Family Symphony.
Claxton, Guy, ed. Cognitive Psychology: New Directions.
Clay, Patrick. Firebolt.
--Sergeant Hawk: Under Attack.
--Sgt. Hawk.
--Tiger Island.
Clay, Phillip L. Neighborhood Renewal: Trends & Strategies.
Clay, Phillip L. & Hollister, Robert M., eds. Neighborhood Policy & Planning.
Clay, Reginald S. & Court, T. H. The History of the Microscope.
Clay, Rotha M. Hermits & Anchorites of England.
Clay, Theresa, jt. auth. see Rothschild, Miriam.
Clay, Willard. Illinois Images of the Landscape.
Claybrook, Billy G. File Management Techniques.
Clayes, Stanley A. & Gerrietts, John. Ways to Poetry.
Clayman, Henry M., et al. Intraocular Lens Implantation: Techniques & Complications.
Claypool, et al. How Did We Get Clocks & Calendars?
--How Do We Smell?
--How Do We Talk?
--What's Skin For?
Claypool, Jane. Jasmine Finds Love.
--Why Do Some People Get Fat?
Claypool, John. Glad Reunion.
--The Light Within You: Looking at Life Through New Eyes.
Clayre, Alasdair. The Heart of the Dragon.
Clayton, Aileen. The Enemy Is Listening.
Clayton, Bernard, Jr. The Complete Book of Breads.
--The Complete Book of Pastry: Sweet & Savory.
--The Complete Book of Soups & Stews.
Clayton, Bruce D. Life after Doomsday: A Survivalist Guide to Nuclear War & Other Disasters.
--Mosby's Handbook of Pharmacology in Nursing.
Clayton, C. R. & Preece, C. M., eds. Corrosion of Metal Processed by Directed Energy Beams: Proceedings TMS-AIME Fall Meeting, Louisville, KY, 1981.
Clayton, E. S. Agrarian Development in Peasant Economies.
Clayton, Gary E. Worker Productivity: A Challenge for Voc Ed.
Clayton, Hugh. Royal Faces: Nine Hundred Years of British Monarchy.
Clayton, John J. The Heath Introduction to Fiction.
Clayton, Joseph F. The Personal History of Douglas F. Roby.
Clayton, Keith, jt. auth. see Straw, Allan.
Clayton, Michael. The Chase: A Modern Guide to Foxhunting.
--A Hunting We Will Go.
Clayton, Philip T., jt. auth. see Smolin, Pauline.
Clayton, R. M. & Truman, D. E., eds. Stability & Switching in Cellular Differentiation.
Clayton, Stanley & Newton, John R. A Pocket Obstetrics.
Clayton, Thompson. Young Wrestler.
Clayton, Vista. The Phantom Caravan or Abd el Kader, Emir of Algeria (1808-1883)
Clear, Todd R. & O'Leary, Vincent. Controlling the Offenders in the Community: Reforming the Community Supervision Function.
Clearman, Brian. Transportation Markings: A Study in Communication.
Cleary, et al. Computed Tomography: Techniques & Procedures.
Cleary, Beverly. Ramona Quimby Diary.
Cleary, Christopher, tr. see Hui, Ta.
Cleary, Donna M., ed. Thinking Thursdays: Language Arts in the Reading Lab.
Cleary, Edward W. & Strong, John W. Evidence, Cases Materials, Problems.
Cleary, James P. & Levenbach, Hans. The Professional Forecaster: The Forecasting Process Through Data Analysis.
Cleary, Jon. City of Fading Light.
--The Sundowners.
Cleary, Jonathan C., tr. from Chinese. Zen Dawn.
Cleary, Patti, ed. see Lander, Jack.
Cleary, Robert E., ed. The Role of Government in the United States-Practice & Theory: A Report of a Conference at the College of Public & International Affairs of the American University, Washington, D. C.. March 2-3. 1984.
Cleary, Thomas, ed. The Original Face: An Anthology of Rinzai Zen.
Cleary, Thomas, tr. from Chinese. Flower Ornament Scripture.
Cleary, Thomas, tr. Sayings & Doings of Pai-Chang.
Cleary, Vincent J. & Wells, Theodore W., eds. The Pervigilium Veneris: A Late Latin Poem of Love & Springtime.
Cleave, T. Fat Consumption & Coronary Disease.
Cleave, William R. van see Cohen, S. T. & Van Cleave, William R.
Cleaver, Bill, jt. auth. see Cleaver, Vera.
Cleaver, Claire M. Step into Sales: Six Weeks to Successful Direct Selling from Your Home.
Cleaver, Dale G. Art: An Introduction.
--Art: An Introduction.
--Art: An Introduction.
Cleaver, Dale G. & Eddins, John M. Art & Music: An Introduction.
Cleaver, David S., jt. auth. see Hsiao, James C.
Cleaver, Harry, tr. see Negri, Antonio.
Cleaver, Kevin M. Economic & Social Analysis of Projects & of Price Policy: The Morocco Fourth Agricultural Credit Project.
Cleaver, Vera & Cleaver, Bill. A Little Destiny.
--The Whys & Wherefores of Littabelle Lee.
Clebsch, William A. Christian Interpretations of the Civil War. Wolf, Richard C., ed.
Cleckley, Hervey. The Mask of Sanity.
Cleef, E. Van see Van Cleef, E.
Cleef, Monique Von see Von Cleef, Monique & Waterman, William.
Cleeland, Caryn L., jt. auth. see Castelli, Louis.
Cleese, John, jt. auth. see Skynner, Robin.
Cleeve, Brian. Nineteen Thirty-Eight: A World Vanishing.
Cleeve, Roger. Daughters of Jerusalem.
Cleevely, R. J. World Palaeontological Collections.
Clegg, Chris W., jt. ed. see Kelly, John E.
Clegg, James S., jt. ed. see Crowe, John H.
Clegg, Joan. Dictionary of Social Services: Policy & Practice.
Clegg, Stewart, et al. Class, Politics & the Economy.
Cleghorn, Reese, jt. auth. see Watters, Pat.
Cleland & King. Project Management Handbook.
Cleland, David I. & King, William R. Management: A Systems Approach.
Cleland, David I. & Kocaoglu, Dundar F. Engineering Management.
Clemeau, Carol. The Ariadne Clue.
Clemen, Wolfgang. English Tragedy Before Shakespeare.
--Shakespeare's Dramatic Art.
Clemen, Wolfgang H. The Development of Shakespeare's Imagery.
Clemens, J. H. Balance Sheets & the Lending Banker.
Clemens, James A., et al. Non-Sexual Hormonal Influences on the Electrophysiology of the Brain.
Clemens, Samuel. The Adventures of Huckleberry Finn.
Clemens, Samuel L. The Adventures of Tom Sawyer.
--The Celebrated Jumping Frog of Calaveras County.
--Mark Twain-Howells Letters: The Correspondence of Samuel L. Clemens & William D. Howells, 1872-1910. Smith, Henry N. & Gibson, William M., eds.
--Personal Recollections of Joan of Arc by the Sieur Louis De Conte.
Clemens, Samuel L. see Twain, Mark.
Clemens, Virginia P. A Horse in Your Backyard?
Clemens, William A., jt. ed. see Woodburne, Michael.
Clement & Du Viver. Topical Steroids for Skin Disorders.
Clement, Clara E. Handbook of Legendary & Mythological Art.
--Saints in Art.
Clement, Francois. The Birth of an Island.
Clement, Fred. The U. S. Nuclear Regulatory Commission.
Clement, Hal. Cycle of Fire.

Authors

--Needle.
--Still River.
Clement, M. A. Transmission.
Clementi, E. Determination of Liquid Water Structure, Coordination Numbers for Ions & Solvation for Biological Molecules.
Clementi, F., ed. see International Symposium on Cell Biology & Cytopharmacology Staff.
Clementi, Muzio. Gradus ad Parnassum: Twenty-Nine Selected Studies for Piano.
Clements, Barbara & Shulman, Colette. Women of the Soviet Union.
Clements, Bruce. From Ice Set Free.
Clements, D. J. & Anderson, B. D. Singular Optimal Control: The Linear-Quadratic Problem.
Clements, Kath. Why Vegan.
Clements, Kendrick A. William Jennings Bryan: Missionary Isolationist.
Clements, R. E. Prophecy & Tradition.
Clements, Ronald E. Old Testament Theology.
Clements, William M. Care & Counseling of the Aging. Clinebell, Howard J. & Stone, Howard W., eds.
Clementson, Alan & Clewett, A. J., eds. Management, Operational Research & the Micro.
Clemeny, Hal. Ice World.
Clemes, Harris, jt. auth. see Bean, Reynold.
Clemett, Arthur R., jt. auth. see Berk, Robert N.
Clemmensen, J., ed. Quantitative Aspects of Risk Assessment in Chemical Carcinogenesis.
Clendenning, Sheila T. Emily Dickinson: A Bibliography, 1850-1966.
Clermont, Kevin M. Civil Procedure.
--Federal Rules of Civil Procedure-1984.
Cleugh, James, tr. see Flaceliere, Robert.
Cleugh, M. F. Psychology in the Service of School.
--The Slow Learner.
Cleve, John. The Crusader No. 2: The Passionate Princess.
--The Crusader No. 3: Julanar the Lioness.
Cleveland, Allan, ed. see Means, R. S., Company, Inc. Staff.
Cleveland, Charles, jt. auth. see Zender, Bob.
Cleveland Museum of Art Staff. Handbook of the Cleveland Museum of Art.
Cleveland Public Library Editors - John G. White Department. Catalogue of the Chess Collection, Including Checkers.
Cleveland, William A. Britannica Atlas.
Cleven, Harry T., tr. see Jervell, Jacob.
Clever. Argon: Gas Solubilities.
--Helium & Neon.
--Krypton, Xenon, & Radon: Gas Solubilities.
Clever, H. L. & Young, C. L., eds. Methane.
Cleverley, John F. The First Generation: The School & Society in Early Australia.
Cleverly, John F. & Wescombe, Christabel. Papua New Guinea: Guide to Sources in Education.
Clevett, Kenneth J. Handbook of Process Stream Analysis.
Clew, Jeff. Harley Davidson Owners Workshop Manual: Sportster '70 Thru '76.
--Honda 250 Elsinore '73 - '75.
--Velocette Singles '53 - '70.
--Yamaha 250 & 350 Twins '70 - '79.
Clew, Jeff & Rogers, Chris. Puch Maxi Mopeds '69 - '80.
Clew, Kenneth R. The Kennet & Avon Canal.
Clewes, Dorothy. Missing from Home.
Clewett, A. J., jt. ed. see Clementson, Alan.
Clewlow, Carol. Hong Kong, Macau & Canton-A Travel Survival Kit.
Clews, F. H. Heavy Clay Technology.
Cleyre, Voltairne de see De Cleyre, Voltairine.
Cliatt, Mary J. & Shaw, Jean M. Junk Treasures: A Sourcebook for Using Recycled Materials with Children.
Cliatt, Mary Jo P., jt. auth. see Shaw, Jean M.
Clibborn, Edward B., ed. European Illustration: 1983.
--European Photography: 1983-84.
Clidero, Robert K. & Sharpe, Kenneth H. Applied Electrical Systems for Construction.
Clief, Sylvia Van see Heide, Florence P. & Van Clief, Sylvia.
Cliff, A. D. & Ord, J. K. Spatial Autocorrelation.
--Spatial Processes: Models & Applications.
Cliff, A. D., et al. Spatial Aspects of Influenza Epidemics.
Cliff, Anne, tr. see Dourlein, Peter.
Cliff, Freda & Cliff, Philip. A Diary for Teachers of Young Children.
Cliff, K. S., jt. auth. see Waters, W. E.
Cliff, Kenneth S. Accidents: Causes, Prevention & Services.
Cliff, Michelle, ed. see Smith, Lillian.
Cliff, Philip, jt. auth. see Cliff, Freda.
Cliffe, J. T. The Puritan Gentry: The Great Puritan Families of Early Stuart England.
Clifford, Brian & Bull, Ray. The Psychology of Person Identification.
Clifford, C. R., ed. Lace Dictionary: Including Historic & Commercial Terms, Technical Terms, Native & Foreign.
Clifford, Denis. Plan Your Estate, Wills, Probate, Avoidance, Trusts & Taxes: California Edition.
--Power of Attorney Book.
Clifford, Denis & Curry, Hayden. A Legal Guide for Lesbian & Gay Couples. Warner, Ralph, ed.
Clifford, Denis & Warner, Ralph. The Partnership Book.
Clifford, Denis, jt. auth. see Pladsen, Carol.
Clifford, Eth. The Curse of the Moonraker.
--The Killer Swan.
--Search for the Crescent Moon.
Clifford, Francis. Drummer in the Dark.
Clifford, H. T. & Ludlow, Gwen. Keys to the Families & Genera of Queensland.
Clifford, H. T. & Specht, R. L. The Vegetation of North Stradbroke Island.
Clifford, J. G., jt. auth. see Paterson, Thomas G.
Clifford, J. Garry, jt. ed. see Dimond, Mary C.
Clifford, Joseph A. Administrative Law.
Clifford, Laurie B. The Peppermint Gang & the Impossible Houseboat.
Clifford, M. N. & Willson, K. C., eds. Coffee: Botany, Biochemistry & Production of Beans & Beverage.
Clifford, Margaret A. & Drummond, Ann E. Radiographic Techniques Related to Pathology.
Clifford, Margaret M. Practicing Educational Psychology.
Clifford, Martin. The Complete Guide to Security.
--The Complete Guide to Video.
--Master Handbook of Electronic Tables & Formulas.
--Your Telephone: Operation, Selection & Installation.
Clifford, Mike. The Harmony Illustrated Encyclopedia of Rock.
--The Harmony Illustrated Encyclopedia of Rock.
Clifford, Nicholas R. Shanghai, Nineteen Twenty-five: Urban Nationalism & the Defense of Foreign Privilege.
Clifford, P. Motocourse 1984-1985.
Clifford, Richard J. & Rockwell, Hays H. Holy Week. Achtemeier, Elizabeth, ed.
Clifford, Sandy. The Smartest Person in the World.
Clifford, William G. Books in Bottles: The Curious in Literature.
Clifford, William K. Lectures & Essays.
Clift, S., jt. auth. see Greenfield, S.
Clifton, Chester V., jt. auth. see Stoughton, Cecil.
Clifton, H. D. Systems Analysis for Business Data Processing.
Clifton, Jack. The Eye of the Artist.
Clifton, James A., retold by. Star Woman & Other Shawnee Tales.
Clifton, Lucille. Everett Anderson's Friend.
--Everett Anderson's Nine Month Long.
--Everett Anderson's Year.
--Everett Anderson's 1-2-3.
--The Times They Used to Be.
Clifton, Merritt, ed. see Ilgen, Jon, et al.
Clifton-Taylor, Alec. The Cathedrals of England.
Climate Review Panel, Climate Research Committee, National Research Council. Carbon Dioxide & Climate: A Second Assessment.
Clinch, Minty. Harrison Ford.
Cline, C. Terry, Jr. The Attorney Conspiracy.
--Missing Persons.
Cline, Gloria G. Exploring the Great Basin.
Cline, Howard F. U. S. & Mexico.
Cline, Hugh F. & Sinnott, Loraine T. The Electronic Library: Automation in Academic Libraries.
Cline, Martin J. & Haskell, Charles M. Cancer Chemotherapy.
Cline, Ray S. U. S. Power in a World of Conflict.
Cline, Richard, et al. Planning in the United States & the United Kingdom 1970-1985: An Annotated Bibliography.
Clineball, Howard J., ed. see Clinebell, Charlotte H.
Clinebell, Charlotte H. Counseling for Liberation. Clineball, Howard J. & Stone, Howard W., eds.
Clinebell, Howard J. Growth Counseling for Marriage Enrichment: Pre-Marriage & the Early Years. Stone, Howard W., ed.
--Growth Counseling for Mid-Years Couples. Stone, Howard W., ed.
Clinebell, Howard J., ed. see Augsburger, David W.
Clinebell, Howard J., ed. see Clements, William M.
Clinebell, Howard J., ed. see Cobb, John B., Jr.
Clinebell, Howard J., ed. see Colston, Lowell G.
Clinebell, Howard J., ed. see Irwin, Paul B.
Clinebell, Howard J., ed. see Leas, Speed & Kittlaus, Paul.
Clinebell, Howard J., ed. see Pattison, E. Mansell.
Clinebell, Howard J., ed. see Stone, Howard W.
Clines, David J. The Esther Scroll: Its Genesis, Growth, & Meaning.
Clinic on Library Applications of Data Processing Proceedings, 1974. Applications of Minicomputers to Library & Related Problems. Lancaster, F. W., ed.
Clinic on Library Applications of Data Processing Staff. The Economics of Library Automation: Proceedings of the Clinic on Library Applications of Data Processing, 1976. Divilbiss, J. L., ed.
Clinic on Library Applications of Data Processing Proceedings, 1973. Networking & Other Forms of Cooperation. Lancaster, F. W., ed.
Clinic on Library Applications of Data Processing Staff. Proceedings of the Clinic on Library Data Processing, 1969. Carroll, Dewey E., ed.
Clinic on Library Applications of Data Processing, Proceedings, 1975. The Use of Computers in Literature Searching & Related Reference Activities in Libraries. Lancaster, F. W., ed.
Clinton, Alan. The Trade Union Rank & File: Trades Councils in Britain, 1900-1940.
Clinton, Kevin. The Sacred Officials of the Eleusinian Mysteries.
Clissold, Stephen. Whirlwind.
Clive, John, ed. see Buckle, Henry T.
Clive, John, ed. see Macaulay, Thomas B.
Clizbe, John A., et al. A Chance for Change: Confronting Student under Achievement.
Clocksin, W. F. & Mellish, C. S. Programming in Prolog.
--Programming in Prolog.
Clodd, Edward. Magic in Names & in Other Things.
--Myths & Dreams.
--Tom Tit Tot.
Cloete, Stuart. Rags of Glory.
Clor, Harry M. The Mass Media & Democracy.
Close, Angela E., jt. ed. see Wendorf, Fred.
Close, Arthur C. & Bologna, Gregory, eds. Washington Representatives 1988.
Close, Arthur C. & Gregg, John P., eds. Washington Representatives, 1987.
Close, Burt E. How to Create Super Slide Shows.
Close, Charles M. Analysis of Linear Circuits.
Close, K. J. & Yarwood, J. Experimental Electronics for Students.
Close, Paul D. Sound Control & Thermal Insulation of Buildings.
Close, Reg A. A Reference Grammar for Students of English.
Close, Robert. Europe Without Defense? Forty-Eight Hours That Could Change the Face of the World.
Close, Sylvia. Sex During Pregnancy & after Childbirth.
--The Toddler & the New Baby.
Close Up Foundation Staff. The Citizen Bee Guide to American Studies.
--The Congress: Perspectives on Representation in American Government.
--International Relations: Understanding the Behavior of Nations.
--The Media: Perspectives on the People's Right to Know.
--The Citizen Bee Guide to American Studies: The Citizen Bee Sourcebook of American Studies.
Clotfelter, Cecil F. & Clotfelter, Mary L., eds. Camping & Backpacking: A Guide to Information Sources.
Clotfelter, Mary L., jt. ed. see Clotfelter, Cecil F.
Cloud, Preston. Oasis in Space: Earth History from the Beginning.
Clough, Arthur H. The Bothie: The Text of 1848. Scott, Patrick, ed.
Clough, B. W. The Crystal Crown.
Clough, John. Scales, Intervals, Keys & Triads: A Self-Instruction Program.
Clough, Rosa T. Futurism.
Clough, Shepard B. European Economic History.
--The Life I've Lived.
Clouse, Robert, et al. Church in History Series.
Clouser, K. Danner. Teaching Bioethics: Strategies, Problems & Resources.
Clouston, John S. CILA: A New Approach to Problems in the Acquisition of Latin American Library Materials.
Clouston, William A. Book of Noodles: Stories of Simpletons.
Clout, Hugh D. The Geography of Post-War France: A Social & Economic Approach.
Clout, Hugh D., ed. Regional Development in Western Europe.
Cloverdale Press Staff & Passell, Peter. Where to Put Your Money.
Clow, C. A. & MacDonald, R. D. Punched-Card Data Processing System.
Clow, Duane J. & Urguhart, N. Scott. Mathematics in Biology: Calculus & Related Topics, Preliminary Edition.
Cloward, Richard & Piven, Frances. Democracy Thwarted.
Clowers, Myles L. & Letendre, Lorin. Understanding American Politics Through Fiction.
Clowers, Myles L., jt. auth. see Beck, Warren A.
Clowes, William L. Black America: A Study of the Ex-Slave - His Late Master.
Clowse, Converse D. Measuring Charleston's Overseas Commerce, 1717-1767: Statistics from the Port's Naval Lists.
Cloyd, Betty S. Glory Beyond All Comparison.
Clubb, Bruce E. United States Foreign Trade Law.
Clubb, Elizabeth & Knight, Jane. Fertility: A Comprehensive Guide to Natural Family Planning.
Clugston, Donald L. All That Money & No Cash.
Clugston, George A. A Looking Glasse for London & England by Thomas Lodge & Robert Greene: A Critical Edition. Orgel, Stephen, ed.
Cluley, John C. Computer Interfacing & On-Line Operation.
Clum, J. A., ed. see AIME Staff.
Clum, Woodworth. Apache Agent: The Story of John P. Clum.
Clune, Frank. Somewhere in New Guinea.
Clurman, Harold. All People Are Famous.
--The Fervent Years: The Group Theatre & the Thirties.
--The Fervent Years: The Story of the Group Theatre & the Thirties.
Clute, Robin & Andersen, Juel. Juel Andersen's Tempeh Primer.
Clute, Robin & Andersen, Sigrid. Carob Primer.
--Juel Andersen's Carob Primer.
--Tempeh Primer.
Clutter, Mary E., ed. Dormancy & Developmental Arrest: Experimental Analysis in Plants & Animals.
Clutterbuck, David. How to Be a Good Corporate Citizen.
Clymer, Eleanor. Santiago's Silver Mine.
--A Search for Two Bad Mice.
Clymer, Floyd. Floyd Clymer's Historical Motor Scrapbook: Ford Model T Edition. Clymer Publications, ed.
Clymer, Floyd, ed. Ford Model A Album.
Clymer Publications. Buick Skylark, 1980.
--Chevrolet Complete Owner's Handbook of Repair & Maintenance: 1929-1955.
--The Complete Ford Owner's Handbook of Repair & Maintenance: 1932-1955.
--Handbook of Engine Swapping.
--Johnson Service-Repair Handbook: 1.5 to 35 Hp, 1965-1983.
--Montesa Service-Repair Handbook: 123-360cc Singles, 1965-1975.
--Plymouth Owner's Handbook, 1946-1955.
--Toyota Service Repair Handbook: Corolla & Carina, 1968-78.
Clymer Publications & Hoy, Ray. Mercury Service-Repair Handbook: 50 to 200 Hp, 1964-1982.
Clymer Publications, ed. Bridgestone Singles & Twins, 50-175cc.
--Corvair Owners Handbook of Maintenance & Repair: 1960-1965.
--Datsun Sports Car Handbook: 1600 & 2000cc.
Clymer Publications, ed. see Bell, Doug.
Clymer Publications, ed. see Clymer, Floyd.
Clymer Publications, ed. see Henry, Les.
Clymer Publications, ed. see Henry, Leslie R.
Clymer Publications, ed. see Hopper, Gordon E.
Clymer Publications, ed. see Page, Victor W.
Clymer Publications Ser. Porsche Owners Handbook & Service Manual: Covers All Porsche Models up to 356c.
Clymer Publications Staff. Corvette, 1955-62: Complete Owner's Handbook.
--Honda Service-Repair Handbook: 250-350cc Scrambler Twins, All Years.
--Jeep Service, Repair Handbook: Covers Willy-Overland Model MB & Ford Model GPW.
--Stern Drive Service-Repair Handbook: OMC, MerCruiser, Stern-Powr, Berkeley, Jacuzzi.
--Triumph Spitfire Owner's Handbook: 1962-1970.
--Volvo Service-Repair Handbook: 122s Series & P 1800, All Years.
--Yamaha: 250-400cc Piston Port Singles, 1968-76, Service, Repair, Performance.
--Yamaha: 250-400cc, 1965-1979 - Service, Repair, Performance.
CMG Imformation Services, Inc. Staff, ed. Faculty Directory of Higher Education, Vol. 10: Science & Mathematics.
CMG Information Services, Inc. Staff, ed. Faculty Directory of Higher Education.
--Faculty Directory of Higher Education, Vol. 11: Social Sciences.
--Faculty Directory of Higher Education, Vol. 2: Communications.
--Faculty Directory of Higher Education, Vol. 3: Computer Science & Data Processing.
--Faculty Directory of Higher Education, Vol. 4: Education.
--Faculty Directory of Higher Education, Vol. 5: Engineering.
--Faculty Directory of Higher Education, Vol. 6: Fine & Applied Arts.
--Faculty Directory of Higher Education, Vol. 7: Hummanities.
--Faculty Directory of Higher Education, Vol. 8: Language & Literature.
--Faculty Directory of Higher Education, Vol. 9: Medicine & Nursing.

Co-operative Union of Canada Staff & MacPherson, Ian. Building & Protecting the Co-operative Movement: A Brief History of the Co-operative Union of Canada, 1909-1984.
Coad, William J. Energy Engineering & Management for Building Systems.
Coakley, Carolyn G., jt. auth. see Wolvin, Andrew D.
Coakley, Davis, ed. Establishing a Geriatric Service.
Coakley, Mary L. How to Live Life to the Fullest: A Handbook for Seasoned Citizens.
Coal Age Magazine Editors. Coal Age Operating Handbook of Coal Preparation.
--Coal Age Operating Handbook of Underground Mining.
Coan. BASIC Microsoft: Basic for the Macintosh.
Coan & Coan. Microsoft BASIC for the Macintosh.
Coan, James S. Basic Microsoft BASIC.
Coase, R. H., ed. see Kessel, Reuben A.
Coate, Roger A., jt. auth. see Feld, Werner J.
Coates, A. P. & Coates, Zelda K. Soviets in Central Asia.
Coates, Belle. Mak.
Coates, D. R., ed. Environmental Geomorphology & Landscape Conservation: Non-Urban.
--Environmental Geomorphology & Landscape Conservation: Prior to 1900.
Coates, Donald R. Environmental Geology.
Coates, Donald R., ed. Environmental Geomorphology & Landscape Conservation.
--Gas Chromatography.
Coates, G. E., et al. Principles of Organometallic Chemistry.
Coates, Gary J., ed. Alternative Learning Environments.
Coates, Jennifer. The Semantics of the Modal Auxiliaries.
Coates, John, tr. see Stoll, Gaby.
Coates, Marie E. Germ-Free Animal in Research.
Coates, Peter & Niklaus, Thelms. The Little Fellow.
Coates, R., et al. Structural Analysis.
Coates, Robert M. The Outlaw Years: The History of the Land Pirates of the Natchez Trace.
--Wisteria Cottage.
Coates, Robert M., ed. Organic Syntheses.
Coates, S. D., et al, eds. Electronic Maintenance.
Coates, William A., tr. see Eliade, Mircea.
Coates, Zelda K., jt. auth. see Coates, A. P.
Coatesville-Jefferson Conference on Addiction, 1st, October 1977. Addiction Research & Treatment Converging Trends: Proceedings. Gottheil, E. L., et al, eds.
Coats, George W. Saga, Legend, Tale, Novella, Fable.
Coats, George W. & Long, Burke O., eds. Canon & Authority: Essays in Old Testament Religion & Theology.
Coats, J. & P. Ltd. Staff. Fifty Counted Thread Embroidery Stitches.
Coats, J & P Staff. Crochet Stitches & Edgings.
Coatsworth, David, jt. ed. see Coatsworth, Emerson.
Coatsworth, Elizabeth. The Werefox.
Coatsworth, Emerson & Coatsworth, David, eds. The Adventures of Nanabush: Ojibway Indian Stories.
Cobb, Buell E., Jr. The Sacred Harp: A Tradition & Its Music.
Cobb, Charles R. & Jefferies, Richard W. Archaeological Investigations at the Milar Site, Alexander County, Illinois.
Cobb, D. Starting to Sail.
Cobb, Douglas. Mastering Symphony.
--Mastering Symphony.
Cobb, Douglas, jt. auth. see Andersen, Dick.
Cobb, Douglas, et al. One-Two-Three for Business.
--Douglas Cobb's 1-2-3 Handbook: The Complete Guide for Power Users. Phifer, Marjorie & Baughman, Linda, eds.
--The Paradox Companion. Phifer, Marjorie & Baughman, Linda, eds.
Cobb, Douglas F. & LeBlond, Geoffrey. Using 1-2-3.
Cobb, Edwin L. No Cease Fires: The War on Poverty in Roanoke Valley.
Cobb, Irvin S. Exit Laughing.
Cobb, James C. The Selling of the South: The Southern Crusade for Industrial Development, 1936 - 1980.
Cobb, John B., Jr. Beyond Dialogue: Toward a Mutual Transformation of Christianity & Buddhism.
--Christ in a Pluralistic Age.
--Christian Natural Theology: Based on the Thought of Alfred North Whitehead.
--Liberal Christianity at the Crossroads.
--Theology & Pastoral Care. Clinebell, Howard J. & Stone, Howard W., eds.
--To Pray or Not to Pray.
Cobb, John B., Jr., jt. auth. see Tracy, David.
Cobb, John B., Jr., jt. ed. see Griffin, David R.
Cobb, Nancy J., jt. auth. see Stevens-Long, Judith.
Cobb, Richard. Armees Revolutionnaires.
Cobb, Roger W., jt. auth. see Elder, Charles D.
Cobb, Russell L., jt. auth. see Rice, Marion J.
Cobb, Steven S., et al. Hands-on Paradox. Phifer, Marjorie M. & Baughman, Linda, eds.
Cobban, J. Maclaren. Master of His Fate.
Cobbett, William. Year's Residence in the United States of America.
Cobbold, Diana. Evenings Faces.
Cobden, Richard, ed. see Chevalier, Michel.
Coben & Ferster. Japanese Cloisonne: History, Technique & Appreciation.
Cobey, Katharine E. Thrift.
Cobham, Rosemary. Kaleidoscope Plus.
Coble, Charles & Hounshell, Paul. Mainstreaming Language Arts & Social Studies: Special Activities for the Whole Class.
Coblentz, W. W. From the Life of a Researcher.
Coburn, Andrew. The Babysitter.
--Off Duty.
Coburn, Edward J. Advanced BASIC: Structured Programming for Microcomputers.
--An Introduction to BASIC.
--Learning about Microcomputers: Hardware & Application Software.
--Microcomputer BASIC: Structures, Concepts, & Techniques.
Coburn, Jack W. & Klein, Gordon L., eds. Metabolic Bone Disease in Total Parenteral Nutrition.
Coburn, John B. A Diary of Prayers-Personal & Public.
--Prayer & Personal Religion.
Coburn, Louisa V., jt. ed. see Anderson, Scarvia B.
Coburn, Oliver, tr. see Sabet, Huschmand.
Coburn, Thomas. Devi Mahatmya.
Cocchi, John. The Westerns: A Picture Quiz Book.
Coche, Andre G., ed. Coastal Aquaculture: Development Perspectives in Africa & Case Studies from Other Regions.
Cochran, Alexander S., Jr. Magic Diplomatic Summary: A Chronological Finding Aid.
Cochran, Alister. Man, Cancer & Immunity.
Cochran, Judith. Education in Egypt.
Cochran, L., jt. auth. see Whitcomb, Helen.
Cochran, Molly. Dressing Sexy.
Cochran, Molly, jt. auth. see Goday, Dale.
Cochran, Norman A., et al. A Teacher's Guide to Elementary School Physical Education.
Cochran, Susan Hill. The Population of Thailand: Its Growth & Welfare.
Cochran, William G. Contributions to Statistics.
Cochrane, A. L., ed. see Migraine Symposium, 3rd, London, 1969.
Cochrane, Arthur C. Eating & Drinking with Jesus: An Ethical & Biblical Inquiry.
Cochrane, Charles C. The Gospel According to Genesis.
Cochrane, Diane. This Business of Art.
Cochrane, Hugh F. Gateway to Oblivion: The Great Lakes Vortex.
Cochrane, Luther P., jt. auth. see Practising Law Institute Staff.
Cochrane, Lydia G., tr. see Klapisch-Zuber, Christiane.
Cochrane, Pauline A., jt. auth. see Markey, Karen.
Cochrane, Roy. Golden Days in Egypt: A Beginner's History of Rights & Duties.
Cochrane, Shirley. Burnsite.
Cochrane, Susan H. & Zachariah, K. C. Infant & Child Mortality As a Determinant of Fertility: The Policy Implications.
Cock, M. J., ed. Bemisia Tabaci.
Cock, Valerie. Dressmaking Simplified.
Cockayne, B. & Jones, D. W., eds. Modern Oxide Materials: Preparation, Properties & Device Applications.
Cockburn, Alexander & Ridgeway, James. The Age of Reagan.
Cockburn, Patricia. The Years of the Week.
Cockburn, Victor & Steinbergh, Judith. The Troubadour Songbook.
Cockburn, W., jt. auth. see Street, H. E.
Cockcroft, James D. Outlaws in the Promised Land: Mexican Immigrant Workers & America's Future.
Cockerell, Douglas. Bookbinding & the Care of Books.
Cockerell, H. A. & Green, Edwin. The British Insurance Business 1547-1970: An Introduction & Guide to Historical Records in the United Kingdom.
Cockerell, Hugh. Lloyd's of London: A Portrait.
Cockerell, T. D. African Bees of the Genera Ceratina, Halictus & Megachile.
Cockerham, William C. Medical Sociology.
Cockett & Hilton. Basic Chemistry of Textile Coloring & Finishing.
--Basic Chemistry of Textile Preparation.
Cockett, A. H., et al. The Chemistry of Monatomic Gases.
Cockett, Frank B., jt. auth. see Dodd, Harold.
Cockle, Paul, jt. auth. see Chandler, John.
Cock-Morgan, Liliane De see Balsys, Algis & De Cock-Morgan, Liliane.
Cockrell, Amanda. The Legions of the Mist.
Cockrill, W. Ross. Antarctic Hazard.
Cockrum, E. Lendell. Mammals of the Southwest.
Cocks, Charles, tr. see Michelet, Jules.
Cockshut, A. O. Truth to Life.
--Truth to Life: The Art of Biography in the Nineteenth Century.
Cockshut, A. O., intro. by. The Novel to Nineteen Hundred.
Cocoris, G. Michael. Making Evangelism Personal.
--Making Evangelsim Personal.
Cocozzoli, Gary, jt. ed. see Keresztesi, Michael.
Cocteau, Jean. Le Bel Indifferent.
--La Belle et la Bete.
--Cahiers Jean Cocteau.
--Colette.
--La Comtesse de Noailles: Oui et Non.
--Le Cordon Ombilical.
--Entre Picasso et Radiquet.
--L' Impromptu Du Palais Royal.
--Jean Cocteau En Verve.
--Lettres a Andre Gide: Avec: Responses d'Andre Gide.
--Maalesh: Journal d'une Tournee de Theatre.
--Opera.
--Opera: Avec: Plain-Chant.
--Opium: The Diary of a Cure. Crosland, Margaret & Road, Sinclair, trs.
--Les Parents Terribles: Avec: La Machine a Ecrire.
--Picasso: Avec: Le Potomak, Le Grand Ecart.
--Poesie Critique.
--Poesie Graphique.
--Le Potomak.
--La Princess de Cleves. Delannoy, ed.
--Le Rappel a l'Ordre.
--Saint-Blaise-Des-Simples.
--Theatre. Incl. Antigone; Les Maries de la Tour Eiffel; Les Chevaliers de la Table Ronde; Les Parents Terribles. French & Eur.
--Theatre. Incl. Les Monstres Sacres; La Machine a Ecrire; Renaud et Armide; L' Aigle a Deux Tetes. French & Eur.
Coda-Messerle, Margaret, jt. auth. see Covino, William A.
CODATA, ed. Scientific Program & Abstracts: International CODATA Conference, 10th, July 14-17, 1986, Ottawa, Canada.
CODATA Staff, ed. Data in Modern Biology: Selected Papers from the 9th International CODATA Conference, Jerusalem, Israel, June 1984.
--Evaluation of Thermophysical Property Measurement Methods & Standard Reference Materials.
--Nutrition: Codata Directory of Data Sources for Science & Technology, Chapter Twelve.
--Thermodynamic Databases: Selected Papers from the First CODATA Symposium on Chemical Thermodynamic & Thermophysical Properties Databases, Paris, France, September 1985.
--Thermophysical Properties of Some Key Solids: Heat Capacity, Thermal Expansion, Electrical Resistivity, Thermal Conductivity & Absolute Thermopower.
Codd, L. W., jt. auth. see Terpstra, P.
Codding, George, Jr. & Rutkowski, Anthony M. The ITU in a Changing World.
Codevilla, Angelo. Modern France.
Codlin, Ellen M., ed. ASLIB Directory: Information Sources in the Social Sciences, Medicine & the Humanities.
Codrescu, Andrei. For Max Jacob.
Cody, Al. West from Abilene.
Cody, Jess. Devil's Gold.
Cody, John. After Great Pain: The Inner Life of Emily Dickinson.
Cody, John F. Loving to Be Loved.
Cody, Liza. Bad Company.
--Dupe.
--Headcase: An Anna Lee Mystery.
--Stalker: A Mystery.
--Under Contract: An Anna Lee Mystery.
Cody, William. The Life of Buffalo Bill.
Coe, Boyer & Summer, Bob. Getting Strong, Looking Strong: A Guide to Successful Bodybuilding.
Coe, Brian, jt. auth. see Millward, Michael.
Coe, Charles K. Consulting Engineer.
Coe, Charles P. & Louviere, Michael L. Preparing the Pharmacy for a JCAH Survey.
Coe, Frances & Coe, Ivan. Insearch: Discovering the Real You.
Coe, Ivan, jt. auth. see Coe, Frances.
Coe, Jacques. Fame, Fraud & Fortune: Seventy-four Years in Wall Street.
Coe, Michael D. The Maya.
Coe, Rodney M. & Brehm, Henry P. Preventive Health Care for Adults: A Study of Medical Practice.
Coe, Tucker. Don't Lie to Me.
Coe, Wesley R. Biology of the Nemerteans of the Atlantic Coast of North America.
Coekin, J. A. High Speed Pulse Technique. Hammond, P., ed.
Coel, Margeret, jt. auth. see Speas, Sam.
Coetzer, P. W. & Le Roux, J. H., eds. Index to Periodical Articles on South African Political & Social History Since 1902: Vol. 3-Bibliographies on South African Political History.
Cofacci, Gino, jt. auth. see Carmack, Robert.
Coffee, Frank. The Complete House Kit.
--The Self-Sufficient House.
Coffen, Richard W., ed. see Bradford, Charles E.
Coffen, Richard W., ed. see Orser, Evelyn.
Coffen, Richard W., ed. see Van Dolson, Leo R.
Coffen, Richard W., ed. see Van Pelt, Nancy L.
Coffey, Barbara. Beauty Begins at Forty: How to Look Your Best for a Lifetime.
--Glamour's Success Book.
Coffey, David. A Veterinary Surgeon's Guide for Cat Owners.
Coffey, Michael. Roman Satire.
Coffey, Robert E., et al. Behavior in Organizations: A Multi-Dimensional View.
Coffey, Thomas M. The Long Thirst: Prohibition in America 1920-1933.
Coffey, William, et al. Molecular Diffusion & Spectra.
Coffin, Charles M. John Donne & the New Philosophy.
Coffin, David R. The Villa in the Life of Renaissance Rome.
Coffin, Tristram P. Great Game for a Girl.
--Uncertain Glory: Folklore & the American Revolution.
Coffin, Tristram P., ed. Indian Tales of North America: An Anthology for the Adult Reader.
Coffin, William S. Once to Every Man.
Coffin, William S., Jr. The Courage to Love.
Coffinberger, Richard L. & Samuels, Linda B. Business & Its Legal Environment: Study Guide & Workbook.
Coffman, C. V. & Fix, G. J. Constructive Approaches to Mathematical Models.
Coffman, James P. Introduction to Professional Food Service.
Coffman, Mary E., jt. auth. see Butturff, Diane.
Coffman, Sara J. How to Improve Your Test-Taking Skills.
--How to Survive at College.
Coffman, Virginia. The Dark Palazzo.
--Dark Winds.
--Dinah Faire.
--Fire Dawn.
--The Gaynor Women.
--House at Sandalwood.
--Hyde Place.
--The Lombard Cavalcade.
--The Lombard Heiress.
--Marsanne.
--Mistress Devon.
--The Orchid Tree.
--Pacific Cavalcade.
--Veronique.
Coffron, James W. The Apple Connection.
--The Commodore 64 Connection.
Cofield, Roger E., Jr. Design Manual for High Temperature Hot Water & Steam Systems.
Cogan, Morris L. Clinical Supervision.
Coger, Dalvan M., jt. auth. see Hess, Robert L.
Coggan, W. Readings in Child Psychology.
Cogger, Harold G. Reptiles & Amphibians of Australia.
Coggeshall, R. E., jt. ed. see Willis, W. D.
Coggin, P. A. Education for the Future: The Case for Radical Change.
Coggin, Philip, jt. ed. see Semper, Edward.
Coggins, Frank W. Clocks: Construction, Maintenance & Repair.
--The Woodturner's Handbook.
Coggins, George C. & Wilkinson, Charles F. Federal Public Land & Resources Law.
Coggins, Jack. Horseman's Bible.
Coggins, Paul. Lady Is the Tiger.
Coggins, R. J. Samaritans & Jews: The Origins of Samaritanism Reconsidered.
Coghill, Neville. The Collected Papers of Neville Coghill: Shakespearian & Medievalist.
Coghlan, Richard T., jt. ed. see Boeckh, J. Anthony.
Cogoli, John, et al. Graphic Arts Photography: Black & White.
Cogswell, James A. Response: The Church in Mission to a World in Crisis.
Cogswell, James A., ed. The Church & the Rural Poor.
Cogswell, William R., jt. auth. see Hutchinngs, Mary H.
Cohalan, John P., Jr. Saga of Aaron Burr.
Cohan, Christopher J. & Olstad, Walter B. Space Transportation Systems: 1980-2000, AAS1.
Cohan, Joel, ed. see Palmer, Jim.
Cohan, John R., ed. Drafting California Irrevocable Inter Vivos Trusts.
Cohan, Robert. The Dance Workshop: A Guide to the Fundamentals of Movement.
Cohan, Steven, ed. see Boaden, James.
Cohan, Tony. Opium.
Cohen & Hansel. Risk & Gambling.
Cohen, jt. auth. see Neal.
Cohen, A. Deviance & Control.
Cohen, A., ed. see Dynamic Aspects of Speech Perception Symposium Staff.
Cohen, Aaron & Cohen, Elaine. Planning the Electronic Office.
Cohen, Alan B., jt. auth. see Steinberg, Carl P.
Cohen, Allan R., et al. Effective Behavior in Organizations: Learning from the Interplay of Cases, Concepts & Student Experiences.

Authors

Cohen, Arnold W. Emergencies in Obstetrics & Gynecology.
Cohen, Arthur A. Acts of Theft.
--Artists & Enemies: Three Novellas.
--The Natural & the Supernatural Jew: An Historical and Theological Introduction.
Cohen, Barbara. Benny.
--Gooseberries to Oranges.
--Here Come the Purim Players!
--I Am Joseph.
--Unicorns in the Rain.
Cohen, Barbara & Lovejoy, Bahija. Seven Daughters & Seven Sons.
Cohen, Barbara, retold by. Lovely Vassilisa.
Cohen, Barry, jt. ed. see Mohamed A. El-Khawas.
Cohen, Benjamin J. The European Monetary System: An Outsider's View.
Cohen, Bernard L. Introduction to the New Economics.
Cohen, Beth. Attic Bilingual Vases & Their Painters.
Cohen, Betsy. The Snow White Syndrome: All about Envy.
Cohen, Caron Lee. Renata, Whizbrain, & the Ghost.
Cohen, Charles P., et al. Psychotherapy & Drug Addiction I: Diagnosis & Treatment.
Cohen, D. E. Groups of Cohomological Dimension One.
Cohen, Dan. The Mystery of the Hidden Camera.
--The Mystery of the Locked Door.
--The Mystery of the Mellafeller Elephant.
--The Mystery of the Missing Ring.
Cohen, Daniel. Bigfoot: America's Number One Monster.
--Computers. Barish, Wendy, ed.
--ESP: The Search Beyond the Senses.
--ESP: The Search Beyond the Senses.
--Famous Curses.
--Ghostly Terrors.
--Horror in the Movies.
--Missing: Stories of Strange Disappearances.
--The Science of Spying.
--The Tomb Robbers.
Cohen, Daniel & Cohen, Susan. How to Get Started in Video.
--Rock Video Superstars II.
--Wrestling Superstars II.
--Young & Famous: Hollywood's Newest Superstars.
Cohen, David. Psychologists on Psychology.
--Sleep & Dreaming: Origin, Nature & Functions.
Cohen, David, jt. auth. see Smolan, Rick.
Cohen, Dian & Shannon, Kristin. The Next Canadian Economy.
Cohen, Doron J. & Brillinger, Peter C. Introduction to Data Structures & Non-Numeric Computation.
Cohen, E. G., ed. see Boltzmann Equation Symposium Staff.
Cohen, Edie L. & Emery, Sherman R., eds. Dining by Design.
Cohen, Edmund D. C. G. Jung & the Scientific Attitude.
Cohen, Elaine, jt. auth. see Cohen, Aaron.
Cohen, Eve, jt. auth. see Erickson, Mary A.
Cohen, Gary G. Biblical Separation Defended.
Cohen, Hayyim J. Jews of the Middle East (1860-1972)
Cohen, Helen L., ed. One-Act Plays by Modern Authors.
Cohen, J. M. Stable Homotopy.
Cohen, J. M., tr. see Cervantes de Saavedra, Miguel.
Cohen, J. W. On Regenerative Processes in Queueing Theory.
Cohen, Jack S., jt. auth. see Portugal, Franklin H.
Cohen, Jacob. Statistical Power Analysis for the Behavioral Sciences.
Cohen, Jay O. The Staphylococci.
Cohen, Jerome A., et al, trs. from Chinese. The Criminal Law & the Criminal Procedure Law of China.
Cohen, Jerome B. Personal Finance.
--Personal Finance.
Cohen, Joel & Snitzer, Herb. Reprise: The Extraordinary Revival of Early Music.
Cohen, Joel, jt. auth. see Philip, David.
Cohen, Joel, jt. auth. see Seixas, Vic, Jr.
Cohen, Joel C., ed. see Friedman, Arthur.
Cohen, Joel E. A Model of Simple Competition.
Cohen, Joel H., jt. auth. see Harrelson, Bud.
Cohen, Joel H., ed. Inside Corner: Talks with Tom Seaver.
Cohen, Joel H., ed. see Balukas, Jean.
Cohen, Joel H., ed. see Morgan, Joe.
Cohen, Jon, jt. auth. see Scaravelli, Paola.
Cohen, Joyce T., compiled by. Insights: Self-Portraits by Women.
Cohen, Judith H. Handbook of Resource Room Teaching.
Cohen, L. Readings in Education & Psychology.
Cohen, Leo & Erickson, Ralph J. Race & Culture: A Psychological Insight into the Present & Past.
Cohen, Leo J. Creating & Planning the Corporate Data Base System Project.
Cohen, Leon J. Say It in French.
--Say It in Spanish.
Cohen, Louis & Manion, Lawrence. Multicultural Classrooms: Perspectives for Teachers.
--Research Methods in Education.
Cohen, M. Bruce, jt. auth. see Jones, Seymour.
Cohen, M. D., ed. Organic Solid-State Chemistry-2: Proceedings of An International Symposium, Rehovot, Israel, 1970.
Cohen, M. M. Notices of Florida & the Campaigns. Tyler, O. Z., Jr., ed.
Cohen, Marcia, jt. auth. see Simon, Gil.
Cohen, Marilyn. Reginald Marsh's New York: Paintings, Drawings, Prints & Photographs.
Cohen, Marjorie A., jt. auth. see Council on International Educational Exchange Staff.
Cohen, Marshall J. Charles Horton Cooley & the Social Self in American Thought.
Cohen, Martin, jt. auth. see Anderson, James L.
Cohen, Michele, tr. see Broyelle, Claudie.
Cohen, Mitch, ed. Berlin: Contemporary Writing from Berlin.
Cohen, Monroe D., ed. see Ballenger, Marcus, et al.
Cohen, Monroe D., ed. see Gillies, Emily.
Cohen, Nurit, jt. auth. see Cohen, William A.
Cohen, Peter Z. Bee.
--Bull in the Forest.
--Calm Horse, Wild Night.
--Foal Creek.
Cohen, Philip. Control of Enzyme Activity.
Cohen, Richard. Congressional Leadership: Seeking a New Role.
--Say You Want Me.
Cohen, Richard, tr. see Levinas, Emmanuel.
Cohen, Richard M., jt. auth. see Neft, David S.
Cohen, Robert. The Theatre.
--Theatre: Brief Edition.
Cohen, Robert, et al, eds. Psych City.
Cohen, Robert S., ed. see Schaff, Adam.
Cohen, Rudolf. Patterns of Personality Judgement. Schaeffer, Dirk L., tr.
Cohen, S. Just Juggle.
Cohen, S. H. Police-Community Problems: Essays on Malice in Blunderland.
Cohen, S. T. & Van Cleave, William R. Nuclear Weapons, Policies & the Test Ban Issue.
Cohen, Sara K. Whoever Said Life Is Fair?
Cohen, Scott. Jocks.
--Zap! The Rise & Fall of Atari.
Cohen, Sherry S. Quizzical Pursuits: Test Yourself & Discover the Real You.
Cohen, Sherry S., jt. auth. see Bruce, Jeffrey.
Cohen, Sherry S., jt. auth. see DeLorean, Cristina F.
Cohen, Sidney. Beyond Within: The LSD Story.
Cohen, Sidney, ed. Clinical Gastroenterology: A Problem-Oriented Approach.
Cohen, Stan B. & Miller, Donald C. Big Burn: The Northwest's Forest Fire of 1910.
Cohen, Stanley, et al, eds. Biology of the Lymphokines.
Cohen, Stanley B. & Denniston, Denie. The Administrator's Guide to Equitable Opportunity in Vocational Educational.
Cohen, Stanley J. & Wool, Robert. How to Survive on Fifty Thousand to One Hundred Fifty Thousand Dollars a Year.
Cohen, Stephen & Burns, Richard C. Pathways of the Pulp.
Cohen, Stephen F. Sovieticus: American Myths & Soviet Realities.
Cohen, Stephen F., ed. see Medvedev, Roy A.
Cohen, Stephen P. Heartless.
Cohen, Stephen P. & Park, Richard L. India: Emergent Power?
Cohen, Susan, jt. auth. see Cohen, Daniel.
Cohen, Susan E., jt. ed. see Johnson, William S.
Cohen, William & Kaplan, John. Constitutional Law, Civil Liberty & Individual Rights: 1985 Supplement.
Cohen, William A. Building a Mail Order Business: A Complete Manual for Success.
--The Executive's Guide to Finding a Superior Job.
Cohen, William A. & Cohen, Nurit. Top Executive Performance: Eleven Keys to Success & Power.
Cohen, William A. & Reddick, Marshall E. Successful Marketing for Small Business.
Cohen, William B. Rulers of Empire: The French Colonial Service in Africa.
Cohen, William S. A Baker's Nickel. Guarnaschelli, Maria D., ed.
Cohen, Y. Radionuclides in Pharmacology.
Coherent, Inc., Laser Division Staff. Lasers: Operation; Equipment; Practical Application; Design.
Cohler, Bertram J. & Grunebaum, Henry U. Mothers, Grandmothers & Daughters: Personality & Child-Care in Three Generation Families.
Cohn. Silent Myocardial ISC-INFR.
Cohn, Alfred & Udolf, Roy. Criminal Justice System & Its Psychology.
Cohn, Alvin W., jt. auth. see Viano, Emilio.
Cohn, David L. Life & Times of King Cotton.
Cohn, Davis L., jt. auth. see Melsa, James L.
Cohn, Don J., tr. see Lao She.
Cohn, Don J, tr. see She, Lao.
Cohn, Jeff. Saturday Night at Daisy's.
Cohn, Jill W. Writing: The Personal Voice.
Cohn, Keith, et al. Coming Back: A Guide to Recovering from Heart Attack & Living Confidently with Coronary Disease.
Cohn, M. Z. Limit Design for Reinforced Concrete Structures.
Cohn, Marjorie B. Wash & Gouache.
Cohn, Norman S. Elements of Cytology.
Cohn, P. M., ed. see Csasar, A.
Cohn, Priscilla, ed. Transparencies: Philosophical Essays in Honor of J. Ferrater Mora.
Cohn, Robert M. & Roth, Karl. Metabolic Disease: A Guide to Early Recognition.
Cohn, Roy M. How to Stand Up for Your Rights & Win!
Cohn, Ruby. New American Dramatists, 1960-1980.
Cohn, Ruby, ed. A Casebook on Waiting for Godot.
Cohn, Ruby, ed. see Beckett, Samuel.
Cohn, Stanley H. Economic Development in the Soviet Union.
Cohn, Stanton H., jt. auth. see Smith, Wendy.
Cohn, William. Chinese Painting.
Cohoon, James P. Algorithms for Some Design Automation Problems. Stone, Harold, ed.
Coid, C. R. Infections & Pregnancy.
Coil, Henry W. Freemasonry Through Six Centuries.
Coit, Charles S. Introduction to Real Estate Law.
Coit, Margaret L. Andrew Jackson.
--Fight for Union.
Coke, Desmond. Art of Silhouette.
Coker, Carolyn. The Other David.
Coker, John B. & Martin, John P. Licensed to Live.
Colaianne, A. J. Piers Plowman: An Annotated Bibliography of Editions & Criticism, 1550-1977.
Colander, David C., jt. auth. see Lerner, Abba P.
Colander, David C., ed. Solutions to Inflation.
Colangelo, Nicholas, et al. Multicultural Nonsexist Education: A Human Relations Approach.
Colarusso, Calvin A. & Nemiroff, Robert A. Adult Development.
Colbert, Edwin. Dinosaurs of the Colorado Plateau.
Colbert, Edwin H. Age of Reptiles.
Colbert, J. C., ed. Modern Coating Technology: Radiation Curing, Electrostatic, Plasma, & Laser Methods.
Colbert, James. Profit & Sheen.
Colbert-Thornton, Mollie. God's Purpose for Man: The Spirit & the Flesh.
Colbourn, H. Trevor, ed. & intro. by see Adair, Douglass.
Colbourn, Trevor, jt. auth. see Bedford, Henry F.
Colbrunn, Ethel B., jt. auth. see Allen, Eliot D.
Colburn, Alan. Squash: The Ambitious Player's Guide.
Colburn, Bettye V. A Tapestry of Childhood.
Colburn, C. William, jt. auth. see Martin, Howard H.
Colby, C. B. Fighting Gear of World War One: Equipment & Weapons of the American Doughboy.
--Fighting Gear of World War Two: Equipment & Weapons of the American G. I.
Colby, John K. A Latin Crossword Puzzle Book.
Colby, Marvelle S. Test Your Management I. Q.
Colby, Marvelle S., jt. auth. see Straughn, Charles T.
Colchie, Thomas, tr. see Angelo, Ivan.
Colchie, Thomas, tr. see Rubiao, Murilo.
Colclasure, Chuck. Proverbs, God's Powerhouse of Wisdom.
Cold Spring Harbor Symposia on Quantitative Biology Staff. Heredity & Variation in Microorganisms: Proceedings.
--Nucleic Acids & Nucleoproteins: Proceedings.
Coldrey, C. Courses for Horses.
Coldsmith, Don. Medicine Knife.
--Return to the River.
--River of Swans.
Cole, Allison. Back Toward Lisbon.
Cole, B. R., jt. auth. see Hume-Rothery, W.
Cole, Babette. Nungu & the Hippopotamus.
--The Trouble with Mom.
Cole, Bill. John Coltrane.
--John Coltrane.
Cole, Bonnie C. see Tennessee. Supreme Court Staff & Michie Company Staff.
Cole, Brock. Alpha & the Dirty Baby.
--The Winter Wren.
Cole, C. Donald. Basic Christian Faith.
Cole, C. Robert & Moody, Michael E., eds. The Dissenting Tradition: Essays for Leland H. Carlson.
Cole, Charles L. Microeconomics: A Contemporary Approach.
Cole, David, ed. History of Rockland County N. Y.
Cole, David E., et al, eds. Strategic & Product Planning for the Automotive Industry.
Cole, David R. Helping: Origins & Development of the Major Psychotherapies.
Cole, Dermot, ed. Frank Barr, Bush Pilot in Alaska & the Yukon.
Cole, Don, ed. Economics 1988-89.
Cole, Donald W. Professional Suicide.
Cole, Elizabeth. Permanency Planning: Past, Present, & Future.
Cole, Evan T. Poems.
Cole, Everett B., jt. auth. see Pruett, Jakie L.
Cole, F. J. A History of Comparative Anatomy: From Aristotle to the Eighteenth Century.
Cole, G. H. An Introduction to the Statistical Theory of Classical Simple Dense Fluids.
Cole, G. H. & Watton, W. G. The Structure of Planets.
Cole, G. H., jt. auth. see Killingbeck, J.
Cole, George D. The British Co-operative Movement in a Socialist Society.
Cole, George F. Criminal Justice: Law & Politics.
Cole, George F., et al, eds. Major Criminal Justice Systems.
Cole, Gerald A. Textbook of Limnology.
Cole, H. A., ed. Petroleum & the Continental Shelf of North-West Europe: Environmental Protection.
Cole, Harry B. The British Labour Party: A Functioning Participatory Democracy.
Cole, Harry E. Stage Coach & Tavern Tales of the Old Northwest. Kellogg, Louise P., ed.
Cole, Henri. The Marble Queen.
Cole, Herbert. Heraldry & Floral Forms As Used in Decoration.
Cole, J. D., jt. auth. see Bluman, G. W.
Cole, J. P. The Development Gaps: A Spatial Analysis of World Poverty & Inequality.
Cole, Jack T., jt. auth. see Cole, Martha L.
Cole, Jacquelyn M. & Cole, Maurice F. Advisory Councils: A Theoretical & Practical Guide for Program Planners.
Cole, John W. & Wolf, Eric R. The Hidden Frontier: Ecology & Ethnicity in an Alpine Valley.
Cole, Johnathan O., jt. auth. see Evans, Wayne O.
Cole, Johnetta B., ed. Anthropology for the Eighties: Introductory Readings.
Cole, Margaret A. The Welsh Corgi.
Cole, Martha L. & Cole, Jack T. Effective Intervention with the Language Impaired Child.
Cole, Maurice F., jt. auth. see Cole, Jacquelyn M.
Cole, Michael, ed. The Selected Writings of A. R. Luria.
Cole, Richard C. Irish Booksellers & English Writers: 1740-1800.
Cole, Richard L. Introduction to Political Research.
Cole, Robert, jt. auth. see Stralen, D. Van.
Cole, Sam. Global Models & the International Economic Order.
Cole, Sam, ed. Models, Planning & Basic Needs: Conference on the Applicability of Global Modelling to Integrated Planning & Developing Countries.
Cole, Sandy, ed. see Grayson, Don, et al.
Cole, Sandy, ed. see Ives, Ronald, et al.
Cole, Sandy, ed. see Lee, James, et al.
Cole, Sonia. Leakey's Luck: The Life of Louis Seymour Bazett Leakey.
Cole, Stephen. The Sociological Method.
--The Sociological Orientation.
Cole, Terrence. E. T. Barnette: The Strange Story of the Man Who Founded Fairbanks.
Cole, Toby, ed. Florence: A Traveler's Anthology.
--Venice: A Portable Reader.
Cole, Wayne S. Senator Gerald P. Nye & American Foreign Relations.
Cole, William. A Boy Named Mary Jane, & Other Silly Verse.
--Give Up?
Cole, William & Thaler, Mike. Monster Knock Knocks.
Cole, William E., jt. auth. see Harris, Diana K.
Coleberd, Frances. Hidden Country Villages of California.
Colebourne, R., jt. auth. see Town, H. C.
Colebrook. Basic Mathematics for Radio & Electronics.
Coleman, jt. auth. see Gaines.
Coleman, Antony & Hammond, Antony, eds. Poetry & Drama, Fifteen Seventy to Seventeen Hundred: Essays in Honor of Harold F. Brooks.
Coleman, B. D. Money: How to Save It, Spend It, & Make It.
Coleman, B. D., ed. see CISM (International Center for Mechanical Sciences), Department of Mechanics of Solids Staff.
Coleman, B. D., et al. Wave Propagation in Dissipative Material: A Reprint of Five Memoirs.
Coleman, Bob. The Later Adventures of Tom Jones.
--The Small Business Survival Guide: A Handbook.
Coleman, Charles G. Divine Guidance: That Voice Behind You.
--Shining Sword.
Coleman, D. A., ed. Demography of Immigrants & Minority Groups in the United Kingdom.
Coleman, Dale & Naiman, Arthur. The Macintosh Bible.

Coleman, Daniel, ed. see American Health Magazine Editors, et al.
Coleman, David, jt. auth. see Gaines, George.
Coleman, David, jt. ed. see Sors, Andrew I.
Coleman, David S., jt. auth. see Gaines, George, Jr.
Coleman, Dorothy G., jt. ed. see Bayley, Peter.
Coleman, Elizabeth A. The Genius of Charles James.
Coleman, Francis X. The Harmony of Reason: A Study in Kant's Aesthetics.
Coleman, Freada A., jt. ed. see McDermott, Beatrice S.
Coleman, Gary J. How Great Will Be Your Joy!
Coleman, James C. & Butcher, James N. Abnormal Psychology & Modern Life.
Coleman, James S. Resources for Social Change: Race in the United States.
Coleman, James S., ed. Education & Political Development.
Coleman, John C. Nature of Adolescence.
Coleman, John C., ed. The School Years: Current Issues in the Socialization of Young People.
Coleman, Jonathan. At Mother's Request: A True Story of Money, Murder, & Betrayal.
Coleman, Joseph. TRS-80 Model 100: A User's Guide.
--Word Processing Simplified & Self-Taught.
Coleman, Jules & Paul, Ellen F., eds. Philosophy & Law.
Coleman, Laurence V. Historic House Museums.
Coleman, Lee. The Reign of Error: Psychiatry, Authority, & Law.
Coleman, Lonnie. Beulah Land.
Coleman, Lyman. Serendipity New Testament for Groups: New International Version.
Coleman, Patricia R., jt. auth. see Coleman, William V.
Coleman, Peter & Shrubb, Lee, eds. Quadrant: Twenty-Five Years.
Coleman, R. G. Ophiolites: Ancient Oceanic Lithosphere.
Coleman, Robert. The New Covenant.
Coleman, Robert E. Evangelism in Perspective.
--The Heartbeat of Evangelism.
Coleman, Stephen F. Streetcops.
Coleman, Thomas G., ed. Computer Simulation of Physiological Systems.
Coleman, Thomas R., ed. Abnormal Psychology.
Coleman, Thomas W. English Mystics of the Fourteenth Century.
Coleman, Vernon. A Guide to Child Health: A Practical Guide.
Coleman, William. Bouncing Back: Finding Acceptance in the Face of Rejection.
--How, Why, When, Where Book.
--How, Why, When, Where Book.
--Peter.
--The Who, What, When, Where Bible Busy Book.
--The Who, What, When, Where Book about the Bible.
Coleman, William L. Escucha a los Animales.
--Getting Ready for My First Day of School.
--Mi Maquina Maravillosa.
Coleman, William V. & Coleman, Patricia R. The Church.
--Jesus, Our Brother.
--The Saints: Heroes to Follow.
Coleman, William V. & McLemore, Patricia R. God Believes in Me, Director Guide.
Colenso, Frances E. History of the Zulu War & Its Origin.
Coleoni, Angelo. U. S. Interventions: A Brief History.
Coleridge, Christabel. Charlotte Mary Yonge, Her Life & Letters.
Coleridge, Henry N. Six Months in the West Indies in Eighteen Twenty-Five.
Coleridge, Nicholas. Around the World in Seventy-Eight Days.
Coleridge, Samuel Taylor. Philsophical Lectures (1818-19)
--Rime of the Ancient Mariner. Hallenborg, Walter, ed.
Colerus, Egmont. Mathematics for Everyman: From Simple Numbers to Calculus.
Coles, Adrian, jt. auth. see Boleat, Mark.
Coles, Clarence W. & Glenn, Harold T. Glenn's Complete Bicycle Manual: Selection, Maintenance, Repair.
Coles, G. H., jt. ed. see Porges, S. W.
Coles, H. M. Paediatrics.
Coles, John. Field Archaeology in Britain.
Coles, Manning. Drink to Yesterday.
Coles, Michael, et al. Psychophysiological Perspectives: Festchrift for Beatrice & John Lacey.
Coles, Robert. Erik Erikson: The Growth of His Work.
--Flannery O'Connor's South.
--Headsparks.
--The Old Ones of New Mexico.
Coles, Robert, et al. Drugs & Youth.
Coles, William A., ed. Classical America IV.
Coletta, Paolo E. The American Naval Heritage in Brief.
--The American Naval Heritage in Brief.
Colette. Betes Libres et Prisonnieres.
--Break of Day.
--Dialogues de Betes.
--Histoire et Absolu: Essai Sur Kierkegaard.
--Lettres a Helene Picard.
--Lettres a Marguerite Moreno.
--Lettres Au Petit Corsaire.
--My Apprenticeship. Beauclerk, Helen, tr. from Fr.
--Paris de ma Fenetre.
--The Pure & the Impure. Briffault, Herma, tr. from Fr.
--Ripening Seed. Senhouse, Roger, tr.
--Trois, Six, Neuf.
Colette, Sidonie G. La Maison de Claudine.
Coletti, Ralph M. Using the Timex-Sinclair 1000 & 1500.
Cole-Whittaker, Terry. The Inner Path from Where You Are to Where You Want to Be: A Spiritual Odyssey.
Coley, Betty A., ed. see Browning, Vivienne.
Colfer, George R. Handbook for Coaching Cross-Country & Running Events.
Colgan, Betsy & Johnson, Eleanor, eds. Directory of Editorial Resources, 1987-88.
Colgate, Craig & Evans, Laurie A., eds. National Recreational, Sporting & Hobby Organizations of the United States, 1981.
Colgate, Craig, Jr. & Evans, Laurie A., eds. National Recreational, Sporting & Hobby Organizations of the United States, 1982.
Colgate, Craig, Jr. & Freedman, Stephany J., eds. National Recreational Sporting & Hobby Organizations of the United States, 1983.
--National Recreational, Sporting & Hobby Organizations of the United States, 1984.
Colgate, Craig, Jr. & Germain, Regina, eds. National Recreational, Sporting & Hobby Organizations of the U. S., 1985.
Colgin, Mary L. Chants for Children.
Colimore, Vincent J., ed. Selected Readings in Modern Language Teaching.
Colin, ed. see Townsley, David & Bjork, Russell.
Colin, Jean L. The Transformations of War.
Colin, Paul & Lippman, Deborah. Craft Sources: The Ultimate Catalogue for Crafts People.
Colin, Paul, jt. auth. see Lippman, Deborah.
Colin, Sid. Ella: The Life & Times of Ella Fitzgerald.
Colina, Tessa. You & Me. Buerger, Jane, ed.
Colina, Tessa, jt. auth. see Moncure, Jane B.
Collacott, R. A. Mechanical Fault Diagnosis & Condition Monitoring.
Collard, David, ed. see Slater, Martin & Lecomber, Richard.
Collard, Jean, jt. auth. see Brannen, Julia.
Collatz, L. Numerical Treatment of Differential Equations.
Collective Editorial Staff. Critical Social Policy, Vol. 1.
Collective Work Staff. Forty-Fourth Electric Furnace Conference Proceedings.
Collectors Club Library Editors, New York. Philately: The Catalog of the Collectors Club Library.
College Board, College Scholarship Service. The College Cost Book, 1984-85.
College Board College Scholarship Service Staff. The College Cost Book, 1987-88.
College Board Staff. Index of Majors, 1984-85.
College Entrance Examination Board. The College Handbook, 1984-85.
College Scholarship Service of the College Board. The College Cost Book 1983-84.
Collet, P. & Eckmann, J. P. A Renormalization Group Analysis of the Hierarchical Model.
Collets Staff. Introducing the GDR.
Collett, George. Suzuki GT 380, 550 '72 - '77.
Collett, George & Witcomb, John. Honda 500 & 450 Twins '66 - '78.
Colletti, Anthony B. Cosmetology: The Keystone Guide to Beauty Culture.
Colley, Ann C. & Moore, Judith K. Starting with Poetry.
Colley, Iain. Dos Passos & the Fiction of Despair.
Colli, Carlo. The Spirit of Mornese.
Colliander, Tito. Way of the Ascetics: The Ancient Tradition of Discipline & Inner Growth.
Collias, Elsie C., jt. ed. see Collias, Nicholas E.
Collias, Nicholas E. & Collias, Elsie C., eds. External Construction by Animals.
Collie, M. J., ed. Corrosion Inhibitors: Developments since 1980.
--Etching Compositions & Processes.
--Extractive Metallurgy: Developments since 1980.
--Industrial Abrasive Materials & Compositions.
Collier, Ann. The Art of Lacemaking.
Collier, C. Patrick. Geometry for Teachers.
Collier, Francis, et al. Quantitative Laboratory Experiments in General Chemistry.
Collier, George. The Years & Me.
Collier, Gerald, ed. Evaluating the New Bed.
--The Management of Peer-Group Learning: Syndicate Methods in Higher Education.
Collier, Gordon, jt. auth. see Matthews, Julian.
Collier, Harry R., et al, eds. Electronic Publishing Review: The International Journal of the Transfer of Published Information via Videotex & Online Media.
Collier, Herbert L. Homework: How to Study & Remember.
--What's Psychotherapy...& Who Needs It?
Collier, J. W. Wood Finishing.
Collier, James L. The Making of Jazz: A Comprehensive History.
Collier, Keith. Fundamentals of Construction Estimating & Cost Accounting.
Collier, Peter & Horowitz, David. The Kennedys: An American Drama.
Collier, Peter, ed. Dilemmas of Democracy: Readings in American Government.
Collier, Peter, jt. ed. see Chace, William.
Collier, Richard. The Freedom Road: 1944-1945.
--The Rainbow People: A Gaudy World of the Very Rich & Those Who Serve Them.
--The Road to Pearl Harbor: Nineteen Forty-One.
Collier, Richard B. Pleneurethic: A World Class Philosophy.
--Pleneurethic: Its Evolution & Scientific Basis.
--Pleneurethic: Way of Life, System of Therapeutics.
Collier, Rod. The Ecology of Steak & Eggs: A Homo Sapiens' Viewpoint.
Colligan, Douglas. Creative Insomnia.
Collignon, Jean, ed. see Mauriac, Francois.
Colligon, J. S., ed. Directory of Manufacturers of Vacuum Plant, Components & Associated Equipment in the U. K., 1982.
Collin, David R. The One Bad Thing about Birthdays.
--The One Bad Thing about Birthdays.
Collin, Rodney. The Mirror of Light.
--The Theory of Celestial Influence: Man, The Universe, & Cosmic Mystery.
--The Theory of Eternal Life.
Colling, Gene. The Bicyclist's Guide to Yellowstone National Park.
Colling, Susan. Frogmorton.
Collings, Ellsworth & England, Alma. The One Hundred & One Ranch.
Collings, Judith, jt. auth. see Collings, Michael.
Collings, Merle D. Projects in Electricity.
Collings, Michael. Season of Calm Weather.
Collings, Michael & Collings, Judith. Whole Wheat Harvest-Recipes for Unground Wheat.
Collingwood, Peter. Techniques of Rug Weaving.
Collingwood, Robin G. Outlines of a Philosophy of Art.
Collins, et al. Aleutian Islands: Their People & Natural History.
--Business Law.
--Handbook for Dental Hygienists.
Collins, A. Frederick. Rapid Math Without a Calculator.
Collins, A. J. Manuale ad usum percelebris ecclesie Sarisburensis.
Collins, Adela Y. & Rice, Charles. Pentecost Two.
Collins, Anthony. A Discourse on the Grounds & Reasons of the Christian Religion. Wellek, Rene, ed.
Collins, Arthur & Collins, Michael. Finder's Keepers.
Collins, Barbara J. Keys to Costal & Chaparral Flowering Plants of Southern California.
Collins, Barry E., ed. Public & Private Conformity: Competing Explanations by Improvisation, Cognitive Dissonance & Attribution Theories.
Collins, Bruce, jt. ed. see Jeffreys-Jones, Rhodri.
Collins, C. C., jt. ed. see Bach-Y-Rita, Paul.
Collins, Carol C., ed. Black Progress: Reality or Illusion.
Collins, Charles, jt. auth. see Doucette, Joseph.
Collins, Charles M. A Feast of Blood.
--Harvest of Fear.
Collins, Charles M., ed. A Walk with the Beast.
Collins, Christiane C., jt. auth. see Collins, George R.
Collins, Colette. Touched by Diamonds.
Collins, D. Aspects of British Politics, 1904-1919.
Collins, D. H., ed. Power Sources Five: Research & Development in Non-Mechanical Electrical Power Sources.
--Power Sources Six.
--Power Sources Two: Proceedings, International Symposium on Batteries, 6th.
Collins, Dan S. Andrew Marvell: A Reference Guide.
Collins, David & Witter, Evelyn. The Golden Circle.
Collins, David R. Super Champ.
Collins, Doreen. The Operation of the European Social Fund.
Collins, Eliza G. Going, Going, Gone: A Mystery Introducing Helen Greene.
Collins, Emily C., jt. auth. see Karnes, Frances A.
Collins, Floyd. Scarecrow.
Collins, Frank A. Bits O' This & That.
Collins, Gary. Beyond Easy Believism.
--The Hour Magazine Cookbook.
--The Hour Magazine Cookbook.
Collins, Gary R. The Magnificent Mind.
--The Sixty-Second Christian.
Collins, Gary R., et al. Changes: Becoming the Best You Can Be. Resnik, Hank, ed.
Collins, George R. & Collins, Christiane C. Camillo Sitte: The Birth of Modern City Planning.
Collins, George R. see O'Neal, William B.
Collins, H. M. & Pinch, T. J. Frames of Meaning: The Social Construction of Extraordinary Science.
Collins, Henry H. & Boyajian, Ned R. Familiar Garden Birds of America: An Illustrated Guide to the Birds in Your Own Backyard.
Collins, Jackie. Hollywood Wives.
--Lucky: A Novel.
Collins, Joan. Past Imperfect: An Autobiography.
Collins, Jodie. Codeword: Catherine.
Collins, John G. Types of Injuries & Impairments Due to Injuries, United States.
Collins, John J. Primitive Religion.
Collins, Joseph, jt. auth. see Lappe, Frances M.
Collins, Joseph, jt. auth. see Lappe, Francis M.
Collins, Joseph T., ed. see Clark, Tim W. & Stromberg, Mark S.
Collins, Judy. Judy Collins Song Book.
Collins, Larry. Fall from Grace.
Collins, Leighton. Takeoffs & Landings.
Collins, M. B., et al, eds. Industrialised Embayments & Their Environmental Problems - a Case Study of Swansea Bay: Proceedings of an Interdisciplinary Symposium Held at University College, Swansea, 26-28 Sept. 1979.
Collins, Marilyn C. Child Abuser: A Study of Child Abusers in Self-Help Group Therapy.
Collins, Marjorie A. Manual for Missionaries on Furlough.
Collins, Max A. The Dark City.
--Midnight Haul.
Collins, Meghan R. Maiden Crown.
Collins, Michael. Freak.
Collins, Michael, jt. auth. see Bullard, Scott R.
Collins, Michael, jt. auth. see Collins, Arthur.
Collins, Norman. The Husband's Story.
Collins, Patrick. Living in Troubled Lands: The Complete Guide to Personal Security Abroad.
Collins, Philip, ed. Dickens: Interviews & Recollections.
Collins, Randall & Markel, Geraldine. Sociology of Marriage & Family: Gender, Love & Property.
Collins, Raymond A., ed. The GIANT Handbook of Electronic Circuits.
Collins, Raymond F. Christian Morality: Biblical Foundations.
--Introduction to the New Testament.
Collins, Robert F. Basic Training: What to Expect & How to Prepare. Rosen, Ruth, ed.
Collins, Robert O. & Nash, Roderick. The Big Drops: Ten Legendary Rapids.
Collins, Shelia, jt. auth. see Golden, Renny.
Collins Staff. Collins French-English Dictionary.
Collins, Stanley N. Man's Only Hope: A Study of the Life & Ministry of Jesus Christ.
Collins, Stephanie. A Page a Day Advent & the Christmas Season, 1988.
--A Page a Day for the Advent & the Christmas Season, 1987.
Collins, Susan B. Ohio Bank Law & Regulation Manual.
Collins, T. & Bruce, T. Staff Support & Staff Training.
Collins, Val. Microwave Fish Cookbook.
--The Microwave Fruit & Vegetable Cookbook.
Collins, Vere H. A Book of English Proverbs, with Origins & Explanations.
Collins, Vincent J. Principles of Anesthesiology.
Collins, Wilkie. Woman in White.
--Woman in White. Tillotson, Kathleen, ed.
--The Woman in White: T. V. Edition. Symons, Julian, ed.
Collins, William, jt. auth. see Holstrum, Gary L.
Collins, William C. Collins: Correctional Law 1987.
Collinson, Francis. The Traditional & National Music of Scotland.
Collinson, Patrick. The Elizabethan Puritan Movement.
Collis, Kevin F. Language Development & Intellectual Functioning.
Collis, Maurice. Cortez & Montezuma.
--Foreign Mud: The Opium Imbroglio at Canton in the 1830's & the Anglo-Chinese War.
Collison, Mary, jt. auth. see Collison, Robert.
Collison, R. L. A History of Foreign-Language Dictionaries.
Collison, Robert. Dictionary of Dates & Anniversaries.
Collison, Robert & Collison, Mary. Dictionary of Foreign Quotations.
Collison, Robert L. Library Assistance to Readers.
Collister, Edward A. The Preservation & Restoration of Library Materials: A Basic & Practical Reading List.
Collmer, H., ed. see Huygens, L., et al.
Collmer, H., tr. see Huygens, L., et al.
Collodi, C., pseud. The Adventures of Pinocchio: Tale of a Puppet. Rosenthal, M. L., tr.
Collodi, Carlo. Adventures of Pinocchio.
Collomb, R. G. Dictionary of Mountaineering.
Collons, Roger D., ed. see Del Mar, Donald.

Colloque Sur la Programmation, Paris, 9-11 April, 1974. Programming Symposium: Proceedings. Robinet, B., ed.
Colloquium of Linguistics Association of Great Britain, Historical Section, University of London Staff. Hamito-Semitica: Proceedings of the Colloquium of the Linguistics Association of Great Britian, Historical Section, Univsity of London, March 18-20, 1970. Bynon, James & Bynon, Theodora, eds.
Colloquium of the Gesellschaft Fuer Biologische Chemie Staff. Molecular Basis of Motility: Proceedings of the Colloquium of the Gesellschaft fuer Biologische Chemie, 26th, Mosbach, Baden, Germany, April 10-12, 1975. Heilmeyer, L., ed.
Colloquium on Automata, Languages & Programming, 2nd, University of Saarbrucken, 1974. Proceedings. Loeckx, J., ed.
Colls, Robert, jt. ed. see Dodd, Philip.
Collyer, Roxanne M. Poems of the Soul & the Sprit.
Collymore, Peter. The Architecture of Ralph Erskine.
Colman. Triangle of Love.
Colman, A. Game Theory & Experimental Games: The Study of Strategic Interaction.
Colman, Bernard H., jt. auth. see Hall, Ian S.
Colman, Carol & Perelman, Michael. Late Bloomers: How to Achieve Your Potential at Any Age.
Colman, E. A., ed. King Lear.
Colman, George the Younger. The Plays of George Colman, the Younger. Tasch, Peter A., ed.
Colman, Hila. Family Trap.
--Hanging on.
--My Friend, My Love.
--What's the Matter with the Dobsons.
Colman-Porter, C. A. Science for Chemical Process Operators.
Colmer, John. E. M. Forster: The Personal Voice.
--E. M. Forster: The Personal Voice.
--Patrick White.
Colmer, Michael. The Stars & Your Baby.
Colmjon, Godert van see Schampers, Karel & Van Colmjon, Godert.
Colmore, Gertrude. Suffragettes: Sally.
Colodny, Robert G. The Struggle for Madrid: The Central Epic of the Spanish Conflict, 1936-1937.
Colodny, Robert G., ed. Frontiers of Science & Philosophy.
--Logic, Laws, & Life: Some Philosophical Complications.
Colombo, F., et al, eds. Epidemiological Evaluation of Drugs.
Colombo, John R. Windigo: An Anthology of Fact & Fantastic Fiction.
Colonial Williamsburg Foundation Staff. The Williamsburg Collection of Antique Furnishing.
Colonnese, Tom & Owens, Louis. Native American Indian Novelists: An Annotated Critical Bibliography.
Colorado School of Mines Editors. Subject Catalogue of the Arthur Lakes Library of the Colorado School of Mines.
Colosi, Thomas R. & Berkeley, Arthur E. Collective Bargaining: How It Works & Why: A Manual of Theory & Practice.
Colosi, Thomas R., jt. auth. see American Arbitration Association Staff.
Colowick, Sidney P., et al, eds. Glutathione: A Symposium.
Colquhoun, A., tr. see Lampedusa, Giuseppe Di.
Colquhoun, Archibald, tr. see Manzoni, Alessandro.
Colquhoun, Frank. Family Prayers.
Colquhoun, W. P., ed. Biological Rhythms & Human Performance.
Colson, Charles, et al. Christianity in Conflict: The Struggle for Christian Integrity & Freedom in Secular Culture. Williamson, Peter S. & Perrotta, Kevin, eds.
Colson, John C. Academic Ambitions & Library Development: The American Bureau of Industrial Research & the State Historical Society of Wisconsin, 1904-18.
Colston, Lowell G. Pastoral Care with Handicapped Persons. Clinebell, Howard J. & Stone, Howard W., eds.
Colston, Stephanie, jt. auth. see Carr, T. R.
Colter, Janet, jt. auth. see Colter, Rudyard.
Colter, John S. & Paranchych, William. Molecular Biology of Viruses.
Colter, Rudyard & Colter, Janet. Favorite Vermont Ski Inns & Lodging Guide.
Coltheart, Max, et al, eds. Deep Dyslexia.
--Deep Dyslexia.
Coltman, Derek, tr. see Pierrot, Jean.
Coltman, M. Cost Control for Hospitality Industry.
--Hospitality Management Account.
Coltman, Michael M. Buying & Selling a Small Business.
--Cost Control for the Hospitality Industry.
--Franchising in the U. S. Pros & Cons.
--Hospitality Management Accounting.
Colton, Calvin. The Life & Times of Henry Clay.
Colton, Timothy J. The Dilemma of Reform in the Soviet Union.
Colum, Padraic, ed. Anthology of Irish Verse: The Poetry of Ireland from Mythological Times to the Present.
Columbe, Bob. Honeymooners Illustrated Trivia.
Columbia University College of Physicians & Surgeons Staff. The Columbia University College of Physicians & Surgeons Complete Home Medical Guide.
Columbia University, East Asian Library Staff. Index to Learned Chinese Periodicals.
Columbia University Editors. Avery Index to Architectural Periodicals.
--Avery Index to Architectural Periodicals, First Supplement.
--Avery Index to Architectural Periodicals: Third Supplement.
--Catalog of the Avery Memorial Architectural Library.
--Catalogue of the Avery Memorial Architectural Library, First Supplement.
--Catalogue of the Avery Memorial Architectural Library, Second Edition, Fourth Supplement.
--Cataloue of the Avery Memorial Architectural Library, Columbia University, Second Supplement.
--Dictionary Catalogue of the Teachers College Library.
--Dictionary Catalogue of the Teachers College Library, First Supplement.
--Dictionary Catalogue of the Teachers College Library, Second Supplement.
Columbia University Law Library, New York Staff. Dictionary Catalogue of the Columbia University Law Library, First Supplement.
Columbia University Law Library Staff. Dictionary Catalogue of the Columbia University Law Library.
Columbia University, New York Staff. Cumulative Author Index to Psychological Index, 1894 to 1935, & Psychological Abstracts, 1927 to 1958.
Columbia University Staff. Spinoza Bibliography. Oko, Adolph S., compiled by.
Columbia University, Teachers College Library Staff. Dictionary Catalogue of the Teachers College Library, Columbia University Third Supplement.
Columbu, Franco, et al. Weight Training for Young Athletes.
Colver, Anne. Bread-&-Butter Indian.
--Bread & Butter Journey.
Colvert, James B. Stephen Crane.
--Stephen Crane.
Colville, John. The Fringes of Power: Ten Downing Street Diaries, 1939-1955.
Colvin, F. H. Machinist Dictionary.
Colvin, Geoffrey, jt. auth. see Prendergast, Curtis.
Colvin, Ian. Chamberlain Cabinet: How the Meetings in 10 Downing Street, 1937-9, Led to the Second World War.
Colvin, Robert, et al. Keeping It off: Winning at Weight Loss.
Colvin, Ruth J. I Speak English.
Colvin, Ruth J. & Root, Jane. Tutor. Lawson, V. K. & Carlin, Chip, eds.
Colvin, Thomas E. Cruising Designs from the Board of Thomas E. Colvin.
Colwell, A. R., Jr. Understanding Your Diabetes.
Colwell, Eileen. Round about & Long Ago.
Colwell, Stella. Tracing Your Family Tree.
Colwin, Laurie. Another Marvelous Thing.
--Family Happiness.
--Passion & Affect.
Colyer, Penrose. I Can Read Spanish.
Coman. Endless Adventure.
Coman, Dale R. Pleasant River.
Comaromi, John P. & Warren, Margaret J. Dewey Decimal Classification: Manual on the Use of the DDC: Edition 19.
Combe, E. C. Notes on Dental Materials.
Comber, Leon. Favourite Stories from Asia.
--Further Favourite Stories from Asia.
--More Favourite Chinese Stories.
--More Favourite Stories from Asia.
Comber, Leon & Shuttleworth, Charles. Favourite Stories from Taiwan.
Comber, Leon, retold by. Favourite Chinese Stories.
--Favourite Stories from Borneo.
--Favourite Stories from Hong Kong.
--Favourite Stories from Malaysia.
--Favourite Stories from the Philippines.
Combinational Theory Seminar Staff. Proceedings of the Combinational Theory Seminar, Eindhoven University of Technology. Van Lint, J. H., ed.
Comblin, Jose. Sent from the Father: Meditations on the Fourth Gospel. Kabat, Carl, tr. from Port.
Combs, Alec. Hearing Loss Help: How You Can Help Someone with Hearing Loss & How They Can Help Themselves.
Combs, Ann. We'll Laugh about This... Someday.
Combs, Arthur W. & Avila. Perspectives on Helping Relationships.
Combs, Arthur W., et al. Humanistic Education: Objectives & Assessment.
Combs, David. Sleepwalker.
--The Surrogate.
Combs, Harry B. & Caidin, Martin. Kill Devil Hill: Discovering the Secret of the Wright Brothers.
Combs, Helen H. The Longest Living Snowflake: A Story in Verse for Children.
Combs, Homer C., ed. see Donne, John.
Combs, Roger. Holsters & Other Gun Leather: Gun Digest Bk.
Comeau, Raymond F. & Lamoureux, Normand J. Echanges.
Comeau, Raymond F., et al. Ensemble: Culture et Societe.
--Ensemble: Grammaire.
--Ensemble: Literature.
Comes, Natalis. Mythologiae.
Comici, Luciano. The Heart Is No Stranger.
Comins, N. R. & Clark, J. B., eds. Specialty Steels & Hard Materials: Proceedings of the International Conference (Materials Development '82), Pretoria, South Africa, 9-12 November 1982.
Comiskey, Kate, ed. see Baird, Chuck, et al.
Comiskey, Kate, ed. see Blattner, John W., et al.
Comiskey, Kate, ed. see Blechman, Fred, et al.
Comiskey, Kate, ed. see Domuret, Allan J., et al.
Comiskey, Kate, jt. ed. see Putnam, Katherine.
Comito, Terry. The Idea of the Garden in the Renaissance.
Commager, Henry S. & Doherty, Stephen M., eds. The American Spirit.
Commager, Henry Steele & Ward, Lynd. America's Robert E. Lee.
Commager, Steele, ed. see Bae Hrens, Aemilius.
Commager, Steele, ed. see Bridges, Robert, et al.
Commager, Steele, ed. see Brinton, Anna C.
Commager, Steele, ed. see Daryusl, A. A., et al.
Commager, Steele, ed. see Deutsch, Rosamund E.
Commager, Steele, ed. see Fowler, H. W., et al.
Commager, Steele, ed. see Lier, Bruno, et al.
Commager, Steele, ed. see Lilja, Saara.
Commager, Steele, ed. see Onions, C. T., et al.
Commager, Steele, ed. see Robinson, Ellis.
Commager, Steele, ed. see Smith, Logan P., et al.
Commager, Steele, ed. see Sparrow, John.
Commager, Steele, ed. see Wagenvoort, Hendrik.
Commager, Steele, ed. see Winbolt, Samuel E.
Commercial Trades Institute Staff. Automatic Transmissions.
Commision International de Redaccion & Ibarruri, Dolores. La Solidaridad de los Pueblos con la Republica Espanola 1936-1939.
Commission for Investigation of Health Hazards of Chemical Compounds in the Work Area Staff. Maximum Concentrations at the Workplace & Biological Tolerance Values for Working Materials 1983.
Commission of Architecture of AEA. Architecture for Adult Education.
Commission of the European Communities, jt. ed. see Amavis, R.
Commission of the European Communities, Luxembourg. Fusion Technology Nineteen Seventy-Eight: Proceedings.
--Fusion Technology: Proceedings of the 11th Symposium, Oxford, England, Sept. 15-19, 1980.
Commission of the European Communities, Luxembourg, ed. Fusion Technology: Proceedings of the 12th Symposium (SOFT), Julich Laboratory, Federal Republic of Germany, 13-17 Setember 1982.
Commission of the European Communities, Joint Varenna-Grenoble International Symposium on Heating in Toroidal Plasmas, Grenoble, July 1978. Heating in Toroidal Plasmas: Proceedings.
Commission of the European Communities. Law & Practice Relating to Pollution Control in the Member States of the European Communities: Italy.
Commission of the European Communities, et al, eds. New Technologies for the Exploration & Exploitation of Oil & Gas Resources.
Commission of the European Communities. Plasma Wall Interaction: Proceedings of the International Symposium EUR 5782e, Kernsfoschungsanlage Julich, 1976.
--Public Health Risks of Exposure to Asbestos. Zielhuis, R. L., ed.
Commission on Cancer Control, Cancer Detection Committee. Cancer Detection.
Commission on Chicago Historical & Architectural Landmarks. Landmark Neighborhoods in Chicago.
Commission on Engineering & Technical Systems, National Research Council. Toward Safer Underground Coal Mines.
Commission on English Staff, ed. Twelve Thousand Students & Their English Teachers: Tested Units in Teaching Literature, Language, Composition.
Committe, Thomas C., et al. Managerial Finance for the Seventies.
Committee for Corporate Responsibility, Stanford University. Corporations & the Environment: How Should Decisions Be Made?
Committee on Classroom Practices Staff & Golub, Jeff. Classroom Practices in Teaching English: Activities to Promote Critical Thinking in English, 1986.
Committee on Pattern Jury Charges. Texas Pattern Jury Charges: (Workmen's Compensation), 1976 Cumulative Supplement.
Committee on Pattern Jury Charges of the State Bar of Texas. Texas Pattern Jury Charges.
Commoner, Barry. The Failure of the Environmental Movement.
Commoner, Barry, ed. see Brodine, Virginia.
Commoner, Barry, ed. see McCaull, Julian & Crossland, Janice.
Commonwealth Relations Office, Great Britain Staff. Catalogue of European Printed Books, India Office Library.
--Index of Post-Nineteen Thirty Seven European Manuscript Accessions. India Office Library.
Commonwealth Scientific & Industrial Research Organization, Australia Staff, ed. Soils: An Australian View Point.
Communications Library Staff. BCTV: Bibliography on Cable Television 1983.
--CINCOM: Courses in Communications - 1987.
--Cincom: Courses in Communications, 1985.
Communist Labor Party of America Staff. Communist: Series 1 & 2.
--National Issues: A Survey of Politics & Legislation.
--Revolutionary Age (Weekly Organ of the Communist Party U. S. A., Majority Group)
Community Kitchens Staff. The Community Kitchens' Complete Guide to Gourmet Coffee.
Compaine, Benjamin M. & Litro, Robert F. Business: An Introduction.
Compass, jt. auth. see Assecuranz.
Comprone, Joseph J. From Experience to Expression: A College Rhetoric.
Compton & Ellis. Leisure & the American Dream.
Compton, Beulah R. Introduction to Social Welfare & Social Work: Structure, Function, & Process.
Compton, Beulah R. & Galaway, Burt. Social Work Processes.
Compton, James V., ed. America & the Origins of the Cold War.
Compton, Norma & Hall, Olive. Foundation of Home Economics Research: A Human Ecology Approach.
Compton, Rae. Complete Book of Traditional Knitting.
Compton, Robert R. Interpreting the Earth.
Compton-Burnett, I. The Mighty & Their Fall.
--Pastors & Masters.
Compton-Burnett, Ivy. Darkness & Day.
--Two Worlds & Their Ways.
Compute! Magazine Staff, ed. Compute's First Book of Atari Games.
--Compute's First Book of PET-CBM.
--Compute's Second Book of Atari.
--Compute's VIC-20 Collection.
Compute! Magazine Staff & Regena, C., eds. Compute's First Book of TI Games.
Compute! Magazine Staff, ed. see Kidd, Clark & Kidd, Kathy H.
Compute! Magazine Staff, ed. see Levitan, Arlan R. & Leemon, Sheldon.
Compute! Magazine Staff, ed. see Mansfield, Richard, et al.
Compute! Magazine Staff, ed. see Standage, Blaine D., et al.
Compute! Publications, Inc. Staff, ed. see Carlson, Edward H.
Compute! Publications, Inc. Staff, ed. see Chamberlain, Craig.
Computer Center of Muenster University with Collaboration of H. Bachmann & W. A. Slaby, jt. ed. see Institute for New Testament Textural Research.
Computer Consultants Ltd. European Computer Survey Nineteen Sixty-Eight to Nineteen Sixty-Nine.
--European Computer Survey Nineteen Sixty-Nine to Seventy.
--European Computer Users Handbook, 1969-70.
Computer Law Institute Staff & ALI-ABA, Committee on Continuing Professional Education. Acquiring & Serving Computer Clients.
Computer Partners, Inc. Handbook of COBOL Techniques & Programming Standards.
Computer Partners, Inc. Staff. Handbook of COBOL Techniques.
Computer Resources International Staff, ed. The CRI Directory of Expert Systems.
Computers in Aerodynamics Symposium Staff. Computers in Aerodynamics: Proceedings of the Symposium, Polytechnic Institute of New York, Aerodynamics Laboratories, 1979. Rubin, S. G. & Bloom, M. H., eds.
Comroe, Julius H., Jr. Exploring the Heart: Discoveries in Heart Disease & High Blood Pressure.
Comstock, John H. Spider Book. Gertsch, W. J., ed.

Comstock, M. B. & Vermeule, C. C. Sculpture in Stone: Museum of Fine Arts Boston.
Comte, Edward Le see Le Comte, Edward.
Comtex Staff. Artificial Intelligence Reports from Bolt, Beranek & Newman.
--Artificial Intelligence Reports from Carnegie Mellon University.
--Artificial Intelligence Reports from Carnegie Mellon University.
--Artificial Intelligence Reports from Carnegie Mellon University.
--Artificial Intelligence Reports from the University of Pennsylvania.
--Artificial Intelligence Reports from Yale University.
Comyn, J. & Johnson, R. Wills & Intestacies.
Conaghan, John, ed. Dryden: A Selection.
Conahan, Judith M. Helping Your Elderly Patients: A Guide for Nursing Assistants.
Conant, James C. All Dreams Never Die.
Conant, Robert, jt. auth. see Bedford, Frances.
Conard, Alfred F., et al. Enterprise Organization: Cases, Statutes & Analysis on Licensing, Employment, Agency, Partnerships, Associations, & Corporations.
--Agency, Associations, Employment, Licensing & Partnerships: Cases, Statutes & Analysis.
Conaway, James. The Kingdom in the Country.
Conaway, Judith. The Discovery Book of Size.
--The Discovery Book of up & Down.
Concannon, Joe, jt. auth. see Rodgers, Bill.
Concha, Joseph. Chokecherry Hunters & Other Poems.
Concone, J. Twenty-Five Easy & Progressive Melodic Studies for Piano. Eckstein, Maxwell, ed.
Conde Nast, ed. see Bride's Magazine Editors.
Conder, Susan. Terence Coran's Decorating with Plants.
Condie, Carol J. & Fowler, Don D., eds. Anthropology of the Desert West: Essays in Honor of Jesse D. Jennings.
Condit, Carl W. Chicago. Incl. Nineteen Ten to Nineteen Twenty-Nine - Building, Planning, & Urban Technology; Nineteen Thirty to Nineteen Seventy - Building, Planning & Urban Technology. U of Chicago Pr.
--The Pioneer Stage of Railroad Electrification.
Condit, Kay, ed. see Owen, Ray.
Condominas, Georges. We Have Eaten the Forest: The Story of a Montagnard Village in the Central Highlands of Vietnam. Foulke, Adrienne, tr. from Fr.
Condon, Arnold & Lloyd, Alan C. Transcribing Speed Studies.
Condon, Arnold, et al. Transcription Thirty-Six.
Condon, Dave, et al. Notre Dame Football: The Golden Tradition.
Condon, Richard. Inuit Youth: Growth & Change in the Canadian Arctic.
--Prizzi's Family.
Condon, Robert E. & Nyhus, Lloyd M. Manual of Surgical Therapeutics.
Condon, Robert E. & De Cosse, Jerome J., eds. Surgical Care I: A Physiologic Approach to Clinical Management.
Condry, Dorothea. The Latter Days.
Condry, William. Thoreau.
Cone, Edward T., jt. ed. see Boretz, Benjamin.
Cone, Ferne G. Crazy Crocheting.
--Knit with Style.
Cone, Molly. Annie Annie.
--Call Me Moose.
--Crazy Mary.
--Mishmash & the Substitute Teacher.
--Mishmash & The Venus Flytrap.
--Number Four.
--Other Side of the Fence.
--Promise Is a Promise.
--Reeney.
--Simon.
Cone, Polly, ed. see Harper, Prudence O. & Meyers, Pieter.
Cone, Poly, et al, eds. see Ettesvold, Paul M.
Conel, J. LeRoy. Life as Revealed by the Microscope.
Coney, Michael. The Celestial Steam Locomotive.
--Gods of the Greataway.
Confer, Grayce. Faith & Fried Potatoes.
Conference Held at Battelle Seattle Research Center, 1975. Structural Stability, the Theory of Catastrophes, & Applications in the Sciences: Proceedings. Hilton, P., et al, eds.
Conference Held at the Univ. of Paris-Sud, Orsay, 12-13 June 1975. Turbulence & Navier Stokes Equations: Proceedings. Temam, R. M., ed.
Conference of ASME, 1976. Present Status & Research Needs in Energy Recovery from Wastes: Proceedings. Matula, Richard A., ed.
Conference of the British Educational Research Association 1980. Microcomputers in Secondary Education: Proceedings. Howe, Jim & Ross, Peter, eds.
Conference of U.S. Schools of Pharmacy, Oct. 1975. Guidelines for Pharm.D Programs.
Conference on Aerospace Adhesives & Elastomers, NSTC 2, Dallas, Texas, Oct. 6-8, 1970. Proceedings.
Conference on Applications of Numerical Analysis, Dundee, Scotland, 1971. Proceedings. Morris, J. L., ed.
Conference on Blood Viscosity in Heart Disease, Thromboembolism & Cancer, Sydney Australia, May, 1978. Health Needs & Health Services in Rural Ghana. De Kadt, E., et al, eds.
Conference On Categorical Algebra - La Jolla - 1965. Proceedings. Eilenberg, S., et al, eds.
Conference on Commutative Algebra. Proceedings. Brewer, J. W. & Rutter, E. A., eds.
Conference on Federal Taxation & Land Use. Proceedings.
Conference on Graph Theory Staff. Graph Theory & Applications: Proceedings of Conference on Graph Theory, Western Michigan University, Kalamazoo, 1972. Alavi, Y., et al, eds.
Conference on Hyperfunctions & Pseudo-Differential Equations Staff. Proceedings of Conferenceon Hyperfunctions, Katata, 1971. Komatsu, H., ed.
Conference on K-Theory & Operator Algebras, University of Georgia, Athens, Ga., Apr. 21-25, 1975. K-Theory & Operator Algebras: Proceedings. Morrel, B. B. & Singer, I. M., eds.
Conference on Local Fields - NUFFIC Summer School - Driebergen - 1966. Proceedings. Springer, T. A., ed.
Conference on Numerical Solution of Ordinary Differential Equations. Proceedings. Bettis, D. G., ed.
Conference on Operator Theory, Dalhousie Univ., Halifax, 1973. Proceedings. Fillmore, P. A., ed.
Conference on Optimization Techniques, 5th. Proceedings. Ruberti, A., ed.
--Proceedings. Ruberti, A., ed.
Conference on Origins of Life, 3rd, California, 1970. Planetary Astronomy: Proceedings. Margulis, L., ed.
Conference on Plant Growth Substances, 9th. Plant Growth Regulation: Proceedings.
Conference on Race Relations in World Perspective, Honolulu, 1954. Race Relations in World Perspective: Papers. Lind, Andrew W., ed.
Conference on Recombinant DNA, Committee on Genetic Experimentation (COGENE) & the Royal Society of London, Wye College, Kent, UK, April, 1979. Recombinant DNA & Genetic Experimentation: Proceedings. Morgan, Joan & Whelan, W. J., eds.
Conference on Science-Philosophy & Religion in Their Religion to the Democratic Way of Life, 17th New York. Ethics & Bigness: Proceedings.
Conference on Science-Philosophy & Religion in Their Relation to the Democratic Way of Live, 12th, New York. Freedom & Authority in Our Time: Proceeding.
Conference on the Public Land Law Review Commission Report, Dec. 1970. America's Public Lands: Politics, Economics, & Administration. Nathan, Harriet, ed.
Confino, Michael. Daughter of a Revolutionary: Natalie Herzen & the Bakunin-Nechayev Circle.
Conford, Ellen. Anything for a Friend.
--Eugene the Brave.
--Hail, Hail, Camp Timberwood.
--Impossible Possum.
--The Luck of Pokey Bloom.
--Me & the Terrible Two.
Conforti, Michael, et al. English Ceramics from Northern California Collections.
Confucius. Confucian Analects, the Great Learning & the Doctrine of the Mean. Legge, James, tr.
--Wisdom of Confucius.
Cong, Ding. Wit & Humour from Ancient China: One Hundred Cartoons by Ding Cong. Mingtong, Ma, tr. from Chinese.
Congdon, Don. Combat WW II: Pacific.
Congdon, Don, ed. Combat World War II. Incl. European Theater of Operations; Pacific Theater of Operations. Morrow.
Conger, Amy. Edward Weston in Mexico: Nineteen Twenty-Three to Nineteen Twenty-Six.
Conger, Amy, jt. ed. see Newhall, Beaumont.
Conger, Shirley & Moore, Kay. Social Work in Long-Term Care Facilities.
Congo, David & Congo, Janet. Less Stress.
Congo, Janet, jt. auth. see Congo, David.
Congress of Illinois Historical Societies & Museums. Historical & Cultural Agencies & Museums in Illinois, 1985.
Congressional Quarterly Inc. Staff. Congressional Roll Call, 1977.
--Congressional Roll Call 1979.
Congressional Quarterly, Inc. Staff. Federal Regulatory Directory: 1983-1984.
--National Party Conventions 1831-1980.
--Presidential Elections since 1789.
--Regulation: Process & Politics.
--State Politics & Redistricting.
--Supreme Court & Individual Rights.
--Supreme Court, Justice & the Law.
--Washington Information Directory, 1984-85.
--Washington Information Directory, 1985-86.
--Washington Information Directory 1986-87.
--Washington Information Directory 1987-88.
--The Washington Lobby.
Congreve, William. Love for Love. Avery, Emmett L., ed.
Coni, et al. The Geriatric Prescriber.
Coniglio, Jamie W. Decentralization of Municipal Services: A Selected Bibliography.
--Marketing & the Small Design Firm: A Selected Checklist of Resources.
--Neighborhood Associations: A Selected Checklist.
--Performance Measurement & Municipalities: A Selected Bibliography.
--Private Consultants & Municipalities: A Selected Checklist.
--Richard Meier, Architect: A Selected Bibliography.
--The Staffing of Congress: A Selected Bibliography.
Coninx, Raymond G. Foreign Exchange Dealer's Handbook.
Conisbee, Philip. Painting in Eighteenth-Century France.
Conkin, Barbara M. & Conkin, James E. Stratigraphy: Foundation & Concepts.
Conkin, James E., jt. auth. see Conkin, Barbara M.
Conkin, Paul K. Prophets of Prosperity: America's First Political Economists.
Conkling, Edgar C., jt. auth. see Berry, Brian J.
Conley, Diane, ed. Graduate & Professional Programs: An Overview 1985.
--Summer Opportunities for Kids & Teenagers, 1984.
--Summer Opportunities for Kids & Teenagers 1985.
Conley, Diane & Goldstein, Amy J., eds. Graduate Programs in the Humanities & Social Sciences, 1985.
Conley, Diane & Granade, Charles, eds. Graduate Programs in Engineering & Applied Sciences, 1985.
--Graduate Programs in the Physical Sciences & Mathematics, 1985.
Conley, Diane & Ready, Barbara C., eds. Graduate Programs in the Biological, Agricultural, & Health Sciences, 1985.
Conley, Effie, jt. auth. see MacDowell, Jeanne.
Conley, Ellen A. Soho Madonna.
Conley, John A., ed. Theory & Research in Criminal Justice: Current Perspectives.
Conley, Robert J. Actor.
Conley, Robert J. see Cherry, Richard L., et al.
Conley, Robert J., ed. see Tahlequah Indian Writer's Group Staff.
Conley, Virginia C. Curriculum & Instruction in Nursing.
Conlin, Joseph R. The American Past: A Survey of American History. Incl. Pt. One. A Survey of American History to 1877; Pt. Two. A Survey of American History Since 1865. HarBraceJ.
--Big Bill Haywood & the Radical Union Movement.
Conlin, Mary L. Concepts of Communication: Reading, Ideas Module, Inferences Module.
--Concepts of Communication: Writing Skills Module.
--Concepts of Communication: Writing: Summary, Paragraph, Essay-Test, Theme Module.
Conlin, Mary Lou. Concepts of Communication: Reading Vocabulary Module.
--Concepts of Communication: Writing.
--Instructor's Guide.
Conmilit Press Staff. PLA Forces.
Conn, Charles P., jt. auth. see Eckerd, Jack.
Conn, Charles P., jt. auth. see Miller, Barbara.
Conn, David. A Theory of Economic Systems.
Conn, G. K. & Fowler, G. N., eds. Essays in Physics.
Conn, Harvie M., ed. Reaching the Unreached: The Old-New Challenge.
Conn, Martha O. Crazy to Fly.
Conn, Paul, jt. auth. see Moore, Pat.
Conn, Walter E. Conscience: Development & Self-Transcendence.
Connally, Andrew M. & Hicks, Olan. Connally-Hicks Debate on Divorce & Remarriage.
Connecticut Board of Education Staff. A Guide to Curriculum Development in Social Studies.
Connell, Charles. They Gave Us Shakespeare: John Heminge & Henry Condell.
Connell, Elizabeth B. & Tatum, Howard J. Barrier Methods of Contraception.
--Sexually Transmitted Diseases: Diagnosis & Treatment.
Connell, Evan S. A Long Desire.
--White Lantern.
Connell, G. Spanish Poetry of the Grupo Poetico de 1927.
Connell, John. New Caledonia or Independent Kanaky?
Connell, John, jt. ed. see Moore, Mick.
Connell, Jon. The New Maginot Line: A Documented Expose of Our Fatally Flawed Defense System & What We Can Do about It.
Connell, Stephen & Galbraith, Ian A. Electronic Mail: A Revolution in Business Communications.
Connellan, Colm. Why Does Evil Exist? A Philosophical Study of the Contemporary Presentation of the Question.
Connell-Smith, Gordon. Forerunners of Drake.
Connell-Tatum, Elizabeth & Tatum, Howard J. Managing Patients with IntrauterineDevices: A Clinic Manual.
Connelly, Marc. Green Pastures.
Conner, David A., jt. auth. see Winter, John V.
Conner, Dennis. No Excuse to Lose: Winning Yacht Races.
Conner, P. E. Differentiable Periodic Maps.
--Notes on the Witt Classification of Hermitian Innerproduct Spaces over a Ring of Algebraic Integers.
Conner, Susan. Artist's Market '87.
Conner, Susan, ed. Artist's Market 88.
Connery, Donald S. The Inner Source: Exploring Hypnosis with Dr. Herbert Spiegel.
--The Inner Source: Exploring Hypnosis with Dr. Herbert Spiegel.
Conniff, Michael, ed. Latin American Populism in Comparative Perspective.
Conning, D. M., jt. ed. see Goldberg, L.
Connochie, T. D. Tv in Education & Industry.
Connolly, B. W., jt. ed. see Oliveira-Pinto, F.
Connolly, Cyril. The Evening Colonnade.
Connolly, Cyril, jt. auth. see Zerbe, Jerome.
Connolly, F. G. Science v Philosophy.
Connolly, Finbarr. God & Man in Modern Spirituality.
Connolly, Francis X., jt. ed. see Blehl, Vincent.
Connolly, John S. Photochemical Conversion & Storage of Solar Energy.
Connolly, Paul M. Entrepreneurs in Corporations.
Connolly, Ray. Newsdeath.
--The Sun Place.
Connolly, Vivian. Five Ports to Danger.
Connor, A. B. Monumental Brasses in Somerset.
Connor, Ann W. & Kohs, Gerald. Microcosm: College & the World.
Connor, Chris, jt. auth. see Farmer, Penelope.
Connor, Frank. Sky Pilot.
Connor, H., et al, eds. The Foot in Diabetes: Proceedings of the First National Conference on the Diabetic Foot, Malvern, 1986.
Connor, John J., ed. Petroleum Training Directory, 1988.
Connor, Patrick E. Dimensions in Modern Management.
Connor, Ralph. Black Rock.
Connor, Susan, jt. auth. see Kendig, Lane H.
Connors, Kenneth A., et al. Chemical Stability of Pharmaceuticals: A Handbook for Pharmacists.
Connors, Marie. Chickasaw Gardens.
Connors, Tracy D. The Nonprofit Organization Handbook.
Conolly, Violet. Siberia Today & Tomorrow.
Conover. Exercises in Diagnosing ECG Tracings.
Conover, Mary. Understanding Electrocardiography: Arrhythmias & the 12 Lead ECG.
Conover, Mary H., jt. auth. see Marriott, Henry J.
Conover, Robert, jt. auth. see Futcher, Jane.
Conquest, Ned. The Gun & the Glory of Granite Hendley.
Conrad, Agnes C., jt. auth. see Gast, Ross H.
Conrad, Alfred F., et al. Enterprise Organization: Corporation & Partnership Statutes, Rules & Forms to Accompany 3rd. ed.
Conrad, Barnaby. A Revolting Transaction.
Conrad, Clifford L., et al. Computer Mathematics.
Conrad, Eva E. & Maul, Terry. Introduction to Experimental Psychology.
Conrad, George L. Prayers for Little Ones.
Conrad, Glenn R. & Baker, Vaughan B., eds. Louisiana Gothic.
Conrad, Glenn R., ed. see De Villiers du Terrage, Marc.
Conrad, J. David. The Steam Locomotive Directory of North America.
Conrad, Jean. Golden Gates.
Conrad, John P. The Dangerous & the Endangered.
--Justice & Consequences.
Conrad, John W. Contemporary Ceramic Techniques.
Conrad, Joseph. Arrow of Gold.
--Chance.
--Chance.
--Heart of Darkness. Kimbrough, Robert, ed.
--The Heart of Darkness & the Secret Sharer.
--Lord Jim.
--Lord Jim.
--Nigger of "Narcissus", Typhoon, Falk, & Other Stories. Sherry, Norman, ed.
--Nostromo.
--Nostromo.
--A Personal Record.
--Rescue.
--Secret Agent.

Authors

Conrad, Lawrence I., et al, eds. see Buheiry, Marwan R.
Conrad, Leo, jt. auth. see Zimmerman, Steven.
Conrad, Leo M., jt. auth. see Zimmerman, Steven M.
Conrad, Les. Desperate Remedies: The Tragedy of Santa Maria, CA.
Conrad, M., et al, eds. Physics & Mathematics of the Nervous Systems.
Conrad, Peter. Imagining America.
Conrad, Peter, ed. Television: The Medium & Its Manners.
Conrad, Sharon. Separate Worlds.
Conrad, Tony & Broughel, Barbara. The Animal.
Conradt, David P. The German Polity.
Conran, Caroline. English Country Cooking.
Conran, Shirley. Lace.
--Lace II.
Conran, Terence. Terence Conran's New House Book.
Conrat, Maisie & Conrat, Richard. The American Farm.
Conrat, Richard, jt. auth. see Conrat, Maisie.
Conroy, Jack. The Weed King & Other Stories.
Conroy, Jack, jt. auth. see Bontemps, Arna.
Conroy, Jack & Johnson, Curt, eds. Writers in Revolt: The Anvil Anthology, 1933-1940.
Conroy, Lawrence E., et al. General Chemistry Laboratory Operation.
Conroy, Pat. The Great Santini.
--The Lords of Discipline.
--The Water Is Wide.
--The Water Is Wide.
Conser, Eugene P. Real Estate European Style or What You Should Know About Real Estate in 32 Countries.
Considine, Douglas M. Chemical & Process Technology Encyclopedia.
--Energy Technology Handbook.
Considine, Shaun. Barbra Streisand: The Woman, the Myth, the Music.
Consolazio, C. F. Nutrition & Performance.
Consolloy, Patricia, ed. Who Offers Part-Time Degree Programs? A National Survey of Postsecondary Institutions Offering Daytime, Evening, Weekend, Summer & External Degree Programs - 1981 Edition.
Constable, Giles, jt. ed. see Benson, Robert L.
Constance, Diana, jt. auth. see Crossland, John.
Constance, J. D. Mechanical Engineering for Professional Engineers' Examinations.
Constandinidou, Loula D. The Anthologized Poetry of Loula D. Constandinidou. Hogan, Maria, tr.
Constandse, William. How to Select Your Own Computer.
Constandse, William J. Dewi.
Constant, Benjamin. De la Perfectibilite de l'Espece Humaine.
--Ecrits et Discours Politiques.
--Journal Intimes.
--Journaux Intimes.
--Memoires sur les Cent Jours.
Constant, Benjamin & Constant, R. de. Correspondance 1786-1830.
Constant, Benjamin & Derre, Jean Rene. Wallstein: Edition Critique.
Constant, Benjamin & Goyet de la Sarthe, Charles L. Correspondance 1818-1822.
Constant, Benjamin & Harpaz, Ephraim. Recueil d'Articles.
Constant, Benjamin, et al. Lettres a un Ami: Cent Onze Lettres Inedites a Claude Hochet.
Constant, Constantine. Student Earth Scientist Explores Changing Earth.
--The Student Earth Scientist Explores Weather.
Constant, Jules. Learning Electrocardiography: A Complete Course.
Constant, Paul. Ephraim of Israel: The Unknown Apostle.
Constant, R. de, jt. auth. see Constant, Benjamin.
Constantin, James A., et al. Marketing Strategy & Management.
Constantine, Albert J. Know Your Woods.
Constantine, Greg. Picasso Visits Chicago.
Constantine, K. C. The Man Who Liked to Look at Himself & a Fix Like This.
Constantinides, A. G., jt. ed. see Bogner, R. E.
Constantinides, P., et al. Immunity & Atherosclerosis.
Constantino, Anthony. Fight City Hall.
Consulting Staff. The CIA & the NSA.
Consumer Guide Editors. Atari Software: Rating the Best.
--Book of Personal Computers & Games.
--Easy-to-Understand Guide to Home Computers.
--Family Medical Guide: The Illustrated Medical & Health Advisor.
--The Fastest, Cheapest, Best Way to Clean Everything.
--Favorite Brand Name Recipes, Appetizers, Dips & Snacks.
--Favorite Brand Name Recipes: Desserts.
--Favorite Brands Name Recipes, Soups & Sandwiches.
--How to Win at Video Games.
--The User's Guide to Apple II, II Plus & IIe Computers, Software & Peripherals.
--The Whole House Catalog.
--Whole Sewing Catalog.
--Your Home Is Money: Managing Your Home for Profit.
Consumer Guide Editors & Adams, Roe R., III. Apple Software: Rating the Best.
Consumer Guide Editors & Goodman, Danny. A Parent's Guide to Personal Computers & Software.
Consumer Guide Editors & Kay, Sophie. The Chicken Cookbook.
Consumer Guide Editors & Kuntzleman, Beth A. The Complete Guide to Aerobic Dancing.
Consumer Guide Staff. Complete Book of the Porsche.
--Italian Cooking Class Cookbook.
--Mexican Cooking Class Cookbook.
--More Favorite Brand Name Recipes Cookbook.
--Prescription Drugs & Their Side Effect, 1985.
--Rating the Movies.
Consumer Report Book Editors, ed. FlyRide Europe 1986. Perkins, Ed.
--Guide to Electronics in the Home: 1986. Florman, Monte.
--Guide to Used Cars 1986. Markovich, Alex.
--I'll Buy That! Fifty Small Wonders & Big Deals That Revolutionized the Lives of Consumers.
Consumer Reports, ed. Funerals: Consumers' Last Rights.
Consumer Reports Book Editors. The Buying Guide Issue 1987.
--Buying Guide Issue, 1988.
--The Consumers Union Report on Life Insurance: A Guide to Planning & Buying the Protection You Need.
Consumer Reports Books Editors, jt. auth. see Levine, Robert.
Consumer Reports Books Editors, jt. auth. see Markovich, Alex.
Consumer Reports Editors. Drug Information for the Consumer.
Consumer Reports Editors, ed. Consumer Reports Buying Guide 1988.
Consumer Union. Consumer Reports Buying Guide 1983.
Consumers Cooperative Publishing Association Staff, et al. Consumer Cooperation: The Heritage & the Dream.
Consumer's Union. Consumer Reports Buying Guide, 1985.
Contat, Michel, ed. see Sartre, Jean-Paul.
Conti, C., et al. Research on Steroids.
Conti, Flavio. Homes of the Kings: The Grand Tour.
--Individual Creations: The Grand Tour. Creagh, Patrick, tr.
--Shrines of Power: The Grand Tour. Creagh, Patrick, tr.
--Splendor of the Gods: The Grand Tour.
Conti, R. Institutiones Mathematicae: Linear Differential Equations & Control.
Conti, Vittorio. The Gem in the Wire. Lewis, Barbara E., tr. from Ital.
Contractor, Farok J., jt. auth. see Sagafi-Nejad, Tagi.
Contreras, Arnoldo H., jt. auth. see Gregerson, Hans.
Contreras, Jose E. The Pervert.
Contributors to Family Festivals Magazine Staff. Winter Festivals.
Controlled Reproduction of Cultivated Fishes Workshop Staff. Reports & Relevant Papers of the Workshop on Controlled Reproduction of Cultivated Fishes.
Convention of Friends of Agricultural Education, Chicago Staff. Early View of the Land-Grant Colleges.
Converse, Jim. Beginning Blacksmithing, with Projects.
Converse, Mary E., ed. see Skurka, Margaret F.
Conversi, M., ed. Evolution of Particle Physics.
--Selected Topics on Elementary Particle Physics.
Conveyor Equipment Manufacturers Association Staff. Belt Conveyors for Bulk Materials.
Conway, Anne. How to Know Everthing about Anyone Through Handwriting.
Conway, Arthur L. Walking Through the Mist of Life.
Conway, B. E. Theory & Principles of Electrode Processes.
Conway, Flo & Siegelman, Jim. Holy Terror: The Fundamentalist War on America's Freedoms in Religion, Politics, & Our Private Lives.
Conway, James. Night of the Wolf.
Conway, M. Margaret, jt. auth. see C. Q. Press Staff.
Conway, Mary, jt. ed. see Hardy, Margaret E.
Conway, P. Development of Volitional Competence: Selected Readings.
Conway, Richard A. & Ross, Richard D. Handbook of Industrial Waste Disposal.
Conway, Theresa. Paloma.
Conway-Rutkowski, Barbara L. Carini & Owens' Neurological & Neurosurgical Nursing.
Conyers, D. Rural Regional Planning: Towards an Operational Theory.
Conyngham, William J. Industrial Management in the Soviet Union: The Role of the CPSU in Industrial Decision-Making, 1917-1970.
Conze, Edward. Buddhism: Its Essence & Development.
--Buddhist Texts Through the Ages.
Coogan, Michael D., ed. Stories from Ancient Canaan.
Coogan, William H. & Woshinsky, Oliver H. The Science of Politics: An Introduction to Hypothesis Formation & Testing.
Cook, A. J. & Ross, Jacquelene. A. J.'s Tax Court - Who Won, Who Lost & Why.
Cook, Albert S. Concordance to Beowulf.
Cook, Alice & Kirk, Gwyn. Greenham Women Everywhere: Dreams, Ideas & Actions from the Womens' Peace Movement.
Cook, Alicia S. Contemporary Perspectives on Adulthood & Aging.
Cook, Allen. Akin to Slavery: Prison Labor in South Africa.
Cook, Alta L., tr. see Tougas, Gerard.
Cook, Anna M. History of Baldwin County Georgia.
Cook, Arlene. Forever Yours.
Cook, Blanche. Max & Crystal Eastman on Peace, Revolution & War. Chatfield, Charles & Cooper, Sandi, eds.
Cook, Bruce. Brecht in Exile.
--God's Secret for Getting Things Done.
Cook, Chris & Wroughton, John. English Historical Facts: 1603-1688.
Cook, Christopher. History of the Great Trains.
--The Lion & the Dragon.
Cook, Clarence. Art & Artists of Our Time. Weinberg, H. Barbara, ed.
Cook, Clifford A. Essays of a String Teacher: Come Let Us Rosin Together.
--Suzuki Education in Action: A Story of Talent Training from Japan.
Cook, Colin see Phillips, Alan, pseud.
Cook, Curtis W., jt. auth. see Basil, Douglas.
Cook, David. Sunrising.
--Sunrising.
--Thinking about Faith: An Introductory Guide to Philosophy & Religion.
--Warlords.
Cook, David, jt. auth. see Spence, Robin.
Cook, David E. Living Victoriously with Illness & Death: Suggestions for Family & Friends.
Cook, Davis R. The Wars of the Roses: Lancastrians & Yorkists.
Cook, Don. Charles de Gaulle: A Biography.
Cook, Earleen H. Desertification & Deforestation: A Selected Bibliography of English Language Sources.
--Divorce, Support & Community Property.
Cook, Earleen H. & Cook, Joseph L. Halfway Houses & Group Homes.
--Same-Day Surgical & Medical Care.
Cook, Earleen H., jt. auth. see Cook, Joseph L.
Cook, Fred J. Ku Klux Klan: America's Recurring Nightmare.
Cook, G. C. & Phipps, Lloyd J. Six Hundred More Things to Make for the Farm & Home.
Cook, George A. John Wise, Early American Democrat.
Cook, Graeme. Commandos in Action.
Cook, Harry E., III & Hine, Albert C. Platform Margin & Deep Water Carbonates.
Cook, Hugh. The Women & the Warlords.
Cook, J. E. & Earlley, Elsie C. Remediating Reading Disabilities: Simple Things That Work.
Cook, John W. & Winkle, Gary M. Auditing: Philosophy & Technique.
--Auditing: Philosophy & Technique.
Cook, Joseph L. & Cook, Earleen H. Employment-at-Will.
--Industrial Spying & Espionage.
Cook, Joseph L., jt. auth. see Cook, Earleen H.
Cook, Judith. Close to the Earth: Living the Social History of the British Isles.
Cook, L., jt. ed. see Gordy, W.
Cook, L. M. Population Genetics: Outline Studies in Biology.
Cook, Laurel, jt. auth. see Cooper, Patricia.
Cook, Lyndon W. & Cannon, Donald Q. A New Light Breaks Forth.
Cook, Lyndon W. & Cannon, Donald W. Exodus & Beyond.
Cook, Madison D. Biographical Concordance of the New Testament.
Cook, Margaret J. The Anatomy of the Laboratory Mouse.
Cook, Marilyn G. Hospital on the Move: The Story of an Army Nurse.
Cook, Mark. Levels of Personality.
Cook, Mark, ed. Issues in Personal Perception.
Cook, Michael L. The Jesus of Faith: A Study in Christology.
Cook, Michael L., jt. auth. see Miller, Harvey R.
Cook, N. G. Problems in Rock Mechanics.
Cook, Olive & Kersting, A. F. The English Country House: An Art & Way of Life.
Cook, Peter, ed. see Graphic-Sha Editorial Staff.
Cook, Richard J. Rails Across the Midlands.
--Super Power Steam Locomotives.
Cook, Rick & Vaughan, Frank. All about Home Satellite Television.
Cook, Robin. Mindbend.
--Mutation.
--Outbreak.
--Outbreak.
--The Year of the Intern.
Cook, Scott & Diskin, Martin, eds. Markets in Oaxaca.
Cook, Shirley. The Marriage Puzzle.
--Through the Valley of Love.
Cook, Stanley A. An Introduction to the Bible.
Cook, Stephanie. Second Life.
Cook, Susanne. The Open Goal of My Life.
Cook, Sy & Moffett, Martha. The Sharing.
Cook, Thomas H. Elena.
--The Orchids.
Cook, Walter A. Case Grammar: Development of the Matrix Model (1970-1978).
Cook, Wanda D. Adult Literacy Education in the United States.
Cook, William J. Confidence in Fact.
Cook, William J., Jr. Security Systems: Considerations, Layout, Performance.
Cooke. Dependent Development in United Kingdom Regions with Particular Reference to Wales.
--Routines in Neonatal Care.
Cooke, Alan, ed. see Universite Laval, Centre d'Etudes Nordiques, Quebec Staff.
Cooke, Bernard. Formation of Faith.
--Ministry to Word & Sacraments: History & Theology.
Cooke, Charles. Playing the Piano for Pleasure.
Cooke, Donald E. Atlas of the Presidents.
--Atlas of the Presidents.
Cooke, Dorian, tr. see Djilas, Milovan.
Cooke, Dorian, tr. see Jukic, Ilija.
Cooke, E. M. & Gibson, G. L. Essential Clinical Microbiology: An Introductory Text.
Cooke, Edward F. & Janosik, G. Edward. Guide to Pennsylvania Politics.
Cooke, Edward I., jt. auth. see Gardner, William.
Cooke, G. Dennis, et al. Lake & Reservoir Restoration.
Cooke, Geoffrey, et al. Youth & Justice: Young Offenders in Ireland.
Cooke, Jacob E. Alexander Hamilton: A Biography.
Cooke, James J. The New French Imperialism, 1880-1910: The Third Republic & Colonial Expansion.
Cooke, James J., ed. see French Colonial Historical Society Staff.
Cooke, John B. The Snowblind Moon: A Novel of the West.
Cooke, John E. Wearing the Grey: Being Personal Portraits, Scenes & Adventures of the War.
Cooke, Melinda W., jt. ed. see Bunge, Frederica M.
Cooke, Miriam. The Anatomy of an Egyptian Intellectual: Yahya Haqqi.
Cooke, Nelson M. & Adams, Herbert F. Arithmetic Review for Electronics.
Cooke, P. Region, Class & Gender: A European Comparison.
Cooke, R. D. Applied Finite Element Analysis: An Apple II Implementation.
Cooke, R. V. & Johnson, J. H. Trends in Geography: An Introductory Survey.
Cooke, Terence E. International Mergers & Acquisitions.
Cooke, W. T. & Holmes, G. K. Coeliac Disease.
Cooking Committee of Concord Alternative Residence, Inc., ed. Family Occasions: A Cookbook.
Cooksley, Peter G. Flying Bomber.
--Wellington: Mainstay of Bomber Command.
Cookson, Catherine. The Bannaman Legacy.
--The Black Velvet Gown.
--The Moth.
--The Whip.
Cookson, R. F., jt. ed. see Chesseman, G. W.
Cool, J. & Smith, E. L., eds. Frontiers in Visual Science: Proceedings of the University of Houston College of Optometry Dedication Symposium, Houston Texas, March, 1977.
Cool, Lisa C. How to Sell Every Magazine Article You Write.
Coole, Arthur B. Ch'i Heavy Sword Coins of the Chou Dynasty.
--The Earliest Round Coins of China.
--The Early Coins of the Chou Dynasty.
--Pointed Spade Coins of the Chou Dynasty.
--Spade Coin Types of the Chou Dynasty.
--State of Ming Coin Knives & Minor Knife Coins.
Cooley, Adelaide N. The Monument Maker: A Biography of Frederick Ernst Triebel.
Cooley, Rossa B. School Acres: An Adventure in Rural Education.
Cooley, Stella G., jt. auth. see Jensen, Joyce D.
Cooley, Susan D. Country Walks in Connecticut.
Cooley, Thomas, ed. The Norton Sampler: Short Essays for Composition.
--The Norton Sampler: Short Essays for Composition.
Coolidge, Guy O. The French Occupation of the Champlain Valley: From 1609-1759 with Added Index.
Coolidge, Olivia. Caesar's Gallic War.

--Come by Here.
--Gandhi.
--Legends of the North.
--Lives of Famous Romans.
--Roman People.
--The Three Lives of Joseph Conrad.
Cooling, W. Colebrook. Simplified Low-Cost Maintenance Control.
Coomaraswamy, A. K. & Noble, M. E. Myths of the Hindus & Buddhists.
Coomaraswamy, Ananda. Buddha & the Gospel of Buddhism.
--Hinduism & Buddhism.
Coomaraswamy, Ananda K. The Transformation of Nature in Art.
Coombes, B., ed. Vehicle Body Building, Pt. 2.
Coombes, B., et al, eds. Vehicle Body Building: Pt. 1.
Coombes, R. H. Soil Warming by Electricity.
Coombs, Charles I. Auto Racing.
Coombs, Clyde F. Printed Circuits Handbook.
Coombs, Clyde H. A Theory of Psychological Scaling.
Coombs, J. Biotechnology Directory 1986.
Coombs, J. & Alston, Y. R. The Biotechnology Directory 1988.
Coombs, Jim. The Biotechnology Directory 1985.
--The International Biotechnology Directory 1984: Products, Companies, Research & Organizations.
Coombs, Margaret. Charlotte Mason & the Parents' National Educational Union.
Coombs, Philip H., ed. Meeting the Basic Needs of the Rural Poor: The Integrated, Community-Based Approach.
Coombs, Roy E. Violets.
--Violets: The History & Cultivation of Scented Violets.
Coomer, James C., ed. Quest for a Sustainable Society.
Coon, Carleton S. A Reader in Cultural Anthropology.
--The Seven Caves: Archaeological Explorations in the Middle East.
Coon, Dennis. Essentials of Psychology.
Coon, Susan. Chiy-une.
--Rahne.
Cooney, Barbara. Little Brother & Little Sister.
Cooney, Caroline. Invasion of the Mutants.
--Racing to Love.
Cooney, Caroline B. I'm Not Your Other Half.
--Sand Trap.
Cooney, Ellen. Small Town Girl.
Cooney, Linda A. Deadly Design.
--Don't Look Now.
Cooney, Nancy E. The Blanket That Had to Go.
Cooney, T. Ultimate Desires.
Cooney, Thomas J., et al. Dynamics of Teaching Secondary Mathematics.
Coontz, Otto. Isle of the Shapeshifters.
Coop, Richard H., jt. auth. see McCandless, Boyd R.
Cooper, jt. auth. see Walker.
Cooper, Alexander A. Shura.
Cooper, Alison & Tusenius, Micheline. International Investment in South Africa.
Cooper, Anne, compiled by. Ishmael My Brother.
Cooper, B. E. Statistics for Experimentalists.
Cooper, Barry. Merleau-Ponty & Marxism: From Terror to Reform.
Cooper, Bobbi G., jt. auth. see Erskine, Jim.
Cooper, C. L. & Marshall, J., eds. White Collar & Professional Stress.
Cooper, C. L. & Payne, R., eds. Stress at Work.
Cooper, Carolyn. Creative Computer-Video.
Cooper, Cary L., jt. auth. see Freedman, Richard D.
Cooper, Cary L. & Alderfer, Clayton, eds. Advances in Experiential Social Processes.
Cooper, Charles. English Table in History & Literature.
--Policy Interventions for Technological Innovation in Developing Countries.
Cooper, Charles W. Arts & Humanity.
Cooper, Darien B. The Christian Woman's Planner.
Cooper, David D. The Lesson of the Scaffold: The Public Execution Controversy in Victorian England.
Cooper, David E. Authenticity & Learning: Nietzsche's Educational Philosophy.
Cooper, David J. Brooks Range Passage.
Cooper, Derek. The Road to Mingulay.
--Skye.
Cooper, Donald, jt. auth. see Murdick, Robert G.
Cooper, Donald, photos by. Theatre Year.
Cooper, Doug & Clancy, Michael. Oh! Pascal!
Cooper, Douglas. Living God's Joy.
--Living We've Just Begun.
Cooper, Douglas & Tinterow, Gary. Essential Cubism.
Cooper, Ed, photos by. Portrait of Seattle.
Cooper, Edwin & Brazier, Mary. Developmental Immunology: Clinical Problems & Aging.
Cooper, Edwin L., ed. see International Symposium of the American Society of Zoologists, Toronto, December 27-30, 1977.
Cooper, Eli L. Am Seguliah: A Treasured People.
Cooper, Elizabeth. Harim & the Purdah: Studies of Oriental Women.
Cooper, Elizabeth K. And Everything Nice: The Story of Sugar, Spice & Flavoring.
--Discovering Chemistry.
--Insects & Plants: The Amazing Partnership.
--Science in Your Own Back Yard.
--Science in Your Own Back Yard.
--Science on the Shores & Banks.
--Science on the Shores & Banks.
--Silkworms & Science: The Story of Silk.
Cooper, Elizabeth K., et al. Fish from Japan.
Cooper, Emanuel. The Potter's Book of Glaze Recipes.
Cooper, Emmanuel. The Sexual Perspective: Homosexuality & Art in the Last 100 Years in the West.
Cooper, Frederick T., jt. auth. see Maurice, Arthur B.
Cooper, Gale. Animal People.
Cooper, George R. & McGillem, Clare D. Probabilistic Methods of Signal & System Analysis.
Cooper, Gordon. Along the Great Rivers.
--Dead Cities & Forgotten Tribes.
--Forbidden Lands.
Cooper, Guy H. Development & Stress in Navajo Religion.
Cooper, Henry S., Jr. Imaging Saturn.
--Imaging Saturn: The Voyager Flights to Saturn.
--The Search for Life on Mars.
--The Search for Life on Mars.
Cooper, I. S. It's Hard to Leave While the Music's Playing.
--Living with Chronic Neurologic Disease: A Handbook for Patient & Family.
--The Vital Probe: My Life As a Brain Surgeon.
Cooper, Ian, jt. ed. see Powell, James A.
Cooper, Irving S. Theosophy Simplified.
Cooper, J. C. Symbolism: The Universal Language.
Cooper, J. I. & MacCallum, F. O. Viruses & the Environment.
Cooper, J. R., jt. ed. see Rose, J. W.
Cooper, James Fenimore. The Crater: Or, Vulcan's Peak.
--Deerslayer.
--The History of the Navy of the United States.
--The Last of the Mohicans.
--The Last of the Mohicans.
--The Last of the Mohicans.
--Leatherstocking Saga. Nevins, Allan, ed.
--Satanstoe.
--Sea Lions. Walker, Warren S., ed.
--Spy: A Tale of the Neutral Ground.
--The Ways of the Hour.
Cooper, James M., jt. auth. see Ryan, Kevin.
Cooper, James N., jt. auth. see Rustgi, Vinod K.
Cooper, Jeff. Principles of Personal Defense.
Cooper, Jerry & Smith, Glenn. Citizens As Soldiers: A History of the North Dakota National Guard.
Cooper, Jilly. Bella.
Cooper, Joe. The Mystery of Telepathy.
Cooper, John C. Throwing the Sticks: Occult Self-Therapy - The Arts of Self-Transcendence in Post-Freudian Modes of Thought.
Cooper, John M. Reason & Human Good in Aristotle.
--The Warrior & the Priest: Woodrow Wilson & Theodore Roosevelt.
Cooper, Laura G. & Smith, Marilyn Z. Standard FORTRAN: A Problem-Solving Approach.
Cooper, M., et al, eds. Current Topics in Microbiology & Immunology.
Cooper, M. A. Fundamentals of Survey Measurement & Analysis.
--Modern Theodolites & Levels.
Cooper, M. D., et al, eds. Immune Deficiency.
Cooper, M. H. Prices & Profits in the Pharmaceutical Industry.
Cooper, M. J., jt. auth. see Hanley, W. S.
Cooper, Mark. Bibliography of C Language.
Cooper, Michael D. California's Demand for Librarians: Projecting Future Requirements.
Cooper, Miriam. Snap! Photography.
Cooper, P., jt. ed. see Gopalakrishnan, S.
Cooper, Pamela J. Speech Communication for the Classroom Teacher.
Cooper, Patricia & Cook, Laurel. Hots Springs & Spas of California.
Cooper, Paulette, ed. Growing up Puerto Rican.
Cooper, Peter. The Secret Papers of Julia Templeton.
Cooper, Richard N. Economic Policy in an Interdependent World.
Cooper, Richard N., et al. Towards a Renovated International System.
Cooper, Robert D. Health Care Cost Survey Results.
Cooper, Robert M. Lost on Both Sides, Dante Gabriel Rossetti: Critic & Poet.
Cooper, Robert W. Investment Return & Property-Liability Insurance Ratemaking.
Cooper, Rodney H., jt. auth. see Johnson, Leroy F.
Cooper, Rosaleen & Palmer, Ann. Games from an Edwardian Childhood.
Cooper, S. J., jt. auth. see Levens, A. S.
Cooper, Sandi. Soups & Salads. Lawrence, Betsy, ed.
Cooper, Sandi, ed. Internationalism in Nineteenth Century Europe.
Cooper, Sandi, ed. see Cook, Blanche.
Cooper, Sandra F., jt. auth. see Mertens, Thomas R.
Cooper, Sonni. Black Fire.
Cooper, Stephanie. Public Housing & Private Property.
Cooper, Susan. The Dark Is Rising.
--The Grey King.
--Over Sea, under Stone.
Cooper, Susan & Heenan, Cathy. Preparing, Designing, Leading Workshops.
Cooper, V. Student's Manual of Auditing.
Cooper, W. C. Physics of Selenium & Tellurium.
Cooper, William. Scenes from Married Life & Scenes from Later Life.
--Scenes from Provincial Life & Scenes from Metropolitan Life.
Cooper, William R. Archaic Dictionary.
Cooperberg, Peter L., jt. ed. see Winsberg, Fred.
Cooperman, David N. Fascinations.
Cooperman, Jehiel B., ed. America in Yiddish Poetry: An Anthology. Cooperman, Sarah C., tr.
Cooperman, Sarah C., tr. see Cooperman, Jehiel B.
Cooperrider, Edward A., tr. see Rommel, Kurt.
Cooperrider, Edward A., tr. see Steinwede, Dietrich.
Cooperrider, Edward A., tr. see Thielicke, Helmut.
Coordinating Committee for Continuing Education in Thoracic Surgery. Self-Education-Self Assessment in Thoracic Surgery.
Coordinating Council of Literary Magazines Staff. Directory of Literary Magazines, 1987.
Coortice, F. C., jt. auth. see Yoffey, J. M.
Coote, Jack. North Sea Harbours & Pilotage: Calais to Den Helder.
Coote, Jack H. Monochrome Darkroom Practice.
Coote, Robert, jt. auth. see Stott, John R.
Coote, Robert B. Amos among the Prophets: Composition & Theology.
Coover, Robert. Gerald's Party: A Novel.
--Spanking the Maid.
Copa, G. & Moss, J. Planning & Vocational Education.
Cope, jt. auth. see Goldman.
Cope, David, jt. auth. see Goldman, Myer.
Cope, Emma E. How to Decipher & Study Old Documents: Being a Guide to the Reading of Ancient Manuscripts, the Key to the Family Deed Chest.
Cope, Lloyd. Astrologer's Forecasting Workbook.
Cope, Mike. Righteousness Inside Out: The Heart of the Problem & the Problem of the Heart.
Cope, Oliver. Breast: Its Problems-Benign & Malignant-How to Deal with Them.
Cope, R. & Sawko, F. Computer Methods for Civil Engineering.
Cope, Thom K. Executive Guide to Employment Practices.
Copeland, Bonnie C. Lady of Moray.
Copeland, Carole, jt. auth. see De La Croix, J. M.
Copeland, Gloria. God's Will Is Prosperity.
Copeland, J. E., ed. see Linguistic Association of Canada & the U. S. Staff.
Copeland, John A. A Study of the Revelation.
Copeland, John G., et al. Intermediate Spanish: Civilizacion y Cultura.
--Intermediate Spanish: Conversacion y Repaso.
Copeland, Tom. Tax Workbook 1987.
Copeland, Tom & Roach, Megan. Successful Strategies for Recruiting Family Day Care Providers. Hix, Jill, ed.
Copeland, Tom, ed. Parents in the Workplace: A Management Resource for Employers.
Copeland, Tom, ed. see Toys 'n Things Press Staff.
Copeland, Vince, ed. see Anderson, Osborne P.
Copeman, George. Managing Director.
Coping with Crisis Research & Training Group, the Open University Staff. Running Workshops: A Guide for Trainers in the Helping Professions.
Copland, Aaron. What to Listen for in Music.
Copland, Douglas. The Changing Structure of the Western Economy.
Copland, Ian. Jawaharlal Nehru of India Eighteen Eighty-Nine to Nineteen Sixty-Four.
Copland, J. W., ed. Goat Production & Research in the Tropics.
Coplans, John, jt. auth. see Bell, Robert.
Copleston, F. W., et al, eds. Advanced Pipe & Tube Welding.
Copleston, Frederick C. Medieval Philosophy.
Copleston, Frederick J. History of Philosophy: Modern Philosophy: Descartes to Leibnitz.
Copley, jt. auth. see Gelbier, S.
Copley, A., ed. Biorheology: Abstracts of the Second International Congress.
--Biorheology: Proceedings of the Second International Congress.
--Hemorheology: Proceedings of the First International Conference.
Copley, A. & Okamoto, S., eds. Hemorheology & Thrombosis: Proceedings of the U. S. Japan Seminar, Kobe Japan.
Copley, A. L., ed. see International Society of Hemorheology, 2nd International Conference, Heidelberg, 1969.
Copley, Frank O. Menaechmi: Plautus.
Copley, Frank O., ed. see Terence.
Copley, Stephen. Literature & the Social Order in Eighteenth Century England.
Coplin, William D. & O'Leary, Michael K. Effective Participation in Government: A Policy Skills Manual.
--Public Policy Study Skills Manual.
Coplin, William D., et al. Power Persuasion: A Surefire System to Get Ahead in Business.
Copp, Dewitt S. A Different Kind of Rain.
Coppa & Avery Consultants Staff. The Administration of the Federal Reserve System: A Bibliographical Overview of Its Board of Governors, Federal Reserve Banks & Monetary Policy.
--Agricultural Administration in the United States: A Bibliographical Overview of Administrative Practices, Price Supports & Models.
--An Architectural Guide to Wood Construction, Preservation, Conservation, Restoration & Framing.
--The Architecture of Embassies.
--Automobile Garages: A Bibliographic Overview.
--A Bibliographical Guide to Disaster Planning, Management, Insurance & the Case of Bhopal, India.
--Bus Terminals: An Architectural Overview.
--Community Centers: An Architectural Guide.
--Contingency Planning & Management: A Bibliographical Guide.
--Cost-Benefit Analysis: A Bibliography.
--The Design of Chemical Plants.
--The Design of Nuclear Reactors.
--The Design of Petroleum Offshore Drilling Structures.
--The Design of Sewage Disposal Plants: A Bibliography.
--The Design of Storage Facilities for Radioactive Substances.
--A Guide to Warehouse Design, Conservation & Restoration.
--Labor Productivity: A Bibliographical Guide to Productivity, Mathematical Models & Case Studies.
--Laboratory Design.
--Medical Care: A Bibliographical Overview of Cost Control.
--Metallurgical Plant Design: A Bibliographical Overview.
--Museum Architecture: A Guide to Design, Conservation & Museum Architecture in the United States.
--Occupational Safety & Health: An Administrative Overview.
--Reservoir Design: A Bibliography.
--Sign & Billboard Design: An Architectural Approach.
--Smoke Detectors: A Bibliographical Overview.
--Subway Design: An Architectural Guide.
Coppel, Alfred. The Apocalypse Brigade.
--Between the Thunder & the Sun.
--The Burning Mountain: A Novel of the Invasion of Japan.
--The Dragon.
--The Hastings Conspiracy.
Coppen, H. E. Aids to Teaching & Learning.
Coppens, Peter R. de see De Coppens, Peter R.
Copper, Basil. The Further Adventures of Solar Pons.
Copper, Marcia S. The Horseman's Etiquette Book.
Copperman, Lois F. & Keast, Frederick D. Adjusting to An Older Work Force.
Coppersmith, Sylvia B. Travelling Jobs for Women: A Guide to Exciting Career Opportunities.
Coppi, B., ed. Theory of Magnetically Confined Plasmas: Proceedings.
Coppi, B., et al, eds. Physics of Plasma Close to Thermonuclear Conditions.
Coppleson, M. & Reid, B. Pre-Clinical Carcinoma of the Cervix Uteri.
Copplestone, Trewin, jt. auth. see Myers, Bernard L.
Coppock, J. T. & Sewell, W. D. The Spatial Dimensions of Public Policy.
Coppock, J. T., ed. Second Homes: Curse or Blessing.
Coppock, J. T., jt. ed. see Maunder, W. F.
Copson, David A. Microwave Heating.
Corballis, Richard & Harding, J. M. A Concordance to the Works of John Webster.
Corbeil, Richard L., Sr. Tele-Robotics: The New Medium for Marketing, Sales, & Politics.
Corbeiller, Clare Le see Parker, James & Le Corbeiller, Clare.
Corben, Richard. Den: Neverwhere.
--Werewolf.
Corben, Richard, et al. Underground Two.
Corbet, H. & Robertson, D. Europe's Free Trade Area Experiment.

Corbett. The Great McGoniggle Rides Shotgun.
Corbett, Bayliss, compiled by. Spectrum: A Guide to the Independent Press & Informative Organizations.
Corbett, Bernard. Boston Sports Trivia.
Corbett, Edmund V. Illustrations Collection: Its Formation, Classification & Exploitation.
Corbett, Edward P. The Little Rhetoric.
Corbett, J. Elliott. Prophets on Main Street.
Corbett, J. Elliott & Smith, Elizabeth S. Becoming a Prophetic Community.
Corbett, James A. Praepostini Tractatus De Officiis.
Corbett, James A., ed. De Instructione Puerorum of William of Tournai.
Corbett, James A. & Garvin, Joseph N., eds. Summa Contra Haereticos.
Corbett, Jane V. Diagnostic Procedures in Nursing Practice.
Corbett, Julian S. Sir Francis Drake.
Corbett, Kathleen, jt. auth. see Borgin, Karl.
Corbett, Michael. Political Tolerance in America: Freedom & Equality in Political Attitudes.
Corbett, Nancy A. & Beveridge, Phyllis. Clinical Simulations in Nursing Practice.
Corbett, Robin. Guerilla Warfare: From Nineteen Thirty-Nine to the Present Day.
Corbett, Scott. Captain Butcher's Body.
--The Case of the Ticklish Tooth.
--The Foolish Dinosaur Fiasco.
--The Great McGoniggle's Gray Ghost.
--Here Lies the Body.
--The Hockey Trick.
--The Mailbox Trick.
--The Mysterious Zetabet.
--Run for the Money.
Corbett, W. J. Pentecost & the Chosen One.
Corbett, William A., ed. Medical Applications of Microcomputers.
Corbierre, Anne. Paris.
Corbin, Cheryl. Nutrition.
Corbin, David A. Life, Work, & Rebellion in the Coal Fields: Southern West Virginia Miners, 1880-1920.
Corbin, Henry. Avicenna & the Visionary Recital. Trask, Willard R., tr. from Fr.
Corbin, Peter, jt. auth. see Thoman, Richard S.
Corbitt, Helen L. Helen Corbitt Cooks for Company.
Corbitt, Joan, illus. The Gary Coleman Show: What If Elephants Had Pink Stripes?
Corbo, Margaret E. & Barras, Diane M. Arnie, the Darling Starling.
Corbo, Margarete S. & Barras, Diane M. Arnie & a House Full of Company.
--Arnie & a House Full of Company.
--Arnie, the Darling Starling.
Corbo, V. & De Melo, J. Liberalization with Stabilization in the Southern Cone of Latin.
Corchado, Veronica & McHugh, Kathleen. Selecting the Right Word Processing Software for the IBM PC.
Corchado, Veronica, jt. auth. see McHugh, Kathleen.
Corcoran, Barbara. All the Summer Voices.
--August, Die She Must.
--Axe-Time, Sword-Time.
--Child of the Morning.
--Don't Slam the Door When You Go.
--The Faraway Island.
--Hey, That's My Soul You're Stomping on.
--Long Journey.
--Make No Sound.
--Me & You & a Dog Named Blue.
--Meet Me at Tamerlane's Tomb.
--Rising Damp.
--A Row of Tigers.
--Sasha, My Friend.
--The Shadowed Path.
--This Is a Recording.
--Trick of Light.
Corcoran, Barbara, jt. auth. see Angier, Bradford.
Corcoran, Eileen L. Know Your Signs - Be a Better Driver: Driving Interstate & Superhighways.
--Rights & Duties of Citizens: Practice Materials for Foundations of Citizenship.
--Weather & Us.
--Weather & Us.
Corcoran, Thomas B., jt. auth. see Wilson, Bruce L.
Cordasco, Francesco, jt. auth. see Pitkin, Thomas M.
Cordasco, Francesco & Alloway, David N., eds. Medical Education in the United States: A Guide to Information Sources.
Cordasco, Francesco, et al. The Puerto Rican Experience: A Sociological Sourcebook.
Cordell, Benjamin. The World Truth Bible.
Corder, A. S. Maintenance Management Techniques.
Corder, Jim W. & Ruszkiewicz, John J. Handbook of Current English.
Cordesman, Anthony. Western Strategic Interests in Saudi Arabia.
Cordingley, Patrick, jt. auth. see Limb, Sue.
Cordner, J. W. Manual of Operating Room Management.
Cordon, Faustino. An Introduction to the Biological Basis of Feeding: Essential Biological Ideas Necessary to a Study of Living Beings from the Evolutionary Standpoint.
--The Origin, Nature & Evolution of Protoplasmic Individuals & their Associations: Protoplasmic Action & Experience.
Cordova, Efren, intro. by see International Labour Office Staff, et al.
Cordoze, Rita C. The Street Soldier's Handbook of Poetry.
Cordry, Donald. Mexican Masks.
Cords, Nicholas & Gerster, Patrick. Myth & the American Experience.
Cordy, Peter, ed. Creative Source: Seventh Annual.
Core, Lucy & Calhoun, David, eds. The Louisiana Almanac, 1984-85 Edition.
Corea, Nicholas J. Cleaner Breed.
Corelli, A. La Folio for Violin & Piano. David, Ferd & Auer, Leopold, eds.
Corelli, Marie. A Romance of Two Worlds. Wolff, Robert L., ed.
Coren, Alan. Arthur & the Purple Panic.
--Arthur Versus the Rest.
--Arthur's Last Stand.
--Bumf.
--The Cricklewood Diet.
Coren, Alan, ed. The Punch Book of Dogs.
--The Punch Book of Kids.
Coren, Stanley, et al. Sensation & Perception.
Corey. Guide to Postal Exam.
Corey, E. Raymond. Procurement Management: Strategy, Organization & Decision-Making.
Corey, E. Raymond & Star, Steven H. Organization Strategy: A Marketing Approach.
Corey, Lee. The Abode of Life.
Corfiato, Hector O., jt. auth. see Richardson, A. E.
Cork, Barbara & Morris, R. Mysteries & Marvels of Nature.
Corke, D. K. Production Control in Engineering.
Corkill, W. A. Railway Modelling: An Introduction.
Corle, Edwin. Billy the Kid.
Corlett, D. Shelby. God in the Present Tense.
Corlett, William T. Medicine Man of the Early American Indian & His Cultural Background.
Corley, Nora T., ed. Travel in Canada: A Guide to Information Sources.
Corlin, Judith R. & Miller, Mary S. The Scarsdale Nutritionist's Weight Loss Cookbook.
--The Scarsdale Nutritionist's Weight-Loss Program for Teenagers.
Corliss, Clark E. Patten's Elements of Embryology.
Corliss, Hazel B. Hilltop Housewife Cookbook.
Corliss, J. O. The Ciliated Protozoa: International Students Edition.
Corliss, John O. The Ciliated Protozoa: Characterization, Classification & Guide to the Literature.
Corliss, Richard, ed. The Hollywood Screenwriter.
Corliss, William R. Strange Artifacts: A Sourcebook on Ancient Man.
--Strange Life: A Sourcebook on the Mysteries of Organic Nature.
--Strange Phenomena: A Sourcebook of Unusual Natural Phenomena.
--The Unfathomed Mind: A Handbook of Unusual Mental Phenomena.
Cormack, Desmond F. Psychiatric Nursing Described.
Corman, Cid. Auspices.
Cormier, Ramona & Pallister, Janis L. Waiting for Death: The Philosophical Significance of Beckett's En Attendant Godot.
Cormier, Robert. After the First Death.
--A Little Raw on Monday Mornings.
--Now & at the Hour.
--Take Me Where the Good Times Are.
Corn, Ira G. Foreword by see Martin, Ira.
Cornaby, W. Arthur. A String of Chinese Peach-Stones.
Cornacchia, Harold J. & Barrett, Stephen. Consumer Health: A Guide to Intelligent Decisions.
Cornacchia, Harold J., et al. Health in Elementary Schools.
Corneille, Pierre see Bentley, Eric.
Cornelisen, Ann. Any Four Women... Could Rob the Bank of Italy.
--Strangers & Pilgrims.
--Strangers & Pilgrims: The Last Italian Migration.
Cornelison, Zona H. Fatness to Fitness.
Cornelius, Hal & Lewis, William. A Career Blazer Guide to Word Processing.
Cornelius, Michael, ed. Teaching Mathematics.
Cornelius, Wayne A. & Craig, Ann L. Politics in Mexico: An Introduction & Overview.
Cornelius, Wayne A., pref. by. Current Research Inventory (Spring 1982)
Cornelius, William L. Beginning & Intermediate Gymnastics.
Cornell, A. D., jt. auth. see Gauld, Alan.
Cornell, Claire P., jt. auth. see Gelles, Richard J.
Cornell, Gary. ProDOS & Beyond: Applesoft File Techniques.
Cornell, James. The First Stargazers: An Introduction to the Origins of Astronomy.
--The Great International Disaster Book.
--The Great International Disaster Book.
Cornell, James & Carr, John, eds. Infinite Vistas: New Tools for Astronomy.
Cornell, Julien. Conscience & the State. Bd. with Conscientious Objector & the Law. Cornell, Julien. Garland Pub.
Cornell University, New York State School of Industrial & Labor Relations Staff. Cumulation of the Library Catalog Supplements of Martin P. Catherwood Library of the New York State School of Industrial & Labor Relations.
--Library Catalog of the Martin P. Catherwood Library of the New York State School of Industrial & Labor Relations.
--Library Catalog of the Martin P. Catherwood Library of the New York State School of Industrial & Labor Relations, First Supplement.
Corner, Desmond, ed. Directory of Unit Trust Management.
Corner, George W. Hormones in Human Reproduction.
Cornes, Phil. Commodore 64: Step by Step Programming Guides.
Cornetto, Anna M., jt. auth. see Bettoja, Jo.
Corney, G., jt. auth. see Strong, S. J.
Cornfield, Jim. Electronic Flash.
Cornfield, Robert, jt. auth. see Martins, Peter.
Cornford, A., tr. see Thimme, Jurgen.
Cornford, F. M. From Religion to Philosophy. A Study of the Origins of Western Speculation.
Cornforth, Maurice. Rebels & Their Causes: Essays in Honour of A. L. Morton.
Cornillie, O., jt. auth. see Lammineur, P.
Cornish, Edward, ed. Careers Tomorrow: The Outlook for Work in a Changing World.
Cornish, Robert L & Mabry, Aleta M. Arkansas: Learning Activities for Elementary Students.
Cornish, Sam. Grandmother's Pictures.
--Your Hand in Mine.
Corns, Albert R. Bibliography of Unfinished Books in the English Language. Sparke, Archibald, ed.
Cornuelle, Richard. The Healing of America.
Cornwall, John. Modern Capitalism: Its Growth & Transformation.
Cornwall-Jones, A. T. Education for Leadership: The International Administrative Staff Colleges, 1948-1984.
Cornwell, jt. auth. see Davis.
Cornwell, Bernard. Sharpe's Sword: The Salamanca Campaign.
Cornwell, Clifton, jt. auth. see Gibson, James W.
Cornwell, Debbie, jt. auth. see Cornwell, Stephen.
Cornwell, Debbra, jt. auth. see Cornwell, Stephen.
Cornwell, Elmer E., Jr., jt. ed. see Seligman, Lester G.
Cornwell, Patricia D. A Time for Remembering: The Ruth Graham Bell Story.
Cornwell, Peter. Church & the Nation: The Case for Disestablishment.
Cornwell, Robert C. & Manship, Darwin W. Applied Business Communication.
Cornwell, Rupert. God's Banker: Account of the Life & Death of Roberto Calvi.
Cornwell, Stephen & Cornwell, Debbie. The Playful Gourmet: For Ladies Only.
--The Playful Gourmet: For Men Only.
--The Playful Gourmet: Quickies.
Cornwell, Stephen & Cornwell, Debbra. Cooking in the Nude: For Playful Gourmets.
Corr, Michael. To Leave the Standing Grain.
Corradini, M. L. & Bishop, A. A., eds. Fuel-Coolant Interactions.
Corrall, Alice E. & Glass, Justine. The Story of Biochemistry.
Correns, C. W., et al. Introduction to Mineralogy: Crystallography & Petrology. Johns, W. D., tr.
Correu, Larry M., ed. The Best of These Days.
Corrick, Marshall, ed. Handicapped Students Science: Teaching.
Corrie, J. E. T., jt. auth. see Hunter, W. M.
Corriere, Richard & Hart, Joseph. Psychological Fitness: Twenty-One Days to Feeling Good.
Corrigan, B. C. A Profile of General Meade & the Four Military Installations Named for the Victor at Gettysburg.
Corrigan, John T. Guide for the Organization & Operation of a Religious Resource Center.
--Librarian-Educator Interdependence.
Corrigan, John T., jt. auth. see Cargas, Harry J.
Corrigan, John T., ed. Anglo-American Cataloging Rules: One Year Later.
--What Today's Youth is Reading & Why.
Corrigan, John T., ed. see Brown, James, et al.
Corrigan, L. Luan, ed. APHA Drug Names. Shoff, Janet.
Corrigan, Robert W., ed. New American Plays. Incl. Mister Biggs. Barlow, Anna M; The Hundred & First. Cameron, Kenneth; A Summer Ghost. Fredericks, Claude; Blood Money. Jasudowicz, Dennis; Socrates Wounded. Levinson, Alfred; Constantinople Smith. Mee, Charles L., Jr; Pigeons. Osgood, Lawrence; The Death & Life of Sneaky Fitch. Rosenberg, James L; Ginger Anne. Washburn, Deric; The Golden Bull of Boredom. Yerby, Lorees. Hill & Wang.
Corrigan, Robert W. & Loney, Glenn M., eds. Forms of Drama.
Corrin, Jay P. G. K. Chesterton & Hilaire Belloc: The Battle Against Modernity.
Corris, Michael. Typographic Samples, Pictures & Polemics.
Corry, J. A. Farewell the Ivory Tower: Universities in Transition.
Corry, John. Golden Clan: The Murrays, the McDonnells, & the Irish American Aristocracy.
--TV News & the Dominant Culture. Media Institute Staff, ed.
Corry, Will. Voyage of Sea Lion.
Corsaro, Maria & Korzeniowsky, Carole. STD: A Common Sense Guide to Sexually Transmitted Diseases.
--A Woman's Guide to a Safe Abortion.
Corsellis, Jane. Painting Figures in Light.
Corsey, Mark, ed. see Patton, Deborah.
Corsini, Ray P., ed. see Loos, Anita.
Corsini, Raymond J. & Marsella, Anthony J. Personality Theories, Research & Assessment.
Corsini, Raymond J., jt. auth. see Gazda, George M.
Corsini, Raymond J., ed. Current Psychotherapies.
Corsini, Raymond J., jt. ed. see Wedding, Dan.
Corson, E. O'Leary, jt. auth. see Corson, Samuel A.
Corson, John J. The Governance of Colleges & Universities: Modernizing Structure & Processes.
Corson, Richard. Stage Makeup.
Corson, Samuel A. & Corson, E. O'Leary. Ethology & Nonverbal Communication in Mental Health: An Interdisciplinary Biopsychosocial Exploration.
Corson, Samuel A., tr. see Anokhin, Peter K.
Cort, John C. Christian Socialism: Moses to Gutierrez.
Cort, Margaret. Little Oleg.
Cortada, James W. Spain & the American Civil War: Relations at Mid-Century, 1855 to 1868.
Cortazar, Julio. Cronopios & Famas. Blackburn, Paul, tr. from Span.
--Hopscotch.
Cortesi, David, jt. auth. see Arnold, David E.
Cortesi, David E. Inside CP-M Plus.
--Inside CP-M-86.
Cortesi, David E., jt. auth. see Zussman, John.
Cortesi, Lawrence. Gunfight at Powder River.
--Justice at Iritara.
--The Last Outlaw.
Corti, Egon C. Maximilian & Charlotte of Mexico.
Cortina, Lynn E. Spanish-American Women Writers: A Bibliographical Research Checklist.
Cortland, Philip Van see Van Cortlandt, Philip.
Corvan, Thomas G. The Best of Gracian.
Corwen, Leonard. There's a Job for You In: Advertising, Commercial Art, Fashion, Films, Public Relations & Publicity, Publishing, Television & Radio, Travel & Tourism.
--Your Resume: Key to a Better Job.
Corwin, Charles H. Basic Chemistry: Laboratory Experiments.
Corwin, Edward S. Supplement to Edward S. Corwin's Constitution & What It Means Todays. Chase, Harold W. & Ducat, Craig R., eds.
Corwin, Harry O. & Jenkins, John B. Conceptual Foundation of Genetics: Selected Readings.
Corwin, Ronald G. Reform & Organizational Survival.
Corwin, Stanley J. How to Become a Bestselling Author.
Corwin, T. K., et al. International Technology for the Nonferrous Smelting Industry.
Coscia, Joseph F. Reincarnation of Bridgett.
Cosell, Howard & Bonventre, Peter. I Never Played the Game.
Cosell, Howard & Bonventure, Peter. I Never Played the Game.
Cosell, Howard & Bonvenure, Peter. I Never Played the Game.
Cosentino, Alfred S. California Ferraris.
--California Ferraris.
Cosenza & Boone. Marketing Compuprobs with IBM disk.
Coser, Lewis A. Masters of Sociological Thought: Ideas in Historical & Social Context.
Coser, Lewis A. & Rosenberg, Bernard. Sociological Theory.
Coser, Lewis A., ed. The Idea of Social Structure: Papers in Honor of Robert K. Merton.
Coser, Lewis A., et al. Introduction to Sociology.
Cosgrove, Francis M. Essentials of Discipleship.

Authors

Cosgrove, Patrick & Hussar, Lawrence. Abuse This Word.
Cosgrove, Stephen. Bangalle.
--Cap'n Smudge.
--Catundra. Manoni, Mary H., ed.
--Flutterby.
--Jake O'Shawnasey.
--Kartusch Book Cassette. Manoni, Mary H., ed.
--Little Mouse on the Prairie. Manoni, Mary H., ed.
--Mumkin.
--Nitter Pitter. Manoni, Mary H., ed.
--Trafalgar True.
Cosic, Dobrica. A Time of Death. Heppell, Muriel, tr.
Cosio Villegas, Daniel. American Extremes. Paredes, Americo, tr. from Span.
Cosminsky, Sheila, jt. auth. see Harrison, Ira E.
Cosofret, V. V. Membrane Electrodes in Drug-Substances Analysis. Thomas, J. D., ed.
Cospar Committee on the International Reference Atmosphere. CIRA Nineteen Seventy-Two.
COSPAR-IAU-IAG-IUGG-IUTAM Staff. Dynamics of Satellites: Proceedings, May 20-24, 1969. Morando, B., ed.
COSPAR-IAU-IUTAM Symposium Staff. Trajectories of Artificial Celestial Bodies As Determined from Observations: Proceedings of the COSPAR-IAU-IUTAM Symposium, Paris, 1965. Kovalevsky, J., ed.
COSRIMS Staff, ed. Mathematical Sciences: A Collection of Essays.
Cossaboom, Sterling P. Fundamentals of Music Theory.
Costa, Barbara C. & Ron, Judith S. The Pregnancy Planner: What You Have to Know, Remember, & Track Each Week of Your Pregnancy.
Costa, E., jt. ed. see Bradley, P. B.
Costa, Michael L. Master Trust: Simplifying Employee Benefits Trust Fund Administration.
Costa, Nicoletta. The Birthday Party.
--The New Puppy.
Costa, Roberto. Sweet Language: The Adventures of a Roman Lover.
Costa, S. Glossary of Harpsichord Terms: English-Deutch, Deutch-English.
Costabel, Eva D. A New England Village.
Costantini, Humberto. Gods, the Little Guys & the Police. Talbott, Toby, tr.
Costas, Orlando E. The Integrity of Mission: The Inner Life & Outreach of the Church.
Costello, Andrew, ed. Thomas More Engagement Calendar, 1989.
Costello, C. G. Psychology for Psychiatrists.
Costello, Charles G. Anxiety & Depression: The Adaptive Emotions.
Costello, D. P., tr. see Hedayat, Sadegh.
Costello, Dennis. New Venture Analysis: Research, Planning & Finance.
Costello, John J., et al. Finite Mathematics with Applications.
Costello, Joseph. Can Modern Man Survive Modern Government?
Costello, Marjorie & Katz, Cynthia. Breaking into Video.
Costello, R. B. American Expressions.
Coster, J., jt. ed. see Lewis, S. M.
Costigan, Giovanni. History of Modern Ireland: With a Sketch of Earlier Times.
Costikyan, Edward N. Behind Closed Doors: Politics in the Public Interest.
--How to Win Votes: The Politics of Nineteen Eighty.
Costonis, John J., et al. Regulation V. Compensation in Land Use Control: A Recommended Accommodation, a Critique, & an Interpretation.
Cote, Richard N. The Genealogists Guide to Charleston County, South Carolina.
Cote, Roxanne D. Sammy's Missing Blanket.
Cote, Wilfred A., ed. Biomass Utilization.
Cotes, Peter. Handbook for the Amateur Theatre.
Cotes, Peter & Niklaus, Thelma. Little Fellow: The Life & Work of Charles Chaplin.
Cotliar, William, jt. auth. see Riordan, John J.
Cotman, C. W., jt. ed. see Tapia, R.
Cotman, Carl W. & Jenson, Robert. Behavioral Neuroscience: An Introduction.
Cotner, Robert C. Readings in American History.
Cotran, Ramzi, ed. Tubulo-Interstitial Nephropathies.
Cotrell, Alvin, et al. Arms Transfers & U. S. Foreign & Military Policy.
Cott, Jonathan. Visions & Voices.
Cott, Jonathan, jt. auth. see Rolling Stone Press Staff.
Cott, Jonathan & Gimbel, Mary, eds. Wonders: Writings & Drawings for the Child in Us All.
Cottam, Philippa J. & Sutton, Andrew, eds. Conductive Education: A System for Overcoming Motor Disorder.
Cottenie, A. Soil & Plant Testing As a Basis of Fertilizer Recommendations.
Cotterell, Arthur. The First Emperor of China: The Greatest Archeological Find of Our Time.
Cotterman, W. W., et al, eds. Systems Analysis & Design: A Foundation for the 1980's.
Cotterman, William W., jt. auth. see Mize, Jan L.
Cotterrell, G. P., tr. see Jakubke, Hans-Dieter & Jeschkeit, Hans.
Cottier, H., et al, eds. see Symposium on Germinal Centers in Immune Responses - University Of Bern-Switzerland - 1966.
Cottle, Ronald E. The Lord's Prayer.
Cottle, Thomas J. Busing.
--Children in Jail.
--Perceiving Time: A Psychological Investigation with Men & Women.
--Private Lives & Public Accounts.
Cotton, F. Albert & Wilkinson, Geoffrey. Advanced Inorganic Chemistry: A Comprehensive Text.
Cotton, James H. Royce on the Human Self.
Cottrell, Alvin J. & Bray, Frank. Military Forces in the Persian Gulf.
Cottrell, Alvin J. & Hanks, Robert J. The Military Utility of the U. S. Facilities in the Philippines.
Cottrell, Alvin J., jt. auth. see Burrell, R. M.
Cottrell, Beekman W., jt. auth. see Slack, Robert C.
Cottrell, Jack. What the Bible Says about God the Ruler.
Cottrell, Leonard. The Lost Pharoahs.
Cottrell, Martha C., jt. auth. see Kushi, Michio.
Cottrell, Ron. The Remarkable Spaceship Earth.
Cottrell, Stan. To Run & Not Be Weary.
Cottrell, Sue. Hoof Beats North & South: Horses & Horsemen of the Civil War.
Cottress, Allin. Social Classes in Marxist Theory.
Cotzias, George & McDowell, Fletcher, eds. Developments in Treatment for Parkinson's Disease.
Couch, William T. The Human Potential: An Essay on Its Cultivation.
Coudroglou, Aliki. Work, Women & the Stuggle for Self-Sufficiency: The Win Experience.
Coudurier, L. & Wilkomirsky, I. Fundamentals of Metallurgical Processes.
Coughlan & Franke Staff. Going Co-op.
Coughlan, Neil. Young John Dewey: An Essay in American Intellectual History.
Coughlan, Peter. Holy Year Prayer Book.
Coughlan, William & Franke, Monte. Going CO-OP: The Complete Guide to Buying & Owning Your Own Apartment.
Coughlin, Mary T., jt. auth. see Brinckloe, William D.
Coughlin, Patrick J. Computing Strategies in Small Universities & Colleges.
Coughlin, T. Glen. The Hero of New York.
Coulbois, Paul, ed. Le Systeme monetaire international face aux Desequilibres: Report & Proceedings of a Seminar Held in Paris, November 23-25, 1981.
Coulby, David & Harper, Tim. Preventing Classroom Disruption: Policy, Practice & Evaluation in Urban Schools.
Coulling, Sidney. Matthew Arnold & His Critics: A Study of Arnold's Controversies.
Coulomb, J. & Caputo, M., eds. Mantle & Core in Planetary Physics.
Coulson, David & Clarke, James. The Roof of Africa.
Coulson, Robert. Arbitration in the Schools.
--Arbitration of Drug & Alcohol Disputes: A Casebook.
--Business Arbitration: What You Need to Know.
--Business Mediation: What You Need to Know.
--High Spy.
--How to Stay Out of Court.
--Labor Arbitration: What You Need to Know.
--Professional Mediation of Civil Disputes.
Coulson, Robert, jt. auth. see DeWeese, Gene.
Coulson, William D. An Annotated Bibliography of Greek & Roman Art, Architecture, & Archaeology.
Coulston, F. & Korte, F., eds. Environmental Quality: Global Aspects of Chemistry, Toxicology & Technology As Applied to the Environment.
Coulston, Frederick, ed. Regulatory Aspects of Carcinogenesis & Food Additives: The Delaney Clause.
Coulter, Carol. Are Religious Cults Dangerous?
Coulter, Jeff. Approaches to Insanity: A Philosophical & Sociological Study.
Coulter, M. O. Modern Chlor-Alkali Technology.
Coulter, Merle C. Story of the Plant Kingdom.
Coulter, N. Arthur, Jr. Leaping into Being.
Coulton, G. G. Medieval Panorama: The English Scene from Conquest to Reformation.
Coulton, George G. Art & the Reformation.
Council, Jon D. Profitable People Planning: A Guide to Effective Human Resource Management.
Council of Better Business Bureaus, Inc. Staff. How to Protect Your Business.
Council on Education in the Geological Sciences Staff & Wright, F. F. Estuarine Oceanography.
Council on Foreign Relations, Inc. Staff. Catalog of the Foreign Relations Library, First Supplement.
Council on Foreign Relations, Inc., Staff. Catalog of the Foreign Relations Library.
Council on International Educational Exchange Staff. Where to Stay U. S. A.
Council on International Educational Exchange Staff & Cohen, Marjorie A. Where to Stay U. S. A., 1984-85.
Council on Interracial Books for Children, Inc. Staff. Guidelines for Selecting Bias-Free Textbooks & Storybooks.
--Guidelines for Selecting Bias-Free Textbooks & Storybooks.
--Stereotypes, Distortions & Omissions in U. S. History Textbooks: A Content Analysis Instrument for Detecting Racism & Sexism.
--Unlearning "Indian" Stereotypes.
Coundakis, Anthony L. Mannerism on Space Communication: Some Methods & Some Reflections.
Counihan, Martin. A Dictionary of Energy.
Counsel, June. But Martin!
--A Dragon in Class Four.
Counter Information Services. Buying Time in South Africa.
Countryman, Vern, et al. Law in Contemporary Society: The Orgain Lectures.
Counts, George S. Education & American Civilization.
Coupe, Judith D. & Porter, Jill, eds. The Education of Children with Severe Learning Difficulties: Bridging the Gap Between Theory & Practice.
Couper, Alastair, ed. The Times Atlas of the Oceans.
Couper, Heather. The Planets.
Couper, Heather, jt. auth. see Henbest, Nigel.
Courcy, Pol Potier De see Potier De Courcy, Pol.
Courlander, Harold. King's Drum & Other African Stories.
--King's Drum: And Other African Stories.
--People of the Short Blue Corn: Tales & Legends of the Hopi Indians.
--Piece of Fire & Other Haitian Tales.
--Tiger's Whisker & Other Tales & Legends from Asia & the Pacific.
Courlander, Harold & Eshugbayi, Ezekiel A. Olode the Hunter & Other Tales from Nigeria.
Courlander, Harold & Prempeh, Albert K. Hat-Shaking Dance & Other Ashanti Tales from Ghana.
Courlander, Harold, ed. Hopi Voices: Recollections, Traditions, & Narratives of the Hopi Indians.
Cournos, John, tr. from Rus. see Biely, Andrei.
Cournoyer, Norman G. & Marshall, Anthony G. Hotel, Restaurant & Travel Law.
Courrier, Kathleen, ed. Journal '86.
Course, A. G. Dictionary of Nautical Terms.
Court, John M. Helping Your Diabetic Child: A Guide to Parents & to Their Children Who Have Diabetes.
--Myth & History in Revelation: The Book of Revelation.
Court, Rosemary. Sam's System: A Guide to Computers.
Court, T. H., jt. auth. see Clay, Reginald S.
Court, Wesli. Courses in Lambents.
Courteline, Georges. Ah! Jeunesse.
--Boubouroche, Lidoire et Potiron.
--Les Femmes d'Amis.
--Le Gendarme Est Sans Pitie: Avec: La Peur des Coupes, Theodore Cherche des Allumettes, La Couche.
--Hortense, Couche-toi: Avec: La Conversion d'Alceste, Monsieur Badinet, Les Boulingrin.
--Les Linottes.
--Theatre Complet.
Courteline, Georges & Pruner, Francis. Les Gaietes de l'Escadron.
--Messieurs les Ronds-de-cuirt.
Courter, Gay. The Beansprout Book.
--Code Ezra.
--River of Dreams.
Courtin, Nicholas, tr. see De Hoyos, Ladislas.
Courtin, Robina, ed. see McDonald, Kathleen.
Courtine, Robert J. Madame Maigret's Recipes.
--Madame Maigret's Recipes. Manheim, Mary, tr.
Courtney, Alice E. & Whipple, Thomas W. Sex Stereotyping in Advertising.
Courtney, Caroline. Libertine in Love.
--The Masquerading Heart.
Courtney, Donald. Simba Gold.
Courtney, E. Wayne, ed. Applied Research in Education.
Courtney, James F., Jr. & Jensen, Ronald. The Systems Laboratory for Information Management.
Courtney, Nicholas. Diana, Princess of Wales.
Courtney, William P. Secrets of Our National Literature: Chapters in the History of the Anonymous & Pseudonymous Writings of Our Countrymen.
Courts, Andrew B. Betcha Didn'tNo.
Courvoisier, Jaques. Zwingli: A Reformed Theologian.
Couse, G. S., jt. ed. see Mudroch, Vaclav.
Couser, G. Thomas. American Autobiography: The Prophetic Mode.
Cousins, Ewert H., ed. Hope & the Future of Man.
Cousins, M. F. Engineering Drawing form the Beginning.
--Engineering Drawing from the Beginning.
Cousins, Norman. Albert Schweitzer's Mission: Healing & Peace.
--The Improbable Triumvirate: Kennedy-Khrushchev-Pope John, an Asterisk to the History of a Hopeful Year, 1962-3.
Cousins, Norman, ed. The Physician in Literature.
Cousse, Raymond. Death Sty: A Pig's Tale.
--Death Sty: A Pig's Tale.
Cousseau, Henry-Claude, ed. Colour since Matisse.
Coustillas, Pierre, ed. see Gissing, George.
Coutchie, Mariann. Jewelry on Display.
Couthen, Charles E., Jr. Evaluation of Statistical Planning & Acquisitions for Small Businesses.
Coutinho, Elisman M., et al. Prostaglandins II: Clinical Aspects.
Coutts, Lyn C. & Hardy, Leslie K. Teaching for Health: The Nurse As Health Educator.
Couturier, Maurice & Durand, Regis. Donald Barthelme.
Couvveur, F. S. Dictionnaire Classique de la Langue Chinoise.
Covannier, Henry. St. Francis De Sales.
Covell, Jon Carter & Yamada, Abbot S. Unraveling Zen's Red Thread: Ikkyu's Controversial Way.
Covell, Mara, et al. The Home Alternative to Hospitals & Nursing Homes.
Covello, Leonard & D'Agnostino, Guido. Teacher in the Urban Community.
Coveney, J., ed. International Organization Documents for Translation from French.
Cover, Arthur B., et al, eds. Harlan Ellison Presents the Best of the New Wave.
Cover, Nelson, compiled by. A Guide to Successful Phonathons.
Coverdale, G. M. Planning Education in Relation to Rural Development.
Coverdale, Gerald D. Snowflakes in the Desert.
Covernton, Mary, et al. Bali & Lombok: A Travel Survival Kit.
Covey, Frances A. The Earl Covey Story.
Covi, Dario A. The Inscription in Fifteenth-Century Florentine Painting. Freedberg, S. J., ed.
Covill, William E., Jr. Ink Bottles & Inkwells.
Covin, Theron M., ed. Readings in Human Development: A Humanist Approach.
--Readings in the Psychology of Early Childhood.
Covington, A. K., ed. Ion Selective Electrode Methodology.
Covington, A. K. & Dickinson, T., eds. Physical Chemistry of Organic Solvent Systems.
Covington, Jim. Confessions of a Single Father.
Covino, Frank. Controlled Painting.
Covino, Willam A., jt. auth. see Weber, Loraine J.
Covino, William A. & Coda-Messerle, Margaret. GED Reading Skills Test Preparation Guide: High School Equivalency Examination.
Covvey, et al. Computers in the Practice of Medicine: Survey of Medical Computing.
Cowan, D. O. & Drisko, R. L., eds. Elements of Organic Photochemistry.
Cowan, Elizabeth, jt. auth. see Cowan, Gregory.
Cowan, Evelyn. Spring Remembered: A Scottish Jewish Childhood.
Cowan, Geoffrey. See No Evil.
Cowan, Gregory & Cowan, Elizabeth. Writing.
Cowan, H. J., jt. auth. see Gero, J. S.
Cowan, Henry J. The Design of Reinforced Concrete in Accordance with the Metric SAA Concrete Structures Code.
--Design of Reinforced Concrete Structures.
--A Dictionary of Architectural Science.
Cowan, Richard O. Doctrine & Covenants: Our Modern Scripture.
Cowan, Thomas. Beyond the Bath: A Dreamer's Guide.
--Beyond the Kitchen: A Dreamer's Guide.
Cowan, Thomas D. How to Tap into Your Own Genius.
Coward, Noel. Plays: Four.
--Plays: One.
--Plays: Three.
--Plays: Two.
Coward, Rosalind. Female Desires: How They Are Sought, Bought, & Packaged.
Cowart, Jack, ed. Roy Lichtenstein.
Cowden-Guido, Richard. Report from the Synod: John Paul II & the Battle for Vatican II.
Cowdry, E. V. & Seno, S. Nucleic Acid Metabolism, Cell Differentiation & Cancer Growth.
Cowel, Lucinda, jt. auth. see Gilliam, Terry.
Cowell, F. R. The Garden As Fine Art.
Cowell, Sally. Happy Times with Happy Seeds.
Cowen, Emory L., jt. auth. see Zax, Melvin.
Cowen, Robert & McLean, Martin, eds. International Handbook of Education Systems: Asia, Australasia & Latin America.
Cowen, Zelman. A Touch of Healing: Speeches by Sir Zelman Cowen As Governor General, 1977-1982. Walker, W. G., ed.

Cowhey, Peter F., jt. auth. see Aaronson, Jonathan D.
Cowie, Ian. Growing Knowing Jesus.
Cowie, Peter. Ingmar Bergman: A Critical Biography.
--Ingmar Bergman: A Critical Biography.
Cowie, V. A Study of the Early Development of Mongols.
Cowie, Vera. Games.
--Rich & the Mighty.
--The Rich & the Mighty.
Cowin, S. C., ed. Mechanical Properties of Bone.
--Mechanics Applied to the Transport of Bulk Materials AMD.
Cowle, Hazel L. Gilagae.
Cowles, Fleur, jt. auth. see Vavra, Robert.
Cowles, George. The Accessible Wilderness.
Cowles, Ginny. Nicholas.
Cowles, V. Phantom Major.
Cowley, Abraham. Essays, Plays & Sundry Verses.
Cowley, Alan H., ed. Compounds Containing Phosphorus-Phosphorus Bonds.
Cowley, David. Molded & Slip Cast Pottery & Ceramics.
--Moulded Slip Cast Pottery.
--Moulded Slip Cast Pottery.
Cowley, G., jt. auth. see MacPhee, I.
Cowley, Hannah. The Plays of Hannah Cowley. Link, Frederick M., ed.
Cowley, R. A., jt. auth. see Bruce, A. D.
Cowling, Elizabeth. The Cello.
--The Cello.
Cowling, K., et al. Resource Structure of Agriculture: An Economic Analysis.
Cowling, Keith. Monopoly Capitalism.
Cowling, T. M. & Steeley, G. C. Sub-Regional Planning Studies: An Evaluation.
Cowman, Mrs. Charles E. Mountain Trailways for Youth: Devotions for Young People.
--Streams in the Desert.
--Streams in the Desert.
--Streams in the Desert.
Cowper, Ann & Young, Cyril. Family Planning: Fundamentals for Health Professionals.
Cox, jt. auth. see Enis.
Cox, Alwyn see Milne, John.
Cox, Andrew W., jt. auth. see McKay, David.
Cox, Archibald. Law & the National Labor Policy.
Cox, Arthur M. The Dynamics of Detente.
Cox, Bryan. The Law of Special Educational Needs: A Guide to the Education Act 1981.
Cox, Charles, jt. ed. see Beck, John.
Cox, D. R. Analysis of Binary Data.
Cox, D. R. & Smith, W. L. Queues: Receptors & Recognition Series B. Incl. Vol. 13. Receptor Regulation; Vol. 12. Purinergic Receptors; Vol. 11. Membrane Receptors; Vol. 10. Neurotransmitter Receptors, Part 2: Biogenic Amines; Vol. 9. Neurotransmitter Receptors, Part 1: Amino Acids, Peptides & Benzodiazepines; Vol. 8. Virus Receptors, Part 2: Animal Viruses; Vol. 7. Virus Receptors, Part 1: Bacterial Viruses; Vol. 6. Bacterial Adherence; Vol. 5. Taxis & Behavior; Vol. 4. Specificity of Embryological Interactions; Vol. 3. Microbial Interactions; Vol. 2. Intercellular Junctions & Synapses; Vol. 1. The Specificity & Action of Animal, Bacterial & Plant Toxins. Routledge Chapman & Hall.
Cox, Earnest S. Lincoln's Negro Policy.
Cox, Edwin. Problems & Possibilities for Religious Education.
Cox, Elizabeth. Familiar Ground.
Cox, Eugene L. The Eagles of Savoy: The House of Savoy in Thirteenth Century Europe.
Cox, Evelyn & Sandberg, Janet, eds. Nutrition & the Elderly: A Selected Annotated Bibliography for Nutrition & Health Professionals.
Cox, Geoffrey, tr. see Okte, Faik.
Cox, Gerald. Seashore Life.
Cox, Harold. Aging, 1988-89.
--Annual Editions: Aging.
Cox, Harold G. Later Life: The Realities of Aging.
Cox, Harvey. Religion in the Secular City: Toward a Post-Modern Theology.
--Religion in the Secular City: Toward a Postmodern Theology.
--Seduction of the Spirit.
--Turning East: The Promise & Peril of the New Orientalism.
Cox, Harvey & Fletcher, Joseph, eds. Situation Ethics Debate.
Cox, Helen. Cooking under Pressure.
--The Floral Art Book of Reference.
Cox, James H. Confessions of a Moonlight Writer: A Freelancer's Guide to the Church Market.
Cox, James W., ed. The Minister's Manual for Nineteen Eighty-Five.
--The Ministers Manual for Nineteen Eighty-Four.
--The Ministers Manual for Nineteen Eighty-Six.
Cox, James W., tr. see Windisch, Hans.
Cox, Jerome R., Jr., jt. ed. see Larson, Kenneth B.
Cox, Joan. Mindsong.
--Star Web.
Cox, John H. & Cox, Lawanda. Politics, Principle & Prejudice 1865-1866: Dilemma of Reconstruction in America.
Cox, John L., ed. Transcultural Psychiatry.
Cox, Kevin R. & Golledge, Reginald G., eds. Behavioural Problems in Geography Revisited.
Cox, Lawanda, jt. auth. see Cox, John H.
Cox, Murray. Coding the Therapeutic Process: Emblems of Encounter.
--Structuring the Therapeutic Process: Compromise with Chaos - a Therapist's Response to the Individual & the Group.
Cox, O. C. Foundations of Capitalism.
Cox, Oliver C. Capitalism & American Leadership.
Cox, Palmer. The Brownies: Their Book.
Cox, Peter R., et al, eds. see Eugenics Society Annual Symposium Staff.
Cox, R. A., ed. Offshore Medicine: Medical Care of Employees in the Offshore Oil Industry.
Cox, R. J., ed. Photographic Gelatin II.
Cox, R. J., ed. see Photographic Gelatin Symposium Staff.
Cox, Richard A. Technicians Guide To Programmable Controllers.
Cox, Samuel. Pilgrim Psalms: Exp.-Songs of Degrees.
Cox, Steve, tr. see Waldberg, Michael.
Cox, T. Motor Boat & Yachting Manual.
Cox, Tom. Damned Englishman: A Study of Erskine Childers (1870-1922)
Cox, Victoria, jt. auth. see Applebaum, Stan.
Coxe, Weld. Marketing Architectural & Engineering Services.
Coxeter, H. S. Unvergangliche Geometrie.
Coxhead, David & Hiller, Susan. Dreams: Visions of the Night.
Coxon, Margaret E. Gardening as Therapy: A Resource Manual of Horticultural Therapy Programs for the Summer Season.
Coxon, Margaret E., et al. Gardening as Therapy: A Resource Manual for Development of Horticultural Therapy Programs for the Spring Season.
Coyle, John J. & Bardi, Edward J. The Management of Business Logistics.
Coyle, Karen. RLIN II Processing for UC Online Catalog Input: Bibliographic Specifications.
Coyle, R. G. Management System Dynamics.
Coyle, Wallace. Stanley Kubrick: A Guide to Reference & Resources.
Coyle, Wallace, jt. ed. see Fowler, William.
Coyle, Wallace, jt. ed. see Fowler, William M.
Coyne. Readings in Managerial Economics.
Coyne, John. The Hunting Season.
--The Piercing.
Coyne, John & Wright, Mike. Management Buy-Outs.
Coyne, Thomas J. Managerial Economics: Analysis & Cases.
--Readings in Managerial Economics.
Coysh, A. W. Dictionary & Picture Postcards in Britain 1894-1939.
Cozby, Paul C. Methods in Behavioral Research.
--Using Computers in the Behavioral Sciences.
Cozzens, James G. Ask Me Tomorrow.
--By Love Possessed.
--Castaway.
--Castaway.
--The Just & the Unjust.
--Men & Brethren.
--Morning Noon & Night.
--S. S. San Pedro.
CQ Inc. Staff. Aging in America.
Crabb, George. English Synonyms.
Crabbe, John. Hector Berlioz: Rational Romantic.
Crabbe, Pierre. ORD & CD in Chemistry & Biochemistry: An Introduction.
Crabbe, Pierre, ed. Prostaglandin Research.
Crabill, Calvin, jt. auth. see Stein, Sherman.
Crabtree, T. T. The Zondervan Nineteen Eighty-Seven Pastor's Annual: A Planned Preaching Program for the Year.
Cracknell, A. P. Applied Group Theory.
Cracraft, James. The Soviet Union Today: An Interpretive Guide.
Craddock, Fred & Keck, Leander. Pentecost 3.
Craddock, Fred B., jt. auth. see Saunders, Ernest W.
Craft, Ann & Craft, Michael. Handicapped Married Couples: A Welsh Study of Couples Handicapped from Birth by Mental, Physical or Personality Disorder.
--Sex & the Mentally Handicapped.
Craft, Christine. An Anchorwoman's Story.
Craft, James E. Wheels on the Mountains.
Craft, M. & Miles, L. Patterns of Care for the Mentally Subnormal.
Craft, M., ed. Psychopathic Disorders.
Craft, Maurice, ed. Teaching in a Multicultural Society: The Task for Teacher Education.
Craft, Michael, jt. auth. see Craft, Ann.
Craft, Paul E. Cats & Other People.
Craft, Robert. A Stravinsky Scrapbook.
Crafton, Roy L., jt. auth. see Kramer, Jack.
Crafts, Kathy & Hauther, Brenda. How to Beat the System: The Student's Guide to Good Grades.
Crafts, Roger C. Textbook of Human Anatomy.
Crafts, Roger C. & Binhammer, Robert T. A Guide to a Regional Dissection & Study of the Human Body.
Crafts-Lighty, Anita. Information Sources in Biotechnology.
Cragg, Dan. The Guide to Military Installations.
Cragg, Ernest E. The Cragg Commentaries.
Cragg, Gerald R. Freedom & Authority: A Study of English Thought in the Early Seventeenth Century.
Cragg, Gordon M., jt. ed. see Pettit, George R.
Cragin, Valerie. Method Modeling.
--Photographic Modeling.
Craig, Albert M., ed. Japan: A Comparative View.
Craig, Alisa. A Dismal Thing to Do.
Craig, Ann L., jt. auth. see Cornelius, Wayne A.
Craig, Barbara G., ed. The Individual Investor's Guide to No-Load Mutual Funds.
Craig, C. Y., ed. Geology of Scotland.
Craig, Charles P. Fundamentals of Infection Control: An In-Service Orientation Program.
Craig, D. H. Sir John Harington.
Craig, E. T. An Irish Commune: The Experiment of Ralahine, County Clare 1831-1833.
Craig, Eleanor. If We Could Hear the Grass Grow.
Craig, Gary & Derricourt, Nick, eds. Community Work & the State: Towards a Radical Practice-Community Work Eight.
Craig, Gordon. Gordon Craig's Paris Diary 1932 - 1933. Franklin, Colin, ed.
Craig, Gordon A. & Gilbert, Felix, eds. Diplomats, Nineteen Nineteen to Nineteen Thirty-Nine.
Craig, Grace J. Human Development.
Craig, Grace J., jt. auth. see Specht, Riva.
Craig, Hardin. English Religious Drama of the Middle Ages.
Craig, Hardin, Jr., ed. Rededication of Fondren Library of Rice University.
Craig, Howard A. Sunward I've Climbed.
Craig, Isabel, jt. auth. see Blaustein, Saul J.
Craig, James. Phototypesetting: A Design Manual. Malmstrom, Margit, ed.
Craig, James D., ed. The Care & Feeding of New Converts.
Craig, Linda, jt. auth. see Holabird, Katherine.
Craig, M. Jean. Dinosaurs & More Dinosaurs.
Craig, M. S. The Third Blonde: A Novel of Suspense.
--To Play the Fox.
Craig, Mary. Pope John Paul II.
Craig Norback & Co. Staff. The Gerber Baby Encyclopedia.
Craig, R. F. Soil Mechanics.
Craig, R. G. & Labovitz, M. L., eds. Future Trends in Geomathematics.
Craig, Richard A. Upper Atmosphere: Meteorology & Physics.
Craig, Robert G. Restorative Dental Materials.
Craig, Ruth H. Learning the Nemeth Braille Code: A Manual for Teachers.
Craig, Tom, jt. ed. see Christodolou, Anastasios.
Craig, W. Lawrence & Park, William W. International Chamber of Commerce Arbitration.
Craiger-Smith, Alan. Tin-Glaze Pottery.
Craighead, Donna. Fifth Annual Microcomputers in Education Conference.
Craighead, Donna & Bitter, Gary G., eds. The Best of the Proceedings Microcomputers in Education Conferences 1982-84.
Craighead, T. W. Sneaking Through Sociology: An Instructional System for the Introductory Course.
Craighead, W. Edward, et al. Behavior Modification.
--Behavior Modification: Principles, Issues & Applications.
Craigmyle, Marshall B. The Aprocrine Glands & the Breast.
--The Mixed Cranial Nerves.
Craik. Big Book of Classic Fairy Stories.
Crain, Jim. Historic Country Inns of California.
Crain, Mary B., ed. see L. A. Weekly Staff.
Crain, Robert L. & Weisman, Carlos S. Discrimination, Personality & Achievement: A Survey of Northern Negroes.
Crais, Robert. The Monkey's Raincoat.
Cramer, Gail L. & Jensen, Clarence W. Agricultural Economics & Agribusiness.
Cramer, J. B. Fifty Selected Piano Studies. Von Bulow, Hans, ed.
Cramer, Kenneth R. & Pai, Shi I. Magnetofluid Dynamics for Engineers & Applied Physicists.
Cramer, Phebe. Word Association.
Cramer, Robert F. Hunger Fighter in Burma: The Story of Brayton Case.
Cramer, Stanley H., jt. auth. see Herr, Edwin L.
Cramer, William & Kane, Gerry. The Sixty-Eight Thousand Microprocessor Handbook.
Cramer, William D., jt. auth. see Erickson, Jonathan.
Cramond, Mike. Killer Bears.
Crampton, C. Gregory. The Zunis of Cibola.
Crampton, Esme. A Handbook of the Theatre.
Crampton, Norman. How to Get from the Airport to the City.
Crampton, Patricia. My Little Bear.
--My Little Bunny.
--My Little Cat.
--My Little Duck.
--My Little Lamb.
--My Little Panda.
--My Little Pig.
--My Little Puppy.
Crampton, Patricia, tr. see Bomans, Godfried.
Crampton, Patricia, tr. see Klink, J. L.
Crampton, Richard. The Hollow Detente: Anglo-German Relations in the Balkans, 1911-1914.
Cramton, Roger C., et al. Conflict of Laws, Cases, Comments, Questions.
Crandall, Chuck. What's Wrong with My Plant?
Crandall, Jo Ann. Adult Vocational ESL.
Crandall, N. Emily Bronte, a Psychological Portrait.
Crandall-Stotler, Barbara & Jacobson, Katherine, eds. Bios: Process & Diversity.
Crandell, Clifton E., ed. Comprehensive Care in Dentistry.
Crane, A. & Lemoine, J. An Introduction to the Regenerative Method for Simulation Analysis.
Crane, Caroline. Someone at the Door.
--Something Evil.
--Woman Vanishes.
--Woman Vanishes.
Crane, Dale. Airframe Mechanic.
--General Mechanic: A Capstan Guide: Fast-Track Method Ser.
--Private Pilot: Airplane.
Crane, Diana. Invisible Colleges: Diffusion of Knowledge in Scientific Communities.
Crane, Donald P. Personnel Management: A Situational Approach.
Crane, Frederick. Extant Medieval Musical Instruments: A Provisional Catalogue by Types.
Crane, John. Annual Editions: Biology.
Crane, John K. The Legacy of Ladysmith.
Crane, John W., ed. Contemporary Readings for General Biology.
Crane, Keith, tr. see Pecsi, Kalman.
Crane, Nancy. Working with the Pregnant Teenager: A Guide for Nutrition Educators.
Crane, Nick & Crane, Richard. Bicycles up Kilimanjaro.
Crane, P. W. Electronics for Technicians.
--Worked Examples in Basic Electronics.
Crane, Peter du see Du Crane, Peter.
Crane, R. S. & Kaye, F. B. Census of British Newspapers & Periodicals, 1620-1800.
Crane, Richard, jt. auth. see Crane, Nick.
Crane, Stephen. The Red Badge of Courage.
--The Red Badge of Courage. Binder, Henry, ed.
--The Red Badge of Courage.
--Red Badge of Courage: An Annotated Text with Critical Essays.
--Red Badge of Courage: An Annotated Text with Critical Essays. Bradley, Sculley, et al, eds.
Crane, Stephen W., jt. ed. see Betts, C. W.
Crane, Thomas F. Italian Popular Tales.
Crane, Walter. The Baby's Opera.
Crane, William. Oom-Pah.
Crank, Harriet P. Empty Boxes.
Crankshaw, Edward. Gestapo: Instrument of Tyranny.
Cranor, Phoebe. Why Doesn't God Do Something?
Cranston, Edwin A., tr. see Okada, Barbara T.
Cranston, Maurice. What Are Human Rights?
Cranstoon, James, ed. see Scott, Alexander.
Crapo, et al. Introduction to Medicine.
Crase, Douglas. The Revisionist.
Crassweller, Robert. Peron & the Enigmas of Argentina.
Craston, Alan, ed. Open to the Spirit.
Crater, Flora. Woman Activist Guide for Women Candidates.
--The Woman Activist Guide to Lobbying, 1977.
Craton, Michael. Roots & Branches: Current Directions in Slave Studies.
Cratty, Bryant J. Developmental Games for Physically Handicapped Children.
Crauder, Renee C. & Etter-Lewis, Gwendolyn E. A Short Course in Remedial English Composition.
Cravalho, Ernest G. Critical Issues in Medical Technology. McNeil, Barbara J., ed.
Craven, Avery O. Rachel of Old Louisiana.
Craven, B. D. Functions of Several Variables.
--Lebesgue Measure & Intergral.
--Mathematical Programming & Control Theory.
Craven, John. A Nation's Choice.
Craven, Wayne, text by. Two Hundred Years of American Art: The Munson-Williams-Proctor Institute.
Craven, Wesley F. White, Red, & Black: The Seventeenth-Century Virginian.
Craver, Elena B. The Bulgarian Longevity: Clues to a Long Life.
Craver, John. VisiCalc for Apple II, II Plus, & IIe.
Cravey, R. H., jt. auth. see Gottschalk, L. A.
Cravey, Robert H. & Baselt, Randall C., eds. Introduction to Forensic Toxicology.
Craw, Julia & French, Bernada. Family Fun with Rocks.

Crawford, A. Berry & Peterson, Dean F. Environmental Management in the Colorado River Basin.
Crawford, Anne, ed. Europa Biographical Dictionary of British Women.
Crawford, Arch. A Doll Named Moses.
Crawford, Charles P. Letter Perfect.
Crawford, D. F., jt. auth. see Messel, H.
Crawford, E. David & Borden, Thomas A., eds. Genitourinary Cancer Surgery.
Crawford, Elisabeth T. The Sociology of the Social Sciences: A Trend Report & Bibliography.
Crawford, Elizabeth D., tr. see Grimm, Jacob & Grimm, Wilhelm K.
Crawford, Elizabeth D., tr. see Schaad, Hans P.
Crawford, G. Cullen, jt. auth. see Rayne, John.
Crawford, H. W. & McDowell, Milton C. Math Workbook for Foodservice-Lodging.
Crawford, H. Warren & Rodgers, John F. Maryland Supplement for Modern Real Estate Practice.
Crawford, Irene. Aids to Independence: A Guide to Products for the Disabled & Elderly.
Crawford, James P. Spanish Drama Before Lope de Vega.
Crawford, Joanna. Primrose.
Crawford, John T., III & Hustrulid, William A., eds. Open Pit Mine Planning & Design.
Crawford, Linda. Ghost of a Chance.
Crawford, Marguerite C. & Fuller, Marietta C. Cornshuck Crafts.
Crawford, Mary C. Little Pilgrimages Among Old New England Inns: Being an Account of Little Journeys to Various Quaint Inns & Hostelries of Colonial New England.
Crawford, Max. The Bad Communist.
--Six Key Cut.
Crawford, Oliver. Done This Day: The European Idea in Action.
Crawford, Peter. The Living Isles: A Natural History of Britain & Ireland.
Crawford, R. J. Plastics Engineering.
Crawford, R. M. A Bit of a Rebel: The Life & Work of George Arnold Wood (1865-1928)
Crawford, Richard. The Civil War Songbook.
--A Historian's Introduction to Early American Music.
Crawford, Robert. But I'm Only a Social Drinker: A Guide to Coping with Alcohol.
Crawford, Shirley O. Is God Dead Within You?
Crawford, Tad. Legal Guide for the Visual Artist.
Crawford, William P. Sea Marine Atlas: Southern California.
Crawley, Brian E., jt. ed. see Feldman, Stanley A.
Crawley, Ernest. Mystic Rose: A Study of Primitive Marriage & of Primitive Thought in Its Bearing on Marriage. Besterman, Theodore, ed.
Crawley, Gerald M. Energy.
Cray, Ed. Levi's.
Crayder, Dorothy. Ishkabibble!
--Pluperfect of Love.
--She & the Dubious Three.
--She, the Adventuress.
Craz, Albert G. & Mavragis, Edward P. Writing: The Business Letter.
CRDI, Ottawa. Le Role des Arbres au Sahel: Compte Rendu du Colloque tenu a Dakar (Senegal) du 5 au 10 Novembre 1979.
Creagh, Patrick, tr. see Conti, Flavio.
Creagh-Osborne, Richard. This Is Racing.
--This Is Sailing.
Creamer, Don. Student Development in Higher Education.
Creamer, Robert W. Stengel: His Life & Times.
Crean, Michael J. Principles of Real Estate Analysis.
Crean, Patrick & Kome, Penney, eds. Peace: A Dream Unfolding.
Crease, J., et al, eds. Essays on Oceanography: A Tribute to John Swallow.
Crease, R., tr. see Taminiaux, J.
Crease, Robert P. & Mann, Charles C. The Second Creation: Makers of the Revolution in Twentieth Century Physics.
Creasey, John see also Marric, J. J.
Creasey, William A., ed. Clinical Pharmacology: Symposium Proceedings.
Creasman, William T., jt. auth. see DiSaia, Philip J.
Creason, Sam. How to Build a Microcomputer & Really Understand It. DeTray, Jeffrey D., ed.
Creasy, Robert K. & Resnik, Robert. Maternal-Fetal Medicine: Principles & Practice.
Creative Concepts. Bluegrass Complete: Complete Words, Music & Guitar Chords for Eighty-Nine Songs.
Creative Homeowner Press Editors. Best Baths.
Crebillon, Claude P. The Wayward Head & Heart. Bray, Barbara, tr.
Crede, Charles E., jt. auth. see Harris, Cyril M.
Credit Research Foundation. Cash Application Using MICR Number.
--Cash Application Using Remit Card.
--Customer Deductions: Evaluation & Resolution.
--Customer Deductions Impact on Receivables.
--DSO As a Management Tool.
--Electronic Funds Transfer System for Business Payments.
--Failure Forecasting.
--How to Evaluate Changes in Credit Policy.
Creed, Virginia. France.
Creed, Virginia & Douglas Jackson, W. A. France & Soviet Union.
Creedy, Judith & Wall, Norbert. Real Estate Investment by Objective.
Creek, Eddie J., jt. auth. see Smith, J. Richard.
Creekmore, W. & Behasa, S. Through the MicroMaze: A Visual Guide to Getting Organized.
Creekmore, Wayne. Through the Micromaze: A Visual Guide from Ashton-Tate.
Creel, Austin. Dharma in Hindu Ethics.
Creel, Catherine. The Yankee & the Belle.
--The Yankee & the Belle.
Creeley, Robert. Selected Poems.
--Was That a Real Poem & Other Essays. Allen, Donald, ed.
Creemers, B. & Verloop, N., eds. Educational Evaluation in the Netherlands.
Cregan, Ailsa, jt. auth. see Jones, Philip R.
Cregg, J. S., jt. ed. see Burges, A.
Creighton, Breen & Gunningham, Neil, eds. The Industrial Relations of Occupational Health & Saftey.
Creighton, Ethel S. The Soul of the City.
Creighton, Joanne V. Margaret Drabble.
Creighton, W. B. Working Women & the Law.
Creishton, H. Campbell, tr. see Rezanov, I. A.
Crenshaw. Bedside Manners.
Crenshaw, A. H., jt. auth. see Edmonson, A. S.
Crenshaw, James. Gerhard von Rad.
Crenshaw, James L. Samson: A Secret Betrayed, a Vow Ignored.
Crenshaw, James L., ed. Theodicy in the Old Testament.
Crepaldi, G., et al, eds. Diabetes, Obesity & Hyperlipidemias.
Crepax, Guido. Illustrated Emanuelle: Based on the Novel by Emmanuelle Arsan.
Crepax, Guido, illus. The Illustrated Justine: Based on the Novel by the Marquis De Sade.
Crescimbeni, Joseph. Arithmetic Enrichment Activities for Elementary School Children.
--Language Enrichment Activities for the Elementary School.
Crespelle, Jean-Paul. Monet: The Masterworks.
Cress, Donald A., tr. see Rousseau, Jean-Jacques.
Cress, Lawrence D. Citizens in Arms: The Army & Militia in American Society to the War of 1812.
Cress, P., et al. FORTRAN IV with WATFOR & WATFIV.
Cress, Sheila S., jt. auth. see Loxley-Taylor, Cynthia M.
Cressey, William W. Spanish Phonology & Morphology: A Generative View.
Cresswell, Helen. The Beachcombers.
Creston, Paul. Rational Metric Notation: The Mathematical Basis of Meters, Symbols, a Note-Values.
Cretcher, Dorothy. Steering Clear: Helping Your Child Through the High-Risk Drug Years.
Cretti, Luciano & Bosisio, Gina B. House Plants: A Color Guide.
Creutzfeld, O., ed. Apparent & Intrinsic Organization of Laminated Structures in the Brain.
Creutzfeldt, W. & Schauder, P., eds. Mittelkettige Triglyzeride in der Parenteralen Ernaehrung.
Creutzfeldt, W., et al, eds. The Genetics of Diabetes Mellitus.
Crew, Michael A., ed. Analyzing the Impact of Regulatory Change in Public Utilities.
--Regulatory Reform & Public Utilities.
Crewe. Parasitic Diseases: Their Biology, Clinical Diagnosis & Therapy.
Crews, Clyde F. Fundamental Things Apply: Reflecting on Christian Basics.
Crews, Donald. Truck.
Crews, Harry. A Feast of Snakes.
Cribb, A. B. & Cribb, J. W. Plant Life of the Great Barrier Reef & Adjacent Shores.
Cribb, J. W., jt. auth. see Cribb, A. B.
Cribbin, James J. Effective Managerial Leadership.
Crichton, Michael. Congo.
--Five Patients.
--The Terminal Man.
Crick, Bernard. George Orwell: A Life.
Crick, Bernard, ed. Unemployment.
Crick, Francis. Life Itself.
Crick, Michael. The March of Militant.
--Militant.
Crick, Paul A. Living Abroad & Sailing.
Crider, Andrew B., et al. Psychology.
Crider, Janet. Quick & Easy Wordstar 2000.
--Word for Word: A Comparative Guide to Word Processing Software.
Crider, Virginia. The Lost God.
Cridland, Nancy C., jt. auth. see Wiltz, John E.
Crigorieff, R. D., jt. ed. see Alefeld, G.
Criley, J. Michael, jt. auth. see French, William J.
Crim, Keith, tr. see Gollwitzer, Helmut.
Crim, Keith, tr. see Westermann, Claus.
Crim, Keith R., tr. see Gese, Hartmut.
Crim, Keith R., tr. see Wolff, Hans W.
Crim, Lottie R. Come Care with Me.
Crippen, G. M. Distance Geometry & Conformational Calculations.
Crippen, Raymond C. The Waste of Money.
Cripps, E. L. Regional Science: New Concepts & Old Problems.
Cripps, E. L., ed. Space-Time Concepts in Urban & Regional Models.
Cripps, Stafford. Towards Christian Democracy.
Criscoe, Betty L. & Gee, Thomas C. Content Reading: A Diagnostic Prescriptive Approach.
Crisp, Michael G., ed. see Manning, Marilyn.
Crispin, A. C. V.
--Yesterday's Son.
Crispin, A. C. & Weinstein, Howard. V: East Coast Crisis.
Crispin, Edmund. Buried for Pleasure. Barzum, Jacques & Taylor, Wendell H., eds.
--The Case of the Gilded Fly.
--Fen Country: Twenty-Six Stories.
--The Glimpses of the Moon.
--Holy Disorders.
--Swan Song.
Crissy, William J., et al. Effective Selling: A Short Course for Professionals.
Crist, jt. auth. see Krause.
Crist, Donald G., et al. Computer Aided Drafting, Programming & Plotting Using the Tektronix 4051.
Crist, Ed, jt. auth. see Krause, John.
Crist, Lynda L. The Papers of Jefferson Davis, 1853-1855.
Crist, Nola P. Mother Cee.
Crist, Raymond F., jt. auth. see Burrill, Harry.
Crist, Steven. The Horse Traders.
Cristini, Ermanno & Puricelli, Luigi. Cristini-Puricelli Nature Set.
Cristofer, Michael. The Shadow Box.
Criswell, Ann. Dining In - Houston.
Critchfield, Howard J. General Climatology.
Critchfield, Margot, jt. auth. see Dwyer, Thomas A.
Critchfield, Richard L. How to Play Slo-Pitch Softball.
Critchley, Deanne L. & Mauring, Judith T., eds. The Clinical Specialist in Psychiatric Mental Health Nursing: Theory, Research, & Practice.
Critchley, John. Feudalism.
Critchley, Julian. Warning & Response.
Critchlow, Keith. Islamic Patterns: An Analytical & Cosmological Approach.
Crittenden, H. Temple. Maine Scenic Route.
Crittenden, R. J., jt. auth. see Bishop, Richard L.
Crittenden, Roger. The Thames & Hudson Manual of Film Editing.
CRM Books Staff. Readings in "Psychology Today"
Cro, Stelio. Realidad y Utopia en el Descubrimiento y Conquista de la America Hispana, 1492-1682.
Croatto, J. Severino. Exodus: A Hermeneutics of Freedom.
Croce, Benedetto. Politica & Moral.
--What Is Living & What Is Dead in the Philosophy of Hegel.
Crocetti, Gino & Clarke, B. M. Law School Admission Test: Preparation for the New Test.
Crocetti, Gino & Ellis, David. Graduate Management Admission Test (GMAT)
Crocker, Chris. Cyndi Lauper.
Crocker, Chris, ed. see Brickner, Dave, et al.
Crocker, Chris, ed. see Glau, Gregory R., et al.
Crocker, Chris, ed. see Vick, Bill, et al.
Crocker, Chris, et al, eds. see Young, George & Stark, Peter.
Crocker, Mary W. Historic Architecture in Mississippi.
Crocker, Sturgis. Sam Crockers Boats: A Design Catalog.
Crocket, James U. & Allen, Oliver E. The Time-Life Book of Annuals.
--The Time-Life Book of Pruning & Grafting.
--The Time-Life Book of Shade Gardens.
--The Time-Life Book of Vegetables & Fruits.
--The Time-Life Book of Wildflower Gardening.
Crocket, James U. & Time-Life Books Editors. The Time-Life Book of Perennials.
Crockett, A. Money Theory Policy & Institutions.
Crockett, Andrew D. International Money: Issues & Analysis.
Crockett, Desda. Sensational Vegetarian Salads - Crisp, Colorful & Delicious: Dishes for All Seasons.
Crockett, Fred E. Special Fleet: The History of the Presidential Yachts.
Crockett, Jim, ed. The Guitar Player Book.
Croffoot, George F. The Last Pursuit.
Crofford, Emily. A Matter of Pride.
Croft, Doreen J. & Hess, Robert D. Activities Handbook for Teachers of Young Children.
Croft, Doreen J., jt. auth. see Hess, Robert D.
Croft, J. H. Going Metric in Catering.
Croft, K. Science Readings for Students of English As a Second Language, with Exercises for Vocabulary Development.
Croft, L. R. Introduction to Protein Sequence Analysis.
Croft, Robert J., jt. auth. see Hess, Robert D.
Croft, Steven J. The Identity of the Individual in the Psalms.
Croft, Terrell, et al. American Electrician's Handbook.
Croft-Cooke, Rupert. Conduct Unbecoming.
Crofton, H. D., ed. Nematode Parasite Population in Sheep & on Pasture.
Crofts, Marylee, jt. auth. see Wiley, David.
Crofut, William. The Moon on the One Hand: Poetry in Song.
Croghan, Anthony. Code for Cataloging Non Book Media.
Croix, Don La see Kaufman, Peter B. & La Croix, Don.
Croix, Horst De La see De La Croix, Horst & Tansey, Richard G.
Croix, J. M. De La see De La Croix, J. M. & Copeland, Carole.
Croke, B. F. & Harris, J. D. Religious Conflict in Fourth Century Rome.
Croll, Elisabeth. Chinese Women since Mao.
Croll, Elisabeth J. Feminism & Socialism in China.
Croll, N. A., ed. The Organisation of Nematodes.
Croll, Paul & Moses, Diana. One in Five: The Assessment & Incidence of Special Educational Needs.
Croman, Dorothy Y. Danger in Sagebrush Country.
--The Mystery of Steamboat Rock.
--The Secret of the Poison Ring.
--Trouble on the Blue Fox Island.
Crombie, I. M. An Examination of Plato's Doctrines. Incl. Vol. 1. Plato on Man & Society; Vol. 2. Plato on Knowledge & Reality. Humanities.
Cromblehome, Roger, jt. auth. see Kirtland, Terry.
Cromer, Alan. Experiments in Physics.
Crompton, Anne E. The Ice Trail.
--The Winter Wife.
Crompton, Don. A View from the Spire: William Golding's Later Novels.
Crompton, John, jt. auth. see National Park Service Staff.
Crompton, T. R. Additive Migration from Plastics into Food.
--The Analysis of Organoaluminium & Organozinc Compounds.
--Chemical Analysis of Additives in Plastics.
--Chemical Analysis of Organometallic Compounds.
Cromwell, Paul F., Jr. & Keefer, George. Readings on Police-Community Relations.
Cron, Leslie M. Le see Le Cron, Leslie M.
Cronan, Edward. Dignity of the Human Person.
Cronbach, Abraham. Stories Made of Bible Stories.
Cronbach, L. J. & Drenth, P. J. Mental Tests & Cultural Adaptation.
Cronbach, Lee J. Educational Psychology.
--Educational Psychology.
Crone, Robert A. Diplopia.
Croner, Helga, ed. Stepping Stones to Further Jewish Relations.
Cronin, A. J. Adventures in Two Worlds.
Cronin, Anthony. Forty-One Sonnet-Poems Eighty-Two.
--Reductionist Poem.
Cronin, Edward W., Jr. The Arun: A National History of the World's Deepest Valley.
Cronin, Etain. Contact Dermatitis.
Cronin, Gaynell B. Activities for the Christian Family Handbook (Paths of Life)
Cronin, Morton J. Vocabulary One Thousand.
Cronley, Jay. Cheap Shot.
Cronyn, George W., ed. American Indian Poetry: An Anthology of Songs & Chants.
Crook, B. M., tr. see Thenius, E.
Crook, Barbara, tr. see Denoix, Pierre.
Crook, Beverly C. Fair Annie of Old Mule Hollow.
--Invite a Bird to Dinner: Simple Feeders You Can Make.
Crook, John H., jt. ed. see Michael, Richard P.
Crook, N., jt. ed. see Dyson, T.
Crook, Roger H. Serving God with Mammon: The Economic Ministry of the Family.
Crook, William. Four Days: A Novel of Burma 1945.
Crookall, Robert. During Sleep.
Crooke, S. T. & Prestayko, A. W., eds. Cancer & Chemotherapy: Antineoplastic Agents.
Crooke, Stanley T. & Prestayko, Archie W. Cancer & Chemotherapy: Introduction to Clinical Oncology.
Crooke, Stanley T. & Prestayko, Archie W., eds. Cancer & Chemotherapy, Vol. 1: Introduction to Neoplasia & Antineoplastic Chemotherapy.
Crooke, Stanley T. & Reich, Steven D., eds. Anthracyclines: Current Status & New Developments.
Crookes, William. Researches in Spiritualism.
Crooks, J. E. The Spectrum in Chemistry.
Crooks, Thomas C. & Hancock, Harry L. Basic Technical Mathematics.
Crookse, Mark. Achieving Wellness Through Risk Taking: The End of Boredom.
Croom, Emily A. Unpuzzling Your Past: A Basic Guide to Genealogy.

Authors

Croom, F. H. Basic Concepts of Algebraic Topology.
Croome, D. J. & Sherratt, A. F., eds. Condensation in Buildings.
Cropley, A. J. & Ravindra, H, eds. Lifelong Education & the Training of Teachers.
Cropsey, Joseph, jt. auth. see Strauss, Leo.
Cropsey, Joseph, ed. see Hobbes, Thomas.
Crosbie, A. L., ed. Journal of Thermophysics & Heat Transfer.
Crosbie, Michael J. The Jersey Devil Design-Build Book.
Crosby, Allan J., ed. Accounts & Papers Relating to Mary Queen of Scots.
Crosby, Donald A. Horace Bushnell's Theory of Language: In the Context of Other Nineteenth-Century Philosophies of Language.
Crosby, Nina, jt. auth. see Marten, Elizabeth.
Crosby, Sumner M., et al. The Royal Abbey of Saint-Denis in the Time of Abbot Suger (1122-1151) Shultz, Ellen, ed.
Crosignani, P. G. & Mishell, D., eds. Ovulation in the Human.
Crosland, Andrew, compiled by. Concordance to F. Scott Fitzgerald's the Great Gatsby.
Crosland, Margaret. Beyond the Lighthouse: English Women Novelists in the 20th Century.
--Women of Iron & Velvet: French Women Writers After George Sand.
Crosland, Margaret, tr. see Cocteau, Jean.
Crosland, Margaret, tr. see Jankelevitch, Vladimir.
Cross. Gingivitis.
Cross, Amanda. In the Last Analysis. Barzun, J. & Taylor, W. H., eds.
--The Question of Max.
Cross, Audrey T. Nutrition for the Working Woman.
--Nutrition for the Working Woman.
Cross, B. H. Arithmetic on Elliptic Curves with Complex Multiplication.
Cross, Beryl. Living Alone.
Cross, D. T. & Bristow, M. R., eds. English Structure Planning: A Commentary on Procedure & Practice in the Seventies.
Cross, Donna W. Mediaspeak: How Television Makes up Your Mind.
Cross, Frank L., Jr., jt. auth. see Hesketh, Howard E.
Cross, Gilbert B. A Hanging at Tyburn.
Cross, Gordon R. The Psychology of Learning: An Introduction for Students of Education.
Cross, Harold H. Lust Market.
Cross, Helen R. The Real Tom Thumb.
Cross, J. P. In Ghurka Company.
Cross, Jack. For Art's Sake.
Cross, James E. Conflict in the Shadows.
Cross, Jeff, ed. see European Syndicate of Soccer Experts Staff.
Cross, K. Patricia. The Missing Link: Connecting Adult Learners to Learning Resources.
Cross, L., et al. Readings in Sociology.
Cross, L. C. & Klyne, W., eds. Nomenclature of Organic Chemistry, Sect. E: Sterochemistry.
Cross, Luther S. Growing in Faith: Devotions for Parent-Child Interaction.
Cross, Mary & Cross, Theodore. Behind the Great Wall: A Photographic Essay on China.
Cross, Michael. New Firm Formation & Regional Development.
Cross, Michael, ed. Grow Your Own Energy.
Cross, N. The Automated Architect.
Cross, R. C., ed. see Symposium On Relaxation Methods In Relation To Molecular Structure - Aberystwyth - 1965.
Cross, Robert R., jt. auth. see Dornette, W. Stuart.
Cross, Theodore, jt. auth. see Cross, Mary.
Cross, Theodore L. Black Capitalism: Strategy for Business in the Ghetto.
Cross, Wilbur. Petroleum.
Cross, Wilbur & Moses, John. Presidential Courage.
Cross, Wilbur, jt. auth. see Pace, Nicholas A.
Crossan, John. In Parables.
Crossan, John D. Finding Is the First Act: Trove Folktales & Jesus' Treasure Parable. Beardslee, William E., et al, eds.
--Sayings Parallels: A Workbook for the Jesus Tradition.
Crosscup, Richard. Classical Speeches.
Crossen, Kendra, ed. Up from Eden.
Crosser, Paul. The Nihilism of John Dewey.
Crosser, Paul K. Economic Fictions.
Crossick, Geoffrey. An Artisan Elite in Victorian Society: Kentish London 1840-1880.
Crossick, Geoffrey, ed. Shopkeepers & Master Artisans in Nineteenth-Century Europe.
Crossing, William. Crossing's Guide to Dartmoor.
Crossland, Janice, jt. auth. see McCaull, Julian.
Crossland, Jill, jt. auth. see Clarke, David D.
Crossland, John & Constance, Diana. Macedonian Greece.
Crossley, Frederick H. The English Abbey: Its Life & Work in the Middle Ages.
Crossley, Patricia G. Let's Learn Astrology: The First Astrology Workbook for Beginners.
Crossley, Robert N. Luther & the Peasants' War: Luther's Actions & Reactions.
Crossley-Holland, Kevin. Exeter Book Riddles.
Crossley-Holland, Kevin, ed. The Anglo-Saxon World.
Crossley-Holland, Kevin C. Green Blades Rising: The Anglo-Saxons.
--Pedlar of Swaffham.
--The Sea Stranger.
Crossman, Elizabeth, jt. auth. see Bouterin, Antoine.
Crosson, Frederick J., ed. Science & Contemporary Society.
Crosswait, C. Bruce, jt. auth. see Wilkes, Mary.
Croswell, Anne. Sidekicks: Or a Merger of Marvelous Magnitude.
Crotwell, Helen G., ed. Women & the Word: Sermons.
Crouch, Bruce R. & Chamala, Shankarish, eds. Extension Education & Rural Development, Vol. 1: International Experience in Communication & Innovation.
Crouch, Colin, ed. British Political Sociology Yearbook: Participation in Politics.
Crouch, James & Carr, Micheline. Anatomy & Physiology: A Laboratory Manual.
Crouch, Marcus & Ellis, Alec. Chosen for Children.
Crouch, Robert L. Macroeconomics.
Croucher, Michael & Reid, Howard. The Fighting Arts.
Crounse, Helen W., pseud. What Is Wrong with the Truth?
Crouse, Betty, tr. see Jonas, Ilsedore B.
Crouse, David B., et al. Web Offset Press Operating.
Crouse, Maurice. The Public Treasury of Colonial South Carolina.
Crouse, Nellis M. French Struggle for the West Indies, 1665-1713.
Crouse, Richard & Sloyer, Clifford. Mathematical Questions from the Classroom.
Crouse, William H. Automotive Electronics & Electrical Equipment.
--Small Engines: Operation & Maintenance.
Crouse, William H. & Anglin, Donald L. Automotive Body Repair & Refinishing.
--Automotive Engines.
--Automotive Mechanics.
--Motor Vehicle Inspection.
Crouthers, David D. Flags of American History.
Crouzet, Maurice. The European Renaissance Since 1945.
Crow, D. R. Principles & Applications of Electrochemistry.
Crow, Donna F. Brandley's Search.
--To Be Worthy.
Crow, G. D., jt. auth. see Crow, John A.
Crow, Jeffrey J. & Hatley, Flora J., eds. Black Americans in North Carolina & the South.
Crow, John A. & Crow, G. D. Panorama de las Americas.
Crow, Lester D. New Approaches to the Psychology of Childhood & Adolescence.
Crow, Mary, ed. Woman Who Has Sprouted Wings: Poems by Contemporary Latin American Women Poets. Felstiner, John & Walsh, Donald, trs.
Crow, Ron, jt. auth. see Glass, Dick.
Crow, Todd, ed. Bartok Studies.
Crow, W. B. Occult Properties of Herbs & Plants.
Crowder, Anne S., jt. auth. see Skydell, Barbara.
Crowder, M., jt. auth. see Brokensha, D.
Crowder, Michael. The Flogging of Phineas McIntosh: A Tale of Colonial Folly & Injustice, Bechuanaland 1933.
--The Story of Nigeria.
Crowdis, David G. & Wheeler, Brandon W. Precalculus Mathematics.
Crowdis, David G., et al. Concepts of Calculus with Applications to Business & Economics.
Crowe & Laseau. Visual Notes for Architects & Designers.
Crowe, Cameron. Fast Times at Ridgemont High: A True Story.
Crowe, Catherine. The Night-Side of Nature: Of Ghosts & Ghost-Seers.
Crowe, Clayton T., jt. auth. see Roberson, John A.
Crowe, Gregory D., jt. auth. see Crowe, Patrick H.
Crowe, John H. & Clegg, James S., eds. Anhydrobiosis.
--Dry Biological Systems.
Crowe, Linda, jt. ed. see Kronus, Carol L.
Crowe, Patrick H. & Crowe, Gregory D. Money-Grubbing: A Student's Guide to Part-time Jobs & Self-Run Businesses.
Crowell, H. Laurence. Scriptural Cloning.
Crowell, Lynda & Mariotti, Maryanne. The Parents' Guide to Austin, 1986.
Crowell, Michael. The Precinct Manual: 1984.
--Search Warrants in North Carolina.
Crowell, Michael, ed. State of North Carolina Extradition Manual.
Crowell, Pers. King Moo, the Wordmaker.
Crowhurst, Jim. Making Lampshades.
Crowhurst, Norman H. Basic Electronics Course.
Crowl, Paul E. Stimulating Poetry II.
Crowle, Alfred J. Immunodiffusion.
Crowley, Aleister. The World's Tragedy. Regardie, Israel, ed.
Crowley, Arthur. Bonzo Beaver.
--The Boogey Man.
--The Ugly Book.
--The Wagon Man.
Crowley, James B., ed. Modern East Asia: Essays in Interpretation.
Crowley, Mary. String of Pearls.
Crowley, Mary C. Decorate Your Home with Love.
Crowley, Robert. The IBM-PC: VisiCalc.
Crowley, T. E. Beam Engines.
Crowley, William J. Grow Strong with Words.
Crown, Francis J., Jr., ed. Confederate Postal History.
Crown, W. The Heritage of Buddhist Poetry.
Crowningshield, Gerald & Gorman, Kenneth A. Cost Accounting: Principles & Managerial Applications.
Crownover, Richard. Lover's Language Guide to Japan.
Crowson, Philip. Minerals Handbook 1986-87.
Crowson, Phillip. Minerals Handbook: 1982-83.
Crowther, Bruce. Robert Redford.
Crowther, C. Edward & Stone, Gayle. Intimacy: Strategies for Successful Relationships.
Crowther, Duane S. A Guide to Effective Scripture Study.
--Prophetic Warnings to Modern America.
--Prophets & Prophecies of the Old Testament.
Crowther, Geoff. Africa on a Shoestring.
--Africa on a Shoestring.
--Korea & Taiwan-A Travel Survival Kit.
--Korea & Taiwan Travel Survival.
--South America on a Shoestring.
Crowther, Geoff & Wheeler, Tony. Malaysia, Singapore & Brunei-A Travel Survival Kit.
Crowther, Geoff, et al. India: A Travel Survival Kit.
Crowther, J. G. & Whiddington, R. Science at War.
Crowther, S. J. & Fawcett, Marion. Science & Medicine to Eighteen-Seventy: Pamphlets in the Library.
Crowther-Hunt, Norman. Two Early Political Associations: The Quakers & the Dissenting Deputies in the Age of Sir Robert Walpole.
Croxton, Clive A. Statistical Mechanics of the Liquid Surface.
Crozier, Brian, ed. see Gladwyn, Hubert M.
Crozier, Emmet. American Reporters on the Western Front, 1914 to 1918.
Cru, Jean N. War Books: A Study of Historical Criticism. Pincetl, Stanley J. & Marchand, Ernest, eds.
Cruden, Robert. Many & One: A Social History of the United States.
Crue, Benjamin L., Jr., ed. Pain: Research & Treatment.
Cruikshank, George. The Tragical Comedy or Comical Tragedy of Punch & Judy.
Cruikshank, James. Soil Geography.
Cruikshank, Margaret. The Lesbian Path.
Cruise, Boyd. Index to the Louisiana Historical Quarterly.
Crum, J. K. Art of Inner Listening.
Crum, Mason. Gullah: Negro Life in the Carolina Sea Islands.
Crum, Milton, Jr., jt. auth. see Reid, Richard.
Crumbaker, Marge & Tucker, Gabe. Up & down with Elvis Presley.
Crumbley, D. L., jt. auth. see Milam, Edward.
Crumbley, D. Larry & Milam, Edward E. Estate Planning: A Guide for Advisors & Their Clients.
Crumley, James. The Muddy Fork.
Crump, Donald J., ed. American Mountain People.
--Exploring America's Valleys: From Shenandoah to the Rio Grande.
--Nomads of the World.
Crump, Donald J., ed. see Keating, Bern.
Crump, Donald J., ed. see Stuart, George.
Crump, Fred, Jr. Missy & the Duke: Missy y el Duque. Woyde, Horst, tr.
Crump, R. W. Christina Rossetti: A Reference Guide.
Crump, Ralph W., ed. The Design Connection: Energy & Technology in Architecture. Harms, Martin J.
Crump, Thomas. The Phenomenon of Money.
Crumpacker, Emily, jt. auth. see Logan, Muriel B.
Crunkilton, John R., jt. auth. see Finch, Curtis R.
Crunock, Nehemiah, abridged by. John Wesley's Journal.
Cruse, Harold. The Crisis of the Negro Intellectual.
Crusoe, Robinson. Robinson Crusoe: My Journals & Sketchbooks.
Crutchfield, James, ed. Georgia Almanac.
--North Carolina Almanac: And Book of Facts.
Crutchfield, James A. The North Carolina Almanac & Book of Facts.
Cruz, J. B., Jr., ed. System Sensitivity Analysis.
Cruz, Rosa M., jt. ed. see Sanchez, Rosaura.
Cryer, Pat, ed. Training Activities for Teachers in Higher Education.
Crynes, Billy L. Chemical Reactions As a Means of Separation.
Crystal, David, ed. see Elliott, Ralph W.
Crystal, M., jt. auth. see Totty, P.
Crystal, Michael R., jt. auth. see Carris, Joan D.
CSAAT. What to Tell Your Child about Sex.
Csasar, A. General Topology. Cohn, P. M., ed.
Csillik, B., ed. see International Society for Neurovegetative Research Staff.
Csiszar, I. & Elias, P. Topics in Information Theory.
Csokits, Janos, tr. see Pilinszky, Janos.
Csovanyos, Margaret F. A New Bouquet.
--Widow Julia.
Cuadra, Carlos A., ed. The Annual Review of Information Science & Technology, 1968.
Cuadra, Carlos A. & Luke, Ann W., eds. The Annual Review of Information Science & Technology, 1969.
--The Annual Review of Information Science & Technology, 1972.
--The Annual Review of Information Science & Technology, 1973.
--The Annual Review of Information Science & Technology, 1974.
--The Annual Review of Information Science & Technology, 1970.
Cua-Lim, Felicidad, et al. Asthma Research: Clinical Studies.
Cuatrecasas, P. & Greaves, M. F., eds. Receptors & Recognition, Series A. Incl. Vol. 1; Vol. 2; Vol. 3; Vol. 4; Vol. 5; Vol. 6. Routledge Chapman & Hall.
Cuatrecasas, P. & Jacobs, S., eds. Membrane Receptors.
Cubitt, J. M., ed. Mathematical Models in the Earth Sciences: Proceedings of the 7th Geochautauqua, Syracuse University, Oct. 1978.
Cubitt, J. M. & Henley, S., eds. Statistical Analysis in Geology.
Cuca, Roberto. Family Planning Programs: An Evaluation of Experience.
Cucco, Ulisse, jt. auth. see Joseph, Lou.
Cudahy, Sheila, tr. see Ginzburg, Natalia.
Cuddihy, John M. The Ordeal of Civility: Freud, Marx, Levi-Strauss, & the Jewish Struggle with Modernity.
Cuddihy, Michael. Celebrations.
Cude, Wilfred. A Due Sense of Differences: An Evaluative Approach to Canadian Literature.
Cudjoe, Selwyn R. Resistance & Caribbean Literature.
Cudlip, David R. Comprador.
Cudworth, Ralph. The True Intellectual System of the Universe. Wellek, Rene, ed.
Cuenod, M. A., ed. see IFAC Symposium, Zurich, Switzerland, 29-31 Aug. 1979.
Cuff, E. C. & Payne, G. C., eds. Crisis in the Curriculum.
Cuffee, James W. Spiritual Automobile. Knickerbocker, Charles, ed.
Cufley, C. F. Ocean Freights & Chartering.
Cugini, John V. Programming Languages for Knowledge-Based Systems.
Cugy, Andre & Page, Kogan. Industrial Robot Specifications. Ioannou, Adrian, ed.
Culbert, Elizabeth, tr. see Alegria, Ricardo E.
Culbert, T. Patrick, jt. auth. see Schusky, Ernest L.
Culbert, T. Patrick, ed. The Classic Maya Collapse.
Culbertson, J. M., jt. ed. see Smith, W. L.
Culbertson, Paul. Living Portraits from the Old Testament.
Culbreath, Myrna, jt. auth. see Marshak, Sondra.
Culin, Stewart. Chinese Games with Dice & Dominoes.
Culinary Arts Institute Staff. The Culinary Arts Institute French Cookbook.
Cullen, Allen. Stirrings in Sheffield on Saturday Night.
Cullen, G. W. & Wang, C. C., eds. Heteroepitaxial Semiconductors for Electronic Devices.
Cullen, I. G., ed. Analysis & Decision in Regional Policy.
Cullen, Ian. Applied Urban Analysis: A Critique & Synthesis.
Cullen, John B. & Watkins, Floyd C. Old Times in the Faulkner Country.
Cullen, M. O. How to Carve Meat, Game & Poultry.
Cullen, Tony, jt. auth. see Foss, Christopher.
Culler, Jonathan. Framing the Sign: Criticism & its Institutions.
Culleton, R. Gerald. The Reign of AntiChrist.
Culley, James, jt. auth. see Lazer, William.
Culley, M. B. The Pilchard.
Culley, Margo & Portuges, Catherine, eds. Gendered Subjects: The Dynamics of Feminist Teaching.
Culley, Robert C. Studies in the Structure of Hebrew Narrative.
Culligan, Emmett. Fatima Secret.
Culligan, Emmett J. The Last World War & the End of Time.
Cullinan, Bernice E., et al. Literature & the Child.
Cullinan, Elizabeth. A Change of Scene.
Cullinan, Thomas. The Bedeviled.
--The Beseiged.
Cullinan, Tim. Visual Disability in the Elderly.

Authors

Cullingford, R. A., et al. Timescales in Geomorphology.
Culliton, J. W., jt. auth. see Lewis, H. T.
Cullmann, Oscar. Baptism in the New Testament.
--Christ & Time: The Primitive Christian Conception of Time & History.
--Christology of the New Testament.
--Early Christian Worship.
--The Johannine Circle. Bowden, John, tr.
Cullmann, Oscar & Leenhardt, Franz J. Essays on the Lord's Supper.
Cully, Iris V. Ways to Teach Children.
Cully, Iris V. & Cully, Kendig B. Introductory Theological Wordbook.
Cully, Kendig B., jt. auth. see Cully, Iris V.
Cully, Kendig B., ed. Westminster Dictionary of Christian Education.
Culp, George & Nickles, Herbert. An Apple for the Teacher: Fundamentals of Instructional Computing.
Culp, Russell L. & Wesner, George M. Handbook of Advanced Wastewater Treatment.
Culpeper, Nicholas. Culpeper's Complete Herbal & English Physician.
Culpepper, R. Alan. Pentecost Two.
Culpin, Claude. Farm Machinery.
--Farm Machinery.
Cultural Alliance of Greater Hampton Roads. Cultural Resources Directory, 1987-88.
Cultural & Social Centre, Asian & Pacific Council, compiled by. Asian & Pacific Short Stories.
Culver, Carmen M. & Hoban, Gary J. Power to Change: Issues for the Innovative Educator. Goodlad, John I., ed.
Culver, Louisa C. Peggy & Her Boyfriend: A True Love Story.
--Peggy & Pete: A Story of Lasting Love & Success.
Culver, Robert D. The Peacemongers. Carpenter, Mark, ed.
Culverhouse, Cecil. Confronted by Christ.
Culverwell, J. P., ed. see Faucher, L.
Cumberland, Richard. The Plays of Richard Cumberland: Eighteenth Century English Drama Ser. Borkat, Roberta F., ed.
Cumes, J. W. The Indigent Rich: A Theory of General Equilibrium in a Keynesian System.
--Inflation: A Study in Stability.
Cumings, Art. There's a Monster Eating My House.
Cumings, J. N., ed. see Migraine Symposium, 4th, London, 1971.
Cumings, J. N., ed. see Migraine Symposium, 5th, London, 1972.
Cumley, Russell W., jt. auth. see Clark, R. Lee.
Cumming, Doug, jt. auth. see Cumming, Joe.
Cumming, Duncan. The Gentleman Savage: The Life of Mansfield Parkyns, 1823-1894.
Cumming, Gordon & Bonsignore, Giovanni, eds. Cellular Biology of the Lung.
Cumming, Joe & Cumming, Doug. The Family Secret.
Cummings, Bart, intro. by. Advertising Career Directory, 1986: 24 Top Industry Leaders.
Cummings, Betty S. Hew Against the Grain.
--Let a River Be.
--Now, Ameriky.
--Turtle.
Cummings, Catherine M. & Smith, B. R. Speech One Hundred & Three Handbook.
Cummings, David, ed. The Purpose of a Christian School.
Cummings, Des, Jr., jt. auth. see Dudley, Roger L.
Cummings, Donald W. & Herum, John, eds. Tempo: Life, Work & Leisure.
Cummings, e. e. Collected Poems.
--Enormous Room.
--The Enormous Room.
--Ninety-Five Poems.
--One Hundred Selected Poems.
--One Times One.
--Selected Letters of e. e. Cummings. Dupee, F. W. & Stade, George, eds.
--Seventy-Three Poems.
Cummings, H. M. Defense of the Supreme God.
Cummings, H. Wayland, et al. Managing Communication in Organizations: An Introduction.
Cummings, J. & Osborn, H., eds. Hadronic Interactions of Electronics & Photons.
Cummings, Jack. Complete Guide to Real Estate Financing.
Cummings, Joe. Thailand: A Travel Survival Kit.
Cummings, L. L. & Dunham, Randall B. Introduction to Organizational Behavior: Text & Readings.
Cummings, Merilyn L. The Diet to Lose & Win.
--The Diet to Lose & Win: Self-Help System.
Cummings, Michael. On the Point of My Pen: The Best of Cummings.
Cummings, Milton C. Democracy Under Pressure.
Cummings, Milton C., Jr. & Wise, David. Democracy Under Pressure: An Introduction to the American Political System.
--Democracy under Pressure: An Introduction to the American Political System.
Cummings, O. R. Street Cars of Boston: Closed Horse & Electric Cars to 1900.
Cummings, P. Howard & Porter, Stephen R. Quick Reference of Common Emergency Drugs.
Cummings, Parke & Lapin, Nora. Fairfield County: An Insider's Guide.
Cummings, Paul, jt. auth. see Bame, E. Allen.
Cummings, Paul, et al. Willem de Kooning: Drawings-Paintings-Sculpture, A Whitney Museum Book.
Cummings, Richard. Contemporary Selling.
--The Pied Piper: Allard K. Lowenstein & the Liberal Dream.
--Proposition Fourteen: A Secessionist Remedy.
Cummings, William, ed. Scott Standard Postage Catalogue, 1985.
--Scott Standard Postage Stamp Catalogue, 1985.
--Scott Standard Postage Stamp Catalogue, 1985.
--Scott Standard Postage Stamp Catalogue, 1985.
Cummings, William W. & Weinfeld, Barbara A., eds. Scott Standard Postage Stamp Catalogue, 1984.
Cummings, William W. & Weinfield, Barbara A., eds. Scott Standard Postage Stamp Catalogue, 1984.
--Scott Standard Postage Stamp Catalogue 1984.
--Scott Standard Postage Stamp Catalogue 1984.
Cummings, William W., jt. ed. see Sine, Richard L.
Cummins, D. Duane & White, William G. Contrasting Decades: The Nineteen Twenties & Nineteen Thirties.
Cummins, G. B. Rust Fungi of Cereals, Grasses & Bamboos.
Cummins, Jack, jt. auth. see Wartell, Michael.
Cummins, Maria. The Lamplighter.
Cummins, Ralph. Coaching Football's Attack & Pursuit.
Cummins, Virginia R. Rookwood Pottery Potpourri.
Cummmings, William W., ed. Scott U. S. Pocket Catalogue & Checklist 1988.
Cumper, G. E. Determinants of Health Levels in Developing Countries.
Cunard, Nancy. Negro Anthology.
Cundall, R. B., jt. ed. see Jennings, K. R.
Cundiff, M. Kinesics: The Power of Silent Command.
Cundiff, W. E. & Reid, Mado. Issues in Canadian-U. S. Transborder Computer Data Flows.
Cuneo, Mary L. Inside a Sand Castle & Other Secrets.
Cunha, Deborah, ed. Public Welfare Directory, 1980-1981.
Cunliffe, Barry. Danebury: Anatomy of an Iron Age Hillfort.
--Roman Bath Discovered.
Cunliffe, John W., et al, eds. Century Readings in English Literature.
Cunliffe, Lesley, jt. auth. see Brown, Craig.
Cunliffe-Jones, Hubert & Drewery, Benjamin, eds. A History of Christian Doctrine.
Cunningham, Alastair J., jt. ed. see Sercarz, Eli E.
Cunningham, Bill. On Bended Knees: The Night Rider Story.
Cunningham, Chet. Beloved Rebel.
--Die of Gold.
--The Gold & the Glory.
--The Gold Wagon.
--The Power & the Prize.
--Rainbow Saga.
--This Splendid Land.
Cunningham, Cliff & Sloper, Patricia. Helping Your Exceptional Baby: A Practical & Honest Approach to Raising a Mentally Handicapped Baby.
Cunningham, E. V. The Case of the Angry Actress.
--The Case of the Kidnapped Angel.
--The Case of the Murdered MacKenzie.
--The Case of the One-Penny Orange.
--The Case of the Russian Diplomat.
--The Case of the Russian Diplomat.
--The Wabash Factor.
Cunningham, Frank E., jt. auth. see Suderman, Darrel R.
Cunningham, G. The Management of Aid Agencies.
Cunningham, Hugh. The Volunteer Force: A Social & Political History, 1859-1908.
Cunningham, John, jt. auth. see Hanckel, Frances.
Cunningham, John E. & Horn, Delton T. Handbook of Remote Control & Automation Techniques.
Cunningham, Joyce I. & Wilson, W. D. A Concordance to Andre Gide's "La Symphonie Pastorale"
Cunningham, Julia. Come to the Edge.
--Dear Rat.
--Dorp Dead.
--Flight of the Sparrow.
Cunningham, Lawrence, ed. Mother of God.
Cunningham, Marilyn. Forbidden Passion.
--Under the Northern Lights.
Cunningham, Mary & Schumer, Fran. Powerplay: What Really Happened at Bendix.
Cunningham, Michael. Intelligence: Its Organization & Development.
Cunningham, Phyllis F. My Godmother: Theodate Pope Riddle & Reminiscences of Creativity.
Cunningham, Randy, et al. Fox Two! America's First Ace in Vietnam.
Cunningham, Richard, tr. see Bombal, Maria L.
Cunningham, Sarah C. Beyond the Flames.
Cunningham, W. P., ed. see Resource Publications, Inc. Staff.
Cunningham, W. Patrick, ed. The Music Locator.
Cunningham, William B., ed. Canada, the Commonwealth & the Common Market: Report of the 1962 Summer Institute, Mount Allison University.
Cunningham, William P. The Music Locator.
Cunnington, P. Children's Costume in England.
Cuns. Strategic Planning.
Cunynghame, Henry H. Time & Clocks: A Description of Ancient & Modern Methods of Measuring Time.
Cunz, Dieter, ed. see Huch, Ricarda.
Cupitt, Don. The Leap of Reason.
Cupps, Thomas R. & Fauci, Anthony S. The Vasculitides.
Cuppy, Will. How to Tell Your Friends from the Apes.
Curatola, Anthony P. State Income Tax Consequences of Retirement Plan Distributions.
Curators of the Israel Museum. Treasures of the Holy Land: Ancient Art from the Israel Museum.
Curators of the Israel Museum, Jerusalem, Staff. Treasures of the Holy Land: Ancient Art from the Israel Museum.
Curcio, Louis L. & Galanti, Marie E. Nouveau Visage Du Monde Francais.
Curds, C. R. & Hawkes, H. A., eds. Ecological Aspects of Used Water Treatment.
Cureton, T. K. Physical Fitness Workbook for Adults.
Curie, Marie. Radioactive Substances: A Translation from the French of the Classical Thesis Presented to the Faculty of Sciences in Paris.
Curl, Donald W. Palm Beach County: An Illustrated History.
Curlee-Salisbury, Joan. When the Woman You Love Is an Alcoholic.
Curley, Daniel. Hilarion.
--Mummy.
Curley, Ed. Saints for Young Christians.
Curley, Jayme, et al. The Balancing Act II: A Career & a Family.
Curnou, Susan, jt. auth. see Curnow, Ray.
Curnow, R. N., jt. auth. see Mead, R.
Curnow, Ray & Curnou, Susan. Games, Graphics & Sound.
Curnow, Ray & Curran, Susan. First Steps in BASIC.
--Learning with Your Home Computer.
Curns, Elleen B. Stress.
Curr, Rosemary, jt. auth. see Cutts, Paddy.
Curran, Charles E. Politics, Medicine & Christian Ethics: A Dialogue with Paul Ramsey.
Curran, David K. Adolescent Suicide.
Curran, Dolores. In the Beginning There Were the Parents: Discussion Guide.
--In the Beginning There Were the Parents.
Curran, James & Smith, Anthony, eds. Impacts & Influences.
Curran, Jan, et al. The Statue of Liberty Is Cracking Up: A Guide to Loving, Leaving, & Living Again.
Curran, Joseph M. The Birth of the Irish Free State, 1921-1923.
Curran, Mona. Collecting Antique Jewelry.
Curran, Raymond J. Architecture & the Urban Experience.
Curran, Susan & Norman, Margaret. Business Applications on the BBC Micro.
Curran, Susan, jt. auth. see Curnow, Ray.
Curran, Valerie. Nigerian Children: Developmental Perspectives.
Curran, Valerie & Golombok, Susan. Pill Popping: How You Can Get Clear.
Currell, David. Learning with Puppets.
Current Digest of the Soviet Press Staff, tr. see Gruliow, Leo.
Current Digest of the Soviet Press Staff, tr. see Gruliow, Leo & Neuweld, Mark.
Current Digest of the Soviet Press Staff, tr. see Saikowski, Charlotte, et al.
Current Digest of the Soviet Press Staff, tr. see Schulze, Fred.
Current, Richard N. Old Thad Stevens: A Story of Ambition.
Currey, C. Brothers Bent.
Currie, D., et al, eds. Macroeconomic Analysis: Essays in Macroeconomics & Econometrics.
--Microeconomic Analysis: Essays in Microeconomics & Economic Development.
Currie, David, ed. Advances in Monetary Economics.
Currie, David R. On the Way!
Currie, Donald J. Abdominal Pain.
Currie, Elliot, et al. America's Problems: Social Issues & Public Policy.
Currie, Elliott, jt. auth. see Skolnick, Jerome H.
Currie, Heather, et al. The New Zealand Fish & Shellfish Cookbook.
Currie, Janice K., jt. auth. see Heyneman, Stephen P.
Currie, S., jt. auth. see Behan, P. O.
Currie, Stuart D. Beginnings of the Church.
Currier & Ives Portfolios. Firefighting & Fires.
--Hunting & Fishing.
Currier, Chet & Associated Press Staff. The Investor's Annual, 1985.
Currier, Chet, jt. auth. see Associated Press.
Currier, Richard L., ed. see Meshorer, Ya'akov.
Curry, Cathy B., tr. & illus. see Havrevold, Finn.
Curry, E. R. Hoover's Dominican Diplomacy & the Origins of the Good Neighbor Policy. Freidel, Frank, ed.
Curry, Estell H., jt. auth. see Silvius, George H.
Curry, Hayden, jt. auth. see Clifford, Denis.
Curry, Jane L. The Birdstones.
--Daybreakers.
--Ghost Lane.
--The Ice Ghosts Mystery.
--The Lost Farm.
--The Magical Cupboard.
--Mindy's Mysterious Miniature.
--Over the Sea's Edge.
--Parsley, Sage, Rosemary & Time.
--Shadow Dancers.
--The Watchers.
Curry, Nigel, jt. ed. see Blunden, John.
Curry, Theresa K. Never-to-Be-Forgotten Adventures with God.
Curry-Lindahl, Kai. Wildlife of the Prairies & Plains.
Curtain, R. F. & Pritchard, A. J. Infinite Dimensional Linear Systems Theory.
Curtain, Ruth & Pritchard, A. J., eds. Functional Analysis in Modern Applied Mathematics.
Curteis, A., jt. auth. see Given-Wilson, C.
Curti, Merle. Roots of American Loyalty.
Curti, Merle E. Bryan & World Peace.
Curtice, Robert M. Planning for Data Base Systems.
Curtice, Robert M. & Jones, Paul E., Jr. Logical Data Base Design.
Curtice, Robert M., ed. see Carroll, John M.
Curtin, Bernadette M., jt. auth. see Hecklinger, Fred J.
Curtin, Daniel J. & Merritt, Robert E. California Subdivision Map Act Practice.
Curtin, Dennis P. The WordStar Handbook.
Curtin, Philip D. Two Jamaicas.
Curtin, Sharon R. Nobody Ever Died of Old Age.
Curtin, W. G., et al. Structural Masonry Designer's Manual.
Curtis, A. S. Cell Surface: Its Molecular Role in Morphogenesis.
Curtis, Adrian H. Ugarit.
Curtis, Alan R. Practical Math for Business.
--Practical Math for Business.
Curtis, Anthony. The Lyle Official Antiques Review 1986.
Curtis, Anthony, compiled by. The Lyle Official Antiques Review, 1985.
Curtis, Arnold. Kenya: A Visitor's Guide.
Curtis, Bob. Retail Security: Controlling Loss for Profit.
Curtis, C. Michael, ed. see Burke, Alan D.
Curtis, Charles K., jt. auth. see Shaver, James K.
Curtis, Charles P., Jr. & Greenslet, Ferris. Practical Cogitator.
Curtis, Charles W. & Reiner, Irving. Representation Theory of Finite Groups & Associative Algebras.
Curtis, D. R. & McIntyre, A. K., eds. Studies in Physiology Presented to John C. Eccles.
Curtis, Eugene W. Saint-Just, Colleague of Robespierre.
Curtis, Gerald L., jt. auth. see Ushiba, Nobuhiko.
Curtis, Gerald L. & Han, Sung-Joo, eds. The U. S.-South Korean Alliance.
Curtis, Helena. Biology.
Curtis, James. Between Flops: A Biography of Preston Sturges.
Curtis, Joyce. Pickle-Ball: For Player & Teacher.
Curtis, Leonard T., jt. auth. see L'Abate, Luciano.
Curtis, Lindsay. Making of a Prophet.
Curtis, Lindsay, et al. Pregnant & Beautiful.
Curtis, Michael, ed. Nature of Politics.
Curtis, Neal, jt. auth. see Pichel, Mervyn.
Curtis, Nelson. Butterflies of Idaho & the Northern Rockies.
Curtis, Patricia. The Urban Dog: How to Understand, Enjoy, & Care for a Dog in the City.
Curtis, R. K. Evolution or Extinction: The Choice Before Us-A Systems Approach to the Study of the Future.
Curtis, Susannah. The Monk's Retreat.
Curtis, Tony. Lyle Official Arms & Armour Review, 1983.
Curtis, Tony, ed. Bronze.
--Lyle Official Arms & Armour Review, 1982.
--Lyle Official Books Review, 1982.
Curtis, William J., et al, eds. Insights: Readings in Children's Literature.

Curtiss Aeroplane & Motor Corp. Curtiss Standard JN-4D Military Tractor (Aircraft) Handbook. Rice, M. S., ed.
Curtiss, Harriette & Homer, F. Four-Fold Health.
--The Truth about Evolution & the Bible.
Curtiss, John S. The Russian Church & the Soviet State, 1917-1950.
Curtiss, Mina. Other People's Letters: A Memoir.
Curtler, Hugh M. Eliseo Vivas: A Bibliography.
Curwen, C. A., tr. see Chesneaux, Jean.
Curwen, Henry. History of Booksellers, the Old & the New.
Curwin & Slater. Quantitative Methods in Business.
Cusa, Noel, ed. Tunnicliffe's Birds: Measured Drawings by C. N. Tunnicliffe.
Cusack, Dymphna. Chinese Women Speak.
Cusack, Isabel L. Mr. Wheatfield's Loft.
Cusack, Margaret. The Christmas Carol Sampler.
Cuschieri, A., et al. Essential Surgical Practice.
Cusens, A. R. & Pama, R. P. Bridge Deck Analysis.
Cushenbery, Donald C. Guide to Meeting Reading Competency Requirements: Effective Diagnosis & Correction of Difficulties.
Cushing, C. E., Jr., ed. see Ecological Society of America Radioecology Symposium Staff.
Cushing, D. H. Detection of Fish.
--Fisheries Biology: A Study in Population Dynamics.
Cushing, George M., Jr. Great Buildings of Boston.
Cushing, Harvery Society Staff. Harvey Cushing's Seventieth Birthday Party, April 8, 1939: Speeches, Letters, & Tributes.
Cushing, Richard C. Mission of the Teacher.
--St. Martin de Porres.
Cushing, Richard J. Eternal Thoughts from Christ the Teacher.
Cushing, William. Initials & Pseudonyms: A Dictionary of Literary Disguises.
Cushion, John. Continental Porcelain.
--English Porcelain.
Cushman, Doug. Mickey Takes a Bow.
Cushman, Jerome. Tom B. & the Joyful Noise.
Cushman, Joseph D., Jr. Goodly Heritage, the Episcopal Church in Florida, 1821-1892.
Cushman, Ralph S., compiled by. Pocket Prayer Book: Large-Type Edition.
Cushman, Robert F. Cases in Civil Liberties.
--Cases in Constitutional Law.
--Leading Constitutional Decisions.
Cushman, Robert F., et al, eds. High Tech Real Estate: Planning, Adapting & Operating Buildings in the Computer & Telecommunications Age.
--Construction Litigation: Representing the Contractor, 1986 Cumulative Supplement.
Cushnir, Howard. The Secret Spinner: Tales of Rav Gedalia.
Cusick, John. First Steps.
Cuss, Gladys. Hidden Manna Revealed by the Comforter.
--I Have Been Before the Judgement Seat of Christ: A Religious Autobiography.
Cuss, T. P. The Story of Watches.
Cussen, Joseph A. World Youth & the Family.
Cussianovich, Alejandro. Religious Life & the Poor: Liberation Theology Perspectives. Drury, John, tr. from Span.
Cussler, Clive. Cyclops.
--Deep Six.
Custance, Arthur C. Doorway Papers: The Virgin Birth & the Incarnation.
Custer, Dan. The Miracle of Mind Power.
Custer, George A. My Life on the Plains.
Cutajar, M. Zammit, ed. UNCTAD & the South-North Dialogue: The First Twenty Years.
Cuthbert, A. R. Architecture, Society & Space-The High-Density Question Re-Examined.
Cuthbert, A. W., et al, eds. Amiloride & Epithelial Sodium Transport.
Cuthbert, C. R. Science & the Detection of Crime.
Cuthbert, Robert E., jt. auth. see Birch, Derek W.
Cuthbertson, Gilbert M. Political Power.
Cuthbertson, Keith. Macroeconomic Policy: New Cambridge, Keynesian & Monetarist Controversies.
Cuthertson, Keith, jt. auth. see Brooks, Simon.
Cuthwillis, Edgar, ed. Lewis Carroll's Bedside Book.
Cutler, Carol. The Woman's Day Low-Calorie Dessert Cookbook.
Cutler, David, jt. auth. see Alston, Edith.
Cutler, Ebbitt. I Once Knew an Indian Woman.
Cutler, G. Ripley. Of Battles Long Ago: Memoirs of an American Ambulance Driver in World War I. Knickerbocker, Charles H., ed. & intro. by.
Cutler, Jane P. Adjudicating Alleged Unethical Conduct: A Simulation.
Cutler, Katherine N. & Bogle, Kate C. Crafts for Christmas.
Cutler, M. E., tr. see Nickl, Peter.
Cutler, Melvin. Liquid Semiconductors.
Cutler, Paul H. & Lucas, A. A., eds. Quantum Metrology & Fundamental Physical Constants.
Cutler, Roland. The Gates of Sagittarius.
Cutler, Wayne & Harris, Michael H., eds. Justin Winsor: Scholar-Librarian.
Cutler, Winnifred B., et al. Menopause: A Guide for Women & the Men Who Love Them.
Cutlip, Glen W., jt. auth. see Shockley, Robert.
Cutter, Susan L., et al. Exploitation, Conservation, Preservation: A Geographic Perspective on Natural Resource Use.
Cutter, Tom. Barbary Coast Tong.
--The Blue Cut Job.
--Chinatown Chance.
--Huntsville Breakout.
--Lincoln County.
--The Oklahoma Score.
--The Winning Hand.
Cutting, C. L. Fish Saving.
Cutting, C. V, ed. see Long Ashton Research Station Symposium Staff.
Cutting, Edith see Kruse, Donald W.
Cutting, John. The Psychology of Schizophrenia.
Cutts, Edward L. Scenes & Characters of the Middle Ages.
Cutts, Paddy & Curr, Rosemary. Creative Techniques in Stage & Theatrical Photography.
Cutts, Paddy, jt. auth. see Payne, Christian.
Cuyler. Sir William & the Pumpkin Monster.
Cuyler, Louise. The Symphony.
Cuyler, Margery. Jewish Holidays.
Cuyler, Susanna. The Shortest Shorter: A Distillation of the Shorter Oxford English Dictionary A - M.
Cuyvers, Luc. Ocean Uses & Their Regulation.
Cuzner, M. L., jt. ed. see Davison, A. N.
CWL. Mail Drops.
Cybernetics & Systems Research Staff. Structure & Dynamics of Socioeconomic Systems, Cybernetics in Organization & Management, Engineering Systems Methodology, Systems Research on Science & Technology: Proceedings of the European Meeting on Cybernetics & Systems Research, Linz, Austria, March 1978.
Cyclic AMP, Cell Growth, & the Immune Response Symposium Staff. Proceedings of the Cyclic AMP, Cell Growth, & the Immune Response Symposium, Marco Island, Fla., 1973. Braun, W., et al, eds.
Cycon, H. L., et al, eds. Schrodinger Operators.
Cyr, Arthur I. Liberal Party Politics in Britain.
Cyr, John & Sobeck, Joan. Real Estate Brokerage: A Success Guide.
Cyras, A. A. Mathematical Models for the Analysis & Optimization of Elastoplastic Structures.
Cyriax, G. R., ed. Liability in Trans-European Road Transport.
--Planning Employee Share Schemes.
Cyriax, James. The Slipped Disc.
Cyrs, Thomas E., Jr., ed. Handbook for the Design of Instruction in Pharmacy Education.
--Handbook for the Design of Instruction in Pharmacy Education.
Cytron. Fire! The Library Is Burning!
Czanderna, A. W., ed. Methods of Surface Analysis.
Czanderna, Al. Silver-Glass Mirrors for Solar Thermal Systems.
Czech, Josef. Oscilloscope Measuring Technique: Principles & Applications of Modern Cathode Ray Oscilloscopes.
Czeh, C., jt. ed. see Szabo, T.
Czerny, Carl. School of Velocity for Piano.
Czerny, Carl, ed. see Bach, J. S.
Czestochowski, Joseph S., ed. see Hassam, Childe.
Czihak, G. & Peter, R., eds. The Sea Urchin Embryo: Biochemistry & Morphogenesis.
Czudnowski, Moshe M. & Landau, Jacob M. The Israeli Communist Party.

D

D. Bradford Barton Ltd., ed. American Flying Boats: A Pictorial Survey.
D. C. Institute for Careers in Tourism. Washington: Eine Den Besucher Faszinierende Stadt (A Guide to Washington in German)
Daalder, Joost, ed. see Heywood, Jasper.
Dabberdt, Walter. Weather for Outdoorsmen.
Dabey, John, ed. see Achebe, Chinua.
Dabney, Lewis M. The Indians of Yoknapatawpha: A Study in Literature & History.
Dabney, Virginius. The Jefferson Scandals: A Rebuttal.
Dabney, Virginius, ed. The Patriots: The American Revolution, Generation of Genius.
D'Abro, A. The Rise of the New Physics: Its Mathematical & Physical Theories.
Dabrowski, Roman. Mussolini, Twilight & Fall.
Dabydeen, Cyril. Still Close to the Island.
DaCal, Ernesto G. & Ucelay, Margarita. Literature del Siglo XX.
Dacey, John. Where the World Is: Teaching Basic Skills Outdoors.
Dacey, Norman F. How to Avoid Probate.
--How to Avoid Probate: Updated!
Dacey, Philip. Gerard Manley Hopkins Meets Walt Whitman in Heaven & Other Poems.
D'Achille, Gino, illus. King Solomon's Mines.
Dada, Victor B. Choose the Sex of Your Baby: A Psychological Approach.
Dadant & Sons Inc., Staff. First Lessons in Beekeeping.
Dadant & Sons, Inc., Staff. The Honey Kitchen: The Best Honey Recipes in the World.
Dadant & Sons, Inc., Staff & Dadant, C. P. First Lessons in Beekeeping.
Dadant & Sons Inc., Staff, ed. The Hive & the Honey Bee.
Dadant, C. P., jt. auth. see Dadant & Sons, Inc., Staff.
Daddad, Wadi D. Educational & Economic Effects of Promotion & Repetition Practices.
D'Adolf, Steven, ed. Capacitors.
--PC Board Connectors.
--Rack & Panel Connectors.
Dadoo, Y. M., et al. South African Communists Speak, 1915-1980.
Daemmrich, Horst. The Shattered Self: E. T. A. Hoffmann's Tragic Vision.
Daeschner, C. William, ed. Pediatrics: An Approach to Independent Learning.
Daetz, Pantell, ed. Environmental Modeling: Analysis & Management.
Da Free, John. The Eating Gorilla Comes in Peace.
--What to Remember to Be Happy.
Da Free John. Love of the Two-Armed Form.
Dage, John H. La see La Dage, John H.
Dagel, John F. Diesel Engine Repair.
Daggett, Harriet S., jt. ed. see Charmatz, Jan P.
Daggett, Stephen & Husbands, Jo. L. Achieving an Affordable Defense: A Military Strategy to Guide Military Spending.
Daggett, Stuart. Principles of Inland Transportation.
Dagher, Joseph P. Writing a Practical Guide.
Dagless, Erik, jt. ed. see Aspinall, David.
Dagless, Erik L. & Aspinall, David. Introduction to Microcomputers.
D'Agnostino, Guido, jt. auth. see Covello, Leonard.
Daguang, Zhou, jt. ed. see Zhongmin, Xu.
Daheim, Mary R. Destiny's Pawn.
--Love's Pirate.
--Pride's Captive.
Daher, Paul. A Cedar of Lebanon.
Dahl, Arlene. Beyond Beauty.
Dahl, B. Consumer Legislation in Denmark.
Dahl, C. Food & Menu Dictionary.
Dahl, Curtis, ed. see Ely, Ben-Ezra S.
Dahl, Gordon. Work, Play, & Worship in a Leisure-Oriented Society.
Dahl, Nils A. The Crucified Messiah.
--Jesus in the Memory of the Early Church.
--Studies in Paul.
Dahl, Roald. My Uncle Oswald.
--Roald Dahl's Revolting Rhymes.
Dahl, V. I. Dahl's Russian Dictionary.
--Dahl's Russian Dictionary.
--Dahl's Russian Dictionary.
--Dahl's Russian Dictionary.
Dahl, Vladimir I. Dahl's Russian Dictionary.
Dahlberg, Arthur. How to Reduce Interest Rates & Poverty.
Dahlberg, Charles C. & Jaffe, Joseph. Stroke: A Doctor's Personal Story of His Recovery.
Dahlby, Edith L. My Own Book of Secrets.
Dahlitz, Julie. Nuclear Arms Control: With Effective International Agreements.
Dahlstrand, Ingemar. Software Portability & Standards.
Dahmer, Sondra & Kahl, Kurt. The Waiter & Waitress Training Manual.
Dahrendorf, Ralf. Life Chances: Approaches to Social & Political Theory.
Daiches. Literary Essays.
Daiches, David. Milton.
Daigneault, Ernest A., jt. auth. see Brown, R. Don.
Daigon, Arthur, et al. Put It in Writing.
Dailey, Charles A. & Madsen, Ann M. How to Evaluate People in Business: The Track-Record Method of Making Correct Judgments.
Dailey, Janet. The Best Way to Lose.
--Calder Born, Calder Bred.
--Difficult Decision.
--For the Love of God.
--Foxfire Light.
--The Glory Game.
--The Great Alone.
--Low Country Liar.
--The Mating Season.
--Northern Magic.
--Pride of Hannah Wade.
--Ride the Thunder.
--The Rogue.
--Silver Wings, Santiago Blue.
--Silver Wings, Santiago Blue.
--Terms of Surrender.
--Touch the Wind.
Dailey, Timothy E., jt. auth. see Wickman, Peter M.
Daily, James M. Interpersonal Skills for the Manager.
Daimler, Harriet, pseud. Darling.
Daimler, Harriet. Innocence.
Dain, Martin J., jt. auth. see Robinson, Barry.
Dainard, J. A. Editing Correspondence: Papers Given at the Fourteenth Annual Conference on Editorial Problems, University of Toronto, 3-4 November 1978.
Dainty, J., jt. ed. see Zimmermann, U.
Daisne, Johan, pseud. The Man Who Had His Hair Cut Short. Sackett, S. J. N, tr. from Flemish.
Daitch, Susan. L. C.
Dajani, M. S., jt. auth. see Daoudi, M. S.
Dakers, Caroline. The Blue Plaque Guide to London.
Dakin, C., jt. auth. see Archer, M.
Dakin, John. Feedback from Tomorrow.
Dal, Bjorn. The Butterflies of Northern Europe. Morris, Michael, ed. Littleboy, Roger, tr.
D'Albert, Joseph L. & Herbert, Richard A. You & the Psychic Within.
Dale, A. M., jt. auth. see Smith, Edwin W.
Dale, Alan. Making Sense of Our World: A Guide to Reading the Bible.
Dale, Alan T. The Bible in the Classroom.
--New World.
--The Winding Quest.
Dale, Allen. The Soft of Pisces.
Dale, Anthony. Historic Preservation in Foreign Countries: France, England, Ireland, the Netherlands, & Denmark. Stipe, Robert E., ed.
Dale, Brian. Ascent to Power: Wran & the Media.
Dale, Celia. A Spring of Love.
Dale, David. The Offical Liars' Handbook.
Dale, Edgar. The Word Game: Improving Communications.
Dale, Edgar & O'Rourke, J. The Living Word Vocabulary: A 44,000 Word Vocabulary Inventory.
Dale, Jack, & Associates, Staff. Energy Audits Manual.
Dale, Jennifer, jt. auth. see Taylor-Gooby, Peter.
Dale, Johannes. Stereochemistry & Conformational Analysis.
Dale, Kathleen, tr. see Redlich, Hans F.
Dale, Nell & Lilly, Susan C. Pascal Plus Data Structures, Algorithms, & Advanced Programming.
Dale, Peter. Mortal Fire.
D' Alembert, Jean L. Traite De Dynamique.
D'Alessio, Gregory J., jt. auth. see Schiffman, Yale M.
Daley, H. W. Manual of Pack Transportation.
Daley, Henry O. Fundamentals of Microprocessors.
Daley, Joseph C. A Guide to Municipal Official Statements.
Daley, Kit. Dance for Two.
--Danger in Paradise.
--Dangerous Highway.
Daley, Michael. Angels.
Daley, Robert. The Dangerous Edge: A Novel.
--Hands of a Stranger.
--Hands of a Stranger.
--Prince of the City: The True Story of the Cop Who Knew Too Much.
Dalfabbro. How to Make Built-in Furniture.
Dal Fabbro, Mario. How to Make Children's Furniture & Play Equipment.
Dalglish, Garven. Of This Man: The Biography of William A. Hillenbrand.
Dalhousie University Staff. Accounting & Information Systems Study Manual: Canadian CEBS Course 6.
Dali, T., ed. see Al Fateh Staff & IFAC Staff.
Dalis, Gus T., jt. auth. see Fodor, John T.
Dallas, Georgia. This Band of Gold.
Dallas, Ian. The Ten Symphonies of Gorka Konig.
Dallas Morning News Staff. Dallas Restaurants: One Hundred Fifty of the Best Places to Eat in Dallas-Fort Worth.
D'Allemagne, Henry R. Decorative Antique Ironwork: A Pictorial Treasury.
Dallemagne, Pierre G., ed. Oceanographic Data Reduction Manual.
Dallery, Arlene B., jt. ed. see Carse, James P.
Dallin, Alexander, compiled by. Soviet Conduct in World Affairs.
Dallin, Leon, jt. auth. see Winslow, Robert W.
Dallinger, Nat. Unforgettable Hollywood.
--Unforgettable Hollywood.
Dallman, Martha. Teaching the Language Arts in the Elementary School.
Dallmayr, Fred R. & McCarthy, Thomas A. Understanding & Social Inquiry.
Dallmeyer, Andrew. The Boys in the Backroom.
Dallmeyer, R. David. Physical Geology Laboratory Text & Manual: A Guide for the Study of Earth.
D'Allonnes, Olivier R. Musical Variations on Jewish Thought. Greenberg, Judith, tr.
Dally, Peter. The Fantasy Games.
Dalmais. Crazy Animal Stories.
D'Alonzo, Bruno J. Educating Adolescents with Learning & Behavior Problems.
D'Alpuget, Blanche. Turtle Beach.
--Winter in Jerusalem.
D'Alquen, Richard J. Gothic Ai & Av.

Dalquest, Walter W., jt. auth. see Hall, E. Raymond.
Dalrymple, Douglas J. Sales Management: Concepts & Cases.
Dalrymple, John. Living the Richness of the Cross.
Dalrymple, Paul, et al. A Year of Snow Accumulation at Plateau Station; Thermal Properties & Heat Transfer Processes of Low-Temperature Snow; Radiative Heat Transfer; Process in Snow & Ice; Papers 1, 2, 3 & 4: Meteorological Studies at Plateau Station, Antarctica. Businger, Joost A., ed.
Dalsass, Diana. Cashews & Lentils, Apples & Oats.
Dalton. The Miracle of Flight.
Dalton, A. J. & Haguenau, Francis. Ultrastructure of the Kidney.
Dalton, B. J., et al, eds. Theory & Applications of Moment Methods in Many-Fermion Systems.
Dalton, Bill. Indonesia Handbook. Deke, Castleman, ed.
Dalton, Bill, ed. see Willliams, George, III.
Dalton, C., jt. ed. see Morel, T.
Dalton, David. The Rolling Stones in Their Own Words.
--The Rolling Stones: The First Twenty Years.
Dalton, John. A New System of Chemical Philosophy.
Dalton, Katharina. Once a Month.
--Once a Month.
D'Alton, Martina. The Runner's Guide to the U. S. A.
Dalton, Pat. Winds of Destiny.
Dalven, Rae, tr. see Cavafy, C. P.
Dalven, Richard. Introduction to Applied Solid State Physics: Topics on the Applications of Semiconductors, Superconductors, & the Nonlinear Optical Properties of Solids.
Daly, Dorothy. Italy.
Daly, Elizabeth. The Book of the Lion.
Daly, Glenn F. Easy Way of Doing Things.
Daly, Howell V., et al. An Introduction to Insect Biology & Diversity.
Daly, John C., et al. How Long Should They Serve? Limiting Terms for the President & the Congress.
Daly, Kathleen N. The Simon & Schuster Question & Answer Book. Barish, Wendy, ed.
Daly, Lowrie J. The Political Theory of John Wyclif.
Daly, M. W. Sudan.
Daly, Marsha. Michael Landon.
Daly, Mary. Beyond God the Father.
--Beyond God the Father: Toward a Philosophy of Women's Liberation.
Daly, Robert J. The Origins of the Christian Doctrine of Sacrifice.
Daly, Robert J., jt. auth. see Helgeland, John.
Daly, Thomas A. Painting Nature's Quiet Places.
Dalyell, Tam. Misrule.
Dam, Kenneth W. America's Near West: U. S. - Japan Relations in Perspective.
Dam, Kenneth W., jt. auth. see Shultz, George P.
D'Amato, Alex & D'Amato, Janet. Italian Crafts: Inspirations from Folk Art.
D'Amato, Alex, jt. auth. see D'Amato, Jane.
D'Amato, Alex, jt. auth. see D'Amato, Janet.
D'Amato, Anthony. How to Understand the Law.
--Litigating International Law.
D'Amato, Jane & D'Amato, Alex. Algonquian & Iroquois Crafts for You to Make.
D'Amato, Janet & D'Amato, Alex. African Animals Through African Eyes.
--American Indian Craft Inspirations.
D'Amato, Janet, jt. auth. see D'Amato, Alex.
D'Amato, Janet P. Who's a Horn? What's an Antler? Crafts of Bone & Horn.
D'Amboise, Jaques, et al. Teaching the Magic of Dance.
D'Ambrosio, Bruce, jt. auth. see Klemperer, Katharina.
D'Ambrosio, Jack. Mr. Jack & Big Ed.
Damer, Eyre. When the Ku Klux Rode.
Damerst, William A. Clear Technical Reports.
Dames & Moore. Alternative Siting Requirements & Practices for Nuclear Power Plants (AIF-NESP 018)
--Generic Methodology for Assessment of Radiation Doses from Groundwater Migration of Radionuclides in LWR Wastes in Shallow Land Burial Trenches (AIF-NESP-013)
Dameton, Joseph, ed. The Professional Counselor: Competencies, Performance Guidelines & Assessment.
Damiani, Cosmo E. Surrender & Other Poems.
Damiani, Rodolfo V. The Stock Market Theory of the Circulation of the Classes: How to Apply & Interpret it Properly for the Maximization of Profits.
Damian-Knight, Guy. Karma & Destiny in the I Ching.
Damiano, David B. & Little, John B. A Course in Linear Algebra.
D'Amico, Michael, jt. auth. see Zikmund, William G.
Damirus. Der Longobardischen Koenigin Rosemundae, Wahrhaffte Lebens & Liebesgeschicht.
Damis, John. Conflict in Northwest Africa: The Western Sahara Dispute.
Damkohler, E. E. Estero, Florida 1882.
Dammann, George H., ed. see Butler, F. Donald.
Dammann, George H., ed. see Gunnell, John.
Dammann, George H., ed. see Moloney, James.
Damme, E. van see Van Damme, E.
Damon, Albert, et al. Human Body in Equipment Design.
Damon, Phillip. Modes of Analogy in Ancient Medieval Verse.
Damon, S. Foster. A Blake Dictionary: The Ideas & Symbols of William Blake.
Damore, Leo. Cache.
--The Crime of Dorothy Sheridan.
--In His Garden: The Anatomy of a Murderer.
Damour, Jacques. One Hundred & One Tips & Hints for Your Boat. Howard-Williams, Jeremy, tr. from Fr.
Damren, Betty R., et al. Training Effective Teachers: A Competency-Based Practicum Model for Teachers of Emotionally Disturbed Children.
Dams, R., jt. auth. see Adams, F.
Dana, Bill. Cowboy-English, English-Cowboy Dictionary.
Dana, Doris, tr. The Elephant & His Secret: Based on a Fable by Gabriela Mistral.
Dana, Doris, tr. see Mistral, Gabriela.
Dana, Mitchell. Beware the Smiling Stranger.
Dana, Richard, ed. Readings in Abnormal Behavior: Toward a Sociopsychological Model.
Dana, Robert. Some Versions of Silence.
Danadian, R., ed. NMR in Medicine.
Danae, Ediciones. Spanish Cooking.
Danaher, Brian G. & Lichtenstein, Edward. Become an Ex-Smoker.
Danbury, Hazel. Teaching Practical Social Work.
Dance in Canada Annual Conference, 7th, Waterloo, Ontario, June 27-July 2, 1979. New Directions in Dance: Proceedings. Taplin, ed.
Dance Notation Bureau Staff, compiled by. Ballet Collection.
Dance, S. Peter. The Collector's Encyclopedia of Shells.
--The World's Shells.
Dance, Stanley, jt. auth. see Ellington, Mercer.
Danckaerts, Jasper & Sluyter, Peter. Journal of a Voyage to New York & a Tour in Several of the American Colonies in Sixteen Seventy-Nine to Sixteen Eighty. Murphy, Henry C., ed.
Dandekar, Hemalata C., ed. The Planner's Use of Information: Techniques for Collection, Organization & Communication.
D'Andrea, Jeanne. Ancient Herbs in the J. Paul Getty Museum.
Daneault, Roland R. Poetic Meditations.
Daneliuk, F. A. Un Systeme Interactif sur Mini-Ordinateur pour la Recherche Documentaire et la Gestion de Bibliotheques.
Danella, Utta. Those Von Tallien Women.
Daneman, Meredith. A Chance to Sit Down.
Danenshyar, M. One-Dimensional Compressible Flow.
Daner, Francine J. The American Children of Krsna: Case Studies in Cultural Anthrology.
Daneshvar, Simin. Daneshvar's Playhouse - (Five Stories) Mafi, Maryam, tr. from Persian, Modern. & intro. by.
Daneshvari, Abbas, ed. Essays in Islamic Art & Architecture (In Honor of Katharina Otto-Dorn)
Danford, John W. Wittgenstein & Political Philosophy: A Re-Examination of the Foundation of Social Science.
--Wittgenstein & Political Philosophy: A Re-Examination of the Foundations of Social Science.
Danga, F., tr. see Gauze, G. F.
Dange, S. A. Legends in the Mahabharata.
Dangeard, P. Le Vacuome de la Cellule Vegetale: Morphologie. Bd. with Le Vacuome Animal. Hovasse, R; Contractile Vacuoles of Protozoa; Food Vacuoles: Food Vacuoles. Kitching, J. A. Springer-Verlag.
D'Angelo, Edward. Problem of Freedom & Determinism.
D'Angelo, Edward, et al. Contemporary East European Marxism.
--Contemporary East European Marxism.
D'Angelo, Gary A., jt. auth. see Stewart, John.
D'Angelo, Jean. Ketone Enolates: Regiospecific Preparation & Synthetic Uses.
Dangerfield, George. The Era of Good Feelings.
Dang-Tan, Chau & Dang-Tan, Hau. How to Automate Your Office.
Dang-Tan, Hau, jt. auth. see Dang-Tan, Chau.
Daniel, Abraham. Labor Enterprises in Israel: The Cooperative Economy.
Daniel, Becky & Daniel, Charlie. Oh, My Word!
--Ready, Set...Read!
--Rhyming & Reading.
Daniel, Becky, jt. auth. see Daniel, Charlie.
Daniel, Charles, jt. auth. see Smith, Page.
Daniel, Charlie & Daniel, Becky. My Very Own Dictionary.
Daniel, Charlie, jt. auth. see Daniel, Becky.
Daniel, Cletus E. Bitter Harvest: A History of California Farmworkers, 1870-1941.
Daniel, Clifton. Lords, Ladies, & Gentlemen: A Memoir.
Daniel, Clifton, et al, eds. Chronicle of the Twentieth Century.
Daniel, Donald C. & Herbig, Katherine L., eds. Strategic Military Deception.
Daniel, Donnie L., jt. auth. see Black, Tyrone.
Daniel, Edwin E. & Paton, David M. Methods in Pharmacology, Vol. 3: Smooth Muscle.
Daniel, James W., jt. auth. see Noble, Ben.
Daniel, John. Spilt Milk.
Daniel, Lee. Dragon Mountain.
Daniel, R. P. Outlines for Christian Youth.
Daniel, R. P., ed. see Hole, F. B.
Daniel, Robert L. American Philanthropy in the Near East, 1820-1960.
Daniel, Timothy M. General License Study Guide. Dunn, Si, ed.
Daniel, Timothy M., ed. Novice License Study Guide.
Daniel, W. H. & Freeborg, R. P. Turf Managers' Handbook.
Daniel, W. W. & Millward, Neil. Workplace Industrial Relations in Britain.
Daniel, Walter G. Ambrose Caliver: Adult Education & Civil Servant.
Daniel, Wayne W. Applied Nonparametric Statistics.
--Essentials of Business Statistics.
--Introductory Statistics with Applications.
Daniel, Wayne W. & Terrell, James C. Business Statistics: Basic Concepts & Methodology.
--Business Statistics: Basic Concepts & Methodology.
Daniele, Anthony, jt. auth. see Clair, Bernard.
Daniele, Joseph W. Early American Metal Projects.
Daniele, R. Anthony, jt. auth. see Clair, Bernard E.
Daniell, Rosemary. Fatal Flowers: On Sin, Sex & Suicide in the Deep South.
--Sleeping with Soldiers: In Search of the Macho Man.
Danielle, Maria. Fieldwork.
Danielli, J. F., jt. auth. see Bourne, G. H.
Danielli, James F., jt. ed. see Bourne, Geoggrey H.
Danielou, Jean. The Angels & Their Mission.
--Prayer As a Political Problem. Kirwan, J. R., ed.
--Salvation of the Nations.
Daniels, Anthony. Coups & Cocaine: Journeys in South America.
Daniels, Diane & Barron, Anne D. The Professional Secretary: Skills & Techniques for Recognition & Success.
Daniels, Dorothy. Juniper Hill.
Daniels, Elizabeth A. Jessie White Mario: Risorgimento Revolutionary.
Daniels, Guy, tr. see Casals, Felipe G.
Daniels, Guy, tr. see Vishnevskaya, Galina.
Daniels, Guy Trans. by see Carrera, Liane.
Daniels, James M. Oriented Nuclei: Polarized Targets & Beams.
Daniels, Josephus. The Wilson Era: Years of Peace, 1910-1917.
--The Wilson Era: Years of War & After, 1917-1923.
Daniels, Kate, jt. ed. see Jones, Richard.
Daniels, Kay & Murnane, Mary, eds. Uphill All the Way: A Documentary History of Women in Australia.
Daniels, Lee. Radical Moves.
Daniels, M. J. & Markham, P. G. Plant & Insect Mycoplasma Techniques.
Daniels, M. J. & Markham, P. G., eds. Plant & Insect Mycoplasma Techniques.
Daniels, Mary F., jt. ed. see Bowe, Forrest.
Daniels, P. W., ed. Spatial Patterns of Office Growth & Location.
Daniels, Pamela & Weingarten, Kathy. Sooner or Later: The Timing of Parenthood in Adult Lives.
--Sooner or Later: The Timing of Parenthood in Adult Lives.
Daniels, Paul R. Teaching the Gifted-Learning Disabled Child.
Daniels, Philip. Alibi of Guilt.
--Cinderella Spy.
--The Dracula Murders.
--Nice Knight for Murder.
Daniels, Rebecca. Book IX-Prophacies Fulfilled.
Daniels, Richard. Jimi Hendrix: Note for Note.
Daniels, Robert L. Lawrence Olivier: Theater & Cinema.
Daniels, Robert V., ed. Documentary History of Communism: Volume 1, Communism in Russia.
Danielsen, Albert L. The Evolution of OPEC.
Danielsen, John A. Winter Hiking & Camping.
Danielson, Albert L. & Kamerschen, David R., eds. Current Issues in Public-Utility Economics: Essays in Honor of James C. Bonbright.
Danielson, Edward E. Missionary Kid, MK.
Danielson, Henry. Arthur Machen: A Bibliography.
Danielson, Peter. Children of the Lion.
--The Lion in Egypt.
--The Shepherd Kings.
--Vengeance of the Lion.
Danielson, Rodger, jt. auth. see Stein, William I.
Danielsson, Bror. Engelsk-Svensk Ordbok (Prisma Modern)
Danilova, E. Z., et al. Las Mujeres Sovieticas.
Danilova, Y. Z., et al. Soviet Women.
Daninos, Pierre. The Notebooks of Major Thompson.
Danker, Frederick W. Luke. Krodel, Gerhard, ed.
--Multipurpose Tools for Bible Study.
Danker, Harold, jt. auth. see Steinberg, Richard M.
Dankert, Clyde E. Adam Smith: Man of Letters & Economist.
Dann, Penny. Why Not Stay for Breakfast?
Danna, Jo. It's Never Too Late to Start Over.
Dannat, Trevor. Architect's Yearbook.
--Architect's Yearbook.
Dannecker, Martin. Theories of Homosexuality.
Dannen, Donna, jt. auth. see Dannen, Kent.
Dannen, Kent & Dannen, Donna. Rocky Mountain National Park Hiking Trails: Including Indian Peaks.
Danner, Ronald P. & Daubert, Thomas E., eds. Manual for Predicting Chemical Process Design Data: Chapter 9: Thermal Conductivity.
Dannhauser, Werner J. Nietzsche's View of Socrates.
Da Nobrega, J. C. The Perils of Cultism.
Danois, Vivian De see De Danois, Vivian.
Danon, Susan, tr. see Mendes France, Pierre.
Danos, Paul P. & Imhoff, Eugene A., Jr. Intermediate Accounting.
Dansereau, Pierre. Inscape & Landscape: The Human Perception of Environment.
Dante, Alighieri. The Last James Dean Book.
Dante Alighieri. La Divina Comedia.
--The Inferno.
--De Monarchia.
--La Vita Nuova. Mathews, J. Chelsey, ed. Emerson, R. W., tr.
Danto, Arthur C. The State of the Art.
--The Transfiguration of the Commonplace: A Philosophy of Art.
D'Antonio, William V. & Form, William H. Influentials in Two Border Cities: A Study in Community Decision-Making.
Danusugondo, Purwanto. Bahasa Indonesia for Beginners.
Danzig, Fred, jt. auth. see Klein, Ted.
Danziger, Dennis. Daddy: The Diary of an Expectant Father.
Danziger, James, ed. & text by. Beaton.
Danziger, Kurt. Interpersonal Communication.
--Readings in Child Socialization.
Danzin, A. Science & the Second Renaissance of Europe.
Daoud, Hesham O. Daoud's Aviation Dictionary.
Daoudi, M. S. & Dajani, M. S. Economic Sanctions: Ideals & Experience.
Da Palestrina, Giovani P. see Palestrina, Giovani Pierluigi da.
DAR Systems International Staff, ed. see Seiden, Eric A.
Darbey, Jill, jt. auth. see Welles, Sigourney.
Darby, Daniel R., jt. auth. see Steffy, Wilbert.
Darby, J. B., jt. ed. see Freeman, A. J.
Darby, M. R. Macroeconomics: The Theory of Income, Employment & the Price Level.
Darby, Michael R. Labor Force, Employment & Productivity in Historical Perspective.
Darbyshire, Tom & Underhill, Stefan. If Wishes Were Saabs & Other Nursery Rhymes for Modern Times.
D'Arcais, Giovanni B., jt. ed. see Levelt, Willem J.
D'Arcangelo, Bartholomew, et al. Blueprint Reading for Plumbers: Residential & Commercial.
Darch, Colin, ed. Africa Index to Continental Periodical Literature: Covering 1979-1980.
D'Arcy, jt. auth. see Griffin.
D'Arcy, Margaretta & Arden, John. The Non-Stop Connolly Show.
--The Non-Stop Connolly Show.
--The Non-Stop Connolly Show: Professional 1986-1903.
--The Non-Stop Connolly Show: The Great Lockout, 1910-1914.
--The Non-Stop Connolly Show: World War & the Rising.
D'Arcy, Margaretta, jt. auth. see Arden, John.
D'Arcy, Martin C. Of God & Man.
Darden, Carole, jt. auth. see Darden, Norma J.
Darden, Carole, jt. auth. see Jean, Norma.
Darden, Ellington. The Darden Technique For Weight Loss, Body Shaping & Slenderizing.
--How to Look Terrific in a Bathing Suit.
--The Nautilus Bodybuilding Book.
--The Nautilus Diet: Ten Weeks to a Brand-New Body.
--The Nautilus Handbook for Young Athletes. Barish, Wendy, ed.
--The Nautilus Woman: For a Slimmer, Stronger, Sexier Body.
--No More Fat.

Authors

Darden, Norma J. & Darden, Carole. Spoonbread & Strawberry Wine: Recipes & Reminiscences of a Family.
Dardess, George, jt. auth. see Rosenthal, Peggy.
Dardis, Tom. Keaton: The Man Who Wouldn't Lie Down.
Darey-Bembe, Francoise & Bembe, John P. Day by Day with God.
Darga, Bert. The Executive Sourcebook.
Dargan, Marion. Guide to American Biography.
D'Argence, Rene-Yvon L. Chinese Jades in the Avery Brundage Collection.
Da Rif, Andrea. The Blueberry Cake That Little Fox Baked.
Daringer, Helen F. Adopted Jane.
--Adopted Jane.
--Mary Montgomery, Rebel.
--Pilgrim Kate.
--Stepsister Sally.
--Yesterday's Daughter.
Dario, Rafaela Contreras de. Short Stories.
Dario, Rafaela Contreras Del see Dario, Rafaela Contreras de.
Dark, Sheila L., jt. auth. see Schultz, Judithm.
Dark, Sidney & Grey, Rowland. W. S. Gilbert, His Life & Letters.
Darke, Diane. Guide to Aegean & Mediterranean Turkey.
Darke, Marjorie. The First of Midnight.
Darkenwald, Gordon G. Retaining Adult Students.
Darling, Joan, jt. auth. see Shaw, Evelyn.
Darling, Lowell. One Hand Shaking: A California Campaign Diary.
--One Hand Shaking: A California Campaign Diary.
Darling, Sharon S. Chicago Ceramics & Glass: An Illustrated History, 1871-1933.
Darling, Wendy. Sex Straight up with a Twist of Lemon.
Darlington, David. In Condor Country.
Darlington, Mansur. Gilera 50: Mopeds '72 Thru '78.
--Honda 125 Elsinore & MR175 '73 - '76.
--Husqvarna Competition Models '72 - '75.
--Mobylette Motobecane Mopeds '66 - '76: '65 Thru '76.
--Suzuki GT750 (3-cyl) Models '71 - '77.
Darnay, Brigitee T., ed. Subject Directory of Special Libraries & Information Centers 1988: Business & Law Libraries.
Darnay, Brigitte T., ed. Directory of Special Libraries & Information Centers.
--Directory of Special Libraries & Information Centers.
--Subject Directory of Special Libraries & Information Centers 1988.
--Subject Directory of Special Libraries & Information Centers 1988: Science & Engineering Libraries.
--Subject Directory of Special Libraries & Information Centers 1988: Education & Information Science Libraries.
--Subject Directory of Special Libraries & Information Centers 1988: Health Sciences Libraries.
--Subject Directory of Special Libraries & Information Centers 1988: Social Sciences & Humanities Libraries.
Darnay, Brigitte T. & Nimchuk, John, eds. Newsletters Directory.
Darnell, Eric, jt. auth. see Ruhe, Benjamin.
Darnton, Robert. Mesmerism & the End of the Enlightenment in France.
Darras, Jacques. Joseph Conrad & the West: Signs of Empire.
Darrow, Peter H. & Mestres, Ricardo A. Creative Financing in the 1980's.
Dart, Dorothy. Jo's Search.
Darter, Tom, ed. The Whole Synthesizer Catalogue.
Dartford, Gerald P. The British Constitution.
--The French Revolution.
Dartmouth College Library, Hanover, N. H. Staff. Dictionary Catalog of the Stefansson Collection on the Polar Regions.
Darton, William E. Quips & Quotes.
Darveniza, M. Electrical Properties of Wood & Line Design.
Darvi, A. Pretty Babies: An Insider's Look at the World of the Hollywood Child Star.
Darwin, Charles. Diary of the Voyage of H. M. S. Beagle. Barlow, Nora, ed.
--Expression of the Emotions in Man & Animal.
--Foundations of the Origin of Species. Darwin, Francis, ed.
--A Monograph of the Sub-Class Cirripedia: 1851-54.
--The Origin of Species.
--Origin of the Species.
Darwin, Charles & Wallace, Alfred R. Evolution by Natural Selection.
Darwin, Francis, ed. see Darwin, Charles.
Darwish, Mahmoud. The Music of Human Flesh. Johnson-Davies, Denys, tr. from Arabic.
Dary, David. The Buffalo Book.
--Cowboy Culture.
Dary, David A. The Buffalo Book: The Full Saga of the American Animal.
Daryabadi, A. Majid. Tafsir-ul-Quran.
Daryusl, A. A., et al. Persian Words in English. Commager, Steele, ed. Incl. The German Influence on the English Vocabulary; H.W. Fowler; The Dutch Influence on English Vocabulary; American Variations; Fine Writing; Names, Designations, & Appelations; Linguistic Self-Criticism; The Formation & Use of Compound Epithets in English Poetry; Northern Words in Modern English. Garland Pub.
Das, Braja. Advanced Soil Mechanics.
Das, Braja M. Soil Mechanics Laboratory Manual.
Das, G. D. & Kreutzberg, G. W. Evaluation of Interstitial Nerve Cells in the Central Nervous System: A Correlative Study Using Acetylcholinesterase & Golgi Techniques.
Das, Hari H. Subhas Chandra Bose & the Indian National Movement.
Das, J., jt. auth. see Dutta Majumdar, D.
Das, J. P. Puri Paintings.
--Verbal Conditioning & Behavior.
Das, Kamala. My Story.
Das, Man S. & Jesser, Clinton J., eds. The Family in Latin America.
Das, Man S., jt. ed. see Cavan, Ruth S.
Das, Manas M. Thomas Hardy-Poet of Tragic Vision: A Study of Hardy's Poetic Sensibility.
Das, R. J. Joseph Conrad: A Study in Existential Vision.
Das, Robert & Schwarzlose, Harald. Practical Seamanship Illustrated.
Das, Singh M. Contemporary Sociology in the United States.
Dasen, P. R., jt. auth. see Berry, J. W.
Dasen, Pierre. Piagetian Psychology.
Dasent, George W. Popular Tales from the Norse: With an Introductory Essay on the Origin & Diffusion of Popular Tales.
Dasent, George W., tr. Story of Burnt Njal.
Das Goswami, Hridayananda, jt. auth. see Bhaktivedanta Swami.
Dasgupta, Ajit K., jt. auth. see Chaudhri, D. P.
Das Gupta, Chidananda. The Cinema of Satyajit Ray.
Das Gupta, D. K. Molybdenum Nutrition in Rice.
Dash, J. G. & Ruvalds, J., eds. Phase Transitions in Surface Films.
Dash, Michael, jt. auth. see Bailey, Joyce.
Dash, V. & Kashyap, L., eds. Materia Medica of Ayurveda.
Dashefsky, Arnold. Ethnic Identity in Society.
Dashew, Linda, jt. auth. see Dashew, Steve.
Dashew, Steve & Dashew, Linda. The Circumnavigators' Handbook.
Da Silva, J. R., jt. ed. see Williams, R. J.
DaSilva, Leon. Mercenary-Green Hell.
DaSilva, Major. Breakout in Angola.
Dasmann, Raymond F., et al. Ecological Principles for Economic Development.
Dasmann, William. Deer Range: Improvement & Management.
Dass, Ram. The Only Dance There Is.
Dassonville, G., ed. Water Supply: The Decade-Half Way: Part of the Proceedings of the Regional Conference of the IWSA Held in Conjunction with the 3rd Congress of the UADE in Libreville, Gabon, 10-15 June, 1985.
Datapro Research Corporation Staff. Who's Who in Microcomputing.
Datar, Kiran K. Malaysia: Quest for Politics or Consensus.
Dathorne, O. R., ed. Caribbean Verse.
Datta, V. N. Madan Lal Dhingra & the Revolutionary Movement.
Datz, I. Mortimer. Power Transmission & Automation for Ships & Submersibles.
Daub, Guida H., jt. auth. see Seese, William S.
Daube, David. Forms of Roman Legislation.
Dauben, William G. Organic Reactions.
Dauben, William G., ed. Organic Reactions.
Daubenspeck, G. Walker. Occupational Health Hazards.
Daubert, Thomas E., jt. ed. see Danner, Ronald P.
Daudel, R. The Fundamentals of Theoretical Chemistry.
Daudon, Rene. French in Review.
Daudon, Rene, ed. see Simenon, Georges.
Dauenhauer, Richard. Glacier Bay Concerto.
Dauer, Manning, Jr. The Adams Federalists.
Dauer, Rosamond. The Three Hundred Pound Cat.
Daughters Of St. Paul. Christ of Vatican Two.
--Every Man's Challenge.
--My Prayerbook.
Daughters of St. Paul, ed. Bible Stories for Everyone.
--Dimensions of the Priesthood.
--Jesus in the Gospels.
--One Family under God.
Daughters of St. Paul Staff, ed. see Pope Paul VI.
Daughtry, Jolyne, jt. auth. see McConnell, Sharon.
D'Aulaire, Edgar P., jt. auth. see D'Aulaire, Ingri.
D'Aulaire, Ingri & D'Aulaire, Edgar P. Benjamin Franklin.
Daum. Extrahepatic Biliary Atresia.
Daum, Eadeth. Color Your Self Beautiful.
DauNe, Michele. Chicken Town.
Daunt, W. J. A Life Spent for Ireland.
D'Auria, Antonio, jt. auth. see Baroni, Daniele.
Dauten, Dale. Taking Chances: Lessons in Putting Passion & Creativity into Your Work Life.
D'Auvergne, Martial. Amant Rendu Cordelier a l'Observance d'Amours.
Daval, Jean-Luc. Oil Painting: From Van Eyck to Rothko.
Davar, Dhun R., jt. auth. see Davar, Rustom S.
Davar, Rustom S. & Davar, Dhun R. The Art of Damaging: A Sequel.
Dave, J. The Human Predicament in Hardy's Novels.
Dave, Ravindra H., ed. Foundations of Life-Long Education.
Davenport, A. T., ed. see TMS Staff & AIME Staff.
Davenport, Charles, jt. auth. see O'Byrne, John C.
Davenport, Cyril. The Book: Its History & Development.
--Cameos.
Davenport, Diana. Wild Spenders.
Davenport, H. M, jt. auth. see Felidae, Thomas.
Davenport, John. How to Make Miniature Furniture.
Davenport, Marcia. The Valley of Decision.
Davenport, May, ed. see Kruse, Donald W.
Davenport, May, ed. see McClelland, Herbert L.
Davenport, Michael. Trade Policy, Protectionism & the Third World.
Davenport, Robert. King John & Matilda: A Critical Edition. Davis, Joyce O., ed.
Davenport, W. G., jt. auth. see Peacey, J. G.
Davenport, W. H. The One Culture.
Daventry, Paula. Sasakawa, the Warrior for Peace: Global Philanthropist.
Davey, D. Mackenzie & Harris, Marjorie. Judging People: A Guide to Orthodox & Unorthodox Methods of Assessment.
Davey, Graham, ed. Applications of Conditioning Theory.
Davey, Jocelyn. Murder in Paradise.
--A Treasury Alarm.
Davey, R., et al, eds. Electrical Inspection.
Davey, W. G. & Redman, W. C. Techniques in Fast Reactor Critical Experiments.
David. The Politics of Law: A Progressive Critique.
David, Andrew. Famous Criminal Trials.
David, Elizabeth. French Provincial Cooking.
--Mediterranean Food.
David, Ferd, ed. see Corelli, A.
David, H. Submicroscopic Ortho- & Patho-Morphology of the Liver.
David, H. A., ed. Contributions to Survey Sampling & Applied Statistics: Papers in Honor of H. O. Hartley.
David, John R., jt. ed. see Bloom, Barry R.
David, Joyce B. What You Should Know If You're Accused of a Crime.
David, Marjorie. Primavera.
David, Miriam E. The State, the Family, & Education.
David, P. & Voge, J. Propagation of Waves.
David, Paul A. & Reder, Melvin W., eds. Nations & Households in Economic Growth: Essays in Honor of Moses Abramovitz.
David, Rosalie. Cult of the Sun: Myth & Magic in Ancient Egypt.
Davidman, Joy. Smoke on the Mountain: An Interpretation of the Ten Commandments.
David-Neel, Alexandra. Buddhism.
--Magic & Mystery in Tibet.
David-Neel, Alexandra & Yongden, Lama. The Power of Nothingness. Van de Wetering, Janwillem, tr.
Davidoff, Zino. The Connoisseur's Book of Cigar.
Davidovici, Sorin, ed. see Sydenham, Peter H.
Davidovitch, David. The Ketuba: Jewish Marriage Contracts Through the Ages.
Davidow, M. Third Soviet Generation.
Davidow, Mike. Cities Without Crisis.
Davids, Kenneth. Coffee: A Guide to Buying, Brewing & Enjoying.
Davids, Kenneth & Duniec, M. L. Coffee: A Revised Guide to Buying, Brewing & Enjoying.
Davids, Lewis E. Dictionary of Insurance.
Davids, Peter H. James: A Good News Commentary.
Davidson, Alan. Seafood of South-East Asia.
Davidson, Alice J. Because I Love You.
--Beware When Elephants Sneeze.
--Monkeys Never Say Please.
--The Twenty-Third Psalm.
--Twenty Third Psalm.
Davidson, Amanda. Teddy at the Seashore.
--Teddy Cleans the House.
--Teddy Goes Outside.
--Teddy Goes Shopping.
--Teddy in the Garden.
--Teddy's Birthday.
--Teddy's Favorite Food.
Davidson, Angus, tr. see Praz, Mario.
Davidson, Art. Minus One Hundred Forty Eight Degrees: The Winter Ascent of Mt McKinley.
Davidson, Audrey & Fay, Judith. Phantasy in Childhood.
Davidson, Avram. Vergil in Averno.
Davidson, Basil, et al, eds. Behind the War in Eritrea.
Davidson, Ben. The Skateboard Book.
Davidson, Billee, jt. auth. see Short, Pat.
Davidson, Bruce, et al. Bruce Davidson: World Champion of Eventing.
Davidson, C. W. Transmission Lines for Communications.
Davidson, Caroline. The Ham House Kitchen.
Davidson, Cathy N. Critical Essays on Ambrose Bierce.
Davidson, Daniel V., et al. Business Law: Principles & Cases.
Davidson, Donald. Tennessee: The Old River, Frontier to Secession.
Davidson, Donald, intro. by. The Fugitive - A Magazine of Verse: April 1922 to December 1925.
Davidson, Ellen P. For Always Only.
Davidson, Eric H. Gene Activity in Early Development.
Davidson, Frank P., jt. ed. see Salkeld, Robert.
Davidson, G. Genetic Control of Insect Pests.
Davidson, George. The ABC's of Air Travel.
Davidson, Gregory, jt. auth. see Poole, Lon.
Davidson, H. W., et al. Manufactured Carbon.
Davidson, Hugh M., jt. auth. see Dube, Pierre H.
Davidson, I., et al, eds. Electronic Maintenance.
Davidson, I. A. Receiving Aeriel Systems.
Davidson, Isobel. Real Stories from Baltimore County History.
Davidson, James D. The Squeeze.
Davidson, James J. The Vision of an Artist & Writer.
Davidson, James J., ed. Creative Children of God.
Davidson, Jeffrey P. Blow Your Horn.
Davidson, John & Lloyd, Richard, eds. Conservation & Agriculture.
Davidson, John H. Agricultural Law.
Davidson, John P. Collective Models of the Nucleus.
Davidson, Josephine, jt. auth. see Reggio, Kathryn.
Davidson, Laurie & Gordon, Laura K. The Sociology of Gender.
Davidson, Marion & Blue, Martha. Making It Legal: A Law Primer for the Craftmaker, Visual Artist, & Writer.
Davidson, Marshal B., intro. by see Smith, G. E.
Davidson, Marshall. Life in America.
Davidson, Marshall B. The American Wing: A Guide.
Davidson, Marshall B. & Stillinger, Elizabeth. The American Wing in the Metropolitan Museum of Art.
Davidson, Mayer B. Diabetes Mellitus: Diagnosis & Treatment.
Davidson, Melvin G. PL-One Programming with PL-C.
Davidson, Muriel. The Thursday Woman.
Davidson, Neil. Neurotransmitter Amino Acids.
Davidson, Neil A. & Gulick, Frances F. Abstract Algebra: An Active Learning Approach.
Davidson, Norman. Astronomy & the Imagination: A New Approach to Experience of the Stars.
Davidson, Philip. Propaganda & the American Revolution.
Davidson, Rebecca, jt. auth. see Kitchen, Jo.
Davidson, Robert L., jt. auth. see Clarke, Loyal.
Davidson, Robert M. Coronary Heart Disease.
Davidson, Roger H. The Role of the Congressman.
Davidson, Ronald C. & Marion, Jerry B. Mathematical Methods for Introductory Physics with Calculus.
Davidson, Sam R. Engineering Economics: Problems & Solutions.
Davidson, Sidney & Schinder, James. Fundamentals of Accounting.
Davidson, Sidney, et al. Intermediate Accounting: Concepts, Methods & Uses.
--CPA Exam Booklet: Intermediate Accounting.
--Financial Accounting.
Davidson, Sidney I., ed. Recent Advances in Ophthalmology.
Davidson, William R., et al. Retailing Management.
Davidson Pratt, J., jt. auth. see Hardie, D. W.
Davidsson, Ake. Catalogue of the Gimo Collection of Italian Manuscript Music in the University of Uppsala.
Davie, Donald. Collected Poems: 1970-1983.
Davie, Donald & Livingstone, Angela, eds. Pasternak.
Davie, Maurice, ed. see Sumner, William G.
Davie, Maurice R., ed. see Sumner, William G.
Davie, Michael, ed. The Diaries of Evelyn Waugh.
Davies, A. Donald. Adventure in Renewal.
Davies, A. Mervyn. Presbyterian Heritage.
Davies, Alan, ed. Language & Learning in Home & School.
Davies, Alan T., ed. Antisemitism & the Foundations of Christianity.
Davies, Alice I. Allart van Everdingen.

Davies, Annette. Industrial Relations & New Technology.
Davies, Arthur L. Death Plays a Duet.
Davies, B. String of Amber: The Heritage of the Mennonites.
Davies, Barbara S. & Davies, J. Clarence, 3rd. The Politics of Pollution.
Davies, Bleddyn. Variations in Children's Services among Urban Authorities.
Davies, Bleddyn P. Variations in Services for the Aged.
Davies, Brian. Social Control & Education.
Davies, C. S. Peace, Print & Protestantism: 1450 to 1558.
Davies, C. Stella & Levitt, John. What's in a Name?
Davies, Charles M. Broad Church. Wolff, Robert L., ed.
--Philip Paternoster: A Tractarian Love Story, 1858. Wolff, Robert L., ed.
--Verts; or, the Three Creeds, 1876. Wolff, Robert L., ed.
Davies, Charles N., ed. Aerosol Science.
Davies, Chase M. Ohio Probate Practice 1973-1985.
Davies, D. R. & Schackleton, V. J. Psychology & Work.
Davies, David, jt. auth. see Bussink, Willem.
Davies, Derek A. C. The Greek Islands.
--Ireland.
Davies, E. J. & Simpson, P. G. Induction Heating Handbook.
Davies, Eirlys. The English Imperative.
Davies, Frederick. Signs of the Stars.
Davies, G. J., jt. auth. see Padmanabham, K. A.
Davies, Gary. Managing Export Distribution.
Davies, Geoffrey, ed. Forensic Science.
Davies, Geoffrey M. Office Diagnosis & Management of Chronic Obstructive Pulmonary Disease.
Davies, Glyn A. Virtual Work in Structural Analysis.
Davies, Graham I., ed. Megiddo.
Davies, Graham I., ed. see Bartlett, John A.
Davies, Helen, ed. Libraries in West Africa.
Davies, Horton. Christian Deviations.
--Christian Deviations: The Challenge of the New Spiritual Movements.
Davies, Hugh. Repertoire International des Musiques Electroacoustiques.
Davies, Hugh M. Francis Bacon: The Early & Middle Years, 1928-1958.
Davies, Hugh W. Catalog of Early German Books in the Library of C. Fairfax Murray.
Davies, Hunter. William Wordsworth: A Biography.
Davies, Ivor K. Competency Based Learning: Management, Technology, & Design.
Davies, J., ed. Esenin: A Biography in Memoirs, Letters, & Documents.
Davies, J. Clarence, 3rd, jt. auth. see Davies, Barbara S.
Davies, J. E., ed. see Saliwanchik, R.
Davies, J. G. Temples, Churches & Mosques: A Guide to the Appreciation of Religious Architecture.
Davies, J. Gordon. The Origin & Development of Early Christian Church Architecture.
Davies, J. H. Musicalia: Sources of Information in Music.
Davies, J. T. Turbulence Phenomena: An Introduction to the Eddy Transfer of Momentum, Mass & Heat, Particularly at Interfaces.
Davies, John E., jt. auth. see Beck, J. Walter.
Davies, John G. The Early Christian Church.
Davies, John P., Jr. Dragon by the Tail: American, British, Japanese, & Russian Ecounters with China & One Another.
Davies, K. G. Royal African Company.
Davies, Laurence. Franck.
Davies, M. Functions of Biological Membranes.
Davies, Margaret L., ed. Maternity: Letters from Working Women.
Davies, Martin. Meaning, Quantification, Necessity.
Davies, Martin, ed. see Jones, R. & Kerslake, A.
Davies, Martin, ed. see Wendelken, Claire.
Davies, Nicholas B., jt. auth. see Krebs, John R.
Davies, Nicholas B., jt. ed. see Krebs, John R.
Davies, P. C. The Physics of Time Asymmetry.
Davies, Paul. Fireball.
--God & the New Physics.
--Other Worlds: Space, Superspace & the Quantum Universe.
--Superforce: The Search for a Grand Unified Theory of Nature.
Davies, Peter. Roots: Family Histories of Familiar Words.
--The Truth about Kent State.
--The Truth about Kent State.
Davies, Phillip R., jt. auth. see Martin, James D.
Davies, R. & Grant, M. D. Railway History in Pictures: Chilterns & Cotswolds.
Davies, R., jt. ed. see Lovelock, D. W.
Davies, R. G., jt. auth. see Richards, O. W.
Davies, Robertson. The Mirror of Nature.
Davies, Ross. Retail Planning in the European Community.
Davies, Ross L. & Champion, Anthony G., eds. The Future for the City Centre.
Davies, Russell D. Doubting Thomas Today.
Davies, Samuel & Pilcher, George W., eds. The Reverend Samuel Davies Abroad: The Diary of a Journey to England & Scotland, 1753-55.
Davies, Sumiko. Kittymouse.
Davies, Thomas L. Supplementary English Glossary.
Davies, Thomas M., Jr., jt. ed. see Loveman, Brian.
Davies, Valentine. Miracle on Thirty-Fourth Street.
Davies, Vicki R. Adventures of Gingerbee.
Davies, W. D. Jewish & Pauline Studies.
--Paul & Rabbinic Judaism: Some Rabbinic Elements in Pauline Theology.
Davies, W. H. Young Emma.
Davies, W. X., jt. auth. see Strategic Operations Group Staff.
Davies, William R. Gathered into One.
Davila, Angelamaria. Animal Fiero y Tierno.
Da Vinci, Leonardo. Anatomical Drawings from the Royal Library Windsor Castle.
--The Art of Painting.
--Didone Abbandonata.
--Philosophical Diary.
Davinson, D. E. Commercial Information.
Davio, Marc, et al. Discrete & Switching Functions.
Davis. World Urbanization, Nineteen Fifty to Nineteen Eighty.
Davis & Cornwell. Introduction to Environmental Engineering.
Davis, A., tr. see Graeff, H. & Kuhn, W.
Davis, A. E. & Bolin, T. D. Physical Diagnosis in Medicine.
Davis, A. R., ed. Modern Japanese Poetry. Kirkup, James, tr. from Japanese.
Davis, Adelle. Let's Cook It Right.
--Let's Cook It Right.
--Let's Eat Right to Keep Fit.
--Let's Eat Right to Keep Fit.
--Let's Get Well.
--Let's Get Well.
--Let's Stay Healthy: A Guide to Lifelong Nutrition. Gildroy, Ann, ed.
Davis, Alan. Children in Clinics: A Sociological Analysis of Medical Work with Children.
Davis, Albert R. & Rawls, Walter C., Jr. The Magnetic Blueprint of Life.
--The Magnetic Effect.
--The Rainbow in Your Hands.
Davis, Alice V. Timothy Turtle.
--Timothy Turtle.
Davis, Allen. Jane Addams on Peace & Freedom, 1914-1935.
Davis, Allison. Leadership, Love & Aggression.
Davis, Arthur P. & Redding, Saunders, eds. Cavalcade: Negro American Writing from 1760 to the Present.
Davis, Barbara. Edward S. Curtis: The Life & Times of a Shadow Catcher.
Davis, Barbara, jt. auth. see Musbach, Alice.
Davis, Barbara, jt. auth. see Stuart, Richard B.
Davis, Barbara, ed. The Cruising World Best of People & Food Cookbook.
Davis, Bernard & Davis, Elizabeth, eds. Poets of the Early Seventeenth Century.
Davis, Bertha & Arnof, Dorothy. How to Fix What's Wrong with Our Schools: A Toolkit for Concerned Parents.
Davis, Bette & Herskowitz, Michael. This 'n That.
Davis, Bill C. Mass Appeal.
Davis, Boyd H., jt. auth. see Bryan, Margaret B.
Davis, Brian, ed. see National Computing Centre, Ltd. Staff.
Davis, Bruce. The Drawings of Ciro Ferri. Freedberg, S. J., ed.
Davis, Bruce & Davis, Genny W. The Heart of the Healing.
Davis, Bruce, jt. auth. see Feinblatt, Ebria.
Davis, Burke. Three for Revolution.
Davis, Calvin V. & Sorensen, K. E. Handbook of Applied Hydraulics.
Davis, Charles G. Rigs of the Nine Principal Types of American Sailing Vessels.
--Shipping & Craft in Silhouette.
Davis, Christopher. A Peep into the Twentieth Century.
Davis, Christopher M., jt. ed. see Stern, Robert M.
Davis, Coralie G. The Folk Architecture of Louisiana: A Selected Bibliography.
Davis, Courtney. The Celtic Art Source Book.
Davis, Craig, jt. auth. see Clark, Buddy.
Davis, Creath. How to Win in a Crisis.
Davis, D. L. Understanding Judaism.
Davis, Daniel S. Struggle for Freedom: The History of Black Americans.
Davis, Daphne. Stars.
Davis, David E. Behavior As an Ecological Factor.
Davis, Dean, jt. auth. see Martin, Vaughn.
Davis, Deborah. Katharine the Great: The Life of Katharine Graham.
Davis, Denny C., jt. auth. see Hall, Carl W.
Davis, Devra, jt. ed. see Ng, Lorenz K.
Davis, Diane W. Call Back the Dawn.
Davis, Donald G., Jr. Comparative Historical Analysis of Three Associations of Professional Schools.
Davis, Dorothy S. A Death in the Life.
--Lullaby of Murder.
--The Pale Betrayer.
--Scarlet Night.
--Tales for a Stormy Night.
Davis, Douglas F. The Lion's Tail.
Davis, Drew. On the Other Side of Anger.
Davis, Dwight & Borgen, Joe. Planning, Implementing & Evaluating Career Preparation Programs.
Davis, Dwight F., jt. auth. see Bramble, Donna L.
Davis, E. A. La Placebo Play.
Davis, E. H. & Campbell-Allen, D. The Profession of a Civil Engineer: Studies in Honour of John Roderick.
Davis, E. H., jt. auth. see Poulos, H. G.
Davis, E. Wades. The Serpent & the Rainbow.
Davis, Edward E. Into the Dark: A Beginner's Guide to Developing & Printing Black & White Negatives.
Davis, Edward Z. Translations of German Poetry in American Magazines, 1741-1810.
Davis, Elizabeth, jt. ed. see Davis, Bernard.
Davis, Enid. Liberty Cap.
Davis, F. T. Business Acquisitions Desk Book.
Davis, Fei-Ling. Primitive Revolutionaries of China: A Study of Secret Societies in the Late Nineteenth Century.
Davis, Frank T., Jr. Business Acquisitions Desk Book, with Checklists & Forms.
Davis, Frederick G., jt. ed. see Robertson, Jack C.
Davis, Gary A. & Rimm, Sylvia. Education of the Gifted & Talented.
Davis, Gene, jt. auth. see Baldwin, Deirdra.
Davis, Genny W., jt. auth. see Davis, Bruce.
Davis, George A. & Donaldson, O. Fred. Blacks in the United States: A Geographic Perspective.
Davis, George F., Sr. Dynamo Davis: A Memoir of a Multi-Faceted Life.
Davis, George L. & Shannon, Samuel H. Institutions of American Government.
Davis, George R. The Local Network Handbook.
Davis, Glenn B., jt. auth. see Bradford, W. Murray.
Davis, Gordon. Directory of Engineering Societies & Related Organizations.
Davis, Gordon B. & Everest, Gordon. Readings in Management Information Systems.
Davis, Grania. Moonbird.
Davis, Gwen. Marriage.
--Romance.
Davis, Harold B. & Gottlieb, Sybil, eds. Current Trends in Dynamic Personality Theory: Problems of Normal & Disturbed Development.
Davis, Harold E. History & Power: The Social Relevance of History.
Davis, Hazel R., jt. auth. see Davis, James E.
Davis, Howard H. Beyond Class Images: Explorations in the Structure of Social Consciousness.
Davis, I., ed. Disasters & the Small Dwelling.
Davis, J. Madison. Stanislaw Lem. Schlobin, Roger C., ed.
Davis, Jack & Loveless, E. E. The Administrator & Educational Facilities.
Davis, James C. A Venetian Family & Its Fortune, 1500-1900: The Dona & the Conservation of Their Wealth.
Davis, James E. & Davis, Hazel R. Women's Studies.
Davis, James W. National Conventions: Nominations Under the Big Top. Dillon, Mary E., ed.
Davis, Jane. The Dynamics of Prostar.
Davis, Jean, jt. auth. see Kahn, Sandra S.
Davis, Jennie. In God's Great Way.
--Praise Him! Praise Him!
Davis, Jennie, jt. auth. see Buerger, Jane.
Davis, Jerome. Disarmament: A World View.
--Religion in Action.
--World Leaders I Have Known.
Davis, Jerome D. High-Cost Oil & Gas Resources.
Davis, Jinni E. Death & Life.
Davis, Joan E. & Mason, Celestine B. Neurologic Critical Care.
Davis, Joan T. Cara Mia.
Davis, John. The Evasive Peace.
--Strike a Giant Bell.
--Technology for a Changing World. England, Roger, compiled by.
Davis, John A., ed. Gramsci & Italy's Passive Revolution.
Davis, John H., ed. Summary of the Colloquium on Public Law 94-210.
Davis, John H., Jr. The Peat Deposits of Florida, Their Occurrence, Development, & Uses.
Davis, John J. Abortion & the Christian: What Every Believer Should Know.
--The Christian's Guide to Pregnancy & Childbirth: Choosing the Best for You & Your Child, from Conception to Delivery.
--Theology Primer.
--Your Wealth in God's World.
--Your Wealth in God's World: Does the Bible Support the Free Market?
Davis, John M., et al. An Atlas of Pedodontics.
Davis, Joyce O., ed. see Davenport, Robert.
Davis, Judy, jt. auth. see Liberatore, Dan.
Davis, Julia F; see O'Neal, William B.
Davis, K. Roscoe & McKeown, Patrick G. Quantitative Models for Management.
Davis, Katie. Sentence Combing & Paragraph Construction.
Davis, Keith. Human Behavior at Work.
Davis, Keith, et al. Business & Society: Concepts & Policy Issues.
Davis, Kenn. Dead to Rights.
Davis, Kenneth P. Land Use.
Davis, L. M., jt. auth. see Winn, Charles S.
Davis, Larry, jt. auth. see Bard, Ray.
Davis, Lawrence M., et al. Studies in Linguistics in Honor of Raven I. McDavid Jr.
Davis, Leslie. The Splintered Moon.
--A Touch of Scandal.
Davis, Levi, jt. auth. see Scott, Stanley.
Davis, Linda. Technical Mathematics.
Davis, Louise L. Snowball Fight in the White House.
Davis, Lydia, tr. see Detrez, Conrad.
Davis, Lynn L., ed. see Dillon, Richard.
Davis, Mackenzie L. Air Resource Management Primer.
Davis, Maggie. Hustle, Sweet Love.
Davis, Maggie S. The Best Way to Ripton.
--Choices of a Growing Woman.
--Grandma's Secret Letter.
--Rickety Witch.
Davis, Marilyn. The Little Fly.
Davis, Marsha, ed. Greenberg's Guide to Marx Trains.
Davis, Martyn. The Effective Use of Advertising Media.
Davis, Marvin A. Turnaround: The No-Nonsense Guide to Corporate Renewal.
Davis, Mary. Careers in a Bank.
--Careers in a Medical Center.
--Careers in Baseball.
--Careers in Printing.
--Careers with a Telephone Company.
Davis, Mary L. & Pack, Greta. Mexican Jewelry.
Davis, Mel, jt. auth. see Bottcher, Betty.
Davis, Mitchell P. Talk Show Guest Directory.
Davis, Monte, jt. auth. see Woodcock, Alexander.
Davis, Morton. Mathematically Speaking.
Davis, Neil M. Medication Error.
Davis, O. B. Introduction to Biblical Literature.
Davis, P. W., ed. see Linguistic Association of Canada & the U. S. Staff.
Davis, P. William & Solomon, E. P. The World of Biology.
Davis, Paxton. A Flag at the Pole.
--Ned.
Davis, Peter, jt. auth. see Jones, Frank.
Davis, Phil. The Dancer's Death.
--Nemesis.
Davis, Philip. And Crown Thy Good.
Davis, Phyllis E. Medical Terminology: A Programmed Text.
Davis, Phyllis E., jt. auth. see Smith, Genevieve L.
Davis, Polly. English Structure in Focus.
Davis Publications Staff & Queen, Ellery. Ellery Queen's Memorable Characters.
--Ellery Queen's Prime Crimes Two.
Davis, R. & Wells, C. H. J. Spectral Problems in Organic Chemistry.
Davis, R. F., et al, eds. Processing of Crystalline Ceramics.
Davis, R. Harvard. General Practice for Students of Medicine.
Davis, Randall & Winston, Patrick. Introduction to AI & Expert Systems One: Their Application & Consequences.
Davis, Raymond E. & Kelly, J. W. Elementary Plane Surveying.
Davis, Rene V. & Lofquist, Lloyd H. Job Satisfaction & Work Adjustment: Implications for Vocational Education.
Davis, Richard B., ed. see Foster, Augustus J.
Davis, Richard C. & Miller, Linda A., eds. Guide to the Cataloged Collections in the Manuscript Department of the William R. Perkins Library, Duke University.
Davis, Robert C. Contemporary Literary Criticism.
Davis, Robert C., ed. The Grapes of Wrath: A Collection of Critical Essays.
Davis, Robert E. American Negro Dilemma.
Davis, Robert S., Jr. Georgia Citizens & Soldiers of the American Revolution.
Davis, Ron L. The Healing Choice.
Davis, S. Race Relations in Ancient Egypt.
Davis, Sally A. Artist's Market, 1985.
Davis, Sally A., ed. Artist's Market, 1983.
--Artist's Market, 1984.
Davis, Sam. The Form of Housing.
Davis, Stephen. Hammer of the Gods: The Led Zeppelin Saga.
Davis, Stephen & Simon, Peter. Reggae Bloodlines.
Davis, Stephen T. The Debate about the Bible: Inerrancy Vs. Infallibility.

Authors

Davis, Sue, ed. see CARASA Collective Staff.
Davis, Suzannah. Deception & Desire.
Davis, Ted J., ed. Development of Rainfed Agriculture under Arid & Semiarid Conditions: Proceedings of the Sixth Agriculture Sector Symposium.
--Proceedings of the Fourth Agricultural Symposium.
Davis, Ted J., ed. see Agricultural Sector Symposium Staff.
Davis, Thadious M. Faulkner's "Negro" Art & the Southern Context.
Davis, Thomas. The Exe Estuary: Wildlife in Camera.
Davis, Thomas A. Algebra & Trigonometry.
Davis, Timothy C. The Indian's Ruby.
Davis, W. Hints to Philanthropists.
Davis, W. N. California Indians Five: Sagebrush Corner - Opening of California's Northeast.
Davis, W. T., ed. Bradford's History of Plymouth Plantation 1606-1646.
Davis, William. Language of Money: An Irreverent Dictionary of Business & Finance.
Davis, William, ed. World's Best Business Hotels.
Davis, William C., ed. Touched by Fire: A Photographic History of the Civil War.
--Touched by Fire: A Photographic Portrait of the Civil War.
Davis, William C., ed. see National Historical Society Staff.
Davis, William H. see Golf Digest Editors.
Davis, William M. Nimrod of the Sea.
Davis, William S., et al, eds. Anasazi Subsistence & Settlement on White Mesa, San Juan County, Utah.
Davis-Friedmann, Deborah. Long Lives: Chinese Elderly & the Communist Revolution.
Davison, A., et al, eds. New Concepts Two.
--Three-Membered Rings.
Davison, A. N., ed. Biochemical Correlates of Brain Structure & Function.
Davison, A. N. & Cuzner, M. L., eds. The Suppression of Experimental Allergic Encephalomyelitis & Multiple Sclerosis.
Davison, Alex M. A Synopsis of Renal Diseases.
Davison, D. J. The Environmental Factor: An Approach for Managers.
Davison, Jane. The Fall of a Doll's House: Three Generations of American Women & the Houses They Lived In.
--The Fall of a Doll's House: Three Generations of American Women & the Houses They Lived In.
Davison, June & Schaub, Ardella. Piano Progress. Podolsky, Leo, ed.
--Piano Progress for the Partially Sighted. Podolsky, Leo, ed.
--Piano Progress for the Partially Sighted. Podolsky, Leo, ed.
--The Piano Way to Music Reader. Podolsky, Leo, ed.
Davison, L., jt. ed. see Aifantis, E. C.
Davison, Marshall B. A History of Art: From Twenty-Five Thousand B.C. to the Present.
Davison, Peter. Praying Wrong: New & Selected Poems, 1957-1984.
--Pretending to Be Asleep.
--A Voice in the Mountain.
Davison, Peter, ed. see Jacobson, Dan.
Davison, Peter, ed. see Jonnes, Jill.
Davison, Peter, ed. see Kunitz, Stanley.
Davison, Peter, ed. see MacLeish, William H.
Davison, Peter, ed. see Mowat, Farley.
Davison, Peter, ed. see Reilly, Robert.
Davison, S. G., ed. Progress in Surface Science.
--Progress in Surface Science.
--Progress in Surface Science.
--Progress in Surface Science.
--Progress in Surface Science.
--Progress In Surface Science.
--Progress in Surface Science.
--Progress in Surface Science.
--Progress in Surface Science.
Davisson, L. D., jt. auth. see Berger, T.
Davisson, Lee D., jt. ed. see Gray, Robert M.
Davitz, Joel R. & Davitz, Lois L. Evaluating Research Plans in the Behavioral Sciences: A Guide.
Davitz, Lois L., jt. auth. see Davitz, Joel R.
Davson, H., jt. ed. see Bito, L.
Davy, A. J., jt. ed. see Jefferies, R. L.
Davy, Don. Anatomy & Life Drawing.
--Drawing Animals & Birds.
--Drawing Boats & Water.
--Drawing Buildings.
Davy, Yvonne. Trail of Peril. Wheeler, Gerald, ed.
Davydoff, Mariamna. Memoirs of a Russian Lady: Drawings & Tales of Life Before the Revolution. Dax, Olga D., tr.
Davydov, A. S. Theory of Molecular Excitations.
Davye, Arnold, et al. Lagonga: A History of the Marque.
Daw, Ednah. How I Grow African Violets.
Daw, George. Gun Patents 1864.
Dawe, Donald G. Jesus: Lord for All Times.
Dawes, Anna, jt. auth. see Trevern, Dawes.
Dawes, Frank. Not in Front of the Servants: A True Portrait of English Upstairs-Downstairs Life.
Dawes, I. W. & Sutherland, I. W. Microbial Physiology.
Dawes, William M. The Circle & the Conic Curves.
Dawidowicz, Lucy. The Jewish Presence: Essays on Identity & History.
Dawidowicz, Lucy S. On Equal Terms: Jews in America, 1881-1981.
--On Equal Terms: Jews in America 1881-1981.
--The War Against the Jews 1933-1945.
Dawihl. Handbook of Hard Metals.
Dawis, Rene V. & Lofquist, Lloyd. A Psychological Theory of Work Adjustment: An Individual-Differences Model & Its Applications.
Dawisha, Karen & Hanson, Philip, eds. Soviet-East European Dilemmas.
Dawkins, Darryl & Wirt, George. Chocolate Thunder: The In-Your-Face, All-Over-the-Place, Death-Defyin', Mesmerizin', Slam-Jam Adventures of Double D.
Dawkins, Lee. The Beast of Revelation Thirteen: The Number of a Man Six Threescore & Six? or Six Threescore to the Power & Six? Equals Nine?
--The Mystery Babylon - Revelation 17-5: Is It America?
Dawkins, Louisa. Natives & Strangers.
Dawley, Alan. Class & Community: The Industrial Revolution in Lynn.
Dawley, Donald L. What Auditors Should Know about Data Processing. Farmer, Richard N., ed.
Dawley, Powel M. Our Christian Heritage: Revised & Expanded.
Daws, Gavan. A Dream of Islands.
Dawson, A. J. Finn the Wolfhound.
Dawson, Adele G. James Franklin Gilman: Nineteenth Century Painter.
Dawson, Anthony B. Indirections: Shakespeare & the Art of Illusion.
Dawson, Barbara. White Work Embroidery 1987.
Dawson, Chandler, jt. auth. see Schachter, Julius.
Dawson, Clayton L., et al. Modern Russian I.
Dawson, Frances, tr. see Steiner, Rudolf.
Dawson, Gene. No Little Plans: Fairfax County's PLUS Program for Managing Growth.
Dawson, Glen. Hungarians in the United States.
Dawson, Glen, jt. auth. see Helen, Mary.
Dawson, J. K. & Long, G. Chemistry of Nuclear Power.
Dawson, James. Superspill.
Dawson, Jim. Whitetail Hunting.
Dawson, John W. The Cancer Patient.
Dawson, Lawrence, ed. see Licht, Hans.
Dawson, Nadine. Light of Truth Beaming on the Human Race.
Dawson, Owen L. Studies of Relief & Rehabilitation in China.
Dawson, P. S., ed. Microbial Growth.
Dawson, Peter E. Evaluation, Diagnosis, & Treatment of Occlusal Problems.
Dawson, Robert O. Sentencing: The Decision As to Type, Length, & Conditions of Sentence.
Dawson, Roger. You Can Get Anything You Want: But You Have to Do More Than Ask.
Dawson, Rosemary B., jt. auth. see Hardgrove, Carol B.
Dawson, S. W. Drama & the Dramatic.
Dawson, Thomas & Skiff, F. J. The Ute War: A History of the White River Massacre.
Dawson, Townes L. Mounce's Legal Forms Workbook.
Dax, Olga D., tr. see Davydoff, Mariamna.
Day. High Density Lipoproteins.
Day, A. Grove, ed. see Becke, Louis.
Day, Alan E. J. B. Priestley: An Annotated Bibliography.
Day, Alan E., ed. Archaeology: A Reference Handbook.
Day, Albert E. An Autobiography of Prayer.
Day, Albert E. & Wagner, James K. Letters on the Healing Ministry.
Day, Clarence. Life with Father.
Day, Cyrus L., ed. see D'Urfey, Thomas.
Day, D. W. Biopsy Pathology of the Oesophagus, Stomach & Duodenum.
Day, David, jt. auth. see Jackson, Albert.
Day, Donald, ed. see Rogers, Will.
Day, Donald L., jt. auth. see Philipp, Ernie.
Day, Douglas. Journey of the Wolf.
Day, Fraser, jt. auth. see Carriere, Dean.
Day, Gene G. Is Any Among You Sick? The Dynamics of a Healing Ministry.
Day, J. H. The Polychaeta of Southern Africa.
Day, J. Laurence. Press Coverage of the Falklands Conflict.
Day, J. S. Subcontracting Policy in the Airframe Industry.
Day, J. Wentworth. Poison on the Land.
Day, Jerry, jt. auth. see Peck, Dave.
Day, John. Works of John Day. Bullen, A. H., ed.
Day, Kenneth, intro. by. William Caxton & Charles Knight.
Day, Kent C., jt. ed. see Moseley, Michael E.
Day, Lewis F. Alphabets Old & New for the Use of Craftsmen.
--Nature & Ornament: Nature the Raw Material of Design.
--Nature in Ornament.
--Ornament & Its Application.
--Pattern Design.
Day, Lewis F. & Buckle, Mary. Art in Needlework: A Book about Embroidery.
Day, Michael H. Guide to Fossil Man.
Day, Millard F. Basic Bible Doctrines.
Day, N. K. & Good, R. A., eds. Biological Amplification Systems in Immunology.
Day, P. R. Genetics of Host-Parasite Interaction.
Day, Paul. The Burns Book.
Day, Peter R. Communication in Social Work.
--Methods of Learning Communication Skills.
Day, S. R. & Good, R. A., eds. Membranes & Viruses in Immunopathology: Proceedings.
Day, Sherman R. & McCane, Mel R. Vocational Education in Corrections.
Day, Stacey B., ed. Intergrated Medicine.
--Life Stress.
Day, Stacey B. & Brandejs, Jan F., eds. Computers for Medical Office & Patient Management.
Day, Virgil. The Equal Employment Compliance Manual.
Dayan, Rodney S., jt. auth. see Practising Law Institute Staff.
Dayan, Ruth & Dudman, Helga. And Perhaps: The Story of Ruth Dayan.
Dayananda, James Y., ed. Eden Phillpotts (Eighteen Sixty-Two to Nineteen Sixty) Selected Letters.
Day-Lewis, Cecil. A Hope for Poetry.
Day-Lewis, Cecil & Lehmann, John, eds. The Chatto Book of Modern Poetry: Nineteen Fifteen to Nineteen Fifty-Five.
Daynes, Byron W. & Tatalovich, Raymond. Contemporary Readings in American Government.
Daynes, Byron W., jt. auth. see Tatalovich, Raymond.
Dayrell, Elphinstone. Why the Sun & the Moon Live in the Sky.
Dayton, Brandt. The Swami & Sam: A Yoga Book.
Dayton, Donald W. Discovering an Evangelical Heritage.
Dayton, Edward & Wagner, C. Peter. Unreached Peoples '80.
Dayton, Edward, jt. auth. see Wagner, C. Peter.
Dayton, Edward R. & Engstrom, Ted W. Strategy for Leadership.
De, Nitish, et al. Managing & Developing New Forms of Work Organization.
Deacon, Alan. In Search of the Scrounger.
Deacon, G. E. & Deacon, Margaret B., eds. Modern Concepts of Oceanography.
Deacon, Margaret B. Oceanography: Concepts & History.
Deacon, Margaret B., jt. ed. see Deacon, G. E.
Deacon, Richard. A History of the British Secret Service.
--The Israeli Secret Service.
Deacon, Robert T. & Johnson, M. Bruce. Forestlands: Public & Private.
Deacon, Ruth E. & Firebaugh, Francille M. Home Management Context & Concepts.
Deagon, Ann. There Is No Balm in Birmingham.
Deakin, Joan. Scuba Diving.
De Alcega, Juan. A Tailor's Pattern Book: From Spain in the Year 1589.
Dealey, Ted. Diaper Days of Dallas.
Dealy, Glenn C. The Public Man: An Interpretation of Latin American & Other Catholic Cultures.
Deamer, D. W., jt. auth. see Branton, D.
Deamer, David. Being Human.
Dean & Carrell. Dust for the Dancer.
Dean, Alan H., jt. auth. see McDonald, Jack R.
Dean, Alexander & Carra, Lawrence. Fundamental of Play Directing.
Dean, Anabel. Submerge: The Story of Divers & Their Crafts.
--Up, up, & Away! The Story of Ballooning.
Dean, Ann, jt. auth. see Schechter, Alan N.
Dean, Bessie. Let's Love One Another.
Dean, Blanche E. Trees & Shrubs of the Southeast.
Dean, D. L. Discrete Field Analysis of Structural Systems.
Dean, Dave & Hefley, Marti. Now Is Your Time to Win.
Dean, J. & Padarathsingh, M. The Biological Relevance of Immune Suppression Induced by Therapeutic & Environmental Chemicals.
Dean, James & Bryan, Bill. Alcohol Programs for Higher Education.
Dean, James S. Robert Greene: A Reference Guide.
Dean, James W. & Schwindt, Richard, eds. Accounting.
--Bargaining & Dispute Resolution Curricula: A Sourcebook.
--Business, Government & Society.
--Business Policy & Strategy.
--International Business.
--Organizational Behavior.
Dean, Janet. Call Me Angie.
Dean, Jennifer B. Careers in a Department Store.
--Careers with an Airline.
Dean, Jill, jt. ed. see McCoy, Sue.
Dean, Jill W., ed. Wisconsin.
Dean, Joan. Managing the Primary School.
--Managing the Primary School.
Dean, Karen S. Between Dances: Maggie Adams' Eighteenth Summer.
--Mariana.
--Stay on Your Toes, Maggie Adams!
Dean, Leigh, jt. auth. see Lisker, Sonia O.
Dean, Lillia. These Special Ones.
Dean, Michael. English for the Business World.
Dean, R. T. Cellular Degradative Processes.
Dean, Stanley R., jt. ed. see Cancro, Robert.
Dean, Susan, jt. auth. see Kennedy, Adele P.
Dean, Thomas & Hedden, Jay. How to Solarize Your House.
Dean, Thomas & Shoham, Yoav. Planning & Reasoning about Time.
Dean, W. G., ed. Economic Atlas of Ontario: Atlas Economique de l'Ontario.
Dean, Warren, pref. by see Fernandes, Florestan.
Dean, William D. Love Before the Fall.
Dean, Winton. Bizet.
DeAndrea, William L. Killed in Paradise.
--Killed on the Ice.
DeAndrea, William L., et al. Edgar Award-Winning Mysteries.
Deane, John F., ed. The Cold Heaven: Irish Religious Poetry of Faith & Doubt.
Deane, Philip. I Should Have Died.
Deanesly, Margaret. The Pre-Conquest Church in England.
De Angeli, Arthur C. & De Angeli, Marguerite. Empty Barn.
De Angeli, Marguerite. Friendship & Other Poems.
De Angeli, Marguerite, jt. auth. see De Angeli, Arthur C.
DeAngelis, Richard A. Blue-Collar Workers & Politics: A French Paradox.
De Angioy, Rosella. Exotic Pasta: Seventy New Recipes for Very Different Pasta Dishes.
Deans, Alan, ed. Australian Mining, Minerals & Oil.
Deans, Alexander S. The Bee Keepers Encyclopedia.
Dear, Michael J. & Taylor, S. Martin. Not on Our Street: Community Attitudes to Mental Health Care.
Dear, William. Dungeon Master: The Disappearance of James Dallas Egbert, III.
Dearborn, Elwyn. The Down East Printmaker: Carroll Thayer Berry.
Dearden, John & Shank, John. Financial Accounting & Reporting: A Contemporary Emphasis.
Dearden, R. F. Problems in Primary Education.
--Theory & Practice in Education.
Dearden, R. F., et al. Educational & the Development of Reason. Incl. Pt. 1. Critique of Current Educationl Aims; Pt. 2. Reason; Pt. 3. Education & Reason. Routledge Chapman & Hall.
DeArdo, A. J. & Ratz, G. A. Thermomechanical Processing of Microalloyed Austenite: Proceedings. Pittsburgh, 1981.
De Arenas, Bibi Armas see Armas de Arenas, Bibi.
De Armas, Frederick, et al, eds. Critical Perspectives on Calderon de la Barca.
DeArmond, Robert N. Alaska: Eighteen Sixty-Seven to Nineteen Fifty-Nine.
Dearn, Robert. Island Cruising Club Book of Ropework for Yachtsmen.
Dearnaley, E. J. & War, P. B., eds. Aircrew Stress in Wartime Operations.
Dearstyne, Howard. Inside the Bauhaus. Spaeth, David, ed.
De Assis, Machado. Epitaph of a Small Winner.
De'ath, Richard. The Best of Tombstone Humor.
Deaton, Angus. Three Essays on a Sri Lanka Household Survey.
Deaux, Kay & Wrightsman, Lawrence C. Social Psychology in the Eighties.
De Azevedo, Carlos. Churches of Portugal.
Deb, B. M. The Force Concept in Chemistry.
De Bakker, M. Mathematical Theory of Program Correctness.
De Balzac, Honore. Beatrix: Le Livre de Poche Classique.
--Le Centenaire ou les Deux Beringheld.
--Chant Funebre.
--Le Chef - d'Oeuvre Inconnu.
--Les Chouans. Regard, ed.
--Les Chouans. Regard, ed.
--Clotilde De Lusignan Ou le Beau Juif.
--Correspondance avec Zulma Carraud.
--Droll Stories. Boyd, Ernest, ed.
--Etudes de Femmes.
--Eugenie Grandet. Marriage, Ellen, tr.
--Exposition Commemorative du 150e Anniversaire de la Mort de Balzac.
--Les Grandes Ecoles, Pourquoi Faire?
--L' Heritier de Biraque.
--L' Histoire de l'Empereur.
--Honorine: Avec: Albert Savarus, La Fausse Maitresse.
--Jean-Louis Ou Lafille Trouvee.
--Mademoiselle du Vissard.

Authors

--Oeuvres Completes Illustrees. Ducourneau, ed.
--Old Goriot. Marriage, Ellen, tr.
--Peau de Chagrin.
--Physiology of Marriage.
--Romans de Jeunesse: Avec: L'Heritiere de Biraque, Jean-Louis ou la Fille Trovee, Clotilde de Lusignan ou le beau Juif, Le Vicaire des Ardennes.
--The Unknown Masterpiece. Neff, Michael, tr. from Fr.
De Balzac, Honore & Meininger, Anne-Marie. Les Celibataires: Avec: Le Cure de Tours, Pierrette.
De Balzac, Honore & Pierrot, Roger. Lettres a Madame Hanska.
De Balzac, Honore & Richard, Marie Helene. Balzac En Sa Touraine.
DeBands, Henward M. & Ginalski, William. Franchise Option: Expanding Your Business Through Franchises.
De Barry, Brett, jt. auth. see Nee, Victor G.
De Bary, Anton. Comparative Morphology & Biology of the Fungi, Mycetozoa, & Bacteria. Balfour, I. B., ed. Garnsey, E. H., tr.
DeBastiani, Richard J. Computers on the Battlefield: Can They Survive?
De Bat, Alfred, ed. Advertising Photography in Chicago, 1985.
DeBat, Don. Home Refinancing: How You Can Cash in on Today's Low Rates.
Debease, Gloria, jt. auth. see Forbes, Adrienne.
De Beauclair, Inez. Studies on Botel Tobago & Yap.
De Beaufort, Simon. Yellow Earth, Green Jade: Constants in Chinese Political Mores.
De Beaumarchais, Pierre A; see Bentley, Eric.
De Beauvoir, Simone. Adieux: A Farewell to Sartre. O'Brian, Patrick, tr.
--L' Amerique au Jour le Jour: Voyages.
--Ethics of Ambiguity.
--Mandarins: Roman.
--Memoires d'une Jeune Fille Rangee.
--Mort Tres Douce.
--Sang Des Autres.
--Tous les Hommes Sont Mortels: Roman.
--Tout Compte Fait.
De Beer, G. R. Sir Hans Sloane & the British Museum.
DeBelleroche, J. Presynaptic Receptors: Mechanisms & Functions.
De Bellis, Jack, ed. Sidney Lanier, Henry Timrod & Paul Hamilton Hayne: A Reference Guide.
De Bercy, Drouin. L' Europe et L'Amerique Comparees.
De Berg, Jean. The Image. Southgate, Patsy, tr.
De Berg, Jeanne. Women's Rites: Essays in the Erotic Imagination. Hollo, Anselm, tr. from Fr.
DeBernardis, Amo. Use of Instructional Materials.
Debertin, K. & Mann, W. B. Gamma & X-Ray Spectrometry Techniques & Applications.
De Beus, J. G. Tomorrow at Dawn.
De Bhardraithe, T. English-Irish Dictionary.
DeBlanc, H. J. & Sorenson, J. A. Noninvasive Brain Imaging: Computed Tomography & Radionuclides.
De Blasis, Celeste. Wild Swan.
De Bliek, Ruth see Pena, Alberto & Bliek, Ruth de.
De Blij, Harm J. The Earth: A Topical Geography.
De Blij, Harm J. & Muller, Peter O. Geography: Regions & Concepts.
De Blumenthal, Vera. Folk Tales from the Russian.
Debnam, Betty. All New Best of the Mini Page.
--The Mini Page Kids' Cookbook.
Debo, Darrell. Burnet County History.
Debo, Richard K. Revolution & Survival: The Foreign Policy of Soviet Russia, 1917-1918.
DeBoer, C. H., jt. auth. see Harrison, R. G.
DeBoer, J. B. & Fischer, D. Interior Lighting.
De Boer, Jan & Baillie, Thomas W., eds. Disasters: Medical Organization.
De Bokx, ed. Viruses of Potatoes & Seed-Potato Production.
De Boor, Carl, ed. Mathematical Aspects of Finite Elements in Partial Differential Equations.
De Boor, W. & Grossarth-Maticek, R., eds. Radikalismus Untersuchungen Zur Persoenlichkeitsentwicklung Westdeutscher Studenten in den Jahren-1973.
De Borchgrave, Arnaud, jt. auth. see Moss, Robert.
De Boyer Argens, Jean Baptiste see Baptiste De Boyer Argens, Jean.
De Brabander, M., et al, eds. Cell Movement & Neoplasia: Proceedings of the Annual Meeting of the Cell Tissue & Organ Culture Study Group, Held at the Janssen Research Foundation, Beerse, Belgium, May 1979.
De Bray, Reginald G. Guide to the East Slavonic Languages: Guide to the Slavonic Languages, Part 3.
--Guide to the South Slavonic Languages: Guide to the Slavonic Languages, Part 1.
DeBray, Reginald G. Guide to the West Slavonic Languages: Guide to the Slavonic Languages, Part 2.
Debreczeni, L. A., jt. ed. see Hutas, I.
Debreczeny, Paul & Eekman, Thomas, eds. Chekhov's Art of Writing: A Collection of Critical Essays.
Debreczeny, Paul & Zeldin, Jesse, eds. Literature & National Identity: Nineteenth-Century Russian Critical Essays.
De Breffny, Brian. Castles of Ireland.
--In the Steps of St. Patrick.
De Breffny, Brian & Mott, George. The Churches & Abbeys of Ireland.
Debrer, M. Riga: A Guide.
Debretts Peerage Editors & Ashe, Geoffrey. The Discovery of King Arthur.
De Broglie, Marie-Blanche & Zukas, Harriet. The Cuisine of Normandy: French Regional Cooking with Princess Marie-Blanche de Broglie.
De Brouker, Jose, ed. see Camara, Dom H.
DeBruin, Jerry. Cardboard Carpentry.
De Brunhoff, Jean. Babar the King.
DeBruyn, Monica. Lauren's Secret Ring. Fay, Ann, ed.
Debry, G., ed. Nutrition, Food & Drug Interactions in Man.
Debry, R. K. Communicating with Display Terminals.
DeByle, Norbert V. & Winokur, Robert P. Aspen: Ecology & Management in the Western United States.
De Camp, Catherine C., jt. auth. see De Camp, L. Sprague.
De Camp, L. Sprague & De Camp, Catherine C. Science Fiction Handbook: How to Write & Sell Imaginative Stories.
De Camp, L. Sprague & Pratt, Fletcher. The Compleat Enchanter.
DeCampoli, Giuseppe. Strength of Structural Materials: Understanding Basic Structural Design.
De Campos, Deoclecio R. Michelangelo: The Last Judgment.
De Carli, Franco. The World of Fish. Richardson, Jean, tr.
De Carlo, Andrea. Macno. Weaver, William, tr.
De Carvalho-Neto, Paulo. My Uncle Atahualpa. Valle, Victor, tr. from Span. Miller, Yvette E., ed.
De Caso, Jacques, jt. auth. see Pratt, James N.
Decaudin, ed. see Apollinaire, Guillaume.
Decaurcel, Martine, ed. Malraux: Life & Work.
De Caussade, Jean-Pierre. The Sacrament of the Present Moment: Self Abandonment to the Divine Providence. Muggeridge, Kitty, tr. from Fr.
Decembre-Alonnier. Dictionnaire de la Revolution Francaise.
De Cervantes, Miguel. Don Quixote.
De Cervantes Saavedra, Miguel. Don Quijote De la Mancha.
De Chamblain De Marivaux, Pierre C. Le Paysan Parvenu: Or, the Fortunate Peasant.
De Chambrun, Rene. Pierre Laval: Traitor or Patriot? Stein, Elly, tr.
De Chardin, Pierre Teilhard see Teilhard De Chardin, Pierre.
De Chiara, Joseph. Site Planning Standards.
Dechter, Rina & Fox, Mark. Constraint Directed Reasoning.
Deci, Edward L., jt. auth. see Gilmer, B. V.
Decius, J. C. & Hexter, R. M. Molecular Vibrations in Crystals.
Decker, Clarabelle D. Common-Sense English Grammar.
Decker, David L. & Shichor, David. Urban Structure & Victimization.
Decker, Donald M. Mastering the International Phonetic Alphabet.
Decker, Harold A. & Herford, Julius, eds. Choral Conducting: A Symposium.
Decker, J., tr. see Taminiaux, J.
Decker, Kurt & Backmund, Herbert. Paediatric Neuroradiology.
Decker, Larry E., jt. ed. see Schoeny, Donna H.
Decker, Margaret S. Mr. Billiwicket's Burro: Ten Stories.
Decker, Natasha. Seventy-Six Ways to Save Our Nation.
Decker, Peter R. Fortunes & Failures: White-Collar Mobility in 19th-Century San Francisco.
Decker, R. Windows on the U. S. A. 1000 Word Level. Incl. Windows on the U. S. A. 1500 Word Level; Windows on the U. S. A. 500 Word Level. Decker, R; Windows on the U. S. A. 750 Word Level. McGraw.
Decker, Randall E. & Schwegler, Robert A. Decker's Patterns of Exposition.
--Decker's Patterns of Exposition.
Decker, Robert J. Effective Psychotherapy: The Silent Dialog.
Decker, Scott H., jt. auth. see Academy of Criminal Justice Sciences Staff.
Deckinger, Larry, jt. auth. see Singer, Jules.
De Clerq, C., jt. auth. see Johl, S. S.
De Cleyre, Voltairine. The First Mayday: The Haymarket Speeches 1895-1910.
Decock, Jean-Pierre. Mirage.
De Cock-Morgan, Liliane, jt. auth. see Balsys, Algis.
De Coppens, Peter R. The Nature & Use of Ritual.
DeCosse, Jerome J., ed. Large Bowel Cancer: Clinical Surgery International.
De Cosse, Jerome J., jt. ed. see Condon, Robert E.
Decoster, Don T. & Schafer, Eldon L. Management Accounting: A Decision Emphasis. Incl. Study Guide to Accompany Management Accounting. Wiley.
De Coursey, R. The Human Organism.
DeCoursey, Russell M. The Human Organism.
--Laboratory Manual of Human Anatomy & Physiology.
DeCrow, Karen, jt. auth. see Seidenberg, Robert.
DeCrow, Roger, ed. Adult Education Dissertation Abstracts 1963-1967. League, Nehume.
De Danois, Vivian. Abortion, The Claims of the Body & the Deceit of "Choice"
--God & Abortion.
Dede, Christopher J., et al. Communications Technologies: Their Effect on Adult, Career, & Vocational Education. Singer, Norman M., ed.
Dedera, Don. Navajo Rugs: How to Find, Evaluate, Buy & Care for Them.
Dedmon, Emmett. Fabulous Chicago.
Deduck, Patricia A. Realism, Reality & the Fictional Theory of Alain Robbe-Grillet & Anais Nin.
Dee, Margaret. Face the Music.
--Face the Music.
--Get Acquainted Book.
--More to Learn.
--On We Go.
--Ready to Play.
--Tips for Junior Pianists.
--Tips for Pianists.
--Touch Technique for Every Pianist.
Deedat, A. Quran, the Ultimate Miracle.
Deedy, Joyce see McClelland, Herbert L.
Deegan, Paul J. Dan Moves Up.
Deeks, Joslin. Prochronisms - Anachronisms.
Deeley, T. A Guide to the Radiotherapy & Oncology Department.
Deem, Rosemary, ed. Schooling for Women's Work.
Deeming, Bill, jt. auth. see Deeming, Sue.
Deeming, Sue & Deeming, Bill. Soups & Sandwiches.
Deen, Edith. Bible's Legacy for Womanhood.
--Wisdom from Women in the Bible.
Deeny, Kevin J., jt. auth. see Junkins, David R.
Deer, Harriet A., jt. ed. see Deer, Irving.
Deer, Irving & Deer, Harriet A., eds. Selves: Drama in Perspective.
Deerforth, Daniel. Knock Wood! Superstition Through the Ages.
Dees, Jerome S. Sir Thomas Elyot & Roger Ascham: A Reference Guide.
Dees, Mary R. So Near, Yet So Far Away. Penoi, Mary, ed.
Deese, David A., jt. ed. see Williams, Frederick C.
Deese, James. Psychology As Science & Art.
Deese, James, jt. auth. see Szalay, Lorand B.
Deeter, Allen C. Heirs of a Promise.
Deetjen, P., et al. Physiology of the Kidney & of Water Balance.
Defaux, Gerard. Le Curieux, le glorieux et la sagesse du monde dans la premiere moitie du XVIe siecle: L'exemple de Panurge.
De Feldy, L. Elizabeth. Common Sense Etiquette: For Business Women, Wives, Mistresses.
De Felice, Renzo. Fascism: An Informal Introduction to Its Theory & Practice.
--Interpretations of Fascism. Everett, Brenda H., tr.
De Felitta, Frank. Golgotha Falls.
Deferrari, Roy J. Latin-English Dictionary of St. Thomas Aquinas.
Deffner, Donald. I Hear Two Voices, God!
--Please Talk to Me, God!
--Voices & Choices.
Deffner, Donald L. Please Change Me, God!
DeFleur, Melvin L. Social Problems in American Society.
DeFleur, Melvin L. & Dennis, Everette E. Understanding Mass Communication.
--Understanding Mass Communication.
De Flumiani, Carlo M. The Cylinder Theory in Dynamic Exhibitional Charts Depicting the Traumatic Extremes of the Stock Market: The Excesses of the National Economy & the Dangerous Extravagances of History from Which New Nations Are Born & Old Nations Die.
Defoe, Daniel. Memoirs of a Cavalier.
--Moll Flanders.
--Robinson Crusoe.
--Robinson Crusoe.
De Fontenay, Elisabeth. Diderot: Reason & Resonance. Mehlman, Jeffrey, tr. from Fr.
Deford, Frank. The Spy in the Deuce Court.
De Fraga Frangipane, E., jt. auth. see Pearson, E. A.
Defrain, John, jt. auth. see LeMasters, E. E.
DeFrain, John, jt. auth. see Stinnett, Nick.
DeFrance, J. J. General Electronic Circuits.
De France, Marie. Shadow of the Hawk & Other Stories. Reeves, James, ed.
DeFranco, Ellen B. TV On-Off: Better Family Use of Television.
DeFreitas', Stan. Stan DeFreitas Complete Guide to Florida Gardening.
Defren, Burton J. Partnership Desk Book.
Deganello, G. Transition Metal Complexes of Cyclic Polyolefins.
De Ganiez, Tana. Simon & Schuster's Concise International Dictionary: English-Spanish, Spanish-English.
De Gautel, Beatrice see Carillon, Annie & Goutel, Beatrice de.
De Gaviria, Maria C., ed. see National Library of Peru Staff.
Degen, Clara, ed. Communicator's Guide to Marketing.
Degen, Marie L. History of the Women's Peace Party.
Degen, Paula, jt. ed. see Wescott, Lynanne.
Degenhardt, Alan J., jt. ed. see Degenhardt, Henry W.
Degenhardt, Henry W., ed. Revolutionary & Dissident Movements: An International Guide.
Degenhardt, Henry W. & Degenhardt, Alan J., eds. Political Dissent: An International Guide to Dissident, Extra-Parliamentary, Guerrila & Illegal Political Movements.
De Gennaro, Angelo A. The Philosophy of Benedetto Croce.
--Philosophy of Benedetto Croce, an Introduction.
Degens, E. T., et al. Inorganic Biochemistry.
De George, Frances V., jt. auth. see Osborne, Richard H.
DeGeorge, R. T. Classical & Contemporary Metaphysics: A Source Book.
Degh, Linda, ed. Folktales of Hungary. Halasz, Judit, tr.
De Giorgio, A., ed. see IFAC Symposium Staff.
Degler, Carl, ed. Social Reform & Reaction in America: An Annotated Bibliography.
Degler, Carl N., ed. see Gilman, Charlotte P.
De Gomez, Madeleine Angelique Poisson see Poisson De Gomez, Madeleine Angelique.
De Gonzalez, Nelly, jt. ed. see Diaz, Jorge.
DeGraaf, Donald E. Macrophysics.
De Gramont, Sanche. The Strong Brown God: The Story of the Niger River.
--Strong Brown God: The Story of the Niger River.
Degras, Jane, tr. see Monnerot, Jules.
DeGrave, Philip. Keep the Baby, Faith.
--Keep the Baby, Faith.
DeGraw, Linda & Wallin, Barbara J. Favorite Children's Parties.
Degrazia, Joseph. Math Is Fun.
De Grazia, Sebastian. Of Time, Work & Leisure (20th Cent. Fund)
DeGrazia, Victoria, tr. see Hobsbawm, Eric.
De Gregory, Augustus. What Everyone Should Know about Death.
DeGregory, Jerry L., jt. auth. see Galliher, John F.
De Groer, Leon. Decorative Arts in Europe Seventeen Ninety to Eighteen Fifty.
DeGroot, Leslie J., et al. The Thyroid & Its Diseases.
De Groot, Roy A. Cooking with the Cuisinart Food Processor.
--The Wines of California, the Pacific Northwest & New York: First Classification of the Wineries & Vineyards.
De Grouchy, Jean & Turleau, Catherine. Clinical Atlas of Human Chromosomes.
De Gruchy. Drug: Induced Blood Disorders.
DeGruson, Gene, ed. & intro. by see Sinclair, Upton.
DeGuzman, Videa P. Syntactic Derivation of Tagalog Verbs.
De Haan, Stefan. Abenteuer Im Wattenmeer. Brown, John H., ed.
De Haas, Frank see Haas, Frank De.
DeHaller, Rodolphe, jt. ed. see Junod, Alain F.
Dehan, Vici. Hiking Trails of the Boulder Mountain Area.
De Harpporte. Northeast & Great Lake Wind Atlas.
--South & Southeast Wind Atlas.
--West & Southwest Wind Atlas.
DeHart, Allen. North Carolina Hiking Trails.
--South Carolina Hiking Trails.
De Hart, Don. Oh, for the Life of a Guide.
De Hartog, Jan. Artist.
--Call of the Sea: Lost Sea, Distant Shore, & Sailor's Life.
--Captain.
--Little Ark.
--Peaceable Kingdom.
DeHaven, Edna P. Teaching & Learning the Language Arts.
DeHaven, Martha L., jt. auth. see Walker, Jacilyn G.
De Haven, Tom. The Freedom Force.
DeHaven, Tom. U. S. S. A. Book 1.
Dehejia, Vidya. Living & Dying: An Inquiry into the Enigma of Death & After-Life.

Authors

Dehio, Ludwig. Germany & World Politics in the Twentieth Century.
De Hoyos, Ladislas. Klaus Barbie: The Untold Story. Courtin, Nicholas, tr.
De Huszar, George B. Fundamentals of Voluntary Health Care.
DeHuszar, William I. Mortgage Loan Administration.
Deighton, Lee C. Handbook of American English Spelling.
Deighton, Len. Berlin Game.
--The Berlin Game.
--Catch a Falling Spy.
--Spy Story.
Deignan, Margaret C., jt. auth. see Tolor, Alexander.
Deily, R. L., ed. IISS Commentary Special Reports I: Steel Plants U. S. A., 1960-1980.
--Steel Industry in Brief: Japan.
Deimling, K. Ordinary Differential Equations in Banach Spaces.
Deimling, Paula. Writer's Market, 1985.
Deimling, Paula, ed. Writer's Market '86.
Deindorfer, Robert G., ed. America's One Hundred One Most High Falutin', Big Talkin' Knee Slappin', Golly Whoppers & Tall Tales: The Best of the Burlington Liars' Club.
Deitchman, Seymour J. New Technology & Military Power: General Purpose Military Forces for the Nineteen Eighties & Beyond.
Deitering, Carolyn. The Liturgy As Dance & the Liturgical Dancer.
Deitrich, Jeff. Reluctant Resister.
Deitz, Reginald W. What the Bible Can Mean for You.
DeJarnette, Harriette. Follow the North Star.
--The Passion Stone.
DeJay, Ralph. Guitar-Plus.
DeJean, Louis. Junior Citizen.
De Jesus, Ed. C., jt. ed. see McCoy, Alfred W.
Dejon, William L. Policy Formulation.
DeJong, Benjamin. God's Promise for Today.
DeJong, Gerald, ed. Explanation-Based Learning.
DeJong, Gerben. Independent Living & Disability Policy in the Netherlands: Three Models of Residential Care & Independent Living.
De Jong, H. G. Bungenberg see Booij, H. L. & Bungenberg De Jong, H. G.
De Jong, J. L., jt. auth. see Falb, P. L.
De Jong, Marvin. Programming & Interfacing the Sixty-Five Two, with Experiments.
De Jong, Marvin L. Apple II Assembly Language.
DeJong, Norman. Christian Approaches to Learning Theory: A Symposium; Major Papers Delivered at the First Annual Conference at Trinity Christian College, November 11-12, 1983.
De Jong, Norman. Christian Approaches to Learning Theory: A Symposium; Major Papers Delivered at the First Annual Conference at Trinity Christian College, November 11-12, 1983.
DeJong, Norman. Education in the Truth.
DeJong, Norman, ed. Christian Approaches to Learning Theory: The Nature of the Learner - Major Papers Delivered at the Second Annual Conference, Trinity Christian College, Palos Heights, Illinois, Nov. 2-3, 1984.
DeJonghe, Marty & Earhart, Caroline. Power Up! Kids' Guide to the Apple IIe-IIc.
--Power Up! Kids' Guide to the Commodore 64.
DeJose, Grace. The Hempstead Plan: Sensible Approach to Dieting & Nutrition.
De Jouvenel, Bertrand. Sovereignty: An Inquiry into the Political Good. Huntington, J. F., tr.
De Kadt, E., et al, eds. see Conference on Blood Viscosity in Heart Disease, Thromboembolism & Cancer, Sydney Australia, May, 1978.
Deke, Castleman, ed. see Dalton, Bill.
DeKeijzer, Arne J. & Kaplan, Fredric M. The China Guidebook, 1982-1983.
DeKeijzer, Arne J., jt. auth. see Kaplan, Fredric M.
De Kerchove, Rene. International Maritime Dictionary.
Dekin, Albert A., Jr. Arctic Archaeology: An Annotated Bibliography & History.
Dekker, Thomas, ed. see Middleton, Thomas.
Dekko, Dottie. The Fast Lane Diet: The Fourteen-Day Weight Loss Program for Everyone on the Fast Track to Success.
Dekobra, Maurice. Shanghai Honeymoon.
Dekock, Carroll W. Thermodynamic Properties of Selected Metal Sulfates & Their Hydrates.
DeKock, Roger L. & Gray, Harry B. Chemical Structure & Bonding.
De Kort, Kees, illus. What the Bible Tells Us: Third Series. Incl. A Baby Called John; Jesus & a Little Girl; The Son Who Left Home; Jesus Goes Away. Augsburg Fortress.
DeKosky, Robert K. Knowledge & Cosmos: Development & Decline of the Medieval Perspective.
DeKovner-Mayer, Barbara, jt. auth. see Harris, Godfrey.
De Kruif, Paul. Hunger Fighters.
Delaat, Adrian N. Microbiology for the Allied Health Professions.
De Lacey, D. R. Expansion of Christianity.
--Jesus & the Gospels.
De la Cierva, Patronato J. Diccionario Ruso-Espanol de la Ciencia y la Tecnica.
De Laclos, Choderlos. Dangerous Acquaintances. Aldington, Richard, tr. from Fr.
Delacorta, pseud. Diva. Bair, Lowell, tr. from Fr.
--Lola: A Novel.
--Luna. Reiter, Victoria, tr.
--Vida. Reiter, Victoria, tr. from Fr.
Delacorte, Peter. Levantine.
Delacorte, Toni, et al. How to Get Free Press: A Do It Yourself Guide to Promote Your Interests, Organization or Business.
--How to Get Free Press: The Step-By-Step Guide to Successful Media Coverage for Your Business, Organization, or Political Campaign.
Delacroix, Eugene. The Journal of Eugene Delacroix. Wellington, Herbert, ed. Norton, Lucy, tr.
De La Croix, Horst & Tansey, Richard G. Gardener's Art Through the Ages.
--Gardner's Art Through the Ages.
De La Croix, J. M. & Copeland, Carole. Directory of United States Adult & Continuing Postsecondary Education.
--Directory of United States Postsecondary Education: Directory of American Colleges & Universities Legally Empowered to Grant Academic Degrees (The Best & Worst American Colleges & Universities)
--Worldwide Encyclopedia of Study & Learning Opportunities Abroad.
De La Fuente, Julio, ed. see Malinowski, Bronislaw.
Delagran, Louise, ed. see Meadowbrook Reference Group.
Delagran, Louise, et al, eds. see Masters, M.
De Laguna, Frederica. Voyage to Greenland: A Personal Initiation into Anthropology.
De la Harpe, P. Classical Banach-Lie Algebras & Banach-Lie Groups of Operators in Hilbert Space.
Delahaye, Brian L., jt. auth. see Smith, Barry J.
Delaisement, ed. see De Maupassant, Guy.
De La Lavoissier, Gaston. Europe, Italy & the Rebuilding of the Holy Roman Empire.
De la Mare, Walter. Stories from the Bible.
--The Voice.
De La Mothe, Francois De Salignac see Fenelon & De Salignac De La Mothe, Francois.
Delamotte, Yves. Grievance Procedure in an American Enterprise.
DeLancy, Elaine. Quiltcraft: New Dimensions from Past Traditions.
Delancy, Patrick R., jt. auth. see Gleim, Irvin N.
DeLand, Antoinette. Fielding's Worldwide Cruises.
--Fielding's Worldwide Guide to Cruises.
De Land, E. C., ed. Information Technology in Health Science Education.
Delaney, Anita J., ed. Black Task Force Report.
Delaney, Anita J., jt. ed. see Mizio, Emelicia.
Delaney, Daniel J., jt. auth. see Eisenberg, Sheldon.
Delaney, Edmund. The Connecticut River: New England's Historic Waterway.
Delaney, Frank. Silver Apples, Golden Apples: Best-Loved Irish Verse.
Delaney, Frank & Lewinski, Jorge. James Joyce's Odyssey: A Guide to the Dublin of Ulysses.
Delaney, John P. & Varco, Richard L., eds. Controversies in Surgery, Two.
Delaney, Matilda S. Whitman Massacre.
Delaney, Ned. Bert & Barney.
--One Dragon to Another.
--Two Strikes, Four Eyes.
--A Worm for Dinner.
Delaney, Patrick R. & Adler, James R. GAAP: A Transaction Approach.
Delaney, Patrick R. & Gleim, Irvin N. CPA Examination Review: Auditing.
--CPA Examination Review: Auditing, Business Law & Theory & Practice.
--CPA Examination Review: Business Law.
--CPA Examination Review: Theory & Practice.
--CPA Examination Review 1984 Edition: Theory & Practice.
Delaney, Patrick R., et al. GAAP 1987: Interpretation & Application.
DeLaney, Ronald A., jt. auth. see Lancaster, Kevin.
Delaney, Shelagh. The Lion in Love.
Delaney, W. How to Run a Growing Company.
--The Thirty Most Common Problems in Management & How to Solve Them.
Delaney, William A. Micromanagement: How to Solve the Problems of Growing Companies.
De Lange, Nicholas, tr. see Oz, Amos.
DeLange, Nicholas, tr. see Oz, Amos.
De Lange, Nicholas, tr. see Oz, Amos.
DeLange, Samuel A., jt. auth. see DeVlieger, Marinus.
Delanglez, Jean, ed. see Garraghan, Gilbert J.
Delannoy, ed. see Cocteau, Jean.
Delano, Hugh. Eddie.
Delano, Kenneth J. Many Worlds, One God.
DeLano, Sharon, jt. auth. see Tracy, Robert.
Delany, M. J. Mammal Ecology.
Delany, Samuel R. Wagner-Artaud: A Play of 19th & 20th Century Critical Fictions.
De la Pena, Augustin. The Psychobiology of Cancer: Automatization & Boredom in Health & Disease.
De La Ramee, Louise see OUIDA.
De La Ree, Gerry. The Book of Virgil Finlay.
De La Roche, Mazo. The Building of Jalna.
--Centenary at Jalna.
--Finch's Fortune.
--Master of Jalna.
--Wakefield's Course.
--The Whiteoak Brothers.
--Whiteoak Harvest.
--Whiteoak Heritage.
--Young Renny.
De La Rochefoucauld, Francois see also La Rochefoucauld, Francois.
De La Rosa, Angeles & Fernandez, C. Gandia. Flavors of Mexico: Authentic Recipes from South of the Border.
De Larrabeiti, Michael. Jeeno, Heloise & Igamor, The Long, Long Horse.
De la Rue. Man & the Winds.
De Las Heras, F. G. see Heras, F. G. de las & Vega, S.
De La Torriente, Donna D. Of Our Soup, Of Our People.
De la Tour du Pin. Memoirs of Madame De La Tour Du Pin.
Delattre, Pierre. Tales of a Dalai Lama.
--Walking on Air.
Delaunay, Charles. Django Reinhardt.
Delaunois, A. L., ed. Biostatistics in Pharmacology.
De Lautreamont, Comte & Ducasse, Isidore. Maldoror. Rodker, John, tr. from Fr.
De la Valdene, Guy. Making Game: An Essay on Woodcock.
De La Vega, Garcilasco. Incas.
Delbanco, Nicholas. Possession.
Del Carmen, Rolando. Criminal Procedure & Evidence.
Delcorta, pseud. Nana. Reiter, Victoria, tr. from Fr.
Del Dario, Rafaela Contreras see Dario, Rafaela Contreras de.
Del Deo, Josephine C., jt. auth. see Tod, Osma G.
Delderfield, Eric R. Eric Delderfield's Book of True Animal Stories.
--West Country Historic Houses & Their Families, Vol. 2: Dorset, Wiltshire & N. Somerset.
De Leeuw, Adele. Carlos P. Romulo: The Barefoot Boy of Diplomacy.
DeLeeuw, Adele & DeLeeuw, Cateau. Anthony Wayne, Washington's General.
DeLeeuw, Cateau, jt. auth. see DeLeeuw, Adele.
De Leeuw, S., jt. auth. see Southworth, R.
Delehanty, Suzanne & Harithas, James. The Philadelphia Houston Exchange.
De Leon, George, ed. Phoenix House: Studies in a Therapeutic Community (1968-1973)
De Leon, Sherry. The Basketry Book.
De Lerma, Dominique-Rene. Igor Fedorovitch Stravinsky, 1882-1971: A Practical Guide to Publications of His Music.
Delft, Pieter Van see Van Delft, Pieter & Botermans, Jack.
Delhaye, J. M., et al. Thermohydraulics of Two-Phase Systems for Industrial Design & Nuclear Engineering.
Deligne, P., et al. Hodge Cycles, Motives, & Shimura Varieties.
Deliman, Tracy & Smolowe, John. Holistic Medicine.
De Lint, Charles. Moonheart.
DeLisser, H. G. Jane's Career.
Delitzsch, Franz & Gloag, P. J. The Messiahship of Christ.
Delius, W., et al, eds. Catecholamines & the Heart: Recent Advances in Experimental & Clinical Research Symposium Proceedings.
Dell, Catherine, jt. auth. see Paton, John.
Dell, David J., et al. Guide to Hindu Religion.
Dell, Sidney. On Being Grandmotherly: The Evolution of IMF Conditionality.
Dell, Susanne. Silent in Court.
Della Cava, Olha. A Guide to the Archives.
De Llano, Rodriguez. Falta una Pagina Que Trate de Eso.
Dell'Antonio, G., et al, eds. Mathematical Problems in Theoretical Physics: International Conference, Held in Rome, June 6-15, 1977.
Della Porta, P., jt. ed. see Giorgi, T. A.
Dellenbrant, Jan-Ake. Soviet Regional Policy: A Quantitative Inquiry into the Social & Political Development of the Soviet Republics.
Dellinger, Ann M. Legal Guide for North Carolina School Board Members.
Delliquadri, Lyn, ed. Drawings: Eighty-First Exhibition by Artists of Chicago & Vicinity.
Dellis, A. N., tr. see Lominadze, D. G.
Dell'Isola, Alphonse & Kirk, Stephen J. Life Cycle Cost Data.
Dell'Isola, Alphonse J. Value Engineering in the Construction Industry.
Dell'Isola, Frank. Thomas Merton: A Bibliography.
Delloff, Linda M., ed. see Sittler, Joseph A.
Dell'Osso, Bernardino. Of Human Values.
Delmage, Lewis, tr. see St. Ignatius.
Delman, David. Dead Faces Laughing.
Del Mar, Donald. Classics in Scientific Management. Collons, Roger D., ed.
Del Mar, Norman. Anchor Companion to the Orchestra.
Del Mar, Norman R. Richard Strauss: A Critical Commentary on His Life & Works.
Delmar, Vina. Freeways.
--McKeever.
Delmonte, John. Technology of Carbon & Graphite Fiber Composites.
--Technology of Carbon & Graphite Fiber Composites.
Deloache, Michel, jt. auth. see St. John's Episcopal Church Staff.
DeLone, Richard, jt. auth. see Carnegie Council Staff.
Delone, Richard P., et al. Aspects of Twentieth Century Music.
Delong, Fred J. Aim for a Job in Drafting.
DeLong, Marilyn F. Medical Acronyms & Abbreviations.
De Longueville, Thomas see Longueville, Thomas de.
De Looff, James L. Commuter Airlines: A Study of the History & Operational Requirements.
De Lopez, Graciela C., jt. auth. see Rohmer, Harriet.
Delora, Joann S., et al. Understanding Human Sexuality.
--Understanding Sexual Interaction.
De Lord, Melvene. Fifty-Fifth Avenuers.
DeLorean, Cristina F. & Cohen, Sherry S. Cristina Ferrare's Style: How to Have It in Every Part of Your Life.
DeLorean, Donna. Passions of the Heart.
DeLorean, John. DeLorean.
Deloria, Vine, Jr. Custer Died for Your Sins.
De Loyola Brandao, Ignacio. Zero. Watson, Ellen, tr.
Delp, Mahlon H. & Manning, Robert T., eds. Major's Physical Diagnosis.
Del Pozo, Cal. The Back Book: The Complete Health & Exercise Program to Cure Your Aching Back.
Del Prado, Oscar Nunez see Nunez Del Prado, Oscar & Whyte, William F.
Del Ray, Lester, ed. see Fletcher, George U.
Del Ray, Lester, ed. see Kuttner, Henry.
Del Ray, Lester, ed. see Smith, Cordwainer.
Del Ray, Lester, ed. see Stasheff, Christopher.
Del Ray, Lester, ed. see Taine, John.
Del Rey, Judy-Lynn, ed. Stellar Science Fiction Stories.
Del Rey, Lester, ed. The Best of C. L. Moore.
Del Rey, Lester, ed. see Farmer, Philip Jose.
Del Rey, Lester, ed. see Fort, Charles.
Del Rey, Lester, ed. see LeGuin, Ursula K.
Del Rey, Lester, ed. see Piper, H. Beam.
Del Rey, Lester, ed. see Smith, Edward E.
Del Rey, Lester, ed. see Smith, Edward E. & Garby, Lee H.
Del Rio, Angel, ed. Responsible Freedom in the Americas.
Delsohn, Gary, jt. auth. see English, Alex.
Delsohn, Steve, jt. auth. see Dickerson, Eric.
Delsohn, Steve, jt. auth. see Trope, Mike.
Delteil, Loys, ed. Le Peintre-Graveur Illustre. Incl. Vol. 17. Camille Pissaro, Alfred Sisley, Auguste Renoir; Vol. 18. Theodore Gericault; Vol. 19. Henri Leys, Henri de Braekeleer, James Ensor; Vols. 20-29. Honore Daumier; Vol. 30. Albert Besnard; Vol. 31. Jean Frelaut; Vol. 32. Appendix. Wechsler, Herman J. Da Capo.
Delton, Judy. Groundhog's Day at the Doctor.
--Near Occasion of Sin.
De Lubac, Henri. Christian Faith.
De Luca, Anthony J. Freud & Future Religious Experience.
DeLuca, Helen. Mountains to Climb.
Deluca, Michael, jt. auth. see Michaelides, Stephen.
De Luca, Stuart M. Television's Transformation, the Next Twenty-Five Years.
Deluca, Stuart M., jt. auth. see Stone, Alfred R.
DeLuca, Virginia & Wolfson, Randy. Couples with Children.
DeLurgio, Stephen A., jt. auth. see Kwak, No Kyoon.
Delve, Eric. To Boldly Go.
Delvin, John P., ed. Pulmonary & Antiallergic Drugs.
Delworth, Ursula, et al. Student Paraprofessionals: A Working Model for Higher Education.
De Lys, Claudia. A Treasury of American Superstitions.
--Treasury of Parenthood & Its Folklore.
--Treasury of Superstitions.
De Lys, Claudia, jt. auth. see Batchelor, Julie F.
Delzell, Robert F. Finding a Position: Strategies for Library School Graduates.
De Maistre, Joseph. Considerations on France. Lebrun, Richard A., ed. & tr. from Fr.
De Malave, Florita Z. Charles W. Moore, North American Architect.
De Malave, Florita Z. Louis see Louis de Malave, Florita Z.

DeMallie, Raymond J., et al. Vestiges of a Proud Nation. Markoe, Glenn E., ed.
Demand, Nancy H. Thebes in the Fifth Century.
De Mandiargues, Andre P. The Girl Beneath the Lion. Howard, Richard, tr. from Fr.
--The Girl on the Motorcycle. Howard, Richard, tr. from Fr.
Demaray, Donald. How Are You Praying?
Demaray, Donald E. Proclaiming the Truth.
DeMarco, Ginilou. It's about Love.
De Marco, Guy. Third from the Sun.
Demare, G. & Summerfield, Joanne. One Hundred & One Ways to Protect Your Job.
Demarest, Arthur J. Resettlement.
Demarest, Bruce, jt. ed. see Lewis, Gordon R.
Demarest, Chris L. Clemens' Kingdom.
Demarest, Kathy K., ed. see Miller, William J., Jr.
De Maria, Robert. Stone of Destiny.
DeMaria, Robert, jt. ed. see Short, Raymond W.
DeMaria, Rusel & Fontaine, George R. Public-Domain Software: Untapped Resources for the Business User.
De Marivaux, Pierre C. De Chamblain see De Chamblain De Marivaux, Pierre C.
De Marne, Henri. Entering the Remodeling Field: A Manual for Small-Volume Builders.
De Marquette. Introduction to Comparative Mysticism.
De Marr, jt. auth. see Bakerman.
De Martin, Elena L., jt. auth. see Marshall, William H.
Demas, William G. The Economics of Development in Small Countries with Special Reference to the Caribbean.
De Massy, Christian & Higham, Charles. Palace: My Life in the Royal Family of Monaco.
DeMasters, Carol. Christmas & Holiday Cooking.
De Maupassant, Guy. Bel Ami. Delaisement, ed.
--Contes Choisis. Price, W. R., ed.
De Maupassant, Guy De. Contes Choisis. Price, William R., ed.
De Mause, Lloyd, et al. A Bibliography of Psychohistory.
Demb, A. Computer Systems for Human Systems.
Dembo, Myron. Teaching for Learning.
Dembofsky, Thomas J., ed. see Dorf, Richard C.
Dembofsky, Thomas J., ed. see Trafalgar House Publishing, Inc. Staff.
Dembowski, P. Finite Geometries.
Dembrow, Mari. Better Sweaters: The Step-by-Step Guide to Drafting Your Own Patterns.
Demby, William. Beetlecreek.
DeMeer, Van see Van DeMeer.
DeMeis, Leopoldo. The Sarcoplasmic Reticulum: Transport & Energy Transduction.
De Mejo, Oscar. My America.
Demel, John T. & Miller, Michael J. Introduction to Computer Graphics.
De Melo, J., jt. auth. see Corbo, V.
De Mente, Boye, ed. see Fournier, Mark E.
Demerast, Kathy K., ed. see Miller, William J., Jr.
De Mercado, Maria A., tr. see Twitchell, Paul.
Demers, Jan. What Do You Do with a...?
--What Do You Do with a...?
Demers, Jan, jt. auth. see Holland, Margaret.
Demers, Jocelyn. Suffer the Little Children: The Battle Against Childhood Cancer. Parry, James, tr. from Fr.
Demers, Laurence & Shaw, Leslie, eds. Evaluation of Liver Function: A Multifaceted Approach to Clinical Diagnosis.
Demeter, Richard L. Primer, Presses, & Composing Sticks: Women Printers of the Colonial Period.
Demetrakopoulos, George H. Dictionary of Orthodox Theology.
Demetrakopoulos, Stephanie. Listening to Our Bodies: The Rebirth of Feminine Wisdom.
Demetrulias, Diana & Deutsch, Alleen. New Audiences for Teacher Education.
De Meur, Gisele. New Trends in Mathematical Anthropology.
DeMeyer, F. & Ingraham, E. Separable Algebras over Commutative Rings.
Demi. The Adventures of Marco Polo.
--Cinderella on Wheels.
--Follow the Line.
--Hide & Seek with Wilma Worm.
Demianski, M., ed. Physics of the Expanding Universe.
Demidovich, B. P., jt. auth. see Kudryavtsev, V. A.
D'Emilio, John. Sexual Politics, Sexual Communities: The Making of a Homosexual Minority in the United States, 1940-1970.
Demille. By the Rivers of Babylon.
DeMille, Nelson. Word of Honor.
Demirchian, K. S. Soviet Armenia. Ludwick, Percy, tr.
Demko, George J. Russian Colonization of Kazakhstan, 1896-1916.
Demling, L. & Classen, M., eds. Endoscopic Sphincterotomy of the Papilla of Vater.
Demolen, Richard L., et al. Meaning of the Renaissance & Reformation.
--One Thousand Years: Western Europe in the Middle Ages.
Demong, Phyllis. Celebearties & Other Bears.
--It's a Pig World Out There.
--Rare & Undone Saints.
--Rare & Undone Saints.
De Montbrial, Thierry. Energy: The Countdown: A Report to the Club of Rome.
De Monte, Alpha. In Return For...
De Montfort, Louis. True Devotion.
De Montherlant, Henri. Bestiaires.
--Les Celibataires.
--Le Chaos et la Nuit.
--Fils De Personne. Bd. with Un Incompris. Schoenhof.
--Guerre Civile.
De Montherlant, Henry. Le Cardinal D'Espagne. Johnson, Robert B. & Johnson, Patricia J., eds.
--Don Juan.
--Don Juan.
--Les Garcons.
--Maitre de Santiago.
--Malatesta.
--Les Olympiques.
--Port-Royal.
--La Rose de Sable.
--Voyageur Solitaire Est Un Diable.
--Un Voyageur Solitaire est un Diable.
De Montoux, Pierre Guillet see Guillet de Montoux, Pierre.
De Morgan, Augustus. Elementary Illustrations of the Differential & Integral Calculus.
--On the Study & Difficulties of Mathematics.
Demory, Richard, jt. auth. see Megill, Donald D.
De Moubray, Jocelyn see Moubray, Jocelyn de.
DeMouy, Jane K. Katherine Anne Porter's Women: The Eye of Her Fiction.
DeMoya, Dorothy, et al. RN's Sex Q & A: Candid Advice for You & Your Patients.
Dempsey, David & Zimbardo, Philip G. Psychology & You.
Dempsey, James. Mission of the Nile.
Dempsey, Michael W., ed. Illustrated Fact Book of Science.
Dempsey, P. E., jt. ed. see Sluzalis, L. I.
Dempsey, Paul. How to Convert Your Car, Van or Pickup to Diesel.
--How to Repair Diesel Engines.
Demtroeder, W. Laser Spectroscopy.
De Mundo Lo, Sara. Index to Spanish American Collective Biography: Vol. 2-Mexico.
De Mundo Lo, Sara see Lo, Sara de Mundo.
De Muralt, Andre. The Idea of Phenomenology: Husserlian Exemplarism. Breckon, Garry L., tr. from Fr.
Demus, Otto. The Mosaics of Norman Sicily.
De Musset, Alfred. La Confession d'un Enfant du Siecle. Allem, ed.
Demuth, Norman. Cesar Franck.
Denaes, Raymond. General Guide to Paris Street Atlas.
De Nangis, Guillaume. Chronique Latine de Guillaume De Nangis 1113 a 1300. Geraud, H., ed.
Denbeaux, Fred J. Understanding the Bible.
Denber, Herman, ed. Schizophrenia: Theory, Diagnoses & Treatment.
Denber, Herman C., ed. Psychopharmacological Treatment: Theory & Practice.
Denbigh, K. G. An Inventive Universe.
Denborough, M. A., ed. Australia & Nuclear War.
Den Brul, Caroline Van see Van Den Brul, Caroline & Spindler, Susan.
Denby, Carol, ed. see National Retail Merchants Association Staff.
Denby, Charles. Indignant Heart: A Black Worker's Journal.
Dence, Joseph B. Steroids & Peptides: Selected Chemical Aspects for Biology, Biochemistry & Medicine.
Dence, Thomas P. The FORTRAN Cookbook.
Dendel, Esther W. African Fabric Crafts: Sources of African Design & Technique.
--The Basic Book of Fingerweaving.
--Designing from Nature: A Source Book for Artists & Craftsmen.
Dendurent, H. O. John Clare Reference Guide.
Dendurent, H. O., ed. Thomas De Quincey: A Reference Guide.
Dendy, P., ed. Human Tumour in Short Term Culture: Techniques & Clinical Applications.
Deng, Ming-Dao. The Wandering Taoist.
Deng, Xiaoping. Fundamental Issues in Present-day China.
--Speeches & Writings.
Dengler, Sandy. This Rolling Land.
Deng Xiaoping. Selected Works of Deng Xiaoping, 1975-1982.
Denham, H. M. The Adriatic: A Sea-Guide to Venice, the Italian Shore & the Dalmatian Coast.
--The Aegean: A Sea-Guide to Its Coasts & Islands.
--Dardanelles: A Midshipman's Diary.
--The Tyrrhenian: A Sea-Guide to Its Coasts & Islands.
Denham, Robert D., intro. by see Frye, Northrop.
Denham, Robert D., ed. see Frye, Northrop.
Denhard, J. G. & Grider, John D. Complete Guide to Fiduciary Accounting.
Denhoff, Eric & Feldman, Steven A. Developmental Disabilities: Management Through Diet & Medication.
Deniker, P., ed. Collegium Internationale Neuro-Psychopharmacologicum, 10th Congress: Proceedings.
Denis, Christopher. The Films of Shirley Maclaine.
Denis, L., et al, eds. Clinical Bladder Cancer.
Denisoff, Serge R. The Sociology of Dissent.
Denisov, P. N., ed. see Lenin, V. I.
Denisyuk, Yu. N. Fundamentals of Holography.
De Nitto, Elisabeth B. Needlepoint on Plastic Canvas.
Denker, Arnold S. My Best Games of Chess 1929-75.
Denker, H. W. Implantation: The Role of Proteinases, & Blockage of Implantation Through Proteinase Inhibitors.
Denker, Henry. The Director.
--The Healers.
--Judge Spencer Dissents.
--Kincaid.
--Outrage.
Denker, M., et al. Ergodic Theory on Compact Spaces.
Denkstein, Vladimir, et al, eds. Prague.
Denlinger, Milo G. Complete Boxer.
Denlinger, William, et al. Complete Chihuahua.
Dennehy, Henry E; see Sheehan, Patrick A.
Dennenberg, Herb. Herb Denenberg's Smart Shopper's Guide.
Denneny, Michael. Lovers: Story of Two Men.
Dennery, Phyllis. Dining In - New Orleans.
--Dining In - New Orleans.
Dennett, Jane & James, Edward. Europe Against Poverty.
Denney, Myron K. A Matter of Choice: An Essential Guide to Every Aspect of Abortion.
Denney, Reuel. In Praise of Adam.
Denney, Richard J., Jr., et al, eds. California Environmental Law Handbook.
Denney, Richard J., Jr., et al, eds. see McCutchen, et al.
Dennis. Extractive Metallurgy.
Dennis, Barbara, jt. auth. see Skilton, David.
Dennis, Deborah E., jt. ed. see Zikmund, Joseph.
Dennis, Everette E., jt. auth. see DeFleur, Melvin L.
Dennis, G. E. International Financial Flows: A Statistical Handbook.
Dennis, J. G., ed. Orogeny.
Dennis, J. Richard & Kansky, Robert. Instructional Computing: An Action Guide for Educators.
Dennis, John. The Plays of John Dennis. Backscheider, Paula R., ed.
Dennis, Landt. Catch the Wind: A Book of Windmills & Windpower.
Dennis, Larry, jt. auth. see Geiberger, Al.
Dennis, Laurie B., jt. auth. see Dennis, Terry L.
Dennis, Lawrence. The Dynamics of War & Revolution.
Dennis, Lawrence & Martin, James J. The Dynamics of War & Revolution.
Dennis, Lisl. Travel Photography: Developing a Personal Style.
Dennis, Patrick. Paradise.
Dennis, Peggy. The Autobiography of an American Communist: A Personal View of a Political Life, 1925-1975.
Dennis, Stephen N., ed. see National Trust for Historic Preservation Staff.
Dennis, Terry L. & Dennis, Laurie B. Microcomputer Models for Management Science: Text.
Dennison, George. Shawno: Large Print Books.
Dennison, W. F. Educational Finance & Resources.
Denniston, Denie, et al. It Isn't Easy Being Special - Let's Help Special Needs Learners: A Resource Guide for Vocational Education Teachers.
Denniston, Denie, jt. auth. see Cohen, Stanley B.
Denniston, K. J. & Enquist, L. W., eds. Recombinant DNA.
Dennon, Jack. CP-M Revealed.
Denny, Don. The Annunciation from the Right: From Early Christian Times to the Sixteenth Century.
Denny, Norman, tr. see Ayme, Marcel.
Denny, Norman, tr. see Renoir, Jean.
Denny, Norman, tr. see Simenon, Georges.
Dennys, Joyce. Henrietta's War: News from the Home Front.
Dennys, Nicholas B. The Folk-Lore of China, & Its Affinities with That of the Aryan & Semitic Races.
De Nogent, Guibert. The Autobiography of Guibert, Abbot of Nogent-Sous-Coucy. Bland, C. C., tr. from Lat.
Denoix, Pierre. Treatment of Malignant Breast Tumors - Indications & Results: A Study Based on 1174 Cases Treated at the Institute Gustave-Roussy Between 1954 & 1962. Crook, Barbara, tr. from Fr.
Denoix, Pierre, ed. Mechanisms of Invasion in Cancer.
Denon, Lester. Bertrand Russell's Dictionary of Mind, Matter, & Morals.
De Noriega, L. A. & Leach, F. Broadcasting in Mexico.
Densmore, Frances. How Indians Use Wild Plants for Food, Medicine & Crafts.
Dent, Alan. Animals & Monsters.
--Mrs. Patrick Campbell.
--The World of Shakespeare.
Dent, David, jt. auth. see Young, Anthony.
Dent, E. J. The Future of Music.
Dentler, Robert A., jt. auth. see Baltzell, D. Catherine.
Denton, D. A. The Hunger for Salt: An Anthropological, Physiological, & Medical Analysis.
Denton, Geoffrey. Economic & Monetary Union in Europe: The Economic Implications of Monetary Integration.
Denton, J. C. Energy Use Management.
Denton, John A. Medical Sociology.
Denton, R. M. & Pogson, C. I. Metabolic Regulation.
Denton, Wallace. Family Problems & What to Do About Them.
D'Entreves, Alexander P. Medieval Contribution to Political Thought: Thomas Aquinas, Marsilius of Padua, Richard Hooker.
Denvir, John. The Life Story of an Old Rebel.
Denzin, Norman K. The Research Act.
--Sociological Methods: A Sourcebook.
Denzin, Norman K., jt. auth. see Spitzer, S. P.
De Oliveira, Fernandes E., et al. Building Energy Management--Conventional & Solar Approaches: Proceedings of the International Congress, 12-16 May 1980, Povoa de Varzim, Portugal.
D'Eon, Leonard J. The Cavalier.
DeOreo, Joellen K., jt. auth. see Boger, Ann C.
De Palacios, Alicia Puyana see Puyana De Palacios, Alicia.
DePaola, Dominick P., et al, eds. Preventive Dentistry.
DePaola, T., jt. auth. see Jennings, M.
De Paola, Tomie. Charlie Needs a Cloak.
--Charlie Needs a Cloak.
DePaola, Tomie. The Cloud Book.
--The Family Christmas Tree Book.
De Paola, Tomie. Flicks.
DePaola, Tomie. The Kids' Cat Book.
--The Popcorn Book.
De Paola, Tomie. The Prince of the Dolomites.
DePaola, Tomie. The Quicksand Book.
De Paola, Tomie. Strega Nona.
--Things to Make & Do for Valentine's Day.
--Watch Out for the Chicken Feet in Your Soup.
Department of the Air Force. Survival! Air Force Manual 64-5.
De Pascale, Marc. Book of Spells.
DePasquale, Michael, Jr. Martial Arts for Young Athletes. Schwartz, Betty, ed.
DePasquale, Nicholas P. & Bruno, Michael S. Cardiology Case Studies.
Depaul & Mount St. Vincent Center. Administrative Manual of Policies & Procedures for Long Term Care Facilities.
Depauw, Karen, jt. auth. see Seaman, Janet.
D'Epinay, Christian L. Haven of the Masses: A Study of the Pentecostal Movement in Chile. Sandle, Marjorie, tr.
De Pisan, Christine. Oeuvres Poetiques. Roy, M., ed.
De Pizan, Christine. The Book of the City of Ladies. Richards, E. J., tr. from Fr.
De Pomaine, Edouard. Cooking in Ten Minutes.
De Ponceau, Arthur. The Golden Door.
DePonceau, Arthur. Kill the Envious Moon.
De Pourtales, Guy. Richard Wagner: The Story of an Artist. May, Lewis, tr. from Fr.
DePree, Gladis. Festival! An Experiment in Living.
De Pree, Max. Leadership Is an Art.
De Prez, Caroline S. & De Prez, Richard J. Resume & Job Hunting Guide for Present & Future Veterans: How to Make Your Military Training Count in Civilian Job Markets.
De Prez, Richard J., jt. auth. see De Prez, Caroline S.
DeProft, Melanie. American Family Cookbook.
Depta, Victor. The Creek.
De Purucker, G. Golden Precepts: A Guide to Enlightened Living. Todd, Helen & Small, W. Emmett, eds.
Depuy, Charles H., jt. ed. see Shapiro, Robert H.
De Queiroz, Rachel. The Three Marias.
Derailleur. How to Maintain & Repair Five, Ten, & Fifteen Speed Bicycles.
Der Beets, Richard Van see Bowen, James K. & Van Der Beets, Richard.
De Recondo, A. M., ed. New Approaches In Eukaryotic DNA Replication.
De Reed, Alicia C., tr. see Hoover, John P.
De Regniers, Beatrice S. A Bunch of Poems & Verses.
--Catch a Little Fox.
--Red Riding Hood.
De Regniers, Beatrice S. & Gordon, Isabel. Shadow Book.
De Regniers, Beatrice S. & Haas, Irene. Something Special.

De Regniers, Beatrice S. & Pierce, Leona. Who Likes the Sun.
Deregowski, J. B. Distortion in Art: The Eye & the Mind.
Derek, Bo & Derek, John. Bo.
Derek, John, jt. auth. see Derek, Bo.
De Renzi, Ennio. Disorders of Space Exploration & Cognition.
Derevitzky. Fiddleheads & Mustard Blossoms.
De Reyna, Rudy. Creative Painting from Photographs.
De Rico, Ul. The Ring of the Nibelung.
Derigs, U., jt. auth. see Burkhard, R. E.
De Rijk, Lambertus M. Logica Modernorum.
Dering, Edward H. Sherborne; or, the House at the Four Ways, 1875. Wolff, Robert L., ed.
Deringer, Janice L., jt. auth. see Armbrust, Steven.
De Rios, Marlene D. Hallucinogens: Cross-Cultural Perspectives.
Derivaux, Don, jt. auth. see Lee, Eddie H.
Deriye, Abdulkadir H. The Role of the Public Sector in Developing Countries: Somalia.
Derksen, Sandy & Nash, Connie. The Other Side of Sorrow.
Derleth, August. Some Notes on H. P. Lovecraft.
Derleth, August, ed. see Lovecraft, H. P., et al.
Derman, Cyrus. Finite State Markovian Decision Processes.
Der Meid, Louise B. Van see Van Der Meid, Louise B.
Dermer, Otis C., jt. auth. see Waller, George R.
Dernberger, Robert F. Economic Consequences & Future Implications of Population Growth in China.
Dernberger, Robert F. & Hartwell, Robert M. Coterminal Characteristics of Political Units & Economic Regions in China.
DeRobertis, E. D. & DeRobertis, E. M., Jr. Cell & Molecular Biology.
--Essentials of Cell & Molecular Biology.
DeRobertis, E. M., Jr., jt. auth. see DeRobertis, E. D.
De Rocco, Jovan. I Was Once a Tree.
DeRocco, Jovan. Legend of the Truant Tree.
De Roche, Joseph. The Heath Introduction to Poetry.
De Rohan Barondes, R. China Lore, Legends, & Lyrics.
Deroin, Nancy. Jataka Tales.
De Rola, Klossowski. Alchemy: The Secret of Art.
De Roo, Ann. Scrub Fire.
DeRoo, Sally. Exploring Our Environment: Animals Student Materials One.
DeRosa, Paul & Stern, Gary H. In the Name of Money: A Professional's Guide to the Federal Reserve, Interest Rates & Money.
DeRosier, Arthur H., Jr. Removal of the Choctaw Indians.
Derossi, Flavia. The Technocratic Illusion: A Study of Managerial Power in Italy. LoBello, Susan, tr. from Ital.
Der Osten-Sacken, Peter Von see Von Der Osten-Sacken, Peter.
De Rougemont, Denis, ed. The State of the Union of Europe: Report of the CADMOS Group to the European People.
De Roussy De Sales, Raoul, ed. see Hitler, Adolph.
De Routisie, Albert see Routisie, Albert de.
Der Pijl, L. Van see Van der Pijl, L.
Derr, Thomas S. Barriers to Ecumenism: The Holy See & the World Council on Social Questions.
--Ecology & Human Need.
Derre, Jean Rene, jt. auth. see Constant, Benjamin.
Derrett, D. R. Ship Stability for Masters & Mates.
Derrick, Christopher. C. S. Lewis & the Church of Rome.
Derricotte, Toi. Natural Birth.
Derricourt, Nick, jt. ed. see Craig, Gary.
Derrida, Jacques. Dissemination. Johnson, Barbara, tr.
--Edmund Husserl's The Origin of Geometry: An Introduction. Leavey, John P., tr. from Fr.
--Writing & Difference. Bass, Alan, tr. from Fr.
Derthick, Martha A. National Guard in Politics.
Dertinger, H. & Jung, H. Molecular Radiation Biology. Action of Ionizing Radiation on Elementary Biological Objects. Hueber, R. P. & Gresham, P. A., trs. from Ger.
Dertouzos, Michael. Threshold Logic: A Synthesis Approach.
Derucher, Kenneth N. & Heins, Conrad. Materials for Civil & Highway Engineers.
DeRuiter, James A. & Wansart, William L. Psychology of Learning Disabilities: Applications & Educational Practice.
Der Vat, Dan van see Van der Vat, Dan.
Derzhavina, M. Central V. I. Lenin Museum.
De Sabbath, Venzo, jt. ed. see Bergmann, Peter G.
De Sade, Marquis see Marquis de Sade.
Desai & Christian. Numerical Methods in Geotechnic Engineering.
Desai, Anita. Games at Twilight.
Desai, Kalpana. Treasures of the Heras Institute.
Desai, Megnad. Applied Econometrics.
De St. Jorre, John. The Brothers' War: Biafra & Nigeria.
De St. Martin, Victor, ed. Full Color Collection of Modern Art in Its Most Representative Offerings.
De Sainte-Beuve, Charles-Agustin. Oeuvres. Incl. Portraits Litteraires (Fin; Portraits de Femmes. Schoenhof.
De Sainte-Beuve, Charles-Augustin. Oeuvres. Incl. Premiers Lundis; Portraits Litteraires. Schoenhof.
De Saint-Exupery, Antoine. Citadelle.
--Courrier Sud.
--Oeuvres.
--Petit Prince.
--Petit Prince.
--Pilote De Guerre.
--Terre des Hommes.
--Vol De Nuit.
De Saint-Exupery, Antoine see Saint-Exupery, Antoine de.
De Saint-Mery, Mederic L. Moreau see Moreau De Saint-Mery, Mederic L.
De Sales, Saint Francoise. Treatise on the Love of God. Mackey, Henry B., tr.
De Sales, Raoul De Roussy see Hitler, Adolph.
De Salignac De La Mothe, Francois, jt. auth. see Fenelon.
Desalve, Louise & Leaska, Mitchell A., eds. The Letters of Vita Sackville-West to Virgina Woolf.
DeSalvo, Louise & Leaska, Mitchell A., eds. The Letters of Vita Sackville-West to Virginia Woolf.
De Santi, Roger J., ed. Teacher's Needs & Concerns Regarding Reading Instruction: Findings, Strategies, & Applications.
De Santiago, Carmen R. El Gobierno De Puerto Rico.
De Santis, Marie. California Currents: An Exploration of the Ocean's Pleasures, Mysteries & Dilemmas.
--Neptune's Apprentice: Adventures of a Commercial Fisherwoman.
De Santis, Zerlina. A Child's Story of Past & Present Saints.
De Sarlo, Carmine R. TV Commercial Film Editing: Professional Motion Picture Pre-& Post-Production Including Animation, Rotoscoping, & Video Tape.
DeSaulniers, Lawrence B. The Response in American Catholic Periodicals to the Crises of the Great Depression, 1930-1935.
De Saussine, Renee. Paganini. Laurie, Marjorie, tr.
De Saussure, Ferdinand. Course in General Linguistics.
Desbarats, Peter. Gabrielle & Selena.
--Gabrielle & Selena.
Desberg, Dan & Kenan, Lucette R. Modern French.
Descartes, Rene. Discourse on Method: Meditations on a First Philosophy, & Principles of Philosophy.
--Philosophical Letters. Kenny, Anthony, ed. & tr.
--Treatise of Man. Hall, Thomas S., tr. & commentary by.
Deschamps, Benoit & Dileep, Mehta. The Chief Financial Officer.
De Schryver, F. C., jt. ed. see Smets, G.
Descotes, J. Immunotoxicology of Drugs & Chemicals.
De Selincourt, Aubrey. Six Great Poets: Chaucer, Pope, Wordsworth, Shelley, Tennyson, the Brownings.
De Selincourt, Basil. William Blake.
DeSerpa. Microeconomic Theory.
De Serres, Frederick J., et al, eds. Utilization of Mammalian Specific Locus Studies in Hazard Evaluation & Estimation of Genetic Risk.
Desh Bandhu & Chauhan, Eklavya. Current Trends in Indian Environment.
Desheng, Zhang. Two Hundred Recipes for the Doufu Devotee.
Desheplo, Linda M. Two Sewers for a Tennis Court: Or What I Got Out of & Into.
DeShong, Barbara R. The Special Educator: Stress & Survival.
Deshpande, Gauri. An Anthology of Indo-English Poetry.
Deshpande, Pradeep B. & Ash, Raymond H. Elements of Computer Process Control with Advanced Control Applications.
Desiderato, O. Readings in General Psychology.
Desiderato, O., ed. Introduction to Psychology: Selected Readings.
Design Bulletins. Housing the Family.
De Silva, M. A. & Siriwardenc, Reggie. Communication Policies in Sri Lanka: A Study Carried Out by a Committee Appointed by the Secretary to the Ministry of Education, Sri Lanka.
De Silva, S. B. The Political Economy of Underdevelopment.
DeSilva, S. B. The Political Economy of Underdevelopment.
DeSimone, Diane, jt. auth. see Durden-Smith, Jo.
Desk Top Seminar Staff. How to Improve Writing Skills.
Desk Top Seminars Staff. Handling Problem Employees: How to Take Corrective Action, Trainer's Edtion.
Desloge, Edward A. Classical Mechanics.
Deslongchamps, Pierre. Stereoelectronic Control in the Cleavage of Tetrahedral Intermediates in the Hydrolysis of Esters & Amides. Barton, et al, eds.
Des Lozieres, Baudry & Narcisse, Louis. Voyage a la Louisiane, et Sur le Continent De L'amerique Septentrionale Fait Dans les Annees Seventeen Ninety-Four to Seventeen Ninety-Eight.
Desmarchelier, J. M., et al. Residue Reviews.
Desmond, Kevin. Richard Shuttleworth.
Desmond, Ray. A Celebration of Flowers.
Desmore, Mary J., jt. auth. see Emanuelson, Kathy L.
De Sola, Carla. Learning Through Dance.
De Sola, Ralph. Crime Dictionary.
DeSola, Ralph. Worldwide What & Where.
De Sola, Ralph, tr. Beethoven by Berlioz.
De Sola Sola de Pool, Ithiel see Pool, Ithiel de Sola.
De Sormo, Maitland C. Summers on the Saranacs.
De Sormo, Maitland C., ed. see Stoddard, Seneca R.
De Sousa, Daniel. A Critical Evaluation of Contemporary "New Left" Sociology.
--Sociological Formalism & Structural-Functional Analysis: The Nature of the "Social" Reality Sui Generis? Form? System?
De Sousa, Maria S., et al. The Effects of Hormones on Immunity.
DeSouza, Glenn R. Energy Policy & Forecasting: Economic, Financial, & Technological Dimensions.
Desov, A. English-Bulgarian Concise Technical Dictionary.
Desowitz, Robert S. New Guinea Tapeworms & Jewish Grandmothers: Tales of Ecology, Parasites, & Progress.
De Spelder, Charles. The Court of Domestic Revelation.
Despland, Michel. Kant on History & Religion.
Desrosier. Elements of Food Technology.
Desrosier, John N., jt. auth. see Desrosier, Norman W.
Desrosier, Norman W. & Desrosier, John N. Technology of Food Preservation.
Desrosier, Norman W. & Tressler, Donald K. Fundamentals of Food Freezing.
Dessent, Michael H. Baseball Becky.
--California Corporation Manual.
Dessi, Guiseppe. The Forests of Norbio.
Dessoir, Max. Aesthetics & Theory of Art. Emery, Stephen A., tr.
De Stevens, George. Diuretics.
De Stevens, George, ed. Analgetics.
Destler, I. M., et al. Our Own Worst Enemy: The Unmaking of American Foreign Policy.
Destombes, Marcel. Selected Contributions to the History of Cartography & Scientific Instruments.
D'Estree, Sabine, tr. see Reage, Pauline.
Destutt De Tracy, A. Treatise on Political Economy.
De Sua, William J. Dante into English: A Study of the Translation of the Divine Comedy in Britain & America.
De Suassure, Eric, ed. Taize Picture Bible.
De Surgy, Paul. Mystery of Salvation. Sheed, Rosemary, tr.
Detacuden, Nam U. The Simplest Explanation of God Ever Explained.
De T. Alvim, Paulo, ed. Ecophysiology of Tropical Crops.
DeTar, C., jt. ed. see Ball, J.
Detar, Delos F., ed. Computer Programs for Chemistry.
--Molecular Mechanics: A Symposium.
Detection Club. The Floating Admiral.
Detering, Alberta M. Of Times & People from Ohio: Distant Cousins.
Dethier, V. G. Man's Plague? Insects & Agriculture.
Detlaf, A., jt. auth. see Yavorsky, B.
Detlaf, A. A., jt. auth. see Yavorski, B. M.
Detmold, M. J. The Unity of Law & Morality: A Refutation of Legal Positivism.
De Tocqueville, Alexis. Democracy in America.
Detorie, Rick. Catholics: An Unauthorized, Unapproved, Illustrated Guide.
De Tracy, A. Destutt see Destutt De Tracy, A.
DeTray, Jeffrey D., ed. see Creason, Sam.
De Trevino, Elizabeth B. see Trevino, Elizabeth B. De.
Detrez, Conrad. A Weed for Burning. Davis, Lydia, tr.
--Zone of Fire. Davis, Lydia, tr.
Detroit Institute of Arts Staff & Museum Practice Program Students. Paris & the American Avant-Garde, 1900-1925.
Detroit Public Library Staff. Automotive History Collection of the Detroit Public Library: A Simplified Guide to Its Holdings.
--Catalog of the E. Azalia Hackley Memorial Collection of Negro Music, Dance & Drama.
De Troyes, Chretien. Perceval: The Story of the Grail. Bryant, Nigel, tr.
Detwiler, Donald S. & Burdick, Charles B., eds. Defense of the Homeland & the End of the War: Japanese Military Studies 1937-1949.
--Japan & the Soviet Union.
--Japan & the Soviet Union.
--Japanese Military Studies Nineteen Thirty-Seven to Nineteen Forty-Nine, Naval Armament Program & Naval Operations: Japanese & Chinese Studies & Documents.
--Japanese Military Studies Nineteen Thirty-Seven to Nineteen Forty-Nine, Naval Armament Program & Naval Operations: Japanese & Chinese Studies & Documents.
--Japanese Military Studies: The Southern Area: Japanese & Chinese Studies & Documents.
--Japanese Military Studies 1937-1949: Command, Administration, & Special Operations; Japanese & Chinese Studies & Documents.
--Japanese Military Studies 1937-1949: China, Manchuria, & Korea.
--Japanese Military Studies 1937-1949: China, Manchuria, & Korea.
--Japanese Military Studies, 1937-1949: Political Background of the War: Japanese & Chinese Studies & Documents.
--Japanese Military Studies, 1937-1949: The Southern Area: Japanese & Chinese Studies & Documents.
--Japanese Military Studies, 1937-1949: The Sino-Japanese & the Chinese Civil Wars.
--Japanese Military Studies, 1937-1949: The Sino-Japanese & the Chinese Civil Wars.
--Japanese Military Studies, 1939-1949: The Sino-Japanese & the Chinese Civil Wars.
Detwiler-Zapp, Diane & Dixon, William C. Lay Caregiving.
Deuchar, Margaret. British Sign Language.
Deudney, Daniel & Flavin, Christopher. Renewable Energy: The Power to Choose.
Deur, Lynne. Doers & Dreamers: Social Reformers of the 19th Century.
Deuring, M. Lectures on the Theory of Algebraic Functions of One Variable.
Deutch, John M. Prospects for Synthetic Fuels in the United States.
Deutcsh, Arthur V. Starett.
Deutrich, Mabel E. & Purdy, Virginia C., eds. Clio Was a Woman: Studies in the History of American Women.
Deutsch. Models of the Nervous System.
Deutsch, Alleen, jt. auth. see Demetrulias, Diana.
Deutsch, David J., ed. see Chemical Engineering Magazine Editors.
Deutsch, E., jt. ed. see Kleinberger, G.
Deutsch, J. A., ed. The Physiological Basis of Memory.
Deutsch, Jordan. Avon Superstars: Kevin McHale, Michael Jordan.
--Avon Superstars: Marcus Allen, Jim McMahon.
Deutsch, Karl W. Analysis of International Relations.
--Politics & Government: How People Decide Their Fate.
Deutsch, Kenneth L., jt. auth. see Kemerer, Frank R.
Deutsch, Marilyn W., jt. ed. see Leland, Henry.
Deutsch, Morton. From Whence Came You?
Deutsch, Otto E. Schubert: Memoirs by His Friends.
--The Schubert Reader: A Life of Franz Schubert in Letters & Documents.
Deutsch, Richard R. Northern Ireland, Nineteen Twenty-One to Nineteen Seventy-Four: A Select Bibliography.
Deutsch, Robert W. Nuclear Power.
Deutsch, Rosamund E. The Pattern of Sound in Lucretius. Commager, Steele, ed.
Deutsch, Yvonne, ed. Painting in Watercolors.
Deutsche Gesellschaft Fuer Neurochirurgie Staff. Proceedings of the Deutsche Gesellschaft fuer Neurochirurgie, 25th Bochum, Germany, Sept. 1974. Klug, W., et al, eds.
Deutsche Gesellschaft Fur Biophysik, Annual Meeting, Konstanz, October 1979. Abstracts of Presentations: Proceedings. Adam, G. & Stark, G., eds.
Deutscher, Isaac. Marxism in Our Time. Deutscher, Tamara, ed.
Deutscher, Tamara, ed. Not by Politics Alone: The Other Lenin.
Deutscher, Tamara, ed. see Deutscher, Isaac.
Deutschman, Alan. Winning Money for College: The High School Student's Guide to Scholarship Contests.
Deutsh, Jordon. Dwight Gooden & Dale Murphy.
Dev, Kalipada. Rural Development in India Since Independence.
Devadutt, Vinjamuri E. Bible & the Faiths of Men.
De Vane, Lenchen Coleman. The Adventures of Tony, David & Marc: Reading from A-Z.
Devane, Richard S. The Failure of Individualism: A Documented Essay.

DeVane, William C. Higher Education in Twentieth-Century America.

Devaney, John. Blood & Guts: The True Story of General George S. Patton, U. S. A.

Devaney, Kathleen, ed. Building a Teachers' Center.

Devas, M., ed. Geriatric Orthopaedics.

De V. Brunkow, Robert see Brunkow, Robert de V.

DeVeaugh-Geiss, Joseph. Tardive Dyskinesia & Related Involuntary Movement Disorders.

De Vecchia, Giorgio. Justice.

De Vecellius, Anthony. Full Color Most Beloved Paintings of Flowers in the Art History of Mankind.

De Vega, Lope see Lope de Vega.

Devellard, Jean-Paul, jt. auth. see Dolce, Donald.

Developmental Research & Programs, Inc. Staff & Roberts, Fitzmahan & Associates Staff. Preparing for the Drug (Free) Years: A Family Activity Book.

De Ven, Andrew H. Van see Van De Ven, Andrew H.

Deverall, Brian J., jt. auth. see Bailey, John A.

Deveraux, Jude. Casa Grande.

--Casa Grande.

--Counterfeit Lady.

--Highland Velvet.

--Lost Lady.

--River Lady.

--Sweetbriar.

--The Temptress.

--Velvet Angel.

--The Velvet Promise.

--Velvet Song.

De Vere, Gaston Du C., tr. see Vasari, Giorgio.

Deverell, C. Business Administration & Management.

--Communication: A Book for Students.

--Management Studies: Questions & Answers.

--Office Administration.

Devereux, Frederick L., Jr. Practical Navigation for the Yachtsman.

Devereux, Owen F. Topics in Metallurgical Thermodynamics.

Devereux, Stephen E., jt. auth. see McGregor, Rob R.

De Veubeke, B. F. Advanced Problems & Methods for Space Flight Optimization.

De Veubeke, B. F., et al, eds. see CISM (International Center for Mechanical Sciences) Staff.

Devi, Gayatri & Rau, Santha R. Princess Remembers.

Devi, Indira & Roy, Dilip K. Pilgrims of the Stars.

De Vicente-Gella, Pilar. The Man with White Slacks.

De Vigny, Alfred. Stello: A Session with Doctor Noir. Massey, Irving, tr.

Devilbiss, M. C. Women in the Armed Forces.

DeVillez, Randy. Step by Step: College Writing.

De Villiers du Terrage, Marc. The Last Years of French Louisiana. Brasseaux, Carl A. & Conrad, Glenn R., eds. Phillips, Hosea, tr.

Devin, Flanna. Alien Encounter.

DeVine, Bob. Uncle Bob Talks with My Central Nervous System.

--Uncle Bob Talks with My Circulatory System.

--Uncle Bob Talks with My Digestive System.

--Uncle Bob Talks with My Respiratory System.

Devine, Elizabeth, et al, eds. Thinkers of the Twentieth Century: A Biographical, Bibliographical & Critical Dictionary.

Devine, Laurie. Nile.

--Saudi.

Devine, Michael J. John W. Foster: Politics & Diplomacy in the Imperial Era, 1873-1917.

Devine, Michael J., ed. see Illinois State Historical Society Staff.

Devine, P. J., et al. An Introduction to Industrial Economics.

De Vito, Alfred. Creative Wellsprings for Science Teaching.

DeVito, Joseph. The Psychology of Speech & Language: An Introduction to Psycholinguistics.

DeVito, Joseph A. Communication: Concepts & Processes.

DeVito, Michael. The Church's Worship.

DeVlieger, Marinus & DeLange, Samuel A. Brain Edema.

Devlin, Ellen. Hide & Seek.

Devlin, John F. The Bacth Party: A History from Its Origins to 1966.

Devlin, K. J. Aspects of Constructibility.

--The Axiom of Constructibility: A Guide for the Mathematician.

Devlin, Mark. Stubborn Child.

Devlin, Mary. Astrology & Past Lives.

Devlin, William. We Crown Them All: An Illustrated History of Danbury.

Devoe, Charles D. Maine Workers' Compensation Act: Practice & Procedure.

De Voe, Thomas F. The Market Assistant.

De Volpi, Alexander. Proliferation, Plutonium & Policy: Institutional & Technological Impediments to Nuclear Weapons Propogation.

Devon, D. G. Shattered Mask.

--Temple Kent.

Devon, Marjorie, text by. Tamarind: Twenty-Five Years.

DeVoney, Chris. MS-DOS User's Guide.

--MS-DOS User's Guide.

--Using PC DOS.

Devor, Barbara. Aunt Maude & le Faisan d'Or.

Devorah-Leah. Lost in the Zoo.

De Vore, Jack B., Jr. & Rolloff, John A. The Methodology of Mass Production in Career Education: A System for Successful Teaching.

Devore, Jay. Probability & Statistics for Engineering & the Physical Sciences.

De Vore, M. Susan. Individualized Learning Program for the Profoundly Retarded.

DeVore, Nicholas. New Frontiers in Psychology.

De Vore, R. A. The Approximation of Continuous Functions by Positive Linear Operators.

Devore, Ulric. Zarine.

De Vorss, Patricia, jt. auth. see Smith, Beverly B.

De Voto, Bernard. Journals of Lewis & Clark.

--Year of Decision.

De Voto, Mark, ed. see Piston, Walter.

Devoy, J. Recollections of an Irish Rebel.

Devreese, J. T. & Van Doren, V. E., eds. Ab Initio Calculation of Phonon Spectra.

Devreese, J. T., et al, eds. Recent Developments in Condensed Matter Physics, Vol. 2: Metals, Disordered Systems, Surfaces & Interfaces.

--Recent Developments in Condensed Matter Physics, Vol. 3: Impurities, Excitons, Polarons, & Polaritons.

--Recent Developments in Condensed Matter Physics, Vol. 4: Low-Dimensional Systems, Phase Changes, & Experimental Techniques.

--Recent Developments in Condensed Matter Physics, Vol. 1: Invited Papers.

De Vries, A. Dictionary of Symbols & Imagery.

De Vries, Barend A. Transition Toward More Rapid & Labor-Intensive Industrial Development: The Case of the Philippines.

De Vries, Barend A. & Brakel, Willem. Restructuring of Manufacturing Industry: The Experience of the Textile Industry in Pakistan, Philippines, Portugal & Turkey.

De Vries, Dawn. Servant of the Word.

De Vries, G., jt. auth. see Norrie, D. H.

DeVries, Gerard, jt. ed. see Norrie, Douglas H.

De Vries, H., jt. auth. see Van Bekkum, O.

DeVries, James E. Race & Kinship in a Midwestern Town: The Black Experience in Monroe Michigan, 1900-1915.

DeVries, Louis & Hochman, Stanley. French-English Science & Technology Dictionary.

DeVries, Louis & Jacolev, Leon. German-English Science Dictionary.

De Vries, Mary. New Century Vest-Pocket Secretary's Handbook.

DeVries, Mary A. see Prentice-Hall Editorial Staff.

DeVries, Peter. Peckham's Marbles.

--The Prick of Noon.

De Vries, Piet Penning see Penning De Vries, Piet.

De Vries, Simon J. The Achievements of Biblical Religion: A Prolegomenon to Old Testament Theology.

De Vries, Tom. On the Meaning & Future of the European Monetary System.

Dew, Philip L. The Trial.

Dew, Robb F. Dale Loves Sophie to Death.

--The Time of Her Life.

De Waal, Ronald B. The International Sherlock Holmes: A Companion Volume to the World Bibliography of Sherlock Holmes & Dr. Watson.

De Waal Malefijt, Anne X. see Malefijt, Anne M.

De Waard, Jan see Waard, Jan de & Nida, Eugene A.

De Waard, Romke. From Music Boxes to Street Organs.

Dewar, Deborah. Breast Cancer: A Woman's Handbook.

Dewar, Donald L. Quality Circle Handbook for Financial Institutions.

--Quality Circle Handbook for Health Care Facilities.

--Quality Circle Leader Manual & Instructional Guide for Financial Institutions.

--Quality Circle Member Manual for Financial Institutions.

--Quality Circle Member Manual for Health Care Facilities.

--The Quality Circle: What You Should Know about It - Financial Institutions.

--The Quality Circle: What You Should Know about It - Health Care Facilities.

--Quality Circles Guidebook: How to Install Quality Circles in Your Organization.

Dewar, Jeffrey D. Quality Circles at Work & Spreading in Utility Systems of Today.

Dewar, M. J. & Jones, R. Computer Compilation of Molecular Weights & Percentage Compositions for Organic Compounds.

Dewar, Michael. The British Army in Northern Ireland, 1969-Present.

Dewart, Joanne. The Theology of Grace of Theodore of Mopsuestia.

De Wayne, M. L., ed. Water, Human Values & the Eighties.

Dewbury, K. C., jt. auth. see Guyer, P. B.

Dewe, Michael, jt. ed. see Fuhlrott, Rolf.

De Weck, Alain L., et al, eds. Biochemical Characterization of Lymphokines: Proceedings of the Second International Lymphokine Workshop.

Dewees, Eleanor. Those Four & Plenty More. Van Dolson, Bobbie J., ed.

DeWeese. Rob & Smith's Operative Surgery: Vascular Surgery.

Deweese, Charles W. Prayer in Baptist Life.

DeWeese, David F. & Saunders, William H. Textbook of Otolaryngology.

DeWeese, Gene & Coulson, Robert. Nightmare Universe.

De Wetering, Janwillem van see David-Neel, Alexandra & Yongden, Lama.

De Wetering, Janwillem Van see Van de Wetering, Janwillem.

De Wetering, Janwillen Van see Van de Wetering, Janwillem.

Dewey, Barbara. As You Believe.

Dewey, Donald, jt. auth. see Acocella, Nick.

Dewey, J. F., et al, eds. Tectonics: A Selection of Papers.

Dewey, John. Human Nature & Conduct.

--The Influence of Darwin on Philosophy & Other Essays.

--Moral Principles in Education.

--Philosophy of Education.

--Problems of Men.

Dewey, Mary. Space-Crafting: Invent Your Own Flying Spaceships.

Dewey, Melvil. Classification Decimale de Dewey et Index. Incl. Vol. 1. Tables Generales; Vol. 2. Index. Forest Pr.

--Dewey Decimal Classification & Relative Index.

--Dewey Decimal Classification & Relative Index. Incl. Vol. 1. Introduction & Tables; Vol. 2. Schedules; Vol. 3. Index. Forest Pr.

--Dewey Decimal Classification & Relative Index.

--Dewey Decimal Classification: 004-006 Data Processing & Computer Science, & Changes in Related Disciplines. Beall, Julianne, et al, eds.

Dewey, Patrick R. Public Access Microcomputers: A Handbook for Librarians.

Dewey, Robert E. & Gould, James A. Freedom: Its History, Nature & Varieties.

De Weydenthal, Jan B. Poland: Communism Adrift.

De Weydenthal, Jan B., et al. Poland Nineteen Eighty to Nineteen Eighty-Two: The Making of the Revolution.

Dewhurst, D. J. An Introduction to Biomedical Instrumentation.

Dewhurst, Eileen. Playing Safe.

--Private Prosecution.

--There Was a Little Girl.

Dewhurst, John, et al, eds. Basic Science in Obstetrics & Gynaecology: A Textbook for MRCOG, Pt. 1.

Dewhurst, Kenneth. John Locke, Physician & Philosopher.

De Windt, Gaye. Poems Beyond Reality.

Dewine, Sue, jt. auth. see Phelps, Lynn.

De Winter, F., ed. Sun: Mankind's Future Source of Energy.

De Wire, Elinor. Guide to Florida Lighthouses.

De Wit, Wim, ed. The Amsterdam School: Dutch Expressionist Architecture 1915-1930.

Dewitt, Steve. The Golden Kingdom.

Dewitt, Steve, tr. see Twitchell, Paul.

DeWitt, Steve, et al, trs. see Twitchell, Paul.

DeWitt, William H. Hi Res-Double Hi Res Graphics for the Apple IIc & Apple II Family.

DeWolf, L. Harold. Eternal Life: Why We Believe.

--What Americans Should Do about Crime.

De Wolf, Paul P. The Noun-Class Systems of Proto-Benue-Congo.

DeWolf, Rose. How to Raise Your Man: The Problems of a New Style Woman in Love with an Old Style Man.

Dews, D., jt. ed. see Fildes, R.

Dews, Peter B., et al. Marijuana: Biochemical, Physiological, & Pathological Effects.

Dewsbury, D. Mammalian Sexual Behavior.

Dewsbury, Donald. A Comparative Psychology in the Twentieth Century.

Dexeus, Santiago, Jr., et al. Colposcopy. Austin, Karl L., tr. from Span.

Dexter, Margaret & Harbert, Wally. The Home Help Service.

Dexter, N. C. & Rayner, E. G. Liberal Studies: An Outline Course.

Dexter, W. A. Field Guide to Astronomy Without a Telescope.

DeYoung, Gordon. Dial-a-Word from the Bible.

Dhake, Arvind M. Television Engineering.

Dhanji, Farid. El Salvador: Demographic Issues & Prospects.

Dhar, R. N. Computer Aided Power System Operation & Analysis.

Dhar, Sheila. Children's History of India.

Dharmalingam, T., jt. auth. see Ramachandran, L.

Dhingra, A. K. & Fishman, S. G., eds. Interfaces in Metal Matrix Composites.

Dhiravamsa. Way of Non-Attachment.

D'Hyon, Jeanine C. The Painted Sky.

Diabetes Education Center, Nassau Hospital Staff, et al. Diabetes: The Comprehensive Self-Management Handbook.

Diaboli, Advocatus. Fifty Years in the Law Business.

Diacon, Diane. Residential Housing & Nuclear Attack.

Diagram Group. The Brain: A User's Manual.

--The Parent's Emergency Guide: An Action Handbook for Childhood Illness & Accidents.

Diagram Group Staff. Maze Puzzles.

--Number Puzzles.

--Picture Puzzles.

--The Scribner Guide to Orchestral Instruments.

--Sex: A User's Manual.

Dial, Hertha & Richter, Catherine. Little Blue Heaven.

Diamant, Anita. The New Jewish Wedding.

Diamant, R. M. Total Energy.

Diamant, Rolf, et al. A Citizen's Guide to River Conservation.

Diamond, A. R. The Confessions of Jeremiah in Context: Scenes of Prophetic Drams.

Diamond, A. S. History & Origin of Language.

Diamond, Arlyn & Edwards, Lee, eds. The Authority of Experience: Essays in Feminist Criticism.

Diamond, D. R. & McLoughlin, J. B. Progress in Planning.

Diamond, D. R., ed. Progress in Planning.

--Progress in Planning.

Diamond, D. R. & McLoughlin, J. B., eds. Progress in Planning.

--Progress in Planning.

--Progress in Planning.

--Progress in Planning.

--Progress in Planning.

--Progress in Planning.

--Progress in Planning.

--Progress in Planning.

--Progress in Planning.

--Progress in Planning.

Diamond, Edwin & Bates, Stephen. The Spot: The Rise of Political Advertising on Television.

Diamond, Harriet & Dutwin, Phyllis. Grammar in Plain English.

Diamond, Irene. Families, Politics, & Public Policy: A Feminist Dialogue on Women & the State.

Diamond, Jay, jt. auth. see Pintel, Gerald.

Diamond, Malcolm L. Martin Buber: Jewish Existentialist.

Diamond, Marian C. & Korenbrot, Carol C., eds. Hormonal Contraceptives, Estrogens & Human Welfare.

Diamond, Seymour & Furlong, William B. More Than Two Aspirin: Hope for Your Headache Problem.

Diamond, Sigmund, ed. The Nation Transformed: The Creation of an Industrial Society.

Diamond, Stanley. In Search of the Primitive.

Diamond, Stephen. Panama Red.

Diamonstein, Barbaralee. Fashion: The Inside Story.

--Handmade in America: Conversations with Fourteen Craftmasters.

DiAntonio, Steve. Making Time: The Resourceful Woman's Guide to Delegating Household Tasks.

Diara, Schavi M. Zora Neale Hurston & Jessie Redmond Fauset: Glistening Reflections from a Bygone Day.

Dias, C. J., et al, eds. Lawyers in the Third World: Comparative & Developmental Perspectives.

Dias-Blue, Anthony. American Wine.

Diaz, Arcadio. Conversacion con Jose Luis Gonzalez.

Diaz, Jorge & De Gonzalez, Nelly, eds. La Biblia lo Dice.

Diaz, Modesto, jt. auth. see Aguera, Helen.

Diaz, Olimpia, tr. see Tickle, John.

Diaz, Olimpia, Sr., tr. see Tickle, John.

Diaz Del Castillo, Bernal. Discovery & Conquest of Mexico.

Diaz Quinones, Arcadio. El Almuerzo en la Hierba.

Dib, Albert & Grant, James K., eds. Legal Handbook for Architects, Engineers & Contractors.

Diba, Farhad. Mohammad Mossadegh: A Political Biography.

Di Bartolo, Baldassare, ed. Radiationless Processes.

Dibb, Paul. The Soviet Union: The Incomplete Superpower.

Dibelius, Martin. Paul. Kuemmel, W. G., ed.

Dibello, C., jt. ed. see Offord, R. E.

DiBernardi, Dominic, tr. see Navarre, Yves.

Dibert, Ken. Photography: Three Generations.

Di Biumo, Panza. Panza Collection.

Dible, Donald. Up Your Own Organization.

--Up Your Own Organization! A Handbook on How to Start & Finance a New Business.

DiCapua, Rinaldo. Vologeso Re De Parti. Brown, Howard M., ed.
DiCastri, F. & Mooney, H. A., eds. Mediterranean-Type Ecosystems: Origin & Structure.
Di Certo, Joseph. The Wall People: In Search of a Home.
Dichgans, J., ed. see International Congress on Physiological Sciences Staff.
Dichter, Ernest. Getting Motivated: The Secret Behind Individual Motivations by the Man Who Was Not Afraid to Ask "Why?"
--Packaging: The Sixth Sense.
Dichter, Harry & Shapiro, Elliot. Handbook of Early American Sheet Music: 1768-1889.
Dicicco, Philip P., jt. auth. see Krutza, William J.
Dick, B., jt. auth. see Dunphy, D. C.
Dick, Carson W., jt. auth. see Moll, J.
Dick, Donald, intro. by see Hawker, Margot, et al.
Dick, Everett. From Horses to Horsepower: Life in Kansas, 1900-1925.
--The Sod-House Frontier, 1854-1890: A Social History of the Northern Plains from the Creation of Kansas & Nebraska to the Admission of the Dakotas.
Dick, Ginger, jt. auth. see Smith, Richard D.
Dick, Philip K. Time Out of Joint.
--The Transmigration of Bishop Timothy Archer.
--UBIK: The Screenplay. Thornhill, Ira M., ed.
Dick, Susan M., ed. Confessions of a Young Man, by George Moore: An Annotated Critical Edition.
Dick, Trevor J. Economic History of Canada: A Guide to Information Sources.
Dick, W. E. Atomic Energy in Agriculture.
Dick, W. M., et al, eds. Contributions to Mycology: A Tribute to Professor C. T. Ingold on His Eightieth Birthday.
Dick, Walter, jt. auth. see Singer, Robert M.
Dick, Walter, jt. auth. see Singer, Robert N.
Dickason, C. Fred. Demon Possession & the Christian.
Dickason, Clifford, jt. auth. see Sloggett, Gordon.
Dicke, K., jt. auth. see Goeldner, C. R.
Dickens, Charles. A Christmas Carol.
--A Christmas Carol Christmas Book.
--David Copperfield. Fuller, Edmund, ed.
--David Copperfield.
--David Copperfield.
--Dickens on America & the Americans. Slater, Michael, ed.
--George Silverman's Explanation. Stone, Harry, ed.
--Great Expectations.
--Great Expectations.
--Hard Times.
--Hard Times.
--The Haunted Man & the Haunted House.
--Mickey's Christmas Carol. Disney Studio Staff, ed.
--Nicholas Nickleby.
--The Old Curiosity Shop.
--The Old Curiousity Shop: T. V. Tie-In. Easson, Angus, ed.
--Oliver Twist.
--Oliver Twist.
--Oliver Twist.
--Pickwick Papers.
--A Tale of Two Cities.
Dickens, Frank, et al, eds. Carbohydrate Metabolism & Its Disorders.
Dickens, Milton & McBath, James H. Guidebook for Speech Practice.
Dickens, Peter, et al. Housing, States & Localities.
Dickens, Robert. Thoreau: The Complete Individualist-His Relevance, & Lack of It, for Our Time.
Dickens, Suzanne, jt. auth. see Knox-Thompson, Elaine.
Dickenson, A. F. see Trotman-Dickenson, A. F. & Parfitt, G. D.
Dickenson, D. I. Trotman see Trotman-Dickenson, D. I.
Dickenson, Mary. Democracy in Trade Unions: Studies in Membership Participation & Control.
Dickenson, Rosalind E. Communication Nil!
--Who Laughs Last.
Dickenson, Rosalind Earnest. The Land Baron Mirage.
Dicker, Marvin, jt. auth. see Sunshine, Jonathan H.
Dicker, Terence F. Computer Programs for the Kitchen.
Dickerman, Alexandra & Dickerman, John. Discovering Hydroponic Gardening: Beginner's Guide to the Pleasures of Soil-Less Gardening.
Dickerman, John, jt. auth. see Dickerman, Alexandra.
Dickerman, Pat. Adventure Travel Abroad.
--Adventure Travel in North America.
Dickerson, Charles L. The Poems of Charles.
Dickerson, Charles S. Commercial Lending by Thrift Institutions.
Dickerson, Eric & Delsohn, Steve. On the Run.
Dickerson, F. Reed. Legislative Drafting.
Dickerson, John W. & Booth, Elizabeth M. Clinical Nutrition for Nurses, Dieticians & Other Health Care Professionals.
Dickerson, R. E. Molecular Thermodynamics.
Dickerson, R. E. & Geis, I. Hemoglobin: Structure, Function, Evolution & Pathology.
Dickerson, Reed. The Fundamentals of Legal Drafting (1965)
Dickerson, Richard E. & Geis, Irving. The Structure & Action of Proteins.
Dickerson, Robert C., jt. auth. see Goldstein, Louis A.
Dickert, Rev. Roy E. Our Trails to Triumphant Living.
Dickey, Bill. The DBASE III for Sales Professionals.
Dickey, Charley & Moses, Fred. Charley Dickey & Fred Moses Trout Fishing.
Dickey, Christopher. With the Contras: A Reporter in the Wilds of Nicaragua.
Dickey, Glenn. America Has a Better Team: The Remarkable Story of Bill Walsh & San Francisco's Super Bowl Champion 49ers.
Dickey, John, jt. ed. see Stanton, Jeffrey.
Dickey, John W. Metropolitan Transportation Planning. Verma, Kiran, ed.
Dickey, John W. & Watts, Thomas M. Analytic Techniques in Urban & Regional Planning: With Applications in Public Administration & Affairs.
Dickey, Nancy, ed. see Perkins, Clifford A.
Dickey, William. The Rainbow Grocery.
Dickey, William, jt. auth. see Schadewald, Robert J.
Dickie, Lois G. No Respecter of Persons.
Dickie, Margaret. Family Microcomputer-Microprocessor User's Manual: M 6805 HMOS-M 146805 CMOS.
Dickinson, Alyce M., jt. ed. see O'Brien, Richard.
Dickinson, C., ed. Microbiology of Aerial Plant Surfaces.
Dickinson, C. H. & Pugh, G. J., eds. Biology of Plant Litter Decomposition.
Dickinson, Emily. For Love of Her.
--Love Poems & Others.
Dickinson, G. A. Introduction to Geometry.
Dickinson, George T. Jeremiah: The Iron Prophet.
Dickinson, H. T. British Radicalism & the French Revolution 1789-1815.
Dickinson, J. C. The Later Middle Ages: From the Norman Conquest to the Eve of the Reformation.
Dickinson, June M., ed. & intro. by. Reminiscences of Clara Schumann As Found in the Diary of Her Grandson Ferdinand Schumann.
Dickinson, Mary. New Clothes for Alex.
Dickinson, Mike. My Brother's Silly.
Dickinson, Mike, illus. Smudge.
Dickinson, Peter. The Gift.
--Healer.
--Hepzibah.
--Tefuga.
Dickinson, Robert E. & Howarth, O. J. R. The Making of Geography.
Dickinson, Robert L. & Beam, Lura. Thousand Marriages: A Medical Study of Sex Adjustment.
Dickinson, Roger A. Retail Management: A Marketing Channels Approach.
Dickinson, T., jt. ed. see Covington, A. K.
Dickinson, W. Calvin. James Harrington's Republic.
Dickinson, W. J. & Sullivan, D. T. Gene-Enzyme Systems in Drosophila.
Dickinson, W. M., ed. Tectonics & Sedimentation.
Dickler, H. The DBASE III Plus Trail Guide.
Dickler, Howard. The DBASE III Trail Guide.
Dickman, Irving R. & Gordon, Sol. One Miracle at a Time: How to Get Help for Your Disabled Child from the Experience of Other Parents.
--One Miracle at a Time: Understanding Your Disabled Child.
Dickman, Tom, tr. see Beaud, Michel.
Dickmeyer, Lowell A. Soccer Is for Me.
--Swimming Is for Me.
Dickmeyer, Nathan & Hughes, K. Scott. Financial Self-Assessment: A Workbook for Colleges.
Dicks, W. Groups, Trees & Projective Modules.
Dickson, Carter. And So to Murder.
Dickson, David. The Politics of Alternative Technology.
Dickson, Elizabeth & Peterson, George. Public Employee Compensation: A Twelve City Comparison.
Dickson, G. W. & Smith, H. R. Introduction to FORTRAN IV Programming: A Self-Paced Approach.
Dickson, Gary, ed. see Jenkins, A. Milton.
Dickson, Gordon. Secrets of the Deep.
Dickson, H., et al, eds. Thin Plate Working.
--Thin Plate Working.
Dickson, Harry E. Arthur Fiedler & the Boston Pops.
Dickson, James F., jt. ed. see Brown, J. H.
Dickson, John. Victoria Hotel.
Dickson, Leonard E. Studies in the Theory of Numbers.
Dickson, Lovat. H. G. Wells: His Turbulent Life & Times.
Dickson, Margaret. Maddy's Song.
--Octavia's Hill.
Dickson, Paul. The Future File.
Dickson, Ron R. Weather & Flight: An Introduction to Meteorology for Pilots.
Diczfalusy, E., ed. Pharmacology of Reproduction.
Didactic Systems staff. Resource Manual for How to Be a Nurse's Aide in a Nursing Home.
Didday, Rich. Home Computers: Two to the Tenth Question & Answers, Vol. 1: Hardware.
Didday, Richard. Home Computers: Two to the Tenth Power Questions & Answers, Vol. 2: Software.
Didion, Joan. Democracy.
--Salvador.
DiDonato, Georgia. Woman of Justice.
--Woman of Justice.
Diebel, Terry L. & Gaddis, John L., eds. Containment: Concept & Policy.
--Containment: Concept & Policy.
Diebold, John. Automation.
--Business in the Age of Information.
--Making the Future Work: Unleashing Our Powers of Innovation for the Decades Ahead.
Diebolt, Thomas, et al. California Elections Code: 1988.
Dieck, T. tom see Tom Dieck, T.
Diedrich, Richard C. & Dye, H. Allan. Group Procedures: Purposes, Processes, & Outcomes.
Diedrich, William M. & Bangert, Jeff. Articulation Learning.
Diegmueller, Karen S., jt. auth. see Schoenfeld, A. Clay.
Diehl, Bernhard, jt. auth. see Schwinn, Monika.
Diehl, George M. Machinery Acoustics.
Diehl, Kemper & Jarboe, Jan. Cisneros: Portrait of a New American.
Diehl, Lorraine B. The Late Great Pennsylvania Station.
Diehl, P., et al. Computer Assistance in the Analysis of High-Resolution NMR Spectra.
Diehl, P., et al, eds. Natural & Synthetic High Polymers: Lectures Presented at the 7th Colloquium on NMR Spectroscopy.
Diehl, William E. Christianity & Real Life.
Diehm, William J. Staying in Love.
Diekman, Norman & Pile, John. Drawing Interior Architecture: A Guide to Rendering & Presentation.
--Sketching Interior Architecture.
Diel, Paul. Symbolism in Greek Mythology: Human Desire & Its Transformations. Stuart, Vincent, et al, trs. from Fr.
Dieleman, Dale, compiled by. Taking Charge.
Dielman, Heinz J. United States-German Economic Survey 1986.
DiElsie, et al. Programming Macintosh BASIC.
Diem, Bui & Chanoff, David. In the Jaws of History.
Diem, Liselott. Children Learn Physical Skills.
Diem, Richard. How to Use Computers as a Resource.
Diener, T. O. Viroids & Viroid Diseases.
Dienes, C. Thomas. Law, Politics, & Birth Control.
Dienes, Thomas, jt. auth. see Barron, Jerome.
Dienstbier, Sharon & Hendricks, Sybil D. Natural Foods Storage Bible: Secrets of Storing, Cooking & Enjoying Natural Foods.
Dieppe, P. & Calvert, P. Crystals & Joint Disease.
Dierker, E. Topological Methods in Walrasian Economics.
Dies, Edward J. Titans of the Soil: Great Builders of Agriculture.
Diesing, Paul R. Patterns of Discovery in the Social Sciences.
Diestel, J. Geometry of Banach Spaces - Selected Topics.
Dieter, William. Beyond the Mountain.
--The Cactus Garden.
--Hunter's Orange.
--Hunter's Orange.
Diethelm, L., ed. see European Association of Radiology Symposium, Mainz, 1970.
Diethrich, Edward B., ed. Noninvasive Assessment of the Cardiovascular System.
--Noninvasive Cardiovascular Diagnosis.
Dietiker, Simone R. En Bonne Forme.
Dietmeyer. Logic Design of Digital Systems.
Dietrich, D. E., ed. Pressure Vessels & Piping - Computer Program Evaluation & Qualification, Series PVP-PB-024.
Dietrich, John & Waggoner, Susan. The Complete Health Club Handbook.
Dietrich, Richard V. Geology & Virginia.
Dietz, Albert G., ed. Composite Engineering Laminates.
Dietz, Beverley. Birdseye Writing Skills: Punctuation.
Dietz, J. B., Jr., jt. auth. see Yalisove, I. L.
Dietz, K., ed. see Theoretical Physics International Summer Institute, Bonn, 1974.
Dietz, Lew. Touch of Wildness: A Maine Woods Journal.
Dietz, Thomas, jt. auth. see McEvoy, James, III.
Di Ferrante, R. K. Trace Metals: Exposure & Health Effects.
DiFiore, Frank. The Mask.
Di Fiore, Mariano S. Atlas of Human Histology.
DiFiori, Lawrence. My Toys, My First Book, Baby Animals, the Farm. Incl. My Toys; My First Book; Baby Animals; The Farm. Macmillan.
Difonzo, Luigi. St. Peter's Banker: Michele Sindona.
DiFranco, Anthony. Italy: Balanced on the Edge of Time.
DiFranco, Anthony & DiFranco, JoAnn. Mister Rogers: Good Neighbor to America's Children.
DiFranco, JoAnn, jt. auth. see DiFranco, Anthony.
DiGaetani, John L. & Harbert, Earl N. Writing Out Loud: A Self-Help Guide to Clear Business Writing.
DiGaetani, John L., jt. auth. see Harbert, Earl N.
DiGangi, Mariano. I Believe in Mission.
Digby, John. Sailing Away from Night.
Digges, Deborah. Vesper Sparrows.
Diggins, John P. The American Left in the Twentieth Century.
Di Giacomo, James. When Your Teenager Stops Going to Church.
Digman, Lester A. Strategic Management: Concepts, Decisions & Cases.
D'Ignazio, Fred. Commodore 64 in Wonderland.
--The Commodore 64 Playground.
--The Creative Kid's Guide to Home Computers.
DiGregorio, G. John, ed. see PreTest Service, Inc. Staff, et al.
DiIorio. Watching Through Tall Windows.
Di Iorio, Paolo. Poems: The Touch of Love.
Di'Itri, F. M. A Systems Approach to Conservation Tillage.
Dijk, J. van see Van Dijk, J.
Dijkstra, Bram. Hieroglyphics of a New Speech: Cubism, Stieglitz, & the Early Poetry of William Carlos Williams.
Dijkstra, Gerard. Self-Steering for Sailboats.
Dijs, Carla & Moerbeek, Kees. Bee Says Buzzzz.
--Let's Play.
--Peek-A-Boo.
Dike, R. Architectural Common Sense Site.
Dikens, Nathaniel A. The Gospel Singer.
Diket, A. L. Senator John Slidell & the Community He Represented in Washington, 1853-1861.
Dikstein, S., ed. see International Society for Eye Research Staff.
Dilcher, D. L. & Taylor, T. N., eds. Biostratigraphy of Fossil Plants: Sucessional & Paleoecological Analyses.
Dileep, Mehta, jt. auth. see Deschamps, Benoit.
DiLiello, Leo R. Clinical Microbiology.
Dilker, Barbara. Stage Management Forms & Formats.
Dilks, David. Curzon in India. Incl. Vol. 1. Achievement; Vol. 2. Frustration. Taplinger.
Dillard, Clyde R. & Goldberg, David E. Chemistry: Reactions, Structure, & Properties.
Dillard, David H., jt. auth. see Mohri, Hitoshi.
Dillard, Mabel M., jt. auth. see Benson, Brian J.
Dille, Carolyn, jt. auth. see Belsinger, Susan.
Dille, Flint & Marconi, David. The Serpentine Assassin.
Dille, Flint, jt. auth. see Gygax, Gary.
Dillenback, Marsden & Schweitzer, John C. Seven Novellas.
Diller, Angela. First Theory Book.
--Keyboard Harmony Course.
Dillett, Eric S. What Is Man?
--Why Were We Born?
Dilley, Romilda. Silhouette Crafts.
Dilligan, Robert J., et al. A Concordance to Ezra Pound's Cantos.
Dillingham, William B., jt. auth. see Watkins, Floyd C.
Dillistone, Frederick W. The Christian Understanding of Atonement.
Dillman, Richard W. Problem Solving with FORTRAN 77.
Dillner, Martha H. & Olson, Joanne P. Personalizing Reading Instruction in Middle Junior & Senior High Schools.
Dillon, Barbara. Mr. Chill.
--Who Needs a Bear?
Dillon, George L. Introduction to Contemporary Linguistic Semantics.
Dillon, J. T. Questioning & Teaching: A Manual of Practice.
Dillon, John L. The Analysis of Response in Crop & Livestock Production.
Dillon, Mark & Haigh, Frank. International Race Car Drivers.
Dillon, Mary E., ed. see Davis, James W.
Dillon, Millicent. A Little Original Sin: The Life & Work of Jane Bowles.
--A Little Original Sin: The Life & Work of Jane Bowles.
Dillon, Myles. Early Irish Literature.
Dillon, Richard. North American Indian Wars.
--North Beach: The Italian Heart of San Francisco. Davis, Lynn L., ed.

--We Have Met the Enemy: The Life of Commodore Oliver Hazard Perry.
Dillon, Richard S. Handbook of Endocrinology: Diagnosis & Management of Endocrine & Metabolic Disorders.
Dillon, Roy. Working with Animal Supplies & Services. Lee, Jasper S., ed.
Dillon, William. Business Mathematics.
Dillon, William, et al. Marketing Research in a Marketing Environment.
Dillow, Rex O., ed. Facilities Management: A Manual for Plant Administration.
Dilman, Ilham. Freud & the Mind.
Dilworth, D. A., tr. see Nishida, Kitaro.
Dilworth, J. R. Log Scaling & Timber Cruising.
--Variable Plot Cruising.
Dimai, Peter A., tr. see Bardon, Franz.
Dimand, M. S. & Mailey, Jean. Oriental Rugs in the Metropolitan Museum of Art.
Dimarco, Susan, jt. auth. see Fishkin, Lois.
DiMarco, Susan, jt. auth. see Fishkin, Lois.
DiMascio, A. & Goldberg, H. Emotional Disorders: An Outline Guide to Diagnosis & Pharmacological Treatment.
DiMascio, Alberto & Shader, Richard, eds. Clinical Handbook of Psychopharmacology.
Dimbleby, Nick. Range Rover Conversions.
Dimbleby, Richard. Elizabeth Our Queen.
Dimen-Schein, Muriel. The Anthropological Imagination.
Di Michael, Eleanor M., jt. auth. see King, Robert G.
Dimitriev, P. P., jt. auth. see Gusev, N. G.
Dimitt, Richard. Red & the Green.
Dimmitt, Cornelia, ed. Classical Hindu Mythology: A Reader in the Sanskrit Puranas. Van Buitenen, J. A., tr.
Dimmock, N. J., jt. auth. see Primrose, S. B.
Dimock, Anthony Weston & Dimock, Julian A. Florida Enchantments.
Dimock, Julian A., jt. auth. see Dimock, Anthony Weston.
Dimon, jt. auth. see Carton.
DiMona, Joseph, jt. auth. see Noguchi, Thomas T.
Dimond, E. Grey. Inside China Today: A Western View.
--More Than Herbs & Acupuncture.
Dimond, Mary C. & Clifford, J. Garry, eds. Memoirs of a Man: Grenville Clark.
Dimroth, K. Delocalized Phosphorus-Carbon Double Bonds: Phosphamethin-Cyanines Lambda to the Third Power - Phosphorins & Lambda to the Fifth Power - Phosphorins.
Dimsdale, Jeffrey M., jt. auth. see Brightman, Richard W.
Dinamarca, Maria L., et al. Biological Effect of DDT in Lower Organisms.
Dinan, Dennis, ed. see Finn, Molly.
Dinan, Dennis, ed. see Mitchell, Don.
Di Napoli, Joseph. Pearls, Points, & Poems for My Lady.
Dinca, F. & Teodosiu, C. Nonlinear & Random Vibrations.
Dinculeanu, N. Vector Measures.
Dine, Jim. Jim Dine: Recent Work (Hearts) Pace Gallery Publications, ed.
Dine, S. S. Van see Van Dine, S. S.
Dineen, Betty. Striped Horses: The Story of a Zebra Family.
Diner, Hasia R., ed. Women & Urban Society: A Guide to Information Sources.
Dinerstein, Nelson T. The Dynamics of Framework.
Dines, Aaron, jt. auth. see Institute for Continuing Legal Education (New Jersey) Staff.
Dinesen, Betzy, ed. Rediscovery: Three Hundred Years of Stories by & about Women.
Dinesen, Isak. The Angelic Avengers.
--Out of Africa.
--Out of'Africa.
--Out of Africa & Shadows on the Grass.
--Seven Gothic Tales.
--Shadows on the Grass.
Dinges, John & Landau, Saul. Assassination on Embassy Row.
Dinges, W. Ray. Natural Systems for Water Pollution Control.
Dingle, David. I've Served My Time in Hell.
Dingle, H., ed. Evolution of Insect Migration & Diapause.
Dingle, Herbert. The Scientific Adventure.
Dingley, Fay, et al. Fidelity of Protein Synthesis & Transfer RNA During Aging.
Dingman, Roger. Power in the Pacific: The Origins of Naval Arms Limitation, 1914-1922.
Ding Shu De, et al. The Chinese Book of Table Tennis.
Dingus, Anne, ed. The Book of Texas Lists.
Dingus, Rick. The Photographic Artifacts of Timothy O'Sullivan.
Dingwall, William O. Language & the Brain.
Dinkel, John. The Road & Track Illustrated Auto Dictionary.
--The "Road & Track" Illustrated Auto Dictionary.
Dinkmeyer, Don & McKay, Gary D. Raising a Responsible Child: Practical Steps to Successful Family Relationships.
Dinner, Joan, jt. auth. see Riddle, Janet T.
Dinoff, Michael, jt. auth. see Rickard, Henry C.
Dinsmoor, William B. The Architecture of Ancient Greece.
Dinsmore, William. Hear Me, White Man!
Dintenfass, L. & Dintenfass, L., eds. Blood Viscosity in Heart Disease & Cancer: Proceedings.
Dintenfass, Leopold, et al, eds. Heart Perfusion, Energetics, & Ischemia.
Diop, Cheikh A. Black Africa: The Economic & Cultural Basis for a Federated State.
--Precolonial Black Africa.
DiOrio, Louis P. Clinical Preventive Dentistry.
DiOrio, Ralph A. Called to Heal: Releasing the Transforming Power of God.
--Miracle to Proclaim: First-Hand Experience of Healing.
Diosdado, Ana. Olvida los Tambores. Maroto, Angel R., ed.
Dioumoulen, I. I., et al. For a Restructuring of International Economic Relations.
Di Paliano, Guido C., et al. Directions for World Trade in the Nineteen-Seventies.
Di Palma, Giuseppe. Political Syncretism in Italy: Historical Coalition Strategies & the Present Crisis.
Di Paolo, J. A. see Ts'o, P. O.
DiPerna, Paula. Cluster Mystery: Epidemic & the Children of Woburn, Mass.
--Juries on Trial: Faces of American Justice.
Di Pietro, Robert J., jt. auth. see Agard, Frederick B.
Di Pietro, Robert J., ed. see Linguistic Association of Canada & the U. S. Staff.
Di Pillo, G. Control Applications of Non-Linear Programming & Optimization: Proceedings of the IFAC Workshop, Capri, Italy, 11-14 June 1985.
Dippel, Horst. Germany & the American Revolution: A Sociohistorical Investigation of Late Eighteenth-Century Political Thinking. Uhlendorf, Bernhard A., tr.
Dipple, Elizabeth. Plot.
Di Prima, Diane. Loba.
DiPrima, Richard C., jt. auth. see Boyce, William E.
Director, Mark D., jt. auth. see Ginsburg, Douglas H.
Director, S. W. Circuit Theory: The Computational Approach.
Director, S. W., ed. Computer-Aided Circuit Design: Simulation & Optimization.
Dirheimer, Y. The Craniovertebral Region in Chronic Inflammatory Rheumatic Diseases.
Diringer, David. The Alphabet.
Diringer, David & Freeman, H. A History of the Alphabet.
Dirksen, D. J. & Reeves, R. A. Recreation Lakes of California.
Dirksen, Ellen R., et al, eds. Cell Reproduction: In Honor of Daniel Mazia.
Di Rocco, C., ed. Brain Tumors in Children.
DiSaia, Philip J. & Creasman, William T. Clinical Gynecologic Oncology.
DiSaisa, Philip J., jt. auth. see Brown, Stephen G.
Di San Lazzaro, G. Painting in France Eighteen Ninety-Five to Nineteen Forty-Nine.
Disch, Thomas M. ABCDEFGHIJKLMNOPQRSTUVWXYZ.
--Dan de Lion.
--Three Hundred Thirty-Four.
Disch, Thomas M. & Naylor, Charles, eds. Strangeness.
Dischert, Dave, jt. auth. see Keen, Dan.
Dise, Craig A., ed. see PreTest Service, Inc. Staff.
Disease Control Centers, for Atlanta, Georgia Staff. Author-Title & Subject Catalogs of the Centers for Disease Control Library.
Dishon, Daniel, ed. Middle East Record, 1969-70.
Disick, Renee S. Individualizing Language Instruction: Strategies & Methods.
Disick, Renee S., jt. auth. see Valette, Rebecca M.
Diski, Jenny. Nothing Natural.
Diskin, Lahna. Theodore Sturgeon: A Primary & Secondary Bibliography.
Diskin, Martin, jt. ed. see Cook, Scott.
Disney, Diane M., et al. Partners in Public Service: Government & the Nonprofit Sector in Rhode Island.
Disney Studio Staff, ed. see Dickens, Charles.
Disney Studios & Disney, Walt. Mickey Mouse Says I Can, Can You? Klimo, Kate, ed.
Disney, Walt. Disney Flash Ahead with ABC's.
--Disney Flash Ahead with Numbers.
--Disney Flash Ahead with Phonics.
--Disney Flash Ahead with Time Telling.
Disney, Walt, jt. auth. see Disney Studios.
Disney, Walt, Productions Staff. How to Draw Donald Duck. Klimo, Kate, ed.
--How to Draw Goofy. Klimo, Kate, ed.
--How to Draw Mickey Mouse. Klimo, Kate, ed.
--How to Draw Pluto. Klimo, Kate, ed.
--Mickey's Pop-Up Book of Colors.
--Mickey's Pop-Up Book of Numbers.
--Mickey's Pop-Up Book of Shapes.
Dison, Norma. Simplified Drugs & Solutions for Nurses, Including Arithmetic.
Di Stasi, Lawrence. Mal Occhio: The Underside of Vision.
DiStasio, J. I., ed. Epoxy Resin Technology: Developments Since 1979.
--Surfactants, Detergents & Sequestrants: Developments since 1979.
Distelhorst, David F. How to Prepare for the Texas Real Estate Exam: A Study Manual for Brokers & Salespeople.
--How to Prepare for the Texas Real Estate Exam.
Ditchburn, R. W. Light.
Ditchfield, P. H. Old English Customs Extant at the Present Time.
Ditewig, William, jt. auth. see Brinkmann, William.
Ditfurth, Hoimar. The Origins of Life: Evolution As Creation. Heinegg, Peter, tr. from Ger.
Ditlea, Steve. The Osborne-McGraw-Hill Home Computer Guide.
--Using WordStar.
Ditmanson, Harold H. Grace in Experience & Theology.
Ditmars, Raymond L. Strange Animals I Have Known.
--Strange Animals I Have Known.
D'Itri, F. M., jt. auth. see Prince, H. H.
Dittenhofer, Mortimer A., ed. Concepts of Government Auditing: A Book of Readings from the Internal Auditor.
Dittes, James E. Bias & the Pious: The Relationship Between Prejudice & Religion.
--When the People Say No.
Dittmer, Bernice. Let There Be Light.
Dittrich, John E. & Zawacki, Robert A. People & Organizations: Cases in Management & Organizational Behavior.
Dittrich, S. Atari ST Peeks & Pokes.
Dittrick, Diane K., jt. auth. see Dittrick, Mark.
Dittrick, Mark. The Bed Book.
Dittrick, Mark & Dittrick, Diane K. Misnomers: One Hundred Fifty Misnamed Words & Their Twisted Definitions.
Di Tullo, Frank. Hypno Weight Control: How to Lose Weight & Discover Yourself Through Self-Hypnosis.
Ditzion, Sidney. Marriage, Morals, & Sex in America: A History of Ideas.
Divac, Ivan, et al, eds. The Neostriatum: Proceedings of a Workshop Sponsored by the European Brain & Behaviour Society, Denmark, 17-19 April 1978.
Dively, George S. Power of Professional Management.
Divilbiss, J. L., ed. Clinic on Library Applications of Data Processing, Proceedings: 1977: Negotiating for Computer Services.
Divilbiss, J. L., ed. see Clinic on Library Applications of Data Processing Staff.
Divilkovsky, S. & Ognetov, I. The Road to Victory.
Divine, Robert A. Second Chance: The Triumph of Internationalism in America During World War II.
Divis, B., ed. see Mahler, K.
Division of Chemistry & Chemical Technology. Specifications & Criteria for Biochemical Compounds.
Diwan, Romesh & Lutz, Mark, eds. Essays in Gandhian Economics.
Diwan, Romesh K. & Livingston, Dennis. Alternative Development Strategies & Appropriate Technology: Science Policy for an Equitable World Order.
Dix, Carol. The New Mother Syndrome.
Dix, George E. & Sharlot, M. Michael. Criminal Law Cases & Materials.
Dix, M. C. & Layzell, A. D. Road Users & the Police.
Dix, M. R. & Hood, J. P. Vertigo.
Dixhoorn, J. van see Van Dixhoorn, J. & Karnopp, D.
Dixhoorn, Jan J. Van see Karnopp, Dean, et al.
Dixon, A. E., ed. see Solar Energy Conversion Course, 5th, University of Waterloo, Ontario, August 6-19, 1978.
Dixon, Adrian K. Body C. T.
Dixon, Bernard. Magnificent Microbes.
Dixon, Bob. Searching for Aboriginal Languages: Memoirs of a Field Worker.
Dixon, C. W. Society, Schools & Progress in Scandinavia.
Dixon, Christa K. Negro Spirituals: From Bible to Folk Song.
Dixon, Conrad. Navigation by Pocket Calculator.
Dixon, D. Can You Retire?
Dixon, D. N. & Glover, J. A. Counseling: A Problem Solving Approach.
Dixon, Don. Universe.
Dixon, Dorothy. Teaching Children to Care.
Dixon, E. J. see Taliaferro, W. H. & Humphrey, J. H.
Dixon, Eileen. The Theatre Nurse & the Law.
Dixon, F. J., Jr. see Taliaferro, W. H. & Humphrey, J. H.
Dixon, Frank J. & Miescher, Peter A. Immunopathology: Eighth International Symposium.
Dixon, Franklin W. The Clue in the Embers.
--Crisscross Shadow.
--Deathgame.
--Figure in Hiding.
--Footprints under the Window.
--Ghost at Skeleton Rock.
--Missing Chums.
--Mystery at Devil's Paw.
--Mystery of the Aztec Warrior.
--Mystery of the Flying Express.
--Secret of the Lost Tunnel.
--Secret of Wildcat Swamp.
--Shore Road Mystery.
--Short-Wave Mystery.
--Sinister Sign Post.
--Viking Symbol Mystery.
Dixon, Franklin W., jt. auth. see Keene, Carolyn.
Dixon, G., ed. Undergraduate Obstetrics & Gynaecology.
Dixon, G. R. Vegetable Crop Diseases.
Dixon, J. L. Community of the Mind.
Dixon, James R. The Neotropical Colubrid Snake Genus Liophis. I. The Generic Concept.
Dixon, Jeane. Horoscopes for Dogs.
Dixon, Jeanne. Lady Cat Lost.
Dixon, John W., Jr. Art & Theological Imagination.
--The Physiology of Faith: A Theory of Theological Relativity.
Dixon, Michael E. Bread of Blessing, Cup of Hope. Lambert, Herbert H., ed.
Dixon, P. F., et al, eds. High Pressure Liquid Chromatography in Clinical Chemistry.
Dixon, Paige. Lion on the Mountain.
--The Loner.
--Pimm's Cup for Everybody.
--Promises to Keep.
--Skipper.
--Summer of the White Goat.
--Walk My Way.
--Young Grizzly.
Dixon, Peter, ed. Writers & Their Background: Alexander Pope.
Dixon, Peter, jt. ed. see Rudrum, Alan.
Dixon, Peter L. The Olympian.
Dixon, R. A. Spain.
Dixon, Raoul M. Way of the Hunters: An Illustrated Commentary & Prehistoric Record.
Dixon, Reginald A. Portugal.
Dixon, Robert T. Dynamic Astronomy.
Dixon, S. L. Worked Examples in Turbomachinery: Fluid Mechanics & Thermodynamics.
Dixon, Terence & Lucas, Martin. The Human Race.
Dixon, W. J. & Nicholson, W. L. Exploring Data Analysis: The Computer Revolution in Statistics.
Dixon, W. J. & Brown, M. B., eds. BMDP-83: Biomedical Computer Programs, P-Series.
Dixon, W. M. & Price, Susan M., eds. Aspects of Occupational Health.
Dixon, William C., jt. auth. see Detwiler-Zapp, Diane.
Dixson. Mi primer diccionario ilustrado de ingles.
Dixson, et al. My First English-Japanese Picture Dictionary.
Dixson, Anne, jt. auth. see Pinkus, Charles E.
Dixson, Robert J. Easy Reading Selections in English.
--Elementary Reader in English.
--Essential Idioms in English.
--Everyday Dialogues in English.
--Graded Exercises in English.
--Modern American English. Incl. Bk. 1; Bk. 2; Bk. 3; Bk. 4; Bk. 5; Bk. 6. Prentice ESL.
--Modern Short Stories in English.
--Second Book in English.
--Tests & Drills in English Grammar.
Dixson, Robert J. & Fisher, Isobel. Beginning Lessons in English.
Dixson, Robert J., jt. auth. see Angel, Juvenal L.
Dixter, Charles, et al. Pediatric Radiographic Interpretation.
Dizard, W. P. The Comming Information Age: An Overview of Technology, Economics, & Politics.
Dizenzo, Patricia. Phoebe.
Dizer, John T., Jr. Tom Swift & Company: "Boys' Books" by Stratemeyer & Others.
Dizikes, John. Sportsmen & Gamesmen: American Sporting Life in the Age of Jackson.
Djedje, Jacqueline C. American Black Spiritual & Gospel Songs from Southeast Georgia: A Comparative Study.
Djenev, Kiril, jt. auth. see Katzarova-Kukudova, Raina.
Djerassi, Carl. The Politics of Contraception, Nineteen Eighty.
Djerassi, Norma L. Glimpses of China from a Galloping Horse (a Woman's Journal).
Djilas, Milovan. Conversations with Stalin. Petrovich, Michael B., tr.
--Land Without Justice.
--The Leper & Other Stories. Edwards, Lovett F., tr.
--Memoir of a Revolutionary.
--Njegos: Poet, Prince, Bishop. Petrovich, Michael B., tr.

--Of Prisons & Ideas. Petrovich, Michael B., tr. from Serbo-Croatian.
--Parts of a Lifetime.
--Rise & Fall. Loud, John, tr.
--The Stone & the Violets.
--Tito: The Story from Inside.
--Under the Colors.
--The Unperfect Society: Beyond the New Class. Cooke, Dorian, tr.
--The Unperfect Society: Beyond the New Class. Cooke, Dorian, tr.
--Wartime. Petrovich, Michael B., tr.
Djindjian, R., jt. ed. see Pia, H. W.
DLW Corporation Staff. My Computer Guide: An Introduction to the IBM-PC.
Doan, Cortland C. Design, Drafting, & Construction Practices for Electronics.
Doan, Marlyn. Hiking Light.
Doan, Rebecca M., et al. Local Institutional Development for Primary Health Care.
--Mobilizing & Managing Economic Resources for Local Institutional Development.
Doane, D. V., ed. see TMS Staff & AIME Staff.
Doane, Jim. Great Smoky Mountains Picture Book. Castaldo, George, ed.
Dobb, Maurice. Capitalism, Yesterday & Today.
Dobb, Maurice, et al. The Transition from Feudalism to Capitalism.
Dobbin, John V. Topographic Terms: English & Spanish.
Dobbin, Muriel. Joe's World.
Dobbins, Austin C. Milton & the Book of Revelation: The Heavenly Cycle.
Dobbins, Bill. High Tech Training.
Dobbins, Bill, jt. auth. see Schwarzenegger, Arnold.
Dobbins, John, ed. see Hegel, G. W.
Dobbins, Richard A. Atmospheric Motion & Air Pollution: An Introduction for Students of Engineering & Science.
Dobbins, Richard D. You Can Find a Good Mate.
Dobbs, Charles M. The Truman Doctrine.
--The Unwanted Symbol: American Foreign Policy, the Cold War, & Korea, 1945-1950.
Dobbs, Michael, et al. Poland-Solidarity-Walesa.
Dobbyn, John F. So You Want to Go to Law School.
Dobell, Bertram. Catalogue of Books Printed for Private Circulation.
Dober, Richard P. Environmental Design.
Dobereiner, Peter. Down the Nineteenth Fairway.
--The World of Golf: The Best of Peter Dobereiner.
Dobereiner, Peter, jt. auth. see Palmer, Arnold.
Doberstein, John W., tr. see Girgensohn, Herbert.
Doberstein, John W., tr. see Thielicke, Helmut.
Dobie, M. R., tr. see Grenier, Albert.
Dobinson, B., et al. The Determination of Epoxide Groups.
Dobkin, Kaye. Desire & Dream.
--Promise Me Tomorrow.
Dobkins, David H. & Kneller, Richard. Workbook for Speech Fundamentals.
Dobler, Donald W., jt. auth. see Lee, Lamar, Jr.
Doblin, Alfred. Berlin, Alexanderplatz. Jolas, Eugene, tr.
Dobree, Bonamy. Alexander Pope.
Dobretsov, L. N. & Gomoyunova, M. V. Emission Electronics.
Dobrev, V. K., et al. Harmonic Analysis.
Dobrian, Walter A. & Jeffers, Coleman R., eds. Spanish Readings for Conversation.
Dobrin, Arnold. Make a Witch, Make a Goblin: A Book of Halloween Crafts.
Dobrotworsky, N. V. Mosquitoes of Victoria.
Dobrozemsky, R., ed. Vacuum-Industry-Energy: Proceedings of Second Joint Meeting of the Roland Eotvos Physical Society (Vacuum Physics & Thin Films Section) & the Austrian Vacuum Society, held Niederosterreich, Austria, 27-29 October, 1981.
Dobschiner, Johanna R. Selected to Live.
Dobson, Austin. Samuel Richardson.
--Thomas Bewick & His Pupils.
Dobson, Danae. Woof!
Dobson, Dorothy. The Parting.
Dobson, E. Foundations & Concrete Works.
Dobson, James. Dare to Discipline.
--Preparing for Adolescence.
Dobson, P. J., ed. Interdisciplinary Surface Science: Proceedings of the ISSC6 Conference, Warwick, U. K., April 18-21, 1983.
Dobson, R. B. & Taylor, J. Rymes of Robyn Hood: An Introduction to the English Outlaw.
Dobson, W. A. Early Archaic Chinese: A Descriptive Grammar.
Doby, John T. Introduction to Social Psychology.
Doby, T. Development of Angiography & Cardiovascular Catheterization.
Dobyns, Roy A. Programmed Guide to Accompany Fundamentals of Algebra & Trigonometry.
Dobyns, Stephen. Black Dog, Red Dog.
--Concurring Beasts.
--Heat Death.
--Saratoga Swimmer.
Dockens, William S., jt. ed. see Thompson, Travis.
Dockrell, W. B. & Hamilton, David. Rethinking Educational Research.
Docks, Les R. American Premium Record Guide Identification & Values: 1915-1965.
Dockstader, Frederick J. Indian Art of the Americas.
Doctor, Jan. The Mystery of Marriage: A Challenge to Forced Divorce.
Dr. Williams' Library, London Staff, ed. Early Nonconformity, Fifteen Sixty-Six to Eighteen Hundred: A Catalogue of Books in Dr. Williams' Library, London. Incl. Pt. 1. Author Catalogue; Pt. 2. Subject Catalogue; Pt. 3. Chronological Catalogue. G K Hall.
Doctoroff, Michael. Synergistic Management: Creating the Climate for Superior Performance.
Doctorow, E. L. Lives of the Poets: Six Stories & a Novella.
--Loon Lake.
--Welcome to Hard Times.
--World's Fair.
Dodd, A. E. Dictionary of Ceramics.
Dodd, Donald B. Historical Atlas of Alabama.
Dodd, E. E. Atlas of Histology.
Dodd, George. Days at the Factories: Manufacturing in the Nineteenth Century.
Dodd, Harold & Cockett, Frank B. The Pathology & Surgery of the Veins of the Lower Limb.
Dodd, Henry P. Epigrammatists: A Selection from the Epigrammatic Literature of Ancient, Mediaeval & Modern Times.
Dodd, Lawrence C. & Schott, Richard L. Congress & the Administrative State.
Dodd, Philip & Colls, Robert, eds. Englishness: National Identity in Arts, Politics & Society 1880-1920.
Dodd, W. A., jt. auth. see Cameron, J.
Dodd, Wayne. A Time of Hunting.
Dodd, William, jt. auth. see Presley, John.
Dodd, William E., Foundation Staff. U. S. Week.
Dodderidge, Esme. New Gulliver.
--The New Gulliver.
Doddridge, Philip. Exposition of the Gospels.
Dodds. Tissue Culture of Trees.
Dodds, Elizabeth D. Marriage to a Difficult Man: The Uncommon Union of Jonathan & Sarah Edwards.
Dodds, J. C. The Investment Behaviour of British Life Insurance Companies.
Dodds, J. C., jt. auth. see Bridge, John.
Doden, Imogene Moats, jt. auth. see Casper, Georgia Moats.
Doder, Dusko. Shadow & Whispers: Power Politics Inside the Knowledge from Brezhnev to Gorbachev.
Dodes, Irving A. Finite Mathematics with BASIC: A Liberal Arts Approach.
--Mathematics: A Liberal Arts Approach with Basic.
Dodge, jt. auth. see Kneedler.
Dodge Building Cost Services Staff. Dodge Manual for Building Construction Pricing & Scheduling, 1979.
Dodge, Clayton W. Numbers & Mathematics.
Dodge Cost Information Systems Staff. Dodge Assemblies Cost Data, 1987.
--Dodge Construction Systems Costs, 1985.
--Dodge Guide to Public Works & Heavy Construction.
--Dodge Heavy Construction Cost Data, 1988.
--Dodge Heavy Construction Costs, 1987.
--Dodge Manual for Building Construction Pricing & Scheduling.
--Dodge Remodeling & Retrofit Cost Data, 1987.
--Dodge Remodeling & Retrofit Cost Data, 1988.
--Dodge Unit Cost Data, 1987.
Dodge, Ernest S., ed. Thirty Years of the American Neptune.
Dodge, H. Robert. Field Sales Management: Text & Cases.
Dodge, Howard. How to Prepare for the College Board Achievement Test - Mathematics Level II.
Dodge, Jim. FUP.
Dodge, Joseph M. Federal Taxation of Estates, Trusts & Gifts: Principles & Planning.
Dodge, Peter, ed. A Documentary Study of Hendrik De Man, Socialist Critic of Marxism.
Dodge, R. N., jt. auth. see Clark, S. K.
Dodge, R. V. Rails of the Silver Gate.
Dodge, Robert J. Isolated Splendor: Put-in-Bay & South Bass Island.
Dodge, Susan E., jt. auth. see Givens, Janet E.
Dodge, Tom. A Literature of Sports.
Dodgshon, R. A. & Butlin, R. A., eds. An Historical Geography of England & Wales.
Dodgson, Charles L. see Carrol, Lewis.
Dodin, Jean-Daniel. Enter. Jarett, Keith, ed. Dodin, Mary-Denise, tr. from Fr.
Dodin, Mary-Denise, tr. see Dodin, Jean-Daniel.
Dodrill, William. Moccasin Tracks & Other Imprints.
Dodson, Daniel B., jt. auth. see Barranger, M. S.
Dodson, Fitzhugh. Give Your Child a Head Start in Reading.
Doelken, Dr. Theodor, jt. ed. see Strute, Karl.
Doelle, H. W., ed. Microbial Metabolism.
Doenecke, Justus D., compiled by. The Diplomacy of Frustration: The Manchurian Crisis of 1931-1933 As Revealed in the Papers of Stanley K. Hornbeck.
Doenges, E. Marilynn, et al. Nursing Care Plans: Nursing Diagnoses in Planning Patient Care.
Doenicke, A., ed. Etomidate: An Intravenous Hypnotic Agent. First Report on Clinical & Experimental Experience.
Doerffler, Alfred. The Yoke Made Easy.
Doering, Jeanne. Your Power of Encouragement.
Doern, G. Bruce. Science & Politics in Canada.
Doerner, Max. The Materials of the Artist: And Their Use in Painting with Notes on the Techniques of the Old Masters. Neuhaus, Eugen, tr.
Doerr, W., et al. Atlas of Pathologic Anatomy.
Doerr, Wilhelm, ed. see Borchard, Franz.
Doerr, Wilhelm, ed. see Tillmann, Bernhard.
Doezema, Linda P., ed. Dutch Americans: A Guide to Information Sources.
Doggett, G. The Electronic Structure of Molecules: Theory & Application to Inorganic Molecules.
Doggett, Joella, jt. auth. see Scheick, William J.
Doggett, LeRoy & Guertler, Helena I. Almanac for Computers, 1987.
Doggett, R. G., ed. Pseudomonas Aeruginosa: Clinical Manifestations of Infection & Current Therapy.
Dogin, Yvette. Teen-Agers at Work.
Dogo, Giuliano. Treasures of Italy.
Doherty. Rehabilitation of the War Injured.
Doherty, Barbara. I Am What I Do: Contemplation & Human Experience.
Doherty, Cecelia & Ilyin, Donna. Technical Manual for ELSA: English Language Skills Assessment in a Reading Context.
Doherty, Frank. The Stalker Affair.
Doherty, Ivy D. Rainbows of Promise. Wheeler, Gerald, ed.
Doherty, Joan F. Hudson County: The Left Bank.
Doherty, Joseph F. & Stephenson, William. The Inward Journey.
Doherty, Katherine M., ed. History Highlights: Bridgewater, Massachusetts, a Commemorative Journal.
Doherty, Paul. Atlas of the Planets.
--Building & Using an Astronomical Observatory.
Doherty, Paul G., jt. auth. see Mann, Stephen G.
Doherty, Robert E. Industrial & Labor Relations Terms: A Glossary.
Doherty, Stephen M., jt. ed. see Commager, Henry S.
Dohr, Donald A. Camino Hacia el Amor.
Dohrman, Richard. Vonda Rosegood.
Doi, Masaru. Cook Japanese.
Doig, Ivan. The Sea Runners.
--This House of Sky: Landscapes of a Western Mind.
--Winter Brothers: A Season at the Edge of America.
Doig, Jameson W. Criminal Corrections: Ideals & Realities.
Doig, Peter. Concise History of Astronomy.
Doiron, John & Hyde, Cornelius J., III. Louisiana Supplement to Modern Real Estate Practice.
Dolak, Frank J. American Indian Culture: A Selective Bibliography of Bibliographies.
--Architectural Education: A Selective Bibliography, 1961-1984.
Dolan. Personal Finance Four Cassette Pak.
Dolan, Edward E., Jr. Calling the Play: A Beginner's Guide to Amateur Sports Officiating.
Dolan, Edward F., Jr. Calling the Play: A Beginner's Guide to Amateur Sports Officiating.
--Great Moments in the Indy 500.
--It Sounds Like Fun: How to Use & Enjoy Your Tape Recorder & Stereo.
--The Simon & Schuster Sports Question & Answer Book. Arico, Diane, ed.
Dolan, Edward F., Jr. & Finney, Shan. Youth Gangs.
Dolan, Edwin G. Basic Macroeconomics.
--Basic Microeconomics.
--Economics.
--Macroeconomics.
--Microeconomics.
Dolan, Jay P. American Catholic Experience: A History from Colonial Times to the Present.
Dolan, John P. Catholicism.
Dolan, Maryanne. Collecting Rhinestone Jewelry.
Dolan, Sheila. The Wishing Bottle.
Dolan, Steve. Decision at Burlington.
Dolan, Walter. The Classical World Bibliography of Greek & Roman History.
Dolbeare, Kenneth M. American Public Policy: A Citizen's Guide.
Dolby, J. L. Evaluation of the Utility & Cost of Computerized Library Catalogues.
Dolby, William, tr. see Sima Qian.
Dolce, Donald & Devellard, Jean-Paul. The Consumer's Guide to Menswear.
Dolciani, Mary P. & Sorgenfrey, Robert H. Elementary Algebra for College Students.
Dolciani, Mary P., et al. Intermediate Algebra for College Students.
Dold, Gaylord. Hot Summer, Cold Murder.
Dolder, Eugene J. & Durrer, Gustav T. The Bar Joint Denture.
Dole, Charles E. Flight Theory for Pilots.
Dole, Malcolm, ed. The Radiation Chemistry of Macromolecules.
Dolesh, Daniel J. & Lehman, Sherelynn. Love Me, Love Me Not: How to Survive Infidelity.
Dolgoff, Ralph, jt. auth. see Loewenberg, Frank.
Dolgoff, Ralph, jt. auth. see Loewenberg, Frank M.
Doll, R., et al, eds. Cancer Incidence in Five Continents Vol. 1.
Doll, T. E., jt. auth. see Jackson, B. R.
Dollar, Bruce & Kleinbard, Peter. Youth Participation in Documenting CETA Youth Employment Programs.
Dollar, Truman. What Went Right, What Went Wrong?
Dollard, J. D., ed. see Drechsler, W. & Mayer, M. E.
Dollard, John & Horton, Donald. Fear in Battle.
Dollen, Charles. John F. Kennedy. American.
Dollenmayer, David, et al. Neue Horizonte.
Dolley, Janice, jt. auth. see Burton, Ursula.
Dollfus, A., jt. ed. see Florkin, M.
Dolman, Anthony J. Resources, Regimes, World Order.
Dolmetsch, Paul & Mauricette, Gail, eds. Teens Talk about Alcohol & Alcoholism.
Dolot, Miron. Execution by Hunger: The Hidden Holocaust.
Dolphin, David & Wick, Alexander. Tabulation of Infrared Spectral Data.
Dolson, Bobbie J. Van see Dewees, Eleanor.
Dolson, Bobbie J. Van see Hills, Desmond B.
Dolson, Bobbie J. Van see Irland, Nancy B.
Dolson, John. Black Canyon of the Gunnison: A Guide & Reference Book.
Doman, Glenn. How to Multiply Your Baby's Intelligence.
Domandi, Agnes K. & Guilloton, D. S. Deutsche Literatur Von Heute: An Intermediate German Course.
Domatilla, John. The Last Crime.
Domb, C. & Green, M., eds. Phase Transitions & Critical Phenomena: Series Expansion for Lattice Models.
Dombroff. Dombroff on Demonstrative Evidence: 1987 Cumulative Supplement.
Dombroff, Mark A. Dombroff on Unfair Tactics: 1987 Cumulative Supplement.
--Dynamic Closing Arguments.
--U. S. A. Products Liability Litigation Institute.
Dombroff, Mark A., et al. Negligence Litigation Handbook: Federal & State.
Dombroski, Thomas. Creative Problem Solving: The Door to Progress & Change.
Domcroft, Mark A., jt. auth. see Practice Law Institute Staff.
Domenet, J. G., jt. ed. see Mitchell, J. R.
Domer, Larry R., jt. auth. see Snyder, Thomas L.
Domingo, Placido. My First Forty Years.
Dominguez, Henry. The Ford Agency: A Pictorial History.
Dominguez, Jorge & Lindenberg, Marc. Central America: Current Crisis & Future Prospects.
Dominguin, Luis M. & Boudaille, George. Picasso: Toros Y Toreros.
Dominiak, Geraldine F., jt. auth. see Louderback, Joseph G.
Dominiak, Geraldine F., jt. auth. see Louderback, Joseph G., 3rd.
Dominic, Annette. We Loved While We Died.
Dominic, Annette V. Why Didn't He Tell Me?
Dominik, Janet B. Christian Von Schneidau: 1893-1976. Stern, Jean, ed.
Domke, Noelle, tr. see Navarre, Yves.
Domling, W., jt. ed. see Schwendowius, B.
Dommen, Edward & Hein, Philippe, eds. States, Microstates & Islands.
Domsky, I. & Perry, J., eds. Recent Advances in Gas Chromatography.
Domuret, Allan J., et al. Encyclopedia for the TRS-80. Putnam, Katherine & Comiskey, Kate, eds.
Domville, Eric, ed. Editing British & American Literature: 1880-1920.
Don, Consultants Staff. EMC Technology: 1982 Anthology.
Donaghey, Robert & Ruddel, JoAnna. Fundamentals of Algebra: An Integrated Text-Workbook.
Donaho, Meyer. How to Get the Job You Want.
Donahoe, Peter M., jt. auth. see Clancy, Ambrose.
Donahue, Bob & Donahue, Marilyn. Don't Be a Puppet on a String.
--Getting Your Act Together.
--How to Make People Like You When You Know They Don't.
--Things That Go Bump in the Night, & Other Fears.
Donahue, J. E. Complementary Definitions of Programming Language Semantics.
Donahue, Jack. The Lady Loved Too Well.
Donahue, Jack & Halbouty, Michel T. Grady Barr.

Authors

Donahue, John R., jt. auth. see Sleeth, Ronald E.
Donahue, John R., ed. see Bailey, Lloyd R., Sr.
Donahue, John R., ed. see Hamerton-Kelly, Robert.
Donahue, John R., ed. see Harrington, Daniel J.
Donahue, John R., ed. see Johnson, Luke T.
Donahue, John R., ed. see Patrick, Dale.
Donahue, John R., ed. see Westermann, Claus.
Donahue, Kenneth, ed. see Pignatti, Terisio.
Donahue, Marilyn. To Catch a Golden Ring.
--To Catch a Golden Ring.
Donahue, Marilyn, jt. auth. see Donahue, Bob.
Donahue, Marilyn C. Music Play Past Midnight.
--Violets Grow in Secret Places.
Donahue, Phil. The Human Animal.
Donald, A. L. Mac see Mac Donald, A. L.
Donald, H. P., jt. auth. see Lerner, I. M.
Donald, Kay. Creative Feltmaking.
Donald, Ted M. Laugh-It's Good for the Jaws.
Donaldson, A. M., jt. ed. see Steltz, W. E.
Donaldson, Christine F., jt. auth. see Flynn, Elizabeth A.
Donaldson, E. Talbot. Speaking of Chaucer.
Donaldson, Fred. Crooked Trail.
Donaldson, Gerald. The Grand Prix of Canada.
Donaldson, Gordon. Scotland: Shaping of a Nation.
--Strategy for Financial Mobility.
Donaldson, Ian, ed. Transformations in Modern European Drama.
Donaldson, Jim. The Official Fantasy Football League Manual: How to Own Your Own Pro Football Team, Coach Your Players, Outsmart Your Friends, & Win Big.
Donaldson, O. Fred, jt. auth. see Davis, George A.
Donaldson, Robert H., jt. auth. see Nogee, Joseph L.
Donaldson, Stephen R. The One Tree.
--The Second Chronicle of Thomas Covenant.
--White Gold Wielder.
--The Wounded Land: Book One of the Second Chronicles of Thomas Covenant.
Donaldson, Terence L. Jesus on the Mountain: A Study in Matthean Theology.
Donalson, George W. The Doughty Scot: An Autobiographical Fragment. Ford, Frank R., Jr., ed.
Donatelli, Gary, jt. auth. see Armentani, Andy.
Donders, Joseph G. The Peace of Jesus: Reflections on the Gospel for the A-Cycle.
Dondes, Seymour & Lurie, Steven W. General Chemistry Laboratory Manual.
Dondo, Mathurian. French Faust: Henri De Saint Simon.
Donegan, William L. & Spratt, John S., Jr. Cancer of the Breast.
Donelson, Kenneth L., jt. auth. see Nilsen, Alleen Pace.
Doner, Dean B., jt. ed. see Bugliarello, George.
Donfried, Karl P., ed. The Romans Debate: Essays on the Origin & Purpose on the Epistle.
Dongen, R. J. Van see Van Dongen, R. J.
Donges, Gregory S. Policymaking for the Mentally Handicapped.
Doniach, D., jt. ed. see Pinchera, A.
Donington, Robert. The Interpretation of Early Music.
--Music & Its Instruments.
--A Performer's Guide to Baroque Music.
Donizetti, Gaetano. Lucia di Lammermoor. Bleiler, Ellen H., tr.
Donkin, R. A. Spanish Red: An Ethnogeographical Study of Cochineal & the Opuntia Cactus.
Donlan, Walter, intro. by. The Classical World Bibliography of Roman Drama & Poetry & Ancient Fiction.
--The Classical World Bibliography of Vergil.
Donleavy, J. P. A Fairy Tale of New York.
--The Ginger Man.
--Singular Man.
Donley, Diana, jt. ed. see Burkhalter, Pamela K.
Donnachie, A. & Shaw, G., eds. Electromagnetic Interactions of Hadrons.
Donnay, Albert, ed. The Investor's Guide to the Military Industry: Fiscal Year 1987.
Donnay, Gabrielle & Donnay, J. D., eds. The M. A. C. Crystallographic Laboratory Manual: Mineralogical Association of Canada, Montreal 1984.
Donnay, J. D., jt. ed. see Donnay, Gabrielle.
Donne, John. Complete Poems.
--Donne: Concordance to the Poems. Combs, Homer C. & Sullins, Z. R., eds.
Donnellan, T. Lattice Theory.
Donnelly. Coping with Stress: RN's Survival Sourcebook.
Donnelly, jt. auth. see Peter.
Donnelly, Austin S. The Three Rs of Investing: Return, Risk & Relativity.
Donnelly, Dody. Team.
Donnelly, Elizabeth A., jt. auth. see Beckmann, David M.
Donnelly, G. F., et al. The Nursing System: Issues, Ethics & Politics.
Donnelly, Honoria M. & Billings, Richard N. Sara & Gerald: Villa America & After.
Donnelly, I. Ragnarok-the Age of Fire & Gravel.
Donnelly, James, et al. Fundamentals of Management: Functions, Behavior, Models.
Donnelly, James H., Jr., jt. auth. see Peter, J. Paul.
Donnelly, James H., Jr., et al, eds. Fundamentals of Management: Selected Readings.
Donnelly, John & Lyons, Leonard, eds. Conscience.
Donnelly, Joseph P. Thwaites' Jesuit Relations, Errata & Addenda.
Donnelly, Judy. True-Life Treasure Hunts.
Donnelly, Marian. A Short History of Observatories.
Donnelly, Mark & Fenton, Nina. Search Heaven & Hell. Rappaport, Jon, ed.
Donnelly, Mary C., jt. auth. see Miller, Bruce W.
Donnelly, Michael. Managing the Mind: A Study of Medical Psychology in Early 19th-Century Britain.
Donnelly, Milly L. Me Spik English.
Donnelly, Morwenna. Founding the Life Divine: An Introduction to the Integral Yoga of Sri Aurobindo.
Donnelly, William J. The Confetti Generation: American Social Character in the Age of the New Electronic Communications.
Donner, Art, ed. see Gross, Rosalind L.
Donner, Barbara, et al. Now You Know About: Animals. Incl. Animal Coverings; Animal Homes; How Animals Stay Alive; Many Animals; Where Animals Live; Where Animals Live. Ency Brit Ed.
Donner, Florinda. The Witch's Dream.
Donner, Neal, tr. see Sueno, Akira.
Donner, Stanley T., jt. ed. The Meaning of Commercial Television.
Donnersberger, Anne B., et al. A Manual of Anatomy & Physiology Laboratory Animal: The Cat.
Donnet, Stoeckl, ed. see Bansal.
Donnison, David & Middleton, Alan. Regenerating the Inner City.
Donoghue, Denis. The Sovereign Ghost: Studies in Imagination.
Donoghue, William F. Distributions & Fourier Transforms.
Donohue, James F. Spitballs & Holy Water.
Donohue, Joseph W., Jr., ed. Theatrical Manager in Britain & America.
Donoughe, Carol, et al. In-Service: The Teacher & the School.
Donovan. Open Road.
Donovan, Arthur & Prentiss, Joseph. James Hutton's Medical Dissertation.
Donovan, D. Once a Warrior King: Memories of an Officer in Vietnam.
Donovan, Dolores A. Prosecutorial & Judicial Misconduct.
Donovan, Frank & Henry, Seth. Headlights & Markers.
Donovan, George S. & Gimmestad, Beverly B. Trigonometry.
Donovan, John. Advanced Techniques in WordStar 2000.
--Wild in the World.
Donovan, John C., et al. People, Power & Politics: An Introduction to Political Science.
Donovan, Mary E., jt. auth. see Sanford, Linda T.
Donovan, Michael & Appleby, Harrison. Planning & Controlling Manufacturing Resources.
Donovan, P. F. At the Other End of Australia: The Commonwealth & the Northern Territory 1911-1978.
--A Land Full of Possibilities: A History of South Australia's Northern Territory.
Donovan, Robert, jt. auth. see Bignell, James.
Donovan, Robert J. Tumultuous Years: The Presidency of Harry S. Truman, 1949-1953.
Donovan, Timothy P. & Gatewood, Willard B., Jr., eds. The Governors of Arkansas: Essays in Political Biography.
Donson, Cyril. Dakota Feud.
--Unsmiling Gun.
Dont, J. Etudes & Caprices for Violin.
Donze, M. Terese, Sr. The Kingdom Lost & Found: A Fable for Everyone.
Doob, Anthony, jt. auth. see Freedman, Jonathan N.
Doohovskoy, A. P., tr. see Landkof, N. S.
Dooley, et al. Imaging in Hepatobiliary Disease.
Dooley, David, jt. auth. see Goodman, Gerald.
Dooley, J. The Wonderful World of Oprah.
Dooley, John. Trump: The Building of an Empire.
Dooley, Roger. From Scarface to Scarlett: American Films in the 1930s.
--From Scarface to Scarlett: American Films in the 1930s.
Dooley, Thomas W. Real Estate Brokerage in the Eighties: Survival among the Giants.
Doolin, Dennis J., tr. Communist China: The Politics of Student Opposition.
Doolittle, Hilda see H. D., pseud.
Doolittle, Hilda see H. D.
Doolittle, Jesse S. & Hale, Francis J. Thermodynamics for Engineers.
--Thermodynamics for Engineers, SI Version.
Doornik, N. Van see Van Doornik, N.
Doornkamp, J. C., et al, eds. Atlas of Drought in Britain Nineteen Seventy-Five to Nineteen Seventy-Six.
Doppo, Kunikida. River Mist & Other Stories. Chibbett, David G., tr. from Japanese.
Dopuch, Nicholas, et al. Cost Accounting: Accounting Data for Management's Decisions.
Doran, Adelaide L. Pieces of Eight Channel Islands: A Bibliographical Guide & Source Book.
Doran, George T. How to Be a Better Manager in Ten Easy Steps.
Dordick, B. F., jt. ed. see Babb, Janice B.
Dore, Gustave. History of Holy Russia. Weissbort, Daniel, tr. from Fr.
Doreian, Raymond, jt. auth. see McCord, Thomas I.
Doren, Carl C. Van see Van Doren, Carl C.
Doren, Mark Van see Bartram, William.
Doren, V. E. Van see Devreese, J. T. & Van Doren, V. E.
Dorf, Martin E. The Role of the Major Histocompatibility Complex in Immunobiology.
Dorf, Richard C. The Energy Factbook. Dembofsky, Thomas J., ed.
--The Energy Factbook.
Dorfles, Gillo. Kitsch: The World of Bad Taste.
Dorfman, Gerald & Duignan, Peter, eds. Politics of Western Europe.
Dorfman, John. Consumer Tactics Manual: How to Get Action on Your Complaints.
--Family Investment Guide.
Dorfman, Mark S. Introduction to Insurance.
Dorfman, Nancy S., jt. auth. see Dorfman, Robert.
Dorfman, Robert & Dorfman, Nancy S. Economics of the Environment: Selected Readings.
Doria, G. & Eshkol, A. The Immune System: Functions & Therapy of Dysfunction.
Dorian, Marguerite, tr. see Caraion, Ion.
Dorin, Patrick C. Yesterday's Trains.
Dorje, Gyurme, ed. see Rinpoche, Dudjom.
Dorland, Gilbert N. & Van Der Wal, John. The Business Idea: From Birth to Profitable Company.
--The Business Idea from Birth to Profitable Company.
Dorling, Ian P., ed. see International Symposium on Stability in Coal Mining Staff.
Dorman, R. G. Dust Control & Air Cleaning.
Dorman, Sonya. Stretching Fence.
Dorman, William A. & Farhang, Mansour. The U. S. Press & Iran Foreign Policy & the Journalism of Deference.
Dorn, Edward. Yellow Lola.
Dorn, Nicholas. Alcohol, Youth & the State: Drinking Practices, Controls & Health Education.
Dornan, Peter. Sporting Injuries: A Trainer's Guide.
Dornburgh, Henry. Why the Wilderness Is Called Adirondack: The Earliest Account of Founding of the MacIntyre Mine.
Dorner, G. Hormones & Brain Differentiation.
Dorner, G. & Kawakami, M., eds. Hormones & Brain Development.
Dornette, W. Stuart & Cross, Robert R. Federal Judiciary Almanac 1986.
Dornette, William H. L. Stedman's Medical Dictionary: Fifth Unabridged Lawyers' Edition.
Dornfeld, Ernst. Butterflies of Oregon.
Dornhoff, Larry L. & Hohn, Franz E. Applied Modern Algebra.
Dornoy, Myriam. Politics in New Caledonia.
Doroghazi, Robert M. & Slater, Eve E. Aortic Dissection.
Doroski, Michael C. More Lives Than a Cat.
Dorozynski, A., ed. Recherche-Operation, Application: Deroulement d'un Seminair-Atelier sur la Recherche Operationelle dans le Domaine de la Sante Publique, tenu au Centre Universitaire des Sciences de la Sante a Yaounde, Cameroun, 6-11 Decembre 1976.
Dorr, John A., Jr., et al. Deformation & Deposition Between a Foreland Uplift & an Impinging Thrust Belt: Hoback Basin, Wyoming.
Dorris, Pearl. Step by Step We Climb to Freedom & Victory.
Dorsari, George R., jt. auth. see Practising Law Institute Staff.
Dorsen, Norman, et al. Political & Civil Rights in the United States: 1981 Supplement to Vol. II.
Dorsett, Judy. Bulletin Board Builders.
--Bulletin Board Builders.
--Handbook of Creativity.
Dorsett, Lyle W., jt. auth. see Brown, A. Theordore.
Dorsey, Anne G., jt. auth. see Sciarra, Dorothy J.
Dorsey, Joan. Introducing Your Kids to the Outdoors.
Dorsey, Mary E. Reading Games & Activities.
Dorsey, Michael, jt. auth. see Calabrese, Edward.
Dorso, Richard. Thicker Than Water.
Dorson, Richard M. Negro Folktales in Michigan.
Dorst, Jean. Field Guide to the Larger Mammals of Africa.
Dorszynski, ed. see Eisen, Jon, et al.
Dorter, Tom & Armbruster, Greg, eds. The Art of Electronic Music.
Dortzbach, Deborah, jt. auth. see Dortzbach, Karl.
Dortzbach, Karl & Dortzbach, Deborah. Kidnapped.
Dorward, Donald L. Words about Words: Nonconventional Methods of Handling Chemical Information.
Dorwart, Reinhold A. Administrative Reforms of Frederick William First of Prussia.
Doscher, David, ed. see Tarnowski, S.
Doscher, Paul, et al. Intensive Gardening Round the Year.
Dose, Klaus, jt. auth. see Fox, Sidney W.
Dos Passos, John. First Encounter.
--Journeys Between Wars.
--Tour of Duty.
--U. S. A. The Forty-Second Parallel, Nineteen Nineteen, The Big Money.
Doss, M., ed. Diagnosis & Therapy of Porphyrias & Lead Toxication.
Dossey, jt. auth. see Guzzetta.
Dossick, Jesse J. Doctoral Research on Russia & the Soviet Union: 1960-1975.
Dostal, John, jt. auth. see Gillette, Ned.
Dostert, P., jt. ed. see Tipton, Keith.
Dostoevsky, Anna. Dostoevsky: Reminiscences. Stillman, Beatrice, tr. from Rus.
Dostoevski, Fedor see Dostoyevsky, Fedor.
Dostoyevsky, Anna. Dostoyevsky: Reminiscences. Stillman, Beatrice, ed. & tr.
Dostoyevsky, Fyodor. Crime & Punishment. Garnett, Constance, tr.
--Crime & Punishment. Gibian, George, ed.
--Crime & Punishment.
--Diary of a Writer. Brasol, Boris, tr. from Rus.
--The Idiot. Garnett, Constance, tr.
--The Notebooks for "Crime & Punishment" Wasiolek, Edward, ed. & tr. from Rus.
--The Possessed. Garnett, Constance, tr. Yarmolinsky, Avrham, ed.
--Village of Stepanchikovo. Avsey, Ignat, tr. from Rus.
Dotson, Bill, et al. Concepts in Coaching Wrestling.
Dotson, Bob. In Pursuit of the American Dream.
Dotter, Pam. Miniature Desserts.
Dotterer, Ray H. Postulates & Implications.
Dottori, D. Mathematics for Today & Tomorrow.
Doty, et al. Practical Bronchoscopy.
Doty, C. Stewart. From Cultural Rebellion to Counterrevolution: The Politics of Maurice Barres.
Doty, Jean S. Can I Get There by Candlelight?
--Summer Pony.
Doty, Leonard. Reliability for the Technologies.
Doty, R. H. Indecent Deception.
Doty, Richard L., ed. Mammalian Olfaction: Reproductive Processes, & Behavior.
Doty, Robert & Watts, Melvin, eds. Eagles, Urns, & Columns: Decorative Arts in the Federal Period.
Doty, Roy. Eye Fooled You.
Doty, Walter & Sinnes, A. Cort. All about Tomatoes. Susan, ed.
Doubiago, Sharon. Hard Country.
Doubleday, Opal A. Whilst Thy Tower Crumbles.
Doucet, Jacques. Catalogue de Fonds Speciaux de la Bibliotheque Litteraire Jacques Doucet, (Paris, France)
--Catalogue de Fonds Speciaux de la Bibliotheque Litteraire Jacques Doucet, (Paris, France)
--Catalogue de Fonds Speciaux de la Bibliotheque Litteraire Jacques Doucet, (Paris, France)
Doucette, Joseph & Collins, Charles. Collecting Antique Toys: A Practical Guide.
Doudna, Lyn. The Odds Against Them.
Doudoroff, M., jt. auth. see Stanier, Roger.
Dougall, Herbert E. & Gaumnitz, Jack E. Capital Markets & Institutions.
Douge, Daniel. Caribbean Pilgrims: The Plight of the Haitian Refugees.
Dougherty, Dale, ed. see Strang, John.
Dougherty, Dale, ed. see Tim, O'Reilly & Todins, Grace.
Dougherty, David M. & Barnes, E. B., eds. La Geste De Monglane.
Dougherty, Flavian, ed. The Deprived, the Disabled & the Fullness of Life.
Dougherty, James L. Union-Free Labor Relations: A Step-by-Step Guide to Staying Union Free.
--The Union-Free Supervisor.
Dougherty, John W. Summer School: A New Look.
Dougherty, Bro. Patricius & Leifer, Sr. Carmel. Review Text in Health.
Dougherty, Samuel A. Call the Big Hook.
Dougherty, Thomas A. The Enigma of the Eighties: Environment, Economic, Energy.
Dougherty, Thomas J., jt. ed. see Hayata, Yoshihiro.
Doughty, Charles M. Travels in Arabia Deserta.
Doughty, Louise G. Smiles Make Fewer Wrinkles.
Doughty, Robin W., jt. ed. see Hugill, Peter J.

Doughty, W. L. Prayers of Susanna Wesley.
Douglas, jt. auth. see Taylor.
Douglas, A G. & Maxwell, J. R., eds. Advances in Organic Geochemistry 1979: Proceedings of the 9th International Meeting on Organic Geochemistry Held at Newcastle-Upon-Tyne, England, Sept. 1979.
Douglas, A. H. An Approach to Engineering Mathematics.
Douglas, Alfred, jt. auth. see Shaw, George Bernard.
Douglas, Ann. The Feminization of American Culture.
Douglas, Brodie E., ed. Inorganic Syntheses.
Douglas, C. A. Love & Politics: Radical Feminist Theories.
Douglas, Carole N. Lady Rogue.
Douglas, Colin. Bleeders Come First.
--The Greatest Breakthrough since Lunchtime.
--The Intern's Tale.
--Sickness & Health: A Novel.
Douglas, Drake. Undertow.
Douglas, Ellen. The Rock Cried Out.
Douglas, Evan J. Managerial Economics: Theory, Practice, & Problems.
Douglas, Frank. Dust Bunnies.
--Dust Bunnies & the Rescue of Buttons the Bear.
Douglas, G. H., ed. The Teaching of Business Communication.
Douglas, George H. Women of the Twenties.
Douglas, Gertrude. Linked Lives. Wolff, Robert L., ed.
Douglas, J. D., ed. The Calling of an Evangelist.
Douglas, J., Jr. & Dupont, T. Collocation Methods for Parabolic Equations in a Single Space Variable: Based on C to the First Power-Piecewise-Polynomial Spaces.
Douglas, J. Leonard. Zaza's Seventh Husband & Some Others.
Douglas, J. M. & Lomo, A., eds. Divry's New Spanish-English & English-Spanish Handy Dictionary.
Douglas, Jack. What Do You Hear from Walden Pond?
Douglas, John. Bacteriophages.
Douglas, Kate. Captive of the Heart.
Douglas, Kathryn. Amelia.
Douglas, Lillie B. Cape Town to Cairo.
Douglas, Marilyn K., jt. auth. see Shinn, Julie A.
Douglas, Mary. In the Active Voice.
Douglas, Mary & Isherwood, Baron. The World of Goods: Towards an Anthropology of Consumption.
Douglas, Mary, ed. Essays in the Sociology of Perception.
--Food in the Social Order: Studies of Food & Festivities in Three American Communities.
Douglas, Mary A. Secretarial Dental Assistant.
Douglas, Norman. London Street Games.
--Old Calabria.
Douglas, Paul H. In the Fullness of Time: The Memoirs of Paul H. Douglas.
Douglas, Randall C., III. The Joy of Stuffed Preppies.
Douglas, Tom. Groups: Understanding People Gathered Together.
Douglas, W. M. Andrew Murray & His Message.
Douglas, William O., jt. ed. see Weinberg, Arthur.
Douglas Jackson, W. A., jt. auth. see Creed, Virginia.
Douglass, Amanda H. Jamaica.
Douglass, Barbara. THe Great Town & Country Bicycle Balloon Chase.
Douglass, David & Krieger, Joel. A Miner's Life.
Douglass, Donna N. Choice & Compromise: A Woman's Guide to Balancing Family & Career.
Douglass, H. E. Hello Neighbor.
Douglass, Jane, ed. Trustable & Preshus Friends.
Douglass, Joseph D., Jr. Soviet Military Strategy in Europe.
Douglass, Joseph D., Jr., ed. Selected Readings from Military Thought: 1963-1973. Hoeber, Amoretta M.
Douglass, Laura M. The Effective Nurse: Leader & Manager.
Douglass, Paul. Guide to Planning the Farm Estate: With Checklists & Forms.
--Guide to Planning the Farm Estate, with Checklists & Forms.
Douglass, Stephen B. & Roddy, Lee. Making the Most of Your Mind.
Douglass, William A. & Etulain, Righard W., eds. Basque Americans: A Guide to Information Sources.
Douglass, William A., as told to see Paris, Beltran.
Douma, George. My Doctrine Book.
Doumato, Lamia. Aldo Van Eyck.
--The American Home: A Historical Background of General Works.
--Architectural Aesthetics.
--Chinese Architecture: A Bibliography.
--Dankmar Adler, Eighteen Forty-Four to Nineteen Hundred.
--Gregory Ain.
--Henry Bacon's Lincoln Memorial.
--John Andrews.
--John Merven Carrere: Eighteen Fifty-Eight to Nineteen Eleven.
--Publications by Women on American Domestic Architecture.
--Russell Sturgis: Eighteen Thirty-Six to Nineteen Nine.
--William Strickland.
Dourado, Autran. Voices of the Dead: A Novel. Parker, John M., tr. from Port.
Dourlein, Peter. Classics of World War Two - The Shadow War: Inside North Pole. Renier, F. G. & Cliff, Anne, trs. from Dutch.
Douthwaite, Graham. Attorney's Guide to Restitution.
--Jury Instructions on Damages in Tort Actions.
Douty, Esther M. Hasty Pudding & Barbary Pirates: A Life of Joel Barlow.
Douville, Leone. Patient Care Services Policy Manual for the Nursing Department.
Douzou, P. Cryobiochemistry: An Introduction.
Doves, Doyle C., jt. auth. see Voelter, Wolfgang.
Dovring, Karin. Road of Propaganda.
Dow, A. B. Reflections.
Dow, Dorothy. Eleanor Roosevelt, an Eager Spirit: The Letters of Dorothy Dow, 1933-45. McClure, Ruth K., ed.
Dow, Gwyneth, ed. Teacher Learning.
Dow, Gwyneth M. Samuel Terry: The Botany Bay Rothschild.
Dow, Philip, ed. Nineteen New American Poets of the Golden Gate.
--Nineteen New American Poets of the Golden Gate.
Dow, Roger W. Business English.
Dow, Ula, jt. auth. see Heseltine, Marjorie.
Dowd, Ben, ed. Some Dimensions of the Formal Organization.
Dowdall, Mike & Welch, Pat. Humans.
Dowdell, Dorothy. Hawk Over Hollyhedge Manor.
Dowden, C. James. Creating a Community Association: The Developer's Role in Condominium & Homeowner Associations.
Dowden, Tony, jt. auth. see Tymes, Elna.
Dowdey, Clifford. The Land They Fought for.
Dowdle, Wade. One Hundred & One Ideas to Help You Sell More Typesetting.
Dowell, Arlene T. AACR Two Headings: A Five-Year Projection of Their Impact on Catalogs.
Dowell, Arlene T., ed. see Frost, Carolyn O.
Dowell, Coleman. The Houses of Children.
Dowell, J., jt. auth. see Greenwood, B.
Dowey, Edward A., Jr. A Commentary on the Confession of Nineteen Sixty-Seven & an Introduction to the Book of Confessions.
Dowie, J. Iverne. Prairie Grass Dividing.
Dowley, Tim. High above the Holy Land. Roe, Earl O., ed.
Dowling, Colette. The Cinderella Complex: Women's Hidden Fear of Independence.
Dowling, David, ed. Novelists on Novelists.
Dowling, Emilia & Osborne, Elsie. The Family & the School: A Joint Systems Approach to Problems with Children.
Dowling, Gregory. Double Take.
Dowling, Jerry L. Criminal Investigation.
Dowling, John R. Developing & Administering an Industrial Training Program.
Dowling, M. & Glahe, F. R., eds. Readings in Econometric Theory.
Dowling, Pamela. My Special Play Group.
Dowling, Shirley. Love Needs No Reason.
Dowman, Keith. The Power-Places of Central Tibet: A Pilgrim's Guide.
Dowman, Keith, ed. Sky Dancer: The Secret Life & Songs of the Lady Yeshe Tsogyel.
Down, P. G. Heating & Cooling Load Calculations.
Downer, Alan S., ed. American Drama & Its Critics: A Collection of Critical Essays.
Downer, Ann H. Physical Therapy Procedures: Selected Techniques.
Downes, John see Wright, James.
Downes, Paul. C-Lect Occupational Module User's Guide.
--Chronicle Math & Science Occupations Guidebook.
Downes, Paul, ed. C-Lect Educational & Financial Aid User's Guide.
--Chronicle Career Index: 1987.
--Chronicle Four-Year College Databook: 1987.
--Chronicle Student Aid Annual: 1987.
--Chronicle Two-Year College Databook: 1987.
--Chronicle Vocational School Manual: 1987.
Downes, Rackstraw. Fairfield Porter: Art in Its Own Terms-Selected Criticism 1935-1975.
Downes, Robert C. & Bartman, William J. International Safe Travel Guide.
Downey, Bob. V-Bombers.
Downey, Douglas W., et al, eds. see Standard Educational Corporation Staff.
Downey, J. A. U. S. Federal Official Publications: The International Dimension.
Downey, James, ed. see Papers from the Thomas Gray Bicentenary Conference at Carleton University.
Downey, Matthew T., jt. ed. see Linden, Glenn M.
Downie, Don. Cockpit Navigation Guide.
Downie, Don, rev. by. Flight Facts for Private Pilots. Rodney, Morgan R.
Downie, Don & Rodney, Morgan R., eds. Flight Facts for Private Pilots.
Downie, J. A. Jonathan Swift: Political Writer.
--Jonathan Swift: Political Writer.
Downie, Jill. Turn of the Century.
Downie, R. S. Roles & Values.
Downie, R. S. & Telfer, Elizabeth. Caring & Curing: A Philosophy of Medicine & Social Work.
Downing, A. F. & Scully, V. J., Jr. Architectural Heritage of Newport, Rhode Island: 1640-1915.
Downing, Andrew J. Victorian Cottage Residences.
Downing, David. The Red Eagles.
Downing, Douglas. Calculus.
Downing, Jean. Peaches, Cream & Sour Apples.
Downing, John & Leong, Che Kan. Psychology of Reading.
Downing, M. E. Landscape Construction.
Downs, A. J. & Adams, C. J. The Chemistry of Chlorine, Bromine, Iodine & Astatine.
Downs, A. M., jt. auth. see Burghes, David N.
Downs, Anthony. Urban Problems & Prospects.
Downs, Barnabus. A Brief & Remarkable Narrative on the Life & Extreme Suffering of Barnabus Downs.
Downs, Florence & Brooten, Dorothy. New Careers in Nursing.
Downs, Frederick, Jr. Aftermath: A Soldier's Return from Vietnam.
Downs, Harold, ed. Theatre & Stage: An Encyclopedic Guide to the Performance of All Amateur Dramatic, Operatic, & Theatrical Work.
Downs, Hugh. On Camera: My Ten Thousand Hours on Television.
Downs, Robert B. Australian & New Zealand Library Resources.
--Books & History.
Downs, Rose G. Dietary Policy & Procedure Manual.
Downs, Thomas. The Parish As Learning Community.
Downstate Medical Center Conference, Brooklyn, 1971. Basic Thalamic Structure & Function: Proceedings of the Downstate Medical Center Conference, Brooklyn, 1971 Staff. Riss, W., et al, eds.
Downton, A. C. Computers & Microprocessors: Components & Systems.
Dowrick, Stephanie & Grundberg, Sibyl, eds. Why Children?
Dowsett, David J., jt. auth. see Ennis, Joseph T.
Dowsett, Dick. Is God Really Fair?
Dowson, Duncan & Higginson, Gordon R. Elasto-Hydrodynamics Lubrication: SI Edition.
Dowson, H. R. Spectral Theory of Linear Operators.
Doxey, William S. E.S.P. Ionage.
Doxiadis, C. A. Building Entopia.
Doxiadis, C. A. & Papaioannou, J. G. Ecumenopolis: The Inevitable City of the Future.
Doxiadis, C. I. Action for Human Settlements.
Doxiadis, Spyros, ed. Improving Public Health: Ethical Dilemmas.
Doyle, A. C. The Ingredient Substitution Recipe.
Doyle, Arthur Conan. Adventures of Sherlock Holmes.
--Great Works of Sir Arthur Doyle: The Illustrated Sherlock Holmes Treasury.
--The Return of Sherlock Holmes.
--Sherlock Holmes: The Published Apocrypha. Tracy, Jack W., ed.
--A Study in Scarlet. Bd. with The Hound of the Baskervilles. RD Assn.
--The Wanderings of a Spiritualist.
Doyle, Barbara. The Hunted Heart.
Doyle, Darrell J., jt. ed. see Segal, Harold.
Doyle, Dickie. Diary by Dickie Doyle.
Doyle, Francis R. Searching the Law: The States.
Doyle, James A. Catholic Press Directory.
--The Male Experience.
Doyle, Joan, jt. auth. see Reilly, Nancy.
Doyle, M. P. & West, C. T., eds. Stereoselective Reductions.
Doyle, Margaret, ed. see American Arbitration Association Staff.
Doyle, P J. & McDiarmid, E. W., eds. The Baker Street Dozen: Sir Arthur Conan Doyle's Thirteen Favorite Sherlock Holmes Stories.
Doyle, Robert J. Gainsharing & Productivity: A Guide to Planning, Implementation & Development.
Doyle, Rodger P. & Redding, James L. The Complete Food Handbook.
Doyle, Winifred. Up the I. R. A.
Dozier, Marc, ed. see Cimino, Louis.
Drabbe, P. Spraakkunst Van Het Marind.
Drabble, Margaret. Arnold Bennett: A Biography.
--For Queen & Country: Victorian England.
Drabek, Anne G. & Knapp, Wilfred. The Politics of African & Middle Eastern States: An Annotated Bibliography.
Drabek, Gordon, jt. ed. see Sinha, Radha.
Drachkovitch, Milorad, ed. East Central Europe: Yesterday, Today, Tomorrow.
Drachman, Theodore S. The Deadly Dream.
Drackett, Phil. Car Makers.
Drage, Charles, ed. Respiratory Medicine for Primary Care Physicians.
Drago, R. S; see Dunitz, J. D., et al.
Dragonwagon, Crescent & Brown, Jan. The Dairy Hollow House Cookbook: Over 400 Delectable Recipes from America's Famed"Nouveau 'Zarks" Cuisine.
Dragunsky, D. Soldier's Life.
Drakakis-Smith, David. Urbanisation in the Developing World.
Drake, Asa. The Lair of Ancient Dreams.
Drake, C. L., jt. ed. see Burk, C. A.
Drake, Christopher, tr. see Ryuichi, Tamura.
Drake, David. Hammer's Slammers.
Drake, Francis S. Tea Leaves: Being a Collection of Letters & Documents Relating to the Shipment of Tea to the American Colonies in the Year 1773, by the East India Tea Company.
Drake, Gertrude C., ed. see Vida, Marco G.
Drake, John D. Interviewing for Managers: A Complete Guide to Employment Interviewing.
Drake, Lewis E. & Oetting, Eugene R. MMPI Codebook for Counselors.
Drake, Marvia, jt. auth. see Drake, Terrance.
Drake, Michael, ed. Applied Historical Studies.
Drake, Nicholas. The Fifties in Vogue.
Drake, R. A., ed. Instrumentation & Control of Water & Wastewater Treatment & Transport Systems: Proceedings of the IAWPRC Workshop, 4th, Houston & Denver, April 27 - May 4, 1985.
Drake, Raleigh M. Abnormal Psychology.
Drake, Robert. The Home Place: A Memory & a Celebration.
Drake, St. Clair & Cayton, Horace R. Black Metropolis.
--Black Metropolis.
Drake, Samuel A. Nooks & Crannies of the New England Coast.
--Old Boston Taverns & Tavern Clubs.
--Old Landmarks & Historic Personages of Boston.
Drake, Stillman. Galileo at Work: His Scientific Biography.
Drake, Stillman, tr. from Lat. Galileo Galilei: "Two New Sciences"
Drake, Terrance & Drake, Marvia. Teaching Your Child about Sex.
Drake, Terri. Singing in A Dark Language.
Drake, William. Connoisseurs Handbook of Marijuana.
--International Cultivator's Handbook.
--Marijuana Food: A Handbook of Marijuana Extract Cooking.
Drake, William, ed. see Teasdale, Sara.
Drakeford, John W. & Drakeford, Robina. Mothers Are Special.
Drakeford, Robina, jt. auth. see Drakeford, John W.
Dramatists Guild Foundation Editors. The Young Playwrights Festival Collection.
Dramesi, John A. Code of Honor.
Drane, James F. A New American Reformation: A Study of Youth Culture & Religion.
Dransfield, P. Hydraulic Control Systems: Design & Analysis of the Dynamics.
Draper, Ann M. Mastering SAMNA Word IV.
Draper, James T. The Conscience of a Nation.
Draper, James T., Jr. The Unveiling.
Draper, John W. Othello of Shakespeare's Audience.
--The Tempo-Patterns of Shakespeare's Plays.
Draper, Judith. Show Jumping Records, Facts & Champions.
Draper, Maurice L. Isles & Continents.
Draper, Perry L. Parents, Take Charge!
Drasar, D. R. & Hill, M. J. Human Intestinal Flora.
Drauglis, E., et al. Molecular Processes on Solid Surfaces.
Draviczki, Lajos. A Minute to Live!
Dray, William. Perspectives on History.
Drazan, Frank. The Sheetfed Pressroom Manager's Training Guide.
Drazil, J. V. Quantities & Units of Measurement: A Dictionary & Handbook.
Draznin, Boris. Marshmellowterra: The Land of Marshmallow People & Whimsical Animals.
Dreamer, Sue. Animal Walk: Make Way for the Horses, Lions, Camels, & Bears in This Spectacular Grand-Entry Parade!
--Circus ABC.
--Circus Train: This Lovable Locomotive Is a Book & Toy All in One!
--Lucy Makes It Big.
Drebin, Allan R., jt. auth. see Bierman, Harold, Jr.
Drechsel, D., jt. ed. see Arenhovel, H.
Drechsler, W. & Mayer, M. E. Fiber Bundle Techniques in Gauge Theory: Lectures in Mathematical Physics at the University of Texas at Austin. Boehm, A. & Dollard, J. D., eds.
Dreeben, Robert, jt. auth. see Barr, Rebecca.
Dreger, Ralph M., jt. ed. see Miller, Kent S.

Dreher, E., ed. see Schweizerische Gesellschaft fuer Gynaekologie Staff.
Dreher, Emil. Chemistry of Synthetic Substances.
Dreier, et al. Three Lectures on Modern Art.
Dreier, Ted. Take Your Life Off Hold.
Dreifuss, Kurt. Other Side of the Universe.
Dreiser, Theodore. Selected Poems from Moods. Saalbach, Robert Palmer, ed.
Dreisewerd, Edna. The Catcher Was a Lady: The Clem Dreisewerd Story.
Dreishpoon, Douglas, jt. auth. see Kline, Katy.
Dreman, David N. Psychology & the Stock Market.
Drennan, James C. Legal Aspects of Chemical Testing for Intoxication.
Drennan, James C., jt. auth. see University of North Carolina at Chapel Hill Institute of Government.
Drennan, Robert E., ed. The Alquonquin Wits.
Drenth, P. J., jt. auth. see Cronbach, L. J.
Drenth, Wiendelt & Kwart, Harold. Kinetics Applied to Organic Reactions.
Drerup, Engelbert. Demosthenes Im Urteile Des Altertums.
Drescher, Henrik. Look-alikes.
--Looking for Santa Claus.
--The Strange Appearance of Howard Cranebill Jr.
Drescher, Joan. The Marvelous Mess.
Drescher, John, jt. auth. see Drescher, Sandra.
Drescher, John M. Seven Things Children Need.
--When Opposites Attract.
--You Can Know It's True Love.
--You Can Plan a Good Marriage.
Drescher, Sandra & Drescher, John. When You Think You're in Love.
Dresher, Melvin, et al, eds. Advances in Game Theory.
Dresner, Joanne, ed. see Martin, Andy & Greene, Joseph.
Dresser, Louisa. Background of Colonial American Portraiture.
Dresser, Peter, ed. New Research Centers.
Dresser, Peter D., ed. Research Center Directory.
Dreusedow, Jean R. see Burn, Barbara.
Dreves, G. M., ed. see Von Lilienfeld, Christian.
Drew, C. J. & Hardman, M. L. Designing & Conducting Behavioral Research.
Drew, Elizabeth A. Novel.
--Poetry: A Modern Guide.
Drew, Katherine F., et al. Studies in History.
Drew, Rodney. Microcomputers for Financial Planning.
Drew, Walter F., et al. Motivating Today's Students.
Drewal, Henry J. African Artistry: Technique & Aesthetics in Yoruba Sculpture. Morris, Kelly, ed.
Drew Connor, Melody, et al. Dynamics of Utilization Management.
Drewery, Benjamin, jt. ed. see Cunliffe-Jones, Hubert.
Drewes, C. F. Introduction to the Books of the Bible.
Drewett. The Nature of Surrey.
--The South East to AD 1000: A Regional History of England.
Drewry, Gavin. The Civil Service Today.
Drews, J., ed. see Symposium, Vienna, Sept. 4-6, 1974.
Drexler, David A. & Sparks, A. Gilchrist, III. The Delaware Corporation: Legal Aspects of Organization & Operation.
Drexler, Eric. Engines of Creation.
Dreyer, Philip H., jt. ed. see Havighurst, Robert J.
Dreyfus, B., jt. auth. see Dreyfus, J. C.
Dreyfus, Bertrand, ed. International Codata Conference, 6th Biennial, Santa Flavia, Italy, 1978: Proceedings.
Dreyfus, J. C. & Dreyfus, B. Hematopoietic Agents.
Dreyfus, M. Bertrand, ed. International Codata Conference on Generation, Compilation, Evaluation & Dissemination of Data for Science & Technology, 4th: Proceedings.
Dreyfus, S., jt. auth. see Bellman, Richard E.
Dreyfuss, Barbara, ed. Prospective Payments: Health Care Revolution.
Dreyfuss, Henry, ed. Symbol Sourcebook: An Authoritative Guide to International Graphic Symbols.
Dreyfuss, Joel & Lawrence, Charles, III. The Bakke Case: The Politics of Inequality.
--The Bakke Case: The Politics of Inequality.
Drez, David, Jr., ed. Knee Braces: Seminar Report.
Drickamer, H. G. Electronic Transitions & the High Pressure Chemistry & Physics of Solids.
Drickamer, Lee C. & Vessey, Stephen H. Animal Behavior: Concepts, Processes, & Methods.
Driessche, P. Van Den see Victoria Conference on Mathematical Problems in Biology Staff.
Drillien & Drummond. Neurodevelopmental Problems in Early Childhood: Assessment & Management.
Drinka, George F. The Birth of Neurosis: Myth, Malady & the Victorians.
--The Birth of Neurosis: Myth, Malady & the Victorians.
Drinker, Henry S. Legal Ethics.
Drinker, Henry S., tr. see Schubert, Franz.
Drinker, Sophie, jt. auth. see Leonard, Eugenie A.
Drinnon, Doris J. Seedlin' Poems of Poet Tree.
Driscoll, Edward J & Musil, Thomas A. Minnesota Supplement for Modern Real Estate Practice.
Driscoll, Frederick F. Microprocessor-Microcomputer Technology.
Driskell, Jeanette. A Guide to Tutoring.
Driskill, Frank. Davy Crockett: The Untold Story.
--Free the North Wind.
Drisko, R. L., jt. ed. see Cowan, D. O.
Driss Ben Hames Charhadi, see Layachi, Larbi, pseud.
Driver, C. J. Patrick Duncan.
Driver, Edwin D. Differential Fertility in Central India.
Driver, Edwin D., ed. see Dubois, W. E. B.
Driver, Harold E. & Driver, Wilhelmine. Ethnography & Acculturation of the Chichimeca-Jonaz of Northeast Mexico.
Driver, R. Ordinary & Delay Differential Equations.
Driver, S. R. Notes on the Hebrew Text of Samuel.
Driver, Tom F. Patterns of Grace: Human Experience As Word of God.
Driver, Walter E. Plastics Chemistry & Technology.
Driver, Wilhelmine, jt. auth. see Driver, Harold E.
Drizari, Nelo. Albanian-English, English-Albanian Dictionary.
Drizd, Terence. Blood Pressure Levels in Persons 18-74 Years of Age in 1974-80 & the Trends in Blood Pressure from 1960-1980 in the United States.
Droge, Dennis & Glander-Bandyk. Woman's Day Book of Calligraphy.
Droge, Dennis, jt. auth. see Bandyk-Glander, Janice.
Drogheda, Lord, et al. The Covent Garden Album: Two Hundred Fifty Years of Theatre, Opera & Ballet.
Drogin, Marc. Biblioclasm.
--Yours Truly, King Arthur: How Medieval People Wrote... & How You Can, Too.
Drongowski, Paul J. A Graphical Engineering Aid for VLSI Systems. Stone, Harold, ed.
Droop, M. & Wood, F., eds. Advances in Microbiology of the Sea.
Drooyan, Irving & Wooton, William. Elementary Algebra for College Students.
Drop, Mark & Spiegel, Steven. Hamper & Trivet Catalog.
Dropkin, Ruth, ed. The Teacher As Learner: Highlights of Work at the Center & Summer Institutes.
--Teachers with Children: Curriculum in Open Classrooms.
Drosnin, Michael. Citizen Hughes.
--Citizen Hughes: In His Own Words-How Howard Hughes Tried to Buy America.
Drossman, Melvyn, jt. auth. see Belove, Charles.
Drost-Hansen, W., ed. Cell-Associated Water.
Droz, Jacques. Europe Between Revolutions, 1815-1848.
Drozdov, V. & Korkeshkin, A. The Soviet Soldier.
Drozdova, T. V., jt. auth. see Manskaya, S. M.
Dr. Seuss. If I Ran the Zoo.
--Thidwick, the Big-Hearted Moose.
Drucker, Malka & Foster, George. The George Foster Story.
Drucker, Malka & James, Elizabeth. Series TV: How a Show Is Made.
Drucker, Peter. The Zen Expressionists: Paintings of the Japanese Counterculture 1600-1800.
Drucker, S., jt. auth. see Georgia Technical Research Institute Staff.
Drucker, Trudy, ed. see Lillo, George.
Drucker-Brown, Susan, ed. see Malinowski, Bronislaw.
Drucker- Colin, R. R. & McGaugh, J. L. Neurobiology of Sleep & Memory.
Druckman, Daniel & Swets, Johns A., eds. Enhancing Human Performance: Issues, Theories, & Techniques.
Drudy, P. J., ed. Anglo-Irish Studies, No. 3.
Druks, Herbert. The U. S. & Israel.
Drum, Priscilla A., jt. ed. see Calfee, Robert C.
Drumm, D. B. To Kill a Shadow.
Drummond, jt. auth. see Drillien.
Drummond, Ann E., jt. auth. see Clifford, Margaret A.
Drummond, Hugh. Dr. Drummond's Spirited Guide to Health Care in a Dying Empire.
Drummond, Lewis A. & Baxter, Paul R. How to Respond to a Skeptic.
Drumwright, Huber L. & Vaughan, Curtis, eds. New Testament Studies: Essays in Honor of Ray Summers in His Sixty-Fifth Year.
Drury. Management & Cost Accounting.
--Management & Cost Accounting: Student Manual.
--Management & Cost Accounting: Teacher's Manual.
Drury, Allen. Advise & Consent.
--The Roads of Earth.
--The Throne of Saturn.
Drury, G. H. Perspectives on Geomorphic Processes.
Drury, John. Old Chicago Houses.
--Old Illinois Houses.
--Tradition & Design in Luke's Gospel.
Drury, John, tr. see Cussianovich, Alejandro.
Drury, John, tr. see Segundo, Juan L.
Drury, Michael, jt. ed. see Hull, Helen R.
Drury, Nevill. Don Juan, Mescalito & Modern Magic: The Mythology of Inner Space.
--The Shaman & the Magician.
--The Shaman & the Magician: Journeys Between the Worlds.
Drury, Robert F., jt. auth. see Duren, Ryne.
Drust, Joseph. You're Next.
Druten, John Van see Van Druten, John.
Drutman, Irving, ed. see Flanner, Janet.
Druxman, Michael B. Merv.
Drvodelic, M. Croatian Serbian-English Dictionary.
--English Serbian Croation Dictionary.
Dryakhlov, N. Scientific & Technological Revolution: Its Role in Today's World.
Dryden, John. Complete Poetical Works. Noyes, George R., ed.
Dryden, Windy. Rational-Emotive Therapy: Fundamentals & Innovations.
Dryfoos, Susan W. Iphigene: My Life & The New York Times, the Memoirs of Iphigene Ochs Sulzberger.
Drygas, H. Coordinate-Free Approach to Gauss-Markov Estimation.
Dryhurst, G. Periodate Oxidation of Diol & Other Functional Groups.
Dryhurst, G., jt. auth. see Frey, A. J.
Drysdale, Ann. Faint Heart Never Kissed a Pig.
--Pearls Before Swine.
Drysdale, James, jt. ed. see Catsimpoolas, Nicholas.
Drysdale, Peter & Shibata, Hirofumi, eds. Federalism & Resource Development: The Australian Case.
Drysdale, Rosemary. The Art of Blackwork Embroidery.
Drysdall, A. R., et al, eds. Felsic Plutonic Rocks & Associated Mineralization of the Kingdom of Saudi Arabia.
Dryuk, V. G. The Mechanism of Epoxidation of Olefins by Pelacids.
Drzewiecki, T. M. & Franke, M. E., eds. Twentieth Anniversary of Fluidics Symposium.
Drzewiecki, T. M., jt. ed. see Franke, M. E.
Duane, Diane. The Door into Fire.
--The Wounded Sky.
Dub, M., ed. see Bauer, K. & Haller, G.
Dubach, U. C. & Schmidt, U., eds. Diagnostic Significance of Enzymes & Proteins in Urine.
Dubacher, H., ed. see Ladewig, D. & Hobi, V.
Dubal, David. Reflections from the Keyboard: The World of the Concert Pianist.
DuBar, Jules R., jt. ed. see Oaks, Robert Q., Jr.
Dubard, Etoile. Teaching Aphasics & Other Language Deficient Children: Theory & Application of the Association Method.
Dubarle. Scientific Humanism & Christian Thought.
DuBarry, Michele. Into Passion's Dawn.
--Toward Love's Horizon: The Loves of Angela Carlyle.
DuBay, Sandra. Fidelity's Flight.
--Fidelity's Flight.
--Mistress of the Sun King.
Dubay, Thomas. Philosophy of the State As Educator.
Dube, Anthony, et al. Structure & Meaning: An Introduction to Literature.
Dube, Pierre H. & Davidson, Hugh M. A Concordance to Pascal's "Les Provinciales"
Dube, S. C. Development Perspectives for the 1980s.
Du Bellay, Joachim. Poemes Choisis.
--Poesies.
Duberman, Lucile, et al. Gender & Sex in Society.
Duberman, Martin, ed. Antislavery Vanguard: New Essays on the Abolitionists.
Dubey, Leon B., Jr. No Need to Count.
Dubin, Fred S. & Long, Chalmers G., Jr. Energy Conservation Standards: For Building Design, Construction & Operation.
Dubin, Robert. Handbook of Work, Organization & Society.
Dubinskaya, L. Moscow-Leningrad-Kiev: A Guide.
Dubner, Ronald, et al, eds. The Neural Basis of Oral & Facial Function.
Dubnick, M. J. & Bardes, B A. Thinking about Public Policy: A Problem Solving Approach.
Dubnow, Simon. Nationalism & History: Essays on Old & New Judaism. Pinson, Koppel S., ed.
Dubofsky, Melvyn. We Shall Be All: A History of the Industrial Workers of the World.
Dubois, Edward N. Essential Methods in Business Statistics.
Dubois, J. Dictionnaire du Francais Contemporain.
DuBois, J. Harry. Plastics History, U. S. A.
DuBois, J. Harry & Pribble, Wayne I., eds. Plastics Mold Engineering Handbook.
Dubois, Rochelle. Second Skin.
Du Bois, W. E. B. The Education of Black People: Ten Critiques, 1906-1960. Aptheker, Herbert, ed.
Dubois, W. E. B. W. E. B. Dubois on Sociology & the Black Community. Green, Dan S. & Driver, Edwin D., eds.
Dubois, W. E. B., ed. Atlanta University Publications.
Dubos, Rene. Beast or Angel? Choices That Make Us Human.
--Celebrations of Life.
--Celebrations of Life.
--The Resilience of Ecosystems.
Dubos, Rene & Escande, Jean-Paul. Quest: Reflections on Medicine, Science & Mankind.
Dubovik, A. S. Photographic Recording of High-Speed Processes.
Dubovsky, E. V., et al. Nuclear Medicine Technology Continuing Education Review.
Dubowski, Cathy E. Escape to Third Earth: A Thundercats Adventure.
Dubpernell, George. Electrodeposition of Chromium from Chromic Acid Solutions.
DuBrey, Rita J. Promoting Wellness in Nursing Practice: A Step-by-Step Approach in Patient Education.
DuBrin. Contemporary Applied Management.
Dubrin, Andrew J. Personnel.
--The Practice of Managerial Psychology.
--The Practice of Supervision: Achieving Results Through People.
Dubrovin, M. I. A Book of Russian Idioms Illustrated.
Dubrovsky, V. B. Construction of Nuclear Power Plants.
Dubsky, Dora. Sing & Dance.
Dubsky, Marie. Tom Pilgrims Progress.
Dubus, Elizabeth N. Marguerite Tanner.
--To Love & to Dream.
Duby, Georges. Rural Economy & Country Life in the Medieval West. Postan, Cynthia, tr.
Ducan, S. Blackwell. The Home Insulation Bible.
Ducanis, Alex J., jt. auth. see Golin, Anne K.
Du Cann, Charlotte. Vogue Modern Style: How to Achieve It.
Ducasse, C. J. Nature, Mind & Death.
Ducasse, Isidore, jt. auth. see De Lautreamont, Comte.
Ducat, Craig R. Modes of Constitutional Interpretation.
Ducat, Craig R., ed. see Corwin, Edward S.
Du Chaillu, Paul. Land of the Long Night.
--Lost in the Jungle.
Duchaine, Fawn, jt. ed. see Stokes, Lynette.
Duchan, Judith F., jt. auth. see Lund, Nancy J.
Ducharme, Gertrude Libby. Odes of Feeling.
Duchein, Michel. Archive Buildings & Equipment.
Duchene, Francois, et al. The Crisis of International Cooperation.
Duchesneau, David, jt. auth. see Pacer Business Automation Staff.
Duchess of Devonshire. The House: Living at Chatsworth.
Duchossior, Andre. Fender Stratocaster.
Du Choul, Guillaume. Discours de la Religion des Anciens Romains Illustre.
Duck. Teaching with Charisma.
Duck, S. & Gilmour, R., eds. Personal Relationships, Vol. 2: Developing Personal Relationships.
Ducker, Richard D., et al. Dedicating & Reserving Land to Provide Access to North Carolina Beaches.
Duckert, Audrey, jt. ed. see Roseler, Robert.
Duckert, Mary. Help: I Run a Sunday School.
--Open Education Goes to Church.
--Tailor-Made Teaching in the Church School.
Duckett, Eleanor. Wandering Saints of the Early Middle Ages.
Duckett, J. G. & Racey, P. A., eds. The Biology of the Male Gamete: Linnean Society Supplement No. 1 to the Biological Journal.
Duckworth, Eleanor, tr. see Piaget, Jean.
Duckworth, Marion. When Your Child Becomes Your Friend.
Duckworth, Walter E. & Hoyle, G. Electro-Slag Refining.
Duckworth, Walter E., et al. A Guide to Operational Research.
Duckworth, William. A Creative Approach to Music Fundamentals.
Ducornet, Rikki. The Stain.
Ducote, Darryl, jt. auth. see McKenna, Megan.
Ducourneau, ed. see De Balzac, Honore.
Du Crane, Peter. High Speed Small Craft.
Duda, Deborah. Coming Home: A Guide to Home Care for the Terminally Ill.
Duda, E., jt. auth. see Whyburn, G.
Duddington, Alexander. The Enemy Within-Without.
Duddington, Natalie, tr. see Pushkin, Alexander.
Dudek, Lee. Professional Broadcast Announcing.
Dudin, M. Nightingales.
Dudley. An Aid to Clinical Surgery.
--Emergency Surgery.
Dudley, Barbara H. Where Is God? Three Church Dramas.

Dudley, Carl S. Where Have All Our People Gone? New Choices for Old Churches.
Dudley, Cliff, jt. auth. see Baker, Tammy.
Dudley, Cliff, jt. auth. see Tari, Mel.
Dudley, Elwood. This Trivial Harp.
Dudley, Ernest. For Love of a Wild Thing.
Dudley, L. Architectural Illustration.
Dudley, R. M. Lectures in Modern Analysis & Applications. Taam, C. T., ed.
Dudley, Roger L. & Cummings, Des, Jr. Adventures in Church Growth. Wheeler, Gerald, ed.
Dudman, Helga, jt. auth. see Dayan, Ruth.
Dudovitz, R. L., ed. Women in Academe.
Due, Jean M. Costs, Returns & Repayment Experience of Ujamaa Villages in Tanzania, 1973-1976.
Due, John F. The Role & Structure of Customs Duties, Exercises, & Sales Taxes.
Duedall, Iver W. Wastes in the Ocean, Vol. 4: Energy Wastes in the Ocean. Ketchum, Bostwick H., et al, eds.
Dueker, Marilynn, jt. auth. see Spirer, Herbert F.
Duell, Donna, jt. auth. see Smith, Sandra F.
Duelli-Klein, R., ed. So Far, So Good, So What? Women's Studies in the U. K.
Duellman, William E. On the Classification of Frogs.
Duelo, Gerardo. Diccionario de Grupos, Fuerzas, y Partidos Politicos Espanoles.
Duenewald, Doris, ed. see Hoch, Edward D.
Duenewald, Doris, ed. see Mumford, Thad & Muntean, Michaela.
Duensing, Edward. Plant Closing Legislation in the United States: A Bibliogrphy.
Duer, Clara E. Pittsburgh Gazette Abstracts, 1797-1803.
Duerr, Hans-Peter, jt. auth. see Breitenlohner, Peter.
Duesberg, Peter, et al. Rous Sarcoma: Current Research I.
Dueuzeide, H., jt. auth. see Becker, H. A.
Dufay, Jean. Galactic Nebulae & Interstellar Matter.
Duff, Annis, jt. auth. see Adshead, Gladys L.
Duff, C. Introducing the Macintosh.
Duff, David. Victoria & Albert.
Duff, David, ed. Queen Victoria's Highland Journals.
Duff, Gerald. William Cobbett & the Politics of Earth.
Duff, J. D., tr. see Rostovtsev, Mikhail.
Duff, Karl J. Martial Arts & the Law. Lee, Mike, ed.
Duff, Maggie. Dancing Turtle.
Duff, Margaret, tr. see Simenon, Georges.
Duff, Susan. Miss Universe Beauty Book.
Duff, William G. Mobile Communications.
Duff, William G., jt. auth. see White, Donald R.
Duffala, Sharon L. Rocky Mountain Cache: Western Wild Game Cookbook.
Duffy, Christopher. The Military Experience in the Age of Reason.
--Russia's Military Way to the West: Origins & Nature of Russian Military Power 1700-1800.
--Siege Warfare: The Fortress in the Early Modern World, 1494-1660.
Duffy, Clinton T. San Quentin Story, As Told to Dean Jennings.
Duffy, Dave, jt. auth. see Lamb, Tony.
Duffy, George H., ed. see Duffy, Nicholas.
Duffy, Gloria, ed. Intermediate-Range Nuclear Forces in Europe: Issue & Approaches.
Duffy, Gloria C. & Scheck, Jennifer. The Soviet Approach to National Security.
Duffy, J. I., ed. Electroless & Other Nonelectrolytic Plating Techniques: Recent Developments.
Duffy, James J. Color Historic Atlanta. Mueller, Phyllis, ed.
--Color Historic Florida.
--Color Historic Georgia. Mueller, Phyllis, ed.
Duffy, John. Epidemics in Colonial America.
--Under the Goldwood Tree.
--Vermont: An Illustrated History.
Duffy, Joseph. Power: Prime Mover of Technology.
Duffy, Karen G., ed. Personal Growth & Behavior 1988-89.
Duffy, Maureen. The Erotic World of Faery.
Duffy, Nicholas. Poems from the Eighteen-Thirties by a Poor Son of Ireland. Duffy, George H., ed.
Duffy, Regis A. A Roman Catholic Theology of Pastoral Care.
Duffy, Reid. Indianapolis Dining.
Duffy, Robert E. Art Law: Representing Artists, Dealers & Collectors.
Dufresne, Francine. Cooking Fish & Wild Game.
DuFresne, Jim. Alaska: A Travel Survival Kit.
--Tramping in New Zealand.
Dugan, LeRoy. The Uncomplicated Christian.
Dugan, Patrick. Biochemical Ecology of Water Pollution.
Dugan, Patrick R. Biochemical Ecology of Water Pollution.
Dugard, John. Human Rights & the South African Legal Order.
Dugdale, D. S. Elements of Elasticity.
Duggal, K. S. Sikhgurus: Their Lives & Teachings.
Duggan, Joseph B. & Duggan, Sandra. Edgar Cayce's Massage, Hydrotherapy & Oils.
Duggan, Sandra, jt. auth. see Duggan, Joseph B.
Duggan, William. Lovers of the African Night.
Duggar, Gordon E. Jehovah's Witness: Not Just Another Denomination.
Dugger, Ronnie. On Reagan: The Man & His Presidency.
--Our Invaded Universities: Form, Reform & New Starts.
Dugger, William E., Jr., jt. auth. see Gerrish, Howard H.
Duhe, Camille, jt. auth. see Von Furstenberg, Egon.
Duhem, Pierre. Aim & Structure of Physical Theory.
--Medieval Cosmology: Theories of Infinity, Place, Time, Void, & the Plurality of Worlds. Ariew, Roger, ed.
Duignan, Peter, jt. ed. see Dorfman, Gerald.
Duignan, Peter, ed. see University of the State of New York, Foreign Area Materials Center Staff.
Dukas, Peter. Planning Profits in the Food & Lodging Industry.
Duke, C. B. Tunneling in Solids.
Duke, Cecil Edward. How to Be Young at Sixty: The Fountain of Youth.
Duke, Chris, ed. Combatting Poverty Through Adult Education: National Development Strategies.
Duke, Chris, ed. see Smith, Barry, et al.
Duke, Daniel L. Decision Making in an Era of Fiscal Instability.
Duke, David N. The Biblical View of Reality: The Bible & Christian Ethics.
Duke, Donald. Pacific Electric Railway.
Duke, James T. Issues in Sociological Theory: Another Look at the "Old Masters"
Duke, Judith S. Religious Publishing & Communications.
Duke, Judith S., ed. Knowledge Industry Two Hundred: America's Two Hundred Largest Media Companies.
Duke, Madelaine. The Bormann Receipt.
Duke, Mathilde W. God Is in Control.
Duke, Maurice. James Branch Cabell: A Reference Guide.
Duke, Neville & Lanchberry, Edward. Sound Barrier.
Dukelow, W. Richard, et al. Laparoscopic Techniques in Studies of Reproductive Physiology.
Duker, Sam. Individualized Reading.
Dukes, H. N. The Bible: Fact, Fiction, Fantasy, Faith.
Dukore, Bernard F. Harold Pinter.
Dukore, Bernard F., ed. American Dramatists Nineteen Eighteen to Nineteen Forty.
--American Dramatists 1918-1945.
--Documents for Drama & Revolution.
Dulakis, Carrie C. Freedom Plays the Flute: A Selection from the Folk Poetry of Modern Greece.
Duller, H. J. Development Technology.
Dulles, Avery. History of Apologetics.
Dulles, Foster R. China & America: The Story of Their Relations Since 1784.
Dulmatovskaya, G. & Shilova, I. Who's Who in Soviet Cinema.
Dulong, Marthe, jt. auth. see Moore, Philip S.
Dumain, Harold J. A Synthesis of Philosophy.
Duman, Daniel. The English & Colonial Bars in the Nineteenth Century.
Dumas, Alexandre. Journal of Madame Giovanni. Wilbur, M. E., tr.
--La Reine Margot.
Dumas, Andre. Political Theology & the Life of the Church. Bowden, John, tr.
Dumas, Charles E. The Effects of Government Deficits: A Comparative Analysis of Crowding Out.
Dumas, Philippe. Laura, Alice's New Puppy.
Dumas, T. & Bulani, W. Oxidation of Petrochemicals: Chemistry & Technology.
Du Maurier, Daphne. Flight of the Falcon.
--Frenchman's Creek.
--The House on the Strand.
--Kiss Me Again, Stranger.
--Kiss Me Again, Stranger.
--The Loving Spirit.
--Rule Britannia.
Du Maurier, Daphne, jt. auth. see Quiller-Couch, Arthur.
Du Maurier, Daphne, ed. see Du Maurier, George L.
Du Maurier, George L. Young George Du Maurier: A Selection of His Letters, 1860-67. Du Maurier, Daphne, ed.
Dumbach, Annette E., jt. auth. see Newborn, Jud.
Dumbrajs, T. Y., tr. see Barbashov, B. M. & Nesterenko, V. V.
Dumbrell, W. J. Covenant & Creation: A Theology of Old Testament Covenants.
Dumezil, Georges. The Destiny of the Warrior. Hiltebeitel, Alf, tr.
Dummer, G. W. Modern Electrical Components.
Dummer, G. W. & Wells, Malvern, eds. Semiconductor & Microprocessor Technology 1980: Selected Papers Presented at the Annual SEMINEX Technical Seminar & Exhibition, London, U. K.
Dummer, G. W. A., ed. Semiconductor & Microprocessor Technology 1981: Selected Papers Presented at the 1981 Annual Seminex Technical Seminar & Exhibition, London, U. K.
Dummer, G. W. A., ed. see SEMINEX Staff.
Dummer, Geoffrey W. Electronic Reliability Electronics. Griffin, N. B., ed.
--Semiconductor Technology 1975.
--Semiconductor Technology 1977.
--Semiconductor Technology 1978.
Dummer, Geoffrey W. & Winton, R. C. An Elementary Guide to Reliability.
Dummer, Geoffrey W., ed. Semiconductor Technology 1976.
Dummer, Geoffrey W. & Robertson, J. M., eds. Electronic Connection Techniques & Equipment, 1968-69.
--Fluidic Components & Equipment, 1968-69.
Dummer, Geoffrey W., et al, eds. Banking Automation, 1970-71.
Dummer, Tom. Tibetan Medicine & Other Holistic Health-Care Systems.
Dummett, Michael. Frege Philosophy of Language.
Dummett, Nanci L. Self-Paced Business Mathematics.
Dumond, Dwight L. Antislavery: The Crusade for Freedom in America.
Dumond, Dwight L., ed. Southern Editorials on Secession.
Dumond, Michael. Coping with Life after High School.
--Coping with the Dating Game.
Dumont, J. & Nunez, J., eds. Hormones & Cell Regulation.
Dumont, Jacques E., jt. ed. see Swillens, Stephane.
Dumont, Jean-Paul. The Headman & I: Ambiguity & Ambivalence in the Fieldworking Experience.
Du Mont, Paul F., jt. auth. see Du Mont, Rosemary R.
Du Mont, Rosemary R. & Du Mont, Paul F. Assessing the Effectiveness of Library Service.
Dunaev, M. Novgorod: A Guide.
Dunas, Jeff. Mademoiselle, Mademoiselle.
--Mademoiselle, Mademoiselle!
Dunas, Jeff, photos by. Captured Women.
Dunaway, D. How Can I Keep from Singing: Pete Seeger.
Dunaway, David K. How Can I Keep from Singing: Pete Seeger.
--How Can I Keep from Singing: Pete Seeger.
Dunaway, Diane. Desire & Conquer.
Dunaway, Kate A., jt. auth. see Knopf, Howard.
Dunayavskaya, Raya. Rosa Luxemburg, Women's Liberation & Marx's Philosophy of Revolution.
Dunayevskaya, R. Women's Liberation & the Dialectics of Revolution Reaching for the Future: A 35-Year Collection of Essays - Historic, Philosophic, Global.
Dunbar, Clement. A Bibliography of Shelley Studies: 1823-1950.
Dunbar, George. India & the Passing of Empire.
Dunbar, Ida. Let There Be Light.
Dunbar, Nancy J., compiled by. Images of Sport in Early Canada: Les images du sport dans le Canada d'autrefois.
Dunbar, Paul L. Folks from Dixie.
Dunbar, Robert E. A Doctor Discusses a Man's Sexual Health.
--A Doctor Discusses Learning to Cope with Arthritis Rheumatism & Gout.
Dunbar-Nelson, Alice. Give Us Each Day: The Diary of Alice Dunbar-Nelson. Hull, Gloria T., ed.
Duncan, A. B. Rydberg Series in Atoms & Molecules.
Duncan, Alastair. Art Deco Furniture: The French Designers.
Duncan, Barbara & Woods, Diane, eds. Social Security Disability Programs: An International Perspective.
Duncan, David. Pedaling the Ends of the Earth.
Duncan, David D. Magic Worlds of Fantasy.
--The Silent Studio.
--Sunflowers for Van Gogh.
--The World of Allah.
Duncan, David D. & Forss, George. New York-New York: Masterworks of a Street Peddler.
Duncan, Delbert J., et al. Modern Retailing Management.
Duncan, Denis. Victorious Living: A Thought & a Prayer a Day at a Time.
Duncan, Denis, ed. see Barclay, William.
Duncan, Doris G. & Aviel, S. David. Computers & Remote Computing Services.
Duncan, Edmondstoune. Story of Minstrelsy.
Duncan, Elmer H. Soren Kierkegaard. Patterson, Bob E., ed.
Duncan, F. Microprocessor Programming & Software Development.
Duncan, Francis, jt. auth. see Hewlett, Richard G.
Duncan, George. Every Day with Jesus.
Duncan, George B. The Person & Work of the Holy Spirit in the Life of the Believer.
Duncan, Gordon W., et al, eds. Female Sterilization: Prognosis for Qualified Outpatient Procedures.
--Fertility Control Methods.
Duncan, Harry. Doors of Perception.
Duncan, Ida R. American Woman's Complete Sewing Book.
Duncan, J. W. Statistical Services in Ten Years' Time.
Duncan, James P., Jr. Your Future in Foreign Service Careers.
Duncan, Jane. Janet Reachfar & Chickabird.
Duncan, John, jt. auth. see Webb, Brian.
Duncan, Joseph E. Revival of Metaphysical Poetry.
Duncan, Juanita. Nothing's Wrong with Me! Penoi, Mary, ed.
Duncan, Judy & McCance, Allison. Clock Watcher's Cookbook.
Duncan, Lois. Hotel for Dogs.
--Terrible Tales of the Happy Days School.
--They Never Came Home.
Duncan, Patricia D. Tallgrass Prairie: The Inland Sea.
Duncan, R. S. A History of the Baptists in Missouri.
Duncan, Ray. Advanced MS-DOS Programming: The Microsoft Guide for Assembly Language & C Programmers.
Duncan, Robert. The Noise: Notes from a Rock 'n' Roll Era.
--Peiping Municipality & the Diplomatic Quarter.
Duncan, Thomas. A Taxonomic Study of the Ranunculus Hispidus: Complex in the Western Hemisphere.
Duncan, W., ed. Prostate Cancer.
Duncan, W. A., jt. ed. see Plaa, Gabriel L.
Duncan, W. Jack. Essentials of Management.
--Organizational Behavior.
--Organizational Behavior.
Duncan, William. Colorectal Cancer.
Duncann, Geraldine. Some Like It Hotter.
Duncker, H. R. The Lung Air Sac System of Birds.
Duncombe, Beverly. Need I Say More.
Duncombe, Sydney, et al. Idaho State & Local Government.
Dunegan, H. L., jt. auth. see Hartman, W. F.
Duner, Anders, ed. Research into Personal Development: Educational & Vocational Choice.
Dunfee, Thomas W. & Bellace, Janice. Business & Its Legal Environment.
Dunford, Martin & Holland, Jack. The Rough Guide to Amsterdam.
--Rough Guide to Amsterdam & Holland.
Dunford, Martin, jt. auth. see Holland, Jack.
Dunford, Michael F. Capital, the State, & Regional Development.
Dunford, Nelson & Schwartz, Jacob T. Linear Operators. Incl. Pt. 1. General Theory; Pt. 2. Spectral Theory, Self Adjoint Operators in Hilbert Space; Pt. 3. Spectral Operators. Wiley.
Dunham, Arthur L. The Industrial Revolution in France, 1815-1848.
Dunham, Katherine. A Touch of Innocence.
Dunham, Randall, jt. auth. see Smith, Frank J.
Dunham, Randall B., jt. auth. see Cummings, L. L.
Dunham, Sam C. The Alaskan Gold Fields.
Duniec, M. L., jt. auth. see Davids, Kenneth.
Dunitz, et al, eds. Structure & Bonding.
Dunitz, J. D., et al, eds. Alkali Metal Complexes with Organic Ligands.
--Coordinative Interactions. Incl. Metal Complexes of Chelating Olefin-Group V Ligands. Williams, R. J., et al.; Structural Radii, Electron-Cloud Radii, Ionic Radii & Solvation. Baughan, E. C; Quantitative Evaluation & Prediction of Donor-Acceptor Interactions. Drago, R. S; Redox Properties: Changes Affected by Coordination. Gutmann, V; Thermodynamics of the Stepwise Formation of Metal-Ion Complexes in Aqueous Solution. Ahrland, S. Springer-Verlag.
--Inorganic Chemistry.
--Novel Aspects.
Dunkels, Marjorie. Training Your Donkey.
Dunkerley, Joy. Trends in Energy Use in Industrial Societies: An Overview.
Dunkerly, W. A. see Oxenham, John.
Dunkl, C. F. & Ramirez, D. E. Representations of Communicative Semitopological Semigroups.
Dunkling, Leslie A. The Guinness Book of Names.
Dunlap, A. Basic Cases in Public International Law.
--Readings on National & Regional Foreign Policies.
Dunlap, W. Crawford, ed. see International Conference on Hot Electrons in Semiconductors Staff.
Dunlap, William. A History of the Rise & Progress of the Arts of Design in the U. S. Weiss, Rita, ed.
Dunlop, Burton, jt. auth. see Durman, E. C.

Dunlop, Eileen. The Maze Stone.
Dunlop, Ian. The Cathedrals' Crusade.
--Palaces & Progresses of Elizabeth First.
--Royal Palaces of France.
Dunlop, J. & Smith, D. G. Telecommunications Engineering.
Dunlop, Janice. Charles & Diana.
Dunlop, John T. The Secular Outlook: Wages & Prices.
Dunlop, Neil. Rapidfile Simplified.
Dunmore, Charlotte, compiled by. Poverty, Participating, Protest, & Black Americans: A Selected Bibliography for Use in Social Work Education.
Dunn, A. & Knight, M. Export Finance.
Dunn, C. D., ed. Current Concepts in Erythropoiesis.
Dunn, Charles W. Highland Settler: A Portrait of the Scottish Gael in Nova Scotia.
Dunn, Charles W. & Byrnes, Edward T. Middle English Literature.
Dunn, Charles W., ed. Chaucer Reader: Selections from the Canterbury Tales.
Dunn, Donald H. The Making of 'No, No, Nanette'
Dunn, Edgar S., Jr. Recent Southern Economic Development as Revealed by the Changing Structure of Employment.
Dunn, Edith B. The Lady from Long Boat Key.
Dunn, G., jt. auth. see Everitt, B. S.
Dunn, J. C. The War the Infantry Knew, 1914-1919: A Chronicle of Service in France & Belgium.
Dunn, James T., jt. ed. see Poatgieter, A. Hermina.
Dunn, Jean. Astronomy for the Younger Set.
Dunn, Jean, ed. Seeds of Consciousness: The Wisdom of Sri Nisargadatta Maharaj.
Dunn, Joyce E. Riding on a School Bus.
Dunn, Katherine. Truck.
Dunn, Leslie C. Heredity & Evolution in Human Populations.
--Heredity & Evolution in Human Populations.
Dunn, Martha D. Fundamentals of Nutrition.
Dunn, Michael. Walking Through the Lake District.
Dunn, Michael, III. Easy Going: Vilas & Oneida Counties.
Dunn, Nell. Different Drummers.
Dunn, Paul H. The Osmonds: The Official Story of the Osmond Family.
Dunn, Philip. A Practical Guide to Press Photography.
Dunn, Richard J., ed. see Bronte, Charlotte.
Dunn, Richard S. Puritans & Yankees: The Winthrop Dynasty of New England, 1630-1717.
Dunn, S. Watson & Barban, Arnold M. Advertising: Its Role in Modern Marketing.
Dunn, Seamus & Morgan, Valerie. The Apple IIe Personal Computer for Beginners.
--BBC Microcomputer for Beginners.
Dunn, Si. The Challenge of One Hundred-Sixty (160) Force, Richard C., ed.
Dunn, Si, ed. see Daniel, Timothy M.
Dunn, Stephen P., ed. see Klibanov, A. I.
Dunn, W. E. The Sex Tax: A Political Fantasy.
Dunnahoo, Terry. Before the Supreme Court: The Story of Belva Ann Lockwood.
Dunne, Agnes C., jt. auth. see Le Gros, F.
Dunne, Dominick. The Two Mrs. Grenvilles.
--The Winners: Part II of Joyce Haber's the Users.
Dunne, John. The House of Wisdom.
--How God Created.
Dunne, John G. Dutch Shea, Jr.
Dunne, John S. The City of the Gods: A Study in Myth & Mortality.
Dunne, Mary C. Hoby & Stub.
Dunne, P. M. Engineering Drawing for Advanced Students.
Dunne, Patrick M., ed. see Theory Conference Staff.
Dunne, Pete & Sutton, Clay. Hawks in Flight: A Guide to the Identification of Migrant Raptors.
Dunne, Philip. Take Two: A Life in Movies & Politics.
Dunne, Thomas A. Do This in Memory of Me.
Dunner, Joseph. Baruch Spinoza & Western Democracy.
Dunnett, Peter J. The Decline of the British Motor Industry: The Effects of Government Policy, 1945-1979.
Dunnette, Marvin D. Handbook of Industrial & Organizational Psychology.
Dunnigan, Brian L. Fort Holmes. Armour, David A., ed.
Dunnigan, James F. How to Make War: A Comprehensive Guide to Modern Warfare.
Dunnigan, James F. & Bay, Austin. A Quick & Dirty Guide to War: Briefings on Present & Potential Wars.
Dunnigan, James F. & Martel, William. How to Stop a War: Lessons of Two Hundred Years of War & Peace.
Dunnill, Mary. Siamese Cats.
Dunning, A. Count Unico Wilhelm van Wassenaer 1692-1766: A Master Unmasked or The Pergolesi-Ricciotti Puzzle Solved.
Dunning, Dorothy C. General Biology Laboratory Manual Biology I.
Dunning, Eric, jt. auth. see Williams, John.
Dunning, Glenna. The American Amusement Park: An Annotated Bibiography.
--The Amtrak Railway System: A Periodical Bibliography of an Inter-City Transportation Network.
--National Parks & Forests: The Administration of the National Park Service & Forest Service, 1977-1984.
--The Olympic Games of 1932 & 1984: The Planning & Administration of the Los Angeles Games.
--Planetariums: A Bibliography on Their Architecture, Construction & Development.
Dunning, H. Ray. Fruit of the Spirit.
Dunning, Harrison C. Water Allocation in California: Legal Rights & Reform Needs.
Dunning, John. Arbor House Treasure of True Crime.
Dunning, John H. International Production & the Multinational Enterprise.
--Japanese Participation in British Industry: Trojan Horse or Catalyst for Growth.
Dunning, Lawrence. Keller's Bomb.
--Neutron Two Is Critical.
Dunning, Rachel. Eagle Butte, U. S. A.
Dunning, Stephen. Teaching Literature to Adolescents: Poetry.
Dunning, William A. A History of Political Theories.
Dunn-Meynell, Hugo, jt. auth. see Salmon, Alice W.
Dunphy, D. C. & Dick, B. Organizational Change by Choice.
Dunrea, Olivier. Ravena.
Dunsany. Selections from the Writings of Lord Dunsany.
Dunsany, Lord. Gods, Men, & Ghosts.
--Gods, Men & Ghosts: The Best Supernatural Fiction of Lord Dunsany. Bleiler, E. F., ed.
Dunseath, T. K. Spenser's Allegory of Justice in Book Five of "The Faerie Queene"
Dunsing, R. You & I Have Simply Got to Stop Meeting This Way.
Dunsing, Richard J. You & I Have Simply Got to Stop Meeting This Way.
Dunstan, Bernard. Composing Your Paintings.
--Starting to Paint Portraits.
--Starting to Paint Still Life.
Dunstan, Florene J., tr. see Pena, Carlos G.
Dunstan, Simon. British Army Fighting Vehicles, Nineteen Forty-Five to the Present.
--British Combat Vehicles Today.
--The Modern British Soldier.
--Tank War Vietnam.
Dunstanx, Simon. Scorpion: The CVR(T) Range.
Dunsterville, E., jt. auth. see Dunsterville, G. C.
Dunsterville, G. C. & Dunsterville, E. Orchid Hunting in the Lost World (& Elsewhere in Venezuela)
Dunston, Danny C. Days of My Life.
Dunthorne, Kirstine B. Artists Exhibited in Wales, Nineteen Forty-Five to Nineteen Seventy-Four.
Dunwell, Steve. Extraordinary Boston. Patrick, James, ed.
--Massachusetts: A Scenic Discovery. Patrick, James B., ed.
Duo Publishing Staff. French Farm & Village Holiday Guide.
Duong, Danh R. English Grammar for the Vietnamese.
Dupain, Max & Johnson, Peter. Leslie Wilkinson: A Practical Idealist.
Dupaquier, J., et al, eds. Marriage & Remarriage in Populations of the Past.
Dupayrat, Jaques. Dictionary of Biomedical Acronyms & Abbreviations.
Dupee, F. W., ed. see Cummings, e. e.
Dupin, Amandine A. see Sand, George.
DuPlessis, D. Synopsis of Surgical Anatomy.
DuPlessis, D. J. Principles of Surgery.
Du Plessis, Menan. A State of Fear.
Du Plessix Gray, Francine. October Blood.
Duplissey, Claude, jt. auth. see Khailany, Asad.
DuPont, Diana, et al. San Francisco Museum of Modern Art: The Painting & Sculpture Collection.
Dupont, J. L. Curvature & Characteristic Classes.
Dupont, Paul. Histoire de l'Imprimerie.
Dupont, T., jt. auth. see Douglas, J., Jr.
Dupre, Irma, et al. The Romance of Dundee.
Dupree, A. Hunter. Asa Gray.
Dupree, Nathalie. Cooking of the South. Atcheson, Richard, ed.
Dupuy, Ernest, ed. see Melick, Arden D.
Dupuy, Ernest, ed. see Wilkinson, Stephan.
Dupuy, R. E. & Dupuy, T. N. Brave Men & Great Captains.
--Compact History of Civil War.
Dupuy, Rene J. & Tunkin, Gregory. Comparability of Degrees & Diplomas in International Law: A Study of the Structural & Functional Aspects.
Dupuy, T. N., jt. auth. see Dupuy, R. E.
Durachko, Michael. Poetry from Heaven.
Duran, B. S. & Odell, P. L., eds. Cluster Analysis: A Survey.
Duran, Bonte. The Adventures of Arthur & Edmund: A Tale of Two Seals.
Duran Duran. Duran Duran: Arena.
Duran, Gloria & Duran, Manuel, eds. El Mundo del mas alla.
--Vivir Hoy.
Duran, Manuel, jt. ed. see Duran, Gloria.
Durand, J. N. & Vidler, Anthony. Recueil et Parallele des Edifices de Tout Genre Anciens et Modernes.
Durand, Regis, jt. auth. see Couturier, Maurice.
Durand-Drouhin, J. L. & Szwengrub, L. M., eds. Rural Community Studies in Europe, Vol. II: Trends, Selected & Annotated Bibliographies, Analyses.
Durand-Drouhin, Jean-Louis & Szwengrub, Lili-Marie, eds. Rural Community Studies in Europe: Trends, Selected & Annotated Bibliographies, Analyses.
Duran Duran. Duran Duran. Lammers, Charmain, ed.
Durang, Christopher. Christopher Durang Explains It All for You.
--A History of the American Film.
Durant, Cheryl. Allure.
Durant, David. Ralegh's Lost Colony.
Durant, David, et al. Programmer's Guide to Windows.
Durant, David N. Bess of Hardwick.
Durant, Jack D. Richard Brinsley Sheridan: A Reference Guide.
Durant, Mary. American Heritage Guide to Antiques.
Durant, Will. Story of Philosophy.
Duranti, Francesca. The House on Moon Lake. Sartarelli, Stephen, tr. from Ital.
DuRapau, Gladys W. When You Went Away.
Duras, Marguerite. Destroy, She Said. Bray, Barbara, tr. from Fr.
--Hiroshima, Mon Amour. Seaver, Richard, tr. from Fr.
--India Song. Bray, Barbara, tr. from Fr.
--The Lover.
--The Malady of Death. Bray, Barbara, tr.
--Marin de Gibraltar.
--Outside. Goldhammer, Arthur, tr. from Fr.
--Ravissement de Lol V. Stein.
--Vice-Consul.
Duray, Paul, ed. see Pretest Service Inc.
Duray, Paul H., ed. Pathology: PreTest Self-Assessment & Review.
Durbin, Elizabeth. New Jerusalem: The Labour Party & the Economics of Democratic Socialism.
Durbin, Enoch & McGeer, Patrick L., eds. Methane: Fuel for the Future.
Durbin, Harold. Color Separation Scanner Comparison Charts: 1985 Edition.
--Color Separation Scanner Comparison Charts: 1988 Edition.
--Graphic Imaging Device Comparison Charts: 1987 Edition.
--Interactive Layout System Comparison Charts: 1985 Edition.
--Photo Typesetter Comparison Charts: 1988 Edition.
--Text Processing Computer System Comparison Charts: 1985 Edition.
Durbin, Harold C. Camera Comparison Charts: 1986 Edition.
--Desktop Publishing Systems.
--Phototypesetter Comparison Charts: 1985 Edition.
Durbin, Paula, ed. see Jussawalla, Meheroo.
Durcan, Paul. Ark of the North.
--Jumping the Train Tracks with Angela.
Durckheim, Karlfried G. The Way of Transformation: Daily Life As Spiritual Exercise.
Durckheim, Karlfried von see Von Duerckheim, Karlfried.
Durden, Charles. No Bugles, No Drums.
--No Bugles, No Drums.
Durden, Robert F. The Climax of Populism: The Election of 1896.
Durden-Smith, Jo & DeSimone, Diane. Sex & the Brain.
Durdin, Tillman. Southeast Asia.
Durdin, Tillman, et al. New York Times Report from Red China.
Duren, James W. Trekking Across the Mind.
Duren, Ryne & Drury, Robert F. The Comeback.
Durette-Desset, M. C., ed. CIH Keys to the Nematode Parasites of Vertebrates, No. 10: Keys to Genera of the Superfamily Trichostrongyloidea (with an Index to Taxa for the Whole Series)
Durey, Michael. The Return of the Plague: British Society & the Cholera 1831-32.
Durey, Peter. Staff Management in University & College Libraries. Chandler, C., ed.
Durfee, Walter. Alphabetic As a Science.
D'Urfey, Thomas. Songs of Thomas D'Urfey. Day, Cyrus L., ed.
Durgnat, Raymond. Franju: Movie Edition.
Durham, Jackie, jt. ed. see Joyner, Nelson T., Jr.
Durham, John. Apache Moon.
--Border Guns.
Durham, Marilyn. Dutch Uncle.
--Flambard's Confession.
--The Man Who Loved Cat Dancing.
Durham, Philip & Jones, Everett L. The Western Story: Fact, Fiction & Myth.
Durham, Philip, ed. see Schorer, Mark, et al.
Durham, T. R. Introduction to Benefit-Cost Analysis for Evaluating Public Programs.
During, Ingemar. Aristotle's De Partibus Animalium: Critical & Literary Commentaries.
--Die Harmonienlehre des Klaudios Ptolemaios. Bd. with Porphyrios Kommentar zur Harmonienlehre des Ptolemaios. Garland Pub.
--Ptolemaios und Porphyrios Uber Die Musik.
Durka, Gloria & Smith, Joanmarie. Aesthetic Dimensions of Religious Education.
Durkee Staff. Durkee Spice & Herb Cookbook.
Durkin, Catherine A., et al. So You Want to Plan a Birthday Party.
Durkin, Dolores. Teaching Them to Read.
Durkin, Sr. Mary B. Dorothy L. Sayers.
Durkin, Thomas A., jt. auth. see Polakoff, Murray E.
Durlacher, J. Direct Mail Databook.
Durman, E. C. & Dunlop, Burton. Volunteers in Social Services: Consumer Assessment of Nursing Homes.
Durney, Charles M. Building Free-Form Furniture.
Durniak, John, jt. auth. see Heyman, Ken.
Durning-Lawrence, Edwin. Bacon Is Shake-Speare.
Duroska, Lud, jt. auth. see Schiffer, Don.
Durova, N. Your Turn.
Durphy, Michael, jt. auth. see Sonkin, Daniel J.
Durr, Eleanor. Lakeside Lore: Ohio's Chautauqua Vacationland.
Durr, Frank, jt. auth. see Greene, Orville.
Durr, Karl. The Propositional Logic of Boethius.
Durr, Michael. Networking IBM PCs: A Practical Guide.
Durran, I. M., jt. auth. see Cashell, G. T.
Durrell, Gerald. Golden Bats & Pink Pigeons: A Journey to the Flora & Fauna of a Unique Island.
--How to Shoot an Amateur Naturalist.
--The Stationary Ark.
--The Stationary Ark.
Durrell, Gerald & Durrell, Lee. Durrell in Russia.
Durrell, Lawrence. Sappho: A Play in Verse.
--Sauve Qui Peut.
Durrell, Lee, jt. auth. see Durrell, Gerald.
Durrenmatt, Friedrich. Play Strindberg. Kirkup, James, tr.
--Der Verdacht. Gillis, William, ed.
--The Visit. Bowles, Patrick, tr. from Ger.
Durrer, Gustav T., jt. auth. see Dolder, Eugene J.
Durst, H. Dupont & Gokel, George W. Experimental Organic Chemistry.
Durstewitz, Claire W. Conscience Plays.
Dury, G. H. Environmental Systems.
Dusek-Girdano, Dorothy. Drugs: A Factual Account.
Dusenberry, William H. The Waynesburg College Story, 1849-1974.
Dushkin Publishing Group Staff. The Encyclopedia of American History.
--The Study of American History.
Dutcher, Nadine. The Use of First & Second Languages in Primary Education: Selected Case Studies.
du Terrage, Marc de Villiers see De Villiers du Terrage, Marc.
Duthie, J. F. The Orchids of the Western Himalaya.
Dutoit, Claire-Lise. Music Movement Therapy.
Dutourd, Jean. The Horrors of Love. Chancellor, Robin, tr. from Fr.
Dutt, Ashok K., ed. Medical Geography South & Southeast Asia.
Dutt, Indu, tr. see Tagore, Rabindrath.
Dutt, K. Guru. Existentialism & Indian Thought.
Dutta, S. & Kanunga, R. N. Affect & Memory: A Reformulation.
Dutta Majumdar, D. & Das, J. Digital Computer's Memory Technology.
Dutton, Frank. Turbo Pascal Toolbox.
Dutwin, Phyllis, jt. auth. see Diamond, Harriet.
DuVal, John, tr. Cuckolds, Clerics & Countrymen: Medieval French Fabliaux.
Duval, Paul-Marie & Hawkes, Christopher, eds. Celtic Art in Ancient Europe - Five Protohistoric Centuries: Proceedings.
Duval, Shelley & Wicklund, Robert A. A Theory of Objective Self Awareness.
Duvall, Charles R., jt. auth. see Krepel, Wayne J.
Du Vall, Stephen. The Song of Hero.
Duveen, Dennis I. & Klickstein, H. S. Bibliography of the Works of Antoine Lavoisier: Bibliography of the Works of Antoine Lavoisier: Seventeen Forty-Three to Seventeen Ninety-Four.
Duverger, Maurice. Political Parties: Their Organization & Activity in the Modern State. North, Barbara & North, Robert, trs.
Duvernoy, J. B. Elementary Studies for Piano. Seifert, Hans T., ed.
Du Viver, jt. auth. see Clement.
Duvoisin, Roger. The Importance of Crocus.
--The Petunia, Beware!
Duvoisin, Roger, jt. auth. see Lipkind, William.

Duyn, Janet Van see Van Duyn, Janet.
Duyn, Julia Van see Van Duyn, Julia.
Duyn, Mona Van see Van Duyn, Mona.
Duyneveldt, A. J. Van see Carlin, R. L. & Van Duyneveldt, A. J.
Dvinov, Boris. Ot Legal 'nostik Podpol'-Iu (From Legality to the Underground)
Dvorak, Eileen M. & Showalter, Ray. NCLEX-LPN Examination.
Dvorak, J., jt. auth. see Otcenasek, M.
Dvorak, M. Submicroscopic Cytodifferentiation.
Dvorak, Max. The History of Art As a History of Ideas.
Dvornik, Francis. Early Christian & Byzantine Political Philosophy: Origins & Background.
Dvosin, Andrew J., ed. see Rahv, Philip.
Dwarkai, Leela, jt. auth. see Blumberg, Rhoda L.
Dwiggins, Don. The Barnstormers.
--Welcome to Flying: A Primer for Pilots.
Dwivedi, A. N., ed. Indian Poetry in English: A Literary History & Anthology.
Dwivedi, S. Hindi on Trial.
Dwivedi, T. D., jt. auth. see Bedford, F. W.
Dworaczek, Marian. Industrial Management: A Bibliography.
--Wages: A Bibliography of Statistical Sources.
--Women in Banking: A Bibliography.
Dworetzky, John P. Psychology.
Dworkin, Andrea. Ice & Fire.
Dworkin, Daniel M., jt. ed. see Baumann, Duane D.
Dworkin, Florence, jt. auth. see Dworkin, Stanley.
Dworkin, Gerald, et al, eds. Markets & Morals.
Dworkin, Stanley & Dworkin, Florence. The Good Goodies.
Dwyer, Dale E., ed. see Marlowe, Lynn G., et al.
Dwyer, J. M., jt. auth. see PreTest Service, Inc. Staff.
Dwyer, M. J., ed. The Performance of Off-Road Vehicles & Machines: Proceedings of the 8th International ISTVS Conference, Cambridge, August 1984.
Dwyer, T. Ryle. Irish Neutrality & the U. S. A. 1939-1947.
Dwyer, Thomas A. & Critchfield, Margot. CP-M & the Personal Computer: Popular.
Dwyre, Bill, ed. see Los Angeles Times Sports Staff.
Dyachenko, V. F. Basic Computational Math.
Dyal, Donald H. Addison Mizner: The Palm Beach Architect.
Dycko, Iryna, tr. see Orwell, George.
Dye, Dwight L. A Kingdom of Servants.
Dye, H. Allan, jt. auth. see Diedrich, Richard C.
Dye, Jacob, jt. auth. see Dye, Rex J.
Dye, Nancy S. As Equals & As Sisters: Feminism, the Labor Movement, & the Women's Trade Union League of New York.
Dye, Rex J. The Hospital Medical Racket & You.
Dye, Rex J. & Dye, Jacob. Lumber Camp Life in Michigan: An Autobiographical Account.
Dye, Thomas R. Power & Society: An Introduction to the Social Sciences.
Dyer, C. Pizza Cookery.
Dyer, Ceil. Best Recipes from the Backs of Boxes, Bottles, Cans & Jars.
--The Chopped, Minced & Ground Meat Cookbook.
--Freezer to Oven to Table.
Dyer, Charles, jt. ed. see Toussaint, Stanley D.
Dyer, Dewey A. So You Want to Start a Restaurant?
Dyer, Edwin A., ed. Gas Chemistry in Nuclear Reactors & Large Industrial Plants.
Dyer, Gwynne. War.
Dyer, Heather. Stories Jesus Told. Incl. The Good Samaritan; The Good Shepherd; The Great Feast; The House Built on Sand; The Prodigal Son; The Rich Man. Cook.
Dyer, Homer L., III. The Life & Dreams of You & Me.
Dyer, James S. & Shapiro, Roy D. Management Science-Operations Research: Cases & Readings.
Dyer, Janell G. The Australian Christian Play.
Dyer, Jon C. Handbook of Industrial Wastes Pretreatment.
Dyer, Jon C. & Mignone, Nicholas A. Handbook of Industrial Residues.
Dyer, Lee, ed. Merchandising in Action.
Dyer, Nancy A., jt. auth. see Starr, John B.
Dyer, Richard, et al. Coronation Street.
Dyer, Wayne. Gifts from Eykis.
Dyer, Wayne W. What Do You Really Want for Your Children?
Dyer, William G. & Kunz, Phillip R. Effective Mormon Families.
Dyhouse, Carol. Girls Growing up in Late Victorian & Edwardian England.
Dyk, Timothy B., jt. auth. see Practising Law Institute Staff.
Dyke, Henry van. The Story of the Other Wise Man.
Dyke, P. P. & Heaps, N. S., eds. Jonsmod Eighty-Two: A Workshop of the Joint North Sea Modelling Group on Mathematical Models of the North Sea & Surrounding Continental Shelf Seas, Heriot-Watt University, Edinburgh, U. K., Sept. 1-3, 1982.
Dykeman, Wilma. Tennessee.
Dykman, Thomas & Swieringa, Robert. Cases in Financial Accounting.
Dykstra, Len & Nobel, Marty. Nails: The Inside Story of an Amazin Season.
Dykstra, Linda A., jt. auth. see Seiden, Lewis S.
Dykstra, Robert R. Cattle Towns.
Dykyjova, D. & Kvet, J., eds. Methods & Results of Quantitative Ecosystem Research in the Czechoslovakian IBP Project: Methods & Results of Quantitative Ecosystem Research in the Czechoslovakian IBP Project Ser.
Dyller, Fran, jt. auth. see Mason, David.
Dym, Clive L. Introduction to the Theory of Shells.
Dym, Clive L., jt. auth. see Shames, Irving H.
Dyment, John. Meet the Men Who Sailed the Seven Seas.
Dymond, David. Writing Local History: A Practical Guide.
Dymsza, W. Multinational Business Strategy.
Dynamic Aspects of Cerebral Edema International Workshop Staff. Dynamics of Brain Edema: Proceedings of Dynamic Aspects of Cebral Edema International Workshops, 3rd, Montreal, June 25-29, 1976. Pappius, H. M., et al, eds.
Dynamic Aspects of Speech Perception Symposium Staff. Structure & Process in Speech Perception: Proceedings of the Dynamic Aspects of Speech Perception Symposium, I. P. O. Eindhoven, the Netherlands, Aug. 4-6, 1975. Cohen, A. & Nooteboom, S. G., eds.
Dynamics of Fluids & Plasmas Symposium Staff. Dynamics of Fluids & Plasmas: Proceedings. Pai, S. I., ed.
Dyne, Susan Van see Van Dyne, Susan.
Dynes, Wayne R. The Illuminations of the Stavelot Bible.
Dynkin, E. B. Markov Processes. Fabius, J., et al, trs.
Dyos, H. J. & Wolff, Michael. The Victorian City-Images & Realities, Vol. 1: Past & Present & Numbers of People.
Dyos, H. J. & Wolff, Michael, eds. Victorian City: Images & Realities.
--The Victorian City-Images & Realities, Vol. 2: Shapes on the Ground & a Change of Accent.
Dyrness, W. A. Christian Art in Asia.
Dyroff, Adolf. Der Peripatos Uber das Greisenalter.
Dysard, Dorothy L. God Made Me: I'm Glad.
Dyson, George. Baidarka.
Dyson, Henry V. & Butt, John E. Augustans & Romantics, Sixteen Eighty-Nine to Eighteen Thirty.
Dyson, J. E. & Williams, D. A. Physics of the Interstellar Medium.
Dyson, R. W. A Ninth Century Political Tract: The De Institutione Regia of Jonas of Orleans.
Dyson, Roger. The National Health Service: Professionals or Militants?
Dyson, Rosamund Shuter see Shuter-Dyson, Rosamund & Gabriel, Clive.
Dyson, S. L. The Stories of the Trees.
Dyson, Stephen L. The Creation of the Roman Frontier. Barb, S., ed.
Dyson, T., ed. India's Historical Demography, Vol. II: Studies in Famine, Disease & Social Change.
Dyson, T. & Crook, N., eds. India's Demography: Essays on the Contemporary Population.
Dzhavad-Zade, M. D. Surgery of Kidney & Ureteral Anomalies.
Dziech, Billie W. & Weiner, Linda. The Lecherous Professor: Sexual Harassment on Campus.
Dzieduszycka, Teresa, tr. see Mrozek, Slawomir.
Dziewanowski, M. K. A History of Soviet Russia.
Dziobek, Linda, ed. Proceedings of the Annual Congress of Correction of the American Correctional Association, 115th.
Dzyubenko, G. Land of the Soviets in Verse & Prose.
Dzyubenko, G. & Kondratovich, A., eds. Land of the Soviets in Verse & Prose.

E

E, Liu. Travels of Lao Can.
E. William, JFK School of Government, Harvard University, jt. ed. see Sven B. Lundstedt, Ohio State University.
Eade, Deborah, jt. auth. see Jackson, Tony.
Eadie. Statistical Methods in Experimental Physics.
Eadie, John W., ed. The Conversion of Constantine.
Eadie, John W. & Ober, Josiah, eds. The Craft of the Ancient Historian: Essays in Honor of Chester G. Starr.
Eadie, Mervyn, jt. auth. see Sutherland, John M.
Eagan, Andrea B. Why Am I So Miserable If These Are the Best Years of My Life?
Eagan, James M. Maximilien Robespierre: Nationalist Dictator.
Eagen, Andrea B. The Newborn Mother: Stages of Her Growth.
Eager, Edward. Half Magic.
--Knight's Castle.
--Knight's Castle.
--Magic or Not.
--Magic or Not?
--Time Garden.
--Well-Wishers.
Eager, Irene F. Margaret Anna Cusack: One Woman's Campaign for Women's Rights.
Eager, Renee. Dining In - Phoenix.
Eagleman, Joe R. Severe & Unusual Weather.
Eagleson, John & Scharper, Philip J., eds. Puebla & Beyond.
Eagleson, John, tr. see Gutierrez, Gustavo.
Eagleson, John, tr. see Miranda, Jose P.
Eaglestein, William H., jt. auth. see Pariser, David M.
Eagleton, Mary & Pierce, David. Attitudes to Class in the English Novel: From Walter Scott to David Storey.
Eaker, D. Natural Toxins: Proceedings of the 6th International Symposium on Animal, Plant & Microbial Toxins, Uppsala, August, 1979. Wadstrom, T., ed.
Eakins, Barbara & Eakins, R. Gene. Sex Differences in Human Communication.
Eakins, R. Gene, jt. auth. see Eakins, Barbara.
Eakins, William J., jt. auth. see Ryan, Elizabeth B.
Eakle, Arlene H. Checklist of German Emigrant Sources.
--Tracing Ancestors with Common Surnames.
--Your Research Dollar.
Eakle, Arlene H., et al. English Collection, 1979.
--New York Collection, 1980.
Eames, Charles & Ray, Staff, et al. Powers of Ten: About the Relative Size of Things in the Universe.
Eames, Marian. Dancing in Prints: A Portfolio Assembled from the Archives of the Dance Collection, 1634-1870.
Eames, Wilberforce. Early New England Catechisms.
Eanes, H. Ray. Interpreting Financial Statements of Life & Health Insurance Companies.
Eargle, John. Sound Recording.
Earhart. Last Flight.
Earhart, Caroline, jt. auth. see DeJonghe, Marty.
Earl, Polly A., jt. ed. see Quimby, Ian M.
Earle, Alice M. China Collecting in America.
--Sun Dials & Roses of Yesterday.
Earle, Allic M., ed. see Winslow, Anna G.
Earle, Edward M., ed. Makers of Modern Strategy: Military Thought from Machiavelli to Hitler.
Earle, M. D. & Malahoff, A., eds. Ocean Wave Climate.
Earle, Peter. The World of Defoe.
Earle, Ralph. Peloubet's Sunday School Notes 1988-1989 September - August.
--Word Meanings in the New Testament: Hebrews-Revelation.
--Word Meanings in the New Testament, Vol. 3: Romans.
--Word Meanings in the New Testament, Vol. 1: Matthew, Mark, Luke.
--Word Meanings in the New Testament, Vol. 5: Philemon-Philippians.
--Word Meanings in the New Testament: 1 & 2 Corinthians, Ephesians.
Earle, Richard A. Teaching Reading & Mathematics.
Earle, W. Hubert. Cacti of the Southwest.
--Cacti of the Southwest.
Earley, Lawrence E. & Gottschalk, Carl W. Strauss & Welt's Diseases of the Kidney.
Earlley, Elsie C., jt. auth. see Cook, J. E.
Early, Jack. A Creative Kind of Killer.
Early, Richard E. Weavers & War: A True Story.
Early, Robert. Powers & Dominations.
Earman, John S., et al, eds. Foundations of Space-Time Theories.
Earney, Fillmore C. Petroleum & Hard Minerals from the Sea.
Earnhardt, Crystal. Annie's Secret. Woolsey, Raymond H., ed.
Earnshaw, Pat. Needle-Made Laces: Materials, Designs, Techniques.
Earnst, Elizabeth. Hummy & the Wax Castle.
Easen, Patrick. Making School-Centered INSET Work: A School of Education Pack for Teachers.
Easley, J. A., jt. ed. see Gallagher, J. M.
Eason, Thomas F. & Manzler, David L. Why Universal Life.
Easson, Angus. Elizabeth Gaskell.
Easson, Angus, ed. see Dickens, Charles.
Easson, Roger R. & Essick, Robert N. William Blake: Book Illustrator.
--William Blake: Book Illustrator.
Easson, Roger R., ed. see Osing, Gordon T.
East African Subcommittee for Soil Correlation & Land Evaluation. Report of the Second Meeting of the Eastern African Sub-Committee for Soil Correlation & Land Evaluation: Addis-Ababa, Ethiopia, 25-30 October 1976.
East, Frank Reynolds. The Entity Process: The Accumulation of a Physical Property as a Function of Mortality & Magnitude of Rank.
East, G. C., jt. auth. see Margerison, D.
East, Reginald. Heal the Sick.
East, Wo. Catfish Cookbook.
Easterbrook, David L., jt. auth. see Myrick, Bismarck.
Easterbrook, James. The Determinants of Free Will: A Psychological Analysis of Responsible, Adjustive Behavior.
Easterlin, Richard A., ed. Population & Economic Change in Developing Countries.
Easterling, Jerry. Country Chaff.
Easterling, K., ed. Mechanisms of Deformation & Fracture: Proceedings of the Interdisciplinary Conference, Held at the University of Lulea-Sweden, 20-22, September 1978.
Easterman, Daniel. The Last Assassin.
Eastham. Biochemical Values in Clinical Medicine.
--Clinical Haematology.
--Pocket Guide to Differential Diagnosis.
Eastham, Scott T. Wisdom of the Fool: Stories & Poems.
Eastlake, William. Bamboo Bed.
Eastland, Jonathan. Creative Techniques in Marine & Seascape Photography.
--Great Yachts & Their Designers.
Eastman, Addison. This Is Southeast Asia Today.
Eastman Arbitration Library. Basic Documents on Commercial Arbitration.
Eastman, Arthur, et al, eds. The Norton Reader.
Eastman, Arthur M. A Short History of Shakespearean Criticism.
Eastman, Arthur M., et al, eds. Norton Anthology of Poetry.
--Norton Anthology of Poetry, Shorter Edition.
--The Norton Reader.
--Norton Anthology of Poetry.
Eastman, Hope. Lobbying: A Constitutionally Protected Right.
Eastman Kodak Co., ed. see Horrell, C. William.
Eastman Kodak Co. Editors. The Joy of Photographing People.
Eastman Kodak Company. Analysis, Treatment & Disposal of Ferricyanide in Photographic Effluents - A Compendium: A Compenchum.
--Fire & Arson Photography.
--KODAK Complete Darkroom DATAGUIDE: Processing & Printing Information for Black-&-White & Color.
--Photolab Design.
--Using Photography to Preserve Evidence.
--Using Process EM-26.
Eastman Kodak Company, ed. Introduction to Color Photographic Processing.
--Photography Through the Microscope.
--Using Kodak Ektachrome R-3 & R-3000 Chemicals.
Eastman Kodak Company Editors. Kodak Pocket Guide to Nature Photography.
--Kodak Pocket Guide to Photographing Cats.
--Kodak Pocket Guide to Photographing Dogs.
Eastman Kodak Company Staff. Black-&-White Processing Using Kodak Chemicals.
--Kodak Guide to 35 MM Photography.
--Kodak Guide to 35mm Photography (AC-95S)
--Printing Color Negatives (E-66)
--Using Filters.
Eastman Kodak Company Staff, ed. The Business of Filmmaking.
--Images, Images, Images: The Book of Programmed Multi-Image Production (S-12)
Eastman, Lester F., ed. Gallium Arsenide Microwave Bulk & Transit-Time Devices.
Eastman, Moira & Poussard, Wendy. The Christmas Book.
Eastman, Robert. Pendulum.
Eastman, Susan T., et al. Broadcast-Cable Programming: Strategies & Practices.
Easton, Brian & Thomson, Norman. An Introduction to the New Zealand Economy.
Easton, David. A Framework for Political Analysis.
Easton, M. G. Illustrated Bible Dictionary.
Easton, Nina, jt. auth. see Brownstein, Ronald.
Easton, Phoebe J. Marbling: A History & Bibliography.
Easton, Stewart C. Man & World in the Light of Anthroposophy.
--Man & World in the Light of Anthroposophy.
Easton, Susan, et al. Popular Culture, Leisure & Social Order.
Easton, Thomas A. Working for Life: Careers in Biology.
Easton, Violet. Elephants Never Jump.
Eastwood, Dana A. Gravity Park.
Eastwood, J. J. & Smith, F. B. Historical Studies: Selected Articles.
Eastwood, Susan. Prisling.
Easwaran, Eknath. Mantram Handbook.
Easyriders Staff, ed. Best Biker Fiction.
Eaton, Carl J., jt. auth. see Yorgason, Blaine M.
Eaton, David. The Potential for Appropriate Water Resource Technology in Guinea, West Africa.
Eaton, Howard O. Happinism: A Goal for All Humanity.
--Happinism Revisited.

Authors

Eaton, Jan & Mundie, Liz. Cross Stitch & Sampler Book.

Eaton, Jeanette. Leader by Destiny.

--Lone Journey: The Life of Roger Williams.

--Lone Journey: The Life of Roger Williams.

Eaton, Jonathan & Gersovitz, Mark. Poor-Country Borrowing in Private Financial Markets & the Repudiation Issue.

Eaton, Roy. Trout & Salmon Fishing.

Eaton, Samuel D. The Forces of Freedom in Spain 1974-1979.

Eaton, Theodore H. Evolution.

Eauclaire, Sally. The New Color Photography.

Eaves, Mary L. The Truth Will Make You Free.

Eayrs, James. In Defence of Canada, Vol. II: Appeasement & Rearmament.

--In Defence of Canada, Vol. III: Peacemaking & Deterrence.

Eban, Abba. The New Diplomacy: International Affairs in the Modern Age.

Ebbels, D. L. & King, J. E., eds. Plant Health: The Scientific Basis for Administrative Control of Plant Diseases & Pests.

Ebbing, Darrell D. General Chemistry.

Ebel, A. & Simon, P. C., eds. Middle Atmosphere Sciences: A Selection of Papers from the Symposium Organised by the IAMAP & IAGA on the Occasion of the XVIII General Assembly of the IUGG, Hamburg, Federal Republic of Germany, August 1983.

Ebeling, Gerhard. Introduction to a Theological Theory of Language. Wilson, R. A., tr. from Ger.

--Luther: An Introduction to His Thought. Wilson, R. A., tr. from Ger.

--The Nature of Faith. Smith, Ronald G., tr. from Ger.

--On Prayer: The Lord's Prayer in Today's World. Leitch, James W., tr. from Ger.

--The Study of Theology. Priebe, Duane A., tr. from Ger.

--Truth of the Gospel: An Exposition of Galatians.

Ebeling, Nancy & Hill, Deborah, eds. Child Abuse-Intervention & Treatment.

Ebenstein, William. The Nazi State.

Eberhard, Eldon W. The Rumrunners.

Eberhard, W. Conquerors & Rulers: Social Forces in Medieval China.

--Social Mobility in Traditional China.

Eberhard, Wolfram. A Dictionary of Chinese Symbols: Hidden Symbols in Chinese Life & Thought.

--Life & Thought of Ordinary Chinese: Collected Essays.

--Studies in Hakka Folktales.

Eberhart, George M. Monsters: A Guide to Information on Unaccounted for Creatures, Including Bigfoot, Many Water Monsters, & Other Irregular Animals.

Eberhart, Mignon G. A Fighting Chance.

Eberhart, Stephen, tr. see Adams, George.

Eberle, Bob. Help! In Solving Problems Creatively at Home & School.

Eberle, Irmengarde. Picture Stories for Children: A Rebus.

Ebershoff-Coles, Susan & Leibenguth, Charla, eds. Motorsports: A Guide to Information Sources.

Ebersole, Frank B. Language & Perception: Essays in the Philosophy of Language.

--Things We Know: Fourteen Essays on Problems of Knowledge.

Eberson, Frederick. Apostles & Prophets: Medicine for Society's Ills.

Eberson, L. Organic Electrochemistry.

Eberson, Lennart & Nyberg, Klas. Synthetic Uses of Anodic Substitution Reactions.

Ebert, Frances H. & Cheatum, Billye A. Basketball.

Ebert, Friedrich A. General Bibliographical Dictionary.

Ebert, James D. & Sussex, Ian M. Interacting Systems in Development.

Ebert, M., ed. Pulse Radiolysis.

Ebert, Roger. Roger Eberts Movie Home Companion: Full-Length Reviews of 600 Films on Cassette--1989.

--Roger Ebert's Movie Home Companion: 1988 Edition.

--Roger Ebert's Movie Home Companion: 400 Films on Cassette, 1980-85.

Ebertin, Elsbeth. Astrology & Romance. Nelson, D. G., tr. from Ger.

Ebinger, Charles K. Pakistan: Energy Planning in a Strategic Vortex.

Eble, Kenneth E. The Craft of Teaching: A Guide to Mastering the Professor's Art.

--F. Scott Fitzgerald.

Eble, Kenneth E., ed. Howells: A Century of Criticism.

Eblin, Lawrence P. Chemistry: A Survey of Fundamentals.

--Chemistry: A Survey of Laboratory Techniques & Procedures.

Ebling, Gerhard. Word & Faith.

Ebling, Ruth, jt. auth. see Reardon, Jean.

Ebon, Martin. The Andropov File.

--Cloning of Man: A Brave New Hope-or Horror?

--Psychic Warfare: Threat or Illusion?

Ebon, Martin, ed. The Riddle of the Bermuda Triangle.

Ebsworth, E. A., et al. The Chemistry of Oxygen.

Ebury Press, ed. Containerisation International Yearbook, 1987.

Eby, Edwin H. Concordance of Walt Whitman's Leaves of Grass & Selected Prose Writings.

Eby, Lloyd, jt. ed. see Berger, Rene.

Eca de Queiroz. Letters from England. Stevens, Ann, tr. from Port.

Eccles, John C. Facing Reality: Philosophical Adventures by a Brain Scientist.

--The Understanding of the Brain.

Eccles, John C., jt. ed. see Karczmar, A. G.

Eccles, Marjorie. Cast a Cold Eye.

Echeverria, Durand. Mirage in the West: A History of the French Image of American Society to 1815.

Echewa, T. Obinkaram. The Land's Lord.

Echezonam, Osodi E. Anioma's Attainment of Humanity.

Echlin, Edward P. Deacon in the Church.

Echols, Edvardus C. Freddus Elephantus et Horatius Porcus Saltans Cincinnatis.

Echols, Edward. Human Fantasy.

--Voidism.

Echols, John M. & Shadily, Hassan. An Indonesian-English Dictionary.

Eck, B. Fans: Design & Operation of Centrifugal, Axial Flow & Cross Flow Fans.

Eck, Laurence, jt. auth. see Buzzard, Lynn R.

Eckankar Studiengruppe Munchen, tr. see Twitchell, Paul.

Eckard, Helen M. Statistics of Public Libraries, 1974 (LIBGIS I)

Eckblad, Edith. Danny's Orange Christmas Camel.

--God Listens & Knows.

--Soft As the Wind.

Eckbo, Garrett. Home Landscape: The Art of Home Landscaping.

--Public Landscape: Six Essays on Government & Environmental Design in the San Francisco Bay Area.

Ecke, Wolfgang. The Face at the Window.

--The Stolen Paintings.

Eckel, Malcolm W. Case Studies from the Ethics of Decision Making.

--The Ethics of Decision Making.

Eckelman, W. C., ed. Technetium Ninety-Nine-M: Generators, Chemistry, & Preparation of Radiopharmaceuticals.

Eckels, Jon. Pursuing the Pursuit-the Black Plight in White America: The Black Plight in White America.

Eckenfelder, W. W. & Englander, A. J. Effluent Variability from Waste Water Treatment Processes & Its Control.

Eckenhoff, James E. Controversies in Anesthesiology.

Eckenhoff, James E., et al, eds. Year Book of Anesthesia, 1980.

Eckenrode, Hamilton J. The Revolution in Virginia.

Eckenstein, Lina. Spell of Words: Studies in Language Bearing on Custom.

Ecker, B. A. Independence Day.

Ecker, Gunter. Theory of Fully Ionized Plasmas.

Eckerd, Jack & Conn, Charles P. Eckerd.

Eckern, U., et al. Proceedings of the Seventeenth International Conference on Low Temperature Physics.

Eckert, Allan W. The Dark Green Tunnel.

--The Scarlet Mansion.

--Song of the Wild.

--The Wand.

Eckert, E. R. & Irvine, T. F., Jr. Heat Transfer Reviews, Nineteen Seventy to Nineteen Seventy-One.

Eckert, Ross D., jt. auth. see Leftwich, Richard H.

Eckhardt, Caroline D. & Stewart, David H. The Wiley Reader: Designs for Writing.

Eckhart, Meister, et al. Treatises & Sermons of Meister Eckhart. Clark, James M. & Skinner, John V., trs. from Ger. & Lat.

Eckhaus, W. New Developments in Differential Equations: Proceedings of the Scheveningen Conference, 2nd, the Netherlands, 1975.

Eckholm, Erik & Brown, Lester R. Spreading Deserts: The Hand of Man.

Eckholm, Erik P. Down to Earth: Environment & Human Needs.

Eckholm, Erik P. & Record, Francis. The Two Faces of Malnutrition.

Eckley, Wilton. The American Circus.

Eckman, Fred, et al. Universals of Second Language Acquisition.

Eckmann, J. P., jt. auth. see Collet, P.

Eckols, Steve. DOS-VSE JCL: Instructor's Guide.

Eckstein, Eleanor F. Food, People & Nutrition.

Eckstein, Everett E. Sunrise on the Mohican.

Eckstein, F., jt. ed. see Sundaram, P. V.

Eckstein, Fay, jt. auth. see Eckstein, Warren.

Eckstein, Joan. Fun with Making Things: An Activity Book for Kids.

Eckstein, Joan & Gleit, Joyce. Fun with Growing Things.

Eckstein, Maxwell, ed. see Concone, J.

Eckstein, O., et al. The DRI Report on U. S. Manufacturing Industries.

Eckstein, P. & Knowles, F., eds. Techniques in Endocrine Research.

Eckstein, Peter, jt. auth. see Sichel, Werner.

Eckstein, Warren & Eckstein, Fay. Pet Aerobics: How to Solve Your Pets Behavior Problems, Improve Their Health, Lengthen Their Lives & Have Fun Doing It.

--Understanding Your Pet: The Eckstein Method of Pet Therapy & Behavior Training.

--Yes, Dog, That's Right!

Eckstorm, Fanny. Minstrelsy of Maine.

Eco, Umberto. Postscript to the Name of the Rose. Weaver, William, tr. from Ital.

Ecodyne Corporation Staff. Weather Data Handbook.

Ecological Society of America Radioecology Symposium Staff. Radioecology & Energy Resources: Proceedings of the Ecological Society of America Radioecology Symposium, Oregon State University, May 12-14, 1975. Cushing, C. E., Jr., ed.

Economic Conference. The Theory & Practice of Corporate Mergers.

Economides, Chris. Earned International Reserve Units: The Catalyst of Two Complementary World Problems - Monetary & Development.

Edagawa, Naoyushi, jt. auth. see Friedmann, Lawrence W.

Edberg, Stephen J. International Halley Watch Amateur Observers' Manual for Scientific Comet Studies.

Eddie, G. The Harvesting of Krill.

Eddins, John M., jt. auth. see Cleaver, Dale G.

Eddleman, H. Leo. By Life or By Death: A Practical Commentary on Paul's Letter to the Philippians.

--Hail Mary.

--Hail Mary, Are You Heeding the Blessed Virgin? In Defense of Public Schools.

--Schools & Churches in American Democracy: In Defense of Public Schools.

Eddy, Donald D. A Bibliography of John Brown.

Eddy, James M. & Alles, Wesley F. Death Education.

Eddy, John. The Teacher & the Drug Scene.

Eddy, Mary Baker. Pulpit & Press.

Eddy, R. Lee, III. What You Should Know about Marriage, Divorce, Annulment, Separation & Community Property in Louisiana.

Eddy, Samuel K. The Minting of Antoniniani A. D. 238-249 & the Smyrna Hoard.

Edel, Abraham & Edel, May. Anthropology & Ethics: The Quest for Moral Understanding.

Edel, Leon. Bloomsbury: A House of Lions.

--Henry James: The Master.

--Henry James: The Untried Years.

--Stuff of Sleep & Dreams: Experiments in Literary Psychology.

Edel, Leon, ed. see James, Henry.

Edel, Leon, ed. see Wilson, Edmund.

Edel, Leon, ed. & intro. by see Wilson, Edmund.

Edel, Matthew & Rothenberg, Jerome. Readings in Urban Economics.

Edel, May, jt. auth. see Edel, Abraham.

Edelfelt, Roy A. & Orvell, Tamar. Teacher Centers: Where, What, Why?

Edelhart, Mike. Getting from Twenty to Thirty: Surviving Your First Decade in the Real World.

Edelhart, Mike & Strom, David. Managing OS-2: Profiting from Changing Standards.

Edelhertz, Herbert, et al. The Containment of Organized Crime.

Edelhoch, H., jt. ed. see Chen, R. F.

Edelman, Bernard. Ownership of the Image. Kingdom, Elizabeth, tr. from Fr.

Edelman, Elaine. I Love My Baby Sister (Most of the Time)

Edelman, Lily. Japan in Story & Pictures.

Edelman, M. Political Languages: Words That Succeed & Policies That Fail.

Edelman, Murray. Politics As Symbolic Action: Mass Arousal & Quiescence.

Edelman, Rosemary. Fireworks.

Edelson, Edward. ABC's of Prescription Drugs.

--Who Goes There: The Search for Intelligent Life in the Universe.

Edelson, Marshall. Sociotherapy & Psychotherapy.

Edelson, Paul J., et al. Immunological Deficiency Syndromes.

Edelstein, Andrew J. The Pop Sixties: A Personal & Irreverent Guide.

Edelstein, N. M., ed. Actinides in Perspective: Proceedings of the Conference Held at Pacific Grove, CA, Sept. 10-15, 1981.

Edelstein, Tilden G. Strange Enthusiasm: A Life of Thomas Wentworth Higginson, 1823-1911.

Edelston. The Problems of Adolescents.

Edem, D. A. Introduction to Educational Administration in Nigeria.

Eden, Dorothy. Death Is a Red Rose.

--An Important Family.

Eden, Horatia K. Juliana Horatia Ewing & Her Books.

Eden, Jerome. Animal Magnetism & the Life Energy.

--Orgone Energy: The Answer to Atomic Suicide.

--Planet in Trouble: The UFO Assault on Earth.

--View from Eden: Talks to Students of Orgonomy.

Eden, Jill, et al. AIDS & Health Related Issues, an OTA Survey.

Edens, Cooper. If You're Afraid of the Dark Remember the Night Rainbow.

Ederer, Bernard F. Bingo, Gallant Reindeer Dog.

Edgar, A. H. John Bull & the Papists; or, Passages in the Life of an Anglican Rector, 1846. Wolff, Robert L., ed.

Edgar, David. Mary Barnes.

--Maydays.

Edgar, David & Todd, Susan. Teendreams.

Edgar, Neal L. & Ma, Wendy Y., eds. Travel in Asia: A Guide to Information Sources.

Edgar, Patricia & Rahim, Syed A. Communication Policy in Developed Countries.

Edge, C. T. Small Computer Systems for Solicitors.

Edge, Findley B. Helping the Teacher.

Edge, L. L. Run the Cat Roads: A True Story of Bank Robbers in the Thirties.

Edge, Sharon M., ed. Acquisitions-Circulation Interface.

Edgell, David P. William Ellery Channing: An Intellectual Portrait.

Edge-Partington, James & Heape, Charles. Ethnological Album of Weapons, Tools, Ornaments & Articles of Dress Etc. of the Natives of the Pacific Island.

Edgerton, Eleanor. A Year in Benares.

Edgerton, Gary R. American Film Exhibition & an Analysis of the Motion Picture Industry's Market Structure, 1963-1980. Jowett, Garth S., ed.

Edgerton, Michael, jt. auth. see Heise, Kenan.

Edgerton, V. Reggie, jt. auth. see Edington, Dee.

Edgerton, William F., ed. Medinet Habu Graffiti.

Edgeworth, Maria. Belinda.

--Helen.

--Patronage.

Edgeworth, Maria & Edgeworth, Richard L. Practical Education. Luria, Gina, ed.

Edgeworth, Richard L., jt. auth. see Edgeworth, Maria.

Edgin, Ruth, jt. auth. see Pugh, Emerson M.

Edgley, Charles, jt. auth. see Brissett, Dennis.

Edgmand, Michael R. Macroeconomics: Theory & Policy.

Edinburgh University Library Staff. Index to Manuscripts.

Edinburgh University Staff. Pharmacological Experiments on Isolated Preparations.

Edinburgh University, Tourism & Recreation Unit Staff. Recreation Site Survey Manual.

Edinger, Lois V. & Nelson, Roland H. Leadership Training for Directors of Group Seminars Abroad: A Japan Model.

Edinger, Lois V., et al, eds. Curricular Challenges.

Edinger, T. Paleoneurology Eighteen-Four to Nineteen Sixty-Six: An Annotated Bibliography.

Edington, jt. auth. see Wilson.

Edington, Andrew. The Word Made Fresh, Vol. 1: Genesis - Kings.

--The Word Made Fresh, Vol. 2: Chronicles - Malachi.

--The Word Made Fresh, Vol. 3: New Testament.

Edington, Dee & Edgerton, V. Reggie. Biology of Physical Activity.

Edington, J. M. & Edington, M. A. Ecology & Environmental Planning.

Edington, M. A., jt. auth. see Edington, J. M.

Edkins, Diana E., jt. auth. see Newhall, Beaumont.

Edkins, Joseph. The Revenue & Taxation of the Chinese Empire.

Edles, Gary J. & Nelson, Jerome. Federal Regulatory Process: Agency Practices & Procedures.

Edlin, Herbert L. The Tree Key.

Edlosi, Mario. Which Way the Wind Blows: Part II of Valley of Many Winds.

Edmands, Allan, jt. auth. see Edmands, Dodie.

Edmands, Dodie & Edmands, Allan. Child Signs: Understanding Your Child Through Astrology.

Edminister, Joseph A. Electric Circuits.

Edminster, Alice W. We Are the Fallen Angels.

Edmond, J. B. The Magnificent Charter: The Origin & Role of the Morrill Land-Grant Colleges & Universities.

Edmonds, Chris W. A Quilt for All Seasons.

Edmonds, Francis. Rudolf Steiner Education: The Waldorf Schools.

Edmonds, I. G. Funny Car Racing for Beginners.

--The Kings of Black Magic.

Edmonds, Michael. Lytton Strachey: A Bibliography.

Edmonds, Robert L., ed. Aerobiology: The Ecological Systems Approach.

--Analysis of Coniferous Forest Ecosystems in the Western United States.

Edmonds, Robin. Setting the Mould: The United States & Britain, 1945-50.

Edmonds, Walter D. The Night Raider & Other Stories.
Edmondson, Jolee, jt. auth. see Argea, Angelo.
Edmondson, Madeleine. The Witch's Egg.
Edmondson, William, ed. see Cherry, Colin.
Edmonson, A. S. & Crenshaw, A. H. Campbell's Operative Orthopaedics.
Edmonson, James B. Textbook in American Education.
Edmunds, Andy. Let the Good Times Roll: The Complete Cajun Handbook.
Edmunds, F. H. Geology & Ourselves.
Edmunds, M. G., jt. auth. see Solomon, P. M.
Edmundson, David, jt. auth. see Johns, Bruce.
Edney, A. T., ed. Dog & Cat Nutrition: A Handbook for Students, Veterinarians, Breeders & Owners.
Edney, Margon & Grimm, Ede. The Elegant Hors d'Oeuvre. Rand, Elizabeth & Polster, Diane, eds.
Edric, Robert. A New Ice Age.
Edsman, C. M., jt. auth. see Hartman, Sven S.
Edson, Billy D. Lone's Christmas Boots & Other Tales from the Mother Lode.
Edson, J. T. The Law of the Gun.
Educational Broadcasting Corp. Staff. V. D. Blues.
Educational Research Council of America Staff. Baker. Ferris, Theodore N. & Marchak, John P., eds.
--Instrument Repairer. Ferris, Theodore N. & Marchak, John P., eds.
--Police Team. Ferris, Theodore N. & Marchak, John P., eds.
--Research Scientist. Ferris, Theodore N. & Marchak, John P., eds.
--Seaman. Braverman, Jack R. & Marchak, John P., eds.
Edvinsson, Lars, jt. ed. see Owman, Christer.
Edward, Derek, jt. auth. see Tilbury, Fred.
Edward, Herbert. First Baron Herbert of Cherbury. Wellek, Rene, ed.
Edwardes, A. Michael. A Season in Hell.
Edwards. Irish Language: An Annotated Bibliography.
Edwards, et al. Advances in the Management of Cleft Palate.
Edwards, A. & Wohl, G. The Picture Life of Muhammad Ali.
--The Picture Life of Stevie Wonder.
Edwards, A. S. & Pearsall, Derek, eds. Middle English Prose: Essays on Bibliographical Problems.
Edwards, Allen L. Techniques of Attitude Scale Construction.
Edwards, Amelia B. A Thousand Miles up the Nile.
Edwards, Andrea. All Too Soon.
--Now Come the Spring.
--Power Play.
Edwards, Anne. Matriarch: Queen Mary & the House of Windsor.
--The Road to Tara: The Life of Margaret Mitchell.
Edwards, Arthur C. Art of Melody.
--Beginning String Class Method.
Edwards, Betty. Drawing on the Artist Within.
Edwards, Brian H. Shall We Dance?
Edwards, C. H. & Penney, David E. Calculus & Analytic Geometry.
Edwards, Cassie. Heart Strings.
--Savage Obsession.
--Secrets of the Heart.
Edwards, Cecile P. King Philip.
Edwards, Charles C. Advanced Techniques in Turbo Pascal.
Edwards, Charles L. Understanding Biblical Symbols.
Edwards, Charlotte W. Let Yourself Go: Try Creative Sunday School.
Edwards, Chris. Developing Microcomputer-Based Business Systems.
Edwards, Cliff. Biblical Christian Marriage.
Edwards, Clifford H. & Fisher, Robert L. Teaching Elementary School Science: A Competency-Based Approach.
Edwards, Colin. Delphiniums.
Edwards, D. K., et al. Transfer Processes.
Edwards, David V. The American Political Experience: An Introduction to Government.
--The American Political Experience: Learning Guide.
Edwards, Don A. Paths to Writing: Developing Prose Power.
Edwards, Dudley. Daniel O'Connell & His World.
Edwards, Eliezer E. Words, Facts & Phrases: A Dictionary of Curious, Quaint, & Out-of-the-Way Matters.
Edwards, Ellis. Operation Golden Buddha.
Edwards, Elwyn H., ed. A Standard Guide to Horse & Pony Breeds.
Edwards, Everett E. Bibliography of the History of Agriculture in the U. S.
Edwards, Francis. Ritual & Drama: The Mediaeval Theater.
Edwards, Fred E. The Role of the Faith Mission: A Brazilian Case Study.
Edwards, G., jt. ed. see Edwards, R. A.
Edwards, Gabrielle. Man & Woman: Inside Homo Sapiens.
Edwards, Gabrielle & Cimmino, Marion. Barron's How to Prepare for the Advanced Placement Examination - Biology. Bleifeld, Maurice, ed.
Edwards, George. Pioneer-at-Law: A Legacy in the Pursuit of Justice.
Edwards, Gwynne. The Discreet Art of Luis Bunuel.
Edwards, Harvey. Skiing to Win.
Edwards, Henry, jt. auth. see Pang, May.
Edwards, Hugh. Surrealism & Its Affinities: The Mary Reynolds Collection.
Edwards, J. Gordon. A Climbers Guide to Glacier National Park.
Edwards, J. H. Human Genetics.
Edwards, J. Michael, jt. auth. see Weiss, Ulrich.
Edwards, Jacqueline, tr. see Trifonov, Yuri.
Edwards, James D., jt. ed. see Black, Homer A.
Edwards, James D., et al. Intermediate Accounting.
Edwards, Jane, jt. auth. see Martinez, Gilbert T.
Edwards, Jaroldeen. A Woman Between.
Edwards, Jim L., jt. auth. see Ottaway, Hal N.
Edwards, John. Exploring Electricity & Electronics With Projects.
Edwards, John & Batley, Richard. The Politics of Positive Discrimination: An Evaluation of the Urban Programme, 1967-1977.
Edwards, John A. see Gale, Anthony.
Edwards, Jonathan. The Philosophy of Jonathan Edwards, from His Private Notebooks. Townsend, Harvey G., ed.
Edwards, Joshua F. A Promise Made, A Promise Kept.
Edwards, Lee, jt. ed. see Diamond, Arlyn.
Edwards, Lenora F. Somebody That Nobody Knows.
Edwards, Lovett F., tr. see Djilas, Milovan.
Edwards, Lovett F., tr. see Pekic, Borislav.
Edwards, Mark & Tavard, George H. Luther: A Reformer for the Churches; An Ecumenical Study Guide.
Edwards, Myrtle. First Course in Geometry: A Modern Textbook for the High School.
Edwards, N. A. & Hassall, K. A. Biochemistry & Physiology of the Cell: An Introductory Text.
Edwards, Nancy M., ed. Office Automation.
Edwards, Nick H. The Inevitable.
Edwards, O. C., jt. auth. see Abbey, Merrill R.
Edwards, O. C., jt. auth. see Bennett, Robert A.
Edwards, O. C., Jr. & Taylor, Gardner C. Pentecost 3. Achtemeier, Elizabeth, et al, eds.
Edwards, Owen. Pete Turner Photographs.
Edwards, Owen D., jt. auth. see Ransom, Bernard.
Edwards, Paul M. Preface to Faith: A Philosophical Inquiry into RLDS Beliefs.
Edwards, Perry. Flowcharting & FORTRAN IV.
Edwards, Perry & Broadwell, Bruce. Flowcharting & BASIC.
Edwards, Peter. Making Silver Jewelry.
Edwards, Philip. Shakespeare & the Confines of Art.
Edwards, R. A. Physics for O.N.C. Courses.
Edwards, R. A. & Edwards, G., eds. Pedro Calderon de la Barca: Los Cabellos de Absalon.
Edwards, R. N., jt. ed. see Zipkin, M A.
Edwards, R. W., jt. ed. see Pascoe, D.
Edwards, Raymond. Chess Tactics & Attacking Techniques.
--Practical Chess Playing.
Edwards, Richard A. A Theology of Q: Eschatology, Prophecy & Wisdom.
Edwards, Richard L., ed. Breaking the Poverty Cycle: Readings on Income Maintenance.
Edwards, Robert R. The Dream of Chaucer: Representation & Reflection in the Early Narratives.
Edwards, Rod. The Technique of Jewelry.
Edwards, Rosemary W. Build Beautiful Bulletin Boards. Wallace, Mary E., ed.
Edwards, Ross. Microcomputer Art.
Edwards, Ruth D. An Atlas of Irish History.
--Patrick Pearse: The Triumph of Failure.
Edwards, Ruth N. Stories Never Heard Before.
Edwards, S., jt. ed. see Edwards, W.
Edwards, Sam, jt. auth. see Renko, Hal.
Edwards, Samuel. The Vidocq Dossier: The Story of the World's First Detective.
Edwards, Sarah A., jt. ed. see Berkey, Robert F.
Edwards, Sebastian. Order of Liberalization of the Balance of Payments: Should the Current Account Be Opened Up First?
Edwards, Stewart H. Critics & Composers: Lectures & Radio Talks.
Edwards, Susan, ed. Gender, Sex & the Law.
Edwards, T., jt. auth. see Hicks, Tyler G.
Edwards, Tryon, ed. New Dictionary of Thoughts.
Edwards, W. & Edwards, S., eds. Letter Tracking: Reusable Edition.
--Manuscript Tracking: Reusable Edition.
Eekman, Thomas, jt. ed. see Debreczeny, Paul.
Eells, J., ed. Complex Analysis Trieste: Proceedings, 1981.
Eells, John M. LAFCO Spheres of Influence: Effective Planning for the Urban Fringe.
Eells, Walter C. & Haswell, Harold A. Academic Degrees.
Eells, Walter C., ed. see United States Office of Education, Division of Higher Education Staff.
Eesley, G. L. Coherent Raman Spectroscopy.
Effendi, Shoghi, tr. see Baha'u'llah.
Effland, Richard W., et al. Archaeology of Powell Plateau: Regional Interaction at Grand Canyon.
Effrat, Andrew, ed. Perspectives in Political Sociology.
Effron, Joel, jt. auth. see Zendex Corporation Staff.
Effros, Richard, et al, eds. The Microcirculation: Current Concepts.
Efimov, A. V. Mathematical Analysis, Advanced Topics, Pt. 1: Functional Series & Their Application.
--Mathematical Analysis, Advanced Topics, Pt. 2: Application of Some Methods of Mathematical & Functional Analysis.
Efimov, N. V. Higher Geometry.
Efremova, Vera. Bistrota: Collection of Stories.
Efron, Daniel H., jt. auth. see Usdin, Earl.
Efron, Edith. The Apocalyptics: Cancer & the Big Lie - How Environmental Politics Controls What We Know About Cancer.
Eftekhar, Nas Ser. Infection in Joint Replacement Surgery: Prevention & Management.
Efvergren, Carl J. Names of Places in a Transferred Sense in English: A Sematological Study.
Egami, F. & Nakamura, K. Microbial Ribonucleases.
Egan, Clifford L. & Knott, Alexander W., eds. Essays in Twentieth Century American Diplomatic History Dedicated to Professor Daniel M. Smith.
Egan, Eileen. Such a Vision of the Street: Mother Teresa; The Spirit & The Work.
Egan, Ferol. The El Dorado Trail: The Story of the Gold Rush Routes Across Mexico.
--The Taste of Time.
Egan, H. & West, T. S., eds. Harmonization of Collaborative Analytical Studies: International Symposium on Harmonization of Collaborative Analytical Studies, Helsinki Finland, 20-21 September 1981.
Egan, Howard T. Gassendi's View of Knowledge: A Study of the Epistemological Basis of His Logic.
Egan, Judith. Elena: A Love Story of the Russian Revolution.
Egan, Katherine. Beginnings: The Orientation of New Teachers.
Egan, Kieran. Structural Communication.
Egan, M. David. Concepts in Architectural Acoustics.
Egan, M. Winston, jt. auth. see Landau, Elliott D.
Egan, Robert. Bookstore Book.
Egan, Robert S. Topics Aids: Biology: A Catalog of Instructional Media.
Egar, Margaret, et al. Regeneration in Lower Vertebrates & Invertebrates.
Egardt, B. Stability of Adaptive Controllers. Balakrishnan, A. V. & Thoma, M., eds.
Egdahl, R. H., ed. Background Papers on Industry's Changing Role in Health Care Delivery.
Egdahl, R. H., jt. ed. see Walsh, D. C.
Egdahl, Richard H. & Gertman, Paul M., eds. Quality Assurance in Health Care.
Egejuru, Phanuel A. Black Writers-White Audience: A Critical Approach to African Literature.
Egelstaff, P. A. & Poole, M. J. Experimental Neutron Thermalization.
Egelstaff, P. A., ed. Thermal Neutron Scattering.
Egelstaff, Peter A., ed. Introduction to the Liquid State.
Egelston, G., jt. auth. see Goldberg, M.
Egendorf, Arthur. Healing from the War: Trauma & Transformation after Vietnam.
Egerton, Clement, tr. from Chinese. The Golden Lotus: A Translation of the Chinese Novel, Chin P'ing Mei.
Egerton, George. Keynotes. Fletcher, Ian & Stokes, John, eds.
Egerton, John. Generations.
Egerton, Margaret. The Red Velvet Mansion.
Egerton-Thomas, Christopher. Royal Singles.
Eggan, Fred, et al. Social Anthropology of North American Tribes.
Egge, Mandus A., ed. Worship: Good News in Action.
Egge, Mandus A. & Moede, Janet, eds. Hymns, How to Sing Them.
Eggen, Paul, jt. auth. see Kauchak, Donald P.
Egger, Rowland. The President of the United States.
Eggers, O. Occupational Therapy in the Treatment of Adult Hemiplegia.
Eggers-Lura, A. Solar Energy for Domestic Heating & Cooling.
--Solar Energy in Developing Countries.
Eggert, Arthur A. Electronics & Instrumentation for the Clinical Laboratory.
Egginton, Joyce. The Poisoning of Michigan.
Egginton, Mary, et al. The Older Woman's Health Guide.
Eggleston, George C., ed. American War Ballads & Lyrics.
Eggleston, John, ed. Contemporary Research in the Sociology of Education.
--Work Experience in Secondary Schools.
Eggleston, Wilfrid. The Road to Nationhood: A Chronicle of Dominion-Provincial Relations.
Egglishaw, John J., tr. see Hansen, Martin A.
Eggum, B. O., jt. ed. see Adler-Nissen, J.
Egle, K. Entscheidungstheorie.
Egleson, Janet F. Design for Writing Workbook.
Egleton, Clive. Backfire.
--A Conflict of Interests.
--The Eisenhower Deception.
--The Mills Bomb.
--The Russian Enigma.
--Troika.
Egly, T. W., Jr. History of the First New York Regiment 1775-1783.
Egorov, I. Right to Fly.
Egret, Jean. The French Pre-Revolution, 1787-1788. Camp, Wesley D., tr. from Fr.
Egri, Lajos. Art of Creative Writing.
Ehinger, R., et al. The Pawcatuck River Estuary & Little Narragansett Bay.
Ehle, John. The Changing of the Guard.
Ehlers, Anita, tr. see Ferris, Timothy.
Ehlers, Chad, photos by. Sentinels of Solitude: West Coast Lighthouses.
Ehlers, Henry J. Crucial Issues in Education.
Ehlers, J., et al, eds. see Simms, D. J.
Ehman, Lee H., et al, eds. Toward Effective Instruction in Secondary Social Studies.
Ehmann, James. Chattey's Island.
Ehmert, A., jt. ed. see Pfotzer, G.
Ehninger, Douglas & Gronbeck, Bruce E. Principles of Speech Communication.
Ehninger, Douglas, et al. Principles & Types of Speech Communication.
Ehrenberg, Miriam & Ehrenberg, Otto. The Intimate Circle: The Sexual Dynamics of Family Life.
Ehrenberg, Miriam, jt. auth. see Ehrenberg, Otto.
Ehrenberg, Otto & Ehrenberg, Miriam. The Psychotherapy Maze: A Consumer's Guide to Getting In & Out of Therapy.
Ehrenberg, Otto, jt. auth. see Ehrenberg, Miriam.
Ehrenberg, Ronald G. & Smith, Robert S. Modern Labor Economics.
Ehrenburg, A., jt. auth. see Akeson, A.
Ehrenburg, I. Second Day.
Ehrendorfer, F., jt. ed. see Nagl, W.
Ehrenhalt, Alan & Glennon, Michael. Politics in America: Members of Congress in Washington & at Home, 1984.
Ehrenpreis, S. & Neidel, A, eds. Methods in Narcotics Research.
Ehrenzweig, Albert A., et al. Jurisdiction in a Nutshell.
Ehret, Walter, jt. auth. see Trusler, Ivan.
Ehrhardt, Roy. Marion Watches Price Guide. Meggers, William F., ed.
--Trademarks.
--Violin Identification & Price Guide.
Ehrhardt, Roy & Rabeneck, Malvern. Clock Identification & Price Guide.
Ehrig, H., et al, eds. Graph-Grammars & Their Application to Computer Science.
Ehringer, H., jt. ed. see Strub, A. S.
Ehrlich, Amy, ed. see Brown, Dee.
Ehrlich, Ann. Business Administration for the Dental Assistant.
--Managing Insurance Claims in the Dental Office.
Ehrlich, Anne H., jt. auth. see Ehrlich, Paul R.
Ehrlich, David, ed. The Health Care Cost Explosion.
Ehrlich, Eugene & Murphy, Daniel. Concise Index to English.
Ehrlich, Everett M., jt. auth. see Scheppach, Raymond C.
Ehrlich, Jeffrey & Mannheimer, Marc. The Carpenter's Manifesto.
Ehrlich, Max. The Big Boys.
--Shaitan.
Ehrlich, Paul R. The Machinery of Nature.
Ehrlich, Paul R. & Ehrlich, Anne H. The End of Affluence: A Blueprint for Your Future.
Ehrlich, Paul R., et al. The Process of Evolution.
Ehrlich, Robert. Physics & Computers: Problems, Simulations, & Data Analysis.
Ehrlich, Ruth A. & Givens, Ellen M. Patient Care in Radiography.
Ehrlich, Shelley. How the Rooted Travel.
Ehrlich, Virginia. Gifted Children: A Guide for Teachers & Parents.
Ehrlichman, John D. The China Card.
Ehrly, A. M., ed. Determination of Tissue Oxygen Pressure in Patients.
Ehrman, Kenneth & Flavin, Sean. Taxing California Property.
Ehrmann, Henry W. Comparative Legal Cultures.
Ehrmann, Lee & Omenn, Gilbert S., eds. Genetics, Environment & Behavior: Implications for Educational Policy.

Eibl-Eibesfeldt, Irenaus. Love & Hate: The Natural History of Behavior Patterns.

Eichberger, J., jt. auth. see Siebert, H.

Eichenberg, Fritz. Dancing in the Moon: Counting Rhymes.

--Lithography & Silkscreen Art & Technique.

Eichengreen, Barry, jt. auth. see Cairncross, Alec.

Eichengreen, Barry, ed. The Gold Standard in Theory & History.

Eichengreen, Barry J. Sterling & the Tariff, Nineteen Twenty-Nine to Nineteen Twenty-Two.

Eicher, T., et al. Cyclic Compounds.

Eichholz, Alice & Rose, James M., eds. Free Black Heads of Households in the New York State Federal Census, 1790 to 1830.

Eichholz, G. G. & Poston, J. W. Principles of Nuclear Radiation Detection.

Eichhorn see Steer, Donald R., et al.

Eichhorn, W., et al, eds. Production Theory: Proceedings of the International Seminar, University of Karlsruhe, May-July, 1973.

Eichler, Margrit & Scott, Hilda, eds. Women in Futures Research.

Eichler, Marie H. Developing Basic Writing Skills in English As a Second Language.

Eichler, Martin. Introduction to the Theory of Algebraic Numbers & Functions.

--Projective Varieties & Modular Forms.

Eichler, Victor, et al. Regeneration in Lower Vertebrates & Invertebrates.

Eichner, Alfred S. The Megacorp & Oligopoly.

Eichner, Hans, ed. see Behler, Ernst, et al.

Eichner, James. First Book of the Cabinet of the President of the U. S.

Eickelman, Dale F. Moroccan Islam: Tradition & Society in a Pilgrimage Center.

Eickman, J. C. The Ford Y-Block.

Eidelberg, Lawrence, ed. The Videolog: Programs for General Interest & Entertainment.

--The Videolog: Programs for the Health Sciences.

Eidelberg, Martin. Watteau's Drawings: Their Use & Significance.

Eidenberg, Eugene & Morey, Roy D. Act of Congress.

Eidenier, Connie, ed. Photographer's Market 1987.

--Photographer's Market 88.

Eigen, M. & Schuster, P. The Hypercycle: A Principle of Natural Self-Organization.

Eiger, Marvin S., jt. auth. see Olds, Sally W.

Eighme, Lloyd. Insects You Have Seen.

Eighmy, John L. Churches in Cultural Captivity: A History of the Social Attitudes of Southern Baptists.

Eighty Micro Editors. Eighty Micro's Review Guide.

Eignmann, Carl H. A Revision of the South American Nematognathi or Catfishes.

Eijk Van Voorthuijesn, M. E. Van see Van Eijk Van Voorthuijsen, M. E.

Eijndhover, J. Van see Van Eijndhover, J.

Eiken, M. Roentgen Diagnosis of Bones.

Eikenbary, R. D., jt. ed. see Boethal, D. J.

Eikhenbaum, Boris. Tolstoi in the Sixties. White, tr. from Rus.

Eikner, Allen V., ed. Religious Perspectives & Problems: An Introduction to the Philosophy of Religion.

Eik-Nes, K. B. & Horning, E. C. Gas Phase Chromatography of Steroids.

Eilenberg, S., et al, eds. see Conference On Categorical Algebra - La Jolla - 1965.

Eilis, Grace. The Rhinehart Reader Companion.

Eilon, S. & King, J. R. Industrial Scheduling Abstracts: 1950-1966.

Eilon, S. & Lampkin, W. Inventory Control Abstracts: 1953-1965.

Eimbinder, Jerry, ed. Designing with Linear Integrated Circuits.

Eims, Leroy. Keeping off the Casualty List.

--Laboring in the Harvest.

--The Lost Art of Disciple Making.

--Prayer: More Than Words.

Einaudi, Paula F. A Grammar of Biloxi.

Einaudi, R., tr. see Nervi, Pier L.

Einon, Dorothy. Play with a Purpose: Learning Games for Children Six Weeks to Ten Years.

Einsele, G. & Soilacher, A., eds. Cyclic & Event Stratification.

Einstein, Albert. Essays in Science.

--Out of My Later Years.

--The World As I See It.

Einstein, C. The Baseball Reader: Favorites from the Fireside Book of Baseball.

Einstein Centennial Celebration Staff. After Einstein: Proceedings of the Einstein Centennial Celebration, Memphis State University, March 14-16, 1979. Barker, Peter & Shugart, Cecil G., eds.

Einstein, Charles. How to Coach, Manage & Play Little League Baseball.

Einstein, David G. Emperor Frederick Second.

Einstein, Gertrude, ed. Learning to Apply New Concepts to Casework Practice.

Einstein, Stanley. Beyond Drugs.

Einstein, Stanley, ed. Drugs in Relation to the Drug User.

Einstein, Susan, ed. see Selz, Peter.

Einzig, Hetty, jt. auth. see Cannon, Geoffrey.

Eisberg, Robert M. & Lerner, Lawrence S. Physics: Foundations & Applications.

Eischen, Martha. Does Your Small Business Need a Computer?

Eisele, Carol. Christ in You.

Eiseley, Loren. All the Strange Hours: The Excavation of a Life.

--Darwin & the Mysterious Mr. X: New Light on the Evolutionists.

--The Invisible Pyramid.

--The Night Country.

--Unexpected Universe.

Eiseman, Alberta. From Many Lands.

--Manana Is Now.

--The Sunday Whirling.

Eiseman, Alberta & Eiseman, Nicole. Gift from a Sheep.

Eiseman, Nicole, jt. auth. see Eiseman, Alberta.

Eisen, Carole, jt. auth. see Eisen, Martin.

Eisen, Johnathan, jt. auth. see Chandler, David L.

Eisen, Jon, et al. Unknown California. Dorszynski, ed.

Eisen, Martin & Eisen, Carole. Finite Mathematics.

Eisenberg, ed. Radiation Protection: A Systematic Approach to Safety: Proceedings of the 5th Congress of the International Radiation Protection Society, March 1980, Jerusalem.

Eisenberg, Arlene, et al. The Pregnancy Organizer.

Eisenberg, Azriel. Jewish Historical Treasures.

Eisenberg, Azriel & Globe, Leah A. The Secret Weapon & Other Stories.

Eisenberg, C. G. History of the First Dakota-District of the Evangelical-Lutheran Synod of Iowa & Other States. Richter, Anton H., tr. from Ger.

Eisenberg, Frank, Jr., jt. ed. see Wells, William W.

Eisenberg, Gerson G. Learning Vacations.

Eisenberg, Howard & Sehnert, Keith W. How to Be Your Own Doctor Sometimes: 10th Anniversary Edition.

Eisenberg, Howard, jt. auth. see Sehnert, Keith W.

Eisenberg, J. M. & Greiner, W. Nuclear Theory, Vol. 1: Nuclear Models.

Eisenberg, James & Kafka, Francis J. Silk Screen Printing.

Eisenberg, Judah M. & Koltun, Daniel S. Theory of Meson Interactions with Nuclei.

Eisenberg, Lawrence B. The Villa of the Ferromonte.

Eisenberg, Lee & Taylor, Decourcy. The Ultimate Fishing Book.

Eisenberg, Melvin, jt. auth. see Cary, William L.

Eisenberg, Mickey, jt. auth. see Larson, Eric.

Eisenberg, Phyllis R. Don't Tell Me a Ghost Story.

Eisenberg, Seymour & Elting, L. Melvin. Nine Day Wonder Diet.

Eisenberg, Sheldon & Delaney, Daniel J. The Counseling Process.

Eisenberg, Terry., et al. Police-Community Action: A Program for Change in Police-Community Behavior Patterns.

Eisenberg, Theodore, et al. Commercial & Debtor-Creditor Law: Selected Statutes.

Eisenbud, Merril. Environmental Radioactivity.

Eisenhower, Julie N. Pat Nixon: The Untold Story.

Eisenman, George, ed. Membranes: Lipid Bilayers & Biological Membranes: Dynamic Properties.

--Membranes, Vol. 2: Lipid Bilayers & Antibiotics.

Eisenreich, S., ed. Physical Behavior of PCBs in the Great Lakes.

Eisenreighler, E. & Pincus, P. Polymers at Surfaces & Colloid Stability.

Eisenson, Jon & Boase, Paul H. Basic Speech.

Eisenstadt, Melvin M. Introduction to Mechanical Properties of Materials: An Ecological Approach.

Eisenstadt, S. N., ed. Post-Traditional Societies.

--Readings in Social Evolution & Development.

Eisenstadt, Samuel N. & Bar-Yosef, Rivkah. Integration & Development in Israel.

Eisenstein, Sergei. The Battleship Potemkin.

Eisenstein, Toby K., et al, eds. Host Defenses to Intracellular Pathogens.

Eiser, J. R. & Strobe, Wolfgang, eds. Categorization & Social Judgment.

Eisert, Martin P., jt. auth. see Imundo, Louis V.

Eisert, W. G. & Mendelsohn, M. L., eds. Biological Dosimetry: Cytometric Approaches to Mammalian Systems.

Eisler, Colin. Sculptors' Drawings over Six Centuries.

Eisler, Robert. Man into Wolf.

Eisner, Bruce. Ecstasy: The MDMA Story.

Eison, Charles L., jt. auth. see Ray, Charles M.

Eitel, Alta W. Yon Mountain: A Doctor of Faith Walks with God.

Eitel, Ernest J. Feng-Shui: The Science of Sacred Landscape.

Eiteman, Wilford J. Essentials of Accounting Theory.

Eitner, Robert, ed. see Vecchi, Orazio.

Eitzen. Social Problems.

--Social Problems.

Eitzen, D. Stanley. In Conflict & Order: Understanding Society.

Eitzen, K. Military Eitzen.

Ejaz, Moina. Reaching for the Stars.

Ejiogu, C. N., jt. ed. see Ominde, S. H.

Ejxenbaum, B. M. O. Henry & the Theory of the Short Story. Titunik, I. R., tr.

Ek, Jan A. Van see Van Ek, Jan A. & Robat, Nico J.

Ekdale, A. A., et al. Ichnology: Trace Fossils in Sedimentology & Stratigraphy.

Ekelund, Robert B. & Hebert, R. H. A History of Economic Theory & Method.

Ekelund, Robert B. & Tollison, Robert D. Economics.

--Macroeconomics.

--Microeconomics.

Ekirch, Arthur A., Jr. Decline of American Liberalism.

Ekkart, R. F., ed. University of Leiden (Athenae Batavae) 1575-1975.

Eklund, Sigvard, ed. see International Atomic Energy Agency Staff.

Ekman, Paul. The Face of Man: Expressions of Universal Emotions in a New Guinea Village.

--Telling Lies: Clues to Deceit in the Marketplace, Politics & Marriage.

Eksborg, S., et al, eds. Liquid Chromatography in the Biomedical Sciences: Invited Papers from the 15th International Symposium Held in , Ronneby, Sweden, 18-21 June 1984.

Eksell, Olle, jt. auth. see Rand, Ann.

Eksten, Jim. The Lord & Me: A Personal Testimony.

Ekstrom, M. P., jt. ed. see Mitra, S. K.

Ekstrom, Margareta. Death's Midwives. Claeson, Eva, tr.

Ekwall, Per, et al, eds. Surface Chemistry: Proceedings.

Ekwensi, Cyprian. People of the City.

El-Agraa, Ali. Trade Theory & Policy: Some Topical Issues.

Elam, Houston G. & Paley, Norton. Marketing for the Non-Marketing Executive.

Eland, J. H. Photoelectron Spectroscopy.

El-Ansary, Adel I., jt. auth. see Stern, Louis W.

Elazar, Daniel J., jt. ed. see Kincaid, John.

Elazo-Ayala, Cast & MacGregor, C., eds. Gynecology & Obstetrics: Abstracts from the 8th World Congress Held in Mexico, 1976.

El-Badry, Hamed M. Micromanipulators & Micromanipulation.

Elbaz, Robert. The Changing Nature of the Self: A Critical Study of the Autobiographic Discourse.

Elbe, Guenther Von see Lewis, Bernard & Von Elbe, Guenther.

Elbert, Joyce. Drunk in Madrid.

--Getting Rid of Richard.

--The Three of Us.

Elbow, Margret. The Rootomom Tree.

Elcock, Howard. Local Government.

Eldefrawi, A. T., jt. ed. see Albuquerque, E. X.

Elder, Carl A. Youth & Values: Getting Self Together.

Elder, Charles D. & Cobb, Roger W. The Political Uses of Symbols. Rockwood, Irving, ed.

Elder, Frank. The Book of the Hackle.

Elder, Glen H. Children of the Great Depression: Social Change in the Life Experience.

Elder, James B., jt. ed. see Chantler, Eric N.

Elder, Lloyd. Blueprints.

Elder, Mark. The Prometheus Operation.

Elder, N. C. Government in Sweden: The Executive at Work.

Elder, Neil & Thomas, Alastair H. The Consensual Democracies? The Government & Politics of the Scandinavian States.

--Consensual Democracies? The Government & Politics of the Scandinavian States.

Elder, Rob & Elder, Sarah. Crash.

Elder, Robert E. Information Machine: The United States Information Agency & American Foreign Policy.

Elder, Sarah, jt. auth. see Elder, Rob.

Elder, T. & Neill, W., eds. Biomedical Technology in Hospital Diagnosis.

Elderfield, John. The Drawings of Henri Matisse.

Elderfield, John, jt. auth. see Golding, John.

Eldot, Paula. Governor Alfred E. Smith: The Politician As Reformer. Freidel, Frank, ed.

Eldred, Patricia M. Donny & Marie.

--What Happens When We Sleep?

Eldredge, Niles. Time Frames: The Re-thinking of Darwinian Evolution & the Theory of Punctuated Equilibria.

Eldred-Grigg, Stevan Treleaven. Of Ivory Accents.

Eldridge, Franklin E. Cytogenetics of Livestock.

Eldridge, G. C. Victorian Imperialism.

Eldridge, Niles. Fossil Factory.

--Time Frames: The Rethinking of Darwinian Evolution & the Theory of Punctuated Equilibria.

Eldridge, Richard, jt. auth. see Kerman, Cynthia E.

Electa-Rizzoli Staff & Whitehill, Walter M. Palladio in America.

Electro-Craft Corp. Staff. DC Motors, Speed Controls, Servo Systems: An Engineering Handbook.

Electronic Industries Association Staff & Zbar, Paul B. Electricity-Electronics Fundamentals: A Text-Lab Manual.

Electronics Magazine Editors. Design Techniques for Electronics Engineers.

--Large Scale Integration.

--Microelectronics Interconnection & Packaging.

--Microprocessors.

--New Product Trends in Electronics Number One.

--Personal Computing: Hardware & Software Basics.

Electronics Magazine Editors & Weber, Samuel. Electronic Circuits Notebook: Proven Designs for Systems Applications.

Elegant, Robert. Mandarin.

Elementary Science Study Staff. Animals in the Classroom: A Book for Teachers.

--The Balance Book: A Guide for Teachers.

--Batteries & Bulbs Two: Student's Book.

--Bones.

--Clay Boats.

--Crayfish.

--Gases & Airs.

--Life of Beans & Peas.

--Light & Shadows.

--Pendulums.

--Spinning Tables.

--Starting from Seeds.

--Tangrams.

--Tracks.

--Whistles & Strings.

Elert, Werner. Law & Gospel. Sherman, Franklin, ed. Schroeder, Edward H., tr. from Ger.

El-Fattah, Y. M. & Foulard, C. Learning Systems: Decision, Simulation, & Control.

El Fattal, David. Successful Selling Strategies.

Elfenbein, Hiram. Organized Religion.

Elfers, Robert A. A Sojourn in Mosaic.

Elfman, Blossom. Butterfly Girl.

--The Girls of Huntington House.

--A House for Jonnie O.

--The Return of the Whistler.

Elfner, Lynn E., jt. auth. see King, Charles C.

Elfring, Gary C. Microcomputer Assembly Language Programming.

Elgaroy, O. Solar Noise Storms. Ter Harr, D., ed.

Elger, C. E., jt. ed. see Speckmann, E. J.

Elgin, Duane. Voluntary Simplicity: Toward a Way of Life That Is Outwardly Simple, Inwardly Rich.

Elgin, Suzette H. The Grand Jubilee.

Elgood, Chris. Handbook of Management Games.

El Guindy, M. I., ed. Precious Metals 1982: Proceedings of the 6th International Precious Metals Institute Conference, Newport Beach, California, June 7-11, 1982.

El Hares, H., ed. see Al Fateh Staff & IFAC Staff.

El-Hifnawi, M., jt. auth. see Fareed, A.

El-Hinnawi, Essam E., ed. Nuclear Energy & the Environment.

Elhmann, Paul W., jt. auth. see White, Trentwell M.

El-Hodiri, M. A. Constrained Extrema: Introduction to the Differentiable Case with Economic Applications.

Eliach, Yaffa. Hasidic Tales of the Holocaust.

Eliade, Mircea. Autobiography: Journey East, Journey West, 1907 to 1937. Ricketts, Mac L., tr.

--Autobiography: Volume I, Journey East, Journey West 1907-1937.

--No Souvenirs: Journal, 1957-1969.

--Two Strange Tales. Coates, William A., tr. from Romanian.

Eliakim, M., ed. International Symposium on Hepatotoxicity.

Elian, G. International Court of Justice.

Elias. Elias Practical Grammar.

Elias, Albert J. The Sonora Mutation.

Elias, Christopher. The Beginner's Investment Handbook: One Hundred & Two Ways to Invest One Thousand or Less...& Make It Pay.

Elias, H. & Sherrick, Joseph C. Morphology of the Liver.

Elias, John L. Conscientization & Deschooling: Freire's & Illich's Proposals for Reshaping Society.

Elias, Michael & Eustis, Michael. Young Doctors in Love.

Elias, Norbert. The Loneliness of Dying.

Elias, P., jt. auth. see Csiszar, I.

Elias, Patrick & Ewing, K. D. Trade Union Democracy, Members' Rights & the Law.

Elias, Robert H. & Finch, Eugene D., eds. Letters of Thomas Attwood Digges (1742-1821)

Elias, Stephen, ed. see Pressman, David.

Eliason, K., et al. Everything but the Kitchen Sink: A Plan Ahead Cookbook.

Eliason, Karine, et al. More Make-A-Mix Cookery.

Eliasson, Rune, jt. ed. see Von Euler, Ulf S.

Eliis, R. A., jt. auth. see Engineering Manpower Commission.
Elimelech, Baruch. A Tonal Grammar of Etsako.
Eliot, Charles W. John Gilley of Baker's Island.
Eliot, George. Adam Bede.
--Daniel Deronda.
--Felix Holt, the Radical.
--Silas Marner.
--Silas Marner.
--Silas Marner: The Weaver of Raveloe.
Eliot, Philip, et al. Televising Terrorism: Political Violence in Popular Culture.
Eliot, R. C., ed. Coal Desulfurization Prior to Combustion.
Eliot, T. S. The Complete Plays of T. S. Eliot.
--The Confidential Clerk.
--The Cultivation of Christmas Trees.
--The Elder Statesman.
--The Family Reunion.
--Four Quartets.
--Four Quartets.
--Notes Towards the Definition of Culture.
--The Use of Poetry & the Use of Criticism Studies in the Relation of Criticism to Poetry in England.
--The Waste Land: Facsimile & Transcript. Eliot, Valerie, ed.
Eliot, Valerie, ed. see Eliot, T. S.
Eliovson, Sima. Proteas for Pleasure.
Elisofon, Eliot & Fagg, William. The Sculpture of Africa.
Elizondo, Sergio D., jt. auth. see Tyler, Richard W.
Elizondo, Virgilio P. La Morenita: Evangelizadora de las Americas.
Elkan, Peter G. The New Model Economy: Economic Inventions for the Rest of the Century.
Elkana, Yehuda, ed. The Interaction Between Science & Philosophy: Sambursky Festschrift.
Elkann, Alain. Piazza Carignano. Weaver, William, tr. from Ital.
El-Khawas, Mohamed A., jt. auth. see Serapiao, Luis B.
El-Khawas, Mohamed A. see Mohamed A. El-Khawas & Cohen, Barry.
Elkin, Stanley. The Franchiser.
--Searches & Seizures: Three Novellas.
Elkin, Stanley & Ravenel, Shannon, eds. The Best American Short Stories Nineteen Eighty.
Elkins, Carolyn. Community Health Nursing: Skills & Strategies.
Elkins, Dov P., ed. Glad to Be Me: Building Self-Esteem in Yourself & Others.
Elkins, Garland, jt. ed. see Warren, Thomas B.
Elkins, John C. Ginger's Star.
Elkins, Norman. Weather & Bird Behaviour.
Elkins, Patricia. Weekday Early Education: Art Idea Book.
Elkoff, Marvin. After the Race.
Ellard, Gerald. Master Alcuin, Liturgist.
Ellard, Palmer T. The Wonder of His Love.
Elle Magazine Staff. The Elle Knitting Book.
Elledge, Scott, ed. see Hardy, Thomas.
Ellen, Roy F. A Guide to the General Conduct of Ethnographic Research.
Ellenberg, H., ed. Progress in Botany.
Ellenberg, H., et al, eds. Progress in Botany.
--Progress in Botany.
--Progress in Botany.
--Progress in Botany.
--Progress in Botany: Vol. 40.
--Progress in Botany.
Ellenberger, J. S. & Mahar, Ellen P., eds. Legislative History of the Securities Act of 1933 & Securities Exchange Act of 1934.
Ellenbogen, Eileen, ed. see Simenon, Georges.
Ellenbogen, Eileen, tr. see Simenon, Georges.
Ellenbogen, Eileen, tr. see Weintraub, Stanley.
Eller, Clyde H., jt. auth. see Swanson, Elizabeth E.
Ellerbach, Richard. Tax Reduction Strategies for Small Business: Planning Techniques for Wealth Accumlation in the Eighties.
Ellerman, David P. Economics, Accounting, & Property Theory.
Ellersieck, Mark R., jt. auth. see Mayer, Foster L., Jr.
Ellerstein, Norman S. Child Abuse & Neglect: A Medical Reference.
Elles, Gertrude L. & Wood, Ethel M. British Graptolites.
Ellin, Stanley. Very Old Money.
--Very Old Money.
Elling, Ray, ed. Traditional & Modern Medical Systems.
Elling, Ray H., ed. Cross National Study of Health Systems by Countries & World Region, & Special Problems: A Guide to Information Sources.
Ellinger, H. Automotive Systems Fuel Lubrication & Cooling.
Ellinger, Herb. Automechanics.
Ellingham, Mark & Fisher, John. Rough Guide to Spain.
Ellingham, Mark, et al. Rough Guide to Greece.
--Rough Guide to Portugal.
--The Rough Guide to Greece.
Ellingsen, Mark. Doctrine & Word.
Ellingson, David R. & Jensen, Darcy D. My Body, My Life.
Ellingson, Marnie. The Wicked Marquis.
Ellington, C. D. Professional Apartmenteering.
Ellington, H. I., et al. Games & Simulations in Science Education.
Ellington, Henry, jt. auth. see Addinall, Eric.
Ellington, Henry, jt. auth. see Percival, Fred.
Ellington, Mark & McVeigh, Shaun. Rough Guide to Morocco.
Ellington, Mercer & Dance, Stanley. Duke Ellington in Person: An Intimate Memoir.
Elliot, A. M., tr. see Vidali, Vittorio.
Elliot, Alfred M. Biology of Tetrahymena.
Elliot, B. J. Western Europe after Hitler.
Elliot, Douglass. Bold Destiny.
Elliot, Elisabeth. As We Forgive Those.
--The Glory of God's Will.
--Love Knows No Limit.
--Marriage Is a Gift.
--Notes on Prayer.
--These Strange Ashes.
--What God Has Joined.
Elliot, Geoff. Video Production in Education & Training.
Elliot, Janice. Dr. Gruber's Daughter.
Elliot, Jeffrey M. Reader's Guide to A. E. van Vogt. Schlobin, Roger C., ed.
--Urban Society.
Elliot, Jeffrey M., ed. Annual Editions: Third World 1988-89.
Elliot, John F., jt. ed. see Tien, John K.
Elliot, John H. A Home for the Homeless: A Sociological Exegesis of 1 Peter, Its Solution & Strategy.
Elliot, Kit. Benin: An African Kingdom & Culture.
Elliot, Nem & Elliot, Percy. The Complete German Shepherd Dog.
Elliot, Percy, jt. auth. see Elliot, Nem.
Elliot, Wallace W. The History of San Bernardino & San Diego Counties.
Elliot-Binns, Christopher. Too Much Tenderness: An Autobiography of Childhood & Youth.
Elliott, A. M., tr. see Carrillo, Santiago.
Elliott, Bill. Plum Cobbler.
Elliott, Bob & Goulding, Ray. From Approximately Coast to Coast...It's the Bob & Ray Show.
--From Approximately Coast to Coast...It's the Bob & Ray Show.
--The New! Improved! Bob & Ray Book.
Elliott, Brian, tr. see Levy-Bruel, Lucien.
Elliott, Charles. Sinfulness of American Slavery. Tefft, Benjamin F., ed.
Elliott, Charles, ed. see Rosenfeld, Albert.
Elliott, Cheri. Backpacker's Digest.
Elliott, Cheri, ed. Archer's Digest.
Elliott, Colleen M., jt. auth. see Alexander, Virginia.
Elliott, D., jt. ed. see Walton, R. G.
Elliott, D. J. Integrated Circuit Fabrication Technology.
Elliott, David. Tradition & Renewal: Contemporary Art in the German Democratic Republic.
Elliott, David, ed. Reconstructions: Avant-Garde Art in Japan 1945-1965.
Elliott, David, ed. & pref. by. Tierra & Libertad! Photographs of Mexico, 1900-1935.
Elliott, Dietlinde, tr. see Stegemann, Wolfgang.
Elliott, Douglas. As You Recover.
Elliott, E. N., ed. Cotton Is King & Pro-Slavery Arguments.
Elliott, Godfrey. Film & Education.
Elliott, J., jt. auth. see Williams, R.
Elliott, J. H., jt. auth. see Briggs, S. R.
Elliott, James F., jt. auth. see Tanzik, David A.
Elliott, Janice. The Sadness of Witches.
Elliott, John E. Comparative Economic Systems.
Elliott, John E. & Grey, Arthur. Economic Issues & Policies: Readings in Introductory Economics.
Elliott, John H., jt. auth. see Vawter, Bruce.
Elliott, Katherine, jt. ed. see Skeet, Muriel.
Elliott, R. W. Runes: An Introduction.
Elliott, Ralph W. Thomas Hardy's English. Crystal, David, ed.
Elliott, Raymond. Fundamentals of Music.
Elliott, Robert C. The Shape of Utopia: Studies in a Literary Genre.
Elliott, Roth & Savage, Jim. The Complete Guide to Affordable In-Home Childcare.
Elliott, S. R. Physics of Amorphous Materials.
Elliott, Scott. Story of Atlantis & the Lost Lemuria.
Elliott, Sumner L. Signs of Life.
Elliott, Thomas C., jt. ed. see O'Keefe, William.
Elliott, W. W. The History of San Bernardino & San Diego Counties.
Elliott, Ward E. The Rise of Guardian Democracy: The Supreme Court's Role in Voting Rights Disputes, 1845-1969.
Elliott, William M., Jr. Cure for Anxiety.
Elliott-Binns, Leonard E. From Moses to Elisha: Israel to the End of the Ninth Century B. C.
Ellis & Campbell. Essential Anaethesia.
Ellis, jt. auth. see Compton.
Ellis, A. E. British Freshwater Bivalve Mollusca: Keys & Notes for the Identification of the Species.
Ellis, A. R., ed. Under Scott's Command: Lashly's Antarctic Diaries.
Ellis, Adrian & Kumar, Krishan. Dilemmas of Liberal Democracies: Studies in Fred Hirsch's Social Limits to Growth.
Ellis, Albert & Abrahms, Eliot R. Brief Psychotherapy in Medical & Health Practice.
Ellis, Albert & Knaus, William J. Overcoming Procrastination.
Ellis, Albert & Whiteley, John M. Theoretical & Empirical Foundations of Rational-Emitive Therapy.
Ellis, Alec. A History of Children's Reading & Literature.
--How to Find Out about Children's Literature.
--Library Services for Young People in England & Wales, 1830-1970.
Ellis, Alec, jt. auth. see Crouch, Marcus.
Ellis, Ann, jt. ed. see Van Gorder, Barbara.
Ellis, Anthony E. Fish & Shellfish Pathology.
Ellis, Bret E. Less Than Zero: A Novel.
Ellis, Brian. Rational Belief Systems.
Ellis, Brobury P., ed. & tr. see Beaumarchais, Pierre-Augustin.
Ellis, C. Douglas & Schachter, Albert. Ancient Greek: A Structural Programme.
Ellis, C. Hamilton. Engines That Passed.
Ellis, Catherine J. Aboriginal Music: Education for Living: Cross Cultural Experiences from South Australia.
Ellis, Charles M. Essay on Transcendentalism.
Ellis, Christopher, jt. auth. see Bishop, Denis.
Ellis, D. & Pekar, P. Planning Basics for Managers.
Ellis, Darryl J. & Pekar, Peter P. Planning for Non-Planners.
Ellis, David. Let's Look at Indonesia.
Ellis, David, jt. auth. see Crocetti, Gino.
Ellis, E. Earle. Eschatology in Luke. Reumann, John, ed.
--Prophecy & Hermeneutics in Early Christianity: New Testament Essays.
Ellis, Ed. Hotel Security Officer.
Ellis, Ella T. Celebrate the Morning.
--Sleepwalker's Moon.
--Where the Road Ends.
Ellis, Ella Thorp. Hallelujah.
Ellis, Florence H. Pueblo Indians, Vol. Two: Archaeologic & Ethnologic Data: Acoma-Laguna Land Claims.
Ellis, Garrison, ed. see Krick, Robert, et al.
Ellis, George, jt. auth. see Neelon, Francis A.
Ellis, Gwynn P. & Lockhart, Ian M., eds. Chromans & Tocopherols.
Ellis, Harold. Varicose Veins.
Ellis, Havelock. Psychology of Sex.
--The Psychology of Sex.
Ellis, Howard S. Notes on Stagflation.
Ellis, J. R. Philip the Second & Macedonian Imperialism.
Ellis, J. R., jt. auth. see Milns, R. D.
Ellis, Jack, jt. auth. see Harwood, Bruce M.
Ellis, Janice R. & Nowlis, Elizabeth A. Nursing: A Human Needs Approach.
--Nursing: A Human Needs Approach.
Ellis, Janice R., et al. Modules for Basic Nursing Skills.
Ellis, Jeffery W. & Beckmann, Charles R. A Clinical Manual of Gynecology.
Ellis, Jeffrey W. & Beckmann, Charles R. A Clinical Manual of Obstetrics.
Ellis, John. Cassino: The Hollow Victory-The Battle for Rome, January-June 1944.
--The Sharp End.
Ellis, John & Ferrara, Sergio, eds. Unification of Fundamental Particle Interactions II.
Ellis, John M. One Fairy Story Too Many: The Brothers Grimm & Their Tales.
Ellis, John T. & Trisco, Robert. A Guide to American Catholic History.
Ellis, Joseph J. After the Revolution: Profiles of Early American Culture.
Ellis, Julia. Glorious Morning.
Ellis, Julie. East Wind.
--Maison Jennie.
--The Only Sin.
--The Poles.
--Rich Is Best.
Ellis, Leigh. Green Lady.
--The Quick.
--Tessa of Destiny.
Ellis, Lynn W. The Financial Side of Industrial Research Management.
Ellis, Marc H. Toward a Jewish Theology of Liberation.
Ellis, Mark & Ellis, Robert. Atari User's Guide: BASIC & Graphics for the Atari 400, 800, 1200.
Ellis, Mark, et al. Professional English.
Ellis, Mary L. Jesus Christ, Son of God.
Ellis, Mel. An Eagle to the Wind.
Ellis, R. A. Engineering & Technology Degrees Fall 1986.
Ellis, R. A. & Engineering Manpower Commission Staff. Engineers' Salaries: Special Industry Report, 1987.
--Professional Income of Engineers, 1987.
Ellis, R. A., jt. auth. see Engineering Manpower Commission.
Ellis, R. A., ed. see Engineering Manpower Commission.
Ellis, Rhoda. Dictionary of Dietetics.
Ellis, Richard. The Book of Sharks: A Complete Illustrated Natural History of the Sharks of the World.
Ellis, Robert & Gulick, Denny. Calculus with Analytic Geometry.
--Calculus with Analytic Geometry.
--College Algebra.
--College Algebra & Trigonometry.
--Fundamentals of College Algebra & Trigonometry.
Ellis, Robert, jt. auth. see Ellis, Mark.
Ellis, Roger & Whittington, Dorothy, eds. New Directions in Social Skill Training.
Ellis, Wesley. Lone Star & the Renegade Comanches.
Ellis-Fermor, Una. Shakespeare's Drama. Muir, Kenneth, ed.
Ellison, Curtis W. & Metcalf, E. W., Jr. Charles W. Chesnutt: A Reference Guide.
Ellison, Emily. First Light: A Novel of a Daughter's Reluctant Understanding of Her Mother's Life.
Ellison, Gordon N. Thermal Computation for Electrical Equipment.
Ellison, H. L. From Babylon to Bethlehem: The People of God from the Exile to the Messiah.
--The Prophets of Israel: From Ahijah to Hosea.
--Understanding the New Testament: 1 Peter-Revelation.
Ellison, Harlan. Shatterday.
Ellison, John W. Nelson's Complete Concordance of the Revised Standard Version.
Ellison, Joseph W. Opening & Penetration of Foreign Influence in Samoa to 1880.
Ellison, Marvin M. The Center Cannot Hold: The Search for a Global Economy of Justice.
Ellison, Mary. Support for Secession: Lancashire & the American Civil War.
Ellison, Suzanne P. Sycamore Steeple.
Elliston, Frederick & McCormick, Peter, eds. Husserl: Expositions & Appraisals.
Ellman, Edgar. Recruiting & Selecting Profitable Sales Personnel.
Ellman, Michael. Collectivization, Convergence & Capitalism: Political Economy in a Divided World.
Ellman, Richard. Four Dubliners: Wilde, Yeats, Joyce & Beckett.
Ellmann, Richard see Joyce, James.
Ellner, Paul D. Current Procedures in Clinical Bacteriology.
Ellory, J. C. & Lew, V. L., eds. Membrane Transport in Red Cells.
Ellos, William J. Linguistic Ecumenism: A Barthian Road Back from Babel.
Ells, Ernest E. Eells Family History in America: Sixteen Thirty-Three to Nineteen Fifty-Two.
Ellsberg, Edward. Under the Red Sea Sun.
Ellsworth, Donald P. Christian Music in Contemporary Witness: Historical Antecedents & Contemporary Practices.
Ellsworth, J. W. & Stahnke, A. A. Politics & Political Systems.
Ellsworth, Liz. Frederick Wiseman: A Guide to References & Resources.
Ellsworth, Ralph, ed. see Norlin, George.
Ellul, Jacques. In Season, Out of Season: An Introduction to the Thought of Jacques Ellul.
--Living Faith.
--The Technological System.
Ellwood, D. C., jt. ed. see Berkeley, R. C.
Ellwood, John, jt. auth. see Webster, Alec.
Ellwood, Robert S., Jr. The Eagle & the Rising Sun: Americans & the New Religions of Japan.
--Many Peoples, Many Faiths.
Ellwood, Roger. Demon Kind.
Ellyson, Mary H. The Little Forecaster.
Elmaghraby, S. E. Some Network Models in Management Science.
Elmaghraby, S. E., ed. see Symposium on the Theory of Scheduling & Its Applications.
El Mallakh, Ragaei. Economic Development & Regional Cooperation: Kuwait.
Elmasry, Mohamed I. Digital Bipolar Integrated Circuits.
Elmen, Paul. Wheat Flour Messiah: Eric Jansson of Bishop Hill.
--Wheat Flour Messiah: Eric Jansson of Bishop Hill.
Elmes, David G. Readings in Experimental Psychology.
Elmes, David G., et al. Methods in Experimental Psychology.
Elmont, Nancy. A Knife for All Seasons.
Elmore, Inez. Children, Our Greatest Treasure.
Elmore, Inez K. The Story of a Great Pioneer in Black Education: Bennie Carl Elmore, 1909-1973.
--Times to Remember: A Dynamic Autobiography.
Elmore, Patricia. Susannah & the Blue House Mystery.
Elmore, Richard F., jt. ed. see Williams, Walter.
Elmore, Theo V. Lost Profits.
Elms, Alan C. Personality in Politics.

Elon, Menachem, ed. The Principles of Jewish Law.
Elonka, Stephen M. Standard Basic Math & Applied Plant Calculations.
Elonka, Stephen M. & Kohan, Anthony L. Standard Boiler Operators' Questions & Answers.
Elonka, Stephen M. & Minich, Quaid W. Standard Refrigeration & Air Conditioning: Questions & Answers.
Elonka, Stephen M., jt. auth. see Higgins, Alex.
Elphinstone, Margaret & Langley, Julia. The Holistic Gardener.
Elprince, Adel M., ed. Chemistry of Soil Solutions.
Elsaesser, H. & Fechtig, H., eds. Interplanetary Dust & Zodiacal Light.
Elsasser, Albert B., jt. auth. see Heizer, Robert.
Elsasser, Nan, et al. Las Mujeres: Conversations from a Hispanic Community.
Elsby, F. H. Marketing & the Sales Manager.
--Marketing Cases.
Elsden, Judy & Elsden, Lary. The Rottweiler.
Elsden, Lary, jt. auth. see Elsden, Judy.
Else, Gerald F. The Origin & Early Form of Greek Tragedy.
Elsea, Janet G. The Four-Minute Sell.
Elsen, Albert E. The Partial Figure in Modern Sculpture, from Rodin to 1969.
--Paul Jenkins.
Elsevier Science Publishing Company Staff, ed. Engineering & Technology Catalog, 1984.
Elsgolc, L. E. Calculus of Variations.
El-Sherbini, A A. Food Security Issues in the Arab Near East: A Report of the United Nations Economic Commission for Western Asia.
Elskamp, Karen K. & Munzert, Alfred W. Test Your Sex Appeal.
Elsner, Norbert, jt. auth. see Kalmring, Klaus.
Elsom, John. Erotic Theatre.
--Post-War British Theatre.
Elson, Diane, ed. Value: The Representation of Labour in Capitalism.
Elson, Lawrence. It's Your Body.
Elson, Louis C. Elson's Music Dictionary.
--The National Music of America & Its Sources.
Elson, Reginald, jt. auth. see Hardy, Alan G.
Elson, Robert T. Time Inc. The Intimate History of a Publishing Enterprise, 1923-1941.
Elspeth. Bedroom in a Country Cottage.
--Country Store.
--Victorian Christmas: Eighteen Seventy-Six.
Elst, E. Vander, ed. Societe International De Chirurgie Orthopedique et de Traumatology: Fifty Years of Achievement.
Elstein, M., ed. Gestodene: The Development of a New Gestodene - Containing Low Dose Oral Contraceptive.
Elster, Robert J., ed. Small Business Sourcebook.
--Trade Shows & Professional Exhibits Directory: Supplement.
--Trade Shows & Professional Exhibits Directory.
Elstob, Winston. Birds: A Brief Anthology of Poems & Prose.
Eltherington, L. G., jt. auth. see Barnes, C. D.
Elting, John R. American Army Life: An Historic Portrait of the American Soldier from Colonial Times to the Present.
--The Superstrategists: Great Captains, Theorists, & Fighting Men Who Have Shaped the History of Warfare.
Elting, John R., et al. A Dictionary of Soldier Talk.
Elting, L. Melvin, jt. auth. see Eisenberg, Seymour.
Elting, Mary & McKown, Robin. A Mongo Homecoming.
Elting, Mary & Wyler, Rose. A New Answer Book.
Elton, C. S. Animal Ecology.
--The Ecology of Animals.
--The Pattern of Animal Communities.
Elton, G., ed. Annual Bibliography of British & Irish History: Publications of 1982 Vol. 8.
Elton, Oliver, compiled by. Verse from Pushkin & Others.
Eltringham, S. K. Wildlife Resources & Economic Development.
Eluard, Paul. Pablo Picasso.
Elvenstar, Diane. Children: To Have or Have Not: A Guide to Making & Living with Your Decision.
Elving, Philip J., jt. auth. see Kolthoff, I. M.
Elwart, Joan P., jt. auth. see Pitrone, Jean M.
Elwell, D. & Scheel, H. J. Crystal Growth from High Temperature Solutions.
Elwell, Dennis. Man-Made Gemstones.
Elwell, Peter. The King of the Pipers.
Elwell, W. T. & Gidley, J. A. Atomic Absorption Spectrophotometry.
Elwell, W. T. & Wood, D. F. Analytical Chemistry of Molybdenum & Tungsten.
El-Wifati, Bashir, jt. ed. see Khader, Bichara.
Elwood. Invitation to Japanese Civilization.
Elwood, Douglas J., ed. Asian Christian Theology: Emerging Themes.
Elwood, John W. Elwood's Stories of the Old Ringgold Cavalry, 1847-1865.
Elwood, Roger. Historias Extranas de Brujeria. Lockward, George, tr. from Eng.
Elwood, Roger, ed. Future Quest.
--Night of the Sphinx & Other Stories.
--Tomorrow, New Worlds of Science Fiction.
Elwood, Roger, ed. see Giles, Gordon, et al.
Elwood, Roger, ed. see Holly, J. Hunter, et al.
Elwood, Roger, ed. see Orgill, Michael, et al.
Elwood, Roger, ed. see Zebrowski, George, et al.
Ely, Alex. A Destiny at Dawn.
Ely, Ben-Ezra S. There She Blows: A Narrative of a Whaling Voyage, in the Indian & South Atlantic Oceans. Dahl, Curtis, ed.
Ely, Carolanne. Love Wounds & Multiple Fractures: Poems.
Ely, Scott. Pit Bull. Herman, John, ed.
--Starlight.
El'yasberg, P. E. Introduction to the Theory of Flight of Artificial Earth Satellites.
Elz, Dieter. Agricultural Marketing: Strategy & Pricing Policy.
Elzey, Freeman F. Introductory Statistics: A Microcomputer Approach.
--Statistics: A Microcomputer Approach with Utility Supporting Software.
Elzinga, Kenneth G., jt. auth. see Breit, William.
Elzinga, Richard J. Fundamentals of Entomology.
Emanuel, N. M. Kinetics of Experimental Tumour Processes.
Emanuel, N. M., et al. Oxidation of Organic Compounds: Solvent Effects in Radical Reactions.
Emanuelson, Kathy L. & Desmore, Mary J. Acute Respiratory Care.
Emata, Bienvenido, Sr. Whispers of Living Memories: Poetry & Prose.
Ember, Carol R. & Ember, Melvin. Anthropology.
--Cultural Anthropology.
Ember, Melvin, jt. auth. see Ember, Carol R.
Emberley, Barbara. Drummer Hoff.
Emberley, Ed. Ed Emberley Little Drawing Book of Birds.
--Ed Emberley Little Drawing Book of Farms.
--Ed Emberley Little Drawing Book of Trains.
--Ed Emberley Little Drawing Book of Weirdoes.
--Ed Emberley Little Drawing Books.
Emberlin, J. C. Introduction to Ecology.
Emblen, D. L., jt. auth. see Hall, Donald.
Embree, John F. Suye Mura: A Japanese Village.
Embry, Bob. Tole'n.
Emelus, K. G. & Woolsey, G. A., eds. Discharges in Electronegative Gases.
Emenheiser, Daniel A. Professional Discotheque Management.
Emerick, Robert H. Troubleshooters Handbook for Mechanical Systems.
Emerson, Connie. How to Make Money Writing Fillers.
Emerson, David, jt. auth. see Taylor, Cliff.
Emerson, Edward W. Emerson in Concord.
Emerson, Ellen T. The Life of Jackson Emerson. G. K. Staff, ed.
Emerson, Everett. Puritanism in America.
Emerson, Everett & Bernhard, Winfred E., eds. Letters from New England: The Massachusetts Bay Colony, 1629-1638.
Emerson, Geraldine M., ed. Aging.
Emerson, Gloria. Some American Men.
Emerson, Jill. Week As Andrea Benstock.
Emerson, Kathy L. The Mystery of Hilliard's Castle.
Emerson, Nathaniel B. Pele & Hiiaka: A Myth from Hawaii.
Emerson, O. B. Faulkner's Early Literary Reputation in America. Litz, A. Walton, ed.
Emerson, Oliver F. History of the English Language.
Emerson, R. W., tr. see Dante Alighieri.
Emerson, Ralph Waldo. Essays: First & Second Series.
--Nature: A Facsimile of the First Edition.
Emerson, Robert M. Judging Delinquents: Context & Process in Juvenile Court.
Emerson, W. K., jt. auth. see Jacobson, M. K.
Emerson, William A., ed. see Aston, Athina.
Emerton, E., tr. see Gregory Seventh, Pope.
Emerton, Ephraim, tr. see Boniface.
Emery, Alan E. Elements of Medical Genetics.
Emery, Alan E. & Rimoin, David L., eds. Principles & Practice of Medical Genetics.
Emery, Anne. Carey's Fortune.
--First Love, True Love.
--First Orchid for Pat.
--Free Not to Love.
--Going Steady.
--High Note, Low Note.
--Popular Crowd.
--Scarlet Royal.
--Senior Year.
--Sky Is Falling.
Emery, Clayton & Wajenberg, Earl. The Four-D Funhouse.
Emery, Donald W. Variant Spellings in Modern American Dictionaries.
Emery, Gary. A New Beginning: How You Can Change Your Life Through Cognitive Therapy.
Emery, Glenice M. Come, Search with Me.
Emery, John. Summer Ends Now.
Emery, K. O. & Skinner, Brian J. Mineral Deposits of the Deep-Ocean Floor.
Emery, Malcolm J. Promoting Nature in Cities & Towns.
Emery, Richard D., jt. auth. see Ennis, Bruce J.
Emery, Robert E. The Japanese Money Market.
Emery, Sherman R., jt. ed. see Cohen, Edie L.
Emery, Stephen A., tr. see Dessoir, Max.
Emett, Charlie & Hutton, Mick. Walking Though Northern England.
Emig, P., tr. see Nevanlinna, R.
Emiller, Elaine C., ed. see CIBA Foundation.
Emin, G. Seven Songs about Armenia.
--Songs of Armenia.
Emiohe, Matthew O. Search for Love.
Emlen, John M. Population Biology.
Emley, E. F. Principles of Magnesium Technology.
Emmanuel, Arghiri. Unequal Exchange: A Study of the Imperialism of Trade. Pearce, Brian, tr. from Fr.
Emmanuel, W. D. Cameras: The Facts, a Collector's Guide, 1957-1964. Matheson, Andrew, ed.
Emmel, Thomas C. Worlds Within Worlds: An Introduction to Biology.
Emmelin, N. & Zotterman, Yngve. Oral Physiology.
Emmelin, N., jt. ed. see Holton, Pamela.
Emmelot, P., ed. see International Conference on Environmental Carcinogensis, Amsterdam, May 1979.
Emmens, Carol A., ed. Children's Media Market Place.
Emmens, Clifford W. & Axelrod, Herbert. Catfishes for the Advanced Hobbyist.
Emmerich, Herbert. Federal Organization & Administrative Management.
Emmerson, Bryan T. Hyperuricaemia & Gout in Clinical Practice.
Emmerson, George S. Rantin' Pipe & Tremblin' String: A History of Scottish Dance Music.
--A Social History of Scottish Dance: Ane Celestial Recreatioun.
Emmerson, Grace I. Hosea: An Israelite Prophet in Judean Perspective.
Emmert, Philip & Brooks, William D. Methods of Research in Communication.
Emmert, Roger A. A Competition Course in Speech.
Emmet, Dorothy M. Whitehead's Philosophy of Organism.
Emmet, E. R. Learning to Philosophize.
Emmett, Kathleen & Machamer, Peter. Perception: An Annotated Bibliography of Philosophical & Related Writings.
Emmons, Frances C. Poems from the Heart.
Emmons, Michael L., jt. auth. see Alberti, Robert E.
Emmons, Nuel. Manson in His Own Words.
Emory, Eric S. When to Sell Stocks Portfolio Liquidation: The Key to Superior Performance Without Stock Selection.
Emory, John M. The Source Book of World War Two Aircraft.
Empie, Paul C. Lutherans & Catholics in Dialogue: Personal Notes for a Study.
Employee Benefit Research Institute Staff. Analysis of Alternative Vesting Requirements for Private Pensions.
--A Bibliography of Research: Health Care Programs.
--A Bibliography of Research: Retirement Income & Capital Accumulation Programs.
--Fundamentals of Employee Benefit Programs.
Emrick, Roy, jt. ed. see Tomizuka, Carl.
Emroiderers' Guild. Designer Textiles: Stitching for Interiors.
Emshoff, James R. Managerial Breakthroughs: Action Techniques for Strategic Change.
Emshoff, James R. & Sisson, Roger L. Design & Use of Computer Simulation Models.
Emsley & Miyazawa, T. NMR Analyses of Molecular Conformations & Conformational Equilibria with the Lanthanide Probe Method.
Emsley, Clive, ed. Conflict & Stability in Europe.
Emsley, Clive & Walvin, James, eds. Artisans, Peasants & Proletarians 1760-1860: Essays Presented to Gwyn A. Williams.
Emsley, J. W. Progress in NMR Spectroscopy.
Emsley, J. W. & Lindon, J. C. NMR Spectroscopy Using Liquid Crystal Solvents.
Emsley, J. W. & Feeney, J., eds. Progress in Nuclear Magnetic Resonance Spectroscopy.
Emsley, J. W. & Sutcliffe, L. H., eds. Progress in NMR Spectroscopy: Vol. 11 Complete.
Emsley, J. W., et al. High Resolution Nuclear Magnetic Resonance Spectroscopy.
Emsley, J. W., et al, eds. Progress in Nuclear Magnetic Resonance Spectroscopy.
--Progress in Nuclear Magnetic Resonanance Spectroscopy.
Emslie, jt. auth. see MacLean.
Enabling Technologies Staff. Decision Modeling.
--Project Analysis.
Enabling Technology Staff & Ashton-Tate Staff. Timeframe.
Enby, Gunnel. Let There Be Love: Sex & the Handicapped.
Encarnacao, J. Computer Aided Design Modelling, Systems Engineering, CAD Systems.
Encel, Sol, jt. ed. see Bell, Colin.
Enchi, Fumiko. Masks.
Encinas, Lydia P., jt. auth. see Tovar.
Encisco, Jorge. Designs from Pre-Columbian Mexico.
Enck, John J., et al, eds. Comic in Theory & Practice.
Ende, Michael. The Neverending Story: Official Tie-In Edition. Manheim, Ralph, tr. from Ger.
Endell, Fritz A. Old Tavern Signs: An Excursion into the History of Hospitality.
Enderle, G. Computer Graphics Programming.
Enders, Alexandra & Hall, Marion G. The Rehabilitation Technology Sourcebook.
Enderwick, Peter, jt. auth. see Buckley, Peter J.
Endicott, Lane D. God Sends the Rain.
Endicott, Norman J., ed. see Browne, Thomas.
Endo, Russell, jt. ed. see Munoz, Faye U.
Endo, Shusaku. Golden Country. Mathy, Francis, tr.
Endres, Gunter G., ed. World Airline Fleets, 1987-88.
Endres, Joseph G. Opportunities in Food Science & Technology.
Enehjelm, Curt A. Australian Finches. Friese, U. Erich, tr. from Ger.
Energy Impact Associates, Inc. Staff. Social Impact Assessment, Monitoring, & Management by the Electric Energy Industry: State-of-the-Practice (AIF-NESP-012)
Energy Resources Center Staff. Illustrated Guide to Home Retrofitting for Energy Savings. Knight, et al, eds.
Enet, Daniel. Exporting for Small & Medium Sized Firms.
Eng, E., tr. see Straus, E. W., et al.
Engdahl, Sylvia L. Beyond the Tomorrow Mountains.
--Enchantress from the Stars.
--The Planet-Girded Suns.
--This Star Shall Abide.
Engdahl, Sylvia L. & Roberson, Rick. The Subnuclear Zoo.
--Tool for Tomorrow: New Knowledge about Genes.
--Universe Ahead: Stories of the Future.
Engdahl, Sylvia L., ed. Anywhere: Anywhen.
Engel, Arthur & Larsson, Tage, eds. Aging of Connective & Skeletal Tissue.
Engel, Bernard T., et al. Hemodynamics & Aging.
Engel, Beverly. The Right to Innocence: Healing the Trauma of Child Sexual Abuse.
Engel, Charles E., ed. Photography for the Scientist.
Engel, Frederic A., ed. Lomas.
Engel, Herbert. Handbook of Creative Learning Exercises.
Engel, James F. & Blackwell, Roger D. Consumer Behavior.
Engel, James P. & Talarzyk, W. Wayne. Cases in Promotional Strategy.
Engel, Mary. Psychopathology in Childhood: Social, Diagnostic, & Therapeutic Aspects.
Engel, Monroe. Fish.
Engel, Paul C. Enzyme Kinetics: The Steady-State Approach.
Engelbarts, Rudolf. Librarian Authors: A Biobibliography.
Engelbrecht, A., ed. see Rufinius, Tyrannius.
Engeler, Erwin. Introduction to the Theory of Computation.
Engelfriet, J. Simple Program Schemes & Formal Languages.
Engelhardt, H. High Performance Liquid Chromatography. Gutnikov, G., tr. from Ger.
Engell, H. J., jt. auth. see Bogdandy, L. V.
Engelmann, F. The Physiology of Insect Reproduction.
Engelmann, Siegfried & Carnine, Douglas. Theory of Instruction: Principles & Applications.
Engelmann, Siegfried & Engelmann, Therese. Give Your Child a Superior Mind.
Engelmann, Therese, jt. auth. see Engelmann, Siegfried.
Engeln, Oscar Dedrich Von & Urquhart, Jane M. The Story Key to Geographic Names.
Engels, Frederick. Condition of the Working Class in England.
--Dialectics of Nature.
--Socialism: From Utopia to Science. Aveling, Edward, tr.
Engels, Frederick, jt. auth. see Marx, Karl.
Engels, Friedrich. The German Revolutions.
Engels, Friedrich, jt. auth. see Marx, Karl.
Engels, W. & Pohl, H., eds. German Yearbook on Business History, 1983. Martin, E., tr. from Ger.
Engelsman. Engelsman's General Construction Cost Guide.
--Residential Cost File.
Engelsman, Coert. Engelsman's General Construction Cost Guide, 1984.
--Heavy Construction Cost File 1984: Unit Prices.
--Heavy Construction Cost File, 1985: Unit Prices.

--Residential Cost Manual, 1984.
Engelsman, Joan C. The Feminine Dimension of the Divine.
Engemann, Joseph G. & Hegner, Robert W. Invertebrate Zoology.
Engen, Gavin. Kit Cars.
Engen, S. Stochastic Abundance Models: With Emphasis on Biological Communities & Species Diversity.
Enger, Eldon D., et al. Concepts in Biology.
Enger, Norman L. Management Standards for Developing Information Systems.
Engerman, Stanley L., jt. auth. see Fogel, Robert W.
Enggass, Robert & Brown, Jonathan. Italy & Spain: 1600-1750.
Engh, Rohn. Sell & Re-Sell Your Photos.
Engholm, Eva. Bird Infirmary.
Engineering & Mining Journal Editors. E-MJ Operating Handbook of Mineral Processing.
--Operating Handbook of Mineral Underground Mining.
Engineering Concepts Curriculum Project, State University of New York Staff. Man & His Technology.
Engineering Industry Training Board, London Staff, ed. Static Electrical Equipment Winding & Building.
Engineering Industry Training Board Staff, ed. Training for Capstan, Turret, & Sequence Controlled Lathe Setters & Operators.
--Training for Drilling Machine Operators.
--Training for Fixed Headstock Single Spindle Automatic Lathe Setters & Operators.
--Training for Industrial Site Radiography. Incl. Vol. 1. Introduction to Radiography; Vol. 2. Ionizing Radiations; Vol. 4. Image Formation; Vol. 5. Safety; Vol. 6. X-Ray Equipment; Vol. 7. Gamma-Ray Equipment; Vol. 8. Exposure; Vol. 9. Operations; Vol. 10. Pipe-Crawler Equipment. Trans-Atl Phila.
--Training for Manual Metal-Arc Welders. Incl. Vol. 1. Metal-Arc Welding; Vol. 2. Welding Electrodes; Vol. 3. Joints & Weld Symbols; Vol. 4. Limiting Distortion; Vol. 5. Basic Welding; Vol. 6. Plate Surfaces; Vol. 7. Fillet Joints; Vol. 8. Single Vee Butt Joints; Vol. 9. Pipe Welding; Vol. 10. Fault Diagnosis; Vol. 11. Branch Connections. Trans-Atl Phila.
--Training for Milling Machine Operators & Setters.
--Training for Multi-Spindle Automatic Lathe Setters & Operators.
--Training for Operators of Numerically Controlled Machines. Incl. Vol. 1. Introduction to NC Machine Tool; Vol. 2. Rotating Tool; Vol. 3. Rotating Work; Vol. 4. Milling Cutters; Vol. 5. Tape NC Machines; Vol. 6. Automatic Tool & Work Exchanging; Vol. 7. X, Y, & Z Axes; Vol. 8. Positioning of the Tool & Workpiece; Vol. 9. Emergency Stop & Switching Operations; Vol. 10. Operation. Trans-Atl Phila.
Engineering Industry Training Board Staff. Training for Pipe Fitters.
Engineering Industry Training Board Staff, ed. Training for Power Press Setters & Operators.
--Training for Riggers-Erectors.
--Training for Sliding Headstock Single Spindle Automatic Lathe (Swiss Auto) Setters & Operators.
Engineering Manpower & Engineering Manpower Commission Staff. Engineers' Salaries: Special Industry Report 1985.
Engineering Manpower Commission. Engineering & Technology Enrollments Fall 1985: Pt. I, Engineering Enrollments. Ellis, R. A., ed.
--Engineering & Technology Enrollments, Fall 1985: Pt. II-Technology Enrollments. Ellis, R. A., ed.
--Salaries of Engineers in Education 1984. Sheridan, P. J., ed.
Engineering Manpower Commission & Ellis, R. A. Engineering & Technology Degrees 1985: By Curriculum.
--Engineering & Technology Degrees, 1986: By Curriculum.
--Engineering & Technology Degrees, 1985: Complete Set.
--Engineering & Technology Degrees 1985: Pt. II by Minorities.
--Engineering & Technology Degrees 1985: Pt. I by School.
--Engineering & Technology Enrollments, Fall 1985.
Engineering Manpower Commission & Eliis, R. A. Professional Income of Engineers 1985.
Engineering Manpower Commission & Ellis, R. A. Salaries of Engineers in Education 1986.
Engineering Manpower Commission Staff, jt. auth. see Ellis, R. A.
Engineering Manpower Commission Staff, jt. auth. see Engineering Manpower.
Engineering Societies Library Staff, ed. Classed Subject Catalog of the Engineering Societies Library, New York City, 9th Supplement.
England, Alma, jt. auth. see Collings, Ellsworth.
England, George W., et al. The Manager & the Man: A Cross-Cultural Study of Personal Values.
--Organizational Functioning in Cross-Cultural Perspective.
England, Kathy. What Is Faith?
England, Robert E., jt. auth. see Brudney, Jeffrey L.
England, Roger, compiled by. How to Make Basic Hospital Equipment.
England, Roger, compiled by see Davis, John.
England, Wendy. In the Shadow of the Cat.
Englander, A. J., jt. auth. see Eckenfelder, W. W.
Englander, W., jt. auth. see Saxon, J.
Engle, William B. The Last Loud Cry.
Englebardt, Leland S. You Have a Right: A Guide for Minors.
Englebardt, Stanley L. Miracle Chip: The Microelectronic Revolution.
Englebert, Victor. Camera on Africa: The World of an Ethiopian Boy.
--Camera on the Sahara: The World of Three Young Nomads.
--The Goats of Agadez.
Engler & Boquist. Cases in Managerial Finance.
Engler, Barbara O. Personality Theories: An Introduction.
Engler, George N. Business Financial Management.
Englesman, Coert. Engelsman's Maintenance Manual for Condominiums: Cooperatives & Rental Apartment Complexes.
English, Adrian J. Armed Forces of Latin America: Their Histories, Development, Present Strength & Military Potential.
English, Alex & Delsohn, Gary. The English Language.
English Association Staff, ed. Poems of To-Day: First & Second Series.
English, Ava C., jt. auth. see English, Horace B.
English, D. Anthony, ed. see Thune, Ensaf & Prigozy, Ruth.
English, Darrel S., et al. Genetic & Reproductive Engineering.
English Folk Dance & Song Society Staff. The Folk Directory: 1987.
English, Horace B. & English, Ava C. A Comprehensive Dictionary of Psychological & Psychoanalytical Terms.
English, James, Jr., et al. Principles of Organic Chemistry.
English, John, ed. The Future of Council Housing.
English, John A. & Addicott, James, eds. The Mechanized Battlefield: A Tactical Analysis.
English, Mary S. Aunt Mary's Wonderland: Short Stories for Children.
--One-Way Street.
English, Maurice. Midnight in the Century.
English, Morley J., ed. Economics of Engineering & Social Systems.
English, Robert D. & Halperin, Jonathan J. The Other Side: How Soviets & Americans Perceive Each Other.
English, T. Malcolm. RAF Colour Album.
Englund, Harold M., ed. see International Clean Air Congress, 2nd.
Engman, E. T., jt. ed. see Carter, W. D.
Engs, Robert F. Freedom's First Generation: Black Hampton, Virginia, 1861-1890.
Engs, Ruth & Wantz, Molly. Teaching Health Education in the Elementary School.
Engstrom, Arne & Strandberg, Bror, eds. Symmetry & Function of Biological Systems at the Macromolecular Level: Proceedings of the Eleventh Nobel Symposium.
Engstrom, Robert E. & Putman, Marc. Planning & Design of Townhouses & Condominiums.
Engstrom, Ted W. Motivation to Last a Lifetime.
Engstrom, Ted W. & MacKenzie, Alex. Managing Your Time.
Engstrom, Ted W., jt. auth. see Dayton, Edward R.
Engstrom, W. A. Multi-Media in the Church: A Beginner's Guide for Putting It All Together.
Enis & Chonko. Selling: Concepts & Techniques for Today.
Enis & Cox. Marketing Classics: A Selection of Influential Articles.
Enis, jt. auth. see Chonko.
Enis, Ben. Marketing Principles.
--Personal Selling: Foundations, Process, & Management.
Enlander, Derek, ed. Computers in Laboratory Medicine.
Enloe, Cynthia. Does Khaki Become You? The Militarization of Women's Lives.
Ennis, Bruce. Prisoners of Psychiatry.
Ennis, Bruce J. Prisoners of Psychiatry.
Ennis, Bruce J. & Emery, Richard D. The Rights of Mental Patients.
Ennis, Carla M. & Lowry, Eve. Living Lean & Loving It: Classic Flavors Without the Fat.
Ennis, Joseph T. & Dowsett, David J. Vascular Radionuclide Imaging: A Clinical Atlas.
Eno, Brian & Mills, Russell. More Dark Than Shark.
Enoeda, K. & Chisholm, J. Karate: Defence & Attack.
Enoeda, K., jt. auth. see Mack, C.
Enquist, L. W., jt. ed. see Denniston, K. J.
Enquist, Per Olov. The Night of the Tribades: A Play from 1889. Shideler, Ross, tr. from Swedish.
Enrick, Norbert L. Industrial Engineering Manual: For the Textile Industry.
--Management Planning: A Systems Approach.
Enrico, Roger & Kornbluth, Jesse. The Other Guy Blinked: How Pepsi Won the Cola Wars.
Enright, D. J. Academic Year: A Novel.
--The Typewriter Revolution & Other Poems.
Enright, Elizabeth. Doublefields.
--Tatsinda.
Enriquez & Bautista. English-Tagalog-Visayan Pocket Dictionary.
Enriquez, Antonio. Dance a White Horse to Sleep: And Other Stories.
Enriquez, Antonio R. Surveyors of the Liguasan Marsh.
Enselme, J. Unsaturated Fatty Acids in Atherosclerosis.
Enser, A. G. Filmed Books & Plays: 1928-1974.
Ensign, John & Ensign, Ruth S. Camping Together As Christians.
Ensign, Marie & Adler, Laurie N. Strategic Planning: Contemporary Viewpoints.
Ensign, Marie S. & Adler, Laurie, eds. International Trade: Contemporary Viewpoints.
Ensign, Marie S. & Adler, Laurie N., eds. The Employee: Contemporary Viewpoints.
Ensign, Ruth S. Make That Story Live!
Ensign, Ruth S., jt. auth. see Ensign, John.
Enslein, Kurt, et al, eds. Statistical Methods for Digital Computers.
Enslin, Theodore. The Fifth Direction.
Ensor, D. M. The Comparative Endocrinology of Prolactin.
Ensor, Richard & Antl, Boris, eds. The Management of Foreign Exchange Risk.
Ensrud, Barbara. Wine with Food: A Guide to Entertaining Through the Seasons.
Enthoven, Alain C. & Freeman, A. Myrick, 3rd, eds. Pollution, Resources & the Environment.
Entmacher, Paul S. & Lew, Edward A. Underwriting the Physical Risk.
Entrekin, Leland, jt. auth. see Everett, James.
Entwhistle, Noel & Ramsden, Paul. Understanding Student Learning.
Entwisle, Frank. Abroad in England.
Entwistle, Beverly M., jt. auth. see Lange, Brian M.
Entwistle, Dean, ed. see Means, R. S., Company, Inc. Staff.
Entwistle, Harold. Antonio Gramsci: Conservative Schooling for Radical Politics.
Entwistle, Noel J. Styles of Learning & Teaching: An Integrative Outline of Educational Psychology for Students, Teachers & Lecturers.
Entwistle, Richard. Do-It-Yourself Designer Furniture.
Environmental Communications Staff. Musical Houses: Homes & Secret Retreats of Music Stars.
Environmental Design Press Staff. How to Make Cities Liveable: Design Guidelines for Urban Homesteading. Robinette, Gary O., ed.
Environmental Protection Agency Staff. N. P. D. E. S. Compliance Inspection Manual.
Environmental Research & Technology, Inc. Staff. Atmospheric Dispersion Modeling for Emergency Preparedness.
Environmental Resources, Ltd. Staff. Environmental Impact of Energy Strategies within the EEC.
Environmental Systems Corporation Staff. Environmental Effects of Cooling Towers: AIF-NESP-026.
Envirosphere Company Staff. NEPA Decision Criteria for Operating License Reviews: AIF-NESP-024.
Enyedi, Gyorgy & Volgyes, Ivan, eds. The Effect of Modern Agriculture on Rural Developement.
Enyingi, Peter, et al. Cataloging Legal Literature: A Manual on AACR2 & Library of Congress Subject Headings for Legal Material with Illustrations.
Enz, Cathy A. Power & Shared Values in the Corporate Culture. Farmer, Richard, ed.
Enzensberger, Hans M. The Consciousness Industry: On Literature Politics & the Media.
--The Sinking of the Titanic: A Poem.
Enzer, Michael J. Selling by Seminar.
Enzinger, Franz M. & Weiss, Sharon W. Soft Tissue Tumors.
Eoyang, Eugene C., et al, eds. see Ai Qing.
EPA Staff & State Labs Staff, eds. EPA Manual of Chemical Methods for Pesticides & Devices.
Epes, Mary, et al. The Comp-Lab Exercises: Self-Teaching Exercises for Basic Writing.
Ephremides, A., ed. Random Processes: Multiplicity & Canonical Decompositions.
Ephron, Amy. Cool Shades.
Ephron, Henry. We Thought We Could Do Anything: Hollywood's Glamorous Days - Behind the Scenes.
Ephrussi, Boris. Hybridization of Somatic Cells.
Epictis, N. B., et al. Unified Valence Bond Theory of Electronic Structure.
Epiotis, N. D., et al. Structural Theory of Organic Chemistry.
Epp, Donald J. & Malone, John W., Jr. Introduction to Agricultural Economics.
Eppard, Philip, jt. auth. see Monteiro, George.
Eppen, et al. M.B.A. Degree.
Eppen, Gary D. & Gould, Floyd J. Introductory Management Science.
Eppenbach, Sarah. Alaska's Southeast: Touring the Inside Passage.
--Alaska's Southeast: Touring the Inside Passage.
Epperson, Arlin, et al. Leisure Counseling: An Aspect of Leisure Education.
Epple, Anne O. Amphibians of New England.
Epps, Garrett. The Floating Island: A Tale of Washington.
Epstein see Steer, Donald R., et al.
Epstein, et al. Barron's Guide to Law Schools.
Epstein, A. L. Ethos & Identity.
Epstein, A. L., ed. The Craft of Social Anthropology.
Epstein, Anne M. Good Stones.
Epstein, Beryl, jt. auth. see Epstein, Samuel.
Epstein, Charlotte. An Introduction to the Human Services: Developing Knowledge, Skills, & Sensitivity.
Epstein, David & Stutman, Suzanne. Torah with Love: A Guide for Strengthening Jewish Values Within the Family.
Epstein, David G. Debtor-Creditor Law in a Nutshell.
Epstein, David G. & Landers, Jonathan M. Debtors & Creditors Cases & Materials.
Epstein, David G. & Martin, James A. Basic Uniform Commercial Code Teaching Materials.
Epstein, Dena J. Music Publishing in Chicago Before 1871: The Firm of Root & Cady, 1858-1871.
Epstein, Edward Z., jt. auth. see Morella, Joe.
Epstein, Elliot M., et al, eds. Profiles of American Colleges.
Epstein, Elliott M., et al. Barron's Guide to Law Schools.
Epstein, Ervin. Controversies in Dermatology.
Epstein, Ervin & Epstein, Ervin, Jr., eds. Techniques in Skin Surgery.
Epstein, Eugene & Freund, William C. People & Productivity: The New York Stock Exchange Guide to Financial Incentives & the Quality of Work Life.
Epstein, Gloria. Divorce Guide for Ontario: A Step-by-Step Guide to Obtaining Your Own Divorce.
Epstein, Henry F. & Wolf, Stewart, eds. Genetic Analysis of the X Chromosome: Studies of Duchenne Muscular Dystrophy & Related Disorders.
Epstein, Herman. Traumatic Dislocation of the Hip.
Epstein, I., ed. Tractate Baba Kamma.
Epstein, Israel. Notes on Labor Problems in Nationalist China.
Epstein, James. The Lion of Freedom: Feargus O'Connor & the Chartist Movement, 1832-1842.
Epstein, Jerome & Gaines, John. Clinical Respiratory Care of the Adult Patient.
Epstein, L. M., jt. auth. see Johnson, K. J.
Epstein, Laurence, jt. auth. see Loney, Glenn.
Epstein, Leon D. Political Parties in Western Democracies.
Epstein, Leslie. Regina.
--Regina.
Epstein, Lewis C. Thinking Physics Is Gedanken Physics.
Epstein, M. A. & Achong, B. G., eds. The Epstein-Barr Virus.
Epstein, O., ed. Molecular Aspects of Primary Billiary Cirrhosis.
Epstein, Paul D. Using Performance Measurement in Local Government: A Guide to Improving Decisions, Performance & Accountability.
Epstein, Perle. Pilgrimage: Adventures of a Wandering Jew.
Epstein, Samuel & Epstein, Beryl. Kids in Court: The ACLU Defends Their Rights.
--She Never Looked Back: Margaret Mead in Samoa.
Epstein, Samuel S. The Politics of Cancer.
Epstein, Saul T. The Variation Method in Quantum Chemistry.
Epstein, Seymore. Caught in That Music.
Epstein, Seymour. The Dream Museum.
Epstein, Sherrie S. Penny the Medicine Maker: The Story of Penicillin.
Epstein, T. Scarlett & Jackson, Darrell, eds. The Feasibility of Fertility Planning: Micro Perspectives.
Epton, Nina. Josephine: The Empress & Her Children.
ERA Staff. The Engineering of Microprocessor Systems: Guidelines on System Development.
Erades, P. A. Points of Modern English Syntax. Robat, N. J., ed.
Erasmus. Christian Humanism & the Reformation: Selected Writings with the Life of Erasmus by Beatus Rhenanus. Olin, John C., ed.

Erasmus, Desiderius. Colloquies of Erasmus. Thompson, Craig R., tr.
Erb, Thomas. Middle School Research Studies, 1983.
Erbe, Ron. The American Premium Guide to Baseball Cards, 1880-1981.
Erber, Thomas & Fowler, Clarence M., eds. Francis Bitter: Selected Papers & Commentaries.
Erbsloeh, F., et al, eds. see Symposium on Neuroglia, 12th Meeting, Berlin, 1966.
Erbstein, Albert, jt. auth. see Erbstein, Julius.
Erbstein, Julius & Erbstein, Albert. Die Ritter Von Schulthess-Rechberg'sche Munz-U. Medaillen Sammlung.
Erdlen. Where Are the Jobs.
--Where Are The Jobs.
Erdman, Charles R. Commentaries on the New Testament Books: Colossians & Philemon.
--Commentaries on the New Testament Books: Corinthians I & II.
--Commentaries on the New Testament Books: Acts.
--Commentaries on the New Testament Books.
--Commentaries on the New Testament Books: Ephesians.
--Commentaries on the New Testament Books: Galatians.
--Commentaries on the New Testament Books: Hebrews.
--Commentaries on the New Testament Books: John.
--Commentaries on the New Testament Books: Luke.
--Commentaries on the New Testament Books: Mark.
--Commentaries on the New Testament Books: Matthew.
--Commentaries on the New Testament Books: Romans.
--Commentaries on the New Testament Books: Philippians.
--Commentaries on the New Testament Books: Pastoral Epistles of Paul: Timothy 1 & 2, Titus.
--Commentaries on the New Testament Books: Revelation of John.
--Commentaries on the New Testament Books: Thessalonians.
--Commentaries on the New Testament Books: The General Epistles: James, Peter 1 & 2, John 1 & 2 & 3, Jude.
Erdman, David V. The Romantic Movement: A Selective & Critical Bibliography for 1981.
Erdman, David V., ed. A Concordance to the Writings of William Blake.
Erdman, J. Complete Guide to the Marital Deduction in Estate Planning.
Erdman, Nicolai. The Suicide.
Erdman, Paul E. Crash of Seventy-Nine.
--The Last Days of America.
--The Last Days of America.
Erdozain, Placido. Archbishop Romero: Martyr of Salvador. McFadden, John & Warner, Ruth, trs. from Span.
Erdrich, Louise. The Beet Queen.
--Love Medicine.
Erdtmann, Gerhard. Neutron Activation Tables.
Eremo, Judie & Guitar Player & Frets Magazine Staff, eds. Country Musicians: The Carter Family, Charlie Daniels, Waylon Jennings, Bill Monroe, Willie Nelson, Ricky Skaggs, Merle Travis, & 27 Other Great American Artists-Their Music & How they Made It.
Ergang, Robert & Rohr, Donald G. Europe since Waterloo.
Ergang, Robert R. The Myth of the All-Destructive Fury of the Thirty Years' War.
Ergodic Theory Symposium Staff. Ergodic Theory: Proceedings of the Symposium, New Orleans, 1961. Wright, Fred B., ed.
Erhard, Ludwig. Prosperity Through Competition. Roberts, Edith T. & Wood, John B., trs.
Erhardt, Ludwik. Music in Poland (1975)
ERIC Clearinghouse on Adult, Career, & Vocational Education Staff. Adult Basic Education.
--Agricultural Education Curriculum.
--Career Assessment Instruments.
--Computerized Career Information System.
--Health Occupations Education Curriculum.
--Improving Vocational Education Curriculum.
--Lifelong Learning.
--Marketing & Distributive Education Curriculum.
--Postsecondary Vocational Education.
--Vocational Education for High Technology.
Ericcson, Samuel, jt. auth. see Buzzard, Lynn.
Erichsen, Heino R., jt. auth. see Nelson-Erichsen, Jean.
Ericksen, Robert P. Theologians under Hitler: Gerhard Kittel, Paul Althaus, & Emmanuel Hirsch.
Erickson, A. J., Jr., ed. Applied Mining Geology.
Erickson, Carlton W. Administering Instructional Media Programs.
Erickson, Carolly. The First Elizabeth.
--Great Harry.
--Our Tempestuous Day.
Erickson, Gerald & Schwartz, Harold L., eds. Social Class in the Contemporary United States.
Erickson, J. Gunnar & Hearn, Edward R. Musician's Guide to Copyright.
Erickson, J. Wayne. The Mountain's Hostage.
Erickson, John. Dada: Performance, Poetry & Art.
Erickson, John R. The Modern Cowboy.
Erickson, Jonathan. C-64 Telecommunications.
Erickson, Jonathan & Baran, Nicholas. Using R: Base: Base 4000.
Erickson, Jonathan & Cramer, William D. The Apple Graphics & Sound Book.
--The IBM-PCjr Image Maker: Graphics on the IBM-PCjr.
--MacTelecommunications.
Erickson, Jonathan & Sayre, Robert. The Model 100 Book: A Guide to Portable Computing.
Erickson, Keith V., ed. Plato: True & Sophistic Rhetoric.
Erickson, Marilyn T. Child Psychopathology: Behavior Disorders & Developmental Disabilities.
Erickson, Mary A. & Cohen, Eve. Creative Knitting: Complete Sourcebook to Patternmaking & Design.
Erickson, Milton H. & Rossi, Ernest, eds. Hypnotic Investigation of Psychodynamic Processes.
Erickson, Paul R. Growing Pains.
Erickson, Ralph J., jt. auth. see Cohen, Leo.
Erickson, Steve. Days Between Stations: A Novel.
Erickson, V. L. & Julien, H. L., eds. Gas Turbine Heat Transfer: 1978.
Erickson, V. Lois & Whiteley, John M. Developmental Counseling & Teaching.
Ericksson, C. Maillard Reactions in Food: Proceedings of the International Symposium, Uddevalla, Sweden, September 1979.
Ericson, Edward E., Jr. Radicals in the University.
Ericson, Edward L. American Freedom & the Radical Right.
Ericson, Robert. AppleWorks: Tips & Techniques.
Ericson, Robert & Moskol, Ann. Mastering Reflex.
Ericson, T. E., ed. Interaction of High-Energy Particles with Nuclei.
Ericson, Tim & Finzer, William. Desktop Publishing with Microsoft WORD on the Macintosh.
Ericsson, Samuel E. Clergy Malpractice: An Illegal Legal Theory.
Eriksen, Ronald G. How to Get I. D. in Canada.
Erikson, Erik H. Childhood & Society.
--Life History & the Historical Moment.
--Toys & Reasons: Stages in the Ritualization of Experience.
Eriksson, Eva. Jealousy.
--The Tooth Trip.
Eriksson, K., ed. see International Conference Held in Helsinki Staff, et al.
Eriksson, Paul S. The Bird Finder's Three Year Notebook.
Eriksson, Paul S., jt. ed. see Krutch, Joseph W.
Eringer, Robert. Strike for Freedom! The Story of Lech Walesa & Polish Solidarity.
Erisbie, Charlotte, ed. Explorations in Ethnomusicology: Essays in Honor of David Mcallister.
Eriye, Enewe. I'm a Nigerian.
Erk, Rien Van see Van Erk, Rien.
Erlandson, Keith. Gundog Training.
Erlanger, B. F., jt. ed. see Montagnoli, G.
Erlich, et al. Business Administration for the Medical Assistant.
Erlich, Gloria C. Family Themes & Hawthorne's Fiction: The Tenacious Web.
Erlich, Haggai. The Struggle over Eritrea, 1962-1978: War & Revolution in the Horn of Africa.
Erlich, Henry, et al. Molecular Biology of Rifomycin.
Ermans, A. M., jt. auth. see Bastenie, Paul A.
Ermentrout, Robert A. Forgotten Men: The Civilian Conservation Corps.
Ernenwein, Leslie. Ambush at Jubilo Junction.
--Boss of Panamint.
--Bullet Barricade.
Ernest, Charlotte, jt. auth. see Ernest, John.
Ernest, John & Ernest, Charlotte. Basic Business Mathematics.
Ernotte, Andre & Tiber, Elliott. High Street.
Ernst & Whinney. Quick Reference Guide to the Tax Reform Act, 1988.
Ernst, Alice H. Trouping in the Oregon Country.
Ernst, David. The Evolution of Electronic Music.
Ernst, Eldon G. Without Help or Hindrance: Religious Identity in American Culture.
Ernst, George W. & Newell, Allen. G. P. S. A Case Study in Generality & Problem Solving.
Ernst, Kathryn. ESP McGee & The Mysterious Magician.
Ernst, Lisa C. The Prize Pig Surprise.
Ernst, Morris L. & Schwartz, Alan U. Privacy: The Right to Be Let Alone.
Ernst, W. G. Amphiboles: Crystal Chemistry, Phase Relations & Occurence.
Ernst, W. G., ed. The Geotectonic Development of California.
--Subduction Zone Metamorphism.
Ernster, L., jt. auth. see Lindberg, O.
Ernster, L. & Ernster, L., eds. Mitochondria, Structure & Function.
Erodes, E. G., ed. see International Symposium On Hypotensive Peptides - Florence - 1965.
Erofeev, Venedikt. Moscow to the End of the Line. Tjalsma, William, tr. from Rus.
Errickson, Yvonne T. The Life & Loves of Hattie.
Errington, Lindsay. Social & Religious Themes in English Art, 1840-1860.
Ersevim, Ismail. Prophet Eshref & Other Short Stories: A Panorama of Psychic Adventures.
Er Si, tr. see Er Si, et al.
Er Si, et al. Inside Stories of the Forbidden City. Shuhan, Zhao & Er Si, trs. from Chinese.
Erskine, Jim & Boldman, Craig. Scrambled Chickens & Seventy Four Other Eccentric How-To's.
Erskine, Jim & Cooper, Bobbi G. The Ultimate Fat Book.
Erte. Erte's Fashion Designs: Harper's Bazaar, 1918-1932.
--Erte's Theatrical Costumes in Full Color.
Erugin, Nikolai P. Linear Systems of Ordinary Differential Equations.
Eruvbetine, Agwonorobo E. Intellectualized Emotions & the Art of James Joyce.
Erven, Lawrence W. Handbook of Emergency Care & Rescue.
--Techniques of Fire Hydraulics.
Ervin, Jane. Reading with Your Child: A Number One Priority.
Ervin, Paula A. Women Exploited: The Other Victims of Abortion.
Ervin, Sam J., Jr. & Clark, Ramsey. Role of the Supreme Court: Policymaker or Adjudicator.
Ervin, Thomas. Real Estate Revolution! Who Will Survive.
Ervin, Thomas & Hart, Don. The Homeowner's Almanac.
Erway, E. A. Listening: A Programmed Approach.
Erwin, Gayle D. The Jesus Style.
Erwin, Joseph, et al. Captivity & Behavior: Primates in Breeding Colonies, Laboratories, & Zoos.
Esaias, W. E., jt. ed. see Bowman, M. J.
Esanu, Warren H., et al. Guide to Income Tax Preparation: 1988 Edition.
Esau, Truman & Burch, Beverly. Partners in Process.
Escande, Jean-Paul, jt. auth. see Dubos, Rene.
Esch, Gerald W. & Nikol, Brent B., eds. Regulation of Parasite Populations.
Escherich, Peter. Social Biology of the Bushy-Tailed Woodrat, Neotoma Cinerea.
Escriva de Balaguer, Josemaria. The Way.
Esenin, S. Selected Poetry.
Eshel, David. The U. S. Rapid Deployment Forces.
Eshkol, A., jt. auth. see Doria, G.
Eshleman, J. Ross & Cashion, Barbara G. Sociology: An Introduction.
Eshleman, Paul. I Just Saw Jesus, Still Doing Miracles, Still Touching Lives.
Eshleman, Ruthe, jt. ed. see Winston, Mary.
Eshugbayi, Ezekiel A., jt. auth. see Courlander, Harold.
Eskapa, Shirley. Woman Versus Woman: The Extra Marital Affair.
Eskenazi, Gerald. There Were Giants in those Days.
Eskinazi, Salamon, ed. Vector Mechanics of Fluids & Magneto-Fluids.
Esko, Wendy. Introducing Macrobiotic Cooking.
Esler, Anthony. Bastion.
Esler, Mary K., jt. auth. see Esler, William K.
Esler, William K. & Esler, Mary K. Teaching Elementary Science.
Esmay, Merle L. Principles of Animal Environment.
Espejel, Carlos. Mexican Folk Ceramics.
Espeland, Pamela. The Story of Pygmalion.
--Why Do We Eat?
Espeland, Pamela & Waniek, Marilyn. The Cat Walked Through the Casserole: And Other Poems for Children.
Espenshade, Abraham H. Pennsylvania Place Names.
Espenshade, Edward B. & Morrison, Joel L., eds. The World Book Atlas.
Espenshade, Edward B., Jr., ed. Goode's World Atlas. Morrison, Joel.
Espenshade, Edward B., Jr. & Morrison, Joel L., eds. Rand McNally Goode's World Atlas.
Esperabe De Artega, Enrique. Diccionario Enciclopedico y Critico De los Hombres De Espana.
Esperti, Robert A. & Peterson, Renno L. Incorporating Your Talents: A Guide to the One-Person Corporation, or How to Lead a Sheltered Life.
Espinosa, Carmen G. Shawls, Crinolines & Filigree: Dress & Adornment of the Women of New Mexico.
Espinosa, G., et al, eds. Solid State Nuclear Track Detectors: Proceedings of the 12th International Conference, Mexico, 4-10 September 1983.
Espinosa, Maria. Longing.
Esplen, Mike see Milne, John.
Esposito, Anthony. Fluid Power with Applications.
Espy, Willard. Have a Word on Me.
--Have a Word on Me: A Celebration of Language.
Espy, Willard R. An Almanac of Words at Play.
--The Life & Works of Mr. Anonymous.
Esquire Editors & Laskin, David. Esquire's Wine & Liquor Handbook.
Esquire Magazine Editors. Man at His Best: The Esquire Guide to Style.
--The Soul of America.
Esser, Cajetan & Grau, E. Love's Reply.
Esser, K., ed. see International Congress of Botany Staff.
Esser, Volkmar. Henri Matisse: Master of Color.
Essex, Mary, pseud. An Apple for the Doctor.
--I Love My Love.
Essex-Cater. Manual of Public Health & Community Medicine.
Essick, Robert N., jt. auth. see Easson, Roger R.
Esslin, Martin. Brecht: The Man & His Work.
--Mediations: Essays on Brecht, Beckett & the Media.
--Pinter: A Study of His Plays.
--Theatre of the Absurd.
Esslinger, M. & Geier, B. Postbuckling Behavior of Structures.
Essoe, Gabe. Films of Clark Gable.
Estabrook, Ronald W., jt. ed. see Srere, Paul A.
Estarellas, Juan. Spanish One-Two-One.
--Spanish One-Two-One.
--Spanish One Two-One: From Sound to Letter.
--Spanish 1-2-1: Level 3.
--Spanish 1-2-1: Level 4.
Esterly, Diana. Early One-Design Sailboats.
Estes, Eleanor. The Coat Hanger Christmas Tree.
--The Lost Umbrella of Kim Chu.
--Middle Moffat.
--The Middle Moffat.
--Miranda the Great.
--Sleeping Giant & Other Stories.
--Tunnel of Hugsy Goode.
--Witch Family.
Estes, Nolan & Waldrip, Donald R., eds. Magnet Schools: Legal & Practical Implications.
Estes, Richard J., jt. auth. see Sanders, Daniel S.
Estes, Rose. The Trail of Death.
Estes, Steve & Estes, Verna. Called to Die: The Story of American Linguist Chet Bitterman, Slain by Terrorists.
Estes, Verna, jt. auth. see Estes, Steve.
Estes, William K. Learning Theory & Mental Development.
Esteves, Roberto, jt. ed. see Burk, Leslie Chamberlin.
Estey, Marten. Unions: Structure, Development, & Management.
--The Unions: Structure Development, & Management.
Estleman, Loren D. Angel Eyes.
--Any Man's Death.
--Every Brilliant Eye.
--The Glass Highway.
--The Midnight Man.
--Motor City Blue.
--This Old Bill.
Estrella, Gregorio & Shell, Olive, eds. Cuentos del Hombre Cacataibo (Cashibo) II.
Estrello, Francisco E. Senderos de Comunion.
Estrogen Therapy Workshop Staff. Estrogen Therapy: Proceedings of the Workshop Conference, Geneva, October 1977. Lauritzen, Ch & Van Keep, P. A., eds.
Etchemendy, Nancy. Strangers From the Stars.
Etchison, Dennis. Cutting Edge.
Etgen, William M., jt. auth. see Trimberger, George W.
Ethell, Jeff & Christy, Joe. B-52 Strato Fortress at War.
Ethell, Jeffrey. Mustang: A Documentary History.
--U. S. Army Air Forces in World War II.
Ethell, Jeffrey & Price, Alfred. Target Berlin: Mission Two Hundred Fifty: Sixth of March Nineteen Forty-Four.
Ethell, Jeffrey L. Moving Up to Twin-Engine Airplanes.
Etheredge, Edward E., ed. Management Techniques in Surgery: Bedside Care of the Surgical Patient.
Etherington, J. W. Another Life: A Novel in Two Parts.
Etherington, Norman. Rider Haggard.
Ethington, Evelyn C. Creative Wheat Cookery: Three Hundred Easy Tips, Tasty Recipes & Low Cost Ideas for Using Wheat & Gluten in the Home.
Etkin, William, ed. Social Behavior & Organization Among Vertebrates.
Etler, Alvin. Making Music: An Introduction to Theory.
Ets-Hokin, Judith. The San Francisco Dinner Party Cookbook.

--The San Francisco Dinner Party Cookbook.
Etten, Mary J., jt. auth. see Saxon, Sue V.
Etter, D. M. Structured FORTRAN 77 for Engineers & Scientists.
Etter, Don. Curtis Park.
Etter, Don D. Auraria: Where Denver Began.
Etter, Roberta & Schneider, Stuart. Halley's Comet: Memories of 1910.
Etter-Lewis, Gwendolyn E., jt. auth. see Crauder, Renee C.
Ettesvold, Paul M. La Belle Epoque Exhibition Checklist. Horbar, Amy, ed.
--The Eighteenth Century Woman. Cone, Poly, et al, eds.
Ettinger, Elzbieta. Kindergarten.
Ettinger, R. C. Man into Superman: The Startling Potential of Human Evolution... & How to Be a Part of It.
Ettinger, Richard P. & Golieb, D. E. Credits & Collections.
Ettinghausen, Richard. Ancient Glass in the Freer Gallery of Art.
Ettinghausen, Richard & Yarshater, Ehsan, eds. Highlights of Persian Art.
Ettlinger, Catherine, jt. auth. see Jacobson, Carlotta K.
Ettre, L. S. & Zlatkis, A. Seventy-Five Years of Chromatography: A Historical Dialogue.
Etukudo, Akanimo J. Waging Industrial Peace in Nigeria.
Etulain, Righard W., jt. ed. see Douglass, William A.
Etzel, Michael J. & Woodside, Arch G. Cases in Retailing Strategy.
Etzioni, A. An Immodest Agenda: Rebuilding America Before the 21st Century.
--An Immodest Agenda: Rebuilding America Before the 21st Century.
Etzioni, Amitai. Capital Corruption: An Assault on American Democracy.
--Political Unification: A Comparitive Study of Leaders & Forces.
Etzioni-Halevy, Eva. Political Manipulation & Administrative Power: A Comparative Study.
Eu, March K. Sons of Chong. McFadden, S. Michele, ed.
Eubank, H. & Sindoni, E., eds. Course on Plasma Diagnostics & Data Acquisition Systems.
Eubank, Keith, ed. The Road to World War II: A Documentary History.
Eubank, Nancy. A Living Past: Fifteen Historic Places in Minnesota.
Eubanks. Comprehensive Respiratory Care.
Eubanks, Cecil L. Karl Marx & Friedrich Engels, an Analytical Bibliography.
Eubanks, David L. & Shannon, Robert C. Hebrews.
Eugard, Athol, ed. see Bruton, Sheila.
Eugene, P. Marie. I Want to See God - I Am a Daughter of the Church.
Eugenics Society Annual Symposium Staff. Equalities & Inequalities in Education: Proceedings of the Eugenics Society Annual Symposium, 11th, London, 1973. Cox, Peter R., et al, eds.
Eugippius. Leben Des Heiligen Severin. Rodenbery, C., tr.
Eulenberger, Peter. Anwendung des Simulationsmodells BAYMO 70 auf die Stadtentwicklungsplanung.
Eulenberger, Peter, jt. auth. see Schuclein, Werner.
Euler, C. Von see Von Euler, C. & Lagercrantz, H.
Euler, U. S. Von see Von Euler, U. S., et al.
Euler, Ulf S. Von see Von Euler, Ulf S. & Eliasson, Rune.
Eunson, Dale. The Day They Gave Babies Away.
Eurakia. The Book.
EURATOM Advisory Group on Fusion Reactor Technology, 1972. Survey of Fusion Reactor Technology: Definition of Problems.
Eure, James Bruce. Joey & DeVon.
Euripides see Weiss, Samuel A.
Euromonitor Publications, Ltd. Staff, ed. World Energy: The Facts & the Future.
European Association of Radiology Symposium, Mainz, 1970. Angiography-Scintigraphy: Proceedings. Diethelm, L., ed.
European Congress of Anaesthesiology of the World Federation of Societies of Anaesthesiologists, 1st, Vienna, 1962. Hypnosis in Anaesthesiology: Proceedings. Lassner, J., ed.
--Resuscitation Controversial Aspects: Proceedings. Safar, P., ed.
European Congress Of Neurosurgery - Rome - 1963. Hypothermia in Neurosurgery: Proceedings. Maspes, P. E. & Hughes, B., eds.
European Congress of Sleep Research Staff. Sleep: Physiology, Biochemistry, Psychology, Pharmacology, Clinical Implications, Proceedings of the European Congress of Sleep Research, 1st, Basel, October 1972. Koella, W. P., et al, eds.
European Congress on Electron Microscopy Staff. Image Processing & Computer-Aided Design in Electronics: Proceedings of the European Congress on Electron Microscopy, 5th. Hawkes, P. W., ed.
European Congress on Perinatal Medicine, Sixth, Vienna, 1978. Perinatal Medicine: Proceedings. Thalhammer, O., et al, eds.
European Consortium for Political Research Staff & Rokkan, Stein. The Politics of Territorial Identity: Studies in European Regionalism.
European Institute of Social Security Staff. EISS Yearbook, Nineteen Seventy-Eight to Nineteen Eighty: The Retirement Age in Europe.
European Molecular Biology International Workshop, Fifth, Marine Biological Laboratory of the University of Malta, Malta, August 2-4, 1976. Structure & Function of Haemocyanin: Proceedings in Life Sciences. Bannister, J. V., ed.
European Nutritionists Staff. Complete Intravenous Nutrition: Proceedings of the Europen Nutritionists, 10th Meeting, Saltsjoebaden, 1971. Wretlind, A., ed.
European Society for the Study of Drug Toxicity. Proceedings.
European Symposium on Calcified Tissues Staff & Menczel. Calcified Tissue: Proceedings of the European Symposium on Calcified Tissues, 8th, Jerusalem, 1971.
European Symposium on Calcified Tissues, 3rd, Davos, 1965. Proceedings. Fleisch, H. J., et al, eds.
European Symposium on Marine Biology, 12th. Physiology & Behaviour of Marine Organisms: Proceedings. McLusky, D. S. & Berry, A. J., eds.
European Syndicate of Soccer Experts Staff. Soccer: Techniques & Tactics. Cross, Jeff, ed. Gill, Wendy, tr. from Ger.
Eusden, John. Zen & Christian: The Journey Between.
Eustace, Rowland, jt. auth. see Moodie, Graeme C.
Eustis, Helen. The Horizontal Man.
Eustis, Michael, jt. auth. see Elias, Michael.
Evaluation Consultants, Inc. Staff. Realval: IBM Personal Computer Version.
Evans & Berman, Barry. Essentials of Marketing.
Evans, Abbie H. Fact of Crystal.
Evans, Alfred S., ed. Viral Infections of Humans: Epidemiology & Control.
--Viral Infections of Humans: Epidemiology & Control.
Evans, Alice F. & Evans, Robert A. Introduction to Christianity: A Case Method Approach.
Evans, Allan R. Energy & Environment.
Evans, Alvis J., et al. Basic Electronics Technology. Luecke, Gerald & Krone, Kenneth M., eds.
Evans, B., jt. auth. see Knapton, J.
Evans, Barbara L., jt. auth. see Evans, Gareth L.
Evans, Barbara L., jt. ed. see Evans, Gareth.
Evans, Barrie, et al, eds. Changing Design.
Evans, Benjamin. Daylight in Architecture.
Evans, Beth, jt. auth. see Evans, Ginny.
Evans, Carol, jt. ed. see Johnson, Walter.
Evans, Christopher. Landscapes of the Night.
Evans, Christopher, tr. see Falassi, Alessandro & Catoni, Guiliano.
Evans, Coleen. Living True.
Evans, D. & Body, R. Freedom & Stability in the World Economy.
Evans, D. A., jt. ed. see Lumsden, W. H. R.
Evans, David R., ed. see Bass, William M.
Evans, Derek & Fulwiler, David. Who's Nobody in America.
Evans, Donald. Struggle & Fulfillment: The Inner Dynamics of Religion & Morality.
Evans, Dorothy & Claiborn, William, eds. Mental Health Issues & the Urban Poor.
Evans, Douglas K. Sabre Jets over Korea: A Firsthand Account.
Evans, E. A. Tritium & Its Compounds.
Evans, E. G. V. & Gentles, J. C. Essentials of Medical Mycology.
Evans, E. J. The Great Reform Act of 1832.
Evans, Eli. The Provincials.
Evans, Ellen. Convention Girls.
Evans, Ellen L. The German Center Party, 1870-1933: A Study in Political Catholicism.
Evans, Ellis D. Contemporary Influences in Early Childhood Education.
Evans, Erastus. A Pilgrims' Way Between Psychotherapy & Religion.
Evans, Eugene D. Golgotha.
Evans, F. J., jt. ed. see Van Dixhoorn, J. J.
Evans, Faith, ed. see Marx, Jenny, et al.
Evans, Frances G., ed. Studies on the Anatomy & Function of Bone & Joints.
Evans, Frank B., compiled by. Modern Archives & Manuscripts: A Select Bibliography.
Evans, G., ed. War on Want.
Evans, G. Edward, et al. Bibliography of Language Arts Materials for Native North Americans, 1965-74.
Evans, Gareth & Evans, Barbara L., eds. Plays in Review: 1956-1980.
Evans, Gareth L. & Evans, Barbara L. The Scribner Companion to the Brontes.
Evans, George E. The Horse in the Furrow.
Evans, Ginny & Evans, Beth. The Vancouver Guide Book: The Definitive Guide to Western Canada's Greatest Metropolis.
Evans, H. H., ed. see Society of American Foresters Staff.
Evans, Harold. Good Times, Bad Times.
Evans, Harold, ed. see Searle, Ronald.
Evans, Howard, jt. auth. see Thody, Philip.
Evans, Hywell. Governmental Regulation of Industrial Relations: A Comparative Study of United States & British Experience.
Evans, I. L., tr. see Parvan, Vasile.
Evans, J. A. Herodotus.
Evans, J. M., ed. Community Leaders of the World: First Commemorative Issue.
--The Directory of Distinguished Americans.
--Five Thousand Personalities of the World.
--Grand Ambassadors of Achievement Internation.
--International Book of Honor.
--Personalities of the West & Midwest.
--Two Thousand Notable Americans.
Evans, Jacob, ed. see Los Alamos Historical Society Staff.
Evans, James E. & Wall, John E. A Guide to Prose Fiction in the Tatler & the Spectator.
Evans, Jean, jt. auth. see Hornsby, June.
Evans, Jeffrey. Practica Musica: A Music Fundamentals Textbook & Software fo the Macintosh.
Evans, Jeffrey C., ed. Toxic & Hazardous Wastes: Proceedings of the 19th Mid-Atlantic Industrial Waste Conference.
Evans, Jeremy. The Complete Guide to Windsurfing.
Evans, Joan. Magical Jewels of the Middle Ages & the Renaissance.
--Magical Jewels of the Middle Ages & the Renaissance Particularly in England.
Evans, John B. Works on Facility Management: A Bibliography.
Evans, John G. The Environment of Early Man in the British Isles.
Evans, John W. Kennedy Round in American Trade Policy: The Twilight of the GATT.
Evans, Jonathan S. The Psychology of Deductive Reasoning.
Evans, Katherine. Boy Who Cried Wolf.
Evans, Keith. The Development & Structure of the English School System.
Evans, Larry. Chess Catechism.
--How to Draw Robots & Spaceships.
--Three-D Maze Art.
--Three-D Monster Mazes.
Evans, Laurie A., jt. ed. see Colgate, Craig.
Evans, Laurie A., jt. ed. see Colgate, Craig, Jr.
Evans, Lee. Basic Pen & Ink Sketching for Pathfinders: A Youth Enrichment Skill.
Evans, M. I., jt. auth. see Pretest Services Inc.
Evans, M. J. Progress of God's People.
Evans, M. Stanton. Clear & Present Dangers: A Conservative View of America's Government.
Evans, M. W., et al, eds. Memory Function Approaches to Stochastic Problems in Condensed Matter.
Evans, Martin J., jt. auth. see Piercy, Nigel.
Evans, Mary. Garden Books, Old & New.
Evans, Mary & Morgan, David. Work on Women: A Guide to Literature.
Evans, Mary & Ungerson, Clare, eds. Sexual Divisions: Patterns & Processes.
Evans, Mary Anne see Eliot, George.
Evans, Mary C. A Decade of Dreams.
Evans, Maurice, ed. see Chapman, George, et al.
Evans, Mike. The Return.
Evans, N. Dean, jt. auth. see Neagley, Ross L.
Evans, Patricia R., jt. auth. see Hogencamp, Jane E.
Evans, Peter. Cystitis.
--The Englishman's Daughter.
Evans, Peter, jt. auth. see Barnard, Christiaan.
Evans, Phil. Motivation.
Evans, Philip R., jt. auth. see Sudhalter, Richard M.
Evans, Pierette. Love Thy Neighbor.
Evans, R., jt. auth. see Kong, F.
Evans, R. E. The American War of Independence.
Evans, R. G. & Williamson, M. F. Extending Canadian Health Insurance: Options for Pharmacare & Denticare.
Evans, Rhonda, et al. The Rough Guide to China.
Evans, Richard, jt. auth. see Pray, Lawrence M.
Evans, Richard I. Konrad Lorenz: The Man & His Ideas.
Evans, Richard, III, jt. auth. see Pray, Lawrence M.
Evans, Robert A., jt. auth. see Evans, Alice F.
Evans, T. The Challenge of Change.
Evans, Tabor. Longarm & the Boot Hillers.
--Longarm on the Nevada Line.
Evans, Tricia. Drama in English Teaching.
--Teaching English.
Evans, Virden, et al. Physical Education Activities: For Lifetime Sports Participation.
Evans, W. H. A Catalogue of the American Hesperiidae Indictating the Classification & Nomenclature Adopted in the British Museum (Natural History), Pt. I: Pyrrhopyginae.
--A Catalogue of the American Hesperiidae Indicating the Classification & Nomenclature Adopted in the British Museum (Natural History), Pt. II: Pyrginae, Sect. 1.
--A Catalogue of the American Hesperiidae Indicating the Classification & Nomenclature Adopted in the British Museum (Natural History), Pt. III: Pyrginae, Sect. 2.
--A Catalogue of the American Hesperiidae Indicating the Classification & Nomenclature Adopted in the British Museum (Natural History), Pt. IV: Hesperiinae & Megathyminae.
Evans, W. McKee. Ballots & Fence Rails: Reconstruction on the Lower Cape Fear.
Evans, Walker, jt. auth. see Agee, James.
Evans, Wayne O. & Cole, Johnathan O. Your Medicine Chest: A Consumer's Guide to the Effects of Prescription & Non Prescription Drugs.
Evans, Zelia S. Tricks of the Trade for Teachers of Language Arts.
Evaristi, Marcella. Commedia.
Evarts, Prescott, Jr. How to Prepare for the American College Test: ACT.
Evatt, Herbert V. The Task of Nations.
Eveland, Wilbur C. Ropes of Sand: America's Failure in the Middle East.
Eveleigh, Virgil. Introduction to Control Systems Design.
Eveleth, P. B., et al, eds. see Fernandes, Florestan.
Eveling, Stanley. The Buglar Boy & His Swish Friend.
Evelyn, John see Lodge, James P., Jr.
Evens, Peter, jt. auth. see Barnard, Christiaan.
Evensen, Ken L. Healing Love: The Inner Power of All Things.
Evenson, Flavis, ed. see Music Educators National Conference Staff.
Evenson, Norma. Le Corbusier: The Machine & the Grand Design.
Everard, Kenneth, jt. auth. see McCullough, Robert J.
Everard, Margaret P., ed. An Approach to Teaching Autistic Children.
Everdell, M. H. Statistical Mechanics & Its Chemical Applications.
Evered, James F. A Motivational Approach to Selling.
--Shirt-Sleeves Management.
Everest, F. Alton. The Master Handbook of Acoustics.
Everest, Gordon, jt. auth. see Davis, Gordon B.
Everett, Alexander. Journal of the Proceedings of the Friends of Domestic Industry: In General Convention Met at the City of New York, October 26, 1831. Hudson, Michael, ed. Bd. with British Opinions on the Protecting System. Garland Pub.
Everett, Andre. Moods, Thinks, & Thoughts.
Everett, B. S. An Introduction to Latent Variable Models.
Everett, Brenda H., tr. see De Felice, Renzo.
Everett, David. Rustler's Blood.
Everett, Eileen. Keeping Pets.
--Keeping Pets.
Everett, Frank E. Brierfield: Plantation Home of Jefferson Davis.
Everett, James & Entrekin, Leland. Academics in the Eighties.
--Academics in the Eighties.
Everett, Percival. Cutting Lisa.
--Walk Me to the Distance.
Everett, Walter K. Faulkner's Art & Characters.
Everett, William J. Blessed Be the Bond: Christian Perspectives on Marriage & Family.
Everett-Heath, John. British Military Helicopters.
--Soviet Helicopters: Design, Development & Tactics.
Everhart, Robert B., ed. The Public School Monopoly: A Critical Analysis of Education & the State in American Society.
Everitt, B. S. & Dunn, G. Advanced Methods of Data Exploration & Modelling.
Everitt, W. N. & Sleeman, B. D., eds. Ordinary & Partial Differential Equations: Proceedings of Conference, 4th, Dundee, Scotland, March 30 - April 2, 1976.
Everitt, W. N., ed. see Symposium, Dundee Staff.
Everroad, Jim & Moscow, Lonna. How to Trim Your Hips & Shape Your Thighs.
Evers, Hans & Haegerstam, Glenn. Handbook of Dental Local Anaesthesia.
Evers, Helen, jt. ed. see Isaacs, Bernard.
Evers, Inge. Feltmaking: Techniques & Projects.
Everse, Johannes, et al, eds. The Pyridine Nucleotide Coenzymes.
Everson, I. The Living Resources of the Southern Ocean.
Evert, Judi. Introduction to Hospitality: Recreation Careers.
Evert-Lloyd, Chris & Amdur, Neil. Chrissie, My Own Story.
Everton, Ian. Alienation.
Everts, H. A. Runaway West.
Everwine, Peter. Collecting the Animals.
Every, Dale Van see Van Every, Dale.
Every, Edward Van see Vanevery, Edward.
Eves, Howard. Great Moments in Mathematics Before 1650.
Evett, Marianne B., ed. see Porter, Henry.
Evetts, L. C. Roman Lettering.
Ewald, Hans. Acupressure Techniques: For the Self Treatment of Minor Ailments.

Authors

Ewald, William B., Jr. Rogues, Royalty & Reporters: The Age of Queen Anne Through Its Newspapers.
--Who Killed Joe McCarthy?
Ewan, Christine & White, Ruth. Teaching Nursing: A Self-Instructional Handbook.
Ewan, Joseph. William Bartram: Botanical & Zoological Drawings, 1756-88.
Ewans, Michael. Janacek's Tragic Operas.
Eward, Ronald S. Deregulation of International Telecommunications.
Ewart, Gavin. The Learned Hippopotamus: Poems Conveying Useful Information About Animals, Ordinary & Extraordinary.
Ewart, Nei. Unsafe As Houses: A Guide to Home Safety.
Ewban, Kay, et al. BBC Micro Gamemaster.
Ewbank, Kay, et al. Electron Gamemaster.
Ewbank, Weeb, jt. auth. see Broeg, R.
Ewen & Nelson. Elementary Technical Mathematics.
Ewen, Cecil H. History of Surnames of the British Isles: A Concise Account of Their Origin, Evolution, Etymology & Legal Status.
Ewen, David. George Gershwin: His Journey to Greatness.
Ewen, Robert B. An Introduction to Theories of Personality.
--An Introduction to Theories of Personality.
Ewert, Charles. No Man's Brother.
Ewing, Alfred C. Short Commentary on Kant's Critique of Pure Reason.
Ewing, Barbara. Strangers.
Ewing, Cortez A. Primary Elections in the South: A Study in Uniparty Politics.
Ewing, David & LeBlond, Geoffrey. Using Symphony.
Ewing, David P. One-Two-Three Macro Library.
Ewing, David P. & Langenes, Bill. Using Q&A.
Ewing, David W. Freedom Inside the Organization: Bringing Civil Liberties to the Workplace.
--Writing for Results: In Business, Government, the Sciences & the Professions.
Ewing, George M. Living on a Shoestring: A Scrounge Manual for the Hobbyist.
Ewing, George W. The Well-Tempered Lyre: Songs & Verse of the Temperance Movement.
Ewing, John A. & Rouse, Beatrice A., eds. Drinking: Alcohol in American Society - Issues & Current Research.
Ewing, K. D., jt. auth. see Elias, Patrick.
Ewing, Kathryn. A Private Matter.
--Things Won't Be the Same.
Ewing, Upton. Thresholds of Existence.
Ewing, William A. The Photographic Art of Hoyningen-Huene.
Ewusi, Kodwo. Economic Development Planning in Ghana.
Ewy, Donna & Ewy, Rodger. Preparation for Breast Feeding.
Ewy, Rodger, jt. auth. see Ewy, Donna.
Exley, Helen, jt. ed. see Exley, Richard.
Exley, Richard & Exley, Helen, eds. To Dad: Written by Children.
--To Grandma & Grandpa.
--To Mom: Written by Children.
Exner, Jurgen H., ed. Detoxication of Hazardous Waste.
Experiential Education Advisory Panel Staff. Experiential Education Policy Guidelines. Miguel, Richard J., ed.
Expert Systems Staff. Framework: On-the-Job Applications. Ashton-Tate Staff, ed.
Expert Systems Staff & ProQuest Staff. Framework: On-the-Job Applications.
Exsteens, Maurice. Felicien Rops: The Complete Graphic Work.
Exton, Harold. Handbook of Hypergeometric Integrals: Theory, Applications, Tables, Computer Programs.
--Multiple Hypergeometric Functions & Applications.
Exton-Smith, A. Norman, ed. Practical Geriatric Medicine. Weksler, Marc E.
Eyer, Dianne W., jt. auth. see Gonzalez-Mena, Janet.
Eyerly, Jeannette. If I Loved You Wednesday.
--More Than a Summer's Love.
--See Dave Run.
--See Dave Run.
Eyers, A. S. Practical Woodwork for Laboratory Technicians.
Eykhoff, P., ed. see Pugachev.
Eyler, Jonathan. Muskegon County, Harbor of Promise: An Illustrated History.
Eyles, Desmond. Doulton Burslem Wares.
--The Doulton Lambeth Wares.
Eylon, Daniel, ed. Titanium for Energy & Industrial Applications.
Eyman, Joy S. Prisons for Women: A Practical Guide to Administration Problems.
Eyre, A. G., ed. see Galsworthy, John, et al.
Eyre, Linda & Eyre, Richard. Teaching Children Joy.
--Teaching Children Responsibility.
Eyre, Richard, jt. auth. see Eyre, Linda.
Eyres, D. J. Ship Construction.
Eyring, Henry & Henderson, Douglas, eds. Theoretical Chemistry: Advances & Perspectives, Vol. 4: Periodicities in Chemistry & Biology.
--Theoretical Chemistry: Advances in Perspectives.
Eyring, Henry, jt. ed. see Henderson, Douglas.
Eyring, LeRoy, ed. Advances in High Temperature Chemistry.
Eysenck, H. J. Psychology Is about People.
Eysenck, H. J. & Rachman, S., eds. Advances in Behaviour Research & Therapy.
--Covert Conditioning: A Review & Evaluation.
Eysenck, Hans J. & Wilson, Glenn D. The Experimental Studies of Freudian Theories.
Eysenck, Michael W. Human Memory: Theory, Research & Individual Differences.
Eyton, Audrey. The F-Plus Diet.
Ezekiel, H. Second India Studies: Overview.
Ezekiel, Nissim. Three Plays.
Ezekiel, Tish O. Floaters.
Ezell, Margaret J. The Patriarch's Wife: Literary Evidence & the History of the Family.
Ezelle, Edward C. & Smith, W. H. Small Arms of the World.
Ezerskaya. Bella Mastera.
Ezerskaya, Bella. Mastera: The Artists.
Ezzell, Ben R. & Ezzell, Mary M., eds. The Handbook of Traps & Tricks.
Ezzell, Mary M., jt. ed. see Ezzell, Ben R.
Ezzo, Elsie B. Bought for a Dollar & Other Exciting Stories of China.

F

F A O see Food & Agriculture Organization.
FAA Staff. Federal Aviation Regulations for Aircraft Mechanics: An Extract.
Faas, Larry A. Children with Learning Problems: A Handbook for Teachers.
--Learning Disabilities: A Competency Based Approach.
Fabbri Magazine Editors Staff. Great Sweaters to Knit.
Fabbri, Tony. Animation, Games, & Graphics for the Timex 1000.
--Animation, Games, & Sound for the Apple II-IIe.
--Animation, Games & Sound for the IBM Personal Computer.
--Animation, Games & Sound for the TI 99-4A.
--Animation, Games, & Sounds for the Commodore 64.
--Using & Programming the Apple IIc: Including Ready-to-Run Programs.
Fabbricante, Thomas & Sultan, William J. Practical Meat Cutting & Merchandising, Vol. 1: Beef.
Fabbrini, A. & Steinberger, E., eds. Recent Progress in Andrology.
Faber, Oscar. Constructional Steelwork.
Faber, Rodney B. Essentials of Solid State Electronics.
Faber, Stuart J. Business Transaction Forms.
--California Discovery Handbook.
--Handbook of Family Law.
Fabian, Derek J., ed. Soft X-Ray Band Spectra & the Electronic Structures of Metals & Materials.
Fabian, Derek J., et al, eds. Inner-Shell & X-Ray Physics of Atoms & Solids.
Fabian, Johannes. Jamaa: A Charismatic Movement in Katanga.
Fabian, John. Fishing for the Beginner.
Fabisch, Judith. A Window's Guide to Living Alone.
Fabius, J., et al, trs. see Dynkin, E. B.
Fabos, Julius G., et al. Frederick Law Olmstead, Sr. Founder of Landscape Architecture.
Fabozzi, Frank & Masonson, Leslie N., eds. Corporate Cash Management: Techniques & Analysis.
Fabozzi, Frank J. & Zarb, Frank G. The Handbook of Financial Markets: Securities, Options and Futures.
Fabozzi, Frank J. & Kipnis, Gregory, eds. Stock Index Futures.
Fabozzi, Frank J. & Pollack, Irving M., eds. The Handbook of Fixed Income Securities.
Fabozzi, Frank J, jt. ed. see Nevitt, Peter K.
Fabri, M. A Bibliography of Hispanic Dictionaries: Catalan, Galician, Spanish, Spanish in Latin America & the Philippines.
Fabricant, Michael. Juveniles in the Family Courts.
Fabricant, Solomon. Measuring Productivity: Trends & Comparisons from the 1st International Productivity Symposium.
Fabricating Manufacturers Association Staff, ed. see Society of Manufacturing Engineers Staff.
Fabris, N., et al, eds. Immunoregulation.
Fabrizius, Peter. Lacht am Besten. Bell, Clair H., ed.
Fabry, Joseph B., tr. see Lukas, Elisabeth.
Fabrycky, Walter J. & Thuesen, Gerald J. Engineering Economy.
Fabun, Don. Corporation As a Creative Environment.
--Dimensions of Change.
Facaros, Dana & Pauls, Michael. Florida.
--Italian Islands.
--Mediterranean Island Hopping: The Italian Islands, Corsica & Malta.
--Mediterranean Island Hopping: The Spanish Islands.
--Spain.
Facey, Philip A., tr. see Memmi, Albert.
Fackenheim, Emil L. The Religious Dimension in Hegel's Thought.
Facklam, Margery. Frozen Snakes & Dinosaur Bones: Exploring a Natural History Museum.
--Wild Animals, Gentle Women.
Fackler, John P., Jr. Symmetry in Coordination Chemistry.
Factor, Regis, jt. auth. see Turner, Stephen.
Factus Staff, ed. Uniforms, Badges & Intelligence Data, etc. of the German Force.
Fadala, Sam. Complete Guide to Game Care & Cookery.
--The Complete Shooter.
--Successful Deer Hunting.
Fader, Shirley S. Successfully Ever After: A Young Woman's Guide to Career Happiness.
Faderman, Lillian. Scotch Verdict: Dame Gordon vs. Pirie & Woods.
--Scotch Verdict: Dame Gordon vs. Pirie & Woods.
Fadieev, Aleksandr A. The Nineteen. Charques, R. D., tr. from Rus.
Faelten, Sharon, jt. auth. see Prevention Magazine Editors.
Faessler, A., ed. Progress in Particle & Nuclear Physics.
--Progress in Particle & Nuclear Physics.
--Progress in Particle & Nuclear Physics, Vol. 13: Nuclear & Subnuclear Degrees of Freedom & Lepton Nucleus Scattering.
--Progress in Particle & Nuclear Physics, Vol. 15: Nucleus-Nucleus Collisions from the Coulomb Barrier to the Quark-Gluon Plasma.
Fagan, Brian. Elusive Treasure.
Fagan, Brian M. Archaeology: A Brief Introduction.
--In the Beginning: An Introduction to Archaeology.
--People of the Earth.
Fagan, Patricia L. Principles & Practices of Teaching Young Children.
Fager, Charles. Selma, Nineteen Sixty-Five: The March That Changed the South.
Fages, Jean B. & Pagano, Christian. The Super Eight Book.
Fagg, William, jt. auth. see Elisofon, Eliot.
Fagin, Gerald M., ed. Vatican II: Open Questions & New Horizons.
Fagles, Robert, tr. see Bacchylides.
Faglia, G., et al. Pituitary Microadenomas.
Fahey, Frank & Fahey, Marie, eds. Chapters from the American Experience.
Fahey, Marie, jt. ed. see Fahey, Frank.
Fahim, Hussein M. Dams, People & Development: The Aswan High Dam Case.
Fahlberg, W. J. & Groschal, D., eds. Occurrence Diagnoses & Sources of Hospital-Associated Diseases.
Fahlbusch, Rudolf & Von Werder, Klaus, eds. Treatment of Pituitary Adenomas.
Fahlgren, Greg & Fahlgren, Nancy. Dragonwand of Krynn: A Dragonlance Adventure.
Fahlgren, Nancy, jt. auth. see Fahlgren, Greg.
Fahnestock, Jeanne, jt. auth. see Secor, Marie.
Fahrmann, Willi. The Long Journey of Lukas B. Bell, Anthea, tr. from Ger.
Fa-hsien, Fl. The Travels of Fa-hsien, 399 to 144 A.D. Or Record of the Buddhistic Kingdoms. Giles, M. A. & Giles, H. A., trs. from Fr.
Fahy, Peter C., jt. ed. see Persley, Garrielle J.
Faibisoff, Sylvia G., jt. ed. see Bonn, George S.
Faigley, Lester & Witte, Stephen P. Evaluating College Writing Programs.
Fain, V. M. & Khanin, Ya. Quantum Electronics: Maser Amplifiers & Oscillators.
Fair, A. A. see also Gardner, Erle S.
Fair, Marvin L. & Guandolo, John. Transportation Regulation.
Fair, Marvin L. & Williams, Ernest W., Jr. Transportation & Logistics.
Fair, Ronald L. Hog Butcher.
Fairbairn, J. W., ed. see Anthraquinone Symposium Staff.
Fairbairns, Zoe. Benefits.
--Here Today.
--Stand We At Last.
Fairbank, Alfred. A Book of Scripts.
Fairbank, Ben, jt. auth. see Foster, Nancy H.
Fairbank, John K., ed. Chinese Thought & Institutions.
--Chinese Thought & Institutions.
Fairbanks, Arthur. Greek Art.
Fairbanks, Charles H. Florida Anthropology.
Fairbanks, Charles H., jt. auth. see Milanich, Jerald T.
Fairchild, Betty & Hayward, Nancy. Now That You Know: What Every Parent Should Know About Homosexuality.
Fairchild Book Research Department Staff. Electronic News Financial Fact Book & Directory.
Fairchild Book Research Dept. Fairchild's Financial Manual of Retail Stores.
--Fairchild's Textile & Apparel Financial Directory 1987.
Fairchild Book Research Division Staff. Electronic News Financial Fact Book & Directory, 1985.
--Electronic News Financial Fact Book & Directory.
--Electronic News Financial Fact Book & Directory.
--Fairchild's Financial Manual of Retail Stores, 1984.
--Fairchild's Financial Manual of Retail Stores.
--Fairchild's Financial Manual of Retail Stores.
--Fairchild's Textile & Apparel Financial Directory.
--Fairchild's Textile & Apparel Financial Directory.
--Fairchild's Textile & Apparel Financial Directory, 1984.
Fairchild Books Special Projects Division Staff. Supermarket News Distribution Study of Grocery Store Sales, 1986.
Fairchild, Erika & Webb, Vincent J. The Politics of Crime & Criminal Justice.
Fairchild, Henry P. Anatomy of Freedom.
--Dictionary of Sociology.
--The Prodigal Century.
--Versus: Reflections of a Sociologist.
Fairchild Market Research Division Staff. Consumer Market Developments, 1986.
--Department Store Sale, 1986.
--Department Store Sales, 1985.
--Dresses & Related Apparel: (Women's Misses & Juniors)
--Dresses & Related Apparel: Women's, Misses', Juniors'
--Fashion Accessories: Men's & Women's.
--Footwear (Men's, Women's, Boys' & Girls') Fact File 1985.
--Footwear, Nineteen Eighty-Six: Men's, Women's, Boys' & Girls'
--Furniture & Bedding.
--Home Textiles.
--Hosiery & Legwear: Men's, Women's, Boy's & Girl's.
--Hosiery-Legwear: (Men's, Women's, Children's)
--Infants', Toddlers', Boys' & Girls' Wear.
--Major Appliances & Electric Housewares.
--Men's Furnishings & Work Wear.
--Men's Sportswear, Casual Wear, Jeans.
--Men's Tailored Clothing & Rainwear.
--Sportswear, Casual Wear, Separates, Jeans: Women's, Misses', Juniors'
--Tabletop & Giftwares.
--The Textile-Apparel Industries.
--Toiletries, Cosmetics, Fragrances & Beauty Aids.
--Women's Coats, Suits, Rainwear & Furs.
--Women's Inner Fashions: Nightwear, Daywear, & Loungewear.
Fairchild Marketing Research Division Staff. Consumer Market Developments.
Fairchild, Roy W. Finding Hope Again: A Pastor's Guide to Counseling Depressed Persons.
Fairchild Special Projects Division Staff. SN Distribution of Grocery Store Sales, 1987.
--SN Distribution Study of Grocery Store Sales.
Fairchilds, Cissie C. Poverty & Charity in Aix-en-Provence, 1640-1789.
Faircloth, Dorothy. Fire & Water - A Night at the Bar.
Faires, Barbara, jt. auth. see Faires, Douglas.
Faires, Douglas & Faires, Barbara. Calculus & Analytic Geometry.
Fairfield, Letitia. Epilepsy.
Fairgrieve. London in Your Pocket.
Fairholt, Frederick W., ed. Dictionary of Terms in Art.
Fairleigh, Runa. An Old-Fashioned Mystery. Morse, L. A., ed.
Fairley, John. Great Racehorses in Art.
Fairley, M. C. Materials Handling in the Printing Industry.
--Safety, Health & Welfare in the Printing Industry.
Fairley, R. E., jt. auth. see Riddle, W. E.
Fairlie, Judi, et al. Menopause: A Time for Positive Change.
Fairman, Marion, ed. see Solon, Gidada.
Fairmount Press, Inc. Staff & Thumann, Albert. Fundamentals of Energy Engineering.
Fairpo, C. G., jt. auth. see Fairpo, J. E.
Fairpo, J. E. & Fairpo, C. G. Dental Students Dictionary.
Fairweather, George W. & Tornatzky, Louis G. Experimental Methods for Social Policy Research.
Fairweather, George W., et al. Creating Change in Mental Health Organizations.
Faith, Karlene, ed. Women in Distance Education: International Perspectives.
Faizi, A. Q. Milly: A Tribute to Amelia E. Collins.

Fakhry, Tamer. The Gospel Unified.
Faktor, M. M. & Garrett, I. Growth of Crystals from the Vapour.
Falace, Donald A., jt. auth. see Little, James W.
Falassi, Alessandro & Catoni, Guiliano. Palio: History Rites & Images of Siena's Festival. Evans, Christopher & Borgese, Elizabeth, trs.
Falb, P. L. & De Jong, J. L. Some Successive Approximation Methods in Control & Oscillation Theory.
Falbe, J. Carbon Monoxide in Organic Synthesis. Adams, C. R., tr.
Falcione, Raymond L., jt. auth. see Greenbaum, Howard H.
Falconer, Alex, tr. see Manyoky-Nemeth, Charles.
Falden, Cass. Light in the Jungle.
Faldi, Italo. Pittori Viterbesi Di Cinque Secoli.
Falen, James E. Isaac Babel, Russian Master of the Short Story.
Falencki, Edye & Newman, Margrit. Vague Fuids. Janicaud, Nicole, tr. from Eng.
Falk, Byron A. & Falk, Valerie R. Personal Name Index to the New York Times Index, 1975-1979 Supplement: Vol. 25, N-Z.
Falk, Candace. Love, Anarchy & Emma Goldman.
Falk, Cathy Kennerson Illus. by see Kennerson, Vern.
Falk, Edwin A. From Perry to Pearl Harbor: The Struggle for Supremacy in the Pacific.
Falk, Eugene H. Renunciation As a Tragic Focus: A Study of Five Plays.
Falk, Howard. Microcomputer Communications in Business.
Falk, J. A., et al, eds. Cardiovascular Disease: Rheumatic Fever, Heart Transplantation & Immunological Aspects.
Falk, J. E. & Fiacco, A. V. Mathematical Programming with Parameters & Multi-Level Constraints.
Falk, John R. The Practical Hunter's Dog Book.
Falk, Lee. The Assassins: No. 14.
--The Curse of the Two-Headed Bull.
--Goggle-Eyed Pirates.
--The Golden Circle.
--The Hydra Monster.
--The Island of Dogs.
--Killer's Town.
--Mysterious Ambassador.
--The Mystery of the Sea Horse.
--The Vampires & the Witch.
Falk, Marcia. The Song of Songs: Love Poems from the Bible.
Falk, Minna R. Germany from the Reformation to the Present Day.
Falk, Peter H., ed. The Photograph Collector's Resource Directory.
--The Photographer's Complete Guide to Exhibition & Sales Spaces.
Falk, Richard A. The Vietnam War & International Law. Incl. Vol. 1; Vol. 2; Vol. 3. The Widening Context; Vol. 4. The Concluding Phase. Princeton U Pr.
Falk, Richard A., jt. auth. see Sakamoto, Yoshikazu.
Falk, Richard J. & Barnet, Richard J., eds. Security in Disarmament.
Falk, Robert, ed. Literature & Ideas in America: Essays in Memory of Harry Hayden Clark.
Falk, Toby, ed. Treasures of Islam.
Falk, Valerie R., jt. auth. see Falk, Byron A.
Falkiner, Suzanne, ed. Room to Move: An Anthology of Australian Women Writers.
Falkmer, S., et al. Structure & Metabolism of the Pancreatic Islets - a Centennial of Paul Langerhan's Discovery.
Falkner, David. The Short Season: The Hard Work & High Times of Baseball in the Spring.
Falkner, Murry C. Falkners of Mississippi: A Memoir.
Falkus, Hugh. Master of Cape Horn: W. A. Nelson 1839-1929.
Falla, R. A. & Sibson, R. B. The New Guide to the Birds of New Zealand.
Fallaw, L. M. The Ugglians.
Fallek, Max. How to Set up Your Own Small Business.
--How to Set up Your Own Small Business.
Fallen-Bailey, Darrel G. & Byer, Trevor A. Energy Options & Policy Issues in Developing Countries.
Fallers, Lloyd A. Bantu Bureaucracy: A Century of Political Evolution Among the Basoga of Uganda.
--Bantu Bureaucracy: A Century of Political Evolution Among the Basoga of Uganda.
--Inequality: Social Stratification Reconsidered.
Fallert, Richard. BST & the Dairy Industry: A National, Regional & Farm-Level Analysis.
Fallis, William J. Points for Emphasis.
--Points for Emphasis, Nineteen Eighty-Eight to Nineteen Eighty-Nine.
Fallon, Berlie J., compiled by. Forty Innovative Programs in Early Childhood Education.
Fallon, Daniel. The German University: A Heroic Ideal in Conflict with the Modern World.
Fallon, E. B. The Appraiser's Handbook: A Unique Guide to Appraising Land, Buildings & Machinery with Specialized Information for Industrial Engineers.
Fallon, Patricia, jt. auth. see Rozendal, Nancy.
Fallon, William K., ed. Effective Communication on the Job.
--Leadership on the Job: Guides to Good Supervision.
Fallow, L. M. Second Book of Ugg.
Fallows, Deborah. A Mother's Work.
Fallows, James. Human Capital: The Cultural Sources of America's Economic Decline - & Rebirth.
Falls, Harold B., et al, eds. Foundations of Conditioning.
Fallside, F., ed. Control System Design by Pole-Zero Assignment.
Falola, Eto I. Family Planning for Developing Countries.
Falola, Toyin, jt. ed. see Olanrewaju, S. A.
Falwell, Jerry. Champions for God.
--My Favorite Verse.
Falzone, Mary G. Elder Tastes.
Familia, T. W. The Ordeal of a Latter Day Oedipus.
Family Circle Editors. Family Circle Christmas Treasury, 1987. Hadda, Ceri, ed.
--Family Circle Cookbook, 1986. Billowitz, JoAnn, ed.
--The Nineteen Eighty-Six Family Circle Cookbook. Brett-Billowitz, JoAnn, ed.
Family Circle Staff. Family Circle Cookbook, 1987. Brett-Billowitz, JoAnn, ed.
Family Handyman Magazine Editors. America's Handyman Book.
--The Family Handyman Home Improvement Book.
--Sixty-Six Family Handyman Wood Projects. Newton, Richard, ed.
Famularo, Joe & Imperiale, Louise. The Festive Famularo Kitchen: An International Cookbook with a Continental Flavor.
Famularo, Joseph J. Handbook of Modern Personnel Administration.
Fan, Kok S. Women in Southeast Asia: A Bibliography.
Fanaroff, Avroy A. & Martin, Richard J. Behrman's Neonatal-Perinatal Medicine: Diseases of the Fetus & Infant.
Fancher, Gordon & Myers, Gerald, eds. Philosophical Essays on Dance: With Responses from Choreographers, Critics & Dancers.
Fancher, Paul S. Research in Support of Motor Truck Brake System Design & Development.
Fancher, Raymond E. The Intelligence Men: Makers of the I.Q. Controversy.
Fancisco, Charles, jt. auth. see Saffon, Joe.
Fandel, G. & Gal, T., eds. Multiple Criteria Decision Making: Theory & Application. Proceedings.
Fandel, John. A Morning Answer.
Fandozzi, Phillip R. Nihilism & Technology: A Heideggerian Investigation.
Fane, Julian. Cautionary Tales for Women.
Fane, Pamela La see La Fane, Pamela.
Fanelli, Giovanni & Godoli, Ezio. Art Nouveau Postcards.
Fanfare House Inc., Staff. Arcade Games for the Commodore 64.
Fang, F. Y., jt. ed. see Winterkorn, Hans F.
Fang, Lucy G., jt. auth. see Fang, Percy J.
Fang, Percy J. & Fang, Lucy G. Zhou Enlai: A Profile.
Fani, Kamran & Khoramshahi, Baha. A Subject Index to the Holy Koran.
Faniran, A. & Oje, Oyediran. Man's Physical Environment.
Fannin, Angela & Fannin, Jerry. Between Anvil & Forge: Pictorial Rememberances of the Blacksmith Shop. Roberts, Melissa, ed.
Fannin, Jerry, jt. auth. see Fannin, Angela.
Fanning, Anthony E. Planets, Stars & Galaxies: Descriptive Astronomy for Beginners.
Fanning, David, ed. Handbook of Management Accounting.
Fanon, Frantz. Toward the African Revolution. Chevalier, Haakon, tr.
Fanqin, Yu, tr. see Lanyun, Liu.
Fansler, Homer F. History of Tucker County.
Fant, David J., Jr. A. W. Tozer: A Twentieth Century Prophet.
Fant, Gunnar. Speech Sounds & Features.
Fantapie, Alain, tr. see Fisher, David & Bragonier, Reginald, Jr.
Fantel, Hans. Better Listening.
--Better Listening: A Practical Guide to Stereo Equipment for the Home.
Fantoni, Barry. Mike Dime.
Farago, Ladislas. Aftermath.
Farago, Ladislas & Sinclair, Andrew. Royal Web: The Story of Princess Victoria & Frederick of Prussia.
Farah, Cynthia & Nickerson, Marina. Country Music: A Look at the Men Who've Made It.
Farah, Madelain. Marriage & Sexuality in Islam: A Translation of al-Ghazali's Book on the Etiquette of Marriage from the Ihya'
Faramazian, R. Desarme y La Economia.
Faramazyan, R. U. S. A. Militarism & Economy.
Farb, Peter. Humankind.
--Man's Rise to Civilization, As Shown by the Indians of North America from Primeval Times to the Coming of the Industrial State.
Farb, Peter & Armelagos, George. Consuming Passions: The Anthropology of Eating.
Farb, Robert L. The United States Supreme Court Modifies the Exclusionary Rule: United States v. Leon & Massachusetts v. Sheppard.
Farb, Robert L., ed. North Carolina Legislation, 1982: A Summary of Legislation in the 1982 General Assembly of Interest to North Carolina Public Officials.
Farb, Robert L., jt. ed. see Brannon, Joan G.
Farber, Daniel A., jt. auth. see Findley, Roger W.
Farber, Donald C. Producing Theatre.
Farber, E., ed. The Pathology of Transcription & Translation.
Farber, Lawrence, ed. Medical Economics Encyclopedia of Practice & Financial Management.
Farber, Norma. How to Ride a Tiger.
Farber, Norma & Lobel, Arnold. As I Was Crossing Boston Common.
Farber, Thomas. Curves of Pursuit.
--Who Wrote the Book of Love?
Farberow, Norman L., jt. ed. see Shneidman, Edwin S.
Fardjam, Faridah. Crystal Flower & the Sun.
Fardjam, Faridah & Azaad, Meyer. Uncle New Year.
Fardo, Stephen W., jt. auth. see Patrick, Dale R.
Fareed, A. & El-Hifnawi, M. Industrial Housing Systems, an Evaluation: Proceedings of the IAHS Cairo Workshop, 1976.
Fareed, Jawed, ed. Perspectives in Hemostasis: Proceedings of a Symposium Held at Loyola University, Maywood, Ill., U. S. A. 11 May 1979.
Farewell, R. C. & Bradley, Bill. Rio Grande--Ruler of the Rockies.
Farewell, V., jt. ed. see Matthews, D. E.
Farge, Oliver La see La Farge, Oliver.
Fargo, Gail. Bible Stories & You.
Farhang, Mansour, jt. auth. see Dorman, William A.
Faria, A. J., et al. Compete: A Dynamic Marketing Simulation.
Faria, Anthony J., et al. Compete: A Dynamic Marketing Simulation.
Faricy, Robert. Praying for Inner Healing.
Faricy, Robert S. The End of the Religious Life.
Farid, Abdel M., ed. The Decline of Arab Oil Revenues.
Farid, Nadir R., ed. HLA in Endocrine & Metabolic Disorders.
Farina, John E. Quantum Theory of Scattering Processes.
--Quantum Theory of Scattering Processes, Pt. 1: General Principles & Advanced Topics. McWeeny, R., ed.
Farinas, Maurice E. see O'Neal, William B.
Faris, Alexander. Jacques Offenbach.
Faris, Irwin. The Management of the Diabetic Foot.
Faris, Paul. Ozark Log Cabin Folks: The Way They Were.
Faris, Robert E. Chicago Sociology, Nineteen Twenty to Nineteen Thirty-Two.
Faristzaddi, Millard. Itations of Jamaica & I Rastafari.
Farjeon, Annabel. Morning Has Broken: A Biography of Eleanore Farjeon.
--Siege of Trapp's Mill.
Farkas, Karl. Zurueck ins Morgen.
Farkas, Margaret A. She's Called Tootsie.
Farkas, Tiber. Introduction to Criminal Justice.
Farley, Alice R., jt. auth. see Farley, Eugene J.
Farley, Benjamin W., tr. see Calvin, John.
Farley, Carol. The Garden Is Doing Fine.
--Ms Isabelle Cornell, Herself.
--Mystery in the Ravine.
--Mystery of the Fiery Message.
--Mystery of the Fog Man.
--Twilight Waves.
Farley, Carol J. Settle Your Fidgets.
Farley, Edward. Ecclesial Man: A Social Phenomenology of Faith & Reality.
--Ecclesial Reflection: An Anatomy of Theological Method.
--Requiem for a Lost Piety: The Contemporary Search for the Christian Life.
Farley, Eugene J. & Farley, Alice R. Developing Reading Skills for the High School Equivalency Examination (Ged) in Social Studies, Science, & Literature: In 26 Lessons.
Farley, James A. Behind the Ballots: The Personal History of a Politician.
Farley, James H., tr. see Simon, Marcel.
Farley, Jennie. Affirmative Action & the Woman Worker: Guidelines for Personnel Management.
Farley, John E. Majority-Minority Relations.
Farley, Tom. The Psychobiology of Sex Differences & Sex Roles. Parsons, Jacqueline, ed.
Farley-Hills, David. Rochester.
Farm Journal Editors. Farm Journal's Choice Chocolate Recipes.
Farm Journal Editors & Ward, Patricia A. Farm Journal's Best Ever Pies.
Farmazyan, R. Disarmament & the Economy.
Farmeer, Peter B. & Walker, John M. The Molecular Basis of Cancer.
Farmer. Accounting for Inflation in U. K.
Farmer, A. S. Synopsis of Biological Data on the Norway Lobster: Nephrops Norvegicus (Linnaeus, 1758)
Farmer, Bertram H. Pioneer Peasant Colonization in Ceylon.
Farmer, Charles & Farmer, Kathleen. Family Book of Camping Lists.
Farmer, Charles J. Backpack Fishing.
Farmer, David H. & Taylor, Bernard, eds. Corporate Planning & Procurement.
Farmer, Evan R., jt. auth. see Provost, Thomas T.
Farmer, Evelyn. Second Math Helper.
Farmer, Herbert H. Servant of the Word.
Farmer, Ian. W. Coal Mine Structures.
Farmer, James. Lay Bare the Heart: An Autobiography of the Civil Rights Movement.
Farmer, James H. Celluloid Wings.
Farmer, John S. Merry Songs & Ballads & Musa Pedestris: Musa Pedestris.
--Public School Word-Book.
Farmer, John S. & Henley, W. E. Dictionary of Slang & Its Analogues.
Farmer, John S., ed. Vocabula Amatoria: French-English Dictionary of Erotica.
Farmer, Kathleen, jt. auth. see Farmer, Charles.
Farmer, P., jt. auth. see Gomersall, A.
Farmer, Paul. France Reviews: Its Revolutionary Origins.
Farmer, Penelope. A Castle of Bone.
--Daedalus & Icarus.
--Emma in Winter.
--Summer Birds.
--William & Mary: A Story.
--Year King.
Farmer, Penelope & Connor, Chris. The Serpent's Teeth: The Story of Cadmus.
Farmer, Philip Jose. The Adventure of the Peerless Peer.
--Behind the Walls of Terra.
--The Classic Philip Jose Farmer, 1964-1973.
--Dare.
--Dayworld.
--The Fabulous Riverboat.
--The Gates of Creation.
--The Green Odyssey.
--Inside Outside.
--Lavalite World.
--The Maker of Universes. Del Rey, Lester, ed.
--Mother Was a Lovely Beast.
--Night of Light. Del Rey, Lester, ed.
--A Private Cosmos.
--Riverworld & Other Stories.
--The Stone God Awakens.
--Strange Relations.
--Tarzan Alive.
--To Your Scattered Bodies Go.
--Tongues of the Moon.
--The Wind Whales of Ishmael.
Farmer, Philip Jose, intro. by see Upfield, Arthur W.
Farmer, Richard, ed. see Abdallah, Wagdy M.
Farmer, Richard, ed. see Battat, Joseph Y.
Farmer, Richard, ed. see Betson, Carol L.
Farmer, Richard, ed. see Bhat, Rajendra R.
Farmer, Richard, ed. see Enz, Cathy A.
Farmer, Richard, ed. see Frieder, Larry A.
Farmer, Richard, ed. see Garland, John.
Farmer, Richard, ed. see Gray, Wayne B.
Farmer, Richard, ed. see Green, John H.
Farmer, Richard, ed. see Greene, William N.
Farmer, Richard, ed. see Guithues, Denise M.
Farmer, Richard, ed. see Hamer, John G.
Farmer, Richard, ed. see Harrison, Clifford E.
Farmer, Richard, ed. see Howard, Geoffrey S.
Farmer, Richard, ed. see James, Samuel D.
Farmer, Richard, ed. see Jatusripitak, Somkid.
Farmer, Richard, ed. see Ligon, Helen H.
Farmer, Richard, ed. see McConnell, Donald K., Jr.
Farmer, Richard, ed. see Mangold, Nancy R.
Farmer, Richard, ed. see Morano, Roy W.
Farmer, Richard, ed. see Ramsey, Jackson E.
Farmer, Richard, ed. see Ramsower, Reagan M.
Farmer, Richard, ed. see Safranski, Scott R.
Farmer, Richard, ed. see Takagi, Haruo.
Farmer, Richard, ed. see Van Nest, Dean G.
Farmer, Richard D. T. & Hirsch, Steven R., eds. The Suicide Syndrome.
Farmer, Richard N. Business: A Novel Approach.
Farmer, Richard N., ed. see Amenkhienan, Felix E.
Farmer, Richard N., ed. see Bartlett, Roger W.
Farmer, Richard N., ed. see Bindon, Kathleen R.
Farmer, Richard N., ed. see Chan, T. S.
Farmer, Richard N., ed. see Dawley, Donald L.
Farmer, Richard N., ed. see Hearth, Douglas.
Farmer, Richard N., ed. see Larkins, Ernest R.
Farmer, Richard N., ed. see McKnight, Reed H.
Farmer, Richard N., ed. see Magann, Julia H.
Farmer, Richard N., ed. see St. Pierre, Kent E.
Farmer, W. D. Small Homes for Pleasant Living.

Farmer, William R. Jesus & the Gospel.
--Maccabees, Zealots & Josephus.
Farmers Weekly, ed. Farm Workshop & Maintenance.
Farmworker Justice Fund Staff & Wilk, Valerie A. Occupational Health of Migrant & Seasonal Farmworkers in the United States. Carlozzo, Ann-Therese, ed.
Farnan, Dorothy J. Auden in Love.
Farner, D. S., jt. auth. see Oksche, A.
Farner, D. S., ed. see Leuthold, W.
Farner, Donald S. & Lederis, Karl, eds. Neurosecretion: Molecules, Cells, Systems.
Farner, Oskar. Zwingli the Reformer.
Farnette, Cherrie. Newspaper Know-How.
--The Study Skills Shop.
Farnette, Cherrie, et al. People Need Each Other.
--At Least a Thousand Things to Do.
--Cents-Abilities.
--I've Got Me & I'm Glad.
--Special Kids' Stuff.
Farnham, Fern. Madame Dacier, Scholar & Humanist.
Farnham, Stanley E. Guide to Thermoformed Plastic Packaging: Sales Builder-Cost Cutter.
Farnham-Diggory, Sylvia, ed. Information Processing in Children.
Farnsworth, D., et al, eds. see Regional Conference on Relativity, Univ. of Pittsburgh, July 13-17, 1970.
Farnsworth, Georgia. How I Conquered Agoraphobia: My Story.
Farnsworth, James. Quicksilver.
Farnsworth, Kirk E. & Lawhead, Wendell H. Life Planning.
Farnsworth, Terry. Managing for Success: The Farnsworth Formula.
Farnum, Dorothy, jt. auth. see Rawlinson, Arthur.
Farnworth, Warren. Approaches to Collage.
Farquhar, John W. The American Way of Life Need Not Be Hazardous to Your Health.
Farquhar, Marilyn G., jt. ed. see Tixier-Vidal, A.
Farr, Caroline. House of Illusions. Bd. with Secret of the Chateau. NAL.
Farr, Finis. Margaret Mitchell of Atlanta.
--Rickenbacker's Luck: An American Life.
Farr, James F. & Wright, Jackson W., Jr. Nineteen Eighty-Five Supplement to An Estate Planner's Handbook.
Farr, Roger. Measurement & Evaluation of Reading.
Farr, William & Toole, K. Ross. Montana: Images of the Past.
Farran, Christopher. Infant Colic: What It Is & What You Can Do About It.
--Infant Colic: What It Is & What You Can Do About It.
Farran, Roy. Operation Tombola.
Farrar, Donald R., jt. auth. see Vander Linden, Peter J.
Farrar, F. W. Life of Christ.
Farrar, Helen G. How Evil the Word.
Farrar, Lancelot L., et al, trs. see Fischer, Fritz.
Farrar, Margaret. Pocket Book Crossword.
--Pocket Book Crossword.
--The Pocket Book of Crossword Puzzles.
Farrar, Margaret, ed. Crosswords from the Daily Times.
Farrar, Margaret P. Crosswords from the Times (Daily)
--Crosswords from the Times (Daliy)
Farrar, Margaret P. & Maleska, Eugene. Crossword Puzzle Book.
Farrar, Margaret P. & Maleska, Eugene T. Simon & Schuster Crossword Puzzle Book, No. 120.
--The Simon & Schuster Crossword Puzzle Treasury.
Farrar, Margaret P., jt. auth. see Maleska, Eugene T.
Farrar, Margaret P., ed. Crossword Puzzle Book, No. 100.
--Crossword Puzzle Book, No. 110.
--Crossword Puzzle Book, No. 111.
--Crossword Puzzle Book, No. 112.
--Crosswords from the Times, No. 32.
--Large Type Crosswords, No. 3.
--Simon & Schuster Crossword from the Times, Series 36: A Daily Collection.
--Simon & Schuster Crosswords from the Times, Series 35: A Sunday Collection.
--Simon & Schuster's Large-Type Crosswords.
--Sunday Times Crossword Omnibus.
Farrar, Ronald T. College 101.
Farrell, B. A. Experimental Psychology.
Farrell, B. A. see Smith, B. Babington.
Farrell, J. G. The Siege of Krishnapur.
Farrell, James T. Judgement Day.
--Studs Lonigan.
Farrell, James W. Ohio Municipal Code 1962-1981.
Farrell, John P. Voices Behind the Wall: Ninety Prison Stories.
Farrell, Michael D., jt. auth. see Greer, Gaylon E.
Farrell, Patricia, jt. auth. see Lundegren, Herberta M.
Farrell, Philip, ed. Lung Development: Biological & Clinical Perspectives.
Farrell, Tim. Programming with Windows.
Farrell, Walter. Companion to the Summa.
Farren, Mick. The Black Leather Jacket.
--The Texts of Festival.
Farrer, James A. Literary Forgeries.
--Military Manners & Customs.
Farrier, Denis. Country Vet.
Farrington, Benjamin. Francis Bacon, Philosopher of Industrial Science.
Farrington, David P., jt. ed. see Gunn, John.
Farrior, J. S., jt. ed. see Roberson, R. E.
Farris, Jack. Me & Gallagher.
Farris, Martin T. & McElhiney, Paul T. Modern Transportation: Selected Readings.
Farris, Martin T. & Sampson, Roy J. Public Utilities: Regulation, Management, & Ownership.
Farris, Martin T., jt. auth. see Sampson, Roy J.
Farris, Stephen. The Hymns of Luke's Infancy Narratives: Their Origin, Meaning & Significance.
Farrokhzad, Forugh. Another Birth. Javadi, Hasan & Sallee, Susan, trs. from Farsi.
Farrow, Nigel, jt. ed. see Lock, Dennis.
Farson, Daniel. A Traveller to Turkey.
Farsoun, Samih K., ed. Arab Society: Continuity & Change.
Farthing, S. M. & Fleming, M. C. Housing in Great Britain & Ireland.
Faruqee, Rashid, jt. auth. see Alauddin, Mohammad.
Farwell, Beatrice. Manet & the Nude, a Study in Iconography in the Second Empire.
Farwell, Byron. Eminent Victorian Soldiers: Seekers of Glory.
--Mr. Kipling's Army.
Farzin, Y. Hossein. Food Import Dependence in Somalia: Magnitude, Causes, & Policy Options.
Faseb. Inbred & Genetically Defined Strains of Laboratory Animals 1 & 2.
Faseb, Philip L. & Katz, Dorothy D., eds. Human Health & Disease.
Fasel, George. Edmund Burke.
Fashion Academy Staff. American Teen: 13 Steps to Beauty.
Fashion Group Inc., Friends & Staff. Your Future in the Beauty Business. Le Vathes, Christine, ed.
Fashion Group Inc., Members & Friends Staff. The Last Word: Exploring Careers in Contemporary Communication. Ovesy, Regina, ed.
Fashion Group Members Staff see LeVathes, Christine.
Fasman, Gerald D., ed. CRC Handbook of Biochemistry & Molecular Biology: Cumulative Index.
Fasnacht, H. D., et al. How to Use Business Machines.
Fasold, David. The Ark of Noah.
Fass, Peter M., jt. auth. see Haft, Robert J.
Fassbinder, Rainer Werner. Querelle: The Film Book.
Fassler, D. & Lay, N. Encounter with a New World: A Reading-Writing Text for Speakers of English As a Second Language.
Fast, Heinhold. Quellen zur Geschichte der Taufer in der Schweiz, Vol. 2: Ostschweiz.
Fast, Howard. Citizen Tom Paine.
--The Immigrants.
--The Immigrant's Daughter.
--The Magic Door.
--The Outsider.
--Time & the Riddle: Thirty-One Zen Stories.
Fast, Johan D. Interaction of Metals & Gases.
Fast, Julius. The Omega-3 Breakthrough: The Revolutionary, Medically-Proven Fish Oil Diet.
Fast, R. W., ed. Advances in Cryogenic Engineering.
Fasulo, Amerigo. The Angry People.
Fatchett, Derek. Trade Unions & Politics in the 1980's: The 1984 Act & Political Funds.
Fate, Terry, jt. auth. see Charlotte-Georgi.
Fath, Creekmore, ed. The Lithographs of Thomas Hart Benton.
Fatio, Louise. Happy Lion.
--The Happy Lioness.
Fattorusso, J., ed. Wonders of Italy.
Faucett, Jack, Associates Staff & S C & A Inc. Staff. Characterization of the Temporary Radiation Work Force at U. S. Nuclear Power Plants: AIF-NESP-028.
Faucher, L. Manchester in 1844: It's Present Condition & Future Prospects. Culverwell, J. P., ed.
Fauci, Anthony S., jt. auth. see Cupps, Thomas R.
Fauci, Anthony S., jt. auth. see Lichtenstein, Lawrence M.
Faudel-Phillips, H. Breaking & Schooling Horses.
Faughn, Jerry S., jt. auth. see Kuhn, Karl F.
Faulhaber, Martha & Underhill, Janet. Music: Invent Your Own.
Faulk, Mrs. Hugh L. & Jones, Billy W. The History of Twiggs County, Georgia.
Faulk, John H. The Uncensored John Henry Faulk.
Faulk, Odie B. Oklahoma: Land of the Fair God.
Faulk, Odie B. & Stout, Joseph A., Jr., eds. The Mexican War: Changing Interpretations.
Faulkner, Keith. First Questions about Transport.
Faulkner, Margaret. I Skate!
Faulkner, Peter, ed. William Morris: The Critical Heritage.
Faulkner, R. J. & Impey, O. R. Shino & Oribe Kiln Sites.
Faulkner, Ray & Faulkner, Sarah. Inside Today's Home.
Faulkner, Ray, et al. Art Today: An Introduction to the Visual Arts.
Faulkner, Sarah, jt. auth. see Faulkner, Ray.
Faulkner, Trader. Peter Finch: A Biography.
Faulkner, Trevor. The Thames & Hudson Manual of Direct Metal Sculpture.
Faulkner, William. As I Lay Dying.
--Light in August.
--Light in August.
--Mosquitoes.
--Mosquitoes.
--Sound & the Fury *32490.
Faulkner, William, jt. auth. see Foote, Horton.
Faulring, Scott H., ed. An American Prophet's Record: The Diaries & Journals of Joseph Smith.
Faupel, Charles E., et al. Disaster Beliefs & Emergency Planning.
Faurot, Jeannette L., ed. Chinese Fiction from Taiwan: Critical Perspectives.
Fauset, Jessie. Plum Bun: A Novel Without a Moral.
Fausold, Martin L. The Presidency of Herbert C. Hoover.
Faust, Aly. Chemistry of Natural Waters.
Faust, Augustus F. Brazil: Education in an Expanding Economy.
Faust, Irvin. The File on Stanley Patton Buchta.
--Foreign Devils.
--Newsreel.
--Roar Lion Roar.
--Willy Remembers.
Faust, Norma. Lecciones para el aprendizaje del Idioma Shipibo-Conibo.
Faust, V., ed. see Ladewig, D. & Hobi, V.
Fausto, Nelson, et al. Liver Regeneration, No. 2.
Faux, David D., jt. auth. see Adams, J. Michael.
Faux, Ian, jt. auth. see Heath, Leslie G.
Faux, Marian. The Complete Resume Guide.
Faux, Marion. Childless by Choice: Choosing Childlessness in the Eighties.
Favata, Benedict F. & Pirone, Frank. Nature of Life & Cancer.
Faverty, Frederic E., ed. Victorian Poets: A Guide to Research.
Faw, Terry. Schaum's Outline of Child Psychology.
Fawcett, Anthony. John Lennon: One Day at a Time: A Personal Biography of the Seventies.
Fawcett, B., jt. auth. see Siegel, A.
Fawcett, Don W. & Newburne, James W. Workshop on Cellular & Molecular Toxicology.
Fawcett, Don W. & Bedford, Michael J., eds. Spermatozoon: Maturation, Motility, Surface Properties & Comparative Aspects.
Fawcett, Jacqueline. Analysis & Evaluation of Conceptual Models of Nursing.
Fawcett, James T., jt. auth. see Bulatao, Rodolfo A.
Fawcett, Marion, jt. auth. see Crowther, S. J.
Fawcett, Susan E. & Sandberg, Alvin. Evergreen: A Guide to Basic Writing.
--Evergreen: A Guide to Writing.
--Grassroots: The Writer's Handbook.
--Grassroots: The Writer's Workbook, Form A.
Fawcus, Margaret, ed. Voice Disorders & Their Management.
Fawls, Charlotte. A Book of Poems Dedicated to the Dream...of Love.
Fax, Elton. Hashar.
Faxon, F. W. Co. Staff. Cumulated Dramatic Index. 1909-1949.
Fay, Ann, ed. see Anderson, Leone C.
Fay, Ann, ed. see Aylesworth, Jim.
Fay, Ann, ed. see DeBruyn, Monica.
Fay, Ann, ed. see Green, Phyllis.
Fay, Ann, ed. see Miescke, Lori.
Fay, Ann, ed. see Pape, Donna L.
Fay, Ann, ed. see Smith, Carole.
Fay, Ann, ed. see Vande Velde, Vivian.
Fay, Ann, ed. see Vigna, Judith.
Fay, Dick, jt auth. see Bowen, Rich.
Fay, J. D. Theta Functions of Riemann Surfaces.
Fay, James, et al, eds. California Almanac: 1986-1987.
Fay, John. Approaches to Criminal Justice Training.
Fay, Judith, jt. auth. see Davidson, Audrey.
Fay, Leo, compiled by. Reading in the Content Fields.
Fay, Martha. A Mortal Condition: Eight Stories of Survival, Hope & Loss.
Faye, Sarah. God Related.
Fayen, Emily G. The Online Catalog: Improving Public Access to Library Materials.
Fayers, F. J. Enhanced Oil Recovery.
Fayerweather Street School Staff & Rofes, Eric E. The Kids' Book about Parents.
Fayod, V. Prodrome d'Une Histoire Naturelle des Agaricinees.
Fazenbaker, Jack. Greenberg's American Flyer Numerical Pocket Guide.
--Greenberg's American Flyer S Gauge Pocket Guide.
--Greenberg's Guide to American Flyer S Gauge.
Fazio, C., ed. see Round Table Conference, Rome, Oct. 30-31, 1974.
Fazio, G. G., et al, eds. Astronomy from Space: Proceedings of the Topical Meeting of the COSPAR Interdisciplinary Scientific Commission E (Meetings E3, E4, & E5) of the COSPAR 25th Plenary Meeting held in Graz, Austria, 25 June - 7 July 1984.
Fazzolare, Rocco & Smith, C. B., eds. Energy Use Management: Proceedings of the International Conference.
Fazzolari, R., jt. auth. see International Conference on Energy Use Management Staff.
Fea, Allan. Secret Chambers & Hiding-Places.
Feagin, Joe. The Urban Real Estate Game: Playing Monopoly With Real Money.
Feagles, Anita M. Sophia Scarlotti & Ceecee.
--The Year the Dreams Came Back.
Fear, Gene, jt. auth. see LaValla, Rick.
Fear, Richard A. The Evaluation Interview.
--McGraw-Hill Course in Effective Interviewing.
Fear, Richard A. & Ross, James F. Jobs, Dollars & EEO: How to Hire More Productive Entry-Level Workers.
Fearing, Dean. The Mansion on Turtle Creek Cookbook.
Fearnley, Alan. Railway Paintings of Alan Fearnley.
Fearnside, et al. Applied Atomic Energy.
Fearon, Mary & Tully, Mary J. Wonder-Filled.
Fearon, William R. Introduction to Biochemistry. Jessop, William J., ed.
Fears, J. Wayne. Cooking the Wild Harvest.
Fearson, Daniel. A Traveller in Turkey.
Featherstone, Bonnie, jt. auth. see Reilly, Jill.
Featherstone, David. Doris Ulmann: American Portraits.
Featherstone, Donald F. Sports Injuries Manual.
Featherstone, John C. Battle of the Crater: Eyewitness Accounts of the Civil War.
Featherstone, Joseph. What Schools Can Do.
Featherstone, R. E. & Nalluri, C. Civil Engineering Hydraulics: Essential Theory with Worked Examples.
Featherstone, Vaughn J. Charity Never Faileth.
FEBS Symposium on DNA, Liblice, 24-29 September, 1979. DNA: Recombination, Interactions & Repair. Zadrazil, S. & Sponar, J., eds.
Febure. Amour Sacre, Amour Profane; Autour de l'Heptameron.
Febvre, Lucien. The Problem of Unbelief in the Sixteenth Century: The Religion of Rabelais. Gottlieb, Beatrice, tr. from Fr.
Febvre, Lucien & Bataillon, Lionel. Geographical Introduction to History. Mountford, E. G. & Paxton, J. H., trs.
Fecher, Constance. The Link Boys.
Fecht, Gerald. The Complete Parent's Guide to Soccer.
Fechtig, H., jt. ed. see Elsaesser, H.
Fechtman, Bernard, tr. see Mauriac, Francois.
Fechtner, Leopold. Galaxy of Funny Gags, Puns, Quips & Putdowns.
Fedden, Robin & Kenworthy-Browne, John. The Country House Guide to England Scotland & Wales.
Fedden, Robin & Joekes, Rosemary, eds. The National Trust Guide to England, Wales, & Northern Ireland.
Fedder, Ruth. Girl Grows Up.
Feddes, R. A., et al. Simulation of Field Water Use & Crop Yield.
Feder, A., ed. see Hilarius, Saint.
Feder, Gershon & Slade, Roger. Experiences with the Monitoring & Evaluation of Training & Visit Extension in India.
Feder, Gershon, et al. Impact of Agricultural Extension: A Case Study of the Training & Visit Systems in Haryana, India.
Feder, Happy Jack. Mime Time: Forty-Five Complete Routines for Everyone.
Feder, Jack & Merrick, Kathryn W. Zen of Cubing: In Search of the Seventh Side.
Feder, Joseph & Tolbert, William R., eds. Large-Scale Mamalian Cell Culture.
Federal Aviation Administration. Type Rating (Airplane) Flight Test Guide (AC 61-57A)
Federal Aviation Administration Staff. A&P Mechanics Airframe Question Book.
--Advanced Ground Instructor Written Test Guide.
--Aircraft Inspection, Repair & Alterations: AC 43.13-1A & 43.13-2A.
--Airframe & Powerplant Mechanics Airframe Writen Test Guide.
--Airframe & Powerplant Mechanics General Written Test Guide.
--Airframe & Powerplant Mechanic's Powerplant Written Test Guide.
--Airline Transport Pilot, Airplane, Practical Test Guide (Ac 61-77)

Authors

--Airline Transport Pilot-Airplane Written Test Guide: Air Carrier.
--Airman's Information Manual. Winner, Walter P., ed.
--Aviation Mechanic Powerplant Question Book.
--Aviation Mechanics General Question Book.
--Basic Ground Instructor Written Test Guide.
--Commercial Pilot-Airplane Written Test Guide.
--Commercial Pilot-Practical Test Standards-ASMEL.
--FAR 121 & 63.
--Federal Aviation Regulations: Air Taxi Operators & Commerical Operators of Small Aircraft. Aviation Book Company, ed.
--Federal Aviation Regulations for Pilots. Winner, Walter P., ed.
--Flight Engineer Turboset-Basic Written Test Guide.
--Flight Instructor Airplane Written Test Guide.
--Flight Instructor Instrument-Airplane Written Test Guide.
--Flight Instructor Practical Test Guide.
--Flight Instructor Practical Test Guide (AC 61-58A)
--Fundamentals of Instructing Flight & Ground Instructors Written Test Guide.
--How to Become a Pilot: The Step-by-Step Guide to Flying.
--Instrument Flying Handbook.
--Instrument Flying Handbook: Ac 61-27c.
--Instrument Rating Practical Test Standards, Airplane-Helicopter.
--Instrument Rating-Written Test Guide.
--Private Pilot-Airplane Written Test Guide.
--Private Pilot-Practical Test Standards-ASMEL.
Federal Bar Association, Securities Law Committee, jt. auth. see United States Securities & Exchange Commission.
Federal Institute for Biology in Agriculture & Forestry Staff & Institute for Plant Protection Agent Research Staff. Gaschromatographie der Pflanzenschutzmittel: Tabellarische Literaturreferate Berlin-Dahlem.
Federico, Pat A., et al. Management Information Systems & Organizational Behavior. Brun, Kim & McCalla, Douglas B., eds.
Federlin, K. & Federlin, K., eds. Immunological Methods in Endocrinology.
Federman, Raymond, jt. ed. see Graver, Lawrence.
Federspiel, Howard. Persatuan Islam: Islamic Reform in Twentieth Century Indonesia.
Fedi, Peter, Jr., ed. The Periodontic Syllabus.
Fedina, L., et al, eds. Mathematical & Computational Methods in Physiology: Proceedings of a Satellite Symposium of the 28th International Congress of Physiological Sciences, Budapest, Hungary, 1980.
Fedler, Fred. An Introduction to the Mass Media.
--Reporting for the Print Media.
--Reporting for the Print Media.
--Reporting for the Print Media: A Workbook.
Fedoroff, S. & Hertz, L., eds. Advances in Cellular Neurobiology.
Fedoroff, S. & Hertz, Leif, eds. Cell, Tissue & Organ Cultures in Neurobiology.
Fedorov, V. V. Theory of Optimal Experiments.
Fedoseyev, P. & Timofeyev, T. Social Problems of Man's Environment: Where We Live & Work.
Fedoseyev, P., ed. What Is "Democratic Socialism"?
Fedosov, V. & Fyodorov, A. We Choose Peace.
Feegel, John R. The Dance Card.
--Death Sails the Bay.
Feehan, John M. Operation Brogue.
Feeley, Terence. Limelight.
Feeling, Durbin, tr. see Ziegenfuss, Mary Lou.
Feelings, Muriel L. Zamani Goes to Market.
Feely, T. J. Rich Little Poor Girl.
Feeman, William E., Jr. Preventing Hardening of the Arteries: The Bowling Green Study.
Feenberg, E. Theory of Quantum Fluids.
Feeney, Floyd, Jr. The Police & Pretrial Release.
Feeney, J., jt. ed. see Emsley, J. W.
Feeney, Mary, tr. see Boissard, Janine.
Feerick, John D. From Failing Hands: The Story of Presidential Succession.
Feerick, John D., et al. NLRB Representation Elections: Law, Practice & Procedure.
Feerick, John D., jt. auth. see Barbash, Joseph.
Feest, Christian. The Art of War.
Feher, Ferenc & Heller, Agnes. Eastern Left, Western Left: Totalitarianism, Freedom & Democracy.
--Hungary, Nineteen Fifty-Six Revisited: The Message of a Revolution a Quarter of a Century After.
Feher, K., ed. Satellite Communications: Proceedings of the Canadian Domestic & International Conference, 1st, June 15-17, Ottawa, Canada.
Feher, Kamilo. Digital Modulation Techniques in an Interference Environment. White, Donald R., ed.
Feher, O. & Joo, F., eds. Cellular Analogues of Conditioning & Neural Plasticity: Proceedings of a Satellite Symposium of the 28th International Congress of Physiological Sciences, Szeged, Hungary, 1980.
Feher, Z. D. & Pogany, G. O. Twentieth Century Hungarian Painting.
Fehr, Lawrence A. Introduction to Personality.
Fehr, Terry, jt. auth. see Petersen, W. P.
Fehrenbach, T. R. Texas: A Salute from Above.
Fehrenbacher, Don E., jt. ed. see Brown, Richard E.
Fehsenfeld, Martha, jt. auth. see McMillan, Dougald.
Fei, Hsiao-Tung. Peasant Life in China: A Field Study of Country Life in the Yangtze Valley.
Feibleman, James. From Hegel to Terrorism & Other Essays on the Dynamic Nature of Philosophy.
Feiblemen, Peter. Charlie Boy.
Feidel, Frank & May, Ernest, eds. The Boston Economy During the Civil War.
Feidel, Jan, tr. see Jaquiera, Joaquim & Mansa, Manuel B.
Feifer, George, jt. auth. see Panov, Valery.
Feiffer, Jules. Ackroyd.
Feigenbaum, Edward D., jt. auth. see Palmer, James A.
Fei Hsiao Tung. Toward a People's Anthropology.
Fei Hsiao-T'Ung, jt. ed. see Shih Kuo-Heng.
Feil, D. K. Ways of Exchange: The Enga Tee of Papua New Guinea.
Feil, Hila. The Ghost Garden.
Feilchenfeld, Ernst H. The International Economic Law of Belligerent Occupation.
Feild, Reshad. The Invisible Way.
Fein, Albert. Frederick Law Olmsted & the American Environmental Tradition.
Fein, Cheri. How to Get Your Child into Modeling & Commercials.
Feinberg, Gerald. Solid Clues: Quantum Physics, Molecular Biology & the Future of Science.
--Solid Clues: Quantum Physics, Molecular Biology, & the Future of Science.
Feinberg, J. G. The Atom Story.
Feinberg, Joel. Doing & Deserving: Essays in the Theory of Responsibility.
Feinberg, Joel see McMurring, Sterling M.
Feinberg, Joel, ed. Reason & Responsibility: Readings in Some Basic Problems of Philosophy.
Feinberg, Leonard. The Secret of Humor.
Feinberg, Michael, tr. see Troyat, Henri.
Feinberg, Richard E. The Intemperate Zone: The Third World Challenge to U. S. Foreign Policy.
Feinblatt, Ebria & Davis, Bruce. Los Angeles Prints: 1883-1980.
Feineman, Neil, jt. auth. see Forsythe, Kenneth.
Feiner, Benjamin, jt. auth. see Sax, N. Irving.
Feingold, Ben F. Introduction to Clinical Allergy.
Feingold, Carl. Fundamentals of Structured COBOL Programming.
Feingold, M. J., jt. auth. see Perrin, E. V.
Feingold, S. Norman. Counseling for Careers in the Nineteen Eighties.
Feingold, S. Norman & Hansard-Winkler, Glenda A. Nine Hundred Thousand Plus Jobs Annually: Published Sources of Employment Listings.
Feingold, S. Norman & Miller, Norma. Your Future: A Guide for the Handicapped Teenager.
Feingold, S. Norman & Perlman, Leonard. Making It on Your Own: The American Dream.
Feingold, Stanley, jt. auth. see McKenna, George.
Feininger, Andreas. Nature Close Up: A Fantastic Journey into Reality.
Feinschreiber, Robert, jt. auth. see Bischel, Jon E.
Feinsilver, Lillian M. The Taste of Yiddish.
Feinsod, Ethan. Awake in Nightmare - Jonestown: The Only Eyewitness Account.
Feirer, John. Bench Woodwork.
Feirer, John L. Cabinetmaking & Millwork.
--Machine Tool Metalworking. Gilmore, D. E., ed.
--Wood Materials & Processes.
--The Woodworker's Reference Guide & Sourcebook.
Feirer, John L. & Hutchings, Gilbert R. Carpentry & Building Construction.
Feis, Herbert. Contest Over Japan: The Soviet Bid for Power in the Far East, 1945-1952.
--Diplomacy of the Dollar, 1919-1932.
Feisner, Edith. Needlepoint & Beyond: Twenty Seven Lessons in Advanced Canvaswork.
Feisner, Edith A. Needlepoint & Beyond: Twenty-Seven Lessons in Advanced Canvas Work.
Feist, Raymond E. Darkness at Sethanon: The Finale of the Riftwar Saga.
--Silverthorn.
Feist, Uwe & Hirsch, R. S. Heinkel 177 "Greif"
Feist, Uwe, jt. auth. see Maloney, Edward T.
Feit, Edward. African Opposition in South Africa: The Failure of Passive Resistance.
--Governments & Leaders: An Approach to Comparative Politics.
Feit, Marvin D. Management & Administration of Drug & Alcohol Programs.
Feix, Irmgard & Schlant, Ernestine. Junge Deutsche Prosa.
Fekete, John. The Critical Twilight: Explorations in the Ideology of Anglo-American Literary Theory from Eliot to McLuhan.
Fekrat, M. Ali, jt. auth. see Amuzegar, Jahangir.
Feld, Bernard T. A Voice Crying in the Wilderness: Essays on the Problem of Science & World Affairs.
Feld, Werner & Boyd, Gavin, eds. Comparative Regional Systems: West & East Europe, North America, the Middle East & Developing Countries.
Feld, Werner J. & Coate, Roger A. The Role of International Nongovernmental Organizations in World Politics.
Feld, Werner J., jt. ed. see Link, Werner.
Feldbaum, A. A. Optimal Control Systems.
Feldbrugge, J. T. Commitment to the Committed: Treatment As Interaction in a Forensic Mental Hospital.
Felderhof, M. C. Religious Education in a Pluralistic Society.
Feldherr, C. M., et al. Nuclear Membrane & Nucleocytoplastic Interchange.
Feldman, Anthony & Ford, Peter. Scientists & Inventors.
Feldman, David M. Birth Control in Jewish Law: Marital Relations, Contraception, & Abortion As Set Forth in the Classic Texts of Jewish Law.
Feldman, Edwin B. Housekeeping Handbook for Institutions, Business & Industry.
--How to Use Your Time to Get Things Done.
Feldman, Edwin B. & Wright, George B. The Supervisor's Handbook.
Feldman, Frances L. The Family in Today's Money World.
Feldman, Fred. Israel.
Feldman, George B. & Felshman, Anne. The Complete Handbook of Pregnancy.
Feldman, Herman, jt. auth. see Chamberlin, Roy B.
Feldman, Herman, jt. ed. see Chamberlin, Roy B.
Feldman, Lawrence H. Riverine Maya: The Torquegua & Other Chols of the Lower Motagua Valley.
Feldman, Lawrence H. & Walters, Garry R., eds. Excavations in Southeastern Guatemala: 1976-1978.
Feldman, M. Basic Principles of Genetics.
Feldman, M. P. & Macculloch, M. J. Homosexual Behaviour: Therapy & Assessment.
Feldman, Phil, jt. auth. see Rugg, Tom.
Feldman, Philip & Orford, Jim, eds. Psychological Problems: The Social Context.
Feldman, Richard S., jt. auth. see Salzinger, Kurt.
Feldman, Ron, ed. The Jew As Pariah: Jewish Identity & Politics in the Modern Age.
Feldman, S. Shirley, jt. ed. see Sears, Robert R.
Feldman, Seth R. Dziga Vertov: A Guide to References & Resources.
Feldman, Stanley A. & Crawley, Brian E., eds. Trachaeostomy & Artificial Ventilation in the Treatment of Respiratory Failure.
Feldman, Steven A., jt. auth. see Denhoff, Eric.
Feldman, William T. Philosophy of John Dewey: A Critical Analysis.
Feldmeth, Joanne, jt. auth. see Larson, Jim.
Feldstein, Sandy, ed. see Zorn, Jay & Hanshumaker, James.
Feldstein, Stanley, jt. auth. see Jaffe, Joseph.
Felger, Donna H., compiled by. Boys' Fashions Eighteen Eighty-Six to Nineteen-Five.
Felheim, Marvin, ed. Comedy: Plays, Theory & Criticism.
Felice, Renzo de see De Felice, Renzo.
Felidae, Thomas & Davenport, H. M. Don't Let Them Kiss You: A Cat's Guide to Choosing & Training People.
Felig, Philip, et al. Endocrinology & Metabolism.
Felimeister, Charles J., jt. ed. see Snyder, Thomas L.
Felitta, Frank de see De Felitta, Frank.
Felix, David. Marx As Politician.
Felix, Monique. The Further Adventures of the Little Mouse Trapped in a Book.
Felkenes, George T. Michigan Criminal Justice Law Manual.
Felkin, H. & Swierczewski, G. Activation of Grignard Reagents by Transition Metal Compounds.
Felkner. Microbial Testers: Probing Carcinogenesis.
Fell, A. F., ed. Drug Analysis: Keynote & Plenary Papers from the First International Symposium, June 1983, Brussels, Belgium.
Fell, Derek. How I Planned to Plant the White House Vegetable Garden.
Fell, J. M, et al. Induced Representations & Banach-Algebraic Bundles.
Fell, John L. A History of Film.
Fell, Peter J. & Skees, William D. The Doctors' Computer Handbook.
Feller-Roth, Barbara. Country Inns: A Selection of Maine's Distinctive Accommodations.
Fellman, Gordon. The Deceived Majority.
Fellner, Rudolph. Opera Themes & Plots.
Fellowes, E. H., jt. ed. see Buck, P. C.
Fellowes, Edmund H. Appendix with Supplementary Notes.
Fellows, B. J. The Discrimination Process & Development.
Fellows, Len. Crossfacts.
--Tri-Play Crosswords. Hook, Henry, ed.
Fellows, Paul. Blue Book of American Antiques: A Price Guide to Americana Collectibles.
Felmeister, Charles J., jt. ed. see Snyder, Thomas L.
Felperin, Howard M. Dramatic Romance: Plays, Theory, Criticism.
Felsen, Jerry. Cybernetic Approach to Stock Market Analysis: Versus Efficient Market Theory.
Felsenstein, Joseph. Bibliography of Theoretical Population Genetics.
Felshman, Anne, jt. auth. see Feldman, George B.
Felstiner, John, tr. see Crow, Mary.
Felt, Robert L., ed. see Fratkin, Jake.
Feltenstein, Tom. Restaurant Profits Through Advertising & Promotion: The Indispensable Plan.
Feltner, Hellen A., jt. auth. see Smith, Ruth E.
Felton, Gilbert R. Evaluation of Population Estimation Procedures for Counties: 1980.
Felton, W. Sidney. Masters of Equitation.
Felts, William J. & Harrison, Richard J., eds. International Review of General & Experimental Zoology.
Fenady, Andrew J. The Man with Bogart's Face.
Fencl, Shirley & Jager, Susan G. The Two R's: Paragraph to Essay.
Fencl, Zdenek, jt. ed. see Malek, Ivan.
Fendell, Bob. How to Make Your Car Last a Lifetime.
Fenech, Henri, ed. Heat Transfer & Fluid Flow in Nuclear Systems.
Fenellosa, Ernest. Certain Noble Plays of Japan. Pound, Ezra, ed.
Fenelon & De Salignac De La Mothe, Francois. The Adventures of Telemachus. Paulson, Ronald, ed.
Fenelon, Fania. Playing for Time.
Feng, Da Hsuan, et al, eds. Contemporary Research Topics in Nuclear Physics.
Feng Jicai. Chrysanthemums & Other Stories. Chen, Susan W., tr. from Chinese.
--Miraculous Pigtail.
Fenichel, Carol H. & Hogan, Thomas H. Online Searching: A Primer.
Fenley, David C. & Petty, Thomas L. Recent Advances in Respiratory Medicine.
Fenn, Donna, jt. ed. see Trueblood, Carol.
Fenn, Henry C. Review Exercises in Chinese Sentence Structure.
Fenn, Henry C., ed. Chinese Characters Easily Confused.
Fenn, J. B., jt. ed. see Shuler, K. E.
Fennell, Francis L., Jr., ed. The Rossetti-Leyland Letters: The Correspondence of an Artist & His Patron.
Fennell, Frederick. Basic Band Repertory: British Band Classics from the Conductor's Point of View.
Fennema, Ilona & Apol, Georgette. Dirk's Wooden Shoes.
Fenner, Carol. Christmas Tree on the Mountain.
Fenner, Frank J. & White, David O. Medical Virology.
Fenner, James, jt. auth. see Mullings, Llewellyn M.
Fenner, Peter G., jt. auth. see Hutch, Richard A.
Fennie, Ziner. The Little Sailor's Biglet.
Fenno, Brooks, Jr. Helping Your Business Grow: One Hundred One Dynamic Ideas in Marketing.
Fensom, Rod. America's Grand Resort Hotels: Eighty Classic Resorts in the United States & Canada.
Fenten. Greenhousing for Purple Thumbs.
Fenten, D. X. Ms. M. D.
Fenton, Alexander & Owen, Trefor. Food in Perspective: Third International Conference of Ethnological Food Research.
Fenton, Edward. The Morning of the Gods.
Fenton, Fred R., et al. Home & Hospital Psychiatric Treatment: An Interdisciplinary Experiment.
Fenton, John. A-Z Industrial Salesmanship.
Fenton, Joseph. Hybrid Buildings.
Fenton, Nina, jt. auth. see Donnelly, Mark.
Fenton, Pat & Williams, Brian. Structured COBOL: Programming & Problem Solving.
Fenton, Thomas P. & Heffron, Mary J., eds. Third World Resource Directories.
Fenwick, Agnes M. My Journey into God's Realm of Light.
Fenwick, Charles G. American Neutrality, Trial & Failure.
Fenwick, Damon C. The Boatman's Bible.
Fenwick, Sara I., ed. Critical Approach to Children's Literature.
--New Definitions of School-Library Service: Proceedings of the 24th Annual Conference of the Graduate Library School.

Fenwick, William A. & Practising Law Institute. Computer Litigation 1984, Resolving Computer Related Disputes & Protecting Proprietary Rights.
Fenzler, Otto, et al, eds. see Roseman, Mill.
Feramisco, James, et al, eds. Cancer Cells Three: Growth Factors & Transformation.
Feraru, Anne T. International Conflict.
Ferazani, Larry. The Last Spartans.
Ferbel, Thomas, ed. Techniques & Concepts of High-Energy Physics I.
--Techniques & Concepts of High-Energy Physics II.
Ferber, A. C. We Are Immortal.
Ferber, Andrew, et al. The Book of Family Therapy.
Ferber, Richard. Solve Your Child's Sleep Problems.
Ference, Michael, Jr., et al. Analytical Experimental Physics.
Ferendeci, A. M., jt. ed. see McDowell, M. R.
Ferguson & Adams. Guide to the Antique Shops of Great Britain 1986.
Ferguson, Adam. Institutes of Moral Philosophy.
Ferguson, Albert B. & Bender, Jay. ABC's of Athletic Injuries & Conditioning.
Ferguson, Clyde L. The Stars & the Bible.
Ferguson, D. R., tr. see Lembeck, F., et al.
Ferguson, Dale V., jt. auth. see Buffaloe, Neal D.
Ferguson, E. James. Power of the Purse: A History of American Public Finance.
Ferguson, George A. Nonparametric Trend Analysis.
Ferguson, Giovonnia. Handling Small Pets: Step by Step.
Ferguson, Gregor. Coup D'Etat: A Practical Manual.
Ferguson, I. K. & Muller, J., eds. The Evolutionary Significance of the Exine.
Ferguson, James M. Habits, Not Diets: The Real Way to Weight Control.
Ferguson, James M. & Taylor, C. Barr. A Change for Heart: Your Family & the Food You Eat.
Ferguson, Jean & Solomon, Rowena. A Toddler in the Family: A Practical Australian Guide for Parents.
Ferguson, John. Bibliographical Notes on Histories & Inventions & Books of Secrets.
--Biblioteca Chimica; Catalog of the Alchemical & Pharmaceutical Books in the Library of James Young.
--The Heritage of Hellenism: The Greek World from 323 to 31 BC.
Ferguson, Lucy R., jt. auth. see Young, Harben B.
Ferguson, M. Carr, jt. auth. see Practising Law Institute Staff.
Ferguson, M. Carr, et al. Federal Income Taxation of Estates & Beneficiaries: 1984 Supplement.
Ferguson, Marjorie. Forever Feminine: Women's Magazines & the Cult of Femininity.
Ferguson, Mary A. Images of Women in Literature.
Ferguson, Mary Ann. Images of Women in Literature.
Ferguson, Pamela. Dominion.
--The Sacrifice.
Ferguson, Patricia. Indefinite Nights: And Other Stories.
Ferguson, Phil M. Reinforced Concrete Fundamentals.
Ferguson, R. & Adams, C., eds. Guide to the Antique Shops of Britain 1987.
Ferguson, Robert W. & Stokke, Allan H. Legal Aspects of Evidence.
Ferguson, Rosemary & Adams, Carol, eds. The Guide to the Antique Shops of Britain 1988.
Ferguson, Rosemary & King, Stella, eds. Guide to the Antique Shops of Britain, 1982.
--Guide to the Antique Shops of Great Britain 1985.
Ferguson, Sherry D., jt. auth. see Ferguson, Stewart.
Ferguson, Sinclair. A Heart for God.
Ferguson, Sinclair B. Kingdom Life in a Fallen World: Living out the Sermon on the Mount.
Ferguson, Stewart & Ferguson, Sherry D. Intercom: Readings in Organizational Communication.
Ferguson, Suzanne. Critical Essays on Randall Jarrell.
Ferguson, Sybil. The Diet Center Cookbook.
Ferguson, Walter W. Living Animals of the Bible.
Fergusson, Erna. Mexican Cookbook.
Fergusson, William E. The Internal Audit Training Program: How to Organize & Administer a Continuing Education Plan for Your Internal Audit Team.
Ferlazzo, Paul J. Emily Dickinson.
Ferlin, Guy R. Techniques du Reboisement dans les Zones Subdesertiques d'Afrique.
Ferlinghetti, Lawrence & Peters, Nancy J. Literary San Francisco: A Pictoral History from the Beginnings to the Present.
Ferm, Deane W. Profiles in Liberation: Thirty-Six Portraits of Third World Theologians.
Ferm, Vergilius. Ancient Religions.
--Brief Dictionary of American Superstitions.
--Dictionary of Pastoral Psychology.
--Encyclopedia of Morals.
--A History of Philosophical Systems.
--The Protestant Dictionary.
--Religion in the Twentieth Century.
Ferm, Vergilus. The American Church.
Fermi, Enrico. Notes on Thermodynamics & Statistics.
Fermi, Laura. Mussolini.
Fernald, L. Dodge & Fernald, Peter S. Basic Psychology.
--Introduction to Psychology.
Fernald, Peter S., jt. auth. see Fernald, L. Dodge.
Fernandes, Florestan. Negro in Brazilian Society. Eveleth, P. B., et al, eds. Skiles, J. D., tr.
--Reflections on the Brazilian Counterrevolution. Dean, Warren, pref. by. Vale, Michel & Hughes, Patrick M., trs. from Port.
Fernandes, Praxy, ed. Financing of Public Enterprises in Developing Countries.
Fernandes, Ron. Come to Think of It, Lord: Personal & Prayerful Reflections.
Fernandez, C. Gandia, jt. auth. see De La Rosa, Angeles.
Fernandez, Fernando. Zora & the Hibernauts.
Fernandez, Genevieve. American Traditional: A Comprehensive Guide to Home Decorating the Ethan Allen Way.
Fernandez, J., jt. auth. see Fitzgibbons, R.
Fernandez, Judi N., jt. auth. see Ashley, Ruth.
Fernandez, Rafael. Eastern Winds: The Imprint of Japan on Nineteenth- & Early Twentieth-Century Western Graphics.
Fernandez, Ronald. Los Macheteros: The Violent Struggle for Puerto Rican Independence.
Fernandez-Caballero, Carlos & Fernandez-Caballero, Marianne, eds. Emergency Medical Services Systems: A Guide to Information Sources.
Fernandez-Caballero, Marianne, jt. ed. see Fernandez-Caballero, Carlos.
Fernandez-Santamaria, J. A. Reason of State & Statecraft in Spanish Political Thought: 1595-1640.
Fernando, Lloyd, ed. Malaysian Short Stories.
Fernando, Tissa & Kearney, Robert N., eds. Modern Sri Lanka: A Society in Transition.
Fernbach, D, jt. ed. see McKay, L.
Fernbaugh, Ralph E. The Dandelion on the Ball.
Fernbaugh, Ralph Emerson. The Rocks around the Crucifix.
Fernett, Gene. American Film Studios.
Ferntheil, Carol. Noah's Ark Diorama Book.
Ferrando, R., ed. see Toxicology & Nutrition Symposium Staff.
Ferrante, Jon, et al. The Shin Tzu Heritage.
Ferrara, Peter L. & Nordin, Margareta C., eds. Muscloskeletal Injuries in the Workplace: Proceeding of International Conference Second Copenhagen, Denmark May 27-29 1986.
Ferrara, Sergio, jt. ed. see Ellis, John.
Ferrara, Sergio, et al, eds. Unification of the Fundamental Particle Interactions.
Ferrari, C., ed. see CISM (International Center for Mechanical Sciences) Staff.
Ferrari, Gustavo E., jt. auth. see Paz, Alberto C.
Ferrari, Paul L., et al. U. S. Arms Exports: Policies & Contractors.
Ferrari, R. L. & Jonscher, A. K., eds. Problems in Physical Electronics.
Ferrari, T. J. Elements of System-Dynamics Simulation.
Ferrarini, Elizabeth M. Confessions of an Infomaniac.
Ferraro, E. You Can Find Anyone: A Missing Persons Search Manual.
Ferraro, Geraldine A. & Francke, Linda B. Ferraro: My Story.
Ferraro, John R. & Ziomek, Joseph S. Introductory Group Theory & Its Applications to Molecular Structure.
Ferrarotti, Franco. Max Weber & the Destiny of Reason.
Ferrars, E. X. Come to be Killed.
--Other Devil's Name.
--Root of All Evil.
--Something Wicked.
Ferrars, Elizabeth. The March Hare Murders.
--Remove the Bodies.
Ferrary, Jeannette & Fiszer, Louise. The California-American Cookbook: Innovations on American Regional Dishes.
Ferrater, Mora. Diccionario de Filosofia.
Ferrater Mora, Jose. Unamuno: A Philosophy of Tragedy. Silver, Philip, tr. from Span.
Ferre see Proust, Marcel.
Ferre, Nels F. The Finality of Faith, & Christianity Among the World Religions.
Ferre, Rosario. Cuentos de Juan Bobo.
--Mona que le Pisaron la Cola.
--Muneca Menor.
Ferreira, J. A. Portuguese-English, English-Portuguese Dictionary.
Ferreira, T. Gomes & Proddow, Mary P. Art Nouveau Jewelry by Rene Lalique. Bradley, B. J., ed. Freeman, Nancy, tr.
Ferrel, Robert H., ed. see Smith, Gaddis.
Ferrell, John M., et al, eds. YMCA Competitive Swimming & Diving Coaches Manual.
Ferrell, Joseph S., ed. County Government in North Carolina.
Ferrell, Mallory H. Rails, Sagebrush & Pine.
Ferrell, O. C., jt. auth. see Pride, William M.
Ferrell, Robert H. American Diplomacy.
--American Diplomacy in the Great Depression: Hoover-Stimson Foreign Policy, 1929-1933.
--George C. Marshall Nineteen Forty-Seven to Nineteen Forty-Nine.
Ferrell, Robert H., ed. The Diary of James C. Hagerty: Eisenhower in Mid-Course, 1954-1955.
Ferrero, Guglielmo. Militarism.
--The Principles of Power: The Great Political Crises of History.
Ferres, John H. Arthur Miller: A Reference Guide.
Ferretti, Val S. & Scott, David L. Death in Literature.
Ferri, Enrico. Criminal Sociology.
Ferrier, Carole, ed. Gender, Politics & Fiction: Twentieth Century Australian Women's Novels.
Ferrier, J. M. French Prose Writers of the Fourteenth & Fifteenth Centuries.
Ferrier, James F. Philosophical Works: Phenomenology-Background, Foreground & Influences. Natanson, Maurice, ed.
Ferrington, Anne. The Adventures of Ricky the Brave.
Ferris, Byron, jt. auth. see Nelson, Roy P.
Ferris, Elvira & Skelley, Esther G. Body Structures & Functions.
Ferris, Elvira B. & Skelley, Esther G. Body Structures & Functions.
Ferris, Haldon. The Meaning of the Covenant.
Ferris, Jean. Music: The Art of Listening.
Ferris, John. Participation in Urban Planning.
Ferris, Lucy. The Gated River.
Ferris, Rose M. Dare to Love Again.
Ferris, Roxana S., ed. see Parsons, Mary E.
Ferris, Theodore N. Spectrum.
Ferris, Theodore N., ed. see Educational Research Council of America Staff.
Ferris, Theodore P. This Is the Day: Selected Sermons.
Ferris, Timothy. Galaxien. Ehlers, Anita, tr. from Eng.
--Galaxies.
Ferris, Valerie. Promises to Keep.
Ferro, Marc. The Bolshevik Revolution: A Social History of the Russian Revolution.
--October Nineteen Seventeen.
--The Use & Abuse of History or How the Past Is Taught.
Ferrone, J., ed. see Chiaromonte, Nicola.
Ferrone, J., ed. see Nance, John.
Ferrone, J., ed. see Woolf, Virginia.
Ferruzzi, Donald R. Human Anatomy & Physiology: A Laboratory Manual of.
Ferry, Anne D. Milton & the Miltonic Dryden.
Ferry, Charles. O Zebron Falls.
--Up in Sister Bay.
Ferry, Douglas J. Cost Planning of Buildings.
Ferry, Douglas J. & Brandon, Peter S. Cost Planning of Buildings.
Ferry, Ted S. Modern Accident Investigation & Analysis: An Executive Guide to Accident Investigation.
--Safety Management Planning Manual.
Ferster, jt. auth. see Coben.
Fertig, Paul E., et al. Using Accounting Information: An Introduction.
Feruson, David. The Complete Moving Planner.
Fesenmaier, Daniel R., jt. ed. see Lieber, Stanley R.
Feshback, Norma D., et al. Early Schooling in England & Israel.
Fesquet, Henri. Has Rome Converted. Salemson, Harold J., tr.
Fess, Elaine, et al. Hand Splinting: Principles & Methods.
Fessenden, Joan S., jt. auth. see Fessenden, Ralph J.
Fessenden, Ralph J. & Fessenden, Joan S. Basic Chemistry for the Health Sciences.
--Techniques & Experiments for Organic Chemistry.
Fessl, Helmut. The Scio Syndrome.
Fessler, Daniel W., jt. auth. see Haar, Charles M.
Fessler, George R. & Westcott, Ray D. The Insurance Primer: Fire & Casualty.
Fest, Joachim. Hitler. Winston, Richard & Winston, Clara, trs.
Fetros, John G. Dictionary of Factual & Fictional Riders & Their Horses.
Fett, Evelyn M. Cooking for Two.
Fetter, Bruce. The Creation of Elizabethville, Nineteen Ten to Nineteen Forty.
Fetter, F. W. & Gregory, D. Monetary & Financial Policy in Nineteenth Century Britain.
Fetter, Richard. Mountain Men of Wyoming.
Fetter, Robert B., ed. see Stair, Ralph M., Jr.
Fetter, Theodore J., jt. auth. see Cashman, Victoria S.
Fetters, Thomas T. & Swanson, Peter W. The Piedmont & Northern Railway.
Fettner. The Truth about AIDS.
Fettner, Ann G. & Check, William A. The Truth about AIDS: Evolution of an Epidemic.
Fetyko, David F. Financial Accounting: Concepts & Principles.
Fetyko, David F., et al. CPA Review, 1981-82: Volume II: Problems & Solutions.
--CPA Review: Theory, Practice, & Auditing.
Fetzer, John. Clemens Brentano.
Feuchtinger, Eugene. Your Voice: Methods for Strengthening & Developing the Voice.
Feuchtwanger, E. J., jt. ed. see Bessel, Richard.
Feuer, Janice. Sweets for Saints & Sinners.
Feuer, Lewis. Imperialism & the Anti-Imperialist Mind.
Feuerstein, Georg. The Essence of Yoga.
Feuerwerker, Albert. China's Early Industrialization: Sheng-Hsuan-Huai, 1844-1916 & Mandarin Enterprise.
--Economic Trends in the Republic of China, 1912-1949.
Feutry, Michel, et al, eds. Dictionary of Industrial Technology: English-French-German-Portuguese-Spanish.
Feville, Peter. Final Offer Arbitration - Concepts, Developments, & Techniques.
Fevold, Eugene L., jt. auth. see Nelson, Clifford.
Fevre, P. G. Le see Le Fevre, P. G.
Fewell, Rebecca R., jt. auth. see Garwood, S. Gray.
Fey, Harold E., ed. Ecumenical Advance: A History of the Ecumenical Movement.
Fey, James T. Mathematics Teaching Today: Perspectives from Three National Surveys.
Feydeau, Georges. The Lady from Maxim's. Mortimer, John, tr.
Feydy, Ann L. Osprey Island.
Feyerabend, Cessa. Diseases of Budgerigais.
Fezler, Lloyd. Adventures at Mountain Haven.
--African Adventures.
--More African Adventures.
Fforde, Adam & Paine, Suzanne H. The Limits of National Liberation: Problems of Economic Management in the Democratic Republic of Vietnam, with a Statistical Appendix.
Ffrench, G. E. & Hill, A. G. Kuwait: Urban & Medical Ecology, a Geomedical Study.
Ffrench, Heather, jt. auth. see Ffrench, Jonathan.
Ffrench, Jonathan & Ffrench, Heather. Country Enterprise: Pleasure & Profit from Home Produce.
Fiacco, A. V., jt. auth. see Falk, J. E.
Fiat, D., ed. International Symposium on Magnetic Resonance, 4th, Rehovot-Jerusalem, 1971: Proceedings.
Fiberarts Magazine Staff, ed. The Fiberarts Design Book Two.
Fibush, Esther & Morgan, Martha. Forgive Me No Longer: The Liberation of Martha.
Ficarra. Medicolegal Handbook: A Guide for Winning Verdicts.
Fichte, Johann G. Vocation of Man. Smith, William, tr. from Ger.
Fichter, Joseph H. The Holy Family of Father Moon.
Fichtner, Hans & Garff, Michael. How to Build Sailboards: Step-by-Step Custom-Made Designs.
Ficini, Jacqueline, ed. Ynamine: A Versatile Tool in Organic Synthesis.
Ficken, Carl. God's Story & Modern Literature: Reading Fiction in Community.
Fickett, Reginald N. Four, Oh! A Change of Values.
Fideler, Raymond & Kvande, Carol. South America.
Fideler, Ruth E., ed. Families.
Fidler, jt. auth. see Wagstaffe.
Fidler, Gail S. Design of Rehabilitation Services in Psychiatric Hospital Settings.
Fidler, Isiah & White, Richard. Design of Models for Testing Cancer Therapeutic Agents.
Fidler, J. Havelock, jt. auth. see Wagstaffe, Reginald.
Fido, Martin. Oscar Wilde.
--Rudyard Kipling.
--Shakespeare.
Fieandt, Kai Von see Von Fieandt, Kai & Mousgaard, I. K.
Fiechter, A. Space & Terrestrial Biotechnology.
Fiechter, A., ed. Biotechnology.
--Microbial Processes.
--Plant Cell Cultures.
Fiechter, A., jt. ed. see Ghose, T. K.
Fiechter, A., et al, eds. Advances in Biochemical Engineering.
Fiedler, Jean. The Year the World Was Out of Step with Jancy Fried.
Fiedler, Leslie A. Freaks, Myths & Images of the Secret Self.
--Freaks: Myths & Images of the Secret Self.
--What Was Literature?
--What Was Literature? Class Culture & Society.
Fiedorowicz, Z. & Priddy, S. Homology of Classical Groups Over Finite Fields & Their Associated Infinite Loop Spaces.

Authors

Fieg, V. P. Why There Aren't Witches & Other Tales.
Field, Barry C. & Willis, Cleve E., eds. Environmental Economics: A Guide to Information Sources.
Field, Claud H. Dictionary of Oriental Quotations.
Field, David. Projects in Wood.
Field Day Theatre Company. Ireland's Field Day.
Field, Edward. Stand Up, Friend, with Me.
Field, F. H. & Franklin, J. L. Electron Impact Phenomena.
Field, Frank, ed. The Wealth Report Two.
Field, Frederick V. From Right to Left: An Autobiography.
Field, G. Lowell & Higley, John. Elitism.
Field, George, et al. Cosmic Evolution: An Indroduction to Astronomy.
Field, Joan R., jt. ed. see Brown, Robert A.
Field, John. The King's Nurseries.
Field, John P. Richard Wilbur: A Bibliographical Checklist.
Field, Lawrence. High Performance.
Field, Louise F. Child & His Book.
Field, M. & Fordtran, J. S., eds. Secretory Diarrhea.
Field, Michael. Cooking with Michael Field. Scobey, Joan, ed.
--The Merchants: The Big Business Families of Saudi Arabia & the Gulf States.
--Michael Field's Cooking School.
Field Research Corporation Staff. Public Opinion of Criminal Justice in California: A Survey Conducted by Field Research Corporation.
Field, Richard H., et al. Civil Procedure, Fifth Edition, Basic Course, 1987 Supplement.
Field, Syd. Screenplay: The Foundations of Screenwriting.
Field, Timothy F., et al. Readings in Rehabilitation Counseling.
Fielder, John. California Images of the Landscape.
--Colorado, Images of the Alpine Landscape.
--Washington Magnificent Wilderness.
Fieldhouse, David K. Unilever Overseas: The Anatomy of a Multinational.
Fieldhouse, David K., jt. ed. see Madden, Frederick.
Fieldhouse, W. L. Gun Lust.
Fielding, Anthony J. & Cavanagh, Darol M. Curriculum Priorities in Australian Higher Education.
Fielding, Henry. Joseph Andrews.
--Joseph Andrews & Shamela.
Fielding, Joy. Life Penalty.
Fielding, Kathy. Having Your Baby at Home.
Fielding, L. P., jt. auth. see Todd, Ian P.
Fielding, Sarah. The Governess: Or Little Female Academy.
Fields, Annie, ed. James T. Fields: Biographical Notes & Personal Sketches with Unpublished Fragments & Tributes from Men & Women of Letters.
Fields, Armond. George Auriol.
Fields, Carl. Exploring Careers in Tool & Die Making.
Fields, Dorothy & Kitakoji, Isamitsu. Cherry Blossoms.
Fields, Howard. High Crimes & Misdemeanors: The Untold & Dramatic Story of the Rodino Committee.
Fields, Jeff. Cry of Angels.
Fields, Kent T., jt. auth. see Bonno, John A.
Fields, L. J. Pharmacologic Review for Intensive Cardiopulmonary Therapy.
Fields, Marion L. Laboratory Manual in Food Preservation.
Fields, Nina S. The Well-Seasoned Marriage.
Fields, Phyllis, tr. see Oliveira, Nuno.
Fields, Piggie. Why Me?
Fields, Rick. How the Swans Came to the Lake: A Narrative History of Buddhism in America.
Fields, Sidney Jacob. The Person Circle: A First Book on Group Psychotherapy & the Small Group Field.
Fienberg, S. E. & Hinkley, D. H., eds. R. A. Fisher: An Appreciation.
Fiennes, R. N., ed. Biology of Nutrition. Incl. Pt. 1. The Evolution & Nature of Living Systems; Pt. 2. The Organizations & Nutritional Methods of Life Forms. Pergamon.
Fiennes, Ranulph. To the Ends of the Earth: The Transglobe Expedition, the First Pole-to Pole Circumnavigation of the Globe.
Fieser. Reagents for Organic Synthesis.
Fiesta, Janine. The Law & Liability: A Guide for Nurses.
Fife, Alta, jt. auth. see Fife, Austin.
Fife, Austin & Fife, Alta. Saints of Sage & Saddle: Folklore Among the Mormons.
Fife, Austin, et al, eds. Forms upon the Frontier: Folklife & Folk Arts in the United States.
Fife, Jonathan D., ed. & frwd. by see Brookes, Michael C. & German, Katherine L.
Fifield, William. Modigliani.
Fifoot, Richard. A Bibliography of Edith, Osbert & Sacheverell Sitwell.
--A Bibliography of Edith, Osbert, & Sacherevell Sitwell.
Figge, Frank H., ed. see Sobotta, Johannes.
Figgie, Harry E. The Cost Reduction & Profit Inprovement Handbook.
Figh, Margaret G., jt. auth. see Windham, Kathryn T.
Figler, Howard. The Complete Job Search Handbook.
Figley, Grace E., et al. Elementary School Physical Education: An Educational Experience.
Figueroa, Ed & Harshman, Dorothy. Yankee Stranger.
Figueroa, John J. Society, Schools & Progress in the West Indies.
Figueroa, Oscar & Winkler, Charles. A Business Information Guidebook.
Figueroa, William G., ed. Hematology.
Fike, Linus. No Nation Alone.
Fike, Richard. The Bottle Book.
Fikhtengol'ts, G. M. Fundamentals of Mathematical Analysis.
Fikrig, Senih M., ed. Handbook of Immunology for Students & House Staff.
Filatov, V. P., et al. Lenin the Revolutionary.
Filby, P. William, ed. Passenger & Immigration Lists Bibliography, 1538-1900: Supplement.
Filby, P. William, jt. ed. see Meyer, Mary K.
Filby, Royston H., et al, eds. Atomic & Nuclear Methods in Fossil Energy Research.
Fildes, R. & Dews, D., eds. A Bibliography of Business & Economic Forecasting.
Filene, Peter G. Americans & the Soviet Experiment, 1917-1933.
Filippone, Samuel R. & Williams, Michael Z. Elementary Mathematics: A Fundamentals & Techniques Approach.
Filippov, S. Theory of Metallurgical Processes.
Fillard, J. P. & Van Turnhout, J., eds. Thermally Stimulated Processes in Solids - New Prospects: Proceedings of an International Workshop, Montpellier, June, 1976.
Filler, Louis. Dictionary of American Social Reform.
Filler, Ronald C., jt. auth. see Alexander, J. Estill.
Filler, Witold. Contemporary Polish Theatre (1977)
Filley, Alan C. Interpersonal Conflict Resolution.
Filley, Richard D. & Szoka, Kathryn. Communicating with Graphics: A Series from Industrial Engineering.
Fillmore, Charles F., et al, eds. Individual Differences in Language Ability & Language Behavior.
Fillmore, P. A., ed. see Conference on Operator Theory, Dalhousie Univ., Halifax, 1973.
Filmer, Robert. Patriarcha & Other Political Works of Sir Robert Filmer.
Filmus, Tully. Tully Filmus: Selected Drawings.
Filon, S. P. L. National Central Library: An Experiment in Library Co-Operation.
Filson, Floyd V., jt. ed. see Wright, G. Ernest.
Financial Accounting Standards Board. Accounting Standards: Complete 1984 Edition.
--Accounting Standards: Current Text (as of June 1, 1985), Complete Edition.
--Accounting Standards: Current Text (as of June 1, 1985) General Standards.
--Accounting Standards: Current Text-General Standards.
--Accounting Standards: Original Pronouncements-Complete Edition.
--Accounting Standards: Original Pronouncements; July 1973-June 1, 1984.
--Accounting Standards: Original Pronouncements-Through June 1973.
--Financial Accounting Standards Board Current Text 1982-1984: International.
Financial Consulting Staff. Investment Banking.
Financial Publishing Co. Staff. Car Loan Payment Tables.
--Monthly Mortgage Loan Payment Table.
--Net Yield Table After Forty-Six Percent Capital Gains Tax.
--Net Yields Table after Twenty Percent Capital Gains Tax.
--Personal Financial Planner.
--Renegotiable Rate: Mortgage Handbook.
Financial Publishing Co. Staff, ed. Family Financial Planner.
Financial Publishing Company Staff. FHA & FHA-GPM Mortgage Payment Tables.
Financial Times Staff, ed. Industrial Companies.
--Mining.
--Oil & Gas.
--Oil & Gas.
--World Hotel Directory.
--World Insurance.
Finazzo, Giancarlo. The Notion of Tao in Lao Tzu & Chuang Tsu.
Finch, A., et al. Chemical Applications of Far Infrared Spectroscopy.
Finch, Bernard. Passport to Paradise.
Finch, C. A. An Approach to Technical Translation.
Finch, Christopher. Making of the Dark Crystal.
--Norman Rockwell's America.
--Norman Rockwell's America.
Finch, Christopher & Ramachandran, Srinivasa. Matchmaking: Science Technology & Manufacturing.
Finch, Curtis R. & Crunkilton, John R. Curriculum Development in Vocational & Technical Education: Planning Content, & Implementation.
Finch, Eugene D., jt. ed. see Elias, Robert H.
Finch, F. E., et al. Managing for Organizational Effectiveness: An Experiential Approach.
Finch, Henry, jt. ed. see Munslow, Barry.
Finch, Henry L. Wittgenstein, the Early Philosophy: An Exposition of the Tractatus.
--Wittgenstein-the Later Philosophy: An Exposition of the Philosophical Investigations.
Finch, I. J. General Studies: First Handbook for Technical Students.
Finch, John D. Aspects of Law Affecting the Paramedical Professions.
Finch, Robert. The Primal Place.
Finch, Roger. Suite from the Ivory Rooming House.
Finck, Henry T. Musical Laughs: Jokes, Tittle-Tattle, & Anecdotes, Mostly Humorous, About Musical Celebrities.
Finder, Jan H., ed. Alien Encounters.
Finder, Joseph. Red Carpet.
Findlater, Richard. The Player Queens.
Findlater, Richard, ed. Author! Author!
Findlay, Christopher, jt. ed. see Garnaut, Ross.
Findlay, J. N. Wittgenstein: A Critique.
Findlay, James V. Safety & the Executive. Stephenson, Bette & Hassel, William, eds.
Findlay, James V. & Morrison, Richard G. Supervisory Control of Absenteeism.
Findlay, John N. Hegel: A Re-Examination.
Findlay, M. Chapman, III, et al. Real Estate Portfolio Analysis.
Findlay, R., jt. auth. see Brockett, O.
Findleton, Jack, jt. auth. see Tiede, Tom.
Findley, D. F., ed. Applied Time Series Analysis.
Findley, Roger W. & Farber, Daniel A. Environmental Law in a Nutshell.
Findley, Warren G., ed. Impact & Improvement of School Testing Programs.
Fine, Ben. Marx's Capital.
--Marx's Capital.
Fine, Carla. Married to Medicine: An Intimate Portrait of Doctor's Wives.
Fine, David, ed. Los Angeles in Fiction: A Collection of Original Essays.
Fine, H. A. & Gaskell, D. R., eds. Second International Symposium on Metallurgical Slags & Fluxes.
Fine, H. Alan & Geiger, Gordon H. Handbook on Material & Energy Balance Calculations in Metallurgical Processes.
--Handbook on Material & Energy Balance Calculations in Metallurgical Processes.
Fine, H. Alan, ed. Extractive Metallurgy Laboratory Exercises.
Fine, Leonard W. Chemistry.
Fine, Ralph A. Escape of the Guilty: A Trial Judge Speaks out Against Crime.
Fine, Reuben. The Logic of Psychology: A Dynamic Approach.
Fine, Richard N. & Gruskin, Alan. Treatment of End Stage Renal Disease in Children.
Fine Woodworking Magazine. Fine Woodworking Techniques One.
Finegan, Jack. Archeology of the New Testament: The Life of Jesus & the Beginning of the Early Church.
Fineman, Stephen. White Collar Unemployment: Impact & Stress.
Fingar, Thomas, ed. Higher Education in the People's Republic of China: Report of the Stanford University Delegation.
Finger, Ben, Jr. Concise World History.
Finger, Seymour M., jt. ed. see Alexander, Yonah.
Finger, Stanley, ed. Recovery from Brain Damage.
Fingerhut, Bruce M. & Haskin, Steve. Read That Label: How to Tell What's Inside a Wine Bottle from What's on the Outside.
Fingerhut, Eugene R. Survivor: Cadwallader Colden II in Revolutionary America.
Fingesten, Peter. Eclipse of Symbolism.
Fingleton, David. Kiri Te Kanawa: A Biography.
Finifter, Ada. Using the IBM Personal Computer: IBM Easywriter.
Finitskaya, Z. Samarkand.
Fink, A. M. Almost Periodic Differential Equations.
Fink, Albert & Kokaska, Charles J., eds. Career Education for Behaviorally Disordered Students.
Fink, Arthur E. The Field of Social Work.
Fink, Carole, tr. see Bloch, Marc.
Fink, Donald G. & Beaty, H. Wayne. Standard Handbook for Electrical Engineers.
Fink, Edward J. Building a Career in the Business World.
Fink, Eugen, jt. auth. see Heidegger, Martin.
Fink, Sr. Harold S., ed. see Foucher Of Chartres.
Fink, Karl J. & Baeumer, Max L., eds. Goethe As a Critic of Literature.
Fink, Michael, jt. auth. see Lofland, John.
Fink, Robert S., jt. auth. see Frankel, Sandor.
Fink, Sam. Constitution.
Fink, Stephen L., et al. Designing & Managing Organizations.
Fink, Stuart, jt. auth. see Burian, Barbara.
Finke, Hubert R. Understanding: How It Grows on You & How You Grow on It.
Finkel, Donald. Adequate Earth.
--Answer Back.
--The Detachable Man.
--Joyful Noise.
--A Mote in Heaven's Eye.
--What Manner of Beast.
Finkel, Jules. Computer-Aided Experimentation: Interfacing to Mini-Computers.
Finkel, Lawrence S., et al. Learning English As a Second Language: Level 1, 2, 3, 4, 5.
Finkel, LeRoy. Learning Word Processing Concepts Using AppleWriter.
Finkel, Norman J. Mental Illness & Health: Its Legacy Tensions, & Changes.
Finkel, Robert. The Brainbooster: Your Guide to Rapid Learning & Remembering.
Finkelhor, David & Yllo, Kersti. License to Rape: Sexual Abuse of Wives.
Finkelstein, Abe & Holtje, Bert. Handbook of Woodworking Plans, Patterns & Projects.
Finkelstein, Honora, jt. auth. see Gross, Gail.
Finkelstein, Miriam. Domestic Affairs.
Finkler, Steven A. The Complete Guide to Finance & Accounting for Non-Financial Managers.
Finks, Lee. Is This a Put-on?
Finlay, Patrick, ed. Jane's Freight Containers, 1986.
Finlayson, Brian, jt. auth. see Statham, Ian.
Finlayson, Geoffrey. Decade of Reform: England in the Eighteen Thirties.
Finlayson, Niall D., jt. ed. see Shearman, David J.
Finletter, Gretchen. The Dinner Party.
Finley, George, ed. see Industrial Design Magazine Staff.
Finley, James & Pennock, Michael. Your Faith & You.
Finley, John, jt. auth. see Sehlinger, Bob.
Finley, John H., Jr. Three Essays on Thucydides.
Finley, K. T. Triazoles.
Finley, M. I. Early Greece: The Bronze & Archaic Ages.
Finley, M. I., ed. see Garlan, Yvon.
Finley, M. I., ed. see Sandbach, F. H.
Finley, Moses I. Ancient Greeks.
Finley, P. J., ed. Progress in Aerospace Sciences.
Finley, P. J., jt. ed. see Bagley, J. A.
Finley, Patrick. Diamond in the Rough.
Finley, Ruth E. Old Patchwork Quilts.
Finn, David, et al. Teaching Manual for Tutor-Librarians.
Finn, Geraldine, jt. ed. see Miles, Angela.
Finn, Michael. Art of Shuriken Jutsu: The Samurai Skill of Throwing Stars & Spikes.
--Jodo: Way of the Stick.
--Kendo No Kata: Forms of Japanese Kendo.
Finn, Molly. Feasts for a Farthing. Dinan, Dennis, ed.
--Summer Feasts.
Finn, Nancy B. The Electronic Office.
--Writing Dynamics: A Guidebook for Communications in the Office of the 80's.
Finnegan, John R. & Hirl, Patricia A. Law & the Media in the Midwest.
Finneran, Richard J. Critical Essays on W. B. Yeats.
Finnerty, Kathleen. Anthology of Verse.
Finney, Charles G. The Circus of Dr. Lao.
Finney Company. Finding Your Job. Incl. Unit IC; Unit 2B; Unit 3B; Unit 4B; Unit 5B; Unit 6B. Finney Co.
Finney, David. The Power Thyristor & Its Applications.
Finney, David J. Introduction to the Theory of Experimental Design.
Finney, Horace M., tr. see Ibsen, Henrik.
Finney, Humphrey S. A Stud Farm Diary.
Finney, Shan, jt. auth. see Dolan, Edward F., Jr.
Finney, Susan, jt. auth. see Kindle, Patricia.
Finocchiaro, Mary. Let's Talk.
Finsand, Mary J. Diabetic Breakfast & Brunch Cookbook.
Finstad, Suzanne. Heir Not Apparent. Rodriquez, Barbara, ed.
Finsterbusch, Kurt & McKenna, George. Taking Sides: Clashing Views on Controversial Social Issues.
Finsterbusch, Kurt, ed. Sociology 1988-89.
Finsterbusch, Kurt & Wolf, Charles P., eds. Methodology of Social Impact Assessment.
Finsterbush, Kurt. Annual Editions: Sociology, 1985-86.
Finzer, William, jt. auth. see Ericson, Tim.
Fiore, Evelyn, jt. auth. see Mickel, John.
Fiore, Mariano S. di see Di Fiore, Mariano S.
Fiore, Michele. Welfare of Nations.
Fiore, N. F. & Berkowitz, B. J., eds. Advanced Techniques for Characterizing Hydrogen in Metals: Proceedings. TMS-AIME Fall Meeting, Louisville, 1981.
Fiore, Robert L. Lazarillo de Tormes.

Fiorenza, Elisabeth S. In Memory of Her: A Feminist Theological Reconstruction of Christian Origins.
Fiorenza, Elisabeth S. & Holmes, Urban T. Lent. Achtemeier, Elizabeth & Krodel, Gerhard, eds.
Fiori, Benjamin, tr. see Tischner, Joseph.
Fiorini, Ettore, ed. Neutrino Physics & Astrophysics.
Fiorito, Len, jt. auth. see Marazzi, Rich.
Firby, P. A. & Gardiner, C. F. Surface Topology.
Firebaugh, Francille M., jt. auth. see Deacon, Ruth E.
Firebaugh, W. C., tr. see Petronius Arbiter.
Fireman, Janet R. The Spanish Royal Corps of Engineers in the Western Borderlands: Instrument of Bourbon Reform, 1764-1815.
Fireman, Judy, ed. The TV Book.
Fireman, Peter. Justice in Plato's Republic.
--Perceptualistic Theory of Knowledge.
Fireside, Harvey. Soviet Psychoprisons.
--Soviet Psychoprisons.
Firestone, David B. & Reed, Frank C. Environmental Law for Non-Lawyers.
Firestone, Ross, jt. auth. see Carroll, Diahann.
Firm, C. Connie. Winning Collection Strategies.
Firmage, Edwin B., jt. auth. see Wormuth, Francis D.
Firmage, Edwin B., et al, eds. Religion & Law: Biblical-Judaic & Islamic Perspectives.
Firmin, Peter. Basil Brush Goes Boating.
Firsoff, V. A. The New Face of Mars.
--Our Neighbor World.
First, Julia. Flat on My Face.
Firth, Peter. Lord of the Seasons.
Firth, Raymond. Elements of Social Organization.
--History & Traditions of Tikopia.
Firth, Raymond, ed. Themes in Economic Anthropology.
Fisch, Max H., jt. auth. see Anderson, Paul R.
Fisch, U., ed. Aktuelle Probleme der Otorhinolaryngologie.
Fischel, Sharon H. The Day-Night Circus Clowns.
Fischer, jt. ed. see Pike.
Fischer, Al, jt. auth. see Fischer, Mildred M.
Fischer, Asma Q., et al. Pediatric Neurosonography: Clinical Tomographic & Neuropathologic Correlates.
Fischer, C. P., et al. Classic Cooking Made Easy.
Fischer, Chris. Coal & the State.
Fischer, Clare B., et al, eds. Women in a Strange Land: A Search for a New Image.
Fischer, Claude S. The Urban Experience.
Fischer, Constance T. & Brodsky, Stanley L., eds. Client Participation in Human Services: The Prometheus Principle.
Fischer, D., jt. auth. see DeBoer, J. B.
Fischer, D. W., ed. Managing Technological Accidents: Two Blowouts in the North Sea: Proceedings of an IIASA Workshop on Blowout Management.
Fischer, E. H., ed. see International Symposium on Metabolic Interconversion of Enzymes Staff.
Fischer, Eberhard & Homberger, Lorenz. Masks in Guro Culture, Ivory Coast. Mullin, Jeanne, et al, eds. Lauf, Cornelia & Isler, Andrea, trs. from Ger.
Fischer, Frank & Sirianni, Carmen, eds. Critical Studies in Organization & Bureaucracy.
Fischer, Fritz. Germany's Aims in the First World War.
--War of Illusions: German Policies, 1911-1914. Jackson, Marion, tr. from Ger.
--World Power or Decline: The Controversy Over Germany's Aims in the First World War. Farrar, Lancelot L., et al, trs. from Ger.
Fischer, G. Complex Analytic Geometry.
Fischer, George. Ways to Self Rule: Beyond Marxism & Anarchism.
Fischer, Gretl. In Search of Jerusalem: Religion & Ethics in the Writings of A. M. Klein.
Fischer, H., ed. see Gesellschaft Fuer Biologische Chemie, 22nd Colloquium, Mossbach Baden, 1971.
Fischer, Kuno. A Commentary on Kant's Critick of Pure Reason. Beck, Lewis W., ed.
Fischer, L. Afghanistan.
Fischer, Lewis A. & Uren, Philip E. The New Hungarian Agriculture.
Fischer, Louis. Men & Politics: An Autobiography.
--Soviet Journey.
Fischer, Mary, jt. auth. see Boulgarides, James.
Fischer, Michael. Assembly Language Programming for the 65816 & 65802.
Fischer, Mildred. London Theatre Today: A Guide for Travelers.
Fischer, Mildred M. & Fischer, Al. Arizona Museums.
Fischer, N. & Georgopoulos, N., eds. Continuity & Change in Marxism.
Fischer, Raymond P. An Aged Man Remembers April.
--The Four Hazardous Journeys of Reverend Jonathan Blanchard.
Fischer, Robert. Hot Dog!
Fischer, Robert B. Chemical Equilibrium.
Fischer, Robert E., ed. see Architectural Record Magazine Editors.
Fischer, Roger A. Successful Air Conditioning & Refrigeration Repair.
Fischer, Ruth. Stalin & German Communism.
Fischer, Theodore. Cheap-Smart Travel: Dependable Alternatives to Travelling Full Fare.
Fischer, W. & Hureau, J. C., eds. Southern Ocean, CCAMLR Convention Area, Fighting Areas 48, 58 & 88.
Fischer-Nagel, Andreas, jt. auth. see Fischer-Nagel, Heiderose.
Fischer-Nagel, Heiderose & Fischer-Nagel, Andreas. A Kitten Is Born.
Fischer-Theurer, Annette, tr. see Peltzer, Martin & Treumann, Walter.
Fischl, Viktor, ed. Antonin Dvorak, His Achievement.
Fischler, Stan, jt. auth. see Cherry, Don.
Fischman, Sheila, tr. see Beauchemin, Yves.
Fischman, Sheila, tr. see Kattan, Naim.
Fischman, Sheila, tr. see Tardivel, Jules-Paul.
Fischnaller, Steve. Northwest Shore Dives.
Fischnich, O. E., jt. auth. see Manshard, W.
Fish, Debra, ed. Home-Based Training Resource Handbook.
Fish, Hamilton. F D R: The Other Side of the Coin.
--FDR: The Other Side of the Coin.
Fish, Hamilton, Sr. The Tragic Deception.
Fish, Peter G. The Politics of Federal Judicial Administration.
Fish, Robert L. The Incredible Schloch Homes.
Fishbein, Lawrence, et al. Chemical Mutagens: Environmental Effects on Biological Systems.
Fishbein, Warren H. Wage Restraint by Consensus: Britain's Search for an Income Policy Agreement, 1965-1979.
Fishburn, Angela. Creating Your Own Soft Furnishing: How to Decorate with Fabric.
Fishburn, Janet F. The Fatherhood of God & the Victorian Family: The Social Gospel in America.
Fishburn, Peter C. The Theory of Social Choice.
Fishel, Elizabeth. The Men in Our Lives: Fathers, Lovers, Husbands, Mentors.
Fishelson, Lev. Mysteries of the Red Sea.
Fisher, Aimee, tr. see Olesha, Yury.
Fisher, Alan. AMC Guide to Country Walks Near Boston.
--Country Walks Near Baltimore.
--Three Passions of Countess Natalya.
Fisher, Andrea. Let Us Now Praise Famous Women: Women Photographers for the U. S. Government, 1935 to 1944.
--Let Us Now Praise Famous Women: Women Photographers for the U. S. Government, 1935 to 1944.
Fisher, Anna Marie. Omits for Obits: Memoirs.
Fisher, Anne B. Stories California Indians Told.
--Stories California Indians Told.
Fisher, Anthony C. Economic Efficiency & Air Pollution Control.
Fisher, Barbara & Spiegal, Richard, eds. Waterways: Poetry in the Mainstream, 1987 Index.
Fisher, Bob & Ross, Bob. The America's Cup, 1987: The Official Record.
Fisher Broadcasting Staff. Cooking with Katherine Wise. Wise, Katherine, ed.
Fisher, Charles O. & Murray, Richard C. Guide to Maryland Negligence Cases.
Fisher, Chris. Coal & the State.
--Custom, Work & Market Capitalism: The Forest of Dean Colliers, 1788-1888.
--Innovation & Australian Industrial Relations.
Fisher, Chris, jt. ed. see Rawson, Don.
Fisher, Clarence S. The Minor Cemetery at Giza.
Fisher, Clay. Black Apache.
Fisher, David. The War Magician.
Fisher, David, jt. auth. see Lasorda, Tommy.
Fisher, David, jt. auth. see Luciano, Ron.
Fisher, David & Bragonier, Reginald, Jr., eds. Qu'est-ce Que C'est. Fantapie, Alain & Brule, Marcel, trs. from Fr.
--What's What in Sports: The Visual Glossary of the Sports World.
Fisher, David E. The Third Experiment: Is There Life on Mars?
Fisher, Dorothy C. Understood Betsy.
Fisher, Elizabeth. Woman's Creation.
Fisher, Eric, jt. auth. see Scott, John.
Fisher, Eunice, jt. ed. see Lock, Andrew.
Fisher, Franklin M. & Shell, Karl. The Economic Theory of Price Indices: Two Essays on the Effects of Taste, Quality & Technological Change.
Fisher, Frederick. China Adventures.
Fisher, G., jt. auth. see Jeffries, J. R.
Fisher, Gary E. Functional Model for Fourth Generation Languages.
Fisher, George. God Would Have Done It If He'd Had the Money.
Fisher, H. J., jt. auth. see Hart, F. L.
Fisher, Hank. The Floater's Guide to Montana.
Fisher, Helen E. The Sex Contract: The Evolution of Human Behavior.
Fisher, Hilda B. Improving Voice & Articulation.
Fisher, Howard. Mapping Information.
Fisher, Isobel, jt. auth. see Dixson, Robert J.
Fisher, Jack. Rough Guide to Mexico.
Fisher, Jack & Gatland, Bruce. Electronics: From Theory into Practice.
Fisher, James, ed. Thorburn's Birds.
Fisher, Jeffrey D. & Nadler, Arie, eds. New Directions in Helping: Vol. 1: Recipient Reactions to Aid.
Fisher, Johanna. A Parent's Guide to Learning Disabilities.
Fisher, John, jt. auth. see Ellingham, Mark.
Fisher, John H., ed. see Chaucer, Geoffrey.
Fisher, John J. Victorious Journey: A Physician-Pilot Battles Cancer During a Worldwide Tour.
Fisher, Katherine & Kay, Elizabeth. Quilting in Squares.
Fisher, Leonard E. The Railroads.
--Star Signs.
Fisher, M. F., tr. see Brillat-Savarin, Jean.
Fisher, M. M. & Roy, C. C., eds. Pediatric Liver Disease.
Fisher, M. Roy. Titian's Assistants During the Later Years.
Fisher, Margaret, et al. Colonial America.
Fisher, Margaret E., jt. auth. see O'Brien, Edward L.
Fisher, Mary L. Guide to State Legislative Materials.
Fisher, Mathias J. see Laurence, Robert, pseud.
Fisher, Mike, et al. Mental Health Social Work Observed.
Fisher, Pat, jt. auth. see Gitter, Kurt A.
Fisher, Paul. The Ash Staff.
--The Princess & the Thorn.
Fisher, Phyllis K. Los Alamos Experience.
Fisher, Richard B. AIDS: Your Questions Answered.
Fisher, Rick, jt. auth. see Yanda, Bill.
Fisher, Robert, ed. Amazing Monsters: Verses to Thrill & Chill. Allen, Rowena, tr. & illus.
Fisher, Robert C., ed. see McNair, Sylvia T.
Fisher, Robert J. Learning How to Learn: The English Primary School & American Education.
Fisher, Robert L., jt. auth. see Edwards, Clifford H.
Fisher, Robert M. Twenty Years of Public Housing.
Fisher, Rod, jt. auth. see Pavord, Tony.
Fisher, Seymour. Body Consciousness.
Fisher, Stephen. GED Social Studies Test Preparation Guide: High School Equivalency Examination.
Fisher, Stephen H. Commonwealth Caribbean.
Fisher, Wallace E. Because God Cares: Messages 1980.
--Who Dares to Preach? The Challenge of Biblical Preaching.
Fisher, Walter, et al. Power, Greed & Stupidity in the Mental Health Racket.
Fisher, Wesley A., jt. ed. see Yanowitch, Murray.
Fisheries Advisory Commission, Major Communicable Fish Diseases in Europe & Their Control Symposium Staff. Panel Reviews & Relevant Papers.
Fishkin, Howard. Taxpayers Survival Manual.
Fishkin, Lois & Dimarco, Susan. The Not-Strictly Vegetarian Cookbook.
--The Super Natural Dessert Cookbook.
Fishlock, David. New Ways of Working Metals.
Fishlock, Trevor. Gandhi's Children.
Fishlow, Albert, et al. Trade with Manufacturers in Developing Countries: Reinforcing North-South Partnership.
Fishman, Alfred P. Pulmonary Diseases & Disorders.
Fishman, Alfred P., ed. Assessment of Pulmonary Function.
--Heart Failure.
--Pulmonary Diseases & Disorders: Update 1.
Fishman, Bernard, jt. auth. see Fleming, Stuart.
Fishman, George S. Spectral Methods in Econometrics.
Fishman, Hertzel. American Protestantism & a Jewish State.
Fishman, Joanne A., jt. auth. see Bartlett, Michael.
Fishman, Joshua A., tr. see Weinreich, Max.
Fishman, K. D. The Computer Establishment.
Fishman, Meryl & Horwich, Kathleen. Living with Your Teenage Daughter & Liking it.
Fishman, Robert A. Cerebrospinal Fluid in Diseases of the Nervous System.
Fishman, S. G., jt. ed. see Dhingra, A. K.
Fishman, William H., ed. On Codevelopmental Markers: Biologic Diagnostic & Monitoring Aspects.
Fishman, William H. & Sell, Stewart, eds. Onco-Developmental Gene Expression.
Fishman, William J. & Breach, N. The Streets of East London.
Fishtein, Ruth. Classroom Psychology.
Fisk, Alan, jt. auth. see Fisk, Margaret C.
Fisk, Edward R. Construction Engineer's Form Book.
--Construction Project Administration.
Fisk, Jim & Barron, Robert. The Official MBA Handbook of Great Business Quotations.
Fisk, Margaret C. & Fisk, Alan. The Paradise Rehearsal Club.
Fisk University Library Editors, Nashville. Dictionary Catalog of the Negro Collection of the Fisk University Library.
Fiske, Donald W., jt. auth. see Kelly, Everett L.
Fiske, Dorsey. Academic Murder.
Fiske, Kenneth & Harter, James H. Direct Current Circuit Analysis Through Experimentation.
Fiske, Patricia, ed. see Archaeological Textiles Staff.
Fiske, Patricia, ed. see Lamb, Venice & Lamb, Alastair.
Fiske, Roger. Beethoven's Missa Solemnis.
Fiske, Thomas S. Low Cost Costing: Product Costing with Your Microcomputer.
Fison, J. E. Understanding the Old Testament: The Way of Holiness.
Fissan, H., ed. Aerosols in Science, Medicine & Technology: Proceedings of the Tenth Annual Conference of the Association for Aerosol Research (Gesellschaft fur Aerosolforschung), Bologna, Italy, 14-17 September 1982.
Fiszel, H. Investment Efficiency in a Socialist Economy.
Fiszer, Louise, jt. auth. see Ferrary, Jeannette.
Fitch, Alger. Claiming God's Promises.
Fitch, Alger M., Jr. Revelation.
Fitch, James M. American Building: The Historical Forces That Shaped It.
--American Building Two: The Environmental Forces That Shape It.
--Historic Preservation.
Fitch, Robert M., ed. Polymer Colloids I.
--Polymer Colloids II.
Fitler, William, jt. auth. see Balma, Phillip.
Fitter & Richardson. Collins Pocket Guide to British Birds.
Fitter, A. H. & Hay, R. K. Environmental Physiology of Plants.
Fitter, A. H., ed. Ecological Interactions in the Soil Environment.
Fitti, Charles J. A Philosophy of Creation.
Fitton, Mary, tr. see Lanez, Manuel M.
Fitts, Dudley. Birds of Aristophanes.
Fitz, Franklin H. A Gardener's Guide to Propagating Food Plants.
Fitzerald, Jim, ed. Transistor Replacement & Alternate Source Guide.
Fitzgerald. ABC.
--Animal Friends.
--Rainbow.
Fitzgerald, Betty J., tr. see Kammer, Reinhard.
Fitzgerald, David, photos by. Oklahoma.
Fitzgerald, Ed. A Nickel an Inch: A Memoir.
Fitzgerald, Edward, tr. see Khayyam, Omar.
Fitzgerald, Ernest A. God Writes Straight with Crooked Lines.
--How to Be a Successful Failure.
Fitzgerald, F. Scott. The Basil & Josephine Stories. Kuehl, John & Bryer, Jackson R., eds.
--Flappers & Philosophers.
--Great Gatsby.
--The Notebooks of F. Scott Fitzgerald. Bruccoli, Matthew J., ed.
--The Notebooks of F. Scott Fitzgerald. Bruccoli, Matthew J., ed.
--The Romantic Egoists: A Pictorial Autobiography from the Albums of Scott & Zelda Fitzgerald. Smith, Scottie F., et al, eds.
Fitzgerald, F. Scott & Fitzgerald, Zelda. Bits of Paradise.
Fitzgerald, F. Scott, jt. auth. see Fitzgerald, Zelda.
Fitzgerald, Frank J. Of Roses & Other Poems.
Fitzgerald, Garret, et al. The Middle East & the Trilateral Countries.
Fitzgerald, George. A Practical Guide to Preaching.
Fitzgerald, Hiram & Walraven, Michael G., eds. Psychology 1988-89.
Fitzgerald, Hiram, jt. ed. see Walraven, Michael G.
Fitzgerald, Hiram E. Annual Editions: Human Development, 1985-86. Wairawen, Michael, ed.
Fitzgerald, Hiram E. & Walraven, Michael. Annual Editions: Psychology, 1985-86.
FitzGerald, James A. For Fear of Little Men.
Fitzgerald, Jerry. Business Data Communications: Basic Concepts, Security, & Design.
Fitzgerald, Jim. Boxing for Beginners.
--Boxing for Beginners.
--The Joys of Smoking Cigarettes.
Fitzgerald, Jim & Boswell, John. The First Family Paper Doll & Cut Out Book.
Fitzgerald, Jim, ed. Engineering Application Software.
--IC Functional Equivalence Guide.
--International Directory of Discontinued ICs & Discrete Semiconductors.
--Memory Discontinued Devices.
--Thyristor Discontinued Devices.
Fitzgerald, Lee A. Time Wounds All Heels.
Fitzgerald, Nancy. Down Into the Water.
Fitzgerald, Robert. Enlarging the Change: The Princeton Seminars in Literary Criticism, 1949-1951.
Fitzgerald, T. J., jt. auth. see Lee, H.
Fitzgerald, W. L., et al. Advertising & Promotion for Professional Pharmacy Practice.

Fitzgerald, Walter. The New Europe: An Introduction to Its Political Geography.
Fitzgerald, William, jt. auth. see Brackin, Ivan L.
Fitzgerald, Zelda & Fitzgerald, F. Scott. Bits of Paradise.
Fitzgerald, Zelda, jt. auth. see Fitzgerald, F. Scott.
Fitz-Gibbon, Carol T. & Morris, Lynn L. How to Calculate Statistics.
--How to Design a Program Evaluation.
Fitz-Gibbon, Carol T., jt. auth. see Morris, Lynn L.
FitzGibbon, Constantine. The Golden Age.
--Man in Aspic.
Fitzgibbon, Dan. All about Your Money.
FitzGibbon, Theodora. Taste of Ireland.
--Your Favorite Recipes.
Fitzgibbons, R. & Fernandez, J. Latin America: Political Culture & Development.
Fitzlyon, April. A Month in the Country.
--The Price of Genius.
FitzPatrick, E. A. Micromorphology of Soils.
Fitzpatrick, John C. George Washington Himself.
Fitzpatrick, Merrilyn. Zhou Enlai.
Fitzpatrick, Paul. Shopacheck's Rugby League Review, Nineteen Eighty-Four to Nineteen Eighty-Five.
Fitzpatrick, Thomas B., et al. Dermatology in General Medicine.
--Dermatology in General Medicine: Update One.
Fitz-Randolph, Jane, jt. auth. see Jespersen, James.
Fitz-Simon, Christopher. The Arts in Ireland: A Chronological Survey.
Fitz-Simon, Christopher, jt. auth. see Morrison, Robin.
Fitzsimons, Christopher. Reflex Action.
Fitzsimons, M. A., jt. ed. see Kertesz, Stephen D.
FitzSimons, Raymund. Death & the Magician.
Fix, G. J., jt. auth. see Coffman, C. V.
Fixico, Donald L. Termination & Relocation: Federal Indian Policy, 1945-1960.
Fixman, Adeline. Aim for a Job in Cartooning.
Fixx, James F. More Games for the SuperIntelligent.
Fizdale, Robert, jt. auth. see Gold, Arthur.
Flaceliere, Robert. Love in Ancient Greece. Cleugh, James, tr.
Flachmann, Kim. Focus: A College English Handbook.
Flack, Dora D. Dry & Save.
Flack, Marjorie. William & His Kitten.
Flagg, Mildred Evelyn. The Silent Murder.
Flagler, John J. Modern Trade Unionism.
Flagstad, Kirsten. The Flagstad Manuscript (by) Louis Biancolli.
Flaherty, Cornelia M. Go with Haste into the Mountains.
Flaherty, E. J. Hermitian & Kahlerian Geometry in Relativity.
Flaherty, Frances H. Odyssey of a Film-Maker: Robert Flaherty's Story.
Flaherty, Joseph. Tin Wife.
Flaig, W., et al. Organic Materials & Soil Productivity.
Flaim, Stephen & Zelis, Robert F., eds. Calcium Blockers: Mechanisms of Action & Clinical Applications.
Flake, Carol. Tarnished Crown: The Quest for a Racetrack Champion.
Flake, Janice L., et al. Fundamentals of Computer Education.
Flakierski, Henryk. Economic Reform & Income Distribution.
Flamma, Thomas. Metaphysics, a Bridge to ECKANKAR.
Flammarion, Camille. Haunted Houses.
Flanagan, Bernard J. A Lenten Pastoral Letter.
Flanagan, Bob. Fuck Journal.
Flanagan, Geraldine L. First Nine Months of Life.
Flanagan, Geraldine L. & Morris, Sean. Window into a Nest.
Flanagan, J. L. & Rabiner, L. R., eds. Speech Synthesis.
Flanagan, Mary. Bad Girls.
Flanagan, Mike. Out West.
Flanagan, Padraig, ed. A New Missionary Era.
Flanagan, Robert. Naked to Naked Goes.
Flanagan, Terrence, jt. auth. see Milman, David.
Flanders, H. Calculus.
Flanders, H. & Price, J. Calculus with Analytic Geometry.
Flanders, Harley & Price, Justin J. Algebra.
--Algebra.
--A Second Course in Calculus.
Flanders, Helen H. & Brown, George. Vermont Folk-Songs & Ballads.
Flanders, Henry J., Jr., et al. Introduction to the Bible.
Flanner, Janet. Janet Flanner's World: Uncollected Writing's 1932-1975. Drutman, Irving, ed.
--Paris Journal: Vol. II, 1965-1971. Shawn, William, ed.
Flannery, Kent V., ed. see Lees, Susan.
Flannigan, Arthur. Me De Villedieu's Les Desordres Del L'amour: History, Literature & the Nouvelle Historique.
Flantz, Richard, tr. see Tammuz, Benjamin.
Flasschoen, Marie. Fires at Midnight.
Flast, Lauren, jt. auth. see Flast, Robert.
Flast, Robert & Flast, Lauren. Macintosh Spreadsheets: Using Microsoft Multiplan, Chart, & File.
Flast, Robert H. Fifty-Four SuperCalc Models: Finance, Statistics, Mathematics.
Flaste, Richard, jt. auth. see Franey, Pierre.
Flaster, Donald J. Malpractice: A Guide to the Legal Rights of Doctors & Patients.
Flatauer, Susanne, tr. see Schneede, Uwe M., et al.
Flaten, Essye P. Come Ride "The Rails " with Me: All over the United States & Norway, England & Wales.
Flaten, Essye Price. All Aboard for Wales!
--Our Farm Years.
Flathman, Richard E. Political Obligation.
Flato, Anne & Schiff, Marilyn. Shop by Mail Worldwide.
Flatt & Scruggs. Folk Music with an Overdrive.
Flatt, Adrian E. Care of the Arthritic Hand.
Flatto, Edwin. Look Younger, Think Clearer, Live Longer.
Flaubert, Gustave. Letters.
--Madame Bovary.
--Sentimental Education.
Flaud, J. M. & Camy-Peyret, C. Water Vapour Line Parameters from Microwave to Medium Infrared: An Atlas of H2 to the Sixteenth, O; H2 to the Seventeenth, O; H2 to the Eighteenth, O; Line Positions & Intensities Between O & 4350 Cm to the -1.
Flavin, Christopher. Electricity from Sunlight: The Future of Photovoltaics.
Flavin, Christopher, jt. auth. see Deudney, Daniel.
Flavin, Martin. Criminal Code.
Flavin, Sean, jt. auth. see Ehrman, Kenneth.
Flaws, Bob. Path of Pregnancy.
Flayerman, Norm, ed. Flayderman's Guide to Antique American Firearms...& Their Values.
Flayhart, William H., III, jt. auth. see Shaum, John H., Jr.
Fleck, James N., ed. see TMS Staff & AIME Staff.
Fleck, Richard F., ed. see Muir, John.
Fleenor, C. Patrick, jt. auth. see Knudson, Harry R.
Fleenor, Juliann, ed. The Female Gothic.
Fleet, David D. van see Albanse, Robert & Van Fleet, David D.
Fleet Owner Magazine Staff. Fleet Owners Maintenance Shop Design Book.
Fleetcroft, C. The Musculo-Skeletal System.
Fleetwood, Hugh. The Beast.
--The Past.
--The Redeemer.
--Roman Magic.
Flegg, Jim, annotations by. Just a Lark!
Flegmann, Vilma. Called to Account: The Public Accounts Committee of the House of Commons.
Fleisch, H. J., et al, eds. see European Symposium on Calcified Tissues, 3rd, Davos, 1965.
Fleischer, Arthur, Jr. Tender Offers: Defenses, Responses, & Planning.
Fleischer, Arthur, Jr., et al, eds. Twelfth Annual Institute on Securities Regulation.
Fleischer, G. Evolutionary Principles of the Mammalian Middle Ear.
Fleischer, G. A., ed. Risk & Uncertainty: Non-Deterministic Decision Making in Engineering Economy.
Fleischer, Leonore. Annie.
Fleischer, Max. Betty Boop.
Fleischer, Richard. The Narrow Margin.
Fleischer, Sidney & Tonomura, Yuji. Structure & Function of Sarcoplasmic Reticulum (Symposium)
Fleischman, Harry. Norman Thomas.
Fleischman, Sid. The Hey Hey Man.
--Jingo Django.
--Kate's Secret Riddle Book.
--McBroom the Rainmaker.
--McBroom's Ear.
--McBroom's Ghost.
--McBroom's Zoo.
Fleischmann, Kaspar M., jt. auth. see Gernsheim, Helmut.
Fleisher, Belton M. & Kniesner, Thomas J. Economics.
Fleisher, Martin, ed. Machiavelli & the Nature of Political Thought.
Fleisher, Nat & Andre, Sam. A Pictorial History of Boxing.
Fleishman, Joel L. & Payne, Bruce L. Ethical Dilemmas & the Education of Policymakers.
Fleishman, Seymour. Printcrafts for Fun & Profit. Rubin, Caroline, ed.
Flemans, R. J., jt. auth. see Hayhoe, F. G.
Fleming, Alex. Private Capital Flows to Developing Countries & Their Determinations: Historical Perspective, Recent Experience, & Future Prospects.
Fleming, Alice. America Is Not All Traffic Lights: Poems of the Midwest.
Fleming, Berry. The Make-Believers.
Fleming, Bruce C. E. Contextualization of Theology: An Evangelical Assessment.
Fleming, David L. The Spiritual Exercises of St. Ignatius: A Literal Translation & a Contemporary Reading. Ganss, George E., ed.
Fleming, Denna F. Treaty Veto of the American Senate.
Fleming, Doris R. This Day.
Fleming, Esther, jt. auth. see Fleming, Robert E.
Fleming, G. H. The Unforgettable Season.
Fleming, Garry. Face of the City.
Fleming, Harold, jt. auth. see Glatthorn, Allan A.
Fleming, I., jt. auth. see Williams, D. H.
Fleming, Ian. Casino Royale.
--Diamonds Are Forever.
--Doctor No.
--For Your Eyes Only.
--Goldfinger.
Fleming, James, ed. see Negri, Antonio.
Fleming, Jean. Between Walden & the Whirlwind.
Fleming, M. C. Construction & the Related Professions.
Fleming, M. C., jt. auth. see Farthing, S. M.
Fleming, Macklin. Of Crimes & Rights.
Fleming, Mary M. Managerial Accounting & Control Techniques for the Non-Accountant.
Fleming, Patricia H. Villagers & Strangers: An English Proletarian Village over Four Centuries.
Fleming, Quentin W. A Guide to Doing Business on the Arabian Peninsula.
--Put Earned Value into Your Management Control System.
Fleming, Robert E. & Fleming, Esther. Sinclair Lewis: A Reference Guide.
Fleming, Robert E., ed. James Weldon Johnson & Arna Wendell Bontemps: A Reference Guide.
Fleming, Robert L. Justice League of America.
Fleming, Spencer. The Twenty Most Valuable Books for Speculative Success in the Stock Market with Elucidations Sufficient to Master the Content of Each Single Book.
--Why You Should Invest in Bank Stocks Now.
Fleming, Steve, ed. Official Professional Rodeo Guide 1987.
Fleming, Stuart & Fishman, Bernard. The Egyptian Mummy: Secrets & Science.
Fleming, Susan. Trapped on the Golden Flyer.
Fleming, Thomas. One Small Candle: The Pilgrims' First Year in America.
--Seventeen-Seventy-Six: Year of Illusions.
Fleming, Walter & Varberg, Dale E. Algebra & Trigonometry.
--Algebra & Trigonometry.
--College Algebra.
Fleming, Walter L. Documentary History of Reconstruction: Political, Military, Social, Religious, Educational & Industrial.
Fleming, William. Arts & Ideas.
Fleming-Holland, Susan, jt. auth. see Camden, Thomas M.
Flemming, Arthur S. Community Colleges: The Untold American Story.
Flemming, Kurt, jt. ed. see Locker, Alfred.
Flemming, Laraine. Reading for Results.
--Reading for Results.
Flenley, J., jt. ed. see Neale, J.
Flere, W. A. Handy Guide to Stowage.
Flerko, B., et al, eds. Reproduction & Development: Proceedings of the 28th International Congress of Physiological Sciences, Budapest, 1980.
Flesch, Janos. Planning in Chess.
Flesher, Dale L. & Flesher, Tonya K. Accounting for the Middle Manager.
Flesher, Dale L., jt. auth. see Flesher, Tonya K.
Flesher, Tonya K. & Flesher, Dale L. Accounting Principles for Midmanagement.
Flesher, Tonya K., jt. auth. see Flesher, Dale L.
Fletcher. Pascal & the Mystical Tradition.
Fletcher, A. F. Mostly Motor Racing: A Pictorial Autobiography.
Fletcher, Aaron. Cowboy.
--Outback.
--Outback.
--Outback.
Fletcher Aircraft Company Staff. Standard Aircraft Workers' Manual.
Fletcher, Alan D. & Jugenheimer, Donald W. Problems & Practices in Advertising Research: Readings & Workbook.
Fletcher, Arnold. Afghanistan: Highway of Conquest.
Fletcher, C. A., jt. auth. see Shackleton, V. J.
Fletcher, D. L., jt. auth. see Rhodes, A.
Fletcher, David B. Social & Political Perspectives in the Thought of Soren Kierkegaard.
Fletcher, Ella A. The Law of the Rhythmic Breath.
Fletcher, George U. The Well of the Unicorn. Del Ray, Lester, ed.
Fletcher, Helen. Bishops & Bluestockings.
Fletcher, Ian, ed. see Allen, Grant.
Fletcher, Ian, ed. see Egerton, George.
Fletcher, Ian, ed. see Harland, Henry.
Fletcher, Ian, ed. see O'Shaughnessy, Arthur.
Fletcher, J. M., jt. auth. see Ott, H.
Fletcher, J. R., jt. auth. see Charlesworth, A. S.
Fletcher, John. Alain Robbe-Grillet.
--The Wild-Goose Chase: A Modern Critical Edition with Commentary and Notes Based on the 1652 Folio. Lister, Rota H. & Orgel, Stephen, eds.
Fletcher, Joseph. Moral Responsibility: Situation Ethics at Work.
Fletcher, Joseph, jt. ed. see Cox, Harvey.
Fletcher, Kenneth, et al. Extend: Youth Reaching Youth.
Fletcher, Leonard, et al. Construction Contract Dictionary.
Fletcher, Max E. Economics & Social Problems.
Fletcher, Merton D. Workers & Commissars: Trade Union Policy in the People's Republic of China.
Fletcher, Mike & Ross, Bob. Tuning a Racing Yacht.
--Tuning a Racing Yacht.
Fletcher, R. Practical Methods of Optimization: Constrained Optimization.
--Practical Methods of Optimization: Unconstrained Optimization.
Fletcher, Rivers. MG: Past & Present.
Fletcher, Ronald. Sociology: The Study of Social Systems.
Fletcher, S. G., et al, eds. Turning.
Fletcher, Sarah. Stewardship: Taking Care of God's World.
Fletcher, Stevenson W. Pennsylvania Agriculture & Country Life: 1640-1840.
Fletcher, W. W. & Kirkwood, R. C. Herbicides & Plant Growth Regulation.
Fletcher, William. The Second Greatest Commandment.
Fletcher, William, jt. ed. see Lenihan, John.
Fletcher, William M. The Triumph of Surrender.
Fletcher, Wyndham. Port: An Introduction to Its Histroy & Delights.
Flett, D. S., ed. Ion Exchange Membranes.
Flett, J. P., jt. auth. see Flett, T. M.
Flett, T. M. & Flett, J. P. Traditional Dancing in Scotland.
Flew, A. G. Logic & Language.
Flexner, James T. An American Saga: The Story of Helen Thomas & Simon Flexner.
--The Light of Distant Skies: 1760-1835.
--Lord of the Mohawks: A Biography of Sir William Johnson.
Flexner, Stuart B. I Hear America Talking.
--Listening to America.
--Listening to America: An Illustrated History of Words & Phrases from Our Lively & Splendid Past.
Flick, Art. Art Flick's Master Fly Tying Guide.
Flick, Ernest W. Handbook of Paint Raw Materials.
Flick, Shockley. How to Be a Successful Song Leader.
Flicke, Wilhelm F. War Secrets in the Ether.
Fliegel, Dorian. The Fix.
Flieger, Wilhelm & Pagtolun-an, Imelda. An Assessment of Fertility & Contraception in Seven Philippine Provinces: 1975.
Flinn, J. E., ed. Membrane Science & Technology: Industrial, Biological, & Waste Treatment Processes.
Flinn, Richard A. & Trojan, Paul K. Engineering Materials & Their Applications.
--Engineering Materials & Their Applications.
Flint, D. A True & Fair View in Company Accounts.
Flint, Emily P., ed. Creative Editing & Writing Workbook.
Flint, Homer E., jt. auth. see Hall, Austin.
Flint, John, ed. Lifetime-Value Packagetion Package.
Flint, Kate. Impressionists in England: The Critical Reception.
--The Victorian Novel & Social Problems.
Flint, Russ, jt. auth. see Mason, Alice L.
Flint, Russ, illus. Christmas with Little Women.
Flipovic, R., et al. Yugoslavic Pocket Dictionary: Croatian-English.
Flippo, Chet. David Bowie's Serious Moonlight: The World Tour.
Flippo, Edwin B. Principles of Personnel Management.
Flipse, J. E., ed. Deep Ocean Mining.
Floan, Howard R. William Saroyan.
Floc'h, F., jt. ed. see Werner, G. H.
Flohn, N. Climate & Weather.
Flomenbaum, Neal & Goldfrank, Lewis, eds. Diagnostic Testing in the Emergency Department.
Flomenhaft, Kalman, jt. ed. see Christ, Adolph E.
Flood, E. A., ed. The Solid-Gas Interface.
Flood, J. The Moth Hunters: Aboriginal Prehistory of the Australian Alps.
Flood, J. E. & Hughes, C. J., eds. The Impact of High Speed & VLSI Technology on Communication Systems: Related Conference Proceedings.
--The ISDN & Its Impact on Information Technology: Related Conference Proceedings.
--Satellite Systems for Mobile Communications & Navigation: Related Conference Proceedings.

--Secure Communication Systems: Related Conference Proceedings.
Flood, Kenneth U., ed. Research in Transportation: Legal-Legislative & Economic Sources & Procedures.
Flood, Robert. Faith for All Generations.
Flood, W. E. Dictionary of Chemical Names.
Floore, Frances Berkeley. Bread of the Oppressed: An American Women's Experiences in War-Disrupted Countries from the Journal & Letters.
Flora, James. Day the Cow Sneezed.
--The Day the Cow Sneezed.
--Fishing with Dad.
--Grandpa's Farm.
--Kangaroo for Christmas.
--Leopold, the See-Through Crumbpicker.
--Little Hatchy Hen.
--My Friend Charlie.
--Pishtosh, Bullwash & Wimple.
--Sherwood Walks Home.
--Stewed Goose.
Flora, Philip C. International CAD-CAM Software Directory.
--International Engineering-Scientific Software Directory.
--International Industrial Sensor Directory.
Floren, Lee. The Bushwhackers.
--Powdersmoke Lawyer.
Florence, Gene. Collector's Encyclopedia of Depression Glass.
--Collectors' Encyclopedia of Depression Glass.
--Elegant Glassware of the Depression Era.
--Pocket Guide to Depression Glass.
Florence, P. S. Atlas of Economic Structure & Policies.
Florence, Ronald. Zeppelin.
Flores, Angel, ed. Anthology of German Poetry from Holderlin to Rilke.
Flores, Ernesto F. Flores en la Tarde. Hernandez, Juan, tr. Fricker, Richard L., ed.
Flores, Janis. Cynara.
Flores, Juan. Insularismo e Ideologia Burguesa.
Flores, Miguel C. El Charro en U. S. A.
Flores, Philip J. How to Conquer Your Addiction Through Group Therapy: A Practical Guide to Changing Your Addiction Habits with Group Help.
Flores, Xavier. Agricultural Organizations & Economic & Social Development in Rural Areas.
Floret, K. Weekly Compact Sets.
Florian, M. A., ed. Traffic Equilibrium Methods.
Florian, Michael & Gaudry, Marc, eds. Transportation Supply Models.
Florida Bar Staff. Basic Creditors' & Debtors' Rights in Florida.
--Employees' Benefits in Florida.
--Evidence in Florida.
--Extraordinary Writs in Florida.
--Florida & Federal Securities Regulation.
--Florida Real Property Practice II.
--Florida Zoning & Land Use Planning.
--Guide to Florida Legal Research.
Florida Clipping Service. Florida Media List.
Floridi, Alexis. Moscow & the Vatican.
Floridis, Ronald G. Comprehensive Split Dollar.
Florio, Carol. Collegiate Programs for Older Adults: A Summary Report on a 1976 Survey.
Florio, Carol, jt. auth. see Murphy, Judith.
Floris-Soltesz, Elizabeth, jt. auth. see Szabo.
Florkin, M. & Dollfus, A., eds. Life Sciences & Space Research.
Florkin, Marcel & Schoffeniels, Ernest. A Molecular Approaches to Ecology.
Florman, Monte see Consumer Report Book Editors.
Flory, Jane. The Bear on the Doorstep.
--The Golden Venture.
--It Was a Pretty Good Year.
--The Liberation of Clementine Tipton.
--The Lost & Found Princess.
--Miss Plunkett to the Rescue.
--The Unexpected Grandchildren.
--We'll Have a Friend for Lunch.
Floss, Heinz C., ed. Biosynthesis of Ergot Alkaloids & Related Compounds.
Floumey, Theodore. From India to the Planet Mars.
Flournoy, Francis R. British Policy Towards Morocco in the Age of Palmerston, 1830-1865.
Flournoy, Valerie. Until Summer's End.
Flower, Dean. Henry James in Northampton: Vision & Revision.
Flower, Dean S., ed. see Thoreau, Henry David.
Flower, J. E. Literature & the Left in France.
Flower, J. E., ed. France Today: Introductory Studies.
Flower, Linda. Problem-Solving Strategies for Writing.
--Problem-Solving Strategies for Writing.
Flower, Raymond. The Old Ship: A Prospect of Brighton.
Flower, Robin, tr. Love's Bitter Sweet.
Flower, Sibylla J. Debrett's Stately Homes of Britian.
Flower, Sybilla J., compiled by. Debrett's Stately Homes of Great Britain.
Flowers, Charles. It Never Rains in Los Angeles.
Flowers, James L., et al. A Complete Preparation for the MCAT.
Flowers, John V., jt. auth. see Whiteley, John M.
Floyd, Beth, jt. ed. see Floyd, Steve.
Floyd, Jesse M. International Fish Trade of Southeast Asian Nations.
Floyd, John A., Jr., jt. auth. see Southern Living Magazine Gardening Editors.
Floyd, Nancy. Essentials of Data Processing.
Floyd, Steve & Floyd, Beth, eds. Handbook of Interactive Video.
Fluck, E., et al. Inorganic Chemistry. Boschke, F., ed.
Fluckiger, W. Lynn. Unique Advantages of Being a Mormon.
Flude, Michael, jt. ed. see Ahier, John.
Fluegge, W. Viscoelasticity.
Flugel, E., ed. Fossil Algae: Recent Results & Developments.
Fluke, Joanne. Cold Judgement.
--The Stepchild.
Flumiani, C. M. Gaining Consistent Profits in Stock Market Charts.
--The Iron Laws of the Historical Inevitabilities.
Flumiani, Carlo Maria de see De Flumiani, Carlo M.
Flusche, Della M. & Korth, Eugene H. Forgotten Females: Women of African & Indian Descent in Colonial Chile, 1535-1800.
Flygt, Sten G. Review of German.
Flying Magazine Editors, jt. auth. see Sorensen, Chris.
Flying Magazine Editors, ed. America's Flying Book.
Flynn, Brian. Easy BASIC Programs for the IBM PC & PCjr.
--Thirty-Three Programs for the TI 99-4A.
Flynn, Elizabeth A. & Donaldson, Christine F. Alternative Careers for Ph.D.s in the Humanities: A Selected Bibliography.
Flynn, Jay. Bannerman.
--Bannerman.
--Bannerman Border Incident.
Flynn, Jean P., jt. auth. see Mahoney, Elizabeth A.
Flynn, Leslie B. Dare to Care Like Jesus.
--The Sustaining Power of Hope.
Flynn, Nancy. Pearl.
Flynn, Norman, et al. Abolition or Reform? The Metropolitan Counties & the GLC.
Flynn, Patricia, jt. auth. see Burbach, Roger.
Flynn, Suzanne K. How to Save Your Hair: A Complete Guide to the Prevention & Treatment of Baldness.
Flynn, Thomas. Tales for My Brothers' Keepers.
Flynt, J. Wayne. Dixie's Forgotten People: The South's Poor Whites.
Fo, Dario. Accidental Death of an Anarchist.
--We Can't Pay? We Won't Pay!
Fo, Dario & Rame, Franca R. Female Parts: One Woman Plays.
Focillon, Henri. The Art of the West in the Middle Ages, Vol. 1: Romanesque. King, Donald, tr. from Fr.
Fock, V. Fundamentals of Quantum Mechanics.
Foderaro, Anthony. Elements of Neutron Interaction Theory.
Fodor, John T. & Dalis, Gus T. Health Instruction: Theory & Application.
Fodor, Nandor. Freud, Jung & Occultism.
--The Search for the Beloved: A Clinical Investigation of the Trauma of Birth & Pre-Natal Conditioning.
Fodor, Ronald V. Earth Afire! Volcanoes & Their Activity.
--Earth in Motion: The Concept of Plate Tectonics.
Foehn, Carla. Directions.
Foell, Wesley K. Small-Sample Reactivity Measurements in Nuclear Reactors.
Foerst, W. Newer Methods of Preparative Organic Chemistry.
Foerster, Friedrich W. Christ & Human Life.
Foerster, K. Beitrag zur Desmidieenflora von Sued-Holstein und der Hansestadt Hamburg.
--Desmidieen aus dem Suedosten der Vereinigten Staaten von Amerika.
Foerster, Norman & Lampe, M. Willard, eds. College Bible.
Foerster, Norman, et al, eds. Eight American Writers.
Foerster, Werner. From the Exile to Christ: Historical Introduction to Palestinian Judaism. Harris, Gordon E., ed.
Fogarty, Marna S. The Cat Yellow Pages: The Cat Owner's Guide to Goods & Services.
Fogarty, Michael. Forty to Sixty-How We Waste the Middle Aged.
Fogarty, Robert S. The Righteous Remnant: The House of David.
Fogel, David & Hudson, Joe, eds. Justice As Fairness: Perspectives on the Justice Model.
Fogel, Robert W. Essays in Econometric History.
Fogel, Robert W. & Engerman, Stanley L. Time on the Cross. Incl. Vol. 1. The Economics of American Negro Slavery; Vol. 2. Evidence & Methods-a Supplement. Little.
--Time on the Cross: The Economics of Negro Slavery. Incl. The Economics of American Negro Slavery; Vol. 2. Evidence & Methods, a Supplement. Little.
Fogelin, Robert J. Understanding Arguments: An Introduction to Informal Logic.
--Understanding Arguments: An Introduction to Informal Logic.
Fogelson, Raymond D. & Adams, Richard N., eds. The Anthropology of Power: Ethnographic Studies from Asia, Oceania & New World.
Fogelson, Robert M. Big-City Police: An Urban Institute Study.
Foget, Karen, ed. Arnold Flaten: Sculptor.
Fogg, A. S. Australian Town Planning: Uniformity & Change.
Fogg, H. Witham. Salad Crops All Year Round.
Fogg, Walter. One Thousand Sayings of History, Presented as Pictures in Prose.
Fogg, Walter L. & Richter, Peyton E. Philosophy Looks to the Future: Confrontation, Commitment & Utopia.
Fogh, Jorgen, et al. Transformation of Tissue Culture Cells by SV - 40 Viruses.
Fogle, Sonja, jt. auth. see Harpers, Ferry W.
Fogleman, William J. I Live in the World.
Foher, E. Europe by Rail.
Fohner, John U. Mana Taboo.
Foin, Theodore C., Jr. Ecological Systems & the Environment.
Fokkema, D. W. Report from Peking: Observations of a Western Diplomat on the Cultural Revolution.
Folami, Takiu. A History of Lagos, Nigeria: The Shaping of an African City.
Folan, Lilias. Lilias, Yoga & Your Life.
Folberth, O. G., jt. ed. see Balk, P.
Folco, G., jt. ed. see Berti, F.
Foley, Charles & Scobie, W. I. The Struggle for Cyprus.
Foley, Frederic J. The Great Formosan Imposter.
Foley, Helen S. Marriage & Death Notices from Alabama Newspapers & Family Record 1819 to 1890.
Foley, James W., jt. auth. see Hunter, John M.
Foley, Leo A. Art, Wisdom & the Pursuit of Excellence.
Foley, Leonard. Signs of Love: The Sacraments of Christ.
Foley, Leonard, ed. Saint of the Day.
Foley, Martha. The Best American Short Stories.
--The Story of Story Magazine.
Foley, Martha, ed. Best American Short Stories 1973.
--The Best American Short Stories 1974.
--Two Hundred Years of Great American Short Stories.
Foley, Martha & Burnett, David, eds. Best American Short Stories, 1971.
--Fifty Best American Short Stories 1915-1965.
Foley, Rae. Call It Accident.
Foley, Robert. Hominid Evolution & Community Ecology.
Foley, Sue, jt. auth. see Ingrassia, Sara.
Foley, Winifred. As the Twig Is Bent: Sketches of a Bittersweet Life.
--A Child in the Forest.
Folger, Joseph P. & Poole, Marshall S. Working Through Conflict.
Folger Shakespeare Library Editors, Washington, D. C. Catalog of Manuscripts of the Folger Shakespeare Library.
--Catalog of Printed Books of the Folger Shakespeare Library.
Folinsbee, Lawrence J., et al, eds. Environmental Stress: Individual Human Adaptations.
Folio, M. Rhonda. Physical Education Programming for Exceptional Learners.
Folio Magazine. Nineteen Eighty Edition Folio: Annual.
Folio Magazine Editors, ed. Handbook of Magazine Publishing.
--Magazine Publishing Management.
Folk, Ernest L., III. The Delaware General Corporation Law: A Commentary & Analysis.
Folk, Jerry. Worldly Christians: A Call to Faith, Prayer & Action.
Folk, Jerry L., jt. auth. see Lutz, Charles P.
Folk St. John, Wylly. The Secrets of the Pirate Inn.
Follain, James & Struyk, Raymond. Homeownership Effects of Alternative Mortgage Instruments.
Follain, James, et al. Place to Place Indexes of the Price of Housing: Some New Estimates & a Comparative Analysis.
Follett, James. Churchill's Gold.
Follett, Ken. Lie down with Lions.
--The Modigliani Scandal. Golbitz, Pat, ed.
--Modigliani Scandal.
--On Wings of Eagles.
--Under the Streets of Nice.
Follett, Ken, jt. auth. see Maurice.
Follett, Muriel. New England Year: A Journal of Vermont Farm Life.
Follin, Marion G., III & Smith, Norman B. Collections: A North Carolina Law Practice System.
Follis, Anne B. I'm Not a Women's Libber, But...
Follmann, Joseph F., Jr. Alcoholics & Business: Problems, Costs, Solutions.
Folon, Jean M. Flowers by Giorgio Morandi.
Folse, Lois J., jt. auth. see Ingram, Marilyn W.
Folsom, Anne & Von Frisch, Otto. The American Bestiary.
Folsom, Merrill. More Great American Mansions: And Their Stories.
Foltin, L. B. Aus Nah und Fern.
Folts, F. Introduction to Industrial Management.
Fonda, Afdera. Never Before Noon.
Fonda, Jane. Jane Fonda's Workout Book.
--Jane Fonda's Year of Fitness & Health 1984.
--Jane Fonda's Year of Fitness, Health & Nutrition, 1985.
Fonda, Jane & McCarthy, Mignon. Women Coming of Age.
Fonda, L., ed. Undulator Magnets for Synchrotron Radiation & Free Electron Lasers: Symposium in the Adriatico Conference Series, Trieste, Italy, 23-26 June 1987.
Fondaneche, Pierre, jt. auth. see Brosset, Raymond.
Fondation Nationale des Sciences Politiques, Paris, France Staff. Bibliographie Courante D'Articles de Periodiques Posterieurs a 1944 Sur les Problems Politiques, Economiques et Sociaux: Dixieme Supplement.
Foner, Philip S. Mark Twain: Social Critic.
Foner, Simon & Schwartz, Brian B., eds. Superconductor Materials Science: Metallurgy, Fabrication, & Applications.
Fong, Elizabeth N. & Goldfine, Alan H., eds. Data Base Directions, Information Resource Management: Making It Work.
Fong, J. T., ed. Inservice Data Reporting & Analysis: PVP-Vol. 35.
Fong, Leo, jt. auth. see Marchini, Ron.
Fong, Pang E., jt. auth. see Lim, Linda.
Fong, Wen, jt. auth. see Fu, Marilyn.
Fonken, G. & Johnson, R. Chemical Oxidations with Microorganisms.
Fonstad, Karen W. The Atlas of the Land.
Fontaine & Bourgoignie. Consumer Legislation in Belgium & Luxemburg.
Fontaine, George R., jt. auth. see DeMaria, Rusel.
Fontana, M. G. & Staehle, R. W., eds. Advances in Corrosion Science & Technology. Incl. Vol. 1; Vol. 2; Vol. 3; Vol. 4; Vol. 5; Vol. 6; Vol. 7. Plenum Pub.
Fontanay, Elisabeth de see De Fontenay, Elisabeth.
Fontanille, Jacques. Le Savoir Partage: Semiotique it Theorie de la Connaissance Dans l'Oeuvre de Marcel Proust.
Fontbrune, Jean-Charles de. Nostradamus: Countdown to Apocalypse.
Fontein Jan. Museum of Fine Arts, Boston.
Fontenot, Peggy Joan. I Almost Burned in Hell.
Fonvielle, William H. From Manager to Innovator: Using Information to Become an Ideal Entrepenuer.
Food & Drug Administration Staff. Macroanalytical Procedures Manual.
Food & Drug Book Company Inc. Staff. The Pill Book of Arthritis.
--The Pill Book of Headaches.
--The Pill Book of High Blood Pressure.
Food & Nutrition Board - Division of Biology & Agriculture Staff. Maternal Nutrition & the Course of Pregnancy.
Food & Wine Magazine Editors. Best of "Food & Wine"
Food Processors Institute Staff. Canned Foods: Principles of Thermal Process Control, Acidification & Container Closure Evaluation.
Food Products & Drink Industries, Second Tripartite Technical Meeting Staff. Appropriate Technology for Employment Creation in the Food Processing & Drink Industries of Developing Countries: Report III of the Food Products & Drink Industries, 2nd Tripartite Technical Meeting, Geneva, 1978.
Foord, Archibald S. His Majesty's Opposition, Seventeen Fourteen to Eighteen Thirty.
Foorman, V. Olympic Stamps.
Foose, Sandra L. Scrap Saver's Stitchery Book: A Farm Journal Book.
Foot, David K. Public Employment in Canada.
Foot, Hugh C., jt. auth. see Chapman, Antony J.
Foot, M. R. Resistance: European Resistance to Nazism 1940-45.
Foote, Caleb, et al. Cases & Materials on Family Law.
Foote, Estelle. The Mender's Manual: Repairing & Preserving Garments & Bedding.
Foote, Geoffrey. The Labour Party's Political Thought: A History.
Foote, Henry S. Casket of Reminiscences.
Foote, Horton & Faulkner, William. Three Plays. Incl. Roots in a Parched Ground; Old Man; Tomorrow. HarBraceJ.
Foote, John T. The Look of Eagles.
--Look of Eagles: Racing Story.
Foote, Mary H. A Victorian Gentlewoman in the Far West: The Reminiscences of Mary Hallock Foote. Paul, Rodman, ed.
Foote, Nancy, et al. Drawings: The Pluralist Decade.

Authors

Foote, Timothy. The Great Ringtail Garbage Caper.
Footman, David. The Alexander Conspiracy: A Life of A. I. Zhelybov.
Foran, Heather M., jt. auth. see Foran, Max.
Foran, Mary, tr. see Aletrino, L.
Foran, Max & Foran, Heather M. Calgary: Canada's Frontier Metropolis.
Forbes, Adrienne & Debease, Gloria. Regents Competency Tests.
Forbes, Brian. The Rewrite Man.
Forbes, Christopher, ed. see Von Solodkoff, Alexander, et al.
Forbes, Clarence A., ed. see Vida, Marco G.
Forbes, Colin. The Leader & the Damned.
--Terminal.
Forbes, David, jt. auth. see Shumway, Nicholas.
Forbes, Dee, jt. auth. see Solie, Gordon.
Forbes, Duncan see Milne, John.
Forbes, Eric G., et al. Greenwich Observatory.
Forbes, Esther. America's Paul Revere.
Forbes, Esther see Levin, David.
Forbes, Gordon. Goodbye to Some.
Forbes, Grace P., ed. see Azbel, Mark Y.
Forbes, Harold M. West Virginia History: Bibliography & Guide to Studies.
Forbes, Harriette M. Gravestones of Early New England: And the Men Who Made Them.
Forbes, J. A., jt. auth. see Clark, Ewen M.
Forbes, Leslie. A Taste of Provence.
Forbes, Leslie, compiled by. & illus. A Taste of Tuscany: Classic Recipes from the Heart of Italy.
Forbes, Margaret S. Coaching Synchronized Swimming Effectively.
Forbes, Mary J. A Practical Guide to Word Processing & Office Management Systems.
Forbes, R. J. Studies in Ancient Technology. Incl. Vols. 1-7; Vols. 8-9. Metallurgy in Antiquity. E J Brill USA.
Forbes, Stanton. Don't Die on Me, Billie Jean.
Forbis, William H. Fall of the Peacock Throne: The Story of Iran.
Forbush, Edward H. Natural History of American Birds of Eastern & Central North America. May, John R., ed.
Force, J. E., ed. see Popkin, Richard H.
Force, Rich, ed. I-C Test Equipment.
Force, Rich, ed. see Grove, Bob.
Force, Rich, ed. see Lee, James, et al.
Force, Rich, ed. see Leventhal, Lawrence A., et al.
Force, Richard C., ed. see Dunn, Si.
Forchheimer, Paul, tr. see Hoffmann, David.
Ford, Alice, ed. see Audubon, John J.
Ford, Alice E. Edward Hicks, Painter of the Peaceable Kingdom.
Ford, Anna. Little Wrinkle & the Baby.
Ford, Arthur C. Words & Wonders: A Collection of Proverbs, Poems & Song Lyrics.
Ford, B. G., retold by. Little Red Riding Hood.
Ford, Charles H. The Super Executive's Guide to Getting Things Done.
Ford, Daniel F. The Button: The Pentagon's Strategic Command & Control System.
--The Button: The Pentagon's Strategic Command & Control System.
--The Cult of the Atom: The Secret Papers of the Atomic Energy Commission.
--Meltdown: The Secret Papers of the Atomic Energy Commission.
Ford, E. B. Ecological Genetics.
Ford, Edward. Bibliography of Australian Medicine Seventeen Ninety to Nineteen Hundred.
Ford, Eileen & Heilman, Joan. The Ford Models' Crash Course in Looking Great.
Ford, Ford Madox. The English Novel, from the Earliest Days to the Death of Joseph Conrad.
--Portraits from Life.
--The Queen Who Flew.
Ford, Frank R., Jr., ed. see Donalson, George W.
Ford, Franklin L. Strasbourg in Transition, 1648-1789.
Ford, G. A., jt. auth. see Ford, P.
Ford, George A. & Lippitt, Gordon L. Planning Your Future: A Workbook for Personal Goal Setting.
Ford, Gerald R. Global Stability.
Ford, Gordon, Jr., tr. see Mayrhofer, Manfred.
Ford, Henry, jt. auth. see Heneage, Simon.
Ford, Henry J. Cleveland Era.
Ford, Herbert. Flee the Captor.
Ford, Hildegarde. Baby's Animal Book.
Ford, Hugh. Published in Paris.
Ford, Ian. Buying & Running Your Own Business.
Ford, Jessie. The Burning Woman.
Ford, Jill. Human Behavior: Towards a Practical Understanding.
Ford, John. The Broken Heart. Morris, Brian, ed.
Ford, John M. The Dragon Waiting: A Masque of History.
--The Final Reflection.
--Web of Angels.
Ford, John S. Rip Ford's Texas.
Ford, Julienne, et al. Special Education & Social Control: Invisible Disasters.
Ford, Katherine & Buskirk, Phyllis. Selected Population, Housing & Economic Characteristics in Kalamazoo County by Tracts: 1960-1970.
Ford, LeRoy. Using Problem Solving in Teaching & Training.
--Using the Case Study in Teaching & Training.
--Using the Panel in Teaching & Training. McCormick, Joe, tr.
Ford, Lewis S. The Lure of God: A Biblical Background for Process Theism.
Ford, Martin. Death of a Marriage.
Ford, Michael J. & Nicol, E. Fiona, eds. MCQ's for MRCP.
Ford Motor Company, ed. Ford Model T Manual: 1922.
Ford, Nelson. Business Graphics for the IBM PC.
Ford, Norman D. America by Car.
--Natural Ways to Relieve Pain.
--Where to Retire on a Small Income.
Ford, P. & Ford, G. A. Breviate of Parliamentary Papers 1900-1916.
--Breviate of Parliamentary Papers 1917-1939.
Ford, Patrick K. & Borst, Karen G., eds. Connections Between Old English & Medieval Celtic Literature: Three Essays by Daniel Frederick Melia, Joseph Falaky Nagy, & Sarah Lynn Higley.
Ford, Paul F. Companion to Narnia, a Complete Illustrated Guide to the Themes, Characters & Events of C. S. Lewis Imaginary World.
Ford, Peter, jt. auth. see Feldman, Anthony.
Ford, Richard. The Ultimate Good Luck.
Ford, Richard & Andersen, Juel. Juel Andersen's Sea Green Primer.
Ford, Thomas I. Pro Techniques of Making Home Video Movies.
Ford, Tommy. Bama under Bear: Alabama's Family Tides.
Forde, Gerhard O. Justification by Faith: A Matter of Death & Life.
Forde, Hugo J., ed. & illus. Jargon Signals - Whistle Talk - Signs of the American Railroad: American Railroadiana.
Forde, Thomas H. Principles & Practice of Oral Dynamics.
Forde-Johnston, J. Prehistoric Britain & Ireland.
Forder, Anthony, et al. Theories of Welfare.
Forder, Anthony, ed. see Hall, Penelope.
Fordham. Silicones.
Fordham, Monroe. Major Themes in Northern Black Religious Thought, 1800-1860.
Fordham, S. High Explosives & Propellants.
Fords, et al. Poganuc People.
Fordtran, J. S., jt. ed. see Field, M.
Fordwor, Kwame D. The African Development Bank: Problems of International Cooperation.
Fordyce, Rachel, ed. Caroline Drama: A Bibliographic History of Criticism.
Fordyce, Richard A., jt. auth. see Tingle, Donald A.
Forefront Corporation Staff. Framework: A Developer's Handbook.
--Framework: A Programmer's Reference. Ashton-Tate, ed.
--Framework: A Programmer's Reference.
--Framework: An Introduction to Programming.
Forehand, Mary A. Love Lives Here.
Foreht, Catherine & Foreht, Peter. Frommer's Dollarwise Guide to Skiing in Europe: The Top Resorts in Austria, France, Italy & Switzerland.
Foreht, Peter, jt. auth. see Foreht, Catherine.
Foreign Affairs Staff & Bundy, William P., eds. America & the World, 1982.
Foreign & Commonwealth Office Editors, London. Catalogue of the Colonial Office Library, London.
--Catalogue of the Foreign Office Library, 1926-1968.
Foreign Policy Association Staff. Great Decisions, 1983.
--Great Decisions, 1985.
--Great Decisions 1986.
--Trade & the Dollar: Coping with Interdependence.
Forell, George W. Augsburg Confession: A Contemporary Commentary.
--Christian Lifestyle: Reflections on Romans 12-15.
--Ethics of Decision: An Introduction to Christian Ethics.
--Faith Active in Love.
--The Luther Legacy: An Introduction to Luther's Life & Thought for Today.
--The Proclamation of the Gospel in a Pluralistic World: Essays on Christianity & Culture.
Forell, George W. & McCue, James F. Confessing One Faith: A Joint Commentary on the Augsburg Confession by Lutheran & Catholic Theologians.
Forell, George W. & Lazareth, William H., eds. Corporation Ethics: The Quest for Moral Authority.
--Crisis in Marriage.
--God's Call to Public Responsibility.
--Human Rights: Rhetoric or Reality.
--Population Perils.
--Work As Praise.
Foreman, Dave, ed. Ecodefense: A Field Guide to Monkeywrenching.
Foreman, Gail H., jt. auth. see Zollers, Frances E.
Foreman, J. K. & Stockwell, P. B., eds. Topics in Automatic Chemical Analysis.
Foreman, John, jt. auth. see Zizmor, Jonathan.
Foreman, Ken. Track & Field.
Foreman, Laure, jt. auth. see Mirkin, Gabe.
Foreman, Lewis, ed. From Parry to Britten: British Music in Letters 1900-1945.
Foreman, Michael. Land of Dreams.
--Panada & the Bushfire.
Foreman, Nancy. Bound for Success.
Foren, R. & Bailey, R. Authority in Social Casework.
Forer, Bruce, jt. ed. see Atwan, Robert.
Foresi, Joseph, Jr. Administrative Leadership in the Community College.
Foresi, Pascal. Celibacy Put to the Gospel Test.
Forest, James H. Thomas Merton: A Pictorial Biography.
Forest, John. Warriors of the Political Arena: The Presidential Election of 1984.
Forest, Ray & Murie, Alan. The Selling of the Welfare State: The Privatisation of Council Housing.
Forestell, J. T., jt. auth. see Macleod, Donald.
Forester, Bruce. Signs & Omens.
Forester, C. S. Hunting the Bismarck.
Foreyt, John P. & Rathjen, Diana P. Cognitive Behavior Therapy: Research & Application.
Foreyt, John P., ed. Behavioral Treatments of Obesity: A Practical Handbook.
Forfar, John O. & Arneil, Gavin C. Textbook of Paediatrics.
Forgan, Harry W. Reading Skillbuilder: Comprehension Skills.
--Reading Skillbuilder: Word Recognition Skills.
Forgey, William W. Wilderness Medicine.
Forgie, George B. Patricide in the House Divided: A Psychological Interpretation of Lincoln & His Age.
Forgione, Albert G. & Bauer, Frederic M. Fearless Flying: The Complete Program for Relaxed Air Travel.
Forgione, Albert G., et al. Fear: Learning to Cope.
Foris, Andreas. Charted Folk Designs for Cross-Stitch Embroidery.
Forkner, Irvine F. BASIC Programming for Business.
Forkner, Irvine H. Pascal Programming Business, Management Science, & Social Science Applications.
Forleo, Romano & Pasini, Willy, eds. Medical Sexology, Third International Congress.
Forliti, John E. Program Planning for Youth Ministry.
--Reverence for Life & Family Program: Parent-Teacher Resource.
Form, William H., jt. auth. see D'Antonio, William V.
Formacek, V. & Kubeczka, K. H. Essential Oils Analysis by Capillary Gas Chromatography & Carbon-13 NMR Spectroscopy.
Forman & Weeks. Whey Cookery (Treats Made with Milk Sugar)
Forman, Barb. Pizzazz for Pennies: Designer Clothes for Children.
Forman, Brenda. America's Place in the World Economy.
Forman, H. Buxton. The Books of William Morris.
Forman, James. The Survivor.
Forman, James D. Call Back Yesterday.
Forman, Max L., ed. World's Greatest Quotations.
Forman, Peter N. Flying Hawaii: A Pilot's Guide to the Islands.
Forman, Rachel Z. Let Us Now Praise Obscure Women: A Comparative Study of Publicly Supported Unmarried Mothers in Government Housing in the United States & Britain.
Formanek, Ruth & Gurian, Anita. Why? Children's Questions: What They Mean & How to Answer Them.
Formations Editorial Collective Staff, ed. Formations of Nations & People.
Fornander, Abraham. An Account of the Polynesian Race: Its Origin & Migration.
Forner, Jose, et al. A Story with No End.
Forner, Sampedro, et al. A Story with No End.
Forness, Steven R., jt. auth. see Hewett, Frank M.
Forney, Matthias N. The Railroad Car Builders Pictorial Dictionary.
Foroulis, Z. A., ed. Environment-Sensitive Fracture of Engineering Materials.
Forpe, Will. The Best of the Old Farmer's Almanac.
Forpe, Will, ed. The Best of the Old Farmer's Almanac.
Forrest, A. P., et al. Principles & Practice of Surgery: A Surgical Supplement to Davidson's Principles & Practice of Medicine.
Forrest, Anthony. The Pandora Secret: A Captain Justice Story.
Forrest, D. W. Francis Galton: The Life & Work of a Victorian Genius.
Forrest, Gary. How to Live with a Problem Drinker & Survive.
Forrest, Herbert E., jt. auth. see Practising Law Institute Staff.
Forrest, James, jt. ed. see Burnley, Ian.
Forrest, Mary & Olson, Margot. Exploring Speech Communication: An Introduction.
Forrest, Richard. The Death at Yew Corner.
Forrest, Roberta. The Lushai Girl.
Forrest, Rose A. Welcome to Paradise.
Forrester, Donald J., et al, eds. Pediatric Dental Medicine.
Forrester, Glenn C. Niagara Falls & the Glacier.
Forrester, Rex. The Chopper Boys: New Zealand's Helicopter Hunters.
--Rex Forrester's True Hunting Adentures.
Forrester, Victoria. The Magnificent Moo.
Forrest-Thompson, Veronica. On the Periphery.
Forsberg. Long Distance Swimming.
Forsell, Mary. The Book of Flower Arranging: For Fresh, Dried, & Artificial Flowers.
Forshaw, Joseph M. Australian Parrots.
Forsky, V., ed. see Romen, A. S.
Forsman, Bettie. From Lupita's Hill.
Forsman, John, ed. Recipe Index, Nineteen Seventy-One: The Eater's Guide to Periodical Literature.
--Recipe Index, Nineteen Seventy: The Eater's Guide to Periodical Literature.
Forss, George, jt. auth. see Duncan, David D.
Forster, A. S., tr. see Bedarida, Francois.
Forster, Arthur B. & Lenoir, Lucille, eds. French Songs, Poems & Proverbs.
Forster, D. F. see Pickersgill, J. W.
Forster, E. M. Albergo Empedocle & Other Early Writings. Thomson, George H., ed.
--Aspects of the Novel.
--Goldsworthy Lowes Dickinson.
--The Life to Come & Other Stories.
--New Collected Short Stories.
Forster, Klaus. Pronouncing Dictionary of English-Place Names.
Forster, Margaret. The Bride of Lowther Fell.
--Marital Rites.
Forster, Werner, et al. Prostaglandins & Thromboxins: Proceedings of the Third International Symposium on Prostaglandins & Thromboxanes in the Cardiovascular System, Hale-Salle, GDR, 5-7 May 1980.
Forsyth, Adrian & Miyata, Ken. Tropical Nature: Life & Death in the Rain Forests of Central & South America.
Forsyth, Robert A., jt. auth. see Blommers, Paul J.
Forsythe, Kenneth & Feineman, Neil. Athletics for Life: Sports Doctor's Program for Safe & Enjoyable Aerobic Conditioning.
Forsythe, Richard. Bishop's Landing.
Fort, Charles. LO! Del Rey, Lester, ed.
Fort, Joel. The Addicted Society.
--The Addicted Society: Pleasure-Seeking & Punishment Revisited.
Forte, Cecile, jt. auth. see Lewis, Stephen.
Forte, Imogene. Comprehension Corral.
--Get Set for Math Success.
--Punctuation Power.
--Rainbow Incentive Collection I.
--Rainbow Incentive Collection II.
--Read about It Series.
--Wordly Wise.
--Writing Away.
Forte, Imogene & MacKenzie, Joy. Dictionary Dynamite.
--Kids' Stuff: Reading & Language Experiences-Primary.
--Skillstuff-Reasoning.
--The Yellow Pages for Students & Teachers.
Forte, Imogene & Pangle, Mary A. Mini-Center Stuff.
Forte, Imogene, et al. Kids' Stuff: Reading & Language Experiences, Intermediate-Jr High.
Fortenberry, Charles N., jt. auth. see Highsaw, Robert B.
Forth, Inc. Staff & Brodie, Leo. Starting FORTH: An Introduction to the FORTH Language & Operating Systems for Beginners & Professionals.
Forth, W. & Rummel, W., eds. Pharmacology of Intestinal Absorption: Gastrointestinal Absorption of Drugs.
Fortiner, Virginia J. Science-Hobby Book of Archaeology.
Fortini, Peter, et al, trs. see Sobol, I. M.
Fortino, Andres, jt. auth. see Bates, William.
Fortman, Edmund J. The Triune God.
Fortuin, Nicholas J. Current Therapy in Cardiovascular Disease 1984-1985.
Fortunato, Connie. Music Is for Children.
Fortune, J. J., et al. Duel for the Samurai Sword.
Fortune, Nigel, jt. ed. see Arnold, Denis.
Forty, George. Chieftain.
--Fifth Army at War.
Forward, Robert L. The Flight of the Dragonfly.
Forward, Susan & Torres, Joan. Men Who Hate Women & the Women Who Love Them.
FOSECO, see Foundry Services, Ltd. Staff.
Foskett, Daphne. Collecting Miniatures.
Fosler, Scott & Berger, Renee A. Public-Private Partnership in American Cities: Seven Case Studies.

Foss, Christopher. Armoured Fighting Vehicles of the World.
Foss, Christopher & Cullen, Tony. Jane's Battlefield Air Defence, 1988-89.
Foss, Christopher & Gander, Terry, eds. Jane's Military Vehicles & Ground Support Equipment, 1986.
Foss, Christopher F. Jane's Main Battle Tanks.
--Jane's Main Battle Tanks.
Foss, Christopher F., ed. Jane's Armour & Artillery 1986-87.
--Jane's Armoured Personnel Carriers.
Foss, F. F. Ragweed the Pixie & Other Tales.
Fossum, John A. Labor Relations: Development, Structure, Process.
Fossum, R. M., et al. Trivial Extensions of Abelian Categories: Homological Algebra of Trivial Extensions of Abelian Categories with Applications to Ring Theory.
Fossum, Robert H. Hawthorne's Inviolable Circle: The Problem of Time.
Foster, jt. auth. see Whitford.
Foster, Alan D. With Friends Like These...
Foster, Augustus J. Jeffersonian America: Notes on the United States of America Collected in the Years 1805-1807 & 1811-1812. Davis, Richard B., ed.
Foster, Bill. The Fernpickers.
Foster, Carol, et al. Growing up in America.
Foster, Carol, et al, eds. Social Welfare: Help or Hindrance.
Foster, Carol D., et al. Gun Control: Restricting Rights or Protecting People?
Foster, Carrie W. I Won't Be Home for Christmas & Other Short Stories.
Foster, Catharine O. The Organic Gardener.
Foster, Caxton C. Computer Architecture.
--Content Addressable Parallel Processors.
Foster, Charles R., ed. Comparative Public Policy & Citizen Participation: Energy, Education, Health & Local Governance in the U. S. A. & Germany.
Foster, David. Innovation & Employment.
Foster, David W., ed. Chilean Literature: A Working Bibliography of Secondary Sources.
Foster, Donald L. The Classification of Nonbook Materials in Academic Libraries: A Commentary & Bibliography.
Foster, Elizabeth R., ed. Proceedings in Parliament Sixteen Ten. Incl. Vol. 1. The House of Lords; Vol. 2. The House of Commons. Yale U Pr.
Foster, Eugene S. Understanding Broadcasting.
Foster, George. Financial Statement Analysis.
Foster, George, jt. auth. see Drucker, Malka.
Foster, Gerald. Harley Davidson: The Cult Lives On.
Foster, Hal & Kardon, Janet. Connections: Bridges-Ladders-Ramps-Staircases-Tunnels.
Foster, Hannah W. The Coquette.
Foster, J. B., jt. ed. see Horler, A. R.
Foster, John. The Case for Idealism: International Library of Philosophy.
Foster, John L., jt. auth. see Henderson, Thomas A.
Foster, John L., et al. National Policy Game: A Simulation of the American Political Process.
Foster, Julia. Julia Foster's Patchwork: Her Own Ideas for You to Make.
Foster, Lawrence, jt. auth. see Foster, Lynn V.
Foster, Lee. Beautiful California Missions. Shangle, Robert D., ed.
Foster, Leslie. Rand McNally Mathematics Encyclopedia.
Foster, Lewis. The True Life.
Foster, Lynn V. & Foster, Lawrence. Fielding's Mexico 1984.
--Fielding's Mexico, 1985.
--Fielding's Mexico, 1986.
--Fielding's Mexico, 1987: Maps, Hotels & Photos.
Foster, Michael. Freedom's Thunder.
Foster, Michael B. Mystery & Philosophy.
--The Political Philosophy of Plato & Hegel.
Foster, Mike, ed. see Rhoda, Franklin.
Foster, Nancy H. & Fairbank, Ben. San Antonio: The Texas Monthly Guidebook. Rodriguez, Barbara, ed.
Foster, Norman G., jt. auth. see Hamming, Mynard C.
Foster, Pearl B. Classic American Cooking.
--Classic American Cooking.
Foster, Philip E. A Study of Lorenzo De'Medici's Villa at Poggio a Caiano.
Foster, Pops. Pops Foster: The Autobiography of a New Orleans Jazzman As Told to Tom Stoddard.
Foster, R. R. Charles Stewart Parnell: The Man & His Family.
Foster, Ria. The Adventures of Wee Willy Wiley.
Foster, Robert D. The Navigator.
Foster, Stephanie. Star Light, Star Bright.
Foster, Stephen. Notes from the Caroline Underground: Alexander Leighton, the Puritan Triumvirate, & the Laudian Reaction to Nonconformity.
Foster, Stephen, ed. see Brown, Marilyn R.
Foster, Stephen, ed. see Charernbhak, Wichit.
Foster, Stephen, ed. see Frank, Suzanne S.
Foster, Stephen C., ed. see Teilhet-Fisk, Jehanne.
Foster, Steven & Little, Meredith. Sun Bear's Book of the Vision Quest: Personal Transformation in the Wilderness.
Foster, Timothy R. Word Processing for Executives & Professionals.
Foster, Tony. The Money Burn.
Foster, Vanda. A Visual History of Costume: The Nineteenth Century.
Foster, William Z. History of the Communist Party of the United States.
Foster, Winston L. Death Whispers.
Foth, H. & Jacobs, H. S. Field Guide to Soils.
Fothergill, Philip G. Historical Aspects of Organic Evolution.
Fothergill, R. & Anderson, J. S. Microelectronics Education Programme Policy & Guidelines.
Fothergill, Stephen & Gudgin, Graham. Unequal Growth: Urban & Regional Employment Change in the U. K.
Fotinos, S. Douglas, jt. auth. see Carver, Tina K.
Foucault, Michel. The Foucault Reader. Rabinow, Paul, ed.
--The History of Sexuality, Vol. 1: An Introduction. Hurley, Robert, tr. from Fr.
--Language, Counter-Memory, Practice: Selected Essays and Interviews. Bouchard, Donald F., ed. & tr. from Fr.
--Politics, Philosophy, Culture: Interviews & Other Writings, 1977-1984. Kritzman, Lawrence D., ed. Sheridan, Alan, tr.
Foucher Of Chartres. A History of the Expedition to Jerusalem, 1095-1127. Fink, Sr. Harold S., ed.
Fought, Sharon G. & Throwe, Anita N. Psychosocial Nursing Care of the Emergency Patient.
Foulard, C., jt. auth. see El-Fattah, Y. M.
Foulds, L. R. Neoplastic Development.
Foulke, Adrienne, tr. see Condominas, Georges.
Foulke, Adrienne, tr. see Sciascia, Leonardo.
Foulke, Arthur T. Mr. Typewriter.
--Picture-Book for Proud Lovers of Danville, Montour County & Riverside, PA.
Foulke, Jan. Blue Book of Dolls & Values.
--Blue Book of Dolls & Values.
--Kestner: King of Dollmakers.
Foulke, Patricia & Foulke, Robert. Daytrips, Getaway Weekends, & Budget Vacations in the Mid-Atlantic States.
Foulke, Robert & Smith, Paul. An Anatomy of Literature.
Foulke, Robert, jt. auth. see Foulke, Patricia.
Foulkes, A. Peter & Lohner, Edgar, eds. Das Deutsche Drama von Kleist bis Hauptmann.
--Deutsche Novellen Von Tieck Bis Hauptmann.
Foulkes, Fred K. & Livernash, E. Robert. Human Resources Management: Text & Cases.
Foulks, James G., jt. ed. see Perry, Thomas L.
Foulsham, W., & Co. Staff. The Bumper Book of Things a Boy Can Make.
Foundation Center Staff. COMSEARCH: Subjects.
--The Foundation Grants Index. Kovacs, Ruth, ed.
--Foundation Grants to Individuals. Renz, Loren, ed.
--National Data Book. Buzan, Barbara, ed.
Foundry Services, Ltd. Staff. Foundryman's Handbook.
Fountain, Charles. Another Man's Poison: The Life & Writings of Columnist George Frazier.
Fountain, Clayton W. The Forces of Love.
Fountain, Rosanna B. Learning from Jesus.
Four by Four's & Off-Road Vehicles & Travelin' Vans Editors. The RV-Truck-Van Conversion Guide.
Fourah Bay College, Library University of Sierra Leone Staff. Catalog of the Sierra Leone Collection.
Fourez, Gerard M. End of the Taboos: An Ethics of Encounter.
Fournier, Jane, ed. see Fournier, Mark E.
Fournier, Mark E. How to Get on the Barter Bandwagon. Fournier, Jane & De Mente, Boye, eds.
Fourtner, Charles R., jt. ed. see Herreid, Clyde F., II.
Foust, Paul. Reborn to Multiply.
Fowler, Charles B. Dance As Education.
Fowler, Charles W. & Smith, Tim D. Dynamics of Large Mammal Populations.
Fowler, Clarence M., jt. ed. see Erber, Thomas.
Fowler, David G. Dream Turf Ravers.
Fowler, Don D., ed. Photographed All the Best Scenery: Jack Hillers's Diary of the Powell Expeditions 1871-1875.
Fowler, Don D., jt. ed. see Condie, Carol J.
Fowler, Doreen & Abadie, Ann J., eds. Fifty Years of Yoknapatawpha: Faulkner & Yoknapatawpha, 1979.
Fowler, Douglas. S. J. Perelman.
Fowler, Elizabeth M. Choosing Your Future: The New York Times Guide to the 101 Best Career Opportunities of Tomorrow.
Fowler, F. Parker, Jr. & Sandberg, E. W. Basic Mathematics for Administration.
Fowler, Flora C. Materials Book for Reading Games for Middle & Upper Grades.
Fowler, Floyd J. Survey Research Methods.
Fowler, Frank. Southern Lights & Shadows.
Fowler, G. N., jt. ed. see Conn, G. K.
Fowler, Gene. Father Goose.
Fowler, H. Ramsey, jt. auth. see Little, Brown Editors.
Fowler, H. W., et al. Metaphor. Commager, Steele, ed. Incl. English Idioms; English Influence on the French Vocabulary; Briton, British, Britisher; The Split Infinitive; Logic & Grammar; Four Words; Subjunctives; Medium Aevum & the Middle Age; Index to Tracts I-XIX. Garland Pub.
Fowler, Harlan D. Three Caravans to Yuma: The Untold Story of Bactrian Camels in Western America.
Fowler, Harold N. Greek Coins.
Fowler, Jeaneane D. Theophoric Personal Names in Ancient Hebrew: A Comparative Study.
Fowler, John M. Energy & the Environment.
Fowler, Kathryn M. Hunger: The World Food Crisis, An NSTA Environmental Materials Guide.
Fowler, Raymond E. UFOs-Interplanetary Visitors: A UFO Investigator Reports on the Facts, Fables & Fantasies of the Flying Saucer Conspiracy.
Fowler, Richard. Bear's Story.
--Inspector Smart Gets the Message!
--Mouse about the House.
Fowler, Roger. Literature as Social Discourse: The Practice of Linguistic Criticism.
Fowler, Virginie. Christmas Crafts & Customs Around the World.
Fowler, William & Coyle, Wallace, eds. The American Revolution: Changing Perspectives.
Fowler, William L. Take Another Look at the Keyboard.
Fowler, William M. The Baron of Beacon Hill: A Biography of John Hancock.
Fowler, William M. & Coyle, Wallace, eds. The American Revolution: Changing Perspectives.
Fowler, William M., Jr. Jack Tars & Commodores: The American Navy, 1783-1815.
Fowler, William S. A Study in Radicalism & Dissent.
Fowler, William W. Woman on the American Frontier.
Fowles, A. J., jt. auth. see Jones, Kathleen.
Fowles, G. W. A., jt. auth. see Cartnell, E.
Fowles, Grant R. Analytical Mechanics.
Fowles, John. Cinderella.
Fowles, John, et al. Britain: A World by Itself; Reflections on the Landscape by Eminent British Writers.
Fowlie, Wallace. Guide to Contemporary French Literature from Valery to Sartre.
Fowlie, Wallace, tr. from Fr. & see Moliere.
Fowlkes, Frank. Majendie's Cat.
Fox. Chronically Ill.
Fox, Adam. Plato & the Christians.
Fox, Aileen. Roman Britain.
Fox, Allan M., jt. ed. see Horman, Richard E.
Fox, B. W., ed. Techniques of Sample Preparation for Liquid Scintillation Counting.
Fox, C. A., jt. auth. see Holmes, R. L.
Fox, C. Fred, jt. ed. see Alberts, Bruce.
Fox, C. Fred, jt. ed. see Gale, Robert P.
Fox, C. Lynn. Communicating to Make Friends: A Program for the Classroom Teacher.
Fox, C. Lynn & Weaver, Francine L. Unlocking Doors to Friendship.
Fox, Charles P. Circus Baggage Stock: A Tribute to the Percheron Horse.
Fox, Cyril S. Water.
Fox, Dan, ed. see Okun, Milton.
Fox, Dan, jt. ed. see Okun, Milton.
Fox, David & Waite, Mitchell. Computer Animation Primer.
--Pascal Primer.
Fox, Donna R. & Blechman, Mark. Clinical Management of Voice Disorders.
Fox, Douglas A. Mystery & Meaning: Personal Logic & the Language of Religion.
--The Vagrant Lotus: An Introduction to Buddhist Philosophy.
Fox, Emmet. Make Your Life Worthwhile.
Fox, Frank, et al. Beginner's Guide to Zen & the Art of Windsurfing.
Fox, Fred K., jt. auth. see Cannon, William A.
Fox, Gardner. The Bold Ones.
--Hurricane.
Fox, Gardner F. The Liberty Sword.
Fox, George. George Fox's Book of Miracles. Cadbury, Henry J., ed.
Fox, H. & Langley, F. A. Postgraduate Obstetrical & Gynaecological Pathology.
Fox, Harland. Top Executive Compensation: 1985 Edition.
Fox, Harold. Pathology of the Placenta.
Fox, Harrison W., Jr., ed. Contemporary Issues in Civil Rights & Liberties.
Fox, Hugh. Happy Deathday.
Fox, Ira L. Ins & Outs of Ups & Downs.
Fox, J. D., jt. ed. see Robson, D.
Fox, J. Ronald. Managing Business-Government Relationships.
Fox, James J., tr. see Mauss, Marcel & Beuchat, Henri.
Fox, John, Jr. Little Shepard of Kingdom Come.
Fox, John P., et al. Epidemiology: Man & Disease.
Fox, K. A., et al, eds. Economic Models, Estimation & Risk Programming: Essays in Honor of Gerhard Tintner.
Fox, L., ed. Advances in Programming Non-Numerical Applications to Computing Machines.
Fox, Larry. The New England Patriots: Triumph & Tragedy.
Fox, Lilla M. Folk Costume of Eastern Europe.
Fox, Mark, jt. auth. see Dechter, Rina.
Fox, Mary V. Lady for the Defense.
--The Skating Heidens.
Fox, Mem. Hattie & the Fox.
Fox, Michael, ed. Schopenhauer: His Philosophical Achievement.
Fox, Michael W. The Healing Touch.
--Love Is a Happy Cat.
--The Soul of the Wolf.
Fox, Mike & Smith, Steve. Rolls-Royce: The Complete Works-The Best 599 Rolls-Royce Stories.
Fox, Paul. Reformation in Poland, Some Social & Economic Aspects.
Fox, Paula. The Western Coast.
Fox, R. M., jt. ed. see Tattersall, M. H.
Fox, Richard G., ed. Political Economy.
Fox, Robert. The Last American Revolution: Confessions of A Dead Politician.
Fox, Robert F. Catechism of the Catholic Church.
Fox, Robert J. Religious Education: Its Effects, Its Challenges Today.
Fox, Ross. Presentation Pieces & Trophies from the Henry Birks Collection of Canadian Silver.
Fox, Ross C. Quebec & Related Silver at the Detroit Institute of Arts.
Fox, Samuel. Management & the Law.
Fox, Sidney. Labor Law.
Fox, Sidney W. & Dose, Klaus. Molecular Evolution & the Origins of Life.
Fox, Sol. Thinking Big: The Education of a Gambler.
Fox, Stephen R. Guardian of Boston: William Monroe Trotter.
Fox, Thomas C., jt. auth. see Lifton, Betty J.
Fox, Vernon, jt. auth. see Wright, Burton.
Fox, William & Stein, Emanuel. Cardiac Rhythm Disturbances: A Step by Step Approach.
Fox, William L., jt. ed. see Walsh, Richard.
Foxall, Gordon. Marketing Behaviour: Issues in Managerial & Buyer Decision Making.
Foxall, Gordon R. Strategic Marketing Management.
Foxcroft, Ezechiel, tr. see Green, Deirdre & Mclean, Adam.
Foxe, John. Foxe's Book of Martyrs.
Foxglove, Lady. We've got the Power: Witches among Us.
Fox-Hutchinson, Juliet. Remembering Vernon.
Foxley, A., et al. Redistributive Effects of Government Programmes: The Chilean Case.
Foxley, Alejandro & Whitehead, Laurence, eds. Economic Stabilization in Latin America: Political Dimensions.
Foy, Felician A. & Avato, Rose M., eds. Catholic Almanac, 1986.
--Catholic Almanac 1987.
Foy, George, jt. auth. see Lawrence, Sidney.
Foyster, John, jt. auth. see Proud, Keith.
Foyt, D. C. The ZX81-TS1000 Home Computer Book.
Fraas, Arthur P. Energy Evaluation of Energy Systems.
Fracchia, Charles A. Living Together Alone: The New American Monasticism.
Frackenpohl, Arthur. Harmonization at the Piano.
Fraenkel, Peter. Food from Windmills.
Fraenkel-Conrat, Heinz & Wagner, Robert R., eds. Comprehensive Virology, Vol. 11: Genetics of Plant Viruses.
--Comprehensive Virology, Vol. 12: Newly Characterized Protist & Invertebrate Viruses.
Fragomen, Austin T. & Bell, Steven C. Immigration Employment Compliance Handbook: How to Comply with Immigration Reporting Requirements When Hiring New Employees.
Fragomen, Austin T., et al. Immigration Procedures Handbook.
Fragomen, Austin T., Jr. & Bell, Steven C. Immigration Primer.
Frakes, G. E. & Adams, W. Royce. From Columbus to Aquarius: An Interpretive History.
Fraknoi, Andrew, et al. Return of Halley's Comet.
Fraleigh, John B., jt. auth. see Beauregard, Raymond A.
Fram, Eugene H., jt. ed. see Vernon, J. Peter.
Frame, Donald M. Francois Rabelais.
--Montaigne: A Biography.
--Montaigne in France, 1812-1852.
Frame, Donald M., tr. Marthe.
Framen, Carl. Rolling Wheels.
Frampton, Muriel. Agoraphobia: Coping with the World Outside.
Francastel, Pierre. Frontieres Du Gothique: Librairie De Medicis 1945.

France, Anatole. Romans et Contes.
--Romans et Contes. Incl. Tome I. Thais; Tome II. Le Lys Rouge; Tome III. Les Dieux Ont Soif; Tome IV. Le Crime de Sylvestre Bonnard; Tome V. La Rotisserie de la Reine Pedauque; Tome VI. Les Contes de Jacques Tournebroche, Histoire Contemporaine; Tome VII. L' Orme du Mail; Tome VIII. Le Mannequin d'Osier; Tome IX. L' Anneau d'Amethyste; Tome X. Monsieur Bergeret a Paris. French & Eur.
France, Ministry of Culture Staff, compiled by. France, Historic Houses, Castles & Gardens, Open to the Public.
Frances, Carol, ed. Successful Responses to Financial Difficulty.
Franceschetti, A., et al. Chorioretinal Heredodegenerations: An Updated Report of La Societe Francaise d'Ophtalmologie.
Franchak, Stephen J. & Kean, Michael H. Using Evaluation Results: Guidelines & Practice for Using Vocational Evaluation Effectively.
Franchak, Stephen J. & Smiley, Larry L. Evaluating Employer Satisfaction: Measurement of Satisfaction with Training & Job Performance of Former Vocational Education Students.
Franchak, Stephen J. & Spirer, Janet E. Evaluation Handbook: Guidelines & Practices for Follow-Up Studies of Former Vocational Students.
Franchak, Stephen J., jt. auth. see Ponce, Eliseo R.
Franchere, Ruth. Hannah Herself.
Franchimont, P., jt. auth. see Van Cauwenberge, H.
Francia, Arthur J., et al. Managerial Accounting.
Francin, Rudy. The Turbulent History of the North Adriatic Archipelago.
Francis. Nutrition for Children.
Francis, intro. by. Child Labour: Extract from the Report of the Director-General to the International Labour Conference, 69th Session, 1983.
Francis, A. J. Introducing Structures.
Francis, Anna B. Pleasant Dreams.
Francis, Anne F. Hieronimus Bosch: The Temptation of Saint Anthony.
--Voyage of Re-Discovery: The Veneration of St. Vincent.
Francis, Dave & Woodcock, Mike. The Unblocked Boss: A Guidebook for Managers.
Francis, Dave, jt. auth. see Woodcock, Mike.
Francis, Dick. Banker.
--Dead Cert. Barzun, J. & Taylor, W. H., eds.
--Proof.
Francis, Fred O. & Sampley, J. Paul, eds. Pauline Parallels.
Francis, G. W. Electrostatic Experiments: Encyclopedic Description of 417 Classical Experiments from the Golden Age of Electrostatics.
Francis, Gloria A. & Lozynsky, Artem, eds. Whitman at Auction: 1899-1972.
Francis, Gloria M. & Munjas, Barbara A. Promoting Psychological Comfort.
Francis, Jack C. Readings in Investments.
Francis, John & Abrecht, Paul, eds. Facing up to Nuclear Power.
Francis, Ken. The New Zealand Kiwi.
Francis, Nelson. English Language: An Introduction.
Francis, Ray, jt. ed. see Pons, Valdo.
Francis, Richard. Swansong.
Francis, Robert. Robert Francis: Collected Poems, 1936-1976.
Francis, Ronald D. Migrant Crime in Australia.
Francis, Samuel T. Power & History: The Political Thought of James Burnham.
Francis, W. & Peters, M. C. Fuels & Fuel Technology.
Francis, W., jt. auth. see Martin, G. W.
Francis, W. W., et al, eds. Bibliotheca Osleriana.
Francis, William H., jt. auth. see Choate, Robert A.
Francis Clare, Sr. Wow God.
Francisco, Albert K. & Smith, Kenneth A. Accounting Theory & Practice.
--Auditing.
--Business Law.
--CPA Exam Questions on Auditing.
--Tax Law.
Francis-Williams, Jesse. The Diagnostic Use of Rorschach with Children.
Franck, Irene M., jt. auth. see Brownstone, David M.
Francke, Linda B. Growing up Divorced: Children of the Eighties.
Francke, Linda B., jt. auth. see Ferraro, Geraldine A.
Franco. Cuentos Escogido H Quiroga. Franco, Jean, ed.
Franco, Jean, ed. see Franco.
Franco, Joseph & Hammer, Richard. Hoffa's Man: The Rise & Fall to James R. Hoffa as Witnessed by His Strongest Arm.
Franco, Lawrence G., et al. The Petroleum Industry in Western Europe: A Guide to Information Sources.
Franco, Marjorie. Genevieve & Alexander.
--So Who Hasn't Got Problems?
Franco, R. R. & Leprevost, A. Minerals of Brazil.
Francoeur, Robert T. Eve's New Rib: Twenty Faces of Sex, Marriage, & Family.
--Taking Sides: Clashing Views on Controversial Issues in Human Sexuality.
Francois, Antoine. Memoirs of a Man of Honour, 1747.
Francois, Bernard & Perrin, Paul. Urinary Infections.
Francois, D. Advances in Fracture Research: Proceedings of the 5th International Conference on Fracture, 1981, Cannes, France.
Francois, D., jt. ed. see Sih, G. C.
Francom, Lane A. Lanes One Walks Thru.
Francq, H. G. Louis the Seventeenth: The Unsolved Mystery.
Franda, Marcus. Bangladesh: The First Decade.
--Bangladesh: The First Decade.
Franda, Marcus F. Radical Politics in West Bengal.
Franey, Pierre. More Sixty-Minute Gourmet.
--The New York Times Sixty-Minute Gourmet.
Franey, Pierre & Flaste, Richard. Pierre Franey's Kitchen.
Franey, Pierre, jt. auth. see Claiborne, Craig.
Frangiamore, Roy & Grady, James. A Thing of Beauty: Art Nouveau, Art Deco, Arts & Crafts Movement, & Aesthetic Movement Objects in Atlanta Collections. Morris, Kelly, ed.
Frangipane, E. De Fraga see Pearson, E. A. & De Fraga Frangipane, E.
Frank, Andre G. The European Challenge: From Atlantic Alliance to Pan-European Entente for Peace & Jobs.
--World Accumulation, Fourteen Ninety-Two to Seventeen Eighty-Nine.
--World Accumulation, 1492-1789.
Frank, Elke, jt. auth. see Irish, Marian D.
Frank, George. Psychiatric Diagnosis: A Review of Research.
Frank, Gerald W. Gerry Frank's "Where to Find It, Buy It, Eat It in New York"
Frank, Harriet, Jr. Single.
--Special Effects.
Frank, Isaiah. Graduation Issue in Trade Policy Towards LDCs.
Frank, Joseph. You.
Frank, Leonhard. Dream Mates.
Frank, Marge & Linton, Nancy. Better, Better Body Book.
Frank, Marjorie. Kids' Stuff Math.
Frank, Mel & Rosenthal, Ed. The Indoor-Outdoor Highest Quality Marijuana Grower's Guide.
Frank, Mel, jt. auth. see Rosenthal, Ed.
Frank, Michael R. The Effective EDP Manager.
Frank, P. El Alcohol y la Familia.
Frank, Perry & Moore, Michele, eds. Public Welfare Directory, 1975.
--Public Welfare Directory, 1976-1977.
Frank, Peter. Nineteen Artists: Emergent Americans-1981 National Exhibition.
Frank, Robert & Model, Lisette. Charles Pratt: Photographs.
Frank, Roberta & Cameron, Angus, eds. A Plan for the Dictionary of Old English.
Frank, Suzanne S. Michel de Klerk, 1884-1923: An Architect of the Amsterdam School. Foster, Stephen, ed.
Frank, Waldo D. The Re-Discovery of America: An Introduction to the Philosophy of American Life.
Frank, Wolfgang. The Sea Wolves.
Franke, Christopher. Title.
Franke, David. The Torture Doctor.
Franke, Lois & Udell, William L. Handwrought Jewelry.
Franke, M. E. & Drzewiecki, T. M., eds. Fluid Transmission Line Dynamics.
Franke, M. E., jt. ed. see Drzewiecki, T. M.
Franke, Monte, jt. auth. see Coughlan, William.
Franke, W., et al. Progress in Botany.
Franke, Wolfgang. A Century of Chinese Revolution, 1851-1949. Rudman, Stanley, tr. from Ger.
--China & the West. Wilson, R. A., tr.
Frankeburg, William K. & Thornton, Susan M., eds. Pediatric Developmental Diagnosis.
Frankel, Charles. Pleasures of Philosophy.
Frankel, Edward. DNA: The Ladder of Life.
Frankel, Eric, jt. auth. see Merkin, Lisa.
Frankel, F. H. & Zamansky, H., eds. Hypnosis at Its Bicentennial.
Frankel, Francine R. India's Green Revolution.
Frankel, Hermann. Early Greek Poetry & Philosophy. Hadas, Moses & Willis, James, trs.
Frankel, Mark S., ed. Value & Ethics in Organization & Human Systems Development: An Annotated Bibliography.
Frankel, Richard B., jt. auth. see Freeman, Arthur J.
Frankel, Sandor & Fink, Robert S. How to Defend Yourself Against the I.R.S.
Frankel, Saul J. Staff Relations in the Civil Service: The Canadian Experience.
Frankel, Sheila, ed. Guidance on Software Package Selection.
Frankel, Tamar. Nineteen Eighty-Five Supplement to Regulation of Money Managers.
Frankena, Frederick. Directories for Small-Scale Hydropower Development.
--The Economist-Business Professional As Expert Witness: A Bibliography.
--The Expert Medical Witness: A Bibliography.
--The Expert Witness: A General, Mostly Legal Bibliography.
--Funds for Decentralized Energy Systems RD&D: An Annotated Bibliography.
--The Mental Health Professional As Expert Witness: A Bibliography.
--The Scientist-Technician As Expert Witness: A Bibliography.
--The Social Science Practitioner As Expert Witness: A Bibliography.
Frankena, William K. Philosophy of Education.
Frankenberg, Lloyd. The Stain of Circumstance: Selected Poems.
Frankenstein, Carl. They Think Again: Restoring Cognitive Abilities Through Teaching.
Franket, Martin M. Directory of Postsecondary Institutions, 1986: Four-Year & Two-Year, Vol. 1.
Frankfort, Hans, tr. see Schafer, Harald.
Frankfurt am Main, jt. ed. see Stadt und Universitatsbucherei.
Frankie, G. W. & Koehler, C. S., eds. Perspectives in Urban Entomology.
Frankis, G. G., jt. auth. see Anderson, R. C.
Frankl, Ludwig A. The Jews in the East. Beaton, P., tr.
Frankl, Victor. The Unconscious God.
Frankl, Victor E. Man's Search for Meaning: An Introduction to Logotherapy.
--Psychotherapy & Existentialism.
Frankl, Viktor E. The Doctor & the Soul: From Psychotherapy to Logotherapy.
Frankle, John T., jt. auth. see Klapper, Jacob.
Franklin. Climate in Miniature.
Franklin, A. White, ed. see International Congress on Child Abuse & Neglect, 2nd, London 1978.
Franklin, Allan. The Principle of Inertia in the Middle Ages.
Franklin, Benjamin. On the Choice of a Mistress.
Franklin Co., Chapter OGS Staff & Martin, W. I. Franklin County, Ohio, History.
Franklin, Colin, ed. see Craig, Gordon.
Franklin, Elizabeth. Shortcuts.
Franklin, Eric. Christ the Lord: A Study in the Purpose & Theology of Luke-Acts.
Franklin, George E. From Cotswolds to High Sierras.
Franklin, H. Bruce. American Prisoners & Ex-Prisoners: Their Writings: An Annotated Bibliography of Published Works, 1798-1981.
Franklin, J. L. Ion-Molecule Reactions.
Franklin, J. L., jt. auth. see Field, F. H.
Franklin, James. New German Cinema.
--Present State of Haiti: Saint Domingo-with Remarks on Its Agriculture, Commerce, Laws, Religion, Finance & Population.
Franklin, Jerome L., ed. Human Resources Development in the Organization: A Guide to Information Sources.
Franklin, Jill. The Gentleman's Country House & Its Plan 1835-1914.
Franklin, Joe. Classics of the Silent Screen.
Franklin, Joel N. Matrix Theory.
Franklin, John H. George Washington Williams: The Massachusetts Years.
--Militant South, Eighteen Hundred to Eighteen Sixty-One.
--Racial Equality in America.
Franklin, John H., ed. see Levy, Eugene.
Franklin, Joseph. African: A Photographic Essay on Black Women of Ghana & Nigeria.
Franklin, Linda C. Library Display Ideas.
Franklin, Marian P., ed. Classroom Centers & Stations in America & Britain.
Franklin, Michael, et al. A Reader's Guide to Fantasy.
Franklin, Miles. On Dearborn Street.
Franklin, Olga, tr. see Vassilyeva, Larissa.
Franklin, Paula. The Unwatched Pot.
Franklin, Peter J. & Woodhead, Caroline. The U. K. Life Assurance Industry: A Study in Applied Economics.
Franklin, R., jt. auth. see Cantor, G.
Franklin, Rena. Soups of Hakafri Restaurant: Original Version.
Franklin, S. Harvey. Trade, Growth & Anxiety: New Zealand Beyond the Welfare State.
Franklin, Steven C., jt. auth. see Fulmer, Robert M.
Franklin, T. J. & Snow, G. A., eds. Biochemistry of Antimicrobial Action.
Franko, Lawrence G. The Threat of Japanese Multinationals: How the West Can Respond.
Franko, Lawrence G. & Seiber, Marilyn J. Developing Country Debt.
Franks, Betty B. & Howard, Mary K. People, Law & the Futures Perspective.
Franks, Hugh. Will to Live.
Franks, L. M. & Wigley, C. B., eds. Neoplastic Transformation in Differentiated Epithelial Cell Systems in Vitro.
Franks, Lynne R. Israel & the Occupied Territories.
Franks, Norman. Aircraft Versus Aircraft: The Illustrated Story of Fighter Pilot Combat since 1914.
Franks, R. & Swartz, H. Simplified Medical Dictionary.
Fransella, F. & Bannister, D. A Manual for Repertory Grid Technique.
Fransella, F., jt. auth. see Beech, H. R.
Fransella, Fay. Need to Change.
--On Being a Woman.
--Personality.
Fransella, Fay, jt. auth. see Bannister, Don.
Fransen, L., jt. auth. see Cardon, A.
Franson, Gwyn, jt. auth. see Bradshaw, Annette.
Franson, Robert W. The Shadow of the Ship.
Frantz, Angelina. The Well Adult.
Frantz, Ray W. English Traveller & the Movement of Ideas, 1660-1732.
Frantzis, Nicholas. The Seven Popular Games of Backgammon.
Franz, Carl. Color Me Macho.
--The People's Guide to Camping in Mexico.
--The People's Guide to Mexico.
--People's Guide to Mexico.
Franz, Carol. If Not for Love.
Franz, Marie-Louise Von see Von Franz, Marie-Louise.
Franz, Marion, et al. Opening the Door to Good Nutrition.
Franz, Marion J. Fast Foods Facts.
Franz, Martin & Good, Phillip I. Writing Business Programs in C Language.
Franzen, H. F. Second-Order Phase Transitions & the Irreducible Representation of Space Groups.
Franzen, Lavern G. Smile God Loves You: 59 Gospel Talks for Children to See & Hear.
--Smile! Jesus Is Lord: Fifty Messages for Children to See & Hear.
Franzero, Carlo M. The Life & Times of Cleopatra.
Franzero, Carolo M. The Life & Times of Nero.
Franzwa, Gregory M., ed. see Start, Clarissa.
Frascino, Edward. My Cousin the King.
Frascona, Joseph L. C. P. A. Law Review: Under the 1978 Uniform Commercial Code: Text, Previous C. P. A. Law Examination Questions, & the Author's Model Answers.
Frascona, Joseph L., et al. Principles of Business Law & the Legal Environment: Brief.
Frasconi, Antonio. House That Jack Built: A Picture Book in Two Languages.
--Kaleidoscope in Woodcuts.
--See & Say.
--See & Say: A Picture Book in Four Languages.
--Snow & the Sun: A South American Folk Rhyme in Two Languages.
Frasconi, Antonio, jt. auth. see Neruda, Pablo.
Fraser. Interpretation of Clinical Chemistry Laboratory Data.
Fraser, Allan. Animal Husbandry Heresies.
Fraser, Andrew F. Reproductive Behaviour in Ungulates.
Fraser, Anthea. Death Speaks Softly.
--Pretty Maids All in a Row.
Fraser, Antonia. Cool Repentance: A Jemima Shore Mystery.
--A Splash of Red.
Fraser, Barry J. Classroom Environment.
Fraser, Colin. Tractor Pioneer: The Life of Harry Ferguson.
Fraser, David. Alanbrooke.
--The Fortunes of War.
Fraser, Donald C., ed. Journal of Guidance, Control, & Dynamics.
Fraser, Donald R. & Rose, Peter S. Financial Institutions & Markets in a Changing World.
Fraser, Donald R., jt. auth. see Rose, Peter S.
Fraser, Donald R. & Rose, Peter S., eds. Financial Institutions & Markets in a Changing World.
Fraser, F. Clark, jt. auth. see Nora, James J.
Fraser, G. S. Metre, Rhyme, & Free Verse.
Fraser, George M. Mr. American.
Fraser, J. M. Psychology: General - Industrial - Social.
Fraser, J. T., et al, eds. Study of Time I: 1st Conference of the International Society for the Study of Time.
Fraser, James, jt. auth. see Scott, Ronald B.
Fraser, James R. & Weber, Renee K., eds. Children's Authors & Illustrators: A Guide to the Manuscript Collections in United States Research Libraries.
Fraser, John. Italy: Society in Crisis-Society in Transformation.
Fraser, John M. Employment Interviewing.
Fraser, Morris. E. C. T. A Clinical Guide.
Fraser, Mowat G. Education & Western Civilization-the Long View: An Attempt to Gain Perspective.
Fraser, Nicholas & Navarro, Marysa. Eva Peron.
Fraser, R. D. & MacRae, T. P. Conformation in Fibrous Protein & Related Synthetic Polypeptides.
Fraser, Ralph S., tr. see Talbert, Charles H. & Keck, Leander E.

Fraser, Ronald. In Search of a Past: The Rearing of an English Gentleman 1933-45.
Fraser, Russel A., ed. Essential Shakespeare: Nine Major Plays & the Sonnets.
Fraser, Russell. The Dark Ages & the Age of Gold.
--The War Against Poetry.
Fraser, Russell A. A Mingled Yarn: The Life of R. P. Blackmur.
--The Three Romes.
Fraser, Thomas G. Captain Fraser's Voyages. Gee, Marjory, ed.
Fraser, W. R. Residential Education.
Frater, Alexander, ed. Great Rivers of the World.
Frates, Jeffrey E. & Molrup, William. Introduction to the Computer: An Integrative Approach.
Fratkin, Jake. WQ-Ten Electro Acupuncture Machine. Felt, Robert L., ed.
Frattolillo, Salmieri. American Grilles.
Frauenfelder, P. & Huber, P. Introduction to Physics, Vol. 1: Mechanics, Hydrodynamics, Thermodynamics.
Fraunce, Abraham see Batman, Stephen.
Fraunfelder, F. T. Drug-Induced Ocular Side Effects & Drug Interactions.
Frayer, W. E., et al, eds. Inventory Design & Analysis.
Frayn, Michael. Alphabetical Order & Donkeys' Years.
--Frayn: Plays One.
Frayn, Michael, tr. see Tolstoy, Leo.
Frazee, Steve. He Rode Alone.
Frazer, A. C., et al. Current Topics in Microbiology & Immunology.
Frazer, James E. Tales of Pudding Hill: True Animal Stories from New Hampshire.
Frazer, Joan, et al. Forty-Thousand Selected Words Organized by Letter, Sound & Syllable.
Frazer, Joan M. & Smith, Cynthia J. Verbs.
Frazer, Joan M., jt. auth. see Blockcolsky, Valeda.
Frazer, John. Artificially Arranged Scenes: The Films of Georges Meiles.
Frazer, Robert W. Forts & Supplies: The Role of the Army in the Economy of the Southwest, 1846-1861.
Frazer, William. Expectations, Forecasting & Control: A Provisional Textbook of Macroeconomics: Vol. II, Prices, Market & Turning Points.
--Expectations, Forecasting & Control: A Provisional Textbook of Macroeconomics, Vol. I: Monetary Matters, Keynesian & Other Models.
Frazetta, Vallejo, et al, illus. Masterpieces of Fantasy Art.
Frazier, Alexander. Values, Curriculum & the Elementary School.
Frazier, Alton E. Good Taste Begins with You. Ide, Arthur F., ed.
Frazier, Bessie. Poems, Short Stories & Plays for Youth.
Frazier, Claude A. Occupational Asthma.
Frazier, Claude A., ed. What Faith Has Meant to Me.
Frazier, Dianne M., jt. auth. see Frazier, James R.
Frazier, Greg. San Francisco Scenes.
Frazier, James R. & Frazier, Dianne M. Exceptional Children: Biological & Psychological Perspectives.
Frazier, James R. & Routh, Donald K., eds. Readings on the Behavior Disorders of Childhood.
Frazier, Kendrick. People of Chaco: A Canyon & Its Culture.
Frazier, Neta L. Stout-Hearted Seven.
Frazier, Thomas R. The Underside of American History.
Frazier, Thomas R., ed. Afro-American History: Primary Sources.
--The Underside of American History, Other Readings. Incl. Vol. 1. To 1877; Vol. 2. Since 1865. HarBraceJ.
Frazier, Thomas R., jt. ed. see Nash, Gary B.
Fream, William C. Notes on Medical Nursing.
Freas, Kelly, ed. see Bradley, Marion Zimmer.
Freas, Polly, ed. see Bradley, Marion Zimmer.
Frech, Francis. Population Primer.
Frechtman, Bernard, tr. see Genet, Jean.
Frechtman, Bernard, tr. see Simenon, Georges.
Frede, Richard. The Nurses.
Fredenslund, et al. Vapor-Liquid Equilibria Using UNIFAC: A Group Contribution Method.
Frederick, J. George. Pennsylvania Dutch Cookbook.
Frederick, John, tr. see Chardenon, Ludo.
Frederick, Norris, jt. auth. see Moore, Thomas.
Frederick, Stella. I Can Be a Machinist. McFadden, S. Michele, ed.
--I Can Be a Marine Biologist. McFadden, S. Michele, ed.
Frederick, Wayne A. & Lyons, Thomas T. The Expansion of the Federal Union Eighteen Hundred One to Eighteen Forty-Eight.
Fredericks, Carlton. Carlton Fredericks' Program for Living Longer.
--Eat Well, Get Well, Stay Well.
--Look Younger, Feel Healthier: A Safe, Professional, Step-by-Step Guide to Total Nutritional Health.
Fredericks, Carlton & Goodman, Herman. Low Blood Sugar & You.
Fredericks, Claude see Corrigan, Robert W.
Fredericks, Karen. Modern Love.
Fredericksen, Burton B. Alma Tadema's Spring.
Frederickson, F. M., ed. Snubber Design Applications & Minimization Methods.
Frederick Van, Der Meer see Van Der Meer, Frederick.
Fredericq, P; see Luria, S. E.
Frederiks, E. Vascular Pattern in Embryos with Clefts of Primary & Secondary Palate.
Frederiksen, A. K. The Finer Points of Riding.
Frederiksen, N., et al. Prediction of Organizational Behavior.
Fredette, Jean, ed. Fiction Writer's Market, 1984-1985.
Fredette, Jean M., ed. Fiction Writer's Market 1986.
Fredette, Raymond H. The Sky on Fire: The First Battle of Britain.
Fredgant, Don. Collecting Art Nouveau, Identification & Values.
Fredrick, Len. Fast Food Gets an "A" in School Lunch.
Free, John Da see Da Free, John.
Free, John Da see John, Da Free.
Free Library of Philadelphia Staff. Catalog of the Hampton L. Carson Collection Illustrative of the the Growth of the Common Law.
Free Stuff Editors. Free Stuff for Kids.
Freeborg, R. P., jt. auth. see Daniel, W. H.
Freeborn, Richard. Turgenev: The Novelist's Novelist, a Study.
Freed, Donald. China Card.
--Spymaster.
Freed, Donald & Landis, Fred S. Death in Washington: The Murder of Orlando Letelier.
Freed, Donald, ed. see Citizens Research & Investigation Committee Staff & Tackwood, Louis.
Freed, Lewis. T. S. Eliot: Aesthetics & History.
Freed, Lynn. Home Ground.
Freed, Rita. Ramesses the Great.
Freedberg, S. J., ed. see Amishai-Maisels, Ziva.
Freedberg, S. J., ed. see Benezra, Neal D.
Freedberg, S. J., ed. see Blumenthal, Arthur.
Freedberg, S. J., ed. see Boyd, Sterling.
Freedberg, S. J., ed. see Burr Carter, Jane.
Freedberg, S. J., ed. see Ceen, Allan.
Freedberg, S. J., ed. see Cheney, Liana.
Freedberg, S. J., ed. see Covi, Dario A.
Freedberg, S. J., ed. see Davis, Bruce.
Freedberg, S. J., ed. see Gibert, Creighton E.
Freedberg, S. J., ed. see Grove, Nancy.
Freedberg, S. J., ed. see Kowal, David M.
Freedberg, S. J., ed. see Lieberman, Ralph E.
Freedberg, S. J., ed. see Martone, Thomas.
Freedberg, S. J., ed. see Quint Platt, Arlene.
Freedberg, S. J., ed. see Schreiber-Jacoby, Beverly.
Freedberg, S. J., ed. see Trilling, James.
Freedberg, S. J., ed. see Wilkins, David G.
Freedberg, S. J., ed. see Yard, Sally.
Freedberg, Sydney J., ed. see Lamoureux, Richard E.
Freedberg, Sydney J., ed. see Lichtenstein, Sara.
Freedberg, Sydney J., ed. see Sale, J. Russell.
Freedman. Yearbook of Psychiatry & Applied Mental Health, 1985.
Freedman, Alan. The Computer Glossary, It's Not Just a Glossary.
--The Computer Glossary: It's Not Just a Glossary.
--The DBASE II for the First-Time User.
--The DBASE II for the First-Time User: A Visual Guide.
Freedman, Alfred M. & Kaplan, Harold I., eds. Child: His Psychological & Cultural Development.
--Diagnosing Mental Illness: Evaluation in Psychiatry & Psychology.
--Human Behavior: Biological, Psychological & Sociological.
--Interpreting Personality: A Survey of Twentieth-Century Views.
--Treating Mental Illness: Aspects of Modern Therapy.
Freedman, Ariva & Pringle, Ian, eds. Reinventing the Rhetorical Tradition.
Freedman, David Noel, ed. see Tyson, Joseph B. & Longstaff, Thomas R. W.
Freedman, G. S. Tomographic Imaging in Nuclear Medicine.
Freedman, Gabriel & Haller, M. A. Verbal Workbook for the S.A.T. College Entrance Examinations.
Freedman, Gordon L., jt. auth. see Boettcher, Robert.
Freedman, Jonathan. Happy People: What Happiness Is, Who Has It & Why.
Freedman, Jonathan N. & Doob, Anthony. Deviancy: The Psychology of Being Different.
Freedman, Lawrence. The Price of Peace: Living with the Nuclear Dilemma.
Freedman, Leonard, ed. Looking at Modern Painting.
Freedman, Matt, jt. auth. see Hoffman, Paul.
Freedman, Morris. Moral Impulse: Modern Drama from Ibsen to the Present.
Freedman, Ralph. Lyrical Novel: Studies in Hermann Hesse, Andre Gide, & Virginia Woolf.
Freedman, Richard D. & Cooper, Cary L. Management Education: Issues in Theory, Research & Practice.
Freedman, Robert, ed. Marx on Economics.
--Marxist Social Thought.
Freedman, Robert O., ed. World Politics & the Arab-Israeli Conflict.
Freedman, Russell. The First Days of Life.
--Getting Born.
Freedman, Stephany J., jt. ed. see Colgate, Craig, Jr.
Free John, Da. Breath & Name: The Initiation & Foundation Practices of Free Spiritual Life.
Freeley, Austin J. Argumentation & Debate: Critical Thinking for Reasoned Decision Making.
Freeling, Nicolas. No Part in Your Death.
Freely, J., jt. auth. see Sumner-Boyd, H.
Freely, John. Istanbul.
Freely, Maureen. The Life of the Party.
Freeman. Baby's Lullabies.
Freeman, A. J. & Darby, J. B., eds. The Actinides: Electronic Structure & Related Properties.
Freeman, A. J., et al, eds. International Conference on Magnetic Alloys & Oxides: Haifa, Israel, August 1977.
Freeman, A. Myrick, 3rd, jt. ed. see Enthoven, Alain C.
Freeman, Arthur. Apollonian Poems.
Freeman, Arthur J. & Frankel, Richard B. Hyperfine Interactions.
Freeman, Arthur M., III, et al, eds. Psychiatry for the Primary Care Physician.
Freeman, Charles. Defence.
Freeman, Cortlandt. Steve Rieschl's Ski Touring for the Fun of It.
Freeman, Cynthia. Come Pour the Wine.
--Cynthia Freeman: A World Full of Strangers, the Days of Winter, Portraits, & Come Pour the Wine.
--The Days of Winter.
--Fairytales.
--No Time for Tears.
--Portraits.
--A World Full of Strangers.
Freeman, David. Choosing the Right School: A Parents' Guide.
--A Hollywood Education: Tales of Movie Dreams & Easy Money.
--The Last Days of Alfred Hitchcock.
Freeman, Denne H. Hook'em Horns: A Story of Texas Football.
Freeman, Douglas S. Lee's Lieutenants.
Freeman, Elinor Illus. by see Patterson, William H.
Freeman, Elizabeth W. You'll Never Come Back.
Freeman, Eugene & Sellars, Wilfrid, eds. Basic Issues in the Philosophy of Time.
Freeman, Eugene, jt. ed. see Reese, William L.
Freeman, Farley. And the Angels Wept.
Freeman, Frank H., et al. Leadership Education: A Source Book.
Freeman, H., jt. auth. see Diringer, David.
Freeman, H. G. Christopher or Notes of a Father to His Son: The Formative Years.
--The Lady in Jade Green.
Freeman, Henry G., compiled by. DIM Definitions: German-English with an English-German Vocabulary.
Freeman, Howard E. & Jones, Wyatt C. Social Problems.
Freeman, Howard E., et al. Handbook of Medical Sociology.
Freeman, Hugh, ed. Mental Health & the Environment.
Freeman, J. W., ed. Solar Power Satellites: Proceedings of the International Symposium, Toulouse, France, June 1980.
Freeman, James A. & Beeler, Myrton F., eds. Laboratory Medicine-Urinalysis & Medical Microscopy.
Freeman, Jo. Women: A Feminist Perspective.
Freeman, Jo, ed. Social Movements of the Sixties & Seventies.
Freeman, Joan. Lettering & Calligraphy.
Freeman, John. Beautiful Ireland.
Freeman, Kathleen. Greek City-States.
--Murder of Herodes & Other Trials from the Athenian Law Courts.
Freeman, Leslie G., jt. ed. see Tax, Sol.
Freeman, Linton C. Patterns of Local Community Leadership.
Freeman, Lucy. The Case on Cloud Nine.
--Freud Rediscovered.
--The Psychiatrist Says Murder.
--Who Is Sylvia?
Freeman, Margaret. Hidden Treasure: Parables for Kids.
Freeman, Margaret H., ed. see Patterson, Rebecca.
Freeman, Marion H. Whispering Wind.
Freeman, Mary E. Wilkins. A Humble Romance & Other Stories.
--A New England Nun.
--The Shoulders of Atlas.
--Wind in the Rose Bush & Other Stories of the Supernatural.
Freeman, Max H., et al. Accounting Ten-Twelve. Incl. Pt. 1. Elements of Financial Records; Pt. 2. Accounting Systems & Procedures; Pt. 3. Special Accounting Procedures; Pt. 4. Business Data Processing Fundamentals. McGraw.
Freeman, Michael. Photo School: A Step by Step Course in Photography.
--The State, the Law & the Family: Critical Perspectives.
Freeman, Michael & Aldcroft, Derek. Atlas of British Railway History.
Freeman, Nancy, tr. see Ferreira, T. Gomes & Proddow, Mary P.
Freeman, Nona. Box 44, Monrovia. Wallace, Mary H., ed.
Freeman, P. The Deaf-Blind Baby: A Programme of Care.
Freeman, R. Austin. The Singing Bone.
Freeman, R. B. British Natural History Books from the Beginning to Nineteen Hundred: A Handlist.
Freeman, R. B., jt. ed. see Barrett, Paul H.
Freeman, R. D., ed. Developmental Neurobiology of Vision.
Freeman, R. G. & Knox, J. M. Treatment of Skin Cancer.
Freeman, Richard B. Charles Darwin: A Companion.
Freeman, Robert. Yesterday-the Beatles 1963-1965.
Freeman, Robert J., jt. auth. see Lynn, Edward S.
Freeman, Roger. Thunderbolt: A Documentary History of the Republic P-47.
Freeman, Roger A. Mighty Eighth.
--Mighty Eighth War Diary.
--Mighty Eighth War Manual.
Freeman, Ronald G. Intercambios: An Activities Manual.
Freeman, Rosemary. English Emblem Books.
Freeman, Russell. Animal Superstars: Biggest, Strongest, Fastest, Smartest.
Freeman, T. Field Guide to Layered Rocks.
Freeman, T. W., et al, eds. Geographers Biobibliographical Studies. Oughton, Marguerita & Pinchemel, Philippe.
--Geographers: Biobibliographical Studies.
Freeman, Tony. Beginning Backpacking.
Freeman, Vicki & Adams, Suzy. Why Won't My Teeter-Totter?
Freeman, Victoria. You Thought I Would Never Leave You.
Freeman, William. Concise Dictionary of English Slang.
--Oliver Goldsmith.
--Physical Education in a Changing Society.
Freemantle, Brian. Charlie M.
--Charlie Muffin U. S. A.
--KGB.
Freemesser, George F. Learning to Live from Within: A Glimpse of Jesus As Healer.
Freer, John. Systems Design with Advanced Microprocessors.
Freese, Arthur S. The Bionic People Are Here.
--The End of Senility.
--The Prime of Your Life: The Book That Makes Old Age Obsolete.
Freese, Artur S., jt. auth. see Lauton, Barry.
Freese, J. H., tr. see Licht, Hans.
Freestone, David & Harrison, Scott. The Institutional Framework of the European Communities.
Freeze, Allan, jt. ed. see Back, William R.
Freeze, R. A. & Back, W., eds. Physical Hydrogeology.
Frege, Gottlob. Philosophical Writings.
--Posthumous Writings. Hermes, Hans, et al, eds. White, Roger & Long, Peter, trs.
Fregel, Louis E., Jr. & Fregel, Louis E. Compaq Users Handbook.
Fregert, S., et al. Patch Testing.
Fregert, Sigfrid. Manual of Contact Dermatitis.
Frei, Beatrice, ed. see Matthews, Peter.
Frei, Daniel. Risks of Unintentional Nuclear War.
Frei, Emil, 3rd, jt. ed. see Holland, James F.
Frei, Hans W. The Identity of Jesus Christ: The Hermeneutical Bases of Dogmatic Theology.
Freiberg, H. Jerome. Those Who Can, Teach: Learning Guide.
Freiberg, J. W., ed. Critical Sociology.
Freiberg, Marcos A. Snakes of South America.
Freiberger, W. & Grenander, U. A Course in Computational Probability & Statistics.
Freidberg, Ardy, jt. auth. see Lunden, Joan.
Freidel, Frank, jt. auth. see Minton, John D.
Freidel, Frank, ed. see Chapman, Richard N.
Freidel, Frank, ed. see Curry, E. R.
Freidel, Frank, ed. see Eldot, Paula.
Freidel, Frank, ed. see Moley, Raymond.
Freidel, Frank, ed. see O'Sullivan, John.
Freidel, Frank, ed. see Patenaude, Lionel V.
Freidel, Frank, ed. see Smith, Glenn H.
Freidel, Frank, ed. see Wickens, James F.
Freidmann, H. Enzymes.
Freidrich, Otto. Going Crazy.

Freidson, Eliot. Professional Dominance: The Social Structure of Medical Care.

--Professional Powers: A Study of the Institutionalization of Formal Knowledge.

Freier, Esther, jt. ed. see Blume, Philip.

Freifelder, D. Recombinant DNA: Readings from Scientific American.

Freiji, I., jt. auth. see Ziadeh, Farhat J.

Freilich, Robert H. & Levi, Peter S. Model Subdivision Regulations: Text & Commentary.

Frel, Jiri. Death of a Hero.

Frel, Jiri, ed. Greek & Roman Portraits in the J. Paul Getty Museum 1.

Frellick, Francis I. Helping Youth in Conflict.

Fremont, Herbert. Teaching Secondary Mathematics Through Applications.

Fremont, John C. The Expeditions of John Charles Fremont Supplement: Proceedings of the Court Martial. Spence, Mary L. & Jackson, Donald, eds.

French, A. The Athenian Half-Century, 478-431 B.C. French, A., tr.

--Sixth-Century Athens: The Sources.

French, Bernada, jt. auth. see Craw, Julia.

French, Charles F. American Guide to U. S. Coins 1986.

--The American Guide to U. S. Coins, 1988 Edition.

--Guide to U. S. Coins, 1987.

French Colonial Historical Society Staff. Proceedings of the French Colonial Historical Society, 5th Meeting. Cooke, James J., ed.

French, Curtis. Winning Words: Devotions for Athletes.

French, Fiona. Future Story.

French Foreign Legion Staff. French Foreign Legion Mines & Booby Traps.

French Government Tourist Office Staff. Hotel Guide: The Country Hotel Tradition.

--The Official Guide to the Small Country Hotels & Inns of France, 1985.

French, Helen P. Wind on the Prairies: How the West Was Really Won.

French, Jack. Up the EDP Pyramid: The Complete Job Hunting Manual for Computer Professionals.

French, James C. IDAM File Organizations. Stone, Harold, ed.

French, Janine. Rhapsody.

French, Judith E. By Love Alone.

--Starfire.

--Tender Fortune.

French, Marilyn. Beyond Power: On Women, Men & Morals.

--The Bleeding Heart.

--The Bleeding Heart.

--The Women's Room.

French, Michael. Soldier Boy.

French, P. M., jt. ed. see McCall, J. L.

French, Peter A. Ethics in Government.

French, Philip, jt. ed. see Sissons, Michael.

French, Ray. The Rugby League Lions Australia & New Zealand Nineteen Eighty-Four. Oxley, David, intro. by.

French, Ruth M. Nurse's Guide to Diagnostic Procedures.

French, Thomas E. & Svensen, C. L. Familiar Problems in Mechanical Drawing.

French, Warren. J. D. Salinger.

--J. D. Salinger.

--John Steinbeck.

French, Warren, intro. by. Twentieth Century American Literature.

French, Wendell. The Personnel Management Process: Cases in Human Resources Administration.

French, Wendell L. The Personnel Management Process.

French, Wendell L. & Hellriegel, Don, eds. Personnel Management & Organization Development: Fields in Transition.

French, Wendell L., et al. The Personnel Management Process: Cases on Human Resources Administration.

French, Wendell L., Jr., et al. Organizational Development: Theory, Practice, Research.

French, William J. & Criley, J. Michael. Practical Cardiology.

French, Ylva. London.

French-Hodges, Peter F., jt. auth. see Althaus, Catherine.

Frenkel, Rene A. & McGarry, J. Denis. Carnitine Biosynthesis, Metabolism & Functions.

Frenyo, V. L., jt. auth. see Pethes, G.

Frenz, Horst, jt. ed. see Stallknecht, Newton P.

Frenzel, Louis E. Digital Counter Handbook.

Frenzel, Louis E., Jr., et al. IBM Personal Computer Handbook.

Frere, R. B. Maxwell's Ghost.

Frere, Walter H. The Anaphora or Great Eucharistic Prayer: An Eirenical Study in Liturgical History.

Frerichs, Wendell W. Take It to the Lord: Prayer Laments for the Afflicted.

Freris, T., jt. auth. see Laithwaite, L.

Frerking, Marvin E. Crystal Oscillator Design & Temperature Compensation.

Fresan, Juan. New York.

Freschet, Bernice. Owl in the Garden.

Freschner, Leonard. Universal Blessings.

Fresenius, W & Luderwald, I., eds. Environmental Research & Protection: Inorganic Analysis.

Freshman, Ron. System Design Guide, Featuring dBASE II.

Fretheim, Terence E. Creation, Fall & Flood.

--The Message of Jonah: A Theological Commentary.

Fretz, Bruce R. & Mills, David H. Licensing & Certification of Psychologists & Counselors: A Guide to Current Policies, Procedures, & Legislation.

Fretz, Bruce R., jt. auth. see Whiteley, John M.

Fretz, Sada. Going Vegetarian: A Guide for Teenagers.

Freud, Ernst L., ed. Letters of Sigmund Freud & Arnold Zweig.

Freud, G. Orthogonale Polynome.

Freud, Sigmund. Complete Introductory Lectures on Psychoanalysis. Strachey, James, ed. & tr.

--Dictionary of Psychoanalysis.

--General Selections from the Works of Sigmund Freud. Rickman, John, ed.

--Introductory Lectures on Psychoanalysis. Strachey, James, tr.

Freudenberg, K. & Neish, A. C. Constitution & Biosynthesis of Lignin.

Freudenberger, C. Dean. Food for Tomorrow.

Freudenthal, Alfred M., et al, eds. Structural Safety & Reliability: Proceedings of the International Conference.

Freudenthal, Juan R. & Katz, Jeffrey. Index to Anthologies of Latin American Literature in English Translation.

Freud-Loewenstein, Andrea. This Place.

Freund, E. Hans. The Balanced Life.

Freund, Edith. Chicago Girls.

Freund, John E. & Walpole, Ronald E. Mathematical Statistics.

Freund, John E. & Williams, Frank J. Elementary Business Statistics: The Modern Approach.

Freund, Paul A., et al. Constitutional Law: Cases & Other Problems. Incl. Vol. 1; Vol. 2. Little.

Freund, William C., jt. auth. see Epstein, Eugene.

Freundlich, Charles I. College Vocabulary Builder.

Freundlich, Irwin, jt. auth. see Friskin, James.

Freundlich, Irwin, ed. see Hinson, Maurice.

Freus'N, Anthony. One Hundred Years of Science Fiction Illustration.

Frevert, Patricia D. Beatrix Potter, Children's Storyteller. Redpath, Ann, ed.

--Mark Twain, an American Voice. Redpath, Ann, ed.

--Pablo Picasso, Twentieth Century Genius. Redpath, Ann, ed.

Frew, David R., jt. auth. see Frew, Mary A.

Frew, Marian L., jt. auth. see Vermeer, Jackie.

Frew, Mary A. & Frew, David R. Comprehensive Medical Assisting: Administrative & Clinical Procedures.

--Medical Office Administrative Procedures.

Frew, Robert, et al. Survival-A Sequential Program for College Writing.

Frew, Robert M., et al. Writer's Workshop: A Self-Paced Program for Composition Mastery.

Frewer, Glyn see Milne, John.

Frey, A. J. & Dryhurst, G. Organic Electrochemistry.

Frey, Albert R. Sobriquets & Nicknames.

Frey, Donald G., jt. auth. see Selby, John B.

Frey, Frank. RDF Sourcebook.

Frey, Hank & Frey, Shaney. One Hundred Thirty Feet Down: Handbook for Hydronauts.

Frey, Jeffrey & Bhasin, Kul, eds. Microwave Integrated Circuits.

Frey, R., et al, eds. see World Congress of Anaesthesiology, 3rd, Sao Paulo, 1964.

Frey, Richard L., ed. According to Hoyle.

Frey, Robert L. Railroads in the Nineteenth Century.

Frey, Shaney, jt. auth. see Frey, Hank.

Frey, Thomas L. & Behrens, Robert H. Lending to Agricultural Enterprises.

Freyhardt, H. C., ed. Growth & Properties.

Freytag, Bruno B. von see Von Freytag, Bruno B. & General Loringhoff.

Freytag, Helen. Living in Taiwan: A Handbook for Housewives.

Frey-Wyssling, A. Comparative Organellography of the Cytoplasm.

Friberg, Ingegerd. Moving Inward: A Study of Robert Bly's Poetry.

Frichman-McKenzie, Deborah. Sexy Legs in Twenty Days: Spot Reducing the Aerobics Way.

Frick, C. H. Comeback Guy.

--Comeback Guy.

--Five Against the Odds.

--Patch.

--Tourney Team.

Frick, G. William, jt. auth. see Arbuckle, J. Gorden.

Frick, G. William, ed. Environmental Glossary.

Frick, Henry C., II, jt. ed. see Nahas, Gabriel G.

Fricke, Robert. Die Elliptischen Funktionen und Ihre Anwendungen.

Fricke, Rolf, tr. see Osterloh, Gunter.

Fricker, Richard L., ed. see Flores, Ernesto F.

Fricrichsen, A., et al. Root of the Vine.

Friday, Nancy. My Mother, My Self: Tenth Anniversary Edition.

Friday, Sandra K. & Hurwitz, Heidi S. The Food Sleuth Handbook.

Fridrichsen, Anton. Problem of Miracle in Primitive Christianity. Harrisville, Roy A. & Hanson, John S., trs. from Fr.

Frieberg, Karen, ed. Educating Exceptional Children 1988-89.

Fried, Albert. The Rise & Fall of the Jewish Gangster in America.

Fried, Alfred H. Les Bases Du Pacifisme.

Fried, Benjamin S., ed. Film Index of Work Measurement & Methods Engineering Subjects.

Fried, Bryan A., jt. auth. see Hibbard, Jack.

Fried, Edrita. The Courage to Change: From Insight to Self-Innovation.

Fried, Emanuel. Big Ben Hood.

--Drop Hammer.

--Elegy for Stanley Gorski.

--Meshugah & Other Stories. Walsh, Joy, ed.

Fried, Ilana. The Chemistry of Electrode Processes.

Fried, Isaac. Numerical Solution of Differential Equations.

Fried, Jonathan L. & Gettleman, Marvin E., eds. Guatemala in Rebellion: Unfinished History.

Fried, Marc B. Tales from the Shawangunk Mountains: A Naturalist's Musings, a Bushwhacker's Guide.

Fried, Martha N. & Fried, Morton H. Transitions: Four Rituals in Eight Cultures.

Fried, Morton H. Fabric of Chinese Society.

Fried, Morton H., jt. auth. see Fried, Martha N.

Fried, Richard M. Men Against McCarthy.

Friedan, Betty. The Feminine Mystique.

--The Feminine Mystique.

--It Changed My Life: Writings on the Women's Movement.

--The Second Stage.

Friedberg, Ardy. Reach for It.

Friedberg, Ardy, jt. auth. see Blye, Irwin.

Friedberg, Felix. Thoughts about Life.

Friede, Goldie, et al. The Beatles A-Z: John Lennon, Paul McCartney, George Harrison & Ringo Starr.

Friede, R. L. Developmental Neuropathology.

Friede, R. L., ed. see Symposium on Pathology of Axons & Axonal Flow, Vienna, 1970.

Frieden, Bernard J. The Environmental Protection Hustle.

Frieden, Edward H. Chemical Endocrinology.

Frieden, Julian & Rubin, Ira L. ECG Case Studies.

Frieder, David. Algebra Simplified & Self-Taught.

Frieder, Larry A. Commercial Banking & Interstate Expansion: Issues, Prospects, & Strategies. Farmer, Richard, ed.

Friederici, George. Ein Beitrag Z. Kenntnis D. Trutzwaffen D. Indonesier, Suedseevoelker U. Indianer.

Friedewald, Vincent E. Textbook of Echocardiography.

Friedland, B., jt. auth. see Schwarz, Ralph.

Friedland, Lois. Dollarwise Guide to Skiing U. S. A. West.

Friedland, Martin L. The Case of Valentine Shortis: A True Story of Crime & Politics in Canada.

Friedland, Ronald, jt. auth. see Malatesta, Anne.

Friedland, Susan R. Caviar.

Friedland, William H. Vuta Kamba: The Development of Trade Unions in Tanganyika.

Friedlander, Albert. Out of the Whirlwind.

Friedlander, C. P. Insects & Spiders.

Friedlander, Ernst. Psychology of Scientific Thinking.

Friedlander, Henry & Milton, Sybil, eds. The Simon Wiesenthal Center Annual.

Friedlander, Saul. Pius XII & the Third Reich.

--Reflections of Nazism.

Friedman, Albert L. Prospecting to Riches in Real Estate.

Friedman, Arthur. The World of Sports Statistics. Cohen, Joel C., ed.

Friedman, Avner. Stochastic Differential Equations & Applications.

Friedman, Avner & Pinsky, Mark, eds. Stochastic Analysis.

Friedman, Benjamin M., ed. The Changing Roles of Debt & Equity in Financing U. S. Capital Formation.

Friedman, Bruce J. Stern.

Friedman, E. H. & Moshy, R. Medicine: The Bare Bones.

Friedman, Ellen G., ed. Joan Didion: Essays & Conversations.

Friedman, Emanual A., et al, eds. Uterine Physiology: Proceedings of the Brook Lodge Workshop.

Friedman, Emanuel A., jt. auth. see Beth Israel Hospital Staff.

Friedman, G. M., jt. ed. see Mueller, G.

Friedman, Gary D. Primer of Epidemiology.

Friedman, H. Harold. Diagnostic Electrocardiography & Vectorcardiography.

Friedman, Herbert. Sun & Earth.

Friedman, Herman, jt. ed. see Ceglowski, W. S.

Friedman, Herman, et al, eds. Immunomodulation by Bacteria & Their Products.

Friedman, Ina, tr. see Halibi, Rafik.

Friedman, Ina, tr. see Schiff, Ze'ev & Ya'ari, Ehud.

Friedman, Ina R. Black Cop: A Biography of Tilmon O'Bryant.

Friedman, Irving M., jt. auth. see Viscardi, Henry, Jr.

Friedman, Irving S. Inflation: A World-Wide Disaster.

Friedman, Jack P., jt. auth. see Lindeman, J. Bruce.

Friedman, Jessie J. A New Air Transport Policy for the North Atlantic.

Friedman, Joel W. & Strickler, George M., Jr. Employment Discrimination Law: Cases & Materials, Teacher's Manual.

--Employment Discrimination Law: Cases & Materials, 1985 Supplement.

Friedman, Joel Wm., et al. Employment Discrimination Law: Cases & Materials.

Friedman, John S., ed. First Harvest: An Institute for Policy Studies Reader, 1963-1983.

--First Harvest: An Institute for Policy Studies Reader, 1963-1983.

Friedman, Joy T. The Important Thing About.

--Sounds All Around.

Friedman, Kinky. Greenwich Killing Time: A Thrilling Murder Mystery.

Friedman, L., et al. Fundamentals of Clinical Trials.

Friedman, Lawrence J. Psychoanalysis.

--The Traveling Psychoanalyst.

Friedman, M. D., jt. auth. see Byrd, P. F.

Friedman, Martin, et al. The Frozen Image: Scandinavian Photography.

Friedman, Maurice. The Human Way.

Friedman, Maurice, ed. The Worlds of Existentialism.

Friedman, Mendel. Chemistry & Biochemistry of the Sulfhydryl Group in Amino Acids, Peptides & Proteins.

Friedman, Mickey. Hurricane Season.

--Venetian Mask.

Friedman, Milton. An Adult Guide to Beginning Piano & Basic Musicianship.

--The Invisible Hand in Economics & Politics.

--The Suicidal Impulse of the Business Community.

Friedman, Milton & Friedman, Rose. Free to Choose: A Personal Statement.

--Tyranny of the Status Quo.

Friedman, Milton R. Friedman on Leases.

--Friedman on Leases.

--Friedman on Leases: 1987 Supplement.

Friedman, Moshe F. Recent Developments in Inventory Theory.

Friedman, Murray, et al, eds. New Perspectives on School Integration.

Friedman, Nathaniel A. Calculus & Mathematical Models.

Friedman, Norman. History of Antisubmarine Warfare.

Friedman, P. Readings in Social Problems & Deviance.

Friedman, Paul. The Life-Stories Interview: Creating Portraits on Tape.

--The Rights of Mentally Retarded Persons.

Friedman, Philip, jt. ed. see Blinder, Alan S.

Friedman, Robert M., jt. ed. see Merigan, Thomas C.

Friedman, Rose, jt. auth. see Friedman, Milton.

Friedman, Roslyn & Nussbaum, Annette. Coping with Your Husband's Retirement.

Friedman, S. H. I. B. I. Guide Bearings.

--I. D. B. I. Guide Drive Belts.

--I. D. L. I. Guide Drive Lines.

--I. S. I. Guide Seals.

Friedman, S. Marvin, ed. Biochemistry of Thermophily.

Friedman, Sanford. Rip Van Winkle.

Friedman, Sara A. & Jacobs, David. Police! A Precinct at Work.

Friedman, Sonya. A Hero Is More Than Just a Sandwich.

Friedman, Stanford & Hoekelman, Robert A. Behavioral Pediatrics: Psychological Aspects of Child Health Care.

Friedman, Thomas, jt. auth. see Solman, Paul.

Friedman, Warner, jt. auth. see Gelman, Rita G.

Friedman, William F. Elements of Cryptanalysis.

Friedman, Wolfgang see Jessup, Philip C.

Friedmann, Lawrence W. & Edagawa, Naoyushi. Treatment of Disordered Function from Pain to Sexual Complaints: An Introduction to the Edagawa Method.

Friedmann, Theodore, ed. Gene Therapy: Fact & Fiction.

Friedrich, Carl J. Inevitable Peace.

Friedrich, Gustav W., jt. auth. see Brooks, William D.

Friedrich, M., jt. ed. see Riedler, W.

Friedrich, Otto. Before the Deluge.

Friedrich, Otto, jt. auth. see Friedrich, Priscilla.

Friedrich, Paul. Proto-Indo-European Syntax: The Order of Meaningful Elements.

Friedrich, Pia. Pier Paolo Pasolini.

Friedrich, Priscilla & Friedrich, Otto. The Easter Bunny That Overslept.
Friedrichs, K. O. Spectral Theory of Operators in Hilbert Space.
Friel, Brian. The Communication Cord.
Friend, Charles, ed. Actions & Remedies.
Friend, G. E., et al. Understanding Data Communications.
Friend, Hilderic. Flower Lore.
Friend, J. A., ed. Australian Conference on Electrochemistry, 1st.
Friend, Nellie E. The Tapestry of Eternity.
Friendlich, Dick. Backstop Ace.
--Baron of the Bull Pen.
--Pinch Hitter.
--Relief Pitcher.
Frier, John P. & Frier, Mary E. Industrial Lighting Systems.
Frier, Mary E., jt. auth. see Frier, John P.
Frierson, William C. English Novel in Transition, Eighteen Eighty Five to Nineteen Forty.
Fries, Elias M. Epicrisis Systematis Mycologici, Seu Synopsis Hymenomycetum.
--Systema Mycologicum, Sistens Fungorum Ordines, Genera et Species.
Fries, James F., jt. auth. see Calin, Andrei.
Fries, James F., jt. auth. see Lorig, Kate.
Fries, Judith E. American Indian in Higher Education, 1975-76 to 1984-85.
Friese, Ralf, tr. see Kiefer, H. & Maushart, R.
Friese, U. Erich, tr. see Enehjelm, Curt A.
Friesen International, Inc. Staff. The Ready Foods Systems for Health Care Facilities.
Friesen, John W., et al. The Teacher's Voice: A Study of Teacher Participation in Educational Decision-Making in Three Alberta Communities.
Frieser, Hellmut. Photographic Information Recording.
Friesner, Arlyne. Maternity Nursing. Raff, Beverly, ed.
Friesner, Arlyne, jt. auth. see Yura, Helen.
Frigone, Albert. Growing Pains. McFadden, S. Michele, ed.
--School Survival Junior-Senior High: You're It-It's Up to You. McFadden, S. Michele, ed.
Friis, Babbis. Kristy's Courage. McKinnon, Lise S., tr.
--Wanted! A Horse! McKinnon, Lise S., tr. from Norwegian.
Friis, Erik J., ed. see Johnson, Eyvind.
Friis-Hansen, Dana & Randolph, Jeanne. Visionary Apparatus: Michael Snow & Juan Geuer.
Frings, Virginia S. Fashion: From Concept to Consumer.
Frisbee, John L., ed. Makers of the United Studies.
Frisch, Karl. Animal Architecture. Gombrich, Lisbeth, tr.
--Dancing Bees: An Account of the Life & Senses of the Honey Bee.
Frisch, Karl Von. Man & the Living World. Lowenstein, Elsa B., tr.
Frisch, Karl Von see Von Frisch, Karl.
Frisch, Kurt C., et al. Polyelectrolytes.
Frisch, Max. Bluebeard. Skelton, Geoffrey, tr.
--Man in the Holocene. Skelton, Geoffrey, tr.
--Montauk. Skelton, Geoffrey, tr.
--Sketchbook 1946-1949. Skelton, Geoffrey, tr.
--Sketchbook 1966 to 1971. Skelton, Geoffrey, tr.
Frisch, Robert A. The Magic of ESOPs & LBOs: The Definitive Guide to Employee Stock Ownership Plans & Leveraged Buyouts.
Frisch, Ulla. Pictures to Play With.
Frish, S. Problems of Wave Optics.
Frishkoff, Patricia A., jt. auth. see Gibson, Charles H.
Frishman, Austin M. & Schwartz, Arthur P. The Cockroach Combat Manual.
Frishman, William H. Clinical Pharmacology of the B-Adrenoceptor Blocking Agents.
Frisinger, Nellie. Jeff & Jenny & the Kidnapping.
--Jeff & Jenny at Camp Pinecrest.
--Jeff & Jenny on the Chinchilla Ranch.
--Jeff & Jenny Winter in Alaska.
Friskin, James & Freundlich, Irwin. Music for the Piano: A Handbook of Concert & Teaching Material from 1580 to 1952.
Frist, Betty. My Neighbors, the Billy Grahams.
Frith, G. Terry. Secrets Parents Should Know about Public Schools.
Frith, James & Andrews, Ronald. Antique Pistols Collection, Fourteen Hundred to Eighteen Sixty.
Frith, James R., ed. Measuring Spoken Language Proficiency.
Frith, Owen, jt. auth. see Venning, Muriel.
Frith, Penelope. The Stick It, Stitch It & Stuff It Toybook.
Frith, Terry. Secrets Parents Should Know about Public Schools.
Frith, William P. John Leech: His Life & Work.
Fritschen, L. J. & Gay, L. W. Environmental Instrumentation.
Fritts, William. House of Another Kind.
Fritz, Dorothy B. Child & the Christian Faith.
--Christian Teaching of Kindergarten Children.
--Growing Old Is a Family Affair.
--Ways of Teaching.
Fritz, Eugene. Energies of Universe.
Fritz, H., et al, eds. see Bayer Symposium, 5th - Proteinase Conference, 2nd, Cologne, Germany, 1973.
Fritz, Hans, et al, eds. Kinins III.
Fritz, Jean. Brady.
Fritz, M. Future Energy Consumption of the Third World-with Special Reference to Nuclear Power: An Individual & Comprehensive Evaluation of 156 Countries.
Fritz, Maxine. With an Oriental Flavor.
Fritz, Paul & Morton, Richard. Woman in the Eighteenth Century & Other Essays.
Fritz, Paul & Williams, David. The Triumph of Culture: Eighteenth Century Perspectives.
Fritz, Roger. Creating Success: A Master Plan.
Fritzhand, James. Dream Babies.
--The New Body.
--Son of the Great American Novel.
--Starring.
Fritzsche, K., jt. auth. see Grauert, H.
Frizzi, Ernest. Ein Beitray Zur Ethrologie Von Bouganville und Buka.
Frobish, Nestle J., jt. auth. see Waldie, Jerome.
Froehlich, Allan F. Managing the Data Center.
--The Software Buyer's Guidebook: Strategies for Selecting Business Software.
Froehlich, Margaret W. Reasons to Stay.
Froehlich, Walter. Spacelab: An International Short-Stay Orbiting Laboratory.
Froehling, Lorene. Quick Meals Cookbook.
Froer, Hans. I Will Tell You about God. Bachmann, E. Theodore, tr. from Ger.
Froeschels, Emil. Philosophy in Wit.
--Twentieth Century Speech & Voice Correction.
Froh, Alfred & King, Margaret. Games for Young People.
Frohlich, A., ed. Algebraic Number Field: L Functions & Galois Properties.
Frohlich, A., jt. ed. see Cassels, J. W.
Frohne, Victor & Frohne, Mrs. Victor. God Calls Us Together.
Frohock, Wilbur M. Novel of Violence in America.
--Strangers to This Ground: Cultural Diversity in Contemporary American Writing.
Froissard, Jean & Froissard, Lilly P. The Horseman's International Book of Reference.
Froissard, Lilly P., jt. auth. see Froissard, Jean.
Frolich, Paul. Rosa Luxemburg: Her Life & Work. Hoornweg, Johanna, tr. from Ger.
Frolkin, V. Pulse Circuits.
Frolov, A. Petrozavodsk & Kizhi: A Guide.
Frome, Michael. America's Favorite National Parks.
Fromentin, Eugene. Dominique. Hoog, ed.
Fromherz, Hans & King, Alexander. English-German Chemical Terminology: An Introduction to Chemistry in English & German.
--French-English Chemical Terminology: An Introduction to Chemistry in French & English.
Fromhold, A. T. Quantum Mechanics for Applied Physics & Engineering.
Froming, William J., jt. auth. see Levy, C. Michael.
Fromm, Alan & Soames, Nicolas. Judo: The Gentle Way.
Fromm, Erich. The Anatomy of Human Destructiveness.
--Dogma of Christ, & Other Essays on Religion, Psychology, & Culture.
--The Forgotten Language.
--The Forgotten Language.
--Man from Himself: An Inquiry into the Psychology of Ethics.
--The Sane Society.
Fromm, Gary, ed. Studies in Public Regulation.
Frommer, Arthur. Europe on Twenty-Five Dollars a Day, 1985-86.
--Frommer's Europe on Five Dollars a Day.
--Frommer's Europe on Twenty-Five Dollars a Day.
--Frommer's Europe on Twenty-Five Dollars a Day.
--The New World of Travel.
Frommer, E. A. Voyage Through Childhood to the Adult World.
Frommer, Harvey. Baseball's Greatest Records, Streaks & Feats.
--The Great American Soccer Book.
--The Martial Arts: Judo & Karate.
--Sports Lingo: A Dictionary of the Language of Sports.
--Sports Roots: How Nicknames, Namesakes, Trophies, Competitions & Expressions Came to Be in the World of Sports.
Frommer, Harvey & Weinmann, Ronald. A Sailing Primer.
Frommer, Harvey, jt. auth. see Lieberman, Nancy.
Frommer, Herbert H. Radiology for Dental Auxiliaries.
Frontier Press Company Staff. Lincoln Library of Essential Information.
--Lincoln Library of Sports Champions.
Fronza, G., ed. Mathematical Models for Planning & Controlling Air Quality: Proceedings.
Frosch, P. J., jt. auth. see Wendt, H.
Frost, Carolyn O. Cataloging Nonbook Materials: Problems in Theory & Practice. Dowell, Arlene T., ed.
Frost, G. Howard. The Reason Why.
Frost, Gerhard E. Color of the Night: Reflections on the Book of Job.
--Homing in the Presence: Meditations for Daily Living.
Frost, Gerhard E., ed. see Bickel, Margot & Steigert, Hermann.
Frost, J. M. World Radio & TV Handbook, 1984.
--World Radio & TV Handbook, 1985.
--World Radio & TV Handbook, 1986.
--World Radio TV Handbook, 1987.
Frost, Joan V. Portrait in Black.
Frost, Joan Van E. A Masque of Chameleons.
Frost, Joe L. & Hawkes, Glenn R. Disadvantaged Child: Issues & Innovations.
Frost, John. A Drop Too Many.
Frost, Lawrence A., ed. With Custer in Seventy-Four: James Calhoun's Diary of the Black Hills Expedition.
Frost, R. A. Database Management Systems.
Frost, Reuben B. & Marshall, Stanley J. Administration of PE & Athletics.
Frost, Richard. The Circus Villains: Poems.
Frost, Robert. In the Clearing.
--Road Not Taken: An Introduction to Robert Frost.
--Selected Letters of Robert Frost. Thompson, L., ed.
--You Come Too.
Frost, S. E. Masterworks of Philosophy.
Frost, Stanley B. Patriarchs & Prophets.
--Standing & Understanding.
Frost, T. W. The Price Guide to Old Sheffield Plate.
Froud, Brian & Jones, Terry. The Goblins of Labyrinth.
Froude, James A. Short Studies on Great Subjects.
--Thomas Carlyle's Life in London at the End of the 19th Century.
Fruchier, A., ed. Physical Organic Chemistry-Three.
Fruchter, Yaakov, jt. auth. see Gewirtz, Eliezer.
Fruehling, Rosemary T. & Bouchard, Sharon. Business Correspondence-Thirty. Tinervia, Joseph, ed.
Fruehling, Rosemary T., jt. auth. see Poe, Roy W.
Frumkin, Mitch. Son of Muscle Car Mania.
Frumkin, Paul, jt. auth. see Guermont, Claude.
Frushell, Richard C., ed. see Centlivre, Susanna.
Fruttero, Carl & Lucentini, Franco. The Sunday Woman.
Fruttero, Carlo & Lucentini, Franco. The Sunday Woman. Weaver, William, tr. from Ital.
Fruzzetti, Lina M. The Gift of a Virgin: Women, Marriage & Ritual in a Bengali Society.
Fry, Anna M. Memories of Old Cahaba.
Fry, Barbara, et al, eds. Eastern Churches Review.
Fry, Daniel W. Verse & Worse.
Fry, E. A., jt. auth. see Phillimore, William P.
Fry, Earl H. Financial Invasion of the U. S. A. A Threat to American Society?
--The Politics of International Investment.
Fry, Edmund. Pantographia: Containing Accurate Copies of All the Known Alphabets in the World, Together with an English Explanation of the Peculiar Force or Power of Each Letter.
Fry, Edward. Elementary Reading Instruction.
--Reading Instruction for Classroom & Clinic.
Fry, G. K. The Administrative "Revolution" in Whitehall: A Study in the Politics of Administrative Change in British Central Government since the 1950's.
Fry, Gary & Berra, Kathy. YMCArdiac Therapy.
Fry, Geoffrey. The Changing Civil Service.
Fry, Henry P. Modern Ku Klux Klan.
Fry, J., et al. A Textbook of Medical Practice.
Fry, James. Employment & Income Distribution in the African Economy.
Fry, John, et al. Prescribing: What, When & Why?
Fry, John A. Industrial Democracy & Labour Market Policy in Sweden.
Fry, L. & Seah, P. Immunological Aspects of Skin Disease.
Fry, Philip. Pluralities-Nineteen Eighty-Pluralite. Bradley, Jessica, ed.
Fry, R. J., et al, eds. Normal & Malignant Cell Growth.
Fry, Ron, ed. Advertising Career Directory: 1987.
--Book Publishing Career Directory: 1987.
--Magazines Career Directory: 1987.
--Marketing & Sales Career Directory, 1987.
--Newspapers Career Directory: 1987.
Fry, Ronald W. Your First Resume.
Fry, Ronald W., ed. Public Relations Career Directory: 1987.
Fry, Ruth T. & Hall, Joyce. Symbolic Profile.
Fry, William C. The Progression of Consciousness.
Frye, Fredric. Husbandry, Medicine & Surgery in Captive Reptiles.
Frye, Northrop. The Great Code: The Bible & Literature.
--Northrop Frye on Culture & Literature: A Collection of Review Essays. Denham, Robert D., intro. by.
--Northrop Frye on Culture & Literature: A Collection of Review Essays. Denham, Robert D., ed.
Frye, Roland M. Shakespeare's Life & Times: A Pictorial Record.
Fryer, Bob, et al, eds. Law, State & Society.
Fryer, M. J. An Introduction to Linear Programming & Matrix Game Theory.
Fryer, P. Staying Power.
Fryer, T. B. & Miller, H. A., eds. Biotelemetry III.
Fryer, William T. & Orentlicher, Herman. Cases & Materials on Legal Method & Legal System.
Fryklund, Verne C. & Kepler, Frank R. General Drafting.
Fryklund, Verne C. & LaBerge, Armand J. General Shop Woodworking.
Fryman, Sarah. The Measure of a Woman.
Fu, K. S., jt. ed. see Chang, S. K.
Fu, King-Sun, jt. ed. see Zadeh.
Fu, Marilyn & Fong, Wen. The Wilderness Colors of Tao-Chi.
Fuchs, Daniel. The Williamsburg Trilogy.
Fuchs, Fred. Introduction to HUD-Subsidized Housing Programs: A Handbook for the Legal Services Advocate.
Fuchs, Jacob, tr. Horace's Satires & Epistles.
Fuchs, Jerome H. Making the Most of Management Consulting Services.
Fuchs, Lawrence H. Hawaii Pono: A Social History.
Fuchs, M., jt. auth. see Bass, F. G.
Fuchs, Roland J. Population Distribution Policies in Asia & the Pacific: Current Status & Future Prospects.
Fucik, S., et al. Spectral Analysis of Nonlinear Operators.
Fudenberg, H. H. & Melnick, V. L., eds. Biomedical Scientists & Public Policy.
Fudge, Colin, jt. ed. see Barrett, Susan.
Fuelling, Daniel & Rothmaler, Audrey. Congregational Outreach & Care: A Manual for Mini-Parish Leadership.
Fuente, Julio De La see Malinowski, Bronislaw.
Fuentes, Carlos. Terra Nostra. Peden, Margaret S., tr.
Fuentes, Carmen. Learning the ABC's with Animals.
Fuerstenau, M. C. & Miller, J. D. Chemistry of Flotation.
Fuerstenau, M. C., ed. Flotation.
Fuerstenau, Maurice C. & Palmer, R. B., eds. Gold, Silver, Uranium & Coal - Geology, Mining, Extraction, & Environment.
Fueter, R. Analytische Geometrie der Ebene und Des Raumes.
Fugard, Athol. Notebooks, Nineteen Sixty to Nineteen Seventy-Seven.
Fugate, James K. Programming Tools for the IBM PC: Screen Design, Code Generator & High Memory Access.
Fugate, Wilbur L. Foreign Commerce & the Antitrust Laws: 1985 Supplement.
--Foreign Commerce & the Antitrust Laws: 1986 Supplement.
Fuhlrott, Rolf & Dewe, Michael, eds. Library Interior Layout & Design.
Fuhrer, Eberhard. Europe by Rail.
Fuhrhop, J. H., et al. Large Molecules.
Fuhrmann, Barbara S. & Grasha, Anthony F. A Practical Handbook for College Teachers.
Fuhrmann, P. A. Linear Operators & Systems: Operator Theory, Mathematical Systems Theory, Control Process.
Fuhs, G. W. Nuclear Structures of Protocaryotic Organisms.
Fujii, Satoru, ed. Outstanding American Illustrators Today.
Fujii, Satoru, tr. see Buronson & Hara, Tetsuo.
Fujii, Satoru, tr. see Hara, Buronson & Hara, Tetsuo.
Fujii, Satoru, tr. see Takahashi, Rumiko.
Fujikawa, Gyo. Shags Finds a Kitten.
--That's Not Fair.
--A Tiny Word Book.
Fujikawa, Gyo, illus. Poems for Children.
Fujimura, Kobon. The Tokyo Puzzles. Gardner, Martin, ed.
Fujimura, Thomas H. The Restoration Comedy of Wit.
Fujino, Yukio, ed. Modern Japanese Literature in Translation: A Bibliography.
Fujioka, Michio. Angkor Wat.
--Kyoto Country Retreats: The Katsura & Shugakuin Palaces.
Fujita, Tsuneo, et al. S. E. M. Atlas of Cells & Tissues.
Fukasaku, Mitsusada. Philippines.
Fukuda, Tetsuo & Mitsuda, Hisatoshi, eds. World Issues in the Problems of Schizophrenic Psychoses.
Fukui, Saburo, jt. ed. see Chibata, Ichiro.
Fukushima, Sho & Russell, Wrio. Men's Gymnastics.
Fulbright, Norma, et al. Young Children & Their Environments... A Readings Book Approach.

Authors

Fulbrook, Julian. Administrative Justice & the Unemployed.
Fulcher, A., et al. Painting & Decorating: An Information Manual.
--Painting & Decorating: An Information Manual.
Fulcher, Alf, et al. Basic Building Craft Science.
Fuld, James J. The Book of World-Famous Music Classical, Popular & Folk.
Fulgham, Barbara. Fifty Simple Ready-To-Run VIC-20 Programs.
Fulginiti, Vincent A., jt. auth. see Stiehm, E. Richard.
Fulks, Danny G. Informal Learning in Elementary Schools.
Fullbrook, Gladys. Apple Island.
Fuller, B. Frank, jt. auth. see Fuller, Benjamin J.
Fuller, Barry, et al. Single-Camera Video Production Handbook: Techniques, Equipment, & Resources for Producing Quality Video Programs.
Fuller, Benjamin J. & Fuller, B. Frank. Physician or Magician: The Myths & Realities of Patient Care.
Fuller, Chet. I Hear Them Calling My Name: A Journey Through the New South.
Fuller, David O., ed. Counterfeit or Genuine?
Fuller, Dorothy M. Strength for the Soul: Wisdom from Past & Present.
Fuller, E. G. & Hayward, E., eds. Photonuclear Reactions.
Fuller, Edmund, ed. see Dickens, Charles.
Fuller, Edward C. Chemistry & Man's Environment.
Fuller, Elizabeth G., jt. auth. see Swanson, Susan C.
Fuller, Eugene T. Priceless Possesion of a Few.
Fuller, Gordon. Plane Trigonometry with Tables.
Fuller, Ilse, tr. see Bornkamm, Gunther.
Fuller, Iola. Loon Feather.
Fuller, Jack. Convergence.
--Mass.
Fuller, John. The Sonnet.
Fuller, John & Renold, Edward. The Chef's Compendium of Professional Recipes.
Fuller, John L., jt. ed. see Scott, John P.
Fuller, Joy. The Glorious Presence.
Fuller, K. R., jt. auth. see Anderson, W.
Fuller, Margaret. Trails of the Sawtooth & White Cloud Mountains.
Fuller, Marietta C., jt. auth. see Crawford, Marguerite C.
Fuller, Millard. No More Shacks: The Daring Vision of Habitat for Humanity.
Fuller, R., jt. ed. see Russell, A. D.
Fuller, R. Buckminster. Operating Manual for Spaceship Earth.
--Utopia or Oblivion: The Prospects for Mankind.
Fuller, R. Buckminster, et al. R. Buckminster Fuller on Education. Wagschal, Peter H. & Kahn, Robert D., eds.
Fuller, Reginald H. Advent-Christmas. Achtemeier, Elizabeth, et al, eds.
--The Formation of the Resurrection Narratives.
--Holy Week. Achtemeier, Elizabeth, ed.
--The Use of the Bible in Preaching.
Fuller, Reginald H., jt. auth. see McFadden, William C.
Fuller, Reginald H., ed. & tr. see Schottroff, Luise, et al.
Fuller, Reginald H., tr. see Bornkamm, Gunther.
Fuller, Reginald H., et al. Hebrews, James, 1 & 2 Peter, Jude, Revelation. Krodel, Gerhard, ed.
Fuller, Richard R. Constipation Control: An Exercise Program to Achieve Regularity.
--Stop Insomnia: How to Sleep Well Through Bed Exercises.
Fuller, Robert. Inflation: The Rising Cost of Living on a Small Planet.
Fuller, Robert & Stevens, Scott. Termpaper.
Fuller, Samuel. Crown of India.
--The Dark Page.
Fuller, Steven & Schmidt, Jeremy. Snow Country, Autumn, Winter & Spring in Yellowstone.
Fuller, Theodore, jt. auth. see Lightfoot, Paul.
Fuller, W. R. FORTRAN Programming: A Supplement for Calculus Course (Universitext)
Fuller, Wayne E. The Old Country School: The Story of Rural Education in the Middle West.
Fullerton, George S. System of Metaphysics.
Fullerton, Georgiana. Grantley Manor: A Tale, 1847. Wolff, Robert L., ed.
--Mrs. Gerald's Niece: A Novel, 1869. Wolff, Robert L., ed.
Fullman, James B. Construction Safety, Security, & Loss Prevention.
Fulmer, jt. auth. see Koontz.
Fulmer, Robert M. Practical Human Relations.
Fulmer, Robert M. & Franklin, Steven C. Supervision: Principles of Professional Management.
Fulmer, Robert M. & Herbert, Theodore T. Exploring the New Management.
Fulop-Miller, Rene. Lenin & Ghandi.
Fulton, Carol A. Dictation of the Law.
Fulton, George P., jt. auth. see Shepro, David.
Fulton, John F. The Great Medical Bibliographers: A Study in Humanism.
Fulton, O. & Gordon, A. Higher Education & Manpower Planning: A Comparative Study of Planned & Market Economies.
Fulton, Robin, et al, trs. see Transtromer, Tomas.
Fulton, William & MacPherson, Robert. Categorical Framework for the Study of Singular Spaces.
Fulton, William F., ed. see McKenney, Carlton N.
Fulwiler, David, jt. auth. see Evans, Derek.
Fulwiler, Kyle D. The Berry Cookbook.
Funabashi, Yoichi. Managing the Dollar: From the Plaza to the Louvre.
Funazaki, Yasuko. Baby Owl.
Funck, R. Recent Developments in Regional Science.
Funck, R. & Parr, J. B., eds. The Analysis of Regional Structure: Essays in Honour of August Losch.
Funcken, Fred, jt. auth. see Funcken, Liliane.
Funcken, Liliane & Funcken, Fred. Arms & Uniforms: The Age of Chivalry.
Fundudis, Trian, et al, eds. Speech Retarded & Deaf Children: Their Psychological Development.
Fung, Edmund S. & Mackerras, Colin. From Fear to Friendship: Australia's Policies Towards the People's Republic of China 1966-1982.
Funk, Jerry. Sportset: A Math Practice Set.
Funk, Rainer. Erich Fromm: The Courage to Be Human.
Funk, Robert W. Jesus As Precursor. Beardslee, William A., ed.
--New Gospel Parallels.
--New Gospel Parallels.
--Parables & Presence.
--The Poetics of Biblical Narrative.
Funke, Lewis & Booth, John, eds. Actors Talk about Acting.
Funke, U. H., ed. Mathematical Models in Marketing: A Collection of Abstracts.
Funkhouser, Charles W., et al. Classroom Applications of the Curriculum: A Systems Approach.
Funston, John. Malay Politics in Malaysia: A Study of Umno & Pas.
Funston, Richard. A Vital National Seminar: The Role of the Supreme Court in American Political Life.
Funt, Tobias R. Diary of a Spy Pilot.
Fuori & Aufiero, Lawrence J. Computers & Information Processing.
Fuori, William M. COBOL: Elements of Programming Style.
Fuori, William M., et al. FORTRAN 77: Elements of Programming Style.
Fu Pei Mei. Chinese Cookbook.
--Chinese Cookbook.
--Chinese Cookbook.
Fuqua, Paul & Wilson, Jerry. Security Investigator's Handbook.
Furan Illustrators Staff & Reece, Collen L. The Outsider. Schroeder, Howard, ed.
Furay, Conal & Salevouris, Michael J. History: A Workbook of Skill Development.
Furbank, P. N. E. M. Forster: A Life.
Furbee-Losee, Louanna. The Correct Language, Tojolabal: A Grammar with Ethnographic Notes.
Furen, Wang, et al. Highlights of Tibetan History. Jian, Xu, tr.
Furer-Haimendorf, Christoph Von see Von Furer-Haimendorf, Christoph.
Furgurson, Ernest B. Hard Right: The Rise of Jesse Helms.
Furlan, M. Israel Defence Forces Insignia.
Furlong, Barry, jt. auth. see Palmer, Arnold.
Furlong, Charles W. Let'er Buck: A Story of the Passing of the Old West.
Furlong, Monica. Merton: A Biography.
--Zen Effects: The Life of Alan Watts.
Furlong, Patrick J. Indiana: An Illustrated History.
Furlong, William B., jt. auth. see Diamond, Seymour.
Furlow, Herb, ed. Pocket Book of Pro Football, 1980.
Furman, A. L., ed. More Horse Stories.
Furman, Abraham L., ed. Teen-Age Space Adventures.
Furman, S., jt. ed. see Schaldach, M.
Furmanov, D. Chapayev.
Furnas, jt. auth. see Buncke.
Furneaux, Barbara, jt. ed. see Roberts, Brian.
Furnell, Dennis. Health from the Hedgerow: Encyclopedia of Medicinal Plants.
Furness, R. S. Expressionism.
Furnish, Victor P. & Thulin, Richard L. Pentecost 3. Achtemeier, Elizabeth, et al, eds.
Furnish, Victor P., jt. auth. see Snow, John H.
Furniss, Norman, ed. Futures for the Welfare State.
Furniss, Norman F. The Mormon Conflict, 1850-1859.
Furniss, Tim. Manned Spaceflight Log.
--Manned Spacelight Log.
--Space Flight: The Records.
--Space Shuttle Log.
Furniture Development Council. Design Manual for Cabinet Furniture.
Furse, Chris. Antarctic Year: Brabant Island Expedition.
Furse, Margaret L., et al. The Problem of Religious Knowledge.
Furst, Lillian R. & Skrine, Peter N. Naturalism.
Furst, M. Lawrence, jt. auth. see Morse, Donald R.
Furst, Viktor. The Architecture of Sir Christopher Wren.
Furstenberg, H. Stationary Processes & Prediction Theory.
Furth, George, jt. auth. see Sondheim, Stephen.
Furutan, A. Mothers, Fathers, & Children: Practical Advice to Parents.
Fury, Kathleen, jt. auth. see CBS, Inc. Staff.
Fusaro, Ramon M., jt. auth. see Lynch, Henry T.
Fusfeld, Daniel R. Economics: Principles of Political Economy.
Fusfeld, Herbert I. & Haklisch, Carmela S., eds. University-Industry Research Interactions.
Fusino, S. A Neo-Keynesian Theory of Inflation & Economic Growth.
Fuss, Peter, ed. see Hegel, G. W.
Fussell, Betty H. Mabel.
Fussell, G. E. Farms, Farmers & Society.
Fussell, Paul. Class: A Guide Through the American Status System.
Fussler, Herman H. Research Libraries & Technology.
Fussner, F. Smith. The Historical Revolution: English Historical Writing & Thought 1580-1640.
Futcher, Jane. Crush.
--Marin-the Place, the People: Profile of a California County.
Futcher, Jane & Conover, Robert. Marin-the Place, the People: Profile of a California County.
Futrell, Charles. ABC's of Selling.
Futrell, Charles M. Contemporary Cases in Sales Management.
--Sales Management.
Futuko, T. R., et al. Residue Reviews. Gunther, F. A., ed.
Future Studies, Secretariat, Stockholm, Sweden. Sweden in World Society: Thoughts about the Future.
Fuwa, K., ed. see International Conference on Atomic Spectroscopy Staff.
Fuwa, K., et al, eds. Atomic Spectroscopy in Japan.
Fux, Johann J. Orfeo ed Euridice. Brown, Howard M., ed.
Fuxe, K., et al. Steroid Hormone Regulation of the Brain: Proceedings of an International Symposium, 27-28 October 1980, Wenner-Gren Center, Stockholm, Sweden.
Fuxe, K., et al, eds. Dynamics of Degeneration & Growth in Neurons.
Fuxe, Kjell, et al, eds. Central Adrenaline Neurons: Basic Aspects & Their Role in Cardiovascular Disease: Proceedings of an International Symposium 27-28 August 1979, Wenner-Gren Center, Stockholm.
--Excitotoxins.
Fyfe, Henry H. Sir Arthur Pinero's Plays & Players.
Fyffe, Don, jt. auth. see Adams, Sexton.
Fynn. Mister God, This Is Anna.
Fynn, compiled by. Anna's Book.
Fyodorov, A., jt. auth. see Fedosov, V.
Fyre, H. R., jt. auth. see Minor, Edward O.
Fyson, Marna. Stinkerbelle the Nark: An Otter's Story.
Fyson, Nance L. The Development Puzzle.
Fyson, P. F. The Flora of the South Indian Hill Stations Ootacamund Coonoor, Kotagiri.

G

G. K. Hall Library Catalogs Staff. Index to Black Periodicals: 1985.
--Index to Black Periodicals: 1986.
--Index to Black Periodicals: 1987.
G. K. Staff, ed. see Emerson, Ellen T.
Gaal, O., et al. Electrophoresis in the Separation of Biological Macromolecules.
Gaan, Margaret. Last Moments of a World.
--Last Moments of a World.
Gaarder, Kenneth R. Eye Movements, Vision & Behavior: A Hierarchical Visual Information Processing Model.
Gabain, Marjorie, tr. see Piaget, Jean.
Gabarro, John J. Taking Charge: The/Dynamics of Taking Charge.
Gabbard, Fred E. Make the Eagle Mount Up.
Gabbay, Rony. Communism & Agrarian Reform in Iraq.
Gabbott, Mabel J. Have a Very Merry Christmas! Skits for Elementary Schools & Families.
Gabe, D. R. Principles of Metal Surface Treatment & Protection.
Gabe, M. Histological Techniques. Blackith, R. E. & Kovoor, A., trs. from Fr.
Gabel, John. Beach Glass.
Gabel, Katherine, et al. The Legal Issues of Female Inmates.
Gabella, G. Structure of the Autonomic Nervous System.
Gabert. Racquetball.
Gabler, MaryJean & Augustine, Lloyd. Carryover: A Maintenance Program for Language Impaired Adolescents.
Gabler, Robert E. & Sager, Robert J. Essentials of Physical Geography.
Gabo, Naum. Gabo: Constructions, Structure, Paintings, Drawings & Engravings.
Gabriel, Astrik L. Skara House at the Mediaeval University of Paris.
Gabriel, Clive, jt. auth. see Shuter-Dyson, Rosamund.
Gabriel, Cynthia M., jt. auth. see Gabriel, Roger.
Gabriel, D. M., jt. auth. see Milwidsky, B. M.
Gabriel, J. W., tr. see Spies, Werner.
Gabriel, Jonathan. The Angel Speaks Again.
--Twenty Eighty-Four - the Philosophy of Oneness.
--Voice of the Angel.
Gabriel, Joyce & Baldwin, Bettye. Having It All: A Practical Guide to Overcoming the Career Woman's Blues.
Gabriel, Leah, jt. ed. see Lyons, Deborah.
Gabriel, Pierre & Zisman, M. Calculus of Fractions & Homotopy Theory.
Gabriel, Richard A. The Ethnic Factor in the Urban Polity.
Gabriel, Roger & Gabriel, Cynthia M. Medical Lists for Examinations.
Gabriel, Yiannis. Freud & Society.
Gabrilovich, E. Fifth Quarter.
Gabriol, Solomon I. Fountain of Life. Wedeck, Harry E., tr.
Gackenbach, Dick. Arabella & Mr. Crack.
--The Leatherman.
--More from Hound & Bear.
--Pepper & All the Legs.
--The Pig Who Saw Everything.
Gackenbach, Dick, retold by. & illus. The Perfect Mouse.
--The Princess & the Pea.
Gad, Shayne & Weil, Carrol S. Statistics & Experimental Design for Toxicologists.
Gadd, David. The Loving Friends: A Portrait of Bloomsbury.
Gaddis, Ben. How to Repair Home Laundry Appliances.
Gaddis, John L., jt. ed. see Diebel, Terry L.
Gaddis, Thomas E. Birdman of Alcatraz.
Gaddis, William. The Recognitions.
Gaddy, C. D., et al. Behavioral Science & Human Factors in Power Plant Applications.
Gadgil, D. R. Writings & Speeches of Professor D. R. Gadgil on Planning & Development: 1967-71. Kamat, A. R., ed.
Gadney, Reg. Cry Hungary!
--Kennedy.
Gadol, E. T., ed. Rationality & Sciences: A Memorial Volume for Moritz Schlick.
Gadourek, Ivan. The Political Control of Czechoslovakia.
Gadzuk, Marilyn W., tr. see Lionel, Frederic.
Gaebelein, Arno C. The Conflict of the Ages: The Mystery of Lawlessness, Its Origin, Historic Development & Coming Defeat.
Gaeddert, Louann. Noisy Nancy Norris.
Gaehler, Heinz V., jt. auth. see Kraus, Emil.
Gaerny, Arnold. Removable Closure of the Interdental Space.
Gaertner, W. & Wenig, A., eds. The Economics of the Shadow Economy.
Gae'tane. Cache of Pearls.
Gaffin, Richard B., Jr., ed. see Vos, Geerhardus.
Gaffney, Judith H., jt. auth. see Toye, Randall.
Gaffney, P. J. Fibrinolysis: Current Fundamental & Clinical Concepts. Balkuv-Ulutin, S., ed.
Gag, Wanda. Snippy & Snappy.
--Three Gay Tales from Grimm.
Gagala, Kenneth. Economics of Minorities: A Guide to Information Sources.
Gage, Nathaniel L. & Berliner, David C. Educational Psychology.
--Educational Psychology.
Gage, Nicholas. Hellas: A Portrait of Greece.
Gage, Richard, tr. see Toynbee, Arnold J.
Gage, Wilson. The Ghost of Five Owl Farm.
Gagetta, Vince. Pittsburgh: Fulfilling Its Destiny.
Gagiati, Annie. Peace Where Is It?
Gagliardi, Robert M. Satellite Communications-An Introduction.
Gagliardo, John G. Reich & Nation: The Holy Roman Empire As Idea & Reality, 1763-1806.
Gagnacci-Schwicker, A. & Schwicker. International Dictionary of Metallurgy, Mineralogy, Geology & the Mining & Oil Industries.
Gagnier, Edmund W. Adventure in Analysis.
Gagnon, Dennis, illus. Exploring the Santa Barbara Back Country.
Gahan, P. B., ed. Autoradiography for Biologists.
Gahart, Betty L. Intravenous Medications: A Handbook for Nurses & Other Allied Health Personnel.
Gahris, Cindi. Good Apple & Career Education.
Gaidar, A. The Deathless Trumpeter & Other Stories about Young Heroes.

Authors

--School.
Gailey, Harry A. Sir Donald Cameron: Colonial Governor.
Gailey, Kenneth D., jt. auth. see Whitten, Kenneth W.
Gaillard, Dawson & Mosier, John. Women & Men Together: An Anthology of Short Fiction.
Gaillard, Frye. Race, Rock & Religion: Profiles from a Southern Journalist.
Gaine, Penelope, jt. auth. see Hollest, Angela.
Gaines & Coleman. Continuing Education for Real Estate Brokers & Salespersons.
Gaines, Brian R., jt. auth. see Boose, John.
Gaines, Charles & Butler, George. Pumping Iron.
--Staying Hard.
Gaines, Charles, jt. auth. see Butler, George.
Gaines, Ernest J. The Autobiography of Miss Jane Pittman.
Gaines, George & Coleman, David. Florida Real Estate Principles, Practices & Law.
Gaines, George, Jr. & Coleman, David S. Continuing Education for Real Estate Brokers & Salespersons: 1987 Edition.
--Florida Real Estate Principles, Practices & Law.
--Florida Real Estate Principles, Practices & Law.
--Salesman Review Outline.
--Salesman Review Outline & Exam Guide.
Gaines, James R. Wit's End: Days & Nights of the Algonquin Round Table.
--Wit's End: Days & Nights of the Algonquin Round Table.
Gaines, John, jt. auth. see Epstein, Jerome.
Gaines, Larry K. & Ricks, Truett A. Managing the Police Organization: Selected Readings.
Gaines, Marion T. Mobile: West Florida to Alabama.
Gaines, Pierce W. Political Works of Concealed Authorship: Relating to the United States 1789-1810.
Gaines, Price, ed. Disability Income & Health Insurance.
--Life Financial Reports.
--Life Rates & Data, 1987.
--Who Writes What - 1988 Edition.
--Who Writes What, 1987.
Gaines, Rayvond. Dreamers Are Thinkers.
Gaines, Steven, jt. auth. see Brown, Peter.
Gainham, Sarah. Habsburg Twilight.
--A Place in the Country.
Gainsborough, J. A. Personal Computing & C.
Gainsborough, John A. Personal Computing & C.
Gainsbrugh, Jonathan. Take Him to the Streets.
Gair, Reavley, ed. see Marston, John.
Gairaud, Yves. Le Guidargus de L'Antiquite.
Gaither, Gerald H. Blacks & the Populist Revolt: Ballots & Bigotry in the "New South"
Gaitskell, Charles D. & Hurwitz, Al. Children & Their Art: Methods for the Elementary School.
Gajda, Walter J., Jr. & Biles, William E. Engineering: Modeling & Computation.
Gajdusek, Robert E. Hemingway's Paris.
--Hemingway's Paris.
Gajendra, Verna K., jt. auth. see Stenhouse, Lawrence.
Gal, Hans. Franz Schubert & the Essence of Melody.
--The Musician's World: Great Composers in their Letters.
Gal, T., jt. ed. see Fandel, G.
Galagotis, Nicholas. Psychiatry in Psychoperception.
Galambos, J. Representations of Real Numbers by Infinite Series.
Galambos, John T. Cirrhosis.
Galantay, Ervin Y., ed. The Metropolis in Transition.
Galante, Jorge O., jt. ed. see Lewis, Jack.
Galanti, Marie. En Mouvement.
Galanti, Marie E. Lectures et Fantaisies.
Galanti, Marie E., jt. auth. see Curcio, Louis L.
Galantiere, Lewis, tr. see Saint-Exupery, Antoine de.
Galasiewicz, Z. M. Helium Four.
--Superconductivity & Quantum Fluids.
Galasko. Neurological Problems in Orthopaedics.
Galasso, F. S. Structure & Properties of Inorganic Solids.
Galaty, Fillmore W., et al. Modern Real Estate Practice.
Galaway, Burt, jt. auth. see Compton, Beulah R.
Galaway, Burt, jt. ed. see Hudson, Joe.
Galbraith, Ian A., jt. auth. see Connell, Stephen.
Galbraith, John Kenneth. The Affluent Society.
--The Age of Uncertainty.
--Ambassador's Journal: A Personal Account of the Kennedy Years.
--American Capitalism: The Concept of Countervailing Power.
--Economic Development.
--Economics & the Art of Controversy.
--Economics & the Public Purpose.
--Economics, Peace & Laughter.
--The Great Crash, Nineteen Twenty-Nine.
--The Great Crash of Nineteen Twenty-Nine.
--Money: Whence It Came, Where It Went.
--The New Industrial State.
--The Scotch.
--The Triumph.
--A View from the Stands: Of People, Politics, Military Power & the Arts.
Galbraith, John Kenneth & Salinger, Nicole. Almost Everyone's Guide to Economics.
Galbraith, Kathryn O. Come Spring.
--Spots Are Special.
Galdieri-Wilcox, Sandra & Sutton, Marilyn, eds. Understanding Death & Dying: An Interdisciplinary Approach.
Galdone, P., jt. auth. see Armour, Richard.
Galdone, Paul. Over in the Meadow.
--Three Wishes.
Galdone, Paul, jt. auth. see Titus, Eve.
Galdone, Paul, retold by. & illus. Hans in Luck.
Galdos, Benito Perez see Rodgers, Eamon J.
Gale, Anthony, ed. Physiological Correlates of Human Behaviour. Edwards, John A.
Gale, Barry & Gale, Linda. Discover Your High-Tech Talents.
Gale, Brent, jt. auth. see Baylin, Frank.
Gale, David. Theory of Linear Economic Models.
Gale, Dennis E. Neighborhood Revitalization & the Postindustrial City: A Multinational Perspective.
Gale, J., jt. ed. see Poljakoff-Mayber, A.
Gale, Jack. How about a Career in Real Estate?
Gale, Jay, jt. auth. see Voss, Jacqueline.
Gale, Linda, jt. auth. see Gale, Barry.
Gale Research Company Staff. National Union Catalogue Author Lists, 1942-1962: A Master Cummulation.
Gale, Robert L. Charles Marion Russell.
Gale, Robert P. & Fox, C. Fred, eds. Biology of Bone Marrow Transplantation.
Gale, Stephen H. Harold Pinter: An Annotated Bibliography.
Gale, Steven H. Butter's Going up: A Critical Analysis of Harold Pinter's Work.
Galen, Robert S. & Gambino, S. Raymond. Beyond Normality: The Predictive Value & Efficiency of Medical Diagnosis.
Galeno, Joseph J. Plumbing Estimating Handbook.
--Plumbing Estimating Handbook.
Galich, Alexander. Songs & Poems. Smith, Gerry, tr. from Rus.
Galin, Joseph J. A Bibliography of Technology for the Law Firm: Computers & the Law.
--Computers & the Law: A Selected Bibliography.
--Industrial Policy: A Bibliography.
--The Political Socialization of Children & Adolescents: A Bibliography.
--Transportation for the Elderly, Handicapped & Disadvantaged: An Annotated Bibliography of Technical Reports.
--Transportation for the Elderly, Handicapped & Disadvantaged: A Bibliography of Articles.
Galindo, Sergio. The Precipice. Brushwood, John & Brushwood, Carolyn, trs. from Span.
Galinsky, Ellen & Hooks, William. The New Extended Family: Day Care Programs That Work.
Galiuski, Christian, ed. Terminological Data Banks: Proceedings of the First Conference Convened 2 & 3 April, 1979 by Infoterm.
Galkin, A., et al. Genocide.
Gall, James. Bible Student's English-Greek Concordance & Greek-English Dictionary.
Gall, Meredith D., jt. auth. see Borg, Walter S.
Gall, Sally M., ed. see Guthrie, Ramon.
Gallager, R., ed. see CISM (International Center for Mechanical Sciences), Dept. of Automation & Information, Cambridge, 1970.
Gallagher, A. P. Coordinating Australian University Development: A Study of the Australian Universities Commission, 1959-1970.
Gallagher, Dolores, ed. Depression in the Elderly: A Selected Bibliography. Kronauer, Margaret.
Gallagher, Dolores & Thompson, Larry W., eds. Depression in the Elderly: A Behavioral Treatment Manual.
Gallagher, Frank. The Indivisible Island: The Story of the Partition of Ireland.
Gallagher, J. M. & Easley, J. A., eds. Knowledge & Development, Vol. 2: Piaget & Education.
Gallagher, J. M., jt. ed. see Overton, Willis F.
Gallagher, James, ed. Impasse Resolution in Public Sector interest Disputes.
Gallagher, James J., jt. auth. see Kirk, Samuel A.
Gallagher, Joseph. Painting on Silence: An Orchestra of Poems.
Gallagher, Joseph, ed. East African Culture History.
Gallagher, Mary. Spend It Foolishly.
--Spend It Foolishly.
Gallagher, Maureen. The Cathedral Book.
Gallagher, Patricia. All for Love.
--Castles in the Air.
--Echoes & Embers.
--The Thicket.
Gallagher, Patricia A. Teaching Students with Behavior Disorders: Techniques for Classroom Instruction.
Gallagher, Patrick. Selected Poetry.
Gallagher, Rita. Passion Star.
Gallagher, Steve, ed. see Kruger, Barbara, et al.
Gallagher, Tess. Instructions to the Double.
--Willingly.
Gallagher, Thomas. Assault in Norway.
--The X-Craft Raid.
Gallagher, William J. Writing the Business & Technical Report.
Gallaher, Robert E., Jr. How to Use the HP12C.
Gallahue, David L., jt. auth. see Vannier, Maryhelen.
Galland, Frank J., ed. Dictionary of Computing: Data Communications, Hardware & Software Basics, Digital Electronics.
Gallant, G. Blake & the Assimilation of Chaos.
Gallant, Mavis. A Fairly Good Time.
--From the Fifteenth District.
--The Other Paris.
Gallatin, A. E., ed. A. E. Gallatin Collection: Museum of Living Art.
Gallatin, Judith E. Abnormal Psychology.
Gallatin, Mike. Piano Peek-a-Boo: Opus-One Note Learner.
Gallaudet College Library Editors, Washington, D. C. Dictionary Catalog on Deafness & the Deaf.
Gallawa, Robert L. On the Viability of 1300 Operation in the MX-C3 Program.
Galle, William P., Jr., jt. auth. see Level, Dale A., Jr.
Gallegly, J. S., et al, eds. Essays in the Humanities.
Gallego, A., ed. see International Symposium on Fosfomycin Staff.
Gallen, Joseph F. Conforming Constitutions to the New Code.
Gallese, Liz R. Women Like Us: A Milestone Study Drawn from Women of the Harvard Business School Class of '75.
Gallet, Jeffrey H., et al. Rent Stabilization & Control Laws in N. Y.
Galli, C. & Avogaro, P., eds. Polyunsaturated Fatty Acids in Nutrition: Proceedings of a Round Table in Polyunsaturated Fatty Acids in Nutrition, Milan, Italy, April 1979.
Gallico, Paul. Thomasina.
Galligan, D. J., jt. ed. see Sampford, Charles.
Galligani, I. & Magenes, E., eds. Mathematical Aspects of Finite Element Methods: Proceedings of the Conference Held in Rome, Dec.10-22, 1975.
Galliher, John F. & DeGregory, Jerry L. Violence in Northern Ireland: Understanding Prostestant Perspectives.
Gallin, D. Intensional & Higher Order Modal Logic PPR.
Gallina, Leonard, jt. auth. see Miller, William C.
Gallinger, Ray. Smoke Rings over the Valley.
Gallison, Kate. Unbalanced Accounts.
Gallo, Anthony E., et al. Food Marketing Review, 1986.
Gallo, Daniel & Kramer, Frederick. The Putnam Division.
Gallo, Donald R., ed. Books for You, 1985: A Booklist for Senior High Students.
Gallo, Joseph D. & Rink, Henry W. Shaping College Writing: Paragraph & Essay.
--Shaping College Writing: Paragraph & Essay.
Gallo, Michael A. & Nenno, Robert B. Computers & Society with BASIC & Pascal.
Gallo, Robert P., jt. auth. see Turk, Frederick J.
Gallon, Arthur J. Coaching: Ideas & Ideals.
--Coaching: Ideas & Ideals.
Galloway, Bruce, ed. Prejudice & Pride: Discrimination Against Gay People in Modern Britain.
Galloway, Dale E. Expect a Miracle.
Galloway, David. Schools, Pupils, & Special Educational Needs.
--Tamsen.
Galloway, David, ed. see Poe, Edgar Allan.
Gallup, Alec M., jt. auth. see Gallup, George, Jr.
Gallup, Barbara & Reich, Deborah. Totally Topiary.
Gallup, Don & Gallup, Jim. Golf Courses of Colorado: A Guide to Public & Resort Courses.
Gallup, Donald, ed. see O'Neill, Eugene.
Gallup, George, Jr. & Gallup, Alec M. The Great American Success Story.
Gallup, George, Jr. & Procter, William. Adventures in Immortality.
Gallup, Jim, jt. auth. see Gallup, Don.
Gallup Organization, Inc. Staff, compiled by. Gallup Study: Images of Community Colleges.
Gallwey, W. Timothy & Kriegel, Robert. Inner Game of Skiing.
Gallwitz, Klaus. Picasso: The Heroic Years.
Galnoor, Itzhak, jt. auth. see Lukes, Steven.
Galonska, Michael L., jt. auth. see University of Connecticut, Center for Real Estate & Urban Economic Studies Staff.
Galot, Jean. The Mystery of Christian Hope.
Galperin, G. Ethiopia: Population, Resources, Economy.
Galperin, I. R. Supplement to the New English-Russian Dictionary: Supplement.
Galphin, Bruce, jt. auth. see Shavin, Norman.
Galpin, A. M. & Milligan, Edward E. French Prose: An Intermediate Reader.
Galsworthy, John. Jocelyn.
--Modern Comedy.
--Plays.
Galsworthy, John, et al. Spine Chillers. Eyre, A. G., ed.
Galt, H. S. A History of Chinese Educational Institutions, Vol. I: To the End of the Five Dynasties (A. D. 960)
Galt, John. Dreams Come Due: Government & Economists As If Freedom Really Mattered.
Galton, Laurence. The Patient's Guide to Surgery.
Galton, Lawrence. One Thousand One Health Tips.
Galton, Lawrence, jt. auth. see Heimlich, Henry J.
Galton, Lawrence, jt. auth. see Miller, Benjamin F.
Galton, Lawrence, jt. auth. see Silberstein, Warren P.
Galton, Maurice & Willcocks, John, eds. Moving from the Primary Classroom.
Galton, Ray & Simpson, Alan. Hancock's Half Hour.
Galtung, J. Peace & Social Structure.
--Peace & World Structure.
Galtung, Johan. Papers on Methodolgy: Theory & Methods of Social Research.
Galuppi, Baldassare. L' Olimpiade. Brown, Howard M., ed.
Galus, Z. Fundamentals of Electrochemical Analysis. Reynolds, G. F., tr. from Pol.
Galvin, jt. auth. see Kent.
Galvin, Brendan. The Minutes No One Owns.
Galvin, Thomas J. & Lynch, Beverly P., eds. Priorities for Academic Libraries.
Gam, Rita. Actress to Actress.
Gambaccini, Paul. Paul McCartney: In His Own Words.
Gambarelli, J., et al. Computerized Axial Tomography.
Gambee, Budd L. Return Engagement: The Role of American Librarians at the Second International Library Conference, London, 1897.
Gambill, Henrietta. Are You Listening?
Gambino, Richard. Bread & Roses.
Gambino, S. Raymond, jt. auth. see Galen, Robert S.
Gamble, Deda R. On Third Thought.
Gamble, Geoffrey. Wikchamni Grammar.
Gamble, Michael & Gamble, Teri K. Communication Works.
Gamble, Teri K., jt. auth. see Gamble, Michael.
Gambling, Trevor. A One Year Accounting Course.
--Positive Accounting: Problems & Solutions.
Gambrell, Don, Jr. Estrogen Replacement Therapy.
Gamer, Helena M., jt. auth. see McNeill, John T.
Gamlin, A. T., et al, eds. Mechanical Maintenance & Installation: Supplementary Training Manual.
Gammel, John L., jt. ed. see Baker, George A., Jr.
Gammell, Stephen. The Story of Mr. & Mrs. Vinegar.
Gammond, Peter. Terms Used in Music.
Gammons, Peter. Beyond the Sixth Game.
Gamson, William A., et al. Encounters with Unjust Authority.
Gamson, Zelda, intro. by. Contexts for Learning: The Major Sectors of American Higher Education.
Gamst, Frederick C. Hoghead.
Gamulin, Grgo. Generalic.
Gamwell, Thomas P., jt. auth. see Slusher, Harold S.
Gamzatov, R. Mi Daguestan.
--Selected Poems.
Ganapol, B. D., ed. New Frontiers in Transport Theory: Selected Papers from the 6th Conference at U. of Ariz, Tuscon, April 1979.
Ganchovski, Nedelcho. The Days of Dimitrov: As I Witnessed & Recorded Them. Maneva, Svelta, tr.
Ganci, David. Desert Hiking.
Gander, Terry. Encyclopedia of the Modern Royal Airforce.
Gander, Terry, jt. ed. see Foss, Christopher.
Gandhi, A. The Morarji Papers: Fall of the Janata Government.
Gandhi, Kishore. Aldous Huxley: Vedantic & Buddhistic Influences.
Gandhi, M. K. Autobiography.
Gandhi, Mohandas K. Nonviolence in Peace & War, 1942. Incl. Nonviolence in Peace & War, 1949. Ghandi, Mohandas K. Garland Pub.
Gandini, A. & Cheradame, H. Cationic Polymerization.
Gandy, Charles D. & Zimmerman-Stidham, Susan. Contemporary Classics: Furniture of the Masters.
Gandy, Tillie H. Of Cabbages & Kings.
Gang, Arthur, jt. auth. see Gang, Miriam.
Gang, Miriam & Gang, Arthur. The Gang's Weigh.
Gangel, Kenneth O. So You Want to Be a Leader.
Gangolli, R. A. & Ylvisaker, Donald. Discrete Probability.

Authors

Gangopadhyay, Sunil. Pratidwandi. Chatterjee, Enakshi, tr. from Bengali.
Gangstad, Edward O. Freshwater Vegetation Management.
Ganguly, J. & Smellie, R. M., eds. Current Trends in the Biochemistry of Lipids: Proceedings.
Gani, J. & Rohatgi, V. K., eds. Contributions to Probability: A Collection of Papers Dedicated to Eugene Lukacs.
Gani, J., et al, eds. Progress in Statistics.
Ganiez, Tana De see De Ganiez, Tana.
Ganikos, Mary, ed. Counseling the Aged, with Index: A Training Syllabus for Educators.
Ganikos, Mary, et al, eds. A Handbook for Conducting Workshop on the Counseling Needs of the Elderly.
Ganley, Gladys D., jt. auth. see Ganley, Oswald H.
Ganley, Oswald H. & Ganley, Gladys D. To Inform or to Control? The New Communications Networks.
Gann, Donald, jt. ed. see Brown, J. H. U.
Gann, Ernest K. The Aviator.
--Fate Is the Hunter.
--Gentlemen of Adventure.
--The Magistrate.
--The Triumph.
Gann, Lewis H., ed. The Defense of Western Europe.
Gann, W. D. Truth of the Stock Tape.
Ganning, London. A Dictionary of Bad Manners.
Gannon, Martin J. Management: Managing for Results.
Gannon, Philip J. Korea.
Ganong, William F., jt. ed. see Martini, L.
Gans, A. I., ed. see California State Library Sutro Branch San Francisco.
Gans, Carl & Parsons, Thomas, eds. Biology of the Reptilia: Morphology D.
Gans, David. Talking Heads.
Ganshof, Francois L. Frankish Institutions under Charlemagne.
Gans-Ruedin, E. Chinese Carpets.
Gans-Ruedin, Erwin. Caucasian Carpets.
Ganss, George E., ed. see Clancy, Thomas H.
Ganss, George E., ed. see Fleming, David L.
Ganssler, P. & Revesz, P., eds. Empirical Distributions & Processes: Selected Papers from a Meeting at Oberwolfach, Mar. 28-Apr. 3, 1976.
Gant, A. Mac. Destiny's Plan: The Story of a Combination Family.
Gantos, Jack. Aunt Bernice.
--Fair-Weather Friends.
--The Perfect Pal.
--Sleepy Ronald.
--The Werewolf Family.
Gantt, Clarence. The Lady on My Right & Other Poems.
Gantt, Robert B., jt. ed. see Lauffer, Richard A.
Gantt, W. H., et al. Pavlovian Approach to Psychopathology.
Ganz, Arthur. George Bernard Shaw.
--George Bernard Shaw.
Gapenski, Louis J., jt. auth. see Brigham, Eugene F.
Gara, Larra & Chatfield, Charles. International War Resistance Through World War II.
Garahan, James C. & Rudman, Jeffrey B. Tax Shelters in Trouble: Private & Public Litigation.
Garan, Dominick. The Paradox of Pleasure & Relativity.
Garattini, S. & Tognoni, G., eds. Biological Markers in Mental Disorders: Proceedings of the Symposium Held in Milan, Italy, June 1983.
Garattini, S., et al. Single Cell Protein--Safety for Animal & Human Feeding: Proceedings of the Protein-Calorie Advisory Group of the United Nations System Symposium, Milan, Italy, March-April 1977.
Garaza, E., tr. see Orozco, R.
Garb, Gerald. Microeconomics: Theory Applications Innovations.
Garb, Paula. They Came to Stay: North Americans in the U. S. S. R.
Garb, Solomon, jt. auth. see Gross, Steven.
Garb, Tamar, jt. auth. see Adler, Kathleen.
Garber, A. Brent, et al. Hospital Crisis Management: A Casebook.
Garber, Judy & Seligman, Martin E., eds. Human Helplessness: Theory & Applications.
Garber, Marjorie. Coming of Age in Shakespeare.
Garber, Max B. & Bond, P. S. A Modern Military Dictionary: Ten Thousand Technical & Slang Terms of Military Usage.
Garbett, Thomas. Corporate Advertising: The What, the Why, & the How.
Garbo, Norman. The Artist.
--Spy.
--Turner's Wife: A Novel.
Garbuny, Max. Optical Physics.
Garbus, Martin. Ready for the Defense.
Garby, Lars & Meldon, Jerry H., eds. Respiratory Functions of Blood.
Garby, Lee H., jt. auth. see Smith, Edward E.
Garcia, Anthony & Myers, Robert. Analogies: A Visual Approach to Writing.
Garcia, Celso-Ramon. Current Therapy of Infertility: Nineteen Eighty-Four to Nineteen Eighty-Five.
Garcia, Florencio O. ISBN, ISSN: A Book's Fingerprints.
Garcia, Gillian G., jt. auth. see Cargill, Thomas F.
Garcia, Hazel D., jt. auth. see Stevens, John D.
Garcia, Joseph R. Wayside Poems.
Garcia, Luis. Mr. Menu.
Garcia, Mario R. Contemporary Newspaper Design: A Structural Approach.
Garcia, R., jt. auth. see Piaget, Jean.
Garcia, Reg see Garcia, Ronda.
Garcia, Reloy, jt. auth. see Hubenka, Lloyd.
Garcia, Ricardo. Learning in Two Languages.
Garcia, Richard. Read-Along with "My Aunt Otilia's Spirits"
Garcia, Richard & Cherin, Robin. My Aunt Otilia's Spirits: Los Espiritus De Mi Tia Otilia.
Garcia, Ronda. Home Centered Care: Designing a Family Day Care Program. Thompson, L. & McDonald, M., eds. Garcia, Reg.
Garcia-Avyens, Francisco. Quien Sabe? A Preliminary List of Chicano Reference Materials.
Garcia Lorca, Federico. Divan & Other Writings. Honig, Edwin, tr.
--Poet in New York.
Garcia Marquez, Gabriel. Leaf Storm & Other Stories.
--No One Writes to the Colonel & Other Short Stories.
Garcia-Prada, Carlos & Wilson, William E. Entendamonos: Manual de Conversacion.
Garcin, F., jt. ed. see Radouco-Thomas, C.
Gard, Michael F. EMI Control in Medical Electronics. White, Donald R., ed.
Gard, Robert E. & Sorden, L. G. Wisconsin Lore.
Gardam, Jane. Crusoe's Daughter.
Gardel, A. Energie: Economie et Prospective.
Garden Center of Greater Cleveland Staff. Flowering Plant Index of Illustration & Information.
Garden, Graeme. A Sense of the Past.
Garden, Nancy. The Kid's Code & Cipher Book.
--The Loners.
Garden, Timothy. Can Deterrence Last? Peace Through a Nuclear Strategy.
Gardener's Catalog Editors. The Gardener's Catalog.
Gardiner, C. F., jt. auth. see Firby, P. A.
Gardiner, C. Harvey. William Hickling Prescott: A Biography.
Gardiner, C. Harvey, ed. see Prescott, William H.
Gardiner, D. E. M. Education of Young Children.
Gardiner, Dorothy, ed. see Chandler, Raymond.
Gardiner, G. & Morris, A. The Price Guide to Metal Toys.
Gardiner, George L. Computer Assisted Indexing in the Central State University Library.
Gardiner, Harvey C., ed. see Koster, Henry.
Gardiner, Harvey C., ed. see Merwin, Mrs. George B.
Gardiner, James J. & Roberts, J. Deotis, eds. Quest for a Black Theology.
Gardiner, John M. & Kaminska, Zofia. First Experiments in Psychology.
Gardiner, John R. Going on Like This.
Gardiner, Samuel R., ed. Documents Relating to the Proceedings Against William Prynne, in 1634 & 1637.
Gardiner, Samuel R., ed. see Great Britain, House of Commons Staff.
Gardiner, Samuel R., ed. see Great Britain, House of Lords Staff.
Gardiner, Stephen. Letters of Stephen Gardiner. Muller, James A., ed.
--Obedience in Church & State: Three Political Tracts. Janelle, Pierre, ed.
Gardiner, W. C., Jr. Rates & Mechanisms of Chemical Reactions.
Gardini, Maria. The Secrets of the Hand.
Gardner. Differential Oral Diagnosis of Systemic Diseases.
Gardner, jt. auth. see Merenstein.
Gardner, Andrew B. The Artist's Silk Screen Manual.
Gardner, David A. & Gardner, Marianne L. Apple BASIC Made Easy.
Gardner, David C. & Beatty, Grace J. Stop Stress & Aging Now: The Methuselah Manual.
Gardner, Dewey D., ed. Bibliography of Theses & Dissertations Relevant to Pharmacy Administration 1970-1974.
Gardner, Donald, tr. see Paz, Octavio.
Gardner, Eileen M. Moral Education for the Emotionally Disturbed Early Adolescent: An Application of Kohlbergian Techniques & Spiritual Principles.
Gardner, Elizabeth E., jt. auth. see Zeri, Federico.
Gardner, Erle S. see also Fair, A. A.
Gardner, Erle Stanley. The Case of the Blonde Bonanza.
--The Case of the Rolling Bones.
Gardner, Gerald H., ed. see Labo, James A.
Gardner, Helen. Art Through the Ages.
Gardner, Jack I. Gambling: A Guide to Information Sources.
Gardner, James E. Training the New Supervisor.
Gardner, James F., et al, eds. Program Issues in Developmental Disabilities: A Resource Manual for Surveyors & Reviewers.
Gardner, Jeanne L. Mary Jemison: Seneca Captive.
Gardner, Jeffery J. Resource Notebook on Planning.
Gardner, Jerome. The Hanging Week.
--The Rawhide Redeemer.
Gardner, John. The Art of Living & Other Stories.
--In the Suicide Mountains.
--No Deals Mr. Bond.
--Nobody Lives Forever.
Gardner, John, ed. Best American Short Stories Nineteen Eighty-Two.
Gardner, John F. Love & the Illusion of Love.
Gardner, John N. & Jewler, A. Jerome, eds. College Is Only the Beginning: A Student Guide to Higher Education.
Gardner, John W. In Common Cause.
--Morale.
--Recovery of Confidence.
--Self-Renewal.
Gardner, John W. & Reese, Francesca G., eds. Know or Listen to Those Who Know.
Gardner, Joseph M., Jr. How to Sell Your Own Home Without a Real Estate Agent & Save Thousands of Dollars.
Gardner, Joy. Healing Yourself.
Gardner, Lloyd C. & O'Neill, William L. Looking Backward: A Reintroduction to American History.
Gardner, M. J, et al. Atlas of Mortality from Selected Diseases in England & Wales 1968-1978.
Gardner, Marianne L., jt. auth. see Gardner, David A.
Gardner, Martin. The Ambidextrous Universe: Mirror Asymmetry & Time-Reversed Worlds.
--The Flight of Peter Fromm.
--Martin Gardner's New Mathematical Diversions from Scientific American.
--Science: Good, Bad & Bogus.
--Unexpected Hanging & Other Mathematical Diversions.
Gardner, Martin, ed. Scientific American Book of Mathematical Puzzles & Diversions.
Gardner, Martin, ed. see Fujimura, Kobon.
Gardner, Mary. Keeping Warm.
Gardner, Michael, jt. auth. see Nace, Ted.
Gardner, Murray B., et al. Physiological Effects of Air Pollution.
Gardner, Philip, ed. E. M. Forster: The Critical Heritage.
Gardner, Philip, et al. The BBC Micro Add-On Guide.
Gardner, Philip W. The Lost Elementary Schools of Victorian England: The People's Education.
Gardner, Richard, et al. A Turning Point in North-South Economic Relations.
Gardner, Richard A. Dr. Gardner's Modern Fairy Tales.
--Doctor Gardner's Stories About the Real World.
Gardner, Richard N. & Glucksmann, Andre. Sovereignty & Intervention.
Gardner, Richard N., et al. OPEC, the Trilateral World, & the Developing Countries-New Arrangements for Cooperation, 1976-1980.
Gardner, Robert. Kitchen Chemistry: Science Experiments to Do at Home.
--Water, the Life Sustaining Resource.
Gardner, Robert W., jt. auth. see Wright, Paul.
Gardner, Roberta. The Bed & Breakfast Guide: East Coast.
--The East Coast Bed & Breakfast Guide: New England & the Mid-Atlantic.
Gardner, Roberta, et al. Country Inns of America: Lower New England.
Gardner, Roberta A. Social Change.
Gardner, Roberta H. Country Inns of America: New York & Mid-Atlantic.
Gardner, Ruth. Graphology Student's Workbook.
Gardner, Ruth, jt. auth. see Inman, Billie A.
Gardner, Thomas J. Criminal Evidence: Principles, Cases & Readings.
Gardner, William & Cooke, Edward I. Chemical Synonyms & Trade Names: A Dictionary & Commercial Handbook.
Gardocki, Gloria J. Use of Antimicrobial Drugs in Office Based Practice: United States, 1980-1981.
Garee, Betty. Accent Onliving Buyers Guide, 1986-87: Your Number One Source of Information on Products for the Disabled.
Gareth Jones, E. B. Recent Advances in Aquatic Mycology.
Garetz, Bruce A. & Lombardi, John R., eds. Advances in Laser Spectroscopy.
Garetz, M., jt. auth. see Libes, S.
Garff, Michael, jt. auth. see Fichtner, Hans.
Garfield. Direct Mail.
--Taking Control Counter Display.
Garfield, Brian. The Threepersons Hunt.
--Valley of the Shadow.
--Valley of the Shadow.
Garfield, Charles A. Psychosocial Care of the Dying Patient.
Garfield, Leon. The King in the Garden.
Garfield, Patricia. Your Child's Dreams.
Garfinkel, Alan & Latorre, Guillermo. Trabajo y Vida.
Garfinkel, Barry H., jt. auth. see Practising Law Institute Staff.
Garfinkel, Charles. Racquetball the Easy Way.
Garfinkel, Herbert. When Negroes March.
Garfinkel, Howard, ed. Five-Star Basketball Drills.
Garg, H. P. Treatise on Solar Energy, Vol. 1: Fundamentals of Solar Energy.
Gargano, James W., ed. Henry James: The Early Novels, The Late Novels.
Gargiulo, Albert F. & Carlucci, Rocco. The Questioned Stock Manual: A Guide to Determining the True Worth of Old & Collectible Securities.
Garin, Eugenio. Astrology in the Renaissance. Jackson, Carolyn & Allen, June, trs. from Ital.
--Astrology in the Renaissance: The Zodiac of Life.
Garitano, Rita. Rainy Day Man.
Garlan, Edwin N. Legal Realism & Justice.
Garlan, Yvon. War in the Ancient World: A Social History. Finley, M. I., ed. Lloyd, Janet, tr.
Garland, Albert N. Infantry in Vietnam.
Garland, Andrew, et al. System 1022 Host Language Interface User's Reference Manual.
Garland, Anne W. Woman Activists.
Garland, Colden. Developing Competence in Teaching Reading: Instructional Modules in Reading Education.
Garland, D. J. & Stainer, F. W. Modern Electronic Maintenance Principles.
Garland, G. D. Earth's Shape & Gravity.
Garland, Hamlin. Rose of Dutcher's Coolly. Pizer, Donald, ed.
--A Son of the Middle Border.
Garland, Joe & Sharp, Jim. Adventure: Queen of the Windjammers.
Garland, John. Industrial Cooperation Between Poland & the West. Farmer, Richard, ed.
Garland, Madge, jt. auth. see Black, J. Anderson.
Garland, Sarah. Going Shopping.
--Having a Picnic.
Garlett, Marti W. Who Will Be My Teacher? The Christian Way to Stronger Schools.
Garlinghouse Co. Staff, ed. Traditional Home Plans.
Garlinghouse Corp. Staff, ed. New Homes for Nineteen Eighty-Nine.
Garlinghouse, L. F., Co., Staff, ed. Multi-Level & Hillside Home Plans.
--Small Home Plans.
--Three Hundred Best Selling Home Plans.
--Vacation & Leisure Home Plans.
Garlinghouse Publication Inc., Staff, ed. Garlinghouse Portfolio of Custom Home Plan.
Garlinski, Jozef. The Swift Corridor: Espionage Networks in Switzerland During World War II.
Garmaise, Freda. Love Bites.
Garman, Tom, et al. Personal Finance.
Garmey, Jane. Great New British Cooking.
Garn, Paul, jt. auth. see Schwenker, Robert F., Jr.
Garnaut, Ross & Findlay, Christopher, eds. The Political Economy of Manufacturing Protection.
Garner, Alan. Alan Garner's Book of British Fairy Tales.
--Conversationally Speaking: Tested New Ways to Increase Your Personal & Social Effectiveness.
--Elidor.
--The Moon of Gomrath.
--The Owl Service.
--The Red Shift.
--The Weirdstone of Brinsingamen.
Garner, J. Dianne & Mercer, Susan O., eds. Women As They Age: Challenge, Opportunity, & Triumph.
Garner, J. F. Practical Planning Law: A Handbook for Planners, Architects & Surveyors.
Garner, John. Modern Deep Sea Trawling Gear.
Garner, John S. The Model Company Town: Urban Design Through Private Enterprise in Nineteenth-Century New England.
Garner, K. C. Introduction to Control Systems Performance Measurements.
Garner, Nathan. A Different Drummer Notes.
Garner, Phillip. Garner's Gizmos & Gadgets.
Garner, R. C., jt. ed. see Norpoth, K. H.
Garner, Richard. Law & Society in Classical Athens.
Garner, S. Paul. Evolution of Cost Accounting.
Garnet, A. H. Maze.
--The Santa Claus Killer.
Garnet, J. Ros. Wild Flowers of Wilson's Promontory National Park.
Garnett, Angelica. Deceived with Kindness: A Bloomsbury Childhood.
Garnett, Constance, tr. see Dostoyevsky, Fyodor.
Garnett, Constance, tr. see Turgenev, Ivan S.
Garnett, Henry. Know about the Armada.

Garnett, J. Analytic Capacity & Measure.
Garnett, Richard & Gosse, Edmund W. English Literature, an Illustrated Record.
Garnham, Alan. Psycholinguistics.
Garnham, Nicholas, tr. see Mattelart, Armand, et al.
Garnir, H. G., et al, eds. Functional Analysis & Its Applications.
Garnsey, E. H., tr. see De Bary, Anton.
Garnweidner, E. Gift Pilze Kompass: Die Giftigen Pilze und Ihre Geniessbaren Doppelgaenger Sicher Bestimmen.
Garon, Philip A., ed. see Gromyko, Anatolii A.
Garoogian, Andrew & Garoogian, Rhoda, eds. Child Care Issues for Parents & Society: A Guide to Information Sources.
Garoogian, Rhoda, jt. ed. see Garoogian, Andrew.
Garr, Doug. WOZ: The Prodigal Son of Silicon Valley.
Garraghan, Gilbert J. A Guide to Historical Method. Delanglez, Jean, ed.
Garrard, John. Mikhail Lermontov.
Garratty, George, ed. Blood Group Antigens & Diseases.
Garraty, John A. Woodrow Wilson: A Great Life in Brief.
Garreau, Joel. The Nine Nations of North America.
Garrels, Robert M. & Mackenzie, Fred T. Evolution of Sedimentary Rocks.
Garret, Maxwell R. Science-Hobby Book of Boating.
Garretson, Warren P. The Roughneck: A Novel.
Garrett. Quantitative Analysis of Drugs.
Garrett, Beatrice. Welfare on Skid Row.
Garrett, Charles, jt. auth. see Lagal, Roy.
Garrett, Charles, et al. Electronic Prospecting. Nelson, Bettye, ed.
Garrett, David & Henderson, Bryn. Legal Terminology Handbook.
Garrett, De Graaf, ed. Duran Duran: The Book of Words.
Garrett, Frank. Killsquad No. 1: Counter Attack.
--Killsquad, No. 10: Mob War.
--Killsquad No. 2: Mission Revenge.
--Killsquad No. 4: The Judas Soldiers.
--Killsquad No. 5: Blood Beach.
--Killsquad No. 6: The Seventh Whore of Babylon.
--Killsquad No. 7: Polar Assault.
--Killsquad, No. 9: Devil's Island.
--Slaughter Zone.
Garrett, G. G. & Marriott, D. L., eds. Engineering Applications of Fracture Analysis: Proceedings of the First National Conference on Fracture Held in Johannesburg, South Africa, 1979.
Garrett, Garet. The Peoples' Pottage.
Garrett, George. An Evening Performance.
--James Jones.
--James Jones.
--The Succession: A Novel of Elizabeth & James.
Garrett, H. E. Surface Active Chemicals.
Garrett, Howard, ed. The Poster Book of Antique Auto Ads.
Garrett, I., jt. auth. see Faktor, M. M.
Garrett, Jane N., jt. ed. see Bailyn, Bernard.
Garrett, John, jt. auth. see Calder, Julian.
Garrett, John G. The World Encyclopedia of Model Soldiers.
Garrett, Joshua H. Come in & Find Your World.
Garrett, Lela G. Papa's Razor Strop.
Garrett, Leonard. Wings of Eagles Feet of Clay.
Garrett, Leonard J. & Silver, Milton. Production Management Analysis.
Garrett, Randall, jt. auth. see Kurland, Michael.
Garrett, Ray & Arthur, Thomas. Corporate Bond Financing.
Garrett, Richard. Atlantic Disaster.
Garrett, Susan E. Test Preparation Guide for Course 1.
Garrett, Willis O. Church Ushers' Manual.
Garrick, Barbara L., ed. Hematology for Medical Technologists: PreTest Self-Assessment & Review.
Garrick, David. The Plays of David Garrick. Berkowitz, Gerald, ed.
Garrido, L., ed. Dynamical Systems & Chaos: Proceedings, Sitges, Barcelona, Spain, 1982.
Garrido, Mar. Eileen Goudges Swept Away, Number Six: Once Upon a Kiss.
Garrigue, Jean. The Ego & the Centaur: Poems.
Garriott, O. K., jt. auth. see Risbeth, Henry.
Garrison. Pilot's Guide to Aviation Insurance.
Garrison, Carolyn L., jt. auth. see Brasher, Ruth E.
Garrison, David. Blue Oboe: A Book of Poems.
Garrison, David, tr. see Aleixandre, Vicente.
Garrison, Fielding H. History of Medicine.
Garrison, Guy, ed. The Changing Role of State Library Consultants.
Garrison, Jayne. A-Z Guide for New Mothers.
Garrison, Linda & Read, Ann K. Fitness for Every Body.
Garrison, Linda, et al. Fitness & Figure Control: The Creation of You.
Garrison, Marc S. Financially Free: Add 30,000 Dollars a Year to Your Income Through Part Time Real Estate Investing.
Garrison, Omar V. The Hidden Story of Scientology.
Garrison, P. Cockpit Computers & Navigation Avionics.
Garrison, Paul. Aircraft Turbocharging.
--Autopilots, Flight Directors & Flight-Control Systems.
--Flying VFR in Marginal Weather.
--One Hundred One Model Railroad Layouts.
--Pilot's Guide to Aviation Insurance.
--Programming the TI-59 & HP-41 Calculators.
--Turbo Pascal for BASIC Programmers.
Garrison, Peter. CV: Carrier Aviation.
Garrison, Ray H. Managerial Accounting.
Garrod, Andrew, et al. Perspectives on Teaching: Learning & Development.
Garrod, Claude, jt. auth. see Hurley, James P.
Garrod, D. R. Cellular Development.
Garrord, Rene J. Wild Rose.
Garshin, M. Stories.
Garside, Charles, Jr. The Origins of Calvin's Theology of Music: 1536-1543.
Garsoian, N. G. Paulician Heresy: A Study of the Origin & Development of Paulicianism in Armenia & the Eastern Provinces of the Byzantine Empire.
Gartenberg, Egon. Mahler: The Man & His Music.
--Mahler: The Man & His Music.
Gartenberg, Michael & Shaw, Barry. Mathematics for Financial Analysis.
Garth, et al, trs. see Ovid.
Garth, John S. & Tilden, J. W. California Butterflies.
Gartling, D. K., jt. ed. see Park, K. C.
Gartner, Alan, ed. College Programs for Paraprofessionals: A Directory of Degree-Granting Programs in the Human Services.
Gartner, Bertil. Iscariot. Reumann, John, ed. Gruhn, Victor I., tr. from Ger.
Garton, Melville. High Profile.
Gartska, Stanley J., jt. auth. see Berney, Paul R.
Garvan, Beatrice B. Federal Philadelphia, 1785-1825: The Athens of the Western World.
Garvan, Fran J., jt. auth. see Brooks, Pat.
Garven, Charles. Student Journalist & Editing. Rosen, Ruth C., ed.
Garver, Thomas H. Christopher Brown: The Painted Room.
--Dennis Nechvatal Painting & Drawings: The Landscape of Anxiety.
--Robert Brady: Ceramic Sculpture.
Garvey, Gerald. Energy, Ecology, Economy: A Framework for Environmental Policy.
--Strategy & the Defense Dilemma.
Garvie, Peter. Music & Western Man.
Garvin, Charles D. Contemporary Group Work.
Garvin, Joseph N., jt. ed. see Corbett, James A.
Garvin, Paul L., ed. see Linguistic Association of Canada & the U. S. Staff.
Garwood, Alfred N., ed. Regional Difference in America: A Statistical Sourcebook.
Garwood, S. Gray & Fewell, Rebecca R. Educating Handicapped Infants: Issues in Development & Intervention.
Garwood, W. R., jt. auth. see Breihan, Carl W.
Gary, Charles L., ed. see Music Educators National Conference Staff.
Gary, Romain. Adieu Gary Cooper.
--Chien Blanc.
--La Danse de Gengis Cohn.
--Education Europeenne.
--Europa.
--Johnnie Coeur.
--Lady L.
--Les Racines du Ciel.
Garza, Catarino, ed. Puerto Ricans in the U. S.
Garza County Historical Society Staff. Garza County History.
Garza, Lucy M. South Texas Mexican Cookbook.
Garzuel, Michel, jt. auth. see Van Ginneken, Wouter.
Gascoigne, George. George Gascoigne's A Hundredth Sundrie Flowres.
Gash, Joe. Newspaper Murders.
--Newspaper Murders.
--Priestly Murders: A Chicago Police Mystery.
Gash, Jonathan. Spend Game.
--The Vatican Rip.
Gasior, Mary A. The Four Prentices of London.
Gaskell. My Lady Ludlow.
Gaskell, D. R., jt. ed. see Fine, H. A.
Gaskell, D. R., et al, eds. Reinhardt Schuhmann International Symposium on Innovative Technology & Reactor Design in Extraction Metallurgy.
Gaskell, David R. Metallurgical Thermodynamics.
Gaskell, Elizabeth. Cranford.
--North & South.
Gaskin, Catherine. The Ambassador's Women.
--Ambassador's Women.
--Promises.
Gaskin, Ina M. Babies, Breastfeeding & Bonding.
Gaskin, Maxwell, ed. The Political Economy of Tolerable Survival.
Gaskin, Stephen. Rendered Infamous: A Book of Political Reality. McClure, Matthew, ed.
Gaskind, Bill. Perspectives on Landscape.
Gasnick, Roy. Francis: Brother of the Universe.
--Francisco: Hermano del Universo.
--Mother Teresa of Calcutta.
Gaspar, Max R. & Barker, Wiley F. Peripheral Arterial Disease.
Gasper, James. The Great Me.
Gasper, JoAnn. What You Need to Know about Planned Parenthood: What Is It? How Does It Affect You & Your Children? What Can You Do about It?
Gasperini, Richard E. Digital Experiments.
--Digital Troubleshooting: Practical Digital Theory & Troubleshooting Tips.
Gass, J. Donald. Stereoscopic Atlas of Macular Diseases: Diagnosis & Treatment.
Gass, S. I., et al, eds. Impacts of Microcomputers on Operations Research.
Gass, Saul I. Illustrated Guide to Linear Programming.
--Linear Programming.
Gass, Susan, jt. auth. see Selinker, Larry.
Gass, Susan & Selinker, Larry, eds. Language Transfer in Language Learning.
Gass, William. On Being Blue.
Gass, William H. The Habitations of the Word: Essays.
--Habitations of the Word: Essays.
Gassen, Chris, jt. auth. see Mittra, Sid.
Gasser, Doris L. Socrates, the Snowman.
Gasser, Michael, jt. auth. see Rossi, Lee D.
Gasset, Jose Ortega Y. see Ortega y Gasset, Jose.
Gasset, Jose Ortega y see Ortega y Gasset, Jose.
Gasset, Jose Ortega Y see Ortega Y Gasset, Jose.
Gasset, Jose Ortega Y. see Ortega Y Gasset, Jose.
Gasset, Jose Ortega Y see Ortega Y Gasset, Jose.
Gassmann, Gunther & Vatja, Vilmos, eds. Oecumenica 1970 Yearbook for Ecumenical Studies.
Gassner, John & Nicholas, Dudley. Best Film Plays Nineteen Forty-Five. Kupelnick, Bruce S., ed.
Gassner, John & Nichols, Dudley. Best Film Plays, Nineteen Forty-Three to Forty-Four.
--Twenty Best Film Plays.
Gast, Ross H. & Conrad, Agnes C. Don Francisco De Paula Marin: A Biography with Letters & Journal.
Gaster. Chronicles of Yerachmiel.
Gastineau, Gary L. The Stock Options Manual.
Gastmans, R., jt. ed. see Basdevant, J. L.
Gaston, jt. auth. see Bender.
Gaston, Georg M. Karel Reisz.
Gaston, Jerry. Originality & Competition in Science: A Study of the British High Energy Physics Community.
Gaston, Jerry, jt. ed. see Merton, Robert K.
Gaston, Thomas E. & Harris, Muriel. Making Paragraphs Work.
Gaston de, la Lavoissier see De La Lavoissier, Gaston.
Gastric Secretion Symposium Staff. Gastric Secretion: Proceedings of the Symposium, Frankfurt Am Main, 1971. Sachs, George, ed.
Gatchel, Robert J., jt. auth. see Mears, Frederick G.
Gately, Robert. The Gods of Bell.
Gates, Anita. Ninety Highest Paying Careers for the 80's.
--Ninety Most Promising Careers for the 80s.
Gates, Charles M., ed. Five Fur Traders of the Northwest.
Gates, Esther B. Softness in the Wind.
Gates, Gary P., jt. auth. see Wallace, Mike.
Gates, George A. Current Therapy in Otolaryngology: Head & Neck Surgery 1984-1985.
Gates, Jean K. Guide to the Use of Books & Libraries.
Gates, John E., jt. auth. see Boatner, Maxine.
Gates, June C. Basic Foods.
Gates, Paul W., et al. Four Persistent Issues: Essays on California's Land Ownership Concentration, Water Deficits, Sub-State Regionalism, & Congressional Leadership.
Gates, Zethyl. Mariano Medina: Colorado Mountain Man.
Gatewood, Willard B., ed. Free Man of Color: The Autobiography of Willis Augustus Hodges.
Gatewood, Willard B., Jr. Black Americans & the White Man's Burden, 1898-1903.
Gatewood, Willard B., Jr., jt. ed. see Donovan, Timothy P.
Gatherer, N. Songs & Ballads of Dundee.
Gathorne-Hardy, Jonathan. The City Beneath the Skin.
Gathrid, Erin B., ed. see Gathrid, Jonathan.
Gathrid, Jonathan. Alphabots. Gathrid, Erin B., ed.
Gati, T., et al, eds. Nutrition-Digestion-Metabolism: Proceedings of the 28th International Congress of Physiological Sciences, Budapest, 1980.
Gatignol, T. Theorie Cinetique des Gaz a Repartition Descrete De Vitesses.
Gatland & Jeffries. Robots.
Gatland, Bruce, jt. auth. see Fisher, Jack.
Gatland, H. B. Electronic Engineering Applications of Two Port Systems.
Gattegno, Caleb. The Mind Teaches the Brain.
--On Being Freer.
--Science of Education. Bd. with Facts of Awareness; Affectivity & Learning; Awareness of Awareness. Ed Solutions.
--Towards a Visual Culture.
Gattin, Dana. God Is the Answer.
Gattis, Lou. Cooking, Basic & Advanced, for Pathfinders: A Youth Enrichment Skill.
Gattis, Lou, III. Basic & Advanced Cooking for Pathfinders: A Youth Enrichment Skill.
Gatto, R., ed. Developments in High-Energy Physics: Italian Physical Society.
Gattozi, R. What's Wrong with My Child?
Gatza, Jim, et al. Decision Making in Administration: Text, Critical Incidents & Cases.
Gatzke, Hans W. Stresemann & the Rearmament of Germany.
Gatzke, Hans W., jt. auth. see Strayer, Joseph R.
Gaubatz, John. The Moot Court Book.
Gauch, Hugh G. Inorganic Plant Nutrition.
Gauch, Patricia L. Dragons on the Road.
--Kate Alone.
--Night Talks.
Gaudet, A. John. Petits Mots Croises.
Gaudet, Marcia G. Tales from the Levee: The Folklore of St. John the Baptist Parish.
Gaudriault, Raymond. La Gravure de Mode Feminine en France.
Gaudry, Marc, jt. ed. see Florian, Michael.
Gaudy, Anthony & Gaudy, Elizabeth. Microbiology for Environment Science Engineers.
Gaudy, Elizabeth, jt. auth. see Gaudy, Anthony.
Gauer, Harold. Bury Me Not.
Gaugas, Joseph M., ed. Polyamines in Biomedical Research.
Gaughan, Pamela, tr. see Trocme, Etienne.
Gauguin, Paul. Noa Noa.
Gaukler, K. H., ed. see International Congress on X-Ray Optics & Microanalysis, 5th, 1968.
Gauld. Differential Topology: An Introduction.
Gauld, Alan & Cornell, A. D. Poltergeists.
Gault, Henri & Millau, Christian. The Best of France.
--The Best of Italy.
--The Best of Los Angeles.
--The Best of New York.
--The Best of New York.
--The Best of Paris.
Gault, Henry & Millau, Christian. The Best of London.
Gault, John C. Public Utility Regulation of an Exhaustible Resource: The Case of Natural Gas.
Gaumnitz, Jack E., jt. auth. see Dougall, Herbert E.
Gauquelin, Francoise, jt. auth. see Gauquelin, Michel.
Gauquelin, Michel & Gauquelin, Francoise. Gauquelin Book of American Charts.
Gaur, Albertine. A History of Writing.
Gauri, K. K., ed. Antiviral Chemotherapy: Design of Inhibitors of Viral Functions.
Gause, Don C. & Weinberg, Gerald M. Are Your Lights On? How to Figure Out What the Problem Really Is.
Gauss, Kathleen M. New American Photography.
Gauss, Lenna. The Egghead & I.
Gaussen, Louis. Divine Inspiration.
Gautam, Vinayshil. Enterprise & Society.
Gautama, Sudargo & Hornick, Robert N. An Introduction to Indonesian Law.
Gautier, Theophile. Le Capitaine Fracasse. Boschot, ed.
--Le Capitaine Fracasse. Boschot, ed.
Gauze, G. F. Problems in the Classification of Antagonistic Actinomycetes. Danga, F., tr.
Gavalas, George R. Nonlinear Differential Equations of Chemically Reacting Systems.
Gaver, Jessyca R. The Golden Dozen.
--How Deep the Cup.
Gavett, Earle E. Fuel Ethanol & Agriculture: An Economic Assessment.
Gavin, James M. Airborne Warfare.
Gaviria, Maria C. de see National Library of Peru Staff.
Gavron, Daniel. Israel after Begin.
--Walking Through Israel.
Gavron, Hannah. The Captive Wife: Conflicts of Housebound Mothers.
Gavronsky, Serge, tr. see Ponge, Francis.
Gaw, Albert, ed. Cross-Cultural Psychiatry.
Gay, Carlo T. E. Xochipala: The Beginnings of Olmec Art.
Gay, Jeanne, ed. Travel & Tourism Audiovisual Guide.
--Travel & Tourism Bibliography & Resource Guide.
Gay, Kathlyn, jt. auth. see Gay, Martin.
Gay, L. W., jt. auth. see Fritschen, L. J.
Gay, Martin & Gay, Kathlyn. Eating What Grows Naturally.
Gay, Michael. Little Truck.
--Rabbit Express.
Gay, Michel. Little Boat.
--Little Plane.
Gay, Oleta. The Gay Bunch.

Gay, Peter. The Dilemma of Democratic Socialism: Edward Bernstein's Challenge to Marx.
--The Enlightenment.
--Style in History.
--Voltaire's Politics: The Poet As Realist.
Gay, Peter, tr. see Voltaire.
Gaya, S. D. Gili see Gili Gaya, S. D.
Gay-Crosier, Raymond, ed. Albert Camus 1980.
Gaydon, A. G. The Spectroscopy of Flames.
Gaydon, A. G. & Wolfhard, H. G. Flames: Their Structure, Radiation & Temperature.
Gaydos, Alice G. Please Quote Me: Selected Poems.
Gaye, Carol. So Dangerous My Love.
--Two Hearts Bid.
Gayford & Haskell. Clinical Oral Medicine.
Gaylin, Willard. The Rage Within: Anger in Modern Life.
Gaylord, Chuck. Working out Without Weights: A Gymnast's Fitness Program You Can Do at Home Without Special Equipment.
Gaylord, Gloria L. & Ried, Glenda E. Careers in Accounting.
Gaynes, Martin J., jt. auth. see Zuckman, Harvey L.
Gaynor, Frank. Aerospace Dictionary.
--Concise Encyclopedia of Atomic Energy.
--Dictionary of Mysticism.
--International Business Dictionary.
Gaynor, Frank, jt. auth. see Pei, Mario.
Gazda, George M. Group Counseling: A Developmental Approach.
Gazda, George M. & Corsini, Raymond J. Theories of Learning: A Comparative Approach.
Gazdar, Adi, jt. auth. see Becker, Kenneth L.
Gaze, Harry. How to Live Forever: The Science & Practice.
Gazey, B. K., jt. auth. see Tucker, D. G.
Gazi, Stephen. History of Croatia.
Gazvoda, Edward A., Jr. & Haney, William M., III. The Harvard Entrepreneurs Society's Guide to Making Money: Or the Tycoon's Handbook.
Geake, R. Robert & Smith, Donald E. Visual Tracking.
Gear, Josephine. Masters or Servants? A Study of Selected English Painters & Their Patrons of the Late 18th & Early 19th Centuries.
Gearing, Winifred. Salvation Patrol.
Geary, Kenneth E. Heart Attack (Mine... & Yours?)
Gebbie, Donald A. Reproductive Anthropology: Descent Through Woman.
Gebelein, H., jt. auth. see Schuler, Max.
Gebert, Gordon, ed. Health-Care.
Gebhardt, Chuck. Inside Death Valley.
Gebhart, B. Heat Transfer.
Gebicki, Janusz M., jt. auth. see Bielski, Benon H.
Gecsei, Jan. Architecture of Videotex Systems.
Geczi, Mike. Futures: The Anti-Inflation Investment.
Gedaliah, Robert. P. E. P.-The Productivity Effectiveness Program.
Gedda, L. Auxology: Human Growth in Health & Disorder. Parisi, P., ed.
Geddes, A. M., jt. ed. see Reeves, David S.
Geddes, Gary. War & Other Measures.
Geddes, James D., ed. Large Ground Movements & Structures.
Geddes, Paul. A State of Corruption.
Geddie, William. Bibliography of Middle Scots Poets.
Gedeon, Charles. Who's Who in Lebanon, 1986-87.
--Who's Who in the Arab World, 1986-1987.
Gedeon, David V., jt. auth. see Tomal, Daniel R.
Gedin, Per. Literature in the Marketplace.
Geduld, Harry, jt. ed. see Gottesman, Ronald.
Geduld, Harry M. Dr. Jekyll & Mr. Hyde: An Anthology of Commentary, Including the Text.
Geduld, Harry M., ed. see Shaw, George Bernard.
Gee, Audrey. Looking at Houses.
Gee, Choy Y. & Choy, Dexter. The Travel Industry.
Gee, E. Gordon & Jackson, Donald W. Legal Education & Lawyer Competency.
Gee, John. Freshwater Studies. Jenkins, Morton, ed.
Gee, K. C. Introduction to Local Area Computer Networks.
Gee, K. C., ed. see National Computing Centre, Ltd. Staff.
Gee, Malcolm. Dealers, Critics, & Collectors or Modern Painting: Aspects of the Parisian Art Market Between 1910 & 1930.
Gee, Marjory, ed. see Fraser, Thomas G.
Gee, S. M., jt. auth. see James, Mike.
Gee, Sue, jt. auth. see Michelson, Joan.
Gee, Thomas C., jt. auth. see Criscoe, Betty L.
Geehr, jt. auth. see Auerbach.
Geehr, Edward C., jt. ed. see Auerbach, Paul S.
Geen, Russell G., et al. Human Motivation: Physiological, Behavioral & Social Approaches.
Geer, Charles see Bitter, Gary G.
Geer, J. C., jt. ed. see Wissler, Robert W.
Geer, Russel M. On Nature Lucretuis.
Geerdes, Harold P. Planning & Equipping Educational Music Facilities.
Geers, T. L. & Tong, P., eds. Survival of Mechanical Systems in Transient Environments.
Geertz, Clifford, ed. Myth, Symbol & Culture.
Geery, Daniel. Wasatch Trails.
Geest, Hans van der see Van Der Geest, Bans.
Gefter, Y. Organophosphorus Monomers & Polymers.
Gefvert, Constance. The Confident Writer: A Norton Handbook.
Gefvert, Constance, et al. Keys to American English.
Gegan, R. A. & Wunderlick, Ray C. The Over Forty Wellness Diet.
Gehani, Narain. ADA: An Advanced Introduction Including Reference Manual for the Ada Programming Language.
--Ada: Concurrent Programming.
--C: An Advanced Introduction.
Gehlert, Sarah. Curation in the Small Museum: Human Bones.
Gehm, John. Bringing It Home.
Gehm, Katherine. Sarah Winnemucca.
Gehman, Walt & Sumner, Lee E., Jr. Advanced Applesoft Techniques with Sound & Graphics.
Gehmlich, D. K., jt. auth. see Hammond, Seymour B.
Gehring, F. W., ed. see Apostol, T. M.
Gehring, F. W., ed. see Grauert, H. & Fritzsche, K.
Gehring, Robert E. Basic Behavioral Statistics.
Gehring, W. J. Genetic Mosaics & Cell Differentiation.
Gehrke, Ralph D., tr. see Wolff, Hans W.
Geiberger, Al & Dennis, Larry. Tempo: Golf's Master Key: How to Find It, How to Keep It.
Geier, B., jt. auth. see Esslinger, M.
Geierhaas, Franz. M. Tomchuk, Graphic Work.
Geiger, Abraham. Judaism & Its History: In Two Parts. Newburgh, Charles, tr. from Ger.
Geiger, Adolph, jt. auth. see Jackson, Eugene.
Geiger, Gordon H., jt. auth. see Fine, H. Alan.
Geijsberts, L. G., jt. auth. see Gribnau, A. A.
Geimer, Reinhold, jt. ed. see Hildegard.
Geiringer, Karl, ed. see Haydn.
Geis, Darlene. Dinosaurs & Other Prehistoric Animals.
Geis, George. Personal Financial Management with dBASE III.
Geis, George L. & Stebbins, William C. Behavior: Reflexes & Conditioned Reflexes.
Geis, I., jt. auth. see Dickerson, R. E.
Geis, Irving, jt. auth. see Dickerson, Richard E.
Geisendorfer, James V., jt. auth. see Melton, James G.
Geiser, Samuel W. Naturalists of the Frontier.
Geisert, Paul. Genes & Populations.
--Understanding the Microscope.
Geisler, Norman L. Christian Apologetics.
Geisler, Norman L. & Watkins, Williams D. Perspectives: Understanding & Evaluating Today's World Views.
Geismar, Ludwig L. & Geismar, Shirley. Families in an Urban Mold: Policy Implications of an Australian-U.S. Comparison.
Geismar, Maxwell. Mark Twain: An American Prophet.
Geismar, Shirley, jt. auth. see Geismar, Ludwig L.
Geismer, Barbara P. & Suter, Antoinette B. Very Young Verses.
Geiss, Immanuel, ed. July 1914 - the Outbreak of the First World War: Selected Documents.
Geissler, E. A. & Wolff, Lise. Legal Dictionary.
Geissler, Eugene S., compiled by. The Spirit Bible.
Geist, Harold. Bahian Adventure.
--Migraine: Psychological, Psychiatric & Physiological Aspects.
--The Psychological Aspects of the Aging Process: With Sociological Implications.
Geist, Harold & Hawkins, C. F. Adults Going to the Hospital.
Geist, Harry, jt. auth. see Pollock, Morris.
Geist, William. The Zucchini Plague: And Other Tales of Suburbia.
Geiwitz, James, jt. auth. see Schaie, Warner K.
Gelb, Alan. Playgrounds.
Gelb, Arthur, jt. ed. see Rosenthal, A. M.
Gelb, Barbara. So Short a Time.
Gelb, Betsy & Gelb, Gabriel. Marketing Is Everybody's Business.
Gelb, Gabriel, jt. auth. see Gelb, Betsy.
Gelb, Joyce & Palley, Marian L. Women & Public Policies.
Gelb, Norman. The Berlin Wall: Kennedy, Khrushchev & a Showdown in the Heart of Europe.
--Scramble: A Narrative History of the Battle of Britain.
Gelbart, S. S. Weil's Representation & the Spectrum of the Metaplectic Group.
Gelber, Jack. The Connection.
Gelber, Leonard, jt. ed. see Martin, Michael.
Gelberg, Steven, ed. Hare Krishna Hare Krishna: Five Distinguished Scholars in Religion Discuss the Krishna Movement in the West.
Gelbier, S. & Copley. Handbook for Dental Surgical Assistants & Other Ancillary Workers.
Gelbuch, F. & Lopata, P. Developed Socialist Society: Basic Features & Place in History.
Geldenhuys, Norval. The Intimate Life.
Gelderman, Carol. Better Writing for Professionals: A Concise Guide.
Gelderman-Curtis, C. Holland-Inside Information: The Complete Guide to Holland.
Geldof, Bob. Is That It?
Geldzahler, Henry, intro. by. Hans Hartung: Paintings, 1971-1975.
--Jean Arp at the Metropolitan Museum of Art.
Gelenbe, E., ed. see International Symposium on Operating Systems, 1974.
Gelfand. The Jeffersons.
--Paul McCartney.
--Wayne Gretzky.
Gelinas, Paul J. Coping with Anger.
Gelineau, P. Songs in Action.
Gell, Heather. Music, Movement, & the Young Child.
Gell, Paul, commentaries by. Flowers from a Painter's Garden: The Watercolors of Paul Gell. King, Ronald, tr.
Gellar, Sheldon, et al. Animation Rurale & Rural Development: The Experience of Senegal.
Geller, Judith. Inner Space: The Wonder of You.
Geller, Lawrence D. & Gomes, Peter J. The Books of the Pilgrims.
Geller, Louis, jt. auth. see Shim, Jae K.
Geller, Michael. Corpse for a Candidate.
--Red Hot & Dangerous.
--Thoroughbreds.
Geller, Norman. David's Seder.
Geller, Robert E. Plain Talk about Grants: A Basic Handbook.
Geller, Ruth. Triangles: A Novel.
Geller, Sidney B. Care & Handling of Computer Magnetic Storage Media.
Geller, Uri & Playfair, Guy L. The Geller Effect.
Gellert, Alexander G. How to Be Your Own Phone Company.
Gellert, W., et al, eds. VNR Concise Encyclopedia of Mathematics.
Gelles, Richard J. & Cornell, Claire P. International Perspectives on Family Violence.
Gelling, Margaret. Signposts to the Past: Placenames & the History of England.
Gellis, Roberta. Alinor.
--Bond of Blood.
--Fire Song.
--Gilliane.
--Joanna.
--Rhiannon.
--Roselynde.
--Sybelle.
Gellner, Ernest. Saints of the Atlas.
Gelman. Lots of Boys.
Gelman, Jan. Boys! Boys! Boys!
--Faraway Loves.
--Take a Chance on Love.
Gelman, Joan, jt. auth. see Rinzler, Carol E.
Gelman, Mitch. Superbowl Sunday.
Gelman, Rita & Richter, Joan. Professor Coconut & the Thief.
Gelman, Rita G. Hey, Kid!
Gelman, Rita G. & Buxbaum, Susan K. Ouch! All about Cuts & Other Hurts.
Gelman, Rita G. & Friedman, Warner. Uncle Hugh: A Fishing Story.
Gelpi, Albert J. Emily Dickinson: The Mind of the Poet.
Gelpi, Ettore. Lifelong Education & International Relations.
Gelpke, R., ed. & tr. see Nizami.
Gelsinger, Michael, tr. from Gr. see Vaporis, Nomikos M.
Gelso, Charles J. & Johnson, Deborah H. Explorations in Time-Limited Counseling & Therapy.
Geltman, Sydney. Topics in Atomic Collision Theory.
Gemery, H. A. & Hogendorn, J. S., eds. The Uncommon Market: Essays in the Economic History of the Atlantic Slave Trade.
Gemme, Leila. Monarch Notes on Mitchell's Gone with the Wind.
Gemme, Robert & Wheeler, C. C., eds. Progress in Sexology.
Gemming, Elizabeth. The Cranberry Book.
Gems, Pam. Queen Christina.
Genazzani, E. & Herken, H., eds. Central Nervous System, Studies on Metabolic Regulation & Function.
Genders, Roy. Complete Book of Herbs & Herb Growing.
Gendrop, Paul, jt. auth. see Heyden, Doris.
Gendzier, Irene L. Frantz Fanon: A Critical Study.
Gene, Chris. Rapid System Development Using Structured Analysis & Relational Technology.
Geneen, Harold & Moscow, Alvin. Managing.
General Agreement on Tariffs & Trade Staff. Basic Instruments & Selected Documents: 1st Through 24th Supplements. Incl. First; Second; Third; Fourth; Fifth; Sixth; Seventh; Eighth; Ninth; Tenth; Eleventh; Twelfth; Thirteenth; Fourteenth; Fifteenth; Sixteenth; Seventeenth; Eighteenth; Nineteenth; Twentieth; Twenty-First; Twenty-Second; Twenty-Third; Twenty-Fourth; Twenty-Fifth; Twenty-Six; Twenty-Seventh; Twenty-Ninth; Thirtieth. UNIPUB.
--Legal Instruments Embodying the Results of the 1964-1967 Trade Conference.
--Third Certification Relating to Rectifications & Modifications of Schedules.
General Conference, Youth Department Staff. Church Heritage: A Course in Church History.
General Dynamics Staff. A Guide to Radiographic Evaluation of Discontinuities in Aluminum Casting.
General Electric Company Staff. Professional Management in General Electric. Incl. Vol. 1. General Electric's Growth; Vol. 2. General Electric's Organization; Vol. 3. The Work of a Professional Manager; Vol. 4. The Work of a Functional Individual Contributor. Hive Pub.
--Responsibilities of Business Leadership: Talks Presented at the Leadership Conference.
General Mills Staff. Betty Crocker's Kitchen Secrets.
General Topology & Its Relations to Modern Analysis & Algebra Symposium Staff. Proceedings of the General Topology & Its General Relations to Modern Analysis & Algebra Symposium, 2nd, Prague, 1967. Novak, J., ed.
Generalized Cosserat Continuum & the Continuum Theory of Dislocations with Applications Symposium Staff. Mechanics of Generalized Continua: Proceedings of the Generalized Cosserat Continuum & the Continuum Theory of Dislocations with Applications, Freudenstadt & Stuttgart, 1967. Kroener, E., ed.
General Loringhoff, jt. auth. see Von Freytag, Bruno B.
Generoso, Edison C. Two Words into One Word Puzzle.
Generoso, W. M., jt. ed. see Lemontt, J. F.
Genet, Jean. Funeral Rites. Frechtman, Bernard, tr. from Fr.
--Haute Surveillance.
--Miracle of the Rose. Frechtman, Bernard, tr. from Fr.
--Notre-Dame-des-Fleurs.
--Our Lady of the Flowers. Frechtman, Bernard, tr. from Fr.
--Our Lady of the Flowers. Frechtman, Bernard, tr. from Fr.
--Querelle. Hollo, Anselm, tr. from Fr.
--The Screens. Frechtman, Bernard, tr. from Fr.
--The Thief's Journal. Frechtman, Bernard, tr. from Fr.
Genetics of Industrial Mangement Symposium Staff. Genetics of Industrial Management: Proceedings of the Symposium, 2nd. Macdonald, K. D., ed.
Genett, Ann. Contributions of Women: Aviation.
Gengle, Dean & Smith, Steven. Mac Access: Information in Motion.
Genis, Alexandr & Vail, Peter. Sovremennaia Russkaia Proza.
Genkang, Hu, tr. see Mei'E, Ren, et al.
Genn, Robert C. Practical Handbook of Solid State Troubleshooting.
Gennaro, Angelo A. De see De Gennaro, Angelo A.
Gennaro, Angelo de see De Gennaro, Angelo A.
Gennaro, L. & Guzzon, F. Kirlian Photography: Research & Prospects.
Genne, Elizabeth S. & Genne, William H. First of All Persons: A New Look at Men-Women Relationships.
Genne, William H., jt. auth. see Genne, Elizabeth S.
Genovesi, Vincent J. Expectant Creativity: The Action of Hope in Christian Ethics.
Gensemer, Robert E. Movement Education.
Genske, Joseph C. Redirecting Farm Policy to Enable Farmers to Do Without Handouts.
Gent, Peter. The Franchise.
Gentil, Pierre Le see Le Gentil, Pierre.
Gentille, Terry. Printed Textiles: A Guide to Creative Design Fundamentals.
Gentle & Riethmaier. Aviation & Space Dictionary.
Gentle, E. J. & Reithmaier, L. W. Aviation-Space Dictionary.
Gentle, Ernest J., ed. see Aero Staff.
Gentle, Ernest J., ed. see Morgan, Len.
Gentle, Ernest J., ed. see Ronnberg, Erik A., Jr.
Gentle, Lionel. Lady of Pleasure & Death.
Gentle, Mary. A Hawk in Silver.
Gentleman, David, jt. auth. see Langstaff, John.
Gentles, J. C., jt. auth. see Evans, E. G. V.
Gentry, Bobby F. Differentiated Staffing for Urban Schools.
Gentry, Christine A., jt. auth. see Rourke, Margaret V.

Gentry, Curt, jt. auth. see Bugliosi, Vincent.
Gentry, Leo. A Country Teacher Tells It.
Gentry, Matthew, ed. see Hurst, Walter E.
Gentry, Patricia. Kitchen Tools: Cooking with a Twist & a Flair.
Gentz, William H. The World of Philip Potter.
Gentz, William H., ed. Religious Writer's Marketplace: The Definitive Sourcebook.
Genuys, F., ed. Programming Languages.
Geoghegan, Richard, tr. see Veniaminov, Ivan.
Georgano, Nick. World Truck Handbook.
--World Truck Handbook.
George, A. S., jt. auth. see Rosser, C.
George, Alan. Resource Based Learning for School Governors.
George, Alan & Liu, Joseph W. Computer Solution of Large Sparse Positive Definite.
George, Barbara. The Wuzzles' Fair.
George, Charles F. & Renwick, Andrew G. Presystemic Drug Elimination (BIMR Clinical Pharmacology & Therapeutics, Vol. 1)
George, D. V. Principles of Quantum Chemistry.
George, Dan & Hirnschall, Helmut. My Spirit Soars.
George, David B. & Taylor, John C., eds. Copper Smelting - An Update: Proceedings AIME Annual Meeting, Dallas, TX, 1982.
George, David L. Freddie Freightliner Goes to Hawaii. Murphy, Carol, ed.
--Freddie Freightliner Goes to Hollywood. Murphy, Carol, ed.
--Freddie Freightliner Goes to Kennedy Space Center. Murphy, Carol, ed.
--Freddie Freightliner Helps the Fire Department. Murphy, Carol, ed.
--Freddie Freightliner Learns to Talk. Murphy, Carol, ed.
--Freddie Freightliner Series. Murphy, Carol, ed.
--Freddie Freightliner to the Rescue. Murphy, Carol, ed.
George, Denise. Dear Daughter.
George, Donald E. Israeli Occupation: International Law & Political Realities.
George, E. Madison. Which Way, Young Americans.
George, Emily, ed. Martha W. Griffiths.
George, F. H. Automation, Cybernetics, & Society.
--The Brain As a Computer.
--Computer Arithmetic.
--An Introduction to Computer Programming.
--An Introduction to Digital Computing.
George, Frances V. De see Osborne, Richard H. & De George, Frances V.
George, Gail. If You Rub a Wrinkle.
George, Gerald S. Biomechanics of Women's Gymnastics.
George, J. David & George, Jennifer. Marine Life: An Illustrated Encyclopedia of Invertebrates in the Sea.
George, James Z. Political History of Slavery in the United States.
George, Jean C. How to Talk to Your Animals.
George, Jennifer, jt. auth. see George, J. David.
George, Michael. The Statue of Liberty.
George, Nelson. Cool It Now: The Authorized Biography of New Edition.
George, Patricia M., jt. auth. see Schieber, Sylvester J.
George, Robert F., photos by. Velo-News Cyclist's Training Diary.
George, Ronald M. California Superior Court Criminal Trial Judges' Benchbook: 1987 Edition.
--California Superior Court Criminal Trial Judges' Deskbook, 1987.
George, Sara. Acid Drop.
George, Susan & Paige, Nigel. Food for Beginners.
George, Uwe. In the Deserts of This Earth. Winston, Richard & Winston, Clara, trs.
George, Vic & Wilding, Paul. The Impact of Social Policy.
George, W. N., jt. auth. see Willis, Arthur J.
George, Wesley C. The Biology of the Race Problem.
George, William M. A Camel on Wheels.
Georgescu-Roegen, Nicholas. Energy & Economic Myths.
Georgetown Law Journal Association Staff. Crisis in Urban Government.
Georgia Hospitality & Travel Association Staff & Smith, Susan H. Chefs' Secrets from Great Restaurants in Georgia.
Georgia Society. Georgian Society Records.
Georgia Technical Research Institute Staff & Drucker, S. The Industrial Wood Energy Handbook.
Georgiou, Hara & Tzedakis, Y. Excavations at Kastelli, Chania, Greece, 1976.
Georgiou, Vassilios J. A Parallel Pipeline Computer Architecture for Speech Processing. Stone, Harold, ed.
Georgopoulos, N., jt. ed. see Fischer, N.
Geoscience Information Society Guidebooks Committee, ed. Union List of Geologic Field Trip Guidebooks of North America.
Gerace, D. T., ed. see Adams, R. W., et al.
Gerada-Azzopardi, E. Malte, Joyau de la Mediterranee.
Geraghty, Tony. Inside the SAS.
Gerald. Apache Indians. Incl. Aboriginal Use & Occupation of Certain Lands by Tigua, Manso & Suma Indians. Gerald, Rex E; History & Administration of the Tigua Indians of Ysleta Del Sur During the Spanish Colonial Period. Jenkins, Myra E; Apache Ethnohistory: Government, Land & Indian Policies Relative to Lipan, Mescalero & Tigua Indians. Neighbours, Kenneth F. Garland Pub.
Gerald, Rex E; see Gerald.
Geramb, H. von, ed. Microscopic Optical Potentials: Proceedings of the Hamburg Topical Workshop on Nuclear Physics, Univ. of Hamburg, Germany, Sept. 25-27, 1978.
Gerard, Alexander. An Essay of Genius.
Gerard, Karen. American Survivors: Cities & Other Scenes.
Gerard, Max. Dali.
Gerard, Philip. Hatteras Light: A Novel.
Geras, Adele. Apricots at Midnight.
--The Girls in the Velvet Frame.
--Other Echos.
--Voyage.
Gerasimov, I. P., ed. International Geography - 76. Incl. Vol. 1. Geomorphology & Paleography; Vol. 2. Climatology, Hydrology, Glaciology; Vol. 3. Geography of the Ocean; Vol. 4. Biogeography & Soil Geography; Vol. 5. General Physical Geography; Vol. 6. General Economic Geography; Vol. 7. Geography of Population; Vol. 8. Regional Geography; Vol. 9. Historical Geography; Vol. 10. Geographical Education, Geographical Literature & Dissemination of Geographical Knowledge; Vol. 11. General Problems of Geography & Geosystems Modelling; Vol. 12. Additional Volume Including Author Index. Pergamon.
--Man, Society & the Environment.
Gerasimov, Ya., ed. Physical Chemistry.
Geraud, H., ed. see De Nangis, Guillaume.
Geraud-Venzac, ed. see Littre.
Geraway, William R. There's Fifty Thousand Dollars on My Head.
Gerber, Albert B., compiled by. The Book of Sex Lists.
Gerber, Ann. Chicago's Classiest Cuisine.
--Chicago's Sweet Tooth.
Gerber, Barbara L. & Storzer, Gerald H. Dictionary of Modern French Idioms.
Gerber, Georg B. see Altman, Kurt I.
Gerber, H., ed. see International Conference on Equine Infectious Diseases Staff.
Gerber, Irving. Albert Einstein: World Scientist.
--Arturo Toscanini: Genius of Conducting.
--Emma Lazarus: Poet of Liberty.
--Felisa Rincon: Woman of the Americas.
--Joe Dimaggio: the Yankee Clipper.
--Puerto Rico: Long Ago.
--Ramon Betances: Father of the Poor.
--Roberto Clemente: The Pride of Puerto Rico.
Gerber, Merrill J. Lady with the Moving Parts.
--Now Molly Knows.
Gerber, Philip L. Robert Frost.
Gerberg, Mort. The Arbor House Book of Cartooning.
Gerboth, Walter. An Index to Musical Festchriften & Similar Publications.
Gerboth, Walter, et al, eds. Introduction to Music: Selected Readings.
Gerbracht, Carl & Robinson, Frank E. Understanding America's Industries.
Gerdeman, D. A. & Hecht, N. L. Arc Plasma Technology in Materials Science.
Gerdine, Leigh, tr. see Keller, Hermann.
Gergely, J., jt. ed. see Baum, H.
Gergen, Michael J., jt. auth. see Pollack, Kenneth.
Gerger, Dawn. Search-a-Word Shapes.
Gerhardsson, Birger. The Ethos of the Bible. Westerholm, Stephen, tr. from Swedish.
--The Origins of the Gospel Traditions. Lund, Gene J., tr. from Swedish.
Gerhardt, Philipp, et al, eds. Manual of Methods for General Bacteriology.
Gericke, Paul. Minister's Filing System.
Gerig, Donald. Leadership in Crisis.
Gerig, J. T. Introductory Organic Chemistry.
Gerin, William & Johnson, Jim. Test Your Parenting Potential.
Geritz, Albert & Laine, Amos L. John Rastell.
Gerke, Wellman E. Music Man of the West.
Gerlach, Wolfgang & Nirenberg, Helgard. The Genus Fusarium: A Pictorial Atlas.
Gerland, Ernst. Geschichte der Physik Von Den Altesten Zeitem Bis Zum Ausgange Des Achtzehnten Jahrhunderts.
Gerling, Helene A. Intuition Through the Ages.
Gerlings, Charlotte & Ives, Suzy. Noah's Ark in Paper & Card.
Gerlock, Larry & Von Schmidt, Carol. Dining In - Salt Lake City.
Germain, Clarence B. Programming the IBM PC & XT: A Guide to Languages.
Germain, D. Saint. The Theory & the Meaning of the Lines of the Hand with Special Emphasis on the Life & the Anticipation of One's Life Span.
Germain, George L. Effective Coaching & Tipping.
--Effective Job Instruction.
--Effective Safe Behavior Reinforcement.
--Effective Safety Talk Technique.
--Safety Performance Management.
Germain, George L. & Kuhlman, Raymond L. The Effective Series Training Program for Supervisors.
Germain, George L., jt. auth. see Clark, M. Douglas.
Germain, J. E. Catalytic Conversion of Hydrocarbons.
Germain, P. & Nayroles, B., eds. Applications of Methods of Functional Analysis to Problems in Mechanics.
Germain, Regina, intro. by. National Avocational Organizations: 1986.
Germain, Regina, jt. ed. see Colgate, Craig, Jr.
Germaine, Elizabeth, et al, eds. Texas the Beautiful Cookbook.
German American Chamber of Commerce Staff, ed. see Peltzer, Martin & Treumann, Walter.
German American Chamber of Commerce Staff, ed. American Subsidiaries of German Firms 1986.
--American Subsidiaries of German Firms-Tochtergesellschaften Deutscher Unternehmen In U. S. A.
German, Jerry B. Managing an Apartment House Profitably.
--Polluted Nursery Rhymes.
German, Katherine L., jt. auth. see Brookes, Michael C.
German Marshall Fund of the United States Staff, et al. Acid Rain in Europe & North America: National Responses to an International Problem - Final Report.
German, R. M. & Lay, K. W., eds. Processing of Metal & Ceramic Powders: Proceedings. TMS-AIME Fall Meeting, Louisville, 1981.
German Society of Metallurgy Staff, ed. Acoustic Emission: Proceedings of the Symposium, held in Bad Nauheim, West Germany, 1979. Nicoll, A. R., tr.
Germanacos, N. C., tr. see Karapanou, Margarita.
Germar, Herb. Student Journalist & Photojournalism.
Germogenova, O. A., tr. see Pozhela, J.
Germond, Jack see Cantril, Albert H., et al.
Gerner, Ken. The Red Dreams.
Gernes, Sonia. The Way to St. Ives.
Gernsback, Hugo. Ultimate Worlds.
Gernsheim, Helmut. Julia Margaret Cameron: Her Life & Photographic Work.
Gernsheim, Helmut & Fleischmann, Kaspar M. Images: The Photographs of Peter Gasser.
Gero, J. S. & Cowan, H. J. Design of Building Frames.
Gero, John S., ed. Computer Applications in Architecture.
Gerould, Gordon H., ed. Old English & Medieval Literature.
Gerow, Josh R. Psychology: An Introduction.
Gerow, Maurice, jt. auth. see Tanner, Paul.
Gerrard, W. Gas Solubilities.
--Organic Chemistry of Boron.
--Solubility of Gases & Liquids: A Graphic Approach.
Gerras, Charlie, ed. see Rodale Food Center Staff & Hurley, Judith.
Gerrietts, John, jt. auth. see Clayes, Stanley A.
Gerrish, B. A. A Prince of the Church: Schleiermacher & the Beginnings of Modern Theology.
Gerrish, H. H. Electricity.
Gerrish, Howard H. & Dugger, William E., Jr. Electricity & Electronics.
Gerrold, David. The War Against the Chtorr: Vol. 1-A Matter for Men.
Gerrond, Carol B. Heartstorm.
Gerry, Chris, jt. ed. see Bromley, Ray.
Gersbach, Jo. Hold Back the Sunset.
Gersh, Harry, et al. Story of the Jew.
Gersh, Isidore, ed. Submicroscopic Cytochemistry. Incl. Vol. 1. Protein & Nucleic Acids; Vol.2. Membranes,Mitochondria, & Connective Tissue. Acad Pr.
Gershenfeld, Matti K., jt. auth. see Napier, Rodney W.
Gershman, Michael. Baseball Card Engagement Book, 1987.
--The Nineteen Eighty-Eight Baseball Card Engagement Book.
Gershon, Karen. Selected Poems.
Gershon-Cohen, J. Atlas of Mammography.
Gershoy, Leo. From Despotism to Revolution, 1763-1789.
Gershuny, Theodore. Soon to Be a Major Motion Picture.
Gershwin, M. Eric, ed. see International Symposium of the American Society of Zoologists, Toronto, December 27-30, 1977.
Gerson, Cyrelle K. More Than Dispensing.
Gerson, Mary-Joan. Why the Sky Is Far Away.
Gersovitz, Mark, jt. auth. see Eaton, Jonathan.
Gersovitz, Mark, et al, eds. The Theory & Experience of Economic Development: Essays in Honor of Sir W. Arthur Lewis.
Gerstein, Arnold & Reagan, James. Win-Win: Approaches to Conflict Resolution at Home, in Business, Between Groups & Across Cultures.
Gerstein, Dean R., ed. Towards the Prevention of Alcohol Problems: Government, Business, & Community Action.
Gerstein, Dean R., jt. ed. see Levison, Peter K.
Gerstell, Richard. The Steel Trap in North America: The Illustrated Story of Its Design, Production, & Use with Furbearing & Predatory Animals, from Its Colorful Past to the Present Controversy.
Gersten, Rita. Fashion Art for the Fashion Industry.
Gersten, Robert. The Spirit of Ole Brant Lake: Or, up at BLC.
Gerstenfeld, Arthur, ed. Science Policy Perspectives U. S. A.: The U. S. & Japan (Symposium)
Gerster, Patrick, jt. auth. see Cords, Nicholas.
Gerstner, John H. Predestination Primer.
--A Primer on the Atonement.
--A Primer on the Deity of Christ.
--Reconciliation Primer.
Gersuny, Carl. Work Hazards & Industrial Conflict.
Gersuny, Carl, et al. Some Effects of Technological Change on New England Fishermen.
Gerszi, Terez, et al. Leonardo to Van Gogh: Master Drawings from Budapest.
Gertman, Paul M., jt. ed. see Egdahl, Richard H.
Gertsch, W. J., ed. see Comstock, John H.
Gertsch, Willis J. American Spiders.
Gervais, Gilbert. Daily Prayer Poems & Words of Wisdom.
Gervasi, Tom. Arsenal of Democracy II: American Military Power in the 1980s & the Origins of the New Cold War.
Gerver, D. & Sinaiko, H. W., eds. Language Interpretation & Communication.
Gerver, Jane, ed. see Hudson, Eleanor.
Geschwender, Arlyne. Real Estate Principles & Practices: A Contemporary Approach.
Gese, Hartmut. Essays on Biblical Theology. Crim, Keith R., tr.
Gesellschaft Fuer Biologische Chemie, 19th Colloquium, Mossbach-Baden, 1968. Biochemistry of Oxygen: Proceedings. Hess, B. & Straudinger, H., eds.
Gesellschaft Fuer Biologische Chemie, 22nd Colloquium, Mossbach Baden, 1971. The Dynamic Structure of Cell Membranes: Proceedings. Wallach, D. F. & Fischer, H., eds.
Gesellschaft Fuer Biologische Chemie, 20th Colloquium, Mossbach-Baden, 1969. Inhibitors: Tools in Cell Research Proceedings. Buecher, T. & Sies, H., eds.
Gesellschaft Fuer Nephrologie, 5th Symposium, Switzerland, 1967. Progress in Nephrology: Proceedings. Peters, G. & Roch-Ramel, F., eds.
Gesellschaft fur Information und Dokumentation Staff, ed. Dictionary of Reprography: German with Definitions in English, French, & Spanish.
Gesner, G., ed. Anthology of American Poetry.
Gessa, G., jt. ed. see Sandler, M.
Gessaman, James A. Ecological Energetics of Homeotherms.
Gessel, Van C., tr. see Shusaku Endo.
Gessell Institute of Human Development Staff, et al. He Hit Me First: When Brothers & Sisters Fight.
Gest, Alexander P. Engineering.
Gest, Howard, ed. see Symposium, Bloomington Staff.
Geste, Justin. Complete Book of Outrageous & Atrocious Practical Jokes.
Getchell, David R., et al, eds. Mariner's Catalog.
Gethers, Peter, ed. see Simon, Roger L.
Gething, Michael J. NATO Air Power Today.
--Tornado.
Getsinger, John. Luis.
Gettings, Fred. Dictionary of Astrology.
--Dictionary of Occult, Hermetic & Alchemical Sigils.
--The Secret Zodiac: The Hidden Art in Medieval Astrology.
Gettleman, Marvin E., et al, eds. Vietnam & America: A Documented History.
--El Salvador: Central America in the New Cold War.
Gettleman, Marvin E., jt. ed. see Fried, Jonathan L.
Gettys, Joseph M. How to Study Acts.
--Living the Gospel: A Study of One Peter.
Getz, Gene. When You Feel Like a Failure...
Getz, Gene A. Measure of a Man.
Getz, Malcolm, jt. auth. see Watson, Donald S.
Getz-Preziosi, P., tr. see Thimme, Jurgen.
Getz-Preziosi, Pat. Early Cycladic Art in North American Collections.
Geuder, Patricia A. The Color Purple: A Language Perspective.
Geutary, Helene & Casanova, Patrice. Skin Deep.
Gever, Larry N., et al, eds. Drugs.
Gevers, R. H., ed. see Boerhaave Course, Univ of Leiden, Netherlands, 1969.
Gevirtz, Eliezer. Shmittah: What It's All About.

Authors

Gewirth, Alan. Political Philosophy.
Gewirtz, Eliezer & Fruchter, Yaakov. Shemittah: What It's All About.
Gey, H. F., et al. Structure & Chemistry of the Aging Heart.
Geyer, Dick. Wreck Diving: A Guide for Sport Divers.
Geyer, Felix R. & Schweitzer, David, eds. Alienation: Problems of Meaning, Theory, & Method.
Geyer, Georgie A. Buying the Night Flight.
Geyer, Nancy. Frailties.
--The Passion Game.
Geyer, R. F. Alienation Theories: A General Systems Approach.
Geyl, Pieter. Debates with Historians.
Ghabbour, I., jt. ed. see Kassas, M.
Ghadar, Fariborz & Stobaugh, Robert. The Petroleum Industry in Oil-Importing Developing Countries.
Ghai, D. P., et al. The Basic-Needs Approach to Development: Some Issues Regarding Concepts & Methodology.
Ghai, Dharam, ed. see International Labour Office Staff.
Ghali, A. Circular Storage Tanks & Silos.
Ghandhi, Sorab K. Semiconductor Power Devices: Physics of Operation & Fabrication Technology.
Ghandi, Mohandas K; see Gandhi, Mohandas K.
Ghanem, Ali. The Seven-Headed Serpent. Sheridan, Alan, tr.
Ghantus, Elias T. Arab Industrial Integration: A Strategy for Development.
Ghareeb, Edmund, ed. Split Vision: The Portrayal of Arabs in the American Media.
Ghatak, A. K., jt. auth. see Sodha, M. S.
Ghazi, A & Watson, R. T., eds. Intercomparison of Stratospheric-Mesospheric Data: Proceedings of the Topical Meeting of the COSPAR Interdisciplinary Scientific Commission A (Meeting A1) of the COSPAR 25th Plenary Meeting, Graz, Austria, 25 June-7 July 1984.
Ghelderode, Michel De. Theatre.
Gherlach, Luther P. & Hine, Virginia H. People, Power, Change.
Gherman, E. M. Stress & the Bottom Line: A Guide to Personal Well-Being & Corporate Health.
Ghey, G., jt. auth. see Barber, N. F.
Ghezzi, Bert. Facing Your Feelings: How to Get Your Emotions to Work for You.
Ghezzi, Bert & Kinzer, Mark. Emotions As Resources: A Biblical & Pastoral Perspective.
Ghidini, Gustavo. Consumer Legislation in Italy.
Ghiotti, et al. Dictionnaire Italien-Francais, Francais-Italien de la Langue d'Aujourd'hui.
Ghiretti, F., ed. Physiology & Biochemistry of Haemocyanins.
Ghiselin, Brewster. Windrose.
Ghista, D. N. Osteoarthromechanics.
Ghodse, H., jt. auth. see Bucknell, P.
Gholson, Ronald E. & Buser, Robert L. Cocurricular Activity Programs in Secondary Schools.
Ghosal, Amitaval. Some Aspects of Queueing & Storage Systems.
Ghose, T. K. & Fiechter, A., eds. Advances in Biochemical Engineering.
Ghose, Zulfikar. Don Bueno.
Ghosh, B. N. Principles of Economic Science.
Ghosh, S. N., ed. Advances in Cement Technology: Critical Reviews & Case Studies on Manufacturing, Quality Control, Optimization & Use.
Ghosh, Sanjib K. Analytical Photogrammetry.
Ghosh, Shubhra. Female Criminals in India.
Ghosh, Suresh C. Dalhousie in India: 1848-1856.
Giacaglia, G. E. Perturbation Methods in Non-Linear Systems.
Giacomo, James Di see Di Giacomo, James.
Giallombardo, Rose. The Social World of Imprisoned Girls.
--Society of Women: A Study of a Women's Prison.
Giamatti, A. Barlett. The University & the Public Interest.
Giamatti, A. Bartlett. Earthly Paradise & the Renaissance Epic.
Gianakaris, C. J. Foundations of Drama.
Giani, Bertha. Homage to My Father, a Pioneer in Central America.
Gianotti, Charles R. The New Testament & the Mishnah.
Gianotti, J. G., jt. ed. see Griffin, O. M.
Gianturco, Franco A., ed. Atomic & Molecular Collision Theory.
Giarchi, George G. Between McAlpine & Polaris: A Social Inscape Study.
Gibaldi, Joseph & Achtert, Walter S. A Guide to Professional Organizations for Teachers of Language & Literature.
--MLA Handbook for Writers of Research Papers.
--MLA Handbook for Writers of Research Papers, Theses & Dissertations.
Gibaldi, M., jt. ed. see Prescott, L. F.
Gibb, Andrew. Glasgow: The Making of a City.
Gibb, D. M., jt. auth. see Studd, John.
Gibb, H. A., et al see Lewis, B., et al.
Gibb, Jocelyn, ed. Light on C. S. Lewis.
Gibb, John & Montgomery, William. The Confessions of Augustine.
Gibb, Terence C. Principles of Mossbauer Spectroscopy.
Gibbany, Etta M. Star Beams.
Gibbard, Mark. Apprentices in Love.
--Twelve Who Prayed: Twentieth Century Models of Prayer.
Gibbings, J. C. Thermomechanics.
Gibbon, Edward. The Decline & Fall of the Roman Empire. Bourne, Frank C., abridged by.
Gibbon, Monk. Red Shoes Ballet & the Tales of Hoffman. Kupelnick, Bruce S., ed.
Gibboney, Jan D., tr. see Management Sciences for Health Staff, et al.
Gibbons, Bob & Wilson, Peter. Night & Low-light Photography: A Complete Guide.
Gibbons, Brian. Jacobean City Comedy.
Gibbons, Euell & Gibbons, Joe. Feast on a Diabetic Diet.
Gibbons, Faye. Some Glad Morning.
Gibbons, Felton. Dosso & Battista Dossi: Court Painters at Ferrara.
Gibbons, Francis M. John Taylor: Mormon Philosopher, Prophet of God.
Gibbons, Gail. Christmas Time.
--Thanksgiving Day.
--Things to Make & Do for Halloween.
--Tool Book.
--Tunnels.
Gibbons, Jean D., et al. Selecting & Ordering Populations: A New Statistical Methodology.
Gibbons, Joe, jt. auth. see Gibbons, Euell.
Gibbons, John H., intro. by. Displaced Homemakers: Programs & Policies, an Interim Report.
--International Cooperation & Competition in Civilian Space Activities.
Gibbons, John H., illus. Federal Government Information Technology: Electronic Surveillance & Civil Liberties.
Gibbons, John T., intro. by. Status of Biomedical Research & Related Technology for Tropical Diseases.
Gibbons, Maurice. The New Secondary Education: A Phi Delta Kappa Task Force Report.
Gibbons, Reginald. The Ruined Motel.
Gibbons, Reginald, ed. The Poet's Work: Twenty-Nine Masters of Twentieth Century Poetry on the Origins & Practice of Their Art.
--The Writer in Our World: A Triquarterly Symposium.
Gibbons, Robert J., et al. Premium Auditing Applications.
Gibbs, C. R. Black American Inventors.
--Great American Inventors.
Gibbs, Emily, jt. ed. see Swank, Jerold.
Gibbs, Emily A. & Perry, Jim, eds. Forty Computer Games.
--Forty Computer Games from Kilobaud Microcomputing.
--Some of the Best from Kilobaud Microcomputing.
Gibbs, Emily A., ed. see Juge, Ed, et al.
Gibbs, Errol A. & Lindo, Marjorie G. The Dilemma of Our Society: A Proposal for Moral Maturity.
Gibbs, George. Dictionary of the Nisqually Indian Language of Western Washington.
Gibbs, George W. New Zealand Butterflies.
Gibbs, Henry. Background to Bitterness.
--Twilight in South Africa.
Gibbs, Jack P. & Martin, Walter T. Status Integration & Suicide: A Sociological Study.
Gibbs, James. Wole Soyinka.
--Wole Soyinka.
Gibbs, James A. Sentinels of the North Pacific.
Gibbs, John A. Unit Steel Band.
Gibbs, Kenneth G. & Hunt, Gordon. California Construction Law.
Gibbs, M. Christians with Secular Power.
Gibbs, M., ed. Structure & Function of Chloroplasts.
Gibbs, Mark, ed. see Mouw, Richard J.
Gibbs, Ronald K., jt. auth. see Taylor, Paul A.
Gibbs, Ronald S. & Weinstein, Alan J. Antibiotic Therapy in Obstetrics & Gynecology.
Gibbs, Sunny, ed. see Hashagen, Werner R.
Gibbs, Tony. Cruising in a Nutshell: The Art & Science of Enjoyable Coastwise Voyaging in Small Auxiliary Yachts.
Gibert, Creighton E. The Works of Girolamo Savoldo: The 1955 Dissertation, with a Review of Research, 1955-1985. Freedberg, S. J., ed.
Gibert, Stephen P. Planning for the Future: Long-Range Planning for Associations.
Gibian, George, ed. & tr. Russia's Lost Literature of the Absurd: Selected Works of Daniil Kharms & Alexander Vvedensky.
Gibian, George, ed. see Dostoyevsky, Fyodor.
Gibilisco, Stan. Violent Weather: Hurricanes, Tornadoes & Storms.
Gibilisco, Stan, jt. auth. see Turner, Rufus P.
Gibney, Frank. Japan: The Fragile Superpower.
--Japan: The Fragile Superpower.
Gibran, Jean, ed. see Gibran, Kahlil.
Gibran, Kahlil. Dramas of Life: Lazarus & His Beloved & the Blind. Gibran, Jean, ed.
--Mirrors of the Soul. Sheban, Joseph, ed.
--Procession.
--Secrets of the Heart.
--Spirits Rebellious.
--Tears & Laughter.
Gibson, A., ed. Controlled Fusion & Plasma Physics: Invited Papers from the Eleventh European Conference of the European Physical Society Plasma Physics Division, 5-9 September 1983, Aachen, Federal Republic of Germany.
Gibson, A. Barbara, et al. Death Education: A Concern for the Living.
Gibson, A. Boyce. The Religion of Dostoevsky.
Gibson, Arthur C., jt. auth. see Brown, James H.
Gibson, Byron H. Word Power: A Short Guide to Vocabulary & Spelling.
Gibson, C. G. & Wirthmuller, K. Topological Stability of Smooth Mappings.
Gibson, Charles H. & Boyer, Patricia A. Financial Statement Analysis.
Gibson, Charles H. & Frishkoff, Patricia A. Cases in Financial Reporting.
Gibson, Constance B. Policy Alternatives for Mobile Homes.
Gibson, Donna K. Lives & Letters from Kiester House.
Gibson, E. Lawrence. Get off My Ship: Ensign Berg vs. the U. S. Navy.
Gibson, Frank, et al. Real Estate Law.
Gibson, Frank, jt. auth. see Golembiewski, Robert T.
Gibson, G. L., jt. auth. see Cooke, E. M.
Gibson, Gerald D., jt. auth. see Gray, Michael H.
Gibson, Gerald W. Mastering Organic Chemistry: A Problem Solving Approach.
Gibson, Glenn A. & Liu, Yu-Cheng. Microcomputers for Engineers & Scientists.
Gibson, H. B. Hypnosis: Its Nature & Therapeutic Uses.
Gibson, Hannah. Honorable Ancestor.
Gibson, J., jt. auth. see Grainger, L.
Gibson, J. B. Histological Typing of Tumors of the Liver, Biliary Tract & Pancreas.
Gibson, J. E. Thin Shells: Computing & Theory.
Gibson, J. R. Electronic Logic Circuits.
Gibson, J. Sullivan, jt. auth. see Batten, J. W.
Gibson, J. Tyrone. Medication Law & Behavior.
Gibson, James J. The Ecological Approach to Visual Perception.
--The Senses Considered As Perceptual Systems.
Gibson, James L., et al. Organizations: Behavior, Structure, Processes.
--Organizations Closeup: A Book of Readings.
Gibson, James W. & Cornwell, Clifton. Creative Speech Communication.
Gibson, Jane, jt. auth. see Padzensky, Herbert R.
Gibson, John C. Great Western Locomotive Design: A Critical Appreciation.
Gibson, John E. Managing Research & Development.
Gibson, Keiko M. Stir Up the Precipitable World.
Gibson, L., jt. auth. see Alexander, John W.
Gibson, Litzkah R. How to Read Palms. Adelman, Sherri, ed.
Gibson, Margaret & McCann, Richard, eds. Landscape & Distance: Contemporary Poets from Virginia.
Gibson, Rex. Critical Theory & Education.
--Structuralism & Education.
Gibson, Roger F. The Philosophy of W. V. Quine: An Expository Essay.
Gibson, Sandra. Beyond the Body.
Gibson, Sheila, jt. auth. see Jarvis, Peter.
Gibson, Shirley. I Am Watching.
Gibson, Walker, jt. auth. see Kierzek, John M.
Gibson, Walter. The Shadow Scrapbook.
Gibson, Walter S. Hieronymus Bosch: An Annotated Bibliography.
--The Paintings of Cornelis Engebrechtsz.
Gibson, William. American Primitive: John & Abigail.
--Cry of Players.
--Dinny & the Witches: Two Plays. Bd. with The Miracle Worker. Macmillan.
--The Distancers.
--Family Life & Morality: Studies in Black & White.
--Golda.
--Mass for the Dead.
--A Season in Heaven.
Gibson, William & Odets, Clifford. Golden Boy.
Gibson, William M., ed. see Clemens, Samuel L.
Giddens, Anthony. Sociology: A Brief but Critical Introduction.
Giddens, Anthony, ed. Positivism & Sociology.
Gidding, Joshua. The Old Girl.
Giddings, Ruth W. Yaqui Myths & Legends.
Giddins, Gary. Celebrating Bird: The Triumph of Charlie Parker.
Gide, Andre. Amyntas.
--Autumn Leaves.
--Cahiers.
--Caves Du Vatican.
--Dostoievesky.
--L' Ecole des Femmes: Avec Robert, Genevieve, le Promethee Mal Enchaine.
--Faux-Monnayeurs: Rompin.
--Immoraliste.
--Journal Nineteen Forty-Two to Nineteen Forty-Nine.
--Journal, Nineteen Thirty-Nine to Nineteen Forty-Two.
--Notes on Chopin.
--Paludes.
--Porte Etroite.
--Retouches a mon Retour de l'U.R.S.S.
--Le Retour du Tchad.
--Return from the U. S. S. R. & Afterthoughts on My Return. Howard, Richard, tr. from Fr.
--Saul.
--La Sequestree de Poitiers.
--Si le Gran ne Meurt: Memoires.
--Symphonie Pastorale: Roman.
--Urien's Voyage. Baskin, Wade, tr.
--White Notebook.
Gidley, J. A., jt. auth. see Elwell, W. T.
Gidley, M. With One Sky above Us: Life on an American Indian Reservation at the Turn of the Century.
Gidley, Mick, ed. The Vanishing Race: Selections from Edward S. Curtis' the North American Indian.
Gidwani, N. W., jt. auth. see Roy, Ashim K.
Giebink, Gerald A., ed. see U. S. Department of the Interior, Federal Water Pollution Control Administration, Committtee on Water Quality Criteria, et al.
Gieck, Kurt. Engineering Formulas.
Gielgud, John. Stage Directions.
Giersch, Herber. The International Debt Problem: Lessons for the Future.
Gies, Miep & Gold, Alison L. Anne Frank Remembered: The Story of Miep Gies, Who Helped to Hide the Frank Family.
Giese, Arthur C. & Pearse, John S., eds. Reproduction of Marine Invertebrates: Acoelomate & Pseudocoelomate Metazoans.
Giese, Frank S. & Wilder, Warren F. French Lyric Poetry: An Anthology.
Giese, Geneva. Camping in Covenant Community.
Gieseking, Audrey, jt. auth. see Joseph, Marjory.
Gieseking, J. E., ed. Soil Components, Vol. One: Organic Components.
--Soil Components, Vol. Two: Inorganic Components.
Giesen, Rosemary, jt. auth. see Thompson, Brenda.
Gieson, Susan Van see Van Gieson, Susan & Kurtz, Regina.
Giet, A. Abacs or Nomograms.
Giffen, Robert. Economic Inquiries & Studies.
Giffin, Paul A. Seasons Come Spring.
Gifford, Barry. Landscape with Traveler: The Pillow Book of Francis Reeves.
Gifford, Courtney D. Directory of U. S. Labor Organizations, 1986-87.
Gifford, Denis. The British Film Catalogue, 1895-1970: A Guide to Entertainment Films.
Gifford, Derek. A Handbook of Physics for Radiologists & Radiographers.
Gifford, Ernest M., jt. ed. see Rost, Thomas L.
Gifford, Frank D. The Christian Way: A Book of Instructions & Devotions for Members of the Episcopal Church.
Gifford, R. W., jt. auth. see Manger, W. M.
Gifford, Terry & Roberts, Neil. Ted Hughes: A Critical Study.
Gifford, Terry, jt. auth. see Roberts, Neil.
Gifford, William C. & Owens, Elisabeth A. International Aspects of U. S. Income Taxation: Cases & Materials.
Gifis, Steven H. Law Dictionary.
Gigihara, Y., jt. ed. see Yoshida, H.
Giglierano, Geoffrey J., et al. The Bicentennial Guide to Greater Cincinnati: A Portrait of Two Hundred Years.
Gihman, I. I. & Skorohod, A. V. The Theory of Stochastic Processes I.
Gihman, L. I. & Skorohod, A. V. The Theory of Stochastic Processes II.
Gikow, Louise. Animal Go Bye-Bye.
--Labyrinth: A Storybook Based on the Movie.
--The Legend of the Doozer Who Didn't.
--Meet the Muppet Babies.
--Sprocket's Christmas Tale.
--Wembley & the Soggy Map.
--Wembley Fraggle & the Magic Stone.
--What's A Fraggle?
Gilbar, Anne. The Lunch Box Book.
Gilbar, Steven. Good Books: A Book Lover's Companion.
Gilberg, Laura S., jt. auth. see Buchholtz, Barbara.
Gilbert, A., jt. auth. see Bryce-Smith, D.
Gilbert, Allan H. On the Composition of Paradise Lost.
Gilbert, Anna. The Long Shadow.
Gilbert, Arthur N., ed. In Search of a Meaningful Past.
Gilbert, B., ed. see Masterman, C. F.
Gilbert, Bil. Westering Man: The Life of Joseph Walker.
Gilbert, Bill, jt. auth. see Wootten, Morgan.
Gilbert, Bob & Theroux, Gary. The Top Ten: Nineteen Fifty-Six to Present.

Gilbert, C. Italian Art: Fourteen Hundred to Fifteen Hundred.
Gilbert, C. Hampton. Here Lies Duffy Baker.
Gilbert, Carolyn A. Communicative Performance of Literature.
Gilbert, Charles, jt. auth. see Krooss, Herman E.
Gilbert, Chris & Williams, Laurie. The ABC's of 1-2-3.
Gilbert, Christopher. Life & Work of Thomas Chippendale. Beard, Geoffrey, ed.
Gilbert, Colleen B. A Bibliography of the Works of Dorothy L. Sayers.
Gilbert, Dennis & Kahl, Joseph A. American Class Structure: A New Synthesis.
Gilbert, Edmund W. Exploration of Western America, Eighteen Hundred to Eighteen Fifty.
Gilbert, Edwin. A Season in Monte Carlo.
Gilbert, Everett E. Sulfonation & Related Reactions.
Gilbert, Felix, ed. Historical Studies Today.
--Norton History of Modern Europe.
Gilbert, Felix, jt. ed. see Craig, Gordon A.
Gilbert, Felix, ed. see Robertson, William.
Gilbert, Glenn. If Television Didn't Have Censorship.
Gilbert, Harold L., ed. A Manual for Classroom Teachers: How to Recognize & Help Children with Mental & Emotional Disorders.
Gilbert, Herman C. The Negotiations: A Novel of Tomorrow.
Gilbert, James B. Another Chance: Post War America, 1945-1985.
Gilbert, Jimmie, jt. auth. see Gilbert, Linda.
Gilbert, Jimmie, et al. College Algebra.
Gilbert, John. Aiki.
Gilbert, John, intro. by. Complete Works of Oscar Wilde.
Gilbert, John T. Documents Relating to Ireland, 1795-1804.
--A Jacobite Narrative of the War in Ireland, 1688-1691.
Gilbert, Katherine E. & Kunn, Helmut. A History of Esthetics.
Gilbert, Kenneth. Alaskan Poker Stories.
Gilbert, Kent S., jt. auth. see Watabe, Masakazu.
Gilbert, Kevin. People Are Legends.
Gilbert, Linda & Gilbert, Jimmie. College Algebra & Trigonometry.
--College Trigonometry.
--Intermediate Algebra.
Gilbert, Lucy & Webster, Paula. Bound by Love: The Sweet Trap of Daughterhood.
Gilbert, Marilyn B. Clear Writing: A Business Guide.
Gilbert, Martin. Auschwitz & the Allies.
--The Holocaust: A History of the Jews of Europe During the Second World War.
--Winston S. Churchill: Companion Vol. III.
--Winston S. Churchill: Companion Vol. V, Part One, The Exchequer Years 1922-1929.
--Winston S. Churchill: Finest Hour, Nineteen Thirty-Nine to Nineteen Forty-One.
--Winston S. Churchill: Vol. V: Pt. 3, The Coming of War 1936-1939.
--Winston S. Churchill, 1916-1922.
Gilbert, Michael. Death Has Deep Roots.
--Inner Landscape.
Gilbert, Michael A. How to Win an Argument.
Gilbert, Miriam. Science-Hobby Book of Shell Collecting.
Gilbert, Nan. The Strange New World Across the Street.
Gilbert, Norma. Statistics.
Gilbert, O. E., jt. auth. see Roeder, D.
Gilbert, R. A. The Golden Dawn: Twilight of the Magicians.
--The Magical Mason.
Gilbert, R. J., jt. ed. see Baillie, A.
Gilbert, R. M. & Sutherland, N. S., eds. Animal Discrimination Learning.
Gilbert, R. P. Constructive Methods for Elliptic Equations.
Gilbert, Rita, jt. auth. see McCarter, William.
Gilbert, Rita K., jt. auth. see Kurzman, Robert G.
Gilbert, Sara. By Yourself.
--What Happens in Therapy.
Gilbert, Scott F. Developmental Biology.
Gilbert, Stuart see Joyce, James.
Gilbert, Stuart, tr. see Malraux, Andre.
Gilbert, Stuart, tr. see Simenon, Georges.
Gilbert, W. Kent, ed. Confirmation & Education.
Gilbert, William E. Great Inns of America.
Gilbertson, Merrill T. Uncovering Bible Times.
--Way It Was in Bible Times.
Gilboa, Amir. Light of Lost Suns. Kaufman, Shirley, tr. from Hebrew.
Gilboy, Robert C. Spell It Fast! The Quick Way to Spell 25,000 Easily Misspelled Words Using Sixty Stimulating Word Lists.
Gilbreath, Glenn H., jt. auth. see Van Matre, Joseph G.
Gilbreth, Frank B., Jr. & Carey, Ernestine G. Cheaper by the Dozen.
Gilbreth, Terry, jt. auth. see Saffell, David C.
Gilchrist, Alexander. The Life of William Blake. Todd, Ruthven, ed.
Gilchrist, Andrew. Russian Professor.
--The Watercress File.
Gilchrist, Cherry. People at Work: Nineteen Thirty to the Nineteen Eighty's.
Gilchrist, Francis G. Survey of Embryology.
Gilchrist, J. D. Fuel, Furnaces & Refractories.
Gilchrist, Jack. Hidden Profits in Stamping: A Creative Materials Management Guide.
Gilchrist, Joelyn S., jt. auth. see Wood, Jacqueline.
Gilder, Eric. The Dictionary of Composers & Their Music.
Gilder, George. The Spirit of Enterprise.
--Wealth & Poverty.
Gilder, Jamison, ed. Modernizing State Policies: Community Colleges & Lifelong Education.
--Policies for Lifelong Education.
Gilder, Jules H. BASIC Computer Programs in Science & Engineering.
Gilder, Rodman. Statue of Liberty Enlightening the World.
Gilder, Stanley S., tr. see Wrage, Karl H.
Gildersleeve, B. L., ed. see Pindar.
Gildon, Charles. The Deist's Manual; or a Rational Enquiry into the Christian Religion. Wellek, Rene, ed.
--The Plays of Charles Gildon. Backscheider, Paula R., ed.
Gildroy, Ann, ed. see Davis, Adelle.
Gilead, Zerubavel & Krook, Dorothea. Gideon's Spring: A Man & His Kibbutz.
Gileadi, Avraham, ed. Israel's Apostasy & Restoration in Prophetic Thought: Essays in Honor of Roland Kenneth Harrison.
Giles, Barbara, jt. auth. see Giles, Carl.
Giles, Carl & Giles, Barbara. Buyer's Guide to Component TV.
Giles, David, jt. ed. see King, Maxwell.
Giles, Floyd. Landscape Construction Procedures, Techniques & Design.
Giles, Floyd A., jt. auth. see Keith, Rebecca M.
Giles, Gordon, et al. Killer Plants & Other Stories. Elwood, Roger, ed.
Giles, H., ed. Language, Ethnicity & Intergroup Relations.
Giles, H. A., tr. see Fa-hsien, Fl.
Giles, Harry. Education & Human Motivation.
Giles, Janice H. Enduring Hills.
--The Enduring Hills.
--Forty Acres & No Mule.
--Johnny Osage.
--Kentuckians.
--The Kinta Years.
--Tara's Healing.
--Wellspring.
Giles, M. A., tr. see Fa-hsien, Fl.
Gilfond, Henry. Journey Without End.
Gilgen, A., jt. auth. see Grandjean, E.
Gilhooly, K. J. Thinking: Directed, Undirected & Creative.
Gili Gaya, S. D. Diccionario de Sinonimos.
Gilioli, R., et al, eds. Neurobehavioral Methods in Occupational Health: Proceedings of an International Symposium on Neurobehavioral Methods in Occupational Health (State of Art & Emerging Trends) Como & Milan, Italy June 1982.
Gilkerson, Seth. Fingerprints & Other Stories.
Gilkerson, William. Maritime Arts by William Gilkerson.
Gill, Anton. Mad about the Boy: The Life & Times of Boy George & Culture Club.
Gill, Arthur. Applied Algebra for the Computer Sciences.
Gill, B. M. Death Drop.
--Nursery Crimes.
--Seminar for Murder.
--The Twelfth Juror.
--Twelfth Juror.
Gill, Bartholomew. McGarr & the Sienese Conspiracy.
Gill, Bob. Forget All the Rules about Graphic Design: Including the Ones in This Book.
Gill, Brendan. Lindbergh Alone.
--Ways of Loving.
--Ways of Loving.
Gill, Brendan, ed. States of Grace: Eight Plays.
Gill, Crispin. Dartmoor: A New Study.
--Plymouth: A New History. Incl. Vol. 1. Ice Age of Elizabethans; Vol. 2. Sixteen Hundred & Three to Present Day. David & Charles.
Gill, Dan & Merriam, Daniel F. Geomathematical & Petrophysical Studies in Sedimentology, an International Symposium: Proceedings of Papers Presented at Sessions Sponsored by the International Association for Mathematical Geology at the Tenth International Congress on Sedimentology in Jerusalem, July 1979.
Gill, Derek, jt. auth. see Graham, Robin.
Gill, Dominic, ed. The Book of the Violin.
Gill, Douglas R., et al. Law of Arrest, Search, & Investigation.
Gill, F. W. & Bates, G. L. Airline Competition: A Study of the Effects of Competition on the Quality & Price of Airline Service & the Self-Sufficiency of the United States Domestic Airlines.
Gill, Jean. Images of My Self: Meditation & Self-Exploration Through the Imagery of the Gospels.
Gill, Jerry H. Toward Theology.
Gill, Kathleen D., jt. ed. see Harris, Anthony A.
Gill, Kay, ed. Business Organizations, Agencies & Publications Directory.
Gill, Kay & Boyden, Donald P., eds. Gale Directory of Publications Update, 1988.
--Gale Directory of Publications Update 1989.
--Gale Directory of Publications, 1988.
Gill, Kay & Tufts, Susan E., eds. Government Research Directory.
--Government Research Directory: Supplement.
Gill, M. S. Himalayan Wonderland: Travels in Lahaul-Spiti.
Gill, Manohar S. Agriculture Cooperatives: A Case Study of Punjab.
Gill, R. D. Gamma-Ray Angular Correlations.
Gill, Richard T. Economics & the Private Interest: An Introduction to Microeconomics.
Gill, Robert. VNR Manual of Rendering with Pen & Ink.
Gill, Roger, jt. ed. see Alexander, Peter.
Gill, Rowland P., ed. see Lawrence, Ken.
Gill, Rowland P., ed. see Sandifer, Kevin W.
Gill, S. S. The Stress Analysis of Pressure Vessels & Pressure Vessel Components.
Gill, T. P. The Doppler Effect: An Introduction to the Theory of the Effect.
Gill, Wendy, tr. see European Syndicate of Soccer Experts Staff.
Gillan, Patricia & Gillan, Richard. Sex Therapy Today.
Gillan, Richard, jt. auth. see Gillan, Patricia.
Gillelan, G. Howard. The Complete Book of the Bow & Arrow.
Gillen, Bob, jt. auth. see Lund, Morten.
Gillen, Bob, jt. ed. see Barlett, Michael.
Giller, Norman. L. A. Eighty-Four.
--The Nineteen Eighty-Four Olympic Handbook.
--The Olympics Handbook, 1984.
Gillers, Stephen, ed. Looking at Law School: A Student Guide from the Society of American Law Teachers.
Gilles, Anthony E. People of Hope: The Story Behind the Modern Church.
Gilles, H. M., jt. auth. see James, D. M.
Gillespie, A., ed. Technological Change & Regional Development.
Gillespie, Alan R., jt. auth. see Siegal, Barry S.
Gillespie, Bryan. Independent Study & Research in Literature.
Gillespie, James. Modern Livestock & Poultry Production.
Gillespie, James H. & Timoney, John F. Hagan & Bruner's Infectious Diseases of Domestic Animals.
Gillespie, Jane. Ladysmead.
Gillespie, Karen R. Creative Supervision.
Gillespie, Neal C. Charles Darwin & the Problems of Creation.
Gillespie, Robert. Daily Crosswords.
Gillespie, Robert H., et al. Adhesives in Building Constrution.
Gillespie, Sheena, et al. The Writer's Craft: A Process Reader.
Gillespie, W. A., jt. auth. see Slade, N.
Gillet, Jean W., jt. auth. see Temple, Charles.
Gillett, Billy E. Methods of Operations Research.
Gillett, Margaret. Dear Grace: A Romance of History.
--We Walked Very Warily: A History of Women at McGill.
Gillett, Mary. Bugles at the Border.
Gillett, Philip. Calculus & Analytic Geometry.
Gillett, Philip W. Introduction to Linear Algebra.
Gillette, J. Michael. Designing with Light: An Introduction to Stage Lighting.
Gillette, Michael. The Cortes Letter.
Gillette, Ned & Dostal, John. Cross-Country Skiing.
Gillette, Paul. Carmela.
--One of the Crowd.
--Three Hundred Five East.
Gilley, Sheridan, jt. ed. see Swift, Roger.
Gillham, Bill. What Can You Do?
Gillham, Bill & Hulme, Susan. Let's Look for Colors.
Gillham, Bill, ed. Handicapping Conditions in Children.
--Problem Behaviour in the Secondary School: A Systems Approach.
--Reconstructing Educational Psychology.
Gilli, Angelo C., Sr. Electrical Principles for Electronics.
Gilliam, Olive K. Living Through the Twentieth Century.
--Qumran & History: The Place of the Teachers in Religion.
--Witness the Power of Woman.
Gilliam, Terry & Cowel, Lucinda. Animations of Mortality.
Gilliatt, Mary. Mary Gilliatt's Mix-&-Match Decorating Book.
Gilliatt, Penelope. Jean Renoir: Essays, Conversations, Reviews.
--Mortal Matters.
Gillies, Emily. Creative Dramatics for All Children. Markun, Patricia M. & Cohen, Monroe D., eds.
Gillies, John, jt. auth. see Price, Walter K.
Gillig, Harry. Gillig's Guide to Turning Unprofitable Real Estate into Moneymakers.
Gillig, Harry S. Real Estate Investment for High Yield & Profit.
Gilligan, Lawrence & Nenno, Robert B. Finite Mathematics: An Elementary Approach.
Gilligan, William J. Our Lady & Vatican II.
Gilliham, Dorothy. Tell Us the Reason Why.
Gilliland, H. Indian Children's Books.
Gilliland, Jean. The Fourteen Day Conspiracy.
Gillin, Donald G. Warlord: Yen Hsi-Shan in Shansi Province, 1911-1949.
Gillingham, F. J., et al, eds. Stereotactic Treatment of Epilepsy.
Gillingham, John & Holt, J. C., eds. War & Government in the Middle Ages: Essays in Honour of J. O. Prestwich.
Gillis, Dan. Crazy Pete.
Gillis, Daniel. Alone.
--Vita.
Gillis, Jack, ed. see Hoffman, Naphtali & Brobreck, Stephen.
Gillis, James C., jt. auth. see Wood, David E.
Gillis, John R. The Development of European Society: 1770-1870.
Gillis, M. Arthur. Microcomputers in Financial Institutions.
Gillis, Malcolm, et al. Economics of Development.
Gillis, Phyllis. Entrepreneurial Mothers.
Gillis, William, ed. see Durrenmatt, Friedrich.
Gillman, Leni, jt. auth. see Gillman, Peter.
Gillman, Leonard & McDowell, Robert. Calculus.
Gillman, Peter & Gillman, Leni. Alias David Bowie.
Gillman, Peter & Peniston, Silvina. Library Automation: A Current Review.
Gillmor, Frances & Wetherill, Louisa W. Traders to the Navajos: The Story of the Wetherills of Kayenta.
Gillon, Edmund V. Art Nouveau: An Anthology of Design & Illustration from the Studio.
Gillon, Edmund V., Jr. Pennsylvania Dutch Farm: To Cut Out & Assemble.
--South Street: A Photographic Guide to New York City's Historic Seaport.
Gillooly, Maryanne. Making Baskets.
Gillott, Edward, tr. see Pouillon, Fernand.
Gillsater, Pia, jt. auth. see Gillsater, Sven.
Gillsater, Sven & Gillsater, Pia. Pia's Journey to the Holy Land. MacMillan, Annabelle, tr.
Gillum, Gary P., compiled by. Of All Things! A Nibley Quote Book.
Gilly, Adolfo. Inside the Cuban Revolution. Gutierrez, Felix, tr.
Gilman, jt. auth. see Sutherland, Robert F.
Gilman, Charlotte P. Women & Economics: A Study of the Economic Relation Between Men & Women As a Factor in Social Evolution. Degler, Carl N., ed.
Gilman, Dorothy. Mrs. Pollifax on Safari.
--Mrs. Pollifax on the China Station.
--The Tightrope Walker.
Gilman, Stephen. The Art of La Celestina.
Gilmartin, Kevin J., et al. Social Indicators: An Annotated Bibliography of Current Literature.
Gilmer, B. V. Applied Psychology: Adjustments in Living & Work.
Gilmer, B. V. & Deci, Edward L. Industrial & Organizational Psychology.
Gilmore, Charles M. Beginner's Guide to Microprocessors.
Gilmore, Christopher C. The Bad Room.
Gilmore, D. E., ed. see Feirer, John L.
Gilmore, Ellen M., jt. auth. see Massachusetts Parole Board Staff.
Gilmore, H. B. Ask Me If I Care.
Gilmore, H. William, et al. Operative Dentistry.
Gilmore, Hobe. Bloody Grass.
Gilmore, James R. Down in Tennessee, Back by Way of Richmond.
Gilmore, Joseph. Blue Flame.
Gilmore, Robert. Catastrophe Theory for Scientists & Engineers.
Gilmour, H. B. Why Wembley Fraggle Couldn't Sleep.
Gilmour, J. S., ed. Thomas Johnson Botanical Journeys in Kent & Hampstead.
Gilmour, John S., tr. see Tournier, Paul.
Gilmour, Pat. Artists in Print: An Introduction to Prints & Printmaking.
--Ken Tyler-Master Printer-& the American Print Renaissance.
Gilmour, Peter. Praying Together.
Gilmour, Peter & Lansbury, Russell D. Marginal Manager: The Changing Role of Supervisors in Australia.
Gilmour, R. Business Systems Handbook: Analysis, Designs & Documentation Standards.
Gilmour, R., jt. ed. see Duck, S.
Gilot, Francoise. Interface: The Painter & the Mask.
Gilpatrick, Lottie, et al, trs. see Twitchell, Paul.
Gilpin. Dictionary of Fuel Technology.
Gilpin, Alan. Environmental Policy in Australia.
Gilpin, Alan & Hartmann, Hanns. Air Pollution & Energy in Australia: Economic & Policy Implications.
Gilpin, D. C., ed. see Anthony, E. J.
Gilpin, Richard O. Moses - Born to Be a Slave, but God...

Authors

Gilreath, Esmarch S. Experimental Procedures in Elementary Qualitative Analysis.
Gilreath, James & Carter, Elizabeth, eds. Federal Copyright Records, Seventeen Ninety to Eighteen Hundred.
Gil-Robles, Jose M. Diccionario de Terminos Electrorales y Parlamentarios.
Gilroy, John, jt. auth. see Holt, Ted.
Gilson, Etienne. The Unity of Philosophical Experience.
Gilson, Etienne H. The Arts of the Beautiful.
Gilstrap, Marie, jt. auth. see Nester, Eugene.
Gimbel, Mary, jt. ed. see Cott, Jonathan.
Gimeno, Jose B. & Ibanez, M. The Education of Primary & Secondary School Teachers.
Gimmestad, Beverly B., jt. auth. see Donovan, George S.
Gimpel, Scott E., jt. auth. see Tondo, Clovis L.
Gin, Maggie. One-Pot Meals.
Gin, Margaret. One-Pot Meals.
--Tomatoes.
Gin, Margaret & Castle, Alfred. Regional Cooking of China.
Gin, Margaret, jt. auth. see Allen, Jana.
Gin, Margaret, jt. auth. see Castle, Coralie.
Ginalski, William, jt. auth. see DeBands, Henward M.
Ginders, James A. A Guide to Napkin Folding.
Ginestet, Bernard. The Great Wines of France: Margaux.
--The Great Wines of France: Saint-Julien.
Ginever, C. A., tr. see Riedl, Frederick.
Ginger, Ann F., jt. auth. see Meiklejohn Civil Liberties Institute Staff.
Gingold, Alfred. Items from Our Catalog.
--More Items from Our Catalog.
--Water in the Basement.
Gingold, Alfred, jt. auth. see Buskin, John.
Gingold, Diane J., jt. auth. see Montgomery Museum of Fine Arts Staff.
Gingold, Diane J., ed. Anne Goldthwaite: Eighteen Sixty-Nine to Nineteen Forty-Four.
--Corporate Collections in Montgomery.
--Master Prints from the Fifteenth Through Eighteenth Centuries.
Gingold, Diane J., ed. see Montgomery Museum of Fine Arts Staff.
Giniger, K. S., ed. Pilgrim of Faith: Words of Inspiration from Pope John Paul II.
Ginn, Helen L., jt. auth. see Kammeyer, Kenneth C.
Ginn, Robert J., Jr. The College Graduate's Career Guide.
Ginneken, J. K. van see Van Ginneken, J. K. & Muller, A. S.
Ginneken, Jaap Van see Van Ginneken, Jaap.
Ginneken, Wouter van see Van Ginneken, Wouter & Garzuel, Michel.
Gino, Carol. The Nurse's Story.
Gins, Madeline H., jt. auth. see Arakawa.
Ginsberg, Allen. Journals: Early Fifties Early Sixties. Ball, Gordon, ed. & intro. by.
--Mostly Sitting Haiku.
Ginsberg, Irving W. Fundamentals of Electro-Optical Remote Sensing.
Ginsberg, Leon H., jt. ed. see Keys, Paul R.
Ginsberg, Matthew & Singh, Narinder. Artificial Intelligence Applications in Hardware Diagnosis.
Ginsberg, Ralph B., jt. ed. see Rejda, George E.
Ginsberg, Ralph B., jt. ed. see Roof, Wade C.
Ginsburg. Cases & Materials on Equal Employment.
--Cases & Materials on Federal Labor Standards.
Ginsburg, David. Propellanes: Structure & Reactions.
Ginsburg, Douglas H. & Director, Mark D. Regulation of Broadcasting: 1983 Supplement.
Ginsburg, Madeleine, intro. by. An Age of Elegance.
Ginsburg, Mirra. How the Sun Was Brought Back to the Sky: Adapted from a Slovenian Folk Tale.
Ginsburg, Mirra, tr. see Bulgakov, Mikhail.
Ginsburg, R. N., jt. auth. see James, N. P.
Ginsburg, R. N., ed. Tidal Deposits: A Case Book of Recent Examples & Fossil Counterparts.
Ginter, Joe. I Wanted to Be Famous.
Ginther, K. & Benedek, W., eds. New Perspectives & Conceptions of International Law: An Afro-American Dialogue.
Ginzberg, Eli & Yohalem, Alice M. Educated American Women: Life-Styles & Self-Portraits.
Ginzberg, Eli, ed. The U. S. Health Care System: A Look to the 1990's.
Ginzberg, Eli, et al. The Negro Potential.
Ginzberg, Louis. Of Jewish Law & Lore.
Ginzburg, Eugenia S. Within the Whirlwind. Boland, Ian, tr.
Ginzburg, L. R. Natural Selection.
Ginzburg, Natalia. No Way.
--No Way. Cudahy, Sheila, tr.
Ginzburg, V. L. Propagation of Electromagnetic Waves in Plasmas.
Ginzburg, V. L. & Lebedev, P. N. Waynflete Lectures on Physics: Selected Topics in Contemporary Physics & Astrophysics. Haar, D. ter, tr.
Ginzburg, V. L., ed. Nonequilibrium Superconductivity.
Giok Po Oey. Checklist of Vietnamese Holdings of the Wason Collection, Cornell University Libraries, As of June 1971.
Giolas, Thomas G. & Randolph, Kenneth. Basic Audiometry: Including Impedance Measurement.
Giolas, Thomas G., jt. auth. see Ross, Mark.
Gionet, Albert. Middle Caraquet: The Lean Years.
Giono, Jean. Accompagnes de la Flute.
--Ames Fortes.
--Chant Du Monde: Roman.
--Le Cheval Fou.
--La Chute des Anges, un Deluge le Coeur Chef.
--Colline.
--Colline.
--Colline: Roman.
--Un De Baumugne.
--Un De Baumugnes: Livre des Conduite du Metteur en Scene (Indications et Dialogues)
--Le Deserteur et Autres Recits.
--Deux Cavaliers de l'Orage.
--L' Eau Vive: Rondeurs des Jours.
--Ennemonde et Autres Caracteres: Roman.
--Le Grand Troupeau.
--Grands Chemins.
--Une Histoire D'Amour.
--Le Hussard sur le Toit: Roman.
--L' Iris de Suse: Roman.
--La Mission.
--Le Poids du Ciel.
--Precisions.
--Provence.
--Que Ma Joie Demeure.
--Recherche de la Purete.
--Recits de la Demi-brigade.
--Regain: Roman.
--Triomphe de la Vie.
--Yves Brayer.
Giono, Jean, et al. Rome.
--Oeuvres Romanesques Completes.
Giordano, Frank. Texas Wines & Wineries. Lubeck, Scott, ed.
Giordano, Gerard. Teaching Writing to Learning Disabled Students.
Giordano, Joseph. Italian-American Catalog.
Giorgi, A., ed. Journal of Phenomenological Psychology.
--Journal of Phenomenological Psychology.
--Journal of Phenomenological Psychology: Fall 1980.
--Journal of Phenomenological Psychology: Fall 1977.
--Journal of Phenomenological Psychology, Fall, 1985.
--Journal of Phenomenological Psychology: Spring 1978.
--Journal of Phenomenological Psychology, Spring, 1985.
Giorgi, A., et al, eds. Journal of Phenomenological Psychology: Studies in the Science of Human Experience & Behavior.
Giorgi, T. A. & Della Porta, P., eds. Residual Gases in Electron Tubes: Proceedings.
Giovanni, Nikki. Black Feeling, Black Talk-Black Judgement.
Giovannoni, Jeanne M., jt. auth. see Billingsley, Andrew.
Gipe, George. Gremlins.
Giraldi, Cinthio. Giraldi Cinthio on Romances. Snuggs, Henry L., tr.
Girard, Joe. How to Sell Yourself.
Girard, Joe & Brown, Stanley H. How to Sell Anything to Anybody.
Girard, Linda W. Earth, Sea & Sky: The Work of Edmond Halley.
Girard, Rene, ed. Proust: A Collection of Critical Essays.
Girard, Weldon. How to Make Big Money Selling Commercial & Industrial Property.
Girardot, R. G., et al, eds. New Directions In International Law: Essays in Honour of Wolfgang Abendroth.
Giraud, Marcel. The Metis in the Canadian West. Woodcock, George, tr.
Giraudoux, Jean. Carnet des Dardanelles.
--La Francaise et la France.
Girault, Maurice. Stochastic Processes.
Girault, V. & Raviart, P. A. Finite Element Approximation of the Navier-Stokes Equations.
Girdler, Allan. Customizing Your Van. Caiati, Carl, rev. by.
Girgensohn, Herbert. Teaching Luther's Catechism. Doberstein, John W., tr. from Ger.
Giri, V. V. My Life & Times.
Girion, Barbara. A Handful of Stars.
--Joshua, the Czar, & the Chicken Bone Wish.
Girl Scouts of the U. S. A. Helping Leaders Help Girls Grow.
Girl Scouts of the U. S. A. Staff. Be an EQ Traveler.
--Cooking Out-of-Doors: For Juniors, Brownies, Cadettes, Seniors & Leaders.
--Feeding a Crowd.
--From Dreams to Reality: Adventures in Careers.
--Let's Make It Happen!
--Moreabouts for Brownie Girl Scout Leaders.
--Mundos a Explorar.
--Mundos a Explorar: Manual para las Brownie y las Junior Girl Scouts.
--Planning Trips with Girl Scouts: A Guide for Leaders.
--Safety-Wise: For Girls (Grade 7-12) & Adults Who Work Directly with Girls.
--Skip to My Lou: For Brownies, Juniors, Cadettes, Seniors & Leaders.
--Training about Girl Scouting.
--Worlds to Explore: Brownie & Junior Leaders' Guide.
--Worlds to Explore Handbook for Brownie & Junior Girl Scouts.
--You Make the Difference: Cadette & Senior Girl Scout Leaders' Guide.
--You Make the Difference: The Handbook for Cadette & Senior Girl Scouts.
Girling, J. S. America & the Third World.
Girls of Lady Eden's School, London. Just How Stories.
Girnau, G. & Haack, A. Tunnelling Research.
Giroux, Henry A. Ideology, Culture & the Process of Schooling.
Giroux, Paul L. God's Plan for the Human Race.
Giroux, Roy F. & Biggs, Donald A., eds. College Student Development Revisited: Programs, Issues & Practices.
Girsanov, I. V. Lectures on Mathematical Theory of Extremum Problems. Louvish, D., tr. from Rus.
Girth, Marjorie. Poor People's Lawyers.
Gisevius, Hans B. To the Bitter End. Winston, Richard & Winston, Clara, trs. from Ger.
Gish, Arthur G. Living in Christian Community.
Gish, Duane T. Up with Creation! Acts, Facts, Impacts.
Gish, Duane T., jt. auth. see Morris, Henry M.
Gish, Duane T., ed. see Bliss, Richard.
Gish, O., ed. Crisis in the Public Sector--Challenge to the Public Health: American Public Health Association 1980 Meeting in Detroit, Michigan.
Gish, Oscar. Doctor Migration & World Health.
Gissing, George. Demos.
--A Life's Morning. Coustillas, Pierre, ed.
--The Nether World.
--Thyrza: A Tale. King, Jacob, ed.
--The Unclassed.
--The Whirlpool. Parrinder, Patrick, ed.
--Workers in the Dawn. Coustillas, Pierre, ed.
Gissing, George R. The Letters of George Gissing to Eduard Bertz: 1887-1903. Young, Arthur C., ed.
Giteau, Cecile. Dictionnaire des Arts du Spectacle: Theatre, Cinema, Cirque, Danse, Radio...
Gitelman, Howard M. Workingmen of Waltham: Mobility in American Urban Industrial Development, 1850-1890.
Gitlin, Todd, ed. Watching Television.
Gitman, Lawrence J. Personal Finance.
Gittell, Marilyn, et al. Local Control in Education: Three Demonstration School Districts in New York City.
Gittelman, Martin, ed. Strategic Intervention for Hyperactive Children.
Gittelman, Philip, jt. auth. see Krefetz, Gerald.
Gittelson, Natalie. Dominus: A Woman Looks at Men's Lives.
Gitter, Kurt A. & Fisher, Pat. Japanese Fan Paintings From Western Collection.
Gitter, Michael. Gitter's Twenty-Four Hour New York.
Gittes, David L. A Practical Guide to Fund Accounting & Auditing.
Gittinger, Mattiebelle. Splendid Symbols: Textiles & Tradition in Indonesia.
Gittings, Clare. Death, Burial & the Individual in Early Modern England.
Gittins, D. The Family in Question: Changing Households & Familiar Ideologies.
Gittleman, Sol. From Shtetl to Suburbia: The Family in Jewish Literary Imagination.
Given, Bruce, et al. Tire Tracks & Tread Marks.
Given, Dave F. The Dave Given Rock 'n' Roll Star's Handbook.
Givens, Bill. Flying with Loran C.
Givens, Ellen M., jt. auth. see Ehrlich, Ruth A.
Givens, Harold. Landscape It Yourself.
Givens, Janet E. & Dodge, Susan E. Something Wonderful Happened.
Givens, John. Living Alone.
--Sons of the Pioneers.
Givens, Mary J., jt. auth. see Blonsky, Richard.
Given-Wilson, C. & Curteis, A. The Royal Bastards of Medieval England.
Givins, John. A Friend in the Police.
Givner, Joan. Katherine Anne Porter: A Life.
Gjersvik, Maryanne. Green Fun.
Gjessing, Lieve. Contribution to the Somatology of Periodic Catatonia. Marshall, H., tr.
Glab, Edward, Jr., ed. Latin American Culture Studies: Information & Materials for Teaching about Latin America.
Glab, Stanislaw, jt. ed. see Hulanicki, Adam.
Glackens, Ira. A Measure of Sliding Sand.
Glackin, James. Elements of Explosives Production.
Glackin, James J. Improvised Munitions Systems.
Glad, Betty. Jimmy Carter: In Search of the Great White House.
Glad, John, tr. see Shalamov, Varlam.
Gladding, Nicholas C., jt. auth. see Bycott, James F.
Glade, Philip R., jt. ed. see Bloom, Barry R.
Gladkov, Alexander. Meetings with Pasternak: A Memoir. Hayward, Max, tr.
Gladman, Donna. It's Sunday Night Again? Zapel, Arthur L., ed.
Gladstone, F. J. Voluntary Action in a Changing World.
Gladstone, Francis. Charity, Law & Social Justice.
Gladstone, M. J. A Carrot for a Nose: The Form of Folk Sculpture on America's City Streets & Country Roads.
Gladstone, Robert M., jt. auth. see Wilburn, Michael D.
Gladstone, W. J. Dictionnaire Anglais-Francais des Sciences Medicales et Paramedicales.
Gladwin, Thomas & Saidin, Ahmad. Slaves of the White Myth: The Psychology of Neocolonialism.
Gladwyn, Hubert M. Europe after De Gaulle. Crozier, Brian, ed.
Glaeser, Dennis, et al. An Invitation to Fly: Basics for the Private Pilot.
Glaeser, W. A., et al, eds. Wear of Materials. Incl. Wear of Materials, 1979. Ludema, K. C. et al., ed; Wear of Materials. Ludema, K. C., ed. ASME.
Glahe, F., ed. Adam Smith & the Wealth of Nations, 1776-1976: Bicentennial Essays.
Glahe, F. R., jt. ed. see Dowling, M.
Glahe, Fred R. Macroeconomics: Theory & Policy.
--Macroeconomics: Theory & Policy.
Glahe, Fred R. & Lee, Dwight R. Microeconomics: Theory & Applications.
Glahe, Fred R., ed. Collected Papers of Kenneth E. Boulding.
Glahe, Fred. R., ed. Collected Papers of Kenneth E. Boulding.
Glaiser, Stephen & Mulley, Corinne. Public Control of the British Bus Industry.
Glander, Deb, ed. see Toys 'n Things Press Staff.
Glander-Bandyk, jt. auth. see Droge, Dennis.
Glansdorff, P., ed. see CISM (International Center for Mechanical Sciences), Department of Mechanics of Solids Staff.
Glantz, Stanton A. Primer of Biostatistics.
Glanville, Brian. The History of the World Cup.
--The Olympian.
Glanville, Joseph. Some Discourse, Sermons & Remains. Wellek, Rene, ed.
Glasby, John S. The Nebular Variables.
Glascock, Raymond. Isotopic Gas Analysis for Biochemists.
Glascoff, Donald G., jt. auth. see Practising Law Institute Staff.
Glaser, Abram. This World of Ours.
Glaser, Barbara, jt. auth. see Kirschenbaum, Howard.
Glaser, Daniel. Handbook of Criminology.
Glaser, Edward M. Productivity Gains Through Worklife Improvement.
Glaser, Edward M., jt. auth. see Greenberg, Paul D.
Glaser, Hermann, ed. The German Mind of the Nineteenth Century: A Literary & Historical Anthology.
Glaser, Hy. How to Write Lyrics That Make Sense & Dollars.
Glaser, Peter E., jt. ed. see Salisbury, John W.
Glaser, Robert. Adaptive Education: Individual Diversity & Learning.
Glaser, Victoria. Training for Musicianship.
Glaser, William A. The Brain Drain: Emigration & Return.
Glasgoleva, Galina, tr. see Vishneva-Sarafanova, N.
Glasgow, Ellen. The Sheltered Life.
Glasgow, G. H. A Modern View of Conveyancing.
Glasgow University, Media Group Staff. Bad News.
Glass, Andrew. My Brother Tries to Make Me Laugh.
Glass, Bill & McEachern, James E. Plan to Win.
Glass, David C. & Singer, Jerome E. Urban Stress: Experiments on Noise & Social Stressors.
Glass, Dick & Crow, Ron. The CET Exam Book.
Glass, Dorothy F. Italian Romanesque Sculpture: An Annotated Bibliography.
Glass, Gene V., jt. auth. see Hopkins, Kenneth D.
Glass, Gene V., et al, eds. Design & Analysis of Time-Series Experiments.
Glass, Justine, jt. auth. see Corrall, Alice E.
Glass, Marion & Atchison, Evelyn. Integrated Studies in Patient Care.
--Integrated Studies in Patient Care.
Glass, Mrs. Quintard. Cemetery Inscriptions from Dyer County, Tennessee.
Glass, Robert L. The Second Coming: More Computing Projects Which Failed.
Glass, Thomas E., ed. Crisis in Urban Schools.
Glasser, Diane, jt. auth. see Pollack, Cecelia.

Authors

Glasser, Ellen. Looking into the Future: An Occupational Worktext.
Glasser, Hannelore. Artist's Contracts of the Early Renaissance.
Glasser, Ronald J. Another War, Another Peace.
Glasser, S., jt. ed. see Balin, H.
Glasser, Selma. Prize-Winning Recipes.
Glassner, Andrew S. Computer Graphics User's Guide.
Glassner, Barry. Essential Interactionism: On the Intelligibility of Prejudice.
Glassock, Richard J. Current Therapy in Nephrology & Hypertension 1984-1985.
Glasstone, Samuel. Energy Deskbook.
Glasstone, Victor. Victorian & Edwardian Theatres: An Architectural & Social Survey.
Glatt, Max. Alcoholic & the Help He Needs.
Glatthorn, Allan A. & Fleming, Harold. Models for Composition.
Glatzer, Hal. Introduction to Word Processing.
Glatzer, Robert. New Advertising: Twenty-One Successful Campaigns from Avis to Volkswagon.
Glau, Gregory. Controlling Your Cash Flow with 1-2-3 or Symphony.
Glau, Gregory R. Business Graphics for the Macintosh.
--Business Graphics with the IBM PC-XT-AT.
--Business Power for Your Apple.
--Controlling Your Cash Flow with Jazz & the Macintosh.
Glau, Gregory R., et al. Annotated BASIC: A New Technique for Neophytes. McCarthy, Nan & Crocker, Chris, eds.
Glauber, R. J., ed. Quantum Optics.
Glavin, John P., ed. Major Issues in Special Education.
--Perceptual - Motor Training for Handicapped Children.
Glaz, Edith & Vecsei, Paul. Aldosterone.
Glaze, Andrew. A Masque of Surgery.
Glaze, Bob, photos by. Portrait of Chicago.
Glazebrook, Philip. Byzantine Honeymoon.
--The Eye of the Beholder.
--Journey to Kars.
--Journey to Kars: A Modern Traveller in the Ottoman Lands.
Glazer, Alan S. & Jaenicke, Henry J. A Framework for Evaluating an Internal Audit Function.
Glazer, Amihai. Managing Money with Your Commodore 64.
--Managing Money with Your VIC-20.
Glazer, Joan & Williams, Gurney, III. Introduction to Children's Literature.
Glazer, Nathan. American Judaism.
Glazer, Nathan, et al, eds. Ethnic Pluralism & Public Policy: Achieving Equality in the United States & Britain.
Glazer, Nona Y. & Waehrer, Helen Y. Woman in a Man-Made World.
Glazer, Tom. America the Beautiful: A Collection of Best-loved Patriotic Songs.
Glazier, Kenneth M. & Hobson, James R. International & English-Language Collections: A Survey of Holdings at the Hoover Institution on War, Revolution & Peace.
Glazier, Richard. A Manual of Historic Ornament: Treating Upon the Evolution, Tradition & Development of Architecture & the Applied Arts.
--A Manual of Historic Ornaments.
Glazier, Teresa F. The Least You Should Know about English, Form A.
--The Least You Should Know About English, Form A.
--The Least You Should Know about English, Form B.
Glazier, Teresa F., ed. Short Stories for Insight.
Glazzard, Peggy. Learning Activities & Teaching Ideas for the Special Child in the Regular Classroom.
Gleasner, Bill & Gleasner, Diana. Kauai: Traveler's Guide.
--Maui: Traveler's Guide.
--Oahu: Traveler's Guide.
Gleasner, Diana, jt. auth. see Gleasner, Bill.
Gleason, Arthur, jt. auth. see Kellogg, Paul U.
Gleason, G. Essentials of FORTRAN.
Gleason, Harold & Becker, Warren. Examples of Music Before Fourteen Hundred.
--Twentieth Century American Composers.
Gleason, Harold, jt. auth. see Marrocco, W. Thomas.
Gleason, Harole. Methods of Organ Playing.
Gleason, John H. The Genesis of Russophobia in Great Britain.
Gleason, Judith. Orisha: The Gods of Yorubaland.
--Santeria: Bronx.
Gleason, S. Everett, jt. auth. see Langer, William L.
Gleason, Venetia. Rattlesnakes.
Gleason, Walter. Essentials of Business Math.
Gleason, Walter J. Moral Idealists, Bureaucracy, & Catherine the Great.
Gleaves, Edwin S. & Tucker, John M., eds. Reference Services & Library Education: Essays in Honor of Frances Neel Cheney.
Gledhill, Alan. Republic of India: The Development of its Laws & Constitution.
Gledhill, David. Gas Lighting.
Gleeson, Bill. Small Hotels of California: A Selective Guide to the Best of California's Most Charming Small Hotels & Inns.
Gleeson, Denis, ed. Youth Training & the Search for Work: A Study of Young People in Crisis.
Gleeson, James & Waldron, Tom. Now It Can Be Told.
Gleim, Irvin N. & Delancy, Patrick R. CPA Examination Review: Outlines & Study Guides.
--CPA Examination Review: Problems & Solutions.
Gleim, Irvin N., jt. auth. see Delaney, Patrick R.
Gleit, Joyce, jt. auth. see Eckstein, Joan.
Gleitman, Henry. Basic Psychology.
Gleitman, Henry, jt. auth. see Gleitman, Lila.
Gleitman, Lila & Gleitman, Henry. Phrase & Paraphrase: Some Innovative Uses of Language.
Glen, Frederick. The Social Psychology of Organizations.
Glen, J. Stanley. Justification by Success: The Invisible Captivity of the Church.
Glen, Jan, jt. auth. see Glen, Simon.
Glen, Simon & Glen, Jan. Sahara Handbook: Algeria, Lybia, Egypt, Niger, Mali.
Glendinning, Carline. Unshared Care: Parents & Their Disabled Children.
Glendinning, Ralph. The Ultimate Game.
Glendinning, Victoria. Vita: The Life of Vita Sackville-West.
Glenesk, Neil, jt. auth. see Houston, Joseph.
Glenn, Allen & Rawitsch, Don. Computing in the Social Studies Classroom.
Glenn, Andrea. Kansas in Color: Photographs Selected by Kansas! Magazine.
Glenn, Constance & Glenn, Jack, eds. Roy Lichtenstein: Landscape Sketches 1984-1985.
Glenn, Constance W., jt. auth. see Barnes, Lucinda.
Glenn, Harold T., jt. auth. see Coles, Clarence W.
Glenn, Jack, jt. ed. see Glenn, Constance.
Glenn, Mel. One Order to Go.
Glenn, Peggy. How to Start & Run a Successful Home Typing Business.
Glenn, Peter, ed. Madison Avenue Handbook.
Glenner, Richard A. The Dental Office: A Pictorial History.
Glennie, K. W., ed. Introduction to the Petroleum Geology of the North Sea.
Glennie, W., jt. ed. see Wilson, Alex.
Glennon, Michael, jt. auth. see Ehrenhalt, Alan.
Glenny & Nelmes. Handbook of Clinical Drug Research.
Glenny, Michael, tr. see Kaminskaya, Dina.
Glenny, Michael, tr. see Schoeck, Helmut.
Glenny, Michael, tr. see Trifonov, Yuri.
Glenton, Bill. Mutiny in Force X.
Gleser, Goldine C., jt. auth. see Gottschalk, Louis A.
Gleser, Goldine G., jt. auth. see Ihilevich, David.
Glezerman, G. Classes & Nations.
GLH, ed. see Balahura, Robert.
Glick. Fundamentals of Human Lymphoid Cell Culture.
Glick, David, ed. Methods of Biochemical Analysis: Analysis of Biogenic Amines & Their Related Enzymes.
Glick, Phyllis. The Mushroom Trail Guide.
Glick, Thomas F. Irrigation & Society in Medieval Valencia.
Glickman, Franklin S. General Dermatology.
Glickman, William G. Winners on the Tennis Court.
Glicksberg, Charles I. Modern Literary Perspectivism.
Glickson, J. D., et al. Vasopressin, I: Chemical & Clinical Aspects.
Glickstein, Mitchell, tr. see Ramon Y Cajal, Santiago.
Gliedman, John & Roth, William. The Unexpected Minority: Handicapped Children in America.
Gligoric, S. & Sokolov, V. The Sicilian Defence.
Glimm, J., et al. Lectures in Modern Analysis & Applications - Two. Taam, C. T., ed.
Glinka, K. D. Treatise on Soil Science.
Glinka, Mikhail I. Memoirs. Mudge, Richard B., tr. from Rus.
Glinka, N. L. General Chemistry.
--Problems & Exercises in General Chemistry.
Glinkov, G. M., jt. auth. see Glinkov, M. A.
Glinkov, M. A. & Glinkov, G. M. A General Theory of Furnaces.
Gloag, Julian. Blood for Blood.
Gloag, P. J., jt. auth. see Delitzsch, Franz.
Gloaguen, Philippe & Josse, Pierre. In & Around Paris.
--Italy.
Gloaguen, Philippe & Josse, Pierre, eds. Hip Pocket Guide to Mexico, Belize, Guatemala & the French Antilles.
--Pocket Guide to Northern & Central Europe.
Global Engineering Documents Staff. Qualified Products List & Sources.
--Source of Supply (SOS) Hook, Carla J., ed.
Globe, Leah A., jt. auth. see Eisenberg, Azriel.
Glockling, Frank. Chemistry of Germanium.
Gloe, jt. auth. see Lieberman.
Gloeden, Wilhelm von see Von Gloeden, Wilhelm.
Glossbrenner, Alfred, jt. auth. see Lau, Charley.
Glossman, Hartmut, et al. Functional & Structural Nature of Biomembranes: I.
Glossop, R. H. Method Study & the Furniture Industry.
Glossop, Ronald J. Confronting War: An Examination of Humanity's Most Pressing Problem.
Glotzer, Arline. Monarch's Complete Guide to Law Schools.
Glotzer, Arline & Sheiman, Bruce. Lovejoy's Guide to Graduate Business Schools.
Gloucester Art Press Editors. A Portfolio of Dramatic & Romantic Illustrations in Full Colours of the Great Railroads of the Past.
Gloucester, Richard & Hobhouse, Hermione. Oxford & Cambridge.
Glovach, Linda. Little Witch's Carnival Books.
Glover, Bob & Shepard, Jack. The Runner's Handbook: A Complete Fitness Guide for Men & Women on the Run.
Glover, J. A., jt. auth. see Dixon, D. N.
Glover, J. D. The Attack on Big Business.
Glover, Jack. The Bobbed Wire VI Bible.
Glover, Jean. Human Sexuality in Nursing Care.
Glover, M., jt. auth. see Keith, G. R.
Glover, R. S., ed. The Bristol Channel & Severn Estuary.
Glover, Robert W. Apprenticeship in the United States: Implications for Vocational Education Research & Development.
Glover, T., et al. A Manual of Underwater Photography.
Glowinski, R. & Lions, J. L., eds. Computing Methods in Applied Sciences & Engineering, 1977, I: Proceedings of the International Symposium, 3rd, December 5-9, 1977.
--Computing Methods in Applied Sciences & Engineering, 1977, II: Proceedings of the International Symposium, 3rd, December 5-9, 1977.
Glowinski, R., et al, eds. Energy Methods in Finite Element Analysis.
Glubok, Shirley, ed. Discovering Tutankhamen's Tomb.
Gluck, Herb, jt. auth. see Lewis, Jerry.
Gluck, Herb, jt. auth. see Mantle, Mickey.
Gluck, Jay & Gluck, Sumi. A Survey of Persian Handicraft.
Gluck, Sherna, ed. From Parlor to Prison: Five American Suffragists Talk About Their Lives.
Gluck, Sherna B. Rosie the Riveter Revisited: Women, the War & Social Change.
Gluck, Sumi, jt. auth. see Gluck, Jay.
Gluckman, Janet. Rite of the Dragon.
Gluckman, P. D., et al, eds. Advances in Fetal Physiology: Reviews in Honor of G. C. Liggins.
Glucksmann, Andre, jt. auth. see Gardner, Richard N.
Glueck, jt. auth. see Ivancevich.
Glueck, Eleanor, jt. auth. see Glueck, S.
Glueck, Eleanor T., jt. auth. see Glueck, Sheldon.
Glueck, Eleanor T., jt. auth. see Glueck, Sheldon S.
Glueck, S. & Glueck, Eleanor. Five Hundred Delinquent Women.
Glueck, Sheldon. Lives of Labor-Lives of Love: Fragments of Friendly Autobiographies.
Glueck, Sheldon & Glueck, Eleanor T. Delinquents & Nondelinquents in Perspective.
Glueck, Sheldon S. Mental Disorder & the Criminal Law.
Glueck, Sheldon S. & Glueck, Eleanor T. Later Criminal Careers.
Glueck, William F. Management Essentials.
--Strategic Management & Business Policy.
Glueck, William F. & Wall, Jerry A. Student Involvement Manual for Personnel Management.
Glueck, William F., jt. auth. see Bedeian, Arthur G.
Glueck, William F., jt. auth. see Ivancevich, John M.
Glueck, William F., jt. auth. see Milkovich, George T.
Glueck, William F., ed. Personnel: A Book of Readings.
Glueck, William F. & Stevens, George E., eds. Cases & Exercises in Personnel & Human Resources Management.
Glusker, David L. & Misner, Peter L. Words for Your Wedding, the Wedding Service Book.
Glusker, Jenny P., ed. Structural Crystallography in Chemistry & Biology.
Glymour, Clark. Theory & Evidence.
Glyn, Caroline. In Him Was Life.
Glynn, James A., jt. auth. see Stewart, Elbert W.
Glynn, Joseph. Construction of Cranes & Machinery, Circa 1850.
Glysson, E. A., et al, eds. Innovations in the Water & Wastewater Fields.
Gmelch, Sharon. Nan: The Life of an Irish Travelling Woman.
--Tinkers & Travellers.
Gnade, Michael. People in My Camera.
--Perfect Nude Photography.
Gnagey, William J. Motivating Classroom Discipline.
Gnedenko, B. V. & Kovalenko, I. N. Introduction to Queueing Theory.
Gnosis, Inc. Staff. Learning LISP.
Goaz, Paul W. & White, Stuart C. Oral Radiology: Principles & Interpretations.
Gobbell, Phyllis & Laster, Jim. Safe Sally Seat Belt & the Magic Click.
Gobbell, Phyllis C. Like a Promise.
Gobel, David. Using Lotus HAL.
Gobel, R., et al, eds. Abelian Groups & Modules.
Gobello, Jose. Diccionario Lunfardo Ilustrado.
Gober, Lasley F. The Christmas Lover's Handbook.
Gobineau, Marceline. Stephanie the Emperor's Agent.
Goble, Frank. Excellence in Leadership.
Goble, Frank & Brooks, B. David. The Case for Character Education.
Gobran, Alfonse. Beginning Algebra.
--Intermediate Algebra.
Gochberg, Herbert S., jt. ed. see Switzer, Richard.
Godana, Bonaya. Africa's Shared Water Resources: Legal & Institutional Aspects of the Nile, Niger & Senegal River Systems.
Godard, James M. Blue Light.
Goday, Dale & Cochran, Molly. Dressing Thin: How to Look up to 35 Pounds Thinner Without Losing an Ounce.
Godbey, Geoffrey, et al. Triples: A New Tennis Game.
Goddard, A. J., ed. Finite Element & Allied Methods for Reactor Physics & Shielding Calculations: Proceedings of a Seminar Held at the Inperial College of Science & Technology, London, U. K., 18-20th September 1985.
Goddard, A. J., ed. see Williams.
Goddard, Alice L. David, My Jewish Friend.
Goddard, Bobbye. Bomber.
Goddard, Carrie L., jt. auth. see Burkholder, Ruth C.
Goddard, Harold C. Meaning of Shakespeare.
Goddard, J. B., ed. Industrial Innovation & Regional Economic Development.
Goddard, J. B. & Champion, A. G., eds. The Urban & Regional Transformation of Britain.
Goddard, John, jt. auth. see Amin, Ash.
Goddard, John, ed. Leisure, Recreation & Tourism.
Goddard, Murray. How to Be Your Own Architect.
Goddard, Pliny E. Indians of the Northwest Coast.
Godden, G. A. Lowestoft Porcelains.
Godden, Geoffrey. Caughly & Worcester Porcelains, 1775-1800.
--Coalport & Coalbrookdale Porcelains.
Godden, Geoffrey A. British Porcelain: An Illustrated Guide.
--British Pottery: An Illustrated Guide.
--Chamberlain-Worcester Porcelain, 1788-1852.
--Encyclopedia of British Pottery & Porcelian Marks.
--Godden's Guide to Mason's China & the Ironstone Wares.
--The Handbook of British Pottery & Porcelain Marks.
--Illustrated Encyclopedia of British Pottery & Porcelain.
--Minton Pottery & Porcelain of the First Period, 1793-1850.
Godel, Howard. Antique Toy Trains: The Hobby of Collecting Old Toy Trains.
Godement, R. & Jacquet, H. Zeta-Functions of Simple Algebras.
Godet, Frederic L. Commentary on Luke.
Godey, John. Fatal Beauty.
Godfrey, A. I. Quantitative Methods for Managers.
Godfrey, D. Modern Technical Communication.
Godfrey, E. Martin, jt. ed. see Bienefeld, Manfred A.
Godfrey, Laurie R., ed. Scientists Confront Creationism.
Godfrey, M. D. Machine Independent Organic Software Tools.
Godfrey, M. D., et al. Machine: Independent Organic Software Tools.
Godfrey, Marie H. Early Settlers of Barbour Co., Ala.
Godfrey, Robert S. Means Man-Hour Standards.
Godfrey, T. & Reichelt, J. Industrial Enzymology.
Goding, James W. Monoclonal Antibodies.
Godley, William P. Cabinets & Vanities: A Builder's Handbook.
Godman, A. & Payne, E. M. F. Longman Dictionary of Scientific Usage.
Godman, David, ed. Be As You Are: The Teachings of Sri Ramana Maharshi.
Godoli, Ezio, jt. auth. see Fanelli, Giovanni.
Godreau, Miguel F. The Holy Nature of Man.
Godschalk, David R & Brower, David J. Constitutional Issues of Growth Management.
--Constitutional Issues of Growth Management.
Godschalk, David R., ed. Planning in America: Learning from Turbulence.

Godsey, John D. Preface to Bonhoeffer: The Man & Two of His Shorter Writings.
Godshalk, William L., ed. Twelfth Night: An Annotated Bibliography.
Godson, Roy. American Labor & European Politics: The AFL As a Transnational Force.
--Labor in Soviet Global Strategy.
Godson, Roy, ed. Analysis & Estimates.
--Clandestine Collection.
--Counterintelligence.
--Covert Action.
--Elements of Intelligence.
--Elements of Intelligence.
Godwin, David. Godwin's Practical Encyclopedia of Cabalistic Magick. Weschcke, Carl L., ed.
Godwin, John. Frommer's Australia on Thirty-Five Dollars A Day.
Godwin, John, et al. Dollarwise Guide to Canada.
Godwin, Joscelyn. Music, Mysticism & Magic: A Source Book.
--Music, Mysticism & Magic: A Source Book.
Godwin, Nadine. Complete Guide to Travel Agency Automation.
Godwin, William. St. Leon: A Tale of the Sixteenth Century.
Gody, Dale & Ross, Monique. How to Dress Rich.
Goebel, Patrice, ed. see Molnar, Paul J.
Goebel, W., ed. Genetic Approaches to Microbial Pathogenicity.
Goebel, W., jt. ed. see Hofschneider, P. H.
Goedert, Jeanne E. Generalizing from the Experimental Housing Allowance Program: An Assessment of Site Characteristics.
Goedicke, Patricia. The Dog That Was Barking Yesterday.
Goehlert, Robert. Concepts of Political & Social Authority: A Selected Bibliography.
--Political & Social Advertising: A Selected Bibliography.
--Political Change & Development: A Selected Bibliography.
--Political Communication & Information: A Selected Bibliography.
--Political Control: A Selected Bibliography.
--Political Corruption: A Selected Bibliography.
--Political Elites: A Bibliography.
--Political Forecasting: A Selected Bibliography.
--Political Legitimacy: A Bibliography.
--Political Modernization: A Selected Bibliography.
--Political Party Organizations: A Bibliography.
--Political Research & Knowledge: A Bibliography.
Goehlert, Robert & Martin, Fenton. The Parliament of Great Britain: A Bibliography.
Goel, N. S., et al. On the Volterra & Other Nonlinear Models of Interacting Populations.
Goel, Narendra & Richter-Dyn, Nira. Stochastic Models in Biology.
Goel, S. L. Public Health Administration.
Goeldner, C. R. & Dicke, K. Bibliography of Skiing Studies.
Goeldner, Christian T. The Thoroughbred Field Hunter.
Goeller, Lee. How to Make an Adding Machine: That Even Adds Roman Numerals.
Goeltz, Judith & Lazenby, Patricia. The Beginner's Natural Food Cookbook.
Goering, Carroll E. Engine & Tractor Power.
Goertler, H., ed. see International Union of Theoretical & Applied Mechanics Staff.
Goertzel, Mildred G., et al. Three Hundred Eminent Personalities: A Psychosocial Analysis of the Famous.
Goertzel, Ted G. Political Society.
Goes, Albrecht. Eine Erzahlung. Loffelchen: Schweitzer, Christoph E., ed.
Goethals, George R., jt. auth. see Worchel, Stephen.
Goethals, Gregor T. The TV Ritual: Worship at the Video Altar.
Goethe. Faust.
--Fausto.
Goethe, Johann Wolfgang von. Faust I & II.
Goetschius, Percy. The Theory & Practice of Tone-Relations.
Goetz, Delia. Neighbors to the South.
Goetz, Elizabeth M., jt. auth. see Allen, K. Eileen.
Goetz, Elizabeth M. & Allen, K. Eileen, eds. Early Childhood Education: Special Environmental, Policy & Legal Considerations.
Goetzl, Edward J. & Kay, A. B., eds. Current Perspectives in Allergy.
Goetzman, Robert. James Anthony Froude: A Bibliography of Studies.
Goetzmann, William H. Army Exploration in the American West, 1803-1863.
Goff, Frederick R. Incunabula in American Libraries: A Supplement to the Third Census of Fifteenth-Century Books Recorded in North American Collections (1964)
Goff, Harry, jt. auth. see Murphy, John D.
Goff, Paul E. Nature, Children & You.
Goff, Victoria. Bargain Hunting in Sacramento.
Goff, Victoria & Sparks-Forrester, Viktoria. Affordable Chic: Tours of Factory Clothing Outlets in San Francisco.
Goffart, M. Function & Form in the Sloth.
Goffe, Thomas. The Courageous Turk. O'Malley, Susan G. & Orgel, Stephen, eds.
Goffee, Robert, jt. auth. see Scase, Richard.
Goffi, Carlos. Tournament Tough: A Guide to Junior Championship Tennis.
Goffman, Erving. Frame Analysis: An Essay on the Organization of Experience.
--Gender Advertisements.
Gogarty, Oliver. Elbow Room.
--An Offering of Swans.
Gogarty, Oliver S. As I Was Going Down Sackville Street.
Goggans, Janice W. & Beavers, Myrtle. The Spider's Touch.
Gogol, N. Nikolai Gogol: A Selection.
Gogol, Nikolai. The Inspector General. Popkin, Henry, ed. MacAndrew, Andrew, tr.
Gogolak, Pete. Kicking the Football Soccer Style with Tips on Playing Soccer. Siegener, Ray, ed.
Gogulan, M. F. & Kusemchenko, L. F. Humorous Stories & Anecdotes.
Goh, Austin. The Secret of Wing Chun Butterfly Knives Form.
Gohagan, N. M. The Singing Heart.
Gohberg, I. & Kal, M., eds. Topics in Functional Analysis: Essays Dedicated to M. G. Krein on the Occasion of His 70th. Birthday.
Gohlke, Annette, ed. Appealing Appetizers.
--Chicken Country Style.
--Country Squash.
--Egg Recipes by the Dozen.
--Harvest of Honey.
--Hearty Helpings.
--Microwave Magic.
--Microwave Magic II.
--My Oh My Country Pies.
--Palate Pleasing Pork.
--Pasta, Please.
--Peanut Butter Favorites.
Gohlke, Mary & Jennings, Max. I'll Take Tomorrow: The Story of a Courageous Woman Who Dared to Subject Herself to a Medical Experiment; The First Successful Heart-Lung Transplant. Heffernen, Maureen, ed.
Goicocchea, Ambrose, et al. Multiobjective Analysis with Engineering & Business Applications.
Goicoecha, Jose M. Elementary Spanish: A First Year College Textbook.
Goicoechea, David, ed. The Great Year of Zarathustra, 1881-1981.
Goilo, E. R. Papiamentu Textbook.
Goin, Coleman J. & Goin, Olive B. Man & the Natural World: An Introduction to Life Science.
Goin, Kenneth L., jt. auth. see Pope, Alan.
Goin, Olive B., jt. auth. see Goin, Coleman J.
Going, Allen J. Bourbon Democracy in Alabama, 1874-1890.
Gojmerac, Walter L. Bees, Beekeeping, Honey & Pollination.
Gokcen, Nev A., ed. Chemical Metallurgy - A Tribute to Carl Wagner: Proceedings. AIME Annual Meeting, Chicago, 1981.
Gokel, G. W., jt. auth. see Weber, W. P.
Gokel, George W., jt. auth. see Durst, H. Dupont.
Golanty, Eric & Harris, Barbara. Marriage & the Family.
Golany, Gideon. Earth-Sheltered Habitat: History, Architecture & Urban Design.
Golany, Gideon S. Design for Arid Regions.
Golay, Frank H. & Lush, Peggy, eds. Directory of the Cornell Southeast Asia Program: 1951-1976.
Golbeck, Amanda. Evaluating Statistical Validity of Research Reports: A Guide for Managers, Planners, & Researchers.
Golbitz, Pat, ed. see Barolini, Helen.
Golbitz, Pat, ed. see Follett, Ken.
Golbitz, Pat, ed. see Hyman, B. D.
Golbitz, Pat, ed. see Littwin, Susan.
Golbitz, Pat, ed. see Lloyd, Sarah.
Golbitz, Pat, ed. see Terrill, Ross.
Golbitz, Pat, ed. see Weber, Eric.
Golbitz, Pat, jt. auth. see Stern, Bert.
Gold, Alison L., jt. auth. see Gies, Miep.
Gold, Arthur & Fizdale, Robert. Misia: The Life of Misia Sert.
Gold, Bela. Productivity, Technology, & Capital Economic Analysis, Managerial Strategies, & Government Policies.
Gold, Bela, et al, eds. Technological Progress & Industrial Leadership: The Growth of the U. S. Steel Industry, 1900-1965.
Gold, Bernard & Rader, Charles M. Digital Processing of Signals.
Gold, Charlotte & Mackenzie, Susan, eds. Wide World of Arbitration: An Anthology.
Gold, Charlotte, ed. see American Arbitration Association Staff & Colosi, Thomas R.
Gold, David, et al. Misguided Expenditures: An Analysis of the Proposed MX Missile System.
Gold, Don. The Intermediate Two Bids in Bridge: A Modern Alternative for Standard American Bidders.
Gold, Edgar. Maritime Transport: The Evolution of International Marine Policy & Shipping Law.
Gold, Herbert. Family: A Novel in the Form of a Memoir.
--Fathers.
--He-She.
--The Man Who Was Not with It.
--Mister White Eyes.
--Slave Trade.
--True Love.
--True Love: A Novel.
--Waiting for Cordelia.
--A Walk on the West Side: California on the Brink.
Gold, Michael. Jews Without Money.
Gold, Ruth, jt. auth. see Siegel, Ernest.
Gold, Sharlya. Amelia Quackenbush.
--Time to Take Sides.
Gold, Steven. State Fiscal Indicators.
Gold, V., jt. auth. see Bethell, Donald.
Goldanskii, V. I. & Herber, R. H., eds. Chemical Applications of Mossbauer Spectroscopy.
Goldbach, Joseph. The Other Mafia.
Goldbarth, Albert. Eurekas.
Goldbeck, David, jt. auth. see Goldbeck, Nikki.
Goldbeck, Nikki & Goldbeck, David. The Good Breakfast Book: A Bringing-Back-Breakfast Cookbook.
Goldbeck, W. B. Mental Illness Programs for Employees.
Goldberg, jt. auth. see Schwarz.
Goldberg, Adele & Robson, David. Smalltalk-Eighty: The Language & Its Implementation.
Goldberg, Andrew C. New Development in Soviet Military Strategy.
Goldberg, B., ed. Solar Radiation Measurements in Developing Countries.
Goldberg, B. B., jt. auth. see Rose, Joseph L.
Goldberg, Barry & Wells, Peter N. Ultrasonics in Clinical Diagnosis.
Goldberg, Barry B., ed. Abdominal Ultrasonography.
Goldberg, Bernard, ed. Communication Channels: Characterization & Behavior.
Goldberg, Carl. Encounter: Group Sensitivity Training Experience.
Goldberg, Carole E. Public Law Two-Eighty.
Goldberg, David E., jt. auth. see Dillard, Clyde R.
Goldberg, David M., ed. Clinical Biochemistry Reviews.
--Clinical Biochemistry Reviews.
Goldberg, Edward D., ed. North Sea Science: Papers Presented at the NATO Science Committee Conference, November 1971.
Goldberg, Gary, jt. auth. see Johner, Martin.
Goldberg, H., jt. auth. see DiMascio, A.
Goldberg, Isaac. Wonder of Words: An Introduction to Language for Every Man.
Goldberg, Israel. Israel: A History of the Jewish People.
Goldberg, Jonathan. James I & the Politics of Literature: Jonson, Shakespeare, Donne, & Their Contemporaries.
Goldberg, Joyce, jt. auth. see McHale, Lucy C.
Goldberg, Kathy E. & Mason, Joan E., eds. Respiratory Emergencies.
Goldberg, Kenneth P., jt. auth. see Weinberg, Sharon L.
Goldberg, L. & Conning, D. M., eds. Saccharin: Current Status.
Goldberg, L., ed. see Bayer Symposium, 4th.
Goldberg, M. & Egelston, G. Mind-Influencing Drugs: Effective Management of Patients with Emotional Illness.
Goldberg, Marshall & Kay, Kenneth. Disposable People.
Goldberg, Marshall, jt. auth. see Kay, Kenneth.
Goldberg, Morton D., jt. auth. see Practising Law Institute Staff.
Goldberg, Moses. Children's Theatre: A Philosophy & a Method.
Goldberg, Nathan, et al. The Classification of Jewish Immigrants & Its Implications: A Survey of Opinion.
Goldberg, Paul. Luminescence of Inorganic Solids.
Goldberg, Philip & Posner, Mitchell J. Strategic Metals Investment Handbook.
Goldberg, S. J. & Chess, V. Adventures of Stanley Kane.
Goldberg, Samuel A. Sales of Real Property.
Goldberg, Steve. Graphiti (Four Quadrants)
--Graphiti (One Quadrant)
Goldberg-Bartura, Maurie, tr. see Oz, Amos.
Goldberger, Ary L. Myocardial Infarction.
Goldblat, J. Agreements for Arms Control: A Critical Survey.
Goldblatt, Howard, tr. from Chinese. Chinese Literature for the Nineteen Eighties: The Fourth Congress of Writers & Artists.
Goldbratt, Howard, tr. see Hong, Xiao.
Goldburg, Arnold, jt. auth. see Pao, Yih-Ho.
Golde, Roger A. Muddling Through: The Art of Properly Unbusinesslike Management.
--Muddling Through: The Art of Properly Unbusinesslike Management.
Golden, Abner. The Kidney.
Golden, Frederic. Colonies in Space: The Next Giant Step.
--Quasars, Pulsars, & Black Holes: A Scientific Detective Story.
Golden, James L., et al. The Rhetoric of Western Thought.
Golden, Lawrence G. & Zimmerman, Donald A. Effective Retailing.
Golden, Renny & Collins, Shelia. Struggle Is a Name for Hope.
Golden, Ursula. Penny Links: A Novel.
Goldenberg, Susan. Trading: Inside the World's Leading Stock Exchanges.
Goldenthal, Allan B. The Teenage Employment Guide.
Goldfarb, Theodore. Taking Sides: Clashing Views on Controversial Environmental Issues.
--Taking Sides: Clashing Views on Controversial Environmental Issues.
Goldfarb, William. Water Law.
Goldfarb, William, et al. A Time to Heal.
Goldfein, Alan. Heads: A Metafictional History of Western Civilization 1762-1975.
Goldfind, Norman. Leisure Fun, No. 17: Find-a-Word.
Goldfind, Norman, ed. Find a Word.
Goldfine, Alan H., jt. ed. see Fong, Elizabeth N.
Goldfrank, Lewis, jt. ed. see Flomenbaum, Neal.
Goldhammer, Arthur, tr. see Bachelard, Gaston.
Goldhammer, Arthur, tr. see Duras, Marguerite.
Goldhammer, Arthur, tr. see Sergent, Bernard.
Goldhammer, Arthur, tr. see Yourcenar, Marguerite.
Goldhor, Herbert. Fact Book of the American Public Library.
--An Introduction to Scientific Research in Librarianship.
Goldhor, Herbert & Sahm, Lawrence A. The Renovation of a Medium-Sized Public Library Building.
Goldhor, Herbert, ed. Education for Librarianship: The Design of the Curriculum of Library Schools.
Goldie, Ian F., tr. see Tillman, K.
Goldin, Albert. Your Guide to Care of the Heart.
Goldin, Augusta. Geothermal Energy: A Hot Prospect.
Goldin, Barbara. The Citizenship Handbook.
Goldin, Nan. The Ballad of Sexual Dependency.
Golding, E. W. The Generation of Electricity by Wind Power.
--Generation of Electricity by Wind Power.
Golding, John & Elderfield, John. The Drawings of Henri Matisse.
Golding, Lawrence, et al, eds. Y's Way to Physical Fitness.
Golding, Patrick. Britain by Train: The Complete Travel Guide to Rail Travel for Pleasure.
Golding, William. Lord of the Flies.
--The Scorpion God.
Golding, William G. The Hot Gates & Other Occasional Pieces.
Goldingay, John. Old Testament Commentary Survey. Hubbard, Robert & Branson, Mark L., eds.
Goldkuhl, G., jt. auth. see Sundburg, M.
Goldlust, John. Playing for Keeps: Sport, the Media, & Society.
Goldman & Cope. Radiographic Index.
Goldman, Albert. Elvis.
--Elvis.
Goldman, Alex J. Child's Dictionary of Jewish Symbols.
Goldman, Bernard S., jt. ed. see Adelman, Allan G.
Goldman, Charlotte & Pozzi-Johnson, David. Daily Living Skills.
Goldman, David. Presidential Losers.
Goldman, I. & Krivchenkov, V. D. Problems in Quantum Mechanics.
Goldman, I. David, et al, eds. Folyl & Antifolyl Polyglutamates.
Goldman, Joshua & Zolotow, Nina. System 1032 Host Language Interface User's Guide.
Goldman, Juliette, jt. auth. see Goldman, Ronald.
Goldman, Larry. Becoming a Professional Model.
Goldman, Larry L., jt. auth. see Aranyi, Laszlo.
Goldman, Laurel. The Part of Fortune.
Goldman, Laurence. Talk Never Dies: The Language of Huli Disputes.
Goldman, Merle R. Literary Dissent in Communist China.
Goldman, Myer & Cope, David. A Radiographic Index.
Goldman, Richard F. Harmony in Western Music.
Goldman, Ron. Design of an Interactive Manipulator Programming Environment. Stone, Harold, ed.
Goldman, Ronald & Goldman, Juliette. Children's Sexual Thinking: A Comparative Study of Children Aged 5 to 15 in Australia, North America, Britain & Sweden.
Goldman, Sherli E. Mary McCarthy: A Bibliography.
Goldman, Shifra M. Contemporary Mexican Painting in a Time of Change.
Goldman, William. No Way to Treat a Lady.
--The Princess Bride.
--Season: A Candid Look at Broadway.
--Wigger.

Goldman-Eisler, F. Psycholinguistics: Experiments in Spontaneous Speech.
Goldmann, Nahum. Online Research & Retrieval with Microcomputers.
Goldoni, Carlo. The Comic Theatre: A Comedy in Three Acts. Miller, John W., tr.
Goldoni, Carolo. Campiello: A Venetian Comedy. Graham-Jones, Susanna, tr. from Ital. Bryden, Bill.
Goldovsky, Boris & Cate, Curtis. My Road to Opera: The Recollections of Boris Goldsovsky As Told to Curtis Cate.
Goldreich. Leah's Journey.
Goldreich, Gloria. Four Days.
--West to Eden.
Goldring, M. S. Economics of Atomic Energy.
Goldring, Mark. Computers & Crafts: A Practical Guide.
Goldsberry, Steven. Maui the Demigod: An Epic Novel of Mythical Hawaii.
Goldsborough, Robert. Murder in E Minor: A Nero Wolfe Mystery.
Goldsbrough, et al. Analog Electronics for Microcomputer Systems.
Goldsby, Richard A. Cells & Energy.
--Race & Races.
Goldscheider, C., jt. auth. see Jianou, Ionel.
Goldscheider, Calvin, jt. auth. see Goldstein, Sidney.
Goldscheider, Robert. Technology Management Handbook 1984.
Goldschieder, Ludwig. Towards Modern Art: Or, King Solomon's Picture Book.
Goldschlager, Nora, jt. auth. see Jacobson, Lester.
Goldschmid, H. J. Business Disclosure: Government's Need to Know.
Goldschmidt, H., ed. Physical Modalities in Dermatologic Therapy: Radiotherapy, Electrosurgery, Phototherapy, Cryosurgery.
Goldschmidt, Lucien & Naef, Weston J. The Truthful Lens.
Goldschmidt, Walter. As You Sow: Three Studies in the Social Consequences of Agribusiness.
Goldschmidt, Yaaqov, jt. auth. see Shashua, Leon.
Goldschmidt-Clermont, Luisella. Unpaid Work in the Household: A Review of Economic Evaluation Methods.
Goldsmid, H. J. Electronic Refrigeration.
Goldsmid, H. J., ed. Problems in Solid State Physics.
Goldsmid, H. J., et al, eds. see Tsidil'Kovskii, I. M.
Goldsmith, Arnold L. The Golem Remembered 1909-1980: Variations of a Jewish Legend.
Goldsmith, Gary, jt. auth. see Mackenzie, Kent.
Goldsmith, Howard. The Twiddle Twins' Haunted House.
Goldsmith, Jay P. & Karotkin, Edward H. Assisted Ventilation of the Neonate.
Goldsmith, Joel. Master Speaks.
Goldsmith, Joel S. The Altitude of Prayer. Sinkler, Lorainne, ed.
--Awakening Mystical Consciousness. Sinkler, Lorraine, ed.
--I Am the Vine.
--Our Spiritual Resources.
--Truth.
Goldsmith, John A. Autosegmental Phonology. Hankamer, Jorge, ed.
Goldsmith, Judith. Childbirth Wisdom: From the World's Oldest Societies.
Goldsmith, Maurice. Frederic Joliot-Curie.
Goldsmith, Melissa. Winter Signs.
Goldsmith, Michael, et al. Today's Father: A Guide to Understanding, Enjoying & Making Things for the Growing Family.
Goldsmith, Oliver. Complete Poetical Works.
--Essays on Goldsmith by Scott, Macaulay & Thackeray, & Selections from His Writings.
Goldsmith, Ulrich, et al, eds. Hypatia: Essays in Classics, Comparative Literature, & Philosophy.
Goldsmith, V. F., jt. auth. see Allison, A. F.
Goldspink, G., ed. Differentiation & Growth of Cells in Vertebrate Tissues.
Goldstein, A. P. & Kanfer, Frederick H., eds. Maximizing Treatment Gains: Transfer Enhancement in Psychotherapy.
Goldstein, A. P., ed. see Hersen, Michel & Barlow, David H.
Goldstein, Al., frwd. by. The Classic Book of Dirty Jokes Anecdota Americana.
Goldstein, Alice, jt. auth. see Goldstein, Sidney.
Goldstein, Alvin H. The Unquiet Death of Julius & Ethel Rosenberg.
Goldstein, Amy J. & Granade, Charles, eds. Graduate Programs in Engineering & Applied Sciences, 1986.
Goldstein, Amy J., jt. ed. see Conley, Diane.
Goldstein, Arnold P. Psychotherapeutic Attraction.
Goldstein, Arnold P. & Stein, Norman. Prescriptive Psychotherapies.
Goldstein, Arnold P., jt. ed. see Kanfer, Frederick H.
Goldstein, Arnold P., et al. In Response to Aggression: Methods of Control & Prosocial Alternatives.
Goldstein, Arnold S. Commercial Transactions Desk Book.
Goldstein, Bernice & Tamura, Kyoko. Japan & America: A Comparative Study in Language & Culture.
Goldstein, Charles. The Bunker.
Goldstein, David S. & Jones, Rhonda A. Metallurgical Engineering Practice Problem Manual.
--Petroleum Engineering Practice Problem Manual.
Goldstein, Donald M., jt. auth. see Prange, Gordon W.
Goldstein, Doris M., ed. Bioethics: A Guide to Information Sources.
Goldstein, E., ed. Consumerism,
--Death & Dying.
--Defense.
--Food.
Goldstein, E. Bruce. Sensation & Perception.
Goldstein, Eleanor, ed. Habitat, Vol. 3 (incl. 1985-1987 Supplements)
--Health, Vol. 3 (incl. 1984-1987 Supplements)
Goldstein, Eleanor C., ed. Aging, Vol. 3 (incl. 1986-87 Supplements)
--The AIDS Crisis, Vol. 1 (Incl. 1986-87 Supplements)
--Alcohol.
--Communication, Vol. 3 (incl. 1985-1987 Supplements)
--Drugs.
--Energy, Vol. 4 (incl. 1985-1987 Supplements)
--Ethics.
--Ethnic Groups, Vol. 3 (incl. 1985-1987 Supplements)
--Mental Health, Vol. 3, (incl. 1984-1987 Supplements)
--Money.
--Pollution, Vol. 4 (incl. 1985-1987 Supplement)
--Population, Vol. 4 (incl. 1985-1987 Supplement)
--Religion, Vol. 3 (Incl. 1986-1987 Supplements)
--School, Vol. 3 (incl. 1984-1987 Supplements)
--Sports, Vol. 3 (incl. 1986-1987 Supplements)
--Technology, Vol. 2 (incl. 1983-1987 Supplements)
--Third World, Vol. 2 (incl. 1983-1986 Supplements)
--Transportation, Vol. 3 (incl. 1985-1986 Supplements)
--Women, Vol. 3 (incl. 1984-1987 Supplements)
--Youth, Vol 3 (Incl. 1986-1987 Supplements)
Goldstein, H. Readings in Family Therapy.
Goldstein, Harold. The Future Role of the New York State Library in Statewide Audiovisual Activities: A Survey with Recommendations.
Goldstein, Harold, ed. The Changing Environment for Library Services in the Metropolitan Area.
Goldstein, Harriet I. & Goldstein, Vetta. Art in Everyday Life.
Goldstein, Harvey, jt. auth. see Moss, Louis.
Goldstein, Irving & Lane, Fred. Goldstein Trial Technique: Nineteen Sixty-Nine to Nineteen Eighty-Four.
Goldstein, Jerome. How to Start a Family Business & Make It Work.
Goldstein, Joseph, et al. Beyond the Best Interests of the Child.
Goldstein, L., ed. see American Physiological Society & American Society of Zoologists, Joint Symposium.
Goldstein, Larry J. The Graphics Generator: Business & Technical Graphics for the IBM Personal Computer.
--Hands-On QuickBASIC.
--TRS-80 Models III & IV: Programming & Applications.
Goldstein, Larry J. & Mosher, F. Commodore 64 BASIC Programming & Applications.
Goldstein, Larry J. & Rensin, Joseph K. Compaq Portable Computer User's Guide.
Goldstein, Larry J. & Schneider, David. Finite Mathematics & Its Applications.
--Microsoft BASIC for the Macintosh.
Goldstein, Larry J., jt. auth. see Rensin, Joseph K.
Goldstein, Larry J., et al. Brief Calculus & Its Applications.
Goldstein, LarryJ., et al. Calculus & Its Applications.
Goldstein, Leon. Introduction to Comparative Physiology.
Goldstein, Louis A. & Dickerson, Robert C. Atlas of Orthopaedic Surgery.
Goldstein, M., et al, eds. Basic Aspects of Receptor Biochemistry: Proceedings, Vienna, Austria, 1982.
Goldstein, Malcolm, ed. see Rowe, Nicholas.
Goldstein, Mark S., jt. auth. see Blum, James D.
Goldstein, Marty & Waldman, Stuart. Black Book: 1987.
--Creative Black Book Portfolio Edition: 1986.
--Creative Black Book Portfolio Edition: 1987.
--Creative Black Book Producer's Volume: 1987.
--Creative Black Book: 1987.
--Creative Black Book: 1987.
--Creative Black Book: 1987.
Goldstein, Milton. The Magnificent West: Yosemite.
Goldstein, Morris. Lift up Your Life.
Goldstein, Nathan. Figure Drawing: The Structure, Anatomy, & Expressive Design of Human Form.
Goldstein, Norm & Associated Press. Henry Fonda.
Goldstein, Norm, jt. auth. see Associated Press Staff.
Goldstein, Paul J. Prostitution & Drugs.
Goldstein, Sidney & Goldscheider, Calvin. Jewish Americans: Three Generations in a Jewish Community.
Goldstein, Sidney & Goldstein, Alice. Population Mobility in the People's Republic of China.
--Surveys of Migration in Developing Countries: A Methodological Review.
Goldstein, Stanley. Troubled Children-Troubled Parents.
Goldstein, Sue. The Underground Shopper's Guide to Health & Fitness.
Goldstein, Thomas. Dawn of Modern Science: From the Arabs to Leonardo Da Vinci.
--Dawn of Modern Science: From the Arabs to Leonardo da Vinci.
Goldstein, Tom. The News at Any Cost: How Journalists Compromise Their Ethics to Shape the News.
Goldstein, Vetta, jt. auth. see Goldstein, Harriet I.
Goldstein, Wallace L. Teaching English As a Second Language: An Annotated Bibliography.
Goldstein-Jackson, Kevin, compiled by. The Dictionary of Essential Quotations.
Goldstein-Jackson, Kevin, et al. Experiments with Everyday Objects: Science Activities for Children, Parents & Teachers.
Goldstern, W. Steam Storage Installations.
Goldstone, A. H. Examination Haematology.
Goldstone, Leonard A. Understanding Medical Statistics.
Goldstone, Richard A. Contexts of the Drama.
Goldwasser, Dan L., jt. auth. see Practising Law Institute Staff.
Goldwasser, Dan L., et al. Directors' & Officers' Liability Insurance 1987.
Goldwasser, M., tr. see Weinreich, Uriel.
Goldwert, Marvin. Psyche & History.
--Psychic Conflict in Spanish America: Six Essays on the Psychohistory of the Region.
Goldzband, Melvin G. Custody Cases & Expert Witnesses: A Manual for Attorneys.
Goleman, Daniel. Vital Lies, Simple Truths: The Psychology of Self-Deception & Shared Illusions.
Golembiewski, Robert T. & Gibson, Frank. Public Administration: Readings in Institutions, Processes, Behavior Policy.
Golembiewski, Robert T. & Hilles, Richard J. Toward the Responsive Organization: The Theory & Practice of Survey Feed.
Golembiewski, Robert T. & White, Michael. Cases in Public Management.
Golembiewski, Robert T., ed. Approaches to Organizing.
Golenbock, Peter, jt. auth. see Johnson, Davey.
Golf Digest, ed. The Golf Digest Almanac, 1984.
Golf Digest Editors. Golf Digest Almanac, 1985.
--Golf Digest Almanac, 1986.
--Tips from the Tour: Professional Lessons from Today's Top Golfers.
Golf Digest Editors, ed. One Hundred Greatest Golf Courses--& Then Some. Davis, William H.
Golfberg, Dick. The Beginner's Guide to Investing.
Golieb, D. E., jt. auth. see Ettinger, Richard P.
Golif, Louis A. Le see Le Golif, Louis A.
Golightly, Henry O. Consultants: Selecting, Using & Evaluating Business Consultants.
Golin, Anne K. & Ducanis, Alex J. The Interdisciplinary Team: A Handbook for the Education of Exceptional Children.
Golino, Carlo L., jt. auth. see Speroni, Charles.
Golka, F. W., ed. see Westerman, Claus.
Gollak, B., ed. see Strogonov, B. P., et al.
Gollay, Elinor, et al. Coming Back: The Community Experiences of Deinstitutionalized Mentally Retarded People.
Golledge, Reginald G., jt. ed. see Cox, Kevin R.
Gollehon, John. Casino Games.
--Winner Take All!
Goller, Karl H., ed. The Alliterative Morte Arthure: A Reassessment of the Poem.
Golley, Frank B., ed. Ecological Succession.
Golley, John. Hurricanes over Murmansk.
Gollihur, Glenn A. Forewordd by see Smith, Lloyd M.
Gollin, James. The Star Spangled Retirement Dream: Why It's Going to Sour & What You Can Do About It.
Gollnick, et al. Multicultural Teacher Education: Case Studies of Thirteen Programs.
Gollock, Georgina A. Sons of Africa.
Gollwitzer, Helmut. Song of Love: A Biblical Understanding of Sex. Crim, Keith, tr. from Ger.
Golomb, Louis. Brokers of Morality: Thai Ethnic Adaptation in a Rural Malaysian Setting.
Golombok, Susan, jt. auth. see Curran, Valerie.
Golos, Ellery B. Patterns in Mathematics.
Golos, Natalie, et al. Coping with Your Allergies.
Golovina, L. & Yaglom, I. Induction in Geometry.
Golstein, Pierre, jt. ed. see Clark, William R.
Golub, Edward S. The Cellular Basis of the Immune Response.
--Immunology.
Golub, Jeff, jt. auth. see Committee on Classroom Practices Staff.
Golub, Sharon, ed. Menarche: The Physiological, Psychological & Social Effects of the Onset of Menstruation.
Golubev, G. N. & Biswas, A. K., eds. Interregional Water Transfers: Projects & Problems: Proceedings of the Task Force Meeting, International Institute for Applied Systems Analysis, Laxenburg, Austria, Oct. 1977.
Golubev, V. V. Lectures on Integration of the Equations of Motion of a Rigid Body about a Fixed Point.
Golz, Judy, jt. auth. see Briscoe, Jill.
Golze, Alfred R., ed. Handbook of Dam Engineering.
Golzen. How Architects Get Work.
Gombrich, E. H. Meditations on a Hobby Horse: And Other Essays on the Theory of Art.
--Norm & Form: Studies in the Art of the Renaissance.
--Symbolic Images: Studies in the Art of the Renaissance.
Gombrich, Ernst H. Art & Illusion: A Study in the Psychology of Pictorial Presentation.
Gombrich, Lisbeth, tr. see Frisch, Karl.
Gomella, C & Mounier, J. P., eds. Eutrophication & Water Supply: Proceedings of the Specialised Conference of the IWSA held in Vienna, Austria, Oct. 7-9, 1981.
Gomer. Svensk Engeldk-Svensk Pocket Dictionary (Prisma Modern) & Grammar.
Gomer, R., ed. Interactions on Metal Surfaces.
Gomersall, A. & Farmer, P. Robotics Bibliography 1970-1981.
Gomes, Alberto G. Ecological Adaptation & Population Change: Semang Foragers & Temuan Horticulturists in West Malaysia.
Gomes, Paulo E. & Gomes, Salles. P's Three Women.
Gomes, Peter. Lent.
Gomes, Peter J., jt. auth. see Geller, Lawrence D.
Gomes, Peter J., jt. auth. see Kee, Howard C.
Gomes, Salles, jt. auth. see Gomes, Paulo E.
Gomez, A. A. & Gomez, K. A. Multiple Cropping in the Humid Tropics of Asia.
Gomez, Alfredo. The Basics of BASIC.
Gomez, Ermilo A. Canek: History & Legend of a Maya Hero.
Gomez, K. A., jt. auth. see Gomez, A. A.
Gomez, Madeleine Angelique Poisson De see Poisson De Gomez, Madeleine Angelique.
Gomez, Monica Villa, tr. see Life in Christ Staff.
Gomez, Thelma J. & Simpson, Elizabeth, eds. Independent Activities for Learning Centers.
Gomez-Ibanez, J. D., ed. Chemical Education: Proceedings of an International Symposium, Sao Paulo, Brazil, 1971.
Gomi, Taro. Hi Butterfly.
--Sharing.
Gomme, A. H., ed. see Middleton, Thomas.
Gomme, George L. Ethnology in Folklore.
--Folklore As A Historical Science.
--Primitive Folk-Moots: Or, Open-Air Assemblies in Britain.
Gomon, Audrey, jt. auth. see Smith, Donald E.
Gomoyunova, M. V., jt. auth. see Dobretsov, L. N.
Gompel, C. Atlas of Diagnostic Cytology.
Gompers, Samuel. Seventy Years of Life & Labour.
Gomperts, B. D. The Plasma Membrane: Models for Its Structure & Function.
Gomperz, Heinrich. Philosophical Studies by Heinrich Gomperz. Robinson, Daniel S., ed.
Gompper, R., ed. Cycloaddition Reactions: Proceedings of a Symposium, Munich, 1970.
Gonchar, O. Cyclone.
Gonen, Rivka. Pottery in Ancient Times.
--Weapons & Warfare in Ancient Times.
Gonick, Jean. Mostly True Confessions: Looking for Love in the Eighties.
Gonser, B. W. see Hausner, Henry.
Gonser, U., ed. Mossbauer Spectroscopy.
Gonzales, Ambrose E. With Aesop along the Black Border.
Gonzales, Laurence. Jambeaux.
--The Last Deal.
--El Vago.
Gonzales, Luis J. & Sanchez Salazar, Gustavo A. The Great Rebel: Che Guevara in Bolivia.
Gonzalez, Carlos F., et al. Computed Brain & Orbital Tomography: Technique & Interpretation.
Gonzalez, Irma, jt. ed. see Wertheim, Bill.
Gonzalez, Jean. Complete Guide to Effective Dictation.
Gonzalez, Jean, jt. auth. see Bergerud, Marly.
Gonzalez, Joe R. & Zufelt, David L., eds. Cognates: Vocabulary Enrichment for Bilinguals.

Authors

Gonzalez, Nelly de see Diaz, Jorge & De Gonzalez, Nelly.
Gonzalez, Richard F., jt. auth. see Harris, Roy D.
Gonzalez, Roseann D., et al. Copy, Combine, & Compose: Controlling Composition.
Gonzalez-del-Valle, Antolin, jt. auth. see Gonzalez-del-Valle, Luis.
Gonzalez-del-Valle, Luis. El Teatro de Federico Garcia Lorca y Otros Ensayos Sobre Literatura Espanola e Hispanoamericana.
Gonzalez-del-Valle, Luis & Gonzalez-del-Valle, Antolin. Ficcion De Luis Romero.
Gonzalez-Echevarria, Robert. Alejo Carpentier: The Pilgrim at Home.
Gonzalez-Echevarria, Roberto. The Voice of the Masters: Writing & Authority in Modern Latin American Literature.
Gonzalez-Mena, Janet & Eyer, Dianne W. Infancy & Caregiving.
Gonzalez-Polio, Edgardo, jt. auth. see Bamberger, Michael.
Gonzalez-Ruiz, Jose-Maria. The New Creation: Marxist & Christian? O'Connell, Mathew J., tr. from Span.
Gonzelez, Carlos F., et al. Head & Spine Imaging. Masdeu, Joseph C. & Grossman, C. Barrie, eds.
Gooberman, Lawrence A. Operation Intercept.
Gooch, Bob. Spinning for Trout.
Gooch, Brison D., ed. & intro. by see Napoleon, Louis, 3rd.
Gooch, Bryan N. & Thatcher, David S. Musical Settings of Early & Mid-Victorian Literature: A Catalogue.
Gooch, G. P., ed. see Great Britain, Foreign Office Staff.
Gooch, Stapleton D; see O'Neal, William B.
Gooch, Steve. Female Transport.
Good, Anthony, jt. auth. see Barnard, Alan.
Good Housekeeping Magazine Editors. The Good Housekeeping Family Health & Medical Guide.
Good Housekeeping Staff. Good Housekeeping International Cookbook.
Good, Phillip I., jt. auth. see Franz, Martin.
Good, R. A. Introduction to Mathematics.
Good, R. A., jt. ed. see Day, N. K.
Good, R. A., jt. ed. see Day, S. R.
Good, R. A., jt. ed. see Twomey, J. J.
Good, Robert A., jt. ed. see Bach, Fritz H.
Good, Robert A., jt. ed. see Lipkin, Martin.
Good, Robert A., jt. ed. see Litman, Gary W.
Good, Ronald G. How Children Learn Science: Conceptual Development & Implications for Teaching.
Good, Thomas L. & Brophy, Jere E. Educational Psychology.
Goodacre, P. Worked Examples in Quantity Surveying Measurement.
Goodacre, P., et al. Cost Factors in Dimensional Co-ordination.
Goodale, Jerry, jt. auth. see Petersen, Daniel C.
Goodale, Thomas & Witt, Peter A., eds. Recreation & Leisure: Issues in an Era of Change.
Goodall, B. & Kirby, A. Resources & Playing.
Goodall, Blake. The Homilies of St. John Chrysostom on the Letters of St. Paul to Titus & Philemon.
Goodall, Charles S. How to Train Your Own Gun Dog.
Goodall, Daphne M., tr. see Mohr, Erna.
Goodall, David W., ed. Evolution of Desert Biota.
Goodall, Homer. James Bond Cookbook.
Goodall, John. Heaven & Earth: Album Leaves from a Ming Encyclopedia.
Goodall, John S. Adventures of Paddy Pork.
--Ballooning Adventures of Paddy Pork.
--An Edwardian Season.
--An Edwardian Summer.
--Jacko.
--Jacko.
--Lavinia's Cottage: A Pop-Up Story.
--Paddy Finds a Job: A Pop-up Story.
--Paddy's New Hat.
--Shrewbetinna's Birthday.
Goodall, John S., illus. Before the War: Nineteen Hundred Eight to Nineteen Thirty-Nine: An Autobiography in Pictures.
Goodban, Dale, jt. auth. see Meyers, Ray C.
Goodchild, Peter J. J. Robert Oppenheimer: Shatterer of Worlds.
Goode, J. E., jt. ed. see Salter, P. J.
Goode, James B. Poets of Darkness.
Goode, Ruth. A Book for Grandmothers.
Goode, Stephen. The New Congress.
--Violence in America.
Goode, William J., jt. auth. see Tavuchis, Nicholas.
Goodefellowe, Robin, jt. auth. see Molin, Sven E.
Goodenough, Ward H. Culture, Language & Society.
Gooder, Glenn G., jt. auth. see Grasham, John A.
Gooders, John. Where to Watch Birds in Europe.
Gooders, John, jt. auth. see Alden, Peter.
Goodey, Brian, jt. auth. see Smales, Lindsay M.
Goodfellow, Barbara. The Complete Make It Now Bake It Later.
Goodfellow, David M. Principles of Economic Sociology: The Economics of Primitive Life as Illustrated from the Bantu Peoples of South & East Africa.
Goodfellow, M., jt. auth. see Jones, D.
Goodfellow, M., ed. The Biology of the Nocardiae.
Goodfellow, P., ed. Genetic Analysis of the Cell Surface.
Goodfield, June. Quest for the Killers.
Goodfriend, Joyce D. Diaries & Letters of American Women: An Annotated Bibliography.
Goodfriend, L., et al, eds. Mechanisms in Allergy: Reagin-Mediated Hypersensitivity.
Goodger, E. M. Alternative Fuels: Chemical Energy Resources.
--Principles of Spaceflight Propulsion.
Goodheart, Eugene. Utopian Vision of D. H. Lawrence.
Goodhew, P. J. Speciman Preparation in Materials Science.
Goodin, Robert E. Political Theory & Public Policy.
Gooding, jt. auth. see Margulis.
Gooding, Charles A., jt. auth. see Margulis, Alexander R.
Gooding, Kathleen. The Festival Summer.
Gooding, Marion F. & Hughes, Bernice. Nursing School Entrance Examinations.
Goodings, Richard & Byram, Michael, eds. Changing Priorities in Teacher Education: An International Survey.
Goodisman, Jerry. Diatomic Interaction Potential Theory. Incl. Vol. 1. Fundamentals; Vol. 2. Applications. Acad Pr.
Goodison-Orr, Wildorf E. Messenger of Love.
Goodlad, John I. & Anderson, Robert H. Nongraded Elementary School.
Goodlad, John I., ed. Changing American School.
Goodlad, John I., ed. see Culver, Carmen M. & Hoban, Gary J.
Goodlad, John I., jt. ed. see Shane, Harold G.
Goodland. General Intensive Care.
Goodman & Mason. Experiencing Accounting: A Study Guide for Personal Computing.
Goodman, A. Harold. Instrumental Music Guide.
Goodman, A. W. Mainstream of Algebra & Trigonometry.
Goodman, A. W., et al. The Mainstream of Algebra & Trigonometry.
Goodman, Allen E., ed. Negotiating While Fighting: The Diary of Admiral C. Turner Joy at the Korean Armistice Conference.
Goodman, Anthony, jt. ed. see Newman, Michael.
Goodman, Clarke E. Preaching the Gospel of Jesus Christ.
Goodman, Danny. Word Processing on the IBM Personal Computer.
Goodman, Danny, jt. auth. see Consumer Guide Editors.
Goodman, David S. China's Provincial Leaders, 1949-1985: Vol. 1, Directory.
Goodman, Ellen. Keeping in Touch.
Goodman, Eric K. High on the Energy Bridge.
Goodman, Eugene B. All the Justice I Could Afford. Sandum, Howard E., ed.
Goodman, Frances S. The Embroidery of Mexico & Guatemala.
Goodman, Frank O & Wachman, Harold Y. Dynamics of Gas-Surface Scattering.
Goodman, G. T., jt. auth. see Chadwick, M. J.
Goodman, G. T. & Rowe, W. D., eds. Energy Risk Management.
Goodman, Gary S. Winning by Telephone: Telephone Effectiveness for the Business Man & Consumer.
--You Can Sell Anything by Telephone.
Goodman, Gerald & Dooley, David. Interpersonal Processes: Introductory Readings.
Goodman, Grant K. An Experiment in Wartime Intercultural Relations: Philippine Students in Japan, 1943-1945.
Goodman, Hanna see Goodman, Philip.
Goodman, Harriet W. & Morse, Barbar. Just What the Doctor Ordered.
Goodman, Herbert I. Japan & the World Energy Problem.
Goodman, Herman, jt. auth. see Fredericks, Carlton.
Goodman, Irving & Schein, Martin, eds. Birds: Brain & Behavior.
Goodman, J. W., ed. Advanced Aluminum & Titanium Structures (AD-02)
Goodman, Joel M., et al. Phylogenetic Development of Vertebrate Immunity, No. 2.
Goodman, John, Jr. Regional Housing Assistance Allocations & Regional Housing Needs.
Goodman, John L. Public Opinion During the Reagan Administration.
Goodman, Joseph I. & Biggers, W. Watts. Diabetes Without Fear.
--Diabetes Without Fear.
Goodman, Kennard E., et al. Today's Business Law.
Goodman, L. Sun Signs.
Goodman, L. J., et al, eds. Low-Cost Housing Technology: An East-West Perspective.
Goodman, Louis J. & Love, Ralph N., eds. Project Planning & Management: An Integrated Approach.
--Small Hydroelectric Projects for Rural Development: Planning & Management.
Goodman, Marcia M., jt. auth. see Roller, Duane.
Goodman, Mark. Hurrah for the Next Man Who Dies.
Goodman, Mark N. The Ninth Amendment: History, Interpretation & Meaning.
Goodman, Martin. State & Society in Roman Galilee, A. D. 132-212.
Goodman, Michael. Dictionary of Collectors Terms.
Goodman, Michael B. William S. Burroughs: An Annotated Bibliography of His Works & Criticism.
Goodman, Michael H. The Last Dalai Lama: A Biography.
Goodman, Mike. How to Win.
Goodman, N., jt. auth. see Belkin, Gary S.
Goodman, Nathan G., ed. The Ingenious Dr. Franklin: Selected Scientific Letters of Benjamin Franklin.
Goodman, Philip, ed. Jewish Marriage Anthology. Goodman, Hanna.
--Purim Anthology.
Goodman, R. W. Nilpotent Lie Groups: Structure & Applications to Analysis.
Goodman, Richard E. & Hueze, Francios E., eds. Issues in Rock Mechanics: Twenty-Third Symposium.
Goodman, Robert. Color TV Case Histories Illustrated: Photo Guide to Troubles & Cures.
--The Last Entrepreneurs: America's Regional Wars for Jobs & Dollars.
Goodman, Robert L. Maintaining & Repairing Videocassette Recorders.
--Practical Troubleshooting with Modern Electronic Test Instruments.
Goodman, Roger B. & Ince, William. How to Prepare for the Reading Skills Test.
--Power Skills in Reading II.
--Power Skills in Writing I.
--Power Skills in Writing II.
Goodman, Sam. Cogiter's Treasury.
Goodman, Sidney, jt. auth. see Schwartz, Seymour.
Goodman, Walter. The Committee: The Extraordinary Career of the House Committee on Un-American Activities.
Goodpasture, B. C. Sermons of B. C. Goodpasture. Thomas, J. D., ed.
Goodreau, William. Many Islands.
Goodrich, Gwenyth B. Bunnechauk: Alaska - Then & Now.
Goodrich, Norma L. Giono: Master of Fictional Modes.
Goodrich, Samuel G. Recollections of a Lifetime, or Men & Things I Have Seen.
Goodridge, Janet. Creative Drama & Improvised Movement for Children.
Goodsell, Jane. Katie's Magic Glasses.
--Katie's Magic Glasses.
Goodsell, John W. On Polar Trails.
Goodson, Aileen. Nudity As Therapy. Kunkin, Art, ed.
Goodson, Barbara D., jt. auth. see Travers, Jeffrey.
Goodson, C. E. & Miertschin, S. L. Technical Algebra with Applications.
--Technical Trigonometry with Applications.
Goodson, Ivor F. School Subjects & Curriculum Change: Case Studies in the Social History of Curriculum.
Goodspeed, Charles E. Yankee Bookseller.
Goodspeed, Donald J. The German Wars Nineteen Fourteen to Nineteen Forty-Five.
Goodspeed, Edgar J., ed. see Smith, John M.
Goodspeed Publishing Company Staff. History of Henderson, Chester, McNairy, Decatur & Hardin Counties, Tennessee.
--History of Lauderdale, Tipton, Haywood & Crockett Counties.
--History of Tennessee Illustrated, History of Thirty East Tenn. Counties.
--Memorial & Genealogical Record of Southwest Texas.
Goodspeed, Robert C. From Greek to Graffiti: English Words That Survive & Thrive.
Goodstein, R. L. Fundamental Concepts of Mathematics.
Goodwin, B., ed. Analytical Physiology of Cells & Developing Organisms.
Goodwin, B. L. Handbook of Intermediate Metabolism of Aromatic Compounds.
Goodwin, Bailey, et al. Subsidised Public Transport & the Demand for Travel.
Goodwin, Bennie E., II. The Effective Teacher.
Goodwin, Brian C. Temporal Organization in Cells.
Goodwin, D. W., ed. Advances in Quantum Electronics.
Goodwin, Derek H. Beef Management & Production: A Practical Guide for Farmers & Students.
Goodwin, Doris K. The Fitzgeralds & the Kennedys.
Goodwin, G. L. New Dimensions of World Politics.
Goodwin, George, Limited Staff, ed. Traffic, Transportation & Urban Planning.
Goodwin, Hope. Shadows over Paradise.
Goodwin, Jean M. Sexual Abuse: Incest Victims & Their Families.
Goodwin, John F., jt. ed. see Yu, Paul N.
Goodwin, John R. & Rovelstad, James M. Travel & Lodging Law: Principles, Statutes & Cases.
Goodwin, Joseph, ed. see Ayensu, Edward S., et al.
Goodwin, Ken. Understanding African Poetry: A Study of Ten Poets.
Goodwin, Mark D. Level II ROMs.
Goodwin, Mary T. & Pollen, Gerry. Creative Food Experiences for Children.
Goodwin, Maud W. Dolly Madison.
Goodwin, Michael, ed. Nineteenth Century Opinion: An Anthology of Extracts from the First 50 Volumes of the Nineteenth Century, 1877-1901.
Goodwin, Paul. Global Studies: Latin America.
Goodwin, Stephen. Blood of Paradise.
Goodwin, T. W. Biosynthesis of Vitamins & Related Compounds.
Goodwin, T. W., ed. Chemistry & Biochemistry of Plant Pigments.
--Chemistry & Biochemistry of Plant Pigments.
Goodwin, T. W. & Goodwin, T. W., eds. Biochemistry of Chloroplasts.
Goodwin, T. W., ed. see Biochemical Society Symposium, 27th.
Goodwin, T. W., ed. see Biochemical Society Symposium, 28th.
Goodwin, T. W., ed. see Biochemical Society Symposium, 29th.
Goodwin, T. W., ed. see Biochemical Society Symposium, 30th.
Goodwin, T. W., ed. see I U B - I U B S Joint Symposium - 1st - Stockholm - 1960.
Goodwin, T. W., ed. see International Symposium on Carotenoids Staff.
Goodwin, T. W., ed. see Phytochemical Society.
Goodwin, Thomas H., tr. see Zander, Maximilian.
Goodwin, Tony. Northern Adirondack Ski Tours: Thirty Selected Tours for the Novice to Expert Skier.
Goodwin, Tony, jt. ed. see Burdick, Neal S.
Goody, Phyllis B. Julio, the Shoeshine Boy.
Goodyear, Imogene, ed. Daily Bread, Nineteen Eighty-Six.
--Daily Bread, 1987.
Goor, Ronald, jt. auth. see Selsam, Millicent E.
Gootlieb, William, ed. see Prevention Magazine Editors.
Gootnick, David. Getting a Better Job.
Goozner, Calman. Computational Skills for College Students.
Gopal, M., jt. auth. see Nagrath, I. J.
Gopal, R., et al, eds. Energy Conservation in Building Heating & Air Conditioning Systems.
Gopalakrishnan, Chennat, ed. Emerging Marine Economy of the Pacific.
Gopalakrishnan, S. & Cooper, P., eds. Performance Prediction of Centifugal Pumps & Compressors.
Gopi Krishna. The Inner World.
--To Those Concerned Citizens.
Gopinathan, V. Plasticity Theory & Its Application in Metal Forming.
Gora, Joel M. The Rights of Reporters.
Gora, Michael H. Blood Coast: A Novel of South Florida.
Goransson, B., ed. Industrial Waste Water & Wastes II.
Gorbach, Sherwood L. & Zimmerman, David R. The Doctor's Anti-Breast Cancer Diet: How the Right Foods Can Reduce Your Risk of Breast Cancer.
Gorbachev, V. M. & Zamyatnin, A. A. Nuclear Reactions in Heavy Elements: A Data Handbook.
Gordan, Gilbert S. & Vaughan, Cynthia. Clinical Management of the Osteoporoses.
Gorder, Christine, jt. auth. see Braithwaite, Julia.
Gordh, Gordon & Trjapitzin, V. Taxonomic Studies of the Encyrtidae with the Descriptions of New Species & a New Genus: Hymenoptera: Chalcidoidea.
Gordis, Philip. How to Stay Ahead Financially.
Gordis, Robert. Faith for Moderns.
--Love & Sex: A Modern Jewish Perspective.
Gordo Guarinos, Francisco. Diccionario Escolar Roble.
Gordon, A., jt. auth. see Fulton, O.
Gordon, Ann & Browne, Kathryn W. Beginnings & Beyond: Foundations in Early Childhood Education.
Gordon, Arthur. A Song Called Hope.
Gordon, B. L. Medieval & Renaissance Medicine.
Gordon, B. L., et al. Apache Indians. Horr, David A., ed.
Gordon, B. Le Roy. Human Geography & Ecology in the Sinu Country of Columbia.
Gordon, Bernard L., ed. Energy from the Sea: Marine Resource Readings.

Gordon, Beverly. Domestic American Textiles: A Bibliographic Sourcebook.
Gordon, Burgess L. Understanding & Promoting the Resources of Aging People: A Guide to Care, Proper Environment & Well-Being.
Gordon, C. W. & Canuto, V. The Earth One: The Upper Atmosphere, Ionisphere & Magnetosphere.
Gordon, C. Wayne, ed. The Uses of Sociology in Education.
Gordon, Caroline. Aleck Maury, Sportsman.
--The Collected Stories.
--Women on the Porch.
Gordon, Cecilia. Resource Organization in Primary Schools.
Gordon, Charles. The Two Tycoons: Charles Clore & Jack Cotton.
Gordon, Clifford K., ed. Coke & Other Solid Fuel Derivatives from Coal.
Gordon, Colin. Beyond the Looking Glass: Reflections of Alice & Her Family.
Gordon, Cyrus H. Common Background of Greek & Hebrew Civilizations.
Gordon, David, tr. from Chinese. Equinox: A Gathering of T'ang Poets.
Gordon, David B., ed. Hypertension: The Renal Basis.
Gordon, David L. Development Finance Companies, State & Privately Owned: A Review.
Gordon, David M. Theories of Poverty & Underemployment.
Gordon, Don E. Electronic Warfare: Element of Strategy & Multiplier of Combat Power.
Gordon, Douglas H. The Pre-Historic Background of Indian Culture. Barrett, D. & Madhuri, Desai, eds.
Gordon, Dudley. The Birch Bark Poems of Charles F. Lummis.
--Charles F. Lummis: Crusader in Corduroy.
Gordon, Emanuel. Uranium Nineteen Eighty.
Gordon, Frank S. & Hemnes, Thomas. The Legal Word Book.
Gordon, G., ed. Active Touch-The Mechanism of Recognition of Objects by Manipulation: A Multidisciplinary Approach.
Gordon, Geoffrey. The Application of GPSS Five to Discrete System Simulation.
Gordon, George K. & Stryker, Ruth. Creative Long-Term Care Administration.
Gordon, Helen H. From Copying to Creating.
Gordon, Herbert. The Canoe Book.
Gordon, Ian, ed. Unemployment, the Regions & Labour Markets: Reactions to Recession.
Gordon, Ira J. Children's Views of Themselves.
Gordon, Ira J., ed. Early Childhood Education.
Gordon, Isabel, jt. auth. see De Regniers, Beatrice S.
Gordon, J. L. Platelets in Biology & Pathology.
Gordon, Jaimy. Rose of the West.
Gordon, John C. Verbal Deficit: A Critique.
Gordon, Judith, jt. auth. see Gordon, Sol.
Gordon, Laura K., jt. auth. see Davidson, Laurie.
Gordon, Leonard. Sociology & American Social Issues.
Gordon, Lincoln. Growth Policies & the International Order.
--Growth Policies & the International Order.
Gordon, Lois. Donald Barthelme.
Gordon, M., ed. Liquid Crystal Polymers I.
Gordon, M. & Plate, N. A., eds. Liquid Crystal Polymers II-III.
Gordon, M. & Ware, W. R., eds. The Exciplex.
Gordon, M., et al. Edinburgh LCF: A Mechanised Logic of Computation.
Gordon, Malcolm R. From Chusan to Sea Princess.
Gordon, Margaret, illus. A Paper of Pins.
Gordon, Mary. Men & Angels.
--Temporary Shelter.
Gordon, Mary & Swinburne, Algernon C. The Children of the Chapel: A Tale. Lougy, Robert E., intro. by.
Gordon, Maxwell, ed. Psychopharmacological Agents. Incl. Vol. 1; Vol. 2; Vol. 3. Acad Pr.
Gordon, Melvin, jt. auth. see Bromberg, Murray.
Gordon, Myron, ed. Pigment Cell Growth: Proceedings.
Gordon, Neil & McKinlay, Ian, eds. Helping Clumsy Children.
Gordon, Noah. The Physician.
Gordon, P., jt. auth. see Guiltinan, Joseph P.
Gordon, P. F. & Gregory, P. Organic Chemistry in Colour.
Gordon, R. & Spaulding, M. L. Numerical Models for Tidal Rivers, Estuaries & Coastal Waters: Bibliography.
Gordon, Rebecca. Letters from Nicaragua.
Gordon, Rex. First on Mars, No. 18.
Gordon, Richard. The Invisible Victory.
--Jack the Ripper.
--The Private Life of Florence Nightingale.
--A Question of Guilt: The Curious Case of Dr. Crippen.
Gordon, Robert & Spaulding, Malcolm. A Bibliography of Numerical Models for Tidal Rivers, Estuaries & Coastal Waters.
Gordon, Ronald D., jt. auth. see Bergland, Glen D.
Gordon, Ronni L., jt. auth. see Stillman, David M.
Gordon, Rue, ed. Conservation Directory, 1988.
Gordon, Ruth. Children of Darkness.
--Shady Lady.
Gordon, Ruth, compiled by. Databases & Clearinghouses: Information Resources for Education.
Gordon, S. D. The Healing Christ.
Gordon, Sol & Gordon, Judith. Raising a Child Conservatively in a Sexually Permissive World.
Gordon, Sol, jt. auth. see Dickman, Irving R.
Gordon, Stephen D., et al. Minnesota Public Sector Labor Law.
Gordon, Stephen L., ed. see American Academy of Orthopedic Surgeons Staff.
Gordon, Suzanne. Off Balance: The Real World of Ballet.
Gordon, Theodore J. Life-Extending Technologies: A Technology Assessment.
Gordon, Thomas F. The History of Pennsylvania, from Its Discovery by Europeans to the Declaration of Independence in 1776.
Gordon, V. O. A Course in Descriptive Geometry.
Gordon, Vivian V. The Self-Concept of Black Americans.
Gordy, W. & Cook, L., eds. Technique of Organic Chemistry: Vol. 9, Pt. 2, Microwave Molecular Spectra.
Gore, Albert. Let the Glory Out.
Gore, Elizabeth. Child Psychiatry Observed. Nursten, Jean, ed.
Gore, Kay, jt. auth. see Bitter, Gary G.
Gore, Marvin & Stubbe, John. Elements of Systems Analysis.
Gore, Marvin R. & Stubbe, John W. Computers & Data Processing.
Gorecki, P. K. & Stanbury, W. T. Perspectives on the Royal Commission on Corporate Concentration.
Gorelik, Mordecai. New Theatres for Old.
Gorelik, S. S. Recrystallization in Metals & Alloys.
Goren, Charles H. & Von der Porten, Ronald P. Introduction to Competitive Bidding.
Gorer, Geoffrey. American People: A Study in National Character.
Gores, Joe. Dead Skip.
--Interface.
Gorev, A. Jawaharlal Nehru.
Gorey, Edward. Amphigorey.
--Amphigorey Too.
--The Sopping Thursday.
Gorham, Nathaniel R. Jackson Browne, Neil Diamond & Elton John: An Analysis of Nineteenth Century Musical Thought.
Goring, Loris. The Care & Repair of Marine Gasoline Engines.
Gorion, Emanuel bin, jt. ed. see Gorion, Micha J. bin.
Gorion, Micha J. bin & Gorion, Emanuel bin, eds. Mimekor Yisrael: Classical Jewish Folktales. Lask, I. M., tr. from Hebrew.
Goritz, John. Mathematics for Welding Trades.
Gorkin, V. Z. Amine Oxidases in Clinical Research.
Gorky, M. Selected Short Stories.
Gorky, M., et al. Anton Makarenko: His Life & His Work in Education.
Gorky, Maxim. The Autobiography of Maxim Gorky. Schneider, Isidore, tr. Incl. My Childhood; In the World; My Universities. Peter Smith.
--Letters.
--Lower Depths. Chwat, Jacques, ed.
--On Literature.
Gorlow, Leon, jt. auth. see Katkosky, Walter.
Gorman, B. S. & Wessman, A. E., eds. The Personal Experience of Time.
Gorman, Ed, ed. The Second Black Lizard Anthology of Crime Fiction.
Gorman, G. E. The South African Novel in English Since 1950: An Information & Resource Guide.
Gorman, George. The Society of Friends.
Gorman, James. First Aid for Hypochondriacs.
Gorman, James E. Simplified Guide to Construction Management for Architects & Engineers.
Gorman, Judy. The Culinary Craft. Taylor, Sandra J., ed.
--Judy Gorman's Vegetable Cookbook. Taylor, Sandra, ed.
Gorman, Kenneth A., jt. auth. see Crowningshield, Gerald.
Gorman, Michael & Height, Frank, eds. Design for Tourism: An I.C.S.I.D. Interdesign Report.
Gorman, Michael & Winkler, Paul W., eds. Anglo-American Cataloguing Rules.
Gormezano, C. & Leotta, G. G., eds. Heating in Toroidal Plasmas III: Proceedings of the 3rd Joint Varenna-Grenoble International Symposium, Grenoble, France, 22-26 March 1982.
Gorn, Janice L. The Writer's Handbook.
Gornick, Vivian. Women in Science: Portraits from a World in Transition.
Gorodetzky, Charles & Christian, Samuel T. What You Should Know About Drugs.
Gorodnov, V., jt. auth. see Buzuev, V.
Gorowara, Krishna, tr. see Pritam, Amrita.
Gorr, Alan, ed. Problems in Todays Education.
Gorrell, Robert M., jt. auth. see Laird, Charlton.
Gorris, Greg. Bible for Bartenders.
Gorski, Andrew, tr. see Manteuffel, Tadeusz.
Gorski, Roger A. & Whalen, Richard E., eds. Brain & Behavior Vol. III: Brain & Gonadal Function.
Gorsky, Susan R. Virginia Woolf.
Gorsline, Douglas, illus. Nursery Rhymes.
Gortner, Harold F. Administration in the Public Sector.
Gorton, Richard A. & McIntyre, Kenneth E. The Senior High School Principalship: The Effective Principal. Koerner, Thomas F., ed.
Gorton, Ron. The Lawyers of Hell.
Gorwen, Leonard. How to Find & Land Your First Full-Time Job.
Gorwood, Brian T. School Transfer & Curriculum Continuity.
Gorzalka, Ann L. The Saddlemakers of Sheridan County, Wyoming.
Gorzelany, James A. Nevada Supplement for Modern Real Estate Practice.
Gose, Elliott B., Jr. The Transformation Process in Joyce's Ulysses.
Gosepath, J., jt. auth. see Reisner, K.
Goshgarian, Gary. Atlantis Fire.
--Exploring Language.
Goslin, David A. Handbook of Socialization Theory & Research.
Gosline, William A. Functional Morphology & Classification of Teleostean Fishes.
Gosling, David & Musschenga, Bert, eds. Science Education & Ethical Values: Introducing Ethics & Religion into the Classroom & Laboratory.
Gosling, E. M., jt. ed. see Wilkins, N. P.
Gosling, Paula. Solo Blues.
Gosling, William G. Life of Sir Humphrey Gilbert, England's First Empire Builder.
Gosner, Robert W. & Pluth, James M. Gas Turbine System Technician, Electrical 3 & 2.
Gosovic, B. United Nations Council on Trade & Development (UNCTAD) Conflict & Compromise.
Gosovic, Branislav. Global Environmental Monitoring.
Goss, Clav see Harrison, Paul C.
Goss, James, jt. ed. see Martin, Luther H.
Goss, Madeleine. Modern Music-Makers: Contemporary American Composers.
Goss, R. J., jt. ed. see Nowinski, W. W.
Goss, Ralph. Roofing Ready Reckoner for Timber Roofs of Any Span or Pitch.
Goss, Robert C. The San Xavier Altarpiece.
Gosse, Edmund W., jt. auth. see Garnett, Richard.
Gossett, Don. How to Conquer Fear.
--How to Cope When You Can't: A How to Manual to Help You Cope with the Stress of Modern Living.
--Praise Avenue.
Gossett, Philip, ed. see Meyerbeer, Giacomo.
Gossett, Phillip, ed. see Rossini, Gioachino.
Gossez, J. P., et al, eds. Nonlinear Operators & the Calculus & Variations: Summer School Held in Bruxelles, 8-19 Sept. 1975.
Gossick, Ben R. Hamilton's Principles & Physical Systems.
Gossip, C. J. An Introduction to French Classical Tragedy.
Gosson, Stephen. The Ephemerides of Phialo.
--Playes Confuted in Five Actions.
Gostelow, Mary. A World of Embroidery.
Goswami, B. C., et al. Textile Yarns: Technology, Structure & Applications.
Goswami, Shyam S. Layayoga: An Advanced Method of Concentration.
Gosz, James R., jt. auth. see Potter, Loren D.
Goth, Andres & Vesell, Elliot S. Medical Pharmacology: Principles & Concepts.
Gotlieb, C. C. & Borodin, A. Social Issues in Computing.
Gotlieb, C. C. & Gotlieb, Leo R. Data Types & Structures.
Gotlieb, Leo R., jt. auth. see Gotlieb, C. C.
Gotlind, Erik. Aspects of Pyschotherapeutic Processes.
Gotoff, Harold C. Cicero's Elegant Style: An Analysis of the Pro Archia.
Gots & Kaufman. People's Hospital Book.
Gotsch, Carl & Brown, Gilbert. Prices, Taxes & Subsidies in Pakistan Agriculture, 1960-1976.
Gotsman, M. S., jt. ed. see Borman, J. B.
Gott, Peter. No House Calls: Irreverent Notes on the Practice of Medicine.
Gottberg, John. Asia 101: History, Art & Culture for the Traveler.
--Australia in Twenty-Two Days.
Gottberg, John, jt. auth. see Steves, Rick.
Gottesman, Ronald & Geduld, Harry, eds. The Girl in the Hairy Paw.
Gottesman, Ronald, et al, eds. The Norton Anthology of American Literature: Shorter Edition.
Gottfredson, Floyd, intro. by. Mickey Mouse.
Gottfried, Byron S. Schaum's Outline of Programming with BASIC.
Gottfried, Herbert & Jennings, Jan. American Vernacular Design, Eighteen Seventy to Nineteen Forty: An Illustrated Glossary.
Gottfried, Martin. In Person: The Great Entertainers.
Gottfried, Nathan, jt. auth. see Seay, Bill M.
Gottfried, Robert S. Doctors & Medicine in Medieval England, 1340-1530.
Gottheil, E. L., et al, eds. see Coatesville-Jefferson Conference on Addiction, 1st, October 1977.
Gottheil, Edward, et al, eds. Substance Abuse & Psychiatric Illness: Proceedings of the Second Annual Coatesville--Jefferson Conference on Addiction.
Gottheil, Fred M. Marx's Economic Predictions.
Gotthilf, Daniel L., jt. auth. see Blecke, Curtis J.
Gottinger, W. Senile Retinoschisis: Morphological Relationship of the Formation of Spaces Within the Peripheral Retina to Senile Retinochisis & to Schisis Detachment. Bayo, J. W., tr.
Gottlieb, Alan. The Rights of Gun Owners.
Gottlieb, Allan, jt. auth. see Almasi, George S.
Gottlieb, Beatrice, tr. see Febvre, Lucien.
Gottlieb, Elaine, ed. see Hemley, Cecil.
Gottlieb, Elaine, tr. see Singer, Isaac Bashevis.
Gottlieb, Leonard. Factory Made: How Things Are Manufactured.
Gottlieb, Robert, ed. see Handl, Irene.
Gottlieb, Robert, ed. see Johnston, Jill.
Gottlieb, Sybil, jt. ed. see Davis, Harold B.
Gotto, A. M., et al, eds. High Density Lipoproteins & Atherosclerosis: Proceedings of the 3rd Argenteuil Symposium Held Under the Auspices of the Foundation Cardiologique Princesse Liliane in Waterloo, Belgium, Nov., 1977.
Gottschalk, Carl W., jt. auth. see Earley, Lawrence E.
Gottschalk, L. A. & Cravey, R. H. Toxicological & Pathological Studies on Psychoactive Drug-Involved Deaths.
Gottschalk, Louis & Bill, Shirley, eds. The Letters of Lafayette to Washington, 1777-1799.
Gottschalk, Louis A. & Gleser, Goldine C. The Measurement of Psychological States Through the Content Analysis of Verbal Behavior.
Gottsegen, Katherine. Cooking is an Act of Love.
Gottstein, G. & Luecke, K., eds. Textures of Materials: Proceedings of the 5th Int'l. Conf. on Texture of Materials, March 29-April 1, 1978, Aachen, Germany.
Gottstein Research Unit Staff & Planck, Max, Society Staff, eds. Directory of Institutions in the Federal Republic of Germany Co-operating with Developing Countries in Science & Technology.
Gotz, Ignacio L. No Schools.
Goudge, Eileen. Eileen Goudge's Swept Away Number One: Gone with the Wish.
--Gone with the Wish.
Goudge, Elizabeth. Little White Horse.
Goudie, Andrew, ed. The Encyclopedic Dictionary of Physical Geography.
Goudket, Michael. Audiovisual Primer.
Goudsblom, Johan. Nihilism & Culture.
Goudy, Frederic W. Alphabet & Elements of Lettering.
Goudzwaard, Bob. Idols of Our Time. Vennen, Mark V., tr. from Dutch.
Gouedy, Terrence. Everything You Never Wanted to Know about Yourself or, the Cancer Syndrome.
Gouge, William M. Short History of Paper Money & Banking in the United States.
Gough, Hugh. The Newspaper Press in the French Revolution.
Gough, Irene. Golden Lamb.
Gough, Vera & Grier, B. R. Better Telephoning: A Plan to Improve Your Telephone Technique.
--Planned Speaking & Your Career.
Gough, W. James, ed. see Seiden, Rudolph.
Goulart, Francis S. Beyond Baby Fat: Weight-Loss Plans for Children & Teenagers.
Goulart, Ron. The Prisoner of Blackwood Castle.
Gould, Byrant P. Planning the New Corporate Headquarters.
Gould, Charles. Mythical Monsters.
Gould, Christopher & Morgan, Richard P. South Carolina Imprints, 1731-1800: A Descriptive Bibliography.
Gould, Dana, jt. auth. see Sanders, J. Oswald.
Gould, David J. Bureaucratic Corruption in the Third World.
Gould Editiorial Staff. Penal Law of New York: Spanish Edition.
Gould Editorial Staff. Bailments Law of New York, 1962.
--Conservation Law of Illinois.
--Criminal Laws of Florida.
--Criminal Laws of Massachusetts.
--Customs Law Handbook (Titles 18, 19 U.S.C. & Related Statutes)
--Evidence Code-Federal.
--Evidence Law of New York Quizzer 1981.

--Law Enforcement Handbook of Connecticut.
--Massachusetts Motor Vehicle Laws.
--New York Family Court Act.
--New York Insurance Law.
--Penal Code of Michigan.
--Penal Law of New York Question & Answers.
--Pennsylvania Civil Procedure Law & Rules.
--UCC State Service.
Gould, Elaine Westall. Look Behind You, Thomas Wolfe: Ghosts of a Common Tribal Heritage.
Gould, Floyd J., jt. auth. see Eppen, Gary D.
Gould, G. & Hurst, A. Bacterial Spore.
Gould, G. W., jt. ed. see Barker, A. N.
Gould, James A., jt. auth. see Dewey, Robert E.
Gould, James W. United States & Malaysia.
Gould, Jay M. & Paykin, Bentley H. The Structure of U. S. Business. Trinet, Inc. Staff, ed.
Gould, John. The Wines of Pentagoet.
Gould, Joseph C. & Mott, Charles J. Earth Science: An Individualized Approach.
Gould, Mary E. Early American Wooden Ware.
Gould, Meredith, et al. Invertebrate Oogenesis.
Gould, Murray, jt. auth. see Hill, George R.
Gould, P. & Olsson, G., eds. A Search for Common Ground.
Gould, P., et al. The Structure of Television.
Gould, Peter. Spatial Diffusion: The Spread of Ideas & Innovations in Geographic Space.
Gould, Rev. G. K. Faith: A Psalm of Active Trust & Quiet Confidence.
Gould, Roger L. Transformations.
Gould, Rupert R. More Oddities & Enigmas.
Gould, Rupert T. The Case for the Sea Serpent.
--Oddities: A Book of Unexplained Facts.
Gould, Wilbur A. Tomato Production, Processing & Quality Evaluation.
Gould, William, ed. see Urdang, Laurence.
Gould, William B. Japan's Reshaping of American Labor Law.
Goulden, Joseph. Jerry Wurf: Labor's Last Angry Man.
Goulden, Joseph C. Best Years-Nineteen Forty-Five to Nineteen Fifty.
Goulden, Joseph C. & Raffio, Alexander W. The Death Merchant: The Rise & Fall of Edwin P. Wilson.
Goulder, ed. Channel West & Solent Almanac: A Nautical Almanac for Yachtsmen.
Goulder, Michael D. The Song of Fourteen Songs.
Goulding, Ray, jt. auth. see Elliott, Bob.
Gouldner, Alvin W. Coming Crisis of Western Sociology.
Gould-Sachs, Jacqueline Illus. by see Callow, Patricia, et al.
Goulet, Claude B. How to Be a Happy & Successful Investor.
Goulet, Denis. Cruel Choice: A New Concept in the Theory of Development.
Gounaris, John, et al. Dining In - Hampton Road. Lotzgar, Elaine, ed.
Gourd, L. M. Introduction to Engineering Materials.
Gourdie, Tom. Calligraphic Styles.
--Calligraphy for the Beginner: Giant.
--Handwriting for Today.
--Handwriting Made Easy: A Simple Modern Approach.
--Italic Handwriting.
Gourman, Jack. Gourman Report: A Rating of Graduate & Professional Programs in American & International Universities.
Gourse, Leslie. Student Guide to New York.
Goutel, Beatrice de, jt. auth. see Carillon, Annie.
Goveia, Elsa V. Slave Society in the British Leeward Islands at the End of the Eighteenth Century.
Gover, Alan. The Oil & Gas Industry & the Bankruptcy Laws.
Gover, Robert. One Hundred Dollar Misunderstanding.
Government Institutes, Inc. Staff, ed. Energy Technology, No. 15: Repowering America.
Government Institutes Staff, ed. Cogeneration in California, 1984.
Govoni, Laura E. & Hayes, Janice E. Drugs & Nursing Implications.
Gowan, Donald E. Reclaiming the Old Testament for the Christian Pulpit.
--The Triumph of Faith in Habakkuk.
Gowans, Fred R. & Campbell, Eugene E. Fort Bridger: Island in the Wilderness.
--Fort Supply: Brigham Young's Green River Experiment.
Gowar, Antonia. Cashing in.
Gowda, H. H., jt. auth. see Wells, Henry.
Gowen, James A. Progress in Writing: A Learning Program.
Gower, J. F., ed. Oceanography from Space.
Gowin, D. Bob. Educating.
Gowin, Emmet. Emmet Gowin - Petra: In the Hashemite Kingdom of Jordan.
Gowland, David. Controlling the Money Supply.
Goyal, Bhagwat S. The Strategy of Survival.
Goyer, Doreen S. The International Population Census Bibliography: 1945-1977.
Goyet de la Sarthe, Charles L., jt. auth. see Constant, Benjamin.
Goze, M., jt. auth. see Lutz, R.
Gozzini, A., ed. Topics of Radiofrequency Spectroscopy.
GP-Info Symposium Staff. Computers & the General Practitioner: Proceedings of the GP-Info Symposium, London March, 13-15, 1980. Malcolm, A. & Poyser, J., eds.
GPS Summer School, Saarbruecken, F. R. Germany, Jul 10-12, 1974. One-Dimensional Conductors: Proceedings. Schuster, H. G., ed.
Grabar, Oleg. The Alhambra.
Graber, Doris. Mass Media & American Politics.
Graber, Doris A. Processing the News: How People Tame the Information Tide.
Graber, Kay, ed. see Tibbles, Thomas H.
Grabill, Paul. Youth's a Stuff Will Not Endure.
Grabowicz, Paul, jt. auth. see Kotkin, Joel.
Grabowska, J. Polish Amber.
Grace, Gerald, ed. Education & the City: Theory, History & Contemporary Practice.
Grace, Helen K., jt. auth. see Knafl, Kathleen A.
Grace, William J., Jr. The ABC'S of IRA'S: The Complete Guide to Individual Retirement Accounts.
Gracey, Michael, ed. Diarrhoeal Disease & Malnutrition: A Clinical Update.
Grachev, Andrei. In the Grip of Terror.
Gracie, Archibald. Titanic.
Gracie, David M., tr. see Harnack, Adolf.
Gracq, Julien. The Castle of Argol. Varese, Louise, tr. from Fr.
Grad, Burton, et al. Management Systems.
Grad, Frank, ed. Public Health Law Manual.
Grad, Laurie B. Dining In - Los Angeles.
Graddis. Recognitions.
Gradidge, Roderick. Dream Houses: The Edwardian Ideal.
Gradshteyn, I. S. & Ryshik, I. M. Table of Integrals, Series & Products.
Grady, Bo. Resurrection Two.
Grady, James. Six Days of the Condor.
Grady, James, jt. auth. see Frangiamore, Roy.
Grady, James, jt. auth. see Hester, James J.
Grady, James H; see O'Neal, William B.
Grady, Leota A. Island of Nightmares.
Graebe, Chris & Graebe, Julie. The Hornby Gauge O System.
Graebe, Julie, jt. auth. see Graebe, Chris.
Graebner, Norman. Nationalism & Communism in Asia: The American Response.
Graedel, T. E. Chemical Compounds in the Atmosphere.
Graedon, Joe. The People's Pharmacy.
Graeff, H. & Kuhn, W. Coagulation Disorders in Obstetrics: Pathobiochemistry-Pathophysiology-Diagnosis-Treatment. Davis, A., tr. from Ger.
Graetz, Michael J., jt. auth. see Griswold, Erwin N.
Graf, Alfred B. Tropica: Color Cyclopedia of Exotic Plants.
Graf, Dieter. Master Drawings of the Roman Baroque.
Graf, Malvina. The Krankon Ghetto & the Plasjon Camp Remembered.
Graf, Max. From Beethoven to Shostakovich.
--Modern Music.
Graf, Rudolf F. & Whalen, George J. The TAB Handbook of Hand & Power Tools.
Grafe, Joyce. Secreta: Three Methods of Laying Gold Leaf.
Graff, Henry F., jt. auth. see Barzun, Jacques.
Graff, Kent M. van de see Van De Graaff, Kent M.
Graffigny, Francoise. Letters Written by a Peruvian Princess, 1748. Shugrue, Michael F., ed.
Grafftey, Heward. Lessons from the Past: From Dief to Mulroney.
Graffy, Julian, tr. see Jangfeldt, Bengt.
Grafton, C. W. Beyond a Reasonable Doubt.
Grafton, Carol Belanger. Treasury of Art Nouveau Design & Ornament.
Grafton, Sue. A Is for Alibi: A Kinsey Millhone Mystery.
Gragg, Alan. Charles Hartshorhe. Patterson, Bob E., ed.
Graham, A. Richard. An Introduction to Engineering Measurements.
Graham, Ada & Graham, Frank. Busy Bugs.
Graham, Alexander. Matrix Theory & Applications for Engineers & Mathematicians.
Graham, Ann H. & Woods, Richard D., eds. Latin America in English-Language Reference Books: A Selected, Annotated Bibliography.
Graham, Anne D. Bird in My Bed.
Graham, B. Cunninghame. Reincarnation: The Best Short Stories of Cunninghame Graham.
Graham, Billy. The Holy Spirit.
--How to Be Born Again.
--The Secret of Happiness.
--Till Armageddon.
Graham, Bob. Pearl's Place.
--The Wild.
Graham, Clarence H., ed. Vision & Visual Perception.
Graham, David. Down to a Sunless Sea.
Graham, Dom A. The End of Religion: Autobiographical Explorations.
--Zen Catholicism: A Suggestion.
Graham, Dougal. Collected Writings of Dougal Graham, Skellat Bellman of Glasgow.
Graham, E. C., ed. see Ogden, Charles K.
Graham, Edward H. Natural Principles of Land Use.
Graham, Frank, jt. auth. see Graham, Ada.
Graham, Franklinn & Lockerbie, Jeanette. Bob Pierce: This One Thing I Do.
Graham, G. S. Tides of Empire: Discursions on the Expansion of Britain Overseas.
Graham, George J., Jr. & Graham, Scarlett G. Founding Principles of American Government: Two Hundred Years of Democracy on Trial.
Graham, Gordon. Automated Inventory Management for the Distributor.
Graham, H. D. Food Colloids.
Graham, Harold. The Contented Amish: An Inside View.
Graham, Harriet. The Ring of Zoraya.
Graham, Harvey. Surgeons All.
Graham, Heather X. An Angel's Share.
--Arabian Nights.
--Dante's Daughter.
--Red Midnight.
--A Season for Love.
--Sensuous Angel.
--Serena' Magic.
--Tempestuous Eden.
--Tender Deception.
--Tender Taming.
--When Next We Love.
Graham, Horace D. Safety of Foods.
Graham, Horace D., jt. auth. see Telek, Lehel.
Graham, Ian & Varley, Helen. The Home Computer Handbook.
Graham, J. D., ed. Cannabis & Health.
Graham, J. T. Scales & Balances.
--Weights & Measures.
Graham, Jefferson. Come on Down!!! The TV Game Show Book.
Graham, John. I Love You, Mouse.
Graham, John W. & Jones, Susan K. Selling by Mail: An Entrepreneurial Guide to Direct Marketing.
Graham, Jory. In the Company of Others.
Graham, Lawrence & Hamdan, Lawrence. F. L. Y. E. R. S. Fun Loving Youth en Route to Success.
Graham, Lawrence S. Civil Service Reform in Brazil: Principles vs. Practice.
Graham, Leroy. Baltimore: The Nineteenth Century Black Capital.
Graham, Lou. Fanny G.
--Fragments.
Graham, Lou & Bibb, John. Mastering Golf.
Graham, Malcolm. Mathematics: A Liberal Arts Approach.
--Modern Elementary Mathematics.
--Modern Elementary Mathematics.
Graham, Margaret. Anna.
Graham, Martha. The Notebooks of Martha Graham.
Graham, Michael H. Cleary & Graham's Handbook of Illinois Evidence: 1986 Supplement.
--Handbook of Illinois Evidence: 1986 Supplement.
Graham, Neill. Artificial Intelligence.
--Programming the IBM Personal Computer: Pascal.
Graham, Otis L., Jr. & Litwack, Leon. The Great Campaigns--Reform & War in America Nineteen Hundred to Nineteen Twenty-Eight.
Graham, Pamela C., jt. auth. see Caras, Roger.
Graham, Peter. International Herald Tribune Guide to Business Travel & Entertainment in Europe.
Graham, Pierre, ed. see International Symposium on Immunopathology Staff.
Graham, Robin & Gill, Derek. The Boy Who Sailed Round the World Alone.
Graham, Roger, jt. ed. see Heick, Welf H.
Graham, Ruth B. Sitting by My Laughing Fire.
Graham, Scarlett G., jt. auth. see Graham, George J., Jr.
Graham, Sheila Y. Harbrace College Workbook.
--Harbrace College Workbook: Form 8A.
--Harbrace College Workbook: Form 8B.
--Harbrace College Workbook: Form 8C.
--Harbrace College Workbook, Form 9A.
--HarBrace College Workbook: Form 9C, Writing for the World of Work.
Graham, Sheila Y. & Hodges, Mrs. John C. Harbrace College Workbook.
Graham, Stephen, ed. Great Russian Short Stories.
Graham, Susan M. Idaho Divorce Book.
Graham, Thomas R., jt. ed. see Rubin, Seymour J.
Graham, Tim. On the Royal Road: A Decade of Photographing the Royal Family.
--Royal Review.
--The Royal Year.
Graham, Tom M. Biology: The Essential Principles.
Graham, Victor E., ed. Representative French Poetry.
Graham, W. Fred. The Constructive Revolutionary: John Calvin & His Socio-Economic Impact.
Graham, William C., jt. ed. see Sprengling, Martin.
Graham-Barber, Lynda. The Kit Furniture Book.
Graham-Campbell, James. The Viking World.
Grahame. The Reluctant Dragon.
Grahame, Kenneth. Dream Days.
--Dream Days.
--The Golden Age.
--The Wind in the Willows Pop-up-Book.
--Wind in the Willows: The Open Road.
Grahame-White, G. K., ed. see Horner, J. G.
Graham-Jones, Oliver. First Catch Your Tiger.
Graham-Jones, Susanna, tr. see Goldoni, Carolo.
Graham-Yooll, Andrew. A Matter of Fear: Portrait of an Argentinian Exile.
Grahn, Judy. Another Mother Tongue: Gay Words, Gay Worlds.
--The Highest Apple: Sappho & the Lesbian Poetic Tradition.
Grainger, A. J. The Bullring: A Classroom Experiment in Moral Education.
Grainger, J. F., jt. auth. see Clarke, D.
Grainger, L. & Gibson, J. Coal Utilisation: Technology, Economics & Policy.
Gralla, Arthur R., ed. see U. S. Naval Academy, Class of 1934 Staff.
Grambs, David. Words about Words: A Dictionary of 2000 Words - Old, New, & Surprising - for the Styles, Devices, Defects & Oddities of the Craft of Prose Writing.
Gramelsbach, Helen. Seventy-One Creative Bible Story Projects: Patterns for Crafts, Visuals, & Learning Centers.
Gramick, Jeannine, ed. Homosexuality & the Catholic Church.
Gramont, Sanche De see De Gramont, Sanche.
Gran, F. C. & Gran, F. C., eds. Cellular Compartmentalization & Control of Fatty Acid Metabolism.
--Structure & Function of the Endoplasmic Reticulum in Animal Cells.
Granade, Charles. Graduate & Professional Programs: An Overview 1984.
Granade, Charles, jt. ed. see Conley, Diane.
Granade, Charles, jt. ed. see Goldstein, Amy J.
Granch, Ladislav. Room of Errors.
Grand, Janet, jt. auth. see Reid, Ron.
Grand, Rebecca. Labyrinth: A Photo Album.
Grandal, Bjorn, ed. Artificial Particle Beams in Space Plasma Studies.
Grandell, J. Doubly Stochastic Poisson Processes.
Grandfather Drewsen, jt. auth. see Andersen, Hans Christian.
Grandilli, Peter A. Technician's Handbook of Plastics.
Grandjean, E. & Gilgen, A. Environmental Factors in Urban Planning.
Grandjean, E., ed. Ergodesign' Eighty-Four: Proceedings of the International Symposium on Ergonomics & Design in the Electronic Office, Montreaux, Jan. 1984.
--Ergonomic Design of the Electronic Office: A Special Issue of Behavior & Information Technology.
Grandjean, E., et al. Environmental Factors in Urban Planning.
Grandjean, Etienne. Fitting the Task to the Man: An Ergonomic Approach.
Grandle, Julia N. Pot of Gold.
Grandon, Ronald E., jt. auth. see Bergin, Edward J.
Grandsen, James, jt. auth. see Zaloga, Steven J.
Grandville, J. J. The Court of Flora.
Granet, Irving. Fluid Mechanics for Engineering Technology.
Grange, Roger T. Fort Robinson, Outpost on the Plains.
Granger, C. W. Forecasting in Business & Economics.
Granger, C. W., ed. Forecasting Economic Time Series.
Granger, P., jt. auth. see Richard, C.
Granick, Lois. Thesaurus of Psychological Index Terms.
Granier, Jacqueline P., jt. ed. see Kavaas, Igor I.
Granit, Ragnar. Basis of Motor Control.
Granito, Michael R. Bond Portfolio Immunization.
Granitz, Marlene, ed. Report on Domestic & International Loan Charge-offs, 1985.
Granov, V. New Realities & the Struggle of Ideas.
Gransden, Antonia. Historical Writing in England: C. 550 to C. 1307.
Granskou, David. Preaching on the Parables.
Granstrand, Ove & Sigurdson, Jon, eds. Technological Innovation & Industrial Development in Telecommunications: The Role of Public Buying in the Telecommunications Sector in the Nordic Countries.
Grant. Skin Disease in the Dog & Cat: The Library of Veterinary Practice.
Grant, Anne R., ed. Medical Malpractice 1984.
--Products Liability, 1984.
Grant, Audrey & American Contract Bridge League Staff. Bridge: An Introduction.
Grant, Blanche C. The Taos Indians.
Grant, Brian W. From Sin to Wholeness.
--Schizophrenia: A Source of Social Insight.

Grant, Carl A., et al. The Public School & the Challenge of Ethnic Pluralism.
Grant, Charles L. A Quiet Night of Fear.
--Shadows Eight.
--Shadows Nine.
--Shadows Ten.
Grant, Charles W. & Butah, Jon. Introduction to the UCSD p-System.
Grant, Cynthia. Summer Home.
Grant, Damian. Realism.
Grant, Daniel A., et al. Periodontics in the Tradition of Orban & Gottlieb.
Grant, Daniel T. Who Should Survive the Purge in American Education & Why.
Grant, Dave. The Great Lover's Manifesto.
Grant, Edward. A Source Book in Medieval Science.
Grant, Edward F. The Kingdom Within You.
Grant, Ellsworth S. Yankee Dreamers & Doers.
Grant, Eugene L. & Bell, L. F. Basic Accounting & Cost Accounting.
Grant, F. S. & West, G. F. Interpretation Theory in Applied Geophysics.
Grant, H. Roger & Bohi, Charles. The Country Railroad Station in America.
Grant, Harold J., Jr., jt. auth. see Rehn, James A.
Grant, I. S. Walking a Thin Line.
Grant, James. Bernard Baruch: The Adventures of a Wall Street Legend.
--Bernard M. Baruch: The Adventures of a Wall Street Legend.
--Mace.
Grant, James K., jt. ed. see Dib, Albert.
Grant, Jan. Our New Baby.
Grant, John C., jt. auth. see Legros, Lucien.
Grant, Julius. Hackh's Chemical Dictionary.
Grant, Kenneth. Ponderings.
Grant, Kenneth, jt. ed. see Symonds, John.
Grant, M. Makers of Black Basaltes.
Grant, M. D., jt. auth. see Davies, R.
Grant, M. J. Rhode Island's Ocean Sands: Management Guidelines for Sand & Gravel Extraction in State Waters.
Grant, Marion H. In & About Hartford: Tours & Tales.
Grant, Mary K. The Tragic Vision of Joyce Carol Oates.
Grant, Matthew G. Geronimo.
--Osceola.
--Pontiac.
--Squanto.
Grant, Michael. Twelve Caesars.
Grant, Michael & Hazel, John. Gods & Mortals in Classic Mythology: Dictionary.
Grant, Moeller M., jt. auth. see McFarland, Mary B.
Grant, Myrna. Ivan & the Daring Escape.
--Ivan & the Hidden Bible.
--Ivan & the Informer.
--Ivan & the Secret in the Suitcase.
--Vanya.
Grant, P. T. & Mackie, A. M., eds. Chemoreception in Marine Organisms.
Grant, Parks. Music for Elementary Teachers.
Grant, Patrick. The Transformation of Sin: Studies in Donne, Herbert, Vaughan & Traherne.
Grant, Paul B. & Kozlowski, Joseph G. Cutting Health Care Costs.
Grant, Philip C. Employee Motivation: Principles & Practices.
Grant, Richard. Saraband of Lost Time.
Grant, Sea. First Aid for Boaters & Divers.
Grant, Steven, jt. auth. see Malinski, Mieczyslaw.
Grant, Susan T. Beauty & the Beast: The Coevolution of Plants & Animals.
Grant, Ulysses S., IV & Hertlein, L. G. The West American Cenozoic Echinoidea.
Grant, W. A., ed. Low Energy Ion Beams: Proceedings of the LEIB Conference, 3rd, Loughborough, U. K., March 28-31, 1983.
--Vacuum, Eighty-Four: Technological Aspects of Surface Treatment & Analysis: Proceedings of the Conference Held at the University of York, 1-4 April 1984.
Grant, W. A. & Balfour, D., eds. Vacuum Eighty-Two: Proceedings of the Biennial Conference of the Vacuum Group of the Institute of Physics, Chester, 29-31 March 1982.
Grant, W. E., tr. see Zlotin, R. I. & Khodashova, K. S.
Grant, W. L., ed. Voyages of Samuel De Champlain, Sixteen Four to Sixteen Eighteen.
Grant-Adamson, Lesley. The Face of Death.
Grantham, Dewey W. Democratic South.
--The Regional Imagination: The South & Recent American History.
--United States Since Nineteen Forty-Five: The Ordeal of Power.
Grantham, Dewey W., ed. see Bunche, Ralph J.
Grantham, G. J. The Utilization of Krill.
Grantham, Jared J., jt. auth. see Sullivan, Lawrence P.
Granville, W. Sea Slang of the Twentieth Century.
--Theatre Dictionary.
Granzotto, Gianni. Christopher Columbus. Sartorelli, Stephen, tr. from Ital.
Graphic-Sha Editorial Staff. Drawings by Japanese Contemporary Architects. Cook, Peter, ed.
Graphic-Sha Staff. Airbrush Illustrations by Twelve Japanese Illustrators.
Graphic-Sha Staff, ed. Airbrush Art in Japan.
--Airbrush Art in Japan.
--Airbrush Art in Japan.
--Mode Illustration.
Graphic-Sha Staff & Orange Book Co. Staff, eds. Interior Best Selection II.
Grappel, Robert D. & Hemenway, Jack E. Tracer: A 6800 Debugging Program.
Graselli, Jeanette, jt. auth. see Brame, Edward.
Grasha, Anthony F., jt. auth. see Fuhrmann, Barbara S.
Grasham, John A. & Gooder, Glenn G. Improving Your Speech.
Grass, Gunter. Cat & Mouse. Manheim, Ralph, tr.
--Davor: Ein Stuck in 13 Szenen. Lange, Victor & Lange, Frances, eds.
--Dog Years. Manheim, Ralph, tr.
--The Flounder.
--Four Plays. Manheim, Ralph & Willson, A. Leslie, trs. Incl. Flood; Mister, Mister; Only Ten Minutes to Buffalo; The Wicked Cooks. HarBraceJ.
--From the Diary of a Snail. Manheim, Ralph, tr, from Ger.
--Headbirths: Or the Germans Are Dying Out. Manheim, Ralph, tr.
--Inmarypraise. Middleton, Christopher, tr. from Ger.
--Local Anaesthetic. Manheim, Ralph, tr.
--Love Tested. Hamburger, Michael, tr.
--Max: A Play. Wilson, Leslie A., tr. Manheim, Ralph.
--The Plebeians Rehearse the Uprising. Manheim, Ralph, tr.
--Selected Poems.
--Speak Out: Speeches, Open Letters, Commentaries. Manheim, Ralph, tr.
--Speak Out! Speeches, Open Letters, Commentaries. Manheim, Ralph, tr.
Grasselli, A., ed. Automatic Interpretation & Classification of Images.
Grasserbauer, M. & Zacherl, M. K., eds. Progress in Materials Analysis.
Grassman, Peter. Physical Principles of Chemical Engineering.
Grassmann, Hermann. Gesammelte Mathematische und Physikalische Werke.
Grasty, William K & Sheinkopf, Kenneth. Successful Fundraising.
Grastyan, E. & Molnar, P., eds. Sensory Functions: Proceedings of the 28th International Congress of Physiological Sciences, Budapest, 1980.
Grater, Michael. One Piece of Paper.
Gratton, L. High Energy Astrophysics.
Gratton, Livio, ed. Star Evolution.
Gratus, Jack. The False Messiahs: Prophets of the Millennium.
Gratwick, A. S., ed. & tr. Terence: The Brothers (Adelphoi)
Gratz, Kathleen E. Archaeological Excavations along Route 24 Near Zuni, New Mexico.
Gratzner, H. G., jt. ed. see Schultz, J.
Grau, E., jt. auth. see Esser, Cajetan.
Grau, Pamela A. Don't Talk to Strangers.
Graubard, Mark. Astrology & Alchemy: Two Fossil Sciences.
--Witchcraft & the Nature of Man.
Graubard, Stephen R., ed. A New America?
Grauer. Study Guide for Advanced Life: Problem Solving in Cardiac Arrest.
Grauer, Robert G. COBOL: A Vehicle for Information Systems.
Grauert, H. & Fritzsche, K. Several Complex Variables. Gehring, F. W. & Moore, C. C., eds. Mumaw, H. J., tr. from Ger.
Graupner, Martha H. Oscar, Laddie, Came Home.
Graupp, Patrick. The Life of John Japanese: Working in Japan.
Grav, Joseph A. Fanny Burney: An Annotated Bibliography.
Gravas, jt. auth. see Brunner.
Grave, S. A. A History of Philosophy in Australia.
Grave, Stephen. The Florida Burn.
--Vengeance Game.
Gravel, Geary. The Alchemists.
Gravelle, Karen, jt. auth. see Rivlin, Robert.
Graver, Lawrence & Federman, Raymond, eds. Samuel Beckett.
Graves, Algernon. Art Sales: From Early in the 18th Century to Early in the 20th Century.
--A Century of Loan Exhibitions, Eighteen Thirteen to Nineteen Twelve.
--Dictionary of Artists: London Exhibitions 1760-1893.
Graves, C. E. Aristophanes: Acharnians.
Graves, Edmund J. Inpatient Utilization of Short-Stay Hospitals by Diagnosis, United States, 1984.
Graves, Edward C. Our Search for Wilderness: The Story of a Sixty-Year Marriage.
Graves, Frederick. The Big Book of Marine Electronics.
Graves, Harvey W. Nuclear Fuel Management.
Graves, Helen, ed. see Bell, Rose S.
Graves, Helen, ed. see Herrington, Patricia.
Graves, Helen, ed. see Kalashian, Susan W.
Graves, John H. Surviving Retirement.
Graves, Maitland E. Art of Color & Design.
Graves, Michael, et al. Easy Reading: Book Series & Periodicals for Less Able Readers.
Graves, Perceval. A. E. Housman: The Scholar-Poet.
Graves, Richard P. The Brothers Powys.
--Lawrence of Arabia & His World.
Graves, Robert. Occupation Writer.
--Poems, Nineteen Thirty-Eight to Nineteen Forty-Five.
--Wife to Mr. Milton.
Graves, Robert & Patai, Raphael. Hebrew Myths.
Graves, Sharol, jt. auth. see Ortiz, Simon J.
Graves, W. Brooke, ed. see Highsaw, Robert B. & Fortenberry, Charles N.
Graves, Wallace & Leary, William G. From Word to Story.
Graves, Will. Raising Your Own Meat for Pennies a Day. Stetson, Fred, ed.
Graves-Morris, P. R. Pade Approximants & Their Applications.
Graves-Smith, Tom R. Linear Analysis of Frameworks.
Gravetter, Frederick J. & Wallanu, Larry B. Statistics for the Behavioral Sciences: A First Course for Students of Psychology & Education.
Gravrock, Mark. Stewardship Preaching.
Gray, jt. auth. see Rendle-Short.
Gray, Alice & Kasahara, Kunihiko. Magic of Origami.
Gray, Alice & McAuley, Marilyn. Mirror, Mirror.
Gray, Alisdair. The Fall of Kelvin Walker.
Gray, Barbara & Issacs, Bernard. Care of the Elderly Mentally Infirm.
Gray, Bettyanne. Manya's Story.
Gray, Bradford H. Human Subjects in Medical Experimentation: A Sociological Study of the Conduct & Regulation of Clinical Research.
Gray, Charles H. & Bacharach, Alfred L., eds. Hormones in Blood.
Gray, Charles M., ed. see Hale, Matthew.
Gray, D. J. Medical Annual 1983.
Gray, Donald & Leiser, Andrew. Biotechnical Slope Protection: Economic Methods for Earth Support & Erosion Control.
Gray, Donald P. Jesus: The Way to Freedom.
Gray, Dorothy L. Reluctant Memory.
Gray, Douglas. Start & Run a Profitable Consulting Business.
Gray, E. G. The Synapse. Head, J. J., ed.
Gray, Ernest A. Microbiology.
Gray, Frances. John Arden.
Gray, Francine du Plessix see Du Plessix Gray, Francine.
Gray, Fred, jt. auth. see Merrett, Stephen.
Gray, Genevieve. Sore Loser.
--Varnell Roberts, Super-Pigeon.
Gray, H. Peter. International Trade, Investment & Payments.
Gray, Harry B. Electrons & Chemical Bonding.
Gray, Harry B., jt. auth. see DeKock, Roger L.
Gray, Howard L. English Field Systems.
Gray, J., jt. auth. see McPherson, A.
Gray, J. A. Elements of a Two-Process Theory of Learning.
Gray, J. M. & Lowe, J. J., eds. Studies in the Scottish Lateglacial Environment.
Gray, Jack C. & Johnston, Kenneth S. Accounting & Management Action.
Gray, James, jt. auth. see Ochs, Robert.
Gray, James, Jr. The Winning Image.
Gray, James R. Process Ethics.
Gray, Jane & Berry, William. Communities of the Past.
Gray, Janet G. The French Huguenots.
Gray, Jeffrey. Psychology of Fear & Stress.
Gray, Jeremy, jt. auth. see Smith, David J.
Gray, Jerry L. Supervision: An Applied Behavioral Science Approach to Managing People.
Gray, John. First & Second Kings, a Commentary.
--Hayek on Liberty.
--Social System: A Treatise on the Principle of Exchange.
Gray, John, ed. VLSI Eighty-One: Very Large Scale Integration.
Gray, John N. Mill on Liberty: A Defence.
Gray, Lynton & Waitt, Ian, eds. Perspectives on Academic Gaming & Simulation: Simulation in Management & Business Education.
Gray, Malcolm. A Matter of Record.
--Stab in the Back.
Gray, Margaret. The Donkey's Tale.
Gray, Mary Jane, jt. auth. see Lutgendorf, Philip.
Gray, Mary Z. Ah, Bewilderness: Muddling Through Life.
Gray, Michael H. & Gibson, Gerald D. Bibliography of Discographies, Vol. III: Popular Music.
Gray, Mike & Rosen, Ira. The Warning: Accident at Three Mile Island.
Gray, Peter, ed. A. I. B. S. Directory of Bio-Science Departments & Facilities in the United States & Canada.
Gray, Randall, jt. auth. see Campbell, Ross.
Gray, Richard. The Two Nations.
Gray, Richard, ed. American Fiction: New Readings.
--American Verse of the Nineteenth Century.
Gray, Robert. A History of London.
Gray, Robert Emmert. The Bard's Theme.
Gray, Robert M. & Davisson, Lee D., eds. Ergodic & Information Theory.
Gray, Rockwell, tr. see Pino-Saavedra, Yolando.
Gray, Roland P., ed. Songs & Ballads of the Maine Lumberjacks.
Gray, Simon. Stage Struck.
Gray, Spalding. In Search of the Monkey Girl.
Gray, Steven & Steffy, Wilbert. Hospital Cost Containment through Productivity Management.
Gray, Thomas. Correspondence.
--Poems of Gray, Collins, Goldsmith. Lonsdale, Roger, ed.
Gray, Valeria B. Invisible Man's Literary Heritage: Benito Cereno & Moby Dick.
Gray, W. A. & Muller, R. Engineering Calculations in Radiative Heat Transfer.
Gray, W. H., jt. ed. see Akin, J. E.
Gray, Wayne B. Productivity versus OSHA & EPA Regulations. Farmer, Richard, ed.
Gray, William H. Venezuela, Uncle Sam & OPEC: A Story for All Americans.
Gray, William S., ed. Reading in the High School & College.
Graybiel, A., ed. Basic Environmental Problems of Man in Space: Proceedings of the Fifth International Symposium, Washington, D.C., 1973.
Graybill, Nina. R & D in FY 1987: R & D & the Budget Crisis.
Graydon, Nell S. Tales of Edisto.
Grayling, A. C. Berkeley: The Central Arguments.
--An Introduction to Philosophical Logic.
Grayling, Christopher. Land Fit for Heroes: Life in England after the Great War.
Graymore, Clive N., ed. Biochemistry of the Retina.
Grayser, Stephen A., jt. auth. see Bursk, Edward C.
Grayson, Cecil, jt. auth. see Chastel, Andre.
Grayson, David. Adventures in Understanding.
Grayson, Don, et al. Component Testers. Cole, Sandy, ed.
Grayson, Donald K. A Bibliography of the Literature on North American Climates of the Past Thirteen Thousand Years.
Grayson, L. E. National Oil Companies.
Grayson, Richard. Death "En Voyage"
Grayson, Richard A. With Hitler in New York.
Grayson, Stan, ed. Ferrari: The Man, the Machines.
Graywon, J., jt. auth. see Catling, D. M.
Grayzel, Solomon. History of the Contemporary Jews from 1900 to the Present.
Graz, William von see Von Graz, William.
Grazia, Alfred de, ed. Congress: The First Branch of Government.
Graziano, Anthony M. Child Without Tomorrow.
Greanias, George C. The Foreign Corrupt Practices Act: Anatomy of a Statute.
Great Britain, Admiralty Staff. Handbook of German East Africa.
--Handbook of Portuguese Nyasaland.
Great Britain, Challenger Office Staff. Report on the Scientific Results of the Voyage of H. M. S. Challenger During the Years 1873-1876.
Great Britain, Foreign Office Staff. British Documents of the Origin of the War 1898-1914. Gooch, G. P. & Temperley, Harold, eds.
Great Britain, House of Commons Staff. Debates in the House of Commons in 1625. Gardiner, Samuel R., ed.
--Parliamentary Debates in Sixteen Ten.
Great Britain, House of Lords Staff. Notes of the Debates in the House of Lords in 1624. Gardiner, Samuel R., ed.
Great Britain, Parliament Staff. British West Indies at Westminister, 1789-1823.
Greater London Council Department of Architecture & Civic Design Staff. Detailing for Building Construction: A Designer's Manual of Over 350 Standard Details.
--GLC Good Practice Details.
Greater London Council, Department of Architecture & Civic Design Staff. GLC Preferred Dwelling Plans.
Greater New York Fund, Inc. Staff. Boards of Directors: A Study of Current Practices in Board Management & Board Operations in Voluntary Hospitals, Health & Welfare Organizations.
Greaves, C. Desmond. The Easter Rising in Song & Ballad.
Greaves, J. H. Rodent Control in Agriculture: A Handbook on the Biology & Control of Commensal Rodents as Agricultural Pests.
Greaves, M. F., jt. ed. see Cuatrecasas, P.
Grebanier, Bernard D., tr. see Moliere.
Grebene, A. B., ed. Analog Integrated Circuits.

Authors

Greberg, Mort. More All-Jewish Cartoons, Yet: And Just As Kosher As the others.
Grechko, A. A. Armed Forces of the Soviet State: A Soviet View.
Greco, Carlo & Greco, Stefano. Piercing the Surface: X Rays of Nature.
Greco, Eileen M. Ramblings in the Clover-Absorbing Shock.
Greco, Marshall C. Group Life.
Greco, Stefano, jt. auth. see Greco, Carlo.
Greeley, Andrew. The Catholic Why? Book.
--God Game.
--Sexual Intimacy.
Greeley, Andrew M. Angels of September.
--Ascent into Hell.
--Happy Are the Meek.
--Lord of the Dance.
--The Magic Cup.
--The Mary Myth: On the Femininity of God.
Green. A Hobbit's Travels.
Green, Al, jt. auth. see Turner, Roger.
Green, Arnold H. The Tunisian Ulama 1873-1915: Social Structure & Response to Ideological Currents.
Green, Arthur. Tormented Master: A Life of Rabbi Nahman of Bratslav.
Green, B. S. & Johns, E. A. An Introduction to Sociology.
Green, Bernard & Schwarz, Ted. Goodbye, Blues: A Guide to Breaking the Tranquilizer Habit the Natural Way.
Green, Beth. Scientific Value of the First Chapter of Genesis.
Green, Brain, jt. auth. see Jeeves, Malcolm A.
Green, Bryan S. Knowing the Poor: A Case Study in Textual Reality Construction.
Green, C. J., et al, eds. Airframe & Systems Fitting.
Green, Calvin C. Counseling: With the Pastor & CPE Student in Mind.
Green, Clifford, tr. see Bonhoeffer, Dietrich.
Green, D. C. Radio Systems for Technicians.
Green, Dan S., ed. see Dubois, W. E. B.
Green, Dana S., ed. Chasms in the Americas.
Green, David E. & Baum, Harold. Energy & the Mitochondrion.
Green, David E., tr. see Becker, Joachim.
Green, David E., tr. see Hahn, Ferdinand.
Green, David E., tr. see Hengel, Martin.
Green, David E., tr. see Ringgren, Helmer.
Green, David E., tr. see Westermann, Claus.
Green, David E., tr. see Zimmerli, Walther.
Green, Deirdre & Mclean, Adam, eds. Commentary on the Chymical Wedding of Christian Rosenkreutz, with the Text of the Foxcroft Translation Revised & Modernized. Foxcroft, Ezechiel & Mclean, Donald, trs. from Ger.
Green, Edwin & Moss, Michael. Business of National Importance.
Green, Edwin, jt. auth. see Cockerell, H. A.
Green, Ernest J. Personal Relationships: An Approach to Marriage & Family.
Green, Eugene & Sachse, William L. Names of the Land: Cape Cod, Nantucket, Martha's Vineyard & the Elizabeth Islands.
Green, Fitzhugh. A Change in the Weather.
Green, Fred, et al. Strategies for Improving Reading in Social Studies.
Green, G. H., et al. Cervical & Nasopharyngeal Carcinoma.
Green, Gerald. Cactus Pie: Ten Stories.
Green, Hannah. I Never Promised You a Rose Garden.
--In the City of Paris.
Green, J. The Book of Political Quotes.
Green, J. & Short, N. M., eds. Volcanic Land Forms & Surface Features: A Photographic Atlas & Glossary.
Green, James & Lee, John. Positronium Chemistry.
Green, James H. Local Area Networks: A User's Guide for Business Professionals.
Green, Jay P., ed. The Pocket Interlinear New Testament.
Green, Jerald R. Direccion: Moncloa: An Intermediate Cultural Reader.
--Direction: Tacuba: An Introductory Conversational Reader.
Green, Jerry & Scheinkman, Jose A., eds. General Equilibrium, Growth & Trade: Essays in Honor of Lionel McKenzie.
Green, Jerry E. The Planning & Management of Zoological Parks: A Selected Annotated Bibliography.
--Port & Harbor Planning & Management: A Selected Bibliography.
Green, Joey & Handy, Bruce, eds. Hellbent on Insanity.
Green, John H. The Impact on Consumers of a Restructured Personal Federal Tax. Farmer, Richard, ed.
Green, John H. & Kramer, Amihud. Food Processing Waste Management.
Green, Jonathan, ed. Snapshot.
Green, Jonathan H. Secret Band of Brothers: A Full & True Exposition of All the Various Crimese, Villainies, & Misdeeds of This Powerful Organization in the United States.
Green, K. B. Family Life Education: Focus on Student Involvement.
--Test Item Construction in the Cognitive Domain.
Green, Karen & Black, Betty. How to Cook His Goose: And Other Wild Games.
Green, L. F., ed. Developments in Soft Drinks Technology. Houghton, H. W.
Green, Leslie. Law & Society: Essays in the Sociology of Law.
Green, Lewis. The Silence of Snakes.
Green, Lewis W. And Scatter the Proud.
--The High-Pitched Laugh of a Painted Lady.
Green, M., jt. ed. see Domb, C.
Green, Marjorie, tr. see Jahn, Janheinz.
Green, Mark & Waldman, Michael. Who Runs Congress?
Green, Mark, jt. auth. see Nader, Ralph.
Green, Maurice B. & West, T. F. Chemicals for Crop Protection & Pest Control.
Green, Michael. I Believe in Satan's Downfall.
--A Walk Through the Shire: Wherein We Discover Some Rare Drawings of Hobbit Life.
Green, Michael, jt. auth. see Zaloga, Steven J.
Green, Michael, ed. see Kuzmin, Mikhail.
Green, Michael E. & Turk, Amos. Safety in Working with Chemistry.
Green, Nan, tr. see Carrillo, Santiago.
Green, Paul. The Outdoor Leadership Handbook.
Green, Paul & Abbott, Abbe. I Am Eskimo: Aknik My Name.
Green, Paul E. Analyzing Multivariate Data.
Green, Peter. Alexander to Actium: An Essay on the Historical Evolution of Hellenistic Age. Bulloch, Anthony W., et al, eds.
--Beyond the Wild Wood: The World of Kenneth Grahame.
Green, Philip, compiled by. Planning Legislation in North Carolina.
--Planning Legislation in North Carolina: 1982 Replacement Pages.
Green, Philip P. North Carolina Supreme Court Cases on Zoning, Subdivision Regulation & Urban Renewal: Supplements.
Green, Philip P., Jr. Planning Legislation in North Carolina.
Green, Phillip P. Legal Responsibilities of the Local Zoning Administrator in North Carolina.
Green, Phyllis. Gloomy Louie. Fay, Ann, ed.
Green, R. D. Hydrogen Bonding by C-H Groups.
Green, R. Elliot, jt. ed. see Parslow, R. D.
Green, R. N., jt. ed. see Ramsden, E.
Green, Roger L. & Hooper, Walter. C. S. Lewis: A Biography.
--C. S. Lewis: A Biography.
Green, Roland. Wandor's Journey.
--Wandor's Ride.
Green, Rosalie B., jt. ed. see Ragusa, Isa.
Green, S. International Disaster Relief: Toward a Responsive System.
Green, Samuel & Long, John V. Marriage & Family Law Agreements.
Green, Samuel, ed. Eleven Skagit Poets.
Green, Sharon & Siemon, Michael. Barron's How to Prepare for the California High School Proficiency Examination (CHSPE)
--Barron's How to Prepare for the California High School Proficiency Examination (CHSPE)
Green, Stanley. Broadway Musicals: Show by Show.
Green, Stephen. Taking Sides: America's Secret Relations with a Militant Israel.
Green, Stephen A. Mind & Body: The Psychology of Physical Illness.
Green, Suzanne. The Birthday Book.
--Going to School.
--The Little Baby Carriage: Baby's Toys, Baby's Family, Going to Bed.
--Seasons.
Green, Suzanne & Tsuda, Satoru. Busy Day.
Green Tiger Press Staff, ed. see Swann, Brian.
Green, Wayne. Encyclopedia for the TRS-80. McCarthy, Nan, et al, eds.
Green, Wayne, et al. Hobby Computers Are Here!
Green, William. Shakespeare's "Merry Wives of Windsor"
Green, William, ed. see Brown, Eric.
Green, William B. Digital Image Processing: A Systems Approach.
Green, William Brothers Staff, jt. auth. see Benjamin, Allen & Co. Staff.
Green, William H. The Higher Criticism of the Pentateuch.
Greenaway, D. L. & Harbeke, G. Optical Properties & Band Structures of Semiconductors.
Greenaway, Peter van see Van Greenaway, Peter.
Greenbaum, Everett. The Goldenberg Who Couldn't Dance.
Greenbaum, Howard H. & Falcione, Raymond L. Organizational Communication Nineteen Seventy-Seven: Abstracts, Analysis, & Overview.
Greenber, Michael R. Long Range Population Projects for Minor Civil Divisions: Computer Programs & Users Manual.
Greenberg, jt. auth. see Carr.
Greenberg, Alan, tr. see Herzog, Werner.
Greenberg, Alvin. Going Nowhere.
Greenberg, Arnold. South America on Twenty-Five Dollars a Day.
Greenberg, Arnold & Greenberg, Harriet. Rio Alive.
--Rio Alive.
--South America on Twenty-Five Dollars a Day: 1983-84 Edition.
--U. S. Virgin Islands Alive.
--Venezuela Alive.
Greenberg, Arnold, jt. auth. see Greenberg, Harriet.
Greenberg, Arnold L., jt. auth. see Greenberg, Harriet.
Greenberg, Bette, ed. How to Find Out in Psychiatry: A Guide to Sources of Mental Health Information.
Greenberg, Blu. How to Run a Traditional Jewish Household.
Greenberg, Bruce & LaVoie, Roland. Greenberg's Price Guide to Lionel Fundimensions Trains 1970-1985.
Greenberg, Bruce C. Greenberg's Price Guide to Lionel Trains: Prewar & Postwar, 1901-86.
Greenberg, Diane, jt. auth. see Block, Joel D.
Greenberg, Edward S. The American Political System: A Radical Approach.
--Serving the Few: Corporate Capitalism & the Bias of Government Policy.
--Understanding Modern Government: The Rise & Decline of the American Political Economy.
Greenberg, Eliezer, jt. ed. see Howe, Irving.
Greenberg, Gary. C-BIMS: Cassette-Based Information Management System for the PET.
Greenberg, Harold. Integer Programming.
Greenberg, Harold M., jt. auth. see Radin, Stephen.
Greenberg, Harriet. U. S. Virgin Islands Alive.
Greenberg, Harriet & Greenberg, Arnold L. Lebendiges Rio.
Greenberg, Harriet & Greenberg, Arnold. Rio Alive.
Greenberg, Harriet & Greenberg, Arnold L. Venezuela Alive.
Greenberg, Harriet, jt. auth. see Greenberg, Arnold.
Greenberg, Jack, jt. auth. see Hill, Herber.
Greenberg, Jack & Lambert, Richard D., eds. Blacks & the Law.
Greenberg, Jan W. Theatre Business: From Auditions Through Opening Night.
Greenberg, Joanne. The Far Side of Victory.
--High Crimes & Misdemeanors.
--In This Sign.
--In This Sign.
--The Monday Voices.
--A Season of Delight.
--A Season of Delight.
--Simple Gifts.
Greenberg, Judith, tr. see D'Allonnes, Olivier R.
Greenberg, Judith E. & Carey, Helen. How to Participate in a Group.
Greenberg, Judith E., jt. auth. see Carey, Helen.
Greenberg, Kenneth S. Masters & Statesmen: The Political Culture of American Slavery.
Greenberg, Lawrence M. The Hukbalahap Insurrection: A Case Study of a Successful Anti-Insurgency Operation in the Philippines, 1946-1955.
Greenberg, Leonard H. Discoveries in Physics for Scientists & Engineers.
Greenberg, Linda, ed. see Ottley, John.
Greenberg, Linda, ed. see Patterson, Jim.
Greenberg, Linda, ed. see Smith, Philip K. & Shantar, Stan.
Greenberg, Martin H. & Olander, Joseph. Science Fiction of the Fifties.
Greenberg, Martin H. see Pronzini, Bill.
Greenberg, Martin H., ed. The Arbor House Celebrity Book of Horror Stories.
--The Best of Marion Zimmer Bradley.
Greenberg, Martin H. & Olander, Joseph D., eds. Tomorrow, Inc. SF Stories about Big Business.
Greenberg, Martin H. & Silverberg, Robert, eds. The Arbor House Treasury of Modern Science Fiction.
Greenberg, Martin H. & Waugh, Charles G., eds. The Arbor House Celebrity Book of the Greatest Stories Ever Told.
--The Arbor House Treasury of Nobel Prize Winners.
Greenberg, Martin H. & Waugh, Charles, eds. Hollywood Unreel: Fantasies About Hollywood & the Movies.
Greenberg, Martin H., jt. ed. see Olander, Joseph D.
Greenberg, Martin H., ed. see Overholser, Wayne D.
Greenberg, Martin H., jt. ed. see Pronzini, Bill.
Greenberg, Martin H., jt. ed. see Silverberg, Robert.
Greenberg, Martin H., jt. ed. see Waugh, Carol-Lynn R.
Greenberg, Martin H., jt. ed. see Asimov, Isaac.
Greenberg, Michael. British Trade & the Opening of China, Eighteen Hundred to Eighteen Forty-Two.
Greenberg, Michael R., ed. Readings in Urban Economics & Spatial Patterns.
Greenberg, Milton, jt. auth. see Plano, Jack C.
Greenberg, Paul D. & Glaser, Edward M. Some Issues in Joint Union-Management Quality of Worklife Improvement Efforts.
Greenberg, Robert A., ed. see Swift, Jonathan.
Greenberg, Selma. Right from the Start: A Guide to Nonsexist Child Rearing.
--Right from the Start: A Guide to Nonsexist Child Rearing.
Greenberg, Sheldon F. Stress & the Teaching Profession.
Greenberg, Sidney. Likrat Shabbat.
Greenblatt, Bernard S. Doctor's Sex Guide for Patients.
Greenblatt, Stephen. Renaissance Self-Fashioning: More to Shakespeare.
Greenburg, Dan. Confessions of a Pregnant Father.
Greenburg, Herbert J. & Murphy, Charlotte W. Intermediate Algebra.
Greene, Amy & Pomerance, Molly. The Successful Face.
Greene, Annie. Bright River Trilogy.
Greene, Asa. A Yankee among the Nullifiers: An Autobiography.
Greene, Bert. Greene on Grains.
--Kitchen Bouquets.
Greene, Bert & Schulz, Phillip S. Cooking for Giving.
Greene, Bette. Morning Is a Long Time Coming.
Greene, Bob. Cheeseburgers: The Best of Bob Greene.
--Cheeseburgers: The Best of Bob Greene.
--Good Morning, Merry Sunshine.
--Good Morning, Merry Sunshine: A Father's Journal of His Child's First Year.
Greene, Carol. I Am One: Prayers for Singles.
--Welcome the Stranger.
Greene, Caroline, jt. auth. see Greene, Gerald.
Greene, David. Your Incredible Cat: Understanding the Secret Powers of Your Pet.
Greene, David M. Greene's Biographical Encyclopedia of Composers.
Greene, Ellin, ed. see Housman, Laurence.
Greene, Gael. Delicious Sex: A Book for Women & the Men Who Want to Love Them Better.
Greene, Gardiner C. How to Start & Manage Your Own Small Business.
Greene, Gerald & Greene, Caroline. S-M: The Last Taboo.
Greene, Graham. Dr. Fischer of Geneva or the Bomb Party.
--Getting to Know the General: The Story of an Involvement.
--The Human Factor.
--A Sort of Life.
--The Tenth Man.
--Ways of Escape.
Greene, Howard M., jt. auth. see McCurdy, Richard N.
Greene, J. H. Production & Inventory Control Handbook.
Greene, Jack P., ed. Great Britain & the American Colonies, 1606-1763.
Greene, Jack R., ed. Managing Police Work: Issues & Analysis.
Greene, John see Heywood, Thomas.
Greene, John R. The Crusade: The Presidential Election of Nineteen Fifty-Two.
Greene, Joseph, jt. auth. see Martin, Andy.
Greene, Judith. Thinking & Language.
Greene, Laura. Computers in Business & Industry.
--I Am an Orthodox Jew.
--I Am Somebody.
Greene, Lawrence J. Kids Who Underachieve: Strategies for Understanding & Parenting the Academically Troubled Child.
Greene, Liz. The Dreamer of the Vine: A Novel About Nostradamus.
--Looking at Astrology.
--The Puppet Master.
Greene, Lorenzo J. Negro in Colonial New England.
Greene, Mark R. Insurance & Risk Management for Small Business.
Greene, Melvyn. Marketing Hotels into the 90's: A Systematic Approach to Increasing Sales.
Greene, Orville & Durr, Frank. The Practical Inventor's Handbook.
Greene, R. W. The Chemical Engineering Guide to Valves.
--The Chemical Engineering to Compressors.
Greene, Richard M. The Hit Parade, Nineteen Twenty to Nineteen Seventy.
Greene, Robert. Friar Bacon & Friar Bungay. Lavin, J. A., ed.
Greene, Robert Lee. Welfare Economics & Peak Load Pricing: A Theoretical Application to Municipal Water Utility Practices.
Greene, Stephanie, jt. ed. see Hamilton, Russel.
Greene, Victor R. Slavic Community on Strike: Immigrant Labor in Pennsylvania Anthracite.
Greene, Vivien. English Dolls' Houses of the Eighteenth & Nineteenth Centuries.
Greene, Walter H., jt. auth. see Read, Donald A.
Greene, Walter H., et al. Health in the Elementary School: Teaching for Relevance.
Greene, William C., ed. see Plato.

Greene, William N. Strategies of the Major Oil Companies. Farmer, Richard, ed.

Greener, W. W. The Gun & Its Development.

Greene Robertson, Merle, ed. First Palenque Round Table, 1973.

Greenes, Carole E., et al. Problem-Solving in the Mathematics Laboratory.

Greenewalt, Crawford H. The Flight of Birds.

Greenfeld, D., jt. auth. see PreTest Service, Inc. Staff.

Greenfeld, Howard. Chanukah.

--Chanukah, Passover, Rosh Hashanah, Yom Kippur.

--Passover.

--Purim.

--Rosh Hashanah & Yom Kippur.

Greenfield, Eloise. Darlene.

Greenfield, Howard, jt. auth. see Jones, Jo Lynne.

Greenfield, Irving. Barracuda.

Greenfield, Irving A. Tagget.

Greenfield, Joseph D. Practical Transistors & Linear Integrated Circuits, Experiments.

Greenfield, Joseph D. & Wray, William C. Using Microprocessors & Microcomputers: The 6800 Family.

Greenfield, Lazar J. Surgery in the Aged.

Greenfield, Margaret. Meeting the Costs of Health Care: The Bay Area Experience & the National Issues.

Greenfield, Norman S., jt. ed. see Abroms, Gene M.

Greenfield, Robert. Temple.

Greenfield, S. & Clift, S. Analytic Chemistry of the Condensed Phosphates.

Greenfield, Thelma N. The Induction in Elizabethan Drama.

Greenfield, Thelma N., jt. ed. see McNeir, Waldo F.

Greengard, Paul, jt. auth. see Nestler, Erie J.

Greengarten, I. M. Thomas Hill Green & the Development of Liberal-Democratic Thought.

Greenhalgh, G. The Necessity of Nuclear Power.

Greenhall, Vladimir. The Art Book of Pencil Sketching.

Greenhaw, Wayne. Flying High: Inside Big-Time Drug Smuggling.

Greenhouse, Herbert B. The Astral Journey.

Greenhowe, Jean. Costumes for Nursery Tale Characters.

--Making Miniature Toys & Dolls.

--Stage Costumes for Girls.

Greenland, Colin. The Entropy Exhibition: Michael Moorcock & the British "New Wave" in Science Fiction.

Greenland, Cyril. Mental Illness & Civil Liberties.

Greenland, D. J. & Lal, R., eds. Soil Conservation & Management in the Humid Tropics.

Greenland, Jack & Szokolay, Steve. Passive Solar Design in Australia.

Greenlaw, Barry A. New England Furniture at Williamsburg.

Greenleaf, Stephen. Toll Call.

Greenlee, Mark, tr. see Myrtek, Mihcael.

Greenman, David & Talbot-Booth, E. C. Jane's Warsaw Pact Merchant Ships Recognition Handbook.

Greenough, Margaret. Advances on the AIDS Horizon: 1986.

Greenslade-Moore, Dianne, ed. see Kosbab, William H.

Greenslet, Ferris. James Russell Lowell: His Life & Work.

--Under the Bridge.

Greenslet, Ferris, jt. auth. see Curtis, Charles P., Jr.

Greenspan, Donald. Arithmetic Applied Mathematics.

Greensted, C. S. & Jardine, A. K. Essentials of Statistics in Marketing.

Greenstein, Fred I. Personality & Politics: Problems of Evidence, Inference, & Conceptualization.

Greenstein, Jesse L., ed. Stellar Atmospheres.

Greenstein, Jesse P. Biochemistry of Cancer.

Greenstein, Julius S., ed. Contemporary Readings in Biology.

Greenstone, Arthur W. & Harris, Sydney P. Concepts in Chemistry.

Greenstreet, Bob & Greenstreet, Karen. The Architect's Guide to Law & Practice.

Greenstreet, Karen, jt. auth. see Greenstreet, Bob.

Greenthal, Kathryn. Augustus Saint-Gaudens: Master Sculptor.

Greenwald, Anthony G., jt. auth. see Nuttin, Joseph.

Greenwald, Anthony G., et al. Psychological Foundations of Attitudes.

Greenwald, Bruce C. Adverse Selection in the Labor Market.

Greenwald, Dorothy & Greenwald, Robert. Learning to Live with the Love of Your Life.

Greenwald, G. Dale & Superka, Douglas P. Evaluating Social Studies Programs: Focus on Law-Related Education.

Greenwald, Harold & Rich, Elizabeth. The Happy Person.

Greenwald, Jerry. Be the Person You're Meant to Be.

Greenwald, Maurine W. Women, War, & Work: The Impact of World War I on Women in the United States.

Greenwald, Robert, jt. auth. see Greenwald, Dorothy.

Greenwald, Sheila. The Atrocious Two.

--The Secret in Miranda's Closet.

Greenway, James C., Jr. Extinct & Vanishing Birds of the World.

Greenway, John. The Primitive Reader: An Anthology of Myths, Tales, Songs, Riddles, & Proverbs of Aboriginal Peoples Around the World.

Greenwell, Alice B. The House of Young.

Greenwood. Truth & Meaning.

Greenwood, B. & Dowell, J. Masculine Focus in Home Economics.

Greenwood, Jennifer, tr. see Tesch, F. W.

Greenwood, Kathryn M. & Murphy, Mary F. Fashion Innovation & Marketing.

Greenwood, Marjorie. Roads & Canals in the Eighteenth Century. Reeves, Marjorie, ed.

Greenwood, N. N. The Chemistry of Boron.

Greenwood, P. H. The Haplochromine Fishes of the East African Lakes.

Greenwood, P. H., et al, eds. Interrelationships of Fishes: Supplement No. 1 to the Zoological Journal of the Linnean Society, Vol. 53, 1973.

Greenwood, Sadja. Menopause, Naturally: Preparing for the Second Half of Life.

Greenwood, Walter. Love on the Dole.

Greenwood, William T. Issues in Business & Society.

Greenya, John, jt. auth. see Bailey, F. L.

Greenya, John, jt. auth. see Burford, Anne M.

Greenya, John, jt. auth. see Cheshire, Maxine.

Greer, Ben. Halloween.

--Slammer.

Greer, Gaylon E. & Farrell, Michael D. Contemporary Real Estate: Theory & Practice.

--Investment Analysis for Real Estate Decisions.

Greer, Germaine. Female Eunuch.

Greer, Mary & Rubenstein, Bonnie. Will the Real Teacher Please Stand Up?

Greer, Thomas H. A Brief History of the Western World.

--A Brief History of Western Man.

--A Brief History of Western Man.

--Development of Air Doctrine in the Army Air Arm: 1917 Through 1941.

Grefe, Edward A. Fighting to Win: Business Political Power.

Greg, W. W. Jonson's Masque of Gipsies: In the Burley Belvoir & Windsor Versions.

Gregerson, Hans & Contreras, Arnoldo H. Economic Analysis of Forestry Projects: Case Studies.

Gregg, A. L. Tropical Nursing.

Gregg, James R. Your Future in New Optometric Careers.

Gregg, Joan Y. Communication & Culture: A Reading-Writing Text.

Gregg, John. How to Launder Money.

Gregg, John P., jt. ed. see Close, Arthur C.

Gregg, Linda. Too Bright to See.

Gregg, Richard B. Power of Non-Violence.

Gregg, Robert C. & Groh, Dennis E. Early Arianism: A View of Salvation.

Gregg, Robert E. The Ants of Colorado: Their Ecology, Taxonomy & Geographic Distribution.

Gregg, Tosh, jt. auth. see Muir, John.

Gregg, Vernon H. Human Memory.

Grego, Joseph. A History of Parliamentary Elections & Electioneering: From the Stuarts to Queen Victoria.

Gregoire, Reginald, et al. The Monastic Realm.

Gregor, Ian, jt. auth. see Kinkead-Weeks, Mark.

Gregoratos, Gabriel, jt. ed. see Karliner, Joel.

Gregorc, Anthony F. Gregorc Style Delineator, Developmental, Technical, & Administration Manual.

Gregor-Dellin, Martin. Richard Wagner: His Life, His Work, His Century. Brownjohn, J. Maxwell, tr. from Ger.

Gregor-Dellin, Martin, ed. see Wagner, Cosima.

Gregori, Mina, et al. The Age of Caravaggio.

Gregoriadis, Gregory, et al, eds. Targeting of Drugs.

Gregorian, Joyce B. Castledown.

Gregoric, Florence I., jt. ed. see McCarthy, Anne.

Gregorich, Barbara & Waldowski, Therese F. Punctuation Through Proofreading.

--The Research Paper.

Gregorvich, Barbara & Manoni, Mary H. Learning to Spell Correctly.

Gregory. Teaching of Saint Gregory: An Early Armenian Catechism. Thomson, Robert W., et al, trs. from Armenian.

Gregory, Andre, jt. auth. see Shawn, Wallace.

Gregory, Cedric E. Bucolic Bull: Fun on a Farm in Australia.

Gregory, Charles O. & Katz, Harold A. Labor & the Law.

Gregory, Charles O., et al. Cases & Materials on Torts: 1981 Supplement.

Gregory, Chester W., II. Women in Defense Work During World War II: An Analysis of the Labor Problem & Women's Rights.

Gregory, D., jt. auth. see Fetter, F. W.

Gregory, G. Robinson. Forest Resource Economics.

Gregory, George A. Pediatric Anesthesia.

Gregory, Horace, ed. & tr. see Catullus.

Gregory, J. S., jt. auth. see Kai-Shek, Chiang.

Gregory, K. J. & Walling, D. E. Man & Environmental Processes.

Gregory, Lady The Kiltartan Poetry Book.

Gregory, Laura A. A Study of Data Base Processor Technology.

Gregory, Lee. Colorado Scenic Guide: Southern Region.

Gregory, Michael S., et al, eds. Sociobiology & Human Nature: An Interdisciplinary Critique & Defense.

Gregory, P., jt. auth. see Gordon, P. F.

Gregory, Paul, jt. auth. see Ruffin, Roy.

Gregory, Paul R. & Stuart, Robert C. Comparative Economic Systems.

--Comparative Economic Systems.

Gregory, Peter. Deafness & Public Responsibility.

--Polluted Homes.

--Telephones for the Elderly.

Gregory, Philippa. Wideacre.

Gregory, Richard L. Intelligent Eye.

--The Psychology of Seeing.

Gregory, Robert A. Sugar Maple Research: Sap Production, Processing, & Marketing of Maple Syrup.

Gregory, Robin. The Horn: A Comprehensive Guide to the Modern Instrument & Its Music.

Gregory, Thomas W., ed. Adolescence in Literature.

Gregory, Veronica. Heart's Possession.

Gregory, William, tr. see Von Reichenbach, Karl.

Gregory Seventh, Pope The Correspondence of Pope Gregory VII. Emerton, E., tr.

Gregson, Robert. Psychometrics of Similarity.

Greguire, Helen. Carnival in Lights.

Greider, Janice E. & Beadles, William T. Law & the Life Insurance Contract.

--Principles of Life Insurance.

Greider, Ken. Invitation to Physics.

Greider, William. Secrets of the Temple: How the Federal Reserve Runs the Country.

Greiff, Barrie S. & Munter, Preston K. Tradeoffs: The Executive, Family & Organization.

Greiff, Constance M., et al. Princeton Architecture: A Pictorial History of Town & Campus.

Greiffenberg, Fay. English Workshop: First Course.

Greig, J. Y., ed. see Hume, David.

Greig, Noel & Griffiths, Drew. Two Gay Sweatshop Plays.

Greig, W. Smith. Economics & Management of Food Processing.

Greil, Arthur L. Georges Sorel & the Sociology of Virtue.

Greiner, John M., et al. Monetary Incentives & Work Standards in Five Cities: Impacts & Implications for Management & Labor.

Greiner, W., jt. auth. see Eisenberg, J. M.

Greisen, Deanna H., ed. Citizen Evaluation of the Community Development Block Grant Program in Norman, Oklahoma.

Greisman, Bernard, ed. see J. K. Lasser Tax Institute Staff.

Grekova, I. Russian Women: Two Stories. Visson, Lynn, tr. from Rus.

Grell, K. G. Protozoology.

Gremetz, M., et al. Meeting of European Communist Workers' Parties for Peace & Disarmament.

Grempel, V. H. Twigs.

Grenander, U., jt. auth. see Freiberger, W.

Grenander, Ulf. Abstract Inference.

Grenard, jt. auth. see Krause.

Grenby, Mike. Mike Grenby's Money Book: How to Survive Canada's Inflation.

Grene, David. Greek Political Theory: The Image of Man in Thucydides & Plato.

Grenier, Albert. Roman Spirit in Religion, Thought & Art. Dobie, M. R., tr.

Grenier, M. Special Day Prayers for the Very Young Child.

Grenier, Richard. The Marrakesh One-Two.

Grennell, Dean A. ABC's of Reloading.

--ABC's of Reloading.

--Autoloading Pistols: Gun Digest Book Of.

Grenoble, Penelope B., jt. auth. see Soll, Robert W.

Grenoble Public Reference Library Staff, ed. General Catalogue of Printed Books to 1900 Grenoble Public Reference Library.

Grenon, M. The Nuclear Apple & the Solar Orange: Alternatives in World Energy.

Grenon, M., ed. Future Coal Supply for the World Energy Balance.

--Methods & Models for Assessing Energy Resources: First IIASA Conference on Energy Resources, 20-21 May, 1975, Laxenburg, Austria.

Grenville-Grey, Wilfred. All in an African Lifetime.

Gresch, P. Managing Spatial Conflict: The Planning System in Switzerland.

Gresham, G. A., jt. ed. see Peeters, H.

Gresham, Geoffrey A. & Jennings, A. R. Introduction to Comparative Pathology: A Consideration of Some Reactions of Humans & Animal Tissues to Injurious Agents.

Gresham, P. A., tr. see Dertinger, H. & Jung, H.

Gresk, Grace E. Come Holy Spirit-I Need Thee.

Grespi, Irving see Cantril, Albert H., et al.

Gress, James R. & Kerber, James E., eds. Explorations into Teaching & Learning: School Based Teacher Education.

Gresser, Julian. Partners in Prosperity: Strategic Industries in the United States & Japan.

Gressley, Gene M. West by East: The American West in the Gilded Age.

Gresty, Hilary & Lewison, Jeremy, eds. Constructivism in Poland.

Greteman, Jim. Coping with Divorce.

Greten, H., ed. Lipoprotein Metabolism.

Gretes, Frances. John C. Portman, Jr. The Man & His Architecture.

Gretter, Clemens. Chain of Reasoning.

Gretz, Susanna. Teddy Bears' Moving Day.

Gretzky, Wayne & Taylor, Jim. Gretzky: From the Backyard Rink to the Stanley Rink.

Greve, John. London's Homeless.

--Private Landlords in England.

Grevich, J. D. Testing Procedures for Automotive AC & DC Charging Systems.

Greville, R. K. Descriptions of New & Rare Diatoms.

Grevisse, Maurice. Grevisse's Correct French: A Practical Guide. Kendris, Christopher, tr. from Fr.

Grevlich, Richard C., jt. ed. see Slavkin, Harold C.

Grew, Joseph C. Ten Years in Japan: A Contemporary Record Drawn from the Diaries & Private & Official Papers of Joseph C. Grew, United States Ambassador to Japan, 1932-1942.

Grewen, J., ed. see International Symposium Clausthal - Zellerfeld, 1968.

Grey, Anthony. Saigon.

Grey, Arthur, jt. auth. see Elliott, John E.

Grey, Elizabeth & Grey, Michael. The Executive Baby: Creating a Truly Superior Child.

Grey, Jerry. The Facts of Flight.

--Noise, Noise, Noise.

--The Race for Electric Power.

Grey, Jerry, ed. Aeronautics in China, AAS4.

--Space Tracking & Data Systems, AAS8.

Grey, Jerry & Hamdan, Lawrence A., eds. International Aerospace Review, AAS6.

Grey, Jerry, jt. ed. see Newman, Martin.

Grey, Loren, ed. see Grey, Zane.

Grey, Margot. Return from Death: An Exploration of the Near-Death Experience.

Grey, Michael, jt. auth. see Grey, Elizabeth.

Grey, R., et al. Readings in Embryology.

Grey, Romer Z. Zane Grey's Arizona Ames: Gun Trouble in Tonto Basin.

--Zane Grey's Arizona Ames: King of the Outlaw Horde.

--Zane Grey's Buck Duane: King of the Range.

--Zane Grey's Buck Duane: The Rider of Distant Trails.

--Zane Grey's Laramie Nelson: The Lawless Land.

--Zane Grey's Laramie Nelson: The Other Side of the Canyon.

--Zane Grey's Laramie Nelson: The Other Side of the Canyon.

--Zane Grey's Nevada Jim Lacy: Beyond the Mogollon Rim.

--Zane Grey's Yaqui: Siege at Forlorn River.

Grey, Rowland, jt. auth. see Dark, Sidney.

Grey, Viscount. Fly Fishing.

Grey, Zane. Arizona Clan.

--Black Mesa.

--Buffalo Hunter.

--The Fugitive Trail.

--Greatest Indian Stories.

--The Last Trail.

--Lone Star Ranger.

--Rainbow Trail.

--Savage Kingdom.

--Tenderfoot.

--Wilderness Trek.

--Zane Grey's Greatest Western Stories. Grey, Loren, ed.

Greynolds, Elbert B. & Aronfsky, J. S. Financial Analysis Using Calculators: Time Value of Money.

Greywolf, Elizabeth S. The Single Mother's Handbook.

Gribble, Leonard. They Shoot to Slay.

Gribnau, A. A. & Geijsberts, L. G. Developmental Stages in the Rhesus Monkey (Macaca Mulatta)

Grice, Julia. Emerald Fire.

--How to Find Romance after Forty.

--Lovefire.

--Wild Roses.

Grider, Edgar M. Can I Make It One More Year? Overcoming the Hazards of the Ministry.

Grider, J. Kenneth. Born Again & Growing.

Grider, John D., jt. auth. see Denhard, J. G.

Authors

Grieg, Sylvia. Escape Me Never.
--Midnight Gold.
Griehl, Manfred. Junkers Bombers.
Griepp, Frank R. & Griepp, Muriel H. Descendants of Gottfried & Wilhelmine Griepp & Their Hintz & Rathke Kinships.
Griepp, Muriel H., jt. auth. see Griepp, Frank R.
Grier, B. R., jt. auth. see Gough, Vera.
Grier, Eunice, jt. auth. see Grier, George.
Grier, George & Grier, Eunice. Equality & Beyond: Housing Segregation & the Goals of the Great Society.
Grierson, John. I Remember Lindbergh.
Grierson, Philip. Byzantine Coinage.
Griesbach, Heinz. Aktuell & Interessant.
--Deutsch X 3. Incl. Gespraechsbuch I mit Uebungen, "Unterwegs; Glossary I, German-English; Glossary II, German-English; Lehrerheft I; Lehrerheft II; Lernbuch I. Horn, Herbert, illus; Lernbuch II. Horn, Herbert, illus; Lernbuch III; Leseheft I mit Uebungen, "Aktuell und interessant; Leseheft II mit Uebungen, "Aktuell und interessant" Die Laender der Bundesrepublik Deutschland; Loesungsheft I; Loesungsheft II; Sprachlabor-Cassetten, Saemtliche Sprechuebungen, Doppelspur Mitnachsprechpausen, 10 Casetten; Sprachlabor-Tonbaender saemtliche Sprechuebungen, Vollspur mit Nachsprechpausen, 10 Tonbaender; Sprechuebungem I - Textheft. M S Rosenberg.
Griese, Arnold A. Do You Read Me? Practical Approaches to Teaching Reading Comprehension.
Griese, Bob, jt. auth. see Sayers, Gayle.
Griesse, Rosalie. The Crooked Shall Be Made Straight.
Grieve, Gregory P., ed. Common Vertebral Joint Problems.
Grieve, Michael, ed. see MacDiarmid, Hugh.
Grieve, Nichol. The Scottish Metrical Psalter (1650) A Revision.
Grieves, Forest L. Conflict & Order: An Introduction to International Relations.
Grieves, Forest L., ed. Transnationalism in World Politics & Business.
Griffen, Thomas. Untitled Griffen, Thomas.
Griffen, William L. & Marciano, J. D. Education for a Culture in Crisis.
Griffenhagen, George & Stieb, Ernst. Pharmacy Museums & Collections in the United States & Canada.
Griffeth, Bill, ed. see Burke, Dennis R.
Griffin & Beale. World of Electronics.
Griffin & D'Arcy. Manual of Adverse Drug Interactions.
Griffin, Adelaide, jt. auth. see Adams, Sexton.
Griffin, Appleton P. Bibliography of American Historical Societies.
Griffin, Arthur. New England: The Four Seasons.
Griffin, C. F. Haakon.
Griffin, C. J. & McGrath, Philomena. Embryogenesis: Development & Some Anomalies of the Upper Respiratory Tract Including the Septo-Maxillary Syndrome & Its Treatment.
Griffin, C. W., jt. auth. see American Institute of Architects Staff.
Griffin, Charles C. United States & the Disruption of the Spanish Empire, 1810-1822.
Griffin, D. M. Ecology of Soil Fungi.
Griffin, D. R., ed. Animal Mind - Human Mind: Report on the Dahlem Workshop.
Griffin, David R. God, Power, & Evil: A Process Theodicy.
Griffin, David R. & Altizer, Thomas J., eds. John Cobb's Theology in Process.
Griffin, David R. & Cobb, John B., Jr., eds. Mind in Nature: Essays on the Interface of Science & Philosophy.
Griffin, Donald R. Animal Thinking.
--The Question of Animal Awareness: Evolutionary Continuity of Mental Experience.
--The Question of Animal Awareness: Evolutionary Continuity of Mental Experience.
Griffin, Donald R. & Novick, A. Animal Structure & Function.
Griffin, Gary W., jt. auth. see Tsang, Wing-Sum.
Griffin, H. J., ed. Comparative History of Metrology.
Griffin, I. H., et al. Basic Tig & Mig Welding.
Griffin, Ivan H., et al. Basic Arc Welding.
--Basic Oxyacetylene Welding.
Griffin, J. A Manual of Adverse Drug Interactions.
Griffin, James. Physical Agents for Physical Therapists.
Griffin, James B., jt. auth. see Braun, David P.
Griffin, James M. & Teece, David J., eds. OPEC Behavior & World Oil Prices.
Griffin, Jasper. The Mirror of Myth: T. S. Eliot Memorial Lecture 1984.
Griffin, Jeff W. Cold Weather Flying.
--Hangar Tales & War Stories: The Humor & Adventure of Flying.
--Instrument Flying.
--Modular Model Railroading.
Griffin, John H. A Hidden Wholeness: The Visual World of Thomas Merton.
--Twelve Photographic Portraits.
Griffin, Joyanne. Love, Vanity & the Mirage.
Griffin, LaDean. Hierbas al Rescate (Herbs to the Rescue)
--Hyper- & Hypoglycemia.
--Please Dr., I'd Rather Do It Myself with Vitamins & Minerals.
Griffin, N. B., ed. see Dummer, Geoffrey W.
Griffin, Nathaniel E., tr. see Boccaccio, Giovanni.
Griffin, Neil. The Bluegrass Banjo Method.
Griffin, O. M. & Gianotti, J. G., eds. Ocean Engineering for OTEC.
Griffin, Roger C., Jr., jt. auth. see Sacharow, Stanley.
Griffin, Russell M. The Timeservers.
Griffin, Sue, jt. auth. see Shoden, Rebecca.
Griffin, Susan. Rape: The Power of Consciousness.
Griffin, Ted, ed. see Stafford, Bill.
Griffin, Thomas K. Pelican Guide to New Orleans.
Griffin, Victor R. Humor in Human Quirks in Paintings & Rhyme.
Griffin, W. E. The New Breed.
Griffin, William D. A Portrait of the Irish in America.
Griffiss, James E. A Silent Path to God.
Griffith, Ernest S. The American System of Government.
Griffith, Francis, jt. auth. see Mersand, Joseph.
Griffith, H. Winter. Complete Guide to Prescription & Non-Prescription Drugs.
Griffith, J. S. Mathematical Neurobiology: An Introduction to the Mathematics of the Nervous System.
Griffith, Jack S. Laboratory Manual for Man & His Environment.
Griffith, Jane, jt. auth. see Mullen, Edwin.
Griffith, Kathryn M. Evil Stalks the Night.
Griffith, Kelly, Jr. Writing Essays about Literature: A Guide & Style Sheet.
Griffith, Marlene, jt. auth. see Muscatine, Charles.
Griffith, Nancy, jt. auth. see Griffith, Robert.
Griffith, Paddy, et al. Wellington Commander: The Iron Duke's Generalship.
Griffith, Richard & Mayer, Arthur. The Movies.
Griffith, Richard, et al. The Movies.
Griffith, Robert & Griffith, Nancy. Blue Water: A Guide to Self Reliant Sailboat Cruising.
Griffith, Roger, ed. see Kirkpatrick, Frank.
Griffith, Roger, ed. see Simmons, Paula.
Griffith, Susan. Work Your Way Around the World.
--Work Your Way Around the World.
Griffith, Susan, ed. Summer Jobs in Britain.
--Summer Jobs in Britain 1985.
--Summer Jobs in Britain 1987.
Griffithe, Elisabeth. Conceived in Conflict: The Politics of the Women's Movement & the Crusade for the ERA.
Griffiths. Washington, D. C. in Your Pocket.
Griffiths, Antong, jt. auth. see Carey, Frances.
Griffiths, Cynthia, jt. auth. see Griffiths, Glyn.
Griffiths, Daniel E., ed. Behavioral Science & Educational Administration: 63rd Yearbook.
Griffiths, Drew, jt. auth. see Greig, Noel.
Griffiths, Glyn & Griffiths, Cynthia. Aspects of the Kadiweu Language.
Griffiths, H. B. & Hilton, P. J. A Comprehensive Textbook of Classical Mathematics: A Contemporary Interpretation.
Griffiths, Harry J. Radiology of Renal Failures.
Griffiths, Harry J. & Sarno, Robert C. Contemporary Radiology: An Introduction to Imaging.
Griffiths, Helen. Rafa's Dog.
--Running Wild.
--Russian Blue.
Griffiths, J. Color & Constitution of Organic Molecules.
Griffiths, J. M., ed. Local Telecommunications: Into the Digital Era.
Griffiths, J. W., et al, eds. Signal Processing: Proceedings.
Griffiths, M. Echidnas.
Griffiths, Paul. Modern Music: The Avant Garde Since 1945.
Griffiths, Trevor. Comedians.
Grigarick, Albert A. & Schuster, Robert O. Discrimination of Genera of Euplectini of North & Central America: Coleoptera; Pselaphidae.
Grigg, John. Nineteen Forty-Three: The Victory That Never Was.
Griggs, Earl L. Thomas Clarkson: The Friend of Slaves.
Griggs, Earl L., ed. see Christophe, Henri.
Griggs, Irwin & Llewellyn, Robert. Basic Writer & Reader.
Grigsby, Charles, jt. auth. see Brey, Ron.
Grigsby, Wayne, ed. A Toronto Lampoon.
Grigsby, William G. & Rosenburg, Louis. Urban Housing Policy.
Grigson, Geoffrey. The Living Rocks.
--Old Stone Age.
Grigson, Jane. Food with the Famous.
--Jane Grigson's British Cookery.
--Jane Grigson's Fruit Book.
--Jane Grigson's Vegetable Book.
Grigson, Jane & Knox, Charlotte. Cooking with Exotic Fruits & Vegetables.
Grigulevich, I. Historia de la Inquisicion.
Grill, Tom & Scanlon, Mark. The Art of Scenic Photography: Technical & Aesthetic Guidelines for the Creative Photographer.
--Photographic Composition.
Grilley, Kate, jt. auth. see Venderheiden, Gregg C.
Grilli, Enzo R. Italian Commercial Policies in the 1970's.
Grilli, Peter. Furo: The Japanese Bath.
Grilliot, Harold J. Introduction to Law & the Legal System.
Grillo, John P. & Robertson, J. Douglas. Graphics for the Macintosh: An Idea Book.
Grillo, Salvatore. The Gospel According to Barabbas. Cavoto, Nino, tr. from Ital.
Grillo, T. Adesanya, et al. The Evolution of Pancreatic Islets.
Grillo, Virgil. Charles Dickens' Sketches by Boz: End in the Beginning.
Grillparzer, F. The Jewess of Toledo. Burkhard, Arthur, tr.
Grimal, Henri & Moreau, Lucien. Histoire De France.
Grimaldi, John V. & Simonds, Rollin H. Safety Management.
Grimble, Ian. Robert Burns.
Grimes, D. M. Electromagnetism & Quantum Theory.
Grimes, Frances H. Uptown Love.
Grimes, Larry E. The Religious Design of Hemingway's Early Fiction. Litz, A. Walton, ed.
Grimes, Russell N. Carboranes.
Grimes, Seamus, ed. Ireland in Eighteen Hundred & Four.
Grimm, Ede, jt. auth. see Edney, Margon.
Grimm, Gary & Mitchell, Don. Dandylions Never Roar Book.
Grimm, Georg, jt. ed. see Benton, Wilbourn E.
Grimm, Jacob. King Thrushbeard.
Grimm, Jacob & Grimm, Wilhelm K. The Bearskinner.
--The Four Clever Brothers: A Story by the Brothers Grimm.
--Good-for-Nothings.
--Grimm's Fairy Tales.
--Hans in Luck. Hoffmann, Felix, ed.
--Hansel & Gretel. Crawford, Elizabeth D., tr. from Ger.
--Hansel & Gretel.
--Hansel & Gretel.
--Hansel & Gretel, the Seven Ravens, & the Little Red Cap.
--The Little Red Cap.
--Little Red Riding Hood. Pincus, Harriet, ed. & illus.
--Little Red Riding Hood.
--Rapunzel. Hoffmann, Felix, ed. & illus.
--Rapunzel.
--Rapunzel.
--Rumpelstiltskin. Ayer, Jacqueline, ed. & illus.
--Rumpelstiltskin.
--The Seven Ravens.
--The Seven Ravens.
--Sleeping Beauty.
--Tom Thumb. Hoffmann, Felix, ed. & illus.
Grimm, Susan. How to Write Computer Manuals for Users.
Grimm, Wilhelm K., jt. auth. see Grimm, Jacob.
Grimme, Hubert. Altsinaitische Forschungen, Epigraphisches und Historisches.
--Israelitische Pfingstfest und der Plejadenkult.
Grimsted, Patricia K. Archives & Manuscript Repositories in the U. S. S. R., Moscow & Leningrad: Supplement I; Biographical Addenda.
Grimwood, Jonathan. Photohistory of the Twentieth-Century.
Grindal, Harald. Telecare Ministry: Using the Telephone in a Care Ministry.
Grindea, Carola. We Make Our Own Music.
Grindlay, J. An Introduction to the Phenomenological Theory of Ferroelectricity.
Grindley, J. H. Principles of Electrical Transmission Lines in Power & Communication.
Grindrod, Muriel, tr. see Chabod, Federico.
Grinevich, E. & Gvozdariov, B. Washington Contra la Habana.
Grinker, Roy R., Sr. & Werble, Beatrice. The Borderline Patient.
Grinnell, Richard M., Jr. Social Work Research & Evaluation.
Grinols, Anne B., ed. Critical Thinking: Reading Across the Curriculum.
Grinsell, L. V. The Ancient Burial-Mounds of England.
Grinspoon, Lester. Marihuana Reconsidered.
Grinstein, Louise & Michaels, Brenda, eds. Calculus: Readings from the Mathematics Teacher.
Grinter, Lawrence E., jt. ed. see Kihl, Young W.
Grioli, G. Mathematical Theory of Elastic Equilibrium.
Grip, J. P. Sexuality, Love & Immorality.
Grippando, Gloria M. Nursing: Perspectives & Issues.
Grise, Jeanette. Robert Benjamin & the Disappearing Act.
Grisez, Germain & Shaw, Russell. Beyond the New Morality: The Responsibilities of Freedom.
Grishanov, V. M., ed. Man & Sea Warfare.
Grishin, M. Hydraulic Structures.
Grishman, Ralph. Assembly Language Programming for the Control Data 6000 Series & the Cyber Series.
Grismer, Raymond L., ed. see Altamirano, Ignacio M.
Grissum, Marlene & Spengler, Carol. Womanpower & Health Care.
Grist & Urquhart. Diagnostic Methods in Clinical Virology.
Griswold, Erwin N. & Graetz, Michael J. Federal Income Taxation, Principles & Policies: 1983 Supplement.
Griswold, H. E. Catalog of Law Books: Reference Catalogue of Law Books Published Prior to 1894.
Griswold, P. R. Colorado's Loneliest Railroad: The San Luis Southern.
Griswold, Ruth M. Experimental Study of Foods.
Gritsch, Eric W. Born Againism: Perspectives on a Movement.
--Martin - God's Court Jester: Luther in Retrospect.
Gritsch, Eric W., ed. see Haendler, Gert.
Gritsch, Ruth C., tr. see Haendler, Gert.
Gritsch, Ruth C., tr. see Moltmann-Wendel, Elisabeth.
Grivet, P. Electron Optics. Incl. Pt. 1. Optics; Pt. 2. Instruments. Pergamon.
--Physics of Transmission Lines at High & Very High Frequencies.
Grivet, P., ed. The Physics of Transmission Lines at High & Very High Frequencies: Microwave Circuits & Amplifiers.
Grizzard, Lewis. Grizzard Advice Book Floor Dump.
Groak, S., ed. Action Planning & Responsive Design: Issues of Housing, Building, Planning & Development in the Third World.
Grob, Bernard. Basic Electronics.
Grob, Bernard & Kiver, Milton S. Applications of Electronics.
Grob, Paul & Brown, Nina W., eds. Readings in Education & Psychology.
Grobani, Anton, ed. Guide to Baseball Literature.
--Guide to Football Literature.
Grobman, Jerald. Group Psychotherapy for Students & Teachers: A Selective Bibliography, 1946-1979.
Grodecki, Louis & Brisac, Catherine. Gothic Stained Glass: 1200-1300. Boehm, Barbara D., tr. from Fr.
Groden, Michael, ed. Ulysses: "Ithaca" & "Penelope." A Facsimile of Manuscripts & Typescripts for Episodes 17 & 18.
--Ulysses: "Sirens," "Cyclops," "Nausicaa," & "Oxen of the Sun." A Facsimile of Placards for Episodes 11-14.
--Ulysses: "Wandering Rocks," "Sirens," "Cyclops," "Nausicaa": Facsimile of Drafts & Typescripts for Episodes 10-13.
Groden, Michael, ed. see Joyce, James.
Grodzins, Morton. Americans Betrayed.
Grodzinsky, Stephen, jt. auth. see Kirwin, Gerald J.
Groen, A. Dutch Costumes.
Groene, Janet. Cooking on the Go.
Groeneveld, Karl-Ontjes, jt. ed. see Berkowitz, Joseph.
Groenfeldt, John S. We Gather Together: The Church Worships God.
Groer, Leon de see De Groer, Leon.
Groer, Maureen W. & Shekleton, Maureen E. Basic Pathophysiology: A Conceptual Approach.
Grof, Baumann T., jt. auth. see Kamm, G.
Grof, Stanislav. LSD Psychotherapy.
Groff, Betty & Wilson, Jose. Good Earth & Country Cooking.
Groff, Cora M. Crown of Jewels.
Groff, James R., jt. auth. see Weinberg, Paul N.
Grofman, Bernard, et al. Representation & Redistricting Issues.
Grogan, Emmett. Ringolevio.
Groger, Molly. E. A. T. Eating Awareness Training.
Groh, Dennis E. In Between Advents: Biblical & Spiritual Arrivals.
Groh, Dennis E., jt. auth. see Gregg, Robert C.
Grohman, Joann S. Keeping a Family Cow.
Grohskopf, Bernice. Blood & Roses.
--Children in the Wind.
--End of Summer.
--Notes on the Hauter Experiment: A Journey Through the Inner World of Evelyn B. Chestnut.
--Shadow in the Sun.
--The Treasure of Sutton Hoo: Ship Burial for an Anglo-Saxon King.
Grolier Club Staff. Catalog of Original & Early Editions of Some of the Poetical & Prose Works from Langland to Prior.

Grolier, Inc. Staff. Encyclopedia Science Supplement, 1984. Kondo, Herbert, ed.
Grolle, Carl G. Electronic Workshop Manual & Guide.
--Grolle's Complete Guide to Electronic Troubleshooting.
Grollenberg, Lucas. Jesus. Bowden, John, tr.
Grollman, Earl. Living When a Loved One Has Died.
Grollman, Earl A. & Sweder, Gerri L. The Working Parent Dilemma: How to Balance the Responsibilities of Children & Careers.
Grollman, Earl A., ed. Suicide: Prevention, Intervention, Postvention.
Grollman, Sigmund. A Laboratory Manual of Mammalian Anatomy & Physiology.
Gromacki, Robert G. Called to Be Saints.
--Modern Tongues Movement.
--New Testament Survey.
--Stand Bold in Grace: An Exposition of Hebrews.
Gromisch, Donald S., jt. auth. see Wasserman, Edward.
Gromyko, A. A. Only for Peace.
Gromyko, Anatolii A. Through Russian Eyes: President Kennedy's One Thousand Thirty-Six Days. Garon, Philip A., ed.
Gronbeck, Bruce E., jt. auth. see Ehninger, Douglas.
Gronbjerg, Kristen A., et al. Government Spending & the Nonprofit Sector in Cook County - Chicago.
Grone, Linda. Reach for a Different Sky.
Groneman. Gen Ind Ed Training.
--General Ind Ed Sg.
Groner, Judye & Wikler, Madeline. Where is the Afikomen?
Gronlund, Norman E. Constructing Achievement Tests.
--Improving Marking & Reporting in Classroom Instruction.
Gronomov, A. Problems & Exercises in Organic Chemistry.
Gronoset, Dagfinn. Anna.
Gronoswska, R., jt. auth. see Gronowski, T.
Gronowicz, Antoni. Polish Profiles: The Land, the People & Their History.
Gronowski, T. & Gronoswska, R. Poland.
Groom, A. J. R., jt. ed. see Light, Margot.
Grooms, Kathe, ed. see Lansky, Bruce.
Groos, G. W., tr. see Waldstein, Baron.
Groot, Roy A. De see De Groot, Roy A.
Groot, Roy A. de see De Groot, Roy A.
Grootings, Peter, ed. Technology & Work: East West Comparisons.
Groover, Mikell P. Automation, Production Systems & Computer-Aided Manufacturing.
Gropius, Ise see O'Neal, William B.
Gropman, Donald & Mirvis, Kenneth. Comet Fever.
Gropp, Louis. Solar Houses: Vol. 17, Facts & Pictures About Authors & Illustrators of Books for Young Peoples.
Gros, F. Le see Le Gros, F. & Dunne, Agnes C.
Groschal, D., jt. ed. see Fahlberg, W. J.
Groschel. Hospital Associated Infections in the General Hospital Populations & Specific Measures of Control.
Groseclose, Elgin. Ararat.
--The Kiowa.
--Olympia.
Grosjean, Francois. Life with Two Languages: An Introduction to Bilingualism.
Grosman, Brian A. Prosecutor: An Inquiry into the Exercise of Discretion.
Gross, Barbara & Shuman, Bernard. Essentials of Parenting in the First Years of Life.
Gross, Bernard. Last Jews in Berlin.
Gross, Charles W. & Peterson, Robin T. Business Forecasting.
Gross, David. The Writer & Society: Heinrich Mann & Literary Politics in 1890-1940.
Gross, Dorothea A. Recollections of My Immigrant Grandmother.
Gross, E. T., et al, eds. Coil Spring Making.
Gross, Edmund J. How to Get More Sales from Your Advertising.
Gross, Edward & Western, John S., eds. The End of a Golden Age: Higher Education in a Steady State.
Gross, Eugene L. A Nomad's Progress: A Biography of Dr. J. E. Zimmerman.
Gross, F. H. & Inman, W. H., eds. Drug Monitoring.
Gross, Feliks. Foreign Policy Analysis.
--Seizure of Political Power.
Gross, Fletcher, jt. ed. see Scott, William R.
Gross, Gail & Finkelstein, Honora. Beautiful Skin.
Gross, Henry. Pure Magic.
Gross, J. F., et al, eds. Modern Techniques in Physiological Sciences.
Gross, Jim, ed. see Carey, Ken.
Gross, John, ed. see Seeley, John R.
Gross, Joseph, tr. see Konnyu, Leslie.
Gross, Kathleen, jt. auth. see Weiner, Michael A.
Gross, Le Roy. Art of Selling Intangibles: How to Make a Million Investing Other People's Money.
Gross, Leonard, jt. auth. see Belsky, Marvin S.
Gross, Leonard, jt. auth. see Cailliet, Rene.
Gross, Martin. Red President.
Gross, Meir, ed. Pseudoepilepsy: The Clinical Aspects of False Seizures.
Gross, Michael & Jakubowski, Maxim. The Rock Yearbook 1981.
Gross, Nedward, Jr. Elegy Andinforno.
Gross, Polly. Western Motel.
Gross, Rebecca H. Voltaire, Non-Conformist.
Gross, Ronald & Murphy, Judith. The Revolution in the Schools.
Gross, Rosalind L. Child-Resistant Packages for Pesticides. Donner, Art & Wilbur, Charles J., eds.
Gross, Sam. An Elephant Is Soft & Mushy.
--I Am Blind & My Dog Is Dead.
--Love Me, Love My Teddy Bear.
--More Gross.
Gross, Sam, ed. Why Are Your Papers in Order? Cartoons for 1984.
Gross, Seymour L., jt. ed. see Stern, Milton R.
Gross, Shelly. Havana X.
Gross, Stephen H. & Smith, Edward L. Legal & Business Aspects of the Magazine Industry, 1984.
Gross, Steven & Garb, Solomon. Cancer Treatment & Research in Humanistic Perspective.
Grossack, Martin M., ed. Understanding Consumer Behavior.
Grossart, G. S. see Yarwood, J.
Grossarth-Maticek, R., jt. ed. see De Boor, W.
Grossbart, June, et al. An Introductory Textile Manual.
Grossberg, S., ed. The Adaptive Brain.
Grosseck, Joyce. Great Explorers.
Grosser, Alfred. The Western Alliance: European American Relations since 1945.
Grosser, Morton. Diesel: The Man & the Engine.
--Gossamer Odyssey: The Triumph of Human-Powered Flight.
Grossi, John A. Model State Policy, Legislation & State Plan Toward the Education of Gifted & Talented Students: A Handbook for State & Local Districts.
Grossi, Ralph. Reliving Reincarnation Through Hypnosis.
Grossinger, Richard, ed. Baseball.
Grosskopf, Susan A. Fabric Frames from Stretch Bars.
Grossman. Secretary Set.
Grossman, Alan, et al. Diamond: A Biography.
Grossman, Bernard A., ed. Letters Rogatory.
Grossman, Bruce & Keyes, Carol. Helping Children Grow: The Adults Role.
Grossman, C. Barrie, ed. see Gonzelez, Carlos F., et al.
Grossman, David A. The Future of New York City's Capital Plant.
Grossman, Elliott S., jt. auth. see Kendrick, John W.
Grossman, H. L. Practical Bar Management.
Grossman, Harold J. Grossman's Guide to Wines, Beers, & Spirits.
Grossman, Herbert J., jt. ed. see Bernsohn, Joseph.
Grossman, Jeffrey E., jt. auth. see Kravitt, Gregory I.
Grossman, Karl. Power Crazy: How the Long Island Lighting Company Became America's Biggest Utilities Scandal.
Grossman, Kurt R. Michael Wurmbrand: The Man & His Work.
Grossman, Lee. The Change Agent.
Grossman, Mort. The Summer Ends Too Soon.
Grossman, Morton I., et al, eds. Cellular Basis of Chemical Messengers in the Digestive System.
Grossman, Peter Z. American Express: An Unauthorized History.
Grossman, Robert G., jt. auth. see Willis, William D., Jr.
Grossman, Stanley. Calculus: Instructor's Manual.
Grossman, Stanley I. Applied Mathematical Analysis.
--Applied Mathematics for the Management, Life, & Social Sciences.
--Brief Introduction to Linear Algebra.
--Calculus.
--Calculus.
--Calculus.
--Calculus of One Variable.
--Elementary Linear Algebra.
Grossman, Tracy B. Mothers & Children Facing Divorce. Nathan, Peter, ed.
Grossmark, D. R. Leica Price Guide, 1984-85: Pocket Book.
Grossmark, D. R., ed. Leica International Price Guide, 1986-87.
Grosso, Sonny & Rosenberg, Philip. Point Blank.
Grossvogel, David I. Limits of the Novel: Evolutions of a Form from Chaucer to Robbe-Grillet.
Grosswald, Blanche. Statistical Summary Report of the 1979 University of California Union Catalog Data Base.
Grosvenor, Theodore P. Primary Care Optometry: A Clinical Manual.
Groten, Dallas. Will the Real Winner Please Stand Up.
Groth, Alexander J. Major Ideologies: An Interpretative Survey of Democracy, Socialism & Nationalism.
Groth, Alexander J., et al. Contemporary Politics: Europe.
Grothendieck, A. Local Cohomology: A Seminar Given by A. Grothendieck at Harvard University, 1961. Hartshorne, ed.
Grothendieck, A. & Murre, J. P. Tame Fundamental Group of a Formal Neighbourhood of a Divisor with Normal Crossing on a Scheme.
Grotjahn, Martin. Psychoanalysis & the Family Neurosis.
Grotjahn, Martin & Kline, Frank M. A Handbook of Group Therapy.
Grotz, George. Furniture Doctor.
Grounds, Roger, ed. Practical Pruning.
Group for the Advancement of Psychiatry Staff. Death & Dying: Attitudes of Patient & Doctor.
Group for the Advancement of Psychiatry. Diagnosis & Treatment in Child Psychiatry.
--Normal Adolescence: Its Dynamics & Impact.
Group for the Advancement of Psychiatry, Committee on Child Psychiatry. The Process of Child Therapy.
Group for the Advancement of Psychiatry Staff. Psychological & Medical Aspects of the Use of Nuclear Energy.
Grout, Bill, jt. auth. see Hewes, Jeremy.
Grout, Donald J. History of Western Music.
--History of Western Music.
Grout, Donald J. & Palisca, Claude. A History of Western Music.
Grout, Jack. On the Lesson Tee: Basic Golf Fundamentals.
Grout, Jarrell C. Fundamental Computer Programming Using FORTRAN 77.
Grout, P. B., et al, eds. The Legend of Arthur in the Middle Ages.
Grove, Bob. Behind the Dial. Force, Rich, ed.
Grove, E. L., ed. Applied Atomic Spectroscopy. Incl. Vol. 1; Vol. 2. Plenum Pub.
Grove, Edward A. & Ladas, Gerasimbs E. Introduction to Complex Variables.
Grove, Fred. The Great Horse Race.
Grove, Lilly. Dancing: A Handbook of the Terpsichorean Arts in Diverse Places & Times, Savage & Civilized.
Grove, Nancy. Isamu Noguchi: A Study of the Sculpture. Freedberg, S. J., ed.
Grove, Pearce S., ed. Nonprint Media in Academic Libraries.
Grove Press Victorian Library Staff. Love Victorian Style: III.
Grove, Victor. The Language Bar.
Grover, Alan. The Oil & Gas Industry & the Bankruptcy Laws: A Course Handbook.
Grover, Eulalie O. Robert Louis Stevenson: A Teller of Tales.
Grover, J. H. Aircraft Communications Systems.
Grover, Lee, jt. auth. see Grover, Ray.
Grover, Marshall. Feud at Mendoza.
Grover, Philip, jt. auth. see Pound, Omar.
Grover, Ray & Grover, Lee. English Cameo Glass.
Grover, Satish. The Architecture of India-Buddhist & Hindu.
--The Architecture of India: Islamic.
Groves, jt. auth. see Ballantyne.
Groves, Donald G. & Hunt, Lee M. The Ocean World Encyclopedia.
Groves, Ivor D., Jr., ed. Acoustic Transducers.
Groves, Norris A. Christian Devotedness.
Groves, Philip M. & Schlesinger, Kurt. Introduction to Biological Psychology.
Groves, Sheila & Stowell, Gordon. All Change.
Groves, Wanda J. Joey Green Loves Red Balloons.
Groves-Raines, Antony, jt. ed. see Langstaff, John M.
Grow, Douglas, jt. auth. see Barnidge, Thomas.
Grow, Lawrence. The Fourth Old House Catalogue.
Grow, Lawrence, compiled by. The Fifth Old House Catalogue.
Grow, Lucille J. & Shapiro, Deborah. Transracial Adoption Today: Views of Adoptive Parents & Social Workers.
Groymko, A. A., et al, eds. Soviet Peace Efforts on Eve of World War Two.
Groza, Vivian S. Arithmetic.
--College Algebra.
--Elementary Algebra.
Groza, Vivian S. & Sellers, Gene. Algebra & Trigonometry.
Grubb & Ellis Staff, jt. auth. see Real Estate Education Company Staff.
Grubb, C. A. & Phares, M. I. Industrialization: A New Concept for Housing.
Grubb, Jan. The Media Mouse Collection. Sharpe, Sally, ed.
Grubb, R. Genetic Markers of Human Immunoglobulins.
Grubb, R. & Samuelsson, G. Human Anti-Human Gammaglobulins: Their Specificity & Function.
Grube, G. M. On Poetry & Style Aristotle.
Grube, Oswald W., jt. auth. see Bush-Brown, Albert.
Gruber, Bruno & Millman, Richard S., eds. Symmetries In Science I.
Gruber, Clemens. Dictionary of Advertising & Marketing.
Gruber, Edward C., jt. auth. see Strand, Stanley.
Gruber, Gary. Professional & Administrative Career Examination.
Gruber, Gary R. Math Review for the GMAT.
Gruber, Jacob W. A Conscience in Conflict: The Life of St. George Jackson Mivart.
Gruber, James, jt. auth. see Benson, Tedd.
Gruber, U. F. Blood Replacement. Oxtoby, L. & Armstrong, R. F., trs.
Gruchy, Allan G. Comparative Economic Systems: Competing Ways to Stability, Growth & Welfare.
Grudzinskas, J. B. & Seppala, M., eds. Pregnancy Proteins: Biology, Chemistry & Clinical Application (Australia)
Gruen, Victor. The Heart of Our Cities.
Gruenanger, P., jt. auth. see Grundmann, C.
Gruenberg, K. W. Linear Geometry.
Gruendemann, Barbara J. & Meeker, Margaret H. Alexander's Care of the Patient in Surgery.
Gruenfeld, Raymond, jt. auth. see Oaks, Sherry.
Gruening, Ernest H. Mexico & Its Heritage.
Gruenstein, Peter, jt. auth. see Hanrahan, John D.
Gruesser, O. J. & Klinke, R., eds. Pattern Recognition in Biological & Technical Systems: Proceedings-Deutsche Gesellschaft Fuer Kybernetik, 4th Congress, Berlin, 1970.
Grugel, Lee E. Society & Religion During the Age of Industrialization: Christianity in Victorian England.
Gruhl, Jim, ed. see Kirsner, Gary.
Gruhn, Victor I., tr. see Gartner, Bertil.
Grujic, B. Pocket English-Croatian-English Dictionary: Short Grammar.
Gruliow, Leo. Current Soviet Policies I: The Documentary Record of the 19th Communist Party Congress & the Reorganization after Stalin's Death. Current Digest of the Soviet Press Staff, tr. from Rus.
Gruliow, Leo, ed. Current Soviet Policies: The Documentary Record of the Twentieth Communist Party Congress & Its Aftermath. Current Digest of the Soviet Press Staff, tr. from Rus.
Gruliow, Leo & Neuweld, Mark, eds. Current Soviet Policies: The Documentary Record of the Extraordinary Twenty-First Communist Party Congress. Current Digest of the Soviet Press Staff, tr. from Rus.
Grumet, Michael. Images of Libery.
Grummelshausen, Hans J. Von see Von Grimmelshausen, Hans J. C.
Grunbaum, Dorien, jt. auth. see Markstein, Linda.
Grunbaum, E., ed. Vacuum Technology: Selected Proceedings of the 6th Israeli Vacuum Congress, Haifa, Israel, 4-5 April, 1982.
Grunberg, Emanuel, jt. auth. see Schnitzer, Robert J.
Grunberger, Richard. The Twelve Year Reich.
Grundberg, Sibyl, jt. ed. see Dowrick, Stephanie.
Grundfest, Sandra. Engineering, Science & Computer Jobs 1983.
Grundfest, Sandra, ed. Engineering, Science, & Computer Jobs 1984.
Grundfest, Warren, jt. ed. see White, Rodney A.
Grundman, Donna. A Distant Eden.
Grundmann, C. & Gruenanger, P. Nitrile Oxides, Versatile Tools of Theoretical & Preparative Chemistry.
Grundmann, Carol, jt. auth. see Williams, Barbara.
Grundmann, E. & Kirsten, W. H., eds. Current Topics in Pathology.
--Perinatal Pathology.
Grundon, M. F. Biosynthesis of Anematic Isoprenoids.
Grundt, Eugene. A Cocktail of Poems.
Grundt, Leonard. Efficient Patterns for Adequate Library Service in a Large City: A Survey of Boston.
Grundtvig, N. F. What Constitutes Authentic Christianity? Nielsen, Ernest D., ed. & tr. from Ger.
Grundy, J. T. Construction Technology.
--Construction Technology.
--Construction Technology.
Grundy, Philip, tr. see Tsaloumas, Dimitris.
Grunebaum, Gustave E., ed. Mediaeval Islam: A Study in Cultural Orientation.
Grunebaum, Henry U., jt. auth. see Cohler, Bertram J.
Gruneberg, M. M., et al, eds. Practical Aspects of Memory.
Gruneberg, Michael M. Understanding Job Satisfaction.
Gruneberg, Michael M. & Morris, Peter, eds. Aspects of Memory.
Gruner, Mark & Brown, Christopher K. Mark Gruner's Numbers of Life: An Introduction to Numerology.
Grunes, Barbara. Dining In - Chicago.
--Dining In - Chicago.
--The Joy of Baking.
--Mexican Cookbook.

Grunewald, H., ed. Chemistry for the Future: Proceedings of the 29th IUPAC Congress, Cologne, Federal Republic of Germany, 5-10 June 1983.
Grung, B. L., jt. auth. see Warner, R. M.
Grunlan, Stephen A. & Mayers, Marvin K. Cultural Anthropology: A Christian Perspective.
Grunsell, C. S. & Hill, F. W. The Veterinary Annual.
Grunwald, Stefan. Osten und Westen.
Grupenhoff, John T. National Health Directory, 1986.
Grupenhoff, John T., ed. National Health Directory 1987.
Grupp, Fred W., Jr. & Maurer, Marvin, eds. Political Behavior in the United States: Readings in American Government.
Gruppe, Henry, jt. auth. see Time-Life Books Editors.
Gruppo Editoriale Fabbri Staff. Man Ray.
Grusa, Jiri. The Questionnaire.
--The Questionnaire: Or, Prayer for a Town & a Friend. Kussi, Peter, tr. from Czech.
Gruskin, Alan, jt. auth. see Fine, Richard N.
Gruss, Edmond C. Jehovah's Witnesses & Prophetic Speculation.
--We Left Jehovah's Witnesses.
Gruss, Robert. Art of the Aqualung.
Gryniewicz, Deborah L., et al. Nuclear Medicine Technology Examination Review.
Grzebieniowski, T. Polish-English, English-Polish Dictionary.
Grzybowski, Kazimierz. Soviet Public International Law: Doctrines & Diplomatic Practice.
Gschossman, Elke. German Grammar.
Gschwind, H. W. & McCluskey, E. J. Design of Digital Computers.
Gual, Charles, et al. Current Studies on Thyrotropin, II.
Guandolo, John. Transportation Law.
Guandolo, John, jt. auth. see Fair, Marvin L.
Guangxian, Xu & Jimei, Xiao, eds. New Frontiers in Rare Earth Science & Applications.
--New Frontiers in Rare Earth Science & Applications.
Guangyuan, Yu. China's Socialist Modernization.
Guannu, Joseph S. Liberian History Before Eighteen Fifty-Seven: A Reference for Elementary Pupils.
Guannu, Joseph S., ed. & compiled by. The Inaugural Addresses of the Presidents of Liberia: From Joseph Jenkins Roberts to William Richard Tolbert, 1848-1976.
Guannu, Joseph S., ed. A Short History of the First Liberian Republic.
Guare, John. Three Exposures.
Guareschi, Giovanni. The World of Don Camillo.
Guarnaschelli, Maria D., ed. see Boyd, William.
Guarnaschelli, Maria D., ed. see Cohen, William S.
Guarnaschelli, Maria D., ed. see Guernsey, Paul.
Guarnaschelli, Maria D., ed. see Polanski, Roman.
Guarnaschelli, Maria D., ed. see Rosenthal, Peggy & Dardess, George.
Guazzi, G. L., ed. see Symposium on Presenile Spongy Encephalopathies, Vienna, 1965.
Gubarev, A. Russian Museum: A Guide.
Guberman, Igor. Bumerang.
Gubser, Mary. Mary's Bread Basket & Soup Kettle.
Gucker, Frank T. & Seifert, Ralph T. Physical Chemistry.
Gudehus, G. Finite Elements in Geomechanics.
Guder, W. G., jt. ed. see Ross, D. B.
Gudgin, Graham & Taylor, Peter J. Seats, Votes & the Spatial Organization of Elections.
Gudgin, Graham, jt. auth. see Fothergill, Stephen.
Gudiol, Jose. Goya.
Gudmundson, Abel, et al. You Can Control Your Class: A Practical Guide to Classroom Management.
Gudzinowicz. Analysis of Drugs, Vol. 6: Cardiovascular, Antihypertensive, Hypoglycemic & Thyroid-Related Agents.
Gudzinowicz, B. J. Analysis of Drugs & Metabolites by Gas Chromatography-Mass Spectrometry: Antipsychotic, Antiemetic & Antidepressant Drugs.
Gudzinowicz, B. J. & Gudzinowicz, M. J. Analysis of Drugs & Meta-Bolites by Gas Chromotography-Mass Spectometry: Analgesics, Local Anesthetics, & Antibiotics.
Gudzinowicz, B. J., et al. Fundamentals of Integrated GC-Ms, Pt. I: Gas Chromatograpghy.
Gudzinowicz, Benjamin & Gudzinowicz, Michael. Analysis of Drugs & Metabolites by Gas Chromatography-Mass Spectometry: Central Nervous Stimulants.
Gudzinowicz, Benjamin J., jt. auth. see Gudzinowicz, Michael J.
Gudzinowicz, M. J., jt. auth. see Gudzinowicz, B. J.
Gudzinowicz, Michael, jt. auth. see Gudzinowicz, Benjamin.
Gudzinowicz, Michael J. & Gudzinowicz, Benjamin J. Analysis of Drugs & Related Compounds by Gas Chromotography-Mass Spectometry: Hypnotics, Anticonvulsants & Sedatives.
--The Analysis of Drugs & Related Compounds by Gas Chromatography-Mass Spectometry: Respiratory Gases, Volatile Anesthetics, Ethyl Alcohol, & Related Toxicological Materials.
Guenther, Anthony L. Criminal Behavior & Social Systems.
Guenther, John. Fun with the Funnies: Fifty Motivating Activities for Language Arts, Writing, & Social Studies, Grades 4-6.
Guenther, Roy, tr. see Orlova, Alexandra.
Guenther, William B. Chemical Equilibrium: A Practical Introduction for the Physical & Life Sciences.
Guenze, P., jt. ed. see Chambers, P. L.
Guerard. Short History International Language Movement.
Guerard, Albert J. Andre Gide.
Guerard, Albert L. France, a Short History.
Guerard, Michel. Michel Guerard's Cuisine Minceur. Chamberlain, Narcisse & Brennan, Fanny, trs.
Guercio, E., et al. General Mathematical Ability: Preparation & Review for the Mathematics Part of the High School Equivalency Diploma Test.
Guermont, Claude & Frumkin, Paul. The Norman Table: The Traditional Cooking of Normandy.
Guerney, Louise, jt. auth. see Keat, Donald B., II.
Guernsey, Dennis. Thoroughly Married.
Guernsey, Joann B. Room to Breathe.
Guernsey, Paul. Unhallowed Ground: A Young Boy's Search for His Father & Brother. Guarnaschelli, Maria D., ed.
Guerra, F. The Pre-Columbian Mind.
Guerrero, Leon M., tr. see Rizal, Jose.
Guerrier, Yvonne, jt. auth. see Broussine, Michael.
Guerry, Moultrie. Men Who Made Sewanee.
Guertin, Robert P. & Suski, Wojciech, eds. Crystalline Electric Field Effects in f-Electron Magnetism.
Guertler, Helena I., jt. auth. see Doggett, LeRoy.
Guertler, John T. & Newburger, Adele M. The Records of Baltimore's Private Organizations: A Guide to Archival Resources.
Guest, Barbara. The Countess from Minneapolis.
Guest, C. Z. C. Z. Guest's Datebook & Gardener Planner.
Guest, Ivor. Adventures of a Ballet Historian.
Guest, Ivor F. La Fille Mal Gardee.
Guest, John. What I Wish I'd Learned in Seminary.
Guest, Judith. Second Heaven.
Guest, Lisa, jt. auth. see Smoke, Jim.
Guest, Lynn. Yedo.
Guest, Robert H. Innovative Work Practices.
Gueulette, David, jt. auth. see Ohliger, John.
Guevara, Ernesto see also Che Guevara.
Guffey, Mary E. Business English.
Guggenbuehl-Craig, A. Macht als Gefahr beim Helfer.
Guggenheim, E. A. & Stokes, R. H. Equilibrium Properties of Aqueous Solutions of Single Strong Electrolytes.
Guggenheim, Hans G. Around the World in Eighty Ways.
Guggenheim, Peggy. Out of This Century.
Guggenheim, Solomon R., Foundation Staff. Alfred Jensen: Paintings & Works on Paper.
Guhl, Louise. Keyboard Proficiency.
Guiasu, S. & Malitza, M. Coalition & Connection in Games.
Guiasu, Silviu. Information Theory with New Applications.
Guichardet, A. Symmetric Hilbert Spaces & Related Topics.
Guichen, Wang, et al. Smashing the Communal Pot.
Guidos, Barbara & Hamilton, Betty. MASA: Medical Acronyms, Symbols & Abbreviations.
Guidos, Barbara, jt. auth. see Hamilton, Betty.
Guignebert, Charles. Christ.
--Jewish World in the Time of Jesus.
Guignebert, Charles A. Ancient, Medieval, & Modern Christianity.
Guiguet, Jean. Virginia Woolf & Her Works. Stewart, Jean, tr.
Guilbault, G. G. Enzymatic Methods of Analysis.
Guilbault, G. G., ed. Fluorescence: Theory, Instrumentation, & Practice.
Guilcher, J. M. Hidden Life of Flowers.
Guild, Nicholas. The Linz Tattoo.
Guild, Reuben A. The Librarian's Manual: A Treatise on Bibliography, Comprising a Select & Descriptive List of Bibliographical Works; to Which Are Added, Sketches of Public Libraries.
Guild, Robin. Homeworks: The Complete Guide to Displaying Your Possessions.
--Homeworks: The Complete Guide to Displaying Your Possessions.
Guilds, John C., ed. see Simms, William G.
Guilfoyle, Ann. Home Free: The No-Nonsense Guide to House Care.
Guilhamet, Leon. The Sincere Ideal: Studies on Sincerity in Eighteenth Century English Literature.
Guiliani, Dorothy A. Complete Guide to Coaching Women's Basketball.
Guilion, Fanny L. Raoul Dufy: Catalogue Raisonne des Aquarelles, Gouaches, et Pastels.
Guilland, Antoine. Modern Germany & Her Historians.
Guillaud, Jacqueline, jt. ed. see Guillaud, Maurice.
Guillaud, Maurice & Guillaud, Jacqueline, eds. Degas: Form & Space.
Guillaumont, Patrick, ed. Croissance et Ajustement: Les Problemes de L'Afrique de L'Ouest.
Guillemin, Ernest A. Synthesis of Passive Networks: Theory & Methods Appropriate to the Realization & Approximation Problems.
Guillet de Montoux, Pierre. Action & Existence: Anarchism for Business Administration.
Guilloton, D. S., jt. auth. see Domandi, Agnes K.
Guillou, Louis A. Calculus with Analytic Geometry.
Guiltinan, Joseph P. & Gordon, P. Readings in Marketing Strategy.
Guin, Ursula K. le see Le Guin, Ursula K.
Guinane, George E. An Analysis of the SMP Policy: A Line-by-Line Explanation of the Special Multi-Peril Policy.
Guindey, Guillaume. The International Monetary Tangle: Myths & Realities. Hoffman, Michael L., tr.
Guiney, Louise I. Happy Ending: The Collected Lyrics of Louise I. Guiney.
Guinle, R. L. A Modern Spanish-English & English-Spanish Technical & Engineering Dictionary.
Guinot, Jean P., jt. auth. see Romeuf, Jean.
Guins, George C. Communism on the Decline.
Guinsburg, Thomas N. The Pursuit of Isolationism in the United States Senate from Versailles to Pearl Harbor.
Guiraud, Pierre. Semiology.
Guirdham, Arthur. We Are One Another.
--We Are One Another: A Record of Group Reincarnation.
Guirguis, Fouad. The Difficult Years of Survival.
Guisewite, Cathy. Eat Your Way to a Better Relationship.
--How to Get Rich, Fall in Love, Lose Weight, & Solve All Your Problems by Saying "No"
--Stressed for Success.
Guisinger, Stephen E., ed. Trade & Investment Policies in the Americas.
Guisset Poch, Consuelo & Castellanos Alentorn, Prado. Diccionario Infantil Ilustrado Bruguera.
Guitar Player & Frets Magazine Staff, jt. ed. see Eremo, Judie.
Guitar Player Magazine Editors. Basic Guitar.
Guitar Player Magazine Editors, compiled by. Hot Licks.
Guitar Player Magazine Editors, jt. ed. see Keyboard Magazine Editors.
Guither, Harold D. The Food Lobbyists: Behind the Scenes of Food & Agri-Politics.
Guithues, Denise M. Innovative Reporting in Foreign Currency Translation. Farmer, Richard, ed.
Guiton, Margaret, jt. auth. see Bree, Germaine.
Gujarati, Damodar. Pensions & New York City's Fiscal Crisis.
Gukhman, A. A. Introduction to the Theory of Similarity.
Gula, Robert J. Exposition: Critical Writing & Thinking.
Gulati, Basia, tr. see Bringuier, Jean-Claude.
Gulati, Bodh R. A Short Course in Calculus.
Guleck, Charles J., jt. ed. see Paoletti, Rodolfo.
Gulhati, Ravi. Eastern & Southern Africa: Past Trends & Future Prospects.
Gulick, Denny, jt. auth. see Ellis, Robert.
Gulick, Frances F., jt. auth. see Davidson, Neil A.
Gulick, Luther H. & Urwick, Lydall, eds. Papers on the Science of Administration.
Gulick, Sidney L. Chesterfield Bibliography to Eighteen Hundred.
Gulik, R. H. Van see Van Gulik, R. H.
Gulik, Robert H. Van see Van Gulik, Robert H.
Gulik, Robert Van see Van Gulik, Robert.
Gull, Carol W., jt. auth. see Larsen, Judith L.
Gulland, John A. Fish Population Dynamics.
Gullan-Whur, Margaret. What Your Handwriting Reveals.
Gullberg. Swedish-English Technical Dictionary.
Gullberg, Elsa & Astrom, Paul. The Thread of Ariadne: A Study of Ancient Greek Dress.
Gullberg, Ingvar E. Swedish-English Dictionary of Technical Terms Used in Business, Industry, Administration, Education & Research.
--Swedish-English Fact Ordbok (Technical Terms)
Gulledge, Dennis & McWhirter, David. An Index to the Evangelist & the Christian.
Gullick, Etta, jt. auth. see Hollings, Michael.
Gullion, Gordon. Grouse of the North Shore.
Gulliver, Ashbel G. Cases & Materials on Future Interests.
--Introduction to the Law of Future Interests.
Gullon, Ricardo, et al. Antonio Machado.
Gulyaev, A. P. Physical Metallurgy.
Gumbert, Marc. Neither Justice nor Reason: A Legal & Anthropological Analysis of Aboriginal Rights.
Gumerman, G. J., jt. ed. see Schiffer, M. B.
Gumpel, Werner. Energy Policy of the Soviet Union.
Gumr, Charles J. Trade Financing.
Gunatilleke, Godfrey & Tiruchelvan, Nellan, eds. Ethical Dilemmas of Development in Asia.
Gunby, R. A. Sport Parachuting Manual. Jeppesen Sanderson Staff, ed.
Gunchuck, Roberta S. An Educator's Cry.
Gundara, Jagdish, et al, eds. Racism, Diversity & Education.
Gundersen, Roy M. Linearized Analysis of One-Dimensional Magnetohydrodynamic Flows.
Gundrey, Elizabeth. Staying Off the Beaten Track.
Gundry, Stanley N. Love Them In: The Proclamation Theology of D. L. Moody.
Gundy, Arthur B. Van see Van Gundy, Arthur B.
Gundy, John H. Assessment of the Child in Primary Health Care.
Gunkel, Hermann. The Influence of the Holy Spirit: The Popular View of the Apostolic Age & the Teaching of the Apostle Paul. Harrisville, Roy A. & Quanbeck, Philip A., II, trs.
--Psalms: A Form-Critical Introduction. Reumann, John, ed. Horner, Thomas M., tr. from Ger.
Gunn, Aeneas. We of the Never-Never & the Little Black Princess.
Gunn, Alan. Federal Income Taxation Cases & Materials.
--Federal Income Taxation, Cases & Other Materials, 1985 Supplement.
Gunn, Alan M. The Mirror of Love: A Reinterpretation of the "Romance of the Rose"
Gunn, Alexander. Sex & You: The Emotional & Physical Aspects of Growing Up.
Gunn, Angus M. Habitat: Human Settlements in an Urban Age.
Gunn, George W. For Adults Only.
Gunn, Giles, ed. The Bible & American Arts & Letters.
Gunn, James. Christ: The Fullness of the Godhead, a Study in New Testament Christology.
Gunn, James E. The Listeners.
Gunn, James W. A Time & Times & Half a Time.
Gunn, John. The Defeat of Distance: Qantas 1919-1939.
Gunn, John, ed. Epileptics in Prison.
Gunn, John & Farrington, David P., eds. Abnormal Offenders, Delinquency & the Criminal Justice System.
Gunn, Robin. Billy 'n' Bear Series. Incl. Billy 'n' Bear Go to Sunday School; Billy 'n' Bear Go to Church; Billy 'n' Bear Go to the Grocery Store; Billy 'n' Bear Go to a Birthday Party; Billy 'n' Bear Go to the Doctor; Billy 'n' Bear Visit Grandma & Grandpa. Concordia.
Gunn, Rodger S. Mormonism: Challenge & Defense.
Gunn, Thomas G., Jr. Computer Applications in Manufacturing.
Gunnarson, Evy, jt. auth. see Ressner, Ulla.
Gunnell, John. Seventy Five Years of Pontiac-Oakland. Dammann, George H., ed.
Gunnell, John G. Convertibles: The Complete Story.
Gunning, B. E. & Robards, A. W., eds. Intercellular Communication in Plants: Studies on Plasmodesmata.
Gunning, Dennis. The Teaching of History.
Gunning, Robert. Technique of Clear Writing.
Gunningham, Neil, jt. ed. see Creighton, Breen.
Gunsch, Emil. Family Homestead Reflections.
Gunson, Phil, et al. Dictionary of Contemporary Politics of South America.
Gunston, Bill. Aircraft of the Soviet Union.
--An Illustrated Guide to Allied Fighters of World War II.
--The Illustrated Guide to German, Italian & Japanese Fighters of World War II.
--Jane's Aerospace Dictionary.
--World Encyclopedia of Aero Engines.
Gunter, Elizabeth E., jt. ed. see Lowry, Bullitt.
Gunter, F. A. & Gunter, J. Davies, eds. Residue Reviews.
Gunter, J. Davies, jt. ed. see Gunter, F. A.
Gunther, Bernard. Dying for Enlightenment: Living Bhagwan Shree Rajneesh.
Gunther, Carl. Practical Malaria Control.
Gunther, Dick, jt. auth. see Roberts, Jack.
Gunther, Erna. Art in the Life of the Northwest Coast Indians.
--Indian Life on the Northwest Coast of North America As Seen by the Early Explorers & Fur Traders During the Last Decade of the 18th Century.
Gunther, F. A., ed. Residue Reviews.
--Residue Reviews: Residues of Pesticides & Other Contaminants in the Total Environment.

Authors

Gunther, F. A. & Gunther, J. Davies, eds. Residue Reviews.
--Residue Reviews.
--Residue Reviews.
--Residue Reviews: Residues of Pesticides & Other Contaminants in the Total Environment.
--Residue Reviews: Residues of Pesticides & Other Contaminants in the Total Environment.
--Residue Reviews: Residues of Pesticides & Other Contaminants in the Total Environment.
--Residue Reviews: Residues of Pesticides & Other Contaminants in the Total Environment.
--Residues of Pesticides & Other Contaminants in the Total Environment.
Gunther, F. A., ed. see Futuko, T. R., et al.
Gunther, F. A., ed. see Kaemmerer, K. & Buntenkoetter, S.
Gunther, Gerald & Schauer, Fred. Constitutional Law: 1986 Case Supplement to 11th Edition. Bd. with Individual Rights in Constitutional Law: 1986 Supplement 4th Edition. Foundation Pr.
Gunther, J. Davies, jt. ed. see Gunther, F. A.
Gunther, Jack. The Gunther Papers.
Gunther, John. Death Be Not Proud.
Gunther, Max. D. B. Cooper: What Really Happened.
--Doom Wind.
Gunther, Robert T. Astrolabes of the World.
Gunther, Samuel P. Current Issues in Financial Accounting for Lawyers.
Gup, Benton. Guide to Strategic Planning.
Gup, Benton E. Financial Intermediaries: An Introduction.
--Financial Intermediaries: An Introduction.
--Management of Financial Institutions.
Gupta, Amar, jt. auth. see Toong, Hoo-min D.
Gupta, Ayodhya P. Anthropod Phylogeny.
Gupta, B. L., et al. Transport of Ions & Water in Animals.
Gupta, Bhabani Sen. Soviet Perspectives of Contemporary Asia.
Gupta, Chidananda Das see Das Gupta, Chidananda.
Gupta, D. K. Das see Das Gupta, D. K.
Gupta, Derek & Voelter, Wolfgang. Hypothalamic Hormones: Chemistry, Physiology & Clinical Applications.
--Hypothalamic Hormones: Structure, Synthesis, & Biological Activity.
Gupta, Giri Raj, ed. Main Currents in Indian Sociology: Social & Cultural Context of Medicine in India.
Gupta, J. N. D. Postal Applications of Operations Research.
Gupta, K. One Hundred Short Cases for the MRCP.
Gupta, K., jt. auth. see Rao, J. S.
Gupta, K. C., jt. auth. see Wahi, Pradeep.
Gupta, K. L. Finance & Economic Growth in Developing Countries.
Gupta, K. M. Man & Forest: A New Dimension in the Himalaya.
Gupta, K. N., jt. ed. see Rao, J. S.
Gupta, M. M., ed. see Sanchez, E.
Gupta, M. M., et al, eds. Advances in Fuzzy Set Theory & Applications.
Gupta, O. P. & Lamba, P. S. Modern Weed Science.
Gupta, R. C. & Johari, J. C. Indian Freedom Movement & Thought, 1930-1947.
Gupta, Ramesh, jt. ed. see Cheremisinoff, Nicholas P.
Gupta, S. P. The Roots of Indian Art.
Gupta, S. P., jt. auth. see Pandit, G. S.
Gupta, Shanti S. & Panchapakesan, S. Multiple Decision Procedures: Theory & Methodology of Selecting & Ranking Populations.
Gupta, Shanti S. & Yackel, James, eds. Statistical Decision Theory & Related Topics: Proceedings.
Gupta, Shiv C. Delhi: The City of Future.
Gupta, Surendra K. Citizen in the Making.
Gupte, Pranay. The Crowded Earth: People & the Politics of Population.
--Sri Lanka: Unrest in Paradise.
--Vengeance: India after the Assassination of Indira Gandhi.
Gura, Timothy, jt. auth. see Lee, Charlotte I.
Guralink, Nehama & Michaelson, Katherine J. Alexander Archipenko.
Gurau, Peter K. & Lieberthal, E. A. Fingermath.
Gurdjian, E. S., et al, eds. Glossary of Neurotraumatology.
Gureyev, P. P. & Sedugin, P. I. Legislation in the U. S. S. R.
Gurian, Anita, jt. auth. see Formanek, Ruth.
Gurian, Jay. Western American Writing: Tradition & Promise.
Gurin, Arnold, jt. auth. see Perlman, Robert.
Gurin, Phillip. The James Bond Trivia Quiz Book: From Odd Job to Money Penny... Everything You Always Wanted to Know about Agent 007.
Gurion, David B. Rebirth & Destiny of Israel.
Gurland, H. J., et al, eds. Therapeutic Plasma Exchange.
Gurley, John G. Challengers to Capitalism, Marx, Lenin, Stalin & Mao.
Gurman, Alan S. & Razin, Andrew M. Effective Psychotherapy: A Handbook of Research.
Gurnah, Abdulrazak. Memory of Departure.
Gurney, A. R. The Snow Ball.
Gurney, Edmund. The Power of Sound.
Gurney, Jackie. National Trust Book of Picnics.
Guroff. Molecular Neurobiology.
Guroff, Katherine S. Quality in Liberal Learning: Curricular Innovations in Higher Education.
Gurpide, E. Tracer Methods in Hormone Research.
Gurr, David. The Ring Master.
Gursan-Salzmann, Ayse & Salzmann, Laurence. Last Jews of Radauti.
Gurthrie, W. K. The Greek Philosophers.
Gurtin, M. E. On the Thermodynamics of Elastic Materials & of Reacting Fluid Mixtures.
Gurtov, Melvin. China & Southeast Asia-The Politics of Survival: A Study of Foreign Policy Interaction.
Gurudas. Flower Essences & Vibrational Healing.
Gurule, Bill F. Fleeting Shadows & Faint Echoes of Las Huertas.
Gurung, Deu B., et al. Gurung-Nepali-English Glossary.
Guruswami, M. N., jt. auth. see Iswaran, V.
Gurvitch, Georges. Sociology of Law.
Gurwin, Larry. Dirty Money: The Global Financiers of Violence, Revolution, & Crime.
Gurzadyan, G. A. Flare Stars.
Guschlbauer, W. Nucleic Acid Structure: An Introduction.
Gusev, N. G. & Dimitriev, P. P. Quantum Radiation of Radioactive Nuclides.
Gussenhoven, Elma J. & Becker, Anton E. Congenital Heart Disease: Morphologic Echocardiographic Correlations.
Gussow, Don. The New Merger Game: The Plan & the Players.
Gussow, Donald. The New Business Journalism: The People & Corporations Behind America's Business Publications.
Gussow, Joan D., jt. auth. see Birch, Herbert G.
Gustafson. Fundamentals of Electricity for Agriculture.
Gustafson, Anita. Some Feet Have Noses.
Gustafson, James M. Ethics from a Theocentric Perspective: Theology & Ethics.
Gustafson, James M. & Laney, James T., eds. On Being Responsible: Issues in Personal Ethics.
Gustafson, Janie. Celibate Passion.
Gustafson, Karl E. & Reinhardt, William P., eds. Quantum Mechanics in Mathematics, Chemistry, & Physics.
Gustafson, Richard F. The Imagination of Spring: The Poetry of Afanasy Fet.
Gustafson, Robert, jt. auth. see Schmalleger, Frank.
Gustafson, Rosalie. Hollywood's Mother Goose.
Gustason, William & Ulrich, Dolph E. Elementary Symbolic Logic.
Gustavson, Carl G. The Institutional Drive: A Study in Pluralistic Democracy.
Gustavson, Karl H. Chemistry & Reactivity of Collagen.
Gustavus, Susan O., jt. auth. see Nam, Charles B.
Guste, Roy F., Jr. Antoine's Restaurant Cookbook.
--The Restaurants of New Orleans.
Gustorf, Ernest A. Von see Von Gustorf, Ernest A.
Gutcheon, Beth. The New Girls.
--Still Missing.
Gutcho, Marcia, ed. Adhesives Technology: Developments Since 1979.
Gutek, Gerald L. Education & Schooling in America.
Gutelle, Pierre. The Design of Sailing Yachts.
Guterman, Martin M. & Nitecki, Zbigniew H. Differential Equations.
Guterman, Norbert, tr. see Hlasko, Marek.
Guth, David A. Suing in North Carolina Small Claims Court: A Practical Guide.
Guth, Hans P. Concise English Handbook.
--Today: A Text-Workbook for English Language & Composition.
Guth, Hans P. & Schuster, Edgar H. Today: A Text-Workbook for English & Composition.
Gutheil, Emil. Music & Your Emotions.
Gutheim, Frederick, ed. In the Cause of Architecture.
Guthridge, G. L. Revenge Rides High.
Guthrie. Introductory Nutrition.
Guthrie, A. B., Jr. Arfive.
--Fair Land, Fair Land.
--No Second Wind.
Guthrie, Alfred B., Jr. The Big It.
--Big Sky.
--The Way West.
Guthrie, Andrew. Vacuum Technology.
Guthrie, Bennett M. Three Winds of Death: The Saga of the 503rd Parachute Regimental Combat Team in the South Pacific.
Guthrie, Diana W. & Guthrie, Richard A. Nursing Management of Diabetes Mellitus.
Guthrie, G., et al. M R N A: Current Research.
Guthrie, Grace D. Legacy to Lebanon.
Guthrie, Jack S., jt. auth. see Guthrie, Ruby C.
Guthrie, Ramon. Maximum Security Ward & Other Poems. Gall, Sally M!, ed.
Guthrie, Richard A., jt. auth. see Guthrie, Diana W.
Guthrie, Ruby C. & Guthrie, Jack S. A Primer for Pickles & a Reader for Relishes.
Guthrie, Rufus K. Food Sanitation.
Gutierrez, Felix, tr. see Gilly, Adolfo.
Gutierrez, Gustavo. A Theology of Liberation: History, Politics, & Salvation. Inda, Caridad & Eagleson, John, trs. from Span.
Gutierrez, Gustavo & Shaull, Richard. Liberation & Change.
Gutkind, E. A. Community & Environment.
Gutkind, Lee. Bike Fever.
Gutman, Bill. Great Baseball Stories Today & Yesterday.
--The Picture Life of Reggie Jackson.
--Pro Sports Champions.
--Refrigerator Perry & the Super Bowl Bears.
--Summer Dreams.
Gutman, Herbert G. Slavery & the Numbers Game: A Critique of Time on the Cross.
Gutman, Robert W. Richard Wagner: The Man, His Mind, & His Music.
Gutmann, Felix, jt. ed. see Keyzer, Hendrik.
Gutmann, V; see Dunitz, J. D., et al.
Gutmann, Viktor, ed. International Review of Halogen Chemistry.
Gutnikov, G., tr. see Engelhardt, H.
Guttentag, Marcia, jt. ed. see Struening, Elmer L.
Gutter, Mae & Rooks, Nancy. The Maid, the Man, & the Fans: Elvis Is the Man.
Gutteridge, Harold C. & Megrah, Maurice. The Law of Bankers' Commercial Credits.
Gutteridge, Thomas G., jt. auth. see Walker, James W.
Guttmacher, A. see Sanger, Margaret.
Guttman, Julius W., ed. see Maimonides, Moses.
Guttsman, W. L. The German Social Democratic Party, 1875-1933.
Gutwinski, Waldemar, ed. see Linguistic Association of Canada & the U. S. Staff.
Guy, A. G. Essentials of Materials Science.
Guyer, David. Ghana & the Ivory Coast: The Impact of Colonialism in an African Setting.
Guyer, Donna D. Three.
Guyer, Kenneth E., jt. auth. see Seibel, Hugo.
Guyer, P. B. & Dewbury, K. C. Sonomammography: An Atlas of Comparative Breast Ultrasound.
Guynn, Denise Y. Independent Living: Getting Started. Pozzi-Johnson, David, ed.
Guyon, Jeanne. The Autobiography of Madame Guyon.
Guyot, A., ed. International Symposium on Polyvinylchloride, 2nd: Proceedings.
Guyton, Arthur C. Arterial Pressure & Hypertension.
Guzman, Jessie P. Crusade for Civic Democracy: The Story of the Tuskegee Civic Association, 1941-1970.
Guzman, Maria O. Tagalog-English-English-Tagalog Dictionary.
Guzzetta & Dossey. Cardiovascular Nursing: Bodymind Tapestry: American Association of Critical-Care Nurses.
Guzzo, Anthony V. Introductory Chemistry Laboratory Manual.
Guzzo, Sandra E. Fox & Heggie. Tucker, Kathleen, ed.
Guzzon, F., jt. auth. see Gennaro, L.
Guzzwell, John. Trekka Round the World.
Gvishiani, J., ed. Science, Technology & Global Problems: Proceedings of the Symposium on the Role of Science & Technology in Solving Global Problems, Tallinn, U. S. S. R., Jan 1979.
Gvishiani, J. M., ed. Systems Research II: Methodological Problems.
Gvozdariov, B., jt. auth. see Grinevich, E.
Gvozdetsky, N. Soviet Geography Today: Physical Geography.
Gwaltney. The Pennsylvania Old Assyrian Texts.
Gwaltney, John L. The Dissenters: Voices from Contemporary America.
--Drylongso: A Self-Portrait of Black American.
Gwartney, James D. & Stroup, Richard. Economics: Private & Public Choice.
Gwartney, James D., et al. Essentials of Economics.
Gwin, Catherine, jt. auth. see Camps, Miriam.
Gwin, Mary M., jt. auth. see Gwin, William.
Gwin, Paul, jt. auth. see Lionberger, Herbert F.
Gwin, Sherry. The Library: What's in It for You?
Gwin, William & Gwin, Mary M. Semiology, Symbolism & Architecture: A Selected & Partially Annotated Bibliography.
Gwon, Pu Gill. Basic Training for Kicking.
Gwynne, Fred. A Chocolate Moose for Dinner.
--The King Who Rained.
Gwynne, S. C. Selling Money.
Gwynne, Walker. The Christian Year; Its Purpose & Its History.
Gy, P., ed. Mineral Processing: Proceedings of the Sixth International Conference.
Gy, P. M. Sampling of Particulate Materials.
Gyamfi, Enoch A. Success Control: Positive Thinking.
Gyatso, Geshe K. Buddhism in the Tibetan Tradition: A Guide.
Gyford, John. Local Politics in Britain.
--The Politics of Local Socialism.
Gygax, Gary & Dille, Flint. The Crimson Sea.
--The Fire Demon.
Gygax, Gary, et al. Dungeons & Dragons: Basic Rule Book.
Gyldenvand, Lily M. Joy in His Presence: Christian Reflections on Everyday Life.
Gyll, Catherine & Blake, Noel S. Paediatric Dianostic Imaging.
Gyllensvard, Bo. Museum of Far Eastern Antiquities, Stockholm.
Gysbers, N. & Moore, Earl J. Improving Guidance Programs.
Gysin, Brion. The Last Museum.
Gyulay, Jo-Eileen. The Dying Child.
Gzowski, Peter. The Sacrament.

H

H. D. see Doolittle, Hilda.
H P Books Staff, ed. Best of Cold Foods.
Haack, A., jt. auth. see Girnau, G.
Haack, Dennis G. Statistical Literacy: A Guide to Interpretation.
Haack, W. & Wendland, W. Lectures on Partial & Pfaffian Differential Equations.
Haaften, Julia Van see Van Haaften, Julia.
Haag, Michael. Guide to Cairo: Including the Pyramids & Saqqara.
--Guide to Egypt.
--Guide to West Africa.
Haaga & Alfidi. Computed Tomography of the Abdomen.
--Computed Tomography of the Brain, Head & Neck.
Haaga, John R. & Alfidi, Ralph J., eds. Computed Tomography of the Whole Body.
Haagen, Lucy E. & Metzloff, Nancy. Kidsplaces.
Haagensen, Cushman D., et al. The Lymphatics in Cancer.
Haak, Bob. The Golden Age: Dutch Painters of the Seventeenth Century. Willems-Treeman, Elizabeth, tr. from Dutch.
Haaland, A., et al. Gas-Phase Electron Diffraction.
Haan, Walter, ed. Famous Sergeants & Corporals in American History.
Haanappel, Peter P. C. Ratemaking & Capacity Determination in International Air Transport: A Legal Analysis.
Haar, Charles M. & Fessler, Daniel W. Fairness & Justice: Law in the Service of Equality.
--Wrong Side of the Tracks.
Haar, Charles M. & Kayden, Jerold S., eds. Zoning at Sixty: Mediating Public & Private Rights.
Haar, D. Ter see Kapitza, P. L.
Haar, D. Ter see Ter Haar, D.
Haar, D. ter see Ter Haar, D.
Haar, D. ter, tr. see Ginzburg, V. L. & Lebedev, P. N.
Haard, Norman F. & Salunkhe, D. K. Postharvest Biology & Handling of Fruits & Vegetables.
Haarder, Andreas, et al, eds. Medieval Legacy: A Symposium.
Haas & Wotruba. Marketing Management: Concepts, Practice & Cases.
Haas, A. & Hallows, R. W. The Oscilloscope at Work.
Haas, Albert. Doctor & the Damned.
Haas, Ernst. In Germany.
Haas, Frank De. Mr. Single Shot's Gunsmithing-Idea Book.
Haas, Harold I. Pastoral Counseling with People in Distress.
Haas, Irene, jt. auth. see De Regniers, Beatrice S.
Haas, Irene, jt. auth. see Joslin, Sesyle.
Haas, John D. Future Studies in the K-Twelve Curriculum.
Haas, L. A., ed. see AIME Staff.
Haas, Leonard E., ed. see New Pulps for the Paper Industry Symposium Staff.
Haas, Mark, ed. see Schultz, Lawrence.
Haas, Michael. International Organization: An Interdisciplinary Bibliography.
Haas, Pamela. Northwest Coast Photographs of Edward Dossetter.
Haas, Robert. Eat to Win: Sports Nutrition Book.
--Nutritional Guide to Fast Food.
Haas, Robert B., ed. see Still, William G.
Haas, Robert W. Industrial Marketing Management.
Haas, Ronald & Hamel, Lawrence, eds. Readings in Foundations of Education.
Haas, Werner & Mathieu, Gustave B. Deutsch fur Alle: Beginning College German: a Comprehensive Approach Workbook.
Haase, T. & Schonert, H. Solid-Liquid Equilibrium.

Authors

Haase, W., ed. Recent Contributions to Fluid Mechanics.
Haasen, P., jt. ed. see Christian, J. W.
Haast, William E. & Anderson, Robert. Complete Guide to Snakes of Florida.
Habegger, Alfred, ed. The Bostonians.
Habel, K. & Salzman, N. P., eds. Fundamental Techniques in Virology.
Habel, Norman C. Birthquakes.
--For Mature Adults Only.
--Hi! Have a Nice Day.
--Vahweh vs. Baal.
Habel, Norman C., ed. What Are We Going To Do With All These Rotting Fish? & Seven Other Short Plays for Church & Community.
Habel, S. T. Theory & Research in Marriage & the Family.
Habenstein, R. W., jt. ed. see Mindel, C.
Haber, Barbara, ed. The Women's Annual, No. 1: 1980--The Year in Review.
--The Women's Annual, No. 2: 1981--The Year in Review.
Haber, Bernard & Aprison, M. H., eds. Neuropharmacology & Behavior.
Haber, Heinz. Our Blue Planet: The Story of the Earth's Evolution.
Haber, Louis. Women Pioneers of Science.
Haber, Michelle I. & Kantrowitz, Barbara. Ultimate Baby Catalog.
Haberek, Judy. One Hundred Twenty-Five Ways to Cut Your Business Health Costs. Varela, Robert, ed.
--Product Defects & Recalls: What Government Wanted & What Industry Did. Varela, Robert, ed.
Haberl, Art. Guide to Adirondack Trails: West-Central Region. Burdick, Neal S., ed.
Haberler, Gottfried. Economic Growth & Stability: An Analysis of Economic Change & Policies.
--Prosperity & Depression: A Theoretical Analysis of Cyclical Movement.
Haberman, Richard. Elementary Applied Partial Differential Equations.
Haberman, Shelby J. The Analysis of Frequency Data.
Haberman, William L., jt. auth. see John, James E.
Habermas, Gary B., jt. auth. see Stevenson, Kenneth.
Habibi, Mohamad & Warisila, Robert. Mechanics: A Laboratory Manual.
Hachten, William A. Muffled Drums: The News Media in Africa.
Hachtman, Tom. Fun City: Gertrude's Follies Comes to Town.
Hack, J. T. & Morisawa, M., eds. Tectonic Geomorphology.
Hackbarth, Winston. Laboratory Study of Plants.
Hackel, Emanuel, ed. Human Genetics 1984.
Hackel, Roberta J. De Sade's Quantitative Moral Universe: Of Irony, Rhetoric & Boredom.
Hacker, Andrew. End of the American Era.
Hacker, Diana & Renshaw, Betty. Writing with a Voice: A Rhetoric Handbook.
Hacker, Frederick J. Crusaders, Criminals, Crazies: Terror & Terrorism in Our Time.
Hacker, J. B., jt. auth. see Tothill, J. C.
Hacker, J. B., ed. Nutritional Limits to Animal Production from Pastures.
Hacker, Louis M. & Hirsch, Mark D. Proskauer, His Life & Times.
Hacker, Richard C. The Ultimate Pipe Book.
Hackert, A. H. Rediscovering Mathematics.
Hackett, Brian. Planting Design.
Hackett, C. J. Diagnostic Criteria of Syphilis, Yaws & Treponarid (Treponematoses) & of Some Other Diseases in Dry Bones (for Use in Osteo-Archaeology)
Hackett, Charles D., jt. auth. see Harrisville, Roy A.
Hackett, Fuchs & Messing. Recombinant DNA Lab Manual.
Hackett, John W. I Was a Stranger.
Hackett, Pat, jt. auth. see Warhol, Andy.
Hackl, C., ed. see IBM Informatik Symposium Staff.
Hackland, Brian, jt. auth. see Williams, Gwyneth.
Hackle, Sparse G. Fishless Days, Angling Nights.
Hackler, James C. The Prevention of Youthful Crime: The Great Stumble Forward.
Hackman, Sandra, ed. see Hunken, Jorie & Madama, John.
Hackney, Harold, jt. auth. see Bernard, Janine.
Hackwood, Frederick W. Christ Lore: Being the Legends, Traditions, Myths, Symbols, Customs, & Superstitions of the Christian Church.
--Good Cheer: The Romance of Food & Feasting.
Hackworth, Robert D. & Howland, Joseph. Introductory College Mathematics: Consumer Mathematics.
--Introductory College Mathematics: Probability.
--Introductory College Mathematics: Tables & Graphs.
Hackworth, Robert D., jt. auth. see Alwin, Robert H.
Hadas, A., et al, eds. Physical Aspects of Soil, Water & Salts in Ecosystems.
Hadas, Moses, tr. see Frankel, Hermann.
Hadas, Moses, tr. see Heliodorus Of Emesa.
Hadaway, C. Kirk, jt. ed. see Rose, Larry L.
Hadd, H. E. & Blickenstaff, R. T. Conjugates of Steroid Hormones.
Hadda, Ceri, ed. see Family Circle Editors.
Haddad, Abraham H., ed. Nonlinear Systems: Processing of Random Signals-Classical Analysis.
Haddad, C. A. Flowers of the Desert.
Haddad, George M. Revolutions & Military Rule in the Middle East: The Arab States.
Haddad, Heskel M., ed. see International Society on Metabolic Eye Disease Staff.
Haddad, Remy, jt. auth. see Robin, Patrick.
Haddad, W., jt. auth. see Avalos, B.
Haddem, Adam. Poems to Drink By.
Hadden, J., et al. Advances in Immunopharmacology: Proceedings of the First International Conference on Immunopharmacology, 29 July-1 August 1980, Brighton.
Hadden, J. W., et al, eds. Immunopharmacology.
Haddock, Roy P., ed. see Proceedings of the International Conference, Los Angeles, 1972, et al.
Haddock, Sally & Matthews, Kathy. The Making of a Woman Veterinarian.
Haddon, A. C., ed. Reports of the Cambridge Anthropological Expedition to Torres Straits. Incl. General Ethnography; Physiology & Psychology; Linguistics. Ray, S. H; Arts & Crafts; Sociology, Magic & Religion of the Western Islanders; Sociology, Magic & Religion of the Eastern Islanders. Johnson Repr.
Haden, Peter. Elementary Knowledge: A Story of the Creation of the Hebrew Alaphabet.
Haden-Guest, Anthony. Bad Dreams.
Hadfield, Charles. British Canals.
--The Canal Age.
--The Canals of South West England.
--The Canals of the West Midlands.
Hadfield, John. A Book of Beauty.
--A Book of Delights.
--A Book of Love.
Hadfield, Miles, et al, eds. British Gardeners: A Biographical Dictionary.
Hadfield, P. Traits of Divine Kingship in Africa.
Hadik, Laszlo, jt. auth. see Schwarz, Urs.
Hadjimachalakis, Michael G. Monetary Policy & Modern Money Markets: Fixed vs. Market-Determined Deposit Rates.
Hadley, Ernest C. Guide to Federal Sector Equal Employment Law & Practice.
Hadley, Hamilton. A Free Order: National Goal & World Goal.
Hadley, Neil F. Environmental Physiology of Desert Organisms.
Hadley, Richard D., ed. see Bowers, Carolyn.
Hadley, Ronald W., et al. Word Processing Made Simple.
Hadlock, Adah. My Life in the Southwest.
Hadlow, William J., jt. ed. see Prusiner, Stanley B.
Hadni, A. Essentials of Modern Physics Applied to the Study of the Infrared.
Hadorn, E. Experimental Studies of Amphibian Development. Turner, D. C., tr.
Hadsell, Helen. The Name It & Claim It Game.
Hadziselimovic, F. Cryptorchidism.
Hadzsits, George D. Lucretius & His Influence.
Haecker, Theodor. Kierkegaard the Cripple.
Haefner, H., ed. Estimating Needs for Mental Health Care: A Contribution of Epidemiology.
Haegeman, Liliane, jt. auth. see Wekker, Herman.
Haegerstam, Glenn, jt. auth. see Evers, Hans.
Haemmerli, U. P. Jaundice During Pregnancy: With Special Emphasis on Recurrent Jaundice During Pregnancy & Its Differential Diagnosis.
Haendel, Dan. Corporate Strategic Planning: The Political Dimension.
Haendler, Gert. Luther on Ministerial Office & Congregational Function. Gritsch, Eric W., ed. Gritsch, Ruth C., tr. from Ger.
Haenel, H., jt. auth. see Somogyi, J. C.
Haenosh, Zahava. How I Raised Almost Perfect Children.
Haeri, Shaykh F. Beams of Illumination from the Divine Revelation.
--Decree & Destiny.
--Heart of Qu'ran & Perfect Mizan.
--Man in Qur'an & the Meaning of Furqan.
Haeri, Shykh F. The Mercy of Qur'an & the Advent of Zaman.
Haeringer, Jacques E. The Chez Francois Cookbook: The Cuisine of Francois R. Haeringer.
Haessler, H. A. How to Make Sure Your Baby Is Well-& Stays That Way.
Haessler, Herbert & Harris, Raymond. Bodyworkbook.
Hafele, W. & Kirchmayer, L. K., eds. Modeling of Large-scale Energy Systems: Proceedings of the IIASA-IFAC Symposium, Laxenburg, Austria, Feb. 25-29, 1980.
Hafen, Ann W. Campfire Frontier.
Hafen, Brent Q. First Aid for Health Emergencies.
--Medical Self Care & Assessment.
Hafen, Brent Q. & Peterson, Brenda. Medicines & Drugs: Problems & Risks, Use & Abuse.
Hafez, E. S., ed. Scanning Electron Microscope Atlas of Mammalian Reproduction.
Hafez, E. S., ed. see World Conference on Embryo Transfer in Vitro Fertilization & Instrumental Insemination Staff.
Haff, Gerry, jt. auth. see Campbell, Alexander.
Haffenden, John. The Life of John Berryman.
Haffner, James W. Radiation & Shielding in Space.
Hafner, Lawrence E. Developmental Reading in Middle & Secondary Schools.
--Improving Reading in the Secondary Schools.
Hafnor, John. Black Hills Believables.
Hafrey, Leigh, tr. see Schneider, Peter.
Haft, Robert J. & Fass, Peter M. Investment Limited Partnerships Handbook.
--Real Estate Syndications Tax Handbook.
Haft, Rose. Poetry Collection.
Haftmann, Werner. Chagall.
Haga, H., ed. Festivals & Costumes in the World.
Haga, William J. Using Scripsit.
Haga, William James. Using Scripsit: For TRS-80 Model III & Model I.
Hagan, Patricia. Coltrane Saga: Love & Dreams.
--Dark Journey Home.
--Dark Journey Home.
--Love's Wine.
--Raging Hearts.
--This Savage Heart.
--Winds of Terror.
Hagarty, Catherine. Revelations of an Army Nurse.
Hagberg, Lennart, ed. Maritime Law, Vol. 1: Arrest of Vessels.
Hage, Per & Harary, Frank. Exchange in Oceania.
Hagedorn, P., et al, eds. Differential Games & Applications: Proceedings of a Workshop, Enschede, Netherlands, March 16-25,1977.
Hagel, William C., jt. ed. see Sims, Chester T.
Hagelman, Charles W., Jr., ed. see Wollstonecraft, Mary.
Hagelshaw, R. Lee. The Computer User's Legal Guide.
Hagelthorn, Joyce & Ruben, Marilyn. I've Never Told Anyone, but...
Hageman, Elizabeth H. Robert Herrick: A Reference Guide.
Hageman, Howard G. & Beker, J. C. Easter.
Hageman, Howard G. & See, Ruth D. That the World May Know.
Hagen, Lorinda. Amy Jean.
--Amy Jean.
--Bold Blades Flashing.
--Bold Blades Flashing.
Hagen-Ansert, Sandra L. Textbook of Diagnostic Ultrasonography.
Hagenmuller, P., jt. auth. see Bevan, D.
Hager, jt. auth. see Rich.
Hager, Jean. Dangerous Enchantment.
--Promise of Spring.
Hagerman, Frederick C. How to Increase Your Speed & Agility.
Hagerty, Bonnie K. & Packard, Karen L. Psychiatric-Mental Health Assessment.
Hagfors, Tor A., jt. auth. see Hultgvist, Bengt.
Haggar, Reginald & Adams, Elizabeth. Mason Porcelain & Ironstone, Seventeen Ninety-Six to Eighteen Fifty-Three.
Haggard, H. Rider. Ayesha: The Return of She.
--King Solomon's Mines.
Haggard, Lilias R., ed. I Walked by Night.
Haggard, Lilias R., ed. see Baldry, George.
Haggerty, Brian A., et al. We Share New Life (Baptism Program)
Haggerty, James. Aviation's Mr. Sam.
Haggett, P., jt. auth. see Chorley, R. J.
Haggett, Peter see Chorley, Richard J.
Haggett, Peter, jt. ed. see Chorley, Richard J.
Haggin, Bernard H. Music Observed.
Hagglund, Bengt. The Background of Luther's Doctrine of Justification in Late Medieval Theology. Anderson, Charles S., ed.
Hagihara, Yusuke. Celestial Mechanics Vol. 1: Dynamical Principles & Transformation Theory.
Hagin, Kenneth E. Bible Answers to Man's Questions on Demons.
--The Ministry Gifts Study Guide.
Hagin, Kenneth, Jr. Healing: A Forever-Settled Subject.
Hagin, Robert. Modern Portfolio Theory.
Hagler, Louise, ed. Farm Vegetarian Cookbook.
Hagman, Donald G. Public Planning & Control of Urban & Land Development Cases & Materials.
--Public Planning & Control of Urban & Land Development-Cases & Materials: 1982 Supplement to Teacher's Manual.
Hagner, Donald A. Hebrews: A Good News Commentary.
Hagstorm, Julie. What's a Mom to Do?
Hagstrom, Jane. The Young Witness: Evangelism to & by Children & Youth.
Hagstrom, Julie. Let's Pretend.
Hagstrum, Jean H. Sex & Sensibility: Ideal & Erotic Love from Milton to Mozart.
--The Sister Arts: The Tradition of Literary Pictorialism & English Poetry from Dryden to Gray.
Hague, B. Introduction to Vector Analysis.
Hague, Kathleen & Hague, Michael. East of the Sun & West of the Moon.
Hague, Michael, jt. auth. see Hague, Kathleen.
Hague, Michael, selected by. & illus. Mother Goose.
Hague, Rene, tr. see Teilhard De Chardin, Pierre.
Haguenau, Francis, jt. auth. see Dalton, A. J.
Hahn, jt. auth. see Payne.
Hahn, Elise, et al. Basic Voice Training for Speech.
Hahn, F. E., ed. Progress in Molecular & Subcellular Biology.
--Progress in Molecular & Subcellular Biology.
Hahn, F. E., ed. see Symposium, Vienna, Sept. 4-6, 1974.
Hahn, F. E., et al, eds. Progress in Molecular & Subcellular Biology.
Hahn, F. E., et al, eds. see Agranoff, B. W., et al.
Hahn, F. E., et al, eds. see Research Symposium on Complexes of Biologically Active Substances with Nucleic Acids & Their Modes of Action Staff.
Hahn, Ferdinand. Historical Investigation & New Testament Faith. Krentz, Edgar, ed. Maddox, Robert, tr. from Ger.
--The Worship of the Early Church. Reumann, John, ed. Green, David E., tr. from Ger.
Hahn, Harriet. The Plantain Season.
Hahn, James & Hahn, Lynn. Aim for a Job in a Small Business Occupation.
--Aim for a Job in Appliance Repair.
--Aim for a Job in the Printing Trade.
--Aim for a Job with the Telephone Company.
--Exploring a Career in Home Economics.
--Hamsters, Gerbils, Guinea Pigs, Pet Mice & Pet Rats.
Hahn, James, jt. auth. see Hahn, Lynn.
Hahn, Lynn & Hahn, James. Aim for a Job in the Construction Industry.
Hahn, Lynn, jt. auth. see Hahn, James.
Hahn, Lynne C., jt. auth. see McKoski, Martin M.
Hahn, Martin E., et al, eds. Development & Evolution of Brain Size: Behavioral Implications.
Hahn, Mary D. The Sara Summer.
Hahn, Otto. The Macmillan Book of Ornamental Gardening.
Hahn, W. Stability of Motion. Baartz, A. P., tr.
Hahn, Walter F., jt. auth. see Joshua, Wynfred.
Hahn, Walter F. & Pflatzgraff, Robert L., Jr., eds. Atlantic Community in Crisis: A Redefinition of the Transatlantic Relationship.
Haider, Muhiuddin. Village Level Integrated Population Education: A Case Study of Bangladesh.
Haig, Alan. The Victorian Clergy.
Haigh, Basil, tr. see Shimanovskaya, K. & Shiman, Alexander.
Haigh, Frank, jt. auth. see Dillon, Mark.
Haigh, R. H. & Turner, P. W. Not for Glory: A Personal History of the 1914-18 War.
Haigh, Robert W., jt. auth. see McLean, John G.
Haigh, Roger & Radford, Loren. BASIC for Microcomputers: Apple, TRS-80, PET.
Haigh, Roger W. & Radford, Loren E. BASIC for Microcomputers: Apple, TRS-80, PET.
Haight, William. Retail Advertising: Management & Technique.
Haile, Berard. Starlore among the Navaho.
Haile, H. G. Invitation to Goethe's Faust.
Hailes & Hubbard. Small Business Management.
Hailes, William D., Jr. & Hubbard, Raymond T. Small Business Management.
Hailey, Arthur. Wheels.
Hailey, Elizabeth F. Joanna's Husband & David's Wife.
--Joanna's Husband & David's Wife.
Hailey, Rhodalee M. World Catastrophe: Behold He Cometh.
Haill, Catherine. Dear Peter Pan.
Haim, S. Persian-English, English-Persian Shorter Dictionary.
Haimann, Theodore, et al. Management.
--Managing the Modern Organization.
Haimovici, Henry. Vascular Surgery.
Haines, E. Early American Brides.
Haines, George. The Young Photographer's Handbook.
Haines, George, 4th. Essays on German Influence upon English Education & Science, 1850-1919.
Haines, Helen S. & Thoburn, Robert. Seventy Five Years of Dentistry: The Diamond Jubilee Volume of the Florida State Dental Society.
Haines, J. Harry. I'm Only One Person, What Can I Do?
--Ten Hands for God.
Haines, Pamela. The Golden Lion.
Haines, R. G. Food Preparation for Hotels, Restaurants, & Cafeterias.
Haines, Robert E. The Inner Eye of Alfred Stieglitz.

Haines, Roger W. Control Systems for Heating, Ventilating & Air Conditioning.
Haining, jt. auth. see Rosen.
Haining, Peter. A Dictionary of Ghost Lore.
--Warlock's Book.
Haining, Peter, ed. Clans of Darkness: Scottish Stories of Fantasy & Horror.
--Deadly Nightshade: Seventeen Strange Tales of the Dark.
Hainsworth, Marguerite D. Experiments in Animal Behaviour.
Hairston, Maxine C. A Contemporary Rhetoric.
--A Contemporary Rhetoric.
--Successful Writing: A Rhetoric for Advanced Composition.
Hais, Karel & Hodek, Bretislav. English-Czech Dictionary.
Haislip, Barbara. Stars, Spells, Secrets & Sorcery: A Do It Yourself Guide to the Occult.
Haissinsky, M., ed. Chemical & Biological Action of Radiations.
Haitian Refugee Center Staff. Plaintiff's Master Exhibit on Conditions in Haiti.
Hajdu, George, tr. see Pecsi, Kalman.
Hajdu, Steven I. Pathology of Soft Tissue Tumors.
Hajek, O., et al, eds. Global Differentiable Dynamics.
Hajek, Otomar. Dynamical Systems in the Plane.
Hajji, Abdurraham. Andalusian Diplomatic Relations with Western Europe During the Umayyad Period.
Hakansson, Hakan. Industrial Technological Development: A Network Approach.
Hakeda, Yoshito S., ed. Bankei Zen. Haskel, Peter, tr.
--Bankei Zen. Haskel, Peter, tr.
Haken, H., ed. Pattern Formation by Dynamic Systems & Pattern Recognition.
--Synergetics-A Workshop: Proceedings of the International Workshop on Synergetics at Schloss Elmau, Bavaria, Germany, May 2-7,1977.
Haken, H. & Nikitine, S., eds. Excitons at High Density.
Hakim, Catherine. Secondary Analysis in Social Research: A Guide to Data Services & Methods with Examples.
Hakim, Sohrab A. E. Foreword by see Lutzker, Edythe.
Hakki, A-Haddi. Ideal Cardiac Pacing.
Haklisch, Carmela S., jt. ed. see Fusfeld, Herbert I.
Hakluyt, Richard. Hakluyt Voyages.
Hakomori, Sen-Itiroh, et al. Rous Sarcoma: Current Research II.
Hakuseki, Arai. Lessons from History: The Tokushi Yoron. Ackroyd, Joyce, tr. from Japanese.
Hakutani, Yoshinobu. Critical Essays on Richard Wright.
Halabi, Joseph N., ed. The Arab Directory for Commerce, Industry & Liberal Professions in the Arab Countries 1977-1978 (1977)
Halacy, D. S., Jr. The Coming Age of Solar Energy.
Halapy, Lili, tr. see Haraszti-Takacs, Marianne.
Halasz, Ida & Behm, Karen. Evaluating Voc Ed Programs: A Handbook for Corrections Educators.
Halasz, Judit, tr. see Degh, Linda.
Halasz, Nicholas. Captain Dreyfus: The Story of Mass Hysteria.
Halasz, Zoltan. Hungary.
Halata, Z. The Mechanoreceptors of the Mammalian Skin: Ultrastructure & Morphological Classification.
Halbach, Edward C., jt. auth. see Scoles, Eugene F.
Halbach, Edward C., Jr., et al. Estate Planning: 1983.
Halberstam, David. The Amateurs.
Halberstam, H. & Richert, H. E. Sieve Methods.
Halbouty, Michel T., jt. auth. see Donahue, Jack.
Halbritter, Gunter. Multidimensionale Optimierung bei der Standortwahl von Grosstechnischen Anlagen.
Halbrook, Stephen P. That Every Man Be Armed: The Evolution of a Constitutional Right.
Halcomb, Ruth. Women Making It.
Hald, A. Statistical Theory with Engineering Applications.
Hald, Marie M. Hurry Home Again.
--Jesus Jewels.
Haldane, Bernard. Career Satisfaction & Success: A Guide to Job Freedom.
--Career Satisfaction & Success: How to Know & Manage Your Strengths.
--The Young People's Job Finding Guide: Job Power.
Haldar, Hiralal. Neo-Hegelianism.
Haldeman, Joe, ed. Nebula Award Stories Seventeen.
Haldeman, Joe W. Infinite Dreams.
--Study War No More: A Selection of Alternatives.
Haldeman, Mabel Glenn. Heart Echoes in Verse.
Hale. Police Community Relations.
Hale, A. P. Electrical Interference.
Hale, B. M. The Subject Bibliography of the Social Sciences & Humanities.
Hale, Charles D. & Wilson, Wesley R. Personal Characteristics of Assaulted & Non-Assaulted Officers.
Hale, Charles D., jt. auth. see Morrison, Patton N.
Hale, Charles D., jt. auth. see Swanson, Cheryl.
Hale, Dennis, ed. U. S. Congress - Proceedings of Thomas P. O'Neal Jr. Symposium.
Hale, Dorinda, ed. see Hunken, Jorie & Madama, John.
Hale, Francis J. Introduction to Control System Analysis & Design.
Hale, Francis J., jt. auth. see Doolittle, Jesse S.
Hale, Frederick, jt. ed. see Sandeen, Ernest R.
Hale, George E., jt. auth. see L, Marian.
Hale, Glorya. Sourcebook for the Disabled.
Hale, Glorya, ed. The Source Book for the Disabled.
Hale, Irina. Brown Bear in a Brown Chair.
--Chocolate Mouse & Sugar Pig: And How They Ran Away to Escape Being Eaten.
Hale, Janice E. Black Children: Their Roots, Culture, & Learning Styles.
Hale, Jessie. The Quest of Prince Ferdinand.
Hale, Judson, ed. The Old Farmer's Almanac 1987.
Hale, Judson & Trowbridge, Rob, eds. The Old Farmer's Almanac 1983: 191st Anniversary Edition.
Hale, Judson, jt. ed. see Trowbridge, Rob.
Hale, Judson D., jt. ed. see Trowbridge, Rob.
Hale, Judy. Ducks at Third Avenue.
Hale, Katherine. Affinity.
--Madness.
Hale, Lucretia P. Complete Peterkin Papers.
Hale, Matthew. History of the Common Law of England. Gray, Charles M., ed.
Hale, Michael. The Other Child.
Hale, Nancy. The Prodigal Women.
Hale, Nathan, Institute Staff, ed. Intelligence in the War of Independence.
Hale, Nathan, Institute Staff, ed. see Sulc, Lawrence B.
Hale, Nathan, Institute Staff, ed. see Wannall, W. Raymond.
Hale, Norman B., jt. auth. see Rugg, Donald D.
Hale, O. J. Publicity & Diplomacy with Special Reference to England & Germany (1890-1914)
Hale, Philip. Great Concert Music: Philip Hale's Boston Symphont Programme Notes. Burk, John N., ed.
Hale, R., et al. The Principles & Practice of Health Visiting.
Hale, Ralph W. & Krieger, John A. Gynecology: A Concise Textbook.
Hale, Ralph W., jt. ed. see U. S. Olympic Water Polo Team Staff.
Hale, Robert. Canterbury & Rome, Sister Churches: A Roman Catholic Monk Reflects on Reunion in Diversity.
Hale, Sheila. Guide to Florence & Tuscany.
Halecki, Oscar. From Florence to Brest, Fourteen Thirty-Nine to Fifteen Ninety-Six.
Halen, Harry. Handbook of Oriental Collections in Finland: Manuscripts, Xylographs, Inscriptions & Russian Minority Literature.
Hales, Dianne R. & Williams, Brian K. An Invitation to Health.
Hales, E. E. Chariot of Fire.
Hales, J. P., Jr., ed. Precipitation Chemistry.
Hales, Stephen. Vegetable Staticks.
Halet, Sydney S., ed. see Aziz, Harry.
Halevi, Z'ev B. The Annointed.
Halevy, Elie. History of the English People.
--A History of the English People in the Nineteenth Century: The Liberal Awakening.
--History of the English People in the Nineteenth Century, Vol. 3: The Triumph of Reform.
Haley, Charles W. & Schall, Lawrence D. The Theory of Financial Decisions.
Haley, Charles W., jt. auth. see Schall, Lawrence D.
Haley, Gail. Marguerite.
Haley, Gail E. Costumes for Plays & Playing.
--The Post Office Cat.
--A Story.
Haley, James L. Kings of San Carlos.
Haley, Jay. Problem-Solving Therapy: New Strategies for Effective Family Therapy.
--Uncommon Therapy: The Psychiatric Techniques of Milton H. Erickson, M. D.
Haley, John W. Alleged Discrepancies of the Bible.
Haley, K. B., jt. auth. see IFORS International Conference Staff.
Haley, Mary J., ed. see CEP Staff & Boothe, Norris.
Haley, Virginia. International English.
Halfin, Harold & Nelson, Orville. Emerging Skills: Implications for Voc Ed.
Halfmann, Eunice K. Clothespins & Calendars.
Halfyard, Lynda, jt. auth. see Rose, Karen.
Halhuber, M. J., et al. ECG - an Introductory Course.
Halibi, Rafik. The West Bank Story. Friedman, Ina, tr. from Hebrew.
Haliburton, Thomas C. The Clockmaker.
Halka, Chester S. Melquiades, Alchemy & Narrative Theory: The Quest for Gold in 'Cien Anos de Soledad.
Halkin, Hillel, tr. see Orlev, Uri.
Halkin, John. Slime.
--Slither.
Hall. Evaluating & Improving Written Expression: A Practical Guide for Teachers.
--Getting More from Your Bible.
--Plumbing: Cold Water Supplies.
Hall, jt. auth. see Bonoma.
Hall, A. & Hall, M. B., eds. The Correspondence of Henry Oldenburg.
Hall, A. Hamer. Fundamentals of World Peace.
Hall, A. Rupert & Hall, Marie B. Correspondence of Henry Oldenburg: May 1674 - Sept. 1675.
Hall, A. Rupert & Smith, Norman, eds. History of Technology: Fourth Annual Volume, 1979.
Hall, A. Y. & Stenner, R. W. Manual of Fracture Bracing.
Hall, Aileen. Candlelight.
Hall, Al, ed. Pinto Tune-up & Repair.
Hall, Alan & Heard, James. Wood Finishing & Refinishing.
Hall, Austin & Flint, Homer E. The Blind Spot.
Hall, Avery. Twice upon A Time.
Hall, B. Frank. This Company of New Men.
Hall, Basil. Extracts from a Journal Written on the Coast of Chile, Peru, & Mexico in the Years Eighteen Twenty, Eighteen Twenty-One, Eighteen Twenty-Two.
Hall, Benjamin H. Collection of College Words & Phrases.
Hall, Brian & Smith, Maury. Value Clarification As Learning Process: A Handbook for Christian Educators.
Hall, Brian K. Developmental & Cellular Skeletal Biology.
Hall, Bud L. & Kidd, Roby, eds. Adult Learning: A Design for Action: A Comprehensive International Survey.
Hall, C. Polymer Materials.
Hall, C. F., tr. see Saakyan, Gurgen S.
Hall, C. M. Woman Unliberated: Difficulties & Limitations in Changing Self.
Hall, C. William, ed. Biomedical Engineering II: Recent Developments: Second Southern Biomedical Engineering Conference, Proceedings, September 26-27, 1983, San Antonio, Texas, U. S. A.
Hall, Cameron P. Lay Action: The Church's Third Force.
Hall, Carl W. & Davis, Denny C. Processing Equipment for Agricultural Products.
Hall, Carolyn. The A to Z of Soft Animals.
--Does God Give Interviews?
Hall, Carolyn V. The Teddy Bear Craft Book.
Hall, Charles E., jt. auth. see U. S. Bureau of the Census Staff.
Hall, Clayton C., ed. Narratives of Early Maryland, Sixteen Thirty-Three to Sixteen Eighty-Four.
Hall, D. O., et al. Biomass for Energy in the Developing Countries: Current Role-Potential-Problems-Prospects.
Hall, David A. The Aging of Connective Tissue.
Hall, Deborah, jt. auth. see Wilson, Christopher.
Hall, Donald. Fathers Playing Catch with Sons.
--Writing Well.
Hall, Donald & Emblen, D. L. A Writer's Reader.
Hall, Donald, ed. To Read Literature: Fiction, Poetry, Drama.
Hall, Douglas J. God & Human Suffering: An Excercise in the Theology of the Cross.
--Lighten Our Darkness: Toward an Indigenous Theology of the Cross.
--The Reality of the Gospel & the Unreality of the Churches.
Hall, Douglas John. Christian Mission: The Stewardship of Life in the Kingdom of Death.
Hall, Douglas K. The Border.
--Rock & Roll Retreat Blues.
--Working Cowboys.
Hall, Douglas K., jt. auth. see Schwarzenegger, Arnold.
Hall, Douglas T. Careers in Organizations. Porter, Lyman W., ed.
Hall, Douglas T. & Schneider, Benjamin. Organizational Climates & Careers: The Work Lives of Priests.
Hall, Douglas V. Microprocessors & Digital Systems.
Hall, Douglas V. & Hall, Marybelle B. Experiments in Microprocessors & Digital Systems.
Hall, E. Raymond & Dalquest, Walter W. A New Doglike Carnivore, Genus Cynarctus, from the Clarendonian, Pliocene, of Texas.
Hall, Edward N. The Art of Destructive Management: What Hath Man Wrought.
Hall, Elizabeth. From Pigeons to People: A Look at Behavior Shaping.
--Possible Impossibilities: A Look at Parapsychology.
--Stand Up, Lucy.
--Why We Do What We Do: A Look at Psychology.
Hall, Elizabeth S. & Pope, Jerilyn D., eds. Matching Gift Details 1988.
Hall, Elizabeth S. & Whitman, Gweneth G., eds. Profiles: Educational Institutions.
Hall, Eugene J. Practical Conversation in English. Incl. For Beginning Students; For Intermediate Students; For Advanced Students. Prentice ESL.
Hall, Everett W. What Is Value?
Hall, F. Plumbing: Hot Water Supplies.
Hall, Francis J. Theological Outlines.
Hall, Franklin. Many Powerful Methods of Natural Healing.
Hall, Frederick. Bible Quizzes for Everybody.
Hall, G. B. The European Intellectual Revolution & the World of Man.
Hall, G. K. & Co. Staff, compiled by. Cumulated Subject Index to Psychological Abstracts, 1927-1960.
Hall, G. Stanley & Mansfield, John M. Hints Toward a Select & Descriptive Bibliography of Education.
Hall, George. Top Gun Fighters & America's Jet Power.
Hall, George F. The Missionary Spirit in the Augustana Church.
Hall, Gus. Karl Marx: Beacon for Our Times.
Hall, H. W., ed. Science Fiction Book Review Index, 1923-1973.
--Science Fiction Book Review Index, 1974 to 1979.
Hall, Ian S. & Colman, Bernard H. Diseases of the Nose, Throat & Ear.
Hall Institute of Real Estate. Managing a Real Estate Team.
Hall, J. Tillman. Total Fitness for Men.
Hall, J. Tillman, et al. Until the Whistle Blows: A Collection of Games, Dances & Activities for Eight to Twelve Year Olds.
Hall, Jack C. A Review of the North & Central American Species of Paravilla Painter (Diptera: Bombyliidae)
Hall, James B., et al. Women: Portraits.
Hall, James H. Knowledge, Belief & Transcendence: Philosophical Problems in Religion.
Hall, James N., jt. auth. see Nordhoff, Charles.
Hall, John. Puzzlers Gamebook.
Hall, John F. An Invitation to Learning & Memory.
Hall, John H. The Boy Soldier.
Hall, John R., et al. Fire Code Inspections & Fire Prevention: What Methods Lead to Success?
Hall, Joseph. Selections from Early Middle English, 1130-1250.
Hall, Joyce, jt. auth. see Fry, Ruth T.
Hall, Laurence S. How Thinking Is Written: An Analytic Approach to Writing.
Hall, Lynn. Flowers of Anger.
--Gently Touch the Milkweed.
--A New Day for Dragons.
--Ride a Wild Dream.
--Riff, Remember.
--The Shy Ones.
--The Siege of Silent Henry.
--Troublemaker.
Hall, M. B., jt. ed. see Hall, A.
Hall, M. P. Secret Destiny of America.
Hall, M. R., et al. Medical Care of the Elderly.
Hall, M. R. P., jt. auth. see Brearley, Paul C.
Hall, Malcolm. Headlines.
Hall, Manly P. Astrological Keywords.
--The Guru.
--Story of Astrology.
Hall, Margaret, jt. auth. see Wolfram, Sybil.
Hall, Marie B., jt. auth. see Hall, A. Rupert.
Hall, Marion G., jt. auth. see Enders, Alexandra.
Hall, Marjory. The April Ghost.
--Beneath Another Sun.
--The Carved Wooden Ring.
--The Gold-Lined Box.
--Mystery at October House.
--The Other Girl.
Hall, Mary B. More for Your Money: How to Increase Your Spending Power up to Twenty Percent Without Increasing Your Income.
Hall, MaryAnne. The Language Experience Approach for Teaching Reading: A Research Perspective.
Hall, Marybelle B., jt. auth. see Hall, Douglas V.
Hall, Max. The Charles People's River.
Hall, Michael G. Edward Randolph & the American Colonies, 1676-1703.
Hall, Michael G., et al, eds. Glorious Revolution in America: Documents on the Colonial Crisis of 1689.
Hall, Miriam J. Jesus, the Children's Friend.
Hall, Nelson. A Complete Course in Super Ju Jitsu.
Hall, Oakley. Apaches.
--The Bad Lands.
--The Children of the Sun.
--Corpus of Joe Bailey.
--Lullaby.
--Warlock.
Hall, Olive, jt. auth. see Compton, Norma.
Hall, Pauline, ed. Alcoholic Liver Disease: Pathobiology, Epidemiology & Clinical Aspects.

Authors

Hall, Penelope. Penelope Hall's Social Services of England & Wales. Mays, J. B. & Forder, Anthony, eds.
Hall, Phoebe, et al. Change, Choice & Conflict in Social Policy.
Hall, R., jt. auth. see Williams, E. W.
Hall, R. C. & Beresford, T. P., eds. Handbook of Psychiatric Diagnostic Procedures, Volume 1.
--Handbook of Psychiatric Diagnostic Procedures, Volume 2.
Hall, R. M., ed. Air Instrument Surgery, Vol. One: Cranial Surgery, Intracranial Surgery, Temperol Bone Surgery, Vertebral Surgery.
--Air Instrument Surgery, Vol. Three: Facial, Oral & Reconstructive Surgery.
Hall, Richard. Butterscotch Prince.
--Disorganized Crime.
Hall, Ridgway M., Jr., et al. RCRA Hazardous Wastes Handbook.
--Superfund Manual: Legal & Management Strategies.
--Superfund Manual: Legal & Management Strategies.
Hall, Robert A., ed. see Linguistic Association of Canada & the U. S. Staff.
Hall, Robert L. The King Edward Plot.
Hall, Robert W. Plato.
Hall, Rodney. The Most Beautiful World.
--Selected Poems.
Hall, Roger. Cloak & Dagger.
Hall, Roger A. Desert Men.
Hall, Ruth. Passionate Crusader: The Life of Marie Stopes.
Hall, Sandra P. & Hirsch, Felice L. Fingertip Reference for Dental Materials.
Hall, Stuart & Jefferson, Tony, eds. Resistance Through Rituals: Youth Subcultures in Post-War Britain.
Hall, T. E., et al, eds. Semigroups.
Hall, Terry. New Testament Express.
--Old Testament Express.
Hall, Theodore, et al, eds. Microprobe Analysis As Applied to Cells & Tissues.
Hall, Thomas S., tr. & commentary by see Descartes, Rene.
Hall, Thor. Anders Nygren.
--Anders Nygren.
--The Future Shape of Preaching.
Hall, Thor & Price, James L. Advent-Christmas.
Hall, Warner L. Symbols of the Faith.
Hall, Wesley W., jt. auth. see Harpe, Shideler.
Hall, William E. & Murray, Grover E., eds. The Niger Cereals Project: An Experience in Technical Assistance.
Hall, Woodie. The Power of Negative Thinking. Wright, Arlene A., ed.
Halla. Dreamboats & Milestones: Cars of the '50s.
Hallahan, Daniel P. & Kauffman, James M. Exceptional Children: Introduction to Special Education.
Hallahan, Daniel P., jt. ed. see Kauffman, James M.
Hallahan, William H. Catch Me: Kill Me.
--The Dead of Winter.
--Foxcatcher.
--Keeper of the Children.
--The Monk.
--The Ross Forgery.
--The Search for Joseph Tully.
--The Trade.
Hallam, A., ed. Patterns of Evolution: As Illustrated by the Fossil Record.
Hallas, et al. Care & Training of the Mentally Handicapped.
Hallbauer, Rosalie C. & Agrawal, Surendra P. A Survey of Accountants' Views on the Desirability & Method of Inflation Accounting.
Halle, Louis J. The Elements of International Strategy: A Primer for the Nuclear Age.
--Out of Chaos.
--The Sea & the Ice: A Naturalist in Antarctica.
--The Search for an Eternal Norm: As Represented by Three Classics.
--Spring in Washington.
Hallem, H. E. Rural England: 1066-1348.
Hallenbeck, Carol A. Our Child: Preparation for Parenting.
Hallenborg, Walter, ed. see Coleridge, Samuel Taylor.
Haller, G., jt. auth. see Bauer, K.
Haller, John S. & Haller, Robin M. The Physician & Sexuality in Victorian America.
Haller, Lynda. Cheerleader U. S. A. Tryouts to Triumph.
--Pom Pon U. S. A.
Haller, M. A., jt. auth. see Freedman, Gabriel.
Haller, Robin M., jt. auth. see Haller, John S.
Haller, William. Early Life of Robert Southey.
Hallesby, O. Infant Baptism & Adult Conversion.
--Prayer. Carlsen, Clarence J., tr.
--Under His Wings.
--Why I Am a Christian.
Hallett, Garth L. Logic for the Labyrinth: A Guide to Critical Thinking.
Hallett, Graham. The Economics of Agricultural Policy.
Hallett, J. P., jt. auth. see Stewart, J. D.
Hallett, John W., Jr. & Brewster, David C. Manual of Patient Care in Vascular Surgery.
Hallett, Judith P. Fathers & Daughters in Roman Society & the Elite Family.
Hallett, R. People & Progress in West Africa.
Halley, Anne. Between Wars & Other Poems.
Halley, Henry H. Halley's Bible Handbook.
Halley, R. J., ed. Agricultural Notebook.
Halliday, A. M., ed. Evoked Potentials in Clinical Testing.
Halliday, Anne. Decorating with Crochet.
Halliday, B., ed. International Directory of Vacuum Equipment, Manufacturers & Suppliers.
--World-Wide Directory of Manufacturers of Vacuum Plant, Components & Associated Equipment.
Halliday, David A. Air Monitoring Methods for Industrial Contaminants.
Halliday, F. E. Shakespeare & His World.
Halliday, Fred. Ambler.
Halliday, James. Wines & Wineries of New South Wales.
--Wines & Wineries of South Australia.
--Wines & Wineries of Victoria.
--Wines & Wineries of Western Australia.
Halliday, Jill, jt. auth. see Halliday, John.
Halliday, John & Halliday, Jill. Practical Goat-Keeping.
--Practical Goat-Keeping.
Halliday, M. S., jt. auth. see Boakes, R. A.
Hallie Q. Brown Memorial Library Staff, jt. ed. see Central State University Staff.
Halligan, Marion. Self-Possession.
Halligan, Marney, jt. auth. see Jackle, Mary.
Hallinan, P. K. Small Town Children's Christmas.
Halliwell, David. The House.
Halliwell, Leslie. Halliwell's Film & Video Guide.
Halliwell, Leslie L. The Filmgoer's Companion.
--Halliwell's Film & Video Guide.
--Halliwell's Film Guide.
--Halliwell's Film Guide.
--Halliwell's Film Guide.
--Halliwell's Film Guide: And Music.
--Halliwell's Filmgoer's Companion.
--Halliwell's Harvest.
--Halliwell's Hundred: A Nostalgic Choice of Films from the Golden Age.
--Seats in All Parts: Life at the Movies.
Halliwell-Phillipps, James O. Popular Rhymes & Nursery Tales.
Hallman, G. Victor & Rosenbloom, Jerry S. Personal Financial Planning.
Hallman, Ralph J. Psychology of Literature.
Hallman, Ruth. I Gotta Be Free.
--Secrets of a Silent Stranger.
Hallmark, Clayton. Computerist's Handy Databook-Dictionary.
--Electronic Measurements Simplified.
Hallock, Ginny. My Dearest Daughter--I Want You to Know.
Halloran, Jack. Applied Human Relations: An Organizational Approach.
Halloran, Joe. Understanding Homosexual Persons: Straight Answers from Gays.
Halloran, John A., jt. auth. see Lanser, Howard.
Halloran, Richard. To Arm a Nation: Rebuilding America's Endangered Defenses.
Hallowell, Elliott R. Cold & Freezer Storage Manual.
Hallows, R. W., jt. auth. see Haas, A.
Halls, David, jt. auth. see Hudson, Peter.
Halls, W. D. Education, Culture & Politics in Modern France.
--Maurice Maeterlinck: A Study of His Life & Thought.
Hallstead, William F. Ghost Plane of Blackwater.
--Ghost Plane of Blackwater.
--The Launching of Linda Bell.
Hallwood, C. Paul & Sinclair, Stuart W. Oil Debt & Development: OPEC in the Third World.
Halmann, M., ed. Analytical Chemistry of Phosphorus Compounds.
Halme, A., jt. auth. see IFAC Symposium Staff.
Halmos, P. R. Lectures on Boolean Algebras.
--Lectures on Ergodic Theory.
Halmos, Paul. Solitude & Privacy.
Halnam, K. E. Atomic Energy in Medicine.
Halpenny, Francess G., ed. Editing Canadian Texts.
--Editing Twentieth Century Texts.
Halper, Marilyn S. How to Stop Smoking.
Halper, Marilyn S. & Neiger, Ira. Physical Fitness.
Halperin, D. A. Psychodynamic Perspectives on Religion, Sect & Cult.
Halperin, Jack H. Private Placement of Securities: Cumulative Supplement 1986.
Halperin, Jonathan J., jt. auth. see English, Robert D.
Halperin, Mark. A Place Made Fast.
Halperin, S. William. Germany Tried Democracy: A Political History of the Reich, 1918-1933.
Halpern, Daniel, tr. see Mririda.
Halpern, Florence. Survival: Black & White.
Halpern, Frederick H. An African Odyssey on Wheels: Twenty Thousand Miles Through East & Central Africa Without a Plan.
Halpern, Howard M. How to Break Your Addiction to a Person.
Halpern, Jay. The Jade Unicorn.
Halpern, Jeanne, ed. Teaching Business Writing.
Halpern, Jeanne W. & Liggett, Sarah. Computers & Composing: How the New Technologies are Changing Writing.
Halpern, M. G., ed. Polishing & Waxing Compositions: Recent Developments.
Halpern, M. I., ed. Annual Review in Automatic Programming.
Halpern, Stephen C. & Lamb, Charles M. Supreme Court Activism & Restraint.
Halpin, Anne, ed. see Rodale Food Center Staff & Hurley, Judith.
Halpin, Anne, ed. see Rodale Press, Inc. Editors.
Hals, Ronald M. Grace & Faith in the Old Testament.
--Theology of the Book of Ruth.
Halsall, E. The Comprehensive School: Guidelines for the Reorganization of Secondary Education.
Halsall, E., ed. Becoming Comprehensive: Case Histories.
Halsall, Maureen. The Old English Rune Poem: A Critical Edition.
Halse, Albert O. Architectural Rendering: The Technique of Contemporary Presentation.
--The Use of Color in Interiors.
Halsell, Grace. Prophecy & Politics: Militant Evangelists on the Road to Nuclear War.
Halsey, A. H. & Trow, M. A. British Academics.
Halsey, Rosalie V. Forgotten Books of the American Nursery.
Halsman, Philippe. Halsman: Portraits. Halsman, Yvonne, selected by.
Halsman, Yvonne, selected by see Halsman, Philippe.
Halstead, Bruce W. Dangerous Aquatic Animals of the World: A Color Guide.
Halstead, Charles L., et al. Physical Evaluation of the Dental Patient.
Halstead, L. B. The Evolution of Mammals.
Halstead, Ward C. Brain & Intelligence: A Quantitative Study of the Frontal Lobes.
Halter, F., ed. Antacids in the Eighties.
Halter, Marek. The Book of Abraham. Blair, Lowell, tr.
Halty-Carrere, Maximo. Technological Development Strategies for Developing Countries: A Review for Policy Makers.
Halver, J. E., jt. ed. see Neuhaus, O. W.
Halverson, Lolas E., jt. auth. see Roberton, Mary Ann.
Halverson, Richard. We the People.
Halverson, Richard P. How to Achieve Complete Financial Freedom.
Halvorsen, Robert & Ruby, Michael G. Benefit-Cost Analysis of Air-Pollution Control.
Halvorson, Arndt L. Authentic Preaching.
Halvorson, Loren. Peace on Earth Handbook.
Halvorson, Loren E. Grace at Point Zero.
Halvorson, Marilyn. Let It Go.
Ham, G. E., ed. Vinyl Polymerization.
Ham, Marion N. Gifts from a Country Kitchen. Voltz, Jeanne, ed.
Ham, Richard J. Geriatric Medicine Annual, 1986.
Hamachek, Don E. Encounters with the Self.
Hamalian, Leo. D. H. Lawrence in Italy.
Hamann, Donald L. Introduction to the Classical Guitar: An Ensemble Approach for the Classroom.
Hamann, H. P. A Popular Guide to New Testament Criticism.
Hamann, Henry P. The Bible Between Fundamentalism & Philosophy.
--Justification by Faith in Modern Theology.
Hamberger, S. M., ed. see Lominadze, D. G.
Hamblet, Edwin. Marcel Dube & French-Canadian Drama.
Hambleton, Joanne Illus. by see Dahlby, Edith L.
Hambleton, Robin. Policy Planning & Local Government.
Hambley, Edmund C. Bridge Deck Behavior.
Hambley, Harold W. Joshua, a Model for Leadership.
Hamblin, Dora J. That Was the Life.
Hamblin, Robert L. & Miller, Jerry L. Introduction to Mathematical Patterns of Cultural Diffusion.
Hambly, Wilfrid D. The History of Tattooing & Its Significance, with Some Account of Other Forms of Corporal Marking.
Hambrick, John. The High Cost of Indifference: Leader's Guide.
Hambrick-Stowe, Charles E. The Practice of Piety: Puritan Devotional Disciplines in Seventeenth-Century New England.
Hamburg, Joan & Ketay, Norma. New York on Thirty-Five Dollars a Day.
Hamburg, Morris. Basic Statistics: A Modern Approach.
--Basic Statistics: A Modern Approach.
--Statistical Analysis for Decision Making.
--Statistical Analysis for Decision Making.
--Statistical Analysis for Decision Making.
Hamburger, Jean. Discovering the Individual.
Hamburger, Joseph. James Mill & the Art of Revolution.
Hamburger, Michael. Truth of Poetry: Tensions in Modern Poetry from Baudelaire to the 1960s.
--The Truth of Poetry: Tensions in Modern Poetry from Baudelaire to the 1960s.
Hamburger, Michael, ed. German Poetry Nineteen Ten to Nineteen Seventy-Five.
Hamburger, Michael, tr. see Celan, Paul.
Hamburger, Michael, tr. see Grass, Gunter.
Hamburger, Robert. All the Lonely People: Life in a Single Room Occupancy Hotel.
Hamdan, Lawrence, jt. auth. see Graham, Lawrence.
Hamdan, Lawrence A., jt. ed. see Grey, Jerry.
Hameau, Marie-Anne. Je Lis Tu Lis.
Hameed, Hakeem A., ed. Islam at a Glance.
Hamel, Jacqueline, jt. auth. see Pucciani, Oreste.
Hamel, Lawrence, jt. ed. see Haas, Ronald.
Hamel, Marilyn. Sex Etiquette: Should I? Can I? May I? Must I? Or, the Modern Woman's Guide to Mating Manners.
Hamer, Douglas, ed. The Works of Sir David Lindsay of the Mount, 1490-1555.
Hamer, John G. Troubled Debt Restructuring: An Alternative to Bankruptcy? Farmer, Richard, ed.
Hamer, Martyn. Trees.
Hamer, Richard, compiled by. & intro. by. A Choice of Anglo-Saxon Verse.
Hamerton-Kelly, Robert. God the Father: Theology & Patriarchy in the Teaching of Jesus. Brueggemann, Walter & Donahue, John R., eds.
Hamerton-Kelly, Robert G. Sprung Time: Seasons of the Christian Year.
Hamey, J. A., jt. auth. see Hamey, L. A.
Hamey, L. A. & Hamey, J. A. The Roman Engineers.
Hamill, Edson T. The Child Killer.
--Motive for Murder.
Hamilton, A. Maori Art.
Hamilton, Alan. The Royal Handbook.
Hamilton, Alastair. Appeal of Fascism.
Hamilton, Alastair, tr. see Simenon, Georges.
Hamilton, Alice & Hardy, Harriet L. Industrial Toxicology.
Hamilton, Annette. Nature & Nurture: Child-Rearing in North & Central Arnhem Land.
Hamilton, Betty & Guidos, Barbara. MASA: Medical Acronyms, Symbols, & Abbreviations.
Hamilton, Betty, jt. auth. see Guidos, Barbara.
Hamilton, Bruce. Too Much of Water.
Hamilton, Bruce, jt. auth. see Mills, Edwin S.
Hamilton, Bruce, jt. auth. see Osborne, Jerry.
Hamilton, Bruce, jt. auth. see Osbourne, Jerry.
Hamilton, C. H., jt. ed. see Paton, N. E.
Hamilton, C. Howard, jt. ed. see Hasson, Dennis F.
Hamilton, Carl, ed. Pure Nostalgia: Memories of Early Iowa.
Hamilton, Catherine D., et al, eds. Text Retrieval: A Directory of Software.
Hamilton, Charles. The Illustrated Letter.
Hamilton, Charles V. American Government.
Hamilton, Cicely M. Marriage As a Trade.
Hamilton, Dan, ed. see MacDonald, George.
Hamilton, David. Newtonian Classicism & Darwinian Institutionalism.
--The Thames & Hudson Manual of Architectural Ceramics.
Hamilton, David & Robbe-Grillet, Alain. Dreams of a Young Girl.
Hamilton, David, jt. auth. see Dockrell, W. B.
Hamilton, David L. The Interior Designers Handbook on Plants.
Hamilton, Dennis, ed. see International Computer Programs, Inc. Staff.
Hamilton, Dennis L., ed. see International Computer Programs, Inc.
Hamilton, Dennis L., jt. ed. see International Computer Programs, Inc.
Hamilton, Dennis L., ed. see International Computer Programs, Inc.
Hamilton, Dennis L., ed. see International Computer Programs, Inc. Staff.
Hamilton, Dennis L., jt. ed. see International Computer Programs, Inc. Staff.
Hamilton, Dennis L., ed. see International Computer Programs, Inc. Staff.
Hamilton, Donna M., jt. auth. see Nemiro, Beverly A.
Hamilton, Dorothy. Charco.
--Mindy.
Hamilton, E. I. Applied Geochronology.
Hamilton, Earl J. American Treasure & the Price Revolution in Spain, 1501-1650.
Hamilton, Edith. Ever-Present Past.
--The Greek Way.
--Greek Way.
--The Roman Way.
--Roman Way.
--Spokesmen for God.
--Witness to the Truth: Christ & His Interpreters.
Hamilton, Edmond. City at World's End.
Hamilton, Eleanor. Partners in Love.
--Sex, with Love: A Guide for Young People.
Hamilton, F. E., ed. Industrial Change in Advanced Economies: Spatial Perspectives.

Authors

Hamilton, F. E. & Linge, G. J. R., eds. Spatial Analysis, Industry & the Industrial Environment: Progress in Research & Applications. Incl. Vol. 1. Industrial Systems; Vol. 2. International Industrial Systems; Vol. 3. Regional Economies & Industrial Systems. Hamilton, F. E. & Linge, G. J., eds.. Wiley.
Hamilton, Gail. Candle to the Devil.
--Love Comes to Eunice K. O'Herlihy.
--Titantia's Lodestone.
Hamilton, Gene, jt. auth. see Hamilton, Katie.
Hamilton, George H. Manet & His Critics.
Hamilton, Helen, jt. auth. see McVan, Barbara.
Hamilton, Helen & Rose, Minnie B., eds. Endocrine Disorders.
--Gastrointestinal Disorders.
--Immune Disorders.
--Neoplastic Disorders.
--NRL Yearbook 86.
--Professional Guide to Drugs.
--Renal & Urologic Disorders.
--Respiratory Disorders.
Hamilton, Henry, et al. Spiro Mound Copper. Chapman, Carl H., ed.
Hamilton, Henry W. & Willoughby, Charles C. The Spiro Mound. Chapman, Carl H., ed.
Hamilton, Holman. Prologue to Conflict: The Crisis & Compromise of 1850.
Hamilton, Innes. The Beagle Brigade.
Hamilton, James D. The Faces of God.
Hamilton, James R., et al. Readings for an Introduction to Philosophy.
Hamilton, John. War at Sea: Nineteen Thirty-Nine to Nineteen Forty-Five.
Hamilton, John & Sorrell, Alan. Saxon England.
Hamilton, John M. Main Street America & the Third World.
--Main Street America & the Third World.
Hamilton, Joseph H., ed. Internal Conversion Processes.
Hamilton, K. G. Paradise Lost: A Humanist Approach.
Hamilton, K. G., ed. Studies in Recent Australian Novel.
Hamilton, Katie & Hamilton, Gene. Build It Together: Twenty-Seven Easy to Make Woodworking Projects for Adults & Children.
Hamilton, Kellen, jt. auth. see Rose, Minnie.
Hamilton, Lawrence S., jt. auth. see Williams, Julia.
Hamilton, Lawrence S. & Snedaker, Samuel C., eds. Handbook for Mangrove Area Management.
Hamilton, Leonard W., ed. Basic Limbic System Anatomy of the Rat.
Hamilton, Malcolm C., ed. Education Literature, Nineteen Hundred Seven to Nineteen Thirty-Two.
--Education Literature, Nineteen Hundred Seven to Nineteen Thirty-Two.
--Education Literature, Nineteen Hundred Seven to Nineteen Thirty-Two.
--Education Literature Nineteen Hundred Seven to Nineteen Thirty-Two.
--Education Literature, Nineteen Hundred Seven to Nineteen Thirty-Two.
--Education Literature, Nineteen Hundred Seven to Nineteen Thirty-Two.
--Education Literature, Nineteen Hundred Seven to Nineteen Thirty-Two.
Hamilton, Marian. The Best Things in New York Are Free.
Hamilton, Marian W., tr. see Jaspers, Karl.
Hamilton, Mark. My Brother's Image.
Hamilton, Mary. Munster Village.
Hamilton, Michael P. & Montgomery, Nancy S. The Ordination of Women: Pro & Con.
Hamilton, Mike. Autocourse 1984-1985.
Hamilton, Morse. How Do You Do, Mr. Birdsteps?
--Who's Afraid of the Dark?
Hamilton, Nigel. Master of the Battlefield: Monty's War Years, 1942-1944.
--Monty: The Making of a General 1887-1942.
Hamilton, Persis M. Basic Maternity Nursing.
--Basic Pediatric Nursing.
Hamilton, Peter & Macdonald, Keith B., eds. Estuarine & Wetland Processes with Emphasis on Modeling.
Hamilton, Peter J. Colonial Mobile. Summersell, Charles G., ed.
Hamilton, R. S. Harmonic Maps of Manifolds with Boundary.
Hamilton, Robert W. Corporations.
--Corporations: Including Partnership & Limited Partnerships-Cases & Materials, 2nd ed. 1985 Supplement.
Hamilton, Russel & Greene, Stephanie, eds. What Bothers Us About Grownups.
Hamilton, Vernon & Warburton, David M., eds. Human Stress & Cognition: An Information Processing Approach.
Hamilton, Virginia. Hugo Black: The Alabama Years.
--Sweet Whispers, Brother Rush.
Hamilton, Virginia V., ed. Hugo Black & the Bill of Rights: Proceedings of the First Hugo Black Symposium in American History on the Bill of Rights & American Democracy.
Hamilton, Walter. Poets Laureate of England.
Hamilton, William. The Charlatan.
--Discussions on Philosophy & Literature.
--Lectures on Metaphysics & Logic.
--The Love of Rich Women.
--Money Should Be Fun.
Hamilton, William J., Jr. & Whitaker, John O., Jr. Mammals of the Eastern United States.
Hamilton-McRritt, Jane. My First Days of School.
Hamilton-Miller, J. M. & Smith, J. T., eds. Beta Lactamases.
Hamley, Edward B. War in the Crimea.
Hamlin, Anna M. Father Was a Tenor.
Hamlin, Charles H. Propaganda & Myth in Time of War. Bd. with War Myth in U. S. History; Educators Present Arms: The Use of the Schools & Colleges As Agents of War Propaganda, 1914-1918. Garland Pub.
Hamlin, E. John. Comfort My People: A Guide to Isaiah 40-66.
Hamlin, Peter R. A Case Study of the Fairfax County, Virginia, Censorship Controversy.
Hamlin, Sonya B. Communication in the Courtroom: How to Tell, Explain & Persuade.
Hamlin, Talbot. Greek Revival Architecture in America.
Hamlyn, D. W. Psychology of Perception: A Philosophical Examination of Gestalt Theory & Derivative Theories of Perception.
--The Theory of Knowledge.
Hamlyn, David W. Schopenhauer.
Hamm, Charles. Yesterdays: Popular Song in America.
Hamm, Edward, Jr. When Fresno Rode the Rails. Sebree, Mac, ed.
Hammack, Mary L. A Dictionary of Women in Church History.
Hammarberg, Dyan, tr. see Anders, Rebecca.
Hammarberg, Dyan, tr. see Overbeck, Cynthia.
Hammarberg, Dyan, tr. see Pursell, Margaret S.
Hammarberg, Melvin A. & Nelson, Clifford A., eds. My Book of Prayers: A Personal Prayer Book.
Hammel, Eric & Lane, John. Seventy-Six Hours: The Invasion of Tarawa.
Hammel, Faye & Levey, Sylvan. Frommer's Hawaii on Forty-Five Dollars a Day.
--Hawaii on Fifty Dollars a Day.
Hammel, H. T. & Scholander, P. F. Osmosis & Tensile Solvent.
Hammel, William M. The Popular Arts in America: A Reader.
Hammer, Armand & Lydon, Neil. Hammer.
Hammer, Armand & Lyndon, Neil. Hammer: A Witness to History.
Hammer, David E. & Kadlec, Robert H. Wetlands Utilization for Management of Community Wastewater: Concepts & Operations in Michigan.
Hammer, Hy. Mail Handler, U.S. Postal Service.
Hammer, Hy, ed. Mechanical Ability Tests.
--Medical Technician, Medical Assistant, Medical Aide.
--State Trooper: Highway Patrolman, Ranger.
--Stenographer-Typist: U. S. Government Positions GS2 & GS7.
Hammer, Kenneth. The Springfield Carbine on the Western Frontier.
Hammer, Louis. Bone Planet.
Hammer, Mary J., ed. see Williams, Henry H.
Hammer, R. M., et al. Investment Regulation Around the World: 1984 Supplement.
Hammer, Richard. Mr. Jacobson's War.
--The Vatican Connection.
--The Vatican Connection: The Astonishing Account of a Billion-Dollar Counterfeit Stock Deal Between the Mafia & the Church.
Hammer, Richard, jt. auth. see Franco, Joseph.
Hammer, Richard M., et al, eds. Investment Regulation Around the World.
Hammerberg, Kuno. Kuno: One of the Last of the General Practitioners.
Hammerman, Susan & Maikowski, Stephen, eds. The Economics of Disability: International Perspectives.
Hammerman, William M. Fifty Years of Outdoor Resident Education.
Hammersma, Richard J., et al. Personal Involvement in Current Psychological Issues.
Hammerstein, Oscar. Songs of Oscar Hammerstein II.
Hammes, Beverly D. How the Appacorn Came to Be.
Hammes, Gordon G. Investigation of Rate & Mechanisms of Reactions.
Hammett, Theodore M. & Sullivan, Monique. AIDS in Correctional Facilities: Issues & Options.
Hammil, Joel. Limbo.
--The Trident.
Hamming, Mynard C. & Foster, Norman G. Interpretation of Mass Spectra of Organic Compounds.
Hamming, Richard W. Digital Filters.
Hammitt, James E., jt. auth. see Prague, Cary N.
Hammock, Wayne, jt. auth. see Johnson, Jack.
Hammond, Allen, ed. Therapy Under Analysis.
Hammond, Allen L. Newton at the Bat: The Science in Sport.
Hammond, Allen L., ed. A Passion to Know: Twenty Profiles in Science.
Hammond, Antony, jt. ed. see Coleman, Antony.
Hammond, Dorothy & Jablow, Alta. The Africa That Never Was: Four Centuries of British Writing about Africa--an Anthropological View Contrasting the Africa of Fact & the Africa of Fiction.
Hammond, George P., ed. Guide to the Manuscript Collections of the Bancroft Library. Incl. Vol. I. Pacific & Western Manuscripts (Except California) Morgan, Dale L. & Hammond, George P., eds.; Vol. II. Mexican & Central American Manuscripts. Hammond, George P., ed. U of Cal Pr.
Hammond, George P. see Hammond, George P.
Hammond, Gloria, jt. auth. see Kostelanetz, Andre.
Hammond Incorporated Editors. Landmarks of Liberty.
Hammond, Jim. Suzuki A50P, A50 & AS50: '69-'77.
Hammond, Karla M. No Name for Season.
Hammond, Keith, et al, trs. see Ivanov, Vsevolod.
Hammond, Mason. The City in the Ancient World. Bartson, Lester, ed.
--Latin: A Historical & Lingusitic Handbook.
Hammond, P., ed. see Coekin, J. A.
Hammond, Paul Y. Cold War & Detente: The American Foreign Policy Process since 1945.
Hammond, Peter B. An Introduction to Cultural & Social Anthropology.
Hammond, R. Dispersions of Materials.
--Separation & Purification of Materials.
Hammond, Ray. Computers & Your Child.
Hammond, Rolt. Dictionary of Civil Engineering.
Hammond, Samuel H. Wild Northern Scenes or Sporting Adventures with Rifle & the Rod.
Hammond, Seymour B. & Gehmlich, D. K. Electrical Engineering.
Hammond Staff, ed. Diplomat World Atlas.
--Hammond Road Atlas & Vacation Guide 1987.
--Road Atlas America 1983.
--Road Atlas America 1987.
Hammond, Thomas T., ed. Soviet Foreign Relations & World Communism: A Selected, Annotated Bibliography of 7,000 Books in 30 Languages.
Hammonds, Michael. A Gathering of Wolves.
Hammond-Tooke, W. D., ed. The Bantu-Speaking Peoples of Southern Africa.
Hammons, Cornel I. Looking for a Kidnapper.
Hammons, Jim, ed. Organization Development & Management.
Hamner, Charles E., et al. Sperm Capacitation.
Hamner, Clay, jt. auth. see Organ, Dennis W.
Hamner, Earl, Jr. The Homecoming.
Hamner, Robert D. Derek Walcott.
Hamner, W. Clay. Organizational Shock.
Hamner, W. Clay, jt. auth. see Tosi, Henry L.
Hamner, W. Clay, jt. ed. see Tosi, Henry L.
Hamnett, I. Social Anthropology & Law.
Hamori, Laszlo. Dangerous Journey. MacMillian, Annabelle, tr.
--Dangerous Journey. MacMillan, Annabelle, tr.
Hamp, Eric P., ed. Proceedings: Papers on Eskimo & Aleut Linguistics.
Hampden-Turner, Charles. Gentlemen & Tradesmen: The Values of Economic Catastrophe.
Hampe, Johann C. A Book of Christian Faith: Questions & Answers for the Twentieth Century. Robertson, Edwin H., tr.
--To Die Is Gain: The Experience of One's Own Death.
Hampe, Johann C., tr. see Bonhoeffer, Dietrich.
Hampel, Robert L. The Last Little Citadel: American High Schools since 1940.
Hamperl, H. & Ackermann, L. V. Illustrated Tumor Nomenclature.
Hampsch, George H. The Theory of Communism.
Hampshire, Jack. Prams, Bassinets & Mailcarts.
Hampshire, Nick. Commodore 64 Graphics.
Hampson, Anne. The Dawn Is Golden.
--Desire.
--Enchantment.
Hampson, Norman. A Social History of the French Revolution.
Hampson, Sarah E. The Construction of Personality.
Hampton, Christopher. Treats.
Hampton, David. Behavioral Concepts in Management.
Hamre, Leif. Leap into Danger. Ramsden, Evelyn, tr.
--Leap into Danger.
--Operation Arctic. Ryen, Dag, tr. from Norwegian.
Hamrick, Kathy, jt. auth. see Baker, Allen.
Hamsher, Donald H., ed. Communications System Engineering Handbook.
Hamsun, Knut. Hunger.
--Victoria.
--The Women at the Pump. Stallybrass, Oliver & Stallybrass, Gunnvor, trs. from Norwegian.
Han, Henry H., ed. World in Transition: Challenges to Human Rights, Development & World Order.
Han, Man-Chung & Kim, Chu-Wan. Sectional Human Anatomy: Correlated with CT & MRI.
Han, Seong S. Cell Biology.
--Human Microscopic Anatomy.
Han, Sung-Joo, jt. ed. see Curtis, Gerald L.
Hanack, Michael. Conformation Theory. Newmann, H. C., tr.
Hanami, Tadashi. Labor Relations in Japan Today.
--Labor Relations in Japan Today.
Hanamura, E. E., jt. ed. see Kubo, S. R.
Hanan, J. J., et al. Greenhouse Management.
Hanan, Mack. Accelerated Growth Planning: Profit Improvement Strategies for Consumer, Industrial, & Service Business Game Plans.
--Fast-Growth Management: How to Improve Profits with Entrepreneurial Stategies.
--Leading Edge Growth Strategies: New Approaches for Accelerated Business Growth & Premium Profits in the Next Twenty Years.
Hanan, Mack, et al. Success Strategies for the New Sales Manager.
--Systems Selling Strategies: How to Justify Premium Prices for Commodity Products.
Hanawalt, Philip C., jt. auth. see Smith, Kendric C.
Hanby, Jeannette. Lions Share.
Hanchett, Elizabeth J. An Adventure in TV Land.
Hanckel, Frances & Cunningham, John. A Way of Love, a Way of Life: A Young Person's Introduction to What It Means to Be Gay.
Hancock, Edward, jt. auth. see Hancock, Sheila.
Hancock, Harry L., jt. auth. see Crooks, Thomas C.
Hancock, Sir Keith. Professing History.
Hancock, Leslie & Krieger, Morris. The C Primer.
Hancock, Norman N. Matrix Analysis of Electrical Machinery.
Hancock, P. L., ed. Multiple Deformation in Ductile & Brittle Rocks: A Selection of Papers Presented at the International Conference on Multiple Deformation & Foliation Development, Bemagui, NSW, Australia, 4-10 Feb. 1984.
Hancock, P. L., et al, eds. Planar & Linear Fabrics of Deformed Rocks: A Selection of Papers Delivered at an International Conference held at ETH Zurich 30 August to 2 September 1982.
Hancock, Sheila & Hancock, Edward. Connections: Ideas for Writing.
Hancock, Sibyl. Bill Pickett: First Black Rodeo Star.
Hancock, Sibyl & Cauley, Lorinda B. Bill Pickett: First Black Rodeo Star.
Hancock, Virginia. Brahms's Choral Compositions & His Library of Early Music. Buelow, George J., ed.
Hancock, Walton C., jt. auth. see Karger, Delmar W.
Hancock, William A. Saving Money Through Ten-Year Trusts.
--The Small Business Legal Advisor.
Hancock, William K. Country & Calling.
Hand, David. Martha Armstrong-Hand's Living Dolls.
Hand, David, jt. auth. see Martin, Nancy.
Hand, Herbert H., jt. auth. see Hollingsworth, A. Thomas.
Hand, Morton H., jt. ed. see Kurian, Milton.
Hand, Robert. Planets in Synthesis: Interpreting the Whole Horoscope.
--Planets in Youth: Patterns of Early Development.
Hand, Wayland D. Superstitions from North Carolina.
Handa, Hajime & Barnett, H. J., eds. Cerebral Ischemia: Clinical & Experimental Approach.
Handa, R. L. The State of the Nation: Presidential Addresses to Parliament from Dr. Rajendra Prasad to Neelam Sanjiva Reddy.
Handegord, Gustav O., jt. auth. see Hutcheon, Neil B.
Handel, George F. & Brown, Howard M. Tamerlano.
Handel, S. Diccionario De Electronica.
Handel, Warren. Ethnomethodology: How People Make Sense.
Handel, Warren H., jt. auth. see Lauer, Robert H.
Handelman, Howard, ed. The Politics of Agrarian Change in Asia & Latin America.
Handelman, Theodore. The Old People.
Handford, Martin. Find Waldo.
--Where's Waldo Now?
Handisyde, Cecil C. Everyday Details.
Handke, Peter. The Left-Handed Woman. Manheim, Ralph, tr. from Ger.
--A Moment of True Feeling. Manheim, Ralph, tr. from Ger.
--Short Letter, Long Farewell. Manheim, Ralph, tr. from Ger.
--A Sorrow Beyond Dreams. Manheim, Ralph, tr. from Ger.
--Three by Peter Handke.
--Two Novels by Peter Handke.
Handl, Irene. The Sioux. Gottlieb, Robert, ed.
Handleman, Jan S., jt. auth. see Powers, Michael D.

Authors

Handler, Andrew. Dori: The Life & Times of Theodor Herzl in Budapest, 1860-1878.
Handler, Joel F. The Coercive Social Worker: British Lessons for American Social Services.
Handler, Joel F., et al. Lawyers & the Pursuit of Legal Right.
Handlin, Mary, jt. auth. see Handlin, Oscar.
Handlin, Mary F., jt. auth. see Handlin, Oscar.
Handlin, Oscar. Boston's Immigrants.
--Newcomers: Negroes & Puerto Ricans in a Changing Metropolis.
Handlin, Oscar & Handlin, Mary. Dimensions of Liberty.
Handlin, Oscar & Handlin, Mary F. Commonwealth: A Study of the Role of Government in the American Economy, Massachusetts, 1774-1861.
Handly, Robert & Neff, Pauline. Anxiety & Panic Attacks: Their Cause & Cure; The Life Plus Five-Point Program for Conquering Fear.
Handmaker, Hirsch & Lowenstein, Jerold M., eds. Nuclear Medicine in Clinical Pediatrics.
Handoo, Jawaharlal, ed. Folklore of Rajasthan.
Hands, Barbara. The West Highland White Terrier.
Hands, Hargrave. Puppy Sees.
Hands, Hargrave, illus. Duckling Sees.
Hands, Rina, tr. see Thomasson, Henri.
Handy, Bruce, jt. ed. see Green, Joey.
Handy, Carol. The Dragons of Rizvania.
Handy, E. Craighill, et al. Ancient Hawaiian Civilization.
Handy, Robert T. American Religious Depression 1925-1935. Wolf, Richard C., ed.
--Protestant Quest for a Christian America, 1830-1930. Wolf, Richard C., ed.
Handy, Toni. The Play Begins.
Hane, Mikiso, tr. see Maruyama, Masao.
Haney, C. Michele & Boenisch, Edmond W., Jr. StressMap: Finding Your Pressure Points.
Haney, Jack V. From Italy to Muscovy: The Life & Works of Maxim the Greek.
Haney, Joy. The Carpenter. Wallace, Mary, ed.
Haney, Margaret, jt. auth. see Alpaugh, Patricia.
Haney, William M., III, jt. auth. see Gazvoda, Edward A., Jr.
Hanff, Helene. Eighty-Four, Charing Cross Road.
--Q's Legacy.
Hanfmann, George M. The Season Sarcophagus in Dumbarton Oaks.
Hanft, Robert. Pine Across the Mountain: California's McCloud River Railroad.
Hangin, John G. Mongolian Epigraphical Dictionary in Reverse Listing.
Hanh, Thich N. The Miracle of Mindfulness! A Manual on Meditation.
Hanham, H. J., ed. see Buckle, Henry T.
Hanhardt, John G., intro. by. Video Culture: A Critical Investigation.
Hanif, M., jt. auth. see Brewer, K. R.
Hanigan, Maureen. Secrets of Successful Speaking.
Hanin, I., jt. ed. see Usdin, E.
Hank, Mary K., jt. auth. see Smalley, Regina L.
Hankamer, Jorge, jt. auth. see Ladusaw, William A.
Hankamer, Jorge, ed. see Akmajian, Adrian.
Hankamer, Jorge, ed. see Bresnan, Joan W.
Hankamer, Jorge, ed. see Carlson, Greg N.
Hankamer, Jorge, ed. see Goldsmith, John A.
Hankamer, Jorge, ed. see Kroch, Anthony S.
Hankamer, Jorge, ed. see Leben, William.
Hankamer, Jorge, ed. see Milsark, Gary L.
Hankamer, Jorge, ed. see Partee, Barbara H.
Hankamer, Jorge, ed. see Schauber, Ellen.
Hankamer, Jorge, ed. see Shaw, Patricia A.
Hankamer, Jorge, ed. see Stampe, David.
Hanke, Howard. The Thompson Chain Reference Bible Survey.
Hankins, Norman E. How to Become the Person You Want to Be.
Hankinson, R. L. & Hankinson, R. L., Jr. Landman's Encyclopedia.
Hanks, Billy. If You Love Me.
Hanks, Geoffrey. Children of Naples.
--Helen: The Story of Helen Keller.
Hanks, Kurt, jt. auth. see Belliston, Larry.
Hanks, Lindsey. Midnight Deception.
--Savage Surrender.
Hanks, Patrick, ed. see Urdang, Laurence.
Hanks, R. J. & Hill, R. W. Modeling Crop Responses to Irrigation in Relation to Soils, Climate & Salinity.
Hanks, Robert J., jt. auth. see Cottrell, Alvin J.
Hanle, Zack. Cooking Wild Game.
Hanley, Boniface. No Greater Love: Maximilian Kolbe.
Hanley, Hope. Hope Hanley's Patterns for Needlepoint.
--Needlepoint.
--Needlepoint Styles For Period Furniture.
Hanley, Mary. Centralized Processing--Recent Trends & Current Status: A Review & Synthesis of the Literature.
Hanley, Peter C. & Hanley, Rosemary A. America's Best Recipes: State Fair Blue Ribbon Winners.
Hanley, Rosemary A., jt. auth. see Hanley, Peter C.
Hanley, Susan B. & Yamamura, Kozo. Economic & Demographic Change in Preindustrial Japan, 1600-1868.
Hanley, W. S. & Cooper, M. J. Man & the Australian Environment.
Hanlon, Martin D., et al. Quality of Worklife Programs & Organizational Structure & Change: The Case of Parkside Hospital.
Hanmer, Davina. Diana: The Fashion Princess.
Hanna, Betty E. Lantern in the Valley.
Hanna, David. Angel: Gypsy Hustler.
--Bogart.
--The Capri Affair.
--Opera House Murders.
Hanna, David C., tr. see Svelto, Orazio.
Hanna, Erian L. Two Plays: Uncle Viva & the Lost Equilibrium.
Hanna, Frank A. State Income Differentials, 1919-1954.
Hanna, J. Gordon, jt. auth. see Siggia, Sidney.
Hanna, John. How to Build Gulfweed.
Hanna, Ken. In Search of Spiritual Leadership.
Hanna, Robert. Sketches of Nebraska.
Hannah, Barbara. Victims of the Creative Spirits.
Hannah, Donald, jt. ed. see Rutherford, Anna.
Hannah, Evelyn, jt. auth. see Nottingham, Carolyn W.
Hannah, Gail. Classroom Spaces & Places: Sixty-Five Projects for Improving Your Classroom.
Hannah, John, ed. Inerrancy & the Church.
Hannah, W. H. Bobs, Kipling's General: The Life of Field-Marshall Earl Roberts of Kandahar, VC.
Hannaher, William J., tr. see Kis, Danilo.
Hannam, Alan G., jt. ed. see Sessle, Barry J.
Hannan, Kate, jt. auth. see Brugger, Bill.
Hannan, Michael. Peter Schulthorpe: His Music & Ideas 1929-1979.
Hannay, Allen. Love & Other Natural Disasters.
Hanneman, Walter W. Daily Assignment Problems in First Year Chemistry.
Hannibal, Edward & Boris, Robert. Blood Feud.
Hannigan, Frank, jt. auth. see Watson, Tom.
Hannigan, Jane A., jt. ed. see Vandergrift, Kay E.
Hannon, jt. auth. see Thomas, Kurt.
Hannon, Ralph H. Basic Technical Mathematics with Calculus.
Hannula, Reino. Computers & Programming: A System 360-370 Assembler Language Approach.
Hannum, H. G., jt. auth. see Lohner, Edgar.
Hannum, Sara & Chase, John T., eds. To Play Man Number One.
--Wind Is Round.
Hanrahan, John. Government by Contract.
Hanrahan, John D. & Gruenstein, Peter. Lost Frontier: The Marketing of Alaska.
Hanratty, T. J., et al, eds. Two Phase Annular & Dispersed Flow: Proceedings of the International Symposium, University of Pisa, Italy, 24-29 June 1984.
Hansard-Winkler, Glenda A., jt. auth. see Feingold, S. Norman.
Hansberry, Lorraine. Raisin in the Sun. Bd. with The Sign in Sidney Brustein's Window. NAL.
Hansburg, Mary E. Myth, Faith & Hermeneutics.
Hansel, jt. auth. see Cohen.
Hansel, Tim. What Kids Need Most in a Dad.
Hansen, Alvin H. Business Cycles & National Income.
Hansen, Alvin H., jt. auth. see McDonough, Martin.
Hansen, Barbara. Mexican Cookery.
Hansen, Bent. Study in the Theory of Inflation.
Hansen, Caryl. I Think I'm Having a Baby.
--Your Choice: A Young Woman's Guide to Making Decisions about Unmarried Pregnancy.
Hansen, Cindy S., ed. Return of Try This One.
--Try This One Strikes Again.
Hansen, Dennis R. Michigan Cross Country Skiing Atlas.
Hansen, Elo H., jt. auth. see Ruzicka, Jaromir.
Hansen, F. R. The Breakdown of Capitalism: A History of the Idea in Western Marxism.
Hansen, Gary B., jt. auth. see Arrington, Leonard J.
Hansen, George & Anderson, Larry. How the IRS Seizes Your Dollars & How to Fight Back.
Hansen, H. H. & Roth, M., eds. Lung Cancer, 1980: Post-Graduate Course II.
Hansen, H. Morris. The Wealth Transfer of Inflation: How to Compute It, Account for It, & Profit from It.
Hansen, H. Reese & Neeleman, Stanley D. Utah Probate System.
Hansen, J. P. & McDonald, I. R. The Theory of Simple Liquids.
Hansen, James C. Counseling Process & Procedures.
Hansen, John A., jt. auth. see Lund, Robert T.
Hansen, Joseph. Brandstetter & Others.
--Early Graves.
--Job's Year.
--Skinflick.
--Skinflick.
--A Smile in His Lifetime.
Hansen, Klaus J. Mormonism & the American Experience.
Hansen, L. Sunny, jt. auth. see Tennyson, W. Wesley.
Hansen, Lilian L. Rosa: A True Story.
Hansen, Martin A. Lucky Kristoffer. Egglishaw, John J., tr. from Danish.
Hansen, Paul, tr. The Nine Monks.
Hansen, R. Gaurth & Wyse, Bonita W. Nutritional Quality Index of Foods.
Hansen, Robert C. Geometric Theory of Diffraction.
Hansen, Ron. Assassination of Jesse James by the Coward Robert Ford.
--Desperadoes.
Hansen, Rosanna. The Fairytale Book of Ballet.
Hansen, Skylar. Roaming Free: Wild Horses of the American West.
Hanser, James. The Glorious Hour of Lieutenant Monroe.
Hanshumaker, James, jt. auth. see Zorn, Jay.
Han Sin-Fong. The Chinese in Sabah, East Malaysia.
Hanslick, Eduard. The Horn: Music Criticisms.
Hanson. Dictionary of Economics & Commerce.
Hanson, Anne M. Red Tape & Broken Hearts: Tragedy in Veterans Hospitals.
Hanson, Bradley. The Call of Silence: Discovering Christian Meditation.
Hanson, C. Recent Advances in Liquid - Liquid Extraction.
Hanson, Dirk. The Incursion.
--The New Alchemists: Silicon Valley & the Microelectronics Revolution.
--The New Alchemists: Silicon Valley & the Microelectronics Revolution.
Hanson, Eric O. Catholic Politics in China & Korea.
Hanson, Erle C. East Shore & Suburban Railway.
Hanson, F. A. & Hanson, Louise. Counterpoint in Maori Culture.
Hanson, Howard. Harmonic Materials of Modern Music: Resources of the Tempered Scale.
Hanson, J. A. Growth in Open Economics.
Hanson, J. R. Introduction to Steroid Chemistry.
Hanson, James A. & Neal, Craig R. Interest Rate Policies in Selected Developing Countries, 1970-1982.
Hanson, James A. & Rocha, Roberto. High Interest Rates, Spreads & the Costs of Intermediation.
Hanson, Joan. More Synonyms: Shout & Yell & Other Words That Mean the Same Thing but Look & Sound As Different as Loud & Noisy.
--Plurals.
--Similes: As Gentle As a Lamb, Spin Like a Top, & Other "Like" or "As" Comparisons Between Unlike Things.
--Still More Antonyms: Together & Apart & Other Words That Are As Different in Meaning As Rise & Fall.
--Still More Homonyms: Night & Knight & Other Words That Sound the Same but Look As Different As Ball & Bawl.
Hanson, John R. Trade in Transition: Exports from the Third World, Eighteen Forty to Nineteen Hundred.
Hanson, John S., tr. see Fridrichsen, Anton.
Hanson, Judy B. Spirit of the Winding Water: A Novel of the Epic 1877 Wilderness Plight of the Nez Perce Indians.
Hanson, June A. Summer of the Stallion.
Hanson, Kenneth O., tr. see Han Yu.
Hanson, Louise, jt. auth. see Hanson, F. A.
Hanson, Map. Diet Management for Ulcerative Colitis: Menus, Recipes & Methods of Food Preparation for Anti-Inflammatory Treatment.
Hanson, Marilyn & Segura, Robert. To Baby with Love: Your Pre-Natal Nutrition Diary.
Hanson, Mark D. Contemporary Travis Picking: Solo Style.
Hanson, Marvin L. & Barrett, Richard H. Fundamentals of Orofacial Myology.
Hanson, Neil, compiled by. The Best Pubs of Great Britain, 1987-1988.
Hanson, Owen. Design of Computer Data Files.
Hanson, Paul D. The Dawn of Apocalyptic: The Historical & Sociological Roots of Jewish Apocalyptic Eschatology.
--The Diversity of Scripture: Trajectories in the Confessional Heritage.
--Dynamic Transcendence: The Correlation of Confessional Heritage & Contemporary Experience in a Biblical Model of Divine Activity.
Hanson, Paul D., ed. Visionaries & Their Apocalypses.
Hanson, Peter. The Joy of Stress.
Hanson, Philip, jt. ed. see Dawisha, Karen.
Hanson, R. Galen. A New Day.
--A New Day Still Dawning: A Sequel to Surgery in Personal Experience & a Reaffirmation of the Joy of Living.
--Platforms on the Prairies: A Public Speaker's Odyssey from Southside Gym to St. Louis & Beyond.
Hanson, R. P. The Attractiveness of God: Essays in Christian Doctrine.
Hanson, Richard & Reynolds, Rebecca. Child Development: Concepts, Issues, & Readings.
Hanson, Richard E. The Manager's Guide to Copying & Duplicating.
Hanson, Richard S. The Comings of God: Meditations for the Advent Season.
--The Future of the Great Planet Earth: What Does Biblical Prophecy Mean for You?
Hanson, Richard W., jt. ed. see Mehlman, Myron A.
Hanson, Richard W., ed. see University of Nebraska Medical School Symposium Staff.
Hansson, Bjorn A. The Stockholm School & the Development of Dynamic Method.
Hansson, C. B., ed. Prepare for Science.
Hansson, Carola, et al. Moscow Women: Thirteen Interviews. Bothmer, Gerry, tr. Lapidus, Gail W., intro. by.
Hansten, Philip D. Drug Interactions.
Hans-Ulrich, Rieker. The Yoga of Light: The Classic Esoteric Handbook of Kundalini Yoga. Becherer, Elsy, tr.
Hantle, Terry W. & Harris, John. Assessment in American Higher Education: Issues & Contexts. Adelman, Clifford, ed.
Hanvey, Christopher. Social Work with Mentally Handicapped People.
Hanxian, Luo. Economic Change in Rural China.
Han Yu. Growing Old Alive. Hanson, Kenneth O., tr. from Chinese.
Hapgood, David. Africa: From Independence to Tomorrow.
Hapgood, David & Richardson, David. Monte Cassino.
Hapgood, Hatchins. Types from City Streets.
Hapgood, Marilyn. Supporting the Learning Teacher: A Source Book for Teacher Centers.
Happe, Bernard. Dictionary of Audio-Visual Terms.
Happel, et al. Base Metal Oxide Catalysts for the Petrochemical, Petroleum, & Chemical Industries.
Happel, J. & Jordan, D. Chemical Process Economics.
Happel, Stephen & Tracy, David. A Catholic Vision.
Happey, Russell. The Colorado Kid: Memoirs of a Life Nurtured by Faith.
Haq, Bilal U., ed. Calcareous Nannoplankton.
Haq, Bilal U. & Milliman, John D., eds. Marine Geology & Oceanography of Arabian Sea & Coastal Pakistan.
Hara, Buronson & Hara, Tetsuo. Fist of the North Star. Horibuchi, Seiji, ed. Fujii, Satoru & Burke, Fred, trs.
--Fist of the North Star. Horibuchi, Seiji, ed. Fujii, Satoru & Burke, Fred, trs.
--Fist of the North Star. Horibuchi, Seiji, ed. Fujii, Satoru & Burke, Fred, trs.
--Fist of the North Star. Horibuchi, Seiji, ed. Fujii, Satoru & Burke, Fred, trs.
Hara, O. Hashnu. Practical Yoga: Thoroughly Practical Lessons upon the Philosophy & Practice of Yoga.
Hara, Tetsuo, jt. auth. see Buronson.
Hara, Tetsuo, jt. auth. see Hara, Buronson.
Harahan, John, ed. Design in General Education.
Harary, Frank, jt. auth. see Hage, Per.
Harary, Frank & Maybee, John S., eds. Graphs & Applications: Proceedings of the First Colorado Symposium on Graph Theory.
Harasowska, Marta, ed. Ukrainian Political Prisoners in the U. S. S. R. A Directory.
Haraszti-Takacs, Marianna. Spanish Painting from Zurbaran to Goya.
Haraszti-Takacs, Marianne. Spanish Painting from the Primitives to Ribera. Halapy, Lili, tr.
Haraszty, Eszter. The Embroiderer's Portfolio of Flower Designs.
Harbage, Alfred. Shakespeare's Audience.
Harbage, Alfred, ed. see Shakespeare, William.
Harbeke, G., jt. auth. see Greenaway, D. L.
Harben, Philip. Cookery Encyclopedia.
Harbert, Earl N. Critical Essays on Henry Adams.
Harbert, Earl N. & DiGaetani, John L. Writing for Action: A Guide for the Health Care Professional.
Harbert, Earl N., jt. auth. see DiGaetani, John L.
Harbert, John, et al, eds. Textbook of Nuclear Medicine, Vol. 2: Clinical Applications.
Harbert, Wally, jt. auth. see Dexter, Margaret.
Harbert, Wally & Rogers, Pat, eds. Community-Based Social Care: The Avon Experience.
Harbhajan Singh Khalsa. Ancient Art of Self-Healing. Siri Amir Singh Khalsa, ed.
Harbin, J. William. When a Pastor Search Committee Comes... or Doesn't.
Harbinson, W. A. The Illustrated Elvis.
--Stryker's Kingdom.
Harbison, Craig. The Last Judgment in Sixteenth Century Northern Europe: a Study of the Relation Between Art & the Reformation.
Harbison, E. Harris. The Age of Reformation.
Harbison, Samuel P. & Steele, Guy L., Jr. C: A Reference Manual.
Harbison, Winfred, jt. auth. see Kelly, Alfred H.

Authors

Harbo, Ole & Kajberg, Leif, eds. Theory & Application of Information Research: Proceedings of the Second International Research Forum of Information Science, 2nd Royal School Librarianship, Copenhagen, Aug. 1977.
Harbold, Harry. Sanitary Engineering: Problems & Calculations for the Professional Engineer.
Harborne, J. B. Introduction to Ecological Biochemistry.
--Introduction to Ecological Biochemistry.
--Phytochemical Methods.
Harborne, J. B. & Mabry, T. J. The Flavonoids: Advances in Research, 1975-1981.
Harborne, J. B., ed. see Phytochemical Society Staff.
Harborne, J. B., ed. see Phytochemical Society Symposium, No.11, University of Ghent, Belgium, Sept. 1973.
Harborne, Jeffrey B., ed. Comparative Biochemistry of Flavonoids.
Harbottle, Thomas B. Dictionary of Battles.
--Dictionary of Historical Allusions.
Harbury, C. D., ed. Workbook in Introductory Economics.
Harcourt, jt. auth. see Mein.
Hard, Frederick, frwd. by. Henry Lee McFee.
Hard, Walter. Vermont Neighbors.
Hardacre, Helen. Kurozumikyo & the New Religions of Japan.
Hardcastle, Bruce B., jt. ed. see Tinkham, Sandra S.
Hardcastle, Kenneth, jt. auth. see Abrash, Henry.
Hardcastle, Michael. One Kick.
Hardcastle, Michael see Milne, John.
Hardee, Melvene D., ed. Personnel Services in Education.
Harden, M. L., jt. auth. see Lamb, M. W.
Hardenbrook, Harry. Walker's Remodeling Estimator's Reference Book.
Hardenburg, Robert E., et al. Commercial Storage of Fruits, Vegetables & Florist & Nursery Stocks.
Härder, Janet. Letters from Carrie.
Harder, Kelsie B., ed. Illustrated Dictionary of Place Names: United States & Canada.
Harder, Paul, et al. Government Spending & the Nonprofit Sector in San Francisco.
Hardesty, Larry L. Use of Slide-Tape Presentations in Academic Libraries.
Hardgrave, Robert L., Jr. India: Government & Politics in a Developing Nation.
--India: Government & Politics in a Developing Nation.
Hardgrove, Carol B. & Dawson, Rosemary B. Parents & Children in the Hospital: The Family's Role in Pediatrics.
Hardie, C. G. Dante's Comedy As Self-Analysis & Integration.
Hardie, D. W. & Davidson Pratt, J. A History of the Modern British Chemical Industry.
Hardie, Lawrence A. Sedimentation of the Modern Carbonate Tidal Flats of Northwest Andros Island, Bahamas.
Hardie, Sean & Lloyd, John. Prince Harry's First Quiz Book.
Hardiman, George W. & Zernich, Theodore, eds. Foundations for Curriculum Development & Evaluation in Art Education.
Hardiman, N. J. Exploring University Mathematics.
Hardin, James W. & Arena, James W. Human Poisoning from Native & Cultivated Plants.
Harding, Albert. The President's Gold Mine.
Harding, Alison, jt. auth. see Holden, Edith.
Harding, Brian. American Literature in Context II, 1830-1865.
Harding, D. E. On Having No Head: Zen & the Rediscovery of the Obvious.
Harding, D. W. The Iron Age in Lowland Britain.
Harding, J. M., jt. auth. see Corballis, Richard.
Harding, James. Maurice Chevalier: His Life, 1888-1972.
Harding, John. Victims & Offenders: Needs & Responsibilities.
Harding, John, ed. Probation & the Community: A Practice & Policy Reader.
Harding, Neil. Lenin's Political Thought.
Harding, Richard M. & Mills, F. John. Aviation Medicine.
Harding, T. D. The Chess Computer Book.
Harding, Tim. Nimzowitsch Defence.
Harding, Vanessa, jt. ed. see Keene, Derek.
Harding, Vincent, ed. see Thurman, Howard.
Harding, Wade G. The Thing You Love Most.
Harding, Walter, ed. see Thoreau, Henry David.
Harding, Walter A., jt. auth. see Meltzer, Milton.
Harding, William H. Mill Song.
--Rainbow.
--Young Hart.
Hardinge, E. Introduction to Modern American Spiritualism.
Hardis. Titus Andronicus.
Hardison, Richard. Upon the Shoulders of Giants: The Shaping of the Industrial West.
Hardisty, George & Hardisty, Margaret. Successful Financial Planning.
Hardisty, M. W. Biology of the Cyclostomes.
Hardisty, Margaret, jt. auth. see Hardisty, George.
Hardman, M. L., jt. auth. see Drew, C. J.
Hardon, John A. Christianity in the Twentieth Century.
--Holiness in the Church.
Hardwick, Elizabeth. Seduction & Betrayal: Women & Literature.
Hardwick, Michael. A Guide to Jane Austen.
--Literary Atlas & Gazetteer of the British Isles.
--Sherlock Holmes: My Life & Crimes.
Hardwick, Mollie. The Crystal Dove.
Hardwicke, Cedric. A Victorian in Orbit.
Hardy & Rossier. Spinal Cord Injuries.
Hardy, Alan G. & Elson, Reginald. Practical Management of Spinal Injuries for Nurses.
Hardy, Alister. Open Sea: Its Natural History.
Hardy, Atlanta G. Like a Winter Cloud.
Hardy, C. Your Money & Your Life.
Hardy, C. Colburn. Your Money & Your Life: How to Plan Your Long-Range Financial Security.
--Your Money & Your Life: Planning Your Financial Future.
Hardy, C. Colburn & Wiener, Howard J. Personal Pension Plan Strategies for Physicians.
Hardy, Clyde & Martin, Nancy. Your Roles As a Medical Assistant.
Hardy, F. Lane & Youse, Bevan K. Mathematics for the Managerial, Social & Life Sciences.
Hardy, George & Harris, Nathaniel. A D. H. Lawrence Album.
Hardy, Gerry & Hardy, Sue. Fifty Hikes in Connecticut: A Guide to Short Walks & Day Hikes Around the Nutmeg State.
Hardy, H. L., et al, eds. Epidemiology & Detection of Lead Toxicity.
Hardy, Harriet L., jt. auth. see Hamilton, Alice.
Hardy, James D. Critical Surgical Illness.
Hardy, Jean. Values in Social Policy: Nine Contradictions.
Hardy, John. A Guide to Osterley Park House.
Hardy, Lane F. Finite Mathematics for the Managerial, Social, & Life Sciences.
Hardy, Lane F. & Youse, Bevan K. Mathematics for the Managerial, Social, & Life Sciences.
Hardy, Leslie K., jt. auth. see Coutts, Lyn C.
Hardy, M. J. Sea, Sky & Stars: An Illustrated History of Grumman Aircraft.
Hardy, Margaret E. & Conway, Mary, eds. Role Theory: Perspectives for Health Professionals.
Hardy, Max. Two Over One Game Force.
Hardy, Michael, et al. A New Regime for the Oceans.
Hardy, Otto, tr. see Pachman, Ludek.
Hardy, Owen B., jt. auth. see Lifton, James.
Hardy, Peter. Historians of Medieval India: Studies in Indo-Muslim Historical Writing.
Hardy, R. W. Travels in the Interior of Mexico in 1825, 1826, 1827 & 1828: In Baja California & Around the Sea of Cortes.
Hardy, Ralph, et al. The Weather Book.
Hardy, Rhea C. Thoughts for Reflection.
Hardy, Ronald. The Wings of the Wind.
Hardy, Steven & Sterling, Leon. Logic Programming Techniques.
Hardy, Sue, jt. auth. see Hardy, Gerry.
Hardy, Thomas. Jude the Obscure. Slack, Robert C., ed.
--Life's Little Ironies.
--The Mayor of Casterbridge.
--Return of the Native.
--Tess of the D'Urbervilles. Elledge, Scott, ed.
--Tess of the D'Urbervilles.
--Tess of the D'Urbervilles.
Hare, Cyril. When the Wind Blows.
Hare, David. Fanshen.
--Slag.
--Teeth 'n' Smiles.
Hare, Douglas. Single Ticket to China.
Hare, Eric B. Fulton's Footprints in Fiji.
--Treasure from Haunted Pagoda.
Hare, F. K. & Kenneth-Thomas, M. K. Climate Canada.
Hare, Lloyd C. The Greatest American Woman, Lucretia Mott.
Hare, Lorraine. Who Needs Her?
Hare, Maud. Negro Musicians & Their Music.
Hare, Paul, et al, eds. Hungary: A Decade of Economic Reform.
Hare, R. M. see McMurring, Sterling M.
Hare, Ronald. Pomp & Pestilence.
Hare, Van C., Jr. Introduction to Programming: A BASIC Approach.
Harelson, Randy. Amazing Days.
Harf, James E., jt. auth. see Burgess, Philip M.
Harfenist, Sylvan. Refrigeration License Manual.
Harger, R. O. Synthetic Aperture Radar Systems Theory & Design.
Hargie, Owen & McCartan, Patrick J. Social Skills Training & Psychiatric Nursing.
Hargittai, I. Sulphone Molecular Structures: Conformation & Geometry from Electron Diffraction & Microwave Spectroscopy; Structural Variations.
Hargrave, Catherine P. History of Playing Cards & a Bibliography of Cards & Gaming.
Hargrave, Eduard C. The Path to Parnassus.
Hargrave, Harry A. Unasked Questions: Seven Stories & a Novella.
Hargrave, Lydon L. Feathers from Sand Dune Cave: A Basketmaker Cave Near Navajo Mountain, Utah.
Hargreaves, et al. Management of Anterior Traumatized Teeth of Children.
Hargreaves, David. Adult Literacy & Broadcasting: The BBC's Experience.
Hargreaves, David H. The Challenge for the Comprehensive School: Culture, Curriculum & Community.
Hargreaves, Reginald, jt. auth. see Melville, Lewis.
Hargreaves, Roger. Albert the Alphabetical Elephant.
--Hippo Leaves Home.
--Little Miss Helpful Plans a Party: A Pop-Up Book.
--Mr. Daydream.
--Mr. Daydream.
--Mr. Noisy.
--Mr. Noisy.
Hargrove, Ann. Showings, Healing & the Ordinary Person.
Hargrove, Erwin C. Presidential Leadership: Personality & Political Style.
Hargrove, Hondon B. Buffalo Soldiers in Italy: Black Americans in World War II.
Hargrove, John O., jt. auth. see California Continuing Eduacation of the Bar Staff.
Hargrove, John O., jt. auth. see California Continuing Education of the Bar Staff.
Hargrove, June E. The Life & Work of Albert Carrier-Belleuse.
Haried, Andrew A., et al. Advanced Accounting.
Haring, Bernard. Law of Christ.
Haring, C. H. Empire in Brazil: A New World Experiment with Monarchy.
Haring, Firth. Greek Revival.
--The Women Who Went Away.
Haring, Norris G. & Phillips, E. L. Teaching Special Children.
Haring, Norris G., jt. ed. see Lovitt, Thomas C.
Haring, Scott. Green Circle Blues.
Haringer, Monica, jt. auth. see Schwarz, Werner.
Harish-Chandra. Harmonic Analysis on Reductive P-adic Groups.
Harithas, James, jt. auth. see Delehanty, Suzanne.
Hark, Ina R. Edward Lear.
Harkavy, Robert E. Great Power Competition for Overseas Bases.
Harkavy, Robert E. & Neuman, Stephanie G., eds. The Lessons of Recent Wars in the Third World: Approaches & Case Studies.
Harker, Carlton. Self-Funding of Welfare Benefits.
Harker, Margret F. Victorian & Edwardian Photographs.
Harkess, Shirley, jt. ed. see Stromberg, Ann H.
Harkins, Harry L. Basketball's Pro-Set Playbook: The Complete Offensive Arsenal.
Harkins, Philip. The Day of the Drag Race.
Harkins, W. E., ed. see Novak, Arne.
Harkins, William E. Dictionary of Russian Literature.
Harkleroad, J. D. Horse Thief Trail.
Harl, Neil E. Farm Estate & Business Planning.
Harlan, Louis R. Separate & Unequal: Public School Campaigns & Racism in the Southern Seaboard States, 1901-1915.
Harlan, Louis R, et al, eds. see Washington, Booker T.
Harlan, N. E. Management Control in Airframe Subcontracting.
Harland, Henry, pseud. Grandison Mather. Fletcher, Ian & Stokes, John, eds.
Harland, James W. Inspection of Fracture Critical Bridge Members: Supplement to the Bridge Inspector's Training Manual.
Harland, W. A. & Orr, J. S., eds. Thyroid Hormone Metabolism.
Harlech, Pamela. Feast Without Fuss.
--Pamela Harlech's Practical Guide to Cooking, Entertaining & Household Management.
Harlem Youth Group Staff. Listen to the Children.
Harless, Dan. Discoveries.
Harley, Brian. Mate in Two Moves: The Two-Move Chess Problem Made Easy.
Harley, J. B. Maps for the Local Historian- a Guide to the British Sources.
Harley, J. L. & Lewis, D. H. The Flora & Vegetation of Britain: Origins & Change.
Harley, John B., et al, eds. Hematology Case Studies.
Harley, John P. An Elementary Human Anatomy Laboratory Textbook.
Harley, Robert, et al. What's It Worth? A Guide to Current Personal Injury Awards & Settlements.
Harlin, John, III. Climber's Guide to North America, Vol. 1: West Coast Rock Climbs.
Harlow, Jan, et al. The Good Age Cookbook: Recipes from the Institute for Creative Aging.
Harlow, John S. French Economic Planning.
Harlow, Neal. Maps & Surveys of the Pueblo Lands of Los Angeles.
Harlow, S. Ralph. Life After Death.
--Thoughts for Times Like These.
Harman, Gilbert. Change in View: Principles of Reasoning.
Harman, Helen S., ed. see International Association of Cooking Schools Members Staff.
Harman, John D., ed. Volunteerism in the Eighties: Fundamental Issues in Voluntary Action.
Harman, Lois S. Castle on the Prairie.
Harman, M. Clare, jt. auth. see Keatinge, W. R.
Harman, P. M. The Scientific Revolution.
Harman, Thomas L. Guide to the National Electrical Code, 1984.
Harmar, Hilary. Dogs: How to Train & Show Them.
Harmelin, William. Disability Insurance: In the Business Buy-Out Agreement.
Harmeling, Jean. The Incredible Will of H. R. Heartman.
Harmer, J. R., ed. see Lightfoot, J. B.
Harmetz, Aljean. The Making of the Wizard of Oz: Movie Magic & Studio Power in the Prime of MGM & the Miracle of Production No. 1060.
Harmin, Merrill, et al. Clarifying Values Through Subject Matter: Applications for the Classroom.
Harmon, David P., Jr., jt. auth. see Chou, Marylin.
Harmon, Margaret. The Engineering Medicine Man: The New Pioneer.
Harmon, Margaret, ed. Working with Words: Careers for Writers.
Harmon, Maurice. The Poetry of Thomas Kinsella.
Harmon, Maurice, ed. Irish Poetry after Yeats: Seven Poets.
Harmon, N. Paul, jt. auth. see Margolis, Neal.
Harmon, Paul. Small Business Management.
Harmon, Paul & Mayer, Ric. Evaluating Knowledge: Engineering Tools.
Harmon, R. Alec, ed. see Morley, Thomas.
Harmon, R. B. & Burger, M. A. An Annotated Guide to the Works of Dorothy L. Sayers.
Harmon, Robert E., ed. Cell Surface Carbohydrate Chemistry.
Harmon, William, jt. auth. see Rubin, Louis D., Jr.
Harms, E., ed. Drugs & Youth: The Challenge of Today.
Harms, Martin J. see Crump, Ralph W.
Harms, Paul. Presenting the Lessons: A Guide for Lectors.
Harms, Robert T. Finnish Structural Sketch.
Harmuth, H. F. Transmission of Information by Orthogonal Functions.
Harnack, Adolf. Militia Christi: The Christian Religion & the Military in the First Three Centuries. Gracie, David M., tr. from Ger.
Harnack, R. Victor, et al. Group Discussion: Theory & Technique.
Harnden, D. G., jt. ed. see Bridges, B. A.
Harnecker, Marta. Cuba: Dictatorship or Democracy?
Harned, David B. Creed & Personal Identity: The Meaning of the Apostles' Creed.
Harner, James L. Samuel Daniel & Michael Drayton: A Reference Guide.
Harner, Philip B. I Am of the Fourth Gospel: A Study in Johannine Usage & Thought. Reumann, John, ed.
--Understanding the Lord's Prayer.
Harnett, Bertram. Law, Lawyers, & Laymen: Making Sense Out of the American Legal System.
--Put the Law on Your Side: Strategies for Winning the Legal Game.
Harney, H. L., et al, eds. see Classical & Quantum Mechanical Aspects of Heavy Ion Collisions Symposium Staff.
Harney, Thomas E. AMDG--A History of Canisius College 1883-1913: Under the New York State Regents' Charter, on Washington Street, Buffalo.
Harnickell, E., jt. auth. see Walter, H.
Harnik, Peter & Jacobson, Michael F. Voodoo Science, Twisted Consumerism.
Harnish, Robert M., jt. auth. see Bach, Kent.
Harnishfeger, Lloyd C. Hunters of the Black Swamp.
Harnly, Caroline D. Agent Orange & the Vietnam Veteran: An Annotated Bibliography.
Haro, Carlos M. Criticism of Traditional Postsecondary School Admissions Criteria: A Search for Alternatives.
Haro, Michael S., et al. Explorations in Personal Health.
Harold, Frederick. Introduction to Computers Basic.
Harold U & Ribalow, Meir Z. The Great Jewish Chess Champions.
Haroutunian, Joseph. God with Us: A Theology of Transpersonal Life.
Harp, Carl. Love & Rage: Entries in a Prison Diary.
Harpaz, Ephraim, jt. auth. see Constant, Benjamin.
Harpe, P. De la see De la Harpe, P.

Authors

Harpe, Shideler & Hall, Wesley W. What Teenagers Want to Know.
Harper, Ann & Lewis, Glenn. The Big Beauty Book: Glamour for the Fuller-Figure Woman.
--The Big Beauty Book: Glamour for the Fuller-Figure Woman.
Harper, Charles A. Handbook of Components for Electronics.
--Handbook of Materials & Processes for Electronics.
--Handbook of Wiring, Cabling, & Interconnecting for Electronics.
Harper, Dennis O. Computer Education for Developing Nations.
Harper, Dennis O. & Stewart, James H. Run: Computer Education.
Harper, F. Principles of Arable Crop Production.
Harper, George M. Yeats's Golden Dawn.
Harper, J. Russell. Early Painters & Engravers in Canada.
Harper, J. W., ed. see Browning, Robert.
Harper, John C. Elements of Food Engineering.
Harper, Mary-Angela. Ascent to Excellence in Catholic Education: A Guide to Effective Decision-Making.
--Developing Performance Excellence in Catholic Educational Policymaking: A Handbook of Training Programs.
Harper, Michael S. Song: I Want a Witness.
Harper, Mike. Through France to the Med: By Canal to the Sea.
Harper, Nancy L., ed. Human Communication.
Harper, Patricia. Joint Practice: A Selected Annotated Bibliography.
Harper, Paula H. Daumier's Clowns: Les Saltimbanques et Les Parades, New Biographical & Political Functions for a Nineteenth Century Myth.
Harper, Prudence O. & Meyers, Pieter. Silver Vessels of the Sansanian Period: Royal Imagery. Preuss, Anne M. & Cone, Polly, eds.
Harper, Robert A. & Schmudde, Theodore H. Between Two Worlds: An Introduction to Geography.
Harper, Tim, jt. auth. see Coulby, David.
Harper, W. M. Management Accounting (Cost & Management Accounting)
Harper, Wilhemina. The Best of Bret Harte. Peters, Aimee, ed.
Harper, William C., ed. Toward a New Politics.
Harper, William G. The Texas Blue Laws.
Harpers, Ferry W. & Fogle, Sonja. Recent Advances in Leather Conservation: Proceedings of a Refresher Course Sponsored by FAIC, June,1984.
Harpool, Jack D., et al. System Analysis & Design Projects.
Harpporte, De see De Harpporte.
Harpsfield, Nicholas. Life & Death of St. Thomas More.
Harpur, Merrily. The Nightmares of Dream Topping.
Harr, John E. The Professional Diplomat.
Harrap Limited Staff, ed. American Southwest.
Harrell, Irene B., jt. auth. see Smith, B. J.
Harrell, John L. Regimental Steins.
Harrell, Karen F. The Constitutional & Political Aspects of the Legislative Veto.
Harrell, Pauline C., et al. Arrowhead Farm: 300 Years of New England Husbandry & Cooking.
Harrell, Sara G. Tomo-Chi-Chi.
Harrelson, Bud & Cohen, Joel H. How to Play Better Baseball.
Harren, Vince, et al, eds. Facilitating Student's Career Development.
Harri-Augstein, Sheila & Smith, Michael. Reading to Learn.
Harrier, Richard A., jt. auth. see Martin, Michael R.
Harrier, Richard C., ed. Jacobean Drama: An Anthology. Incl. Every Man in His Humour. Jonson, Ben; Malcontent. Marston, John; White Devil. Webster, John; Bussy d'Ambois. Chapman, George. Norton.
Harries, Clive, jt. ed. see Towell, David.
Harries, John. Discovering Stained Glass.
Harriet, Pollack, jt. auth. see Smith, Alexander B.
Harrigan, John J. Political Change in the Metropolis.
--Politics & Policy in States & Communities.
Harrigan, Kathryn R. Strategies for Vertical Integration.
Harrigan, Pamela. Principles of Interpretation in Echocardiography.
Harrigan, Raymond W., jt. auth. see Stine, William B.
Harrigan, Stephen. Jacob's Well: A Novel.
Harrigan, W. C., ed. see TMS Staff & AIME Staff.
Harrigan, W. C., et al, eds. International Conference on Composite Materials Five (ICCM V)
Harriman, P. L. Encyclopedia of Psychology.
--Twentieth Century Psychology.
Harriman, W. Averell, Institute for Advanced Study of the Soviet Union Staff, jt. auth. see National Security Committee.
Harrington & Wilson. Corporate Financial Analysis.
--Corporate Financial Analysis.
Harrington, Alan. Life in a Crystal Palace.
--The Revelations of Dr. Modesto.
Harrington, Avery R. & Zimmerman, Stephen W. Pathophysiology of Renal.
Harrington, Daniel J. God's People in Christ: New Testament Perspectives on the Church & Judaism. Brueggemann, Walter & Donahue, John R., eds.
--Pentecost Two: Proclamation 3B.
Harrington, Eileen. Education for Living: A Common-Sense Program for Grades K-6.
Harrington, Evans & Abadie, Ann J., eds. The Maker & the Myth: Faulkner & Yoknapatawpha, 1977.
Harrington, Geri. The Salad Book.
--Summer Garden, Winter Kitchen.
Harrington, John & Wenzl, Michael. A Suitable Design: How to Organize Your Writing.
Harrington, John W. Discovering Science.
Harrington, Joyce. Family Reunion.
--No One Knows My Name.
Harrington, Michael. Decade of Decision.
--The Next America: The Decline & Rise of the United States.
--The Politics at God's Funeral: The Spiritual Western Civilization.
--Taking Sides: The Education of a Militant Mind.
--The Vast Majority.
Harrington, Milton. Management of the Mind.
Harrington, Thomas F. Handbook of Career Planning for Special Needs Students.
Harriot, Ray. Stories for Around the Campfire.
Harriot, Thomas. A Brief & True Report of the New Found Land of Virginia.
Harris, ed. Recent Advances in Sexually Transmitted Diseases.
Harris, Abram L., jt. auth. see Spero, Sterling D.
Harris, Alexander. Review of the Political Conflict in America, from the Commencement of the Anti-Slavery Agitation to the Close of Southern Reconstruction.
Harris, Ann S., ed. see Marrow, Deborah.
Harris, Anne B. My Darling.
Harris, Anthony. Night's Black Agents: Witchcraft & Magic in Seventeenth-Century English Drama.
Harris, Anthony A. & Gill, Kathleen D., eds. ERISA: The Law & the Code 1987 Edition.
Harris, Arthur S. New York.
Harris, Arthur S., Jr. Boston.
Harris, Aurand. Six Plays for Children: Biography & Play Analyses by Coleman A. Jennings.
Harris, Barbara, jt. auth. see Golanty, Eric.
Harris, Barry C. Organization: The Effect on Large Corporations. Bateman, Fred, ed.
Harris, Bill. Austria.
Harris, Bill, jt. ed. see Marqusee, Mike.
Harris, Bob. Growing Wild Mushrooms.
Harris, C. C. Readings in Kinship in Urban Society.
Harris, C. C., jt. auth. see Rosser, Colin.
Harris, Charlaine. Sweet & Deadly.
Harris, Charles S., et al. Applied Research in Aging: A Guide to Methods & Research.
Harris, Christie. Mouse Woman & the Vanished Princesses.
--Mystery at the Edge of Two Worlds.
--Secret in the Stlalakum Wild.
--Sky Man on the Totem Pole.
Harris, Clement. Hennage: A Social System in Miniature. Spindler, George & Spindler, Louise, eds.
Harris, Curtis C. & Autrup, Herman N., eds. Human Carcinogenesis: Symposium.
Harris, Cyril M. & Crede, Charles E. Shock & Vibration Control Handbook.
Harris, D. J. & Robson, P. D. The Physical Basis of Electronics.
--Vacuum & Solid State Electronics.
Harris, D. J., et al. Coal, Gas & Electricity Industries.
Harris, Dale B. Children's Drawings As Measures of Intellectual Maturity.
Harris, Daniel. The Fence.
--Lotus 1-2-3 Mastery: A Business Guide to 1-2-3 Productivity.
Harris, David. The League: The Rise & Decline of the NFL.
--Planning & Designing the Office Environment.
Harris, Diana K. & Cole, William E. Sociology of Aging.
Harris, Diane. The Woman's Day Book of Great Sandwiches.
--The Woman's Day Guide to Organizing Your Life.
Harris, Dixie L. Twenty Stories of Bible Women.
Harris, Ernest E., ed. Music Education: A Guide to Information Sources.
Harris, Errol E. The Foundations of Metaphysics in Science.
Harris, Eugenie. Monarch Notes on Blake's Poetry.
Harris, F. Ground Engineering Equipment & Methods.
Harris, Frank. Ground Engineering Equipment & Methods.
Harris, Frank & McCaffer, Ronald. Construction Plant: Management & Investment Decisions.
--Modern Construction Management.
--Modern Construction Management.
--Worked Examples in Construction Management.
Harris, Frank E. Numbers & Units for Science.
Harris, Fred R. Potomac Fever.
Harris, George S. The Origins of Communism in Turkey.
Harris, Gertrude. Foods of the Frontier.
--Pasta International.
Harris, Godfrey & DeKovner-Mayer, Barbara. From Trash to Treasure: How to Make Money at the Swaps.
Harris, Gordon E., ed. see Foerster, Werner.
Harris, Graham P. Phytoplankton Ecology: Structure, Function & Fluctuation.
Harris, Harold A. Greek Athletes & Athletics.
Harris, Harry & Hirschhorn, Kurt, eds. Advances in Human Genetics. Incl. Vol. 1; Vol. 2; Vol. 3; Vol. 4; Vol. 5; Vol. 6; Vol. 7; Vol. 8; Vol. 9; Vol. 10. Plenum Pub.
Harris, Helen & Chauhan, Ela. So You Want to Buy a Word Processor?
Harris, Henry, jt. auth. see Rosen, Marcia.
Harris, Henry G. Collecting & Identifying Old Clocks.
Harris, Ian. The Price Guide to Victorian Silver.
Harris, Iverson L. The Wisdom of Laotse.
Harris, J. D., jt. auth. see Croke, B. F.
Harris, J. M. & White, T. D. Evolution of the Plio-Pleistocene African Suidae.
Harris, J. Mel & Scofield, Michael L. IBM-PC Conversion Handbook of BASIC.
Harris, James. High Ideals?
--High Ideals?
Harris, James E. & Weeks, Kent R. X-Raying the Pharaohs.
Harris, Jana. Manhattan As a Second Language & Other Poems.
Harris, Jane B. When We Teach Juniors.
Harris, Janet C. & Park, Roberta J., eds. Play, Games, & Sports in Cultural Contexts.
Harris, Jean. Stranger in Two Worlds.
Harris, Jennifer, et al. Nineteen Hundred and Sixty-Six & All That: Design & the Consumer in Britain, 1960-1969.
Harris, Jessica B. Hot Stuff: A Cookbook in Praise of the Piquant.
Harris, John. Build Your Own Statue of Liberty.
--Violence & Responsibility.
--Without a Trace: A Fresh Investigation of Eight Lost Ships & Their Fates.
Harris, John, jt. auth. see Hantle, Terry W.
Harris, John, ed. see McParland, Edward.
Harris, John, ed. see Willis, Peter.
Harris, John K. Professional Examination Questions & Answers: A Self-Study Approach to Accompany Horngren, Cost Accounting, 5th Edition.
Harris, Judith R., jt. auth. see Liebert, Robert M.
Harris, Jules, ed. see Leukocyte Culture Conference Staff.
Harris, Julian & Leveque, Andre. Basic Conversational French.
--Intermediate Conversational French.
Harris, Ken. World Electric Locomotives.
Harris, Kenneth. Attlee.
--The Wildcatter: A Portrait of Robert O. Anderson.
Harris, Kevin. Education & Knowledge: The Structured Misrepresentation of Reality.
--Teachers & Classes.
Harris, Leon. Moscow Circus School.
Harris, Leon A. The Great Diamond Robbery.
Harris, Lis. Holy Days: The World of a Hasidic Family.
Harris, Louis. American Attitudes Towards Health Maintenance Organizations.
--The Anguish of Change.
--A Survey of Spousal Violence Against Women in Kentucky.
Harris, Louis, & Associates Staff & Westin, Alan F. The Dimensions of Privacy: A National Opinion Research Survey of Attitudes Toward Privacy.
Harris, Louis, & Associates Staff. Fitness in America--the Perrier Study: A National Research Report of Behavior, Knowledge, & Opinions Concerning the Taking up of Sports & Exercise.
--Retirement & Income: A National Research Report of Behavior & Opinion Concerning Retirement, Pensions, & Social Security.
--Victims of Crime: A Research Report of Experiencing Victimization.
Harris, Lucien, Jr. Butterflies of Georgia.
Harris, MacDonald. The Balloonist.
--Herma.
--Pandora's Galley.
--Screenplay.
--Tenth.
--The Treasure of Sainte-Foy.
--Yukiho.
Harris, Maria, ed. The DRE Reader: A Sourcebook in Education & Ministry.
Harris, Marilyn. Bledding Sorrow.
--Runaway's Diary.
--This Other Eden.
--Warrick.
Harris, Marjorie, jt. auth. see Davey, D. Mackenzie.
Harris, Marjorie S. Francisco Romero on Problems of Philosophy.
Harris, Mark. Good Hope Poems.
--It Looked Like for Ever.
--Lying in Bed.
Harris, Mark & Wright, R. Glenn. Index to Birthplaces of United Kingdom Authors.
Harris, Mark J. Confessions of a Prime Time Kid.
--Henry Wiggen's Books.
Harris, Mark J., et al. The Homefront: America During World War II.
Harris, Marshall D. Origin of the Land Tenure System in the United States.
Harris, Martin, jt. auth. see Vincent, Nigel.
Harris, Marvin. America Now.
--Good to Eat: Riddles of Food & Culture.
--Patterns of Race in the Americas.
--Town & Country in Brazil.
Harris, Max. Angry Eye: A Comment on Life & Letters.
Harris, Maz. Bikers: Birth of a Modern-Day Outlaw.
Harris, Michael. Great Western Coaches from the Eighteen Nineties.
Harris, Michael, jt. ed. see Myers, Robin.
Harris, Michael H., jt. ed. see Cutler, Wayne.
Harris, Milton M. The Commissions Are Bigger! the Bonuses Are Higher!
Harris, Muriel, jt. auth. see Gaston, Thomas E.
Harris, N. D. Preparing Educational Materials.
Harris, Nathaniel. The Decisive Battle.
Harris, Nathaniel, jt. auth. see Hardy, George.
Harris, Nell. The Castlemaker.
Harris, Nick. Barry Sheene.
Harris, Norman D. History of Negro Servitude in Illinois & of the Slavery Agitation in That State, 1719-1864.
Harris, P. & Opie, L., eds. Calcium & the Heart.
Harris, P. M. Facies Anatomy & Diagenesis of a Bahamian Ooid Shoal.
Harris, P. M., ed. The Potato Crop: The Scientific Basis for Improvement.
Harris, Paul, ed. Scotland: An Anthology.
Harris, Phil. An Introduction to Law.
Harris, Philip R. New World, New Ways, New Management.
Harris, Philip R. & Moran, Robert T. Managing Cultural Differences.
Harris, Quincy. Understanding the New Telephone Service.
Harris, R. Approaches to Language.
Harris, R. Baine, ed. Authority: A Philosophical Analysis.
Harris, R. J., ed. see International Cancer Congress, 9th, Tokyo, 1966.
Harris, R. J., ed. see International Society for Cell Biology Staff.
Harris, R. T., jt. auth. see Beckhard, R.
Harris, Raymond, jt. auth. see Haessler, Herbert.
Harris, Richard J. A Primer of Multivariate Statistics.
Harris, Richard L. Death of a Revolutionary: The Last Days of Che Guevara.
Harris, Robert. Microanalytic Simulation Models for Analysis of Public Welfare Policies.
Harris, Robert & Webb, David. Welfare, Power, & Juvenile Justice: The Social Control of Delinquent Youth.
Harris, Robert J., ed. Biological Approaches to Cancer Chemotherapy: Proceedings.
--Cellular Basis & Aetiology of Late Somatic Effects of Ionizing Radiations: Proceedings.
--Initial Effects of Ionizing Radiations on Cells.
--Protein Biosynthesis.
--Techniques in Experimental Virology.
Harris, Robert S., ed. Art & Science of Dental Caries Research.
--Feeding & Nutrition of Nonhuman Primates.
Harris, Robin & Mann, Brian, eds. NMR & the Periodic Table.
Harris, Ron & Bloch, Penelope. Aerobicise.
Harris, Rosemary. Janni's Stork.
--The King's White Elephant.
--Zed.
Harris, Roy D. & Gonzalez, Richard F. The Operations Manager.
Harris, Ruth. Kinesiology: Workbook & Laboratory Manual.
Harris, Sandra L., jt. auth. see Nathan, Peter E.
Harris, Sarah. How & Why: The General Strike.
Harris, Stacy. Comedians of Country Music.
Harris, Stacy & Krishef, Robert K. The Carter Family.
Harris, Stuart. European Interests in ASEAN. Bridges, Brian, ed.
Harris, Susan E. Horsemanship in Pictures.
Harris, Susan E., jt. auth. see Traister, Robert J.
Harris, Sydney J. The Best of Sydney J. Harris.
--For the Time Being.
--Pieces of Eight.
--Winners & Losers.
Harris, Sydney P., jt. auth. see Greenstone, Arthur W.
Harris, Toby, jt. ed. see Bradshaw, Jonathan.
Harris, W. E., jt. auth. see Bowerman, William J.

Harris, W. Glen. Toward the Sunrising: A Story about Preaching.
Harris, Walter E. & Kratochvil, Byron. Introduction to Chemical Analysis.
Harris, Warren. The Other Marilyn: A Biography of Marilyn Miller.
Harris, Whitney R. Tyranny on Trial: The Evidence at Nuremberg.
Harris, William W. Taking Root: Israeli Settlement in the West Bank, the Golan & Gaza-Sinai, 1967-1980.
Harris, Wilson. Whole Armor & the Secret Ladder.
Harris-Bowlsbey, JoAnn, et al. Take Hold of Your Future: Leader's Manual.
Harrison. Challenger Crosswords.
Harrison, Allen F. & Bramson, Robert M. Styles of Thinking: Strategies for Asking Questions, Making Decisions & Solving Problems.
Harrison, B. Framework: An Introduction.
--Framework II: An Introduction.
Harrison, Barbara. The Gorlin Clinic.
Harrison, Bennet. Urban Economic Development: Suburbanization, Minority Opportunity, & the Condition of the Central City.
Harrison, Beppie. The Shock of Motherhood: The Unexpected Challenge for the New Generation of Mothers.
Harrison, Beppie, jt. auth. see Romney, Ronna.
Harrison, Betty D. Dial-a-Skill: A Manual of Procedures for Team Members of Special Education & Related Services.
Harrison, Beverly W. Making the Connections: Essays in Feminist Social Ethics. Robb, Carol S., intro. by.
Harrison, Bill. Framework: An Introduction.
Harrison, Brian. The Danger Light & Other Stories.
Harrison, Cliff. Popular Tropical Fish for Your Aquarium.
Harrison, Clifford E. Managing Staff Reductions in Corporations. Farmer, Richard, ed.
Harrison, E. Frank. Management & Organizations.
--The Managerial Decision Making Process.
Harrison, F. Time, Place & Music: An Anthology of Ethnomusicological Observation, C. 1550 to C. 1800.
Harrison, F. L., jt. auth. see Westrup, J. A.
Harrison, F. L., jt. ed. see Westrup, J. A.
Harrison, Frank, ed. see Baker, Theodore.
Harrison, Frank M., ed. see Brown, John.
Harrison, Fred. Hell-Holes & Hangings.
--The Power in the Land: An Inquiry into Unemployment, the Profits Crisis & Land Speculation.
Harrison, Frederic. John Ruskin.
Harrison, G. B. Profession of English.
Harrison, George B. Introducing Shakespeare.
--Major British Writers.
--Shakespeare at Work, Fifteen Ninety-Two to Sixteen Three.
--Shakespeare under Elizabeth.
Harrison, George B., ed. Major British Writers.
Harrison, George B., ed. see Shakespeare, William.
Harrison, George H. Backyard Bird Watcher.
Harrison, George H., jt. auth. see Harrison, Kit.
Harrison, Gilbert A. The Enthusiast: A Life of Thornton Wilder.
--Gertrude Stein's America.
Harrison, Glenna W. Meal Management: Laboratory Manual.
Harrison, H. R. & Nettleton, T. Principles of Engineering Mechanics.
Harrison, Hal H. Wood Warblers' World.
--Wood Warbler's World.
Harrison, Harland, jt. auth. see Rosenzweig, Ed.
Harrison, Harry. The Adventures of the Stainless Steel Rat.
--The QE Two Is Missing.
--Skyfall.
--West of Eden.
--Winter in Eden.
Harrison, Ira E. & Cosminsky, Sheila. Traditional Medicine: Implications of Mental Health, Public Health, Maternal & Child Health & Family Planning.
Harrison, J. A., jt. auth. see Thirsk, H. R.
Harrison, James, ed. Nature's Secret World.
Harrison, James P. Communists & Chinese Peasant Rebellions: A Study in the Rewriting of Chinese History.
--The Endless War: Fifty Years of Struggle in Vietnam.
Harrison, Jamie & Boris, Shelley, eds. The International Mail Order Gourmet: A Sourcebook of Selected Delicacies from Around the World.
Harrison, Jane. Epilegomena to the Study of Greek Religion, & Themis: A Study of the Social Origins of Greek Religion.
Harrison, Jane E. Mythology.
Harrison, Jim. Locations.
--Plain Song.
Harrison, John & Harrison, Shirley. Greece.
--Ireland.
Harrison, John, jt. auth. see Harrison, Shirley.
Harrison, John A. China Since Eighteen Hundred.
--The Chinese Empire.
Harrison, John A., ed. China: Enduring Scholarship Selected from the Far Eastern Quarterly, the Journal of Asian Studies 1941-1971.
Harrison, Joyce M. Instructional Strategies for Physical Education.
Harrison, Kit & Harrison, George H. America's Favorite Backyard Birds.
Harrison, Linda. Design Your Own.
Harrison, M. A. Lectures on Linear Sequential Machines.
Harrison, M. John. The Pastel City.
Harrison, Marc. The Animal Book.
Harrison, Martin, jt. auth. see Bailey, David.
Harrison, Mary. Infertility: A Couple's Guide to Its Causes & Treatments.
Harrison, Max. Jazz Retrospect.
Harrison, P. Ian, jt. ed. see Brodie, Martin J.
Harrison, P. M. & Hoare, R. J. Metals in Biochemistry.
Harrison, Paul. Third World Tomorrow: A Report from the Battlefront in the War Against Poverty.
Harrison, Paul C. The Drama of Nommo: Black Theater in the African Continuum.
Harrison, Paul C., ed. Kuntu Drama. Incl. A Beast Story. Kennedy, Adrienne; Devil's Mask. Brown, Lennox; Great Goodness of Life. Amiri, Imanu; The Great MacDaddy. Harrison, Paul C; Kabnis. Toomer, Jean; Mars. Goss, Clav; The Owl Answers. Kennedy, Adrienne; A Season in the Congo. Cesaire, Aime. Grove.
Harrison, R. G. Clinical Embryology.
Harrison, R. G. & DeBoer, C. H. Sex & Infertility.
Harrison, R. J., ed. Functional Anatomy of Marine Mammals.
Harrison, R. M. & Laxen, D. P. Lead Pollution: Causes & Control.
Harrison, R. M., ed. Endoscopy in Primates & Other Experimental Animals.
Harrison, Randall P. The Cartoon: Communication to the Quick.
Harrison, Ray. Death of a Dancing Lady: A Sargent Bragg-Constable Morton Mystery.
--Death of an Honourable Member.
--Why Kill Arthur Potter?
Harrison, Richard J., jt. ed. see Felts, William J.
Harrison, Sarah. A Flower That's Free: A Novel.
--In Granny's Garden.
Harrison, Scott, jt. auth. see Freestone, David.
Harrison, Shirley & Harrison, John. Austria & Switzerland.
Harrison, Shirley, jt. auth. see Harrison, John.
Harrison, Stephen, jt. ed. see Long, Andrew F.
Harrison, Steve. Fight That Ticket in British Columbia.
Harrison, William J. A Programmer's Guide to COBOL.
Harriss, C. Lowell. Innovations in Tax Policy & Other Essays.
Harriss, Joseph. The Tallest Tower: Eiffel & the Belle Epoque.
Harrisville, Roy. Holy Week.
Harrisville, Roy A. Miracle of Mark.
Harrisville, Roy A. & Hackett, Charles D. Holy Week. Achtemeier, Elizabeth, et al, eds.
Harrisville, Roy A., tr. see Bultmann, Rudolf.
Harrisville, Roy A., tr. see Fridrichsen, Anton.
Harrisville, Roy A., tr. see Gunkel, Hermann.
Harrisville, Roy A., tr. see Kasemann, Ernst.
Harrisville, Roy A., tr. from Ger. see Stuhlmacher, Peter.
Harrod, Howard L. The Human Center: Moral Agency in the Social World.
Harrod, L. M., ed. see Prytherch, Ray.
Harrold, Robert. Cassadaga: An Inside Look at the South's Oldest Psychic Community with True Experiences of People Who Have Been There.
Harrop, Alex. Behaviour Modification in the Classroom.
Harrop, Clayton. History of the New Testament in Plain Language.
Harroun, Catherine, jt. auth. see Teiser, Ruth.
Harrowe, Fiona. Bittersweet Afternoons.
Harry, Bill. Beatlemania: The History of the Beatles on Film.
--Paperback Writers: The History of the Beatles in Print.
Harry, Keith, jt. ed. see Kaye, Anthony.
Harsch, Hilya. Fivescourt: A Novel in Reverse.
Harshananda, Swami. Hindu Gods & Goddesses.
Har-Shefi, Yoella. Beyond the Gunsights: One Arab Family in the Promised Land.
Harshman, Carl L. Quality Circles: Implications for Training.
Harshman, Dorothy, jt. auth. see Figueroa, Ed.
Hart, Albert B. & Chapman, Annie B. How Our Grandfathers Lived.
Hart, Allen de see DeHart, Allen.
Hart, Arthur A., jt. auth. see Wells, Merle.
Hart, Bruce & Hart, Carol. Cross Your Heart.
Hart, Bruce & Hart, Carole. Flare Bestseller.
--Jeux de Patience.
--Sooner or Later.
Hart, Carol, jt. auth. see Hart, Bruce.
Hart, Carole. Delilah.
Hart, Carole, jt. auth. see Hart, Bruce.
Hart, David. The Ait 'Atta of Southern Morocco: Daily Life & Recent History.
Hart, David K., jt. auth. see Scott, William G.
Hart, David M. Banditry in Islam: Case Studies in Morocco, Algeria & the Pakistan North West Frontier.
Hart, Dennis. The Ministry of Sovereign Authority.
Hart, Don, jt. auth. see Ervin, Thomas.
Hart, Don De see De Hart, Don.
Hart, Douglas. Strategic Planning in London: The Rise & Fall of the Primary Road Network. Urban & Regional Planning Advisory Committee, ed.
Hart, Ernest H. Dog Breeding.
Hart, F. D. Practical Problems in Rheumatology.
Hart, F. L. & Fisher, H. J. Modern Food Analysis.
Hart, Glen, jt. auth. see Zimmerman, Larry.
Hart, H. L., jt. auth. see Bentham, Jeremy.
Hart, Harold & Schuetz, Robert D. Organic Chemistry: A Short Course.
Hart, Harold H. Chairs Through the Ages: A Pictorial Archive of Woodcuts & Engravings.
--Weapons & Armor: A Pictorial Archive of Woodcuts & Engravings.
Hart, Hastings H. Plans for City Police Jails & Village Lockups.
Hart, Hendrik & Van Der Hoeven, Johan, eds. Rationality in the Calvinian Tradition.
Hart, Herbert M. Tour Guide to Old Forts of New Mexico, Arizona, Nevada, Utah, Colorado.
--Tour Guide to Old Forts of Texas, Kansas, Nebraska, Oklahoma.
Hart, J. Roger. Effective Chemical Marketing, Advertising & Promotion: A Practical Guide for the Chemical Marketing Professional.
Hart, James A., jt. auth. see Clar, Lawrence M.
Hart, James D., ed. see Norris, Frank.
Hart, Jeanne M. Scareboy.
Hart, John. Regard the Lilies, Regard the Blood: Poems to the Blessed Virgin.
Hart, John M. Anarchism & the Mexican Working Class, 1860-1931.
Hart, Joseph, jt. auth. see Corriere, Richard.
Hart, Julian T. Hypertension.
Hart, Laura K. The Arithmetic of Dosages & Solutions: A Programmed Presentation.
Hart, Leslie A. Human Brain & Human Learning.
Hart, M., ed. Educating the Inner-City Child: Readings in Psychology.
Hart, Max. Strings on a Kite: The Poetry of Max Hart.
Hart, Moss, jt. auth. see Kaufman, George S.
Hart, Nicky. When Marriage Ends: A Study in Status Passage.
Hart, P. J., ed. The Earth's Crust & Upper Mantle.
Hart, Paul J., jt. auth. see Pitcher, Tony J.
Hart, Philip. Conductors: A New Generation.
--Conductors: A New Generation.
--Orpheus in the New World.
Hart, Reed L. Key Thoughts for Talks.
Hart, Robert. The Economics of Non-Wage Labour Costs.
Hart, Roderick P. The Political Pulpit.
Hart, Roger. Children's Experience of Place: A Developmental Study.
--Children's Experience of Place: A Developmental Study.
Hart, Roy. A Position of Trust.
Hart, T., et al. Life Is No Yuk for the Yak.
Hart, T. L., et al. Multi-Media Indexes, Lists, & Review Sources: A Bibliographic Guide.
Hart, Thomas R. Gil Vicente: Farces & Festival Plays.
Hart, Tony. Puppets & Moving Toys.
--Scrap Art.
Hart, W. A., et al. The Chemistry of Lithium, Sodium, Potassium, Rubidium, Cesium & Francium.
Hart, William L. Mathematics of Investment.
Hart, Wilson R. Collective Bargaining in the Federal Civil Service.
Hartbarger, Janie C. & Hartbarger, Neil J. Eating for the Eighties.
Hartbarger, Neil J., jt. auth. see Hartbarger, Janie C.
Hartcup, Guy. Camouflage.
Hart-Davis, Duff. The Heights of Rimring.
--Level Five.
Harte, Samantha. Summersea.
Harten, Jurgen, et al, eds. Neue Malerei in Deutschland.
Harter, Eugene C. The Lost Colony of the Confederacy.
Harter, James H., jt. auth. see Fiske, Kenneth.
Harter, Karl. In the Skin.
Harter, Penny. House by the Sea.
Harter, Penny & Higginson, William J., eds. Between Two Rivers: Union County Literature Today.
Harter, W. G. & Patterson, C. W. A Unitary Calculus for Electronic Orbitals.
Hartert, H., ed. see International Society of Hemorheology, 2nd International Conference, Heidelberg, 1969.
Hartigan, Joe. To Become a Racehorse Trainer.
--To Own a Racehorse.
Hartigan, Richard S. The Forgotten Victim: A History of the Civilian.
Hartjen, Clayton A. Crime & Criminalization.
Hartkaemper, A. & Neumann, H., eds. Foundations of Quantum Mechanics & Ordered Linear Spaces.
Hartkamper, A. & Schmidt, H. J., eds. Structure & Approximation in Physical Theories.
Hartkopf, Roy. Math Without Tears.
Hartl, Daniel L. Principles of Population Genetics.
Hartl, Robert. Basics of Financial Management.
Hartland, Edwin S., ed. English Fairy & Other Folktales.
Hartland, Michael. The Third Betrayal.
Hartland, S. Counter Current Extraction.
Hartle, Douglas G. Public Policy Decision Making & Regulation.
Hartley, Duncan, jt. ed. see Weil, Mildred.
Hartley, F. R., et al. Solution Equilibria.
Hartley, Iris F. Fundamentals of Investing: Student Guide.
Hartley, James, ed. Psychology of Written Communication.
Hartley, Karen. Energy R & D Decision Making for Canada.
Hartley, Keith. NATO Arms Co-Operation: A Study in Economics & Politics.
Hartley, Margaret L., ed. The Southwest Review Reader.
Hartley, Norman. Quicksilver.
--Quicksilver.
--ShadowPlay.
--The Viking Process.
Hartley, Robert F. Retailing: Challenge & Opportunity.
--Retailing: Challenge & Opportunity.
--Sales Management.
Hartley, Robert F., et al. Essentials of Marketing Research Text, Readings, & Cases.
Hartley, W. C. Cash: Planning, Forecasting & Control.
--Introduction to Business Accounting for Managers.
Hartley, William. In the Beginning God: Jottings from Genesis.
Hartman, Carol. The Stress Management Workshop. Jones, Dan, ed.
Hartman, Carol, ed. see Moore, Sandra S.
Hartman, Charles O. Free Verse: An Essay on Prosody.
Hartman, Geoffrey H. Unmediated Vision.
Hartman, Howard L., ed. Rock Mechanics: Key to Energy Production.
Hartman, J. Ted. Fracture Management: A Practical Approach.
Hartman, Joan M. Chinese Jade of Five Centuries.
Hartman, N. Perspectives in Reading.
Hartman, Nancy, jt. ed. see Hartman, Robert K.
Hartman, Robert K. & Hartman, Nancy, eds. Psychology in the Classroom.
Hartman, Sven S. & Edsman, C. M. Mysticism.
Hartman, W. F. & Dunegan, H. L. NDT: Acoustic Emission: Advances in Acoustic Emission.
Hartmann, Frederick H. World in Crisis. Carroll, James J., ed.
Hartmann, G. K., et al. Satellite Beacons, Observations from 1964 to 1970.
Hartmann, H., jt. auth. see Zahradnik, R.
Hartmann, H. F., et al. Nature in the Balance.
Hartmann, Hanns, jt. auth. see Gilpin, Alan.
Hartmann, Hudson T. & Kester, Dale E. Plant Propagation: Principles & Practices.
Hartmann, R. R., ed. Dictionaries & Their Users.
Hartmann, R. T. Palace Politics: An Inside Account of the Ford Years.
Hartmann, Reinhard R. The Language of Linguistics: Reflections on Linquistic Terminology, with Particular Reference to Level & Rank.
Hartmann, William K. Astronomy: The Cosmic Journey.
Hartnett, James P., jt. auth. see Rohsenow, Warren M.
Hartnett, James P., et al. Studies in Heat Transfer: A Festschrift for E.R.G. Eckert.
Hartnett, Ken. A Saving Grace.
Hartnett, Michael. Collected Poems.
Hartnett, Oonagh, jt. ed. see Chetwynd, Jane.
Hartnett, Rodney T., jt. auth. see Baird, Leonard L.
Hartnett, William, tr. see Lubich, Chiara.
Hartnoll, E. G., jt. ed. see Naylor, E.
Hartnoll, Phyllis. Who's Who in George Eliot.
--Who's Who in Shaw.
Hartog, Ina D. Indonesian Cooking: Slamat Makan.
Hartog, Jan De see De Hartog, Jan.
Hartsaw, John W. End Time-God's Glory.
Hartshorn, Leon R. A Mother's Love.
Hartshorne, ed. see Grothendieck, A.
Hartshorne, R. Residues & Duality.
Hartshorne, Thomas L. The Distorted Image: Changing Conceptions of the American Character Since Turner.
Hartstein, Jack. Extended Wear Contact Lenses: For Aphakia & Myopia.

Hartt, Frederick. Art: A History of Painting, Sculpture, Architecture.
Hartt, Frederick N. Art: A History of Painting, Sculpture, Architecture.
--History of Italian Renaissance Art.
Hartung, E. J. Astronomical Objects for Southern Telescopes.
Hartung, Elsie L. Patrimony.
Hartwell, Robert M., jt. auth. see Dernberger, Robert F.
Hartwell, Ronald M., ed. Causes of the Industrial Revolution in England.
Harty, Kevin J. Strategies for Business & Technical Writing.
--Strategies for Business & Technical Writing.
Hartz, Louis. Founding of New Societies.
Hartzog, George B. Battling for the National Parks.
Haruf, Kent. The Tie That Binds.
Harvard Committee. General Education in a Free Society.
Harvard Educational Review Staff. Guidance, an Examination.
Harvard, J. Bilingual Guide to Business & Professional Correspondence: English-French.
Harvard Medical Library Staff & Boston Medical Library Staff. Author-Title Catalog of the Francis A. Countway Library of Medicine for Imprints Through 1959.
Harvard, Stephen. An Italic Copybook: The Cantaneo Manuscript.
Harvard University Center for Italian Renaissance Studies at Villa I Tatti (Florence, Italy) Staff. Catalogues of the Berenson Library.
Harvard University Dumbarton Oaks Research Library Staff. Dictionary Catalogue of the Byzantine Collection of the Dumbarton Oaks Research Library.
Harvard University, Dumbarton Oaks Research Library and Collection, Washington, D.C. Staff. Dumbarton Oaks Papers.
Harvard University, Fogg Art Museum Staff. Catalogue of the Harvard University Fine Arts Library, First Supplement.
Harvard University, Graduate School of Business Administration Staff. Author-Title Catalog of the Baker Library.
Harvard University Graduate School of Design, Laboratory for Computer Graphics & Spatial Analysis Staff. Bibliography & Index, Vol. 18: Part I, Authors.
Harvard University, Graduate School of Design Staff. Catalog of the Library of the Graduate School of Design, Second Supplement.
Harvard University - Graduate School of Design Staff. Catalogue of the Library of the Graduate School of Design.
--Catalogue of the Library of the Graduate School of Design, First Supplement.
Harvard University, Graduate School of Business Administration Staff. Subject Catalog of the Baker Library.
--Subject Catalog of the Baker Library: First Supplement.
Harvard University, Gray Herbarium Staff. Gray Herbarium Index.
Harvard University Library Staff. Catalogue of English & American Chap-Books & Broadside Ballads in Harvard College Library.
--Philosophy & Psychology: Classification Schedule, Author & Title Listing, Chronological Listing.
Harvard University Museum of Comparative Zoology Staff. Catalogue of the Library of the Museum of Comparative Zoology.
Harvard University, Peabody Museum of Archaeology & Ethnology Staff. Author & Subject Catalogues of the Library of the Peabody Museum of Archaeology & Ethnology, Second Supplement.
--Author & Subject Catalogues of the Library of the Peabody Museum of Archaeology & Ethnology.
--Author & Subject Catalogues of the Library of the Peabody Museum of Archaeology & Ethnology, Third Supplement.
Harvard University Staff. Catalog of the Harvard University Fine Arts Library.
--Catalogue of the Library of the Graduate School of Design: Third Supplement.
Harvey, A. E. Jesus & the Constraints of History.
--Jesus on Trial.
--Something Overheard: An Invitation to the New Testament.
Harvey, A. M., et al, eds. The Principles & Practice of Medicine.
Harvey, A. P., ed. European Sources of Scientific & Technical Information.
Harvey, Andrew. The Web.
Harvey, B. J. & Hoar, W. S. La Reproduction Provoquee chez les Poissons: Theorie et Pratique.
--Teoria y Practica de la Reproduccion Inducida en los Peces.
Harvey, Bill. Mind Magic: With Mind Experiments.
Harvey, Bonnie C., ed. see Lee, Laurel.
Harvey, Bonnie C., ed. see Stirrup Associates, Inc. Staff.
Harvey, Bruce. Portfolio of New Zealand Birds.
Harvey, Charles. Analysis of Project Finance in Developing Countries.
--Macroeconomics for Africa.
Harvey, Charles & Jacobs, Jake. Rural Employment & Administration in the Third World.
Harvey, Chris. Austin Seven.
Harvey, Clay. Popular Sporting Rifle Cartridges.
Harvey Comics Staff. Casper & Richie Rich: Million Dollar Fun.
--Casper Far Out Fables.
--Casper in Fun & Monsters.
--Casper in What's Up.
--Casper, No. Four: Casper & Wendy.
--Casper No. Thirteen: Laughquakes.
--Casper, No. Two: TV Tales.
Harvey, D. Society, the City & the Space-Economy of Urbanism.
Harvey, David. Limits to Capital.
--The Limits to Capital.
Harvey, David & Kovar, Ilya, eds. Child Health: A Textbook for THR DCH.
Harvey, David R. Christmas Turkey or Prairie Vulture?
Harvey, Denis. The Gypsies: Waggon Time & After.
Harvey, Donald F. & Brown, Donald R. An Experimental Approach to Organization Development.
Harvey, E. N; see Rothstein, A.
Harvey, E. Newton. History of Luminescence from the Earliest Times Until 1900.
Harvey, Edwin D. The Mind of China.
Harvey, Godfrey E. History of Burma.
Harvey, Greg. Mastering Q & A.
--Mastering SuperCalc 3.
--Understanding HyperCard.
Harvey, H., ed. see Symposium on the Impact of Science on Society, Brussels, 1971.
Harvey, H. R. & Prem, Hanns J., eds. Explorations in Ethnohistory: Indians of Central Mexico in the Sixteenth Century.
Harvey, J. A., ed. Experimental Neutron Resonance Spectroscopy.
Harvey, J. D, jt. ed. see Walls, D. F.
Harvey, J. G. Atmosphere & Ocean: Our Fluid Environments.
Harvey, J. W., et al, eds. Solar-Space Observations & Stellar Prospects: Proceedings of the Topical Meeting of the COSPAR Interdisciplinary Scientific Commission E (Meetings E1, E2 & E6) of the COSPAR 25th Plenary Meeting, Graz, Austria, 25 June-7 July 1984.
Harvey, Joan M. Statistics America: Sources for Social, Economic, & Marketing Research.
Harvey, Joan M., ed. Statistics, Africa: Sources for Social, Economic, & Market Research.
Harvey, John. Coup d'Etat.
Harvey, John H. An Introduction to Tudor Architecture.
Harvey, Katherine A. The Lonaconing Journals: The Founding of a Coal & Iron Community, 1837-1840.
Harvey, Lori & Thomas, W. T. The Nineteen Eighty-Seven Pesticule Directors.
Harvey, Marianne. The Dark Horseman.
Harvey, Michael. Creative Lettering.
Harvey, Nigel. Discovering Farm Livestock.
--Old Farm Buildings.
Harvey, Nigel, ed. Agricultural Research Centers.
Harvey, P. J., tr. see Yatsimirskii, K. B.
Harvey, Paul. Baby Dolphin.
Harvey, Roland. Roland Harvey's Incredible Book of Almost Everything.
Harvey, Virginia I., ed. see Woodsmall, Annabel W., et al.
Harvey, W. J., ed. Discrete Groups & Automorphic Functions.
Harvey, William F., tr. see Vogel-Jorgensen, T.
Harvey, William W. Sketches of Haiti: From the Expulsion of the French to the Death of Christophe.
Harvie, Ron. The Voltaire Smile & Other Stories.
Harwell. British Atomic Energy Research Establishment, 1946-1951.
Harwood, Alan. Ethnicity & Medical Care.
Harwood, Bruce M. & Ellis, Jack. Real Estate Resource Book.
Harwood, Herbert. Blue Ridge Trolly: The Hagerstown & Frederick Railway.
Harwood, Norma. A Woman's Legal Guide to Separation & Divorce in All 50 States.
Harwood, Pearl A. Mr. Bumba & the Orange Grove.
--Very Big Problem of Mr. & Mrs. Bumba.
Harwood, Richard K., jt. auth. see Bachhuber, Thomas D.
Hasan, Khalid, ed. Versions of Truth: Urdu Short Stories from Pakistan.
Hasebe, Gakuji & Hayashiya, Seizo. Tokyo National Museum.
Hasegawa, A. Plasma Instabilities & Nonlinear Effects.
Hasegawa, Goro & Brady, Maxine. How to Win at Othello.
Hasegawa, Nyozekan. The Japanese Character: A Cultural Profile. Bester, John, tr. from Japanese.
Hasegawa, S., ed. Collection of TradeMarks & Logotypes in Japan 1984-85.
Hasegawa, Sumio & Kobayashi, Shigeji, eds. A Collection of Trademarks & Logotypes in Japan, 1982-83.
Hasegawa, T., ed. see IFAC-IFIP Workshop, Kyoto, Japan, Aug. 31-Sept. 2, 1981.
Hasek, Milan, et al, eds. Mechanisms of Immunological Tolerance: Proceedings.
Haselkorn, Avigdor. The Evolution of Soviet Security Strategy: 1965-1975.
Haselmayer, Louis A. Medieval English Episcopal Registers.
Hasenau, J. James. Cecelia's Gerbils.
Hasenkamp, G. Specification & Estimation of Multiple-Output Functions.
Hasenstab, M. Suzanne & Horner, John S. Comprehensive Intervention with Hearing - Impaired Infants & Preschool Children.
Hasenstab, M. Suzanne & Laughton, Joan M. Reading, Writing & the Exceptional Child: A Psycho-socio-linguistic Approach.
Hasenstab, Suzanne, jt. auth. see Laughton, Joan.
Hashagen, Werner R. How to Get it Built. Gibbs, Sunny, ed.
Hashim, Wan. Race Relations in Malaysia.
Hashin, Zvi & Herakovich, Carl T. Mechanics of Composite Materials: Recent Advances. Proceedings of the International Union of Theoretical & Applied Mechanics Symposium, August 16-19, 1982, Blacksburg, Virginia, U. S. A.
Hasija, Nipla. The Bridal Dress (A Romance from Modern India)
Hasin, Bernice Rothman. Consumers, Commissions, & Congresses: Law, Theory, & the Federal Trade Commission, 1968-1985.
Hasitavej, Rasmee. How to Live with & Overcome the Problems of Mental Retardation.
Haskel, Peter, tr. see Hakeda, Yoshito S.
Haskell, jt. auth. see Gayford.
Haskell, Barbara. Blam: The Explosion of Pop, Minimalism & Performance, 1958-1964.
Haskell, Charles M., jt. auth. see Cline, Martin J.
Haskell, Francis. Rediscoveries in Art: Some Aspects of Taste, Fashion, & Collecting in England & France.
Haskell, Martin R. & Yablonsky, Lewis. Crime & Delinquency.
--Criminology.
--Criminology: Crime & Criminality.
--Juvenile Delinquency.
--Juvenile Delinquency.
Haskell, Patricia & Senelick, Laurence. The Cheese Book.
Haskell, Patricia, jt. auth. see Marquis, Vivienne.
Haskell, Thomas L., ed. The Authority of Experts: Studies in History & Theory.
Haskew, Paul & Adams, Cynthia. When Food Is a Four Letter Word: Programs for Recovery from Anorexia, Bulimia, Bulimarexia, Obesity, & Other Appetite Disorders.
Haskin, Georgette see Zuverink, Mary.
Haskin, Steve, jt. auth. see Fingerhut, Bruce M.
Haskins & Sells. Revolving Funds & Business Enterprises of the Government, Exclusive of Lending Agencies.
Haskins, James. The New Americans: Cuban Boat People.
Haslam, E. Chemistry of Vegetable Tannins.
Haslam, Malcolm. Marks & Monograms of the Modern Movement: 1875-1930.
Hasler, A. F., jt. ed. see Yates, H.
Hasluck, Paul N., ed. Manual of Traditional Wood Carving with 1,146 Working Drawings & Photographic Illustrations.
Hasruddin Siddiqui, M. K. Bleaching Earths.
Hass, Robert. The Apple Trees at Olema.
Hass, Robert, ed. see Transtromer, Tomas.
Hassall, A. J. Fielding's Tom Jones.
Hassall, Christopher. Bell Harry & Other Poems.
--Biography of Edward Marsh.
Hassall, John, illus. Old Fashioned Nursery Rhymes & Tales.
Hassall, K. A., jt. auth. see Edwards, N. A.
Hassam, Abdul S. The Learning Process: How to Pass Examinations.
Hassam, Childe. Ninety-One Prints by Childe Hassam. Czestochowski, Joseph S., ed.
Hassan, Aftab, ed. see Blain, Beryl B., et al.
Hassan, Ihab. Radical Innocence: The Contemporary American Novel.
Hassan, Mulhim A. Prevention & Cure of Cancer.
Hassani, N. Ultrasound in Gynecology & Obstetrics.
Hasse, John E., ed. Ragtime: Its History, Composers, & Music.
Hassel, William, ed. see Findlay, James V.
Hasselman, D. P. & Heller, R. A., eds. Thermal Stresses in Severe Environments.
Hasselmeier, H. & Spruth, W. C., eds. Data Base Systems.
Hassenzahl, W. Storage of Energy.
Hassenzahl, W. V., ed. Electrochemical, Electrical & Magnetic Storage of Energy.
--Mechanical, Thermal & Chemical Storage of Energy.
Hassett, jt. auth. see Chapin.
Hassett, William D. Off the Record with F. D. R., Nineteen Forty-Two to Forty-Five.
Hasslam, C. J., jt. auth. see Burton, W. R.
Hassler, Donald M. Reader's Guide to Isaac Asimov. Schlobin, Roger C., ed.
Hassler, Jon. Jemmy.
--Simon's Night.
--Staggerford.
Hasson, D. F., jt. ed. see Baeslack, W. A.
Hasson, Dennis F. & Hamilton, C. Howard, eds. Advanced Processing Methods for Titanium: Proceedings. TMS-AIME Fall Meeting, Louisville, 1981.
Hassoun, M. Nadim. Design of Reinforced Concrete Structures.
Hassrick, Peter H. Frederic Remington: An Essay & Catalog to Accompany a Retrospective Exhibition.
Hastie, John W. High Temperature Vapors: Science & Technology.
Hastie, Stephen M., jt. auth. see Schepp, Brad.
Hastin, Bud. Bud Hastin's Collector's Price Guide: Avon Bottle Encyclopedia.
Hastings, Adrian. Church & Mission in Modern Africa.
Hastings, Cecil. Approximations for Digital Computers.
Hastings, D. E., ed. The Knee: Ligament & Articular Cartilage Injuries.
Hastings, Linda E. Complete Handbook of Activities & Recreational Programs for Nursing Homes.
Hastings, Max. The Korean War.
--Overlord: D-Day, June 6, 1944.
--Das Reich: The March of the Second SS Panzer Division Through France.
Hastings, N. A. & Mello, J. M. Decision Networks.
Hastings, Paul G. Introduction to Business.
Hastings, Phil R. Chicago Great Western.
Hastings, Robert C., ed. Leprosy.
Hastins, Bud. Avon Bottle Encyclopedia.
Hasty, Ronald W., jt. auth. see Burns, Robert W., Jr.
Haswell, Harold A., jt. auth. see Eells, Walter C.
Hata, Kazuo. New Hydrogenating Catalysts: Urushibara Catalysts.
Hatano, Sumi. Home Style Chinese Cooking in Pictures.
Hatch, Mary C. Thirteen Danish Tales.
Hatch, Ronald B. Crabbe's Arabesque: Social Drama in the Poetry of George Crabbe.
Hatch, Stephen. Outside the State: Voluntary Organisations in Three English Towns.
Hatcher, Anne S., jt. auth. see Mumey, Jack.
Hatcher, Harvey B. Holy Nativity.
Hatcher, John. Ali's Dream: The Story of Baha'u'llah.
Hatcher, Robert A., et al. Tecnologia de la Contracepcion: Segunda Edicion en Espanol. Montana, Eduardo, tr. from Eng.
Hatefi, D., ed. The Structural Basis of Membrane Function.
Hatfield, Fred, jt. auth. see Bentley, Stacey.
Hatfield, Frederick C. Weight Training for the Young Athlete.
Hatfield, Henry. From The Magic Mountain: Mann's Later Masterpieces.
Hatfield, James R. Political Effectiveness.
Hatfield, Julie, et al. Guide to the Recommended Thrift Shops of New England: Financial Survival in the 1980s.
Hatfield, Philip M. & Wise, Robert E. Radiology of the Gallbladder & Bile Ducts.
Hatfield, Weston P. The Weekend Real Estate Investor: The New Low-Risk Team Approach That Transforms Everyday Opportunities into Big Profits.
Hatfield, William E., ed. Molecular Metals.
Hathaway, Bo. A World of Hurt: A Novel.
Hathaway, Lulu. Boy Who Couldn't Talk.
Hathaway, Starke R. & Monachesi, Elio D. Adolescent Personality & Behavior: MMPI Patterns of Normal, Delinquent, Dropout & Other Outcomes.
Hatley, Derek J. & Pirhai, Imtiaz A. Strategies for Real-Time System Specification.
Hatley, Flora J., jt. ed. see Crow, Jeffrey J.
Hatry, Harry, et al. Efficiency Measurement for Local Government Services: Some Initial Suggestions.
Hatry, Harry P., et al. Program Analysis for State & Local Governments.
Hattaway, Michael. Elizabethan Popular Theatre: Plays in Performance.
Hatten, John T., et al. Emerging Language Three.
Hattery, Lowell H. Executive Control & Data Processing.
Hattingberg, M. Von see Von Hattingberg, M.
Hatton, E. M. The Tent Book.
Hattori, Akihiko, jt. ed. see Sigleo, Anne C.
Hattori, Tsutonu. The Viable Count: Quantitative & Environmental Aspects.
Hatvary, George E. The Suitor.
Hauber, Donald P., jt. ed. see Jackson, R. C.
Haublein, Ernst. The Stanza.
Hauck, Paul A. & Kean, Edmund S. Marriage & the Memo Method.

Haueisen, Kathy. Married & Mobile: Making a Move That's Right for You.
Hauenstein & Bachmeyer. Introduction to Communications Careers.
Hauer, Mary, et al. Books, Libraries, & Research.
Hauerwas, Stanley. A Community of Character: Toward a Constructive Christian Social Ethic.
--Vision & Virtue: Essays in Christian Ethical Reflection.
Hauf, Harold D., jt. auth. see Parker, Harry.
Haufler, George. Successful Settlement of Large Liabilities: How Annuity Policies Will Work for You.
Haug, E. J., ed. Computer Aided Analysis & Optimization of Mechanical System Dynamics.
Haug, Edward J. & Arora, Jasbir S. Applied Optimal Design: Mechanical & Structural Systems.
Haug, F. M. Heavy Metals in the Brain.
--Sulphide Silver Pattern & Cytoarchitectonics of Parahippocampal Areas in the Rat.
Haugaard, Erik C. Chase Me, Catch Nobody!
--Cromwell's Boy.
--Hakon of Rogen's Saga.
--Hakon of Rogen's Saga.
--Hans Christian Andersen: The Complete Fairy Tales & Stories.
--Little Fishes.
--A Messenger for Parliament.
--Orphans of the Wind.
--Slave's Tale.
--Untold Tale.
Haugen, Einar, tr. see Koht, Halvdan.
Haugh, William J. Everyone's Guide to Preparing a Bill of Lading.
Haughey, John. Personal Values in Public Policy.
Haughton & Williams. Computed Tomography of the Spine.
Haughton, Claire S. Green Immigrants.
--Green Immigrants: The Plants That Transformed America.
Haughwout, Lefferd M. Ways & Teachings of the Church.
Hauglid & Asker. Norway: Native Art.
Hauglie-Hanssen, E. Intrinsic Neuronal Organization of the Vestibular Nuclear Complex in the Cat: A Golgi Study.
Haugse, Vera L., jt. auth. see Lauerhass, Ludwig, Jr.
Hauk, Warren C., ed. Motivating People to Work.
Haule, J. M., ed. A Concordance to Night & Day By Virginia Woolf.
Haultain, Arnold. The Mystery of Golf.
Haupt, Kathryn J., et al. California Real Estate Practices.
Hauptmann, H., et al, eds. Operations Research & Economic Theory: Essays in Honor of Martin J. Beckmann.
Hauptmann, Tatjana. A Day in the Life of Petronella Pig.
Haurowitz, Felix. The Chemistry & Function of Proteins.
Haus, Felice. Beep! Beep! I'm a Jeep! A Toddler's Book of "Let's Pretend"
Hausbrandt, Andrzej. Tomaszewski's Mime Theatre.
Hausch, Donald B., jt. auth. see Ziemba, William T.
Hause, Earl M. Tumble-Down Dick: The Fall of the House of Cromwell.
Hausen, Helmuth. Heat Transfer: In Counterflow, Parallel Flow & Cross Flow. Sayer, M. S., tr. from Ger.
Hauser, Ernest. Italy: A Cultural Guide.
Hauser, Gayelord. Gayelord Hauser's New Treasury of Secrets.
--Mirror, Mirror on the Wall: An Invitation to Beauty.
Hauser, Hillary. Call to Adventure.
Hauser, Thomas. The Black Lights: Inside the World of Professional Boxing.
--The Execution of Charles Horman: An American Sacrifice.
--The Family Legal Companion.
--Missing.
Hausman, Carl, jt. auth. see Benoit, Philip.
Hausman, Gerald. Night Herding Song.
--Sitting on the Blue-Eyed Bear: Navajo Myths & Legends.
Hausman, J. C., ed. Knot Theory: Proceedings, Plans-Sur-Bex, Switzerland 1977.
Hausman, James. Mystery at Sans Souci.
Hausman, Jerome J. Arts & the Schools.
Hausman, Patricia. Jack Sprat's Legacy: The Science & Politics of Fat & Cholesterol.
Hausmann, D., ed. Integer Programming & Related Areas: A Classified Bibliography 1976 - 1978. Compiled at the Institute Fuer Oekonometrie und Operations Research, Univ of Bonn.
Hausmann, Winifred W. Your God-Given Potential.
Hausner, Ernst. Vienna: Introduction & Reminiscence.
Hausner, Henry, ed. Modern Materials: Advances in Development & Applications. Incl. Vol. 1; Vol. 2; Vol. 3; Vol. 4. Gonser, B. W. & Hausner, Henry H., eds.; Vol. 5. Gonser, B. W., ed; Vol. 6; Vol. 7. Acad Pr.
Hausner, Henry H. see Hausner, Henry.
Hausslein, Evelyn B. Children & Divorce: An Annotated Bibliography & Guide.
Hauther, Brenda, jt. auth. see Crafts, Kathy.
Hautzig, Deborah. Second Star to the Right.
Hautzig, Esther. Life with Working Parents: Practical Hints for Everyday Situations.
Havard, William C. & Bernd, Joseph L., eds. Two Hundred Years of the Republic in Retrospect.
Havelock, Eric A. The Literate Revolution in Greece & Its Cultural Consequences.
Havelock, Ronald G., et al. Planning for Innovation Through Dissemination & Utilization of Knowledge.
Haveman, Josepha. Workbook in Creative Photography.
Haveman, Robert. Water Resource Investment & the Public Interest: An Analysis of Federal Expenditures in Ten Southern States.
Havemann, Ernest, jt. auth. see Kagan, Jerome.
Havemann, Joel. Congress & the Budget.
Havemann, K. & Janoff, A., eds. Neutral Proteases of Human Polymorphonuclear Leukocytes: Biochemistry, Physiology & Clinical Significance.
Haven, Beverly. Charlie.
Haven Group Editors. The Electronic Money Machine: Profits from Your Home Computer.
Haven, Tom De see De Haven, Tom.
Haven, Virginia. The Link & the Promise.
Havener. Synopsis of Opthamology: The Opthamology Book.
Havens, Thomas R. Valley of Darkness: The Japanese People & World War Two.
Haverfield, Lyman. To Heaven on Horseback.
Havergal, Frances R. Opened Treasures.
Havergel, Frances. Kept for the Master's Use.
Haverkamp-Begemann, E. Rembrandt: The Nightwatch.
Haverkamp-Begemann, Egbert, et al. Small Paintings of the Masters. Shore, Leslie, ed.
Havers, J. & Stubbs, F. Handbook of Heavy Construction.
Haviaras, Stratis. The Heroic Age: A Novel.
Havighurst, Robert J. & Jansen, Anton J. Community Research.
Havighurst, Robert J., jt. auth. see Levine, Daniel U.
Havighurst, Robert J., ed. Leaders in American Education.
--Metropolitanism: Its Challenge to Education.
Havighurst, Robert J. & Dreyer, Philip H., eds. Youth.
Havighurst, Walter, ed. Midwest & Great Plains.
Havighurst, Walter E., ed. Masters of the Modern Short Story.
Haviland, Robert P. Computer Companion for the Apple II-Apple IIe.
--How To Design, Build & Program Your Own Advanced Working Computer System.
--How to Design, Build & Program Your Own Working Computer System.
Haviland, Virginia. Favorite Fairy Tales Told in India.
--Favorite Fairy Tales Told in Norway.
Haviland, William A. Cultural Anthropology.
Havlicek, Penny L. Medical Groups in the U. S., 1984.
Havlik, Richard J., et al. Health Statistics on Older Pesons: United States, 1986.
Havner, Vance. Pleasant Paths.
Havrevold, Finn. Undertow. Curry, Cathy B., tr. & illus.
Havrilesky, Thomas M. & Boorman, John T. Money Supply, Money Demand, & Macroeconomic Models.
Hawaii, Office of Environmental Quality Control Staff & University of Hawaii, Environomental Center Staff. Hawaii Environmental Laws & Regulations.
Hawdon, David, ed. The Changing Structure of the World Oil Industry.
Hawes, J. L., jt. auth. see Anderson, Christian.
Hawk, Douglas D. Moonslasher.
Hawke, David F. Those Tremendous Mountains: The Story of the Lewis & Clark Expedition.
Hawke, David F., ed. see Rockefeller, John D.
Hawke, Sharryl, jt. auth. see Superka, Douglas P.
Hawken, Paul. The Next Economy.
Hawker, Margot, et al. The Older Patient & the Role of the Physiologist. Dick, Donald, intro. by.
Hawker, Ross W. Notebook of Medical Physiology: Endocrinology with Aspects of Maternal, Fetal & Neonatal Monitoring.
--Notebook of Medical Physiology: Gastroenterology.
Hawkes, Alex D. Encyclopedia of Cultivated Orchids.
--A World of Vegetable Cookery.
--A World of Vegetable Cookery.
Hawkes, Christopher, jt. ed. see Duval, Paul-Marie.
Hawkes, Ellen. Feminism on Trial: The Ginny Foat Case & Its Meaning for the Future of the Women's Movement.
Hawkes, Glenn R., jt. auth. see Frost, Joe L.
Hawkes, H. A., jt. ed. see Curds, C. R.
Hawkes, J. G., et al, eds. Computer Mapped Flora: A Study of the County of Warwickshire.
Hawkes, John. Adventures in the Alaskan Skin Trade.
Hawkes, John D. Doctrine & Covenants & Pearl of Great Price Digest.
Hawkes, Laura M. Favorite Christmas Stories.
Hawkes, N., ed. see International Seminar on Trends in Mathematical Modelling Staff.
Hawkes, P. W., ed. see European Congress on Electron Microscopy Staff.
Hawkesworth, John. Almoran & Hamet: An Oriental Tale 1761. Shugrue, Michael F., ed.
Hawkins, et al. Consumer Behavior.
Hawkins, Anthony A. see Hope, Anthony.
Hawkins, C. F., jt. auth. see Geist, Harold.
Hawkins, Colin & Hawkins, Jacqui. Boo! Who?
Hawkins, D. F., jt. auth. see Ledward, R. S.
Hawkins, David. The Informed Vision: Essays on Learning & Human Nature.
Hawkins, David & Brown, Barbara. Effectiveness of the Annual Reports.
Hawkins, Delbert I., et al. Consumer Behavior: Implications for Marketing Strategy.
Hawkins, Desmond, compiled by. War Report: D-Day to VE-Day.
Hawkins, Donald. Online Information Retrieval Bibliography 1964-1979.
Hawkins, Donald T. Online Information Retrieval Bibliography, 1964-1982.
Hawkins, Edward. Wellspring.
Hawkins, Freda. Canada & Immigration: Public Policy & Public Concern.
Hawkins, Frederick W. French Stage in the Eighteenth Century.
Hawkins, Harry. Residential Wiring: Concepts & Practices.
Hawkins, Jacqui, jt. auth. see Hawkins, Colin.
Hawkins, Jennifer. The Poole Potteries.
Hawkins, Joellen, et al. Protocols for Nurse Practitioners in Gynecologic Settings.
Hawkins, Joellen B. & Higgins, Loretta P. Nursing & the American Health Care Delivery System.
Hawkins, Joellen B. & Thibodeau, Janice A. The Nurse Practitioner: Current Practice Issues.
Hawkins, Joellen W. & Higgins, Loretta P. Nursing & the American Health Care Delivery System.
Hawkins, K. H. & Pass, C. L. The Brewing Industry.
Hawkins, Maxine, jt. auth. see Ogletree, Earl J.
Hawkins, Mel. You Must Die Before You Live.
Hawkins, Nancy, et al. Nantucket & Other New England Cooking.
Hawkridge, David G. New Information Technology in Education.
Hawksley, Rozanne, jt. auth. see Lee, Pamela.
Hawksworth, D. L., ed. The Changing Flora & Fauna of Britain.
Hawley. The True Confessions of a Sunday School Teacher.
Hawley, Amos H., ed. see McKenzie, Roderick D.
Hawley, Cameron. Executive Suite.
Hawley, Don. The Nature of Things.
Hawley, G. S. Spanish-English, English-Spanish Dictionary of Chemistry & Chemical Products.
Hawley, Gessner. Condensed Chemical Dictionary.
Hawley, Henry. Faberge & His Contemporaries: The India Early Minshall Collection of The Cleveland Museum of Art.
Hawley, James. Against the Stream.
Hawley, Leonard, jt. auth. see Steffy, Wilbert.
Hawley, Peggy. Sex Fair Career Counseling.
Hawley, Richard A. Coming Through School.
Hawley, W. M. Chinese Folk Designs: A Collection of 300 Cut-Paper Designs Together with 160 Chinese Art Symbols & Their Meanings.
Hawley, Willis D. Blacks & Metropolitan Governance: The Stakes of Reform.
Hawley, Willis D., ed. Strategies for Effective Desegregation: Lessons from Research.
Haworth-Booth, Mark. Personal Choice: A Celebration of Twentieth Century Photographs.
Haworth-Booth, Mark, et al. The Golden Age of British Photography, 1839-1900, from the Collection of the Victoria & Albert Museum.
Hawthorne, J. & Rolfe, E. J., eds. Low Temperature Biology of Foodstuffs.
Hawthorne, Maurice & Num, Richard. Ear, Nose & Throat.
Hawthorne, Nathaniel. Great Stone Face & Other Tales of the White Mountains.
--House of the Seven Gables.
--The House of the Seven Gables.
--House of the Seven Gables.
--Life of Franklin Pierce.
--Scarlet Letter.
--Scarlet Letter. Levin, H., ed.
--Scarlet Letter. Bradley, Sculley, et al, eds.
--The Scarlet Letter. Bradley, Sculley, et al, eds.
--The Scarlet Letter.
--Scarlet Letter: Text, Sources, Criticism. Lynn, Kenneth S., ed.
--Wonder-Book. Bd. with Tanglewood Tales. HM.
Hawthorne, Nathaniel see Levin, David.
Hawthorne, Rosemary & Want, Mary. From Busk to Bra: A Survey of Women's Corsetry.
Hawthorne, William R. & Olson, W. T., eds. Design & Performance of Gas Turbine Power Plants.
Hawton, Hector. Philosophy for Pleasure.
Haxby, D., jt. ed. see Klare, H. J.
Haxthausen, Charles W. Paul Klee: The Formative Years.
Hay, Elizabeth D., et al, eds. Macromolecules Regulating Growth & Development.
Hay, Eloise K. Political Novels of Joseph Conrad.
Hay, Gilbert. The Buik of Alexander the Conquerour III. Cartwright, John, ed.
Hay, Henry. Learn Magic.
Hay, J. M. Reactive Free Radicals.
Hay, J. Thomas. Five Hundred Thirty-Four Ways to Raise Money.
Hay, Leon E. Accounting for Government & Non-Profit Entities.
Hay, Louise L. Heal Your Body.
--You Can Heal Your Life.
--Your Personal Colors & Numbers.
Hay, R. K., jt. auth. see Fitter, A. H.
Hay, Stephen N. Asian Ideas of East & West: Tagore & His Critics in Japan, China, & India.
Hay, Taylor. Flexease.
Hay, Wendy. Library Services for Handicapped People: An Annotated Bibliography of British Material 1970-1981.
Hayaishi, Osamu, ed. Oxygenases.
Hayakawa, S. I. & Reader's Digest Editors. Use the Right Word.
Hayakawa, Samuel I. Language in Thought & Action.
--Language in Thought & Action.
--Symbol, Status, & Personality.
Hayashi, Tetsumaro. William Faulkner: Research Opportunities & Dissertation Abstracts.
Hayashiya, Seizo, jt. auth. see Hasebe, Gakuji.
Hayat, M. Arif. Electron Microscopy of Enzymes Principles & Methods.
--Electron Microscopy of Enzymes: Principles & Methods.
--Electron Microscopy of Enzymes: Principles & Methods.
--Electron Microscopy of Enzymes: Principles & Methods.
--Electron Microscopy of Enzymes: Principles & Methods.
--Positive Staining for Electron Microscopy.
--Principles & Techniques of Electron Microscopy, Vol. 5: Biological Applications.
--Principles & Techniques of Electron Microscopy, Vol. 8: Biological Applications.
--Principles & Techniques of Electron Microscopy.
--Principles & Techniques of Electron Microscopy.
--Principles & Techniques of Electron Microscopy.
--Principles & Techniques of Electron Microscopy.
--Principles & Techniques of Electron Microscopy.
--Principles & Techniques of Scanning Electron Microscopy.
--Principles & Techniques of Scanning Electron Microscopy.
--Principles & Techniques of Scanning Electron Microscopy.
--Principles & Techniques of Scanning Electron Microscopy: Biological Applications.
--Principles & Techniques of Scanning Electron Microscopy, Vol. 2: Biological Applications.
Hayata, Yoshihiro, ed. Lung Cancer Diagnosis.
Hayata, Yoshihiro & Dougherty, Thomas J., eds. Lasers & Hematoporphyrin Derivative in Cancer.
Haycox, Ernest. Alder Gulch.
--Canyon Passage.
--Free Grass.
--Starlight Rider.
Hayden, Edwin V. Preaching Through the Bible.
Hayden, Eric W. Internationalizing Japan's Financial System.
Hayden, Karen. The Look of Love.
Hayden, Reynolds H. Splendid Murder.
Hayden, Robert. Angle of Ascent: New and Selected Poems.
Hayden, Robert, et al. Afro-American Literature: An Introduction.
Hayden, Sterling. Wanderer: A Reissue with a New Introduction & Illustrations.
Hayden, Thomas C. Handbook for College Admissions.
Hayden, Trudy & Novik, Jack. Your Rights to Privacy.
Haydn. Haydn: Symphony No. One Hundred & Three in E-Flat Major (Drum Roll) Geiringer, Karl, ed.
Haydn, Hiram C. The Counter-Renaissance.
--Words & Faces.
Haydock, Roger S. & Herr, David F. Nineteen Eighty-Six Supplement to Discovery Practice.
Haydock, Tim. Treasure Trove: The Great Undiscovered Treasures of the World.
Haydon, G., tr. see Jeppesen, Knud.

Authors

Hayek, F. A. Law, Legislation & Liberty: Vol. 3: the Political Order of a Free People.
Hayes, Alfred. Just Before the Divorce.
Hayes, Barbara. Dragons.
--Ghosts.
--Giants & Ogres.
--Gnomes.
Hayes, Carrie C. A Miniature Faith.
Hayes, Colin. Robert Buhler.
Hayes, Denis. Energy for Development: Third World Options.
--Pollution: The Neglected Dimensions.
Hayes, E. Kent, jt. auth. see Lazzarino, Alex.
Hayes, Edward. The Florida One-Day Trip Book: Fifty-Two Off-Beat Excursions in & Around Orlando.
Hayes, Ellen M. The Fine Gossoon: Saga of a Proud Irishman.
Hayes, Ernest H., ed. Fifty Favorite Bible Stories.
Hayes, Geoffrey. The Lantern Keeper's Bedtime Book.
Hayes, Harold, jt. ed. see California Magazine Staff.
Hayes, Helen. A Gathering of Hope.
Hayes, Helen & Loos, Anita. Twice over Lightly.
Hayes, Horace M. Veterinary Notes for Horse Owners. Tutt, J. F., ed.
Hayes, J., jt. auth. see Hopson, B.
Hayes, J. A., jt. ed. see Homburger, F.
Hayes, James L. Memos for Management...Leadership.
--Memos for Management...the Manager's Job.
Hayes, Janice E., jt. auth. see Govoni, Laura E.
Hayes, Janice E., jt. auth. see Hoexter, Joan C.
Hayes, John & Wilson, Alex, eds. Proceedings: Ninth National Passive Solar Conference, Columbus.
Hayes, John, jt. ed. see Schwolsky, Rick.
Hayes, John H. & Miller, J. Maxwell, eds. Israelite & Judaean History.
Hayes, Joseph. The Ways of Darkness.
Hayes, Julia. French Cooking for the People Who Can't.
Hayes, Leola G. Come & Get It: Reading for Information, Made Easy Through Recipes.
--I Can Help the Teacher: A Program for Training the Non-Academic Teacher Aide.
Hayes, Louis, jt. auth. see Woodin, J. C.
Hayes, Margaret Calder. Three Alexander Calders: A Family Memoir.
Hayes, Mary. The Memoirs of Emma Courtney.
Hayes, Michael. Money: How to Get It, Keep It, & Make It Grow.
--Pay Yourself First: The High Beta No-Load Way to Stock Market Profits.
--Stock Market Forecasting for Entrepreneurs.
Hayes, Norvel. God's Boot Camp.
--God's Power Through the Laying On of Hands.
--How to Protect Your Faith.
--The Seven Ways Jesus Heals.
--You Can Be a Soulwinner.
--Your Faith Can Heal You.
Hayes, O. William Bill. Personality & Salesmanship, Speedways to Success.
Hayes, Ralph. The Deadly Prey.
--Sheryl.
Hayes, Rick S. & Baker, C. Richard. Simplified Accounting for Non-Accountants.
Hayes, Rick S., jt. auth. see Baker, C. Richard.
Hayes, Ruth. Animal Husbandry.
Hayes, Sue T. God Made Farm Animals.
Hayes, Theresa, compiled by. God Is Everywhere: Fifteen Stories to Help Children Know God.
Hayes, Wayland J., Jr; see Blood, F. R.
Hayes, William C. The Burial Chamber of the Treasurer Sobk-Mose from Er-Rizeikat.
--Most Ancient Egypt. Seele, Keith C., ed.
--Scepter of Egypt: A Background for the Study of Egyptian Antiquities in the Metropolitan Museum of Art. Incl. Vol. 1. From the Earliest Times to the End of the Middle Kingdom; Vol. 2. The Hyksos Period & the New Kingdom (1675-1080 B.C.. Metro Mus Art.
Hayfield, Nancy. Cleaning House.
Hayford, Dolores, jt. auth. see Braemer, Alice.
Hayford, Harrison, ed. see Melville, Herman.
Hayford, Jack. The Visitor.
Haygood, Wil. Two on the River.
Hayhoe, F. G. & Flemans, R. J. A Color Atlas of Hematological Cytology.
Hayhurst, Emma L. I Will!
Hayhurst, G. Mathematical Programming for Management & Business.
Haykin, S., ed. Array Processing.
--Nonlinear Methods of Spectral Analysis.
Hayley, Rodney, ed. see Cibber, Colley.
Hayley, William. Ode, Inscribed to John Howard. Reiman, Donald H., ed. Bd. with An Essay on Painting: in Two Epistles to Mr. Romney...Third Edition Corrected & Enlarged; The Triumphs of Temper; a Poem. In Six Cantos; An Essay on Epic Poetry: in Five Epistles to the Rev. Mr. Mason. With Notes... Garland Pub.
Haymaker, Webb, et al. Hypothalamus.
Hayman, Laura L. & Sporing, Eileen. Handbook of Pediatric Nursing.
Hayman, Patty. BMX Bear.
Hayman, Ronald. Fassbinder.
--Gunter Grass.
--How to Read a Play.
Hayman, Ronald see Thwaite, Ann.
Haymes, Bill. The Bill Haymes Songbook.
Hayne, Catherine C., ed. Food Industry Benefit Plans 1984.
Haynes, Brian, et al. Compliance in Health Care.
Haynes, Cynthia. Raising Chickens.
Haynes, David G., tr. see Akhmanova, O. S., et al.
Haynes, Denys. Greek Art & the Idea of Freedom.
Haynes, Elton. Tales of Poultney.
Haynes, Henry L. Squarehead & Me.
Haynes, J. H. Haynes General Motors J Car Owners Workshop Manual 1982 thru 1987.
--Haynes GM-A Cars Owners Workshop Manual 1982 thru 1987.
Haynes, J. H. & Chalmers Hunt, B. L. Rover 2000 & 2200 '63 - '73.
Haynes, J. H. & Page, S. F. Ford Anglia Owners Workshop Manual: '59 Thru '68.
Haynes, J. H., jt. auth. see Choate, Curt.
Haynes, James Percival. Thunderbolt-Champ of the Patowmack.
Haynes, R., ed. Environmental Science Methods.
Haynes, Stephen L. Computers & Litigation Support.
Haynes, Stephen N. & Wilson, C. Chrisman. Behavioral Assessment: Recent Advances in Methods, Concepts, & Applications.
Haynes, Warren W., jt. auth. see Henry, William R.
Haynes, William W. Nationalization in Practice: The British Coal Industry.
Hays, Donald. The Dixie Association.
Hays, H. R., tr. see Brecht, Bertolt.
Hays, James D. Our Changing Climate.
Hays, Mary. Appeal to the Men of Great Britain on Behalf of Women. Luria, Gina, ed.
Hays, Samuel P. Conservation & the Gospel of Efficiency: The Progressive Conservation Movement, 1890-1920.
--Conservation & the Gospel of Efficiency: The Progressive Conservation Movement, 1890-1920.
Hayt, William H. & Nevdeck, Gerold W. Electronic Circuit Analysis & Design.
Hayter, Concilia, tr. see Mitterand, Francois.
Hayter, Judith. Canary Island Hopping: The Azores Madeira.
Haythornthwaite, Philip. British Infantry of the Napoleonic Wars.
Hayum, Andree. Giovanni Antonio Bazzi - "Il Sodoma"
Hayward, E., jt. ed. see Fuller, E. G.
Hayward, G. G., jt. auth. see Thompson, F.
Hayward, Helena & Kirkham, Pat. William & John Linnell: 18th Century London Furniture Makers.
Hayward, J. F. European Firearms.
Hayward, J. L. & Bulbrook, R. D., eds. Clinical Evaluation in Breast Cancer.
Hayward, Jane & Horbar, Amy, eds. Glass in the Collections of the Metropolitan Museum of Art.
Hayward, Linda. A Phonic Dictionary.
--The Simon & Schuster Picture Dictionary of Phonics from A to Zh.
Hayward, Max. Writers in Russia: 1917-1978. Blake, Patricia, ed. Schapiro, Leonard.
Hayward, Max, ed. see Siniavskii, Andrei D.
Hayward, Max, tr. see Gladkov, Alexander.
Hayward, Nancy, jt. auth. see Fairchild, Betty.
Hayward, W. H. Introduction to Radio Frequency Design.
Haywood, Carolyn. A Christmas Fantasy.
--The King's Monster.
--Two & Two Are Four.
Haywood, Stuart & Alaszewski, Andy. Crisis in the Health Service: The Politics of Management.
Haywood, Trevor. Walking with a Camera in Herries Lakeland.
Hazard, Barbara. Dangerous Lady.
Hazard, Geoffrey C., Jr., ed. Law in a Changing America.
Hazari, Bharat R. Colonialism & Foreign Ownership of Capital: A Trade Theorist's View.
--The Pure Theory of International Trade & Distortions.
Hazel. Yearwood.
Hazel, A. C. & Reid, A. S. Enjoying a Profitable Business.
Hazel, John, jt. auth. see Grant, Michael.
Hazel, Jon, ed. Ovid-The Roman World: Selections from the Poems.
Hazell, Robert. Conspiracy & Civil Liberties.
Hazelton, Roger. Ascending Flame, Descending Dove: An Essay on Creative Transcendence.
--Blaise Pascal: The Genius of His Thought.
--Graceful Courage: A Venture in Christian Humanism.
Hazen, Barbara S. The Fat Cats, Cousin Scraggs & the Monster Mice.
--The Gorilla Did It.
--Gorilla Wants to Be the Baby.
--Step on It, Andrew.
--The Ups & Downs of Marvin.
--The Very Best Name for Baby.
Hazen, Helen. Endless Rapture: Rape, Romance, & the Female Imagination.
Hazen, M. Hindle, jt. ed. see Hazen, R. M.
Hazen, R. M., ed. North American Geology: Early Writings.
Hazen, R. M. & Hazen, M. Hindle, eds. American Geological Literature 1669-1850.
Hazen, Thomas L. Securities Regulation: The Law of 1987 Pocket Part.
Hazleton, Lesley. Jerusalem, Jerusalem. Johnson, Joyce, ed.
Hazlitt, Henry. Economics in One Lesson.
Hazlitt, William. The Hazlitt Sampler: Selections from His Familiar, Literary & Critical Essays. Sikes, H. M., ed.
Hazlitt, William C. English Proverbs & Proverbial Phrases.
--Gleanings in Old Garden Literature.
--Old Cookery Books & Ancient Cuisine.
--Studies in Jocular Literature.
Hazo, Samuel. Inscripts.
--Smithereened Apart: A Critique of Hart Crane.
Hazo, Samuel, tr. see Adonis.
Hazrat Inayat Khan. The Awakening of the Human Spirit.
Hazzard, B. J., et al. Organicum: A Practical Handbook of Organic Chemistry.
H. D. Selected Poems of H. D.
H. D., pseud. Tribute to Freud.
He & Ying. The White Haired Girl.
Heacock, D. A Psychodynamic Approach to Adolescent Psychiatry.
Heacock, John, ed. The Earth's Crust: Its Nature & Physical Properties.
Heacox, Kim. Alaska's Inside Passage.
Head, Brian, ed. Politics & Development.
Head, Diane. Come to the Waters.
Head, J. J., ed. see Adrian, R. H.
Head, J. J., ed. see Chappell, J. B.
Head, J. J., ed. see Gray, E. G.
Head, J. J., ed. see Nachmias, Vivianne T.
Head, J. J., ed. see Neil, Eric.
Head, J. J., ed. see Neville, Charles.
Head, J. J., ed. see Sanders, F. Kingsley.
Head, J. J., ed. see Sidebottom, Eric & Ringertz, Nils.
Head, J. J., ed. see Travers, A. A.
Head, J. J., ed. see Weale, R. A.
Head, J. J., ed. see Whittingham, C. P.
Head, John, jt. ed. see Beatts, Anne.
Head, R. V. A Guide to Packaged Systems.
Head, Robert G. & Nurenberg, Phil. The Enriched Uranium Poems-Bern Porter Interview.
Head, Sydney W. Broadcasting in America.
Head, Sydney W., et al. Broadcasting in America.
Head, Timothy E. Going Native in Hawaii: A Poor Man's Guide to Paradise.
Head, William F., Jr. Pharmaceutical Quality Control.
Headapohl, Betty. Song of Love.
Headapohl, Betty R. Bittersweet Love.
--By Love Renewed.
Headland, Isaac T. Home Life in China.
Headley, Lee. Adults & Their Parents in Family Therapy: A New Direction in Treatment.
Headridge, J. B. Electrochemical Techniques for Inorganic Chemists.
Headstrom, Richard. Adventures with a Hand Lens.
--Memories from a Naturalists' Notebook: A Year of Favorite Observations in the World of Nature.
--Suburban Geology: An Introduction to the Common Rocks & Minerals of Your Back Yard & Local Park.
Heady, Earl O. see Ball, A. Gordon.
Heafford, Philip. The Math Entertainer.
--The Math Entertainer.
Heald, Gordan, ed. The International Values Databooks.
Heald, Gordon & Wybrow, Robert J., eds. The Gallup Survey of Britain, 1985.
Heald, M. A. & Wharton, C. B. Plasma Diagnostics with Microwaves.
Heald, Tim. Caroline R.
--Old Boy Networks: Who We Know & How We Use Them.
--Red Herrings.
--Red Herrings.
Healey, Deryck. New Art of Flower Design.
Healey, Estelle R., tr. see Von Duerckheim, Karlfried.
Healey, Frederick G. Fifty Key Words: Theology.
Healey, Larry. The Hoard of the Himalayas.
Healey, M. Advances in Small Computer Technology.
Healey, M. C. & Wallace, R. R., eds. Canadian Aquatic Resources.
Healey, Martin. Principles of Automatic Control.
Healey, P. & McDougall, G., eds. Planning Theory-Prospects for the Nineteen Eighties: Selected Papers from a Conference Held in Oxford, U. K., 2-4 April 1981.
Healey, R. M. Hertfordshire: A Shell Guide.
Health Care Education Associates Staff. Professional Writing Skills for Health Care Managers.
Healthcare Financial Management Association Staff. Certified Professional Membership Directory.
--Description & Analysis of Medicare Prospective Price Setting Including Changes for Year Three.
--Directions in Healthcare 1985 to 1987.
--HFM Readings.
--Long Term Care: Challenges & Opportunities.
Healy, A. M. Tunku Abdul Rahman.
Healy, Anthony & Yaldwyn, John C. Australian Crustaceans in Colour.
Healy, C., jt. auth. see Winn, Charles S.
Healy, Diana D. America's Vice-Presidents: Our First Forty-Three Vice-Presidents & How They Got to Be Number Two.
Healy, J. W. Plutonium, Health Implications for Man: Proceedings of the 2nd Los Alamos Life Sciences Symposium.
Healy, James T. Winning the High Technology Sales Game.
Healy, Juanita see Summerlin, Lee R.
Healy, Kathleen, jt. auth. see Van Kamm, Adrian.
Healy, Kent T. Performance of the U. S. Railroads since World War II.
--Performance of the U. S. Railroads since World War II.
Healy, M. Tables of Laplace, Heaviside, Fourier & Z Transforms.
Heaney, L. R. & Patterson, B. D., eds. Island Biogeography of Mammals.
Heaney, Seamus. Poems: Nineteen Sixty-Five to Nineteen Seventy-Five.
Heap, A., jt. auth. see Lal, Deepak.
Heap, Ken. Process & Action in Work with Groups: The Preconditions for Treatment & Growth.
Heape, Charles, jt. auth. see Edge-Partington, James.
Heaps, N. S., jt. ed. see Dyke, P. P.
Heaps, Willard A. Juvenile Justice.
--Riots, U. S. A.
--Taxation, U. S. A.
Heard, Alexander, ed. State Legislatures in American Politics.
Heard, Carolyn M. Fast-n-Easy Phrase Book.
Heard, James, jt. auth. see Hall, Alan.
Heard, James E. & Sherman, Howard D. Conflicts of Interest in the Proxy Voting System.
Hearle, J. W., et al. Use of the Scanning Electron Microscope.
Hearn. Peptide & Protein Reviews.
Hearn, Diane D. Uncle Traveling Matt's Adventures in Outer Space.
Hearn, Diane Dawson, illus. Muppet Babies' Mother Goose.
Hearn, E. J. Mechanics of Materials.
Hearn, Edward R., jt. auth. see Erickson, J. Gunnar.
Hearn, Gordon, ed. General Systems Approach: Contributions Toward an Holistic Conception of Social Work.
Hearn, Lafcadio. Tale of the Porcelain God.
Hearn, M. F. Romanesque Sculpture: The Revival of Monumental Stone Sculpture in the Eleventh & the Twelfth Centuries.
Hearn, Milton W., ed. Peptide & Protein Reviews.
Hearne, Betsy & Kaye, Marilyn. Celebrating Children's Books.
Hearne, Betsy G. Choosing Books for Children.
--South Star.
Hearnshaw, F. J., ed. The Social & Political Ideas of Some English Thinkers of the Augustan Age, A.D. 1650-1750. A Series of Lectures Delivered at King's College University of London during the Session 1927-28.
--The Social & Political Ideas of Some Representative Thinkers of the Revolutionary Era: A Series of Lectures Delivered at King's College University of London during the Session 1929-30.
Hearon, Shelby. Painted Dresses.
--A Small Town.
Hearth, Douglas. Federal Intervention in the Mortgage Markets: An Analysis. Farmer, Richard N., ed.
Heasler, Richard. Whispers on the Wind.
Heaslip, L., jt. auth. see McLean, A.
Heat & Mass Transfer in Buildings Summer Seminar Staff. Energy Conservation in Heating, Cooling & Ventilating Buildings: Proceedings of Heat & Mass Transfer in Buildings Summer Seminar, Dubrovnik, Yugoslavia, Aug. 29-Sept. 3, 1977. Hoogendoorn, C. J. & Afgan, N., eds.
Heater, Sandra H. Am I Still Visible? A Woman's Triumph over Anorexia Nervosa.
Heath, C. J. & Jones, E. G. The Anatomical Organization of the Suprasylvian Gyrus of the Cat.
Heath, Carl. Social & Religious Heretics in Five Centuries.
Heath, Catherine. Behaving Badly.
--Lady on the Burning Deck.

Authors

Heath, Charles. The A-Team, No. 3: When You Comin' Back, Range Rider?
--Your Future in Big Business.
Heath, Ed, jt. auth. see Kirk, Kris.
Heath, Edward M. Old World, New Horizons: Britain, Europe, & the Atlantic Alliance.
Heath, G. Louis. The High School Rebel: Readings in Adolescent School Rebellion.
Heath, Helen T., ed. The Letters of Samuel Pepys & His Family Circle.
Heath, I. B., ed. Nuclear Division in the Fungi.
Heath, L., jt. auth. see Winn, Charles S.
Heath, Leslie G. & Faux, Ian. Introductory Phototypesetting.
Heath, Phillip A., jt. ed. see Kristo, Janice V.
Heath, Royton E. Rock Plants for Small Gardens.
Heath, Samuel. Coat & Skirt Making: Skirts, Trousers, Jackets & Coats.
Heath, Sidney. The Romance of Symbolism & Its Relation to Church Ornament & Architecture.
Heath, Thomas. Mathematics in Aristotle.
Heath, Veronica. A Dog at My Heel.
Heath, William L. Most Valuable Player.
Heather, Nick. Radical Perspectives in Psychology.
Heatley, R. V., jt. ed. see Losowsky, M. S.
Heaton, E. W. The Old Testament Prophets.
--Solomon's New Men.
Heaton, Herbert. Productivity in Service Organizations: Organizing for People.
Heaton, Israel C. & Thorstenson, Clark T. Planning for Social Recreation.
Heaton, J. B. Beginning Composition Through Pictures.
Heaton, Willis E., jt. auth. see Waren, Oscar.
Heatter, Justin W. Buying a Condominium.
--The Small Investor's Guide to Large Profits in the Stock Market.
--Take Charge of Your Finances & Win Financial Freedom.
Heatwole, Harold. Reptile Ecology.
Heavey, Susan, jt. auth. see Heavey, Thomas.
Heavey, Thomas & Heavey, Susan. Twenty Bicycle Tours in New Hampshire.
Heavner, Martin L. see Hill, Richard F., et al.
Heavner, Martin L., jt. ed. see Zimmer, Michael J.
Heavyside, G. T. Narrow Gauge into the Eighties.
Hebart, Friedemann. One in the Gospel.
Hebbard, Neysa, ed. More Great New England Recipes: And the Cooks Who Made Them Famous.
Hebbard, Neysa, ed. see Janericco, Terence.
Hebbard, Neysa, ed. see Lazzaro, Bea & Mendelsohn, Lotte.
Hebblethwaite, Peter. In the Vatican.
--The New Inquisition? The Case of Edward Schillebeeckx & Hans Kung.
--Pope John XXIII: Shepherd of the Modern World.
Hebeisen, Ardyth. Peer Program for Youth.
Heberle, Dave, jt. auth. see Wallace, Hal.
Hebert, Albert J. Priestly Celibacy: Recurrent Battle & Lasting Values.
Hebert, F. Ted. Oklahoma Legislative Voting: A Roll Call Analysis for 1970-1974.
Hebert, R. H., jt. auth. see Ekelund, Robert B.
Hechler, Ken. The Bridge at Remagen.
Hecht, Anthony. Hard Hours.
--Obbligati: Essays in Criticism.
--The Venetian Vespers.
Hecht, Ben. Fantazius Mallare: A Mysterious Oath.
--The Kingdom of Evil: A Continuation of the Journal of Fantazius Mallare.
Hecht, Caroline, jt. auth. see Hecht, Miriam.
Hecht, David. Russian Radicals Look to America, 1825-1894.
Hecht, Helen. Cold Cuisine.
--Cold Cuisine.
--Cuisine for All Seasons: A Menu Cookbook.
Hecht, Helen & Mushlin, Linda L. Gifts in Good Taste.
Hecht, Ingeborg. Invisible Walls: A German Family under the Nuremberg Laws. Brownjohn, J. Maxwell, tr. from Ger.
Hecht, Jeff & Teresi, Dick. Laser: Supertool of the Nineteen Eighties.
Hecht, Max K., et al, eds. Evolutionary Biology.
Hecht, Miriam & Hecht, Caroline. Modumath: Arithmetic.
Hecht, Myron. File & Database Management Programs for the IBM-PC.
Hecht, N. L., jt. auth. see Gerdeman, D. A.
Hecht, Robert A. Continents in Collision: Documents.
Hecht, S. H., ed. Bleomycin: Chemical, Biochemical & Biological Aspects.
Hechter, Michael. Principles of Group Solidarity.
Hechtlinger, Adelaide. The Seasonal Hearth: The Woman at Home in Early America.
Heckel, Frederick C. A Tale of Ancient Egypt.
Hecker, S. S., et al, eds. see TMS Staff & AIME Staff.
Hecker, W. C., jt. auth. see Rickham, P. P.
Heckhausen, Heinz. Anatomy of Achievement Motivation.
Hecklinger, Fred J. & Curtin, Bernadette M. Training for Life: A Practical Guide to Career & Life Planning.
Heckman, Marlin L. Overland on the California Trail, 1846-1859.
Heckman, Richard, ed. Yankees under Sail.
Heckman, Richard D., jt. auth. see Chambers, Carl D.
Heckman, Theodore, ed. The Nativity of Christ.
Heckscher, August & Robinson, Phyllis. When LaGuardia Was Mayor: New York's Legendary Years.
Heckscher, August, jt. auth. see Aron, Raymond.
Heckscher, Eli F. Mercantilism.
Hedayat, Sadegh. Blind Owl. Costello, D. P., tr.
Hedberg, Nancy. Rings of Grass.
--A Rooted Sorrow.
Hedden, Jay, jt. auth. see Dean, Thomas.
Heddle, T. Calculations in Fundamental Physics. Incl. Vol. 1. Mechanics & Heat; Vol. 2. Electricity & Magnetism. Pergamon.
Heden, C. G. & King, A., eds. Social Innovations for Development.
Hedgecoe, John. John Hedgecoe's Complete Course in Photographing Children.
--John Hedgecoe's Darkroom Techniques.
--John Hedgecoe's Nude Photography.
--John Hedgecoe's Photographer's Workbook.
--John Hedgecoe's Taking Great Photographs.
Hedges. Fun for the Not So Young.
Hedges, Bob A., jt. auth. see Mehr, Robert I.
Hedges, Elaine & Wendt, Ingrid, eds. In Her Own Image: Women Working in the Arts.
Hedges, Elaine R. & Hedges, William L. Land & Imagination: The Rural Dream in America.
Hedges, Sid G. Games for the Not So Young.
Hedges, William L., jt. auth. see Hedges, Elaine R.
Hedgpeth, Don. Cowboy.
Hedinger, C. Histological Typing of Thyroid Tumours.
Hedley, Arthur. Chopin.
Hedley, R. H. & Adams, C. G., eds. Foraminifera.
--Foraminifera.
Hedlin, Edie. Business Archives: An Introduction.
Hedlund, Douglas E. What Every Potential Homeowner Should Know about Construction, Vol. I, General Construction: Residential Construction Information & Details That Every Potential Homeowner Should Be Familiar With.
Hedlund, Gunnar & Otterbeck, Lars. The Multinational Corporation, the Nation State & the Trade Unions: A European Perspective.
Hedman, Emma. Plow a New Furrow.
Hedman, Richard. Stop Me Before I Plan Again.
--Stop Me Before I Plan Again.
Hedren, Tippi & Taylor, Theodore. The Cats of Shambala.
Hedrick, Hannah H., jt. ed. see Burrows, William R.
Hedrick, U. P. Fruits for the Home Garden.
Hedvig, Peter. Quantum Effects in Organic Chemistry.
Hedwig, J. Species Muscorum Frondosorum.
Heemann, Warren. Criteria for Evaluating Advancement Programs.
Heemst, H. D. Van see Makkink, G. F. & Van Heemst, H. D.
Heen, E. & Kreuzer, R., eds. Fish in Nutrition.
Heenan, Cathy, jt. auth. see Cooper, Susan.
Heeney, Brian. A Different Kind of Gentleman: Parish Clergy As Professional Men in Early & Mid-Victorian England.
Heer, C. V. Statistical Mechanics, Kinetic, Theory & Stochastic Process.
Heere, Wybo P. International Bibliography of Air Law, 1900-1971.
Heeren, Vern E., jt. auth. see Miller, Charles D.
Heerikhuizen, F. W. Van see Van Heerikhuizen, F. W.
Heering, Gerrit J. Fall of Christianity.
Heertje, Arnold, et al. Economics.
Heesakkers, Wim. My First Step.
--My Little Brother.
--My Little Cat Woodbook.
--My Little Goose Woodbook.
Hees-Stauthamer, Jellemieke C. The First Pregnancy: An Integrating Principle in Female Psychology. Nathan, Peter E., ed.
Hefferman, Terry, jt. auth. see Johnson, Brian.
Heffernan, H., jt. auth. see Todd, Vivian E.
Heffernan, James A. & Lincoln, John E. Writing-A College Workbook: Ancillary for Writing a College Handbook.
Heffernan, William. The Corsican.
Heffernen, Maureen, ed. see Gohlke, Mary & Jennings, Max.
Hefford, R. K. Farm Policy in Australia.
Hefford, Ron, et al. An Introduction to the Australian Economy.
Heffron, Dorris. Nice Fire & Some Moonpennies.
Heffron, Mary J., jt. ed. see Fenton, Thomas P.
Hefley, James C. Running with God.
Hefley, James C., jt. auth. see Steinberg, Jeff.
Hefley, Marti. Assignment in the Philippines: Dramatic Accounts from Jared & Marilee Barker.
Hefley, Marti, jt. auth. see Dean, Dave.
Hefner, Philip, jt. auth. see Benne, Robert.
Hefner, Philip, tr. see Ritschl, Albrecht.
Hefter, Richard. Lion Is Down in the Dumps.
--Moody Moose Buttons.
--Stork Spills the Beans.
--Very Worried Walrus.
--Zip Goes Zebra.
Hefter, Richard & Reinach, Jacquelyn. Yakety-Yak-Yak Yak.
Hefter, Richard, et al. Pig Thinks Pink. Perle, Ruth L. & Reinach, Jacquelyn, eds.
Heftmann, E. Steroid Biochemistry.
Heftmann, Erich, ed. Modern Methods of Steroid Analysis.
Hegarty, Edward J. How to Succeed in Company Politics.
Hegde, K. S. Crisis in Indian Judiciary.
Hegedus, Andras. The Structure of Socialist Society.
Hegel. Encyclopedia of Philosophy.
Hegel, G. W. Three Essays, Seventeen Ninety-Three to Seventeen Ninety-Five: The Tubingen Essay, Berne Fragments, The Life of Jesus. Fuss, Peter & Dobbins, John, eds.
Hegel, Georg W. Lectures on the Philosophy of Religion. Speirs, E. B. & Sanderson, J. B., trs.
--Phenomenology of Mind. Baillie, J. B., tr.
Hegel, George W. Political Writings.
Hegel, Richard. Nineteenth Century Historians of New Haven.
Hegener, Karen C. The College Money Handbook.
Hegener, Karen C., jt. auth. see Zuker, R. Fred.
Hegener, Karen C., ed. Peterson's Competitive Colleges.
Heggen, P. M. Solar Concentrating Mirrors.
Heggen, Thomas. Mister Roberts.
Hegner, Robert W., jt. auth. see Engemann, Joseph G.
Heiberg, J. L., tr. see Archimedes.
Heiberg, Milton. Nikon F-Three: Amphoto Pocket Companion.
Heick, Welf H. & Graham, Roger, eds. His Own Man: Essays in Honour of Arthur Reginald Marsden Lower.
Heid, John L. & Joslyn, Maynard A. Fundamentals of Food Processing Operations: Ingredients, Methods & Packaging.
Heide, Florence P. The Key.
--Who Needs Me.
Heide, Florence P. & Heide, Roxanne. The Mystery of the Bewitched Bookmobile.
--Mystery of the Midnight Message.
--Mystery of the Vanishing Visitor.
Heide, Florence P. & Van Clief, Sylvia. Mystery of the Silver Tag.
--Mystery of the Whispering Voice.
Heide, Robert see Hoffman, William M.
Heide, Roxanne, jt. auth. see Heide, Florence P.
Heidegger. Essays in Metaphysics.
Heidegger, Martin. Early Greek Thinking. Krell, David & Capuzzi, Frank, trs.
Heidegger, Martin & Fink, Eugen. Heraclitus Seminar, Nineteen Sixty-Six to Nineteen Sixty-Seven. Seibert, Charles H., tr.
Heidel, William A. Selected Papers. Taran, Leonardo, ed.
Heider, E., et al. Svenska Fur Nyborjaae.
Heidish, Marcy. Witnesses.
Heiges, Donald R. The Christian's Calling.
Height, Frank, jt. ed. see Gorman, Michael.
Heijden, A. H. Van Der see Van Der Heijden, A. H.
Heijenoort, Jean Van see Van Heijenoort, Jean.
Heilborn, John. Atari ST User's Guide.
Heilborn, John & Talbott, Ran. VIC-20 User Guide.
Heilborn, John, ed. Science & Engineering Programs: Apple II Edition.
Heilbron, Bertha L. The Thirty-Second State: A Pictorial History of Minnesota.
Heilbroner, Robert L. Between Capitalism & Socialism: Essays in Political Economics.
--Business Civilization in Decline.
--An Inquiry into the Human Prospect.
--An Inquiry into the Human Prospect.
Heilbroner, Robert L. & Singer, Aaron. The Economic Transformation of America.
Heilbroner, Robert L. & Thurow, L. Economic Problem.
Heilbroner, Robert L. & Thurow, Lester C. The Economic Problem.
--The Economic Problem: (Third CPCU Edition)
Heilbroner, Robert L. & Thurow, Lester. Economics Explained.
--Economics Explained.
Heilbronner, E. & Straub, P. A. HMO-Hueckel Molecular Orbitals.
Heilbrunn, L. V. Viscosity of Protoplasm.
Heilbut, Anthony. Exiled in Paradise: German Refugee Artists & Intellectuals from the 1930's to Present.
Heillig, Roma J. Adolescent Suicidal Behavior: A Family Systems Model. Nathan, Peter E., ed.
Heilman, Gail. The Complete Outfitting & Source Book for Bicycle Touring.
Heilman, Grant, jt. auth. see McManigal, J. W.
Heilman, Joan, jt. auth. see Ford, Eileen.
Heilman, Joan R. Grandma's Large Type Knitting Book.
Heilman, Samuel. The Gate Behind the Wall.
--A Walker in Jerusalem.
Heilmann, Klaus. Therapeutic Systems: Pattern-Specific Drug Delivery: Concept & Development.
Heilmeyer, L., ed. see Colloquium of the Gesellschaft Fuer Biologische Chemie Staff.
Heilpern, John, ed. see Klein, William.
Heim, David, jt. auth. see Carlinsky, Dan.
Heim, Lafcadio. Japan's Religions, Shinto & Buddhism.
Heim, Michael H., tr. see Aksyonov, Vassily.
Heim, Ralph D. Reader's Companion to the Bible.
Heimbold, Noreen & Betts, Jim. New Products.
Heimenz, U. & Schatz, K. W. Trade in Place of Migration.
Heimlich, Henry J. & Galton, Lawrence. Dr. Heimlich's Home Guide to Emergency Medical Situations.
--Dr. Heimlich's Home Guide to Emergency Medical Situations.
Heimlich, Ralph E. & Langner, Linda L. Swampbusting: Wetland Conversion & Farm Programs.
Hein, Peter C. Business Information: Protection & Disclosure.
Hein, Philippe, jt. ed. see Dommen, Edward.
Hein, Ruth, tr. see Bruckner, Christine.
Heinberg, John D., jt. auth. see Carlson, David B.
Heinberg, John D., et al. Housing Allowances in Kansas City & Wilmington: An Appraisal.
Heine, Heinrich. The North Sea. Jones, Howard M., tr.
Heine, Helme. Mr. Miller the Dog.
Heine, Marc. Poland.
Heine, Marc E., tr. see Lem, Stanislaw.
Heine, V. Group Theory in Quantum Mechanics.
Heinecken, Karl H. Von see Von Heinecken, Karl H.
Heinegg, Peter, tr. see Ditfurth, Hoimar.
Heinen, Anton M. Islamic Cosmology.
Heinerman, John. Medical Doctors Guide to Herbs.
Heiney, Donald. America in Modern Italian Literature.
Heinig, Ruth B. & Stillwell, Lyda. Creative Drama for the Classroom Teacher.
Heinl, Nancy G., jt. auth. see Heinl, Robert D., Jr.
Heinl, Robert D., Jr. & Heinl, Nancy G. Written in Blood: The Story of the Haitian People 1492-1971.
Heinlein, Albert C., ed. Decision Models in Academic Administration.
Heinlein, Robert A. A Double Star.
--Friday.
--Job: A Comedy of Justice.
--The Moon Is a Harsh Mistress.
--The Past Through Tomorrow.
--Starship Troopers.
--To Sail Beyond the Sunset.
Heinlein, W. E. & Holmes, W. H. Active Filters for Integrated Circuits.
Heinman, S. A. Scientific & Technical Revolution: Economic Aspects.
Heinonen, O. P., et al. Birth Defects & Drugs in Pregnancy.
Heinrich, Amy V., jt. ed. see Martin, Roberta.
Heinrich, Herbert W. Industrial Accident Prevention.
Heinrich, Milton R., ed. Extreme Environments: Mechanisms of Microbial Adaptation.
Heinrich, Peggy, jt. auth. see Uhlmann, John.
Heinroth, Johann C. Textbook of Disturbances of the Mental Life, or Disturbances of the Psyche & Their Treatment.
Heins, Conrad, jt. auth. see Derucher, Kenneth N.
Heins, M. Hardy Classes on Riemann Surfaces.
Heins, Maurice. Complex Function Theory.
Heintzelman, Donald S. The Birdwatcher's Activity Book.
--Guide to Owl Watching in North America.
--A World Guide to Whales, Dolphins & Porpoises.
Heintzen, Paul H. & Bursch, J. H., eds. Roentgen-Video-Techniques.
Heiny, Robert L., jt. auth. see Bryson, Maurice C.
Heinz, E. Mechanics & Energetics of Biological Transport.
Heinz, E., ed. see International Congress of Physiological Sciences, Satellite Symposium, 1971.
Heinz Foods Editors. The Condiment Cookbook.
Heinz, H. J. & Lee, Marshall. Namkwa: Life Among the Bushmen.
Heinz, W. C. The Professional.
Heinze, S. Fachwoerterbuch des Versicherungswesen.
Heisberger, Jean M., ed. Arise Jerusalem: Parish Advent Program, Advent Family Handbook.
Heise, David R., ed. Sociological Methodology 1976.
Heise, Kenan & Edgerton, Michael. Chicago: Center For Enterprise.
Heisel, W. D. & Skinner, Gordon S. Costing Union Demands.
Heisenberg, Werner. Nuclear Physics.

Heiserman, Arthur. The Novel Before the Novel: Essays & Discussions About the Beginnings of Prose Fiction in the West.
Heiserman, David. Programmers Reference Guide For the Atari 400-800 Computers.
Heiserman, David L. Apple IIe Programmer's Reference Guide.
--Beginner's Handbook of IC Projects.
--Handbook of Digital IC Applications.
--Handbook of Major Appliance Trouble-Shooting & Repair.
--One Hundred One Programming Surprises & Tricks for Your Commodore 64 Computer.
Heisey, Marion J. Clinical Case Studies in Psychodrama.
Heisig, James W., tr. see Waldenfels, Hans.
Heisler, Bernice C. Brook to River, River to Sea.
Heiss, W. D. & Phelps, M. F., eds. Positron Emission Tomography of the Brain.
Heiting, Kenneth. When Your Child Is Hyperactive.
Heitman, Sidney, ed. Nikolai I. Bukharin: A Bibliography.
Heitner, Robert R., ed. The Contemporary Novel in German: A Symposium.
Heitzman & Mueller. Statistics for Business & Economics.
Heitzmann, William R., jt. auth. see National Education Association Staff.
Heizer, Robert & Elsasser, Albert B. A Bibliography of California Indians: Archaelogy, Ethnography, Indian History.
Heizer, Robert F. Man's Discovery of His Past.
Heizer, Robert F., jt. auth. see Hole, Frank.
Hejzlar, Zdenek & Kusin, Vladimir. Czechoslovakia Nineteen Sixty-Eight - Nineteen Sixty-Nine: Annotation, Bibliography, Chronology.
Hekken, P. M. Land Scarcity & Rural Inequality in Tanzania: Some Case Studies from Rungwe District.
Helander, Donald P. Fundamentals of Formation Evaluation.
Helberg, Kristin. Cowboys.
Helbling, Robert E. & Barnett, A. Introduction Au Francais Actuel.
Helbling, Robert E., et al. Aspekte: First-Year German Reader.
Held. IBM-PC User's Reference Manual.
Held, G. IBM-PCjr User's Reference Manual.
Held, Gilbert. Data Communications Procurement Manual.
--Lotus 1-2-3 Models.
--Multiplan Models.
--SuperCalc 3 Models.
Held, Gilbert & Sarch, Ray. Data Communications: A Comprehensive Approach.
Held, Julius S., ed. Rubens & the Book: Title Pages by Peter Paul Rubens (1977)
Held, Shirley E. Weaving: A Handbook of Fiber Arts.
Helden, Albert Van see Van Helden, Albert.
Helen, Mary & Dawson, Glen. Miniature Publications of Dawson's Book Shop. Mundell, E. H., ed.
Helfer, Ray E., jt. auth. see Kempe, C. Henry.
Helfgott, Daniel. The Buried.
Helfman, Elizabeth S. Maypoles & Wood Demons: The Meaning of Trees.
--Signs & Symbols of the Sun.
Helgeland, John & Daly, Robert J. Christians & the Military: The Early Experience. Burns, J. Patout, ed.
Helinandus. Vers de la Mort.
Heliodorus Of Emesa. An Ethiopian Romance. Hadas, Moses, tr.
Hell, Henri. Francis Poulenc.
Hellebust, Lynn. State Legislative Sourcebook, 1986: A Resource Guide to Legislative Information in the Fifty States.
Helleiner, Frederick M., ed. see International Geographical Congress Staff.
Hellekson, Terry. Popular Fly Patterns.
Heller, Agnes, jt. auth. see Feher, Ferenc.
Heller Associates Staff. The Heller Report: The National Plan for Science Abstracting & Indexing Services.
Heller, David. Vortex.
Heller, David & Johnson, John. Dr. C. Wacko Presents Atari BASIC & the Whiz-Bang Miracle Machine.
Heller, David, et al. Dr. C. Wacko's Miracle Guide to Designing & Programming Your Own Atari Computer Arcade Games.
Heller, Denise L. An Analysis of Police Assailants in Albuquerque.
Heller, Erica & Levites, Vicki. Three Hundred Ways to Say No to Your Man.
Heller, Fred I., jt. auth. see Practising Law Institute Staff.
Heller, Gerhard B., ed. Thermophysics & Temperature Control of Spacecraft & Entry Vehicles, PAAS18.
Heller, H., tr. see Lembeck, F., et al.
Heller, Joseph. Catch Twenty-Two.
--Catch 22.
--God Knows.
--Good As Gold.
Heller, Keith. Man's Storm: A Novel of Crime Set in London...1703.
Heller, Lois J. & Mohrman, David E. Cardiovascular Physiology. Mixter, Richard W., ed.
Heller, Mel. So Now You're a Principal. Koerner, T., ed.
Heller, Mikhail & Nekrich, Aleksandr. Utopia in Power.
Heller, R. International Trade: Theory & Empirical Evidence.
Heller, R. A., jt. ed. see Hasselman, D. P.
Heller, Rachelle & Martin, Dianne. Bits 'n Bytes about Computing for Everyone.
Heller, Rachelle S. & Martin, C. Dianne. Bits 'n Bytes about Computing: A Computer Literacy Primer.
--Bits 'n Bytes Gazette.
Heller, Richard M. & Squire, Lucy F. Pediatrics.
Heller, Robert. The Business of Business: Managing with Style.
--Super Self: The Art & Science of Self-Management: A Practical Guide to Getting the Most Out of Your Life.
--The Supermanagers: Managing for Success, the Movers & the Doers, & the Reasons Why.
Heller, Robert, et al, eds. Challenges to Science: Earth Science.
Heller, Robert J. How to Win at Trivial Pursuit.
Heller, Steve. The Automotive History of Lucky Kellerman.
Heller, Steven & Chwast, Seymour, eds. Patient's Revenge.
Heller, Suzanne. Misery Loves Company.
--More Misery.
Heller, Walter. New Dimensions of Political Economy.
Heller, Walter W. The Economy: Old Myths & New Realities.
Heller, Wendy. The Sunshine Tree: And Other Tales From Around the World.
Hellerstein, Herman K., jt. auth. see Wenger, Nanette K.
Hellerstein, Jerome R. & Hellerstein, Walter. State & Local Taxation Cases & Materials.
Hellerstein, Walter, jt. auth. see Hellerstein, Jerome R.
Hellman, Hal. Energy in the World of the Future.
--Feeding the World of the Future.
--Technophobia: Getting Out of the Technology Trap.
--Transportation in the World of the Future.
Hellman, Joan R., jt. auth. see Mirsky, Stanley.
Hellman, John. Simone Weil: An Introduction to Her Thought.
Hellman, K., jt. ed. see Hilgard, P.
Hellman, Lillian. Maybe: A Story.
--Maybe: A Story.
Hellman, Peter. Avenue of the Righteous.
Hellman, R. G. & Rosenbaum, H. J. Latin America: The Search for a New International Role.
Hellmann, Kurt, ed. see Stanford Cade Memorial Symposium Staff.
Hellmuth, James G. Finding Money.
Hellmuth, Theodore H. Missouri Leasing Guide for Nonlawyers.
Hellriegel, Don, jt. ed. see French, Wendell L.
Hellsing, Lennart. The Wonderful Pumpkin.
Hellstedt, Leone M. Women Physicians of the World: Autobiographies of Medical Pioneers.
Hellwege, A. M., ed. see Mitsui, T., et al.
Hellwege, K. H., ed. see Mitsui, T., et al.
Hellwig, Monika. The Christian Creeds.
--What Are the Theologians Saying.
Helm, Alex. The English Mummers' Play.
Helm, MacKinley. Man of Fire: J. C. Orozco, an Interpretive Memoir.
Helm, P. J. England under the Yorkists & Tudors 1471 - 1603.
Helman, Edith F., jt. ed. see Arjona, Doris K.
Helmbold, F. Wilbur. Tracing Your Ancestry: A Step-by-Step Guide to Researching Your Family History.
Helmer, Howard & O'Sullivan, Joan. The Forty-Second Omelet Guaranteed!
Helmericks, Harmon. The Last of the Bush Pilots.
Helmers, Carl, ed. Robotics Age: In the Beginning.
Helmholz, R. H., ed. see Burge, William.
Helmold Priest Of Bosau. Chronicle of the Slavs. Tschan, Francis J., tr.
Helmore, G. A. Piaget: A Practical Consideration.
Helms, Cynthia. Favourite Stories from Persia.
Helms, Donald B., jt. auth. see Turner, Jeffrey S.
Helms, Hal M., ed. see Bunyan, John.
Helms, R. Illumination Engineering for Energy Efficient Luminous Environments.
Helms, Randel. Tolkien & the Silmarils.
Helmstrom, C. W. Statistical Theory of Signal Detection.
Heloise. Heloise's Beauty Book: A Helpful Hints Approach to Looking & Feeling Your Best.
--Heloise's Handy Book: Nineteen Eighty-Four Home & Away Calendar-Organizer.
--Help! From Heloise.
--Help! From Heloise.
--Hints from Heloise.
Helprin, Ben. Photographic Self-Assignments.
Helprin, Mark. Refiner's Fire.
Helsel. BF Draw with Templates.
--BF Lettering.
--BF Mech Drawing Loop.
--BF Revolved Sect.
--BF Sketching Circles.
--BF Surface Devel Par.
--BF 1 Pt Persp Draw.
--BG Sketching Lines.
Helsel, Jay, jt. auth. see Jensen, Cecil H.
Helstrom, Jo, jt. auth. see Metz, Mary S.
Helten, William L. Van, ed. Die Altostniederfraenkischen Psalmenfragmente: Die Lipsius'schen Glossen & Die Altsuedmittelfraenkischen Psalmenfragmente.
Heltne, Paul, ed. see Institute for Laboratory Animal Resources Staff.
Helvey, T. C., ed. Space Trajectories.
Helwig, E. B., jt. auth. see Ten Seldam, R. E.
Hemenway, Jack E., jt. auth. see Grappel, Robert D.
Hemenway, Robert. At the Border.
Hemer, C. J. The Letters to the Seven Churches of Asia in Their Local Setting.
Hemery, David. Another Hurdle: The Making of an Olympic Champion.
Hemery, Eric. Walking the Dartmoor Waterways.
Hemingway, Amanda. Pzyche.
--Tantalus.
Hemingway, Ernest. The Enduring Hemingway: An Anthology of a Lifetime in Literature. Scribner, Charles, ed.
--A Farewell to Arms.
--For Whom the Bell Tolls.
--The Garden of Eden.
--Sun Also Rises.
--The Torrents of Spring.
Hemingway, Gregory H. Papa: A Personal Memoir.
Hemingway, Jack. Misadventures of a Fly Fisherman: My Life With & Without Papa.
Hemingway, Joan & Armstrong, Russ. Dining In - Sun Valley.
Hemingway, Maggie. The Bridge.
Heminway, John. No Man's Land: The Last of White Africa.
Hemker, H. C., ed. Human Blood Coagulation: Proceedings.
Hemker, P. W. & Miller, J. J., eds. Numerical Analysis of Singular Perturbation Problems.
Hemleben, Sylvester J., ed. The Voice of the People.
Hemley, Cecil. Dimensions of Midnight: Poetry & Prose. Gottlieb, Elaine, ed.
Hemlow, Joyce. A Catalogue of the Burney Family Correspondence, 1749-1878.
Hemming, John. Conquest of the Incas.
Hemmings, Gwynneth. Biological Aspects of Schizophrenia & Addiction.
Hemmings, Susan. A Wealth of Experience: The Lives of Older Women.
Hemnes, Thomas, jt. auth. see Gordon, Frank S.
Hemond, Conrad J., Jr. Engineering Acoustics & Noise Control.
Hempel, Carl G. Fundamentals of Concept Formation in Empirical Science.
Hempel, George & Yawitz, Jess B. Financial Management of Financial Institutions.
Hempfing, W. P., ed. Microbial Respiration.
Hemphill, Charles F., Jr. Famous Phrases from History.
Hemphill, Charles F., Jr. & Hemphill, Robert D. Security Safeguards in Computer Operations.
Hemphill, Gary B. Blasting Operations.
Hemphill, John M., jt. auth. see Kuriloff, Arthur H.
Hemphill, John M., II. Virginia & the English Commercial System, 1689-1773: Studies in the Development & Fluctuations of a Colonial Economy under Imperial Control. Bruchey, Stuart, ed.
Hemphill, Phyllis D. Career English: Skill Development for Effective Communication.
Hemphill, Robert D., jt. auth. see Hemphill, Charles F., Jr.
Hempstead, John W. Pay: The Experiences of a Junior Supply Officer During World War II.
Hempstone, Smith. A Tract of Time.
Henbest, Nigel & Couper, Heather. Physics.
--The Restless Universe.
Hench, Larry L. & McEldowney, B. A., eds. Bibliography of Ceramics & Glass.
Hendel, Samuel & Bishop, Hillman. Basic Issues of American Democracy.
Henden, Patrick, intro. by. Beatrice.
--Eveline II.
Henderlite, Rachel. Call to Faith.
--Exploring the New Testament.
--Exploring the Old Testament.
Hendersen, Robert, ed. Learning in Animals.
Henderson. Agricultural Process Engineering.
--The Location of Immigrant Industry Within a U. K. Assisted Area: The Scottish Experience.
Henderson, Algo D. & Henderson, Jean G. Higher Education in America: Problems, Priorities & Prospects.
Henderson, Andrew. Scottish Proverbs.
Henderson, Anne. Anything Goes: An Educator's Guide for Working with Parents & Citizens.
Henderson, Bill, ed. The Pushcart Prize I: Best of the Small Presses.
--Pushcart Prize II: Best of the Small Presses.
--The Pushcart Prize III: Best of the Small Presses.
--Pushcart Prize IV: Best of the Small Presses.
--Pushcart Prize IX: Best of the Small Presses.
--Pushcart Prize V: Best of the Small Presses.
--The Pushcart Prize VI: Best of the Small Presses.
--Pushcart Prize VII: The Best of the Small Presses.
--The Pushcart Prize VIII: The Best of the Small Presses.
--Pushcart Prize XII: Best of the Small Presses, 1987-88 Edition.
Henderson, Bryn, jt. auth. see Garrett, David.
Henderson, Carter. Winners: The Successful Strategies Entrepreneurs Use to Build New Businesses.
Henderson, Charles R. Prison Reform.
Henderson, Davis. McCracken's Removable Partial Prosthodontics.
Henderson, Dion. A Season of Birds.
Henderson, Don. Bomb Two.
Henderson, Dorothy. Creative Living: Memories, Reflections & Dreams.
--I Live & Move.
--Look to This Day for Tomorrow.
Henderson, Douglas, ed. Theoretical Chemistry: Theory of Scattering-Papers in Honor of Henry Eyring.
--Theoretical Chemistry: Theory of Scattering: Papers in Honor of Henry Eyring.
Henderson, Douglas & Eyring, Henry, eds. Theoretical Chemistry: Advances & Perspectives.
Henderson, Douglas, jt. ed. see Eyring, Henry.
Henderson, Edith G. Foundations of English Administrative Law: Certiorari & Mandamus in the Seventeenth Century.
Henderson, Edmund & Beers, James, eds. Developmental & Cognitive Aspects of Learning to Spell: A Reflection of Word Knowledge.
Henderson, Ellen C. Phonics in Learning to Read.
--Teaching Reading to Bilingual Children: A Step-by-Step Guide That Guarantees Reading Success.
Henderson, Faye, jt. ed. see Chase, Leslie R.
Henderson, G. P. E. P. Papanoutsos.
Henderson, G. P. & Henderson, S. P., eds. Directory of British Associations & Associations in Ireland.
Henderson, Gary L., et al. Effects of DDT on Man & Other Mammals II.
Henderson, Gerard C. The Federal Trade Commission: A Study in Administrative Law & Prcedure.
Henderson, Gregory, et al. Public Diplomacy & Political Change: Four Case Studies - Okinaws, Peru, Czechoslavakia, Guinea.
Henderson, Harley, jt. auth. see Small, Lawrence F.
Henderson, Harold G. Handbook of Japanese Grammar.
Henderson, Ian. Rudolf Bultmann. Nineham, D. E. & Robertson, E. H., eds.
Henderson, J. Frank & Paterson, A. R. Nucleotide Metabolism.
Henderson, J. L. Education for World Understanding.
Henderson, J. T., ed. Tioconazole: A New Antifungal in Gynecology.
Henderson, J. V. Economic Theory & the Cities.
Henderson, James M. Michigan Statutes Annotated: Containing the Text of All General Laws of a Permanent Character in Force in Michigan. Callaghan & Company Staff, ed.
Henderson, Jean G., jt. auth. see Henderson, Algo D.
Henderson, Jeff & Lowrey, Robert E., eds. Thor's Hammer: Essays on John Gardner.
Henderson, Jill, jt. ed. see Clark, June.
Henderson, Joe. Running Your Best Race Computerized Edition: IBM-PC Version.
Henderson, Kathryn L., ed. Major Classification Systems: The Dewey Centennial.
--Trends in American Publishing.
Henderson, L. W. The Kingdom.
Henderson, L. W. & Chenoweth, D., eds. Blood-Membrane Internation in Extracorporeal Circuits.
Henderson, Lawrence W. Angola: Five Centuries of Conflict.
Henderson, Lois. A Candle in the Dark.
Henderson, Lois T. Miriam: A Novel.
Henderson, Mae G., jt. auth. see Blassingame, John W.
Henderson, Michael. Inspirations from the Olde Dover House.
Henderson, Nicholas. Inside the Private Office: Memoirs of the Secretary to British Foreign Ministers.
Henderson, Philip. Richard Coeur De Lion: A Biography.
Henderson, Robert T. Joy to the World: An Introduction to Kingdom Evangelism.

Henderson, Robert W. Aggregating Behavior & Exploitation of Subterranean Habitat by Gravid Eastern Mild Snakes (Lampropeltis T. triangulum)
Henderson, S. P., jt. ed. see Henderson, G. P.
Henderson, Simon, jt. auth. see Almansi, Guido.
Henderson, Thomas A. & Foster, John L. Urban Policy Game: A Simulation of Urban Politics.
Henderson, Thomas F. Scottish Vernacular Literature: A Succinct History.
Henderson, Timothy, et al. Groundwater: Strategies for State Action.
Henderson, William D. Cohesion: The Human Element in Combat.
Henderson, Zenna. The Anything Box.
--Holding Wonder.
Hendin, David. Death As a Fact of Life.
Hendler, Nelson H., et al, eds. Diagnosis & Treatment of Chronic Pain.
Hendler, Sheldon S. The Complete Guide to Anti-Aging Nutrients.
Hendley, Jesse M. The Fifth Horseman of the Apocalypse.
Hendra, Tony. Going Too Far.
Hendrich, Paula. Saving America's Birds.
Hendrick, Clyde & Jones, Russell A. Nature of Theory & Research in Social Psychology.
Hendrick, George. Katherine Anne Porter.
Hendrick, John R. Opening the Door of Faith: The Why, When & Where of Evangelism.
Hendrick, Kingsley. Improving Employee Safety & Health Performance: A Managerial Guide.
Hendricks, Donald. Pamphlets on the First World War: An Annotated Bibliography.
Hendricks, Donald D. A Report on Library Networks.
Hendricks, Howard. Las Familias Conviven Mejor con Amor.
Hendricks, Howard & Hendricks, Jeanne. Footprints: Walking Through the Passages of Life.
Hendricks, Howard G. Say It with Love.
Hendricks, Jeanne, jt. auth. see Hendricks, Howard.
Hendricks, Rhoda A. Mythologies of the World: A Concise Encyclopedia. Shapiro, Max S., ed.
Hendricks, Sybil D., jt. auth. see Dienstbier, Sharon.
Hendricks, William C. & Noord, Glenn Van. Bible Word Chain Puzzles.
Hendricks, William L. The Harrowing of Hell.
Hendrickson, Chris, jt. auth. see Wohl, Martin.
Hendrickson, Harvey S., jt. auth. see Burns, T. J.
Hendrickson, Joe. Tournament of Roses-One Hundredth Anniversary Edition.
Hendrickson, Paul. The Seminary: A Search.
--Seminary: A Search.
Hendrickson, William see Summerlin, Lee R.
Hendrie, Don, Jr. Boomkitchwatt.
Hendrix, Don. Polk County Folks.
Hendrix, Farris K. Falling Stars.
--Pinetucky - Lost Trails Echo.
Hendrix, Lee C. Indexes of Edgefield County, South Carolina Vol. 1: Probate Records.
Hendrix, Olan. Management for the Christian Leader.
Hendrix, Scott H. Luther & the Papacy: Stages in a Reformation Conflict.
Hendry, A. W. Elements of Experimental Stress Analysis: SI Edition.
--Structural Brickwork.
Hendry, David F. & Wallis, Kenneth F., eds. Economics & Quantitative Economics.
Hendry, George S. The Westminister Confession for Today.
Hendry, Maurice D. Cadillac, Standard of the World: The Complete History.
Heneage, Simon & Ford, Henry. Sidney Sime: Master of the Mysterious.
Heneghan, Donald A. A Concordance to the Poems & Fragments of Wilfred Owen.
Heneghan, James B., ed. Germfree Research: Biological Effects of Gnotobiotic Environments.
Heneman, Herbert G., Jr., jt. ed. see Yoder, Dale.
Heneman, Herbert G., Jr., jt. ed. see Yoder, Dale, Jr.
Heneman, Herbert G., Jr., et al. Personnel-Human Resource Management.
Henerson, Marlene E., et al. How to Measure Attitudes.
Henfrey, Arthur, ed. Reports & Papers on Botany.
Hengartner, Walter & Theodoresco, Rado. Concentration Functions.
Hengel, Martin. Acts & the History of Earliest Christianity.
--The Atonement: The Origins of the Doctrine in the New Testament. Bowden, John, tr. from Ger.
--Between Jesus & Paul.
--Christ & Power. Kalin, Everett R., tr. from Ger.
--Jews, Greeks & Barbarians: Aspects of the Hellenization of Judaism in the Pre-Christian Period. Bowden, John, tr. from Ger.
--Judaism & Hellenism: Studies in Their Encounter in Palestine During the Early Hellenistic Period. Bowden, John, tr. from Ger.
--Property & Riches in the Early Church: Aspects of a Social History of Early Christianity. Bowden, John, tr. from Ger.
--The Son of God: The Origin of Christology & the History of Jewish-Hellenistic Religion. Bowden, John, tr. from Ger.
--Studies in the Gospel of Mark. Bowden, John, tr.
--Victory over Violence: Jesus & the Revolutionists. Green, David E., tr. from Gr.
--Was Jesus a Revolutionist? Reumann, John, ed. Klassen, William, tr. from Ger.
Hengener, Henri. Fokker, the Man & the Aircraft. Robertson, B., ed.
Hengeveld. Beyond the General Hospital Patient: Investigations in Consultation Psychiatry.
Henggeler, Scott W., ed. Delinquency & Adolescent Psychopathology.
Henglein, F. A. Chemical Technology.
Hengst, Herbert R., jt. auth. see Monahan, William G.
Henig, Harry. I Sold Myself a Dream.
Henig, Robin M. The Myth of Senility: The Truth about the Brain & Aging.
Henin, F., jt. auth. see Ter-Haar, D.
Heninger, S. K., Jr. Touches of Sweet Harmony: Pythagorean Cosmology & Renaissance Poetics.
Henisch, H. K. & Roy, R. Silicon Carbide-1968.
Henisch, H. K., et al, eds. Phase Transitions & Their Applications in Materials Science.
Henke, Emerson O. Accounting for Non-Profit Organizations.
--Introduction to Nonprofit Organization Accounting.
Henke, Emerson O., jt. auth. see Thomas, C. William.
Henke, Emerson O., et al. Managerial Use of Accounting Data.
Henke, Jack. Sylvan Beach, New York.
Henke, James T. Courtesans & Cuckolds: A Glossary of Renaissance Dramatic Bawdy (Exclusive of Shakespeare)
Henke, Thomas R. Managing Your Private Trucking Operation.
Henkel, James G. & Clarke, Frank H., eds. Molecular Graphics on the IBM PC Microcomputer.
Henkel, James G., jt. ed. see Clarke, Frank H.
Henkels, Robert M., Jr. Robert Pinget: The Novel As Quest.
Henken, Louis, ed. Arms Control: Issues for the Public.
Henker, Barbara, jt. ed. see Whalen, Carol K.
Henkes, R. Notes on Art & Education.
Henkes, Robert. Sport in Art: A Guide for Beginning Illustrators.
Henkin, Bill, jt. auth. see Vermiglio, Maria.
Henkin, Bill, jt. auth. see Young, George.
Henkin, L. Disarmament.
Henkin, Leon, et al. Cylindric Algebras.
Henle, James M. Numerous Numerals.
Henley, Beth. Crimes of the Heart.
Henley, Diana, et al. ASPCA Guide to Pet Care.
Henley, E. J., jt. ed. see Calo, J. M.
Henley, Karyn. Hatch!
Henley, Nancy, ed. see Thorne, Barrie.
Henley, S., jt. ed. see Cubitt, J. M.
Henley, Virginia. Bold Conquest.
--The Irish Gypsy.
--Wild Hearts.
Henley, W. & Woodcock, C. Universal Dictionary of Violin & Bow Makers, Vol. 7: Price Guide & Appendix.
Henley, W. E., jt. auth. see Farmer, John S.
Henley, Wallace. City under the Sands.
--The Roman Solution.
Henn, Harry G. Copyright Law: A Practitioners Guide.
Henn, T. R. The Lonely Tower: Studies in the Poetry of W. B. Yeats.
Henn, Thomas R. The Apple & the Spectroscope.
Henneberg, Ulrich & Reinhardt, Hans-Wolfgang, eds. Elektrolyte und Spurenelemente der Intensivmedizin: Colloquium November 11, 1972 in Klinikum Steglitz der Freien Universitaet Berlin.
Hennen, Brian K., jt. auth. see Shires, David B.
Hennes, Aileen, tr. see Skram, Amalie.
Hennessey, E. F., jt. auth. see Stewart, J.
Hennessy, Jeff T. Trampolining.
Hennessy, John F. Hypothyroidism.
Hennessy, Max. Back to Battle.
--Blunted Lance.
--The Bright Blue Sky.
--Challenging Heights.
--The Crimson Wind.
--The Dangerous Years.
--The Iron Stallions.
--The Lion at Sea.
--Once More the Hawks.
--Soldier of the Queen.
Hennig, Willi. Insect Phylogeny.
Henning, Fritz. Concept & Composition: The Basis of Successful Art.
--Drawing & Painting Animals.
Henning, Fritz, ed. see Piersol, Edna W.
Henning, Heinz M., jt. auth. see Strohecker, Rolf.
Henning, Joel. Holistic Running: Beyond the Threshold of Fitness.
Henning, Standish. Fair Em: An Introduction & Critical Edition.
Hennings, Dorothy G. Communication in Action.
--Communication in Action: Teaching the Language Arts.
Hennings, Dorothy G. & Hennings, George. Today's Elementary Social Studies.
Hennings, George, jt. auth. see Hennings, Dorothy G.
Henningsen, B., et al, eds. Endocrine Treatment of Breast Cancer: A New Approach.
Henningsen, Rodney J. Probation & Parole.
Hennock, E. P. Fit & Proper Persons: Ideal & Reality in Nineteenth-Century Urban Government.
Henrichs, Betty. Love's Suspect.
--More Than Friends.
Henrichsen, Walter A. A Layman's Guide to Applying the Bible.
Henrici, Holice H. Shreveport, the Beginnings.
Henrici, Peter. Computational Analysis with the HP-25 Pocket Calculator.
--Discrete Variable Methods in Ordinary Differential Equations.
Henrici, Stanley B. Salary Management for the Nonspecialist.
Henrici-Olive, G., et al. Advances in Polymer Science. Cantow, H. J., ed.
Henricks, Jacalyn. Audit Criteria for Drug Utilization Review.
--Audit Criteria for Drug Utilization Review.
Henriques, Leslie, ed. see Riegert, Ray.
Henry, Bruce. The Henrys: A Family of Artists.
Henry, D. Geometric Theory of Semilinear Parabolic Equations.
Henry, George W., jt. auth. see Zilboorg, Gregory.
Henry, Glenn E. The Christmas Owl.
Henry, J. Tell Me I'm Allowed to Love.
Henry, Jules. Jungle People: A Kaingang Tribe of the Highlands of Brazil.
Henry, Laurie. Fiction Writer's Market 1987.
Henry, Laurie, ed. Fiction Writer's Market '88.
Henry, Lawrence. ABC's. Klimo, Kate, ed.
--E. T. Counting. Klimo, Kate, ed.
--What Is This For. Klimo, Kate, ed.
Henry, Les. Model T Memories. Clymer Publications, ed.
Henry, Leslie R. Henry's Fabulous Model A Ford. Clymer Publications, ed.
--How to Restore the Model a Ford. Clymer Publications, ed.
--Model T Ford Restoration Handbook. Clymer Publications, ed.
Henry, Margaret. Towards Achievement & Acceptance: A Classroom Study of Mildly Intellectually Handicapped Children.
Henry, Matthew. A Commentary on the Whole Bible.
Henry, P. & Henry, P., eds. Konstantin Paustovskii: Selected Stories.
Henry, Patrick & Stransky, Thomas F. God on Our Minds.
Henry, Patrick, ed. Schools of Thought in the Christian Tradition.
Henry, Porter J., jt. auth. see Barry, John W.
Henry, Ralph L. St. Croix Boyhood.
Henry, Seth, jt. auth. see Donovan, Frank.
Henry, Sondra & Taitz, Emily. Written out of History: Our Jewish Foremothers.
Henry, Stuart. Private Justice: Towards Integrative Theorising in the Sociology of Law.
Henry, Vernon J., jt. ed. see Rezak, Richard.
Henry, William A., III. Visions of America: How We Saw the 1984 Election.
Henry, William R. & Haynes, Warren W. Managerial Economics: Analysis & Cases.
Henry Duke of Lancaster. Livre de Seyntz Medicines. Arnould, E. J., ed.
Henry J. Million Memories of You.
Henschell, Todd, ed. see Lin, Willy.
Henshall, S. H. Medium & High Speed Diesel Engines for Marine Use.
Henshall, S. H. & Jackson, G. G. Slow Speed Diesel Engines.
Henshaw, Alex. The Flight of the Mew Gull.
Henshaw, George R. A Scientific Approach to Homeopathy.
Henshaw, Paul & Weemhoff, Harold. Worship in Our Family.
Henshel, Anne-Marie. The Forgotten Ones: A Sociological Study of Anglo & Chicano Retardates.
Hensher, David & Stopher, Peter, eds. Behavioural Travel Modelling.
Henslee, Helen. Pretty Redwing.
Hensley, Jeffrey, ed. The Zero People.
Hensley, Joe L. Fort's Law.
Henslin, James M., ed. Deviant Life-Styles.
Henson Association & Miss Piggy. Miss Piggy's Guide to Life.
Henson, David B. Optometric Instrumentation.
Henson, Kenneth T. Secondary Teaching Methods.
Henson, Kim. Austin A30 & A35.
Henstock, M. & Bever, M. B., eds. New & Better Uses of Secondary Resources: Proceedings of the Second Recycling World Congress, Philippine International Conventional Center, Manila, March 1979.
Henstock, M. E. Recycling & Disposal of Solid Waste.
Henstock, M. E., ed. Reutilization of Waste Materials: Selected Papers from the Third Recycling World Congress, Basle, Switzerland, 29 September-1 October 1980.
Henstock, M. E. & Biddulph, M. W., eds. Solid Waste As a Resource.
Henstock, M. E., jt. ed. see Bever, M. B.
Henstra, Friso. Mighty Mizzling Mouse & the Red Cabbage House.
Hentoff, N., jt. auth. see Shapiro, Nat.
Hentoff, Nat. Jazz Is.
Hentze, Margot. Pre-Fascist Italy: The Rise & Fall of the Parliamentary Regime.
Henwood, James & Muncie, John. Laurel Line: An Anthracite Region Railway.
Henze, Geraldine. From Murk to Masterpiece.
Henze, Paul B. The Plot to Kill the Pope.
--The Plot to Kill the Pope.
Hepburn, Alonzo B. History of Currency in the United States.
Hepburn, Daisy. Be It Ever So Humble.
--Be Mine.
--Color Me Christian.
--Get up & Go.
--Get up & Grow.
--Life with Spice Resource Manual.
--Living Simply.
--Look, You're a Leader.
--Never Underestimate the Power of God's Woman.
Hepburn, James. Arnold Bennett: The Critical Heritage.
Hepburn, Mary A., ed. New Information Technology in Social Science Education: Viewpoints from Europe & the U. S.
Heppell, Muriel, tr. see Cosic, Dobrica.
Heppenheimer, T. A. The Man-Made Sun: The Quest for Fusion Power.
Hepworth, H. How to Find Out in History.
Hepworth, Mike, jt. auth. see Turner, Bryan S.
Her Majesty's Stationery Office, Office of Special Inquiries & Reports Staff. Special Reports on Educational Subjects.
Herak, J. N. & Adamic, K. J., eds. Magnetic Resonance in Chemistry & Biology.
Herak, Janok N., jt. ed. see Pifat, Greta.
Herakovich, Carl T., jt. auth. see Hashin, Zvi.
Herakovich, Carl T., ed. Inelastic Behavior of Composite Materials AMD.
Heras, F. G. de las & Vega, S., eds. Medicinal Chemistry Advances: Proceedings of the International Symposium on Medicinal Chemistry, 7th International Symposium Torremolinos, 2-5 September 1980.
Heraud, B. J. Sociology & Social Work.
Herb Society of America Staff. Herbs for Use & for Delight: An Anthology from the Herbarist.
Herbaty, Frank. Cost-Effective Maintenance Management: Productivity Improvement & Downtime Reduction.
Herber, Bernard P. Modern Public Finance.
Herber, R. H., jt. ed. see Goldanskii, V. I.
Herberg, Will. Faith Enacted As History: Essays in Biblical Theology. Anderson, Bernhard W., ed.
Herberger, Charles F. The Thread of Ariadne.
Herberhold, M. Metal Pi Complexes.
Herberman, Ronald B. Natural Cell-Mediated Immunity Against Tumors.
Herbers, John. No Thank You, Mr. President.
Herbert, A. P. The Secret Battle.
Herbert, A. S. Historical Catalogue of Printed Editions of the English Bible: 1525-1961.
Herbert, Brian. Sudanna, Sudanna.
Herbert, Brian, jt. auth. see Herbert, Frank.
Herbert, D. T. & Johnston, R. J. Geography & the Urban Environment: Progress in Research & Applications.
--Geography & the Urban Environment: Progress In Research & Development.
Herbert, D. T. & Johnston, R. J., eds. Geography & the Urban Environment: Progress in Research & Applications.
Herbert, David T. & Thomas, Colin J. Urban Geography: A First Approach.
Herbert, Eugenia W., jt. auth. see Lopez, Claude-Anne.
Herbert, Frank. The God Makers.
--Whipping Star.
Herbert, Frank & Herbert, Brian. Man of Two Worlds.
Herbert, Frank & Ransom, Bill. The Lazarus Effect.
Herbert, Ian, ed. Who's Who in the Theatre.
Herbert, J. The Interpreter's Handbook: How to Become a Conference Interpreter.
Herbert, John. Fortune & Men's Eyes.
Herbert, Martin. Emotional Problems of Development in Children.
Herbert, Mike. Mike Schmidt: The Human Vacuum Cleaner.

Herbert, R. B. Biosynthesis of Secondary Metabolites.
Herbert, Richard A., jt. auth. see D'Albert, Joseph L.
Herbert, T. Walter, Jr. Moby Dick & Calvinism: A World Dismantled.
Herbert, Theodore T. Dimensions of Organizational Behavior.
Herbert, Theodore T., jt. auth. see Fulmer, Robert M.
Herbert, Theodore T., ed. Organizational Behavior Reading & Cases.
Herbert, W. L. & Jarvis, F. J. Marriage Counselling in the Community.
Herbert-Caesari, E. Vocal Truth: Some of the Things I Teach.
Herbert-Caesari, Edgar F. Science & Sensations of Vocal Tone.
--Tradition & Gigli.
Herbig, Katherine L., jt. ed. see Daniel, Donald C.
Herbst, John. Farm Management: Principles, Planning, Budgets.
Herbst, Robert & Readett, Alan G. The Herbst Dictionaries of Commercial, Financial & Legal Terms.
--The Herbst Dictionaries of Commercial, Financial & Legal Terms: English-German.
--The Herbst Dictionaries of Commercial, Financial & Legal Terms Vol. I.
Herbst, Robert & Readett, Alan G., eds. The Herbst Dictionaries of Commercial, Financial & Legal Terms: Deutsch-Englisch.
--The Herbst Dictionaries of Commercial, Financial & Legal Terms Vol. 2.
--Herbst Dictionary of Commercial, Financial & Legal Terms.
Hercules, D. M., et al, eds. Contemporary Topics in Analytical & Clinical Chemistry.
Hercules, Frank. On Leaving Paradise.
Herd, Harold. The March of Journalism.
Herda, D. J. Dirt Bike Racing. Anderson, Madelyn K., ed.
--Photography Ser. Close-up.
Herdeg, Walter, ed. Graphis Annual: 1986-1987.
--Graphis Posters Eighty-Six: The International Annual of Poster Art.
Herdendorf, Charles E., et al. Ecology of Lake St. Clair Wetlands: A Community Profile.
Herder, Johann Gottfried Institut Staff. Alphabetischer Katalog der Bibliothek des Johann Gottfried Herder-Instituts: Second Supplement.
--Alphabetischer Katalog der Bibliothek.
Herding, R. Job Control & Union Structure.
Heren, Louis. Selections from the New American Commonwealth: American Values Projected Abroad.
Herendeen, James B. The Economics of the Corporate Economy.
Herfarth, C. & Betzler, M., eds. Mammakarzinom.
Herford, Julius, jt. ed. see Decker, Harold A.
Herfurth, M., et al, eds. Social Integration of Migrant Workers & Other Ethnic Minorities: A Documentation of Current Research.
Hergenhahn, B. R. An Introduction to Theories of Learning.
Hergenhan, Laurie. Unnatural Lives: Studies in Australian Fiction about the Convicts from James Tucker to Patrick White.
Hergert, Douglas. BASIC for Business.
--Command Performance: dBASE III.
--Mastering Framework.
--Microsoft QuickBASIC.
--Turbo BASIC Instant Reference.
Hergert, Douglas & Kalash, Joseph T. Apple Pascal Games.
Hergert, Douglas, jt. auth. see Hergert, Richard.
Hergert, Richard & Hergert, Douglas. Doing Business with Pascal.
Herget, J. Barlow, jt. auth. see Reid, Dee.
Herhold, Robert M. Learning to Die, Learning to Live.
Herhold, Robert M., ed. see Sittler, Joseph A.
Hering, Ewald. The Theory of Binocular Vision.
Hering, H. Robert Leroy Platzman Memorial.
Heritage Home Plans, Inc. Luxury Home Plans.
Heritage, P., et al, eds. Machining for Toolmaking & Experimental Work.
Heriteau, Jacqueline. Oriental Cooking the Fast Wok Way.
Herken, H., jt. ed. see Genazzani, E.
Herkes, Richard, ed. Bible for Today.
Herlach, F., jt. ed. see Knoepfel, H.
Herley, Richard. The Stone Arrow.
Herlihy, James L. All Fall Down.
Herlihy, John G. & Herlihy, Myra T. Mainstreaming in the Social Studies.
Herlihy, Myra T., jt. auth. see Herlihy, John G.
Herlin, Hans. Grishin. Brownjohn, J. Maxwell, tr.
--Which Way the Wind.
Herling, Gustav. A World Apart: The Journal of a Gulag Survivor. Ciozkosz, Andrzej, tr. from Pol.
Herman, Barry & Lawren, Bill. The Long Life Gourmet Cookbook.
Herman, E. Edward. Collective Bargaining & Labor Relations.
Herman, Esther, jt. ed. see Wasserman, Paul.
Herman, G. T., ed. Image Reconstruction from Projections Implementation & Applications.
Herman, Gary, tr. see Broyelle, Claudie.
Herman, George, ed. R. D. Mindlin & Applied Mechanics: A Collection of Studies in the Development of Applied Mechanics Dedicated to Prof. R. D. Mindlin by His Former Students.
Herman, H., ed. Treatise on Materials Science & Technology, Vol. 18: Ion Implantation.
Herman, Jerome H., et al. Rheumatoid Arthritis.
Herman, John, ed. see Ely, Scott.
Herman, John R. Electromagnetic Ambients & Manmade Noise. White, Donald R., ed.
Herman, Lloyd. American Porcelain.
Herman, Melvin. Administrative Justice & Supplementary Benefits.
Herman, Roger E. Disaster Planning for Local Government.
Herman, V. & Mendel, F., eds. Parliaments of the World.
Herman, William & Young, Jeffrey M. Troubleshooting: Basic Writing Skills.
Herman, Y., ed. Marine Geology & Oceanography of the Arctic Seas.
Hermann, E. R., et al, eds. Piaget: Dictionary of Terms.
Hermann, Gayl G., et al. What to Do about Bill?
Hermans, Hubert J. Value Areas & Their Development: Theory & Method of Self-Confrontation. Spiekerman, Joseph A., tr. from Dutch.
Hermans, J. J., ed. Polymer Solution Properties: Part I, Statistics & Thermodynamics.
Hermans, Jan, ed. Molecular Dynamics & Protein Structure: Proceedings of a Workshop held 13-18 May 1984 at the University of North Carolina.
Hermans, Theo. The Structure of Modernist Poetry.
Hermansen, Janet. On the Crest of the Wave: Leader's Guide.
Hermansen, Janice. Karen's Choice.
Hermanson, et al. Accounting Principles.
Hermanson, Renee. Here or Nowhere.
Hermanson, Roger H., et al. Financial Accounting.
--Accounting Principles.
--Financial Accounting.
Hermelin, B. & O'Connor, N. Psychological Experiments with Autistic Children.
Hermens, Ferdinand A. Fifth Republic.
Herment, Georges. Pipe.
Hermes, Hans, et al, eds. see Frege, Gottlob.
Hermes, Patricia. Nobody's Fault?
--A Solitary Secret.
--What If They Knew.
Hermet, Guy, et al, eds. Elections Without Choice.
Hermodsson, Ivan. Roentgenological Studies of Traumatic & Recurrent Anterior & Inferior Dislocations of the Shoulder Joint.
Hernandez, Juan, tr. see Flores, Ernesto F.
Herndon, Booton. Mary Pickford & Douglas Fairbanks: The Most Popular Couple the World Has Known.
Herndon, James. How to Survive in Your Native Land.
--Notes from a School Teacher.
Herndon, Terry. We, the Teachers.
--We, the Teachers: Terry Herndon on Education & Democracy.
Hernon, Peter & McClure, Charles R. Public Access to Government Publications.
Herod, F. G. The Gospels: A First Commentary.
Herodes Atticus. Herodon Peri Politeias.
Herold, Mort. You Can Have a Near-Perfect Memory.
Herold, Raymond. Compute's Guide to TI-99-4A Sound & Graphics.
Heron, Jackie. Exploring Careers in Nursing.
Heron, Liz. Changes of Heart: Reflections of Women's Independence.
Heron, S. D., jt. auth. see Schlaifer, R.
Herr, David F., jt. auth. see Haydock, Roger S.
Herr, David F., et al. Nineteen Eighty-Six Supplement to Motion Practice.
Herr, Edward & Pinson, Nancy. Foundations for Policy in Guidance & Counseling.
Herr, Edwin L. Guidance & Counseling in the Schools: Perspective on the Past, Present & Future.
--Vocational Guidance & Human Development.
Herr, Edwin L. & Cramer, Stanley H. Career Guidance Through the Lifespan: Systematic Approaches.
Herr, Michael, jt. auth. see Peellaert, Guy.
Herr, William A. Catholic Thinkers in the Clear: Giants of Catholic Thought from Augustine to Rahner.
Herramann, Frank. A Practical Guide to Portrait Photography.
Herreid, Clyde F. Biology.
Herreid, Clyde F., II & Fourtner, Charles R., eds. Locomotion & Energetics in Anthropods.
Herrero, Stephen. Bear Attacks.
Herrick, Eduard F. Old Indian Temples, Idols & Worship.
Herrick, J. M., jt. auth. see Jones, J. F.
Herrick, Marvin T., compiled by. Italian Plays, 1500-1700, in the University of Illinois Library.
Herrick, Robert. Complete Poetry of Robert Herrick. Patrick, J. Max, ed.
Herrigel, Eugen. The Method of Zen.
Herriges, Greg. Secondary Attachments.
--Someplace Safe.
Herring, Charlanne F. The Cruise Answer Book: A Comprehensive Guide to the Ships & Ports of North America.
Herring, George C., Jr. Aid to Russia, Nineteen Forty-One to Nineteen Forty-Six: Strategy, Diplomacy, the Origins of the Cold War.
Herring, H. J. & Steltz, W. G., eds. Flow in Primary Non-Rotating Passages in Turbomachines.
Herring, James E. School Librarianship.
Herrington, Lee P., jt. ed. see Black, Peter E.
Herrington, Patricia. Don't Miss the Present Moment. Graves, Helen, ed.
Herrington, Robert W., Jr. & Tidwell, Samuel M. Manual for the Employment of Aliens.
Herriot, James. Illustrated Textbook of Dog Diseases.
Herriot, Peter, ed. see Oatley, Keith.
Herriot, Peter, ed. see Turner, Johanna.
Herriot, Peter, ed. see Walker, Stephen.
Herriott, John. Using & Programming the VIC-20, Including Ready-to-Run Programs.
Herriott, Peter. An Introduction to the Psychology of Language.
Herrmann, Dorothy. S. J. Perelman: A Life.
Herrmann, Elizabeth R. & Spitz, Edna H., eds. German Women Writers of the Twentieth Century.
Herrmann, Frank. Sotheby's: Portrait of an Auction House.
Herrmann, Fred. Tricks & Games on the Pool Table.
Herrmann, G. & Perrone, N., eds. The Dynamic Response of Structures.
Herrmann, Lawrence M., ed. see Oldman, Oliver, et al.
Herrmann, Luke. Paul & Thomas Sandby.
Herrmann, Ned. The Creative Brain.
Herrmann, Nina. Go Out in Joy.
Herrmann, Roland, jt. auth. see Alkemade, Cornelis T.
Herrmann, Siegfried. A History of Israel in Old Testament Times. Bowden, John, tr. from Ger.
--A History of Israel in Old Testament Times. Bowden, John, tr. from Ger.
Herrmann, Wilhelm. Communion of the Christian with God. Voelkel, Robert T. & Keck, Leander E., eds. Stanyon, J. Sandys, tr. from Ger.
Herrmanns, Ralph. Children of the North Pole. MacMillan, Annabelle, tr.
Herrnstein, Richard J., jt. auth. see Wilson, James Q.
Herron, Ima H. The Small Town in American Drama.
Herron, R. E., ed. see Society of Photo-Optical Instrumentation Engineers Staff.
Hers, Francois & Chevrier, Jean-Francois. Francois Hers: A Tale.
Hers, H. G. & Van Hoof, F., eds. Lysosomes & Storage Diseases.
Herscher, Uri D. Jewish Agricultural Utopias in America, 1880-1910.
Herschman, A., ed. AAAS Annual Meeting Program - 154th National Meeting, February 1988.
--AAAS Annual Meeting Program - 1987.
Hersen, Michel & Barlow, David H. Single Case Experimental Designs: Strategies for Studying Behavior Change. Goldstein, A. P. & Krasner, L., eds.
Hersen, Michel & Bellack, Alan S., eds. Behavioral Assessment: A Practical Handbook.
Hersen, Michel & Ollendick, Thomas H., eds. Handbook of Child Psychopathology.
Hersey, Bill. Hersey's Executive Memory Program.
Hersey, Harold B. Pulpwood Editor.
Hersey, I., ed. see International Astronautical Congress, 13th, Varna, 1962.
Hersey, John. Aspects of the Presidency.
Hersey, John B., ed. Deep-Sea Photography.
Hersey, Paul & Blanchard, Kenneth H. Management of Organizational Behavior: Utilizing Human Resources.
Hersh, Seymour. The Price of Power: Kissinger in the Nixon White House.
Hershberger, W. D. Topics in Solid State & Quantum Electronics.
Hershenson, Herbert M. Infrared Absorption Spectra. Incl. Index for 1945-57. Acad Pr.
--Nuclear Magnetic Resonance & Electron Spin Resonance: Index For 1958-1963.
Hershey, Robert D. Advent Landmarks: From a Preacher's Notebook.
Hershey's Kitchens Staff. Hershey's Cookies, Bars, & Brownies.
--Hershey's Kidsnacks.
--Hersheys Time-Less Desserts.
Herskowitz, Irwin H. The Elements of Genetics.
Herskowitz, Michael, jt. auth. see Davis, Bette.
Herskowitz, Mickey. The Legend of Bear Bryant.
Hersov, L., ed. Children in Turmoil: Tomorrow's Parents.
Hersov, Lionel & Berg, Ian, eds. Out of School: Modern Perspectives in Truancy & School Refusal.
Herstein, H., et al. Challenge & Survival: The History of Canada.
Herstein, I. N. Topics in Ring Theory.
Hertlein, L. G., jt. auth. see Grant, Ulysses S., IV.
Hertz, Grete J. Hi, Daddy, Here I Am.
Hertz, H. G. Electrochemistry: A Reformulation of the Basic Principles.
Hertz, J. H. Affirmations of Judaism.
Hertz, Jacky. Abortion: Sexual Suicide.
Hertz, Joseph H., ed. A Book of Jewish Thoughts.
Hertz, Karl H., ed. Two Kingdoms & One World: A Sourcebook in Christian Social Ethics.
Hertz, L., jt. ed. see Fedoroff, S.
Hertz, Leah. In Search of a Small Business Definition: An Exploration of the Small-Business Definitions of the U. S., the U. K., Israel, & the People's Republic of China.
Hertz, Leif, jt. ed. see Fedoroff, S.
Hertzberg, Hans W. First & Second Samuel, A Commentary.
Herum, John, jt. ed. see Cummings, Donald W.
Herwig, Robert. The Good Housekeeping Encyclopedia of House Plants.
Herwitz, Stanley R. The Regeneration of Selected Tropical Tree Species in Corcovado National Park, Costa Rica.
Herxheimer, H. A Guide to Bronchial Asthma.
Herz, John H. The Government of Germany.
Herz, Judith S. & Martin, Robert K., eds. E. M. Forster: Centenary Revaluations.
Herzberg, Gerhard. Molecular Spectra & Molecular Structure. Incl. Vol.1. Spectra of Diatomic Molecules; Vol. 2. Infrared & Raman Spectra of Polyatomic Molecules; Vol. 3. Electronic Spectra & Electronic Structure of Polyatomic Molecules. Krieger.
Herzberg, R. J., jt. auth. see Thorner, Marvin E.
Herzbrum, Robert. The Perfect Martini Book.
Herzfeld, Judith. Sense & Sensibility in Childbirth: A Guide to Supportive Obstetrical Care.
Herzfeld, Michael & Lenhart, Margot D., eds. Semiotics 1980.
Herzig, Alison C. & Mali, Jane L. A Season of Secrets.
--A Word to the Wise.
Herzog, Arthur. LSITT.
Herzog, Asa S., et al. Herzog's Bankruptcy Forms & Practice.
Herzog, Chaim. The Arab-Israeli Wars: War & Peace in the Middle East, from the War of Independence Through Lebabon.
Herzog, Emile see Maurois, Andre.
Herzog, Frederick. Justice Church: The New Function of the Church in North American Christianity.
Herzog, H. K. European Piano Atlas.
Herzog, Werner. Screenplays. Greenberg, Alan, tr. from Ger.
Hesburgh, Theodore M. Patterns for Educational Growth.
Heschel, Abraham J. Man's Quest for God: Studies in Prayer & Symbolism.
Heseltine, Marjorie & Dow, Ula. Revised Basic Cookbook.
Hesketh, H. E., ed. Integrated Environmental Control for Coal-Fired Power Plants.
Hesketh, Howard E. & Cross, Frank L., Jr. Fugitive Emissions & Controls.
Heskett, John. German Design 1870-1918.
Hesla, Stephen. The Hawthorn Conspiracy.
Heslin, Jo-Ann, jt. auth. see Natow, Annette B.
Heslop, W. G. Nuggets From Numbers.
Heslop, William G. Diamonds From Daniel.
Hess. A-Twenty Havoc at War.
Hess, Adrien L. Four-Dimensional Geometry: Introduction.
--Mathematics Projects Handbook.
Hess, Alfred F. Scurvy: Past & Present.
Hess, B., ed. see Gesellschaft Fuer Biologische Chemie, 19th Colloquium, Mossbach-Baden, 1968.
Hess, Bartlett & Hess, Margaret. Never Say Old.
Hess, Beth B., ed. Growing Old in America.
Hess, C. J. Brother Gander's Rhymes for Adults & Precocious Children.
Hess, Carol, ed. Political Resource Directory: National Edition 1988-1989.
Hess, Clinton W. & Kerschner, Paul A. The Silver Lobby: A Guide to Advocacy for Older Persons.
Hess, D. Plant Physiology.
Hess, David. The Last Flight.
--Whom the Gods Love: A Lyrical Drama in Three Acts.
--Woven Nights & Days: The Like & the Unlike.
Hess, Eckhard H. Imprinting: Early Experience in the Developmental Psychology.
Hess, H. Ober, ed. The Nature of a Humane Society.
Hess, Hans-Jurgen, ed. Annual Reports in Medicinal Chemistry.

Hess, Herbert J. & Tucker, Charles O. Talking about Relationships.
Hess, Joseph C. Night Stick.
Hess, Karen, jt. auth. see Nelson, R. Y.
Hess, Karen M. Introduction to Private Security. Wrobleski, Henry M., ed.
Hess, Karen M., jt. auth. see Quie, Gretchen.
Hess, M. A. & Hunt, A. Pickles & Ice Cream.
Hess, Margaret. Unconventional Women.
Hess, Margaret, jt. auth. see Hess, Bartlett.
Hess, Max W. Experimental Thymectomy, Possibilities & Limitations.
Hess, Moses. Rome & Jerusalem.
Hess, Robert D. & Croft, Doreen J. Teachers of Young Children.
Hess, Robert D. & Croft, Robert J. Teachers of Young Children.
Hess, Robert D., jt. auth. see Croft, Doreen J.
Hess, Robert L. & Coger, Dalvan M. A Bibliography of Primary Sources for Nineteenth Century Tropical Africa, As Recorded by Explorers, Missionaries, Traders, Travelers, Administrators, Military Men, Adventurers & Others.
Hess, Robert P. Desk Book for Setting up the Closely-Held Corporation.
Hess, Stephen. Organizing the Presidency.
--The Presidential Campaign.
Hess, Tom. Let My People Go.
Hessayon, D. G. & Wheatcroft, Harry. Be Your Own Rose Expert.
Hesse, Alice. The Guests at the Villa.
--Terror in Taormina.
Hesse, Alice W. Tropics of Fear.
Hesse, Erich. Narcotics & Drug Addiction.
Hesse, Hermann. Beneath the Wheel. Roloff, Michael, tr. from Ger.
--Glass Bead Game; Magister Ludi.
--Steppenwolf.
Hesse, Jurgen. Mobile Retirement Handbook: A Complete Guide to Living & Traveling in an RV.
Hessel, L. W. & Krans, J. M., eds. Lipoprotein Metabolism & Endocrine Regulation.
Hesselgrave, David J., ed. Dynamic Religious Movements: Case Studies of Rapidly Growing Religious Movement Around the World.
Hession, W. & Rubel, M. Performance Guide to Word Processing Software.
Hestenes, Magnus R. Calculus of Variations & Optimal Control Theory.
--Optimization Theory: The Finite Dimensional Case.
Hestenes, Marshall D. & Hill, Richard O. College Algebra with Calculators.
Hester, James J. & Grady, James. Introduction to Archaeology.
Hester, Jimmy. Personal Soulwinning.
Hester, R. E., jt. ed. see Clark, R. J.
Hester, Ralph, jt. auth. see Jian, Gerard.
Hesterman, R. C. The Role Theory.
Hesterman, Vicki, jt. auth. see Storrer, Carol M.
Heston, Alan W., jt. ed. see Berki, S. E.
Heston, Jean F., et al, eds. Forty-Five Years of Cancer Incidence in Connecticut: 1935-79.
Het PTT-BEDRIJF, the Netherlands Staff. Human Factors in Telephone Communications International Symposium, 3rd.
Heth, Edward H. Wisconsin Country Cookbook & Journal.
Hetherington, A. L., jt. auth. see Hobson, R. L.
Hetherington, John, Jr., jt. auth. see Kolker, Allan E.
Hetherington, Keith. Patrick.
Hetherington, Mavis E. & Parke, Ross D. Contemporary Readings in Child Psychology.
Hetsroni, G., ed. Basic Two Phase Flow Modeling in Reactor Safety & Performance: EPRI Workshop Held at Tampa, Fla. 27 Feb.--2 March 1979.
Hettich, Arthur & Seranne, Ann. The Four-Star Kitchen: Classic Recipes from New York's Great Restaurants.
Hettne, Bjorn. The Political Economy of Indirect Rule: Mysore 1881-1947.
Hetu, Sylvie, jt. auth. see Kleiber, Michael C.
Hetzel, William. The Complete Guide to Software Testing.
Heuckenkamp, P., ed. see Symposium, Muenchen Staff.
Hevelius, Johannes. Machina Coelestis.
Hevenor, Hilary, jt. auth. see Anderson, John.
Hewat, Joanathan, jt. auth. see Hewat, Theresa.
Hewat, Matthew L. Bantu Folklore.
Hewat, Theresa & Hewat, Joanathan. Overland & Beyond.
Hewes, Gordon W., ed. Language Origins: A Bibliography Part One A-K Part Two L-Z.
Hewes, Jeremy & Grout, Bill. Word Processing with the IBM PC.
Hewes, Jeremy J. Build Your Own Playground: A Sourcebook of Play Sculptures, Designs & Concepts from the Work of Jay Beckwith.
Hewetson, David & Miller, David. Christianity Made Simple: Belief.
Hewett & Taylor. The Emotionally Disturbed Child in the Classroom.
Hewett, C. A., jt. auth. see Martin, M. C.
Hewett, Cecil A. English Historic Carpentry.
Hewett, Daniel. Daniel Hewett's List of Newspapers & Periodicals in the United States in 1828.
Hewett, Frank M. & Forness, Steven R. Education of Exceptional Learners.
Hewett, Joan. When You Fight the Tiger.
Hewins, Caroline M. Mid-Century Child & Her Books.
Hewison, C. H. Locomotive Boiler Explosions.
Hewison, Robert, ed. New Approaches to Ruskin: Thirteen Essays.
Hewitt, A., jt. ed. see Burbidge, G.
Hewitt Associates Staff. ESOPS: An Analytical Report.
Hewitt, D., et al, eds. An Anthology of Longer Scottish Poems.
Hewitt, Dick, jt. auth. see Mosenthal, Basil.
Hewitt, E. & Ross, K. A. Abstract Harmonic Analysis: Vol. 1, Structure of Topological Groups, Integration Theory, Group Representations.
Hewitt, Graily. Lettering.
Hewitt, Jean. The N. Y. Times Natural Foods Cookbook.
--The New York Times Large Type Cookbook.
Hewitt, Nancy. Asparagus.
Hewitt, Paul G. Conceptual Physics.
Hewitt, Rosalie. Composing with Wordstar.
Hewlett, Dorothy. Elizabeth Barrett Browning.
Hewlett, Richard G. & Duncan, Francis. Nuclear Navy, Nineteen Forty-Six to Nineteen Sixty-Two.
Hewson, E. W., jt. auth. see Wade, J. E.
Hewton, Eric. Rethinking Educational Change.
Hexter, J. H. On Historians.
Hexter, R. M., jt. auth. see Decius, J. C.
Hey, David. Family History & Local History: A Regional History of England.
Heyden, Doris & Gendrop, Paul. Pre-Columbian Architecture of Mesoamerica.
Heydon, Peter N., ed. see Browning, Elizabeth Barrett.
Heyduck-Huth, Hilde. In the Village.
Heyel, Carl, ed. The Encyclopedia of Management.
Heyer, Anna H. Historical Sets, Collected Editions, & Monuments of Music: A Guide to their Contents.
Heyerdahl, Thor. Kon-Tiki.
--Kon-Tiki.
Heym, Stefan. Queen Against Defoe & Other Stories.
--The Wandering Jew.
--The Wandering Jew.
Heyman, J. Beams & Framed Structures.
Heyman, Jay. The Gourmet Guide to Water Cookery.
Heyman, Ken & Durniak, John. The Right Picture.
Heyman, Marjorie R. Enriching Your Reading Program.
Heymann, C. David. Ezra Pound: The Last Rower.
--Ezra Pound: The Last Rower. A Political Profile.
Heymann, Jaia, jt. ed. see Klein, Nancy.
Heyn, Jean. The Tessie C. Price.
Heyne, Pamela. Today's Architectural Mirror: Interiors, Buildings, & Solar Designs.
Heyneman, Stephen P. Investment in Indian Education: Uneconomic?
Heyneman, Stephen P. & Currie, Janice K. Schooling, Academic Performance & Occupational Attainment in a Non-Industrialized Society.
Heyns, Terry L. American & Soviet Relations Since Detente: The Framework.
Heyrman, Christine L. Commerce & Culture: The Maritime Communities of Colonial Massachusetts, 1690-1750.
Heyward, Edna Earle. The Rehabilitation of the Severely Mentally Retarded Trainable Child.
Heywood Brothers & Wakefield Co. Staff. Classic Wicker Furniture.
Heywood, Chester D. Negro Combat Troops in the World War: The Story of the Three Hundred Seventy-First Infantry.
Heywood, Jasper. Thyestes. Daalder, Joost, ed.
Heywood, John. Assessment in Higher Education.
--Foreign Exchange & the Corporate Treasurer.
--John Heywood's Works & Miscellaneous Short Poems. Milligan, Burton A., intro. by.
--Pitfalls & Planning in Student Teaching.
Heywood, R. B. Photoelasticity for Designers.
Heywood, Thomas. An Apology for Actors. Bd. with A Refutation of the 'Apology for Actors' Greene, John. Garland Pub.
Heywood, V. H. Flowering Plants of the World.
Heywood Broun, May, tr. see Valle-Inclan, Ramon.
Heyworth, Peter. Conversations with Klemperer.
Hezekiah. Hezekiah Speaks the Word of God in the Last Testament.
HFMA Staff. Disproportionate Share & Uncompersated Care.
Hiaasen, Carl, jt. auth. see Montalbano, William D.
Hiaasen, Carl, jt. auth. see Montalbano, William L.
Hiang The, jt. auth. see Sin The.
Hiatt, D. B. Sam Houston: Mid Muddle & Mud.
Hibbard, Don & Kaleialoha, Carol. The Role of Rock: A Guide to the Social & Political Consequences of Rock Music.
Hibbard, Jack & Fried, Bryan A. Weaponless Defense: A Law Enforcement Guide to Non-Violent Control.
Hibbard, W., ed. United States Minerals Issues--the Seventies, a Review; the Eighties, a Preview: 6th Annual Mineral Economics Symposium, November 12, 1980, Washington DC.
Hibbeler, Russell C. Structural Analysis.
--Transparency Acetates to Accompany Engineering Mechanics, Statics & Dynamics.
Hibberd, Robert G. Integrated Circuits: A Basic Course for Engineers & Technicians.
Hibbert, Christopher. Africa Explored: Europeans in the Dark Continent, 1769-1889.
--Cities & Civilizations.
--Cities & Civilizations.
--Days of the French Revolution.
Hibbert, Gerald K., ed. New Pacifism.
Hibbin, Sally, ed. Politics, Ideology & the State: Papers from the Communist University of London.
Hibler, Jane. Fair Game: A Hunter's Cookbook. Lawrence, Betsy, ed.
Hichens, Phoebe. All about the Royal Family.
Hick, John, ed. The Myth of God Incarnate.
--Truth & Dialogue in World Religions: Conflicting Truth Claims.
Hickerson, Harold. Chippewa Indians III. Horr, David A., ed.
Hickethier, Alfred. Hickethier Color Atlas.
Hickey, Albert E., ed. Simulator Training of Nuclear Reactor Operators.
Hickey, Denis. Home from Exile: An Approach to Post-Existentialist Philosophizing.
Hickey, Des & Smith, Gus. Operation Avalanche: The Salerno Landings, 1943.
Hickey, Firmin A., Jr., ed. see State Bar of Texas, Professional Efficiency & Economic Research Committee.
Hickey, Henry V. & Villines, William M., Jr. Elements of Electronics.
Hickey, Joseph E. & Scharf, Peter L. Toward a Just Correctional System: Experiments in Implementing Democracy in Prisons.
Hickey, Marilyn. Motivational Gifts.
Hickey, Mary E., tr. from Fr. Novena of Confidence & Thanksgiving to the Sorrowful & Immaculate Heart of Mary.
Hickey, Raymond. A Case for an Auxiliary Priesthood.
Hickish, Gordon W. Ear, Nose, & Throat Disorders.
Hickman, Cleveland P. & Roberts, Larry S. Integrated Principles of Zoology.
Hickman, Cleveland P., jt. auth. see Hickman, Frances M.
Hickman, Frances M. & Hickman, Cleveland P. Laboratory Studies in Integrated Zoology.
Hickman, Hannah. Robert Musil.
Hickman, Janet. The Thunder Pup.
--Zoar Blue.
Hickman, John. Horse Management.
Hickman, Martha H. Waiting & Loving: Thoughts Occasioned by the Illness & the Death of a Parent.
Hickman, Martha W. The Growing Season.
Hickman, Ronald D., jt. auth. see Wilson, Harold K.
Hickman, W. B. Statistical Measures of Corporate Bond Financing Since 1900.
Hickok, Ralph. The New Encyclopedia of Sports.
Hicks, Bernice E. All the World Is Kin.
Hicks, Bruce & Baron, Sylvia. The IIc BASIC Paint: Graphics for the Apple II Family.
Hicks, Clifford B. Alvin Fernald, Mayor for a Day.
--Alvin Fernald, Superweasel.
--Alvin Fernald, TV Anchorman.
--Alvin's Secret Code.
--Marvelous Inventions of Alvin Fernald.
--The Wacky World of Alvin Fernald.
Hicks, David. David Hicks Garden Design.
Hicks, Donald, ed. see President's Commission for a National Agenda: Panel on Policies & Prospects for Metropolitan & Nonmetropolitan America.
Hicks, George L. Appalachian Valley: Case Studies in Cultural Anthropology.
Hicks, Herbert G., et al. Business: An Involvement Approach.
Hicks, J. Limited Offerings Exemptions: Regulation D.
Hicks, Jocelyn M. & Boeckx, Roger L. Pediatric Clinical Chemistry.
Hicks, John D. Rehearsal for Disaster: The Boom & Collapse of 1919-1920.
Hicks, John D., et al. American Nation.
Hicks, Maynard. Where the Jobs Are: Communications.
Hicks, Olan, jt. auth. see Connally, Andrew M.
Hicks, R. E., jt. auth. see Probstein, R. F.
Hicks, Regina, et al. Dining In - Monterey Peninsula.
Hicks, Robert & Bewes, Richard. The Christian.
--The Church.
--God.
--The Holy Spirit.
--Jesus Christ.
--The Last Things.
--Man.
--Salvation.
Hicks, Roger. Thirty-Five MM Panorama.
Hicks, Roger W. Advanced Portrait Photography.
--Creative Color Photography.
--The Medium Format Handbook: A Guide to Rollfilm Photography.
--Thirty-Five MM Panorama.
Hicks, Shirley. The Oxtail Cocktail: A Modern Western.
Hicks, Tyler G. Business Borrowers Complete Success Kit.
--Business Capital Sources.
--Cash Credit Riches Success System.
Hicks, Tyler G. & Edwards, T. Pump Application Engineering.
Hickson, David J., jt. ed. see Lammers, Cornelius J.
Hickson, Joan. The Seven Sparrows & the Motor Car Picnic.
Hickson, Mark L., III, jt. auth. see Roebuck, Julian B.
Hidalgo, Italo M. Ceramica Tradicional del Oriente de Guatemala.
Hider, George M., jt. auth. see Batten, Robert W.
Hidy, George M., et al, eds. The Character & Origins of Smog Aerosols: A Digest of Results from the California Aerosol Characterization Experiment (ACHEX)
Hieb, Elizabeth, ed. Fund Advisors Institute, July 1980, Williamsburg, Va. Proceedings.
Hieb, Elizabeth A., ed. Collection of Employer Contributions Institute, Las Vegas, Nevada, June 15 to 18, 1980: Proceedings.
--Textbook for Employee Benefit Plan Trustees, Administrators & Advisors 1980: Proceedings.
--Textbook for Employee Benefit Plan Trustees, Administrators & Advisors 1981: Proceedings.
Hiebel, Frederick. The Epistles of Paul & Rudolf Steiner's Philosophy of Freedom.
Hiebert, D. Edmond. First Peter: An Expositional Commentary.
Hiebert, Ray & Reuss, Carol. Impact of Mass Media.
Hiebert, Ray, et al. Mass Media IV.
Hiemenz, Ulrich, et al. The Competitive Strength of European, Japanese, & U. S. Suppliers on Asian Markets.
Hieronymus, Lynn. What the Bible Says about Worship.
Hieronymus, Saint Epistulae.
--In Hieremiam Prophetam Libri 6.
Hiers, Richard H. Jesus & the Future: Unsolved Questions on Eschatology.
Hiers, Richard H., jt. auth. see Riegert, Eduard.
Hiers, Richard H., tr. see Weiss, Johannes.
Hiesinger, Ulrich W. & Percy, Ann, eds. A Scholar Collects: Selections from the Anthony Morris Clark Bequest.
Higaonna, Morio. Goju Ryu.
Higatsberger, M. J., ed. see International Symposium on Electromagnetic Separation of Radioactive Isotopes, Vienna, 1960.
Higbee, Edward C. Farms & Farmers in an Urban Age.
Higbee, Homer & Winters, Margaret K., eds. Admission & Academic Placement of Students from Hong Kong, Malaysia, Philippines & Singapore: Report of the 1979 NAFSA, AACRO & JCOW Workshop.
Higbee, Kenneth L. & Jensen, Larry C. Influence: What It Is & How to Use It.
Higdon, Archie, et al. Mechanics of Materials: Set SI Version.
Higdon, Hal. Horse That Played Center Field.
Higginbotham, Bill. Whittlin' Bill's Folk Characters.
Higginbottom, J. Winslow, tr. see LeRoy, Gen.
Higgins, jt. auth. see Margulis.
Higgins, Alex & Elonka, Stephen M. Boiler Room Questions & Answers.
Higgins, Benjamin. Economic Development.
Higgins, Brian & Parker, Hershel. Critical Essays on Herman Melville's "Pierre; or "the Ambiguities"
Higgins, C. S. & Moss, P. D. Sounds Real: Radio in Everyday Life.
Higgins, Daniel. The Challenge: Life of Dominic Savio.
Higgins, Dick, tr. see Novalis.
Higgins, E. Tory see Kuiper, Nicholas A.
Higgins, F. R. Arable Holdings.
Higgins, George V. A Choice of Enemies.
--Imposters.
--Imposters.
Higgins, Heather & Laiderman, Beth. Bruce! The Ultimate Springsteen Quiz Book.
Higgins, J., ed. Cesar Vallejo: An Anthology of Poetry.
Higgins, J. C. Information Systems for Planning & Control: Concepts & Cases.
Higgins, Jack. Day of Judgement.
Higgins, James E. Beyond Words: Mystical Fancy in Children's Literature.

Authors

Higgins, James M. Organizational Policy & Strategic Management: Text & Cases.
Higgins, James M., et al. Cases in Contemporary Business.
Higgins, John. The Making of an Opera.
Higgins, Jon L., ed. A Metric Handbook for Teachers.
Higgins, Lindley R. & Morrow, L. C. Maintenance Engineering Handbook.
Higgins, Loretta P., jt. auth. see Hawkins, Joellen B.
Higgins, Loretta P., jt. auth. see Hawkins, Joellen W.
Higgins, Mike. A Robot in Every Home: An Introduction to Personal Robots & Brand-Name Buyer's Guide.
Higgins, Paul C., jt. auth. see Albrecht, Gary L.
Higgins, Robert C. Analysis for Financial Management.
--Analysis for Financial Management.
Higgins, Susan J. A Latin American Filmography.
Higgins, Thomas. Comparing Strategies for Reducing Traffic Related Problems: The Potential for Road Pricing.
Higginson, Gordon R., jt. auth. see Dowson, Duncan.
Higginson, Mary T., ed. see Higginson, Thomas W.
Higginson, Thomas W. Letters & Journals of Thomas Wentworth Higginson: 1846-1906. Higginson, Mary T., ed.
--Tales of Atlantis & the Enchanted Islands.
Higginson, William J., jt. ed. see Harter, Penny.
Higginson, William J., tr. see Shiki, et al.
Higgs, Robert J. & Manning, Ambrose N., eds. Voices from the Hills: Selected Readings from Southern Appalachia.
High Fidelity Magazins Staff. The Recordings of Beethoven.
High, Monique R. Encore.
--Thy Father's House.
Higham, Charles. The Adventures of Conan Doyle: The Life of the Creator of Sherlock Holmes.
--Errol Flynn: The Untold Story.
--Kate: The Life of Katharine Hepburn.
--Marlene: The Life of Marlene Dietrich.
--Sisters: The Story of Olivia de Havilland & Joan Fontaine.
Higham, Charles, jt. auth. see De Massy, Christian.
Higham, Florence M. Charles First: A Study.
Higham, John. Send These to Me: Jews & Other Immigrants in Urban America.
Higham, Robin. Air Power: A Concise History.
--Britain's Imperial Air Routes: 1918-1939.
Higham, Robin O. The British Rigid Airship, Nineteen Hundred Eight to Nineteen Thirty-One: A Study in Weapons Policy.
Higher Education Energy Task Force Staff. Energy Cost & Consumption Report, 1980-1981 & 1981-1982.
Highland, Esther, jt. auth. see Highland, Harold.
Highland, Harold & Highland, Esther. CBASIC Programming for Business.
Highsaw, Robert B. & Fortenberry, Charles N. The Government & Administration of Mississippi. Graves, W. Brooke, ed.
Highsmith, Patricia. Little Tales of Mysogyny.
Highsmith, Patrick. Slowly, Slowly in the Wind.
Highstone, John. Victorian Gardens: How to Plan, Plant & Enjoy Them.
Hightower, Florence. Ghost of Follonsbee's Folly.
--The Secret of the Crazy Quilt.
Hightower, James E., Jr. Illustrating Paul's Letter to the Romans.
Highwater, Jamake. Native Land: Sagas of the Indian Americas.
--Ritual of the Wind: North American Indian Ceremonies, Music & Dance.
--Ritual of Wind: North American Indian Ceremonies, Music, & Dance.
Higley, Joan M. Activities Desk Book for Teaching Arithmetic Skills.
Higley, John, jt. auth. see Field, G. Lowell.
Higman, Dennis. Laura Jordan.
Higman, G., ed. see London Mathematical Society Instructional Conference Staff.
Higuchi, Tadahiko. The Visual & Spatial Structure of Landscapes. Terry, Charles, tr. from Japanese.
Hihara, Koho. Misho School.
Hilado, Carlos J., ed. Carbon Reinforced Epoxy Systems.
Hilarius, Saint Opera. Feder, A., ed.
Hilberry, Conrad. Rust.
Hilbers, C. W. & MacLean, C. N M R of Molecules Oriented in Electric Fields. Bd. with N M R & Relaxation of Molecules Absorbed on Solids. Pfeifer, H. Springer-Verlag.
Hilbert, Stephen & Jaffe, Eugene. Barron's How to Prepare for the Graduate Management Admission Test (GMAT)
Hilborn, Ann. Personal Justice.
Hilborn, Nat & Hilborn, Sam. Battleground of Freedom: South Carolina in the Revolution.
Hilborn, Sam, jt. auth. see Hilborn, Nat.
Hilburn, J. L., jt. auth. see Johnson, D. E.
Hilburn, John L. & Julich, Paul M. Microcomputers-Microprocessors: Hardware, Software & Applications.
Hilburn, Robert. Springsteen.
--Springsteen.
Hild, Walter J., ed. see Sobotta, Johannes.
Hildebrand, Alice J. Von see Von Hildebrand, Alice J.
Hildebrand, B. P. & Brenden, B. B. NDT: Holographic Testing: An Introduction to Acoustical Holography.
Hildebrand Editorial Staff. Jamaica.
--Kenya.
--Seychelles.
--South Africa.
--Taiwan.
Hildebrand, Francis B. Methods of Applied Mathematics.
Hildebrand, George H. Postwar Italy: A Study in Economic Contrasts.
Hildebrand, James K. Maintenance Turns to the Computer.
Hildebrand, Joel, et al. Regular & Related Solutions: The Solubility of Gases, Liquids & Solids.
Hildebrand, Milton. Analysis of Vertebrate Structure.
--Laugh & Love.
Hildebrandt, Timothy A., illus. The Unicorn Journal II: An Illustrated Book with Space for Notes.
Hildegard & Geimer, Reinhold, eds. Research Organization & Science Promotion in the Federal Republic of Germany.
Hildeman, Gregory J., jt. ed. see Koczak, Michael J.
Hildemann, W. H., jt. auth. see Snell, George D.
Hilden, Alton H. Alton-Loki: Dual Personality.
Hilder, Frazer F. & Watkins, Thomas W. Regulation of Corporate Political Activity.
Hilder, Rowland. Starting with Watercolour.
Hildesley, C. Hugh. Sotheby's Guide to Buying & Selling at Auction.
Hildick, E. W. The Case of the Bashful Bank Robber.
--The Case of the Bashful Bank Robber.
--The Case of the Condemned Cat.
--The Case of the Felon's Fiddle.
--The Case of the Four Flying Fingers.
--Case of the Invisible Dog.
--Case of the Nervous Newsboy.
--Case of the Phantom Frog.
--The Case of the Phantom Frog.
--Case of the Secret Scribbler.
--The Case of the Snowbound Spy.
--The Case of the Snowbound Spy.
--The Case of the Treetop Treasure.
--The Case of the Vanishing Ventriloquist.
--The Great Rabbit Rip-Off.
--McGurk Gets Good & Mad.
--Manhattan Is Missing.
--The Nose Knows.
Hildick, Wallace. Word for Word: The Rewriting of Fiction.
Hildick-Smith, Gavin Y., jt. auth. see Burke, John F.
Hildyard, R. J., jt. auth. see Oswald, Adrian.
Hiler, Craig. Monkey Mountain.
Hiler, Hilaire. Notes on the Technique of Painting.
Hiley, Jim. Theatre at Work.
Hiley, Michael. Victorian Working Women.
Hilferding, Rudolf. Finance Capital: A Study of the Latest Phase of Capitalist Development. Bottomore, Tom, tr. from Ger.
Hilfiker, David. Healing the Wounds: A Physician Looks at His Work.
Hilgard, Ernest R. Hypnotic Susceptibility.
Hilgard, Ernest R., ed. Theories of Learning & Instruction.
Hilgard, Ernest R., et al. Introduction to Psychology.
--Introduction to Psychology.
Hilgard, Josephine R. Personality & Hypnosis: A Study of Imaginative Involvement.
Hilgard, P. & Hellman, K., eds. Anticancer Drug Development.
Hilgartner, Margaret W., ed. Hemophilia in Children.
Hilger, Inez. Chippewa Child Life & Its Cultural Background.
Hilgert, Raymond L., jt. auth. see Schoen, Sterling H.
Hilgert, Raymond L., et al. Cases & Policies in Human Resource Management.
--Cases & Policies in Personnel-Human Resources Management.
--Cases & Policies in Personal-Human Resources Management.
Hill, A. G., jt. auth. see Ffrench, G. E.
Hill, Adrian. What Shall We Draw?
Hill, Albert, jt. auth. see Hill, David.
Hill, Albert F. Economic Botany.
Hill, Albert F., jt. auth. see Hill, David C.
Hill, Albert F., et al. I'm a Patient, Too. CanSurmount - The Dramatic Support Program for Cancer Patients.
Hill, Alfred, et al. Violin Makers of the Guarneri Family, 1626-1762.
Hill, Archie. Closed World of Love.
Hill, Bennett D., jt. auth. see McKay, John P.
Hill, Brennan. Rediscovering the Sacraments: Approaches to the Sacrament.
Hill, Brian. The Common Agricultural Policy.
Hill, C. J. Introduction to the Law of Carriage of Goods by Sea.
Hill, Calvin. The Art of Power & Control Selling: The Salesman's Bible.
Hill, Carol. The Eleven Million Mile High Dancer.
--An Unmarried Woman.
Hill, Carol, ed. see Hoffman, William.
Hill, Christopher. Century of Revolution, 1603-1714.
Hill, Christopher, jt. auth. see Hines, Lawrence G.
Hill, Christopher T. & Utterback, James M., eds. Technological Innovation for a Dynamic Economy.
Hill, Claire C. Problem Solving: Learning & Teaching.
Hill, Daniel B. Discounting Hospital Services: Some Arithmetic.
Hill, David. New Testament Prophecy.
Hill, David & Hill, Albert. The Deadly Messiah.
Hill, David C. & Hill, Albert F. The Deadly Messiah.
Hill, Debora. Cuts from a San Francisco Rock Journal.
Hill, Deborah, jt. ed. see Ebeling, Nancy.
Hill, Donald L. The Biochemistry & Physiology of Tetrahymena.
Hill, Donna. First Your Penny.
Hill, Donna M. Life Wasn't Meant to Be Easy.
Hill, Elliott M., ed. see Jones, Thomas.
Hill, Eric. At Home.
--My Pets.
--The Park.
--Up There.
Hill, Errol. Shakespeare in Sable: A History of Black Shakespearean Actors.
Hill, Eugenie. More Innocent Time.
Hill, F. W., jt. auth. see Grunsell, C. S.
Hill, Frank W. & Searight, Roland. Study Outline & Workbook in the Elements of Music.
Hill, Geoffrey. Somewhere Is Such a Kingdom: Poems, 1952-1971.
--Tenebrae.
Hill, Geoffrey, jt. auth. see Ibsen, Henrik.
Hill, George H. Black Media in America: A Bibliography & Resource Guide.
Hill, George J. Leprosy in Five Young Men.
Hill, George J., II. Outpatient Surgery.
Hill, George R. A Preliminary Checklist of Research on the Classic Symphony & Concerto to the Time of Beethoven (Excluding Haydn & Mozart)
Hill, George R. & Gould, Murray. A Thematic Locator for Mozart's Works, As Listed in Koechel's Chronologisch Thematisches Verzeichnis.
Hill, George W. The Radiant Universe.
Hill, Grace L. The Enchanted Barn.
--The Man of the Desert.
--The Patch of Blue.
Hill, Graham L. Nutrition & the Surgical Patient.
Hill, Harry G. Interpreting Automotive Systems.
Hill, Herber & Greenberg, Jack. Citizen's Guide to Desegregation: A Study of Social & Legal Change in American Life.
Hill, I. D. & Meek, B. L. Programming Language Standardization.
Hill, Ian. Jet 88.
Hill, Ivan, ed. Ethics of Economics.
Hill, James C. Chemistry: The Central Science.
Hill, John H. Dear God, Pourquoi? Why Did You Born Me in Texas.
Hill, John H. & Hill, Laurita L. Peter Tudebode: Historia De Hierosolymitano Itinere.
--Raymond D'Aguilers: Historia Francorum Qui Ceperunt Iherusalem.
--Raymond IV, Count of Toulouse.
Hill, John W. Chemistry for Changing Times: Student Study Guide.
Hill, Johnson D. & Stuermann, Walter E. Roots in the Soil.
Hill, Judith & Hill, Michael, eds. The Cook's Magazine Cookbook.
Hill, Kenneth. Wine & Beermaking at Home.
Hill, Langdon. Mr. Romance's Book of Love: Passionate Secrets of America's Greatest Lovers.
Hill, Larry B. Parliament & the Ombudsman in New Zealand.
Hill, Laurita L., jt. auth. see Hill, John H.
Hill, Louis B. Joseph E. Brown & the Confederacy.
Hill, M. Anne, jt. ed. see Berkowitz, Monroe.
Hill, M. J., jt. auth. see Drasar, D. R.
Hill, Marvin S. & Rooker, C. Keith. The Kirtland Economy Revisited: A Market Critique of Sectarian Economics.
Hill, Michael. Understanding Social Policy.
Hill, Michael, jt. ed. see Hill, Judith.
Hill, Myron G., Jr., et al. Smith's Review of Torts.
Hill, Nancy K. A Reformer's Art: Dickens' Picturesque & Grotesque Imagery.
Hill, Napoleon. Master-Key to Riches.
--You Can Work Your Own Miracles.
Hill, Norman L. Claims to Territory in International Law & Relations.
Hill, Norwood, jt. ed. see Khan, Amanullah.
Hill, P. Maurice, tr. Poems of Sappho.
Hill, Pamela. The Sisters.
Hill, Patricia R., jt. ed. see Bucher, Glenn R.
Hill, Peter. The Enthusiast.
--The Liars.
Hill, Phyllis M., ed. The Teachers Library.
Hill, R. Principles of Dynamics.
Hill, R. R. & Rendell, D. A. Interpretation of Infrared Spectra: A Programmed Introduction.
Hill, R. W., jt. auth. see Hanks, R. J.
Hill, Ralph, et al. Vermont: A Special World.
Hill, Reba M. A Doctor's Prescription for Gourmet Cooking.
Hill, Rebecca. Among Birches.
Hill, Reginald. An Advancement of Learning.
--A Fairly Dangerous Thing.
--A Killing Kindness.
--Traitor's Blood.
Hill, Renais, ed. see St. Ama, Johnny W.
Hill, Richard F. Synfuels Industry Development.
Hill, Richard F., et al, eds. Synfuels Industry Opportunities. Boardman, Elliot B. & Heavner, Martin L.
Hill, Richard O., jt. auth. see Hestenes, Marshall D.
Hill, Robert A., ed. see Tolbert, Emory J.
Hill, Robert B. Occupational Attainment: Minorities & Women in Selected Industries, 1969-1979.
Hill, Ronald C. & Stanley, Dave. Rails in the Northwest, a Contemporary Glimpse.
Hill, Ruth B. Hanta Yo.
Hill, S. C., jt. auth. see Barber, P. W.
Hill, S. R. The Distributive System.
Hill, Scott, jt. auth. see Playfair, Guy L.
Hill, Stuart & Ott, Pierre. Basic Techniques in Ecological Farming.
Hill, Susan. The Magic Apple Tree: A Country Year.
Hill, T. H. Math for the Layman.
Hill, Thomas see Mountaine, Dydymus, pseud.
Hill, Tom. Color for the Watercolor Painter.
Hill, W. Aber. Ten Million Photoplay Plots. Kupelnick, Bruce S., ed.
Hill, W. C. Primates: Comparative Anatomy & Taxonomy. Incl. Vol. 2; Vol. 3; Vol. 4; Vol. 5; Vol. 6; Vol. 7; Vol. 8. Halsted Pr.
Hill, Walter R. Secondary School Reading: Process-Program-Procedure.
Hill, Winston W., jt. auth. see Atchison, Thomas J.
Hillaby, John. Journey Home.
--Journey Through Love.
--A Walk Through Britain.
Hillary, Edmund & Hillary, Peter. Ascent: Two Lives Explored.
Hillary, Peter, jt. auth. see Hillary, Edmund.
Hillenbrand, Martin, jt. ed. see Yergin, Daniel H.
Hiller, B. B. & Hiller, Neil W. The Best Times.
Hiller, Bevis, compiled by see Betjeman, John.
Hiller, Cathy & Hofler, Robert. The Complete Sexenders Program: The Celibacy Movement That's Cooling off All America.
Hiller, Herbert L. Guide to the Small & Historic Lodgings of Florida.
Hiller, Lejaren A. & Isaacson, Leonard M. Experimental Music: Composition with an Electronic Computer.
Hiller, Neil W., jt. auth. see Hiller, B. B.
Hiller, Susan, jt. auth. see Coxhead, David.
Hillerbrand, Hans. Men & Ideas in the Sixteenth Century.
Hillerbrand, Hans J. Christendom Divided: The Protestant Reformation.
Hillerman, Tony. The Blessing Way.
--Dance Hall of the Dead.
--The Dark Wind.
--The Fly on the Wall. Barzun, J. & Taylor, W. H., eds.
--People of Darkness.
Hillert, Margaret. Rabbits & Rainbows.
Hillery, George A., Jr. Communal Organizations, a Study of Local Societies.
Hilles, Richard J., jt. auth. see Golembiewski, Robert T.
Hillestad, Steven G. & Berkowitz, Eric W. Health Care Marketing Plans: From Strategy to Action.
Hillesum, Etty. Letters from Westerbork. Pomerans, Arnold, tr.
Hillier, Bevis. Greetings from Christmas Past.
--The Simon & Schuster Pocket Guide to Antiques.
Hillier, Caroline. The Bulwark Shore: Exploring Thanet & the Cinque Ports.
Hillier, Caroline, tr. see Simenon, Georges.
Hillier, Sheila & Jewell, John. Health Care & Traditional Medicine in China, 1800-1982.
Hilligoss, Pamela J. & Woodward, Addison E., Jr. The Child: Development from Birth to Adolescence.
Hillila, Bernhard, tr. see Kaukola, Olavi.
Hilling, D., jt. ed. see Hoyle, B. S.
Hillis, Danny, ed. Parallel Models of Intelligence.
Hillis, Dick. Not Made for Quitting.

Authors

Hillis, W. Edward & Brown, Alan G., eds. Eucalypts for Wood Production.
Hillman, H. Cook's Book.
Hillman, Howard. Great Peasant Dishes of the World.
--Kitchen Science: A Compendium of Essential Information for Every Cook.
Hillman, James, ed. Spring 1985: An Annual of Archetypal Psychology & Jungian Thought.
Hillman, Libby. Fresh Garden Vegetables. Beckhardt, Robin, ed.
Hillman, Priscilla. Merry-Mouse Book of Favorite Poems.
--The Merry Mouse Schoolhouse.
Hillman, Priscilla, illus. Merry-Mouse Book of Prayers & Graces.
Hillman, William C. Commercial Loan Documentation.
Hillman, William C., jt. auth. see Practising Law Institute Staff.
Hillmann, Michael C. Persian Carpets.
Hillner, K. P. Learning: Psychology Of.
Hillock, Wilfred M. Involved.
Hills, Christopher. Nuclear Evolution: A Guide to Cosmic Enlightenment.
--Success Is a Way of Life.
Hills, Desmond B. Light for My Life. Van Dolson, Bobbie J., ed.
Hills, E. S. Elements of Structural Geology.
Hills, Jill. Information Technology & Industrial Policy.
Hills, Jill, jt. ed. see Lovenduski, Joni.
Hills, P. J. Educating for a Computer Age.
--Educational Futures.
--Educational Futures.
--The Self-Teaching Process in Higher Education.
Hills, P. J., ed. Dictionary of Education.
Hills, P. J. & McLaren, Margaret, eds. Teaching Communication Skills.
Hills, P. J., ed. see Chibnall, Bernard.
Hills, P. J., ed. see Painter, Derek.
Hills, P. J., ed. see Todd, Frankie.
Hills, Patricia. The Genre Painting of Eastman Johnson: The Sources & Development of His Styles & Themes.
Hills, Rust. Writing in General & the Short Story in Particular.
Hills, Sarah Jane, jt. auth. see Hills, Theo L.
Hills, Theo L. & Hills, Sarah Jane. Canada.
Hillway, Tyrus & Mansfield, Luther S., eds. Moby Dick Centennial Essays.
Hiltebeitel, Alf, tr. see Dumezil, Georges.
Hiltner, William A., ed. Astronomical Techniques.
Hilton, jt. auth. see Cockett.
Hilton, Bruce, et al, eds. Ethical Issues in Human Genetics: Genetic Counseling & the Use of Genetic Knowledge.
Hilton, Della. Who Was Kit Marlow? The Story of the Poet & Playwright.
Hilton, Donna, ed. Springhouse Drug Reference.
Hilton, Edie. Bar & Party Guide, Complete Guide to Mixing Drinks.
Hilton, Hermine. The Executive Memory Guide.
Hilton, Jack & Knoblauch, Mary. On Television: A Survival Guide for Media Interviews.
Hilton, Julian. Georg Buchner.
Hilton, P., et al, eds. see Conference Held at Battelle Seattle Research Center, 1975.
Hilton, P. J. Differential Calculus.
Hilton, P. J., jt. auth. see Griffiths, H. B.
Hilton, P. J., ed. see Algebraic Topology Symposium Staff.
Hilton, Peter J., ed. see Battelle Memorial Institute Conference Staff.
Hilton, R. H. Decline of Serfdom in Medieval England.
Hilton, Suzanne. Beat It, Burn It, Drown It.
--Getting There: Frontier Travel Without Power.
--Here Today & Gone Tomorrow: The Story of World's Fairs & Expositions.
--How Do They Cope with It?
--It's a Model World.
--It's Smart to Use a Dummy.
--The Way It Was-Eighteen Seventy-Six.
--Who Do You Think You Are? Digging for Your Family Roots.
Hilton, W. S. Industrial Relations in Construction.
Hilts, Philip J. Scientific Temperaments.
--Scientific Temperaments: Three Lives in Contemporary Science.
Hiltz. Readings in Introductory Sociology.
Hilvert, John. Blue Pencil Warriors: Censorship & Propaganda in World War II.
Himalayan International Institute Staff. Inner Paths.
--Meditation in Christianity.
--Therapeutic Value of Yoga.
Himes, Chester. The Crazy Kill.
--For Love of Imabelle.
Himmelblau, David M. Basic Principles & Calculations in Chemical Engineering.
Himmelwright, A. Pistol & Revolver Shooting.
Himstreet, William C. & Baty, Wayne M. Business Communications.
--Business Communications: Principles & Methods.
Hince, Kevin. Conflict & Coal: A Case Study of Industrial Relations in the Open-Cut Coal Mining Industry of Queensland.
Hinchliffe, A. P. The Absurd.
Hinchliffe, R. F. & Lilleyman, J. S., eds. Practical Paediatric Haematology: A Laboratory Worker's Guide to Blood Disorders in Children.
Hinchman, Jane. Rendezvous with Love.
Hinckle, Warren, 3rd & Hobbs, Frederic, eds. The Richest Place on Earth: The Story of Virginia City, Nevada, & the Heyday of the Comstock Lode.
Hinckley, Barbara. Coalitions & Politics.
--Congressional Elections.
Hinckley, Helen. Crazy Judah: Father of the Transcontinental Railroad.
Hind, A. M. History of Engraving & Etching: From the Fifteenth Century to the Year 1914.
Hind, W. Carboniferous Lamellibranchiata.
Hinde, Robert A., ed. Primate Social Relationships.
Hinde, Thomas. The Domesday Book: England's Heritage Then & Now.
Hindelang, Thomas J., jt. auth. see Pritchard, Robert E.
Hindenlang, D. M., jt. auth. see Shamma, M.
Hinderer, Karl. Foundations of Non-Stationary Dynamic Programming with Discrete Time Parameter.
Hinderlie, Mary & Hong, Edna. Festival of Christmas.
Hindess, Barry. Freedom, Equality & the Market: Arguments on Social Policy.
--Parliamentary Democracy & Socialist Politics.
Hindess, Barry & Hirst, Paul Q. Pre-Capitalist Modes of Production.
Hindle, Brooke. The Pursuit of Science in Revolutionary America, 1735-1789.
Hindley, jt. auth. see Amery.
Hindman, Margaret H., jt. auth. see McGough, Dixie P.
Hindman, Sandra. Text & Image in Fifteenth-Century Illustrated Dutch Bibles (1977)
Hindmarsh, J. Electrical Machines & Their Applications.
--Worked Examples in Electrical Machines & Drives.
Hinds, Dudley & Carn, Neil. Winning at Zoning.
Hinds, J. A., jt. auth. see Organick, E. I.
Hinds, Richard D., jt. auth. see Practising Law Institute Staff.
Hindson, Edward & Byrd, Walter. When the Road Gets Rough.
Hindus, Milton, ed. Walt Whitman: The Critical Heritage.
Hindwood, Keith. Australian Birds in Colour.
Hine, Al & Alcorn, John. A Letter to Anywhere.
--Where in the World Do You Live?
Hine, Albert C., jt. auth. see Cook, Harry E., III.
Hine, Daryl. Academic Festival Overtures.
--The Homeric Hymns.
Hine, Daryl & Parisi, Joseph, eds. The Poetry Anthology Nineteen Twelve to Nineteen Seventy-Seven: 65 Years of America's Most Distinguished Verse Magazine.
Hine, J. & Wetherill, G. B. Programmed Text in Statistics.
Hine, Robert V. California's Utopian Colonies.
Hine, Virginia H., jt. auth. see Gherlach, Luther P.
Hinerman, Ivan D. Automotive Engine Repair.
Hinerman, Paige S. Teaching Autistic Children to Communicate.
Hines, Al. Signs & Portents.
Hines, Carole P., jt. ed. see Shores, David L.
Hines, Eugene B. Asking the Hard Questions.
--Living in the Presence of God.
Hines, Herman & Stalick, Wayne M. Base Catalyzed Reactions of Hydrocarbons & Related Compounds.
Hines, Lawrence G. & Hill, Christopher. Environmental Issues.
Hines, M. A. How to Prepare for the Real Estate Licensing Exam.
--Real Estate Appraising.
--Real Estate Finance.
--Real Estate Investment.
--Real Estate Principles.
Hines, Mary A. Income-Property Development, Financing, & Investment.
--Shopping Center Development & Investment.
Hines, Neal O. Business Officers in Higher Education: A History of NACUBO. Jacobson, David W., ed.
Hines, Raymond D., jt. auth. see Jensen, Cecil H.
Hines, Robert S. The Orchestral Composer's Point of View: Essays on Twentieth-Century Music by Those Who Wrote It.
Hinger, Charlotte. Come Spring.
Hingson, John H. How to Defend a Drunk Driving Case: A Guide to Practical, Procedural, & Legal Aspects.
Hink, Heinz R., jt. auth. see Mason, Bruce B.
Hinkemeyer, Michael T. A Time to Reap.
Hinkle, Douglas P. Poetry Is You.
Hinkle, Joseph W., et al. Oikos: A Practical Approach to Family Evangelism.
Hinkle, Roscoe C. Founding Theory of American Sociology 1881-1915.
Hinkle, Vernon. Music to Murder by.
Hinkley, ed. Laser Monitoring of the Atmosphere.
Hinkley, D. H., jt. ed. see Fienberg, S. E.
Hinks, Peter. Twentieth Century British Jewellery, 1900-1980.
Hinman, Bob. The Duck Hunter's Handbook.
Hinnebusch, Paul. Friendship in the Lord.
Hinojo, Ida, ed. Vest Pocket Spanish Dictionary.
Hinojosa, Ida N., ed. New Century World-Wide Spanish Dictionary.
Hinrichs, H., jt. auth. see Von Schmidt, W. A.
Hinrichs, John R. Practical Management for Productivity.
Hinrichsen, E. N. Control of Large Wind Turbine Generators Connected to Utility Networks.
Hinrichsen, Gerda. The Body Shop: Scandinavian Exercises for Relaxation.
Hinsdale, Burke A. Horace Mann & the Common School Revival in the U. S.
Hinsdale, Harriett. Be My Love.
Hinsdale, W. B. Distribution of the Aboriginal Population of Michigan.
Hinshaw, Jane S., jt. auth. see Autry, William O., Jr.
Hinshaw, Joseph H. Elements of Truth.
Hinson, Betty S. Smile Worm - Who Am I? What Will I Be?
Hinson, E. Glenn. A Serious Call to a Contemplative Lifestyle.
Hinson, Maurice. Guide to the Pianist's Repertoire. Freundlich, Irwin, ed.
Hinson, Oleen T. Poems & Prayers of Inspiration.
Hinton. Heavy Current Electricity in the United Kingdom.
Hinton, Ann P. How to Keep the Home Fires Burning: Have An Affair with Your Spouse.
Hinton, Ann P., et al. Getting Free: Women & Psychotherapy.
Hinton, Geoffrey E. & Rumelhart, David E., eds. Neural Network Architectures for Artificial Intelligence.
Hinton, James F., jt. auth. see Amis, Edward S.
Hinton, Nicholas. Making Work.
Hintz, Martin. Tons of Fun: Training Elephants.
Hintz, Martin & Hintz, Sandra. Computers in Our World, Today & Tomorrow.
Hintz, Sandra, jt. auth. see Hintz, Martin.
Hinxman, Margaret. The Boy from Nowhere.
Hinz. Baltimore Orioles.
--Houston Astros.
--Minnesota Twins.
--San Diego Padres.
--Seattle Mariners.
Hinz, Earl. Sail Before Sunset.
Hinz, Evelyn J. The Mirror & the Garden: Realism & Reality in the Writings of Anais Nin.
Hinz, Evelyn J., ed. see Williams, Roger.
Hinze, Harry C., et al, eds. Animal Models for the Study of Herpes Virus Associated Malignancy.
Hinze, Juergen. Energy Storage & Redistribution in Molecules.
Hinze, Juergen, ed. Electron-Atom & Electron-Molecule Collisions.
Hip Society. The Hip: Proceedings of the 10th Open Scientific Meeting of the Hip Society,1982.
--The Hip: Proceedings of the 12th Open Scientific Meeting of the Hip Society 1982.
Hip Society, ed. The Hip: Proceedings of the 11th Open Scientific Meeting of the Hip Society, 1983.
Hipkins, Alfred J. A Description & History of the Pianoforte.
Hippchen, Leonard J., jt. auth. see American Correctional Association Staff.
Hippocrates & Kelly, Crosby. Theory & Practice of Medicine.
Hirai, Tomio. Zen & the Mind: A Scientific Approach to Zen Practice.
--Zen Meditation & Psychotherapy.
Hiraki, Akemi & Parlocha, Pamela Kees. Returning to School: The RN to BSN Handbook.
Hirano, Umeyo, tr. see Kindaich, Haruhiko.
Hirasuna, Delphine & Hirasuna, Diane J. Flavors of Japan.
Hirasuna, Diane J., jt. auth. see Hirasuna, Delphine.
Hirchorn, Joel S. Introduction to Powder Metallurgy.
Hirl, Patricia A., jt. auth. see Finnegan, John R.
Hirmer, Oswald & Lobinger, Fritz. Sunday Readers Lectionary: For Lay Ministers.
Hirnle, Robert W. Clinical Simulations in Neonatal Respiratory Therapy.
Hirnschall, Helmut, jt. auth. see Chief Dan George.
Hirnschall, Helmut, jt. auth. see George, Dan.
Hiro, D. Inside the Middle East.
Hiro, Te R. The Coming of the Maori.
Hirohata, Kazushi, et al. Ultrastructure of Bone & Joint Diseases.
Hirono, R., jt. ed. see Xhng, M. K.
Hirono, Ryokichi, jt. auth. see Camps, Miriam.
Hiroshige, Ando. Hiroshige: A Shoal of Fishes.
Hirsch, Barbara. Living Together: A Guide to the Law for Unmarried Couples.
Hirsch, Bernard A. see Cherry, Richard L., et al.
Hirsch, Bob. Houseboating on Lake Powell.
Hirsch, Edith, jt. auth. see Luchins, Abraham S.
Hirsch, Elisabeth. Problems of Early Childhood: An Annotated Bibliography & Guide.
Hirsch, Felice L., jt. auth. see Hall, Sandra P.
Hirsch, Foster. A Method to Their Madness: A History of the Actors Studio.
Hirsch, H. J., tr. see Borchard, Franz.
Hirsch, J. & McGuire, T. R., eds. Behavior-Genetic Analysis.
Hirsch, Jerrold, jt. ed. see Terrill, Tom E.
Hirsch, John D. The Complete Book of Car Maintenance & Repair.
Hirsch, M. W., et al. Invariant Manifolds.
Hirsch, Marcie S., jt. auth. see Wheatly, Meg.
Hirsch, Mark D., jt. auth. see Hacker, Louis M.
Hirsch, Martin S., et al. Investigation of Oncogenic Viruses.
Hirsch, Maurice L., Jr. & Louderback, Joseph G. Cost Accounting: Accumulation, Analysis & Use.
Hirsch, Miriam F. Women & Violence.
Hirsch, Nathaniel. Genius & Creative Intelligence.
Hirsch, R. & Weber, E., eds. Hofmannsthal Issue of Journal of the International A. Schnizler Research Foundation.
Hirsch, R. S., jt. auth. see Feist, Uwe.
Hirsch, Rudolf, ed. Catalog of Manuscripts & Archives in F. Clark Wood Institute at College of Physicians in Philadelphia.
Hirsch, Steven R., jt. ed. see Farmer, Richard D. T.
Hirsch, W. The Contracts Management Deskbook.
Hirsch, Werner Z. Law & Economics: An Introductory Analysis.
--Urban Economics.
--Urban Economics.
Hirschberg, Walter. Woerterbuch der Voelkerkunde.
Hirschfeld, Burt. Acapulco.
--The Big Score.
--Cindy on Fire.
Hirschfeld, Burt, pseud. Doll Baby.
Hirschfeld, Burt. Father Pig.
--Fire in the Embers.
--Fire Island.
--Fun City.
--Generation of Victors.
--The Love Thing.
--Masters Affair.
--Return to Fire Island.
--Tilt!
Hirschfeld, G. Exile in Great Britain: Refugees from Hitler's Germany.
Hirschfeld, Gerhard. An Essay on Mankind.
Hirschfeld, J. & Wheeler, W. H. Forcing, Arithmetic, Division Rings.
Hirschfelder, Arlene B. Annotated Bibliography of the Literature on American Indians Published in State Historical Society Publications: New England & Middle Atlantic States.
Hirschhorn, Bernard. The Perilous Presidency.
Hirschhorn, Joel, jt. auth. see Kasha, Al.
Hirschhorn, Joel S. Introduction to Powder Metallurgy.
Hirschhorn, Kurt, jt. ed. see Harris, Harry.
Hirschhorn, Richard C. Target Mayflower.
Hirschkop, Philip J., jt. auth. see Bronstein, Alvin J.
Hirschman, Albert O. The Strategy of Economic Development.
Hirschmeier, Johannes. Origins of Entrepreneurship in Meiji Japan.
Hirschson, Linda B., jt. auth. see Practising Law Institute Staff.
Hirsh, M. E. Kabul.
Hirsh, Marilyn. Hannibal & His Thirty-Seven Elephants.
Hirson, Roger O. & Schwartz, Stephen. Pippin.
Hirst. Gun & the Olive Branch.
Hirst & Illiff. Sights & Sounds of Ophthamology: Occular & Periocular Trauma.
Hirst, David. Edward Bond. King, Bruce & King, Adele, eds.
--The Gun & the Olive Branch: The Roots of Violence in the Middle East.
Hirst, David & Beeson, Irene. Sadat.
Hirst, David L. Comedy of Manners.
--Tragicomedy.
Hirst, Margaret E. Quakers in Peace & War.
Hirst, Paul Q., jt. auth. see Hindess, Barry.
Hirst, R. J. Problems of Perception.
Hirst, R. J., ed. Philosophy: An Outline for the Intending Student.
Hirt, Geoffrey A., jt. auth. see Block, Stanley B.
Hirt, Howard. The Heat of Winter.
Hirth, Kenneth G., ed. Trade & Exchange in Early Mesoamerica.
Hirtz, J. L., jt. ed. see Societe Francaise des Sciences et Techniques Pharmaceutiques Working Group Staff.
Hirtz, Jean L. Fate of Drugs in the Organism: A Bibliographic Survey.

Authors

Hirvoen, J. K., ed. see Annual Meeting of the Materials Research Society Staff.
Hirzebruch, F. E., et al. Prospects in Mathematics.
Hisatake, Masayuki. Scientific Karatedo: Spiritual Development of Individulality in Mind & Body.
Hishey, David, jt. auth. see Bodo, Peter.
Hisket, J. Brent. Au & Ag Heap & Dump Leaching Practice.
Hislop, Alexander. Proverbs of Scotland.
Hislop, John. Breeding for Racing.
Hiss, Tony. Laughing Last: Alger Hiss.
Historical Division, Department of the Army, ed. Anzio Beachhead Twenty-Second of January to Twenty-Fifth of May 1944.
Hitchcock, Alfred. Death Can Be Beautiful.
--Down by the Old Blood Stream.
--Games Killers Play.
--Hangman's Dozen.
Hitchcock, Alfred, ed. Don't Look a Gift Shark in the Mouth.
Hitchcock, Anthony. Country Inns California.
--Country Inns: Lodges & Historic Hotels, New England States, 1988-89.
Hitchcock, Arthur A. & Nott, Wanda L., eds. Mid-Life Change.
Hitchcock, George. The Piano Beneath the Skin.
Hitchcock, Henry-Russell & Seale, William. Temples of Democracy.
Hitchcock, J. Gareth. Profiles in Innocence by Quentin K. Y. Huang: With an Introduction by Himself.
Hitchcock, John R., jt. ed. see Bourne, Larry S.
Hitchcock, Mary J. Foodservice Systems Administration.
Hitchcock, Thomas H., ed. see Smith, J. Richard, et al.
Hitchcock, W. Readings in Guidance.
Hitchens, Neal, jt. auth. see Riese, Randall.
Hitching, Francis. The Mysterious World: An Atlas of the Unexplained.
--The Neck of the Giraffe: Where Darwin Went Wrong.
Hitchman. The Port of Bellingham: 1919-1979.
Hitchman, Janet. Such a Strange Lady.
Hitchman, Michael L. Measurement of Dissolved Oxygen.
Hitler, Adolf. Hitler's Secret Book.
Hitler, Adolph. My New Order. De Roussy De Sales, Raoul, ed.
Hittinger, F. Russell, ed. Linking the Human Life Issues.
Hittleman, Daniel. Developmental Reading.
--Developmental Reading, K-8: Teaching from a Psycholinguistic Perspective.
Hittleman, Richard. Yoga Way to Figure & Facial Beauty.
Hittman Associates, Inc. General Environmental Guidelines for Evaluating & Reporting the Effects of Nuclear Power Plant Site Preparation, Plant & Transmission Facilities Construction (AIF-NESP-003)
Hiu Lie. Die Mandschu-Sprachkunde in Korea.
Hix, Charles. Man Alive! Dressing the Free Way. 1986.
--Working Out: The Total Shape-Up Guide for Men.
Hix, Jill, ed. see Copeland, Tom & Roach, Megan.
Hix, Jill, ed. see Toys 'n Things Press Staff.
Hix, John. The Glass House.
Hixson. Place Names of the White Mountains.
Hiza, M. J., et al. Equilibrium Properties of Fluid Mixtures, Vol. 1: A Bibliography of Data on Fluids of Cryogenic Interest.
Hjelm, Ingalill H., tr. see Aulen, Gustaf.
Hjelm, Ingalill H., tr. see Lohmann, Hartwig.
Hjelmfelt, David C. Antitrust & Regulated Industries.
Hjertstrand, A., ed. see International Astronautical Congress, 11th, Stockholm, 1960.
Hjertstrand, A. see International Astronautical Congress, 11th, Stockholm, 1960.
Hjorth, Peder, et al, eds. Hydraulic Problems Solved by Stochastic Methods.
Hjortsberg, William. Falling Angel.
Hla, Khin S., ed. The Official Directory of Industrial & Commercial Traffic Executives, 1986.
Hladik, J., ed. Physics of Electrolytes. Incl. Vol. 1. Transport Processes in Solid Electrolytes; Vol. 2. Thermodynamics & Electrode Processes in Solid State Electronics. Acad Pr.
Hlasko, Marek. The Graveyard. Guterman, Norbert, tr. from Pol.
Hlongwane, Themba. The Light of Dark.
Hnatek, Eugene R. A User's Handbook of D-A & A-D Converters.
--A User's Handbook of Semiconductor Memories.
Ho, B. T., et al, eds. Drug Discrimination & State Dependent Learning.
Ho, C. Y., jt. auth. see Touloukian, Y. S.
Ho, Eugene H., jt. auth. see Kong, Bucksam.
Ho, H. C. Y. The Fiscal System of Hong Kong.
Ho, Lucy C., ed. Exhibition Catalogue Manual in Use in the Library of the Metropolitan Museum of Art.
Ho, Sam P. S. Small-Scale Enterprises in Korea & Taiwan.
Hoachlander, Marjorie. Profile of a Museum Registrar.
Hoag, A. Eugene. The Legal Assassination of a Sheriff.
Hoag, Albert L., jt. auth. see McNeese, Donald G.
Hoag, Victor. It's Fun to Teach.
Hoagland, Edward. Cat Man.
--Seven Rivers West.
Hoagland, Jim. South Africa: Civilizations in Conflict.
Hoagland, Mahlon B. Discovery: The Search for the DNA's Secrets.
--The Roots of Life: A Layman's Guide to Genes, Evolution & the Ways of Cells.
--The Roots of Life: A Layman's Guide to Genes, Evolution, & the Ways of Cells.
Hoaglund, Franklin T., jt. auth. see Leach, Robert E.
Hoar, W. S., jt. auth. see Harvey, B. J.
Hoar, W. S. & Randall, D. J., eds. Fish Physiology, Vol. 10: Gills.
Hoard, Laurie, compiled by. Standard Easter Program Book.
Hoare, John, jt. auth. see Anderson, Bruce.
Hoare, Merval. Norfolk Island: An Outline of Its History, 1774-1981.
Hoare, R. J., jt. auth. see Harrison, P. M.
Hoban, Brom. The October Fort.
Hoban, Gary J., jt. auth. see Culver, Carmen M.
Hoban, Russell. Charlie Meadows.
--Jim Frog.
--Lavinia Bat.
--The Little Brute Family.
--Little Brute Family.
--Mouse & His Child.
--A Near Thing for Captain Najork.
--Pilgermann.
--The Twenty-Elephant Restaurant.
Hobart, Donald J. A Practical Dissector & Textbook of Human Anatomy: Emphasizing the Musculoskeletal System.
Hobart, Lois. Mexican Mural: The Story of Mexico, Past & Present.
Hobbes, Thomas. De Cive or the Citizen. Lamprecht, Sterling P., ed.
--Dialogue Between a Philosopher & a Student of the Common Laws of England. Cropsey, Joseph, ed.
--Opera Philosophica Quae Latine Scripsit Omnia. Molesworth, W., ed.
Hobbie, F. Wellford. Easter.
Hobbie, Francis W., jt. auth. see Keck, Leander E.
Hobbie, J. E., ed. Limnology of Tundra Ponds: Barrow, Alaska.
Hobbie, Russell K. Intermediate Physics for Medicine & Biology.
Hobbs, B. E., et al. An Outline of Structural Geology.
Hobbs, Cecil. Southeast Asia Field Trip for the Library of Congress, Nineteen Seventy to Nineteen Seventy-One.
Hobbs, Edward C., ed. Stubborn Faith: Papers on Old Testament & Related Subjects Presented to Honor William Andrew Irwin.
Hobbs, F. D. Traffic Planning & Engineering.
Hobbs, Frederic, jt. ed. see Hinckle, Warren, 3rd.
Hobbs, Graham, tr. see Sollertinsky, Dmitri & Sollertinsky, Ludmilla.
Hobbs, Harry J. Veneer Craft for Everyone.
--Veneering Simplified.
Hobbs, Jack A. Art in Context.
--Art in Context.
Hobbs, Marivin. Modern Communications Switching Systems.
Hobbs, Robert. Teach Yourself Transatlantic.
Hobbs, Walter C., ed. Understanding Academic Law.
Hobday, Geoffrey. In Harm's Way: A RNVR Officer at War, 1940-44.
Hobe, Laura, jt. auth. see Rosner, Stanley.
Hobe, Phyllis. With His Hand in Yours.
Hobhouse, Hermione, jt. auth. see Gloucester, Richard.
Hobhouse, Leonard T. The Metaphysical Theory of the State: A Criticism.
Hobhouse, Penelope, ed. see Jekyll, Gertrude.
Hobi, V., jt. auth. see Ladewig, D.
Hobohm, Freya. Bedeutung Franzoesischer Dichter in Werk und Weltbild Stefan Georges.
Hobsbawm, Eric. The Italian Road to Socialism: An Interview with Giorgio Napolitano of the Italian Communist Party. Cammett, John & DeGrazia, Victoria, trs.
Hobsbawm, Eric J. The Age of Capital.
Hobson, Alan. Symbols of Transformation in Poetry.
Hobson, Anthony. The Art & Life of J. W. Waterhouse RA 1849-1917.
Hobson, Asher. International Institute of Agriculture.
Hobson, C. K. Export of Capital.
Hobson, G. D., ed. Advances in Organic Geochemistry, 1964-1966: Proceedings.
Hobson, G. S. Charge Transfer Devices.
Hobson, James R., jt. auth. see Glazier, Kenneth M.
Hobson, John A. Towards International Government.
Hobson, Laura Z. Gentleman's Agreement.
--Laura Z: A Life.
Hobson, R. L. & Hetherington, A. L. The Art of the Chinese Potter.
Hobson, Richmond P., Jr. Grass Beyond the Mountains.
Hoby, Thomas, tr. see Castiglione, Baldassare.
Hocart, A. M. Kings & Councillors: An Essay in the Comparative Anatomy of Human Society. Needham, Rodney, ed.
Hoch, Edward D. The Monkey's Clue & The Stolen Sapphire. Duenewald, Doris, ed.
Hoch, Edward D., ed. see Mystery Writers of America Members.
Hoch, Paul. Differential Diagnosis in Clinical Psychiatry.
Hochberg, Gary M. Kant: Moral Legislation & Two Senses of "Will"
Hochhuth, Rolf. The Deputy. Winston, Richard & Winston, Clara, trs. from Ger.
--Tell Thirty-Eight.
Ho Chi-Fang. Paths in Dreams: Selected Prose of Ho Chi-Fang. McDougall, Bonnie, tr. from Chinese.
Hochman, S. Readings in Psychology.
Hochman, Sandra. Endangered Species.
Hochman, Stanley. Yesterday & Today: A Dictionary of Recent American History.
Hochman, Stanley, jt. auth. see DeVries, Louis.
Hochman, Stanley, tr. see Bazin, Andre.
Hochman, Stanley, tr. see Signoret, Simone.
Hochreiter, L. E. & Sozzi, G. L., eds. Experimental & Analytical Modeling of LWR Safety Experiments.
Hochstedler, Ellen & Academy of Criminal Justice Sciences Staff. Corporations As Criminals.
Hochstein, Rolaine. Stepping Out: A Love Story.
Hochwalder, Fritz. The Public Prosecutor & Other Plays.
Hock, Alfred. Reason & Genius.
--Reason & Genius: Studies in Their Origin.
Hock, Ronald F. The Social Context of Paul's Ministry: Tentmaking & Apostleship.
Hock, W. & Schittkowski, K. Test Examples for Nonlinear Programming Codes.
Hockerman, Dennis. Springtime in Fraggle Rock.
Hockett, Charles F. Course in Modern Linguistics.
--Progressive Exercises in Chinese Pronunciation.
Hockett, Shirley. Basic Mathematics: What Every College Student Should Know.
Hockett, Shirley O. Barron's How to Prepare for the Advanced Placement Examination-Mathematics.
Hockey, Lisbeth, ed. Primary Care Nursing.
Hockey, Robert V. Physical Fitness: The Pathway to Healthful Living.
Hocking, Barbara, ed. International Law & Aboriginal Rights.
Hocksema, Thomas, tr. Mexican Women Poets: An Anthology of Poetry.
Hocutt, Charles H., et al. Power Plants: Effects on Fish & Shellfish Behavior.
Hodder, B. W. Economic Development in the Tropics.
Hodder, Ian, ed. The Spatial Organisation of Culture.
Hodder, W. R. & Molesworth, S. L. Projects for Design & Technology in Wood, Metal & Plastics.
Hodeir, Andre. Jazz: Its Evolution & Essence. Noakes, David, tr. from Fr.
--The Worlds of Jazz. Burch, Noel, tr. from Fr.
Hodek, Bretislav, jt. auth. see Hais, Karel.
Hodes, W. William. Legal Research: A Self-Teaching Guide to the Law Library.
Hodgart, Matthew. James Joyce: A Student's Guide.
Hodge, A. A. Evangelical Theology.
Hodge, Charles B., Jr. Getting Involved with Jesus.
Hodge, Ian & Whitby, Martin. Rural Employment: Trends, Options, Choices.
--Rural Employment: Trends, Options, Choices.
Hodge, Ken, et al. Power Hockey.
Hodge, Paul W. Concepts of Contemporary Astronomy.
Hodge, Philip G. Plastic Analysis of Structures.
Hodgell, P. C. God Stalk.
Hodgen, Margaret T. Early Anthropology in the Sixteenth & Seventeenth Centuries.
Hodges, Andrew. Alan Turing: The Enigma.
Hodges, C. Walter. Globe Restored: A Study of the Elizabethan Theatre.
Hodges, C. Walter, et al, eds. see Reconstruction of the Globe Playhouse Symposium Staff.
Hodges, Cyril W. The Globe Restored: A Study of the Elizabethan Theatre.
Hodges, Elizabeth J. Song for Gilgamesh.
Hodges, John C. & Whitten, Mary E. Harbrace College Handbook.
--Harbrace College Handbook.
--Harbrace College Handbook: 1984.
Hodges, Mrs. John C., jt. auth. see Graham, Sheila Y.
Hodges, Laurent. Environmental Pollution.
Hodges, Lewis H. Master Craftsman's Illustrated Woodworking Manual with Projects.
--The Woodturning Handbook: With Projects.
Hodges, Peter French- see Althaus, Catherine & French-Hodges, Peter F.
Hodges, R. D. The Histology of the Fowl.
Hodges, R. E. & Rudorf, E. Hugh. Language & Learning to Read: What Teachers Should Know About Language.
Hodges, Raymond W., et al. Basic Studies Reading & Word Skills.
Hodges, Robert E. Nutrition in Medical Practice.
Hodges, Walter C. The Battlement Garden.
Hodgeson, Pat. Growing up with the North American Indians.
Hodgetts, D. Combustion Processes in the Spark Ignition Engine.
Hodgetts, Richard M. Management.
--Management Fundamentals.
--Management: Theory, Process & Practice.
--Modern Human Relations at Work.
Hodgetts, Richard M., jt. auth. see Altman, Steven.
Hodgins. Invention of the World.
Hodgins, Eric. Episode: Report on the Accident Inside My Skull.
Hodgkin, John E., et al, eds. Pulmonary Rehabilitation: Guidelines to Success.
Hodgman, Ann. Attack of the Mutants: A Thundercats Adventure.
Hodgskin, Thomas. Natural & Artificial Right of Property Contrasted.
Hodgson, Adam. Remarks During a Journey Through North America in the Years 1819, 1920 & 1921.
Hodgson, Godfrey. America in Our Time: From World War II to Nixon--What Happened & Why.
Hodgson, John & Richards, Ernest. Improvisation.
Hodgson, Jonathan. Computer Operator Tests.
--Computer Programming Tests.
Hodgson, Julian. Music Titles in Translation: A Checklist of Musical Compositions.
Hodgson, Kenneth W. Deaf & Their Problems.
Hodgson, Moira. The New York Times Gourmet Shopper: A Guide to the Best Foods.
Hodgson, P. E. Growth Points in Nuclear Physics.
--Growth Points in Nuclear Physics.
--Growth Points in Nuclear Physics.
Hodgson, Pat. Home Life.
Hodgson, Peter C. Jesus: Word & Presence.
--New Birth of Freedom: A Theology of Bondage & Liberation.
Hodgson, Peter C., ed. see Strauss, David F.
Hodkinson, I. D. & Hughes, M. K. Insect Herbivory.
Hodkinson, Keith. Muslim Family Law: A Sourcebook.
Hodkinson, M. A. Nursing the Elderly.
Hodlin, Sue, jt. auth. see Jupp, T. C.
Hodnett, Edward, ed. Poems to Read Aloud.
Hodson, H. V., ed. Annual Register, 1981.
Hodson, Henry V., ed. International Foundation Directory.
Hodson, J. H. The Administration of Archives.
Hodupp, Shelley, compiled by. Second Shopper's Guide to Museum Stores.
Hoe, R., & Co. Catalogue of Printing Presses & Printers' Materials, Lithographic Presses, Stereotyping & Electrotyping Machinery, Binders' Presses & Materials. Bidwell, John, ed.
Hoeber, Amoretta M. see Douglass, Joseph D., Jr.
Hoeber, Francis P. How Little Is Enough? Salt & Security in the Long Run.
Hoeber, Francis P., et al. Arms, Men, & Military Budgets: Issues for Fiscal Year 1981.
Hoefer, Hans J., ed. Insight Guides: Pacific Northwest.
Hoefer, J. C., ed. Nouvelle Biographie Generale.
Hoegh-Krohn, R. J., jt. auth. see Albeverio, S. A.
Hoehler, G., ed. see International Summer Institute in Theoretical Physics Staff.
Hoehler, Richard S. Categories of a Racial Mind.
Hoehlman, Conrad H. How Jesus Became God.
Hoehn. The Plain Truth about Seventh Day Adventists.
Hoehn, Matthew, ed. Catholic Authors: Contemporary Biographical Sketches, 1930-1947.
Hoehner, Harold W. Herod Antipas: A Contemporary of Jesus Christ.
Hoek, E. & Imperial College of Science & Technology, Rock Mechanics Section. KWIC Index of Rock Mechanics Literature: Pt. 1, 1870-1968.
Hoek, Kees Van see Van Hoek, Kees.
Hoekelman, Robert A. Principles of Pediatrics Patient Management Cases Pre-Test Self-Assessment.
Hoekelman, Robert A., jt. auth. see Friedman, Stanford.
Hoel. Contemporary Issues & Practices in Marketing.

Authors

Hoel, Paul, et al. Introduction to Stochastic Processes.
Hoel, Paul G. & Jessen, Raymond J. Basic Statistics for Business & Economics.
Hoeldtke, Clyde, jt. auth. see Richards, Lawrence O.
Hoeller, P., ed. New Procedures in Nondestructive Testing: Proceedings, Saarbruecken, FRG, 1982.
Hoellering, Michael F., et al, eds. Arbitration & the Law, 1984.
Hoelscher, Russ von see Von Hoelscher, Russ & Sterne, George.
Hoelzl, J., et al. Solid Surface Physics.
Hoenig, Alan. Guide to PC & MS DOS.
Hoenig, J., tr. see Jaspers, Karl.
Hoenig, Stuart A. How to Build & Use Electronic Devices Without Frustration, Panic, Mountains of Money, or an Engineering Degree.
Hoenigswald, Henry M. Language Change & Linguistic Reconstruction.
Hoerder, Dirk. Crowd Action in Revolutionary Massachusetts, 1765-1780.
Hoerder, Dirk, ed. Plutocrats & Socialists: Reports by German Diplomats & Agents on the American Labor Movement, 1878 to 1917.
--Protest, Direct Action, Repression. Dissent in American Society from Colonial Times to the Present.
Hoerner, Thomas & Bettis, Mervin. Power Tool Safety & Operation.
Hoest, William. Taste of Carrot.
Hoetzsch, Otto. Evolution of Russia.
Hoeven, Johan Van Der see Hart, Hendrik & Van Der Hoeven, Johan.
Hoexter, Joan C. & Hayes, Janice E. Curriculum in Graduate Education in Nursing: Part II - Components in the Curriculum Development Process.
Hoey, Carole C., tr. see Modersohn-Becker, Paula.
Hoferichter, J., ed. see International Congress of Hedrologicum Conlegium, 3rd, Erlangen-Nuremberg Germany, 1968.
Hoff, Benjamin. The Singing Creek Where the Willows Grow: The Rediscovered Diary of Opal Whiteley.
Hoff, Benjamin, ed. The Singing Creek Where the Willows Grow: The Rediscovered Diary of Opal Whiteley.
Hoff, Julian T., jt. auth. see Wilson, Charles B.
Hoff, N. J., ed. see International Union of Theoretical & Applied Mechanics Staff.
Hoff, Syd. Soft Skull Sam.
--Soft Skull Sam.
Hoffenberg, Jack. Anvil of Passion.
--The Desperate Adversaries.
--Forge of Fury.
--A Raging Talent.
--Reap in Tears.
--Thunder at Dawn.
--A Time for Pagans.
Hoffer, Abram & Osmond, Humphry. How to Live with Schizophrenia.
Hoffer, Alice. Gretchen's World.
Hoffer, Charles R. The Understanding of Music.
Hoffer, Jeffrey A., jt. auth. see Clark, Jon.
Hoffer, Marjorie L. Hoofbeats to Harness: Adventures of Jesse Beery, Horse Trainer.
Hoffer, P. B., et al. Semiconductor Detectors in the Future of Nuclear Medicine.
Hoffman, Allen. Kagan's Superfecta & Other Stories.
Hoffman, Banesh. The Strange Story of the Quantum.
Hoffman, Bengt R. Luther & the Mystics: A Re-Examination of Luther's Spiritual Experience & His Relationship to the Mystics.
Hoffman, Betsy. Haunted Places.
Hoffman, Bob. No One Is to Blame: Getting a Loving Divorce from Mom & Dad.
Hoffman, Carolyn. Fifty Hikes in Eastern Pennsylvania: Day Hikes & Backpacks from the Susquehanna to the Poconos.
Hoffman, Daniel. Form & Fable in American Fiction.
--Poe Poe Poe Poe Poe Poe Poe.
Hoffman, Dezo. Beatles Conquer America.
Hoffman, Dietrich, jt. ed. see Wynder, Ernest L.
Hoffman, Donald B., jt. auth. see Warren, Kenneth S.
Hoffman, Donald B., Jr. & Warren, Kenneth S., eds. Schistosomiasis IV: Condensations of the Selected Literature 1963-1975.
Hoffman, Douglas, ed. see Total Environmental Action, Inc. Staff.
Hoffman, Douglas R., ed. see Adams, Jennifer A.
Hoffman, E. & Pfeil, E., eds. Protein: Structure, Function & Industrial Applications.
Hoffman, Edward. The Way of Splendor: Jewish Mysticism & Modern Psychology.
Hoffman, Edward, jt. auth. see Schachter, Zalman M.
Hoffman, Edward G. Practical Problems in Mathematics for Machinists.
Hoffman, Eleanor. The Charmstone.
Hoffman, F. G., jt. ed. see Root, W. S.
Hoffman, Felix. The Wolf & the Seven Little Kids.
Hoffman, Frederick J. William Faulkner.
--William Faulkner.
Hoffman, Frederick J. & Vickery, Olga W. William Faulkner: Three Decades of Criticism.
Hoffman, Gar, jt. auth. see Hoffman, Mable.
Hoffman, Horace Addison. Everyday Greek: Greek Words in English, Including Scientific Terms.
Hoffman, Jeanne, jt. auth. see Prizzi, Elaine.
Hoffman, John. Concrete Mama: Prison Profiles from Walla Walla.
Hoffman, John P. Introduction to Electronics for Technologists.
Hoffman, K., ed. Microelectronics, International Competiton & Development Strategies: The Unavoidable Issues.
Hoffman, K. O., jt. ed. see National Machine Tool Builders Association Staff.
Hoffman, Kenneth. Analysis in Euclidian Space.
Hoffman, Mable & Hoffman, Gar. Make-Ahead Entertaining.
Hoffman, Martin. Hoffman on Pairs Play.
Hoffman, Mary. Animals in the Wild: Elephant.
--Animals in the Wild: Monkey.
--Animals in the Wild: Tiger.
Hoffman, Michael L., tr. see Guindey, Guillaume.
Hoffman, Michael W., et al, eds. Corporate Governance & Institutional Ethics.
Hoffman, Naphtali & Brobreck, Stephen. The Bank Book: How to Get the Most for Your Banking Dollars. Gillis, Jack, ed.
Hoffman, Oswald. The Lord's Prayer.
Hoffman, Paul. Macintosh Paperwork: Integrating Microsoft Products.
--Microsoft Word Made Easy.
--Microsoft Word Made Easy: Macintosh Edition.
--The MSX Book.
Hoffman, Paul & Freedman, Matt. Dictionary, Schmictionary.
Hoffman, Peggy & Biro, Gyuri. The Money Hat & Other Hungarian Folk Tales.
Hoffman, R. A., et al. Analysis of NMR Spectra.
Hoffman, Richard L. & Myers, L. M. Companion to the Roots of Modern English.
Hoffman, Stanley, ed. Contemporary Theory in International Relations.
Hoffman, Stephen A. Under the Ether Dome: One Doctor's Apprenticeship at Massachusetts General Hospital.
Hoffman, Tony. How to Negotiate Successfully in Real Estate.
Hoffman, W. Michael, ed. Proceedings of the Second National Conference on Business Ethics.
Hoffman, Walter J. The Menomini Indians.
Hoffman, Wayne. Letters to the Modern Church.
Hoffman, William. Queen Juliana: The Story of the Richest Woman in the World. Hill, Carol, ed.
Hoffman, William H. Economic Recovery Tax Act of Nineteen Eighty-One: Supplement to Accompany the 1982 Annual Edition of West's Federal Taxation.
Hoffman, William H., Jr. West Federal Taxation: Comprehensive Volume, 1988.
Hoffman, William M., ed. New American Plays. Incl. Slaughterhouse Play. Yankowitz, Susan; At War with the Mongols. Heide, Robert; Captain Jack's Revenge. Smith, Michael; African Medea. Magnuson, Jim; Icarus. Rubenstein, Ken; Moby Tick. Peluso, Emanuel. Hill & Wang.
Hoffmann, Ann. Lives of the Tudor Age, 1485 to 1603.
Hoffmann, David. The First Mishna & the Controversies of the Tannaim. Forchheimer, Paul, tr. from German. Incl. The Highest Court in the City of Sanctuary. Hermon.
Hoffmann, Dezo. The Faces of John Lennon.
Hoffmann, Donald. The Architecture of John Wellborn Root.
Hoffmann, E. Dictionary for the Glass Industry: Fachwoerterbuch fuer die Glasindustrie.
Hoffmann, E. T. The Devil's Elixirs. Taylor, Ronald, tr. from Ger.
--Selected Writings of E.T.A. Hoffmann. Knight, Elizabeth C. & Kent, Leonard J., eds.
Hoffmann, Felix, ed. see Grimm, Jacob & Grimm, Wilhelm K.
Hoffmann, Felix, ed. & illus. see Grimm, Jacob & Grimm, Wilhelm K.
Hoffmann, Gretl. Doors: Excellence in International Design.
Hoffmann, Hans-Christoph. Die Theaterbauten von Fellner und Helmer.
Hoffmann, Heinrich. Adolf Hitler: Faces of a Dictator.
--Struwwelpeter.
Hoffmann, Irene B. The Book of Herb Cookery.
Hoffmann, Johanes. Fachworterbuch Verpackung.
Hoffmann, K. H., jt. auth. see Berglund, J. F.
Hoffmann, Leon F. Essays on Haitian Literature.
Hoffmann, Peggy. My Dear Cousin.
Hoffmann, R., jt. auth. see Woodward, R. B.
Hoffmann, Robert G. Establishing Quality Control & Normal Ranges in the Clinical Laboratory.
--New Clinical Laboratory Standardization Methods.
Hoffmann, Stanley. Primacy or World Order: American Foreign Policy Since the Cold War.
--Primacy or World Order: American Foreign Policy Since the Cold War.
Hoffmann-Ostenhof, O., et al, eds. Affinity Chromatography: Proceedings of an International Symposium Held in Vienna, 1977.
Hoffmeister, F., ed. see Bayer Symposium, 4th.
Hoffmeister, Karel. Antonin Dvorak. Newmarch, Rosa, tr.
Hofheins, Roger, jt. auth. see Tooker, Dan.
Hofheins, Roger, jt. ed. see Tooker, Dan.
Hofinger, Johannes. Art of Teaching Christian Doctrine.
Hofler, Karl A., ed. Geschichtschreiber der Husitischen Bewegung in Bohmen.
Hofler, Robert, jt. auth. see Hiller, Cathy.
Hofler, Robert, jt. auth. see Zarco, Cyn.
Hofmann. History of Mathematics.
Hofmann, J. C. Von see Von Hofmann, J. C.
Hofmann, K. H. Lectures on Rings & Modules Vol. 1: Tulane University Ring & Operator Theory Year, 1970-71, Vol. 1.
Hofmann, K. H. & Mostert, P. S. Cohomology Theories for Compact Abelian Groups.
Hofmann, K. H., ed. Lectures on Operator Algebras: Tulane University Ring & Operator Theory Year, 1970-71.
Hofmann, W. Lead & Lead Alloys: Properties & Technology. Lead Development Association, tr.
Hofmeister, Friedrich, jt. auth. see Whistling, Carl F.
Hofmeister, Richard & Prince, David. Security Dictionary.
Hofmekler, Ori. Hofmekler's People.
Hofner, Naftali. Our Life's Aim.
Hofschneider, P. H. & Goebel, W., eds. Gene Cloning in Organisms Other Than E. Coli.
Hofschneider, P. H. & Starlinger, P., eds. Integration & Excision of DNA Molecules.
Hofsoos, Emil. What Management Should Know about Industrial Advertising.
Hogaboom, George B., jt. auth. see Blum, William.
Hogan, Ben. Five Lessons: The Modern Fundamentals of Golf.
Hogan, David, ed. see White, Jack.
Hogan, David J. Who's Who of Horrors.
Hogan, Desmond. A Curious Street.
--Diamonds at the Bottom of the Sea & Other Stories.
Hogan, Edward. Tight Case.
Hogan, Griff, ed. The Church & Disabled Persons.
Hogan, Jim. Remove Your Shoes.
Hogan, Maria, tr. see Constandinidou, Loula D.
Hogan, Michael J., et al. Histology of the Human Eye.
Hogan, Ray. The Doomsday Canyon.
--The Doomsday Trail.
--The Iron Jehu.
--Outlaw's Empire.
--The Raptors.
--The Rawhiders.
--Solitude's Lawman.
Hogan, Robert. Since O'Casey: And Other Essays on Irish Drama.
Hogan, Robert J. Scourge of the Steel Mask: G-8 & His Battle Aces.
Hogan, Ronald F. The God of Glory.
Hogan, Thom. CP-M User's Guide.
--Discover FORTH: Learning & Programming the FORTH Language.
Hogan, Thomas H., jt. auth. see Fenichel, Carol H.
Hogan, William. The Quartzsite Trip.
--The Year of the Mongoose.
Hogan, William T. Steel in the United States: Restructuring to Compete.
--World Steel in the 1980's: A Case for Survival.
Hogancamp, Ilene. Our African Safari.
Hogarth, Robin M. Judgement & Choice: The Psychology of Decision.
Hogben, Carol. British Art & Design, Nineteen Hundred-Nineteen Sixty.
Hogben, Lancelot. Science for the Citizen.
--Statistical Theory.
Hoge, Dean R. Division in the Protestant House: The Basic Reasons Behind Intra-Church Conflicts.
Hogencamp, Jane E. & Evans, Patricia R. Physical Therapy Licensure Examination Review.
Hogendorn, J. S., jt. ed. see Gemery, H. A.
Hogfoss, Bob, jt. auth. see Zucker, Jeff.
Hogg, Ian & Weeks, John. Military Small Arms of the Twentieth Century.
Hogg, Ian V. Revolvers.
Hogg, Ian V., ed. Jane's Infantry Weapons 1986-87.
--Jane's Military Review.
Hogg, Ivan. Guns & How They Work.
Hogg, James. Private Memoirs & Confessions of a Justified Sinner.
Hogg, James, ed. Staff Training in Mental Handicap.
Hoggart, K., jt. auth. see Buller, H.
Hoggart, Keith & Buller, Henry. Rural Development: A Geographical Perspective.
Hoggart, Keith & Kofman, Eleonore, eds. Politics, Geography & Social Stratification.
Hoggart, Richard & Morgan, Janet, eds. The Future of Broadcasting.
Ho-gia-Huong, D., et al. Deutsch-Vietnamesisches Woerterbuch.
Hogwood, Christopher. Handel.
Hohenberg, John. Parisian Girl.
Hohenstein, Charles L., Jr., jt. auth. see Banks, Jerry.
Hohenstein, Herbert E. Upper Room to Garden Tomb: Messages for Lent & Easter on the Passion Narrative in Mark.
Hohler, G., ed. Solid-State Physics.
Hohlwein, Kathryn J., jt. auth. see Lamb, Patricia F.
Hohman, Elmo P. The American Whaleman: Life & Labor in the Whaling Industry.
Hohmann, D., jt. ed. see Schaldach, M.
Hohn, Franz E. Elementary Matrix Algebra.
Hohn, Franz E., jt. auth. see Dornhoff, Larry L.
Hoiberg, Anne, ed. Women & the World of Work.
Hoigjelle, E. Did Dorit Die in Vain?
Hoijer, Harry, et al. Linguistic Structures of Native America. Osgood, Cornelius, ed.
Hoiriis-Nielson, J., jt. ed. see Kastrup, K. W.
Hoitash, Charles. Achieving Success in Manufacturing Management.
Hokanson, Jack E. Introduction to the Therapeutic Process.
Hoke, Helen, ed. Demons Within: And Other Disturbing Tales.
--Jokes, Jokes, Jokes.
Hokelman, Robert A., jt. auth. see Smith, David H.
Hok-Lam Chan. Li Chih: His Life Works.
Holabird, Katharine. Angelina's Birthday & Address Book.
Holabird, Katherine. The Little Mouse One Two Three.
Holabird, Katherine & Craig, Linda. The Little Mouse ABC.
Holaday, Alan, ed. see Chapman, George.
Holaday, Allan. The Plays of George Chapman: The Comedies.
Holahan, C. J. Environment & Behavior.
Holahan, John & Scanlon, William. Price Controls, Physician Fees, & Physician Incomes from Medicare & Medicaid.
Holahan, John, et al. Altering Medicaid Provider Reimbursement Methods.
Holahan, William L., jt. auth. see Call, Steven T.
Holand, H. R. Norse Discoveries & Explorations in America: 982-1362.
Holberg, Ludvig. The Journey of Niels Klim to the World Underground.
Holborow. Standardization in Immunofluorescence.
Holbrook, David, ed. The Case Against Pornography.
Holbrook, J. G. Laplace Transforms for Electronic Engineers.
Holbrook, Sabra. Canada's Kids.
--The French Founders of North America & Their Heritage.
--Growing up in France.
--Lafayette: Man in the Middle.
Holbrook, Stephen F. Rapid Reading: A Home Study Course.
Holbrook, Stewart. America's Ethan Allen.
Holbrook, Stewart H. The Age of the Moguls.
Holbrook, Wallace W. Contemporary Lamps.
Holburt, Idell. How to Improve Your Reading Comprehension Skills.
--Lovejoy's Preparation for the GED.
Holcomb, Brent. Probate Records of S. C. An Index to Inventories, 1746-1785.
--Probate Records of S. C. Journal of the Court of Ordinary, 1764-1771.
Holcomb, Brent & Parker, Elmer O. Chester County, South Carolina Minutes of the County Court, Seventeen Eighty-Five to Seventeen Ninety-Nine.
Holcombe, Arthur N., jt. auth. see Organization of Peace Commission.
Holcombe, Marya & Stein, Judith. Writing for Decision Makers.
Holcroft, Thomas. Memoirs of Bryan Perdue. Paulson, Ronald, ed.
--The Plays of Thomas Holcroft. Rosenblum, Joseph, ed.
Holde, Arthur. Jews in Music.
Holden, A. N. Dispersion Fuel Elements.
Holden, Anna. The Bus Stops Here: A Study of School Desegregation in Three Cities.
Holden, Anne. In Love & Anger.
Holden, Anthony. Of Presidents, Prime Ministers & Princes: A Decade in Fleet Street.
--Prince Charles.
--Prince Charles: A Biography.
Holden, David & Johns, Richard. The House of Saud: The Rise & Rule of the Most Powerful Dynasty in the Arab World.
Holden, Edith & Harding, Alison. Country Diary Cookery Notes.
Holden, Harriet W. Before Nightfall.
Holden, Matthew, Jr. Cabinet Departments with Domestic Reponsibilities: A Working Note & Bibliography, 1933-1981.
--The Centrality of Administration to Politics.

Holden, Robert B. Ceramic Fuel Elements.
Holder, Maryse. Give Sorrow Words: Maryse Holder's Letters from Mexico.
Holder, Preston, ed. see Boas, Franz.
Holder, Steven L. & Sherman, Chris. A Problem Solving Approach for Business.
Holder, Thomas M. & Ashcraft, Keith W. Pediatric Surgery.
Holder, William G. & Siuru, William D., Jr. General Dynamics F-16.
Holder-Bryant, Lenora Foreword by see Shepherd-Moore, Marie.
Holderness, Graham. Who's Who in D. H. Lawrence.
Holdgate, M. W. & Woodman, M. J., eds. The Breakdown & Restoration of Ecosystems.
Holdgate, Martin W. & White, Gilbert F., eds. Environmental Issues-Scope Report 10.
Holding, D. H. Principles of Training.
Holdridge, L. R., et al. Forest Environments in Tropical Life Zones: A Pilot Study.
Holdstein, Deborah H. On Composition & Computers.
Holdstock, Robert. Mythago Wood.
Hole, F. B. Assembly Principles. Daniel, R. P., ed.
Hole, Frank & Heizer, Robert F. Prehistoric Archaeology: A Brief Introduction.
Hole, John W., Jr. Human Anatomy & Physiology.
Holeman, Jack R. Condominium Management.
Holen, Harold H., jt. auth. see Hoven, Vernon.
Holgate, Jack F., jt. auth. see Broussard, E. Joseph.
Holiday, F. W. Great Orm of Loch Ness.
Holl, Adelaide. Remarkable Egg.
Holl, Karl. The Reconstruction of Morality. Adams, James L. & Bense, Walter F, eds. Meuser, Fred W. & Wietzke, Walter E., trs.
--What Did Luther Understand by Religion? Adams, James L. & Bense, Walter F., eds. Meuser, Fred W. & Wietzke, Walter R., trs. from Ger.
Hollaender, A., et al, eds. Trends in the Biology of Fermentations for Fuels & Chemicals.
Hollaender, Alexander, ed. Genetic Engineering for Nitrogen Fixation.
Hollan, S. R., et al. Genetics, Structure & Function of Blood Cells: Proceedings of the 28th International Congress of Physiological Sciences, Budapest, 1980.
Hollan, S. R., et al, eds. Recent Advances in Haemotology, Immunology & Blood Transfusion.
Holland, C. H. Lower Palaeozoic Rocks of the World: Lower Palaeozoic of the Middle East, Eastern & Southern Africa & Antartica.
Holland, Cecelia. The Belt of Gold.
--Great Maria.
Holland, Celia M. Ellicott City, Maryland: Mill Town, U. S. A.
Holland, Charles D. & Anthony, Raymond G. Fundamentals of Chemical Reaction Engineering.
Holland, David, ed. Encyclopedia Americana.
Holland, David L., tr. see Weiss, Johannes.
Holland, F. A. & Chapman, F. S. Pumping of Liquids.
Holland, Florence. Chronos.
--Summer in Sodom with Kitchen Privileges.
Holland, Gary. Running a Business Meeting.
Holland, Isabelle. Green Andrew Green.
--Journey for Three.
--Perdita.
Holland, J. R. & Mansur, L. K., eds. Phase Stability During Irradiation: Proceedings. TMS-AIME Fall Meeting, Pittsburgh, 1980.
Holland, Jack & Dunford, Martin. The Rough Guide to New York.
Holland, Jack, jt. auth. see Dunford, Martin.
Holland, James F. & Frei, Emil, 3rd, eds. Cancer Medicine.
Holland, John, ed. The Way It Is.
Holland, John M. Basic Robotic Concepts.
Holland, Kevin C. Axe-Age, Wolf-Age: A Selection of Norse Myths.
Holland, L., et al. Vacuum Manual.
Holland, Margaret & Demers, Jan. How Do You Know Who's a Stranger? Book & Cassette.
Holland, Margaret, jt. auth. see McKee, Craig.
Holland, Margaret, jt. auth. see McKee, Craig B.
Holland, Margaret, ed. see Smoke & Isaacsen-Bright.
Holland, Margaret, ed. see Thomas, Sharon K. & Siegal, Marjorie.
Holland, Marjorie & Burk, John. Stone Walls & Sugar Maples: An Ecology for Northeasterners.
Holland, Max. The Militarization of the Middle East.
Holland, Muhtar, tr. Al Ghazali: On the Duties of Brotherhood.
Holland, Norman N. The Dynamics of Literary Response.
--Poems in Persons: An Introduction to the Psychoanalysis of Literature.
Holland, Penny. Looking at BASIC.
--Looking at Computer Graphics.
--Looking at Computer Programming.
--Looking at LOGO.
Holland, Seamas. Rutland Street: The Story of an Educational Experiment for Disadvantaged Children in Dublin.
Holland, Stuart, ed. Out of Crisis: A Project for European Recovery.
Holland, Vicki. We Are Having a Baby.
Holland, Vyvyan. Oscar Wilde & His World.
Hollander, J. H. Studies in State Taxation with Particular Reference to the Southern States.
Hollander, Jacob H. Economic Library of Jacob H. Hollander. Marsh, Elsie A., ed.
Hollander, Joe, tr. see Komarov, Boris.
Hollander, John. Reflections on Espionage.
--Town & Country Matters.
--Untuning of the Sky: Ideas of Music in English Poetry, 1500-1700.
--Visions from the Ramble.
Hollander, L. M. Old Norse Poems.
Hollander, Lee M. The Poetic Edda.
Hollander, Nathan. They've Killed Anna.
Hollander, Neil & Mertes, Harald. Cook Is the Captain.
Hollander, Samuel. Economics of Adam Smith.
Hollander, Zander, ed. see Associated Features Inc. Editors.
Hollenbeck, Beatrice. Esther.
--God's Word & Me.
--God's Word & Me.
Hollender, Louis, et al, eds. Acute Pancreatitis: An Interdisciplinary Synopsis.
Hollenwager, Walter J. The Pentecostals. Wilson, R. A., tr. from Ger.
Hollest, Angela & Gaine, Penelope. Children's Parties.
Holley. Markrich Sportsworld, Inc. An Audit Practice Case.
Holley, William H. & Jennings, Kenneth M. The Labor Relations Process.
Hollick, Ann L. U. S. Foreign Policy & the Law of the Sea.
Holliday, A. K. & Massey, A. G. Inorganic Chemistry in Nonaqueous Solvents.
Holliday, Vance T., ed. Guidebook to the Central Llano Estacado: Friends of the Pleistocene South-Central Cell, 1983 Field Trip.
Hollingdale, R. J. Western Philosophy: An Introduction.
Hollingdale, S. H., ed. Mathematical Aspects of Marine Traffic.
Hollings, Michael & Gullick, Etta. The One Who Listens.
Hollingsworth, A. Thomas & Hand, Herbert H. Guide to Small Business Management.
Hollingsworth, Alan. The Way of the Yacht.
Hollingsworth, Brian. Atlas of the World's Railways.
Hollingsworth, Harold M. & Holmes, William F., eds. Essays on the New Deal.
Hollingsworth, Harold M. & Myres, Sandra L., eds. Essays on the American West.
Hollingsworth, J. R., ed. American Expansion in the Late 19th Century.
Hollingsworth, Jan. Unspeakable Acts: The True Story of One Community's Nightmare.
Hollingsworth, Paul M. & Kelly, Patrick, eds. Basic Reading Instruction.
Hollins, R. J. Production & Planning Applied to Building.
Hollins, Timothy. Beyond Broadcasting: Into the Cable Age.
Hollinshead, Betty, ed. see Society for Academic Gaming & Simulation in Education & Training Staff.
Hollis, D. Animal Identifcation: Insects.
Hollis, John H., ed. Developmental Deficiencies, Vol. 1: A Comparative Approach.
--Developmental Deficiencies, Vol. 2: An Interdisciplinary Approach.
Hollis, Joseph. Status of Guidance & Counseling in the Nation's Schools.
Hollis, Joseph W. & Wantz, Richard. Counselor Preparation Personnel, 1983-85: Programs, Personel, Trends.
Hollis, Nesta. Successful Sewing: A Modern Guide.
Hollis, Shelia S., jt. auth. see Tomain, Joseph P.
Hollister, C. W., ed. see Smith, Lacey B.
Hollister, Leo E. Clinical Pharmacology of Psychotherapeutic Drugs.
Hollister, Robert M., jt. ed. see Clay, Phillip L.
Hollmann, Siegfried. Non-Glycolytic Pathways of Metabolism of Glucose. Touster, Oscar, tr.
Hollo, Anselm, tr. see Arsan, Emmanuelle.
Hollo, Anselm, tr. see De Berg, Jeanne.
Hollo, Anselm, tr. see Genet, Jean.
Hollow, Fern. Busy Times.
--Winter Fun.
Hollow, John. Against the Night, the Stars: The Science Fiction of Arthur C. Clarke.
Hollow, John, ed. The After-Summer Seed.
Holloway, Donald A., jt. auth. see Poe, William D.
Holloway, John. Victorian Sage.
Holloway, Lisabeth M., et al. Medical Obituaries: American Physicans Biographical Notices in Selected Medical Journals before 1907.
Holloway, Milton L., ed. Texas National Energy Modeling Project: An Experience in Large-Scale Model Transfer & Evaluation.
Holloway, Nancy M. Critical-Care: Care Plans.
Holloway, P. J. & Swallow, J. N. Child Dental Health.
Holloway, Richard. Let God Arise.
Holloway, William V. Intergovernmental Relations in the United States.
Hollowell, John. Fact & Fiction: The New Journalism & the Nonfiction Novel.
Hollstein, F. W., ed. Dutch & Flemish Etchings, Engravings & Woodcuts: 1450 to 1700.
--German Engravings, Etchings & Woodcuts: 1400-1700.
Hollwich, F. The Influence of Ocular Light Perception on Metabolism in Man & Animal.
Holly, Douglas M. Seven Eleven.
Holly, J. Hunter, et al. Graduated Robot & Other Stories. Elwood, Roger, ed.
Hollyman, Burnes S. Glauber Rocha & the Cinema Novo in Brazil: A Study of His Films & Critical Writing. Jowett, Garth S., ed.
Hollyn, Lynn. Town & Country Cat.
Hollywood Arts Science & Professions Council. Thought Control in the U. S. A. Kupelnick, Bruce S., ed.
Holm, Anne S. North to Freedom. Kingsland, L. W., tr.
Holm, Bill, annotations by. Soft Gold: The Fur Trade & Cultural Exchange on the Northwest Coast of America.
Holm, Dieter. Energy Conservation in Hot Climates.
Holm, Else, jt. auth. see Holm, Ragnar.
Holm, Leroy, et al. A Geographical Atlas of World Weeds.
Holm, Marilyn F. Tell Me Why: A Guide to Children's Questions about Faith & Life.
Holm, R., jt. auth. see Ohnsorge, J.
Holm, Ragnar & Holm, Else. Electric Contacts: Theory & Application.
Holman, Alan. White River, Brown Water: A Record-Making Kayak Journey Down the Amazon.
Holman, C. Hugh, jt. ed. see Rubin, Louis D., Jr.
Holman, Felice. Professor Diggins' Dragons.
Holman, Glenn P. My Younger Son.
Holman, Mary A., jt. auth. see Watson, Donald S.
Holman, R. J., ed. Progress in Lipid Research: Golden Jubilee International Conference, Minnesota, May 4-7, 1980.
Holman, R. T., ed. Progress in Lipid Research.
--Progress in Lipid Research.
--Progress in Lipid Research.
Holman, Ralph T., ed. New Concepts in Lipid Research in Honor of Stina & Einar Stenhagen.
Holman, Richard, jt. auth. see Anderson, Urton.
Holman, Richard, ed. see Mautz, Robert K., et al.
Holmans, A. E. Housing Policy in Britain.
Holmberg, Bengt. Paul & Power: The Structure of Authority in the Primitive Church Reflected in the Pauline Epistles.
Holmberg, Meg, jt. auth. see Alper, Lynne.
Holmberg, Uno. Finno-Ugric, Siberian Mythology.
Holmberg, Verda. Do Decimals First.
--The Metric System of Measurement.
Holmberg, Verda, et al. Metric Multibase Mathematics.
Holme, Anthea. Housing & Young Families in East London.
Holme, C. Geoffrey, ed. see James, Philip.
Holme, Geoffrey, ed. see Salaman, Malcolm C.
Holme, Thea. Caroline: A Biography of Caroline of Brunswick.
Holmes, et al. Accounting for Control & Decisions.
--Accounting Problem for Manual Solution.
Holmes, Anita. Pierced & Pretty: The Complete Guide to Ear Piercing, Pierced Earrings, & How to Create Your Own.
Holmes, Arthur F. War & Christian Ethics.
Holmes, Arthur W. & Burns, David C. Audit Problem: Crafters, Inc.
--Auditing: Standards & Procedures.
Holmes, Brian, ed. International Handbook of Education Systems: Europe & Canada.
Holmes, Burton. The Olympian Games in Athens: The First Modern Olympics, 1896.
Holmes, Charles S. The Clocks of Columbus: The Literary Career of James Thurber.
Holmes, Deborah A. Survival Prayers for Young Mothers.
Holmes, Edward. An Age of Cameras.
Holmes, Edward M. A Part of the Main.
Holmes, Ernest. The Basic Ideas of Science of Mind.
--Freedom to Live. Kinnear, Willis H., ed.
--Give Us This Day.
--It's Up to You. Kinnear, Willis H., ed.
--Know Yourself! Kinnear, Willis H., ed.
Holmes, Ernest & Barker, Raymond C. Richer Living.
Holmes, Fiona. Tomorrow's World: Medicine.
Holmes, G. K., jt. auth. see Cooke, W. T.
Holmes, Geoffrey. Augustan England.
Holmes, John R. Refuse Recycling & Recovery: A Review of the State of the Art.
Holmes, Jon. Texas: A Self-Portrait.
Holmes, Joseph. Natural Light.
Holmes, King K. & Mardh, Per-Anders. International Perspectives on Neglected Sexually Transmitted Diseases: Impact on Venereology, Infertility, & Maternal & Infant Health.
Holmes, L. P. Hill Smoke.
Holmes, Marjorie. God & Vitamins.
--I've Got to Talk to Somebody, God.
--Three from Galilee.
--Two from Galilee.
Holmes, Max. Writing Your College Application & Essay.
Holmes, Neal J., et al. Gateways to Science, Level 1.
Holmes, Oliver W. The Poetical Works of Oliver Wendell Holmes. Tilton, Eleanor M., intro. by.
--Psychiatric Novels of Oliver Wendell Holmes.
Holmes, Pat. Concepts in Adoption.
Holmes, R. B. A Course on Optimization & Best Approximation.
--Geometric Functional Analysis & Its Applications.
Holmes, R. L. & Fox, C. A. Control of Human Reproduction.
Holmes, Reed M. The Church in Israel.
Holmes, Rolston. The Apostle Paul Speaks to Us Today.
Holmes, Roy. The Characteristics of Mechanical Engineering Systems.
Holmes, S. Market Structure, Conduct, & Foodgrain Pricing Efficiency: An Indian Case Study.
Holmes, S. B. Outline of Plant Classification.
Holmes, Samuel J. Synopsis of California Stalk - Eyed Crustacea.
Holmes, Urban T. & Schutz, Alexander H. A History of the French Language.
Holmes, Urban T., jt. auth. see Fiorenza, Elisabeth S.
Holmes, W. H., jt. auth. see Heinlein, W. E.
Holmes, William C. Antitrust Law Handbook, 1987.
Holmes, William F., jt. ed. see Hollingsworth, Harold M.
Holmgren, Frederick. The God Who Cares: A Christian Looks at Judaism.
Holmquist, Ingrid. From Society to Nature: A Study of Doris Lessing's "Children of Violence"
Holmquist, June D., ed. They Chose Minnesota: A Survey of the State's Ethnic Groups.
Holmstrom, J. E., et al. Trilingual Dictionary for Materials & Structures.
Holmstrom, John. Dan Marino - Joe Montana.
Holmstrom, Lakshmi. The Novels of R. K. Narayan.
Holmyard, E. J. British Scientists.
Holod, Renata & Rastorfer, Darl, eds. Architecture & Community: Building of the Islamic World Today.
Holoien, Renee A., jt. ed. see Patton, Peter C.
Holquist, Michael. Dostoevsky & the Novel: The Wages of Biography.
Holroyd, Michael. The Genius of Shaw.
--Lytton Strachey.
Holroyd, P., jt. auth. see Smith, K. M.
Holroyd, Sam V., jt. auth. see Requa, Barbara.
Holroyd, Sam V., ed. Clinical Pharmacology in Dental Practice.
Holroyd, Stuart. PSI & the Consciousness Explosion.
Holsaert. Dinosaurs.
Holschuh, Albrecht. Leutebuch: Ein Leichtes Lesebuch.
Holst, Imogen. Holst.
Holst, Imogen, jt. auth. see Short, Michael.
Holst, J. J. & Schneider, W., Jr., eds. Why A B M? Policy Issues in the Missile Defense Controversy.
Holst, Lawrence. Hospital Ministry. Marty, Martin E., intro. by.
Holst, Per. Computer Simulation, 1951-1976: An Index to the Literature.
Holst, Spencer. The Language of Cats & Other Stories.
Holstein, Jonathan. American Pieced Quilts.
Holstein, William K. & Seagle, John P. Basic Concepts & Applications.
Holsti, K. J. International Politics: A Framework for Analysis.
Holsti, K. J., et al. Why Nations Realign: Foreign Policy Restructuring in the Post War World.
Holstrum, Gary L. & Collins, William. Operational Audits of Production Control.
Holt, A., ed. Character Recognition.
Holt, Alfred H. American Place-Names.
Holt, Alix, ed. & tr. see Kollontai, Alexandra.
Holt, C. A. & Shore, R. W. Bayesian Analysis in Economic Theory & Time Series Analysis.
Holt Editorial Staff. Holt Intermediate Dictionary of American English.
Holt, Emily S. Ye Olden Time: English Customs in the Middle Ages.
Holt, G. Richard, et al. Decision Making in Otolaryngology: Head & Neck Surgery.
Holt, J. C. Robin Hood.
--Robin Hood.
Holt, J. C., jt. ed. see Gillingham, John.
Holt, M., ed. see Yanenko, N. N.

Holt, Margaret. David McCheever's Twenty-Nine Dogs.
Holt, Mary M. Guide to Apartment House Management.
Holt, Maurice. Curriculum Workshop: An Introduction to Whole Curriculum Planning.
Holt, Pat & Ketterman, Grace. When You Feel Like Screaming: Help for Frustrated Mothers.
Holt, R. F., ed. The Strength of Tradition: Stories of the Immigrant Presence in Australia.
Holt, Robert E. Two Little Devils.
Holt, Robert L. The Complete Book of Bonds: How to Buy & Sell Profitably.
--Publishing: A Complete Guide for Schools, Small Presses, & Entrepreneurs.
Holt, Robert R. Assessing Personality.
Holt, Rochelle L. How to Cope with Depression Psychically.
Holt, Solomon. Dictionary of American History.
Holt, Stephen. Manning Clark & Australian History: 1915-1963.
Holt, Ted & Gilroy, John. A Commentary of Wordsworth's "Prelude"
Holt, Terry. The Universe Next Door: A Complete Guide to Exploring the Skies & Understanding What You See.
Holt, Tonie, ed. see Bairnsfather, Bruce.
Holt, Valmai, ed. see Bairnsfather, Bruce.
Holt, Victoria. The House of a Thousand Lanterns.
--The Indian Fan.
--The Judas Kiss.
--The Pride of the Peacock.
--Road to Paradise Island.
--The Spring of the Tiger.
Holt, Victoria see Carr, Philippa, pseud.
Holt, Virginia. Kermie, Where Are You?
--Nine Little Popples.
--One More Popple.
--Pick a Popple.
Holt, Virginia, tr. see Muir, John.
Holtby, Winifred. Virginia Woolf.
Holter, Doris J. Admission Standards & Admission Processes of Medical Technology Programs.
Holthusen, T. Lance, ed. The Potential of Earth-Shelter & Underground Space: Today's Resource for Tomorrow's Space & Energy Viability: Proceedings of the Underground Space Conference & Exposition, Kansas City, MO, June 8-10, 1981.
Holtje, Bert, jt. auth. see Finkelstein, Abe.
Holton, Gerald. Thematic Origins of Scientific Thought: Kepler to Einstein.
Holton, Gerald, ed. The Twentieth-Century Sciences.
Holton, Gerald & Morison, Robert S., eds. Limits of Scientific Inquiry.
Holton, Pamela & Emmelin, N., eds. Pharmacology of Gastrointestinal Motilation.
Holton, Susan & Jones, David L. Spirit Aflame: Luis Palau's Mission to London.
Holt-Seeland, Inger. Women of Cuba.
Holtz, Frederick. The AT&T 6300: A Comprehensive User's Manual.
--Using & Programming the Macintosh, Including 32 Ready-to-Run Programs.
Holtz, Herman. The Consultant's Edge: Using the Computer As a Marketing Tool.
--How to Buy the Right Personal Computer.
Holtz, Herman R. The One Hundred Billion Dollar Market: How to Do Business with the U. S. Government.
--Profit from Your Money Making Ideas: How to Build a New Business or Expand an Existing One.
--Profit from Your Moneymaking Ideas: How to Build a New Business or Expand an Existing One.
--Profit-Line Management: Managing a Growing Business Successfully.
Holtz, Larry E. Law Enforcement Handbook of Pennsylvania.
Holtz, Matthew. Mastering Microsoft WORD.
--Mastering MS Word.
--Mastering Ventura.
Holtzclaw, William H. Black Man's Burden.
Holtzer, H., jt. ed. see Reinert, J.
Holtzman, Jerome, ed. Fielder's Choice: An Anthology of Baseball Fiction.
Holtzman, Jerry. Fielder's Choice: An Anthology of Baseball Fiction.
Holtzman, Jordan L. Spin Labeling in Pharmacology.
Holtzman, Steven H. & Leich, Christopher M., eds. Wittgenstein: To Follow a Rule.
Holtzschue, Karl B. Real Estate Contracts with 1987 Supplement.
Holub, Allen. A UNIX-Like Shell for MS-DOS.
Holum, J. R. Experiments in General, Organic & Biological Chemistry.
Holum, John R., jt. auth. see Brady, James E.
Holusha, John, jt. auth. see Meyers, Gerald C.
Holway, John. Voices of Great Black Baseball Leagues.
Holz, K. P., jt. ed. see Suendermann, J.
Holz, Loretta. How to Sell Your Arts & Crafts.
Holz, Robert K. The Surveillant Science: Remote Sensing of the Environment.
Holz, Robert K., ed. Surveillant Science: Remote Sensing of the Environment.
Holzel, Tom & Salkeld, Audrey. First on Everest: The Mystery of Mallory & Irvine.
Holzer, Hans. The Entry.
--Houses of Horror.
--Star Ghosts.
--White House Ghosts.
--Yankee Ghosts. Adams, Jennifer, ed.
Holzgang, David A. Understanding PostScript Programming.
Holzhauser, Gillian R. Coping with Being Handicapped.
Holzman, Jan. The Legacy of Chopin.
Holzman, Red & Lewin, Leonard. A View from the Bench.
Holzman, Robert S. Holzman's New Guide to the Accumulated Earnings Tax.
Holzmann, Richard I. Production of the Boranes & Related Research.
Holznecht, Karl J. Outlines of Tudor & Stuart Plays, Fourteen Ninety-Seven to Sixteen Forty-Two.
Hom, Ken & Steiman, Harvey. Chinese Technique: An Illustrated Guide to the Fundamental Techniques of Chinese Cooking.
Hom, Nancy, jt. auth. see Tran-Khanh-Tuyet.
Homan, Beulah. Chadwick the Chipmunk & the Sunflower Seeds.
Homans, George C. English Villagers of the Thirteenth Century.
--Social Behavior: Its Elementary Forms.
Homans, Peter. Jung in Context: Modernity & the Making of a Psychology.
Homans, Peter, ed. Dialogue Between Theology & Psychology.
Ho Man Yee, retold by. More Favourite Chinese Stories.
Homberger, Lorenz, jt. auth. see Fischer, Eberhard.
Homburger, F. & Hayes, J. A., eds. A Guide to General Toxicology.
Homburger, Freddy & Marquis, Judith K., eds. Safety Regulation & Compliance.
Homchaudhuri, S. Shakespeare Criticism: Dryden to Morgann.
Home, Christopher, tr. see Loisy, Alfred.
Home, D. D. Incidents in My Life.
Home, Henry & Kames, Lord. Essays on the Principles of Morality & Natural Religion.
Home Magazine Editors. Kitchens: Creative Ideas for Your Home.
Home Planners Editors. Two Hundred Fifty-Five Home Designs for Family Living.
Home Planners, Inc. Staff. One Hundred Fifty-Two House Plans.
--One Hundred Seventy-Two Most Popular Homes.
--One Hundred Sixty-Six Most Popular Homes.
--One Hundred Twelve Traditional & Contemporary Family Homes.
Home Planners Staff. One Hundred Forty-Four Home Designs for All Americans.
Home, Robert K. Inner City Regeneration.
Homer, F., jt. auth. see Curtiss, Harriette.
Homewood, A. E. The Neurodynamics of Vertebral Subluxation.
Homewood, Harry. Final Harbor.
--Silent Sea.
--Torpedo!
Hommes, E. A. & Van Den Berg, C. J., eds. Normal & Pathological Development of Energy Metabolism.
Hon, David. Trade-Offs: For the Person Who Can't Have Everything.
Honacki, James H. & Kinman, Kenneth E., eds. Mammal Species of the World: A Taxonomic & Geographic Reference.
Honan, Park. Matthew Arnold: A Life.
Hondius, E. Consumer Legislation in the Netherlands.
Hone, Joseph. Africa of the Heart: A Personal Journey.
Hone, Joseph, ed. The Love Story of Thomas Davis.
Hone, William. Ancient Mysteries Described.
--Table Book.
Honea, Charla, compiled by. Family Rituals.
Honegger, Marc, ed. Dictionnaire de la Musique.
Honerkamp, J. & Pohlmeyer, J., eds. Structural Elements in Particle Physics & Statistical Mechanics.
Honey, Martha, jt. auth. see Avirgan, Tony.
Honey, Peter. Solving People-Problems.
Honeyford, R. Starting Teaching.
Hong, Beverly. Situational Chinese.
Hong, Christopher C. To Whom the Land of Palestine Belongs.
Hong, Edna. The Downward Ascent.
--Forgiveness Is a Work As Well As a Grace.
--From This Good Ground.
--The Gaiety of Grace.
--The Gayety of Grace.
--A Nostalgic Almanac.
Hong, Edna, jt. auth. see Hinderlie, Mary.
Hong, Edna, tr. see Kierkegaard, Soren.
Hong, Edna H., tr. see Malantschuk, Gregor.
Hong, H. V., ed. see Kierkegaard, Soren.
Hong, Howard, tr. see Kierkegaard, Soren.
Hong, Howard V., tr. see Malantschuk, Gregor.
Hong, Xiao. Selected Stories of Xiao Hong. Goldbratt, Howard, tr. from Chinese.
Honig, Albert M. China Today: Sin or Virtue?
Honig, Carl R. Modern Cardiovascular Physiology.
Honig, Donald. The National League: An Illustrated History.
Honig, Edwin, tr. see Garcia Lorca, Federico.
Honig, Werner K. & James, Henry, eds. Animal Memory.
Honig, Werner K. & Staddor, J., eds. Handbook of Operant Behavior.
Honigman, John J. Handbook of Social & Cultural Anthropology.
Honigmann, E. A. Shakespeare: Seven Tragedies: the Dramatist's Manipulation of Response.
Honigmann, John J. Culture & Personality.
Honigsbaum, Frank. The Struggle for the Ministry of Health.
Honisch, Dieter. Uecker. Wolf, Robert E., tr.
Honston, Samuel R., et al, eds. Applications in Bayesian Decision Processes.
Honter, John, et al. Food Intolerance: Are the Foods You Eat Making You Sick. Sharkey, Jacqueline, ed.
Honton, Margaret. Take Fire.
Hoobler, Icie G. Boundless Horizons: Portrait of a Pioneer Woman Scientist.
Hoobler, James A., ed. Nashville Memories: Thirty-Two Historic Postcards.
Hood, D., ed. Probes: Processes & Resources of the Bering Sea Shelf.
Hood, Edwin T., et al. Nineteen Eighty-Five Supplement to Closely Held Corporations in Business and Estate Planning: 1985 Supplement.
Hood, H. P. Daring Dairy Recipes.
Hood, J. P., jt. auth. see Dix, M. R.
Hood, Joan. Will It Freeze?
Hood, Mary. How Far She Went.
Hood, Miriam. Gunboat Diplomacy Eighteen Ninety-Five to Nineteen Hundred Five: Great Power Pressure in Venezuela.
Hood, Phil, ed. Artists of American Folk Music: The Legends of Traditional Folk, the Stars of the Sixties, the Virtuosi of New Acoustic Music.
Hood, Roger. Homeless Borstal Boys.
Hood, Roger & Sparks, Richard. Key Issues in Criminology.
Hood, Ronald D. Cacodylic Acid: Agricultural Uses, Biological Effects, & Environmental Fate.
Hood, W. Edmund. Beginner's Guide to Electricity & Electrical Phenomena.
Hood, William. Spy Wednesday: A Novel.
Hoog, ed. see Fromentin, Eugene.
Hoogenboom, Ari & Hoogenboom, Olive. A History of the ICC from Panacea to Palliative.
Hoogenboom, Olive, jt. auth. see Hoogenboom, Ari.
Hoogendoorn, C. J., ed. see Heat & Mass Transfer in Buildings Summer Seminar Staff.
Hook, Carla J., ed. see Global Engineering Documents Staff.
Hook, Diana F. The I Ching & Its Associations.
--I Ching & Mankind.
--The I Ching & You.
Hook, Diane F. The I Ching & You.
Hook, Donald D. Madmen of History.
Hook, Ernest, et al, eds. Monitoring Birth Defects & Environment: The Problem of Surveillance.
Hook, Ernest B., jt. ed. see Porter, Ian H.
Hook, Henry, ed. see Fellows, Len.
Hook, J. N. Spelling 1500: A Program.
Hook, J. Nicholas. A Long Way Together: A Personal View of NCTE's First Sixty-Seven Years.
Hook, Jim, jt. auth. see Trabert, Tony.
Hook, John E. Van see Van Hook, John E.
Hook, Judith. Siena: A City & Its History.
Hook, Peter Edwin. Compound Verb in Hindi.
Hook, Sidney. Education & the Taming of Power.
--The Hero in History: Myth, Power, or Moral Ideal.
--The Paradoxes of Freedom.
Hook, Sidney, ed. John Dewey: Philosopher of Science & Freedom.
Hook, Thom. Shenandoah Saga: A Narrative History of the U. S. Navy's Pioneering Large Rigid Airship. Settle, T. G., ed.
Hooke, Robert. Posthumous Works.
Hooker, Alan. Herb Cookery.
--Vegetarian Gourmet Cookery.
--Vegeterian Gourmet Cookery.
Hooker, J. T. Mycanean Greece.
Hooker, Richard. Two Sermons upon S. Judes Epistle.
Hooker, Ruth & Smith, Carole. The Kidnapping of Anna. Pacini, Kathy, ed.
Hooks, David. The Spoilers.
Hooks, William, jt. auth. see Galinsky, Ellen.
Hooks, William, et al, eds. The Pleasure of Their Company: How to Have More Fun with Your Children.
Hoole, John. The Plays of John Hoole. Siebert, Donald T. & Backscheider, Paula R., eds.
Hoole, John, ed. see Mrazkova, Daniela & Remes, Vladimir.
Hoole, K. A Regional History of the Railways of Great Britain: The North East.
Hooper, A., jt. ed. see Breheny, M.
Hooper, C., jt. auth. see Reader, G. T.
Hooper, H. Paul. Introduction to Financial Accounting.
Hooper, J., jt. ed. see Jalland, P.
Hooper, J. T. & Burland, C. A. Art of Primitive People.
Hooper, Janet see Bruton, Sheila.
Hooper, John. The Circus Boat.
Hooper, Luther. Hand Loom Weaving.
Hooper, Madge. Herbs & Medicinal Plants.
Hooper, Meredith. The Story of Australia.
Hooper, R. Patterns of Acute Head Injury.
Hooper, Robert E. A Call to Remember.
Hooper, Walter, jt. auth. see Green, Roger L.
Hooper, Walter, ed. see Lewis, C. S.
Hoopes, Donelson F. Eakins Watercolors.
Hoopes, Penrose R. Connecticut Clockmakers of the Eighteenth Century.
Hoopes, Robert, jt. ed. see Stone, Wilfred.
Hoopes, Roy. Cain: The Biography of James M. Cain.
--Ralph Ingersoll: A Biography.
Hoopes, Roy, ed. see Cain, James M.
Hoornaert, P. Reverse Osmosis.
Hoornweg, Johanna, tr. see Frolich, Paul.
Hoose, Phillip M. Building an Ark: Tools for the Preservation of Natural Diversity Through Land Protection.
Hoose, William H. Van see Van Hoose, William H., et al.
Hoover. The Professional Teachers Handbook: A Guide for Improving Instruction in Today's Middle & Secondary Schools.
Hoover, Glenn E. Essays in Provocation.
--Twentieth Century Economic Thought.
Hoover, H. M. The Lost Star.
--Return to Earth.
Hoover, Helen. The Gift of the Deer.
Hoover, Herbert. Addresses upon the American Road: 1955-1960.
Hoover, Herbert T. The Sioux: A Critical Bibliography.
Hoover, Irwin H. Forty-Two Years in the White House.
Hoover, John P. Admirable Warrior: Guerrero Admirable; el Mariscal Sucre, Luchador Por la Independencia Sudamericana. De Reed, Alicia C., tr.
Hoover, Marjorie L. Meyerhold: The Art of Conscious Theater.
Hoover, Mary, jt. auth. see Ohashi, Wataru.
Hoover, Mildred B., et al. Historic Spots in California.
Hoover, Rosenna, tr. see Bolliger, Max.
Hoovler, David G., jt. auth. see Alger, Chadwick F.
Hope, Arthur J. Notre Dame: One Hundred Years.
Hope, Christopher. The Dragon Wore Pink.
--A Separate Development.
--A Separate Development.
Hope, Gordon S. Integrated Devices in Digital Circuit Design.
Hope, K. Elementary Statistics: A Workbook.
Hope, Laura L. Bobbsey Twins & the Cedar Camp Mystery.
--Bobbsey Twins & the Four-Leaf Clover Mystery.
--Bobbsey Twins & Their Camel Adventure.
--The Case of the Runaway Money.
Hope, Quentin M. Spoken French in Review.
Hope, Richard, tr. see Aristotle.
Hope, Robert C. Legendary Lore of the Holy Wells of England.
Hopewell, S. One Hundred & Fifty Years of Modern Britain.
Hopf, Alice L. Misplaced Animals, Plants & Other Living Creatures.
Hopf, John T. The Complete Picture Guide to Newport, R. I.
Hopf, Peter S. Designer's Guide to OSHA: A Practical Design Guide to the Occupational Safety & Health Act for Architects, Engineers, & Builders.
Hopgood, Frank R., et al. Introduction to the Graphical Kernel System-GKS.
Hopkin, John A., et al, eds. Financial Management in Agriculture. Barry, Peter J. & Baker, C. B.
Hopkins, Albert A. Magic, Stage Illusions, Special Effects & Trick Photography.
Hopkins, Budd. Intruders: The Incredible Visitations at Copley Woods.
Hopkins, Charles O. A National Prospectus on Vocational Education: Its Impact on Research & Leadership Development.
Hopkins, David. In-Service Training & Educational Development: An International Survey.
Hopkins, David & Reid, Ken, eds. Rethinking Teacher Education.
Hopkins, Donald R. Princes & Peasants: Smallpox in History.
Hopkins, F. N. Lights & Tides of the World.
--Lights & Tides of the World.
Hopkins, Gerald M. Major Poems.

Authors

Hopkins, Gerard Manley. Memoires Interieurs. Mauriac, Francois, tr. from Fr.
--Therese. Mauriac, Francois, tr. from Fr.
--Titans: A Three-Generation Biography of the Dumas. Maurois, Andre, tr. from Fr.
Hopkins, James T. Fifty Years of Citrus: The Florida Citrus Exchange, 1909-1959.
Hopkins, Jeffrey. Meditation on Emptiness. Napper, Elizabeth, ed.
Hopkins, Jeffrey, jt. auth. see Sopa, Geshe L.
Hopkins, Jerry. Bowie.
--Yoko Ono.
Hopkins, John. Losing Time.
Hopkins, Kenneth D. & Glass, Gene V. Basic Statistics for the Behavioral Sciences.
Hopkins, Lee B. The Best of Book Bonanza.
--Kits, Cats, Lions & Tigers. Pacini, Kathy, ed.
--Pups, Dogs, Foxes & Wolves. Pacini, Kathy, ed.
Hopkins, Lee B., ed. Beat the Drum: Independence Day Has Come.
--A Dog's Life.
--Easter Buds Are Springing: Poems for Easter.
--Good Morning to You, Valentine.
--Hey-How for Halloween!
--I Am the Cat.
--Me: A Book of Poems.
--Merrily Comes Our Harvest In: Poems for Thanksgiving.
--Moments: Poems about the Seasons.
--My Mane Catches the Wind: Poems About Horses.
--Sing Hey for Christmas Day!
--To Look at Any Thing.
Hopkins, Lee B., ed. see Behn, Harry.
Hopkins, Paul A. What Next in Mission?
Hopkins, Pauline E. Contending Forces: A Novel.
Hopkins, R. A., jt. auth. see U. S. Department of Commerce Staff.
Hopkins, S. J. Drugs & Pharmacology for Nurses.
Hopkins, Sheila V., jt. auth. see Brown, Henry P.
Hopkins, Vincent C. Dred Scott's Case.
Hopkinson, J., jt. auth. see Cash, J.
Hopkinson, R. G., et al. Daylighting.
Hopkinson, Tom, intro. by. David Hurn: Photographs 1956-76.
Hopkirk, Peter. Foreign Devils on the Silk Road: The Search for the Lost Cities & Treasures of Chinese Central Asia.
--Setting the East Ablaze: Lenin's Dream of an Empire in Asia.
Hopko, Thomas. The Spirit of God.
Hopman, Harry. Better Tennis for Boys & Girls.
Hoppe, Arthur. The Marital Arts.
Hoppe, Joanne. The Lesson Is Murder.
Hoppe, Robert A. Social & Economic Environment of Black Farmers.
Hoppel, Charles L., jt. auth. see Tandler, Bernard.
Hopper, A. G. Einfuehrung in die Statistische Qualitatskontrolle. Berchtold, W., tr. from Eng.
Hopper, David H. A Dissent on Bonhoeffer.
Hopper, Gordon E. Model A Ford Restoration Handbook. Clymer Publications, ed.
Hopper, Nancy S. Whoppers.
Hopper, Stanley R. & Miller, David L., eds. Interpretation: The Poetry of Meaning.
Hoppock, Robert. Occupational Information.
Hopson, B. & Hayes, J. The Theory & Practice of Vocational Guidance.
Hopwood, A. G., ed. Human Resource Accounting.
Hopwood, Derek, ed. Euro-Arab Dialogue: The Relations Between the Two Cultures.
Hora, Heinrich, jt. ed. see Schwarz, Helmut J.
Horace. Complete Works of Horace. Passage, Charles E., tr. from Gr.
Horack, I., jt. ed. see Wecker, E.
Horadam, A. F. A Guide to Undergraduate Projective Geometry.
--Outline Course of Pure Mathematics.
Horan, D., jt. auth. see Stahl, Norman.
Horan, Dennis J. & Oelahoyde, Melinda, eds. Infanticide & the Handicapped Newborn.
Horan, James D. The Blue Messiah.
--The Right Image.
Horan, James F., jt. ed. see Palmer, Kenneth T.
Horan, Kelly, jt. ed. see Naiman, Arthur.
Horan, Michael. Index to Parachuting, Nineteen Hundred to Nineteen Seventy-Five: An Annotated Bibliography.
Horbar, Amy, ed. see Ettesvold, Paul M.
Horbar, Amy, jt. ed. see Hayward, Jane.
Horbar, Amy, ed. see Mathews, Zena P.
Horchem, Sophie K. All about Permanent Hair Removal.
Hord, R. Michael. The Illiac IV: The First Supercomputer.
Horden, William. Experience & Faith.
Horder, John, jt. auth. see Butrym, Zofia.
Hordern, A. Legal Abortion: The English Experience.
Hordern, William & Otwell, John. Lent.
Hordern, William E., jt. auth. see Bruner, Frederick D.
Hordinsky, J. R., ed. see Basic Environmental Problems of Man in Space II, International Symposium Staff & Klein, K. E.
Hore, Brian D. & Plant, Martin A., eds. Alcohol Problems in Employment.
Hore-Lacy, Ian. Creating Common Wealth.
Horewitz, James. Transactional Analysis & Family Therapy.
Horgan, M. Competitive Tendering for Engineering Contracts.
Horgan, Paul. The Centuries of Santa Fe.
--Encounters with Stravinsky.
--Memories of the Future.
--Mountain Standard Time.
--Songs after Lincoln.
--Whitewater.
Hori, J. Spectral Properties of Disordered Chains & Lattices.
Horibuchi, Seiji, ed. see Buronson & Hara, Tetsuo.
Horibuchi, Seiji, ed. see Hara, Buronson & Hara, Tetsuo.
Horibuchi, Seiji, ed. see Takahashi, Rumiko.
Horine, Billie & Channel, Kimberley. Billie & Berley's Best of Quilting.
Horine, Lawrence E. Administration of Physical Education & Sports Programs.
Horine, Ruth, tr. see Jung Institute, Curatorium Staff.
Horkheimer, Patricia. Educators Guide to Free Health, Physical Education & Recreation Materials.
Horler, A. R. & Foster, J. B., eds. Progress in Clinical Medicine.
Horlock, J. H. Actuator Disk Theory: Discontinuities in Thermo-Fluid Dynamics.
Horman, Richard E. & Fox, Allan M., eds. Drug Awareness: Key Documents on LSD, Marijuana & the Drug Culture.
Horn, A. S., et al, eds. The Neurobiology of Dopamine.
Horn, Babette J., jt. auth. see Levin, Richard M.
Horn, Bill Van see Van Horn, Bill.
Horn, Delton T. Basic Electronics Theory with Projects & Experiments.
--Electronic Music Synthesizers.
--Golden Flutes & Great Escapes - Apple.
--Golden Flutes & Great Escapes - Commodore 64.
--Music Synthesizers: A Manual of Design & Construction.
--Thirty Customized Microprocessor Projects.
--Thirty-Four MORE Tested, Ready-To-Run Game Programs in BASIC.
Horn, Delton T., jt. auth. see Cunningham, John E.
Horn, Delton T., jt. auth. see Warring, R. H.
Horn, George, ed. see Robinson, Sharon.
Horn, George F. Cartooning.
Horn, George F., ed. see Brommer, Gerald.
Horn, George F., ed. see Sheaks, Barclay.
Horn, George F., ed. see Wasserman, Burton.
Horn, Jane, jt. auth. see Pappas, Lou S.
Horn, Marilyn J. The Second Skin.
Horn, Richard. Fifties Style: Then & Now.
--Memphis: Objects, Funiture & Patterns.
--Memphis: Objects, Furniture, & Patterns.
Horn, Robert D. Marlborough: A Survey of Panegyrics, Satires & Biographical Writings, 1688-1788.
Horn, Tom. Tom Horn Autobiography.
Horn, Vivian. Composition Steps.
Horn, William Van see Van Horn, William.
Horn, Yvonne. Dozens of Ways to Make Money.
--Sing for Your Supper.
Horn, Yvonne M. Dozens of Ways to Make Money.
Horn, Zsuzanna, tr. see Pataky-Brestyanszky, I.
Hornback, Bert G. The Hero of My Life: Essays on Dickens.
--Noah's Arkitecture: A Study of Dicken's Mythology.
Hornback, Kenneth E., jt. auth. see Morrison, Denton E.
Hornback, Ned B. Self-Assessment of Current Knowledge in Therapeutic Radiology.
Hornbein, Thomas F. Everest: The West Ridge.
Hornbostel, Caleb. Architectural Detailing Simplified.
Hornburger. African Countries & Cultures.
Horne, Chevis. You Can Find Comfort.
Horne, Dennis. Trampolining: A Complete Handbook.
Horne, James C. Van see Van Horne, James C.
Horne, James C. van see Van Horne, James C.
Horne, M. R. Plastic Theory of Structures: In SI-Metric Units.
Horne, R. A. The Chemistry of Our Environment.
Horne, Robert W. Virus Structure.
Horner, A. Musgrave. Speech Training.
Horner, Deborah R. Masks of the World: To Cut Out & Wear.
Horner, I. B. & Jaini, Padmanabh S., trs. Apochryphal Birth Stories.
Horner, J. G. Dictionary of Mechanical Engineering Terms. Grahame-White, G. K., ed.
--Dictionary of Mechanical Engineering Terms.
--Dictionary of Mechanical Engineering Terms.
--Dictionary of Terms in Mechanical Engineering.
Horner, John S., jt. auth. see Hasenstab, M. Suzanne.
Horner, P. C. Earthworks.
Horner, Thomas M., jt. auth. see Gunkel, Hermann.
Horner, Tom. Sex in the Bible.
--Terriers of the World: Their History & Characteristics.
Horner, William R. Bad at the Bijou.
Horngren, Charles T. Cost Accounting: A Managerial Emphasis.
Hornick, Melvyn. The Successful Marketing of Schools.
Hornick, Robert N., jt. auth. see Gautama, Sudargo.
Hornig, Doug. The Dark Side.
--Foul Shot.
--Waterman.
Horning, E. C., jt. auth. see Eik-Nes, K. B.
Hornsby, Beve. Overcoming Dyslexia: A Straightforward Guide for Families & Teachers.
Hornsby, June & Evans, Jean. Apples of Gold.
Hornsey, et al. Mechanics & Materials: An Individualized Approach - Reference Manual-Study Guide.
Hornsey, A. W., ed. see Mann, Thomas.
Hornsey, Alan W., ed. Handbook for Modern Language Teachers.
Hornung, C. P. Handbook of Designs & Devices.
Hornung, William J. Estimating Building Construction.
--Metric Architectural Construction Drafting & Design.
Hornyak, William F. Nuclear Structure.
Hornyak, William F., jt. auth. see Marion, Jerry B.
Hornykiewicz, O., jt. ed. see Livingston, K. E.
Horovitz, C. T., et al. Scandium: Its Occurence, Chemistry, Physics, Metallurgy, Biology & Technology.
Horovitz, J. Law & Logic: A Critical Account of Legal Argument.
Horowitz, D. The Economics of Israel.
Horowitz, David, jt. auth. see Collier, Peter.
Horowitz, E. Fundamentals of Programming Languages.
Horowitz, Ellis. Fundamentals of Programming Languages.
Horowitz, Ellis, ed. Programming Languages: A Grand Tour.
--Programming Languages: A Grand Tour.
Horowitz, Gad. Canadian Labour in Politics.
Horowitz, Gene. Mr. Jack & the Greenstalks.
Horowitz, Harvey. Non-Profit Cultural Organizations.
Horowitz, Herbert. Working with Wood.
Horowitz, I. L. Sociological Self-Images.
Horowitz, Ira, jt. auth. see Spulber, Nicolas.
Horowitz, Irving L. Taking Lives: Genocide & State Power.
Horowitz, Irving L., ed. Cuban Communism.
--Cuban Communism.
--Cuban Communism.
--Cuban Communism.
--Genocide: State Power & Mass Murder.
--The Rise & Fall of Project Camelot: Studies in the Relationship Between Social Science & Practical Politics.
--Sociological Realities: A Guide to the Study of Society. Strong, Mary S.
--The Use & Abuse of Social Science: Behavioral Science & National Policy Making.
--The Use & Abuse of Social Science: Behavioral Science & National Policy Making.
Horowitz, Isaac M. Synthesis of Feedback Systems.
Horowitz, Leonard, jt. ed. see Reiser, H. Joseph.
Horowitz, Lois. Knowing Where to Look: The Ultimate Guide to Research.
Horowitz, Martin, ed. The Glycoconjugates: Glyconproteins, Glycolipides & Proteoglycans.
Horowitz, Martin & Pigman, Ward, eds. Glycoconjugates: Mammalian Glycoproteins & Glycolipids.
Horowitz, P., jt. ed. see Booss, C.
Horowitz, Z. P. Angiotensin Converting Enzyme Inhibitors: Mechanisms of Action & Clinical Implications.
Horowski, R., jt. ed. see Wuttke, W.
Horr, David A., ed. see Bender, Averam B.
Horr, David A., ed. see Gordon, B. L., et al.
Horr, David A., ed. see Hickerson, Harold.
Horrell, C. William. College Instruction in Photography. Eastman Kodak Co., ed.
Horrobin, D. F., ed. see Hume, Wilfred I.
Horrobin, D. F., ed. see Skrabanek, Petr & Powell, David.
Horrobin, David. Medical Hubris: A Reply to Ivan Illich.
Horrobin, David F. Prolactin.
Horrobin, David F., ed. Clinical Uses for Essential Fatty Acids.
Horrobin, Peter. Constructional Mathematics.
Horrocks, D. Feedback Circuits & Op-Amps.
Horrocks, Donald L. & Peng, Chin-Tzu, eds. Organic Scintillators & Liquid Scintillation Counting.
Horrocks, James. My Dear Parents: The Civil War Seen by an English Union Soldier. Lewis, A. S., ed.
Horrocks, John E. The Psychology of Adolescence.
Horsch, John. Principle of Non-Resistance As Held by the Mennonite Church. Bd. with Hutterian Brethren, Fifteen Twenty-Eight to Nineteen Thirty-One. Horsch, John. Garland Pub.
Horsefield, J. Keith. British Monetary Experiments, 1650-1710.
Horsfield, Peter. Religious Television: The Experience in America.
Horsley, F. W. Means Scheduling Manual.
Horsley, Gaye. Commercial Foods Exposed!
Horsley, Jack E. & Carlova, John. Testifying in Court.
Horsley, R. Kent. Highlights of the Watergate Tapes.
Horsley, William, ed. see Means, R. S., Company, Inc. Staff.
Horspool, W. M. Aspects of Organic Photochemistry.
Hort, Greta. Piers Plowman & Contemporary Religious Thought.
Horton, jt. auth. see Byrd.
Horton, Arthur M., Jr., ed. Mental Health Interventions for the Aging: Psychotherapeutic Treatment Approaches.
Horton, Byrne J. Dictionary of Modern Chess.
Horton, C. W., Jr. & Reichl, L. E., eds. Statistical Physics & Chaos in Fusion Plasmas.
Horton, Charles E., ed. Plastic & Reconstructive Surgery of the Genital Area.
Horton, Craig, jt. ed. see Mencke, Claire.
Horton, David. In Celebration of the Discovery of the Abandoned Star Factory.
Horton, Derek & Szarek, Walter A., eds. Anomeric Effect: Origins & Consequences.
Horton, Derek, jt. ed. see Pigman, Ward.
Horton, Donald, jt. auth. see Dollard, John.
Horton, Forest W., Jr., ed. Understanding U. S. Information Policy. Incl. Vol. I. The Resources for the Information Economy; Vol. II. The Participants in the Information Marketplace; Vol. III. The Assets of the Information Society; The Information Policy Primer. Info Indus.
Horton, H. Mack, tr. see Takeda, Tsuneo.
Horton, John. Grieg.
Horton, Karen, jt. auth. see Horton, Tom.
Horton, Michael S. Mission Accomplished: What Today's Christian Must Know About God & Salvation.
Horton, Patricia C. Royal Mistress.
Horton, Paul B. & Horton, Robert L. Personal Learning Aid for Introductory Sociology.
Horton, Paul B. & Hunt, Chester L. Sociology.
Horton, Robert L., jt. auth. see Horton, Paul B.
Horton, Tom & Horton, Karen. Dolphin Guide to Hawaii.
Horuath. Halogenated Benzenes: Mutual Solubility of Liquids.
Horvasse, R; see Satir, P.
Horvat, Branko. The Yugoslav Economic System: The First Labor-Managed Economy in the Making.
Horvat, Dilwyn. Operation Titan.
Horvath, Betty. Jasper & the Hero Business.
Horvath, David G., ed. Roy Stryker Papers Nineteen Hundred Twelve to Nineteen Seventy-Two: A Guide to the Microfilm Edition.
Horvath, J., ed. see International Mathematical Conference, College Park, 1970.
Horvath, Nicholas. Essentials of Philosophy.
Horvath, T. & Berta, I. Static Elimination.
Horwath, jt. auth. see Laventhol.
Horwich, Kathleen, jt. auth. see Fishman, Meryl.
Horwitz, Henry. Welding: Principles & Practice.
Horwitz, Julius. Landfall.
Horwitz, Leonard. Clinical Prediction in Psychotherapy.
Horwood, Richard M. & Katz, Steven J., eds. Real Estate Investments: Tax & Financial Planning.
Horwood, William. The Stonor Eagles.
Horzinger, Manfred, tr. see Mitterauer, Michael & Sieder, Reinhard.
Hosen, Harris. Clinical Allergy Based on Provocative Testing.
Hosford, David H. Nottingham, Nobles, & the North: Aspects of the Revolution of 1688.
Hosford, Zia Wesley see Wesley-Hosford, Zia.
Hoshijo, Kathy. Kathy Cooks...Naturally.
Hosie, Alexander. Manchuria: Its People, Resources & Recent History, London, 1904.
Hosie, Kenneth, jt. auth. see Bullock, Spencer M.
Hoskin, Michael. Mind of the Scientist: Imaginary Conversations with Galileo, Newton, Herschel, Darwin, & Pasteur.
Hoskins, Robert. Jack-in-the-Box Planet.
--To Control the Stars.
--To Escape the Stars.
Hosler, Russell J., et al. Programmed Gregg Shorthand.
Hosley, Richard, ed. Essays on Shakespeare & Elizabethan Drama: In Honor of Hardin Craig.

Hosmer, Steven T. & Wolfe, Thomas W. Soviet Policy & Practice Towards Third-World Conflicts.
Hosner, Sheila, ed. see Bronfman, Sam.
Hosner, Sheila, ed. see Kinssies, Richard.
Hosner, Sheila, ed. see Marter, Marilynn.
Hosner, Sheila, ed. see Wolf, Elliott.
Hosner, Shiela, ed. see Byrn, Anne.
Hosokawa, B. Thirty-Five Years in the Frying Pan.
Hosoya, Chihiro, et al. Collaboration with Communist Countries in Managing Global Problems: An Examination of the Options.
Hospers, John. Human Conduct: Problems of Ethics.
--Introduction to Philosophical Analysis.
Hospital Research & Educational Trust of the AHA. Servicio De Alimentacion (Food Service Worker)
Hossain, Tony. The Nineteen Sixties Supercars: A Repair & Restoration Guide.
Hossu, Alex. Doodling As an Art.
Host. Danish Pocket Dictionary.
Host, P. Danish Made Easy for the Tourist.
Hostage, Jacqueline. Jackie's Kitchen Charts.
Hostalek, Z., jt. ed. see Vanek, Zdenko.
Hostetler, John A. Amish Society.
Hostettler, R. Printer's Terms Dictionary.
Hot Rod Magazine Editors, ed. Engine Swapping.
--History of Drag Racing.
Hotchkis, Katharine B. Christmas Eve at Rancho los Alamitos.
Hotchkiss, Bill. Ammahabas.
--Crow Warriors.
Hotchkiss, Bill & Shears, Judith. The Russians.
Hotchkiss, John F. Hummel Art Two with Prices.
Hotchner, A. E. Papa Hemingway: The Ecstasy & Sorrow.
--Papa Hemingway: The Ecstasy & Sorrow.
Hotchner, Ursula, et al, eds. Newman's Own Cookbook.
Hoteles Camiro Real Chefs. Los Tesoros de la Cocina Mexicana.
Hotema, Hilton. Cosmic Science of the Ancient Masters.
--The Empyreal Sea-Live 1400 Years.
--Kingdom of Heaven.
--Secret of Regeneration.
--Why Do We Age?
Hotham, Gary. This Space Blank.
Hothem, Lar. North American Indian Artifacts: A Collector's Identification & Value Guide.
Hottinger, Arnold. Spain in Transition: Franco's Regime.
Hotton, Peter. So You Want to Build a House.
Hotz, Rudolf. Orthodontics in Daily Practice.
Houart, Victor. Antique Spoons: A Collector's Guide.
--Sewing Accessories: An Illustrated History.
Houck, Carter. Warm As Wool, Cool As Cotton: The Story of Natural Fibers & Fabrics & How to Work with Them.
Houden, Robert. Memoirs. Wraxall, tr.
Hougan, Carolyn. Shooting in the Dark: A Novel.
Hougen, Joel O. Measurements & Control Applications.
Hough, Franklin B. The Siege of Charleston, by the British Fleet & Army Under the Command of Admiral Arbuthnot & Sir Henry Clinton, Which Terminated with the Surrender of That Place on the 12th of May, 1780.
Hough, George A. News Writing.
--News Writing.
Hough, George P., jt. auth. see Raudsepp, Eugene.
Hough, Graham. Essay on Criticism.
Hough, Henry B. Mostly on Martha's Vineyard: A Personal Record.
--Soundings at Sea Level.
--To the Harbor Light.
Hough, J. R. Education & the National Economy.
--Education & the Natonal Economy.
Hough, Jack L. Geology of the Great Lakes.
Hough, Jerry F. Soviet Prefects: The Local Party Organs in Industrial Decision-Making.
Hough, Michael. City Form & Natural Process: Towards a New Urban Vernacular.
Hough, R. E. The Ministry of the Glory Cloud.
Hough, Richard. Edwina: Countess Mountbatten of Burma.
--The Greatest Crusade: Roosevelt, Churchill, & the Naval Wars.
--The Longest Battle: The War at Sea 1939-1945. Cady, Howard, ed.
Hough, William. The Black American.
Houghteling, James L., Jr. Dynamics of Law.
Houghton, Diane & Wallace, Ralph G. Students' Accounting Vocabulary.
Houghton, Eric. Steps Out of Time.
Houghton, H. W. see Green, L. F.
Houghton Mifflin Company Staff, ed. My First Dictionary.
--The Pocket Dictionary.
Houghton, Norris. But Not Forgotten: The Adventure of the University Players.
Houghton, Richard M. Life & Letters of John Keats.
Houk, K. N. & Paquette, L. A. Organic Chemistry.
Houlden, J. L. Patterns of Faith: A Study in the Relationship Between the New Testament & Christian Doctrine.
Houle, Cyril O. The External Degree.
Houle, Georgia B. Learning Centers for Young Children.
Houlihan, Patrick. Lummis in the Pueblos.
Houlihan, William, ed. Indoles.
Houlihan, William J., ed. Indoles.
Hounshell, Paul, jt. auth. see Coble, Charles.
Hounsome, Terry. New Rock Record.
Hounsome, Terry & Chambre, Tim. Rock Record.
Hourani, George F., ed. Essays on Islamic Philosophy & Science.
Housby, Trevor. Dream Fishing the World's Greatest Waters.
Housden, Leslie. Prevention of Cruelty to Children.
House & Garden, ed. Twentieth Century Decorating Architecture & Gardens.
House, Elizabeth Johnson. The Bull by the Horns.
House, Ernest R. Evaluating with Validity.
House, J. W. France: An Applied Geography.
House, Kurt, ed. Texas Archeology: Essays Honoring R. King Harris.
House, M. R. The Origin of Major Invertebrate Groups.
House, Millie B. The Joy of Wildflowers: A Fieldbook of Familiar Flowers of Rural & Urban Habitats in the Eastern United States.
House, Peter A. & Steger, Wilber A. The Modern Federalism: An Analytical Dimension.
Household, Geoffrey. Arrows of Desire. Weeks, Edward & Brady, Upton, eds.
Householder, Joanne, jt. auth. see Musick, Judith S.
Houseman, Gerald L., jt. auth. see Roelofs, H. M.
Houseman, John. Entertainers & the Entertained: Essays on Theater, Film & Television.
--Final Dress.
--Final Dress.
--Run-Through.
Housen, Sharon L. Of Shadow, Song, & Soul.
Houser, Thomas. Agatha's Friends.
Housley, Trevor. Data Communications & Teleprocessing Systems.
Housman, Alfred E. A Shropshire Lad.
Housman, Laurence. The Rat-Catcher's Daughter. Greene, Ellin, ed.
Housner, J. M., jt. ed. see Noor, A. K.
Houston, Charles S., jt. ed. see Sutton, John R.
Houston, James. Akavak: An Eskimo Journey.
--Eagle Mask: A West Coast Indian Tale.
--Eagle Song.
--Ghost Fox.
--Ghost Fox.
--Ghost Paddle: A Northwest Coast Indian Tale.
--Kiviok's Magic Journey: An Eskimo Legend.
--Spirit Wrestler.
--Spirit Wrestler.
--Tikta'liktak: An Eskimo Legend.
--The White Archer: An Eskimo Legend.
--The White Archer: An Eskimo Legend.
--White Dawn: An Eskimo Saga.
--Wolf Run: A Caribou Eskimo Tale.
Houston, James, ed. & illus. Songs of the Dream People: Chants & Images from the Indians & Eskimos of North America.
Houston, James D., jt. auth. see Houston, Jeanne W.
Houston, Jeanne W. & Houston, James D. Farewell to Manzanar.
Houston, John P. The Shape & Style of Proust's Novel.
Houston, John P. & Benassi, Victor. Invitation to Psychology.
Houston, John P., et al. Essentials of Psychology.
Houston, Joseph & Glenesk, Neil. The Professional Service of Food & Beverage in Britain.
Houston, Martha L. The Eighteen Twenty-Seven Land Lottery of Georgia.
Houston, Rab. Records of a Scottish Village: Lasswade 1650-1750.
Houston, Robert. Ararat.
--Blood Tango.
--Monday, Tuesday, Wednesday.
Houston, Robert J. D-Day to Bastogne: A Paratrooper Recalls World War II.
Houston, Tom. Were You There. Mills, Kathi, ed.
Houston, Victoria. Loving a Younger Man: How Women Are Finding & Enjoying a Better Relationship.
Hou-tien, Cheng. Six Chinese Brothers: An Ancient Tale.
Hovanec, Evelyn A. Henry James & Germany.
Hovanessian, Shahan A. Introduction to Synthetic Array & Imaging Radars.
Hovasse, R; see Dangeard, P.
Hovde, Christian A., jt. auth. see Berry, Charles N.
Hove, M. A. Van see Somorjai, G. A. & Van Hove, M. A.
Hoven, Vernon & Holen, Harold H. Dramatic Tax Savings Through Real Estate Transactions.
Hovenkamp, Herbert, jt. auth. see Areeda, Phillip E.
Hovey, Richard, jt. auth. see Carman, Bliss.
Hoving, Thomas. King of the Confessors.
--Masterpiece.
--Tutankhamen: The Untold Story.
--Two Worlds of Andrew Wyeth.
Hoving, W. Tiffany Table Manners.
Hovis, Gene & Rosenthal, Sylvia. Gene Hovis's Uptown, Down Home Cookbook.
Howard, Alice, jt. auth. see Howard, Walden.
Howard, Anne. Welfare Rights-the Local Authorities Role.
Howard, Audrey. Ambitions.
Howard, C. H., ed. see Chamberlain, Joseph.
Howard, C. Jeriel & Tracz, Richard F. The Paragraph Book.
Howard, Carole & Mathews, Wilma. On Deadline: Managing Media Relations.
Howard, Colin, jt. auth. see Zuckerman, Arie.
Howard, Constance. Inspiration for Embroidery.
--Textile Crafts.
Howard, David. Why World Evangelism.
Howard, David S. Chinese Armorial Porcelain.
Howard, David S. & Ayers, John. China for the West: Chinese Porcelain & Other Decorative Arts for Export Illustrated from the Mottahedeh Collection.
Howard, Dick. The Development of the Marxian Dialectic.
Howard, E. D. Modern Foundry Practice.
Howard, Elizabeth J. Winter on Her Own.
Howard, Elliot J. & Roth, Susan A. Health Risks.
Howard, Fred. Charlie Flowers & the Melody Gardens.
Howard, Geoffrey S. Computer Anxiety & the Use of Microcomputers in Management. Farmer, Richard, ed.
Howard, George. Think It Through.
Howard, Hampton. War Toys.
Howard, Harry N., ed. see University of the State of New York, Foreign Area Materials Center Staff.
Howard, Herbert H. & Kievman, Michael S. Radio & TV Programming.
Howard, I. K., tr. see Al-Din, Shaykh M.
Howard, I. K., tr. see Kattani, Sulayman.
Howard, James. A Child Possessed by Chess.
Howard, James H. Cut-Outs: Native American Art.
Howard, Jane. A Different Woman.
--Margaret Mead: A Life.
Howard, Jean G. Tuk, the Timid: The Story of a Sea Otter.
Howard, Joan R., jt. auth. see Kandzari, Judith H.
Howard, John E. Musings & Reminiscences of A Pseudo-Scientist.
Howard, John R., ed. The Awakening Minorities: American Indians, Mexican Americans & Puerto Ricans.
--An Overview of International Studies.
Howard, Joseph K. Strange Empire, a Narrative of the Northwest.
Howard, Joyce. Basics in Folk Art & Tole.
Howard, Kathleen, ed. The Metropolitan Museum of Art Guide.
Howard, Kathleen, ed. see Okada, Barbara T.
Howard, Kathleen, ed. see Rewald, Sabine.
Howard, Kenneth S. One Hundred Years of the American Two-Move Chess Problem.
Howard, Lauren D. Principles of Biology Laboratory Manual.
Howard, Leon. Victorian Knight-Errant: A Study of the Early Literary Career of James Russell Lowell.
Howard, Leslie G. The Expansion of God.
Howard, Leslie R. Auditing.
Howard, Lisa, jt. auth. see Weiner, Sue.
Howard, Marion. Sometimes I Wonder about Me: Teen-Agers & Mental Health.
Howard, Marshall C. Legal Aspects of Marketing.
Howard, Mary Ann. Blueprint for Health.
Howard, Mary K., jt. auth. see Franks, Betty B.
Howard, Maureen. Expensive Habits.
Howard, Michael & McKim, Patrick C. Contemporary Cultural Anthropology.
Howard, Oliver G. Not in Our Stars.
Howard, Oswald. The Montreal Diocesan Theological College.
Howard, Rev. Fielding T. Sunbeams & Shadows.
Howard, Richard. Findings: A Book of Poems.
--Lining Up.
Howard, Richard, ed. see Roy, Jules.
Howard, Richard, tr. see Barthes, Roland.
Howard, Richard, tr. see Cioran, E. M.
Howard, Richard, tr. see De Mandiargues, Andre P.
Howard, Richard, tr. see Gide, Andre.
Howard, Richard, tr. see Michaux, Henri.
Howard, Richard, tr. see Robbe-Grillet, Alain.
Howard, Richard A. Charles Wright in Cuba, Eighteen Fifty-Six to Eighteen Sixty-Seven.
Howard, Robert & Skjei, Eric. What Makes the Crops Rejoice: An Introduction to Gardening.
Howard, Robert E., jt. auth. see Lovecraft, H. P.
Howard, Roger. Contemporary Chinese Theatre.
Howard, Ross & Perley, Michael. Acid Rain.
Howard, Seymour. Bartolomeo Cavaceppi, Eighteenth-Century Restorer.
Howard, Ted, jt. auth. see Rifkin, Jeremy.
Howard-Tilton Memorial Library Staff. Catalog of the William Ransom Hogan Jazz Archive.
Howard, Velma S., tr. see Lagerloef, Selma O.
Howard, Velma S., tr. see Lagerlof, Selma.
Howard, Virgil P. Pentecost 1.
Howard, Walden & Howard, Alice. Exploring the Road Less Traveled.
Howard, William E., jt. auth. see Baar, James.
Howard-Williams, Jeremy. The Care & Repair of Sails.
Howard-Williams, Jeremy, tr. see Damour, Jacques.
Howarth, David. The Greek Adventure: Byron & Other Characters of the Greek War of Independence.
Howarth, O. J. R., jt. auth. see Dickinson, Robert E.
Howarth, R. G., ed. Minor Poets of the Seventeenth Century.
Howarth, Stephen. The Fighting Ships of the Rising Sun: The Drama of the Imperial Japanese Navy, 1895-1945.
--The Knights Templar.
Howarth-Williams, Martin. R. D. Laing: His Work & Its Relevance to Sociology.
Howatch, Susan. Penmarric.
--The Wheel of Fortune.
Howatson, A. M. An Introduction to Gas Discharges.
Howden, William E., jt. auth. see Miller, Edward.
Howe. Minor Oral Surgery.
Howe, Anna L., ed. Towards an Older Australia: Readings in Social Gerontology.
Howe, Clifford E. Administration of Special Education.
Howe, Daniel W. The Political Culture of the American Whigs.
Howe, Fanny. The Blue Hills.
--Bronte Wilde.
--Radio City.
--Taking Care.
--The White Slave.
--Yeah, But.
Howe, Florence & Bass, Ellen, eds. No More Masks: An Anthology of Poems by Women.
Howe, Frederic C. Confessions of a Reformer.
Howe, Frederick. Why War?
Howe, Glenn. Dinner in the Clouds.
Howe, Helen H. Gentle Americans, Eighteen Sixty-Four to Nineteen Sixty: Biography of a Breed.
Howe, Hubert S., Jr. Electronic Music Synthesis.
Howe, Irving. Decline of the New.
--A Margin of Hope: An Intellectual Autobiography.
--Steady Work: Essays in the Politics of Democratic Radicalism, 1953-1966.
--World of Our Fathers.
Howe, Irving, ed. Classics of Modern Fiction: Ten Short Novels.
--Classics of Modern Fiction: Ten Short Novels.
Howe, Irving & Greenberg, Eliezer, eds. Yiddish Stories Old & New.
Howe, J. P. & Melese-D'Hospital, G. Thorium & Gas Cooled Reactors.
Howe, James R. Marlowe, Tamburlaine, & Magic.
Howe, Janet R. The Mystery of the Marmalade Cat.
Howe, Jeanne, et al, eds. The Handbook of Nursing.
Howe, Jim, ed. see Conference of the British Educational Research Association 1980.
Howe, K. R. The Loyalty Islands: History of Culture Contacts, 1840-1900.
Howe, Louise K. Pink Collar Workers.
Howe, Mark D., ed. Holmes-Laski Letters, the Correspondence of Justice Oliver Wendell Holmes & Harold J. Laski 1916-1935.
Howe, Michael J. Television & Children.
Howe, P. J. Transfer of Nuclear Technology.
Howe, P. J., ed. Advanced Converters & Near Breeders: Proceedings of the Wingspread Conference, Racine, Wisconsin, 1975.
Howe, Reuel L. Miracle of Dialogue.
Howe, Susan W., jt. auth. see Whitney, John R.
Howell, Daisy, et al. Activities for Teaching Mathematics to Low Achievers.
Howell, David C. Statistical Methods for Psychology.
Howell, David W. Northstar One.
Howell, Edward B. & Howell, Richard P. Untangling the Web of Professional Liability.
--Untangling the Web of Professional Liability.
Howell, F. S. Navigation Primer for Fishermen.
Howell, Grace & Perez Y Sabido, Jesus. Spanish-English Handbook.
Howell, J. N., ed. see Acker, Arnold.
Howell, James A., jt. auth. see Boltz, David F.
Howell, James F. & Memering, W. Dean. Brief Handbook for Writers.
Howell, John R., jt. auth. see Siegel, Robert.
Howell, Leonore, jt. auth. see McNamara, Charlotte.
Howell, Rate, et al. Business Law: Alternate Edition.
Howell, Rate A., et al. Business Law: Text & Cases.
--The Legal Environment of Business.

Authors

Howell, Richard D. & Scott, Patrick B. Selected Microcomputer Applications for Teachers: A Hands-on Approach with the Apple.
Howell, Richard P., jt. auth. see Howell, Edward B.
Howell, Robert L. Fish for My People.
Howell, Robert W., et al. Educators, Parents & Micros: How to Help Your School Get & Use Computer Power.
Howell, Ruth. Dome People.
Howell, Ruth R. Splash & Flow.
Howell, Sarah. Home Cooking in a Hurry.
--More Home Cooking in a Hurry.
Howell-Koehler, Nancy, jt. auth. see Baer, Gordon.
Howells, Malcolm, jt. ed. see Kokelaar, B. P.
Howells, Victor. A Naturalist in Palestine.
Howells, William, ed. Ideas on Human Evolution: Selected Essays, 1949-1961.
Howells, William Dean. The Shadow of a Dream & an Imperative Duty.
Howery, D. G., jt. auth. see Marcus, Y.
Howes, M. J. & Morgan, D. V., eds. Microwave Solid State Devices & Applications.
--Variable Impedance Devices.
Howes, Nancy. Fully Human: A Program in Human Sexuality for Use with Persons Who Are Developmentally Disabled.
Howes, Paul G. Mini-Wood Community.
Howeski, Dave. Body Flying for Skydivers. Truffer, Michael, ed.
Howie, J. R. Research in General Practice.
Howington, Nolan P. A Royal Priesthood.
Howitt, Arnold M. Managing Federalism: Studies in Intergovernmental Relations.
Howitt, William. Colonization & Christianity: A Popular History of the Treatment of the Natives by the Europeans in All Their Colonies.
Howkins, Alun. Poor Labouring Men: Rural Radicalism in Norfolk, 1870-1923.
Howkins, John & Hudson, Christopher N. Shaw's Textbook of Operative Gynaecology.
Howland, Joseph, jt. auth. see Hackworth, Robert D.
Howlett, John. The Christmas Spy.
--Tango November.
Howsden, Jackie L. Work & the Helpless Self: The Social Organization of a Nursing Home.
Howse, Ruth. French Cooking Simplified with a Food Processor.
Howson, D. P. Mathematics for Electronic Technology.
Howson, Mark, tr. see Breton, Thierry & Beneich, Denis.
Howson, Susan. Sterling's Managed Float: The Operations of the Exchange Equalisation Account, 1932-39.
Hoy, Michael. Exotic Weapons: An Access Book, 1982 Edition. Where & How to Buy Strange Weapons.
--ID for Sale in the Mail.
Hoy, Ray. Opel Service Repair Handbook: All Models, 1966-1975.
Hoy, Ray, jt. auth. see Clymer Publications.
Hoyaux, M. F. Arc Physics.
--Solid State Plasmas.
Hoyem, George A. The History & Development of Small Arms: British Sporting Rifle.
Hoyem, George A., jt. auth. see Brewster, Melvin.
Hoyer, George W. What Happened Next? Nine Messages on Some of Jesus' Great Acts & Stories.
Hoyer, George W. & Roth, Wolfgang. Pentecost 2.
Hoyer, S., ed. The Aging Brain: Physiological & Pathophysiological Aspects.
Hoyes, Donald J., ed. Advertising Law Anthology Index (1987)
Hoyle. Advanced Accounting.
Hoyle, B. S. & Hilling, D., eds. Seaport Systems & Spatial Change: Technology, Industry & Development Strategies.
Hoyle, Bernard, jt. ed. see Pope, Rex.
Hoyle, Edmund. Hoyle's Card Games.
Hoyle, Eric. The Politics of School Management.
Hoyle, Fred. The Intelligent Universe: A New View of Creation & Evolution.
Hoyle, Fred & Wickramasinghe, Chandra. Evolution from Space: A Theory of Cosmic Creationism.
Hoyle, G., jt. auth. see Duckworth, Walter E.
Hoyle, Graham. Muscles & Their Neural Control.
Hoyles, J. Arthur. Religion in Prison.
--The Treatment of the Young Delinquent.
Hoyos, Ladislas see De Hoyos, Ladislas.
Hoyt, Charles A., ed. Minor American Novelists.
Hoyt, Edwin P. The Kamikazes.
--Pacific Destiny: The Story of America in the Western Sea in the Early 1800's to the 1980's.
--The U-Boat Wars.
--William O. Douglas: A Biography.
Hoyt, Edwin P., jt. auth. see Hoyt, Olga G.
Hoyt, Elizabeth E. Choice & Destiny of Nations.
Hoyt, J. H. Field Guide to Beaches.
Hoyt, Olga G. & Hoyt, Edwin P. Freedom of the News Media.
Hoyt, Patricia. How to Get Started When You Don't Know Where to Begin.
Hoyt, Samuel L. Men of Metals.
Hrapchak, Barbara B., jt. auth. see Sheehan, Denza C.
Hrebenar, Ronald J., jt. auth. see Scott, Ruth K.
HRH Princess Michael of Kent. Crowned in a Far Country: Portraits of Eight Royal Brides.
Hridayananda dasa Goswami Acaryadeva. Srimad-Bhagavatam: Eleventh Canto.
Hroch, Miroslav & Skybova, Anna. Ecclesia Militans: The Inquisition.
Hrones, Stephen. How to Try a Criminal Case.
Hronzny, Bedrich. Ancient History of Western Asia, India, & Crete.
Hrubesh, Lawrence W., jt. auth. see Varma, Ravi.
Hruby, Peter. Fools & Heroes: The Changing Role of Communist Intellectuals in Czechoslovakia.
Hrudey, S. E., jt. ed. see Vandermeulen, J. H.
Hsia, Linda & Wang, Y. C. Speak Chinese: Selections for Memorization.
Hsiang Ju Lin. Chinese Gastronomy.
Hsiao, James C. & Cleaver, David S. Management Science: Quantitative Approaches to Resource Allocation & Decision Making.
Hsieh, Ching-yao, et al. A Short Introduction to Modern Growth Theory.
Hsieh, Pao C. Government of China, 1644-1911.
Hsieh, Winston. Chinese Historiography on the Revolution of 1911: A Critical Survey & a Selected Bibliography.
Hsieh, Yuan-Yu. Elementary Theory of Structures.
Hsien, Lu. Personality & Adjustment.
Hsien, Lu, ed. Behavioral Modification & Cognitive-Affective Processes.
--Major Topics & Issues in Psychology.
--Scientific Studies in Behavioral Development.
Hsu, Chi-Ping. Signal Routing in Integrated Circuit Layout. Stone, Harold, ed.
Hsu, Donald K., et al. Spectral Atlas of Nitrogen Dioxide: 5530a to 6480a.
Hsu, Kenneth J. The Great Dying: A Cosmic Catastrophe Demolishes the Dinosaurs & Rocks the Theory of Evolution.
Hsu, Linda, jt. auth. see Roisen, Fred J.
Hsu, Priscilla L., jt. auth. see Malloy, Ruth L.
Hsu, T. C. & Benirschke, K. An Atlas of Mammalian Chromosomes, Vol. 10.
Hsu, T. C., jt. ed. see Benirschke, K.
Hu, S. Handbook of Industrial Energy Conservation.
Hua, Ellen K. Wisdom from the East: Meditations, Reflections, Proverbs & Chants.
Hua, Ellen Kei see Hua, Ellen K.
Hua, Gu. Pagoda Ridge & Other Stories. Yang, Gladys, tr. from Chinese.
Huang, Al C. Embrace Tiger, Return to Mountain: The Essence of T'ai Chi.
Huang, C. C., et al. Molecular Studies on Halogenated Deoxynucleosides.
Huang, Kerson. I Ching: The Oracle.
--Statistical Mechanics.
Huang, Philip, et al. Chinese Communists & Rural Society, Nineteen Twenty-Seven to Nineteen Thirty-Four.
Huang Po. The Zen Teaching of Huang Po: On the Transmission of the Mind. Blofeld, John, tr.
Huang, Quentin K. Y. Pilgrim from a Red Land.
Huang, Shuan-Fan. A Study of Adverbs.
Huang, T. S., ed. Two-Dimensional Digital Signal Processing I: Linear Filters.
Huang, Walter T. Petrology.
Huazong, H. Li. Fracture Mechanics in China: A Selection of Chinese Papers & Abstracts.
Hub, D. R., jt. auth. see Probert, S. D.
Hubatka, Milton C. & Hull, Frederick. Audio Sweetening for Film & TV.
Hubbard, jt. auth. see Hailes.
Hubbard, Bela. Memorials of a Half-Century in Michigan & the Lake Region.
--Political & Economic Structures.
Hubbard, Clyde, jt. auth. see Buttrey, T. V.
Hubbard, David A. Pentecost One: Proclamation 3B.
Hubbard, Ethan. First Light: Sojourns with People of the Outer Hebrides, the Sierra Madre, the Himalayas & Other Remote Places.
Hubbard, G. Art for Elementary Classrooms.
Hubbard, James L. How to Self Create an Internal-Unity Existence: Essence, Phase One Pursuits One Through Fourteen.
Hubbard, John G. Greenberg's Repair & Operating Manual for Prewar Lionel Trains.
Hubbard, L. Ron. Dianetics: The Modern Science of Mental Health.
--Slaves of Sleep.
Hubbard, Linda S., ed. Publishers Directory.
--Publishers Directory, 1988: Supplement.
Hubbard, Raymond T., jt. auth. see Hailes, William D., Jr.
Hubbard, Robert, ed. see Goldingay, John.
Hubbard, Robert L., et al. Drug Abuse Treatment Client Characteristics & Pretreatment Behaviors.
Hubbard, Stuart. The Computer Graphics Glossary.
Hubbell, J. G. P.O.W.
Hubbell, Patricia. Eight A. M. Shadows.
Hubble, Edwin. The Nature of Science, & Other Lectures.
Hubbs, Don. Home Education Resource Guide.
Hubbuch, Susan M. Writing Research Papers Across the Curriculum.
Hubenka, Lloyd & Garcia, Reloy. The Design of Drama: An Introduction.
Huber, Alfred. Eye Signs & Symptoms in Brain Tumors.
Huber, Frederic V. Apple Crunch.
Huber, J., jt. auth. see Bresinsky, A.
Huber, Michael. Olympus OM-2 Spot-Program.
Huber, P., jt. auth. see Frauenfelder, P.
Hubert, J., jt. auth. see Shapcott, D.
Huberty, Robert & Ludwig, Catherine, eds. The Annual Guide to Public Policy Experts, 1985.
Hubickey, John F. Shards.
Hubig, Chr. & Rahden, W. Van, eds. Kritischer Wissenschafts-Theorie.
Hubinont, P. O., et al, eds. see International Seminar on Reproductive Physiology & Sexual Endocrinology Staff.
Hubler, G. K., et al, eds. Ion Implantation & Ion Beam Processing of Materials: Proceedings of the 3rd Symposium on Ion Implantation & Ion Beam Processing of Materials, Boston, MA, Nov. 1983.
Hubley, Faith & Hubley, John. The Hat.
Hubley, Faith, jt. auth. see Hubley, John.
Hubley, John & Hubley, Faith. Dig: A Journey under the Earth's Crust.
Hubley, John, jt. auth. see Hubley, Faith.
Huch, Ricarda. Der Letzte Sommer. Cunz, Dieter, ed.
Huchton, Laura M. Protect Your Child: A Parent's Safeguard Against Child Abduction & Sexual Abuse.
Huck, Charlotte S. Children's Literature in the Elementary School.
Huck, Gabe. Major Feasts & Seasons: Christmastime.
--Major Feasts & Seasons: Eastertime.
Huck, Gabe, ed. Simple Gifts.
Huck, Gabe & Sloyan, Virginia, eds. Parishes & Families: A Model for Christian Formation Through Liturgy.
Huck, P. M. & Toft, P., eds. Treatment of Drinking Water for Organic Contaminants: Proceedings of the Second National Conference on Drinking Water, Edmonton, Alberta, Canada, 7-8 April 1986.
Hucker, Charles O. The Ming Dynasty: Its Origins & Evolving Institutions.
--Two Studies on Ming History.
Huckins, Sue E. My Life Is Love.
Huckleberry, Alan W., jt. auth. see Strother, Edward S.
Hucknall, D. J. Selective Oxidation of Hydrocarbons.
Huculak, M. When Russia Was in America: The Alaska Boundary Treaty Negotiations, 1824-25.
Hudak, Joseph. Gardening with Perennials.
Huddart, Henry. Comparative Structure & Function of Muscle.
Huddle, David. A Dream with No Stump Roots in It: Stories.
Huddleston, Kenneth F. If Productivity Is the Problem.
Huddleston, Lee E. Origins of the American Indians: European Concepts, 1492-1729.
Huddleston, Sisley. France: The Tragic Years.
Huddlestone, Richard & Leonard, Stanley L., eds. Plasma Diagnostic Techniques.
Hudec, John. An Empirical Analysis of the Circular Dichroism of Chiral Olefins.
Hudiburg, Everett, ed. see International Fire Service Training Association Staff.
Hudiburg, Everett, ed. see International Fire Services Training Association Committee.
Hudlicka, O. Circulation of Skeletal Muscle.
Hudman, Lloyd E., ed. Directory of Tourism Education Programs: Guide to Programs in Aviation, Hospitality & Tourism.
Hudner, H. Kennedy. Heirs of the Kingdom.
Hudnut, Robert K. An Active Man & the Christ.
--Sensitive Man & the Christ.
Hudon, Paul. The Valley & Its Peoples: An Illustrated History of the Lower Merrimack.
Hudson, Anna. Kiss the Tears Away.
--Taking a Chance.
Hudson, B. & Peticolas, W. L., eds. Proceedings of the International Conference on Raman Spectroscopy, 10th.
Hudson, B., jt. ed. see Peticolas, W. L.
Hudson, C. Computer Graphics for Artists.
Hudson, Charles M., ed. Four Centuries of Southern Indians.
Hudson, Christopher. Where the Rainbow Ends.
Hudson, Christopher N., jt. auth. see Howkins, John.
Hudson, Derek. Thomas Barnes of the Times. Child, Harold, ed.
Hudson, Derek, ed. Modern English Short Stories.
Hudson, Eleanor. A Whale of a Rescue. Gerver, Jane, ed.
Hudson, Heather. A Bibliography of Telecommunications & Development.
Hudson, Heather, ed. New Directions in Satellite Communications: Challenges for North & South (Conference Proceedings)
Hudson, Henry T. Papal Power.
Hudson, Herman & Imhoof, Maurice L. From Paragraph to Theme.
Hudson, Howard P. Publishing Newsletters.
Hudson, Jack W., jt. ed. see Wang, Lawrence.
Hudson, James. Two Persons for One Job.
Hudson, James B., et al. Polyoma Virus: Current Research.
Hudson, Jean B. Rivers of Time.
Hudson, Joe & Galaway, Burt, eds. Victims, Offenders, & Alternative Sanctions.
Hudson, Joe, jt. ed. see Fogel, David.
Hudson, Keith. Introducing CAL: A Practical Guide to Writing Computer Assisted Learning Programs.
Hudson, Manley O. Permanent Court of International Justice, 1920-1942: A Treatise.
Hudson, Margaret W. All About Me Books.
Hudson, Margaret W., jt. auth. see Weaver, Ann A.
Hudson, Michael, ed. see Everett, Alexander.
Hudson, Mike, et al. Bicycle Planning: Policy & Practice.
Hudson, Nathaniel. On the Fringe of the Getto.
Hudson, Nora E. Ultra-Royalism & the French Restoration.
Hudson, Peter & Halls, David. Favorite Recipes from Hudson & Halls.
Hudson, R. An Atlas of EEC Affairs.
Hudson, R. & Lewis, J., eds. Regional Planning in Europe.
Hudson, R., jt. ed. see Lewis, J.
Hudson, R. F. Structure & Mechanism in Organo-Phosphorus Chemistry.
Hudson, Ray. State Policies, Party Politics, & Regional Change.
Hudson, Richard. Word Grammar.
Hudson, Ronald, jt. ed. see Kelley, Philip.
Hudson, Van D., ed. Choice Messages from Free Will Baptist Pulpits.
Hudson, W. H. Far Away & Long Ago.
Hudson, W. J. Australia & the Colonial Question at the United Nations.
Hudson, W. J., ed. Australia & the League of Nations.
--Australia, Papua & New Guinea.
Hudson, William H. The Purple Land.
Hudson, Wilson M. Andy Adams: His Life & Writings.
Hudspeth, C. M. Cases on Torts: A Baker's Dozen.
Hudspeth, Ron. Southern Nights & City Lights.
Huebel, Harry R. Jack Kerouac.
--Things in the Driver's Seat.
Hueber, R. P., tr. see Dertinger, H. & Jung, H.
Huebner, S. S. & Black, Kenneth. Life Insurance.
Huebner, S. S., jt. auth. see Black, Kenneth, Jr.
Huebner, Theodore & Voss, Carl. This Is Israel.
Hueckel, Glenn R. The Napoleonic Wars & Their Impact on Factor Returns & Output Growth in England: 1793-1895.
Hueck-Van Der Plas, E. H., ed. Disposal of Chemical Waste in the Marine Environment: Implications of International Dumping Conventions: Proceedings of the International Symposium, Rotterdam, Sept 11-12, 1980.
Huelsberg, Enid L. Sometimes of Children.
Hueper, W. C. Occupational & Environmental Cancers of the Respiratory System.
Huerts, Margie C., jt. auth. see Tchudi, Stephen N.
Huestis, Douglas W., et al. Practical Blood Transfusion.
Huey. Elementary Physical Science.
Hueze, Francios E., jt. ed. see Goodman, Richard E.
Hufbauer, Gary C. & Rosen, Howard F. Domestic Adjustment & International Trade.
Huffaker, C. B., ed. Biological Control.
--Biological Control.
Huffman, Carolyn & Barrow, Lu Ann. Life Between the Questions.
Huffman, D. C. Guidelines for Prescription Pricing Systems.
Huffman, Harry. Programmed Business Mathematics.
Huffman, Jannie B. Physical Science: Introductory Experiments.
Huffman, John W., et al. The Gynecology of Childhood & Adolescence.
Huffmon, Herbert B. Amorite Personal Names in the Mari Texts: A Structural & Lexical Study.
Hufton, Richard A., jt. auth. see Tucker, Ronald D.
Hug, James E., ed. Tracing the Spirit: Communities, Social Action & Theological Reflection.
Hugenberg, Lawrence W., Sr. & Owens, Alfred W., II. Structures for Business & Professional Speech: A Working Resource Manual.
Hugget, Frank. The Land Question & European Society Since 1650.
Huggins, Alice M. The Red Chair Waits.
Huggins, Larry. Believer's Bible Companion.
Huggins, Patricia J. Conquering Disease the Natural Way: Confessions of a Hypoglycemic Victim.

Hughart, David P. Prospects for Traditional & Non-Conventional Energy Sources in Developing Countries.
Hughes. The Elementary Principal's Handbook.
Hughes, A. Daniel. Tombstone Story: The Biography of an Arizona Pioneer.
Hughes, A. I., ed. Lead Nineteen Sixty-Eight: Proceedings, International Conference on Lead - 3rd - Venice - 1968.
Hughes, Andrew. Medieval Manuscripts for Mass & Office: A Guide to Their Organization & Terminology.
Hughes, Ann J. Applied Mathematics: For Business, Economics & the Social Sciences.
Hughes, Arthur F. Aspects of Neural Ontogeny.
Hughes, Arthur H. & Allen, Morse S. Connecticut Place Names.
Hughes, Arthur J. American Government.
Hughes, B., ed. see European Congress Of Neurosurgery - Rome - 1963.
Hughes, B. P. Limit State Theory for Reinforced Concrete Design.
Hughes, Barrie. The Martini-Henry Modification.
Hughes, Bernice, jt. auth. see Gooding, Marion F.
Hughes, C. J., jt. ed. see Flood, J. E.
Hughes, Catharine R., ed. American Theatre Annual, 1978-1979.
--American Theatre Annual, 1979-1980.
--New York Theatre Annual: 1976-77.
--New York Theatre Annual: 1977-78.
Hughes, Catherine A., ed. Economic Education: A Guide to Information Sources.
Hughes, Charles W. The Human Side of Music.
Hughes, Colin A., jt. auth. see Western, J. S.
Hughes, D. J. Science & Starvation.
Hughes, Dana, et al. The Health of America's Children: Maternal & Child Health Data Book.
--Maternal & Child Health Data Book: The Health of America's Children.
Hughes, David. The Joke of the Century.
Hughes, Dean. Brothers.
--Millie Willenheimer & the Chestnut Corporation.
Hughes, Dolores. Bitter Dreams.
Hughes, Edward, et al. Colorectal Surgery.
Hughes, Emmet J. Church & the Liberal Society.
--Ordeal of Power: A Political Memoir of the Eisenhower Years.
Hughes, G. Bernard. Living Crafts.
Hughes, G. M., ed. Respiration of Amphibious Vertebrates.
Hughes, G. R., jt. ed. see Jarman, A. O.
Hughes, Gary E. & Mason, Paul J. Insurance Products under the Securities Laws 1985: New Regulatory Initiatives: A Course Handbook.
Hughes, Glenn. History of the American Theatre, 1700-1950.
Hughes, H. Stuart. Contemporary Europe: A History.
Hughes, J. Donald. In the House of Stone & Light: A Human History of Grand Canyon.
Hughes, J. F. & Johnston, R. J. Geography & the Urban Environment: Progress in Research & Applications.
Hughes, James W. Economic Growth & Residential Patterns: A Methodological Investigation.
--Suburbanization Dynamics & the Future of the City.
--Urban Indicators, Metropolitan Evolution & Public Policy.
Hughes, James W., jt. auth. see James, Franklin J.
Hughes, James W., jt. ed. see Sternlieb, George.
Hughes, Jim. Uncle Sam, Super Cop: A Satirical View of American History.
Hughes, John. Before the Crying Ends.
Hughes, John, jt. auth. see Jordan, W. J.
Hughes, Joseph H., Jr. The Making of a Coast Guard Officer.
Hughes, K. Scott, jt. auth. see Dickmeyer, Nathan.
Hughes, K. Scott, et al. A Management Reporting Manual for Colleges. Nevin, Jeanne, ed.
Hughes, Karrel. God Kind of Marriage.
Hughes, Kathy. A Collector's Guide to Nineteenth Century Jugs.
Hughes, Langston. Good Morning, Revolution: Uncollected Writings of Social Protest. Berry, Faith, ed.
--I Wonder as I Wander: An Autobiographical Journey.
--Simple's Uncle Sam.
Hughes, Langston, et al. Pictorial History of Black Americans.
Hughes, Leo. The Drama's Patrons: A Study of the Eighteenth-Century London Audience.
Hughes, M. K., jt. auth. see Hodkinson, I. D.
Hughes, Mary & Kennedy, Mary, eds. New Futures: Changing Women's Education.
Hughes, Maysie J. & Barnes, Charles D., eds. Neural Control of Circulation.
Hughes, Megan. Yesterday's Music.
Hughes, Megan & Ohrbach, Frank. Givers & Takers.
Hughes, Melba. To You from Me, Folk Verse.
Hughes, Monica. Crisis on Conshelf Ten.
Hughes, Nancie, jt. auth. see Opton, Gene.
Hughes, Norton J. The Airport People.
Hughes, Owen F. Ship Structural Design: A Rationally-Based, Computer Aided, Optimization Approach.
Hughes, P., jt. auth. see Morrison, C.
Hughes, Patrick M., tr. see Fernandes, Florestan.
Hughes, Peter & Williams, David. The Varied Pattern: Studies in the 18th Century.
Hughes, Philip E. Christian Ethics in Secular Society: An Introduction to Christian Ethics.
Hughes, R. D. Living Insects.
Hughes, R. Kent. Behold the Lamb.
--Behold the Man.
Hughes, R. N., jt. auth. see Barnes, R. S.
Hughes, R. R., jt. ed. see Rippin, D. W.
Hughes, Raymond. The Almost Murder.
Hughes, Richard & Brewin, Bob. The Tranquilizing of America: Pill-Popping & the American Way of Life.
Hughes, Richard & Serig, Joseph A., eds. Evangelism: The Ministry of the Church.
Hughes, Robert J., jt. auth. see McKenzie, Jimmy C.
Hughes, Robert J., et al. Business.
Hughes, Samantha. Desert Splendor.
--Diamonds in the Sky.
Hughes, Shirley. Lucy & Tom's Day.
Hughes, Shirley, ed. Over the Moon: A Book of Sayings.
Hughes, Susan. Long Term Care: Options in an Expanding Market.
Hughes, T. J., ed. Finite Element Methods for Convection Dominated Flows.
Hughes, T. J., et al, eds. New Concepts in Finite Element Analysis.
Hughes, Ted, ed. see Shakespeare, William.
Hughes, Ted, jt. ed. see Weissbort, Daniel.
Hughes, Ted, tr. see Pilinszky, Janos.
Hughes, Theodore E. & Klein, David. A Family Guide to Estate Planning, Funeral Arrangements, & Settling an Estate after Death.
--The Parents' Financial Survival Guide.
Hughes, V. W., jt. ed. see Bromley, D. Allan.
Hughes, Vernon & Wu, C. S., eds. Muon Physics. Incl. Vol. 1; Vol. 2. Weak Interactions; Vol. 3. Chemistry & Solids. Acad Pr.
Hughes, W. G. The Magdalene & Other Poems.
Hughes, Walter T. & Buescher, E. Stephen. Pediatric Procedures.
Hughes, William. Aces High.
--Annual Editions: Western Civilization.
--Western Civilization.
--Western Civilization.
Hughes, William F. Introduction to Viscous Flow.
Hughes, Winifred. The Maniac in the Cellar: Sensation Novels of the Eighteen Sixties.
Hughes-Evans, ed. Environmental Education-Key Issues of the Future: Proceedings of the Conference Held at the College of Technology, Farnborough, England.
Hughey, J. D. & Johnson, Arlee W. Speech Communication: Foundation & Challenges.
Hugill, Peter J. & Doughty, Robin W., eds. Field Trip Guide: AAG San Antonio 1982.
Hugill, Stan. Shanties from the Seven Seas.
Huglin, M. B., ed. Light Scattering from Polymer Solutions.
Hugman, Bruce. Act Natural.
Hugo. Computing Economics.
--Fourth Generation.
Hugo, Graeme J. Population Mobility & Wealth Transfers in Indonesia & Other 3rd World Societies.
Hugo, I. S. Marketing & the Computer.
Hugo, Richard. Death & the Good Life.
--Farewell to Russia.
--The Lady in Kicking Horse Reservoir.
--The Real West Marginal Way: A Poet's Autobiography. Hugo, Ripley S. & Welch, James, eds.
--Thirty-One Letters & Thirteen Dreams: Poems.
--The Triggering Town: Lectures & Essays on Poetry & Writing.
--What Thou Lovest Well, Remains American: Poems.
Hugo, Ripley S., ed. see Hugo, Richard.
Hugo, Thomas. Bewick Collector.
Hugo, Victor. Actes et Paroles: Avant et Pendant l'Exil.
--Actes et Paroles: Avant, Pendant et Depuis l'Exil.
Hugo, W. B., ed. Inhibition & Destruction of the Microbial Cell.
Hugo, W. B., ed. see Russell, A. D.
Hugo, W. B., jt. ed. see Skinner, F. A.
Hugunin, John D. Donald Zolan's Oil Paintings of Early Childhood.
Huheey, James E. & Stupka, Arthur. Amphibians & Reptiles of Great Smoky Mountains National Park.
Huhne, Christopher, jt. auth. see Lever, Harold.
Hui, Lee T. The Communist Organization in Singapore: Its Techniques of Manpower Mobilization & Management, 1948-1966.
Hui, Ta. Swampland Flowers: The Letters & Lectures of Zen Master Ta Hui. Cleary, Christopher, tr.
Huijing, F. & Lee, E. Y., eds. Protein Phosphorylation in Control Mechanisms.
Huijing, F., ed. see Miami Winter Symposium Staff.
Huilian, Chen, jt. auth. see Lufeng, Tang.
Huisingh, Donald & Bailey, Vicki, eds. Making Pollution Prevention Pay: Ecology with Economy As Policy.
Huisman, L. Artificial Groundwater Discharge.
Hulanicki, Adam & Glab, Stanislaw, eds. Redox Indicators: Characteristics & Applications.
Hulbert, Archer B. History of the Niagara River.
Hulbert, James R. Dictionaries of British & America.
Huldman. ABC of Ear, Nose & Throat.
Huldt, Bo, ed. see Swedish Institute of International Affairs.
Hulin, Michel, ed. see International Conference on Physics of Semiconductors Staff.
Hull, Betty. Cobwebs & Crystal: Colorado's Grand Old Hotels.
Hull, Beverly W. Spanish Moon.
Hull, Bill. Jesus Christ, Disciplemaker.
--Right Thinking: Insights for Spiritual Growth.
Hull, C. Hadlai, jt. auth. see Nie, Norman H.
Hull, Clark L. A Behavior System.
--Essentials of Behavior.
Hull, Clark L., et al. Mathematico-Deductive Theory of Rote Learning: A Study in Scientific Methodology.
Hull, Denison B., tr. see Babrius, Valerius.
Hull, Frederick, jt. auth. see Hubatka, Milton C.
Hull, Gloria T., ed. Give Us Each Day: The Diary of Alice Dunbar-Nelson.
Hull, Gloria T., ed. see Dunbar-Nelson, Alice.
Hull, Helen R. & Drury, Michael, eds. Writer's Roundtable.
Hull, John, ed. New Directions in Religious Education.
Hull, Judy B. When You Receive a Child.
Hull, Nancy R., et al. High Blood Pressure.
Hull, R. F., ed. see Weber, Alfred.
Hull, R. F., tr. see Jung Institute, Curatorium Staff.
Hull, Raymond H. Hearing Impairment among Aging Persons.
Hull, Richard. Murder of My Aunt.
Hull, Robert., jt. auth. see Van Orman, Ward T.
Hull, Valerie & Simpson, Mayling, eds. Breastfeeding, Child Health & Child Spacing: Cross-Cultural Perspectives.
Hull, Vida J. Hans Memlinc's Paintings for the Hospital of Saint John in Bruges.
Hull, William I. Two Hague Conferences & Their Contributions to International Law.
Hull, Wythe M., Jr. History of Pepsi Cola MBC.
Hullmandel, Charles J. The Art of Drawing on Stone, Giving a Full Explanation of the Various Styles of the Different Methods to Be Employed to Ensure Success, & of the Modes of Correcting, As Well As of the Several Causes of Failure.
Hulls, Mary E. Pretrial Detention: A Bibliography.
Hulme, Charles. Reading Retardation & Multi-Sensory Teaching.
Hulme, F. Edward. The Birth & Development of Ornament.
--Proverb Lore.
Hulme, Kathryn. Undiscovered Country: In Search of Gurdjieff.
Hulme, Susan, jt. auth. see Gillham, Bill.
Hulme, William. Living with Myself.
Hulme, William E. Am I Losing My Faith?
--Building a Christian Marriage.
--Creative Loneliness.
--Dealing with Doublemindedness.
--Two Ways of Caring: A Biblical Design for Balanced Ministry.
--Your Pastor's Problems: A Guide for Ministers & Laymen.
--Your Potential Under God: Resources for Growth.
Hulme, William E., ed. see Vayhinger, John M.
Huls, Mary E. Adaptive Reuse of School Buildings: A Bibliography.
--Agri-Finance: Banks, Farmers, & Agricultural Policy.
--Alternative Sentencing, Nineteen Seventy-Nine to Nineteen Eighty-Four: A Selective Bibliography.
--The Architecture & Interior Design of Beauty Salons: A Periodical Bibliography.
--Citizen Participation - Alternatives in Municipal Services Delivery: A Bibliography.
--Civic Center Architecture: A Bibliography.
--Cladding: A Bibliography.
--Computer Applications in Personnel & Human Resources Management: A Bibliography.
--Computers in Criminal Justice: A Selective Bibliography.
--Computers in Police Work: A Selective Bibliography.
--Contracting-Out - Alternatives in Municipal Services Delivery: A Bibliography.
--Conversion vs. Preservation - America's Farmland: A Bibliography.
--Criminal Justice Reform - Determinate Sentencing: A Bibliography.
--Determining Compensation in the Public Sector: A Bibliography.
--Elevators & Escalators in Architectural Design: A Bibliography.
--Exclusionary & Inclusionary Zoning: A Bibliography.
--Gunnar Birkerts: A Bibliography.
--The History & Implementation of Employee Assistance Programs: A Bibliography.
--Infill: A Selective Bibliography.
--Infrastructure: A Bibliography.
--Interagency & Interstate Cooperation in Criminal Justice: A Select Bibliography.
--Lecture Hall Design: A Bibliography.
--Moshe Safdie, Canadian Architect: A Bibliography.
--Postmodernism: A Bibliography.
--Productivity-Performance Measures for Public Services at the Local Level: A Bibliography.
--Records Management for State & Local Government: A Bibliography.
--Seaside & Lakeside Domestic Architecture: A Bibliography.
--Zoning & Development Rights: A Bibliography.
Hulse, James W. The University of Nevada: A Centennial History.
Hulse, Lisa S., ed. Internships 1985.
--Internships 1986.
Hulsizer, Allan. The Indian Boy's Days: The Indian Then & Now-His Presence & Influence on Our Life-style.
--Our Burro & Other Animal Friends.
Hulsizer, Allan, jt. auth. see Hulsizer, Marion.
Hulsizer, Marion & Hulsizer, Allan. My Pony, Johnny.
Hulten, Pontus, ed. see Breton, Andre, et al.
Hultgren, Arland J. Jesus & His Adversaries: The Form & Function of the Conflict Stories in the Synoptic Tradition.
--Paul's Gospel & Mission: The Outlook from His Letter to the Romans.
Hultgvist, Bengt & Hagfors, Tor A. High-Latitude Space Plasma Physics.
Hults, Dorothy N. New Amsterdam Days & Ways: The Dutch Settlers of New York.
Hulzen, J. A. van see Van Hulzen, J. A.
Human Rights Foundation Staff. Demystifying Homosexuality: A Teaching Guide about Lesbians & Gay Men.
Humble, Richard. Fraser of North Cape: The Life of Admiral of the Fleet Lord Fraser, 1888-1981.
--Napoleon's Peninsular Marshals: A Reassessment.
--U. S. Fleet Carriers of World War II.
Humble, S. Introduction to Particle Production in Hadron Physics.
Hume, Abraham. Learned Societies & Printing Clubs of the United Kingdom.
Hume, David. The Letters of David Hume. Greig, J. Y., ed.
--The New Letters of David Hume. Klibansky, Raymond & Mossner, Ernest C., eds.
Hume, Diane, ed. see Stanley, David.
Hume, George B. Searching for God.
Hume, Leslie, ed. see Kinzer, Bruce L.
Hume, Leslie, ed. see Kruppa, Patricia S.
Hume, Leslie, ed. see Schoenl, William J.
Hume, Margaret L., ed. see Management Sciences for Health Staff, et al.
Hume, Martin A. Philip Second of Spain. Ketcham, Henry, ed.
Hume, Wilfred I. Biofeedback. Horrobin, D. F., ed.
--Biofeedback. Horrobin, D. F., ed.
Humenuk, Stanley. Automatic Shelving & Book Retrieval: A Contribution Toward a Progressive Philosophy of Library Service for a Research Library.
Hume-Rothery, W. & Cole, B. R. Atomic Theory for Students of Metallurgy.
Humes, Charles W., jt. auth. see Hummel, Dean L.
Humes, James C. How to Be a Very Important Person.
Humez, Jean M., ed. Gifts of Power: The Writings of Rebecca Jackson, Black Visionary, Shaker Eldress.
Humfrey, Belinda, ed. Recollections of the Powys Brothers.
Humfrey, Michael. Sea Shells of the West Indies: A Guide to the Marine Molluscs of the Caribbean.
--A Shadow in the Weave.
Humiston, Gerard E., jt. auth. see Brady, James E.
Humm, Harold J. The Marine Algae of Virginia.
Hummel & Seebeck. Mathematics of Finance.
Hummel, Dean L. & Humes, Charles W. Pupil Services: Development, Coordination, Administration.
Hummel, Dean L., et al. Law & Ethics in Counseling.
Hummel, Dieter O. Polymer Spectroscopy.
Hummel, Robert P., Jr. Clinical Burn Therapy: A Management & Prevention Guide.
Humphrey, C. Surgical Nursing.
Humphrey, J. A., jt. ed. see Launder, B.
Humphrey, J. Edward. Emil Brunner. Patterson, Bob E., ed.
Humphrey, J. H., jt. ed. see Taliaferro, W. H.

Authors

Humphrey, J. H. see Taliaferro, W. H. & Humphrey, J. H.
Humphrey, N., et al. The Future of Cincinnati's Capital Plant.
--The Future of Cleveland's Capital Plant.
Humphreys. Search Within.
Humphreys Academy Patrons Staff. Festival.
Humphreys, Alice L. Angels in Pinafores.
--Heaven in My Hand.
--Three Hear the Bells.
Humphreys, C. A Popular Dictionary of Buddhism.
Humphreys, Fisher. Nineteenth Century Evangelical Theology.
Humphreys, J. E. Arithmetics Groups.
Humphreys, Joel D. Vendetta.
Humphreys, K. K. & McMillan, B. G., eds. Transactions of the American Association of Cost Engineers.
--Transactions of the American Association of Cost Engineers, 1980.
--Transactions of the American Association of Cost Engineers, 1981.
Humphreys, K. K. & Novak, T., eds. Transactions of the American Association of Cost Engineers.
Humphreys, Kenneth K. & Leonard, Joseph W., eds. Basic Mathematics & Computer Techniques for Coal Preparation & Mining.
Humphries, Patrick & Hunt, Chris. Bruce Springsteen: Blinded by the Light.
Humphries, Robert G. The Illustrated Apple LOGO Book.
Humphry, Derek & Wickett, Ann. Jean's Way: A Love Story.
Huna, Michael S. Havoc.
Hundley, Norris, Jr. Water & the West: The Colorado River Compact & the Politics of Water in the American West.
Huneke, Douglas K. The Moses of Rovno: The Stirring Story of Fritz Graeve, a German Christian Who Risked His Life to Lead Hundreds of Jews to Safety During the Holocaust.
Huneycutt, C. D. Among the Ashes: Six SF Horror Stories.
--Dinosaurs of North Carolina.
--A N. C. Outdoor Drama: Spanish Autumn.
--North Carolina's Extinct Prehistoric Mammals.
Huneycutt, C. D., ed. & intro. by. N. C. Writers & Writing: Essays.
Huneycutt, C. D., ed. N. C. Writers & Writing: Essays.
Hungerford, D. S., ed. Leg Length Discrepancy: The Injured Knee.
Hungerford, Thomas W. & Mercer, Richard. Algebra & Trigonometry.
Hungness, Carl, jt. ed. see Mahoney, John.
Hungry Wolf, Adolph & Hungry Wolf, Beverly. Shadows of the Buffalo: A Family Odyssey among the Indians.
Hungry Wolf, Beverly, jt. auth. see Hungry Wolf, Adolph.
Hunken, Jorie & Madama, John. Ladybugs & Lettuce Leaves. Hale, Dorinda & Hackman, Sandra, eds.
Hunker, Jeffrey A., ed. Structural Change in the U. S. Automobile Industry.
Hunkins, Dalton & Mugridge, Larry. Applied Finite Mathematics.
Hunnisett, Henry S. Retirement Guide for Canadians: Planning Now for a Comfortable Future.
Hunsacker, Philip & Alessandra, Anthony J. The Art of Managing People.
Hunsinger, George, ed. Karl Barth & Radical Politics.
Hunsinger, Marjorie & McComas, Donna C. Modern Business Correspondence.
Hunsucker, Vivian. Reap, So, & Harvest.
Hunt, A., jt. auth. see Hess, M. A.
Hunt, Albert. Hopes for Great Happenings: Alternatives in Education & Theatre.
Hunt, Alfred L. Corporate Cash Management Including Electronic Funds Transfer.
Hunt, Alice. Archeology of the Death Valley Salt Pan.
Hunt, B. Stather. Primitive Gospel Sources.
Hunt, Bernice, jt. auth. see Sager, Clifford J.
Hunt, Bernice K. Your Ant Is a Which: Fun with Homophones.
--Your Ant Is a Which: Fun with Homophones.
Hunt, Cecil. How to Write a Book.
Hunt, Chester L., jt. auth. see Horton, Paul B.
Hunt, Chris, jt. auth. see Humphries, Patrick.
Hunt, David. Confessions of a Scilly Birdman.
Hunt, David M., jt. auth. see Stewart, Alistair D.
Hunt, Derald D. California Criminal Law Manual.
Hunt, Diana. You, Your Stars & Your Partner.
Hunt, Don. What the Bible Says about the Unfolded Plan of God.
Hunt, Donnell R. Engineering Models for Agricultural Production.
Hunt, Edmund. Johannis Dominici Lucula Noctis.
Hunt, Florine E., ed. Public Utilities Information Sources.
Hunt, G. E., jt. auth. see Kondratyev, K. Y.
Hunt, G. E. & Ballard, J., eds. Atmospheric Spectroscopy: Proceedings of the International Workshop SERC Rutherford Appleton Laboratory, Chilton, Didcot, Oxon, U. K., July 19-21, 1983.
Hunt, G. P. Poems by Olive Hunt.
Hunt, Garry & Moore, Patrick. The Planet Venus.
Hunt, Gary T. Communication Skills in the Organization.
Hunt, George. The Centurion's Shadow.
Hunt, Gerry. The Zone of Silence.
Hunt, Gladys. Family Secrets: What You Need to Know to Build a Strong Christian Family.
Hunt, Gordon, jt. auth. see Gibbs, Kenneth G.
Hunt, Hugh. The Live Theatre: An Introduction to the History & Practice of the Stage.
Hunt, Hugh, et al. Revels History of Drama in English, Vol. 7: 1880 to the Present.
Hunt, Irene. The Lottery Rose.
--Lottery Rose.
--No Promises in the Wind.
Hunt, Irma. Dearest Madame: Handmade, Inexpensive Ways to Make a House a Home.
Hunt, J. M. Intelligence & Experience.
Hunt, J. N. No Higher Calling.
Hunt, J. W. Managing People at Work.
Hunt, James. Selected Readings in Sociobiology.
Hunt, Jeanne, ed. Being a Loving Wife.
--Raising a Joyful Family.
Hunt, John. Lee's Meadow Country.
Hunt, John D., ed. see Attiret, Jean D. & Shenstone, William.
Hunt, John D., ed. see Caus, Isaac.
Hunt, John D., ed. see Johnson, George W.
Hunt, John D., ed. see Kent, William.
Hunt, John D., ed. see Loudon, J. C.
Hunt, John D., ed. see Mavor, William.
Hunt, John D., ed. see Morris, Robert & Trusler, John.
Hunt, John D., ed. see Mountaine, Dydymus.
Hunt, John D., ed. see Walpole, Horace.
Hunt, John D., ed. see Whatley, Thomas.
Hunt, Lee M., jt. auth. see Groves, Donald G.
Hunt, Linda L., jt. auth. see Lubben, Twyla.
Hunt, M. Briggs. Greco-Roman Wrestling.
Hunt, Morton. Gay: What Teenagers Should Know about Homosexuality & the AIDS Crisis.
--Gay: What You Should Know About Homosexuality.
Hunt, Nancy, ed. Mirror Image.
Hunt, R. Multiplication & Division.
Hunt, R. L., jt. auth. see Cain, H. W.
Hunt, Richard A. & Shultz, Richard H., Jr., eds. Lessons from an Unconventional War: Reassessing U. S. Strategies for Future Conflicts.
Hunt, Robert D. Fruit & Vegetable Exports from the Mediterranean Area to the EEC.
Hunt, Robert, jt. auth. see Arras, John.
Hunt, Rockwell D. California in the Making.
Hunt, Rod. Hippo Learns His Name.
Hunt, Ruth, jt. auth. see Linke, Maria Z.
Hunt, S. Polysaccharide-Protein Complexes in Invertebrates.
Hunt, Sara M., et al. Nutrition: Principles & Clinical Practice.
Hunt, Shelby D. Marketing Theory: The Philosophy of Marketing Science.
Hunt, Sonja M., et al. Measuring Health Status.
Hunt, Thomas, jt. auth. see Kreiser, Ralph.
Hunt, Tim, ed. see Jeffers, Robinson.
Hunt, V. Daniel. Energy Dictionary.
--Handbook of Energy Technology: Trends & Perspectives.
Hunt, William R. Dictionary of Rogues.
Hunter, A. M. The New Testament for Today.
Hunter, Alan. Amorous Leander.
--Gently with the Innocents.
Hunter, Allan. James Stewart.
--Joseph Conrad & the Ethics of Darwinism: The Challenges of Science.
Hunter, Archibald M. According to John: The New Look at the Fourth Gospel.
--Gleanings from the New Testament.
--Introducing New Testament Theology.
Hunter, Beatrice T. Consumer Beware!
--Fact-Book on Fermented Foods & Beverages.
--Gardening Without Poisons.
--The Sugar Trap & How to Avoid It.
Hunter, Beverly, et al. Guide to Managing Information with Your Personal Computer.
Hunter, Bob, jt. auth. see Snypp, Wilbur.
Hunter, Brian. Soviet-Yugoslav Relations, 1948-1972: A Bibliography of Soviet, Western & Yugoslav Comment & Analysis.
Hunter, Bruce H. Fifty Pascal Programs.
Hunter, C. Bruce. Masonic Dictionary.
Hunter, Claud, jt. auth. see Weathers, Thomas.
Hunter, Damion. The Centurions II: Barbarian Princess.
--The Emperor's Games.
Hunter, Dard. Paper Making in Pioneer America.
Hunter, David, ed. North Carolina Modern Erotica.
--North Carolina Modern Erotica.
--North Carolina Modern Erotica.
Hunter, Donald. The Diseases of Occupations.
Hunter, Doreen, jt. auth. see Willsher, Betty.
Hunter, Earl D. Out of Heartland Hell.
Hunter, Edith F. Sue Ellen.
Hunter, Elizabeth. The Bonds of Matrimony.
--One More Time.
Hunter, Evan. The Blackboard Jungle.
--The Blackboard Jungle.
--The Blackboard Jungle.
--Far from the Sea.
--Lizzie.
Hunter, G K. Paradise Lost.
Hunter, Grover C., Jr. Dawn at Red Mountain.
Hunter, Harold D. Spirit-Baptism: A Pentecostal Alternative.
Hunter House Staff. Charting Your Way Thru' PMS. Rana, K. S. & Wassil-Grimm, C., eds.
Hunter, Ira. The Epstein-Barr Virus Diet.
Hunter, J. Paul, ed. Norton Introduction to Literature: Poetry.
--The Norton Introduction to Poetry.
--The Plays of Edward Moore.
Hunter, Jack. The Terror Alliance.
Hunter, Jack D. Judgment in Blood.
Hunter, James T. Our Second Revolution.
Hunter, Jillian. Heart of the Storm.
--Shadows of Splendor.
Hunter, Jim. Tom Stoppard's Plays.
Hunter, Jim & Shelley, Marshall. A Man Against the Mountain.
Hunter, Joan H., jt. ed. see Shepherd, Rebecca A.
Hunter, John M. & Foley, James W. Economic Problems of Latin America.
Hunter, Kristin. Boss Cat.
--The Lakestown Rebellion.
--Lou in the Limelight.
--Soul Brothers & Sister Lou.
Hunter, Lea A. & Sienkiewicz, Magdalen. Learning Clubs for the Poor.
Hunter, Norman. Professor Branestawm's Crunchy Crockery.
--Professor Branestawm's Hair-Raising Idea.
Hunter, Norman D. Angels Look the Same.
--Walk in the Sun & Other Stories.
Hunter, Richard S. The Measurement of Appearance.
Hunter, Ronald P. Automated Process Control Systems: Concepts & Hardware.
Hunter, S. Leslie. The Scottish Educational System.
Hunter, Sam. Tony Smith, Ten Elements & Throwback. Pace Gallery Publications Staff, ed.
Hunter, Sam & Jacobus, John. Modern Art from Post Impressionisms to the Present.
Hunter, Samuel D. The Dictionary of Anagrams.
Hunter, Steve. Home Inspection Workbook.
Hunter, Thom. Like Father, Like Sons (And Daughter Too)
Hunter, W. J. & Smeets, G. P., eds. The Evaluation of Toxicological Data for the Protection of Public Health: Proceedings of an International Colloquium, Luxemburg, 1976.
Hunter, W. M. & Corrie, J. E. T. Immunoassays for Clinical Chemistry.
Hunter, William B., Jr., ed. see Jonson, Ben.
Huntford, Roland. Scott & Amundsen: The Race to the South Pole.
Huntingford, Peter J., et al, eds. Perinatal Medicine.
Huntington, Archer M., tr. see Cid Campeador.
Huntington Art Gallery Staff. The Gift of the Greeks: Art & Civilization of Ancient Greece.
Huntington, D. Art & the Excited Spirit: America in the Romantic Period.
Huntington Free Library, Reading Room Staff. Dictionary Catalog of the American Indian Collection.
Huntington, Hillard B. Elastic Constants of Crystals.
Huntington, J. F., tr. see De Jouvenel, Bertrand.
Huntington, Lee P. Maybe a Miracle.
Huntington, Mairi. The Great Game.
Huntington, Samuel P. American Politics: The Promise of Disharmony.
--Soldier & the State: The Theory & Politics of Civil Military Relations.
Huntington, Samuel P. & Nelson, Joan M. No Easy Choice: Political Participation in Developing Countries.
Huntley, Barbara D., tr. see OAS, General Secretariat.
Huntley, C. C. The Life of One Doctor & His Patients.
Huntly, Moira. Draw Still Life.
Huntoon, Irene, tr. see Alovert, Nina.
Hunziker, J. C., ed. see Jaeger, E.
Hunziker, N. Experimental Studies on Guinea Pig's Eczema: Their Significance in Human Eczema.
Hurch, Heidi, et al. Great Decisions 86 Activity Book.
Hurd, David. Home to My Island.
Hurd, F. K., jt. auth. see Paris, D. T.
Hurd, Florence. Legacy.
--Rommany.
--The Secret of Awen Castle.
--Shadows of the Heart.
--Voyage of the Secret Duchess.
Hurd, Jerrie W. Our Sisters in the Bible.
Hurding, Roger F. Christian Care & Counseling: A Practical Guide.
Hurdle, J. Frank. Low Blood Sugar: A Doctor's Guide to Its Effective Control.
Hureau, J. C. & Monod, T., eds. Check-List of the Fishes of the North-Eastern Atlantic & the Mediterranean.
Hureau, J. C., jt. ed. see Fischer, W.
Hurlburt, Allen. Publication Design: A Guide to Page Layout, Typography, Format & Style.
Hurley, A. C. Introduction to the Electron Theory of Small Molecules.
Hurley, Alfred F. Billy Mitchell: Crusader for Air Power.
Hurley, Andrew, tr. see Arrabal, Fernando.
Hurley, Andrew, tr. see Sainz, Gustavo.
Hurley, J. Finley. Sorcery.
Hurley, J. V. Acute Inflammation.
Hurley, James. Intermediate Calculus.
Hurley, James P. & Garrod, Claude. Principles of Physics.
Hurley, John. Assassination American Style.
Hurley, Judith, jt. auth. see Rodale Food Center Staff.
Hurley, Leslie, jt. auth. see Osgood, William.
Hurley, Patrick M. How Old Is the Earth?
Hurley, Robert, tr. see Foucault, Michel.
Hurll, Estelle M. Life of Our Lord in Art: With Some Account of the Artistic Treatment of the Life of St. John the Baptist.
Hurlock, Elizabeth B. Adolescent Development.
--Child Growth & Development.
Hurme, R. & Pesonen, M. Finnish General Dictionary: English-Finnish.
Hurme, R., et al. Finnish-English General Dictionary.
Hurrle, Karl, et al. Technical Dictionary of Vacuum Physics & Vacuum Technology (English, French, German, Russian)
Hurst, A., jt. auth. see Gould, G.
Hurst, J. Willis. Clinical Essays on the Heart. Incl. Vol. 1; Vol. 2; Vol. 3; Vol. 4. McGraw.
--Clinical Essays on the Heart.
--The Heart: Update II.
--The Heart: Update IV.
--The Heart: Update V.
--Medicine for the Practicing Physician.
Hurst, J. Willis & Pretest Services, Inc. Staff. The Heart: Pretest Self-Assessment & Review.
Hurst, J. Willis & Pretest Services, Inc. The Heart: Pretest Self-Assessment & Review with CME Examination.
Hurst, J. Willis, ed. The Heart: Update I.
Hurst, J. Willis & Logue, R. Bruce, eds. The Heart.
Hurst, J. Willis, et al. The Heart.
--The Heart.
Hurst, Leanard L., ed. see U. S. Department of the Interior, Federal Water Pollution Control Administration, Committtee on Water Quality Criteria, et al.
Hurst, Leslie & Hurst, Ronald, eds. Fly & Survive: Safety in General Aviation.
Hurst, Michael E. I Came to the City: Essays & Comments on the Urban Scene.
Hurst, Paul, jt. ed. see Cameron, John.
Hurst, Ronald, jt. ed. see Hurst, Leslie.
Hurst, Vernon W., jt. auth. see Klineburger, Bert.
Hurst, Walter E. Copyright Registration Forms PA & SR: How to Prepare Applications to Register Songs, Movies, Performing Arts Works & Sound Recordings with the U. S. Copyright Office. Gentry, Matthew, ed.
Hurt, Harry, III. Texas Rich: The Hunt Dynasty from the Early Oil Days Through the Silver Crash.
Hurt, Henry. Reasonable Doubt: An Investigation into the Assassination of John F. Kennedy.
Hurtado, Elena, jt. auth. see Scrimshaw, Susan C.
Hurtado, Larry. Mark: A Good News Commentary.
Hurter, Bill. Money-Making Photography.
--Sports Photography.
Hurwicz, Michael. Networking With The IBM Network & Cluster.
Hurwitt, Samuel. Treasury of Epigrams.
Hurwitz, Al. Programs of Promise: Art in the Schools.
Hurwitz, Al & Madeja, Stanley. The Joyous Vision: A Sourcebook for Elementary Art Appreciation.
Hurwitz, Al, jt. auth. see Gaitskell, Charles D.
Hurwitz, Alfred L., et al. Disorders of Esophageal Motility.
Hurwitz, Heidi S., jt. auth. see Friday, Sandra K.
Hurwitz, Johanna. Aldo Applesauce.
--Aldo Ice Cream.
--Anne Frank: A Short Life.
--The Law of Gravity.
Hus, Alain. The Etruscans.
Husband, T. M., ed. The Impact of Technology on Production.
Husbands, Jo L. Defense Choices: Greater Security with Fewer Dollars.
Husbands, Jo. L., jt. auth. see Daggett, Stephen.

Authors

Huseman, Richard C. & Carroll, Archie B. Readings in Organizational Behavior: Dimensions of Management Actions.
Huseman, Richard C., et al. Business Communication.
Husen, Torsten. Psychological Twin Research.
Huser, H. J. Atlas of Comparative Primate Hematology.
Husfloen, Kyle, jt. ed. see Murphy, Catherine.
Hush, Joanne & Wong, Peter. The Chinese Menu Cookbook.
Husik, Isaac. History of Mediaeval Jewish Philosophy.
Huss, Sally M. How to Play Power Tennis with Ease.
Hussain, A. & Tribe, K., eds. Paths of Development in Capitalist Agriculture.
Hussain, Donna & Hussain, K. M. Information Processing Systems for Management.
Hussain, Jassim M. The Occulation of Imam: A Historical Background.
Hussain, K. M., jt. auth. see Hussain, Donna.
Hussar, Lawrence, jt. auth. see Cosgrove, Patrick.
Hussein, Saddam. Social & Foreign Affairs in Iraq. Kishtainy, Khalid W., tr.
Husseiny, A. A., ed. Iceberg Utilization: Proceedings of the First International Iceberg Utilization Conference, Ames, Iowa.
Hussell, C. G. & Laing, A. F. Biological & Psychological Background to Education.
Husserl, Edmund. Cartesian Meditations: An Introduction to a Phenomenology.
Hussey, Christopher. The Life of Sir Edwin Lutyens.
Hussey, Christopher, et al. Early Mid & Late Georgian Houses.
Hussey, D. E. Introducing Corporate Planning.
Hussey, Dyneley. Wolfgang Amadeus Mozart.
Hussey, Joyce. Calf Love.
Hussey, S. S. Chaucer: An Introduction.
Hussian, Richard A. Geriatric Psychology.
Husted, Stewart W., et al. Principles of Modern Marketing.
Hustedt, Friedrich. Bacillariophyta: Diatomeae.
Huston, Ted L., jt. ed. see Burgess, Robert L.
Hustrulid, William A., jt. ed. see Crawford, John T., III.
Huszar, George B. de see De Huszar, George B.
Hutas, I. & Debreczeni, L. A., eds. Respiration: Proceedings of the 28th International Congress of Physiological Sciences, Budapest 1980.
Hutch, Richard A. & Fenner, Peter G. Under the Shade of a Coolibah Tree: Australian Studies in Consciousness.
Hutchens, John K., ed. The Gambler's Bedside Book.
Hutcheon, Neil B. & Handegord, Gustav O. Building Science for a Cold Climate.
Hutcheson, Mark A., et al. Employer's Guide to Strike Planning & Prevention.
Hutcheson, Richard G., Jr. Mainline Churches & the Evangelicals.
--Wheel Within the Wheel.
Hutchings, Arthur. The Baroque Concerto.
--Mozart: the Man - the Musician.
--Schubert.
Hutchings, Bill. The Poetry of William Cowper.
Hutchings, D., ed. Late Seventeenth Century Scientists.
Hutchings, Gilbert R., jt. auth. see Feirer, John L.
Hutchings, James M. Seeking the Elephant, Eighteen Forty-Nine: James Mason Hutchings' Journal of His Overland Trek to California. Sargent, Shirley, ed.
Hutchings, Margaret. What Shall I Do with This?
Hutchings, Mark, jt. auth. see Waud, Clarice.
Hutchinngs, Mary H. & Cogswell, William R. Exercises in Calculus.
Hutchins, Carleen M., ed. Musical Acoustics: Violin Family Functions.
Hutchins, Maude. Victorine.
Hutchins, Victor, jt. auth. see London College of Furniture Staff.
Hutchinson, jt. auth. see Stallings.
Hutchinson, A. & Monahan, P., eds. The Rule of Law.
Hutchinson, C. R., jt. ed. see Trost, Barry M.
Hutchinson, Earl R., jt. ed. see Clark, David G.
Hutchinson, Gloria. Jesus' Saving Questions.
Hutchinson, J. M. & Mann, W. B., eds. Metrology Needs in the Measurement of Environmental Radioactivity: Seminar Sponsored by the International Committee for Radionuclide Metrology.
Hutchinson, J. S., jt. ed. see Jeffcoate, S. L.
Hutchinson, Joyce, tr. see Bebey, Francis.
Hutchinson, Joyce A., tr. see Bebey, Francis.
Hutchinson, Lucy. Memoirs of the Life of Colonel Hutchinson.
Hutchinson, Mary J. Red Ice.
Hutchinson, P. Games Authors Play.
Hutchinson, Ralph, et al. A Dictionary of American Wines.
Hutchinson, Ron. The Dillen.
Hutchinson, Sandra, ed. see Wayne Green Books Editors.
Hutchinson, Sylvester. Guidebook to Revelations.
Hutchinson, Van R. Excelling: High School Superstars & How to Become One.
Hutchinson, Warner, jt. auth. see Abrams, Richard I.
Hutchinson, William A. Plant Propagation & Cultivation.
Hutchinson, William K. History of Economic Analysis.
Hutchinson, William K., ed. American Economic History: A Guide to Information Sources.
Hutchison, Chester. Your Future in Agribusiness.
Hutchison, David. Fundamentals of Computer Logic.
Hutchison, Harold F. The Hollow Crown: A Life of Richard II.
Hutchison, Howard. The Complete Handbook of Sewing Machine Repair.
--The Typewriter Repair Manual.
Hutchison, Michael. The Book of Floating: Exploring the Private Sea.
Huth, F., et al. Aortic Alterations in Rabbits Following Sheathing with Silastic & Polyethylene Tubes. Incl. Radioactively Labeled Iododeoxyuridine in the Study of Experimental Liver Regeneration. Buerki, K., et al.; The Human Placental Villitides: A Review of Chronic Intrauterine Infection. Altshuler, G. & Russel, P.; Ultrastructural Pathology of the Adrenal Glands Incushing's Syndrome. Mitschke, H. & Saeger, W.; DNA in Human Tumors: A Cytophotometric Study. Boehm, N. & Sandritter, W.. Springer-Verlag.
Huth, H. C. Practical Problems in Mathematics for Carpenters.
Huth, Holly Y. Centerplay: Focusing Your Child's Energy.
Huth, Mark W. Basic Construction Blueprint Reading.
Huthmacher, J. Joseph. Massachusetts People & Politics, 1919-1933.
--Senator Robert F. Wagner & the Rise of Urban Liberalism.
Hutner, Herbert H. Larger Than Life!
Hutson, Patsy, jt. auth. see Hutson, Roger.
Hutson, Percival W. Guidance Function in Education.
Hutson, Roger & Hutson, Patsy. A Wider Circle.
Hutt, Allen. The Changing Newspaper: Typographic Trends in Britain & America, 1622-1972.
Hutt, Annel, tr. see Aumiaux, M.
Hutt, C., jt. auth. see Hutt, S. J.
Hutt, Michael D. & Speh, Thomas W. Industrial Marketing Management.
Hutt, S. J. & Hutt, C. Behaviour Studies in Psychiatry.
Hutt, W. H. A Rehabilitation of Say's Law.
--The Theory of Idle Resources.
Hutter, Bridget & Williams, Gillian, eds. Controlling Women: The Normal & the Deviant.
Hutter, K. & Van De Ven, A. A. Field Matter Interactions in Thermoelastic Solids.
Hutterian Society of Brothers Staff, ed. see Arnold, Eberhard.
Hutton, jt. auth. see Blakey.
Hutton, Alfred. Sword & the Centuries: Or Old Sword Days & Old Sword Ways.
Hutton, David. Journey to Love.
Hutton, Graham. Midwest at Noon.
Hutton, John. The Mystery of Wealth: Political Economy, Its Development & Impact on World Events.
Hutton, Mick, jt. auth. see Emett, Charlie.
Hutton, Richard, jt. auth. see Kendig, Frank.
Hutton, William T. & Schwarz, Stephen. Exempt Organizations: Tax Strategies & Legal Problems.
Huxham, Fred A., et al. Using the Macintosh Toolbox with C.
Huxhold, Harry N. Followers of the Cross.
Huxley, Aldous. Brave New World.
--On Art & Artists. Philipson, Morris, ed.
Huxley, Anthony. Green Inheritance: The World Wildlife Fund Book of Plants.
Huxley, Anthony, ed. The World Guide to House Plants: Origins, Care, & Cultivation.
Huxley, Elsepth. Scott of the Antarctic.
Huxley, Elspeth. The African Poison Murders.
--The Flame Trees of Thika.
Huxley, Julian S. Africa View.
Huxley, Julian S., jt. auth. see Huxley, Thomas H.
Huxley, Laura. You Are Not the Target.
Huxley, M. & McLoughlin, J. B. The New Urban Studies Literature: A Review with Special Reference to Australia.
Huxley, Renira, ed. see C. A. S. D. S. Study Group on Mechanisms of Language Development, London, 1968.
Huxley, Thomas H. & Huxley, Julian S. Diary of the Voyage of H. M. S. Rattlesnake.
Huxley-Blythe, Peter J. The East Came West.
Huxtable, Ryan J. & Pasantes-Morales, Herminia, eds. Taurine In Nutrition & Neurology.
Huyette, Summer S. Political Adaptation in Sa'udi Arabia: A Study of the Council of Ministers.
Huygen, Wil, jt. auth. see Poortvliet, Rien.
Huygens, L., et al. The English Journals, 1651-1652. Bachrach, A. G. & Collmer, H., eds. Bachrach, A. G. & Collmer, H., trs.
Hvidt, Kristian. Flight to America: The Social Background of 300,000 Danish Emigrants.
Hvorslev, M. Juul. Subsurface Exploration & Sampling of Soils for Civil Engineering Purposes.
Hwang, C. L. & Masud, A. S. Multiple Objective Decision Making-Methods & Applications: A State-of-the-Art Survey.
Hwang, David H. Broken Promises: Four Chinese American Plays.
Hwang, Kai. Supercomputers - Design & Applications.
Hwang, Ned H. Fundamentals of Hydraulic Engineering Systems.
Hwang, Sun-won. The Stars & Other Korean Short Stories. Poitrass, Edward W., tr.
Hyams, Ario S. Toward a One World Jewry: An Essay in Jewish Identity.
Hyams, Edward. The Millennium Postponed: Socialism from Sir Thomas More to Mao Tse-Tung.
--Pierre-Joseph Proudhon: His Revolutionary Life, Mind & Works.
Hyamson, Albert M. Palestine under the Mandate, 1920-1948.
Hyatt, Carole. The Woman's Selling Game: How to Sell Yourself & Anything Else.
Hyatt, Christopher S., ed. An Interview with Israel Regardie: His Final Thoughts & Views.
Hyatt, James A. A Cost Accounting Handbook for Colleges & Universities. Jacobson, David W., ed.
Hyde, Anthony. The Red Fox.
--The Red Fox.
Hyde, Christopher. The Icarus Seal.
Hyde, Cornelius J., III, jt. auth. see Doiron, John.
Hyde, Dayton O. Don Coyote: The Good & Bad Times of a Maligned American Original.
--One Summer in Montana.
Hyde, Douglas. The Love Songs of Connacht.
Hyde, Eleanor. Those Who Stayed Behind.
Hyde, Frank W. Radio Astronomy for Amateurs.
Hyde, H. Montgomery. The Atom Bomb Spies.
--Lord Alfred Douglas: A Biography.
--A Solitary in the Ranks: Lawrence of Arabia As Airman & Private Soldier.
Hyde, Harry van Zile Foreword by see Floore, Frances Berkeley.
Hyde, Janet S. Understanding Human Sexuality.
Hyde, Kathy. Teaching the Bible to Change Lives.
Hyde, Margaret O. Addictions.
--Everyone's Trash Problem: Nuclear Wastes.
--Fears & Phobias.
--Is the Cat Dreaming Your Dream.
--Mind Drugs.
--My Friend Wants to Run Away.
--The Rights of the Victim.
Hyde, Mary, ed. see Shaw, George Bernard & Douglas, Alfred.
Hyde, Montgomery, ed. The Annotated Oscar Wilde.
Hyde, Stuart W. Television & Radio Announcing.
--Television & Radio Announcing.
--Television & Radio Announcing.
Hyde-Chambers, Audrey, jt. auth. see Hyde-Chambers, Fredrick.
Hyde-Chambers, Frederick R. Lama: A Story of Tibet.
Hyde-Chambers, Fredrick & Hyde-Chambers, Audrey. Tibetan Folk Tales.
Hyde-Pritchard, Marion. Pain, Penance & Peace: A Selection of Poems.
Hyder, Clyde K., ed. Swinburne: The Critical Heritage.
Hyder, O. Quentin. Shape Up.
Hydrick, Janie & Miller, Maurice. ASU's Annual Conference on Micros in Education.
Hydrick, Janie, ed. Sixth Annual Microcomputers in Education Conference: Ethics & Excellence in Computer Education: Choice or Mandate?
Hyer, Nancy, ed. see Society of Manufacturing Engineers Staff.
Hyer, Richard. Riceburner.
Hyland, Drew A. The Virtue of Philosophy: An Interpretation of Plato's "Charmides"
Hyland, William G., ed. America & the World, 1984.
--America & the World 1985.
Hylander, Clarence J. Wildlife Community: From the Tundra to the Tropics in North America.
Hyltin, Tom M. Digital Electronic Watch.
Hylton, John. Reintegrating the Offender: Assessing the Impact of Community Corrections.
Hyman. Economics.
--Modern Microeconomics.
--Modern Microeconomics: Analysis & Applications.
--Principles of Macroeconomics: Theory & Practice.
--Principles of Microeconomics: Theory & Practice.
Hyman, B. D. My Mother's Keeper.
--My Mother's Keeper: A Daughter's Candid Portrait of Her Famous Mother. Golbitz, Pat, ed.
Hyman, David N. Economics of Governmental Activity.
--Public Finance: A Contemporary Application of Theory to Policy.
Hyman, G. M., jt. auth. see Angel, S.
Hyman, Helen K., jt. auth. see Silverstone, Barbara.
Hyman, Isabelle. The Palazzo Medici & a Ledger for the Church of San Lorenzo.
Hyman, Jane & Ruane, Pat. LOGO Activities for the Computer: A Beginner's Guide.
Hyman, Michael. Memory Resident Utilities, Interrupts & Disk Management with MS & PC DOS.
Hyman, Richard. Shell Classification Research.
Hyman, Ronald. Improving Discussion Leadership.
Hyman, Sidney. Marriner S. Eccles: Private Entrepreneur & Public Servant.
Hyman, Stanley. Supplies Management for Health Service.
Hyman, Stanley Edgar. The Critic's Credentials.
--The Tangled Bank.
Hyman, Steven E. Manual of Psychiatric Emergencies.
Hymes, James L., Jr. Early Childhood Education: An Introduction to the Profession.
Hyndman, Donald, jt. auth. see Alt, David.
Hynek, J. Allen Foreword by see Fowler, Raymond E.
Hynes, Kathleen. An Ethical Inquiry. McKenna, Constance & Johnson, Karen, eds.
Hynes, Samuel. Edwardian Turn of Mind.
Hynes, William G. Start & Run a Profitable Craft Business.
Hyslop, N., ed. see Biometerological Congress Staff.
Hyslop, N., ed. see International Biometeorological Congress Staff.
Hyslop, N. St. G., jt. ed. see Zemel, Z.
Hyslop, Theophilus B. Great Abnormals.
Hyson, Athena, jt. auth. see Tawil, Natalie.
Hyvaerinen, L. P. Information Theory for Systems Engineers.
--Mathematical Modeling for Industrial Processes.

I

I. P. R. A. Staff. Proceedings of the Third General Conference.
I U B - I U B S Joint Symposium - 1st - Stockholm - 1960. Biological Structure & Function: Proceedings. Goodwin, T. W. & Lindberg, Olov, eds.
Iachello, F., ed. Interacting Bose-Fermi Systems in Nuclei.
Iacobucci, Albert A. In the Name of Jesus Christ.
Iacone, Salvatore J. Modern Business Report Writing.
IAHO Staff. Directory of Hydrogen Energy Products & Services, 1980-1981.
Iannarelli, S. Joseph. The Third Testament of the Holy Bible.
Iatrides, John O. Revolt in Athens: The Greek Communist "Second Round", 1944-1945.
Ibach, Bob & Panaccio, Tim. The Comeback Kids: The Philadelphia Phillies & the 1980 World Series.
Ibanez, M., jt. auth. see Gimeno, Jose B.
Ibarruri, D. En la Lucha, Tomo I: Palabras y Hechos 1936-1939.
Ibarruri, D., et al. International Solidarity with the Spanish Republic 1936-1939.
Ibarruri, Dolores. El Unico Camino.
Ibarruri, Dolores, jt. auth. see Commision International de Redaccion.
Ibberson, J. The Language of Decision: An Essay in Prescriptivist Ethical Theory.
Ibbetson, J., jt. auth. see Whitmore, D. A.
Ibbotson, Eva. A Countess Below Stairs.
Ibele, Warren E., ed. Modern Developments in Heat Transfer.
Ibero-American Institute Staff, in Berlin. Subject Catalog of the Ibero-American Institute in Berlin, Prussian Cultural Heritage Foundation.
IBM Informatik Symposium Staff. Interactive Systems: Proceedings of the IBM Informatik Symposium, 6th, Bad Homburg, Germany, Sept., 1976. Blaser, A. & Hackl, C., eds.
IBM Staff. Diccionario de Siglas Relacionadas con la Informatica.
Ibn Batutah see Muhammed ibn 'abd Allah.
IBP Research & Editorial Staff. How to Raise Money to Make Money.
--Lawyer's Desk Book.
--Lawyer's Desk Book.
--Real Estate Desk Book.
--Real Estate Desk Book.
--Real Estate Forms Desk Book.
--Successful Techniques That Multiply Profits & Personal Payoff in the Closely - Held Corporation.

--Successful Techniques That Multiply Profits & Personal Payoff in the Closely-Held Corporation.
--Tax Desk Book for the Small Business.
--Tax Desk Book for the Small Business.
--Tax-Free & Tax-Sheltered Investments for the 1980's.
Ibragimbekov, M. There Never Was a Better Brother.
Ibrahim, I., et al. Readings in Managerial Economics.
Ibrahim, M. Z. Glycogen & Its Related Enzymes of Metabolism in the Central Nervous System.
Ibrahim, Sonallah. The Smell of It & Other Stories.
Ibsen, Henrik. Brand. Meyer, Michael, tr. from Norwegian.
--A Doll's House. Meyer, Michael, tr.
--Ghosts.
--Ghosts.
--Hedda Gabler. Popkin, Henry, ed. Jurgensen, Kai & Schenkkan, Robert, trs.
--Peer Gynt. Meyer, Michael, tr.
--Peer Gynt. Finney, Horace M., tr.
--Wild Duck.
Ibsen, Henrik & Hill, Geoffrey. Brand: A Version for the Stage.
Ibsen, Henrik see Weiss, Samuel A.
Ichikawa, H. Double Contrast Radiography of the Stomach.
Ichikawa, Yoshiyuki, et al. Cytochromes: Current Research, I.
Ichimaru, Setsuo. Plasma Physics.
Ickes, Harold L. America's House of Lords: An Inquiry into the Freedom of the Press.
ICLG Conference, 1977 & Burnett, D. International Library & Information Programmes: Proceedings.
ICN-UCLA Symposia Staff. Eukaryotic Genetics Systems: Proceedings of the ICN-UCLA Symposia on Molecular & Cellular Biology. Wilcox, Gary, et al, eds.
--Human Cytogenetics: Proceedings of the ICN-UCLA Symposia on Molecular & Cellular Biology. Sparkes, Robert S., et al, eds.
--T & B Lymphocytes: Proceedings of the ICN-UCLA Symposia on Molecular & Cellular Biology, 1979. Bach, Fritz H., et al, eds.
Idaho Real Estate Commission Staff. Idaho Supplement for Modern Real Estate Practice.
Idahosa, Benson. Fire in His Bones.
Idaikkadar, N. M. Agricultural Statistics: A Handbook for Developing Countries.
Idashkin, Yu & Bondarev, Yu. Yuri Bondarev, Yuri Bondarev on Craftmanship.
Iddings, C., tr. see Kaellen, G.
Ide, Arthur F. AIDS Hysteria.
Ide, Arthur F., ed. see Frazier, Alton E.
Ideals Staff. Christmas Ideals.
--Country Christmas Cookbook.
--Grandma's Country Cooking.
--Homemade Cookies.
--Homemade Desserts.
--Ideals Easter.
Idelsohn, Abraham Z. Jewish Music in Its Historical Development.
--Thesaurus of Hebrew Oriental Melodies.
Idle, Christopher. Stories of Our Favorite Hymns.
Idler, David R., ed. Steroids in Nonmammalian Vertebrates.
Idol-Maestas, Lorna. Special Educator's Consultation Handbook.
Idol-Maestas, Lorna, et al. Collaborative Consultation.
IDRC, Ottawa Staff. Agriculture, Food & Nutrition Sciences Division: The First Five Years.
--International Development Research Centre Projects: 1970-1981.
--Science of the Culture of Freshwater Fish Species in China.
IEAD Staff. Coal Information Report 1984.
IEEE, Inc. Staff. C-Thirty-Seven Complete: 1986.
IFAC-FIP International Conference Staff. Proceedings of the IFAC-FIP International Conference on Digital Computer a 75211. Mansour, M. & Schaufelberger, W., eds.
IFAC-IFIP-IEA-IFORS Symposium Staff & Johannsen, G. Analysis, Design, & Evaluation of Man-Machine Systems: Proceedings of the IFAC-IFIP-IEA-IFORS Symposium, Baden-Baden, Brd, Sept., 1982. Rijnsdorp, J. E., ed.
IFAC-IFIP Workshop, Kyoto, Japan, Aug. 31-Sept. 2, 1981. Real Time Programming, 1981: Proceedings. Hasegawa, T., ed.
IFAC Staff, jt. auth. see Al Fateh Staff.
IFAC Symposium Staff. Case Studies in Automation Related to Humanization of Work: Proceedings of the IFAC Symposium, Enschede, The Netherlands, Oct., 1977. Rijnsdorp, J. E., ed.
--Components & Instruments for Distributed Computer Control Systems: Proceedings of the IFAC Symposium, Paris, France, Dec. 1982. Binder, Z. & Perret, R., eds.
--Control in Power Electronics & Electrical Drives: Proceedings of the IFAC Symposium, 2nd, Dusseldorf, Brd, Oct. 1977. Leonhard, W., ed.
--Criteria for Selecting Appropriate Technologies Under Different Cultural, Technical & Social Conditions: Proceedings of the IFAC Symposium, Bari, Italy, May, 1979. De Giorgio, A. & Roveda, C., eds.
--Pneumatic & Hydraulic Components & Instruments in Automatic Control: Proceedings of the IFAC Symposium, Warsaw, Poland, May, 1980. Leskiewicz, H. J. & Zaremba, M., eds.
IFAC Symposium Staff & Campbell, R. M. Control Aspects of Prosthetics & Orthotics: Proceedings of the IFAC Symposium, Columbus, Ohio, May, 1982.
IFAC Symposium Staff & Halme, A. Modelling & Control of Biotechnical Processes: Proceedings of the Symposium, 1st, Helsink, Finland, Aug., 1982.
IFAC Symposium Staff & Rauch, H. E. Applications of Nonlinear Programming to Optimization & Control: Proceedings of the IFAC Symposium, 4th, San Francisco, California, June, 1983.
IFAC Symposium, Zurich, Switzerland, 29-31 Aug. 1979. Computer Aided Design of Control Systems: Proceedings of the IFAC Symposium, Zurich,Switzerland, Aug. 29-31, 1979. Cuenod, M. A., ed.
Ife, Barry, jt. auth. see Quevedo, Francisco De.
Iffy, Leslie, jt. auth. see Kaminetzky, Harold.
IFI-Plenum Data Company, Staff, compiled by. Political Science Abstracts: 1984 Annual Supplement.
IFIP-TC Working Conference Staff. Modelling & Optimization of Complex Systems: Proceedings of the IFIP-TC Working Conference, 7th, Novosibirsk, U.S.S.R., July 3-9, 1978. Marchuk, G. I., ed.
IFIP Technical Conference Staff. Optimization Techniques: Proceedings the IFIP Technical Conference, Novosibirsk, 1974. Marchuk, G. I., ed.
IFORS International Conference Staff & Haley, K. B. Operational Research 1975: Proceedings of the IFIP International Conference on Operational Research, 7th, Japan, 1975.
IFSTA Committee. Fire Apparatus Practices. Carlson, Gene P. & Orton, Charles, eds.
IFT-Plenum Data Company, Staff, compiled by. Political Science Abstracts: 1983 Annual Supplement.
Iftikhar-Ul-Awwal, A. Z. The Industrial Development of Bengal, 1900-1939.
Igarashi, Takenbou, ed. World Trademarks & Logotypes: A Collection of Symbols & Their Applications.
Igartua, Arturo, tr. see Armstrong, Wm.
Igglesden, Charles. Those Superstitions.
Ignatiev, O. & Borovik, G. La Agonia De una Dictadura: Cronica Nicaraguense.
--The Agony of a Dictatorship.
Ignatin, George & Barra, Allen. Football by the Numbers 1986.
Ignatovsky, P. S., jt. auth. see Jaroszewski, T. M.
Ignatyev, Oleg. Secret Weapon in Africa.
--Secret Weapon in Africa.
Ignition Manufacturers Institute Staff. Automotive Emission Control & Tune-up Procedures.
Ignizio, Bill, jt. auth. see Sternberg, Dick.
Ignoffo, Robert, jt. auth. see See-Lasley, Kay.
Igoe, James, jt. auth. see Igoe, Lynn M.
Igoe, Lynn M. & Igoe, James. Two Hundred Fifty Years of Afro-American Art: An Annotated Bibliography.
Igu Commission on Quantitative Geography, Meeting, 1972. Proceedings. Yeates, Maurice, ed.
Igusa, J. I. Lectures on Forms of Higher Degree.
Ihara, Toni & Warner, Ralph. The Living Together Kit.
Ihara, Toni, jt. auth. see Warner, Ralph.
Ihilevich, David & Gleser, Goldine G. Evaluating Mental-Health Programs: The Progress Evaluation Scales.
Ihirg, Mary A. Emerson's Transcendental Vocabulary: A Concordance.
Ihli, Sr. Jan. Liturgy of the Word for Children.
Iiams, Thomas M. Peacemaking from Vergennes to Napoleon.
Iijima, Kanjitsu. Buddhist Yoga.
Iijima, Nobuku. Pollution Japan: Historical Chronology.
Iino, Norimoto. Hints in Haiku.
--Zeal for Zen.
Iio, M. Nuclear Medicine in Japan.
Iitaka, Y., jt. auth. see Motte, G. A.
Ijere, Martin O. An African in Germany.
--Survey of Afro-American Experience in the U. S. Economy.
Ijiri, Y. & Simon, H. A. Skew Distributions & Sizes of Business Firms.
Ijiri, Yuji & Whinston, Andrew B., eds. Quantitative Planning & Control: In Honor of William W. Cooper.
Ikawa, Yoji & Odaka, Tadeshi, eds. Oncogenic Viruses & Host Cell Genes.
Ikeda, Daisaku. Glass Children & Other Essays. Watson, Burton, tr.
--Life: An Enigma, a Precious Jewel.
Ikeda, Daisaku, tr. see Toynbee, Arnold J.
Ikeda, N. & Watanabe, S. Stochastic Differential Equations & Diffusion Processes.
Ikle, Max. Switzerland: An International Banking & Financial Center. Schiff, Eric, tr. from Ger.
Ikonnikov, A. Mysaskovsky, His Life & Work.
Ilchman, Warren F. Professional Diplomacy in the United States, 1779-1939.
Ilchman, Warren F., jt. ed. see Uphoff, Norman T.
Ilfrey, Jack & Reynolds, Max. Happy Jack's Go-Buggy: A WW 11 Fighter Pilot's Personal Document.
Ilgen, Jon, et al. The Tower Anthology of the San Jose Movement in Fiction. Clifton, Merritt, ed.
Ilich, John. Building a Fortune in Common Stocks.
Iliffe, J. Advanced Computer Design.
Ilk, Craig R. Student's Career Guide to a Future in the Allied Health Professions.
Illich, Ivan. Celebration of Awareness: A Call for Institutional Revolution.
--Gender.
Illiff, jt. auth. see Hirst.
Illingworth. Common Symptoms of Disease in Children.
Illingworth, Frank. Highway to the North.
--North of the Circle.
Illinois Principals Association Staff. Strengthening School Leadership.
Illinois State Historical Society Staff. Annual Report of the Illinois State Historical Library. Devine, Michael J., ed.
Illsley, Raymond & Mitchell, Ross G., eds. Low Birth Weight: A Medical, Psychological & Social Study.
Illyes, Gy & Reismann, Janos. Lake Balaton.
ILO Asian Employment Programme Staff. Poverty in Rural Asia. Khan, Azizur Rahman & Lee, Eddy, eds.
ILO Staff. Bibliography of Published Research of the World Employment Programme.
Ilse, Dora, tr. see Von Frisch, Karl.
Ilyin, Donna. Ilyin Oral Interview Test.
--Listening Comprehension Group Test: Examiner's Test Manual.
Ilyin, Donna & Rubin, Susan. LCGT Technical Guide.
Ilyin, Donna, jt. auth. see Doherty, Cecelia.
Ilyin, Donna, et al. English Language Skills Assessment in a Reading Context (Elsa Test AN)
Ilyin, Olga. The White Road: A Russian Odyssey 1919-1923.
Ilyin, V. A., et al. Analytic Geometry.
Ilyushchenko, Valerii, tr. see Logunov, A. A.
Ilyushin, A. A. & Lenskii, V. S. Strength of Materials. Redshaw, L. C., ed. Loshor, J. K., tr.
Imaeda, Yoshiro, jt. auth. see Pommaret-Imaeda, Francoise.
Image Industry Publications Staff, jt. ed. see Thompson, Jacqueline.
Imam, Zafar, jt. auth. see Balogh, Andras.
Imbiorski, W. Adventure Together: Teacher's Manual.
Imbovitz, E., ed. They Found Their Voice.
Imel, Susan, et al. Career Development in the Workplace: A Guide for Program Developers.
Imelik, B., et al, eds. Catalysis by Zeolites: Proceedings.
Imeson, Sparky. Mountain Flying.
Imhoff, Eugene A., Jr., jt. auth. see Danos, Paul P.
Imhoof, Maurice L., jt. auth. see Hudson, Herman.
Immegart, Glenn L. & Boyd, William L., eds. Problem-Finding in Educational Administration: Trends in Research & Theory.
Immergut, E. H., tr. see Vollmert, B.
Immerman, Leon A., jt. auth. see Buitrago, Ann.
Impagliazzo, John, jt. auth. see Barbasso, Salvatore.
Impagliazzo, M., jt. ed. see Chenoweth, J. M.
Impell Corporation Staff, jt. auth. see Nuclear Safety Associates Staff.
Imperato, Eleanor M., jt. auth. see Imperato, Pascal J.
Imperato, Pascal J. & Imperato, Eleanor M. Mali: A Handbook of Historical Statistics.
Imperial College of Science & Technology, Rock Mechanics Section, jt. auth. see Hoek, E.
Imperiale, Louise, jt. auth. see Famularo, Joe.
Impey, O. R., jt. auth. see Faulkner, R. J.
Imran, Surat A. The Light of Iman from the House of 'Imran.
Imre, Roberta W. Knowing & Caring: Philosophical Issues in Social Work.
Imrie, Alex. Fokker Fighters of World War One.
--German Air Aces of World War One.
Imrie, P. R., jt. auth. see Allen, D. J.
Imundo, Louis V. The Effective Supervisor's Handbook.
Imundo, Louis V. & Eisert, Martin P. Managing Your Human Resources: A Partnership Approach.
Imus, Don. God's Other Son: The Life & Times of the Reverend Billy Sol Hargus.
Imwinkelried, Edward J. Handbook for the Trial of Contract Lawsuits: Strategies & Techniques.
Inabnit, Mark. Roses.
Inamoto, Noboru. Colloquial Japanese.
Inbau, Fred E., et al. Criminal Law & Its Adminstration, 1986 Supplement to.
--Criminal Law, Cases & Comments.
--Criminal Procedures: Cases & Comments.
--Criminal Procedure, Cases & Comments On: 1986 Supplement.
Ince, Basil A., et al, eds. Issues in Caribbean International Relations.
Ince, William, jt. auth. see Goodman, Roger B.
Inch, Dennis, jt. auth. see Keefe, Laurence E., Jr.
Inch, Morris A. The Evangelical Challenge.
--Making the Good News Relevant: Keeping the Gospel Distinctive in Any Culture.
Inchbald, Elizabeth. The Plays of Elizabeth Inchbald. Backscheider, Paula R., ed.
Inciardi, James A. & Siegal, Harvey A. Emerging Social Issues: A Sociological Perspective.
Inciardi, James A., ed. The Drugs-Crime Connection.
Income Opportunities Editors. Income Opportunities Magazine Guide to Family Finance.
Inczedy, J. Analytical Applications of Complex Equilibria.
Inda, Caridad, tr. see Gutierrez, Gustavo.
INDECS Economics Staff. State of Play.
Independent Living Center Staff. Celebrity Cookbook.
Indian Claims Commission. Osage Indians, Vol. Five: Findings of Fact, & Opinion.
Indian Society of Theoretical & Applied Mechanics, 20th Congress, India, 1975. Dynamics of Rotors: Selected Papers. Rao, J. S., ed.
Indiana Public School Study Council Staff. Exploring Junior High School Guidance.
Indiana State University, Department of Foreign Languages, Literature Circle Symposium Staff & Jennermann, Donald L. The Writer & the Past: Proceedings of the Indiana State University, Department of Foreign Languages, Literature Circle Symposium, 1980.
Indiana University, Folklore Institute, Archives of Traditional Music Staff. A Catalog of Phonorecording of Music & Oral Data Held by the Archives of Traditional Music.
Indiana University, Institute for Sex Research Staff. Catalog of Periodical Literature in the Social & Behavioral Sciences Section, Library of the Institute for Sex Research, Including Supplement to Monographs, 1973-1975.
--Catalog of the Social & Behavioral Sciences Monograph Section of the Library of the Institute for Sex Research.
--International Directory of Sex Research & Related Fields.
Indiana University Staff. The Arts of Thailand: A Handbook of the Architecture, Sculpture, & Painting of Thailand.
--Cost-Effectiveness-Benefit Analysis of Postsecondary Vocational Programs.
Industrial Design Magazine Editors & Schmitt, Paul. Packaging Design Two.
Industrial Design Magazine Staff. Designer's Choice: The Best Products, Graphics & Environments of 1980. Finley, George, ed.
Industrial Workers of the World Staff. Industrial Union Bulletin (Industrial Workers of the World)
Inez, Colette. Alive & Taking Names.
Information Center for Hearing, Speech & Disorders of Human Communication of the Johns Hopkins Medical Institution Staff, compiled by. Hearing, Speech & Communication Disorders. Incl. Cumulated Citations: 1973; Cumulated Citations: 1974. Plenum Pub.
Information Concepts, Inc. (ICON) Staff, compiled by. InTech Index: A Cumulative Index of Technical Articles Appearing in Instrumentation Technology (now InTech) 1954-1979.
Information Gatekeepers, Inc. Staff. Fiber Optics & Market Trends in Japan.
Informational Macromolecules Symposium Staff. Informational Macromolecules: Proceedings of the Symposium, Rutgers University, 1962. Vogel, Henry J., et al, eds.
Infotech Staff. International Survey: Structured Programming.
--Management Report.
Ingalls, A. Joy & Salerno, M. Constance. Maternal & Child Health Nursing.
Ingalls, John D. Human Energy: The Critical Factor for Individuals & Organizations.
Ingalls, Rachel. I See a Long Journey: Three Novellas.
--The Pearlkillers: Four Novellas.
Ingalls, Robert. TI Games for Kids.
Ingalls, Robert P. Mental Retardation: The Changing Outlook.
Ingalsbe, Lon, jt. auth. see Manning, William A.
Ingbar, Mary L. & Taylor, Lester D. Hospital Costs in Massachusetts: An Econometric Study.

Inge, M. Thomas, ed. Ellen Glasgow: Centennial Essays.
Ingelfinger, Franz J., ed. Dorland's Medical Dictionary.
Ingells, Douglas J. L-Ten-Eleven Tristar & the Lockheed Story.
Ingerman, Peter Z. Syntax Oriented Translator.
Ingersoll, Ernest. Birds in Legend, Fable & Folklore.
Ingersoll, Fern S., tr. see King Rama, 2nd.
Ingersoll, William B., jt. auth. see Practising Law Institute Staff.
Ingham, A. E., ed. Sea Surveying.
Ingham, Herbert S. Discretus Calculus.
Ingham, John M. Mary, Michael, & Lucifer: Folk Catholicism in Central Mexico.
Ingham, Kenneth. Reformers in India, 1793-1833: An Account of the Work of Christian Missionaries on Behalf of Social Reform.
Ingham, Roger J. Stuttering & Behavior Therapy: Current Status & Experimental Foundations.
Ingle, Dwight J. Is It Really So? A Guide to Clear Thinking.
Inglehart, Margaret L. World Civilization since Seventeen Seventy.
Ingles, James W. The Amazing D. Randall MacRae.
Ingleton, Roy D. Police of the World.
Inglis, Brian. The Forbidden Game: A Social History of Drugs.
--Roger Casement.
Inglis, Craig M., jt. auth. see Sondrup, Steven P.
Inglis, Fred. Radical Earnestness: English Social Theory, 1880-1980.
Inglis, J. K. A Textbook of Human Biology.
Inglis, S. Usborne Guide to Soccer: Skills, Tricks & Tactics.
Ingmanson, Dale E. & Wallace, William J. Oceanography: An Introduction.
Ingold, Beth, jt. auth. see Windt, Theodore O.
Ingoldsby, Mary F. Up & Down Catholic Italy.
Ingpen, Brian & Pabst, Robert. Maritime South Africa: A Pictorial History.
Ingraham, E., jt. auth. see DeMeyer, F.
Ingram, Arthur. The Country Animal Doctor.
Ingram, Arthur & Phippard, Martin. Highway Heavy Metal: The World's Trucks at Work.
Ingram, C. D. Time Warp & a Time to Speak.
Ingram, D. The Commonwealth at Work.
Ingram, Dave. The Radio Amateur's Microwave Communications Handbook.
--Video Electronics Technology.
Ingram, David. David Ingram's Investment Guide.
--The Ultimate Tax Book.
Ingram, Elisabeth, ed. see C. A. S. D. S. Study Group on Mechanisms of Language Development, London, 1968.
Ingram, Helen M., et al. A Policy Approach to Political Representation: Lessons from the Four Corners States.
Ingram, I. M., et al. Notes on Psychiatry.
Ingram, J. B. Curriculum Integration & Lifelong Education.
Ingram, J. E. Spectroscopy at Radio & Microwave Frequency.
Ingram, James C. International Economic Problems.
Ingram, Marilyn W. & Folse, Lois J. Dining In - Dallas.
Ingram, Robert W., ed. Accounting in the Public Sector.
Ingrassia, Sara & Foley, Sue. Teacher Fairs: Counterpoint to Criticism.
Ingres, Jean A., jt. auth. see Rosenblum, Robert.
Inhelder, B., et al, eds. Piaget & His School: A Reader in Developmental Psychology.
Injury Committee. A Voice for All Children: Report of an Independent Committee of Injury.
Inkeles, Alex, jt. auth. see Spencer, Metta.
Inman, Billie A. & Gardner, Ruth. Aspects of Composition.
Inman, Henry. Buffalo Jones Adventures on the Plains.
Inman, James E., jt. auth. see Litka, Michael P.
Inman, Linda. Farms & Farmers.
Inman, W. H., jt. ed. see Gross, F. H.
Inmon, William H. Information Systems Architecture: A System Developer's Primer.
--Managing End User Computing In Information Organizations.
--Technomics: The Economics of Technology & the Computer Industry.
Inner London Council Staff. Educational Gymnastics.
Innes, G. S., ed. The Production & Hazards of a Hyperbaric Oxygen Environment: Proceedings.
Innes, Hammond. High Stand.
Innes, Jocasta. Paint Magic.
Innes, Lowell. Pittsburgh Glass, 1797-1891: A History & Guide for Collectors.
Innes, Michael. Carson's Conspiracy.
Inokuma, Isao & Sato, Nobuyuki. Best Judo.
Inonu, E. & Zweifel, P. F., eds. Developments in Transport Theory.
Inoue, Etsuko. White Embroidery Story: Candlewicking.
Inoue, Ken. Education & Training of Industrial Manpower in Japan.
Insel, Paul M. & Roth, Walton T. Core Concepts in Health.
Insel, Thomas R. New Findings in Obsessive Compulsive Disorders.
Insight Guides Staff. APA Map: Indonesia.
--APA Map: Malaysia.
--APA Map: Nepal.
--APA Map: Sri Lanka.
--Thailand.
Inskip, Hampden. Residential Homes for the Physically Handicapped.
Insko, Chester A. & Schopler, John. Experimental Social Psychology: Commentary & Readings.
In-Sob, Zong, ed. & tr. Folk Tales from Korea.
Institut de Droit International Staff, ed. Session d'Aix-en-Provence Nineteen Fifty-Four.
--Session d'Amsterdam Nineteen Fifty-Seven.
--Session de Bath Nineteen-Fifty.
Institut des Etudes Augustiniennes, Paris Staff. Fichier Augustinien.
--Fichier Augustinien, First Supplement.
Institut Francais de Pertrole Staff. Manual of Economic Analysis of Chemical Processes. Miller, Ryle & Miller, Ethel B., trs.
Institut fuer Konfliktforschung Staff, ed. Politisch motivierte Kriminalitaet-Echte Kriminalitaet.
Institut fuer Spektrochemie und Angewandte Spektroskopie, Germany Staff, jt. auth. see Photoelectric Spectrometry Group, England Staff.
Institut Voor Sociale Geschiedenis Staff. Alfabetische Catalogus Van De Boeken En Brochures Van Het International: Alphabetical Catolog of the Books & Pamphlets of the International Institute of Social History.
Institute, Boulder, Colorado, 1959 Staff. Theory of Numbers.
Institute for Business Planning, Inc. Staff. Lawyer's Desk Book.
Institute for Business Planning Research & Editorial Staff. Business & Financial Tables Desk Book.
Institute for Communication Research, Stanford University Staff. The Role of the Telephone in Economic Development.
Institute for Contemporary History, Munich Staff. Catalog for the Institute for Contemporary History. Incl. Pt. 1. Alphabetical Catalog; Pt. 2. Subject Catalog; Pt. 3. Regional Catalog; Pt. 4. Biographical Catalog. G K Hall.
--Catalog of the Library of the Institute for Contemporary History, First Supplement.
Institute for Continuing Legal Education (New Jersey) Staff & Dines, Aaron. Appellate Advocacy (2-84)
Institute for Continuing Legal Education (New Jersey) Staff. Seminar Material, Filing & Administering a Chapter 13 Proceeding.
Institute for Continuing Legal Education (New Jersey) Staff & Lasser, Lawrence L. Seminar Materials for Local Property Taxes & the New Jersey Tax Court.
Institute for Continuing Legal Education (New Jersey) Staff. Trying the Toxic Tort Case (3-84)
Institute for Economic & Financial Research Editorial Council Staff. Kondratieff's Cycles & the Future of the Stock Market in Its Convulsions & Price Gyrations.
Institute for Environmental Education Staff & Association of New Jersey Environmental Commissions. Tuning the Green Machine, An Integrated View of Environmental Systems.
Institute for Food & Development Policy Staff. Removing the Obstacles. Millikan, Brent & Kinley, David, eds.
Institute for Historical Review Staff. Revisionist Bibliography - 1981. Stimely, Keith, ed.
Institute for Jazz Studies. Studies in Jazz Discography.
Institute for Laboratory Animal Resources Staff. Neotropical Primates: Field Studies & Conservation. Thorington, Richard, Jr. & Heltne, Paul, eds.
Institute for New Testament Textural Research & Computer Center of Muenster University with Collaboration of H. Bachmann & W. A. Slaby, eds. Computer Concordance to the Novum Testamentum Graece of Nestle-Alard, 26th Edition & to the Greek New Testament, 3rd Edition.
Institute for Paralegal Training Staff. Introduction to Real Estate Law. Bellavance, Russell C. & Laden, Caroline S., eds.
Institute for Plant Protection Agent Research Staff, jt. auth. see Federal Institute for Biology in Agriculture & Forestry Staff.
Institute for Real Estate Management Staff. Income-Expense Analysis: Conventional Apartments.
Institute for Research on Public Policy, Canada & Brookings. Conferences on Canadian-U. S. Economic Relations.
Institute for the History of Art, Florence, Kunsthistorischen Institut - Florence Staff. Katalog Des Kunsthistorischen Instituts in Florenz, Catalogue of the Institute for the History of Art, Florence.
Institute for the Study of Conflict Staff, ed. Annual of Power & Conflict, 1979-1980.
Institute for the Study of Conflict, London Staff. Annual of Power & Conflict, 1981-82.
Institute for Urban Design Staff, ed. Education for Urban Design.
Institute for World Economics, Kiel, Germany Staff. Catalog of the Library of the Institute for World Economics. Incl. Pt. 1. Bibliographical Catalog of Persons; Pt. 2. Catalog of Administrative Authorities; Pt. 3. Catalog of Corporations; Pt. 4. Regional Catalog; Pt. 5. Subject Catalog; Pt. 6. Shelf List of Periodical Holdings; Pt. 7. Title Catalog. G K Hall.
Institute of Advanced Legal Studies, University of London Staff. Catalogue of the Library of the Institute of Advanced Legal Studies.
Institute of C. F. A. Staff. Readings in Financial Analysis.
Institute of Ceramics. Health & Safety in Ceramics.
Institute of Continuing Legal Education in Georgia, jt. auth. see Insurance Law Institute.
Institute of Continuing Legal Education in Georgia. Program Materials for Seminar on Federal Practice & Procedure: March 7, 1986, Savannah, March 14, 1986, Atlanta, GA.
--Program Materials for Seminar on Will Drafting & Estate Planning, April 18, 1986, Savannah, April, 25, 1986, Atlanta.
Institute of Criminology, University of Cambridge, England Staff. The Library Catalogue of the Radzinowicz Library. Perry, R., ed.
Institute of Electrical & Electronics Engineers, Inc. (IEEE) Staff. IEEE Recommended Practice for Protection & Coordination of Industrial & Commercial Power Systems.
Institute of Electrical & Electronics Engineers, Inc. Digital Signal Processing Committee. Programs in Digital Signal Processing.
Institute of Electrical & Electronics Engineers, Inc. (IEEE) Staff. Recommended Practice for Electric Power Distribution for Industrial Plants.
Institute of Electrical Electronic Engineers Staff, et al. Foreign Engineers in the United States: Immigration or Importation?
Institute of Electrical Engineers (UK) Staff & Peter Perogrinus, Ltd. Antennas & Propagation (ICAP 83)
Institute of Endocrinology, Gunma Univ., ed. Progress & Prospects in Endocrinology.
Institute of Financial Education Staff. Strategies for Consumer Counselor Training.
Institute of Foreign Policy Analysis Staff. The Warsaw Pact: Arms, Doctrine & Strategy. Lewis, William J., ed.
Institute of Human Nutrition, Columbia University College of Physicians & Surgeons. The Columbia Encyclopedia of Nutrition. Winick, Myron, ed.
Institute of Industrial Relations Staff. Employment Problems in the Defense Industry: Proceedings of the Institute of Industrial Relations Conference.
--Organization & Collective Bargaining in Public Employment: Proceedings of the Institute of Industrial Relations Conference on Employee Relations in Public Agencies.
Institute of Internal Auditors, Inc., Board of Regents Staff. Certified Internal Auditor Examination: May 1982-Questions & Suggested Solutions.
--Certified Internal Auditor Examination May 1984: Questions & Suggested Solutions.
Institute of Internal Auditors Inc., Board of Regents Staff. Compendium - Questions & Suggested Solutions: Certified Internal Auditor Examinations 1980 Through 1983.
Institute of International Education, New York Staff. English Language & Orientation Programs in the United States.
Institute of Labor Law Developments Staff. Labor Law: Twenty-Ninth Annual Institute on Labor Law.
Institute of Laboratory Animal Resources Staff & National Research Council Staff. Animals As Monitors of Environmental Pollutants.
Institute of Laboratory Animal Resources Staff. Research in Zoos & Aquariums.
--Ruminants: Cattle, Sheep & Goats, Guidelines for Breeding, Care & Management of Laboratory Animals.
Institute of Latin American Studies Staff. Latin American Research & Publications at the University of Texas at Austin, 1893-1969.
Institute of Marine Engineers Staff. Glossary of Marine Technology Terms.
Institute of Marketing Staff, ed. Marketing in the Construction Industry.
Institute of Mathematics Staff. Large Spare Sets of Linear Equations: Proceedings of the Institute of Mathematics Oxford Conference, April 1970. Reid, R., ed.
Institute of Mechanical Engineers Staff. Vehicle Structures.
Institute of Medicine. Homeless in America: Health Care & Human Needs.
Institute of Medicine, Division of Health Promotion & Disease Prevention Staff & National Research Council Staff. Alcoholism, Alcohol Abuse & Related Problems: Opportunities for Research.
Institute of Medicine Staff. Ethics of Health Care. Tancredi, Laurence, ed.
--Health Services Research.
--A Manpower Policy for Primary Health Care.
--Pharmaceuticals for Developing Countries.
--Sleeping Pills, Insomnia, & Medical Practice.
Institute of Medicine Staff & National Research Council Staff. Nursing & Nursing Education: Public Policies & Private Actions.
Institute of National Science Staff & Chinese Academy of Science Staff. Ancient China's Technology & Science.
Institute of Pacific Relations Staff. Economic Trends & Problems in the Early Republican Period: 1931.
Institute of Petroleum Staff. Expanding Uses of Petroleum.
--Model Code of Safe Practice, Pt. 12: Pressure Vessel Inspection Safety Code.
--Model Code of Safe Practices for the Petroleum Industry: The Petroleum Pipeline.
--Petroleum Measurement Manual: Fidelity & Security of Measurement - Data Transmission Systems Section 1.
--Petroleum Measurement Manual: Tank Calibration Section I- Liquid Calibration Methods, Pt. II.
--Storage & Piped Distribution of Heating Oil Safety Code.
Institute of Real Estate Management Staff. AMO Profile.
--The CPM Profile, 1986.
--Expense Analysis: Condominiums, Cooperatives, & Planned Unit Developments, 1981. Anderson, Kenneth R., ed.
--Income-Expense Analysis: Office Buildings.
Institute of Recreation Management Staff, ed. Recreational Management Handbook.
Institute of Store Planners' Store Interior Design Competition Staff, jt. auth. see National Retail Merchants Association Staff.
Institute Publishing Company Staff. Thoughts for Buffets.
Institution of Chemical Engineers. Condensers: Theory & Practice.
--The Control of Sulphur & Other Gaseous Emissions.
--Cost Savings in Distillation.
--Distillation - 1979.
--Fluid Mixing.
--Industrial Water Economy.
--Opportunities & Constraints.
Institution of Chemical Engineers, ed. Profitability of Food Processing - 1984 Onwards - the Chemical Engineers' Contribution: Proceedings of the Conference Held at Bath, U. K., 10-12 April 1984.
Institution of Chemical Engineers. Reliable Production in the Process Industries.
--Runaway Reactions.
Institution of Chemical Engineers Staff. The Assessment of Major Hazards.
--Chemical Engineering Education.
--Chemical Process Hazards.
Institution of Chemical Engineers Staff, ed. Coal Liquid Mixtures: Proceedings of the Second European Conference, London, U. K. 16-18 September 1985.
--Coal Liquid Mixtures: Proceedings of the European Conference, 1st, Cheltenham, U. K., October 5-6, 1983.
Institution of Chemical Engineers Staff. Design Eighty-Two: Proceedings of the Symposium Organised by the Institution of Chemical Engineers at the University of Aston in Birmingham, U. K., September 22-23, 1982.
--Energy-Money, Materials & Engineering: Proceedings of the Symposium Organised by the Institution of Chemical Engineers (in Conjunction with the American Institute of Chemical Engineers & Deutsche Vereinigung fur Chemie-und Verfahrenstechnik), London, U. K., October 12-15, 1982.
Institution of Chemical Engineers Staff, ed. Ergonomics Problems in Process Operations: Proceedings of the Symposium, Birmingham, U. K., July 11-13, 1984.
--Eurochem 'Eighty-Three-Chemical Engineering Today: The Challenge of Change.
--Fluid Mixing: Proceedings of the Symposium Held at Bradford University, U. K., 3-5 April 1984.
--Heat Transfer: Proceedings of the U. K. National Conference, 1st, Leeds, U. K., July 3-5, 1984.
Institution of Chemical Engineers Staff. Interflow Eighty.
--The Jubilee Chemical Engineering Symposium: Proceedings of the Symposium Organised by the Institution of Chemical Engineers, Imperial College, London, U. K., April 1982.
--Loss Prevention & Safety Promotion in the Process Industries: Chemical Process Hazards.

--Management & Conservation of Resources: Proceedings of the Conference Organised by the Institution of Chemical Engineers at the University of Salford, U. K., April 1982.
--Mixing of Particulate Solids.
--Particle Technology.
--Powtech: 1983.
Institution of Chemical Engineers Staff, ed. Process Systems Engineering 1985: Computers in Chemical Engineering. Proceedings of the Symposium, Cambridge, U. K., March 31 - April 4, 1985.
--The Protection of Exothermic Reactors & Pressurised Storage Vessels: Proceedings of the Symposium, Chester, U. K., April 25-27, 1984.
Institution of Chemical Engineers Staff. Solids Separation Processes.
--Understanding Process Integration.
Institution of Chemical Engineers Staff & Linhoff, B. User Guide on Process Integration for the Efficient Use of Energy.
Institution of Civil Engineers Staff, ed. Arbitration Procedure.
--Diaphragm Walls & Anchorages.
Institution of Electrical Engineers (UK) Staff & Peter Peregrims, Ltd. Metering Apparatus & Tariffs for Electricity Supply.
Institution of Electrical Engineers (UK) Staff & Peter Peregrinus, Ltd. Network Planning Symposium (Networks 83)
Institution of Electrical Engineers (UK) Staff & Peter Peregrinus, Ltd. Staff. Reliability of Power Supply Systems.
--Road Traffic Signalling.
--Software Engineering for Telecommunication Switching Systems.
Institution of Metallurgists Staff. Progress in Metallurgical Technology.
--The Structure of Metals: A Modern Conception.
Instituto Geografico de Agostini Staff. World Atlas of Agriculture: Europe, U. S. S. R., Asia Minor; South & East Asia, Oceania; the Americas; & Africa.
Institutue Lanfranco, et al, trs. see Twitchel, Paul.
Instituut voor Sociale Geschiedenis Staff. Alfabetische Catalogus Van De Boeken En Brochures Van Het Internationaal Instituut Voor Sociale Geschiedenis (Alphabetical Catalog of the Books & Pamphlets of the International Institute of Social History) Amsterdam, 1st Suppl.
Instructional Aides, Inc. Domestic Violence--No Longer Behind the Curtain.
--Education: Can Success Be Measured?
Instrument Maintenance Management Symposium Staff. Instrument Maintenance Management, Vol. 13: Proceedings of the 13th Instrument Maintenance Management Symposium.
Instrument Society of America Staff. Advances in Instrumentation: Proceedings of the ISA Conference & Exhibit, 39th.
--Advances in Instrumentation: Proceedings of the ISA International Conference & Exhibit, Philadelphia, Pa., Oct., 1982.
--Advances in Instrumentation: Proceedings of the 38th ISA Conference & Exhibit, 1983.
--Aerospace & Test Measurement Proceedings Index: Index of Proceedings from Instrumentation in the Aerospace Industry, Vols. 1-24, Fundamentals of Aerospace Intrumentation, Vols. 1-10 & Advances in Test Measurement, Vols. 11-15, 1980.
--Biomedical Sciences Instrumentation: Proceedings of the Rocky Mountain Bioengineering International Symposium, 18th, Laramie, Wyoming, 1981.
--Biomedical Sciences Instrumentation: Proceedings of the Rocky Mountain Bioengineering International Symposium, 16th, Denver, Colorado, 1979.
--Biomedical Sciences Instrumentation: Proceedings of the Rocky Mountain Bioengineering International Symposium, 17th, Colorado Springs, Colorado, 1980.
--Biomedical Sciences Instrumentation: Proceedings of the Rocky Mountain Bioengineering International Symposium, 19th, 1982.
--Enhancing Productivity: Proceedings of the Pacific Cascade Instrumentation '84 Symposium.
--Instrumentation & Control in the 80's: Proceedings of the 1984 Joint Symposium.
--Instrumentation in the Power Industry, Vol. 23: Proceedings of the 23rd Power Instrumentation Symposium.
Instrument Society of America Staff & University of Pittsburgh Staff. Modeling & Stimulation: Proceedings of the Annual Pittsburgh Conference.
Instrumentation Symposium Staff. Instrumentation Symposium for the Process Industries, Vol. 35: Proceedings of the Annual Instrumentation Symposium for the Process Industries.
--Instrumentation Symposium for the Process Industries, Vol. 34: Proceedings of the Annual Instrumentation Symposium for the Process Industries.
Insurance Law Institute & Institute of Continuing Legal Education in Georgia. Program Materials for Insurance Law Institute: September 25-27, 1986, St. Simons Island, Georgia.
Inte. Table Constants Tables of V17.
Intel Marketing Communications Staff. The Eighty Eighty, Eighty Eighty-Five Microprocessor Book.
Intel Staff. Automotive Handbook.
--Components Quality Reliability Handbook.
--Development Systems Handbook.
--IAPX 286 Programmer's Reference Manual Numeric Supplement.
--IAPX 88.
--An Introduction to the IAPX 286: Concepts & Architecture.
--Memory Components Handbook, 1988.
--Military Handbook.
--Military Handbook Nineteen Eighty-Seven.
--OEM Systems Handbook.
--PASCAL 86 User's Guide for DOS Systems.
--PL-M 286 User's Guide for DOS.
Intentional Educations, Inc. Staff. Practical Problem Solving.
--Practical Problem Solving.
--Practical Problem Solving.
Inter-American Commission of Women Assembly. Comparative Document on the Legislation in Force in the American States in Regard to Family Law.
Inter-American Development Bank, Washington, D. C. Staff. Inter-American Bank Index of Periodical Articles on the Economics of Latin America.
Inter-Parliamentary Union Staff. International Parliamentary Conference: Proceedings, 69th, Rome, 1982.
Interdisciplinary Conference, Ann Arbor, March 1973. Formal Aspects Cognitive Processes: Proceedings. Storer, T. & Winter, D., eds.
InterMatrix Ltd. Staff. Stockton International Business Reports: Egypt.
--Stockton International Business Reports: Malaysia.
--Stockton International Business Reports: Brazil.
--Stockton International Business Reports: Indonesia.
--Stockton International Business Reports: Thailand.
--Stockton International Business Reports: India.
--Stockton International Business Reports: Mexico.
--Stockton International Business Reports: Saudi Arabia.
--Stockton International Business Reports: South Korea.
Internal Revenue Service Staff. Blueprint for Progress in Tax Administration of New York State Tax Laws.
International Academy Of Pathology. Bilharziasis. Mostofi, F. K., ed.
International Advanced Course & Workshop on Thermomechanics of Magnetic Fluids Participants. Thermomechanics of Magnetic Fluids: Theory & Applications Proceedings of the International Advanced Course & Workshop on Thermomechanics of Magnetic Fluids, Udine, Italy, Oct. 3-7, 1977. Berkovsky, Boris, ed.
International African Institute Staff. Cumulative Bibliography of African Studies, International African Institute, London Author Catalog.
--Cumulative Bibliography of African Studies, International African Institute, London Classified Catalog.
--Social Implications of Industrialization & Urbanization in Africa South of the Sahara.
International AIRAPT Conference Staff. High Pressure Science & Technology: Proceedings of the International AIRAPT Conference, Le Creuset, France, July 30-Aug. 3, 1979. Vodar, B. & Marteau, P., eds.
International Association for Educational Assessment Staff. Criteria for Awarding School Leaving Certificates, an International Discussion: Proceedings of the International Association for Education Assessment of the 3rd Annual Conference, Narrobi, May 23, 1977. Ottobre, Frances M., ed.
International Association for Hydrogen Energy Staff. Hydrogen in Metals.
International Association of Business Communicators Staff. No Secrets: Gold Quill Winners Tell All. Allan, Elizabeth, ed.
International Association of Cooking Schools Members Staff. The International Association of Cooking Schools Cookbook. Harman, Helen S., ed.
International Association of Gerontology Staff. Medical & Clinical Aspects of Aging: Proceedings of the International Association of Gerontology, 5th Congress. Blumenthal, H. T., ed.
--Proceedings of the International Congress of the International Association of Gerontology, 10th. Andrews, J., ed.
International Association of Music Libraries Staff. Guide for Dating Early Published Music: A Manual of Bibliographical Practices. Krummel, Don W., ed.
International Association of Universities Staff. International Handbook of Universities. Aitken, D. J. & Taylor, A., eds.
International Association of Universities Staff, compiled by. World List of Universities.
International Astronautical Congress, 28th, Prague, 1977, jt. auth. see Napolitano, Luigi G.
International Astronautical Congress Staff & Napolitano, L. G. Applications of Space Developments II: Selected Papers of the International Astronautical Congress, Tokyo, Japan, September 22-27, 1980.
International Astronautical Congress Staff. Astronautics for Peace & Human Progress: Proceedings of the International Astronautical 29th Congress, Dubrovnik, October 1-8, 1978. Napolitano, L. G., ed.
International Astronautical Congress, 12th, Washington, 1961. Proceedings. Baker, R. M. & Makemson, M. W., eds.
International Astronautical Congress, 13th, Varna, 1962. Proceedings. Boneff, N. & Hersey, I., eds.
International Astronautical Congress, 11th, Stockholm, 1960. Proceedings. Reuterswaerd, C. W. & Hjertstrand, A., eds. Incl. Vol. 1. Main Session. Reuterswaerd, C. W., ed; Vol. 2. Small Sounding Rockets Symposium. Hjertstrand, A., ed. Springer-Verlag.
International Atomic Energy Agency Staff. INIS Reference Series.
--Programming & Utilization of Research Reactors: Proceedings. Eklund, Sigvard, ed.
International Atomic Energy Agency. The Text of the Agreement of 20 July 1978 Between Guatemala & the Agency for the Application of Safeguards in Connection with the Treaty for the Prohibition of Nuclear Weapons in Latin America & the Treaty on the Non-Proliferation of Nuclear Weapons.
International Biological Program Staff & National Research Council Staff. Productivity of World Ecosystems.
International Biometeorological Congress Staff. Biometeorology: Proceedings of the 7th Congress, College Park, MD, 1975. Landsberg, H. E., ed.
--Biometeorology Seven: Proceedings, Supplement to Volume 24, of the International Journal of Biometeorology of the 8th Congress, September 9-15, 1979. Zemel, Z. & Hyslop, N., eds.
International Brain Research Organization. Psychophysiological Mechanisms of Hypnosis: Proceedings. Chertok, L., ed.
International Business Unit, Department of Management Science, University of Manchester Institute of Science & Technology Staff. International Business Bibliography.
International Cancer Congress, 9th, Tokyo, 1966. Proceedings. Harris, R. J., ed.
--Proceedings. Harris, R. J., ed.
International CBF Symposium Staff, et al. Cerebral Circulation & Metabolism: Proceedings of the 6th International CBF Symposium, June 6-9, 1973. Langfitt, T. W., ed.
International Chamber of Commerce Staff, ed. Arbitration Law in Europe.
International City Management Association Staff. Compensation Eighty-Four: Annual Report on Local Government Executive Salaries & Fringe Benefits.
--Effective Supervisory Practices.
--Municipal Year Book 1980.
--The Municipal Year Book 1981.
International Clean Air Congress, 2nd. Proceedings. Englund, Harold M. & Beery, W. T., eds.
International Coal Exploration Symposium Staff. Coal Exploration: Proceedings of the 2nd International Symposium, Denver, Colorado, Oct. 1978. Argall, George O., Jr., ed.
International Commission of Jurists (Geneva, Switzerland) Staff, ed. see Shehadeh, Raja.
International Commission on Irrigation & Drainage, New Delhi, India, ed. The Application of Systems Analysis Irrigation, Drainage & Flood Control: A Manual for Engineers & Water Technologists.
International Commission on Microbial Specifications for Foods. Microbial Ecology of Foods: Vol. 1 Factors Affecting Life & Death of Microorganisms.
International Commission on Radiological Protection. Implications of Commission Recommendations That Doses Be Kept As Low As Readily Achievable.
--Permissible Dose for Internal Radiation.
--Protection of the Patient in X-Ray Diagnosis.
--Radiation Protection in Schools for Pupils up to the Age of 18 Years.
International Committee for Social Science Information & Documentation, ed. International Bibliography of Economics - Bibliographie Internationale de Science Economique.
--International Bibliography of Economics, 1978.
--International Bibliography of Political Science - Bibliographie Internation ale de Science Politique.
--International Bibliography of Political Science, 1978.
--International Bibliography of Political Science 1977.
International Committee on English in the Liturgy, Confraternity of Christian Doctrine for the New American Bible, tr. see Catholic Church-Sacred Congregation of Divine Worship Staff.
International Committee on Taxonomy of Viruses. Classification & Nomenclature of Viruses: Proceedings of the International Committee on Taxonomy of Viruses, 1st Report. Wildy, P., ed.
--Classification & Nomenclature of Viruses: Proceedings of the International Committee on Taxonomy of Viruses, 2nd Report.
International Computer Programs, Inc. Staff. ICP Software Directory. Hamilton, Dennis L., ed.
International Computer Programs, Inc. Staff & Hamilton, Dennis L., eds. ICP Software Directory.
--ICP Software Directory.
--ICP Software Directory.
International Computer Programs, Inc. ICP Software Directory. Hamilton, Dennis L. & Keesling, Monika A., eds.
--ICP Software Directory. Hamilton, Dennis L. & Keesling, Monika A., eds.
--ICP Software Directory. Hamilton, Dennis L. & Keesling, Monika A., eds.
--ICP Software Directory. Hamilton, Dennis L. & Keesling, Monika A., eds.
--ICP Software Directory. Hamilton, Dennis L. & Keesling, Monika A., eds.
--ICP Software Directory. Hamilton, Dennis L. & Keesling, Monika A., eds.
International Computer Programs, Inc. Staff. ICP Software Directory: Banking, Insurance & Finance. Hamilton, Dennis L. & Keesling, Monika A., eds.
International Computer Programs, Inc. & Hamilton, Dennis L., eds. ICP Software Directory: Banking, Insurance & Finance.
International Computer Programs, Inc. ICP Software Directory: Banking, Insurance & Finance. Hamilton, Dennis L. & Keesling, Monika A., eds.
--ICP Software Directory: Banking, Insurance & Finance. Hamilton, Dennis L. & Keesling, Monika A., eds.
International Computer Programs, Inc. Staff. ICP Software Directory: Cross Industry Applications. Spangler, Richard J., ed.
--ICP Software Directory: General Accounting. Hamilton, Dennis L. & Keesling, Monika A., eds.
--ICP Software Directory: General Accounting. Hamilton, Dennis L. & Keesling, Monika A., eds.
International Computer Programs, Inc. Staff & Hamilton, Dennis L., eds. ICP Software Directory: General Accounting.
--ICP Software Directory: General Accounting.
International Computer Programs, Inc. ICP Software Directory: General Accounting. Hamilton, Dennis L. & Keesling, Monika A., eds.
--ICP Software Directory: General Accounting. Hamilton, Dennis L. & Keesling, Monika A., eds.
--ICP Software Directory: General Accounting. Hamilton, Dennis L. & Keesling, Monika A., eds.
--ICP Software Directory: General Accounting. Hamilton, Dennis L. & Keesling, Monika A., eds.
International Computer Programs, Inc. Staff & Hamilton, Dennis L., eds. ICP Software Directory: Industry Specific Applications.
--ICP Software Directory: Industry Specific Applications.
International Computer Programs, Inc. ICP Software Directory: Industry Specific Applications. Hamilton, Dennis L. & Keesling, Monika A., eds.
--ICP Software Directory: Industry Specific Applications. Hamilton, Dennis L. & Keesling, Monika A., eds.
--ICP Software Directory: Industry Specific Applications. Hamilton, Dennis L. & Keesling, Monika A., eds.
International Computer Programs, Inc. Staff. ICP Software Directory: Mainframe-Minicomputer Series. Hamilton, Dennis L. & Keesling, Monika A., eds.

International Computer Programs, Inc. ICP Software Directory: Management & Administration. Hamilton, Dennis L. & Keesling, Monika A., eds.
--ICP Software Directory: Management & Administration. Hamilton, Dennis L. & Keesling, Monika A., eds.
--ICP Software Directory: Management & Administration. Hamilton, Dennis L. & Keesling, Monika A., eds.
International Computer Programs, Inc. & Hamilton, Dennis L., eds. ICP Software Directory: Manufacturing & Engineering.
International Computer Programs, Inc. ICP Software Directory: Manufacturing & Engineering. Hamilton, Dennis L. & Keesling, Monika A., eds.
--ICP Software Directory: Manufacturing & Engineering. Hamilton, Dennis L. & Keesling, Monika A., eds.
--ICP Software Directory: Microcomputer Series. Hamilton, Dennis L. & Keesling, Monika A., eds.
--ICP Software Directory: Office Automation & Business Management. Hamilton, Dennis L. & Keesling, Monika A., eds.
--ICP Software Directory: Office Automation & Business Management. Hamilton, Dennis L. & Keesling, Monika A., eds.
International Computer Programs, Inc. Staff. ICP Software Directory: System Software. Spangler, Richard J., ed.
International Computer Programs, Inc. Staff & Hamilton, Dennis L., eds. ICP Software Directory: Systems & Utilities.
--ICP Software Directory: Systems & Utilities.
International Computer Programs, Inc. ICP Software Directory: Systems & Utilities. Hamilton, Dennis L. & Keesling, Monika A., eds.
--ICP Software Directory: Systems & Utilities. Hamilton, Dennis L. & Keesling, Monika A., eds.
--ICP Software Directory: Systems & Utilities. Hamilton, Dennis L. & Keesling, Monika A., eds.
International Computer Programs, Inc. Staff & Spangler, Richard J. ICP Software Directory-United Kingdom: Software Products, Services & Suppliers.
International Computer Programs, Inc. Staff. ICP Software Directory, Vol. 1: Systems Software. Hamilton, Dennis L., ed.
--ICP Software Directory, Vol. 2: General Accounting Systems. Hamilton, Dennis L., ed.
--ICP Software Directory, Vol. 3: Management & Administration Systems. Hamilton, Dennis L., ed.
--ICP Software Directory, Vol. 4: Banking, Insurance & Finance Systems. Hamilton, Dennis, ed.
--ICP Software Directory, Vol. 5: Manufacturing & Engineering Systems. Hamilton, Dennis L., ed.
--ICP Software Directory, Vol. 6: Specialized Industry Systems. Hamilton, Dennis L., ed.
--ICP Software Directory, Vol. 7: Microcomputer Systems, Specialized Business Applications. Hamilton, Dennis L., ed.
--ICP Software Directory, Vol. 7: Microcomputer Systems, Systems Software & General Business Applications. Hamilton, Dennis L., ed.
International Conference Held in Helsinki Staff, et al. Animal Models in Alcohol Research: Proceedings of the International Conference, June 4-8, 1979. Eriksson, K., ed.
International Conference London Staff. Business Telecom: Proceedings of the International Conference London, 1983.
International Conference, New Haven Staff. Fractional Calculus & Its Applications: Proceedings of the International Conference, June 1974. Ross, B., ed.
International Conference of Selected Papers Staff. Applied Cross-Cultural Psychology: Proceedings of the 2nd Conference, Kingston, Ont., August 6-10, 1974. Berry, J. W. & Lonner, W., eds.
International Conference on Advances in Computer Chess Staff. Advances in Computer Chess in 3 Parts: Proceedings of the International Conference on Advances in Computer Chess, London, UK, April, 1981. Clarke, M. R., ed.
International Conference on Atherosclerosis, Milan Staff. Proceedings of the International Conference on Atherosclerosis, November, 1977. Carlson, Lars A., et al, eds.
International Conference on Atomic Spectroscopy Staff. Recent Advances in Analytical Spectroscopy: Proceedings of the 9th International Conference on Atomic Spectroscopy & 22nd Colloquium Spectroscopicum Internationale, Tokyo, Japan, 4-8 September 1981. Fuwa, K., ed.
International Conference on Automation in Warehousing Staff. Proceedings of the 2nd International Conference on Automation in Warehousing, University of Nottingham, England, April 1975.
--Proceedings of the 2nd International Conference on Automation in Warehousing, Keele, England, March 1977.
International Conference on Cartography Staff. Abstracts of Papers: Proceedings of the 9th International Conference on Cartography, College Park, MD, 1978.
International Conference on Civil Liability for Nuclear Damage, Vienna, 1963. Civil Liability for Nuclear Damage: Official Records.
International Conference on Comparative Mammalian Cytogenetics Staff. Proceedings of the International Conference on Comparative Mammalian Cytogenetics, Dartmouth Medical School, 1968. Benirschke, K., ed.
International Conference on Computational Methods in Nonlinear Mechanics Staff. Computational Methods in Nonlinear Mechanics: Selected Papers of the 2nd Conference, Univ. of Texas at Austin. Oden, J. T., ed.
International Conference on Computing Methods in Optimization Problems - 2nd San Remo, Italy - 1968. Proceedings. Balakrishnan, A. V., ed.
International Conference on Electron Microscopy Staff. Proceedings of the Fourth International Conference on Electron Microscopy, Berlin, 1958. Mollenstedt, G., et al, eds.
International Conference on Energy Use Management Staff & Fazzolari, R. Beyond the Energy Crisis-Opportunity & Challenge: Proceedings of the ICEUM, 3rd, Berlin, October 26-30, 1981.
International Conference on Environmental Carcinogensis, Amsterdam, May 1979. Environmental Carcinogenesis; Occurrence Risk Evaluation & Mechanisms: Proceedings. Emmelot, P. & Kriek, E., eds.
International Conference on Equine Infectious Diseases Staff. Equine Infectious Diseases III: Proceedings of the International Conference, 3rd. Bryans, J. T. & Gerber, H., eds.
International Conference on Hot Electrons in Semiconductors Staff. Hot Electrons in Semiconductors: Proceedings of the International Conference, Denton, TX, July 6-8, 1977. Dunlap, W. Crawford, ed.
International Conference on Industrial Robot Technology Staff & International Symposium on Industrial Robots, 6th, Univ. Nottingham, Eng., Mar. 1976. First Joint Robots Conference: Proceedings of the International Conference on Industrial Robot Technology, 3rd, University of Nottingham, Eng., March 1976. Brock, T. E., ed.
International Conference on Industrial Robot Technology Staff. Proceedings of the International Conference on Industrial Robot Technology, 1st, University of Nottingham, Eng, March 1973.
International Conference on Information Sciences & Systems Staff. Applications & Research in Information Systems & Sciences: Proceedings of the International Conference, 1st, Patras, Greece, August 1976. Lainiotis, Demetrios G. & Tzannes, Nicolaos, eds.
International Conference on Man-Machine Systems Staff. Man-Machine Systems: Proceedings of the International Conference, Manchester, UK, July 1982.
International Conference on Mechanisms of Salivary Secretion & Their Regulation-2nd-Birmingham-Ala.-1966. Secretory Mechanisms of Salivary Glands. Schneyer, Leon H. & Schneyer, Charlotte A., eds.
International Conference on Noise Control Engineering Staff. Inter-Noise '85: Proceedings. Steinhardt, H., ed.
International Conference On Nuclidic Masses - 2nd - Vienna - 1963. Proceedings. Johnson, W. H., Jr., ed.
International Conference on Numerical Methods in Fluid Dynamics Staff. Meningiomas Diagnostic & Therapeutic Problems: Proceedings of the International Conference on Numerical Methods in Fluid Dynamics, 4th, University of Colorado, June 24-28, 1974. Richtmyer, R. D., ed.
International Conference on Numerical Methods in Fluid Mechanics, 3rd. Problems of Fluid Mechanics: Proceedings. Cabannes, H. & Temam, R., eds.
International Conference on Physics of Semiconductors Staff. Physics of Semiconductors: Proceedings. Hulin, Michel, ed.
International Conference on Plant Growth Substances Staff. Plant Growth Substances, 1970: Proceedings of the International Conference, 7th, Canberra. Carr, D. J., ed.
International Conference on Probability in Banach Spaces Staff. Probability in Banach Spaces: Proceedings of the International Conference, First, Oberwolfach, July 20-26, 1975. Beck, A., ed.
International Conference on Secondary Ion Mass Spectrometry Staff. Secondary Ion Mass Spectrometry SIMS IV: Proceedings of the International Conference, 4th, Minoo-Kanko Hotel, Osaka, Japan, November 13-19, 1984. Benninghoven, A., et al, eds.
International Conference on Submillimetre Waves & Their Applications Staff. Submillimetre Waves & Their Applications: Proceedings of the International Conference, 3rd, 1978.
International Conference on the Commercial Applications & Implementations of Biotechnology Staff. Biotech: Proceedings.
International Congress for Energy & the Ecosystem Staff. Ecology & Coal Resource Development: Proceedings of the International Congress for Energy & the Ecosystem, University of North Dakota, June 12-16, 1978. Wali, Mohan K., ed.
International Congress for Hypnosis & Psychosomatic Medicine Staff. Proceedings of the International Congress for Hypnosis & Psychosomatic Medicine, Paris, 1965. Lassner, J., ed.
International Congress for Suicide Prevention Staff, et al. Suicide Prevention: Proceedings of the International Congress for Suicide Prevention, 7th, Amsterdam, August 27-30, 1973.
International Congress of Allergology Staff. Advances in Allergology & Applied Immunology: Proceedings of the International Congress of Allergology, 10th, Jerusalem, Israel, Nov., 1979. Oehling, A., et al, eds.
International Congress of Botany Staff. Incompatability in Fungi: Proceedings of the International Congress of Botany, Edinburgh, 1964. Raper, J. R. & Esser, K., eds.
International Congress of Hedrologicum Conlegium, 3rd, Erlangen-Nuremberg Germany, 1968. Progress in Proctology: Proceedings. Hoferichter, J., ed.
International Congress of Histochemistry & Cytochemistry, 2nd, Frankfurt Am Main, 1964. Proceedings. Schiebler, T. H., et al, eds.
International Congress of Microbiological Standardization Staff. Proceedings of the International Congress of Microbiological Standardization, 11th, Milan, 1968. Regamey, R. H., et al, eds.
International Congress of Physiological Sciences, Satellite Symposium, 1971. Na-Linked Transport of Organic Solutes: The Coupling Between Electrolyte & Nonelectrolyte Transport in Cells, Proceedings. Heinz, E., ed.
International Congress of Physiological Sciences & Annual Meeting of the German Angiological Society, Tuebingen, 1971. Vascular Smooth Muscle: Proceedings. Betz, E., ed.
International Congress of Psychosomatic Obstetrics & Gynecology Staff. Emotion & Reproduction: Proceedings of the International Congress of Psychosomatic Obstetrics & Gynecology, 5th. Carenza, L. & Zinchella, L., eds.
International Congress of Pure & Applied Chemistry 28th, Vancouver, BC, Canada, 16-22 August 1981. Frontiers in Chemistry: Proceedings. Laidler, ed.
International Congress on Analytical Techniques in Environmental Chemistry Staff. Analytical Techniques in Environmental Chemistry: Proceedings of the International Congress, Barcelona, November 27-30, 1978. Albaiges, J., ed.
International Congress on Analytical Techniques in Environmental Chemistry Staff & Albaiges, J. Analytical Techniques in Environmental Chemistry 2: Proceedings of the International Congress, 2nd, Barcelona, Spain, November, 1981.
International Congress on Child Abuse & Neglect, 2nd, London 1978. Abstracts of the Second International Congress on Child Abuse & Neglect. Franklin, A. White, ed.
International Congress on Criminology, 6th, Madrid, 1970. Criminological Research Trends in Western Germany: German Reports. Kaiser, G. & Wuertenberger, T., eds.
International Congress on Medicinal Plant Research, Section A Staff. New Natural Products & Plant Drugs with Pharmacological, Biological or Therapeutical Activity: Proceedings of the International Congress on Medicinal Plant Research, Section A, University of Munich, Germany, Sept. 6-10, 1976. Wagner, H. K. & Wolff, P. M., eds.
International Congress on Physiological Sciences Staff. Cerebral Control of Eye Movements & Motion Perception: Proceedings of the International Congress on Physiological Sciences, 25th, Munich, 1971. Dichgans, J. & Bizzi, E., eds.
International Congress on Suicide Prevention 7th. Proceedings. Speyer, N., et al, eds.
International Congress on X-Ray Optics & Microanalysis, 5th, 1968. Proceedings. Gaukler, K. H. & Moellenstedt, G., eds.
International Council for Building Research & Documentation Staff & International Union of Testing & Research Labs for Materials & Structures Staff, eds. Appropiate Building Materials for Low Cost Housing.
International Council for Building Research Studies & Documentation Staff. Appropriate Building Materials for Low Cost Housing. International Union of Testing & Research Labs for Materials & Structures Staff, ed.
--Directory of Building Research, Information & Development Organizations.
International Council for Philosophy & Humanistic Studies Staff & International Social Science Council Staff. Marx & Contemporary Scientific Thought.
International Council of Aeronautical Sciences Staff. The Congress of the International Council of the Aeronautical Sciences, 15th, London, England, 7-12 September, 1986: Proceedings.
International Council on Archives, Business Archives Committee. Business Archives: Studies on International Practices.
International Council on Health, Physical Education & Recreation Staff. ICHPER Book of Worldwide Games & Dances.
International Court of Justice Staff. Case Concerning Delimitation of the Maritime Boundary in the Gulf of Maine Area: Order of 5 November 1982.
--Western Sahara.
International Defense Images Staff. Power at Sea: A Portrait of U. S. Naval Aviation. Mi Seitelman, ed.
International Fire Service Training Association Staff. Fire Prevention & Inspection. Hudiburg, Everett & Thomas, Charles, eds.
--Water Supplies for Fire Protection. Laughlin, Jerry & Williams, Connie E., eds.
International Fire Services Training Association Committee. Fire Hose Practices. Hudiburg, Everett & Thomas, Charles E., eds.
International Foundation for Theatrical Research Staff. An Advanced College Course on How to Become a Great Actor.
International Franchise Association, jt. auth. see Legal & Government Affairs Symposium.
International Geographical Congress Staff. International Geography 1972: Proceedings of the International Geographical Congress, 22nd, Canada. Adams, W. Peter & Helleiner, Frederick M., eds.
International Glaucoma Symposium, Nara, Japan, May 7-11, 1978. Glaucoma Update: Proceedings. Krieglstein, G. K. & Leydecker, W., eds.
International Heat Pipe Conference Staff & Reay, D. A. Heat Pipes & Thermosyphons for Heat Recovery: Proceedings of the International Heat Pipe Conference, 4th, London, Sept. 7-10, 1981.
International Heat Transfer Conference Staff. Heat Transfer Nineteen Seventy-Four: Proceedings of the International Conference, 5th, Tokyo. Mizushina, T., ed.
International High Technology Machine Tool & Production Engineering Conference Staff. MACH-TECH: Proceedings of the International High Technology Machine Tool & Production Engineering Conference, 1st.
International Institute for Strategic Studies Staff. The Military Balance, 1980-1981.
--The Military Balance, 1981 to 1982.
--The Military Balance, 1987-1988.
--The Military Balance, 1988-89.
International Institute for the Unification of Private Law Staff. Digest of Legal Activities of International Organizations & Other Institutions.
--The Digest of Legal Activities of International Organizations & Other Institutions.
International Institute for Unification of Private Law Staff. Digest of Legal Activities of International Organizations: Other Institutions.
International Institute of Refrigeration. Heat Transfer-Current Application of Air Conditioning. Van Iherbeek, A., ed.
--The New International Dictionary of Refrigeration in English, French, Russian, German, Italian, Spanish, & Norwegian.
--Progress in Refrigeration Science & Technology, Munich Conference.
International Institute of Social History, Amstersdam Staff. Alphabetical Catalog of the Books & Pamphlets of the International Institute of Social History: Library Catalogs-Bibliography Guides 2nd Supplement.
International Institute of Welding Staff, ed. The Physics of Welding.
--Underwater Welding: Proceedings of the Conference, Norway, June 27-28, 1983.

Authors

International Instrumentation Symposium Staff. Fundamentals of Aerospace Instrumentation & Fundamentals of Test Measurement: Tutorial Proceedings of the International Instrumentation Symposium, 28th, 1982.

--Fundamentals of Aerospace Instrumentation & Fundamentals of Test Measurement: Tutorial Proceedings of the 29th International Instrumentation Symposium.

--Fundamentals of Aerospace Instrumentation, Vol. 11 & Fundamentals of Test Measurement, Vol. 6: Tutorial Proceedings of the International Instrumentation Symposium, 25th, Anaheim, California, 1979.

--Fundamentals of Aerospace Instrumentation, Vol. 12 & Fundamentals of Test Measurement, Vol. 7: Tutorial Proceedings of the International Instrumentation Symposium, 26th, Seattle, Washington, 1980.

--Fundamentals of Aerospace Instrumentation, Vol. 15 & Fundamentals of Test Measurement, Vol. 10: Tutorial Proceedings of the International Instrumentation Symposium, 30th.

--Instrumentation in the Aerospace Industry & Advances in Test Measurement: Tutorial Proceedings of the International Instrumentation Symposium, 26th.

--Instrumentation in the Aerospace Industry & Advances in Test Measurement: Proceedings of the International Instrumentation Symposium, 26th.

--Instrumentation in the Aerospace Industry & Advances in Test Measurement: Proceedings of the International Instrumentation Symposium, 28th.

--Instrumentation in the Aerospace Industry, Vol. 30: Proceedings of the International Instrumentation Symposium, 30th, 1984. Bd. with Vol. 21. Advances in Test Measurement. Instru Soc.

International Irrigation Information Center, Bet Dagan, Israel Staff, ed. Irrigation: International Guide to Organizations & Institutions.

International Labor Office, Geneva Staff. Yearbook of Labor Statistics 1980.

International Labour Office. Directory of Workers' Education Institutions & Programmes in Developing Countries.

International Labour Office, ed. see Abdel-Fadil, Mahmoud.

International Labour Office, Central Library, Geneva Staff. International Labour Documentation, Cumulative Edition, 1965-1969.

International Labour Office, Geneva Staff, ed. see Bell, Michael.

International Labour Office, Geneva Staff. Audiovisual, Draughting, Office, Reproduction & Other Ancillary Equipment & Supplies: Equipment Planning Guide for Vocational & Technical Training & Education Programmes.

--Migrant Workers.

International Labour Office, Iron & Steel Committee. The Improvement of Working Conditions & Working Environments in the Iron & Steel Industry: Proceedings of the International Labour Office, Iron & Steel Committee, 10th Session, Geneva, 1981.

International Labour Office Staff. Agrarian Policies & Rural Poverty in Africa: Second Impression, 1985. Ghai, Dharam & Radwan, Samir, eds.

--Apartheid: Proceedings of the International Labour Conference, 64th Session, 1978.

--Collective Bargaining in Industrialised Market Economies.

International Labour Office Staff, et al. Conciliation Services: Structures, Functions & Techniques. Cordova, Efren, intro. by.

International Labour Office Staff. Construction of the International Labour Organisation & Standing Orders of the International Labour Conference, 1980 Edition.

--Employment & Economic Reform - Towards a Strategy for the Sudan: Report of a Mission Financed by the United Nations Development Programme & Organized by the ILO-Jobs & Skills Programme for Africa, August-September 1986.

International Labour Office Staff & Jobs & Skills Programme for Africa Staff. First Things First - Meeting the Basic Needs of the People of Nigeria: Report to the Government of Nigeria by a JASPA Basic Needs Mission - Jobs & Skills Programme for Africa.

International Labour Office Staff. The ILO-Norway African Regional Training Course for Senior Social Security Managers & Administrative Officials.

International Labour Office Staff, ed. see Lim, Linda & Fong, Pang E.

International Labour Office Staff. Making Work More Human: Proceedings of the International Labour Office Conference, 60th Session, 1975.

--New Forms of Work Organisation: German Democratic Republic, India, Italy, U. S. S. R., Economic Costs & Benefits.

International Labour Office Staff, ed. see Paul, Samuel.

International Labour Office Staff. Prosperity for Welfare: Proceedings of the International Labour Conference, 58th Session, Geneva, 1973.

International Labour Office Staff & Shahandeh, Behrouz. Rehabilitation Approaches to Drug & Alcohol Dependence.

International Labour Office Staff. Small-Scale Oil Extraction from Groundnuts & Copra: Technical Memorandum.

--Small-Scale Weaving: Technical Memorandum No. 4.

--Tasks to Jobs: Developing a Modular System of Training for Hotel Occupations.

--Technology & Employment in Industry: A Case Study Approach. Bhallas, A., ed.

--Trade Union Rights & Their Relation to Civil Liberties: Proceedings of the International Labour Conference, 54th Session, Geneva, 1970.

International Labour Office Staff & UN High Commission for Refugees. Tradition & Dynamism Among Afghan Refugees: A Report on Income-Generating Activities for Afghan Refugees in Pakistan.

International Labour Office Staff. The Urban Informal Sector in Developing Countries: Employment, Poverty & Environment. Sethuraman, S. V., ed.

--Vocational Training of Seafarers: Proceedings of the International Labour Conference, 55th Session, 1970.

--World Employment Programme: Proceedings of the International Labour Conference, 56th Session.

--World Employment Programme: Proceedings of the International Labour Conference, 53rd Session, 1969.

International Labour Organisation (ILO) Staff, ed. Yearbook of Labor Statistics, 1982.

International Labour Organisation Staff. Safety & Health Practices of Multinational Enterprises.

International Marine & Shipping Conference Staff. Proceedings of the International Marine & Shipping Conference, 1969.

International Masonry Institute Staff. Masonry Glossary.

International Mathematical Conference, College Park, 1970. Several Complex Variables 1: Proceedings. Horvath, J., ed.

International Mathematical Union Staff, ed. World Directory of Mathematicians 1986.

International Meeting on Solid Electrolytes Staff. Solid Electrolytes: Proceedings of the International Meeting on Solid Electrolytes, 2nd, University of St. Andrews, Sept. 20-22, 1978. Armstrong, R. D., ed.

International Mine Drainage Symposium Staff. Mine Drainage: Proceedings of the International Mine Drainage Symposium, 1st, Denver, Colorado, May, 1979. Argall, George O., Jr. & Brawner, C. O., eds.

International Monetary Fund Staff. Balance of Payments Statistics Yearbook.

--Government Finance Statistics Yearbook.

--Surveys of African Economies. Incl; Vol. 4. Democratic Republic of Congo, (Zaire), Malagasy Republic, Malawi, Mauritius & Zambia; Vol. 5. Botswana, Lesotho, Swaziland, Burundi, Equatorial Guinea, & Rwanda; Vol. 7. Algeria, Mali, Morocco, & Tunisia. Intl Monetary.

International Museum of Photography, George Eastman House Staff. Library Catalog of the International Museum of Photography at George Eastman House.

International Narcotics Control Board Staff. Estimated World Requirements of Narcotic Drugs in 1983: Supplement.

--Estimated World Requirements of Narcotic Drugs in 1983: Supplement.

International Organization for Standardization Staff. Information Transfer: ISO Standards Handbook I.

International Publishing Corporation, Inc. Staff. Individual Investor's Guide to Investment Publications.

International Research Seminar - Berkeley - 1963. Bernoulli Seventeen Thirteen, Bayes Seventeen Sixty-Three, Laplace Eighteen Thirteen: Proceedings, Anniversary Vol. Lecam, Lucien M. & Neyman, Jerzy, eds.

International Resource Development, Inc. Staff. Artificial Intelligence.

--Color Printers.

--Data & Voice Multiplexers.

--Data, Text & Voice Encryption Worldwide Markets.

--European Local Area Network Markets.

--Far Eastern Vendors Strategies for U. S. Microcomputer Markets.

--Fiber Optic Markets.

--Financial Information Services: Online Teledelivery.

--High Resolution Displays & HDTV.

--Integrated Voice-Data Terminals.

--Interactive Video Systems & Services.

--Laser Market Opportunities.

--Local Area Networks: Applications, Technologies & Opportunities.

--Market for Add-On Boards, Systems & Services for the IBM PC.

--Medical Imaging Markets.

--Microcomputer Operating System Strategies.

--Microcomputer Publications Survey.

--Military Electro-Optics Market.

--Non-Impact Printers in the U. S.

--Non-Keyboard Data Entry.

--PABX Peripherals Market.

--Paperless Consumer Information Services.

--PCs vs. CWPs in the Clerical Workstation of the Future.

--Portable Computers.

--Satellite Communications Services & Equipment Markets.

--Software Publishing & Distribution.

--Telecom Bypass Markets.

--Terminals & Network Products for the 3270 Environment.

--Third Party Maintenance of PCs.

--U. K. Telecommunication Market Opportunities.

--Videocassette & Videodisc Hardware & Software Markets.

International School of Fusion Reactor Technology, Erice (Trapani), Italy, Sept. 4-15, 1972. Course on Stationary & Quasi-Stationary Toroidal Reactors.

International School of Mathematical Physics Staff. Invariant Wave Equations: Proceedings of the International School of Mathematical Physics, Erice, Italy, June 27-July 9, 1977. Velo, G. & Wightman, A. S., eds.

International School Of Nonlinear Mathematics & Physics-Munich-1966. Topics in Nonlinear Physics: Proceedings of the Physics Session. Zabusky, N. J. & Kruskal, M. D., eds.

International School of Nuclear Physics, Sept 23-30, 1974. The Investigation of Nuclear Structure by Scattering Processes at High Energies: Proceedings. Schopper, H., ed.

International School of Plasma Physics, Varenna (Como), Italy, 1971. Course on Instabilities & Confinement in Toroidal Plasmas.

International School of Statistical Mechanics Staff. Transport Phenomena: Proceedings of the International School of Statistical Mechanics, Sitges, Barcelona, June, 1974. Kirczenow, G. & Marro, J., eds.

International School on Electro & Photonuclear Reactions Staff. International School on Electro & Photonuclear Reactions I: Proceedings of the International School on Electro & Photonuclear Reactions, 1st Course, Erice, Italy, June 2-17, 1976. Schaerf, C., ed.

International Seaweed Symposium Staff. Proceedings: Proceedings of the International Seaweed Symposium, 7th, Sappora, Japan, Aug., 1971. Science Council of Japan Staff, ed.

International Seminar on Biomechanics Staff. Biomechanics 3: Proceedings of the International Seminar on Biomechanics, 3rd, Rome, 1971. Cerquiglini, S., et al, eds.

International Seminar on Reproductive Physiology & Sexual Endocrinology Staff. Basic Actions of Sex Steroids on Target Organs: Proceedings of the International Seminar on Reproductive Physiology & Sexual Endocrinology, 3rd, Brussels, 1970. Hubinont, P. O., et al, eds.

International Seminar on Trends in Mathematical Modelling Staff. Proceedings of the International Seminar on Trends in Mathematical Modelling, Venice, Dec., 1971. Hawkes, N., ed.

International Social Science Council Staff, jt. auth. see International Council for Philosophy & Humanistic Studies Staff.

International Society for Cell Biology Staff. Cellular Dynamics of the Neuron. Barondes, Samuel H., ed.

--Control Mechanisms in the Expression of Cellular Phenotypes. Padyluka, Helen A., ed.

--Cytogenetics of Cells in Culture. Harris, R. J., ed.

--Differentiation & Immunology. Warren, Katherine B., ed.

--Formation & Fate of Cell Organelles. Warren, Katherine B., ed.

--Intracellular Transport. Warren, Katherine B., ed.

--Use of Radioautography in Investigating Protein Synthesis. Leblond, C. P. & Warren, Katherine B., eds.

International Society for Education through Art Staff. Arts in Cultural Diversity.

International Society for Eye Research Staff. Drugs & Ocular Tissues: Proceedings of the International Society for Eye Research, 2nd Meeeting, Jerusalem, Sept. 12-17, 1976. Dikstein, S., ed.

International Society for Neurovegetative Research Staff. Neurohormones & Neurohumors: Proceedings of the International Society for Neurovegetative Research, Amsterdam, 1967.

--Neurovegetative Transmission Mechanisms: Proceedings of the International Society for Neurovegetative Research, Tinany, 1972. Csillik, B. & Kappers, J. A., eds.

International Society for the Study of Behavioral Development Symposium Staff. Determinants of Behavioral Development: Proceedings of the International Society for the Study of Behavioral Development, University of Nijmegen, the Netherlands, July 1971. Monks, F. J., et al, eds.

International Society of Blood Transfusion Staff. Proceedings of the International Society of Blood Transfusion, 12th Congress, Moscow, 1969. Stampfli, K., ed. Incl. Pt. 1. Immunhematology-Immunology, Transplantation Problems, Leukemia, Coagulation; Pt. 2. Organization & Technical Problems of Transfusion; Clinical Problems of Transfusion. S Karger.

International Society of Hemorheology, 2nd International Conference, Heidelberg, 1969. Theoretical & Clinical Hemorheology: Proceedings. Hartert, H. & Copley, A. L., eds.

International Society on Metabolic Eye Disease Staff. Metabolic & Pediatric Eye Disease: Proceedings of the International Society on Metabolic Eye Disease Symposium, 3rd. Haddad, Heskel M., ed.

International Software Database Staff. The Software Catalog: Business Software.

--The Software Catalog: Minicomputers, 1985.

--The Software Catalog: Science & Engineering.

International Spring School on Crystal Growth Staff. Crystal Growth & Characterization: Proceedings of the International Spring School on Crystal Growth, 2nd, Japan, 1974. Ueda, R. & Mullin, J. B., eds.

International Summer Institute in Theoretical Physics Staff. Photon-Hadron Interactions, 1: Proceedings of the International Summer Institute in Theoretical Physics. Desy, 1971. Hoehler, G., ed.

International Summer School for Theoretical Physics Staff. Modular Functions of One Variable Four: Proceedings of the International Summer School for Theoretical Physics, University of Antwerp, RUCA, July-Aug., 1972. Birch, B. J. & Kuyk, W., eds.

International Summer School on Mathematical Systems Theory & Economics, Varenna, Italy, 1967. Proceedings. Kuhn, H. W. & Szegoe, G. P., eds.

International Symposium, Berlin, Sep, 1973. The Pathology of Cerebral Microcirculation: Proceedings. Cervos-Navarro, J., et al, eds.

International Symposium Biologische Staff. Quantitative Biology of Metabolism: Proceedings of the International Symposium on Models of Metabolism, Metabolic Parameters, Damageto Metabolism, Metabolic Control, 3rd, Anstalt Helgoland, 1967. Locker, A., ed.

International Symposium Clausthal - Zellerfeld, 1968. Textures in Research & Practice: Proceedings. Grewen, J. & Wassermann, G., eds.

International Symposium Held at the Battelle Seattle Research Center Seattle, WA, Nov. 4-6, 1974, et al. Molecular Aspects of Membrane Phenomena. Kabak, H. R. & Neurath, H., eds.

International Symposium of the American Society of Zoologists, Toronto, December 27-30, 1977. Animal Models of Comparative & Developmental Aspects of Immunity & Disease: Proceedings. Gershwin, M. Eric & Cooper, Edwin L., eds.

International Symposium on Atherosclerosis Staff. Proceedings of the International Symposium on Atherosclerosis, 3rd, 1973. Schettler, G. & Weizel, A., eds.

International Symposium On Basic Environmental Problems Of Man In Space - 2nd - Paris - 1965. Proceedings. Bjurstedt, H., ed.

International Symposium On Basic Environmental Problems Of Man In Space - 1st - Paris - 1962. Proceedings. Bjurstedt, H., ed.

International Symposium on Carotenoids Staff. Carotenoids Chemistry & Biochemistry: Proceedings of the International Symposium on Carotenoids, 6th, Liverpool, U. K., July 26-31, 1981. Goodwin, T. W. & Britton, G., eds.

International Symposium on Category Theory Staff. Category Theory Applied to Computation & Control: Proceedings of the International Symposium, 1st, San Francisco, 1974. Manes, E. G., ed.

International Symposium on Cell Biology & Cytopharmacology Staff. Advances in Cytopharmacology: Proceedings of the International Symposium on Cell Biology & Cytopharmacology, 1st. Clementi, F. & Ceccarelli, B., eds.

Authors

International Symposium on Chrionomidae Staff. Chironomidae-Ecology Systematics Cytology & Physiology: Proceedings of the International Symposium, 7th, Dublin, August, 1979. Murray, D. A., ed.

International Symposium On Classification Of Brain Tumors - Cologne - 1961. Proceedings. Zuelch, K. J. & Woolf, A. L., eds.

International Symposium on Control Theory, Numerical Methods & Computer Systems Modelling, June, 1974. Proceedings. Bensoussan, A. & Lions, J. L., eds.

International Symposium on Crytorchidism Staff. Cryptorchidism: Proceedings.

International Symposium on Diagnosis & Treatment of Cardiac Arrhythmias Staff. Diagnosis & Treatment of Cardiac Arrhythmias: Proceedings of the International Symposium on Diagnosis & Treatment of Cardiac Arrhythmias, Barcelona, Spain, Oct 5-8, 1977. Bayes De Luna, A. J., ed.

International Symposium on Diagnosis & Treatment of Disorders Affecting the Intrauterine Patient, Dorado, Puerto Rico, 1967. Diagnosis & Treatment of Fetal Disorders: Proceedings. Adamsons, K., ed.

International Symposium On Echo-Encephalography - Erlangen - 1967. Proceedings. Kazner, E., et al, eds. Lewke, M., tr.

International Symposium on Electromagnetic Separation of Radioactive Isotopes, Vienna, 1960. Proceedings. Higatsberger, M. J. & Viehboeck, F. P., eds.

International Symposium on Epilepsy, 7th, West Berlin. Epileptology: Proceedings. Janz, D., ed.

International Symposium on Feto-Placental Insufficiency, 1st, Italy, 1974. Proceedings. Salvadori, B., ed.

International Symposium on Fosfomycin Staff. Proceedings of the International Symposium on Fosfomycin, Madrid, 1975. Gallego, A. & Rubio, J. M., eds.

International Symposium On Hypotensive Peptides - Florence - 1965. Proceedings. Erodes, E. G., ed.

International Symposium on Immunopathology Staff. Immunopathology: Proceedings of the International Symposium, 3rd. Miescher, Peter A. & Graham, Pierre, eds.

International Symposium on Industrial Robots, 6th, Univ. Nottingham, Eng., Mar. 1976, jt. auth. see International Conference on Industrial Robot Technology Staff.

International Symposium on Industrial Robots Staff & Robots Institute of America Staff. Proceedings of the International Symposium on Industrial Robots, 9th.

International Symposium on Malignant Lymphomas of the Nervous System. Proceedings. Jellinger, K. & Seitelberger, F., eds.

International Symposium on Mathematical Problems Staff. Proceedings of the Interntional Symposium on Mathematical Problems, Kyoto University, Kyoto, Japan, Jan. 23-29, 1975.

International Symposium on Metabolism, Physiology & Clinical Use of Pentoses & Pentitols, Hakone, Japan, 1967, et al. Proceedings.

International Symposium on Metabolic Interconversion of Enzymes Staff. Proceedings of the International Symposium on Metabolic Interconversion of Enzymes, 3rd, Seattle, 1973. Fischer, E. H., ed.

International Symposium on Neurosecretion, Kiel, 1969. Aspects of Neuroendocrinology: Proceedings. Bargmann, W. & Scharrer, B., eds.

International Symposium on Neurosecretion, 4th, Strasbourg, 1966. Neurosecretion: Proceedings. Stutinsky, F., ed.

International Symposium on Operating Systems, 1974. Proceedings. Gelenbe, E. & Kaiser, C., eds.

International Symposium on Renal Transport, West Germany, 1968. Renal Transport & Diuretics. Thurau, K. & Jahrmaerker, H., eds.

International Symposium on Shipboard Acoustics. International Symposium on Shipboard Acoustics: Proceeedings, 1976. Janssen, J. H., ed.

International Symposium on Stability in Coal Mining Staff. Stability in Coal Mining: Proceedings of the International Symposium, 1st, Vancouver, B. C., Canada 1978. Brawner, C. O. & Dorling, Ian P., eds.

International Symposium on Staphylococci & Staphylococcal Infections Staff. Staphylococci & Staphylococcal Infections: Proceedings of the Inernational Symposium, Warsaw, Sept., 1971. Jeljaszewicz, J., ed.

International Symposium on Superheavy Elements, March 9-11, 1978, Lubbock, Texas. Superheavy Elements: Proceedings. Lodhi, M. A., ed.

International Symposium on the Aerodynamics & Ventilation of Vehicle Tunnels Staff. Proceedings of the International Symposium on the Aerodynamics & Ventilation of Vehicle Tunnels, 1st.

International Symposium on the Glomerular Basement Membrane Staff. Proceedings of the International Symposiums on the Glomerular Basement Membrane, 1st, Vienna, Sept., 1980. Lubec, G., ed.

International Symposium on the Transportation & Handling of Minerals Staff. Minerals Transportation: Proceedings of the International Symposium, 3rd, Vancouver, British Columbia, Canada, Oct., 1979. Argall, George O., Jr., ed.

International Symposium on Transport & Handling in the Pulp & Paper Industry Staff. Transport & Handling in the Pulp & Paper Industry, Vol. 3: Proceedings of the International Symposium, 3rd, Vancouver, British Columbia, Canada, Sept., 1978. Kalish, John, ed.

International Symposium on Transport & Handling in the Pulp & Paper Industry, Staff. Transport & Handling in the Pulp & Paper Industry, Vol. 4: Proceedings of the International Symposium, 4th, London, England, Nov., 1980. Kalish, John E., ed.

International Symposium on X-Ray Optics & X-Ray Microanalysis Staff. Proceedings of the International Symposium on X-Ray Optics & X-Ray Microanalysis, 3rd, Stanford, California, 1962. Pattee, Howard H., Jr., et al, eds.

International Symposium on Yersinia, Pasteurella & Francisella Staff. Yersinia, Pasteurella & Francisella: Proceedings of the International Symposium, Malmoe, April, 1972. Winblad, ed.

International Tailing Symposium Staff. Tailing Disposal Today: Proceedings of the International Tailing Symposium, 2nd, Denver, Colorado, 1978. Argall, George O., Jr., ed.

International Technical Information Institute Staff. Practical Quality Control Manual with Eight Simple Chart Systems.

International Transcript of Proceedings, jt. auth. see Legal & Government Affairs Symposium.

International Tunnelling Association. Advances in Tunnelling & Subsurface Technology & Use.

International Union Against Cancer Staff. International Catalogue of Films, Filmstrips & Slides.

International Union Against Cancer - Chemotherapy Panel. Treatment of Burkitt's Tumor: Proceedings. Burchenal, J. H. & Burkitt, D. P., eds.

International Union of Biochemistry, Nomenclature Committee, ed. Enzyme Nomenclature 1978.

International Union of Pure & Applied Chemistry. Atomic Absorption Spectroscopy: Proceedings of an International Conference, Sheffield, U. K., 1969.

--Chemical Thermodynamics: Proceedings of an International Conference, Baden Bei Wien, Austria, 1973.

--Classification & Nomenclature of Electroanalytical Techniques.

--High Temperature Technology-3: Proceedings of an International Symposium, Pacific Grove, Calif., 1967.

--International Congress of Pure & Applied Chemistry, 23rd, Boston, 1971. Proceedings Special Lectures Supplement.

--Nomenclature, Symbols, Units & Their Usage in Spectrochemical Analysis 11, Data Interpretation, 111 Analytical Flame Spectroscopy & Associated Non-Flame Procedures.

--Organosilicon Chemistry--1: Proceedings of an International Symposium, Prague, 1965.

--Pharmaceutical Chemistry-2: Proceedings of an International Symposium, Muenster, 1968.

International Union of Pure & Applied Chemistry Staff. Stability Constants of Metal Complexes: Critical Survey of Stability Constants of EDTA Complexes. Anderegg, G., ed.

International Union of Pure & Applied Chemistry. Symposium on Surface Area Determination: Proceedings, Additional Publication, Bristol, U. K., 16-18 July 1969. Ottewill, R. H., ed.

International Union of Testing & Research Labs for Materials & Structures Staff, jt. ed. see International Council for Building Research & Documentation Staff.

International Union of Testing & Research Labs for Materials & Structures Staff, ed. see International Council for Building Research Studies & Documentation Staff.

International Union of Theoretical & Applied Mechanics Staff. Boundary Layer Research: Proceedings of the International Union of Theoretical & Applied Mechanics Symposium, Freiberg, 1957. Goertler, H., ed.

--Creep in Structures: Proceedings of the International Union of Theoretical & Applied Mechanics Symposium, Stanford University, 1960. Hoff, N. J., ed.

International Union of Theoretical & Applied Mechanics Symposium Vienna 1966. Irreversible Aspects of Continuum Mechanics & Transfer of Physical Characteristics in Moving Fluids: Proceedings. Parkus, H. & Sedov, L. I., eds.

International Universitaetswochen Fuer Kernph Staff. Electromagnetic Interactions & Field Theory: Proceedings of the International Universitaetswochen Fuer Kernphysik, 14, der Karlfranzens Universitaet, Schladming. Urban, P., ed.

International University Courses on Nuclear Physics Staff. Concepts in Hadron Physics: Proceedings of the International University Courses on Nuclear Physics, 10th, Schladming, Austria, 1971.

International University Courses on Nuclear Physics, 9th, Schladming, Austria, 1970. Developments in High Energy Physics: Proceedings.

International University Courses on Nuclear Physics Staff. Elementary Particle Physics (Multiparticle Aspects) Proceedings of the International University Courses on Nuclear Physics, 11th, Schladming, Austria, 1972. Urban, P., ed.

International University Courses on Nuclear Physics, 5th, Schladming, Austria, 1966. Elementary Particle Theories: Proceedings. Urban, P., ed.

International University Courses on Nuclear Physics, 8th, Schladming, Austria, 1969. Particle Physics: Proceedings. Urban, P., ed.

International University Courses on Nuclear Physics, 7th, Schladming, Austria, 1968. Particles, Currents, Symmetries: Proceedings. Urban, P., ed.

International University Courses on Nuclear Physics Staff. Progress in Particle Physics: Proceedings of the International University Courses on Nuclear Physics, 13th, Schladming, Austria, 1974. Basetto, A., et al, eds.

--Recent Developments in Mathematical Physics: Proceedings of the International University Courses on Nuclear Physics, 12th, Schladming, Austria, 1973. Urban, P., ed.

International University Courses on Nuclear Physics, 6th, Schladming, Austria, 1967. Special Problems in High Energy Physics: Proceedings. Urban, P., ed.

International University Courses on Nuclear Physics, 3rd, Schladming, Austria, 1964. Weak Interactions & Higher Symmetries: Proceedings. Urban, P., ed.

International Working Seminar on the Role of the History of Physics in Physics Education Staff. History in the Teaching of Physics: Proceedings. Brush, Stephen G. & King, Allen L., eds.

International Workshop on Ergot Alkaloids Staff. Proceedings of the International Workshop on Ergot Alkaloids, Rome, Dec. 6-7, 1976. Brodie, B. B., et al, eds.

International Workshop on Phosphate & Other Minerals Staff. Phosphate & Other Minerals International Workshop: On Phosphate & Other Minerals, 5th International Workshop Abstracts. Massry, S. G., ed.

Internationalen Jugendbibliothek, (International Youth Library) Staff. Kataloge der Internationale Jugendbibliothek, (Catalogs of the International Youth Library) Incl. Pt. 1. Alphabetischer Katalog, (Alphabetical; Pt. 2. Laenderkatalog, (Language Sections Catalog; Pt. 3. Systematischer Katalog, (Classified; Pt. 4. Titelkatalog, (Title; Pt. 5. Illustratorenkatalog, (Catalog of Illustrators. G K Hall.

Interrante, C. G. & Pressouyre, G. M., eds. Current Solutions to Hydrogen Problems in Steels.

Intersociety Working Group Staff. AAAS Report IX: Research & Development, FY 1985. Shapley & Teich, eds.

--AAAS Report VIII: Research & Development, FY 1984. Shapley, et al, eds.

--AAAS Report X: Research & Development FY 1986. Shapley, et al, eds.

--Congressional Action on Research & Development in the FY 1983 Budget.

--Research & Development in the FY 1984 Budget: A Preliminary Analysis. Shapley & Teich, eds.

Intertec Publishing Corp. Staff. Outboard Motor Maintenance & Tune-up Manual.

--Outboard Motor Maintenance Tune-up Manual.

Intertec Publishing Corporation Staff. Intertec Publishing Corporation Staff: 87-88 Season.

Intertec Publishing Staff. Chain Saw Service Manual.

Intervisual Communications. Viking Circus Block Books: Circus Parade Zoo-A Book in-a-Box with a Performing Picture.

Intervisual Staff. Tron Pop-up Book.

Int'l Resource Development Inc. Diamond Thin Film: The Threshold of Commercialization.

Int'l. Resource Development, Inc. Staff. Military Electro-Optics Markets.

Intravaia, Lawrence. Building a Superior School Band Library.

Intriligator, M. D., ed. Frontiers of Quantitative Economics.

Intriligator, Michael D., jt. ed. see Brito, Dagobert.

Inwood, Kristiaan, jt. auth. see Scott, David.

Ioannou, Adrian, ed. see Cugy, Andre & Page, Kogan.

Iocolano, Mark. Nikon F-Two.

--Nikon FM & FE.

Ionesco, Eugene. La Cantatrice Chauve.

--Ce Formidable Bordel.

--Exit the King. Watson, Donald, tr. from Fr.

--The Hermit. Seaver, Richard, tr. from Fr.

--Hugoliad, or The Grotesque & Tragic Life of Victor Hugo. Milos, Yara, tr. from Fr.

--Hunger & Thirst & Other Plays. Watson, Donald, tr. from Fr. Incl. The Picture; Anger; Salutations. Grove.

--Jeux de Massacre: Theatre.

--Macbett. Marowitz, Charles, tr. from Fr.

--Present Passe, Passe Present, Journal en Miettes.

--Present Past, Past Present. Lane, Helen R., tr. from Fr.

--Rhinoceros & Other Plays: The Leader, The Future Is in Eggs. Prouse, Derek, tr. from Fr.

--Victimes du Devoir. Lee, Vera G., ed.

Ionescu, Ghita. The Break-up of the Soviet Empire in Eastern Europe.

Iooss, Walter & Angell, Roger, Jr. Baseball.

Iooss, Walter, Jr. & Anderson, Dave. Shooting for the Gold: A Portrait of America's Olympic Athletes.

Iorizzo, Luciano J. & Mondello, Salvatore. The Italian-Americans.

Iosifescu, M. & Tautu, P. Stochastic Processes & Applications in Biology & Medicine, Pt. 2: Models.

Iosifescu, Marius. Finite Markov Processes & Applications.

Iozawa, Tomoya. Trekking in the Himalayas. Michiko, U. & Kornhauser, David H., trs. from Japanese.

Ipser, Karl. Vatican Art.

Iracki, K., et al, eds. Optimization Techniques: Proceedings.

Irby, Thomas C. & Ward, Darrell L. Hypergraphics User's Guide: Apple II Version.

Ireland, Alexander. Book-Lover's Enchiridion.

Ireland, Denis. From the Jungles of Belfast: A Footnote to History, 1904-1972.

Ireland, Gordon, ed. The Drug Monitoring Data Pocket Guide.

Ireland, Jill. Life Wish.

Ireland, Karin. Hollywood Stuntpeople.

Ireland, Norma O. Index to Women of the World from Ancient to Modern Times: Biographies & Portraits.

Ireland, Thomas R., jt. auth. see Mitchell, William E.

Ireland, Timothy. Who Lies Inside.

IREM Research Department Staff. Computer Applications in Property Management Accounting.

Ireson, Amy G. & Lipscomb, Shirley F. Cooking for One or Two or More.

--Foods for One or Two - or More.

Ireson, Barbara, ed. In a Class of Their Own.

Iri, M. Network Flow, Transportation & Scheduling: Theory & Algorithms.

Iribarne, Louis, tr. see Lem, Stanislaw.

Irion, Arthur L. Introduction by see Cheers, Arlynne Lake & Carter, Lamore J.

Irion, Mary J., et al. Takeoffs from Tension.

Irion, Paul E. Cremation.

Irion, Ruth H. The Christmas Cookie Tree.

Irish Bishop's Pastoral Staff. Human Life Is Sacred.

Irish Genealogical Foundation Staff. Three Hundred Great Families of Ireland.

Irish, Jerry. The Religious Thought of H. Richard Niebuhr.

Irish, Jerry A. A Boy Thirteen: Reflections on Death.

Irish, Lola. The Place of the Swan.

Irish, Marian D. & Frank, Elke. U. S. Foreign Policy: Context, Conduct, Content.

Iriye, Akira. Across the Pacific: An Inner History of American-East Asian Relations.

--Across the Pacific: An Inner History of American-East Asian Relations.

--After Imperialism: The Search for a New Order in the Far East, 1921-1931.

Iriye, Akira, ed. Mutual Images: Essays in American-Japanese Relations.

Irland, Lloyd C. Wildlands & Woodlots: The Story of New England's Forests.

Irland, Nancy. Baby Jesus' Birthday.

Irland, Nancy B. No More Alphabet Soup. Van Dolson, Bobbie J., ed.

Irmiter, Theodore F., jt. auth. see Morr, Mary L.

Irodov, I. E. Basic Laws of Electromagnetism.

--Fundamental Laws of Mechanics.

--Problems in General Physics.
Ironmaking Conference Staff. Ironmaking Conference: Proceedings of the Forty-Third Conference.
Irons, Keith L., jt. auth. see Appley, Lawrence A.
Irons, Patricia. Psychotropic Drugs & Nursing Intervention.
Ironside, H, A. The Best of H. A. Ironside.
--The Continual Burnt Offering: Daily Meditations on the Word of God.
--Sailing with Paul.
Iroshnikov, M. Genesis of the Soviet Federative State: 1917-1925.
Irsigler, F. J. Neurosurgical Approach to Intracranial Infections: A Review of Personal Experiences 1940-1960.
Irsigler, Karl, et al. Diabetes Treatment with Implantable Insulin Infusion Systems.
Irvin, Carol K. & Irvin, James D. Ohio Real Estate Law.
Irvin, James D., jt. auth. see Irvin, Carol K.
Irvine, Elizabeth E. Social Work & Human Problems: Casework, Consultation & Other Topics.
Irvine, Georgeanne. Bo the Orangutan.
--Elmer the Elephant.
--Georgie the Giraffe.
--Lindi the Leopard.
--The Nursery Babies.
--Tully the Tree Kangaroo.
Irvine, J. M. Nuclear Structure Theory.
Irvine, Lucy. Castaway.
Irvine, Mat. Dr. Who Special Effects.
Irvine, T. F., Jr., jt. auth. see Eckert, E. R.
Irvine, T. N., ed. Chromium: Its Physicochemical Behaviour & Petrologic Significance: Proceedings of the Carnegie Institute of Washington Conference, Geophysical Laboratory.
Irvine, Thomas F., Jr. Steam & Gas Tables with Computer Equations.
Irvine, W. M., tr. see Sobolev, V. V.
Irving, Clifford, jt. auth. see Burkholtz, Herbert.
Irving, Clive. Axis.
Irving, Darrel. A Fingerboard Foundation for the Classical GNR.
--The Keystorn of the Guitar.
Irving, David. History of Scottish Poetry. Carylye, J. A., ed.
--The War Between the Generals: Inside the Allied High Command.
Irving, F. G. An Introduction to the Longitudinal Static Stability of Low-Speed Aircraft.
Irving, H. M., ed. Guide to Trivial Names, Trade Names & Synonyms for Substances Used in Analytical Chemistry.
Irving, J. B. Had You Been Born a Muslim.
Irving, James T. Calcium & Phosphoros Metabolism.
Irving, L. Arctic Life of Birds & Mammals Including Man.
Irving, Pierre M. The Life & Letters of Washington Irving.
Irving, Washington. The Legend of Sleepy Hollow & Other Tales.
--Old Christmas.
--Old Christmas-Bracebridge Hall.
--Voyages & Discoveries of the Companions of Columbus. Tuttleton, James W., ed.
--The Wit & Whimsy of Washington Irving. MacPhail, Bruce D., ed.
Irwin. Young Bess.
Irwin & Tecklin. Cardiopulmonary Physical Therapy.
Irwin, Ann & Reida, Bernice. Until We Reach the Valley.
Irwin, Godfrey. American Tramp & Underworld Slang.
Irwin, John R. The Story of John Rice Irwin's Museum of Appalachia.
Irwin, Margaret E. Elizabeth, Captive Princess.
Irwin, Marty. Words from Within.
Irwin, Mary. Reflections in the Son.
Irwin, Paul B. The Care & Counseling of Youth in the Church. Clinebell, Howard J. & Stone, Howard W., eds.
Irwin, Robert. Mingles: A Home Buying Guide for Unmarried Couples.
--The New Mortgage Game.
--Protect Yourself in Real Estate: The Complete Beginner's Guide.
--Smart Money Real Estate for the 80's: New Profits in Big Properties.
Irwin, Robert & Brickman, Richard. The Real Estate Agent's & Investor's Tax Book.
Irwin, Stevens. Dictionary of Electronic Organ Stops.
Irwin, William A., ed. see Smith, John M.
Isaac, E. D., jt. auth. see Carey, Roy.
Isaac, Irene E. Guide on Selecting ADP Backup Processing Alternatives.
Isaac, Jeffrey A. Consumer Legal Kit: General Contracts.
--Consumer Legal Kit: Setting up a Delaware Corporation.
--Consumer Legal Kit: Starting a Small Business.
Isaac, P. C. River Management.
Isaacs. Maria.
Isaacs, Bernard, ed. Recent Advances in Geriatric Medicine.
Isaacs, Bernard & Evers, Helen, eds. Innovations in the Care of the Elderly.
Isaacs, Neil D. Checking Back: The Story of NHL Hockey.
--Jock Culture, U. S. A.
Isaacs, Susan & Keller, Marti. The Inner Parent: Raising Ourselves, Raising Our Children.
Isaacsen-Bright, jt. auth. see Smoak, Dona V.
Isaacsen-Bright, jt. auth. see Smoke.
Isaacson & Williams. Introduction to Fixed Appliances.
Isaacson, Dean L. & Madsen, Richard W. Markov Chains: Theory & Applications.
Isaacson, Harold J. The Ink-Stone: A P. G. Wodehouse Haiku Book.
Isaacson, Leonard M., jt. auth. see Hiller, Lejaren A.
Isaacson, Max D. How to Conquer the Fear of Public Speaking: And Other Coronary Threats.
Isaacson, Michael, jt. auth. see Sarpkaya, Turgut.
Isaacson, Robert L. & Pribram, Karl H., eds. The Hippocampus. Incl. Vol. 1, Structure & Developmemnt; Vol. 2, Neurophysiology & Behavior. Plenum Pub.
Isaacson, Walter & Thomas, Evan. The Wise Men: Architects of the American Century.
Isaak, Robert A. Individuals & World Politics.
Isachenko, V. P., et al. Heat Transfer.
Isadora, Rachel. The Nutcracker.
--Willaby.
Isayev, Y. Verdict of Memory.
Isbister, W. L. T. Performance & Progress in Working Life.
Isby, David C. Weapons & Tactics of the Soviet Army.
Iseminger, Gary, ed. Logic & Philosophy: Selected Readings.
Isenberg, Anita & Isenberg, Seymour. How to Work in Stained Glass.
Isenberg, Seymour, jt. auth. see Isenberg, Anita.
Isenhour, T. L., jt. ed. see Justice, J. B.
Isermann, R., ed. System Identification Tutorials.
Isern, Margarita S., jt. auth. see Austin, Jacqueline.
ISES Staff, ed. International 85.
Isherwood, Baron, jt. auth. see Douglas, Mary.
Isherwood, Christopher. Christopher & His Kind.
--Down There on a Visit.
--The Memorial: Portrait of a Family.
--Prater Violet.
--A Single Man.
--The World in the Evening.
Isherwood, Christopher & Bachardy, Don. Frankenstein: The True Story.
Ishida, M. The Genus Fields of Algebraic Number Fields.
Ishiguro, Kazuo. An Artist of the Floating World.
Ishii, Y. & Tsutsui, M., eds. Fundamental Research in Homogeneous Catalysis.
Ishii, Yoshio, jt. ed. see Tsutsui, Minoru.
Ishikawa, Eiji, et al. Enzyme Immunoassay.
Ishikawa, Takuboku. A Handful of Sand. Sakanishi, Shio, tr. from Japanese.
Ishimatsu, Lorie, tr. see Machado de Assis, Joaquim M.
Ishimoto, Yasuhiro. Chicago, Chicago.
Ishizawa, Masao & Tanaka, Ichimatsu. The Heritage of Japanese Art.
--The Heritage of Japanese Art.
Isidori, A., et al, eds. see CISM (International Center for Mechanical Sciences), Department of Automation & Information Staff.
Isihara, A. Statistical Physics.
Iskandar, I. K., ed. Modeling Wastewater Renovation: Land Treatment.
Islam, A. K. Introduction to Cultural Anthropology.
Islam, A. K., ed. Our Way-Their Way.
Islam, A. S. Fundamentals of Genetics.
Islam, Nural. Development Strategy of Bangladesh.
Islam, Shamsul. Chronicles of the Raj: A Study of Literary Reaction to the Imperial Idea Towards the End of the Raj.
Island Canoe Co. Staff. The New San Juan Current Guide.
--Puget Sound Current Guide.
Isler, Andrea, tr. see Fischer, Eberhard & Homberger, Lorenz.
Isler, Betty. I'm Still Here Lord!
--Thank You for My Grandchild.
--A Time for Every Purpose.
Ismael, Tareq Y. Arab Left.
Ismay, Lord. The Memoirs of General Lord Ismay.
Isogai, Hiroshi & Matsushima, Shunjiro. Marketplaces of the World.
Ison, Terence G. Credit Marketing & Consumer Protection.
Ison, Walter. The Georgian Buildings of Bath from Seventeen Hundred to Eighteen Thirty.
Isozaki, Arata & Sato, Osamu. Katsura Villa: The Ambiguity of Its Space.
Ispa, Jean. Exploring Careers in Child Care Services.
Israel, Abby, tr. see Chin-Li, C.
Israel, H. & Krebs, A., eds. Nuclear Radiation in Geophysics.
Israel, Jerold, jt. auth. see LaFave, Wayne R.
Israel, Jerold H. & LaFave, Wayne R. Criminal Procedure in a Nutshell.
Israel, Liliane, et al. Evaluations en Gerontologie.
--Evaluations en Gerontologie: Manuel de references des moyens d'Investigation et de Mesure des Fonctions Mentales.
--Evaluations en Gerontologie: Receuil des Instruments Analyses.
--Valutare l'Anziano: Manuale de Riferimento dei Mezzi di Studio e di Misura delle Funzioni Mentali.
Israel, Robert H., jt. ed. see Poe, Robert H.
Israel, Y., et al, eds. Research Advances In Alcohol & Drug Problems.
Israeli, Isaac. Isaac Israeli: A Neoplatonic Philosopher of the Early Tenth Century. Altmann, A. & Stern, S. M., eds.
Israeli, Rafi. Islam in Asia.
Israeli, Raphael, ed. The Crescent in the East.
Israeli Vacuum Congress Staff. Advances in Vacuum Science & Technology: Proceedings of the Israeli Vacuum Congress, 5th, Israel, April, 1978. Yarwood, J. & Margoninski, Y., eds.
ISRM Staff. ISRM List of Members, 1980.
Issacharoff, Michael & Vilquin, Jean-Claude, eds. Sartre et la Mise en Signe.
Issacs, Bernard, jt. auth. see Gray, Barbara.
Issacs, Bernard, ed. Recent Advances in Geriatric Medicine.
Issahakian, A. Selected Works.
Issari, Mohammed Ali & Paul, Doris A. A Picture of Persia.
Issawi, Charles, ed. Economic History of the Middle East: A Book of Readings.
Issawi, Charles, jt. ed. see Wise, George S.
Issel, Dan & Martin, Buddy. Parting Shots.
Isselbacher, Kurt J. & Adams, Raymond D. Harrison's Principles of Internal Medicine: Update 4.
Isselbacher, Kurt J., ed. Medicine, Science & Society: Symposia Celebrating the Harvard Medical School Bicentennial.
Isselbacher, Kurt J., et al. Harrison's Principles of Internal Medicine: Update 2.
--Harrison's Principles of Internal Medicine: Update One.
--Harrison's Principles of Internal Medicine: Update Three.
Issell, Brian F., et al. Etoposide (VP-Sixteen) Current Status & New Developments (Symposium)
ISSS Working Group Staff. Developments in Soil Information Systems: Proceedings of ISSS Working Group Meeting on Soil Information, Varna-Sofia, Bulgaria, May 30-June 4, 1977. Sadovsky, A. D. & Bie, S. W., eds.
Istel, John, ed. Theatre Directory 1987-88.
Istvan, Donald F. & Avery, Clarence G. Accounting Principles.
Iswaran, V. & Guruswami, M. N. Pharmacology & Pharmaco-Therapeutics.
Italiano, Carlo. Sleighs, the Gentle Transportation: Or, Sleighs of Old Montreal.
ITC Information Group Staff. Unquoted Companies, 1986.
Ito, Aiko, tr. see Natsume, Soseki.
Ito, Hirobumi. Commentaries on the Constitution of the Empire of Japan. Ito, Miyoji, tr. from Japanese.
Ito, K. Stochastic Processes.
Ito, K. & McKean, H. P., Jr. Diffusion Processes & Their Sample Paths.
Ito, Miyoji, tr. see Ito, Hirobumi.
Ito, Susuu, jt. auth. see Schlein, Miriam R.
Itoh, Hiroshi, ed. & tr. Japanese Politics - An Inside View: Readings from Japan.
Itoh, S., et al, eds. Advances in Climatic Physiology.
Itoh, Teiji. The Classic Tradition in Japanese Architecture: Modern Versions of the Sukiya Style.
--The Elegant Japanese House: Traditional Sukiya Architecture.
--Imperial Gardens of Japan.
--Kura: Design & Tradition of the Japanese Storehouse. Terry, Charles S., tr. from Japanese.
Itrat, Husain. The Dogmatic & Mystical Theology of John Donne.
IUCN Staff. Proceedings of the IUCN General Assembly & Technical Meeting, 14th, Ashkhabad, 1978.
Ivancevich & Glueck. Foundations of Personnel-Human Resource Management.
Ivancevich, John M. & Glueck, William F. Foundations of Personnel.
Ivancevich, John M. & Matteson, Michael. Management Classics.
Ivancevich, John M. & Matteson, Michael T. Organizational Behavior & Management.
Ivancevich, John M., jt. auth. see Matteson, Michael.
Ivancevich, John M., et al. Managing for Perfomance.
Ivanescu, Petru see Hammer, Petru L.
Ivankovich, Michael. The Price Guide to Wallace Nutting Pictures.
Ivanov, Anatoly. Ol' Jake's Lucky Day.
Ivanov, V. T., jt. auth. see Ovchinniko, Yu A.
Ivanov, Vsevolod. Selected Stories. Hammond, Keith, et al, trs.
Ivanova, O., jt. auth. see Shakhbazyana, M.
Ivanovic, Vane. LX.
Ivens, Virginia, jt. auth. see Levine, Norman D.
Iversen, B. Linear Determinants with Applications to Picard Scheme of a Family of Algebraic Groups.
Iversen, Edwin S. & Skinner, Renate. How to Cope with Dangerous Sea Life.
Iverson, Genie. Margaret Bourke-White.
Iverson, Shari. Worship Leader's Guide.
Ives, Charles E. Charles E. Ives: Memos. Kirkpatrick, John E., ed.
Ives, Jack D. & Barry, Roger G. Arctic & Alpine Environments.
Ives, Jane H. International Occupational Safety & Health Resource Catalogue.
Ives, Ronald, et al. Audio Frequency Testers. Cole, Sandy, ed.
Ives, Suzy, jt. auth. see Gerlings, Charlotte.
Ivey, Allen E. Counseling & Psychotherapy: Skills, Theories & Practices.
--Intentional Interviewing & Counseling.
Ivey, Donald. Sound Pleasure: A Prelude to Active Listening.
Ivins, Dan. Main Events.
--Model for Christian Wholeness.
Ivory, James. Savages & Shakespeare Wallah.
Iwai, Junichi, ed. Salt & Hypertension: Proceedings of the Lewis K. Dahl Symposium.
Iwamura, Kazuo. Ton & Pon: Big & Little.
Iwao, Seiichi, ed. Biographical Dictionary of Japanese History. Watson, Burton, tr. from Japanese.
I.W.W., EmergencyProgram Branches Staff. Industrial Unionist.
Iyas, Ibn. An Account of the Ottoman Conquest of Egypt in the Year A. H. 922 (A. D. 1516) Salmon, W. H., tr. from Arabic.
Iyevleva, Z. N., jt. auth. see Babalova, L. L.
Izawa, Tadasu, illus. Things That Go.
Izay, Victor. Recipes for Starving Actors.
Ize, A. F., ed. Functional Differential Equations & Bifurcations: Proceedings.
Izenberg, Jerry. The Greatest Game Ever Played.
Izmidlian, Georges. Oriental Rugs & Carpets Today: How to Choose & Enjoy Them.
Izzo, Herbert J., jt. ed. see McCormack, William G.

J

J. K. Lasser Tax Institute Staff. How You Can Profit from the New Tax Laws.
--J. K. Lasser's Personal Finance Planner 1988.
--J. K. Lasser's Quick & Easy Taxes 1988.
--J. K. Lasser's Retirement Plan Handbook 1988.
--J. K. Lasser's Tri-State Guide, 1988: New York, New Jersey, Connecticut.
--J. K. Lasser's Your Income Tax. Greisman, Bernard, ed.
--J. K. Lasser's Your Income Tax, 1987.
--Quick & Easy Taxes.
Jaag, O., et al, eds. Water Pollution Research: Proceedings of the Second International Conference.
Jabarin, Dorothy, jt. auth. see Schwartz, Arleen G.
Jaber, Kamel S. Abu see Abu Jaber, Kamel S.
Jaber, William. Whatever Happened to the Dinosaurs?
Jablonski, Edward. Air War: One Volume Edition.
Jablonski, Ronald, jt. auth. see Moore, Franklin G.
Jablow, Alta, jt. auth. see Hammond, Dorothy.
Jabusch, David M. & Littlejohn, Stephen. Elements of Speech Communication: Achieving Competency.
Jaccard, James. Statistics for the Behavioral Sciences.
Jack, George. Wood Carving.
Jackiw, Roman, jt. auth. see Treiman, Sam B.
Jackiw, Roman W., jt. auth. see Bethe, Hans A.
Jackle, Mary & Halligan, Marney. Cardiovascular Problems: A Critical Care Nursing Focus.
Jacklin, Judith. The Blues Brothers: Private.
Jackman, L. M. & Sternhell, S. Applications of Nuclear Magnetic Resonance Spectroscopy in Organic Chemistry.
Jackman, Mary J. & Mahoney, James R. Shoulders to the Wheel: Energy-Related College-Business Cooperative Agreements.
Jackman, Stuart. The Davidson File.
--A Game of Soldiers.
--Sandcatcher.
Jacko, Diane N. Jock Momma.
Jackowski, Karol. Home on the Range.
Jack-Roller & Snodrass, Jon. The Jack-Roller at Seventy.
Jackson & Whitelaw. European Hand Firearms.
Jackson, et al, eds. Student Activities in Secondary Schools: A Bibliography. Battiste.
Jackson, Albert & Day, David. The Antiques Care & Repair Handbook.

Authors

Jackson, B. R. & Doll, T. E. Grumman F8F "Bearcat"
Jackson, Barbara G., jt. auth. see Benward, Bruce.
Jackson, Basil. Crooked Flight.
--Flameout.
--The Night Manhattan Burned.
--State of Emergency, A Novel.
Jackson, Bernard S. Semiotics & Legal Theory.
Jackson, Bobby. The Magic Moments of a Poet.
Jackson, Brian. The Black Flag: A Look Back at the Strange Case of Nicola Sacco & Bartolomeo Vanzetti.
--Streaming: An Educational System in Miniature.
Jackson, C. I., ed. Human Settlements & Energy: A Seminar of the United Nations Economic Commission for Europe.
Jackson, C. Ian & Mabogunje, A. L., eds. Shelter Provision in Developing Countries: The Influence of Standards & Criteria.
Jackson, C. Paul. Junior High Freestyle Swimmer.
Jackson, Carlton. Who Will Take Our Children? The Story of the Evacuation of Britain 1939-1945.
Jackson, Carolyn, tr. see Garin, Eugenio.
Jackson, Charles. The Fall of Valor.
Jackson, Clyde O. Come Like the Benediction: A Tribute to Tuskegee Institute & Other Essays.
--In Old Hollywood: The Movies During Their Golden Years.
--In This Evening Light.
--Let the Record Show.
--We Shall Not Sleep.
Jackson, Clyde Owen. Tomorrow, Night Will Come Again.
Jackson, Constance & Plowman, Judith. The Woolcraft Book: Spinning, Dyeing, & Weaving.
Jackson, D. M. & Vanstone, S. A. Enumeration & Design.
Jackson, Danny. Frankie Say: The Rise of Frankie Goes to Hollywood.
Jackson, Darrell, jt. ed. see Epstein, T. Scarlett.
Jackson, Dave. Storybooks for Caring Parents.
Jackson, David. Encounters with Books: Teaching Fiction 11-16.
Jackson, David & Jackson, Janice. Tibetan Thangka Painting: Methods & Materials.
Jackson, Don D., ed. Communication, Family & Marriage.
Jackson, Donald. Religious Concepts in Ancient America & in the Holy Land: As Illustrated by the Sacred Book of the Quiche Mayans & by the Bible.
--Valley Men: A Speculative Account of the Arkansas Expedition of 1807.
--Voyages of the Steamboat Yellowstone.
Jackson, Donald, ed. see Fremont, John C.
Jackson, Donald W., jt. auth. see Gee, E. Gordon.
Jackson, Douglas W. Soviet Union.
Jackson, Edgar N. A Psychology for Preaching.
--Understanding Loneliness.
--Understanding Prayer.
--Your Health & You: How Awareness, Attitudes, & Faith Contribute to a Healthy Life.
Jackson, Elmore. Middle East Mission: The Story of a Major Bid for Peace in the Time of Nasser & Ben-Gurion.
Jackson, Estelle F. Letters to Thelma: From One Christian Science Sunday School Teacher to Another.
Jackson, Eugene & Geiger, Adolph. German Made Simple.
Jackson, Eugene & Rubio, Antonio. Spanish Made Simple.
Jackson, Felicity & Lopategui, Miren. Cooking with Herbs & Spices.
Jackson, Felix. Secrets of the Blood.
Jackson, Forrest W. Their Story-Our Story.
Jackson, Frank, jt. auth. see Jackson, Jean.
Jackson, G. G., jt. auth. see Henshall, S. H.
Jackson, Gabriel. The Making of Medieval Spain.
Jackson, Geoffrey. Concorde Diplomacy: The Ambassador's Role in the World Today.
Jackson, George. COBOL.
Jackson, George A. A Case Study of Mr. Bird: Mind Over Matter or Matter Over Mind.
--A Case Study of Mr. Cage: Toleration Over Assertion or Assertion Over Toleration.
--A Case Study of Mr. Cough: Justification Over Condemnation or Condemnation Over Justification.
--A Case Study of Mr. Paranoid: Victim Over Victimizer or Victimizer Over Victim.
--A Case Study of the Retarded Prophet: Responses Over Will or Will Over Responses.
Jackson, Graham. The Decline of Western Hill.
--The Haphazard Amorist.
--Square Crib.
Jackson, H. European Hand Firearms of the 16th, 17th & 18th Century, with a Treatise on Scottish Hand Firearms by C. Whitlaw.
Jackson, H. A. Mr. Jackson's Mushrooms. Cazort, Mimi, intro. by.
Jackson, Herbert W. Introduction to Electric Circuits.
--Introduction to Electric Circuits.
Jackson, Holbrook. The Anatomy of Bibliomania.
Jackson, Ian. The Breathplay Approach to Whole Life Fitness.
Jackson, J. A., et al. Discovering Biology.
Jackson, J. Hampden. England since the Industrial Revolution, 1815-1848.
Jackson, J. R. Poetry of the Romantic Period.
Jackson, J. R., ed. Coleridge: The Critical Heritage.
Jackson, James J. Through These Eyes I Saw.
Jackson, James R. Method & Imagination in Coleridge's Criticism.
Jackson, Janice, jt. auth. see Jackson, David.
Jackson, Janice E., jt. auth. see Schantz, William T.
Jackson, Jean & Jackson, Frank. The Making of the Parson Jack Russell Terrier.
Jackson, Joan, illus. Fifty Biking Holidays.
Jackson, John B. American Space: The Centennial Years, 1865-1876.
--The Southern Landscape Tradition in Texas.
Jackson, John G. Introduction to African Civilization.
--Man, God, & Civilization.
Jackson, John H., jt. auth. see Mathis, Robert L.
Jackson, John H., jt. auth. see Musselman, Vernon A.
Jackson, John J. Sport Administration: Learning Designs for Administrators of Sport, Physical Education, & Recreation.
Jackson, Joyce see Crounse, Helen W., pseud.
Jackson, Judith. Scentual Touch: A Personal Guide to Aromatherapy Massage.
Jackson, Julia A., jt. ed. see Bates, Robert L.
Jackson, Julie, jt. auth. see Bates, Robert L.
Jackson, Kenneth T., ed. Encyclopedia of New York City.
Jackson, Laura R. The Poems of Laura Riding.
--A Progress of Stories.
Jackson, Luther P. Free Negro Labor & Property Holding in Virginia, 1830-1860.
Jackson, M. C. & Keys, P., eds. Systems Thinking in Action.
Jackson, Marian, tr. see Leonhard, Wolfgang.
Jackson, Marion, tr. see Fischer, Fritz.
Jackson, Marvin H. The Secret of Life.
Jackson, Mason. Pictorial Press, Its Origin & Progress.
Jackson, Michael, ed. The World Guide to Beer.
Jackson, Michael D. Youth Unemployment.
Jackson, Michael P. Industrial Relations.
--Industrial Relations.
--Industrial Relations: A Textbook.
Jackson, Michael W. Matters of Justice.
Jackson, Paul. Origami & Paper Craft.
Jackson, Peter & Smith, Susan, eds. Social Interaction & Ethnic Segregation.
Jackson, R. C. & Hauber, Donald P., eds. Polyploidy.
Jackson, Reggie & Lupica, Mike. Reggie.
Jackson, Richard. Part of the Story. Pack, Robert, ed.
--Part of the Story. Pack, Robert, ed.
Jackson, Richard L. The Afro-Spanish American Authors, an Annotated Bibliography of Criticism.
Jackson, Robert. Annual Editions: Global Issues, 1985-1986.
--Avro Vulcan.
--Fighter Pilots.
--Fighter Pilots of World War II.
--Hawker Hurricane in Action.
--Plural Societies & New States: A Conceptual Analysis.
--World Military Aircraft Since Nineteen Forty-Five.
Jackson, Robert, ed. Global Issues 1988-89.
Jackson, Robert L. Dostoevsky: New Perspectives.
Jackson, Ronald. The Power of Propaganda: Imagination & Idealism.
Jackson, Rope. Bonfire!
Jackson, Ruth A. Combing the Coast - San Francisco to San Luis Obispo: A Lively Guide to Beaches, Backroads, Parks, Historic Sites & Towns.
--Combing the Coast II: Santa Cruz to Carmel.
Jackson, S. Trevena. Fanny Crosby's Story.
Jackson, Shirley. The Bird's Nest.
Jackson, Steve. Battle Road.
--Fuel's Gold.
Jackson, Sue B. Hooked on Prescription Drugs. Wallace, Mary H., ed.
Jackson, T. J. Radiologic Technology: A Future for You.
Jackson, Terence E. Ain't That Mad.
Jackson, Tony & Eade, Deborah. Against the Grain: The Dilemma of Project Food Aid.
Jackson, W. A. Douglas see Creed, Virginia & Douglas Jackson, W. A.
Jackson, W. G. The Battle for Rome.
--Seven Roads to Moscow.
Jackson, William, jt. auth. see Martin, Joseph H.
Jacob, Bernard & Morphew, Carol. Skyway Typology.
--Skyway Typology Minneapolis.
Jacob, Dorothy. Witch's Guide to Gardening.
Jacob, Francois & Wollman, E. Sexuality & the Genetics of Bacteria.
Jacob, Helen P. The Diary of the Strawbridge Place.
--A Garland for Gandhi.
--The Secret of the Strawbridge Place.
Jacob, Herbert & Weissberg, Robert. Elementary Political Analysis.
Jacob, Kenneth D., ed. Fertilizer Technology & Resources in the United States.
Jacob, M., ed. Dual Theory.
Jacob, Margaret C. The Newtonians & the English Revolution, 1689-1720.
Jacob, Mary J., jt. ed. see Belloli, Jay.
Jacob, Max. The Dice Cup: Selected Prose Poems. Brownstein, Michael, ed. Ashbery, John, et al, trs.
Jacob, Mira. Paul Delvaux: Graphic Work.
Jacob, Richard C., ed. United States-German Economic Yearbook, 1987: Deutsch-Amerikanisches Wirtschaftsjahrbuch, 1987.
Jacob, S. Children's Massage Workshop, for Kids 10-90.
Jacobi, C. Vocabulaire Forestier Francais, Allemand, Danois.
Jacobi, Charles T. The Printers' Vocabulary.
Jacobi, John E. A Professor's Odyssey: A Portrait of a Profession.
Jacobi, Otto, et al, eds. Economic Crisis, Trade Unions & the State.
Jacobowitz, Ellen S., et al. New Art on Paper, Acquired with Funds from the Hunt Manufacturing Co.
Jacobs & Kasten. Laboratory Test Handbook with DRG Index.
Jacobs, A. & Worwood, M., eds. Iron in Biochemistry & Medicine.
Jacobs, Alexandra. Minneapolis-St. Paul Epicure. Keating, Isabel & Weidenbach, Gretchen, eds.
Jacobs, Alfred & Sachs, Lewis B. Psychology of Private Events.
Jacobs, Allan, jt. auth. see Jacobs, Leland.
Jacobs, Arthur. Diccionario de Musica.
Jacobs, Barbara, ed. Law Dictionary: Fachwoerterbuch der anglo-amerikanischen Rechtssprache, Englisch-Deutsch.
Jacobs, Carrie, jt. auth. see Mason, Robert L.
Jacobs, David, jt. auth. see Friedman, Sara A.
Jacobs, Ernest, ed. see Vakman, D. E.
Jacobs, Flora G. Doll's Houses in America.
--Dolls' Houses in America: Historic Preservation in Miniature.
--A History of Doll Houses.
Jacobs, Frank. Alvin Steadfast on Vernacular Island.
Jacobs, Gabriel. When Children Think: Using Journals to Encourage Creative Thinking.
Jacobs, H. Donald, jt. auth. see Searfoss, Lyndon W.
Jacobs, H. S., jt. auth. see Foth, H.
Jacobs, Harold, ed. Weatherman.
Jacobs, Henry E. & Johnson, Claudia D. An Annotated Bibliography of Shakespearean Burlesques, Parodies & Travesties.
Jacobs, Holly, et al. Testing ESL Composition: A Practical Approach.
Jacobs, Howard, jt. auth. see Wilson, Justin.
Jacobs, J. A. The Earth's Core.
--The Earth's Core & Geomagnetism.
Jacobs, Jake, jt. auth. see Harvey, Charles.
Jacobs, Jay. Cooking for All It's Worth: Making the Most of Every Morsel of Food You Buy.
Jacobs, John A., et al. Physics & Geology.
Jacobs, Jon D. International Tax Summaries 1987: A Guide for Planning & Decisions.
Jacobs, Joseph. Coo-My-Dove, My Dear.
Jacobs, Kenneth C., jt. auth. see Smith, Elske P.
Jacobs, Leland & Jacobs, Allan. Behind the Circus Tent.
Jacobs, Leo M. A Deaf Adult Speaks Out.
Jacobs, Lewis. The Movies As Medium.
Jacobs, Lou, Jr. Basic Guide to Photography. Stensvold, Mike, ed.
Jacobs, Louis. The Book of Jewish Values.
Jacobs, Louis L. Fossil Rodents from the Neogene Siwalik Deposits, Pakistan.
Jacobs, M. Herman Johannes Lam 1892-1977: The Life & Work of a Dutch Botanist.
Jacobs, Milton C. Outline of Theatre Law.
Jacobs, Monty. Birth of the Israel Air Force.
Jacobs, Nancy R., jt. ed. see Siegel, Mark A.
Jacobs, Nancy R., et al. Into the Third Century: A Profile of America.
Jacobs, O. L. R., et al, eds. Analysis & Optimization of Stochastic Systems.
Jacobs, Robert L. Wagner.
--Wagner.
Jacobs, Roderick A., jt. auth. see Jacobs, Suzanne.
Jacobs, Ruth H. Life after Youth: Female, 40, What Next?
Jacobs, S. The Handbook for No-Load Fund Investors, 1987.
Jacobs, S., jt. ed. see Cuatrecasas, P.
Jacobs, Sidney J. The Jewish Word Book.
Jacobs, Suzanne & Jacobs, Roderick A. The College Writer's Handbook.
Jacobs, Travis B., jt. auth. see Berle, Beatrice B.
Jacobs, Valerie. Black & White Shaded Drawing.
Jacobs, Vernon K. Taxwise Investing.
Jacobs, William J. Search for Freedom: America & Its People.
Jacobsen, Antonio N., illus. Antonio Jacobsen: The Checklist.
Jacobsen, Bruce. Europe.
Jacobsen, Bruce & Riggs, Rollin. The Rites of Winter: A Skier's Budget Guide to Making It on the Slopes.
Jacobsen, Bruce, jt. auth. see Riggs, Rollin.
Jacobsen, Thorkild. Sumerian King List.
--Toward the Image of Tammuz & Other Essays on Mesopotamian History & Culture. Moran, William L., ed.
Jacobson, Alex & Caufield, Page, eds. Introduction to Radiographic Cephalometry.
Jacobson, Beverly. Young Programs for Older Workers: Case Studies in Progressive Personnel Policies.
Jacobson, Carlotta K. & Ettlinger, Catherine. How to Be Wrinkle-Free: Look Younger Longer Without Plastic Surgery.
Jacobson, D. H. Extensions of Linear-Quadratic Control, Optimization & Matrix Theory.
Jacobson, Dan. The Rape of Tamar.
--Time & Time Again: Autobiographies. Davison, Peter, ed.
Jacobson, David W., ed. see Hines, Neal O.
Jacobson, David W., ed. see Hyatt, James A.
Jacobson, Gary C. The Politics of Congressional Elections 1983.
Jacobson, George. The Alcoholisms: Detection, Diagnosis & Assessment.
Jacobson, Gertrude T. Haviland China, Vol. 2: A Pattern Identification Guide.
Jacobson, Harold G., jt. auth. see Murray, Ronald O.
Jacobson, Howard. Peeping Tom.
Jacobson, James R. How to Grow Today's Children: A Guide for Modern Parents.
Jacobson, Joseph S., tr. see Nesin, Aziz.
Jacobson, Katherine, jt. ed. see Crandall-Stotler, Barbara.
Jacobson, Laurie. Hollywood Heartbreak: The Tragic & Mysterious Deaths of Hollywood's Most Remarkable Legends.
Jacobson, Lester & Goldschlager, Nora. Arrhythmias Case Studies.
Jacobson, M. K. & Emerson, W. K. Shells from Cape Cod to Cape May: With Special Reference to the New York City Area.
Jacobson, Michael F., jt. auth. see Harnik, Peter.
Jacobson, Michael F., et al. Salt: The Complete Brand Name Guide to Sodium Content.
Jacobson, Mildred. Guptill Geneology.
Jacobson, N. PI-Algebras: An Introduction.
Jacobson, R. E., et al, eds. The Manual of Photography.
Jacobson, Steve. The Best Team Money Could Buy.
Jacobson, Willard J. Population Education: A Knowledge Base.
Jacobstabal, Paul. Early Celtic Art.
Jacobstein, Helen L. The Segregation Factor in the Florida Democratic Gubernatorial Primary of 1956.
Jacobstein, J. Myron, jt. ed. see Mersky, Roy M.
Jacobstein, Neil, jt. auth. see Kahn, Gary.
Jacobus, Donald L. & Boyer, Carl, III. Index to Genealogical Periodicals.
Jacobus, John, jt. auth. see Hunter, Sam.
Jacobus, Lee A. Developing College Reading.
--Developing College Reading.
--Improving College Reading.
--Improving College Reading.
--Improving College Reading.
--The Paragraph & Essay Book.
--The Sentence Book.
--The Sentence Book.
Jacobus, Lee A. & Moynihan, William T. Poems in Context.
Jacobus, Melancthon W., jt. auth. see Turner, Gregg M.
Jacoby, Beverly Schreiber see Schreiber-Jacoby, Beverly.
Jacoby, Florence G. Nursing Care of the Patient with Burns.
Jacoby, Helmut, compiled by. New Techniques of Architectural Rendering.
Jacoby, J. E. Across the Night.
Jacoby, Oswald. How to Win at Gin Rummy.
Jacoby, Oswald, jt. auth. see Benson, William H.
Jacoby, Sidney B. Jacoby, Ohio Civil Practice: A Guide to Civil Practice in Ohio Under the Rules of Civil Procedure.
Jacolev, Leon, jt. auth. see DeVries, Louis.
Jacolliot, Louis. Occult Science in India & Among the Ancients.
Jacot, Louis. An Heretical Cosmology: The Catastrophic Dislocations of Galaxies, Stars & Planets.
Jacoway, Elizabeth. Yankee Missionaries in the South: The Penn School Experiment.
Jacquemont, Guy & Mereaud, Paul. Beaujolais: The Complete Guide.
Jacques Cattell Press Staff, ed. American Men & Women of Science.
Jacques, Elliott. The Health Services.
Jacques, Eve. My String of Pearls.
Jacques, Fredonia F. Verdict Pending: A Patient Representative's Intervention.

Authors

Jacquet, H., jt. auth. see Godement, R.
Jacqz, Jane W. Africa Policy Update.
Jacy Of Chickdedee Land. Our Challenging World: Food for Christians, Food for Thinkers.
Jaeger, Doris, jt. ed. see Meiss, Harriet.
Jaeger, E. Lectures in Isotope Geology. Hunziker, J. C., ed.
Jaeger, L. G. Cartesian Tensors in Engineering Science.
--Elementary Theory of Elastic Plates.
Jaeggli, Osvaldo. Topics in Romance Syntax.
Jaenicke, Henry J., jt. auth. see Glazer, Alan S.
Jaenicke, L., ed. see Symposium on the Biochemistry of Sensory Functions, Colloquium Mosbach, Apr. 1974.
Jafek, Bruce W., jt. auth. see Sasaki, Clarence T.
Jaffe. A Clear Introduction to FORTRAN IV.
Jaffe, A. & Carleton, R. O. Occupational Mobility in the United States, 1930-1960.
Jaffe, Alfred I. Insurance Producer's Handbook.
--Insurance Producer's Handbook: Vol. 1-Personal Lines.
--Insurance Producer's Handbook: Vol. 2-Commercial Lines.
Jaffe, Alfred I. & Miller, Jerome S. Business Building Letters: Ready-to-Use Letters That Build Premiums & Goodwill.
Jaffe, Bernard & Behrman, Harold, eds. Methods of Radioimmunoassay.
Jaffe, C. Carl, ed. Vascular & Doppler Ultrasound.
Jaffe, Dan & Knoepfle, John, eds. Frontier Literature: Images of the American West.
Jaffe, Eugene, jt. auth. see Hilbert, Stephen.
Jaffe, Frederick S., et al. Abortion Politics: Private Morality & Public Policy.
Jaffe, H. H. & Orchin, Milton M. Symmetry in Chemistry.
Jaffe, Joseph & Feldstein, Stanley. Rhythms in Dialogue.
Jaffe, Joseph, jt. auth. see Dahlberg, Charles C.
Jaffe, Louis L. & Nathanson, Nathaniel L. Administrative Law: Cases & Materials.
Jaffe, Marie & Skidmore, Linda. Diagnostic & Laboratory Cards for Clinical Use.
Jaffe, Norman, et al, eds. Bone Tumors in Children.
Jaffe, Rona. After the Reunion.
--The Best of Everything.
--The Fame Game.
Jaffe, Sandra S. & Viertel, Jack. Becoming Parents: Preparing for the Emotional Changes of First-Time Parenthood.
Jaffee, Cabot. Assessing & Developing Management Skills: Perception.
Jager, Grace, jt. auth. see Jager, Ronald.
Jager, Ronald & Jager, Grace. New Hampshire: An Illustrated History of the Granite State.
Jager, Susan G., jt. auth. see Fencl, Shirley.
Jagersma, Henk. A History of Israel from Alexander the Great to Bar Kochba. Kok, J. H., tr.
--A History of Israel in the Old Testament Period. Bowden, John, tr.
Jagiellonian University Staff. History of Polish Emigration & Polish Communities in North & South Americas in the 19th & 20th Century.
Jagoda, Robert. A Friend in Deed.
Jagtiani, Duru, ed. Fruit Preservation.
Jahan, Rounaq & Papanek, Hanna, eds. Women & Development: Perspectives from South & Southeast Asia.
Jahn, Janheinz. Muntu: An Outline of the New African Culture. Green, Marjorie, tr.
--Neo-African Literature: A History of Black Writing.
Jahn, Larry A. & Anderson, Richard V. Ecology of Pools 19 & 20, Upper Mississippi River: A Community Profile.
Jahn, O. & Michaelis, A. The Acropolis of Athens As Described by Pausanias & Other Writers: Inscriptions & Archaeological Evidences.
Jahn, Raymond. Tobacco Dictionary.
Jahnel, Franz. Manual of Guitar Technology.
Jahoda, Gustav. The Psychology of Superstition.
Jahoda, Marie, jt. ed. see Christie, Richard.
Jahrmaerker, H., ed. see International Symposium on Renal Transport, West Germany, 1968.
Jailtly, Anam. International Politics: Major Contemporary Trends & Issues.
Jain, D., ed. Indian Women.
Jain, Mahendra K. Handbook of Enzyme Inhibitors (1965-1977)
Jain, R. K. U. S.-South Asian Relations, 1947-1982.
--The U. S. S. R. & Japan.
Jain, S. K. An Introduction to Metallurgical Analysis: Chemical & Instrumental.
Jain, S. K., jt. auth. see Kumar, Dharmenora.
Jain, Sagar C., ed. Policy Issues in Personal Health Services: Current Perspectives.
Jain, Subhash C. & Tucker, Lewis R. International Marketing: Managerial Perspectives.
Jain, Sunita. Eunuch of Time & Other Stories.
Jain, V. V. W. B. Yeats As Literary Critic.
Jaini, Padmanabh S. Lokaneyya-Pakarana.
Jaini, Padmanabh S., jt. tr. see Horner, I. B.
Jairazbhoy, Nazir A. & Marzac-Holland, Nicole, eds. Selected Reports in Ethnomusicology: Essays in Honour of Peter Crossley-Holland on His 65th Birthday.
Jaiswal, N. K. Priority Queues.
Jakab, Irene, ed. see Annual Meeting of the American Society of Psychopathology, 4th, Belmont, Mass., October 1969.
Jakes, jt. auth. see Kane.
Jakes, John. North & South.
--Time Gate.
Jaki, Stanley L. Relevance of Physics.
Jakimowicz, Irena. Contemporary Polish Graphic Art.
Jakob, W., jt. auth. see Blume, C.
Jakobiec, Frederick A. & Sigelman, Jesse. Advanced Techniques in Ocular Surgery.
Jakobovitz, Immanual. Jewish Medical Ethics.
Jakoubek, B. Brain Function & Macromolecular Synthesis.
Jakubke, Hans-Dieter & Jeschkeit, Hans. Aminoacids, Peptides & Proteins: An Introduction. Cotterrell, G. P. & Jones, J. H., trs.
Jakubowski, Maxim, jt. auth. see Gross, Michael.
Jalland, Michael, jt. auth. see Channon, Derek F.
Jalland, P. & Hooper, J., eds. Women From Birth to Death: The Female Life Cycle in Britain 1830-1914.
Jamaica Assembly Staff. Proceedings of the Jamaica Assembly, 1795-1796: In Regard to the Maroon Negroes.
Jamal, Michele, ed. Shape Shifters: Shaman Women in Contemporary Society.
James, A. Everette, ed. Legal Medicine with Special Reference to Diagnostic Imaging.
James, Bill. The Bill James Baseball Abstract 1983.
James, Bruce A., jt. auth. see Shapiro, Keith J.
James, C. L. Nkrumah & the Ghana Revolution.
James, C. V., ed. see Rozental, D. E.
James, Carol, et al. Tyee Cookbook of the University of Washington.
James, Clive. Falling Towards England: Unreliable Memoirs II.
James, D. M. & Gilles, H. M. Human Antiparasitic Drugs: Pharmacology & Usage.
James, David. Protecting the Working Man: The Quest for Safety in Logging & Milling in the State of Oregon.
James, David G. Scepticism & Poetry: An Essay on the Poetic Imagination.
James, Don L., et al. Retailing Today: An Introduction.
James, Edward, jt. auth. see Dennett, Jane.
James, Edwin, compiled by. Account of An Expedition from Pittsburgh to the Rocky Mountains, Performed in the Years 1819 & 1820.
James, Elizabeth & Barkin, Carol. What Do You Mean by "Average"? Means, Medians, & Modes.
James, Elizabeth, jt. auth. see Barkin, Carol.
James, Elizabeth, jt. auth. see Drucker, Malka.
James, Frank L. Wild Tribes of the Soudan.
James, Franklin J. & Hughes, James W. Modeling State Growth: New Jersey Nineteen Eighty.
James, Franklin J., ed. Models of Employment & Residence Location.
James, G. D. The Representation Theory of the Symmetric Groups.
James, Garry, ed. Guns for Home Defense.
James, George G. Stolen Legacy.
James, George W., ed. Airline Economics.
James, Henry. The Ambassadors.
--Awkward Age.
--Henry James: Stories of the Supernatural. Edel, Leon, ed.
--A London Life.
--Madam Varnish & the Golden Era.
--Roderick Hudson.
--Seven Was the Padre's Number.
--Turn of the Screw.
James, Henry, jt. ed. see Honig, Werner K.
James, Herbert. Survivor.
James, J. R., et al. Microstrip Antenna Theory & Design.
James, Jennifer. Success Is the Quality of Your Journey.
James, John. Chartres: The Masons Who Built a Legend.
--The Contractors of Chartres.
--The Contractors of Chartres.
--Talleyman.
James, John H., jt. auth. see Champion, John M.
James, Lawrence. Mutiny: In the British & Commonwealth Forces, 1797-1956.
James, Leonard F. Following the Frontier: American Transportation in the Nineteenth Century.
James, M. R. Bowhunting for Whitetail & Mule Deer.
--Medieval Manuscripts: Part 3 of Biblioteca Pepysiana, a Descriptive Catalogue of the Library of Samuel Pepys.
James, M. R., tr. see Andersen, Hans Christian.
James, Marquis. Biography of a Bank: The Story of Bank of America N. T. & S. A.
James, Michael. The Second Quiltmaker's Handbook.
James, Michael, jt. auth. see Beck, Simone.
James, Mike & Gee, S. M. Advanced Programming for the BBC Micro.
James, Mike, et al. The Atari Book of Games.
James, N. P. & Ginsburg, R. N. The Seaward Margin of Belize Barrier & Atoll Reefs.
James, P. D. Cover Her Face. Barzun, J. & Taylor, W. H., eds.
--Innocent Blood.
--The Skull Beneath the Skin.
--Trilogy of Death: Three Complete Novels.
James, Paul. California Superquake, Nineteen Seventy-Five to Nineteen Seventy-Seven: Scientists, Cayce, Psychics Speak.
James, Philip. Children's Books of Yesterday. Holme, C. Geoffrey, ed.
James, Richard & Plant, Richard M. Study Guide to the Multiple Choice Examinations for Third & Second Mates.
James, Richard H. Reality & Other Writings.
James, S. E., jt. ed. see Robinson, D. J.
James, Samuel D. The Impact of Cybernation Technology on Black Automotive Workers in the U. S. Farmer, Richard, ed.
James, Sian. Another Beginning.
James, Stuart. Lacrosse for Beginners.
James, Susannah. The Jeweled Birdcage.
James, Sydney. Farm Accounting & Business Analysis Workbook.
James, Sydney V. People among Peoples: Quaker Benevolence in Eighteenth Century America.
James, Thomas N. These Beautiful Hills: A Natural History of the U. S. Air Force Academy.
James, Tom, et al. Dream of the Highway.
James, V. H. & Pasqualini, J. R., eds. Hormonal Steroids: Proceedings of the Fourth International Congress.
James, V. H., et al, eds. The Endocrine Function of the Human Adrenal Cortex.
James, V. H., et al, eds. see Symposium at University of Florence, Italy Staff.
James, V. H. T., et al, eds. Endocrine Function of the Human Ovary.
James, Vanessa. Try to Remember.
James, Walene. Handbook for Educating in the New Age.
James, Walter. Love & Joy.
James, Warren St. see St. James, Warren.
James, William. The Meaning of Truth: A Sequel to Pragmatism. Burkhardt, Frederick, et al, eds.
--The Principles of Psychology.
--Varieties of Religious Experiences.
Jameson, Anna B. The History of Our Lord As Exemplified in Works of Art; with That of His Type; St. John the Baptist; & Other Persons of the Old & New Testament.
--Legends of the Madonna, As Represented in the Fine Arts.
Jameson, C. W. & Walters, Douglas B. Chemistry for Toxicity Testing.
Jameson, C. W., jt. auth. see Walters, Douglas.
Jameson, G. J. Topology & Normed Spaces.
Jameson, J. The Picture Life of O. J. Simpson.
Jameson, J. Franklin. Dictionary of United States History: Alphabetical, Chronological, Statistical. McKinley, Albert E., ed.
Jameson, J. Franklin, ed. Johnson's Wonder-Working Providence, 1638-1651.
Jameson, K. P., jt. ed. see Wilber, C. K.
Jameson, Kenneth. Flower Painting for Beginners.
--You Can Draw.
Jameson, Samuel H. Flirting with Destiny.
James Second King of Great Britain. The Memoirs of James Second: His Campaigns As Duke of York, 1652-1660. Sells, A. Lytton, tr.
Jamgotch, Nish, Jr. Soviet-East European Dialogue: Relations of a New Type?
Jamieson & Shumway. Cardiac Surgery: Rob & Smith's Operative Surgery Ser.
Jamieson, Howard S. Funtastic Tales for Young People.
Jamieson, John A., ed. see SPIE - International Society for Optical Engineering Staff.
Jamieson, Paul. Adirondack Canoe Waters: North Flow.
--Adirondack Pilgrimage.
Jamieson, Tulitas. Tulitas of Torreon.
Jamison, Bonnie. Take Me Home.
Jamison, Dean T., et al. The Cost of Educational Media: Guidelines for Planning & Evaluation.
Jamison, Leland. Light for the Gentiles: Paul & the Growing Church.
Jamison, P. L. & Zegura, S. L., eds. The Eskimo of Northwestern Alaska: A Biological Perspective.
Jamison, Robert V. FORTRAN IV Programming: Based on the IBM System 1130.
Jamison, Ronald D. Modern College Algebra & Trigonometry: With Applications.
--Modern College Algebra: With Applications.
Jammer, Max. Concepts of Space: The History of Theories of Space in Physics.
Jamsa, Kris. Using SPRINT: The Professional Word Processor.
Jamsa, Kris & Nameroff, Steven. Turbo Pascal Programmer's Library.
Jan. Amazing Home Remedy: The Natural Hot Water Washing Method for Relief from Hemorrhoid.
Jana, Patricia O. Lovejoy's Preparation for the GRE.
Janacek, Leos. Janacek: Leaves from His Life. Tausky, Vilem & Tausky, Margaret, trs. from Czech.
Jancel, R. Foundations of Classical & Quantum Statistical Mechanics.
Jandrell, R., jt. auth. see Piercy, B.
Janelle, Pierre, ed. see Gardiner, Stephen.
Janericco, Terence. The Book of Great Breakfasts & Brunches.
--The Complete Book of Sandwiches for the Professional Chef.
--Fabulous Fruit Desserts. Hebbard, Neysa & Smith, Sharon, eds.
Janerich, Dwight T., et al, eds. Congenital Defects: New Directions in Research.
Janes, Ann. Everyday Death: The Case of Bernadette Powell.
Janetta, Phillip, jt. auth. see Kushi, Michio.
Janeway, Charles, et al. Immunoglobulin Idiotypes.
Janger, Kathie, jt. auth. see Korenblit, Joan.
Jangfeldt, Bengt, ed. Love Is the Heart of Everything: Correspondence Between Vladimir Mayakovsky & Lili Brik 1915-1930. Graffy, Julian, tr.
Janiak, Jane M. & Lovelock, Marty H. Sources of Information in Transportation: Part 2, Air Transportation.
Janicaud, Nicole, tr. see Falencki, Edye & Newman, Margrit.
Janick, Jules, ed. Horticultural Reviews.
--Horticultural Reviews.
Janicke, Jack. How to Make Better QSLs.
Janicki, Paul & Konikowsky, Jerzy. Flohy-Mikenas System, English Opening.
Janicki, Paul, tr. see Konikowski, Jerzy.
Janifer, Laurence M. Knave & the Game: A Collection of Short Stories.
Janik, Carolyn. The Woman's Guide to Selling Residential Real Estate Successfully.
Janik, Del Ivan, jt. ed. see Rhodes, Robert E.
Janis, Irving. Psychological Stress.
--Victims of Groupthink: A Psychological Study of Foreign-Policy Decisions & Fiascoes.
Janis, Irving L. Stress & Frustration.
Janis, Irving L., et al. Personality: Dynamics, Development & Assessment.
Janis, J. Harold. Writing & Communication in Business.
Jankelevitch, Vladimir. Ravel. Crosland, Margaret, tr.
Jankowski, James P. Egypt's Young Rebels: "Young Egypt", 1933-1952.
JanMohamed, Abdul R. Manichean Aesthetics: The Politics of Literature in Colonial Africa.
Janner, Greville. Know Your Law.
Janner, James T. Guide to the Study of Animal Pysulations.
Jannis, C. Paul, et al. Managing & Accounting for Inventories: Control, Income Recognition, & Tax Strategy.
Jannott, Paul F. Improving Bank Profits: How to Decrease Operating Expenses & Increase Income.
Janoff, A., jt. ed. see Havemann, K.
Janos, Andrew C. & Slottman, William B., eds. Revolution in Perspective: Essays on the Hungarian Soviet Republic.
Janosik, G. Edward, jt. auth. see Cooke, Edward F.
Janossy, James. Commercial Software Engineering: For Productive Program Design.
Janota, M. S., jt. auth. see Watson, N.
Janov, Arthur. Feeling Child.
--Imprints: The Life Long Effects of the Birth Experience.
Janovy, John, Jr. Yellowlegs.
Janowitz, Morris & Wright, D. Public Administration & the Public: Perspectives Toward Government in a Metropolitan Community.
Janowitz, Morris, ed. see Park, Robert W. & Burgess, Ernest W.
Janowitz, Morris, ed. see Thomas, William I.
Janowsky, David S., et al. Psychopharmacology Case Studies.
Jansen, Anton J., jt. auth. see Havighurst, Robert J.
Jansen, C. J. Readings in the Sociology of Migration.
Jansen, Elly. The Therapeutic Community.
Jansen, John F. Let Us Worship God: An Interpretation for Families.
Jansen, Scott. The Right to Kill.
Jansky, Donald M. Spectrum Management Techniques. White, Donald R., ed.
Janson, Anthony F. Great Paintings from the Ringling Museum of Art: Fortieth Anniversary Celebration.
Janson, Anthony F., rev. by see Janson, H. W. & Cauman, Samuel.
Janson, H. W. & Cauman, Samuel. History of Art for Young People. Janson, Anthony F., rev. by.
Janson, H. W., et al. A Basic History of Art.

Janson, Lone. Mudhole Smith: Alaska Flier.
Janson, Lone E. The Copper Spike.
Janss, Edmund W. Making the Second Half the Best Half.
Janssen, Al, jt. auth. see Winters, Ted.
Janssen, J. H., ed. see International Symposium on Shipboard Acoustics.
Janssen, Martha. Silent Scream.
Janssen, Pierre. A Moment of Silence. Tyler, William R., tr.
Jansson, Tove. The Exploits of Moominpappa.
--Moominstroll. Incl. Comet in Moominland; Finn Family Moomintroll; Moominland Midwinter; Moominpappa at Sea; Moomin's Summer Madness; Moominvalley in November; Tales from Moominvalley. Avon.
--The Sculptor's Daughter.
--Sun City.
Jansz, Litza, jt. auth. see Jansz, Natania.
Jansz, Natania & Jansz, Litza. Prudie Finds Out.
Jantzen, Steven L. Winning Ideas in the Social Studies.
Januz, Lauren R. & Jones, Susan K. Time Management for Executives.
--Time Management for Executives: A Handbook from the Editors of Execu-Time.
Janz, D., ed. see International Symposium on Epilepsy, 7th, West Berlin.
Janz, Denis. Luther & Late Medieval Thomism: A Study in Theological Anthropology.
Janz, George J. Thermodynamic Properties of Organic Compounds.
Janz, George J. & Tompkins, R. P. T. Non-Aqueous Electrolytes Handbook.
Janzen, Donald E. The Naomikong Point Site & the Dimensions of Laurel in the Lake Superior Region.
Japan Chamber of Commerce & Industry Staff. Standard Trade Index of Japan.
--Standard Trade Index of Japan, 1982-83.
--Standard Trade Index of Japan, 1983-84.
Japan External Trade Organization (JETRO) Staff, ed. White Paper on International Trade: Japan 1980.
Japan Graphic Designers Association Staff. Graphic Design in Japan.
--Graphic Design in Japan.
Japan Industrial Robot Association Staff, ed. The Specifications & Applications of Industrial Robots in Japan 1984.
Japan Institute of International Affairs Staff, ed. White Papers of Japan, 1978-79: Annual Abstract of Official Reports & Statistics of the Japanese Government, Tokyo.
--White Papers of Japan, 1979-80: Annual Abstract of Official Reports & Statistics of the Japanese Government, Tokyo.
Japan Institute of International Affairs Staff. White Papers of Japan, 1980-81: Annual Abstract of Official Reports & Statistics of the Japanese Government, Tokyo.
Japan National Preparatory Committee. A Call from Hibakusha of Hiroshima & Nagasaki: Proceedings of the International Symposium on the Damage & After-Effects of the Atomic Bombing of Hiroshima & Nagasaki, 21 July - 9 August 1977, Tokyo, Hiroshima & Nagasaki.
Japan Society Staff. Spectacular Helmets of Japan: 16th-19th Century.
Japan Textile Color Design Center Staff. Textiles Designs of Japan, Vol. III: Okinawan, Ainu, & Foreign Designs.
Japrisot, Sebastien. One Deadly Summer. Sheridan, Alan, tr.
Jaques Cattell Press, ed. American Library Directory, 1980.
Jaques Cattell Press Staff, ed. American Art Directory.
--American Men & Women of Science: Physical & Biological Sciences.
--Energy Research Programs Directory.
--Who's Who in American Art.
Jaques Cattell Press Staff, compiled by. Who's Who in American Politics.
Jaques, David. Learning in Groups.
Jaques, Elliott. The Form of Time.
--Free Enterprise, Fair Employment.
Jaques, Faith. Tilly's House.
Jaques, Florence P. Canoe Country.
Jaques-Dalcroze, Emile. Rhythm Music & Education. Rubenstein, Harold F., tr. from Fr.
Jaquiera, Joaquim & Mansa, Manuel B. The Warriors. Feidel, Jan, tr.
Jara, Joan. An Unfinished Song: The Life of Victor Jara.
Jarass, L., et al. Wind Energy.
Jarboe, Jan, jt. auth. see Diehl, Kemper.
Jarchow, Stephen P. Real Estate Syndications - Tax, Securities & Business Aspects: 1986 Cumulative Supplement.
--Real Estate Syndications: Tax, Securities & Business Aspects.
Jardine, A. K., jt. auth. see Greensted, C. S.
Jardine, Samuel. Anchor of the Soul.
Jaret, Peter, jt. auth. see Mizel, Steven B.
Jarett, Irwin M. Computer Graphics & Reporting Financial Data.
Jarett, Keith, ed. see Dodin, Jean-Daniel.
Jarman, A. O. & Hughes, G. R., eds. A Guide to Welsh Literature.
Jarman, Christopher. Fun with Pens.
Jarman, John. Junior Soccer.
Jarman, Rufus. Energy Merchant.
Jarman, T. R. Landmarks in the History of Education.
Jarmul, Seymour. The Architect's Guide to Energy Conservation.
Jarnagin, Roy C. Christianity & the Narrow Way.
--UFO's: The Extrauniveral Connection.
Jarnow, Jill, jt. auth. see Potter, Betsy.
Ja Roma. The Sex Lure: Cartoons.
Jaroszewski, T. M. & Ignatovsky, P. S. Socialism as a Social System.
Jarrat, Vernon, jt. auth. see Jarratt, Enrica.
Jarratt, Enrica & Jarrat, Vernon. The Complete Book of Pasta.
Jarrell, Randall. Pictures from an Institution.
--The Third Book of Criticism.
Jarrett, W. S., ed. Shooters Bible, 1988.
Jarrett, William S., ed. Shooter's Bible, No. 77: 1986.
--Shooter's Bible: 1985 Edition.
Jarrette, Peter & Rose, Dorothy. I Am Five!
--I Am Four!
--I Am Three!
--I Am Two!
Jarrow, Robert & Rudd, Andrew. Option Pricing.
Jarves, James J. Art Thoughts: The Experiences & Observations of an American Amateur in Europe. Weinberg, H. Barbara, ed.
Jarvi, Edith, jt. auth. see McLean, Isabel.
Jarvie, Grant. Class, Race & Sport in South Africa's Political Economy.
Jarvis, D. C. Arthritis & Folk Medicine.
--Folk Medicine.
Jarvis, Debra. Take It Again from the Top.
Jarvis, F. J., jt. auth. see Herbert, W. L.
Jarvis, F. Washington. Prophets, Poets, Priests, & Kings: The Old Testament Story.
Jarvis, Gilbert A. Invitation: French Communication & Cultural Awareness.
Jarvis, Gilbert A., et al. Connaitre et Se Connaitre.
--Nous Tous.
Jarvis, Lance P., jt. auth. see Mayo, Edward J.
Jarvis, M. Todd, ed. Molecular Electronics: Beyond the Silicon Chip.
Jarvis, Peter & Gibson, Sheila. Teacher Practitioner in Nursing, Midwifery & Health Visiting.
Jarvis, Peter, jt. auth. see Long, Huey.
Jarvis, W. H., jt. auth. see Jenkins, J.
Jarzebski, Z. M. Oxide Semiconductors.
Jaschke, Richard. English-Arabic Conversational Dictionary.
Jasen, David A. P. G. Wodehouse: A Portrait of a Master.
Jason, Heda. Studies in Jewish Ethnopoetry.
Jason, Philip, ed. Anais Nin Reader.
Jasper, David. The New Testament & the Literary Imagination.
Jasper, Ronald & Winstone, Harold, eds. Prayers We Have in Common.
Jaspers, Karl. Anaximander, Heraclitus, Parmenides, Plotinus, Lao-Tzu, Nagarjuna. Arendt, Hannah, ed. Manheim, Ralph, tr. from Ger.
--Anselm & Nicholas of Cusa. Arendt, Hannah, ed. Manheim, Ralph, tr. from Ger.
--The Atom Bomb & the Future of Man. Ashton, E. B., tr.
--The Nature of Psychotherapy: A Critical Appraisal. Hoenig, J. & Hamilton, Marian W., trs.
--Perennial Scope of Philosophy.
--Spinoza. Arendt, Hannah, ed. Manheim, Ralph, tr. from Ger.
Jastram, Roy W. Silver: The Restless Metal.
Jastrow, R. & Cameron, A. G., eds. Origin of the Solar System: Proceedings.
Jastrow, Robert. The Enchanted Loom.
--How to Make Nuclear Weapons Obsolete.
--Red Giants & White Dwarfs.
Jastrzebski, Zbigniew T. Scientific Illustration: A Guide for the Beginning Artist.
Jasudowicz, Dennis see Corrigan, Robert W.
Jatusripitak, Somkid. Exporting Behavior of Manufacturing Firms. Farmer, Richard, ed.
Jauch, Lawrence R., et al. The Managerial Experience: Cases, Exercises & Readings.
Javadi, Hasan, tr. see Farrokhzad, Forugh.
Javaherian, K., jt. ed. see Bradbury, E. M.
Javid, M., jt. auth. see Brenner, Egon.
Javitch, Daniel. Poetry & Courtliness in Renaissance England.
Javits, Jacob K. & Steinberg, Rafael. Javits: The Autobiography of a Public Man.
Jawetz, Ernest, et al. Review of Medical Microbiology.
Jawitsch, L. S. The General Theory of Law.
Jaworowsky, J., tr. see Bronshtein, I. N. & Semendyayev, K. A.
Jaworski, Irene D. & Joseph, Alexander. Atomic Energy: The Story of Nuclear Science.
Jaworski, Leon. After Fifteen Years.
--The Right & the Power: The Prosecution of Watergate.
Jaxitron. Cybernetic Music.
Jay, Carroll E. Gretchen, I Am.
Jay, Eric G. The Church: Its Changing Image Through Twenty Centuries.
Jay, Jon C., ed. Basic Ignition & Electrical Systems.
Jay, K. E. Atomic Energy Research at Harwell.
Jay, Roma & Oberman, Phyllis. Room for Improvement: Kitchens.
Jayant, N. S., ed. Waveform Quantization & Coding.
Jayarajah, Carl A. Bangladesh: Current Trends & Development Issues.
Jaynes, Austin. Yamagata.
Jaynes, Julian. The Origin of Consciousness in the Breakdown of the Bicameral Mind.
Jayson, Malcolm I. & Black, Carol M., eds. Systemic Sclerosis, Scleroderma.
Jayson, Malcoln, ed. Still's Disease: Juvenile Chronic Polyarthritis.
JDR 3rd Fund Staff. Arts in Education Partners: Schools & Their Communities.
Jean, M., ed. Nuclear Structure & Nuclear Reactions.
Jean, Norma & Darden, Carole. Spoonbread & Strawberry Wine.
Jeanmart, L., jt. ed. see Baeft, A.
Jeans, D. N., ed. Australia - A Geography: Space & Society.
--Australia - A Geography: The Natural Environment.
Jeans, Marylu T. Moonset.
Jeansonne, Louis O., jt. auth. see Waring, William W.
Jeanty, P. & Romero, R. Obstetrical Ultrasound.
Jeavons, Clyde. A Pictorial History of War Films.
Jech, T. J. Lectures in Set Theory with Particular Emphasis on the Method of Forcing.
Jedrey, Christopher M. The World of John Cleaveland: Family & Community in Eighteenth-Century New England.
Jeejeebhoy, Khursheed N. Gastrointestinal Diseases: Focus on Clinical Diagnosis.
Jeeves, Malcolm A. & Green, Brain. Analysis of Structural Learning: Monograph.
Jeeves, Terry, jt. auth. see Ashley, Michael.
Jeffares, A. Norman. W. B. Yeats: Man & Poet.
Jeffares, A. Norman, jt. ed. see Brewer, Derek.
Jeffcoate, S. L. The Lutheal Phase.
Jeffcoate, S. L., ed. Androgens & Anti-Androgen Therapy.
Jeffcoate, S. L. & Hutchinson, J. S., eds. The Endocrine Hypothalamus.
Jefferies, R. L. & Davy, A. J., eds. Ecological Processes in Coastal Environments: Nineteenth Symposium of the British Ecological Society.
Jefferies, Richard W., jt. auth. see Cobb, Charles R.
Jeffers, Coleman R., jt. ed. see Dobrian, Walter A.
Jeffers, H. Paul. Rubout at the Onyx.
Jeffers, J. N. Modelling.
Jeffers, Jeff. Rally: The Twelve Greatest Notre Dame Football Comebacks.
Jeffers, P. E., jt. auth. see Svec, J. J.
Jeffers, Robinson. The Collected Poetry of Robinson Jeffers. Hunt, Tim, ed.
--Not Man Apart: Photographs of the Big Sur Coast. Brower, David, ed.
Jeffers, Susan. All the Pretty Horses.
--Little People's Book of Baby Animals.
Jefferson, Brian T. Profitable Crafts Marketing: A Complete Guide to Successful Selling.
Jefferson, Roland S. Five Fifty-Nine to Damascus.
Jefferson, Thomas, Center Foundation Staff & Shields, Roger E. Aspects of Current International Debt Comebacks: Is the Problem Insolvency or Illiquidity?
Jefferson, Tony, jt. ed. see Hall, Stuart.
Jefferson, Travis, ed. see Lee, Jack.
Jeffery, Graham. Bush Brother.
Jefferys, Margot & Sachs, Bessie. Rethinking General Practice: Dilemmas in Primary Care.
Jefferys, William H. & Robbins, R. Robert. Discovering Astronomy: With Discovery Kit.
Jeffree, Dorothy & McConkey, Roy. Let Me Speak: Learning Games for the Retarded Child.
Jeffrey, A. Asymptotic Methods in Nonlinear Wave Theory.
Jeffrey, Alan & Taniuti, T., eds. M H D Stability & Thermonuclear Containment.
Jeffrey, Betty. White Coolies.
Jeffrey, Carol. As It Happenith to the Fool.
Jeffrey, J. W. Methods in X-Ray Crystallography.
Jeffreys, Alan E. Michael Faraday: A List of His Lectures & Published Writings.
Jeffreys, Sheila. The Spinster & Her Enemies: Feminism & Sexuality, 1880 to 1930.
Jeffreys-Jones, Rhodri & Collins, Bruce, eds. The Growth of Federal Power in American History.
Jeffries, jt. auth. see Gatland.
Jeffries, Clark. Mathematical Modelling Workbook for Students of Ecology.
Jeffries, J. R. & Bates, J. D. The Executives Guide to Meetings, Conferences & Audiovisual Presentations.
Jeffries, J. R. & Fisher, G. PET Fun & Games.
Jeffries, Ronald, et al. Commodore 64 Fun & Games.
Jeffus, Larry & Johnson, Harold. Welding: Principles & Applications.
Jefkins, F. W. Marketing & PR Media Planning.
Jefkins, Frank. Public Relations for Management Success.
Jegede, Oluremi. Bibliography on the Constitutions of Nigeria.
Jegen, Mary E. How You Can Be a Peacemaker.
Jehle, Faustin F. The Complete & Easy Guide to Social Security & Medicare.
--Complete & Easy Guide to Social Security & Medicare.
Jehu, Derek. Sexual Dysfunction: A Behavioral Approach to Causation, Assessment & Treatment.
Jekyll, G. Flower Decoration in the House.
Jekyll, Gertrude. Children & Gardens.
--Flower Decoration in the House.
--Gertrude Jekyll on Gardening. Hobhouse, Penelope, ed.
Jelavich, Barbara, ed. see Otto, Robert C.
Jelen, F. C., ed. Project & Cost Engineers' Handbook.
Jelinek, Arthur. A Pre-Historic Sequence in the Middle Pecos Valley, New Mexico.
Jelinek, Mariann, et al. Organizations by Design.
Jeljaszewicz, J., ed. see International Symposium on Staphylococci & Staphylococcal Infections Staff.
Jellicoe, Ann, tr. see Chekhov, Anton.
Jelliffe, D. B. Child Health in the Tropics.
Jellinek, Frank, tr. see Brunschwig, Henri.
Jellinek, Frank, tr. see Sartre, Jean-Paul.
Jellinger, K., ed. see International Symposium on Malignant Lymphomas of the Nervous System.
Jellinger, K., et al, eds. Neurotransmitters in Cerebral Coma & Stroke: Proceedings of the Workshop, Vienna, July 11, 1978.
Jellins, Jack & Kobayashi, Joshiji, eds. Ultrasonic Examination of the Breast.
Jellison, Holly, ed. Directory of Administrators of Community, Technical & Junior Colleges, 1984.
--Higher Education & the Older Volunteer: A Place for Everyone.
Jellison, Molly M., ed. Interface in Retrospect: 1978-1980.
Jemmali, M., ed. Mycotoxins in Foodstuffs.
Jena, P. & Satterthwaite, C. B., eds. Electronic Structure & Properties of Hydrogen in Metals.
Jencks, Beata. Your Body - Biofeedback at Its Best.
Jencks, William P. Catalysis in Chemistry & Enzymology.
Jene-Hagan Bookcorp Staff & Ayer, Eleanor, eds. Colorado Books in Print: 1984 Supplement.
Jenkin, P. M. Animal Hormones, Pt. 1: Control of Growth & Metamorphosis.
Jenkins, A. D., ed. Progress in Polymer Science.
--Progress in Polymer Science.
Jenkins, A. D. & Stannett, V. T., eds. Progress in Polymer Science.
--Progress in Polymer Science.
Jenkins, A. Milton. MIS Design Variables & Decision Making Performance: A Simulation Experiment. Dickson, Gary, ed.
Jenkins, Alphonse, Sr. Black Struggles.
Jenkins, Barbara, jt. auth. see Jenkins, Peter.
Jenkins, C. & Mortimer, J. E. British Trade Unions Today.
Jenkins, C., et al. How to Prepare for the New High School Equivalency Examination.
Jenkins, Christie. Buns: A Woman Looks at Men's.
Jenkins, Clare, jt. auth. see Jenkins, Dilwyn.
Jenkins, Claude. Bishop Barlow's Consecration & Archbishop Parker's Register: With Some New Documents.
Jenkins, Clive. Power at the Top: A Critical Survey of the Nationalized Industries.
Jenkins, Colleen M. The Home Owner's Journal: What I Did & When I Did It.
Jenkins, D. Graham & Murray, John W., eds. Stratigraphical Atlas of Fossil Foraminifera.
Jenkins, Dan. Baja Oklahoma.
--Dead Solid Perfect.
--Life Its Ownself: The Semi-Tougher Adventures of Billy Clyde Puckett.
Jenkins, Dan & Shrake, Edwin. Limo.
Jenkins, Daniel. Believing in God.
--Christian Maturity & Christian Success.
Jenkins, David. Black Zion.
Jenkins, Dilwyn & Jenkins, Clare. Rough Guide to Peru.
Jenkins, Edward L. You Can't Take It with You: Plan Your Estate Now.
Jenkins, Farish A., ed. Primate Locomotion.
Jenkins, Frances C. Hey Girls, Let's Go Fishing.
Jenkins, G. Curtis & Newton, R. The First Year of Life.
Jenkins, Gladys G. Helping Children Reach Their Potential: A Teachers' Resource Book.
Jenkins, Iredell. Social Order & the Limits of Law: A Theoretical Essay.
Jenkins, Irving. Hawaiian Furniture & Hawaii's Cabinetmakers 1820-1940.

Authors

Jenkins, J. & Jarvis, W. H. Basic Principles of Electronics, Vol. 2: Semiconductors.
Jenkins, J. Geraint. The English Farm Wagon: Origins & Structure.
Jenkins, J. P. & Brown, E. T., eds. KWIC Index of Rock Mechanics Literature: Pt. 2, 1969-1976.
Jenkins, James A. Univalent Functions & Conformal Mapping.
Jenkins, Jean, ed. International Directory of Musical Instrument Collections.
Jenkins, Jerry. Blizzard!
--The Clubhouse Mystery.
--Daniel's Big Surprise.
--Fourteen Days to Midnight.
--Good Sport, Bad Sport.
--In Deep Water.
--The Kidnapping.
--Two Runaways.
Jenkins, Jerry, jt. auth. see Lemon, Meadowlark.
Jenkins, Jerry, jt. auth. see Williams, Pat.
Jenkins, Jerry B. Before the Judge.
--Daniel's Big Decision.
--The Jennifer Grey Mysteries.
--Mystery at Raider Stadium.
Jenkins, Jim & Quick, Dave. Motion, Motion: Kinetic Art.
Jenkins, Jo-An see Bowman, Leona.
Jenkins, John & Smith, Jon. Electric Music: A Practical Manual.
Jenkins, John B. Genetics.
Jenkins, John B., jt. auth. see Corwin, Harry O.
Jenkins, Jordan. Learning About Love.
Jenkins, Joseph R. & Jenkins, Linda M. Cross Age & Peer Tutoring: Help for Children with Learning Problems.
Jenkins, Linda M., jt. auth. see Jenkins, Joseph R.
Jenkins, Mildred R. Fundamentals of English Grammar.
Jenkins, Morton, ed. see Gee, John.
Jenkins, Myra E; see Gerald.
Jenkins, Peter. The Tennessee Sampler.
Jenkins, Peter & Jenkins, Barbara. The Road Unseen.
--The Road Unseen.
Jenkins, Ray. Taking Time for Marriage.
Jenkins, Reese V. Images & Enterprise: Technology & the American Photographic Industry, 1839-1925.
Jenkins, Robin. Fergus Lamont.
--A Would-Be Saint.
Jenkins, Roy, ed. Britain & the EEC.
Jenkins, S. H. Advanced Treatment & Reclamation of Wastewater.
--A Consolidated Approach to Activated Sludge Process Design.
--Design-Operation Interactions at Large Waste Water Treatment Plants.
--Instrumentation & Control for Water & Wastewater Treatment & Transport Systems.
--Kinetics of Wastewater Treatment, Copenhagen, Denmark, June 1979.
--Nitrogen As a Water Pollutant.
--Proceedings of the International Conference on Water Pollution Research, 8th, Sydney, Australia, 1978.
--Water Quality: Management & Pollution Control Problems.
Jenkins, S. J., ed. New Developments in River Basin Management.
Jenkins, Stephen, ed. Fritz Lang.
Jenkins, T. M., jt. ed. see Nelson, Walter R.
Jenkins, W. Basic Computing for Civil Engineers 0685.
Jenkinson, Edwin B. Censors in the Classroom.
Jenkinson, J. R., ed. see Persius.
Jenkinson, M., et al, eds. see Smith, Nila B.
Jenks, William A. Francis Joseph & the Italians: 1849-1859.
Jenner, James R. Discovery.
Jenner, W. J., tr. see Wu Cheng'en.
Jenner, W. J. F., tr. see Cheng'en, Wu.
Jennermann, Donald L., jt. auth. see Indiana State University, Department of Foreign Languages, Literature Circle Symposium Staff.
Jenness, Diamond. The Economics of Cyprus: A Survey to 1914.
Jennett, Sean. The West of Ireland.
Jennings. Reaction Kinetics Progress.
Jennings, A. & Weiss, T. G., eds. The Challenge of Development in the Eighties: Our Response.
Jennings, A. R., jt. auth. see Gresham, Geoffrey A.
Jennings, C. Wade, jt. auth. see Trimmer, Joseph F.
Jennings, Edward H., ed. see Stevenson, Richard A.
Jennings, Eugene E. An Anatomy of Leadership: Princes, Heroes & Supermen.
--Mobile Manager.
Jennings, Francis. The Ambiguous Iroquois Empire.
Jennings, Gary. Aztec.
--Sow the Seeds of Hemp.
--Sow the Seeds of Hemp.
--The Terrible Teague Bunch.
--The Terrible Teague Bunch.
--The Treasure of Superstition Mountains.
--World of Words: The Personalities of Language.
Jennings, Jan, jt. auth. see Gottfried, Herbert.
Jennings, Jerry, ed. The Northeast.
Jennings, Jerry E. The West.
Jennings, Jerry E. & Smith, Marion H. The South.
Jennings, Joseph, jt. auth. see Theriault, Jean Y.
Jennings, K. R. & Cundall, R. B., eds. Progress in Reaction Kinetics.
--Progress in Reaction Kinetics: Vol. 9 Complete.
Jennings, K. R., et al, eds. Progress in Reaction Kinetics.
--Progress in Reaction Kinetics.
Jennings, Kenneth M., jt. auth. see Holley, William H.
Jennings, M. & DePaola, T. Robin Goodfellow & the Giant Dwarf.
Jennings, Max, jt. auth. see Gohlke, Mary.
Jennings, Thelma. The Nashville Convention: Southern Movement for Unity, 1849 to 1850.
Jennings, Theodore W., Jr. Introduction to Theology: An Invitation to Reflection Upon the Christian Mythos.
Jennings, Theodore W., Jr., ed. Vocation of the Theologian.
Jennison, Keith & Pratt, William A. Year-Around Conditioning for Part-Time Golfers.
Jennison, Peter, jt. auth. see Tree, Christina.
Jennison, Peter S., jt. auth. see Tree, Christina.
Jens, Arlen J. I Am the Lord Thy Sex: An Interpretation of Genesis & Exodus.
Jensen. A Managerial Experience with the IBM PC.
Jensen & Cherrington. The Business Management Laboratory.
Jensen, ed. Plasma Chemistry: Proceedings of an International Symposium, Kiel, Germany, 1973.
Jensen, Adolf E. Myth & Cult Among Primitive Peoples.
Jensen, Albert C. Wildlife of the Oceans.
Jensen, Alfred E. & Chenoweth, Harry H. Statics & Strength of Materials.
Jensen, Andrew. The Trial of Chaplain Jensen.
Jensen, Andrew, jt. auth. see Jensen, Mary.
Jensen, Arthur R. Educational Differences.
Jensen, Arthur R., jt. auth. see Symonds, Percival M.
Jensen, Cecil H. & Helsel, Jay. Fundamentals of Engineering Drawing.
Jensen, Cecil H. & Hines, Raymond D. Interpreting Engineering Drawings.
Jensen, Clarence W., jt. auth. see Cramer, Gail L.
Jensen, Clayne R. & Schultz, Gordon W. Applied Kinesiology.
Jensen, Clayne R., jt. auth. see Jensen, Mary B.
Jensen, Darcy D., jt. auth. see Ellingson, David R.
Jensen, DeLamar, et al. World of Europe to Eighteen Fifteen.
Jensen, Dwight W. Visiting Boise: A Personal Guide.
Jensen, Finn, jt. auth. see Becker, Peter W.
Jensen, Irving L. Acts: An Inductive Study.
Jensen, J. Trygve. Physics for the Health Professions.
Jensen, John, compiled by. The Human Development Program for Institutionalized Teenagers.
Jensen, Joyce D. & Cooley, Stella G. A Handbook of Career Education Activities: For Use by Secondary Counselors & Classroom Teachers.
Jensen, Larry C., jt. auth. see Higbee, Kenneth L.
Jensen, M. C. Parenting Education at Medford & Churchill High Schools.
Jensen, Marcus M. & Wright, Donald N. Introduction to Medical Microbiology.
Jensen, Margaret & Bobak, Irene. Handbook of Maternity Care: A Guide for Nursing Practice.
Jensen, Margaret D. & Bobak, Irene M. Maternity & Gynecologic Care: The Nurse & the Family.
Jensen, Margaret D., jt. auth. see Bobak, Irene M.
Jensen, Marlene. Women Who Want to Be Boss: Business Revelations & Success Strategies from America's Top Female Executives.
Jensen, Mary & Jensen, Andrew. Audiovisual Idea Book for Churches.
--Making Your Marriage Work.
Jensen, Mary B. & Jensen, Clayne R. Folk Dancing.
Jensen, Mary J., ed. U. S. & Worldwide Travel Accommodations Guide: For 6 to 18 Dollars per Day.
Jensen, Merrill. New Nation: A History of the United States During the Confederation 1781-1789.
Jensen, Niels. Days of Courage. Stallybrass, Oliver, tr.
Jensen, Oliver. Revolt of American Women.
Jensen, Oliver, et al. American Album.
Jensen, Oliver O., ed. & frwd. by see Turner, Gregg M. & Jacobus, Melancthon W.
Jensen, Randall W. & Watkins, Bruce O. Network Analysis: Theory & Computer Methods.
Jensen, Richard A. Touched by the Spirit: One Man's Struggle to Understand His Experience of the Holy Spirit.
Jensen, Robert G., jt. auth. see Patton, Stuart.
Jensen, Ronald & Cherrington, David J. The Business Management Laboratory: Participants' Manual.
Jensen, Ronald, jt. auth. see Courtney, James F., Jr.
Jensen, Rosalie S. & Spector, Deborach C. Teaching Mathematics to Young Children: A Basic Guide.
Jensen, Ruby J. Hear the Children Cry.
Jensen, Timothy S. VLA Guide to Copyright Series.
Jenson, Jorgen. The Prehistory of Denmark.
Jenson, Robert, jt. auth. see Cotman, Carl W.
Jenson, Robert W. Story & Promise: A Brief Theology of the Gospel About Jesus.
--The Triune Identity: God According to the Gospel.
--Visible Words: The Interpretation & Practice of Christian Sacraments.
Jenson, Ron & Stevens, Jim. Dynamics of Church Growth.
Jenson, Ronald & MacDonald, Chuck. Together We Can Deal with Life in the 80's.
Jentoft, Clyde W. Sir Thomas Wyatt & Henry Howard, Earl of Surrey: A Reference Guide.
Jentz, Barry C. Entry: The Hiring, Start-up & Supervision of Administrators.
Jenyns, Soame. Japanese Pottery.
Jeor, Sachiko St. see St. Jeor, Sachiko, et al.
Jephcott, Edmond, tr. see Benjamin, Walter.
Jephson, Robert. The Plays of Robert Jephson. Maynard, Temple & Backscheider, Paula R., eds.
Jeppesen, Knud. Counterpoint: The Polyphonic Vocal Style of the Sixteenth Century. Haydon, G., tr.
--The Style of Palestrina & the Dissonance.
Jeppesen Sanderson Staff, ed. see Gunby, R. A.
Jeppson, J. O. The Last Immortal.
Jepsen, Dee. Women: Beyond Equal Rights.
Jepsen, Glenn L., et al, eds. Genetics, Paleontology & Evolution.
Jerd, Russell F. Industrial Metric Conversion.
Jerdee, Thomas H., jt. auth. see Rosen, Benson.
Jeremiah, David. Overcoming Loneliness.
Jeremias, Joachim. The Central Message of the New Testament.
--The Eucharistic Words of Jesus. Perrin, Norman, tr. from Ger.
--Jesus' Promise to the Nations.
--The Lord's Prayer. Reumann, John, ed. & tr. from Ger.
--Problem of the Historical Jesus. Reumann, John, ed. Perrin, Norman, tr. from Ger.
--Sermon on the Mount. Reumann, John, ed. Perrin, Norman, tr. from Ger.
Jergensen, Gerald V., II, jt. ed. see Spisak, John F.
Jergensen, Gerald V., III, jt. ed. see Mular, Andrew L.
Jerger, James, jt. auth. see Jerger, Susan.
Jerger, James, ed. Modern Development in Audiology.
Jerger, Susan & Jerger, James. Auditory Disorders.
Jerin, Richard E. Chronicles & Ice Cream.
Jerina, Carol. Tropic Gold.
Jerison, Harry J. Evolution of the Brain & Intelligence.
Jerlov, N. G. Optical Aspects of Oceanography.
Jernigan, Anna K. Food Sanitation: Study Course.
Jernigan, E., et al. Lead Poisoning in Man & the Environment.
Jerome. On Mountains.
Jerome, John. On Mountains: Thinking About Terrain.
Jerome, Judson. On Being a Poet.
--Plays for an Imaginary Theater.
--Poet's Market 88.
Jerome, Judson, ed. Poet's Market 1986.
--Poet's Market 1987.
Jerrold, Walter C. A Book of Famous Wits.
Jerrold, Walter C. & Leonard, R. M. Century of Parody & Imitation.
Jerse, Dorothy W. & Calvert, Judith, eds. On the Banks of the Wabash: A Photograph Album of Greater Terre Haute, 1900-1950.
Jersey, Stanley C. Postal History of the United States Forces in British Solomon Islands Protectorate During World War 2.
Jersild, Arthur T. In Search of Self: An Exploration of the Role of the School in Promoting Self-Understanding.
--Psychology of Adolescence.
Jersild, P. C. After the Flood. Blecher, Lone T. & Blecher, George, trs. from Swedish.
Jersild, Paul T. & Johnson, Dale A. Moral Issues & Christian Responses.
Jerusalem Conference on Impaired Vison in Childhood Staff. Impaired Vision in Childhood: Proceedings of the Jerusalem Conference, May 1977. Nawratzki, I. & Merin, S., eds.
Jerusalem Symposia on Quantum Chemistry & Biochemistry Staff. The Purines. Bergmann, E. D. & Pullman, B., eds.
Jervell, Jacob. Jesus in the Gospel of John. Cleven, Harry T., tr.
--Luke & the People of God: A New Look at Luke-Acts.
--Luke & the People of God: A New Look at Luke-Acts.
--The Unknown Paul: Essays on Luke-Acts & Early Christian History.
Jervis, Alice, tr. see Mazzini, Giuseppe.
Jervis, Robert. Logic of Images in International Relations.
Jervis, Robert, et al. Psychology & Deterrence.
Jeschke, Herbert, tr. see Muir, John.
Jeschke, Susan. Sidney.
--Tamar & the Tiger.
Jeschkeit, Hans, jt. auth. see Jakubke, Hans-Dieter.
Jeshurun, Chandran, ed. Government & Rebellions in Southeast Asia.
Jeske, Richard L. & Barr, Browne. Holy Week. Achtemeier, Elizabeth, et al, eds.
Jespersen, James & Fitz-Randolph, Jane. Time & Clocks for the Space Age.
Jespersen, Otto. Philosophy of Grammar.
Jesperson, Otto. International Dictionary.
Jesse, F. Tennyson. The Lacquer Lady.
Jessen, Kenneth C. Railroads of Northern Colorado.
Jessen, Raymond J., jt. auth. see Hoel, Paul G.
Jesser, Clinton J., jt. ed. see Das, Man S.
Jessop, T. E. A Bibliography of David Hume & of Scottish Philosophy from Francis Hutcheson to Lord Balfour.
Jessop, William J., ed. see Fearon, William R.
Jessor, R. Problem Behavior & Psychological Development.
Jessup, B., et al. University of Oregon Centennial Lectures.
Jessup, Bertram & Rader, M. Art & Human Values.
Jessup, Claudia & Chipps, Genie. The Woman's Guide to Starting a Business.
Jessup, F. W., ed. Lifelong Learning.
Jessup, Myrtle S. Gems of Truth.
Jessup, Philip C. United States & the World Court. Incl. What's Wrong with International Law? Friedman, Wolfgang; Foreign Policy of a Free Democracy. Jessup, Philip C; Fallacy of a "Preventive" War. Jessup, Philip C; Legal Process & International Order. Kelsen, Hans. Garland Pub.
Jester, Pat. Microwave Cookbook: The Complete Guide.
Jesuit Missionaries Staff. China.
Jesus, Ed. C. de see McCoy, Alfred W. & De Jesus, Ed. C.
Jeter, James R., Jr., jt. ed. see Cameron, Ivan L.
Jett, Claudia. Elmer's Diet.
Jetter, Judy & Kadlec, Nancy. The Arthritis Book of Water Exercise.
Jetter, R. I., et al, eds. Metallic Bellows & Expansion Joints.
Jevsevar, Frederick. Scintilla & the Fall of the Children of Seth.
Jewell, Derek. Frank Sinatra: A Celebration.
Jewell, Geri & Weiner, Stewart. Geri.
Jewell, John, jt. auth. see Hillier, Sheila.
Jewell, John B., jt. auth. see Starzyk, Lawrence J.
Jewell, Peter & Spiers, Barbara. Early Retirement on Medical Grounds.
Jewett, Ann, jt. auth. see Nixon, John.
Jewett, Ann E., jt. auth. see Knapp, Clyde G.
Jewett, Robert. The Captain America Complex: The Dilemma of Zealous Nationalism.
--Christian Tolerance: Paul's Message to the Modern Church.
--A Chronology of Paul's Life.
Jewett, Sarah O. The Country of the Pointed Firs.
Jewkes, John. A Return to Free Market Economics.
Jewkes, John, et al. Sources of Invention.
Jewler, A. Jerome. Creative Strategy in Advertising.
Jewler, A. Jerome, jt. ed. see Gardner, John N.
Jezewski, W., jt. auth. see Blok, C.
Jha, Akhileshwar. The Imprisoned Mind: Guru Shisya Tradition in Indian Culture.
Jha, L. K. North South Debate.
Jhabvala, Ruth P. Out of India: Selected Stories.
Jhaveri, S. & Montecalvo, J., Jr. Abstracts of Methods Used to Assess Fish Quality.
Jhingan, M. L. Advanced Economic Theory.
--Microeconomic Theory.
Jian, Gerard & Hester, Ralph. Decouvert et Creation.
Jian, Xu, tr. see Furen, Wang, et al.
Jianou, Ionel & Goldscheider, C. Rodin.
Jick, Leon A. The Americanization of the Synagogue, 1820-1870.
Jim, Brian. Mitchell (The All-Around Good Guy)
Jimei, Xiao, jt. ed. see Guangxian, Xu.
Jimenez, Irene Z. Thoughts in Time, Whispers & Roars.
Jimenez, Juan R. Platero & I. Roach, Eloise, tr. from Span.

Jin, Cheng, ed. A Chronology of the People's Republic of China 1949-1984.
Jingwen, Liao. Xu Beihong: Life of a Master Painter. Peiji, Zhang, tr. from Chinese.
Jinks, Harold. Ronald Reagan: Smile, Style & Guile.
Jinks, William. The Celluloid Literature: Film in the Humanities.
Jipp, Lester F. & Miguel, Richard J. Priority Concerns of Five Groups Involved in Experiential Education Programs.
Jippensha, Ikku. Shank's Mare.
Jirat-Wasiutynski, Vojtech. Paul Gauguin in the Context of Symbolism.
Jiryis, Sabri. The Arabs in Israel. Bushnaq, Inea, tr.
Joachain, Charles J. & Post, Douglas E., eds. Atomic & Molecular Physics of Controlled Thermonuclear Fusion.
Joachim Pillai, C. A. The Apostolic Interpretation of History: A Commentary on Acts 13: 16-41.
--Early Missionary Preaching: A Study of Luke's Report in Acts 13.
Joad, C. E. Decadence (A Philosophical Inquiry)
--The Pleasure of Being Oneself.
Joad, Cyril E. Guide to Philosophy.
--The Present & Future of Religion.
Joan, jt. auth. see Willadeene.
Joaquin, Nick. Tropical Baroque: Four Manileno Theatricals.
--Tropical Gothic.
Job, John. Job Speaks to Us Today.
Jobe, Frank W. & Moynes, Diane R. The Official Little League Guide to Fitness.
Jobling, David. The Sense of Biblical Narrative II: Stuctural Analyses in the Hebrew Bible.
Jobs & Skills Programme for Africa Staff, jt. auth. see International Labour Office Staff.
Jobst, Katherine, ed. Internships Nineteen Eighty-Eight.
--Internships, Nineteen Eighty-Seven.
Jochelson, Vladimir I. Peoples of Asiatic Russia.
Jocher, Willy. Spawning Problem Fishes. Incl. Book 1; Book 2. TFH Pubns.
Jochim, H. & Ziegler, B. Interaction Studies in Nuclei.
Jodock, Darrell, tr. see Kirchner, Hubert.
Joe, Barbara. Public Policies Toward Adoption.
Joedicke, Harry W. Arthritis: Its Cause & Cure.
Joekes, Rosemary, ed. & rev. by. The National Trust Guide.
Joekes, Rosemary, jt. ed. see Fedden, Robin.
Joergens, K. & Weidmann, J. Spectral Properties of Hamiltonian Operators.
Joerns, Consuelo. The Forgotten Bear.
Joes, Anthony J. Mussolini.
Joesten, Joachim. Nasser: The Rise to Power.
Joffe, Ellis. Between Two Plenums: China's Intraleadership Conflict, 1959-1962.
Joffe, Irwin L. Achieving Success in College.
Jogn, Norman de see DeJong, Norman.
Johannessen, Jan V. Diagnostic Electron Microscopy.
--Electron Microscopy in Human Medicine: The Skin.
--Electron Microscopy in Human Medicine: Vol. I, Instrumentation & Techniques.
--Electron Microscopy in Human Medicine, Vol. 10: Endocrine Organs.
--Electron Microscopy in Human Medicine: Vol. 2, Cellular Pathology.
--Electron Microscopy in Human Medicine: Vol. 3, Infectious Agents.
--Electron Microscopy in Human Medicine: Vol. 4, Soft Tissues, Bones & Joints.
--Electron Microscopy in Human Medicine: Vol. 5, Cardiovascular System, Lymphoreticular & Hematopoietic System.
--Electron Microscopy in Human Medicine: Vol. 6, Nervous System, Sensory Organs, & Respiratory Tract.
--Electron Microscopy in Human Medicine, Vol. 7: Digestive System.
--Electron Microscopy in Human Medicine: Vol. 8, the Liver, Gallbladder & Biliary Ducts.
--Electron Microscopy in Human Medicine, Vol. 9: Urogenital System & Breast.
Johannessen, Jan V., ed. Electron Microscopy in Human Medicine, Vol. 11: The Skin - Special Applications.
Johannessen, Jan V., jt. ed. see Lapis, Karoly.
Johanningmeier, E. V. Americans & Their Schools.
Johannis, Theodore B., Jr., jt. auth. see Avery, Curtis E.
Johannsen, Elizabeth, ed. The Alaska Catalog: Living, Working & Traveling in the Northland.
Johannsen, G., jt. auth. see IFAC-IFIP-IEA-IFORS Symposium Staff.
Johannsen, G., jt. ed. see Sheridan, T. B.
Johannson, K. Homotopy Equivalence of Three-Manifolds with Boundaries.
Johansen, Donald A. Plant Microtechnique.
Johansen, L. Lectures on Macroeconomic Planning.
Johanson, Brenda C. Standards for Critical Care.
Johanson, Gregory J., ed. Feed My Sheep: Sermons on Contemporary Issues in Pastoral Care.
Johansson, Rune. The Dynamic Psychology of Early Buddhism.
Johany, Ali D. The Myth of the OPEC Cartel: The Role of Saudi Arabia.
Johari, J. C., jt. auth. see Gupta, R. C.
Johari, J. C., ed. see Bahadur, Lal.
Johl, S. S. Essentials of Farm Financial Management.
Johl, S. S. & De Clerq, C. Irrigation & Agricultural Development.
John, Angela V. By the Sweat of Their Brow: Women Workers at Victorian Coal Mines.
John, Anthony. The Predator.
John, B. & Lewis, K. R. Chromosome Complement.
--Chromosome Cycle.
--Meiotic System.
John, B. S. Scandinavia: A New Geography.
John Carter Brown Library Staff. Bibliotheca Americana: Catalogue of the John Carter Brown Library in Brown University, Short-Title List of Additions, Books Printed 1471-1700.
John, Colin. The Witching.
John Crerar Library Staff. Author-Title Catalog.
--Classified Subject Catalog.
--List of Books on the History of Industry & the Industrial Arts.
John, Da Free. The Dawn Horse Testament.
--Do You Know What Anything Is?
--The Fire Gospel.
--Forehead, Breath & Smile: An Anthology of Devotional Readings from the Spiritual Teaching of Master Da Free John.
--God Is Not a Gentleman & I Am That One.
--I Is the Body of Life.
--The Liberator, Eleutherios.
--Nirvanasara.
--What Is the Conscious Process?
John, Da Free see John, Da Free.
John, E. Roy. Mechanisms of Memory.
John, Edith. Creative Stitches.
John, Elizabeth A. H. Storms Brewed in Other Men's Worlds: The Confrontation of Indians, Spanish, & French in the Southwest, 1540-1795.
John, Erwin E. Key to a Successful Church Library.
John G. Finch Symposium on Psychology & Religion Staff & Oden, Thomas C. After Therapy What? Proceedings of the John G. Finch Symposium on Psychology & Religion, 1nd.
John Hay Library, Brown University Staff. Catalog of Broadsides of American Verse in the Harris Collection of American Poetry & Plays.
John, James E. & Haberman, William L. Introduction to Fluid Mechanics.
John, Jeffrey St. see St. John, Jeffrey.
John, Laurie, ed. Cosmology Now.
John M. Wing Foundation, Newberry Library Staff. Dictionary Catalogue of the History of Printing from the John M. Wing Foundation, Second Supplement.
John, Nancy. Make-Believe Bride.
John, P. K., jt. ed. see McGowan, J. W.
John, P. W. Statistical Design & Analysis of Experiments.
John, Wylly F. St. see St. John, Wylly F.
Johner, Martin & Goldberg, Gary. Successful Parties: Simple & Elegant. Atcheson, Jean, ed.
Johnk, Carl T. Engineering Electromagnetic Fields & Waves.
John Of Salisbury. Frivolities of Courtiers & Footprints of Philosophers. Pike, Joseph B., tr.
John Paul II, Pope Day by Day With Pope John Paul II.
John-Roger. A Consciousness of Wealth: Creating a Money Magnet.
--Dream Voyages.
Johns, Bruce & Edmundson, David. Motorcycles: Fundamentals, Service Repair.
Johns, D. J. Thermal Stress Analysis.
Johns, E. A. The Social Structure of Modern Britain.
--The Sociology of Organizational Change.
Johns, E. A., jt. auth. see Green, B. S.
Johns, Edward B., et al. Health for Effective Living.
Johns, Gary. Organizational Behavior: Understanding Life at Work.
Johns, Glover S., Jr. The Clay Pigeons of St Lo.
Johns, Jerry L. Advanced Reading Inventory: Grade Seven Through College.
Johns, Karen. Proud Surrender.
Johns, Richard, jt. auth. see Holden, David.
Johns, S., jt. ed. see Sideri, S.
Johns, T., jt. auth. see Ross, C. T.
Johns, Virginia J. Dining In - Vancouver, B.C.
Johns, W. D., tr. see Correns, C. W., et al.
Johnsen, Carsten & Johnsen, Sylvi. The Writing in the Sand.
Johnsen, Frederick A. Bombers in Blue: PB4Y-2 Privateers & PB4Y-1 Liberators.
Johnsen, Henry. Freedom For the Gods.
Johnsen, Kenneth G. Apple Country Interurban.
Johnsen, Sylvi, jt. auth. see Johnsen, Carsten.
Johnsgard, Paul A. A Guide to North American Waterfowl.
Johnson. Encyclopedia for Boys & Girls.
--Physical Research.
--Soul of the Black Preacher.
--Young American's Dictionary.
Johnson, A. Modelling & Control of Biotechnological Processes: Proceedings of the 1st IFAC Symposium, Noorwijkerhout, The Netherlands, 11-13 December 1985.
Johnson, A. F., jt. auth. see Berry, Turner W.
Johnson, A. S. Marketing & Financial Control.
Johnson, A. William. Ylide Chemistry.
Johnson, Alan. How to Restore & Improve Your Victorian House.
Johnson, Albert. Roger Williams & Mary.
Johnson, Alex R. Living among the Bedouin Arabs.
Johnson, Alexander B. Treatise on Language. Rynin, David, ed.
Johnson, Ann J. Hearts in the Clouds.
Johnson, Arlee W., jt. auth. see Hughey, J. D.
Johnson, Arnold H., jt. auth. see Peterson, Martin S.
Johnson, Arthur H. & Atkinson, C. T. The Age of the Enlightened Despot: Sixteen Sixty to Seventeen Eighty-Nine.
Johnson, Artis. Oliver Wants a Pony.
Johnson, B. Connor, ed. Postranslational Covalent Modification of Proteins: MS Repro Symposium.
Johnson, B. L. India: Resources & Development.
--Pakistan.
--South Asia.
Johnson, B. Lamar, ed. General Education in Two-Year Colleges.
Johnson, Barbara. The Critical Difference: Essays in the Contemporary Rhetoric of Reading.
--Private Consulting: How to Turn Experience into Employment Dollars.
Johnson, Barbara, tr. see Derrida, Jacques.
Johnson, Barbara F. Delta Blood.
--The Heirs of Love.
--Homeward Winds the River.
--Lionors.
--Tara's Song.
Johnson, Barbara M. Saying Yes to Change.
Johnson, Ben, jt. auth. see Stevick, Daniel B.
Johnson, Bernard, tr. see Pekic, Borislav.
Johnson, Bert. Credit: Get It, Use It, Stretch It, Save It.
Johnson, Bev. Drama in the Church: Planning & Staging Dramatic Productions.
Johnson, Brian & Hefferman, Terry. A Most Secret Place: Boscombe Down 1939-45.
Johnson, Broderick H., ed. see Mason, Bruce B. & Hink, Heinz R.
Johnson, Bruce. A Child's Comfort: Baby & Doll Quilts in American Folk Art.
--A Child's Comfort: Baby & Doll Quilts in American Folk Art.
Johnson, Bruce, ed. The American Catalogue.
Johnson, C. Amos. The Computer Buyer's Survival Manual.
Johnson, C. E., ed. Hyperbaric Diving Systems & Thermal Protection.
Johnson, Carl L. Professor Longfellow of Harvard.
Johnson, Carolyn E. & Thew, Carol L., eds. Proceedings of the Second International Congress for the Study of Child Language.
Johnson, Catherine, jt. auth. see Cazort, Mary.
Johnson, Charlene. Altogether Lovely.
Johnson, Charles. A General History of the Robberies & Murders of the Most Notorious Pyrates.
--Language of Painting.
--The Sorcerer's Apprentice.
Johnson, Charles S. Shadow of the Plantation.
Johnson, Claudia D., jt. auth. see Jacobs, Henry E.
Johnson, Clifton, ed. The Oak-Tree Fairy Book.
Johnson, Crockett. Barnaby: Wanted: A Fairy Godmother.
--Ellen's Lion: Twelve Stories.
--J. J. O'Malley Goes Hollywood.
--Jackeen J. O'Malley for Congress.
--Mr. O'Malley & the Haunted House.
--Mr. O'Malley Goes for the Gold.
--Mr. O'Malley, Wizard of Wall Street.
Johnson, Curt, jt. ed. see Conroy, Jack.
Johnson, Curtis. Network Analysis for Technology.
Johnson, Curtis D. Process Control Instrumentation Technology.
Johnson, D. E. & Hilburn, J. L. Rapid Practical Designs of Active Filters.
Johnson, Dale A., jt. auth. see Jersild, Paul T.
Johnson, Daniel L. Starting Right, Staying Strong: A Guide to Effective Ministry.
Johnson, Daphne & Ransom, Elizabeth. Family & School.
Johnson, Davey & Golenbock, Peter. Bats.
Johnson, David, et al, eds. Popular Culture in Late Imperial China.
Johnson, David E., et al. Basic Electric Circuit Analysis.
Johnson, David W. Educational Psychology.
--Human Relations & Your Career: A Guide to Interpersonal Skills.
Johnson, David W. & Johnson, Frank P. Joining Together: Group Theory & Group Skills.
Johnson, David W. & Johnson, Roger T. Learning Together & Alone: Cooperation, Competition, & Individualization.
Johnson, David W., jt. auth. see Tjosvold, Dean.
Johnson, Deborah, jt. auth. see National Association of Home Builders Staff.
Johnson, Deborah H., jt. auth. see Gelso, Charles J.
Johnson, Denis. Angels.
Johnson, Derek. Victorian Shooting Days: East Anglia 1810-1910.
Johnson, Don. Body.
Johnson, Donald C. Index to Southeast Asian Journals, 1975-1979: A Guide to Articles, Book Reviews, & Composite Works.
Johnson, Donald C., ed. see University of the State of New York, Foreign Area Materials Center Staff.
Johnson, Donald L., ed. Australian Architecture, 1901 to 1951: Sources of Modernism.
Johnson, Dorothy E. & Vestermark, Mary J. Barriers & Hazards in Counseling.
Johnson, Douglas & Johnson, Madeleine. The Age of Illusion: Politics & Art in France, 1918-1940.
Johnson, Douglas, jt. auth. see Mettam, Roger S.
Johnson, Douglas W. The Challenge of Single Adult Ministry.
--Managing Change in the Church.
Johnson, Douglass W., jt. auth. see Johnson, R. Winifred.
Johnson, E. A. Organization of Space in Developing Countries.
Johnson, E. D., ed. The Poetry of Earth: A Collection of English Nature Writings.
Johnson, Edna, et al. Anthology of Children's Literature.
Johnson, Elden. Prehistoric Peoples of Minnesota.
Johnson, Eleanor, jt. ed. see Colgan, Betsy.
Johnson, Elizabeth S. & Johnson, Harry G. The Shadow of Keynes: Understanding Keynes, Cambridge, & Keynesian Economics.
Johnson, Elizabeth S. & Williamson, John B. Growing Old: The Social Problems of Aging.
Johnson, Ellen, ed. The Toy Library: A How-To Handbook.
Johnson, Ellen H. Jackie Winsor.
Johnson, Elliot. The Point After: Advice from God's Athletes.
Johnson, Elmer C. Survey of American Law.
Johnson, Elvera. Design: Without a Designer?
Johnson, Eric W. An Introduction to Jesus of Nazareth.
Johnson, Ethel B. Monte & the Coons.
Johnson, Eugene. The Beginnings.
Johnson, Eva M. I, too, Shall Wear Purple.
Johnson, Evelyne. The Cow in the Kitchen.
Johnson, Eyvind. Dreams of Roses & Fire. Friis, Erik J., ed.
Johnson, F. N. Lithium Research & Therapy.
Johnson, Frank A., ed. Alienation: Concept, Term, & Meaning.
Johnson, Frank P., jt. auth. see Johnson, David W.
Johnson, Franklin P. Lysippos.
Johnson, Fridolf, ed. Rockwell Kent.
--A Treasury of Bookplates from the Renaissance to the Present.
Johnson, G. I. & Wilson, J. R. Ergonomics in Advanced Manufacturing Technology.
Johnson, G. P. I Was Fighting for Peace, but, Lord, There Was Much More.
Johnson, George W. A History of English Gardening, Chronological, Biographical, Literary & Critical. Hunt, John D., ed.
Johnson, Glen R. & Walker, Fred M. Army Staff Officer's Guide.
Johnson, Guion G., jt. auth. see Johnson, Guy B.
Johnson, Guy B. & Johnson, Guion G. Research in Service to Society: The First Fifty Years of the Institute for Research in Social Science at the University of North Carolina.
Johnson, Harold, jt. auth. see Jeffus, Larry.
Johnson, Harry G. & Swoboda, Alexander K. The Economics of Common Currencies.
Johnson, Harry G., jt. auth. see Johnson, Elizabeth S.
Johnson, Haynes. Bay of Pigs.
Johnson, Hazel A., compiled by. A Checklist of New London, Connecticut, Imprints 1709-1800.
Johnson, Henry C., Jr. The Public School & Moral Education.
Johnson, Hewlett. Soviet Russia Since the War.
Johnson, Hilda A. Box Two Hundred Four.
Johnson, Homer H., ed. The HRD Professional's Bibliography of Resources & References.
Johnson, Howard A. Windows of the Mind.
Johnson, Hugh. Hugh Johnson's Cellar Book.
--Hugh Johnson's Modern Encyclopedia of Wine.
--Hugh Johnson's Pocket Encyclopedia of Wine, 1984.
--Hugh Johnson's Pocket Encyclopedia of Wine, 1985.
--Hugh Johnson's Pocket Encyclopedia of Wine 1986.
--Hugh Johnson's Pocket Encyclopedia of Wine: 1982 Edition.
--The Principles of Gardening.

--Wine.
Johnson, Ian. MCQ's in Undergraduate Obstetrics & Gynaecology.
Johnson, Isabel, jt. auth. see Ridenour, Nina.
Johnson, Ivan C. & Roberts, William. Money & Banking: A Market Oriented Approach.
Johnson, J. & Kassel, S. The Multibus Design Guidebook.
Johnson, J. C., ed. Plant Growth Regulators & Herbicide Antagonists: Recent Advances.
Johnson, J. H., jt. auth. see Cooke, R. V.
Johnson, Jack & Hammock, Wayne. Installing Heat Pumps.
Johnson, Jacquelyn & Benegar, John. Global Issues in the Intermediate Classroom, Grades 5-8.
Johnson, James A. Automotive Diagnosis & Tune-up: A Text-Workbook.
Johnson, James A., et al. Introduction to Foundations of American Education.
Johnson, James C. Readings in Contemporary Physical Distance & Logistics.
Johnson, James C., jt. auth. see Boone, Louis E.
Johnson, James C., jt. auth. see Wood, Donald F.
Johnson, James E. The Irish in America.
Johnson, James H. SALT: The Primary Cause of Disease?
Johnson, James L., jt. auth. see McDaniel, Eugene B.
Johnson, James M. Handbook of Depreciation Methods, Formulas & Tables.
Johnson, James T., ed. The Bible & American Law, Politics, & Political Rhetoric.
Johnson, James Weldon. Black Manhattan.
--Prose in Practice: A Rhetorical Reader.
--Prose in Practice: A Rhetorical Reader.
Johnson, Jan. Mary Bethune & Her Somedays.
Johnson, Jane A., jt. ed. see Bryant, Peter S.
Johnson, Jerah & Percy, William A. The Age of Recovery: The Fifteenth Century.
Johnson, Jim, jt. auth. see Gerin, William.
Johnson, Joan D. & Xanthos, Paul. Tennis.
Johnson, Joe, compiled by. A Field of Diamonds.
Johnson, John, jt. auth. see Heller, David.
Johnson, John W. How You Can Manage Your Money: A Christian's Guide to Personal & Family Financial Decision Making.
--Political Christians: A Guide for Christians in Public Service.
Johnson, Joseph, jt. auth. see Pegram, Samuel.
Johnson, Joyce. Minor Characters.
Johnson, Joyce, ed. see Hazleton, Lesley.
Johnson, Joyce, ed. see Lambton, Lucinda.
Johnson, Joyce, ed. see Nicholson, Louise.
Johnson, Joyce, ed. see Smart, Richard.
Johnson, Joyce, ed. see Thompson, Sandra.
Johnson, Joyce, ed. see Thubron, Colin.
Johnson, Judi, compiled by. Green Corn & Violets: Amerindian Recipes for Camp & Kitchen. King, Frances.
Johnson, Julian & Porter, Roger, eds. Liquid Crystals & Ordered Fluids. Incl. Vol. 1; Vol. 2; Vol. 3. Plenum Pub.
Johnson, K., et al. Biology: An Introduction.
Johnson, K. J. & Epstein, L. M. General Chemistry Examination Questions.
Johnson, Karen, ed. see Hynes, Kathleen.
Johnson, Keith. Communicate in Writing: A Functional Approach to Writing Through Reading Comprehension.
Johnson, Kenneth A., ed. see American Academy of Orthopaedic Surgeons Staff.
Johnson, Kent L. Paul the Teacher: A Resource for Teachers in the Church.
Johnson, L. How to Restore & Repair Practically Everything.
Johnson, L. G. Statistical Treatment of Fatigue Experiments.
Johnson, L. Murphy & Steffensen, Arnold R. Elementary Algebra.
--Intermediate Algebra.
Johnson, L. Murphy, jt. auth. see Steffensen, Arnold R.
Johnson, L. W. Colonial Sunset: Australia & Papua New Guinea 1970-74.
Johnson, Larry, jt. auth. see Toboldt, William K.
Johnson, Laura S., ed. Reading & the Adult Learner.
Johnson, Leland G. Biology.
Johnson, Leon J. Introductory Soil Science: A Study Guide & Laboratory Manual.
Johnson, Leonard, et al, eds. Physiology of the Gastrointestinal Tract.
Johnson, Leroy F. & Cooper, Rodney H. File Techniques for Data Base Organization in COBOL.
Johnson, Linda, jt. auth. see Ross, Sally.
Johnson, Lloyd. Highlights from Drugs & American High School Students, 1975-1983.
Johnson, Lois. Lollipop Lexicon.
Johnson, Lois H. Cornflakes.
Johnson, Lois W. Aaron's Christmas Donkey.
--Either Way, I Win: A Guide for Growth in the Power of Prayer.
--Falling Apart or Coming Together: How You Can Experience the Faithfulness of God.
--Hello, God! Prayers for Small Children.
--Songs for Silent Moments: Prayers for Daily Living.
Johnson, Lonnell E. Ears Near to the Lips of God.
Johnson, Luke T. Decision Making in the Church: A Biblical Model.
--Sharing Possessions: Mandate & Symbol of Faith. Brueggemann, Walter & Donahue, John R., eds.
Johnson, Lynn, et al. Pittsburgh Moments.
Johnson, Lynn, jt. auth. see Child, Arodel.
Johnson, Lynn Ann, ed. see Schulz, James H. & Leavitt, Thomas D.
Johnson, Lynwood A., jt. auth. see Montgomery, Douglas C.
Johnson, M., ed. Developments in Mammals.
Johnson, M. Bruce, jt. auth. see Deacon, Robert T.
Johnson, M. Clemens. A Review of Research Methods in Education.
Johnson, Madeleine, jt. auth. see Johnson, Douglas.
Johnson, Malcolm. David Claypool Johnston: American Graphic Humorist, 1798-1865.
Johnson, Margaret. After the Storm.
Johnson, Margaret, jt. auth. see Christian, Sharon.
Johnson, Margaret H. God's Rainbow.
--Living Faith: Mastectomy or Partial? Ask Jesus.
Johnson, Margery M. Hand in Hand.
Johnson, Marian S. Promoting Your Church Library.
Johnson, Marion. The Borgias.
Johnson, Marion L. Functional Administration in Physical & Health Education.
Johnson, Marion T., et al. Bridges to Employment: Practices for Job Development, Placement & Follow-Through of Unemployed Youth for Vocational Education & Manpower Training.
Johnson, Mark, jt. auth. see Lakoff, George.
Johnson, Marlys C. & Thompson, Linda J. Dollars for Scholars Student Aid Catalog: Minnesota Edition. Citizen's Scholarship Foundation of America Staff, ed.
Johnson, Marlys C., jt. auth. see Thompson, Linda J.
Johnson, Marsha P. How to Make & Cook with Gourmet Vinegars.
Johnson, Mary. Reflex for the MAC: Database Design & Applications.
Johnson, Mary E. & Pearson, Katherine. NatureCrafts: Seasonal Projects from Natural Materials.
Johnson, Melvin W. The Cobblestone Architecture of the Great Lake Region: An Annotated Bibliography.
Johnson, Michael & Mackworth-Young, Robin. Tune & Repair Your Own Piano.
Johnson, Mildred D. Problem Solving & Chemical Calculations.
Johnson, Miriam, jt. auth. see Wegmann, Robert.
Johnson, Morris, et al. From Freedom to Freedom: A Student's Guide.
Johnson, Myrtle E. & Snook, Harry J. Seashore Animals of the Pacific Coast.
Johnson, Nancy K. Alone & Beginning Again.
Johnson, Nevil. In Search of the Constitution: Reflections on State & Society in Britain.
Johnson, Nora. Tender Offer: A Novel.
--The Two of Us: A Novel.
Johnson, Norman, ed. Marital Violence.
Johnson, Oliver A. & Beatty, John L. Heritage of Western Civilization.
Johnson, Pamela H. An Avenue of Stone.
--The Good Husband.
Johnson, Patricia. Memoirs of a Mom.
Johnson, Patricia J., ed. see De Montherlant, Henry.
Johnson, Paul. The Aerofilms Book of London from the Air.
--The Civilization of Ancient Egypt.
--Civilizations of the Holy Land.
--Enemies of Society.
Johnson, Paul C. Alaska.
--San Francisco.
Johnson, Paul E. The Middle Years.
Johnson, Pauline. Creative Bookbinding.
--Marxist Aesthetics: The Foundations Within Everyday Life for an Emancipated Consciousness.
Johnson, Penelope D., ed. & Medieval History: Selected Course Outlines & Reading Lists from Leading American Colleges & Universities in History.
Johnson, Peter, jt. auth. see Dupain, Max.
Johnson, Peter D., ed. Painting with Pastel.
Johnson, Peter H. Parker, America's Finest Shotgun.
Johnson, Philip C. see O'Neal, William B.
Johnson, Philip M. How to Maximize Your Advertising Investment.
Johnson, R. Condemned to Die: Life Under Sentence of Death.
Johnson, R., jt. auth. see Comyn, J.
Johnson, R., jt. auth. see Fonken, G.
Johnson, R., et al. Readings in American Social Studies.
Johnson, R. Charles. Draft Registration & the Law. Sherman, Charles E., ed.
Johnson, R. E. Existential Man: The Challenge of Psychotherapy.
Johnson, R. H. & Blair, J. A. Logical Self Defense.
Johnson, R. M. & Siddiqi, I. W. The Determination of Organic Peroxides.
Johnson, R. P. & Buckby, R. J. Composite Structures of Steel & Concrete, Vol. 11: Bridges with a Commentary on BS 5400.
Johnson, R. Winifred & Johnson, Douglass W. Introduction to Nursing Care.
Johnson, Reginald. Celebrate, My Soul.
Johnson, Richard, jt. ed. see Stuart, Robert.
Johnson, Richard A. & Wichern, Dean W. Applied Multivariate Statistical Analysis.
Johnson, Richard A., et al. Theory & Management of Systems.
--Production & Operations Management: A systems Concept.
Johnson, Richard B., ed. New Perspectives for Bank Directors.
Johnson, Richard E. Flexible Benefits: A How-to-Guide.
Johnson, Robert. Elementary Statistics.
Johnson, Robert A. We: Understanding the Psychology of Romantic Love.
Johnson, Robert A. & Pease, Ralph W. Police Report Writing.
Johnson, Robert B. The Black Resource Guide.
Johnson, Robert B., ed. see De Montherlant, Henry.
Johnson, Robert C. John McLoughlin: Father of Oregon.
Johnson, Robert F. & Shimshak, Robert H. The Power of Light: Daguerreotypes from the Robert Harshorn Shimshak Collection.
Johnson, Robert F., jt. auth. see Mills, Paul.
Johnson, Robert W. & Melicher, Ronald W. Financial Management.
Johnson, Roger A., ed. Psychohistory & Religion: The Case of Young Man Luther.
--Views from the Pews: Christian Beliefs & Attitudes.
Johnson, Roger T., jt. auth. see Johnson, David W.
Johnson, Ronald. Valley of the Many-Colored Grasses.
Johnson, Ross H. & Winn, Paul R. Quantitative Methods for Management.
Johnson, Rossiter, ed. A Dictionary of Biographies of Authors Represented in the Authors Digest Series: With a Supplemental List of Later Titles & a Supplementary Biographical Section.
Johnson, Samuel. Lives of the English Poets: Selection.
--The Plays of Samuel Johnson of Cheshire. Backscheider, P. R. & Rudolph, Valerie C., eds.
--The Prince of Abissinia: A Tale, 1759. Bd. with Candide; or, All for the Best, 1759. Voltaire. Garland Pub.
Johnson, Sara E., jt. auth. see National Housing Law Project Staff.
Johnson, Scott D. A Computer System for Checking Proofs. Stone, Harold, ed.
Johnson, Shirley A., ed. Circulating Platelet.
Johnson, Siskin. Elementary Statistics for Business.
Johnson, Stancil E. Frisbee.
Johnson, Sue. Little Green Monster: Story Book For Young Children in Sign Language.
Johnson, Sylvia A. Animals of the Deserts.
--Animals of the Polar Regions.
Johnson, T. B. & Barnes, R. J., eds. Application of Computers & Operations Research in the Mineral Industry: 17th International Symposium.
Johnson, T. C. Doctor! What You Should Know About Health Care Before You Call a Physician.
Johnson, Ted, jt. auth. see Case, Christine.
Johnson, Thomas. The Ice Futures.
Johnson, Thomas M. & Omsby, John R. Swords of WWII Germany.
Johnson, Tom. You Are Always Your Own Experience!
Johnson, Una. Alice Trumbull Mason.
Johnson, Uwe. Third Book about Achim.
Johnson, V. A. Karl Lark-Horovitz, Pioneer in Solid State Physics.
Johnson, W., ed. Pressure Vessels Analysis for Design: Proceedings of the Conference in Honour of Emeritus Professor Sidney Gill, held at UMIST, Manchester, U. K., April 1981.
Johnson, W. C. Citizen Participation in Local Planning in the U. K. & U. S. A.
Johnson, W. H. If You Must Write.
Johnson, W. H., Jr., ed. see International Conference On Nuclidic Masses - 2nd - Vienna - 1963.
Johnson, Walter & Evans, Carol, eds. The Papers of Adlai E. Stevenson, Vol. 1: Beginnings of Education, 1900-1941.
--The Papers of Adlai E. Stevenson, Vol. 2: Washington to Springfield 1941-1948.
--The Papers of Adlai E. Stevenson, Vol. 3: Governor of Illinois 1949-1953.
--The Papers of Adlai E. Stevenson, Vol. 7: Continuing Education & the Unfinished Business of American Society 1957-1961.
Johnson, Walter, et al, eds. The Papers of Adlai E. Stevenson, Vol. 6: Toward a New America, 1955-1957.
--The Papers of Adlai E. Stevenson, Vol. 8: Ambassador to the United Nations 1961-1965.
Johnson, Walter S. Maxims of the Civil Law: Essays in the Evolution of Law.
Johnson, Warren T. & Lyon, H. H. Insects That Feed on Trees & Shrubs: An Illustrated Practical Guide.
Johnson, Wesley M. & Maxwell, John A. Rock & Mineral Analysis.
Johnson, Will S. For the Love of St. Maarten.
Johnson, William. Sketches of the Life & Correspondences of Nathanael Green.
Johnson, William, jt. auth. see Whitman, William.
Johnson, william G. Mort Safety Assurance Systems Book.
Johnson, William S. & Cohen, Susan E., eds. International Photography Index: 1979.
--International Photography Index: 1981.
Johnson, William W. Addition & Subtraction Logarithms: Gaussian Tables.
--Heroic Mexico.
Johnson-Davies, Denys, tr. see Darwish, Mahmoud.
Johnson-Laird, Philip N., jt. auth. see Miller, George A.
Johnson-McHenry, Martha K. Golden Book of Original Contemporary Poems for Adults & Children.
Johnsson, William. Religion in Overalls.
Johnston, Arthur, ed. Selected Poems of Thomas Gray & William Collins.
Johnston, Brenda A. Between the Devil & the Sea: The Life of James Forten.
Johnston, Chris. The Microcomputer Builder's Bible.
Johnston, Douglas M. Environmental Management in the South China Sea: Legal & Institutional Developments.
Johnston, F. E., et al, eds. Human Physical Growth & Maturation: Methodologies & Factors.
Johnston, Francis E. & Selby, Henry A. Anthropology: The Biocultural View.
Johnston, Fred S. Fundamental Relationships & Their Logical Formulations.
Johnston, Gordon. Which Way Out of the Men's Room?
Johnston, Hank. Thunder in the Mountains.
--The Whistles Blow No More: Railroad Logging in the Sierra Nevada, 1874-1942. Sebree, Mac, ed.
Johnston, Harry H. History of the Colonization of Africa by Alien Races.
--Liberia.
Johnston, Howard. Learning to Program.
Johnston, James, Jr., jt. ed. see Turk, Amos.
Johnston, James P. A Hundred Years Eating: Food, Drink, & the Daily Diet in Britain Since the Late Nineteenth Century.
Johnston, Jennifer. Shadows on Our Skin.
Johnston, Jill. Lesbian Nation: The Feminist Solution.
--Paper Daughter: Paper Daughter. Gottlieb, Robert, ed. Kaplan, Martha.
Johnston, Kenneth S., jt. auth. see Gray, Jack C.
Johnston, Linda G., jt. ed. see Warbick-Cerone, Ann.
Johnston, Mary. Roman Life.
--To Have & to Hold.
Johnston, Mary T. & Lipscomb, Elizabeth J. Amelia Gayle Gorgas: A Biography.
Johnston, Norma. The Crucible Year.
--Gabriel's Girl.
--Glory in the Flower.
--If You Love Me, Let Me Go.
--The Keeping Days.
--A Mustard Seed of Magic.
--Myself & I.
--A Nice Girl Like You.
--Of Time & of Seasons.
--Pride of Lions.
--Strangers Dark & Gold.
--A Striving After Wind.
Johnston, Norman, jt. ed. see Savitz, Leonard D.
Johnston, Ollie, jt. auth. see Thomas, Frank.
Johnston, P. & Roots, B. Nerve Membranes: A Study of the Biological & Chemical Aspects of Neuron Glia Relationships.
Johnston, Philip M. & Liebowitz, Murray. Advanced Sheet Metal Skills.
Johnston, R., ed. Marine Pollution.
Johnston, R. F. Lion & Dragon in Northern China.
Johnston, R. J. Dictionary of Human Geography.
--The Geography of English Politics: The 1983 British Election.
Johnston, R. J., jt. auth. see Herbert, D. T.
Johnston, R. J., jt. auth. see Hughes, J. F.
Johnston, R. J. & Taylor, P. J., eds. A World in Crisis? Geographical Perspectives.
Johnston, R. J., jt. ed. see Herbert, D. T.
Johnston, R. L. TEAPACK Users' Manual.

Johnston, Robert K. Evangelicals at an Impasse: Biblical Authority in Practice.
Johnston, Ronald. Sea Story.
Johnston, Ronald J. Residential Segregation: The State & Constitutional Conflict in American Urban Areas.
Johnston, Ruby F. Development of the Negro Religion.
--The Religion of Negro Protestants.
Johnston, Russ & Rank, Maureen. Dynamic Praying for Exciting Results.
Johnston, Valerie J. Diet in Workhouses & Prisons: Eighteen Thirty-Five to Eighteen Ninety-Five. Mathias, Peter & Bruchey, Stuart, eds.
Johnston, Velda. Along a Dark Path.
--The Crystal Cat: A Novel of Suspense.
--Fatal Affair.
--House above Hollywood.
--A Howling in the Woods.
--The Light in the Swamp.
--The Mourning Trees.
--Shadow Behind the Curtain.
--Voice in the Night.
Johnston, Verna. Sierra Nevada.
Johnston, W. Ross. Great Britain Great Empire.
Johnston, William. England As It Is: Political, Social & Industrial in the Middle of the Nineteenth Century.
Johnstone, Charles. Chrysal: Or, the Adventures of a Guinea. Paulson, Ronald, ed.
--The Pilgrim; or, a Picture of Life, 1775.
Johnstone, Henry W., Jr. Problem of the Self.
Johnstone, Judith, jt. auth. see Williston, Glenn.
Johnstone, Kathleen Y. Sea Treasure.
Johnstone, Margaret. Home Care for the Stroke Patient.
--The Restoration of Motor Function in the Stroke Patient.
--The Stroke Patient: Principles of Rehabilitation.
Johnstone, Mark, intro. by. Contemporary American Photography.
Johnstone, P. T. Topos Theory.
Johnstone, P. T., et al. Indexed Categories & Their Application.
Johnstone, Parker L. A Religious Science Book.
--Russia's New Religion.
Johnstone, Simen, tr. see Shentao, Ye.
Johnstone, William W. Rig Warrior.
Joiner, Beth. Gotta Dance!
Joiner, Charles A. The Politics of Massacre: Political Processes in South Vietnam.
Joiner, Lee M., et al. Microcomputers in Education.
Joint Bank-Fund Library (Washington, D. C.) Staff. The Developing Areas: A Classed Bibliography of the Joint Bank-Fund Library, World Bank Group & International Monetary Fund. Incl. Vol. 1. Latin America & the Caribbean; Vol. 2. Africa & the Middle East; Vol. 3. Asia & Oceania. G K Hall.
--Economics & Finance: Index to Periodical Articles, 1947-1971.
--Economics & Finance: Index to Periodical Articles, 1975-1976-1977.
Joint Comittee on Continuing Legal Education, et al. Federal Taxation of Estates, Gifts, & Trusts.
Joint Expedition to Khirbet Shema Staff & Meyers, Eric M. Ancient Synagogue Excavations at Khirbet Shema, Upper Galilee, Israel, 1970-1972.
Joint Steering Committee for Revision of AACR2. Anglo-American Cataloguing Rules: Revisions 1985.
Joint Steering Group on Uranium Resources of the OECD Nuclear Energy Agency & the International Atomic Energy Agency Staff. World Uranium Geology & Resource Potential.
Joint Working Party of the BMA, the Bar Council, & the Law Society Staff. Medical Evidence.
Joklik, Wolfgang, ed. Zinsser Microbiology.
Jolas, Eugene, tr. see Doblin, Alfred.
Joliffe, Jill. East Timor, Nationalism & Colonialism.
Jolivet, Pierre. Insects & Plants.
Joll, Caroline & McKenna, Chris. Developments in Labour Market Analysis.
Joll, Evelyn, jt. auth. see Butlin, Martin.
Jolles, P. & Paraf, A. Chemical & Biological Basis of Adjuvants.
Jolley, Jerry L., jt. auth. see Newcomb, Robert D.
Jolley, Miesje. A Crack in Time.
Jolley, Robert L., ed. Water Chlorination: Environmental Impact & Health Effects.
Jolley, Robert L., et al, eds. Water Chlorination: Environmental Impact & Health Effects.
--Water Chlorination: Environmental Impact & Health Effects.
Jolly, Brad. Videotaping Local History.
Jolly, Constance S., tr. see Schindler, Anton F.
Jolly, Grace, ed. see Linguistic Association of Canada & the U. S. Staff.
Jolly, Hugh. The Book of Child Care: The Complete Guide for Today's Parents.
--The First Five Years: Dr. Hugh Jolly Answers Questions from Parents.
--The Grandparents' Handbook: A Practical Guide to Enjoying the New Generation.
Jolly, Richard, ed. Disarmament & World Development.
Jolly, Stephen, tr. see Langer, Jiri.
Jolly, William, ed. Metal-Ammonia Solutions.
Jolly, William L. Encounters in Experimental Chemistry.
Joly, H. L. & Tomita, K. Japanese Art & Handicraft.
Joly, Henri L. & Tomita, Kumasaku. Japanese Art & Handicraft.
Jonah, Kathleen, jt. auth. see Barice, E. Joan.
Jonas, Carl. The Observatory.
Jonas, George. Cities.
--Vengeance: The True Story of an Israeli Counter-Terrorist Team.
Jonas, Ilsedore B. Thomas Mann & Italy. Crouse, Betty, tr.
Jonas, Steven. Medical Mystery: The Training of Doctors in the United States.
Jones. I Speak Basic to My Apple.
--I Speak BASIC to My Computer.
--Introduction to Modern Theories of Economic Growth.
--Love in the Afternoon Cookbook.
--World According to Robo the Robot.
Jones & Woodward. Clinical Paediatric Surgery: Diagnosis & Management.
Jones, A. H. Were Ancient Heresies Disguised Social Movements? Lee, Clarence L., ed.
Jones, A. H., ed. Mining Technology for Energy Resources Advances for the Eighties.
Jones, A. J. & Barlow, N. Twenty-Four Worked Engineering Drawing Examples.
Jones, Aaron & DeMarco, Lis, photos by. The Scott Madsen Poster Book.
Jones, Aaron I. Conquering the Night Season.
Jones, Aaron Isaiah. God's Promises to Preachers.
Jones, Adrienne. So, Nothing Is Forever.
Jones, Alan & Botsford, Keith. Driving Ambition.
Jones, Alan L., et al. Occupational Hygiene: An Introductory Guide.
Jones, Allen H. Essenes: The Elect of Israel & the Priests of Artemis.
Jones, Alwyn. Rural Housing.
Jones, Anita W. Door to Chinese Festivals, Feasts, Fortunes.
Jones, Arnold H. The Cities of the Eastern Roman Provinces. Avi-Yonah, M., et al, eds.
Jones, Arthur. Illustrated Dictionary of World Religions.
Jones, Aubrey. I Speak BASIC to My PET.
Jones, Aubrey B., Jr. I Speak BASIC to My VIC.
Jones, B. W. & Milns, R. D. The Use of Documentary Evidence in the Study of Roman Imperial History.
Jones, B. W., ed. Energy & Housing: Symposium - Open University, Milton Keynes, Building Science, Suppl.
Jones, Barry, tr. from Rus. Zionism: Enemy of Peace & Social Progress Issue.
Jones, Ben, ed. see Papers from the Thomas Gray Bicentenary Conference at Carleton University.
Jones, Betsy B. Edwin Romanzo Elmer: Eighteen Fifty to Nineteen Twenty-Three.
Jones, Billy W., jt. auth. see Faulk, Mrs. Hugh L.
Jones, Boisfeuillet, ed. Health of Americans.
Jones, Brian G., jt. auth. see Phillips-Jones, Linda.
Jones, Bronwyn & Braver, John M. Essentials of Gastrointestinal Radiology.
Jones, C. A., ed. Lope de Vega: El Castigo sin Venganza.
Jones, C. E. Science & the Car. Thomas, R. W. & Lowrie, R. S., eds.
Jones, C. Eugene, jt. auth. see Little, R. John.
Jones, C. W. Biological Energy Conservation.
Jones, Calvin, et al. National Longitudinal Study of the High School Class of 1972: Postsecondary Education Transcript Study, Data File User's Manual, Contractor Report.
Jones, Calvin C., et al. Four Years after High School: A Capsule Description of 1980 Senior.
Jones, Carl. Sharing Birth: A Father's Guide to Giving Support During Labor.
Jones, Carol. Painting Classes.
Jones, Catherine. Immigration & Social Policy in Britain.
Jones, Catherine & Stevenson, June. The Yearbook of Social Policy, 1983.
Jones, Catherine, jt. auth. see Stevenson, June.
Jones, Catherine & Stevenson, June, eds. The Yearbook of Social Policy in Britain 1980-1981.
Jones, Catherine, jt. ed. see Brenton, Maria.
Jones, Charles C., Jr. Negro Myths from the Georgia Coast.
Jones, Charles P. Investments: Analysis & Management.
Jones, Chester L. Readings on Parties & Elections in the United States.
Jones, Christopher G., jt. auth. see Timm, Paul R.
Jones, Chuck. A Cricket in Times Square.
--Rikki-Tikki-Tavi.
Jones, Chuck, ed. see Kipling, Rudyard.
Jones, Clara, jt. auth. see Wood, Brenda.
Jones, Clinton R. Homosexuality & Counseling.
Jones, Craig. Blood Secrets.
Jones, Crate H. Tall Truths from Short Stories.
Jones, D. & Goodfellow, M. Bacterial Taxonomy.
Jones, D., jt. auth. see Searle, W.
Jones, D. L., ed. War Poetry: An Anthology.
Jones, D. W., ed. Introduction to the Spectroscopy of Biological Polymers.
Jones, D. W., jt. ed. see Cockayne, B.
Jones, Dallas L., et al, eds. Reducing Worker Absenteeism.
Jones, Dan. Counseling Adults: Life Cycle Perspectives. Moore, Sandra S., ed.
Jones, Dan, ed. see Hartman, Carol.
Jones, Dan B. The Prints of Rockwell Kent.
Jones, David. Crime, Protest, Community, & Police in Nineteenth Century Britain.
Jones, David & Mayo, Marjorie. Community Work: One.
Jones, David, ed. The Shaping of Southern England.
--Soviet Armed Forces Review Annual 1986-1987.
Jones, David A. The Law of Criminal Procedure: An Analysis & Critique.
Jones, David A., jt. auth. see O'Donnell, William J.
Jones, David B., jt. auth. see Rhys, John.
Jones, David C. Municipal Accounting for Developing Countries.
Jones, David K., ed. The Impact of North Sea Hydrocarbons.
Jones, David K. C. Southeast & Southern England.
Jones, David L. Books in English on the Soviet Union, 1917-73: A Bibliography.
Jones, David L., jt. auth. see Holton, Susan.
Jones, David P. see Pryce-Jones, David.
Jones, David R., ed. Soviet Armed Forces Review Annual, 1977-1985.
Jones, Delbert S., jt. auth. see Lord, Kenniston W., Jr.
Jones, Delmos J., jt. auth. see King, William S.
Jones, Dennis. Barbarossa Red.
Jones, Derek C. & Svejnar, Jan, eds. Participatory & Self-Managed Firms: Evaluating Economic Performance.
Jones, Dewitt & Bradley, David. Robert Frost: A Tribute to the Source.
Jones, Diana. Patterns for Canvas Embroidery.
Jones, Diana W. Cart & Cwidder.
--Drowned Ammet.
--The Spellcoats.
Jones, Dolores B., ed. Children's Literature Awards & Winners: A Directory of Prizes, Authors, & Illustrators.
Jones, Don. Miss Liberty Meet Crazyhorse.
Jones, Donald G. A Bibliography of Business Ethics, 1971-1975.
Jones, Douglas C. The Barefoot Brigade.
--The Court Martial of George Armstrong Custer.
--Elkhorn Tavern.
--Elkhorn Tavern.
--Gone the Dreams & Dancing.
--Season of Yellow Leaf.
--Weedy Rough.
--Winding Stair.
Jones, E. & Sinclair, D. J. Atlas of London.
Jones, E. Anthony, jt. ed. see Thomas, Howard C.
Jones, E. G., jt. auth. see Heath, C. J.
Jones, Edgar. Accountancy & the British Economy, Eighteen Forty to Nineteen Eighty: The Evolution of Ernst & Whitney.
Jones, Edward. Using Rapid File.
Jones, Elizabeth B. Let the Children Come.
Jones, Erin B. Law of the Sea: Oceanic Resources.
Jones, Ernest, ed. see Balint, Michael.
Jones, Esmor, jt. auth. see Adams, Anthony.
Jones, Eugene W. & Brown, Lyle C. Practicing Texas Politics.
Jones, Eugene W., et al. Practicing Texas Politics.
--Practicing Texas Politics: A Brief Survey.
Jones, Evan. Left at the Post.
Jones, Evan, jt. auth. see Brady, Terence.
Jones, Everett L., jt. auth. see Durham, Philip.
Jones, Everett L., ed. see Schorer, Mark, et al.
Jones, F. C. The Far East: A Concise History.
Jones, F. C., et al. Nineteen Forty-Two to Nineteen Forty-Six.
Jones, Frank & Davis, Peter. Models of Society: Class, Stratification & Gender in Australia & New Zealand.
Jones, Franklin. Painting Nature.
Jones, Franklin D., jt. auth. see Amiss, John M.
Jones, G., jt. auth. see Williams, D. A.
Jones, G. A. Modern Applied Photography.
Jones, Gareth. Anglo-American Trends in Restitution.
Jones, Gareth L. Railway Walks: Exploring Disused Railways in Britain.
Jones, Gavin W. Structural Change & Prospects for Urbanization in Asian Countries.
Jones, Genevieve. Seeds of Movement: Philosophy of Movement with Techniques Applied to the Beginner.
Jones, George & Stewart, John. The Case for Local Government.
--The Case for Local Government.
Jones, Geraint V. Christology & Myth in the New Testament.
Jones, Gerard, tr. see Takahashi, Rumiko.
Jones, Girault M. That Reminds Me.
Jones, Gordon. Footprints: Chilling Drama of Two Bigfoot.
Jones, Gwendolyn, ed. Packaging Information Sources.
Jones, Gwyn. The Mabinogion. Jones, Thomas, tr.
Jones, Gwyn E. & Rolls, Maurice J., eds. Progress in Rural Extension & Community Development, Vol. 1: Extension & Relative Advantage in Rural Development.
Jones, Harold. There & Back Again.
Jones, Harold E. Adolescence.
Jones, Helen. Nothing Seemed Impossible: Women's Education & Social Change in South Australia 1875-1915.
Jones, Henry J. The Egotistical Sublime: A History of Wordsworth's Imagination.
Jones, Howard. Crime, Race & Culture: A Study in a Developing Country.
Jones, Howard A. Hooked on Horses: Bits of This & That about People & Horses after 21 Years in the Racing Game.
--Hooked on Horses: Bits of This & That about People & Horses after 21 Years in the Racing Game.
Jones, Howard M., tr. see Heine, Heinrich.
Jones, I. S. The Effect of Vehicle Characteristics on Road Accidents.
Jones, Ian, jt. auth. see Binns, Bronwyn.
Jones, Idris W. The Superintendent Plans His Work.
Jones, Iris. Early North American Dollmaking.
Jones, J., jt. auth. see Campbell, R. D.
Jones, J., jt. auth. see Joshua, D.
Jones, J. Benton. A Guide for the Hydroponic & Soilless Culture Grower.
Jones, J. Charles. Learning.
Jones, J. Christopher. Design Methods: Seeds of Human Futures - 1980 Edition - A Review of New Topics.
--Essays in Design.
Jones, J. D. Frequency Modulation Receivers.
--Transistor Audio Frequency Amplifiers.
Jones, J. F. & Herrick, J. M. Citizens in Service: Volunteers in Social Welfare During the Depression, 1929-1941.
Jones, J. H., tr. see Jakubke, Hans-Dieter & Jeschkeit, Hans.
Jones, J. Mervyn. Organisational Aspects of Police Behaviour.
Jones, J. R. The Ionization of Carbon Acids.
Jones, J. Sydney. Tramping in Europe: A Walking Guide.
Jones, James. From Here to Eternity.
--Go to the Widowmaker.
--The Thin Red Line.
--The Thin Red Line.
Jones, James H. & Peterson, Joseph L. Evidence Technician Program Manual.
Jones, James P. Yankee Blitzkrieg: Wilson's Raid Through Alabama & Georgia.
Jones, James R. Britain & Europe in the Seventeenth Century.
Jones, Jane & Swajeski, Donna. The Love in the Afternoon: Recipes from Your Favorite ABC-TV Soap Operas: Ryans Hope, All My Children, One Life to Life, General Hospital.
Jones, Jean G. Time Out for Grief: A Practical Guide to Passing Through Grief to Happiness.
Jones, Jean R. Woman on Her Own. Beasley, Jim, ed.
Jones, Jeanne. The Calculating Cook.
--Diet for a Happy Heart.
--Diet for a Happy Heart: A Low-Cholesterol, Low-Saturated Fat, Low Calorie Cookbook.
--The Fabulous Fiber Cookbook.
--Jeanne Jones Party Planner & Entertaining Diary.
--More Calculated Cooking: Practical Recipes for Diabetics & Dieters.
--Secrets of Salt-Free Cooking: A Complete Low Sodium Cookbook.
Jones, Jeanne & Swajeski, Donna. The Love in the Afternoon Cookbook: Recipes from Your Favorite ABC-TV Soap Operas- Ryan's Hope, One Life to Live, All My Children, General Hospital.
Jones, Jim. If You Can Count to Four.
Jones, Jo Lynne & Greenfield, Howard. Applesoft BASIC Primer for the Apple II Plus, IIe, & IIc.
Jones, Johanna, jt. auth. see Jones, Joseph.
Jones, Joseph & Jones, Johanna. New Zealand Fiction.
Jones, Judy, jt. auth. see Smith, Kathy.
Jones, K. The Chemistry of Nitrogen.
Jones, Katherine M., ed. Heroines of Dixie: Confederate Women Tell Their Story of the War.
Jones, Kathleen. The Teaching of Social Studies in British Universities.
Jones, Kathleen & Brown, John. Issues in Social Policy.

Jones, Kathleen & Fowles, A. J. Ideas on Institutions: Analysing the Literature on Long-Term Care & Custody.
Jones, Leslie W., tr. see Cassiodorus Senator.
Jones, Lewis P. Books & Articles on South Carolina History: A List for Laymen.
Jones, Linda, et al, eds. Proceedings of the Eleventh World Conference on Nondestructive Testing.
Jones, Lloyd. U. S. Fighters.
Jones, Lucille. History of Mineola.
Jones, M. J. A Guide to Metrication.
Jones, Mablen, jt. auth. see Silberstein-Storfer, Muriel.
Jones, Madeline. Finding Out about Life in Britain in the Second World War.
Jones, Maggie. Government Grants: A Guide for Voluntary Organisations.
Jones, Marc E. Astrology: How & Why It Works.
--How to Learn Astrology.
Jones, Marilyn. Exploring Careers As a Carpenter.
--Exploring Offbeat Jobs. Rosen, Ruth, ed.
--Getting High on Creativity.
Jones, Mark M., et al. Chemistry, Man & Society.
--Laboratory Manual for Chemistry, Man & Society.
Jones, Martin R. Our Love Reachin' Out to Earth.
Jones, Mary Ann, jt. auth. see Beck, Dorothy F.
Jones, Mary E. The Eastern Way of Love.
Jones, Mary G. & Reynolds, Lily. Coweta County, Georgia: Chronicles.
Jones, Max. Louis: The Louis Armstrong Story 1900-1971.
Jones, Maxwell. The Process of Change: From a Closed to an Open System in a Mental Hospital.
Jones, Melissa, jt. auth. see Miller, Grover C.
Jones, Mervyn. The Pursuit of Happiness.
Jones, Mortyn, et al, eds. Interaction Within the Brain-Pituitary Adrenocortical System.
Jones, N., ed. Impact Crashworthiness: First International Symposium on Structural Crashworthiness, University of Liverpool, September 14-16, 1983.
--Structural Crashworthiness: Proceedings of the Structural Crashworthiness Conference, Liverpool University, 14-16 September 1983.
Jones, N. V. & Wolff, W. J., eds. Feeding & Survival Strategies of Estuarine Organisms.
Jones, Neville, jt. ed. see Sayer, John.
Jones, Norman F. & Peters, D. K., eds. Recent Advances in Renal Medicine.
Jones, O. C., Jr. & Bankoff, S. G., eds. Symposium on the Thermal & Hydraulic Aspects of Nuclear Reactor Safety - Light Water Reactors.
Jones, Olive, ed. see Cervantes de Saavedra, Miguel.
Jones, Olive, tr. see Rettich, Margret.
Jones, Owen. Chinese Design & Pattern in Full Color.
Jones, Page H. Evolution of a Valley: The Androscoggin Story.
Jones, Paul E., Jr., jt. auth. see Curtice, Robert M.
Jones, Philip R. & Cregan, Ailsa. Sign & Symbol Communication for Mentally Handicapped People.
Jones, Philip T. Racial Hybridity.
Jones, Preston. A Texas Trilogy.
Jones, R. & Kerslake, A. Intermediate Treatment & Social Work. Davies, Martin, ed.
Jones, R., jt. auth. see Dewar, M. J.
Jones, R. A. Introduction to Gas-Liquid Chromatography.
Jones, R. A. & Bean, G. P. The Chemistry of Pyrroles.
Jones, R. B., jt. ed. see Brey, J.
Jones, R. D. The Fenris Option.
Jones, R. F., Jr see Armen, Harry.
Jones, R. F., Jr., jt. ed. see Park, K. C.
Jones, R. F., Jr., et al, eds. Numerical Modeling of Manufacturing Processes, PVP-PB-025.
Jones, R. M. Application of the Geometrical Theory of Diffraction to Terrestrial LF Radio Wave Propagation.
Jones, R. M., ed. Current European Anaesthesiology, 1986: The Yearbook of the European Academy of Anaesthesiology.
Jones, R. S. Asthma in Children.
Jones, R. T., jt. auth. see Trump, B. F.
Jones, R. V., et al. Running a Practice: A Manual of Practice Management.
Jones, Raymond T., jt. ed. see Trump, Benjamin F.
Jones, Reginald & Trentin, H. George. Budgeting.
Jones, Reginald L. Problems & Issues in the Education of Exceptional Children.
Jones, Rhonda A., jt. auth. see Goldstein, David S.
Jones, Richard & Daniels, Kate, eds. Of Solitude & Silence: Writings on Robert Bly.
Jones, Richard M. The Dream Poet.
--Introduction to Pascal & Computer Applications.
Jones, Richard M., ed. Poetry & Politics: An Anthology of Essays.
--Poetry & Politics: An Anthology of Essays.
Jones, Richard M. & Smith, Barbara L., eds. Against the Current: Reform & Experimentation in Higher Education.
Jones, Richard W. Principles of Biological Regulation: An Introduction to Feedback Systems.
Jones, Robert B. & Mendiones, Ruchira C. Thai Cultural Reader.
Jones, Robert M. Mechanics of Composite Materials.
Jones, Robin & Stewart, Ian. Timex-Sinclair 1000: Programs, Games, & Graphics.
Jones, Robin R., jt. auth. see Rutter, Michael.
Jones, Rodney W., ed. Small Nuclear Forces & U. S. Security Policy: Threats & Potential Conflicts in the Middle East & South Asia.
Jones, Roger. Freestyle Windsurfing with Gary Eversole.
Jones, Roger M. The Platonism of Plutarch & Selected Papers. Taran, Leonardo, ed.
Jones, Ron. The Christmas Coat.
Jones, Russell. One Hundred & One Uses of a Condom.
Jones, Russell A., jt. auth. see Hendrick, Clyde.
Jones, Russell K. & Norton, C. McKim. New Cruising Cookbook.
Jones, Ruth A., jt. auth. see Jones, William M.
Jones, RuthAnn & Melton, Emily, eds. ALA Publications Checklist 1988.
Jones, Sandy. Good Things for Babies.
--Good Things for Babies.
--Learning for Little Kids: Parents' Sourcebook for the Years 3 to 8.
Jones, Seymour & Cohen, M. Bruce. The Emerging Business: Managing for Growth.
Jones, Stanleigh H., tr. see Oka, Isaburo.
Jones, Stanley F., tr. see Luedemann, Gerd.
Jones, Stephen. Harbor of Refuge.
--Short Voyages.
Jones, Susan K., jt. auth. see Graham, John W.
Jones, Susan K., jt. auth. see Janusz, Lauren R.
Jones, T. Fairy Tales by T. Jones.
Jones, Ted. The Dogwatch.
Jones, Terry & Palin, Michael. Dr. Fegg's Encyclopedia of All World Knowledge.
Jones, Terry, jt. auth. see Froud, Brian.
Jones, Theodore A. Challenge '77: Newport & the America's Cup.
Jones, Thomas. The Tragedy of Nero. Hill, Elliott M. & Orgel, Stephen, eds.
Jones, Thomas, tr. see Jones, Gwyn.
Jones, Thomas F. Rebel Gold.
Jones, Thomas L. When Leisure Is the Lord's.
Jones, Tom, jt. auth. see Schmidt, Harvey.
Jones, Tom B. From the Tigris to the Tiber: An Introduction to Ancient History.
Jones, Tony, jt. ed. see Magne, Lawrence.
Jones, Tristan. Adrift.
--AKA.
--Ice.
--The Incredible Voyage.
--Saga of a Wayward Sailor.
Jones, Vane A. North American Radio-TV Station Guide.
Jones, Walter S. The Logic of International Relations.
Jones, William. Credulities Past & Present.
Jones, William M. & Jones, Ruth A. Two Careers: One Marriage.
Jones, William M., ed. The Present State of Scholarship in Sixteenth-Century Literature.
Jones, William R. Yosemite: The Story Behind the Scenery.
Jones, William R., ed. see Muir, John.
Jones, Wilmer L. Learning to Compute.
Jones, Wyatt C., jt. auth. see Freeman, Howard E.
Jong, Anthony. Dental Public Health & Community Dentistry.
Jong, Erica. At the Edge of the Body.
--Fear of Flying.
--Fruits & Vegetables.
--Half-Lives.
--Loveroot.
--The Poetry of Erica Jong.
Jong, H. G. Bungenberg De see Booij, H. L. & Bungenberg De Jong, H. G.
Jong, Marvin De see De Jong, Marvin.
Jong, Marvin L. De. Apple II Applications.
Jong, Marvin L. De see De Jong, Marvin L.
Jong, Norman de see De Jong, Norman.
Jongman, A. J., jt. auth. see Schmid, Alex P.
Jonnes, Jill. We're Still Here: The Rise, Fall & Resurrection of the South Bronx. Davison, Peter, ed.
Jonscher, A. K., jt. ed. see Ferrari, R. L.
Jonson, Ben. The Alchemist. Mares, F. M., ed.
--Complete Poetry of Ben Jonson. Hunter, William B., Jr., ed.
--Sejanus: His Fall. Bolton, W. F., ed.
--Volpone.
Jonson, Ben see Harrier, Richard C.
Jonsson, B. Topics in Universal Algebra.
Jonvelle, Jean-Francois, photos by. Mistress.
Jonxis, J. H. P. Growth & Development of the Full-Term & Premature Infant.
Joo, F., jt. ed. see Feher, O.
Joo-Jock, Lim. Territorial Power Domains, Southeast Asia, & China: The Geo-Strategy of an Overarching Massif.
Joon-Chien, Doh. Eastern Intellectuals & Western Solutions: Follower Syndrome in Asia.
Joos, Ernest. Lukacs' Last Autocriticism: The Ontology.
Joos, Lawrence J. Valley of the Vultures.
Joos, Martin. The Five Clocks.
Joplin, Norman. British Toy Figures 1900 to the Present.
Jopling, W. H. Handbook of Leprosy.
Joppien, Rudiger & Smith, Bernard. The Art of Captain Cook's Voyages, Vol. III: The Voyage of the Resolution & the Discovery, 1776-1780.
Joranson, Philip N. & Butigan, Ken, eds. Cry of the Environment: Rebuilding the Christian Creation Tradition.
Jorban, E. Meet Your Guru: How to Unlock Your Soul.
Jordan, Alexis H. Summer Stars.
Jordan, Amos A. & Taylor, William J. American National Security: Policy & Process.
Jordan, Brenda, jt. auth. see Leech, Kenneth.
Jordan, Clarence. Cotton Patch Version of Hebrews & the General Epistles.
--Cotton Patch Version of Luke & Acts.
--Cotton Patch Version of Matthew & John.
--Cotton Patch Version of Paul's Epistles.
Jordan, D., jt. auth. see Happel, J.
Jordan, D., tr. see Matussek, P.
Jordan, David P. Gibbon & His Roman Empire.
Jordan, David S. War & Breed.
Jordan, Donaldson & Pratt, Edwin J. Europe & the American Civil War.
Jordan, Ethel T. Scissor Magic.
Jordan, Fred, ed. see Limonov, Edward.
Jordan, Fred, ed. see Nicosia, Gerald.
Jordan, Fred, jt. ed. see Rosset, Barney.
Jordan, Hope D. Haunted Summer.
Jordan, James B. Entangling Alliances: Christianity & Foreign Policy.
--Sabbath Breaking & the Death Penalty: A Theological Investigation.
Jordan, James B., ed. The Failure of the American Baptist Culture.
--The Reconstruction of the Church.
Jordan, Jeanne. Marry Me, Marybeth. Woolsey, Raymond, ed.
Jordan, John. An Illustrated Guide to the Modern Soviet Navy.
Jordan, Joseph A. We Can Make It...Together.
--We Can Make It...Together.
Jordan, June. Civil Wars.
--Passion: New Poems, Nineteen Seventy-Seven to Nineteen Eighty.
Jordan, June B. & Ramirez, Bruce A., eds. Special Education Yearbook 1986.
Jordan, Nina R. American Costume Dolls: How to Make & Dress Them.
--Holiday Handicraft.
--Homemade Dolls in Foreign Dress.
Jordan, P. & Webbe, G. Schistosomiasis: Epidemiology, Treatment & Control.
Jordan, Pascual. The Expanding Earth. Beer, Arthur, ed.
--Physics in the Twentieth Century.
Jordan, Richard M., jt. ed. see Kohler, Peter O.
Jordan, Robert F. Le Corbusier.
Jordan, Robert L. Black Theology Exposed.
Jordan, Robert L. & Warren, William D. Commentary to Commercial Law.
--Commercial Law.
--Commercial Law, 1986 Bankruptcy Supplement to.,
--Commercial Paper.
Jordan, Rudolf. The Autobiography of Rudolf Jordan.
Jordan, Ruth. Daughter of the Waves: Memories of Growing up in Pre-War Palestine.
--George Sand: A Biographical Portrait.
--Nocturne: A Life of Chopin.
Jordan, S. C. Synopsis of Cardiology.
Jordan, Terry G. Texas Graveyards: A Cultural Legacy.
Jordan, V. C., jt. ed. see Sutherland, R. L.
Jordan, W. Bennett, ed. History, People, & Relevancy.
Jordan, W. J. & Hughes, John. Care of the Wild: Family First Aid & Care for All Wild Creatures.
Jordan, William R., Sr. Heat Lighting. Wilson, Sherrian P. & Oliver, Janie W., eds.
--More Than Friends. Wilson, Sherrian, ed.
Jordan, William S., Jr. Community Medicine in the United Kingdom: Medical Education & an Emerging Specialty Within the Reorganized National Health Service.
Jorden, Paul J. & Adair, James R. Surgeon on Safari.
Joreskog, Karl G. & Sorbom, Dag. Simplis.
Jorge, Antonio, et al, eds. Foreign Debt & Latin American Economic Development.
Jorgens, Elise B., ed. The Texts of the Songs.
Jorgensen, C. K. Oxidation Numbers & Oxidation States.
Jorgensen, C. K., et al. Theoretical Inorganic Chemistry.
Jorgensen, C. K., et al, eds. Chemical Bonding in Solids.
Jorgensen, Carolyn. Mastering 1-2-3.
Jorgensen, Dan. Sky Hook.
Jorgensen, Elizabeth W. & Jorgensen, Henry I. Eric Berne, Master Gamesman: A Transactional Biography.
Jorgensen, Eric. Arctic Cat: Snowmobile Service-Repair, 1974-1979.
--Suzuki DS80-250 Singles, 1978-1980: Service, Repair, Maintenance.
Jorgensen, Eric, ed. BMW 500 & 600 cc Twins, 1955-1969: Service-Repair-Performance.
--Capri Nineteen Seventy-Nine to Nineteen Eighty-Two Includes Turbo Shop Manual.
--Chrysler Outboard Service Handbook: 25 to 140 HP, 1966-1983.
--Datsun 810 1977-1980 Shop Manual.
--Dodge & Plymouth 4-Wheel Drive Tune-Up: 4-Wheel Drive Maintenance, 1965-1982.
--Dodge Aspen: 1976-1979 Shop Manual.
--Evinrude Service-Repair Handbook: 40-140 Hp, 1965-1981.
--Fiat Service-Repair Handbook: 131 Series, 1975-1977.
--Fiat: 128 & X1-9, 1971-1982--Service, Repair Handbook.
--Ford Car Tune-Up Maintenance: 1969-1981.
--Honda Express: 1977-1980 Service-Repair-Performance.
--Johnson Service-Repair Handbook: 40-140hp, 1965-1983.
--Kawasaki: 250-750cc Triples 1969-1979--Service, Repair, Maintenance Handbook.
--Mazda GLC Rearwheel Drive Shop Manual: 1977-1980.
--Mazda RX2 & RX3 Service Repair Handbook.
--Mercedes-Benz Tune-up Maintenance: Gas & Diesel, 1958-1978.
--Mercury Service-Repair Handbook: 4 to 40 Hp, 1964-1982.
--Mustang 1979-1982 Includes Turbo Shop Manual.
--Plymouth Arrow: 1976-1980 Shop Manual.
--Plymouth Horizon: 1978-1981 Shop Manual.
--Plymouth Volare: 1976-1979 Shop Manual.
--Polaris Snowmobile Service-Repair: 1973-1977.
--Porsche: 924 Series, 1976-1980. Service Repair Handbook.
--Puch Moped Owner Service-Repair: 1976-1977.
--Ski-Doo Snowmobile Service-Repair: 1970-1979.
--Suzuki GS1000 Chain Drive Fours: 1978-1979 Service-Repair-Performance.
--Suzuki SP-DR 370 & 400 Singles, 1978-1980: Service, Repair, Performance.
--Suzuki: 50-120cc Singles 1964-1981-Service, Repair, Maintenance Handbook.
--Toyota Service-Repair Handbook: Corona, Mark II & Celica, 1970-1978.
--Triumph Service-Repair Handbook: TR 7 Series, 1975-1978.
--Yamaha Service-Repair Handbook: 90-200cc Twins, 1966-1977.
--Yamaha Snowmobiles: Nineteen Seventy-Five to Nineteen Eighty Service, Repair & Maintenance.
--Yamaha: TX500 & XS500 Twins, 1973-1978--Service, Repair, Performance.
--Yamaha: XS360 & XS-400 Twins, 1976-81, Service, Repair, Maintenance.
--Yamaha: 50-100cc Rotary Valve Singles, 1963-1976--Service, Repair, Maintenance.
Jorgensen, Eric & Jorgensen, Eric, eds. Ford Fiesta 1978-1980 Shop Manual.
Jorgensen, Eric, ed. see Bishop, Mike.
Jorgensen, Eric, ed. see Vesely, Anton.
Jorgensen, George W., jt. auth. see Lavi, Abrahim.
Jorgensen, Henry I., jt. auth. see Jorgensen, Elizabeth W.
Jorgensen, Joseph G. The Sun Dance Religion: Power for the Powerless.
Jorgensen, Poul. Modern Fly Dressings for the Practical Angler.
Jorgensen, Richard, jt. auth. see Murphey, Wayne K.
Jorgensen, S. E. State of the Art of Ecological Modelling: Proceedings of the Conference on Ecological Modelling, Copenhagen, 28 August 2, September 1978.
Jorgensen, S. E, ed. Lake Management.
Jorgenson, Eric, ed. Jeep All Models: 1969-1978, 4-Wheel Drive Maintenance.
Jorgenson, Eric, ed. see Sales, David.
Jorstad, Erling. Being Religious in America: The Deepening Crises over Public Faith.
--The Politics of Moralism: The New Christian Right in American Life.
Jortner, J. & Kestner, N. R., eds. Electrons in Fluids: The Natural of Metal-Ammonia Solutions.
Jose, Nicholas. The Possession of Amber.
Joselyn, Bernardine, ed. see National Security Committee & Harriman, W. Averell, Institute for Advanced Study of the Soviet Union Staff.
Joseph, Alexander, jt. auth. see Jaworski, Irene D.
Joseph, Alexander, et al. Teaching High School Science: A Source Book for the Physical Sciences.

Joseph, Bertram L. Conscience & the King: A Study of Hamlet.
Joseph, D. D. Stability of Fluid Motions 1.
Joseph, Elizabeth B. Mosaics & Home, Where Love & Contentment Abide.
Joseph, Frank. Face the Wind: The Art & Science of Motorcycle Riding.
Joseph, Gerda. New Century Instant German Conversation Guide.
Joseph, Jack. New Century Instant Spanish Conversation Guide.
Joseph, Jennifer, ed. The Manic D Sampler.
Joseph, Lou & Cucco, Ulisse. A Doctor Discusses Prepared Childbirth.
Joseph, Marjory & Gieseking, Audrey. Illustrated Guide to Textiles.
Joseph, Marjory L. Essentials of Textiles.
Joseph, Stephen M., ed. The Me Nobody Knows: Children's Voices from the Ghetto.
Joseph, William. Global Studies: China.
--Professional Service Management.
Josephs, Melvin J. & Sanders, Howard J. Chemistry & the Environment.
Josephs, Rebecca. Early Disorder.
Josephson, Emanuel. The Strange Death of Franklin D. Roosevelt.
Josephson, I. Zelig. The Sole Solution. Naiman, Melvin H., ed.
Josephson, Lennart. Role: O'Neill's Cornelius Melody. Blair, Alan, tr. from Swedish.
Josephson, Mark E. & Wellens, Hein J. J., eds. Tachycardias: Mechanisms, Diagnosis, Treatment.
Josephson, Matthew. The Politicos.
Josephy, Alvin M., Jr., ed. see Brandon, William.
Josephy, Alvin M., Jr., ed. see Lavender, David.
Josh, Sohan S. Hindustan Gadar Party: A Short History.
Joshi, Arun. Lala Shri Ram: A Study in Entrepreneurship & Industrial Management.
Joshi, P. C. Madagascar: Recent Economic Development & Future Prospects.
Joshi, S. T., intro. by see Lovecraft, H. P.
Joshi, S. T., ed. see Lovecraft, H. P.
Joshi, Vasant. The Awakened One: The Life & Work of Bhagwan Shree Rajneesh.
Joshi, Vijay. International Adjustment in the 1980's.
Joshua, D. & Jones, J. Reproductive Clinical Problems in the Dog.
Joshua, Wynfred & Hahn, Walter F. Nuclear Politics: America, France, & Britain.
Josipovici, Gabriel. Four Stories.
Joslin, Sesyle. Last Summer's Smugglers.
--Spy Lady & the Muffin Man.
Joslin, Sesyle & Alcorn, John. La Fiesta.
Joslin, Sesyle & Barry, Katharina. There Is a Bull on My Balcony.
Joslin, Sesyle & Haas, Irene. Dear Dragon: And Other Useful Letter Forms for Young Ladies & Gentlemen Engaged in Everyday Correspondence.
--There Is a Dragon in My Bed.
Joslin, Sesyle & Weisgard, Leonard. Baby Elephant & the Secret Wishes.
--Brave Baby Elephant.
Joslyn, Maynard A., jt. auth. see Heid, John L.
Josse, Pierre, jt. auth. see Gloaguen, Philippe.
Josse, Pierre, jt. ed. see Gloaguen, Philippe.
Josselyn, Irene M. Adolescent & His World.
--Psychosocial Development of Children.
Josselyn, John. New England's Rarities Discovered.
Jost, Lee F. & Sutherland, C. Bruce. Guide to Professional Benefit Plan Management & Administration.
Jost, R. Local Quantum Theory.
Jottrand, R., ed. Chemical Reaction Engineering: Proceedings of the Fourth International Symposium.
Joubert, Joseph. The Notebooks of Joseph Joubert: A Selection. Auster, Paul, ed. & tr. from Fr.
Joudry, Patricia. And the Children Played.
Jouklova, Z., ed. Czech-English, English-Czech Concise Technical Dictionary.
Jourard, Sidney. Self Disclosure: An Experimental Analysis of the Transparent Self.
Jourdain, P. E., tr. see Cantor, Georg.
Journal of Nutrition Staff. Nutrition Requirements of Man: A Conspectus of Research.
Jouvenel, Bertrand De see De Jouvenel, Bertrand.
Jovah. The Lord's Hidden Message in Money.
Jovanovich, William, intro. by see Brandwein, Paul F.
Jowell, Frances S. Thore-Buerger & the Art of the Past.
Jowett, B., tr. see Plato.
Jowett, Garth S., ed. see Arzooni, O. G.
Jowett, Garth S., ed. see Edgerton, Gary R.
Jowett, Garth S., ed. see Hollyman, Burnes S.
Jowett, Garth S., ed. see Mould, David H.
Jowett, Garth S., ed. see Nelson, Richard A.
Jowett, Garth S., ed. see Nowotny, Robert A.
Jowett, Garth S., ed. see Roth, Lane.
Jowett, Garth S., ed. see Waller, Gregory A.
Jowitt, D., jt. auth. see Jowitt, R.
Jowitt, R. & Jowitt, D. Discovering Hampshire & the New Forest.
Jowsey, Jennifer, ed. The Bone Biopsy.
Joy, Charles R., ed. Harper's Topical Concordance.
Joy, David. A Regional History of the Railways of Great Britain: Vol. 14: The Lake Counties.
--A Regional History of the Railways of Great Britain, Vol. 8: South & West Yorkshire.
Joy, Donald. Bonding: Relationships in the Image of God.
--Rebonding: Preventing & Restoring Damaged Relationships.
Joy, Edward T. English Furniture, 1800-1851.
Joy, Helene K. A Heroine's Journey.
Joy, Margaret. See You at the Match.
Joyce, Carol. Designing for Printed Textiles: A Guide to Studio & Freelance Work.
Joyce, Cyril. Errant Sleuth.
Joyce, Edward J. Modula-2: Seafarer's Manual & Shipyard Guide.
Joyce, James. Dubliners: A Facsimile of Drafts & Manuscripts. Groden, Michael, ed.
--Dubliners: A Facsimile of Proofs for the 1910 Edition. Groden, Michael, ed.
--Dubliners: A Facsimile of Proofs for the 1914 Edition. Groden, Michael, ed.
--Exiles: A Facsimile of Notes, Manuscripts & Galley Proofs. Groden, Michael, ed.
--Letters of James Joyce. Incl. Vol. 1. Gilbert, Stuart, ed; Vol. 2. Ellmann, Richard, ed; Vol. 3. Ellmann, Richard, ed. Penguin USA.
--Notes, Criticism, Translations, & Miscellaneous Writings: A Facsimile of Manuscripts & Typescripts.
--Notes, Criticism, Translations, & Miscellaneous Writings: A Facsimile of Manuscripts & Typescripts.
--Passages from Finnegans Wake: A Free Adaptation for the Theater. Manning, Mary, ed.
--Poems Pennyeach.
--A Portrait of the Artist As a Young Man: A Facsimile of the Manuscript Fragments of Stephen Hero. Groden, Michael, ed.
--A Portrait of the Artist As a Young Man.
--Ulysses: "Aeolus" "Lestrygonians," & "Scylla & Charybdis" a Facsimile of Page Proofs for Episodes 7-9. Groden, Michael, ed.
--Ulysses: "Circe": A Facsimile of Page Proofs for Episode 15. Groden, Michael, ed.
--Ulysses: "Circe" & "Eumaeus": A Facsimile of Manuscripts & Typescripts for Episodes 15 (Part II) & 16. Groden, Michael, ed.
--Ulysses: "Cyclops" & "Nausicaa", & "Oxen of the Sun": a Facsimile of Page Proofs of Episode 12-14. Groden, Michael, ed.
--Ulysses: "Eumaeus," "Ithaca," & "Penelope": A Facsimile of Page Proofs for Chapters 16-18. Groden, Michael, ed.
--Ulysses: "Oxen of the Sun," & "Circe": A Facsimile of Drafts, Manuscripts, & Typescripts 14 & 15 (Part 1) Groden, Michael, ed.
--Ulysses: "Telemachus," "Nestor," "Proteus" Calypso" "Lotus Eaters," & "Hades": a Facsimile of Placards for Episodes 1-6. Groden, Michael, ed.
--Ulysses: "Wandering Rocks" & "Sirens" A Facsimile of Page Proofs for Episodes 10-11. Groden, Michael, ed.
Joyce, James A. The War Machine: The Case Against the Arms Race.
Joyce, Joan & Anquillare, John. Winning Softball.
Joyce, M. Site Investigation Practice.
Joyce, Marianne. Edge of Reckoning.
Joyce, Marion. The Frugal Shopper: Save Money on Everything with Coupons, Refunds, Rebates & Free Offers.
Joyce, Patrick W. English As We Speak It in Ireland.
Joyce, Robert. The Esthetic Animal: Man, the Art-Created Art Creator.
Joyce, Rosemary. Up to No Good.
Joyce, Rosemary, created by. Bond of Love.
--Love or Glory.
--Tarnished Victory.
Joyce, William, illus. Mother Goose.
--My First Book of Nursery Tales: Five Favorite Bedtime Tales.
Joyner, Nelson T., Jr. & Durham, Jackie, eds. Joyner's Guide to Official Washington for Doing Business Overseas.
Joynes, Monty & Poyer, Dave. Insiders' Guide to the Outer Banks of North Carolina, 1986-87.
--Insider's Guide to the Outer Banks, 1985-86.
Joynson, C. Guide for Games.
Joynson, D. Cyril. Physical Education for Children.
Joys, Joanne. The Wild Animal Trainer in America.
Jozwiak, William G. Meetings with the Master.
Juarroz, Roberto. Ninth Vertical Poetry, Tenth Vertical Poetry. Carmell, Pamela, tr.
--Vertical Poetry. Merwin, W. S., tr.
Juarroz, Roberto, jt. auth. see Merwin, W. S.
Jubb, K. V. & Kennedy, P. C. Pathology of Domestic Animals.
Jubiz, William. Endocrinology: A Logical Approach for Clinicians.
--Endocrinology: A Logical Approach for Clinicians.
Judd, Cameron. Bad Night at Dry Creek.
--Beggar's Gulch.
--Corrigan.
Judd, Denis. Prince Philip, Duke of Edinburgh.
Judd, Dennis R. The Politics of American Cities: Private Power & Public Policy.
Judd, Jacob, ed. see Van Cortlandt, Philip.
Judd, John, jt. ed. see Smith, Dennis.
Judd, Robert, jt. auth. see Phillips, Debora.
Judd, Robert, jt. auth. see Phillps, Debora.
Judd, Stan. Inshore Fishing: Its Skills, Risks, Rewards.
Jude, D. V. Civil Engineering Drawing.
Judge, Bill C. The Agony of Alcholism & How I Overcome It.
Judge, Clark S. The Best, Worst, Least & Most: The U. S. Book of Rankings.
Judge, George G., et al. Introduction to the Theory & Practice of Econometrics.
Judge, Richard D. & Zuidema, George D. Clinical Diagnosis: A Physiologic Approach.
Judge, Richard P., jt. auth. see Sana, Josephine M.
Judicial Conference of the United States, Committee on Rules of Practice & Procedure & United States Supreme Court Staff. Preliminary Draft of Proposed Amendments to the Federal Rules of Civil Procedure.
Judkins, David C. Ben Jonson's Non-Dramatic Works: A Reference Guide.
Judrin, Claudie, ed. Rodin: Drawings & Watercolors.
Judson, Clara I. Green Ginger Jar.
Judson, Franklyn N., jt. ed. see Wentworth, Berttina B.
Judson, Horace & Schaill, William S. The Techniques of Reading: An Integrated Program for Improved Comprehension & Speed.
Judson, Horace F. The Search for Solutions.
Judson, Margaret A. Crisis of the Constitution.
--From Tradition to Political Reality: A Study of the Ideas Set Forth in Support of the Commonwealth Government in England, 1649-1653.
Judson, Sylvia S. The Quiet Eye Engagement Calendar 1988.
Juel, Donald H. & Buttrick, David. Pentecost 2. Achtemeier, Elizabeth, et al, eds.
Juengst, Orah I. Darken Fruits.
Juergens, John L., et al. Allen-Barker-Hines Peripheral Vascular Diseases.
Juergensmeyer, Mark. Fighting with Gandhi: Step-by-Step Strategy for Resolving Everyday Conflicts.
Juge, Ed, et al. Some of the Best from Kilobaud Microcomputing. Gibbs, Emily A. & Perry, Jim, eds.
Jugenheimer, Donald W., jt. auth. see Fletcher, Alan D.
Juhasz, Fernec, jt. auth. see Weores, Sandor.
Juhasz-Nagy, A., jt. ed. see Szentivanyi, M.
Juhl, H., tr. see Krug, S. & Stein, P.
Juillard, E., ed. Recent Orientations of Regional Analysis in French Geography.
Juilliard School of Music - New York Staff. Juilliard Report on Teaching the Literature & Materials of Music.
Jukes, Thomas H., et al. Effects of DDT on Man & Other Mammals I.
Jukic, Ilija. The Fall of Yugoslavia. Cooke, Dorian, tr.
Jul, Mogens & Zeuthen, Peter. Quality of Pig Meat: Progress of Food & Nutrition Science.
Julian & Careymore. Views from the Hollywood Hills.
Julian, Desmond G. Angina Pectoris.
Julian, Jane. Ellen Bray: A Novel of Superb Romance.
Julian, Joseph, jt. auth. see Bates, Alan P.
Julian, Philippe. Collectors.
Julich, Paul M., jt. auth. see Hilburn, John L.
Julien, H. L., jt. ed. see Erickson, V. L.
Julien, M. H., ed. Biological Control of Weeds: A World Catalogue of Agents & Their Target Weeds.
Julme, Willam E., ed. see Becker, Russell J.
Julme, William E., ed. see Mace, David.
July, Robert W. Pre-Colonial Africa: An Economic and Social History.
Jumikis, Alfreds R. Rock Mechanics.
Jump, Dennis N. Programmer's Guide to MS-DOS.
Jump, John D. Burlesque.
--The Ode.
Jumper, Andrew A. Chosen to Serve: The Deacon.
--The Noble Task: The Elder.
Jundt, Dwight W. Buying & Selling Farmland: A Guide to Profitable Investment.
Jung, C. G. Flying Saucers: A Modern Myth of Things Seen in the Sky.
--The Symbolic Life.
Jung, H., jt. auth. see Dertinger, H.
Jung Institute, Curatorium Staff. Conscience. Hull, R. F. & Horine, Ruth, trs.
Jung, John. Understanding Human Motivation: A Cognitive Approach.
Jung, L. Shannon. Identity & Community: A Social Introduction to Religion.
Jung, Leo. Heirloom: Sermons, Lectures & Studies.
Jung, M. A Review of Annulation. Barton, D. H., ed.
Jung, Mary B. The One-Burner Cookbook.
Jung, Richard K., jt. auth. see Kennedy, Mary M.
Jung, Steven M. The Role of Accreditation in Directly Improving Educational Quality.
Junge, C. E. Air Chemistry & Radioactivity.
Jungel, Eberhard. Death: The Riddle & the Mystery.
Junger, Friedrich G. Major Dobsa und Andere Erzahlungen. Kahn, Robert L., ed.
Jungerman, Joan. Mary, Handmaid of the Lord.
Jungk, Robert. The Everyman Project: A World Report on the Resources from Humane Society.
Jungkuntz, Theodore R. Confirmation & the Charismata.
Junior League of Shreveport, Inc. Staff. Revel.
Junior League of Tulsa, Inc. Staff. Cook's Collage: Favorite Fare of the Junior League of Tulsa.
--Tulsa Art Deco: An Architectural Era Nineteen Twenty-Five to Nineteen Forty-Two.
Junior League of Wilmington, Inc. Staff. Nothing Could Be Finer. Nash, Suzanne, tr.
Junior Liaison Organization Annual Conference, London, 1974. Have You Got the Energy? Proceedings.
Juniper, Dean F. Decision-Making for Schools & Colleges.
Junkin, Brock & Junkin, Elizabeth. Eat Cheaper!
Junkin, Elizabeth, jt. auth. see Junkin, Brock.
Junkins, David R. & Deeny, Kevin J. The Activated Sludge Process: Fundamentals of Operation.
Junkins, Donald, ed. The Contemporary World Poets.
Junod, Alain F. & DeHaller, Rodolphe, eds. Lung Metabolism: Proteolysis & Antiproteolysis, Biochemical Pharmacology, Handling of Bioactive Substances.
Junod, Henri P. Bantu Heritage.
Junor, Penny. Diana, Princess of Wales. Woods, Charles R., ed.
Junta del Acuerdo de Cartagena Staff. Andean Pact Technology Policies.
Junusov, M. S., et al. Theory & Practice of Proletarian Internationalism.
Jupp, T. C. & Hodlin, Sue. Industrial English.
Jupp, T. C. & Milne, John. Guided Course in English Composition.
--Guided Paragraph Writing.
Jupp, T. C; see Milne, John.
Juptner, Joseph P. U. S. Civil Aircraft. Incl. ATC 501-600; Vol. 7. ATC 601-700; Vol. 8. ATC 801-817 & Series Index; Vol. 4. ATC 301-400; Vol.5. ATC 401-500; Vol. 9. ATC 701-800; Vol. 6. ATC 501-600. TAB Bks.
Jurado, Roy, jt. auth. see Litwak, Robert.
Juran, Joseph M. Quality Control Handbook.
Jurgensen, Barbara. How to Live Better on Less: A Guide for Waste Watchers.
--The Prophets Speak Again: A Brief Introduction to Old Testament Prophecy.
Jurgensen, Kai, tr. see Ibsen, Henrik.
Jurmain, Robert, jt. auth. see Nelson, Harry.
Jurmain, Suzanne. From Trunk to Tail: Elephants Legendary & Real.
Jury, Eliahu I. Sampled-Data Control Systems.
Jury, Mark. Playtime! Americans at Leisure.
Jury Verdict Research, Inc. Staff. Personal Injury National Verdict Survey.
Jussawalla, Meheroo. Bridging Global Barriers: Two New International Orders: NIEO, NWIO. Durbin, Paula, ed.
Jussawalla, Meheroo & Lamberton, D. M., eds. Communication Economics & Development: Proceedings of an East-West Communication Institute Workshop, Honolulu, Hawaii, June 1980.
Jussawalla, R. J. Natural Dietetics: A Handbook on Food, Nutrition & Health.
Jussim, Estelle. Frederic Remington, the Camera & the Old West.
Just, H. & Bussmann, W. D., eds. Vasidilators in Chronic Heart Failure.
Just, Johannes. Meissen Porcelain of the Art Nouveau Period.
Just, Richard E., et al. Applied Welfare Economics & Public Policy.
Justamond, J. O., tr. see Raynal, Guillaume T.
Justice, J. B. & Isenhour, T. L., eds. Digital Computers in Analytical Chemistry.
Justin, Jules J. How to Manage with a Union.
--Managing Without a Union.
Justman, Dorothy E. German Colonists in Houston.
Juszczak, Wieslaw, et al, eds. Symbolism in Poland: Collected Essays.
Juszli, Frank L. & Rodgers, Charles A. Elementary Technical Mathematics.
Jute, Andre. Designing & Building Special Cars.

Juxon, John. Lewis & Lewis: The Life & Times of a Victorian Solicitor.
JV-Warwick Press Staff, ed. see Rutland, Jonathan.

K

Kaaiakamanu, D. M. & Akina, J. K. Hawaiian Herbs of Medicinal Value. Akana, Akaiko, tr.
Kaam, Adrian van see Van Kaam, Adrian.
Kaapu, Myrtle King. I Married a Prince: A Cinderella Story from Hawaii.
Kabak, H. R., ed. see International Symposium Held at the Battelle Seattle Research Center Seattle, WA, Nov. 4-6, 1974, et al.
Kabalka, George W., jt. auth. see Lane, Clinton F.
Kabat, Carl, tr. see Comblin, Jose.
Kabat, Elvin A. Blood Group Substances: Their Chemistry & Immunochemistry.
Kabbe, Frederick & Kabbe, Lois. Chemistry, Energy, & Human Ecology.
Kabbe, Lois, jt. auth. see Kabbe, Frederick.
Kaberlein, Joseph J. Air Conditioning Sheet Metal Layout.
Kabotie, Fred. Designs from the Ancient Mimbrenos With Hopi Interpretation.
Kacy, W. Thoughts-a-Fleeting.
Kaczmerek, J. Principles of Machining by Cutting, Abrasion & Erosion.
Kadans, Joseph M. Encyclopedia of Medicinal Herbs.
Kadar, L. & Borsy, Z., eds. The Danubian Region.
Kadarkay, Arpad. Human Rights in American & Russian Political Thought.
Kadel, Thomas E., ed. Growth in Ministry.
Kadel, William H. Prayers for Every Need.
Kadlec, Nancy, jt. auth. see Jetter, Judy.
Kadlec, Robert H., jt. auth. see Hammer, David E.
Kadowaki, J. K. Zen & the Bible: A Priest's Experience.
Kaduk, Bruce. Illuminations.
Kadushin, Max. Rabbinic Mind.
--Worship & Ethics: A Study in Rabbinic Judaism.
Kael, Pauline. Five Thousand One Nights at the Movies: A Guide from A to Z.
Kaellen, G. Quantum Electrodynamics. Iddings, C. & Mizushima, M., trs. from Ger.
Kaemmerer, K. & Buntenkoetter, S. Residue Reviews: The Problems of Residues in Meat of Edibles. Gunther, F. A., ed.
Kaempffer, F. A. Concepts in Quantum Mechanics.
Kaestner, Dorothy. Bargello Antics.
--Needlepoint Bargello.
--Needlepoint Bargello.
Kafka, Barbara. American Food & California Wine. Topkis, Gladys, ed.
Kafka, Francis J., jt. auth. see Eisenberg, James.
Kafka, Franz. The Castle.
Kafka, Vincent W. Discovering Career Satisfaction.
Kafkafi, U., ed. see Soil Chemistry, Soil Fertility & Soil Clay Mineralogy Commissions of the International Society of Soil Science, 13-18 July 1976, Jerusalem.
Kafker, Frank A. The French Revolution: Conflicting Interpretations. Laux, James M., ed.
Kafoglis, Milton Z. Welfare Economics & Subsidy Programs.
Kafrissen, Edward & Stephans, Mark. Industrial Robots & Robotics.
Kagan, B. A., jt. auth. see Marchuk, G. I.
Kagan, Carolyn, ed. Interpersonal Skills in Nursing: Research & Applications.
Kagan, Doreen V., jt. ed. see Morgan, John P.
Kagan, Jerome. Personality Development.
--Understanding Children: Behavior, Motives, & Thought.
Kagan, Jerome & Havemann, Ernest. Psychology: An Introduction.
--Psychology: An Introduction.
Kagan, Jerome & Lang, Cynthia. Psychology & Education: An Introduction.
Kagan, Jerome, et al. Psychology: Adapted Readings.
--Psychology: An Introduction.
--Psychology: An Introduction.
Kagwa, Benjamin N. H. A Ugandan: Defiant & Triumphant.
Kahan, Barry D. & Reisfeld, Ralph A., eds. Markers of Biological Individuality: The Transplantation Antigens Immunology.
Kahan, Jane & Stone, Marie K. Writing the Expository Essay.
Kahan, Jane M., et al. Understanding Your Sexuality.
Kahan, Mitchell. Heavenly Visions: The Art of Minnie Evans.
Kahan, Mitchell D. American Paintings of the Sixties & Seventies, the Real-the Ideal-the Fantastic: Selections from the Whitney Museum of American Art.
--David Parrish.
Kahan, Steven. Intermediate Algebra.
Kahana, K. Case for Jewish Civil Law in the Jewish State.
--The Case for Jewish Civil Law in the Jewish State.
Kahaner, Larry. A Guide to Ham Radio.
Kahin, G. M., ed. see Bedlington, Stanley S.
Kahl, Joseph A., jt. auth. see Gilbert, Dennis.
Kahl, Kurt, jt. auth. see Dahmer, Sondra.
Kahle, A. B., et al, eds. Sessions on Remote Sensing 1980.
Kahler, Erich. Rallying Idea.
Kahler, Martin. The So Called Historical Jesus & the Historic Biblical Christ. Braaten, Carl E., tr. from Ger.
Kahn. PC COBOL.
--Power Skills.
Kahn, Arnold D. Family Security Through Estate Planning.
Kahn, David. The Codebreakers.
Kahn, Douglas A. Basic Corporate Taxation - Nineteen Eighty-Two Pocket Part.
Kahn, E. J., Jr. The Problem Solvers: A History of Arthur D. Little, Inc.
--The Staffs of Life.
Kahn, G., ed. Semantics of Concurrent Computation.
Kahn, G., et al, eds. Semantics of Data Types: International Symposium, Sophia-Antipolis, France, June 27-29, 1984 Proceedings.
Kahn, Gary & Jacobstein, Neil. Managing Expert Systems Projects.
Kahn, George N. Thirty Six Biggest Mistakes Salesmen Make & How to Correct Them.
Kahn, Gilbert, jt. auth. see Mulkerne, Donald J.
Kahn, Harold L. Monarchy in the Emperor's Eyes: Image & Reality in the Ch'ien-Lung Reign.
Kahn, Harriet. How Much Do You Tip the Whipper?
Kahn, Herman. The Coming Boom.
--The Coming Boom: Economic, Political & Social.
--Thinking about the Unthinkable in the 1980's.
Kahn, Herman & Pepper, Thomas. Will She Be Right? The Future of Australia.
Kahn, J. H. Job's Illness: Loss, Grief & Integration; a Psychological Interpretation.
Kahn, J. H., jt. auth. see Thompson, S.
Kahn, J. H., ed. see Morrice, J. K.
Kahn, Jane & Trotter, Gwendolyn. Reading in the Content Areas.
Kahn, Joan, ed. Some Things Dark & Dangerous.
--Some Things Fierce & Fatal.
--Some Things Strange & Sinister.
--Trial & Terror.
Kahn, Kathy. Hillbilly Women.
Kahn, Lawrence E. When Couples Part: How the Legal System Can Work for You.
Kahn, Lisa. From My Texan Log Cabin.
Kahn, Lisa, ed. see Behler, Ernst, et al.
Kahn, Lothar, ed. God: What People Have Said about Him.
Kahn, Norma. More Learning in Less Time: A Guide to Effective Study.
Kahn, P. M., ed. Computational Probability.
Kahn, Peggy & Lewis, Norman. Picketing: Industrial Disputes, Tactics & the Law.
Kahn, Raymond H. & Lands, William E. M., eds. Prostaglandins & Cyclic AMP: Biological Actions & Clinical Applications.
Kahn, Robert & Nestler, Herbert. Power Skills in Science II.
Kahn, Robert D., ed. see Fuller, R. Buckminster, et al.
Kahn, Robert L. & Cannell, Charles F. The Dynamics of Interviewing: Theory, Technique, & Cases.
Kahn, Robert L., ed. Studies in German in Memory of Andrew Louis.
Kahn, Robert L., ed. see Junger, Friedrich G.
Kahn, Roger. Good Enough to Dream.
Kahn, S. How People Get Power: Organizing Oppressed Communities for Action.
Kahn, Samuel. Psychology of Love.
Kahn, Sandra S. & Davis, Jean. The Kahn Report on Sexual Preferences.
Kahn, Steven. The Secure Executive: The Secret of Becoming One, Being One, Staying One.
Kahn, T. C., et al. Methods & Evaluation in Clinical & Counseling Psychology.
Kahng, D., ed. Advances in Applied Solid State Science, Supplement, 2A: Silicon Integrated Circuits.
Kahrl, William L. Advanced Modern Food & Beverage Service.
--The Food Service Productivity & Profit Ideabook.
Kaibara, Ekiken. Yojokun: Japanese Secret of Good Health.
Kail, Robert. Swastika.
Kailath, T. Lectures on Linear Least-Squares Estimation.
Kailer, Claude, jt. auth. see Lowndes, Rosemary.
Kain, John F. & Meyer, John R. Essays in Regional Economics.
Kain, Richard M., jt. auth. see Magalaner, Marvin.
Kainz, Howard P. Wittenberg, Revisited: A Polymorphous Critique of Religion & Theology.
Kaiser, Ann, ed. Cookin' for Kids.
Kaiser, C., ed. see International Symposium on Operating Systems, 1974.
Kaiser, G., ed. see International Congress on Criminology, 6th, Madrid, 1970.
Kaiser, Harvey. The Great Camps of the Adirondacks.
Kaiser, Otto. Introduction to the Old Testament: A Presentation of Its Results & Problems. Sturdy, John, tr. from Ger.
Kaiser, Robert G. Russia: The People & the Power.
Kaiser, Walter C., Jr. Classical Evangelical Essays in Old Testament Interpretation.
Kaiser, Walter C., Jr., jt. ed. see Youngblood, Ronald.
Kai-Shek, Chiang & Gregory, J. S. Jiang Jie-Shi: 1887-1975.
Kaissling, B. & Kriz, W. Structural Analysis of the Rabbit Kidney.
Kaiya, H., jt. ed. see Namba, M.
Kajberg, Leif, jt. ed. see Harbo, Ole.
Kajima, Morinosuke. Emergence of Japan As a World Power, Eighteen Hundred Ninety-Five to Nineteen Hundred Twenty-Five.
Kakac, S., et al, eds. Heat Exchangers: Thermal-Hydraulic Fundamentals & Design.
Kakiuchi, Shiro, et al, eds. Calmodulin & Intracellular Ca-Plus-Plus Receptors.
Kakkar, K. C., jt. auth. see Sethi, G. S.
Kaku, Michio & Trainer, Jennifer, eds. Nuclear Power, Both Sides: The Best Arguments for & Against the Most Controversial Technology.
Kal, M., jt. ed. see Gohberg, I.
Kalash, Joseph T., jt. auth. see Hergert, Douglas.
Kalashian, Susan W. Before Divorce: A Handbook for Relationships. Graves, Helen, ed.
Kalat, James W., ed. Foundations of Experimental Psychology.
Kalavros, Philip M. Pose & Jealousy.
Kalb, Jonah. The Kid's Candidate.
Kalberer, Jan, jt. auth. see Krall, Jack.
Kalchman, Lois. Safe Hockey: How to Survive the Game Intact.
Kalckar, H. M., et al, eds. see Benzon, Alfred, Symposium.
Kaldewey, Harald & Vardar, Yusuf. Hormonal Regulation in Plant Growth & Development.
Kaldor, Mary. The Baroque Arsenal.
Kaldor, Mary, et al, eds. Democratic Socialism & the Cost of Defence: The Report & Papers of the Labour Party Defence Study Group.
Kaldor, Nicholas. Economics Without Equilibrium.
Kaledin, Eugenia. The Education of Mrs. Henry Adams.
Kaleialoha, Carol, jt. auth. see Hibbard, Don.
Kalellis, Peter M. Wedded or Wedlocked?
Kalidasa. The Dynasty of Raghu. Antoine, Robert, tr. from Sanskrit.
Kalil, Ford, ed. High-Density Digital Recording. Buschman, Al.
Kalil, Susie & Rose, Barbara. Fresh Paint: The Houston School. Lubeck, Scott, ed.
Kalin, Everett R., tr. see Braun, Herbert.
Kalin, Everett R., tr. see Hengel, Martin.
Kalin, Everett R., tr. see Stuhlmacher, Peter.
Kalinichenko, D. F., jt. auth. see Bitsadze, A. V.
Kalinnikova, Elena J. Indian-English Literature: A Survey.
Kalir, Joseph. Introduction to Judaism.
Kalisch, Isidor, tr. see Munk, S.
Kalish, Donald & Montague, Richard. Logic: Techniques of Formal Reasoning.
Kalish, Harry I. From Behavioral Science to Behavior Modification.
Kalish, John, ed. Transport & Handling in the Pulp & Paper Industry.
Kalish, John, ed. see International Symposium on Transport & Handling in the Pulp & Paper Industry Staff.
Kalish, John, ed. see Miller Freeman Publications, Inc. Staff.
Kalish, John E., ed. see International Symposium on Transport & Handling in the Pulp & Paper Industry, Staff.
Kalish, Robert. Bloodmoon.
--Bloodrun.
--Bloodtide.
Kalish, Susan & Kallish, Nancy. Pillow Talk.
Kaliski, Burton S. Business Mathematics.
--Business Mathematics.
--Business Mathematics.
--Office Management.
--Today's Business Math: A Text Workbook.
Kalita, Dwight K., jt. ed. see Williams, Roger J.
Kall, P. Stochastic Linear Programming.
Kallas, James. Layman's Introduction to Christian Thought.
--The Real Satan.
--Story of Paul.
Kallen, Howard. Handbook of Instrumentation & Controls: A Practical Manual for the Mechanical Services.
Kallen, Lucille. C. B. Greenfield: A Little Madness.
--C. B. Greenfield: No Lady in the House.
Kallenberg, O. Random Measures.
Kalley, Jacqueline A. The Transkei Region of Southern Africa, 1877-1978: An Annotated Bibliography.
Kallfelz, J. M. & Karam, R. A., eds. Advanced Reactors: Physics, Design, & Economics: Proceedings, International Conference, Atlanta, Georgia, Sept. 1974.
Kallich, Martin, et al, eds. Book of the Sonnet: Poems & Criticism.
Kallio, Elmer, jt. auth. see Keiser, James R.
Kallioinen, V. Finnish Conversational Exercises: Elementary Level.
Kallir, Rudolf F. Autographensammler - Lebenslaenglich.
Kallish, Nancy, jt. auth. see Kalish, Susan.
Kalman, David M., ed. The dBASE Language Handbook.
Kalman, Harold. Pioneer Churches.
Kalman, Natalie & Waughfield, Claire. Mental Health Concepts.
Kalman, Yvonne. Greenstone.
--Riversong.
--Silver Shores.
--Silver Shores.
Kalmanson, Daniel, ed. The Mitral Valve: A Pluridisciplinary Approach.
Kalmring, Klaus & Elsner, Norbert. Acoustic & Vibrational Communication in Insects: Proceedings of Two Symposia at the Seventeenth International Congress of Entomology.
Kalmus, Hans. Diagnosis & Genetics of Defective Color Vision.
Kalmus, I. & Ripp, R. Women See Men.
Kalnay, Francis. Chucaro, Wild Pony of the Pampa.
--It Happened in Chichipica.
Kalpakian, Laura. Crescendo.
Kalsner, Stanley. Trends in Autonomic Pharmacology.
Kalsner, Stanley, ed. Trends in Autonomic Pharmacology.
Kalstone, David. Becoming a Poet.
Kaltenbach, M. Exercise Testing of Cardiac Patients.
Kalter, Suzy. How to Take Twenty Pounds Off Your Man.
Kalton, G. Introduction to Statistical Ideas for Social Scientists.
Kalugin, David. For the Loneliest of Reasons.
--The Leaves Still Talk.
--Naturally.
--The Tintinnabulations of Boos & Applause.
--Tomorrow Is So Far from Now.
Kaluzny, Arnold D., jt. auth. see Shortell, Stephen M.
Kamal, A. N., jt. ed. see Boal, D. H.
Kamal, Abdul N., jt. ed. see Capri, Anton Z.
Kamal, Asif & Brocklehurst, J. C. Color Atlas of Geriatric Medicine.
Kamaraju, V., jt. auth. see Naidu, N. S.
Kamat, A. R., ed. see Gadgil, D. R.
Kamath, M. V. Philosophy of Death & Dying.
Kamath, S. H. Clinical Biochemistry for Medical Technologists.
Kambayashi, Yahiko. Database: A Bibliography.
Kameeta, Zephania. Why, O Lord? Psalms & Sermons from Namibia.
Kamel, M. M., ed. see CISM (International Center for Mechanical Sciences) Staff.
Kamen, Betty & Kamen, Si. In Pursuit of Youth: Everyday Nutrition for Everyone over 35.
Kamen, Martin D. Isotopic Tracers in Biology: An Introduction to Tracer Methodology.
--Primary Processes in Photosynthesis.
Kamen, Milton. A Grandparent's Book.
Kamen, Ruth, ed. British & Irish Architectural History: A Bibliography & Guide to Sources of Information.
Kamen, Si, jt. auth. see Kamen, Betty.
Kamenetz, Rodger. Terra Infirma.
Kamerman, Sylvia E., ed. Book Reviewing.
--On Stage for Christmas.
Kamerschen, David R., jt. ed. see Danielson, Albert L.
Kames, Lord, jt. auth. see Home, Henry.
Kamien, R. Music: An Appreciation.
Kamien, Roger. Music: An Appreciation.
--Norton Scores: An Anthology for Listening.
Kamien, Roger, ed. The Norton Scores.
--The Norton Scores: An Anthology for Listening.
--Norton Scores: Standard Edition.
Kamikamica, Esiteri, compiled by. Come to My Place: Meet My Island Family.
Kamil, Jill. The Ancient Egyptians: How They Lived & Worked.
Kamil, Leo. Fuelling the Fire: U. S. Policy & the Western Sahara Conflict.
Kamin, John. Hyperinflation: How You Can Come Out Ahead & Your Personal Financial Success Program.
Kamin, Jonathan. Mastering ThinkTank of the IBM PC.
--Mastering ThinkTank on the 512k Macintosh.
--The MS-DOS Power User's Guide, Vol. I.
--Power User's Guide to Hard Disk Management.

Kamin, Philip. Bryan Adams.
--David Lee Roth.
--Dire Straits.
--Howard Jones.
--Led Zeppelin.
--Madonna.
--Paul Young.
--Phil Collins.
--Tears for Fears.
--Tina Turner.
--Wham!
--ZZ Top.
Kaminer, B. Search & Discovery: A Tribute to Albert Szent Gyorgy.
Kaminetzky, Harold & Iffy, Leslie. Progress in Perinatology.
Kaminkow, Marion J. First Days at School: A Co-operative Reader for Child & Adult.
Kaminska, Zofia, jt. auth. see Gardiner, John M.
Kaminskaya, Dina. Final Judgment: My Life as a Soviet Defense Attorney. Glenny, Michael, tr. from Rus.
Kaminsky, Daniel. Snout to Snout.
Kaminsky, Manfred. Atomic & Ionic Impact Phenomena on Metal Surfaces.
Kaminsky, Marc. The Road from Hiroshima: A Narrative Poem.
Kaminsky, Stuart M. Down for the Count.
--A Fine Red Rain: An Inspector Porfiry Rostnikov Mystery.
--John Huston: Maker of Magic.
--Red Chameleon.
Kamisar, Yale, jt. auth. see Lockhart, William B.
Kamiya, N. Protoplasmic Streaming.
Kamiya, Noburo, jt. ed. see Allen, Robert D.
Kamm, Adrian Van see Van Kamm, Adrian & Healy, Kathleen.
Kamm, G. & Grof, Baumann T. Machame Anaesthesia Notebook for Medical Auxiliaries: With Special Emphasis on the Developing Countries.
Kamman, Madeleine. Dinner Against the Clock.
--When French Women Cook: A Gastronomic Memoir.
Kammer, Charles L., 3rd. The Kingdom Revisited: An Essay on Christian Social Ethics.
Kammer, Reinhard. The Way of the Sword: The Tengu-geijutsu-ron of Chozan Shissai. Fitzgerald, Betty J., tr. from Japanese.
Kammeraad-Campbell, Susan. Doc: The Story of Dennis Littky & His Fight for a Better School.
Kammert, James L. International Commercial Banking Management.
Kammeyer, Kenneth C. & Ginn, Helen L. Introduction to Population.
Kamoroff, Bernard. Small Time Operator: How to Start Your Own Small Business, Keep Your Books, Pay Your Taxes & Stay Out of Trouble.
Kamoroff, Bernard & Krause, Emil. Small Time Operator.
Kampel, Ian. A Practical Introduction to the New Logic Symbols.
Kamshilov, M. M. Evolution of the Biosphere. Brodskaya, Minna, tr.
Kamstra, Douglas, compiled by. Good Times Game Book: Good Things for Youth Leaders.
Kana, D. D. & Butler, T. G., eds. Reliability Design for Vibroacoustic Environments: AMD.
Kanai, E., jt. ed. see Somiya, S.
Kandel, Lenore. Word Alchemy.
Kandel, Michael, ed. see Lem, Stanislaw.
Kandel, Michael, tr. see Lem, Stanislaw.
Kandel, Myron. How to Beat Wall Street.
Kandel, Robert S. Earth & Cosmos.
Kandel, Thelma. What to Name the Cat.
Kandell, Jonathan. Passage Through El Dorado.
Kandias, Kostis. Revelations One: Noah's Flood Was a Result of Nuclear War.
Kandinsky, Wassily. Kandinsky: Complete Writings on Art. Lindsay, Kenneth C. & Vergo, Peter, eds.
Kandzari, Judith H. & Howard, Joan R. The Well Family: A Developmental Approach to Assessment.
Kane & Jakes. Excalibur!
Kane, jt. auth. see Bodie.
Kane, Andy. Jobs That Suck... And Some That Don't.
--Saloon Survival.
Kane, G. Sixty-Eight Thousand Microprocessor Handbook.
Kane, Gerry. The CRT Controller Handbook.
Kane, Gerry, jt. auth. see Cramer, William.
Kane, Gerry, et al. Assembly Language Programming: 68000.
Kane, Henry. The Little Red Phone.
Kane, Israel. In Quest of the Truth: A Survey of Medieval Jewish Thought.
Kane, James C., jt. auth. see Rolnick, Michael.
Kane, Joseph W. & Sternheim, Morton M. Physics.
Kane, Katie. Kept in Stitches.
Kane, Patricia. Food Makes the Difference: A Parent's Guide to Raising a Healthy Child.
Kane, Paula & Short, Patricia. Communicado con Palabras.
--Entretiens avec les Mots.
Kane, Raymond W. & Young, Albert D., Jr. Underground Storage Tank Management: A Practical Guide.
Kane, Robert L. & Kane, Rosalie A., eds. Values & Long-Term Care.
Kane, Robert M. & Vose, Allen D. Air Transportation.
Kane, Rosalie A., jt. ed. see Kane, Robert L.
Kane, Thomas A. Who Controls Me? A Psychotheological Reflection.
Kaneko, Jiro J., ed. Clinical Biochemistry of Domestic Animals.
Kaneko, Lonny. Coming Home From Camp.
Kaner, N., tr. see Vinogradov, A. P. & Udintsev, G. B.
Kanet, Roger E., ed. Soviet Foreign Policy in the 1980's.
Kanfer, Frederick H. & Goldstein, Arnold P., eds. Helping People Change: A Textbook of Methods.
Kanfer, Frederick H., jt. ed. see Goldstein, A. P.
Kanfer, Frederick H., jt. ed. see Karoly, Paul.
Kanfer, Stefan. The International Garage Sale.
Kang, Sugwon. Human Nature in Politics.
Kang, Younghill. The Grass Roof. Bd. with The Yalu Flows. Li, Mirok. Norton.
Kang Rae Cho. Multinational Banks: Their Identities & Determinants. Bateman, Fred, ed.
Kania, Edwin E. Donnager's Cat.
Kanin, Garson. Cordelia?
--Hollywood: Stars & Starlets, Tycoons & Flesh-Peddlers, Moviemakers & Moneymakers, Frauds & Geniuses, Hopefuls & Has-beens, Great Lovers & Sex Symbols.
Kankashian, I. K. Contexts: Strategies for Vocabulary Enrichment.
Kann, Eduard A. The History of China's Internal Loan Issues: Shanghai, 1934. Bd. with China's Currency Reform, 1941. Lin Yu Shen. Garland Pub.
Kann, P. Environs of Leningrad.
Kannady, Paul. Tosh "le Vengeur"
Kannan, C. R. Gastroenterology: A Problem-Oriented Approach.
Kannan, C. T. Inter-Racial Marriages in London: A Comparative Study.
Kannan, Rangacesari, jt. ed. see Cesari, Lamberto.
Kano, Susan. Making Peace with Food: A Step-By-Step Guide to Freedom from Diet-Weight Conflict, with Index & Bibliography.
Kanovasky, E. Economic Development of Syria.
Kansky, Robert, jt. auth. see Dennis, J. Richard.
Kant, Candace. Zane Grey's Arizona.
Kant, Immanuel. Critique of Practical Reason & Other Writings in Moral Philosophy. Beck, Lewis W., tr.
--Critique of Pure Reason.
--Introduction to Logic. Abbot, Thomas K., tr.
Kant, Sharad. Practical Approach to COBOL Programming.
Kantar, Edwin B. Bridge Humor.
Kantar, Edwin B. & Stanley, Jackson. Gamesman Bridge: Play Better with Kantar.
Kantenwein, Louise. The Day Velvet Disappeared.
--Henri & the Crocodile.
--Tasha: Her Middle Name Is Mischief.
--Welcome Home, Charlie.
Kanter, Donald L. & Mirvis, Philip H. The Cynical Americans: Living & Working in an Age of Discontent & Disillusion.
Kanter, H. Libyan: Libya.
Kanter, Harold M. Computer Applications of Educational Measurement Concepts.
Kanter, Rosabeth Moss see Moss Kanter, Rosabeth.
Kantonen, T. A. Life After Death.
Kantor, Frederick W. Information Mechanics.
Kantor, Wallace. Relativistic Propagation of Light.
Kantorowicz. Inlays, Crowns & Bridges.
Kantowitz, Barry & Roediger, Henry, III. Experimental Psychology: Understanding Psychological Research.
Kantowitz, Barry H. & Roediger, Henry L., III. Experimental Psychology.
Kantrowitz, Barbara, jt. auth. see Haber, Michelle I.
Kantzenback, Friedrich W., jt. ed. see Vatja, Vilmos.
Kanuk, Leslie L., jt. auth. see Schiffman, Leon G.
Kanunga, R. N., jt. auth. see Dutta, S.
Kanungo, M. S. Biochemistry of Aging.
Kanzig, Werner. Ferroelectrics & Antiferroelectrics.
Kao, C. K. Optical Fiber Technology II.
Kao, Charles C. Search for Maturity.
Kao, James. Chinese Divination.
Kapachenko, N. E., jt. auth. see Sanakoyev, Sh. P.
Kapantais, G. Gloria. Decennial Census Data for Selected Health Occupations, United States, 1980.
Kapelle, William E. The Norman Conquest of the North: The Region & Its Transformation, 1000-1135.
Kapes, Jerome & Mastie, Marjorie. A Counselor's Guide to Vocational Guidance Instruments.
Kapferer, Bruce. A Celebration of Demons: Exorcism & the Aesthetics of Healing in Sri Lanka.
Kapitza, P. L. Collected Papers of P. L. Kapitza. Ter Haar, D., ed.
Kaplan. Variety International Showbusiness, 1983.
Kaplan & Loughrey. Ins & Outs of On-Track & Off-Track Horse Race Betting.
Kaplan & Waltz. Evidence, Cases on.
Kaplan, Albert S., ed. The Herpesviruses.
--Viral Transformation & Endogenour Viruses.
Kaplan, Arthur M., jt. ed. see Sharpley, J. Miles.
Kaplan, Aryeh. Ethics of the Talmud.
Kaplan, Aryeh, tr. The Book of Esther.
Kaplan, Daile. Lewis Hine in Europe, 1918-1919: The Lost Photographs.
Kaplan, Eugene H. Experiences in Life Science: A Laboratory Guide.
Kaplan, Frances B., ed. see U. S. President's Commission on the Status of Women.
Kaplan, Fred. Miracles of Rare Device: The Poet's Sense of Self in Nineteenth-Century Poetry.
--The Wizards of Armageddon.
--The Wizards of Armageddon: Strategists of the Nuclear Age.
Kaplan, Frederic M., et al. The China Guidebook, 1982.
Kaplan, Fredric M. & DeKeijzer, Arne J. The China Guidebook, 1984.
Kaplan, Fredric M., jt. auth. see DeKeijzer, Arne J.
Kaplan, Fredric M., et al. The China Guidebook 1985.
--The China Guidebook, 1986.
--The China Guidebook: 1988 Edition.
Kaplan, Glenn. The Big Time: How Success Really Works in 14 Top Business Careers.
Kaplan, Harold I., jt. ed. see Freedman, Alfred M.
Kaplan, Helen S. The Illustrated Manual of Sex Therapy.
--Making Sense of Sex.
Kaplan, I. G. Symmetry of Many Electron Systems.
Kaplan, Irving, ed. Angola: A Country Study.
--Zambia: A Country Study.
Kaplan, Irving & Nelson, Harold D., eds. Ethiopia: A Country Study.
Kaplan, Janice. First Ride.
--If You Believe in Me.
Kaplan, John & Skolnick, Jerome H. Criminal Justice: Introductory Cases & Materials.
Kaplan, John & Waltz, Jon R. Evidence, Cases & Materials: Teachers' Manual.
Kaplan, John, jt. auth. see Cohen, William.
Kaplan, Jonathan, ed. International Bibliography of Jewish History & Thought.
Kaplan, Larry. Retiring Right: Planning for Your Successful Retirement.
Kaplan, Louise J. Adolescence: A Farewell to Childhood.
Kaplan, M. L., et al. The Structural Approach in Psychological Testing.
Kaplan, Martha see Johnston, Jill.
Kaplan, Mike. The Complete Book of Major U. S. Show Business Awards.
--Variety Index Film Reviews, 1907-1980.
Kaplan, Mike, ed. Variety Film Reviews: 1907-1920.
--Variety Film Reviews: 1921-1925.
--Variety Film Reviews: 1926-1929.
--Variety Film Reviews: 1930-1933.
--Variety Film Reviews: 1934-1937.
--Variety Film Reviews: 1938-1942.
--Variety Film Reviews: 1943-1948.
--Variety Film Reviews: 1949-1953.
--Variety Film Reviews: 1954-1958.
--Variety Film Reviews: 1959-1963.
--Variety Film Reviews: 1964-1967.
--Variety Film Reviews: 1968-1970.
--Variety Film Reviews: 1971-1974.
--Variety Film Reviews: 1975-1977.
--Variety Film Reviews: 1978-1980.
--Variety: International Motion Picture Marketplace, 1982-1983.
--Variety: International Show Business Reference.
--Variety's Who's Who in Show Business.
Kaplan, Milton. In a Time Between Wars.
Kaplan, Morton A., ed. Global Policy: Challenge of the Eighties.
Kaplan, Nathan O. & Kennedy, Eugene P., eds. Current Aspects of Biochemical Energetics.
Kaplan, Nathan O. & Robinson, Arthur, eds. From Cyclotrons to Cytochromes: Essays in Molecular Biology & Chemistry.
Kaplan, Norman M. Management of Hypertension.
Kaplan, Norman M. & Stamler, Jeremiah. Prevention of Coronary Heart Disease: Practical Management of Risk Factors.
Kaplan, Peter, ed. see Morley, Hilda.
Kaplan, Peter, et al. Pourboire Sixteen: Peter Kaplan's Book.
Kaplan, Roger P., jt. auth. see Loevi, Francis J., Jr.
Kaplan, S. A. & Tsytovich, V. N. Plasma Astrophysics.
Kaplan, Sandra, et al. The Teacher's Choice: Ideas & Activities for Teaching Basic Skills.
Kaplan, Sherman, illus. Best Restaurants Chicago & Suburbs.
Kaplan, Solomon A. Clinical Pediatric & Adolescent Endocrinology.
Kaplan, Sydney J. Feminine Consciousness in the Modern British Novel.
Kaplan, Vladimir. Tournament Checkers: An Introduction to Pool Checkers.
Kaplan, Wendy, ed. The Art That Is Life: The Arts & Crafts Movement in America, 1875-1920.
Kaplan, William L. & Lebowitz, Melvyn. The Student Scientist Explores Energy & Fuels.
Kaplan-Williams, Strephon. Transforming Childhood: A Handbook for Personal Growth.
Kapleau, Phillip. To Cherish All Life: A Buddhist Case for Becoming Vegetarian.
Kaplow, Robert. Alex Icicle: A Romance in Ten Torrid Chapters.
--Two in the City.
Kapoor, A. & McKay, Robert J. Managing International Markets: A Survey of Training Practices & Emerging Trends.
Kapp, Ardeth G. Miracles in Pinafores & Bluejeans.
Kapp, Dan & Leben, Joseph F. IMS Programming Techniques: A Guide to Using DL-1.
Kapp, Robert A., ed. Four Views of China.
Kappa. Bartender's Guide to the Best Mixed Drinks.
Kappeler, Susanne & Bryson, Norman, eds. Teaching the Text.
Kappers, J. A., ed. see International Society for Neurovegetative Research Staff.
Kappos, Demetrios. Probability Algebras & Stochastic Spaces.
Kaps, Helen K. Moral Perspective in La Princesse de Cleves.
Kapstein, Matthew, ed. see Rinpoche, Dudjom.
Kapur, J. C. India: An Uncommitted Society.
Kapur, R. K. Joseph Conrad: Theme & Treatment of Evil.
Kapur, Tribhuwan. Hippies: A Study of Their Drug Habits & Sexual Customs in India.
Kapur, Vijay. Virginia Woolf's Vision of Life & Her Search for Significant Form: A Study in the Shaping Vision.
Kapuscinski, Ryszard. The Emperor: Downfall of an Autocrat. Brand, William R. & Mroczkowska-Brand, Katarzyna, trs.
Kapustka, Lawrence. Plants Humanity & the Environment: Discussion Guide.
Kaputa, Catherine, tr. see Takeda, Tsuneo.
Karagulla, Shafica, jt. auth. see Neal, Viola P.
Karakousis, C. Atlas of Operations in Soft Tissue Sarcomas.
Karam, Emile. Spoken Arabic: The Language of Lebanon.
Karam, R. A. & Weaver, L. E., eds. Risk-Benefit Assessments & Societal Cost of Nuclear & Other Energy Sources.
Karam, R. A., jt. ed. see Kallfelz, J. M.
Karamcheti, K., ed. Rarefield Gas Dynamics.
Karapanou, Margarita. Kassandra & the Wolf. Germanacos, N. C., tr.
Karapetyants, M. Chemical Thermodynamics.
Karas, Thomas. The New High Ground: Strategies & Weapons of Space-Age War.
--The New High Ground: Systems & Weapons of Space Age War.
Karasek, Mirek. The Anatomy of Decision.
Karassik, I. J. Centrifugal Pump Clinic.
Karassik, Igor J. & Krutzch, William C. Pump Handbook.
Karasu, Toksoz B., ed. see APA Commission on Psychiatric Therapies.
Karcher, Joseph T. How to Build a One Hundred Thousand Dollar Law Practice.
--New Guide to Building a One Hundred Thousand Dollar Law Practice.
Karczmar, A. G. Anticholinesterase Agents.
Karczmar, A. G. & Eccles, John C., eds. Brain & Human Behavior.
Kardestuncer, H., ed. see CISM (International Center for Mechanical Sciences), Department of Mechanics of Solids Staff.
Kardiner, A. My Analysis with Freud: Reminiscences.
Kardon, Janet. Photography: A Sense of Order.
Kardon, Janet & Marincola, Paula. Red Grooms: Philadelphia Cornucopia.
Kardon, Janet, jt. auth. see Foster, Hal.
Kardon, Janet, et al. Laurie Anderson: Works from 1969-1983.
Karff. Hebrew Union College-Jewish Institute of Religion at One Hundred Years.
Karfunkel, Thomas & Ryley, Thomas W. The Jewish Seat: Antisemitism & the Appointment of Jews to the Supreme Court.
Kargas, Nicholas A., jt. auth. see Ameiss, Albert P.
Karger, Delmar W. & Hancock, Walton C. Advanced Work Measurement.
Kargere, Audrey. Color & Personality.
Kargilis, G., jt. auth. see Pactor, P.
Karim, Iman B., ed. & intro. by. Malcolm X: The End of White World Supremacy.

Karim, Mehtab S., jt. auth. see Smith, Peter C.
Karim, R. W. Drugs During Pregnancy.
Karki, N., ed. Mechanisms of Toxicity & Metabolism: Proceedings of the 6th International Congress of Pharmacology, Helsinki, 1975.
Karl, Frederick. Biography of William Faulkner.
--Modern & Modernism: The Sovereignty of the Artist 1885-1925.
Karl, John. An Introduction to Digital Signal Processing.
Karl, John C. Scramblings.
Karlen, Arno. Napoleon's Glands & Other Ventures in Biohistory.
--Sexuality & Homosexuality: A New View.
Karlen, Delmar. Procedure Before Trial.
Karlen, Delmar, et al. Cases on Civil Procedure.
Karlic, Tony. My Life Is a Poem.
Karlin, Arthur, et al, eds. Neuronal Information Transfer.
Karlin, Muriel S. Solving Your Career Mystery.
Karlin, Robert. Teaching Elementary Reading: Principles & Strategies.
--Teaching Elementary Reading: Principles & Strategies.
Karlin, Wayne. Crossover.
Karliner, Joel & Gregoratos, Gabriel, eds. Coronary Care.
Karlins, Marvin & Abelson, Herbert. Persuasion: How Opinions & Attitudes Are Changed.
Karlinsky, Simon, tr. see Nabokov, Vladimir.
Karlowich, Robert A. Young Defector.
Karlsson, P. W., jt. auth. see Srivastava, H. M.
Karmel, Louis J. Measurement & Evaluation in the School.
Karmos, Joe, et al. Help for Job Hunters.
Karn, George. Circus Big & Small: And Now, in the Center Ring, Introducing Circus Opposites!
--Circus Colors: Step Right up & Meet a Rainbow of Colors!
Karnes, Frances A. & Collins, Emily C. Handbook of Instructional Resources & References for Teaching the Gifted.
Karnes, Merle B. Learning Language at Home: Level I & II.
--Learning Mathematical Concepts at Home.
Karnes, Merle B., ed. Creative Games for Learning: Parent, Teacher Made Games.
Karnopp, D., jt. ed. see Van Dixhoorn, J.
Karnopp, Dean, et al. Bond Graph Techniques for Dynamic Systems in Engineering & Biology.
Karo, George H. Greek Personality in Archaic Sculpture.
Karo, Wolf, jt. auth. see Sandler, Stanley R.
Karol, K. S. Between Two Worlds: The Life of a Young Pole in Russia 1939-46.
Karoly, Paul & Steffen, John J. Adolescent Behavior Disorders: Foundations & Contemporary Concerns, Advances in Child Behavioral Analysis & Therapy.
Karoly, Paul & Kanfer, Frederick H., eds. Self-Management & Behavior Change: From Theory to Practice.
Karoly, Paul & Steffen, John J., eds. Improving Children's Competence: Advances in Child Behavioral Analysis & Therapy.
Karoly, Paul, jt. ed. see Steffen, John J.
Karotkin, Edward H., jt. auth. see Goldsmith, Jay P.
Karp, Ivan. Fields of Change among the Iteso of Kenya.
Karp, Naomi J. Nothing Rhymes with April.
--The Turning Point.
Karp, Richard A. Proving Operating Systems Correct. Stone, Harold, ed.
Karpeck, John J., jt. auth. see Charlier, Rodger H.
Karpel, Bernard, ed. Arts in America: A Bibliography.
Karpeles, Maud & Sharp, Cecil J., eds. Eighty Appalachian Folk Songs.
Karplus, Curtis M., jt. auth. see California Continuing Education of the Bar Staff.
Karpman, V. I. Non-Linear Waves in Dispersive Media. Cap, Ferdinand, tr.
Karpovich, Peter, jt. auth. see Murray, Jim.
Karpovsky, Mark G. Spectral Techniques & Fault Detection.
Karr, Kathleen. Chessie's King.
Karr, Lee. The Housesitter.
--Tangles Mesh.
Karraker, R., et al. Readings in Classroom Management.
Karran, S. J. & Alberti, K. G. Practical Nutritional Support.
Karreman, George, ed. Cooperative Phenomena in Biology.
Karrenbrock, Marilyn H., jt. auth. see Lucas, Linda.
Karrer, Otto. Meister Eckhart Speaks.
Karsh, Jeff, jt. auth. see Swanson, Jack.
Karssen, Mrs. Gien. Beside Still Waters.
Karstad, Aleta. Wild Habitats.
Kartashev, Steven, jt. auth. see Kartashev, Svetland.
Kartashev, Svetland & Kartashev, Steven. Designing & Programming Modern Computers & Systems.
Kartenbeck, J., et al. The Nuclear Envelope in Freeze-Etching.
Kartini, Raden A. Letters of a Javanese Princess.
Karve, Iravati. Yuganta: The End of an Epoch.
Kasahara, Kunihiko, jt. auth. see Gray, Alice.
Kasanin, J. S., ed. Language & Thought in Schizophrenia.
Kasbah, Mimi. Michael J. Fox Scrapbook.
Kase, Nathan G. & Weingold, Allan B., eds. Principles & Practice of Clinical Gynecology.
Kasem, A., ed. Three Clean Fuels from Coal-Technology & Economics: Synthetic Natural Gas, Methanol, & Medium Btu Gas.
Kasemann, Ernst. Essays on New Testament Themes.
--Jesus Means Freedom. Clarke, Frank, tr. from Ger.
--New Testament Questions of Today. Montague, W. J., tr. from Ger.
--Perspectives on Paul. Kohl, Margaret, tr. from Ger.
--Perspectives on Paul.
--The Testament of Jesus: A Study of the Gospel of John in the Light of Chapter 17.
--The Wandering People of God: An Investigation of the Letter to the Hebrews. Harrisville, Roy A., tr.
Kasevich, Lawrence S. Harvard Project Manager-Total Project Manager: Controlling Your Resources.
Kasha, Al. If They Ask You, You Can Write a Song.
Kasha, Al & Hirschhorn, Joel. Notes on Broadway: Conservations with the Great Songwriters.
--Reaching the Morning After.
Kashyap, L., jt. ed. see Dash, V.
Kasindorf, Jeannie. The Nye County Brothel Wars: A Tale of the New West.
Kasl, Elizabeth, jt. auth. see Anderson, Richard E.
Kasle, Myron J. An Atlas of Dental Radiographic Anatomy.
Kasle, Myron J. & Langlais, Robert. Basic Principles of Oral Radiography.
Kasler, F. Quantitative Analysis by NMR Spectroscopy.
Kasner, Erick. Essentials of Engineering Economics.
Kasoff, Lawrence, jt. auth. see Madigan, Bob.
Kaspar, Herbert. Minolta Maxxum 7000.
Kasparyan, G. M. Domination in 2545 Endgame Studies.
Kass, Edward H. & Platt, Richard. Current Therapy in Infectious Disease: 1983 to 1984.
Kass, Judith M., jt. auth. see Rosenthal, Stuart.
Kass, Louis A. Agency N. Y.
--Enforcement of Money Judgments.
--Mortgages (N.Y.)
--New York Landlord-Tenant.
--Real Property: New York.
Kassakowski & Obudhowski. Progress in the Psychology of Personality.
Kassam, S. A. & Thomas, J. B., eds. Nonparametric Detection: Theory & Applications.
Kassarjian, Harold & Robertson, Thomas. Perspectives in Consumer Behavior.
Kassas, M. & Ghabbour, I., eds. The Nile & Its Environment.
Kassel, Christian. Gun Gamble.
Kassel, S., jt. auth. see Johnson, J.
Kasser, Joe. Microcomputers in Amateur Radio.
--Software for Amateur Radio.
Kassorla, Irene. Nice Girls Do.
Kassorla, Irene C. Go for It: How to Win at Love, Work & Play.
Kast, Andy. Reflections of the Spirit.
Kast, Fremont & Rosenzweig, James. Organization & Management: A Systems & Contingency Approach.
Kaste, Omar, tr. see Westerman, Claus.
Kasten, jt. auth. see Jacobs.
Kastenbaum, Robert. Between Life & Death.
--Is There Life after Death?
Kastens, Merritt. Redefining the Manager's Job: The Proactive Manager in a Reactive World.
Kastens, U., et al. GAG: A Practical Compiler Generator.
Kastle, Herbert. Cross-Country.
--Ladies of the Valley.
--Miami Golden Boy.
--Millionaires.
Kastler, D., ed. C Algebras & Their Applications of Statistical Mechanics & Quantum Field Theory.
Kastner, Jonathan & Kastner, Marianna. Sleep: The Mysterious Third of Your Life.
Kastner, Marianna, jt. auth. see Kastner, Jonathan.
Kastrup, K. W. & Hoiriis-Nielson, J., eds. Growth Factors.
Katayev, V. Rainbow Flower.
Katch, Frank I. & McArdle, William D. Nutrition, Weight Control, & Exercise.
Katch, Frank I., et al. Getting in Shape: An Optimum Approach to Fitness & Weight Control.
Katchadourian, Herant & Lunde, Donald T. Biological Aspects of Human Sexuality.
--Fundamentals of Human Sexuality.
Katchadourian, Herant, et al. Human Sexuality: Brief Edition.
Katchen, Carole. Promoting & Selling Your Art.
Katcher, Aaron, jt. auth. see Beck, Alan.
Katcher, Brian S. & Young, Lloyd Y., eds. Applied Therapeutics: The Clinical Use of Drugs.
Kateb, George, ed. Utopia: Controversy.
Kater, David. Macintosh Graphics & Sound: Programming in Microsoft Basic.
Kater, David A. TRS-80 Word Processing with Scripsit.
Kater, David A. & Thomas, Susan. TRS-80 Graphics.
Kater, S. B. & Nicholson, C., eds. Intracellular Staining in Neurobiology.
Kates, George N. The Years That Were Fat: The Last of Old China.
Kathman, Clemens A., jt. auth. see Berliner, Thomas H., III.
Katkoff, Vladimir. Soviet Economy Nineteen Forty to Nineteen Sixty-Five.
Katkosky, Walter & Gorlow, Leon. The Psychology of Adjustment: Current Concepts & Applications.
Kato, Ichiro. Mechanical Hands Illustrated. Sadamoto, Kuni, ed.
Kato, Junzo, et al. Hormone Receptors in the Brain.
Kato, Shuichi. Form, Style, Tradition: Reflections on Japanese Art & Society. Bester, John, tr. from Japanese.
Katona, G., ed. see CISM (International Center for Mechanical Sciences) Deartment of Automation & Information Staff.
Katona, G., ed. see CISM (International Center for Mechanical Sciences), Department of Automation & Information Staff.
Katona, George. Psychological Analysis of Economic Behavior.
Katritzky, A. R. & Lagowski, J. J. Chemistry of Heterocyclic Oxides.
Katritzky, A. R. & Boulton, A. J., eds. Theoretical Chemistry: Advances & Perspectives.
Katsaros, T., et al. The Western Tradition to Sixteen Sixty.
Katsaros, Thomas & Teluk, John. Capitalism: A Cooperative Venture.
Katsenelinboigen, Aron. Soviet Economic Thought & Political Power in the U. S. S. R.
Katsh, Ethan. Taking Sides: Clashing Views on Controversial Legal Issues.
Katsh, Shelley & Merle-Fishman, Carole. The Music Within You.
Katsoufris, Yannis S. Capetan Konstandis Mavros.
Katsujo, Terayama, jt. auth. see Sogen, Omori.
Kattan, Naim. Farewell, Babylon. Fischman, Sheila, tr. from Fr.
--Reality & Theatre. Brown, Alan, tr.
Kattani, Sulayman. Imam Ali: Source of Light, Wisdom & Might. Howard, I. K., tr.
Kattenburg, Paul M. Diplomatic Practices.
--The Vietnam Trauma in American Foreign Policy 1945-1975.
Katterhenry, Lorraine. Aerobic Pas de Deux.
Kattsoff, L. O. Logic & the Nature of Reality.
--Physical Science & Physical Reality.
Katunuma, Nobuhiko, jt. ed. see Schimke, Robert T.
Katz. Mission of Man.
--Psychological Atlas.
Katz, et al. Construction Claims.
Katz, Arnold, ed. Cardiac Arrhythmias.
Katz, Cynthia, jt. auth. see Costello, Marjorie.
Katz, D. H. Lymphocyte Differentiation, Recognition & Regulation.
Katz, D. L. Handbook of Natural Gas Engineering.
Katz, David & Benacerraf, Baruj, eds. Immunological Tolerance: Mechanisms & Potential Therapeutic Applications.
Katz, Dorothy D., jt. ed. see Faseb, Philip L.
Katz, Harold A., jt. auth. see Gregory, Charles O.
Katz, Harry C. The Impact of Public Employee Unions on City Budgeting & Employee Remuneration: A Case Study of San Francisco.
Katz, Harry S. & Milewski, John V. Handbook of Fillers & Reinforcements for Plastics.
Katz, Harvey A. & Warrick, Patricia. Introductory Psychology Through Science Fiction.
Katz, Helen T., ed. Consolidated Index to Minnesota History 1930-1967.
Katz, Herb, ed. see Scalia, Toni.
Katz, Herbert. Love & Marriage.
Katz, Herbert M. Nicolette.
Katz, Israel J. & Keller, John E., eds. Studies on the Cantigas de Santa Maria: Art, Music & Poetry.
Katz, J. Society, Schools & Progress in Canada.
Katz, J. J., ed. Inorganic & Nuclear Chemistry: H. H. Hyman Memorial Volume.
Katz, J. J., jt. ed. see Spitsyn, V. I.
Katz, Jack L., et al. Gout I: Recent Studies.
Katz, Jane. This Song Remembers: Self-Portraits of Native Americans in the Arts.
Katz, Jane B., ed. Let Me Be a Free Man: A Documentary History of Indian Resistance.
--We Rode the Wind: Recollections of 19th-Century Tribal Life.
Katz, Jeffrey, jt. auth. see Freudenthal, Juan R.
Katz, Melvin & Loeb, Ronald M. Acquisitions & Mergers 1985: Tactics, Techniques, & Recent Developments.
Katz, Melvin, jt. auth. see Practising Law Institute Staff.
Katz, Michael, jt. ed. see Moskowitz, Milton.
Katz, Michael J. Murder of the Glass.
Katz, Molly. Always Keep Him Laughing.
--Heights of Desire.
--Mischief-Maker.
--No Reservations.
--Worth His Weight in Gold.
Katz, Murray A. Calculus for the Life Sciences: An Introduction.
Katz, Neil, jt. auth. see Lawyer, John.
Katz, Phyllis A., ed. Towards the Elimination of Racism.
Katz, Ralph. Career Issues in Human Resource Management.
Katz, Robert. The Spoils of Ararat.
--Ziggurat.
Katz, Robert L. Pastoral Care & the Jewish Tradition: Empathic Process & Religious Counseling.
Katz, Sali. Hispanic Furniture: An American Collection from the Southwest.
Katz, Sheldon F. Business Communications: Theory Structure Form.
--The Research Paper-the Business Report: A Few Ideas.
Katz, Shelley. Family Passions.
Katz, Sidney B., et al. Resources for Writing for Publication in Education.
Katz, Steven J., jt. ed. see Horwood, Richard M.
Katz, William. Open House.
--Surprise Party.
Katz, William A. Collection Development: The Selection of Materials for Libraries.
Katzan, Harry, Jr. Introduction to Computers & Data Processing.
--Office Automation: A Manager's Guide.
Katzander, Howard L. Antiques & Art: How to Know, Buy & Use Them.
Katzarova-Kukudova, Raina & Djenev, Kiril. Bulgarian Folk Dances.
Katzenbach, John. First Born.
--In the Heat of the Summer.
Katzenelbogen, Solomon. Analyzing Psychotherapy.
Katzenellenbogen, Adolf. Allegories of the Virtues & Vices in Medieval Art.
Ka-Tzetnik. Star Eternal.
Katzman, Martin C. Political Economy of Urban Schools.
Katzman, Martin T. Cities & Frontiers in Brazil: Regional Dimensions of Economic Development.
Katzman, Robert & Pappius, Hanna. Brain Electrolytes & Fluid Metabolism.
Katznelson, Ira & Kesselman, Mark. The Politics of Power: A Critical Introduction to American Government.
--The Politics of Power: A Critical Introduction to American Government.
Kauchak, Donald P. & Eggen, Paul. Exploring Science in the Elementary School.
Kaucher, Edgar W. & Miranker, Willard L. Self-Validating Numerics For Function Space Problems: Computation With Guarantees For Differential & Integral Equations.
Kaud, Faisal A. Financial Management of the Hospital Food Service Department.
Kauf, Robert & McCluney, Daniel C. Proben Deutscher Prosa.
Kaufelt, David A. American Tropic.
--Late Bloomer.
--The Late Bloomer.
--Silver Rose.
--Six Months with an Older Woman.
--The Wine & the Music.
Kaufert, Joseph M., jt. ed. see Tuckett, David.
Kauff, Jerome, jt. auth. see Barbash, Joseph.
Kauff, Jerome B. & McClain, Maureen E. Unjust Dismissal Update 1985: How to Evaluate, Litigate, Settle, & Avoid Claims: A Course Handbook.
Kauffman, C. M. Felix H. Man.
Kauffman, Donald T. Ask & It Shall Be Given.
Kauffman, Donald T., compiled by. Baker's Pocket Treasury of Religious Verse.
Kauffman, Elizabeth J., jt. auth. see Kauffman, Nancy J.
Kauffman, George B., ed. Classics in Coordination Chemistry: The Selected Papers of Alfred Werner.
Kauffman, James M., jt. auth. see Hallahan, Daniel P.
Kauffman, James M. & Hallahan, Daniel P., eds. Handbook of Special Education.
Kauffman, Nancy J. & Kauffman, Elizabeth J. Heavy Bread.
Kauffmann, George B. Alfred Werner: Founder of Coordination Chemistry.

Kauffmann, Stanley. Albums of Early Life.
Kaufman, jt. auth. see Gots.
Kaufman, jt. auth. see Kiver.
Kaufman, Allan. Exploring Solar Energy: Principles & Projects.
Kaufman, Barry N. Giant Steps.
--A Sense of Warning.
--To Love Is to Be Happy With.
Kaufman, Bel. Love Etc.
--Up the down Staircase.
Kaufman, Charles. After the Dream.
Kaufman, David J., jt. auth. see Practising Law Institute Staff.
Kaufman, Edward. The Market for Executive Talent.
Kaufman, George G. Money, the Financial System & the Economy.
Kaufman, George S. & Hart, Moss. Once in a Lifetime, You Can't Take It With You, The Man Who Came to Dinner: Three Plays.
Kaufman, Gerald. My Life in the Silver Screen.
Kaufman, Henry R., ed. Book Publishingm 1984.
Kaufman, Herbert, jt. auth. see Sayre, Wallace S.
Kaufman, Leon, ed. Anaesthesia-Review 3.
Kaufman, Leonard, jt. auth. see Massart, D. Luc.
Kaufman, Louis C. Essentials of Advertising.
Kaufman, M. Ralph, et al, eds. Evolution of Psychosomatic Concepts: Anorexia Nervosa: a Paradigm.
Kaufman, Mike. Capital Budgeting Handbook.
Kaufman, Milton. Radio Operator's License Q & A Manual.
--Radio Operator's License Q & A Manual.
Kaufman, Milton & Seidman, Arthur H. Handbook for Electronic Engineering Technicians.
--Handbook of Electronics Calculations.
Kaufman, Milton, jt. auth. see Wilson, J. A.
Kaufman, Milton, et al. Understanding Radio Electronics.
Kaufman, Pamela. Pandora.
Kaufman, Peter B. & La Croix, Don, eds. Plants, People, & Environment.
Kaufman, Richard C. The Age Reduction System: A Complete Program to Help Slow, Halt, or Retard Aging.
Kaufman, Roger. FORTRAN Coloring Book.
Kaufman, Shirley. From One Life to Another.
--Gold Country.
Kaufman, Shirley, tr. see Gilboa, Amir.
Kaufman, Stephen A. The Akkadian Influences on Aramaic.
Kaufman, Wallace, jt. auth. see Rehder, Jessie.
Kaufman, William I., ed. Great Television Plays.
Kaufmann, David J. Franchising in New York 1985: Compliance & Strategies for National & Local Franchisors: A Course Handbook.
--Franchising Nineteen Eighty-Seven: Business Strategies & Legal Compliance.
Kaufmann, E. Lehrbuch der speziellen pathologischen Anatomie. Staemmler, ed.
Kaufmann, Jerome E. Intermediate Algebra.
--Mathematics Is...
Kaufmann, Lori, jt. auth. see Kaufmann, Yadin.
Kaufmann, Myron S. The Love of Elspeth Baker.
Kaufmann, Thomas D. Variations on the Imperial Theme: Studies in Ceremonial Art & Collecting in the Age of Maximilian II & Rudolf II.
Kaufmann, W. & Krause, D., eds. Central Nervous Control of Na plus Balance.
Kaufmann, Walter. Existentialism, Religion & Death.
--Man's Lot.
--Tibetan Buddhist Chant: Musical Notations & Interpretations of a Song Book by the Bkah Brgyud Pa & Sa Skya Pa Sects. Norbu, Thubten Jigme, tr.
--Tragedy & Philosophy.
Kaufmann, Walter, ed. Twenty-Five German Poets: A Bilingual Collection.
Kaufmann, Walter, ed. & tr. from Ger. Twenty-Five German Poets: A Bilingual Collection.
Kaufmann, Walter, tr. see Baeck, Leo.
Kaufmann, Yadin & Kaufmann, Lori. The Boston Ice Cream Lover's Guide: A Heavenly Tour of over 55 of the Hub's Finest Ice Cream Shops.
Kaukola, Olavi. The Riches of Prayer. Hillila, Bernhard, tr.
Kaul, H. K., ed. Urdu Manuscripts; A Descriptive Bibliography.
Kaunda, Kenneth. The Riddle of Violence.
Kaur, Manmohan. Women in India's Freedom Struggle.
Kausch, H. H. & Zachmann, H. G., eds. Characterization of the Polymers in the Solid State I.
Kausch, H. Henning, et al, eds. Deformation & Fracture of High Polymers.
Kaushall, Phillip & Skagen-Munshi, Kiki. The Growing Years: A Study Guide for the Televised Course.
Kautsky, Benedikt. Erinnerungen und Erorterungen Von Karl Kautsky: Quellen und Untersuchungen Zur Geschichte Er Deutschen und Osterreichischen Arbeiterbewegung.
Kautsky, Karl. Class Struggle.
Kauzmann, W. Quantum Chemistry: An Introduction.
Kavaas, Igor I. & Granier, Jacqueline P., eds. Human Rights, the Helsinki Accords & the United States.
Kavaler, Florence & Swire, Margaret R. Foster-Child Health Care.
Kavan, Anna. Ice: A Novel.
--Julia & the Bazooka & Other Stories.
Kavanagh, Aidan, jt. auth. see Tiede, David L.
Kavanagh, Denis, ed. The Politics of the Labour Party.
Kavanagh, James F. & Mattingly, Ignatius G., eds. Language by Ear & by Eye: The Relationships Between Speech & Reading.
Kavanagh, P. J. People & Weather.
Kavanagh, Peter. A Catena of Five Plays: Jerome, Patrick, Melachy, John Scotus, Oliver Plunkett.
--Irish Mythology: A Dictionary.
Kavanagh, Peter, ed. Patrick Kavanagh: Complete Poems.
Kavanaugh, Ian. From the Shamrock Shore.
Kavanaugh, James. The Celibates.
Kavanaugh, Mrs. Russell. Kavanaugh's Juvenile Speaker.
Kavass, Igor I. & Sprudzs, Adolf. Current Treaty Index.
Kavet, Bob. Dirty Boy.
Kavet, Herbert I. I'd Rather Be Forty Than Pregnant.
--Small Busted Women Have Big Hearts.
--You Know When You're over Fifty When...
--You Know When You're over Forty When...
Kavner, Richard S. Your Child's Vision: The Complete Guide to Growth & Development.
Kawahito, Kiyoshi. The Japanese Steel Industry: With an Analysis of the U. S. Steel Import Problem.
Kawai, Keiichi. The Early Diagnosis of Pancreatic Cancer.
Kawakami, M., jt. ed. see Dorner, G.
Kawakita, Michiaki, jt. auth. see Kokei, Kobayashi.
Kawana, Alfred K., jt. ed. see Spahr, Frederick T.
Kawashima, Masaaki. Fundamentals of Men's Fashion Design: A Guide to Tailored Clothes.
--Men's Outerwear Design.
Kay, A. B., jt. ed. see Goetzl, Edward J.
Kay, D. A. The United Nations Political System.
Kay, Drina. All the Desk's a Stage.
Kay, E. A Mathematical Model for Handling in a Warehouse.
Kay, Elizabeth, jt. auth. see Fisher, Katherine.
Kay, Ernest. Arabic Computer Dictionary: English-Arabic, Arabic-English.
--Arabic Dictionary of Civil Engineering: English-Arabic, Arabic-English.
Kay, Ernest, ed. Dictionary of International Biography 1982.
--The World Who's Who of Women.
Kay, F. George. France.
--London.
Kay, Herma H. Sex-Based Discrimination: Cases & Materials, 1986 Supplement.
--Sex-Based Discrimination: Text, Cases & Materials.
Kay, J. Alan. The Nature of Christian Worship.
Kay, J. E., jt. ed. see Ling, N. R.
Kay, Jane H. Lost Boston.
Kay, Kenneth & Goldberg, Marshall. The Man Who Must Not Die.
Kay, Kenneth, jt. auth. see Goldberg, Marshall.
Kay, N. W. Modern Building Encyclopedia.
Kay, Peg & Powell, Patricia, eds. Future Information Processing Technology.
Kay, R., jt. ed. see Baum, M.
Kay, Rob. Tahiti & French Polynesia: A Travel Survival Kit.
Kay, Sophie, jt. auth. see Consumer Guide Editors.
Kay, Terry. After Eli.
--Dark Thirty.
--The Year the Lights Came On.
Kay, Valerie. Biological Sciences.
Kay, William. Moral Education.
Kay, William J., jt. auth. see Animal Medical Center Editors.
Kayden, Jerold S., jt. ed. see Haar, Charles M.
Kaye. Note for the DRCOG.
Kaye, Anthony & Harry, Keith, eds. Using the Media for Adult Basic Education.
Kaye, Bruce & Rogerson, John. Miracles & Mysteries in the Bible.
Kaye, Donald & Rose, Louis F. Fundamentals of Internal Medicine.
Kaye, F. B., jt. auth. see Crane, R. S.
Kaye, G., et al. Tables of Co-efficients for the Analysis of Triple Angular Correlations of Gamma-Rays from Aligned Nuclei.
Kaye, Kim R., ed. Guide to Four-Year Colleges 1984.
--Guide to Two-Year Colleges 1984.
--Peterson's Guide to Colleges in New England.
--Peterson's Guide to Colleges in New York.
--Peterson's Guide to Colleges in the Middle Atlantic States.
--Peterson's Guide to Colleges in the Midwest.
Kaye, M. M. Ordinary Princess.
Kaye, Marilyn. Max Flips Out.
--Max Goes Bad.
--Max on Earth.
--Max on Fire.
Kaye, Marilyn, jt. auth. see Hearne, Betsy.
Kaye, Marvin, ed. Devils & Demons.
Kaye, Susan. The Best of Colorado.
--Small People in Colorado Places.
Kay-Larsen, Mogens, tr. see Moller, Svend E., et al.
Kayle, Marlaine. A Game of Hearts.
Kaylin, Walter. The Power Forward.
Kayne, Richard S. French Syntax: The Transformational Cycle.
Kayne, Ronald C., ed. Drugs & the Elderly.
Kays, John M. The Horse.
Kays, William M. & London, A. L. Compact Heat Exchangers.
Kaysar, Myrna, jt. auth. see Kysar, Robert.
Kayser, Alex. Heads.
Kayser, R. Spinoza, Portrait of a Spiritual Hero.
Kayser, Rudolf. The Life & Times of Jehuda Halevi.
Kayyali, Abdul W., ed. Zionism, Imperialism, & Racism.
Kazan, Elia. Arrangement.
Kazanas, H. C., et al. The Philosophy & Foundations of Vocational Education.
Kazantzakis, Nikos. The Fratricides.
--Freedom or Death.
Kazarian, Edward A. Foodservice Facilities Planning.
--Work Analysis & Design for Hotels, Restaurants & Institutions.
Kazarinoff, N. D., jt. auth. see Bloom, C. O.
Kazee, Buell H. Faith Is the Victory.
Kazemzadeh, Firuz. The Struggle for Transcaucasia.
Kazin, Alfred. On Native Grounds.
--Open Form: Essays for Our Time.
--A Walker in the City.
Kazmer, Daniel R. & Kazmer, Vera, eds. Russian Economic History: A Guide to Information Sources.
Kazmer, Vera, jt. ed. see Kazmer, Daniel R.
Kazmier, Leonard J. Statistical Analysis for Business & Economics.
Kazner, E., et al, eds. see International Symposium On Echo-Encephalography - Erlangen - 1967.
Keach, A. New African Song.
Keagle, Fred. Life's Byways: Poetry & Prose.
Keagle, Fred A. Poetic Justice.
Kealy, J. Kevin. Diagnostic Radiology of the Dog & Cat.
Kean, Eccleston A., ed. see Symposium, Kingston, Jamaica Staff.
Kean, Edmund S., jt. auth. see Hauck, Paul A.
Kean, Michael H., jt. auth. see Franchak, Stephen J.
Kean, P. M. Chaucer & the Making of English Poetry. Incl. Vol. 1. Love Vision & Debate; Vol. 2. The Art of Narrative. Routledge Chapman & Hall.
--Chaucer & the Making of English Poetry.
Keane, Betty W. Sensing: Letting Yourself Live.
Keane, Bil. Any Children?
--Deuce & Don'ts of Tennis.
--Go To Your Room!
--I'm Already Tucked In.
Keane, Bil, jt. auth. see Bombeck, Erma.
Keane, Christopher. The Crossing.
--The Hunter: Tales of a Different Papa.
Keane, John B. Letters of an Irish Publican.
Keane, Molly. Time after Time.
Keane, Molly & Snaffles. Red Letter Days.
Keane, Noel P. & Breo, Dennis L. The Surrogate Mother.
Keaney, Thomas A. Strategic Bombers & Conventional Weapons: Airpower Options.
Kear, Dennis J., jt. aûth. see Silvaroli, Nicholas J.
Kearney, P. C., ed. Ethylenethiourea.
Kearney, Peter J., jt. auth. see Stuempfle, Herman G., Jr.
Kearney, Robert N., jt. ed. see Fernando, Tissa.
Kearney, Tim, jt. auth. see Bowick, Chris.
Kearns, Kevin C. Georgian Dublin: Architectural Restoration.
Kearns, Lewis. Sweetheart, Don't Ask Me to Fix It.
Kearny, Mary Ann & Baker, James. Life, Liberty & the Pursuit of Happiness.
Kearsley, Joseph E. Complete Real Estate Exchange & Acquisition Handbook.
Keast, Frederick D., jt. auth. see Copperman, Lois F.
Keat, Donald B. Fundamentals of Child Counseling.
Keat, Donald B., II & Guerney, Louise. Helping Your Child.
Keates, J. S. Understanding Maps.
Keating. Guidelines.
Keating, Bern. Mighty Mississippi. Crump, Donald J., ed.
Keating, Edward. The Broken Bough: The Solution to the Riddle of Man.
Keating, G. M., et al, eds. The Atmosphere of Venus: Recent Findings: Proceedings of Workshop III of the COSPAR 25th Plenary Meeting Held in Graz, Austria, 28 June-2 July 1984.
Keating, Isabel, ed. see Jacobs, Alexandra.
Keating, Lawrence A. Comeback Year.
--Fleet Admiral: The Story of William F. Halsey.
Keating, P. J. The Working Classes in Victorian Fiction.
Keating, Pat. I'm Doing My Best-but It Isn't Enough: Choices & Coping Steps for Personal Dilemmas & Distress.
Keatinge, W. R. & Harman, M. Clare. Local Mechanisms Controlling Blood Vessels.
Keats, Ezra J. Goggles.
--Goggles.
--Hi, Cat!
--The Little Drummer Boy.
--Regards to the Man in the Moon.
Keats, John. John Keats.
--Keats.
--The Poetical Works of John Keats.
Keats-Shelley Memorial House Staff. Catalog of Books & Manuscripts at the Keats-Shelley Memorial House in Rome.
Keaveney, Arthur. Sulla: The Last Republican.
Keaveney, Sydney S. American Painting: A Guide to Information Sources.
Keay, A. J. & Morgan, D. M. Craig's Care of the Newly Born Infant.
Keay, F. Marketing & Sales Forecasting.
Keay, F. & Wensley, G. F. Marketing Through Measurement.
Kebbe, Charles. Profitable Public Speaking.
Kechris, A. S. & Moschovakis, Y. N., eds. Cabal Seminar, 76-77: Proceedings, Caltech-UCLA Logic Seminar 1976-1977.
Keck, Leander, jt. auth. see Craddock, Fred.
Keck, Leander E. A Future for the Historical Jesus: The Place of Jesus in Preaching & Theology.
--Paul & His Letters. Krodel, Gerhard, ed.
Keck, Leander E. & Hobbie, Francis W. Pentecost One.
Keck, Leander E. & Martyn, J. Louis, eds. Studies in Luke-Acts.
Keck, Leander E., ed. see Herrmann, Wilhelm.
Keck, Leander E., ed. see Mathews, Shailer.
Keck, Leander E., ed. see Schleiermacher, Friedrich.
Keck, Leander E., ed. see Strauss, David F.
Keck, Leander E., jt. ed. see Talbert, Charles H.
Keck, Leander E., ed. see Weiss, Johannes.
Keck, Leander E., tr. & intro. by see Strauss, David F.
Keckhut, John. The Dublin Pawn.
Keddie, Kenneth M. Action with the Elderly: A Handbook for Relatives & Friends.
Keddie, Nikki R., ed. Scholars, Saints & Sufis: Muslim Religious Institutions since 1500.
Keddie, William, ed. Cyclopaedia of Literary & Scientific Anecdote: Illustrative of the Characters, Habits, & Conversation of Men of Letters & Science.
Keddy, David J. Against the Odds.
Kedourie, Elie. Islam in the Modern World.
Kedron, Jane, tr. see Seidler, Barbara.
Kee, Alistair, ed. A Reader in Political Theology.
Kee, Howard C. Community of the New Age: Studies in Mark's Gospel.
--Jesus in History: An Approach to the Study of the Gospels.
--Making Ethical Decisions.
Kee, Howard C. & Gomes, Peter J. Pentecost One. Achtemeier, Elizabeth, et al, eds.
Kee, Howard C., jt. auth. see Sloyan, Gerard S.
Kee, Robert. Nineteen Forty-Five: The World We Fought For.
--Nineteen Thirty-Nine: In the Shadow of War.
Keeble, David & Wever, Egbert, eds. New Firms & Regional Development.
Keeble, Marshall. From Muleback to Super Jet with the Gospel.
Keedy, Mervin L., et al. Geometry for Today.
Keefe, Carolyn B., et al. Introduction to Debate.
Keefe, Eugene F., jt. auth. see Very, Donald.
Keefe, John, jt. auth. see Peirce, Neal R.
Keefe, John E. Aim for a Job As an Electronic Technician.
Keefe, Laurence E., Jr. & Inch, Dennis. The Life of a Photograph: Archival Processing, Matting, Framing & Storage.
Keefe, Michael. Running Away.
Keefe, William J. Congress & the American People.
Keefer, George, jt. auth. see Cromwell, Paul F., Jr.
Keefer, Sarah L. The Old English Metrical Psalter: An Annotated Set of Collation Lists with the Psalter Glosses.
Keeffe, Barrie. Bastard Angel.
--Frozen Assets.
--Gimme Shelter: Three Plays.
Keegan, B. F. & Ceidigh, P. O., eds. Biology of Benthic Organisms: 11th European Symposium on Marine Biology, Galway, Ireland.
Keegan, Desmond. The Foundations of Distance Education.
Keegan, Joanne. Peter the Caterpillar.
Keegan, Marcia. Oklahoma.
Keehn, J. D. The Origins of Madness: The Psychopathology of Animal Life.
Keehn, J. D., ed. Psychopathology in Animals: Research & Clinical Duplications.

Keele, Doman K. The Developmentally Disabled Child: A Manual for Primary Physicians.
Keele, Kenneth & Roberts, Jane. Leonardo Da Vinci: Anatomical Drawings from the Royal Library, Windsor Castle.
Keeler, Clyde E. Cuna Indian Art: The Culture & Craft of Panama's San Blas Islanders.
Keeler, Richard F., et al, eds. Effects of Poisonous Plants on Livestock.
Keeley, Edmund. A Wilderness Called Peace.
Keeley, Edmund, tr. see Ritsos, Yannis.
Keeley, Kim, jt. auth. see Solomon, Joel.
Keeling, D. British Library History, Nineteen Seventy-Three to Nineteen Seventy-Six: A Bibliography.
Keely, Jane. One Thousand One Great Housekeeping Hints.
Keen, A. W. Electronics.
Keen, Benjamin & Wasserman, Mark. A Short History of Latin America.
Keen, Benjamin, ed. Latin American Civilization.
Keen, Benjamin, tr. see Lafaye, Jacques.
Keen, Dan & Dischert, Dave. Mastering the Tandy 2000.
Keen, G. Chest Injuries.
Keen, Gerald, ed. Operative Surgery & Management.
Keen, Martin L. Be a Rockhound.
Keen, Maurice. The Outlaws of Medieval Legend.
Keen, Michael A. Out of the Desert.
Keen, Richard A. Skywatch: The Western Weather Guide.
Keen, Sam. Apology for Wonder.
--Beginnings Without End.
--Gabriel Marcel.
Keenan, Jack. Cincinnati & Lake Erie.
Keenan, Michael & White, Lawrence J., eds. Mergers & Acquisitions: Current Problems in Perspective.
Keenan, P. E. Orchids: A Guide to All Species Found in Maine.
Keene, Carolyn. Clue in the Old Album.
--Clue of the Leaning Chimney.
--Clue of the Velvet Mask.
--Clue of the Whistling Bagpipes.
--Hidden Staircase.
--The Hidden Window Mystery.
--The Invisible Intruder.
--The Message in the Hollow Oak.
--Moonstone Castle Mystery.
--Mystery of the Brass Bound Trunk.
--Mystery of the Tolling Bell.
--Password to Larkspur Lane.
--Phantom of Pine Hill.
--The Secret of the Lost Lake.
--The Secret of the Minstrel's Guitar.
--The Sierra Gold Mystery.
--Sign of the Twisted Candles.
--Whispering Statue.
--The Witch Tree Symbol.
--The Witch's Omen.
Keene, Carolyn & Dixon, Franklin W. The Nancy Drew & the Hardy Boys Super Sleuths: Seven New Mysteries.
Keene, Derek & Harding, Vanessa, eds. A Survey of Documentary Sources for Property Holding in London Before the Great Fire.
Keene, Donald. Japanese Literature: An Introduction for Western Readers.
--World Within Walls: Japanese Literature of the Pre-Modern Era 1600-1867.
Keene, Donald, ed. Anthology of Japanese Literature: Earliest Era to Mid-Nineteenth Century.
Keene, Donald, tr. see Mishima, Yukio.
Keene, Frances, tr. see Simenon, Georges.
Keene, H. G. Hindustan under Free Lances: Seventeen Seventy to Eighteen Twenty.
Keeney, Clifford. An Illustrated Guide to Cat Dissection.
Keep, P. A. Van see Estrogen Therapy Workshop Staff.
Keep, P. A. Van see Van Keep, P. A. & Lauritzen, C.
Keepers, Terry D., jt. auth. see Babcock, Dorothy E.
Keeping, Charles, ed. Charles Keeping's Book of Classic Ghost Stories.
Keepnews, Orrin. A Pictorial History of Jazz: People & Place from New Orleans to Modern Jazz.
Keesey, Ray E. Modern Parliamentary Procedure.
Keesing, Donald B. Trade Policy for Developing Countries.
Keesing, Marie. Hidden Valleys & Unknown Shores.
Keesling, Monika A., ed. see International Computer Programs, Inc.
Keesling, Monika A., ed. see International Computer Programs, Inc. Staff.
Keeton, Page, et al. The Law of Torts Cases & Materials: 1981 Supplement.
Keeton, William R. Equilibrium Credit Rationing.
Keeton, William T. Biological Science.
--Elements of Biological Science.
--Elements of Biological Science.
Keeton, William T., et al. Laboratory Guide for Biological Science.
--Biology in the Laboratory.
Keey, R. B. Drying: Principles & Practice.
--Introduction to Industrial Drying Operations.
Kefalides, Nicholas A., ed. Biology & Chemistry of Basement Membranes.
Kefen, Wang. The History of Chinese Dance.
Keffer, Joseph H., jt. auth. see Watts, Nelson B.
Kegan, Stephanie. Places to Go with Children in Southern California: More Than 350 Attractions Throughout Southern California to Delight Children & Parents.
--Places to Go with Children in Southern California.
Kegley, Jacquelyn A., ed. The Humanistic Delivery of Services to Families in a Changing & Technological Age.
Kehler, P. L. The Lower Zuni Sequence in the Southwestern United States.
Kehoe, Andre J. His Irish Connection.
Keighley, Dr. Dale G. Proctology.
Keightley. The Fairy Mythology.
Keil, A., jt. auth. see Schmidt, W. J.
Keilholz, Peg, ed. Real Estate Sales Handbook.
Keillor, Garrison. Happy to Be Here.
Keim, Charles J. Aghvook, White Eskimo.
Keintz, Rita M., ed. Health Care Costs & Financing: A Guide to Information Sources.
Keir, Jack & Lundy, Carl P. Fundamentals of Estate Planning. Snyder, Bernhart R., rev. by.
Keiser, Bernhard E. EMI Control in Aerospace Systems. White, Donald R., ed.
Keiser, James R. & Kallio, Elmer. Controlling & Analyzing Costs in Food Service Operations.
Keiser, Stephen K. & Lupul, Max E. Marketing Interaction.
Keiser-Nielsen, S. Person Identification by Means of the Teeth: A Practical Guide.
Keisler, H. Jerome. Foundations of Infinitesimal Calculus.
Keith, et al. Chlorinated Dioxins & Dibenzofurans in the Total Environment.
Keith, Arthur. A New Theory of Human Evolution.
Keith, Arthur B. Belgian Congo & the Berlin Act.
Keith, Bill, ed. see Rawlings, Meridel.
Keith, Bruce E., jt. auth. see Lee, Eugene C.
Keith, Elizabeth. Old Korea.
Keith, Eros. Bedita's Bad Day.
Keith, G. R. & Glover, M. Primary Langauge Learning with Microcomputers.
Keith, Gordon. The Ferryboat Islands: A Practical Guide to Washington State's San Juan Islands.
--Voices from the Islands.
Keith, Gordon, jt. auth. see Olzendam, Roderic M.
Keith, Graeme, ed. The Triumph of Humanism: A Visual Survey of the Decorative Arts of the Rennaissance.
Keith, J. Andrew, jt. auth. see Sechi, Stephan M.
Keith, J. Andrew, Jr. Hivers: Alien Module 7.
Keith, Judith. I Haven't a Thing to Wear!
Keith, L. H., jt. ed. see Choudhary, G.
Keith, Lawrence H. Identification & Analysis of Organic Pollutants in the Air.
Keith, Rebecca M. & Giles, Floyd A. Dwarf Shrubs for the Midwest.
Keith, Robert W., ed. Central Auditory & Language Disorders in Children.
Keith, Sam & Proenneke, Richard. One Man's Wilderness: An Alaskan Odyssey.
Keith, William H., Jr. The Free City of Krakow.
--Pirates of the Vistula.
Keithley, George. The Donner Party.
Keith-Lucas, Alan. This Difficult Business of Helping.
Keith-Lucas, Bryan. The Unreformed Local Government System.
Keker, John W., jt. auth. see Brockett, William A.
Kelber, Werner H. The Kingdom in Mark: A New Place & a New Time.
--Mark's Story of Jesus.
--The Oral & the Written Gospel: The Hermeneutics of Speaking & Writing in the Synoptic Tradition, Mark, Paul, & Q.
Kelber, Werner H., jt. auth. see Allison, C. Fitzsimons.
Kelber, Werner H., ed. The Passion in Mark: Studies on Mark 14-16.
Keleher, William A. Violence in Lincoln County, 1869-1881: A New Mexico Item.
Kelemen, E. Physiopathology & Therapy of Human Blood Diseases.
Kelleher, Ed & Vidal, Harriette. Madonna.
Kelleher, Patrick J. Living with Modern Sculpture: The John P. Putnam, Jr. Memorial Collection at Princeton.
Kelleher, Robert F. Industrial Marketing & Sales Management in the Computer Age.
Kelleher, Victor. Africa & After.
--The Beast of Heaven.
Keller, A. G., ed. see Sumner, William G.
Keller, Albert G., ed. see Sumner, William G.
Keller, Allan. Scandalous Lady: The Life & Times of Madame Restell.
Keller, Beverly. No Beasts! No Children!
--When Mother Got the Flu.
Keller, Catherine. From a Broken Web: Separation, Sexism, & Self.
Keller, Charles. Ballpoint Bananas & Other Jokes for Children.
--Smokey the Shark & Other Fishy Tales.
--Still Going Bananas.
Keller, Charles, ed. Colossal Fossils: Dinosaur Riddles.
Keller, Charles R. The Second Great Awakening in Connecticut.
Keller, Cornelius. The Chemistry of Transuranium Elements.
Keller, David N. Cooper Industries, 1833-1983.
Keller, Dick & Keller, Irene. Santa Claus Visits the Thinggumajigs.
Keller, Dick, jt. auth. see Keller, Irene.
Keller, Edmund B. Some Paradoxes of Paul.
Keller, Ernst & Keller, Marie-Luise. Miracles In Dispute: A Continuing Debate.
Keller, Fred, et al. Introduction to Historical Geology.
Keller, Fred B., et al. General Geology Eleven Laboratory Manual.
Keller, Fred S. The Definition of Psychology.
Keller, Fred S. & Ribes-Inesta, Emilio, eds. Behavior Modification: Applications to Education.
Keller, Gary D., jt. ed. see Sobejano, Gonzalo.
Keller, H. H. Differential Calculus in Locally Convex Spaces.
Keller, Hans, jt. auth. see Mitchell, Donald.
Keller, Hans, jt. ed. see Mitchell, Donald.
Keller, Hermann. Thoroughbass Method. Parrish, Carl, tr.
--The Well-Tempered Clavier by Johann Sebastian Bach. Gerdine, Leigh, tr.
Keller, Irene. Benjamin Rabbit & the Fire Chief.
--Benjamin Rabbit & the Stranger Danger.
--Kenny the Kitty.
--The Thingumajig Book of Do's & Don'ts.
--The Thingumajig Book of Manners.
Keller, Irene & Keller, Dick. Benjamin Rabbit & the Bad Dream.
Keller, Irene, jt. auth. see Keller, Dick.
Keller, Irvin A. The Interscholastic Coach.
Keller, J. & Papadakis, J., eds. Wave Propagation & Underwater Acoustics.
Keller, J. J., & Associates, Inc. Staff. Pesticides Guide.
Keller, Janet, jt. auth. see Sword, Randall S.
Keller, John E., jt. ed. see Katz, Israel J.
Keller, Kate V. & Sweet, Ralph. American Country Dances of the Revolutionary Era: Seventeen Seventy-Five to Seventeen Ninety-Five.
Keller, Linda, tr. see Sander, Gunther.
Keller, Marie-Luise, jt. auth. see Keller, Ernst.
Keller, Marion W. Intermediate Algebra: A Text Workbook.
Keller, Marion W. & Zant, James H. Basic Mathematics.
--Basic Mathematics: Second Series-Form A.
Keller, Marti, jt. auth. see Isaacs, Susan.
Keller, Phillip. Elijah: Prophet of Power.
--A Shepherd Looks at Psalm 23.
Keller, Thomas F. & Zeff, Stephen A. Financial Accounting Theory Two: Issues & Controversies.
Keller, W. Phillip. As a Tree Grows: Reflections on Growing in the Image of Christ.
--David II: The Shepherd King.
--Lessons from a Sheepdog.
--Wonder O' the Wind.
Keller, Werner. Diaspora: The Post-Biblical History of the Jews.
Kellerman, J. J., jt. ed. see Raineri, A.
Kellerman, Jonathan. Helping the Fearful Child: A Guide to Everyday & Problem Anxieties.
Kellermann, J. J., ed. Exercise in Diagnosis & Treatment of Coronary Heart Disease.
Kellett, A., ed. Guy De Maupassant: Contes du surnaturel.
Kellett, Atnold. Isms & Ologies.
Kellett, Michael. High-Intensity Memory Power.
Kellett, Michael C. How to Improve Your Memory & Concentration.
Kelley. An Accounting Experience with the Apple II Microcomputer: A Service Firm.
--An Accounting Experience with the IBM Microcomputer: A Service Firm.
Kelley, Ann E. Modern Florida Government.
Kelley, Arleon L. Your Church: A Dynamic Community.
Kelley, Clarence. Kansas City Epicure. Champlin, Kathy & Weidenbach, Gretchen, eds.
Kelley, Colleen. Assertion Training: A Facilitator's Guide.
Kelley, Elizabeth B. John Burroughs, Naturalist.
Kelley, J. Roland, jt. auth. see McKenzie, Jimmy C.
Kelley, James E., Jr. The IBM Personal Computer User's Guide.
Kelley, Jane. An Accounting Experience with the IBM Microcomputer: A Merchandising Firm.
Kelley, Kate, jt. auth. see Shobe, John.
Kelley, Kevin. The Longest War: Northern Ireland & the IRA.
Kelley, Kitty. Elizabeth Taylor: The Last Star.
Kelley, Lee. How to Build a Street Rod.
Kelley, Leo P. Luke Sutton: Hired Gun.
--Morgan.
--Morgan.
Kelley, Martha. A Big Man & Other Stories.
Kelley, Mary, ed. Woman's Being, Woman's Place: Female Identity & Vocation in American History.
Kelley, P. J. So High the Price.
Kelley, Patrick A. Slightly Deceived.
--Slightly Invisible.
--Slightly Lethal.
--Slightly Murder.
Kelley, Philip & Hudson, Ronald, eds. Diary by E. B. B.
Kelley, Philip, ed. see Browning, Elizabeth Barrett.
Kelley, Robert K. Courtship, Marriage, & the Family.
--Courtship, Marriage, & the Family.
Kelley, William N., et al. Textbook of Rheumatology.
Kelling, G., jt. ed. see Stanley, D. J.
Kellman, Martin C. Plant Geography.
Kellman, Peter & Saxon, Burt. Modern Human Sexuality.
Kellner, Douglas, ed. Postmodernism-Jameson-Critique.
Kellner, Douglas, jt. ed. see Bronner, Stephen.
Kellock, Harold. Parson Weems of the Cherry-Tree.
Kellogg, Caroline, jt. auth. see Bard, Rachel.
Kellogg, I. How to Use Financial Statements.
Kellogg, Louise P., ed. Early Narratives of the Northwest, 1634-1699.
Kellogg, Louise P., ed. see Cole, Harry E.
Kellogg, Marion S. Putting Management Theories to Work.
--Talking with Employees: A Guide for Managers.
--What to Do about Performance Appraisal.
Kellogg, Mary A. Fast Track: The Super Achievers & How They Make It to Early Success.
Kellogg, Paul U. & Gleason, Arthur. British Labour & the War: Reconstruction for a New World.
Kellogg, Richard M. The Molecules R2CXCR2 Including Azomethine, Carbonyl & Thiocarbonyl Ylides: Their Syntheses, Properties & Reactions.
Kellough, Jean L., jt. auth. see Kellough, Patrick H.
Kellough, Patrick H. Cable Television & Censorship: A Bibliography.
--Statistical Package for the Social Sciences Bibliography: Selected SPSS Manuals & Research Articles Using SPSS.
Kellough, Patrick H. & Kellough, Jean L. Public Education & the Children of Illegal Aliens.
Kellough, Richard D., ed. Developing Priorities & A Style: Selected Readings in Education for Teachers & Parents.
Kells, Lyman M., et al. Log & Trig Tables.
Kelly. Mosby's Workbook for Nursing Assistants.
Kelly, A. A., jt. auth. see Suanders, Norah.
Kelly, Alfred H. & Harbison, Winfred. American Constitution.
Kelly, Brian & London, Mark. Amazon.
--Amazon.
Kelly, Crosby, jt. auth. see Hippocrates.
Kelly, Edward. Parent-Teacher Interaction: A Special Educational Perspective.
Kelly, Edward F., jt. auth. see Kidder, Ralph D.
Kelly, Everett L. & Fiske, Donald W. Prediction of Performance in Clinical Psychology.
Kelly, Fred C. George Ade: Warmhearted Satirist.
Kelly, Gary. Learning about Sex: The Contemporary Guide for Young Adults.
--Sexuality: The Human Perspective.
Kelly, Gary F. Good Sex: A Healthy Man's Guide to Sexual Fulfillment.
--Sexuality Today: The Human Perspective.
Kelly, Geffrey B. Liberating Faith: Bonhoeffer's Message for Today.
Kelly, George A. The Psychology of Personal Constructs.
Kelly, George W. Rocky Mountain Horticulture.
Kelly-Grimes Corporation Staff. Apple Registered Computer Directory: Hardware, Software & Peripherals.
--DEC Microcomputer Directory: Hardware, Software & Peripherals.
--IBM Personal Computer Directory: Hardware, Software, & Peripherals.
Kelly, Hugh. Memoirs of a Magdalen, or, the History of Louisa Mildmay, 1767.
--The Plays of Hugh Kelly. Carver, Larry, ed.
Kelly, J. & Namioka, I. Linear Topological Spaces.
Kelly, J. W. Metachromatic Reaction.
Kelly, J. W., jt. auth. see Davis, Raymond E.
Kelly, Jack. Escape to the Sea.
--The Unexpected Peace.
Kelly, James. Music from Another Room.
Kelly, James L. & Kelly, Mary J., eds. The Successful Elementary Teacher.
Kelly, James W. The Faust Legend in Music.
Kelly, John, jt. auth. see Sanger, Sirgay.
Kelly, John, jt. auth. see Verny, Thomas.
Kelly, John D., jt. auth. see Rosenberg, Richard.
Kelly, John E. & Clegg, Chris W., eds. Autonomy & Control at the Workplace: Contexts for Job Redesign.
Kelly, Karin. Careers with the Circus.

Authors

Kelly, Kenneth M. When Night the Moon Awakes.
Kelly, Leo P. A Man Called Dundee.
Kelly, Louise. Wichita County Beginnings.
Kelly, Margaret M., ed. see Twelve O'Clock Scholars Staff.
Kelly, Mary. Post-Partum Document.
Kelly, Mary Ann. My Old Kentucky Home, Good-night.
--Rex & the Single Girl.
Kelly, Mary J., jt. ed. see Kelly, James L.
Kelly, Max, ed. Nineteenth-Century Sydney: Studies in Urban History.
Kelly, Patrick, jt. ed. see Hollingsworth, Paul M.
Kelly, Robert. Baseball Trivia Puzzler.
--Micro-Model Railways.
--Sports Trivia Puzzler.
Kelly, Robert, ed. see Blackburn, Paul.
Kelly, Sally, et al, eds. Birth Defects: Risks & Consequences.
Kelly, Selby, ed. see Kelly, Walt.
Kelly, Thomas. History of Public Libraries in Great Britain.
Kelly, Tim. The British Computer Industry: Crisis & Development.
--The British Computer Industry: Crisis & Development.
Kelly, W. Revelation Expounded.
Kelly, Walt. Pogo's Body Politic. Kelly, Selby, ed.
Kelly, Walter K. Curiosities of Indo-European Tradition & Folk-Lore.
Kelly, William W. Irrigation Managament in Japan: A Critical Review of Japanese Social Science Research.
Kelly-Bootle, Stan. Mastering Turbo C.
Kelman, G. R. Physiology: A Clinical Approach.
Kelner, Richard H. An American Story.
Kelsall, H. M., jt. auth. see Kelsall, R. K.
Kelsall, R. K. & Kelsall, H. M. The School Teacher in England & the United States.
Kelsen, Hans see Jessup, Philip C.
Kelsey, David, et al. New Mexico Divorce Manual.
Kelsey, H. W. Bridge: The Mind of the Expert.
--More Killing Defense at Bridge.
--The Needle Match.
--Test Your Match Play.
--The Tough Game.
Kelsey, Hugh. Test Your Safety Play.
Kelsey, Michael. Guide to the World's Mountains.
Kelsey, Morton. The Age of Miracles.
Kelsey, Neal. Respiratory Therapy Review: A Workbook & Study Guide.
Kelso, Leon, tr. see Schmalhausen, Ivan I.
Keltner, Jeanie. The Ballads of the Big California Woman.
Kelton, Christina M. Trends in the Relocation of U.S. Manufacturing. Bateman, Fred, ed.
Kelton, Elmer. After the Bugles.
--Man Who Rode Midnight.
Kemal, Yashar. Seagull.
Kemali, Milena & Braitenberg, Valentino. Atlas of the Frog's Brain.
Kemeny, J. G., et al. Denumerable Markov Chains.
Kemeny, John & Kurtz, Tom. Truebasic: Algebra II.
--Truebasic: CHIPendale.
--Truebasic: Discrete Mathematics.
--Truebasic: Pre-Calculus.
--Truebasic: Probability Theory.
--Truebasic: Trigonometry.
--Truebasic: TrueSTAT Theory.
--TruebasicTM: Calculus.
Kemeny, John G. & Kurtz, Thomas E. BASIC Programming.
Kemeny, John G., ed. The Accident at Three Mile Island: The Need for Change, the Legacy of TMI.
Kemerer, Frank R. & Deutsch, Kenneth L. Constitutional Rights & Student Life: Value Conflict in Law & Education; Cases & Materials.
Kemmer, Elizabeth. Violence in the Family: An Annotated Bibliography.
Kemmer, Elizabeth J. Rape & Rape Related Issues: An Annotated Bibliography.
Kemmerer, Edwin W. ABC of the Federal Reserve System.
Kemmit, R., ed. The Chemistry of Manganese, Technetium & Rhenium. Peacock, R.
Kemnitz, T. M., et al. Kids Working with Robots: The RB5X.
Kemnitz, Thomas M., jt. auth. see Mass, Lynne.
Kemp, Anthony. Springboard for Overlord, Hampshire & the D-Day Landings.
Kemp, C. Gratton. Perspectives on the Group Process: A Foundation for Counseling with Groups.
Kemp, Gene. Mr. Magus Is Waiting for You.
--The Well.
Kemp, Harold. Le Vent du Changement. Martin, Yves D., tr.
Kemp, Jim. The Victorian Revival in Interior Design.
Kemp, John C. Robert Frost & New England: The Poet As Regionalist.
Kemp, John P. God Is a Lousy Strategist.
Kemp, John R., ed. see Mugnier, George F.
Kemp, Lysander, tr. see Paz, Octavio.
Kemp, Lysander, tr. see Rulfo, Juan.
Kemp, Martin. Leonardo da Vinci: The Marvelous Works of Nature & Man.
Kemp, Norman. Conquest of the Antarctic.
Kemp, Paul J. British Submarines in World War II.
Kemp, Sarah. Lure of Sweet Death.
--What Dread Hand.
--What Dread Hand?
Kempczinski, R. F., et al. Organ & Tissue Regeneration in Mammals II.
Kempe, C. Henry & Helfer, Ray E. The Battered Child.
--The Battered Child.
Kempe, Helen, jt. auth. see Calhoun, James.
Kempe, Helen, jt. ed. see Calhoun, James.
Kemper, Alfred. Presentation Drawings by American Architects.
Kemper, Frederick. The Christmas Cycle.
Kemper, Frederick & Bass, George M. You Are My Beloved Sermon Book.
Kemper, Frederick W., jt. auth. see Bauerle, Richard E.
Kemper, R. W. The Pentecost Cycle.
Kemper, Ria. The Tokyo Round: Results & Implications for Developing Countries.
Kemper, Robert V. & Phinney, John F. The History of Anthropology: A Research Bibliography.
Kempf, G., et al. Toroidal Embeddings 1.
Kempner, Alan H., Jr. The Lane.
Kemp-Smith, Norman. Commentary to Kant's Critique of Pure Reason.
--The Philosophy of David Hume.
Kenan, Lucette R. Chez les Francais.
Kenan, Lucette R., jt. auth. see Desberg, Dan.
Kendal, Brian. Manual of Avionics: An Introduction to the Electronics of Civil Aviation.
Kendall, Aubyn. The Art of Pre-Columbian Mexico: An Annotated Bibliography of Works in English.
Kendall, Carol. Gammage Cup.
Kendall, Dorothy S. & Perry, Carmen. Gentilz: Artist of the Old Southwest.
Kendall, E. J., ed. Transistors.
Kendall, Edward C. Cortisone.
Kendall, Henry M., et al. Introduction to Cultural Geography.
--Introduction to Geography.
--Introduction to Physical Geography.
Kendall, Martha. Elizabeth Cady Stanton.
Kendall, Martha B. Selected Problems in Yavapai Syntax: The Verde Valley Dialect.
Kendall, Myra. Physiotherapy & the Asthmatic Child.
Kendall, Paul M. Yorkist Age: Daily Life During the Wars of the Roses.
Kendall, Phillip C., jt. auth. see Lerner, Richard M.
Kendall, Timothy. Kush: Lost Kingdom of the Nile: A Loan Exhibition from the Museum of Fine Arts Boston.
Kendall, Willmoore. John Locke & the Doctrine of Majority-Rule.
Kendeigh, S. Charles. Bird Populations in East Central Illinois: Fluctuations, Variations, & Development over a Half-Century.
Kendig, Frank & Hutton, Richard. Life Spans: Or, How Long Things Last.
Kendig, Lana S. Marketing Essentials: Student Guide.
Kendig, Lane H. & Connor, Susan. Performance Zoning.
Kendrick, Dennis, jt. auth. see Simon, Seymour.
Kendrick, Jan. Cat's Paw.
Kendrick, John W. & Grossman, Elliott S. Trends & Cycles.
Kendrick, John W. & Vaccara, Beatrice N., eds. New Developments in Productivity Measurement & Analysis.
Kendrick, Thomas D. Late Saxon & Viking Art.
Kendris, Christopher, tr. see Grevisse, Maurice.
Keneally, Thomas. A Family Madness: A Novel.
--Gossip from the Forest.
--Ned Kelly & the City of the Bees.
--Ned Kelly & the City of the Bees.
--Passenger.
--Schindler's List.
--Schindler's List.
--Season in Purgatory.
--Victim of the Aurora.
Kenichi, Ohmae. The Mind of the Strategist: Business Planning for a Corporate Advantage.
Keniston, Kenneth. The Uncommitted: Alienated Youth in American Society.
--Young Radicals: Notes on Committed Youth.
--Young Radicals: Notes on Committed Youth.
--Youth & Dissent.
--Youth & Dissent: The Rise of a New Opposition.
Keniston, Kenneth & Carnegie Council on Children Staff. All Our Children: The American Family Under Pressure.
Kenmare, Dallas. Firebird: A Study of D. H. Lawrence.
Kennan, George. Tent Life in Siberia.
Kennan, George F. Realities of American Foreign Policy.
Kennan, Kent. Counterpoint.
Kennaway, James & Kennaway, Susan. The Kennaway Papers.
Kennaway, Susan, jt. auth. see Kennaway, James.
Kenneally, James J. Women & American Trade Unions.
Kennedy, A. C. & Blumgart, L. Essentials of Medicine & Surgery for Dental Students.
Kennedy, Adele P. & Dean, Susan. Touching for Pleasure: A Guide to Sensual Enhancement.
Kennedy, Adrienne see Harrison, Paul C.
Kennedy, Alan. The Psychology of Reading.
Kennedy, Mrs. Alexander, tr. see Mantegazza, Paolo.
Kennedy, Beatrice B. Women Out of Bondage & in Love.
Kennedy, Benjamin H. Kennedy's Revised Latin Primer.
Kennedy, Brendan, jt. auth. see Kennedy, William.
Kennedy, D. B. Paediatric Operative Dentistry.
Kennedy, Daniel B., ed. The Dysfunctional Alliance: Emotion & Reason in Justice Administration.
Kennedy, David W. The Condominium & Cooperative Apartment Buyer's & Seller's Guide.
--Insurance: What Do You Need? How Much Is Enough?
Kennedy, Donald P. Minicomputers: Low-Cost Computer Power for Management.
Kennedy, Doris. Guide to Recommended Country Inns of the Rocky Mountain Region (Colorado, Utah, Idaho, Montana, Nevada & Wyoming)
Kennedy, Eddie C. Methods in Teaching Developmental Reading.
Kennedy, Ellen, tr. see Schmitt, Carl.
Kennedy, Emmet. A Philosophe in the Age of Revolution: Destutt de Tracy & the Origins of "Ideology"
Kennedy, Eugene C. Choice to Be Human: Jesus Alive in the Gospel of Matthew.
--Now & Future Church.
--The Now & Future Church: The Psychology of Being an American Catholic.
--A Sense of Life, a Sense of Sin.
Kennedy, Eugene P., jt. ed. see Kaplan, Nathan O.
Kennedy, Florynce R., jt. auth. see Pepper, William F.
Kennedy, G. E. Paleoanthropology.
Kennedy, Gavin. Doing Business Abroad: Everything the Businessman Needs to Know for Successful Negotiation, Barter, Trade & Business Entertaining Around the World.
--Everything Is Negotiable!
--Military in the Third World.
Kennedy, Gavin, ed. see Barrow, Sir John.
Kennedy, Gavin, et al. Managing Negotiations: A Guide for Managers, Labor Workers, & Everyone Else Who Wants to Win.
Kennedy, George. Art of Persuasion in Greece.
--Electronic Communication Systems.
--Murder on High.
--Murder on Location.
Kennedy, George A. Chinese Reading for Beginners.
--Serial Arrangement of Chinese Characters.
--Simple Chinese Stories.
Kennedy, Grace. Father Clement, 1823. Wolff, Robert L., ed. Bd. with Father Oswald 1842. Garland Pub.
Kennedy, H. E., et al, trs. see Masaryk, Tomas G.
Kennedy, Harry A. Theology of the Epistles.
Kennedy, J. J., tr. see Paz, Alberto C. & Ferrari, Gustavo E.
Kennedy, J. P., et al. Mechanisms of Polyreactions - Polymer Characterization.
Kennedy, James H., ed. Directory of Executive Recruiters.
--How to Seek a New & Better Job.
--International Directory of Executive Recruiters.
Kennedy, James W. Holy Island.
Kennedy, Jimmy. The Teddy Bears' Picnic.
Kennedy, K. & Possehl, G., eds. Studies in the Archaeology & Palaeoanthropology of South Asia.
Kennedy, M. Thomas. European Labor Relations: Text & Cases.
Kennedy, Mary, jt. ed. see Hughes, Mary.
Kennedy, Mary M. Effectiveness of Chapter One Services.
Kennedy, Mary M. & Jung, Richard K. Poverty, Achievement, & the Distribution of Compensatory Education Services.
Kennedy, Michael. Mahler.
--The Works of Ralph Vaughan Williams.
Kennedy, P. C., jt. auth. see Jubb, K. V.
Kennedy, Pam. Swan Lake.
Kennedy, Patrick. Legendary Fictions of the Irish Celts.
Kennedy, Paul M. The Samoan Tangle: A Study in Anglo-German-American Relations 1878-1900.
Kennedy, R. Emmet. Mellows: A Chronicle of Unknown Singers.
Kennedy, Raymond P. Herpes: Identification, Treatment & Prevention.
Kennedy, Robert & Mason, Vivian. Hardcore Bodybuilder's Source Book.
Kennedy, Robert E. Life Choices: Applying Sociology.
Kennedy, S. A. Hey, Didi Darling.
Kennedy, S. C., tr. see Straus, E. W., et al.
Kennedy, Scott & Awad, Mubarak. Nonviolent Struggle in the Middle East.
Kennedy, Stanislaus. One Million Poor: The Challenge of Irish Inequality.
Kennedy, Thomas L., jt. ed. see Mathias, Jim.
Kennedy, Victor S., ed. Esturarine Comparisons: Symposium.
Kennedy, William & Kennedy, Brendan. Charley Malarkey & the Belly-Button Machine.
Kennedy, William H., tr. see Von Franz, Marie-Louise.
Kennedy, X. J. Did Adam Name the Vinegarroon?
--One Winter Night in August & Other Nonsense Jingles.
--The Phantom Ice Cream Man: More Nonsense Verse.
Kennelly, Brendan, ed. Landmarks of Irish Drama.
Kennemore, Tim. Changing Times.
Kenner, Charles T. & Busch, Kenneth W. Quantitative Analysis.
Kenner, Charmain. No Time for Women: Exploring Women's Health: 1930's vs. 1980's.
Kenner, Hugh. Heath-Zenith Z100 User's Guide.
--The Poetry of Ezra Pound.
Kenner, T., et al, eds. Cardiovascular System Dynamics: Models & Measurements.
Kennerson, Vern. Love Stories for Children.
Kenneson, Claude. A Cellist's Guide to the New Approach.
Kenneth, P., tr. see Lions, J. L. & Magenes, E.
Kenneth-Thomas, M. K., jt. auth. see Hare, F. K.
Kennett, Audrey. The Palaces of Leningrad.
Kennett, Frances. Exclusively Yours: Fashion Knits from the World's Top Designers.
Kennett, James P., ed. Magnetic Stratigraphy of Sediments.
Kennett, Lee. For the Duration... The United States Goes to War, Pearl Harbor-1942.
--The G. I. The American Soldier in World War II.
Kenney, Donald P. Minicomputers: Low-Cost Computer Power for Management.
Kenney, James F. Sources for the Early History of Ireland: Ecclesiastical.
Kenney, John P. Police Administration.
Kenney, John P., et al. Police Work with Juveniles & the Administration of Juvenile Justice.
Kenney, Kathryn & Prather, Elizabeth M. Coarticulation Assessment in Meaningful Language.
Kenney, Leon F. Memories & Meditations.
Kenney, Richard. Orrery.
Kenney, William. How to Analyse Fiction.
--How to Analyze Fiction.
Kenny, Adele. Illegal Entries.
Kenny, Anthony, ed. & tr. see Descartes, Rene.
Kenny, David M. & Parrish, Michael E. Power & Responsibility: Case Studies in American Leadership.
Kenny, Dick, jt. auth. see Banks, Bruce.
Kenny, Donald P. Personal Computers in Business.
Kenny, Herbert, jt. auth. see Westman, Barbara.
Kenny, Herbert A. Literary Dublin: A History.
Kenny, James & Kenny, Mary. When Your Marriage Goes Stale.
Kenny, James & Spicer, Stephen. Caring for Your Aging Parent.
Kenny, John. Now That You Are a Catholic.
Kenny, John J. Primer of Labor Relations.
Kenny, Mary, jt. auth. see Kenny, James.
Kenny, Maurice. Dancing Back Strong the Nation.
--I Am the Sun.
Kenny, Rose A. MCQ's in Geriatric Medicine.
Kenny, Shirley S. & Backscheider, P. R., eds. The Performers & Their Plays.
Kenrick, Tony. China White.
Kenschaft, Pat. Childbirth, Cooperative Style: Family Experience with Prepared Childbirth & Prenatal Classes.
Kenseth, Arnold & Unsworth, Richard P. Prayers for Worship Leaders.
Kenstowicz, Michael & Kisseberth, Charles. Generative Phonology: Description & Theory.
Kenstowicz, Michael J., ed. see Urbana Conference on Phonology Staff.
Kent & Galvin. The On Line Revolution in Libraries.
Kent, Alexander. Colours Aloft.
--The Inshore Squadrons.
--Signal-Close Action.
Kent, Arthur. Deadly Medicine: Doctors & True Crime.
Kent, B. Social Work Supervision in Practice.
Kent, Donald, et al, eds. Research Planning & Action for the Elderly.

Authors

Kent, Frank R. The Story of Maryland Politics: An Outline History of the Big Political Battles of the State from 1864 to 1910, with Sketches & Incidents of the Men & Measures That Figured As Factors, & the Names of Most of Those Who Held Office in That Period.
Kent, Frederick C. & Kent, Maude E. Compound Interest & Annuity Tables.
Kent, George C. Comparative Anatomy of the Vertebrates.
Kent, Jack. The Biggest Shadow in the Zoo.
--The Caterpillar & the Polliwog.
--The Caterpillar & the Polliwog.
--Joey Runs Away.
--The Scribble Monster.
Kent, John H. The End of the Line? The Development of Christian Theology in the Last Two Centuries.
Kent, Kate P. Navajo Weaving: Three Centuries of Change.
--Prehistoric Textiles of the Southwest.
Kent, Leonard J., ed. see Hoffmann, E. T.
Kent, Louise A. & Campion, Polly. Mrs. Appleyard's Kitchen Omnibus.
Kent, Marian, ed. The Great Powers & the End of the Ottoman Empire.
Kent, Maude E., jt. auth. see Kent, Frederick C.
Kent, Raymond. A History of British Empirical Sociology.
Kent, Rockwell. N by E.
Kent, Susan. Analyzing Activity Areas: An Ethnoarchaeological Study of the Use of Space.
Kent, William. Landscape Garden Designer. Hunt, John D. & Willis, Peter, eds.
Kent, William W. Hooked Rug.
Kenter, Adriana A. see Baker, Keith A.
Kentish, D. N. Pipework Design Data.
Kenton, Edna. With Hearts Courageous.
Kenton, Leslie. Ageless Ageing: The Natural Way to Stay Young.
Kenton, Warren. Astrology: The Celestial Mirror.
Kentucky Historical Society Staff. Certificate Book of the Virginia Land Commission, 1779 to 1780: The Register for 1923.
Kentwell, Richard G., jt. auth. see Barnes, Mildred J.
Kenworthy, Mary A. & King, Eleanor M. Preserving Field Records: Archival Techniques for Archaeologists & Anthropologists.
Kenworthy-Browne, John, jt. auth. see Fedden, Robin.
Kenyon, Cora & Kenyon, Cory. Sheer Delight.
Kenyon, Cory. Fancy Footwork.
--Fortune Hunter.
--The Quintessential Woman.
Kenyon, Cory, jt. auth. see Kenyon, Cora.
Kenyon Critics. Gerard Manley Hopkins.
Kenyon, D. & Steinman, G. D. Biochemical Predestination.
Kenyon, F. W. The Duke's Mistress.
--The Naked Sword.
--The Naked Sword.
Kenyon, Dame Kathleen. The Bible & Recent Archaeology.
Kenyon, Michael. A Healthy Way to Die.
Keogh, James E. & Suntag, Beu. Handbook of Simplified Radio, Phono & Tape Recorder Repairs: An Illustrated Troubleshooting Guide.
Keogh, Richard N., jt. auth. see Weisz, Paul B.
Keohane, Robert O. & Nye, Joseph S. Power & Interdependence: World Politics in Transition.
Keough, William F., Jr. Declining Enrollments: A New Dilemma for Educators.
Keown. Frommer's Guide to Athens.
Keown, Ian. Ian Keown's Caribbean Hideaways with a Special Supplements on Mexico & Charter Yachts.
Keown, R. An Introduction to Group Representation Theory.
Kepert, D. L. & Vrieze, K. Compounds of the Transition Elements Involving Metal-Metal Bonds.
Kepes, Juliet. Five Little Monkeys.
--Five Little Monkeys.
Kephart, C. I. Races of Mankind.
Kephart, William M. The Family, Society, & the Individual.
--The Family, Society, & the Individual.
Kepler, Ann, et al. The After Fifty Pharmacy: An Easy-to-Understand Guide to Prescription & Nonprescription Medications.
Kepler, Frank R., jt. auth. see Fryklund, Verne C.
Keppel, Geoffrey, jt. ed. see Postman, Leo.
Keppes, Gyorgy, ed. Module, Proportion, Symmetry, Rhythm.
Keramidas, George A. & Brebbia, C. A., eds. Computational Methods & Experimental Measurements, Washington, D.C. 1982: Proceedings.
Keramos Staff. The Westwood Clay National.
Kerber, A. Representations of Permutation Groups, Part 1: Representations of Wreath Products & Applications to the Representations Theory of Symmetric & Alternating Groups.
Kerber, James E., jt. ed. see Gress, James R.
Kerchove, Rene de see De Kerchove, Rene.
Keren, David F. Interpretive Surface Marker Analysis.
Kerensky, Oleg. The New British Drama: Fourteen Playwrights Since Osborne & Pinter.
Keresztesi, Michael & Cocozzoli, Gary, eds. German-American History & Life: A Guide to Information Sources.
Kerin, et al. Contemporary Perspectives on Strategic Market Planning.
Kerin, Roger & Peterson, Robert M. Perspectives on Strategic Marketing Management.
Kerklit, G. A. & Phillis, J. W., eds. Progress in Neurobiology, Vol. 16.
Kerkut, ed. see Matsuda, R.
Kerkut, G. A. Progress in Neurobiology.
Kerkut, G. A., ed. Progress in Neurobiology.
Kerkut, G. A. & Phillis, J. W., eds. Process in Neurobiology.
--Progress in Neurobiology.
--Progress in Neurobiology.
--Progress in Neurobiology.
--Progress in Neurobiology.
--Progress in Neurobiology.
--Progress in Neurobiology.
--Progress in Neurobiology.
--Progress in Neurobiology.
--Progress in Neurobiology.
Kerkut, G. A. & Phillus, J. W., eds. Progress in Neurobiology.
Kerkut, G. A., ed. see Threadgold, L. T.
Kerlin, T. W. Frequency Response Testing in Nuclear Reactors.
Kerlinger, Frederick N. Foundations of Behavioral Research: Educational, Psychological, & Sociological Inquiry.
Kerman, Cynthia E. & Eldridge, Richard. The Lives of Jean Toomer: A Hunger for Wholeness.
Kerman, Joseph. Contemplating Music.
--The Elizabethan Madrigal: A Comparative Study.
Kermani, David K. John Ashbery: A Comprehensive Bibliography.
Kermode, Frank. Shakespeare, Spenser, Donne.
Kermode, Frank, ed. Four Centuries of Shakespearian Criticism.
Kern, Barbara & Kern, Ken. Ken Kern's Masonry Stove.
--The Owner Built Homestead.
Kern, Barbara, jt. auth. see Kern, Ken.
Kern, Guenther & Kern-Bontke, E. Preinvasive Carcinoma of the Cervix: Theory & Practice. Wynn, R. M., tr.
Kern, Ken. The Owner-Built Home.
Kern, Ken & Kern, Barbara. Ken Kern's Homestead Workshop.
Kern, Ken & Magers, Steve. Fireplaces: The Owner-Builder's Guide.
Kern, Ken, jt. auth. see Kern, Barbara.
Kern, Marna E. An Introduction to Breadcraft.
Kern, Mary M. Be a Better Parent.
Kern, Stephen. The Culture of Time & Space, Eighteen Eighty to Nineteen Eighteen.
Kernahan, jt. auth. see Barclay.
Kernan. Set Steps to Engl 1.
Kernan, Alvin B., ed. Modern Satire.
Kernan, Alvin B., et al. Man & His Fictions: An Introduction to Fiction-Making, Its Forms & Uses.
Kernan, Roderick P. Cell Potassium.
Kern-Bontke, E., jt. auth. see Kern, Guenther.
Kerneckel, Edward J., Jr. Wake up, World-We're People Too.
Kerner, John A., ed. Manual of Pediatric Parenteral Nutrition.
Kernicki, Jeanette G. & Weiler, Kathi M. Electrocardiography for Nurses: Physiological Correlates.
Kernighan, Brian W. & Ritchie, Dennis M. The C Programming Language: Convergent Technologies Edition.
--The C Programming Language, Digital Equipment Coporation Edition.
Kernodle, George R. Invitation to the Theatre.
Kernodle, George R. & Kernodle, Portia. Invitation to the Theatre.
--Invitation to the Theatre.
Kernodle, Portia, jt. auth. see Kernodle, George R.
Kerns, D. M. & Beatty, R. W. Basic Theory of Waveguide Junctions & Introductory Microwave Network Analysis.
Kerns, Frances C. A Cold Wild Wind.
Kerns, Virginia. Women & the Ancestors: Black Carib Kinship & Ritual.
Kerola, Dana X. Ultimate Commune: The Universe & Us.
Kerouac, Jack. Doctor Sax.
--Lonesome Traveler.
--Maggie Cassidy.
--Mexico City Blues.
--Pic.
--Satori in Paris.
--Satori in Paris & Pic.
Kerr, A. J. The Common Market & How It Works.
Kerr, Allen. Lao-English Dictionary.
Kerr, Arnold D. & Kornhauser, Alain L., eds. Productivity in Railroads: Proceedings of a Symposium Held at Princeton University, July, 1977.
Kerr, Barbara A. Career Education for the Gifted & Talented.
Kerr, Clark, et al. Conflict, Retrenchment, & Reappraisal: The Administration of Higher Education.
Kerr, Don & Kerr, Vivian. Kerr's Country Kitchen.
Kerr, Donald A., et al. Oral Diagnosis.
Kerr, Elizabeth M. & Aderman, Ralph M. Aspects of American English.
Kerr, George H. Formosa: Licensed Revolution & the Home Rule Movement, 1895-1945.
--Okinawa: The History of an Island People.
Kerr, Hugh T., ed. Sons of the Prophets: Leaders in Protestantism from Princeton Seminary.
Kerr, Hugh T., Jr. Our Life in God's Light: Essays by Hugh T. Kerr.
Kerr, James W. Illustrated Treasury of Budd Railway Passenger Cars.
Kerr, James W., ed. see Kerr, O. M.
Kerr, Jean. Please Don't Eat the Daisies.
Kerr, John S. Adult-Youth Guide on "The Nations of Southern Africa"
--The Mystery & Magic of the Occult.
Kerr, Katharine. Daggerspell.
Kerr, Kathleen, tr. see Spiegel, Rene & Aebi, Hans-J.
Kerr, Mary & Kerr, Nigel. Anglo-Saxon Architecture.
Kerr, Nigel, jt. auth. see Kerr, Mary.
Kerr, O. M. Centennial Treasury of General Electronic Locomotives: Electric-Gas-Turbine-Diesel Electric Locomotives. Kerr, James W., ed.
--Illustrated Treasury of Pullman Standard Railway Passenger Cars Since 1945. Kerr, James W., ed.
--Illustrated Treasury of the American Locomotive Company. Kerr, James W., ed.
Kerr, Vivian, jt. auth. see Kerr, Don.
Kerr, William S. Handbook of the Papacy.
Kerrane, Kevin. Dollar Sign on the Muscle.
Kerrich, G. J., et al, eds. Key Words to the Fauna & Flora of the British Isles & Northwestern Europe.
Kerrigan, Anthony, ed. & intro. by see Borges, Jorge L.
Kerrigan, Anthony, ed. & frwd. by see Borges, Jorge L.
Kerrigan, Anthony, tr. see Unamuno, M. De.
Kerrigan, William, jt. ed. see Smith, Joseph H.
Kerrigan, William J. Writing to the Point: Six Basic Steps.
--Writing to the Point: Six Basic Steps.
--Writing to the Point: Six Basic Steps.
Kerrod, Robin. See Inside a Space Station. Warwick Press, ed.
Kerrod, Robin, et al. Space.
Kerry, Stephen. Ship's Doctor.
Kerry, Trevor, ed. Finding & Helping the Able Child.
Kersaudy, Francois. Churchill & DeGaulle.
Kerschner, Paul A., jt. auth. see Hess, Clinton W.
Kersey, Burt, jt. auth. see Weishaar, Tom.
Kershaw, Alister. The Pleasure of Their Company.
Kershaw, Norma, ed. Ancient Art from Cyprus: The Ringling Collection.
Kershul, Kristine. Russian in Ten Minutes.
Kerslake, A., jt. auth. see Jones, R.
Kersten, H. & Kersten, W. Inhibitors of Nucleic Acid Synthesis: Biophysical & Biochemical Aspects.
Kersten, Karen K., jt. auth. see Kersten, Lawrence.
Kersten, Lawrence & Kersten, Karen K. The Love Exchange.
Kersten, Pete & Kersten, Rick. Burt's Big Day.
--Looking for Zippy.
--A Name for Number Nine.
--Winter Fun.
--Wishes & Dreams.
Kersten, Pete & Lersten, Rick. Gabby's Grand Opening.
Kersten, Rick, jt. auth. see Kersten, Pete.
Kersten, W., jt. auth. see Kersten, H.
Kerstetter, Robert W. Illustrated Ventura 1.1.
Kersting, A. F., jt. auth. see Cook, Olive.
Kert, Bernice. The Hemingway Women.
Kertesz, Stephen. The Last European Peace Conference: Paris 1946-Conflict of Values. Thompson, Kenneth W., ed.
Kertesz, Stephen D. & Fitzsimons, M. A., eds. What America Stands for.
Kertz, George J. The Nature & Applications of Mathematics.
Kertzer, Morris N. What Is a Jew.
Kerwood, Lewis O., jt. ed. see Britton, James A., Jr.
Kerzner. Project Management for Small & Medium Size Businesses.
Kerzner, Harold. Project Management: A Systems Approach to Planning, Scheduling & Controlling.
Kerzner, Harold, jt. auth. see Loring, Roy J.
Kesavan, B. S. The National Bibliography of Indian Literature, 1901-1953. Incl. Vol. 1. Assamese-Bengali-English-Gujaratt. Kulkarni, V. Y., ed; Vol. 2. Hindi-Jannada-Kashmiri-Malayalam. Mulay, Y. M., ed; Vol. 3. Marathi-Oriya-Panjabi-Sanskrit; Vol. 4. Sindhi-Tamil-Teleyu-Urdu. E J Brill USA.
Keschner, Richard L., jt. auth. see Krass, Stephen J.
Kesey, Ken. One Flew Over the Cuckoo's Nest.
Keskemethy, Laszlo, tr. see Vatai, Laszlo.
Kesler, Jay. Family Forum.
--Too Big to Spank.
Kesler, S. E. Our Finite Resources.
Kesling, Amelia B. Tapestry of the North.
Kesling, Peter C., jt. auth. see Begg, P. R.
Kespohl, Ruth C. Geometry Problems My Students Have Written.
Kess, Sidney, jt. auth. see Metz, Robert.
Kessel, Joyce K. Careers in Dental Care.
Kessel, L., jt. auth. see Bayley, J. I.
Kessel, R. G. & Shih, C. Y. Scanning Electron Microscopy in Biology: A Students' Atlas of Biological Organization.
Kessel, Reuben A. Essays in Applied Price Theory. Coase, R. H. & Miller, Merton, eds.
Kessell, John L. The Missions of New Mexico Since 1776.
Kesselman, Judi R. Stopping Out: A Guide to Leaving College & Getting Back In.
Kesselman, Mark. The French Workers' Movement: Economic Crisis & Political Change.
Kesselman, Mark, jt. auth. see Katznelson, Ira.
Kesselman, Wendy. Joey.
Kessler, A. D. A Fortune at Your Feet: How You Can Make Money with Real Estate in Good Times & Bad.
Kessler, Carol F., ed. Daring to Dream: Eighteen Thirty-Six to Nineteen Nineteen.
Kessler, Carolyn. The Acquisition of Syntax in Bilingual Children.
Kessler, D. J., ed. Space Debris, Asteroids & Satellite Orbits: Proceedings of Workshop IV & XIII & of the COSPAR Interdisciplinary Scientific Commission P (Meeting Pl) of the COSPAR Twenty-fifth Plenary Meeting Held i n Graf, Austria, 25 June-7 July 1984.
Kessler, Ethel & Kessler, Leonard. The Sweeneys from 9D.
Kessler, Henry H. Knife Is Not Enough.
Kessler, Leonard, jt. auth. see Kessler, Ethel.
Kessler, Lyle. Orphans.
Kessler, Ronald. The Life Insurance Game.
Kessler, Stephen. Nostalgia of the Fortuneteller.
Kessler, Stephen & Barth, Jack. Tennis, Anyone?
Kest, Lynda F. Detecting Sequences of Events-Level A: Developing Reading Comprehension.
Kestenbaum, Victor. The Phenomenological Sense of John Dewey: Habit & Meaning.
Kester, Dale E., jt. auth. see Hartmann, Hudson T.
Kester, Ralph J. Using Systematic Observation Techniques in Evaluating Career Education.
Kesteven, G. R. The Pale Invaders.
Kestin, J. A Course in Thermodynamics.
Kestner, Joseph A. The Spatiality of the Novel.
Kestner, N. R., jt. ed. see Jortner, J.
Ketay, Norma, jt. auth. see Hamburg, Joan.
Ketcham, Hank. Dennis the Menace: Five Years at the Same Location.
--Dennis the Menace: Good Intenshuns.
--Dennis the Menace: One More Time!
Ketcham, Henry, ed. see Hume, Martin A.
Ketcham, Rodney K. Patterns of French.
Ketcher, Fritzi. Daisy.
Ketchledge, E. H. Trees of the Adirondack High Peak Region.
Ketchum, Bostwick H., et al, eds. see Duedall, Iver W.
Ketchum, Jack. Hide & Seek.
Ketchum, Milo S. Handbook of Standard Structural Details for Buildings.
Ketchum, William. Fortie's & Fiftie's Collectibles.
--Sports Collectibles.
Ketchum, William C., Jr. Hooked Rugs: A Historical Collector's Guide - How to Make Your Own.
Ketchum, William, Jr. Collecting Bottles for Fun & Profit.
Ketefian, Shake, ed. see Stewart Conference on Research in Nursing Staff.
Kets De Vries, Manfred E., jt. auth. see Zaleznik, Abraham.
Kett, P. W. Motor Vehicle Science.
Kettelkamp, Larry. Sixth Sense.
Kettenacker, Lothar & Mommsen, Wolfgang J., eds. The Fascist Challenge & the Policy of Appeasement.
Ketterer, Roman N., ed. E. L. Kirchner: Drawings & Pastels.
Ketterman, Grace, jt. auth. see Holt, Pat.
Kettler, David, et al, eds. see Mannheim, Karl.
Kettler, Robert, jt. auth. see Trimmer, Joseph F.
Kettless, Alonzo W. Designs for Wood: How to Plan & Create Your Own Furniture.
Kettner, James H. The Development of American Citizenship, 1608-1870.
Kettridge, J. O. French for English Idioms & Figurative Phrases.

Authors

--French Idioms & Figurative Phrases: With Many Quotations.
Kety, Seymour S., jt. auth. see Matthysse, Steven.
Keuls, Henry P. Foreign & American Folk Sayings, Realities & Philosophies.
Keun, Irmgard. After Midnight.
Kevan, Ernest F. The Grace of Law.
Keven, Keith McE. Soil Animals.
Kevill-Davies, Sally. Jelly Moulds. Riley, Noel, ed.
Kevorkian, Jack. Story of Dissection.
Kewley, T. H., ed. Australian Social Security Today.
Key, Alexander. The Case of the Vanishing Boy.
--Escape to Witch Mountain.
--The Forgotten Door.
--The Incredible Tide.
--The Magic Meadow.
--The Preposterous Adventures of Swimmer.
--Return from Witch Mountain.
--The Strange White Doves.
--The Sword of Aradel.
Key, Della T. In the Cattle Country: History of Potter County, 1887-1966.
Key, Ellen. War, Peace, & the Future.
Key, Harold. Fonotacticas del Cayuvava.
Key, Marcus M., et al, eds. Pulmonary Reactions to Coal Dust: A Review of the U. S. Experience.
Key, Mike & Thacker, Tony. Fins & the Fifties.
Key, Ted. The Cat from Outer Space.
Keyboard Magazine Editors & Guitar Player Magazine Editors, eds. New Age Musicians.
Keyes, Carol, jt. auth. see Grossman, Bruce.
Keyes, Daniel. The Fifth Sally.
Keyes, Edward. Cocoanut Grove.
--Double Dare.
--Double Dare.
Keyes, Elizabeth & Chivington, Paul K. What's Eating You?
Keyes, Fenton. Aim for a Job in the Allied Health Field.
--Your Future in a Mental Health Career.
Keyes, Frances P. Fielding's Folly.
--Parts Unknown.
--Restless Lady & Other Stories.
--Victorine.
Keyes, John H. Consumer Handbook of Solar Energy for the United States & Canada.
Keyes, Ken, Center Residents. The Methods Work...If You Do.
Keyes, Ken, Jr. & Burkan, Bruce T. How to Make Your Life Work, or Why Aren't You Happy?
Keyes, Margaret N. Nineteenth Century Home Architecture of Iowa City.
Keyes, Paul T. Pastoral Presence & the Diocesan Priest.
Keyes, Ralph. Chancing It: Why We Take Risks.
Keyes, Roger. Outrageous Fortune: The Tragedy of Leopold III of the Belgians, 1901-1941.
Keynes, Geoffrey, intro. by see Blake, William.
Keynes, Geoffrey, ed. see Browne, Thomas.
Keynes, John Maynard. Essays in Biography.
Keys, Donald, jt. ed. see Laszlo, Ervin.
Keys, P., jt. ed. see Jackson, M. C.
Keys, Paul, jt. auth. see Beaumont, John R.
Keys, Paul R. & Ginsberg, Leon H., eds. Modern Social Work Management.
Keysell, Pat. Mime Themes & Motifs.
Keyser, Herbert. Women under the Knife.
Keyserlingk, Robert H. Media Manipulation: A Study of the Press & Bismarck in Imperial Germany.
Keyssar, Helene. Feminist Theatre.
--Feminist Theatre.
Keystone, E. C., jt. auth. see Pruzanski, W.
Keywood, Olive. Personal & Community Health.
Keyworth, C. L. Letters That Get Action.
Keyzer, Hendrik & Gutmann, Felix, eds. Bioelectrochemistry.
Kezdi, P., ed. Baroreceptors & Hypertension.
Kezdi, Paul. You & Your Heart.
Kezirian, Richard. American History: Major Controversies Reviewed.
Kezys, A., ed. A Lithuanian Cemetery.
Kgositsile, Keorapetse. For Melba.
Khabaza, I. M. Numerical Analysis.
Khadduri, Majid. Law of War & Peace in Islam: A Study of Moslem International Law.
Khader, Bichara & El-Wifati, Bashir, eds. The Economic Development of Libya.
Khailany, Asad & Duplissey, Claude. COBOL for Medium & Small Sized Computers.
Khaleolulla, S. M. Counterexamples in Topological Vector Spaces.
Khalfina, R. State Property in the U. S. S. R.
Khalidi, Walid. Before Their Diaspora: A Photographic History of the Palestinians, 1876-1948 (Arabic Edition)
Khalifa, Saida M. The Fifth Pillar: The Story of a Pilgrimage to Mecca & Medina.
Khalil, ed. Flow, Mixing & Heat Transfer in Furnaces.
Khammaan, Khonkhai. The Teachers of Mad Dog Swamp. Wijeyewardene, Gehan, tr. from Thai.
Khan, jt. auth. see Sarma, Y. S.
Khan, A. A., ed. The Physiology & Biochemistry of Seed Dormancy & Germination.
Khan, Amanullah & Hill, Norwood, eds. Human Lymphokines.
Khan, Amanullah, et al, eds. Immune Regulators in Transfer Factor.
Khan, Azizur Rahman, ed. see ILO Asian Employment Programme Staff.
Khan, Hazrat I. Gayan, Vadan, Nirtan.
--Nature Meditations.
Khan, Hazrat Inayat. The Alchemy of Happiness.
--The Bowl of Saki.
--The Development of Spiritual Healing.
--Education from Before Birth to Maturity.
--Gayan.
--The Mysticism of Sound.
--The Palace of Mirrors.
--Sufi Teachings.
--The Unity of Religious Ideals.
Khan, M. A. & Bederka, John, eds. Survival in Toxic Environments.
Khan, M. Y. Indian Financial System.
Khan, Mohammed A. Generals in Politics: Pakistan 1958-1982.
Khan, Muhammad A., tr. The Right Path: Abd al Husyan Sharaf al-Din al Musawi.
Khan, Muhammad S. Islamic Medicine.
Khan, Muhammad Z. Muhammad: Seal of the Prophets.
Khan, S. U., jt. auth. see Bockris, J. O. M.
Khan, Shoaib S. Rural Development in Pakistan.
Khan, Zafar, jt. auth. see Lerner, Judith.
Khan, Zillur R. Leadership in the Least Developed Nation: Bangladesh.
Khandwalla, Pradip N. The Design of Organizations.
Khanin, Ya, jt. auth. see Fain, V. M.
Khan-Magomedov, Selim O. Alexander Vesnisn & Russian Constructivism.
Khanna, K. M. Classical Mechanics.
Kharchev, K., jt. auth. see Bunich, P. C.
Kharkevich, D. A., ed. Ganglion-Blocking & Ganglion-Stimulating Agents.
Kharlamova, L. Armoury in the Moscow Kremlin.
Khatena, Joe. Educational Psychology of the Gifted.
Khatri, Linda A., jt. auth. see Roysdon, Christine M.
Khayyam, Omar. Rubaiyat of Omar Khayyam. Fitzgerald, Edward, tr.
Kherdian, David. Any Day of Your Life.
--Place of Birth.
--Right Now.
--Six Poets of the San Francisco Renaissance: Portraits & Checklists.
Khetrapal, C. L. Lyotropic Liquid Crystals.
Khodasevich, Vladislav. Izbrannaia Proza.
Khodashova, K. S., jt. ed. see Zlotin, R. I.
Khomskaia. Brain & Activation.
Khoramshahi, Baha, jt. auth. see Fani, Kamran.
Khoshkish, A. The Socio-Political Complex.
Khosla, G. D. Never the Twain: A Novel.
Khoury, S. J. & Parsons, T. D. Mathematical Methods in Finance & Economics.
Khozin, G. The Biosphere & Politics.
Khrenov, L. S. Six-Figure Tables of Trigonometric Functions.
Khrushchev, Nikita S. Disarmament & Colonial Freedom.
Khvoinik, P. Trade Among Capitalist Countries.
Kiam, Victor. Going for It! How to Succeed As an Entrepreneur.
Kiang, Yen-Hsiung & Metry, Amir. Hazardous Waste Processing Technology.
Kibbe, Richard R. Grinding Machine Operations.
--Lathe Operations.
--Milling Machine Operations.
Kibbey, D. R., jt. auth. see Moore, H. D.
Kibby, David R. Ark: A Provocative & Challenging Look at Religion.
Kibler, James E., Jr., jt. auth. see Butterworth, Keen.
Kiborne, Benjamin, tr. see Anzieu, Didier.
Kichenside, Geoffrey, jt. auth. see Kingston, Patrick.
Kicklighter, Clois E. Modern Masonry.
Kicknosway, Faye. Asparagus, Asparagus, Ah Sweet Asparagus.
Kiczales, Gregor, jt. auth. see Bobrow, Daniel.
Kidd, Charles V. Manpower Policies for the Use of Science & Technology in Development.
Kidd, Clark & Kidd, Kathy H. VIC Games for Kids. Compute! Magazine Staff, ed.
Kidd, Elizabeth. The Dancers Land.
--My Lord Guardian.
Kidd, Flora. Passionate Stranger.
Kidd, J. Roby, jt. ed. see Smith, Robert.
Kidd, Jane. A Festival of Dressage.
Kidd, Kathy H., jt. auth. see Kidd, Clark.
Kidd, Roby, jt. ed. see Hall, Bud L.
Kidd, Ron. The Littlest Angel: A Pop-Up Book.
Kidd, Russ. Six-Shooter Sod-Buster.
--Trouble Brand.
Kidd, Yasue A. Women Workers in the Japanese Cotton Mills: 1880-1920.
Kidder, Alfred V. The Pottery of Pecos: The Dull Paint Wares.
Kidder, Ralph D. & Kelly, Edward F. Choice for Survival: The Baby Boomer's Dilemma.
Kiddle, Mary E. & Wegmann, Brenda. Perspectivas: Temas de Hoy y de Siempre.
Kidman, Fiona. In the Clear Light.
Kidron, Michael & Segal, Ronald. New State of the World Atlas.
Kids' Stuff People Staff. Arithmefun.
--The Elementary School Kids' Book of Lists.
Kidwell, David S. & Peterson, Richard L. Financial Institutions, Markets, & Money.
Kiefer, H. & Maushart, R. Radiation Protection Measurement. Friese, Ralf, tr.
Kiefer, J., ed. Radiation & Cellular Control Processes.
Kieffer, F., ed. Radiation Physics & Chemistry: Magat Memorial Issue.
--Trapped Charges.
Kielhofner, G., jt. auth. see Barris, R.
Kiene, Richard H., ed. see American Academy of Orthopaedic Surgeons Staff.
Kienzle, O., et al. The Promotion of the Relationship Between Research & Industry in Mechanical Production.
Kienzle, William X. Deadline for a Critic.
--Death Wears a Red Hat.
--Kill & Tell.
--Kill & Tell.
--The Rosary Murders.
--Sudden Death.
Kier, Lemont B., ed. see Battelle Seattle Research Center Symposium Staff.
Kierkegaard, Soren. The Concept of Irony. Capel, Lee M., tr.
--Either-Or. Lowrie, W., tr.
--For Self-Examination. Hong, Edna & Hong, Howard, trs.
--Philosophical Fragments. Hong, H. V., ed. Swenson, David, tr.
Kiernan, jt. auth. see Roback.
Kiernan, Catherine H. Sound Thinking - Basic Learning, the Making & Sharing of Music.
Kiernan, Thomas. Arafat: The Man & the Myth.
--The Intricate Music: A Biography of John Steinbeck.
--Roman Polanski: A Biography.
Kiernan, V. G. From Conquest to Collapse: European Empires from Eighteen Fifteen to Nineteen Sixty.
--State & Society in Europe 1550-1650.
Kiersch, George A., et al, eds. Engineering Geology Case Histories.
Kiersh, Edward. Where Are You Now, Bo Diddley? The Artists Who Made Us Rock & Where They Are Now.
Kierzek, John M. & Gibson, Walker. Handbook of Writing & Revision.
Kies, Paul P., et al. Writer's Manual & Workbook.
Kieselhorst, Daniel C. A Theoretical Perspective of Violence Against Police.
Kiesler, H. Jerome. Elementary Calculus: Student Supplement.
Kiessling, Nicolas. The Incubus in English Literature: Provenance & Progeny.
Kietzman, Mitchell, et al, eds. Experimental Approaches to Psychopathology.
Kievman, Michael S., jt. auth. see Howard, Herbert H.
Kihl, Young W. & Grinter, Lawrence E., eds. Asian-Pacific Security: Emerging Challenges & Responses.
Kihlstrom, B., jt. auth. see Langefors, U.
Kikkert, Lois. Joyful Waiting.
Kikrorian, E., ed. Technical Issues in Infared Detectors & Arrays.
Kilbourn, D. Readings for Resident Assistants.
Kilbourne, Edwin D., ed. The Influenza Viruses & Influenza.
Kilbride, James M., jt. auth. see Napoli, Vince.
Kilby, Clyde S. & Mead, Marjorie L., eds. Brothers & Friends: An Intimate Portrait of C. S. Lewis; the Diaries of Major Warren Hamilton Lewis.
Kilchenman, A., ed. Quantitative & Theoretical Geography.
Kildeberg, Poul. Quantitative Acid-Base Physiology.
Kilduff, Peter, tr. see Von Richthofen, Manfred.
Kiley, Dan. Dr. Dan's Prescriptions.
--The Wendy Dilemma: When Women Stop Mothering Their Men.
Kiley, W. Paul. Human Possibilities.
Kilgore, James. Try Marriage Before Divorce.
Kilgore, James D. Dr. Kilgore's Feel Good Parenting Book.
Kilgore, Kathleen. The Ghost-Maker.
--The Wolfman of Beacon Hill.
Kilgour, John G. Preventive Labor Relations.
Kilias, H. Revision Gesteinsbewohnender Sippen der Flechtengattung Catillaria Mass in Europa(Lecanorales, Lecideaceae)
Kiliper, R. Smith, jt. auth. see Schulz, Charles M.
Killeen, Jacqueline. Country Inns of the Far West: California.
--Country Inns of the Far West: California.
--One Hundred One Secrets of Gourmet Chefs.
Killeen, Jacqueline & Silva, Sharon. Best Restaurants San Francisco Bay Area.
Killeen, Jacqueline, jt. auth. see Castle, Coralie.
Killeen, Jacqueline, et al. Best Restaurants San Francisco Bay Area.
--Country Inns of the Far West: A Guide to the Inns of California, Oregon, Washington & British Columbia.
Killen, Kenneth H. Management: A Middle Management Approach.
Killen, Linda & Lael, Richard. Versailles & After: An Annotated Bibliography of American Diplomatic Relations, 1919-1933.
Killey. Fractures of the Mandible.
Killey, H. & Seward, G. Outline of Oral Surgery.
Killian, H. Cold & Frost Injuries: Rewarming Damages.
Killian, Lewis, jt. auth. see Turner, Ralph H.
Killian, Robert. Winners Without Races.
Killick, Anthony. The Economies of East Africa.
Killingback, Julia. One, Two, Three, Go!
Killingbeck, J. & Cole, G. H. Mathematical Techniques & Physical Applications.
Killinger, John. A Devotional Guide to the Gospels: Three Hundred Sixty-Six Meditations.
--The Fragile Presence: Transcendence in Modern Literature.
--Steeple People & the World: Planning for Mission Through the Church.
Killip, Christopher. The Isle of Man: A Book About the Manx.
Killough, Larry & Leininger, Wayne. Cost Accounting: Concepts & Techniques for Management.
Killough, Lee. Aventine.
Kilman, Gilbert M. & Rosenfeld, Albert. Responsible Parenthood: The Child's Psyche Through the Six-Year Pregnancy.
Kilmann, Ralph H. Managing Beyond the Quick Fix: A Completely Integrated Program for Creating & Maintaining Organizational Success.
Kilmann, Ralph H., jt. auth. see Mitroff, Ian I.
Kilmann, Ralph H., et al. The Management of Organization Design.
Kilmartin, Edward J. Church, Eucharist & Priesthood: A Theological Commentary on "The Mystery & Worship of the Most Holy Eucharist"
Kilmarx, Robert A. Toward a Coherent U. S. Policy on Strategic Materials.
Kilmarx, Robert A. & Alexander, Yonah. Business & the Middle East.
Kilmer, Nicholas, tr. see Petrarch, Francis.
Kilmister, C. W. General Theory of Relativity.
--Special Theory of Relativity.
Kilpatrick, Anna G., jt. auth. see Kilpatrick, Jack F.
Kilpatrick, Anne O. Resolving Community Conflict: An Annotated Bibliography.
Kilpatrick, C. W. Naval Night Battles of the Solomons.
Kilpatrick, Jack F. & Kilpatrick, Anna G. Run Toward the Nightland: Magic of the Oklahoma Cherokees.
Kilpatrick, James J., jt. auth. see McCarthy, Eugene J.
Kilpatrick, James J., Jr. The Writer's Art.
Kilpatrick, John, jt. auth. see Miller, Robert R.
Kilpatrick, John A., Jr., jt. auth. see Aegerter, Ernest E.
Kilson, Martin. Political Change in a West African State: A Study of the Modernization Process in Sierra Leone.
Kilworth, Garry. The Night of Kadar.
Kim & McFarland. Pocket Guide to Nursing Diagnosis.
Kim, Ashida. Dragon Lady of the Ninja.
Kim, C. I. & Koh, B. C., eds. Journey to North Korea: Personal Perceptions.
Kim, Chong Lim, jt. auth. see Boynton, G. R.
Kim, Chu-Wan, jt. auth. see Han, Man-Chung.
Kim, Daeshik & Shin, Kyung Sun. Judo.
Kim, Elaine. With Silk Wings: Asian American Women at Work.
Kim, Hak-Un. A Study on Inflation & Unemployment.
Kim, Hee-Jin. Dogen Kigen - Mystical Realist.
Kim, Hesook S. The Nature of Theoretical Thinking in Nursing.
Kim, Jae T., ed. New Perspectives in Public Administration.
Kim, Kwan & Ruccio, David, eds. Debt & Development in Latin America.
Kim, Scott. Inversions: A Catalog of Calligraphic Cartwheels.
Kim, Seung H. & Miller, Stephen W. Competitive Structure of the International Banking Industry. Miossi, Alfred F., ed.
Kim, W. Chan & Young, Philip K. Y., eds. The Pacific Challenge in International Business.
Kim, Y. Y. & Thompson, R. G. Oil & Gas Supplies in the Lower Forty-Eight States.
Kim, Young C. Japanese Soviet Relations: Interaction of Politics, Economics & National Security.
Kimball, C. P., jt. ed. see Krakowski, A. J.
Kimball, Chase P., jt. ed. see Krakowski, Adam J.
Kimball, Donald L. Many Mansions.
Kimball, George, jt. auth. see Youell, Tessa.
Kimball, Heber C. On the Potter's Wheel: The Diaries of Heber C. Kimball. Kimball, Stanley B., intro. by.

Authors

Kimball, Margot C., jt. auth. see Palmer, Adrian S.
Kimball, Penn. The File.
--File.
Kimball, Robert E. & Simon, Alfred E. The Gershwins.
Kimball, Spencer W., et al. Priesthood.
Kimball, Stanley B. Discovering Mormon Trails.
Kimball, Stanley B., intro. by see Kimball, Heber C.
Kimball, William. What the Bible Says about the Great Tribulation.
Kimball, Yeffe, jt. auth. see Anderson, Jean.
Kimbell Art Museum Staff. Kimbell Art Museum: A Catalogue of the Collection.
Kimbell, Chase P., jt. ed. see Krakowski, Adam J.
Kimbell, Richard. Design Education: The Foundation Years.
Kimber, Edward. The Life & Adventures of Joe Thompson, 1750.
--Maria: The Genuine Memoirs of a Young Lady of Rank & Fortune, 1765.
Kimber, Richard T. & Boyd, A. Automation in Libraries.
Kimberling, William C., ed. Voter Information & Education Programs 1: Designing Effective Voter Information Programs.
Kimberly, John R. & Quinn, Robert E. Managing Organizational Transitions.
Kimble, Gerald W. Information & Computer Science.
Kimbrall, Grady. Introduction to Business & Office Careers.
Kimbrall, Mary E. Introduction to Health Careers.
Kimbrell, Grady & Vineyard, Ben S. Strategies for Implementing Work Experience Programs.
Kimbrough, Emily, jt. auth. see Skinner, Cornelia Otis.
Kimbrough, M. The Joy & Adventure of Growing Younger.
Kimbrough, Mary. The Muny: St. Louis' Outdoor Theater.
Kimbrough, Robert, ed. see Conrad, Joseph.
Kimbrough, S. T., Jr., ed. see Kuske, Martin.
Kimche, David. Afro-Asian Movement: Ideology & Foreign Policy of the Third World.
Kime, Helen R. & Wynkoop, Shari H. Getting Ready for Your Baby.
Kime, Philip. The Seekers.
Kimerling, L. C. & Parsey, J. M., Jr., eds. Thirteenth International Conference on Defects in Semiconductors.
Kimes, Beverly R. The Cars That Henry Ford Built.
--Standard Catalog of American Cars, 1805-1942.
Kim Il Sung. Revolution & Education in People's Korea: Theses on Socialist Education.
Kimmel, H. D., ed. Experimental Psychopathology: Recent Research & Theory.
Kimmel, Karen S. & Blank, Joan C., eds. Technology for Career Information Delivery: Conference Proceedings.
Kimmel, Mark, ed. see Phillips Publishing, Inc. Staff.
Kimmel, Wayne A., et al. Municipal Management & Budget Methods: An Evaluation of Policy Related Research.
Kimmelman, Elaine. Dark Comet.
Kimmelman, Joan, jt. auth. see Krantz, Harriet.
Kimmitt, M. F. Far-Infrared Techniques.
Kimpel, Ben. A Philosophy of the Religions of Ancient Greeks & Israelites.
Kimpel, Ben F. Faith & Moral Authority.
--Moral Principles in the Bible.
--The Symbols of Religious Faith.
Kimura, Jun. Electrodiagnosis in Diseases of Nerve & Muscle: Principles & Practice.
Kimura, Katsumi, et al. Handbook of HeI Photoelectron Spectra of Fundamental Organic Molecules.
Kin, David. Dictionary of American Proverbs.
Kincaid, D. The Sunset Bomber.
Kincaid, John & Elazar, Daniel J., eds. The Covenant Connection.
Kincaid, Nell. Love on Any Terms.
--Turn Back the Dawn.
--Whisper on the Wind.
Kincaid-Smith, P. S. & Whitworth, J. A., eds. Hypertension: Mechanisms & Management.
Kinchlow, Ben & Slosser, Bob. Plain Bread.
Kinchum, Moore E. How to Become a Successful Private Eye.
Kindaich, Haruhiko. The Japanese Language. Hirano, Umeyo, tr.
Kinder, Chuck. The Silver Ghost.
Kinderman, Katherine S., jt. auth. see Lo, Ruth E.
Kindervatter, Suzanne. Women Working Together for Personal, Economic & Community Development.
Kindilien, Carlin. Basic Writing Skills: Preparation for Competency Tests.
Kindle, Patricia & Finney, Susan. Alaska.
--Napoleon.
Kindleberger, Charles P. The World in Depression Nineteen Twenty-Nine to Nineteen Thirty-Nine: History of the World Economy in the Twentieth Century.
Kindred, Dave, jt. auth. see Theismann, Joe.
Kindsfather, William L., jt. auth. see Parish, W. Alton.
King. Intergrated Electronic Circuits & System.
--No Church Is an Island: Study Guide.
King, jt. auth. see Cleland.
King, A., jt. ed. see Heden, C. G.
King, A. B. Self-Hypnosis: The Key to Health & Happiness.
King, Adele, ed. see Hirst, David.
King, Adele, ed. see Knapp, Bettina L.
King, Adele, ed. see Morgan, Margery.
King, Adele, ed. see Senelick, Laurence.
King, Alan & Sheraton, Mimi. Is Salami & Eggs Better Than Sex? Memoirs of a Happy Eater.
King, Alexander. Mine Enemy Grows Older.
--The State of the Planet: A Report Prepared by the International Federation of Institutes for Advanced Study, Stockholm.
King, Alexander, jt. auth. see Fromherz, Hans.
King, Allen L., ed. see International Working Seminar on the Role of the History of Physics in Physics Education Staff.
King, Bert & McGinnies, Elliot, eds. Attitudes, Conflict & Social Change.
King, Brian, jt. auth. see Williams, Robert E.
King, Brian L., jt. auth. see Philips, Sheldon W.
King, Bruce, ed. Literatures of the World in English.
--West Indian Literature.
King, Bruce, ed. see Hirst, David.
King, Bruce, ed. see Knapp, Bettina L.
King, Bruce, ed. see Morgan, Margery.
King, Bruce, ed. see Senelick, Laurence.
King, C. A., ed. Periglacial Processes.
King, Carl. Model T Days: Florida or Bust.
King, Charles C. & Elfner, Lynn E. Organisms & Biological Communities As Indicators of Environmemtal Quality: A Symposium, the Ohio State University, March 25,1974.
King, Cheryl N. see Wah-Be-Gwo-Nese, pseud.
King, Clive. Stig of the Dump.
King, Constance E. Jumeau Prince of Dollmakers.
King, Cuchlaine A. Northern England.
King, David. Fiscal Tiers: The Economics of Multi-Level Government.
King, David, et al. Trotsky.
King, David C. & Koller, Marvin R. Foundations of Sociology.
King, David C., et al. Windows on California.
King, David S. No Church Is an Island.
King, Deborah. Sirius & Saba.
King, Donald, tr. see Focillon, Henri.
King, E. J. The Teacher & the Needs of Society in Evolution.
King, Edmund F., ed. Ten Thousand Wonderful Things.
King, Elaine A. Artists Observed.
King, Eleanor M., jt. auth. see Kenworthy, Mary A.
King, Estelle, jt. auth. see King, Robert.
King Features Staff. Mandrake the Magician Cartoon.
King, Frances. Act of Darkness.
King, Frances see Johnson, Judi.
King, Francis. Magic: The Western Tradition.
--One Is a Wanderer: Selected Stories.
--Voices in an Empty Room.
King, Francis S. Advertising Practices.
King, Frank A. The Missabe Road: The Duluth, Missabe & Iron Range Railway.
King, George. The Day the Gods Came.
King, Gordon, jt. auth. see Spring, Vicky.
King, Gordon J. Color Television Servicing.
King, Graham. Say "Cheese"! Looking at Snapshots in a New Way.
King, H. Gill, jt. auth. see Aceves, Joseph B.
King, Harold. The Hahnemann Sequela.
King, Hazel. Elizabeth Macarthur & Her World.
King, Henry C. The History of the Telescope.
King, Irene M. John O. Meusebach: German Colonizer in Texas.
King, J. E., jt. ed. see Ebbels, D. L.
King, J. Norman. The God of Forgiveness & Healing in the Theology of Karl Rahner.
King, J. R. Production Planning & Control: An Introduction to Quantitative Methods.
King, J. R., jt. auth. see Eilon, S.
King, J. W. & Newman, W. S. Solar Terrestrial Physics.
King, Jack. Concrete Walkways Projects.
King, Jack L. Wings of Man: The Legend of Captain H.T. Dick Merrill.
King, Jacob, ed. see Gissing, George.
King, James E. Science & Rationalism in the Government of Louis Fourteenth, 1661-1683.
King, John A., jt. auth. see Ouellette, Robert P.
King, Jonathan. Mayflower Miracle.
King, Jonathan, ed. Protein & Nucleic Acids Structure.
King, Judith. My Most Marvelous Memory Book.
King, Judy. Evaluation of Database Management Systems.
King, Kamla J., jt. ed. see BNA Library Staff.
King, Ken, ed. see Lefrancois, Guy R.
King, Kenneth. U. S. Monetary Policy & European Responses in the 1980's.
King, Kerryn, intro. by. Public Relations Career Directory 1986: 25 Top PR Professionals.
King, Kimball. Ten Modern Irish Playwrights: A Comprehensive Annotated Bibliography.
King, Larry & Yoffe, Emily. Larry King.
King, Larry L., jt. auth. see Baker, Bobby.
King, Lester S. Growth of Medical Thought.
King, Lincoln, jt. auth. see Sitton, Thad.
King, Linda O., ed. see Mugnier, George F.
King, M. A. Public Policy & the Corporation.
King, Margaret, jt. auth. see Froh, Alfred.
King, Martin Luther, Jr. Stride Toward Freedom.
King, Martin Luther, Sr. & Riley, Clayton. Daddy King.
King, Maxwell & Giles, David, eds. Specification Analysis in the Linear Model.
King, Michael. The Framework of Criminal Justice.
King, Mona. Mexico.
King, Nancy. Traveling.
King, Norman. Past Due: How to Collect Money.
King, Orin C. The Circus World of Willie Sells.
King, P. R. Nine Contemporary Poets: A Critical Introduction.
King, Pat. How to Have All the Energy You Need Every Day.
King, Pauline. Snares of the Enemy.
King, Peter. The Life & Letters of John Locke, with Extracts from His Journals & Common-Place Books.
King, R. A. Electronic Circuits & System Solutions.
King, R. B. Transition-Metal Organometallic Chemistry: An Introduction.
King, R. J. & Young, R. E. A Systematic Sociology of Australian Education.
King, Richard A. IBM PC-DOS Handbook.
--IBM-PC-DOS Handbook.
--The MS-DOS Handbook.
--The MS-DOS Handbook.
King, Richard A. & Trost, Stanley R. Multiplan on the Commodore 64.
King, Robert & King, Estelle. My Church Covenant & I.
King, Robert, et al. Invertebrate Oogenesis, Vol. 1: Interactions Between Oocytes & Their Accessory Cells.
King, Robert B. Ferguson's Castle: A Dream Remembered.
King, Robert G. & Di Michael, Eleanor M. Articulation & Voice: Improving Oral Communication.
King, Robert H. Meaning of God.
King, Robert R. A History of the Romanian Communist Party.
--Minorities under Communism: Nationalities As a Source of Tension Among Balkan Communist States.
King, Roger, ed. Capital & Politics.
King, Ronald. The Sociology of School Organization.
King, Ronald, tr. see Gell, Paul.
King, Ronald W. Tables of Antenna Characteristics.
King, Rufus. The Drug Hang-up: America's Fifty Year Folly.
King, Russell, ed. Return Migration & Regional Economic Problems.
King, Spencer B., Jr. Georgia Voices: A Documentary History to 1872.
King, Stella, jt. ed. see Ferguson, Rosemary.
King, Stephen. Pet Sematary.
King, T. E., et al, eds. Oxidases & Related Redox Systems: Proceedings of a Conference Held in New York, 3-7 July 1979.
King, Tappan, jt. auth. see Polikarpus, Viido.
King, Ted. How to Keep Your Lawyer Honest.
King, Thomas M. & Salmon, James F., eds. Teilhard & the Unity of Knowledge.
King, Timothy, ed. Education & Income.
King, Willard F., tr. see Lope de Vega.
King, William. An Essay on the Origin of Evil. Bd. with Dissertations Concerning the Fundamental Principle & Immediate Criterion of Virtue. Garland Pub.
King, William R., jt. auth. see Cleland, David I.
King, William S. & Jones, Delmos J. Papago Indians, Vol. 2: Papago Population Studies.
King, Winston L. Theravada Meditation: The Buddhist Transformation of Yoga.
Kingdom, Elizabeth, tr. see Edelman, Bernard.
Kinget, G. Marian. On Being Human: A Systematic View.
King-Fitch, Catherine. Bridges to Employment, Bk. III: Practices for Providing Follow-Through Services to Former Employment & Training Clients.
Kinghorn, Alexander M. see Ramsay, Allan.
Kinghorn, Kenneth C. Dynamic Discipleship.
Kinglake, A. W. Eothen.
Kingman, Lee. Break a Leg Betsy Maybe.
--Georgina & the Dragon.
--Head over Wheels.
--Peter Pan Bag.
--The Refiner's Fire.
--Year of the Raccoon.
Kingman, Lee, ed. Newbery & Caldecott Medal Books, 1976-1987.
King Rama, 2nd. Sang Thong: A Dance-Drama from Thailand. Ingersoll, Fern S., tr.
Kingsbury, Donald. Courtship Rite.
Kingsbury, Jack D. The Christology of Mark's Gospel.
--Matthew. Krodel, Gerhard, ed.
--Matthew As Story.
--Matthew: Structure, Christology, Kingdom.
Kingsbury, Jack D. & Pennington, Chester. Lent. Achtemeier, Elizabeth, et al, eds.
Kingsbury, Jack D., jt. auth. see Randolph, David.
Kingsland, Gerald. The Voyager.
Kingsland, L. W., tr. see Brodtkorb, Reidar.
Kingsland, L. W., tr. see Holm, Anne S.
Kingsley, Charles. The Heroes.
--Hypatia; or, New Foes with an Old Face: 1853. Wolff, Robert L., ed.
Kingsley, D. & Taylor, F. Albion in China: The First British Football Tour to China in Pictures.
Kingsley, Henry. Hillyars & the Burtons.
Kingsley, Philip. The Complete Hair Book: The Ultimate Guide to Your Hairs Health & Beauty.
Kingston, Beryl. Lifting the Curse.
Kingston, Maxine H. China Men.
Kingston, Patrick & Kichenside, Geoffrey. Royal Trains: From Queen Victoria to the Present.
King-Yi, Hsu. Political Mobilization & Economic Extraction: Chinese Communist Agrarian Policies During the Kiangi Period.
Kinigsberg, David. Modern Man & An Old-Fashioned God.
Kininmonth, Christopher. The Travellers' Guide to Malta & Gozo.
Kinkead-Weeks, Mark & Gregor, Ian. William Golding: A Critical Study.
Kinley, David. Money: Study of the Theory of the Medium of Exchange.
Kinley, David, ed. see Institute for Food & Development Policy Staff.
Kinley, Harold. The PLL Synthesizer Cookbook.
Kinman, Kenneth E., jt. ed. see Honacki, James H.
Kinmond, Jean. The Coats Book of Modern European Embroidery.
Kinnara Inc. Staff. Pilgrimage.
Kinnear, Thomas C., jt. auth. see Bernhardt, Kenneth L.
Kinnear, Willis H., ed. The Creative Power of Mind.
Kinnear, Willis H., ed. see Holmes, Ernest.
Kinnell, Galway, tr. The Poems of Francois Villon.
Kinnell, Susan, tr. see Chardenon, Ludo.
Kinney, Ann R. Japanese Investment in Manchurian Manufacturing, Mining, Transportation & Communications, 1931-1945. Myers, Ramon H., ed.
Kinney, Arthur F. Dorothy Parker.
Kinney, Cle, jt. auth. see Kinney, Jean.
Kinney, Francis. Skenes Yacht Design.
Kinney, Jean & Kinney, Cle. How to Make Nineteen Kinds of American Folk Art from Maska to TV Commercials.
--Twenty One Kinds of American Folk Art & How to Make Each One.
--Twenty-Three Varieties of Ethnic Art & How You Can Make Each One.
Kinney, Jean & Leaton, Gwen. Loosening the Grip: A Handbook of Alcohol Information.
--Understanding Alcohol.
Kinney, Ralph P. The Complete Book of Furniture Repair & Refinishing.
Kinnison, William A. Springfield & Clark County: An Illustrated History.
Kinsale, Laura. Hidden Heart.
Kinsbourne, Marcel & Caplan, Paula. Children's Learning & Attention Problems.
Kinsella, Paul L. The Techniques of Writing.
--The Techniques of Writing.
Kinsella, Thomas. One & Other Poems.
Kinsella, Thomas, tr. see Tuama, Sean O.
Kinsella, W. P. Shoeless Joe.
Kinser, Charlene. Sewing Sculpture: Sewn Art in Three Dimensions.
Kinsey, Alfred C., et al. Sexual Behavior in the Human Male.
Kinsey, Alfred C., Institute for Sex Research, Indiana University Staff. Sex Studies Index: 1980.
Kinsey, Bill. Creating Rural Employment.
Kinsey, Stephen A., et al. Five Manuscript Newspapers from Early Nevada.
Kinsman, Robert. Low Risk Profits in High Risk Times.
Kinssies, Richard. Seattle Epicure. Hosner, Sheila, ed.
Kintgen, Eugene R. The Perception of Poetry.
Kintner, Earl W. Primer on the Law of Mergers: A Guide for the Businessman.
Kintzer, Frederick C., ed. Improving Articulation & Transfer Relationships.
Kinzer, Bruce L. The Ballot Question in Nineteenth Century English Politics. Stansky, Peter & Hume, Leslie, eds.
Kinzer, Mark. Self-Image of a Christian: Humility & Self-Esteem.

--Taming the Tongue: Why Christians Should Care about What They Say.
Kinzer, Mark, jt. auth. see Ghezzi, Bert.
Kinzey, Bert. F-111 Aardvark in Detail & Scale.
Kip, Jan, jt. auth. see Knyff, Leonard.
Kiparsky, Carol, jt. auth. see Burt, Marina K.
Kipfer, Donald. Of Thee I Sing.
Kipling, Rudyard. Mowgli's Brothers.
--O Beloved Kids: Rudyard Kipling's Letters to His Children.
--Poems & Short Stories.
--Rikki-Tikki-Tavi.
--Second Jungle Book.
--The White Seal.
--The White Seal. Jones, Chuck, ed.
--The White Seal.
Kipnis, David. Character Structure & Impulsiveness.
--The Powerholders.
Kipnis, Gregory, jt. ed. see Fabozzi, Frank J.
Kipp, Thomas E. Starlight.
Kiralyfalvi, Bela. The Aesthetics of Gyorgy Lukacs.
Kirby, A., jt. auth. see Goodall, B.
Kirby, Dan & Liner, Tom. Inside Out: Developmental Strategies for Teaching Writing.
Kirby, Howard R., ed. Personal Travel Budgets.
Kirby, J. C. I Am Two from Kentucky: The Poetry of J. C. Kirby.
--Retrospect.
Kirby, Jack A. Estate Planner's Kit.
Kirby, James C., et al. Congress & the Public Trust: Report of the Association of the Bar of the City of New York - Special Committee on Congressional Ethics.
Kirby, Judy. Work After Work.
Kirby, Lee & Scarry, John. From Writers to Writing.
Kirby, Money Alian. Dr. Jesus Christ & the Sick World.
Kirby, Patricia. Cognitive Style, Learning Style & Transfer Skill Acquisition.
Kirby, Philippa. Creative Gift Wrapping.
--Creative Gift Wrapping: The Complete Guide to Techniques & Ideas.
Kirby, Ronald, et al. An Assessment of Short-Range Transit Planning in Selected U. S. Cities.
Kirby, Sandra. N. U. R. S. E. Nursing Undergraduate Review for Self Evaluation.
Kirby, Susan E. Ike & Porker.
Kirchberger, Michael. Quid Pro Quo: Equity & Claims of Money.
Kircher, John F. & Bowman, Richard E. Effects of Radiation on Materials & Components.
Kirchheimer, Otto. Political Justice: The Use of Legal Procedure for Political Ends.
Kirchmayer, L. K., jt. ed. see Hafele, W.
Kirchner, Corinne. Data on Blindness & Visual Impairment in the U. S. A. A Resource Manual on Characteristics, Education, Employment & Service Delivery.
Kirchner, Hubert. Luther & the Peasants' War. Anderson, Charles S., ed. Jodock, Darrell, tr. from Ger.
Kirchner, Paul. The Bus.
Kirchoff, Mary. Portrait in Blood.
--Vision of Doom.
Kirczenow, G., ed. see International School of Statistical Mechanics Staff.
Kireev, P. S. Semiconductor Physics.
Kiricuta, Ion. Use of the Omentum in Plastic Surgery.
Kirin, V. A., jt. auth. see Yevteyev, M.
Kirk, Eugene P. Menippean Satire: An Annotated Catalogue of Texts & Criticism.
Kirk, Gordon. The Core Curriculum.
Kirk, Gwyn, jt. auth. see Cook, Alice.
Kirk, Gwyneth. Urban Planning in a Capitalist Society.
Kirk, J. Andrew. Liberation Theology: An Evangelical View from the Third World.
Kirk, John E. Enzymes of the Arterial Wall.
Kirk, Kris & Heath, Ed. Men in Frocks.
Kirk, Malcolm. Man As Art.
Kirk, Mildred. The Everlasting Cat.
Kirk, Philip. Hydra Conspiracy.
--Killer Satellites.
--Love Me to Death.
--The Slayboys.
--Smart Bombs.
Kirk, R. M. Basic Surgical Techniques.
Kirk, R. M., et al. Surgery: A Textbook for Students.
Kirk, Ruth. David, Young Chief of the Quileutes: An American Indian Today.
--Desert: The American Southwest.
--Sigemi: A Japanese Village Girl.
--Yellowstone: The First National Park.
Kirk, Samuel A. & Gallagher, James J. Educating Exceptional Children.
--Educating Exceptional Children.
Kirk, Samuel A. & Lord, Francis E. Exceptional Children: Educational Resources & Perspectives.
Kirk, Samuel A. & McCarthy, Jeanne M. Learning Disabilities: Selected ACLD Papers.
Kirk, Samuel A., et al. Teaching Reading to Slow & Disabled Learners.
Kirk, Stephen J., jt. auth. see Dell'Isola, Alphonse.
Kirk, W. Richard. Exploring Careers in Hospital & Health Services Administration.
Kirkaldy, J. F. General Principles of Geology.
Kirkaldy, J. S., ed. see TMS Staff & AIME Staff.
Kirkby, D. One Hundred Questions in Auditing with Suggested Answers for Accountancy Examinees.
Kirkemo, Ronald B. An Introduction to International Law.
Kirkendall, Richard S. United States, Nineteen Twenty-Nine to Nineteen Forty-Five: Years of Crisis & Change.
Kirkendall, Tom & Spring, Vicky. Cross-Country Ski Trails of Washington's Cascades & Olympics.
Kirk-Greene, Anthony. A Biographical Dictionary of the British Colonial Governor, Vol. 1: Africa.
Kirk-Greene, C. W. E. French False Friends.
Kirkham, Margaret. Jane Austen, Feminism & Fiction.
Kirkham, Pat, jt. auth. see Hayward, Helena.
Kirkland, Caroline. A New Home - Who'll Follow? Glimpses of Western Life.
Kirkland, Dianna C. & Morris-Vann, Artie M. Understanding Loss.
Kirkland, Edward C. History of American Economic Life.
Kirkland, James W. & Sanders, F. David. Poetry: Sight & Insight.
Kirkland, John. Crying & Babies: Helping Families Cope.
Kirklin, John W. & Barratt-Boyes, Brian G. Cardiac Surgery: Morphology, Diagnostic Criteria, Natural History, Techniques, Results & Indications.
Kirkman, J., et al, eds. Common Ground: Shared Interests in ESP & Communication Studies.
Kirkman, John, jt. auth. see Turk, Christopher.
Kirkpatrick, C. A., jt. auth. see Littlefield, James E.
Kirkpatrick, Charles A., jt. auth. see Russ, Frederick A.
Kirkpatrick, Charles H. & Burger, Denis R., eds. Immunobiology of Transfer Factor.
Kirkpatrick, D. L., ed. Contemporary Dramatists.
Kirkpatrick, David W. Tuition Vouchers: Adam Smith to Ronald Reagan.
Kirkpatrick, Diane, ed. see Campbell, Russell.
Kirkpatrick, Diane, ed. see Caton, Joseph H.
Kirkpatrick, Donald L. Managing Change.
Kirkpatrick, Frank. Permits, Licenses, & Registrations: New England Edition. Griffith, Roger, ed.
Kirkpatrick, Jeane J. Dictatorships & Double Standards: Rationalism & Reason in Politics.
--Dictatorships & Double Standards: Rationalism & Reason in Politics.
Kirkpatrick, John E., ed. see Ives, Charles E.
Kirkpatrick, Samuel A. & Pettit, Lawrence K. Legislative Role Structures, Power Bases & Behavior Patterns: An Empirical Examination of the U. S. Senate.
--Sources of Organizational & Personal Power in the U. S. Senate: A Test of Alternative Models.
Kirkup, James, tr. see Davis, A. R.
Kirkup, James, tr. see Durrenmatt, Friedrich.
Kirkup, James, tr. see Kpomassie, Tete-Michel.
Kirkwood, Evelyne M. & Lewis, Catriona J. Understanding Medical Immunology.
Kirkwood, James. Good Times, Bad Times.
--There Must Be a Pony.
Kirkwood, Kenneth P. Renaissance in Japan: A Cultural Survey of the Seventeenth Century.
Kirkwood, R. C., jt. auth. see Fletcher, W. W.
Kirlin, John, jt. ed. see Levitt, Rachelle.
Kirman, B. H. Mental Retardation.
Kirman, Brian H. The Mentally Handicapped Child.
Kirn, Elaine, ed. Regents Illustrated Classics Series.
Kirpal, Prem. Voices from the Deep.
Kirpatrick, Donald L. How to Plan & Conduct Productive Business Meetings.
Kirsch, Johann P. Heilige Caecilia in der Roemischen Kirche Des Altertums.
Kirsch, Paul J. We Christians & Jews.
Kirschbaum, Leo. Character & Characterization in Shakespeare.
Kirschenbaum, Howard & Glaser, Barbara. Developing Support Groups: A Manual for Facilitators & Participants.
Kirschenbaum, Michael A., jt. ed. see Bricker, Neal S.
Kirschenblaum. Lifnim Meshurat Hadin.
Kirschke, James J. Henry James & Impressionism.
Kirschman, John C., jt. ed. see Ayres, John C.
Kirschner, Becky, jt. auth. see Wendling, Becky.
Kirschner, E. & Stone, K. M. Electronics Drafting Workbook.
Kirschner, Joseph, et al, eds. Background Studies for History of Education.
Kirsner, Gary. The Mettlach Book: Illustrated Catalog, Current Prices, & Collector's Information. Gruhl, Jim, ed.
Kirsner, Laura T. & Taetzsch, Lyn. Practical Accounting for Small Businesses.
Kirsop, B. E., ed. The Stability of Industrial Organisms.
Kirst, J., ed. Electronic Publishing.
Kirsten, W. H., ed. Malignant Transformation by Viruses.
Kirsten, W. H., jt. ed. see Grundmann, E.
Kirszner, Laurie G. & Mandell, Stephen R. The Holt Handbook.
--Writing: A College Rhetoric.
--Writing: A College Rhetoric, Brief Edition.
Kirtland, G. B. One Day in Aztec Mexico.
Kirtland, Terry & Cromblehome, Roger. Steam British Isles: Minor & Miniature Railway Preservation.
Kirts, Donald K., jt. auth. see Powell, C Randall.
Kirwan, J. R., ed. see Danielou, Jean.
Kirwan, W. E. & Zalcman, L., eds. Advances in Complex Function Theory.
Kirwen, Michael C. African Widows.
Kirwin, Gerald J. & Grodzinsky, Stephen. Basic Circuit Analysis.
Kirzner, Israel M., ed. Method, Process & Austrian Economics: Essays in Honor of Ludwig von Mises.
Kis. Tomb for Boris Daviovch.
Kis, Danilo. Garden, Ashes.
--Garden, Ashes. Hannaher, William J., tr.
--Sandglass. Alcalay, Ammiel & Alcalay, Klara, trs. from Serbo-Croatian.
Kisch, Guido, ed. Pseudo-Philo's Liber Antiquitatum Biblicarum.
--Sachsenspiegel & Bible.
Kiseliov, V. A., et al. Mecanica De Construccion En Ejemplos y Problemas.
Kiser, Wayne. Getting More Out of Church.
Kish, George. Bibliography of International Geographical Congresses, 1871-1976.
Kish, Joseph L. Office Management Problem Solver.
Kish, Joseph L, Jr. Word Processing in the Transitional Office.
Kishel, Gregory F. & Kishel, Patricia G. Dollars on Your Doorstep: The Complete Guide to Home-Based Businesses.
Kishel, Patricia G., jt. auth. see Kishel, Gregory F.
Kishtainy, Khalid W., tr. see Hussein, Saddam.
Kiskaddon, Bruce. Rhymes of the Ranges: A New Collection of the Poems of Bruce Kiskaddon. Cannon, Hal, intro. by.
Kislan, Richard. Hoofing on Broadway: A History of Show Dancing.
Kismaric, Susan. Jan Groover.
Kiso, Akiko. The Lost Sophocles.
Kisseberth, Charles, jt. auth. see Kenstowicz, Michael.
Kisseberth, Charles W., ed. see Urbana Conference on Phonology Staff.
Kisselbach, Theo. Leica CL.
--Leica R-4 Reflex Manual.
Kissinger, Henry A. American Foreign Policy.
--American Foreign Policy: Three Essays.
--For the Record: Selected Statements, 1977 to 1980.
Kissling, Chris, et al, eds. Regional Impacts of Resource Developments.
Kisslo, Joseph, et al, eds. Basis Doppler Echocardiography.
Kister, Kenneth F. Encyclopedia Buying Guide: A Consumer Guide to General Encyclopedia in Print.
Kistler, Don, ed. God's Numbers in Creation, Vol. 1.
Kistler, Richard C. The High Plains Route. Reisdorff, James J., ed.
--The Wymore Story. Reisdorff, James J., ed.
Kistler, Robert. Adventists & Labor Unions in the U. S. Wheeler, Gerald, ed.
Kistner, Robert W., jt. auth. see Patton, Grant W.
Kitahara, S. Interior: S. Kitahara's Modernism.
Kitaigorodsky, A. I. Physics for Everyone: Electrons.
--Physics for Everyone: Photons & Nuclei.
Kitaigorodsky, A. I., jt. auth. see Landau, L.
Kitakoji, Isamitsu, jt. auth. see Fields, Dorothy.
Kitamura, Hiroshi. Psychological Dimensions of U. S.-Japanese Relations.
Kitamura, Satoshi. Paper Jungle.
Kitano, Harry H. Japanese Americans: Evolution of a Subculture.
Kitazono, Oki, ed. Directory of Nature Centers & Related Environmental Education Facilities, 1979.
Kitchen, Jo & Davidson, Rebecca. Shop & Dine.
Kitchen, Margaret. Grandmother Goes up the Mountain.
Kitchen, Martin. A Military History of Germany: From the 18th Century to the Present Day.
Kitchen, Paddy. Gerard Manley Hopkins.
Kitching, J. A; see Dangeard, P.
Kitching, R. L., jt. auth. see Matthews, E. G.
Kitson, Harry D. & Stover, Edgar M. Vocations for Boys.
Kitson, Harry D., jt. auth. see Lingenfelter, Mary R.
Kittel, Charles. Elementary Statistical Physics.
Kittelson, James M. Luther the Reformer: The Story of the Man & His Career.
Kittlaus, Paul, jt. auth. see Leas, Speed.
Kittle, James L. Home Plumbing Made Easy: An Illustrated Manual.
--Mastering Household Electrical Wiring.
Kittredge, George L. Witchcraft in Old & New England.
Kittredge, Henry C. Cape Cod: Its People & Their History.
Kittross, John M., jt. auth. see Sterling, Christopher H.
Kitts, David B. The Structure of Geology.
Kitzing, Donald R. Credit & Collections for Small Business: An Easy-to-Read Guide to Effective Collections.
Kitzinger, Ernst. The Art of Byzantium & the Medieval West: Selected Studies. Kleinbauer, W. Eugene, ed.
Kitzinger, Sheila. The Experience of Breastfeeding.
--The Experience of Childbirth.
Kitzinger, U. The Second Try: Labour & the EEC.
Kitzman, Elizabeth. A Chosen Vessel: The Story of the Very Reverend Harold G. Plume.
Kiver & Kaufman. Television Simplified.
Kiver, Milton S. Transistor & Integrated Electronics.
Kiver, Milton S., jt. auth. see Grob, Bernard.
Kivy, Peter. The Corded Shell: Reflections on Musical Expression.
Kjelgaard, Jim. Boomerang Hunter.
Kjellberg, Pierre. Art deco Les Maitres du Mobilier.
Klaften, E. B. & Allison, F. C. German-English, English-German Patent Terminological Dictionary.
Klager, Karl, jt. ed. see Boyars, Carl.
Klagsbrun, Francine. Freedom Now.
Klahr, David & Wallace, J. F. Cognitive Development: An Information-Processing View.
Klaiman, Henry S. & Chirls, Richard. Tax-Exempt Financing of Non-Governmental Projects.
Klais, Hans G. Reflections on the Organ Stoplist: Theory & Practice from the Organ Workshop. Blanchard, Homer D., tr. from Ger.
Klammer, Enno. Paragraph Sense: A Basic Rhetoric.
--Sentence Sense: A Basic Grammar.
Klammer, Enno, jt. auth. see Willis, Hulon.
Klapisch-Zuber, Christiane. Women, Family, & Ritual in Renaissance Italy. Cochrane, Lydia G., tr. from Fr.
Klapper, Jacob & Frankle, John T. Phase Lock & Frequency Feedback Systems: Principles & Techniques.
Klapper, Marvin. Textile Glossary.
Klapthor, Margaret B. First Ladies.
Klare, H. J. & Haxby, D., eds. Frontiers of Criminology.
Klare, Michael T. Resurgent Militarism.
Klaren, Peter F. Modernization, Dislocation, & Aprismo: Origins of the Peruvian Aprista Party, 1870-1932.
Klarner, David A., ed. Mathematical Gardner.
--The Mathematical Gardner.
Klarner, Walter E., et al. Writing by Design.
Klasen, Edith. Audio-Visual-Motor Training with Pattern Cards.
Klass, Donald L., ed. Biomass As a Nonfossil Fuel Source.
Klassen, William. Love of Enemies: The Way to Peace.
Klassen, William, tr. see Hengel, Martin.
Klatt, Lawrence. Managing the Dynamic Small Firm: Readings.
Klatzkin. Thesaurus Philosophicus Linguae Hebraica.
Klatzo, I., ed. see Brain Edema Symposium Staff.
Klauder, Francis J. The Wonder of the Real: A Sketch in Basic Philosophy.
Klavan, Kate D. American Period Interiors in Miniature.
Kleberger, Ilse. Grandmother Oma.
Klechkovskii, V. M., et al. Radioecology.
Kleczek, Josip. Astronomical Dictionary: In Six Languages.
Klee, Gary A., ed. World Systems of Traditional Resources Management.
Klee, James B. Points of Departure: Aspects of the Tao.
Kleefeld, Carolyn M. Lovers in Evolution.
--Satan Sleeps with the Holy: Word Paintings.
Kleege, Georgina, tr. see Adnan, Etel.
Kleek, Peter E. Van see Van Kleek, Peter E.
Kleek, Peter Van see Van Kleek, Peter.
Kleeman, Charles R., jt. ed. see Maxwell, Morton H.
Kleeman, Leonard. Handbook of Real Estate Mathematics.
Kleeman, Walter B. The Challenge of Interior Design.
Kleeman, Walter B., Jr. The Challenge of Interior Design.
Kleen, Werner J. Electronics of Microwave Tubes. Lindsay, P. A., et al, trs.

Authors

Kleiber, A. W. German-English, English-German Welding Engineering Dictionary.
Kleiber, Michael, jt. auth. see Krummes, Daniel.
Kleiber, Michael C. & Hetu, Sylvie. Sources of Information in Transportation: Part 9, Urban Transportation.
Kleiman, S., jt. auth. see Altmann, A.
Klein, Aaron E. You & Your Body.
Klein, Barbara & Roscow, Judith. Dining In - Pittsburgh.
Klein, Barry. Electronic Music Circuits.
Klein, Benjamin. The Collector's Illustrated Price Guide to Russel Wright Dinnerware.
Klein, Carol. Credo of Maimonides.
Klein, Carole. The Single Parent Experience.
Klein, Charlotte. Anti-Judaism in Christian Theology. Quinn, Edward, tr.
Klein, Dan & Lloyd, Ward, eds. The History of Glass.
Klein, Dave. Vince Lombardi.
--The Vince Lombardi Story.
Klein, David & Klein, Marymae E. Yourself Ten Years from Now: A Career Planning Guide.
Klein, David, jt. auth. see Hughes, Theodore E.
Klein, Dennis A. Peter & Anthony Shaffer: A Reference Guide.
Klein, Don. Help! I Just Found Out I'm a Pig!
Klein, Donald A. Environmental Impacts of Artificial Ice Nucleating Agents.
Klein, Donald F., jt. auth. see Wender, Paul H.
Klein, E. Roseland & Klein, Peter D., eds. Stable Isotopes: Proceedings of the Third International Conference.
Klein, Elizabeth. Reconciliations.
Klein, Fred. The Bisexual Option.
--The Bisexual Option: A Concept of One Hundred Percent Intimacy.
Klein, George & Weinhouse, Sidney, eds. Advances in Cancer Research.
Klein, Gerda. The Blue Rose.
Klein, Gerda W. Promise of a New Spring: The Holocaust & Renewal.
Klein, Gordon L., jt. ed. see Coburn, Jack W.
Klein, H. Arthur, jt. ed. see Klein, Nina C.
Klein, H. P. & Korneck, G., eds. Life Sciences & Space Research XXI (1) Proceedings of the Topical Meeting of the COSPAR Interdisciplinary Scientific Commission F (Meetings F4 & F8) of the COSPAR 25th Plenary Meeting held in Graz, Austria 25 June-7 July 1984.
Klein, Henry. Through Ferrengi Eyes: The Diary of a Peace Corps Volunteer in Ethiopia, 1974-1976.
Klein, Herbert. The Middle Passage: Comparative Studies in the Atlantic Slave Trade.
Klein, Irving. I Remember My Brother Morris.
Klein, Jack. Mod-4.
Klein, Jacob. Plato's Trilogy: Theaetetus, the Sophist & the Statesman.
--Plato's Trilogy: Theaetetus, the Sophist, & the Statesman.
--Royal Hymns of Shulgi, King of Ur: Man's Quest for Immortal Fame.
Klein, James P. Tax Effective Total Compensation: Using 401(K) & 125 Plans.
Klein, John J. Money & the Economy.
Klein, K. E., jt. auth. see Basic Environmental Problems of Man in Space II, International Symposium Staff.
Klein, L. R. & Krelle, W. E., eds. Capital Flows & Exchange Rate Determination.
Klein, Lawrence R. & Young, Richard M., eds. An Introduction to Econometric Forecasting & Forecasting Models.
Klein, M. L. & Venables, J. A., eds. Rare Gas Solids.
--Rare Gas Solids.
Klein, Marcus. After Alienation: American Novels in Mid-Century.
Klein, Marion H. Dynamics of Comprehension: How to Learn from a College Textbook.
Klein, Marymae E., jt. auth. see Klein, David.
Klein, Maxine. Time: Space & Designs for Actors.
Klein, Nancy & Heymann, Jaia, eds. Directory of Government Document Collections & Librarians.
Klein, Nina C. & Klein, H. Arthur, eds. The Kidnapped Saint & Other Stories by B. Traven.
Klein, Norma. Blue Trees, Red Sky.
--Hiding.
--A Honey of a Chimp.
--Mom, the Wolf Man & Me.
--The Queen of the What Ifs.
--Taking Sides.
Klein, Peter D., jt. ed. see Klein, E. Roseland.
Klein, R. Duelli, ed. Rethinking Sisterhood: Unity in Diversity.
Klein, Ralph W. Textual Criticism of the Old Testament: The Septuagint After Qumran. Tucker, Gene M., ed.
Klein, Raymond L., jt. auth. see Clark, Leonard H.
Klein, Renate D. see Arditti, Rita, et al.
Klein, Richard B., ed. see Calvo-Sotelo, Joaquin.
Klein, Richard G., jt. ed. see Martin, Paul S.
Klein, Robert E., et al, eds. Evaluating the Impact of Nutrition & Health Programs.
Klein, Roger & Wolman, William. The Beat Inflation Strategy.
Klein, Sidney. The Economics of Mass Migration in the Twentieth Century.
Klein, Stanley J. How to Avoid Products Liability: A Management Guide.
Klein, Stuart M. & Ritti, Richard R. Understanding Organizational Behavior.
Klein, Ted & Danzig, Fred. Publicity: How to Make the Media Work for You.
Klein, Thomas, et al, eds. Biological Response Modifiers in Human Oncology & Immunology.
Klein, William. William Klein: Photographs. Heilpern, John, ed.
Klein, Zev. Integrating Jerusalem Schools.
Kleinbard, Peter, jt. auth. see Dollar, Bruce.
Kleinbauer, W. Eugene, ed. see Kitzinger, Ernst.
Kleinberg, Susan B. Educating the Chronically Ill Child.
Kleinberger, A. F. Society, Schools & Progress in Israel.
Kleinberger, G. & Deutsch, E., eds. New Aspects of Clinical Nutrition.
Kleindienst, Richard G. Justice: The Memoirs of Attorney General Richard Kleindienst.
Kleinenberg, S. E., et al. Beluga: Investigation of the Species.
Kleinfield, Sonny. The Biggest Company on Earth: A Profile of AT&T.
--The Biggest Company on Earth: A Profile of AT&T.
--The Traders.
--The Traders.
Klein-Helmuth, Barbara C., compiled by. AAAS Annual Meeting Abstracts of Papers: 154th National Meeting, 1988.
Klein-Helmuth, Barbara C. & Savold, David, eds. AAAS Annual Meeting Abstracts of Papers: 153rd National Meeting, 1987.
Kleinman, Carol. Women's Networks.
Kleinpenning, J. M., jt. auth. see Reitsma, H. A.
Kleinpoppen, H. & MacDowell, M. R., eds. Electron & Photon Interactions with Atoms.
Kleinsmith, Lewis J., ed. see Symposium, University of Florida, Gainsville Staff.
Kleinsorge, Paul L., ed. Public Finance & Welfare: Essays in Honor of C. Ward Macy.
Kleist, Friedrich Von see Weiss, Samuel A.
Kleitman, Nathaniel. Sleep & Wakefulness.
Klejment, Anne. The Berrigans: A Bibliography of Published Works by Daniel, Philip, & Elizabeth Berrigan.
Klem, Herbert V. Oral Communication of the Scripture: Insights from African Oral Art.
Klemanov, Y. Racing Driver's Diary.
Klement, A. W. & Schultz, V., eds. Freshwater & Terrestrial Radioecology: A Selected Bibliography.
Klemm, W. R. Animal Electroencephalography.
--Applied Electronics for Veterinary Medicine & Animal Physiology.
Klemme, Marvin. Home Rule on the Range: Early Days of the Grazing Service.
Klemperer, D., tr. see Welder, G.
Klemperer, Katharina. Bibliographic Specifications for Consolidation of Records.
Klemperer, Katharina & Berger, Michael. University of California Prototype On-Line Catalog: Preliminary Specifications for the Patron Interface.
Klemperer, Katharina & D'Ambrosio, Bruce. University of California Union Catalog-Conversion of Catalog Cards to Machine-Readable Form: Phase I-Bibliographic Characteristics of University of California Cataloging.
Klemperer, Katharina & Shih, Kitty M. University of California Union Catalog: Conversion of Catalog Cards to Machine-Readable Form, Phase III-Comparison Study of Existing Data Bases for the Use of Retrospective Conversion.
Klemperer, Otto. Klemperer on Music: Shavings from a Musician's Workbench.
Klen, R. Biological Principles of Tissue Banking.
Kleppe, Kjell, jt. ed. see Seeberg, Erling.
Kleppner, Daniel & Pipkin, Francis M., eds. Atomic Physics 7.
Kleppner, Paul & Burnham, Walter D. The Evolution of American Electoral Systems.
Klerer, Melvin & Reinfelds, Juris, eds. Interactive Systems for Experimental Applied Mathematics.
Klett, Mark, et al. Traces of Eden: Travels in the Desert Northwest.
Klever, Eva & Klever, Ulrich. The Big Book of Fondues.
Klever, Ulrich, jt. auth. see Klever, Eva.
Klewin, Jean & Klewin, Thomas. When the Man You Love Is an Alcoholic.
Klewin, Thomas, jt. auth. see Klewin, Jean.
Kliban, B. Catcalendar Cats.
--Whack Your Porcupine & Other Drawings.
Klibanov, A. I. History of Religious Sectarianism in Russia (1860s-1917) Dunn, Stephen P., ed.
Klibansky, Raymond, ed. see Hume, David.
Klibbe, Lawrence. Monarch Notes on Hemingway's Farewell to Arms.
Klicic, Fadila. It's Fun to Be in Love with an Older Man.
Klickstein, H. S., jt. auth. see Duveen, Dennis I.
Kliebard, Herbert M. The Struggle for the American Curriculum 1893-1958.
Klien, Carole. Mothers & Sons.
Kliever, Lonnie. H. Richard Niebuhr.
Kligman, A. M., jt. auth. see Plewig, G.
Kliiver, Billy & Martin, Julie. Kiki's Paris: Artists & Lovers (Nineteen Hundred to Nineteen Thirty)
Klijnsmit, A. J. Spinoza & Grammatical Tradition.
Klima, Slava, ed. see Spence, Joseph.
Kliman, Gilbert W. & Rosenfeld, Albert. Responsible Parenthood.
Klimisch, Richard L. & Larson, John G., eds. The Catalytic Chemistry of Nitrogen Oxides.
Klimisch, Richard L., jt. ed. see Wolff, George T.
Klimo, Kate, ed. Animals at the Zoo.
--Animals in the Country.
--Animals in the Jungle.
--Animals of the Ocean.
--Animals on the Farm.
--Fly Away with E. T.
--Little Simon ABC.
--Look at Plants with E.T.
--Meet Baby Animals with E. T.
Klimo, Kate, ed. see Alda, Arlene.
Klimo, Kate, ed. see Disney Studios & Disney, Walt.
Klimo, Kate, ed. see Disney, Walt, Productions Staff.
Klimo, Kate, ed. see Henry, Lawrence.
Klimo, Kate, ed. see Knights, Roger.
Klimo, Kate, ed. see Marshall, Ray & Paul, Korky.
Klimo, Kate, ed. see Moskowitz, Stewart.
Klimo, Kate, ed. see Pienkowski, Jan.
Klimo, Kate, ed. see Schongut, Emanuel.
Klimo, Kate, ed. see Smith, Frank.
Klimo, Kate, ed. see Yeatman, Linda.
Klimontovich, Yu L. The Statistical Theory of Non-Equilibrium Processes in a Plasma.
Klimova, V. A. Basic Methods of Organic Microanalysis.
Kline, Draza & Overstreet, Helen-Mary F. Foster Care of Children: Nurture & Treatment.
Kline, Frank M., jt. auth. see Grotjahn, Martin.
Kline, Harvey F., jt. auth. see Wiarda, Howard.
Kline, Herbert, ed. New Theatre & Film 1934 to 1937: An Anthology.
--New Theatre & Film 1934 to 1937: An Anthology.
Kline, John B., et al. Managing the Small Business.
Kline, John M. State Government Influence in U. S. International Economic Policy.
Kline, Katy & Dreishpoon, Douglas. Natural Forms & Forces: Abstract Images in American Sculpture.
Kline, Katy & Lajer-Burcharth, Ewa. Counter Monuments: Krzysztof Wodiczko's Public Projections.
Kline, Katy, et al. Peter Fischli David Weiss.
Kline, Lanning B., rev. by. Neuro-Ophthamology Review Manual.
Kline, Paul. Fact & Fantasy in Freudian Theory.
Kline, Peter. Theatre Student: Diary of Producing a Play.
--The Theatre Student: Gilbert & Sullivan Production.
Kline, Robert D., jt. ed. see Murphy, Thomas P.
Klineberg, I. & Sessle, B., eds. Oro-Facial Pain & Neuromuscular Dysfunction: Mechanisms & Clinical Correlates.
Klineburger, Bert & Hurst, Vernon W. Big Game Hunting Around the World.
Kling, Bill. The ABC's of Lotus 1-2-3: A Step-by-Step Guide.
Klingaman, David C. Study Guide for Auerbach Money, Banking, & Financial Markets.
Klinge, E., ed. Receptors & Cellular Pharmacology: Proceedings of the 6th International Congress of Pharmacology, Helsinki, 1975.
Klingel, Cynthia & Zadra, Dan. Francis Marion.
--Kit Carson.
Klingenberg, M., jt. ed. see Schaefer, G.
Klinger, Bernd, ed. Rifle Shooting As a Sport.
Klinger, Chad. It's How You Play the Game.
Klinger, Fred. Mathematics for Everyone.
Klinger, Georgette & Rowes, Barbara. Georgette Klinger's Skincare.
Klinger, H. P., et al, eds. Chromosome Mutations: Their Potential Relevance to the Genetic Risks in Man.
Klinger, Kathryn. Kathryn Klinger's First Book of Beauty.
Klinger, M., tr. see Schiefer, W., et al.
Klinger, M. I. Problems of Linear Electron Transport Theory in Semiconductors.
Klinger, Ron. Basic Bridge.
--Guide to Better Acol Bridge.
Klinghammer, Erich. The Behavior & Ecology of Wolves.
Klingman, Mildred. The Secret Lives of Fat People.
Klingner, Donald E. Public Personnel Management: Contexts & Strategies.
Klingstedt, John P. & Brock, Horace R. Oil & Gas Taxation Nineteen Eighty-Six.
Klink, J. L. Bible for Children, with Songs & Plays, Vol. 2: New Testament. Crampton, Patricia, tr.
Klink, J. L., ed. Bible for Children, with Songs & Plays, Vol. I, Vol. II: Old Testament, New Testament.
Klink, Johanna. Teaching Children to Pray.
Klink, William. Maxwell Anderson & S. N. Behrman: A Reference Guide.
Klinke, R., jt. ed. see Gruesser, O. J.
Klinzing, James E., jt. auth. see Melograno, Vincent J.
Kliore, A., ed. The Mars Reference Atmosphere.
Kliore, A. J., et al, eds. The Venus International Reference Atmosphere.
Klipping, Gustav & Klipping, Ingrid, eds. Proceedings of the Eleventh International Cryogenic Engineering Conference.
Klipping, Ingrid, jt. ed. see Klipping, Gustav.
Klitz, J. Kenneth. North Sea Oil: Resource Requirements for U. K. Development.
Klitzman, Maurice H. Patent Interference: Law & Practice.
Klitzner, Carol & Klitzner, Herb. Help Your Child Succeed with a Computer: Choosing & Using the Right Computer for Your Child.
Klitzner, Herb, jt. auth. see Klitzner, Carol.
Klochek, V. I. Soviet Foreign Trade: Today & Tomorrow.
Klochkovski, L., ed. Economia de los Paises Latinoamericanos.
Klock, P. Joseph. The Home Team: BA-II & You, Berlin, Helene, ed.
Kloe, Donald R. A Dictionary of Onomatopoeic Sounds, Tones, & Noises in English & Spanish.
Kloefkorn, William. Not Such a Bad Place to Be.
Kloepfel, Don V., ed. Motion Picture Projection & Theatre Presentation Manual.
Kloepfer, Marguerite. But Where Is Love.
--The Heart & the Scarab.
Klohn, LaVonne, jt. auth. see Young, Robert.
Klonglan, Gerald E. & Nan Lo, Chun. Communication Policy & Planning: A Case Study of the American Cancer Society Public Education Program.
Kloomok, Isaac. Marc Chagall.
Klopf, Donald W. & Cambra, Ronald E. Personal & Public Speaking.
Klopfenstein, Charles E. & Wilkins, Charles L., eds. Computers in Chemical & Biochemical Research.
Kloppenburg, Bonaventure. Ecclesiology of Vatican II.
Klopper, A., et al, eds. The Human Placenta: Proteins & Hormones.
--Research on Steroids.
Klores, Dan. Roundball Culture: South Carolina Basketball.
Klos, J., jt. auth. see Wittman, A.
Klos, Sarah. Prayers: Alone, Together.
Klose, Kevin. Russia & the Russians: Inside the Closed Society.
Klossowski, Pierre. Roberte Ce Soir & The Revocation of the Edict of Nantes. Wainhouse, Austryn, tr.
Klott, Gary L. & New York Times Staff. The New York Times Guide to the New Tax Law.
Klotz, Alfred. Appians Darstellung Des Zweiten Punischen Krieges.
Klotz, Ester & Lawton, H. A History of Citrus in the Riverside Area.
Klotz, J. A Christian View of Abortion.
Klotz, Lynn C., jt. auth. see Sylvester, Edward J.
Kloudova, B. & Stakeova, V., eds. Czech-English Technical Dictionary.
Klousky, D. A. Sequential Transmission of Digital Information.
Kluckhohn, Clyde M. To the Foot of the Rainbow.
Klug, Eugene F. Getting into the Formula of Concord.
Klug, John R. The Complete Guide to Running a Business.
Klug, Lyn, jt. auth. see Klug, Ron.
Klug, Ron. Growing in Joy: God's Way to Increase Joy in All of Life.
Klug, Ron & Klug, Lyn. Family Prayers.
--I'm a Good Helper.
--My Christmas ABC Book.
--Please, God: Prayers for Young Children.
--Thank You, God: Prayers for Young Children.
Klug, Ronald. Following Christ: Prayers from Imitation of Christ.
--My Prayer Journal.
Klug, W., et al, eds. Air Pollution-Health & Management: Proceedings of the Joint IIASA-WHO-EURO Workshop, Laxenburg, Austria, 27-30 July, 1982. Suess, M. J.
Klug, W., et al, eds. see Deutsche Gesellschaft Fuer Neurochirurgie Staff.
Kluger, Marilyn. The Joy of Spinning.
--Wild Flavor.
Kluger, Phyllis. Victorian Designs for Needlepoint.
Klushansev, P. All about the Telescope.
Kluver, Heinrich. Mescal & Mechanisms of Hallucinations.
Kluver, Heinrich, ed. see Polyak, Stephen.
Kluyeva, Elena. Svetoten: Poems.
Kluz, Carol. Aura of Roses.

Authors

Klyachko, Y. A., jt. auth. see Lyalikov, Y. S.
Klyde. I Paint with Words...Hope You Like My Pictures.
Klyne, W., jt. ed. see Cross, L. C.
Kmetz, A. R. & Von Willisen, F. K., eds. Nonemissive Electro-Optic Displays.
Knacke, O., jt. auth. see Barin, I.
Knaff, Jean C. Figures.
Knafl, Kathleen A. & Grace, Helen K. Families Across the Life Cycle.
Knafl, Kathleen A., jt. auth. see Kviz, Frederick J.
Knapik, Harold. Knapik Cookbook.
Knapp, B. J. Soil Processes.
Knapp, Bettina L. Contemporary French Theater.
--French Theatre 1918-1939. King, Bruce & King, Adele, eds.
--French Theatre 1918-1939. King, Bruce & King, Adele, eds.
Knapp, Clyde G. & Jewett, Ann E. Physical Education Student Teaching Guide.
Knapp, E. J. The Great Golden Gate Bridge Trivia Book: A Half-Century Compendium of Astounding Facts, Superlative Statistics & Fanciful Lore.
Knapp, Gottfried, ed. Helmut Pfeuffer: Trauma & Drama.
Knapp, Herbert & Knapp, Mary. Red, White, & Blue Paradise: The American Canal Zone.
Knapp, Herbert, jt. auth. see Knapp, Mary.
Knapp, James F. Ezra Pound.
Knapp, James I., et al. Prosecutorial Discretion.
Knapp, Sr. Justina. Christian Symbols & How to Use Them.
Knapp, Mark L. Social Intercourse: From Greeting to Goodbye.
Knapp, Mary & Knapp, Herbert. One Potato, Two Potato: The Secret Education of American Children.
Knapp, Mary, jt. auth. see Knapp, Herbert.
Knapp, Ron. From Prison to the Major Leagues: The Picture Story of Ron Leflore.
Knapp, Ruediger. Gegenseitige Beeinflussung und Temperatur-Wirkung bei tropischen und subtropischen Pflanzen: Bericht ueber neue experimentelle Untersuchungen an Nutzpflanzen und Arten der spontanen Vegetation.
Knapp, W. Unity & Nationalism in Europe since 1945.
Knapp, Wilfred, jt. auth. see Drabek, Anne G.
Knappert, Jan. Malay Myths & Legends.
Knapton, J. & Evans, B. Teaching a Literature-Centered English Program.
Knaster, Scott. How to Write Mac Software.
Knauer, Karl. Bertelsmann Woerterbuch Deutsch-Franzoesisch, Franzoesisch-Deutsch.
Knaupp, Jonathan, et al. Patterns & Systems of Elementary Mathematics.
Knaus, William J., jt. auth. see Ellis, Albert.
Knebel, Fletcher. Poker Game.
Knecht, Ken, jt. auth. see Miller, Merl.
Kneedler & Dodge. Perioperative Patient Care: The Nursing Perspective.
Knell, Heiner. Ullstein Lexikon der Kunst und Architektur.
Kneller, E., jt. ed. see Berkowitz, A. E.
Kneller, George F. The Education of the Mexican Nation.
--Existentialism & Education.
--Logic & Language of Education.
--Movements of Thought in Modern Education.
Kneller, Richard, jt. auth. see Dobkins, David H.
Knepper, William E. & Bailey, Dan A. Liability of Corporate Officers & Directors with 1985 Supplement.
Kneubuhl, F. K. & Moss, T. S., eds. Infrared Physics Three: Papers from the Third International Conference (CIRP 3) Held in Zurich, Switzerland, 23-27 July 1984.
Kneubuhl, Fritz, ed. International Conference on Infrared Physics, 2nd, (CIRP 2), Zurich, 1979.
Knevitt, Charles. Space on Earth: Architecture: People & Buildings.
Knibb, David G. West's Federal Court of Appeals Manual: 1986 Pocket Part.
Knickerbocker, Charles, ed. see Cuffee, James W.
Knickerbocker, Charles H., ed. & intro. by see Cutler, G. Ripley.
Knickerbocker, K. L. & Reninger, H. W. Interpreting Literature: Preliminaries to Literary Judgment.
Knickerbocker, William, ed. Twentieth Century English.
Knief, Ronald A. Nuclear Energy Technology.
Kniesner, Thomas J., jt. auth. see Fleisher, Belton M.
Knight, et al, eds. see Energy Resources Center Staff.
Knight, Alanna. Lament for Lost Lovers.
Knight, Albion. Chariots of God: Biblical Blueprints on Defense.
Knight, Allen W. & Simmons, Mary Ann, eds. Water Pollution: A Guide to Information Sources.
Knight, Bernard. The Coroner's Autopsy: A Guide to Non-Criminal Autopsies for the General Pathologist.
--Legal Aspects of Medical Practice.
Knight, C. A. Chemistry of Viruses.
--Chemistry of Viruses.
Knight, C. A., ed. see National Center for Atmospheric Research Staff.
Knight, C. Gregory. Ecology & Change: Rural Modernization in an American Community.
Knight, C. Gregory & Wilcox, R. Paul. Triumph or Triage? The World Food Problem in Geographical Persective. Natoli, Salvatore J., ed.
Knight, Christopher. Twenty-Five Years of Space Photography.
Knight, D. The Other Foot.
Knight, D. P., jt. auth. see Lewis, P. R.
Knight, Damon. A for Anything.
--Rule Golden & Other Stories.
--Science Fiction in the Thirties.
Knight, Damon, et al, eds. First Voyages.
Knight, David C. Best True Ghost Stories of the 20th Century.
--Dinosaur Days.
--Harnessing the Sun: The Story of Solar Energy.
--The Moving Coffins: Ghosts & Hauntings Around the World.
Knight, David M. Living the Sacraments: A Call to Conversion.
--Meditations for Priests.
Knight, Diane. Bed & Breakfast Homes Directory: Homes Away from Home, West Coast. Blackaby, Suzy, ed.
Knight, Douglas A., ed. Tradition & Theology in the Old Testament.
Knight, Elizabeth C., ed. see Hoffmann, E. T.
Knight, Etheridge. Born of a Woman: Selected & New Poems.
Knight, Everett. The Novel As Structure & Praxis: From Cervantes to Malraux.
Knight, G. Norman, jt. auth. see Pick, Fred L.
Knight, G. Wilson. The Crown of Life: Essays in Interpretation of Shakespeare's Final Plays.
--The Imperial Theme: Further Interpretations of Shakespeare's Tragedies Including the Roman Play.
--Symbol of Man.
Knight, George W. Principles of Shakespearian Production with Special Reference to the Tragedies.
Knight, George W., III. The Role Relationship of Men & Women.
Knight, Harold, tr. see Schoeps, Hans J.
Knight, Harry A. Slimer.
Knight, Hilary. Hilary Knight's the Twelve Days of Christmas.
Knight, J. W. The Starch Industry.
Knight, Jane, jt. auth. see Clubb, Elizabeth.
Knight, John B. & Kotschevar, Lendal H. Quantity Food Production, Planning & Management.
Knight, Kathryn L. Trace Elements.
Knight, Kenneth & McDaniel, Reuben. Organizations: An Information Systems Perspective.
Knight, Kenneth E. & McDaniel, Reuben R., Jr. Organizations: An Information Systems Perspective.
Knight, Kenneth L. & Stone, Alan. A Catalog of the Mosquitoes of the World.
Knight, M., jt. auth. see Dunn, A.
Knight, Max, tr. The Daynight Lamp.
Knight, Norman, jt. auth. see Pick, Fred L.
Knight, Peter. Economic Decision-Making Structures & Processes in Hungary: The Dilemmas of Decentralization.
Knight, R. J., ed. Guide to the Manuscripts in the National Maritime Museum: The Personal Collections.
Knight, Rolf. Along the Number Twenty Line: Reminiscences of the Vancouver Waterfront.
Knight, Thomas J. Technology's Future: The Hague Congress Technology Assessment.
Knight, Tim. Mastering Sound & Music on the Atari ST.
--Understanding Atari ST BASIC Programming.
Knight, Timothy O. BASIC Programs for the ATARI 600XL & 800XL.
--Using & Programming the ADAM: Including Ready-To-Run Programs.
Knight, U. G. Power Systems Engineering & Mathematics.
Knight, Walter W. How to Publish a Church Newsletter.
Knight, Wilfred. Red Fox: Brigadier-General Stand Watie's Civil War Years in Indian Territory.
Knight, William E. The Tiger Game.
Knightley, Phillip. The First Casualty: From the Crimea to Vietnam: The War Correspondent As Hero, Propagandist, & Myth Maker.
Knights, Lionel C. Drama & Society in the Age of Jonson.
Knights, Roger. The Alphabets Go to the Park. Klimo, Kate, ed.
Knille, Robert, ed. As I Was Saying: A Chesterton Reader.
Kniseley, R., ed. Analytical Spectroscopy: Theory & Applications: Dedicated to Velmer Fassel.
Kniveton, Bromley & Towers, Brian. Training for Negotiating.
Knobel, Bruno. Camping-Out: One Hundred & One Ideas & Activities.
Knoben, James E., et al. Handbook of Clinical Drug Data.
Knoblauch, Mary, jt. auth. see Hilton, Jack.
Knoblock, Peter. Teaching Emotionally Disturbed Children.
Knoblock, Peter, jt. auth. see Berres, Michael S.
Knode, Jay C. An Intellectual Primer.
Knoepfel, H. & Herlach, F., eds. Megagauss Magnetic Field Generation by Explosives & Related Experiments: Proceedings of the EUR-CNEN Association Meetings, Frascati, Italy, 1965.
Knoepfle, John. Whetstone.
Knoepfle, John, jt. ed. see Jaffe, Dan.
Knoke, David, jt. auth. see Bohrnstedt, George W.
Knoles, Jere J. Individual Retirement Accounts Handbook.
Knoll, Arthur J. Togo under Imperial Germany 1884-1914: A Case Study in Colonial Rule.
Knoll, Max. Materials & Processes of Electron Devices.
Knoll, Robert E. Ben Jonson's Plays: An Introduction.
--Robert McAlmon: Expatriate Publisher & Writer.
Knop, A. & Scheib, W. Chemistry & Application of Phenolic Resins.
Knopf, Howard & Dunaway, Kate A. Good Apple & Creative Writing Fun.
Knopf, Lucille, ed. Cost of Nursing Education: A Manual for Analysis of Expenditures. Incl. Pt. I. Method, Directions, & Examples: Baccalaureate Program; Pt. I. Methods, Directions, & Examples: Associate Degree Program; Pt. I. Method, Directions, & Examples: Diploma Program; Pt. II. Data-Gathering Instruments. Natl League Nurse.
Knopf, Mildred. The Perfect Hostess Cookbook.
Knopf, Mildred O. Memoirs of a Cook: Yesterday & Today.
Knopp, Anna, tr. see Meslier, Jean.
Knorr, Dietrich. Alterations in Food Production.
--Sustainable Food Systems.
Knorr, Klaus & Rosenau, James N., eds. Contending Approaches to International Politics.
Knorr, Klaus E., ed. What Price Economic Growth? Baumol, William J.
Knorr-Cetina, K. & Cicourel, A., eds. Advances in Social Theory & Methodology: Towards a Integration of Micro & Macro-Sociology.
Knotel, Richard, et al. Uniforms of the World: A Compendium of Army, Navy & Air Force Uniforms, 1700-1937.
Knott, Alexander W., jt. ed. see Egan, Clifford L.
Knott, Bill. Rome in Rome.
Knott, John & Parker, Reeve. Triumph of Style: Modes of Non-Fiction.
Knott, Julie & Prochnow, Dave. Commodore 64 Tutor for Home & School: How to Program in LOGO, PILOT, & BASIC.
--Epson, Epson, Read All about It!
--One Hundred One Projects, Plans & Ideas for the High-Tech Household.
Knott, K., ed. Physics of Planetary Magnetospheres.
Knott, Kim. My Sweet Lord: The Hare Krishna Movement.
Knott, Leonard L. Writing for the Joy of It.
Knotts, Howard. Great-Grandfather, the Baby, & Me.
--The Lost Christmas.
Knowledge Industry Publications Staff & American Society for Information & Science Staff, eds. Database Directory.
Knowledge Industry Publications Staff. Database Directory, Nineteen Eighty-Seven to Eighty-Eight. American Society for Information & Science Staff, ed.
Knowledge Industry Publications Staff, ed. Database Directory: Nineteen Eighty-Seven to Eighty-Eight.
Knowledge Industry Publications Staff. The Video Register & Teleconferencing Resources Directory 1987.
--The Video Register Nineteen Eighty-Five to Nineteen Eighty-Six.
Knowles, A., jt. auth. see Burgess, C.
Knowles, A. & Burgess, C., eds. Practical Absorption Spectrometry.
Knowles, A. V., ed. & tr. see Turgenev, Ivan S.
Knowles, David. The Evolution of Medieval Thought. Luscombe, D. E., ed. Brooke, C. N., tr.
Knowles, David H. Consumer Math Series.
Knowles, F., jt. ed. see Eckstein, P.
Knowles, G. Patterns of Spoken English: An Introduction to English Phonetics.
Knowles, John. Peace Breaks Out.
--A Separate Peace.
--A Stolen Past.
Knowles, K. G. Strikes.
Knowles, Lewis. Encouraging Talk.
Knowles, M. E., jt. ed. see Walker, R.
Knowles, Ralph. Sun Rhythm Form.
Knowles, Ruth S. The First Pictorial History of the American Oil & Gas Industry, 1859-1983.
Knowlson, James & Pilling, John. Frescoes of the Skull: The Later Prose & Drama of Samuel Beckett.
Knowlton, Christopher. The Real World.
Knowlton, John. A Letter for Johanna: Memories of a Massachusetts Boyhood.
Knox, Bernard. Oedipus at Thebes: Sophocles Tragic Hero & His Time.
Knox, Bill. Dead Man's Mooring.
Knox, Charlotte, jt. auth. see Grigson, Jane.
Knox, David. Choices in Relationships: An Introduction to Marriage & Family.
Knox, Donald. Death March: The Survivors of Bataan.
Knox, Donald, jt. auth. see Beckwith, Charlie A.
Knox, Edward C. Rencontres.
Knox, George. Tiepolo Drawings.
Knox, J. Portugese-English (Only) Dictionary of Economy, Finance, Sociology, Commerce & Related Fields.
Knox, J. M., jt. auth. see Freeman, R. G.
Knox, Patty. New Directions in Fair Isle Knitting.
Knox, Vera H., ed. Public Finance Information Sources.
Knox-Thompson, Elaine & Dickens, Suzanne. Guide to Riding & Horse Care.
Knudsen, Baard B. Europe Versus America: Foreign Policy in the 1980's.
Knudsen, James. Playing Favorites.
Knudsen, James G., jt. ed. see Somerscales, Euan F.
Knudsen, Johannes. The Formation of the Lutheran Church in America.
Knudsen, Johannes, ed. N. F. S. Grundtvig: Selected Writings.
Knudsen, Odin K. Economics of Supplemental Feeding of Malnourished Children: Leakages, Costs, & Benefits.
Knudsen, Odin K. & Scandizzo, Pasquale L. Nutrition & Food Needs in Developing Countries.
Knudson, Harry R. & Fleenor, C. Patrick. Organizational Behavior: A Management Approach.
Knudson, R. R. Muscles!
--Punch!
Knudson, Richard L. Fabulous Cars of the 1920s & 1930s.
Knudson, S. J. Culture in Retrospect.
Knudsvig, Glenn M., jt. auth. see Sweet, Waldo E.
Knutsen, Ronald. Japanese Polearms.
Knutson, Andie L. The Individual Society & Health Behavior.
Knutson, D. Algebraic Spaces.
--Lambda-Rings & the Representation Theory of the Symmetric Group.
Knutson, Kent S. His Only Son Our Lord.
--The Shape of the Question: The Mission of the Church in a Secular Age.
Knutson, Marlys & Bender, Lloyd D. Choosing Among Local Impact Models.
Knutton, Harry. Vocational Education for a Changing Society.
Knyff, Leonard & Kip, Jan. Britannia Illustrata.
Kobal, John. Hollywood: The Years of Innocence.
--Rita Hayworth: The Time, the Place, the Woman.
Kobayashi, Akira. Machining of Plastics.
Kobayashi, Joshiji, jt. ed. see Jellins, Jack.
Kobayashi, Shigeji, jt. ed. see Hasegawa, Sumio.
Kobayashi, Tetzuya. Society, Schools & Progress in Japan.
Kobayashi, Toshiji, ed. Clinical Ultrasound of the Breast.
Kobayashi, Yuji. Miss Josephine's Secret Walk.
Koberg, Don & Bagnall, Jim. Values Tech: A Portable School for Self-Assessment & Self-Enhancement.
Kobernick, Sidney D., tr. see Masson, Pierre.
Kobert, Norman. Managing Time.
Kobler, John. Damned in Paradise: A Life of John Barrymore.
Koblyakov, I. K. U. S. S. R.-for Peace Against Aggression Nineteen Thirty-Three to Nineteen Forty-One.
Kobrin, Janet, jt. auth. see Bernstein, Margery.
Kobus, H. E., jt. ed. see Rao Lakshmana, N. S.
Kocan, Peter. The Treatment & the Cure.
Kocaoglu, Dundar F., jt. auth. see Cleland, David I.
Koch, Adrienne, ed. see Madison, James.
Koch, C. J. The Doubleman.
--The Doubleman.
Koch, Caspar, ed. Gradus ad Parnassum.
Koch, E., ed. Non-Isothermal Reaction Analysis.
Koch, E. E., et al, eds. Vacuum Ultraviolet Radiation Physics: Proceedings of the 4th International Conference.
Koch, Edward I. & Rauch, William. Mayor: An Autobiography.
--Politics.
Koch, Frank. Corporate Giving: Policy & Practice.
Koch, Gebhard & Richter, Dietmar. Biosynthesis, Modification & Processing of Cellular & Viral Polyproteins.

Koch, Gerhard & Richter, Dietmar. Biochemical & Clinical Aspects of Neuropeptides: Synthesis, Processing, & Gene Structure.
Koch, Gerhard & Richter, Dietmar, eds. Regulation of Macromolecular Synthesis by Low Molecular Weight Mediators.
Koch, H. W. How to Multiply Top Executive Effectiveness.
Koch, Hal. Pronoia und Paideusis: Studien Uber Origenes und Sein Verhaltnis Zum Platonismus.
Koch, Hans-Albrecht & Koch, Uta, eds. Internationale Germanistische Bibliographie.
Koch, Harry W. California Wills & Probate.
Koch, Helen L. Twins & Twin Relations.
Koch, Howard. Koch: As Time Goes by: Memoirs of a Writer.
Koch, Hugh, ed. Community Clinical Psychology.
Koch, James V. Industrial Organization & Prices.
Koch, James V., jt. auth. see Ostrosky, Anthony L., Jr.
Koch, Jerome. Sycamore Stories.
Koch, Joanne B., jt. auth. see Levande, Diane I.
Koch, Karen. A Special Look.
Koch, Kenneth, tr. see Roussel, Raymond.
Koch, Klaus-Friedrich. War & Peace in Jalemo: The Management of Conflict in Highland New Guinea.
Koch, Lawrence O. Yardbird Suite: A Compendium of the Music & Life of Charlie Parker.
Koch, Manfred. Laugh with Health.
Koch, Paul S. Converting to Phacoemulsification: A Manual for the Surgeon in Transition.
Koch, Peter. Utilization of Hardwoods Growing on Southern Pines Sites.
Koch, Robert. Louis C. Tiffany's Glass, Bronzes & Lamps: A Complete Collector's Guide.
Koch, Robert A. Hans Baldung Grien: Eve, the Serpent & Death.
Koch, Ron. Goodbye, Grandpa.
Koch, S., ed. Psychology: Vol. 6, Investigations of Man As Socius, Their Place in Psychology, in the Social Sciences.
Koch, Uta, jt. ed. see Koch, Hans-Albrecht.
Koch, Walter A. & Schaeck, Elisabeth. Birthplace Tables of Houses.
Kochan, Lionel. Russia & the Weimar Republic.
Kochan, Stephen G. Programming in C.
--Programming in C.
Kochan, Thomas A., et al. Dispute Resolution Under Fact-Finding & Arbitration: An Empirical Analysis.
Kocher, Eric. International Jobs - Where They Are, How to Get Them.
Kocher, Helen R. & Ross, Alec. Success with Sentences.
Kocher, Paul H. Master of Middle-Earth: The Fiction of J. R. R. Tolkien.
--A Reader's Guide to the Silmarillion.
Kocherga, O. D., tr. see Sitenko, A. G.
Kochetkov, N. K. & Budovsky, E. I., eds. Organic Chemistry of Nucleic Acids.
Kochetkov, N. K., et al, eds. Radiation Chemistry of Carbohydrates.
Kochetov, V. The Zhurbins.
Kochhar, S. K. Guidance & Counseling in Colleges & Universities.
Kochina, P. Love & Mathematics: Sofya Kovalevskaya.
Koch-Miramond, L. & Lee, M. A., eds. Particle Acceleration Processes, Shockwaves, Nucleosynthesis & Cosmic Rays: Proceedings of Symposia 6 & 8 & the Joint Sessions 6-8 of the COSPAR Twenty-fifth Plenary Meeting Held in Graz, Austria, 25 June to 7 July 1984.
Koch-Weser, Jan, ed. Reprints of Articles on Drug Therapy. Incl. Vol. 6; Vol. 5; Vol. 4; Vol. 3; Vol. 2; Vol. 1. MA Med Soc.
Kock, Winston E. Engineering Applications of Lasers & Holography.
Kockelmans, Joseph J. Edmund Husserl's Phenomenological Psychology.
Koconda-Brons, Angela, adapted by. & illus. Jorinda & Joringel: Large Print.
Koczak, Michael J. & Hildeman, Gregory J., eds. High-Strength Powder Metallurgy: Aluminum: Proceedings of the AIME Annual Meeting, Dallas, TX, 1982.
Kodak. Recovering Silver from Photographic Materials.
Kodaly, Zoltan. Folk Music of Hungary.
Kodama, Goji, jt. auth. see Parry, Robert W.
Kodera, Takashi J., tr. from Japanese. Dogen's Formative Years in China: Historical Study & Annotated Translation of the Hokyo-ki.
Kodjak, Andrej. Alexander Solzhenitsyn.
Koeberle, S. & Spiegel, R., eds. A Long Term Study with Co. Dergocrine Mesylate (Hydergine) in Healthy Pensioners: Results after Three Years.
Koechlin-Schwartz, Dorothee, jt. auth. see LeComte, Jacques.
Koehler, C. S., jt. ed. see Frankie, G. W.
Koehler, J. K., ed. Advanced Techniques in Biological Electron Microscopy.
Koehler, Jerry W., et al. Public Communication: Behavioral Perspectives.
Koehler, S. R. American Etchings. Bd. with American Art. Garland Pub.
--The United States Art Directory & Year-Book. Weinberg, H. Barbara, ed. Incl. Vol. 1. A Guide for Artists, Art Students, Travellers, Etc; Vol. 2. A Chronicle of Events in the Art World, & a Guide for All Interested in the Progress of Art in America. Garland Pub.
Koehn, Constance, ed. Books for Public Libraries.
Koehn, Peter & Waldron, Sidney R. Afocha: A Link Between Community & Administration in Harar Ethiopia.
Koek, Karin, ed. International Organizations: 1988.
--International Organizations, 1988: Supplement to Vol. 4 of the Encyclopedia of Associations.
Koek, Karin, jt. ed. see Boyles-Martin, Susan.
Koek, Karin, jt. ed. see Martin, Susan B.
Koek, Karin E., ed. Encyclopedia of Associations: International Organizations 1988.
Koekkoek, K. A., et al. On Protectionism in the Netherlands.
Koella, W. P., et al, eds. see European Congress of Sleep Research Staff.
Koelle, D. E., ed. Space Systems Economics: Cost Reductions in Space Operations.
Koelsch, Francine, jt. auth. see Aarons, Trudy.
Koenig, Alfred E., et al, eds. Philosophy of the Humanistic Society.
Koenig, Alma J. Gudrun. Bell, Anthea, tr.
Koenig, Constance R., jt. auth. see Bucher, Charles A.
Koenig, Jack L. Chemical Microstructure of Polymer Chains.
Koenig, John. Charismata: God's Gift for God's People.
--Puff, Wrinkle & Squint.
Koenig, Joseph. Floater.
Koenig, Laird. The Neighbor.
Koenig, Louis W. The Chief Executive.
--Toward a Democracy: A Brief Introduction to American Government.
Koenig, Teresa, jt. auth. see Bell, Rivian.
Koenig, Thomas R., ed. An Introduction to Ethics: A Philosophical Orientation.
Koenig, Walter. Buck Alice & the Actor-Robot.
Koenigsberg, Richard A., ed. The Psychoanalysis of Culture & History.
Koenigsberger, F. & Tlusty, J. Machine Tool Structures.
Koenigsberger, F., jt. ed. see Tobias, S. A.
Koenigsberger, O. H., ed. Housing.
Koenigsberger, T., jt. ed. see Tobias, S. A.
Koenker, Robert H. Simplified Statistics for Students in Education & Psychology.
Koepchen, H. P., et al, eds. Central Interaction Between Respiratory & Cardiovasclar Central Systems.
Koepf, Michael. Save the Whale.
Koepke, Fred T. How to Be Sure of Immortality.
Koepke, Wulf. Die Deutschen: Vergangenheit und Gegenwart.
Koepping, Klaus-Peter. Adolf Bastian & the Psychic Unity of Mankind: The Foundations of Anthropology in Nineteen Century Germany.
Koerner, James. Hoffer's America.
Koerner, T., ed. see Heller, Mel.
Koerner, Thomas, ed. see Lipham, James.
Koerner, Thomas, ed. see McCleary, Lloyd & Thomson, Scott.
Koerner, Thomas F., ed. The Senior High School Principalship: The National Survey.
--Student Learning Styles & Brain Behavior.
Koerner, Thomas F., ed. see Gorton, Richard A. & McIntyre, Kenneth E.
Koertge, Ronald. The Boogeyman.
Koester, Helmut. Introduction to the New Testament: History & Literature of Early Christianity.
--Introduction to the New Testament: History, Culture, & Religion of the Hellenistic Age.
Koester, Helmut, jt. auth. see Robinson, James M.
Koester, Helmut, jt. auth. see Smith, Charles W.
Koester, Rudolf. Ullstein Lexikon der Deutschen Sprache.
Kofele-Kale, Ndiva. Tribesmen & Patriots: Political Culture in a Poly-Ethnic African State.
Koff, Richard. Home Computers: A Manual of Possibilities.
Koff, Richard, jt. auth. see Lerner, Eugene.
Koffka, Kurt. Principles of Gestalt Psychology.
Kofman, Eleonore, jt. ed. see Hoggart, Keith.
Kofmehl, Kenneth. Professional Staffs of Congress.
Kofranek, Anton M. & Larson, Roy A., eds. Growing Azaleas Commercially.
Kofstad, Per. Nonstoichiometry, Diffusion, & Electrical Conductivity in Binary Metal Oxides.
Koga, T. Introduction to Kinetic Theory.
Kogan, Benjamin A. Health.
--Health.
--Health: Man in a Changing Environment.
--Human Sexual Expression.
--Readings in Health Science.
Kogan, J. Fundamentals of Crane Design.
Kogan, Maurice. Educational Policy-Making: A Study of Interest Groups & Parliament.
Kogan, Maurice, et al, eds. School Governing Bodies.
Kogbe, C. A., ed. Geology for Development, Mineral Resources & Exploration Potential of Africs (GSA '82) Proceedings of the General Conference on African Geology, 6th, Nairobi, Africa, December 1982.
Kogge, Peter M. The Architecture of Pipelined Computers.
Kogiku, K. C. Microeconomic Models.
Koh, B. C., jt. ed. see Kim, C. I.
Kohake, Rosanne. Ambrosia.
--Chastity Morrow.
--For Honor's Lady.
Kohan, Anthony L., jt. auth. see Elonka, Stephen M.
Kohavi, Zvi & Paz, Azaria, eds. Theory of Machines & Computations: International Symposium on the Theory of Machines & Computations.
Kohen-Raz, R. Psychobiological Aspects of Cognitive Growth.
Kohfeldt, Mary Lou. Lady Gregory: The Woman Behind the Irish Renaissance.
Kohl, David G. Chinese Architecture in the Straits Settlements & Western Malaya: Temples, Kongsis & Houses.
Kohl, Herbert R. Basic Skills: A Plan for Your Child, A Program for All Children.
Kohl, Herbert R. & Kohl, Judith. The View from the Oak.
Kohl, Judith, jt. auth. see Kohl, Herbert R.
Kohl, M, tr. see Pannenberg, Wolfhart.
Kohl, Margaret, tr. see Kasemann, Ernst.
Kohl, Margaret, tr. see Marxsen, Willi.
Kohl, Margaret, tr. see Moltmann, Jurgen.
Kohl, Margaret, tr. see Soelle, Dorothee.
Kohl, Margaret, tr. see Von Der Osten-Sacken, Peter.
Kohl, Margaret, tr. see Wolff, Hans W.
Kohl, Wilfied L. & Basevi, Giorgio. West Germany: A European & Global Power.
Kohl, Wilfrid L. After the Second Oil Crisis: Energy Policies in Europe, America, & Japan.
Kohlenberger, John R., III. Books about the Book: A Guide to Biblical Reference Works.
Kohler, Christine. My Friend Is Moving.
Kohler, F. Across the Soviet Union.
Kohler, Gernot. The Meaning of Global Apartheid.
Kohler, Heinz. Statistics for Business & Economics.
Kohler, Josef. On the Prehistory of Marriage. Barnes, R. H., ed.
Kohler, Peter O. & Jordan, Richard M., eds. Clinical Endocrinology.
Kohler, Wolfgang. Gestalt Psychology.
Kohli, Suresh, ed. Modern Indian Short Stories.
Kohlman, M. & Vogel, W., eds. Stochastic Control Theory & Stochastic Differential Systems.
Kohn, Clyde F., jt. ed. see Mayer, Harold M.
Kohn, David. More Than Truth.
Kohn, Hans. American Nationalism: An Interpretative Essay.
Kohn, Jacob. Evolution as Revelation.
--Moral Life of Man.
Kohn, Leonard D., jt. ed. see Middlebrook, John H.
Kohn, Melvin L. Class & Conformity: A Study in Values.
Kohner, Hanna, et al. Hanna & Walter.
Kohnert, Gerald V., jt. auth. see Kolstad, C. Kenneth.
Kohnke, Helmut & Bertrand, A. R. Soil Conservation.
Kohnke, Mary F. Advocacy: Risk & Reality.
Kohnstamm, Geldolph, ed. Temperament Discussed: Temperament & Development in Infancy & Childhood.
Kohonen, T. Associative Memory: A System-Theoretical Approach.
Kohout, Jessica L. Concerns for Applied Sociology: A Bibliography.
Kohr, Leopold. The Breakdown of Nations.
Kohs, Ellis B. Musical Form: Studies in Analysis & Synthesis.
Kohs, Gerald, jt. auth. see Connor, Ann W.
Koht, H. Old Norse Sagas.
Koht, Halvdan. Driving Forces in History. Haugen, Einar, tr.
Kohut, Sylvester, Jr. & Range, Dale G. Classroom Discipline: Case Studies & Viewpoints.
Koichi, Iijima see Minoru, Yoshioka.
Koizumi, Kazuko. Traditional Japanese Furniture.
Kojecky, Roger. T. S. Eliot's Social Criticism.
Kojima, Ken-Ichi, ed. Mathematical Topics in Population Genetics.
Kojima, Takashi, tr. see Akutagawa, Ryunosuke.
Kok, J. F. W. Structopathic Children. Incl. Pt. 1. Description of Disturbance Type & Strategies; Pt. 2. Results of Experimental Research of Structuring Group Therapy. CJ Hogrefe Pubs.
Kok, J. H., tr. see Jagersma, Henk.
Kokaska, Charles J., jt. ed. see Fink, Albert.
Kokei, Kobayashi & Kawakita, Michiaki. Library of Japanese Art: Kokei.
Kokelaar, B. P. & Howells, Malcolm, eds. Marginal Basin Geology: Volcanic & Associated Sedimentary & Tectonic Processes in Modern & Ancient Marginal Basins.
Kokeritz, Helge. Shakespeare's Pronunciation.
Kol, Bessel A. van der see Van Der Kolk, Bessel A.
Kolakowski, Leszek. Husserl & the Search for Certitude.
Kolas, Y. On Life's Expanses.
Kolasa, Blair J., jt. auth. see Meyer, Bernadine.
Kolata, Alan L., jt. ed. see Leventhal, Richard M.
Kolata, Gina B., jt. auth. see Marx, Jean L.
Kolatch, Alfred J. Fun-In-Learning about Passover.
Kolb, B. Applied Headspace Gas Chromatography.
Kolb, Burton. Principles of Financial Management.
Kolb, Glen L. Democracy & Dictatorship in Venezuela, 1945-1958.
Kolb, Robert. Andreae & the Formula of Concord.
Kolb, Robert W. Investments.
--Understanding Futures Markets.
Kolber, Alan R., et al, eds. In Vitro Toxicity Testing of Environmental Agents, Current & Future Possibilities: Part A; Survey of Test Systems - Part B-Development of Risk Assessment Guidelines.
Kolby, K. Berenice, Princess of Judea.
Kolchkovsky, L. L. Economic Neocolonialism.
Kolde, Endel-Jakob. Environment of International Business: Concepts, Structures, & Strategies.
Kolden, Marc. Called by the Gospel: An Introduction of the Christian Faith.
Koldjeski, Dixie. Community Mental Health Nursing: New Directions in Theory & Practice.
Kolenda, Konstantin. In Defense of Practical Reason.
Kolenda, Konstantin, ed. Studies in Philosophy: A Symposium on Gilbert Ryle.
Kolenda, Konstantin, et al, eds. Creativity & Openness: Essays in Honor of James S. Fulton.
Kolers, Paul A. Aspects of Motion Perception.
Kolesnik, Eugene M. NATO & Warsaw Pact Submarines since 1955.
Kolisko, Eugen. Zoology for Everybody.
--Zoology for Everybody, Vol. 8: Amphibians & Reptiles.
Kolk, Justin Vander see Vander Kolk, Justin.
Kolker, Allan E. & Hetherington, John, Jr. Becker-Shaffer's Diagnosis & Therapy of the Glaucomas.
Kolkey, Jonathan M. The New Right, Nineteen Sixty to Nineteen Sixty-Eight: With Epilogue, 1969-1980.
Kolko, S. Joel, ed. Family Law Handbook.
Kolle, Kurt. Introduction to Psychiatry.
Koller, Alice. An Unknown Woman: A Journey to Self-Discovery.
Koller, Marvin R., jt. auth. see King, David C.
Kollmann, Wolfgang, ed. Prediction Methods for Turbulent Flows.
Kollock, John. Think Persian.
Kollontai, Alexandra. Alexandra Kollontai: Selected Writings. Holt, Alix, ed. & tr.
--A Great Love. Porter, Cathy, tr.
Kolman, B., jt. auth. see Beck, R. E.
Kolman, Bernard. Calculus for the Management, Life, & Social Sciences.
Kolman, Bernard & Busby, Robert C. Discrete Mathematical Structures for Computer Science.
Kolman, Bernard & Shapiro, Arnold. Algebra for College Students.
--College Algebra.
--College Algebra & Trigonometry.
--College Algebra & Trigonometry.
--Precalculus: Functions & Graphs.
--Test Bank for College Algebra.
Kolman, Bernard, jt. auth. see Anton, Howard.
Kolodin, Irving. The Continuity of Music: A History of Influence.
--The Metropolitan Opera, 1883-1966: A Candid History.
--The Musical Life.
Kolodny, Robert C., et al. How to Survive Your Adolescent's Adolescence.
Kologrivova, S. V. & Zalmanova, T. S. Alphabet Is Fun.
Kolotyrkin, Y. Advances in Physical Chemistry: Current Developments in Electrochemistry & Corrosion.
Kolpas, Norman. Abraham Lincoln. Nichols, Eleanor, ed.
Kolpas, Norman, ed. Britain: The Queen, Cricket, Sherlock Holmes, & Other Things Indubitably British.
Kolstad, C. Kenneth. Rapid Electrical Estimating & Pricing.
Kolstad, C. Kenneth & Kohnert, Gerald V. Rapid Electrical Estimating & Pricing: A Handy, Quick Method of Directly Determining the Selling Prices of Electrical Construction Work.
Koltanowski, George. Chessnicdotes I.

Kolthoff, I. M. & Elving, Philip J. Treatise on Analytical Chemistry.
Koltun, Daniel S., jt. auth. see Eisenberg, Judah M.
Kolve, Carolee N. How to Buy (& Survive!) Your First Computer: A Guide for Small Business Success.
Kolvin, I., et al. Help Starts Here: The Maladjusted Child in the Ordinary School.
Kolvin, Israel, et al. Help Starts Here: The Maladjusted Child in the Ordinary School.
Kolzow, D., jt. ed. see Bellow, A.
Komaiko, Jean, et al. Around Lake Michigan.
Komanoff, Charles. Power Plant Cost Escalation: Nuclear & Coal Capital Costs, Regulation, & Economics.
Komar, John J. The Great Escape from Your Dead End Job.
Komar, Paul D. Beach Processes & Sedimentation.
Komarov, Boris. The Destruction of Nature in the Soviet Union. Vale, Michel & Hollander, Joe, trs. from Rus.
Komarovsky, Mirra. Dilemmas of Masculinity: A Study of College Youth.
--Dilemmas of Masculinity: A Study of College Youth.
Komatsu, H., ed. see Conference on Hyperfunctions & Pseudo-Differential Equations Staff.
Kome, Penney, jt. ed. see Crean, Patrick.
Komkov, V. Optimal Control Theory for the Damping of Vibrations of Simple Elastic Systems.
Komo, Dolores. Clio Brown.
Komoda, Beverly. The Lake Mess Monster.
Kompa, K. L. Chemical Lasers. Boschke, F., ed.
Kompaneyets, A. Course in Theoretical Physics.
Komroff, Manuel, ed. Contemporaries of Marco Polo.
Kon, Abraham. Prayer.
Kondo, Herbert, ed. see Grolier, Inc. Staff.
Kondo, T., jt. ed. see Takahashi, K.
Kondrashov, N. A., ed. see Lenin, V. I.
Kondratiev, V. N. Chemical Kinetics of Gas Reactions.
Kondratov, A. The Riddles of Three Oceans.
Kondratovich, A., jt. ed. see Dzyubenko, G.
Kondratyev, K. Y. & Hunt, G. E. Weather & Climate on Planets.
Kondratyeva, M. & Taborko, V. Children & Sport in the U. S. S. R.
Konenigsber, ed. Technology & Development.
Konev, Ivan. Year of Victory. Mishne, David, tr.
Konferenz der Gesellschaft Deutscher Naturforscher und Aerzte Staff. Metabolic Interconversion of Enzymes: Proceedings of the Konferenz der Gesellschaft Deutscher Naturforscher und Aerzte, 2nd, Rottach-Egern, 1971. Wieland, O., et al, eds.
Kong, Bucksam & Ho, Eugene H. Hung Gar Kung-Fu Chinese Art of Self-Defense. Scurra, John, ed.
Kong, F. & Evans, R. Reinforced & Prestressed Concrete.
Konig, Barbara. Namibia: The Ravages of War.
Konig, E. & Kremer, S. Ligand Field Energy Diagrams.
Konig, Imre. Chess from Morphy to Botwinnik.
Konigsberg, Irwin R., jt. ed. see Subtelny, Stephen.
Konigsburg, E. L. From the Mixed-up Files of Mrs. Basil E. Frankweiler.
--Throwing Shadows.
Konikow, Robert B. & McElroy, Frank E. Communications for the Safety Professional.
Konikowski, Jerzy. Queen's Gambit Declined: Exchange Variation.
--Queen's Gambit: Tartakower System. Janicki, Paul, tr.
Konikowsky, Jerzy, jt. auth. see Janicki, Paul.
Koning, Frederick. Diccionario de Demonologia.
Koning, Hans. De Witt's War.
--Death of a Schoolboy.
--The Kleber Flight.
--A New Yorker in Egypt.
Konings, Chris. The Queen Elizabeth at War.
Konishi, Masatoshi. Afghanistan.
Konkel, Gilbert, jt. auth. see Peck, Phyllis.
Konkel, Gilbert J., jt. auth. see Peck, Phyllis.
Konkle, Gail. Shapes & Perceptions: An Intuitive Approach to Geometry.
Konkor, Laszlo, illus. Cross-Country Skiing.
Konle, Carolyn W. Social Work Day-to-Day: The Experience of Generalist Social Practice.
Konner, Alfred. Olrik.
Konner, Melvin. The Tangled Wing: Biological Constraints on the Human Spirit.
Konnyu, Leslie. Collected Poems. Gross, Joseph, tr.
Konold, et al. WEESKA Patenets.
Kononova, G. Odessa: A Guide.
Konorza, G., tr. see Tillmann, Bernhard.
Konrad, George. Antipolitics. Allen, Richard E., tr.
--The Case Worker.
--The Case Worker. Aston, Paul, tr.
--The City Builder. Sanders, Ivan, tr.
--The Loser. Sanders, Ivan, tr. from Hungarian.
Konrad, George & Szelenyi, Ivan. The Intellectuals on the Road to Class Power: A Sociological Study of the Role of the Intelligentsia in Socialism. Arato, Andrew & Allen, Richard E., trs.
Konsler, Runelle & Mirabella, Lauren. Math Activities with a Porpoise.
Konstantin, Anatole, tr. see Tretyak, Vladislav & Snegirev, V.
Konvisser, Marc. Elementary Linear Algebra with Applications.
Konvitz, Jeffrey. Monster: A Tale of Loch Ness.
--The Sentinel.
Konvitz, Milton R., ed. see Liberia, Republic of.
Konzelman, Robert G. Talking Christmas Tree: Family Doings for Christmas Time.
Konzo, Seichi & Bayne, James W. Opportunities in Mechanical Engineering.
Koo, Hagen & Yu, Eui-Young. Korean Immigration to the United States: Its Demographic Pattern & Social Implications for Both Societies.
Koons, Carolyn. Tony: Our Journey Together.
Koontz & Fulmer. Practical Introduction to Business.
Koontz, Dean R. Night Chills.
Koontz, Harold D., et al. Essentials of Management.
--Management.
Koonz, Claudia, jt. auth. see Bridenthal, Renate.
Koopman, L. Advent & Christmas Resource Book.
Koopmans, Lambert H. An Introduction to Contemporary Statistics.
Koos, W. Th., et al. Clinical Microneurosurgery.
Kopacsi, Sandor. In the Name of the Working Class: The Former Police Chief of Budapest Reveals the Inside Story of the Hungarian Revolution of 1956. Staffman, Daniel & Staffman, Judy, trs. from Fr.
Kopal, Zdenek. Widening Horizons.
Kopal, Zdenek, ed. Physics & Astronomy of the Moon.
Kopay, David & Young, Perry D. The David Kopay Story.
--David Kopay Story.
Kopel, E. Financial & Corporate Public Relations: The Integrated Approach.
Kopelev, Lev. Utoli Moia Pechali.
Kophal, E. E. Blood Relations.
Kopp, Karl. The Juggler.
Kopp, Otto C. An Introduction to Physical Geology.
Kopp, Sheldon B. Here I Am, Wasn't I! The Inevitable Disruption of Easy Times.
Koppelman, Susan, compiled by. Old Maids: A Selection of Short Stories by Nineteenth-Century Women Writers.
Kopperl, Bert. Double Entry: A Spirited Tale.
--With Two Wheels & a Camera.
Koppett, Leonard. Sports Illusion, Sports Reality: A Reporter's View of Sports, Journalism, & Society.
Koppman, Lionel, jt. auth. see Postal, Bernard.
Koprowski, Claude & Koprowski, Hilary. Viruses & Immunity: Toward Understanding Viral Immunology & Immunopathology.
Koprowski, H., jt. ed. see Vogt, P. K.
Koprowski, Hilary, jt. auth. see Koprowski, Claude.
Kops, L., ed. Manufacturing Solutions Based on Engineering Sciences.
Kopycinski, Joseph V., ed. Textile Industry Information Sources.
Kopytkin, Y., tr. see Steinbach, Valeri.
Koral, April. Headlines & Deadlines.
Koralek, Jenny, tr. see Zuber, Rene.
Korbitz, William E. Modern Management of Wastewater Utilities.
Korchari, Abas. Escape from Hell.
Korda, Michael. Queenie.
--Queenie.
--Success!
Kordesch, Karl, ed. Batteries: Lead Acid Batteries & Electric Vehicles.
Kordus, Claude L., ed. Trustees Handbook: A Basic Text on Labor-Management Employee Benefit Plans.
Korelitz, Burton I., ed. Inflammatory Bowel Diseases.
Korem, Danny & Meier, Paul. The Fakers: Exploding the Myths of the Supernatural.
Koren, Edward. Are You Happy? & Other Questions Lovers Ask.
Koren, Henry J. To the Ends of the Earth: A General History of the Congregation of the Holy Ghost.
Koren, Herman. Handbook of Environmental Health & Safety: Principles & Practices.
Koren, J., ed. see Beardsley, Theodore S., Jr.
Korenblit, Joan & Janger, Kathie. Knowing Beans about Coffee. Brown, Suzanne, ed.
Korenbrot, Carol C., jt. ed. see Diamond, Marian C.
Korenman, I. M. Introduction to Quantitative Ultramicroanalysis.
Koretsky, Elaine. Color for the Hand Papermaker.
Korfhage, Robert R. Discrete Computational Structures.
Korg, Jacob. Dylan Thomas.
Korite, J. G. & Sick, H. Atlas of Sectional Human Anatomy: Frontal, Sagittal & Horizontal Planes. Incl. Vol. 1. Head, Neck, Thorax; Vol. 2. Abdomen, Pelvis. Urban & S.
Kork, John O. JKDIGIT, A Program to Control a Digitizing Board for Geologists, Written in Basic for an IBM Personal Computer.
Korkeshkin, A., jt. auth. see Drozdov, V.
Korkhmazian, E. Armenian Miniatures of the Thirteenth & Fourteenth Centuries.
Korkisch, J. M 'ern Methods for the Separation of Rarer Metai Ions.
Korky, Paul, jt. auth. see Marshall, Ray.
Korman, Richard I. Checklist of Government Directorie., Lists & Rosters.
Kormendi, Ferenc. That One Mistake.
Kormov, Yu. Specialisation & Cooperation of the Socialist Economies.
Korn, Berton W. Early Jews of New Orleans.
Korn, Bertram W. American Jewry & the Civil War.
Korn, Ellen, ed. Teach Yourself Calligraphy: For Beginners from Eight to Eighty.
Korn, Granino A. Microprocessors & Small Digital Computer Systems: For Engineers & Scientists.
Korn, Henry, ed. see National Academy of the Avant Garde Staff.
Kornai, J. Anti-Equilibrium.
Kornberg, Warren, ed. see National Science Foundation Staff.
Kornbluth, Jesse, jt. auth. see Enrico, Roger.
Kornbluth, Jesse, jt. auth. see Osborn, Jack R.
Korneck, G., jt. ed. see Klein, H. P.
Korner, E., jt. ed. see Lechner, H.
Korneva, O. Selected Works: Konstantin Stanislavsky.
Kornfeld, Albert. Doubleday Book of Interior Decorating & Encyclopedia of Styles.
Kornfeld, Alfred D. & Schneiderman, Leo, eds. Readings in Psychopathology.
Kornfeld, Melvin, tr. see Becker, Jurek.
Kornfeld, Stuart, et al. Transferrin Biology.
Korngold, Ralph. Citizen Toussaint.
--The Last Years of Napoleon.
Kornhauser, Alain L., jt. ed. see Kerr, Arnold D.
Kornhauser, Arthur W. How to Study.
Kornhauser, David H., tr. see Iozawa, Tomoya.
Kornheiser, Tony. The Baby Chase.
Kornhuber, H. H., ed. The Somatosensory System.
Kornitzer, Margaret. Child Adoption in the Modern World.
Kornstein, Daniel. The Music of the Laws.
Kornup, A. & Wanscher, J. H. Methuen Handbook of Colour.
Korolenko, V. Selected Stories.
Korolenko, Vladimir. In a Strange Land. Zilboorg, Gregory, tr.
Korolyov, B. I. Real Socialism & Ideological Struggle.
Korot, Beryl, jt. auth. see Schneider, Ira.
Korotyukov, Aleksei. Nelegko byt' Ruskim Shpionom.
Korpi, Walter. The Working Class in Welfare Capitalism: Work, Unions & Politics in Sweden.
Korshunov, Y. M. Fundamentos Matematicos de la Cibernetica.
Kort, Kees De, illus. What the Bible Tells Us: A Series for Young Children. Incl. Jesus Is Born; Jesus at the Wedding; The Good Samaritan; Jesus Is Alive. Augsburg Fortress.
Kort, Michael G. The Soviet Colossus: A History of the U. S. S. R.
Kort, Wesley A. Moral Fiber: Character & Belief in Recent American Fiction.
--Narrative Elements & Religious Meaning.
Korte, F., jt. ed. see Coulston, F.
Korteweg, Pieter. Exchange-Rate Policy, Monetary Policy, & Real Exchange-Rate Variability.
Korth, Eugene H., jt. auth. see Flusche, Della M.
Korting, G. W., et al. Diseases of the Skin in Children & Adolescents.
Kortum, Jeanie & Stermer, Dugald. Ghost Vision.
Koryta, J. Medical & Biological Applications of Electrochemical Devices.
Korzeniowsky, Carole, jt. auth. see Corsaro, Maria.
Kosa, John, ed. see Adler, Franx, et al.
Kosbab, William H. Motorcycle & Small Engine: Dictionary-Terminology. Greenslade-Moore, Dianne & Lamont, Daveta, eds.
Koschatzky, Walter. Hundertwasser: The Complete Graphic Work 1951-1986.
Kosel. Chapter 13: Federal Plan Repay Debts.
Kosel, Janice. Bankruptcy, Do It Yourself. Warner, Ralph, ed.
--Bankruptcy: Do It Yourself.
--Bankruptcy: Do It Yourself.
Koshkin, Naomi, jt. auth. see Brower, Millicent.
Kosinski, Jerzy. Blind Date.
--Cockpit.
--The Devil Tree.
--The Painted Bird.
--Pinball.
Kosobud, Richard & Minami, Ryishin, eds. Econometric Studies of Japan.
Kosolapoff, G. M. & Maier, L. Organic Phosphorous Compounds.
Kosow, Irving L., ed. see Power, Thomas C.
Kosoy, Ted. Kosoy Travel Guide to Canada.
--Kosoy Travel Guide to Europe.
Kossak, Howard S. The Ins, Outs & Ups of Venture Capital.
Kossen, Stan, jt. auth. see Straub, Joseph T.
Kossoff, David. Sweet Nutcracker.
Kost, James. Shop Toons.
Kostanoski, John, jt. auth. see Bottom, Norman R.
Kostecka, Andrew. Franchising in the Economy 1985-1987.
Kostecka, Andrew, compiled by. Franchise Opportunities Handbook 1986.
Kostelanetz, Andre & Hammond, Gloria. Echoes: Memoirs of Andre Kostelanetz.
Kostelski, Z. The Yugoslavs.
Kosten, A. How To Conquer Loneliness.
Kosten, L. Stochastic Theory of Service Systems.
Koster, Henry. Travels in Brazil. Gardiner, Harvey C., ed.
Kosterlitz, H. W. & Terenius, L. Y., eds. Pain & Society.
Kostich, Dragos. George Morrison.
Kostick. Getting More from Your Food Processor.
Kostick, Marilyn, ed. see Sunbeam Staff.
Kostick, Marilyn G., ed. see Murphy, Margaret D.
Kostiner, Edward & Rea, Jesse R. Fundamentals of Chemistry.
Kostka, Stefan M. A Bibliography of Computer Applications in Music.
Kostman, Samuel. Women of Valor.
Kostrov, Konstantin A., tr. see Rastyannikov, V. G.
Kostyukhin, D. The World Market Today.
Kosuth, Joan & Minnesang, Sandy. Choices: Organizing & Teaching a Course in Personal Decision-Making.
Koszarowski, Tadeusz. Cancer Surgery.
Koszul, J. L. Fibre Bundles & Differential Geometry.
Koszyk, Kathleen. Who Says You Can't Find Good Help Anymore?
Kot, R. A., ed. see AIME Annual Meeting Staff.
Kot, Richard A. & Bramfitt, Bruce L., eds. Fundamentals of Dual-Phase Steels: Proceedings of the AIME Meeting, Chicago, IL, 1981.
Kotchen, Jane M., jt. auth. see Kotchen, Theodore A.
Kotchen, Theodore A. & Kotchen, Jane M. Clinical Approaches to High Blood Pressure in the Young.
Kotecha, Ken C. & Adams, Robert W. African Politics: The Corruption of Power.
Kotin, Paul, jt. ed. see Lee, Douglas H.
Kotker, Norman, jt. auth. see Whitehill, Walter M.
Kotkin, Amy J., jt. auth. see Zeitlin, Steven J.
Kotkin, Joel & Grabowicz, Paul. California, Inc.
Kotler, Philip. Marketing for Nonprofit Organizations.
--Marketing Management: Analysis, Planning & Control.
Kotler, Philip, et al. Cases & Readings for Marketing for Nonprofit Organizations.
Kotschevar, Lendal. Standards, Principles & Techniques in Quality Food Production.
Kotschevar, Lendal H., jt. auth. see Knight, John B.
Kotter, John P. Power in Management.
Kottke, Frederic J., et al. Handbook of Physical Medicine & Rehabilitation.
Kottler, Jeffrey A. & Blau, Diane S. The Imperfect Therapist: Learning from Failure in Therapeutic Practice.
Kottmeyer. Rd-Sp Cht.
--Rd-Sp Web.
--SMGP Rd-Sp Cht.
--SMGP Rd-Sp Tm.
--SMGP Rd-Sp Tm.
--SMGP Rd-Sp Web.
Kottmeyer, William A. Our Constitution & What It Means.
Kottow, Michael H. Anterior Segment Fluorescein Angiography.
Kotturan, G. The Himalayan Gateway-History & Culture of Sikkim.
Kotz, Mary L., jt. auth. see Bayh, Marvella.
Kotz, Samuel. Russian-English Dictionary & Reader in the Cybernetical Sciences.
Kotzwinkle, William. Doctor Rat.
--Elephant Bangs Train.
--The Fan Man.
--The Leopard's Tooth.
--The Nap Master.
--The Nap Master.
--Nightbook.
Kouba, Dennis M. Software Reference Guide, 1986-87.
Koudelka, Josef. Gypsies.
Koumoulides, John T., ed. Hellenic Perspectives: Essays in the History of Greece.
Koupernik, Cyrille, jt. auth. see Stone, Frederick H.

Authors

Kovach, A. G. B., et al, eds. Cardiovascular Physiology, Microcirculation & Capillary Exchange: Proceedings of the 28th International Congress of Physiological Sciences, Budapest, 1980.
--Cardiovascular Physiology, Heart, Peripheral Circulation & Methodology: Proceedings of the 28th International Congress of Physiological Sciences, Budapest, Hungary, 1980.
--Cardiovascular Physiology-Neural Control Mechanisms: Processings of the 28th International Congress of Physiological Sciences, Budapest, 1980.
Kovach, E. G., ed. Technology of Efficient Energy Utilization: Report, Nato Science Committee Conference, les Arcs, France, Oct. 1973.
--Thermal Energy Storage.
Kovach, Joseph K., jt. auth. see Murphy, Gardner.
Kovach, Kenneth A. Readings & Cases in Contemporary Labor Relations 1980.
Kovacic, Michael L. Calculus: A Tool for Analysis & Decision.
--Mathematics: Fundamentals for Managerial Decision-Making.
Kovacs, E. Biochemistry of the Poliomyelitis Viruses.
Kovacs, Ruth, ed. see Foundation Center Staff.
Kovacs, T. & Zsoldos, L. Dislocations & Plastic Deformations.
Koval, B. Movimiento Obrero en America Latina: 1917-1959.
Kovaleff, Theodore P. Business & Government During the Eisenhower Administration: A Study of the Antitrust Policy of the Antitrust Division of the Justice Department.
Kovalenko, I. N., jt. auth. see Gnedenko, B. V.
Kovalevsky, J., ed. see COSPAR-IAU-IUTAM Symposium Staff.
Kovaly, John J., ed. Synthetic Aperture Radar.
Kovar, Ilya, jt. ed. see Harvey, David.
Kovel, Ralph M. & Kovel, Terry H. Kovels' Advertising Collectibles Price List.
--Kovels' Antique & Collectibles Price List.
--Kovels' Antique Price List.
--Kovel's Antique Price List.
--The Kovels' Antiques & Collectibles Price List.
--Kovels' Antiques & Collectibles Price List.
--Kovels' Antiques & Collectibles Price List.
--Kovels' Antiques Price List.
--Kovels' Antiques Price List.
--Kovels' Antiques Price List.
--Kovels' Antiques Price List.
--The Kovels' Bottle Price List.
--The Kovels' Bottle Price List.
--The Kovels' Collector's Book of Antique Labels.
--The Kovels' Illustrated Price Guide to Depression Glass & American Dinnerware.
--The Kovels' Illustrated Price Guide to Royal Doulton.
--The Kovels' Official Bottle Price List.
--The Kovels' Organizer for Collectors.
Kovel, Terry H., jt. auth. see Kovel, Ralph M.
Kovi, Paul, jt. auth. see Margittai, Tom G.
Kovnedhov, L. A Brush with Hate.
Kovner, Anthony R. & Neuhauser, Duncan, eds. Health Services Management: A Book of Cases.
Kovol, Yu. Purple Bird.
Kovoor, A., tr. see Gabe, M.
Kovrig, Bennett. Communism in Hungary from Kun to Kadar. Staar, Richard F., ed.
Kovtunov, V. Battle of Ideas in the Modern World.
Kowal, David M. Francisco Ribalta & His Followers: A Catalogue Raisonne. Freedberg, S. J., ed.
Kowallis, Jon, tr. from Chinese. Wit & Humor from Old Cathay.
Kowalski, Charles J., jt. ed. see Prahl-Andersen, B.
Kowalski, E. Nuclear Electronics.
Kowalski, R. Logic for Problem Solving.
Kowalsky, Hans J. Topological Spaces. Strum, Jay, tr.
Kowet, Don. Pele.
Kowle, Carol P., et al. Problem-Solving Process: A Planner's Handbook for Program Improvement.
Kownslar, Allan O., ed. Teaching American History: The Quest for Relevancy.
Koyre, Alexander. Newtonian Studies.
Kozar, Andrew J. R. Tait McKenzie: The Sculptor of Athletes.
Kozel, S., et al. Collected Problems in Physics.
Kozesnik, J., ed. Transactions.
Koziakin, Vladimir. The Amazing Amazeman & The Hydrozoid Attack: A Super-Maze Adventure.
--The Amazing Amazeman in a Super Maze Adventure.
--Amazing Amazeman vs. the Spider Queen.
Kozic, T., ed. Contract Writing & Engineering - Pipeline Hydraulics - Offshore Structure Technology: A Workbook for Engineers.
Kozinn, Allan, et al. The Guitar: The History, the Music, the Players.
Kozlowski, Jerzy. Threshold Approach in Urban, Regional & Environmental Planning: Theory & Practice.
Kozlowski, Joseph G., jt. auth. see Grant, Paul B.
Kozlowski, T. T., jt. auth. see Kramer, Paul J.
Kozlowski, T. T., jt. ed. see Marks, G. C.
Kozol, Jonathan. Death at an Early Age: The Destruction of the Hearts & Minds of Negro Children in the Boston Public Schools.
--Illiterate America.
Kozub, Robert M. The Progressivity Issue in Taxation: A Bibliography.
Kozuki, Russell. Junior Karate.
Kpomassie, Tete-Michel. An African in Greenland. Kirkup, James, tr.
Kra, I., ed. see American Mathematical Society Staff.
Kra, Siegfried. Coronary Bypass Surgery: Who Needs It?
Kra, Siegfried J. Examine Your Doctor: A Patient's Guide to Avoiding Medical Mishaps.
Krabbe, Gregors. Operational Calculus.
Krachenberg, A. R. Marketing Bank Services in Business.
Krader, Lawrence, tr. see Nolte, Ernst.
Kraeling, Emil G., ed. The Brooklyn Museum Aramaic Papyri: New Documents of the Fifth Century B. C. from the Jewish Colony at Elephantine.
Kraemer, Richard & Newell, Charldean. Texas Politics.
Kraemer, William P. The Enemy Within-Without Psychotherapy & Morals Psychotherapy-What It Is.
Kraepelin, Emil. Dementia Praecox & Paraphrenia: With Historical Introduction.
--One Hundred Years of Psychiatry. Baskin, Wade, tr.
Kraft, Betsy H. Oil & Natural Gas.
Kraft, Charles H. Hausa Reader: Cultural Materials with Helps for Use in Teaching Intermediate & Advanced Hausa.
Kraft, David A. Ghost Knights of Camelot.
--The Incredible Hulk: The Secret Story of Marvel's Gamma-Powered Goliath.
Kraft, Herbert C., ed. A Delaware Indian Symposium.
Kraft, Lisbeth M., tr. see Ramon Y Cajal, Santiago.
Kraft, Melvin D., jt. auth. see Practising Law Institute Staff.
Kraft, Quentin. Classic Old Car Value Guide.
Kraft, Richard, ed. Educational Issues of the Seventies: Foundations of Education.
Kraft, Robert A., ed. see Bauer, Walter.
Kraft, Victor. The Vienna Circle.
Kraft, William F. Achieving Promises: A Spiritual Guide for the Transitions of Life.
--A Psychology of Nothingness.
--The Search for the Holy.
Kragelsky, I. V. & Alisin, V. V. Friction, Wear, Lubrication.
Kragen, Adrian A. & McNulty, John K. Cases & Materials on Taxation: Individuals, Corporations, Partnerships.
Krahl, Maurice E. Action of Insulin on Cells.
Krahn, Cornelius. Menno Simons: Ein Beitrag zur Geschichte und Theologie der Taufgerinnten.
Krahn, Fernando. The Biggest Christmas Tree on Earth.
--The Creepy Thing.
--Here Comes Alex Pumpernickel.
--Sleep Tight, Alex Pumpernickel.
Kraiss, F. K., jt. ed. see Moraal, J.
Krajeski, Anita, ed. A Taste of the West from Coors.
Krajewska, Anna, ed. see Middle East Economic Digest Staff.
Krajewski, Robert J. & Shuman, R. Baird. The Beginning Teacher: A Practical Guide to Problem Solving.
Krakowski, A. J. & Kimball, C. P., eds. Psychosomatic Practice & Research: International College of Psychosomatic Medicine, 7th. World Congress, Hamburg, July 1983.
Krakowski, Adam J. & Kimball, Chase P., eds. Psychosomatic Research & Practice.
Krakowski, Adam J. & Kimbell, Chase P., eds. Psychosomatic Medicine: Theoretical, Clinical & Transcultural Aspects.
Krali, N. A., ed. see Tidman, D. A.
Krall, Hanna. Shielding the Flame: An Intimate Conversation with Merek Edelman, One of the Last Surviving Leaders of the Warsaw Ghetto Uprising. Stasinska, Joanna & Weschler, Lawrence, trs.
Krall, Jack & Kalberer, Jan. Finding the Clown In Yourself.
Krall, Leo P., ed. Joslin Diabetes Manual.
Kramarae, Cheris. Women & Men Speaking.
Kramarae, Cheris & Treichler, Paula A. A Feminist Dictionary.
Kramarae, Cheris, ed. The Voices & Words of Women & Men.
Kramer. Phonics Crossword Puzzles Series. Incl. Early Phonics Crossword Puzzle Book; Bk. A; Bk. B; Bk. C. Random Sch Div.
Kramer, jt. auth. see Krause.
Kramer, Aaron, tr. see Rilke, Rainer M.
Kramer, Amihud & Twigg, Bernard A. Quality Control for the Food Industry, Vol. 1: Fundamentals.
Kramer, Amihud, jt. auth. see Green, John H.
Kramer, Ann, jt. auth. see Sloan, Liz.
Kramer, Arthur D., jt. auth. see Burke, Ronald S.
Kramer, Barry, ed. Intellectual Property Law Review, 1986.
Kramer, Fred & Krause, John. Long Island Railroad.
Kramer, Frederick, jt. auth. see Gallo, Daniel.
Kramer, Hans. Habsburg und Rom in Den Jahren 1708-1709.
Kramer, I. R., jt. auth. see Pindborg, J. J.
Kramer, Jack. The Everest House Complete Book of Gardening.
--Plants That Grow on Air.
--A Seasonal Guide to Indoor Gardening.
--Silhouettes: How to Make & Use Them.
Kramer, Jack & Crafton, Roy L. Miniature Orchids to Grow & Show.
Kramer, Jack & Sheehan, Larry. How to Play Your Best Tennis All the Time.
Kramer, John E., Jr. The American College Novel: An Annotated Bibliography.
Kramer, John E., Jr. & Kramer, John E., III. College Detective Stories Bibliography.
Kramer, Jonathan. Stepping up: How to Fight Your Boss & Win.
Kramer, Karlheinz. Erdoel Lexicon.
Kramer, M. & Lauterbach, F., eds. Intestinal Permeation: Proceedings of the Fourth Workshop Conference, Oct. 1975.
Kramer, Mollie. A Selected Bibliography on the Aging, & on the Role of the Library in Serving Them.
Kramer, Paul J. & Kozlowski, T. T. Physiology of Trees.
Kramer, Rita. Maria Montessori: A Biography.
Kramer, Rita W. Marriage Happens to the Nicest People.
Kramer, Samuel N. Sumerians: Their History, Culture & Character.
Kramer, Victor A. Thomas Merton.
Kramov, I. The Voice of the Steppe.
Krampen, Martin. Meaning in the Urban Environment.
Krane, Stephen M., jt. ed. see Avioli, Louis V.
Kranes, David. Hunters in the Snow: A Collection of Short Stories.
Krangel, Ida. In the Name of God.
Kranich, Roger E. & Messec, Jerry L. Visual Data.
Kranitz-Sanders, Lillian. Twelve Who Survived: An Oral History of the Jews of Lodz, Poland, 1930-1954.
Krannich, Larry K., ed. Compounds Containing AS-N Bonds.
Krannich, Ronald L. Moving Out of Government: A Guide to Surviving & Prospering in the 1980's.
Krannich, Ronald L. & Banis, William J. High Impact Resumes & Letters.
Krannich, Ronald L. & Bants, William J. Moving Out of Education: The Educator's Guide To Career Management & Change.
Krans, J. M., jt. ed. see Hessel, L. W.
Krantz, Grover S., jt. ed. see Sprague, Roderick.
Krantz, Harriet & Kimmelman, Joan. Keys to Reading & Study Skills.
Krantz, Jeffrey I., jt. auth. see Willen, David C.
Krantz, Les, ed. American Art Galleries: The Illustrated Guide to Their Art & Artists.
Krantz, Sheldon. Law of Corrections & Prisoners' Rights in a Nutshell.
Krantzler, Mel. Creative Marriage.
Kranz, J., et al, eds. Diseases, Pests & Weeds in Tropical Crops.
Kranz, M. K., jt. auth. see Kranz, R. J.
Kranz, R. J. & Kranz, M. K. Professional Selling: A Practical Approach.
Kranzler, David. My Jewish Roots: A Practical Guide to Tracing & Recording Your Genealogy & Family History.
Kranzler, Gershon. Averted Threat.
--Carpets from Baghdad.
--Faded Mezzuzoth.
--Gershon Kranzler's Ten Stories.
--Golden Shames.
--Leather Boots.
--Selichoth Night.
--Silver Matzoth.
--Silver Mezzuzah.
--Smithy of Burgwald.
--Unusual Seder.
Krapels, Edward N., ed. Pricing Petroleum Products: Strategies of Eleven Industrial Nations.
Krappe, Alexander H. Science of Folklore.
Krar, S. F. & Oswald. Drilling Technology.
Krar, S. F. & Oswald, J. W. Grinding Technology.
Krar, Stephen F., et al. Technology of Machine Tools.
Krashen, Stephen D., et al, eds. Child-Adult Differences in Second Language Acquisition.
Krasilovsky, M. William, jt. auth. see Shemel, Sidney.
Krasinski, Zygmunt. Iridion. Noyes, George R., ed. Noyes, Florence, tr. from Pol.
Kraska, Edie. Toys & Tales from Grandmother's Attic.
Kraske, Robert. Is There Life in Outer Space?
--Riddles of the Stars: White Dwarfs, Red Giants, & Black Holes.
--The Sea Robbers.
--The Story of the Dictionary.
Krasner, L. & Ullmann, L. P. Behavior Influence & Personality.
Krasner, L., ed. see Hersen, Michel & Barlow, David H.
Krasner, Michael A. & Chabersky, Stephen G. American Government.
Krasner, William. Death of a Minor Poet.
--Resort to Murder: A Sam Birge Mystery.
--Walk the Dark Streets: A Sam Birge Mystery.
Krasnoselskiy, M. A., et al. Plane Vector Fields.
Krasnov, M. Ordinary Differential Equations.
Krasnov, M. L., et al. Book of Problems in Ordinary Differential Equations.
--Functions of a Complex Variable, Operational Calculus, & Stability Theory.
Krasnov, N. U. Aerodynamics.
Krasnow, Donna C., jt. auth. see Levy, Tedd.
Krasovskaya, Vera. Nijinsky. Bowlt, John E., tr. from Rus.
Krass, Stephen J. & Keschner, Richard L. The Pension Answer Book.
Kratchman, Stanley H., jt. auth. see Benjamin, James J.
Kratcoski, Lucille D., jt. auth. see Kratcoski, Peter C.
Kratcoski, Peter C. & Kratcoski, Lucille D. Juvenile Delinquency.
Kratochvil, Byron, jt. auth. see Harris, Walter E.
Kratz, Charlotte R., jt. ed. see Barber, J. H.
Kratzer, Myron B. Prior Consent & Nuclear Cooperation.
Kraus, et al. Noel the Coward.
Kraus, Allan D. Matrices for Engineers.
Kraus, Bruce, jt. auth. see Kraus, Robert.
Kraus, Chester L. Guidebook of Franklin Mint Issues.
Kraus, Emil & Gaehler, Heinz V. Tropical Fruits & Vegetables Cookbook.
Kraus, George. A Guide to a Year's Reading in Luther's Works.
Kraus, Gerhard. Homo Sapiens in Decline: A Reappraisal of Natural Selection.
Kraus, Henry. Gold Was the Mortar: The Economics of Cathedral Building.
Kraus, John D. Electromagnetics.
Kraus, Karl, ed. Modern Austrian Literature: Special Issue.
Kraus, Michael. The North Atlantic Civilization.
Kraus, Milton N., jt. auth. see Chemical Engineering Magazine Editors.
Kraus, Richard & Scanlin, Margery. Introduction to Camp Counseling.
Kraus, Robert. Come Out & Play, Little Mouse.
--The Hoodwinking of Mrs. Elmo.
--Owliver.
Kraus, Robert & Kraus, Bruce. The Detective of London.
Krause & Crist. Susquehanna: NYS&W.
Krause & Grenard. The Overland Route.
Krause & Kramer. Cumberland & Pennsylvania.
Krause, Cheste, jt. auth. see Lemke, Robert.
Krause, Chester & Mishle, Clifford. Standard Catalog of World Gold Coins.
Krause, Chester & Mishler, Clifford. Standard Catalog of World Coins.
--Standard Catalog World Coins.
Krause, Chester L. & Lemake, Robert. United States Paper Money.
Krause, Chester L. & Lemke, Robert F. Standard Catalog of U. S. Paper Money.
Krause, D., jt. ed. see Kaufmann, W.
Krause, David. Sean O'Casey & His World.
Krause, Dieter K., et al, eds. Radioimmunoassay-Renin-Angiotensin: Principles of Radioimmunoassay & Their Application in Measuring Renin & Angiotensin.
Krause, E. G., et al, eds. Cyclic Nucleotides & Protein Phosphorylation in Cell Regulation: Proceedings of the 12th FEBS Meeting, Dresden, 1978.
Krause, Emil, jt. auth. see Kamoroff, Bernard.
Krause, F. & Radler, K-H. Mean-Field Magnetohydrodynamics & Dynamo Theory.
Krause, Gail. The Encyclopedia of Duncan Glass.
Krause, John. The American Narrow-Gauge.
Krause, John & Crist, Ed. The Final Years: NYO&W.
Krause, John, jt. auth. see Kramer, Fred.
Krause, Kathalyn. Mellona.
Krause, Sonja, ed. Molecular Electro-Optics: Electro-Optic Properties of Macromolecules & Colloids in Solution.
Krause, Walter C. The Sergeant's Colonel.
--So I Was a Sergeant: Memoirs of an Occupation Soldier.
Krause, William H. How to Get Started As a Manufacturers' Representative.
--How to Get Started As a Manufacturer's Representative.
Kraushar, P. New Products & Diversifications-New Edition.

Authors

Krauskopf, Konrad B. & Beiser, Arthur. Fundamentals of Physical Science.
Krausnick, Helmut & Broszat, Martin. Anatomy of the SS State.
Krauss, G. & Banerji, S., eds. Fundamentals of Microalloying Forging Steels.
Krauss, Hans. Backache, Stress & Tension.
Krauss, Helen. Shell Art: A Handbook for Making Flowers, Mosaics, Jewelry & Other Ornaments.
Krauss, Leonard I. SAFE: Security Audit & Field Evaluation for Computer Facilities & Information Systems.
Krauss, Leonard I. & MacGahar, Aileen. Computer Fraud & Countermeasures.
Krauss, Melvyn. How NATO Weakens the West.
Krauss, Melvyn B. Development Without Aid: Growth, Poverty & Government.
Krauss, Michael E. & McGary, Mary Jane. Alaska Native Languages: A Bibliographical Catalogue - Part One: Indian Languages.
Krauss, Ronnie. Mickey Visits the Dentist.
--Mickey's Question & Answer Book.
Krausz, John & Van der Reis Krausz, Vera. Indoor Cycling.
Krauth, Charles P. Conservative Reformation & Its Theology.
Krauth, Nigel. Matilda, My Darling.
--New Guinea Images in Australian Literature.
Krautheimer, R. Lorenzo Ghiberti.
Krautheimer, Richard. Early Christian & Byzantine Architecture.
Kravis, Irving B. Domestic Interests & International Obligations.
Kravitt, Gregory I. & Grossman, Jeffrey E. How to Raise Capital.
Kravitz, William N. Qualified Plans which Invest in Employer Securities.
Krawetz, Michael. Self-Esteem Passport.
Krawzya, L., jt. ed. see Van Stijgeren, E.
Krayenbuehl, H. Cerebral Angiography in Clinic & Practice.
Kraytman, Maurice. The Complete Patient History.
--Guide to Clinical Reasoning.
Krebs, A., jt. ed. see Israel, H.
Krebs, John R. & Davies, Nicholas B. An Introduction to Behavioural Ecology.
Krebs, John R. & Davies, Nicholas B., eds. Behavioural Ecology: An Evolutionary Approach.
Krebs, Richard. Alone Again.
--Creative Conflict.
--How to Bring up a Good Child.
Krebs, Richard L. It's Hard to Tell You How I Feel: Helping Children Express & Understand Their Feelings.
Krech, Hans. Woerterbuch der Deutschen Aussprache.
Krech, Inez M., ed. see Lobel, Leon & Lobel, Stanley.
Kreck, Lothar A. & McCracken, John W., eds. Dimensions of Hospitality Management: An Industry Performance in Seven Acts.
Kredel. Glass Flowers.
Kreeft, Peter. For Heaven's Sake.
--Yes or No? Straight Answers to Tough Questions about Christianity.
Kreeft, Peter J. Heaven: The Heart's Deepest Longing.
Krefetz, Gerald. How to Read & Profit from Financial News.
--How to Read & Profit from Financial News.
--Jews & Money: The Myths & the Reality.
Krefetz, Gerald & Gittelman, Philip. The Book of Incomes.
Kregel, J. A., ed. see Roncaglia, Alessandro.
Kreh, Lefty. Fly Fishing in Salt Water.
Kreh, Lefty & Sosin, Mark. Practical Fishing Knots.
Kreh, Lefty, jt. auth. see Sosin, Mark.
Krehbiel, Edward K. Nationalism, War & Society.
Kreider, Carl. The Christian Entrepreneur.
Kreider, Jan F. The Solar Heating Design Process: Active & Passive.
Kreider, Jan F., jt. auth. see Kreith, Frank.
Kreidl, John F. Jean-Luc Godard.
Kreig, Allan. Last of the Three Foot Loggers.
Kreinin, Mordechai E. International Economics: A Policy Approach.
--International Economics: A Policy Approach.
Kreis, Bernadine. Fodor's Canada, 1984.
Kreisberg, Adolph. The ABC of Democracy.
Kreiser, Ralph & Hunt, Thomas. Kern County Panorama.
Kreish, Marcand H. I Cook As I Please.
Kreith, Frank & Kreider, Jan F. Principles of Solar Engineering.
Kreitman, J. Bread, Peace & Liberty.
Kreitner, Robert. Management: A Problem-Solving Process.
--Management: Basic Concepts & Decisions.
Kreitner, Robert & Sova, Margaret. Understanding Management: Study Guide to Management: A Problem-Solving Process.
Kreitzberg, Charles B. & Shneiderman, Ben. FORTRAN Programming: A Spiral Approach.
Kreitzman, Stephen & Kreitzman, Susan. The Nutrition Cookbook: 123 Gourmet Recipes Computer Analyzed for Your Specific Daily Requirements.
Kreitzman, Susan, jt. auth. see Kreitzman, Stephen.
Krell, David, tr. see Heidegger, Martin.
Krelle, W. E., jt. ed. see Klein, L. R.
Krementz, Jill. Holly's Farm Animals.
--How It Feels When a Parent Dies.
--Lily Goes to the Playground.
--Sweet Pea.
--Zachary Goes to the Zoo.
Kremer, John. One Hundred One Ways to Market Your Books: For Publishers & Authors.
Kremer, Laura, jt. auth. see Kremer, William F.
Kremer, S., jt. auth. see Konig, E.
Kremer, William F. & Kremer, Laura. The Doctors' Metabolic Diet.
Kreml, William P. The Anti-Authoritarian Personalities.
Kremmer, T. & Boross, L. Gel Chromatography: Theory, Methodology & Application.
Krempl, F., jt. ed. see Chang, T. Y.
Kremser, G., et al. X-Ray Measurements in the Auroral Zone from July to October 1964.
Kren, Thomas, ed. Renaissance Painting in Manuscripts: Treasures from the British Library. Backhouse, Janet, et al.
Krencker, Daniel & Schede, Martin. Der Tempel in Ankara.
Krensky, Stephen. A Big Day for Scepters.
--Castles in the Air & Other Tales.
--The Perils of Putney.
--Woodland Crossings.
Krentel, Mildred. I See Four.
Krentz, Edgar. Easter.
Krentz, Edgar & Vogel, Arthur A. Easter. Achtemeier, Elizabeth, et al, eds.
Krentz, Edgar, ed. see Hahn, Ferdinand.
Krentz, Klaus. Integrated Atlas of Gastric Diseases.
Krentzman, Harvey C. Managing for Profits.
Krepel, Wayne J. & Duvall, Charles R. Field Trips: A Guide for Planning & Conducting Educational Experiences.
Kreshkov, jt. auth. see Yaroslarisev.
Kresiman, Lawrence. The Bloedel Reserve: Gardens in the Forest.
Kreskin. Kreskin's Mind Power Book.
Kress, Gunther. Language As Ideology.
Kress, Robert. A Rahner Handbook.
Kressel, Marilyn, ed. Adult Learning & Public Broadcasting.
Kretchmer, Norman, jt. ed. see Quilligan, E. J.
Kretschmar, Freda. Hundestammvater und Kerberos.
Kretschmer, Ernst. Hysteria Reflex & Instinct.
Kretsmann. Industrial Electronics Handbook.
Kretz, Sandra E., jt. auth. see Wallack, Stanley S.
Kretzmann, O. P. & Oldsen, A. C. Voices of the Passion: Meditations for Lent & Easter.
Kreutzberg, G. W., jt. auth. see Das, G. D.
Kreuzer, R., jt. ed. see Heen, E.
Krey, Isabelle A. & Metzler, Bernadette V. Principles & Techniques of Effective Business Communication: A Text-Workbook.
Kreyche, Gerald F., jt. auth. see Mann, Jesse A.
Kreyche, Gerald F., jt. ed. see Mann, Jesse A.
Kreyszig, Erwin. Advanced Engineering Mathematics.
Krich, Aron M. Homosexuals: As Seen by Themselves & Thirty Authorities.
Krich, John. Music in Every Room: Around the World in a Bad Mood.
--One Big Bed.
Krick, Edward V. An Introduction to Engineering: Methods, Concepts & Issues.
Krick, Robert, et al. Virginia Country Civil War. Ellis, Garrison, ed.
Kricka & Carter. Clinical & Biochemical Luminescence.
Kricka, L. J., ed. Analytical Methods in Clinical Chemistry.
Krickeberg, Walter. Altere Ethnographica aus Nordamerika im Berliner Museum fuer Voelkerkunde.
Krider, J. L. & Carroll, W. E. Swine Production.
Krieg, Carl E. What to Believe? The Questions of Christian Faith.
Kriegel, John. Houston Home & Garden's Complete Guide to Houston Gardening.
Kriegel, Leonard. Edmund Wilson.
Kriegel, Robert, jt. auth. see Gallwey, W. Timothy.
Krieger, Daniel. San Luis Obispo County: Looking Backward into the Middle Kingdom.
Krieger, Dorothy T. & Bardin, C. Wayne, eds. Current Therapy in Endocrinology 1985-1986.
Krieger, Joel, jt. auth. see Douglass, David.
Krieger, John A., jt. auth. see Hale, Ralph W.
Krieger, L. C. Mushroom Handbook.
Krieger, Leonard, ed. see Robertson, William.
Krieger, Morris. Homeowner's Encyclopedia of House Construction.
Krieger, Morris, jt. auth. see Hancock, Leslie.
Kriegler, Roy, et al. Data Processing in Australia: A Profile & Forward Perspective of Skills & Usage.
Krieglstein, G. K., ed. see International Glaucoma Symposium, Nara, Japan, May 7-11, 1978.
Kriek, E., ed. see International Conference on Environmental Carcinogenesis, Amsterdam, May 1979.
Krikler, D. M. & McKenna, W. J., eds. Amiodarone & Arrhythmias: Based on the Scientific Symposium Sponsored by the International Society & Federation of Cardiology.
Krill, John. English Artist' Paper.
Krimsky, Joseph. A Doctor's Soliloquy.
--Jesus & the Hidden Bible.
Kring, Michael. Children of the Night.
Krishef, Robert K. Hank Williams.
--Loretta Lynn.
--Playback: The Story of Recording Devices.
Krishef, Robert K., jt. auth. see Harris, Stacy.
Krishman, Kalliana R. How to Beat Your Power Company at Their Own Game.
Krishman, M. S., ed. see Mahadeuan, C.
Krishna, G. & Ranjhan, S. K. Advanced Laboratory Manual for Nutrition Research.
Krishna, Gopi see Gopi Krishna.
Krishna, P. Cable-Suspended Roofs.
Krishna, P., ed. Crystal Growth & Characterization of Polytype Structures.
Krishnaiah. Multivariate Analysis: Proceedings of Third International Symposium.
Krishnaiah, P., ed. Multivariate Analysis.
Krishnamurti, J. The Awakening of Intelligence.
--From Darkness to Light-Poems & Parables: The Collected Works of Krishnamurti.
--Krishnamurti on Education.
--Meditations.
Krishnamurti, Jiddu. Beyond Violence.
Krishnan, R. S., et al. Thermal Expansion of Crystals.
Krishnan, T. N. General Animal Ecology.
Krishnan-Kutty, G. Money & Banking.
Krishnaswamy, S. Musical Instruments of India.
Krislovsky, M. William, jt. auth. see Shemel, Sidney.
Kristeller, Paul. Early Florentine Woodcuts.
Kristinsson, V., jt. ed. see Nordal, J.
Kristjansson, Jonas. Icelandic Sagas & Manuscripts.
Kristo, Janice V. & Heath, Phillip A., eds. Today's Curriculum: An Integrative Approach.
Kristoferson, L. A., jt. ed. see Chadwick, M. J.
Kritsick, Stephen M. Dr. Kritsick's Tender Loving Cat Care.
Kritz, Mary M., et al, eds. Global Trends in Migration: Theory & Research in International Population Movements.
Kritzer, Richard. The Application of Videotape to the Teaching of Reading: Implications for Global Education.
Kritzman, Lawrence D., ed. see Foucault, Michel.
Krivandin, V. & Markov, B. Metallurgical Furnaces.
Krivchenkov, V. D., jt. auth. see Goldman, I.
Krivosheyev, V., jt. auth. see Preobrazhensky, V.
Kriz, Caroline. Convection Cookery.
--Cooking for Men Only.
Kriz, W., jt. auth. see Kaissling, B.
Krizanc, John. Tamara.
Krmpotic, Vesna. Eyes of Eternity: A Spiritual Autobiography.
Kroch, Anthony S. The Semantics of Scope in English. Hankamer, Jorge, ed.
Krodel, Gerhard, jt. auth. see Watermulder, David B.
Krodel, Gerhard, ed. see Bauer, Walter.
Krodel, Gerhard, ed. see Danker, Frederick W.
Krodel, Gerhard, ed. see Fiorenza, Elisabeth S. & Holmes, Urban T.
Krodel, Gerhard, ed. see Fuller, Reginald H., et al.
Krodel, Gerhard, ed. see Keck, Leander E.
Krodel, Gerhard, ed. see Kingsbury, Jack D.
Kroe, Elaine. Less Than-4-Year Awards in Institutions of Higher Education: 1983-85.
Kroeber, A. L. Handbook of the Indians of California.
Kroeber, Alfred L. Anthropology: Biology & Race.
--Nature of Culture.
--Style & Civilizations.
Kroeber, Donald W. & Watson, Hugh J. Instructor's Manual with Transparency Masters: Computer-Based Information Systems: A Managerial Approach.
Kroeber, Donald W., jt. auth. see LaForge, R. Lawrence.
Kroeber, Theodora. Carousel.
--A Green Christmas.
--Ishi, Last of His Tribe.
Kroeck, Patricia C., jt. ed. see Ossenbeck, Frederick J.
Kroeger, Herbert E. Using Discounted Cash Flow Effectively.
Kroeger, Louis J. The Art & Practice of Public Administration: Papers by Louis J. Kroeger. Nathan, Harriet, ed.
Kroener, E., ed. see Generalized Cosserat Continuum & the Continuum Theory of Dislocations with Applications Symposium Staff.
Kroepelin, H., et al. Thermodynamic Diagrams for High Temperature Plasmas of Air-Carbon, Carbon-Hydrogen Mixtures & Argon.
Krog, Carl E. & Tanner, William R., eds. Herbert Hoover & the Republican Era: A Reconsideration.
Krogh, Daniel & McCarty, John. The Amazing Herschell Gordon Lewis & His World of Exploitation Films.
Krogh, P., ed. Control of Mycotoxins: Proceedings of a Symposium, Goteborg, Sweden, 1972.
Krogman, W. M., jt. auth. see Moyers, R. E.
Krogsgaard-Larsen, P., et al, eds. GABA-Neurotransmitters.
Krohn, Michael. Photography for the Hiker & Backpacker.
Krojzlova, Clare, tr. see Loth, Wilfried.
Krokodil Editors. Soviet Humor: The Best of Krokodil.
Krol, John C. God-the Cornerstone of Our Life.
Kroll, Arthur H. Tax Compliance after TEFRA: Dealing with the New Reporting Requirements & Penalties.
Kroll, Barry M. & Wells, Gordon, eds. Explorations in the Development of Writing: Theory, Research, & Practice.
Kroll, Oskar. The Clarinet.
Kroll, Steven. Banana Bits.
--Bathrooms.
--Dirty Feet.
--Giant Journey.
--Gobbledygook.
--Space Cats.
Kroll, Una. Flesh of My Flesh.
Kroll, Woodrow M. It Will Be Worth It All: A Study in the Believer's Rewards.
Krollman, F. Dictionary of Military Terms.
Kromdijk, G. Two Hundred House Plants in Color.
Krome, Ronald L., ed. see American College of Emergency Physicians Staff.
Kromer, Helen. Caught Between.
Kronauer, Margaret see Gallagher, Dolores.
Kronchnabel, Darlene. Ideals Eggs & Cheese Cookbook.
Krone, Kenneth M., ed. see Evans, Alvis J., et al.
Kronenberg, M. Machining Science & Applications.
Kronenthal, Richard L., et al, eds. Polymers in Medicine & Surgery.
Kronhausen, Eberhard, jt. auth. see Kronhausen, Phyllis.
Kronhausen, Phyllis & Kronhausen, Eberhard. Erotic Fantasies.
--Erotic Fantasies: A Study of the Sexual Imagination.
Kronick, D., jt. auth. see Mersky, Roy M.
Kronschnabel, Darlene. The Country Kitchen Cookbook. Kuse, James K., ed.
Kronus, Carol L. & Crowe, Linda, eds. Libraries & Neighborhood Information Centers.
Krook, Dorothea, jt. auth. see Gilead, Zerubavel.
Krook, Hans. Close to Nature: An Exploration of Nature's Microcosm.
Kroon, A. M. & Saccone, C., eds. The Biogenesis of Mitochondria: Transcriptional, Translational & Genetic Aspects, Proceedings.
Krooss, Herman E. & Gilbert, Charles. American Business History.
Kropotkin, Peter. Kropotkin's Revolutionary Pamphlets. Baldwin, Roger, ed.
Kropotkin, Petr A. Fields, Factories & Workshops or Industry Combined with Agriculture & Brain Work with Manual Work.
Kropp, Paul. Getting Even.
Kroptkin, P. Ideals & Realities in Russian Literature.
Kroth, Roger L. & Scholl, Geraldine T. Getting Schools Involved with Parents.
Krotkov, Yuri. The Red Monarch: Scenes from the Life of Stalin. Mairs, Tanya E., tr.
Kroupa, Melanie, ed. see Carillo, Charles.
Kroupa, Melanie, ed. see Nilsson, Ulf.
Kroy, Michael. The Conscience: A Structural Theory.
Krsna devi dasi & Sama devi dasi, eds. The Hare Krishna Cookbook.
Kruberg, Galina. A Handbook for Translating from English into Russian.
Kruchten, Marcia. The Ghost in the Mirror.
--I Don't Want to Be Like Her.
Krueckeberg, Donald A. The American Planner.
Krueckeberg, Donald A. & Silvers, Arthur L. Urban Planning Analysis: Methods & Models.
Krueger, Anne O., ed. Trade & Employment in Developing Countries: Synthesis & Conclusions.
Krueger, Mark A. & Webster, Christopher D., eds. Practicioner Perspectives in Residential Child & Youth Care Work: A Special Issue of Child Care.
Krueger, Treila. All Clear: An Everyday Guide to Total Skin Care.
Krug, S. & Stein, P. Influence Surfaces of Orthogonal Anisotropic Plates. Juhl, H., tr.

Kruger, Arnd & Oberdieck, Helmut. Guide to Track & Field Injuries.
Kruger, Barbara, et al. Picture This: Films Chosen by Artists. Gallagher, Steve, ed.
Kruger, D., jt. auth. see Mullish, H.
Kruger, Gustav O. Textbook of Oral & Maxillofacial Surgery.
Kruger, Hardy. The Upside Down Tree.
Krughoff, Robert, jt. auth. see Center for the Study of Services Staff.
Kruglinski, David. Data Base Management Systems: A Guide to Microcomputer Software.
Krugman, Stanley L., et al. Forest Genetics & Tree Improvement in the People's Republic of China.
Kruif, Paul De see De Kruif, Paul.
Kruk, Z. L., jt. auth. see Williams, R. A.
Krukow, Ira. Project Management with the IBM PC.
Krumm, Donald L. Winning the Second American Revolution, Plus Winning your Personal Battle For Financial Success.
Krumm, Rob. Understanding & Using dBASE II & dBASE III.
Krumm, Robert. DBASE III Plus Power Tools: Communications, Debugging & File Integration.
Krummel, D. W., ed. see Newberry Library, Chicago Staff.
Krummel, Don W., ed. see International Association of Music Libraries Staff.
Krummel, Donald W., ed. Organizing the Library's Support: Donors, Volunteers, Friends.
Krummes, Daniel & Kleiber, Michael. Recent Transportation Literature for Planning & Engineering Librarians (January 1985)
--Recent Transportation Literature for Planning & Engineering Librarians (February 1985)
--Recent Transportation Literature for Planning & Engineering Librarians (March 1985)
--Recent Transportation Literature for Planning & Engineering Librarians: A Selection Based upon the Acquisitions of the Institute of Transportation Studies Library, University of California, Berkeley, (December 1985)
--Recent Transportation Literature for Planning & Engineering Librarians: A Selection Based upon the Acquisitions of the Institute of Transportation Studies Library, University of California, Berkeley, (November 1985)
--Recent Transportation Literature for Planning & Engineering Librarians: A Selection Based upon the Acquisitions of the Institute of Transportation Studies Library, University of California, Berkeley, (October 1985)
--Recent Transportation Literature for Planning & Engineering Librarians: A Selection Based upon the Acquisitions of the Institute of Transportation Studies Library, University of California, Berkeley (September 1985)
--Recent Transportation Literature for Planning & Engineering Librarians: A Selection Based upon the Acquisitions of the Institute of Transportation Studies Library, University of California, Berkeley (August 1985)
--Recent Transportation Literature for Planning & Engineering Librarians: A Selection Based upon the Acquisitions of the Institute of Transportation Studies Library, University of California, Berkeley (July 1985)
--Recent Transportation Literature for Planning & Engineering Librarians: A Selection Based upon the Acquisitions of the Institute of Transportation Studies Library, University of California, Berkeley (June 1985)
--Recent Transportation Literature for Planning & Engineering Librarians: A Selection Based upon the Acquisitions of the Institute of Transportation Studies Library, University of California, Berkeley (May 1985)
--Recent Transportation Literature for Planning & Engineering Librarians: A Selection Based upon the Acquisitions of the Institute of Transportation Studies Library, University of California, Berkeley (April 1985)
Krummes, Daniel C., et al. Sources of Information in Transportation: Part 8, Highways.
Krupa, Viktor. The Polynesian Languages: A Guide.
Krupman, William A., jt. auth. see Lewis, Robert.
Krupp, Marcus A., et al. Current Medical Diagnosis & Treatment.
Krupp, R. A. Saint John Chrysostom: A Scripture Index.
Kruppa, Carole. The Free & Equal Cookbook.
Kruppa, Patricia S. Charles Haddon Spurgeon: A Preachers Progress. Stansky, Peter & Hume, Leslie, eds.
Kruse, Donald W. There's a Skunk in My Trunk. Davenport, May, ed. Bd. with Spotty the Goat. Walker, Robert W; Christopher C. Cat. Cutting, Edith; Night Dancers. Pendleton, Jan. Davenport.
Kruse, John. The Hour of the Lily.
Kruse, Paul, Jr. & Patterson, M. K., eds. Tissue Culture: Methods & Applications.
Kruse, Robert L. Data Structures & Program Design.
Kruse, Ted. Locating Computer Software.
Kruse, Vindling. Community of the Future.
Krusina, A. Czech-Say It in Czech: English-Czech Phrase Book with Pronunciation.
Kruskal, M. D., ed. see International School Of Nonlinear Mathematics & Physics-Munich-1966.
Kruss, James. My Great-Grandfather, the Heroes & I.
Krutch, Joseph W. The Great Chain of Life.
Krutch, Joseph W. & Eriksson, Paul S., eds. A Treasury of Birdlore.
Kruteskii. The Psychology of Mathematical Abilities in School Children.
Krutogolov, M. A. Talks on Soviet Democracy.
Krutz, R. L. Microprocessor for Managers: A Decision Maker's Guide.
Krutza, William J. & Dicicco, Philip P. Facing the Issues.
Krutzch, William C., jt. auth. see Karassik, Igor J.
Kruzas, Anthony T., et al. Medical & Health Information Directory.
Kryder, Christian & Strickland, Stephen P. Americans & Drug Abuse.
Kryger, Meir H. Pathophysiology of Respiration.
Krylov, Ivan. Soviet Staff Officer.
Krylov, V. A. Handbook of Methods of Approximate Fourier Transformation & Inversion of Laplace Transformaton.
Krystal, Henry & Raskin, Herbert A. Drug Dependence: Aspects of Ego Functions.
Krzywick-Herburt, Barbara, tr. see Wyszynski, Stefan.
Krzywoblocki, M. Z. Von see Von Krzywoblocki, M. Z.
Kubeczka, K. H., jt. auth. see Formacek, V.
Kubie, Lawrence S. Neurotic Distortion of the Creative Process.
Kubik, Richard S. Baseball Trades & Acquisitions, Nineteen Fifty to Nineteen Seventy-Nine.
Kubilinskas, K. The Frog Queen.
Kubler-Ross, Elisabeth. Remember the Secret.
Kublin, Hyman. Africa: Regional Study.
--China: Selected Readings. Anderson, Howard R., ed.
--India: Selected Readings.
--Japan: Selected Readings.
Kubo, R. Statistical Mechanics.
Kubo, S. R. & Hanamura, E. E., eds. Relaxation of Elementary Excitations: Proceedings.
Kubo, Sakae. God Meets Man: A Theology of the Sabbath & the Second Advent.
--The Open Rapture.
Kubota, Itchiku. Opulence: The Kimonos & Robes of Itchiku Kubota. Yamanobe, Tomoyuki, ed.
Kubr, Milan, ed. Management Consulting: A Guide to the Profession.
Kubursi, Atif. The Economies of the Arabian Gulf: A Statistical Source Book.
Kubursi, Atif A. Oil, Industrialization & Development in the Arab Gulf States.
Kubursi, Atif A. & Naylor, Thomas, eds. Co-Operation & Development in the Energy Sector: The Arab Gulf States & Canada.
Kucherawy, M. D., jt. auth. see Beer, T.
Kuchler, Robert J., ed. Animal Cell Culture & Virology.
Kuchta, Joseph M. Investigation of Fire & Explosion Accidents in the Chemical, Mining, & Fuel-Related Industries.
Kuchta, Ronald A., ed. see Seckler, Dorothy G.
Kuck, Glen. Help My Faith Grow, Lord!
Kuck, Loraine. The World of the Japanese Garden: From Chinese Origins to Modern Landscape Art.
Kuck, Loraine E. & Tongg, Richard C. Hawaiian Flowers & Flowering Trees.
Kuczynski, Irving. British Offshore Oil & Gas Policy.
Kuczynski, Jurgen. Germany: Economic & Labour Conditions under Fascism.
Kudler, Jacqueline & Stark, Arlene. Walking from Inn to Inn: The San Francisco Bay Area.
Kudlick, Michael D. Assembly Language Programming for the IBM Systems 360 & 370 for OS-DOS.
Kudo, Kazuzo. Judo in Action: Throwing Techniques.
Kudryavtsev, V. A. & Demidovich, B. P. A Brief Course of Higher Mathematics.
Kudryk, V. & Rao, Y. K., eds. Physical Chemistry of Extractive Metallurgy.
Kuechemann, K., tr. see Mori, Y. & Lennert, K.
Kueck, Gary, jt. auth. see Tedeschi, Frank P.
Kuehl. A Taxonomy of Critical Tasks for Evaluating Student Teaching.
Kuehl, John, ed. see Fitzgerald, F. Scott.
Kuehl, Warren F. Dissertations in History: An Index to Dissertations Completed in History Departments of United States & Canadian Universities 1970 - June 1980.
Kuehn, Dick, jt. auth. see RAK Associates Staff.
Kuehne, Robert S. & Baker, R. Jerry. Inventory Management Factomatic-A Portfolio of Successful Forms, Reports, Records & Procedures.
Kuehnemann, Ursula. Cold Enamelling.
--Presents for Dad.
Kuemmel, W. G., ed. see Dibelius, Martin.
Kuenzel, W. & Toman, J., eds. Kinderstomatologie 2.
Kuenzli, Esther Wilcox. The Last Years of Thomas Jefferson, 1809-1826.
Kuesel, Harry N. Kuesel on Closing Sales.
Kuh, George. Evaluation in Student Affairs.
Kuhaulua, Jesse & Wheeler, John. Takamiyama: The World of Sumo.
Kuhl, D. E., ed. Principles of Radionuclide Emission Imaging.
Kuhler, Otto. My Iron Journey: An Autobiography.
Kuhlman, Raymond L. Effective Operator Training-Lift Trucks.
--Effective Operator Training: Motorized Equipment.
Kuhlman, Raymond L., jt. auth. see Germain, George L.
Kuhlmann -Wilsdorf, Doris, ed. see TMS Staff & AIME Staff.
Kuhn, Alvin B. The Red Sea Is Your Blood.
Kuhn, Annette. Women's Pictures: Feminism & Cinema.
Kuhn, Bowie K. Hardball: The Education of a Baseball Commissioner.
Kuhn, Charles L. German & Netherlandish Sculpture, 1280-1800: The Harvard Collections.
Kuhn, H. W., ed. see International Summer School on Mathematical Systems Theory & Economics, Varenna, Italy, 1967.
Kuhn, Harold W. Contributions to the Theory of Games. Tucker, A. W., ed.
Kuhn, Isobel. Second-Mile People.
Kuhn, J. W., jt. auth. see Chamberlain, Neil W.
Kuhn, Karl F. & Faughn, Jerry S. Physics in Your World.
Kuhn, Tillo E. Public Enterprise: Economics & Transport Problems.
Kuhn, W., jt. auth. see Graeff, H.
Kuhne, Gary W. The Change Factor: The Risks & the Joys.
Kuhner, Hans. Encyclopedia of the Papacy.
Kuhner, Herbert. Broadsides & Pratfalls.
Kuhnert-Brandstatter, M. Thermomicroscopy in the Analysis of Pharmaceuticals.
Kuhnmund, Vas I., jt. auth. see Pachman, Ludek.
Kuic, Vukan, ed. see Simon, Yves.
Kuiper, Gerald P. & Middlehurst, Barbara, eds. Telescopes: Stars & Stellar Systems.
Kuiper, Nicholas A., ed. Social Cognition & Depression. Higgins, E. Tory.
Kuiper, Pieter C. The Neuroses.
Kuipers, Benjamin & Williams, Brian. Qualitative Simulation & Causal Models.
Kuipers, L. & Timman, R. Handbook of Mathematics.
Kujawa, Charles C., ed. National YMCA Camping Standards.
Kujawa, Duane. International Dimensions of Industrial Relations. Ricks, David A., ed.
Kukarkin, A. The Passing Age.
Kuklin, Susan. Mine for a Year.
Kukushkin, G. I. System of Physical Education in the U. S. S. R.
Kula, Eric & Weiss, Volker, eds. Residual Stress & Stress Relaxation.
Kulacki, F. & Lyczkowski, R. W., eds. Heat Transfer in Nuclear Waste Disposal: HTD-Vol. 11.
Kuleshov, Vadim, tr. see Artsibasov, A.
Kulik, Stephen, et al. The Audubon Society Field Guide to the Natural Places of the Northeast: Inland.
Kulikov, G., jt. auth. see Medvedev, F.
Kulikowsky, J., ed. see CISM (International Center for Mechanical Sciences), Department of Automation & Inforamation Staff.
Kulka, Erich. Escape from Auschwitz.
Kulkarni, S. V., et al. Composite Materials in the Automobile Industry.
Kulkarni, V. Y. see Kesavan, B. S.
Kullenberg, G. The State of the Baltic.
Kulonen, E., ed. Biology of Fibroblast.
Kulshrestha, S. K. A Textbook of Applied Thermodynamics: Steam & Thermal Engineering.
Kulski, Julian E. Land of Urban Promise: Continuing the Great Tradition.
Kumagai, Kojiro. Fashion & Color.
Kumar, Dharmenora & Jain, S. K. Materials Science & Manufacturing Processes. Shargava, A. K., ed.
Kumar, Joginder. Population & Land in World Agriculture.
Kumar, Krishan. Reference Service.
Kumar, Krishan, jt. auth. see Ellis, Adrian.
Kumar, Ram, jt. auth. see Chopra, M. G.
Kumar, S. & Rathi, M., eds. Perinatal Medicine: Clinical & Biochemical Aspects of the Evaluation, Diagnosis & Management of the Fetus & Newborn.
Kumar, Satish. CIA & the Third World: A Study in Cryptodiplomacy.
Kumar, Shiv K. Nude Before God: A Novel.
Kumar, Sudhir. Biochemistry of the Brain.
Kumar, V., tr. see Samoilenko, A. M., et al.
Kumar, Vinay. Experimental Techniques in Quantitative Chemical Analysis.
Kumchy, Gayle, jt. auth. see Lonnetto, Richard.
Kume, Genichi. Picture Play: Kintaro's Adventures.
Kumin, Libby. Aphasia.
Kumin, Maxine. What Color Is Caesar.
Kummel, P. Formalization of Natural Languages.
Kummer, Fred. Effective Weight Manager.
Kump, Peter. Quiche & Pate. Topkis, Gladys, ed.
Kumpe, Roy & Lester, Jim. The Lion's Share: A History of Arkansas Enterprises for the Blind.
Kumpel, P. G., jt. auth. see Thorpe, J. A.
Kundell, James E. Acid Rain: The Georgia Situation.
--Litter Abatement Measures.
Kundla, E., et al. Magnetic Resonance & Related Phenomena.
Kundu, C. L. Adult Education: Principles, Practice & Prospects.
Kundu, C. L. & Tutoo, D. N. Educational Psychology.
Kunen, James S. Strawberry Statement.
Kunetka, James W. City of Fire: Los Alamos & the Atomic Age, 1943-1945.
Kunetka, James W., jt. auth. see Strieber, Whitley.
Kung, H. T., et al, eds. VLSI Systems & Computations.
Kung, Jeanne L., jt. auth. see Kung, Samuel S.
Kung, Samuel S. & Kung, Jeanne L. Village Life in China.
Kunhardt, Philip B., Jr., ed. Life Smiles Back: More Than Two Hundred Classic Photos From the Famous Back Page of America's Favorite Magazine.
Kuniholm, Bruce R. The Persian Gulf & United States Policy: A Guide to Issues & References.
Kunii, T. L., jt. ed. see Yao, S. B.
Kunin, Robert. Ion Exchange Resins.
Kuninori. Jason in Outer Space.
Kunitz, Stanley. Next-to-Last Things: New Poems & Essays. Davison, Peter, ed.
Kunkel, Francis L. Passion & the Passion: Sex & Religion in Modern Literature.
Kunkel, Henry G. see Taliaferro, W. H. & Humphrey, J. H.
Kunkin, Art, ed. see Goodson, Aileen.
Kunkle, S. H. & Thames, J. L., eds. Hydrological Techniques for Upstream Conservation.
Kunn, Helmut, jt. auth. see Gilbert, Katherine E.
Kunstler, Gustav, ed. Romanesque Art in Europe.
Kunstler, James H. Blood Solstice.
--An Embarrassment of Riches.
--The Life of Byron Jaynes.
Kunstler, William. Trials & Tribulations.
Kuntz, Eugene O., et al. Forms Manual to Accompany Cases & Materials on Oil & Gas Law.
Kuntzleman, Beth A., jt. auth. see Consumer Guide Editors.
Kuntzleman, Charles T. The Well Family Book.
Kunz, Marilyn & Schell, Catherine. Amos (Neighborhood Bible Study)
--Choose Life.
Kunz, Phillip R., jt. auth. see Dyer, William G.
Kunz, Robert, jt. auth. see Weissbach, Herbert.
Kunzle, David. Fashion & Fetishism: A Social History of the Corset, Tight-Lacing & Other Forms of Body-Sculpture in the West.
Kuo, Benjamin C. Automatic Control System.
Kuo, H. H. Gaussian Measures in Banauch Spaces.
Kuong, Javier. Applied Nomography.
Kuong, Javier F. Applied Nomography.
Kupelnick, Bruce S., ed. see Biro, Lajos & Wimperis, Arthur.
Kupelnick, Bruce S., ed. see Boyer, Deena.
Kupelnick, Bruce S., ed. see Brundidge, Harry.
Kupelnick, Bruce S., ed. see Gassner, John & Nicholas, Dudley.
Kupelnick, Bruce S., ed. see Gibbon, Monk.
Kupelnick, Bruce S., ed. see Hill, W. Aber.
Kupelnick, Bruce S., ed. see Hollywood Arts Science & Professions Council.
Kupelnick, Bruce S., ed. see Lathrop, William A.
Kupelnick, Bruce S., ed. see McCoy, Horace.
Kupelnick, Bruce S., ed. see Palmer, Edwin.
Kupelnick, Bruce S., ed. see Patterson, Frances.
Kupelnick, Bruce S., ed. see Pirandello, Luigi.
Kupelnick, Bruce S., ed. see Pollak, James.
Kupelnick, Bruce S., ed. see Rawlinson, Arthur & Farnum, Dorothy.
Kupelnick, Bruce S., ed. see Rotha, Paul.
Kupelnick, Bruce S., ed. see Schary, Dore.
Kupelnick, Bruce S., ed. see Short, William A.
Kupelnick, Bruce S., ed. see Vidor, King.
Kupfer, David J., et al. Mental Health Information Systems: Design & Implementation.
Kupferberg, Herbert. Basically Bach: A Three Hundredth Birthday Celebration.
--Felix Mendelssohn: His Life, His Family, His Music.
--Tanglewood.
Kupperstein, Lenore, et al, eds. Drugs & Social Policy.
Kuprin, A. Miracle Doctor.
Kuralt, Charles. Dateline America.
Kurata, Mamoru. Numerical Analysis for Semiconductor Devices.

Authors

Kuratowski, K. A Half Century of Polish Mathematics: Remembrances & Reflections.
--Introduction to Calculus.
--Introduction to Set Theory & Topology.
Kureishi, R. The Nation of Pakistan.
Kurelek, William. Fields.
--Lumberjack.
--Lumberjack.
Kurfees, M. C. Instrumental Music in Worship.
Kurian, George T. Dictionary of Biography.
Kurian, Milton & Hand, Morton H., eds. Lectures in Dynamic Psychiatry.
Kuriloff, Arthur H. & Hemphill, John M. How to Start Your Own Business & Succeed.
Kuris, Cindy & Kuris, Marc. Every Excuse in the Book.
Kuris, Marc, jt. auth. see Kuris, Cindy.
Kurkin, A. Russkii Narodnye Skazkii: (Russian Fairy Tales)
Kurland, Leonard T., et al. Epidemiology of Neurologic & Sense Organ Disorders.
Kurland, Michael & Barton, S. W. The Last President.
Kurland, Michael & Garrett, Randall. Star Griffin.
Kurland, Philip B. Politics, the Constitution & the Warren Court.
Kuroda, Seiyo. Rome.
Kuroff, Barbara N. Summer Employment Directory of the U. S. 1984.
Kuroff, Barbara N., ed. Songwriter's Market, 1983.
--Songwriter's Market, 1984.
Kurosawa, Akira, et al. Ran.
Kurosch, A. G. Curso de Algebra Superior.
Kursh, Harry. Apprenticeships in America.
Kurstak, C., jt. ed. see Kurstak, E.
Kurstak, Christine, jt. auth. see Kurstak, E.
Kurstak, E. & Kurstak, Christine. Comparative Diagnosis of Viral Diseases: Human & Related Viruses.
--Comparative Diagnosis of Viral Diseases.
Kurstak, E. & Kurstak, C., eds. Comparative Diagnosis of Viral Diseases, Vol. 3: Vertebrate Animal & Related Viruses, DNA Viruses.
--Comparative Diagnosis of Viral Diseases, Vol. 4: Vertebrate Animal & Related Viruses, Part B-BNA Viruses.
Kurstak, E., jt. ed. see Maramorosch, Karl.
Kurstak, Edouard & Maramorosch, Karl. Viruses & Environment.
Kurstak, Edouard, ed. Arctic & Tropical Arboviruses.
Kurstak, Edouard & Maramorosch, Karl, eds. Viruses, Evolution & Cancer.
Kurstak, Edouard & Marqmorosch, Karl, eds. Invertebrate Tissue Culture: Applications in Medicine, Biology & Agriculture.
Kurstak, Edouard & Morisset, Richard, eds. Viral Immunodiagnosis.
Kursunoglu, Behram & Perlmutter, Arnold, eds. Gauge Theories, Massive Neutrinos & Proton Decay.
Kurten, Bjorn. Singletusk.
Kurten, Nancy N. Needlepoint: Stitch by Stitch.
Kurth, Rudolf. Dimensional Analysis & Group Theory in Astrophysics.
--Elements of Analytical Dynamics.
Kurtin, Norman, tr. see Berg, Lasse & Berg, Lisa.
Kurtis, Arlene H. Puerto Ricans: From Island to Mainland.
Kurtz, Agnes B. Women's Lacrosse for Coaches & Players.
Kurtz, David & Marshall, Eldon. Interviewing Skills for Family Assistance Workers.
Kurtz, David L. & Boone, Louis E. Marketing.
Kurtz, David L., jt. auth. see Boone, Louis E.
Kurtz, David L., et al. Professional Selling.
Kurtz, Edwin B. & Shoemaker, Thomas M. The Lineman's & Cableman's Handbook.
Kurtz, Irma. Beds of Nails & Roses: Witty Observations on Enjoying Life As a Modern Woman.
--Loneliness.
Kurtz, Irma & Unger-Hamilton, Clive. The Children's Guide to...Paris.
Kurtz, J. H. Sacrificial Worship of the Old Testament. Martin, James, tr.
Kurtz, John W. & Politzer, Heinz. German: A Comprehensive Course.
Kurtz, Max. Engineering Economics for Professional Engineers' Examinations.
Kurtz, Regina, jt. auth. see Van Gieson, Susan.
Kurtz, Ron & Prestera, Hector. The Body Reveals.
Kurtz, Seymour. Jewish America.
Kurtz, Thomas E., jt. auth. see Kemeny, John G.
Kurtz, Tom, jt. auth. see Kemeny, John.
Kurtz, V. Ray. Metrics for Elementary & Middle Schools.
Kurtzke, J. F. Epidemiology of Cerebrovascular Disease.
Kurtzman, Jeffrey. Essays on the Monteverdi Mass & Vespers of 1610.
Kuruvilla, M. I. Studies in World Literature.
Kury, Gloria. The Early Work of Signorelli: 1465-1490.
Kury, Zaher P. From a Gun to a Flower: Messages Through the Mediumship of Zaher P. Kury.
Kurz, Otto, jt. auth. see Buchtal, Hugo.
Kurzman, Dan. Ben-Gurion: Prophet of Fire.
--Ben Gurion: Prophet of Fire.
--The Day of the Bomb: Countdown to Hiroshima.
Kurzman, Robert G. & Gilbert, Rita K. Paralegals & Successful Law Practice.
Kurzweil, Edith & Phillips, William, eds. Writers & Politics: A Partisan Review Reader.
Kusan, Ivan. The Mystery of Green Hill. Petrovich, Michael B., tr.
--The Mystery of the Stolen Painting. Willen, Drenka, tr.
Kuse, James, ed. see Smith, Catharine P.
Kuse, James A., ed. Bunny Tales.
Kuse, James A., ed. see Brand, Mildred.
Kuse, James A., ed. see Wiersum, Beverly.
Kuse, James K., ed. see Kronschnabel, Darlene.
Kusemchenko, L. F., jt. auth. see Gogulan, M. F.
Kushi, Michio. The Book of Macrobiotics: The Universal Way of Health & Happiness.
Kushi, Michio & Cottrell, Martha C. AIDS & Immune Deficiency: Macrobiotic Approach.
Kushi, Michio & Janetta, Phillip. Macrobiotics & Oriental Medicine: An Introduction.
Kushner, Carol S. Crafts: A Career Alternative.
Kushner, Ervan F. Alferd G. Packer: Cannibal! Victim?
Kushner, Harold S. When All You've Ever Wanted Isn't Enough.
--When Bad Things Happen to Good People.
Kushner, Kenneth. One Arrow, One Life: Zen, Archery & Daily Life.
Kushner, Lawrence. The River of Light: Spirituality, Judaism, & the Evolution of Consciousness.
Kushner, Morton, intro. by. Materials Nineteen Eighty.
Kushner, Rose. Breast Cancer.
Kusin, Vladimir, jt. auth. see Hejzlar, Zdenek.
Kuske, Martin. The Old Testament As the Book of Christ: An Appraisal of Bonhoeffer's Interpretation. Kimbrough, S. T., Jr., ed.
Kuskin, Karla. A Boy Had a Mother Who Bought Him a Hat.
--Herbert Hated Being Small.
Kusniewicz, Andrezej. The King of Two Sicilies. Wieniewska, Celina, tr.
Kuspit, Donald. Samaras, Pastels & Bronzes.
Kuspit, Donald, ed. see Buettner, Stewart.
Kussi, Peter, tr. see Grusa, Jiri.
Kut, D. Heating & Hot Water Services in Buildings.
--Warm Air Heating.
Kutash, S. B., jt. auth. see Branham, V. C.
Kutepov, A. Problems in Geometry.
Kuthumi, et al. Understanding Yourself. Prophet, Mark & Prophet, Elizabeth, eds.
Kutler, Stanley I. Privilege & Creative Destruction: The Charles River Bridge Case.
Kutler, Stanley I., ed. The Supreme Court & the Constitution: Readings in American Constitutional History.
Kutner, Lynn. Bountiful Bread: Basics to Brioches. Spiegel, Barbara, ed.
Kutner, Peter B. & Reynolds, Osborne M. Advanced Torts: Cases & Materials.
Kutsche, Paul & Van Ness, John R. Canones: Values, Crisis, & Survival in a Northern New Mexico Village.
Kutscher, Austin H., et al, eds. Pharmacology for the Dental Hygienist.
Kutsky, Roman J. Handbook of Vitamins, Minerals & Hormones.
Kutter, Peter. Basic Aspects of Psychoanalytic Group Therapy. Molnos, Angela, tr.
Kuttner, Henry. Mutant. Del Ray, Lester, ed.
Kuttner, Robert. The Economic Illusion: False Choices Between Prosperity & Social Justice.
Kuttner, Robert E. Race & Modern Science.
Kuttruff, Heinrich. Room Acoustics.
Kutzelnigg, W., et al. Sigma & PI Electrons in Organic Compounds.
Kuusi, Juha. Host State & the Transnational Corporation.
Kuusi, Matti, et al. Finnish Folk Poetry: Epic.
Kuvas, J., ed. Boss Nineteen Seventy-Six: Proceedings of an International Conference on the Behavior of Off-Shore Structures, Norwegian Institute of Technology, Trondheim, 2-5 August 1976.
Kuwayama, George. Far Eastern Lacquer.
Kuwayama, Yasaburo. Trademarks & Symbols of the World.
Kuyk, W., ed. see International Summer School for Theoretical Physics Staff.
Kuypers, Mary S. Studies in the Eighteenth Century Background of Hume's Empiricism.
Kuzanskaya, A. Calculations of Chemical Equilbria.
Kuzin, N., et al. La Instruccion Publica in la URSS.
Kuzirian, Eugene & Madaras, Larry. Taking Sides: Clashing Views on Controversial Issues in American History.
--Taking Sides: Clashing Views on Controversial Issues in American History.
Kuzman, Y. A. Thematic Dialogue: Mathematics.
Kuzmenko, Yuri. Soviet Literature: Yesterday, Today & Tomorrow. Butler, Jan, tr.
Kuzmich, John, Jr. & Bash, Lee. Complete Guide to Instrumental Jazz Instruction.
Kuzmin, A. D. & Salomonovich, A. E. Radioastronomical Methods of Antenna Measurements.
Kuzmin, L. The Wondrous Apple.
Kuzmin, Mikhail. Selected Prose & Poetry. Green, Michael, ed.
Kuznets, Simon. Economic Growth & Structure.
--Population, Capital & Growth.
--Toward a Theory of Economic Growth.
Kuznetsov, V. V., tr. see Maslov, A. V., et al.
Kuznetzov, B. V. Russian-English Polytechnical Dictionary.
Kvande, Carol, jt. auth. see Fideler, Raymond.
Kvenvolden, K. A., ed. Geochemistry & the Origin of Life.
Kvenvolden, Keith A., ed. Geochemistry of Organic Molecules.
Kvet, J., jt. ed. see Dykyjova, D.
Kviz, Frederick J. & Knafl, Kathleen A. Statistics for Nurses: An Introductory Text.
Kwa Hong Giok. Experimental Study of Pituitary Tumors: Genesis. Cytology & Hormone Content.
Kwak, No Kyoon & DeLurgio, Stephen A. Quantitative Models for Business Decisions.
Kwang, Tan C., ed. see Winstedt, Richard.
Kwan Ha Yim, ed. China Since Mao.
Kwart, Harold, jt. auth. see Drenth, Wiendelt.
Kwasky, Albert. The Old Lady in Dubuque.
Kwitny, Jonathan. Shakedown.
--Vicious Circles: The Mafia in the Marketplace.
Kwizda, R. Vocabularium Nocentium Florae.
Kwok, Samuel. The Path to Wing Chun.
Kwok Man Ho, et al. Lines of Destiny: How To Read Faces, & Hands the Chinese Way.
Kybett, Harry. Video Tape Recorders.
Kyburg, H. E. Studies in Subjective Probability.
Kyd, Thomas. Blood on the Bosom Devine.
Kyle, Duncan. The Dancing Men.
Kyle, James, et al. Amateur Radio Advanced Class License Study Guide.
--Amateur Radio General Class License Study Guide.
Kyle, Jim G. & Woll, Bencie, eds. Language in Sign: An International Perspective on Sign Language.
Kyle, Mabel R. White Caps: Nurse's Training Fifty Years Ago.
Kyle, Robert C. Property Management.
Kyle, William. The Uniqueness of Pastoral Psycholtherapy.
Kynerd, Thomas E. Administrative Reorganization of Mississippi Government: A Study in Politics.
Kyngeston, Richard. Expeditions to Prussia & the Holy Land Made by Henry Earl of Derby. Smith, L. T., ed.
Kynoch, P. A., jt. ed. see Lehmann, H.
Kyper, Frank & Rainey, Lee. East Broad Top Railroad.
Kyrala, A. Theoretical Physics: Applications of Vectors, Matrices, Tensors & Quaternions.
Kysar, Ardis & McLinn, Dianne. New Faces, New Spaces: Helping Children Cope with Change.
Kysar, Ardis & Overstad, Elizabeth, eds. Helping Young Children Cope with Crisis: A Guide for Training Child Care Workers.
Kysar, Robert. The Fourth Evangelist & His Gospel: An Examination of Contemporary Scholarship.
--The Scandal of Lent: Themes for Lenten Preaching in the Gospel of John.
Kysar, Robert & Kaysar, Myrna. The Asundered: Biblical Teachings on Divorce & Remarriage.
Kyte, Dennis. The Last Elegant Bear.
--Puppy Gets Around.
--Puppy in the Garden.
--Puppy Plays a Song.
--Puppy Tidies Up.
--To the Heart of a Bear.
Kyte, Kathy S. Play It Safe: The Kids' Guide to Personal Safety & Crime Prevention.
Kytle, Annette P., jt. auth. see Kytle, Ray.
Kytle, Calvin. Gandhi: Soldier of Nonviolence.
Kytle, Ray & Kytle, Annette P. The Complex Vision: A Collection of Short Stories.

L

L. A. Weekly Staff. The Best of L. A. The L.A. Weekly's Guide to the Very Best That Los Angeles Has to Offer. Crain, Mary B., ed.
L. F. Garlinghouse Co., Inc. Single Level & Underground Home Plans.
L. F. Garlinghouse, Co., Staff, ed. Multi-Level, Hillside & Solar Home Plans.
L. F. Garlinghouse Co., Staff, ed. Small Home Plans.
--Traditional Home Plans.
L, Marian & Hale, George E. Politics of Federal Grants.
L.A. Immigration Committee. Contesting Deportability: Tactics & Issues in Deportation Hearings.
Laband, David N. Foreign Ownership of U. S. Farmland.
Labanna, Wallace D. Groupwork Guide for Discussion Leaders to the Cure Is in the Cause.
La Barba, Richard. Foundations of Developmental Psychology.
Labarca, Angela & Rodriguez, Elmer A. Invitacion: Spanish for Communication & Cultural Awareness.
Labaree, Benjamin W., jt. auth. see Christie, Ian R.
Labarge, Margaret W. Court, Church & Castle.
--Medieval Travellers.
--A Small Sound of the Trumpet: Women in Medieval Life.
L'Abate, Bess, jt. auth. see L'Abate, Luciano.
L'Abate, Luciano. Family Psychology: Theory, Therapy, & Training.
L'Abate, Luciano & Curtis, Leonard T. Teaching the Exceptional Child.
L'Abate, Luciano & L'Abate, Bess. How to Avoid Divorce.
Labedz, Leopold, jt. ed. see Survey Magazine Staff.
Labella, Frank S., et al. Pinocytosis.
LaBelle, Judith & Waugh, Carol. Patchworking: A Quilt Design & Coloring Book.
LaBelle, Judith, jt. auth. see Waugh, Carol.
Labenne, Wallace D. The Cure Is in the Cause: A Humane Approach to Child Discipline.
Labenski, L., jt. auth. see Labenski, R.
Labenski, R. & Labenski, L. TK! Solver the Easy Way.
LaBerge, Armand J., jt. auth. see Fryklund, Verne C.
Labiak, William. Programming the 65816.
LaBier, Douglas. Modern Madness.
Labine, Clem, ed. see Old-House Journal Staff.
Labo, James A. A Practical Introduction to Borehole Geophysics. Mentemeier, Samuel H. & Gardner, Gerald H., eds.
Labor Research Association Staff, ed. Labor Confronts the Transnationals.
Labor Research Front Staff. Labor Bulletin.
Laboratory for Computer Graphics & Spatial Analysis, Harvard University Graduate School of Design Staff. Bibliography & Index, Vol. 19: Part II, Bibliography & Key-Word-in-Context.
--Cartographic & Statistical Data Bases & Mapping Software.
--Cartographic Data Bases & Software.
--Computer Graphics Hardware.
--Computer Graphics Hardware.
--Computer Mapping Applications in Urban, State, & Federal Government: Plus Computer Graphics & Education.
--Computer Mapping in Education, Research, & Medicine.
--Computer Mapping in Natural Resources & Environment: Including Applications of Satellite-Derived Data.
--Computer Mapping of Natural Resources & the Environment: Including Applications of Satellite-Derived Data.
--Computer Mapping of Natural Resources & the Environment: Plus Satellite-Derived Data Applications.
--The Harvard Library of Computer Graphics, Mapping Collection.
--How to Design an Effective Graphics Presentation.
--Management's Use of Computer Graphics.
--Management's Use of Maps: Commercial & Political Applications.
--Management's Use of Maps: Including an Introduction to Computer Mapping for Executives.
--Mapping Software & Cartographic Data Bases.
--Thematic Map Design.
--Urban, Regional, & State Applications: Plus a Special Section on Cadastral Systems.
--Urban, Regional, & State Government Applications of Computer Mapping: Plus Computer Mapping in Education.
Labov, William. Language in the Inner City: Studies in the Black English Vernacular.
Labov, William, ed. Locating Language in Time & Space.
Labovitz, M. L., jt. ed. see Craig, R. G.
Labowitz, Fred. For Love or Money: How to Succeed in Spite of Yourself.
LaBrecque, Ron. Lost Undercover: An FBI Agent's True Story.
LaBrie, Ross. Howard Nemerov.
Labuz, Ronald A. & Altimonte, Paul. The Interface Data Book for Word Processing Typesetting.
Labuza, Theodore P. & Sloan, A. Elizabeth. Food for Thought.
Lacan, Jacques. The Four Fundamental Concepts of Psycho-Analysis.
LaCerva, Victor A. Breastfeeding: A Manual for Health Professionals.
Lacey, A. R. A Dictionary of Philosophy.

Authors

Lacey, Colin & Lawton, Denis, eds. Issues in Evaluation & Accountability.
Lacey, D. R. de see De Lacey, D. R.
Lacey, P. R. Life with the Mentally Sick Child.
Lacey, Robert. The Kingdom: Arabia & the House of Sa'ud.
--Majesty.
--Majesty: Elizabeth II & the House of Windsor.
Lacey, Thomas A., ed. The King's Book, or a Necessary Doctrine & Erudition for Any Christian Man, 1543.
Lacey, William N. & Sage, Bruce H. Thermodynamics of One-Component Systems.
Lachenbruch, David & Norback, Craig. The Complete Book of Adult Toys.
Lacher, Chris, jt. auth. see Bryant, John.
Lacher, Mortimer J. Hodgkin's Disease.
Lachlan, A., et al, eds. Set Theory & Hierarchy Theory 5: Bierutowice, Poland 1976.
Lachmann, Karl, ed. T. Lucreti Cari de Rerum Natura Libri Sex.
Lachtman, Howard. Sherlock Slept Here: A Brief History of the Singular Adventures of Sir Arthur Conan Doyle in America, with Some Observations upon the Exploits of Mr. Sherlock Holmes.
--Sherlock Slept Here: Being a Brief History of the Singular Adventures of Sir Arthur Conan Doyle in America, with Some Observations Upon the Exploits of Mr. Sherlock Holmes.
Lacis, Astra, tr. see Chapman, Jean.
Lackey, Ivan. Who Am I? Asks the Alcoholic: A Study Based on Concepts a Recovering Alcoholic Heard, Heeded & Now Teaches.
Lackey, Larry. How to Start a Small Business.
Lackner, Marie & Paterno, Cynthia. RCT Reading: A Workbook.
Lackner, Stephan. Max Beckmann: Memories of a Friendship.
Lackner, Stephen. Peaceable Nature: An Optimistic View of Life on Earth.
Lackstrom, J. E. & White, R. V. Moving Up: Intermediate Functional English.
Lacocque, Andre. The Book of Daniel.
--But As for Me: The Question of Election for God's People Today.
Lacocque, Andre & Lacocque, Pierre. Jonah Complex.
Lacocque, Andre, jt. auth. see Niedenthal, Morris.
Lacocque, Pierre, jt. auth. see Lacocque, Andre.
Laconte, M. Pierre & Lambert, Richard D., eds. Changing Cities: A Challenge to Planning.
La Croix, Don, jt. ed. see Kaufman, Peter B.
LaCroix, Ernest O. Banking Is Serious Business:(Don't You Believe It)
La Croix, Horst De see De La Croix, Horst & Tansey, Richard G.
Lacroix, Richard L. Integrated Rural Development in Latin America.
La Cuaza, C. & Root, A. W. Problems in Pediatric Endocrinology.
Lacy, Creighton. Coming Home-To China.
Lacy, Dan. The Abolitionists.
--White Use of Blacks in America.
Lacy, Mary L. And God Wants People.
--Springboard to Discovery.
--Woman Wants God.
La Dage, John H. Modern Ships: Elements of Their Design, Construction, & Operation.
Ladas, Alice K. & Whipple, Beverly. The G Spot: & Other Recent Discoveries about Human Sexuality.
Ladas, Gerasimbs E., jt. auth. see Grove, Edward A.
Ladd & Tideman, eds. Tax & Expenditure Limitations.
Ladd, D. Robert, tr. see Pascu, Stefan.
Ladd, Everett C., Jr. Where Have All the Voters Gone? The Fracturing of America's Political Parties.
Ladd, George T., jt. auth. see Brown, George D.
Ladd, M. F. Structure & Bonding in Solid State Chemistry.
Ladd, William. Essays of Philanthropos on Peace & War.
Ladefoged, Peter. A Course in Phonetics.
Laden, Caroline S., ed. see Institute for Paralegal Training Staff.
Ladenheim, J., jt. auth. see Olivecrona, H.
Ladenson, Robert F. A Philosophy of Free Expression & Its Constitutional Applications.
Ladewig, D. & Hobi, V. Drogen unter uns. Dubacher, H. & Faust, V., eds.
Ladimer, Irving, jt. auth. see McCarthy, Jane.
Ladley, Winifred, ed. Federal Legislation for Libraries.
Ladman, Jerry R., et al, eds. U. S.-Mexican Energy Relationships: Realities & Prospects.
Lado, Robert. Lado English Series.
LaDochy, et al. Climate & Landforms: A Laboratory Manual in Physical Geography.
Ladurie, Emmanuel L. Jasmin's Witch: A Case of Possession in Seventeenth-Century France. Pearce, Brian, tr.
Ladusaw, William A. & Hankamer, Jorge. Polarity Sensitivity As Inherent Scope Relations.
Lady Morgan. The Wild Irish Girl.
Lael, Richard, jt. auth. see Killen, Linda.
Laertacher, David V. A Nonbook Cataloguing Sampler.
Laeuchli, Samuel. Religion & Art in Conflict: Introduction to a Cross-Disciplinary Task.
La Fane, Pamela. It's a Lovely Day, Outside.
La Farge, Oliver. Laughing Boy.
La Fauci, H. M. & Richter, P. Team Teaching at the College Level.
LaFave, Wayne R. Modern Criminal Law: Cases, Comments & Questions.
--Principles of Criminal Law.
--Search & Seizure: A Treatise on the Fourth Amendment, 1985 Pocket Parts to Vols. 1-3.
LaFave, Wayne R. & Israel, Jerold. Criminal Procedure, 1986 Pocket Part.
LaFave, Wayne R. & Scott, Austin. Criminal Law.
LaFave, Wayne R., jt. auth. see Israel, Jerold H.
Lafavore, Michael. The Home Gym: A Guide to Fitness Equipment.
Lafaye, Jacques. Quetzalcoatl & Guadalupe: The Formation of Mexican National Consciousness, 1531-1813. Keen, Benjamin, tr. from Fr.
Laffer, Arthur B. & Seymour, Jan P. The Economics of the Tax Revolt: A Reader.
Lafferty, Peter. Introduction to Computing.
Lafferty, R. M. Enzyme Technology.
Lafferty, Sarah R. Standing Ground: Sculpture by American Women.
Laffin, Jack. Rhetoric & Reality: The Arab Mind Considered.
Laffin, John. Arab Mind Considered: A Need for Understanding.
Lafford, Barbara A., ed. Central America & the Caribbean: Today & Tomorrow.
Lafleur & Starr. Exploring Medical Language: A Student-Directed Approach.
Lafore, Robert. Assembly Language Primer for the IBM PC.
--Turbo C Programming for the IBM.
LaForge, R. Lawrence & Kroeber, Donald W. Business Statistics.
LaFray, Joyce. Florida Famous Restaurants.
--Florida Underwater Gourmet.
Lagadec, P. Le Risque Technologique Majeur.
Lagal, Roy. Detector Owner's Field Manual. Nelson, Bettye, ed.
Lagal, Roy & Garrett, Charles. The Complete VLF-TR Metal Detector Handbook: All about Ground Cancelling Metal Detectors. Nelson, Bettye, ed.
Lage, William & Borchard, Edwin M. Neutrality for the U. S.
Lagercrantz, H., jt. ed. see Von Euler, C.
Lagercrantz, Rose. Tulla's Summer. Blecher, George & Thygesen-Blecher, Lone, trs.
Lagerloef, Selma O. The Diary of Selma Lagerloef. Howard, Velma S., tr.
--Memories of My Childhood: Further Years at Marbacka. Howard, Velma S., tr.
Lagerlof, Selma. Marbacka. Howard, Velma S., tr.
Lago, A. M., jt. auth. see Beenhakker, H. L.
Lagos Conference Staff. Outline of a Plan for Scientific Research & Training in Africa: Proceedings of the Lagos Conference, 1964.
Lagowski, J. J., jt. auth. see Katritzky, A. R.
Lagowski, J. J. & Sienko, M. J., eds. Metal-Ammonia Solutions: Proceedings of the International Conference on the Nature of Metal-Ammonia Solution, Ithaca, N.Y., 1969.
LaGrone, Gregory G. Basic Conversational Spanish.
LaGuardia, Robert. Monty.
--Monty: A Biography of Montgomery Clift.
--Soap World.
--Soap World.
LaGumina, Salvatore J., ed. The Immigrants Speak: The Italian Americans Tell Their Story.
Laguna, Frederica De see De Laguna, Frederica.
Laham, Sandra L., jt. ed. see Popovich, Dorothy.
LaHaye, Beverly, jt. auth. see LaHaye, Tim.
LaHaye, Tim & LaHaye, Beverly. Our Favorite Verse.
--Practical Answers to Common Questions about Sex in Marriage.
Lahee, Frederick H. Field Geology.
Lahey, G. F. Gerard Manley Hopkins.
Lahita, Robert, ed. Systemic Lupus Erythematosis.
Lahm, Liz, jt. ed. see Behrmann, Michael M.
Lahren, James A. & Pautler, Albert J., eds. Current Concepts in Occupational Education.
Lahue, Kalton. Mariner Outboard Shop Manual 50-200Hp, 1976-1984.
Lahue, Kalton, ed. Petersen's Big Book of Photography.
Lahue, Kalton C. The Darkroom Guide.
--Mini-Truck Repair Manual.
--Photo Filters & Lens Attachments.
--Photo Retouching & Restoration.
--Wide Angle Photography.
Lahue, Kalton C., jt. auth. see PhotoGraphic Magazine Editors.
Lahue, Kalton C., ed. Basic Tune-up & Test Equipment.
--Big Book of Auto Repair: 1982 Edition.
--Honda Tune-up & Repair.
Lai, W. M., et al. Introduction to Continuum Mechanics.
Laiderman, Beth, jt. auth. see Higgins, Heather.
Laidlaw, John P. & Richens, Alan. A Textbook of Epilepsy.
Laidlaw, John R. The Catholic Church in Oregon and the Work of Its Archbishops.
Laidlaw, W. A. Latin Literature.
Laidler, ed. see International Congress of Pure & Applied Chemistry 28th, Vancouver, BC, Canada, 16-22 August 1981.
Laidler, David. Introduction to Microeconomics.
Laidler, K. J. Reaction Kinetics.
Laidler, K. J., jt. ed. see Back, M.
Laiken, Deidre S. Death among Strangers.
Laine, Amos L., jt. auth. see Geritz, Albert.
Laine, Denny. Denny Laine: How to Play the Guitar.
Laine, I., jt. auth. see Laine, S.
Laine, S. & Laine, I. Promotion in Food Service.
Laing, A. F., jt. auth. see Hussell, C. G.
Laing, Alastair, ed. see McParland, Edward.
Laing, Alastair, ed. see Willis, Peter.
Laing, Anna C. My Father's Reply.
Laing, Donald A. Roger Fry: An Annotated Bibliography.
Laing, Gordon. Survivals of Roman Religion.
Laing, Jennifer, jt. auth. see Laing, Lloyd.
Laing, Lloyd. The Archaeology of Late Celtic Britain & Ireland, c.400-1200 A.D.
--Celtic Britain.
Laing, Lloyd & Laing, Jennifer. Anglo-Saxon England.
--The Origins of Britain.
Laing, Mary, ed. see Reynolds, Graham.
Laing, R. D. The Facts of Life.
--Wisdom, Madness & Folly: The Making of a Psychiatrist, 1927-1957.
Lainiotis, Demetrios G., ed. see International Conference on Information Sciences & Systems Staff.
Lainiotis, Dmitri G., jt. ed. see Mehra, Raman K.
Laiou-Thomadakis, A. E. Peasant Society in the Late Byzantine Empire: A Social & Demographic Study.
Lair, Jess. Ain't I a Wonder & Ain't You a Wonder Too.
--I Don't Know Where I'm Going, but I Sure Ain't Lost.
--Sex: If I Didn't Laugh, I'd Cry.
Laird. Mind & Deity.
--Theism & Cosmology.
Laird, Charlton & Gorrell, Robert M. Reading About Language.
Laird, John. Hume's Philosophy of Human Nature.
Laird, M. Bibliography of the Natural History of Newfoundland & Labrador.
Laithwaite. Exciting Electric Machine Inventions.
Laithwaite, E. R. Linear Motor & Its Application to Tracked Hovercraft.
Laithwaite, L. & Freris, T. Electrical Energy: Its Generation, Transmission & Use.
Lajer-Burcharth, Ewa, jt. auth. see Kline, Katy.
Lake, Brian. British Newspapers: A History & Guide for Collectors.
Lake, Carol L. Pediatric Cardiac Anesthesia.
Lake, John G., jt. auth. see Reidt, Wilford H.
Lake, P. The Cambrian Trilobites.
Lake, Steven R. Hearts & Dollars: How to Beat the High Cost of Falling In & Out of Love.
Lake, Veronica & Bain, Donald. Veronica: The Autobiography of Veronica Lake.
Laker, Rosalind. Fair Wind of Love.
--Silver Touch.
Lakich, Lili. Neon Lovers Glow in the Dark.
Lakin, K. Charlie, jt. ed. see Wood, Frank H.
Lakin, Leonard, jt. auth. see Chaykin C. P. A. Review Staff.
Laklan, Carli. Golden Girls: True Stories of Olympic Women Stars.
Lakland, Carli, jt. auth. see Chadzynski, Martin.
Lakoff, George & Johnson, Mark. Metaphors We Live by.
Lakoff, Robin T. & Scherr, Raquel L. Face Value: The Politics of Beauty.
Lakos, Amos. American Diplomatic Memoirs: A Bibliography.
--Modern Diplomacy: A Bibliography.
--The Nuclear Terrorism Threat: A Bibliography.
Lakovaara, Seppo, ed. Advances in Genetics, Development, & Evolution of Drosophila.
Lakshmikantham, V., ed. Nonlinear Equations in Abstract Spaces.
Lal, B. B. Elements of Income Tax.
--Income Tax Law & Practice.
Lal, Chaman. India: Cradle of Cultures.
Lal, Deepak. A Liberal International Economic Order: The International Monetary System & Economic Development.
Lal, Deepak & Heap, A. Men or Machines: A Philippines Case Study of Labour-Capital Substitution in Road Construction in the Philippines.
Lal, P. The Mahabharata.
Lal, P., jt. ed. see Nopany, Nandini.
Lal, R., jt. ed. see Greenland, D. J.
Lala, P., ed. Satellite Perturbations & Orbital Determination.
Lall, K. B. & Chopra, H. S., eds. EEC & the Third World.
Lall, Sanjaya. The New Multinationals: The Spread of Third World Enterprises.
Lall, Sanjaya, ed. Conflict & Bargaining.
Lallemant, Hans G. Structure of the Canyon Mountain (Oregon) Ophiolite & Its Implication for Sea-Floor Spreading.
Lalli, Sergeo, jt. auth. see Bonanno, Joseph.
Lalli, Victor R. Intermediate Perspective.
Lally, Dick. Pinstriped Summers: Memories of Yankee Seasons Past.
LaLonde, William S. & Stack-Staikidis, William. Professional Engineer's Examination Questions & Answers.
Lalov, I. J. Modern Problems of Surface Physics: Proceedings-Condensed Matter & Statistical Mechanics.
Lam, T. Y. Serre's Conjecture.
Lam, W. Perception & Lighting as Formgivers for Architecture.
Lamadrid, Enrique E., et al. Communicating in Spanish, Level I.
Lamantia, Philip. Blood of the Air.
Lamar, Howard R. Far Southwest, Eighteen Forty-Six to Nineteen Twelve: A Territorial History.
LaMar, Virginia, ed. see Shakespeare, William.
LaMar, Virginia A., ed. see Shakespeare, William.
Lamare, James W. Texas Politics: Economics, Power & Policy.
Lamartine, Alphonse de. La Chute d'un Ange.
Lamb, Alastair. British India & Tibet Seventeen Sixty-Six to Nineteen Hundred Ten.
Lamb, Alastair, jt. auth. see Lamb, Venice.
Lamb, Charles & Lamb, Mary. Poetry for Children.
Lamb, Charles E., jt. auth. see Lamberg, Walter J.
Lamb, Charles M., jt. auth. see Halpern, Stephen C.
Lamb, Charles W., Jr. Marketing: Cases for Analysis.
Lamb, Charles W., Jr., ed. see Theory Conference Staff.
Lamb, Charlotte. Duel of Desire.
Lamb, Eleanor. Ashes of Sin.
Lamb, G. H. Underground Coal Gasification.
Lamb, Gordon H. Choral Techniques.
Lamb, Hugh, ed. Return from the Grave.
--Terror by Gaslight: More Victorian Tales of Terror.
--Victorian Nightmares.
Lamb, J. Modern Food Processing.
Lamb, John W. Saint Wulstan, Prelate & Patriot: A Study of His Life & Times.
Lamb, Linda. Learning the VI Editor.
Lamb, M. W. & Harden, M. L. Meaning of Human Nutrition.
Lamb, Margaret. Colorado High Country.
Lamb, Mary, jt. auth. see Lamb, Charles.
Lamb, Michael E. & Campos, Joseph J. Infancy.
Lamb, Patricia F. & Hohlwein, Kathryn J. Touchstone: Letters Between Two Women 1953-1964.
Lamb, Richard. Montgomery in Europe Nineteen Forty-Three to Nineteen Forty-Five: Success or Failure.
--Whitehall Madness.
Lamb, Robert & Rappaport, Stephen P. Municipal Bonds: The Comprehensive Review of Tax-Exempt Securities & Municipal Finance.
Lamb, Tony & Duffy, Dave. Retirement Threat.
Lamb, Venice & Lamb, Alastair. West African Narrow Strip Weaving. Fiske, Patricia, ed.
Lamb, Warren & Watson, Elizabeth. The Body Code: The Meaning in Movement.
Lamba, P. S., jt. auth. see Gupta, O. P.
Lambard, Greene & Lambard, Sharleen. Badlands Run.
Lambard, Sharleen, jt. auth. see Lambard, Greene.
Lambe, Dwight W., et al, eds. Anaerobic Bacteria: Selected Topics.
Lambe, T. William & Whitman, Robert V. Soil Mechanics, SI Version.
Lambel, R. A., et al. Chemistry in Space Research.
Lamberg, Stanley L. & Rothstein, Robert. Functional Medical Laboratory Technology: Hematology & Urinalysis.
--Histology & Cytology: Functional Medical Laboratory Manual.
Lamberg, Walter J. & Lamb, Charles E. Reading Instruction in the Content Areas.
Lambermont, Paul. Helicopters & Autogyros of the World.
Lambert. Microsoft Word for the MAC.
Lambert, A. M. The Making of the Dutch Landscape: An Historical Geography of the Netherlands.
Lambert, Dennis & Zalkind, Ronald. Producing Hit Records.
Lambert, Herbert H., ed. see Dixon, Michael E.
Lambert, J. L. Police Powers & Accountability.
Lambert, Jack M. Older Soldier.
Lambert, Jacklyn & Samborski, Jeffrey. Mental Blocks: The Block Party.

Authors

Lambert, Jean C. The Human Action of Forgiving: A Critical Application of the Metaphysics of Alfred North Whitehead.
Lambert, Jeffrey M. From Comiskey to the Domes: An Architectural History of the Ball Parks.
Lambert, Joseph B., et al. Organic Structural Analysis.
Lambert, Karel & Brittan, Gordon G., Jr. An Introduction to the Philosophy of Science.
Lambert, Kenneth. Analysis Repair & Individuation.
Lambert, Mark. Plant Life.
Lambert, Nina. A Place in the Sun.
Lambert, Regina. Every Woman Has a Ministry.
Lambert, Richard D., jt. ed. see Greenberg, Jack.
Lambert, Richard D., jt. ed. see Laconte, M. Pierre.
Lambert, Richard D., jt. ed. see Lamberton, Donald M.
Lambert, Richard D., jt. ed. see Martin, L. John.
Lambert, Richard D., jt. ed. see Yarmolinsky, Adam.
Lambert, Ronald D. The Sociology of Contemporary Quebec Nationalism: A Annotated Bibliography & Review.
Lambert, Royston. New Wine in Old Bottles?
Lambert, Steve. Presentation Graphics on the IBM PC & Compatibles: How to Use Microsoft Chart to Create Dazzling Graphics for Professional & Corporate Applications.
Lambert, Steve & Ropiequet, Suzanne, eds. CD ROM: The New Papyrus.
Lambert, Terence. Lambert's Birds of Shore & Estuary.
Lambert, Wallace E., et al. Child Rearing Values: A Cross National Study.
Lamberth, John, et al. Personality: An Introduction.
Lamberton, D. M., jt. ed. see Jussawalla, Meheroo.
Lamberton, Donald M. & Lambert, Richard D., eds. The Information Revolution.
Lambertsen, Christian J., ed. Underwater Physiology.
Lamberty, Kim, ed. see National Security Committee & Harriman, W. Averell, Institute for Advanced Study of the Soviet Union Staff.
Lambeth, M. Discovering Corn Dollies.
Lambi, Ivo N. Free Trade & Protection in Germany, 1868-79.
Lambie, Jack. The Ultralight Kit Book.
Lambie, Jack, jt. auth. see Thomas, Kas.
Lamborn, Kathleen R., jt. auth. see Tashman, Leonard J.
Lambot, Isobel. Past Tense.
Lambrecht, Judith J., et al. Business & Office Education: Review & Synthesis of Research.
Lambrinos, James. Evaluation of Employee Benefits: Theory, Practice & Implication for Tort Practice.
Lambro, Donald. Land of Opportunity: The Entrepreneurial Spirit in America.
--Washington: City of Scandals.
Lambton, Lucinda. Beastly Buildings: Architecture for Animals. Johnson, Joyce, ed.
Lamenek, K., ed. Agreements of International Organizations & the Vienna Convention on the Law of Treaties: Oesterreich, Zeitschrift fuer Oeffentiliches Recht Suppl. 1.
La Mer, Victor K., ed. Retardation of Evaporation by Monolayers.
Lamera, S. Maggiorino, the Little Apostle of the Good Press.
LaMere, Shirley. Seafood Primer: A Practical Book of Fish Cookery.
Lamit, Gary. Industrial Model Building.
Lamitie, Marg. How to Select & Place Your Parents in a Nursing Home.
Lamm. The Royal Reach.
Lamm, Dottie. Second Banana.
Lamm, Kathryn. Ten Thousand Ideas for Term Papers, Projects & Reports.
Lamm, Martin. Modern Drama.
Lamm, Richard D. Megatraumas: America at the Year 2000.
Lamm, Richard D. & McCarthy, Michael. The Angry West: A Vulnerable Land & Its Future.
Lammers, Ann C., tr. see Steiner, Jorg.
Lammers, Charmain, ed. see Duran Duran.
Lammers, Cornelius J. & Hickson, David J., eds. Organizations Alike & Unlike.
Lammie. Partial Dentures.
Lammineur, P. & Cornillie, O. Industrial Robots.
Lamming, G. E., ed. Marshall's Physiology of Reproduction, Vol. 1: Reproductive Cycles of Vertebrates.
Lamming, R. M. In the Dark.
--The Notebook of Gismondo Cavalletti.
Lamoitier, J. P. BASIC Exercises for the IBM Personal Computer.
LaMond, Annette M. Competition in the General-Freight Motor-Carrier Industry.
Lamont, Corliss. Illusion of Immortality.
--Man Answers Death.
--The Philosophy of Humanism.
Lamont, Daveta, ed. see Kosbab, William H.
Lamont, I. M., ed. Water Research Topics.
Lamont, Lansing. Day of Trinity.
Lamont, Marianne. Dark Changeline.
La Monte, Francesca & Welch, Micaela. Vanishing Wilderness.
LaMore, Gregory S. Handicapped...How Does It Feel.
La Mothe, Francois De Salignac De see Fenelon & De Salignac De La Mothe, Francois.
L'Amour, Louis. Bowdrie's Law.
--Jubal Sackett.
--Jubal Sackett.
--Passin' Through.
--The Walking Drum.
Lamoureux, Normand J., jt. auth. see Comeau, Raymond F.
Lamoureux, Richard E. Alberti's Church of San Sebastiano in Mantua. Freedberg, Sydney J., ed.
Lamp, C. O. Gentle Tigress.
Lamparski, Richard. Whatever Became of....? The Best & Newest of the Lamparaki Profiles of Personalities.
Lampe, M. Willard, jt. ed. see Foerster, Norman.
Lampedusa, Giuseppe Di. Leopard. Colquhoun, A., tr.
Lampen, Nevada. Fat-Free Recipes.
Lampert, Eleanor V. Black Bloomers & Han-Ga-Ber.
Lampert, Hope. Behind Closed Doors: Wheeling & Dealing in the Banking World.
--Till Death Do Us Part: Bendix vs. Martin Marietta.
Lampert, Junko, jt. auth. see Barber, Linda L.
Lampert, Lyndon J., jt. auth. see Borneman, Walter.
Lampert, Lyndon J., jt. auth. see McLeod, Robert W.
Lamphear, Lynn. Short Cuts to Affective on the Job Writing.
Lampkin, W., jt. auth. see Eilon, S.
Lampl, Paul. Cities & Planning in the Ancient Near East.
Lampman, Evelyn S. Bargain Bride.
--Cayuse Courage.
--Go up the Road.
--The Potlatch Family.
--Rattlesnake Cave.
--Squaw Man's Son.
--Three Knocks on the Wall.
--Year of Small Shadow.
Lampman, Robert J. Ends & Means of Reducing Income Poverty.
--Social Welfare Spending: Accounting for Changes from Nineteen Fifty to Nineteen Seventy-Eight.
Lamprecht, Sterling P., ed. see Hobbes, Thomas.
Lampton, Christopher. COBOL for Beginners.
--Pascal for Beginners.
Lampton, David M. Paths to Power: Elite Mobility in Contemporary China.
Lamson, Peggy. The Glorious Failure: Black Congressman Robert Brown Elliott & the Reconstruction in South Carolina.
--In the Vanguard: Six American Women in Public Life.
Lamson, Roy & Smith, Hallett, eds. Renaissance England.
Lamy, Steven L., et al. Comparative World Issues for Grades One to Twelve.
Lancashire, Anne, ed. The Editing of Renaissance Dramatic Texts: English, Italian, & Spanish.
Lancaster, Anita S. & Berne, Richard R. Employer-Sponsored Career Development Programs.
Lancaster, Clay, et al. East Hampton's Heritage: An Illustrated Architectural Record.
Lancaster, Don. Assembly Cookbook for the Apple II-IIe.
--Cheap Video Cookbook.
--CMOS Cookbook.
--Enhancing Your Apple II & IIe.
--Enhancing Your Apple Two.
--Micro Cookbook, Machine Language Programming.
--Son of Cheap Video.
Lancaster, F. W. If You Want to Evaluate Your Library...
Lancaster, F. W., ed. Library Automation As a Source of Management Information: Proceedings of the Clinic on Library Applications of Data Processing, 1982.
--Problems & Failures in Library Automation: Proceedings of the Clinic on Library Applications of Data Processing, 1978.
--The Role of the Library in an Electronic Society: Proceedings of the Clinic on Library Applications of Data Processing 1979.
Lancaster, F. W., ed. see Clinic on Library Applications of Data Processing Proceedings, 1974.
Lancaster, F. W., ed. see Clinic on Library Applications of Data Processing Proceedings, 1973.
Lancaster, F. W., ed. see Clinic on Library Applications of Data Processing, Proceedings, 1975.
Lancaster, F. Wilfrid. The Dissemination of Scientific & Technical Information: Toward a Paperless System.
--Evaluation of On-Line Searching in MEDLARS (AIM-TWX) by Biomedical Practitioners.
Lancaster, F. Wilfrid, ed. Clinic on Library Applications of Data Processing, Proceedings, 1979: The Role of the Library in an Electronic Society.
Lancaster, G. T. Programming in COBOL.
Lancaster, Graham. The Nuclear Letters.
Lancaster, Henry C. Sunset: A History of Parisian Drama in the Last Years of Louis XIV, 1701-1715.
Lancaster, Jan, ed. see Sutton, Denys.
Lancaster, Jeanette. Adult Psychiatric Nursing.
Lancaster, Jeannette, jt. auth. see Stanhope, Marcia.
Lancaster, John. Approaches to Printing.
Lancaster, Kevin & DeLaney, Ronald A. Modern Economics: Principles & Policy.
Lance, Kathryn. Sportsbeauty.
Lanchberry, Edward, jt. auth. see Duke, Neville.
Lanciani, Rodolfo. Ancient & Modern Rome.
Lanckton, Alice K. Bar Mitzvah Mother's Manual.
Lancy, David F. & Tindall, B. Allan, eds. Study of Play: Problems & Prospects.
Land, Hilarly. Large Families in London.
Land, Lois B., jt. auth. see Schott, Sally E.
Land, Lois R. & Vaughan, Mary A. Music in Today's Classroom: Creating, Listening, Performing.
Land, Myrick. The Dream Buyers.
--Last Flight.
Land Study Bureau, Univ. of Hawaii Staff. Detailed Land Classification. Incl. Island of Hawaii; Island of Kauai; Island of Lanai; Island of Maui; Island of Molokai; Island of Oahu. UH Pr.
Landa, Robin. Visual Solutions: Activities, Experiments, & Projects for Solving Art & Design Problems.
Landa, S., jt. auth. see Weisser, Otto.
Landau, Anneliese. The Lied: The Unfolding of Its Style.
Landau, Elaine. Growing Old in America.
Landau, Elliott D. & Egan, M. Winston. Guiding Your Child: A 60-Point Checklist for Parents.
Landau, Jacob M., jt. auth. see Czudnowski, Moshe M.
Landau, L. & Kitaigorodsky, A. I. Physics for Everyone: Molecules.
--Physics for Everyone: Physical Bodies.
Landau, M. E. Women of Forty.
Landau, Saul, jt. auth. see Dinges, John.
Landau, Sidney I. International Dictionary of Medicine & Biology.
Landau, Sidney I. & Bogus, Ronald, eds. Doubleday Roget's Thesaurus in Dictionary Form.
Landauer, J. Blowpipe Analysis.
Lande, Alfred. Quantum Mechanics in a New Key.
Lande, Nathaniel. Self-Health: The Lifelong Fitness Book.
Lande, Nathaniel & Slade, Afton. Stages: Understanding How You Make Your Moral Decisions.
Lande, Paul S., jt. ed. see Bell, Michael E.
Landeira, Ricardo, ed. Critical Essays on Gabriel Miro.
Landenau, John C., jt. auth. see Practising Law Institute Staff.
Lander, Eleanor. Science & Technology: A Reader.
Lander, J. R. Crown & Nobility, 1450-1509.
Lander, Jack. Make Money By Moonlighting: Own Your Own Low-Risk Business. Cleary, Patti, ed.
Lander, Mary K. Index in Xenophontis Memorabilia.
Landers, Gunnard. The Hunting Shack.
--Rite of Passage.
Landers, Jonathan M., jt. auth. see Epstein, David G.
Landers, Ray. The Talent Education School of Shinichi Suzuki - An Analysis: The Application of the Suzuki Philosophy & Methods to All Areas of Instruction.
Landers, Robert, jt. ed. see Chase, Leslie R.
Landersdorfer, Simon K., ed. & tr. Altbabylonische Privatbriefe.
Landersdorfer, Simon K., ed. Der Bael Tatpauopoos und Die Kerube Des Ezechiel.
Landes, Alison & Landes, Sonia. Pariswalks.
Landes, Margaret W., ed. see Burthogge, Richard.
Landes, Ruth. Ojibwa Woman.
Landes, Sonia, jt. auth. see Landes, Alison.
Landgraf, Arthur. Commentarius Cantabrigiensis in Epistolas Pauli e Schola Petri Abaelardi. Incl. Vol. 1. In Epistolam Ad Romanos; Vol. 2. In Epistolam Ad Corinthios Iam et Iiam, Ad Galatas et Ad Ephesios; Vol. 3. In Epistolam ad Philippenses, ad Colossenses, ad Thessalonicenses Primam et Secundam, ad Timotheam Priman et Secundam, ad Titum et Philemonem. U of Notre Dame Pr.
Landgraf, John R. Creative Singlehood & Pastoral Care.
Landgraf, Larry S. Dangerous Waters.
Landheer, B. & Robertson, A. H., eds. European Yearbook.
Landis, Charles. Twenty-Two Caliber Varmint Rifles.
Landis, Dan, ed. Handbook of Intercultural Training: Issues in Theory & Design.
Landis, Fred S., jt. auth. see Freed, Donald.
Landis, J. D. Daddy's Girl.
--Daddy's Girl.
Landis, James M. The Administrative Process.
Landis, John L. The Mechanics of Patent Claim Drafting.
Landis, Joseph C., ed. The Great Jewish Plays.
Landis, Judson R. Sociology: Concepts & Characteristics.
Landkof, N. S. Foundations of Modern Potential Theory. Doohovskoy, A. P., tr. from Rus.
Landman, H. B., ed. European & American Art from the Princeton Alumni Collection: Publication of the Art Museum, Princeton University.
Landon, D. H., ed. The Peripheral Nerve.
Landon, Michael deL. The Honor & Dignity of the Profession: A History of the Mississippi State Bar, 1906-1976.
Landone, Brown. Body Purification.
Landorf, Joyce. His Stubborn Love.
--Irregular People.
--Silent September.
Landow, George P. Images of Crisis: Literary Iconology, 1750 to the Present.
--Victorian Types, Victorian Shadows: Biblical Typology in Victorian Literature, Art & Thought.
Landow, Melvin S. Your People Are Your Business: A Manager's Manual for Making Millions in Merchandising.
Landow, R. K. Herpes in Focus.
Landry, J. Paul Newman: An Illustrated Biography.
Landry, Judith, tr. see Benevolo, Leonardo.
Lands, William E. M., jt. ed. see Kahn, Raymond H.
Landsberg, H. E., ed. see International Biometeorological Congress Staff.
Landsberg, P. T., ed. Problems in Thermodynamics & Statistical Physics.
Landsberg, P. T. & Willoughby, A. F, eds. Recombination in Semiconductors: Selected Proceedings of the International Conference Held at the University of Southampton, England. 30 August - 1st September 1978.
Landsberg, Paul L. Experience of Death.
Landscape Architecture Magazine Editors. Water & Landscape.
Landsman, Sandy. Castaways on Chimp Island.
Landy, Alice S., ed. The Heath Introduction to Literature.
Landy, M., jt. ed. see Lawrence, H. S.
Landy, Maurice & Braun, W., eds. Immunological Tolerance.
Landy, Maurice, jt. ed. see McDevitt, Hugh O.
Landy, Maurice, jt. ed. see Smith, Richard T.
Landy, Maurice, jt. ed. see Uhr, Jonathan W.
Lane. Purchase & Sale of Small Businesses: 1987 Cumulative Supplement.
Lane, Arthur L., jt. auth. see Poynter, Margaret.
Lane, Barbara. Tribute to Lotte Brand Philip.
Lane, Barbara M. Architecture & Politics in Germany, 1918-1945.
Lane, Carl D. How to Sail.
--New Boatman's Manual.
Lane, Carolyn. Echoes in an Empty Room: And Other Supernatural Tales.
--The Winnemah Spirit.
Lane, Christy. All That Jazz & More: The Complete Book of Jazz Dancing.
Lane, Clinton F. & Kabalka, George W. A New Hydroboration Reagent.
Lane, D. R. Jones' Animal Nursing.
Lane, Denis. Preach the Word.
Lane, Fred, jt. auth. see Goldstein, Irving.
Lane, Fred, ed. Medical Trial Technique Quarterly: 1955-1983.
Lane, Hana U., ed. World Almanac & Book of Facts 1985.
Lane, Helen R., tr. see Ionesco, Eugene.
Lane, Helen R., tr. see Umbral, Francisco.
Lane, J., jt. auth. see Miller, Madeleine S.
Lane, J. G. ENT & Oral Surgery of the Dog & Cat: Veterinary Practitioner Handbook.
Lane, Jim R. Static.
Lane, John, jt. auth. see Hammel, Eric.
Lane, Maggie. Chinese Rugs Designed for Needlepoint.
--Maggie Lane's Oriental Patchwork: Elegant Designs for Easy Living.
--Needlepoint by Design.
--Needlepoint by Design: Variations on Chinese Themes.
Lane, Maggie & Bartlett, Nigel. Dell Book of Quizzes & Puzzles for Literature Lovers.
Lane, Marc J. Legal Handbook for Small Business.
Lane, Patrick. Beware the Months of Fire.
Lane, Paula. Maine Is Many Things: A Coloring & Game Book.
Lane, Peter. Elizabethan England.
--Norman England.
Lane, Richard. Erotica Japonica: Masterworks of Shunga Painting.

--Library of Japanese Art: Kaigetsudo. Seiichiro, Takahashi, ed.
Lane, Robert S., jt. auth. see Middlekauff, Woodrow W.
Lane, Roger. Policing the City: Boston, Eighteen Eighty-Two to Eighteen Eighty-Five.
Lane, Sharon, et al, eds. The Seattle Times Cookbook.
Lane, W. L. Understanding the New Testament: Ephesians-2 Thessalonians.
Lane, William L. Highlights of the Bible: New Testament.
Lane, Yoti. Psychology of the Actor.
Lanes, Selma. Down the Rabbit Hole: Adventures & Misadventures in the Realm of Children's Literature.
Laney, D. H. Leica Accessory Guide: Pocket Books.
Laney, D. H., jt. auth. see Tompkins, B.
Laney, James T., jt. ed. see Gustafson, James M.
Laney, William R., et al, eds. Diagnosis & Treatment in Prosthodontics.
Lanez, Manuel M. The Wandering Unicorn: A Novel. Fitton, Mary, tr. from Span.
Lang. Absorption Spectra.
--The New York Mets - World Series Edition.
Lang, Andrew. Favorite Andrew Lang Fairy Tale Books in Many Colors: Red, Green, Yellow & Blue Fairy Tale Books.
--More Andrew Lang Fairy Tale Books in Many Colors.
Lang, Andy. Andy Lang's Remodeling Handbook.
--One Hundred & One Select Dream Houses.
--Vacation Dream Homes.
Lang, Anton, ed. see Society for the Study of Developmental Biology Staff.
Lang, Berel. Art & Inquiry.
Lang, Brad. Crockett: Brand of Fear.
--Crockett on the Loose.
--The Perdition Express.
Lang, Cliff. Greenberg's Guide to Lionel Layout Plans.
Lang, Cynthia, jt. auth. see Kagan, Jerome.
Lang, Daniel. A Backward Look.
--A Backward Look: Germans Remember.
--Casualties of War.
Lang, David M. The First Russian Radical: Alexander Radischev, 1749-1802.
Lang, Elizabeth E., jt. auth. see Tighe, Mary Ann.
Lang, Faber B. Terra.
Lang, G. The Cuisine of Hungary.
Lang, Gabrielle M. see Bowen, Marjorie.
Lang, J. Clinical Anatomy of the Head: Neurocranium, Orbita, Craniocervical Regions.
Lang, J., et al, eds. Designing for Human Behavior: Architecture & the Behavioral Sciences.
Lang, J. Stephen. The Complete Book of Bible Trivia.
Lang, Jack, jt. auth. see Simon, Peter.
Lang, James. Anglo-Saxon Sculpture.
Lang, Kurt. Military Sociology 1963-1969: A Trend Report & Bibliography.
Lang, Mabel. The Athenian Citizen.
Lang, Margaret A. Gramma's Stories & Rhymes for Little Christians.
Lang, Paul H. George Frederic Handel.
Lang, Paul H., ed. Creative World of Beethoven.
--Problems of Modern Music.
--Stravinsky: A New Appraisal of His Work.
Lang, Rosalind, jt. auth. see Whitcomb, Helen.
Lang, S. Cyclotomic Fields.
Lang, Serge. Twenty-One Years of World Cup Ski Racing.
Lang, V. Paul. Heating & Cooling Safety.
--Principles of Air Conditioning.
Lang, Varley. Follow the Water.
Langa, Harry. Relative Analgesia in Dental Practice: Inhalation Analgesia & Sedation with Nitrous Oxide.
Langacker, Ronald W. Fundamentals of Linguistic Analysis.
Langacker, Ronald W., ed. Studies in Uto-Aztecan Grammar.
--Studies in Uto-Aztecan Grammar: Southern Uto-Aztecan Grammatical Sketches.
Langan, John. Sentence Skills: A Workbook for Writers.
Langbaum, Robert. Poetry of Experience: The Dramatic Monologue in Modern Literary Tradition.
Langdon, Helen. The Simon & Schuster Pocket Art Museum Guide.
Langdon, Rohen. Lighthouse of Langdon: Presenting 20th Century Jehovah to Doomsday Man.
Lange. Piaf.
Lange, Brian M. & Entwistle, Beverly M. Dental Management of the Handicapped: Approaches for Dental Auxiliaries.
Lange, Frances, ed. see Grass, Gunter.
Lange, Frederick W. & Stone, Doris Z., eds. The Archaeology of Lower Central America.
Lange, Harald. Kilimanjaro: The White Roof of Africa.
Lange, K. Norwegian Music: A Survey.
Lange, K., ed. Simulation of Metal Forming Processes by the Finite Element Method (SIMOP-I)
Lange, Monique. Piaf. Woodward, Richard S., tr. from Fr.
Lange, Nicholas De see Oz, Amos.
Lange, O. L., et al, eds. Water & Plant Life: Problems & Modern Approaches.
Lange, Oskar. Introduction to Economic Cybernetics. Banasinski, Antoni, ed. Stadler, Jozef, tr.
--On Political Economy & Econometrics.
--Optimal Decisions.
--Political Economy.
Lange, Oskar & Taylor, Fred M. On the Economic Theory of Socialism.
Lange, Peter & Ross, George. Unions, Change & Crisis: French & Italian Union Strategy & the Political Economy, 1945-1980.
Lange, Roland A. Two Hundred One Japanese Verbs Fully Conjugated in All the Forms.
Lange, Victor, ed. see Grass, Gunter.
Lange, W., jt. ed. see Masihi, K. N.
Lange, Walter Rudolf. Healing Miracles.
Langefors, U. & Kihlstrom, B. The Modern Technique of Rock Blasting.
Langellier, J. P., jt. auth. see Laughlin, C. P.
Langen, P., jt. ed. see Skoda, J.
Langenbach, Robert & Nesnow, Stephen, eds. Organ & Species Specificity in Chemical Carcinogenesis.
Langenes, Bill, jt. auth. see Ewing, David P.
Langenkamp, Robert. Deluxe Illustrated Petroleum Reference Dictionary.
Langer, Elinor. Josephine Herbst: The Story She Could Never Tell.
Langer, H., ed. see Biochemistry & Physiology of Visual Pigments Symposium Staff.
Langer, Jiri. Nine Gates to the Chassidic Mysteries. Rossel, Seymour, ed. Jolly, Stephen, tr. from Czech. & Fr.
Langer, Maryn. Ride with Wings.
Langer, Paul F. Communism in Japan.
Langer, Richard. Grow It.
Langer, Victor & Thomas, Walter. The Nuclear War Fun Book.
Langer, Walter C. Psychology & Human Living.
Langer, William L. & Gleason, S. Everett. The Undeclared War Nineteen Forty-Nineteen Forty-One.
Langer, William L., ed. see Wolf, John B.
Langeveld, M. J. Columbus Picture Analysis of Growth Towards Maturity: A Series of 24 Pictures & a Manual.
Langevoort, Donald C. Insider Trading Handbook 1987.
Langfitt, T. W., ed. see International CBF Symposium Staff, et al.
Langford, Cameron. Winter of the Fisher.
Langford, Gerald, ed. see Clark, Emily.
Langford, Michael. The Single Lens Reflex Camera Handbook.
Langford, Norman F. Barriers to Belief.
Langford, Sandra. Midnight's Lady.
Langford, Sondra G. Red Bird of Ireland.
Langford, Thomas. Prayer & the Common Life.
Langford, Thomas A. Christian Wholeness.
Langford, W. J., ed. see Neville, Eric H.
Langhaar, Henry L. Energy Methods in Applied Mechanics.
Langhans, Edward A., ed. Restoration Adaptations.
Langhans, Peter, jt. ed. see Bunte, Hermann.
Langie, Andre. Cryptography.
Langlais, Robert, jt. auth. see Kasle, Myron J.
Langlais, Robert P., et al. Oral Diagnosis, Oral Medicine & Treatment Planning.
Langley, Andrew. The Making of the Living Planet.
Langley, Billy C. Electric Controls for Refrigeration & Air Conditioning.
Langley, Dorothy M. & Langley, Gordon E. Dramatherapy & Psychiatry.
Langley, F. A., jt. auth. see Fox, H.
Langley, Gordon E., jt. auth. see Langley, Dorothy M.
Langley, J. Ayo. Ideologies of Liberation in Black Africa, 1856-1970: Documents on Modern African Political Thought from Colonial Times to the Present.
Langley, Julia, jt. auth. see Elphinstone, Margaret.
Langley, L. L., ed. Contraception.
Langley, Lee L. Homeostasis: Origins of the Concept.
Langley, Michael. No Woman's Country.
Langley, Myrtle. Religions.
Langley, Pat & Carbonell, Jaime. Machine Learning.
Lang Li, Wen see Li, Wen L.
Langlois-Berthelot, R. Electromagnetic Machines.
Langmack, Helger C. God & the Universe.
Langman, Jan & Woerdeman, M. W. Atlas of Medical Anatomy.
Langman, Jan & Woerdman, M. W. Atlas of Medical Anatomy.
Langman, M. J. Concise Textbook of Gastroenterology.
Langmeier, J. & Matejcek, Z. Psychological Deprivation in Childhood.
Langmuir, Irving. Phenomena, Atoms & Molecules.
Langnas, Isaac A. One Thousand Two Hundred Russian Proverbs.
Langnas, Isaac A. & List, Jacob S. Major Writers of the World.
Langner, Linda L., jt. auth. see Heimlich, Ralph E.
Langone, John. Bombed, Buzzed, Smashed, or... Sober.
--Goodbye to Bedlam: Understanding Mental Illness & Retardation.
--Human Engineering: Marvel or Menace?
--Like, Love, Lust: A View of Sex & Sexuality.
--Like, Love, Lust: A View of Sex & Sexuality.
Langs, Robert, ed. International Journal of Psychoanalytic Psychotherapy.
--International Journal of Psychoanalytic Psychotherapy, 1983-84.
Langsam, Walter Consuelo. The World & Warren's Cartoons.
Langsam, Yedidyah, et al. Data Structures for Personal Computers.
Langsdale, Richard. Getting Ready for Living Together.
Langseth-Christensen, Lillian. Holiday Cook.
Langsley, Donald G. Legal Aspects of Certification & Accreditation.
Langstaff, John. Hot Cross Buns & Other Old Street Cries.
--The Two Magicians.
Langstaff, John & Gentleman, David. Golden Vanity.
Langstaff, John, ed. Hi Ho the Rattlin' Bog: And Other Folk Songs for Group Singing.
Langstaff, John, compiled by. St. George & the Dragon: A Folk Play.
Langstaff, John, ed. Sweetly Sings the Donkey: Animal Rounds for Children to Sing or Play on Recorders.
Langstaff, John, jt. ed. see Langstaff, Nancy.
Langstaff, John, et al. Swapping Boy.
Langstaff, John M. & Groves-Raines, Antony, eds. On Christmas Day in the Morning.
Langstaff, Nancy & Langstaff, John, eds. Jim Along, Josie: A Collection of Folk Songs & Singing Games for Young Children.
Langton, Jane. Natural Enemy.
Langton, Stuart. Environmental Leadership.
Langton, Stuart, ed. Citizen Participation in America: Essays on the State of the Art.
Language & Orientation Resource Center Staff. Indochinese Students in U. S. Schools: A Guide for Administrators.
--The Peoples & Cultures of Cambodia, Laos & Vietnam.
--Their New Life in the United States.
--Your New Life in the United States, in Chinese.
--Your New Life in the United States, in Hmong.
--Your New Life in the United States, in Khmer.
Language & Orientation Resource Center Staff & Center for Applied Linguistics Staff. Your New Life in the United States, in Lao.
Language & Orientation Resource Center Staff. Your New Life in the United States, in Vietnamese.
Languis, Marlin, et al. Brain & Learning: Directions in Early Childhood Education.
Langwill, L. G. An Index of Musical Wind-Instrument Makers.
Langwill, Lyndesay G. Bassoon & Contrabassoon.
Langworth, R. M. New Complete Book of Collectibles Cars.
Lanham, Edwin M. Murder on My Street.
Lanham, Jan, jt. auth. see Paul, Cecil.
Lanham, Richard A. Analyzing Prose.
--Revising Business Prose.
Lanier, B. V. The World Supply & Demand Picture for Canned Small Pelagic Fish.
Lanier, Mary, ed. see Lanier, Sidney.
Lanier, Pamela. All Suite Hotels.
--The Complete Guide to Bed & Breakfasts, Inns & Guesthouses.
--The Complete Guide to Bed & Breakfasts, Inns & Guesthouses in the U. S. & Canada.
--Complete Guide to Bed & Breakfasts: 1987-88 Edition.
Lanier, Sidney. Poems of Sidney Lanier. Lanier, Mary, ed.
Lanigan, Catherine. Admit Desire.
--Bound by Love.
--Sins of Omission.
Lankenau, John C., jt. auth. see Practising Law Institute Staff.
Lankford, J., jt. ed. see Ritchie, R. O.
Lannie, Vincent P., ed. see Shuster, George.
Lanning, Dave, jt. auth. see Rees, Leighton.
Lannois, Georges, ed. Pages Francaises.
Lannon, John M. Technical Writing.
--The Writing Process.
Lansbury, Coral. Elizabeth Gaskell.
Lansbury, Russell D., jt. auth. see Gilmour, Peter.
Lansdale, Nina. The White Island.
Lansdell, N. Atom & the Energy Revolution.
Lansdown, Brenda, et al. Teaching Elementary Science Through Investigation & Colloquium.
Lansdown, Richard. More Than Sympathy: The Everyday Needs of Sick & Handicapped Children & Their Families.
Lansdowne, James F. Birds of the Eastern Forest.
--Birds of the Northern Forest.
--Birds of the West Coast.
--Birds of the West Coast.
Lanser, Howard & Halloran, John A. Introduction to Financial Management.
Lansing, Alfred. Endurance.
Lansing, John S. Evil in the Morning of the World: Phenomenological Approaches to a Balinese Community.
Lansing, Lambert, jt. ed. see Weiss, Leon.
Lanski, Ralph. Handbook of Bibliographies on Law in the Developing Countries.
Lansky, Bruce. Successful Dieting Tips. Grooms, Kathe, ed.
Lansky, Vicki. Welcoming Your Second Baby.
Lansley, Stewart. Housing & Public Policy.
Lansley, Stewart, jt. auth. see Mack, Joanna.
Lanson & Tuffrau. Manuel Illustre D'histoire De La Litterature Francaise.
Lanstrom, Edith. Christian Parent Burnout.
Lant, Jeffrey. Money Talks: The Complete Guide to Creating a Profitable Workshop or Seminar in Any Field.
Lant, Jeffrey L. Insubstantial Pageant: Ceremony & Confusion at Queen Victoria's Court.
Lant, Jeffrey L., ed. Our Harvard: Reflections on College Life by Twenty-Two Distinguished Graduates.
Lantry, Kimberx. Uncle Uriah & Tad.
Lantz, Fran. Eileen Goudge's Swept Away Number Four: Star Struck.
--Swept Away No. 8: All Shook Up.
Lantzeff, George V. & Pierce, Richard A. Eastward to Empire: Exploration & Conquest on the Russian Open Frontier, to 1750.
Lanwick, Hugo Van see Van Lawick, Hugo.
Lanyun, Liu. Golden Millet Dream & Other Stories Ser. Fanqin, Yu & Mingjie, Wang, trs. from Span.
Lanza, Frank. Gourmet Italian Cooking for Large Appetites & Small Budgets: With Special Sections on Outdoor & Teenage Cooking.
Lanzano, Susan & Abreu, Rosendo. Preparacion Para el Examen de Equivalencia de la Escuela Superior. Ringel, Martin & Banks, William K., eds.
Lanzkowsky, Philip. Pediatric Hematology-Oncology: A Treatise for the Clinician.
--Pediatric Oncology.
Laoghaire, Ida N., jt. auth. see O'Brien, Michael.
Lao She. Beneath the Red Banner. Cohn, Don J., tr. from Chinese.
--Cat Country: A Satirical Novel of China in the 1930's. Lyell, William A., Jr., tr.
Lao Tsu. Tao Te Ching. Wilhelm, Richard, tr.
Lapage, S. P., et al, eds. International Code of Nomenclature of Bacteria.
Lapaglia, Janelle C. Sweet Sounds of Life.
Lapatra, Jack W. Applying the Systems Approach to Urban Development.
La Penta, Barbara L., tr. see Ciucci, Giorgio, et al.
Lapham, Lewis. Money & Class in America: Notes & Observations on the American Character.
Lapide, Pinchas & Moltmann, Jurgen. Jewish Monotheism & Christian Trinitarian Doctrine. Swidler, Leonard, tr. from Ger.
Lapides, Fred. The Raigne of King Edward the Third.
Lapidus, Gail W., intro. by see Hansson, Carola, et al.
Lapidus, Leon & Seinfeld, John H. Numerical Solution of Ordinary Differential Equations.
La Pierre, Dominique. City of Joy. Spink, Kathryn, tr. from Fr.
Lapierre, Dominique. City of Joy.
Lapin, Jackie & Parkhouse, Bonnie L. The Woman in Athletic Administration.
Lapin, Laurence L. Statistics for Modern Business Decisions.
Lapin, Lawrence L. Quantitative Methods for Business Decisions.
--Quantitative Methods for Business Decisions, with Cases.
--Quantitative Methods for Business Decisions: With Cases.
--Statistics for Modern Business Decisions.
--Statistics for Modern Business Decisions.
--Statistics: Meaning & Method.
Lapin, Nora, jt. auth. see Cummings, Parke.
Lapis, Karoly & Johannessen, Jan V., eds. Liver Carcinogenesis.
Lapkin. Money, Banking, & the Nation's Income.
LaPlace, John. Health.
Laplanche, Jean. Life & Death in Psychoanalysis. Mehlman, Jeffrey, tr.
LaPlante, Joseph A., jt. auth. see Tait, Colin C.
Lapointe, Claire C., jt. auth. see Lapointe, Francois H.
Lapointe, Clarie C., jt. auth. see Lapointe, Francois H.
Lapointe, Francois H. & Lapointe, Claire C. Claude Levi-Strauss & His Critics: An International Bibliography (1950-1976)
--Maurice Merleau-Ponty & His Critics: An International Bibliography (1942-1976) Including a Bibliography of His Writings.

Authors

Lapointe, Francois H. & Lapointe, Clarie C. Gabriel Marcel & His Critics: An International Bibliography (1935-1976)

La Pointe, Ken. Hey Joe! The Portrait of a Wisconsin Woodsman.

Laponce, J. A. The Government of the Fifth Republic.

Lapoulide, J. Diccionario Grafico de Arte y Oficios Artisticos.

Lapp, Hannah B. To Belize with Love.

Lapp, Henry. A Craftsman's Handbook: Henry Lapp.

Lapp, Rhonda S. Devotionals for Nurses.

Lapp, Robert A. Developing Effective Telephone Skills.

Lappe, Frances M. & Beccar-Varela, Adele. Mozambique & Tanzania: Asking the Big Questions.

Lappe, Frances M. & Collins, Joseph. World Hunger: Twelve Myths.

Lappe, Francis M. & Collins, Joseph. Food First: Beyond the Myth of Scarcity.

Lappin, Alvin R. Plastics - Projects & Techniques.

Lappin, Peter. Conquistador.

--The Wine in the Chalice.

Lappo, G. Moscow, Capital of the Soviet Union.

Lapsanski, Duane V. The First Franciscans & the Gospel.

Lapsley, James N. Salvation & Health: The Interlocking Processes of Life.

Laptev, I. The Planet of Reason: A Sociological Study of the Interrelation of Society & Nature.

Lapwood, E. R. Ordinary Differential Equations.

Laque, Francis L. Marine Corrosion: Causes & Prevention.

Laquer, Walter, ed. see Thomas, David.

Laqueur, Walter. Germany Today: A Personal Report.

--The Terrible Secret: Suppression of the Truth about Hitlers' Final Solution.

--Terrorism.

Laqueur, Walter & Breitman, Richard. Breaking the Silence.

Lara-Braud, Jorge, ed. Our Claim on the Future: A Controversial Collection from Latin America.

LaRaia, Joseph J. A City under the Influence: A Political Autobiography.

Larcombe, F. A. The Advancement of Local Government in New South Wales, 1906 to the Present.

--The Origin of Local Government in New South Wales 1831-58.

--Stabilization of Local Government in New South Wales, 1858-1906.

Larden, Walter. Estancia Life: Agricultural, Economic, & Cultural Aspects of Argentine Farming.

Lardner, Ring. Ring Lardner's "You Know Me Al" The Comic Strip Adventures of Jack Keefe.

Lareau, William. Conduct Expected: The Unwritten Rules for a Successful Business Career.

--The Inside Track: A Successful Job Search Method.

--Millennium Management: Last Chance for America.

La Ree, Gerry De see De La Ree, Gerry.

Large, Brian. Smetana.

Large, John, ed. Contributions of Voice Research to Singing.

Larionov, V., et al. World War II: Decisive Battles of the Soviet Army.

Lariviere, Marian, jt. auth. see Vermeer, Jackie.

Lariviere, Susan & Schiffman, Ted. Amphoto Guide to Backpacking Photography.

Lark, P. D., et al. The Handling of Chemical Data.

Larkin, David. Dali.

Larkin, George. The Mill Girls.

Larkin, Gerald. Occupational Monopoly & Modern Medicine.

Larkin, J. Practical Problems in Mathematics for Mechanical Drafting.

Larkin, Margaret. Seven Shares in a Gold Mine.

Larkin, Murl A. Evidence Trial Manual for Texas Lawyers.

Larkin, Patricia. Strike!

Larkin, Peter A. Freshwater Pollution, Canadian Style.

Larkin, Philip. Girl in Winter.

--Jill.

Larkins, Ernest R. The Impact of Taxes on U.S. Citizens Working Abroad. Farmer, Richard N., ed.

Larmer, Oscar, jt. auth. see Tomasch, E. J.

Larn, Richard & Whistler, Rex. Commercial Diving Manual.

Larney, Violet H. Abstract Algebra.

La Rochefoucauld see also De La Rochefoucauld, Francois.

Laron, Z., jt. ed. see Chiumello, Giuseppe.

Laron, Z., et al, eds. Clinical Use of Growth Hormone.

Laronne, Jonathan & Mosley, M. Paul, eds. Erosion & Sediment Yield.

Laroque, Ginette. Les Aventures de France et Quelques Autres Contines.

Larose, Paul. Working with Children & the Liturgy.

Larrabee, Edward M. Recurrent Themes & Sequences in North American Indian-European Culture Contact.

Larralde, Carlos, et al, eds. Molecules, Cells & Parasites in Immunology.

Larrick, Nancy & Merriam, Eve, eds. Male & Female under Eighteen.

Larrie, Reginald R. Makin' Free: African-Americans in the Northwest Territory.

Larrowe, Charles P. Shape-up & Hiring Hall.

Larsen, E. John, jt. auth. see Mosich, A. N.

Larsen, Egon. An American in Europe.

Larsen, Ellouise B. American Historical Views on Staffordshire China.

Larsen, Ernest. Not a Through Street.

Larsen, Jens P. Handel's Messiah. Bayliss, Major, et al, trs. from Danish.

Larsen, John A. When a Member of the Family Needs Counseling.

Larsen, Judith L. & Gull, Carol W. The Patchwork Quilt Design & Coloring Book. Brannon, Evelyn, ed.

Larsen, L. S., tr. see Schuler, Max & Gebelein, H.

Larsen, Otto. Nightmare of the Innocents.

Larsen-Freeman, Diane, ed. Discourse Analysis in Second Language Research.

Larson. No Longer Strangers.

Larson, Arthur D., ed. National Security Affairs: A Guide to Information Sources.

Larson, Bruce. My Creator, My Friend.

Larson, Bruce L. Lindbergh of Minnesota: A Political Biography.

Larson, Carl, jt. auth. see Milts, Michael H.

Larson, Charles R. Fulke Greville.

--The Portland Murders.

Larson, Charles U. Persuasion: Reception & Responsibility.

Larson, E. Great Ideas in Engineering.

Larson, Elaine, et al. Development of the Clinical Nephrology Practitioner: A Focus on Independent Learning.

Larson, Eric & Eisenberg, Mickey. Manual of Admitting Orders & Therapeutics.

Larson, Gordon A. Adult Education for the Handicapped.

Larson, Gustave O. Prelude to the Kingdom: Mormon Desert Conquest, a Chapter in American Cooperative Experience.

Larson, James. A Church Guide for Strengthening Families: Strategies, Models, Programs, & Resources.

Larson, Jim. Caring Enough to Hear & Be Heard: Leader's Guide.

--Rights, Wrongs, & In-Betweens: Guiding Our Children to Christian Maturity.

Larson, Jim & Feldmeth, Joanne. Your Spiritual Gifts Can Help Your Church Grow.

Larson, John G., jt. ed. see Klimisch, Richard L.

Larson, Kenneth B. & Cox, Jerome R., Jr., eds. Computer Processing of Dynamic Images from an Anger Scintillation Camera.

Larson, Lane, jt. auth. see Larson, Peggy.

Larson, Martin A. Essence Heritage.

--The Federal Reserve & Our Manipulated Dollar.

--Religion of the Occident.

Larson, Maurice A., jt. auth. see Randolph, Alan D.

Larson, Nora E. The Alphabet of God.

--As a Little Child.

Larson, Norita D. Langston Hughes, Poet of Harlem. Redpath, Ann, ed.

--Why Do We Have Earthquakes?

Larson, Norma. Hospital Patience.

Larson, Peggy & Larson, Lane. Sierra Club Naturalist's Guide to the Deserts of the Southwest.

Larson, Philip M., Jr. Vital Church Management.

Larson, Rebecca. Balancing Act.

Larson, Richard E. Federal Court Awards of Attorney's Fees.

Larson, Robert E., et al. Distributed Control.

Larson, Robert H., et al. Williamsport: Frontier Village to Regional Center.

Larson, Robert L. Bible Stories Reader.

Larson, Robert W. New Mexico Populism: A Study of Radical Protest in a Western Territory.

Larson, Rodger & Meade, Ellen. Young Filmmakers.

Larson, Roy A., jt. ed. see Kofranek, Anton M.

Larson, Sanford J., jt. auth. see Sances, Anthony, Jr.

Larson, W. C., jt. ed. see Schlitt, W. J.

Larson, William R., as told to. & as told see Lewis, Richard H.

Larsson, Tage, jt. ed. see Engel, Arthur.

LaRue, Mabel G. Tiny's Big Umbrella.

Larwood, Laurie G. Organizational Behavior & Management.

Lasagna, Louis, ed. Clinical Pharmacology.

LaSalle, Peter. Strange Sunlight. Lubeck, Scott, ed.

Lasansky, Jeannette. In the Heart of Pennsylvania: Nineteenth & Twentieth Century Quiltmaking Traditions.

--In the Heart of Pennsylvania: Pieced by Mother.

--In the Heart of Pennsylvania: Symposium Papers.

--Pieced by Mother: Over One Hundred Years of Quiltmaking Tradition.

Lasansky, Jeannette, ed. Pieced by Mother: Symposium Papers.

Lasby, Clarence. Project Paperclip: German Scientists & the Cold War.

Lascar, D., jt. ed. see Van Dalen, D.

Lascelle, Joan, jt. auth. see Brown, Howard M.

Lascelles, G. Art of Falconry.

Lasch, Christopher. The Culture of Narcissism: American Life in an Age of Diminishing Expectations.

Laseau, jt. auth. see Crowe.

Laseau, Paul. Graphic Thinking for Architects & Designers.

--Ink-Line Sketching.

Lasell, Fen H. Michael Grows a Wish.

Lash, Joseph P. Helen & Teacher.

--Life Was Meant to Be Lived: A Centenary Portrait of Eleanor Roosevelt.

--Roosevelt & Churchill - 1939-1941: The Partnership That Saved the West.

Lash, Joseph P., ed. From the Diaries of Felix Frankfurter.

Lash, Nicholas. Voices of Authority.

Lashgari, Deirdre, jt. auth. see Bankier, Joanna.

Lashof, R., jt. auth. see Burghelea, D.

Lasinski, Thomas, jt. auth. see Levi-Setti, Riccardo.

Lask, I. M., tr. see Agnon, S. Y.

Lask, I. M., tr. see Gorion, Micha J. bin & Gorion, Emanuel bin.

Lasker, George E., ed. Applied Systems & Cybernetics: Proceedings of the International Congress on Applied Systems Research & Cybernetics, Acapulco, Mexico, Dec. 12-16, 1980. Incl. Vol. 1. The Quality of Life: Systems Approaches; Vol. 2. Systems Concepts, Models & Methodology; Vol. 3. Human Systems, Sociocybernetics, Management & Organizations; Vol. 4. Systems Research in Health Care, Biocybernetics & Ecology; Vol. 5. Systems Approaches to Computer Science & Mathematics; Vol. 6. Fuzzy Sets & Systems, Possibility Theory, & Special Topics in Systems Research. Pergamon.

Lasker, Judith, jt. auth. see Borg, Susan O.

Lasker, Toy. Flashmaps Instant Guide to Chicago.

--Flashmaps Instant Guide to Dallas-Fort Worth.

--Flashmaps Instant Guide to New York.

--Flashmaps Instant Guide to Washington, D. C.

Laski, Audrey. Keeper.

Laski, Harold, ed. see Mornay, Philppe.

Laski, Marghanita. Ecstasy: A Study of Some Secular & Religious Experiences.

Laskin, Allen I. Enzymes & Immobilized Cells in Biotechnology.

Laskin, David, jt. auth. see Esquire Editors.

Laskowski, Lester P., jt. auth. see Tocci, Ronald J.

Lasky, Kathryn. Puppeteer.

Lasky, Michael. The Complete Junk Food Book.

Lasley, John F. Genetics of Livestock Improvement.

Lasley, John F., jt. auth. see Campbell, John R.

Lasnier, Denis R., et al, trs. see Twitchell, Paul.

Lasok, D., et al, eds. Fundamental Duties: A Volume of Essays by Present & Former Members of the Law Faculty of the University of Exeter to Commemorate the Silver Jubilee of the University.

LaSor, William S. The Truth about Armageddon: What the Bible Says about the End of Times.

Lasorda, Tommy & Fisher, David. The Artful Dodger.

Lasry, George. Valuing Common Stock: The Power of Prudence.

Lass, Norman J., ed. Speech & Language: Vol. 11: Advances in Basic Research & Theory.

Lass, William E. A History of Steamboating on the Upper Missouri River.

Lassaigne, Jacques. Rufino Tamayo.

Lassam, Robert. Fox Talbot, Photographer.

Lassan, N. A. Advances & Technical Standards in Neurosurgery.

Lasselle, jt. auth. see Ramsay.

Lasselle, Joan & Ramsay, Carol. The ABC's of the IBM PC.

Lasser. Everyone's 1979 Tax.

Lasser Institute. J. K. Lasser's Managing Your Family Finances.

Lasser, J. K. J. K. Lasser's the Professional Edition of Your Income Tax, 1985.

Lasser, J. K., Tax Institute Staff. J. K. Lasser's One Hundred One Plans to Pay Less Taxes: 1986.

--J. K. Lasser's Your Income Tax, 1986.

Lasser, Jacob K. How to Run a Small Business.

Lasser, Jacob K., ed. Handbook of Cost Accounting Methods.

Lasser, Lawrence L., jt. auth. see Institute for Continuing Legal Education (New Jersey) Staff.

Lassiter, Roy L., Jr. Association of Income & Educational Achievement.

Lassner, J., ed. see European Congress of Anaesthesiology of the World Federation of Societies of Anaesthesiologists, 1st, Vienna, 1962.

Lassner, J., ed. see International Congress for Hypnosis & Psychosomatic Medicine Staff.

Lasswell, Harold D. Political Writings: Psychopathology & Politics; Politics: Who Gets What, When, How; Democratic Character.

Lasswell, Marcia & Lobsenz, Norman M. No-Fault Marriage.

Last, F. T., jt. ed. see Cannell, M. G.

Last, Rex W. Language Teaching & the Microcomputer.

Laster, Jim, jt. auth. see Gobbell, Phyllis.

Lasure, Charles F. Dollars from Washington: An Individual's Share, 1930-81.

Laszlo, Ervin. The Inner Limits of Mankind: Heretical Reflections on Today's Values, Culture & Politics.

Laszlo, Ervin, ed. The New International Economic Order (NIEO) Library.

Laszlo, Ervin & Keys, Donald, eds. Disarmament: The Human Factor: Proceedings of a Colloquim on the Societal Context for Diasarmament.

Laszlo, Ervin & Sellon, Emily B., eds. Vistas in Physical Reality.

Laszlo, Ervin, et al. The Objectives of the New International Economic Order.

--The Obstacles to the New International Economic Order.

Lategan, Bernard & Vorster, Willem. Text & Reality.

Lategan, Bernard C. & Vorster, Willem S. Text & Reality: Aspects of Reference in Biblical Texts.

Latham, A. J., jt. ed. see Anderson, B. L.

Latham, Caroline. The Best Bars of New York: Two Hundred & Fifty of the Most Exciting Watering Holes in Manhattan.

--Life with Rose Kennedy.

Latham, Earl. Communist Controversy in Washington: From the New Deal to McCarthy.

Latham, Edward. Famous Sayings & Their Authors: A Collection of Historical Sayings in English, French, German, Greek, Italian, & Latin.

Latham, J. D., ed. Saracen Archery. Paterson, W. F.

Latham, M. C. Human Nutrition in Tropical Africa.

Latham, Robert, ed. Catalogue of the Pepys Library at Magdalene College Cambridge: Volume 5, Part 2: Modern Manuscripts.

Latham, Roger M. The Complete Book of the Wild Turkey.

Latham, Shyree A. Melange.

Latham, W. Bryan. Management of Medical Cost.

Lathem, Edward. Robert Frost One Hundred.

Lathem, Edward C., ed. Interviews with Robert Frost.

Lathen, Emma. Green Grow the Dollars.

--The Longer the Thread.

--A Place For Murder.

Lathrop, Gilbert. Rio Grande Glory Days.

Lathrop, William A. Little Stories from the Screen. Kupelnick, Bruce S., ed.

Latif, Rebecca C. Using Lotus 1-2-3: A Guide for Non-Programmers.

Latimer, Henry C. Preparing Art & Camera Copy for Printing: A Contemporary Procedures Techniques for Mechanicals & Related Copy.

--Production Planning & Repro Mechanicals for Offset Printing.

Latimer, Hugh. Seven Sermons Before Edward VI, Fifteen Forty-Nine. Arber, Edward, ed.

Latimer, Paul R. The Psychology of Life & the Psychology of Death.

Latin American Collection, Yale University Staff. The Allende Years: A List of Chilean Imprints in Selected U. S. Libraries, 1970-1973.

Latkiewicz, John, et al. Health Occupations.

Latner, Albert L. Cantarow & Trumper Clinical Biochemistry.

Latorre, Guillermo, jt. auth. see Garfinkel, Alan.

Latortue, Regine & Adams, Gleason R., trs. Les Cenelles: A Collection of Poems by Creole Writers of the Early Nineteenth Century.

LaTouche, Robert. The Birth of Western Economy: Economic Aspects of the Dark Ages. Wilkinson, E. M., tr.

La Tourette, Amelie. Ice Dancing.

La Tourette, Jacqueline. The Incense Tree.

Lattimer, John K. Lincoln & Kennedy: Medical & Ballistic Comparisons of Their Assassinations.

Lattimore, Eleanor F. Little Pear.

--Little Pear & His Friends.

Lattimore, Owen. Ordeal by Slander.

Lattimore, Richmond, tr. from Gr. The Four Gospels & the Revelation.

Latymer de Nedham, Hugh. Juggling with Jesus & His Two-Thousand Year Legacy to Mankind.

Latynski, Maya, tr. see Michnik, Adam.

Lau, Charley & Glossbrenner, Alfred. The Winning Hitter: How to Play Championship Baseball.
Lau, Lawrence J., ed. Models of Development: A Comparative Study of Economic Growth in South Korea & Taiwan.
Laubach, Frank C. Forty Years with the Silent Billion.
--The Inspired Letters.
Laube, Ed & Walker, Craig. The Chinese Catalog: Your Source Book for Things Chinese in America.
Laube, Herbert L. How to Have Air-Conditioning & Still Be Comfortable.
Lauber, John. The Making of Mark Twain.
Lauber, Patricia. Home at Last: A Young Cat's Tale.
Laubheim, Charles S., et al. Just Writing.
--Just Writing.
Laucks, Irving F. Speculation in Reality.
Laucks, Peter J. The Legend.
Laude, Theresita & Russo, Raymond M. Dermatologic Disorders in Black Children & Adolescents.
Lauderdale, Michael. Burnout: Strategies for Personal & Organizational Life; Speculations on Evolving Paradigms.
Laudet, M., et al, eds. see Automatic Demonstrations Symposium Staff.
Laudicinda, Susan S. Queens Health Systems Agency District G: A Profile of Health Status & Health Resources.
Laue, Max Von see Von Laue, Max.
Laue, Theodore Von see Von Laue, Theodore.
Lauenstein, Milton. What's Your Game Plan? Creating Business Strategies That Work.
Lauenstein, Milton C. Building & Operating an Effective Board of Directors.
Lauer, Eugene & Mlecko, Joel. A Christian Understanding of the Human Person: Basic Readings.
Lauer, Robert H. & Handel, Warren H. Social Psychology: The Theory & Application of Symbolic Interactionism.
Lauer, Rudolph F. Computer Simulation of Classical Substitution: Cryptographics Systems.
Lauerhass, Ludwig, Jr. & Haugse, Vera L. Education in Latin America: A Bibliography.
Lauersen, Niels & Stukane, Eileen. Listen to Your Body: A Gynecologist Answers Women's Most Intimate Questions.
Lauf, Cornelia, tr. see Fischer, Eberhard & Homberger, Lorenz.
Lauf, Detlef-Ingo. Secret Revelations of Tibetan Thangkas.
Laufer. Lesage ou le Metier de Romancier.
Laufer, Igor. Double Contrast Gastrointestinal Radiology: With Endoscopic Correlation.
Laufer, Robert, jt. ed. see Altbach, Philip G.
Lauffer, Armand. Practice of Continuing Education in the Human Services.
Lauffer, Barbara, jt. auth. see Yasko, Joyce.
Lauffer, Richard A. & Gantt, Robert B., eds. Physical Activities for Fitness & Fun.
Laufman, Harold, jt. auth. see Banks, Sam W.
Laughlin, C. P. & Langellier, J. P. U. S. Army Uniforms: Europe, Nineteen Forty-Four to Nineteen Forty-Five.
Laughlin, Cameron P. U. S. Airborne Forces of World War Two.
Laughlin, David E., jt. ed. see Aaronson, Hubert I.
Laughlin, Eugene J. Financial Accounting.
--Paper Two to Accompany Financial Accounting.
--Practice Set One to Accompany Financial Accounting.
Laughlin, Florence. The Little Leftover Witch.
--Little Leftover Witch.
Laughlin, Jerry, ed. see International Fire Service Training Association Staff.
Laughlin, Ruth. Natural Sweets & Treats.
Laughton, Joan & Hasenstab, Suzanne. Language Learning Process: Implications for Management of Disorders.
Laughton, Joan M., jt. auth. see Hasenstab, M. Suzanne.
Laulicht, I., jt. auth. see Pinchas, S.
Laum, Bernhard. Das Alexandrinische Akzentuationssystem Unter Zugrundelegung der Theoretischen Lehren der Grammatik.
Laumer, Keith. Retief & the Rebels.
--Retief to the Rescue.
Launder, B & Humphrey, J. A., eds. Momentum & Heat Transfer Processes in Recirculating Flows: HTD.
Launder, B. E., ed. Studies in Convection: Theory Measurement & Applications.
Launer, Robert L. & Wilkinson, Graham N., eds. Robustness in Statistics.
Laurance, Alice & Asimov, Isaac. Who Done It?
Laurance, Alice, jt. ed. see Asimov, Isaac.
Laurance, Andrew. The Other You: Develop Your Psychic Potential.
Laure, Ettagale, jt. auth. see Laure, Jason.
Laure, Jason & Laure, Ettagale. Joi Bangla! The Children of Bangladesh.
Laurello, Bartholomew J. Ministering to the Aging.
Lauren, Paul G. Diplomats & Bureaucrats: The First Institutional Responses to Twentieth-Century Diplomacy in France & Germany.
Laurence, D. R. & Bacharach, A. L., eds. Evaluation of Drug Activities: Pharmacometrics.
Laurence, Dan H., ed. see Shaw, George Bernard.
Laurence, John. Seeds of Disaster: A Report on South Africa.
Laurence, Margaret. A Tree for Poverty: Somali Poetry & Prose.
Laurence, Robert, pseud. Democracy vs. Capitalism.
Laurence, Theodor. Foundation Book of Astrology.
Laurenson, R. M. & Yuceoglu, U., eds. Advances in Aerospace Structures & Materials, 1982.
Laurent, J., et al. Hypoglycaemic Tumors.
Laurenti, Luigi. Property Values & Race: Studies in Seven Cities.
Laurentin, Rene. Miracles in El Paso.
Laurents, Arthur. The Way We Were.
Laurie, Bruce, jt. ed. see Cantor, Milton.
Laurie, Greg. Spiritual Survival in the Last Days.
Laurie, Marjorie, tr. see De Saussine, Renee.
Laurin, Anne. Little Things.
Lauritzen, C., jt. ed. see Van Keep, P. A.
Lauritzen, Ch, ed. see Estrogen Therapy Workshop Staff.
Laury, Jean R. A Treasury of Needlecraft Gifts for the New Baby.
--A Treasury of Needlecraft Gifts for the New Baby.
Laury, Jean R. & Aiken, Joyce. The Pantyhose Craft Book: Making Things from Run Pantyhose & Nylons.
Laury, Jean Ray, jt. auth. see Aiken, Joyce.
Lauterbach, F., jt. ed. see Kramer, M.
Lauterstein, Ingeborg. Vienna Girl.
Lauton, Barry & Freese, Artur S. The Healthy Adolescent: A Parents Manual.
Lautreamont, Comte de see De Lautreamont, Comte & Ducasse, Isidore.
Lautz, Terry E. & Willey, Fay, eds. Asia: Half the Human Race, a Viewer's Guide.
Lauwerys, Roberts R. Industrial Chemical Exposure: Guidelines for Biological Monitoring.
Laux, James M. In First Gear: The French Automobile Industry to 1914.
Laux, James M., ed. see Kafker, Frank A.
Lavalla, Patrick, jt. auth. see Stoffel, R.
Lavalla, Rick. Helirescue Manual: Personal Safety & SAR Operations Around Helicopters.
LaValla, Rick & Fear, Gene. Resource Guide for Search & Rescue Training Material.
Lavallee, M., et al. Glass Microelectrodes.
Lavatelli, Celia S. & Stendler, Faith. Readings in Child Behavior & Development.
Lave, Charles, ed. Automobile Choice & Its Energy Implications.
La Vega, Garcilasco De see De La Vega, Garcilasco.
Laveleye, Emile L; see Bastiat, Frederic.
LaVelle. Applied Physiology of the Mouth.
Lavelle, Des. Skellig: Island Outpost of Europe.
Lavender, David. The American Heritage History of the Great West. Josephy, Alvin M., Jr., ed.
--California - A Place, a People, a Dream: A Journey Through California History from Miwok Baskets to Silicon Chips.
--Images from the Southwest.
--The Trans-Canada Canoe Trail.
Laventhol & Horwath. Hotel & Motel Development.
Laver, James, ed. Costume Through the Ages.
Laverghetta, Thomas S. Microwave Materials & Fabrication Techniques.
--Practical Microwaves.
Lavers, Norman. Jerzy Kosinski.
Laverty, Bernard M. The Great Profundo & Other Stories.
LaVey, Anton S. The Satanic Rituals.
--The Satanic Rituals.
Lavi, A. Ocean Thermal Energy Conversion.
Lavi, Abrahim & Jorgensen, George W. Lithographic Pressman's Handbook.
Lavin, Henry. How to Get & Keep!--Good Industrial Customers Through Effective Direct Mail.
Lavin, J. A., ed. see Greene, Robert.
Lavin, Mary. The Shrine & Other Stories.
Lavin, Ronald J., ed. The Human Chain for Divine Grace: Lutheran Sermons for Evangelical Outreach.
Lavine & Scuro. The Wonders of Mules.
Lavine, Harold, jt. auth. see Wechsler, James.
La Vine, Paul. In a Glamorous Fashion.
LaVoie, Roland, jt. auth. see Greenberg, Bruce.
Lavoissier Gaston de, la see De La Lavoissier, Gaston.
LaVor, Marty. Ceramics for Any Hands.
Lavranyov, B. The Courageous Heart.
Lavrentiev, M. M. Some Improperly Posed Problems of Mathematical Physics. Sacker, R. J., tr.
Lavretski, J. Salvador Allende.
Law, Alan G. & Sahney, Badri N., eds. Theory of Approximation: With Applications.
Law, Alexander see Ramsay, Allan.
Law & Business Inc. Staff, ed. Law & Business Directory of Corporate Counsel: 1983-1984 Edition.
--Law & Business Directory of Major U. S. Law Firms.
--Legal Times of Washington D. C. Circuit Handbook.
Law & Economics Center, University of Miami School of Law Staff. The Attack on Corporate America: The Corporate Issues Sourcebook.
Law, Bernard, intro. by. Extraordinary Synod 1985.
Law, Christopher M. British Regional Development since WWI.
Law, Edmund. An Enquiry into the Ideas of Space & Time. Wellek, Rene, ed.
Law, Jane, jt. auth. see Tilson, Marie.
Law, Janice. Death Under Par.
--The Shadow of the Palms.
--Under Orion.
Law, John, ed. Power, Action & Belief: A New Sociology of Knowledge?
Law, Marie H. How to Read German.
Law, Peter. Portrait of My Father: The Wonder of Knowing God.
Law, Preston. Shipboard Antennas.
Law, R. G. Ultrasound in Clinical Obstetrics.
Law, Sylvia. The Rights of the Poor.
Law, William. A Serious Call to Holy Living.
--William Law: Christian Perfection.
Lawall, David B. Asher B. Durand: A Documentary Catalogue of the Narrative & Landscape Paintings.
--Asher Brown Durand: His Art & Art Theory in Relations to His Times.
Lawall, Sarah, et al, eds. Decouverte de l'Essai.
Lawder, Elizabeth A., et al. Five Models of Foster Family Group Homes.
Lawhead, Steve, jt. auth. see Slaikeu, Karl.
Lawhead, Wendell H., jt. auth. see Farnsworth, Kirk E.
Lawick-Goodall, Hugo Van see Van Lawick-Goodall, Jane & Van Lawick-Goodall, Hugo.
Lawick-Goodall, Jane Van see Van Lawick-Goodall, Jane.
Lawick-Goodall, Jane Van see Van Lawick-Goodall, Jane & Van Lawick-Goodall, Hugo.
Lawing, Betty S. Solving Mathematical Word Problems.
Lawler, John. Book Auctions in England in the Seventeenth Century.
Lawler, Michael G. Raid on the Inarticulate: An Invitation to Adult Religion.
Lawless, Gary. Gulf of Maine: First Reader.
--Yellow Dog.
Lawless, Greg, ed. The Harvard Crimson Anthology.
Lawless, Richard, jt. ed. see Niblock, Tim.
Lawless, Richard M. When Love Unites the Church.
Lawlis, Frank, jt. auth. see Achterberg, Jeanne.
Lawlor, Hugh J. The Reformation & the Irish Episcopate.
Lawlor, John J., et al. Real Property Tax Delinquency & Urban Land Policy.
Lawn, Martin, ed. The Politics of Teacher Unionism: International Perspectives.
Lawn, R. J., jt. auth. see Shepard, Merle.
Lawren, Bill, jt. auth. see Herman, Barry.
Lawrence. Breastfeeding: A Guide for the Medical Profession.
Lawrence, Barbara, jt. auth. see Castle, Coralie.
Lawrence, Betsy, ed. see Cooper, Sandi.
Lawrence, Betsy, ed. see Hibler, Jane.
Lawrence, Betsy, ed. see Pressman, Thelma.
Lawrence, Bette. Mike: A Mother's Prayers.
Lawrence, Bill. Nigger, Go Home!
Lawrence, Bill, ed. Then Some Other Stuff Happened.
Lawrence, Bruce B. Notes from a Distant Flute: The Extant Literature of Pre-Mughal Indian Sufism.
Lawrence, Charles, III, jt. auth. see Dreyfuss, Joel.
Lawrence, Christopher W., ed. Induced Mutagenesis: Molecular Mechanisms & Their Implications for Environmental Protection.
Lawrence, D. H. Lady Chatterley's Lover.
--The Rainbow.
--Sons & Lovers: Text & Criticism.
--Women in Love.
Lawrence, D. H., tr. see Verga, Giovanni.
Lawrence, D. H. see also Lawrence, David H.
Lawrence, David, jt. auth. see Lawrence, Lauren.
Lawrence, David H. Lady Chatterley's Lover.
Lawrence, David H. see also Lawrence, D. H.
Lawrence, Elizabeth A. Rodeo: An Anthropologist Looks at the Wild & the Tame.
Lawrence, Elwood P. Henry George in the British Isles.
Lawrence, Evelyn. Friedrich Froebel & English Education.
Lawrence, G. Hugh. Problems of the Pleural Space.
Lawrence, G. R. Cartographic Methods.
Lawrence, Gene H. The Psychology of Successful Living: An Advanced Guide to All Achievement Based on the Laws & Psychology of Right Human Relationship with Oneself, Mankind, & God.
--Right Human Relations: The Only Way to World Peace.
Lawrence, George H. Introduction to Plant Taxonomy.
--Taxonomy of Vascular Plants.
Lawrence, H. S. & Landy, M., eds. Mediators of Cellular Immunity.
Lawrence, Herbert. The Life & Adventures of Common Sense, 1769.
Lawrence, J. A., jt. auth. see Blish, James.
Lawrence, Jim. ESP McGee & the Haunted Mansion.
Lawrence, Jodi. Alpha Brain Waves.
Lawrence, John S. & Timberg, Bernard, eds. Fair Use & Free Inquiry: Copyright Law & the New Media.
Lawrence, John T. History of Russia.
Lawrence, Judy. Common Cents: The Complete Money Management Workbook.
Lawrence, Judy M. Common Cents: The Complete Money Management Workbook.
Lawrence, Kathleen R. Maud Gone.
Lawrence, Ken. Photography Simplified for Archivists. Gill, Rowland P., ed.
Lawrence, Lauren & Lawrence, David. Living with Mirrors: Two Books of Poetry.
Lawrence, Leslie, ed. see Temko, Florence.
Lawrence, Louise D. To Whom the Wilderness Speaks.
Lawrence, Marjorie. Apple Bloom.
Lawrence, Marjorie K. Eider Down.
--Fairy Smoke: Children's Poems.
--Misty Meadows.
--The Singing Wind.
Lawrence, Marjorie Kahl. High on a Hilltop.
--Mother Goose for the Animals' Children.
Lawrence, Mildred. Forever & Always.
--Inside the Gate.
--No Slipper for Cinderella.
--Once at the Weary Why.
--One Hundred White Horses.
--Peachtree Island.
--Sand in Her Shoes.
--Touchmark.
--The Treasure & the Song.
--Walk a Rocky Road.
Lawrence, Nathaniel, jt. auth. see Brumbaugh, Robert S.
Lawrence, Ness. From Justinian to Charlemagne. European Art, 565-787: An Annotated Bibliography.
Lawrence, P. A. Insect Development.
Lawrence, P. Scott, et al. Readings in Abnormal Psychology.
Lawrence, Peter. A Kid's New York.
--Road Belong Cargo: A Study of the Cargo Movement in the Southern Madang District New Guinea.
Lawrence, R. D. The Ghost Walker.
--The North Runner.
--Paddy: A Naturalist's Story of an Orphaned Beaver.
--Secret Go the Wolves.
--Voyage of the Stella.
--The Zoo That Never Was.
Lawrence, Richard D. & Record, Jeffrey. U. S. Force Structure in NATO: An Alternative.
Lawrence, Robert, jt. auth. see Caldwell, Gaylon L.
Lawrence, Robert M. Magic of the Horseshoe.
Lawrence, Roger. Tribunal Representation.
Lawrence, S. So You Want to Be a Rock & Roll Star.
Lawrence, Sidney & Foy, George. Music in Stone: Great Sculpture Gardens of the World. Tompkins, P., ed.
Lawrence, Steven C. The Naked Range.
--North to Montana.
--Slattery Stands Alone.
--Slattery's Gun Says No.
Lawrence, Steven G. With Blood in Their Eyes.
Lawrence, T. E. Mint.
Lawrence, Thomas E. T. E. Lawrence to His Biographers, Robert Graves & Liddell Hart.
Lawrence, V. B. & LoCicero, J. L., eds. IEEE Communications Society's Tutorials in Modern Communication.
Lawrence, Victor J. Easy Steps to Playing Guitar.
--Easy Steps to Playing Guitar.
--Teaching Spanish Guitar: In Advanced Modern Style.
Lawrenson, P. J., jt. auth. see Binns, K. J.
Lawrie, Margaret, ed. Myths & Legends of the Torres Strait.
Lawrie, R. Developments in Meat Science.
Lawrie, R. A. Meat Science.
Lawry, John D. Guide to the History of Psychology.
Laws, Priscilla W., jt. auth. see Public Citizen Health Research Group Staff.
Laws, W. Electricity Applied to Marine Engineering. Tyrell, R., rev. by.
Lawson, Annetta. The Lucky Yak.
Lawson, D. E., ed. Vitamin D.
Lawson, D. Gaynell. Search Within.

Lawson, David H. & Richards, R. Michael. Clinical Pharmacy.
Lawson, Don. The KGB.
Lawson, Douglas E. Wisdom & Education.
Lawson, Harold. Understanding Computer Systems.
Lawson, Jennifer A. A Right to Love.
Lawson, Joan. Mime: The Theory & Practice of Expressive Gesture.
--The Story of Ballet.
Lawson, LeRoy. Cracking the Code.
--God's Word A. D.
--The Lord of Parables: Instructor Edition.
Lawson, Lewis A. Wheeler's Last Raid.
Lawson, Robert. McWhinney's Jaunt.
--Mr. Twigg's Mistake.
--Watchwords of Liberty: A Pageant of American Quotations.
Lawson, Rodger. Allied Health Education in Michigan: Labor Market Information for Counselors & Administrators.
Lawson, Rodger S. Population of Kalamazoo County, Michigan: Estimates As of July 1, 1973 & Projections to 2000.
Lawson, Rodgers. Perspectives on the Development of a Comprehensive Labor Market Information System for Michigan.
Lawson, Ruth C., ed. International Regional Organizations: Constitutional Foundations.
Lawson, V. K., ed. see Colvin, Ruth J. & Root, Jane.
Lawson, William. The Western Scar: The Theme of the Been-to in West African Literature.
Lawton, A. T. A Window in the Sky.
Lawton, Anna. Vadim Shershenevich.
Lawton, C. W. & Seeley, R. R., eds. Fatigue, Creep, & Pressure Vessels for Elevated Temperature Service.
Lawton, Denis. Curriculum Studies & Educational Planning.
--An Introduction to Teaching & Learning.
--School Curriculum Planning.
--Social Class, Language & Education.
Lawton, Denis, jt. ed. see Lacey, Colin.
Lawton, Esther C. & Suskin, Harold. Elements of Position Classification in Local Government.
Lawton, H., jt. auth. see Klotz, Ester.
Lawton, Lynna. Under Crimson Sails.
Lawvere, F. W., ed. Toposes, Algebraic Geometry & Logic.
Lawyer, John & Katz, Neil. Communication Skills for Ministry.
Laxen, D. P., jt. auth. see Harrison, R. M.
Laxness, Halldor. Independent People: An Epic. Thompson, J. A., tr. from Icelandic.
Lay, K. W., jt. ed. see German, R. M.
Lay, N., jt. auth. see Fassler, D.
Lay, S. Houston & Taubenfeld, Howard J. Law Relating to Activities of Man in Space.
Lay, Tracy. Beyond Our Limitations.
Layachi, Larbi, pseud. A Life Full of Holes.
Layamon, jt. auth. see Wace, Robert.
Laybourne. Teaching Science to the Ordinary Pupil.
Laybourne, Kit. The Animation Book.
Laycock, George. Alaska: The Embattled Frontier.
--Deer Hunter's Bible.
--How the Settlers Lived.
Layder, Derek. Structure, Interaction & Social Theory.
Layman, Richard. Shadow Man: The Life of Dashiell Hammett.
Layman, Richard, jt. ed. see Bruccoli, Matthew J.
Layne, Lisa & Sinn, Paul. The Book of Love.
Layton, Thomas N., jt. auth. see Yee, Min S.
Layzell, A. D., jt. auth. see Dix, M. C.
Lazan, Albert. The Secret Life of the Reindeer-Cat.
Lazareff, Helen & Lazareff, Pierre. The Soviet Union after Stalin.
Lazareff, Pierre, jt. auth. see Lazareff, Helen.
Lazareth, William H., jt. ed. see Forell, George W.
Lazareth, William H., et al, eds. The Left Hand of God: Essays on Discipleship & Patriotism.
Lazarevic, B. & Lazarevic, B., eds. Global & Large Scale System Models: Proceedings.
Lazaroff, Allan. The Theology of Abraham Bibago: A Defense of the Divine Will, Knowledge, & Providence in Fifteenth-Century Spanish-Jewish Philosophy.
Lazarus, Arnold A. Behavior Therapy & Beyond.
Lazarus, H. American Business Dictionary.
Lazarus, Sy. Loud & Clear: A Guide to Effective Communication.
Lazell, Barry & Smith, Steve. Rock Day-by-Day.
Lazenby, Patricia, jt. auth. see Goeltz, Judith.
Lazenby, Roland, jt. auth. see Packer, Billy.
Lazer, William & Culley, James. Marketing Management: Foundations & Practices.
Lazzarin, Piero, jt. auth. see Lubich, Gino.
Lazzarini, John & Lazzarini, Roberta. Pavlova: Repertoire of a Legend.
Lazzarini, Roberta, jt. auth. see Lazzarini, John.
Lazzarino, Alex & Hayes, E. Kent. Find a Safe Place.
Lazzarino, Graziana. Da Capo: A Review Grammar.
Lazzarino, Graziana, et al. Prego! An Invitation to Italian.
Lazzaro, Bea & Mendelsohn, Lotte. Italian Provincial Cookery. Hebbard, Neysa, ed.
LDA-Symposium Staff. The Accuracy of Flow Measurements by Laser Doppler Methods: Proceedings of the LDA Symposium, Copenhagen, 1975. Buchhave, P., et al, eds.
Lea. The Leaves Turn Autumn.
Lea, F. A. The Tragic Philosopher.
Lea, Tom. A Picture Gallery.
Leab, Daniel. From Sambo to Superspade: The Black Experience in Motion Pictures.
--From Sambo to Superspade: The Black Experience in Motion Pictures.
Leab, Daniel J., jt. ed. see Leab, Katharine K.
Leab, Katharine K. & Leab, Daniel J., eds. American Book Prices Current.
--American Book Prices Current.
Leacacos, John P. Fires in the in-Basket: The ABC's of the State Department.
Leach, Ben. Worry Free Worry.
Leach, Christopher. Letter to a Younger Son.
--Texas Station.
Leach, Donald P. Experiments in Digital Principles.
Leach, Douglas E. Flintlock & Tomahawk: New England in King Philip's War.
Leach, F., jt. auth. see De Noriega, L. A.
Leach, Graham. South Africa Today: No Easy Path to Peace.
Leach, Jack. Sods I Have Cut on the Turf.
Leach, James A. Reindustrialization: Implications for Voc Ed.
Leach, Michael. Don't Call Me Orphan!
--I Know It When I See It: Pornography, Violence, & Public Sensitivity.
Leach, R. H. see Bissett, D. E., et al.
Leach, R. J. International Schools & Their Role in the Field of International Education.
Leach, Robert E. & Hoaglund, Franklin T. Controversies in Orthopaedic Surgery.
Leach, Sidney J., ed. Physical Principles & Techniques of Protein Chemistry.
Leach, Vickie, tr. see Bonino, Jose M.
Leacock, Stephen. The Social Criticism of Stephen Leacock: The Unsolved Riddle of Social Justice & Other Essays.
Leacroft, Richard. The Development of the English Playhouse.
Lead Development Association, tr. see Hofmann, W.
Leader, Robert W., et al. Diseases of Latent & Slow Growth Viruses.
Leader, Zachery. Reading Blake's "Songs"
League for Social Reconstruction Staff. Social Planning for Canada.
League, Nehume see DeCrow, Roger.
League of American Writers Staff. Black & White.
League of Women Voters Education Fund Staff. Achieving "Due Responsibility" Perspectives on the American Presidency.
--Achieving Sex Equity in Vocational Education: A Crack in the Wall.
--The Bill of Rights Then & Now: Perspectives on Individual Liberty.
League of Women Voters Education Fund. Budget Cuts & Block Grants: Social Needs & the New Federalism.
League of Women Voters Education Fund Staff. Budget Cuts & Block Grants: Social Needs & the New Federalism.
--Campaigning for Fair School Finance: Cases in Point.
--Choosing the President: 1980 Edition.
--The Growth of Judicial Power: Perspectives on "The Least Dangerous Branch"
League of Women Voters Education Fund. Indian Country.
--Instructions for Monitoring the Impact of General Revenue Sharing at the Local Level.
League of Women Voters Education Fund, ed. The National Flood Insurance Program: Is It Working?
League of Women Voters Education Fund Staff. A Nuclear Power Primer: Issues for Citizens.
--Past As Prologue: Present Perspectives.
--Perspectives on Congress: Performance & Prospects.
League of Women Voters Education Fund. School Finance Reform in the Nineteen Eighties: Social Needs & the New Federalism.
League of Women Voters Education Fund Staff. Tell It to Washington.
League of Women Voters Education Fund. The Women's Vote: Beyond the Nineteenth Amendment.
League of Women Voters Education Fund Staff. World Trade at a Crossroads.
--You & Your National Government.
League of Women Voters of New Jersey Staff. New Jersey: Spotlight on Government.
League of Women Voters of New York State Staff. The Health Care Puzzle in New York State: A Citizen Guide. Stuligross, Katherine, ed.
--The Judicial Maze: The System in New York State. Banks, Lenore, ed.
--Toward an Evaluation of the Property Tax System in New York State. Amlung, Susan, ed.
League of Women Voters of the United States Staff. Who Should Elect the President.
Leahey, Thomas H. A History of Psychology.
Leahy, Michael. Privileged Class: Senior Year at Beverly Hills High School.
Leak, J. India: A Practical Guide.
Leake, Mary J. Manual of Simple Nursing Procedures.
Leakey, L. & Savage, R., eds. Fossil Vertebrates of Africa.
Leakey, L. S. By the Evidence: Memoirs, Nineteen Thirty-Two to Nineteen Fifty-One.
Leakey, L. S., et al, eds. Fossil Vertebrates of Africa.
Leakey, Mary. Disclosing the Past: An Autobiography.
--Disclosing the Past: An Autobiography.
Leal, Luis. Cuentistas Hispanoamericanos del Siglo Veinte.
--Juan Rulfo.
Leaman, Arthur, jt. auth. see Wilson, Jose.
Leaming, Barbara. Polanski.
Leane, J. B., tr. see Neudert, Walter & Roepke, H.
Leapman, Michael. Companion Guide to New York.
Lear, Edward. A Book of Nonsense.
--The Owl & the Pussy Cat.
Lear, Edward, et al. A Book of Nonsense.
--A Book of Nonsense.
Learning Achievement Corp. Staff. MATCH Microcomputer Software Program.
Learning Systems Ltd. Break-Even Charts: Their Interpretation & Construction.
--Discounted Cash Flow.
--Effective Communication.
Learning Technology, Inc. Staff. Basic Spelling Skills. Raygor, Alton L., ed.
Leary, Lewis, intro. by. American Literature to Nineteen Hundred.
Leary, O., jt. auth. see Boschke, F.
Leary, Paul M. The Northern Marianas Covenant & American Territorial Relations.
Leary, Timothy. Neuropolitique.
--Psychedelic Prayers.
Leary, William. Shakespeare Plain: The Making & Performing of Shakespeare's Plays.
Leary, William G., jt. auth. see Graves, Wallace.
Leary, William G., et al. Thought & Statement.
Leas, Speed & Kittlaus, Paul. The Pastoral Counselor in Social Action. Clinebell, Howard J. & Stone, Howard W., eds.
Leaska, Mitchell A., jt. ed. see Desalve, Louise.
Leaska, Mitchell A., jt. ed. see DeSalvo, Louise.
Leasor, James. Boarding Party.
--Code Name Nimrod.
--The Unknown Warrior.
Leat, Diana & Smolka, Gerry. Voluntary & Statutory Collaboration.
Leatherman, Donna, ed. see Sturm, Dorothy.
Leatherman, Stephen F. Barrier Island Migration: An Annotated Bibliography.
Leatherman, Stephen P., ed. Overwash Processes.
Lea Thomas, M. Phlebography of the Lower Limb.
Leaton, Anne. Pearl.
Leaton, Gwen, jt. auth. see Kinney, Jean.
Leaver, C. J., ed. Genome Organization & Expression In Plants.
Leavey, John P., tr. see Derrida, Jacques.
Leavitt, Harold J., et al. The Organizational World.
Leavitt, Thomas D., jt. auth. see Schulz, James H.
Leavy, Una. Is Anyone There?
LeBeau, Roy. Rifle River.
LeBeaux, D. J. Love Me, Somebody.
Lebedev, N. N. Chemistry & Technology of Basic Organic & Petrochemical Synthesis.
Lebedev, P. N., jt. auth. see Ginzburg, V. L.
Lebedoff, David. The New Elite: The Death of Democracy.
Leben, Joe & Arnold, Jim. IBM CPU & Storage Architecture: System-370-Mode & 370-XA Mode.
--IBM I-O Architecture & Virtual Storage Concepts: Systems-370-Mode & 370-XA-Mode Processors.
--MVS JCL for Sequential Data Management.
--MVS JCL Library.
Leben, Joseph F., jt. auth. see Kapp, Dan.
Leben, William. Suprasegmental Phonology. Hankamer, Jorge, ed.
Lebens, Ralph M. Passive Solar Heating Design.
Leblond, C. P., ed. see International Society for Cell Biology Staff.
LeBlond, Geoffrey, jt. auth. see Cobb, Douglas F.
LeBlond, Geoffrey, jt. auth. see Ewing, David.
LeBoeuf, Michael. Imagineering: How to Profit from Your Creative Powers.
--Imagineering: How to Profit from Your Creative Powers.
--The Productivity Challenge: How to Make It Work for America & You.
LeBon, Leo. The Adventurous Traveler's Guide.
Lebovitz, Norman, et al, eds. Theoretical Principles in Astrophysics & Relativity.
Lebow, Richard N. Between Peace & War: The Nature of International Crisis.
Lebowitz, Melvyn, jt. auth. see Kaplan, William L.
Lebowitz, Philip W. & Newberg, Leslie A. Clinical Anesthesia Procedures of the Massachusetts General Hospital.
Lebra, Joyce, et al, eds. Women in Changing Japan.
Lebrun, Richard A., ed. & tr. see De Maistre, Joseph.
Lebrun, Yvan & Zangwill, O., eds. Lateralisation of Language in the Child: Proceedings of the International Symposium, St. Ode, Belgium, Oct. 1-3, 1979.
Lebrun, Yvan, et al. The Artificial Larynx.
LeBuffe, Francis P. Ninety Eight Point Six Meditations to Maintain Spiritual Well-Being.
Lecam, Lucien M., ed. see International Research Seminar - Berkeley - 1963.
Le Carre, John. The Looking Glass War.
Lechene, Claude P. & Warner, Ronald, eds. Microbeam Analysis in Biology.
Lechford, Thomas. Note-Book.
Lechner, H. & Korner, E., eds. Sleep & Sleep Disordery, 1986.
Lecht, Charles P. The Waves of Change.
Lechtman, Max D., et al. The Games Cells Play.
Leck, J. H. Theory of Semiconductor Junction Devices.
Lecker, Sidney. Why Women Choose the Wrong Men.
Leckey, Hugo. Floating.
Lecky, Prescott. Self Consistency: A Theory of Personality.
Le Clair, Robert C. Three American Travellers in England: James Russell Lowell, Henry Adams, Henry James.
LeClair, Thomas & McCaffery, Larry, eds. Anything Can Happen: Interviews with Contemporary American Novelists.
Lecler, Rene. The Three Hundred Best Hotels in the World.
Leclercq, Jacques. This Day Is Ours. Livingstone, Dinah, tr. from Fr.
LeClezio, J. M. The Giants.
LeCoff, Albert. Gallery of Turned Objects.
Lecomber, Richard, jt. auth. see Slater, Martin.
Le Comte, Edward. Dictionary of Last Words.
LeComte, Jacques & Koechlin-Schwartz, Dorothee. How to Talk to the Birds & the Beasts.
Le Coq, Albert V. Sprichworter und Lieder Aus der Gegend Von Turfan.
Le Corbeiller, Clare, jt. auth. see Parker, James.
LeCron, Leslie M. Magic Mind Power: Make It Work for You!
Le Cron, Leslie M., ed. Experimental Hypnosis.
Ledbetter, Gordon T. Water Gardens.
Ledbetter, J. O. Air Pollution, Pt. B: Prevention & Control.
Ledbetter, M. C. & Porter, K. Introduction to the Fine Structure of Plant Cells.
Ledeen, Michael, ed. see Thomas, David.
Lederer, Laura, ed. Take Back the Night: Women on Pornography.
Lederer, Richard, jt. auth. see Burnham, Phillip.
Lederer, William J. A Happy Book of Christmas Stories.
--I, Giorghos: A Novel.
--Marital Choices: Forecasting, Assessing & Improving a Relationship.
--A Nation of Sheep.
Lederer, Wolfgang. Fear of Women.
Lederis, Karl, jt. ed. see Farner, Donald S.
Ledermann, Walter. Integral Calculus.
Ledgard, Henry F. & Chmura, Louis J. FORTRAN with Style: Programming Proverbs.
Ledgard, Henry F. & Chmura, Louis J., Jr. COBOL with Style: Programming Proverbs.
Ledgard, Henry F., jt. auth. see Nagin, Paul.
Ledgard, Henry F., et al. Pascal with Style: Programming Proverbs.
Ledin, George, Jr. & Ledin, Victor. The Programmer's Book of Rules.
Ledin, George, Jr., et al. The COBOL Programmer's Book of Rules.
Ledin, Victor, jt. auth. see Ledin, George, Jr.
Ledingham, I., ed. Recent Advances in Intensive Therapy, No. 1.
Ledner, Caryl. The Bondswoman.
Lednicer, Daniel. Central Analgetics.
Ledson, Sidney. Teach Your Child to Read in Sixty Days.
Ledward, R. S. & Hawkins, D. F. Drug Treatment in Obstetrics: A Handbook of Prescribing.
Ledwith, A. & North, A. M., eds. Molecular Behavior & the Development of Polymer Materials.
Lee. Company Auditing U. K.
--The Legend of the Milky Way.
--Modern Financial Accounting.
Lee & Wood, L. J. Adjustment in the Urban System: The Tasman Bridge Collapse & Its Effects on Metropolitan Hobart.
Lee, jt. auth. see Tyrer.
Lee, et al. Guided Weapons.

Lee, A. Robert, ed. William Faulkner: The Yoknapatawpha Fiction.
Lee, Albert & Lee, Carol A. The Total Couple.
Lee, Alfred & Sloan, Timothy. Competition in the Local Exchange Telephone Service Market.
Lee, Alfred M. Electronic-Message Transfer & its Implications.
Lee, Allan W. One Great Fellowship Travels of a Global Minister.
Lee, Amy. Call Him a Man: The Story of Hazzard Parks.
--Throbbing Drums: The Story of James H. Robinson.
Lee, Art. Fishing: Dry Flies for Trout on Rivers & Streams.
Lee, B. Y. Chronic Ulcers of the Skin.
Lee, Benjamin. It Can't Be Helped.
Lee, Bennett & Barme, Geremie. China Traveler's Phrasebook.
Lee, Bennett, tr. see Yang Jiang.
Lee, Betsy. Miracle in the Making.
--Mother Teresa: Caring for All God's Children.
Lee, Bill. Every Day Is Father's Day.
--Have a Good Day at the Office, Dear.
Lee, Billy, jt. ed. see Reginald, R.
Lee, Bob, jt. auth. see Arnold, Henri.
Lee, C. Y. China Saga.
Lee, Carol A., jt. auth. see Lee, Albert.
Lee, Charles A. Aleutian Indian & English Dictionary.
Lee, Charles C., jt. ed. see Chiang, C. Nora.
Lee, Charles H. Divine Direction or Chaos: A Layman Looks at Philosophy, Natural Science, & Devine Metaphysics.
Lee, Charlotte I. Oral Reading of the Scriptures.
Lee, Charlotte I. & Gura, Timothy. Oral Interpretations.
Lee, Clarence L., ed. see Carpenter, H. J.
Lee, Clarence L., ed. see Jones, A. H.
Lee, Clarence L., ed. see Vischer, Lukas.
Lee, D. E. & Brower, Walter A. Secretarial Office Procedures.
Lee, David. Shadow Weaver.
Lee, Dennis. Alligator Pie.
--Garbage Delight.
--Nicholas Knock.
Lee, Donald G. Oxidation of Organic Compounds by Permanganate Ion & Hexavalent Chromium.
Lee, Donald G., ed. see Arndt, Diether.
Lee, Douglas H., ed. Environmental Factors in Respiratory Disease.
--Metallic Contaminants & Human Health: Fogarty International Center Proceedings,
Lee, Douglas H. & Kotin, Paul, eds. Multiple Factors in the Causation of Environmentally Induced Disease.
Lee, Dwight R., jt. auth. see Glahe, Fred R.
Lee, E. C. & Lee, Kenneth. Safety & Survival at Sea.
--Safety & Survival at Sea.
Lee, E. H. & Symonds, P. S., eds. Plasticity: Proceedings, Symposium on Naval Structural Mechanics, 2nd, Brown University, 1960.
Lee, E. Stanley. Quasilinearization & Invariant Imbedding.
Lee, E. Y., jt. ed. see Huijing, F.
Lee, Eddie H. & Derivaux, Don. I Murdered My Love.
Lee, Eddy, jt. auth. see Radwan, Samir.
Lee, Eddy, ed. see ILO Asian Employment Programme Staff.
Lee, Edward. Folksong & Music Hall.
Lee, Edward, jt. auth. see Vulliamy, Graham.
Lee, Elisa T. Statistical Methods for Survival Data Analysis.
Lee, Elizabeth. The Way of Passion.
Lee, Elsie. An Eligible Connection.
--Elsie Lee's Book of Simple Gourmet Cookery.
--Elsie Lee's Party Cookbook.
--The Passions of Medora Graeme.
--A Prior Betrothal.
--Wingarden.
Lee, Ernest M. Story of Opera.
--Story of Symphony.
Lee, Essie E. Alcohol-Proof of What?
--Marriage & Families.
Lee, Eugene C. & Keith, Bruce E. California Votes, Nineteen Sixty to Nineteen Seventy-Two: A Review & Analysis of Registration & Voting.
Lee, Eugene C., jt. auth. see Bowen, Frank M.
Lee, Frederick G. A Glossary of Liturgical & Ecclesiastical Terms.
Lee, G. Modern Financial Accounting.
Lee, Grace Eaton, compiled by. Graduate Research in Arid & Semi-Arid Lands at Texas Tech University: 1928-1972.
Lee, Guy C. Historical Jurisprudence: An Introduction to the Systematic Study of the Development of Law.
Lee, Gypsy Rose. Gypsy: A Memoir.
Lee, H. & Fitzgerald, T. J. Progress in Research & Clinical Applications of Corticosteroids.
Lee, H. A., ed. Parenteral Nutrition in Acute Metabolic Illness.
Lee, H. Alton. Seven Feet Four & Growing.
Lee, H. B. Lost Tales of Appalachia.
Lee, Hanka, jt. auth. see Lee, Michael.
Lee, Harold N. Perception & Aesthetic Value.
Lee, Harper. To Kill A Mockingbird.
Lee, Harris W. Time for Questions: Messages for Lent & Easter.
Lee, Hector. Heroes, Villains, & Ghosts: Folklore of Old California.
Lee, Henry. Anti-Scepticism: Or, Notes upon Each Chapter of Mr. Locke's Essay Concerning Humane Understanding.
Lee, Henry & Neville, Kris. The Handbook of Biomedical Plastics.
Lee, Henry L., et al. New Linear Polymers.
Lee, Hermione. Philip Roth.
Lee, Hermione, pref. by. Stevie Smith: A Selection.
Lee, J. D. Testament of Intent.
Lee, Jack. Sex, Science Fiction, Stage, Screen, Soccer & Other Educational Matters: The Uncensored Letters of a Prep School Freshman. Jefferson, Travis, ed.
Lee, James, et al. Radio Frequency Testers. Cole, Sandy & Force, Rich, eds.
Lee, James M., ed. Catholic Education in the Western World.
Lee, Jasper S., ed. see Dillon, Roy.
Lee, Jerry. Making Wood & Stone Jewelry.
Lee, John, jt. auth. see Green, James.
Lee, John A. Computer Semantics: Studies of Algorithms Processors & Languages.
Lee, Jong K., ed. Interatomic Potentials & Crystalline Defects: Proceedings of the TMS-AIME Fall Meeting, Pittsburgh, 1980.
Lee, Joo B. Hwa Rang Do.
Lee, Joshua A. With Their Ears Pricked Forward, Tales of Mules I've Known.
Lee, Julian C. An Ecogeographic Analysis of the Herpetofauna of the Yucatan Peninsula.
Lee, Jung Y. Death Overcome: Towards a Convergence of Eastern & Western Views.
--Principle of Changes: Understanding the I Ching.
Lee, Karen & Branyon, Alexandra. Chinese Cooking Secrets.
Lee, Kenneth & Mills, Anne. Policy-Making & Planning in the Health Sector.
Lee, Kenneth, jt. auth. see Lee, E. C.
Lee, LaJuanna W., et al. Business Communication.
Lee, Lamar, Jr. & Dobler, Donald W. Purchasing & Materials Management.
Lee, Laurel. To Comfort You. Phillips, Cheryl M. & Harvey, Bonnie C., eds.
Lee, Laurence D., ed. see Oldman, Oliver, et al.
Lee, Lauri E. & Olsen, Roger E. This Is English.
Lee, Laurie. As I Walked out One Midsummer Morning.
--As I Walked Out One Midsummer Morning.
--I Can't Stay Long.
Lee, Lawrence. The Grants Game: How to Get Free Money.
Lee, Leo Ou-fan, ed. see Prusek, Jaroslav.
Lee, Lieng-Huang. Adhesion Science & Technology. Incl. Pt. A; Pt. B. Plenum Pub.
Lee, Linda. Today I Am a Woman?
Lee, Linda, compiled by. Meditate Upon These Things.
Lee, M. A., jt. ed. see Koch-Miramond, L.
Lee, M. J. The United Nations & World Realities.
Lee, M. J., jt. auth. see Bunting, G. R.
Lee, Marion H. The Sea at Montauk & Other Poems.
Lee, Marshall, jt. auth. see Heinz, H. J.
Lee, Martin A. & Shlain, Bruce. Acid Dreams: The CIA, LSD & the Sixties Rebellion.
Lee, Mary P. Exploring Careers in Research & Development in Industry.
--Money & Kids: How to Earn It, Save It, & Spend It.
--The Team That Runs Your Hospital.
Lee, Michael & Lee, Hanka. Cyprus.
Lee, Mike, ed. see Bryne, Richard.
Lee, Mike, ed. see Cheung, William.
Lee, Mike, ed. see Duff, Karl J.
Lee, Mike, ed. see Yamashita, Tadashi.
Lee, Mildred. Fog.
--The People Therein.
--Sycamore Year.
Lee, Molly K., ed. East Asian Economies: A Guide to Information Sources.
Lee, Nanci. Self Paced Business Mathematics.
Lee, Nancy. Targeting the Top.
Lee, Pamela & Hawksley, Rozanne. Pattern Designing & Adaptation for Beginners.
Lee, Philip R., jt. ed. see Cater, DouglasS.
Lee, R. G. An Introduction to Battlefield Weapons Systems & Technology.
Lee, R. Shao-Lin, tr. see Stupochenko, Y. V., et al.
Lee, Raymond L. & Palmer, Dorothy A. Government by the People: National, State, & Local.
Lee, Rebecca S. Mary Austin Holley: A Biography.
Lee, Reginald. Building Maintenance Management.
Lee, Rex E. A Lawyer Looks at the Constitution.
--A Lawyer Looks at the Equal Rights Amendment.
Lee, Robert. Faith & the Prospect of Economic Collapse.
Lee, Robert A. Orwell's Fiction.
Lee, Robert C. It's a Mile from Here to Glory.
Lee, Robert E. The Dialogues of Lewis & Clark: A Narrative Poem.
--The Joy of Bach.
Lee, Robert M. Man & Me, M. D.
Lee, Ronald D., jt. auth. see Bulatao, Rodolfo A.
Lee, Ruth W. Sandwich Glass: The History of the Boston & Sandwich Glass Company.
Lee, S. C. Auburn-Alabama Joke Book.
--Best Basketball Booster.
--Georgia-Georgia Tech Joke Book.
--Little League Baseball Leader.
--North Carolina-North Carolina State Joke Book.
--Texas-Texas A & M Joke Book.
--University Jokes Told with Class.
Lee, S. D., et al. Aerosols: Research, Risk Assessment & Control Strategies.
Lee, Sammy & Lehrman, Steve. Diving.
Lee, Samuel C. Digital Circuits & Logic Design.
Lee, Sang M. Introduction to Management Science.
Lee, Seungho H. & Rao, Krishna C. Cranial Computed Tomography.
Lee, Sharon. When the Time Had Fully Come: Christmas Service for Church Schools.
Lee, Stan, jt. auth. see Marvel Comics Staff.
Lee, Stan, intro. by. The Marvel Comics Illustrated Version of Star Wars.
Lee, Stephen J. Aspects of European History, 1494-1789.
--Aspects of European History: 1789-1980.
Lee, Stewart. A Growing.
Lee, Suk B. Impact of United States Forces in Korea.
Lee, Susan. Signet Book of Inexpensive Wine.
Lee, T. & Parker, R. The Evolution of Corporate Financial Reporting.
Lee, T. D., ed. Weak Interactions & High Energy Neutrino Physics.
Lee, Terence. Psychology & the Environment.
Lee, Thomas B., ed. Modern History of China & Japan.
Lee, Vera G., ed. see Ionesco, Eugene.
Lee, Vernon. The Handling of Words & Other Studies in Literary Psychology.
Lee, Virginia. The Magic Moth.
Lee, W. R., ed. Current Research in Ophthalmic Electron Microscopy, 3.
Lee, Warren F., et al. Agricultural Finance.
Lee, William T. Understanding the Soviet Military Threat: How C. I. A. Estimates Went Astray.
Leebron, Elizabeth, jt. auth. see Lynn, Gartley.
Leech, Bryan J. Lift My Spirits, Lord: Prayers of a Struggling Christian.
Leech, J. Computational Problems in Abstract Algebra.
Leech, Jay, jt. auth. see Spencer, Zane.
Leech, John & Wing, John. Helping Destitute Men.
Leech, Kenneth. True Prayer: An Invitation to Christian Spirituality.
Leech, Kenneth & Jordan, Brenda. Drugs for Young People: Their Use & Misuse.
Leeds, C. A. European History Seventeen Eighty-Nine to Nineteen Fourteen.
Leeds, Wendy. Cameo.
--Cameo.
Leedy, Paul D. Key to Better Reading.
Leek, Sybil. Star Speak: Your Body Language from the Stars.
Leeker, Robert, ed. The Annotated Bibliography of Canada's Major Authors, Vol. 2: Margaret Atwood, Leonard Cohen, Archibald Lampman, E. J. Pratt, & Al Purdy.
Leeman, Wayne A. Centralized & Decentralized Economic Systems.
Leeming, David A. Flights: Readings in Magic, Mysticism, Fantasy & Myth.
Leeming, Glenda. Who's Who in Henry James.
--Who's Who in Jane Austen & the Brontes.
--Who's Who in Thomas Hardy.
Leemon, Sheldon. Mapping the Commodore 64.
Leemon, Sheldon, jt. auth. see Levitan, Arlan R.
Leemon, Thomas A. The Rites of Passage in a Student Culture.
Leen, Jason. The Death of the Prophet.
Leen, Nina. The Bat.
--Cats.
--Monkeys.
--Rare & Unusual Animals.
--Snakes.
--Taking Pictures.
--What Kind of a Dog Is That?
--Women, Heroes, & a Frog.
Leen, Nina, ed. Taking Pictures.
Leenders, Michael R., et al. Purchasing & Materials Management.
Leenhardt, Franz J., jt. auth. see Cullmann, Oscar.
Leerburger, Benedict A. The Complete Consumer's Guide to the Latest Telephones.
Lees, Brian. A Handbook of the Al Sa'ud Ruling Family of Saudi Arabia.
Lees, Carlton B. New Budget Landscaping.
Lees, David & Singer, Albert. Color Atlas of Gynecological Surgery, Vol. 2: Abdominal Operations for Benign Conditions.
Lees, David H. & Singer, Albert. A Color Atlas of Gynecological Surgery, Vol. 5: Infertility Surgery.
Lees, John D. Political System of the United States.
Lees, Ray & Mayo, Marjorie. Community Action for Change.
Lees, Susan. Sociopolitical Aspects of Canal Irrigation in the Valley of Oaxaca. Flannery, Kent V., ed.
Leese, See & Packer, Moira. Creative Dance for Schools.
Lees-Haley, Paul R. Evaluation Indoctrination.
Lees-Milne, James. The Age of Adam.
--The Age of Inigo Jones.
--The Last Stuarts: British Royalty in Exile.
Leeson, George, tr. see Martinsant.
Leeson, George, tr. see Sartre, Jean-Paul.
Leeson, Sylvia, tr. see Sartre, Jean-Paul.
Leestma, Sanford & Nyhoff, Larry. Programming with Pascal.
Leestma, Sanford, jt. auth. see Nyhoff, Larry R.
Leete-Hodge, L. Royal Family Pop-Up.
Leeuw, Adele De see De Leeuw, Adele.
Leeuw, Frank de, et al. The Web of Urban Housing.
Leeuw, S. De see Southworth, R. & De Leeuw, S.
Leeuwenhoek, Anthony Van. Anthony Van Leeuwenhoek & His Little Animals.
Lee-Warner, William. The Life of the Marquis of Dalhousie.
Lefcoe, George. When Governments Become Land Developers: Notes on the Public-Sector Experience in the Netherlands & California.
Lefcoe, George, ed. Respective Roles of State & Local Governments in Land Policy & Taxation.
Lefebure, Marcus, ed. Conversation on Counseling Between a Doctor & a Priest.
Lefebvre, Anny, tr. see Beaud, Michel.
Lefebvre, Arthur H. Gas Turbine Combustion.
Lefebvre, Claire. Syntaxe de l'Haitien. Magloire-Holly, Helene & Piou, Nanie, eds.
Lefebvre, G. The Great Fear of 1789.
LeFever, Marlene & Weyna, Kathy. Creative Kid Books.
--Creative Kid Books.
Lefevre, Carl A. & Lefevre, Helen E. Reading Power & Study Skills for College Work.
Lefevre, Helen E., jt. auth. see Lefevre, Carl A.
Lefevre, M. J., ed. First Aid Manual for Chemical Accidents: For Use with Nonpharmaceutical Chemicals. Solvay American Corporation & Becker, Ernest I., trs. from Fr.
Le Fevre, P. G. Active Transport Through Animal Cell Membranes.
LeFevre, Perry. Understandings of Man.
Leffin, et al. Basic Technical Mathematics.
Leffin, Walter W. Going Metric: Guidelines for the Mathematics Teacher, Grades K-8.
Leffler, John F. Short Course in Modern Organic Chemistry. Smith, James, ed.
Lefkovitz, David. Data Management for On-Line Systems.
Lefkowitz, M. M., et al. Growing up to Be Violent: A Longitudinal Study of the Development of Agression.
Lefler, Hugh T. & Newsome, Albert R. North Carolina: The History of a Southern State.
LeFort, David, tr. see Rein, Gerhard.
LeFort, Emilio, ed. World-Wide Spanish Dictionary.
Lefrancois, Guy R. The Lifespan. King, Ken, ed.
--Of Children: An Introduction to Child Development.
Lefroy, H. Maxwell. Indian Insect Life: A Manual of the Insects of the Plains (Tropical India)
--Indian Insect Pests.
Lefschetz, S. Applications of Algebraictopology, Graphs & Networks: The Picard-Lefschetz Theory & Feynman Integrals.
--Lectures on Differential Equations.
--Topics in Topology.
Lefschetz, Solomon. Topology.
Leftwich, Adrian. Redefining Politics: People, Resources & Power.
Leftwich, Joseph, tr. see Lehmann, Marcus.
Leftwich, Richard H. A Basic Framework for Economic Analysis.
--A Basic Framework for Economics.
Leftwich, Richard H. & Eckert, Ross D. The Price System & Resource Allocation.
Leftwich, Richard H. & Sharp, Ansel M. Economics of Social Issues.
--Economics of Social Issues.
Legal Aid Foundation of L.A. Labor Defense Network Operations Manual.
Legal & Government Affairs Symposium & International Transcript of Proceedings. The International Franchise Association Presents "Cultivating the Franchise Relationship," A Play in Three Acts: Official Transcript of Proceedings.
Legal & Government Affairs Symposium & International Franchise Association. The International Franchise Association Presents "Management & Law," A Play in Three Acts: Official Transcript of Proceedings.

Authors

Legator, Marvin S., et al, eds. The Health Detective's Handbook: A Guide to the Investigation of Environmental Health Hazards by Nonprofessionals.
Legenfelder, Helga, et al, eds. World Guide to Libraries.
Le Gentil, Pierre. Chanson De Roland. Beer, Frances F., tr.
Leger, Robert G. & Stratton, John R. The Sociology of Corrections: A Book of Readings.
Legg, Alicia, ed. Painting & Sculpture in the Museum of Modern Art with Selected Works on Paper: A Catalog.
--Sol LeWitt.
Legg, Alicia & Smalley, Mary B., eds. Painting & Sculpture in the Museum of Modern Art: Catalog of the Collection, 1987.
Legg, John. Cheyenne Lance.
--Cheyenne Lance.
Legg, N., ed. Neurotransmitter Systems & Their Clinical Disorders.
Legg, Robin. Revenge, My Friend.
Leggatt, Alexander. Ben Jonson: His Visión & Art.
--Shakespeare's Comedy of Love.
--Shakespeare's Political Drama: The History Plays & the Roman Plays.
Leggatt, Timothy W. The Evolution of Industrial Systems: The Forking Paths.
Legge, David & Barber, Paul J. Information & Skill.
Legge, David, jt. auth. see Barber, Paul J.
Legge, James, tr. see Confucius.
Legget, Jane. Local Heroines: A Women's History Gazetteer to England, Scotland & Wales.
Leggett, B. J. Houseman's Land of Lost Content: A Critical Study of "A Shropshire Lad"
Leggett, H. W. Bertrand Russell.
Leggett, John. Gulliver House.
Leggett, S., et al. Planning Flexible Learning Places.
Leggett, Trevor. The Chapter of the Self.
--Encounters in Yoga & Zen.
--The Warrior Koans: Early Zen in Japan.
Leghorn, Lisa & Parker, Katherine. Woman's Worth: Sexual Economics & the World of Women.
Leghorn, Lisa & Roodkowsky, Mary. Who Really Starves? Women & World Hunger.
Legisoft Staff. Willmaker.
Le Golif, Louis A. Memoirs of a Buccaneer.
LeGrand, Francoise. Boatopia.
LeGrande, James L., jt. auth. see Pomerance, Rocky.
Legrenzi, Giovanni. Totila. Brown, Howard M., ed.
Le Gros, F. & Dunne, Agnes C. Ageing in Industry.
Legros, Lucien & Grant, John C. Typographical Printing-Surfaces: The Technology & Mechanism of Their Production. Bidwell, John, ed.
LeGros, Lucy C. Activities & Games.
--Reading Success for School & Home.
Le Guin, Ursula K. The Beginning Place.
--The Compass Rose.
LeGuin, Ursula K. Rocannon's World. Del Rey, Lester, ed.
Legum, Colin. Africa: The Year of the Students.
--Africa: Year of Great Decision.
Lehane, Brendan, jt. auth. see Time-Life Books Editors.
Lehigh, Dwayne, ed. see Means, R. S., Company, Inc. Staff.
Lehman, Anthony. Quiltmaker's Big Book of Twelve Inch Patterns.
Lehman, Carolyn. God's Wonderful World: Twenty Six Lessons for Primary Church.
Lehman, Ernest. The French Atlantic Affair.
Lehman, H. Eugene. Laboratory Studies in General Zoology.
Lehman, Harry. Biology in Transition: A Critical Inquiry.
Lehman, Hohn M., et al. S-V Forty Viruses: Molecular Structure.
Lehman, Israel O., tr. see Auerbach, Elias.
Lehman, Jerry D. Three Approaches to Classroom Management: Views From a Psychological Perspective.
Lehman, John W. Operational Organic Chemistry: A Laboratory Course.
Lehman, June M., ed. EDP: Applications for Employee Benefit Plans.
--EDP: Applications for Employee Benefit Plans.
Lehman, Sherelynn, jt. auth. see Dolesh, Daniel J.
Lehman, Yvonne. Fashions of the Heart.
Lehmann. Sea-Grape Tree.
Lehmann, Dietrich & Callaway, Enoch, eds. Human Evoked Potentials: Applications & Problems.
Lehmann, Donald R. Market Research & Analysis.
Lehmann, H. & Kynoch, P. A., eds. Human Hemoglobin Variants & Their Characteristics.
Lehmann, Irvin J. & Mehrens, William A. Educational Research: Readings in Focus.
Lehmann, John. Edward Lear & His World.
--In the Purely Pagan Sense.
--The Strange Destiny of Rupert Brooke.
--Three Literary Friendships: Byron & Shelley, Rimbaud & Verlaine, Robert Frost & Edward Thomas.
--Virginia Woolf & Her World.
Lehmann, John, jt. ed. see Day-Lewis, Cecil.
Lehmann, Joseph. The First Boer War.
Lehmann, Marcus. Akiba. Leftwich, Joseph, tr.
Lehmann, Michael B. The Dow Jones-Irwin Guide to Using the Wall Street Journal.
Lehmann, Rosamond. The Ballad & the Source.
--Dusty Answer.
--Echoing Grove.
--Invitation to the Waltz.
Lehmann, Val W. Forgotten Legions: Sheep in the Rio Grande Plain of Texas.
Lehmann, Winfred P. Proto-Indo-European Syntax.
Lehmann-Hartleben, Karl, jt. auth. see Noack, Ferdinand.
Lehmann-Haupt, Hellmut. The Terrible Gustave Dore.
Lehner, T. & Barnes, C. G., eds. Behcet's Syndrome: Clinical & Immunological Features.
Lehninger, Albert L. Bioenergetics: The Molecular Basis of Biological Energy Transformations.
Lehnus, Donald J. A Comparison of Panizzi's 91 Rules & the AACR of 1967.
Lehr, Helene M. Capture the Dream.
--A Gallant Passion.
Lehr, Jay H., et al. Domestic Water Treatment.
Lehrer, James. We Were Dreamers.
Lehrer, Keith, ed. Freedom & Determinism.
Lehrer, Oscar J. Complete Method for Voice & Guitar: Instruction Manual in Accompaniment Playing & Singing.
Lehrman, Albert M. The Complete Book of Wills & Trusts.
--Tax Desk Book for the Closely-Held Corporation.
Lehrman, Steve. Your Career in Harness Racing.
Lehrman, Steve, jt. auth. see Lee, Sammy.
Lehrman, Steve, jt. auth. see Shapiro, Neal.
Leib, Steven, jt. auth. see Renneker, Mark.
Leibenguth, Charla, jt. ed. see Ebershoff-Coles, Susan.
Leibenstein, Margaret, jt. auth. see Wurtman, Judith J.
Leiber, Fritz. The Worlds of Fritz Leiber.
Leibert, A. The Benefit of Environmental Satellites to Offshore Industries.
Leibfried, G., tr. see Becker, R.
Leibling, Louis, jt. auth. see Riemer, Edwin.
Leibniz, Gottfried W. Leibniz Philosophical Writings. Parkinson, G. H., ed. Morris, Mary, tr.
Leibniz, Gottfried W. & Parkinson, G. H. Leibniz Philosophical Writings. Morris, Mary, tr. from Ger.
Leibovic, K. N. Nervous System Theory: An Introductory Study.
Leibowitz. Religious Guidance.
--Studies in the Shemoth.
Leibowitz, Rene. Schoenberg & His School.
Leibowitz, Uri, ed. Progress in Multiple Sclerosis: Research & Treatment.
Leibson, Steve. The Handbook of Microcomputer Interfacing.
Leibzon, B. M. Unity, Solidarity, Internationalism.
Leich, Christopher M., jt. ed. see Holtzman, Steven H.
Leichman, Seymour. Shaggy Dogs & Spotty Dogs & Shaggy & Spotty Dogs.
--The Wicked Wizard & the Wicked Witch.
Leichtentritt, Hugo. Serge Koussevitsky, the Boston Symphony Orchestra & the New American Music.
Leichter. Public School & the Family.
Leichter, Hope. Families & Communities As Educators.
Leidecker, Kurt F. Yankee Teacher.
Leider, Anna. College Grants from Uncle Sam: Am I Eligible & for How Much?, 1988-89.
Leider, Anna, ed. Scholarships for International Students: A Complete Guide to U. S. Colleges & Universities.
Leider, Robert. Your Own Financial Aid Factory: The Guide to Locating College Money.
--Your Own Financial Aid Factory: The Guide to Locating College Money.
Leifer, Sr. Carmel, jt. auth. see Dougherty, Bro. Patricius.
Leifer, Neil. Neil Leifer's Sports Stars.
--Neil Leifers Sports Stars.
Leifson, Einar. Atlas of Bacterial Flagellation.
Leigh, C. H., jt. auth. see Aiken, S. R.
Leigh, D. An Analysis of the Determinants of Occupational Upgrading.
Leigh, J. R. Applied Control Theory.
--Applied Digital Control: Theory, Design & Implementation.
Leigh, L. H. The Control of Commercial Fraud.
Leigh, Lori. On the Winds of Love.
Leigh, Michael. European Integration & the Common Fisheries Policy.
Leigh, Michael B. The Rising Moon: Political Change in Sarawak.
Leigh, Mick. Junior Judo.
Leigh, Oretta. The Merry-Go-Round.
Leigh, Stephen. The Bones of God.
--The Crystal Memory.
Leighly, John, ed. see Sauer, Carl O.
Leight, Warren, et al. One Hundred One Ways to Answer the Request: Would You Please Put Out That Cigar!
Leighton, Ann. American Gardens in the Eighteenth Century: "For Use or for Delight"
--Early American Gardens: For "Meate & Medicine"
Leighton, George R., jt. auth. see Brenner, Anita.
Leighton, Isabel. Aspirin Age: 1919-1941.
Leighton, Robert. Commentary on First Peter.
Leighton, Walter L., tr. see Soil Survey Staff.
Leiman, Arnold L., jt. auth. see Rosenzweig, Mark R.
Leimanis, E. General Problem of the Motion of Coupled Rigid Bodies About a Fixed Point.
Leimberg, Stephan R. Section Three Hundred & Three Stock Redemptions Buy the Numbers.
Leimberg, Stephan R., et al. The Tools & Techniques of Estate Planning.
Lein, Laura. Families Without Villains: American Families in an Era of Change.
Leinbaugh, Harold P. & Campbell, John D. The Men of Company K: The Autobiography of a World War II Rifle Company.
Leininger, Madeleine. Transcultural Nursing: Concepts, Theories & Practices.
Leininger, Wayne, jt. auth. see Killough, Larry.
Leininger, Wayne E. Quantitative Methods in Accounting.
Leinsdorf, Erich. Cadenza: A Musical Career.
Leipholz, H. H., ed. Stability of Elastic Structures.
Leipnitz, jt. ed. see Wenzel, E.
Leipnitz, Walter, et al, eds. Oil Refining & Petroleum Chemistry Multi-Lingual Dictionary: English-French-German-Russian.
Leipunskii, O. I., et al. The Propagation of Gamma Quanta in Matter.
Leiris, Michael & Mourlot, Fernand. Joan Miro, Lithographs.
Leiser, Andrew, jt. auth. see Gray, Donald.
Leiser, Joseph. American Judaism: The Religion & Religious Institutions of the Jewish People in the United States.
Leiserson, Mark, jt. auth. see Anderson, Dennis.
Leisi, Ernst, ed. see Shakespeare, William.
Leisk, Alan. The Tommy Knockers.
Leistad, Einar. The Man with the White Horse.
Leitch, James W., tr. see Ebeling, Gerhard.
Leitenberg, Milton, jt. auth. see Burns, Richard D.
Leiter, Marcia. Collecting Comic Books.
Leites, Nathan. Depression & Masochism: An Account of Mechanisms.
--Interpreting Transference.
Leites, Nathan, jt. auth. see Wolfenstein, Martha.
Leith, Carol. Runaway Maggie.
--Wally's Walk.
Leith, John H. Assembly at Westminster: Reformed Theology in the Making.
--Introduction to the Reformed Tradition: A Way of Being the Christian Community.
Leith, John H., jt. auth. see Ramsay, William M.
Leith, John H., ed. Creeds of the Churches: A Reader in Christian Doctrine from the Bible to the Present.
Leith, Prue & Tyrer, Polly. Entertaining with Style.
Leithauser, David. Programs for Electronic Circuit Design.
--Programs for Electronic Circuit Design.
--Programs for Electronic Circuit Design: Package with Software for TRS-80 Model I-Model III Computers.
Leitmann, George, jt. ed. see Blaquriere, Austin.
Leitner, Dina. A Precious Love.
Leitner, Stuart, jt. auth. see Stark, Robin.
Leive, Loretta, ed. Bacterial Membranes & Walls.
Leive, Loretta, et al, eds. Microbiology 1986.
Lejins, Atis, ed. see Swedish Institute of International Affairs.
Lekachman, Robert. The Age of Keynes.
Lekich, Kata. The Polluted Pond: The Myth about Aging.
Leklem, James E. & Reynolds, Robert D., eds. Methods In Vitamin B-6 Nutrition: Analysis & Status Assessment.
Lelama, Homero. Diccionario de Mitologia.
Leland, Charles G. English Gypsies & Their Language.
--Legends of Florence.
--Memoirs.
Leland, Christopher T. Mrs. Randall.
Leland, Henry & Deutsch, Marilyn W., eds. Abnormal Behavior: A Guide to Information Sources.
Leland, Mary. The Killeen.
Lelchuk, V. Historica de la Sociedad Sovietica.
Leliavsky, S. Arches & Short Span Bridges.
--Dams.
--Hydroelectric Engineering for Civil Engineers.
Lely, James A. Star Trek.
Lem, Stanislaw. The Chain of Chance.
--The Cosmic Carnival of Stanislaw Lem: An Anthology of Entertaining Stories by the Modern Master of Science Fiction. Kandel, Michael, ed.
--The Cyberiad: Fables for the Cybernetic Age.
--The Futurological Congress.
--His Master's Voice. Kandel, Michael, tr.
--Imaginary Magnitude. Heine, Marc E., tr.
--Memoirs of a Space Traveler: Further Reminiscences of Ijon Tichy. Stern, Joel & Swiecicka-Ziemianek, Maria, trs.
--Microworlds: Writings on Science Fiction & Fantasy. Rottensteiner, Franz, ed.
--More Tales of Pirx the Pilot. Iribarne, Louis, tr.
--Mortal Engines. Kandel, Michael, tr.
--A Perfect Vacuum. Kandel, Michael, tr.
--Return from the Stars. Marszal, Barbara & Simpson, Frank, trs.
--Return from the Stars.
--The Star Diaries. Kandel, Michael, tr.
--Tales of Pirx the Pilot.
--Tales of Pirx the Pilot. Wolff, Helen, ed. Iribarne, Louis, tr.
Lemake, Robert, jt. auth. see Krause, Chester L.
Leman, Kevin. Bonkers Is a Preventable Disease.
Leman, Martin. Ten Cats & Their Tales.
Lemann, Nicholas. The Fast Track: Texans & Other Strivers.
--Out of the Forties.
LeMaster, J. R. Jesse Stuart: A Reference Guide.
LeMasters, E. E. & Defrain, John. Parents in Contemporary America: A Sympathetic View.
Le May, Alan. The Unforgiven.
LeMay, H. Eugene, jt. auth. see Brown, Theodore L.
LeMay, H. Eugene, Jr., jt. auth. see Brown, Theodore L.
Lemay, Harding. Eight Years in Another World.
Lembeck, F., et al. Pharmacological Facts & Figures. Heller, H. & Ferguson, D. R., trs.
Lembke, R. Langenscheidts Sportwoerterbuch.
Lembourn, Hans J. Diary of a Lover of Marilyn Monroe.
Leme, J. Garcia, jt. auth. see Rocha E Silva, M.
Le Mehante, B. An Introduction to Hydrodynamics & Water Waves.
Lemerise, Bruce. Sheldon's Lunch.
Le Mesurier, John. A Jobbing Actor.
Lemire, Robert A. Creative Land Development: Bridge to the Future.
Lemke, Bob, jt. auth. see Albaugh, Dan.
Lemke, Elmer & Wiersma, William. Principles of Psychological Measurement.
Lemke, Robert & Krause, Cheste. Standard Catalog of United States Paper Money. Wilhite, Bob, ed.
Lemke, Robert F., jt. auth. see Krause, Chester L.
Lemlech, Johanna K. Classroom Management.
Lemlich, Robert. Adsorptive Bubble Separation Techniques.
Lemmen, Hans van see Van Lemmen, Hans.
Lemmerz, A. H. & Schmidt, R. R. Auswertung und Deutung des EKG 11. Auflage.
Lemoine, J., jt. auth. see Crane, A.
Lemon, H. How to Find Out about the Wool Textile Industry.
Lemon, Meadowlark & Jenkins, Jerry. Meadowlark.
Lemon, Richard. The Probity Chorus.
Lemon, Roy R. Stratigraphy.
Lemontt, J. F. & Generoso, W. M., eds. Molecular & Cellular Mechanisms of Mutagenesis.
Lempel, Blanche. Storm over Paris.
Lempert, Richard O. & Sanders, Joseph. An Invitation to Law & Social Science: Deserts, Disputes, & Distribution.
Lempriere, J. Lempriere's Classical Dictionary Writ Large.
Lenanton, Carola M. Nelson.
Lenarcic, R. J. As Long As the Grass Shall Grow.
Lenard, A., ed. Statistical Mechanics & Mathematical Problems.
Lenard, Yvone. Elan.
Lenard, Yvonne, tr. see Robbe-Grillet, Alain.
Lenburg, Carrie. The Clinical Performance Examination: Development & Implementation.
Lenczner, D. Elements of Loadbearing Brickwork.
Lendal H., jt. auth. see National Institute for Food Service Industry Staff.
Leneman, Leah. Soya Foods Cookery.
--Vegetarian Pita Bread Recipes: Delicious Wholefood Meal-In-A-Pocket.
Lenfest, ed. see Woods, Linda K.
Lengenfelder, Helga. Libraries, Information Centers & Databases in Science & Technology: A World Guide.
L'Engle, Madeleine. Everyday Prayers.
--Prayers for Sunday.
Lenglet, Philippe, jt. ed. see Vasudev, Aruna A.
Lengyel, Bela A. Lasers.
Lenhardt, G., tr. see Adorno, T. W.
Lenhart, Margot D., jt. ed. see Herzfeld, Michael.
Lenhart, Phil. Till Death Do Us Part.
Lenica, Jan, jt. auth. see Bolliger, Max.

Authors

Lenier, Minnette & Maker, Janet. Keys to a Powerful Vocabulary: Level I.
Lenier, Minnette, jt. auth. see Maker, Janet.
Lenihan, J. M. & Thomson, S. J., eds. Advances in Activation Analysis.
Lenihan, John & Fletcher, William, eds. Environment & Man: The Built Environment.
Lenin. What Is to Be Done?
Lenin, V. I. Against Liquidationism.
--Against Revisionism.
--Lenin on Language. Denisov, P. N. & Kondrashov, N. A., eds.
Lenin, V. I., et al. Soviet Legal Philosophy. Babb, Hugh W., tr.
Lenin, Vladimir I. El Imperialismo, Fase Superior Del Capitalismo.
--The Proletarian Revolution & the Renegade Kautsky.
--Selected Works.
--What Is Soviet Power?
Lenin, Vladimir I., jt. auth. see Marx, Karl.
Lenk, John D. Handbook of Controls & Instrumentation.
--Handbook of Practical Solid State Troubleshooting.
Lenk, Torsten. Flintlock: Its Origin & Development.
Lenker, J. M., tr. see Luther, Martin.
Lenman, Bruce. The Jacobite Risings in Britain 1689-1746.
Lenneberg, E. H. Foundations of Language Development a Multidisciplinary Approach. Lenneberg, Elizabeth, ed.
Lenneberg, Elizabeth, ed. see Lenneberg, E. H.
Lennerstrand, G. & Bach-Y-Rita, P., eds. Basic Mechanisms of Ocular Motility & Their Clinical Implications.
Lennert, K. Histopathology of Non-Hodgkin Lymphomas: Kiel Classification.
Lennert, K., jt. auth. see Mori, Y.
Lennett, David J. The McGraw-Hill Hazardous Waste Monitor: A Quarterly RCRA Update.
Lennette, Edwin H. & Schmidt, Nathalie J., eds. Diagnostic Procedures for Viral, Rickettsial & Chlamydial Infections.
Lennox, B. Medical Terms: Their Origin & Construction.
Lennox, Charlotte. The Female Quixote.
Lennox, Daphne. Residential Group Therapy for Children.
Lenoir, Lucille, jt. ed. see Forster, Arthur B.
Le Noury, Daniel. Computer Crazy.
Lenski, Lois, et al. Christmas Comes to Blueberry Corners: And Other Christmas Stories for Children.
Lenskii, V. S., jt. auth. see Ilyushin, A. A.
Lent, Henry B. The Peace Corps: Ambassadors of Good Will.
Lent, Patricia A. Sport with Terriers.
Lenta, Clementine. What Can I Do for Christ?
Lenthall, Patricia R. Carlotta & the Scientist.
Lentz, Andrea D. The James M. Comley Papers: An Inventory to the Microfilm Edition.
Lenz, Karl & Patzer, W. Nordamerika im Kartenbild.
Lenz, Marjorie & Shaevitz, Marjorie. So You Want to Go Back to School.
Lenz, Matthew. Risk Management: College Edition. Merritt Company Staff, ed.
Lenz, Siegfried. Das Wrack & Other Stories. Russ, C. A., ed.
Leocha, Charles. Skiing America: Winter 1989.
Leocha, Charles & Walker, William. Ski Europe: Winter 1987.
--Ski Europe: Winter 1987-88.
--Ski Europe: Winter 1989.
Leon, D. Kibbutz: New Way of Life.
Leon, Dan, tr. see Zamir, Yaron.
Leon, Dorothy. The Secret World of Underground Creatures.
Leon, George De see De Leon, George.
Leon, Judene. Bible Games for Teams & Groups.
Leon, Vicki. California Wineries: A Photographic Profile.
Leon, Vicki, ed. see Wilson, Lynn & Wilson, Jim.
Leonard. Mosby's Rad-Tech Assesstest.
Leonard, Alan. Kid Gloves.
Leonard, B. J., ed. Toxicological Aspects of Food Safety: Proceedings of the European Society of Toxicology.
Leonard, Bill. In the Storm of the Eye: A Lifetime at CBS.
Leonard, David C. & McGuire, Peter J. Readings in Technical Writing.
Leonard, Eileen B. Women, Crime, & Society: A Critique of Theoretical Criminology.
Leonard, Elizabeth. Painting the Landscape.
Leonard, Elmore. Cat Chaser.
--Cat Chaser.
--City Primeval.
--City Primeval: High Noon in Detroit.
--Double Dutch Treat.
--Elmore Leonard's Dutch Treat.
--Glitz.
--LaBrava.
--Split Images.
--Split Images.
--Stick.
--Stick.
Leonard, Eugenie A. & Drinker, Sophie. The American Woman in Colonial & Revolutionary Times, 1565-1800.
Leonard, George. The Ice Cathedral.
--The Ultimate Athlete.
Leonard, Henry A., jt. auth. see Olvey, Lee D.
Leonard, John, intro. by. Soho: A Picture Portrait by Carl Glassman.
Leonard, Jonathan N. Early Japan.
Leonard, Joseph W., jt. ed. see Humphreys, Kenneth K.
Leonard, Ken, jt. auth. see Berman, Lee.
Leonard, Patricia. Seashells & Laughing Gulls.
Leonard, Peter. Personality & Ideology.
Leonard, R. M., jt. auth. see Jerrold, Walter C.
Leonard, Stanley L., jt. ed. see Huddlestone, Richard.
Leonard, William L. & Toeppe, William F. Comprehensive Examination Review in Radiography.
Leonards, G. A., ed. Foundation Engineering.
Leon-Dufour, Xavier. Death & Life in the New Testament: The Teaching of Jesus & Paul. Prendergast, Terrance, tr.
--Dictionary of the New Testament. Prendergast, Terrence, tr.
Leone, Bruno, ed. Nuclear Arms: 1984 Annual.
Leone, Bruno, et al, eds. Criminal Justice: 1984 Annual.
--Criminal Justice, 1985 Annual.
--Criminal Justice, 1986 Annual.
--Death-Dying, 1985 Annual.
--Death-Dying, 1986 Annual.
--Foreign Policy, 1985 Annual.
--Foreign Policy, 1986 Annual.
--Nuclear Arms: 1985 Annual.
--Nuclear Arms, 1986 Annual.
Leong, Che Kan, jt. auth. see Downing, John.
Leonhard, Karl. Classification of Endogenous Psychoses. Berman, Russell, tr. from Gr.
Leonhard, W., ed. see IFAC Symposium Staff.
Leonhard, Wolfgang. The Kremlin & the West: A Realistic View of Relations With the Soviet Union.
--The Kremlin Since Stalin. Wiskemann, Elizabeth & Jackson, Marian, trs. from Ger.
Leonhardt, F. Prestressed Concrete Design & Construction.
Leonor, M., jt. auth. see Richards, P.
Leonor, M. D., ed. Unemployment, Schooling & Training in Developing Countries: Tanzania, Egypt, the Philippines & Indonesia.
Leontief, Wassily, et al. The Future of Nonfuel Minerals in the U. S. & World Economy: Input-Output Projections, 1980 to 2030.
Leontovich, M. A., ed. Reviews of Plasma Physics.
--Reviews of Plasma Physics.
--Reviews of Plasma Physics, Vol. 7.
Leontyev, L. Political Economy: A Condensed Course.
Leopold, A., et al. Plant Growth & Development.
Leopold, A. Starker, et al. North American Game Birds & Mammals.
--North American Game Birds & Mammals.
Leopold, Aldo. Sand County Almanac Illustrated.
Leotta, G. G., jt. ed. see Brunelli, B.
Leotta, G. G., jt. ed. see Gormezano, C.
LePage, Portia Conrad. A String of Pearls.
Le Page, William, ed. see Baba, Meher.
Lepanto, Paul. Return to Reason: An Introduction to Objectivism.
Lepawsky, Albert, ed. The Prospect for Presidential-Congressional Government.
Lepman, Jella. How Children See Our World.
LePore, Ernest & McLaughlin, Brian, eds. Actions & Events: Perspectives on the Philosophy of Donald Davidson.
Le Postre, Pierre. Rude Food.
Lepow, Irwin H. & Ward, Peter A. Inflammation: Mechanisms & Control.
Lepper, F. A. Trajan's Parthian War.
Lepper, John H. Famous Secret Societies.
Leppik, E. E. Floral Evolution in Relation to Pollination Ecology.
Leppzer, Robert. Voices from Three-Mile Island: The People Speak Out.
Leprevost, A., jt. auth. see Franco, R. R.
Lerch, et al. Perceptual - Motor Learning: Theory & Practice.
Lerch, Harold H. Teaching Elementary School Mathematics: An Active Learning Approach.
Lerche, Charles, jt. auth. see Said, Abdul A.
Lerche, Hans-Werner. Luftwaffe Test Pilot.
Lerma, Dominique-Rene De see De Lerma, Dominique-Rene.
Lerman, A., et al, eds. Lakes: Chemistry, Geology, Physics.
Lerman, Annie. Salad & Soup Book: More Than Two Hundred & Fifty Delectable Recipes from Annie's Kitchen.
Lerman, F. & Weinbert, R. Drug Interactions Index.
Lerman, Rhoda. The Book of the Night.
--Eleanor: A Novel.
Lermontov, Mihail. A Hero of Our Time. Nabokov, Vladimir & Nabokov, Dmitri, trs. from Rus.
Lerner, Aaron B. Einstein & Newton: A Comparison of the Two Greatest Scientists.
Lerner, Abba P. & Colander, David C. MAP: A Market Anti-Inflation Plan.
Lerner, Adam. Fantasy Football.
Lerner, Alan J. The Street Where I Live.
--The Street Where I Live.
Lerner, Anne L. Passing the Love of Women: A Study of Gide's Saul & Its Biblical Roots.
Lerner, Arthur, ed. Poetry in the Therapeutic Experience.
Lerner, Eugene & Koff, Richard. Increasing Your Wealth: A Professional Portfolio Manager Tells You How To.
Lerner, Eugene M. Managerial Finance: A Systems Approach.
Lerner, I. M. & Donald, H. P. Modern Developments in Animal Breeding.
Lerner, Janet W. Children with Learning Disabilities.
--Learning Disabilities: Theories, Diagnosis, & Teaching Strategies.
Lerner, Joel J. Financial Planning for the Utterly Confused.
Lerner, Joel J., jt. auth. see Cashin, James A.
Lerner, Judith & Khan, Zafar. Mosby's Manual of Urologic Nursing.
Lerner, Lawrence S., jt. auth. see Eisberg, Robert M.
Lerner, Marguerite R. Peter Gets the Chickenpox.
--Twins: The Story of Twins.
Lerner, Mark. Careers at a Zoo.
--Careers in a Restaurant.
--Careers in a Supermarket.
--Careers in Basketball.
--Careers in Beauty & Grooming.
--Careers in Hotels & Motels.
--Careers in Toy Making.
--Careers in Trucking.
--Careers with a Newspaper.
Lerner, Norbert, jt. auth. see Sobel, Max A.
Lerner, Richard M. & Kendall, Phillip C. Instructor's Manual for Psychology.
Lerner, Richard M. & Spanier, Graham B. Adolescent Development.
Lerner, S. W., et al. Workshop Wage Determination.
Lerner, Sharon. I Like Vegetables.
Lerner, Stephen A., et al. Aminoglycoside Ototoxicity.
Leroi-Gourhan, A. Prehistoric Man.
Le Roux, J. H., jt. ed. see Coetzer, P. W.
LeRoy, Gen. Billy's Shoes. Higginbottom, J. Winslow, tr.
Leroy, Maurice. Main Trends in Modern Linguistics. Price, Glanville, tr. from Fr.
Leroy-Beaulieu, A. Un Homme d'etat russe, Nicolas Miliutine, d'apres sa correspondance inedite.
Le Roy-Ladurie, Emmanuel. The Territory of the Historian.
Lerski, George J. Origins of Trotskyism in Ceylon.
Lersten, Rick, jt. auth. see Kersten, Pete.
Le Sage, Alain R; see Bentley, Eric.
Lesage, Julia. Jean-Luc Godard: A Guide to References & Resources.
Le Sage, Laurence. Metaphor in the Nondramatic Works of Jean Giraudoux.
Lesberg, Sandy, & intro. by. American Recipe Collection.
Lesberg, Sandy, ed. The Great American Chefs Institute.
Lesce, J., jt. auth. see Lesce, T.
Lesce, T. The Shotgun in Combat.
Lesce, T. & Lesce, J. Checklist for Survival: Supplies, Preparations, Investments, Stockpiles, Weapons, Tools, Rural Retreats.
Leserman, D. MacFonts.
Le Serve, A., et al. Chemical, Work & Cancer.
LeShan, Eda J. Oh, to Be Fifty Again: On Being Too Old for a Mid-Life Crisis.
--The Roots of Crime: What You Need to Know about Crime & What You Can Do about It.
LeShan, Lawrence & Margenau, Henry. Einstein's Space & Van Gogh's Sky: Physical Reality & Beyond.
Leshem, Y. The Molecular & Hormonal Basis of Plant Growth Regulation.
Lesher, Janie. Experimental Control of Mitosis, 1: Radiation Effects on Mitosis.
Lesher, Stephen. Media Unbound: The Impact of Television Journalism on the Public.
Leshowitz, Barry. Apple Writer Tutor: A Step-by-Step Tutorial on Apple Writer IIe-II-III.
Le Sieg, Theodore. Maybe You Should Fly a Jet! Maybe You Should Be a Vet!
Lesikar, Raymond V. Business Communication: Theory & Application.
--Report Writing for Business.
Lesikar, Raymond V., jt. auth. see Perlick, Walter W.
Leskiewicz, H. J., ed. see IFAC Symposium Staff.
Lesko, Matthew. The Computer Data & Database Source Book.
--Information U. S. A.
Leskov, N. S. The Enchanted Wanderer & Other Stories.
Leskov, Nikolai. Selected Tales. Magarshack, David, tr. from Rus.
Lesky, Erna. The Vienna Medical School in the Nineteenth Century.
Leslie. The Physical Metallurgy of Steels.
Leslie, Clare W. Notes from a Naturalist's Sketchbook.
Leslie, Donald D. The Survival of the Chinese Jews: The Jewish Community of Kaifeng.
Leslie, Donald D., et al, eds. Essays on the Sources for Chinese History.
Leslie, Douglas L. Statutory Supplement to Cases & Materials on Labor Law.
Leslie, J. D., ed. see Solar Energy Conversion Course, 5th, University of Waterloo, Ontario, August 6-19, 1978.
Leslie, Julian C., jt. auth. see Millenson, J. R.
Leslie, Louis A. Twenty Thousand Words.
Leslie, Louis A. & Zoubek, Charles E. Dictation for Transcription.
--Gregg Shorthand, Functional Method.
Leslie, Louis A., et al. College Dictation for Transcription.
Leslie, Mary, jt. auth. see Seltz, David D.
Leslie, Michael. Spenser's "Fierce Warres & Faithfull Loves" Martial & Chivalric Symbolism in "The Faerie Queene"
Leslie, Peter. The Liberation of the Riviera.
Leslie, Robert F. In the Shadow of a Rainbow: The True Story of a Friendship Between Man & Wolf.
--Lorenzo the Magnificent: The Story of an Orphaned Blue Jay.
Leslie, Tim, jt. auth. see Purdum, Jack.
Leslie, William C. The Physical Metallurgy of Steels.
Leslie-Melville, Betty. A Falling Star: A True Story of Romance in the Wilds of Africa.
Lesly, Philip. How We Discommunicate.
Lesner, Patricia A. Pediatric Nursing.
Lesnevskii, Stanislav. TA K Vam Pridu.
Lesnick, Henry, ed. Guerilla Street Theatre.
Lesnikowski, W. Rationalism & Romanticism in Architecture: A Selected Inquiry into the Nature of Both Trends.
Lesnoff-Caravaglia, Gari, ed. Perspectives on Aging.
Lesobre, J. & Sommer, H. Vocabulaire Technique Des Assurances: Anglais-Francais, Francais-Anglais.
L'Esperance. Ophthalmic Lasers: Photocoagulation, Photoradiation & Surgery.
L'Esperance, W. L. Structure & Control of State Economy.
Lesser, M. L. Using the Microsoft Business BASIC Compiler on the IBM PC.
Lesser, Michael. Nutrition & Vitamin Therapy.
Lessing, Doris. Briefing for a Descent into Hell.
--Golden Notebook.
--A Man & Two Women.
--Particularly Cats.
Lessing, Karin. The Spaces of Sleep in Midsummer.
Lessley, Merrill J., jt. auth. see Sellman, Hunton D.
Lessner, ed. Medical Oncology.
Lessnoff, Michael. The Structure of Social Science.
Lessof, M. H. Allergy.
--Clinical Reactions to Food.
Lessof, M. H., et al. Allergy: Immunological & Clinical Aspects.
Lester, C. Edwards. The Glory & Shame of England.
Lester, David, jt. auth. see Murrell, Mary.
Lester, Gordon J. When Its Time to Talk about Sex.
Lester, Jim. The People's College: Little Rock Junior College & Little Rock University, 1927-1969.
Lester, Jim, jt. auth. see Kumpe, Roy.
Lester, Malcom. Anthony Merry Redivivus: A Reappraisal of the British Minister to the United States, 1803-6.
Lester, Marilyn A. Some Recent Government Publications of Professional Interest to School Librarians: A Bibliographic Essay.
Lester, Michael & Subtle, Susan. How To Have Fun with Your Body.
Lester, Richard A. Manpower Planning in a Free Society.
Lesur, Rosalynde, jt. auth. see Putterman, Jaydie.
Lesure, Francois. Music & Art in Society.
Lesy, Michael. Real Life: Louisville in the Twenties.
--Wisconsin Death Trip.
Le-Tan, Pierre. Happy Birthday Oliver!
Letarouilly, Paul. Letarouilly on Renaissance Rome: An American Student Edition. Bayley, John B., ed.
Letchford, S. Statistics.
Letelier, Orlando & Moffitt, Michael. The International Economic Order.
Letendre, Lorin, jt. auth. see Clowers, Myles L.
Leteurtre, J. & Quere, Y. Irradiation Effects in Fissile Materials.
Leth, Kathy, ed. see Spies, Joseph R.
Lethaby, W. R. Medieval Art, Three Hundred Twenty-One to Thirteen Fifty.
Lethbridge, Alice. Through the Years in Genesee: An Illustrated History.

Authors

Lethbridge, David G., ed. Government & Industry Relationships: The Lubbock Memorial Lectures, 1975.
Lethbridge, T. C. The Legend of the Sons of God: A Fantasy.
--The Painted Men.
--The Power of the Pendulum.
Letmanyi, Helen. Guide on Workload Forecasting: National Bureau of Standards Special Publication 500-123.
Letnansky, Karl. Biology of the Cancer Cell.
Letwin, Oliver. Ethics, Emotion & the Unity of Self.
Letwin, William, ed. A Documentary History of American Economic Policy Since 1789.
Leu, Olaf, illus. Typography Six.
Leubling, Harry, jt. auth. see Bleiberg, Aaron H.
Leuchtenburg, W. E., et al. Britain & the United States.
Leuchtenburg, William E. In the Shadow of FDR: From Harry Truman to Ronald Reagan.
Leuchtmann, H., ed. Dictionary of Musical Terms in Seven Languages: English-German-French-Italian-Spanish-Hungarian-Russian.
Leuchtmann, Horst, ed. Dictionary of Terms in Music: English-German, German-English.
Leukart, R. H., jt. auth. see Otis, Jay L.
Leukefeld, Carl G., jt. ed. see Tims, Frank M.
Leukocyte Culture Conference Staff. Immune Recognition: Proceedings of the Leukocyte Culture Conference, 9th. Rosenthal, Alan S., ed.
--Proceedings of the Leukocyte Culture Conference, 5th. Harris, Jules, ed.
--Proceedings of the Leukocyte Culture Conference, 6th. Schwarz, M. Roy, ed.
Leupp, Francis E. In Red Man's Land: A Study of the American Indian.
Leuthold, W. African Ungulates: A Comparative Review of Their Ethology & Behavioral Ecology. Farner, D. S., ed.
Leuven, Hendrick Van see Van Leuven, Hendrick.
Levande, Diane I. & Koch, Joanne B. Marriage & the Family.
Levant, Leonid, tr. see Bugrov, Y. S. & Nikolsky, S. M.
Levanthal, Lance, et al. Understanding & Programming Microcomputers.
Levarie, Siegmund. Fundamentals of Harmony.
Levashov, E. A. Dictionary of New Words & Meanings in Russian.
LeVathes, Christine, ed. Your Future in the New World of American Fashion. Fashion Group Members Staff.
Le Vathes, Christine, ed. see Fashion Group Inc., Friends & Staff.
Levchev, Lyubomir. The Mysterious Man. Phillipov, Vladimir, tr.
Levcik, Friedrich & Stankovsky, Jan. Industrial Cooperation Between East & West.
Level, Dale A., Jr. & Galle, William P., Jr. Business Communication: Theory & Practice.
Levelt, Willem J. & D'Arcais, Giovanni B., eds. Studies in the Perception of Language.
Leven, Merwin. Accounting for Owners & Managers.
Levenbach. Forecasting Process Leader's Guide.
Levenbach, Hans, jt. auth. see Cleary, James P.
Levens, A. S. & Cooper, S. J. Problems in Mechanical Drawing.
Levens, Alexander & Chalk, William. Graphics in Engineering Design.
Levens, Peter. Manipulus Vocabulorum: A Dictionary of English & Latin Words, Arranged in the Alphabetical Order of the Last Syllables.
Levenson. Politics: How to Get Involved.
Levenson, Dorothy. The First Book of the Civil War.
Levenson, Goldie. A Guide for Time Studies.
Levenson, L. L., ed. Surface Properties of Materials: Proceedings from the Conference on Surface Properties of Materials, Held at the University of Missouri, Rolla, June 24-27, 1974.
Levenson, Marc. Introduction to Nonlinear Laser Spectroscopy.
Levenspiel, Octave. Chemical Reactor Omnibook Plus.
Leventhal, Lance, et al. Assembly Language Programming: 6502.
Leventhal, Lance A., et al. Z-8000 Assembly Language Programming.
Leventhal, Lawrence A., et al. The New Hobby Computers. Force, Rich, ed.
Leventhal, Richard M. & Kolata, Alan L., eds. Civilization in the Ancient Americas: Essays in Honor of Gordon R. Willey.
Leventhal, Richard M., jt. ed. see Vogt, Evon Z.
Leventhal, Ruth & Cheadle, Russell F. Medical Parasitology: A Self-Instructional Text.
Leveque, Andre, jt. auth. see Harris, Julian.
Le Veque, W. J., ed. see Mahler, K.
Lever, Harold & Huhne, Christopher. Debt & Danger: The World Financial Crisis.
Lever, J. W. Tragedy of a State: A Study of Jacobean Drama.
Lever, O. W., ed. New Horizons in Carbonyl Chemistry: Reagents for Nucleophilic Acylation.
Lever, Walter F., et al, eds. Dermatomyositis & Polymyositis.
Leverenz, Jon. Rand McNally Contemporary World Atlas.
Leverenz, Jon, ed. The New Rand McNally College World Atlas.
--Rand McNally New Century World Atlas.
Leverette, Bill. On Edgar Bergen's Lap: An Ironic History of the Human Condition.
Levering, Johnson. Out of the Night, Into the Wind.
LeVert, Suzanne, ed. Horse Story Collection.
Levertov, Denise. Footprints: Poems.
--To Stay Alive.
Lever-Tracy, Constance & Quinlan, Michael. A Divided Working Class: Worker Migration in Australia.
Leveson. Electronic Business Machines.
Levey, Gerald S. Hormone Receptor Interaction: Molecular Aspects.
Levey, Michael. Durer.
Levey, Sylvan. Frommer's Guide to New York.
Levey, Sylvan, jt. auth. see Hammel, Faye.
Levey, SYlvan, jt. auth. see Hammel, Faye.
Levi, Albert W. Philosophy & the Modern World.
Levi, Arrigo. Journey among the Economists.
Levi, Edward H. Point of View: Talks on Education.
Levi, Peter S., jt. auth. see Freilich, Robert H.
Levi, Primo. If Not Now, When? A Novel. Weaver, William, tr.
Levi, Werner. Australia's Outlook on Asia.
Leviant, Curt. The Yemenite Girl.
Levick. Breakfast of Champions.
Levick, Myra & Wheeler, Diana S. Mommy, Daddy, Look What I'm Saying.
Levicki, Cyril, ed. Small Business: Theory & Policy.
Levie, Robert C. & Ballard, Lou E. Writing Effective Reports on Police Investigations: Concepts, Procedures, Samples.
Levin. Petroleum Encyclopedia.
Levin, Alexander A. Solid State Quantum Chemistry: The Chemical Bond & Energy Bands in Tetrahedral Semiconductors.
Levin, B. & Radlova, Lidia. Astronomia para los Ninos.
Levin, Beatrice. Creative Games for Teaching English: Fun & Wonderful Sourcebook of Knowledge, Vocabulary & Grammar Games to Supplement Your English Lessons for Gifted Elementary, English As a Second Language & Jr. High Through Jr. College Level Students. Alaxander, Frank, ed.
Levin, Benjamin H. Black Triumvirate.
Levin, Betty. The Beast on the Brink.
--Landfall.
--The Zoo Conspiracy.
Levin, Cecile T. Cooking for Regeneration: Macrobiotic Relief from Cancer, AIDS, & Degenerative Diseases.
Levin, David. What Happened in Salem? Incl. Mirror for Witches. Forbes, Esther; Young Goodman Brown. Hawthorne, Nathaniel. HarBraceJ.
Levin, Donald A., ed. Hybridization: An Evolutionary Perspective.
Levin, Edith. The Penetrating Beam: Reflections on Light.
Levin, Gail. Edward Hopper: The Art & the Artist.
--Hopper's Places.
Levin, Gerald. Prose Models.
--Prose Models.
--Prose Models.
--Richardson the Novelist: The Psychological Patters.
--Short Essays.
--Short Essays: Models for Composition.
--Short Essays: Models for Composition.
--Styles for Writing: A Brief Rhetoric.
Levin, Gerald, ed. Prose Models.
--Short Essays: Models for Composition.
Levin, H., ed. see Hawthorne, Nathaniel.
Levin, Harold. Earth Through Time.
Levin, Harry. Contexts of Criticism.
Levin, Ira. The Boys from Brazil.
Levin, James. The Gay Novel: The Male Homosexual Image in America.
--The Gay Novel: The Male Homosexual Image in America.
Levin, Jane W. Star of Danger.
Levin, Jane W. & Steiner, Mary M. Bringing up Puppies: A Child's Book of Dog Breeding & Care.
Levin, Jennifer. Snow.
--Water Dancer.
Levin, Juliette, tr. see Odent, Michael.
Levin, Lawrence M. The Political Doctrine of Montesquieu's Esprit Des Lois: Its Classical Background.
Levin, Leo A. & Wheeler, Russell R., eds. The Pound Conference: Perspectives on Justice in the Future.
Levin, Malinda. Psychology: A Biographical Approach.
Levin, Marcia, jt. auth. see Bendick, Jeanne.
Levin, Martin, ed. Hollywood & the Great Fan Magazines.
Levin, Marvin E. & O'Neal, Lawrence W. The Diabetic Foot.
Levin, Marvin T. & Nichols, Barbara. How to Profit on the Real Estate Roller Coaster: An Investor's Guide to Avoiding Big Mistakes.
Levin, Meyer. Compulsion.
Levin, Michael R. see Blinn, James D.
Levin, Murray B. & Repak, T. A. Edward Kennedy: The Myth of Leadership.
Levin, Peter J., jt. auth. see Wolfson, Jay.
Levin, Richard I., et al. Production-Operations Management.
Levin, Richard M. & Horn, Babette J. Pediatric Anesthesia Handbook.
Levin, Simon A., jt. ed. see Whittaker, Robert H.
Levinas, Emmanuel. Ethics & Infinity. Cohen, Richard, tr. from Fr.
Levine, Alan H. The Rights of Students.
Levine, Andrew. Arguing for Socialism: Theoretical Considerations.
--The Politics of Autonomy: A Kantian Reading of Rousseau's "Social Contract"
Levine, Betty K. Hawk High.
Levine, Carol. Taking Sides: Clashing Views on Controversial Bioethical Issues.
--Taking Sides: Clashing Views on Controversial Bioethical Issues.
Levine, Daniel U. & Havighurst, Robert J. Society & Education.
--Society & Education.
Levine, Daniel U., jt. auth. see Ornstein, Allan C.
Levine, David. Economic Theory: The System of Economic Relations As a Whole.
--No Known Survivors: David Levine's Political Plank.
Levine, David P. Economic Studies: Contributions to the Critique of Economic Theory.
--Economic Theory: The Elementary Relations of Economic Life.
Levine, Donald N. Greater Ethiopia: The Evolution of a Multiethnic Society.
Levine, Erwin L. & Wexler, Elizabeth. PL 94 - 142: An Act of Congress.
Levine, George & Thomas, Owen P., eds. Scientist vs. the Humanist.
Levine, Gustav. Introductory Statistics for Psychology: The Logic & the Methods.
Levine, Howard. Life Choices: Confronting the Life & Death Decisions Created by Modern Medicine.
Levine, Howard, jt. auth. see Rheingold, Howard.
Levine, James P., et al. Criminal Justice: A Public Policy Approach.
Levine, Jerry, ed. see Burton, Nelson, Jr.
Levine, John R., et al. Understanding Javelin PLUS.
Levine, Joseph, jt. auth. see Pine, Tillie S.
Levine, Lawrence, ed. see Cell in Mitosis Symposium Staff.
Levine, Lawrence W. & Middlekauff, Robert, eds. The National Temper: Readings in American History.
Levine, Linda & Barbach, Lonnie. The Intimate Male: Candid Discussions About Women, Sex & Relationships.
Levine, Mark L. Real Estate Exchanges. Allen, Pat, ed.
--Real Estate Tax-Shelter Desk Book.
--Real Estate Tax Shelter Desk Book.
--Real Estate Transactions, Tax Planning & Consequences: 1987 Edition.
Levine, Martin P., jt. auth. see Markisz, John A.
Levine, Marvin J., ed. Public Personnel Management: Readings, Cases & Contingency Plans.
Levine, Michael. The Address Book: How to Reach Anyone Who's Anyone.
--The Address Book: How to Reach Anyone Who's Anyone.
Levine, Michael W. & Shefner, Jeremy M. Fundamentals of Sensation & Perception.
Levine, Mindy N., jt. auth. see Off Off Broadway Alliance Staff.
Levine, Nathan. Typing Made Simple.
Levine, Norman D. & Ivens, Virginia. The Coccidian Parasites of Carnivores.
Levine, Norman G. How to Build a One Hundred Million Dollar Agency in Five Years or Less.
Levine, Pamela, et al. The Complete Guide to Home Video Programming.
Levine, Paul. E. L. Doctorow.
Levine, Philip. Pili's Wall.
Levine, R. & Pfeiffer, E. F., eds. Lipid Metabolism, Obesity & Diabetes Mellitis.
Levine, Renee. How to Get a Job in Boston, or Anywhere Else.
Levine, Richard A., intro. by. The Victorian Experience: The Prose Writers.
Levine, Robert & Consumer Reports Books Editors. Guide to Opera & Dance on Videocassette.
Levine, Ruth R. Pharmacology: Drug Actions & Reactions.
Levine, Saul V. Radical Departures: Desperate Detours to Growing Up.
Levine, Seymour. Cyclist's Guide to Overnight Stops: Western States.
--Hormones & Behavior.
Levine, Stuart. Edgar Poe: Seer & Craftsman.
Levine, Suarti & Stuart-Fox, David, eds. Favourite Stories from Bali.
Levine, Summer N., ed. Financial Analyst's Handbook. Incl. Vol. 1. Portfolio Management; Vol. 2. Analysis by Industry. Dow Jones-Irwin.
Levine, Sumner N. The Dow Jones-Irwin Business & Investment Almanac, 1986.
Levine, Sumner N., ed. The Dow Jones-Irwin Business & Investment Almanac, 1987.
--The Dow Jones-Irwin Business & Investment Almanac, 1988.
Levine, Suzanne, ed. She's Nobody's Baby: A History of American Women in the 20th Century.
Levine, Suzanne J., tr. see Cabrera Infante, G.
Levine, Talya. Chronic Cholecystitis: Its Pathology & the Role of Vascular Factors in Its Pathogenesis.
Levine, Victor T. The Cameroons from Mandate to Independence.
Le Vine, Victor T. Political Corruption: The Ghana Case.
--Political Leadership in Africa.
Levine, W. G., ed. The Chelation of Heavy Metals.
Levings, Pat. Profit from Foodservice: A Q & A Approach.
Levins, Richard A. & Walden, W. Charles. Agricultural Computer Programming: A Practical Guide.
Levinsohn, Florence H. Harold Washington: A Political Biography.
Levinson, A. A. & Taylor, Ross. Moon Rocks & Minerals.
Levinson, Alfred see Corrigan, Robert W.
Levinson, David & Sherwood, David. The Tribal Living Book: One Hundred Fifty Things to Do & to Make from Traditional Cultures Around the World.
Levinson, Nanette S., ed. New Federal Policies for R & D: Impacts on Government, Industry & Academy - Proceedings of the 38th National Conference on the Advancement of Research.
Levinson, Norma. The Room Upstairs.
Levinson, Paul, ed. In Pursuit of Truth: Essays on the Philosophy of Karl Popper on the Occasion of His 80th Birthday.
Levinson, Robert E. The Decentralized Company: Making the Most of Entrepreneurial Management.
Levinson, Salmon O; see Morrison, Charles C.
Levi-Setti, Riccardo & Lasinski, Thomas. Strongly Interacting Particles.
Levi-Setti, Trilobites. A Photographic Atlas.
Levisohn, Steven R. & Simon, Harvey B. Tennis Medic.
Levison, Peter K. & Gerstein, Dean R., eds. Commonalities in Substance Abuse & Habitual Behavior.
Levi-Strauss, Claude. Savage Mind.
Levitan, Arlan R. & Leemon, Sheldon. Compute's Telecomputing on the IBM. Compute! Magazine Staff, ed.
Levitan, Donald. Grants Survival Library.
Levitan, Herbert. Cell Biology & Physiology.
Levitan, S. A. Big Brother's Indian Programs: With Reservations.
Levitan, Sar A. & Zickler, Joyce K. The Quest for Federal Manpower Partnership.
Levitan, Sar A. & Mangum, Garth L., eds. CETA Training: A National Review & Eleven Case Studies.
Levites, Vicki, jt. auth. see Heller, Erica.
Levitin, Sonia. All the Cats in the World.
--The Fisherman & the Bird.
--Jason & the Money Tree.
--The No-Return Trail.
--Nobody Stole the Pie.
--Reigning Cats & Dogs.
--Roanoke.
--A Single Speckled Egg.
--A Sound to Remember.
--Who Owns the Moon?
--Who Owns the Moon?
--The Year of Sweet Senior Insanity.
Levitine, George. Girodet-Trioson: An Iconographical Study.
Levitt, B. P., ed. Physical Chemistry of Fast Reactions, Vol. 1: Gas Phase Reactions of Small Molecules.
Levitt, Cyril. Children of Privilege: Student Revolt in the Sixties.
Levitt, Harry & Pickett, James M., eds. Sensory Aids for the Hearing Impaired.
Levitt, I. M. & Marshall, Roy K. Star Maps for Beginners.
Levitt, J. Frost, Drought & Heat Resistance.
--Responses of Plants to Environmental Stresses.
Levitt, John, jt. auth. see Davies, C. Stella.
Levitt, Kari. Silent Surrender.
Levitt, Leonard. The Healer.
Levitt, Michael & Lloyd, Barbara. Upset: Australia Wins the America's Cup.
Levitt, Morris & Belforte, David. Industrial Laser Annual Handbook.
Levitt, Mortimer. The Executive Look.

Authors

Levitt, Morton P. Modernist Survivors: The Contemporary Novel in England, France, the United States, & Latin America.
Levitt, Rachelle & Kirlin, John, eds. Managing Development Through Public-Private Negotiations.
Levitt, Raymond E., jt. auth. see Bourdon, Clinton C.
Levitt, Ruth. Implementing Public Policy.
--The Reorganised National Health Service.
Levitt, Ruth & Wall, Andrew. The Reorganised National Health Service.
Levitt, Ruth, jt. auth. see Simpson, Peter.
Levitt, Seymour H. & Tapley, Norah, eds. Technological Basis of Radiation Therapy: Practical Clinical Applications.
Levitzki, Alexander. Receptors: A Quantitative Approach.
Levitzky, M. G. Pulmonary Physiology.
Levt, Claude-Frederic. Capitalistes et Pouvoir Au Siecle Des Lumieres: Les Fondateurs Des Origines a 1715.
Levy, jt. auth. see Berne.
Levy, Alex, jt. auth. see Marcus, William.
Levy, Allan. Century of Model Trains.
Levy, Azriel. A Hierarchy of Formulas in Set Theory.
Levy, Barbara. The Language Master.
--The Language Master.
--The Language Master: CB.
Levy, Barbara W. The Comprehension Master Level 1.
--The Comprehension Master Level 2.
--The Comprehension Master Level 3.
--The Comprehension Master Level 4.
Levy, Barry S. & Wegman, David H., eds. Occupational Health: Recognizing & Preventing Work-Related Diseases.
Levy, Bill. Sam, Sipe, & Company: The History of the Cleveland Browns.
Levy, Bruce A., jt. auth. see Matsumoto, Teruo.
Levy, C. Michael & Froming, William J. Statmaster: Exploring & Computing Statistics.
Levy, Charles J. Voluntary Servitude: Whites in the Negro Movement.
Levy, Clarence A. World Survey of Drug & Narcotic Control: A Medical Subject Analysis & Research Index with Bibliography.
Levy, D. Gods of Foxcroft.
Levy, Darline G., et al, eds. Women in Revolutionary Paris, 1789-1795.
Levy, David. Chess & Computers.
--U. S. Computer Chess Championship: 1975.
Levy, David & Newborn, Monroe. All about Chess & Computers.
--More Chess & Computers: The Microcomputer Revolution, the Challenge Match.
Levy, David, jt. auth. see O'Connell, K. J.
Levy, David, et al, eds. The Double King's Pawn, 1982.
--The King's Indian, 1982.
--The Queen's Indian, 1982.
--The King's Indian.
Levy, E., jt. auth. see World Association of Societies of Pathology Staff.
Levy, Edward. The Beast Within.
--Came a Spider.
Levy, Elizabeth. The Case of the Counterfeit Racehorse.
--The Case of the Fired-up Gang.
--The Case of the Frightened Rock Star.
--The Case of the Wild River Ride.
--Dani Trap.
--The Shadow Nose.
Levy, Emanuel. Passive Solar Construction Handbook.
Levy, Eugene. James Weldon Johnson: Black Leader, Black Voice. Franklin, John H., ed.
--James Weldon Johnson: Black Leader, Black Voice. Franklin, John H., ed.
Levy, Faye. The La Varenne Tour Book.
Levy, Gerald M., ed. Arbitration of Real Estate Valuation Disputes.
Levy, Howard S. Oriental Sex Manners.
--Two Chinese Sex Classics.
Levy, Howard S., tr. Illusory Flame: Chinese Love Stories.
--Japan's Best Loved Poetry Classic: Hyakunin Isshu.
--Korean Sex Jokes in Traditional Times: 206 Stories.
--Warm-Soft Village: Chinese Essays on Love.
Levy, Jay A., et al. Oncogenesis & Other Pathological Results of Herpesvirus Infection II.
Levy, Jean-Philippe. Economic Life of the Ancient World. Biram, John G., ed.
Levy, Joanne P. Ouch! My Back Is Killing Me!
Levy, John & McCarthy, Kyle. Greece on Twenty-Five Dollars a Day: Including Istanbul & Turkey's Aegean Coast.
Levy, Judith & Pelikan, Judy. Grandmother Remembers Family Recipes.
Levy, Lawrence S. Trigonometry with Calculators.
Levy, Leon, et al. The Consumer in the Marketplace.
Levy, Leonard W. & Peterson, Merrill D., eds. Major Crises in American History: Documentary Problems.
Levy, Marion J. Modernization & the Structure of Societies: A Setting for International Affairs.
Levy, Mark. Intonation in North Indian Music.
Levy, Matthew N., jt. ed. see Berne, Robert M.
Levy, Mervyn. Carel Weight.
--Ruskin Spear.
--Whistler Lithographs.
Levy, Micheline, tr. see Williams, G.
Levy, Norman. The Foundations of the South African Cheap Labour System.
Levy, Paul, jt. auth. see Barr, Ann.
Levy, Reuben. The Persian Language.
Levy, Robert I. Tahitians: Mind & Experience in the Society Islands.
--Tahitians: Mind & Experience in the Society Islands.
Levy, Samuel & Wilkinson, John P. Component Element Method in Dynamics.
Levy, Stephen J. Managing the Drugs in Your Life: A Commonsense Personal & Family Guide.
Levy, Steven. Hackers: Heros of the Computer Revolution.
Levy, Stuart B., et al, eds. Molecular Biology, Pathogenicity, & Ecology of Bacterial Plasmids.
Levy, Tedd & Krasnow, Donna C. A Guidebook for Teaching United States History: Earliest Times to the Civil War.
Levy, Valerie, ed. A Guide to Shakespeare's Best Plays.
Levy, Walter A., jt. auth. see Summer, Claire.
Levy-Bruel, Lucien. Primitive Mythology: The Mythic World of the Australian & Papuan Natives. Elliott, Brian, tr.
Levyns, J. E. The Disciplines of War: Memories of the War of 1914-18.
Levytsky, Borys. The Soviet Political Elite: Brief Biographies.
Lew, Edward A., jt. auth. see Entmacher, Paul S.
Lew, J. & Stanbrook, C., eds. International Trade: Law & Practice.
Lew, V. L., jt. ed. see Ellory, J. C.
Lewak, Richard W., jt. auth. see Nelson, Gerald E.
Lewallen, Joyce. Galaxy of Games & Activities for the Kindergarten.
Lewandowski, J. Swedish Contributions to the Polish Resistance Movement During World War II.
Lewandowski, Stephen, ed. Farmer's & Housekeeper's Cyclopaedia of 1888.
Lewanski, Richard C. Eastern Europe & Russia-Soviet Union: A Handbook of West European Archival & Library Resources.
Lewenhak, Sheila. The Role of the European Investment Bank.
Lewery, A. J. Narrow Boat Painting: A History & Description of the English Narrow Boats' Traditional Paintwork.
Lewicki, Paul. Nonconscious Social Information Processing.
Lewin, Arie Y. & Shakum, Melvin F., eds. Policy Science: Methodologies & Cases.
Lewin, Benjamin. Genes.
Lewin, David, et al. Public Sector Labor Relations: Analysis & Readings.
Lewin, Ellen, ed. Women, Health & Healing: Toward a New Perspective. Olesen, Virginia.
Lewin, Gordon, ed. Car-Free in Boston: The Guide to Public Transit in Greater Boston & New England.
Lewin, John, ed. British Rivers.
Lewin, Kurt. Field Theory in Social Science.
Lewin, Lauri. Naked Is the Best Disguise: My Life As a Stripper.
Lewin, Leonard, jt. auth. see Holzman, Red.
Lewin, M. & Bonfils, S., eds. Regulatory Peptides in Digestive, Nervous & Endocrine Systems: Proceedings of the International Symposium on Regulatory Peptides, Mode of Action on Digestive, Nervous & Endocrine Systems held in Gouvieux-Chantilly, France, 9-11 May. 1985.
Lewin, Marsha D., jt. auth. see Rosenau, Milton D.
Lewin, Menachem, et al, eds. Flame-Retardant Polymeric Materials.
--Flame-Retardant Polymeric Materials.
Lewin, Ralph A., ed. Physiology & Biochemistry of Algae.
Lewin, Roger. Bones of Contention: Controversies in the Search for Human Origins.
Lewin, Ronald. The American Magic: Codes, Ciphers & the Defeat of Japan.
--Hitler's Mistakes.
--Rommel: As Military Commander.
Lewin, S. Vitamin C: Its Molecular Biology & Medical Potential.
Lewin, Virginia B. One of Benny's Faces: A Study of Benjamin Bufano (1886-1970) the Man Behind the Artist.
Lewins, J. Nuclear Reactor Kinetics & Control.
Lewinski, Jorge, jt. auth. see Delaney, Frank.
Lewis, A. S., ed. see Horrocks, James.
Lewis, A. S., ed. see Romen, A. S.
Lewis, Alan J. Software Sourcebook.
Lewis, Albert B. Decorative Art of New Guinea.
Lewis, Alfred A. & MacDonell, Herbert L. The Evidence Never Lies: The Casebook of a Modern Sherlock Holmes.
Lewis, Alfred B. A Political Odyssey: Alone & Together.
Lewis, Alvin G. Teach Me, Lord: Devotions on Basic Christian Teachings.
Lewis & Clark College Staff & Beaverton School District Staff. Comprehensive Classroom Management: Creating Positive Learning Environments & Solving Problems.
Lewis, Ann C. & Bambrey, Thomas E. Four Concepts: An English Workbook.
Lewis, Anne. A Guide to Basic Riding Instruction.
Lewis, Anthony J. Mechanisms of Neurological Disease.
Lewis, Ardron B. Our Money & Our Misery: A Diagnosis & Prescription.
Lewis, Arnold. American Country Houses of the Guilded Age.
Lewis, Arnold & Morgan, Keith. American Victorian Architecture: A Survey of the 70's & 80's in Contemporary Photographs.
Lewis, Arthur H. Dark Side of the Millennium: The Problem of Evil in Revelation 20: 1-10.
Lewis, B., et al, eds. Encyclopedia of Islam. Incl. Vol. 1. A-B: Fasc. 1-22. Gibb, H. A., et al, eds.; Vol. 2. C-G: Fasc. 23-40. Lewis, B., et al, eds.; Vol. 3. H-Iram: Fasc. 41-60; Vols. 4 & 5. I-Ram &K-Ha: Fasc. 61-78. Humanities.
Lewis, Barbara E., tr. see Conti, Vittorio.
Lewis, Bernard & Von Elbe, Guenther. Combustion, Flames, & Explosions of Gases.
Lewis, Bernard, et al. Aspects-Radar Signal Processing.
Lewis, Bernard T. & Marron, J. P. Facilities & Plant Engineering Handbook.
Lewis, Bessie. Walks of Jesus.
Lewis, Betty. Watsonville: Memories That Linger.
Lewis, Beverley A. Roo!
Lewis, Bobby, illus. Home Before Midnight: A Traditional Verse.
Lewis, Brian. Planning Your First Vacation to Australia.
Lewis, Bryan. Data Management for Professionals.
Lewis, C. D., ed. Operations Management in Practice.
Lewis, C. I. Analysis of Knowledge & Valuation.
Lewis, C. L. & Ott, L. Analytical Chemistry of Nickel.
Lewis, C. S. The Chronicles of Narnia.
--The Dark Tower & Other Stories. Hooper, Walter, ed.
--The Four Loves.
--The Horse & His Boy.
--The Joyful Christian: One Hundred Readings from the Works of C. S. Lewis.
--The Last Battle.
--Literary Impact of the Authorized Version. Reumann, John, ed.
--On Stories & Other Essays on Literature.
--Prince Caspian.
--The Screwtape Letters.
--Till We Have Faces: A Myth Retold.
--The Voyage of the "Dawn Treader"
Lewis, C. S. see also Lewis, Clive S.
Lewis, Catriona J., jt. auth. see Kirkwood, Evelyne M.
Lewis, Chris, jt. auth. see Slesser, Malcolm.
Lewis, Clive S. see also Lewis, C. S.
Lewis, Colin. Managing with Micros: Management Uses of Microcomputers.
--Managing with Micros: Management Uses of Microcomputers.
Lewis, Collin A. Hunting in Ireland.
Lewis, D. H., jt. auth. see Harley, J. L.
Lewis, D. H., ed. Controlled Release of Pesticides & Pharmaceuticals.
Lewis, D. Sclater. The Royal College of Physicians & Surgeons of Canada, 1920-1960.
--Royal Victoria Hospital Eighteen Eighty-Seven to Nineteen Forty-Seven.
Lewis, Daniel E. At the Crossroads.
Lewis, David. Fascinating Facts: Weird Bits of Information on Practically Everything.
--How to Be a Gifted Parent: Realize Your Child's Full Potential.
--Ice Bird.
--Sexpionage: The Exploitation of Sex by Soviet Intelligence.
--The Voyaging Stars.
Lewis, David, tr. see Lochman, Jan M.
Lewis, David B. Eureka! Math Fun from Many Angles.
Lewis, David L. King: A Biography.
Lewis, David V. Secrets of Successful Writing, Speaking, & Listening.
Lewis, Dorothy, jt. ed. see Piper, Charlotte.
Lewis, Douglas. The Late Baroque Churches of Venice.
Lewis, E. E. Nuclear Power Reactor Safety.
Lewis, E. G. & Massad, C. E. The Teaching of English as a Foreign Language in Ten Countries.
Lewis, E. Glyn. Bilingualism & Bilingual Education: A Comparative Study.
Lewis, Edward S., ed. Investigation of Rates & Mechanisms of Reactions.
Lewis, Edward W. Comes the Revolution.
Lewis, Eils M. The Snug Little House.
Lewis, Emmanuel R. Seacoast Fortifications of the United States: An Introductory History.
Lewis, Ernest A. The Fremont Cannon: High Up & Far Back.
Lewis, Ernest L., jt. auth. see Beggs, Donald L.
Lewis, Ewart. Medieval Political Ideas.
Lewis, Frank R., Jr., jt. ed. see Trunkey, Donald D.
Lewis, Gaspar J. Cabinetmaking, Patternmaking, & Millwork.
Lewis, Geoffrey. Quantitative Methods in Economics.
Lewis, George, ed. Biomedical Aspects of Botulism.
Lewis, Gerald E. So Long, Scout, & Other Stories of Maine.
Lewis, Gladys S. On Earth As It Is...
--Two Dreams & a Promise.
Lewis, Glenn, jt. auth. see Harper, Ann.
Lewis, Gogo, jt. auth. see Manley, Seon.
Lewis, Gordon. Bible, Christian & Latter Day Saints.
--Bible, Christians & Jehovah's Witnesses.
Lewis, Gordon R. & Demarest, Bruce, eds. Challenges to Inerrancy: A Theological Response.
Lewis, Griselda. The Collectors' History of English Pottery.
Lewis, H. Gregg. Unionism & Relative Wages in the United States.
Lewis, H. Spencer. Symbolic Prophecy of the Great Pyramid.
Lewis, H. T. & Culliton, J. W. Role of Airfreight in Physical Distribution: Including Two Cases by J. D. Steele.
Lewis, Hal M. Arthur Frommer's Guide to Philadelphia & Atlantic City, 1983-84.
Lewis, Harriet. The Tempter.
Lewis, Henry W. Property Tax in North Carolina: An Introduction.
Lewis, Herschell G. How to Make Your Advertising Twice As Effective at Half the Cost.
Lewis, Howard R. & Lewis, Martha E. The Electronic Confessional: A Sex Book of the Eighties. Arbeiter, Jean, ed.
Lewis, Hywel D. Freedom & History.
Lewis, Ian. The Student Experience of Higher Education.
Lewis, Ira M. The Tock Book: Poetry for the Last Days.
Lewis, J. & Hudson, R., eds. Uneven Development in Southern Europe.
Lewis, J., jt. ed. see Hudson, R.
Lewis, J. G. Therapeutics.
Lewis, J. R. Cases for Discussion.
Lewis, Jack. Gun Digest Book of Modern Gun Values.
--Gun Digest Book of Modern Gun Values.
--The Hunting Rifle: Gun Digest Book.
--Modern Gun Values.
Lewis, Jack & Mitchell, Jack. Combat Handgunnery.
Lewis, Jack & Galante, Jorge O., eds. Bone Implant Interface: Workshop Report.
Lewis, Jack, jt. ed. see Bow & Arrow Magazine Staff.
Lewis, Jane, ed. Women's Welfare-Women's Rights.
Lewis, Janet. The Ancient Ones.
Lewis, Jeffrey D., jt. auth. see Stern, Joseph J.
Lewis, Jerry & Gluck, Herb. Jerry Lewis: In Person.
Lewis, Jerry M. How's Your Family?
Lewis, Jerry M., jt. ed. see Usdin, Gene.
Lewis, Jessica, et al. Bleeding Disorders.
Lewis, Jim. Finding the Treasure Within You.
Lewis, John C., jt. ed. see Ong, Helen H.
Lewis, John N. Architecture of the Caribbean.
Lewis, John W., ed. The Security Challenge in Northeast Asia: Report of a Conference.
Lewis, K. R., jt. auth. see John, B.
Lewis, Kay O. Church Wedding Handbook.
Lewis, L. J. Society, Schools & Progress in Nigeria.
Lewis, Lee O. SKCALB.
Lewis, Leslie L., jt. auth. see Altenbernd, Lynn.
Lewis, Lloyd. Captain Sam Grant.
Lewis, Luevester. Jackie.
Lewis, M. F., ed. Current Research in Marijuana.
Lewis, Marcia & Warden, Carol D. Law & Ethics in the Medical Office Including Bioethical Issues.
Lewis, Martha E., jt. auth. see Lewis, Howard R.
Lewis, Mary J., ed. Directory of North American Fisheries Scientists.
Lewis, Matthew. The Monk.
Lewis, Melvin. Clinical Aspects of Child Development: An Introductory Synthesis of Developmental Concepts & Clinical Experience.
Lewis, Michael, jt. ed. see Pervin, Lawrence A.
Lewis, Myrna I., jt. auth. see Butler, Robert N.
Lewis, Naomi. Puffin.
Lewis, Naomi, ed. see Andersen, Hans Christian.
Lewis, Norman. The New Roget's Thesaurus in Dictionary Form.
--The Sicilian Specialist.

Lewis, Norman, jt. auth. see Kahn, Peggy.
Lewis, O. Physical Constants of Linear Homopolymers.
Lewis, P., et al. Visual Blight in America.
Lewis, P. R. & Knight, D. P. Staining Methods for Sectioned Material.
Lewis, Patricia A. Of Other Realms: A Journey of the Soul.
Lewis, Paul G. & Potter, David C., eds. The Practice of Comparative Politics: A Reader.
Lewis, Paul H. Paraguay under Stroessner.
Lewis, Paul M. Beautiful Idaho.
--Beautiful Oregon Coast.
Lewis, Peter, jt. auth. see Wright, Jack.
Lewis, Peter W. Criminal Procedure: The Supreme Court's View Cases.
Lewis, R., ed. Computers in the Life Sciences: Applications in Research & Education.
Lewis, R. W. Emblem For an Era: Selected Images of American Victorian Womanhood.
Lewis, Richard, ed. Miracles: Poems by Children of the English-Speaking World.
Lewis, Richard H. Hell above & Hell Below: A Real Life Story of an American Airman. Larson, William R., as told to. & as told to.
Lewis, Richard L. & Sweet, Doris, eds. Registry of Toxic Effects of Chemical Substances, 1983-84 Cumulative Supplement to the 1981-82 Edition.
Lewis, Robert. South of Tiburon.
Lewis, Robert & Krupman, William A. Winning NLRB Elections: Management's Strategy & Preventive Programs.
Lewis, Robert A. & Sussman, Marvin B., eds. Men's Changing Roles in the Family.
Lewis, Robert T. Taking Chances: The Psychology of Losing & How to Profit from It.
Lewis, Roger. How to Tutor in an Open-Learning Scheme: Group-Study Version.
--How to Tutor in an Open-Learning Scheme: Self-Study Version.
Lewis, Roger & Paine, Nigel. How to Communicate with the Learner.
Lewis, Roger, ed. Open Learning in Action.
Lewis, Roy H. Fine Book Binding in the Twentieth Century.
Lewis, Russell. Margaret Thatcher.
Lewis, S. M. & Verwilghen, R. Dyserythropoiesis.
Lewis, S. M. & Coster, J., eds. Quality Control in Haematology.
Lewis, Samella. Art: African American.
Lewis, Shari. The Do-It-Better Book.
--Magic Show in a Box.
Lewis, Shari & Reinach, Jacquelyn. Headstart Book of Knowing & Naming.
Lewis, Sinclair. Arrowsmith.
--Dodsworth.
Lewis, Stephen. The Best Sellers.
--The Regulars.
Lewis, Stephen & Forte, Cecile. Discovering Process.
Lewis, Stephen R., Jr. Economic Policy & Industrial Growth in Pakistan.
Lewis, Steven. Exits off a Toll Road.
Lewis, T. M. & McNicoll, I. H. North Sea Oil & Scotland's Economic Prospects.
Lewis, Taylor B., Jr. & Young, Joanne B. Christmas in Williamsburg.
Lewis, Theodore G. & Smith, Brian J. Computer Principles of Modeling & Simulation.
Lewis, Theodore G. & Smith, Marilyn Z. Applying Data Structures.
Lewis, Thomas R. Near the Long Tidal River: Readings in the Historical Geography of Central Connecticut.
Lewis, Vivienne. Keep Young after Forty!
Lewis, W. Arthur. The Theory of Economic Growth.
Lewis, William. Gala.
--Resumes for College Graduates.
Lewis, William, jt. auth. see Cornelius, Hal.
Lewis, William J., ed. see Institute of Foreign Policy Analysis Staff.
Lewis, William P. Foreword by see Cohen, Leo & Erickson, Ralph J.
Lewis, Wyndham. Collected Poems & Plays. Munton, Alan, ed.
Lewisohn, Ludwig. The Island Within.
Lewison, Jeremy, jt. ed. see Gresty, Hilary.
Lewison, Lawrence. You & Your Eyes.
Lewis-Steere, Cynthia. Stepping Lightly: An A to Z Guide for Stepparents.
Lewitt, Fil. Hi Hai High: Zen & the Art of Backpacking.
Lewitt, S. N. U. S. S. A.
--U. S. S. A. Book 1.
Lewke, M., tr. see International Symposium On Echo-Encephalography - Erlangen - 1967.
Lewus, William, tr. see Zlotin, R. I. & Khodashova, K. S.
Lewy, A. Studies in Educational Evaluation.
Lewytzkyj, Borys, ed. The Soviet Union: Facts, Figures, Data.
Lexau, Joan M. Come! Sit! Stay!
Ley, David & Samuels, M. Humanistic Geography.
Leyda, Si-lan C. Footnote to History.
Leydecker, W., ed. see International Glaucoma Symposium, Nara, Japan, May 7-11, 1978.
Leyden, Rudolph von see Von Leyden, Rudolph.
Leyden, Wolfgang von see Von Leyden, Wolfgang.
Leyland, Eric. Libraries in Schools.
Leyland-DiBlasi, Sharon, illus. My Color Book.
Leymarie, Jean, jt. auth. see Skira-Rizzoli Staff.
Leys, Simon. The Burning Forest: Essays on Chinese Culture & Politics.
Leyssac, Paul, tr. see Andersen, Hans Christian.
Lezra, Giggy. Mechido, Aziza, & Ahmed.
Lhalungpa, Lobsang P., tr. see Takpo Tashi Namgyal.
Lhande, Pierre. Dictionnaire Basque Francais.
Lherbier, L. W., jt. ed. see Wells, M. G. H.
L'Heureux, John. Desires.
L'Heureux, Marc. How to Write a Love Letter.
L'Heureux, Maurice. Into the Back Country.
L'Hommedieu, Toni. The Divorce Experience of Working & Middle Class Women. Nathan, Peter, ed.
L'Hote, Jean. Communale. Torrens, Robert W. & Sanders, James B., eds.
Lhuyd, Edward. Archaeologia Britannica: An Account of the Languages, Histories & Customs of the Original Inhabitants of Great Britain from Collections: Glossography.
Li, Charles N., ed. see Symposium, University of California, Santa Barbara Staff.
Li, David K., jt. auth. see Burhenne, H. Joachim.
Li, Hsueh Jei, ed. Chromatin & Chromosome Structure.
Li, Liu, tr. see Yuan, Tian.
Li, Mirok see Kang, Younghill.
Li, S. T., et al. Microcomputer Tools for Communication Engineering.
Li, Tien-Min. Liu Shao-chi: Mao's First Heir-Apparent.
Li, Wen-Hsiung, ed. Stochastic Models in Population Genetics.
Li, Wen L. The Measurement & Analysis of Internal Migration: Testing Models with Korean Data.
Li, Xu. The Beginnings of Monkey.
--Trouble on Black Wind Mountain.
Lial, Margaret L. & Miller, Charles D. Beginning Algebra.
--Calculus with Applications.
--College Algebra.
--Finite Mathematics.
--Intermediate Algebra.
--Mathematics & Calculus with Applications.
--Trigonometry.
Liancheng, Duan, ed. & tr. see Tsomin, Wang.
Liang Fang-Chung. Single-Whip Method of Taxation in China.
Liang Hsi-Huey. The Berlin Police Force in the Weimar Republic, 1918-1933.
Liao Wen-Kuei. The Individual & the Community.
Lias, Geoffrey, tr. see Benes, Edward.
Liazos. Sociology: A Liberating Perspective.
Libanio, J. B. Spiritual Discernment & Politics: Guidelines for Religious Communities. Morrow, Theodore, tr. from Port.
Libby, Bill. Joe Louis: The Brown Bomber.
--The Reggie Jackson Story.
--The Young Swimmer.
Libby, Bill, jt. auth. see Roseboro, John.
Libby, L. M. Carbon Dioxide & Climate: Dedicated to Williard F. Libby & Hans E. Suss.
Liberatore, Dan & Davis, Judy. Shape up for Sex.
Liberatore, Karen. The Complete Guide to the Golden Gate National Recreation Area.
Liberia, Republic of. Opinions of the Attorney General of the Republic of Liberia, September, 1964-August 1968. Konvitz, Milton R., ed.
Liberia, Republic of, Staff. Reports & Opinions of the Attorney General of the Republic of Liberia: December 1922-July 1930.
Liberman, Cy & Liberman, Pat. The Crab Book.
Liberman, Pat, jt. auth. see Liberman, Cy.
Libert, Lutz. Tobacco, Snuff Boxes & Pipes.
Libes, S. & Garetz, M. Interfacing to the S-100 Microcomputers.
Libman. Moses Malone.
Libman, Lillian. And Music at the Close: Stravinsky's Last Years, a Personal Memoir.
Liboff, Richard L. Introduction to the Theory of Kinetic Equations.
Libowitz, G. G. & Whittingham, M. S., eds. Materials Science in Energy Technology.
Library Administration & Management Association Preconference Staff. Library Effectiveness: State of the Arts.
Library Association, London Staff. British Humanities Index 1979.
--Report of the Commission on the Supply of & Demand for Qualified Librarians.
Library Association, London Staff, ed. British Humanities Index, 1980.
--British Technology Index, 1977.
--British Technology Index, 1978.
Library of Congress, Research Libraries Staff, jt. auth. see New York Public Library, Research Libraries Staff.
Library of Congress Staff. Africa South of the Sahara: Index to Periodical Literature, First Supplement.
--Africa South of the Sahara: Index to Periodical Literature, 1900-1970.
--Catalog of Broadsides in the Rare Book Division.
--Far Eastern Languages Catalog.
--Index to Latin American Legislation, 1950-1960.
--Southeast Asia Subject Catalog.
Library of Congress Staff, jt. auth. see New York Public Library Staff.
Library of Congress, Washington, D. C., Geography & Map Division Staff. The Bibliography of Cartography.
--The Bibliography of Cartography, First Supplement.
Library of Congress, Washington, D. C., Staff. Catalog of Brazilian Acquisitions of the Library of Congress, 1964-1974.
Licciardi, David D. Beginnings & Other Poems.
Lichardus, R., et al, eds. Hormonal Regulation of Sodium Excretion.
Lichine, Alexis. Alexis Lichine's Guide to the Wines & Vineyards of France.
--Alexis Lichine's Guide to the Wines & Vineyards of France.
--Alexis Lichine's New Encyclopedia of Wines & Spirits.
Lichner, H. Nine Sonatinas for Piano.
Lichstein, Herman C., ed. Bacterial Nutrition.
Licht, Hans, pseud. Sexual Life in Ancient Greece. Dawson, Lawrence, ed. Freese, J. H., tr. from Gr.
Licht, Sidney, ed. Massage, Manipulation & Traction.
--Therapeutic Electricity & Ultraviolet Radiation.
Lichtenberg, Betty K., jt. auth. see Troutman, Andria P.
Lichtenberg, D. B. Meson & Baryon Spectroscopy.
Lichtenberg, Jacqueline. City of a Million Legends.
--Molt Brother.
Lichtenfels, J. R., ed. CIH Keys to the Nematode Parasites of Vertebrates, No. 7: Keys to Genera of the Superfamily Strongyloidea.
--CIH Keys to the Nematode Parasites of Vertebrates, No. 8: Keys to Genera of the Superfamilies Ancylostomatoidea & Diaphanocephaloidea.
Lichtensteiger, Walter, jt. ed. see Schlumph, Margret.
Lichtenstein, Edward, jt. auth. see Danaher, Brian G.
Lichtenstein, L. M., et al, eds. Asthma: Physiology, Immunopharmacology & Treatment.
Lichtenstein, Lawrence M. & Fauci, Anthony S. Current Therapy in Allergy Immunology & Rheumatology 1985-1986.
Lichtenstein, Sara. Delacroix & Raphael. Freedberg, Sydney J., ed.
Lichtlen, P. R. Coronary Angiography & Angina Pectoris.
Lichtman, Marshall A. Hematology for Practitioners.
Lick, D. R., jt. ed. see Alavi, Y.
Lick, Rainer F. Color Atlas of Surgical Diagnosis.
Lickley, W. A. Malachi: Lessons for Today.
Lickteig, Mary J. An Introduction to Children's Literature.
Liddell, Louise A. Clothes & Your Appearance.
Liddell Hart, B. H., ed. Rommel Papers.
Liddell-Hart, Basil H. The Red Army: The Red Army 1918-1945; The Soviet Army 1946 to the Present.
Liddle, Peter. The Airman's War 1914-1918.
Lidgren, H., jt. auth. see Bridgewater, A.
Lidgren, K. & Butlin, J. Container Costs.
Lidgren, K., jt. auth. see Bridgwater, A. V.
Lidicker, W. Z., Jr. & Caldwell, R. L., eds. Dispersal & Migration.
Lidz, Carol S. Improving Assessment of Schoolchildren: A Guide to Evaluating Cognitive, Emotional & Physical Problems.
Lieb, Sandra R. Mother of the Blues: A Study of Ma Rainey.
Liebb, Julius, jt. auth. see Bromberg, Murray.
Liebeck, Pamela. Vectors & Matrices.
Lieber, Hugh G. & Lieber, Lillian R. The Education of T. C. Mits.
--Human Values & Science, Art & Mathematics.
Lieber, Lillian R., jt. auth. see Lieber, Hugh G.
Lieber, Michael. Street Life: Afro-American Culture in Urban Trinidad.
Lieber, Stanley R. & Fesenmaier, Daniel R., eds. Recreation Planning & Management.
Lieberman & Gloe. Microsoft Word for the IBM PC.
Lieberman & Schimmel. Typing the Easy Way.
Lieberman, Carl, ed. Institutions & Processes of American National Government.
Lieberman, Chaim. Christianity of Sholem Asch.
Lieberman, Herbert. City of the Dead.
--The Green Train.
--Green Train.
--Nightbloom.
Lieberman, Jethro K. Crisis at the Bar: The Unethical Ethics of Lawyers (and What to Do About It)
Lieberman, Jethro K. & Rhodes, Neil S. The Complete 1980 CB Handbook.
Lieberman, Jethro K. & Siedel, George J. Business Law & the Legal Environment.
Lieberman, L. The Emergence of Man.
Lieberman, Maurice. Elementary Keyboard Harmony.
Lieberman, Michael, jt. ed. see Stollak, Gary E.
Lieberman, Morton A., jt. auth. see Whitaker, Dorothy S.
Lieberman, Nancy & Frommer, Harvey. Basketball My Way.
Lieberman, Ralph E. The Church of Sainta Maria Dei Miracoli in Venice. Freedberg, S. J., ed.
Lieberman, Sima. The Contemporary Spanish Economy: A Historical Perspective.
Lieberman, Stuart. Transgenerational Family Therapy.
Lieberman, William S., ed. An American Choice: The Muriel Kallis.
Liebers, Arthur & Sheppard, Georgie M. How to Raise & Train a Pomeranian.
Lieberson, Stanley, ed. Explorations in Sociolinguistics.
Liebert, Robert M. & Harris, Judith R. The Child: Development from Birth through Adolescence.
Liebert, Robert M., et al. The Early Window: Effects of Television on Children & Youth.
Lieberthal, E. A., jt. auth. see Gurau, Peter K.
Lieberthal, Kenneth & Oksenberg, Michel. Bureaucratic Politics & Chinese Energy Development.
Liebgott, Bernard. The Anatomical Basis of Dentistry.
Liebhafsky. The Nature of Price Theory.
Lieblich, Jerome H., ed. Instructions for the Preparation of Specifications, Standards & Technical Manuals.
--Military Aerospace Standard Drawings.
--Military Fastener Standard Drawings.
Liebow, Averill A. Encounter with Disaster: A Medical Diary of Hiroshima, 1945.
Liebowitz, Burt H. & Carson, John H. Distributed Processing.
Liebowitz, H., ed. Combined Nonlinear & Linear (Micro & Macro) Fracture Mechanics: Applications to Modern Engineering Structures - Selected Papers, U.S.-Japan Seminar.
--Progress in Fatigue & Fracture.
Liebowitz, Murray, jt. auth. see Johnston, Philip M.
Liechty, Richard D. & Soper, Robert T. Synopsis of Surgery.
Liederman, Judith. The Moneyman.
--The Pleasure-Dome.
Liedermann, David, jt. auth. see Urvater, Michele.
Liedlich, Raymond D., jt. auth. see Smith, William F.
Liedloff, Helmut, jt. auth. see Moeller, Jack R.
Liehm, Antonin J. The Milos Forman Stories.
Lien, Arnold J. Concurring Opinion: The Privileges or Immunities Clause of the Fourteenth Amendment.
Lien, David A. The IBM BASIC Handbook.
--Learning Commodore 64 BASIC.
Liener, I. Toxic Constituents in Plant Foodstuffs.
Lienhard, John. A Heat Transfer Textbook.
Lienhard, John H., jt. auth. see Tieu, Chang L.
Lienhard, Marc. Luther: Witness to Jesus Christ: Stages & Themes of the Reformer's Christology. Robertson, Edwin H., tr.
Lientz & Rea. Data Communications for Business.
Liepmann, Kate K. The Journey to Work.
Lier, Bruno, et al. Bruno Lier: Ad Topica Carminum Amatorium Symbolae. Commager, Steele, ed. Bd. with Keith Preston: Studies in the Diction of the Sermo Amatorius in Roman Comedy; Alfons Spies: Militat Omnis Amons. Garland Pub.
Liestol, Knut. The Origin of the Icelandic Family Sagas.
Lieth, H., jt. ed. see Schnitzler, H.
Lieth, Helmut F., ed. Patterns of Primary Production in the Biosphere.
Lietmann, G., ed. see CISM (International Center for Mechanical Sciences) Dept. of Automation & Information, 1973.
Lieverman, Theodore & Schneider, Peter. Memorandum of Law on the United States Policy Toward Nicaragua.
Life in Christ Staff, ed. Guia Para Leer el Antiguo Testamento: Segunda Parte, el Esenario Esta Puesto. Gomez, Monica Villa, tr.
Life Office Management Association Staff, ed. Life Company Operations.
--Life Insurance Investments: Readings.
--Pension Planning: Readings.
--Student Guide for Canadian.
--Student Guide for Management Principles.
--Student Guide to Accounting for Life Insurance Companies.
--Teaching Part Two: Life Company Operations.
Life Sciences Symposium Staff. Public Health Risks of the Dioxins: Proceedings of the Life Sciences Symposium, New York, October 19-20, 1983. Lowrance, William W., ed.
Liffick, Blaise W. Bits & Pieces.

Liffick, Blaise W., ed. Numbers in Theory & Practice.
--Program Design.
Lifflander, Matthew. Final Treatment: The File on Dr. X.
Lifshitz. Commom Pediatric Problems.
--Shock Waves in Chemistry.
Lifshitz, Fima, ed. Common Pediatric Disorders: Metabolism, Heart Disease, Allergies, Substance Abuse & Trauma.
Lifshitz, Samuel & Buchsbaum, Herbert. Gynecologic Oncology Case Studies.
Liftig, Rick. The Frugal Woodworker.
Lifton, Bernice. Bugbusters: Getting Rid of Household Pests Without Dangerous Chemicals.
Lifton, Betty J. Contemporary Children's Theater.
--Good Night, Orange Monster.
Lifton, Betty J. & Fox, Thomas C. The Children of Vietnam.
Lifton, David. Best Evidence.
Lifton, James & Hardy, Owen B. Site Selection for Health Care Facilities.
Lifton, Robert J. Psycho-Birds.
--Thought Reform & the Psychology of Totalism.
Liggett, Sarah, jt. auth. see Halpern, Jeanne W.
Light, Caroline. Gift in Secret.
--Minor Royalty.
Light, Donald. Becoming Psychiatrists: The Professional Transformation of Self.
Light, Donald, Jr. Becoming Psychiatrists.
Light, Margot & Groom, A. J. R., eds. International Relations: A Handbook of Current Theory.
Light, Mary. God: Incidences or Divine Providence.
--God's Guidance at Dawn.
--Joy of the Lord.
--Rejoice & Be Exceeding Glad.
--Signs & Wonders.
Light, Richard W. Pleural Diseases.
Lightbody, Andy. The Terrorism Survival Guide: 101 Travel Tips on How Not to Become a Victim.
Lightbody, Mark. Canada-A Travel Survival Kit.
--Canada Travel Survival Kit.
Lightfoot, A. Socio-Psychological Dimensions of Education: Teaching & Learning.
Lightfoot, Albert. Urban Education in Social Perspectives.
Lightfoot, Alfred. American Urban Education: Inquiries into Changing Patterns.
Lightfoot, Frederick S., ed. Nineteenth-Century New York in Rare Photographic Views.
Lightfoot, J. B. Notes on Epistles of Saint Paul. Harmer, J. R., ed.
Lightfoot, Neil. The Parables of Jesus.
Lightfoot, Neil R. How We Got the Bible.
Lightfoot, Paul & Fuller, Theodore. Circulation & Interpersonal Networks Linking Rural & Urban Areas: The Case of Roi-et, Northeastern Thailand.
Lighthouse Publishing Staff, et al. The Complete Book of Symphony Macros.
Lightman, Alan P. Time Travel & Papa Joe's Pipe: Essays on the Human Side of Science.
Lightman, Sidney, ed. The Jewish Travel Guide, 1986.
--The Jewish Travel Guide 1988.
Lightner, Robert P. Neoevangelicalism Today.
Lightstone, A. H. Linear Algebra.
Lightwood, Martha B., ed. Public & Business Planning in the United States: A Bibliography.
Ligon, Helen H. Successful Mangement Information Systems. Farmer, Richard, ed.
Liguori, Fred, ed. Automatic Test Equipment: Hardware, Software & Management.
Lihani, John, pref. by. Global Demands on Language & the Mission of the Language Academies.
Likens, Gene E., jt. auth. see Wetzel, Robert G.
Likhanov, A. The Maze.
Liler, M. Reaction Mechanisms in Sulphuric Acid & Other Strong Acid Solutions.
Liles, Bruce L. Basic Grammar of Modern English.
Lilienfeld, Christian Von see Von Lilienfeld, Christian.
Liliom, Tom C. Legion of the Dark. Penoi, Lois & Penoi, Jon, eds.
Lilipaly, Hendrik Th. Experiences with God & His Messengers: The Key to God's Kingdom.
Lilja, Saara. The Roman Elegists' Attitude Towards Women. Commager, Steele, ed.
Lilje, Hanns. The Valley of the Shadow.
Liljedahl, John B., et al. Tractors & Their Power Units.
Liljefors, Bruno. Peerless Eye: The Art of Bruno Lilefors.
Lillard, Louise, jt. auth. see Poletti, Jacques.
Lillesand, Thomas M., intro. by. Thermosense I: Proceedings.
Lilley, A. E. & Midgley, W. A Book of Studies in Plant Form: With Some Suggestions for Their Application to Design.
Lilley, T. Problems of Accelerating Aircraft Production During World War II.
Lilleyman, J. S., jt. ed. see Hinchliffe, R. F.
Lillibridge, G. D. Images of American Society: A History of the United States.
Lillington, Kenneth. Isabel's Double.
--What Beckoning Ghost?
Lillis, Carol. Brady's Introduction to Medical Terminology.
Lillis, Kevin, jt. auth. see Sinclair, M. E.
Lillis, Kevin M., ed. School & Community in Less Developed Areas.
Lillo, George. The Plays of George Lillo. Drucker, Trudy, ed.
Lilly, Fred. Word Gifts: Keys to Charismatic Power.
Lilly, Fred, jt. auth. see Osburn, Charlie.
Lilly, John C. Programming & Metaprogramming in the Human Biocomputer.
Lilly, Kenneth. Animal Builders.
--Animal Climbers.
--Animal Jumpers.
--Animal Runners.
--Animal Swimmers.
Lilly, Luella J. An Overview of Body Mechanics.
Lilly, M. Stephen. Children with Exceptional Needs.
Lilly, Susan C., jt. auth. see Dale, Nell.
Lilly, Susan C., tr. see Megged, Aharon.
Lim, C. Y., jt. auth. see You, P. S.
Lim, Linda & Fong, Pang E. Technology Choice & Employment Creation: A Case Study of Three Multinational Enterprises in Singapore. International Labour Office Staff, ed.
Lim, Pacifico A. A Guide to Structured COBOL with Efficiency Techniques & Special Algorithms.
--A Guide to Structured COBOL with Efficiency Techniques & Special Algorithms.
Lim, R. K., ed. Pharmacology of Pain: Proceedings - Vol. 9.
Lim, Rolland M. The Effects of Negative Conditioning on Children.
Lim, Willie. Mahjong Made Easy: Standard Chinese Rules Simplified.
Lima, Frank. Angel: New Poems.
Limaye, Dilip R. Planning Cogeneration Systems.
Limb, Sue & Cordingley, Patrick. Captain Oates: Soldier & Explorer.
Limburg, James. Old Stories for a New Time.
--The Prophets & the Powerless.
Limburg, Val E. Workbook for Mass Communication & Society.
Limerick, Patricia Nelson. Desert Passages: Encounters with the American Deserts.
Liming, Roy A. Math for Computer Graphics.
Limmer, Ruth, ed. What the Woman Lived: Selected Letters of Louise Bogan, 1920-1970.
Limonov, Edward. His Butler's Story. Jordan, Fred, ed. Rosengrant, Judson, tr. from Rus.
Lin, Ching-Yuan. Japanese & U. S. Inflation: A Comparative Analysis.
Lin, N. Foundations of Social Research.
Lin, Nan. The Study of Human Communication.
Lin, Paul J. A Translation of Lao Tzu's "Tao Te Ching" & Wang Pi's "Commentary."
Lin, Sein. Land Reform Implementation: A Comparative Perspective.
Lin, Sein, ed. Readings in Land Reform.
Lin, Sein & Ramakrishnan, S., eds. Land Management Issues & Development Strategies in Developing Countries.
Lin, Sheng H., ed. Radiationless Transition.
Lin, Willy. Chin-Na: The Grappling Art of Self Defense. Henschell, Todd, ed.
Linchevsky, B. Methods of Metallurgical Experiment.
Lincoln, Eleanor T. Through the Grecourt Gates.
Lincoln, Eleanor T. & Pinto, John A. This, the House We Live In.
Lincoln, John C. Ground Rent, Not Taxes: The Natural Source of Revenue for the Government.
--Should Land Have Selling Value?
--Stop Legal Stealing.
Lincoln, John E., jt. auth. see Heffernan, James A.
Lincoln, Nina, jt. auth. see Schalkwijk, Bob.
Lincoln, W. Bruce. Passage Through Armageddon: The Russians in War & Revolution 1914-1918.
Lind, Andrew W., ed. see Conference on Race Relations in World Perspective, Honolulu, 1954.
Lindahl & Osaba, David, eds. Lymphocyte Recognition & Effector Mechanisms.
Lindahl, Judy. Decorating with Fabric.
Lindbeck, John R. Designing Today's Manufactured Products.
Lindberg, Jana H. Counted Cross-Stitch Designs for All Seasons.
--Counted Cross-Stitch Designs for the Home.
Lindberg, John. Three Steps to the Essay: An Expository Handbook.
Lindberg, Leon N. & Scheingold, Stuart A., eds. Regional Integration: Theory & Research.
Lindberg, O. & Ernster, L. Chemistry & Physiology of Mitochondria & Microsomes.
Lindberg, Olov, ed. see I U B - I U B S Joint Symposium - 1st - Stockholm - 1960.
Lindbergh, Anne. Nobody's Orphan.
Lindbergh, Anne M. Bring Me a Unicorn: Diaries & Letters of Anne Morrow Lindbergh, 1922-1928.
--Dearly Beloved: A Theme & Variations.
--Earth Shine.
--Earth Shine: Shine.
--The Flower & the Nettle: Diaries & Letters of Anne Morrow Lindbergh 1936-1939.
--Hour of Gold, Hour of Lead.
--Listen! The Wind.
--War Within & Without: Diaries & Letters 1939-1944.
Lindbergh, Charles A. Boyhood on the Upper Mississippi: A Reminiscent Letter.
--The Spirit of St. Louis.
Lindblom, J. The Bible: A Modern Understanding. Wahlstrom, Eric H., tr. from Swedish.
--Prophecy in Ancient Israel.
Lindblom, Steven. The Fantastic Bicycle Book.
Lindburg, Donald G. The Macaques: Studies in Ecology, Behavior & Evolution.
Lindeburg, Franklin A. Teaching Physical Education in the Secondary School.
Lindeburg, Michael R. Engineering Fundamentals Quick Reference Cards.
--Expanded Interest Tables.
--Seismic Design for the Professional Engineering Examination.
Lindegren, Erik. ABC of Lettering & Printing Types.
Lindeke, W. Four-Language Technical Dictionary of Heating, Ventilation & Sanitary Engineering: English, German, French, Russian.
Lindell, Paul J. The Mystery of Pain.
Lindeman, Carla G., jt. auth. see Nystuen, David W.
Lindeman, Carol, ed. Alternate Conceptions of Work in Society & the Nursing Profession.
Lindeman, J. Bruce & Friedman, Jack P. Barron's How to Prepare for the Real Estate Licensing Examination -- Salesperson & Broker.
Lindeman, Richard, et al. Introduction to Bivariate & Multivariate Analysis.
Linden, Eugene, jt. auth. see Patterson, Francine.
Linden, Geoffrey. Jigsaw.
Linden, Glenn M. & Downey, Matthew T., eds. Teaching American History: Structured Inquiry Approaches.
Linden, Jonathan, jt. ed. see Rosenbaum, Lawrence.
Linden, M. L., tr. see Murail, Elvire.
Linden, Peter J. Van der see Vander Linden, Peter J. & Farrar, Donald R.
Linden, Stanton J. William Cooper's - A Catalogue of Chymicall Books, 1673-88: A Verified Version.
Lindenauer, Nancy & Selman, Edythea G. School & Me.
Lindenberg, Marc, jt. auth. see Dominguez, Jorge.
Lindenburg, Katja & West, Bruce J. Open & Closed Systems: The Nonequilibrium Statistical Mechanics of Nonlinear Processes.
Linder, Elisha & Raban, Avner. Introducing Underwater Archaeology.
Linder, Fredric & McMillan, James. Educational Psychology, 1987-88.
Linder, Fredric & McMillan, James H. Annual Editions: Educational Psychology, 1985-1986.
Linder, Leslie, ed. see Potter, Beatrix.
Linder, Marc. The Supreme Labor Court in Nazi Germany.
Linder, Maria C., ed. Nutritional Biochemistry & Metabolism, with Clinical Applications.
Linderman, Larry, jt. auth. see Sills, Beverly.
Linders, B. E. Strategic Planning in South East England 1968-78: A Case Study.
Lindfield, Michael. The Dance of Change: An Eco-Spiritual Approach to Transformation.
Lindfors, Bernth, ed. Research Priorities in African Literature.
Lindfors, Judith W. Children's Language & Learning.
Lindfors, Judith W., jt. auth. see Campbell, Russell N.
Lindgren, Astrid. Children on Troublemaker Street. Bothmer, Gerry, tr.
--I Want a Brother or Sister. Lucas, Barbara, tr. from Swedish.
Lindgren, Henry C. Great Expectations: The Psychology of Money.
Lindgren, I., et al, eds. Atomic Physics 8.
Lindgren, Linda L. Decorations from Nature: Growing, Preserving, & Arranging Naturals.
Lindholm, Richard W. The Economics of VAT: Preserving Efficiency, Capitalism & Social Progress.
Lindholm, U. S., ed. see Symposium on Mechanical Behavior of Materials Under Dynamic Loads, San Antonio, 1967.
Lindl, Ernest. Das Priester und Beamtentum der Altbabylonischen Kontrakte.
Lindley, Craig A. TRS-80 Z80 Assembly Language Library.
Lindley, David. Lyric.
Lindley, K. Appreciation of Architecture: Landscape & Buildings.
Lindman, N., jt. ed. see Chadwick, M. J.
Lindmark, Sture. Swedish America, 1914-1932.
Lindner, R. M. Correctional Psychology.
Lindo, David K. Supervision Can Be Easy.
Lindo, Marjorie G., jt. auth. see Gibbs, Errol A.
Lindon, Edmund. Cuba.
Lindon, J. C., jt. auth. see Emsley, J. W.
Lindon, John A., ed. The Psychoanalytic Forum.
Lindop, Grevel. The Opium-Eater: A Life of Thomas De Quincey.
Lindow, Ch. W. Historic Organs in France. Blanchard, Homer D., tr.
Lindquist, Donald. Berlin Tunnel, Twenty-One.
Lindquist, Linnea M. West's Comprehensive Cosmetology Outline.
Lindquist-Cock, Elizabeth. The Influence of Photography on American Landscape Painting, 1839-1880.
Lindqvist, I., jt. ed. see Bendz, G.
Lindroos, Maria. Me & My Life.
Lindsay, A. D., tr. see Plato.
Lindsay, Alexander D. Kant.
Lindsay, B. R., ed. Applications of Energy: Nineteenth Century.
Lindsay, C. School & Community.
Lindsay, Cecile, tr. see Lyotard, Jean-Francois.
Lindsay, Cotton M. Applied Price Theory.
Lindsay, David. The Violet Apple & the Witch. Pick, J. B., ed. & intro. by.
Lindsay, Geoff, ed. Problems of Adolescence in the Secondary School.
--Screening for Children with Special Needs: Multidisciplinary Approaches.
Lindsay, Gillian. The Toffee Apple Tree.
Lindsay, Gordon. Fire over the Holy Land.
Lindsay, Jack. Ancient Egyptian Alchemy. O'Quinn, John, ed.
--The Blood Vote.
--Charles Dickens.
--Hogarth: His Art & His World.
--William Blake.
--William Morris: His Life & Work.
Lindsay, Jack, ed. & tr. from Rus. Russian Poetry, Nineteen Seventeen to Nineteen Fifty-Five.
Lindsay, John V. City.
--The Edge.
Lindsay, Jon. Indroduction to CP-M Assembly Language.
Lindsay, Kenneth C., ed. see Kandinsky, Wassily.
Lindsay, Leslie & Aron, John. The Great Bazaar.
Lindsay, P. A., et al, trs. see Kleen, Werner J.
Lindsay, R. B. Julius Robert Mayer, Prophet of Energy.
--Lord Rayleigh, the Man & His Work.
Lindsay, R. Bruce. The Control of Energy.
--Physical Acoustics.
Lindsay, R. Bruce, ed. Acoustics.
--Energy: Historical Development of the Concept.
Lindsay, Rae S. Crisis Theory: A Critical Overview.
Lindsay, Robert, ed. Computer Analysis of Neuronal Structures.
Lindsay, Thomas. Plant Names.
Lindsay, Vachel. Adventures, Rhymes & Designs.
Lindsell, Sheryl L. Word Processing Mastery for Everyone: Typewriter Drills for Learning Keyboarding.
Lindsey, Darry. The Design & Drafting of Printed Circuits.
Lindsey, David. Americans in Conflict: The Civil War & Reconstruction.
Lindsey, David L. Spiral.
Lindsey, Johanna. Brave the Wild Wind.
--A Gentle Feuding.
--A Heart So Wild.
--Love Only Once.
--Tender Is the Storm.
Lindsey, John. Robert Burns: Rantin' Dog, Poet of the Common Man.
--Wren: His Life & Times.
Lindsey, Robert. The Falcon & the Snowman.
--The Flight of the Falcon.
Lindsey, Treska. When Batistine Made Bread.
Lindskoog, John & Lindskoog, Kathryn. How to Grow a Young Reader: A Parent's Guide to Kids & Books.
Lindskoog, Kathryn. The Gift of Dreams: A Christian View.
Lindskoog, Kathryn, jt. auth. see Lindskoog, John.
Lindskoog, Kathryn, ed. Around the Year with C. S. Lewis & His Friends.
Lindsley, Mary F. Grand Tour & Other Poems.
Lindstrom, C. E. The Fading American Newspaper.
Lindvall, C. Mauritz & Nitko, Anthony J. Measuring Pupil Achievement & Aptitude.
Lindvall, Ella K. Jonah & the Great Fish.
Line, David. Screaming High.
Line, Francis & Line, Helen. Our Road to Prayer.
Line, Helen, jt. auth. see Line, Francis.
Line, Les & Reiger, George. The Audubon Society Book of Marine Wildlife.
Lineback, Richard H., ed. see Philosophy Documentation Center Staff.
Lineberry, Robert L. Government in America: People, Politics & Policies.

Linecar, Howard A. The Commemorative Medal: Its Appreciation & Collection.
Linehan, Mary & Tucker, Vincent. Workers' Cooperatives: Potential & Problems. Bank of Ireland Centre for Co-op Studies Staff, ed.
Liner, Tom, jt. auth. see Kirby, Dan.
Lines, James. Beyond the Balance Sheet: Evaluating Profit Potential.
Lines, Judy L., jt. auth. see Mertens, Thomas R.
Lines, Kathleen, ed. The Haunted & the Haunters: Tales of Ghosts & Other Apparitions.
Lines, M. Vardell, jt. auth. see Boeing Computer Service Co. Staff.
Linet, Beverly. Ladd: The Life, the Legend, the Legacy of Alan Ladd.
--Star-Crossed: The Story of Robert Walker & Jennifer Jones.
--Susan Hayward: Portrait of a Survivor.
Lineweaver, Thomas H., III & Backus, Richard H. The Natural History of Sharks.
Linfert, Carl. Bosch.
Linfield, Warner M., ed. Anionic Surfactants.
Ling, Betty, jt. auth. see Ling, Charlie.
Ling, Charlie & Ling, Betty. Speak Chinese by Singing.
Ling, Ding. The Sun Shines over the Sanggan River. Xianyi, Yang & Yang, Gladys, trs.
Ling, Edgar R. A Textbook of Dairy Chemistry.
Ling, Hsien C. The Petroleum Industry of the People's Republic of China.
Ling, Miao, tr. see Zhongmin, Xu & Daguang, Zhou.
Ling, N. R. & Kay, J. E., eds. Lymphocyte Stimulation.
Ling, Pan. Old Shanghai: Gansters in Paradise.
Ling, Robert F. & Roberts, Harry V. IDA: A User's Guide to the IDA Interactive Data Analysis & Forecasting System.
Ling, Robert F., jt. auth. see Roberts, Harry V.
Ling, T. O. A Dictionary of Buddhism.
Linge, G. J. see Hamilton, F. E. & Linge, G. J. R.
Linge, G. J. R., jt. ed. see Hamilton, F. E.
Lingeman, C. H., ed. Carcinogenic Hormones.
Lingeman, Richard. Small Town America: A Narrative History Sixteen Twenty to the Present.
Lingenfelter, Mary R. & Kitson, Harry D. Vocations for Girls.
Lingenfelter, Richard E. Death Valley & the Amargosa.
Lingens, Barbara, jt. auth. see Lingens, Hans G.
Lingens, Hans G. & Lingens, Barbara. Education in West Germany: A Quest for Excellence.
Linguistic Association of Canada & the U. S. Staff. Eleventh Lacus Forum. Hall, Robert A., ed.
--Fifth LACUS Forum: Proceedings. Woelck, Wolfgang & Garvin, Paul L., eds.
--The First LACUS Forum: Proceedings. Makkai, Adam & Makkai, Valerie, eds.
--The Fourth LACUS Forum: Proceedings. Paradis, Michel, ed.
--LACUS Forum, 3rd: Proceedings. Di Pietro, Robert J. & Blansitt, Edward L., Jr., eds.
--LACUS Forum, 8th: Proceedings. Gutwinski, Waldemar & Jolly, Grace, eds.
--The Second LACUS Forum: Proceedings. Reich, Peter A., ed.
--Seventh Lacus Forum: Proceedings. Copeland, J. E. & Davis, P. W., eds.
--Tenth Lacus Forum: Proceedings. Manning, Alan, et al, eds.
Linhart, J. F., ed. Plasma Physics: Proceedings of the EUR-CNEN Association Meeting, 1969.
Linhoff, B., jt. auth. see Institution of Chemical Engineers Staff.
Linington, Elizabeth. Strange Felony.
--Strange Felony.
Link, Arthur S. Wilson: The Road to the White House.
--Wilson: The Struggle for Neutrality, 1914-1915.
Link, Arthur S., et al. Crucial American Elections.
Link, F. Eclipse Phenomena in Astronomy.
Link, Frederick M. Aphra Behn.
Link, Frederick M., ed. see Cowley, Hannah.
Link, Frederick M., ed. see O'Keefe, John.
Link, Frederick M., ed. see Scott, Walter.
Link, Mark. Breakway: Twenty-Eight Steps to a More Reflective Life.
--You: Prayer for Beginners & Those Who Have Forgotten How.
Link, Michael. Nature's Classroom: A Manual for Teaching Outdoor Education.
Link, Mike & Blacklock, Craig. Black Hills Badlands.
Link, Peter K. Basic Petroleum Geology.
--Basic Petroleum Geology.
Link, Ruth. House Full of Mice.
Link, Werner & Feld, Werner J., eds. The New Nationalism: Implications for Transatlantic Relations.
Linke, Maria Z & Hunt, Ruth. East Wind.
Linker, Robert, tr. Misfortunes of Ogier the Dane. Butts, M., ed.
Linkert, Lo. Laugh off the Pounds.
--Lo Linkert's Golftoons.
Linkert, Lo, jt. auth. see Olson, Bill.
Linkh, Richard M. American Catholicism & European Immigrants (1900-1924)
Linklater, Eric. White Man's Saga.
Linkletter, Art & Bishop, George. Hobo on the Way to Heaven.
Linkugel, Wil A., et al. Contemporary American Speeches.
Linn, Bill. Missing in Action.
Linn, Don. U. S. Naval & Marine Aircraft Today.
Linn, Don & Spering, Don. Tactical Air Command.
Linn, Ed. Steinbrenner's Yankees: An Inside Account.
Linnard, W., jt. auth. see Ussovsky, B. N.
Linnaus, Vernon F. Modern College Accounting.
Linnick, Stuart, et al, eds. Developing Labor Law Third Supplement, 1982-86.
Linowitz, Sol M. The Making of a Public Man.
Lins, David A., jt. auth. see Penson, John B., Jr.
Linsell, Tony. Mr. Ferdinand Fisk, Cat Detective.
Linskens, H. F., jt. auth. see Stanley, R. G.
Linsky, Benjamin, ed. Chicago Association of Commerce & Industry, Committee of Investigatin or Smoke Abatement: Smoke Papers of the Chicago Association of Commerce Collected 1911-1915 for Preparation of Report Entitled Smoke Abatement & Electrification of Railway Terminals.
Linsky, Leonard. Referring.
Linsley, E. G. & MacSwain, J. W. Nesting Biology & Associates of Melitoma (Hymenoptera, Anthrophoridae)
Linsley, E. G., jt. auth. see Chemsak, John A.
Linsley, Leslie. First Steps in Counted Crosstitch.
--First Steps in Quilting.
--First Steps in Stenciling.
Lin Songying. Rag Doll Looks for a House.
Linssen, John. Tabitha Ffoulkes.
--Yellow Pages.
Linssen, Robert. Living Zen. Abrahams-Curiel, Diana, tr.
Lint, Charles de see De Lint, Charles.
Lint, J. H. Van see Combinational Theory Seminar Staff.
Lint, J. Van see Van Lint, J. H.
Linthorst, Ann T. Gift of Love: Marriage As a Spiritual Journey.
Lintner, K., ed. see CISM (International Center for Mechanical Sciences), Department for Mechanics of Defamable Bodies Staff.
Linton, Eliza L. The True History of Joshua Davidson, 1872. Wolff, Robert L., ed.
Linton, Nancy, jt. auth. see Frank, Marge.
Linton, Ralph, ed. Most of the World: The Peoples of Africa, Latin America & the East Today.
Linton, Sydney, tr. see Sjogren, Per-Olof.
Linver, Sandy. Speak Easy: How to Talk Your Way to the Top.
Lin Yu Shen see Kann, Eduard A.
Lin Yutang. A Leaf in the Storm.
--Vermilion Gate.
Linz, Peter. Programming Concepts & Problem Solving: An Introduction to Computer Science Using Pascal.
Linzey, Stanford E. Why I Believe in the Baptism with the Holy Spirit.
Lionberger, Herbert F. & Gwin, Paul. Communication Strategies: A Guide for Agricultural Change Agents.
Lionel, Frederic. The Magic Tarot: Vehicle of Eternal Wisdom. Gadzuk, Marilyn W., tr.
--Revolution in Consciousness.
Lionni, Leo. Colors.
--Let's Make Rabbits.
--Numbers.
--Swimmy.
--Words.
Lions, J. L. & Magenes, E. Non-Homogeneous Boundary Value Problems & Applications. Kenneth, P., tr.
Lions, J. L., jt. ed. see Bensoussan, A.
Lions, J. L., jt. ed. see Glowinski, R.
Lions, J. L., ed. see International Symposium on Control Theory, Numerical Methods & Computer Systems Modelling, June, 1974.
Lipatov, Glanys A., tr. see Mikhailov, N.
Lipatov, V. A Village Detective.
Lipatov, Vil. Stoletov Dossier. Miller, Alex, tr.
Lipham, James. Effective Principal, Effective School. Koerner, Thomas, ed.
Lipinski, Andrew J., jt. auth. see Amara, Roy C.
Lipke, Jean. Marriage.
Lipke, Jean C. Loving.
--Puberty & Adolescence.
--Sex Outside of Marriage.
Lipke, Paul. Plank on Frame: The Who, What & Where of 150 Boatbuilders.
Lipkin, Martin & Good, Robert A., eds. Gastrointestinal Tract Cancer.
Lipkin, R., jt. auth. see Vetrova, N.
Lipkind, William. Boy of the Islands.
--Boy with a Harpoon.
Lipkind, William & Duvoisin, Roger. Nubber Bear.
Lipkind, William & Mordvinoff, Nicolas. Little Tiny Rooster.
Lipking, Lawrence I., jt. ed. see Litz, Walton A., Jr.
Lipman, Andrew D., et al, eds. Teleports & the Intelligent City.
Lipman, Beata. We Make Freedom: Women in South Africa Speak.
Lipman, Bernard. Clinical Electrocardiography.
Lipman, Bernard S., et al. Clinical Scalar Electrocardiography.
Lipman, Burton E. How to Control & Reduce Inventory.
--Professional Job Search Program: How To Market Yourself.
Lipman, Jean. American Primitive Painting.
Lipman, Jean & Warren, Elizabeth V. Young America: A Folk-Art History.
Lipman, Zev, illus. Baruch Ata Befi Hataf: Illustrated Prayers & Blessings for Young Children.
Lipnack, Jessica & Stamps, Jeffrey. The Networking Book: People Connecting with People.
Lipp, Frederick J. Some Lose Their Way.
Lipp, Solomon. Three Argentine Thinkers.
Lipp, Sylvia E., tr. see Wenckheim, Nicholas.
Lippe, Iris. The Accident Case & Family Law Guide: A Dialogue & Translation Between Attorney & the Spanish Client.
Lipphardt, Walther, ed. Die Lateinische Osterfeiern und Osterspiele.
Lippincott, Henry. Military Bachelor Chef: A Guide for Getting Started in the Kitchen.
Lippitt, Gordon L., jt. auth. see Ford, George A.
Lippitt, Ronald, et al. Dynamics of Planned Change: A Comparative Study of Principles & Techniques.
Lippitt, Vernon G. The National Economic Environment.
Lippman, Deborah & Colin, Paul. Amulets, Charms & Talismans, How to Make: What They Mean & How to Use Them.
--Craft Sources: The Ultimate Catalog for Craftspeople.
Lippman, Deborah, jt. auth. see Colin, Paul.
Lippman, Marc E., ed. National Institutes of Health Consensus Development Conference on Adjuvant Chemotherapy & Endocrine Therapy for Breast Cancer.
Lippmann, F. Sedimentary Carbonate Minerals.
Lippmann, H., ed. Engineering Plasticity: Theory of Metal Forming Processes.
Lipscomb, Elizabeth J., jt. auth. see Johnston, Mary T.
Lipscomb, Shirley F., jt. auth. see Ireson, Amy G.
Lipscomb, Susan D. & Zuanich, Margaret A. BASIC Beginnings.
--BASIC Fun with Adventure Games.
--BASIC Fun with Graphics: The Apple Computer Way.
--BASIC Fun with Graphics: The Atari Computer Way.
--BASIC Fun with Graphics: The IBM-PC Computer Way.
Lipscomb, Terry W., ed. The Journal of the Commons House of Assembly, November 20, 1755-July 6, 1757.
Lipset, Seymour M. Rebellion in the University.
Lipset, Seymour M. & Bendix, Reinhard. Social Mobility in Industrial Society: A Study of Political Sociology.
Lipsett, Suzanne. Coming Back Up.
--Out of Danger.
Lipsitt, Paul D. & Sales, Bruce D., eds. New Directions in Psychologal Research.
Lipsitz, Lou. Reflections on Samson.
Lipsky, Richard. How We Play the Game: Why Sports Dominate American Life.
Lipson, Benjamin. How to Collect More on Your Insurance Claims.
--How to Collect More on Your Insurance Claims.
Lipson, Shelley. It's BASIC.
--It's BASIC: The ABC's of Computer Programming.
--More BASIC: A Guide to Intermediate Level Computer Programming.
Liptak, David Q. More Saints for Our Time.
Lipton, Benjamin. Aim for a Job in Watchmaking.
Lipton, Eunice. Looking into Degas.
Lipton, Judith E., jt. auth. see Barash, David P.
Lipton, Lawrence. Bruno in Venice West & Other Poems.
Lipton, Lenny. Super Eight Book.
Lipton, Mark, jt. auth. see Solomon, Neil.
Lipton, Michael. Labor & Poverty.
Lipton, Werner J., jt. auth. see Ryall, A. Lloyd.
Liria, Pilar, tr. see OAS, General Secretariat.
Lischer, Richard. Speaking of Jesus: Finding the Words for Witness.
Liscio, Mary A., ed. A Guide to Colleges for Learning Disabled Students.
--A Guide to Colleges for Learning Disabled Students.
Liscio, Mary Ann. A Guide to Colleges for Hearing Impaired & Deaf Students.
--A Guide to Colleges for Mobility Impaired Students.
--A Guide to Colleges for Visually Impaired Students.
Lish, Gordon. Dear Mr. Capote.
--Dear Mr. Capote.
--English Grammar.
--What I Know So Far.
--What I Know So Far: Short Stories.
Lish, Gordon, ed. All Our Secrets Are the Same: New Fiction from Esquire.
Lisiero, Dario. People Ideology-People Theology: New Perspectives on Religious Dogma.
Lisk, R. D., et al. Neonatal Hormone Treatment & Adult Sexual Behavior in Rodents.
Liska, Catherine. Black Is Beautiful but Grey Is Gorgeous.
Liska, Ken & Pryde, Lucy T. Introductory Chemistry for Health Professionals.
Lisker, R., jt. auth. see Armendares, S.
Lisker, Sonia O. Lost.
Lisker, Sonia O. & Dean, Leigh. Two Special Cards.
Liskov, Barbara. CLU Reference Manual.
Liss, Howard. Picture Story of Dave Winfield.
--Strange But True Basketball Stories.
Lissak, Moshe. The Structure of Stratification in Thailand.
Lissner, H. R., jt. auth. see Perry, C. C.
List, Jacob S. Education of Living.
--Living a Day at a Time.
List, Jacob S., jt. auth. see Langnas, Isaac A.
Listar, Glenn S. Technology Activity Guides.
Lister, Harry J. Your Guide to IRAs & Fourteen Other Retirement Plans.
Lister, Laurie, ed. see Cannon, Taffy.
Lister, Raymond. Little Treasury of Familiar Prose.
Lister, Rota H., ed. see Fletcher, John.
Listokin, David. The Dynamics of Housing Rehabilitation: Macro & Micro Analyses.
--Funding Education: Problems, Patterns, Solutions.
Listokin, David, jt. auth. see Burchell, Robert W.
Liston, Mary D., jt. ed. see Stapp, William B.
Liston, Maureen. Gertrude Stein: An Annotated Critical Bibliography.
Liston, Robert. We the People: Congressional Power.
Litchfield, Ada B. It's Going to Rain.
Litchfield, C. D. Marine Microbiology.
Litchfield, Carter. Analysis of Triglycerides.
Litchfield, Thorndike, jt. auth. see Ward, Sol A.
Litero. Diccionario de Crucigramas.
Litka, Michael P. & Inman, James E. The Legal Environment of Business: Public & Private Laws.
Litka, Michael P., jt. auth. see Pearson, Karl G.
Litman, Gary W. & Good, Robert A., eds. Immunoglobulins.
Litro, Robert F., jt. auth. see Compaine, Benjamin M.
Litsky, Frank. Winners in Gymnastics.
Littauer, Florence. Lives on the Mend.
Littauer, U. Z., jt. auth. see Weizman Institute of Science Conference Staff.
Littel, Robert. Mother Russia.
Littell, John, jt. auth. see Caleel, Richard.
Littell, Robert. The Amateur.
--The Debriefing.
--The October Circle.
Littke, Lael. Trish for President.
Little, Arthur D. The Funds Statement.
Little, Brown & Co. College Division Staff. Author's Guide.
Little, Brown Editors & Fowler, H. Ramsey. The Little, Brown Handbook.
Little, C. Challenge of the Land.
Little, Carol Handley. Sewing Easy Garments Without a Pattern.
Little, Charles E. Historical Lights.
Little, Craig B. Understanding Deviance & Control: Theory, Research & Social Policy.
Little, David & Twiss, Sumner B., Jr. Comparative Religious Ethics.
Little, E. C. Handbook of Utilization of Aquatic Plants: A Review of World Literature.
Little, Elbert L., Jr. Checklist of United States Trees: Native & Naturalized.
Little, Geoffrey, jt. ed. see Abbott, Graham.
Little, Geraldine C. Endless Waves.
Little, Gerry Paul. Come to Me Warmly.
Little, Henry. YHWH: Tetragrammaton.
Little, I. M. Aid to Africa.
Little Inc., et al. Corporate Director.
Little, J. M. The Gospel in the Last Days.
Little, J. Wesley, jt. auth. see Anderson, Jack A.
Little, James W. & Falace, Donald A. Dental Management of the Medically Compromised Patient.
Little, Jane. Philosopher's Stone.
Little, Jean. Mine for Keeps.
Little, Jeffrey B. & Rhodes, Lucien. Understanding Wall Street.
Little, John B., jt. auth. see Damiano, David B.
Little, Keith, jt. ed. see Robertson, Colin.
Little, Mary. ABC for the Library.
Little, Mary E. One, Two, Three for the Library.
Little, Mary L. A Woman in a World of Men: An Autobiography of a Farmer's Daughter.
Little, Meredith, jt. auth. see Foster, Steven.
Little, Paul E. How to Give Away Your Faith.

Authors

Little, R. John & Jones, C. Eugene. A Dictionary of Botany.
Little, Richard L. Welding & Welding Technology.
Little, Roger, tr. see Bleikasten, Andre.
Little, Royal. How to Lose One Hundred Million Dollars & Other Valuable Advice.
Little, Sara. Language of the Christian Community.
--Learning Together in the Christian Fellowship.
--Youth, World, & Church.
Little, Stuart W. & Cantor, Arthur. Playmakers.
Little, Wallace I. Transportation-Logistics Dictionary 1977.
Littleboy, Roger, tr. see Dal, Bjorn.
Littledale, Freya. Magic Fish.
Littledale, Freya & Littledale, Harold. Timothy's Forest.
Littledale, Harold, jt. auth. see Littledale, Freya.
Littlefair, Duncan E. The Glory Within You: Modern Man & the Spirit.
--Sin Comes of Age.
Littlefield, James E. & Kirkpatrick, C. A. Advertising: Mass Communication in Marketing.
Littlefield, Mark G. A Bibliographic Index to Romance Philology, Vols. 1-25.
Littlejohn, David. Architect: The Life & Work of Charles W. Moore.
Littlejohn, Nigel. The Intelligent Investor's Guide to IRAs & Keogh Plans.
Littlejohn, Stephen, jt. auth. see Jabusch, David M.
Littlejohn, Stephen W. Theories of Human Communication.
Littlepage, Layne. Murder-by-the-Sea.
Littlepage, Loyd. Why David Can.
Littler, Craig R. The Development of the Labour Process in Capitalist Societies.
Littleton, Taylor, ed. see Richardson, Alan, et al.
Littlewood, John, ed. see Pachman, Ludek.
Littlewood, John, tr. see Pachman, Ludek.
Littman, Connie. Practical Problems in Mathematics for Consumers.
Littman, Robert J. Greek Experiment: Imperialism & Social Conflict, 800-400 B. C. Barraclough, Geoffrey, ed.
Littner, Ner. Five More.
Littre. Dictionnaire de la Langue Francaise. Beaujean & Geraud-Venzac, eds.
Littre, Emile. Dictionnaire de La Langue Francaise.
Littwin, Susan. The Postponed Generation: Why America's Grown-Up Kids Are Growing Up Later. Golbitz, Pat, ed.
Litvak, Lawrence, et al. South Africa: Foreign Investment & Apartheid.
Litvan, Gyorgy, ed. see Szabo, Ervin.
Litvinoff, Barry, jt. auth. see Solomon, Flora.
Litvinov, Ivy, tr. see Pisemskii, Aleksei F.
Litwack, Georgia, jt. auth. see Avery, Mary E.
Litwack, Leon. The American Labor Movement.
Litwack, Leon, jt. auth. see Graham, Otis L., Jr.
Litwak, Robert & Jurado, Roy. Care of the Cardiac Surgical Patient.
Litwiniszyn, J. Stochastic Methods in Mechanics of Granular Bodies.
Litz, A. Walton, ed. see Emerson, O. B.
Litz, A. Walton, ed. see Grimes, Larry E.
Litz, Walton A., Jr. & Lipking, Lawrence I., eds. Modern Literary Criticism: Nineteen Hundred to Nineteen Seventy.
Liu, Aimee & Rottmamn, Meg. Shoe Time.
Liu, Alan P. Communications & National Integration in Communist China.
Liu, Bede, ed. Digital Filters & the Fast Fourier Transform.
Liu, Chung L. & Liu, J. W. Linear Systems Analysis.
Liu, H. Mei. Biology & Pathology of Nerve Growth.
Liu, J. W., jt. auth. see Liu, Chung L.
Liu, James J. The Interlingual Critic: Interpreting Chinese Poetry.
--Poetry of Li Shang-Yin, Ninth-Century Baroque Chinese Poet.
Liu, Joseph W., jt. auth. see George, Alan.
Liu, Wu-Chi & Yucheng Lo, Irving, eds. Sunflower Splendor.
Liu, Yu-Cheng, jt. auth. see Gibson, Glenn A.
Liubavskii, M. K. Obrazovanie Osnovnoi Gosudarstvennoi Territorii Velikorusskoi Narodnosti.
Live, Anna H. & Sandkowsky, Suzanne H. American Mosaic: Intermediate-Advanced ESL Reader.
Lively, Penelope. Boy Without a Name.
--Ghost of Thomas Kempe.
--Judgement Day.
Liverani, Giuseppe. Italian Ceramics. Charleston, Robert J., ed.
Livermore, Elaine. Find the Cat.
--Follow the Fox.
--Lost & Found.
--One to Ten, Count Again.
Livernash, E. Robert, jt. auth. see Foulkes, Fred K.
Liverpool Town Planning & Housing Exhibition Staff. Liverpool Town Planning & Housing Exhibition: Transactions of Conference Held March 9-13, 1914 at Liberty Buildings Liverpool. Adshead, S. D., et al, eds.
Livesay, Herbert B. The American Express Pocket Guide to Spain.
Livesley, R. K. Matrix Methods of Structural Analysis.
Livgren, Kerry & Boa, Kenneth. Seeds of Change.
Livingood, James W. A History of Hamilton County, Tennessee.
Livings, Henry. Honour & Offer.
--This Jockey Drives Late Nights.
Livingston, Bernard. Their Turf.
--Zoo: Animals, People, Places.
Livingston, Dennis, jt. auth. see Diwan, Romesh K.
Livingston, Dorothy M. The Master of Light: A Biography of Albert A. Michelson.
Livingston, G. Herbert. The Pentateuch in Its Cultural Environment.
Livingston, James C. Anatomy of the Sacred: An Introduction to Religion.
Livingston, Jane. Wisconsin Biennial, 1982.
Livingston, K. E. & Hornykiewicz, O., eds. Limbic Mechanisms: The Continuing Evolution of the Limbic System Concept.
Livingston, Marco. David Hockney.
Livingston, Myra C. A Circle of Seasons.
--A Learical Lexicon: A Magnificent Feast of Boshblobberbosh & Fun from the Works of Edward Lear.
--The Moon & a Star: And Other Poems.
--When You Are Alone It Keeps You Capone: An Approach to Creative Writing with Children.
--Wide Awake: And Other Poems.
Livingston, Myra C. & Blegvad, Erik. Happy Birthday.
--I'm Hiding.
Livingston, Myra C., ed. Listen, Children, Listen: An Anthology of Poems for the Very Young.
--One Little Room, an Everywhere.
--Speak Roughly to Your Little Boy: A Collection of Parodies & Burlesques.
--Tune Beyond Us: A Collection of Poetry.
--What a Wonderful Bird the Frog Are: An Assortment of Humorous Poetry-Verse.
Livingston, R. J., ed. Ecological Processes in Coastal & Marine Systems.
Livingstone, Angela, jt. ed. see Davie, Donald.
Livingstone, Dinah, tr. see Leclercq, Jacques.
Livingstone, I., jt. auth. see Ord, H. W.
Livingstone, Ian & Ord, H. W. Economics for Eastern Africa.
Livingstone, Marco. David Hockney Faces.
Livingstone, S. E. The Chemistry of Ruthenium, Rhodium, Palladium, Osmium, Iridium & Platinum.
Li Wei, jt. ed. see Tang Guang You.
Liyong, Taban L. Frantz Fanon's Uneven Ribs with Poems More & More.
Ljung, L., jt. ed. see Anderson, B. D.
Ljungmark, Lars. For Sale: Minnesota: Organized Promotion of Scandinavian Immigration, 1866-1873.
L. K. Tao, jt. auth. see Simon Yang.
Llano, George, ed. Adaptations Within Antarctic Ecosystems: Proceedings of the Third SCAR Symposium on Antarctic Biology.
Llano, Rodriguez de see De Llano, Rodriguez.
Llaurado, J. G., et al, eds. Biologic & Clinical Effects of Low-Frequency Magnetic & Electric Fields.
Lless, Andreas. Carl Orff.
Llewellyn, David T. International Financial Integration: The Limits of Sovereignty.
Llewellyn, Meyer. The Stray Cow.
Llewellyn, P. J., jt. auth. see Ratcliffe, N. A.
Llewellyn Publications Staff. Llewellyn's Sun Sign Book, Annual 1987. Buske, Terry, ed.
--Llewellyn's Sun Sign Book, 1985. Wood, Matthew, ed.
--Llewellyn's 1987: Astrological Calendar. Buske, Terry, ed.
--Llewellyn's 1987: Daily Planetary Guide & Astrologer's Date Book. Buske, Terry, ed.
--Llewellyn's 1987: Moon Sign Book. Buske, Terry, ed.
Llewellyn, Robert, jt. auth. see Griggs, Irwin.
Llewelyn, John. Beyond Metaphysics? The Hermeneutic Circle in Contemporary Continental Philosophy.
Llosa, Mario V. Contra Viento y Marea.
--The Green House.
Lloyd, jt. auth. see Phelps.
Lloyd, A. R. The Boy & the Otter.
Lloyd, Alan C., jt. auth. see Condon, Arnold.
Lloyd, Alan C., et al. Gregg Typing for Colleges: Intensive Course.
--Typing Power Drills.
Lloyd, Alan C., et al, eds. Typing Seventy Five: Basic.
Lloyd, Barbara, jt. auth. see Levitt, Michael.
Lloyd, Christopher. Nation & the Navy.
Lloyd, D. G. Modern Syllabus Algebra.
Lloyd, D. H. & Sellers, K. C., eds. Dermatophilus Infection in Animals & Man.
Lloyd, Dana. The Sex Cure.
Lloyd, David. Ball.
--Bathtime.
--Boots.
--Cat & Dog.
--Hello, Goodbye.
Lloyd, E. J., jt. ed. see Megaw, E. D.
Lloyd, Eva B. Annie: Herald of Home Missions.
Lloyd, Frances. Education of the Sub Normal Child.
Lloyd, Glenn T., ed. see University of Tennessee, 1979, Knoxville, Tenn. Staff.
Lloyd, H. The Legal Limits of Journalism.
Lloyd, H. Alan. Some Outstanding Clocks over Seven Hundred Years 1250-1950: 1250-1950.
Lloyd, Howell. The State, France, & the Sixteenth Century.
Lloyd, Janet, tr. see Garlan, Yvon.
Lloyd, John, jt. auth. see Hardie, Sean.
Lloyd, John B., jt. ed. see Beck, Felix.
Lloyd, Richard, jt. ed. see Davidson, John.
Lloyd, Richard G. The Bar Code Book.
Lloyd, Sarah. An Indian Attachment. Golbitz, Pat, ed.
Lloyd, Seton. The Archaeology of Mesopotamia: From the Old Stone Age to the Persian Conquest.
--Foundations in the Dust: The Story of Mesopotamian Exploration.
Lloyd, Tom. Dinosaur & Co. Studies in the Corporate Evolution.
Lloyd, Ward, jt. ed. see Klein, Dan.
Lloyd Evans, Barbara, jt. auth. see Lloyd Evans, Gareth.
Lloyd Evans, Gareth & Lloyd Evans, Barbara. The Shakespeare Companion.
Lloyd-Still, J. D. Malnutrition & Intellectual Development.
Llywelyn, Morgan. Bard: The Odyssey of the Irish.
--The Horse Goddess.
--The Wind from Hastings.
LM Ericson Telephone Company Staff, jt. auth. see Swedish Telecommunications Administration Staff.
Lo, Chun Nan see Klonglan, Gerald E. & Nan Lo, Chun.
Lo, Jung-Pang. K'ang Yu-Wei: A Biography & a Symposium.
Lo, Kenneth H. Quick & Easy Chinese Cooking.
Lo, Kuan-Chung. Romance of the Three Kingdoms. Brewitt-Taylor, C. H., tr.
Lo, R. E., ed. Earth Observation & Remote Sensing by Satellites: Proceedings of the Symposium on Earth Observation & Remote Sensing by Satellites, Hannover, West Germany, 21 May 1982.
Lo, Ruth E. & Kinderman, Katherine S. In the Eye of the Typhoon.
Lo, Sara de Mundo see De Mundo Lo, Sara.
Lo, Sara de Mundo, ed. Index to Spanish American Collective Biography: The Andean Countries.
Loach, Jennifer, jt. ed. see Tittler, Robert.
Load-Curve Coverage in Future Electrical Power Generating Systems Symposium Staff. Electrical Load-Curve Coverage: Proceedings of the Symposium, Rome, Oct. 1977. United Nations Economic Commission for Europe, ed.
Loban, Walter, et al. Teaching Language & Literature: Grades Seven to Twelve.
Lobb, Charlotte. Exploring Careers Through Part-Time & Summer Employment.
--Exploring Careers Through Volunteerism.
Lobb, M. O., jt. auth. see Beazley, J. M.
Lobb, Nancy. Basic Health.
Lobbenberg, Susan. Using Urban Wasteland: A Guide for Community Groups.
Lobel, Arnold. Gregory Griggs & Other Nursery Rhyme People.
--Ming Lo Moves the Mountain.
Lobel, Arnold, jt. auth. see Farber, Norma.
Lobel, J. Foiling the System Breakers: Computer Security & Access Control.
Lobel, Jules & Ratner, Michael. Is United States Military Intervention in Central America Illegal?
Lobel, Jules & Wolvovitz, Barbara. Statement before the House Committee on the Judiciary Subcommittee on Civil & Constitutional Rights, April 3, 1985.
Lobel, Leon & Lobel, Stanley. All about Meat. Krech, Inez M., ed.
--Meat.
Lobel, Stanley, jt. auth. see Lobel, Leon.
Lobell, Carl D., jt. auth. see Practising Law Institute Staff.
Lo Bello, Nino. European Detours: A Travel Guide to Unusual Sights.
LoBello, Susan, tr. see Derossi, Flavia.
LoBianco, Joseph R. What Happened to the Donkey After Christmas?
Lobinger, Fritz, jt. auth. see Hirmer, Oswald.
Lobiondo, et al. Nursing Research: Critical Appraisal & Utilization.
Lobitz, Walter C., Jr., jt. ed. see Montagna, William.
Lobley, Priscilla. Your Book of Patchwork.
Lobo, F. L., et al. Offshore Structures Engineering.
Lobos, Amilcar & Mellot, Leland. Quetzal. Castellon, Rolando & Perez, Carlos, eds.
Lobsenz, Norman M., jt. auth. see Lasswell, Marcia.
Lobstein, Tim, ed. Namibia: Reclaiming the People's Health.
Lobuglio, A. E. Clinical Immunotheraphy.
Locher-Ernst, L. Einfuehrung in die Freie Geometrie Ebener Kurven.
Lochhead, Liz. Blood & Ice.
Lochhead, Marion. Renaissance of Wonder: The Fantasy Worlds of J. R. R. Tolkein, C. S. Lewis, George MacDonald, E. Nesbit, & Others.
Lochman, Jan. Living Roots of Reformation.
Lochman, Jan M. Encountering Marx: Bonds & Barriers Between Christians & Marxists. Robertson, Edwin H., tr. from Ger.
--Reconciliation & Liberation: Challenging a One-Dimensional View of Salvation.
--Signposts to Freedom: The Ten Commandments of Christian Ethics. Lewis, David, tr.
--The Theology of Praise: The Kingdom, the Power, & the Glory.
Lochmoeller, Donald C. Industrial Development Handbook. Spink, Frank H., Jr., ed. Muncy, Dorothy A. & Thorne, Oakleigh H.
Lochner, W., et al. Internatioanl Nifedipine Adalat Symposium, 2nd.
Lochte, Dick. Sleeping Dog.
LoCicero, J. L., jt. ed. see Lawrence, V. B.
Lock, Andrew, ed. Action, Gesture & Symbol: The Emergence of Language.
Lock, Andrew & Fisher, Eunice, eds. Language Development.
Lock, D. Project Management.
Lock, D. S. Engineers' Metric Manual & Buyers' Guide.
Lock, Dennis & Farrow, Nigel, eds. Gower Handbook of Management.
Lockaby, George W. Sermon Outlines on the Person & Work of Christ.
Lockard, L. Desk Reference for Neuroanatomy: A Guide to Essential Terms.
Lockard, William K. Design Drawing.
--Drawing As a Means to Architecture.
Locke, Don. A Fantasy of Reason: The Life & Thought of William Godwin.
Locke, Don, jt. auth. see Weinreich-Haste, Helen.
Locke, Edwin A. A Guide to Effective Study.
Locke, Flora M., jt. auth. see Busche, Don.
Locke, John. An Essay Concerning Human Understanding.
--Locke's Essay Concerning Human Understanding.
Locke, Michael & Locke, Michael, eds. Cellular Membranes in Development.
--Control Mechanisms in Developmental Processes.
Locke, Michael, ed. see Society for the Study of Developmental Biology Staff.
Lockemann, Georg. Story of Chemistry.
Locker, A., ed. Biogenesis-Evolution-Homeostasis: A Symposium by Correspondence.
Locker, A., ed. see International Symposium Biologische Staff.
Locker, Alfred & Flemming, Kurt, eds. Radioprotection: Chemical Compounds - Biological Means.
Locker, David. Symptoms & Illness.
Lockerbie, D. Bruce. Asking Questions: A Classroom Model for Teaching the Bible.
Lockerbie, D. Bruce, jt. auth. see Bell, Robert W.
Lockerbie, Jeanette. Forgive, Forget & Be Free.
--Twenty-Four Women's Programs: Please Pass the Fruit.
Lockerbie, Jeanette, jt. auth. see Graham, Franklinn.
Lockerby, Robert W. District Heating.
Lockerman, George. Story of Chemistry.
Lockert, Lacy, tr. see Racine, Jean.
Lockhart, Bruce. Jan Masaryk.
Lockhart, Carol A., jt. auth. see Werther, William B.
Lockhart, Darrell C. Blueprint Reading for the Welding Trade.
Lockhart, Ian M., jt. ed. see Ellis, Gwynn P.
Lockhart, J. A. & Wiseman, A. J. Introduction to Crop Husbandry.
Lockhart, J. C. Redistribution Reactions.
Lockhart, James. The Men of Cajamarca: A Social & Biographical Study of the First Conquerors of Peru.
Lockhart, James, jt. ed. see Altman, Ida.
Lockhart, Terence. Housing Adaptations for Disabled People.
Lockhart, William B. & Kamisar, Yale. Constitutional Law, the American Constitution, Constitutional Rights & Liberties: 1986 Supplement.
Lockhart, William B., et al. Constitutional Law, American Constitution, Cases & Material on Constitutional Rights & Liberties Cases, Comments, Questions: 1984 Supplement.
--Constitutional Law: Cases-Comments-Questions.

--Constitutional Rights & Liberties Cases & Materials.

Lockhart, William E. Mathematics Response Sheets & Prescription Sheets.

--Mathematics Study Material: High School Equivalency-GED.

Lockheed, Marlaine E. Computer Literacy: Definition & Survey Items for Assessment in Schools.

Locklear, Edmond, Jr. Aids Package.

Lockley, R. M. The Private Life of the Rabbit.

Lockley, Ronald. Seal-Woman.

--Seal Woman.

Lockley, Ronald M. Whales, Dolphins, & Porpoises.

Lockmiller, David A. Sir William Blackstone.

Lockridge, Frances, jt. auth. see Lockridge, Richard.

Lockridge, Kenneth A. A New England Town: The First Hundred Years.

Lockridge, Preston J. Educational Displays & Exhibits.

Lockridge, Richard. A Plate of Red Herrings.

Lockridge, Richard & Lockridge, Frances. Death on an Aisle.

Lockridge, Ross, Jr. Raintree County.

--Raintree County.

Lockspeiser, Edward, jt. auth. see Blunt, Anthony.

Lockward, George, tr. see Elwood, Roger.

Lockwood, Charles. The Guide to Hollywood & Beverly Hills: The Best Driving Tours, Walks, Restaurants, Homes, Shopping, Sights & Architecture.

--Manhattan Moves Uptown: An Illustrated History.

Lockwood, Craig, ed. The Whole Ocean Catalog.

Lockwood, David G. Introduction to Stratificational Linguistics.

Lockwood, Guy. Raising & Caring for Animals, a Handbook of Animal Husbandry & Veterinary Care.

Lockwood, Lewis, ed. see Palestrina, Giovani Pierluigi da.

Lockwood, Tim. Motorcycle Repair Encyclopedia. Robinson, Jeff, ed.

Lockyear, Fredick E. Iran.

Lockyer, Herbert. All the Divine Names & Titles in the Bible.

--Daily Promises.

--Sins of Saints.

Lode, H., et al, eds. Cefotetan: A Long-Acting Antibiotic.

Loder, James E. The Transforming Moment: Understanding Convictional Experiences.

Lodge, Arthur S. Body Tensor Fields in Continuum Mechanics.

Lodge, David. The British Museum Is Falling Down.

--The Language of Fiction.

--Small World.

--Working with Structuralism: Essays & Reviews on Nineteenth & Twentieth Century Literature.

Lodge, Don. Radio Control Model Helicopter Handbook.

Lodge, Henry C. As It Was: An Inside View of Politics & Power in the Fifties & Sixties.

Lodge, James P., Jr., ed. The Smoke of London: Two Prophecies. Incl. Fumifugium or, The Inconvience of the Aer-Smoake of London Dissipated. Evelyn, John; The Doom of London. Barr, Robert. Pergamon.

Lodge, Ken. Studies in the Phonology of Colloquial English.

Lodge, Thomas. Complete Works of Thomas Lodge: 1580-1623.

Lodhi, M. A., ed. see International Symposium on Superheavy Elements, March 9-11, 1978, Lubbock, Texas.

Loeb, Anthony, ed. Filmmakers in Conversation.

Loeb, Ben F., compiled by. Materials Relating to Legal Aspects of Dental Practice.

Loeb, Ben F., Jr., annotations by. Motor Vehicle Law.

Loeb, Catherine, jt. auth. see Stineman, Esther.

Loeb, D., et al, eds. A Dream Compels Us: Voices of Salvadoran Women.

Loeb, Gerald M. Battle for Investment Survival.

Loeb, Jeffrey, jt. auth. see Arnold, Eric H.

Loeb, Jo & Loeb, Paul. You Can Train Your Cat.

Loeb, Leonard B. Static Electrification.

Loeb, Lester. Better Photography.

Loeb, Louis E. From Descartes to Hume: Continental Metaphysics & the Development of Modern Philosophy.

Loeb, M. H., ed. see Summer School in Logic, Leeds, 1967.

Loeb, Marshall. Marshall Loeb's Money Guide 1986.

--Marshall Loeb's 1987 Money Guide.

--Marshall Loeb's 1988 Money Guide.

Loeb, Paul, jt. auth. see Loeb, Jo.

Loeb, Robert H., Jr. Marriage: For Better or for Worse?

Loeb, Ronald M., jt. auth. see Katz, Melvin.

Loebenstein, E. International Mutual Assistance in Administrative Matters.

Loebl, Eugen. My Mind on Trial.

--My Mind on Trial.

Loeckx, J. Computability & Decidability.

Loeckx, J., ed. see Colloquium on Automata, Languages & Programming, 2nd, University of Saarbrucken, 1974.

Loeffke, Bernard, jt. ed. see Cheston, Stephen T.

Loehr, Raymond. Agricultural Waste Management.

Loeks, Mary F. Good Morning, Lord: Devotions for Young Mothers.

Loelhoeffel, Dieter von see Von Loelhoeffel, Dieter & Schimanke, Dieter.

Loen, R. O. Manage More by Doing Less.

Loengard, John. Pictures under Discussion.

Loening, K. L., ed. List of Standard Abbreviations, (Symbols) for Synthetic Polymers & Polymeric Materials: Basic Definitions of Terms Relating to Polymers.

--Nomenclature of Regular Single-Strand Organic Polymers.

Loening, Sarah L. Joan of Arc.

Loeper, John J. The Flying Machine: A Stagecoach Journey in 1774.

--Galloping Gertrude.

--The Golden Dragon: By Clipper Ship Around the Horn.

--Mr. Marley's Main Street Confectionery.

--The Shop on High Street: Toys & Games of Early America.

Loero, Guido. Boundary Conditions & Global Management.

Loertscher, David V. A School Library Media Center Taxonomy.

Loertscher, David V., jt. auth. see Roper, Paul M.

Loesch, Larry C. & Wheeler, Paul T. Principles of Leisure Counseling. Sorenson, Don L., ed.

Loescher, Ann D., jt. auth. see Loescher, Gil.

Loescher, Gil & Loescher, Ann D. China: Pushing Toward the Year Two Thousand.

--The Chinese Way: Life in the People's Republic of China.

--The World's Refugees: A Test of Humanity.

Loeschke, H. H., ed. Acid Base Homeostasis of the Brain Extracellular Fluid & the Respiratory Control System.

Loesser, Arthur. Humor in American Song.

Loest, Erich. The Monument.

Loether & McTavish. Descriptive & Inferential Statics: An Introduction.

Loetscher, Lefferts A. A Brief History of the Presbyterians.

--Problem of Christian Unity in Early 19th Century America. Wolf, Richard C., ed.

Loevi, Francis J., Jr. & Kaplan, Roger P. Arbitration & the Federal Sector Advocate: A Practical Guide.

Loewe, Michael. Chinese Ideas of Life & Death.

Loewenberg, Bert J. Darwinism Comes to America: 1859-1900. Wolf, Richard C., ed.

Loewenberg, Frank & Dolgoff, Ralph. Teaching of Practice Skills in Undergraduate Programs in Social Welfare & Other Helping Services.

Loewenberg, Frank M. & Dolgoff, Ralph. Ethical Decisions for Social Work Practice.

Loewenberg, Jacob. Hegel's Phenomenology: Dialogues on the Life of Mind.

--Reason & the Nature of Things.

Loewenfeld, Claire. Herb Gardening.

Loewenfeld, Claire & Back, Philippa. The Complete Book of Herbs & Spices.

--The Complete Book of Herbs & Spices.

Loewenich, Walter von see Von Loewenich, Walter.

Loewus, Frank, ed. see American Chemical Society Staff.

Loewy, Herta. The Retarded Child.

--Training the Backwards Child.

Loewy, Raymond. Industrial Design.

Lof, H. Water Use Efficiency & Competition Between Arid Zone Annuals, Especially the Grasses Phalaris Minor & Hordeum Murinum.

Loffler, Ernst. Papua New Guinea.

Lofland, John & Fink, Michael. Symbolic Sit-Ins: Protest Occupations at the California Capitol.

Lofquist, Lloyd, jt. auth. see Dawis, Rene V.

Lofquist, Lloyd H., jt. auth. see Davis, Rene V.

Loft, Abram. Violin & Keyboard: The Duo Repertoire. Incl. Vol. 1. From the Seventeenth Century to Mozart; Vol. 2. From Beethoven to the Present. Penguin USA.

Lofthouse, William F. Israel after the Exile: Sixth & Fifth Centuries B. C.

Loftin, Jack. Archer County History.

Lofts, Norah. The Old Priory.

Lofts, Pamela, retold by. & illus. How the Birds Got Their Colors.

Loftus, David J. Boston College High School: 1863-1983.

Lo Fu-Chen & Salih, K., eds. Growth Pole Strategy & Regional Development Policy: Asian Experiences & Alternative Approaches.

Logan, Arthur L. Remembering Made Easy.

Logan, Ben. The Land Remembers.

Logan, Christopher. So Grand.

Logan, Dan P., Sr. Do You Want Me to Do All That & Plow Too?

Logan, Gerald E. German Conversational Practice.

Logan, Gerald E. & Braswell, David. Hallo Deutschland!

Logan, James K. & Martin, Alson R. Kansas Corporation Law & Practice.

Logan, Jane. The Very Nearest Room.

Logan, Jo. The Prediction Book of Palmistry.

Logan, Jo, ed. see Montalban, Madeline.

Logan, Margaret. Happy Endings.

Logan, Muriel B. & Crumpacker, Emily. Dining In - Portland.

Logan, Tom, jt. auth. see Schostak, John F.

Logan, William H. Pedlar's Pack of Ballads & Songs.

Logan, William S. The Gentrification of Inner Melbourne: A Political Geography of Inner City Housing.

Loghry, Lizabeth. An Uncertain Chime.

Logic Conference Staff. Proceedings of the Logic Conference, Kiel, 1974. Muller, G. H., et al, eds.

Logica, Ltd. Staff. Introducing Communications Protocols.

Logie, K. Structures: Basic Theory with Worked Examples.

Logsdail, D. H. & Mills, A. L., eds. Solvent Extraction & Ion Exchange in the Nuclear Fuel Cycle.

Logsdon, Gene. Last Days of the Farmer: A Personal Account.

Logsdon, John M. The Decision to Go to the Moon: Project Apollo & the National Interest.

Logsdon, Thomas. Computers & Social Controversy.

Logue, Christopher, compiled by. The Children's Book of Comic Verse.

Logue, John. Boats Against the Current.

--Replay: Murder.

Logue, Patrick E. Understanding & Living with Brain Damage.

Logue, R. Bruce, jt. ed. see Hurst, J. Willis.

Logunov, A. A., ed. Gravitation & Elementary Particle Physics. Ilyushchenko, Valerii, tr.

Loh, Stan. Start & Run a Profitable Video Stores: A Complete Step-by-Step Business Plan.

Loh, W. H. Jet, Rocket, Nuclear, Ion & Electric Propulsion.

Lohff, Wenzel, jt. ed. see Spitz, Lewis W.

Lohkamp, Nicholas. Living the Good News: An Introduction to Moral Theology.

Lohmann, Hartwig. I Can Tell You Anything, God. Hjelm, Ingalill H., tr. from Ger.

Lohmuller, Keith. Introduction to Business Programming & Systems Analysis.

Lohner, Edgar & Hannum, H. G. Modern German Drama.

Lohner, Edgar, jt. ed. see Foulkes, A. Peter.

Lohnes, Paul R., jt. auth. see Ackerman, Winona B.

Lohr, Charles H. St. Thomas Aquinas: Scriptum Super Sententiis - An Index of Authorities Cited.

Lohre, Heinrich. Von Percy Zum Wunderhorn: Beitraege Zur Geschichte der Wolksliedforschung in Deutschland.

Lohrer, Alice, ed. The School Library Materials Center: Its Resources & Their Utilization.

Lohse, Eduard. The First Christians: Their Beginnings, Writings, & Beliefs.

Lohsen, J. G. Weep Not for Anger: A Novel of a Slavic-American Family in New England.

Loi, Lee A. Tomiki Aikido: Book One: Randori.

Loiseau, Maurice, jt. auth. see Miller, J. Dale.

Loisy, Alfred. The Gospel & the Church. Home, Christopher, tr. from Ger.

Lojda, Z., et al. Enzyme Histochemistry: A Laboratory Manual.

Loken, Newt. Cheerleading.

Loken, Palmer, tr. see Lunde, Johan.

Lomas, Gillian, jt. ed. see Reed, John.

Lomask, Martha. Pancakes, Crepes & Waffles.

--Pizzas, Hamburgers & Relishes.

Lomasney, Eileen. Timmy Greenthumb.

Lomax & Schonbaum. Body Temperature: Regulation, Drug Effects, & Theraputic Implications.

Lomax, Alan. Hard Hitting Songs for Hard-Hit People.

--The Penguin Book of American Folk Songs.

Lomax, J. D., ed. see National Computing Centre, Ltd. Staff.

Lomax, John, III. Nashville: Music City, U. S. A.

Lomax, Joseph F., ed. see Bright, Susan.

Lomax, W. R. & Saul, A. J. Laboratory Work in Hydraulics.

Lombardi, Estelle J., jt. auth. see Lombardi, Thomas P.

Lombardi, John R., jt. ed. see Garetz, Bruce A.

Lombardi, John V. Venezuelan History: A Comprehensive Bibliography.

Lombardi, Thomas P. Career Adaptive Behavior Inventory Complete Battery.

Lombardi, Thomas P. & Lombardi, Estelle J. ITPA: Clinical Interpretation & Remediation.

Lombardo, Frank, jt. auth. see Schroeder, Donald.

Lombardo, Frank A., jt. auth. see Schroeder, Donald J.

Lombrosso, Caesar. Female Offender.

Lominadze, D. G. Cyclotron Waves in Plasma. Hamberger, S. M., ed. Dellis, A. N., tr.

Lomnitz, C. & Rosenblueth, E. Seismic Risk & Engineering Decisions.

Lomo, A., jt. ed. see Douglas, J. M.

London, A. L., jt. auth. see Kays, William M.

London, A. L., jt. auth. see Shah, Ramesh.

London, Barbara. A Short Course in Minolta Photography.

--A Short Course in Photography.

London College of Furniture Staff & Hutchins, Victor. The Woodworker's Handbook: A Complete Course for Craftsmen, Do-It-Yourselfers & Hobbyists.

London, Hannah R. Miniatures & Silhouettes of Early American Jews.

London, Jack. Before Adam.

--Burning Daylight.

--Call of the Wild. Bd. with White Fang. RD Assn.

--The Call of the Wild & White Fang.

--The Dream of Debs, Together with An Account of the San Francisco Cooks & Waiters Strike.

--Jack London Stories.

--Jack London's Klondike Tales.

--Love of Life.

--Martin Eden.

--The Son of the Wolf.

--War of the Classes.

--White Fang.

London, Keith. Introduction to Computers.

London, Kurt. Seven Soviet Arts.

London, Laura. A Heart Too Proud.

London, Mark, jt. auth. see Kelly, Brian.

London Mathematical Society Instructional Conference Staff. Finite Simple Groups: Proceedings. Powell, M. B. & Higman, G., eds.

London, Mel. The Bread Winners' Cookbook.

London Missionary Society Staff. London Missionary Society's Report of the Proceedings Against the Late Rev. J. Smith of Demerara, Who Was Tried Under Martial Law & Condemned to Death, on a Charge of Aiding & Assisting in a Rebellion of Negro Slaves.

London Netsuke Committee. Contrasting Styles: A Catalogue of the Exhibition of Netsuke & Kizeruzutsu from Private English Collections.

London, P. S., jt. auth. see Tubbs, N.

London - St. Paul's Cathedral Staff. Domesday of Saint Paul of the Year Twelve Twenty-Two.

--Visitations of Churches Belonging to St. Paul's Cathedral in 1297 & 1458.

London, Sheryl. Eggplant & Squash.

London Stationers' Company Staff. An Analytical Index to the Ballad-Entries (1557-1709) in the Registers of the Company of Stationers of London.

--An Analytical Index to the Ballad-Entries, 1557-1709, in the Register of the Company of Stationers London.

London Stock Exchange Staff. International Stock Exchange Official Yearbook 1987-88.

--The Stock Exchange Official Yearbook 1985-1986.

--The Stock Exchange Official Yearbook, 1986-87.

Lonergan, Bernard. Insight.

--The Way to Nicea: The Dialectical Development of Trinitarian Theology.

Lonergan, Bernard J. Philosophy of God, & Theology.

--A Second Collection.

Loney, Glenn & Epstein, Laurence. Your Future in the Performing Arts.

Loney, Glenn M., jt. ed. see Corrigan, Robert W.

Long. Current Therapy in Neurological Surgery, 1985-1986.

Long & Reim. The American Forecaster, 1986.

Long, Andrew F. & Harrison, Stephen, eds. Health Services Performance: Effectiveness & Efficiency.

Long Ashton Research Station Symposium Staff. Fungal Pathogenicity & the Plant's Response: Proceedings of the Long Ashton Research Station Symposium, University of Bristol, September 1971. Byrde, R. J. & Cutting, C. V, eds.

Long Ashton Symposium - Fourth, University of Bristol, September, 1974. Lactic Acid Bacteria in Beverages & Food: Proceedings. Carr, J. G., et al, eds.

Long, Barry. The Origins of Man & the Universe: The Myth That Came to Life.

Long, Basil. British Miniaturists. 1520-1860.

Long, Burke O., jt. ed. see Coats, George W.

Long, Chalmers G., Jr., jt. auth. see Dubin, Fred S.

Long, Charles. The Backyard Stonebuilder: Fourteen Projects for the Weekend Mason.

--How to Survive Without a Salary.

Long, Charles H., ed. Anglican Cycle of Prayer, 1988.

Long, D. T., jt. ed. see Angino, E. D.

Long, Dani, ed. see Morton, Gene.

Long, Frank, ed. The Political Economy of EEC Relations with African, Caribbean & Pacific States: Contributions to the Understanding of the Lome Convention on North-South Relations.

Long, Frank B. Rim of the Unknown.

Long, Franklin A. & Reppy, Judith, eds. The Genesis of New Weapons: Decision Making for Military R&D.
Long, G., jt. auth. see Dawson, J. K.
Long, Huey & Jarvis, Peter. New Perspectives on the Education of Adults in the United States: International Perspectives on Adult & Continuing Education.
Long, J., et al, trs. see Raspe, G.
Long, James D., jt. auth. see Williams, Robert L.
Long, Jeff. Outlaw: The Saga of Claude Dallas.
Long, John. Modern Russia.
Long, John H., jt. auth. see Smith Center for the History of Cartography Staff.
Long, John L. Introduced Birds of the World.
Long, John V., jt. auth. see Green, Samuel.
Long, Kate. Johnny's Such a Bright Boy, What a Shame He's Retarded.
Long, Kim. The American Forecaster Nineteen Eighty-Eight: The First No-Nonsense Authority on the Future.
Long, Kim, jt. auth. see Reim, Terry.
Long, Larry A. The Gentle Tyrant.
Long, Leslie, et al. Design Mix Manual for Concrete Construction. Allen-Browne, Patricia, ed.
Long, Lucy, et al. Food Products Formulary, Vol. 1: Meats, Poultry, Fish & Shellfish.
Long, Lyda B. Crucible of Evil.
Long, Lynette & Long, Thomas. The Handbook for Latchkey Children & Their Parents: A Complete Guide for Latchkey Kids & Their Working Parents.
Long, Marguerite. At the Piano with Faure.
Long, Marvin R. God's Works Through Elvis.
Long, Orma F. Eskimo Legends & Other Stories of Alaska.
Long, Patricia. The Nutritional Ages of Women: A Lifetime Guide to Eating Right for Health, Beauty, & Well-Being.
Long, Paul. All the Answers to All Your Questions About Training Pointing Dogs.
Long, Paul B. The Man in the Leather Hat.
Long, Peter, tr. see Frege, Gottlob.
Long, Raphael. Red Car Days: Pacific Electric Memories. Walker, Jim, ed.
Long, Rosemary. Systematic Nursing Care.
Long, S. P. & Mason, C. F. Saltmarsh Ecology.
Long, Thomas, jt. auth. see Long, Lynette.
Long, William G. Asses vs. Jackasses.
Long, William S. The Colonists.
--The Exiles.
--The Goldseekers.
--The Settlers.
--The Traitors.
Longacre, Robert E. Joseph: A Story of Divine Providence: A Text Theoretical & Textlinguistic Analysis of Gensis 37 & 39-48.
Longenecker, Martha, commentary by. Ikat of India.
--Serizawa: A Living Treasure of Japan.
Longest, Beaufort B., Jr. Principles of Hospital Business Office Management.
Longest, George C., ed. Three Virginia Writers: A Reference Guide.
Longfellow, Henry Wadsworth. Evangeline.
Longford, Elizabeth. The Queen Mother.
Longhurst, Thomas M., ed. Functional Language Intervention.
Longland, Stella, jt. auth. see Osborn, Marijane.
Longley, Dennis & Shain, Michael, eds. Dictionary of Information Technology.
Longley, Edna, ed. see Thomas, Edward.
Longman, David, ed. The Instant Guide to Healthy Cacti.
--The Instant Guide to Healthy Flowering Houseplants.
--The Instant Guide to Healthy Flowering Houseplants.
--The Instant Guide to Healthy Foliage Houseplants.
--The Instant Guide to Healthy Foliage Houseplants.
--The Instant Guide to Healthy Indoor Bulbs & Annuals.
--The Instant Guide to Healthy Palms & Ferns.
--The Instant Guide to Healthy Succulents.
Longman, Debbie, jt. auth. see Atkinson, Rhonda H.
Longman, Francis, tr. from Rus. Zionism: Enemy of Peace & Social Progress Issues.
Longman, Harold. The Fox in the Ball Park.
Longman, Jan & Woerdeman, M. W. Atlas of Medical Anatomy.
Longman, Kenneth A. Advertising.
Longman, Lester D. & Maurice, Bloch. Joyce Treiman. Solomon, Denise, ed.
Longman, Phillip. Born to Pay: The New Politics of Aging in America.
Longmate, Elizabeth & Reeves, Marjorie. Children at Work, Eighteen Thirty to Eighteen Eighty-Five.
Longmeyer, Carole M. The Best of the Outer Banks.
--The Lost Colony Colorbook.
--The Lost Colony Cookbook.
--The Lost Colony Garden Book.
Longmore, Jane. Humpty Dumpty & Other Favorite Nursery Rhymes.
Longmore, Jane, illus. Jack & Jill & Other Nursery Rhymes.
Longnecker, Nancy, ed. see Bonge, Dusti.
Longo, G., ed. Coding & Complexity.
Longo, G., ed. see CISM (International Center for Mechanical Sciences), Department of Automation & Information Staff.
Longo, Stephen A. Introduction to DECsystem 20 Assembly Programming.
Longstaff, Thomas R. W., jt. auth. see Tyson, Joseph B.
Longstreet, Augustus. Georgia Scenes, Characters, Incidents, &c., in the First Half Century of the Republic.
Longstreet, Stephen. The Canvas Falcons.
--The Kingston Fortune.
--Pedlock & Sons.
--Real Jazz, Old & New.
--She Walks in Beauty.
Longsworth, Polly. Austin & Mabel: The Amherst Affair & Love Letters of Austin Dickinson & Mabel Loomis Todd.
Longtin, Ray C. Three Writers of the Far West: A Reference Guide.
Longueville, Thomas de. The Life of a Prig. Wolff, Robert L., ed.
Longyear, Barry B. Sea of Glass.
Loniello, Mariann, et al. The Job Game: A Career Handbook.
Lonigan, Paul R. The Early Irish Church: From the Beginnings to the Two Doves.
--Early Irish Church: From the Beginnings to the Two Doves.
Lonner, W., ed. see International Conference of Selected Papers Staff.
Lonnetto, Richard & Kumchy, Gayle. Back to Normal: Living Your Life to Prevent Back Pain.
Lonnroth, Mans & Steen, Peter. Energy in Transition: A Report on Energy Policy & Future Options.
Lonnroth, Mans, jt. auth. see Walker, William.
Lonsdale, Richard E. & Seyler, H. L., eds. Nonmetropolitan Industrialization.
Lonsdale, Roger, ed. see Gray, Thomas.
Lonsted, K., ed. Algebraic Geometry: Proceedings: Summer Meeting, Copenhagen, August 7-12, 1978.
Loo, F. T., ed. Failure Prevention & Reliability, 1981.
Loo, Shirley, ed. Management by Design: Library Management.
Loogen, F. & Seipel, L., eds. Detection of Ischaemic Myocardium with Exercise: Symposium.
Loogen, Franz, jt. ed. see Breithardt, Gunter.
Loomba, jt. auth. see Turban.
Loomba, N. Paul, jt. ed. see Turban, Efraim.
Loomie, Albert J. The Spanish Elizabethans: The English Exiles at the Court of Philip II.
Loomis. Paris in Your Pocket.
Loomis, Burdett, jt. auth. see Cigler, Allan.
Loomis, Evarts G. & Paulson, Sig. Healing for Everyone.
Loomis, Kristin S., et al, eds. National Directory of Addresses & Telephone Numbers.
Loomis, Louise R., tr. Book of the Popes.
Loomis, Noel M. & Nasatir, Abraham P. Pedro Vial & the Roads to Santa Fe.
Loomis, Roger S. Development of Arthurian Romance.
Loomis, Stanley. Paris in the Terror.
Loomis, William F. Dictyostelium Discoideum: A Developmental System.
Loon, Hendrick W. Van see Van Loon, Hendrik W.
Loon, Hendrik W. van see Van Loon, Hendrik W.
Loon, Hendrik W. Van see Van Loon, Hendrik W.
Looney, Jackie N., jt. auth. see Britton, Susan M.
Looney, Martin. Community Against Government: The British Community Development Project 1968-78.
Looney, Robert E. Saudi Arabia's Development Potential: Application of an Islamic Growth Model.
Loos, Anita. Fate Keeps on Happening: Adventures of Lorelei Lee & Other Writings. Corsini, Ray P., ed.
--Gentlemen Prefer Blondes.
Loos, Anita, jt. auth. see Hayes, Helen.
Loos, Bob. The Way Grampa Tells Stories.
Loos, H. Van Der see Molliver, M. E. & Van Der Loos, H.
Loos, M., ed. Bacteria & Complement.
Loos, M., et al, eds. Molecular Mechanisms of Complement.
Loose, Gert. Towards a Cross-National Model for Cooperation in Vocational Education: Implications for Research & Development.
Loose, Helmut. The Macmillan Book of Berry Gardening.
Loose, K. E. & Van Dongen, R. J. A. M., eds. Atlas of Angiography.
Loose, S. & Ramb, R. Southeast Asia Handbook: Singapore, Burma, Brunei, Borneo, Malaysia, Thailand.
Loose, Warren. Bodie Bonanza: The True Story of a Flamboyant Past.
Lopata, P. Communism as a Social Formation.
Lopata, P., jt. auth. see Gelbuch, F.
Lopate, Phillip. Bachelorhood: Tales of the Metropolis.
Lopategui, Maren. Salads & Summer Dishes.
Lopategui, Miren, jt. auth. see Jackson, Felicity.
Lope de Vega. The Knight of Olmedo (El Caballero de Olmedo) The Spanish Text with a Facing English Translation. King, Willard F., tr.
Lopez, Agustin. Taming of a Dream.
Lopez, Anthony, intro. by. A Complete Course in Canning.
Lopez, Barry H. Winter Count.
Lopez, Claude-Anne. Benjamin Franklin's "Good House"
Lopez, Claude-Anne & Herbert, Eugenia W. The Private Franklin: The Man & His Family.
Lopez, Felix M. Personnel Interviewing: The Working Woman's Resource Book.
Lopez, R. A. & Moser, C. L., eds. Rods, Bundles & Stiches: A Century of Southern California Indian Basketry.
Lopez, Robert S. & Raymond, Irving W., eds. Medieval Trade in the Mediterranean World: Illustrative Documents.
Lopez, Tomas. Chicano, Go Home! The Life of Alfonso Rodriguez.
Lopez-Gonzaga, Violeta. Peasants in the Hills.
Lopez-Reyes, Ramon R. Power & Immortality.
Lopinot, N. H., et al. Archaeological Investigations at the Kingfish Site, St. Clair County, Illinois.
Lopshire, Robert. The Beginner Book of Things to Make.
Loram, Ian & Phelps, Leland, eds. Aus Unserer Zeit.
Lorant, Stefan. Pittsburgh: The Story of an American City.
Lorant, Terry, jt. auth. see Carroll, Jon.
Lorant, Tessa. Hand & Machine Knitting.
Loranth, Alice N., ed. Catalog of Folklore, Folklife & Folk Songs.
Lorayne, H. The Magic Book: A Beginner's Guide to Anytime, Anywhere, Sleight-of-Hand Magic.
Lorayne, Harry, jt. auth. see Lucas, Jerry.
Lorch, Robert S. Colorado's Government.
Lorch, Walter. Handbook of Water Purification.
Lord, Albert B. The Singer of Tales.
Lord, Bette B., as told to see Sansan.
Lord, Daniel A. Played by Ear.
Lord, Eda. Matter of Choosing.
Lord, Ernest E. Shrubs & Trees for Australian Gardens.
Lord, Francis E., jt. auth. see Kirk, Samuel A.
Lord, Frederic M. & Novick, Melvin R. Statistical Theories of Mental Test Scores.
Lord, George D., ed. Andrew Marvell: Complete Poetry.
Lord, Harold W., et al. Noise Control for Engineers.
Lord, Harvey G. Programming for Real.
Lord, James. Giacometti: A Biography.
Lord, Kenniston, Jr. Using Apple Business Computer.
Lord, Kenniston W. The Data Center Disaster Consultant.
Lord, Kenniston W., Jr. ACP Review Manual: Foundations of an Information System Career.
--Graphics with the IBM PC.
--Using the Compaq Portable Computer.
--Using the Eagle PC & 1600 Series.
--Using the IBM PCjr Personal Computer.
--Using the IBM Personal Computer.
--Using the Kaypro II Personal Computer.
--Using the Osborne Personal Computer.
--Using the Radio Shack TRS-80 in Your Home.
--Using the TI Professional Personal Computer.
Lord, Kenniston W., Jr. & Jones, Delbert S. The Dynamics of Symphony.
Lord, Kenniston W., Jr. & Steiner, James B. CDP Review Manual: A Data Processing Handbook.
Lord, Melvene De see De Lord, Melvene.
Lord, Peter. The Nine Hundred Fifty-Nine Plan.
Lord, Richard A. Complete Preparation for the Multi-State Bar Examination.
Lord, Robert. Russian Literature: An Introduction.
Lord, Tom. Ash Tallman, the Wages of Sin: No. 3.
--Crossfire.
--The Highbinders.
Lord, Walter. The Dawn's Early Light.
--Day of Infamy.
--Night to Remember.
Lordahl, Daniel S. Modern Statistics for Behavioral Sciences.
Lordahl, Jo Ann. Argentine Journal.
Lorde, Audre. Coal.
Lord Horder. Fifty Years of Medicine.
Lord Montague. Jaguar.
Lord Russell. The Source of the Swastika.
Loree, Sharron. The Sunshine Family & the Pony.
Lorenz, Bob. Fifty Best of Baltimore & Ohio Railroad.
Lorenz, Ed B. Jesus: A Biography.
Lorenz, J. D. Jerry Brown: Man on the White Horse.
Lorenz, Konrad. Behind the Mirror: A Search for a Natural History of Human Knowledge. Taylor, Ronald, tr.
--Evolution & Modification of Behavior.
--The Foundations of Ethology.
--On Aggression. Wilson, Marjorie K., tr.
--The Year of the Greylag Goose. Wolff, Helen, ed. Martin, Robert, tr.
Lorenz, Lee. Big Gus & Little Gus.
Lorenz, Oscar A. & Maynard, Donald N. Knott's Handbook for Vegetable Growers.
Lorenz, Rita, jt. auth. see Adolph, L.
Lorenzen, Evelyn J., ed. Dietary Guidelines.
Lorenzini, Carlo see Collodi, C., pseud.
Lorenzini, Jean. Medical Phrase Index.
Lorge, Irving, jt. auth. see Thorndike, Edward L.
Lorian, Nicole. A Birthday Present for Mama.
Lorie, James & Brealy, Richard. Modern Developments in Investment Management.
Lorig, Kate & Fries, James F. Arthritis Helpbook: What You Can Do for Your Arthritis.
Lorimer, David. Survival: Body, Mind & Death in the Light of Psychic Experience.
Lorimer, Larry. The Simon & Schuster United States Question & Answer Book.
Lorin, Amii. Breeze off the Ocean.
--Come Home to Love.
Lorin, Martin I. The Febrile Child: Clinical Management of Fever & Other Types of Pyrexia.
--The Parents' Book of Physical Fitness for Children.
Loring, Gloria. Kids, Food, & Diabetes: A Book of Recipes, Menus, & Practical Advice.
--Kids, Food & Diabetes: A Book of Recipes, Menues, & Practical Advice.
Loring, John & Acton, David. Jones Road Print Shop & Stable 1971-1981: A Catalogue Raisonne. Myers, Trent, ed.
Loring, Marion. A Christian View of Economics.
Loring, Rosalind K. & Otto, Herbert A. New Life Options.
Loring, Roy J. & Kerzner, Harold. Proposal Preparation & Management Handbook.
Loring, Trevor. Million Dollar Burn.
Lornell, R. & Schaller, D. A. Wind Energy & Small Power Production.
Lorrain, Paul, et al. Electromagnetic Fields & Waves.
Lorrimer, Claire. Frost in the Sun.
--Last Year's Nightingale.
--The Secret of Quarry House.
--The Shadow Falls.
--A Voice in the Dark.
--The Wildering.
Lorwin, Madge. Dining with William Shakespeare.
Los Alamos Historical Society Staff. Los Alamos: The First Forty Years. Lyon, Fern & Evans, Jacob, eds.
Los Altos Writers Roundtable Staff. Borrowed Water: A Book of American Haiku.
Los Angeles County Museum of Art Curatorial Staff. Los Angeles County Museum of Art Report, July 1, 1977-June 30, 1979.
Los Angeles County Museum of Art Staff. Los Angeles County Museum of Art Report, July 1, 1981-June 30, 1983.
Los Angeles Police Department Staff. Daily Training Bulletin of the Los Angeles Police Department: Consisting of Bulletins 1-173. Parker, W. H., ed.
--Daily Training Bulletin of the Los Angeles Police Department: Consisting of Bulletins from Vols. II, III, IV. Parker, W. H., ed.
Los Angeles Public Library Staff. Catalog of the Police Library of the Los Angeles Public Library.
Los Angeles Times Food Staff. The Los Angeles Times California Cookbook.
Los Angeles Times Sports Staff. The Los Angeles Times Book of the 1984 Olympic Games. Dwyre, Bill, ed.
Lose, M. Phyllis & Mannix, Daniel. No Job for a Lady.
Loshin, Ronald S. & McCathren, Randall R. Essentials of Bank Consumer Leasing.
--Essentials of Consumer Vehicle Leasing.
Loshor, J. K., tr. see Ilyushin, A. A. & Lenskii, V. S.
Losoncy, Larry. When Your Child Needs a Hug.
Losowsky, M. S. & Heatley, R. V., eds. Gut Defences in Clinical Practice.
Lossing, Benson J. Pictorial Field-Book of the Revolution or, Illustrations, by Pen & Pencil, of the History, Biography, Scenery, Relics, & Traditions of the War for Independence.
Loth, Wilfried. The Division of the World, Nineteen Forty-One to Nineteen Fifty-Five. Krojzlova, Clare, tr. from Ger.
Lothian, Elizabeth. Devonshire Flavour: A Devonshire Treasury of Recipes & Personal Notes.
Lothrop, Gloria, ed. see Mengarini, Gregory.
Lothrop, Harriet M. see Sidney, Margaret.
Lothstein, Leslie M. Female-to-Male Transsexualism: Historical, Clinical, Theoretical Issues.

Lotstra, Hans. Abortion: The Catholic Debate in America.
Lott, George M. The Story of Human Emotions.
Lott, James E. Practical Protocol: A Guide to International Courtesies.
Lott, R. E., ed. Juan Valera: Pepita Jimenez.
Lott, Richard W. Auditing the Data Processing Function.
Lottery Player's Magazine Staff, ed. Almanac & Traveler's Guide to Lotteries.
Lottman, Herbert R. The Left Bank: Writers, Artists, & Politics from the Popular Front to the Cold War.
--The Purge: The Fate of French Collaborators after World War II.
Lotz, Agnes M., jt. auth. see Bruno, Joseph A., Jr.
Lotz, Preston R., jt. auth. see Quisling, Ronald G.
Lotze, Hermann. Logic. Natanson, Maurice, ed.
Lotzgar, Elaine, ed. see Gounaris, John, et al.
Lou, Y. K., ed. Deepwater Mooring & Drilling.
Loud, John, tr. see Djilas, Milovan.
Louderback, Joseph G. & Dominiak, Geraldine F. Managerial Accounting.
Louderback, Joseph G., jt. auth. see Hirsch, Maurice L., Jr.
Louderback, Joseph G., jt. auth. see Manners, George E., Jr.
Louderback, Joseph G., 3rd & Dominiak, Geraldine F. Managerial Accounting.
Loudon, David L. Consumer Behavior: Concepts & Applications.
Loudon, J. C. An Encyclopaedia of Gardening. Hunt, John D., ed.
--The Suburban Gardener & Villa Companion. Hunt, John D., ed.
Loudon, Nancy & Newton, John, eds. Handbook of Family Planning.
Lough, John. France Observed: In the Seventeenth Century by British Travellers.
--France on the Eve of Revolution: British Travellers' Observations 1763-1788.
--Locke's Travels in France, Sixteen Seventy-Five to Sixteen Seventy-Nine: As Related in His Journals, Correspondence & Other Papers.
Loughrey, jt. auth. see Kaplan.
Loughridge, Nancy. Dictionary of Etiquette.
Lougy, Robert E., intro. by see Gordon, Mary & Swinburne, Algernon C.
Louis, Joe, et al. Joe Louis: My Life.
Louis de Malave, Florita Z. Alfred Mansfeld, Architect (Israel)
--Egon Eiermann, Architect.
--Ettore Sottsass, Jr. Architect.
--Harald Deilmann, Architect.
Louisiana Restaurant Association Staff & Smith, Susan H. Chefs-Secrets from Great Restaurants in Louisiana: 1984 World Exposition Edition.
Louisiana State University Medical Center, Subrata Saha Staff. Biomedical Engineering I: Recent Developments. Proceedings of the First Southern Biomedical Engineering Conference, Shreveport, Louisiana, U. S. A., June 7-8, 1982.
Loulan, JoAnn G., et al. Period.
Loulis, John C. The Greek Communist Party, 1940-1944.
Lounibos, John, jt. ed. see Smith, Robert C.
Lounsbury, Ralph G. The British Fishery at Newfoundland, 1634-1763.
Lour, John. The Education of Adults: A World Perspective.
Lourie, Eugene. My Work in Films.
Lourie, Richard, tr. see Spasowski, Romuald.
Louth, Andrew L. Von see Von Louth, Andrew L.
Louttit, James R. The New-Skipper's Bowditch: Piloting from Here to There-& Home Again-with Maximun Pleasure & Minimun Trauma.
Louvau, Gordon E., et al. Systems Specifications for a Micro-or Mini-Computer Based Accountant's Client Write-up Systems.
Louviere, Michael L., jt. auth. see Coe, Charles P.
Louvish, D., tr. see Girsanov, I. V.
Louvish, Misha, tr. see Agnon, S. Y.
Louw, J. P. Semantics of New Testament Greek.
Lovari, Sandro, ed. The Biology & Management of Mountain Ungulates.
Lovasik, Lawrence. Our Lady's Knight.
Lovasz, L. Combinatorial Problems & Exercises.
Love, A. W., ed. Reflector Antennas.
Love, Barbara, ed. Handbook of Circulation Management.
Love, Glen A. & Love, Rhoda M. Ecological Crisis: Readings for Survival.
Love, Harold D., jt. auth. see Walthall, Joe E.
Love, Harriet. Harriet Love's Guide to Vintage Chic.
Love, Judith Anne. Thirty Thousand Kicks: What's It Like to Be a Rockette?
Love, R. The Chemical Biology of Fishes: With a Key to Literature.
Love, Ralph N., jt. ed. see Goodman, Louis J.
Love, Rhoda M., jt. auth. see Love, Glen A.
Love, Robert Emmett. Hell No.
Love, S., et al. Electroweak Interactions-Theory & Phenomenology: Proceedings of the Lectures Held at Trieste, Italy, Summer 1982.
Love, Sandra. But What About Me.
--Dive for the Sun.
--Melissa's Medley.
Love, William D. The Colonial History of Hartford: Bicentennial Edition.
Lovecraft, H. P. In Defence of Dagon. Joshi, S. T., intro. by.
--The Lurking Fear & Other Stories.
--The Tomb & Other Tales.
--Uncollected Letters. Joshi, S. T., ed.
Lovecraft, H. P. & Howard, Robert E. The Illustrated Challenge from Beyond.
Lovecraft, H. P., et al. Horror in the Museum & Other Revisions. Derleth, August, ed.
--The Boiling Point.
Loveday, Alexander. Reflections on International Administration.
Loveday, George C. Electronic Testing & Troubleshooting.
Lovegrove, H. T. Crop Production Equipment: A Practical Guide for Farmers, Operators, & Trainees.
Lovejoy. Lovejoy's College Guide.
Lovejoy, Arthur O. The Thirteen Pragmatisms, & Other Essays.
Lovejoy, Arthur O. & Boas, George. Primitivism & Related Ideas in Antiquity.
Lovejoy, Bahija, jt. auth. see Cohen, Barbara.
Lovelace, Dennis J. The Internal Consultant.
Lovelady, Janet. SOAR: A Program for the Gifted Using Bloom's Taxonomy - Student's Workbook.
Lovelady, Janet, ed. see Reid, Charlotte & Reid, John D.
Loveland, D. W., ed. Automated Deduction Conference: Proceedinngs of Conference, 6th, New York, 1982.
Loveland, W., jt. ed. see Seaborg, G. T.
Loveless, E. E., jt. auth. see Davis, Jack.
Lovell. Educational Psychology & Children.
Lovell, D. J. Optical Anecdotes.
Lovell, David W. Trotsky's Anaylysis of Soviet Bureaucratization: A Critical Essay.
Lovell, Helen, ed. see Olson, Kenneth J.
Lovell, J., jt. auth. see Bryant, T. H. E.
Lovell, John P. The Challenge of American Foreign Policy.
--Neither Athens nor Sparta? The American Service Academies in Transition.
Lovell, Marc. The Spy Who Barked in the Night.
Lovell, Robert E., jt. auth. see Beakley, George C.
Lovelock, D. W., jt. auth. see Skinner, F. A.
Lovelock, D. W. & Davies, R., eds. Techniques for the Study of Mixed Populations.
Lovelock, Marty H., jt. auth. see Janiak, Jane M.
Loveman, Brian & Davies, Thomas M., Jr., eds. The Politics of Antipolitics: The Military in Latin America.
Lovenberg, Walter & Yamori, Yukio, eds. Nutritional Prevention of Cardiovascular Disease.
Lovenduski, Joni & Hills, Jill, eds. The Politics of the Second Electorate: Women & Public Participation: Britain, U. S. A., Canada, Australia, France, Spain, West Germany, Italy, Sweden, Finland, Eastern Europe, U. S. S. R., & Japan.
Lovesey, Peter. The False Inspector Dew.
--Keystone.
Lovett, D. R. Semimetals & Narrow-Bandgap Semiconductors.
Lovett, D. R., jt. auth. see Ballentyne, D. W.
Lovett, James E. Nuclear Materials: Accountability Management Safeguards.
Lovett, Tom. Radical Approaches to Adult Education.
Lovett, Tom, ed. Radical Approaches to Adult Education.
Lovett, William A. Banking & Financial Institutions Law in a Nutshell.
Lovill, J. E., jt. ed. see McCormick, M. P.
Lovin, Robin W. Christian Faith & Public Choices: The Social Ethics of Barth, Brunner, & Bonhoeffer.
Loving, Waldon, jt. auth. see Bowling, W. Kerby.
Lovitt, Carl R., tr. see Pierssens, Michel.
Lovitt, Thomas C. & Haring, Norris G., eds. Classroom Application of Precision Teaching.
Lovoos, Janice. Sculpting in Clay.
Lovorn, Janie, jt. auth. see Lovorn, Tom.
Lovorn, Tom & Lovorn, Janie. Building a Caring Church.
Low, Alfred D. The Anschluss Movement in Austria & Germany, 1918-1919 & the Paris Peace Conference.
Low, Alice. All Around the Farm.
--All Through the Town.
Low, David. Low's Autobiography.
Low, Donald A. Thieves' Kitchen: The Regency Underworld.
Low, Jane G. The Acquisition of Maps & Charts Published by the United States Government.
Low, Janet. Understanding the Stock Market: A Guide for Young Investors.
Low, Jean. Star Showers.
Low, Joseph. Beastly Riddles: Fishy, Flighty & Buggy, Too.
--Boo to a Goose.
--Five Men under One Umbrella: And Other Ready-to-Read Riddles.
Low, N. P. & Power, J. M. Policy Systems in An Australian Metropolitan Region: Political & Economic Determinants of Change in Victoria.
Low, Peter W., et al. Criminal Law: Cases & Materials, 1983 Supplement.
--Criminal Law: Cases & Materials.
Low, William, ed. Paramagnetic Resonance.
Lowden, Desmond. Sunspot.
Lowder, Wayne M., jt. ed. see Adams, John A.
Lowdin. Proceedings of the International Symposium on Quantum Chemistry.
Lowdin, Per-Olov, ed. Quantum Theory of Atoms, Molecules & the Solid State.
Lowe, C. W. Project Control by Critical Pathanalysis: A Basic Guide of CPA.
Lowe, Charles H., Jr., ed. The Vertebrates of Arizona: With Major Section on Arizona Habitats.
Lowe, David. KKK: The Invisible Empire.
--Lost Chicago.
--Lost Chicago.
Lowe, Don & Lowe, Roberta. Forty-One Hiking Trails, Northwest California.
--Sixty-Two Hiking Trails, Northern Oregon Cascades. Worcester, Thomas K., ed.
--Thirty Five Hiking Trails, Columbia River Gorge. Bullard, Oral, ed.
Lowe, Eileen M., tr. see Simenon, Georges.
Lowe, G. The Cysteine Proteinases.
Lowe, Hal. The World's First Female Flattery Book.
Lowe, J. F., jt. auth. see Atkins, M. H.
Lowe, J. J., jt. ed. see Gray, J. M.
Lowe, J. J., et al, eds. Studies in the Lateglacial of North-West Europe: Including Papers Presented at a Symposium of the Quaternary Research Association Held at University College London, January 1979.
Lowe, James L. Standard Postcard Catalog.
Lowe, John C. & Moryadas, S. Spatial Interaction: The Geography of Movement.
Lowe, John S. Oil & Gas in a Nutshell.
Lowe, John W. The Dynamics of Apocalypse: A Systems Simulation of the Classic Maya Collapse.
Lowe, Josiah B. The Cross Prefigured & Fulfilled.
Lowe, Mary, jt. auth. see Walsh, E. G.
Lowe, Robert W. Bibliographical Account of English Theatrical Literature.
Lowe, Roberta, jt. auth. see Lowe, Don.
Lowell, Amy. Complete Poetical Works of Amy Lowell.
Lowell, Amy, jt. tr. see Ayscough, Florence.
Lowell, Charles J. The Persistent Dominion in History of the Theory of Masters & Slaves & Its Significance for the Human Race.
Lowell, Dorothy. The Farm.
Lowell, Mark, jt. auth. see Potter, Jack.
Lowell, R. P., jt. auth. see Rona, P. A.
Lowell, Robert. History.
--Mills of the Kavanaughs.
--Near the Ocean.
--Prometheus Bound.
--The Voyage & Other Versions of Poems by Baudelaire.
Lowenfeld, Viktor. The Nature of Creative Activity.
Lowenhardt, Werner. Amsterdam, Twelve Seventy-Five - Nieuw Amsterdam, Sixteen Twenty-Five - New York, Nineteen Seventy-Five.
Lowenhaupt, Cecile K., jt. auth. see Baer, J. A.
Lowenheim, Frederick A. & Moran, Marguerite K. Faith, Keyes, & Clark's Industrial Chemicals.
Lowenkamp, William. Of Life & Love: Contemporary Poems.
Lowenkopf, Martin. Politics in Liberia: The Conservative Road to Development.
Lowensohn-Lessing, V. Rembrandt: Paintings from Soviet Museums.
Lowenstein, Elsa B., tr. see Frisch, Karl Von.
Lowenstein, Elsa B., tr. see Von Frisch, Karl.
Lowenstein, Jerold M., jt. ed. see Handmaker, Hirsch.
Lowenstein, O. E., ed. Advances in Comparative Physiology & Biochemistry.
Lowenthal, A. & Mori, A., eds. Urea Cycle Diseases.
Lowenthal, Abraham F., ed. Armies & Politics in Latin America.
Lowenthal, James. The Hidden Sun: Solar Eclipses & Astrophotography.
Lowenthal, Mark M. Crispan Magicker.
Lowenthal, Max. Federal Bureau of Investigation.
Lower, Arthur R. Canada & the Far East-Nineteen Forty.
--Great Britain's Woodyard: British America & the Timber Trade 1763-1867.
Lower, Mark A. English Surnames.
Lowery, Andrew & Rivera, Richard J. Device Good Manufacturing Practices Manual.
Lowery, James L., Jr. Peers, Tents, & Owls: Some Solutions to Problems of the Clergy Today.
Lowery, James L., Jr., ed. Case Histories of Tentmakers.
Lowery, Joan, jt. auth. see Nixon, Hershell H.
Lowery, Marilyn M. How to Write Romance Novels that Sell.
Lowes, John L. Road to Xanadu: A Study in the Ways of the Imagination.
Lowi, Theodore J. American Government: Incomplete Conquest.
Lowi, Theodore J., ed. Private Life & Public Order.
Lowie, Robert H. The German People: A Social Portrait to 1914.
--Primitive Religion.
--Toward Understanding Germany.
Lowith, Karl. From Hegel to Nietzsche.
Lowman, Al. Printing Arts in Texas.
Lowman, P. D., Jr. Lunar Panorama: A Photographic Guide to the Geology of the Moon.
--Space Panorama.
Lowman, Paul D., Jr. The Third Planet.
Lown, Elizabeth M., jt. ed. see Strausz, Otto P.
Lowndes, D. Marketing: The Uses of Advertising.
Lowndes, Rosemary & Kailer, Claude. Make Your Own Noah's Arc.
Lowndes, William T. Bibliographer's Manual of English Literature.
Lownds, Camille & August, Tony. Foil Around & Stay Fit: Exercise Secrets of a Fencer.
--Foil Around & Stay Fit: Exercise Secrets of a Fencer.
Lowrance, William W. Of Acceptable Risk: Science & the Determination of Safety.
Lowrance, William W., ed. Assessment of Health Effects at Chemical Waste Disposal Sites.
Lowrance, William W., ed. see Life Sciences Symposium Staff.
Lowrey, Robert E., jt. ed. see Henderson, Jeff.
Lowrie, Donald A. Rebellious Prophet: A Life of Nicolai Berdgaev.
Lowrie, R. S., ed. see Jones, C. E.
Lowrie, W., tr. see Kierkegaard, Soren.
Lowrie, Walter. Action in the Liturgy.
--Art in the Early Church.
--Enchanted Island.
Lowry, Albert J. Hidden Fortunes: How to Profit from the New Opportunities of the 1980s.
--How to Become Financially Independent by Investing in Real Estate.
--How to Successfully Manage Real Estate in Your Spare Time.
--How You Can Become Financially Independent by Investing in Real Estate.
Lowry, Bullitt & Gunter, Elizabeth E., eds. The Red Virgin: Memoirs of Louise Michel.
Lowry, Eve, jt. auth. see Ennis, Carla M.
Lowry, Gertrude S. The Wheel of Truth: An Ancestral Saga.
Lowry, Heath W., ed. Early Reading Experiences for Young Children: A Book of Selected Readings for Students, Interns & Teachers.
Lowry, Helen. The Wonderful World of Ginkel Bugs.
Lowry, Samuel. Should You Be Psychoanalyzed?
Lowry-Corry, Elizabeth. Let's Have a Conference.
Lowther, H. An Introduction to Organic Chemistry.
Lowy, Martin E. & Muckenfuss, Cantwell F. The Glass-Steagall Act: Banks & the Securities Business.
Loxley, Janet C. & Whiteley, John M. Character Development in College Students, Vol. II: The Curriculum & Longitudinal Results.
Loxley-Taylor, Cynthia M. & Cress, Sheila S. Nursing 88 Nursing Diagnosis Cards.
Loxton, John. Practical Map Production.
Loyd, Mary, tr. see Waliszewski, Kazimierz.
Loyola Brandao, Ignacio De see De Loyola Brandao, Ignacio.
Lozano, Wendy. Sweet Abandon.
Lozansky, Edward. For Tatiana: When Love Triumphed over the Kremlin.
Lozynsky, Artem, jt. ed. see Francis, Gloria A.
Lu. Introduction to the Mechanics of Viscous Fluids.
Lu, Cary. The Apple Macintosh Book.
Lu, Hsien, ed. Major Topics & Issues in Psychology: Scientific Studies in Behavioral Development.
Lu, James C., et al. Leachate from Municipal Landfills: Production & Management.
Lu, P. Introduction to the Mechanics of Viscous Fluids.
Lu, P., jt. auth. see Opella, S. J.
Lu, Y. C. Singularity Theory & Introduction to Catastrophe Theory.
Lu, Yong-Zai & Williams, Theodore J. Modelling, Estimation & Control of the Soaking Pit: An Example of the Development & Application of Some Modern Control Techniques to Industrial Processes.
Luard, E. Human Rights & Foreign Policy.
Luard, Evan. The Control of the Sea-Bed: An Updated Report.
Luard, Nicholas. The Orion Line.
--The Shadow Spy.
Lubac, Henri de see De Lubac, Henri.
Lubben, Twyla & Hunt, Linda L. Christina's World.
Lubbock, Basil. The China Clippers.

Authors

Lubbock, Sir John. A Contribution to Our Knowledge of Seedlings.
Lubec, G., ed. see International Symposium on the Glomerular Basement Membrane Staff.
Lubeck, Scott, ed. see Ashby, Lynn.
Lubeck, Scott, ed. see Giordano, Frank.
Lubeck, Scott, ed. see Kalil, Susie & Rose, Barbara.
Lubeck, Scott, ed. see LaSalle, Peter.
Lubeck, Scott, ed. see Zelade, Richard.
Lubell, Samuel. The Future While It Happened.
--Hidden Crisis in American Politics.
Lubetski, Edith & Lubetski, Meir. Building a Judaica Library Collection: A Resource Guide.
Lubetski, Meir, jt. auth. see Lubetski, Edith.
Lubich, Chiara. The Eucharist.
--Jesus in the Midst: Spiritual Writings.
--Journey: Spiritual Insights. Moran, Hugh & Hartnett, William, trs. from Ital.
--Our Yes to God. Moran, Hugh J., tr. from Ital.
Lubich, Gino & Lazzarin, Piero. Joan Antida Thouret: When God Hear the voice of the Poor. Brody, Joel, tr. from Ital.
Lubin, Bernard, jt. ed. see O'Connor, William A.
Lubin, Leonard B., illus. This Little Pig: A Mother Goose Favorite.
Lubin, Martin. Good Guys, Bad Guys.
Lubitz, Wolfgang. Trotsky Bibliography.
Lubke, Kraus, jt. ed. see Schroder, Eberhard.
Lubkoll, Hans-Georg & Wiesnet, Eugen. Getting to Know Your Bible. Scheidt, David L., tr. from Ger.
Lubow, Martha. Working Out with AutoCAD.
Luby, Barry J., jt. auth. see Brown, Robert B.
Luby, Sue & St. Onge, Richard A. Bodysense: The Hazard Free Fitness Program for Men & Women.
Luc, H., jt. ed. see Mercier, C.
Luca, Stuart M. De see De Luca, Stuart M.
Lucarini, Spartaco. The Difficult Role of a Father. Moran, Hugh, tr. from Ital.
Lucas, A. A., jt. ed. see Cutler, Paul H.
Lucas, Amy & Marcaccio, Kathleen Y. New Information Systems & Services.
Lucas, Amy, ed. Encyclopedia of Information Systems & Services, International Volume.
--Encyclopedia of Information Systems & Services, United States Volume.
--Encyclopedia of Information Systems & Services: United States, International & Index Volume.
Lucas, Amy & Novallo, Annette, eds. Encyclopedia of Information Systems & Services, 1988.
--Encyclopedia of Information Systems & Services, 1988: International Volume.
--Encyclopedia of Information Systems & Services, 1988: United States, International & Index.
--New Information Systems & Services.
Lucas, Barbara, tr. see Lindgren, Astrid.
Lucas, Charles, ed. see Brinkley, F.
Lucas, D. O., ed. Regulatory Mechanism in Lymphocyte Activation.
Lucas, Ethel G., jt. auth. see Mansfield, Evelyn A.
Lucas, George. Star Wars.
Lucas, George R., Jr. & Ogletree, Thomas W., eds. Lifeboat Ethics: The Moral Dilemma of World Hunger.
Lucas, Georges. Transfer Theory for Trapped Electromagnetic Energy.
Lucas, Harry. Pensions & Industrial Relations: A Practical Guide for All Involved in Pensions.
Lucas, J. R. Weeping in Ramah.
Lucas, Jack A. & Park, Michael A. Workbook in General Anthropology.
Lucas, Jerry & Lorayne, Harry. The Memory Book.
Lucas, John. Moderns & Contemporaries: Novelists, Poets, Critics.
Lucas, Laddie, ed. Out of the Blue: Role of Luck in Air Warfare.
Lucas, Linda & Karrenbrock, Marilyn H. The Disabled Child in the Library.
Lucas, Martin, jt. auth. see Dixon, Terence.
Lucas, Peter J., ed. Exodus.
Lucas, Ronald J. Pension Planning Within a Major Company.
Lucas, Rosemary, jt. auth. see Armstrong, Eric.
Lucas, Silas E., Jr. Davidson County Marriage Record Book I: 1789-1837.
--The Eighteen Hundred Seven Land Lottery of Georgia.
--The Third or Eighteen-Twenty Land Lotteries of Georgia.
Lucas, Stephen E. Portents of Rebellion: Rhetoric & Revolution in Philadelphia, 1765-1776.
Lucasfilm, Ltd. Staff. The Star Wars Intergalactic Passport.
Lucassen, Jan. Migrant Labour in Europe, Sixteen Hundred to Nineteen Hundred: The Drift to the North Sea.
Lucchese, Jean. Alphabet for Young Eckists.
Luce, Clare Booth, jt. auth. see Mabardi, Georges.
Luce, Marnie. One Is Unique.
--Zero Is Something.
Luce, T. J. Livy: The Composition of His History.
Luce, William. The Belle of Amherst.
Lucentini, Franco, jt. auth. see Fruttero, Carl.
Lucentini, Franco, jt. auth. see Fruttero, Carlo.
Luchins, Abraham S. & Hirsch, Edith. Rigidity of Behavior: A Variational Approach to the Effect of Einstellung.
Luchting, Johanna. The Birds of Paradise.
Luciani, Vince. Amateur Radio, Super Hobby.
Luciano, Ron & Fisher, David. Strike Two.
Lucid, Dan, ed. see Markham, Gervase.
Lucier, Ruth. Tim: A Baby's Odyssey.
Lucie-Smith. Thinking about Art.
Lucie-Smith, Edward. Art of the 1930's: The Age of Anxiety.
--The Body: Images of the Nude in Art.
--Eroticism in Western Art.
--Joan of Arc.
--Lives of the Great Twentieth Century Artists.
--Movements in Art since 1945.
Lucie-Smith, Edward, jt. auth. see Smith, Paul J.
Lucifer of Cagliari. Opvuscula.
Luck, jt. auth. see Simmons.
Luck, David J., et al. Marketing Research.
Luck, Werner A. Structure of Water & Aqueous Solutions.
Lucken, E. A. Nuclear Quadrupole Coupling Constants.
Luckey, Carl F. Collector Prints Old & New: An Identification & Value Guide.
--Collector Prints Old & New: An Identification & Value Guide.
--Old Fishing Lures & Tackle: Identification & Value Guide.
Luckey, T. D., jt. auth. see Venugopal, B.
Luckey, Thomas D. Germfree Life & Gnotobiology.
Luckhardt, C. G., tr. see Wittgenstein, Ludwig.
Luckner, M., jt. ed. see Schreiber, K.
Luckner, Martin. The Secondary Metabolism of Plants & Animals.
Luckock. Simon de Montfort: Reformer & Rebel.
Lucky, Carl F. Depression: Era Glassware.
--Hummel Figurines & Plates: A Collectors Identification & Value Guide.
Lucky, Luretha F. & Miller, Nancy O. Engineering Learning Through Creativity: Recycling Instructional Resources.
Luckyj, George. Before the Storm: Soviet Ukrainian Fiction of the 1920s. Tkacz, Yuri, tr. from Ukrainian.
Luckyj, George S. Between Gogol & Sevcenko: Polarity in the Literary Ukraine, 1798-1847.
Lucovsky, et al. The Physics of MOS Insulators.
Lucy, J. A., et al. Mammalian Cell Hybridization, II.
Ludanyi, Andrew, jt. ed. see Cadzow, John F.
Ludema, K. C. see Glaeser, W. A., et al.
Ludema, K. C. et al. jt. ed. see Glaeser, W. A., et al.
Ludena, E. V., et al, eds. Computers in Chemical Education & Research.
Luderwald, I., jt. ed. see Fresenius, W.
Ludlam, Harry, ed. Elliott O'Donnell's Casebook of Ghosts.
Ludlow, Edmund. Edmund Ludlow: A Voyce from the Watch Tower 1660-1662. Worden, A. B., ed.
Ludlow, Gwen, jt. auth. see Clifford, H. T.
Ludlow, Norman, Jr. Potpourri: Clipbook Number Two of Line Artwork.
Ludlum, David M. The American Weather Book.
--The Country Journal New England Weather Book.
Ludlum, Robert. The Aquitaine Progression.
--The Holcroft Covenant.
--The Parsifal Mosaic.
Ludman, Joan, jt. ed. see Mason, Lauris.
Ludolphy, Ingetraut. From Luther to Fifteen Eighty: A Pictorial Account.
Ludvigsen, Karl. Mercedes-Benz Racing Cars.
Ludwick, Percy, tr. see Demirchian, K. S.
Ludwig, Catherine, jt. ed. see Huberty, Robert.
Ludwig, Charles. Levi Coffin & the Underground Railroad.
Ludwig, David. The Spirit of Your Marriage.
Ludwig, David J. In Good Spirits.
Ludwig, Emil. Abraham Lincoln.
--Of Life & Love.
--Son of Man: The Story of Jesus.
Ludwig, G. Wave Mechanics.
Ludwig, H. & Tauber, P. F., eds. Human Fertilization.
Ludwig, Lyndell. The Shoemaker's Gift.
--Ts'ao Chung Weighs an Elephant.
Ludwig, Otto. Between Heaven & Earth. Almon, Muriel, tr.
Ludwig, Stephen. Out of Work.
Ludz, Peter C. Alienation As a Concept in the Social Sciences: A Trend Report & Bibliography Prepared for the International Sociological Association Under the Auspices of the International Committee for Social Science Information & Documentation.
Luebbers, D. W., et al, eds. Progress in Enzyme & Ion-Selective Electrodes.
Luecke, Gerald, jt. auth. see Cannon, Don L.
Luecke, Gerald, ed. see Evans, Alvis J., et al.
Luecke, Gerald, ed. see Mishkoff, Henry C.
Luecke, Gerald, et al, eds. see Ribbens, William B. & Mansour, Norman P.
Luecke, K., jt. ed. see Gottstein, G.
Luedemann, Gerd. Paul, Apostle to the Gentiles: Studies in Chronology. Jones, Stanley F., tr. from Ger.
Luederitz, B., ed. Cardiac Pacing: Diagnostic & Therapeutic Tools.
Lueders, Edward. The Clam Lake Papers: A Winter in the North Woods.
Luedtke, D. Ralph, ed. see Smith, Catharine P.
Luedtke, Peter. Computers for Grocery Stores & Supermarkets.
--Computers for Insurance Agencies: Computer Selection Ser.
--Computers for Membership Organizations.
--Computers for Retailers: Computer Selection Ser.
Luedtke, Peter & Luedtke, Rainer. Computers for Law Offices.
Luedtke, Rainer, jt. auth. see Luedtke, Peter.
Luening, Otto. The Odyssey of an American Composer.
Luenn, Nancy. The Dragon Kite.
--The Dragon Kite.
--The Ugly Princess.
Luepke, Gretchen, ed. Stability of Heavy Minerals in Sediments.
Luepnitz, Deborah A. Child Custody: A Study of Families After Divorce.
Luetkeholter, G. W., tr. see Von Campenhausen, Hans & Chadwick, Henry.
Luettge, U., ed. Microautoradiography & Electron Probe Analysis: Their Application to Plant Physiology.
Luetzow, Robert H. Interfacing Test Circuits with Single-Board Computers.
--Practical Interfacing Projects with the Commodore Computers.
Lufeng, Tang & Huilian, Chen. Four Seasons of the Year.
Luffberry, Henry B. A New Manual for Vestrymen.
Luft & Yalow. Radioimmunoassay: Methodology & Applications in Physiology & in Clinical Studies.
Luft, Anita. Diccionario de Palabras Anticuadas y en Desuso.
Luginbuhl, Geraldine. General Microbiology Laboratory Manual.
Lugton, Robert C. American Topics: A Reading Vocabulary Text for Speakers of ESL.
Luh, B. S. & Woodroof, J. G. Commercial Vegetable Processing.
Luh, Bor S. Rice: Production & Utilization.
Luibheid, Colm. Eusebius of Caesarea & the Arian Crisis.
Luijpen, W. A. Existential Phenomenology.
Luikov, A. V. Heat & Mass Transfer.
Luisi, Billie. Overlook Guide to Smallscale Goatkeeping.
Luitjters, Guus & Timmer, Gerard. Sexbombs: The Life & Death of Jayne Mansfield. Pachter, Josh, tr.
Luk, Charles. The Transmission of the Mind Outside the Teaching.
Lukacs, George. Historical Novel.
Lukacs, John A. Decline & Rise of Europe: A Study in Recent History with Particular Emphasis on the Development of a European Consciousness.
Lukas, Elisabeth. Meaningful Living: Logotherapy Guide to Health. Fabry, Joseph B., tr.
Lukas, Ellen, jt. auth. see Lukas, Mary.
Lukas, Mary & Lukas, Ellen. Teilhard.
Lukashin, Y. National Folk Sports in the U. S. S. R.
Lukasiewicz, J. Elements of Mathematical Logic.
Luke, Ann W., jt. ed. see Cuadra, Carlos A.
Luke, Barbara. Maternal Nutrition.
Luke, Gladys L. Tales from the Midwest.
Luke, Mary. The Nine Days' Queen: A Portrait of Lady Jane Grey.
Luke, Robert A. Teacher-Centered In-Service Education: Planning & Products.
Lukeman, Tim. Witchwood.
Lukenbill, jt. auth. see Stokes.
Lukenbill, W. Bernard. A Working Bibliography of American Doctoral Dissertations in Children's & Adolsecents' Literature, 1930-1971.
Lukens, R. J. Chemistry of Fungicidal Action.
Lukerman, Barbara, et al. The Twin Cities Nonprofit Sector in a Time of Government Retrenchment.
Lukes, Steven & Galnoor, Itzhak. No Laughing Matter: A Collection of Political Jokes.
Luke the Physician. On Trial: Being a Summary of Eyewitness Reports Concerning the Early Church.
Luks, Alan, ed. Having Been There.
Lula, R. A., ed. Duplex Stainless Steels.
Lull, Ramon. The Book of the Beasts. Peers, E. Allison, tr. from Catalan.
Lulow, Kalia, jt. auth. see Anastas, Robert.
Lumb, jt. auth. see Mitchell.
Lumb, D. Teaching Mathematics, Five to Thirteen.
Lumholtz, Carl. New Trails in Mexico: Travels among the Papago, Pima & Cocopa Indians.
Lumley, Brian. Beneath the Moors.
Lumley, J. P., et al. Essential Anatomy.
Lumley, Judith, jt. auth. see Chamberlain, Geoffrey.
Lummis, Charles. General Crook & the Apache Wars.
--General Crook & the Apache Wars.
Lumsden, jt. auth. see Attiyeh.
Lumsden, D. B., jt. ed. see Sherron, R. H.
Lumsden, George J. Impact Management: Personal Power Strategies for Success.
Lumsden, W. H., ed. Advances in Parasitology.
Lumsden, W. H. R. & Evans, D. A., eds. Biology of the Kinetoplastida.
Luna, Severino N. Born Primitive in the Philippines. Murphy, Irene, ed. & frwd. by.
Lunar & Planetary Institute Staff, compiled by. The Ancient Sun: Proceedings of the Conference on the Ancient Sun: Fossil Record in the Earth, Moon & Meteorites, Boulder Colorado, October 16-19, 1979.
Lunar & Planetary Institute Staff. Basaltic Volcanism on Terrestrial Planets: Proceedings of the Lunar & Planetary Institute, Houston, Texas.
Lunar & Planetary Institute Staff, ed. Mare Crisium: The View from Luna Twenty-Four, Houston, Texas.
Lunar & Planetary Institute Staff. Proceedings of the Conference on the Lunar Highlands Crust: Houston, Texas, U. S. A., 14-16 November 1979.
Lunar Science Conference, 8th, Houston, 1977. Proceedings. Lunar Science Institute, Houston, Texas, compiled by.
Lunar Science Institute, Houston, Texas, compiled by see Lunar Science Conference, 8th, Houston, 1977.
Lunardini, Virgil J. Heat Transfer in Cold Climates.
Lund, Gene J., tr. see Gerhardsson, Birger.
Lund, Gerald N. The Alliance.
Lund, H. F. Industrial Pollution Control Handbook.
Lund, Morten & Gillen, Bob. The Ski Book.
Lund, Nancy J. & Duchan, Judith F. Assessing Children's Language in Naturalistic Contexts.
Lund, Philip R. Compelling Selling.
--Compelling Selling: A Framework for Persuasion.
Lund, Robert T. & Hansen, John A. Keeping America at Work: Strategies for Employing the New Technologies.
Lunday, Berneice. Unblessed.
Lundberg, Donald E. The Hotel & Restaurant Business.
--The Tourist Business.
Lundborg, Louis B. Up to Now.
Lunde, Anders S. Whirligigs: Design & Construction.
Lunde, Donald T. Murder & Madness.
Lunde, Donald T. & Morgan, Jefferson. The Die Song: A Journey into the Mind of a Mass Murderer.
Lunde, Donald T., jt. auth. see Katchadourian, Herant.
Lunde, Johan. Light at Eventide: Devotions for the Autumn. Loken, Palmer, tr.
Lundegren, Herberta M. & Farrell, Patricia. Evaluation for Leisure Service Managers.
Lundell, A. T. & Weingram, S. The Topology of CW Complexes.
Lunden, Joan & Freidberg, Ardy. Good Morning, I'm Joan Lunden.
Lundevall, E., ed. see Welle-Strand.
Lundgren. Across the High Frontier.
Lundgren, Hal. Earl Campbell: The Texas Tornado, Sports Stars.
Lundin, Frank E., jt. ed. see Chiazze, Leonard, Jr.
Lundin, Jack W. A Church for an Open Future: Biblical Roots & Parish Renewal.
Lundkvist, Artur. Agadir. Smith, William Jay & Sjoberg, Leif, trs. from Swedish.
Lundquist, Carl H. Silent Issues of the Church.
Lundquist, Helmer C. & Pendorf, James G. Church Organization: A Manual for Effective Local Church Administration.
Lundqvist, Bengt & Lundqvist, Stig, eds. Collective Properties of Physical Systems: Proceedings.
Lundqvist, Lennart J. From Tenancy to Home Ownership: A Comparative Study of Tenure Conversions & Their Effects.
Lundqvist, Stig, jt. ed. see Lundqvist, Bengt.
Lundstrom, Lowell. Heaven's Answer for the Home.
--How You Can Pray with Power & Get Results.
Lundy, Carl P., jt. auth. see Keir, Jack.
Lunin, Lois F., ed. Health Sciences & Services: A Guide to Information Sources.
Lunn. Lecture Notes on Anaesthetics.
Lunn, Eugene. Prophet of Community: The Romantic Socialism of Gustav Landauer.
Lunn, Hugh. Queenslanders.
Lunn, Simon. Burden-Sharing in NATO.
Lunny, Robert M. Early Maps of North America.
Lunsford, M. Rosser. Thoughts of Life.
Lunsford, Ronald F., jt. auth. see Bridges, Charles W.
Lunstrum, John P. & Taylor, Bob L. Teaching Reading in the Social Studies.

Authors

Lunt, Dudley C., ed. see Thoreau, Henry David.
Lunt, Horace G. Fundamentals of Russian.
Lunt, Horace G., ed. Accented Russian Reader.
Lunt, James. John Burgoyne of Saratoga.
Lunt, Peter. Udo Fahrt Nach Koln.
Lunt, Susanne. A Handbook for the Disabled.
Luo Guanzhong, jt. auth. see Shi, Nai'an.
Luoma, Jon. Introduction on Environmental Issues.
Lupica, Mike, jt. auth. see Jackson, Reggie.
Lupis, Claude H. Chemical Thermodynamics of Materials.
Lupoff, Richard A. Circumpolar: A Novel.
Lupold, Harry F. The Forgotten People: The Woodland Erie.
Lupton, Leonard. Canyon Country.
Lupton, Martha. They Tell a Story.
Lupul, Max E., jt. auth. see Keiser, Stephen K.
Lurani, G. Mille Miglia: The Fabulous Story of the Great Road Race.
Luria, Gina, ed. see Edgeworth, Maria & Edgeworth, Richard L.
Luria, Gina, ed. see Hays, Mary.
Luria, S. E. The Multiplication of Viruses. Bd. with Virus Inclusions in Plant Cells. Smith, K. M; Virus Inclusions in Insect Cells. Smith, K. M; Antibiotika Erzeugende Virus-Ahnliche Faktoren in Bakterien. Fredericq, P. Springer-Verlag.
Lurie, Adolph G. Business Segments: A Guide for Managers & Accountants.
Lurie, Alison. The Language of Clothes.
--Love & Friendship.
Lurie, Steven W., jt. auth. see Dondes, Seymour.
Lusch, Robert F. Management of Retail Enterprises.
Luscher, Martin, ed. Phase & Caste Determination in Insects - Endocrine Aspects: Proceedings of the International Congress of Entomology, 15th, Washington, D.C., 1976.
Luscher, Max. The Luscher Color Test. Scott, Ian, ed. & tr.
Luscombe, D. E., ed. see Knowles, David.
Lush, Peggy, jt. ed. see Golay, Frank H.
Lusk, Graham. The Elements of the Science of Nutrition.
Luska, Sidney see Harland, Henry, pseud.
Lussier, Ernest. Adore the Lord: Adoration Viewed Through the Old Testament.
Lustbader, Eric Van see Van Lustbader, Eric.
Lustig, Arnost. The Unloved: From the Diary of Perla S.
Lustig, Herbert, jt. auth. see Allen, Carol.
Lutgendorf, Philip. Addition & Subtraction.
Lutgendorf, Philip & Gray, Mary Jane. Sentence Structure.
Lutgens, Frederick K. & Tarbuck, Edward J. The Atmosphere: An Introduction to Meteorology.
--The Atmosphere: An Introduction to Meteorology.
Luthans, Fred. Introduction to Management: A Contingency Approach.
Luthans, Fred, jt. auth. see Wortmen, Max S., Jr.
Luther, Martin. Commentary on the Epistle to the Galatians. Watson, P. S., tr. from Ger.
--Luther's Large Catechism. Lenker, J. M., tr.
Luther, William M. The Marketing Plan: How to Prepare & Implement It.
Lutheran Church of America. Yearbook.
Luthin, Reinhard H. The First Lincoln Campaign.
Luton, M. J. & Polizzotti, R. S., eds. High Temperature Structural Composites: Synthesis, Characterization & Properties.
Lutters, Valerie A. The Haunting of Julie Unger.
Luttrell, Ida. Not Like That, Armadillo.
--Not Like That, Armadillo.
--One Day at School.
--One Day at School.
Luttrell, Wanda. In the Shadow of the White Rose.
--The Legacy of Drennan's Crossing.
Luttwak, Edward N. On the Meaning of Victory: Essays on Strategy.
--On the Meaning of Victory: Essays on Strategy.
--The Pentagon & the Art of War: The Question of Military Reform.
--Strategy & Politics.
Lutz, Charles P. Abounding in Hope: A Family of Faith at Work through the Lutheran World Federation.
--Farming the Lord's Land: Christian Perspectives on American Agriculture.
Lutz, Charles P. & Folk, Jerry L. Peaceways: Sixteen Christian Perspectives on Security in a Nuclear Age.
Lutz, Charles P., ed. Church Roots: Stories of Nine Immigrant Groups That Became the American Lutheran Church.
--God, Goods & the Common Good: Eleven Perspectives on Economic Justice in Dialog with the Roman Catholic Bishops' Pastoral Letter.
Lutz, Cora E. Essays on Manuscripts & Rare Books.
--The Oldest Library Motto & Other Library Essays.
Lutz, Donald S. & Warren, Jack D. A Covenanted People: The Religious Tradition & the Origins of American Constitutionalism.
Lutz, Giles A. The Feud.
--Outcast Gun.
--The Trespassers.
Lutz, H. O., et al, eds. Fundamental Processes in Energetic Atomic Collisions.
Lutz, John. Tropical Heat.
Lutz, Mark, jt. ed. see Diwan, Romesh.
Lutz, Nancie A. The Doll Directory & Buying Guide, 1986.
Lutz, Paul E. & Santmire, H. Paul. Ecological Renewal.
Lutz, R. & Goze, M. Nonstandard Analysis: A Practical Guide with Applications.
Lutz, Ralph H., jt. ed. see Burdick, Charles B.
Lutz, Richard J. Contemporary Perspectives in Consumer Research.
Lutz, Robert D. Photographer's Market, 1985.
Lutzeler, H. Bonn: The Capital of West Germany in Photographs.
Lutzer, Erwin. Failure: The Back Door to Success.
Lutzer, Erwin, jt. auth. see Orr, Bill.
Lutzeyer, W. & Melchior, H., eds. Urodynamics.
Lutzker, Edythe. Edith Pechey-Phipson, M.D. The Story of England's Foremost Pioneering Woman Doctor.
Luur, A., et al. Songs from the Baltic Coast.
Luurie, Donald A., tr. see Berdiaer, Nicolaii.
Luvaas, William. The Seductions of Natalie Bach.
Lux, Don. Introduction to Construction Careers.
Lux, Thomas. Sunday.
Luxemburg, Rosa & Bukharin, Nikolai. The Accumulation of Capital--An Anti-Critique: Imperialism & the Accumulation of Capital. Tarbuck, Kenneth J., ed. Wichmann, Rudolf, tr. from Ger.
Luxton, Richard. The Mystery of the Mayan Hieroglyphs: The Vision of an Ancient Tradition. Balam, Pablo, ed.
Luza, Radomir. Austro-German Relations in the Anschluss Era.
LW, LC, ed. see Balahura, Robert.
Lwoff, Andre & Ullman, Agnes, eds. Origins of Molecular Biology: A Tribute to Jacques Monod.
Lyalikov, Y. S. & Klyachko, Y. A. Theoretical Foundations of Modern Chemical Analysis.
Lyall, Leslie T. New Spring in China.
Lycholat, Tony. Shape Your Body, Shape Your Life: The Weight Training Ways to Total Fitness.
Lyczkowski, R. W., jt. ed. see Kulacki, F.
Lydecker, Beatrice. Stories the Animals Tell Me.
Lydecker, Garrit D. Sign Carving.
Lydekker, John W. The Life & Letters of Charles Inglis: His Ministry in America & Consecration As First Colonial Bishop from 1759 to 1787.
Lyden, Fremont J. & Miller, Ernest G. Public Budgeting.
Lydenberg, H. M., tr. see Blum, Andre.
Lydenberg, Steve. Bankrolling Ballots: The Role of Business in Financing State Ballot Question Campaigns.
Lydersen, Aksel L. Fluid Flow & Heat Transfer.
Lydon, Neil, jt. auth. see Hammer, Armand.
Lyell, William A., Jr., tr. see Lao She.
Lyko, James J., jt. auth. see Sweeney, Dennis M.
Lyle, Carl & Bianchi, Raymond. Common Clinical Perplexities.
Lyle, Dorothy S. Performance of Textiles.
Lyle, Joseph L., Jr., jt. auth. see Carrington, Frank.
Lyle, Peter. Rolind of Meru.
Lyle, Sandy. Learning Golf: The Lyle Way.
Lyles, J. B. The Preacher's Outline & Sermon Bible, Vol. 9: Galatians, Eph., Phil., Col.
Lyles, John S. Youth & Alcoholic Beverages.
Lyles, W. H. Mary Shelley: An Annotated Bibliography.
Lyman, Darryl. The Animal Things We Say.
Lyman, Donald E. Making the Words Stand Still: How to Rescue the Learning Disabled Child.
Lyman, George R. The Art & Science of Effective Thinking.
Lyman, Henry, jt. auth. see Woolner, Frank.
Lyman, Raymond R. Military History Calendar, 1989.
Lyman, Tom & Riviere, Bill. The Field Book of Mountaineering & Rock Climbing.
Lyman, W. J. & Reehl, W. F. Handbook of Chemical Property Estimation Methods.
Lynch, jt. auth. see Barron.
Lynch, Barbara S. & Chapman, Charles F. Writing for Communication in Science & Medicine, or Out of Your Mind with Comprehensive Assurance.
Lynch, Beverly P., jt. ed. see Galvin, Thomas J.
Lynch, Bohun. A History of Caricature.
--Max Beerbohm in Perspective.
Lynch, Dorothea, jt. auth. see Richards, Eugene.
Lynch, Frederick H. Christian in Wartime.
Lynch, Henry T. Genetics & Breast Cancer.
Lynch, Henry T. & Anton-Guirgis, Hoda. Biomarkers, Genetics & Cancer.
Lynch, Henry T. & Fusaro, Ramon M. Cancer-Associated Genodermatoses.
Lynch, Henry T., et al. Colon Cancer Genetics.
Lynch, James. Reform of Teacher Education in the U. K.
Lynch, John. The Spanish American Revolutions, 1808-1862.
Lynch, John D. Evolutionary Relationships, Osteology & Zoogeography of Leptodactyloid Frogs.
--The Species Groups of South American Frogs of the Genus Eleutherodactylus: (Leptodactylidae)
Lynch, Kathleen A., et al, eds. see Newman, Sasha M.
Lynch, Mary J. ALA Survey of Librarian Salaries, 1986.
Lynch, Michael, ed. The Early Modern Town in Scotland.
Lynch, Nancy. The Old-Fashioned Garden: Four Delightful Pop-Up Plans.
Lynch, Patricia. The Grey Goose of Kilnevin.
Lynch, Regina, jt. auth. see Austin, Martha.
Lynch, Regina H. Cookbook - Chiyaan iitini Binaaltsoos.
--A History of Navajo Clans.
Lynch, Richard. Precision Management: How to Build & Manage the Winning Organization.
--Secret of Health.
Lynch, Robert, jt. ed. see Teglovic, Steve.
Lynch, Robert E. & Rice, John A. Computers: Their Impact & Use-BASIC Language.
Lynch, Thomas. The Printer's Manual, a Practical Guide for Compositors & Pressmen.
Lynch, Thomas, ed. Contemporary Public Budgeting.
Lynch, Thomas F., ed. Guitarrero Cave: Early Man in the Andes.
Lynch, Wilfred. Handbook of Silicone Rubber Fabrication.
Lynche, Richard see Batman, Stephen.
Lynd. Middletown in Transition.
Lynd, Alice, jt. ed. see Lynd, Staughton.
Lynd, Helen M. On Shame & the Search for Identity.
Lynd, Staughton & Lynd, Alice, eds. Rank & File: Personal Histories by Working Class Organizers.
Lyndon, Neil, jt. auth. see Hammer, Armand.
Lynds, Beverly T., ed. Dark Nebulae, Globules, & Protostars.
Lyne, G. M., tr. see Anglund, Joan W.
Lyne, G. M., tr. see Travers, Pamela L.
Lynes, Russell. The Tastemakers: The Shaping of American Popular Taste.
Lynes, Tony. French Pensions.
Lyness, Dody. Potpourri...Easy As One, Two, Three.
Lyng, Merwin J., et al. Applied Technical Mathematics.
Lynge, Richard & Trowbridge, Keith W. The Real Estate Broker's Guide to Resort Timesharing.
Lynn, Chester. The Road Back.
Lynn, Conrad. There Is a Fountain: The Autobiography of a Civil Rights Lawyer.
Lynn, Diana, jt. auth. see Abernethy, Rose.
Lynn, Edward S. & Freeman, Robert J. Fund Accounting: Theory & Practice.
Lynn, Elizabeth A. The Red Hawk.
Lynn, Gartley & Leebron, Elizabeth. Walt Disney: A Guide to References & Resources.
Lynn, J. Daniel, et al. New Methods of Automated Sequence Analysis of Proteins.
Lynn, Jack. The Professor.
Lynn, John A. Living in the Eye of the Storm.
--Will the Real You Please Remain Standing!
--Will the Real You Please Stand Up!
Lynn, Karen. The Rake.
Lynn, Kenneth S., ed. see Hawthorne, Nathaniel.
Lynn, Lou, jt. auth. see Russ, Joel.
Lynn, R. Attention, Arousal & the Orientation Reaction.
--Personality & National Character.
Lynn, Richardson R. Appellate Litigation.
Lynn, Robert A. & O'Grady, James P. Elements of Business.
Lynn, Robert J. The Pension Crisis.
Lynn, Theodore A. Introductory Musicianship: A Workbook.
--Introductory Musicianship: A Workbook.
Lynne, James B. Rogue Diamond.
Lynott, John. Loaded & Rollin' Trucks & Their Drivers.
Lyon, A. J. Dealing with Data.
Lyon, Bruce & Rowen, Herbert H. A History of the Western World.
Lyon, Christopher, ed. The International Dictionary of Films & Filmmakers, Vol. II: Directors - Filmakers.
Lyon, David. The Brave Little Computer.
--Karl Marx: A Christian Assessment of His Life & Thought.
Lyon, Eugene. The Search for the Atocha.
Lyon, Fern, ed. see Los Alamos Historical Society Staff.
Lyon, G., jt. auth. see Adams, Raymond D.
Lyon, George E. Father Time & the Day Boxes.
Lyon, H. H., jt. auth. see Johnson, Warren T.
Lyon, Jean. Yarn Art Projects.
Lyon, Jeff. Playing God in the Nursery.
Lyon, Judith, ed. see Sutton, Denys.
Lyon, K. Brynolf. Toward a Practical Theology of Aging.
Lyon, Larry. Community in Urban Society.
Lyon, Phyllis, jt. auth. see Martin, Del.
Lyon, William. A Pew for One, Please.
Lyon-Caen, Robert. Diodes, Transistors, & Integrated Circuits for Switching Systems.
Lyons, Albert S. & Petrucelli, R. Joseph. Medicine: An Illustrated History.
Lyons, Arthur. All God's Children.
--At the Hands of Another.
--At the Hands of Another.
--Castles Burning.
--The Dead Are Discreet.
--Dead Ringer.
--Hard Trade.
--The Killing Floor.
--Three with a Bullet.
Lyons, Barbara, et al. Departs: An Introductory (French) Course.
Lyons, C. G., et al. Concise Textbook of Organic Chemistry.
Lyons, Charles. Samuel Beckett.
Lyons, Deborah & Gabriel, Leah, eds. Cardiac Crises.
Lyons, Dorothy. Blue Smoke.
--Dark Sunshine.
--Pedigree Unknown.
--Red Embers.
Lyons, Grant. Mustangs, Six-Shooters & Barbed Wire: How the West Was Really Won.
Lyons, Ivan, jt. auth. see Lyons, Nan.
Lyons, J. M., et al, eds. Genetic Engineering of Symbiotic Nitrogen Fixation & Conservation of Fixed Nitrogen.
Lyons, Jerry L. The Designer's Handbook of Pressure Sensing Devices.
Lyons, John W. Fire.
Lyons, Ken. Complete Guide to Winning Slot-I Football.
Lyons, Len. The One Hundred One Best Jazz Albums: A History of Jazz on Records.
Lyons, Len, et al. Using the Commodore 64: A Hand Guide to Getting the Most from the Bestselling Microcomputer.
Lyons, Leonard, jt. ed. see Donnelly, John.
Lyons, Nan & Lyons, Ivan. Someone Is Killing the Great Chefs of Europe.
Lyons, Ruth, ed. see American Arbitration Association Staff & Colosi, Thomas R.
Lyons, T. P., ed. A Step to Energy Independence: Gasohol.
Lyons, Thomas T., jt. auth. see Frederick, Wayne A.
Lyons, Timothy J. Charles Chaplin Film Guide.
Lyons, William. Gilbert Ryle: An Introduction to His Philosophy.
Lyotard, Jean-Francois. The Wall of the Pacific. Lindsay, Cecile, tr. from Fr.
Lype, E. J., pseud. Behind the Door.
Lys, Claudia De see Batchelor, Julie F. & De Lys, Claudia.
Lys, Claudia De see De Lys, Claudia.
Lys, Claudia de see De Lys, Claudia.
Lysaght, Brian. Special Circumstances.
Lysne, Mary E. Bible Activity Fun for Kids.
--Bible Learning Fun for Kids.
Lystak, Mary, ed. Innovations in Mental Health Services to Disaster Victims.
Lytle, Charles F., jt. auth. see Wodsedalek, J. E.
Lytle, R. J. American Metric Handbook.
--Farm Builder's Handbook.
Lytle, R. J. & Reschke, R. C. Component & Modular Techniques: A Builder's Handbook.
Lyttelton, Humphrey. The Best of Jazz: Basin Street to Harlem.
--The Best of Jazz I: Basin Street to Harlem, 1917-1930.
--Best of Jazz II: Enter the Giants, 1931-1944.
Lyttle, Peter T., ed. Central Appalachian Geology: NE-SE GSA '82 Field Trip Guidebook.
Lyttle, Richard B. Computers in Government & the Military.
--The Games They Played.
--People of the Dawn.
Lyttleton, Humphrey. The Best of Jazz II: Enter the Giants, 1931-1944.

M

M. D. Anderson Annual Clinical Conference of Cancer Staff & M. D. Anderson Hospital & Tumor Institute. Immunotherapy of Human Cancer: Proceedings of the M. D. Anderson Annual Clinical Conference of Cancer, 22nd.
M. D. Anderson Hospital & Tumor Institute, jt. auth. see M. D. Anderson Annual Clinical Conference of Cancer Staff.
Ma, John T. East Asia: A Survey of Holdings at the Hoover Institution on War, Revolution & Peace.
Ma, Laurence J. & Noble, Allen G., eds. The Environment: Chinese & American Perspectives.
Ma, Wendy Y., jt. ed. see Edgar, Neal L.

Authors

Maanen, Marj van see Van Maanen, Paul & Van Maanen, Marj.
Maanen, Paul van see Van Maanen, Paul & Van Maanen, Marj.
Maanum, Armand & Montgomery, Herb. The Complete Book of Swedish Massage.
Ma'Arri, Abu Ala Al. Saqt Al Zand (the Spark from the Flint) Wormhoudt, Arthur, tr.
Maas, James W., ed. MHPG (3-Methoxy 4-Hydroxyphenethyle Neglycol) Basic Mechanisms & Psychopathology.
Maas, Peter. Serpico.
Maass, H. Modular Functions of One Complex Variables.
--Siegel's Modular Forms & Dirichlet Series.
Mabardi, Georges & Luce, Clare Booth. Vanity Fair's Backgammon to Win.
Mabbett, Ian W., ed. Patterns of Kingship & Authority in Traditional Asia.
Mabbutt, Fred R. Paths to the Present.
Mabbutt, Fred R., jt. auth. see Osborne, Thomas J.
Mabert, Vincent A. & Showalter, Michael J. Cases in Operations Management.
Mabey, David. Jordan's Real Food Guide.
Mabey, Richard. Plantcraft: A Guide to the Everyday Use of Wild Plants.
Mabire, Jean & Breheret, Yves. The Samurai.
Mabley, Jack. Halas, Hef, the Beatles, & Me.
Mabogunje, A. L., jt. ed. see Jackson, C. Ian.
Mabogunje, Akin L. Regional Mobility & Resource Development in West Africa.
Mabry, Aleta M., jt. auth. see Cornish, Robert L.
Mabry, T. J., jt. auth. see Harborne, J. B.
Mabry, T. J., ed. see Phytochemical Society of North America Symposium Staff.
Mabry, T. J., et al. Systematic Identification of Flavonoids.
Mabry, T. J., et al, eds. Creosote Bush.
Mabus, Eileen L. Music for Tiny Tots: A Teacher's Manual for Group Teaching of Four-&-Five-Year-Olds.
MAC Staff. A Cup of Butterflies & Birdsongs.
Macadam, Alta. Florence.
--Northern Italy: From the Alps to Rome.
--Rome & Environs.
--Venice.
MacAdam, Preston. Michael Sheriff: Arabian Assault.
--Michael Sheriff, the Shield: African Assignment.
McAdams. Law, Business & Society.
--Law, Business & Society.
McAdams, Cliff. Yellowstone National Park: Guide & Reference Book.
MacAdams, Michael. Osteoporosis.
McAdams, Phyllis J. The Parent in the Shadows.
MacAdams, Preston. Island Intrigue.
McAfee, Annalena. Kirsty Knows Best.
McAfee, Ward. California's Railroad Era, Eighteen-Fifty to Nineteen-Eleven.
McAleer, John. Ralph Waldo Emerson: Days of Encounter.
McAlister, Linda, ed. The Philosophy of Brentano.
McAllen, Audrey E. The Extra Lesson: Exercises in Movement, Drawing & Painting for Helping Children in Difficulties with Writing, Reading & Arithmetic.
McAllen, Michael. Chandeliers in the Bathroom: Verses & Lyrics from the Seventies.
McAllester, David & McDermott, Drew. Truth Maintenance Systems.
McAllister, Annabelle C. Estes Famlies of Old Clay County, Missouri: Their Ancestors & Their Descendants.
McAllister, Chris. Planes & Airports.
McAllister, Constance, compiled by. Further Phonics Fun.
--Getting Ready for Phonics.
--Learning More about Phonics.
--Phonics Combinations.
--Phonics Fun for Beginners.
McAllister, Harry E. Elements of Business & Statistics: Learning by Objectives.
McAllister, Mick. Illustrated VP-Info. 1.2.
McAloon, Kenneth & Tromba, Anthony. Calculus of One Variable.
McAlpin, Heller. Nostalgia.
McAlpine, Thomas H. Sleep, Divine & Human, in the Old Testament.
MacAndrew, Andrew, tr. see Gogol, Nikolai.
MacAndrew, Andrew R., tr. see Olesha, Yuri.
McAndrew, Patricia, tr. see Bournonville, August.
MacAndrews, C. & Chia, L. S. Developing Economies & the Environment: The Southeast Asia Experience.
MacAndrews, Colin & Sien, Chia Lin, eds. Too Rapid Rural Development: Perceptions & Perspectives from Southeast Asia.
MacArdle, Donald W., ed. see Schindler, Anton F.
McArdle, Lois. Portrait Drawing: A Practical Guide for Today's Artists.
McArdle, William D., jt. auth. see Katch, Frank I.
Macaree, David, jt. auth. see Macaree, Mary.
Macaree, Mary & Macaree, David. One Hundred Three Hikes in Southwestern British Columbia.
McArthur, Colin, ed. Scotch Reels: Scotland in Cinema & Television.
MacArthur, John. My Favorite Verse.
MacArthur, John, Jr. Your Family.
McArthur, Kathleen. The Bush Blooms Again.
McArthur, Robert. Four Creeks.
McArthur, Tom. Unitive Thinking.
Macartney, Anne, jt. auth. see Briggs, Asa.
Macaulay, J. B., jt. auth. see Brookes, Edgar H.
Macaulay, Ranald & Barrs, Jerram. Being Human: The Nature of Spiritual Experience.
Macaulay, Rose. The Towers of Trebizond.
Macaulay, Susan S. Something Beautiful from God.
Macaulay, Thomas B. History of England.
--History of England.
--History of England: From the Accession of James II.
--Selected Writings. Clive, John & Pinney, Thomas, eds.
McAuley, Marilyn. Let's Count.
--My Bible Says.
--What Did God Make?
McAuley, Marilyn, jt. auth. see Gray, Alice.
Macauley, Ted. Yamaha Revised & Updated.
McAuley, W. F. Concept of Schizophrenia.
MacAuliffe, W. R. Modern Asia Explained.
McAuslan, Patrick. The Ideologies of Planning Law.
McAvin, Margaret. Edible Landscaping.
McAvoy, Katherine T. Seymore Snake & Friends: Chester Does His Chores Speech Reinforcement for the Ch Sound.
--Seymore Snake & Friends: Freddy the Frog Speech Reinforcement for the R Sound.
--Seymore Snake & Friends-Liam the Leprechaun: Speech Reinforcement for the L Sound.
--Seymore Snake & Friends: S Sound Reinforcement.
--Seymore Snake & Friends: Shadra O'Shay: Speech Reinforcement for the Sh Sound.
--Seymore Snake & Friends: Theodore Throughly: Speech Reinforcement for the Th Sound.
McAvoy, Thomas T. Formation of the American Catholic Minority, 1820-1860. Wolf, Richard C., ed.
McBain, Ed. Beauty & the Beast.
--Cinderella.
--Cinderella.
--The Con Man.
--Eight Black Horses.
--Eight Black Horses.
--Goldilocks.
--Ice.
--Jack & the Beanstalk.
--Lightning.
--Lightning: An Eighty-Seventh Precinct Novel.
--The McBain Brief.
--The Pusher.
--Snow White & Rose Red.
McBain, Gordon. Quest of the Dawnstar.
McBath, James H., jt. auth. see Dickens, Milton.
McBean, Janet, jt. auth. see Anderson, Dick.
McBeath, Gerald A. Political Integration of the Philippine Chinese.
McBeen, Janet, jt. auth. see Andersen, Dick.
MacBeth, George. Buying a Heart.
--Collected Poems, Nineteen Fifty-Eight to Nineteen Seventy.
--Night of Stones.
--Poems from Oby.
--The Samurai.
--The Seven Witches.
--Shrapnel & the Poet's Year.
--The Survivor.
McBirnie, William S. How to Motivate Your Child Toward Success.
M'Bow, Amadou-Mahtar, ed. see UNESCO General Conference Staff.
McBoyle, Geoffrey. Climate in Review.
McBride, Alfred. Saints Are People: Church History Through the Saints.
McBride, Claude D. Cyrock.
McBride, Earle F., ed. Diagenesis of Sandstone: Cement-Porosity Relationships.
McBride, Henry. The Flow of Art.
McBride, Kelly A., jt. auth. see Nuccio, Richard.
McBride, L. R. Pele, Volcano Goddess of Hawaii.
McBride, Neal. Equipping Adults Through Bible Study.
McBride, Robert L. Art of Instructing the Jury.
McBride, Vearl G. Damn the School System Full Speed Ahead.
McBurney, William J., Jr. College Recruitment.
McCabe, Charles. The Charles McCabe Reader: The Best & the Last of Charles McCabe Himself.
--The Fearless Spectator: A Selective Collection of the Columns of the Late Charles McCabe.
McCabe, Charles R., ed. see Scripps, Edward W.
McCabe, Helen M. & Popham, Estelle L. Word Processing: A Systems Approach to the Office.
McCabe, Joseph. Rationalist Encyclopaedia: A Book of Reference on Religion, Philosophy, Ethics, & Science.
McCabe, Joseph E. Handel's Messiah: A Devotional Commentary.
McCabe, Robert & Anthony, Sally, eds. Ghettos & Barrios.
McCabe, Trisha, jt. ed. see McRobbie, Angela.
McCaffer, Ronald, jt. auth. see Harris, Frank.
McCaffery, Carlyn S., jt. auth. see Practising Law Institute Staff.
McCaffery, Jerry & Mikesell, John, eds. Urban Finance Policy & Administration: A Guide to Information Sources.
McCaffery, Larry, jt. ed. see LeClair, Thomas.
McCaffery, Robert M. Managing the Employee Benefits Program.
McCaffrey, Anne. The Girl Who Heard Dragons.
--Killashandra.
--Nerilka's Story: A Pern Adventure.
MacCaffrey, Isabel G. Spenser's Allegory: The Anatomy of Imagination.
McCaffrey, R. G., et al. The Civil Engineering Standard Method of Measurement in Practice.
McCaig, Donald. Nop's Trials.
McCain, William D., Jr. Properties of Petroleum Fluids.
McCall. Example of Richard Wright.
McCall, Chester H., Jr. Sampling & Statistics Handbook for Research in Education.
McCall, Dan. Queen of Hearts.
McCall, G. J., ed. The Archean: Search for the Beginning.
McCall, G. J. H., ed. Astroblemes-Cryptoexplosion Structures.
McCall, J. L. & French, P. M., eds. Interpretive Techniques for Microstructural Analysis.
--Metallography As a Quality Control Tool.
McCall, James A., et al. Software Maintenance Management.
McCall, Robert B. Fundamental Statistics for Psychology.
--Fundamental Statistics for Psychology.
McCalla, Douglas B., ed. see Federico, Pat A., et al.
McCalla, Thomas R. Introduction to Structured COBOL: With Business Applications.
McCall's Editors. McCall's Big Book of Country Needlecrafts.
--McCall's Big Book of Cross Stitch.
McCall's Editors, ed. McCall's Big Book of Christmas Knit & Crochet.
--McCall's Big Book of Knit Crochet.
McCall's Food Staff. The New, Revised & Updated McCall's Cookbook.
McCall's Pattern Company Staff. The McCall's Book of Quilts.
McCallum, Brian K. Breaking the Bread of Revelation.
MacCallum, F. O., jt. auth. see Cooper, J. I.
McCallum, Jack. Making It in America: Life & Times of Rocky Aoki, Benihana's Pioneer.
McCallum, Pamela. Literature & Method: Towards a Critique of I. A. Richards, T. S. Eliot & F. R. Leavis.
McCameron, Fritz A. COBOL Logic & Programming.
McCammon, R. B., ed. Concepts in Geostatistics.
McCammon, Robert R. Mystery Walk.
--Usher's Passing.
McCance, Allison, jt. auth. see Duncan, Judy.
McCandless, Boyd R. & Coop, Richard H. Adolescents: Behavior & Development.
McCandless, J. Bardarah. An Untainted Saint....Ain't.
McCandless, Ruth S. & Senzaki, Nyogen. Buddhism & Zen.
McCane, Mel R., jt. auth. see Day, Sherman R.
McCann, Eileen. The Two-Step: Dancing Toward Intimacy.
McCann, John M. The Marketing Workbench: Using Computers for Better Performance.
McCann, John S. The Critical Reputation of Tennessee Williams: A Reference Guide.
McCann, Larry D., ed. Heartland & Hinterland: A Geography of Canada.
McCann, Patricia S., jt. auth. see Romans, Robert C.
McCann, Phillip & Young, Francis A. Samuel Wilderspin & the Infant School Movement.
McCann, Richard, jt. ed. see Gibson, Margaret.
McCann, Roger C. Introduction to Linear Algebra.
McCants, Louise. The Womanchange!
McCardell, John M., Jr. The Idea of a Southern Nation: Southern Nationalists & Southern Nationalism, 1830-1860.
McCarl, Henry N. & McConnell, David. Bibliography on Economic Analysis for Parks & Recreation.
McCarn, Joan O. A General Handbook for the Dental Office.
McCarroll, Jesse C., jt. auth. see Adler, Marvin S.
McCarroll, John D. Computer-Aided Part Programming for Numerical Control: An Industry Study.
McCarry, Charles. The Miernick Dossier.
McCartan, Dominic. Operation Emerald.
McCartan, Patrick J., jt. auth. see Hargie, Owen.
McCarter, Neely D. Hear the Word of the Lord.
--Help Me Understand, Lord: Prayer Response to the Gospel of Mark.
McCarter, William & Gilbert, Rita. Living with Art.
McCarthy. A Death in the Family: A Self-Help Guide to Coping with Grief.
McCarthy, Abigail. Circles: A Washington Story.
McCarthy, Abigail & Muskie, Jane G. One Woman Lost.
McCarthy, Anne & Gregoric, Florence I., eds. International Symposium on Labeled & Unlabeled Antibody in Cancer Diagnosis & Therapy.
McCarthy, B. Eugene. William Wycherley: A Biography.
McCarthy, Bridget B. Where to Find the Oregon in Oregon 1988-89.
McCarthy, Charles. Elements in a Theory of Industrial Relations.
McCarthy, Charles, jt. auth. see McCarthy, Estelle.
McCarthy, Constance F. & Sheehy, Ann D. Easy As One-Two-Three.
McCarthy, Dennis B. The Great Chicago Bar & Saloon Guide.
McCarthy, Dennis J. Old Testament Covenant: A Survey of Current Opinions.
McCarthy, Estelle & McCarthy, Charles. The Power Picture.
McCarthy, Eugene, et al. The Second Opinion Handbook: A Guide for Medical Self Defense.
McCarthy, Eugene J. Gene McCarthy's Minnesota.
McCarthy, Eugene J. & Kilpatrick, James J. A Political Bestiary.
McCarthy, Frank M. Emergencies in Dental Practice: Prevention & Treatment.
--Medical Emergencies in Dentistry: Emergencies in Dental Practice.
McCarthy, Gary. Mustangers.
--Powder River.
--Wind River.
McCarthy, Gillian T. The Physically Handicapped Child: An Interdisciplinary Approach to Management.
McCarthy, Gregory J., ed. Scientific Basis for Nuclear Waste Management.
McCarthy, Gregory J., et al, eds. Advances in X-Ray Analysis.
McCarthy, I. E. Introduction to Nuclear Theory.
--Nuclear Reactions.
McCarthy, J. E. & Shapiro, Stanley J. Basic Marketing: A Managerial Approach. Canadian Edition.
McCarthy, Jane & Ladimer, Irving. Resolving Faculty Disputes.
McCarthy, Jane E., jt. auth. see American Arbitration Association Staff.
McCarthy, Jeanne M., jt. auth. see Kirk, Samuel A.
McCarthy, John F. The Science of Historical Theology: Elements of a Definition.
McCarthy, John J. John J. McCarthy's Secrets of Super Selling.
--Secrets of Management Excellence.
--Why Managers Fail.
McCarthy, Joseph M. An International List of Articles on the History of Education Published in Non-Educational Serials, 1965-1974.
McCarthy, Kyle, jt. auth. see Levy, John.
McCarthy, Mary. Birds of America.
--Cannibals & Missionaries.
--A Charmed Life.
--The Company She Keeps.
--The Company She Keeps.
--The Group.
--The Groves of Academe.
--The Groves of Academe.
--Hanoi.
--The Hounds of Summer & Other Stories.
--Medina.
--Memories of a Catholic Girlhood.
--The Oasis.
--The Seventeenth Degree.
--Social Change & the Growth of British Power in the Gold Coast: The Fante States Eighteen Hundred & Seven to Eighteen Seventy-Four.
--Vietnam.
--The Writing on the Wall & Other Literary Essays.
McCarthy, Michael. Campaigning for the Poor.
--Mastering DisplayWrite 3.
McCarthy, Michael, jt. auth. see Lamm, Richard D.
McCarthy, Michael, et al. Proficiency Plus.
McCarthy, Mignon, jt. auth. see Fonda, Jane.
McCarthy, Nan, ed. see Brickner, Dave, et al.
McCarthy, Nan, ed. see Glau, Gregory R., et al.
McCarthy, Nan, ed. see Vick, Bill, et al.
McCarthy, Nan, ed. see Young, George.
McCarthy, Nan, et al, eds. see Green, Wayne.
McCarthy, Patricia, ed. License to Steal: Secrets of Acquiring Distress Property.
McCarthy, Ruth. Katie & the Smallest Bear.
McCarthy, Shawna, ed. see Asimov, Isaac.
McCarthy, Thomas A., jt. auth. see Dallmayr, Fred R.

McCartney, Eugene S. Warfare by Land & Sea.
McCartney, Hazel S. Saga of Seven Sisters.
McCartney, Thomas L. The Zone System: Testing Procedures for All Formats.
McCartney, W. Olfaction & Odours: An Osphresiological Essay.
McCarty, Betsy. A Passionate Flower.
McCarty, Clifford. Published Screenplays: A Checklist.
McCarty, Daniel J., ed. Arthritis & Allied Conditions: A Textbook of Rheumatology.
McCarty, J. W. & Schedvin, C. B. Australian Capital Cities: Historical Essays.
McCarty, J. W., jt. auth. see Scheduin, C. B.
McCarty, John, jt. auth. see Krogh, Daniel.
McCarty, Marilu. Dollars & Sense: Introduction to Economics.
McCarty, Teresa, jt. auth. see Materials Development Staff.
McCary, James L. Freedom & Growth in Marriage.
McCary, James L. & McCary, Stephen P. Human Sexuality.
McCary, Stephen P., jt. auth. see McCary, James L.
MacCaskey, Michael R. All about Lawns. Ortho Books Editorial Staff, ed.
Mc Caslin, N. L. & Walker, Jerry P. A Guide for Improving Locally Developed Career Education Measures.
McCaslin, N. L., et al. Career Education Measures: A Compendium of Evaluation Instruments.
McCathren, Randall R., jt. auth. see Loshin, Ronald S.
McCauley, Kirby E. Night Chills.
McCauley, Lois B. A. Hoen on Stone: E. Weber & Co. & A. Hoen & Co. Exhibition Catalogue.
McCauley, Martin. The Stalin File.
McCauley, Stephen. The Object of My Affection.
McCauley, Sue. Then Again.
McCaull, Julian & Crossland, Janice. Water Pollution. Commoner, Barry, ed.
McCavitt, William E. Broadcasting Around the World.
McCaw, Mabel. What Is Loving?
McCaw, Mabel N. What God Can Do.
McCawley, James D. Adverbs, Vowels, & Other Objects of Wonder.
McCawley, Patricia. Glass Paperweights.
McChesney, et al. Guide to Language & Study Skills, for College Students of English As a Second Language.
Macchia, Donald D. Weight Training in Sports: A Bibliography with Special Reference to Body-Building & Olympic Power Lifting.
McClain, Elissa L. Rest from the Quest.
McClain, Maureen E., jt. auth. see Kauff, Jerome B.
McClain Printing Company Staff. The Flood of November Fourth, 1985.
McClanahan, Richard. Cadence--Key to Musical Clarity.
--Harmonic Study Editions of Six Early Keyboard Classics.
McClane. Fisherman's Diary.
McClane, Kenneth. To Hear the River.
McClaskey, Marilyn J., jt. auth. see Simonton, Wesley.
McClatchy, J. D. Stars Principal.
McClave, James, jt. auth. see Scheaffer, Richard.
McClave, James T., jt. auth. see Mendenhall, William.
McClave, Randy. The Works.
McClean, Adam. The Western Mandala: A Survey of the Mandala in the Western Esoteric Tradition.
McCleary, Julia C. Cooking Metric Is Fun.
McCleary, Lloyd & Thomson, Scott. The Senior High School Principalship: The Summary Report. Koerner, Thomas, ed.
McCleary, Richard. Dangerous Men: The Sociology of Parole.
McClellan, James, jt. auth. see Redden, Kenneth R.
McClelland, Herbert L. The Magga Birds of Ranatan. Davenport, May, ed. Bd. with Why Do We Not See Little People, Miss Wintergreen? Zimelman, Nathan; Spots & Splashes & a Million Butterflies. Deedy, Joyce. Davenport.
McClelland, Mark W. The Artistic Applications of Classical Criteria to the Decoration of Walls.
McClelland, Trish. Dynamics of Reflex.
--The Dynamics of Wordperfect.
McClennan, Brad. Birth to Rebirth.
McClernan, John B. Slade's Wells Fargo Colt.
MacClintock, Carol. The Solo Song, Fifteen Eighty to Seventeen Thirty.
McClintock, David L. Formula Budgeting: An Approach to Facilities Funding.
MacClintock, Dorcas. A Natural History of Raccoons.
MacClintock, Dorcas & Mochi, Ugo. A Natural History of Giraffes.
McClintock, James C. & Caroline, Nancy L. Workbook for Emergency Care in the Streets.
McClintock, Marsha H. The Middle East & North Africa on Film: An Annotated Filmography.
McClintock, Michael. Homeowner's Handbook: What You Need to Know about Buying, Maintaining, Improving, & Running Your Home Successfully.
McClintock, Mike. The Home How-to Sourcebook.
--Home Sense.
--Popular Science Do-It-Yourself Yearbook 1985.
--Popular Science Woodworking Projects Yearbook.
McClinton, Katharine M. Changing Church.
McClinton, Katherine M. Antique Cats for Collectors.
McClelland, Harold F., jt. auth. see Benson, George C.
McCloskey, A. L., jt. ed. see Steinberg, H.
McCloskey, H. J. Ecological Ethics & Politics.
McCloskey, Paul N. United States Constitution.
MacCloud, Malcolm. A Gift of Mirrorvax.
--The Tera Beyond.
McCloy, D. Control of Fluid Power: Analysis & Design.
McCloy, Shelby T. The Negro in the French West Indies.
McCluney, Daniel C., jt. auth. see Kauf, Robert.
McClung, Robert M. Rajpur: Last of the Bengal Tigers.
McClure, Charles R., jt. auth. see Hernon, Peter.
McClure, Donald S., ed. see Brome, Richard.
McClure, Ethel. A Historical Directory of Minnesota Homes for the Aged.
McClure, James. The Artful Egg.
--The Blood of an Englishman.
--The Caterpillar Cop.
--Cop World: Policing the Streets of San Diego.
--The Steam Pig.
--The Sunday Hangman.
McClure, Matthew, ed. see Gaskin, Stephen.
McClure, Michael. The Beard & Victims: Two Plays.
McClure, Rhyder. Fast Access Wordperfect 5.0.
McClure, Robert M., ed. Curriculum, Retrospect & Prospect.
McClure, Ruth K., ed. see Dow, Dorothy.
McClurg, Eunice. Your Down's Syndrome Child: Everything Today's Parents Need to Know about Raising Their Special Child.
McCluskey, E. J., jt. auth. see Gschwind, H. W.
McClymont, John. Laboratory Manual for General Botany.
McCoard, R. W. English Perfect: Tense-Choice & Pragmatic Inferences.
Maccoby, Eleanor E. & Zellner, Miriam. Experiments in Primary Education: Aspects of Project Follow-Through.
Maccoby, Michael. The Leader: A New Face for American Management.
McColl, Patricia, ed. see Bowman, Leona.
McCollough, Albert. The Complete Book of Buddy "L" Toys: A Greenberg Guide.
McComas, Donna C., jt. auth. see Hunsinger, Marjorie.
McComas, Tom & Tuohy, James. Lionel: A Collector's Guide & History: Advertising & Art.
--Lionel: A Collector's Guide & History: Standard Guage.
McComb, H. G., Jr., jt. auth. see Noor, A. K.
McCombs, Maxwell, et al. Handbook of Reporting Methods.
McConahay, John B., jt. auth. see Sears, David O.
McConkey, Clarence. When Cancer Comes.
McConkey, Dale D. How to Manage By Results.
--No-Nonsense Delegation.
--No-Nonsense Delegation.
McConkey, Roy, jt. auth. see Jeffree, Dorothy.
McConkie, Joseph F. His Name Shall Be Joseph: Ancient Prophecies of the Latter-Day Seer.
McConnel, Malcolm L. The Essence of Fiction: A Practical Handbook for Successful Writing.
McConnell, Adeline P. & Anderson, Beverly. Single After Fifty: How to Have the Time of Your Life.
McConnell, Carol & McConnell, Malcolm. The Mediterranean Diet: Optimal Nutrition for a Long Healthy Life.
--Middle Sea Autumn.
McConnell, Carol, jt. auth. see McConnell, Malcolm.
McConnell, Charles R. The Effective Health Care Supervisor.
McConnell, D. Apatite: Its Crystal Chemistry, Mineralogy, Utilization, & Biologic Occurrences.
McConnell, David, jt. auth. see McCarl, Henry N.
McConnell, Donald K., Jr. Public Company Auditor Changes & Big Eight Firms: Disagreements & Other Issues. Farmer, Richard, ed.
McConnell, Edwina A. Burnout in the Nursing Profession: Causes, Costs & Coping Strategies.
McConnell, Grant. Decline of Agrarian Democracy.
McConnell, J. Knox. How to Get a Loan from Your Bank, Credit Union, or Finance Company.
McConnell, James. English Public Schools.
McConnell, James G. Comparative Negligence Defense Tactics.
McConnell, James V. Understanding Human Behavior: An Introduction to Psychology.
McConnell, Joan, tr. see Mazzolani, Lidia S.
McConnell, Josephine. Who Are We Americans?
McConnell, Malcolm. Stepping Over: Personal Encounters with Young Extremists.
McConnell, Malcolm & McConnell, Carol. First Crossing: A Personal Log.
McConnell, Malcolm, jt. auth. see McConnell, Carol.
McConnell, Sharon & Daughtry, Jolyne. Your Guide to the Seventh Edition of James M. McCrimmon's: Writing with a Purpose.
McConnell, Thomas R. General Education.
--Psychology of Learning.
McConnor, Vincent. I Am Vidocq.
--The Paris Puzzle.
McConochie, Jean, ed. see Messec, Jerry L.
MacConomy, Alma D., ed. see Borland, Hal.
MacConomy, Alma D., ed. see Robinson, David F.
McCool, Audrey C. & Posner, Barbara M. Nutrition Services for Older Americans: Foodservice Systems & Technologies: Administrative Guidelines.
--Nutrition Services for Older Americans: Foodservice Systems & Technologies: Program Management Strategies.
McCord, David T. In Sight of Sever: Essays from Harvard.
McCord, Howard. Maps.
McCord, Jean. Bitter is the Hawk's Path.
McCord, Thomas I. & Doreian, Raymond. Erisa Plan Administrators Desk Book with Checklists & Guidelines for Successful Communications.
McCord, William, et al. Life Styles in the Black Ghetto.
McCorduck, Pamela. The Universal Machine: Confessions of a Technological Optimist.
McCorkle, Donald M., ed. Brahms: Variations on a Theme of Haydn.
McCormack, Lily. I Hear You Calling Me.
McCormack, Mark H. The Wonderful World of Professional Golf.
--The World of Professional Golf Annual, 1974.
--The World of Professional Golf Annual, 1975.
--The World of Professional Golf: Golf Annual 1972.
--The World of Professional Golf: Golf Annual 1973.
--The World of Professional Golf: Golf Annual 1976.
--The World of Professional Golf: Golf Annual 1977.
McCormack, Michael K., ed. Prevention of Mental Retardation & Other Developlmental Disabilities.
McCormack, Robert, jt. auth. see Ward, Richard H.
McCormack, William C. & Wurm, Stephen A., eds. Language & Man: Anthropological Issues.
--Language & Thought: Anthropological Issues.
McCormack, William G. & Izzo, Herbert J., eds. Sixth LACUS Forum Proceedings, Linguistic Association of Canada & the U. S.
McCormick, E. Allen, jt. auth. see Ryder, Frank G.
McCormick, Edith, tr. see Winterfeld, Henry.
McCormick, Harry & Carey, Mary. Bank Robbers Wrote My Diary.
McCormick, Harvey L. Social Security Claims & Procedures: 1986 P.P.
McCormick, J. J., et al. Experimental Control of Mitosis, 2.
McCormick, James. The Doctor: Father Figure or Plumber?
McCormick, Joe, tr. see Ford, LeRoy.
McCormick, M. P. & Lovill, J. E., eds. Space Observations of Aerosols & Ozone: Proceedings of the Topical Meeting of the COSPAR Interdisciplinary Scientific Commission A (Meetings A1 & A2) of the COSPAR 24th Plenary Meeting held in Ottawa, Canada, 16 May-2 June, 1982.
McCormick, Mark, jt. auth. see Starr, V. Hale.
McCormick, Mary J. Enduring Values in a Changing Society.
McCormick, Michael E., ed. Anchoring Systems.
--Port & Ocean Engineering under Arctic Conditions: Selected Papers from the 3rd International Conference.
McCormick, Mike, jt. auth. see Schwartz, Bill.
McCormick, N. J. see Williams, M. M.
McCormick, N. J., jt. ed. see Williams, M. M.
McCormick, N. J., jt. ed. see Williams, M. R.
McCormick, Peter, jt. ed. see Elliston, Frederick.
McCormick, Richard P. Experiment in Independence: New Jersey in the Critical Period 1781-1789.
McCormick, Rose-Marie & Parkavich, Tamar J. Patient & Family Education: Tools, Techniques & Theory.
McCormick, Ruth, tr. from Ger. Fassbinder.
McCormick, Thomas J; see O'Neal, William B.
McCormick, William F., jt. auth. see Bell, William E.
McCormick-Ray, M. G., jt. auth. see Ray, G. Carleton.
McCowen, Alec. Double Bill.
--Young Gemini.
McCoy, Alfred W. & De Jesus, Ed. C., eds. Philippine Social History: Global Trade & Local Transformations.
McCoy, Esther. Case Study Houses, 1945-1962.
--Five California Architects.
McCoy, Floyd, jt. auth. see McCoy, Lois.
McCoy, Horace. I Should Have Stayed Home. Kupelnick, Bruce S., ed.
McCoy, J. J. In Defense of Animals.
--A Sea of Troubles.
McCoy, John H. Livestock & Meat Marketing.
McCoy, K. Landscape Planning for a New Australian Town.
McCoy, Kathy & Wibbelsman, Charles. The Teenage Body Book.
McCoy, L. M., tr. see Alves, Rubem.
McCoy, Lois & McCoy, Floyd. Science under Sail: The Story of Oceanography.
McCoy, Maureen. Walking after Midnight.
McCoy, R. D., et al. Current Research in Petroleum Fuels, I.
McCoy, Richard B., jt. auth. see Baum, Lloyd.
McCoy, Robert A. Practical Photography.
McCoy, Seth. Not Quite Human! Batteries Not Included.
McCoy, Sue & Dean, Jill, eds. Yarns of Wisconsin.
McCoy, Sue W., ed. see Nonken, Pam, et al.
McCoy, Vivian & Cassell, Phyllis, eds. Career Exploration Workshop for Women: Leader's Manual.
--Career Exploration Workshop for Women: Participant's Personal Portfolio.
McCoy, Vivian, jt. ed. see Rozzelle, Robert W.
McCoy, Vivian R., et al. The Adult Life Cycle Trainer Manual & Reader.
McCoy, Vivian R., et al, eds. Create: A New Model for Career Change - Participants Manual.
--Create: A New Model for Career Change - Trainers Manual.
McCracken, Alexander W. & Cawson, Broderick A. Clinical & Oral Microbiology.
McCracken, Alexander W., jt. auth. see Cawson, Roderick A.
McCracken, Daniel D. Computing for Engineers & Scientists with FORTRAN 77.
McCracken, John W., jt. ed. see Kreck, Lothar A.
McCracken, Karen H. Connie Hagar: The Life History of a Texas Birdwatcher.
McCracken, Sylvia. My Silent Obligato.
McCraken, jt. auth. see Nelson.
McCraken, J. L. Representative Government in Ireland: A Study of Dail Eireann, 1919-48.
McCraney, William L., ed. Readings in Criminal Psychology.
McCrank, Lawrence J. Education for Rare Book Librarianship: A Reexamination of Trends & Problems.
McCrary, William & Madrigal, Jose A., eds. Studies in Honor of Everett W. Hesse.
McCray, Walter A. Reaching & Teaching Black Young Adults.
--Solid: Nine Vital Lessons on Settling, Saving & Solidifying the Black Marriage.
McCready, Richard R. Business Mathematics.
--Learning Business Math with Electronic Calculators.
--Learning Business Mathematics with Electronic Calculators.
--Solving Business Problems with Calculators.
McCreary, Alf. Survivors: Documentary Account of the Victims of Northern Ireland.
McCree, Cree. Flea Market America: The Bargain Hunter's Guide.
McCreight, L. R., et al. Ceramic & Graphic Fibers & Whiskers: A Survey of Technology.
McCreight, Tim, et al. John Prip: Master Metalsmith.
McCrerey, Linda. Fabulous Makeovers for Ultimate Beauty. Incl. Blonde; Brunette; Redhead. Macmillan.
McCrickard, Eleanor F., ed. Alessandro Stradella's "Esule dalle sfere" Cantata for the Souls of Purgatory. Scaglione, Aldo, tr. from Ital.
McCrimmon, Barbara. Antonio Panizzi As Administrator.
McCrimmon, James M. Teaching with a Purpose.
--Writing with a Purpose.
--Writing with a Purpose.
McCrimmon, James M., et al. Writing with a Purpose.
--Writing with a Purpose: Short Edition.
McCrohan, Donna. The Second City.
McCrone, Carole N. & Rose-Hancock, Marga, eds. Fresh, Fast, & Fabulous.
McCrossen, V. A. The New Renaissance of the Spirit.
McCrossen, Vincent A. Empty Room.
McCrum, Robert. The Fabulous Englishman.
--A Loss of Heart.

McCrum, Sean. Changing Images: Figurative Painting by Irish Artists since 1970.
McCue, James F., jt. auth. see Forell, George W.
McCue, Lisa, illus. They Call Me Boober Fraggle.
McCuen, Gary, ed. Illiteracy in America.
--Treating the Mentally Disabled.
McCuen, Jo R. & Winkler, Anthony C. Readings for Writers.
McCuen, Jo R., jt. auth. see Winkler, Anthony C.
McCuen, Jo Ray & Winkler, Anthony C. Readings for Writers.
--Readings for Writers.
--Rhetoric Made Plain.
McCuen, Jo Ray, jt. auth. see Winkler, Anthony C.
McCuen, JoRay & Winkler, Anthony C. Rhetoric Made Plain.
McCullagh, A., jt. auth. see Marsden, P.
McCullagh, Suzanne F., jt. auth. see Brettell, Richard R.
McCullen, Maurice & Sawin, Lewis. A Dictionary of the Characters in George Meredith's Fiction.
McCullers, Carson. Collected Short Stories. Bd. with The Ballad of the Sad Cafe. HM.
--Member of the Wedding.
McCullers, Carson, jt. auth. see Albee, Edward A.
McCullo, Marion. Student Journalist's Proofreader's Manual.
McCulloch, Alan. Encyclopedia of Australian Art.
McCulloch, J. In the Twilight of the Revolution: The Political Theory of Amilcar Cabral.
McCulloch, J. W. & Philip, A. E. Suicidal Behavior.
McCulloch, J. W., et al. Social Work Research & the Analysis of Social Data.
McCulloch, James E., ed. see Southern Sociological Congress Staff.
McCulloch, John R., ed. Select Collection of Scarce & Valuable Tracts & Other Publications on the National Debt & the Sinking Fund.
McCulloch, Lou W. Paper Americana: A Collector's Guide.
Macculloch, M. J., jt. auth. see Feldman, M. P.
McCulloch, Walter F. Woods Words.
McCulloh, Judith, jt. ed. see Malone, Bill.
McCullough. First of All.
McCullough, C. Sue. Computers in School Psychology: An Overview.
McCullough, Colleen. The Ladies of Missalonghi.
--The Thorn Birds.
McCullough, Constance M., ed. Inchworm, Inchworm: Persistent Problems in Reading Education.
McCullough, David. Mornings on Horseback: The Story of an Extraordinary Family, a Vanquished Way of Life, & the Unique Child Who Became Theodore Roosevelt.
McCullough, David W. The Great Bridge.
--Mornings on Horseback.
McCullough, George H. Washington Square Poems: Bicentennial Edition.
McCullough, Mamie. I Can, You Can Too!
McCullough, Newton C., III, ed. Critical Needs of the Child with Long Term Orthopaedic Impairment: Conference Report.
McCullough, Robert J. & Everard, Kenneth. Bank Reconciliation Projects.
McCullough, W., jt. auth. see Munro, A.
McCully, Marilyn, intro. by. Homage to Barcelona: The City & Its Art 1888-1936.
McCully, Mary, ed. History Of Genesee County, New York 1890-1982.
McCumber, W. E. The Good News: Mark.
McCumsey, Janet. A Magical Menagerie.
McCune, George. Blessings of Temple Marriage.
McCunn, Ruthanne L. Thousand Pieces of Gold: A Biographical Novel.
McCurdy, David W., jt. auth. see Spradley, James P.
McCurdy, David W. & Spradley, James P., eds. Issues in Cultural Anthropology: Selected Readings.
McCurdy, Michael. The Illustrated Harvard: Harvard University in Wood Engravings & Words.
McCurdy, Richard M. Qualities & Quantities: Preparation for College Chemistry.
McCurdy, Richard N. & Greene, Howard M. Qualities & Quantities in the Laboratory.
McCurley, Foster, tr. see Wolff, Hans W.
McCurley, Foster R. Ancient Myths & Biblical Faith.
--Genesis, Exodus, Leviticus, Numbers.
McCurley, Foster R., ed. see Achtemeier, Elizabeth.
McCurley, Foster R., ed. see Anderson, Bernhard W.
McCurley, Foster R., ed. see Mays, James L.
McCurley, Foster R., ed. see Rast, Walter E.
McCurley, Foster R., Jr. Proclaiming the Promise: Christian Preaching from the Old Testament.
McCurtin, Peter. Battle Pay.
--Death Dance.
--Gold Strike.
--Hangman's Knot.
--Los Olvidados.
--Scorpion.
--Sundance: The Marauders.
McCutchan, Kenneth P. At the Bend in the River: The Story of Evansville.
McCutchen, et al. California Environmental Law Handbook. Denney, Richard J., Jr., et al, eds.
McCutcheon, Ernest P., ed. Chronically Implanted Cardiovascular Instrumentation.
McCutcheon, James M. China & America: A Bibliography of Interactions, Foreign & Domestic.
McDade, Charlie. Almost Dark.
McDaniel, Burruss. How to Know the Mites & Ticks.
McDaniel, D. W., ed. see American Fisheries Society Fish Health Section Staff.
McDaniel, Deborah. Foster Care in the 1980s.
McDaniel, E. F. Discovering the Real Self.
McDaniel, Earl W. The Mobility & Diffusion of Ions in Gases.
McDaniel, Eugene B. & Johnson, James L. Before Honor.
McDaniel, Genevieve S. Mrs. Spratt's Buffet Cookbook.
McDaniel, James W. Physical Disability & Human Behavior.
McDaniel, Johnnie. True Tales of a Soul Traveler.
McDaniel, Karl S. On the Rise.
McDaniel, Lurlene. Head over Heels.
--More Than Just a Smart Girl.
--Peanut Butter for Dinner Again?
McDaniel, Reuben, jt. auth. see Knight, Kenneth.
McDaniel, Reuben R., Jr., jt. auth. see Knight, Kenneth E.
McDaniels, Carl. Leisure: Integrating a Neglected Component in Life Planning.
McDarrah, Fred W., ed. Stock Photo & Assignment.
McDarrah, Gloria S. Frommer's Guide to Atlantic City & Cape May.
McDermott, A. Cytogenetics of Man & Other Animals.
McDermott, Annella, ed. & tr. see Salcedo-Bastardo, J. L.
Mcdermott, Austin, jt. auth. see Shavin, Norman.
McDermott, Barry, jt. auth. see Bollettieri, Nick.
McDermott, Beatrice S. & Coleman, Freada A., eds. Government Regulation of Business Including Antitrust Information Sources.
McDermott, Drew, jt. auth. see McAllester, David.
McDermott, J. How to Get Lost & Found in Fiji.
McDermott, Robert. Hypnosis, Is It For You?
McDermott, William V., Jr., ed. Atlas of Standard Surgical Procedures.
McDevitt, David, ed. Cell Biology of the Eye.
McDevitt, Hugh O., ed. Ir Genes & Ia Antigens (Symposium) (MS-Repro)
McDevitt, Hugh O. & Landy, Maurice, eds. Genetic Control of Immune Responsiveness: Relationship to Disease Susceptibility.
McDiarmid, ed. see Zoological Society of London Symposium Staff.
McDiarmid, E. W., jt. ed. see Doyle, P J.
MacDiarmid, Hugh. The Hugh MacDiarmid Anthology: Poems in Scots & English. Grieve, Michael & Scott, Alexander, eds.
McDiarmid, Norma J., et al. Loving & Learning: Interacting with Your Child from Birth to Three.
--Loving & Learning: Interacting with Your Child from Birth to Three.
McDicken, W. N. Diagnostic Ultrasonics: Principles & Use of Instruments.
McDonagh, et al. Engineering Science for Technicians.
McDonagh, Francis, tr. see Theissen, Gerd.
McDonagh, I., et al. Engineering Science for Technicians.
MacDonagh, Oliver. The Inspector-General: Sir Jeremiah Fitzpatrick & the Politics of Social Reform 1783-1802.
MacDonagh, Oliver & Mandle, W. F., eds. Ireland & Irish-Australia: Studies in Cultural & Political History.
McDonald, jt. auth. see Skobel.
Macdonald, A. G. & Wann, K. T. Physiological Aspects of Anaesthetics & Inert Gases.
McDonald, A. G., ed. Selective Studies in Health & Social Services.
Mac Donald, A. L. Agricultural Technology in Developing Countries.
MacDonald, Alastair, tr. see Malraux, Andre.
MacDonald, Angus J. Power: Mechanics of Energy Control.
McDonald, Archie P. In Celebration of Texas. Wells, Susan, ed.
McDonald, Archie P., ed. Make Me a Map of the Valley: The Civil War Journal of Stonewall Jackson's Topographer.
Macdonald, Argus J. Wind Loading on Buildings.
McDonald, Boyd. Smut: True Experiences from "Straight to Hell"
Macdonald, Charles B. Company Commander.
Macdonald, Charles R. Sixty Ways, Sixty Days & Twenty Four Ways to Greater Business Productivity.
--Twenty-Four Ways to Greater Business Productivity: Master Checklists for Marketing, Advertising, Sales, Distribution & Customer Service.
MacDonald, Chuck, jt. auth. see Jenson, Ronald.
McDonald, Cleveland. Creating a Successful Christian Marriage.
Macdonald, Cynthia. Transplants.
Macdonald, D., jt. ed. see Amlaner, C.
MacDonald, David, et al. The Complete Book of the Dog.
Macdonald, David S. Harris Postage Stamp Catalog: 1987 Edition.
Macdonald, Donald Ian & Newton, Miller. Drugs, Drinking, & Adolescents.
McDonald, Durstan, et al. Scripture Today.
McDonald, Durstan R., et al, eds. The Myth: Truth of God Incarnate. Nineham, Dennis & Sano, Roy.
Macdonald, Dwight. The Responsibility of Peoples & Other Essays in Political Criticism.
McDonald, Elvin. Making Your Lawn & Garden Grow.
McDonald, Eugene T. A Deep Test of Articulation: Picture.
--A Screening Deep Test of Articulation.
Macdonald, Fergus. The Catholic Church & the Secret Societies in the United States.
McDonald, Forrest. The Presidency of George Washington.
--The Presidency of George Washington.
--We the People.
MacDonald, Frank. Chicago Bulls.
--Golden State Warriors.
McDonald, Frank. Provenance.
MacDonald, George. The Last Castle.
--The Lost Princess.
--Macdonald Fairy Tales Gift Set.
--The MacDonald Trilogy.
--On Tangled Paths. Hamilton, Dan, ed.
--Princess & Curdie.
--The Prodigal Apprentice.
--A Quiet Neighborhood.
--The Seaboard Parish.
--The Shopkeeper's Daughter.
--The Vicar's Daughter.
McDonald, Gerald W., jt. auth. see Nass, Gilbert D.
McDonald, Gregory. Carioca Fletch.
McDonald, H. D. The Atonement of the Death of Christ.
--The God Who Responds.
--Theories of Revelation.
MacDonald, Hugh, ed. see Marvell, Andrew.
McDonald, I. R., jt. auth. see Hansen, J. P.
McDonald, Irene B. Language: All About It.
McDonald, Jack R. & Dean, Alan H. Electrostatic Precipitator Manual.
McDonald, Jan. The New Drama 1900-1914.
--The New Drama 1900-1914.
Macdonald, Janet W. The Right Horse: An Owner's & Buyers' Guide.
McDonald, Jean G. Legislators & Patronage in Oklahoma.
MacDonald, John D. Bright Orange for the Shroud.
--Bright Orange for the Shroud.
--Darker Than Amber.
--Dead Low Tide. Barzun, J. & Taylor, W. H., eds.
--The Deep Blue Good-by.
--The Deep Blue Good-by.
--The Dreadful Lemon Sky.
--Dress Her in Indigo.
--Dress Her in Indigo.
--The Empty Copper Sea.
--Free Fall in Crimson.
--Girl in the Plain Brown Wrapper.
--The Green Ripper.
--The Long Lavender Look.
--One Fearful Yellow Eye.
--The Only Girl in the Game.
--Pale Gray for the Guilt.
--Pale Grey for Guilt.
--The Quick Red Fox.
--The Scarlet Ruse.
--A Tan & Sandy Silence.
--The Turquoise Lament.
McDonald, John F. Economic Analysis of an Urban Housing Market.
MacDonald, Joseph A., ed. see Professional Publications Staff.
Macdonald, K. D., ed. see Genetics of Industrial Mangement Symposium Staff.
McDonald, Kathleen. How to Meditate: A Practical Guide. Courtin, Robina, ed.
Macdonald, Keith B., jt. ed. see Hamilton, Peter.
McDonald, Leslie E., jt. auth. see Booth, Nicholas H.
MacDonald, Lisa, ed. National Gallery of Art Early American Guest Book.
--The National Gallery of Art Small French Paintings: A Book of Days.
McDonald, M., ed. see Garcia, Ronda.
MacDonald, Malcolm. Schoenberg.
--The Symphonies of Havergal Brian.
--Symphonies of Havergal Brian.
Macdonald, Margaret, ed. see Wittgenstein, Ludwig.
McDonald, Mary R. Little Stories about God.
MacDonald, Maurice. Food Stamps, & Income Maintenance.
Macdonald, Michael C. & Bane, John, Jr. Street Cop.
McDonald, P., et al. Animal Nutrition.
McDonald, P. W., jt. auth. see Tisdell, C. A.
McDonald, Perry & Odell, William. Laws of Christian Living: The Commandments.
MacDonald, Philip. Murder Gone Mad.
McDonald, Phyllis. Law Enforcement Education in the Middle Grades: Police-Student Relations.
MacDonald, R., jt. ed. see Bailey, D. K.
MacDonald, R. D., jt. auth. see Clow, C. A.
MacDonald, R. P. see Reiner, Miriam, et al.
McDonald, Ralph E. & Avery, David R. Dentistry for the Child & Adolescent.
MacDonald, Robert D. Summit Conference.
McDonald, Robert J. Basic Upholstery Repair & Restoration.
--Upholstery Repair & Restoration: A Complete Guide to Fabric & Leather Upholstery Repair.
McDonald, Robert P. Syndicated Loans.
MacDonald, Robert W. Control Your Future: Find Your Fortune in the Financial Services Revolution.
McDonald, Rod, jt. auth. see Bond, David.
McDonald, Roger. First Paperback Poets Anthology.
MacDonald, Ronald R., ed. Scientific Basis of Obstetrics & Gynecology.
Macdonald, Ross. The Barbarous Coast.
--The Drowning Pool. Barzun, Jacques & Taylor, Wendell H., eds.
Macdonald, Shelagh. No End to Yesterday.
McDonald, Stephen L. Federal Tax Treatment of Income from Oil & Gas.
Macdonald, Susan & Mottram, Maxine. Preparation for Cosmetology Licensing Examinations.
McDonald, T. Marll. Mathematical Methods for Social & Management Scientists.
McDonald, Tom. Next of Kin in Jail.
McDonald, Travis C. Emporia: A Centennial Retrospective, 1897-1987.
MacDonald, William. Enjoying the Psalms.
MacDonald, William C. Ghost Town Gold.
--Roaring Lead.
--Six-Gun Melody.
McDonald, William F., ed. Criminal Justice & the Victim.
--The Prosecutor.
McDonald, William J. The Elect.
MacDonell, Herbert L., jt. auth. see Lewis, Alfred A.
MacDonlad, Frank. Cleveland Cavaliers.
McDonnall, Sarah J. Our Precious Heritage.
McDonnel. Introduction to Map Projections.
Macdonnell, J. D. Hunter-Killer.
Macdonnell, John & Manson, Edwards, eds. Great Jurists of the World: From Gaius to Von Ihering.
McDonnell, Lois Eddy. Susan Comes Through the Fire.
McDonnell, Robert F., ed. see Shakespeare, William.
McDonough, Martin & Hansen, Alvin H. Practice for the SAT (Scholastic Aptitude Test)
McDonough, Mary Lou, ed. Poet Physicians: An Anthology of Medical Poetry Written by Physicians.
McDonough, Steven H. Psychology in Foreign Language Teaching.
McDorman, Ted L. & Beauchamp, Kenneth P. Maritime Boundary Delimitation: An Annotated Bibliography.
McDougal. One Hundred & One Great Golf Jokes' & Stories.
McDougal, Weldon A., III. The Michael Jackson Scrapbook: The Early Days of the Jackson 5.
McDougall, Bonnie, tr. see Ho Chi-Fang.
McDougall, Bonnie S., ed. & tr. Notes from the City of the Sun: Poems by Bei Dao.
MacDougall, Elisabeth B. & Miller, Naomi. Fons Sapientiae: Garden Fountains in Illustrated Books, Sixteen-Eighteenth Centuries.
McDougall, G., jt. ed. see Healey, P.
Mc Dougall, J. Lorne. Canadian Pacific: A Brief History.
McDougall, John A. McDougall's Medicine: A Challenging Second Opinion.
MacDougall, Ruth D. The Flowers of the Forest.
--A Lovely Time Was Had by All.
McDougall, T. W., jt. auth. see MacNaughton, E. G.
McDougall, Williams. Janus: The Conquest of War, a Psychological Enquiry.
McDowall, Robert M. New Zealand Freshwater Fishes: A Guide & Natural History.
McDowell, Bart. Journey Across Russia: The Soviet Union Today.
McDowell, Bart, jt. auth. see National Geographic Society Staff.
MacDowell, Douglas M. The Law in Classical Athens.
McDowell, Fletcher, jt. ed. see Cotzias, George.
McDowell, Frank, et al. Surgical Rehabilitation in Leprosy.

McDowell, Gordon. Jesus Christ Returns by 1988?
MacDowell, Jeanne & Conley, Effie. The New England Inns Christmas Traditions.
McDowell, M. R. & Ferendeci, A. M., eds. Atomic & Molecular Processes in Controlled Thermonuclear Fusion.
MacDowell, M. R., jt. ed. see Kleinpoppen, H.
McDowell, Michael. The Amulet.
--Blackwater, I: The Flood.
--Blackwater, II: The Levee.
--Blackwater, III: The House.
--Blackwater, IV: The War.
--Blackwater, VI: Rain.
--Cold Moon over Babylon.
--Elementals.
--Fortune.
--Gilded Needles.
--Katie.
McDowell, Milton C., jt. auth. see Crawford, H. W.
McDowell, Robert. Quiet Money.
McDowell, Robert, jt. auth. see Gillman, Leonard.
McDowell, Robert B. British Conservatism, 1832-1914.
McDowell, William L., Jr., ed. Documents Relating to Indian Affairs, May 21, 1750-August 7, 1754.
MacDuff, John R. Footsteps of St. Peter.
McDuffie, Norman M., ed. Heparin: Structure, Cellular Functions, & Clinical Applications.
Mace. Men, Women, & God.
Mace, David. Sexual Difficulties in Marriage. Julme, William E., ed.
Mace, David R. Hebrew Marriage.
--Whom God Hath Joined.
Mace, Myles L. Directors: Myth & Reality.
Mace, Rodney. Trafalgar Square: Emblem of Empire.
MacEachen, Dougald B. The Ten-Dollar Bill.
McEachern, Alton H. Dramatic Monologue Preaching.
--The Lord's Presence.
McEachern, James E., jt. auth. see Glass, Bill.
McElderry, B. R., Jr., ed. see Shelley, Percy Bysshe.
McEldowney, B. A., jt. ed. see Hench, Larry L.
McElhiney, Paul T., jt. auth. see Farris, Martin T.
McElrath, William N. Indian Treasure on Rockhouse Creek.
MacElrevey, Daniel H. Shiphandling for the Mariner.
McElroy, Bernard. Shakespeare's Mature Tragedies.
McElroy, Frank E., jt. auth. see Konikow, Robert B.
McElroy, W. D., jt. auth. see Seliger, Howard H.
McElroy, William Francis, Jr. One Better.
McEneney, John. Albany: Capital City on the Hudson.
McEnroe, Colin. Swimming Chickens & Other Half-Breasted Accounts of the Animal World.
McEnvoy, Gerald K., ed. AHFS Drug Information, Nineteen Eighty-Seven.
McEuen, Kathryn A. Classical Influence upon the Tribe of Ben.
McEvedy, Colin. Atlas of Ancient History.
--Atlas of Modern History to Eighteen Fifteen.
--The Penguin Atlas of Recent History: Europe Since 1815.
McEvoy, Gerald K., ed. AHFS Drug Information, 1988.
McEvoy, James, III & Dietz, Thomas. Handbook for Environmental Planning: The Social Consequences of Environmental Change.
McEvoy, Marjorie. Camelot Country.
--Camelot Country.
McEvoy, Seth. Creating Arcade Games on the Timex-Sinclair.
--Find the Kirillian.
--Killer Robot.
McEwan, Ian. The Imitation Game & Other Plays.
McEwan, P., ed. Some Case Studies in Latin America.
McEwan, P. J., ed. Second Special Conference Issue.
McEwan, Peter J., ed. International Conference on Social Science & Medicine, 6th, Amsterdam, 1979: Second Special Conference Issue.
--Social Science & Medicine: Seventh International Conference Background Papers.
McEwen, F. L. & Stephenson, G. R. The Use & Significance of Pesticides in the Environment.
McEwen, John. Escape.
McEwen, John, jt. auth. see Sylvester, David.
McEwen, June H. The Gift of Simplicity.
MacEwen, W. A. Blue Book of Questions & Answers for Second Mate, Chief Mate & Master.
McEwen, W. E. & Berlin, K. D., eds. Organophosphorous Stereochemistry. Incl. Pt. 1. Origins of P(3&4) Compounds; Pt. 2. P(5) Compounds. Acad Pr.
McEwen, William P. Enduring Satisfaction.
McEwin, Kenneth, jt. auth. see Allen, Michael G.
Macey, Samuel C., ed. see Carey, Henry.
McFadden, John & Brooks, David K., Jr., eds. Counselor Licensure Action Packet.
McFadden, John, tr. see Erdozain, Placido.
McFadden, Max W., et al. Forest Pest Management in the People's Republic of China.
McFadden, Michael. Bachelor Fatherhood.
McFadden, S. Michele, ed. see Eu, March K.
McFadden, S. Michele, ed. see Frederick, Stella.
McFadden, S. Michele, ed. see Frigone, Albert.
McFadden, Sybill. Fawn Zeller's Porcelain Dollmaking Techniques.
McFadden, W. H. Techniques of Combined Gas Chromatography - Mass Spectrometry: Applications in Organic Analysis.
McFadden, William C. & Fuller, Reginald H. Holy Week.
MacFadyen, J. Tevere. Gaining Ground: The Renewal of America's Small Farms.
McFadyen, Mary J. Earth Is the Lord's.
McFadyen, Mary J., et al. Reconciling.
McFadyen, Stuart, et al. Canadian Broadcasting.
McFall, Waddy F. Taxidermy Step by Step.
McFarlan, Donald M. Who & What & Where in the Bible.
McFarlan, F. Warren & McKenney, James L. Corporate Information Systems Management: The Issues Facing Senior Executives.
McFarland. The Exploding Frog.
McFarland, jt. auth. see Kim.
MacFarland, C. S., jt. auth. see Bell, H. F.
Macfarland, Charles S. Lyman Pierson Powell.
McFarland, D. J., ed. Motivational Control Systems Analysis.
McFarland, Dalton E. Management: Foundations & Practices.
McFarland, Mary B. & Grant, Moeller M. Nursing Implications of Laboratory Tests.
McFarland, Philip. Sojourners: A Narrative of the Human Adventure As Lived by Some Historic Dreamers & Sufferers.
McFarland, Philip J., et al. Forms in English Literature.
--Perceptions in Literature.
--Themes in American Literature.
--Themes in World Literature.
McFarland, Ronald E., ed. Eight Idaho Poets: An Anthology.
McFarland, Wilma, ed. For a Child: Great Poems Old & New.
Macfarlane, D. I. Safety in Industry.
McFarlane, Gavin. A Practical Introduction to Copyright Law.
MacFarlane, Janet R. Hudson Valley Paintings, 1700-1750.
MacFarlane, Katherine N. Isidore of Seville on the Pagan Gods.
MacFarlane, Lynne, jt. auth. see Wylie, Betty J.
MacFarlane, W. V., ed. see Zoological Society of London Symposium Staff.
McFarquhar, A. M., ed. Europe's Future Food & Agriculture.
McFather, Nelle. Ecstasy's Captive.
McFayden, Mary Jean, et al. Giving & Receiving.
McFeat, Tom. Small-Group Cultures.
McFeely, William S. Grant: A Biography.
McFie, J. Assessment of Organic Intellectual Impairment.
MacGaffey, Wyatt. Custom & Government in the Lower Congo.
--Modern Kongo Prophets: Religion in a Plural Society.
MacGahar, Aileen, jt. auth. see Krauss, Leonard I.
McGann, Mary. Enjoying the Arts: Theatre.
McGarigle, Bob. Baseball's Great Tragedy: The Story of Carl Mays, Submarine Pitcher.
McGarrah, Robert E., jt. auth. see Chen, K. C.
McGarry, Daniel D. Medieval History & Civilization.
McGarry, J. Denis, jt. auth. see Frenkel, Rene A.
McGarry, James. Place Names in the Writings of William Butler Yeats. Malins, E., ed.
McGarvey, Patrick J. Visions of Victory: Selected Vietnamese Communist Military Writings, 1964-1968.
McGary, Grace L. Black Dragon River.
McGary, Mary Jane, jt. auth. see Krauss, Michael E.
McGaugh, J. L., jt. auth. see Drucker- Colin, R. R.
McGaugh, James L., ed. Psychobiology: Behavior from a Biological Perspective.
McGaughan, James P. Vatican Two, A Satanic Victory.
McGauhey, P. H. Engineering Management of Water Quality.
McGavin, Gary L. Earthquake Protection of Essential Building Equipment: Design, Engineering, & Installation.
McGaw, Charles J. & Blake, Gary. Acting Is Believing: A Basic Method.
McGaw, Jessie B. The Aztec Downfall.
McGeachy, D. P. Help Lord! a Guide to Public & Private Prayer.
McGeachy, D. P., 3rd. Common Sense & the Gospel: A Study of the Wisdom Books.
--The Gospel According to Andy Capp.
McGeachy, Pat. Beyond the Facts, Acts.
McGeary, David, jt. auth. see Plummer, Charles C.
McGee, J. Vernon. My Favorite Verse.
McGee, James P., jt. auth. see Pope, Benjamin.
McGee, L. Randolph. The Kentucky Supplement to Modern Real Estate Practice.
McGee, Michael H. Separation & Divorce in North Carolina: How to Do It with or Without a Lawyer.
McGee, Oliver, Jr Poor Boy Is the Name.
McGee, Robert W. Accounting for Software.
McGee, Terence G. Labor Markets, Urban Systems, & the Urbanization Process in Southeast Asian Countries.
McGeer, Patrick L., jt. ed. see Durbin, Enoch.
McGehee, Brad M. The Complete Guide to Writing Software User Manuals.
--Programmer's Market, 1985.
McGervey, John D. Introduction to Modern Physics.
McGhee, Paul E. & Chapman, Antony J., eds. Children's Humour.
McGhee, Robert. The Tuniit: First Explorers of the High Arctic.
McGhie, John, et al. Rough Guide to Yugoslavia.
MacGibbon, James & Caldwell, Stanley, eds. The New Glenans Sailing Manual.
McGiffert, Michael. The Higher Learning in Colorado: A Historical Study, 1860-1940.
McGiffert, Michael, ed. God's Plot: The Paradoxes of Puritan Piety, Being the Autobiography & Journal of Thomas Shepard.
McGill, Michael. The McGill Report on Male Intimacy.
McGill, Michael E. THe Forty to Sixty Year Old Male: A Guide for Men & the Women in Their Lives to See Them Through the Crises of the Male Middle Years.
MacGill, Sally. The Politics of Anxiety: Sellafield's Cancer-Link Controversy.
McGill, Shirley L. & Smith, Jean R. IV Therapy.
McGill, T. E., et al. Sex & Behavior: Status & Prospect.
McGill University, Blacker - Wood Library of Zoology & Ornithology Staff. A Dictionary Catalogue of the Blacker - Wood Library of Zoology & Ornithology.
McGillan, J. J., et al. Consumer Product Safety Law.
McGillem, Clare D., jt. auth. see Cooper, George R.
MacGillivray, Ian, jt. ed. see Beller, Fritz.
McGilvary, Evander B. Toward a Perspective Realism. Ramsperger, Albert G., ed.
McGinley, Patrick. Bogmail.
McGinley, Ronald J. Systematics of the Colletidae Based on Mature Larvae with Phenetic Analysis of Apoid Larvae (Hymenoptera, Apoidea)
MacGinley, T. J. Steel Structures: Practical Design Studies.
McGinn, Colin. Wittgenstein on Meaning.
McGinnies, Elliot, jt. ed. see King, Bert.
McGinnis, Marilyn. Give Me a Child Until He's Two: Then You Take Him till He's Four!
McGinty, Brian. Haraszthy at the Mint.
McGinty, Sarah M. Writing Your College Application Essay.
McGivern, William P. Matter of Honor.
--Soldiers of Forty-Four.
--Summitt.
McGlashan, N. D., ed. Health Problems in Australia & New Zealand.
McGlashen, Alan. Gravity & Levity.
McGloin, Joseph T. How to Get More Out of the Mass.
McGlone, Mary E. & Mayer, Gloria G. Kids' Chic: Great Looks for Kids & How to Put Them Together.
McGoldrick, Monica, jt. ed. see Carter, Elizabeth A.
McGonagle, John J., Jr. Managing the Consultant: A Corporate Guide.
McGough, Dixie P. & Hindman, Margaret H. Guide to Planning Alcoholism Treatment Programs.
McGovern, Ann. Hee Haw.
--Mr. Skinner's Skinny House.
--Sharks.
--Stone Soup.
McGowan. Maxillary Sinus.
McGowan, Daniel A. Consumer Economics.
--Contemporary Personal Finance.
McGowan, Harold. The Incorrigibles.
McGowan, J. W. & John, P. K., eds. Gaseous Electronics.
McGowan, Jan. Winds of Enchantment.
McGowan, Joan Y. Waiting: The Hope & Frustrations of a Childless Couple.
McGowan, Prudence P. Loper Longears.
McGowan, Robert F. Kate: A Divorced Mother's Story.
MacGowen, Kenneth & Melnitz, W. Living Stage: A History of the World Theatre.
McGown, Jill. An Evil Hour.
McGrail, Sean. Ancient Boats.
McGran, Philip. The Individual Inventor: What He Should Know about the U. S. Patent System.
McGranahan, David A., et al. Social & Economic Characteristics of the Population in Metro & Nonmetro Counties, 1970-80.
McGrath, Ann S. Tony's Tunnel.
McGrath, Charles M., et al, eds. Cell Biology of Breast Cancer.
McGrath, Cynthia, et al, eds. Pesticides: A Community Action Guide.
McGrath, J. B., jt. auth. see Weiss, Harold.
McGrath, Lawrence H. Student Access to Libraries & Library Resources in Secondary Schools.
McGrath, Nancy. Dollarwise Guide to California & Las Vegas.
--Dollarwise Guide to Egypt.
McGrath, Philomena & Mills, P. Atlas of Sectional Anatomy.
McGrath, Philomena, jt. auth. see Griffin, C. J.
McGrath, Robert. Emergency Removal of Patients & First Aid Fire Fighting in Hospitals.
McGrath, Rory & O'Donoghue, Denise, eds. Who Dares Wins.
McGrath, William. Watch Out for These Three Leavers.
McGraw, Eloise J. Greensleeves.
--Master Cornhill.
McGraw-Hill Editors. Basic Bibliography of Science & Technology.
--Encyclopedia of Environmental Science.
--McGraw-Hill Encyclopedia of Science & Technology.
--McGraw-Hill Yearbook of Science & Technology 1984.
McGraw Hill Editors. McGraw-Hill Yearbook of Science & Technology, 1982-83: Annual Supplement.
McGraw-Hill Editors. Yearbook of Science & Technology, 1986.
McGraw-Hill Encyclopedia of Science & Technology Editors. McGraw-Hill Encyclopedia of Science & Technology.
McGraw-Hill Management Awareness Program Editors. McGraw-Hill Management Awareness Program No. 8.
--McGraw-Hill Management Awareness Program No. 7.
McGraw, Tug. Lumpy: A Baseball Fable.
McGreane, Meagon. On Stage with John Denver.
McGreevey, William P., ed. Third-World Poverty: New Strategies for Measuring Development Progress.
MacGreevy, Thomas. Collected Poems.
MacGregor, C., jt. ed. see Elazo-Ayala, Cast.
McGregor, Donald R. The Inertia of the Vacuum: A New Foundation for Theoretical Physics.
MacGregor, Ellen & Pantell, Dora. Miss Pickerell & the Supertanker.
--Miss Pickerell on the Trail.
--Miss Pickerell Tackles the Energy Crisis.
--Miss Pickerell to the Earthquake Rescue.
McGregor, Geddes. The Bible in the Making.
McGregor, Georgette F. & Robinson, Joseph A. The Communication Matrix: Ways of Winning with Words.
McGregor, Gordon, jt. auth. see Bright, John.
Macgregor, Gordon, et al. Warriors Without Weapons: A Study of the Society & Personality Development of the Pine Ridge Sioux.
McGregor, Graham & White, Robert S., eds. The Art of Listening: The Creative Hearer in Language, Literature & Popular Culture.
McGregor, Ian A. Fundamental Techniques of Plastic Surgery.
MacGregor, J. Geddes. So Help Me God: A Calendar of Quick Prayers for Half-Skeptics.
MacGregor, M. H. The Nature of the Elementary Particle.
McGregor, Malcolm. Paul McLean.
McGregor, R. Diffusion & Sorption in the Fibers & Films: An Introduction with Particular Reference to Dyes.
McGregor, Rob R. & Devereux, Stephen E. The McGregor Solution for Managing the Pains of Fitness.
McGuffey. McGuffey Display Carton Six Address Book Set.
McGuiness, B., tr. see Waismann, Friedrich.
McGuinness, B. F., tr. see Wittgenstein, Ludwig.
McGuinness, Brian. Wittgenstein: A Life, Young Ludwig, 1889-1921.
McGuinness, Brian, ed. see Waismann, Friedrich.
McGuire, jt. auth. see Rayshich, Hale.
McGuire, Carolyn, ed. see Zagat, Eugene H., Jr. & Zagat, Nina S.
Mc Guire, Edna, jt. auth. see Montgomery, Ruth.
McGuire, James, jt. auth. see Priestley, Philip.
McGuire, James D. Becoming Myself.
MacGuire, Jillian. Threshold to Nursing.
McGuire, Peter J., jt. auth. see Leonard, David C.
McGuire, Phillip. Taps for a Jim Crow Army: Letters from Black Soldiers in World War II.
McGuire, Robert A. An Empirical Investigation of Farmers' Behavior under Uncertainty: Income, Price, & Yield Variability for Late 19th Century American Agriculture. Bruchey, Stuart, ed.
--Treasure Train.
McGuire, T. R., jt. ed. see Hirsch, J.

Authors

McGuire, William, ed. see Spiegel, Lawrence.
McGuire, William J. & Scrocco, Joseph D., Jr., eds. The Complete, Easy to Read, Medical Handbook.
McGurk, Harry, ed. Issues in Childhood Social Development.
Mach, Elyse. Contemporary Class Piano.
Machado de Assis, Joaquim M. The Devil's Church & Other Stories. Schmitt, Jack & Ishimatsu, Lorie, trs. from Span.
MacHale, Des. The Official Kerryman Joke Book.
McHale, John & McHale, Magda C. Women in World Trends: Facts & Trends.
McHale, Kenneth W., et al, eds. Evaluating Transnational Programs in Government & Business.
McHale, Lucy C. & Goldberg, Joyce. The All American Chinese Cookbook.
McHale, Magda C., jt. auth. see McHale, John.
Machamer, Peter, jt. auth. see Emmett, Kathleen.
Machen, Elizabeth M. Christian Education Public Schools: A Teacher's Interpretation.
McHenry, Dean E. The Third Force in Canada: The Cooperative Commonwealth Federation,1932-1948.
McHenry, Paul G. Adobe & Rammed Earth Buildings: Design & Construction.
Machi, S., ed. Radiation Processing for Environmental Conservation.
Machiavelli, Niccolo. The Discourses. Walker, Leslie J., tr.
Machin, John L. The Expectations Approach: Improving Managerial Communication & Performance.
Machin, Patricia, ed. Browning.
Machin, Patricia, illus. Keats.
--Shakespeare.
--Shelley.
--Tennyson.
--Wordsworth.
Machina, Kenton. Basic Applied Logic.
Machine Tool Design & Research International Conference Staff, et al. Proceedings of the Machine Tool Design & Research International Conference, 12th. Tobias, S. A., ed.
Machleidt, H., ed. Contributions of a Chemistry to Health.
Machleidt, H., et al, eds. Contributions of Chemistry to Health: Perspectives & Recommendations Compiled at the Fifth CHEMRAWN Conference Heidelberg, 1986.
Machlin, E. S. & Rowland, T. J., eds. Synthesis & Properties of Mestastable Phases: Proceedings. TMS-AIME Fall Meeting in Pittsburgh, 1980.
Machlin, Milt. Atlanta.
--Libby.
--The Michael Jackson Catalog: A Comprehensive Guide to Records, Videos, Clothing, Posters, Toys & Millions of Collectible Souvenirs.
--Pipeline.
Machlin, Milt, jt. auth. see Minsky, Morton.
Machlin, Milt, jt. auth. see Moore, Robin.
Machlis, Joseph. Introduction to Contemporary Music.
Machlowitz, Marilyn. Whiz Kids: Success at an Early Age.
Machlup, Fritz. Knowledge: Its Creation, Distribution, & Economic Significance.
Machol, R. E., et al, eds. Management Science in Sports.
Machotka, Otakar. Stories of an Expatriate.
McHoul, A. W. Telling How Texts Talk: Essays on Reading & Ethnomethodology.
Machovec, Milan. A Marxist Looks at Jesus.
McHoy, Peter. Container Gardening.
--Rock Gardening.
McHugh, Heather. Dangers.
--A World of Difference.
McHugh, Kathleen & Corchado, Veronica. Selecting the Right Data Base Software for the IBM PC.
--Selecting the Right Spreadsheet Software for the IBM PC.
McHugh, Kathleen, jt. auth. see Corchado, Veronica.
McHugh, P., jt. auth. see Blum, A.
McHugh, Robert C. Working Drawing Handbook.
McHugh, Vincent. Caleb Catlum's America.
McIlroy, Brian. Sweden.
McInerney, Judith W. Judge Benjamin: Superdog.
--Judge Benjamin: The Superdog Rescue.
McInerny, Paul M., jt. auth. see Thomsen, Gregory.
McInerny, Ralph. Gate of Heaven.
--Leave of Absence.
--The Noonday Devil.
--The Priest.
McInerny, Ralph M. History of Western Philosophy: Philosophy from St. Augustine to Ockham.
MacInnes, David & MacInnes, Kathleen. Hiking from Inn to Inn: Wilderness Walking Tours with Comfortable Overnight Lodging from Maine to Virginia.
MacInnes, Helen. Agent in Place.
--Assignment: Suspense.
--Double Image.
--Friends & Lovers.
--The Hidden Target.
--Home Is the Hunter.
--Message from Malaga.
--Prelude to Terror.
--Prelude to Terror.
--Ride a Pale Horse.
--The Salzburg Connection.
--The Snare of the Hunter.
--Triple Threat.
--The Venetian Affair.
MacInnes, Kathleen, jt. auth. see MacInnes, David.
MacInnis, Donald, jt. auth. see Martin, Mary L.
McIntire, Sue N. & Cioppa, Anne L., eds. Cancer Nursing: A Developmental Approach.
McIntosh, D. H., et al. Essentials of Meteorology.
McIntosh, D. M. Statistics for the Teacher.
Macintosh, H. G., ed. Techniques & Problems of Assessment for Teachers.
McIntosh, J. T. The Suiciders.
McIntosh, Michael. The Best Shotguns Ever Made in America: Seven Vintage Doubles to Shoot & to Treasure.
MacIntosh, Olding C. Use & Abuse of Diagnostic Services: The Canadian Experience.
MacIntyre. Difficulties in Christian Belief.
McIntyre, A. K., jt. ed. see Curtis, D. R.
MacIntyre, Alasdair C. Unconscious: A Conceptual Analysis.
McIntyre, C. F. Ann Radcliffe in Relation to Her Time.
McIntyre, D., et al. Investigations of Microteaching.
McIntyre, Joan. Mind in the Waters: A Book to Celebrate the Consciousness of Whales & Dolphins.
McIntyre, Kenneth E., jt. auth. see Gorton, Richard A.
McIntyre, Neil, jt. ed. see Petrie, J. C.
Macintyre, Stuart. Little Moscows: Communism & Working Class Militancy in Inter-War Britain.
McIntyre, Thomas J. & Obert, John C. The Fear Brokers.
McIntyre, Vonda N. The Bride.
--Dreamsnake.
--The Entropy Effect.
--Fireflood & Other Stories.
--The Search for Spock.
Macione, Alberta, jt. auth. see Adams, Catherine G.
MacIsaac, David. Strategic Bombing in World War II: The Story of the United States Strategic Bombing Survey.
McIsaac, Mary, jt. auth. see Morris, Allison.
McIver, Colin. Case Studies in Marketing, Advertising & Public Relations.
MacIver, Joyce. The Exquisite Thing.
--The Frog Pond.
McIver, N. J. Assasin Prepares.
McJunkins, Robert F., jt. auth. see Perry, James T.
Mack, A. Full Dentures.
Mack, C. & Enoeda, K. Shotokan Karate: Free Fighting Techniques.
Mack, Dietrich, ed. see Wagner, Cosima.
Mack, Gerstle. Nineteen Hundred Six: Surviving the Great Earthquake & Fire.
Mack, Helen. Unpacking a Bundle.
Mack, J. M., jt. auth. see Barnes, D. W.
Mack, James. Psychological Examination & Report Writing.
Mack, Joanna & Lansley, Stewart. Poor Britain.
Mack, John, jt. auth. see Picton, John.
Mack, Maynard, ed. see Pope, Alexander.
Mack, Maynard, et al, eds. World Masterpieces.
--World Masterpieces.
--World Masterpieces, Continental Edition.
--World Masterpieces, Continental Edition.
--World Masterpieces Continental Comp.
Mack, Nancy, ed. see Walz-Chojnacki, Greg.
Mack, R. L. The Klan Killer.
Mack, Stan. Runaway Road.
Mack, Walter S. & Buckley, Peter. No Time Lost.
Mack, Wayne. How to Pray Effectively.
McKale, Donald M. The Swastika Outside Germany.
Mackall, Lucy. Lucy's Bag Book.
Mackarness, Richard. Eating Dangerously: The Hazards of Hidden Allergies.
McKaughan, Howard P., ed. see Bunye, Maria V. & Yap, Elsa P.
Mackay, Charles. Dictionary of Lowland Scotch.
McKay, Claude. Harlem: Negro Metropolis.
Mackay, D., jt. ed. see Afghan, B. K.
McKay, David & Cox, Andrew W. Politics of Urban Change.
Mackay, David, ed. Flock of Words: An Anthology of Poetry for Children & Others.
McKay, Ernest. Undersea Terror: U-Boat Wolf Packs in World War II.
McKay, Ernest A. Carrier Strike Force: Pacific Air Combat in World War II.
McKay, Gary D., jt. auth. see Dinkmeyer, Don.
McKay, George L., ed. American Book Auction Catalogues, 1713-1934.
McKay, Henry D., jt. auth. see Shaw, Clifford R.
McKay, John P. & Hill, Bennett D. A History of Western Society.
--A History of Western Society.
--A History of Western Society.
McKay, John P., et al. A History of Western Society.
McKay, Johnston R. & Miller, James F., eds. Biblical Studies: Essays in Honor of William Barclay.
McKay, Kathleen, jt. auth. see Stern, Loraine.
McKay, L. & Fernbach, D, eds. Nuclear-Free Defence.
Mackay, Mary see Corelli, Marie.
McKay, Nellie Y. Critical Essays on Toni Morrison.
McKay, Robert. The Running Back.
McKay, Robert & Traynor, Carol. Between Ocean & Empire: An Illustrated History of Long Island.
McKay, Robert J., jt. auth. see Kapoor, A.
Mackay, Ronald, et al. Reading in a Second Language: Hypotheses, Organization & Practice.
McKay, Sandra & Wong, Sau-Ling. Language as Resource: A Social & Educational Perpective on Language Minorities in the United States.
McKay, Vernon. Africa in World Politics.
McKay-Smith, Alexander, et al. Man & the Horse: An Illustrated History of Equestrian Apparel.
McKeag, Malcolm. Cudmore & the America's Cup.
McKeague, Charles P. Elementary Algebra.
McKean, H. P., Jr., jt. auth. see Ito, K.
McKean, Hugh F. The Lost Treasures of Louis Comfort Tiffany.
McKean, Thomas. Moroccan Mystery.
McKearin, George S., jt. auth. see McKearin, Helen.
McKearin, Helen & McKearin, George S. American Glass.
McKechnie, Al, jt. auth. see Roblee, Charles L.
McKee, Alexander. King Henry VIII's Mary Rose: Its Fate & Future: the Story of One of the Most Exciting Projects in Marine Archaeology.
McKee, Craig & Holland, Margaret. Time to Swim.
--Time to Swim.
McKee, Craig B. & Holland, Margaret. A Peacock Ate My Lunch.
McKee, David. King Rollo & King Frank.
--King Rollo & the Balloons.
--King Rollo & the Bath.
--King Rollo & the Dishes.
--King Rollo & the Dog.
--King Rollo & the Masks.
--King Rollo & the Playroom.
--King Rollo & the Search.
--King Rollo & the Tree.
--The Magician & the Balloon.
--The Magician & the Petnapping.
--Two Admirals.
McKee, David & Woo, Nancy E. Ecclesiastes in A. S. L. - Chapter Three, Verses 1-4: Written in Sutton Sign Writing.
McKee, Delber. Chinese Exclusion Versus the Open Door Policy, 1900-1906: Clashes Over China Policy in the Roosevelt Era.
McKee, James B. Introduction to Sociology.
McKee, James L. Lincoln: The Prairie Capital.
McKee, Judy S. Annual Editions: Early Childhood Education, 1985-86.
McKee, Judy S. & Paciorek, Karen M. Annual Editions: Early Childhood Education, 1988-1989.
McKee, Judy S. & Paciorek, Karen M., eds. Early Childhood Education 1988-89.
McKee, Lorna & O'Brien, Margaret, eds. The Father Figure.
McKee, Richard L. Machining with Abrasives.
Mckee, Russell, ed. Michigan Hiking Opportunities.
--Michigan's Snow Trails.
McKeehan, Wallace L., jt. ed. see Boynton, Alton L.
McKeen, Gregory B., jt. auth. see American Institute of Certified Public Accountants. Continuing Professional Education Division Staff.
McKeever, Harry. Hell above Water.
McKeever, J. Ross. Shopping Center Zoning.
McKeever, Michael. Start-Up Money: How to Finance Your New Small Business.
McKelvey, John J., jt. ed. see Metcalf, Robert L., Jr.
McKelvey, Robert, ed. Lectures on Ordinary Differential Equations: A Symposium Vol.
McKelvy, James. Music for Conducting Class.
McKelway, Alexander J. & Willis, E. David, eds. The Context of Contemporary Theology: Essays in Honor of Paul Lehmann.
MacKendrick, Louise. Natchez.
MacKendrick, Paul. The Greek Stones Speak: The Story of Archaeology in Greek Lands.
McKenna, Brian, jt. auth. see Maltby, Arthur.
McKenna, Chris, jt. auth. see Joll, Caroline.
McKenna, Constance, ed. see Hynes, Kathleen.
McKenna, Constance, et al, eds. My Conscience Speaks.
McKenna, George. Media Voices: Debating Critical Issues in Mass Media.
--Taking Sides: Clashing Views on Controversial Political Issues.
McKenna, George & Feingold, Stanley. Taking Sides: Clashing Views on Controversial Political Issues.
McKenna, George, jt. auth. see Finsterbusch, Kurt.
McKenna, George L. Repeated Exposure: Photographic Imagery in the Print Media.
McKenna, Harold, Jr. We Are the Targets: Environmental Impacts.
McKenna, J. J. Ask of the Wind.
--Sarah & Joshua.
McKenna, J. James. Trial Advocacy: Passion & Preparation.
McKenna, James. ICIAM '87: Proceedings of the First International Conference on Industrial & Applied Mathematics.
McKenna, John F., jt. auth. see Siklua, Andrew F.
McKenna, Joseph P. Aggregate Economic Analysis.
McKenna, Marian. Concise History of Catholicism.
McKenna, Megan & Ducote, Darryl. Beginnings of the Church.
--Jesus Living the Father's Values.
--New Testament Understanding of Jesus.
--Old Testament Journeys in Faith.
--Sacraments, Liturgy & Prayer.
--The Spirit in the Church.
McKenna, Virginia. Some of My Friends Have Tails.
McKenna, Virginia & Travers, Bill. On Playing with Lions.
McKenna, W. J., jt. ed. see Krikler, D. M.
McKenney, Carlton N. Rails in Richmond. Fulton, William F., ed.
McKenney, Jack. Sharks, Wrecks, & Movie Stars: The Adventures of an Underwater Photographer.
McKenney, James L., jt. auth. see McFarlan, F. Warren.
McKenney, Kenneth. The Moonchild.
McKenney, Ruth. My Sister Eileen.
Mackensen, G., ed. see Ophthalmic Microsurgery Study Group Symposium Staff.
MacKenzie. District Heating Thermal Generation & Distribution.
Mackenzie, Alastair, jt. auth. see Benson, Jeffrey.
MacKenzie, Alex, jt. auth. see Engstrom, Ted W.
MacKenzie, Andrew. Riddle of the Future: A Modern Study of Precognition.
MacKenzie, Andrew, ed. A Gallery of Ghosts: An Anthology of Reported Experience.
MacKenzie, Charles H., et al. Liner Shipping Conferences: An Annotated Bibliography.
McKenzie, David. Wolfhart Pannenberg & Religious Philosophy.
McKenzie, Donald. Nobody Here by That Name.
MacKenzie, Donald. Raven & the Paperhangers.
--Raven Settles a Score.
--Raven's Revenge.
--Savage State of Grace.
Mackenzie, Donald A. Migration of Symbols & Their Relations to Beliefs & Customs.
Mackenzie, Fred T., jt. auth. see Garrels, Robert M.
McKenzie, George J., et al. The Special Senses.
McKenzie, Hugh A., ed. Milk Proteins.
McKenzie, J. M. The Partition of Africa.
MacKenzie, Jeanne, jt. auth. see MacKenzie, Norman.
McKenzie, Jimmy C. & Hughes, Robert J. Office Machines: A Practical Approach.
McKenzie, Jimmy C. & Kelley, J. Roland. Business Mathematics.
MacKenzie, John. Be Good to Yourself.
McKenzie, John L. The Civilization of Christianity.
McKenzie, John L., jt. auth. see Wylie, Samuel.
McKenzie, John L., jt. ed. see Walter, Eugen.
Mackenzie, John P. Birds in Peril: A Guide to the Endangered Birds of the United States & Canada.
--Complete Outdoorsman's Guide to Birds of Eastern North America.
MacKenzie, Joy, jt. auth. see Forte, Imogene.
Mackenzie, Joy, jt. auth. see Forte, Imogene.
Mackenzie, K. K. Keys to the North American Species of Carex.
McKenzie, Kenneth, ed. see Aesopus.
Mackenzie, Kent & Goldsmith, Gary. Saturday Morning.
MacKenzie, Lewis, tr. Autumn Wind: A Selection from the Poems of Issa.
McKenzie, Michael. Madonna: Lucky Star.
MacKenzie, Norman & MacKenzie, Jeanne. H. G. Wells.
Mackenzie, R. Auditorium Acoustics.
Mackenzie, R. Alec. The Time Trap.
MacKenzie, R. C. Differential Thermal Analysis, Vol. 1: Fundamental Aspects.
McKenzie, Richard B., jt. auth. see Tullock, Gordon.

Authors

McKenzie, Roderick D. Roderick D. McKenzie on Human Ecology. Hawley, Amos H., ed.
Mackenzie, Ross. The Word in Action: The Acts of the Apostles for Our Time.
MacKenzie, Steve. Blackbird.
--SEALS No. 3: Rescue!
--Seals, No. 5: Breakout.
--Seals No. 6: Desert Rain.
Mackenzie, Susan, jt. ed. see Gold, Charlotte.
McKeon, Clare & McKeon, Joseph P. Oakville: A Place of Some Importance.
McKeon, Joseph P., jt. auth. see McKeon, Clare.
McKeone, Dermot. Small Computers for Business & Industry.
McKeough, D. Michael. The Coloring Review of Neuroscience.
McKeown. Living with Computers.
McKeown, Beverly. Guitar Songbook with Instructions.
McKeown, James M. & McKeown, Joan C. Price Guide to Antique & Classic Cameras: 1985-1986.
McKeown, Joan C., jt. auth. see McKeown, James M.
McKeown, Martha F. Trail Led North.
McKeown, Neil. Case Studies & Projects in Communication.
McKeown, Patrick G., jt. auth. see Davis, K. Roscoe.
McKercher, R. M., ed. Potash Mining Processing Transportation: Proceedings of the International Potash Technology Conference, Saskatoon, Saskatchewan, Canada, October 3-5, 1983.
McKernan, Michael, jt. ed. see Cashman, Richard.
McKerns, K. W. Hormones & Cancer.
McKerns, Kenneth W., ed. Structure & Function of the Gonadotropins.
Mackerras, Colin. The Performing Arts in Contemporary China.
Mackerras, Colin, jt. auth. see Fung, Edmund S.
McKerrow, W. Stuart, ed. The Ecology of Fossils: An Illustrated Guide.
Mackey, Daniel. Employment at Will & Employer Responsibility.
Mackey, G. W. Unitary Group Representations.
Mackey, George W. Lectures on the Theory of Functions of a Complex Variable.
Mackey, Henry B., tr. see De Sales, Saint Francoise.
Mackey, James P. Jesus, the Man & the Myth.
Mackey, Joan, jt. auth. see Abraham, Paul.
Mackey, M. C. Ion Transport Through Biological Membranes: An Integrated Theoretical Approach.
Mackey, Mary. A Grand Passion.
Mackey, Richard T. Bowling.
Mackey, Samson A. Mythological Astronomy of the Ancients Demonstrated. Bd. with Pt. 2. The Key to Urania. Wizards.
Mackey, Sandra. The Saudis: Inside the Desert Kingdom.
Mackey, William, Jr. American Bird Decoys.
Mackie, A. M., jt. ed. see Grant, P. T.
Mackie, Annebeth, tr. Bible Speaks Again.
Mackie, J. L. Hume's Moral Theory.
Mackie, Robert L. King James Fourth of Scotland: A Brief Survey of His Life & Times.
McKie, Roy, jt. auth. see Beard, Henry.
McKillip, Patricia. Stepping from the Shadows.
McKillip, Patricia A. The Forgotten Beasts of Eld.
--Heir of Sea & Fire.
--The House on Parchment Street.
--The Riddle-Master of Hed.
--The Throme of the Erril of Sherill.
McKillop, Alan D. English Literature from Dryden to Burns.
McKim, Patrick C., jt. auth. see Howard, Michael.
McKinlay, A. P., ed. Arator: The Codices.
McKinlay, Ian, jt. ed. see Gordon, Neil.
McKinley, Albert E., ed. see Jameson, J. Franklin.
McKinley, Daniel, jt. ed. see Shepard, Paul.
McKinley, Edward H. Marching to Glory: The History of the Salvation Army in the United States, 1880 to 1980.
McKinley, John, jt. auth. see Bergevin, Paul.
McKinley, Robin. The Door in the Hedge.
McKinley, Robin, ed. Imaginary Lands.
McKinnell, R. G., ed. Differentiation & Neoplasia.
Mackinney, Archie A., Jr., ed. Pathophysiology of Blood.
McKinney, Kevin, jt. auth. see Schafer, Mike.
McKinney, Lois. Writing for Theological Education by Extension.
McKinney, R. E. Microbiology for Sanitary Engineers.
McKinney, Ruth, jt. auth. see Wirt, Sherwood E.
McKinney, Whitney. A History of the Shoshone-Paiutes of the Duck Valley Indian Reservation.
MacKinnon, Colin. Finding Hoseyn.
MacKinnon, Jan, ed. see Smedley, Agnes.
Mackinnon, L. Eliot, Auden, Lowell: Aspects of the Baudelairean Inheritance.
McKinnon, Lise S., tr. see Friis, Babbis.
McKinnon, Ronald I. & Mathieson, Donald J. How to Manage a Repressed Economy.
MacKinnon, Steve, ed. see Smedley, Agnes.
Mackintosh, H. R., ed. see Schleiermacher, Friedrich.
MacKintosh, N. J., jt. auth. see Sutherland, N. S.
McKitrick, Eric L. Andrew Johnson & Reconstruction.
Macklem, Francesca. Tomorrow & Forever.
Mackler, Ian. Pattern for Profit in Southern Africa.
McKnight, Daniel L., Jr. The Complete Partnership Manual & Guide with Tax, Financial & Managerial Strategies.
McKnight, Edgar V. The Bible & the Reader: An Introduction to Literary Criticism.
--Meaning in Texts: The Historical Shaping of a Narrative Hermeneutics.
McKnight, Hugh. Canal & River Craft in Pictures.
Macknight, James. Macknight on the Epistles.
McKnight, Mid. Vestibules of Heaven.
McKnight, Pete C., frwd. by. Kays Gary, Columnist.
McKnight, Reed H. Measurement Error & Banks' Reported Earnings. Farmer, Richard N., ed.
McKnight Staff. Exploring Careers in Child Care.
--Exploring Careers in Hospitality & Food Service.
--Exploring Fabrics.
--Exploring Living Environments.
McKnight Staff & Miller, Wilbur R. Graphic Arts.
--Photography.
McKoski, Martin M. & Hahn, Lynne C. The Developing Writer: A Guide to Basic Skills.
McKowen, K. D. Wildlife: Activity Book.
McKown, Robin, jt. auth. see Elting, Mary.
McKoy, Vincent & Suzuki, H., eds. Electron-Molecule Collisions & Photoionization Processes.
Mackrodt, W. C., jt. ed. see Catlow, C. R.
Macksey, Kenneth. The Tank Pioneers.
McKuen, Rod. Another Beautiful Day: The All-New 1986 Rod McKuen Book of Days, Databook & Diary.
--The Beautiful Strangers.
--Come to Me in Silence.
--The Outstretched Hand: Poems, Prayers, & Meditations.
--Rod McKuen's Book of Days.
--Rod McKuen's Book of Days: And a Month of Sundays.
--We Touch the Sky.
McKusick, Victor A. Mendelian Inheritance in Man: Catalogs of Autosomal Dominant, Autosomal Recessive, & X-Linked Phenotypes.
Mackworth-Young, Robin, jt. auth. see Johnson, Michael.
McLachlan, Christopher A. Inflation-Wise: How to Do Almost Everything for Less.
McLachlan, Elizabeth P. The Scriptorium of Bury St. Edmunds in the Twelfth Century.
McLachlan, K. D. Sulphur in Australasian Agriculture.
McLachlan, K. S. & Whittaker, W. A Bibliography of Afghanistan.
McLachlan, Keith, jt. auth. see Al-Moosa, Abdulrasool.
Maclagan, Eric R. Italian Sculpture of the Renaissance: The Charles Eliot Norton Lectures for the Years 1927-1928.
MacLaine, Allan, intro. by. The Beginnings to Fifteen Fifty-Eight.
McLanathan, Richard. American Tradition in the Arts.
--American Tradition in the Arts.
--Pageant of Medieval Art & Life.
McLane, Helen J. Selecting, Developing & Retaining Women Executives.
--Selecting, Developing & Retaining Women Executives: A Corporate Strategy for the Eighties.
MacLane, S., ed. see Midwest Category Seminar Staff.
McLaren, A. D. & Shugar, D. Photochemistry of Proteins & Nucleic Acids.
Maclaren, Alexander & Swete, H. B. Post-Resurrection Ministry of Christ.
McLaren, Dell. The Seduction of Lucy.
McLaren, Donald S., ed. Nutrition & Its Disorders.
McLaren, Margaret, jt. ed. see Hills, P. J.
McLaughlin. Modern Science & God.
McLaughlin & Westphal, eds. Southern California Anthology.
McLaughlin, Arthur J. Manual of Infection Control in Respiratory Care.
McLaughlin, Brian, jt. ed. see LePore, Ernest.
McLaughlin, Clara J. The Black Parents Handbook: A Guide to Healthy Pregnancy, Birth & Child Care.
--The Black Parents Handbook: A Guide to the Facts of Pregnancy, Birth & Child Care.
McLaughlin, Frank S. & Pickhardt, Robert C. Quantitative Techniques for Management Decisions.
McLaughlin, Kenneth. Cambridge: The Making of a Canadian City. Wells, Susan, ed.
McLaughlin, Patrick J. The Church & Modern Science.
McLaughlin, R. A., jt. auth. see Monds, F. C.
McLaughlin, Robert E., jt. auth. see Carron, Harold.
McLaughlin, W. L., ed. Trends in Radiation Dosimetry.
McLaurin, R. D., et al. Foreign Policy Making in the Middle East: Domestic Influences on Policy in Egypt, Iraq, Israel, & Syria.
Mac Laverty, Bernard see Laverty, Bernard M.
MacLean & Emslie. Accidental Hypothermia.
McLean, A. & Heaslip, L. Continuous Casting.
McLean, A. J., et al. Organization Development in Transition: Evidence of an Evolving Profession.
Mclean, Adam. The Triple Goddess: An Exploration of the Archetypal Feminine.
Mclean, Adam, commentary by. A Commentary on the Mutus Liber.
Mclean, Adam, ed. The Magical Calendar: A Synthesis of Magical Symbolism from the Seventeenth Centry Renaissance of Medieval Occultism.
Mclean, Adam, jt. ed. see Green, Deirdre.
Mclean, Adam, ed. see Rudd.
MacLean, Alistair. Goodbye, California.
--San Andreas.
--Santorini.
--Where Eagles Dare.
MacLean, C., jt. auth. see Hilbers, C. W.
Maclean, Charles. Island on the Edge of the World: The Story of St. Kilda.
--The Watcher.
McLean, Colleen J., jt. auth. see Woollerton, Henry.
Mclean, Donald, tr. see Green, Deirdre & Mclean, Adam.
MacLean, Douglas, ed. The Security Gamble: Deterrence Dilemmas in the Nuclear Age.
MacLean, Douglas, jt. ed. see Brown, Peter G.
McLean, Eric & Wilson, R. D. The Living Past of Montreal: Le Passe Vivant de Montreal.
Maclean, F., et al. Person from England.
McLean, F. C. & Budy, A. M. Radiation, Isotopes, & Bone.
Maclean, Fitzroy. Holy Russia.
MacLean, Gilmour, tr. see Schleiermacher, Friedrich.
McLean, Gordon. Danger at Your Door.
MacLean, Helene. Caring for Your Parents: A Sourcebook of Options & Solutions for Both Generations.
McLean, Hugh. Nikolai Leskov: The Man & His Art.
McLean, Hugh & Vickery, Walter N., eds. The Year of Protest, 1956.
Maclean, Hugh, ed. see Spenser, Edmund.
McLean, Hugh A. There is a Better Way to Manage.
McLean, Isabel & Jarvi, Edith. Canadian Selection: Books & Periodicals for Libraries (Supplement) 1977-79.
McLean, J. Michael. The Impact of the Microelectronics Industry on the Structure of the Canadian Economy.
McLean, Janice, ed. Consultants & Consulting Organizations Directory.
--Consultants & Consulting Organizations Directory.
--New Comnsultants & Consulting Organizations Directory, 1988: New Consultants - Inter-Edition Supplement.
--New Consultants.
--New Training Organizations.
McLean, John G. & Haigh, Robert W. The Growth of Integrated Oil Companies.
MacLean, Katherine & West, Carl. Dark Wing.
MacLean, Kenneth. John Locke & English Literature of the Eighteenth Century. Schouls, Peter A, ed.
McLean, Martin, jt. ed. see Cowen, Robert.
McLean, Mervyn. Oceanic Music & Dance: An Annotated Bibliography.
Maclean, N. Control of Gene Expression.
Maclean, Norman. A River Runs Through It.
McLean, Ruari. Reynolds Stone.
--The Thames & Hudson Manual of Typography.
Maclean, Virginia. Much Entertainment: A Visual & Culinary Record of Johnson & Boswell's Tour of Scotland in 1773.
McLeave, Hugh. Icarus Threat.
McLeavey, Dennis W. & Narasimhan, Seetharama L. Production Planning & Inventory Control.
MacLehose, J. H. The Burnished Sword.
McLeish. Myths & Legends of Ancient Rome.
MacLeish, Archibald. The Human Season: Selected Poems, 1926-1972.
--Poetry & Experience.
--Scratch.
McLeish, Kenneth. The Theatre of Aristophanes.
McLeish, Kenneth, ed. see Sargent, Michael.
McLeish, Robert. The Technique of Radio Production.
McLeish, Valerie, ed. see Sargent, Michael.
MacLeish, William H. Oil & Water: The Struggle for Georges Bank. Davison, Peter, ed.
McLellan, Dave, jt. auth. see Warrick, Bill.
McLellan, Diana. Ear on Washington: A Chrestomathy of Scandal, Rumor & Gossip among the Capital's Elite.
McLellan, Gerald D. Equitable Distribution Law & Practice.
McLellan, H. J. Elements of Physical Oceanography.
McLellan, Joyce. Days of the Year.
McLellan, Thomas A. Guide to the Addiction Severity Index: Background, Administration, & Field Testing Results.
McLelland, Ernestine B. Angie: The Story of a Mischievous Scottie.
McLemore, Clinton W. Good Guys Finish First: Success Strategies from the Book of Proverbs for Business Men & Women.
McLemore, Lelan E. Behavioral Orientations Toward Party Leadership & System Norms: An Exploratory Analysis.
--Task-Related Norms in a State Legislature: The Case of Oklahoma.
McLemore, Patricia R., jt. auth. see Coleman, William V.
McLemore, W. P. Social Studies Strategies for Today's Learners.
MacLennan, Bruce J. Principles of Programming Languages.
McLennan, D. J. A Revised Transition State Spectrum for Concerted Bimolecular B - Eliminations.
McLennan, John F. Primitive Marriage. Riviere, Peter, ed.
MacLennan, W. J., jt. auth. see Paterson, C. R.
McLeod & Welford. Classical Guitar Design & Construction.
McLeod, et al. Metallurgical Progress.
MacLeod, A. B., jt. auth. see Allen, P. C.
McLeod, Alex N. The Principles of Financial Intermediation.
MacLeod, Charlotte. King Devil.
--Maid of Honor.
--Something the Cat Dragged In.
McLeod, David D. Machine Language Subroutines for the Color Computer.
MacLeod, Dawn. Herb Handbook.
Macleod, Donald. Presbyterian Worship: Its Meaning & Method.
Macleod, Donald & Forestell, J. T. Pentecost 2.
McLeod, Eileen. Women Working: Prostitution Now.
MacLeod, Hilary & Boden, Robin. Tools of Their Trade: The Book of Professional Fiascos.
McLeod, Jesse T. Is It Worth Remembering.
MacLeod, John, ed. Davidson's Principles & Practice of Medicine.
Macleod, Joseph. Sister D'Aranyi.
McLeod, Kristy. Drums & Trumpets: The House of Stuart.
Macleod, R. M., jt. ed. see Polleri, A.
McLeod, Robert W. & Lampert, Lyndon J. Little Book Cliff Railway: The Life & Times of a Colorado Narrow Gauge.
McLeod, Robin J. & Wachspress, Eugene L., eds. Frontiers of Applied Geometry: Proceedings of a Symposium, Las Cruces, New Mexico, 1980.
MacLeod, Roy M. Treasury Control & Social Administration.
Macleod, Ruth. Mendocino Menace.
McLeod, William E. Tax Shelters in Canada: Choose with Care.
McLinn, Dianne, jt. auth. see Kysar, Ardis.
MacLochlainn, Alf, ed. see National Library of Ireland Staff.
McLoone, Margo & Siegel, Alice. Sports Cards: Collecting, Trading & Playing.
McLoone, Margo, jt. auth. see Siegel, Alice.
McLoone-Basta, Margo & Siegel, Alice. The Kids' Book of Lists.
McLoone-Basta, Margo, jt. auth. see Siegel, Alice.
McLoughlin, J. B., jt. auth. see Diamond, D. R.
McLoughlin, J. B., jt. auth. see Huxley, M.
McLoughlin, J. B., jt. ed. see Diamond, D. R.
McLoughlin, Wayne. Space Freighter - Future Supply Ship: A Complete Kit in a Book.
MacLow, Jackson. A Vocabulary for Annie Brigitte Gilles Tardos.
McLuhan, Marshall. Counterblast.
--Counterblast.
Maclure, W. Observations on the Geology of the United States of America.
McLusky, D. S., ed. see European Symposium on Marine Biology, 12th.
McLyman, C. Transformer & Inductor Design Handbook.
McLynn, Frank. Invasion.
McMahan, Ian. ESP McGee & the Ghost Ship.
--Footwork.
--The Fox's Lair.
--Lake Fear.
McMahan, John W. Property Development: Effective Decision Making in Uncertain Times.
McMahan, Mike. Graphics & Sound for Your Personal Computer.
Macmahon, Brian & Pugh, Thomas F. Epidemiology: Principles & Methods.
McMahon, Edward J., jt. auth. see Bhar, Tarak N.
McMahon, Edwin & Campbell, Peter. Please Touch.
McMahon, Marilyn, et al. Report Writing in dBASE II.

McMahon, Sarah L., jt. ed. see Carney, Clarke G.
McMahon, Thomas. Principles of American Nuclear Chemistry: A Novel.
McManigal, J. W. & Heilman, Grant. Farm Town: A Memoir of the Nineteen Thirties.
McManis, Charles R. Unfair Trade Practices in a Nutshell.
McMann, Evelyn, ed. The Royal Canadian Academy of Arts: Exhibitions & Members, 1880-1979.
McManus. Improbable World of Veteran Outdoorsman.
McManus, Edgar J. Black Bondage in the North.
McManus, James. Chin Music.
McManus, Patrick F. A Fine & Pleasant Misery.
--The Grasshopper Trap.
--Never Sniff a Gift Fish.
--They Shoot Canoes, Don't They?
Macmanus, Sheila. The Adoption Book.
MacManus, Yvonne. The Presence.
McMartin, Arthur. Public Servants & Patronage: The Foundation & Rise of the New South Wales Public Service, 1786-1859.
McMartin, Barbara. Fifty Hikes in the Adirondacks: Short Walks, Day Trips & Backpacks Throughout the Park.
--Guide to the Eastern Adirondacks: Lake George, Pharaoh Lake & Beyond.
McMenamin, Kevin. Glory Days: Alex Wyllie & the Canterbury Ranfurly Shield Team 1982-85.
MacMichael, D. B., jt. auth. see Reay, D. A.
McMichael, James. Four Good Things.
--The Lover's Familiar.
McMichael, Joan K. Handicap: A Study of Physically Handicapped Children & Their Families.
McMicheal, Scot R. Historical Perspective on Light Infantry.
MacMillan, Annabelle, tr. see Anckarsvard, Karin.
MacMillan, Annabelle, tr. see Gillsater, Sven & Gillsater, Pia.
MacMillan, Annabelle, tr. see Hamori, Laszlo.
MacMillan, Annabelle, tr. see Herrmanns, Ralph.
McMillan, B. G., jt. ed. see Humphreys, K. K.
McMillan, Bruce. Ghost Doll.
--Making Sneakers.
--The Remarkable Riderless Runaway Tricycle.
Macmillan, C. Wright, jt. auth. see Villaverde, Manuel M.
McMillan, Carl H., intro. by. The East-West Business Directory: A Guide to Commercial Contacts with Eastern European Countries in OECD States.
McMillan, Claude, ed. see Stair, Ralph M., Jr.
MacMillan, D. H., jt. auth. see Russell, R. C.
Macmillan, Diane D. The Portable Feast: A Cookbook for Food on the Move.
McMillan, Dougald & Fehsenfeld, Martha. Beckett in the Theatre: The Author as Practical Playwright & Director.
MacMillan Editorial Staff. Cubs: The Complete Record of Chicago Cubs Baseball.
--Dodgers: The Complete Record of Dodger Baseball.
McMillan, James, jt. auth. see Linder, Fredric.
McMillan, James H. & Schumacher, Sally. Research to Education: A Conceptual Introduction.
McMillan, James H., jt. auth. see Linder, Fredric.
McMillan, L. G. How to Make Money with Stock Options.
McMillan, Lawrence G. Options As a Strategic Investment.
MacMillan, Michael, ed. Cattulus.
Macmillan Publishing Company Staff. Macmillan Dictionary for Children.
McMillan, R. Bruce, jt. ed. see Wood, W. Raymond.
McMillen, Harlow. History of Staten Island, New York, During the American Revolution.
McMillen, S. I. None of These Diseases.
MacMillian, Annabelle, tr. see Hamori, Laszlo.
McMillon, Bill. Volunteer Vacations.
McMinn, Curtis J., ed. Light Metals 1980: Proceedings. AIME Annual Meeting, Las Vegas, 1980.
McMinnies, William G. Premier Hotels of Great Britain.
McMurdie, Howard F., ed. Advances in X-Ray Analysis.
McMurrey, David A. & Campman, M. S. Writing Fundamentals.
McMurrin, Sterling M., ed. Liberty, Equality, & Law.
McMurrin, Sterling M., et al. The Tanner Lectures on Human Values, Vol. III: 1982.
McMurring, Sterling M., ed. The Tanner Lectures on Human Values, Vol. I: 1980. Feinberg, Joel & Hare, R. M.
McMurry, John. Organic Chemistry.
McMurtrie, P., jt. auth. see Skimin, E.
McMurtry, Larry. Cadillac Jack: A Novel.
--The Desert Rose: A Novel.
--Film Flam: Essays on Hollywood.
--Terms of Endearment.
McNab, Barbara. Yindala: An Original Australian Story.
McNab, Jessie, jt. auth. see Wilkinson, Charles K.
McNab, Oliver. Horror Story.
McNab, Tom. Flanagan's Run.
McNair, James. Power Food: Exciting New Recipes for Vigorous Good Health, Energy & Strength.
McNair, Sylvia. Vacation Places Rated.
McNair, Sylvia T. Florida & the Southeast 1985. Fisher, Robert C., ed.
McNaire, Robert M., jt. auth. see Practising Law Institute Staff.
McNally, Kenneth. The Islands of Ireland.
--Standing Stones: And Other Monuments of Early Ireland.
McNally, R. T. Dracula was a Woman.
McNally, Robert E. Council of Trent, the Spiritual Exercises & the Catholic Reform. Anderson, Charles S., ed.
McNamara, Charlotte & Howell, Leonore. The Before & After Dinner Cookbook.
McNamara, John. Magic in Frosting.
McNamara, Joseph D. Safe & Sane: The Sensible Way to Protect Yourself, Your Loved Ones, Your Property & Possessions.
McNamara, Martin. Targum & Testament: Aramaic Paraphrases of the Hebrew Bible: a Light on the New Testament.
McNary, Arthur H. The Way Men Love: A Study into the Emotional Subconscious.
McNaught, Brian R. A Disturbed Peace: Selected Writings of an Irish Catholic Homosexual.
MacNaughton, E. G. & McDougall, T. W. A New Approach to Latin.
McNaughton, Kenneth J. The Chemical Engineering Guide to Pumps.
McNaughton, Kenneth J., ed. see Chemical Engineering Magazine Editors.
McNaughton, Kenneth J., et al. Controlling Corrosion in Process Industry.
McNaughton, S. J. & Wolf, Larry L. General Ecology.
McNeer, May. America's Mark Twain.
--Bloomsday for Maggie.
--My Friend Mac: The Story of Little BAptiste & the Moose.
--Stranger in the Pines.
McNeese, Donald G. & Hoag, Albert L. Engineering & Technical Handbook.
McNeil, Barbara, ed. Author Biography Master Index 2nd Edition Supplement.
McNeil, Barbara J., ed. see Cravalho, Ernest G.
McNeil, Donald R. Interactive Data Analysis: A Practical Primer.
MacNeil, Duncan. The Red Daniel.
--The Subaltern.
McNeil, Linda M. Contradictions of Control: School Structure & School Knowledge.
McNeil, W. K., compiled by. Ghost Stories from the American South.
MacNeilage, Linda, jt. auth. see Adams, Kathleen.
McNeile, A. H. Gospel According to St. Matthew.
McNeill, Desmond. The Contradictions of Foreign Aid.
McNeill, John T. A History of the Cure of Souls.
McNeill, John T. & Gamer, Helena M. Medieval Handbooks of Penance.
McNeill, John T. & Nichols, James H. Ecumenical Testimony: The Concern for Christian Unity Within the Reformed & Presbyterian Churches.
McNeill, Joseph. Principles of Home Inspection: A Guide to Residential Construction, Inspection & Maintenance.
McNeill, Patrick. Research Methods.
McNeill, Patrick, jt. auth. see O'Donnell, Mike.
McNeill, Patrick, ed. see Wilson, Adrian.
McNeill, William H., ed. see Otto, Robert C.
McNeillie, Andrew, ed. see Woolf, Virginia.
McNeir, Waldo F. & Greenfield, Thelma N., eds. Pacific Coast Studies in Shakespeare.
McNeish, James. Lovelock.
McNellis, Bob, jt. auth. see McNellis, Cathy.
McNellis, Cathy & McNellis, Bob. You Can Still Own a Home: A Strategy for Stretching Your Housing Dollar.
MacNelly, Jeff. Directions.
--The Greatest Shoe on Earth.
--The New Shoe.
--On with the Shoe.
--One Shoe Fits All.
--The Other Shoe Book.
--A Shoe for All Seasons.
--The Shoe Must Go On.
--The Very First Shoe Book.
McNelly, Theodore. Politics & Government in Japan.
McNelly, Theodore, ed. Sources in Modern East Asian History & Politics.
McNemee, Andrew J. Brother Mack, the Frontier Preacher.
McNichols, Joan & Purkiss, Gerri. Word Ways.
McNickle, D'Arcy. Wind from an Enemy Sky: A Novel.
Macnicol, Malcolm F. Aids to Orthopaedics.
McNicoll, I. H., jt. auth. see Lewis, T. M.
MacNiece, Louis. The Last Ditch.
MacNitt. How to Use Astral Power: Key to a Miraculous New Life.
McNitt, J. I. Livestock Husbandry Techniques.
McNitt, Jim. The Art of Computer Management: How Small Firms Can Increase Their Productivity & Profits with Personal Computers.
McNulty, A. J. Road of the Dashing Commuter.
McNulty, Charles. China.
McNulty, Edward N. When TV Is a Member of the Family.
McNulty, Faith. The Burning Bed.
McNulty, J. Bard. Modes of Literature.
McNulty, John K. Federal Estate & Gift Taxation in a Nutshell.
--Federal Income Taxation of Individuals in a Nutshell.
McNulty, John K., jt. auth. see Kragen, Adrian A.
McNulty, Kenneth K., Sr. Street or Pulpit? The Witness of Activist Monsignor Charles Owen Rice of Pittsburgh.
McNulty, Paul J. The Origins & Development of Labor Economics.
McNutt, Dan J. The Eighteenth Century Gothic Novel: An Annotated Bibliography of Criticism & Selected Texts.
MacNutt, William S. Days of Lorne: Impressions of a Governor-General.
McOmie, J. F., ed. Protective Groups in Organic Chemistry.
McParland, Edward. James Gandon: Vitruvius Hibernicus. Harris, John & Laing, Alastair, eds.
McPartland, John M. The March Toward Matter.
McPartland, Joseph F. McGraw-Hill's National Electrical Code Handbook.
McPartland, Joseph F. & Novak, W. J. Practical Electricity.
McPeck, Helen. Shalom, My Marty...
McPeek, Mary, tr. & intro. by. Bobbin Lace, First Series: Les Dentelles Aux Fuseaux.
MacPhail, Bruce D., ed. see Irving, Washington.
McPhail, David. Bumper Tubbs.
MacPhee, I. & Cowley, G. Essentials of Periodontology & Periodontics.
McPhee, John. The Pine Barrens.
McPherson, A. & Gray, J. Reconstruction of Secondary Education: Theory, Myth & Practice Since the War.
MacPherson, Alan & MacPherson, Sue. Edible & Useful Wildplants of the Urban West.
McPherson, Alan & McPherson, Sue. Wild Food Plants of Indiana & Adjacent States.
McPherson, Alexander. Preparation & Analysis of Protein Crystals.
McPherson, Bruce. Between Two Worlds: Victorian Ambivalence about Progress.
McPherson, Dorothy. Authority Control in the University of California Union Catalog.
--Bibliographic Specifications for Processing Campus OCLC Records.
--Bibliographic Specifications for Processing Campus RLIN Records.
McPherson, Dorothy W. Mathematics Applied to Business Problems, 1981.
McPherson, E. & Ashton, D. L. Metric Engineering Drawing Examples.
McPherson, Edward. Handbook of Politics from 1868-94. Incl. Vol. 1. 1868; Vol. 2. 1870; Vol. 3. 1872; Vol. 4. 1874; Vol. 5. 1876; Vol. 6. 1878; Vol. 7. 1880; Vol. 8. 1882; Vol. 9. 1884; Vol. 10. 1886; Vol. 11. 1888; Vol. 12. 1890; Vol. 13. 1892; Vol. 14. 1894. Greenwood.
Macpherson, Hectar. Guide to the Stars.
MacPherson, Ian, jt. auth. see Co-operative Union of Canada Staff.
McPherson, Ian & Sutton, Andrew, eds. Reconstructing Psychological Practice.
MacPherson, J. C., jt. auth. see Neilson, W. A.
MacPherson, James. The Feral Classroom: High School Students' Construction of Reality.
McPherson, James A. Elbow Room: Stories.
MacPherson, Malcolm C. The Blood of His Servants: The True Story of One Man's Search for His Family's Friend & Executioner.
MacPherson, Margaret M. Ponies for Hire.
--Rough Road.
MacPherson, Robert, jt. auth. see Fulton, William.
Macpherson, Ruth. Discover Brunch: A New Way of Entertaining.
MacPherson, Stewart, jt. ed. see Bean, Philip.
McPherson, Sue, jt. auth. see McPherson, Alan.
MacPherson, Sue, jt. auth. see MacPherson, Alan.
McPherson, William. Testing the Current.
McPhillips, Martin. The Solar Energy Almanac.
McQuade, Donald & Atwan, Robert. Thinking in Writing.
McQuaid, Patrick, jt. auth. see Stahl, Barbara J.
McQuaig, Douglas J. Career Accounting Fundamentals.
--College Accounting Fundamentals.
--College Accounting Fundamentals. Incl. Westside Lanes: A Sole-Proprietorship Service Business for Chapters 1-10; Driscoe's Rugs: A Sole-Proprietorship Merchandising Business for Chapters 1-15; Claverton Outdoor Store: A Voucher System for Business for Chapters 22-29; Denton Appliance; CW Hale; Accounting Stationery; Transparencies for Problem Solutions; Instructor's Annotated Ed., Accounting Stationery; Mt. Chandler Legal Practice Set; CW Hale Medical Practice Set; Computer-Assisted Practice Set (Denton Appliance & Air Conditioning; Achievement Tests; Achievement Tests; Answer Key for Achievement Tests. HM.
Macquarrie, John. Christian Unity & Christian Diversity.
--God-Talk: An Examination of the Language & Logic of Theology.
--The Humility of God.
--Martin Heidegger.
--New Directions in Theology Today: God & Secularity, Vol. 3.
--Studies in Christian Existentialism.
--Twentieth Century Religious Thought.
Macquarrie, John, ed. Dictionary of Christian Ethics.
McQuay, Earl. John-Apostle of Love.
McQuay, Mike. Memories.
McQueen, jt. auth. see Bowman.
McQueen, Ian. Japan-A Travel Survival Kit.
MacQueen, John. Allegory.
--The Enlightenment & Scottish Literature: Progress & Poetry.
McQuigg, R. Bruce. Tools of the Trade.
McQuiston, Faye C. & Parker, Jerald D. Heating, Ventilating & Air Conditioning: Analysis & Design.
McQuiston, Frank W., Jr. & Shoemaker, Robert S. Primary Crushing Plant Design.
McQuiston, L., jt. ed. see Bicknell, J.
McRae, Bobbi A. The Fireworks Source Book: Your Mail Order Guide to Supplies & Services for the Fiber Arts.
McRae, Bradley C. Practical Time Management - How to Get More Done in Less Time.
MacRae, C. Duncan, jt. auth. see Andreassi, Michael W.
MacRae, Donald L., et al. You & Others: An Introduction to Interpersonal Communication.
MacRae, George W. & Price, Charles P. Easter.
Macrae, Norman. America's Third Century.
Macrae, R. HPLC in Food Analysis.
McRae, R. & Walker, D. Foreign Exchange Management.
MacRae, T. P., jt. auth. see Fraser, R. D.
McReynolds, Helen. Microforms of United States Government Publications.
Macridis, Roy C. Contemporary Political Ideologies: Movements & Regimes.
--Foreign Policy in World Politics.
McRobbie, Angela & McCabe, Trisha, eds. Feminism for Girls: An Adventure Story.
MacRobbie, Bill. Enjoying the Signery.
McRoberts, Darlene. Family Fare: Christian Activities for Every Season of the Year.
--Second Marriage: The Promise & the Challenge.
Macrorie, Ken. Searching Writing.
Macrory, Patrick, ed. see Sale, Florentia.
Macrosty, Henry W. The Trust Movement in British Industry: A Study of Business Organization.
MacShane, Frank. The Life of Raymond Chandler.
MacShane, Frank, ed. Collected Stories of John O'Hara.
McShane, Mark. Just a Face in the Dark.
McShane, Philip. Searching for Cultural Foundations.
--Wealth of Self & Wealth of Nations: Self Axis of the Great Ascent.
McShine, Kynaston. An International Survey of Recent Painting & Sculpture.
McSorley, Harry J., Jr. Luther: Right or Wrong.
MacSwain, J. W., jt. auth. see Linsley, E. G.
Mactaggart & Chambers. Plastics & Building.
McTaggart, Ellis, jt. auth. see McTaggart, John.
McTaggart, John & McTaggart, Ellis. Studies in Hegelian Cosmology.
McTaggart, Lynne. Kathleen Kennedy: Her Life & Times.
--Kathleen Kennedy: Her Life & Times.
McTague, John J., Jr. British Policy in Palestine: Nineteen Seventeen to Nineteen Twenty-Two.
McTavish, jt. auth. see Loether.
McTavish, David. Giuseppe Porta.
McTeigue, Michael, jt. auth. see Merrins, Eddie.
McTighe, James. Roadside History of Colorado.
Maculaitis, Jean D. & Scheraga, Mona. What to Do Before the Books Arrive.
McVan, Barbara & Hamilton, Helen. Nursing Yearbook, 1987.
McVan, Barbara, jt. ed. see Carey, Katherine W.
McVan, Barbara, jt. ed. see Robinson, Jean.
McVan, Barbara, jt. ed. see Urosevich, Patricia R.
McVan, Barbara, jt. ed. see Urosevich, Patti.
McVan, Barbara, jt. ed. see West, Richard.
McVan, Barbara, jt. ed. see Williams, Susan.

McVan, Barbara, jt. ed. see Williams, Susan R.
McVann, Barbara, jt. ed. see Robinson, Jean.
McVann, Barbara, jt. ed. see Urosevich, Patti.
MacVaugh, Gilbert S. Frigidity: Its Cure with Hypnosis.
McVayne, Jean. The Open Gate.
McVeagh, John. Tradeful Merchants: The Portrayal of the Capitalist in Literature.
McVeigh, Patrick. Scottish East Coast Potteries, 1750-1840.
McVerry, V. Early Warning Health Guide.
Macvey, John W. Interstellar Travel: Past, Present & Future.
McVey-Gill, Mary, et al. En Contacto: Gramatica en Accion.
--En Contacto: Lecturas Intermedias.
McViegh, Shaun, jt. auth. see Ellington, Mark.
McVoy, D. Stevens, jt. auth. see Baldwin, Thomas F.
McWade, Patricia. Financial Aid for Graduate & Professional Education 1987.
--Financial Aid for Graduate & Professional Education 1988.
McWaters, Marcus M. & Reed, James H. Elements of Calculus: With Contemporary Applications.
McWatters, Ann R. Financing Capital Formation for Local Governments.
McWeeny, R. Spins in Chemistry.
McWeeny, R. & Sutcliffe, B. T. Methods of Molecular Quantum Mechanics.
McWeeny, R., ed. see Farina, John E.
McWhinney, Edward. Quebec & the Constitution: Nineteen Sixty to Nineteen Seventy-Eight.
McWhinnie, M. A., et al. Euphausiacea Bibliography: A World Literature Survey.
McWhirter, David, jt. auth. see Gulledge, Dennis.
McWhirter, Norris. Guinness Book of World Records.
--Guinness Book of World Records 1984.
--Guinness Book of World Records 1986.
McWhorter, Kathleen T. College Reading & Study Skills.
--A Guide to College Reading.
McWhorter, Lucullus. Tragedy of the Wahk-Shum.
McWhorter, Margaret L., ed. see Andrecht, Venus C.
McWilliams, Donald A. Myth of Evolution.
McWilliams, J. & Steel, R. J. Gas! The Battle for Ypres, 1915.
McWilliams, James R. Brother Artist: A Psychological Study of Thomas Mann's Fiction.
McWilliams, Margaret. Experimental Foods Laboratory Manual.
--Illustrated Guide to Food Preparation.
MacWilliams, Margaret. Queenscote.
McWilliams, Margaret & Paine, Harriett. Modern Food Preservation.
McWilliams, Michael. TV Sirens.
McWilliams, Peter A. Personal Computer in Business Book.
--Personal Computers & the Disabled.
--Peter McWilliams Personal Computer Buying Guide.
Macy, John. Story of the World's Literature.
Madama, John, jt. auth. see Hunken, Jorie.
Madan, T. N. Way of Life: King, Householder, Renouncer; Essays in Honour of Louis Dumont.
Madan, T. N., et al. Doctors & Society: Three Asian Case Studies.
Madara, Lynda, jt. auth. see Adams, Leigh.
Madaras, Area, jt. auth. see Madaras, Lynda.
Madaras, Larry. Taking Sides: Clashing Views on Controversial Issues in American History.
--Taking Sides: Clashing Views on Controversial Issues in American History.
Madaras, Larry, jt. auth. see Kuzirian, Eugene.
Madaras, Lynda & Madaras, Area. What's Happening to My Body? Book for Girls: A Growing-up Guide for Parents & Daughters.
Madaras, Lynda & Saavedra, Dane. The "What's Happening to My Body?" Book for Boys: A Growing-up Guide for Parents & Sons.
Madaras, Lynda, jt. auth. see Patterson, Jane.
Madaus, George F., et al. School Effectiveness: A Reassessment of the Evidence.
Madden. Guide to Alcohol & Drug Dependence.
Madden, Chris C. The Summer House Cookbook.
Madden, David. The Suicide's Wife.
Madden, Deirdre. Hidden Symptoms. Brady, Upton B., ed.
Madden, Edward J. Fundamental Harmony Workbook.
Madden, Frederick & Fieldhouse, David K., eds. Oxford & the Idea of Commonwealth.
Madden, L. How to Find Out about the Victorian Period.
Madden, Lionel, ed. Robert Southey: The Critical Heritage.
Madden, Lorring. How to Cope with Your Child's Teacher.
Madden, Michael. Lifestyles of Library Users & Nonusers.
Madden, Palmer B., et al. The Law of Politics: Federal & California Fair Political Practices & Election Laws.
Maddison, Angus. Economic Growth in Japan & the U. S. S. R.
Maddison, R. E., tr. see Schmidt, Helmut & Von Stackelberg, Mark.
Maddocks, Melvin & Time-Life Books Editors. The Atlantic Crossing.
Maddocks, Peter. How to Be a Super Cartoonist.
Maddow, Ben. A Sunday Between Wars.
Maddox, Brenda. Married & Gay: An Intimate Look at a Different Relationship.
Maddox, Gaynor, ed. Cookbook for Diabetics.
Maddox, James H., Jr. Joyce's Ulysses & the Assault upon Character.
Maddox, Richard. Troubleshooting & Repairing Satellite TV Systems.
Maddox, Robert, tr. see Hahn, Ferdinand.
Maddox, Robert J. American History, 1987-88.
--American History, 1987-88.
--Annual Editions: American History.
--Annual Editions: American History.
--William E. Borah & American Foreign Policy.
Maddux, Rachel. Abel's Daughter.
--The Orchard Children.
--A Walk in the Spring Rain.
Maddux, Robert. Quality Interviewing.
Maddy, Yulisa A. No Past, No Present, No Future.
Madej, W. Victor, ed. Japanese Armed Forces Order of Battle, 1937-1945.
Madeja, Stanley, jt. auth. see Hurwitz, Al.
Madeja, Stanley S. Arts & Aesthetics: An Agenda for the Future.
Madeja, Stanley S., ed. The Arts, Cognition, & Basic Skills.
Madeja, W. Victor, ed. Russo-German War: Autumn 1941.
Madeley, J. Human Rights Begin with Breakfast.
Mader, Andreas E. Altchristliche Basiliken und Lokaltraditionen in Sudjudaa.
Mader, Chris & Bortz, John. Dow Jones-Irwin Guide to Real Estate Investing.
Mader, Sylvia S. Inquiry into Life.
Madge, Nicola, ed. Families at Risk.
Madge, Violet. Children in Search of Meaning.
Madhuri, Desai, ed. see Gordon, Douglas H.
Madigan, Bob & Kasoff, Lawrence. The First-Time Investor.
Madigan, Thomas F. Word Shadows of the Great: The Lure of Autograph Collecting.
Madison, Arnold. How to Play Girls' Softball.
--Vandalism: The Not-So-Senseless Crime.
--Vandalism: The Not-So-Senseless Crime.
--Vigilantism in America.
Madison, Arnold, jt. auth. see Wyndham, Lee.
Madison, J. J. The Thing.
Madison, James. Notes of Debates in the Federal Convention of 1787 Reported by James Madison. Koch, Adrienne, ed.
Madison, Louis E. San Francisco on a Shoestring: The Intelligent Traveller's (& Natives) Guide to Budget Living in San Francisco.
Madison, Winifred. Growing up in a Hurry.
Madlee, Dorothy, jt. auth. see Norton, Andre.
Madow, Leo. Love: How to Understand & Enjoy It.
--Love: How to Understand & Enjoy It.
Madrick, Jeffrey, ed. see Boesky, Ivan F.
Madrigal, Ezequias, jt. auth. see Madrigal, Margarita.
Madrigal, Jose A., jt. ed. see McCrary, William.
Madrigal, Margarita. Invitation to Italian.
--Open Door to Spanish.
Madrigal, Margarita & Madrigal, Ezequias. Invitation to Spanish.
Madrigal, Margarita & Meyer, Ursula. An Invitation to German.
Madron. Local Area Networks in Large Organzitions.
Madron, Thomas W. The Micro-Mainframe Connection.
Madsen, Ann M., jt. auth. see Dailey, Charles A.
Madsen, Axel. Open Road: Truckin' on the Biting Edge.
--Sixty Minutes: The Power & the Politics.
Madsen, Brigham D. The Northern Shoshoni.
Madsen, K. B., jt. auth. see Berlyne, D. E.
Madsen, Norman P. Lord, Teach Us to Pray.
Madsen, Richard W., jt. auth. see Isaacson, Dean L.
Madsen, Susan A. Christmas: A Joyful Heritage.
Madson, John. Where the Sky Began: Land of the Tallgrass Prairie.
Maeda, Mana, jt. auth. see Richie, Donald.
Maeda, Robert J. Two Sung Texts on Chinese Painting & the Landscape Styles of the 11th & 12th Centuries.
--Two Twelfth Century Texts on Chinese Painting.
Maeder, Edward, et al. Elegant Art: Fashion & Fantasy in the Eighteenth Century.
Maeder, Herbert & Och, Armin, eds. Beautiful Switzerland-Merveillevse Suisse.
Maehl, William H. Germany in Western Civilization.
--World History Syllabus: Ancient & Medieval Times.
--World History Syllabus: Early Modern Times.
--World History Syllabus: Modern Times.
Maeland, A., jt. ed. see Andresen, A. F.
Maeroff, Gene I. Don't Blame the Kids: The Trouble with America's Public Schools.
Maestri, Vic. Little Eva, Baby Doll, & Blondy Ryan: Sports Trivia, Nicknames & Real First Names.
Maestro, Marcello. The Deep Freeze & Other Stories.
Maeterlinck, Maurice. The Great Beyond.
Mafeje, Archie. Science, Ideology & Development-Three Essays on Development Theory.
Maffei, Paolo. Beyond the Moon.
--Monsters in the Sky.
Maffezzoni, C., ed. Modeling & Control of Electric Power Plants: Proceedings of the IFAC Workshop, Como, Italy, 22-23 September 1983.
Mafi, Maryam, tr. Daneshvar's Playhouse: Five Stories.
Mafi, Maryam, tr. from Persia see Daneshvar, Simin.
Magagna, Anna M., illus. First Prayers.
Magalaner, Marvin & Kain, Richard M. Joyce: The Man, the Work, the Reputation.
Magallona, E. D., et al. Residue Reviews.
Magann, Julia H. Municipal Financial Disclosure: An Empirical Investigation. Farmer, Richard N., ed.
Magarick, Pat. Successful Handling of Casualty Claims.
Magaro, Peter A. Construction of Madness: Emerging Conceptions & Interventions into Psychotic Process.
Magarshack, David. Stanislavsky, a Life.
Magarshack, David, tr. see Leskov, Nikolai.
Magarshack, David, tr. see Schneider, Ilya I.
Magarshack, David, tr. & intro. by see Stanislavsky, Konstantin.
Magaziner, Ira C. & Reich, Robert C. Minding America's Business: The Decline & Rise of the American Economy.
Magee, J. O. Basic Accounting.
--Company Accounts.
--Company Accounts.
Magee, R. J. Selected Readings in Chromatography.
Magee, Susan F. MesoAmerican Archaeology: A Guide to the Literature & Other Information Sources.
Magenes, E., jt. auth. see Lions, J. L.
Magenes, E., jt. ed. see Galligani, I.
Mager, N. H. & Mager, S. K. What Business Can Get from the Government.
Mager, Nathan H. & Mager, Sylvia K. The Morrow Book of New Words: 8500 Terms Not Yet in Standard Dictionaries.
Mager, S. K., jt. auth. see Mager, N. H.
Mager, Sylvia K., jt. auth. see Mager, Nathan H.
Magerman, W. D. Zay Jeffries.
Magers, Steve, jt. auth. see Kern, Ken.
Maggin, Elliot S. Batman.
Maggiolo, Walter A. Techniques of Mediation in Labor Disputes.
Maggs, Christopher J. The Origins of General Nursing.
--The Origins of General Nursing.
Magill, Frank N., ed. Magill Surveys - American Literature: Colonial Age to 1890.
--Magill Surveys - American Literature: Realism to 1945.
--Magill Surveys - English Literature: Middle Ages to 1800.
--Magill's Bibliography of Literary Criticism.
Magill, M. J. On a General Economic Theory of Motion.
Magill, Richard A., et al, eds. Children in Sport.
Magilova, R. Ethnic Problems of Tropical Africa: Can They Be Solved?
Maginley, C. J. America in Miniatures: How to Make Models of Early American Houses & Furniture.
--Historic Models of Early America, & How to Make Them.
--Historic Models of Early America: & How to Make Them.
--Make It & Ride It.
--Models of America's Past & How to Make Them.
--Toys to Make & Ride.
Magliola, Robert R. Phenomenology & Literature: An Introduction.
Maglione, Sabatino G. Lope de Vega Los Celos de Rodamonte, Edicion Critica.
Magloire-Holly, Helene, ed. see Lefebvre, Claire.
Magne, Lawrence & Jones, Tony, eds. Passport to World Band Radio.
--Radio Database International.
--Radio Database International.
--Radio Database International: Tropical Bands Edition.
--Radio Database International: Worldwide Broadcasting Edition.
Magnifico, Giovanni. European Monetary Unification.
Magnum Photos, Inc. Staff. The Fifties: Photographs of America.
Magnus, K., ed. see CISM (International Center for Mechanical Sciences) Staff.
Magnus, Laurie. A Dictionary of European Literature, Designed As a Companion to English Studies.
Magnus, Leonard A. Russian Folk-Tales with Introduction & Notes.
Magnus, P. D., jt. auth. see Chapman, Dennis.
Magnus, W., et al. Formulas & Theorems for the Special Functions of Mathematical Physics.
Magnuson, Jim see Hoffman, William M.
Magnusson, Magnus. Lindisfarne: The Cradle Island.
Magnusson, Sigurdur A. Northern Sphinx: Iceland & the Icelanders from the Settlement to the Present Day.
Magocsi, Paul R. Galicia: A Historical Survey & Bibliographic Guide.
Magon, Ricardo F. Land & Liberty: Anarchist Influences in the Mexican Revolution. Poole, David, ed.
Magonon, P. L., jt. ed. see Bramfitt, B. L.
Magoon, Paul M. & Richards, John B. Discipline or Disaster: Management's Only Choice.
Magoon, T. M., et al. Mental Health Counsellors at Work.
Magowan, Robin. Persian Notes.
Magrath, C. Peter. Yazoo: Law & Politics in the New Republic, Case of Fletcher V. Peck.
Magriel, Paul. An Introduction to Backgammon: A Step-by-Step Guide.
Magruder, Jeb S. An American Life.
Maguglin, Robert O. The Queen Mary: The Official Pictorial History.
Maguidovich, I. P. Historia del Descubrimiento y Exploracion De Latinoamerica.
Maguire, Cecilia. Excelling: The Nutritional Way to Good Health.
Maguire, Doris D. French Ensor Chadwick: Selected Letters & Papers.
Maguire, Gregory. The Lightning Time.
Maguire, Jack. Head Sharp: Step-by-Step Exercises to Develop Your Brain Power.
--What Does Childhood Taste Like? Mental Workouts That Will Stretch, Bend, & Energize the Way You Think, Respond, Dream, & Create.
Maguire, Jane. On Shares: Ed Brown's Story.
Maguire, Mike, jt. ed. see Vagg, John.
Maguire, R. J., tr. see Mihardja, Achdiat.
Maguire, Robert A. Red Virgin Soil: Soviet Literature in the Late 1920's.
Magyary-Kossa, Ilona von. A Medical Librarian? What's That?
Mahadeuan, C. Mahadevan Volume: A Collection of Geological Papers in Commeration of the Sixty-First Birthday of Pr. C. Mahadevan. Krishman, M. S., ed.
Mahadevan, A., ed. Physiology of Host Pathogen Interaction, 1977.
Mahan, Aline, jt. auth. see Mahan, Thomas.
Mahan, Benton, illus. Circus Baby.
Mahan, Bruce H. Elementary Chemical Thermodynamics.
Mahan, Thomas & Mahan, Aline. Assessing Children with Special Needs: A Practical Guide for the Use of Psychological, Behavioral, & Educational Measures.
Mahaney, W. C., ed. see Quarternary Stratigraphy Symposium Staff.
Mahaney, William E. Workbook of Current English.
Mahanthappa, K. T. & Randa, James, eds. Quantum Flavordynamics, Quantum Chromodynamics & Unified Theories.
Mahanthappa, K. T., et al, eds. see Boulder Conference on High Energy Physics Staff.
Mahanty, J. & Ninham, B. W., eds. Dispersion Forces.
Mahany, Patricia. Stories Jesus Told.
Mahany, Patricia, ed. Bible Animals.
--Bible Babies.
--Jesus Is Born.
Mahany, Patricia, ed. see Claire, Anne.
Mahany, Patricia, ed. see Truitt, Gloria.
Mahany, Patricia S. Bible Who Am I?
--Clint's "Be Cheerful" Day.
Mahar, Ellen P., jt. ed. see Ellenberger, J. S.
Mahathera, A. P., compiled by. English-Pali Dictionary.
Mahdihassan, S. Indian Alchemy or Rasayana: In the Light of Asceticism & Geriatrics.
Mahedy, William P. Out of the Night: The Spiritual Journey of Vietnam Vets.
Maher, Tom & Schwartz, Malcolm. Doctor Discusses Cancer.
Mahesh, Vivenda B., ed. see Pituitary Symposium Staff.
Maheshwari, B. L. Decision Styles & Organizational Effectiveness.
Mahln, Philip W. Entrepreneurial Skills: Cases in Small Business Management.
Mahl, George F. Psychological Conflict & Defense.
Mahler, Clarence A. Group Counseling in the Schools.
Mahler, K. Lectures on Transcendental Numbers. Divis, B. & Le Veque, W. J., eds.
Mahlqvist, Stefan. I'll Take Care of the Corcodiles.
Mahmood, K., et al, eds. Unsteady Flow in Open Channels.

Mahmoud, Adel A. see Warren, Kenneth S.
Mahnke, Susan, ed. Index to Yankee Magazine, 1935-1978.
Mahnken, Jan. A Cook's Garden.
Mahoney, Dorothy. The Craft of Calligraphy.
Mahoney, Elizabeth A. & Flynn, Jean P. The Handbook of Medical-Surgical Nursing.
Mahoney, Eugene F. Fire Department Hydraulics.
Mahoney, James R. Community College Centers for Contracted Programs.
Mahoney, James R., jt. auth. see Jackman, Mary J.
Mahoney, John & Hungness, Carl, eds. The Indianapolis Five Hundred Yearbook: 1969-1972.
Mahoney, John L. The Enlightenment & English Literature: Prose & Poetry of the Eighteenth Century with Selected Modern Critical Essays.
Mahoney, Marjorie C. The Wit & Wisdom of Anon: Humor.
Mahoney, Michael J. Self-Change: Strategies for Solving Personal Problems.
--Self-Change: Strategies for Solving Personal Problems.
Mahoney, Robert, jt. auth. see Rizzo, Betty.
Mahoney, Susan, ed. see Manoni, Mary H.
Mahoney, William, ed. see Means, R. S., Company, Inc. Staff.
Mahoney, William, ed. see R. S. Means Company, Inc. Staff.
Mahoney, William D., ed. see R. S. Means Company, Inc. Staff.
Mahoney, William F., ed. see R. S. Means Company, Inc. Staff.
Mahood, M. M. Shakespeare's Wordplay.
Mahowald, M. E., jt. ed. see Barratt, M. B.
Mahr, Adolph R. Christian Art in Ancient Ireland.
Mahr, August C. Cyprus Passion Cycle.
Mahre, Phil & Mahre, Steve. No Hill Too Fast.
Mahre, Steve, jt. auth. see Mahre, Phil.
Mahrenholtz, O, ed. Dynamics of Rotors: Stability & System Identification.
Mahy, B. W. & Barry, R. D., eds. Negative Strand Viruses & the Host Cell.
Mai, Ludwig H. Approach to Economics.
Maibach, Howard, jt. auth. see Reeves, John.
Maibach, Howard I., jt. ed. see Marzulli, Francis N.
Maichel, Karol. Soviet & Russian Newspapers at the Hoover Institution: A Catalog.
Maidens, Ena. The Techniques of Crocheted & Openwork Lace.
Maidment, Fred, ed. Human Resources, 1988-89.
Maidment, Susan. Child Custody & Divorce: The Law in Social Context.
Maier, Charles S. Recasting Bourgeois Europe: Stabilization in France, Germany, & Italy in the Decade After World War One.
Maier, Charles S., ed. The Origins of the Cold War & Contemporary Europe.
Maier, Johann. The Temple Scroll: An Introduction, Translation & Commentary.
Maier, L. & Mislow, V. Chemistry of Organophosphorous Compounds, 1.
Maier, L., jt. auth. see Kosolapoff, G. M.
Maier, Norman R. Psychology in Industrial Organizations.
Maier, Norman R. F., et al. The Role-Play Technique: A Handbook for Management & Leadership Practice.
Maier, Paul A. Caspar Schwenckfeld on the Person & Work of Christ.
Maier, Paul L. The Best of Walter A. Maier.
--First Christmas: The True & Unfamiliar Story in Words & Pictures.
--First Easter: The True & Unfamiliar Story in Words & Pictures.
Maier, Walter A. The Book of Nahum.
Maikowski, Stephen, jt. ed. see Hammerman, Susan.
Maile, Anne. Tie-Dyed Paper: An Easy New Craft.
Mailer, Norman. The Deer Park.
--The Executioner's Song.
--Of a Fire on the Moon.
--St. George & the Godfather.
Mailey, Jean, jt. auth. see Dimand, M. S.
Maillie, H. David, jt. ed. see Berg, George G.
Maillol, Aristide. Maillol Woodcuts: Three Hundred & Three Great Book Illustrations.
Mails, Thomas E. Fool's Crow.
Maimon, Salomon. Gesammelte Werke.
Maimonides. Preservation of Youth.
Maimonides, Moses. Guide of the Perplexed. Guttman, Julius W., ed. Rabin, Chaim, tr.
Main, Alex. Educational Staff Development.
Main, Earl D. A Nationwide Evaluation of M.D.T.A. (Manpower Development & Training Act) Institutional Job Training Programs.
Maine, Henry J. Ancient Law.
Maine Historical Society Staff. Province & Court Records of Maine.
Maingyou, Gao, ed. True & False Monkey.
Mainhood, Beth. Reaching Your World.
Mainichi Newspapers Staff. Japan & the Japanese.
Mainis, G. Introducing ProDOS.
Mains, David. A Closer Walk with God.
--Getting to Know the Holy Spirit.
--Making Church More Enjoyable.
--Making Scripture Yours.
--Praying More Effectively.
--Psalms That Touch Us Where We Live.
Mains, David & Mains, Karen. Our Favorite Verse.
Mains, Karen, jt. auth. see Mains, David.
Mainstream Access, Inc. Staff. The Publishing Job Finder.
--The Real Estate Job Finder.
Mair, George. Inside Home Box Office: The Billion-Dollar War Between HBO, Hollywood, & the Home Video Revolution.
Mair, L. Witchcraft.
Mairowitz, David Z. The Radical Soap Opera.
Mairs, Tanya E., tr. see Krotkov, Yuri.
Maisel, E. The Alexander Technique.
Maisel, Edward, ed. see Alexander, F. Matthias.
Maisel, Sherman J. & Roulac, Stephen E. Real Estate Investment & Finance.
Maisel, Sherman J., ed. Risk & Capital Adequacy in Commercial Banks.
Maisels, Ziva Amishai see Amishai-Maisels, Ziva.
Maistre, Joseph De see De Maistre, Joseph.
Maitland, David. Against the Grain: Coming through Mid-Life Crises.
Maitland, Derek, ed. Hong Kong in Focus.
Maitland, Ernest Y. Exporting: A Practical Manual for Developing Export Markets & Coping with Foreign Customs.
--Importing: A Practical Manual for Coping with Canadian Customs.
Maitland, Ian. The Causes of Industrial Disorder: A Comparison of a British & a German Factory.
Maitland, J. A., ed. see Byrd, William, et al.
Maitland-Jones, J. F. Politics in Africa: The Former British Territories.
Maity, S. K. Cultural Heritage of Ancient India.
Major, Alan. Maritime Antiques.
Major, Beverly. Porcupine Stew.
Major, Charles. Bears of Blue River.
Majors, William R. End of Arcadia: Gordon Browning & Tennessee Politics.
Majstorovic, Stevan. Cultural Policy in Yugoslavia: Self-Management & Culture.
Majumdar, A. K. N-Benzoylphenylhydroxylamine & Its Analogues.
Majumdar, B. Joyce Cary: An Existentialist Approach.
Majumdar, Sachindra K. Introduction to Yoga Principles & Practices.
Mak, W. & Molijn, H. Introduction to Trade-Mark Law in the Benelux.
Makaleris, Thanasis. Poems & Translations.
Makanna, Philip, photos by. Ghosts: Vintage Aircraft of World War II.
Makarenko, Anton. La Colectividad y la Educacion De la Personalidad.
Makay, John J. Speaking with an Audience.
Makemson, M. W., ed. see International Astronautical Congress, 12th, Washington, 1961.
Maker, C. June. Curriculum Development for the Gifted.
Maker, C. June, jt. auth. see Whitmore, Joanne R.
Maker, C. June, ed. Defensible Programs for the Gifted: Critical Issues in Gifted Education.
Maker, Janet & Lenier, Minnette. College Reading.
Maker, Janet, jt. auth. see Lenier, Minnette.
Makgetla, Neva S., jt. auth. see Seidman, Ann.
Makhrenko, A. Kh. The State Law of the Socialist Countries.
Makinodan, T. & Yunis, Edmond, eds. Immunology & Aging.
Makinson, D. C. Topics in Modern Logic.
Makinson, Randell L. Greene & Greene.
Makiyama, Hideko, ed. A New International Economic Order: Selected Documents, 1977.
Makkai, Adam, ed. see Boatner, Maxine & Gates, John E.
Makkai, Adam, ed. see Linguistic Association of Canada & the U. S. Staff.
Makkai, M. & Reyes, G. First-Order Categorical Logic: Model-Theoretical Methods in the Theory of Topoi & Related Categories.
Makkai, Valerie, ed. see Linguistic Association of Canada & the U. S. Staff.
Makkink, G. F. & Van Heemst, H. D. Simulation of the Water Balance of Arable Land & Pastures.
Makky, Ghazy A. Mecca, the Pilgrimage City: A Study of Pilgrim Accomodation.
Makowski, Z. S. Analysis Design & Construction of Double Layer Grids.
Makridakis, S. Forecasting. Wheelwright, S. C., ed.
Makris, Demetra. First Prize Quilts.
Maksakovsky, V., ed. The Economic Geography of the World.
Malahoff, A., jt. ed. see Earle, M. D.
Malak, Sharon, et al. Assessing Experimental Learning in Career Education.
Malalasekera, G. P., compiled by. Dictionary of Pali Proper Names.
Malamed, Stanley F. Handbook of Medical Emergencies in the Dental Office.
Malamud, Bernard. Dubin's Lives.
--The Magic Barrel.
--A New Life.
--A New Life.
--Pictures of Fidelman: An Exhibition.
--The Tenants.
--The Tenants.
Malandrino, Carmen P. The Italian Textbook: Ci Divertiamo con la Famiglia Tatasure.
Malanga, Gerard, ed. Scopophilia: The Love of Looking.
Malantschuk, Gregor. Kierkegaard's Thought. Hong, Howard V. & Hong, Edna H., trs. from Danish.
Malasky, Sol. Systems Safety: Technology & Application.
Malatesta, Anne & Friedland, Ronald. The White Kikuyu.
Malatesta, Li & Cenini, S. Zerovalent Compounds of Metals.
Malaurie, Jean, ed. Le Peuple Esquimau Aujourd'hui et Demain-The Eskimo People Today & Tomorrow: Quatrieme Congres International De la Fondation Francaise D'etudes Nordiques.
Malave, Florita Z. de see De Malave, Florita Z.
Malave, Florita Z. Louis De see Louis de Malave, Florita Z.
Malcolm, A., ed. see GP-Info Symposium Staff.
Malcolm, Aleen. Ride Out the Storm.
Malcolm, Janet. Diana & Nikon: Essays on the Aesthetic of Photography.
Malcolm, John. A Back Room in Somers Town.
--The Godwin Sideboard.
--Gothic Pursuit.
--The Gwen John Sculpture.
--A Memoir of Central India, Including Malwa, & Adjoining Provinces: With the History, & Copious Illustrations, of the Past & Present Condition of That Country.
--Whistler in the Dark.
--Whistler in the Dark: A Tim Simpson Mystery.
Malcolme-Lawes, David J. Microcomputers & Laboratory Instrumentation.
Malcolmson, Anne. Yankee Doodle Cousins.
Malcolmson, Anne, ed. A Taste of Chaucer: Selections from the Canterbury Tales.
Malcome, D. J. Programming ALGOL.
Male, Robert A., jt. auth. see Perrone, Philip.
Maleady, Antoinette O. Index to Record & Tape Reviews: A Classical Music Buying Guide Nineteen Eighty-Two.
--Index to Record & Tape Reviews: A Classical Music Buying Guide 1980.
--Index to Record & Tape Reviews: A Classical Music Buying Guide, 1977.
--Index to Record & Tape Reviews: A Classical Music Buying Guide, 1979.
--Index to Record & Tape Reviews: A Classical Music Buying Guide, 1975.
--Index to Record & Tape Reviews: A Classical Music Buying Guide, 1978.
--Index to Record & Tape Reviews: A Classical Music Buying Guide, 1976.
--Index to Record & Tape Reviews: A Classical Music Buying Guide, 1981.
--Record & Tape Reviews Index Nineteen Seventy-Four.
--Record & Tape Reviews Index Nineteen Seventy-Two.
--Record & Tape Reviews Index Nineteen Seventy-Three.
Maleady, Eugene L., jt. auth. see O'Donnell, Paul T.
Malefijt, Anne M. Religion & Culture: An Introduction to Anthropology of Religion.
Malefijt, Anne X. De Waal see Malefijt, Anne M.
Malehorn, Hal. Complete Book of Illustrated Learning Aids, Games & Activities.
Malek, Ivan & Fencl, Zdenek, eds. Continuous Cultivation of Microorganisms: Proceedings.
Malek, P. & Bartos, V., eds. Lymphology: Proceedings of the Sixth International Conference.
Maleska, Eugene. A Pleasure in Words.
Maleska, Eugene, jt. auth. see Farrar, Margaret P.
Maleska, Eugene T. Book of Cryptic Puzzles.
Maleska, Eugene T. & Farrar, Margaret P. Crossword Puzzle Book.
Maleska, Eugene T., jt. auth. see Farrar, Margaret P.
Maleska, Eugene T., ed. The Simon & Schuster Book of Cryptic Crossword Puzzles.
--The Simon & Schuster Book of Cryptic Crossword Puzzles.
--The Simon & Schuster Book of Cryptic Puzzles.
--Simon & Schuster Crossword Book of Quotations.
--Simon & Schuster's Crossword Puzzle Book: Series No. 136.
Malgrange, B. Lectures on the Theory of Functions of Several Complex Variables.
Malhortra, D. & Riggs, W. F., eds. Chemical Reagents in the Mineral Processing Industry.
Malhotra, P. L. Administration of Lord Elgin in India, Eighteen Ninety-Four to Eighteen Ninety-Nine.
Malhotra, S, et al. Foundation in Physics.
Mali, Jane L., jt. auth. see Herzig, Alison C.
Malickson, David L. & Nason, John W. Advertising: How to Write the Kind That Works.
Malik, Harji, jt. ed. see Singh, Patwant.
Malik, S. C. Introduction to Convergence.
Malin, Irving. New American Gothic.
Malin, Nigel, et al. Services for the Mentally Handicapped in Britain.
Malina, F. J. Applied Sciences Research & Utilization of Lunar Resources.
Malina, Frank J., ed. Visual Art, Mathematics & Computers: Selections from the Journal Leonardo.
Malina, Judith, ed. The Diaries of Judith Malina 1947-1957.
Malinin, T. I., et al, eds. Microcirculation, Perfusion & Transplantation of Organs.
Malinin, Theodore. Surgery & Life: The Extraordinary Career of Alexis Carrel.
Malino, Frances. The Sephardic Jews of Bordeaux: Assimilation & Emancipation in Revolutionary & Napoleonic France.
Malinova, Libuse, ed. Czech-English, English-Czech Dictionary of Electrical Engineering & Electronics.
Malinowski. Sex, Culture & Myth.
Malinowski, Bronislaw. Father in Primitive Psychology.
--Malinowski in Mexico: The Economics of a Mexican Market System. Drucker-Brown, Susan & De La Fuente, Julio, eds.
--Sexual Life of Savages in North-Western Melanesia.
Malinowski, Janet S. Nursing Care of the Labor Patient.
Malinowsky, H. Robert & Richardson, Jeanne M. Science & Engineering Literature: A Guide to Reference Sources.
Malins, Donald C., ed. Effects of Petroleum on Arctic & Subarctic Marine Environments & Organisms: Biological Effects.
Malins, E., ed. see McGarry, James.
Malinski, Mieczyslaw & Grant, Steven. The Life of John Paul II.
Malinvaud, Edmond. Mass Unemployment.
Malisoff. Dictionary of Biochemistry.
Malitza, M., jt. auth. see Guiasu, S.
Malkiel, Burton G. A Random Walk down Wall Street.
Malkin, Leonard I., et al. Liver Regeneration, No. 1.
Malkin, Michele. Blanche & Smitty.
--Blanche & Smitty's Summer Vacation.
Malkinson, A. M. Hormone Action.
Mallakh, Ragaei E. Qatar: Energy & Development.
Mallakh, Ragaei El see El Mallakh, Ragaei.
Mallalieu, H. L. The Dictionary of British Watercolour Artists Up to 1920: Vol. 1, The Text.
Mallalieu, Huon, ed. The Popular Antiques Yearbook.
Mallan, Chicki. Guide to Catalina Island.
Mallary, Peter. Houses of New England.
Mallen, Bruce E. The Marketing Channel: A Conceptual Viewpoint.
Mallen, Ronald E. Legal Malpractice.
Mallery, D. Garrick. Sign Language Among North American Indians Compared with That among Other Peoples & Deaf Mutes. (with Articles by A. L. Kroeber & C. F. Vogelin)
Mallet, R. H., et al, eds. Effects of Piping Restraints on Piping Integrity: PVP.
Mallett, Jerry J., jt. auth. see Bartch, Marian R.
Mallett, R. H. & Nair, B. R., eds. Coolant Boundary Integrity Considerations in Breeder Reactor Design, PVP-PB-027.
Malley, I. Educating the User.
Mallick, Netar, jt. auth. see Brooks, David.
Mallinson, Jeremy. Okavango Adventure.
Malliol, William. Slave.
Mallison, John. Building Small Groups in the Christian Community.
--Creative Ideas for Small Group in the Christian Community.
Malloch, David. Moulds: Their Isolation, Cultivation, & Identification.
Mallon, Marvin C. Exploring the NEC PC 8201A.
Mallon, Thomas. A Book of One's Own: People & Their Diaries.
Mallonee, Helen. How to Write Themes for English & Humanities.
Mallory, James D. & Baldwin, Stanley C. The Kink & I: A Psychiatrist's Guide to Untwisted Living.
Mallos, Tess. The Complete Middle East Cookbook.
Mallow, Alex & Chabot, Leon. Laser Safety Handbook.
Mallow, Vernon. The Demonic: A Selected Theological Study: An Examination into the Theology of Edwin Lewis, Karl Barth, & Paul Tillich.
Mallowe, Mike. The Meatman.

Mallows, D. F. & Pickering, W. J. Stress Analysis Problems in SI Units.
Mallows, Wilfrid. The Mystery of the Great Zimbabwe: A New Solution.
Malloy, James M. & Thorn, Richard S., eds. Beyond the Revolution: Bolivia Since 1952.
Malloy, John F., jt. auth. see Turner, William C.
Malloy, Ruth L. & Hsu, Priscilla L. Fielding's People's Republic of China, 1987.
Malm, Donald G. A Computer Laboratory Manual for Number Theory.
Malmaud, Roslyn K. Work & Marriage: The Two-Profession Couple. Nathan, Peter, ed.
Malmberg, B. Structural Linguistics & Human Communication.
Malmin, Kenneth P. Bible Research.
Malmstrom, Margit, ed. see Craig, James.
Malmstrom, Ruth, jt. auth. see Malmstrom, Vincent.
Malmstrom, Vincent & Malmstrom, Ruth. British Isles.
Malmstrom, Vincent H., et al. British Isles & Germany.
Malnati, Richard J. & Trembley, Edward L. Group Procedures for Counselors in Educational & Community Settings.
Maloff, Chalda & Zears, Russell. Computers in Nutrition.
Maloiy, C. M. O., ed. see Zoological Society of London Symposium Staff.
Maloiy, G. M., ed. Comparative Physiology of Osmoregulation in Animals.
Maloiy, G. W., ed. Comparative Physiology of Osmoregulation in Animals.
Malone. Robot Book.
Malone, Bill & McCulloh, Judith, eds. Stars of Country Music.
Malone, Dolores M. God's Covenant: The One Story of the Bible.
Malone, E. T. Tapestry Maker: Poems by Ted Malone.
Malone, H. E. The Determination of Hydrazine-Hydrazide Groups.
Malone, John W., Jr., jt. auth. see Epp, Donald J.
Malone, Maggie. Heirloom Quilts You Can Make.
Malone, Margaret G. Cowboys & Computers: Life on a Modern Ranch.
Malone, Michael. Dingley Falls.
Malone, Robert A., jt. auth. see Acquaviva, Francis A.
Malone, Ruth. Here No Evil.
--Mystery of the Golden Ram.
Malone, Thomas P., jt. auth. see Whitaker, Carl A.
Malone, Tom. Rejoicing with Creation.
Malone, William F., ed. Tissue Management in Restorative Dentistry.
Maloney, Albert S. Dutton's Navigation & Piloting.
Maloney, Edward. Boeing P-26 "Peashooter"
Maloney, Edward T. Luftwaffe Aircraft & Aces.
Maloney, Edward T. & Feist, Uwe. Chance Vought F4U-Corsair.
Maloney, Elbert S. Chapman Piloting, Seamanship, & Small Boat Handling.
Maloney, Elbert S., jt. auth. see Chapman, Charles F.
Maloney, Frank R. How to Eat a Slug & Other Poems.
Maloney, Ralph. Fish in a Stream in a Cave.
Maloney, Roy T. Real Estate Quick & Easy.
Maloney, Timothy J. Industrial Solid State Electronics: Devices & Systems.
Maloney, William F. Productivity Bargaining: A Study in Contract Construction.
Malory, Thomas. Le Morte D'Arthur.
--Le Morte D'Arthur.
--Tales of King Arthur. Senior, Michael, ed.
Malouf, Pyrrha. Metamassage: How to Massage Your Way to a Beautiful Complexion - All Over.
Malraux, Andre. Antimemoires.
--Les Chenes qui'on abat.
--La Condition Humaine.
--The Conquerors. Becker, Stephen, tr. from Fr.
--L' Espoir.
--Lazare: Le Miroir des Limbes.
--Man's Hope. Gilbert, Stuart & MacDonald, Alastair, trs. from Fr.
--Le Musee Imaginaire.
Maltbaek, J. C. Essential Engineering Dynamics.
Maltby, Arthur & McKenna, Brian. Irish Official Publications: A Guide to Republic of Ireland Papers, with a Breviate of Reports 1922-1972.
Maltby, Arthur & Maltby, Jean. Ireland in the Nineteenth Century: A Breviate of Official Publications.
Maltby, Jean, jt. auth. see Maltby, Arthur.
Malterner, Virginia M. Circles.
Malthus, Thomas R. An Essay on the Principle of Population.
--Inquiry into the Nature & Progress of Rent & the Principles by Which It Is Regulated: A Greenwood Archival Edition.
Maltz, Albert. Tale of One January.
Maltz, Maxwell. Magic Power of Self-Image Psychology.
Maluccio, Anthony N. & Sinanoglu, Paula A., eds. The Challenge of Partnership: Working with Parents of Children in Foster Care.
Maly, Kenneth, jt. auth. see Sallis, John.
Malyar, I. Alma-Ata: A Guide.
Malyusz, Edith C. The Theatre & National Awakening. Szendrey, Thomas, tr.
Malzberg, Barry. Everything Happened to Susan.
--The Social Worker.
--The Spread.
Malzberg, Barry, jt. auth. see Pronzini, Bill.
Malzberg, Barry, jt. ed. see Pronzini, Bill.
Malzberg, Barry N., jt. ed. see Pronzini, Bill.
Maman, Andre, et al. France: Ses Grandes Heures Litteraires.
Mamantov, Ilya A., ed. see Altman, Moses.
Mamatey, Victor S. Rise of the Habsburg Empire: 1526-1815.
Mamet, David. American Buffalo.
--Edmond.
--Edmond.
--Glengarry Glenn Ross.
--Goldberg Street: Short Plays & Monologues.
--House of Games: Screenplay.
--Lakeboat.
--Lakeboat.
--A Life in the Theatre.
--Three Children's Plays: The Poet & the Rent; The Frog Prince & the Revenge of the Space Pandas or Binky Rudich & the Two-Speed Clock.
--The Water Engine & Mr. Happiness.
Mamonova, Tatyana, ed. Women & Russia: Feminist Writings from the Soviet Union.
Management Roundtable, Inc. Staff. CAD-CAM Databases: Gaining Control.
--The Complete CAD-CAE Electronics Marketplace Directory.
Management Sciences for Health Staff, et al. Managing Drug Supply: The Selection, Procurement, Distribution, & Use of Pharmaceuticals in Primary Health Care. Quick, Jonathan D. & Hume, Margaret L., eds.
--El Suministro de Medicamentos: La Seleccion, Adquisicion, Distribucion y Uso de Productos Farmaceuticos en la Atencion Primaria de Salud. Quick, Jonathan D. & Hume, Margaret L., eds. Gibboney, Jan D. & Petit, Adrian M., trs. from Eng.
Manaker, George H. Interior Plantscapes: Installation Maintenance & Management.
Manassah, Jamal T., ed. Innovations In Telecommunications.
Mance, Joan. A Comparison Between Counselling & Analysis.
Manceron, Claude. The Wind from America.
Manchester, William. The Death of a President.
Mancini, Henry. Sounds & Scores.
Mancini, Janet K. & Robbins, Franklyn A. Encountering Society: Introductory Readings in Sociology.
Mancini, M., et al. Medical Complications of Obesity.
Mancino, Douglas M., jt. auth. see Burns, Linda A.
Mancuso, Anthony. California Non-Profit Corporation Book.
--How to Form Your Own California Corporation. Warner, Ralph, ed.
--How to Form Your Own Texas Corporation.
Mancuso, Anthony & Rosenbluth, Lewis. How to Form Your Own New York Corporation.
Mancuso, James C., jt. auth. see Sarbin, Theodore R.
Mancuso, Joseph. How to Write a Winning Business Plan.
Mancuso, Joseph R. How to Prepare & Present a Business Plan.
--How to Start, Finance & Manage Your Own Small Business.
--How to Start, Finance & Manage Your Own Small Business.
Mancuso, Joseph R., jt. auth. see Baumback, Clifford M.
Mandal & Mayon. Lecture Notes on the Infectious Diseases.
Mandel, Bea & Mandel, Byron. Play Safe: How to Avoid Getting Sexually Transmitted Diseases.
Mandel, Byron, jt. auth. see Mandel, Bea.
Mandel, Eli. Contexts of Canadian Criticism.
--Crusoe: Poems Selected & New.
Mandel, Eli & Taras, David. A Passion for Identity: An Introduction to Canadian Studies.
Mandel, Elias, jt. auth. see Meilach, Dona Z.
Mandel, Ernest. Formation of the Economic Thought of Karl Marx. Pearce, Brian, tr. from Fr.
--Marxist Economic Theory. Pearce, Brian, tr. from Fr.
Mandel, Ernest, et al. Fifty Years of World Revolution, An International Symposium. Pual, Gerald, tr.
Mandel, George. Crocodile Blood.
Mandel, J. & Brun, L., eds. Mechanical Waves in Solids.
Mandel, Janice K. Biotechnology Emerges: The Key Years, 1973-1980.
Mandel, L. & Wolf, E., eds. Coherence & Quantum Optics III.
--Coherence & Quantum Optics IV.
Mandel, Morris. A Complete Treasury of Stories for Public Speakers.
Mandel, Robert. Perception, Decision Making & Conflict.
Mandel, Ruth B. In the Running: The New Woman Candidate.
--In the Running: The New Woman Candidate.
Mandel, Siegfried, ed. see Rilke, Rainer M.
Mandelbaum, Maurice, et al, eds. Philosophic Problems.
Mandelbaum, Seymour J. Community & Communications.
Mandelberg, Cynthia, jt. auth. see Sutton, Michael.
Mandelker, Jacob. New Theory of Gravitation.
Mandelker, Jakob. Matter-Energy Mechanics.
--Principles of a New Energy Mechanics.
Mandell, A. J. & Mandell, M. P., eds. Psychochemical Research in Man: Methods, Strategy & Theory.
Mandell, Fran G. Dr. Mandell's Allergy-Free Cookbook.
Mandell, Gerald, et al, eds. Principles & Practice of Infectious Diseases.
Mandell, Gerald L., et al, eds. Anti-Infective Therapy.
Mandell, M. P., jt. ed. see Mandell, A. J.
Mandell, Maurice I. & Rosenberg, L. Marketing.
Mandell, Robert B. Contact Lens Practice.
Mandell, Sally. Change of Heart.
Mandell, Stephen R., jt. auth. see Kirszner, Laurie G.
Mandell, Steven L. Computers & Data Processing Today.
Mandelstam, Osip. Osip Mandelstam: Fifty Poems. Meares, Bernard, tr.
Mandelstam, S. L., ed. Spectrochemical Analysis in the U. S. S. R.
Mander, A. E. Logic for the Millions.
Mander, Rosalie. Mrs. Browning: The Story of Elizabeth Barrett.
Manderson, Lenore, ed. Australian Ways.
Mandeville, Glenn A., jt. auth. see Axe, John.
Mandiargues, Andre P. de see De Mandiargues, Andre P.
Mandis, M. George. The Aero Aviation College Directory.
Mandle, W. F., jt. ed. see MacDonagh, Oliver.
Mandyczewski, Eusebius, ed. see Brahms, Johannes.
Maneesha, Ma Prem, ed. see Rajneesh, Bhagwan Shree.
Maner, Jerome H., jt. auth. see Pond, Wilson G.
Manera, Anthony S. Solid-State Electronic Circuits for Engineering Technology.
Manes, E. G. Algebraic Theories.
Manes, E. G., ed. see International Symposium on Category Theory Staff.
Manes, Esther & Manes, Stephen. The Bananas Move to the Ceiling.
Manes, Stephen. The Boy Who Turned into a TV Set.
--Slim Down Camp.
Manes, Stephen, jt. auth. see Manes, Esther.
Maness, Bill. Recreation Ministry: A Guide for all Congregations.
Maneva, Svelta, tr. see Ganchovski, Nedelcho.
Manfred, A. Z., ed. A Short History of the World.
--Short History of the World.
Mangan, Frank, ed. see Metz, Leon C.
Mangan, G. The Biology of Human Personality.
Mangasarian, O. L., et al, eds. Nonlinear Programming Three.
Mange, Arthur P. & Mange, Elaine J. Genetics: Human Aspects.
Mange, Elaine J., jt. auth. see Mange, Arthur P.
Mangen, Steen P., ed. Mental Health Care in the European Community.
Manger, W. M. & Gifford, R. W. Pheochromocytoma.
Mangham, E. & Peace, A. Jet Engine Manual.
Mangilli-Climpson, Massimo. Men of Heart of Red, White & Green: The Italian Antifascists in the Spanish Civil War.
Mangin, Clare A. Imagination.
Mangione, Jerre. The Dream & the Deal: The Federal Writers Project.
Mangold, Nancy R. Changing Auditors & the Effect on Earnings, Auditors' Opinions & Stock Prices. Farmer, Richard, ed.
Mangone, Gerard J. The Future of Gas & Oil from the Sea.
Mangonon, P. L., Jr. & Bramfitt, B. L., eds. Metallurgy of Continuous-Annealed Sheet Steel: Proceedings. AIME Annual Meeting, Dallas, 1982.
Mangonon, P. L., Jr., ed. see AIME Staff.
Mangrum, Charles T., II, et al. Fell's Guide to College Money: For the Asking in Florida.
Manguel, Alberto, tr. see Yourcenar, Marguerite.
Mangum, Garth L., jt. ed. see Levitan, Sar A.
Mangurian, David. Lito the Shoeshine Boy.
Manheim, Jarol B. & Wallace, Melanie. Political Violence in the United States, 1875-1974: A Bibliography.
Manheim, Mary, tr. see Courtine, Robert J.
Manheim, Ralph see Grass, Gunter.
Manheim, Ralph, ed. see Brecht, Bertolt.
Manheim, Ralph, tr. see Ende, Michael.
Manheim, Ralph, tr. see Grass, Gunter.
Manheim, Ralph, tr. see Handke, Peter.
Manheim, Ralph, tr. see Jaspers, Karl.
Manheim, Ralph, tr. see Mrozek, Slawomir.
Manheim, Ralph, tr. see Remarque, Erich M.
Manheim, Ralph, tr. see Schwarz-Bart, Andre.
Manheim, Ralph, tr. see Simenon, Georges.
Mani, M. S. Ecology & Phytogeography of High Altitude Plants of the Northwest Himalayas.
Manicas, Peter T. A History & Philosophy of the Social Sciences.
Manifold, Laurie F. Christmas Window.
Manion, Lawrence, jt. auth. see Cohen, Louis.
Maniotes, John & Quasney, James. Computer Careers: Planning, Prerequisites, Potential.
Maniscalco, Joe. Bible Hero Stories.
Manisco, Francesca, ed. All Italy: The Book of Everything Italian.
Manitto, P. Biosynthesis of Natural Products Polylketides, Terpenoids, Steroids & Phenepropanoids.
Manjone, Joseph A. & Bowen, Robert T. Co-Rec Intramural Sports Handbook.
Manjunath, Shri S., jt. auth. see Adke, S. R.
Mank, Gregory W. It's Alive! the Classic Cinema Saga of Frankenstein.
Mankabady, Samir. The International Maritime Organisation: Accidents at Sea.
Mankabady, Samir, ed. The International Maritime Organisation.
Mankbady, Samir. The International Maritime Organisation: International Shipping Rules.
Mankiewicz, Rene H., ed. Yearbook of Air & Space Law, 1965.
--Yearbook of Air & Space Law, 1966.
--Yearbook of Air & Space Law, 1967.
Mankin, Jim. Prescription for Troubled Hearts.
Manko, Howard H. Effective Technical Speeches & Sessions: A Guide for Speakers & Program Chairmen.
Mankoff, Robert. Elementary: The Cartoonist Did It.
Manley, Frank H. A Veterinary Odyssey.
Manley, Seon & Lewis, Gogo. The Haunted Dolls.
Manley, Victor J. Authentic Arthritis Diet & the Problem of Alkalosis.
Manley-Casimir, Michael E., ed. Family Choice in Schooling: Issues & Dilemmas.
Manly, Brian F. The Statistics of Natural Selection.
Manly, Richard S., ed. Adhesion in Biological Systems.
Mann. The Art in a Democratic Society.
Mann, Alfred. Study of Fugue.
Mann, Arthur. Immigrants in American Life: Selected Readings.
--La Guardia: A Fighter Against His Times, 1882-1933.
--Yankee Reformers in the Urban Age: Social Reform in Boston, 1880-1900.
Mann, Brian, jt. ed. see Harris, Robin.
Mann, Catherine. Tinsel Town.
--Tinsel Town: A Novel.
Mann, Charles C., jt. auth. see Crease, Robert P.
Mann, David, ed. see Cibber, Tehophilus & Cibber, Susanna.
Mann, David R. Tears in the Rainbow: The Fannie Korsun Story.
Mann, G. C., et al, eds. Applied Radionuclide Metrology: Proceedings of the International Committee for Radionuclide Metrology Seminar, Geel, Belgium, 16-17 May 1983.
Mann, H. K. Radiation Sterilization of Plastic Medical Devices: Seminar under the Auspices of the University of Lowell, Mass., March 1979.
Mann, J. Y. & Milligan, I. S., eds. Aircraft Fatigue: Design, Operational & Economic Aspects.
Mann, James K., ed. see American Association of Critical Care Nurses Staff.
Mann, Jesse A. & Kreyche, Gerald F. Reflections on Man: Readings in Philosophical Psychology from Classical Philosophy to Existentialism.
Mann, Jesse A. & Kreyche, Gerald F., eds. Approaches to Morality: Readings in Ethics from Classical Philosophy to Existentialism.
Mann, Jim. Solving Publishing's Toughest Problems.
Mann, Jim, jt. auth. see Oxford Dietetic Group Staff.
Mann, Jim, ed. see Bloch, Robert.
Mann, Joan S. Washington.
Mann, John A. Secrets of Life Extension.
Mann, Karl O., ed. Readings in Labor Relations.
Mann, Lawrence, Jr. Applied Engineering Statistics for Practicing Engineers.
Mann, Lester & Sabatino, David A. Foundations of Cognitive Process in Remedial & Special Education.
Mann, Lester, jt. auth. see Sabatino, David.
Mann, Lester, et al. Teaching the Learning-Disabled Adolescent.
Mann, Marty. Marty Mann Answers Your Questions about Drinking & Alcoholism.
Mann, Maybelle. Francis William Edmonds: Mammon & Art.

Mann, Michael, ed. The International Encyclopedia of Sociology.
Mann, Peggy. My Dad Lives in a Downtown Hotel.
Mann, Peter. From Author to Reader: A Social Study of Books.
Mann, Philip H., et al. Teachers Handbook of Diagnostic Inventories: Spelling, Reading, Handwriting, Arithmetic -- a Practical Guide with Duplicator Masters.
Mann, Phillip. The Eye of The Queen.
Mann, Roger, ed. Exotic Species in Mariculture.
Mann, Stella T. How to Live in the Circle of Prayer & Make Your Dreams Come True.
Mann, Stephen G. Tourism Theory: A Selected Bibliography.
Mann, Stephen G. & Doherty, Paul G. Case Studies in Tourism: A Selected Bibliography.
Mann, T. C., et al. Born to Live.
Mann, Thomas. The Black Swan. Trask, Willard R., tr.
--Tod in Venedig. Hornsey, A. W., ed.
Mann, W. B., jt. auth. see Debertin, K.
Mann, W. B., jt. ed. see Hutchinson, J. M.
Mann, W. Edward. Orgone, Reich & Eros.
Mann, W. P. How to Get the Best Buy from Your Car Dealer: An Inside View of What to Watch for in Buying a New or Used Car.
Mann, William S. Richard Strauss: A Critical Study of the Operas.
Mann, Willie. The Discjockies Good Dance Guide.
Mannari, Hiroshi & Befu, Harumi. The Challenge of Japan's Internationalization: Organization & Culture.
Manners, George E., Jr. & Louderback, Joseph G. Managing Return on Investment: Implications for Pricing, Volume, & Funds Flow.
Manners, William. Patience & Fortitude: Fiorello la Guardia.
Mannes, Willibald. Designing Staircases.
Mannheim. Regeln und Sprache Des Sports.
Mannheim, Karl. Man & Society in an Age of Reconstruction.
--Structures of Thinking. Kettler, David, et al, eds. Shapiro, Jeremy & Weber, Shierry, trs.
--Systematic Sociology.
Mannheimer, Marc, jt. auth. see Ehrlich, Jeffrey.
Manni, Alvin S. Brother Peter Ferraris.
Manniche, P. & Porter, J. F., eds. Rural Development & the Changing Countries of the World.
Manninen, Talvikki. Refuge under the Boot.
Manning, A. B. Exporting from the U. S. A. How to Develop Export Markets & Cope with Foreign Customs.
Manning, Al G. Miracle of Universal Psychic Power: How to Build Your Way to Prosperity.
Manning, Alan, et al, eds. see Linguistic Association of Canada & the U. S. Staff.
Manning, Ambrose N., jt. ed. see Higgs, Robert J.
Manning, Clarence. Soldier of Liberty: Casimir Pulasky.
Manning, Clarence A. Forgotten Republics.
--The Story of the Ukraine.
Manning, Clarence A. & Smal-Stocki, Roman. History of Modern Bulgarian Literature.
Manning, D. J. & Robinson, T. J. The Place of Ideology in Political Life.
Manning, Doug. Comforting Those Who Grieve: A Guide for Helping Others.
Manning, Francis, jt. auth. see Canjar, Lawrence.
Manning, Francis F., ed. Medical Group Practice Management.
Manning, Frederic. The Middle Parts of Fortune.
Manning, Gerry. Advanced COBOL: A Structured Approach.
Manning, Harvey. Footsore One: Walks & Hikes Around Puget Sound.
--Footsore Two: Walks & Hikes Around Puget Sound.
Manning, Harvey & O'Hara, Pat. Washington Wilderness: The Unfinished Work.
Manning, Harvey, jt. auth. see Spring, Ira.
Manning, Jane. New Vocal Repertory: An Introduction.
Manning, Jerome A. Estate Planning Plus 1985 Supplement.
Manning, John, ed. Rand McNally Interstate Road Atlas: United States, Canada, Mexico.
Manning, Jonathan R., ed. Propaganda of Adolf Hitler.
Manning, Kaye. The Baker's Flower Quick Mix Cookbook.
Manning, Leonard F. The Law of Church-State Relations in a Nutshell.
Manning, Marilyn. Leadership Skills for Women. Crisp, Michael G., ed.
Manning, Mary, ed. see Joyce, James.
Manning, Olivia. The Danger Tree.
--The Remarkable Expedition: The Story of Stanley's Rescue of Emin Pasha from Equatorial Africa.
--The Sum of Things.
Manning, Ric, ed. National Directory of Bulletin Board Systems, 1986-87.
Manning, Robert T., jt. ed. see Delp, Mahlon H.
Manning, William, jt. auth. see Willis, Jerry.
Manning, William A. & Ingalsbe, Lon. Get Personal with Your TI 99.
Mannix, Daniel, jt. auth. see Lose, M. Phyllis.
Mannix, Daniel P. The Wolves of Paris.
Mano, D. Keith. War Is Heaven.
Manocha, H. L., jt. auth. see Srivastava, H. M.
Manocha, S. L., et al. Macaca Mulatta Enzyme Histochemistry of the Nervous System.
Manoff, Robert K. & Schudson, Michael, eds. Reading the News.
Manoni, Mary H. Cynthia's Great Paint Adventure. Mahoney, Susan, ed.
--The Kite Ride.
--Scotty & the Kittens. Mahoney, Susan, ed.
Manoni, Mary H. & Cienkus, Robert. Phonetic Rules in Reading.
Manoni, Mary H., jt. auth. see Gregorvich, Barbara.
Manoni, Mary H., ed. see Cosgrove, Stephen.
Manor, Oded & Bell, David, eds. Family Work in Action: A Handbook for Social Workers.
Manougian, M. N. Basic Algebra.
Manougian, Manoug, jt. auth. see Ratti, Jogindar.
Mansa, Manuel B., jt. auth. see Jaquiera, Joaquim.
Manschreck, Clyde L. & Petry, Ray C., eds. History of Christianity.
Manschreck, Clyde L. & Zikmund, Barbara B., eds. The American Religious Experiment: Piety & Practicality.
Manschreck, Clyde L., ed. & tr. see Melanchthon, Philip.
Mansel, H. L. The Limits of Religious Thought.
Mansell, Gilbert. Working with the Computer.
Manser, Anthony. Bradley's Logic.
Manser, Gordon & Cass, Rosemary H. Voluntarism at the Crossroads.
Manser, Nancy. Older People Have Choices: Information for Decisions about Health, Home, & Money.
Mansfield, Bruce. Phoenix of His Age: Interpretations of Erasmus, Fifteen Fifty to Seventeen Fifty.
Mansfield, Don L. & Buckley, Gary J. Conflict in American Foreign Policy: The Issues Debated.
Mansfield, Edwin. Economics of Technological Change.
--Economics: Principles, Problems, Decisions.
--Economics: Principles, Problems, Decisions.
--Economics Problems: Concepts, Essays, Tests, Workbook.
--Microeconomic Problems.
--Microeconomic Problems: Case Studies and Exercises for Review.
--Microeconomics: Theory & Applications.
--Microeconomics: Theory & Applications.
--Microeconomics: Theory & Applications.
--Principles of Macroeconomics.
--Principles of Macroeconomics.
--Principles of Microeconomics.
--Principles of Microeconomics.
--Principles of Microeconomics.
--Statistics for Business & Economics: Methods & Applications.
--Statistics for Business & Economics.
--Technological Change.
Mansfield, Edwin, ed. Defense, Science & Public Policy.
--Industrial Research & Technological Innovation.
--Managerial Economics & Operations Research.
--Managerial Economics & Operations Research.
--Managerial Economics & Operations Research.
--Micro-Economics: Selected Readings.
--Microeconomic Problems.
--Microeconomics: Selected Readings.
--Microeconomics: Selected Readings.
--Monopoly Power & Economic Performance.
--Principles of Macroeconomics. Incl. Reading, Issues, & Cases. Norton.
Mansfield, Edwin, et al. Research & Innovation in the Modern Corporation.
Mansfield, Evelyn A. & Lucas, Ethel G. Clothing Construction.
Mansfield, Harvey C., Jr. Machiavelli's New Modes & Orders: A Study of the Discourses on Livy.
Mansfield, Harvey C., Jr., jt. ed. see Burke, Edmund.
Mansfield, Helene. Some Women Dance.
Mansfield, Jerry W. The Nuclear Power Debate: A Guide to the Literature.
Mansfield, John M., jt. auth. see Hall, G. Stanley.
Mansfield, Katherine. Novels & Novelists.
Mansfield, Luther S., jt. ed. see Hillway, Tyrus.
Mansfield, Richard, et al. The Beginner's Guide to Buying a Personal Computer. Compute! Magazine Staff, ed.
Manshard, W. & Fischnich, O. E. Man & Environment.
Manship, Darwin W., jt. auth. see Cornwell, Robert C.
Manskaya, S. M. & Drozdova, T. V. Geochemistry of Organic Substances.
Manso, Peter. Mailer: His Life & Times.
Manson, Christopher. The Rails I Tote: A Collection of Short Stories.
Manson, Edwards, jt. ed. see Macdonnell, John.
Manson, Richard. The Theory of Knowledge of Giambattista Vico: On the Method of the New Science Concerning the Common Nature of the Nations.
Manson, T. W. Only to the House of Israel? Jesus & the Non-Jews. Reumann, John, ed.
Manson-Hing, Lincoln R. Fundamentals of Dental Radiography.
Manson-Hing, Lincoln R., jt. auth. see Wuehrmann, Arthur H.
Mansour, M., ed. see IFAC-FIP International Conference Staff.
Mansour, Norman, jt. auth. see Ribbens, William B.
Mansour, Norman P., jt. auth. see Ribbens, William B.
Manston, Peter B. Manston's Travel Key--Europe '88: How to Make a Phone Call, Do Your Laundry, Find a Toilet, Get Around Easily & Much More.
--Manston's Travel Key Europe.
Mansur, L. K., jt. ed. see Holland, J. R.
Mantegazza, Paolo. The Legends of Flowers. Kennedy, Mrs. Alexander, tr.
Mantell, David M. True Americanism: Green Berets & War Resisters: A Study of Commitment.
Manteuffel, Tadeusz. The Formation of the Polish State: The Period of Ducal Rule, 963-1194. Gorski, Andrew, tr.
Mantinband, Gerda B. Papa & Mama Biederbeck.
Mantinband, James. Dictionary of Latin Literature.
Mantis, Elizabeth M. A Legacy of Womanhood.
Mantle, Margaret. Some Just Clap Their Hands: Raising a Handicapped Child.
Mantle, Mickey & Gluck, Herb. Mick.
Manton, Richard, ed. The Victorian Imagination: A Sampler.
--The Victorian Imagination: A Sampler.
--The Victorians in the Harem: Grove Press Victorian Library.
Manuel, Dino. Paragraph of Life: Killer-Your Friend?
Manuel, Frank E. The Realities of American-Palestine Relations.
Manunder, W. F., ed. see Munby, Denys & Watson, A. H.
Manusch, Dorothea. The Unicorn.
Manushkin, Fran. Moon Dragon.
--The Tickle Tree.
Manyoky-Nemeth, Charles. The Hunted. Falconer, Alex, tr.
Manzano, R. Whitney, jt. auth. see Cho, Paul Y.
Manzler, David L., jt. auth. see Eason, Thomas F.
Manzo, L., ed. Advances in Neurotoxicology: Proceedings of the International Congress on Neurotoxicology, Varese, 27-30 September 1979.
Manzo, Salvatore E., jt. auth. see Williams, Edward E.
Manzoni, Alessandro. The Betrothed. Colquhoun, Archibald, tr.
Mao Dun. Midnight.
Mao Tse-Tung. Five Articles: Serve the People.
--Quotations from Chairman Mao Tse-Tung.
Ma'oz, Moshe. Asad - The Sphinx of Damascus: A Political Biography.
--Palestinian Arab Politics.
Mapel, Eugene B. Banking & Financial Deregulation: A Blessing or a Curse?
Maquarrie, John. In Search of Deity.
Mar, James W., ed. Structures Technology for Large Radio & Radar Telescope Systems.
Mar, Norman R. Del see Del Mar, Norman R.
Maraccini, Jim. Read & Do with Professor Riddle.
Maragos, G. D., ed. Seminar on Childhood Poisoning.
--Seminar on Office Pediatrics, Part I.
Marai, Sandor. Naplo: 1945-1957.
Marais, Johan. Snake Versus Man.
Maraist, Frank L. Admiralty in a Nutshell.
Maramorosch, K., ed. see Symposium of the Entymological Society of America - Atlantic City - 1960.
Maramorosch, Karl, jt. auth. see Kurstak, Edouard.
Maramorosch, Karl, ed. Insect & Plant Viruses: An Atlas.
--Invertebrate Immunity: Mechanisms of Invertebrate Vector-Parasite Relations.
Maramorosch, Karl & Kurstak, E., eds. Comparative Virology.
Maramorosch, Karl & Mitsuhashi, Jun, eds. Invertebrate Cell Culture Applications.
Maramorosch, Karl, jt. ed. see Kurstak, Edouard.
Marandel, Patrice, intro. by. Symbolism in Polish Painting 1890-1914.
Marazzi, Rich & Fiorito, Len. Aaron to Zipfel.
Marbach, Ethel & Walker, Mary Lu. Cranberries, Fireflies, & Rhubarb Pie: The Adventures of Grandma Bagley & Her Friends.
Marbeck, John see Buck, P. C. & Fellowes, E. H.
Marble, Duane F., et al. Basic Readings in Geographic Information Systems.
Marcaccio, Kathleen Y., jt. auth. see Lucas, Amy.
Marcavage, Susan C., et al. Revitalizing Neighborhoods & Downtowns: A Selective, Annotated Bibliography on Urban Ecology.
Marceau, Claude, jt. auth. see Stone, Leroy O.
Marcel, Gabriel. Decline of Wisdom.
Marcellino, Ralph, tr. see Martial.
March, Jerry. Advanced Organic Chemistry.
March, Jerry, jt. auth. see Bettelheim, Frederick A.
March, Norman H. Liquid Metals.
March, William. Company K.
Marchak, John P., ed. see Educational Research Council of America Staff.
Marchalonis. Cancer Biology Reviews.
Marchalonis, John J., ed. The Lymphocyte: Structure & Function.
--The Lymphocyte: Structure & Function.
Marchand, Ernest, ed. see Cru, Jean N.
Marchand, L., et al, trs. see Twitchell, Paul.
Marchand, Leslie A. Byron's Poetry: A Critical Introduction.
Marchant, James. Anthology of Jesus. Wiersbe, Warren W., ed.
Marchant, Jill, jt. auth. see Marchant, Ralph.
Marchant, Ralph & Marchant, Jill. Little Painter.
Marchant, W. T. In Praise of Ale, or Songs, Ballads, Epigrams & Anecdotes Relating to Beer Malt, & Hops.
Marchese, R. Critical Review of the Effects of Synthetic Detergents on Aquatic Life.
Marchesini, G. & Mitter, S. K., eds. Mathematical Systems Theory.
Marchington, John. The Natural History of Game.
--Shooting: A Complete Guide for Beginners.
Marchington, M. Managing Industrial Relations.
--Responses to Participation at Work.
Marchini, Ron & Fong, Leo. Advanced Power Training.
Marchman, Watt. Rutherford B. Hayes State Memorial, Fremont, Ohio.
Marchuk, G. I. Numerical Methods in Weather Prediction.
Marchuk, G. I. & Kagan, B. A. Ocean Tides: Mathematical Models & Numerical Experiments. Cartwright, D. E., tr.
Marchuk, G. I. & Nisevich, N. I., eds. Mathematical Methods in Clinical Practice.
Marchuk, G. I., ed. see IFIP-TC Working Conference Staff.
Marchuk, G. I., ed. see IFIP Technical Conference Staff.
Marciano, J. D., jt. auth. see Griffen, William L.
Marckwardt, Albert, jt. auth. see Rosier, James L.
Marckwardt, Albert H., ed. Linguistics in School Programs.
Marco, Guy A., tr. see Zarlino, Gioseffo.
Marco, Guy de see De Marco, Guy.
Marco Da Nizza, tr. The Journey of Fray Marcos de Niza, by Cleve Hallenbeck.
Marconi, David, jt. auth. see Dille, Flint.
Marconi, R., jt. ed. see Cappellini, V.
Marcs, Les. Bedtime Story.
Marcum, David. The Dow Jones-Irwin Guide to Fine Gems & Jewelry.
Marcum, John A. The Angolan Revolution: Exile Politics & Guerrilla Warfare, 1962-1976.
Marcus, Eric H. & Barton, William A. Litigating Psychological Injury Claims.
Marcus, Genevieve G. & Smith, Robert L. Equal Time: Maintaining a Balance in Today's Intimate Relationships.
Marcus, Jacob R. Critical Studies in American Jewish History.
Marcus, Jacob R. & Peck, Abraham J., eds. Studies in the American Jewish Experience II: Contributions from the Fellowship Programs of the American Jewish Archives.
Marcus, Jane, ed. Virginia Woolf & Bloomsbury: A Centenary Celebration.
Marcus, Melanie. Cooking with a Harvard Accent: A Collection of International Recipes from the Harvard Community.
Marcus, Morton. The Armies Encamped in the Fields Beyond the Unfinished Avenues: Prose Poems.
--Big Winds, Glass Mornings, Shadows Cast by Stars: Poems, 1972-1980.
--Origins.
Marcus, Stanley. Minding the Store.
Marcus, William & Levy, Alex. Elements of Radio Servicing.
--Practical Radio Servicing.
Marcus, Y. & Howery, D. G. Ion Exchange Equilibrium Constants.
Marcus, Y., ed. Solvent Extraction Reviews.
Marcuse, Dietrich. Light Transmission Optics.
Marcuse, Sibyl. Musical Instruments: A Comprehensive Dictionary.
Marcuss, Stanley J., ed. Effective Washington Representation.
Marcy, Barton C., Jr., jt. ed. see Schubel, Jerry R.
Marcy, Carl M., jt. auth. see Wilcox, Francis O.
Marcy, Sam. Chrysler & the UAW.
Marden, Fay. The Almond Blossom Fairy.
--The Midsummer Ball.
--A Midwinter Tale.
--The Missing Hazelnuts.

Authors

Marden, Margaret A. The Bargain Shopper's Guide to Northern New England.

Marder, A. R. & Stephenson, E. T., eds. Energy Efficient Electrical Steels: Proceedings TMS-AIME Fall Meeting, Pittsburgh, PA, 1980.

Marder, Simon. The Forty-Nine Year Old Rookie.

Marder, Tod A., ed. The Critical Edge: Controversy in Recent American Architecture.

Mardh, Per-Anders, jt. auth. see Holmes, King K.

Mardsen, David, et al. The Car Industry: Labour Relations & Industrial Adjustment.

Mare, Walter De La see De la Mare, Walter.

Mare, Walter de la see De la Mare, Walter.

Marechal, Joseph. Studies in the Psychology of the Mystics.

Mareieb, Elaine N; see Marieb, Elaine N.

Marek, W. & Srebrny, M., eds. Set Theory & Hierarchy Theory.

Marelli, Leonard R., jt. auth. see Nadler, Harvey.

Marer, Paul, ed. U. S. Financing of East-West Trade: The Political Economy of Government Credits & the National Interest.

Marer, Paul & Montias, John M., eds. East European Integration & East-West Trade.

Marer, Paul, ed. see Pecsi, Kalman.

Mares, F. M., ed. see Jonson, Ben.

Marett, Robert R. Psychology & FolkLore.

Marfleet, H. F. Pictorial Guide to Woodworking Tools & Joints.

Marfuggi, Joseph, jt. auth. see Pearson, Craig.

Margaris, N. S., et al, eds. Adaptations to Terrestial Environments.

Margenau, Henry, jt. auth. see LeShan, Lawrence.

Margerison, Charles. How to Assess Your Managerial Style.

Margerison, D. & East, G. C. An Introduction to Polymer Chemistry.

Marghescour, Mircea. Le Concept de Litterarite: Essai sur les Possibilities Theoriques d'une Science de la Litterature.

Margison, G. P., jt. ed. see Canonico.

Margittai, Tom G. & Kovi, Paul. The Four Seasons Cookbook.

--The Four Seasons: Splendid Recipes from the World-Famous Restaurant.

Marglin, Stephen A. Growth, Distribution & Prices.

Margolies, Barbara L. Princes of the Earth: Subcultural Diversity in a Mexican Municipality.

Margolies, Eva L. The Best of Friends, the Worst of Enemies: Womens Hidden Power over Women.

--Sensual Pleasure: A Woman's Guide.

Margolin, David, jt. auth. see Wylie, Jonathan.

Margolin, Edythe. Teaching Young Children at School & Home.

Margolin, Harriet & Nicklaus, Carol. Busy Bear's Refrigerator: A Book about Colors.

Margolin, Malcolm. The Earth Manual.

Margolis, Adele P. Encyclopedia of Sewing.

Margolis, Art. Computer User's Guide to Electronics.

--Troubleshooting & Repairing Personal Computers.

Margolis, Bette S., tr. see Sheriff, Margaret L.

Margolis, Diane R. The Managers: Corporate Life in America.

Margolis, John D. T. S. Eliot's Intellectual Development, 1922-1939.

Margolis, John S. Joseph Wood Krutch.

Margolis, Joseph. Art & Philosophy.

Margolis, Matthew & Siegal, Mordecai. Good Dog, Bad Dog.

Margolis, Neal & Harmon, N. Paul. Accounting Essentials.

Margolis, Richard J. Wish Again, Big Bear.

Margoninski, Y., ed. see Israeli Vacuum Congress Staff.

Margulis & Gooding. Diagnostic Radiology, 1984.

Margulis & Higgins. Clinical Magnetic Resonance Imaging.

Margulis, Alexander R. & Gooding, Charles A. Innovations in Diagnostic Radiology.

Margulis, Joel, jt. auth. see Richardson, Jerry.

Margulis, L., ed. see Conference on Origins of Life, 3rd, California, 1970.

Margulova, R. Nuclear Power Stations.

Maria, Constantino de. Enciclopedia de la Magia y de la Brujeria.

Maria, Jack Santa see Santa Maria, Jack.

Maria, Robert De see De Maria, Robert.

Mariacher, B. C., jt. ed. see Rausch, D. O.

Mariani, Emilia C. My Heart, My Temple.

Mariani, John F. The Dictionary of American Food & Drink.

--The Dictionary of American Food & Drink.

--Mariani's Coast-To-Coast Dining Guide.

Mariani, Michael P. & Palmer, David F. Distributed System Design.

Mariani, Paul. Crossing Cocytus & Other Poems.

--Crossing Cocytus & Other Poems.

--Prime Mover. Pack, Robert, ed.

--Prime Mover. Pack, Robert, ed.

Marie, Olaus. Alaska Yukon Caribou.

Marie, Susan. Never Bring Her Roses.

--When the Spotlight Fades.

Marieb, Elaine. Essentials of Human Anatomy & Physiology.

Marieb, Elaine N. Human Anatomy & Physiology Laboratory Manual. Incl. Human Anatomy & Physiology Laboratory Manual: The Pig Version. Mareieb, Elaine N; Human Anatomy & Physiology: Cat Version. Benjamin-Cummings.

Marijnissen, Roger H. Hieronymus Bosch: The Complete Works.

--Hieronymus Bosch: The Complete Works.

Marill, Alvin H. Movies Made for Television.

Marin, B. R., et al. Pion-Pion Interactions in Physics.

Marin, G., jt. auth. see Westerveld, A.

Marinacci, Barbara & Marinacci, Rudy. California's Spanish Place-Names: What They Mean & How They Got There.

Marinacci, Rudy, jt. auth. see Marinacci, Barbara.

Marinaro, Vincent. In the Ring of the Rise.

Marincola, Paula, jt. auth. see Kardon, Janet.

Marindin, Hope, ed. The Handbook for Single Adoptive Parents.

Marine Aquaculture Association Staff & Northeast Regional Coastal Information Center Staff. Directory of Aquaculturists in the Northeast.

Marine Biological Laboratory Staff & Woods Hole Oceanographic Institution, Woods Hole, Massachusetts Staff. Catalog of the Library of the Marine Biological Laboratory & the Woods Hole Oceanographic Institution.

Marine Board, Asembly of Engineering Staff & National Research Council Staff. Mining in the Outer Continental Shelf & in the Deep Ocean.

Marine Board, Assembly of Engineering Staff & National Research Council Staff. Outer Continental Shelf Frontier Technology.

Marine Board Staff. Responding to Casualties of Ships Bearing Hazardous Cargoes.

Marine, Gene. America the Raped.

Mariner, James L. Human Reproduction & Development.

Mariners Museum Library - Newport News - Virginia Staff. Catalog of Maps, Ships' Papers & Logbooks.

--Dictionary Catalog of the Library of the Mariners Museum.

Marino, Andrew A., jt. auth. see Becker, Robert O.

Marino, James. The Asgard Solution.

Mariological Society of America. North Palm Beach, Fla. Convention, 1983. Marian Studies: Proceedings.

Mariological Society of America Staff. Marian Studies: Proceedings of the Mariological Society of America, Atlanta Convention, 1975.

--Marian Studies: Proceedings of the Mariological Society of America, Dayton Convention, 1968.

--Marian Studies: Proceedings of the Mariological Society of America, Detroit Convention, 1960.

--Marian Studies: Proceedings of the Mariological Society of America, Dayton Convention, 1985.

--Marian Studies: Proceedings of the Mariological Society of America, Kansas City, MO. Convention, 1964.

--Marian Studies: Proceedings of the Mariological Society of America, North Palm Beach Convention, 1967.

--Marian Studies: Proceedings of the Mariological Society of America, San Antonio, Texas, Convention, 1982.

Marion, Jerry B. Physical Science in the Modern World.

Marion, Jerry B. & Hornyak, William F. Physics for Scientists & Engineers: Combined Volume.

--Principles of Physics.

Marion, Jerry B. & Roush, Marvin L. Energy in Perspective.

Marion, Jerry B., jt. auth. see Davidson, Ronald C.

Marion, Jerry B. & Van Patter, Douglas M., eds. Nuclear Research with Low Energy Nuclear Accelerators.

Marion, Norman. Last Town.

Marion, Robert. Born Too Soon.

Marion, Ruth. Through a Child's Looking Glass.

Mariotti, Maryanne, jt. auth. see Crowell, Lynda.

Marique, Pierre J. Philosophy of Christian Education.

Maris, C. W. Critique of the Empiricist Explanation of Morality: Is There a Natural Equivalent of Categorical Morality?

Maris, Ronald, jt. ed. see Battin, Margaret P.

Marishall, Jean. The History of Miss Clarinda Cathcart & Miss Fanny Renton, 1765.

Maritain, Jacques. Art & Faith.

--Art & Poetry.

--An Essay on Christian Philosophy.

--The Philosophy of Nature.

Maritain, Jacques & Maritain, Raissa. The Situation of Poetry.

Maritain, Jacques, et al. Wisdom: A Manifesto.

Maritain, Jacquest. Dream of Descartes.

Maritain, Raissa, jt. auth. see Maritain, Jacques.

Maritime & Transport Law Committee. Arrest of Vessels.

Maritime Transportation Research Board Staff & National Research Council Staff. Alternative Fuels for Maritime Use.

--Critical Issues in Coal Transportation Systems.

--Port Development in the United States.

--Public Involvement in Maritime Facility Development.

Marivaux, Pierre C; see Bentley, Eric.

Marivaux, Pierre C. De Chamblain De see De Chamblain De Marivaux, Pierre C.

Mark-Age Staff. Evolution of Man: Two Hundred & Six Million Years on Earth.

--How to Do All Things: Your Use of Divine Power.

Mark, Alane. An Ethical Man.

Mark, Alexandra. Astrology for the Aquarian Age.

Mark, Charles, ed. Research Studies in Comparative Sociology.

Mark, Charles & Mark, Paula F., eds. Sociology of America: A Guide to Information Sources.

Mark, H. F., et al. Man-Made Fibers: Science & Technology.

Mark, Jan. Nothing to Be Afraid Of.

Mark, Mary E. Streetwise.

Mark, Michael L. Contemporary Music Education.

Mark, Norman. Norman Mark's Chicago.

Mark, Paula F., jt. ed. see Mark, Charles.

Marke, Julius J. & Bander, Edward J. Commercial Law Information Sources.

Markel, Geraldine & Wolter, Daniel. Designing & Using Feedback Forms.

Markel, Geraldine, jt. auth. see Collins, Randall.

Markel, J. D., jt. ed. see Schafer, R. W.

Markels, Robin B. A New Perspective on Cohesion in Expository Paragraphs.

Markey, John F. The Symbolic Process & Its Integration in Children: A Study in Social Psychology.

Markey, Karen & Cochrane, Pauline A. ONTAP: Online Training & Practice Manual for ERIC Data Base Searchers.

Markham, Clements R. History of Peru.

Markham, Felix. The Bonapartes.

Markham, Gervase. The Art of Archerie.

--The Compleat Horseman. Lucid, Dan, ed.

Markham, Jordon J. F-Centers in Alkali Halides.

Markham, P. G., jt. auth. see Daniels, M. J.

Markham, P. G., jt. ed. see Daniels, M. J.

Markides, Andreas. Binaural Hearing Aids.

Markides, Kyriacos C. Homage to the Sun.

--The Magus of Strovolos: The Extraordinary World of a Spiritual Healer.

Markis, Dimetra. First Prize Quilts.

Markisch, Robert. Die Altenglische Bearbeitung der Erzahlung von Appolonius von Tyrus.

Markisz, John A. & Levine, Martin P. Applied Contemporary Chemistry.

Markl, Julia. The Battle of Britain.

Markle, Sandra & Markle, William. In Search of Graphics: Adventures in Computer Art.

Markle, William, jt. auth. see Markle, Sandra.

Markley, N. G., et al, eds. The Structure of Attractors in Dynamical Systems: Proceedings, North Dakota, June 20-24, 1977.

Markley, O. W., jt. ed. see Center for the Study of Social Policy-SRI International Staff.

Markmann, Charles L., tr. see Mucchielli, Roger.

Markoe, Arnie, jt. auth. see Phillips, Louis.

Markoe, Glenn E., ed. see DeMallie, Raymond J., et al.

Markoe, Karen & Phillips, Louis. Nuttier Knock Knocks.

--Nutty Knock Knocks.

--Sneakers.

Markoe, Karen, jt. auth. see Phillips, Louis.

Markov, B., jt. auth. see Krivandin, V.

Markov, D. Socialist Literature: Problems of Development.

Markov, Georgi. The Truth That Killed. Brisby, Liliana, tr.

Markov, Vladimir. The Longer Poems of Velimir Khlebnikov.

Markova, Alicia. Markova Remembers.

Markovic, V., ed. Radiation Processing: Fourth International Meeting on Radiation Processing, Dubrovnik, Yugoslavia, October 1982.

Markovich, Alex & Consumer Reports Books Editors. Guide to Used Cars, 1987.

Markovich, Alex see Consumer Report Book Editors.

Markowitz, Hal. Behavioral Enrichment in the Zoo.

Markowitz, Marvin D. Cross & Sword: The Political Role of Christian Missions in the Belgian Congo, 1908-1960.

Markowitz, Randi & Noble, Charles R., III. L. A. Lunch - Downtown Dining: A Selective Guide to the Best Luncheon Spots in Downtown Los Angeles.

Marks. Analyzing Research Data: The Basics of Biomedical Research.

--Common Facial Dermatoses.

Marks, Betty & Schechter, Lucille H. The International Menu Diabetic Cookbook.

Marks, Bobbi, ed. see Buten, Howard.

Marks, Claude. Journeys into Paintings.

Marks, Copeland & Soeharjo, Mintari. The Indonesian Kitchen.

Marks, Elaine. Colette.

Marks, Elaine, jt. ed. see Stambolian, George.

Marks, G. C. & Kozlowski, T. T., eds. Ectomycorrhizae: Their Ecology & Physiology.

Marks, Holly L. Mrs. McDillydally's Candy Store.

Marks, Isaac M. Living with Fear: You As a Therapist.

Marks, Janet. Home Help.

Marks, John. The Search for the "Manchurian Candidate" The CIA & Mind Control.

Marks, Myles H. Basic Integrated Circuits.

Marks, R. Practical Problems in Dermatology.

Marks, Russell. The Idea of I.Q.

Marks, Thomas J. More Bible Study Puzzles.

Marks, V. & Alberti, K. H., eds. Clinical Biochemistry Nearer the Patient.

Marks, Walter & Nystrand, Raphael O. Strategies for Educational Change.

Marks, William C. The Corporate Tax Caper.

Markson, Elizabeth & Batra, Gretchen, eds. Public Policies for an Aging Population.

Markstein, George. Ferret.

Markstein, Linda & Grunbaum, Dorien. Stranger on the Road.

Markstein, Selma S. Humorous & Dramatic Poetry.

Markun, Patricia M., ed. see Gillies, Emily.

Markus, John. Electronic Circuits Manual.

--Electronics Style Manual.

--Sourcebook of Electronic Circuits.

Markus, Julia. American Rose.

--Friends along the Way.

--Uncle.

Markus, Rixi. More Deadly Than the Male: First Lady of Bridge.

Marland, Michael, ed. Sex Differentiation & Schooling.

Marland, Sidney P., Jr. Career Education: A Proposal for Reform.

Marlette, Jerry. Interstate Railroad.

Marlin, J. Appeal to the Heart.

Marlin, John T. Revenue Sharing Renewal.

Marlor. History of the Brooklyn Art Association with an Index of Exhibitions.

Marlow, A. R. Quantum Theory & Gravitation.

Marlow, Cecilia A., ed. Directory Information Service.

--Directory of Directories.

Marlow, Curtis. Star Address Book.

Marlow, David. Yearbook.

Marlow, W. H. Mathematics for Operations Research.

Marlowe, Christopher. Doctor Faustus.

--Edward the Second. Chwat, Jacques, ed.

Marlowe, Lynn G., et al. California State Capitol Restoration, a Pictorial History. Worsley, John C. & Dwyer, Dale E., eds.

Marlowe, Olwen C. Outdoor Design: A Handbook for the Architect & Planner.

Marlowe, Stephen. The Memoirs of Christopher Columbus.

--Nineteen Fifty-Six.

Marmion, Shakerly. A Fine Companion. Sonnershein, Richard & Orgel, Stephen, eds.

Marmont, Auguste F. Spirit of Military Institutions. Schaller, Frank, tr.

Marne, Henri de see De Marne, Henri.

Marnes, Larry E. Doubling Over.

Marnham, Patrick. Fantastic Invasion: Notes on Contemporary Africa.

Marois, M. Towards a Plan of Actions for Mankind.

Marois, Maurice, ed. Towards a Plan of Actions for Mankind. Incl. Vol. 1. Long Range Mineral Resources & Growth; Vol. 2. Long Range Energetic Resources & Growth; Vol. 3. Biological Balance & Thermal Modification; Vol. 4. Design of Global System Models & Their Limitations; Vol. 5. Conclusions & Perspectives. Pergamon.

Marol, Jean-Claude. Vagabul & His Shadow.

--Vagabul Escapes.

--Vagabul in the Clouds.

--Vagabul Skis.

Marolli, G. Italian-English, English-Italian Technical Dictionary.

Marom, E., et al, eds. Applications of Holography & Optical Data Processing: Proceedings of an International Conference, Jerusalem, 1976.

Maron, Melvin J. Applied Numerical Analysis.

Maroto, Angel R., ed. see Diosdado, Ana.

Marotta, Gary, jt. auth. see Miller, Joan V.

Marotta, Kenny. A Piece of Earth.

Marotta, Toby. The Politics of Homosexuality.

Marotta, Toni, et al. One Month Lighter: The Lean Line Way to 30 Day Slimness.

Marotz, Lynn, et al. Health, Safety, & Nutrition for the Young Child.

Marowitz, Charles. The Act of Being: Towards a Theory of Acting.

Marowitz, Charles, tr. see Ionesco, Eugene.

Marple, Hugo D. The Beginning Conductor.

Marqmorosch, Karl, jt. ed. see Kurstak, Edouard.

Marquand, John P. Last Laugh, Mr. Moto.

--Mr. Moto Is So Sorry.

Authors

--Right You Are, Mr. Moto.
--Thank You, Mr. Moto.
--Think Fast, Mr. Moto.
--Your Turn, Mr. Moto.
Marquardt, Brigitte. Schmuck, Seventeen Eighty to Eighteen Fifty.
Marquardt, Charles E., jt. auth. see Swanson, Richard W.
Marquez, Ely & Bowen, J. Donald. English Usage.
Marquez, Jaime R. Oil Prices Effects & OPEC's Pricing Policy: An Optimal Control Approach.
Marquez, Robbie. Through My Memory's Window.
Marquez Garcia, Gabriel. Cien Anos De Soledad.
Marquez Villegas, Luis. Vocabulario Del Espanol Hablado.
Marquis, Bill. The Fencin' Tool Bible.
Marquis, Judith K., jt. ed. see Homburger, Freddy.
Marquis, Vivienne & Haskell, Patricia. Cheese Book.
Marquis de Sade. Juliette. Wainhouse, Austryn, tr. from Fr.
Marqusee, Mike & Harris, Bill, eds. New York: An Anthology.
Marrett, Michael M. The Lambeth Conferences & Women Priests: The Historical Background of the Lambeth Conferences & Their Impact on the Episcopal Church in America.
Marriage, Ellen, tr. see De Balzac, Honore.
Marriage Encounter Communities Staff. Marriage Enrichment: Resource Manual.
Marric, J. J. see also Creasey, John.
Marrin, Albert. Overlord: D-Day & The Invasion of Europe.
Marriner. Nursing Theorists & Their Work.
Marriner, Ann. Contemporary Nursing Management: Issues & Practice.
--Guide to Nursing Management.
Marriner, Sheila. The Economic & Social Development of Merseyside.
Marriott, Alice. Osage Indians, Vol. Two: Osage Research Report, & Bibliography of Basic Research References.
Marriott, D. L., jt. ed. see Garrett, G. G.
Marriott, F. H. Basic Mathematics for the Biological & Social Sciences.
Marriott, Henry J. & Conover, Mary H. Advanced Concepts in Arrhythmias.
Marriott, J. Disaster at Sea.
Marriott, James W., ed. One-Act Plays of Today: Second Series.
Marriott, McKim, ed. Village India: Studies in the Little Community.
Marriott, N. G. Principles of Food Sanitation.
Marris, Peter. Community Planning & Conceptions of Change: Dilemmas of Inner City Planning.
--Family & Social Change in an African City: A Study of Rehousing in Lagos.
Marris, Robin. A Survey & Critique of World Bank Supported Research in International Comparisons of Real Product.
Marro, J., ed. see International School of Statistical Mechanics Staff.
Marrocco, W. Thomas & Gleason, Harold. Music in America: An Anthology from the Landing of the Pilgrims to the Close of the Civil War 1620-1865.
Marron, J. P., jt. auth. see Lewis, Bernard T.
Marrow, Deborah. The Art Partronage of Maria de' Medici. Harris, Ann S., ed.
Marrs, Edwin W., Jr., ed. see Carlyle, Thomas.
Marrs, Texe. The Personal Robot Book.
--You & the Armed Forces: Career & Educational Opportunities for a Secure Future.
Marrs, Texe & Marrs, Wanda. Perfect Name for Your Pet.
Marrs, Texe W. Careers in Computers.
--High Technology Careers.
Marrs, Wanda, jt. auth. see Marrs, Texe.
Marrus, R., ed. Atomic Physics of Highly Ionized Atoms.
Mars, Gerald. Cheats at Work: An Anthology of Workplace Crime.
Mars, Gerald, jt. auth. see Binns, David.
Mars, Gerald, jt. auth. see Burns, David.
Marsac, J., jt. ed. see Chretien, J.
Marschak, Marianne. Parent-Child Interaction & Youth Rebellion.
Marsden, C. D., jt. ed. see Bradford, H. F.
Marsden, J. E., jt. auth. see Chernoff, P. R.
Marsden, Kate. On Sledge & Horseback to Outcast Siberian Lepers.
Marsden, Neville. Diagnosis Before First Aid.
Marsden, P. & McCullagh, A. Endocrinology.
Marsden, Victor E., tr. from Rus. The Protocols of the Meetings of the Learned Elders of Zion.
Marsella, Anthony J., jt. auth. see Corsini, Raymond J.
Marsella, Anthony J., et al, eds. Culture & Self: Asian & Western Perspectives.
Marsh. Comparative Sociology.
Marsh, Arthur, ed. Trade Union Handbook.
Marsh, Carole. Bath Color & Activity Book.
--Bath Cookbook.
--Bugs & Bytes: Computer for Kids.
--Copperbritches: Your ForeBear.
--How to Produce a Good-Looking Book Fast & Cheap.
--Kids Ask: Carole Marsh Answers Kids Questions about Writing & Writers.
Marsh, Dave. Elvis.
--Elvis.
Marsh, Dave & Stein, Kevin. The Book of Rock Lists.
Marsh, Derick R., ed. The Recurring Miracle.
Marsh, Elsie A., ed. see Hollander, Jacob H.
Marsh, G., ed. The Local Plan Inquiry: The Role in Local Plan Preparation.
Marsh, Geoffrey. Patch of the Odin Soldier.
Marsh, Harold, Jr. Marsh's California Corporation Law.
Marsh, J. B. Story of the Jubilee Singers, with Their Songs.
Marsh, Jan. Jane & May Morris: A Biographical Story 1839-1938.
Marsh, Jeri. Hurrah for Alexander!
Marsh, John. Saint John.
Marsh, Margaret. Anarchist Women: Eighteen Seventy to Nineteen Twenty.
Marsh, Michael N. Immunopathology of the Small Intestine.
Marsh, Ngaio. Colour Scheme.
--Colour Scheme.
--Final Curtain.
--Off with His Head.
--Tied up in Tinsel.
Marsh, Nicky, illus. Snow White & the Seven Dwarfs.
Marsh, P. D. Contract Negotiation Handbook.
Marsh, Reginald. Anatomy for Artists.
Marsh, Robert C., ed. see Russell, Bertrand.
Marsh, Robert W. MacLaren's Men.
--McLaren's Men.
--A Taste of Steel.
Marsh, William M. Environmental Analysis: For Land-Use & Site Planning.
Marshak, R. T., jt. auth. see Seybold, P. B.
Marshak, Sondra & Culbreath, Myrna. The Prometheus Design.
--Triangle.
--Triangle.
Marshall, Agnes. Victorian Ices & Ice Cream: 117 Delicious & Unusual Recipes Updated for the Modern Kitchen.
Marshall, Alan. Changing the Word: The Printing Industry in Transition.
Marshall, Alexandra. Brass Bed.
Marshall, Anthony G., jt. auth. see Cournoyer, Norman G.
Marshall, Carherine. Julie.
Marshall, Catherine. Catherine Marshall's Story Bible.
--Christy.
--Christy.
--Friends with God.
--God Loves You.
--Julie.
--Julie.
--Something More.
Marshall, Edison. American Captain.
--Caravan to Xanadu.
--Gypsy Sixpence.
--The Infinite Woman.
Marshall, Edward. Edward Marshall.
Marshall, Edward M. The Marshall Plan for Lifelong Weight Control.
Marshall, Eldon, jt. auth. see Kurtz, David.
Marshall, F. Ray. Labor Economics: Wages, Employment & Trade Unionism.
Marshall, George C. Memoirs of My Services in the World War: 1917-1918.
Marshall, George N. An Understanding of Albert Schweitzer.
Marshall, H., ed. Yevgeny Yevtushenko: Bilingual Edition.
Marshall, H., tr. see Gjessing, Lieve.
Marshall, I. Howard. Understanding the New Testament: Mark.
Marshall, J., jt. ed. see Cooper, C. L.
Marshall, J. D. The Old Poor Law 1795-1834.
Marshall, J. F., jt. ed. see Weisz, P. B.
Marshall, J. John, ed. Mechanisms of Saccharide Polymerization & Depolymerization.
Marshall, James. Four Little Troubles. Incl. Eugene; Someone Is Talking About Hortense; Sing Out Irene; Snake - His Story. HM.
--The Guest.
--Miss Dog's Christmas Treat.
--Portly McSwine.
Marshall, James V. Walkabout.
Marshall, Jeff. The Bicycle Rider's Bible.
Marshall, Joanne. Flower of Silence.
Marshall, Joseph. Poems for the Fireside.
Marshall, Kenneth, ed. see Newbourne, Malcolm J.
Marshall, Martha. What Child Is This?
--The Wonderful Surprise.
Marshall, Mary R., jt. auth. see Baker, Pat.
Marshall, Mel. The Care & Repair of Fishing Tackle.
--Steelhead.
Marshall, Muriel. Uncompahgre.
Marshall, Myrna. Something Worth Saving.
Marshall, N. B. Aspects of Deep Sea Biology.
Marshall, Norton L., jt. auth. see Mason, William H.
Marshall, Paul W., et al. Operations Management: Text & Cases.
Marshall, Ray & Korky, Paul. Crocodile & the Dumper Truck.
Marshall, Ray & Paul, Korky. Hey Diddle Diddle. Klimo, Kate, ed.
--Humpty Dumpty. Klimo, Kate, ed.
--Jack & Jill. Klimo, Kate, ed.
--Sing a Song of Sixpence. Klimo, Kate, ed.
Marshall, Richard, jt. auth. see Rosenblum, Robert.
Marshall, Robert L., ed. Studies in Renaissance & Baroque Music in Honor of Arthur Mendel.
Marshall, Roger. Designed to Win.
--Race to Win.
Marshall, Roger G., jt. auth. see Skitok, J.
Marshall, Roy K., jt. auth. see Levitt, I. M.
Marshall, S. L. Crimsoned Prairie.
Marshall, S. M. & Orr, A. P. The Biology of a Marine Copepod: Calanus Finmarchicus (Gunnerus)
Marshall, Samuel L. Ambush.
--Battles in the Monsoon: Campaigning in the Central Highlands, Vietnam, Summer 1966.
--Night Drop: The American Airborne Invasion of Normandy.
Marshall, Stanley J., jt. auth. see Frost, Reuben B.
Marshall, Sybil. The Silver New Nothing.
Marshall, Walter H. I've Met Them All.
Marshall, William. Head First: A Yellowthread Street Mystery.
--Perfect End.
--Perfect End.
--Roadshow.
--Sci-Fi.
--Sci Fi.
--Skulduggery.
--Skulduggery.
--Thin Air.
Marshall, William H. & De Martin, Elena L. La Vida en Espana.
Marshalla. Analysis Cartel Market.
Marshall-Stoneking, Billy. Lasseter: The Making of a Legend.
Mars-Jones, Adam, ed. Mae West Is Dead: Recent Lesbian & Gay Fiction.
Marston, Alwyn. Time Out for Murder.
Marston, Claire. Financial Reporting in India.
Marston, John. Antonio's Revenge. Gair, Reavley, ed.
--The Plays of John Marston.
Marston, John see Harrier, Richard C.
Marston, John E. Modern Public Relations.
Marszal, Barbara, tr. see Lem, Stanislaw.
Marteau, P., ed. see International AIRAPT Conference Staff.
Martech Strategies, Inc. Staff. Present & Projected Business Utilization of International Telecommunications.
Marteena, Constance H. The Lengthening Shadow of a Woman: A Biography of Charlotte Hawkins Brown.
Martel, Leon. Mastering Change.
Martel, Myles. Before You Say a Word: The Executive Guide to Effective Communication.
--Political Campaign Debates: Images, Strategies, & Tactics.
Martel, Sheila. Direct Work with Children: Social Work Practice in Family Service Units.
Martel, Sheila, ed. Supervision & Team Support.
Martel, William, jt. auth. see Dunnigan, James F.
Martello, Aileen M. The Yorkshire Terrier: Origin, History & Complete Care.
Marten, Elizabeth & Crosby, Nina. Creative Writing in Action.
Marten, Gerald & Matsuda, Yoshiaki. A Strategic Goal Analysis of Options for Tuna Longline Joint Ventures in Southeast Asia: Indonesia-Japan Case Study.
Marten, Gerald G. & Babor, Daryl. Environmental Considerations for Biomass Energy Development: Hawaii Case Study.
Marteniuk, R. G. Information Processing in Motor Skills.
Martens, Robert W., jt. auth. see Sisson, James E.
Marter, Marilynn. Dining in Philadelphia. Hosner, Sheila, ed.
Marth, Del. Florida Almanac, 1986-1987.
Marth, Del & Marth, Martha. Field Guide to Florida Media.
Marth, Del & Marth, Martha, eds. Florida Almanac, 1986-1987.
Marth, Del & Marth, Martha J., eds. The Florida Almanac, 1983-84 Edition.
Marth, Martha, jt. auth. see Marth, Del.
Marth, Martha, jt. ed. see Marth, Del.
Marth, Martha J., jt. ed. see Marth, Del.
Marthaler, Berard L. An Official Commentary for Sharing the Light of Faith.
Marthe. As Lonely As Franz Kafka.
Marti, Margaret, ed. see Vaness-Ann Collection Staff.
Marti, Margaret, ed. see Vanessa-Ann Collection Staff.
Martial. Selected Epigrams. Marcellino, Ralph, tr. from Lat.
Martimort, A. G., ed. The Church at Prayer: Part One-The Liturgy.
--The Church at Prayer Part Two: The Eucharist.
Martin. Atlanta Braves.
--Boston Red Sox.
--Chicago Cubs.
--Detroit Tigers.
--Kansas City Royals.
--Milwaukee Brewers.
--New York Mets.
--Oakland A'S.
--Philadelphia Phillies.
--Pittsburgh Pirates.
--St. Louis Cardinals.
--That Man from Smyrna.
Martin & Martin, Donald. Apple LOGO Programming Primer.
Martin, jt. auth. see Walls.
Martin, Alexander C. & Barkely, William D. Seed Identification Manual.
Martin, Alexander C., et al. American Wildlife & Plants: A Guide to Wildlife Food Habits.
Martin, Alice A. & Tenenbaum, Frances. Diet Against Disease: A New Plan for Safe & Healthy Eating.
Martin, Alson R., jt. auth. see Logan, James K.
Martin, Alvin. American Realism: Twentieth-Century Drawings & Watercolors.
Martin, Andy & Greene, Joseph. Blues for Julie.
--Doris Diamond-Private Eye. Dresner, Joanne, ed.
Martin, Anna, jt. auth. see Women's Co-operative Guild.
Martin, Anthony & Camm, A. John, eds. Heart Disease in the Elderly.
Martin, B. R. Statistics for Physicists.
Martin, Ben. Shipmaster's Handbook on Ship's Business.
Martin, Billy & Pepe, Phil. Billyball.
Martin, Bob. Hiking Trails of Central Colorado.
Martin, Brian W. John Keble: Priest, Professor & Poet.
Martin, Brone. Dreams & Reality.
--The Wandering Sea Gull. Zdanys, Jonas, tr. from Lithuanian.
Martin, Buddy, jt. auth. see Issel, Dan.
Martin, Burns see Ramsay, Allan.
Martin, C. Dianne, jt. auth. see Heller, Rachelle S.
Martin, C. Dianne, ed. see Association of Educational Data Systems.
Martin, C. L. Geometrical Optics.
Martin, C. Leslie. Architectural Graphics.
Martin, Catherine. Building Christian Community.
Martin, Charles C. Project Management: How to Make It Work.
Martin, Chester. Empire & Commonwealth.
Martin, Chryssee P., jt. auth. see Martin, Esmond B.
Martin, David. The Crying Heart Tattoo.
--Final Harbor.
--Tethered.
Martin, David, intro. by. Patriot or Traitor: The Case of General Mihailovich.
Martin, David L., jt. auth. see Morlan, Robert L.
Martin, Dean F. Marine Chemistry, Vol. 2: Theory & Applications.
Martin, Del & Lyon, Phyllis. Lesbian-Woman.
Martin, Dianne, jt. auth. see Heller, Rachelle.
Martin, Don & Martin, Jennifer. Eighty-Eight Apple LOGO Programs.
Martin, Don, jt. auth. see Osborn, George C.
Martin, Donald, jt. auth. see Martin.
Martin, Donald, et al. IBM PC & PCjr LOGO Programming Primer.
Martin, Donald F., jt. auth. see Blake, Clarence N.
Martin, Dorothy. Chapter Closed.
--Faith at Work.
--Heart's Surrender.
--Hopes Fulfilled.
--More Answers.
--Mystery Solved.
--New Life.
--Open Doors.
--Prayer Answered.
--Wider Horizons.
Martin, E., tr. see Engels, W. & Pohl, H.
Martin, E. A. A Dictionary of Life Sciences.
Martin, E. Wainwright, Jr. Basic Algebra.
Martin, Edward G. Using Applications Software: Tutorials & Activities.
Martin, Edward J. A History of the Iconoclastic Controversy.
Martin, Esmond B. & Martin, Chryssee P. Cargoes of the East: The Ports, Trade & Culture of the Arabian Seas & Western Indian Ocean.
Martin, F. R. The Miniature Paintings & Painters of Persia, India & Turkey from the 8th to the 18th Century.
Martin, Fenton, jt. auth. see Goehlert, Robert.
Martin, Florence. Observing National Holidays & Church Festivals: A Weekday Church School Unit in Christian Citizenship Series for Grades Three & Four.
Martin, Frederick N., ed. Medical Audiology: Disorders of Hearing.

Authors

Martin, G. W. & Francis, W. Industrial & Manufacturing Chemistry.
Martin, Garry & Pear, Joseph. Behavior Modification: What It Is & How to Do It.
Martin, Ged. Bunyip Aristocracy: The New South Wales Constitution Debate of 1853 & Hereditary Institutions in the British Colonies.
--Bunyip Aristocracy: The New South Wales Constitution Debate of 1853 & Hereditary Institutions in the British Colonies.
Martin, Gene. Library Services for Adults.
Martin, George. Lost Souls.
--Madam Secretary: Frances Perkins.
--To Pray As Jesus.
Martin, George, ed. Making Music: The Guide to Writing, Performing & Recording.
Martin, George R. The Armageddon Rag.
--Fevre Dream.
Martin, Gerhard M. Fest: The Transformation of Everday. Meeks, M. Douglas, tr.
Martin, Gib, jt. auth. see Richards, Lawrence.
Martin, Graham D. Catchfire.
--Giftwish.
Martin, Graham D., ed. & tr. see Valery, Paul.
Martin, Grant. Transformed by Thorns.
Martin, Greg. Spiritus Contra Spiritum: The Struggle of an Alcoholic Pastor.
Martin, H. G. Mathematics for Engineering Technology & Computing.
Martin, H. V. Kierkegaard, the Melancholy Dane.
--The Wings of Faith.
Martin, Harry. Contemporary Homes of the Pacific Northwest.
Martin, Howard H. & Colburn, C. William. Communication & Consensus: An Introduction to Rhetorical Discourse.
Martin, Ian K. Billions.
Martin, Ira. The Ins & Outs & Wins of Contract Bridge.
Martin, J. C. Managing Technological Innovation & Entrepreneurship.
Martin, J. R., jt. auth. see Wallace, Hugh A.
Martin, James. A Pilgrim's Guide to the Holy Land.
Martin, James, tr. see Kurtz, J. H.
Martin, James A., jt. auth. see Epstein, David G.
Martin, James D. & Davies, Phillip R. A Word in Season: Essays in Honour of William McKane.
Martin, James D., tr. see Noth, Martin.
Martin, James I., ed. Proceedings of the San Diego Biomedical Symposium.
Martin, James J., jt. auth. see Dennis, Lawrence.
Martin, Jane. Global Studies: Africa, 1984.
Martin, Jay. Winter Dreams: An American in Moscow.
Martin, Jennifer, jt. auth. see Martin, Don.
Martin, John. Feudalism to Capitalism: Peasant & Landlord in English Agrarian Development.
--Modern Dance.
Martin, John F. In the Way of the Whale: The Whaling Journal of John F. Martin, 1841 to 1844. Martin, Kenneth R., ed.
Martin, John P., jt. auth. see Coker, John B.
Martin, John R. Riding the Rails: Reminiscences of a Railway Career.
Martin, John R., ed. see Rubens.
Martin, John T. Positioning in Anesthesia & Surgery.
Martin, Joseph H. Real Estate License Examinations: Salesperson & Broker.
Martin, Joseph H. & Jackson, William. New Jersey Supplement for Modern Real Estate Practice.
Martin, Judith. Common Courtesy: In Which Miss Manners Solves the Problem That Baffled Jefferson.
--Miss Manners' Guide to Rearing Perfect Children.
--Style & Substance.
Martin, Julie, jt. auth. see Kliiver, Billy.
Martin, Kenneth R., ed. see Martin, John F.
Martin, L. John & Lambert, Richard D., eds. Role of the Mass Media in American Politics.
Martin, Laurence. NATO & the Defense of the West.
--The Two-Edged Sword: Armed Force in the Modern World, The Reith Lectures 1981.
Martin, Laurence W., ed. Neutralism & Nonalignment: The New States in World Affairs.
Martin, Lee. The Invisible Castle. Spinner, Stephanie, ed.
Martin, Luther H. & Goss, James, eds. Essays on Jung & the Study of Religion.
Martin, M. C. & Hewett, C. A. Elements of Classical Physics.
Martin, Malachi. There Is Still Love.
Martin, Margaret. Colleagues or Competitors.
Martin, Margaret J. & Chapman, Peter. Succulents & Their Cultivation.
Martin, Margaret J., jt. auth. see Ausberger, Carolyn.
Martin, Mary L. & MacInnis, Donald. Values & Religion in China Today: A Teaching Workbook & Lesson Series.
Martin, Mary L., jt. auth. see Bowers, Q. David.
Martin, Mayer. Grandissimo Pavarotti.
Martin, Melody. Off to College: The Survival Manual for High School Students & Their Parents.
Martin, Michael & Gelber, Leonard, eds. New Dictionary of American History.
Martin, Michael R. & Harrier, Richard A. Concise Encyclopedic Guide to Shakespeare.
Martin, Mike W. Self-Deception & Morality.
Martin, Minnie. Basutoland: Its Legends & Customs.
Martin, Molly. New York Knicks.
--Portland Trailblazers.
Martin, Nancy. John Lennon & Julian Lennon.
Martin, Nancy & Hand, David. Today Is Yesterday, Tomorrow!
Martin, Nancy, jt. auth. see Hardy, Clyde.
Martin, Nancy, ed. Prayers for Children & Young People.
Martin, P. G. Shopping Centre Management.
Martin, P. W. Experiment in Depth: A Study of the Work of Jung, Eliot & Toynbee.
Martin, Paul. Good Morning, Lord: More Devotions for Teens.
--Good Night, Lord.
Martin, Paul S. & Klein, Richard G., eds. Quarternary Extinctions: A Prehistoric Revolution.
Martin, Paul S., et al. Indians Before Columbus: Twenty Thousand Years of North American History Revealed by Archaeology.
--Indians Before Columbus: Twenty Thousand Years of North American History Revealed by Archaeology.
Martin, Peter, jt. ed. see Toon, Peter.
Martin, Peter, et al. Towards Better Practice.
Martin, Phyllis. Turn on the Dark.
Martin, Phyllis M. & O'Meara, Patrick, eds. Africa.
Martin, R. L., ed. Regional Wage Inflation & Unemployment.
Martin, R. L., et al, eds. Towards the Dynamic Analysis of Spatial Systems.
Martin, Rafe. The Hungry Tigress & Other Traditional Asian Tales.
Martin, Ralph. Fire on the Earth.
--Hungry for God.
Martin, Ralph & Toon, Peter, eds. Reconciliation: A Study of Paul's Theology.
Martin, Ralph, ed. see Avis, Paul D.
Martin, Ralph G. Charles & Diana.
Martin, Ralph P. The Spirit & the Congregation: Studies in I Corinthians 12-15.
--Understanding the New Testament: Acts.
--Understanding the New Testament: 1 Corinthians-Galatians.
Martin, Richard J., jt. auth. see Fanaroff, Avroy A.
Martin, Richie, ed. Judgment in the Gate.
Martin, Robert, tr. see Lorenz, Konrad.
Martin, Robert B. Tennyson: The Unquiet Heart.
--With Friends Possessed: A Life of Edward FitzGerald.
Martin, Robert E., et al, eds. Fire & Forest Meteorology Conference, 6th: Proceedings.
Martin, Robert J. High-Tech Bits.
Martin, Robert J. & Chagnon, Napoleon. Toward the Ph.D for Dogs.
Martin, Robert K., jt. ed. see Herz, Judith S.
Martin, Robert L. The City Moves West: Economic & Industrial Growth in Central West Texas.
Martin, Roberta & Heinrich, Amy V., eds. Contemporary Japan: A Teaching Workbook.
Martin, Roderick & Undy, Roger. Ballots & Trade Union Democracy.
--Ballots & Trade Union Democracy.
Martin, Ronald T. Six Wheel Drive.
Martin, Roy E., et al. Chemistry & Biochemistry of Marine Food Products.
Martin, Russell. The Color Orange: A Supper Bowl Season with the Denver Broncos.
--Matters Gray & White: A Neurologist, His Patients, & the Mysteries of the Brain.
Martin, Russell, jt. auth. see Allen, Joseph P.
Martin, Sarah S., jt. auth. see Seal, Robert A.
Martin, Sheila. The Spy Who Never Was.
Martin, Susan B. & Koek, Karin, eds. Encyclopedia of Associations, Vol. 1: National Organizations of the U. S.
--Encyclopedia of Associations, Vol. 2: Geographic & Executive Index.
Martin, Sylvia P. Ride On, Ride On.
Martin, T. T. Dear Heavenly Father: Letters from an Adopted Son.
Martin, Theodora P. The Sound of Our Own Voices: Women's Study Clubs, 1860-1900.
Martin, Thomas L., Jr. Malice in Blunderland.
--Malice in Blunderland.
Martin, Tom. Long Lance.
--Rappelling.
Martin, Toni. How to Survive Medical School.
Martin, Trevor. The Terminal Transfer.
Martin, Vaughn & Davis, Dean. Electronic & Microprocessor - Controlled Security Projects.
Martin, Victor de St. see De St. Martin, Victor.
Martin, Virginia H., jt. auth. see Nollen, Stanley D.
Martin, W. I., jt. auth. see Franklin Co., Chapter OGS Staff.
Martin, Walter T., jt. auth. see Gibbs, Jack P.
Martin, Warner, ed. Verzeichnis der Nobelpreistrager 1901-1984.
Martin, Wayne W., tr. The Gospel of Mark: A Translation for Children.
Martin, Werner, ed. Verzeichnis der Nobelpreistrager, 1901-1984.
Martin, Whitney G. Verdi: His Music, Life & Times.
Martin, William. Nerve Endings.
Martin, Yves, tr. see Twitchell, Paul.
Martin, Yves D., tr. see Kemp, Harold.
Martin, Yves D., tr. see Twitchell, Paul.
Martindale, Chris. Curse of the Werewolf.
--Prince of Thieves.
Martindale, Don A. Nature & Types of Sociological Theory.
--The Nature & Types of Sociological Theory.
Martindale, Joanna, ed. English Humanism: Wyatt to Cowley.
Martin-Doyle, J. A Synopsis of Ophthalmology.
Martin du Gard, Roger. Jean Barois.
--Notes sur Andre Gide.
Martineau, ed. see Stendhal.
Martineau, Jane, jt. ed. see Whitfield, Clovis.
Martinello, Gilda. Sources of Information in Transportation: Part 4, Railroads.
Martinez, A. R., ed. Solar Cooling & Dehumidifying: Proceedings of the First International Solar Cooling & Dehumidifying Conference (Solar 80), Held in Caracas, 3-6 August 1980.
Martinez, Al. Jigsaw John.
Martinez, Alberto & Nory, Jean-Loup. American Automobiles of the Fifties & Sixties.
Martinez, Emanuel J. Aggression & Criminality of Adolescence.
Martinez, Gilbert T. & Edwards, Jane. The Mexican American: His Life Across Four Centuries.
Martinez, J. N. Man in Nature & His Behavior.
Martinez, Joseph, jt. auth. see Martinez, Nancy.
Martinez, Nancy & Martinez, Joseph. The Holt Workbook.
Martinez, Oscar J. Border Boom Town: Ciudad Jaurez since 1848.
--Troublesome Border.
Martinez, Oscar J., ed. Fragments of the Mexican Revolution: Personal Accounts from the Border.
Martinez-Maldonado, Manuel, ed. Methods in Pharmacology, Vol. 4A: Renal Pharmacology.
--Methods in Pharmacology, Vol. 4B: Renal Pharmacology.
Martinez Sierra, Gregorio. Sueno de una Noche de Agosto. Walsh, Donald, ed.
Martin-Hoffman, Diana L., ed. Artist's Market, 1986.
Martini, Frederic. Exploring Tropical Isles & Seas: An Introduction for the Traveler & Amateur Naturalist.
Martini, G. A. & Bode, Ch., eds. Metabolic Changes Induced by Alcohol.
Martini, G. A. & Siegert, R., eds. Marburg Virus Disease.
Martini, L. & Ganong, William F., eds. Neuroendocrinology.
Martini, L. & Meites, J., eds. Neurochemical Aspects of Hypothalmic Function.
Martini, L. & Pecile, A., eds. Hormonal Steroids, Biochemistry, Pharmacology, Therapeutics.
Martini, L., et al, eds. Hypothalamus.
Martini, Luciano & Besser, G. M., eds. Clinical Neuroendocrinology.
Martini, Teri. All Because of Jill.
--John Marshall.
--The Lucky Ghost Shirt.
--The Mystery of the Woman in the Mirror.
--The Mystery Waters of Tonbridge Wells.
--Patrick Henry, Patriot.
Martin-Loef, A. Statistical Mechanics & the Foundations of Thermodynamics.
Martino, A. A., jt. auth. see Ciampi, C.
Martino, Joseph P. A Fighting Chance: The Moral Use of Nuclear Weapons.
Martino, R. L. Resources Management.
Martins, Peter & Cornfield, Robert. Far from Denmark.
Martins, Richard. The Cinch.
Martinsant. Time of Silence. Leeson, George, tr.
Martinson, Arthur. Wilderness above the Sound: The Story of Mount Rainer National Park.
Marto, P. J. & Nunn, R. H. Power Condenser Heat Transfer Technology: Computer Modeling-Design-Fouling.
Martof, Bernard S., et al. Amphibians & Reptiles of the Carolinas & Virginia.
Marton, Kati. An American Woman.
Marton, L., ed. Advances in Electronics & Electron Physics.
Martone, Thomas. The Iconography of the Conversion of Saint Paul. Freedberg, S. J., ed.
Marts, J. A. Paying Your Way.
Marty, Martin E. Christian Churches in the United States, 1800-1983.
--The Kingdom of God in America.
--A Short History of Christianity.
--The Word: People Participating in Preaching.
Marty, Martin E. & Vaux, Kenneth L. Health, Medicine & the Faith Traditions: An Inquiry into Religion & Medicine.
Marty, Martin E., ed. The Place of Trust: Martin Luther.
--Where the Spirit Leads: Seventeen American Denominations Today.
Marty, Martin E., intro. by see Holst, Lawrence.
Martyn, J. Louis, jt. auth. see Rice, Charles.
Martyn, J. Louis, jt. ed. see Keck, Leander E.
Martyn, T. Company Law Study Book.
Martynov, Ivan. Shostakovich: The Man & His Work.
Martynov, L. A Book of Poems.
Martz, Larry. Ministry of Greed: The Inside Story of the Televangelists & Their Holy Wars.
Martzlufft, Nancy. Gift of Life.
Maruyama, Masao. Studies in the Intellectual History of Tokugawa Japan. Hane, Mikiso, tr. from Japanese.
Marvel. Decepticon Hijack.
Marvel Comics Staff & Lee, Stan. Hulk.
Marvell, Andrew. The Poems of Andrew Marvell. MacDonald, Hugh, ed.
Marwil, Jonathan. The Trials of Counsel: Francis Bacon in 1621.
Marwood, Pamela, tr. see Borsi, Franco.
Marx, Jean L. & Kolata, Gina B. Combating the Number One Killer: The Science Report on Heart Research.
Marx, Jenny, et al, trs. The Daughters of Karl Marx: Family Correspondence 1866-98. Evans, Faith, ed.
Marx, K., et al. The General Council of the First International.
Marx, Karl. Das Kapital.
--Letters to Dr. Kugelmann.
--Wage, Labour & Capital.
--Wages, Price & Profit.
Marx, Karl & Engels, Frederick. On Historical Materialism.
Marx, Karl & Engels, Friedrich. Anarchism & Anarcho-Syndicalism: Selections.
--Communist Manifesto.
--On Colonialism: Selections.
Marx, Karl & Lenin, Vladimir I. The Civil War in France: The Paris Commune.
Marx, Karl, et al. The Woman Question: Selections from the Writings of Karl Marx, Frederick Engels, V. I. Lenin, Joseph Stalin.
--The Essential Left: Four Classic Texts on the Principles of Socialism.
Marx, Robert F. Robert Marx: Quest for Treasure. Nelson, B. J., ed.
Marx, Walter H. Thus Spake the Kings.
Marx, Werner. Hegel's Phenomenology of Spirit.
Marxer. Elements of Data Processing.
Marxhausen, Evelyn. The Man Who Slept Through a Sermon.
Marxhausen, Joanne. Thank God for Circles.
Marxhaussen, Joanne. Thank God for Circles.
Marxist-Worker's Party Staff. Marxist Review.
Marxsen, Willi. The Beginnings of Christology, together with The Lord's Supper. Achtemeier, Paul J. & Nieting, Lorenz, trs. from Ger.
--Introduction to the New Testament: An Approach to Its Problems. Buswell, G., tr. from Ger.
--Lord's Supper As a Christological Problem. Reumann, John, ed. Nieting, Lorenz, tr. from Ger.
--New Testament as the Church's Book. Mignard, James E., tr. from Ger.
--Resurrection of Jesus of Nazareth. Kohl, Margaret, tr. from Ger.
Maryon, Herbert. Metalwork & Enamelling: A Practical Treatise on Gold & Silversmiths' Work & Their Allied Crafts.
Marzac-Holland, Nicole, jt. ed. see Jairazbhoy, Nazir A.
Marzano, Tony & Powell, Painter E. The Big Steal.
Marzollo, A., ed. Topics in Artificial Intelligence.
Marzollo, Jean & Savage, Beth. Big Fearon Early Learning Book.
Marzulli, Francis N. & Maibach, Howard I., eds. Dermatotoxicology.
Masaryk, Tomas G. Modern Man & Religion. Kennedy, H. E., et al, trs.
Masatoshi. The Art of Netsuke Carving.
Mascall, Eric L. Theology & the Future.
Mascetta, Joseph. Barron's How to Prepare for the College Board Achievement Tests -- Chemistry.
Mascetta, Joseph A. Chemistry: The Easy Way.
Maschke, Ruby. Blinkety Blanks. Zapel, Arthur L., ed.
Maschler, Fay & Oxenbury, Helen. A Child's Book of Manners.
Masdeu, Joseph C., ed. see Gonzelez, Carlos F., et al.
Masefield, John. John M. Synge: A Few Personal Recollections.
Maser, Jack D., ed. Efferent Organization & the Integration of Behavior.
Mashaw, Bijan. BASIC: Programming Byte-by-Byte.
Masi, Dale A. Human Services in Industry.
Masia, Seth. The Ski Maintenance & Repair Handbook.
Masia, Seth, jt. auth. see Bennet, John.
Masie, Elliott & Stein, Michele. Handbook for Youth & Student Leadership.

Authors

Masih, L. Educational & Psychological Measurement: Selected Readings.
Masihi, K. N. & Lange, W., eds. Immunomodulators & Non-Specific Host Defence Mechanisms Microbial Infections: International Symposium, 6-8 May, 1987, West Berlin, FRG.
Maskus, Keith E. The Changing Structure of Comparative Advantage in American Manufacturing. Bateman, Fred, ed.
Maslach, Christina, jt. auth. see Zimbardo, Philip.
Masland, Anne C. The Witch Who Became Someone Else.
Maslinski, C., ed. Histamine: Mechanisms of Regulation of the Biogenic Amines Level in the Tissues with Special Reference to Histamine.
Maslov, A. V., et al. Geodetic Surveying. Kuznetsov, V. V., tr.
Maslow, Jonathan E. Bird of Life, Bird of Death: A Naturalist's Journey Through a Land of Political Turmoil.
Mason, jt. auth. see Goodman.
Mason, et al. Mathematics for Business & Consumers.
--Statistics: An Introduction.
Mason, Alice L. Larry the Lion.
--Maggie the Mink.
--Oscar the Otter.
--Sammy the Sloth.
--Simon the Snake.
Mason, Alice L. & Flint, Russ. Katie the Camel.
Mason, Alice L., jt. auth. see Moore, Clement.
Mason, Alpheus T., et al. American Constitutional Law: Introductory Essays & Selected Cases.
Mason, Anita. The Illusionist: A Novel.
Mason, Brian & Moore, Carleton B. Principles of Geochemistry.
Mason, Bruce B. & Hink, Heinz R. Constitutional Government in Arizona. Johnson, Broderick H., ed.
Mason, C. F., jt. auth. see Long, S. P.
Mason, Celestine B., jt. auth. see Davis, Joan E.
Mason, Charles, jt. auth. see Melges, Buddy.
Mason, Connie. Tender Fury.
Mason, David. Frank C. Laubach: Teacher of Millions.
--Reaching the Silent Billion.
Mason, David & Dyller, Fran. Bitter Pills.
Mason, David T. & Wellbank, J. H. John Rawls & His Critics.
Mason, Dean T., ed. Cardiac Emergencies.
Mason, Dorothy E. Music in Elizabethan England.
Mason, E. A. & Spurling, T. H. The Viral Equation of State.
Mason, Edward S. Economic Concentration & the Monopoly Problem.
Mason, Edward S., ed. Corporation in Modern Society.
Mason, Edwin. Collaborative Learning.
Mason, Elizabeth J., ed. NCLEX-RN Sample Tests from American Nursing Review.
Mason, Eugene, tr. see Wace, Robert & Layamon.
Mason, F. Van Wyck see Van Wyck Mason, F.
Mason, Francis K. Lockheed Hercules.
--Tornado.
Mason, George E., et al. Computer Applications in Reading.
Mason, Germaine. Concise Survey of French Literature.
Mason, Harriett S. Miss Mason Remembers.
Mason, Haydn. Voltaire: A Biography.
Mason, Herbert M., Jr. To Kill the Devil: The Attempts on the Life of Adolph Hitler.
Mason, Herbert W., et al, eds. Humaniora Islamica: An Annual Publication of Islamic Studies & the Humanities.
Mason, Herman L. Touch Me in the Morning.
Mason, Hilary. Morisco.
Mason, J. Barry & Mayer, Morris L. Foundations of Retailing.
--Modern Retailing: Theory & Practice.
--Modern Retailing: Theory & Practice.
Mason, J. Barry, et al. Cases & Problems in Contemporary Retailing.
--Retailing.
Mason, J. David, ed. Proceedings of the Conference on Stochastic Differential Equations & Applications.
Mason, J. E. Gentlefolk in the Making: Studies in the History of English Courtesy Literature & Related Topics from 1531 to 1774.
Mason, J. K. Forensic Medicine for Lawyers.
Mason, Jackie. Jackie Mason's America.
Mason, Jess. One Hundred Thousand Dollars a Year Selling Real Estate! The 5000 System.
Mason, Jill, ed. see Clark, Bruce.
Mason, Joan E., jt. ed. see Goldberg, Kathy E.
Mason, John M. Financial Management of Commercial Banks.
--The Fourth Generation: A Call for New Understanding for the Growing Numbers over Age 75.
Mason, Joseph B. History of Housing in the U. S., 1930-1980.
Mason, L. F. Photographic Processing Chemistry.
Mason, Lauris & Ludman, Joan, eds. Print Collector's Quarterly: An Anthology of Essays on Eminent Printmakers of the World.
Mason, Linda. Linda Mason's Sun-Sign Makeovers.
Mason, Mary Ann. An Introduction to the Use of Computers in Law.
Mason, Mercia. Oxford & Cambridge.
Mason, Michael, ed. The Country Music Book.
Mason, Miriam E. Yours with Love, Kate.
Mason, Otis. Basket Work of the Aborigines.
Mason, Paul J., jt. auth. see Hughes, Gary E.
Mason, R. Essentials of Statistics.
Mason, R. H., ed. Photograms of the Year.
Mason, Ralph. Native Clays & Glazes for North American Potters: A Manual for the Utilization of Local Clay & Glaze Materials.
Mason, Rita A. A Guide to Dental Radiography.
Mason, Robert L. & Jacobs, Carrie. How to Choose the Wrong Marriage Partner & Live Unhappily Ever After.
Mason, Shirlene. Daniel Defoe & the Status of Women.
Mason, Vivian, jt. auth. see Kennedy, Robert.
Mason, William H. & Marshall, Norton L. General Biology Laboratory Manual.
Masonson, Leslie N., jt. ed. see Fabozzi, Frank.
Masooduzzafar, Translated by see Nejand, Farghaneh.
Masor, Nathan. The New Psychiatry.
Masoro, E. J., ed. Pharmacology of Lipid Transport & Atherosclerotic Processes.
Maspes, P. E., ed. see European Congress Of Neurosurgery - Rome - 1963.
Mass, Lynne. Kids Working with Word Processors: Apple Writer.
--Kids Working with Word Processors: Bank Street Writer.
Mass, Lynne & Kemnitz, Thomas M. The Acorn BASIC Manual.
--The Apple BASIC Manual.
--The Apple LOGO Manual.
--The Atari BASIC Manual.
--The Commodore BASIC Manual.
--The Commodore LOGO Manual.
--The IBM BASIC Manual.
--The IBM LOGO Manual.
--The Texas Instruments BASIC Manual.
--The Texas Instruments LOGO Manual.
--The TRS-80 BASIC Manual.
--The TRS-80 Color LOGO Manual.
Massachusetts Anti-Slavery Society. First to Twenty-First Annual Reports.
Massachusetts Bar Association Staff, ed. Massachusetts Corporate Tax Manual.
Massachusetts Continuing Legal Education, Inc. Staff, jt. auth. see New England Bankruptcy Conference Staff.
Massachusetts Continuing Legal Education, Inc. Staff, jt. auth. see Nexon, Phillip J.
Massachusetts Continuing Legal Education-New England Law Institute Staff, jt. auth. see Massachusetts Continuing Legal Education-New England Law Institute, Inc. Staff.
Massachusetts Continuing Legal Education, Inc. Staff. Commercial Real Estate from Purchase & Sale to Closing.
--Commercial Real Estate Loans.
Massachusetts Continuing Legal Education Staff. Divorce Judgements & Post Divorce Problems.
Massachusetts Continuing Legal Education-New England Law Institute, Inc. Staff. Estate Planning for Family Lawyers.
Massachusetts Continuing Legal Education, Inc. Staff. Fundamentals of Civil Litigation Preparation: Research, Pleadings, & Paper Discovery.
--Fundamentals of Civil Motion Practice.
--Fundamentals of Corporate Organization.
Massachusetts Continuing Legal Education-New England Law Institute, Inc. Staff. Fundamentals of Income Tax Return Preparation with Related Planning Considerations.
Massachusetts Continuing Legal Education, Inc. Staff. How to Handle Debt Collection Matters: Before & After Judgement.
Massachusetts Continuing Legal Education-New England Law Institute, Inc. Staff. Landmark Changes in Divorce Taxation Rules.
Massachusetts Continuing Legal Education-New England Law Institute, Inc. Staff & American Law Institute-American Bar Association Committee on Continuing Professional Education. Litigating Medical Malpractice Claims: ALI-ABA Course of Study Materials.
Massachusetts Continuing Legal Education, Inc. Staff. Living with Environmental Law.
Massachusetts Continuing Legal Education-New England Law Institute, Inc. Staff. Martial Deduction Planning After ERTA.
Massachusetts Continuing Legal Education, Inc. Staff. Medical Testimony in a Worker's Compensation Case.
Massachusetts Continuing Legal Education-New England Law Institute, Inc. Staff. Motions, Discovery, & Negotiated Agreements.
--Planning for the Second Marriage.
Massachusetts Continuing Legal Education, Inc. Staff. Post-Mortem Estate Planning.
Massachusetts Continuing Legal Education-New England Law Institute, Inc. Staff & Massachusetts Continuing Legal Education-New England Law Institute Staff. Practical Answers to Everyday Zoning Problems.
Massachusetts Continuing Legal Education Inc. & American Law Institute-American Bar Association Committee for Continuing Professional Education. Real Estate Financing.
Massachusetts Continuing Legal Education-New England Law Institute, Inc. Staff. Representing the Tenant in Commercial Leasing.
--Residential Real Estate for Those Who More Than Dabble.
Massachusetts Continuing Legal Education-New England Law Institute, Inc. Staff & American Law Institute-American Bar Association Committee on Continuing Professional Education. Sophisticated Estate Planning Techiques: ALI-ABA Course of Study Materials.
Massachusetts Continuing Legal Education-New England Law Institute, Inc. Staff. Superior Court Judicial Profiles.
Massachusetts Continuing Legal Education, Inc. Staff. Tax Aspects of Real Estate Transactions.
Massachusetts Continuing Legal Education-New England Law Institute, Inc. Staff. Trial of a Toxic Tort Case.
Massachusetts Continuing Legal Education, Inc. Staff. Trial of an Eminent Domain Case.
Massachusetts Continuing Legal Education-New England Law Institute, Inc. Staff. Trial Skills: Twentieth Annual Practical Skills Series.
--The Use of Expert Witnesses.
Massachusetts Continuing Legal Education, Inc. Staff. Wetlands Regulations.
Massachusetts General Hospital Department of Nursing Staff. Department of Nursing Staff Education Manual. Stetler, Cheryl B., et al, eds.
Massachusetts General Hospital Department of Nursing, et al, eds. Manual of Nursing Procedures.
Massachusetts General Hospital Department of Nursing Staff. Massachusetts General Hospital Department of Nursing Operating Room Procedure Manual.
Massachusetts Historical Society Staff. Catalog of Manuscripts of the Massachusetts Historical Society: First Supplement.
--Historical Index to the Pickering Papers.
Massachusetts Horticultural Society, Boston Staff. Dictionary Catalog of the Library of the Massachusetts Horticultural Society.
--Dictionary Catalog of the Library of the Massachusetts Horticultural Society, First Supplement.
Massachusetts Parole Board Staff & Gilmore, Ellen M. Parole Board Votes, County Houses of Correction, 1982.
Massachusetts-Rhode Island Guidebook Committee, ed. AMC Massachusetts-Rhode Island Trail Guide.
Massad, C. E., jt. auth. see Lewis, E. G.
Massam, Thomas, ed. Computer Frontiers.
Massar, Phyllis D. Presenting Stefano della Bella: Seventeenth-Century Printmaker.
Massart, D. Luc & Kaufman, Leonard. The Interpretation of Analytical Chemical Data by the Use of Cluster Analysis.
MassCOSH Legal Committee. Injured on the Job: A Handbook for Massachusetts Workers. Schwartz, Robert M., ed.
Masse, W. B., jt. ed. see Wilcox, D.
Masser, D. W., jt. auth. see Baker, A.
Masser, I. Theory & Practice in Regional Science.
Massey. Nuclear Explosions & Their Effects.
Massey, A. G., jt. auth. see Holliday, A. K.
Massey, B. Mechanics of Fluids.
Massey, Doreen. Spatial Divisions of Labour: Social Structures & the Geography of Production.
Massey, Doreen & Meegan, Richard. Anatomy of Job Loss: The How, Why & Where of Employment Decline.
Massey, Doreen B. & Batey, P. W., eds. Alternative Frameworks for Analysis.
Massey, H. S. Atoms & Energy.
Massey, Irving. Posthumous Poems of Shelley: Mary Shelley's Fair Copy Book.
Massey, Irving, tr. see De Vigny, Alfred.
Massey, J., jt. auth. see Meredith, W.
Massey, James E. Spiritual Disciplines: Growth Through the Practice of Prayer, Fasting, Dialogue, & Worship. Allison, Joseph D., ed.
Massey, Reginald, et al. The Music of India.
Massie, Allan. The Death of Men.
--Let the Emperor Speak: A Novel of Caesar Augustus.
Massie, Joseph L. Essentials of Management.
Massie, Larrie B., jt. auth. see Schmitt, Peter J.
Massie, Sonya. Dream Carver.
Massignon, Genevieve. Folktales of France.
Massillon Society Staff & Walsh, John, eds. Inside Football, 1984.
Massimino, S. How to Master the Art of Closing Sales.
--How to Sell to the People's Republic of China.
Massimino, Sal T. The Complete Book of Closing Sales.
Massimo, L. Physics of High Temperature Reactors.
Massinger, Philip. City Madam.
Massman, Patti, jt. auth. see Beck, Pamela.
Masson, Alison & Steiner, Robert L. Generic Substitution & Prescription Drug Prices: Economic Effects of State Drug Product Selection Laws.
Masson, C. R. Metallurgical Slags.
Masson, G. M., jt. auth. see Thurber, Kenneth J.
Masson, Georgina. Frederick II of Hohenstaufen.
Masson, Pierre. Human Tumors: Histology, Diagnosis, & Technique. Kobernick, Sidney D., tr. from Fr.
Massry, S. G., ed. see International Workshop on Phosphate & Other Minerals Staff.
Massry, Shaul G., et al, eds. Regulation of Phosphate & Mineral Metabolism.
Massy, Christian de see De Massy, Christian & Higham, Charles.
Massy, William F., jt. auth. see Boyd, Harper W., Jr.
Mast, Gerald. A Short History of the Movies.
Mastaglia, F. L. & Walton, John. Skeletal Muscle Pathology.
Master Hua, Tripitaka. Great Compassion Dharma Transmission Verses of the 42 Hands & Eyes. Buddhist Text Translation Society, tr. from Chinese.
Master Hua, Triptaka. Herein Lies the Treasure-Trove. Buddhist Text Translation Society, tr. from Chinese.
Masterman, C. F. From the Abyss of Its Inhabitants by One of Them.
--The Heart of the Empire: Discussions of Problems of Modern City Life in England with an Essay on Imperialism. Gilbert, B., ed.
Masterman, Eric V. The Auto Compendium.
Masterman, Len. Teaching the Media: An Introduction to Media Education.
Masterman, Len, ed. see Wilson, Elizabeth, et al.
Masters, Anthony. Nancy Astor.
--Napoleon.
Masters, Charles O. The Encyclopedia of Live Foods.
Masters, Edgar L. Spoon River Anthology.
Masters, H. Last Stands: Notes from Memory.
Masters, Janet F., tr. see Smith, Joyce M.
Masters, John. Heart of War.
--Now, God Be Thanked.
Masters, Lowell F. & Mori, Allen A. Adapted Physical Education: A Practitioner's Guide.
--Teaching Secondary Students with Mild Learning & Behavior Problems: Methods, Materials, Strategies.
Masters, Lowell F., jt. auth. see Mori, Allen A.
Masters, M. The Case of the Clever Computer Crooks & Other Mysteries. Delagran, Louise, et al, eds.
--The Case of the Famous Chocolate Chip Cookies & Other Mysteries. Delagran, Louise, et al, eds.
Masters, Marcia L. Wind Around the Moon.
Masters, Olga. A Long Time Dying.
--A Long Time Dying.
--Loving Daughters.
Masters, Roy. Hypnosis of Life.
--The Letter Killeth... Baker, Dorothy, ed.
--No One Has to Die.
Masters, S. Black-White Income Differentials: Empirical Studies & Policy.
Masters, T. W. Hairdressing in Theory & Practice.
Masters, William H., et al. Crisis: Heterosexual Behavior in the Age of AIDS.
--Human Sexuality.
--Human Sexuality.
--Masters & Johnson on Sex & Human Loving.
Masterson, Amanda R., ed. Index to the Proceedings of the Lunar & Planetary Science Conferences, Houston, Texas, 1970-1978.
Masterson, John. A Case for a Triangle.
Masterton, Graham. Corroboree.
Masterton, R. Bruce, ed. Sensory Integration: Handbook of Behavioral Neurobiology.
Masterton, William & Slowinski, Emil. Chemical Principles.
Masterton, William, et al. Chemical Principles, Using S. I. Units.
Masterton, William L., et al. Chemical Principles.
Mastie, Marjorie, jt. auth. see Kapes, Jerome.
Masud, A. S., jt. auth. see Hwang, C. L.
Masuda, Masasuke, ed. Pancreatic Function Diagnostant.
Matane, Paulias. Aimbe, the Pastor.
Matantle, Ivor. Collecting & Using Classic Cameras.
Matchette, Franklin J. Outline of Metaphysics.
Mate, Ferenc. From a Bare Hull.
Matejcek, Z., jt. auth. see Langmeier, J.
Matejka, Ladislav, ed. Cross Currents, No. 4.
--Cross Currents, No. 5.
Matejka, Ladislav & Stolz, Benjamin A., eds. Cross Currents.

Authors

Materials Development Staff & McCarty, Teresa. Navajo Changes: A History of the Navajo People.
Materka, Pat R. Time in, Time Out, Time Enough: A Time Management Guide for Women.
Mates, Antonio. Guide to Reviews of Books from & about Hispanic America 1981.
Mateu, Julio. Olivos y Abedules.
Mateus, Abel. Targeting Food Subsidies for the Needy: The Use of Cost-Benefit Analysis & Institutional Design.
Mateveyev, L. Fundamentals of Sports Training.
Mathe, G. Cancer Active Immunotherapy, Immunoprophylaxis & Immunorestoration: An Introduction.
Mathe, G. & Rappaport, H. Histological & Cytological Typing of Neoplastic Diseases of Haematopoietic & Lymphoid Tissues.
Mathematical Foundations of Computer Science Symposium Staff. Mathematical Foundations of Computer Science: Proceedings of the Symposium, 3rd, Jadwisin, June 17-22, 1974. Blikle, A., ed.
Mathematics & Computation Division Staff. Nuclear Science & Engineering-Improved Methods for Analysis of Nuclear Systems: Proceedings, American Nuclear Society Topical Meeting.
--Nuclear Science & Engineering-Improved Methods for Analysis of Nuclear Systems: Proceedings, American Nuclear Society Topical Meeting.
Matheny, Fred. Beginning Bicycle Racing. Pavelka, Ed, ed.
--Beginning Bicycle Racing. Pavelka, Ed, ed.
Mather, Arthur. Easy Money.
Mather, Christine, ed. Colonial Frontiers: Art & Life in Spanish New Mexico, the Fred Harvey Collection.
Mather, Frank J. History of Italian Painting.
Mather, J. Y. & Speitel, H. H., eds. The Linguistic Atlas of Scotland: Scots Section, Vol. III, Phonology.
Mather, J. Y., et al, eds. The Linguistic Atlas of Scotland: Scots Section.
--The Linguistic Atlas of Scotland: Scots Section.
Mather, John R. The Birds of Yorkshire.
Mather, K. Genetical Structures of Populations.
Mather, Kirtley F. The Permissive Universe.
Mather, Melissa. Damian.
Mathers, Michael. Sheepherders.
Mathes, Joachim, et al, eds. The Annual Review of the Social Sciences of Religion.
Matheson, Andrew, ed. see Emmanuel, W. D.
Matheson, Douglas W. Introductory Psychology: The Modern View.
Matheson, Maureen, ed. The College Handbook, 1987-88.
Matheson, Neil. The Rules of the Game of Superpower Military Intervention in the Third World: 1975-1980.
Matheson, Richard C. Scars.
Matheson, Roy. Loving God's Family.
Mathew, Brian & Baytop, Turhan. The Bulbous Plants of Turkey.
Mathew, David. Ethiopia, the Study of a Polity, 1540-1935.
Mathews, Alice E. Society in Revolutionary North Carolina.
Mathews, Boots, jt. auth. see Rieger, James.
Mathews, Donald K. Measurement in Physical Education.
Mathews, Harry. Cigarettes.
Mathews, J. Chelsey, ed. see Dante Alighieri.
Mathews, Jan. Thief of Hearts.
Mathews, Jay & Mathews, Linda. One Billion.
Mathews, Jay, et al, trs. see Andors, Stephen.
Mathews, John, ed. At the Table of the Grail: Magic & the Use of Imagination.
Mathews, Linda, jt. auth. see Mathews, Jay.
Mathews, M. B. Connective Tissue: Macromolecular Structure & Evolution.
Mathews, Marcia M. Henry Ossawa Tanner: American Artist.
Mathews, Mervyn. Education in the Soviet Union: Policies & Institutions since Stalin.
Mathews, P. M. & Venkatesan, K. A Textbook of Quantum Mechanics.
Mathews, R. Arthur. Born for Battle.
Mathews, Shailer. Jesus on Social Institutions. Cauthen, Kenneth & Keck, Leander E., eds.
Mathews, Shailer & Smith, Gerald B., eds. Dictionary of Religion & Ethics.
Mathews, Walter M., ed. Monster or Messiah? The Computer's Impact on Society.
Mathews, Wilma, jt. auth. see Howard, Carole.
Mathews, Zena P. Color & Shape in American Indian Art. Aspinwall, Margaret & Horbar, Amy, eds.
Mathewson, G. Construction of an Astronomical Telescope.
Mathewson, Hugh S. Pharmacology for Respiratory Therapists.
Mathewson, Joseph. Alicia's Trump.
--Death Turns Right.
Mathewson, R. Duncan, III. Treasure of the Atocha.
Mathias, A. R., ed. see Cambridge Summer School in Mathematical Logic Staff.
Mathias, Jim & Kennedy, Thomas L., eds. Computers, Language Reform, & Lexicography in China.
Mathias, Peter. The First Industrial Nation: An Economic History of Britain, 1700-1914.
Mathias, Peter, ed. see Johnston, Valerie J.
Mathias, Peter, ed. see Sacks, David H.
Mathiasen, Carolyn, ed. see Newman, Anne & Bowers, Cathy.
Mathiesen, Thomas J. A Bibliography of Sources for the Study of Ancient Greek Music.
Mathieson, Donald J., jt. auth. see McKinnon, Ronald I.
Mathieson, Margaret. Teaching Practical Criticism: An Introduction.
Mathieu, G., ed. Advances in the Teaching of Modern Languages.
Mathieu, Gustave B., jt. auth. see Haas, Werner.
Mathieu, Jean & Weill-Raynal, Jean. Introduction of an Alpha-Functional Carbon Chain & Special Condensation Reactions: Formation of C-C Bonds.
Mathieu, Jean P. Optics. Incl. Pt. 1. Electromagnetic Optics; Pt. 2. Quantum Optics. Pergamon.
Mathieu, Pierre-Louis. Gustave Moreau: The Watercolors.
Mathis, Edward. Dark Streaks & Empty Places: A Dan Roman Mystery.
--From a High Place.
--Natural Prey.
Mathis, Harry R. The Accounting Cycle: A Self-Study Review Program.
Mathis, Mary E. A Scriptural Treasury of Eternal Life.
--A Scriptural Treasury of Forgiveness.
--A Scriptural Treasury of Guidance.
--A Scriptural Treasury of Hope.
--A Scriptural Treasury of Joy.
--A Scriptural Treasury of Love.
--A Scriptural Treasury of Peace.
Mathis, Ray. In the Land of the Living: Wartime Letters by Confederates from the Chattahoochee Valley of Alabama & Georgia.
Mathis, Robert L. & Jackson, John H. Personnel: Human Resource Management.
Mathis, Sharon B. Sidewalk Story.
--Teacup Full of Roses.
Mathur, N. K. & Narang, C. K. Determination of Organic Compounds with N-Bromosuccinimide & Allied Reagents.
Mathy, Francis, tr. see Endo, Shusaku.
Matich, Olga. Paradox in the Religious Poetry of Zinaida Gippius.
Matijevic, Egon, ed. Surface & Colloid Science.
Matisoff, Bernard S. Handbook of Electronics Packaging Design & Engineering.
Matkovick, V. I., ed. Boron & Refractory Borides.
Matlack. Statistics for Public Policy & Management.
Matley, Jay & Chemical Engineering Magazine Editors. Practical Process Instrumentation & Control.
Matlin, Margaret. Perception.
Matlin, Samuel, jt. auth. see Neimark, Paul.
Matlis, E. One-Dimensional Cohen-Macaulay Rings.
Matlock, Bill J., jt. auth. see Schell, Frank R.
Matlock, James. Open Book.
Matonti, Charles. Celebrate with Song.
Matos, Antonio. Guide to Reviews of Books from & about Hispanic America, 1982.
--Guide to Reviews of Books from & About Hispanic America, 1975: Guia a las Resenas de Libros de y Sobre Hispanoamerica, 1975.
--Guide to Reviews of Books from & About Hispanic America, 1979: Guia a las Resenas de Libros de y Sobre Hispanoamerica, 1979.
--Guide to Reviews of Books from & About Hispanic America, 1978: Guia a las Resenas de Libros de y sobre Hispanoamerica, 1978.
--Guide to Reviews of Books from & About Hispanic America, 1974: Guia a las Resenas de Libros de y Sobre Hispanoamerica, 1974.
--Guide to Reviews of Books From & About Hispanic America, 1977: Guia a las resenas de libros de y sobre Hispanoamerica, 1977.
Matos, Antonio, ed. Guide to Reviews of Books from & about Hispanic America, 1980.
--Guide to Reviews of Books from & About Hispanic America, 1972: Guia a las Resenas De Libros De y Sobre Hispanoamerica, 1972.
--Guide to Reviews of Books from & About Hispanic America 1973: Guia a las Resenas De Libros De y Sobre Hispanoamerica 1973.
--Guide to Reviews of Books from & About Hispanic America, 1976: Guia a las Resenas de Libros de y sobre Hispanoamerica.
Matossian, Mary A. The Impact of Soviet Policies in Armenia, Nineteen Twenty to Nineteen Thirty-Six: A Study of Planned Cultural Transformation.
Matossian, Nouritza. Xenakis.
Matoth, Yehuda, ed. see Tel Aviv University Conference on Erythropoiesis Staff.
Matox, R. B. & Miller, W. D., eds. Special Report Number Thirty-Nine: Ogallala Aquifer Symposium, 1979.
Matranga, Frances. My Book of Prayers.
Matranga, Frances C. Secret Behind the Blue Door.
Matre, Joseph G. Van see Van Matre, Joseph G. & Gilbreath, Glenn H.
Matre, Steve Van see Van Matre, Steve.
Matsch, Charles L. North America & the Great Ice Age.
Matson, Carl E. Thirty Instruction Units in Basic Electricity.
Matson, Esther. Adventures in Tranquility.
Matson, Floyd, jt. auth. see Ashley Montagu.
Matson, Floyd, jt. auth. see Ashley-Montagu.
Matson, Floyd, jt. auth. see Ashley Montagu.
Matson, J. L. Philosophy & Care of the Mentally Retarded: A Worldwide Status Report.
Matson, Peter H. A Place in the Country: A Narrative on the Imperfect Art of Homesteading & the Value of Ignorance.
Matsubara, Hisako. Cranes at Dusk. Vennewitz, Leila, tr. from Ger.
Matsuda, R. Morphology & Evolution of the Insect Abdomen. Kerkut, ed.
Matsuda, Yoshiaki, jt. auth. see Marten, Gerald.
Matsumoto, Teruo. Acupuncture for Physicians.
Matsumoto, Teruo & Levy, Bruce A. Acupuncture for Patients.
Matsushima, Shunjiro, jt. auth. see Isogai, Hiroshi.
Matsushita, Konosuke. Japan at the Brink. Terry, Charles, tr. from Japanese.
Matsuya Piece-Goods Store Staff. Japanese Design Motifs: 4260 Illustrations of Heraldic Crests. Adachi, Fumie, tr. & illus.
Matt, Stephen R. Electricity & Basic Electronics.
Matta, Michael, jt. auth. see Wilbraham, Antony.
Mattam, Donald. Vital Approach.
Mattar, E. P. & Ball, M. Handbook for Corporate Directors.
Mattelart, Armand. Multinational Corporations & the Control of Culture: The Ideological Apparatuses of Imperialism. Chanan, Michael, tr.
Mattelart, Armand, et al. International Image Market: In Search of an Alternative Perspective. Garnham, Nicholas, tr. from Fr.
Mattelart, Michele. Women, Media, Crisis: Femininity & Disorder.
Matter, Frank. The Biography of a Bar Harbor Summer Cottage.
Matter, Joseph A. Love, Altruism, & World Crisis: The Challenge of Pitirim Sorokin.
Matter, Roxana M., ed. Group Insurance: Readings.
Matteson, David R. Adolescence Today: Sex Roles & the Search for Identity.
Matteson, Marilee, ed. Simple Feasts: Appetizers, Main Dishes & Desserts.
Matteson, Michael & Ivancevich, John M. Management Classics.
Matteson, Michael, jt. auth. see Ivancevich, John M.
Matteson, Michael T., jt. auth. see Ivancevich, John M.
Matthais, John, tr. see Ostergren, Jan.
Matthee, Dalene. Circles in a Forest.
Mattheisen, Paul F. & Millgate, Michael, eds. Transatlantic Dialogue: Selected American Correspondence of Edmund Gosse.
Matthes, Joachim, et al, eds. The Annual Review of the Social Sciences of Religion.
--The Annual Review of the Social Sciences of Religion.
Matthew Bender Publishers Staff. Court Awarded Attorney Fees: Report 3.
--Private Investors Index.
Matthew Bender Publishers Staff, ed. see Waren, Oscar & Heaton, Willis E.
Matthew, Christopher. The Long-Haired Boy.
Matthew, Donald. The Norman Monasteries & Their English Possessions.
Matthews, Ann. Earthquake.
Matthews, Anne. The Vogue Dictionary of Knitting Stitches.
Matthews, Bill & Matthews, Dawn. The Pitcher Mountain Inn Cookbook.
Matthews, Brander. Historical Novel & Other Essays.
Matthews, Brander, ed. Ballads of Books.
--The Oxford Book of American Essays.
Matthews, C. M. Words, Words, Words.
Matthews, Caitlin. Mabon & the Mysteries of Britain.
Matthews, Caitlin & Matthews, John. The Western Way: A Practical Guide to the Western Mystery Tradition.
Matthews, Carol B. & Matthews, Martin S. Word Processing for the IBM PC & PCjr & Compatible Computers.
Matthews, Catlin & Matthews, John. The Western Way: A Practical Guide to the Western Mystery Tradition.
Matthews, Clayton. The Negotiator.
--The Power Seekers.
--The Proud Castles.
Matthews, Clyde. The Ides of March Conspiracy.
Matthews, D. E. & Farewell, V., eds. Using & Understanding Medical Statistics.
Matthews, David L., jt. auth. see Baley, James A.
Matthews, Dawn, jt. auth. see Matthews, Bill.
Matthews, Dee, et al. The You Can Do It! Kids Diet.
Matthews, Denis, ed. Keyboard Music.
Matthews, Donald R. U. S. Senators & Their World.
Matthews, Donald R. & Prothro, James W. Negroes & the New Southern Politics.
Matthews, Douglas. Sue the B-St-Rds: The Victim's Handbook.
--Sue the B-st-rds: The Victim's Handbook.
Matthews, Douglas, et al. Second Hand Is Better.
Matthews, E. G. & Kitching, R. L. Insect Ecology.
Matthews, E. N. Colonial Organs & Organ Builders.
Matthews, Ellen. Putting up with Sherwood.
Matthews, G. A. Polymer Mixing Technology.
Matthews, G. M., ed. Keats: The Critical Heritage.
Matthews, Gordon. Prince.
Matthews, Greg. Heart of the Country.
Matthews, Herbert L. Revolution in Cuba.
Matthews, J. E., et al, eds. Automatic Turning Machines.
Matthews, J. I. Experiments in Solid State Electronics.
Matthews, J. L. Solid State Electronics Concepts.
Matthews, Jack. Charisma Campaigns.
Matthews, John. At the Table of the Grail: Magic & the Use of Imagination.
Matthews, John, jt. auth. see Matthews, Caitlin.
Matthews, John, jt. auth. see Matthews, Catlin.
Matthews, John F., ed. see Shaw, George Bernard.
Matthews, Joseph L. & Berman, Dorothy M. Social Security, Medicare & Pensions: A Sourcebook for Older Americans.
Matthews, Julian & Collier, Gordon. The New Zealander's Garden.
Matthews, Kathy, jt. auth. see Haddock, Sally.
Matthews, Kay. Going Potty.
Matthews, Laura. Emotional Ties.
Matthews, Lawrence M. Estimating Manufacturing Costs: A Practical Guide for Managers & Estimators.
Matthews, Martin S., jt. auth. see Matthews, Carol B.
Matthews, Mervyn, ed. Soviet Government: A Selection of Official Documents on Internal Policies.
Matthews, Patricia. Gambler in Love.
--Tides of Love.
Matthews, Peter. Track & Field Athletics: The Records. Frei, Beatrice, ed.
Matthews, Phoebe. Honeymoon House.
Matthews, R. C. & Sargent, J. R., eds. Contemporary Problems of Economic Policy: Essays from the Clare Group.
Matthews, T. S. Angels Unawares: Twentieth Century Portraits.
Matthews, Thomas S. O My America.
Matthews, W. H. Mazes & Labyrinths.
Matthews, William. Ruining the New Road.
Matthews, William C. King Cobra.
Matthias, F. R. Blood Coagulation Disorders.
Matthias, Lee A. The Pandora Plague.
Matthiesen, Thomas, photos by. ABC, an Alphabet Book.
Matthiessen, A. B. The Singing & the Gold.
Matthiessen, Peter. Far Tortuga.
--The Tree Where Man Was Born. Bd. with The African Experience. Porter, Eliot. Avon.
Matthysse, Steven & Kety, Seymour S. Catecholamines & Their Enzymes in the Neuropathology of Schizophrenia.
Mattick, Paul. Anti-Bolshevik Communism.
Mattick, Paul, Jr. Social Knowledge: An Essay on the Nature & Limits of Social Science.
Mattingly, David, jt. auth. see Seward, Charles.
Mattingly, Garrett. Renaissance Diplomacy.
Mattingly, Harold. The Imperial Civil Service of Rome.
Mattingly, Ignatius G., jt. ed. see Kavanagh, James F.
Mattingly, Joan. The Rose & the Sword.
Mattingly, Joseph G., Jr. Annual Editions: Business-Management, 1985-86.
Mattison, Judith. Facing Up.
--From a Woman's Heart.
--Help Me Adapt, Lord: Discovering New Blessings While Learning to Live with Less.
--I'm Worried about Your Drinking: Feelings of Family & Friends Who Care.
--Mom Has a Second Job: Prayer Thoughts for Working Mothers.
--Prayers from a Mother's Heart.
--Prayers from a Woman's Heart.
Matto, Edward A. A Manager's Guide to the Antitrust Laws.
Matton, E. Market for Frozen Small Pelagic Fish.
Mattox, Beverly. Help! I'm a Woman!
Mattsson, May. Five Plays about King John.
Matula, Richard A., ed. see Conference of ASME, 1976.
Matura, Mustapha. Nice Rum An' Coca-Cola & Welcome Home Jacko.
Maturin, Charles R. Melmoth the Wanderer: A Tale.
Matusow, Allen J. Farm Policies & Politics in the Truman Years.

Authors

Matusow, Barbara. The Evening Stars: The Making of the Network News Anchor.
Matussek, P. Internment in Concentration Camps & Its Consequences. Jordan, D., tr. from Ger.
Matwes, George & Matwes, Helen. Loss Control Safety Guidebook for Trades & Services.
Matwes, Helen, jt. auth. see Matwes, George.
Matyjaszkiewicz, Krystyna, ed. James Tissot.
Matz, Samuel A. Snack Food Technology.
Matza, D. Deliquency & Drift.
Matzke, Gordon. Wildlife in Tanzanian Settlement Policy: The Case of the Selous.
Mau, Ernest E. Getting the Most from Your Micro.
--Getting the Most from Your Personal Computer.
Mauch & Birch. Guide to the Successful Thesis & Dissertation.
Mauer, Jim, ed. see Teyler.
Mauer, Shelley M., jt. auth. see Morford, Ted R.
Maugham, W. Somerset. The Razor's Edge: Television Edition.
Maughon, Martha. Why Am I Crying?
Maul, Terry, jt. auth. see Conrad, Eva E.
Mauldin, Bill. The Brass Ring.
--A Sort of a Saga.
Maunder, L., frwd. by. Engineering Challenges in the 1980's.
Maunder, W. F. & Coppock, J. T., eds. Land Use & Town & Country Planning.
Maunder, W. F., ed. see Baxter, R. E. & Phillips, C.
Mauner, George. The Nabis: Their History & Their Art, 1888-1896.
Mauntz, Alfred Von see Von Mauntz, Alfred.
Maupassant, Guy De see De Maupassant, Guy.
Maupassant, Guy De see De Maupassant, Guy De.
Maupin, B. Blood Platelets in Man & Animals.
Maupin, Robert N. Passage from Russia: A Personal History.
Maurer, Allan. Lasers: The Light Wave of the Future.
Maurer, C. & Wraith, G. C., eds. Model Theory & Topoi.
Maurer, David J., ed. United States Politics & Elections: A Guide to Information Sources.
Maurer, Harry, jt. auth. see Mirow, Kurt R.
Maurer, Marvin, jt. ed. see Grupp, Fred W., Jr.
Maurer, W. C. Novel Drilling Techniques.
Maurer, W. Douglas. Commodore 64 Assembly Language.
Maurer, Warren R. The Naturalist Image of German Literature: A Study of the German Naturalists - Appraisal of Their Literary Heritage.
Mauriac, Francois. Letters on Art & Literature.
--Men I Hold Great.
--Proust's Way.
--Saint Margaret of Cortona. Fechtman, Bernard, tr.
--The Stumbling Block.
--Therese Desqueyroux. Collignon, Jean, ed.
--Words of Faith.
Mauriac, Francois, tr. see Hopkins, Gerard Manley.
Maurice. Unpublished Letters of H. M. Stanley.
Maurice & Follett, Ken. The Gentlemen of Sixteen July.
Maurice, Arthur B. & Cooper, Frederick T. History of the Nineteenth Century in Caricature.
Maurice, Bloch, jt. auth. see Longman, Lester D.
Mauricette, Gail, jt. ed. see Dolmetsch, Paul.
Maurier, Daphne Du see Du Maurier, Daphne.
Maurier, Daphne Du see Du Maurier, George L.
Maurier, Daphne du see Quiller-Couch, Arthur & Du Maurier, Daphne.
Maurier, George L. Du see Du Maurier, George L.
Mauring, Judith T., jt. ed. see Critchley, Deanne L.
Mauro, Phillip. God's Pilgrims.
Maurois, Andre, tr. see Hopkins, Gerard Manley.
Mauron, J., ed. Nutrition, Neurotransmitter Function & Behavior.
Maus, Francis L. Economics of Abundance: A Primer of Economic Law.
Maus, John A. Adolescents with Reading Disability-- A Search for Early Causes: Warning: Educational Theory May Be Dangerous to Your Child's Reading Development.
Mause, Lloyd de see De Mause, Lloyd, et al.
Mauser, Ferdinand F. Salesmanship: A Contemporary Approach.
--Selling: A Self-Management Approach.
Mauser, Ferdinand F. & Schwartz, David J. American Business: An Introduction.
--American Business: An Introduction.
Maushart, R., jt. auth. see Kiefer, H.
Mauskopf, Seymour. Crystals & Compounds: Molecular Structure & Composition in Nineteenth-Century French Science.
Mauss, Marcel. A General Theory of Magic.
Mauss, Marcel & Beuchat, Henri. Seasonal Variations of the Eskimo: A Study in Social Morphology. Fox, James J., tr. from Fr.
Mausteller, J. W. Alkali Metal Handling & Systems Operating Techniques.
Mautz, Robert K., et al. Internal Auditing: Directions & Opportunities. Holman, Richard, ed.
Mauvais-Jarvis, P., et al, eds. Percutaneous Absorption of Steroids.
Mauzey, Merritt. An Artist's Notebook: The Life & Art of Merritt Mauzey. Weaver, Gordon, ed.
Maver, Thomas N. Building Services Design: A Systemic Approach to Decision Making.
Maves, Paul B. A Place to Live in Later Years.
Mavor, J. M. O. S. T. Integrated-Circuit Engineering.
Mavor, William. New Description of Blenheim. Hunt, John D., ed.
Mavragis, Edward P., jt. auth. see Craz, Albert G.
Maw-Cheng Yang, jt. auth. see Thigpen, M. Elton.
Mawdesley-Thomas, Lionel E., ed. see Zoological Society of London Symposium Staff.
Maxey, Chester C. Bipartisanship in the United States.
Ma Xiaoqing, et al. Contemporary Chinese Photographs.
Maxim, John R. Abel-Baker-Charley.
Maximillian, Omar. Words, Conversation & Poetry: From the Musical, "Omar, Man of Fire"
Maximin, Jacques. The Cuisine of Jacques Maximin.
Maximovitch, John. The Orthodox Veneration of the Mother of God. Rose, Seraphim, tr.
Maxman, Jerrold S. A Good Night's Sleep: A Step-by-Step Program for Overcoming Insomnia & Other Sleep Problems.
Maxmen, Jerrold S. The New Psychiatry: How Modern Psychiatrists Think about Their Patients, Theories, Diagnoses, Drugs, Psychotherapies, Power, Training, Families & Private Lives.
Maxtone-Graham, Katrina. Pregnant by Mistake: The Stories of Seventeen Women.
--Pregnant by Mistake: The Stories of Seventeen Women.
Maxwell. Just Another Day in Paradise.
Maxwell, A. E. Basic Statistics for Medical & Social Science Students.
--The Frog & the Scorpion.
Maxwell, Baldwin. Studies in the Shakespeare Apocrypha.
Maxwell, J. R., jt. ed. see Douglas, A G.
Maxwell, John A., jt. auth. see Johnson, Wesley M.
Maxwell, L. E. Women in Ministry.
Maxwell, M. Shaping a Library: William L. Clements As Collector.
Maxwell, Morton H. & Kleeman, Charles R., eds. Clinical Disorders of Fluid & Electrolyte Metabolism.
Maxwell, Ruth. The Booze Battle.
Maxym, Lucy. Russian Lacquer, Legends & Fairy Tales.
--Russian Lacquer, Legends & Fairy Tales.
May, Alan Le see Le May, Alan.
May, Antoinette. Helen Hunt Jackson: A Lonely Voice of Conscience.
May, Arthur J. Hapsburg Monarchy: 1867-1914.
May, Brian. Russia, America, the Bomb & the Fall of Western Europe.
May, C. & Tanaka, Y., eds. Epoxy Resins: Chemistry & Technology.
May, Charles P. The Uprooted.
May, Dean, intro. by see Arrington, Leonard J. & Alexander, Thomas G.
May, Donald C., Jr., jt. auth. see Burington, Richard S.
May, Elizabeth E., et al. Independent Living for the Handicapped & the Elderly.
May, Ernest & Blaney, D. Careers for Humanists.
May, Ernest, jt. ed. see Feidel, Frank.
May, Gerald. Pilgrimage Home.
May, Howard K., ed. The Fifty Front Pages of the Rarest & Most Valuable Books on Wall Street & the Stock Market.
May, J. P. The Geometry of Iterated Loop Spaces.
May, Jill P. Films & Filmstrips for Language Arts: An Annotated Bibliography.
May, John, et al. Curious Facts.
May, John R., ed. The Bent World: Essays on Religion & Culture.
May, John R., ed. see Forbush, Edward H.
May, Judith V. & Wildavsky, Aaron B., eds. The Policy Cycle.
May, Julian. The Cincinnati Bengals.
--The Denver Broncos.
--The Golden Torc.
--The Kansas City Chiefs.
--Los Angeles Rams.
--Miami Dolphins.
--The Miami Dolphins.
--New York Giants.
--Oakland Raiders.
--The San Diego Chargers.
--San Francisco Forty Niners.
--The Student Chemist Explores Computations.
--Washington Redskins.
May, Lewis, tr. see De Pourtales, Guy.
May, Phillip T. Programming Business Applications in FORTRAN IV.
May, R. M., ed. Exploitation of Marine Communities.
May, Robert. Sex & Fantasy: Patterns of Male & Female Development.
May, Robert, et al. Perforating Veins.
May, Robert M., ed. Theoretical Ecology.
May, Robin. Indians.
--Who's Who in Shakespeare.
--The World of Ballet. Barish, Wendy, ed.
May, Rollo. The Courage to Create.
--Man's Search for Himself.
--The Meaning of Anxiety.
--Power & Innocence.
--Psychology & the Human Dilemma.
May, Rollo, et al, eds. Existence: A New Dimension in Psychiatry & Psychology.
May, Someth. Cambodian Witness: The Autobiography of Someth May.
May, Trevor. An Economic & Social History of Britain, 1760-1970.
Maybee, John S., jt. ed. see Harary, Frank.
Mayer. Adelasia Ed Aleramo & Exve.
Mayer, Andre & Wheeler, Michael. The Crocodile Man: A Case of Brain Chemistry & Criminal Violence.
Mayer, Anna. El Mundo de Santiago.
Mayer, Arthur, jt. auth. see Griffith, Richard.
Mayer, Bernadette, jt. auth. see Worsley, Dale.
Mayer, David, 3rd. Harlequin in His Element: The English Pantomime, 1806-1836.
Mayer, E. International Auction Records: Volume 22-1988.
Mayer, Edgar N. Structure of French.
Mayer, Edmund. Introduction to Dynamic Morphology.
Mayer, Foster L., Jr. & Ellersieck, Mark R. Manual of Acute Toxicity: Interpretation & Data Base for 410 Chemicals & 66 Species of Fresh Water Animals.
Mayer, G. Roy, jt. auth. see Sulzer-Azaroff, Beth.
Mayer, G. Roy, ed. see Sulzer-Azaroff, Beth.
Mayer, Gloria G., jt. auth. see McGlone, Mary E.
Mayer, Hans. Portrait of Wagner: An Illustrated Biography.
Mayer, Harold M. & Kohn, Clyde F., eds. Readings in Urban Geography.
Mayer, Herbert T. Pastoral Care: Its Roots & Renewal.
Mayer, John E., jt. auth. see Rosenthal, Bernard G.
Mayer, Joseph, Jr Escape to Freedom.
Mayer, Karel, tr. see Stanek, Jaroslav, et al.
Mayer, Lyle V. Fundamentals of Voice & Diction.
Mayer, M. E, jt. auth. see Drechsler, W.
Mayer, Marianna. Alley Oop!
Mayer, Martin. The Builders: Houses, People, Neighborhoods, Government, Money.
--Making News.
Mayer, Mercer. Bubble Bubble.
--Trouble in Tinktonk Land.
Mayer, Morris L., jt. auth. see Mason, J. Barry.
Mayer, N. Keys to the Growth of Neighborhood Development Organizations.
Mayer, Nancy K. Rainy Day Activities for the Atari.
Mayer, Paul. Vegetable Cookbook. Walsh, Jackie, ed.
Mayer, R. J. & Walker, J. H. Immunological Methods in the Biological Sciences: Enzymes & Proteins.
Mayer, Ric, jt. auth. see Harmon, Paul.
Mayer, Richard, jt. auth. see Tarpy, Roger.
Mayer, Robert H., jt. auth. see Stark, Robert M.
Mayer, Thomas, et al. Money, Banking & the Economy,
Mayers, Lewis. Shall We Amend the Fifth Amendment?
Mayers, Marlene, jt. auth. see Watson, Annita.
Mayers, Marvin K., jt. auth. see Grunlan, Stephen A.
Mayers, Ronald. Both-And: A Balanced Apologetic.
Mayers, William F. Chinese Reader's Manual.
Mayerson, Charlotte. Home Fires.
Mayes, Janet. Writing & Rewriting.
Mayfield, James L. Up with Marriage.
Mayhall, Carole. Lord, Teach Me Wisdom.
Mayhall, Jack. Discipleship: The Price & the Prize.
Mayhew, Harry E. & Rodgers, Leroy A., eds. Basic Procedures in Family Practice: An Illustrated Manual.
Mayhue, Richard. Divine Healing Today.
Mayleas, D. S. A Man of Property.
Maynard, Alan. Health Care in the European Community.
Maynard, Donald N., jt. auth. see Lorenz, Oscar A.
Maynard, Geoffrey & Van Ryckeghem, W. A World of Inflation.
Maynard, Harold B. Handbook of Modern Manufacturing Management.
Maynard, Joyce. Baby Love: Too Young for Love But Not for Making Babies.
Maynard, Leslie-Jane. When Your Child Is Overweight.
Maynard, Mary, jt. auth. see Brittan, Arthur.
Maynard, Richard. The Coconut Book.
Maynard, Russell. The Complete Guide to Fighting Folders.
Maynard, Temple, ed. see Jephson, Robert.
Mayne, A. J. Fever, Squalor & Vice: Sanitation & Social Policy in Victorian Sydney.
Mayne, Lynn. Fabric Games.
Mayne, R. W. & Ragsdell, K. M., eds. Progress in Engineering Optimization, 1981.
Mayne, Richard. The Europeans.
Mayne, William. Drift.
Mayo Clinic Staff. Clinical Examinations in Neurology.
Mayo, Edward J. & Jarvis, Lance P. The Psychology of Leisure Travel: Effective Marketing & Selling of Travel Services.
Mayo, Herbert B. Basic Finance: An Introduction to Money & Financial Management.
--Basic Investments.
--Finance.
--Investments: An Introduction.
Mayo, J. K. The Hunting Season.
Mayo, Margaret. A Taste of Paradise.
Mayo, Marjorie, jt. auth. see Jones, David.
Mayo, Marjorie, jt. auth. see Lees, Ray.
Mayo, Mary A. Parents' Guide to Sex Education.
Mayo, Patricia T. The Sugarless Baking Book: The Natural Way to Prepare America's Favorite Breads, Pies, Cakes, Puddings & Desserts.
Mayo, S. M. The Relevance of the Old Testament for the Christian Faith: Biblical Theology & Interpretive Methodology.
Mayoh, Brian H. Problem Solving with Ada.
Mayon, jt. auth. see Mandal.
Mayor, A. Hyatt. Rembrandt & the Bible.
Mayr, Ernst. Principles of Systematic Zoology.
Mayrhofer, Manfred. Sanskrit Grammar, with Comparative Indo-European Explanations. Ford, Gordon, Jr., tr. from Ger.
Mays, Benjamin. Negro's God As Reflected in His Literature.
Mays, Benjamin E. Lord, the People Have Driven Me On.
Mays, Buddy. Guide to Western Wildlife.
Mays, J. B., ed. see Hall, Penelope.
Mays, James L. Ezekiel, Second Isaiah. McCurley, Foster R., ed.
Mays, James L., ed. Interpreting the Gospels.
Mays, James L., jt. ed. see Westermann, Claus.
Mays, Laura. Genetics: A Molecular Approach.
Mays, Lucinda. The Candle & the Mirror.
--The Other Shore.
Mays, Pamela. Teaching Children Through the Environment.
Maz, Veronica. The Stick-Carrier.
Mazas, F. Seventy-Five Melodious & Progressive Studies for Violin. Saenger, G., ed.
Mazda, F. F. Components of Computers (1977)
Mazel, David. Arizona Trails.
Mazer, Norma F. Mrs. Fish, Ape, & Me, the Dump Queen.
Mazlack, L. J. PL-C Essentials.
Mazlish, Bruce. The Revolutionary Ascetic.
Mazmanian, Daniel A. & Nienaber, Jeanne. Can Organizations Change? Environmental Protection, Citizen Participation, & the Army Corps of Engineers.
Mazon, Mauricio. The Zoot-Suit Riots: The Psychology of Symbolic Annihilation.
Mazor, Emma S. Tears & Laughters in My Poetry.
Mazor, L. Analytical Chemistry of Organic Halogen Compounds.
Mazour, Anatole G. Writing of History in the Soviet Union.
Mazrui, Ali A. The Africans: A Triple Heritage.
Mazumdar, Dipak. The Issue of Small Versus Large in the Indian Textile Industry: An Analytical & Historical Survey.
Mazumder, J., jt. ed. see Mukherjee, Kali.
Mazzei, George. Moving Up: Digging In, Taking Charge, Playing the Power Game & Learning to Like It.
--The New Office Etiquette: A Guide to Getting along in the Corporate Age.
Mazzeo, Joseph A. Medieval Cultural Tradition in Dante's Comedy.
Mazzini, Giuseppe. Mazzini's Letters. Jervis, Alice, tr.
Mazzola, jt. auth. see Zabinski.
Mazzolani, Federico, jt. auth. see Ballio, Giulio.
Mazzolani, Lidia S. Empire Without End. McConnell, Joan & Pel, Mario, trs.
Mazzolini, R. Government Controlled Enterprises: International Strategic & Policy Decisions.
Mazzoni, Giacopo. On the Defense of the Comedy of Dante: Introduction & Summary. Montgomery, Robert L., tr. from Ital.
Mburu, F. M. Ocular Needs in Africa.
MC Publishing Company Staff. McCutcheon's Emulsifiers & Detergents North American & International: 1988. Allured, Michael, ed.
MCP Test & Research Bureau Staff, et al. DART: Test A-4.
--DART: Test B-1.
--DART: Test B-2.

--DART: Test B-3.
--DART: Test C-1.
--DART: Test C-2.
--DART: Test C-3.
Meacham, John A., ed. Action Theory.
--Family & Individual Development.
Meacham, John A. & Santilli, Nicolas R., eds. Social Development in Youth.
Mead, C. A. Symmetry & Chirality.
Mead, Carl D. Yankee Eloquence in the Middle West: The Ohio Lyceum, 1850-1870.
Mead, Charles W. Old Civilizations of Inca Land.
Mead, Chris. Champion: Joe Louis.
Mead, Christopher. Bird Migration.
Mead, D. Eugene. Six Approaches to Child Rearing: Models from Psychological Theory.
Mead, G. R. Fragments of a Faith Forgotten.
Mead, G. R. S., tr. see Trismegistos, Hermes.
Mead, George H. George Herbert Mead on Social Psychology. Strauss, Anselm, ed.
--Philosophy of the Present. Murphy, Arthur E., ed.
Mead, Jean. Wyoming in Profile.
Mead, Jude C. St. Paul of the Cross: A Source-Workbook in Paulacrucian Studies.
Mead, Lauren R. Foreword by see Witt, Twylla.
Mead, Leon & Newell, Gilbert F. Manual of Forensic Quotations.
Mead, Lucia A. Law or War?
Mead, Margaret. An Anthropologist at Work.
--Blackberry Winter.
Mead, Margaret & Bunzel, Ruth L., eds. The Golden Age of American Anthropology.
Mead, Margaret, ed. see U. S. President's Commission on the Status of Women.
Mead, Marjorie L., jt. ed. see Kilby, Clyde S.
Mead, Philip. This River Is in the South.
Mead, R. & Curnow, R. N. Statistical Methods in Agriculture & Experimental Biology.
Mead, Shepherd, jt. auth. see Williams, Dakin.
Mead, Sidney. The Old Religion in the Brave New World: Reflections on the Relation Between Christendom & the Republic.
Mead, William B., jt. auth. see Strassels, Paul N.
Meade, Chris. Careers with a Railroad.
Meade, Ellen, jt. auth. see Larson, Rodger.
Meade, Richard. Gaylord's Badge.
Meade, T. W., ed. Anticoagulants & Myocardial Infraction: A Reappraisal.
Meader, Robert E. Iranxe: Notas Gramaticais e Lista Vocabular.
Meader, Stephen W. Boy with a Pack.
--Buckboard Stranger.
--Cedar's Boy.
--Clear for Action.
--Keep 'em Rolling.
--Lumberjack.
--Muddy Road to Glory.
--Red Horse Hill.
--Sparkplug of the Hornets.
--Voyage of the Javelin.
--Whaler Round the Horn.
--Who Rides in the Dark?
Meador, Billie. Critical Care Nursing Review & Self-Test.
Meador, Billie C. The Critically Ill.
Meador, Roy. Guidlines for Preparing Proposals.
Meadow, Charles T. Sounds & Signals: How We Communicate.
Meadowbrook Reference Group. Economy Motel Guide. Delagran, Louise, ed.
Meadows, A. J. Early Solar Physics.
Meadows, Alicia. Opposites Attract.
Meadows, Cecil A. Discovering Oil Lamps.
Meadows, Jack. Space Garbage: Comets, Meteors & Other Solar-System Debris.
Meadows, Sara, ed. Developing Thinking: Approaches to Children's Cognitive Development.
Meagher, Robert E. Cave Notes: First Reflections on Sense & Spirit.
Meagher, Robert F. International Redistribution of Wealth & Power: A Study of the Charter of Economic Rights & Duties of States.
Meals, Robert W. Careers, Incorporated.
--Thou Shalt Not Kill.
Meaney, Neville. The Search for Security in the Pacific, 1901-14.
Means, Florence C. The Moved-Outers.
--Our Cup Is Broken.
--Reach for a Star.
--Shuttered Windows.
Means, Gardiner. Administrative Inflation & Public Policy.
Means, Gardiner C., jt. auth. see Berle, Adolf A.
Means, R. S., Company, Inc. Staff. Building Construction Cost Data, 1986. Mahoney, William, ed.
--Concrete & Masonry Cost Data, 1986. Thornely, Arthur, ed.
--Historical Cost Indexes, 1986. Entwistle, Dean, ed.
--Interior Cost Data, 1986. Smit, Kornelis, ed.
--Labor Rates for the Construction Industry, 1986. Mahoney, William, ed.
--Means Assemblies Cost Data, 1986. Horsley, William, ed.
--Means Electrical Cost Data, 1986. Mahoney, William, ed.
--Means Mechanical Cost Data, 1986. Mossman, Melville, ed.
--Means Site Work Cost Data Annual, 1986. Smit, Kornelis, ed.
--Means Square Foot Costs, 1986. Mahoney, William, ed.
--Open-Shop Building Construction Cost Data, 1986. Lehigh, Dwayne, ed.
--Repair & Remodeling Cost Data, 1986. Cleveland, Allan, ed.
--Residential - Light Commercial Cost Data, 1986. Lehigh, Dwayne, ed.
Means, Robin & Smith, Randall. The Development of Welfare Services for Elderly People.
Meara, David. Victorian Memorial Brasses.
Meares, Bernard, tr. see Mandelstam, Osip.
Mears, Frederick G. & Gatchel, Robert J. Fundamentals of Abnormal Psychology.
Mears, Peter. Introduction to Apple Keyboarding.
--Introduction to Apple Keyboarding.
--Introduction to the IBM Personal Computer: Keyboarding.
Measurement, Mapping, & Management in the Coastal Zone from Virginia to Maine Symposium Staff. Technical Papers of the Measurement, Mapping & Management in the Coastal Zone from Virginia to Maine Symposium, New York, 1979.
Mebust, J. Leland, jt. auth. see Achtemeier, Paul J.
Mech, Doris. Joy with Honey.
Mecham, Merlin J. & Willbrand, Mary L. Language Disorders in Children: A Resource Book for Speech-Language Pathologists.
Mechanic, David. Mental Health & Social Policy.
Mechlin, Stuart & Bonanno, Ellen. Without a Thorn: A Guide to Rose Gardening in the Pacific Northwest.
Meck, Stuart & Netter, Edith M., eds. A Planner's Guide to Land Use Law.
Meckler, Milton. Energy Conservation in Buildings & Industrial Plants.
Medawar. Major Histocompatibility System: The Gorer Symposium.
Medcalf, G. Marketing & the Brand Manager.
Medcof, John & Roth, John, eds. Approaches to Psychology.
Meddaugh, Susan. Too Short Fred.
--Too Short Fred.
Medearis, Mary. Big Doc's Girl.
Meder, Albert E., Jr., ed. see Buchanan, O. Lexton, Jr.
Medges, G. A. Der? Die? Das? The Gender of German.
Medgyessy, Pal. Decomposition of Superpositions of Density Functions & Discrete Distributions.
Medhurst, Kenneth M. Government in Spain: The Executive at Work.
Media Institute Staff. Economic Forecasts: Election Years & the Media.
Media Institute Staff & Brown, Timothy G. International Communications Glossary.
Media Institute Staff & Sussman, Leonard R. Glossary for International Communications.
Media Institute Staff, ed. see Corry, John.
Medical Branch of the University of Texas Staff. The University of Texas Medical Branch at Galveston: A Seventy-five Year History.
Medical Economics Company. Pediatricks.
Medical Economics Company Staff. Drug Identification Guide from PDR.
Medical Group Management Association Staff. The Superbill: Guide to a Uniform Billing & Claims System.
Medical Sciences Division Staff. Manganese.
Medina, H. R., jt. auth. see Association of the Bar of the City of New York Staff.
Medina Tellez, Gabriel. Arara: The Capital of the Ticuna Indians of the Colombian Amazon.
Medjati, Z. M. & Trice, J. E. English & Continental Systems of Adminstrative Law.
Medley, Frank, jt. auth. see Smith, Wm. Flint.
Medley, Margaret. Percival David Foundation of Chinese Art, London.
Medley, Richard, ed. The Politics of Inflation: A Comparative Analysis.
Medlicott, W. N. Contemporary England: 1914-1964.
Medlicott, W. N., ed. From Metternich to Hitler: Aspects of British & Foreign History, 1814-1939.
Medlicott, William N. Bismarck, Gladstone, & the Concert of Europe.
Mednick, M. S., et al, eds. Women & Achievement: Social & Motivational Analyses.
Medved, Michael. Hospital: The Hidden Lives of a Medical Center Staff.
Medvedev, F. & Kulikov, G. Human Rights & Freedoms in the U. S. S. R.
Medvedev, Roy A. An End to Silence: Uncensored Opinion in the Soviet Union from Roy Medvedev's Underground Magazine Political Diary. Cohen, Stephen F., ed.
Medvedkov, Yuri, ed. Amelioration of the Human Environment: IGU Congress, Moscow, 1976, Proceedings.
--Regional Systems: IGU Congress, Moscow, 1976, Proceedings.
--Urbanization: IGU Congress, Moscow, Proceedings.
Medvevdev, Roy A. Nikolai Bukharin: The Last Years. Briggs, A. D., tr.
Medway, William, et al. Textbook of Veterinary Clinical Pathology.
Mee, Arthur. Staffordshire.
Mee, Charles L., Jr. The Marshall Plan.
--The Ohio Gang: The World of Warren G. Harding.
Mee, Charles L., Jr; see Corrigan, Robert W.
Mee, Margaret. Flowers of the Amazon.
Meech, D. W. Learn That Language: Principles of Language Learning.
Meegan, Richard, jt. auth. see Massey, Doreen.
Meehan, Betty. Shell Bed to Shell Midden.
Meehan, Eugene J. Public Housing Policy.
Meehl, Paul E. Psychodiagnosis: Selected Papers.
Meek, Alexander B. Romantic Passages in South-Western History: Including Orations, Sketches, & Essays.
Meek, B. L., jt. auth. see Hill, I. D.
Meek, M. R. Hang the Consequences.
--In Remembrance of Rose: A Lennox Kemp Mystery.
--The Split Second: A Lennox Kemp Mystery.
Meek, Margaret, et al. The Cool Web: The Pattern of Children's Reading.
Meek, Martyn. Honda CD-CM 185, 200 & 250 Twins '77-'80.
--Honda CD-CM 185, 200 & 250 Twins '78-'80.
--Suzuki FZ50 Suzy '79 - '80.
Meek, Pauline P. God Speaks to Me.
Meek, Ronald L. Smith, Marx & After: Ten Essays in the Development of Economic Thought.
Meek, V. Lynn. The University of Papua New Guinea: A Case Study in the Sociology of Higher Education.
Meeker, Amy, ed. see Carillo, Charles.
Meeker, Margaret H., jt. auth. see Gruendemann, Barbara J.
Meeker, Richard H. Newspaperman: S. I. Newhouse & the Business of News.
Meekings, B. A., jt. auth. see Berry, R. E.
Meeks, John E. The Fragile Alliance: An Orientation to the Psychiatric Treatment of the Adolescent.
Meeks, Linda B., jt. auth. see Burt, John J.
Meeks, M. Douglas. Origins of the Theology of Hope.
Meeks, M. Douglas, tr. see Martin, Gerhard M.
Meeks, M. Douglas, tr. & intro. by see Moltmann, Jurgen.
Meeks, M. Douglas, tr. from Ger. see Moltmann, Jurgen.
Meeks, M. Douglas, tr. see Moltmann, Jurgen.
Meeks, M. L. Explorations in Space & Time: A Series of Computer-Generated Astronomy Films, Filmnotes.
Meer, Antonia Van der see Van der Meer, Antonia.
Meer, Charles Vander see Vander Meer, Charles.
Meer, Ron Van Der see Smith, Richard & Van Der Meer, Ron.
Meer, Ron van der see Van der Meer, Ron.
Meer Frederick Van, Der see Van Der Meer, Frederick.
Meeropol, Michael & Meeropol, Robert. We Are Your Sons: The Legacy of Ethel & Julius Rosenberg.
Meeropol, Robert, jt. auth. see Meeropol, Michael.
Meers, Gary, et al. Handbook of Special Vocational Needs Education.
Meese, J. M., ed. Neutron Transmutation Doping in Semiconductors.
Meesook, Oey Astra. Income, Consumption & Poverty in Thailand, 1962-63 to 1975-76.
Meeter, Merle. Country of the Risen King: Anthology of Christian Poetry.
Meetham, A. R. Atmospheric Pollution.
--Encycolpedia of Linguistics, Information & Control.
Meeting on Hemoperfusion, Kidney & Liver Supports & Detoxification Staff. Hemoperfusion: Kidney & Liver Support & Detoxification, Proceedings of the Meeting, Haifa, August 25-26, 1979. Sideman, Samuel & Chang, T. M., eds.
Meezan, William, et al. Adoptions Without Agencies: A Study of Independent Adoptions.
Meffen, John. A Guide to Tuning Musical Instruments.
Megahan, Darlene, jt. ed. see Millard, Patricia.
Megarry, Jacquetta, ed. Aspects of Simulation & Gaming: An Anthology of SAGSET Journal Volumes.
--Perspectives on Academic Gaming & Simulation: Human Factors in Games & Simulation.
Megaw, E. D. & Lloyd, E. J., eds. Human-Computer Interaction.
Megaw, H. David. Quick Reference Guide to the Tax Reform Act of 1986.
Megged, Aharon. Asahel: A Novel. Whitehill, Robert & Lilly, Susan C., trs. from Hebrew.
--The Short Life: A Novel. Arad, Miriam, tr. from Hebrew.
Meggers, William F., ed. see Ehrhardt, Roy.
Megginson, Leon C. Human Resources: Cases & Concepts.
--Personnel & Human Resources Administration.
Meggs, Brown. Aria.
--War Train.
Megill, Donald D. & Demory, Richard. Introduction to Jazz History.
Megill, R. E. An Introduction to Exploration Economics.
Megrah, Maurice, jt. auth. see Gutteridge, Harold C.
Megson, T. Aircraft Structures for Engineering Students.
--Strength of Materials for Civil Engineers.
Mehan, Hugh. Learning Lessons: Social Organization in the Classroom.
Mehan, Richard L., ed. see TMS Staff & AIME Staff.
Mehl, Dieter. The Elizabethan Dumb Show.
Mehl, Duane. At Peace with Failure.
--No More for the Road: One Man's Journey from Chemical Dependency to Freedom.
--You & the Alcoholic in Your Home.
Mehl, Roger. Catholic Ethics & Protestant Ethics.
Mehler, Alan H. Introduction to Enzymology.
Mehlman, Jeffrey, tr. see De Fontenay, Elisabeth.
Mehlman, Jeffrey, tr. see Laplanche, Jean.
Mehlman, Myron A. & Hanson, Richard W., eds. Control Processes in Neoplasia.
--Energy Metabolism & the Regulation of Metabolic Processes in Mitochondria.
Mehlman, Myron A., ed. see University of Nebraska Medical School Symposium Staff.
Mehlman, Stanley, jt. auth. see Brescia, Frank.
Mehmet, Ozay. Development in Malaysia: Poverty, Wealth & Trusteeship.
Mehnert, Klaus. Twilight of Young: The Radical Movements of the 1960's & Their Legacy.
Mehr, Robert I. Life Insurance: Theory & Practice.
Mehr, Robert I. & Hedges, Bob A. Risk Management: Concepts & Applications.
Mehr, Robert I., et al. Principles of Insurance.
Mehra, Raman K. & Lainiotis, Dmitri G., eds. System Identification: Advances & Case Studies.
Mehrabi, Jacqueline. Remember the Rainbow.
Mehrabian, Albert. Nonverbal Communication.
Mehren, Arthur T. Von see Von Mehren, Arthur T.
Mehrens, William A., jt. auth. see Lehmann, Irvin J.
Mehring, M. High Resolution NMR in Solids.
Mehrotra, S. R. The Commonwealth & the Nation.
Mehta, A. Perception of Asian Personality.
Mehta, Balraj. India's Political Economy.
Mehta, Dina. The Other Woman & Other Stories.
Mehta, J. L., tr. see Biemel, Walter.
Mehta, Jeroo. One Hundred & One Parsi Recipes.
Mehta, Mark. Intractable Pain.
Mehta, Rama. Inside the Haveli.
--Inside the Haveli.
Mehta, Vinod. Soviet Economic Policy: Income Differentials in the U. S. S. R.
Meichenbaum, Donald. Cognitive Behavior Modification: An Integrative Approach.
Meid, Louise B. Van Der see Van Der Meid, Louise B.
Meiden, Walter, jt. auth. see Carlut, Charles.
Meidl, James H. Hazardous Materials Handbook.
Mei'E, Ren, et al, eds. An Outline of China's Physical Geography. Tingquan, Zhang & Genkang, Hu, trs. from Chinese.
Meier & Brudney. Applied Statistics & Analytic Techniques for Public Administrators.
Meier, August & Rudwick, Elliott M., eds. Making of Black America.
Meier, G., et al. Applications of Liquid Crystals.
Meier, H. Organic Semiconductors: Dark & Photoconductivity of Organic Solids.
Meier, Hans W. Construction Specifications Handbook.
Meier, John P. The Vision of Matthew: Christ, Church & Morality in the First Gospel.
Meier, Kenneth J. Predicting Oklahoma Elections: An Inexpensive & Accurate Method.
Meier, Marie. The Development & Evaluation of A Pre-School Curriculum For Severely Disabled Children.
Meier, Paul, jt. auth. see Korem, Danny.
Meigs, Walter B., et al. Principles of Auditing.
--Modern Advanced Accounting.
Meijer, J. G. Librarianship: A Definition.
Meijers, J. J. Problem-Solving Therapy with Socially Anxious Children.
Meiklejohn Civil Liberties Institute Staff & Ginger, Ann F. The Pentagon Papers Case Collection: Annotated Procedural Guide & Index.
Meilach, Dona Z. & Mandel, Elias. Doctor Talks to Five to Eight Year Olds.
Meilach, Dona Z. & Seiden, Donald. Direct Metal Sculpture: Creative Techniques & Appreciation.
Meilach, Dona Z., jt. auth. see Birch, William G.

Authors

Meilaender, Gilbert C. Friendship: A Study in Theological Ethics.
Meilakh, M., ed. see Vvedenskii, Aleksandr.
Mein & Harcourt. Diagnosis & Management of Ocular Motility Disorders.
Meinecke, Friedrich. Historism: The Rise of a New Historical Outlook.
Meiners, Roger E. & Ringleb, Al H. The Legal Environment of Business.
Meinig, Donald W. The Great Columbia Plain: A Historical Geography, 1805-1910.
Meininger, Anne-Marie, jt. auth. see De Balzac, Honore.
Meir, Menahem. My Mother Golda Meir: A Son's Evocation of Life with Golda Meir.
Meirill Library Staff. Name Index to the Library of Congress Collection of Mormon Diaries.
Meiring, Desmond. The Girl with the Golden Lion.
Meir van Praag, Herman, jt. auth. see Mendlewicz, Julien.
Meisel, Irwin B. Saturday Always Comes: The Relaxed Way to Sales Success.
Meisel, Tony. Nautical Emergencies: Seamanship for the Unexpected.
Meiseles, Meir. Judaism, Thought & Legend. Schonfeld-Brand, Rebecca & Newman, Aryeh, trs. from Hebrew.
Meisels, Samuel J. Developmental Screening in Early Childhood: A Guide.
Meisenholder, Robert, jt. auth. see Broun, Kenneth S.
Meisler, Richard. Trying Freedom: The Case for Liberating Education.
Meislin, Jack. Rehabilitation Medicine & Psychiatry.
Meisner, Arnold & Russell, Lee. Modern American Soldier.
Meisner, Maurice. Li Ta-Chao & the Origins of Chinese Marxism.
Meiss, Harriet & Jaeger, Doris, eds. Information to Authors: Editorial Guidelines Reprinted from 246 Medical Journals.
Meissl, H., jt. ed. see Zrenner, E.
Meissner, Gunter, jt. auth. see Buttner, Horst.
Meister, Alton. Advances in Enzymology & Related Areas of Molecular Biology.
Meister, Alton, ed. Advances in Enzymology & Related Areas of Molecular Biology.
Meister, Barbara. An Introduction to the Art Song.
Meister, Charles W. The Year of the Lord: A. D. 1844.
Meister, Peter W. & Reber, Hort. European Porcelain of the 18th Century.
Meister, Robert. Hypochondria: Toward a Better Understanding.
Meites, J., jt. ed. see Martini, L.
Meites, Louis & Zuman, Petr. Electrochemical Data.
Meites, S. see Reiner, Miriam, et al.
Mejetta, Mirko & Spada, Simonetta. Creating Interiors for Unusual Spaces.
Melahn, Martha. Wave of Destiny.
Melanchthon, Philip. Melanchthon on Christian Doctrine: Loci Communes 1555. Manschreck, Clyde L., ed. & tr.
Meland, Bernard E. Fallible Forms & Symbols: Discourses on Method in a Theology of Culture.
Meland, Sam. Electrical Project Management.
Melaniphy, John C., Jr. Commercial & Industrial Condominiums.
Melbourne House Publishers Staff. Programs for Your Timex-Sinclair 1000.
Melcher, Arlyn J., ed. General Systems & Organization: Methodological Aspects.
Melcher, James R. Field-Coupled Surface Waves: A Comparative Study of Surface-Coupled EHD & MHD Systems.
Melchers, F. & Potter, M., eds. Lymphocyte Hybridomas: Second Workshop on "Functional Properties of Tumors of T & B Lymphocytes" Sponsored by the National Cancer Institute (NIH) April 3-5, 1978, Bethesda, MD.
Melchers, F., ed. see Workshop for Biological Chemistry Staff.
Melchior, H., jt. ed. see Lutzeyer, W.
Melchiori, Barbara A. Terrorism in the Late Victorian Novel.
Meldal-Johnsen, Trevor. Always.
--This Cruel Beauty.
Melden, A. I., ed. Human Rights.
Melden, A. I., ed. see Murphy, Arthur E.
Meldman, Monte J., et al. Occupational Therapy Manual.
Meldon, Jerry H., jt. ed. see Garby, Lars.
Meldrum, Brian S., jt. ed. see Pedley, Timothy A.
Melendy, H. Brett. Asians in America.
Melese-D'Hospital, G., jt. auth. see Howe, J. P.
Melges, Buddy & Mason, Charles. Sailing Smart: Winning Techniques, Tactics & Strategies.
Melhotra, H. L. Design of Fire Resisting Structures.
Melia, Kath M., jt. auth. see Thompson, Ian E.
Melicher, Ronald W., jt. auth. see Johnson, Robert W.
Melick, Arden D. Wives of the Presidents. Dupuy, Ernest, ed.
--Wives of the Presidents. Dupuy, Ernest, ed.
Melin, John S. Libraries & Data Processing--Where Do We Stand?
Melin, Nancy Jean, ed. Publisher's Catalogs Annual, 1983-84.
Melin, Per, et al. Oxytocin: Current Research.
Melinkoff, Ellen. L.A. Picnincs: The Complete Guide to Picnic Sites & Styles in & Around Los Angeles.
Mell, George. Writing Antiques.
Mellan, Eleanor, jt. auth. see Mellan, Ibert.
Mellan, Ibert & Mellan, Eleanor. Dictionary of Poisions.
Mellars, Paul, ed. The Early Postglacial Settlement of Northern Europe: An Ecological Perspective.
Melle, Gerte & Redies, Rainer. The Cat's Party.
Mellen, Rachael. A Practical Guide for the Genealogist in English.
Meller, Walter C. Old Times.
Meller, Winfrid H. Music & Society: England & the European Tradition.
Mellers, Wilfred H. The Sonata Principle.
Mellers, Wilfrid. The Twilight of the Gods: The Music of the Beatles.
Mellersh, H. E. From Ape Man to Homer.
Mellersh, N. Discoverers of the Universe.
Mellett, Peter, ed. Learning & Psychosomatic Approach to the Nature & Treatment of Illness: 18th Annual Conference of the Society for Psychosomatic Research.
Mellichamp, Josephine. Senators from Georgia.
Mellin, Jeanne. The Morgan Horse Handbook.
Mellini, Peter. Sir Eldon Gorst: The Overshadowed Proconsul.
Mellinkoff, David. Lawyers & the System of Justice.
--Legal Writing: Sense & Nonsense.
Mellish, C. S., jt. auth. see Clocksin, W. F.
Mello, A. DeSilva. Man.
Mello, J. M., jt. auth. see Hastings, N. A.
Mellon, James. African Hunter.
Mellon, W. Giles, jt. auth. see Bernstein, Samuel J.
Mellor, Hugh W. The Role of Voluntary Organizations in Social Welfare.
Mellor, J. W. & Parkes, G. D. A Comprehensive Treatise on Inorganic & Theoretical Chemistry. Incl. Vol. 1; Vol. 3; Vol. 4; Vol. 5; Vol. 6; Vol. 7; Vol. 8; Vol. 10; Vol. 11. A Comprehensive Treatise on Inorganic & Theoretical Chemistry. Mellor, Joseph W; Vol. 12; Vol. 13; Vol. 14; Vol. 15; Vol. 16. Halsted Pr.
Mellor, John. The Motor Cruising Manual.
Mellor, Joseph W; see Mellor, J. W. & Parkes, G. D.
Mellor, Stuart, jt. auth. see Read, Michael D.
Mellors, Colin & Pijnenburg, Bert, eds. Local Coalitions in Europe.
Mellot, Leland, jt. auth. see Lobos, Amilcar.
Mellow, James R. Charmed Circle: Gertrude Stein & Company.
--Invented Lives: The Marriage of F. Scott & Zelda Fitzgerald.
--Nathaniel Hawthorne & His Times.
--Nathaniel Hawthorne in His Times.
Mellspaugh, Ben P. The Private Pilot's License Program.
Melluzzo, Paul J. & Nealon, Eleanor. Living with Surgery: Before & After.
--Living with Surgery, Before & After.
Melman, Seymour. The Permanent War Economy.
Melnick, J. L., ed. see Cheville, N. F.
Melnick, Michael, ed. Clinical Dysmorphology of Oral-Facial Structures. Shields, Edward D. & Burzynski, Norbert J.
Melnick, V. L., jt. ed. see Fudenberg, H. H.
Mel'nik, B. D. & Mel'nikov, F. B. Technology of Inorganic Compounds: Chemical Engineers' Handbook.
Mel'nikov, F. B., jt. auth. see Mel'nik, B. D.
Melnitz, W., jt. auth. see MacGowen, Kenneth.
Melnyk, Myron. Principles of Applied Statistics.
Melnyk, P. L., et al. Meiosis: Current Research.
Melo, J. de see Corbo, V. & De Melo, J.
Melograno, Vincent J. & Klinzing, James E. An Orientation to Total Fitness.
Melsa, J., jt. auth. see Schultz, Donald.
Melsa, James L. & Cohn, Davis L. Decision & Estimation Theory.
Melson. Transition Metal Chemistry.
Melton, Emily, jt. ed. see Jones, RuthAnn.
Melton, J. Gordon, ed. Encyclopedia of American Religions.
--Encyclopedia of American Religions: Supplement.
Melton, James G. & Geisendorfer, James V. A Directory of Religious Bodies in the United States.
Meltzer, Alan. The ABC's of S.T.D. A Guide to Sexually Transmitted Diseases.
Meltzer, Alan S. Sexually Transmitted Disease: Guidelines for Physicians & Health Workers.
Meltzer, Allan & Reynolds, Alan. Towards a Stable Monetary Policy: Monetarism vs. the Gold Standard.
Meltzer, David, ed. Birth: An Anthology of Ancient Texts, Songs, Prayers & Stories.
Meltzer, H. & Stagner, Ross, eds. Industrial-Organizational Psychology: 1980 Overview.
Meltzer, Ida. Fiorello LaGuardia.
Meltzer, Ida S. Frederick Douglass, Great Abolitionist. Thomas, Nestina, ed.
--Montgomery Bus Story. Thomas, Nestina, ed.
Meltzer, Milton. The Human Rights Book.
--The Right to Remain Silent.
Meltzer, Milton & Harding, Walter A. A Thoreau Profile.
Meltzer, Milton, ed. see Thoreau, Henry David.
Melvill, Harry, tr. see Bakst, Leon.
Melville, Annabelle M. Elizabeth Bayley Seton.
Melville, Cuthbert. The Rolling Files: A Study of the Bible.
Melville, Dorothy Sutherland. Tyler-Browns of Brattleboro.
Melville, Herman. Billy Budd & Typee.
--Billy Budd, Sailor, & Other Stories. Beaver, Harold, ed. Incl. Bartlby; Cock-a-Doodle-Doo; Encantada; Bell Tower; Benito Cereno; John Marr; Daniel Orme. Penguin.
--Journal up the Straits: Oct. 11, 1856-May 5, 1857. Weaver, Raymond, ed.
--Moby Dick, or the Whale. Hayford, Harrison & Parker, Hershel, eds.
Melville, Joy. Ellen & Edy: A Biography of Ellen Terry & Her Daughter, Edith Craig, 1847-1947.
Melville, K. E. Stay Alive in the Desert.
Melville, Lewis & Hargreaves, Reginald. Famous Duels & Assassinations.
Melvin, Lawrence S., Jr., jt. auth. see Trost, Barry M.
Melwood, Mary. Nettlewood.
--The Watcher Bee.
Melzack, Ronald, jt. ed. see Wall, Patrick D.
Memering, W. Dean, jt. auth. see Howell, James F.
Memmi, Albert. Dependence. Facey, Philip A., tr. from Fr.
Mena, Flavio & Valverde, Carlos M., eds. Prolactin Secretion: A Multidisciplinary Approach.
Mena, Janet Gonzalez see Gonzalez-Mena, Janet & Eyer, Dianne W.
Menaker, Michael, ed. Extraretinal Photoreception in Circadian Rhythms & Related Phenoma: Proceedings of a Symposium, Vancouver.
Menard, Russell R. Economy & Society in Early Colonial Maryland. Bruchey, Stuart, ed.
Mencher, A. G., ed. Management & Technology: An Anglo-American Exchange of Views.
Mencher, Samuel. Private Practice in Britain.
Mencke, Claire, ed. Solar Energy Update: A Select Guide to Federal & State Government Agencies, Trade & Professional Associations Information Systems, Centers & Publications.
Mencke, Claire & Horton, Craig, eds. Energy Information Locator: A Select Guide to Information Centers, Systems, Data Bases; Abstracing Services, Directories, Newsletters, Binder Services, & Journals.
Mencken, H. L. Mencken Chrestomathy.
--The Philosophy of Friedrich Nietzsche.
Menczel, jt. auth. see European Symposium on Calcified Tissues Staff.
Menczel, J., et al, eds. Osteoporosis: Proceedings of an International Symposium Held at the Jerusalem Osteoporosis Center in June, 1981.
Mendax, F. Art Fakes & Forgeries. Whitman, H. S., tr.
Mendel, Douglas H. Japanese People & Foreign Policy: A Study of Public Opinion in Post-Treaty Japan.
Mendel, F., jt. ed. see Herman, V.
Mendels, Ora. Mandela's Children.
Mendelsohn, Lotte, jt. auth. see Lazzaro, Bea.
Mendelsohn, M. The Guide to Franchising.
Mendelsohn, M. L., jt. ed. see Eisert, W. G.
Mendelsohn, M. Stefan. Money on the Move: The Modern International Capital Market.
Mendelsohn, Robert S. How to Raise a Healthy Child: In Spite of Your Doctor.
Mendelson & Whitehouse. Self-Assessment in Radiology.
Mendelson, Bert. A First Course in Programming with Pascal.
Mendelson, J., jt. ed. see Weijnen, J. A.
Mendelssohn, K. The World of Walther Nernst: The Rise & Fall of German Science, 1864-1941.
Menden, Fred R. Von der see Bender, Stephen O., et al.
Mendenhall, William. Introduction to Linear Models & the Design & Analysis of Experiments.
Mendenhall, William & McClave, James T. Statistics for Psychology.
Mendenhall, William & Ott, Lyman. Understanding Statistics.
Mendenhall, William & Reinmuth, James. Statistics for Management & Economics.
Mendenhall, William & Reinmuth, James E. Statistics for Management & Economics.
Mendenhall, William & Scheaffer, Richard L. Mathematical Statistics with Applications.
Mendenhall, William, jt. auth. see Beaver, Robert J.
Mendenhall, William, et al. Elementary Survey Sampling.
Mendenhall, Wm., jt. auth. see Scheaffer, R. L.
Mendershausen, Horst. Two Postwar Recoveries of the German Economy.
Mendes France, Pierre. Face to Face with Asia. Danon, Susan, tr.
Mendez, ed. Diccionario Tecnico de la Industria del Petroleo y Derivados.
Mendiones, Ruchira C., jt. auth. see Jones, Robert B.
Mendl. Divine Quest in Music.
Mendlewicz, Julien & Meir van Praag, Herman. Biological Rhythms & Behavior.
Mendoskin, Joseph & Mendoskin, Margaret. The Adventures of John-John the Mouse That Turned into a Puppy.
Mendoskin, Margaret, jt. auth. see Mendoskin, Joseph.
Mendoza, Luis E., tr. see Richardson, P. N.
Mendoza, Luis E., tr. see Weir, C. I.
Menendez, Albert J. Church-State Relations: An Annotated Bibliography.
--Religion at the Polls.
Menendez Pidal, Ramon. Spaniards in Their History. Starkie, Walter, tr.
Mengarini, Gregory. Recollections of the Flathead Mission. Lothrop, Gloria, ed.
Menges, Constantine C. Spain: The Struggle for Democracy Today.
Menn, Julius J., ed. see Chemistry & Action of Insect Juvenile Hormones Symposium Staff.
Mennel, Robert M. Thorns & Thistles: Juvenile Delinquents in the United States, 1825-1940.
Mennell, John M., jt. auth. see Zohn, David A.
Mennell, Robert L. Community Property in a Nutshell.
Mennell, S. Sociological Theory.
Menninger Foundation, Topeka, Kansas Staff. Catalog of the Menninger Clinic Library.
Menninger, Jeanetta L., jt. auth. see Menninger, Karl A.
Menninger, Karl A. Man Against Himself.
Menninger, Karl A. & Menninger, Jeanetta L. Love Against Hate.
Menolascino, Frank J. Challenges in Mental Retardation: Progressive Ideology & Services.
Menovschchikov, G. Singing Rabbit.
Mensah, Joseph A. Ghana: History & Traditional Customs of a Proud People.
Mensch, Gerhard O. & Niehaus, Richard J., eds. Work, Organizations, & Technological Change.
Mensendiek, Mark. Grace to You.
Menshikov, S. The Economic Cycle: Postwar Developments.
--Millionaires & Managers.
Mensing, Steve. Gold in the Black Hills.
Mente, Boye De see Fournier, Mark E.
Mentemeier, Samuel H., ed. see Labo, James A.
Menten, Ted. The Teddy Bear Lovers Catalog: A Treasury of Bearfaced Pleasure.
Menten, Theodore. Art Nouveau Decorative Ironwork: 137 Photographs.
Menter, Ian. The Kids Next Door.
Mentzer, Frank & Ward, James M., eds. Game Buyer's Guide.
Menuhin, Yehudi. The Compleat Violinist.
--Violin: Six Lessons with Yehudi Menuhin.
Menuhin, Yehudi, et al. The King, the Cat & the Fiddle.
Menut, Albert D. Maistre Nicole Oresme: Le Livre de Politiques D'Aristote.
--Maistre Nicole Oresme: Le Livre De Yconomique D'Aristote.
Menzel, R., jt. ed. see Snyder, A. W.
Menzies, Elizabeth G. Passage Between Rivers: A Portfolio of Photographs with a History of the Delaware & Raritan Canal.
Menzies, Ken. Sociological Theory in Use.
Menzies, Robert G. Central Power in the Australian Commonwealth: An Examination of the Growth of Commonwealth Power in the Australian Federation.
Mepham, John, ed. see Bettelheim, Charles.
Mer, Victor K. La see La Mer, Victor K.
Mera, H. P. Spanish-American Blanketry: Its Relationship to Aboriginal Weaving in the Southwest.
Meranus, Leonard S., jt. ed. see Polking, Kirk.
Meras, Phyllis. Miniatures: How to Make Them, Use Them & Sell Them.
--Vacation Crafts.
--A Yankee Way with Wood.
Meras, Phyllis & Tenenbaum, Frances. Cārry-Out Cuisine.
Meras, Phyllis & Turkevich, Julianna. Christmas Angels.
Mercado, A., tr. see Strogonov, B. P., et al.
Mercado, Maria A. De see Twitchell, Paul.
Mercer, David. Bankrupt & Other Plays.
--Huggy Bear & Other Plays: Huggy Bear, The Arcata Promise, A Superstition.
Mercer, James L. & Philips, Ronald J., eds. Public Technology: Key to Improved Government Productivity.
Mercer, James L., et al. Managing Urban Government Services: Strategies, Tools, & Techniques for the Eighties.
Mercer, John. The Canary Islanders: Their Prehistory, Conquest & Survival.

Authors

Mercer, Michael W. How Winners Do It: High Impact People Skills for Your Career Success.
Mercer, Peggy. Strangers in Eden.
Mercer, Richard, jt. auth. see Hungerford, Thomas W.
Mercer, Susan O., jt. ed. see Garner, J. Dianne.
Merchant, Kenneth A. Fraudulent Financial Reporting: A Corporate Perspective.
Merchant, Moelwyn. Comedy.
Merchant, Paul. Epic.
Merchant, Ronald. Basic Business Math & Electronic Calculators.
Mercier, C. & Luc, H., eds. Lectures in Plasma Physics: The Magnetohydrodynamic Approach to the Problem of Plasma Confinement in Closed Magnetic Configurations.
Mercier, J., ed. Anticonvulsant Drugs.
Mercier, Jean. Lexique Anglais-Francais des Appareils de Mesures Electriques.
Mercier, M., ed. Criteria (Dose Effect Relationships) for Organichlorine Pesticides: Report of a Working Group of Experts Prepared for the Commission of the European Communities.
Mere, Shirley La see LaMere, Shirley.
Mereaud, Paul, jt. auth. see Jacquemont, Guy.
Meredith & Turban. Essentials of Management Science.
Meredith, jt. auth. see Turban.
Meredith, Arthur, jt. auth. see Meredith, Roy.
Meredith, Char, jt. auth. see Oraker, James.
Meredith, Christabel, tr. see Philippovich Von Philippsberg, Eugen.
Meredith, D. R. Sheriff & the Panhandle Murders.
Meredith, George. Diana of the Crossways.
Meredith, George & Sutro, Alfred. The Egoist: A Play from the Novel by George Meredith. Sawin, Lewis, ed.
Meredith, Jack, jt. auth. see Turban, Efraim.
Meredith, John. Learn to Talk Old Jack Lang: A Handbook of Australian Rhyming Slang.
Meredith, Lucy, selected by see Uttley, Alison.
Meredith, P. Instruments of Communication.
Meredith, Peter, ed. The Mary Play: From the N. Town Manuscript.
Meredith, Philip & Thomas, Lyn, eds. Planned Parenthood in Europe: A Human Rights Perspective.
Meredith, Robert, jt. auth. see Smith, E. Brooks.
Meredith, Roy. Matthew Brady's Portrait of an Era.
--Mr. Lincoln's Camera Man: Matthew B. Brady.
Meredith, Roy & Meredith, Arthur. Mr. Lincoln's Military Railroads: A Pictorial History of the United States Civil War Railroads.
Meredith, W. & Massey, J. Fundamental Physics of Radiology.
Merenstein & Gardner. Handbook of Neonatal Intensive Care.
Merhav, M. Technological Dependence, Monopoly & Growth.
Meriam, James L. Engineering Mechanics, SI Version: Dynamics.
Merian, Maria S. Leningrad Watercolors.
Merickel, Mark. Stepping into CAD Professional Edition.
Merigan, Thomas C. & Friedman, Robert M., eds. Interferons: Symposium.
Merin, S., ed. see Jerusalem Conference on Impaired Vison in Childhood Staff.
Merino, Barbara D., jt. auth. see Previts, Gary J.
Merinoff, Linda. The Glorious Noodle: A Culinary Tour Around the World.
Meriwether, Crystal K. & Sippel, Curtis L. The Record Keeper: The Workbook That Helps You Organize Your Life.
Merk, Frederick. Oregon Question: Essays in Anglo-American Diplomacy & Politics.
Merkel, James A. Basic Engineering Principles.
--Managing Livestock Wastes.
Merkel, Jayne & Rudd, William J. Drawn by Cincinnati: Architectural Drawings in the Collection of the Cincinnati Historical Society.
Merken, Mel. Physical Science, with Modern Applications.
Merker, Hans J., jt. ed. see Neubert, Diether.
Merker, M. Die Masai: Ethnographische Monographie Eines Ostafrikanischen Semitenvolkes.
Merkin, Leon. Human Behavior in Daily Life.
Merkin, Lisa & Frankel, Eric. Trivial Conquest: The Smart Reference Source for Trivial Pursuit.
Merkin, Victor. Petroleum Conservation in Eastern Europe. Tamberg, Andreas, ed.
Merkl, Peter H. The Making of a Stormtrooper.
--Modern Comparative Politics.
--The Origin of the West German Republic.
Merkx, Gilbert W., jt. ed. see Remmer, Karen L.
Merla, G., et al. Geological Map of Ethiopia & Somalia.
Merle, Robert. The Virility Factor.
Merle-Fishman, Carole, jt. auth. see Katsh, Shelley.
Merlen, R. H. De Canibus: Dog & Hound in Antiquity.
Merlin, Jan. Brocade.
Merlini the Great. How to Entertain Children with Magic You Can Do.
Merlonghi, Ferdinando, et al. Oggi in Italia: A First Course in Italian.
Merlonghi, Ferninando, et al. Oggi in Italia: A First Course in Italian.
Merlonghi, Franca, jt. auth. see Valencia, Pablo.
Mermaid, Vanessa. Little Simon One Two Three.
Mermin, N. David. Space & Time in Special Relativity.
Meroff, Deborah. Captain, My Captain.
Merono, F. En el Cielo De Espana.
Merrell, David J. An Introduction to Genetics.
Merrell, Lloyd F. Flowering Dust.
Merrett, C. E. A Selected Bibliography of Natal Maps.
Merrett, Christopher E. Map Classification: A Comparison of Schemes, with Special Reference to the Continent of Africa.
Merrett, Frank, jt. ed. see Whendall, Kevin.
Merrett, Stephen & Gray, Fred. Owner Occupation in Britain.
Merriam, D. Random Processes in Geology.
Merriam, D. F., ed. Capture, Management & Display of Geological Data: With Special Emphasis on Energy & Mineral Resources.
--Computer Applications in the Earth Sciences: An International Symposium.
--Computer Applications in the Earth Sciences: An Update of the Seventies.
--Computer Assisted Instruction in Geology: Proceedings of the 4th Geochautauqua, Syracuse University, 1975.
--Computer Software for the Geosciences: Proceedings of the Geochautauqua, 5th, 1976.
--Management, Analysis & Display of Geoscience Data: Proceedings of the First Annual Conference, Golden, CO, January 27-29, 1982.
--Quantitative Stratigraphic Correlation: Proceedings of the 6th Geochautauqua, Syracuse University, October 1977.
--Quantitative Techniques for the Analysis of Sediments.
Merriam, Daniel F., jt. auth. see Gill, Dan.
Merriam, Eve. The Double Bed.
--It Doesn't Always Have to Rhyme.
--There Is No Rhyme for Silver.
--A Word or Two with You.
Merriam, Eve, jt. ed. see Larrick, Nancy.
Merriam, Lawrence C., Jr., jt. auth. see Brockman, C. Frank.
Merriam, Sharon, ed. Linking Philosophy & Practice.
Merrick, Gordon. Forth into Light.
--The Great Urge Downward.
--An Idol for Others.
--The Lord Won't Mind.
--Now Let's Talk About Music.
--One for the Gods.
--Perfect Freedom.
--The Quirk.
Merrick, James, tr. see Al-Majilisi, Muhammad B.
Merrick, Kathryn W., jt. auth. see Feder, Jack.
Merrifield, D. Bruce. Strategic Analysis, Selection, & Management of R & D Projects.
Merrigan, Joseph A. Sunlight to Electricity: Prospects for Solar Energy Conversion by Photovoltaics.
Merril, Judith, ed. Annual of the Year's Best Science Fiction, 6th.
Merrill, Boynton, Jr. Jefferson's Nephews: A Frontier Tragedy.
Merrill, Fredric R. Merrill's Oregon Rules of Civil Procedure: 1988 Handbook.
Merrill, Gary F. & Weiss, Harvey R., eds. CA 2t Entry Blockers, Adenosine, & Neurohumors.
Merrill, Grayson. Managing a Defense Company: For Growth & Profit.
Merrill, James. Mirabell: Books of Number.
Merrill, Jean. Maria's House.
Merrill, John J. Study Guide for General Physics.
Merrill, John R. Using Computers in Physics.
Merrill, R. B. Proceedings of the Sixth Lunar Science Conference.
Merrill, Robert, et al. New Rochelle: Portrait of a City.
Merrill, Susan. Washday.
Merrill, Vic. Can You Hear Me God?
Merrill, William K. The Survival Handbook.
Merriman, Paul A., et al. Market Timing with No-Load Mutual Funds.
Merrins, Eddie & McTeigue, Michael. Golf for the Young.
Merris, Mary, jt. auth. see Tobias, Doris.
Merrit Company Staff, ed. see Vaughn, Emmett.
Merritt, Abraham. The Fox Woman & Other Stories.
--The Metal Monster.
--Seven Footprints to Satan.
--The Ship of Ishtar.
Merritt, Abraham & Bok, Hannes. The Black Wheel.
Merritt Company Staff, ed. Georgia Life & Accident & Sickness Insurance.
--Texas Life & Health Insurance.
Merritt Company Staff, ed. see Lenz, Matthew.
Merritt, D. H., ed. Infant Nutrition.
Merritt, Frank S. Listen Metaphysics.
Merritt, Frederick S., ed. Structural Steel Designer's Handbook.
Merritt, George. Truth for Today.
Merritt, John. Refrigeration on Fishing Vessels.
Merritt, Robert A. Appomattox & Other Poems.
Merritt, Robert E., jt. auth. see Curtin, Daniel J.
Merrium. Boys & Girls, Girls & Boys.
Mersand, Joseph & Griffith, Francis. Spelling Your Way to Success.
Mersenne, Marin. Harmonie Universelle: The Books on Instruments.
Merser, Cheryl. Honorable Intentions: The Manners of Courtship in the Eighties.
--Honorable Intentions: The Manners of Courtship in the 80's.
Mersky, Peter & Polmar, Norman. The Naval Air War in Vietnam.
--The Naval Air War in Vietnam.
Mersky, Roy M. & Kronick, D. A Manual on Medical Literature for Law Librarians: A Handbook & Annotated Bibliography.
Mersky, Roy M. & Jacobstein, J. Myron, eds. Ten Year Index to Periodical Articles Related to Law (1959-1968)
Mersky, Roy M., et al, eds. Index to Periodical Articles Related to Law, Five Year Cumulation, 1969-73.
Merson, A. Communist Resistance in Nazi Germany.
Merte, H. J., ed. Metipranolol: Pharmacology of Beta-blocking Agents & Use of Metipranolol in Opthalmology, Contributions to the First Metipranolol Symposium, Berlin 1983.
Mertens, Joan R., jt. auth. see Von Bothmer, Dietrich.
Mertens, Thomas & Robinson, Sandra K., eds. Human Genetics & Social Problems.
Mertens, Thomas R. & Cooper, Sandra F. Probability & Chi Square.
Mertens, Thomas R. & Lines, Judy L. Principles of Biosystematics.
Mertes, Harald, jt. auth. see Hollander, Neil.
Merton, Robert K. & Gaston, Jerry, eds. The Sociology of Science in Europe.
Merton, Robert K. & Nisbet, Robert A., eds. Contemporary Social Problems.
Merton, Robert K., ed. see Bassis, Michael S., et al.
Merton, Robert K., jt. ed. see Riley, Matilda W.
Merton, Thomas. Contemplation in a World of Action.
--Last of the Fathers: Saint Bernard of Clairvaux & the Encyclical Letter, Doctor Mellifluus.
--The Silent Life.
--What Is Contemplation?
Mervyn, Leonard. Rheumatism & Arthritis.
Merwin, Henry C. Life of Bret Harte, with Some Account of the California Pioneers.
Merwin, Mrs. George B. Three Years in Chile. Gardiner, Harvey C., ed.
Merwin, W. S. The First Four Books of Poems: Including a Mask for Janus, the Dancing Bear, Green with Beasts, the Drunk in the Furnace.
Merwin, W. S. & Juarroz, Roberto. Vertical Poems.
Merwin, W. S., tr. from Fr. Four French Plays.
Merwin, W. S., jt. tr. see Brown, Clarence.
Merwin, W. S., tr. see Juarroz, Roberto.
Meryman, Richard. Broken Promises, Mended Dreams: An Alcoholic Woman Fights for Her Life.
Merz, Harold, jt. auth. see Starr, Harold.
Merz, Rollande. Pictures: Life & Still Life.
Merzer, Meridee. Winning the Diet Wars.
Merzkirch, Wolfgang. Flow Visualization.
Merzkirch, Wolfgang, ed. Flow Visualization Two.
Mesa Research Staff. The Lisa Connection.
Mesarovic, M. D. & Takahara, Y. General Systems Theory: Mathematical Foundations.
Mesarovic, M. D., ed. see Systems Symposium - 4th - Case Western Reserve University, Institute of Technology.
Mesavoric, M. D., ed. see Systems Symposium Staff.
Meschery, Joanne. In a High Place.
Meselson, Matthew S. Chemicals & Cancer.
Meserole, Harrison T., ed. Seventeenth-Century American Poetry.
Meserve, Bruce E. & Sobel, Max. Introduction to Mathematics.
Meserve, Bruce E. & Sobel, Max A. Contemporary Mathematics.
Meserve, Robert L., jt. auth. see Camp, Thomas.
Meserve, Walter J. An Emerging Entertainment: The Drama of the American People to 1828.
Meshii, M., ed. Mechanical Properties of BCC Metals: Proceedings of a Meeting at Honolulu, HI, 1981.
Meshorer, Ya'akov. Coins of the Ancient World. Currier, Richard L., ed.
Mesick, Jane L. English Traveller in America, 1785-1835.
Mesko, A. Fundamentals of Digital Filtering with Applications in Geophysical Prospecting for Oil.
Meslier, Jean. Superstition in All Ages. Knopp, Anna, tr.
Mesnard, Jean. Pascal: His Life & His Works.
Messec, Jerry L. A Southern Childhood. McConochie, Jean, ed.
Messec, Jerry L., jt. auth. see Kranich, Roger E.
Messel, H. & Crawford, D. F. Electron-Photon Shower Distribution Function: Tables for Lead, Copper & Air Absorbers.
Messel, H., ed. Science Update.
Messenger, R. W. Patty Cannon Administers Justice.
Messent, Jan. Embroidery & Nature.
Messer, Alfred. When You Are Concerned with Homosexuality.
Messer, Thomas M. Fifty Years of Collecting: An Anniversary Selection. Painting by Modern Masters.
Messerli, Douglas. Some Distance.
Messimer, Dwight R. Pawns of War: The Loss of the U. S. S. Langley & the U. S. S. Pecos.
Messinesi, X. L. Meet the Ancient Greeks.
Messing, jt. auth. see Hackett, Fuchs.
Messing, G. L., et al, eds. Ceramic Powder Science.
Messing, Ralph A., ed. Immobilized Enzymes for Industrial Reactors.
Messing, W. The Crystals Associated to Barsotti-Tate Groups: With Applications to Abelian Schemes.
Messinger, Lisa. Biting the Hand That Feeds Me: Days of Binging, Purging, & Recovery.
Messner. The Science of Society.
Messner, Julian. Julian Messner Book of Dates & Events.
Messner, Mary B. East & West.
Mesthene, Emanuel G. Technological Change: Its Impact on Man & Society.
Mestinsek, Erma & Mestinsek, Minnie G. Discoveries of the Hidden Things of God.
Mestinsek, Minnie G., jt. auth. see Mestinsek, Erma.
Mestres, Ricardo A., jt. auth. see Darrow, Peter H.
Metabooks, Inc. Staff. Escape.
Metalious, Grace. Peyton Place.
Metcalf, Amanda, tr. see Vampilov, A., et al.
Metcalf, C. E. An Econometric Model of Income Distribution.
Metcalf, D. Homopoietic Colonies.
Metcalf, E. W., Jr., jt. auth. see Ellison, Curtis W.
Metcalf, John, ed. Making It New.
Metcalf, Kenneth N., ed. Transportation Information Sources.
Metcalf, Robert L., Jr. & McKelvey, John J., eds. The Future for Insecticides: Needs & Prospects.
Metcalfe, W. M., ed. Legends of the Saints, in the Scottish Dialect of the Fourteenth Century.
Metchenko, A., et al. Vladimir Mayakovsky: Innovator.
Metelka, Charles J. The Dictionary of Tourism.
Metelka, Charles J., ed. The Dictionary of Tourism.
Meter, Donald Van see Sharkansky, Ira & Van Meter, Donald.
Meter, Margaret Van see Yacone, Linda A.
Meter, Margaret Van see Van Meter, Margaret.
Metford, John C. San Martin.
Metheny, Elenor. Moving & Knowing: Sport, Dance, Physical Education.
Methuen-Campbell, James. Chopin Playing: From the Composer to the Present Day.
Methven, Barbara. Basic Microwaving.
Metman, Philip. Around & Beyond the Confines of Art.
Metos, Thomas H. Robots A Two Z.
Metras, Gary. Destiny's Calendar.
Metraux, Guy P. Western Greek Land: Use & City-Planning in the Archaic Period.
Metress, James, ed. Man in Ecological Perspective.
Metress, Seamus P. The Irish-American Experience: A Guide to the Literature.
Metropolitan Emilianos Timiadis Staff. The Nicene Creed: Our Common Faith.
Metropolitan Museum of Art, Curatorial Staff. Metropolitan Museum of Art: Notable Acquisitions, 1965-1975.
Metropolitan Museum of Art, New York Staff, ed. Library Catalog of the Metropolitan Museum of Art, New York.
--Library Catalog of The Metropolitan Museum of Art (New York), Suppl. 6.
--Library Catalog of the Metropolitan Museum of Art.
Metropolitan Museum of Art Staff. Going Places: A Traveller's Journal.
--Guest Book.
Metropolitan Museum of Modern Art, New York Staff, ed. Catalog of the Robert Goldwater Library of Primitive Art.
Metropolitan Washington Council of Governments Staff & Reilly, Scott W. Subsidized Housing Information File.
Metropulos, Lyman. The Illustrated Book of the Great Ancient Temples.
Metry, Amir, jt. auth. see Kiang, Yen-Hsiung.
Mets, David R. NATO: Alliance for Peace.

Mettam, Roger S. & Johnson, Douglas. French History & Society: The Wars of Religion to the Fifth Republic.
Mettling, Stephen R. Assumptions & Purchase Money Mortgages (A plus PMM)
--An Autopsy of Traditional Real Estate Financing.
--Buydown Agreements.
--Installment Sales Tax Reporting.
--The Language of Creative Financing.
Metz, Don, ed. The Compact House Book: Thirty-Three Prize Winning Designs one thousand square feet or less.
Metz, Leon C. Fort Bliss, An Illustrated History. Mangan, Frank, ed.
Metz, Mary S. & Helstrom, Jo. Le Francais a Vivre, Learning French the Modern Way.
Metz, Robert & Kess, Sidney. Cut Your Own Taxes & Save, 1988.
Metzbower, E. Source Book on Applications of the Laser in Metalworking.
Metzbower, E. A., ed. Lasers in Materials Processing.
Metzbower, Edward A., ed. Applications of Lasers in Materials Processing.
Metzger, Barbara. Bething's Folly.
--The Earl & the Heiress.
Metzger, Daniel L. Electronic Components, Instruments & Troubleshooting.
Metzger, Henri. Saint Paul's Journey in the Greek Orient.
Metzger, Michael B., et al. Business Law & the Regulatory Environment.
Metzger, Norman. The Health Care Supervisor's Handbook.
Metzler, Bernadette V., jt. auth. see Krey, Isabelle A.
Metzloff, Nancy, jt. auth. see Haagen, Lucy E.
Metzner, H. Die Ascorbinsaeure in der Pflanzenzelle. Bd. with Vitamin C in the Animal Cell. Bourne, G. H. Springer-Verlag.
Metzner, H., ed. Photosynthetic Oxygen Evolution.
Meulen, Henk Van Der see Baudet, Henri & Van Der Meulen, Henk.
Meulen, Jan van der see Van Der Meulen, Jan, et al.
Meur, Gisele De see De Meur, Gisele.
Meuser, Fred W. Luther the Preacher.
Meuser, Fred W., tr. see Holl, Karl.
Meuwissen, Hilaire J., et al, eds. Combined Immunodeficiency Disease & Adenosine Deaminase Deficiency: A Molecular Defect-Proceedings.
Meves, Christa. The Bible Answers Us with Pictures. Taussig, Hal, tr. from Ger.
Mew, James. Traditional Aspects of Hell.
Mew, James & Ashton, John. Drinks of the World.
Mewshaw, Michael. Blackballed.
--Land Without Shadow.
--Life for Death.
--Short Circuit: Inside the World of Professional Tennis.
--The Toll.
--Waking Slow.
--Year of the Gun.
Meye, Robert P. Foreword by see Miller, David J.
Meyen, Edward L., ed. Exceptional Children & Youth.
Meyendorff, et al. The Primacy of Peter.
Meyer, Alfred G., ed. see Casals, Felipe G.
Meyer, Annie & Munro, Mary Lynn. A Coloring Cookbook for Children.
Meyer, B. J. The Organization of Prose & Its Effects on Memory.
Meyer, Ben F. & Sanders, E. P., eds. Jewish & Christian Self-Definition, Vol. 3: Self-Definition in the Greco-Roman World.
Meyer, Bernadine & Kolasa, Blair J. Legal Systems.
Meyer, C. Kenneth, jt. auth. see Morrison, Patton N.
Meyer, C. Kenneth, et al. An Analysis of Officer Characteristics & Police Assaults Among Selected South Central Cities.
--A Social-Psychological Analysis of Police Assailants.
Meyer, Carolyn. Amish People: Plain Living in a Complex World.
--The Bread Book.
--Bread Book: All about Bread & How to Make It.
--Eskimos: Growing up in a Changing Culture.
--Lots & Lots of Candy.
--Mask Magic.
--Miss Patch's Learn to Sew Book.
--The Needlework Book of Bible Stories.
--People Who Make Things: How American Craftsmen Live & Work.
--Rock Band: Big Men in a Great Big Town.
--Stitch by Stitch: Needlework for Beginners.
--Yarn: The Things It Makes & How to Make Them.
Meyer, Donald H. The Instructed Conscience: The Shaping of the American National Ethic.
Meyer, Edwin W. & Oldfield, Molly. WordStar for the IBM PC: A Self-Guided Tutorial.
Meyer, Ellen T., ed. see Association for Information & Image Management Staff.
Meyer, Ernst H. Early English Chamber Music: From the Middle Ages to Purcell. Poulton, Diane, ed.
Meyer, Eugene & Brady, Joseph V. Research in the Psychobiology of Human Behavior.
Meyer, F. B. F. B. Meyer Bible Commentary.
--New Testament Men of Faith.
--Old Testament Men of Faith.
Meyer, F. V., ed. Prospects for Recovery in the British Economy.
Meyer, Genevieve R. Tenderness & Technique: Nursing Values in Transition.
Meyer, Gunther H. Initial Value Methods for Boundary Value Problems: Theory & Applications of Invariant Imbedding.
Meyer, Hans H. Die Barundi Eine Volkerkundliche Sudie aus Deutch-Ostafrika.
Meyer, Howard N. The Amendment That Refused to Die: Amendment XIV.
Meyer, J. Toward an Urban Strategy.
Meyer, J., jt. ed. see Sreebny, L. M.
Meyer, J. S., et al, eds. Cerebral Vascular Disease.
Meyer, Jack A., ed. Market Reforms in Health Care: Current Issues, New Directions, Strategic Decisions.
Meyer, Jerome S. The Handwriting Analyzer.
Meyer, Jerry. How to Catch Trout Between the Hatches.
Meyer, John C. Christian Beliefs & Teachings.
Meyer, John R., jt. auth. see Kain, John F.
Meyer, John W., et al. Organizational Environments: Ritual & Rationality.
Meyer, Kathleen A. Ireland: Land of Mist & Magic.
Meyer, Lester. The Message of Exodus.
Meyer, Lorenzo. Mexico & the United States in the Oil Controversy, 1917-1942. Vasconcellos, Muriel, tr. from Span.
Meyer, Lorenzo, jt. auth. see Vazquez, Josefina Z.
Meyer, Luc. Left Bank Celebrity Cookbook.
Meyer, Marvin C. & Olsen, O. Wilford. Essentials of Parasitology.
Meyer, Mary Jane. Bits of Faith & Love & Fun.
Meyer, Mary K. & Filby, P. William, eds. Who's Who in Genealogy.
Meyer, Michael. Lunatic & Lover: A Play about Strindberg.
Meyer, Michael, tr. see Ibsen, Henrik.
Meyer, Nathan M. From Now to Eternity: Sermons from Revelation.
--Noah's Ark, Pitched & Parked.
Meyer, P. A. Martingales & Stochastic Integrals I.
Meyer, Peter. Awarding College Credit for Non-College Learning: A Guide to Current Practices.
--Jews in the Soviet Satellites.
Meyer, Philip. Editors, Publishers & Newpaper Ethics.
Meyer, Priscilla. How to Make Your IRA Grow: Investing under the New Tax Law.
Meyer, Ray & Sons, Ray. Coach.
Meyer, Richard. The Fate of the Badger.
Meyer, Robert A., Jr. Microeconomic Decisions.
--Problems in Macroeconomics.
--Problems in Price Theory.
Meyer, Robert G. The Clinician's Handbook: The Psychopathology of Adulthood & Late Adolescence.
Meyer, Sheila, ed. see Shiplett, Gary R.
Meyer, Stewart. The Lotus Crew.
Meyer, Susan E. A Treasury of the Great Children's Book Illustrators.
Meyer, Ted. Body Count.
Meyer, Ursula, jt. auth. see Madrigal, Margarita.
Meyerbeer, Giacomo. Les Huguenots. Rosen, Charles & Gossett, Philip, eds.
Meyerer, Margaret R. Heartbreak: The Losing Struggle of the Middle Years.
Meyerhoff, Hans, tr. see Scheler, Max.
Meyerink, George. Appliance Service Handbook.
Meyerowitz, Patricia. Making Jewelry & Sculpture Through Unit Construction.
Meyers, Alan. Composing with Confidence.
--Writing with Confidence.
Meyers, Carole T. Weekend Adventures for City-Weary People: Overnight Trips in Northern California.
Meyers, Craig, jt. auth. see Schroeder, Frederick.
Meyers, Eric M., jt. auth. see Joint Expedition to Khirbet Shema Staff.
Meyers, Gerald C. & Holusha, John. When It Hits the Fan: Managing the Nine Crises of Business.
Meyers, Jeffrey. T. E. Lawrence: A Bibliography.
Meyers, Jeffrey, ed. The Craft of Literary Biography.
Meyers, Joan, jt. auth. see Whitaker, George O.
Meyers, Joel, jt. auth. see Alpert, Judith L.
Meyers, Joel, et al. School Consultation: Readings about Preventive Techniques for Pupil Personnel Workers.
Meyers, Kenneth, jt. auth. see Balassa, Bela.
Meyers, L. D. Chilton's Complete Home Wiring & Lighting Guide.
Meyers, L. Donald. The Complete Backyard Planner.
Meyers, Lewis. Seeing Writing.
Meyers, Marvin H., ed. The Multiply Injured Patient with Complex Fractures.
Meyers, Pieter, jt. auth. see Harper, Prudence O.
Meyers, Ray C. & Goodban, Dale. Spell It Right!
Meyers, Robert. Like Normal People.
Meyers, Susan. P. J. Clover, Private Eye: The Case of the Stolen Laundry.
Meyers, Walter D. The Young Landlords.
Meyers, Walter E. Handbook of Contemporary English.
Meyerson, Adam, jt. ed. see Asman, David.
Meylan, B., jt. auth. see Butterfield, B. G.
Meynard, Virginia G. The Venturers: The Hampton, Harrison & Earle Families of Virginia, South Carolina & Texas.
Meynell, Laurence W. Virgin Luck.
Meynen, E. Multilingual Dictionary of Technical Terms in Cartography.
Meynen, Emil. Bibliography on German Settlements in Colonial North America.
Meyners, Robert & Wooster, Claire. Sexual Style: Facing & Making Choices About Sex.
Meyrink, Gustav. Some Taoist Alchemical Legends.
Mezhuev, V. Cultura y Historia.
Mezo, Francine. The Fall of Worlds.
--No Earthly Shore.
--Unless She Burn.
Mial, L. C. Sirenoid Ganoids.
Miami Winter Symposium Staff. Molecular Basis of Biological Transport. Woessner, J. F., Jr. & Huijing, F., eds.
--The Molecular Basis of Electron Transport. Schultz, Julius & Cameron, Bruce F., eds.
Mian, Mary. The Net to Catch War.
Mibar, Ltd. Staff. NRCSA Directory of Special Interest Programs, 1982-1983: Britain-Ireland.
--NRCSA Program Directory Europe, 1982-83.
Micali, Paul J. Success Handbook for Salespeople.
Micallef, Mary. Times to Treasure.
Micewski, Andrzej. Cardinal Wyszynski: A Biography. Brand, William R. & Mroczkowska-Brand, Katarzyna, trs.
Michael, Colette V. Choderlos De Laclos, the Man, His Works, & His Critics: An Annotated Bibliography.
Michael, Donald N. On Learning to Plan & Planning to Learn: The Social Psychology of Changing Toward Future-Responsive Societal Learning.
Michael, George. The Overlook Treasury of Federal Antiques.
Michael, Henry N., ed. Lieutenant Zagoskin's Travels in Russian America, 1842-1844: The First Ethnographic & Geographic Investigations in the Yukon & Kuskokwim Valleys of Alaska.
Michael, Henry N., ed. see Chernetsov, V. N. & Moszynska, W. I.
Michael, Henry N., ed. see Okladnikov, A. P.
Michael J., jt. auth. see Adams, Robert Lang, & Associates Staff.
Michael, J., jt. auth. see Adams, Robert Lang, & Associates Staff.
Michael, Jerome & Adler, Mortimer J. Crime, Law & Social Science.
Michael, Judith. Possessions.
--Private Affairs.
Michael, Mary E. Continuing Professional Education in Librarianship & Other Fields: A Classified & Annotated Bibliography, 1965-1974.
Michael, Nancy. Forget the Dust: Let's Paint.
Michael Prince of Greece. Sultana.
Michael, Richard P. & Crook, John H., eds. Comparative Ecology & Behaviour of Primates.
Michaelides, Stephen & Deluca, Michael. Dining In - Cleveland.
Michaelis. Portuguese-English, English-Portuguese Dictionary.
Michaelis, A., jt. auth. see Jahn, O.
Michaelis, A., ed. see Symposium on the Impact of Science on Society, Brussels, 1971.
Michaelis, Anthony R. Research Films in Biology, Anthropology, Psychology & Medicine.
Michaelis, Carol T. Home & School Partnerships in Exceptional Education.
Michaelis, David T. The Best of Friends: Profiles of Men & Friendship.
Michaelis, L. S. Orthopaedic Surgery of the Limbs in Paraplegia.
Michaelis, L. S., tr. see Miehlke, Adolf.
Michaelis, L. S., tr. see Reisner, K. & Gosepath, J.
Michaels, Barbara. The Grey Beginning.
--Shattered Silk.
--Someone in the House.
Michaels, Brenda, jt. ed. see Grinstein, Louise.
Michaels, Cheri. Defiant Dreams.
Michaels, Fern. Beyond Tomorrow.
--Captive Embraces.
--Captive Innocence.
--Captive Splendors.
--Golden Lasso.
--Nightstar.
--Whisper My Name.
Michaels, J. Ramsey. John: A Good News Commentary.
--Servant & Son: Jesus in Parable & Gospel.
Michaels, John G., jt. auth. see Bloch, Norman J.
Michaels, Jonathan, jt. auth. see Stern, Ellen.
Michaels, Joseph. Joe, the First Thirty Years.
Michaels, Judith. Deceptions.
Michaels, L. & Chissick, S. S. Asbestos Properties, Applications & Hazards: (Properties of Materials: Saftey & Environmental Factors)
Michaels, Leonard. The Men's Club.
Michaels, Lynn. Like a Lover.
--Lover's Gift.
--Tainted Gold.
Michaels, Philip. Come, Follow Me.
--Grail.
Michaels, Rhoda M. & Brown, G. R., eds. Drug Consultant 1985-86: The Pocket Clinical Guide to Drugs & Their Usefulness.
Michaels, Rick. Canon AE1, AT-1, AV-1: Amphoto Pocket Companion.
Michaels, Walter B. & Pease, Donald E., eds. Selected Papers from the English Institute 1982-83.
Michaelsen, James A. How You Can Stop Smoking Now As I Did After 33 Years.
Michaelsen, Katherine J. Archipenko: A Study of the Early Works, 1908-1920.
Michaelson, I. C. & Berman, Elaine R., eds. Causes & Prevention of Blindness.
Michaelson, Katherine J., jt. auth. see Guralink, Nehama.
Michaelson, Mike. Weekend Getaway Guide: Chicago.
Michaelson, Mike, ed. Weekend Escapes: Southeast.
--Weekend Escapes: Southeast Texas.
--Weekend Escapes: Southern California.
Michalopoulos, Andre. Homer.
Michalos, James & Wilson, E. N. Structural Mechanics & Analysis.
Michal-Smith, Harold Foreword by see Hayes, Leola G.
Michaud, Joseph F. Biographie universelle ancienne et moderne.
Michaud, Regis. The American Novel To-Day: A Social & Psychological Study.
Michaud, Stephen G. & Aynesworth, Hugh. The Only Living Witness.
Michaudon, A., et al, eds. Nuclear Fission & Neutron-Induced Fission Cross-Sections.
Michaux, Henri. The Major Ordeals of the Mind & the Countless Minor Ones. Howard, Richard, tr. from Fr.
Michel, Allen & Shaked, Israel. Takeover Madness: Corporate America Fights Back.
Michel, Beth. When a Parent Imposes Limits: Discipline, Authority, & Freedom in Today's Family.
Michel, Francois, compiled by. Stendhal Fichier.
Michel, Sally. Animals & Pets in Pastel.
--Painting Animals in Watercolor.
Michel, Scott. Journey into Limbo.
Michelet. Histoire de la Revolution Francaise: Livres I a VIII.
--Histoire de la Revolution Francaise: Livres IX a XXI-Tableau Chronologique.
Michelet, Jules. History of the French Revolution. Wright, Gordon, ed. Cocks, Charles, tr.
Michelin. Paris Index Plan.
Michelin Guides & Maps. Dictionnaire des Communes de France (Guide to French Townships)
--Michelin Red Guide to Paris Annual: Paris Hotels & Restaurants.
--Paris Index & Map.
Michelin Guides & Maps Department Staff. Michelin Green Guide Rome.
--Michelin Green Guide to Alpes.
--Michelin Green Guide to Auvergne.
--Michelin Green Guide to Bourgogne.
--Michelin Green Guide to Canada.
--Michelin Green Guide to Causses-Cevennes.
--Michelin Green Guide to Corse.
--Michelin Green Guide to Cote D'Azur.
--Michelin Green Guide to Cote De L'Atlantique.
--Michelin Green Guide to Dordogne.
--Michelin Green Guide to Environs De Paris.
--Michelin Green Guide to Hollande.
--Michelin Green Guide to London.
--Michelin Green Guide to Normandy.
--Michelin Green Guide to Nouvelle Angleterre.
--Michelin Green Guide to Switzerland.
Michelin Guides & Maps Dept. Michelin Green Guide Belgique et Grand Duche du Luxembourg.
--Michelin Green Guide to Autriche.
--Michelin Green Guide to French Riviera.
--Michelin Green Guide to Londres.
--Michelin Green Guide to Provence Eng.
--Michelin Green Guide to Vosges.
--Michelin Red Guide to Deutschland, 1986: Annual.
--Michelin Red Guide to Great Britain & Ireland, 1985: Annual.
--Michelin Red Guide to Italia, 1985: Annual.

--Michelin Red Guide to London: Annual.
--Michelin Red Guide to "Main Cities in Europe" Annual.
--Michelin Red Guide to Spain & Portugal.
Michelin Guides & Maps Division. France Motorway Atlas.
Michelin Travel Publications Staff. Michelin Green Guide to England, the West Country.
Michell, John. Eccentric Lives & Peculiar Notions.
Michell, John & Rickard, Robert J. Living Wonders: Mysteries & Curiosities of the Animal World.
Michell, S. J. Introduction to Fluid & Particle Mechanics.
Michelle, Arthur A. You Don't Have to Ache: Orthotherapy.
Michelman, Irving S. The Roots of Capitalism in Western Civilization.
Michelmore, Peter. The Pigkeeper's Guide.
Michelmore, Peter, jt. auth. see Barracato, John.
Michelozzi, Betty N. Coming Alive from Nine to Five: The Career Search Handbook.
Michels, et al. Physics: Principles & Applications.
Michels, Barbara & White, Bettye. Apples on a Stick.
Michels, Caroll. How to Survive & Prosper As an Artist.
Michels, Joseph W. Dating Methods in Archaeology.
Michels, Timothy I. Solar Energy Utilization.
Michelsen, Neil F. American Ephemeris for the 20th Century: 1900 to 2000.
--The American Ephemeris 1971 to 1980.
Michelson, Herb. Almost a Famous Person.
Michelson, Joan & Gee, Sue. Coming Late to Motherhood: Twenty Women Tell Their Stories.
Michener, Dorothy & Muschlitz, Beverly. First Place: Skills & Activities for Early Learning.
Michener, James A. The Drifters.
--Fires of Spring.
--Kent State: What Happened & Why.
--A Michener Miscellany, 1950-1970.
--Poland.
--Selected Writings.
Michener, James A., frwd. by. Cosmep.
Michie Company Editorial Staff. Alabama Criminal Code.
--Alabama Rules Annotated.
--Arkansas Court Rules.
--Arkansas Criminal Code.
--Delaware Advance Annotation Service.
--Federal Ethics Handbook.
--General Statutes of North Carolina, Rules Volume.
--Illinois Civil Practice, 1987 & Illinois Criminal Practice, 1987.
--Indiana Alcoholic Beverage Laws: Annotated.
--Kentucky Rules of Court.
--Maryland Rules.
--Michie's Texas Tort Reporter.
--North Carolina Criminal Law & Procedure.
--Police, Crimes & Offenses & Motor Vehicle Laws of Virginia.
--Police, Crimes & Offenses & Motor Vehicle Laws of Virginia.
--Rules of the U. S. Bankruptcy Court for the Eastern District of Virginia.
--Supreme Court Rules of the State of Delaware.
--Utah Rules of Court.
--Virginia Rules Annotated.
--Virginia Rules Annotated: 1985 Edition.
--West Virginia Rules Annotated.
Michie Company Staff, ed. Drugs in Litigation: Damage Awards Involving Prescription & Nonprescription Drugs.
Michie Company Staff, jt. ed. see Tennessee. Supreme Court Staff.
Michigan State University, East Lansing Staff. Dictionary Catalog of the G. Robert Vincent Library.
Michigan United Conservation Clubs Staff. Michigan Hiking & Skiing Trails.
Michiko, U., tr. see Iozawa, Tomoya.
Michnik, Adam. Letters from Prison & Other Essays. Latynski, Maya, tr.
Michon, J. A., et al, eds. Handbook of Psychonomics.
Michon, John A. Traffic Education for Young Pedestrians: A Selection of Papers Adapted from the Proceedings of the 1978 OECD Workshop on Training Objectives for Child Pedestrians.
Mick, Colin K. & Ball, Jerry. The Financial Planner's Guide to Using a Personal Computer.
Mickel, John & Fiore, Evelyn. The Home Gardener's Book of Ferns.
Mickelsen, A. Berkeley & Mickelsen, Alvera. Understanding the Scriptures.
Mickelsen, Alvera & Mickelsen, Berkley. Family Bible Encyclopedia. Incl. Volume I (A-K; Volume II (L-Z. Cook.
Mickelsen, Alvera, jt. auth. see Mickelsen, A. Berkeley.
Mickelsen, Berkley, jt. auth. see Mickelsen, Alvera.
Mickens, Ronald E. Difference Equations.
Micklem, Niel. Playing Consequences.
Micks, Marianne H. Epiphany.
--Future Present: The Phenomenon of Christian Worship.
--Our Search for Identity: Humanity in the Image of God.
Micks, Marianne H. & Ridenhour, Thomas E. Lent. Achtemeier, Elizabeth, et al, eds.
Mickwitz, Ann-Mari & Miekkavaara, Leena, eds. The A. E. Nordenskiold Collection in Helsinki University Library: Annotated Catalogue of Maps Made up to 1800.
Mico, Paul, jt. auth. see Ross, Helen S.
Microform Review, Inc. Staff. The Micropublishers' Trade List Annual, 1976.
Microforms in Print Staff, ed. Subject Guide to Microforms in Print, 1987.
Micronesian Community College Students Staff. Never & Always: Micronesian Stories of the Origin of Islands, Landmarks, & Customs. Ashby, Gene, ed.
--Some Things of Value: Micronesian Customs as Seen by Micronesians. Ashby, Gene, ed.
Micue, Donald E. Valiant Hearts.
Mid-Hudson Chapter of the Guild. Action Against Abuse: Handbook for Battered Women & their Advocates.
Middelhoek, S., et al. Physics of Computer Memory Devices.
Middendorf, William H. What Every Engineer Should Know about Inventing.
Middione, Carlo. Pasta! Cooking It, Loving It. Atcheson, Richard, ed.
Middle East Economic Digest Staff. AED African Financial Directory.
--Bahrain. Whelan, John, ed.
--The Dictionary of Professional Business Terms: English-Arabic.
--Images of Bahrain.
--Jordan. Mostyn, Trevor, ed.
--Kuwait. Whelan, John, ed.
--MEED-TAIC Middle East Financial Directory. Krajewska, Anna, ed.
--The Middle East Business Information Guide.
--Oman. Whelan, John, ed.
--Qatar. Whelan, John, ed.
--Saudi Arabia. Mostyn, Trevor, ed.
--UAE. Mostyn, Trevor, ed.
Middle East Executive Reports, High-Level Staff, ed. Middle East Government Directory & Guide to Purchasing Agencies.
Middle East Research Institute Staff. MERI Report: Egypt.
--MERI Report: Iran.
--MERI Report: Israel.
--MERI Report: Kuwait.
--MERI Report: Saudi Arabia.
--MERI Report: Turkey.
--MERI Report: United Arab Emirates.
--MERI Reports on the Middle East: Saudi Arabia, Kuwait, United Arab Emirates, Israel, Turkey, Iran, & Egypt.
Middle, P., tr. see Schmidt, W. J. & Keil, A.
Middlebrook, Diane. Worlds into Words: Understanding Modern Poems.
Middlebrook, John H. & Kohn, Leonard D., eds. Receptor-Mediated Binding & Internalization of Toxins & Hormones.
Middlebrook, Martin. The Battle of Hamburg: Allied Forces Against a German City in 1943.
Middlehurst, Barbara, jt. ed. see Kuiper, Gerald P.
Middlekauff, Robert, jt. ed. see Levine, Lawrence W.
Middlekauff, Woodrow W. & Lane, Robert S. Adult & Immature Tabanidae (Diptera) of California.
Middlemass, Tom. Irish Standard Gauge Railways.
Middleton, Alan, jt. auth. see Donnison, David.
Middleton, Christopher, tr. see Grass, Gunter.
Middleton, Christopher, tr. see Nietzsche, Friedrich.
Middleton, Elliott, Jr., et al, eds. Allergy: Principles & Practice.
Middleton, John, ed. Gods & Rituals: Readings in Religious Beliefs & Practices.
Middleton, Kathleen, jt. auth. see Pollock, Marion B.
Middleton, Robert G. Digital Logic Circuits: Tests & Analysis.
--Know Your Oscilloscope.
--Troubleshooting with the Oscilloscope.
Middleton, Sallie & Sibley, Celestine. The Magical Realm of Sallie Middleton.
Middleton, Susan, ed. Blueprints: Building Educational Programs for People Who Care for Children.
Middleton, Thomas. The Ghost of Lucrece.
--The Roaring Girl. Dekker, Thomas & Gomme, A. H., eds.
--Three Plays. Muir, Kenneth, ed.
Middleton, Thomas H. Crostics Omnibus.
--Crostics 88.
--Simon & Schuster Crostics.
--Simon & Schuster's Crostics.
--Simon & Schuster's Crostics Omnibus, No. 9.
Middleton, Thomas H., ed. Double-Crostics by Fans, No. 5.
--Double-Crostics by Fans, No. 6.
--Simon & Schuster Crostics, No. 72.
--Simon & Schuster Crostics, No. 80.
--Simon & Schuster's Crostic Omnibus.
--Simon & Schuster's Crostics No. 93.
Middleton, William. South Shore: America's Last Interurban.
Middleton, William D. China by Rail. Bradley, Bill, ed.
--Grand Central...the World's Greatest Railway Terminal.
--Railroad Scene.
Midgeley, David. Barron's How to Prepare for the College Board Achievement Tests - Social Studies - American History.
Midgely, Charles, tr. see Sollertinsky, Dmitri & Sollertinsky, Ludmilla.
Midgley, W., jt. auth. see Lilley, A. E.
Midkiff, Pat. The Complete Book of Stenciling: Furniture Decoration & Restoration.
Midwest Autumn Immunology Conference Staff. Immunologic Tolerance & Macrophage Function: Proceedings of the Midwest Autumn Immunology Conference, 7th Meeting, Michigan, November, 1978. Baram, R., et al, eds.
Midwest Category Seminar Staff. Reports of the Midwest Category Seminar, Fourth. MacLane, S., ed.
Midwest Category Seminar, 3rd. Reports. Barr, M., ed.
Midwest Plan Service Engineers Staff. Beef Housing & Equipment Handbook.
--Planning Grain-Feed Handling for Livestock & Cash-Grain Farms.
Midwest Plan Service Engineers Staff & Northeast Regional Agricultural Engineering Service Staff. Small Farms--Livestock Buildings & Equipment.
Midwest Plan Service Engineers Staff. Structures & Environment Handbook.
Midwest Securities Commissioners Association. Guidelines for Preparation of the Uniform Franchise Offering Circular & Related Documents.
Miehl, James A., Jr. Refugee's Vision.
Miehlke, Adolf. Surgery of the Facial Nerve. Michaelis, L. S., tr.
Miekkavaara, Leena, jt. ed. see Mickwitz, Ann-Mari.
Miele, Philip, jt. auth. see Silva, Jose.
Mielke, Arthur W. Through the Valley.
Mierow, Christopher, tr. see Otto of Freising.
Miers, Earl S. The Web of Victory: Grant at Vicksburg.
Miertschin, S. L., jt. auth. see Goodson, C. E.
Miescher, Peter A., jt. auth. see Dixon, Frank J.
Miescher, Peter A., ed. see International Symposium on Immunopathology Staff.
Miescke, Lori. Shaggy Dog Riddles. Fay, Ann, ed.
Mieszkowski, P. & Peterson, G., eds. Public Sector Labor Markets.
Mieszkowski, Peter & Oakland, William, eds. Fiscal Federalism & Grants-in-Aid.
Mignard, James E., tr. see Marxsen, Willi.
Mignone, Nicholas A., jt. auth. see Dyer, Jon C.
Migraine Symposium, 2nd, London, 1967. Background to Migraine: Proceedings. Smith, R., ed.
Migraine Symposium, 3rd, London, 1969. Background to Migraine: Proceedings. Cochrane, A. L., ed.
Migraine Symposium, 4th, London, 1971. Background to Migraine: Proceedings. Cumings, J. N., ed.
Migraine Symposium, 5th, London, 1972. Background to Migraine: Proceedings. Cumings, J. N., ed.
Miguel, Richard J., ed. see Experiential Education Advisory Panel Staff.
Miguel, Richard J., jt. auth. see Jipp, Lester F.
Miguel, Richard J., jt. auth. see Wasson, Louise E.
Mihailescu, V., ed. One Hundred Years of Geosciences in Romania.
Mihalich, Joseph C. Existentialism & Thomism.
Mihalik, John. Thirty-Five Amazing Games for Your Commodore 128.
Mihalyka, Jean M. & Wilson, Faye D. Graven Stones of Lower Accomack County, VA.
Mihankhah, Kianpour, jt. auth. see Barber, Sandra.
Mihardja, Achdiat. Atheis. Maguire, R. J., tr.
Mihich, Enrico, ed. Drug Resistance & Selectivity: Biochemical & Cellular Basis.
--Immunity Cancer Chemotherapy.
--Regulation of Cell Metabolism: Organizational & Pharmacological Aspects on the Molecular Level.
Mihina, Joseph S. Joe-Pye & Delphinium.
Mihram, G. Arthur. An Epistle to Dr. Benjamin Franklin.
--Simulation: Statistical Foundations & Methodology.
Mikaelian, M. Art Gallery of Armenia.
Mikellides, Byron, ed. Architecture for People.
Mikes, George. How to Be Seventy.
--Switzerland for Beginners.
Mikesell, John, jt. ed. see McCaffery, Jerry.
Mikeshin, N. History vs. Anti-History.
Mikhailov, N. Panorama of the Soviet Union. Lipatov, Glanys A., tr.
Mikhailovskii, A. B. Theory of Plasma Instabilities. Incl. Vol. 1. Instabilities of a Homogeneous Plasma; Vol. 2. Instabilities of an Inhomogeneous Plasma. Plenum Pub.
Mikhalkov, S. From Carriage to Spaceship.
--Jolly Hares.
Miklos, Frantisek, jt. ed. see Uhlir, Ludvik.
Miklouho-Maclay, N. Travels to New Guinea.
Miklowitz, Gloria D. Love Story, Take Three.
--Movie Stunts & the People Who Do Them.
--Movie Stunts & the People Who Do Them.
--Natalie Dunn: World Roller Skating Champion.
--Save That Raccoon!
--Secrets Not Meant to Be Kept.
Miklowitz, Gloria D. & Yates, Madelein. The Young Tycoons.
Mikola, P., jt. ed. see Romberger, J. A.
Mikoloski, Pavel. The Warrior Who Walked Home: A Young Man Learns to Conquer Himself.
Miksche, J. P., ed. Modern Methods in Forest Genetics.
Miksell. Modern Abnormal Psychology.
Mikulsky, K. I., ed. CMEA: International Significance of Socialist Integration.
Milady Editors. Supplement to the Standard Textbook of Cosmetology.
--Theory Workbook for Practice & Science of Standard Barbering.
Milam, Edward & Crumbley, D. L. Estate Planning.
Milam, Edward E., jt. auth. see Crumbley, D. Larry.
Milan, Deanne K. & Rattner, Naomi C. Forms of the Essay: The American Experience.
Milan, Victor. Cybernetic Samurai. Silverberg, Robert, ed.
Milan, Victor, jt. auth. see Vardeman, Robert E.
Milanich, Jerald T. & Fairbanks, Charles H. Florida Archaeology.
Milano, et al. SYBEX WordPerfect Study Guide.
Milazzo, Guilio. Elektrochemie: Vol. 1 Grundlagen & Anwendungen.
Milbauer, Barbara & Obrentz, Bert N. The Law Giveth: Legal Aspects of the Abortion Controversy.
Milburn, Ellen. Wings of Darkness.
Milburn, JoAnne F., jt. ed. see Cartledge, Gwendolyn.
Milburn, Josephine & Schuck, Victoria, eds. New England Politics.
Mild, Warren. Strangers Outside the Feast: A Choral Reading.
Mildvan, A. S., et al. Biochemistry.
Milepost Staff. The Milepost: All-the-North Travel Guide Annual, 1985.
--The Milepost: All-the-North Travel Guide, 1986.
Miles, compiled by. The Beatles in Their Own Words.
Miles, A., jt. ed. see Chandler, M.
Miles, A. J., ed. see Chandler.
Miles, Angela & Finn, Geraldine, eds. Feminism in Canada: From Pressure to Politics.
Miles, Betty. The Trouble with Thirteen.
--The Trouble With Thirteen.
Miles, C. W. & Seabrooke, W. Recreational Land Management.
Miles, Curtis & Rauton, Jane. Thinking Tools. Pitkin, Doree, ed.
Miles, Derek. A Manual on Building Maintenance: Management.
--A Manual on Building Maintenance: Methods.
Miles, Donald, tr. see Piaget, Jean & Garcia, R.
Miles, E., jt. auth. see Wesner, Maralene.
Miles, Elton. Tales of the Big Bend.
Miles, H. B. Some Factors Affecting Attainment at 18: A Study of Examination Performance in British Schools.
Miles, L., jt. auth. see Craft, M.
Miles, Lawrence D. Techniques of Value Analysis & Engineering.
Miles, Marguerite, tr. see Piaget, Jean & Garcia, R.
Miles, Marshall. All Fifty-Two Cards: How to Reconstruct the Concealed Hands at the Bridge Table.
--How to Win at Duplicate Bridge.
--Marshall Miles Teaches Logical Bridge.
Miles, Michael. Love Is Always.
Miles, Michael W. The Radical Probe: The Logic of Student Rebellion.
Miles, P. A., jt. ed. see Townes, C. H.
Miles, Philip G., jt. ed. see Schwalb, Marvin N.
Miles, Robert H. Coffin Nails & Corporate Strategies.
Milestone, W. D., ed. Reliability Stress Analysis & Failure Prevention Methods in Mechanical Design.
Miletich, John S., ed. Hispanic Studies in Honor of Alan D.Deyermond: A North American Tribute.
Milewski, John V., jt. auth. see Katz, Harry S.
Milford, Lee. The Hand.
Milford, Nancy. Zelda.
Milford, T. R. Christian Decision in the Nuclear Age. Sherman, Franklin, ed.

Authors

Authors

Miller, Michael B. The Bon Marche: Bourgeois Culture & the Department Store, 1869 to 1920.
Miller, Michael J., jt. auth. see Demel, John T.
Miller, Mitchell, ed. & illus. One Misty Moisty Morning: Rhymes from Mother Goose.
Miller, Monte. Snowshoe.
Miller, Nancy E. & Petersen, Charles G. File Structures Using Ada.
Miller, Nancy G. Managing Your Money.
Miller, Nancy O., jt. auth. see Lucky, Luretha F.
Miller, Naomi. French Renaissance Fountains.
Miller, Naomi, jt. auth. see MacDougall, Elisabeth B.
Miller, Nathan. The Child in Primitive Society.
Miller, Ned A. The Complete Guide to Employee Benefit Plans.
--Nonsalary Compensation for Employees of Independent Schools.
Miller, Nick. Battered Spouses.
Miller, Norma, jt. auth. see Feingold, S. Norman.
Miller, Norman N. & Spitzer, Manon L., eds. Faces of Change: Five Rural Societies in Transition: Bolivia, Kenya, Afghanistan, Taiwan, China Coast.
Miller, Ovvie, et al. Changes in California Marital Dissolution under the Tax Reform Act of 1984.
Miller, P. M. Behavioral Treatment of Alcoholism.
Miller, P. M. & Wilson, M. J. A Dictionary of Social Science Methods.
Miller, Patrick D., Jr. Pentecost 2.
Miller, Paul F., jt. ed. see Baderschneider, Earl R.
Miller, Paul W., ed. see Whitlock, Brand.
Miller, Peggy, jt. auth. see Bremner, Joseph.
Miller, Perry, ed. Major Writers of America.
Miller, Peter & Nelson, Janet. The Photographer's Almanac.
Miller, Phyllis, jt. auth. see Norton, Andre.
Miller, R. Baxter. Langston Hughes & Gwendolyn Brooks: A Reference Guide.
Miller, R. C. Soviets Begin War in the Middle East-U. S. Counters.
--Successful Job Hunting for Managers, Professionals & Graduates.
Miller, Rene Fulop see Fulop-Miller, Rene.
Miller, Richard. Snail.
--Snail.
Miller, Richard, tr. see Sarde, Michele.
Miller, Richard L. Truman: The Rise to Power.
Miller, Richard U. Hospital Labor Relations.
Miller, Robert J., ed. Robotics: Future Factories, Future Workers.
Miller, Robert K. The Informed Argument: A Multi Disciplinary Reader & Guide.
Miller, Robert R. & Kilpatrick, John. Private International Investment: An Exercise in Theory & Policy.
Miller, Robert W. Clock Guide Identification.
--Flea Market Price Guide.
--Wallace-Homestead Price Guide to Dolls, 1982-1983 Prices.
--Wallace-Homestead Price Guide to Dolls: 1984-1985 Prices.
Miller, Robert W., ed. Wallace-Homestead Price Guide to Antiques & Pattern Glass.
Miller, Roger L. Intermediate Microeconomics.
Miller, Ronald D., jt. auth. see Stoelting, Robert K.
Miller, Ronald E. Dynamic Optimization & Economic Applications.
Miller, Ronald J. The Demolition of Skid Row.
Miller, Rosalind & Terwillegar, Jane. Commonsense Cataloging: A Cataloger's Manual.
Miller, Ruby M., jt. auth. see Miller, E. Willard.
Miller, Rupert G., et al, eds. Biostatistics Casebook.
Miller, Russell. Bunny: The Real Story of Playboy.
--Continents in Collision.
--The House of Getty.
Miller, Russell, jt. auth. see Time-Life Books Editors.
Miller, Russell, Inc. Staff. Supergrowth: Buying & Selling Agencies for Profit.
Miller, Rusty. The Jedi Master's Quizbook.
Miller, Ruth. The City Rose.
Miller, Ryle, tr. see Institut Francais de Pertrole Staff.
Miller, S. M. & Tomaskovic-Devey, Donald. Recapitalizing America: Alternatives to the Corporate Distortion of National Policy.
Miller, Samuel H. Religion in a Technical Age.
--What Child Is This? Readings & Prayers for Advent-Christmas.
Miller, Sarah W. Devotional Dramas for Easter.
--Devotional Dramas for the Christian Life.
Miller, Saul. After Law School? Finding a Job in a Tight Market.
--New York City Street Smarts.
--Super Traveler: The Complete Handbook of Essential Facts, Regulations, Rights & Remedies for Trouble-Free International Travel.
Miller, Serene. Painting on Fabric.
Miller, Shelby M., jt. auth. see Zitner, Rosalind.
Miller, Sidney R. & Schloss, Patrick J. Career-Vocational Education for Handicapped Youth.
Miller, Sigmund S., ed. Symptoms: The Complete Home Medical Encyclopedia.
Miller, Sonja, tr. see Rzhevsky, Leonid D.
Miller, Stanley, et al. New York's Chinese Restaurants: A Guide.
Miller, Stanton S., ed. Solid Wastes.
Miller, Stella. Two Groups of Thessalian Gold.
Miller, Stephen A. General Zoology Laboratory Manual.
Miller, Stephen H., et al. Practical Points in Plastic Surgery.
Miller, Stephen W., jt. auth. see Kim, Seung H.
Miller, Stuart. Men & Friendship.
Miller, Stuart W. Library Use Instruction in Selected American Colleges.
Miller, Ted, ed. On Being a Caring Father.
--On Meeting Life's Challenges.
Miller, Theodore J., ed. Make Your Money Grow.
Miller, Thomas E. California Construction Defect & Land Subsidence Litigation: 1987 Supplement.
Miller, Thomas W. Business & Industry Perspectives on U. S. Production: Implications for Vocational Education.
Miller, Timothy S. The Birth of the Hospital in the Byzantine Empire.
Miller, Tom. World of the California Gray Whale.
Miller, Tom & Baxter, Elmar. The Baja Book.
--The Baja Book II.
Miller, Tom, jt. auth. see Rodriguez, Barbara.
Miller, Vincent A. The Guidebook for International Trainers in Business & Industry: Co-Published with the American Society for Training & Development, Inc.
Miller, W. D., jt. ed. see Matox, R. B.
Miller, W. Maureen. The French.
Miller, W. R. & Rose, H. C. Instructors & Their Jobs.
Miller, Walter G. Treasure of Brewsters Neck or a Busy Little Summer.
Miller, Walter M., Jr. A Canticle for Leibowitz.
Miller, Warren & Sorel, Edward. King Carlo of Capri.
Miller, Wilbur R., jt. auth. see McKnight Staff.
Miller, William. Trebizond: The Last Greek Empire.
Miller, William A. Big Kids' Mother Goose: Christian Counselor Finds New Insights in Old Stories.
--Prayers at Midpoint: Conversations with God for Those in Life's Second Half.
--Why Do Christians Break Down?
--You Count-You Really Do!
Miller, William B. America's Management Challenge: Capitalizing on Change.
Miller, William C. Estimating & Cost Control in Electrical Construction Design.
Miller, William C. & Gallina, Leonard. Estimating & Cost Control in Plumbing Design.
Miller, William D. A Harsh & Dreadful Love: Dorothy Day & the Catholic Worker Movement.
Miller, William E. Basic Drafting for Interior Designers.
Miller, William H., Jr. The Great Luxury Liners, Nineteen Twenty-Seven to Nineteen Fifty-Four: A Photographic Record.
Miller, William J., Jr. Crossing the Delaware: The Story of the Delaware Memorial Bridge, the Longest Twin Suspension Bridge in the World. Demerast, Kathy K., ed.
--A Ferry Tale: Crossing the Delaware on the Cape May-Lewes Ferry. Demarest, Kathy K., ed.
Miller, William, Jr. Luxury Liner Row-Passenger Ships at New York.
Miller, Wilma H. The First R: Elementary Reading Today.
--The Reading Activities Handbook.
Miller, Yvette E., ed. see De Carvalho-Neto, Paulo.
Miller, Yvonne A. Through My Eyes.
Miller, Zane L. The Urbanization of Modern America: A Brief History.
Millers Editors. Miller's CPA Exam Solutions: May 1978 Through November 1982.
--Miller's Solutions to the Uniform CPA Exam, November 1982.
Milles, Jim. International Court of Law Justice: A Selected Bibliography of Law Review Articles.
Millet, Mrs. Edward. An Australian Parsonage: The Settler & the Savage in Western Australia.
Millet, Robert. Perfected Millenial Kingdom.
Millett, Esther Lee. Togetherness Is Love: A Manual of Creative Teaching Ideas.
--What? Four Little Surprises!
Millett, K. C., ed. Algebraic & Geometric Topology: Proceedings of a Symposium Held at Santa Barbara in Honor of Raymond L. Wilder, July 25-29, 1977.
Millett, Kate. Sita.
Milley, C. Ross. The Prophets of Israel.
Millgate, Jane, ed. Editing Nineteenth-Century Fiction.
Millgate, Linda. The Almanac of Dates.
Millgate, Michael. Thomas Hardy: A Biography.
Millgate, Michael, jt. ed. see Mattheisen, Paul F.
Millhauser, Steven. From the Realm of Morpheus: A Mesmerizing Tour of the Human Imagination.
Millhone, J. P. & Willis, E. H., eds. New Energy Conservation Technologies & Their Commercialization: Proceedings.
Milliband, Ralph & Saville, J., eds. Socialist Register: Annuals: Nineteen Sixty-Eight to Nineteen Seventy-Eight.
Milligan, Burton A., intro. by see Heywood, John.
Milligan, Edward A. Dakota Twilight: The Standing Rock Sioux, 1874-1890.
Milligan, Edward E. Beginning Readings in French.
Milligan, Edward E., jt. auth. see Galpin, A. M.
Milligan, I. S., jt. ed. see Mann, J. Y.
Millikan, Brent, ed. see Institute for Food & Development Policy Staff.
Milliken, Mary E. Understanding Human Behavior.
Milliman, J. D. & Qingming, J., eds. Sediment Dynamics on the Changjiang Estuary & the Adjacent East China Sea: A Selection of Edited Papers from the International Symposium Held in Hangzhou, People's Republic of China, April 1983.
Milliman, J. D., et al. Recent Sedimentary Carbonates, Part 1: Marine Carbonates.
Milliman, John D., jt. ed. see Haq, Bilal U.
Milling, Bryan E. Handbook of Accounts Receivable Financing: A Dynamic Approach to Cash Flow & Profits.
Millingen, J. G. Curiosities of Medical Experience.
Millington, Ada, jt. auth. see Bershadsky, Luba.
Millington, Herbert. American Diplomacy & the War of the Pacific.
Millington, William G. Law & the College Student: Justice in Evolution.
Milliren, Alan, jt. auth. see Anderson, Karen.
Millis, W. Arms & the State: Civil-Military Elements in National Policy.
Millkie, Ron & Carlson, Ray. How You Can Appear in TV Commercials.
Millman, Dan. Way of the Peaceful Warrior: A Basically True Story.
Millman, Lawrence. Our Like Will Not Be There Again: Notes from the West of Ireland.
Millman, Marcia. Such a Pretty Face: Being Fat in America.
Millman, Richard S., jt. ed. see Gruber, Bruno.
Millner, Cork. Sherry: The Golden Wine of Spain.
Millner, R., et al, eds. Ultrasound Interaction in Biology & Medicine.
Millon, Henry, ed. Studies in Italian Art & Architecture: 15th Through 18th Centuries.
Millon, Rene, ed. Urbanization at Teotihuacan, Mexico, Vol. 1, Pts. 1 & 2: The Teotihuacan Map.
Millonzi, Joel C. Citizenship in Africa: The Role of Adult Education in the Political Socialization of Tanganyikans, 1891-1961.
Millot, N., ed. see Zoological Society of London Symposium Staff.
Mills, A. L., jt. ed. see Logsdail, D. H.
Mills, Anne, jt. auth. see Lee, Kenneth.
Mills, Clark, tr. see Breton, Andre.
Mills, D. C. & Pareti, F. I., eds. Platelets & Thrombosis.
Mills, D. Quinn. Labor-Management Relations.
Mills, David H., jt. auth. see Fretz, Bruce R.
Mills, David W., jt. auth. see Bloom, Herschel M.
Mills, David W., jt. auth. see Practising Law Institute Staff.
Mills, Desmond & Barnes, Mike. Amateur Gunsmithing.
Mills, Edward D. Architect's Detail Sheets: First Series.
--Architect's Detail Sheets: Second Series.
--Architect's Detail Sheets: Third Series.
Mills, Edwin S. & Hamilton, Bruce. Urban Economics.
Mills, F. John, jt. auth. see Harding, Richard M.
Mills, Gordon. Optimization in Economic Analysis.
Mills, Gussie. Cannery Kid.
Mills, John. Up in the Clouds, Gentlemen Please.
Mills, John, jt. auth. see Atcheson, Mack.
Mills, John F. Paint!
Mills, Kathi, ed. see Houston, Tom.
Mills, Mark. Strange & Scary Ghosts.
Mills, P. Managing for Profit.
Mills, P., jt. auth. see McGrath, Philomena.
Mills, Paul & Johnson, Robert F. Mark Adams: A Retrospective.
Mills, Richard C. The Colonization of Australia (1829-42) The Wakefield Experiment in Empire Building.
--Workbook on the Four Gospels.
Mills, Robert B. Offender Assessment: A Casebook in Corrections.
Mills, Robert E. The Cheyenne's Woman.
Mills, Russell, jt. auth. see Eno, Brian.
Mills, Sonya, jt. ed. see Sperling, Veronica.
Mills, W. Jay, ed. see Paterson, William.
Mills, William R., jt. auth. see West, Gary.
Millward, Michael & Coe, Brian. Victorian Townscape: The Work of Samuel Smith.
Millward, Neil, jt. auth. see Daniel, W. W.
Milman, David. Educational Conflict & the Law.
Milman, David & Flanagan, Terrence. Modern Partnership Law.
Milman, Harry A. & Sell, Stewart, eds. Application of Biological Markers to Carcinogen Testing.
Milman, Miriam, jt. auth. see Skira-Rizzoli Staff.
Milne, A. A. Once a Week.
--Pooh's Birthday Book.
--Toad of Toad Hall.
Milne, A. D. MOS Devices: Design & Manufacture.
Milne, Bruce G. Vocational Education for Gifted & Talented Students.
Milne, Dennis W. & Turner, Simon. An Atlas of Surgical Approaches to the Bones of the Horse.
Milne, Gordon. Stephen Crane at Brede: An Anglo-American Literary Circle of the Eighteen Nineties.
Milne, J. S. Clinical Effects of Aging: A Longitudinal Study.
Milne, John. Queen of Death.
Milne, John, jt. auth. see Jupp, T. C.
Milne, John, ed. Heinemann Guided Readers. Incl. Beginner Level. Rich Man, Poor Man. Jupp, T. C; Beginner Level. Death of a Soldier. Prowse, Philip; Beginner Level. Marco. Esplen, Mike; Dangerous Journey. Cox, Alwyn; Beginner Level. Money for a Motorbike. Milne, John; Beginner Level. The Truth Machine. Whitney, Norman; Elementary Level. Road to Nowhere. Milne, John; Elementary Level. The Black Cat. Milne, John; Elementary Level. Star for a Day. Prowse, Philip; Intermediate Level. Bristol Murder. Prowse, Philip; Intermediate Level. The Smuggler. Plowright, Piers; Intermediate Level. Football. Forbes, Duncan; Intermediate Level. The Woman Who Disappeared. Prowse, Philip; Intermediate Level. The Raid. Frewer, Glyn; Upper Level. Money for Sale. Hardcastle, Michael; Upper Level. The Story of Pop. Byrne, John; Upper Level. The Olympic Games. Tulloh, Bruce. Heinemann Ed.
Milne, John S. Surgical Instruments in Greek & Roman Times.
Milne, Joseph G. Greek & Roman Coins & the Study of History.
Milne, Lorus & Milne, Margery. Because of a Flower.
--The How & Why of Growing.
--Senses of Animals & Men.
--Water & Life.
--When the Tide Goes Far Out.
Milne, Lorus J. & Milne, Margery. Behavior in the Insect World.
--Gadabouts & Stick-at-Home: Wild Animals & Their Habitats.
Milne, Margery, jt. auth. see Milne, Lorus.
Milne, Margery, jt. auth. see Milne, Lorus J.
Milne, Patricia M., tr. Selected Short Stories of Thein Pe Myint.
Milne, R. & Strachey, C. The Theory of Programming Language Semantics.
Milne, R. D. Building Estate Maintenance Administration.
Milne, Teddy. Peace Porridge, No. 2: Russia, to Begin With.
Milne, Tom. The Cinema of Carl Dreyer.
Milner, Anita C. Newspaper Genealogical Column Directory.
Milner, G. W. & Phillips, G. Coulometry in Analytical Chemistry.
Milner, Marion. On Not Being Able to Paint.
Milner, Max, jt. auth. see Nerval, Gerard de.
Milner, R. A Calculus of Communicating Systems.
Milner, Wanda. How to Use Your Bible.
Milner, Wendy L. Personal Money Management with Your Micro.
Milne-Thomson, L. M. Antiplane Elastic Systems.
--Plane Elastic Systems.
Milnor, John. Introduction to Algebraic K-Theory.
Milns, R. D. & Ellis, J. R. Spectre of Phillip.
Milns, R. D., jt. auth. see Jones, B. W.
Milo, Mary. A Different Music.
Milos, Yara, tr. see Ionesco, Eugene.
Milosevich, Vincent. Toward Excellence: A Reader.
Milovanov, E. L. & Veistman, E. A., eds. English-Russian Dictionary of Environmental Control.
Milovsky, A. Mineralogy & Petrography.
--Suzdal: A Guide.
Milroy, M. E., ed. Church Lace: Being Eight Ecclesiastical Patterns in Pillow Lace.
Milsark, Gary L. Existential Sentences in English. Hankamer, Jorge, ed.
Milstead, William W., ed. Lizard Ecology: A Symposium.
Milsten, Richard. Male Sexual Function: Myth, Fantasy, Reality.
Milton, David. The Hyte Maneuver.

Milton, David & Milton, Nancy D. The Wind Will Not Subside: Years in Revolutionary China,1964-1969.
Milton, David S. Kabbalah.
Milton, Hilary. Fun House Terrors. Schwartz, Betty, ed.
--The Gitaway Box.
--Horror Hotel. Schwartz, Betty, et al, eds.
--Plot It Yourself Horror Stories, No. 8: Dungeon Demons. Arico, Diane, ed.
--Plot-Your-Own Horror Stories: Craven House Horrors. Schneider, Meg, ed.
--Shutterbugs & Car Thieves.
--Space Age Terrors! Schwartz, Betty, ed.
--Two from the Dead.
Milton, John. Milton.
--Paradise Lost.
Milton, John P. Prophecy Interpreted.
Milton, Joyce. Secrets of the Mummies.
Milton, Joyce, jt. auth. see Radosh, Ronald.
Milton, Mary Lee. The Poetry of Samuel Taylor Coleridge: An Annotated Bibliography of Criticism, 1935 to 1970.
Milton, Nancy D., jt. auth. see Milton, David.
Milton, Octavia. Assist One, Two & Three.
Milton, Ohmer & Shoben, Edward J., Jr., eds. Learning & the Professors.
Milton, R. C. & Nelder, J. A., eds. Statistical Computation.
Milton, Roger, et al. Unemployment, Poverty & Social Policy in Europe.
Milton, Sybil, jt. ed. see Friedlander, Henry.
Milts, Michael H. & Larson, Carl. Only a Gringo Would Die for an Anteater: The Adventures of a Veterinarian.
Milunsky, Aubrey. Know Your Genes.
Milward, John. The Beach Boys Silver Anniversary. Cherna, Ilene, ed.
Milwaukee Brewers Staff. Major League Baseball Manual.
Milwaukee County Welfare Rights Organization. Welfare Mothers Speak Out: We Ain't Gonna Shuffle Anymore.
Milwaukee Labor Committee & National Labor Law Center. Strategy Memo on Legal Issues & Strategies in Plant Closings.
Milwaukee Team Staff. Image One.
Milwidsky, B. M. & Gabriel, D. M. Detergent Analysis: A Handbook for Cost-Effective Quality Control.
Milyukova, M. S. Analytical Chemistry of Plutonium.
Mims, Amy, tr. see Ritsos, Yannis.
Mims, Cedric A. Pathogenesis of Infectious Disease.
Mims, Forrest M., III. Forrest Mims's Computer Projects.
Mims, Sam. Trail to a Pot of Gold.
Minahan, John. Eyewitness.
--The Face Behind the Mask: A Novel.
--Nine-Thirty-Fifty-Five.
Minahan, John, jt. auth. see Tress, Arthur.
Minami, Ryishin, jt. ed. see Kosobud, Richard.
Minar, Edwin L., Jr., tr. see Burkert, Walter.
Minasian, Stanley, et al. The World's Whales: The First Complete Illustrated Guide.
Minchew, Michael & Minchew, Norma. Oral Communication: The Essential Skill.
Minchew, Norma, jt. auth. see Minchew, Michael.
Mincoff, Marco K. Die Bedeutungsentwicklung der.
Mindel, C. & Habenstein, R. W., eds. Ethnic Families in America.
Mindell, Arnold. City Shadows: Psychological Interventions in Psychiatry.
--River's Way: The Process of Science & the Dreambody.
--Working with the Dreaming Body.
Minden, Shelley see Arditti, Rita, et al.
Mindess, et al. Antioch Humor Test.
Mindlin, R. D., ed. see CISM (International Center for Mechanical Sciences) Staff.
Mindszenty, Josef. Face of the Heavenly Mother.
Minear, Larry. New Hope for the Hungry? The Challenge of the World Food Crisis.
Minear, Paul S. I Pledge Allegiance: Patriotism & the Bible.
--Images of the Church in the New Testament.
Minear, Paul S. & Adams, Harry B. Pentecost 2. Achtemeier, Elizabeth, et al, eds.
Minear, Richard H. Japanese Tradition & Western Law: Emperor, State, & Law in the Thought of Hozumi Yatsuka.
--Victors' Justice: The Tokyo War Crimes Trial.
Miner, Alan E. That's a Good Idea!
Miner, Craig. West of Wichita: Settling the High Plains of Kansas, 1865-1890.
--West of Wichita: Settling the High Plains of Kansas, 1865-1890.
Miner, Dorothy E., et al. Two Thousand Years of Calligraphy.
Miner, Dwight C. Fight for the Panama Route.
Miner, Earl, ed. Writers & Their Background: John Dryden.
Miner, John B. The Management Process: Theory, Research, & Practice.
Miner, Malcolm. Healing & the Abundant Life.
Minford, Patrick, et al. Unemployment: Cause & Cure.
Ming, W. Mao's Betrayal.
Ming, Xiao. Two Rats Helping the Kitten.
Mingay, G. E., ed. The Victorian Countryside.
Mingjie, Wang, tr. see Lanyun, Liu.
Mingo, Jack, et al. The Couch Potato Guide to Life.
Mingqui, Cui, jt. auth. see Chinnery, John D.
Mings, Turley. The Study of Economics.
--The Study of Economics: Principles, Concepts & Applications.
--Working with the Study of Economics: Principles, Concepts & Applications.
Mingst, Karen. The Political Economy of International Commodity Trade.
Mingtong, Ma, tr. see Cong, Ding.
Minh-ha, Trinh Thi. Art Sans Oeuvre ou L'Anonymat dans les Arts Contemporains.
Minich, Quaid W., jt. auth. see Elonka, Stephen M.
Minifie, Bernard W. Chocolate, Cocoa & Confectionery: Science & Technology.
Mining & Metallurgy Instrumentation Symposium Staff. Instrumentation in the Mining & Metallurgy Industries, Vol. 7: Proceedings of the 8th Mining & Metallurgy Instrumentation Symposium.
Mining & Metallurgy Instrumentation Symposium. Instrumentation in the Mining & Metallurgy Industries, Vol. 8: Proceedings of the 9th Mining & Metallurgy Instrumentation Symposium.
Mining & Metallurgy Instrumentation Symposium Staff. Instrumentation in the Mining & Metallurgy Industries, Vol. 9.
Mining Informational Services Staff. World Demand for Raw Materials in 1985-2000.
Minisci, F., et al. Synthetic & Mechanistic Organic Chemistry.
Ministry of Light Industry, Scientific & Technical Information Institute Staff. Directory of International Consumer Goods Industries-1986.
Mink, Louis O. A Finnegans Wake Gazetteer.
Mink, Nelson. Pocket Gems.
Mink, Stephen. Insuring Your Home: How to Choose the Right Policy & Get the Most Benefit from Your Claim.
Minkin, Steve. A No Doubt Mad Idea. Nathan, Stella, ed.
Minkoff, Eli. C. A Laboratory Guide to Frog Anatomy.
Minn, Lorretta B. Rhymes, Riddles & Research.
Minnery, Tom, ed. Pornography: A Human Tragedy.
Minnesang, Sandy, jt. auth. see Kosuth, Joan.
Minnesota Trade Office Staff. Minnesota Medical & Healthcare Resources Guide: The 1986 Medical Alley Directory. Bolton, Urgil, ed.
Minnich, Jerry A. The Wisconsin Garden Guide.
Minnick, Wayne C. Art of Persuasion.
--Public Speaking.
Minnis, A. J. Chaucer & Pagan Antiquity.
Mino-Garces, Fernando. Early Reading Acquisition: Six Psycholinguistic Case Studies.
Minor, Edward O. & Fyre, H. R. Techniques for Producing Visual Instructional Media.
Minor, James. A Measure of Light.
Minor, Lewis J. Nutrition Additive & Flavor Standards.
Minoru, Yoshioka. Celebration in Darkness. Tadayoshi, Onuma, tr. from Japanese. Bd. with Strangers' Sky. Koichi, Iijima. U of Wash Pr.
Minot, Stephen. Surviving the Flood.
Minshull, Evelyn. Dune Witch.
Minshull, Evelyn W. Firebug!
--Madame Pastry & Meow.
--The Steps to My Best Friends House.
Minski. Deafness, Mutism, & Mental Deficiency in Children.
Minsky, Hyman P. Can "IT" Happen Again? Essays on Instability & Finance.
Minsky, Marvin. The Society of Mind.
Minsky, Morton & Machlin, Milt. Minsky's Burlesque.
Minter, D. W., jt. auth. see Cannon, P. F.
Minters, Frances C., jt. auth. see Sands, Harry.
Minto, C. S. Scotland Yesterday.
Minton, Arthur J. Philosophy: Paradox & Discovery.
Minton, John D. & Freidel, Frank. The New Deal in Tennessee, Nineteen Thirty-Two to Nineteen Thirty-Eight.
Minton, Madge R., jt. auth. see Minton, Sherman A.
Minton, Michael H. & Block, Jean L. What Is a Wife Worth? A Leading Expert Places a High Dollar Value on Homemaking.
Minton, Sherman A. & Minton, Madge R. Venomous Reptiles.
Mints, Fredrick E. Behavioral Patterns in Internal Audit Relationships.
Mints, Lloyd W. History of Banking Theory in Great Britain & the United States.
Mintz, Elizabeth E. Marathon Groups: Reality & Symbol.
Mintz, Harold K., jt. auth. see Vasile, Albert J.
Mintz, Jerome R. Anarchists of Casa Viejas.
Mintz, Lorelie M. How to Grow Fruits & Berries.
--Vegetables in Patches & Pots: A Child's Guide to Organic Vegetable Gardening.
Minugh, Carol J. & Tiger, Miller R. Extending the Benefits of Vocational Education to Indian Populations: Integrated Planning Package.
Miossi, Alfred F., ed. see Kim, Seung H. & Miller, Stephen W.
Mirabai & Nandy, Pritish. Krishna: Devotional Songs of Mirabai.
Mirabella, Lauren, jt. auth. see Konsler, Runelle.
Miranda, Jose P. Being & the Messiah: The Message of St. John. Eagleson, John, tr. from Span.
Miranda, Miguel Dario Cardinal Foreword by see Abeloe, William N.
Miranker, Willard L., jt. auth. see Kaucher, Edgar W.
Mirchandani, G. G. The People's Verdict: DCM Computer-Based Study.
Mirer, Thad W. Principles of Statistics & Econometrics.
Miri, Sujata. Religion & Society of North-East India.
Mirikitani, Janice, et al, eds. Time to Greez! Incantations from the Third World.
Miringoff, Marc L. Management in Human Service Organizations.
Mirkin, Gabe & Foreman, Laure. Getting Thin: All about Fat-How You Get it, How You Lose It, How You Keep It Off for Good.
Mirkovic, Irene. The Greedy Shopkeeper.
--The Greedy Shopkeeper.
Mirny, P. Written in the Book of Life.
Miroff, Franklin I., jt. auth. see Smith, Jerome.
Mirow, Kurt R. & Maurer, Harry. Webs of Power: International Cartels & the World Economy.
Mirsha, Jagannath & Sinha, R. K. Financing of State Plans.
Mirsky, G. Radio Electronic Measurements.
Mirsky, L., ed. Studies in Pure Mathematics.
Mirsky, Stanley & Hellman, Joan R. Diabetes: Controlling It the Easy Way.
Mirus, Jeffrey. The Divine Courtship: A History of Our Salvation.
Mirvis, Kenneth, jt. auth. see Gropman, Donald.
Mirvis, Philip H., jt. auth. see Kanter, Donald L.
Mirviss, Joan B., tr. see Burn, Barbara.
Mirza, Jerome. Illinois Tort Law & Practice.
Miscall, Peter D. The Workings of Old Testament Narrative.
Mische, Gerald & Mische, Patricia. Toward a Human World Order: Beyond the National Security Straitjacket.
Mische, Patricia, jt. auth. see Mische, Gerald.
Mischel, Theodore, ed. Human Action: Conceptual & Empirical Issues.
Mischel, Walter. Introduction to Personality.
Mischenko, A. S., et al. Problems in Differential Geometry & Topology.
Mise, David W. Algeria.
Mi Seitelman, ed. see International Defense Images Staff.
Misell, D. L. Image Analysis, Enhancement & Interpretation.
Miser, A. & Pennypincher, A. Factory Store Guide to All New England.
Miserez-Schira, Georges. The Art of Painting on Porcelain.
Mises, Richard Von see Von Mises, Richard.
Mishan, E. J. The Economic Growth Debate.
--Making the World Safe for Pornography.
Mishell, D., jt. ed. see Crosignani, P. G.
Mishell, Daniel R. & Brenner, Paul F., eds. Management of Common Problems in Obstetrics & Gynecology.
Mishima, Yukio. Madame de Sade. Keene, Donald, tr. from Japanese.
--Sun & Steel. Bester, John, tr. from Japanese.
Mishkoff, Henry C. Understanding Artificial Intelligence. Stevens, Jan & Luecke, Gerald, eds.
Mishle, Clifford, jt. auth. see Krause, Chester.
Mishler, Clifford, jt. auth. see Krause, Chester.
Mishlove, Jeffrey. PSI Development Systems.
Mishne, David, tr. see Konev, Ivan.
Mishra, R. K., ed. The Living State.
Mishra, S. N. Politics & Society in Rural India: A Case Study of Darauli Gram Panchayat, Siwan District, Bihar.
Mishra, V. B. From the Vedas to the Manu-Samhita: A Cultural Study.
Miskimin, Harry A. Money, Prices, & Foreign Exchange in Fourteenth Century France.
Miskin, J. Robert. Among Lions: The Battle for Jerusalem, June 5-7, 1967.
Misko, James A. Creative Financing of Real Estate.
Mislevy, Robert & Bock, R. Darrell. Bilog 2.
--PC-Bilog.
Mislow, V., jt. auth. see Maier, L.
Misner, Peter L., jt. auth. see Glusker, David L.
Misra, K. P. Afghanistan in Crisis.
Misra, K. P., jt. ed. see Narayanan, K. R.
Misra, K. S. Twentieth-Century English Poetic Drama: A Reevaluation.
Misra, R. S., jt. ed. see Bilgrami, K. S.
Misra, Raghunath P. & Sanusi, I. Daniel. An Atlas of Skin Biopsy: Diagnosis by Light & Immuno Microscopy of Vesico-Bullous, Connective Tissue Disorders & Vasculitis of the Skin.
Misra, S. P., jt. auth. see Shukla, A. C.
Missett, Judi S. The Jazzercise Workout Book: Your Customized Fitness Program-for Life.
Missildine, W. Hugh. Your Inner Child of the Past.
Missionary Research Library Staff. New York Dictionary Catalog of the Missionary Research Library.
Miss Piggy, jt. auth. see Henson Association.
Mr. X Staff. Double Eagle.
Mr. 1047. Classic Diet: The Way to Be Well.
Misterly, John, Jr. Over & Under.
Mistral, Gabriela. Crickets & Frogs: A Fable in Spanish & English. Dana, Doris, tr. from Span.
Mistrik, Josef. Basic Slovak.
MIT Conference on Advanced Research in VLSI Staff. Proceedings of MIT Conference on Advanced Research in VLSI, Cambridge, Massachusetts, Jan. 1982. Penfield, Paul, Jr., ed.
MIT Faculty Staff, ed. Nuclear Almanac: Confronting the Atom in War & Peace.
Mitcalfe, Ann & Wilson, Doug. Himalaya: Trekking from Sikkim to Pakistan.
Mitchard, Jacquelyn. Mother Less Child.
Mitchell. Urology for Nurses.
Mitchell & Lumb. Handbook of Surgical Diathermy.
Mitchell, A. Scottish Travel Books: List of Travels, Tours, Journeys - Relating to Scotland.
Mitchell, Adrian. Man Friday & Mind Your Head.
Mitchell, Andrew. The Enchanted Canopy: A Journey of Discovery to the Last Unexplored Frontier, the Rainforests of the World.
Mitchell, Anita M. Career Development Needs of Seventeen-Year Olds.
Mitchell, Arthur. Five Hundred Years of Travel Books about Scotland, 1296-1796.
Mitchell, Barbara. The Old Fasnacht.
--Tomahawks & Trombones.
Mitchell, Betty L. Edmund Ruffin: A Biography.
Mitchell, Bob. Color Printing.
Mitchell, Breon. James Joyce & the German Novel, 1922-1933.
Mitchell, Bruce M., et al. Planning for Creative Learning.
Mitchell, Carleton. Passage East.
Mitchell, Charles, jt. auth. see Bodnar, Edward W.
Mitchell, Charles W. & Riley, Joseph E. Beginning Model Rocketry.
Mitchell, Curtis. Getting in Shape for Skin & Scuba Diving.
Mitchell, Dan. The Souls of Lambs: A Fable.
Mitchell, David I., ed. New Mission for a New People: Voices from the Caribbean.
Mitchell, Dick. Mountaineering First Aid: A Guide to Accident Response & First Aid Care.
Mitchell, Don. Living Upcountry: A Pilgrim's Progress. Dinan, Dennis, ed.
--Moving UpCountry: A Yankee Way of Knowledge.
Mitchell, Don, jt. auth. see Grimm, Gary.
Mitchell, Don, jt. auth. see Wayman, Joe.
Mitchell, Donald. The Language of Modern Music.
Mitchell, Donald & Keller, Hans. Benjamin Britten.
Mitchell, Donald & Keller, Hans, eds. Music Survey: New Series, 1949-1952.
Mitchell, Donald G. About Old Story-Tellers.
Mitchell, Edwin V. Horse & Buggy Age in New England.
Mitchell, Everett R., ed. Management of Insect Pests with Semiochemicals: Concepts & Practice.
Mitchell, Ewan. The Director's Lawyer & the Company Secretary's Legal Guide.
Mitchell, Faith. Hoodoo Medicine.
Mitchell, G. Behavioral Sex Differences in Non-Human Primates.
--Human Sex Differences: A Primatologist's Perspective.
Mitchell, G. D., jt. auth. see Snowden, R.
Mitchell, Harold H. Comparative Nutrition of Man & Domestic Animals.
Mitchell, Harold P. Europe in the Caribbean.
Mitchell, Henry H. The Recovery of Preaching.
Mitchell, Hubert. Putting Your Faith on the Line.
Mitchell, J. L. Three Go Back.
Mitchell, J. R. & Domenet, J. G., eds. Thromboembolism: A New Approach to Therapy.
Mitchell, Jack, jt. auth. see Lewis, Jack.
Mitchell, Jesse C. The Ecstasy of Victory & the Agony of Defeat.
Mitchell, John. The Earth Spirit: Its Ways, Shrines & Mysteries.
Mitchell, John J., jt. auth. see Nightingale, Demetra S.
Mitchell, John W. Energy Engineering.
Mitchell, Joseph, jt. auth. see Wilson, Edmund.
Mitchell, Joseph B. Decisive Battles of the Civil War.
Mitchell, Joyce S. The Classroom Teacher's Workbook for Career Education.

Authors

--How to Make Ends Meet: Fifty-Five Special Job-Hunting Strategies for Retirees.
--My Mommy Makes Money.
--See Me More Clearly: Career & Life Planning for Teens with Physical Disabilities.
--Stopout! Working Ways to Learn.
--Taking on the World: Empowering Strategies for Parents of Children with Disabilities.
--What's Where: The Official Guide to College Majors.
--Your Job in the Computer Age: The Complete Guide to the Computer Skills You Will Need to Get the Job You Want.
Mitchell, Laura. Simple Relaxation.
Mitchell Library, Sydney, Australia Staff. Dictionary Catalog of Printed Books.
Mitchell, M. E. The Message & the Sequel.
Mitchell, M. J., jt. auth. see Cava, Michael P.
Mitchell, Margaret. Margaret Mitchell: A Dynamo Going to Waste (Letters to Allen Edee 1919-1921) Peacock, Jane B., ed.
Mitchell, Mozella G. Spiritual Dynamics of Howard Thurman's Theology.
Mitchell, Nance. Skin Sense: The Complete Guide to Skin Care for Men.
Mitchell, Osvald W. Keynes, Schumpeter & the Effort to Save Capitalism from Total Collapse.
Mitchell, Peter. Great Flower Painters: Four Centuries of Floral Art.
Mitchell, Richard. The Graves of Academe.
--The Leaning Tower of Babel.
--The Leaning Tower of Babel: And Other Outrages from the Underground Grammarian.
Mitchell, Richard M. The Steam Launch.
Mitchell, Richard S. Mineral Names: What Do They Mean?
Mitchell, Ross G., jt. ed. see Illsley, Raymond.
Mitchell, Simon. The Logic of Poverty: The Case of the Brazilian Northeast.
Mitchell, Stephen, jt. ed. see Seaby, H. A.
Mitchell, Stephen, tr. see Sahn, Seung.
Mitchell, Steven. Geology of Great Exuma Island: Field Guide for Second Symposium on the Geology of the Bahamas.
Mitchell, Susan. Entertaining Fast & Fresh.
--Fast & Fresh Cooking Basics.
Mitchell, Tony. Dario Fo: People's Court Jester.
Mitchell, W. J. Iconology: Image, Text, Ideology.
Mitchell, Walter. Unopened Letters & a Virgin Page.
Mitchell, Walter, tr. Christian Asceticism.
Mitchell, Wesley C. Gold, Prices & Wages Under the Greenback Standard.
Mitchell, William E. The Bamboo Fire: An Anthropologist in New Guinea.
--Mishpokhe: A Study of New York City Jewish Family Clubs.
Mitchell, William E. & Ireland, Thomas R. Common Stocks for Common Sense Investors.
Mitchell, William E., et al. Exercises in Macroeconomics: Development of Concepts.
Mitchell, Yvonne. Colette: A Taste for Life.
Mitchiner, Michael. Oriental Coins & Their Values: The Ancient & Classical World.
Mitchison, N. Avrion, ed. Manipulation of the Immune Response in Cancer.
Mitchison, R. A History of Scotland.
Mitchum, Hank. Cimarron.
--Santa Fe.
--Station, No. 22: Devil's Canyon.
--Virginia City.
Mitgang, Herbert. Get These Men Out of the Hot Sun.
--Kings in the Counting House.
--Kings in the Counting House.
--The Montauk Fault.
--The Montauk Fault.
--The Return.
Mitgutsch, Waltraud A. Three Daughters. Mueller, Lisel, tr.
Mithal, C. P. Miracles of Urine Therapy: A Practical Guide to Auto-Urine Therapy for Every Man, Woman & Child.
Mitooka, E. Illustration & Perspective.
Mitooka, Eiji. Airbrushing in Rendering.
Mitra, Devi. The Leaves of Autumn.
Mitra, Jayati D. Capital Goods Sector in LDCs: A Case for State Intervention.
Mitra, S. K. & Ekstrom, M. P., eds. Two-Dimensional Digital Signal Processing.
Mitra, S. S., jt. ed. see Nudelman, S.
Mitra, Sanjit K., jt. ed. see Temes, Gabor C.
Mitre Corp. Staff. Military Communications System Control Symposium.
Mitrevski, Paul. Can the English Language Become Phonetic?
Mitroff, Ian I. & Kilmann, Ralph H. Methodological Approaches to Social Science: Integrating Divergent Concepts & Theories.
Mitrokhina, V. I. & Motovilova, O. G. Russian for Scientists.
Mitrovic, George. Atlan Revisited: The War of the Gods.
Mitscherlich, Alexander & Mitscherlich, Margarete. The Inability to Mourn: Principles of Collective Behavior.
--The Inability to Mourn: Principles of Collective Behavior.
Mitscherlich, Margarete, jt. auth. see Mitscherlich, Alexander.
Mitschke, H. see Huth, F., et al.
Mitsuda, Hisatoshi, jt. ed. see Fukuda, Tetsuo.
Mitsuhashi, Jun, jt. ed. see Maramorosch, Karl.
Mitsuhashi, S., et al, eds. Plasmids: Medical & Theoretical Aspects.
Mitsuhashi, S., et al, eds. see Symposium on Antibiotics Resistance, 2nd, Smolenice Castle, Czechoslovakia, Jun 5-8, 1974.
Mitsui, T., et al. Ferro & Antiferroelectric Substances. Hellwege, K. H. & Hellwege, A. M., eds.
Mittal, S. P. The Aesthetic Venture: Virginia Woolf's Poetics of the Novel.
Mitter, S. K., jt. ed. see Marchesini, G.
Mitter, Wolfgang. Secondary School Graduation: University Entrance Qualification in Socialist Countries.
Mitterand. Wheat & Chaff.
Mitterand, Francois. The Wheat & the Chaff. Woodward, Richard & Hayter, Concilia, trs. from Fr.
Mitterauer, Michael & Sieder, Reinhard. The European Family: Patriarchy to Partnership from the Middle Ages to the Present. Oosterveen, Karla & Horzinger, Manfred, trs.
Mitterling, Philip I., ed. United States Cultural History: A Guide to Information Sources.
Mittins, W. H. A Grammar of Modern English.
Mittman, Charles, ed. Pulmonary Emphysema & Proteolysis.
Mitton, Simon. Daytime Star.
--Exploring the Galaxies.
Mittra, R., ed. Numerical & Asymptotic Techniques in Electromagnetics.
Mittra, R. A., ed. Computer Techniques for Electromagnetics.
Mittra, Sid & Gassen, Chris. Investment Analysis & Portfolio Management.
Mittwoch, Ursula. Genetics of Sex Differentiation.
--Sex Chromosomes.
Mityayev, U., jt. auth. see Apalin, G.
Mitz, Rick. Aim for a Job in the Record Business.
--Your Future As a Writer.
--Your Future Career in the American Government.
Miura, Akira, tr. see Suzuki, Takao.
Miura, N. & Chikazumi, S., eds. Physics in High Magnetic Fields: Proceedings.
Miura, R. M., ed. Baelund Transformations, the Inverse Scattering Method, Solutions, & Their Applications.
Miura, Y., et al. Advances in Biomedical Engineering.
Mix, Floyd M. House Wiring Simplified.
--Housewiring Simplified.
Mixon, S. R. Handbook of Data Processing Administration, Operations, & Procedures.
Mixter, Richard W., ed. see Heller, Lois J. & Mohrman, David E.
Miyamoto, H., et al, eds. Alkaline Earth Metal Halates.
Miyata, Ken, jt. auth. see Forsyth, Adrian.
Miyazawa, K. Input-Output Analysis & the Structure of Income Distribution.
Miyazawa, Kenji. Spring & Asura. Sato, Hiroaki, tr.
Miyazawa, T., jt. auth. see Emsley.
Mize, Jack P., jt. auth. see Carr, William N.
Mize, Jan L. & Cotterman, William W. Essential of Structured COBOL Programming.
Mizel, Steven B. & Jaret, Peter. The Human Immune System: The New Frontier in Medicine.
--In Self-Defense.
Mizell, M., ed. Biology of Amphibian Tumors.
Mizener, Arthur. The Far Side of Paradise: A Biography of F. Scott Fitzgerald.
Mizener, Arthur, ed. Modern Short Stories.
Mizener, Sharon Fusselman. Manhattan Transients.
Mizher, George H. Not Too Dusty.
Mizio, Emelicia, ed. Puerto Rican Task Force Report.
Mizio, Emelicia & Delaney, Anita J., eds. Training for Service Delivery to Minority Clients.
Mizrahi, Abe & Sullivan, Michael. Calculus & Analytic Geometry.
Mizuki, John. The Growth of Japanese Churches in Brazil.
Mizushima, M., tr. see Kaellen, G.
Mizushima, San-Ichiro. Structure of Molecules & Internal Rotation.
Mizushina, T., ed. see International Heat Transfer Conference Staff.
Mjelde, K. M. Methods of the Allocation of Limited Resources.
Mjos, Ole D., jt. ed. see Refsum, Helge.
Mladjenovic, M. Development of Magnetic B-Ray Spectroscopy.
--Radioisotope & Radiation Physics: An Introduction.
Mlecko, Joel, jt. auth. see Lauer, Eugene.
Mlinaric, Christina. Poetry of Love & Life.
Mlodozeniec, Juventyn M. I Knew Blessed Maximilian.
Mo, Timothy. An Insular Possession.
Moat, Albert G. Microbial Physiology.
Moberg, David A. The Church As a Social Institution.
Moberly, Robert B. Three Mozart Operas: Figaro, Don Giovanni, the Magic Flute.
Moberly, Walter. Legal Responsibility & Moral Responsibility. Sherman, Franklin, ed.
Mobil Corporation Staff. The Clock Is Running.
Mobiley, Arieta E. The Educational Crisis.
Mobley, George F., photos by. Alaska: High Roads to Adventure. Crump, Donald J., ed.
Moch, Cheryl, jt. auth. see Tannenhauser, Carol.
Mochalov, B. Requirements of Developed Socialist Society.
Moche, Dinah. Astronomy.
Mochi, Ugo, jt. auth. see MacClintock, Dorcas.
Mock, Ruth. Principles of Art Teaching.
Mocker, Donald W. & Spear, George E. Lifelong Learning: Formal, Nonformal, Informal, & Self-Directed.
Mockingbird, John. The Wokosani Road: A Novel of Indian Love in the Southwest.
Modak, E. S. The Guru & the Policemen: A Novel.
Model, Lisette, jt. auth. see Frank, Robert.
Modersohn-Becker, Paula. Paula Modersohn-Becker: The Letters & Journals, 1876-1907. Busch, Gunter & Von Reinken, Liselotte, eds. Wensinger, Arthur S. & Hoey, Carole C., trs.
Modesitt, L. E., Jr. Hammer of Darkness.
Modgil, Celia, jt. ed. see Modgil, Sohan.
Modgil, Sohan & Modgil, Celia, eds. Jean Piaget: An Interdisciplinary Critique.
Modigliani, Piero. Journals of a Scientician.
Modjeska, Lee. Handling Employment Discrimination Cases.
Mody, N. H. A Collection of Nagasaki Colour Prints & Paintings: Showing the Influence of Chinese & European Art on That of Japan.
Moe, Barbara. Pickles & Prunes.
Moe, J. Melvin, tr. see Ruud, Erling.
Moe, Terry M. The Organization of Interests: Incentives & the Internal Dynamics of Political Interest Groups.
Moede, Janet, jt. ed. see Egge, Mandus A.
Moehle, Natalia R. The Dimensions of Evil & Transcendence: A Sociological Perspective.
Moellenstedt, G., ed. see International Congress on X-Ray Optics & Microanalysis, 5th, 1968.
Moeller, Bill, jt. auth. see Moeller, Jan.
Moeller, F. H. Fungi of the Faeros. Incl. Pt. 1. Basidiomycetes; Pt. 2. Myxomycetes, Archimycetes, Phycomycetes, Asomycetes, & Fungi Imperfecti (with Appendix to Pt. 1. Lubrecht & Cramer.
Moeller, Jack R. & Liedloff, Helmut. Deutsch Heute: Grundstufe.
Moeller, Jan & Moeller, Bill. The Intracoastal Waterway.
Moeller, T. The Chemistry of the Lanthanides.
Moen, Daryl R. Newspaper Layout & Design.
Moerbeek, Kees. Patrick's Problem.
Moerbeek, Kees, jt. auth. see Dijs, Carla.
Moer Chen, Barbara D., jt. auth. see Blankenship, Martha L.
Moeri, Louise. First the Egg.
--The Girl Who Lived on the Ferris Wheel.
--How the Rabbit Stole the Moon.
Moerman, Daniel E. American Medical Ethnobotany: A Reference Dictionary.
Moertel, C. G. Multiple Primary Malignant Neoplasms: Their Incidence & Significance.
Moeslein, M. E. The Plays of Henry Medwall: A Critical Edition.
Moestro, Betsy. A More Perfect Union.
Moffat, C. A., jt. ed. see Moffat, E. A.
Moffat, David V. Common Algorithms in Pascal with Programs for Reading.
Moffat, E. A. & Moffat, C. A., eds. Highway Collision Reconstruction.
Moffatt & Mottram. Anatomy & Physiology for Physiotherapists.
Moffett, George D., Jr. So You Are Looking for a New Job... Now What?
Moffett, James. Coming on Center: English Education in Evolution.
--Teaching the Universe of Discourse.
Moffett, Martha, jt. auth. see Cook, Sy.
Moffit, Kathleen, et al. Archaeological Investigations along the Navajo-McCullough Transmission Line, Southern Utah & Northern Arizona.
Moffitt, John. Escape of the Leopard.
Moffitt, Michael. The World's Money.
--The World's Money: International Banking from Bretton Woods to the Brink of Insolvency.
Moffitt, Michael, jt. auth. see Letelier, Orlando.
Moffitt, Oleta S. Arranging Flowers for the Church.
Moger, Art. The Complete Pun Book.
Moger, Victoria. The Favour of Your Company: Invitations to London Social Events, 1750 to 1850.
Mogey, John, ed. Sociology of Marriage & Family Behavior 1957-1968: A Trend Report & Bibliography.
Moghissi, A. A., ed. Oil Spills.
Moghissi, A. A., et al, eds. Nuclear Power Waste Technology.
Moglen, Helene. Charlotte Bronte: The Self Conceived.
Mohamed, Ethel W. Ethel Wright Mohamed. Wilson, Christine, ed.
Mohamed, Ramli. Communication Planning Processes in the MUDA Agricultural Development Authority (MADA).
Mohamed A. El-Khawas & Cohen, Barry, eds. The Kissinger Study of Southern Africa: National Security Study Memorandum 39(Secret)
Mohammed, Rasheed. Animals I Love & Other Stories.
Mohan, Kshitij. Ashes of Gold.
Mohapatra, Surya N. Non-Invasive Cardiovascular Monitoring by Electrical Impedance Technique.
Mohler, James A. Dimensions of Faith.
--The Origin & Evolution of the Priesthood.
Mohler, R. R. & Ruberti, A. Theory & Applications of Variable Structure Systems with Emphasis on Modeling & Identification.
Mohler, R. R. & Shen, C. N. Optimal Control of Nuclear Reactors.
Mohonk Conference on the Negro Question Staff. Mohonk Conference on the Negro Question: Proceedings of the First & Second Conferences, 1890-1891.
Mohr, Charles E. & Poulson, T. Life of the Cave.
Mohr, Dolores V., tr. see Akhmanova, O. S., et al.
Mohr, Erna. The Asiatic Wild Horse. Goodall, Daphne M., tr.
Mohr, H. Lectures on Structure & Significance of Science.
Mohri, Hideo, jt. ed. see Sakai, Hikoichi.
Mohri, Hitoshi & Dillard, David H. Hypothermia for Cardiovascular Surgery.
Mohrig, Jerry R. & Neckers, Douglas C. Laboratory Experiments in Organic Chemistry.
Mohrman, David E., jt. auth. see Heller, Lois J.
Mohrmann, Gerald P., jt. auth. see Vohs, John L.
Mohtadi, M. F. Man & His Environment: Proceedings of the Third International Banff Conference, May 1980.
Mohtadi, M. F., ed. Man & His Environment, Vol. 2: Proceedings of the Second Banff Conference.
Moir, G., ed. Into Television.
--Teaching & Television: ETV Explained.
Moir, Lyn, tr. see Simenon, Georges.
Moise, E. E. Geometric Topology in Dimensions 2 & 3.
Moiser, Jeremy, tr. see Boecker, Hans J.
Moiseyev, N. N. & Rumyantsev, V. V. Dynamic Stability of Bodies Containing Fluid.
Mojena, Richard, jt. auth. see Ageloff, Roy.
Mojtabai, A. G. Autumn.
Mojzes, Paul. Christian-Marxist Dialogue in Eastern Europe.
Mokherjee, Sal, jt. auth. see Allen, Michael.
Mokrzycki, E. Philosophy of Science & Sociology: From the Methodological Doctrine to Research Practice.
Mokwa, Michael P., et al, eds. Marketing the Arts.
Mokyr, Joel. Why Ireland Starved: A Quantitative & Analytical History of the Irish Economy, 1800-1850.
Molarsky, Osmond. The Peasant & the Fly.
--The Peasant & the Fly.
Moldea, Dan E. The Hunting of Cain: A True Story of Money, Greed & Fratricide.
Moldenhauer, Hans. Death of Anton Weber.
Mole, John. Once There Were Dragons.
Mole, Robert L. Montagnards of South Vietnam: A Study of Nine Tribes.
--Thai Values & Behavior Patterns.
Mole, Winifred A. So Dear to Me.
Molenaar, Pete. Stradivari-Cremona Mystery Disclosed.
Molesworth, S. L., jt. auth. see Hodder, W. R.
Molesworth, W., ed. see Hobbes, Thomas.
Moley, Raymond. First New Deal.
--Realities & Illusions Eighteen Eighty-Six to Nineteen Thirty-Two. Freidel, Frank, ed.
Moliere. Don Juan. Fowlie, Wallace, tr. from Fr. & intro. by.
Moliere, pseud. Don Juan.
Moliere. Misanthrope. Grebanier, Bernard D., tr. from Fr.
--Pretentious Young Ladies. Briffault, Herma, tr. from Fr.
Moliere see Bentley, Eric.
Moliere see Weiss, Samuel A.
Molijn, H., jt. auth. see Mak, W.
Molin, Sven E. & Goodefellowe, Robin. Dion Boucicault, the Shaughraun.
Molitor, Joseph W. Architectural Photography.
Moll, Celeste. Dionne: A Novel.
Moll, J. & Dick, Carson W. Recent Advances in Rheumatology.
Molland, Einar. Christendom.
Mollard, F. R., jt. ed. see Murty, Y. V.
Mollenhoff, Clark R. Game Plan for Disaster.
Mollenstedt, G., et al, eds. see International Conference on Electron Microscopy Staff.
Moller, Aage R. & Boston, Pamela, eds. Basic Mechanisms in Hearing.

Authors

Authors

Moody, Graham B. Petroleum Exploration Handbook: A Practical Manual Summarizing the Application of Earth Sciences to Petroleum Exploration.
Moody, John. Truth about Trusts.
Moody, Michael E., jt. ed. see Cole, C. Robert.
Moody, Paul A. Genetics of Man.
--Genetics of Man.
Moody, Penderel, ed. Devon Pillow Lace: Its History & How to Make It.
Moody, Peter R., Jr. Opposition & Dissent in Contemporary China.
--The Politics of the Eighth Central Committee of the Communist Party of China.
Moody, Ralph. Come on Seabiscuit.
--Little Britches.
--Man of the Family.
Moody, Raymond A., Jr. Elvis after Life: Unusual Psychic Experiences Surrounding the Death of a Superstar.
Moody, Richard. The World of Dinosaurs.
Moody, Ron. Very Very Slightly Imperfect.
Moody, Sophy. What Is Your Name: A Popular Account of the Meaning & Derivations of Christian Names.
Moody, Williams J. How to Probate an Estate: A Handbook for Executors & Administrators.
Mook, Jane D. Probe Probe.
Moon, Brenda E., compiled by. Periodicals for South-East Asian Studies: A Union Catalogue of Holdings in British & Selected European Libraries.
Moon, Cliff. Pigs on the Farm.
--Poultry on the Farm.
--Sheep on the Farm.
Moon, Doug. Gardening for People: Who Think They Don't Know How.
Moon, F. C., ed. Mechanics of Superconducting Structures.
Moon, Jan. Living with Nature in Hawaii.
Moon, Jay. Chancellor of Mars.
Moon, Lawrence D. God's Fool.
Moon, M. L. & Smolensky, Eugene, eds. Augmenting Economic Measures of Well-Being.
Moon, Sonia. Poppy Visits Holiday Lane.
Moon, William L. Blue Highways.
--Blue Highways: A Journey into America.
Moonan, Willard. Martin Buber & His Critics: An Annotated Bibliography of Writings in English through 1978.
Mooney, Christopher F. Religion & the American Dream: The Search for Freedom Under God.
Mooney, Elizabeth C. Men & Marriage: The Changing Role of Husbands.
Mooney, Gavin H. International Perspectives in Health Economics: Selected Papers from the World Congress in Health Economics, Leiden, the Netherlands, September 1980.
Mooney, H. A., jt. ed. see DiCastri, F.
Mooney, Hal. A, jt. ed. see Chabot, Brain F.
Mooney, Harold A., ed. Convergent Evolution in Chile & California: Mediterranean Climate Ecosystems.
Mooney, James. Ghost Dance Religion: Shakers of Puget Sound - Extracts.
Mooney, James L. Dictionary of American Naval Fighting Ships.
Mooney, Patrick. A Gift of Love: Remembering the Old Anew.
Mooney, Peter, jt. auth. see Bown, Colin.
Mooney, Thomas. Arithmetic That We Need.
--The Getting along Series of Skills. Incl. Vol. I. After School Is Out; Vol. II. Al Looks for a Job; Vol. III. A Job at Last; Vol. IV. Money in the Pocket; Vol. V. From Tires to Teeth. Pendergrass Pub.
Moor, James & Nelson, Jack. A Manual for Bertie.
Moorat, Joseph. Nursery Songs.
Moorat, Joseph & Woodroffe, Paul. Nursery Songs.
Moorcock, Michael. An Alien Heat.
--Behold the Man.
--The End of All Songs.
--The Hollow Lands.
--The Knight of the Swords.
--The War Hound & the World's Pain.
Moore. Two-Phase Steam Flow in Turbines & Separators.
Moore, jt. auth. see Dames.
Moore, et al. Swingin' Texas Fiddlin'
Moore, Albert C. Iconography of Religions: An Introduction.
Moore, Alma C. How to Clean Everything.
--How to Clean Everything.
Moore, Anne S. Breeding Purebred Cats.
Moore, Arthur. The Kid from Rincon.
--Trackdown.
Moore, B. Workers in World News.
Moore, Barrington, Jr Soviet Politics - The Dilemma of Power: The Role of Ideas in Social Change.
Moore, Basil, ed. The Challenge of Black Theology in South Africa.
Moore, Bradley G. Philosophy Applied to Controversial Issues in a Democratic Society.
Moore, Brian. Cold Heaven.
--The Doctor's Wife.
--The Great Victorian Collection.
Moore, Brooke & Parker, Richard. Critical Thinking: Evaluating Claims & Arguments in Everyday Life.
Moore, C. B. Meteorites.
Moore, C. C., ed. see Apostol, T. M.
Moore, C. C., ed. see Grauert, H. & Fritzsche, K.
Moore, C. H. Uber Deutschland: A Reader on German Affairs.
Moore, Carl H. WWII: Flying the B-26 Marauder over Europe.
Moore, Carleton B., jt. auth. see Mason, Brian.
Moore, Charles & Allen, Gerald. The Place of Houses.
Moore, Chris. How to Handle Customer Complaints.
Moore, Clancy, jt. auth. see Tuten, Rich.
Moore, Clare, ed. The Visual Dimension: Aspects of Jewish Art.
Moore, Clement & Mason, Alice L. Christmas Twin Pack.
Moore, Clement C. The Night Before Christmas Coloring Book.
Moore, Clement H. Images of Development: Egyptian Engineers in Search of Industry.
Moore, Colin & Brown, John. Community Versus Crime.
Moore, D. F. Principles & Applications of Tribology.
Moore, D. M. Plant Cytogenetics.
Moore, Dan H. see Oster, Gerald, et al.
Moore, David S. & Yackel, James W. Applicable Finite Mathematics.
Moore, David W. & Readence, John E. Prereading Activities for Content Area Reading & Learning.
Moore, Dennis, jt. auth. see Simon, Michael.
Moore, Derry & Pick, Michael. The English Room.
Moore, Dorothy, jt. auth. see Moore, Raymond.
Moore, Douglas. Listening to Music.
Moore, Earl J., jt. auth. see Gysbers, N.
Moore, Edward. Studies in Dante, First Series: Scriptures & Classical Authors in Dante.
--Studies in Dante, Third Series: Miscellaneous Essays.
Moore, Eleanor I. And the Truth Shall Set You Free.
Moore, Elisabeth. Bend with the Wind.
Moore, Elizabeth C. An Almanac for Music Lovers.
Moore, Emily. Whose Side Are You On?
Moore, Eva. Clarion Cook Book for Boys & Girls.
--The Cookie Book.
Moore, Franklin G. & Jablonski, Ronald. Production Control.
Moore, Gary. The Gift of God. Wallace, Mary H., ed.
Moore, George. Brook Kerith.
--Esther Waters.
--Hail & Farewell. Cave, Richard, ed.
--Heloise & Abelard.
Moore, Georgie. Reaching Out - How to Love & Be Loved.
Moore, Gerald. Twelve African Writers.
--The Unashamed Accompanist.
Moore, Glover. A Calhoun County, Alabama, Boy in the 1860s. Moore, Glover, Jr., ed.
Moore, H. D. & Kibbey, D. R. Manufacturing: Materials & Processes.
Moore, H. Frazier. Public Relations: Principles, Cases & Problems.
Moore, Harry E. Tornadoes over Texas: Waco & San Antonio in Disaster.
Moore, Howard W. Plowing My Own Furrow.
Moore, Inge, tr. see Baader, Juan.
Moore, J. E. Design for Good Acoustics & Noise Control.
Moore, J. R. Principles of Oral Surgery.
Moore, James, jt. auth. see Baylor, J.
Moore, James E. The Pelican Guide to the Bahamas.
Moore, James F. Sexuality & Marriage.
--Situation Analyst: Stategic Manager.
Moore, James T., jt. ed. see Younger, Edward.
Moore, Jane A., ed. Cry Sorrow, Cry Joy: Selections from Contemporary African Writers.
Moore, Jean, ed. Roads to Recovery: A National Directory of Alcohol & Drug Addiction Treatment Centers.
Moore, Jennie Douglass. Rhyme of a Race & Other Poems.
Moore, Jerrold N. A Matter of Records: Fred Gaisberg & Golden Era of the Gramophone.
Moore, Jim. Atlanta Hawks.
--Dallas Mavericks.
--Detroit Pistons.
--Houston Rockets.
--Indiana Pacers.
--Kansas City Kings.
--Los Angeles Lakers.
--Milwaukee Bucks.
--New Jersey Nets.
--Phoenix Suns.
--San Antonio Spurs.
--San Diego Clippers.
--Utah Jazz.
--Washington Bullets.
Moore, Joan W. Mexican Americans.
Moore, John, ed. Jane's Fighting Ships 1986-87.
--Jane's NATO Warships Handbook.
--Jane's Naval Review.
--Jane's Naval Review.
Moore, John, tr. see Stevenson, William.
Moore, John E. Warships of the Royal Navy.
--Warships of the Soviet Navy.
Moore, John E., jt. ed. see Anderson, Stanley V.
Moore, John G., ed. Scientific Basis for Nuclear Waste Management.
Moore, John H. Over-Sexed, Over-Paid & Over Here: Americans in Australia 1941-1945.
--The South Carolina Highway Department, 1917-1987.
Moore, John N. How to Teach Origins.
--Should Evolution Be Taught?
Moore, John N., ed. see Bliss, Richard.
Moore, John N., et al. National Security Law.
Moore, John W. Moore's Historical, Biographical, & Miscellaneous Gatherings.
Moore, Judith K., jt. auth. see Colley, Ann C.
Moore, Kathleen, ed. Vegetarian Times Guide to Dining in the U. S. A.
Moore, Kay, jt. auth. see Conger, Shirley.
Moore, Keith L. The Developing Human.
--Study Guide & Review Manual of Human Embryology.
Moore, Kristin A., et al. Teenage Motherhood: Social & Economic Consequences.
Moore, Kurt R. Archaeology & Cultural Resources Management: Selected Topics.
Moore, L. P. Does This Mean My Kid's a Genius.
Moore, Lilian. Go with the Poem.
--I Thought I Heard the City.
--Papa Albert.
--Sam's Place.
--See My Lovely Poison Ivy.
Moore, Lilian, compiled by. To See the World Afresh. Thurman, Judith.
Moore, Linda P. You're Smarter Than You Think: At Least 500 Fun Ways to Expand Your Intelligence.
Moore, Lloyd. The Jury: History of the Trial Jury.
Moore, M. J. & Sieverding, C. H. Two-Phase Steam Flow in Turbines & Separators: Theory, Instrumentation, Engineering.
Moore, Mabel. Carthage of the Phoenicians: In the Light of Modern Excavation.
Moore, Marcia, jt. auth. see Alltounian, Howard S.
Moore, Marie. Portrait of Essex.
Moore, Marsha E. The Teddy Bear Book.
Moore, Marvin. Where Is Bobby Now?
Moore, Marvin G. Insight into Relativity.
Moore, Maurice. The Maurice Moore-Betty Cooking School Book of Fine Cooking.
Moore, Merrill. Poems of American Life.
Moore, Michele, ed. Public Welfare Directory, 1977-1978.
--Public Welfare Directory, 1978-1979.
--Public Welfare Directory, 1979-1980.
Moore, Michele, jt. ed. see Frank, Perry.
Moore, Mick & Connell, John, eds. Village Studies: Data Analysis & Bibliography: Africa, Middle East & North Africa, Asia (Excluding India), Pacific Islands, Latin America, West Indies & the Caribbean, 1950-1975.
Moore, Neil F. What's Next.
Moore, P. D. & Bellamy, D. J. Peatlands.
Moore, Pat & Conn, Paul. Disguised.
Moore, Patricia G., ed. see Schulz, James H. & Leavitt, Thomas D.
Moore, Patrick. The A-Z of Astronomy.
--Can You Speak Venusian?
--Can You Speak Venusian? A Guide to Independent Thinkers.
--Guide to Mars.
--Naked-Eye Astronomy.
--New Guide to the Moon.
--New Guide to the Planets.
--The New Guide to the Stars.
--The Next Fifty Years in Space.
Moore, Patrick & Cattermole, Peter J. Craters of the Moon: An Observational Approach.
Moore, Patrick, jt. auth. see Hunt, Garry.
Moore, Patrick, ed. Astronomical Telescopes & Observatories for Amateurs.
--Yearbook of Astronomy, 1970.
--Yearbook of Astronomy, 1975.
--Yearbook of Astronomy, 1976.
--Yearbook of Astronomy 1977.
--Yearbook of Astronomy, 1978.
--Yearbook of Astronomy, 1980.
--Yearbook of Astronomy, 1981.
--Yearbook of Astronomy, 1982.
--Yearbook of Astronomy, 1983.
--Yearbook of Astronomy, 1984.
--Yearbook of Astronomy, 1987.
Moore, Patrick, tr. see Charon, Jean.
Moore, Philip S. Century of Law at Notre Dame.
Moore, Philip S. & Dulong, Marthe. Sententiae Petri Pictaviensis 1.
Moore, Philip S., et al. Sententiae Petri Pictaviensis 2.
Moore, Phyllis S. Illustrated PageMaker 1.0a.
Moore, R. I., ed. Atlas of World History.
Moore, Randy, jt. auth. see Vodopich, Darrell.
Moore, Raymond & Moore, Dorothy. Homespun Schools.
Moore, Rebecca. A Sympathetic History of Jonestown: The Moore Family Involvement in Peoples Temple.
Moore, Richard D. & Webb, George D. The K Factor: Reversing & Preventing High Blood Pressure Without Drugs.
Moore, Robert. The Social Impact of Oil: The Case of Peterhead.
Moore, Robin. The Big Paddle.
Moore, Robin & Machlin, Milt. The Family Man.
Moore, Roger E. Jason's First Quest.
--Nightmare Realm of Baba Yaga.
Moore, Ruth. Niels Bohr: The Man, His Science, & the World They Changed.
Moore, Ruth N. Hiding the Bell.
Moore, Sally F. Law As Process: An Anthropological Approach.
Moore, Sally F. & Myerhoff, Barbara G., eds. Symbol & Politics in Communal Ideology: Cases & Questions.
Moore, Sandra S. The Turning Point: A Program for Women in Transition Participant Packet. Welborn, Andrea & Hartman, Carol, eds.
Moore, Sandra S., ed. see Jones, Dan.
Moore, Sandra S., et al, eds. The Turning Point: A Program for Women in Transition Trainer Manual.
Moore, Susan R. The Drama of Discrimination in Henry James.
Moore, Susanna. My Old Sweetheart.
Moore, Thomas. Lyrics & Satires from Tom Moore. O'Faolain, Sean, ed.
Moore, Thomas & Frederick, Norris. The Saturday Notebook: A Diary for Children & Adults to Use Together.
Moore, Vardine. Mice Are Rather Nice.
Moore, W. Basic Physical Chemistry: Solutions Manual.
Moore, W. G. The Tutorial System & Its Future.
Moore, Walter J. Basic Physical Chemistry.
Moore, Ward. Bring the Jubilee.
Moore, Wilbert E. Creative & Critical Thinking.
Moore, Wilbur E., jt. auth. see Black, John W.
Moore, William & Berlitz, Charles. The Philadelphia Experiment.
Moore, William T. Dateline Chicago: A Veteran Newsman Recalls Its Heyday.
Moore-Betty, Maurice, jt. auth. see Travers, P. L.
Moorehead, Caroline. Hostages to Fortune.
Moorehead, Cleatus. Math Made Fun for the Young Child.
Moores, B. M., et al. Practical Guide to Quality Assurance in Medical Imaging.
Moores, Dick. Gasoline Alley.
Moores, Donald F. Educating the Deaf: Psychology, Principles & Practices.
--Educating the Deaf: Psychology, Principles, & Practices.
Moorey, P. R. Ancient Persian Bronzes in the Adam Collection.
Moorhouse, Geoffrey. Calcutta: The City Revealed.
--India Britannica.
--To the Frontier.
Moorman, Phyllis. Attracting, Feeding & Housing Wild Birds: With Project Plans.
Moorman, Thomas. How to Make Your Science Project Scientific.
--How to Work Toward Agreement.
Moorsom, Richard. Namibia: Transforming a Wasted Land.
Moos, R. H. & Brownstein, R. Environment & Utopia: A Synthesis.
Moos, Rudolf & Brownstein, Robert. Environment & Utopia: A Synthesis.
Mooser, Stephen. Funnyman & the Penny Dodo.
--The Ghost with the Halloween Hiccups.
--Invasion of the Mutants.
--The Mind Bandits.
--Monster Fun.
Mooth, Verla A. The Spirit-Filled Life.
Moo-Young. Advances in Biotechnology: Fermentation & Yeasts--Proceedings of the 6th International Fermentation Symposium-5th International Symposium on Yeasts, London, Canada, July 20-25, 1980.
Moo-Young, M., jt. auth. see United Nations Environment Programme Staff.
Mora, George & Brand, Jeanne L. Psychiatry & Its History: Methodological Problems in Research.
Mora, Jaime & Palacios, Rafael, eds. Glutamine: Metabolism, Enzymology & Regulation.
Moraal, J. & Kraiss, F. K., eds. Manned Systems Design: Methods, Equipment, & Applications.
Morad, Martin & Smith, Susan, eds. Biophysical Aspects of Cardiac Muscle.
Morain, Stanley. Systematic & Regional Biogeography.
Morain, Stanley A., pref. by. Thermosense II: Proceedings.
Morais, Vamberto. A Short History of Anti-Semitism.
Morales, Juan-Antonio. Bayesian Full Information Structural Analysis.
Morales, Pablo. Big Deal in Veragua.

Authors

Moran, Deborah, et al. GED Mathematics Test Preparation Guide: High School Equivalency Examination.
Moran, Gabriel. Interplay: A Theory of Religion & Education.
Moran, Hugh, tr. see Lubich, Chiara.
Moran, Hugh, tr. see Lucarini, Spartaco.
Moran, Hugh J., tr. see Lubich, Chiara.
Moran, Marguerite K., jt. auth. see Lowenheim, Frederick A.
Moran, Martha M. Sugar & Mr. Duck.
--Sugar Gets the Skunk.
Moran, Maya. Down to Earth: An Insider's View of a Frank Lloyd Wright Prairie House.
Moran, Peg. Invest in Yourself: A Woman's Guide to Starting Her Own Business.
Moran, Peter. A Speck in the Sky.
Moran, Richard. Cold Sea Rising.
--Cold Sea Rising.
Moran, Robert. A Hiking Guide to Acadia National Park & Mount Desert Island.
Moran, Robert D. OSHA Handbook.
Moran, Robert T., jt. auth. see Harris, Philip R.
Moran, Theodore H. Oil Prices & the Future of OPEC: The Political Economy of Tension & Stability in the Organization of Petroleum Exporting Countries.
Moran, Tom, illus. Cyclist's Training Diary.
Moran, William L., ed. see Jacobsen, Thorkild.
Morando, B., ed. see COSPAR-IAU-IAG-IUGG-IUTAM Staff.
Morano, Roy W. The Protestant Challenge to Corporate America: Issues of Social Responsibility. Farmer, Richard, ed.
Moransee, Jesse R., ed. Children's Prize Books: An Int'l Listing of 193 Children's Literature Prizes.
Morash, Merry, jt. auth. see Trojanowicz, Robert C.
Moravcsik, Julius & Temko, Phillip, eds. Plato on Beauty, Wisdom & the Arts.
Morawetz, Thomas. Wittgenstein & Knowledge: The Importance of "On Certainty"
Morch, J., ed. Calcium Ion Antagonists in Cardiovascular Disease: Proceedings of an International Conference, 12-13 October 1979, Toronto, Canada.
Mordden, Ethan. Demented: The World of the Opera Diva.
--The Splendid Art of Opera: A Concise History.
Mordell, L. J. Diophantine Equations.
Mordvinoff, Nicolas, jt. auth. see Lipkind, William.
More, A. I., tr. see Sander, U., et al.
More, Carey, jt. auth. see More, Julian.
More, Daphne. Discovering Country Winemaking.
More, Julian & More, Carey. Views from a French Farmhouse.
More, Paul E. Platonism.
Morea, Peter. Guidance, Selection, & Training: Ideas & Applications.
Moreau, Claude. Moulds, Toxins & Food.
Moreau, James F. Effective Small Business Management.
Moreau, Lucien, jt. auth. see Grimal, Henri.
Moreau, R. E. Bird Faunas of Africa & Its Islands.
Moreau De Saint-Mery, Mederic L. A Civilization That Perished: The Last Years of White Colonial Rule in Haiti. Spencer, Ivor D., abridged by. & tr. from Fr.
Moreby, D. H. Personnel Management in Merchant Ships.
Morecki, A., ed. Robotics & Manipulators: Theory & Practice.
Morecki, A. & Bianchi, G., eds. Theory & Practice of Robots & Manipulators, III: Proceedings of the 3rd Symposium.
Moreen. Miniature Paintings.
Morehead, Richard. Richard Morehead's Texas.
Morehouse, Clifford P., jt. auth. see Wilson, Frank E.
Morehouse, Cynthia T., jt. ed. see Williamsen, Marvin.
Morehouse, Ward & Chopra, Ravi. Chicken & Egg: Electronics & Social Change in India.
Morehouse, Ward, ed. Handbook of Tools for Community Economic Change.
Morel, Julian. Pullman.
Morel, T. & Dalton, C., eds. Aerodynamics of Transportation.
Morell, R. W. Administrative Finance.
Morella, Joe & Epstein, Edward Z. Jane Wyman: A Biography.
--Jane Wyman: A Biography.
--Loretta Young: An Extraordinary Life.
Morelli, George, ed. Basic Psychology: Selected Readings.
Morelli, Remo, et al, eds. Clinical Studies of Complement.
Moreno, Harriet N., et al. Test of English As a Foreign Language: TOEFL.
Moreno, J. L. The First Psychodramatic Family.
--Theater of Spontaneity.
Morey, Charles R. Christian Art.
--Medieval Art.
Morey, Robert. A Christian Handbook for Defending the Faith.
Morey, Robert A. Worship Is All of Life.
Morey, Roy D., jt. auth. see Eidenberg, Eugene.
Morfey, Wallace. Painting the Day: Thomas Chruchyard of Hoodbridge.
Morfill, G. E., ed. Dust in Space & Comets: Proceedings of the Topical Meeting of the COSPAR Interdisciplinary Scientific Commission B (Meetings B1 & B2) of the COSPAR 25th Plenary Meeting, Graz, Austria, 25 June-7 July 1984.
Morford, Ted R. & Mauer, Shelley M. The Job World Workbook.
Morgado, Fernando, et al. T & B Cell Cooperation.
Morgan. Labor Economics.
Morgan, ed. Ergogenic Aids & Muscular Performance.
Morgan, Arthur, jt. auth. see Morgan, Griscom.
Morgan, Arthur E. Observations.
Morgan, Barbara, ed. Problems in Obstetric Anaesthesia.
Morgan, Brian & Wright, Margaret. Essentials of Plastic & Reconstructive Surgery with Notes on Clinical, Nursing & General Management.
Morgan, Campbell G. Analyzed Bible.
--Analyzed Bible.
Morgan, Charles H. George Bellows: Painter of America.
Morgan, Clifford T., et al. Introduction to Psychology.
Morgan, Cynthia. If You Love Somebody Who Smokes: Confessions of a Nicotine Addict.
Morgan, D. H. The Family, Politics & Social Theory.
Morgan, D. J. The Official History of Colonial Development. Incl. Vol. 1. The Origins of British Aid Policy 1924-1945; Vol. 2. Developing British Colonial Resources 1945-1951; Vol. 3. Reassessment of British Aid Policy 1951-1965; Vol. 4. Changes in British Aid Policy 1951-1970; Vol. 5. Guidance Towards Self-Government on British Colonies 1941-1971. Humanities.
Morgan, D. M., jt. auth. see Keay, A. J.
Morgan, D. V., jt. ed. see Howes, M. J.
Morgan, Dale L. see Hammond, George P.
Morgan, David, jt. auth. see Evans, Mary.
Morgan, David H. Harvesters & Harvesting, Eighteen Forty to Nineteen Hundred: A Study of the Rural Proletariat. Nuti, Frances, ed.
Morgan, David R. Legislative Attitudes Toward State Constitutional Revision: The Oklahoma Case.
Morgan, David R., jt. auth. see Whorton, Joseph W., Jr.
Morgan, Donn F. Wisdom in the Old Testament Traditions.
Morgan, Douglas H., et al. Diseases of the Temporomandibular Apparatus: A Multidisciplinary Approach.
Morgan, Dudley E. Living, Dealing, Learning & Growing with Your Children.
Morgan, E. Philip, jt. ed. see Carter, Gwendolen M.
Morgan, Edmund S. The Genius of George Washington.
--So What About History.
Morgan, Edward, tr. see Weores, Sandor & Juhasz, Fernec.
Morgan, Elizabeth. Custody: A True Story.
Morgan, Florence H. & Morgan, Fred. Experiences.
Morgan, Fred, jt. auth. see Morgan, Florence H.
Morgan, G. Campbell. The Parable of the Father's Heart.
--Practice of Prayer.
Morgan, Griscom & Morgan, Arthur. Small Community As Educator & Human Scale in Schools.
Morgan, Hal & Symmes, Daniel. Amazing 3-D.
Morgan, Harry, jt. ed. see Mueller, Jeanne.
Morgan, Henry & Booth, George. Dogs.
Morgan, Henry H. The Interviewer's Manual.
Morgan, Henry J. Bibliotheca Canadensis: A Bio-Bibliographical Manual of Canadian Literature.
Morgan, J. B., jt. auth. see Snell, K. S.
Morgan, James. Computer Power for Your Accounting Firm.
Morgan, Jan. From Holland with Love: Delicious Dutch Recipes.
Morgan, Jane, et al. Nicknames: Their Origins & Social Consequences.
Morgan, Janet, jt. ed. see Hoggart, Richard.
Morgan, Jefferson, jt. auth. see Lunde, Donald T.
Morgan, Jeremy. Draw Dogs.
Morgan, Jimmie N. A Doll Without Hands.
Morgan, Jimmy. How the World Looks to a Georgian.
Morgan, Joan, ed. see Conference on Recombinant DNA, Committee on Genetic Experimentation (COGENE) & the Royal Society of London, Wye College, Kent, UK, April, 1979.
Morgan, Joe. Baseball, My Way. Cohen, Joel H., ed.
Morgan, John. Complete History of Algiers.
Morgan, John H. Who Becomes a Bishop? A Study of Priests Who Become Bishops in the Episcopal Church (1960 to 1980)
Morgan, John H., ed. Aging in Developing Societies: A Reader in Third World Gerontology.
--Coleridge in Memoriam: A Poetry Anthology to Samuel Taylor Coleridge (1834-1984)
Morgan, John P. & Kagan, Doreen V., eds. Society & Medication: Conflicting Signals for Prescribers & Patients.
Morgan, John S. The Wolf Strikes.
Morgan, Joseph. Introduction to Geometrical & Physical Optics.
Morgan, Keith, jt. auth. see Lewis, Arnold.
Morgan, Kenneth O. The Age of Lloyd George: The Liberal Party & British Politics, 1880-1929.
Morgan, Len. The AT-6 Harvard. Gentle, Ernest J., ed.
--Crackup.
Morgan, Lewis B. A Casebook for School Counselors.
Morgan, Lyndon, ed. see National Computing Centre, Ltd. Staff.
Morgan, Margery. August Strindberg. King, Bruce & King, Adele, eds.
--August Strindberg. King, Bruce & King, Adele, eds.
Morgan, Margery M. The Shavian Playground: An Exploration of the Art of George Bernard Shaw.
Morgan, Marilyn A. Managing Career Development.
Morgan, Martha, jt. auth. see Fibush, Esther.
Morgan, Mary & Mosteller, Dee. Trapunto & Other Forms of Raised Quilting.
--Trapunto Quilting.
Morgan, Mary H. How to Dress an Old-Fashioned Doll.
Morgan, Murray & Morgan, Rosa. South on the Sound: An Illustrated History of Tacoma & Pierce County.
Morgan, P. Glass Reinforced Plastics.
Morgan, Patrick M. Theories & Approaches to International Politics.
Morgan, Philip. Progress in Plastics.
Morgan, Prys, jt. auth. see Thomas, David.
Morgan, R. Fort Ancient.
Morgan, Richard P., jt. auth. see Gould, Christopher.
Morgan, Robert & Pye, Michael, eds. Ernst Troeltsch: Writings on Theology & Religion.
Morgan, Robin. Dry Your Smile.
Morgan, Roland. Honolulu Then & Now.
Morgan, Rosa, jt. auth. see Morgan, Murray.
Morgan, Ted. FDR.
--On Becoming American.
--Rowing Toward Eden.
Morgan, Thomas B. Snyder's Walk.
Morgan, Valerie, jt. auth. see Dunn, Seamus.
Morgan, W. Hospitality Personnel Management.
Morgan, W. B. & Parkin, B. R., eds. International Symposium on Cavitation Inception.
Morgan, W. Robert, ed. Twenty-Four Dramatic Cases of the International Academy of Trial Lawyers.
Morganstern, Stanley. Legal Regulation of Consumer Credit.
Morganston, Charles E. The Appointing & Removal Power of the President of the United States.
Morgan-Witts, Max, jt. auth. see Thomas, Gordon.
Morgenroth, Anton. Splendor of the Faith: Meditations on the Credo of the People of God.
Morgenroth, Barbara. Demons at My Door.
--In Real Life I'm Just Kate.
--Last Junior Year.
--Ride a Proud Horse.
--Tramps Like Us.
--Will the Real Renie Lake Please Stand up.
Morgenroth, Robert L., jt. auth. see Valette, Rebecca M.
Morgenrothy, Anton. Mediations on the Rosary.
Morgenstein, Gary. The Man Who Wanted to Play Center Field for the New York Yankees.
Morgenstern. Dimensional Structure of Time.
Morgenstern, Dan, ed. & tr. see Berendt, Joachim.
Morgenthau, Hans W. Politics in the Twentieth Century.
Morgulis, Sergius, tr. & annotations by see Oparin, A. I.
Morholt, Evelyn, et al. Sourcebook for the Biological Sciences.
Mori, A., jt. ed. see Lowenthal, A.
Mori, Alan A. Families of Children with Special Needs: Early Intervention Techniques for the Practitioner.
Mori, Allen A. & Masters, Lowell F. Teaching the Severely Mentally Retarded: Adaptive Skills Training.
Mori, Allen A. & Olive, Jane E. Handbook of Preschool Special Education: Programming, Curriculum, Training.
Mori, Allen A., jt. auth. see Masters, Lowell F.
Mori, Joseph E., jt. auth. see Pahler, Arnold J.
Mori, Y. & Lennert, K. Electron Microscopic Atlas of Lymph Node Cytology & Pathology. Kuechemann, K., tr.
Moriarty, Denis, ed. Alec Clifton-Taylor's Buildings of Delight.
Moriarty, F., ed. Ecotoxicology: The Study of Pollutants in Exosystems.
--Organochlorine Insecticides: Persistent Organic Pollutants.
Moriarty, Rowland T. Industrial Buying Behavior: Concepts, Issues, & Applications.
Moriarty, Tim. Hockey's Hall of Fame.
Morice, Anne. Death & the Dutiful Daughter.
--Getting Away with Murder?
--Murder Post-Dated.
Morice, Dave. A Visit from St. Alphabet.
Morienus. A Testament of Alchemy: Being the Revelations of Morienus, Ancient Adept & Hermit of Jerusalem, to Khalid ibn Yazid ibn Mu'awiyya, King of the Arabs, of the Divine Secrets of the Magisterium & Accomplishment of the Alchemical Art. Stavenhagen, Lee, ed. & tr. from Lat.
Morin, F. A. Serpent & the Satellite.
Morin, Jack. Anal Pleasure & Health.
Morin, William J. & Cabrera, James C. Parting Company: How to Survive the Loss of a Job & Find Another Successfully.
Morin, William J. & Yorks, Lyle. Outplacement Techniques: A Positive Approach to Terminating Employees.
Morina, Michael, jt. auth. see Black, J. Thomas.
Morinaga, H. Developments & Borderlines of Nuclear Physics.
Morinigo, Marcos A. Diccionario de Americanismos.
Moris, Jon R. Managing Induced Rural Development.
Morisawa, Jackson S. The Secret of the Target.
Morisawa, M. Rivers.
Morisawa, M., jt. ed. see Hack, J. T.
Morishima, A. & Catephores, G. Value, Exploitation & Growth.
Morison, James. Gospel According to Matthew.
Morison, Robert S., jt. ed. see Holton, Gerald.
Morison, Samuel E. Builders of the Bay Colony.
--Harvard College in the Seventeeth Century.
--Three Centuries of Harvard, 1636-1936.
Morison, Samuel E., et al. Dissent in Three American Wars.
Morison, Stanley. John Fell, the University Press & the Fell Types.
Morisset, Richard, jt. ed. see Kurstak, Edouard.
Morissey, Kirkie. In His Name.
Moristo, Dennis, jt. auth. see Allen, Jack.
Morita, Edward K., et al. Group Practice Administration: Current & Future Roles.
Morlan, Robert L. Capitol, Courthouse & City Hall.
Morlan, Robert L. & Martin, David L. Capital, Courthouse & City Hall.
Morland, Nigel. An Outline of Scientific Criminology.
Morland, Nigel, ed. The Criminologist.
Morlee, jt. auth. see Baglee.
Morley. Ratio Analysis.
Morley, jt. auth. see Barnett.
Morley, Andrew P., Jr. Dr. Andy Answers Your Everyday Medical Questions.
Morley, Christopher. The Haunted Bookshop.
--Parnassus on Wheels.
Morley, David. The Missing Links: Golf & the Mind.
--Nationwide Audience.
Morley, David, jt. auth. see Brunsdon, Charlotte.
Morley, Henry. Memoirs of Bartholomew Fair.
Morley, Hilda. A Blessing Outside Us. Kaplan, Peter, ed.
Morley, I. W. Black Sands: A History of the Mineral Sand Mining Industry in Eastern Australia.
Morley, John, ed. Bronchial Hyperactivity.
Morley, John D. In the Labyrinth. Brady, Upton, ed.
--Pictures from the Water Trade: Adventures of a Westerner in Japan.
Morley, Peter & Wallis, Roy, eds. Culture & Curing: Anthropological Perspectives on Traditional Medical Beliefs & Practices.
Morley, Samuel A. Macroeconomics.
Morley, Sheridan. Ingrid Bergman: Legends.
--Katharine Hepburn.
--A Talent to Amuse: A Biography of Noel Coward.
Morley, Sheridan, jt. ed. see Payn, Graham.
Morley, Thomas. A Plain & Easy Introduction to Practical Music. Harmon, R. Alec, ed.
Morley, William F. Ontario & the Canadian North.
Morley-Pegge, R. The French Horn.
--French Horn.
Morling, K. Geometric & Engineering Drawing.
Morlock-Rahn, G. Wassim-Countersimulation Von Wasserversorgung Ung Abwasserentsorgung in Verdichtungsraeumen.
Mornay, Philippe. Defense of Liberty Against Tyrants. Laski, Harold, ed.
Morneau, Robert F. Principles of Preaching.
Morningstar, Mona, jt. auth. see Suppes, Patrick.
Morovskin, V. V., ed. Lexical Basis of Russian: An Integrated Students Dictionary.

Morowitz, Harold J. Cosmic Joy & Local Pain: Musings of a Mystic Scientist.
--Mayonnaise & the Origin of Life: Thoughts of Minds & Molecules.
Morowitz, Harold J. & Morowitz, Lucille S. Life on the Planet Earth.
Morowitz, Lucille S., jt. auth. see Morowitz, Harold J.
Moroz, E., ed. Home Fires: Stories by Writers from Byelorussia.
Moroz, Harold R. The Republic of Vietnam: An In-Depth Study of Indochina's Fortress under Attack & the Roots of U. S. Involvement.
Morphet, Edgar L. Citizens Co-Operation for Better Public Schools.
Morphew, Carol, jt. auth. see Jacob, Bernard.
Morpurgo. Last Days of Shelley & Byron.
Morpurgo, G., ed. Quarks & Hadronic Structure.
Morpurgo, Jack. Allen Lane: King Penguin.
Morr, Mary L. & Irmiter, Theodore F. Introductory Foods: A Laboratory Manual of Food Preparation & Evaluation.
Morra, Marion & Potts, Eve. Choices: Realistic Alternatives in Cancer Treatment.
Morrah, Patrick. Prince Rupert of the Rhine.
Morral, J. E., ed. see TMS-AIME Fall Meeting Symposium Staff.
Morran, Michelle, jt. auth. see Ollivier, Jacqueline.
Morrel, B. B., ed. see Conference on K-Theory & Operator Algebras, University of Georgia, Athens, Ga., Apr. 21-25, 1975.
Morrell, David. John Barth: An Introduction.
--The Last Reveille.
Morrell, Gloria G. The Dare.
--Lying...Not a Very Fun Thing.
--Sally's Calendar Book.
Morrell, Gordon. Computer-Ease: A Guide to Selecting Your Personal Computer.
Morrell, James. Britain Through the Nineteen Eighties.
Morrell, Patrick. Design of Reinforced Concrete Elements.
Morrice, J. K. Crisis Intervention: Case Histories. Kahn, J. H., ed.
Morrill, Chester, Jr. Computers & Data Processing Information Sources.
Morrill, Chester, Jr., ed. Systems & Procedures Including Office Management Information Sources.
Morrill, Dexter. The Little Book of Computer Music Instruments.
Morrill, Harriet H. BASIC Programming for the IBM Personal Computer.
Morrill, L. G., et al. Organic Compounds in Soils: Sorption, Degradation & Persistence.
Morrill, Richard L. Teaching Values in College: Facilitating Development of Ethical, Moral & Value Awareness in Students.
Morrin, Peter, jt. auth. see Agee, William C.
Morris & Rohrer. Decade of Creation: Acts-Facts-Impacts.
Morris, A., jt. auth. see Gardiner, G.
Morris, A. J. The Scaremongers: The Advocacy of War & Rearmament 1896-1914.
Morris, Alfred E. The Last Viking: A Fable.
Morris, Allison & McIsaac, Mary. Juvenile Justice?
Morris, Alton C., et al. College English: The First Year.
--Imaginative Literature: Fiction, Drama, Poetry.
--College English: The First Year.
--Imaginative Literature.
Morris, Alvin L., ed. Dental Specialties in General Practice. Bohannan, Harry M.
Morris, Anita. Writing Study Guides.
Morris, Ann. Short Guide to Writing Better Themes.
Morris, Ben & Morris, Elizabeth. Making Clothes in Leather.
Morris, Brian, ed. Art Directors Index to Illustrators.
Morris, Brian, ed. see Ford, John.
Morris, Brian, et al. The European Community: A Guide for Business & Government.
Morris, C. R. The Cost of Good Intentions: New York & the Liberal Experiment.
Morris, Carl & Rolph, John. Introduction to Data Analysis & Statistical Inference.
Morris, Charles. Signs, Language & Behavior.
Morris, Charles R. The Cost of Good Intentions: New York City & the Liberal Experiment.
Morris, Charles W. Foundations of the Theory of Signs.
Morris, Colin. Bugles in the Afternoon.
Morris, Daniel. Beatitude Saints.
Morris, Danny E. Any Miracle God Wants to Give.
Morris, Desmond. The Human Zoo.
Morris, Don. Elementary Physical Education: Toward Inclusion.
Morris, Dwight A. & Morris, Lynne D., eds. Health Care Administration: A Guide to Information Sources.
Morris, Edward E. Austral English.
Morris, Edward P., ed. Horace: Satires & Epistles.
Morris, Edwin T. Fragrance: The Story of Perfume from Cleopatra to Chanel.
Morris, Eleanor. Guide to the Recommended Country Inns of Arizona, New Mexico & Texas.
Morris, Elizabeth, jt. auth. see Morris, Ben.
Morris, Elizabeth A. see Smith, Watson & Breternitz, David A.
Morris, Eric. Churchill's Private Armies: British Special Forces in Europe, 1939-42.
Morris, Frank T. Field Guide to Birds of Prey of Australia.
Morris, G. Dimensions of Psychology.
--Where Human Rights Are Real.
Morris, George E. Engineering: A Decision Making Process.
Morris, Gilbert. Barney Buck & the Flying Solar Cycle.
--Barney Buck & the Phantom of the Circus.
--Barney Buck & the Rough Rider Special.
--Barney Buck & the World's Wackiest Wedding.
--The Runaway.
Morris, H. Creation & Its Critics.
Morris, Harriet. Art of Korean Cooking.
Morris, Henry M. Education for the Real World.
--King of Creation.
--Men of Science, Men of God.
--The Remarkable Birth of Planet Earth.
--The Remarkable Birth of Planet Earth.
--Science, Scripture & the Young Earth.
--The Scientific Case for Creation.
--The Troubled Waters of Evolution.
--What Is Creation Science.
Morris, Henry M. & Gish, Duane T. The Battle for Creation: Acts, Facts, Impacts.
Morris, Henry M., et al. Scientific Creationism: Public School Edition.
Morris, Henry M., et al, eds. Creation: The Cutting Edge-Acts, Facts, Impacts.
Morris, Henry, 3rd. Explore the Word!
Morris, Hughlett, ed. The Bratislava Project: Some Cleft Palate Surgical Results.
Morris, J. L., ed. see Conference on Applications of Numerical Analysis, Dundee, Scotland, 1971.
Morris, J. W., ed. see AIME Annual Meeting Staff.
Morris, James. Farewell the Trumpets: The Decline of an Empire.
--The Great Port: A Passage Through New York.
--Heaven's Command: An Imperial Progress.
--Pax Britannica: The Climax of an Empire.
--Places.
--The World of Venice.
--The World of Venice.
Morris, James A., jt. ed. see Ropp, Steve C.
Morris, James G., ed. Thermomechanical Processing of Aluminum Alloys.
Morris, James G., ed. see TMS Staff & AIME Staff.
Morris, Jan. Conundrum.
--Travels.
--The Venetian Empire.
Morris, Jill. The Dream Workbook.
--Time & Timelessness in Virginia Woolf.
Morris, Jim. Silvernail.
Morris, John. The Checkerboard Caper.
Morris, John D. Tracking Those Incredible Dinosaurs & the People Who Know Them.
Morris, John R. Davis H. Waite: The Ideology of a Western Populist.
Morris, Johnny, ed. The Faber Book of Animal Stories.
Morris, Keeton T., & Associates Staff. Experiential Learning: Rationale, Characteristics, & Assessment.
Morris, Kelly, ed. see Drewal, Henry J.
Morris, Kelly, ed. see Frangiamore, Roy & Grady, James.
Morris, Kenneth T. & Cinnamon, Kenneth M. A Handbook of Non-Verbal Group Exercises.
--A Handbook of Verbal Group Exercises.
Morris, L. W. Critical Path: Construction & Analysis.
Morris, Larry W. Extraversion & Introversion: An Interactional Perspective. Spielberger, C. D. & Sarason, I. G., eds.
Morris, Leavitt F. Travel Editor's Diary.
Morris, Lee. Clown Confessions.
--Ladies of the Sun: Three Modern Comedies Adapted from the Work of Euripides.
Morris, Leon. Understanding the New Testament: 1 Timothy-James.
Morris, Lloyd R. Celtic Dawn: A Survey of the Renaissance in Ireland, 1889-1916.
Morris, Lois B. Talking Sex with Your Kids.
Morris, Lynn L. & Fitz-Gibbon, Carol T. Evaluator's Handbook.
--How to Deal with Goals & Objectives.
--How to Measure Achievement.
--How to Measure Program Implementation.
--How to Present an Evaluation Report.
Morris, Lynn L., jt. auth. see Fitz-Gibbon, Carol T.
Morris, Lynn L., et al. Program Evaluation Kit.
Morris, Lynne D., jt. ed. see Morris, Dwight A.
Morris, Mary. The Bus of Dreams.
Morris, Mary, tr. see Leibniz, Gottfried W.
Morris, Mary, tr. see Leibniz, Gottfried W. & Parkinson, G. H.
Morris, Michael, ed. see Dal, Bjorn.
Morris, Noel M. Advanced Industrial Electronics.
Morris, Norma A. How to Set Up a Business Office: The Complete Guide to Locating, Outfitting & Staffing.
Morris, Peter. Embattled Shadows: A History of Canadian Cinema, 1895-1939.
--Rough Guide to Tunisia.
Morris, Peter, jt. ed. see Gruneberg, Michael M.
Morris, R., jt. auth. see Cork, Barbara.
Morris, Reginald O. Foundations of Practical Harmony & Counterpoint.
Morris, Richard. Time's Arrows: Scientific Attitudes Toward Time in Western Culture.
Morris, Richard B. Dismantling the Universe: The Nature of Scientific Discovery.
--Evolution & Human Nature.
--Government & Labor in Early America.
Morris, Robert. Country Inns of the Great Lakes.
--Country Inns of the Great Lakes: A Guide to Inns, Lodges, & Historic Hostelries of the Upper Midwest.
Morris, Robert & Trusler, John. An Essay upon Harmony As It Relates Chiefly to Situation & Building with Elements: The Art of Laying Out of Pleasure Grounds. Hunt, John D., ed.
Morris, Robert, Associates Staff. An Integrated Approach to Foreign Bank Analysis.
Morris, Roger. The Devil's Butcher Shop: The New Mexico Prison Uprising.
Morris, Ronald. Success & Failure in Learning to Read.
Morris, Ronald L. Wait until Dark.
Morris, Sally M. Favorite Seafood Recipes.
Morris, Sean, jt. auth. see Flanagan, Geraldine L.
Morris, Suzanne. Wives & Mistresses.
Morris, Thomas D. Free Men All: The Personal Liberty Laws of the North, 1780-1861.
Morris, Thomas R. The Virginia Supreme Court: An Institutional & Political Analysis.
Morris, Timothy. Innovations in Banking: Business Strategies & Employee Relations.
Morris, William H., ed. Rules for Admission to the Bar in the United States & Territories: 1982 Edition.
Morris, William O. Dental Litigation.
--The Law of Domestic Relations in West Virginia.
Morris, Winifred. With Magical Horses to Ride.
Morris, Wright. The Home Place.
--In Orbit.
--Wright Morris: A Reader.
Morrisby, Ted. The Golden Spike.
Morrisey, T. J. Selected Readings on American Industry.
Morrisey, T. J., ed. Pollution Control Problems & Related Federal Legislation.
Morrison, jt. auth. see Ballantyne.
Morrison, Adrian R. & Strick, Peter L., eds. Changing Concepts of the Nervous Systems: University of Pennsylvania School of Medicine Symposia in Anatomy.
Morrison, Arthur. A Child of the Jago.
--The Hole in the Wall.
--The Hole in the Wall.
--Tales of Mean Streets.
Morrison, Bill. Louis James Hates School.
--Simon Says.
Morrison, Blake. The Movement: English Poetry & Fiction of the 1950's.
Morrison, C. & Hughes, P. Professional Engineering Practice: Ethical Aspects.
Morrison, Carl & Morrison, Dorothy V. Can I Help How I Feel?
Morrison, Charles C. Outlawry of War: A Constructive Policy for World Peace. Bd. with Outlawry of War. Levinson, Salmon O. Garland Pub.
Morrison, Charles E. Threats to Security in East Asia-Pacific: National & Regional Perspectives.
Morrison, Clinton D. & Barnes, David H. New Testament Word Lists.
Morrison, David R. Education & Politics in Africa: The Tanzanian Case.
Morrison, Denton E. Energy: A Bibliography of Social Science & Related Literature.
--Energy II: A Bibliography of 1975-1976 Social Science & Related Literature.
Morrison, Denton E. & Hornback, Kenneth E. Collective Behavior: A Bibliography.
Morrison, Dorothy N. The Eagle & the Fort: The Story of John McLoughlin.
--Ladies Were Not Expected: Abigail Scott Duniway & Women Rights.
Morrison, Dorothy V., jt. auth. see Morrison, Carl.
Morrison, Hugh. Louis Sullivan: Prophet of Modern Architecture.
Morrison, James. Expanding & Maintaining Your Apple Personal Computer.
Morrison, James W. Psychology: Advanced Test for the G. R. E.
Morrison, James W., et al. Advanced Placement & College Level Examinations in English: Analysis & Interpretation of Literature.
Morrison, Joan & Morrison, Robert K. From Camelot to Kent State: The Sixties Experience in the Words of Those Who Lived It.
Morrison, Joel see Espenshade, Edward B., Jr.
Morrison, Joel L., jt. ed. see Espenshade, Edward B.
Morrison, Joel L., jt. ed. see Espenshade, Edward B., Jr.
Morrison, Joseph L. Governor O. Max Gardner: A Power in North Carolina & New Deal Washington.
Morrison, L. Jed & Morrison, M. K. The Onset of Parenthood: A Comprehensive, Illustrated Guide to Pregnancy, Birth & Infant Care.
Morrison, Lillian. The Sidewalk Racer & Other Poems of Sports & Motion.
Morrison, M. K., jt. auth. see Morrison, L. Jed.
Morrison, Malcolm H., ed. Economics of Aging: The Future of Retirement.
Morrison, Patton N. & Hale, Charles D. Perceptions of the Police Organization: A Sociometric Analysis.
Morrison, Patton N. & Meyer, C. Kenneth. A Microanalysis of Assaults on Police in Austin, Texas.
Morrison, Philip, et al, eds. see NASA Staff.
Morrison, Phyllis C. & Twing, J. W. The Business Office.
--The Business Office, Office Career Guide.
Morrison, Richard G., jt. auth. see Findlay, James V.
Morrison, Robert H., ed. Tax Navigation.
Morrison, Robert K., jt. auth. see Morrison, Joan.
Morrison, Robin & Fitz-Simon, Christopher. The Irish Village.
Morrison, S. Roy. The Chemical Physics of Surfaces.
Morrison, Samuel L. & Rowe, John S. Warships of the U. S. Navy.
Morrison, Theodore. Chautauqua.
--Leave of Absence: A Novel.
Morrison, Tony. Pathways to the Gods: The Mystery of the Andes Lines.
Morrison, W. I., jt. auth. see Smith, P.
Morrissey, Kirkie. On Holy Ground.
Morrissey, L. J. Henry Fielding: A Reference Guide.
Morrissey, Robert, Jr., jt. auth. see Barrett, Thomas.
Morris-Suzuki, Tessa. Showa: An Inside History of Hirohito's Japan.
Morris-Vann, Artie M., jt. auth. see Kirkland, Dianna C.
Morrow, C. Paul & Townsend, Duane E. Synopsis of Gynecologic Oncology.
Morrow, Carolyn C. A Conservation Policy for Research Libraries.
--Conservation Treatment Procedures: A Manual of Step-by-Step Procedures for the Maintenance & Repair of Library Materials.
Morrow, E. Frederic. Forty Years a Guinea Pig.
--Way down South, up North.
Morrow, James. The Continent of Lies: A Novel.
--This Is the Way the World Ends.
--The Wine of Violence.
Morrow, James & Suid, Murray. Media & Kids: Real-World Learning in the Schools.
Morrow, L. C., jt. auth. see Higgins, Lindley R.
Morrow, Linda & Morrow, Ray. Go Fly a Sailplane.
Morrow, Mary L. Help! For Elementary School Substitutes & Beginning Teachers.
Morrow, Ray, jt. auth. see Morrow, Linda.
Morrow, Skip. Don't Laugh, You're Next.
--The End.
--For the Birds.
--For the Birds.
--The Official I Hate Cats Book.
--The Official I Hate Love Book.
--The Second Official I Hate Cats Book.
Morrow, Theodore, tr. see Libanio, J. B.
Morse, A. R. Tennis Champion: Billie Jean King.
Morse, Ann, jt. auth. see Morse, Charles.
Morse, Barbar, jt. auth. see Goodman, Harriet W.
Morse, Charles & Morse, Ann. John Denver.
Morse, Christopher. The Logic of Promise in Moltmann's Theology.
Morse, D. E., et al. Recent Innovations in Cultivation of Pacific Molluscs.
Morse, Dan F. & Morse, Phyllis A. Archaeology of the Central Mississippi Valley.
Morse, Donald R. & Furst, M. Lawrence. Stress for Success.
Morse, Flo. Yankee Communes: Another American Way.
Morse, L. A. The Big Enchilada.
Morse, L. A., ed. see Fairleigh, Runa.
Morse, Lois. Two Blocks from Happiness.
Morse, Peter, et al. The Essential Guide to Timex-Sinclair Home Computers: The Only Book You'll Ever Need to Become an Expert at the Timex-Sinclair 1000 & 2000.
Morse, Philip M., et al. Nuclear, Particle & Many Body Physics.
Morse, Phyllis A., jt. auth. see Morse, Dan F.
Morse, Randy. The Mountains of Canada.
Morse, Roger A. Making Mead (Honey Wine) History, Recipes, Methods.
--A Year in the Beeyard.
Morse, S. A. Basalts & Phase Diagrams: An Introduction to the Quantitative Use of Phase Diagrams in Igneous Petrology.

Authors

Morse, Sanford M., ed. Reporter Services & Their Use.
Morse, Stephen. Management Skills in Marketing.
Morse, William C., et al, eds. Affective Education for Special Children & Youth.
Morsley, Peter. Modern Sociology.
Morson, B. C. Histological Typing of Intestinal Tumours.
Morson, Bosil C. The Pathogenesis of Colorectal Cancer.
Morson, Lillian I. An English Guide for Court Reporters.
Mort, Margaret. Retraining for the Elderly Disabled.
Mortensen, C. David. Communication: The Study of Human Interaction.
Mortensen, Ralph, tr. see Yeh Ch'ing.
Mortensen, V. Harvey. It's Time to Backdate.
Mortensen, Vern C. The Making of a Cowboy.
Morthland, John. Best of Country Music: A Guide to 750 Great Albums.
Mortimer, Edward. The Rise of the French Communist Party.
Mortimer, G., et al, eds. Coach (Automobile) Trimming: Part One.
--Coach (Automobile) Trimming: Part Two.
Mortimer, J. E., jt. auth. see Jenkins, C.
Mortimer, John. Clinging to the Wreckage: A Part of Life.
--A Voyage Round My Father.
Mortimer, John, tr. see Feydeau, Georges.
Mortimer, Martin, jt. auth. see Begon, Michael.
Mortimer, Mildred P., ed. Contes Africains.
Mortimer, Ruth, ed. The Landscape Alphabet.
Mortimore, Eugene P. Amiga's Programmer's Handbook.
Mortimore, G. W., jt. ed. see Benn, S. I.
Mortimore, Peter, et al. Behaviour Problems in Schools: An Evaluation of Support Centres.
Mortman, Doris. Circles.
Morton, A. L. People's History of England.
Morton, Alexander C. The Official Guide to Food Service & Hospitality Management.
Morton, Andrew. Inside Kensington Palace.
Morton, Barbara. VD: A Guide for Nurses & Counselors.
Morton, Brenda. Sleeve Puppets.
--Your Book of Knitted Toys.
Morton, Frederic. Rothschilds: A Family Portrait.
Morton, Frederick. The Crosstown Sabbath: Autobiography.
Morton, Gene. Principles of Life & Health Insurance. Long, Dani, ed.
Morton, Henry. St. Croix, St. Thomas, St. John: Danish West Indian Sketchbook & Diary, 1843-44.
Morton, I. & Rhodes, D. N., eds. Contribution of Chemistry to Food Supplies: Proceedings of a Symposium, Hamburg, 1973.
Morton, J. Analytical Potential of the Current Population Survey for Manpower & Employment Research.
--Handbook for Community Manpower Surveys.
--On the Evolution of Manpower Statistics.
Morton, J. E. On Manpower Forecasting.
Morton, Joyce. Legal Secretarial Procedures.
Morton, Kati. Wallenberg.
Morton, Lena B. My First Sixty Years.
Morton, Leslie T. How to Use a Medical Library.
Morton, Leslie T., ed. Garrison's & Morton's a Medical Bibliography: An Annotated Check-List of Texts Illustrating the History of Medicine.
Morton, Miriam. Pleasures & Palaces: After-School Activities of Russian Children.
Morton, N. Structural Engineering Design Programs: Software Project.
Morton, Patricia. The Province of Darkness.
Morton, Phyllis. Pathways of Life: Poems by Phyllis Morton.
Morton, Richard, jt. auth. see Browning, John.
Morton, Richard, jt. auth. see Fritz, Paul.
Morton, Richard A., et al. Cytochromes: Current Research, II.
Morton, T. Ralph. God's Moving Spirit.
Morton, Tom J. Texas Real Estate Finance.
Moruzzi, V. L., et al. Calculated Electronic Properties of Metals: Designing Our Career Machines.
Morwood, John. Sailing Aerodynamics.
Moryadas, S., jt. auth. see Lowe, John C.
Mosberg, Lewis. Tax Shelter Desk Book.
Mosby. Mosby's Assesstest: Basic Science.
--Mosby's Assesstest: Drugs & Solutions.
--Mosby's Assesstest: Fundamentals - Application.
--Mosby's Assesstest: Fundamentals - Basic Concepts.
--Mosby's Assesstest: Maternity Nursing.
--Mosby's Assesstest: Medical - Surgical Nursing.
--Mosby's Assesstest: Nutrition.
--Mosby's Assesstest: Pediatric Nursing.
--Mosby's Assesstest: Pharmacology.
--Mosby's Assesstest: Psychiatric Nursing.
Mosby, Dewey F. Alexandre-Gabriel Decamps (1803-1860).
Mosbysorts. Apple.
--IBM-PC.
Moscheles, Ignace, tr. see Schindler, Anton.
Moschovakis, Y. N., jt. ed. see Kechris, A. S.
Moschytz, G. S. & Neirynck, J., eds. Circuit Theory & Design.
Moschytz, G. S., ed. see Brayton, R. K., et al.
Moschytz, George. Linear Integrated Networks: Fundamentals.
Moscove, Stephen A. & Simkin, Mark G. Accounting Information Systems: Concepts & Practice for Effective Decision Making.
Moscovici, Serge. Social Influence & Social Change.
Moscovitz, Judy. The Rice Diet Report: How I Lost up to 12 Pounds a Week on the World-Famous Weight-Loss Plan.
Moscow, Alvin, jt. auth. see Geneen, Harold.
Moscow, Lonna, jt. auth. see Everroad, Jim.
Moseley, George V., 3rd. Consolidation of the South China Frontier.
Moseley, H. F. Recurrent Dislocation of the Shoulder.
Moseley, Keith. The Flight of the Pterosaurs.
Moseley, Keith, designed by see Seymour, Peter.
Moseley, L. G. Research for Social Welfare: Six Case Studies in Cyprus.
Moseley, Malcolm. Growth Centres in Spatial Planning.
Moseley, Malcolm J. Accessibility: The Rural Challenge.
Moseley, Michael E. & Day, Kent C., eds. Chan Chan: Andean Desert City.
Mosenkis, Robert & Wood, Dorothy. Health Devices Sourcebook, 1987.
Mosenkis, Robert & Wood, Dorothy, eds. Health Devices Sourcebook, 1988.
Mosenthal, Basil & Hewitt, Dick. Ready for Sea: Check Your Boat.
Moser, jt. auth. see Spangenburg.
Moser, C. L., jt. ed. see Lopez, R. A.
Moser, Charles. Dimitrov of Bulgaria.
Moser, Dian, jt. auth. see Spangenburg, Ray.
Moser, Diane, jt. auth. see Spangenburg, Raymond.
Moser, Don. A Heart to the Hawks.
Moser, Hans J. Heinrich Schutz: His Life & Work.
Moser, J. Dynamical Systems, Theory & Applications.
Moser, Joy, jt. auth. see Rootman, Irving.
Moser, Jurgen. Stable & Random Motions in Dynamical Systems: With Special Emphasis on Celestial Mechanics.
Moser, Robert H. Diseases of Medical Progress, a Study of Iatrogenic Disease: A Contemporary Analysis of Illness Produced by Drugs & Other Therapeutic Procedures.
Moses, A. J. Nuclear Techniques in Analytical Chemistry.
Moses, Bernard. Establishment of Spanish Rule in America.
Moses, Diana, jt. auth. see Croll, Paul.
Moses, Frank, jt. auth. see Berry, Roland.
Moses, Fred, jt. auth. see Dickey, Charley.
Moses, H. Weston & Taylor, George J. A Practical Guide to Cardiac Pacing.
Moses, John, jt. auth. see Cross, Wilbur.
Moses, Louis J. Call for JCS Reform: Crucial Issues.
Moses, Montrose J. Children's Books & Reading.
Moses, Robert A. Adler's Physiology of the Eye: Clinical Application.
Mosher, Bruce & Mosher, Dottie. How Do You Spell TV.
Mosher, Dottie, jt. auth. see Mosher, Bruce.
Mosher, F., jt. auth. see Goldstein, Larry J.
Mosher, Frederick C., jt. ed. see Stillman, Richard.
Mosher, Jerry, ed. see Armstrong, Frederick.
Mosher, Jerry, ed. see Ashmore, Nancy V.
Mosher, Ralph L., et al. Supervision: The Reluctant Profession.
Moshy, R., jt. auth. see Friedman, E. H.
Mosich, A. N. & Larsen, E. John. CPA Review Manual.
Mosich, Donna. WordPerfect 4.2 Macros.
Mosier, John, jt. auth. see Gaillard, Dawson.
Moskalenko, Yu E., ed. Biophysical Aspects of Cerebral Circulation.
Moskin, J. Robert. Among Lions: The Definitive Account of the 1967 Battle for Jerusalem.
--The U. S. Marine Corps Story.
Moskin, Marietta. In Search of God.
Moskin, Marietta D. Dream Lake.
--Rosie's Birthday Present.
Moskol, Ann, jt. auth. see Ericson, Robert.
Moskovitz, Myron & Warner, Ralph. Tenants Rights: California Tenants' Handbook.
Moskow, Michael H., et al. Collective Bargaining in Public Employment.
Moskowitz, Joel. The Working Clock-Timer.
Moskowitz, Milton & Katz, Michael, eds. Everybody's Business Scoreboard: Corporate America's Winner's, Loosers & Also-Rans.
Moskowitz, Sam. Science Fiction by Gas Light.
Moskowitz, Stewart. Fred's Pyramid. Klimo, Kate, ed.
--Fred's Pyramid.
--The Legend of the American Rabbit. Klimo, Kate, ed.
--The Legend of the American Rabbit.
--A Patchwork Fish Tale.
--Too-Loose the Chocolate Moose.
--Tooloose the Chocolate Moose. Klimo, Kate, ed.
Moskvichov, L. N. The End of Ideology Theory: Illusions & Reality.
Moskvin, L. The Working Class & Its Allies.
Moskvitin, Jurij. Essay on the Origin of Thought.
Mosler Anti-Crime Bureau Staff. Security Risk Management: A Practitioners Guide. Rosberg, Robert, ed.
Mosley, Jean B. The Deep Forest Award.
Mosley, Leonard. Blood Relations.
--Druid.
--Zanuck: The Rise & Fall of Hollywood's Last Tycoon.
Mosley, M. Paul, jt. ed. see Laronne, Jonathan.
Mosley, M. Paul, jt. ed. see Schumm, Stanley A.
Moss, Brian. The Ecology of Fresh Waters.
Moss, Cynthia. Portraits in the Wild: Behavior Studies of East Africa Mammals.
Moss, D. W. Isoenzymes.
Moss, Gillian. Printed Textiles: Seventeen Sixty to Eighteen Sixty. Aakre, Nancy, ed.
Moss, Howard. Buried City.
--Selected Poems.
--Two Plays: The Palace at 4 A. M., the Folding Green.
Moss, Howard & Belli, Frederick. Tigers & Other Lilies.
Moss, Howard, ed. New York: Poems.
Moss, J., jt. auth. see Copa, G.
Moss, Jan. Onyx Flame.
Moss, Joel, jt. ed. see Sekura, Ronald.
Moss, Joyce, jt. auth. see Wilson, George.
Moss, Louis & Goldstein, Harvey. Recall Methods in Social Surveys.
Moss, Mary W. A Profile of the Dixon Family.
Moss, Michael, jt. auth. see Green, Edwin.
Moss, P. D., jt. auth. see Higgins, C. S.
Moss, R., et al. Animal Population Dynamics.
Moss, Ralph W. The Cancer Syndrome.
--The Cancer Syndrome.
--The Cancer Syndrome.
Moss, Robert. Moscow Rules.
--Valiant Witness: A Novel of Moroni.
Moss, Robert & De Borchgrave, Arnaud. Monimbo.
Moss, Robin. Video: The Educational Challenge.
Moss, Roger. The Game of the Pink Pagoda.
Moss, Roger W., jt. auth. see Tatman, Sandra L.
Moss, Scott J. An Economic Theory of Business Strategy: An Essay in Dynamics.
Moss, Sylvia, jt. auth. see Tubbs, Stewart L.
Moss, T. S. & Stenholm, S. Progress in Quantum Electronics.
Moss, T. S., jt. ed. see Kneubuhl, F. K.
Moss, T. S., jt. ed. see Schultz, G.
Moss, T. S., ed. see U. S. Specialty Group on Infrared Detectors.
Moss, T. S., et al, eds. Progress in Quantum Electronics.
Moss, W. Stanley. ILL Met by Moonlight.
Moss, William T., et al. Radiation Oncology: Rationale, Technique, Results.
Mosse, George & Vago, Bela, eds. Jews & Non-Jews in Eastern Europe, 1918-1945.
Mosse, George L. The Crisis of German Ideology: Intellectual Origins of the Third Reich.
--The Holy Pretence.
Mosse, Hilda L. The Complete Handbook of Children's Reading Disorders: A Critical Evaluation of Their Clinical, Educational & Social Dimensions.
Mosse, W. E. European Powers & the German Question, 1848-1871.
Moss Kanter, Rosabeth. The Change Masters: Innovation for Productivity in the American Corporation.
Mossman, Elliot, ed. Correspondence of Boris Pasternak & Olga Freidenberg: Russian Edition.
Mossman, Elliot, compiled by. The Correspondence of Boris Pasternak & Olga Friedenberg, 1910-1954. Wettlin, Margaret, tr.
Mossman, Melville, ed. see Means, R. S., Company, Inc. Staff.
Mossner, Ernest C., ed. see Hume, David.
Most, Glenn W. & Stowe, William W., eds. The Poetics of Murder: Detective Fiction & Literary Theory.
Most, Konrad. Training Dogs: A Manual.
Mosteller, Dee, jt. auth. see Morgan, Mary.
Mostert, P. S., jt. ed. see Hofmann, K. H.
Mosti, Francisco H. Suppression.
Mostofi, F. K. Histological Typing of Testis Tumours.
Mostofi, F. K., ed. see International Academy Of Pathology.
Mostofi, F. K., jt. ed. see Pearson, Carl M.
Mostowski, J. & Stark, M. Introduction to Higher Algebra.
Mostyn, Trevor, ed. United Arab Emirates: A Middle East Economic Digest Guide.
Mostyn, Trevor, ed. see Middle East Economic Digest Staff.
Moszkowski, Steven A., ed. see Proceedings of the International Conference, Los Angeles, 1972, et al.
Moszynska, W. I., jt. auth. see Chernetsov, V. N.
Motamen, H., jt. auth. see Brookes, L. G.
Motani, Nizar. On His Majesty's Service: The Origins of Uganda's African Civil Service, 1912-1940.
Mote, Max E. Soviet Local & Republic Elections.
Motes, R. Andrew. Electronic Design & Construction of Alternate Energy Projects.
Motherwell, William. Minstrelsy Ancient & Modern.
Motil, John. Programming Principles: Modula II.
Motil, John M. Digital System Fundamentals. Truxal, John G. & Rohrer, R. A., eds.
Motion, Andrew. Philip Larkin.
Motley, R. W. Q Machines.
Motor Auto Engines & Electrical Staff. Motor Auto Engines & Electrical Systems.
Motor Auto Repair Manual Staff. Motor Auto Repair Manual.
--Motor Auto Repair Manual.
--Motor Auto Repair Manual, 1985.
Motor Carriers Lawyers Association Staff, jt. auth. see University of Denver, College of Law Staff.
Motor Vehicle Manufacturers Association of the United States Staff. Automobiles of America: Milestones, Pioneers, Roll Call, Highlights.
Motorola, Inc. Staff. MC68020 32-Bit Microprocessor: User's Manual.
--M68000 8-, 16-, 32-Bit Microprocessor's Programmer's Reference Manual.
--M6816 32-Bit Microprocessor: Programmer's Reference Manual.
Motovilova, O. G., jt. auth. see Mitrokhina, V. I.
Mott, Charles J., jt. auth. see Gould, Joseph C.
Mott, George, jt. auth. see De Breffny, Brian.
Mott, J. J., jt. ed. see Tothill, J. C.
Mott, Nevill & Berry, M. Elementary Quantum Mechanics.
Mott, Pearle G. History of Davis & Canaan Valley.
Mott, Stephen C., jt. auth. see Bruland, Esther B.
Motta, M., et al. Hypothalamic Hormones: Chemistry, Physiology, Pharmacology & Clinical Uses.
Motta, Pietro, jt. auth. see Blerkom, Jonathan Van.
Mottahedeh, Roy. The Mantle & the Prophet: Learning & Power in Modern Iran.
Motte, G. A. & Iitaka, Y. Evaluation of Trawl Performance by Statistical Inference of the Catch.
Motte, R. Weather Routing of Ships.
Motteler, Zane C. Introduction in Ordinary Differential Equations.
Motter, Alton M. Preaching on National Holidays.
Motter, Alton M., ed. Preaching about Death: Eighteen Sermons Dealing with the Experience of Death from the Christian Perspective.
Mottola, H. A., ed. Henry Freisher: "Talanta" Issue.
Mottram, jt. auth. see Moffatt.
Mottram, Maxine, jt. auth. see Macdonald, Susan.
Mottram, Ron. Inner Landscapes: The Theater of Sam Shepard.
Mott-Smith, Morton. The Concept of Energy Simply Explained.
--Concept of Heat & Its Workings.
Motulsky, A. G., et al, eds. Human Genetic Variation in Response to Medical & Environmental Agents: Pharmacogenetics & Ecogenetics.
Motulsky, Arno G., et al. Genetic Counseling.
Mouat, Kit. Fighting for Our Lives.
Moubray, Jocelyn de. The Thoroughbred Business.
Moudgal, N. R. Gonadotropins & Gonadal Function.
Moudon, Anne V., ed. Public Streets for Public Use.
Moudud, Hasna J. Women in China.
Moughtin, James C. Hausa Architecture in Northern Nigeria.
Moul, Keith R. Theodore Roethke's Career: An Annotated Bibliography.
Mould, Daphne Pochin see Pochin-Mould, Daphne.
Mould, David H. American Newsfilm, 1914-1919: The Underexposed War. Jowett, Garth S., ed.
Moule, C. F. Meaning of Hope: A Biblical Exposition with Concordance. Reumann, John, ed.
Moulton, D. G., ed. Methods in Olfactory Research.
Moulton, Gary. John Ross, Cherokee Chief.
Moulton, Harold G. Can Inflation Be Controlled.
Moulton, Jenni H., ed. The Random House Basic Dictionary: German.
Moulton, Nancy. Crosswinds.
--Defiant Destiny.
--Tempest of the Heart.
Mounce, Robert. A Living Hope: A Commentary on I & II Peter.
Mounce, Robert H. Matthew: A Good News Commentary.
Mounier, J. P., jt. ed. see Gomella, C.

Authors

Mount, Ferdinand. The Subversive Family: An Alternative History of Love & Marriage.
Mount, Graeme S. The Sudbury Region: An Illustrated History.
Mountaine, Dydymus, pseud. The Gardeners Labyrinth. Hunt, John D., ed.
Mountbattan. Southeast Asia.
Mountcastle, Vernon B. Medical Physiology.
Mountfield, David. The Railway Barons.
Mountford, E. G., tr. see Febvre, Lucien & Bataillon, Lionel.
Mourad, Samiha. Understanding & Programming Computers.
Mourlot, Fernand, jt. auth. see Leiris, Michael.
Moursund, Dave. Collected Editorials.
Moursund, David. Computers & Problem Solving: A Workshop for Educators.
--The Parent's Guide to Computers in Education.
Mousgaard, I. K., jt. auth. see Von Fieandt, Kai.
Mousset-Jones, Pierre F. Geostatistics.
Mouton, Jane S., jt. auth. see Blake, Robert R.
Mouw, Richard J. Called to Holy Worldliness. Gibbs, Mark, ed.
Movsessian, Vahe. Student's World Atlas.
Mow, Anna B. Springs of Love.
Mow, V. C., ed. Nineteen Hundred & Eighty Advances in Bioengineering.
Mowat, Farley. Sea of Slaughter.
--The World of Farley Mowat: A Selection from His Works. Davison, Peter, ed.
Mowlam, Marjorie, jt. ed. see Clarke, Michael.
Mowrer, Donald E. & Case, James L. Clinical Management of Speech Disorders.
Mowschenson, P. M. Aids to Undergraduate Surgery.
Mowvley, Harry. Reading the Old Testament Prophets Today.
Moxey, Keith P. Pieter Aertsen, Joachim Beuckelaer & the Rise of Secular Painting in the Context of the Reformation.
Moxley & Woods. Illustrated Directory of Architects 1986.
Moxon, P. R. Training the Roughshooter's Dog.
Moyar, Gerald J. & Pilkey, Walter D., eds. Track Train DYNMC & DESGN.
Moye, H. Anson. Analysis of Pesticide Residues.
Moyer, Charles, et al. Contemporary Financial Management (International Edition)
Moyer, Charles R., et al. Contemporary Financial Management.
Moyer, D. David. Land Information Systems: An Annotated Bibliography.
Moyer, Roy, et al. Dogancay.
Moyer, T. & Boeckx, R., eds. Applied Therapeutic Drug Monitoring.
Moyers, R. E. & Krogman, W. M. Craniofacial Growth in Man.
Moyes, Gordon. Discovering Jesus.
Moylan, Charles E., Jr. The Right of the People to Be Secure: An Examination of the Fourth Amendment.
Moyle, Peter B. & Cech, Joseph J. Fishes: An Introduction to Ichthyology.
Moynahan, J. McCauslin, Jr. Police Ju Jitsu.
Moynahan, John K. Designing an Effective Sales Compensation Program.
Moynahan, Michael E. God of Untold Tales.
Moynes, Diane R., jt. auth. see Jobe, Frank W.
Moynihan, Cornelius J. Introduction to Real Property.
Moynihan, William T. Essays Today Seven.
Moynihan, William T., jt. auth. see Jacobus, Lee A.
Mozart, Wolfgang A. Don Giovanni. Bleiler, Ellen H., tr. &
Mozes, Lee & Schultz, Julius, eds. Cellular Responses to Molecular Modulators.
Mozina, Stane, ed. Guide to Planning for Manpower Development.
Mozine, Stane, jt. ed. see Armstrong, Aubry.
Mozsik, Gy., et al, eds. Gastrointestinal Defence Mechanisms: Proceedings of a Satellite Symposium of the 28th International Congress of Physiological Sciences, Budapest, 1980.
Mozzer, Patricia. Vegetarian Cooking for Diabetics.
Mozzochi, C. J. Foundations of Analysis: Landau Revisited.
--On the Pointwise Convergence of Fourier Series.
Mozzochi, C. J., et al. Symmetric Generalized Topological Structures.
Mozzochi, D. J. Everything You Ever Need to Know to Enhance the Sexual Response by Hypnosis but Didn't Know Whom to Ask.
Mrazkova & Remes, eds. The Russian War: Nineteen Forty One Nineteen Forty Five.
Mrazkova, Daniela & Remes, Vladimir. Early Soviet Photographers. Hoole, John, ed.
MRC Symposium Staff. Contributions to Nonlinear Functional Analysis: Proceedings of the MRC Symposium, 1971. Zarantonello, Eduardo H., ed.
Mririda. Songs of Mririda. Halpern, Daniel & Paley, Paula, trs.
Mrkvicka, Edward F., Jr. Battle Your Bank & Win.
--Moving Up: Proven Strategies for Career Success.
Mroczkowska-Brand, Katarzyna, tr. see Kapuscinski, Ryszard.
Mroczkowska-Brand, Katarzyna, tr. see Micewski, Andrzej.
Mroczkowski, George & Bishop, Chara. Professional Treasure Hunter. Nelson, B. J., ed.
Mrozek, Slawomir. Tango. Manheim, Ralph & Dzieduszycka, Teresa, trs. from Pol.
--Vatzlav. Manheim, Ralph, tr. from Pol.
MSDS Staff. MSDS Reference for Crop Protection Chemicals: Update One.
MTV Staff. Who's Who in Rock Video.
Mu Alpha Theta Staff. Mathematical Buds.
Mucchielli, Roger. Introduction to Structural Psychology. Markmann, Charles L., tr.
Muchnick, David M. Urban Renewal in Liverpool.
Muchnick, David M. & Weinstein, Martin, eds. The Construction & Reconstruction of Democratic Societies.
Mucibabich, Darlene. Life in Western Mining Camps: Social & Legal Aspects, 1848-1872.
Muckenfuss, Cantwell F., jt. auth. see Lowy, Martin E.
Muckle, W. Modern Naval Architecture.
Mudge, Jean M. Emily Dickinson & the Image of Home.
Mudge, Lewis S., ed. see Ricoeur, Paul.
Mudge, Richard B., tr. see Glinka, Mikhail I.
Mudie-Smith, Richard, ed. Handbook of the Daily News Sweated Industries Exhibition.
Mudrick, Marvin. Nobody Here But Us Chickens.
Mudroch, Vaclav & Couse, G. S., eds. Essays on the Reconstruction of Medieval History.
Muecke, D. C. The Compass of Irony.
Mueller, jt. auth. see Heitzman.
Mueller, Arno. Internationaler Riechstoff Kodex.
Mueller, Charles S. Words of Faith: A Devotional Dictionary.
Mueller, Charles S. & Bardill, Donald R. Thank God I'm a Teenager.
Mueller, David. Karl Barth. Patterson, Bob E., ed.
Mueller, David L. Karl Barth.
Mueller, E. Hydraulic Forging Presses.
Mueller, Frank P. The Burdick Family Chronology.
Mueller, G. & Friedman, G. M., eds. Recent Developments in Carbonate Sedimentology in Central Europe.
Mueller, G. H. & Scott, D. S., eds. Higher Set Theory: Proceeding, Oberwolfach Germany, April 13-23, 1977.
Mueller, G. O., jt. auth. see Wise, E. M.
Mueller, Gerhard & Adler, Freda. Outlaws of the Ocean: The Complete Book of Crime on the High Seas.
Mueller, Gustav E. Plato: The Founder of Philosophy as a Dialectic.
Mueller, Gustave E. Philosophy of Literature.
Mueller, J. Regulation of Aldosterone Biosynthesis.
Mueller, Jeanne & Morgan, Harry, eds. Social Services in Early Education: Head Start, Day Care & Early Education Schools.
Mueller, Jo. Cooking Your Own Mushrooms.
Mueller, John H., et al. Statistical Reasoning in Sociology.
Mueller, Kimberly J., ed. California Museum Directory.
Mueller, Lisel, tr. see Mitgutsch, Waltraud A.
Mueller, Marge. The San Juan Islands: Afoot & Afloat.
Mueller, Marlies, jt. auth. see Slack, Anne.
Mueller, Phyllis, ed. see Duffy, James J.
Mueller, Robert A. Automated Microcode Synthesis. Stone, Harold, ed.
Mueller-Deham, Albert. Human Relations: Power & Politics.
Mueller-Dombois, Dieter, ed. Island Ecosystems: Biological Organization in Selected Hawaiian Communities. Bridges, Kent W. & Carson, Hampton L.
Mueller-Merbach, H. On Round-off Errors in Linear Programming.
Muench, David, jt. auth. see Abbey, Edward.
Muench, David, photos by. California.
--Colorado.
--This Great Land.
--Washington Shores.
Muench, I. Von. Voelkerrecht in programmierter Form mit Vertiefungshinweisen.
Muench, Josef, photos by. Arizona II.
Muenchow, Charles A., tr. see Westermann, Claus.
Muenscher, Walter C. & Rice, Myron A. Garden Spice & Wild Pot-Herbs: An American Herbal.
Mueser, Anne M. The Picture Story of Jockey Steve Cauthen.
--The Picture Story of Rod Carew.
Muessig, Paul, et al. The Builders Guide to Bathroom Design.
Muff, Janet. Socialization, Sexism & Stereotyping, Women's Issues in Nursing.
Mufti, I. H. Computational Methods in Optimal Control Problems.
Muggenberg, James see O'Neal, William B.
Muggenburg, Frederico. The Catholic Church in Mexican Political Life.
Muggeridge, Kitty & Adam, Ruth. Beatrice Webb: A Life.
Muggeridge, Kitty, tr. see De Caussade, Jean-Pierre.
Muggeridge, Malcolm. The Green Stick.
--The Infernal Grove.
Muggeridge, Richard, jt. auth. see Reed, Philip.
Mugnier, George F. Louisiana Images, 1880-1920: A Photographic Essay, by George Francois Mugnier. Kemp, John R. & King, Linda O., eds.
Mugridge, Larry, jt. auth. see Hunkins, Dalton.
Muhaiyaddeen, Bawa R. Gems of Wisdom.
Muia, Joseph, jt. auth. see Alexander, Patricia.
Muir, Andrew F., ed. Texas in Eighteen Thirty-Seven.
Muir, Bernice L. Pathophysiology: An Introduction to Mechanisms of Disease.
Muir, Dorothy E. Machiavelli & His Times.
Muir, Dorothy Troth. Presence of a Lady: Mount Vernon 1861-1868.
Muir, Edward. The Social Studies Student Investigates American Law.
Muir, Edwin. The Structure of the Novel.
Muir, Frank. Christmas Customs & Traditions.
Muir, John. Como Mantener Tu Volkswagen Vivo. Holt, Virginia, tr. from Eng.
--Es Lebe Mein Volkswagen. Shamai, Ruth & Jeschke, Herbert, trs.
--How to Keep Your Volkswagen Alive.
--Mountaineering Essays. Fleck, Richard F., ed.
--The Velvet Monkeywrench.
--Wilderness Essays. Buske, Frank, ed.
--The Yellowstone National Park. Jones, William R., ed.
Muir, John & Gregg, Tosh. How to Keep Your Volkswagen Alive: A Manual of Step by Step Procedures for the Compleat Idiot.
Muir, Kenneth. Shakespeare's Sonnets.
Muir, Kenneth, intro. by. The Romantic Period: Excluding the Novel.
Muir, Kenneth, ed. see Ellis-Fermor, Una.
Muir, Kenneth, ed. see Middleton, Thomas.
Muir, M. Palynology, Pt. 1& 2.
Muir, Percy H., ed. see National Book League Staff.
Muir, Richard, jt. auth. see Taylor, Christopher.
Muir, Wellesley. Faith under Fire. Woolsey, Raymond H., ed.
Muirhead, H. Notes on Elementary Particle Physics.
Muirhead-Thomson, E. C. Behaviour Patterns of Blood-Sucking Flies.
Mujeeb, M. Akbar.
--The Indian Muslims.
Mujumdar, Arun S., ed. Drying Eighty: Developments in Drying.
Mukerjee, Radhakamal. Social Function of Art.
Mukerjee, Radhakamal, tr. The Song of the Self Supreme: Astavakra Gita.
Mukhamedzhanov, Kaltai, jt. auth. see Aitmatov, Chingiz.
Mukherjea, A. & Tserpes, N. A. Measures on Topological Semi-Groups: Convolution Products & Random Walks.
Mukherjee, B. N. East Indian Art Styles: A Study in Parallel Trends.
Mukherjee, Bharati. Wife.
Mukherjee, Kali & Mazumder, J., eds. Lasers in Metallurgy.
Mukherjee, Kanai L. Introductory Mathematics for the Clinical Laboratory.
Mukherjee, Pranab. Beyond Survival: Emerging Dimensions of Indian Economy.
Mukherji, A. K. Analytical Chemistry of Zirconium & Hafnium.
Mukhlyonov, I., ed. Chemical Technology.
Mukhlyonov, I. P., ed. Calculations of Chemical Technological Processes.
Mukhopadhyay, Amar, ed. Recent Developments in Switching Theory.
Mukhoti, Bela. International Monetary Fund & Low-Income Countries.
Mukohata, Yusuo & Packer, Lester, eds. Cation Flux Across Biomembranes.
Muktananda, Swami. Play of Consciousness.
Mular, A. L. & Anderson, M. A., eds. Design & Installation of Concentration & Dewatering Circuits.
Mular, A. L., jt. ed. see Bhappu, R. B.
Mular, Andrew L. & Bhappu, Roshan B., eds. Mineral Processing Plant Design.
Mular, Andrew L. & Jergensen, Gerald V., III, eds. Design & Installation of Communication Circuits.
Mulay, Y. M. see Kesavan, B. S.
Mulcahy, B. To Speak True: A Study of Poetry As a Spoken Art.
Mulcahy, Charles C. & Smith, Marion C. Problems & Solutions Resulting from Inability to Pay in the Public Sector.
Mulcahy, Patrick D. Survival on Atlantis.
Muldoon, Joseph A. & Berdie, Mitchell. Effective Employee Assistance: A Comprehensive Guide for the Employer.
Mule, S. J. & Brill, Henry. Chemical & Biological Aspects of Drug Dependence.
Mulford, Wendy. This Narrow Place: Sylvia Townsend Warner & Valentine Ackland-Life, Letters & Politics, 1930-1951.
Mulgan, John, jt. auth. see Bolitho, Hector.
Mulhearn, Daniel & Taibi, John. General Motors F Units the Locos: That Revolutionized Railroading.
Mulholland, James A. A History of Metals in Colonial America.
Mulholland, John. Book of Magic.
Mulholland, Joyce, jt. auth. see Brown, Meta.
Mulkay, Michael. Science & the Sociology of Knowledge.
Mulkeen, Anne. Wild Thyme, Winter Lightning: The Symbolic Novels of L. P. Hartley.
Mulkerne, Donald J. & Kahn, Gilbert. The Term Paper: Step by Step.
Mull, Martin & Rucker, Allen. A Paler Shade of White: The History of White People in America.
Mullahy, Patrick. The Beginnings of Modern American Psychiatry: The Ideas of Harry Stack Sullivan.
Mullaly, Edward J. Archibald Macleish: A Checklist.
Mullan, Bob. Life As Laughter: Following Bhagwan Shree Rajneesh.
--The Mating Trade.
Mullen, Edward J., jt. auth. see Castillo-Feliu, Guillermo I.
Mullen, Edwin & Griffith, Jane. Short Bike Rides in Connecticut.
Mullen, John. In a Year of Our Lord: A Memoir of American Innocence.
Mullen, K. & Pregosin, P. S. Fourier Transform Nuclear Magnetic Resonance Techniques: A Practical Approach.
Mullen, Tom. Laughing Out Loud & Other Religious Experiences.
Muller. Nutrition & Food Processing.
Muller, A. S., jt. ed. see Van Ginneken, J. K.
Muller, Achim & Newton, William E., eds. Nitrogen Fixation: The Chemical-Biochemical-Genetic Interface.
Muller, Antal. Quantum Mechanics: A Physical World Picture.
Muller, B. Navier-Stokes Solution for Laminar Transonic Flow over a NACA0012 Airflow. Aeronautical Research Institute of Sweden Staff, ed.
Muller, David J., et al. Language Assessment for Remediation.
Muller, Edward J. Architectural Drawing & Light Construction.
Muller, Eugenio E., et al. Neurotransmitters & Anterior Pituitary.
Muller, F. Max see also Mueller, F. Max.
Muller, G. H., et al, eds. see Logic Conference Staff.
Muller, Gilbert H. John A. Williams.
Muller, H. J. Thomas Wolfe.
Muller, I., ed. see CISM (International Center for Mechanical Sciences), Department of Mechanics of Solids Staff.
Muller, J., jt. ed. see Ferguson, I. K.
Muller, James A., ed. see Gardiner, Stephen.
Muller, James E., ed. see Vikhert, Anatolii M. & Zhdanov, Valentin S.
Muller, Julian P., ed. see West, Jessamyn.
Muller, Marcia. The Cheshire Cat's Eye.
Muller, Marcia & Pronzini, Bill. The Deadly Arts.
Muller, Marcia & Pronzini, Bill, eds. The Web She Weaves: An Anthology of Mystery & Suspense Stories by Women.
Muller, Marion, jt. auth. see Ormond, Brande.
Muller, Max. Wortkritik und Sprachbereicherung in Adelungs Worterbuch.
Muller, O. & Roy, R. The Major Ternary Structure Families.
Muller, Olga E. Mind & Soul.
Muller, P. Economy & Ecological Equilibrium.
Muller, P. C., ed. see CISM (International Center for Mechanical Sciences), Department for General Mechanics Staff.
Muller, Peter. Essentials of Treasury Management.
Muller, Peter O. Contemporary Suburban America.
--The Outer City: Geographical Consequences of the Urbanization of the Suburbs. Natoli, Salvatore J., ed.
Muller, Peter O., jt. auth. see De Blij, Harm J.
Muller, R., jt. auth. see Gray, W. A.
Muller, Ralph, jt. ed. see Taylor, Angela E.
Muller, Rudolf O. Spectrochemical Analysis by X-Ray Fluorescence.
Muller, Steven. Mastering Omnis Three.
Muller, Thomas. Automated Guided Vehicle Systems.
--Growing & Declining Urban Areas: A Fiscal Comparison.
Muller, W. & Blank, H., eds. Heavy Element Properties: Proceedings of the Joint Session of the Baden Meetings, Sept. 1975.
Muller, W., et al, eds. Rheumatoid Arthritis: Pathogenetic Mechanisms & Consequences in Therapeutics.
Muller-Schwarze, Dietland, ed. Evolution of Play Behavior.
Mulley, Corinne, jt. auth. see Glaiser, Stephen.
Mulligan, Joseph F. Practical Physics: The Production & Conservation of Energy.

Mulliken, Frances H. A Bite of Eve's Apple: And Other Stories.
--First Ladies of the Restoration.
Mulliken, Ruth K. & Buckley, John J. Assessment of Multihandicapped & Developmentally Disabled Children.
Mullin, Arthur. Spy: Dr. Bancroft, America's First Double Agent.
Mullin, Glen H. Death & Dying: The Tibetan Tradition.
Mullin, J. B., ed. see International Spring School on Crystal Growth Staff.
Mullin, Jeanne, et al, eds. see Fischer, Eberhard & Homberger, Lorenz.
Mullin, Ray C. Electrical Wiring-Residential.
--Electrical Wiring-Residential.
Mullin, Ray C. & Smith, Robert L. Electrical Wiring-Commercial.
--Electrical Wiring: Commercial.
Mullin, Raymond & Smith, Robert. Electrical Wiring-Commercial.
Mullin, Ronald C., jt. auth. see Blake, Ian F.
Mullin, Timothy J. Training the Gunfighter.
Mullings, Llewellyn M. & Fenner, James. Economic Development.
Mullins, B. P., ed. see Shtern, V. Y.
Mullins, L. J., compiled by. Annual Reviews Reprints. Incl. Cell Membranes, 1975-1977. Annual Reviews.
Mullins, Phil, et al, eds. Political Reform in California: Evaluation & Perspective.
Mullish, H. & Kruger, D. Applesoft BASIC: From the Ground Up.
Mullish, Henry. A Basic Approach to Structured BASIC.
Mulloy, Paul, jt. auth. see Switzer, Kenneth A.
Mulock, Dinah M. John Halifax, Gentleman.
Mulry, Ray C. & White, Arthur H. The Portable Back School.
Multer, H. Gray. Field Guide to Some Carbonate Rock Environments: Florida Keys & Western Bahamas, 1977.
Multhauf, Robert P. The Origins of Chemistry.
Multhauf, Robert P., ed. see American Philosophical Society.
Multinational Executive Inc. Nineteen Seventy-Nine Multinational Executive Travel Companion.
Multinational Executive, Inc. Staff. Nineteen Eighty-One Multinational Executive Travel Companion.
Mulvaney, D. J. & Calaby, J. H. So Much That Is New: Baldwin Spencer.
Mulvihill, Deanna L., jt. auth. see Ney, Philip G.
Mulvihill, Margaret. Natural Selection.
Mumaw, H. J., tr. see Grauert, H. & Fritzsche, K.
Mumey, Jack & Hatcher, Anne S. Good Food for a Sober Life: A Diet & Nutrition Book for Recovering Alcoholics- & Those Who Love Them.
Mumford. Herman Melville.
Mumford, Alan. Making Experience Pay: Management Success Through Effective Learning.
Mumford, Amy R. Help Me Understand.
--When Divorce Ends Your Marriage...It Hurts.
Mumford, D. Geometric Invariant Theory.
Mumford, Edwin. The Five Flights of the Starfire.
--Flight of the Starfire.
--The Fourth Flight of the Starfire.
--Memories of the Past since Snooksie Died.
--The Second Flight of the Starfire.
--Some of Snooksie's Sayings, Stories & Pictures: Words of Wisdom.
--The Third Flight of the Starfire.
--The Voyage of the Starfire to Atlantis.
--What's the Fair Ward? Psychiatric Humor.
--What's the Funny Ward? Or My Last Ten Years with Snooksie the Guinea Pig.
--What's the Good Ward? Caustic Cartoons.
Mumford, J. M. Orofacial Pain: Aetiology, Diagnosis & Treatment.
Mumford, Lewis. City Development: Studies in Disintegration & Renewal.
--The City in History: Its Origins, Its Transformations, & Its Prospects.
--Highway & the City.
--In the Name of Sanity.
--Interpretations & Forecasts Nineteen Twenty-Two to Nineteen Seventy-Two.
--My Works & Days: A Personal Chronicle, 1895-1975.
--Technics & Human Development: The Myth of the Machine.
--The Urban Prospect.
Mumford, Thad & Muntean, Michaela. How to Make Your Own TV Show. Duenewald, Doris, ed.
Mumphrey, Anthony, jt. auth. see Atherton, J. C.
Mumtaz, Kamil K. Architecture in Pakistan.
Munasinghe, Mohan & Schramm, Gunther. Energy Policy & Demand Management Policy.
Munby, Denys & Watson, A. H. Road Passenger Transport & Road Goods Transport. Manunder, W. F., ed.
Munch, James C., Jr. Nineteen Eighty-Five Supplement to Life Insurance in Estate Planning.
Munch, Theodore W. Man the Engineer: Nature's Copycat.
Munch, Theodore W. & Winthrop, Robert D. Thunder on Forbidden Mountain.
Muncheryan, Hrand M. Patent It: A Do It Yourself Handbook.
Muncie, John, jt. auth. see Henwood, James.
Munck, Johannes. Paul & the Salvation of Mankind.
Muncy, Dorothy A. see Lochmoeller, Donald C.
Mundell, E. H. Erle Stanley Gardner: A Checklist.
Mundell, E. H., ed. see Helen, Mary & Dawson, Glen.
Mundell, Jacqueline. Current Literature on Communication in Personnel Management, 1980-1984.
--Intergovernmental Fiscal Relations During the First Reagan Administration: A Bibliography.
--Job Satisfaction: A Bibliography.
--Risk Management in the Public Sector: Recent Writings.
Mundell, Marvin E. Improving Productivity & Effectiveness.
Mundhenk, Robert T. & Siebenschuh, William R. Contact: A Guide to Writing Skills.
Mundie, Liz, jt. auth. see Eaton, Jan.
Mundis, Jerrold. Gerhardt's Children.
Mundis, Jerrold, ed. The Dog Book.
Mundt, Carlos S. Stars & Outer Space Made Easy.
Munford, Clarence J. Production Relations, Class & Black Liberation: A Marxist Perspective in Afro-American Studies.
Munford, W. A. History of the Library Association 1877-1977.
Mungazi, Dickson A. The Underdevelopment of African Education: A Black Zimbabwean Perspective.
Munger, Evelyn M. & Bowdon, Susan J. Beyond Peek-a-Boo & Pat-a-Cake: Activities for Baby's First Year.
Mungham, Geoff & Bankowski, Zenon, eds. Essays in Law & Society.
Mungo, Raymond. Mungobus.
Mungo, Raymund. Return to Sender.
Mungoshi, Charles. Waiting for the Rain.
Municipal Art Society of New York Staff. Design Arts Two.
Municipal Finance Officers Association Staff. A Guidebook to Improved Financial Management for Small Cities & Other Governmental Units.
Municipal Law Conference Staff. Open Meeting & Conflict of Interest Laws.
Munis, Richard H. Thermography: A New Way to Profit from the Energy Crisis.
Munjas, Barbara A., jt. auth. see Francis, Gloria M.
Munk, S. Philosophy & Philosophical Authors of the Jews: A Historical Sketch With Explanatory Notes. Kalisch, Isidor, tr.
Munn, Norman L. Evolution of the Human Mind.
--The Growth of Human Behavior.
Munoz, Faye U. & Endo, Russell, eds. Perspectives on Minority Group Mental Health.
Munro, A. & McCullough, W. Psychiatry for Social Workers.
Munro, Craig, ed. New Australian Short Stories.
Munro, Douglas. Alexandre Dumas Pere: A Bibliography of Works Published in French, 1825-1900.
--Alexandre Dumas Pere: A Bibliography of Works Translated into English to 1910.
Munro, H. H. see also Saki.
Munro, Ian S. Island of Bute.
Munro, Jim L. Classes, Conflict & Control: Studies in Criminal Justice Management.
Munro, John A., Associates, Inc. Staff, ed. see Munro, Robert A.
Munro, Mary Lynn, jt. auth. see Meyer, Annie.
Munro, Robert A. Real Estate Periodicals Index, 1983. Munro, John A., Associates, Inc. Staff, ed.
--Real Estate Periodicals Index, 1983. Munro, John A., Associates, Inc. Staff, ed.
Munro, Roxie. Color New York.
Munroe, John A. Federalist Delaware: 1775-1815.
Munroe, Ruth H., et al. Handbook of Cross-Cultural Human Development.
Munro-Smith, R. Elements of Ship Design.
--Ships & Naval Architecture (S. I. Units)
Munsell, Joel. Chronology of the Origin & Progress of Paper & Paper-Making. Bidwell, John, ed.
Munsinger, Harry. Fundamentals of Child Development.
Munslow, Barry & Finch, Henry, eds. Proletarianisation in the Third World: Studies in the Creation of a Labour Force under Dependent Capitalism.
Munson, Albe E. Construction Design for Landscape Architects.
Munson, Ken. U. S. Commercial Aircraft.
Munson, Ronald. The Way of Words: An Informal Logic.
Munson, Thomas N. The Essential Wisdom of George Santayana.
Munson-Williams-Proctor Institute Staff. Charles Baurchfield: Catalogue of Paintings in Public & Private Collections.
Munster, Sebastian. Cosmography.
Munsterberg, Hugo. A Short History of Chinese Art.
--Twentieth Century Painting.
Muntean, Michaela. The Tale of Traveling Matt.
--What Do Doozers Do?
Muntean, Michaela, jt. auth. see Mumford, Thad.
Munter, Paul H., jt. auth. see Ratcliffe, Thomas A.
Munter, Preston K., jt. auth. see Greiff, Barrie S.
Munton, Alan, ed. see Lewis, Wyndham.
Muntz, Hope. Golden Warrior.
Muntz, T. G. Overseas Economic Survey, Turkey, April 1950.
Muntzing, L. Manning, ed. Nuclear Power & Its Regulation in the United States.
Munves, James. The FBI & the CIA: Secret Agents & American Democracy.
--Thomas Jefferson & the Declaration of Independence.
Munz, Elizabeth. Happily Appley: A Leader's Guide to Food Fun with Young Children.
Munzert, Alfred. Test Your Computer I. Q.
Munzert, Alfred W. Analyze Your Personality Through Color.
--Test Your E. S. P.
--Test Your I. Q.
Munzert, Alfred W., jt. auth. see Elskamp, Karen K.
Mur, Jan. A Prisoner of Martial Law: Camp Journal-Poland, 1981-1982. Vallee, Lillian, tr.
Murach, Mike, jt. auth. see Noll, Paul.
Murail, Elvire. Stairway C. Linden, M. L., tr.
Murakami, Hyoe. Japan: The Years of Trial 1919-52.
Muralt, A. Von see Nestle Foundation Symposium Staff.
Muramatsu, Takashi, et al, eds. Teratocarcinoma & Embryonic Cell Interactions.
Muraoka, T. Modern Hebrew for Biblical Scholars: An Annotated Chrestomathy with an Outline Grammar & Glossary.
Murasaki, Lady. The Tale of Genji-One.
Murata, Kenji. Practical Bonsai for Beginners.
Muratov, M. Origin of Continents & Ocean Basins.
Murch. Development of the Detective Novel.
Murch, Arvin W., ed. Environmental Concern: Personal Attitudes & Behavior Toward Environmental Problems.
Murch, M., jt. auth. see Borowski, M.
Murchie, Guy. The Seven Mysteries of Life: An Exploration in Science & Philosophy.
Murchison, Irene, et al. Legal Accountability in the Nursing Process.
Murchison, Thomas M., ed. Prose Writings of Donald Lamont, 1874-1958.
Murdick, Robert G. & Cooper, Donald. Business Research: Concepts & Guides.
Murdick, Robert G., et al. Business Policy: A Framework for Analysis.
Murdin, P., jt. ed. see Beers, P.
Murdoch, Alexander. The People Above: Politics & Administration in Mid-18th Century Scotland.
Murdoch, Burn. From Edinburgh to the Antarctic.
Murdoch, John. Forty-Two British Watercolours.
Murdoch, Joseph S. & Seagle, Janet, eds. Golf: A Guide to Information Sources.
Murdock, Bruce K. Handbook of Electronic Design & Analysis Procedures Using Programmable Calculators.
Murdock, Doris B. Journey into Light: Lessons of Pain & Joy to Renew Your Energy & Strengthen Your Faith.
Murdock, James. Fluid Mechanics & Its Applications.
Murdock, M. S. The Web of the Romulans.
Mure, David. The Last Temptation: A Novel of Treason.
Murfree, Mary N. In the Tennessee Mountains.
Murger, Henri. The Bohemians of the Latin Quarter.
Murgo, John D., ed. Readings in the Economics of Education.
Murie, Alan, jt. auth. see Forest, Ray.
Murin, William J., et al, eds. Public Policy: A Guide to Information Sources.
Murison, R., jt. ed. see Ursin, H.
Murken, J. D., et al, eds. see Third European Congress.
Murnane, Gerald. The Plains.
Murnane, Mary, jt. ed. see Daniels, Kay.
Murnane, Richard J., ed. see National Research Council.
Murnane, William J. The Road to Kadesh: A Historical Interpretation of the Battle Reliefs of King Sety I at Karnak.
Muro, Diane P. Police Careers for Women.
Muro, Lisa. A Taste of Hate.
Muroga, Saburo. Threshold Logic & Its Applications.
Murphey, Cecil. Comforting Those Who Grieve.
--Seven Daily Sins & What to Do about Them.
Murphey, Cecil B. Somebody Knows I'm Alive.
--When in Doubt, Hug 'em: How to Develop a Caring Church.
Murphey, Cecil B., compiled by. The Encyclopedia for Today's Christian Woman.
Murphey, Dwight D. Liberal Thought in Modern America.
Murphey, Rhoads. Fading of the Maoist Vision.
--Patterns on the Earth.
--The Treaty Ports & China's Modernization: What Went Wrong?
Murphey, Wayne K. & Jorgensen, Richard. Wood As an Industrial Arts Material.
Murphy, et al. Algebra & Trigonometry.
Murphy, Angeline, Sr. Mother Florence: A Biographical History.
Murphy, Arlene W., jt. auth. see Murphy, Jack W.
Murphy, Arthur. The Plays of Arthur Murphy. Backscheider, Paula R., ed.
Murphy, Arthur E. Theory of Practical Reason. Melden, A. I., ed.
Murphy, Arthur E., ed. see Mead, George H.
Murphy, B. Dictionary of Australian History.
Murphy, Bill, et al, eds. see National Computing Centre, Ltd. Staff.
Murphy, Brian. The World Wired Up: Unscrambling the New Communications Puzzle.
Murphy, Carol, ed. see George, David L.
Murphy, Carol, ed. see Wright, Glen.
Murphy, Catherine, ed. The Antique Trader Antiques & Collectibles Price Guide.
--The Antique Trader Antiques & Collectibles Price Guide.
--Antique Trader Antiques & Collectibles Price Guide.
Murphy, Catherine & Husfloen, Kyle, eds. The Antique Trader Antiques & Collectibles Price Guide.
Murphy, Charles F. Working Decoy Plans: Kit I.
--Working Decoy Plans: Kit II.
Murphy, Charlotte W., jt. auth. see Greenburg, Herbert J.
Murphy, Chet. Advanced Tennis.
Murphy, Christopher. Dance for a Diamond.
Murphy, Clive. A Stranger in Gloucester.
Murphy, D. J., et al, eds. Labor in Power: The Labor Party & Governments in Queensland, Nineteen Fifteen to Nineteen Fifty-Seven.
Murphy, Dallas. Lover Man: A Mystery Introducing Artie Deemer.
Murphy, Daniel, jt. auth. see Ehrlich, Eugene.
Murphy, Dennis K. The Ravel'd Sleave of Care.
Murphy, Dervla. Nuclear Stakes: Race to the Finish.
Murphy, G. J. The Transport Operators Guide to Professional Competence.
Murphy, Gardner. Psychological Thought from Pythagoras to Freud: An Informal Introduction.
Murphy, Gardner & Kovach, Joseph K. Historical Introduction to Modern Psychology.
Murphy, Gardner, et al. Experimental Social Psychology.
Murphy, Haughton. Murder for Lunch.
Murphy, Henry C., ed. see Danckaerts, Jasper & Sluyter, Peter.
Murphy, Irene, ed. & frwd. by see Luna, Severino N.
Murphy, J. A., jt. auth. see Society of Manufacturing Engineers Staff.
Murphy, J. M. Thyristor Control of A. C. Motors.
Murphy, Jack W. & Murphy, Arlene W. Catechetics from A to Z.
Murphy, James F. Concepts of Leisure.
Murphy, James F., Jr. The Mill.
--Quonsett.
--They Were Dreamers: A Saga of the Irish in North America.
Murphy, James J. Renaissance Rhetoric: A Short Title Catalogue.
Murphy, James M. The Gabby Hartnett Story: From a Mill Town to Cooperstown.
Murphy, Jim. The Indy 500.
Murphy, John. The Origins & History of Religions.
Murphy, John D. Luganda-English Dictionary.
Murphy, John D. & Goff, Harry. A Bibliography of African Languages & Linguistics.
Murphy, John W. The Social Philosophy of Martin Buber: The Social World as a Human Dimension.
Murphy, Joseph. Healing Power of Love.
--Infinite Power for Richer Living.
--Miracle Power for Infinite Riches.
Murphy, Joseph P., jt. auth. see Rumney, Jay.
Murphy, Judith & Florio, Carol. Never Too Old to Teach.
Murphy, Judith, jt. auth. see Gross, Ronald.
Murphy, Karen. A House Full of Kids: Running a Successful Day Care Business in Your Own Home.
Murphy, Leona S. Miracles & the Sumrall Family.
Murphy, M. J., Jr., ed. In Vitro Aspects of Erythropoiesis.
Murphy, Marcy. Networking Practices & Priorities of Special & Academic Librarians: A Comparison.

Murphy, Margaret D. The Boston Globe Cookbook. Perrin, Gail, ed.
--Food Processor Cookery: Step-by-Step Guide to Success.
--Meat Makes the Meal.
--Wonderful Ways with Food. Kostick, Marilyn G., ed.
Murphy, Mary A., jt. auth. see Brown, Marie S.
Murphy, Mary F., jt. auth. see Greenwood, Kathryn M.
Murphy, Michael G. & Oberhoff, Kenneth E. Algebra for College Students.
Murphy, Pat & Murphy, Shirley. Mrs. Tortino's Return to the Sun.
Murphy, Patricia. Healing with Time & Love: A Guide for Visiting the Elderly.
Murphy, Pender. Bleeding Orange.
Murphy, Peter. The Moving Shadow Problem.
Murphy, Richard. Selected Poems.
Murphy, Robert. The Peregrine Falcon.
Murphy, Robert C. Fish-Shape Paumanok.
Murphy, Robert D. Mass Communication & Human Interaction.
Murphy, Robert F. Cultural & Social Anthropology: An Overture.
Murphy, Roland E. The Psalms, Job.
Murphy, Shirley, jt. auth. see Murphy, Pat.
Murphy, Shirley R. The Castle of Hape.
--Caves of Fire & Ice.
--Caves of Fire & Ice.
--Elmo Doolan & the Search for the Golden Mouse.
--The Flight of the Fox.
--The Grass Tower.
--The Joining of the Stone.
--The Pig Who Could Conjure the Wind.
--The Ring of Fire.
--The Ring of Fire.
--Silver Woven in My Hair.
--Soonie & the Dragon.
--The Wolf Bell.
--The Wolf Bell.
Murphy, Thomas P. & Kline, Robert D., eds. Urban Law: A Guide to Information Sources.
Murphy, Timothy F. Nietzsche As Educator.
Murphy, Walter F. Congress & the Court.
--Upon This Rock: The Life of St. Peter.
Murray, A., jt. ed. see Campbell, R. W.
Murray, A. R. An Introduction to Political Philosophy.
Murray, Amelia J. A Regency Lady's Faery Bower.
Murray, Andrew. Absolute Surrender: A Guide to the Spirit-Filled Life.
--The Blood of the Cross: Understanding the Mystery of Redemption.
--Confession: The Road to Forgiveness.
--Every Day with Andrew Murray.
--The Full Blessing of Pentecost.
--God's Best Secrets.
--Humility: The Beauty of Holiness.
--The Inner Life.
--The Ministry of Intercession: A Plea for More Prayer.
--Not My Will. Schoolland, Marian, tr.
--La Nueva Vida.
--The Prayer Life: A Guide to the Inner Chamber.
Murray, Charles S., jt. auth. see Carr, Roy.
Murray, D. A., ed. see International Symposium on Chrionomidae Staff.
Murray, Donald M. Write to Learn.
--Writer Teaches Writing.
Murray, Douglas P. International Relations Research & Training in the People's Republic of China.
Murray, E. C. Side-Lights on English Society: Sketches from Life, Social & Satirical.
Murray, Francis X. Energy: A National Issue.
Murray, Frank, jt. auth. see Adams, Ruth.
Murray, Frank B., ed. see Waller, T. Gary.
Murray, George. Caribbean Gold.
Murray, Grover E., jt. ed. see Hall, William E.
Murray, Henry A. Golf Secret.
Murray, Henry V. & Sluder, Troy B. Fixed Restorative Techniques.
Murray, Ian. New Penguin Book of Scottish Short Stories.
Murray, Jane W. Walk the High Horizon.
Murray, Janet H. & Clark, Anna K., eds. The Englishwoman's Review of Social & Industrial Questions: An Index.
Murray, Jerry. Moped: The Wonder Vehicle.
Murray, Jim & Karpovich, Peter. Weight Training in Athletics.
Murray, John. Daily Life of the Christian.
Murray, John W., jt. ed. see Jenkins, D. Graham.
Murray, Katherine. Anthropology & Education: A Selected Bibliography.
Murray, Lindley. Memoirs.
Murray, Margaret. Genesis of Religion.
Murray, Margaret A. The Splendor That Was Egypt.
Murray, Mary E., jt. auth. see Atkinson, Leslie D.
Murray, Merrill G. The Duration of Unemployment Benefits.
Murray, Michele. The Crystal Nights.
--Nellie Cameron.
Murray, Peter. Renaissance Architecture.
Murray, R. C. & Tedrow, John C. Forensic Geology: Earth Sciences & Criminal Investigation.
Murray, R. L. Nuclear Energy: In SI Metric Units.
Murray, Randall, ed. Mutagens & Carcinogens.
Murray, Raymond L. Understanding Radioactive Waste. Powell, Judith A., ed.
Murray, Rebecca, ed. History of the Public School Kindergarten in North Carolina.
Murray, Richard C., jt. auth. see Fisher, Charles O.
Murray, Robb. Batter My Heart.
Murray, Robert A. The Army on the Powder River.
Murray, Robert D., et al. The Natural Coumarins: Occurence, Chemistry & Biochemistry.
Murray, Robert K. The Politics of Normalcy: Governmental Theory & Practice in the Harding-Coolidge Era.
--Red Scare: A Study in National Hysteria, 1919-1920.
Murray, Robert W., jt. ed. see Wasserman, Harry H.
Murray, Ronald O. & Jacobson, Harold G. The Radiology of Skeletal Disorders: Exercises in Diagnosis.
Murray, Roy H. The Way Prayer Works: A Space Age View of the Timeless Substance of the Lord's Prayer.
Murray, Sheilagh. The Peacock & the Lions.
Murray, Spence. Trucking Trends.
Murray, Spence, ed. Basic Auto Repair Manual.
--Basic Cams, Valves & Exhaust Systems.
--Chevrolet Tune-up & Repair.
--Chevy-GMC Pickup Repair.
--Complete Book of Plymouth, Dodge, Chrysler.
--Creative Customizing.
--Dodge Pickup Repair.
--Ford Pickup Repair.
--How to Tune Your Car.
--Vanning Trends.
--VW Rabbit Tune-up & Repair.
Murray, Tom, ed. All Time All Stars.
Murray, William J. My Life Without God.
Murray-Aynsley, Harriet G. Symbolism of the East & West.
Murre, J. P., jt. auth. see Grothendieck, A.
Murrell, Hywel. Men & Machines.
--Motivation at Work.
Murrell, Jim. Way Howe to Lymne: Tudor Miniatures Observed.
Murrell, K. F. Ergonomics: Man In His Working Environment.
Murrell, Mary & Lester, David. Juvenile Delinquency.
Murry, John M. D. H. Lawrence: Son of Woman.
Murry, Kathleen see Mansfield, Katherine.
Murstein, Bernard I. Love, Sex & Marriage Through the Ages.
Murtha & Petrie. PC-DOS Companion.
Murtha, Stephen M. & Waite, Mitchell. CP-M Primer.
Murthy, M. K., jt. auth. see Cea, J.
Murthy, V. Rama, jt. ed. see Pollack, H. N.
Murton, Thomas O. The Dilemma of Prison Reform.
Murty, A. S., ed. Toxicity of Pesticides to Fish.
Murty, Y. V. & Mollard, F. R., eds. Continuous Casting of Small Cross Sections.
--Continuous Casting of Small Cross Sections: Proceedings TMS Fall Meeting, Pittsburgh, 1980.
Murtz, Harold A. Guns Illustrated 1984.
Murtz, Harold A., ed. Guns Illustrated 1985.
--Guns Illustrated 1986.
--Guns Illustrated, 1987.
--Guns Illustrated, 1988.
Murwin, Susan A., jt. auth. see Payne, Suzzy C.
Musashi, Miyamoto. Book of Five Rings.
Musbach, Alice & Davis, Barbara. Flight Attendant.
Muscarella, Oscar W. Bronze & Iron: Ancient Near Eastern Artifacts in the Metropolitan Museum of Art.
Muscatine, Charles & Griffith, Marlene. The Borzoi College Reader.
Muschg, Adolph. Besprechungen.
Muschlitz, Beverly, jt. auth. see Michener, Dorothy.
Museum of American Folk Art Staff. American Folk Art: Expressions of a New Spirit.
Museum of Fine Arts, Boston. Albert Durer Master Printmaker.
Museum of Fine Arts, Boston Staff. An Illustrated Handbook: The Museum of Fine Arts, Boston.
Museum of Modern Art, New York Staff, ed. Catalog of the Library of the Museum of Modern Art, New York.
Museum of Science & Industry Staff. Paper Dolls of China.
Museum Publications Staff. The Recreation Guide to Chicago & Suburbs.
Musgrave, Gerald L., ed. The Galbraith Viewpoint in Perspective: Critical Commentary on "The Age of Uncertainty" Television Series.
Musgrave, P. W. From Brown to Bunter: The Life & Death of the School Story.
Musgrave, Peggy B., jt. auth. see California Policy Seminar Staff.
Musgrove, Frank. Education & Anthropology: Other Cultures & the Teacher.
Musgrove, Gordon. Operation Gomorrah.
Mushlin, Linda L., jt. auth. see Hecht, Helen.
Musial, Stan & Buck, Jack. We Saw Stars.
Music Educators National Conference Staff. Documentary Report of the Ann Arbor Symposium: Applications of Psychology to the Teaching & Learning of Music, Sessions I & II.
Music Educators National Conference. Documentary Report of the Ann Arbor Symposium.
Music Educators National Conference Staff. Power of Music.
--Selective Music Lists, 1979: Instrumental Solos & Ensembles.
--Study of Music in the Elementary School: A Conceptual Approach. Evenson, Flavis & Gary, Charles L., eds.
Musick, Judith S. & Householder, Joanne. Infant Development: From Theory to Practice.
Musil, Thomas A., jt. auth. see Driscoll, Edward J.
Muske, Carol. Camouflage.
Muskie, Jane G., jt. auth. see McCarthy, Abigail.
Musleah, Ezekiel N. On the Banks of the Ganga: The Sojourn of Jews in Calcutta.
Musoff, Lloyd D. Uncle Sam's Private, Profitseeking Corporations: Comsat, Fannie Mae, Amtrak, & Conrail.
Musschenga, Bert, jt. ed. see Gosling, David.
Mussell, Harry & Staples, Richard C. Stress Physiology in Crop Plants.
Musselman, Donald & Musselman, Vernon. Lesson Plans in Accounting.
Musselman, Vernon, jt. auth. see Musselman, Donald.
Musselman, Vernon A. & Jackson, John H. Introduction to Modern Business.
Musselman, Virginia. The Day Camp Program Book.
Musselwhite, James C., Jr. & Saunders, Lauren K. Government Spending & the Nonprofit Sector in Two Michigan Communities: Flint - Genesee County & Tuscola County. Salamon, Lester, ed.
Musset, Alfred de & Barrier, Gerard. La Confession d'un Enfant du Siecle.
Musset, Alfred De see De Musset, Alfred.
Mussner, Franz. Tractate on the Jews: The Significance of Judaism for the Christian Faith. Swidler, Leonard, tr. from Ger.
Musson, James, jt. ed. see Robinson, Eric H.
Mustafa, Ahmed. Benzofurans.
Mustarde, John C. Repair & Reconstruction in the Orbital Region.
Mustarde, John C., ed. Plastic Surgery in Infancy & Childhood.
Muston, John. Survival Training & Techniques.
Muswick, Gary J., jt. auth. see Nowak, Stephen F.
Muthiani, Joseph. Akamba from Within: Egalitarianism in Social Relations.
Mutiso, Gideon-Cyprus. Socio-Political Thought in African Literature.
Mutloatse, Mothobi, ed. Africa South: Contemporary Writings.
Muto, Susan. The Journey Homeward.
Mutoh, Nancy W., jt. auth. see Pifer, George W.
Mutrux, Robert. Great New England Churches: Sixty-Five Houses of Worship That Changed Our Lives.
Mutschler, E. & Winterfeldt, E., eds. Trends in Medicinal Chemistry: Proceedings of the 9th International Symposium on Medicinal Chemistry.
Mutter, K. H. & Schilling, K., eds. Current Topics in Elementary Particle Physics.
Mutuwka, Kasuka S. Politics of the Tanzania-Zambia Railproject.
Muuss, Rolf E. Theories of Adolescence.
Muzzaffar, Muhammed R. Al see Al-Muzaffar, Muhammed R.
Muzzarelli, Riccardo A. Chitin.
--Natural Chelating Polymers.
Muzzey, Artemas B. Reminiscences & Memorials of Men of the Revolution.
Mvungi, Martha. Three Solid Stones.
Mwangi, Meja. Carcase for Hounds.
Mydans, Carl. More Than Meets the Eye.
Myddleton, D. R., jt. auth. see Reid, Walter.
Myer, Alma M. The Golden Page.
Myer, Elizabeth Gallup. The Social Situation of Women in the Novels of Ellen Glasgow.
Myerhoff, Barbara G., jt. ed. see Moore, Sally F.
Myers. Izzy Manheim's Reunion.
Myers, A. R. Parliaments & Estates in Europe: To 1789.
Myers, Albert & Andersen, Christopher. Success over Sixty.
Myers, Albert & Andersen, Christopher P. Success over Sixty.
Myers, Albert & Anderson, Christopher. Success over Sixty.
Myers, Andrew B., ed. Century of Commentary on the Works of Washington Irving, 1860-1974.
--Washington Irving: A Tribute.
--The Worlds of Washington Irving, 1783-1859: An Anthology Exhibition from the Collections of The New York Public Library.
Myers, Bernard L. & Copplestone, Trewin. Family Encyclopedia of Art.
Myers, Bernard S. Art & Civilization.
Myers, Bill, ed. see Redinger, David H.
Myers, Carol, jt. ed. see Myers, Dwight.
Myers, Carole R. A Primer of Left-Handed Embroidery.
Myers, Charles A. & Schultz, George P. The Dynamics of a Labor Market: A Study of the Impact of Employment Changes on Labor Mobility, Job Satisfactions, & Company & Union Policies.
Myers, David C. The Human Puzzle: Psychological Research & Christian Belief.
Myers, David G. The Inflated Self: Human Illusions & the Bibical Call to Hope.
Myers, David R. Samuel Gompers: A Selected List of References about the Man & His Times.
Myers, Denys P. Origin & Conclusion of the Paris Pact. Bd. with Renunciation of War. Page, Kirby. Garland Pub.
Myers, Desaix, III, et al. U. S. Business in South Africa: The Economic, Political & Moral Issues.
Myers, Don A. Sole Prints: A Reference Guide for Law Enforcement Personnel.
Myers, Donald G., et al. The Right-to-Education Child: A Curriculum for the Severely & Profoundly Mentally Retarded.
Myers, Drew G. To Kill a Witch.
Myers, Dwight & Myers, Carol, eds. In Celebration of the Book: Literary New Mexico.
Myers, Emily R. Automated Financial Systems: How to Computerize a Business.
Myers, Forrest D. Sam Myers (Eighteen Five to Eighteen Eighty-Three) & Lydia Horner (Eighteen Thirty-Three to Nineteen Seven) Their Ancestors & Descendants.
Myers, Franklin S. The Clarinets: A Story of Teenage Friendship & Courage.
Myers, Gerald, jt. ed. see Fancher, Gordon.
Myers, Glenford J. Digital System Design with LSI Bit-Slice Logic.
--Reliable Software Through Composite Design.
Myers, J. M. Grace & Torah.
Myers, Jack, compiled by. A Trout in the Milk: A Composite Portrait of Richard Hugo.
Myers, James H. & Reynolds, William H. Consumer Behavior & Marketing Management.
Myers, John G., jt. auth. see Aaker, David A.
Myers, John J., ed. Handbook of Ocean & Underwater Engineering.
Myers, John M. The Last Chance: Tombstone's Early Years.
Myers, K. A., et al. Principles of Pathology in Surgery.
Myers, Katherine. Dark Soldier.
--Ribbons of Silver.
--Winter Flame.
Myers, Kathy. Understains: The Sense & Seduction of Advertising.
Myers, Kenneth A., ed. NATO-the Next Thirty Years: The Changing Political, Economic, & Military Setting.
Myers, L. M., jt. auth. see Hoffman, Richard L.
Myers, Larry L. How to Create Your Own Computer Bulletin Board.
Myers, M. Scott. Every Employee a Manager. Newton, William R., ed.
Myers, Mary R. Friday's Daughter.
--Love Unspoken.
Myers, Norman. The Primary Source: Tropical Forests & Our Future.
Myers, Oma L., jt. auth. see Welch, Rosa P.
Myers, Philip. Patterns of Reproduction of Four Species of Vespertiliohia Bats in Paraguay.
Myers, Ramon, ed. see Nankai University Committee on Social & Economic Research.
Myers, Ramon H. The Japanese Economic Development of Manchuria, 1932-1945.
Myers, Ramon H., jt. auth. see Arnold, Julean.
Myers, Ramon H., ed. see Buck, John L.
Myers, Ramon H., ed. see Bush, Richard C.
Myers, Ramon H., ed. see Chen, Han-Seng A.
Myers, Ramon H., ed. see Cheng Wang.
Myers, Ramon H., ed. see Kinney, Ann R.
Myers, Ramon H., ed. see Simon Yang & L. K. Tao.
Myers, Ramon H., ed. see Sung-Ho Lin.
Myers, Ramon H., ed. see Wiens, Thomas B.
Myers, Ramon H., ed. see Wilhelm, Richard.
Myers, Raymond H., jt. auth. see Walpole, Ronald E.
Myers, Robert, jt. auth. see Garcia, Anthony.
Myers, Robert E. Jack Williamson: A Primary & Secondary Bibliography.
Myers, Robert M., ed. A Georgian at Princeton.
Myers, Robin & Harris, Michael, eds. Sale & Distribution of Books from Seventeen Hundred.

Myers, Ruth, jt. auth. see Myers, Warren.
Myers, Trent. Dewain Valentine: Double Pyramid.
--The Eiler Collection...Now.
--Owen Morrel Works: Nineteen Seventy-Six to Nineteen Eighty-Four.
Myers, Trent, jt. auth. see Adrian, Dennis.
Myers, Trent, ed. see Adrian, Dennis.
Myers, Trent, ed. see Loring, John & Acton, David.
Myers, W. Fast Sam, Cool Clyde, & Stuff.
Myers, Warren & Myers, Ruth. Pray: How to Be Effective in Prayer.
Myers, William, ed. Restoration & Revolution: Political, Social & Religious Writings 1660-1700.
Myerson, Joel. The Brook Farm Book: A Collection of First-Hand Accounts of the Community.
--Theodore Parker: A Descriptive Bibliography.
Myerson, Joel, ed. Critical Essays on Margaret Fuller.
Mylander, Maureen. The Great American Stomach Book.
Myler, Charles E., Jr. Arizona Supplement for Modern Real Estate Practice.
Mylius, Ralph. The Complete PFS Book.
Myller, Rolf. How Big Is a Foot?
--Symbols & Their Meaning.
Myra, Harold. The New You.
Myrdal, Gunnar. Asian Drama: An Inquiry into the Poverty of Nations.
Myrdal, Jan. Return to a Chinese Village.
Myres, R. W. Out, Out, Brief Candle!
Myres, Sandra L., jt. ed. see Hollingsworth, Harold M.
Myrick. Ninety-Nine Pockets.
Myrick, Arthur B., tr. see Boccaccio, Giovanni.
Myrick, Bismarck & Easterbrook, David L. Three Aspects of Crisis in Colonial Kenya.
Myrick, David F. Montecito & Santa Barbara. Walker, Jim, ed.
Myrick, Kenneth. Sir Philip Sidney As a Literary Craftsman.
Myrtek, Mihcael. Constitutional Psychophysiology: Research in Review (Monograph) Greenlee, Mark, tr. from Ger.
Myskis, A. D. Advanced Mathematics for Engineers.
Myslobodsky, M. Petit Mal Epilepsy: A Search for the Precursors of Spike-Wave Activity.
Mysse, Janet. Fisherman Knits: The Classics.
Mysse, Janet W. Affordable Furs: Combining Fur & Leather with Knitting.
Mystery Writers of America Members. All but Impossible! An Anthology of Locked Room & Impossible Crime Stories. Hoch, Edward D., ed.

N

N. F. L. Staff, compiled by. Official Nineteen Eighty-Seven NFL Record & Fact Book.
Nabb, Magdalen. Death in Autumn: A Florentine Mystery.
--Death in Springtime: A Florentine Mystery.
--Death of an Englishman.
Nabel, Norman C. The Form & Meaning of the Fall Narrative.
Nablo, S. Progress in Radiation Processing: Proceedings of the International Meeting, 5th, San Diego, California, October 24-26, 1984.
Nabokov, Dmitri, tr. see Lermontov, Mihail.
Nabokov, Dmitri, tr. see Nabokov, Vladimir.
Nabokov, Vladimir. Ada or Ardor: A Family Chronicle.
--Annotated Lolita. Appel, Alfred, Jr., ed. & intro. by.
--Bend Sinister.
--Dar.
--The Enchanter.
--Glory.
--Glory.
--King, Queen, Knave.
--King, Queen, Knave.
--Lectures on Don Quixote. Bowers, Fredson, ed.
--Lectures on Russian Literature. Bowers, Fredson, ed.
--Lolita.
--Lolita: A Screenplay.
--Look at the Harlequins.
--Look at the Harlequins.
--The Man from the U. S. S. R. & Other Plays. Nabokov, Dmitri, tr.
--Mary.
--Nabokov's Dozen.
--Pnin.
--Poems & Problems.
--Priglashenie Na Kazn.
--A Russian Beauty & Other Stories. Nabokov, Dmitri & Karlinsky, Simon, trs. from Rus.
--Strong Opinions.
--Strong Opinions.
--Transparent Things.
--Tyrants Destroyed & Other Short Stories. Nabokov, Dmitri, tr. from Rus.
--Tyrants Destroyed & Other Stories.
Nabokov, Vladimir, tr. see Lermontov, Mihail.
Nace, Ted & Gardner, Michael. LaserJet Unlimited: How to Get the Most from Your Hewlett-Packard LaserJet or LaserJet Plus Printer.
Nachazel, Delbert P., jt. auth. see Smith, Joan F.
Nachbar. American Language Today.
--American Language Today.
--American Language Today.
--American Language Today L-4 Te.
--American Language Today L-5 Te.
--American Language Today Lev 6.
--American Language Today LV3 Te.
Nachbar, Jack. Popular Culture Reader.
Nachbar, John. Western Films: An Annotated Critical Bibliography.
Nachmansohn, David. Chemical & Molecular Basis of Nerve Activity.
Nachmias, Vivianne T. Microfilaments. Head, J. J., ed.
Nachtigall, W. Biological Mechanisms of Attachment: The Comparative Morphology & Bioengineering of Organs for Linkage, Suction, & Adhesion. Biederman-Thorson, M. A., tr.
Naczi, Frances D. Without Bombast & Blunders: An Executive's Guide to Effective Writing.
Nadawi, Abul H. Madha Khasira al-Alam bi-Inhtat al-Muslimin.
Nadeau, Maurice. The Greatness of Flaubert. Bray, Barbara, tr.
Nadeau, Roland. Symphony: Structure & Style.
Nadel, Mark V. The Politics of Consumer Protection.
Nadel, Max & Sherrer, Arthur. Barron's How to Prepare for the Advanced Placement Examination - English.
Nadelhoffer, Hans. Cartier: Jewelers Extraordinary.
Nadell, Bonnie & Small, John. Break Dance.
Nader, Ralph & Abbotts, John. The Menace of Atomic Energy.
Nader, Ralph & Green, Mark. Taming the Giant Corporation.
Nader, Ralph, ed. The Consumer & Corporate Accountability.
Nader, Ralph, et al. The Lemon Book.
Nader, Ralph, et al, eds. Who's Poisoning America: Corporate Polluters & Their Victims in the Chemical Age.
Nadkarni, Meena. Citizenship in Canada: A Retrospective Bibliography.
Nadler, Arie, jt. ed. see Fisher, Jeffrey D.
Nadler, Bob. Advanced B & W Darkroom Book.
--The Commodore 64 Illustrated.
Nadler, Gerald. Work Simplification.
Nadler, Gerald, et al. Design Concepts for Information Systems.
Nadler, Harvey & Marelli, Leonard R. American English: Grammatical Structure.
--American English: Guided Composition Paper.
--American English: Pronunciation & Dictation.
Nadler, Leonard. Corporate Human Resource Development.
--Personal Skills for the Manager.
Nadolsky, Julien M., ed. see Vocational Evaluation & Work Adjustment Association Staff.
Nadvi. An Easy History of the Prophet of Islam.
Naef, Weston J. Counterparts: Form & Emotion in Photographs.
Naef, Weston J., jt. auth. see Goldschmidt, Lucien.
Naeslund, B. & Sellstedt, B. Neo-Ricardian Theory: With Applications to Some Current Economic Problems.
Naeve, Milo M., ed. Winterthur Portfolio.
Nag, B. R. Theory of Electrical Transport in Semi-Conductors.
Nag, Kalidas. Tolstoy & Gandhi.
Nagakansara Rao, Dittakavi. Legal Ethics, Professional Responsibility: A Selected Bibliography of Articles.
Nagashima, Kei, jt. auth. see Watanabe, Masahiro.
Nagatake, Takeshi. Imari.
Nagaya, Miyo. Russian Cooking.
Nagel, Ernest. Structure of Science: Problems in the Logic of Scientific Explanation.
Nagel, G. A., jt. ed. see Brunner, K. W.
Nagel, M. R., et al. Illumination, Color, A Contrast Tables: Naturally Illuminated Objects.
Nagel, Paul C. This Sacred Trust: American Nationality, Seventeen Ninety-Eight to Eighteen Ninety-Eight.
Nagel, Stuart, et al. The Political Science of Criminal Justice.
Nagell, John R. van see Van Nagell, John R., Jr. & Barber, Hugh R.
Nagin, Paul & Ledgard, Henry F. BASIC with Style: Programming Proverbs.
Nagl, W. & Ehrendorfer, F., eds. Genome & Chromatin - Organization, Evolution, Function: Symposium, Kaiserslautern, October 13-15, 1978.
Nagle, D. Brendan. The Ancient World: A Social & Cultural History.
Nagle, James J. Heredity & Human Affairs.
Nagle, John D. Introduction to Comparative Politics: Comparing Political System Performance in Three Worlds.
Nagle, Mercita C. I Look to the Mountain for Strength & Love.
Nagle, Walter H. Five Straight Errors on Ladies Day.
Naglee, David I. In Praise of More Folly.
Nagornyi, et al. Povest' OB Ugolovnom Rozyske.
Nagorski, Andrew. Reluctant Farewell: An American Reporter's Candid Look Inside the Soviet Union.
Nagrath, I. J. & Gopal, M. Control Systems Engineering.
Na Greine, Donal. A Bottle of Psychology.
Nagy, Margarita E., jt. ed. see White, Philip L.
Nagy, P. J. Country Risk.
Naha, Ed. Horrors: From Screen to Scream!
Nahas, G. G., ed. Marihuana: Chemistry, Biochemistry, & Cellular Efffects.
Nahas, Gabriel G. & Frick, Henry C., II, eds. Drug Abuse in the Modern World: A Perspective for the Eighties: Proceedings of a Symposium Held at the College of Physicians & Surgeons of Columbia University, New York, N.Y.
Nahmias, A. J., jt. ed. see Schinazi, R. F.
Nahum, Peter. Victorian Painters Monograms: A Pocket Identification Guide.
Naidich, T. P. & Quencer, R. M., eds. Clinical Neurosonography.
Naidu, N. S. & Kamaraju, V. High Voltage Engineering.
Naidu, V. N. Tandava Laksanam or the Fundamentals of Ancient Hindu Dancing.
Naifeh, Steven & Smith, Gregory W. The Best Lawyers in America.
Naik, J. A. India & the Communist Countries: Documents 1979.
--India & the West: Documents, 1979.
--Russia & the Communist Countries: Documents.
--Russia & the Western World: 1946-1971 Documents.
Naik, J. A., ed. India & the West: Documents 1976-78.
--India in Asia & Africa: Documents, 1976-78.
--India in Asia & Africa: Documents, 1979.
--Russia & the West: Documents 1972-1975.
--Russia in Asia & Africa Documents, 1972-75.
Naik, M. K. The Ironic Vision: A Study of the Fiction of R. K. Narayan.
--Perspectives on Indian Prose in English.
Naim, C. M., ed. Iqbal, Jinnah, & Pakistan: The Vision & the Reality.
Naiman. MacBook.
Naiman, Arthur. Every Goy's Guide to Common Jewish Expressions.
--IBM Personal Computer Made Easy.
--Introduction to WordStar.
--Mastering WordStar on the IBM-PC.
--Word Processing Buyer's Guide.
Naiman, Arthur, jt. auth. see Coleman, Dale.
Naiman, Arthur & Horan, Kelly, eds. Supercharging WordStar.
Naiman, J. Lawrence, jt. auth. see Oski, Frank A.
Naiman, Melvin H., ed. see Josephson, I. Zelig.
Naimark, Susan, ed. see Boston Urban Gardeners.
Naimy, Mikhail. Memoirs of a Vagrant Soul.
Naine, D. T. Sundiata: An Epic of Old Mali.
Naipaul, V. S., et al. Island Voices: Stories from the West Indies. Salkey, Andrew, ed.
Nair, B. R., jt. ed. see Mallett, R. H.
Nair, N. K. Purchasing & Materials Management.
Nair, Sreedhar, ed. Computers in Critical & Pulmonary Medicine.
Nairn, A. E., tr. see Braitsch, O.
Nairne, Sandy & Serota, Nicholas. British Sculpture in the Twentieth Century.
Naisbitt Group Staff & Naisbitt, John. The Year Ahead: 1985.
Naisbitt, John, jt. auth. see Naisbitt Group Staff.
Naito, Akira. Katsura: A Princely Retreat. Terry, Charles S., tr. from Japanese.
Najita, Tetsuo. Hara Kei in the Politics of Compromise 1905-1915.
Najita, Tetsuo & Scheiner, Irwin, eds. Japanese Thought in the Tokugawa Period (1600-1868) Methods & Metaphors.
Nakadate, Neil, ed. Robert Penn Warren: A Reference Guide.
Nakagawa, Tsuyoshi. El Salvador.
Nakajima, Heitaro & Ogawa, Hiroshi. Compact Audio Disc: Understanding the New Digital Technology.
Nakamura, Hajime. Parallel Developments: A Comparative History of Ideas.
Nakamura, Julia & Nakamura, Massy. Your Future in Medical Illustrating: Art & Photography.
Nakamura, K., jt. auth. see Egami, F.
Nakamura, Massy, jt. auth. see Nakamura, Julia.
Nakano, Ann. Broken Canoe: Conversations & Observations in Micronesia.
Nakano, Toru. Trekking in Nepal. Ooka, D. T., tr. from Fr. & Japanese.
Nakarai, Toyozo W. An Elder's Public Prayers.
Nakata, Yuri & Strange, Michele. Classification Scheme for Illinois State Publications.
Nakayama, Masatoshi. Best Karate: Kata: Heian & Tekki.
Nakayama, Shigeru, et al, eds. Science & Society in Modern Japan.
Nakhjavan, Fred K. Cardiac Catheterization: Diagnostic Interventions.
Nakon, Robert. Chemical Problem Solving Using Dimensional Analysis.
Nalanda Translation Committee, tr. see Trungpa, Chogyam.
Nalbandian, Carol & Ryan, Colleen, eds. Planning Your Career Pathways: Employee's Career Development Workbook.
Nalbandian, Carol, jt. ed. see Ryan, Colleen.
NALCO Chemical Company Staff. NALCO Water Handbook.
Nale, Sharon A. A Cry for Help: For Families of Alcohol & Other Drug-Dependent Persons.
Nalluri, C., jt. auth. see Featherstone, R. E.
Nam, Charles B. & Gustavus, Susan O. Population: The Dynamics of Demographic Change.
Nama, P. G., et al. Breast Self Examination & You.
Nama, Prabharathie G., jt. auth. see Tetzleff, Judith.
Namath, Joe. Joe Namath's Football Basics.
Namba, M. & Kaiya, H., eds. Psychobiology of Schizophrenia, In Memory of C. & O. Vogt & M. Hayashi: Proceedings of a Satellite Symposium to the 8th International Congress of Pharmacology, Gifu, Japan, June 27-29, 1981.
Nameroff, Steven, jt. auth. see Jamsa, Kris.
Names, Jerry. Mindblock.
Names, Larry D. Cowboy Conspiracy.
Namikawa, Banri. Iran.
Namioka, I., jt. auth. see Kelly, J.
Namm, Diane, ed. Favorite Nursery Rhymes.
Nancarrow, Peter. Early China & the Wall.
Nance, Gusta B., tr. see Pena, Carlos G.
Nance, Harold. Office Work Measurement.
Nance, John. The Gentle Tasaday: A Stone Age in the Philippine Rain Forest.
--The Gentle Tasaday: A Stone Age People in the Philippine Rain Forest. Ferrone, J., ed.
Nance, John J. Blind Trust: The Human Crisis in Airline Safety.
Nance, Joseph M. Attack & Counterattack: The Texas-Mexican Frontier, 1842.
Nanda, B. R. The Nehrus: Motilal & Jawaharlal.
--Science & Technology in India.
Nandy, Pritish, jt. auth. see Mirabai.
Nandy, Pritish, ed. Modern Indian Stories.
Nangis, Guillaume de see De Nangis, Guillaume.
Nangle, Benjamin. The Gentleman's Magazine Biographical & Obituary Notices, 1781-1819: An Index.
Nankai University Committee on Social & Economic Research. Wholesale Prices & Price Index Numbers in North China: 1913-1929. Myers, Ramon, ed.
Nankani, Gobindram T. Development Problems of Mineral Exporting Countries.
Nan Lo, Chun, jt. auth. see Klonglan, Gerald E.
Nanney, T. Ray. Computing: A Problem-Solving Approach Using FORTRAN 77.
Nanry, Charles. The Jazz Text.
Napier. Blood Transfusion Therapy: A Problem Oriented Approach.
Napier, Annie R. Sing Out: For the Reader Who Loves to Explore Life.
Napier, B. W., et al, eds. Comparative Dismissal Law.
Napier, Davie. Song of the Vineyard: A Guide Through the Old Testament.
--Word of God, Word of Earth.
Napier, Davie, jt. auth. see Borsch, Frederick H.
Napier, Miles. Blood Will Tell.
--Breeding a Racehorse.
--Breeding a Racehorse.
Napier, Rodney W. & Gershenfeld, Matti K. Groups: Theory & Experience.
--Groups: Theory & Experience.
Napoleon, Louis, 3rd. Napoleonic Ideas. Gooch, Brison D., ed. & intro. by.
Napoli, illus. Life of Jesus.
Napoli, Vince & Kilbride, James M. Adjustment & Growth in a Changing World.
Napolitano, L., ed. Space Two Thousand-Activities to Be Performed for the Next Decade: Selected Papers from the 33rd IAF Congress, Paris, France, 27 September - 2 October 1982.
Napolitano, L. G. Microgravity Sciences & Processes.
--Space Developments for the Future of Mankind.
--Using Space, Today & Tomorrow, Vol. 2: Communications Satellite Symposium.
Napolitano, L. G., jt. auth. see International Astronautical Congress Staff.
Napolitano, L. G., ed. Space Developments: Applications of Space & Energy: Selected Proceedings of the XXXI International Astronautical Congress, Tokyo, Japan, 21-28 September 1980.

Authors

--Space Developments for the Future of Mankind-II: Proceedings of the Thirtieth International Astronautical Congress, Munich, FRG. September 16-23 1979.
--Space, Mankind's Fourth Environment: Selected Proceedings of the XXXII IAF Congress, Rome, September 6-12, 1981.
Napolitano, L. G., ed. see International Astronautical Congress Staff.
Napolitano, Luigi G. & International Astronautical Congress, 28th, Prague, 1977. Using Space--Today & Tomorrow: Proceedings.
Napper, Elizabeth, ed. see Hopkins, Jeffrey.
Nappi, Carmine. Commodity Market Controls.
Narada, U. Guide to Conditional Relations Part I: Being a Guide to Pages 1-12 of "Conditional Relations" Patthana.
Narang, C. K., jt. auth. see Mathur, N. K.
Narasimhaiah, C. D., ed. Awakened Conscience: Studies in Commonwealth Literature.
Narasimhan, R. Introduction to the Theory of Analytic Spaces.
Narasimhan, Seetharama L., jt. auth. see McLeavey, Dennis W.
Narayan, R. K. Lawley Road & Other Stories.
--Reluctant Guru.
Narayanan, K. R. & Misra, K. P., eds. Nonalignment in Contemporary International Relations.
Narayananda, Swami. The Primal Power in Man: The Kundalini Shakti Yoga.
Narayan Prasad Jain. Conversational Hindi.
Narazaki, Muneshige. The Japanese Print: Its Evolution & Essence.
Narcisse, Louis, jt. auth. see Des Lozieres, Baudry.
Nardi, Fred, jt. auth. see Nardi, Vincent.
Nardi, G., et al. Exceptionality: Selected Readings.
Nardi, V., et al, eds. Energy Storage, Compression, & Switching.
Nardi, Vincent & Nardi, Fred. Color Your Hair Like A Pro.
Nardone, Nancy K., ed. Secular Choral Music in Print: 1982 Supplement.
Nardone, Thomas R., ed. Classical Vocal Music in Print.
Narka, Ryan. My Place in God's World.
Narmour, Eugene. Beyond Schenkerism: The Need for Alternatives in Music Analysis.
Narovchatov, S. Selected Verse.
Narramore, Bruce. Parenting with Love & Limits.
Narramore, Bruce S. Why Children Misbehave: A Guide To Positive Parenting.
Narramore, Clyde M. Counseling Youth.
--Twenty Danger Signals.
--Why a Christian Leader May Fall.
Narramore, S. Bruce. An Ounce of Prevention: A Parent's Guide to Moral & Spiritual Growth in Children.
Narveson, Paul R. Theory of Melody: A Complete General Presentation of the Practical Materials, Resources, & Phenomena.
Nary, R. William, compiled by. Documents on Disarmament.
NASA Staff. The Search for Extraterrestrial Intelligence. Morrison, Philip, et al, eds.
Nasar, Syed A. Power System & Electric Machines.
Nasatir, Abraham P., jt. auth. see Loomis, Noel M.
Nash, Bruce. So You Think You Know Your Boyfriend-Girlfriend? Schneider, Meg, ed.
--So You Think You Know Your Brother-Sister? Schneider, Meg, ed.
Nash, Connie, jt. auth. see Derksen, Sandy.
Nash, Edward L. Direct Marketing: Strategy, Planning, Execution.
Nash, Gary B. & Frazier, Thomas R., eds. The Private Side of American History: Readings in Everyday Life.
--The Private Side of American History: Readings in Everyday Life. Incl. Vol. 1. To 1877; Vol. 2. Since 1865. HarBraceJ.
Nash, Jay R. Murder America.
Nash, Jean. Golden Reckoning.
--The Golden Thread.
--The Silver Web.
Nash, N. Richard. Aphrodite's Cave.
--The Last Magic.
Nash, Ogden. There's Always Another Windmill.
Nash, Richard. East Wind, Rain.
Nash, Roderick, jt. auth. see Collins, Robert O.
Nash, Ronald H., ed. Liberation Theology.
--Liberation Theology.
Nash, S. Elizabeth. Cooking Craft.
Nash, Suzanne, tr. see Junior League of Wilmington, Inc. Staff.
Nash, Thomas. Pierce Penilesse, His Supplication to the Divell.
Nash, Tony, jt. auth. see Bender, Arnold.
Nash, Walter. English Usage: A Guide to First Principles.
Nashelsky, Louis, jt. auth. see Boylestad, Robert L.
Nashif, Huda. Pre-School Education in the Arab World: The Experience of Kuwait.
Nasir, Pir. The Faceless Enemy: A True Story of Injustice.
Nasman, Leonard. Postsecondary Business & Industry Needs Assessment Model.
Nason, John W., jt. auth. see Malickson, David L.
Nasr, Seyyed H. Muhammed: Man of Allah.
Nasr, Seyyed H., ed. Nasir-I Khusraw: Forty Poems from the Divan. Wilson, Peter L. & Aavani, Gholam R., trs.
Nasri, William Z. & Rizzo, John R., eds. Legal Issues for Library & Information Managers.
Nass, Gilbert D. & McDonald, Gerald W. Marriage & the Family.
Nassaney, Michael S. Archaeological Investigations at the Riebling Site, Monroe County, Illinois.
Nassour, Ellis. Patsy Cline.
Nastick, Sharon. So You Think You've Got Problems: Twelve Stubborn Saints & Their Pushy Parents.
Nastuk, William L. see Oster, Gerald, et al.
Natanson, ed. see Celms, Theodor.
Natanson, I. P. Problemas Elementales de Maximo y Minimo y Suma de Cantidades Infintamente Pequenas.
Natanson, M., ed. see Straus, E. W., et al.
Natanson, Maurice, ed. see Ferrier, James F.
Natanson, Maurice, ed. see Lotze, Hermann.
Natanson, Maurice, ed. see Osborn, A. D.
Natelson, Ethan A., jt. ed. see Natelson, Samuel.
Natelson, Samuel & Natelson, Ethan A., eds. Principles of Applied Clinical Chemistry: Chemical Background & Medical Applications. Incl. Vol. 1, Maintenance of Fluid & Electrolyte Balance; Vol. 2, The Erythrocyte Chemical Composition, Normal & Aberrant Metabolism. Plenum Pub.
Nath, R. An Annotated Bibliography of Indian Painting Through the Ages.
--The Art of Chanderi: A Study of the Fifthteen Century Monuments of Chanderi.
--History of Mughal Architecture Akbar (1556-1605) The Age of Personality Architecture Vol. II.
Nath, R., et al. Molecular Aspects of Idiopathic Urolithiasis.
Nath, Sanjiva K., et al. Buyer's Guide to Computer Printers.
Nathan, Andrew J. Modern China, 1840-1972: An Introduction to Sources & Research Aids.
Nathan, D. Lionel Richie: An Illustrated Biography.
Nathan, Harold D. GED Science Test Preparation Guide: High School Equivalency Examination.
Nathan, Harriet, ed. see Conference on the Public Land Law Review Commission Report, Dec. 1970.
Nathan, Harriet, ed. see Kroeger, Louis J.
Nathan, Harriet, jt. ed. see Scott, Stanley.
Nathan, James A. & Oliver, James K. United States Foreign Policy & World Order.
Nathan, Joan. International Pasta Cookbook.
Nathan, John, tr. see Oe, Kenzaburo.
Nathan, John, tr. from Japane see Oe, Kenzaburo.
Nathan, Leonard, tr. see Sen, Ramprasad.
Nathan, Peter, ed. see Grossman, Tracy B.
Nathan, Peter, ed. see L'Hommedieu, Toni.
Nathan, Peter, ed. see Malmaud, Roslyn K.
Nathan, Peter, ed. see Ochberg, Richard L.
Nathan, Peter, ed. see Steinberg, Jill A.
Nathan, Peter E. & Harris, Sandra L. Psychopathology & Society.
--Psychopathology & Society.
Nathan, Peter E., ed. see Hees-Stauthamer, Jellemieke C.
Nathan, Peter E., ed. see Heillig, Roma J.
Nathan, Peter E., ed. see Prince, Robert M.
Nathan, Peter E., ed. see Weissbourd, Katherine.
Nathan, Ronald G., jt. auth. see Charlesworth, Edward A.
Nathan, Stella, ed. see Minkin, Steve.
Nathan-Neher, Barbara. Chaissac.
Nathanson, Bernard N. The Abortion Papers: Inside the Abortion Mentality.
--The Abortion Papers: Inside the Abortion Mentality.
Nathanson, Larry, ed. Management of Advanced Melanoma.
Nathanson, Nathaniel L., jt. auth. see Jaffe, Louis L.
Nathanson, S. The Ideal of Rationality.
Nathanson, Virginia. Making Bead Flowers & Bouquets.
Nation, Earl F., et al. An Annotated Checklist of Osleriana.
Nation, Jim G., jt. auth. see Page, John S.
National Academy of Science, Academy Forum. Experiments & Research with Humans: Values in Conflicts.
National Academy of Sciences. Feasibility of a Global Observation & Analysis Experiment.
National Academy of Sciences Staff, ed. see Chinese Academy of Sciences Staff.
National Academy of Sciences Staff. Permafrost Fourth International Conference: Final Proceedings.
--Rapid Population Growth, Consequences & Policy Implications. Incl. Vol. I. Summary & Recommendations; Vol. II. Research Papers. Johns Hopkins.
National Academy of the Avant Garde Staff. Proceedings of the National Academy of the Avant Garde. Korn, Henry, ed.
National Advisory Committee on Mathematical Education. Overview & Analysis of School Mathematics.
National Alliance for Optional Parenthood Staff. Exploring the Parenthood Choice: An Activities Guide for Educators.
National Army Museum, London Staff. War & Weapons.
National Assessment of Educational Progress Staff. Career & Occupational Development Objectives.
--Career & Occupational Development Objectives.
--Citizenship Objectives.
--Citizenship Objectives.
--Citizenship-Social Studies Released Exercise Set.
--The First Assessment of Reading, 1970-71: Assessment, Released Exercise Set.
--Male-Female Achievement in Eight Learning Areas.
--Science Objectives.
--Science Objectives: Third Assessment, 1976-77.
--The Second Assessment of Mathematics, 1977-78: Released Exercise Set.
--Social Studies Exercise Set.
--The Third Assessment of Science, 1976-1977: Released Exercise Set.
--What Students Know & Can Do: Profiles of Three Age Groups.
--Writing Exercise Set.
National Association for Foreign Students Affairs Staff. NAFSA Directory of Institutions & Individuals in International Educational Exchange, 1985.
National Association for Public Continuing & Adult Education Publications Committee, ed. Tested Techniques for Teachers of Adults.
National Association for the Advancement of Colored People. Crisis, A Record of the Darker Races. Incl. Greenwood.
National Association for Women Deans, Administrators & Counselors. Another Look at the Campus Culture.
National Association for Women Deans, Administrators, & Counselors. Aspects of the K Through Twelve Culture.
National Association for Women Deans, Administrators & Counselors. Counseling Women.
National Association for Women Deans, Administrators, & Counselors. Global Communication & Understanding.
National Association for Women Deans, Administrators & Counselors. Looking Toward the 1980's.
National Association for Women Deans, Administrators & Counselors Staff. On Being a Woman in 1976: Selected Issues & Research.
National Association for Women Deans, Administrators & Counselors. Potpourri of Ideas for Student Development Specialists.
National Association for Women Deans, Administrators & Counselors Staff. Professional Status, Concerns, & Reflections.
National Association for Women Deans, Administrators & Counselors. Sensitivity to Social Change.
--Some Considerations for Counselors.
--Students Older Than Average.
National Association for Women Deans, Administratos & Counselors. Two Symposia: Ethnic Minority Feminism & Two Sides of the Coin.
National Association for Women Deans, Administrators & Counselors. University Student Services.
National Association for Women Deans, Administrators & Counselors Staff. Values, Employment & Status of Professional Women.
National Association for Women Deans, Administrators & Counselors. Vocational Development.
--What, Then, Is a Human Being...?
National Association of College & University Business Officers Staff, et al. A Planning Manual for Colleges. Nevin, Jeanne, ed.
National Association of Computer Dealers (NACD) Staff. SYBEX Computer Blue Book.
--SYBEX Computer Blue Books.
National Association of Home Builders Staff. Accounting & Financial Management.
--Buying a New Home: A Step-by-Step Guide.
--Construction Cost Control.
--Cost of Doing Business for the Single-Family Home Builder, 1986.
--Data Processing for Builders.
--Designing, Building & Selling Energy Conserving Homes.
--Energy Saver Homes: Design Energy Consumption Versus Measured Energy Consumption of the 10 NAHB Energy Saver Homes.
--Financing Rental Construction After Tax Reform: A Builder's Guide.
National Association of Home Builders Staff & Johnson, Deborah. Home Builders Publicity Manual - A-Step-by-Step Guide for Successful Public Relations.
National Association of Home Builders Staff. Home Building after Tax Reform: A Builder's Guide.
--Homes & Homebuilding 1984.
--Homes & Homebuilding 1986.
--Housing America--The Challenges Ahead: The Long Range Planning Report of the National Association of Home Builders.
--Management Manual for the Small-Volume Home Builder.
--Productivity Improvement Manual.
--Software Catalog for Home Builders, 1986. Stroh, Robert C., ed.
--Solar Energy for Homes Current Status.
--Suretyship & the Builder.
--Yes, Today's Mortgages Make Home Buying Easier.
National Association of Legal Assistants, Inc. Staff. Manual for Legal Assistants. Park, William R., ed.
National Association of Legal Secretaries (NALS) Staff, ed. The Career Legal Secretary.
National Association of Secondary School Principals Staff. Student Council Handbook.
National Association of Women Deans & Counselors. Alternative Roles.
--Redefining Personnel Services.
--Students View the Campus Culture.
--Understanding Student-Parent Expectations.
National Associations of Women Deans & Counselors. The Educator in an Era of Social Change - Evolutionist or Revolutionist?
National Book League Staff. Children's Books of Yesterday. Muir, Percy H., ed.
National Business Institute Staff. Creditor Rights & Bankruptcy in State.
National Center for Atmospheric Research Staff. National Hail Research Experiment: Hailstorms of the Central High Plains. Knight, C. A. & Squires, P., eds.
National Center for Research in Vocational Education Staff. Business & Office Education Curriculum.
National Center for Research in Vocational Education. Career & Vocational Education Programs for Female, Handicapped & Disadvantaged Students.
National Center for Research in Vocational Education Staff. Home Economics Education Curriculum.
--Methods & Techniques of Teaching Adults.
--Productivity Primer.
--Vocational Education & Economic Development.
National Center for State Courts Staff. Indiana Judicial System.
--San Bernardino County: Prototype Courtroom Design.
--Trial Court Administrator: A Brochure.
National College of Education Staff. Young People's Science Encyclopedia.
National College of the State Judiciary Staff. Directory of State & Local Judges.
National Committee for Clinical Laboratory Standards. Calibration & Control Materials for Neonatal Hypothyroid Screening Programs: Proposed Guideline.
--Control Materials in Clinical Chemistry: Tentative Guideline.
--Kinetic Analysis of Enzyme Reaction: Tentative Guideline.
--Labeling of Clinical Laboratory Materials: Approved Standard.
National Committee on Careers for Older Americans. Older Americans: An Untapped Resource.
National Computing Centre, Ltd. Staff. Batch One: Computer Programming Problems.
--COBOL Reference Summary.
National Computing Centre, Ltd. Staff, ed. Commodity Coding: Its Effects on Data Recording & Transfer.
--Computer Appreciation for the Majority.
--Computers in Civil Engineering Design.
National Computing Centre, Ltd. Staff. Computers in the Creative Arts: A Studyguide. Lomax, J. D., ed.
--Computers in the Social Sciences: A Study Guide. Penney, G., ed.
--Computing Practice: Security Aspects.
--Control of DP Production. Walker, G. S., ed.
--Data Base in Perspective. Davis, Brian, ed.
--Distributed Database Technology.
National Computing Centre, Ltd. Staff, ed. Documenting Systems (the User's View)
National Computing Centre, Ltd. Staff. Elements of BASIC.
--Ensuring Program Quality. Murphy, Bill, et al, eds.
--Guidelines for Computer Managers.
--High-Level Languages for Microprocessor Projects. Taylor, David & Morgan, Lyndon, eds.
--Impact of Microprocessors on British Business.

--Introducing Computerized Telephone Switchboards (PABXs)
--Introducing Data Processing.
--Introduction to On-Line Systems. Pritchard, J. A., ed.
--Managing Distributed Systems. Gee, K. C., ed.
National Computing Centre, Ltd. Staff, ed. Microprocessors in Industry.
--Production Control Packages.
--Program Testing Aids.
National Computing Centre, Ltd. Staff. Systems Documentation Manual.
--Technical Documentation Standards for Computer Programs & Computer-Based Systems Used in Engineering.
National Computing Centre, Ltd. Staff, ed. Thesaurus of Computing Terms.
National Computing Centre, Ltd. Staff. The Uses of Microprocessors. Simons, G. L., ed.
--Working with Computers: A Guide to Jobs & Careers.
National Conference of Lawyers & CPA's Staff. Lawyers & Certified Public Accountants: A Study of Interprofessional Relations: Statements on Practice in the Field of Federal Income Taxation & Estate Planning.
National Conference of State Legislatures Staff. Directory of Legislative Leaders, 1987-88.
--The Homeless Mentally Ill: No Longer Out of Sight & Out of Mind.
National Conference on Social Welfare Staff, ed. The Social Welfare Forum Nineteen Seventy-Nine.
National Conference on Social Welfare Staff. The Social Welfare Forum: Official Proceedings. Incl. Ninety Fourth Annual Forum; Ninety Fifth Annual Forum; Ninety Sixth Annual Forum; Nintey Seventh Annual Forum; Nintey Eighth Annual Forum. Columbia U Pr.
--Social Work Practice: Proceedings. Incl. Ninety-Third Annual Meeting; Ninety-Fourth Annual Meeting; Ninety-Fifth Annual Meeting; Ninety-Sixth Annual Meeting; Ninety-Seventh Annual Meeting; Ninety-Eighth Annual Meeting. Columbia U Pr.
National Consumer Law Center. Consumer Bankruptcy Law & Practice: 1982 & 1984 Supplement.
National Consumer Law Center Staff. Consumer Bankruptcy Law & Practice: 1985 & 1987 Supplement.
--Consumer Usury & Credit Overcharges: 1982 & 1986 Supplement.
--Debt Collection Harassment: 1982 & 1986 Supplement.
--Equal Credit Opportunity Act: 1982 & 1986 Supplement.
--Fair Credit Reporting Act: 1982 & 1986 Supplement.
National Council for the Social Studies Staff. National Assessment & Social Studies Education.
National Council of Churches Corporate Information Center Staff. Church Investments, Corporations, & Southern Africa.
National Council of Social Service. Right to Know: A Review of Advice Services in Rural Areas.
National Council of State Boards of Nursing Staff. The National Council Licensure Examination for Registered Nurses.
National Council of Teachers of English Staff & Stanford, Gene, eds. Classroom Practices in Teaching English, 1980-1981: Dealing with Differences.
National Council of Teachers of English Task Force on Measurement & Evaluation in the Study of English Staff & Purves, Alan. Common Sense & Testing in English.
National Council of Teachers of Mathematics Staff. Directory of NCTM Individual Members, 1987.
--Experiences in Mathematical Ideas.
--Geometry in the Mathematics Curriculum: 36th Yearbook.
--Historical Topics in Algebra.
--Instructional Aids in Mathematics, 34th Yearbk.
--The Slow Learner in Mathematics: 35th Yearbook.
--The Teaching of Secondary School Mathematics, 33rd Yearbk.
National Deans, Administrators & Counselors. Fortieth Anniversary Issue.
National Deviancy Conference Staff, ed. Permissiveness & Control: The Fate of the Sixties Legislation.
National Education Association Computer Services Staff. The Yellow Book: A Parent's Guide to Teacher-Tested Educational Software.
National Education Association Staff & Union of Concerned Scientists. Choices: A Unit on Conflict & Nuclear War.
National Education Association Staff & Heitzmann, William R. Educational Games & Simulations.
National Education Association Staff. Helping Your Child Read.
--How to Prepare Your Child for School.
--Learning the Alphabet.
--NEA Handbook for Local, State, & National Associations 1985-86.
--Numbers & Counting.
National Equivalence Information Center Staff. International Guide to Qualifications in Education.
National Federation of Community Assoc. Creative Living.
National Food Processors Association Staff, ed. Laboratory Manual for Food Canners & Processors.
National Football League Staff, compiled by. The Official National Football League Record & Fact Book,1985.
--The Official National Football League Record & Fact Book, 1986.
National Football League Staff, photos by. Giants: An Unforgettable Season.
National Foundation for Long Term Care Staff. Pharmacy Issues in Long Term Care.
National Gallery of Canada (Ottawa) Staff. Catalogue of the Library of the National Gallery of Canada.
National Gallery Staff. The Book of Days.
National Geographic Society Staff & McDowell, Bart. Gypsies.
National Geographic Society Staff, ed. Life in Rural America.
National Health Publishing Staff. Health Administration: Laws, Regulations, & Guidelines.
National Historical Society Staff. The Embattled Confederacy: Eighteen Sixty-One to Eighteen Sixty-Five.
--End of an Era. Davis, William C. & Wiley, Bell I., eds.
--Fighting for Time. Davis, William C. & Wiley, Bell I., eds.
--Guns of Sixty-Two. Davis, William C., ed.
--Shadows of the Storm. Davis, William C. & Wiley, Bell I., eds.
--South Besieged. Davis, William C. & Wiley, Bell I., eds.
National Housing Law Project Staff & Johnson, Sara E. Preserving HUD-Assisted Housing for Use by Low-Income Tenants: An Advocate's Guide.
National Immigration Project. Asylees & Refugees: Strategies for Representation.
--Immigration Law & Defense.
National Information Center for Special Education Materials (NICSEM) Staff. NICSEM Mini-index to Special Education Materials: Functional Communication Skills.
--NICSEM Mini-Index to Special Education Materials: Family Life & Sex Education.
--NICSEM Mini-index to Special Education Materials: High Interest, Controlled Vocabulary Supplementary Reading Materials for Adolescents & Young Adults.
--NICSEM Mini-index to Special Education Materials: Independent Living Skills for Moderately & Severely Handicapped Students.
--NICSEM Mini-index to Special Education Materials: Personal & Social Development for Moderately & Severely Handicapped Students.
--NICSEM Source Directory.
--Special Education Index to Assessment Materials.
--Special Education Index to Parent Materials.
National Institute for Food Service Industry Staff. Applied Foodservice Sanitation.
National Institute for Food Service Industry Staff, et al. Financial Ingredient in Foodservice Management.
National Institute for Food Service Industry Staff & Lendal H. Management by Menu.
National Institute for Urban Wildlife Staff, et al. A Guide to Urban Wildlife Management.
National Interracial Conference Staff. Toward Interracial Cooperation.
National Judicial College (U. S.) Staff. Significant State Appellate Decisions.
National Labor Law Center. Employee & Union Member Guide to Labor Law.
National Labor Law Center, jt. auth. see Milwaukee Labor Committee.
National Lawyers Guild, NYC Chapter Staff. Analysis of the Report of the New York State Bar Association for Implementing the American Bar Association's Proposal Relative to Loyalty Among Lawyers.
National Legal Aid & Defender Association Staff. Reaching the People: A Public Affairs Training Manual for Civil Legal Services Programs.
National Libraries Symposium Staff. National Libraries: Their Problems & Prospects, Proceedings of the Symposium, Vienna, 1958.
National Library of Anthropology & History Staff, Mexico City. Catalogo de la Biblioteca Nacional de Antropologia y Historia - Catalogs of the National Library of Anthropology & History.
National Library of Australia Staff. Australian National Bibliography, 1981.
National Library of Ireland Staff. Manuscript Sources for the History of Irish Civilisation: First Supplement. MacLochlainn, Alf, ed.
National Library of Ireland Staff, Dublin. Manuscript Sources for the History of Irish Civilisation.
--Sources for the History of Irish Civilization: Articles in Irish Periodicals.
National Library of Peru Staff. Author Catalog of the Peruvian Collection of the National Library of Peru. De Gaviria, Maria C., ed.
National Machine Tool Builders Association Staff & Hoffman, K. O., eds. Basic Shop Measurement.
National Machine Tool Builders Association Staff. Shop Theory.
National Materials Advisory Board, National Research Council Staff. Rapid Inexpensive Tests for Determining Fracture Toughness.
National Medical Series for Independent Study Staff. Pharmacology.
National Monetary Commission. Statistics for Great Britain, Germany & France, 1867-1909.
National Museum of Natural Sciences, Canada Staff. A Natural History Notebook of North American Animals.
National Notary Magazine Editors. California Notary Law Primer.
National Park Service Staff. Winning Support for Parks & Recreation.
National Park Service Staff & Crompton, John. Marketing Parks & Recreation.
National Press Photographers Association Staff. The Best of Photojournalism, 5: People, Places, & Events of 1979.
National Public Radio Staff & Stamberg, Susan. Every Night at Five: Susan Stamberg's "All Things Considered" Book.
National Real Estate Institute Staff. How to Pass the California Real Estate Exam.
--Washington Real Estate Review Questions.
National Register Publishing Co. Staff. The Corporate Finance Bluebook.
--The Corporate Finance Sourcebook.
--Directory of Corporate Affiliations.
--Directory of Leading Private Companies.
--The Official Catholic Directory.
--Standard Directory of Advertisers: Classified Edition.
--Standard Directory of Advertisers: Geographical Edition.
--The Standard Directory of Worldwide Marketing.
National Register Publising Co. Staff. International Directory of Corporate Affiliations.
National Research Council. Advanced Nuclear Systems for Portable Power in Space.
--Architectural Fabric Structures: The Use of Tensioned Fabric Structures by Federal Agencies.
--Controlled Nuclear Fusion: Current Research & Potential Progress.
--Counting the People in 1980: An Appraisal of Census Plans.
--Directory of Atomic, Molecular & Optical Scientists.
--Disposal of Chemical Munitions & Agents.
--Domestic Potential of Solar & Other Renewable Energy Sources.
--Estimating Population & Income of Small Areas.
--Fifty-Five: A Decade of Experience.
--Geochronology of North America.
--Guide to Infectious Diseases of Mice & Rats.
--Improved Indicators of Science & Mathematics in Grades 1-12. Murnane, Richard J. & Raizen, Senta A., eds.
--Improving Energy Demand Analysis.
--Job Evaluation: An Analytical Review.
--Learning from Experience: Evaluating Early Childhood Demonstration Programs.
--Nutrient Requirements of Dairy Cattle, 1978.
--On the Theory & Practice of Voice Identification.
--Pesticide Decision Making.
--Plant & Animal Products in the U. S. Food System.
--Postdoctoral Appointments & Disappointments.
--Principles of Plant & Animal Pest Control.
--Principles of Plant & Animal Pest Control.
--Principles of Plant & Animal Pest Control, Vol. 6: Effects of Pesticides on Fruit & Vegetable Physiology.
--Procedures & Standards for a Multipurpose Cadastre.
--Rehabilitation of Criminal Offenders: Problems & Prospects.
--Research Priorities in Tropical Biology.
--Scientific & Technological Cooperation among Industrialized Countries: The Role of the United States.
--Technology & Agricultural Policy.
National Research Council Advisory Board on Military Personnel Supplies. Hospital Patient Feeding Systems.
National Research Council, Assembly of Life Sciences Staff. The Health Effects of Nitrates, Nitrites, & N-Nitroso Compounds.
National Research Council Assembly of Life Sciences. Indoor Pollutants.
--Marine Invertebrates.
National Research Council, Astronomy Survey Committee. Challenges to Astronomy & Astrophysics: Working Documents of the Astronomy Survey Committee.
National Research Council, Board on Science & Technology for International Development & Shay, Griff. Alcohol Fuels: Options for Developing Countries.
National Research Council, Board on Toxicology & Environmental Health Hazards. Identifying & Estimating the Genetic Impact of Chemical Mutagens.
National Research Council Board on Agriculture & Renewable Resources. Nutrient Requirements of Swine.
National Research Council, Board on Toxicology & Environmental Health Hazards. Odors from Stationary & Mobile Sources.
National Research Council Board on Toxicology & Environmental Health Hazards. Quality Criteria for Water Reuse.
National Research Council Commission on Natural Resources. Surface Mining: Soil, Coal, & Society.
--Testing for Effects of Chemicals on Ecosystems.
National Research Council Committee on Animal Nutrition. Nutrients & Toxic Substances in Water for Livestock & Poultry.
National Research Council Committee on Program Evaluation in Education. Program Evaluation in Education: When? How? to What Ends?
National Research Council, Committee on Food Protection. The Use of Chemicals in Food Production, Processing, Storage & Distribution.
National Research Council Diesel Impact Study Committee. Diesel Technology.
National Research Council, Division of Medical Sciences Medical & Biologic Effects of Environmental Pollutants, ed. Ozone & Other Photochemical Oxidants.
National Research Council Institute of Medicine Staff. Behavioral Science & the Secret Service: Toward the Prevention of Assassination.
National Research Council, Institute of Medicine. Health Care in a Context of Civil Rights.
National Research Council Institute of Medicine. Health Planning in the U. S.
National Research Council, Institute of Medicine. Health Planning in the U. S.
National Research Council, Ocean Sciences Board Staff. Continental Margins: Geological & Geophysical Research Needs.
--The Continuing Quest: Large Scale Ocean Science for the Future.
--Doctoral Scientists in Oceanography.
--Tropospheric Transport of Pollutants & Natural Substances to the Ocean.
National Research Council Ocean Waste Transportation Committee. Ocean Disposal Systems for Sewage Sludge & Effluent.
National Research Council, Space Science Board Staff. Human Factors in Long-Duration Space Flight.
--Space Research: Directions for the Future.
National Research Council Staff. Economic Facts.
--Effects of Fluorides in Animals.
--Polychlorinated Biphenyls.
--Rock-Mechanics Research in the U. S.
--Solar Variability, Weather & Climate.
--Toxic Shock Syndrome.
National Research Council Staff, jt. auth. see Institute of Laboratory Animal Resources Staff.
National Research Council Staff, jt. auth. see Institute of Medicine, Division of Health Promotion & Disease Prevention Staff.
National Research Council Staff, jt. auth. see Institute of Medicine Staff.
National Research Council Staff, jt. auth. see International Biological Program Staff.
National Research Council Staff, jt. auth. see Marine Board, Asembly of Engineering Staff.
National Research Council Staff, jt. auth. see Marine Board, Assembly of Engineering Staff.
National Research Council Staff, jt. auth. see Maritime Transportation Research Board Staff.
National Research Council, Toxicology & Environmental Health Hazards Board Staff. Protection Against Trichothecene Mycotoxins.
National Research Council (U. S.) Transportation Research Board. Atmospheric Emergencies: Existing Capabilities & Future Needs.
--Traffic Records, Accident Analysis & Traffic Law Enforcement.
National Research Council U. S. Committee on a National Strategy for Biotechnology in Agriculture. Agriculture Biotechnology: Strategies for National Competitiveness.

National Resource Center for Consumers of Legal Services Staff. Group Legal Service Plans: Organization, Operation & Management.
National Resources Committee. Working Group Meeting on Energy Planning: Proceedings, 5th Session.
National Restaurant Association Staff. Franchise Restaurants: A Statistical Appendix to Foodservice Trends.
--Restaurant Industry Operations Report, 1986.
--Restaurant Industry Operations Report, 1985.
National Retail Merchant Association Staff. Retailing Job Analysis & Job Evaluation.
National Retail Merchants Association Staff & Institute of Store Planners' Store Interior Design Competition Staff. The Best of Store Designs.
National Retail Merchants Association Staff. The Best of Store Designs Two. Denby, Carol, ed.
--Personnel Practices of the Retail Industry.
National Rural Electric Cooperative Association Staff, ed. Wind Energy in Rural United States.
National Safety Council. Guards Illustrated.
--Meat Industry Safety Guidelines.
National Science Foundation, Division of Science Information Staff. Current Research on Scientific & Technical Information Transfer.
National Science Foundation Staff. The Cell: Inter & Intra-Relationships. Kornberg, Warren, ed.
--DNA: The Master Molecule. Kornberg, Warren, ed.
National Security Committee & Harriman, W. Averell, Institute for Advanced Study of the Soviet Union Staff. A Guide to Films about the Soviet Union. Lamberty, Kim & Joselyn, Bernardine, eds.
National Society for the Study of Education Staff. Graduate Study in Education: 50th Yearbook. Tyler, Ralph W., ed.
National Society of Colonial Dames of America Staff. American War Songs.
National Standards Association Staff. Walker's Manual Incorporated.
National Student Forum of the Paris Pact Staff. New Student.
National Telecommunications Administration, Office of International Affairs Staff. Profiles of International Private Lease, DATEL & Packet Switched Service Markets for the Years 1976 to 1979.
National Training Systems Staff. Inside dBASE III.
--Inside Symphony.
National Trust for Historic Preservation Staff. Directory of American Preservation Commissions. Dennis, Stephen N., ed.
National Trust for Historic Preservation in the United States & American Law Institute-American Bar Association Committee for Continuing Professional Education. Historic Preservation Law & Tax Planning for Old & Historic Buildings.
National Underwriter Co. Staff & Thomas, William W., III. All about Medicare.
National Video Clearinghouse, Inc. Staff, ed. The Video Tape & Disc Guide to Home Entertainment.
National Video Clearinghouse, Inc. Staff. The Video Tape & Disc Guide to Home Entertainment.
Nations, D. The Record of Geologic Time: A Vicarious Trip.
Natke, H. G., ed. Identification of Vibrating Structures.
NATO Advanced Study Institute Staff & Skiathos, Greece. Police Selection & Training: The Role of Psychology.
NATO Staff. Economic Reforms in Eastern Europe & Prospects for the 1980s: NATO Colloquium, Brussels, 1980.
Natoli, Salvatore J., ed. see Knight, C. Gregory & Wilcox, R. Paul.
Natoli, Salvatore J., ed. see Muller, Peter O.
Natoli, Salvatore J., ed. see Platt, Rutherford H.
Natow, Annette B. & Heslin, Jo-Ann. No-Nonsense Nutrition from Toddlers to Pre-Teen.
--Nutrition for the Prime of Your Life.
Natsume, Soseki. Ten Nights of Dream, Hearing Things, the Heredity of Taste. Ito, Aiko & Wilson, Graeme, trs.
Natural Resources & Energy Division, U. N. Dept. of Technical Co-Operation for Development. The Development Potential of Precambrian Mineral Deposits.
Natvig, Paul. Jacques Joseph: Surgical Sculptor.
Natwar-Singh, K., ed. E. M. Forster: A Tribute with Selections from His Writings on India.
Nauman, Ann K. A Handbook of Latin American & Caribbean National Archives.
Naumann, H. H. Head & Neck Surgery.
--Head & Neck Surgery: Indications, Techniques & Pitfalls.
Naumes, William, jt. auth. see Paine, Frank T.
Naunton, Ralph F., ed. Evoked Electrical Activity in the Auditory Nervous System.
Naur, Peter. Concise Survey of Computer Methods.
Naval Hydrodynamics Symposium Staff. Naval Hydrodynamics: Proceedings of the Symposium, 12th, Naval Studies Board.
Navarantham, V. The Human Heart & Circulation.
Navarick, Douglas J. Principles of Learning: From Laboratory to Field.
Navarra, John G. Atmosphere, Weather & Climate.
--Contemporary Physical Geography.
--Superplanes.
Navarre, Monte, ed. see Airguide Publications Staff.
Navarre, Yves. Our Share of Time. DiBernardi, Dominic & Domke, Noelle, trs. from Fr.
Navarro, Marysa, jt. auth. see Fraser, Nicholas.
Navas, Deb, ed. New Fiction from New England.
Navas, Deborah. Giving Good Food.
Navasky, Victor S. Kennedy Justice.
Nave, Gary, jt. auth. see Zembrosky-Barkin, Patti.
Navia, Juan M. Animal Models in Dental Research.
Navia, Luis E. A Bridge to the Stars: Our Ancient Cosmic Legacy.
Naviasky, Laurence M. A Directory of Independent Workers' Clinics.
Navon, David H. Electronic Materials & Devices.
Navratil, James D., jt. ed. see Schultz, Wallace W.
Navy Times Editors, jt. ed. see Slinkman, John.
Nawratzki, I., ed. see Jerusalem Conference on Impaired Vison in Childhood Staff.
Nayak, Debi, ed. The Molecular Biology of Animal Virus.
--The Molecular Biology of Animal Viruses.
Nayak, Debi S., ed. Genetic Variation among Influenza Viruses.
Naylor, Charles, jt. ed. see Disch, Thomas M.
Naylor, Chris. Build Your Own Expert System.
Naylor, E. & Hartnoll, E. G., eds. Cyclic Phenomena in Marine Plants & Animals.
Naylor, Gloria. Linden Hills.
Naylor, Henry D. Horace, Odes & Epodes: A Study in Poetic Word-Order.
Naylor, K. Africa: The Nile Route.
Naylor, Phyliss R. No Easy Circle.
Naylor, Phyllis R. The Boy with the Helium Head.
--Change in the Wind.
--Faces in the Water.
--How I Came to Be a Writer.
--How to Find Your Wonderful Someone.
--In Small Doses.
--A String of Chances.
--A Triangle Has Four Sides: True-to-Life Stories Show How Teens Deal with Feelings & Problems.
--Unexpected Pleasures.
--Walking Through the Dark.
--The Witch Herself.
--Witch Water.
Naylor, Thomas. Hot Money: Peekaboo Finance & the Politics of Debt.
Naylor, Thomas, jt. ed. see Kubursi, Atif A.
Nayroles, B., jt. ed. see Germain, P.
Nazzaro, Jean, ed. Computer Connections.
Nazzaro, Lovel. Pesto Manifesto.
Neace, James C. George Washington Noble.
Neagle, Larry. Underground Manual for Spiritual Survival.
Neagley, Ross L. & Evans, N. Dean. Handbook for Effective Supervision of Instruction.
Neal. Medical Pharmacology at a Glance.
Neal & Cohen. Nursing Care Planning Guides from Nurseco.
Neal, Arthur G. Social Psychology: A Sociology Perspective.
Neal, B. G. Structural Theorems & Their Applications.
Neal, B. G., ed. see Cheung, Y. K.
Neal, Bill. Bill Neal's Southern Cooking.
Neal, Craig R., jt. auth. see Hanson, James A.
Neal, Emily G. Reporter Finds God Through Spiritual Healing.
Neal, Harry E. Before Columbus: Who Discovered America?
Neal, James E., Jr. Effective Phrases for Performance Appraisals: A Guide to Successful Evaluations.
Neal, James M. & Brown, Suzanne S. Newswriting & Reporting.
Neal, James T., ed. Playas & Dried Lakes: Occurrence & Development.
Neal, Viola P. & Karagulla, Shafica. Through the Curtain.
Neale, J. & Flenley, J., eds. The Quaternary in Britain: Essays Reviews & Original Work on the Quarternary Published in Honour of Lewis Penny on His Retirement.
Neale, John M. & Oltmanns, Thomas F. Schizophrenia.
Neale, John M., et al. Contemporary Readings in Psychopathology.
Nealey, Stanley, et al. Public Opinion & Nuclear Energy.
Nealon, Eleanor, jt. auth. see Melluzzo, Paul J.
Nealon, Thomas F., ed. Management of the Patient with Cancer.
Neaman, J. S. & Silver, C. G. Kind Words: A Dictionary of Euphemisms.
Neame, Alan, tr. The Hermitage Within: Spirituality of the Desert.
Neame, Alan, tr. see Camara, Dom H.
Neary, Donal. Masses with Young People.
Neasom, Mike & Sanders, Murray. Going Up! Pompey Season, 1986-1987.
Neasom, Mike, et al. Pompey: The History of Portsmouth Football Club.
Neave, Edwin H. & Wiginton, John C. Financial Management: Theory & Strategies.
Neave, H. R. Statistics Tables.
Nebeker, Helen. Jean Rhys: Woman in Passage.
Nebel, Bernard J. Environmental Science: The Way the World Works.
Neblett, Otis Evelyn. The Gift of Poverty.
Neborak, Sonja. Thoughts in the Atomic Age.
Nebraska Curriculum Development Center Staff. Nebraska Curriculum for English, Grade 8: Units 82-84, the Hero.
Neckers, Douglas C., jt. auth. see Mohrig, Jerry R.
Nedderman, R. M., jt. auth. see Blackadder, D. A.
Nederhof, Anton J. Artifact in Social Science Research.
Nedobeck, Don. Nedobeck's Twelve Days of Christmas.
Nee, Victor G. & De Barry, Brett. Longtime Californ' A Documentary Study of an American Chinatown.
Needham, D. Barrie. How Cities Work: An Introduction.
Needham, Paul. Twelve Centuries of Bookbindings: Four Hundred to Sixteen Hundred.
Needham, Peter, tr. see Cappellanus, George.
Needham, Richard, & Associates Staff & Swaim, John. In Search of Excellence.
Needham, Rodney, ed. Right & Left: Essays on Dual Symbolic Classification.
Needham, Rodney, ed. see Hocart, A. M.
Needleman, Carla. The Work of Craft.
--The Work of Craft.
Needleman, Jacob. A Sense of the Cosmos: The Encounter of Modern Science with Ancient Truth.
Needleman, John, ed. The Sword of Gnosis: Metaphysics, Cosmology, Tradition, Symbolism.
Needles, Belverd E. & Williams, Doyle Z. The Complete CPA Examination Review.
Needles, Belverd E., et al. Principles of Accounting.
--Principles of Accounting. Incl. Instructor's Handbook; Study Guide & Selected Readings; Working Papers; Tranparencies; Checklist of Key Figures; Achievement Tests 1-7A; Achievement Tests 1-7B; Achievement Tests 8-14A; Achievement Tests 8-14B; Computer Casebook of Accounting Problems. HM.
Needles, Belverd E., Jr. Financial Accounting.
Needles, Belverd E., Jr. & Williams, Dayle Z. The Complete CPA Examination Review.
--The Complete CPA Examination Review.
Neel, Jasper P., jt. ed. see Brod, Richard I.
Neeleman, Stanley D., jt. auth. see Hansen, H. Reese.
Neelon, Francis A. & Ellis, George. A Syllabus of Problem Oriented Patient Care.
Neels, Betty. Hannah: Nightingale Ser.
--Polly.
Neely, Ester J. South Wind.
Neely, Esther J. Chateau Laurens.
Neely, F. L. The Genes of Ambition.
Neely, James A. & Olson, Alan P. Archaeological Reconnaissance of Monument Valley in Northeastern Arizona.
Neely, Mary, jt. auth. see Seay, Davin.
Neely, Richard. Why the Courts Don't Work.
Neely, William, jt. auth. see Petty, Richard.
Nef, John U. Cultural Foundations of Industrial Civilization.
Nef, W. Lehrbuch der Linearen Algebra.
Neff, Alan H., jt. auth. see Westin, Richard A.
Neff, Donald. Warriors for Jerusalem: The Six Days That Changed the Middle East.
Neff, Glenda T. Writer's Market 88.
Neff, Michael, tr see De Balzac, Honore.
Neff, Pauline, jt. auth. see Handly, Robert.
Neff, Robert & Plaisted, Elinor. Laboratory Manual in Anatomy & Physiology.
Neff, Thomas L. The Social Costs of Solar Energy: A Study of Photovoltaic Energy Systems.
Neff, William D. Contributions to Sensory Psychology.
Neft, David S. & Cohen, Richard M. The Sports Encyclopedia: Pro Football the Modern Era, 1960 to the Present.
Negandhi, Anant, jt. ed. see Burack, Elmer H.
Negandhi, Anant R. & Prasad, Benjamin S. The Frightening Angels: A Study of U. S. Multinationals in Developing Nations.
Negandhi, Anant R. & Wilpert, Bernhard. Work Organization Research: American & European Perspectives.
Negandhi, Anant R., ed. Modern Organizational Theory: Contextual, Environment & Socio-Cultural Variables.
Negele, John W. & Orland, Henri. Quantum Many Particle Physics.
Negev, Avraham, ed. Archaeological Encyclopedia of the Holy Land.
Neggers, Carla. Dancing Season.
--The Knotted Skein.
--The Uneven Score.
--The Venus Shoe.
Negi, Jagmohan. Hotels for Tourism Development.
Negin, Elliott. Celebrities Sweepsteaks.
Negishi, Ei-Ichi. Organometallics in Organic Synthesis: General Discussions & Organometallics of Main Group Metals in Organic Synthesis.
Negri, Antonio. Marx Beyond Marx: Lessons on the Grundrisse. Fleming, James, ed. Cleaver, Harry & Ryan, Michael, trs. from Ital. & Fr.
Negron-Portillo, Mariano. Autonomismo Puertorriqueno.
Negulesco, Jean. Things I Did... & Things I Think I Did.
Negus, James. Good Bibliographic Practice.
Negwer, Martin. Organic Chemical Drugs & Their Synonyms.
Nehemkis, Peter. Latin America: Myth & Reality.
Neher. Public Speaking: A Rhetorical Approach.
Neher, William W. & Waite, David H. Nuts & Bolts: A Manual for Effective Professional Communication.
Nehrling, Arno & Nehrling, Irene. Peonies, Outdoors & in.
Nehrling, Irene, jt. auth. see Nehrling, Arno.
Neibauer, Alan. MacWrite: Guide for Students & Business Professionals.
Neibauer, Alan R. The ABC's of Microsoft WORD.
--Advanced Techniques in Microsoft WORD.
--Applications in Word & Information Processing.
--Practical Techniques in MS Word.
--WordPerfect Tips & Tricks.
--WordPerfect Tips & Tricks.
Neidel, A, jt. ed. see Ehrenpreis, S.
Neider, Charles, ed. & intro. by. Mark Twain at His Best.
Neiderman. Imp.
Neidermeier, William, et al. Phylogenetic Development of Vertebrate Immunity.
Neidle, M. Electrical Installation Theory & Practice.
Neier, Henri M. Swiss Capital Market.
Neifert, Marianne & Price, Anne. Dr. Mom: A Guide to Baby & Child Care.
Neiger, Ira, jt. auth. see Halper, Marilyn S.
Neighbour, Ralph W., Jr. The Seven Last Words of the Church.
Neighbours, Kenneth F; see Gerald.
Neihardt, John G. River & I: A Voyage Down the Missouri River in 1908.
Neikirk, William R. Volcker: Portrait of the Money Man.
Neil, Charles, jt. ed. see Wright, Charles.
Neil, Eric. The Human Circulation. Head, J. J., ed.
Neil, J. Meredith see O'Neal, William B.
Neil, William. The Difficult Sayings of Jesus.
Neilands, J. B. Microbial Iron Metabolism: A Comprehensive Treatise.
Neill, Kenneth. Irish People: An Illustrated History.
Neill, Stephen. Call to Mission.
Neill, Stephen C. & Weber, Hans-Ruedi, eds. The Layman in Christian History.
Neill, Stephen C., jt. ed. see Rouse, Ruth.
Neill, W., jt. ed. see Elder, T.
Neilson, Francis. The Tragedy of Europe.
Neilson, Jack. The Moon Is Mine & Other Tales.
--Schooner Bay.
Neilson, Stefan & Thoelke, Shay. Personality Language: Power Pack.
--Personality Language: Youth's Road to Excellence.
Neilson, W. A. & MacPherson, J. C. The Legislative Process in Canada: The Need for Reform.
Neilson, William A. & Thorndike, Ashley H. The Facts About Shakespeare.
Neiman, Joseph C. Coordinators: A New Focus in Parish Religious Education.
Neimark, Anne E. Sigmund Freud: The World Within.
--Touch of Light: The Story of Louis Braille.
Neimark, Paul & Berkowitz, Gerald. A Doctor Discusses Care of the Back.
Neimark, Paul & Matlin, Samuel. Doctor Discusses Female Surgery.
Neimark, Paul, jt. auth. see Scheimann, Eugene.
Neirynck, J., ed. see Brayton, R. K., et al.
Neirynck, J., jt. ed. see Moschytz, G. S.
Neish, A. C., jt. auth. see Freudenberg, K.
Neisworth, John T. Assessment in Special Education.
Neisworth, John T. & Smith, Robert M. Guiding the Mentally Retarded Person to Success: Basic Behavior Principles & Practice.
--Modifying Retarded Behavior.

Authors

Neisworth, John T., jt. auth. see Bagnato, Stephen J.
Nejand, Farghaneh. If a Black Were President of the U. S. A.
Nekrasov, B. V. Quimica General.
Nekrich, Aleksandr, jt. auth. see Heller, Mikhail.
Nekrich, Aleksandr M. The Punished Peoples: The Deportation & Fate of Soviet Minorities at the End of the Second World War.
Nekrich, Aleksandr M., tr. see Petrov, Vladimir.
Nelder, J. A., jt. ed. see Milton, R. C.
Nelkin, Dorothy. The Creation Controversy: Science or Scripture in the Schools?
--Selling Science: How the Press Covers Science & Technology.
Nellis, Muriel. The Female Fix.
Nellis, Robert L. How I Survived to Be Ninety-Five.
Nelmes, jt. auth. see Glenny.
Nelms, Henning. Magic & Showmanship: A Handbook for Conjurers.
Nelms, Walter. Feathers on the Wind.
Nelsen, William C. Renewal of the Teacher-Scholar: Faculty Development in the Liberal Arts College.
Nelsen, William C. & Siegel, Michael E., eds. Effective Approaches to Faculty Development.
Nelson & McCraken. Clinical Reviews in Pediatric Infectious Disease.
Nelson, jt. auth. see Bennett.
Nelson, jt. auth. see Ewen.
Nelson, A. Dictionary of Mining.
Nelson, A. & Nelson, K. D. Dictionary of Applied Geology.
Nelson, Alvar, jt. auth. see United Nations Congress on the Prevention of Crime & the Treatment of Offenders Staff.
Nelson, Anne. Murder under Two Flags: The U. S., Puerto Rico & Cerro Maravilla Cover-Up.
Nelson, B. J., ed. see Marx, Robert F.
Nelson, B. J., ed. see Mroczkowski, George & Bishop, Chara.
Nelson, Barbara J. American Women in Politics.
Nelson, Bettye, ed. see Garrett, Charles, et al.
Nelson, Bettye, ed. see Lagal, Roy.
Nelson, Bettye, ed. see Lagal, Roy & Garrett, Charles.
Nelson, Bettye, ed. see Poteet, G. Howard.
Nelson, Bill. On Seeing Things.
Nelson, Bruce. Land of the Dacotahs.
Nelson, Byron C. After Its Kind.
Nelson, Carl & Nelson, Martha. The Ministering Couple.
Nelson, Charles. The Boy Who Picked the Bullets Up.
Nelson, Charles T. After-Tax Money Income Estimates of Households 1984.
Nelson, Clarence, jt. auth. see Nelson, Ruth Y.
Nelson, Clemens A., jt. auth. see Zumberge, James H.
Nelson, Clifford & Fevold, Eugene L. Lutheran Church among Norwegian Americans.
Nelson, Clifford A., jt. ed. see Hammarberg, Melvin A.
Nelson, Cordner. Excelling in Sports: How to Train.
Nelson, D. G., tr. see Ebertin, Elsbeth.
Nelson, Daniel J. Wartime Origins of the Berlin Dilemma.
Nelson, Darrell. Little Millard Mustardseed.
Nelson, Dean, jt. auth. see Spencer, Dean.
Nelson, Don. Mines & Mining Equipment & Service Companies Worldwide, 1984-85.
--Oil & Oilfield Equipment & Service Companies Worldwide Nineteen Eighty-Five.
Nelson, Don, compiled by. Mines & Mining Equipment & Service Companies Worldwide, 1986.
Nelson, Don H. The Adrenal Cortex: Physiological Function & Disease.
Nelson, Dorothy W. Cases & Materials on Judicial Administration & the Administration of Justice.
Nelson, E. Clifford. The Rise of World Lutheranism: An American Perspective.
Nelson, Elof G. Keeping Love Alive.
Nelson, Emily M. Frontier Crossroads II: The People of Newport, Vermont.
Nelson, Esther L. Dancing Games for Children of All Ages.
--Singing & Dancing Games for the Very Young.
Nelson, Florence. The Astrological Let Me Be Book.
--How to Teach a Demonstration-Type Subject.
--How to Teach a Lecture-Type Subject.
--How to Use the Basic Seven Professional Teaching Techniques.
--How to Write a Lesson Plan for Adult Classes.
--Teaching for Craft Retailers.
--Yes You Can Teach.
Nelson, George W., Jr. Expressions of Love & Nature.
Nelson, Gerald E. The One-Minute Scolding.
Nelson, Gerald E. & Lewak, Richard W. Who's the Boss? Love, Authority & Parenting.
--Who's the Boss? Love, Authority, & Parenting.
Nelson, Grant & Whitman, Dale. Land Transactions & Finance.
Nelson, Harold D., ed. Kenya: A Country Study.
--Liberia: A Country Study.
--Libya: A Country Study.
Nelson, Harold D., jt. ed. see Kaplan, Irving.
Nelson, Harold H. Medinet Habu - Epigraphic Survey: The Calendar, the Slaughterhouse, & Minor Records of Ramses III.
Nelson, Harry & Jurmain, Robert. Introduction to Physical Anthropology.
Nelson, Horatio. Letters of Lord Nelson.
Nelson, J. Craig, ed. see PreTest Service, Inc. Staff.
Nelson, J. H. The Propagation Wizard's Handbook.
Nelson, J. Robert. Human Life: A Biblical Perspective for Bioethics.
--Science & Our Troubled Conscience.
Nelson, Jack, jt. auth. see Moor, James.
Nelson, James. Everybody's Guide to Great Wines under Five Dollars.
Nelson, James B. Human Medicine: Ethical Perspective on New Medical Issues.
--Rediscovering the Person in Medical Care: Patient, Family, Physician, Nurse, Chaplain, Pastor.
Nelson, James E. The Practice of Marketing Research.
--What We Know about Heaven.
Nelson, Janet, jt. auth. see Miller, Peter.
Nelson, Jerome, jt. auth. see Edles, Gary J.
Nelson, Joan M., jt. auth. see Huntington, Samuel P.
Nelson, John A. How to Read & Understand Blueprints.
Nelson, John L. The Pilot's Complete Computer Book.
Nelson, K. D., jt. auth. see Nelson, A.
Nelson, Kay S. Cooking with Mushrooms.
--Mediterranean Cooking for Everyone.
Nelson, Kay Y. Advanced Techniques in WordPerfect.
Nelson, Keith L. Victors Divided: America & the Allies in Germany, 1918-1923.
Nelson, Lee H. Century of Oregon Covered Bridges, 1851-1952.
Nelson, Lindsey. Hello Everybody, I'm Lindsey Nelson.
Nelson, Louise E. Project-Readiness: A Guide to Family Emergency Preparedness.
Nelson, Mark & Bonner, Miller. The Semi-Official Dallas Cowboys Haters' Handbook.
Nelson, Mark, jt. auth. see Allen, John.
Nelson, Martha, jt. auth. see Nelson, Carl.
Nelson, Michael, jt. auth. see Peters, Charles.
Nelson, Michael, ed. The Presidency & the Political System.
Nelson, Murry. Law in the Curriculum.
Nelson, Nici. Why Has Development Neglected Rural Women? A Review of the South Asian Literature.
Nelson, Nickola W. Planning Individual Speech & Language Intervention Programs.
Nelson, Nina. Canada.
--Malta.
Nelson, Orville, jt. auth. see Halfin, Harold.
Nelson, Patricia Limerick see Limerick, Patricia Nelson.
Nelson, Philip F. Frisky in the Morning.
Nelson, R. Guidance & Counseling in the Elementary School.
Nelson, R. Y. & Hess, Karen. God's Joy in My Heart.
Nelson, Ralph, tr. Popol Vuh: The Great Mythological Book of the Ancient Maya.
Nelson, Randy F. The Almanac of American Letters.
Nelson Reference Books Staff, ed. The Basic Meeting Manual: For Officers & Members of Any Organization.
Nelson, Richard A. Florida & the American Motion Picture Industry, 1898-1980. Jowett, Garth S., ed.
Nelson, Richard D. The Double Redaction of the Deuteronomistic History.
Nelson, Richard K. Shadow of the Hunter: Stories of Eskimo Life.
Nelson, Richard R. The Moon & the Ghetto.
Nelson, Richard R. & Schultz, T. P. Structural Change in a Developing Economy.
Nelson, Richard R., ed. Government & Technical Progress: Cross-Industry Analysis.
Nelson, Robert H. Zoning & Property Rights.
Nelson, Roberta. Creating Community Acceptance for Handicapped People.
Nelson, Roland H., jt. auth. see Edinger, Lois V.
Nelson, Rosella, et al. English at Your Fingertips.
Nelson, Roy P. & Ferris, Byron. Fell's Guide to Commercial Art.
Nelson, Ruth A. Plants of Rocky Mountain National Park.
Nelson, Ruth Y. God's Song in My Heart: Daily Devotions.
--A Grandma's Letters to God.
--You Can Make a Difference: American Mother of the Year Shares the Secret of Dynamic Christian Living.
Nelson, Ruth Y. & Nelson, Clarence. Cast Your Bread Upon the Waters.
Nelson, Sheila M. The Violin & the Viola.
Nelson, Steve & Rollins, Jack. Here Comes Peter Cottontail.
Nelson, Steven M. & Starkey, Frank L. Becoming One Flesh.
Nelson, Susan. Community Colleges & Their Share of Student Financial Assistance.
Nelson, T. M., et al. Non-Sighted & Sighted Adults' Volumetric Perceptions of Functional Objects.
Nelson, Trena T. Scramble: Sunshine, Rainfall, Sunshine-Such Is Life.
Nelson, Vivian L. By Special Request: Words of Love.
Nelson, Walter R. & Jenkins, T. M., eds. Computer Techniques in Shielding & Dosimetry.
Nelson, William. On Justifying Democracy.
Nelson, William E. Dispute & Conflict Resolution in Plymouth County, Massachusetts, 1725-1825.
Nelson-Erichsen, Jean & Erichsen, Heino R. Gamines: How to Adopt from Latin America.
Nelson-Jones, Richard. The Theory & Practice of Counselling Psychology.
Nelson-Raney, Steve, jt. auth. see Rosenblum, Martin J.
Nelson-Richards, M. Social Change & Rural Development: Intervention or Participation - A Zambian Case Study.
Nemec, Dulci. White Fury.
Nemec, Ludvik. Antonin Cyril Stojan: Apostle of Church Unity.
Nemecek, Otto. Virginity.
Nemeck, Francis K. Receptivity.
Nemenyi, R. Controlled Atmospheres for Heat Treatment.
Nemerov. Scientific Stream Pollution Analysis.
Nemerov, Howard. The Collected Poems of Howard Nemerov.
--New & Selected Essays.
Nemerow. Stream, Lake, Estuary, Ocean Pollution.
Nemes, Sylvester. The Soft-Hackled Fly: A Trout Fisherman's Guide.
Nemeth, Charles P. Legal Research.
Nemetz, Peter N. Energy Policy: The Global Challenge.
Nemiah, John. Foundations of Psychopathology.
Nemiro, Beverly A. & Hamilton, Donna M. High Altitude Cookbook.
Nemiroff, Robert A., jt. auth. see Colarusso, Calvin A.
Nemirovskii, P. E. Contemporary Models of the Atomic Nucleus.
Nemoshkalenko, V. V. & Aleshin, V. G. Electron Spectroscopy of Crystals.
Nenner, Howard. By Colour of Law: Legal Culture & Constitutional Politics in England, 1660-1689.
Nenno, Robert B., jt. auth. see Gallo, Michael A.
Nenno, Robert B., jt. auth. see Gilligan, Lawrence.
Nenot, J. C. & Stather, J. W. The Toxicity of Plutonium, Americium & Curium.
Nephele, Maria. Odysseus Elytis: A Poem in Two Voices. Anagnostopoulos, Athan, tr. from Gr.
Nequatewa, Edmund. Truth of a Hopi.
Nerbonne, J. J. A Foreign Correspondent Looks at Taiwan.
Neri, U. Singular Integrals.
Nerney, Catherine. The Experience of Lent with the Risen Christ.
Neruda, Pablo. Five Decades: Poems, Nineteen Twenty-Five to Nineteen-Seventy. Belitt, Ben, ed. & tr. from Span.
--Let the Rail-Splitter Awake.
--New Decade (Poems 1958-1967) Belitt, Ben & Reid, Alastair, trs. from Span.
--New Poems (1968-1970) Belitt, Ben, ed. & intro. by.
Neruda, Pablo & Frasconi, Antonio. Bestiary-Bestiario. Neuberger, Elsa, tr.
--Bestiary-Bestiario. Neuberger, Elsa, tr. from Span.
Nerval, Gerard de. Les Chimeres.
Nerval, Gerard de & Milner, Max. Les Illumines.
Nervi, Pier L. Aesthetics & Technology in Building. Einaudi, R., tr.
NES Division of Science Applications, Inc. Potential Benefits of Reducing Occupational Radiation Exposure (AIF-NESP-010R)
Nesbit, E. The Last of the Dragons.
--Story of the Amulet.
Nesbitt, Gene H. Canine & Feline Dermatology: A Systematic Approach.
Nesbitt, George. Praise of Worthy Women & Other Poems.
Nesbitt, William A. Getting Nations Together: A Case Study of the European Community.
Nesheim, Margaret. From the Hinterland of Ecuador to the Shores of Galapagos.
Nesi, Ruth, jt. auth. see Stalberg, Roberta.
Nesin, Aziz. Istanbul Boy: Boyle Gelmis Boyle Gitmez (That's How It Was But Not How It's Going to Be) The Autobiography of Aziz Nesin. Jacobson, Joseph S., tr.
Nesmeyanov, A. N. Guide to Practical Radio Chemistry.
--Guide to Practical Radio Chemistry.
--Selected Works in Organic Chemistry.
Nesnow, Stephen, jt. ed. see Langenbach, Robert.
Ness, Frederic W. The Use of Rhyme in Shakespeare's Plays.
Ness, John R. Van see Kutsche, Paul & Van Ness, John R.
Nessmith, William C., jt. auth. see Sloshberg, Willard.
Nester, Eugene & Gilstrap, Marie. Microbiology Experiments.
Nester, Eugene & Pearsall, Nancy. The Microbial Perspective.
Nesterenko, I. F., jt. auth. see Brekhman, I. I.
Nesterenko, V. V., jt. auth. see Barbashov, B. M.
Nestingen, James A. The Faith We Hold: The Living Witness of Luther & the Augsburg Confession.
--Martin Luther: His Life & Teachings.
Nestle Foundation Symposium Staff. Protein-Calorie Malnutrition: Proceedings. Von Muralt, A., ed.
Nestler, Erie J. & Greengard, Paul. Protein Phosphorylation in the Nervous System.
Nestler, Herbert, jt. auth. see Kahn, Robert.
Nestor, William P. Into Winter: Discovering a Season.
Nesvadba, Josef. Lost Face: Best Science Fiction from Czechoslovakia.
Netboy, Anthony. The Salmon: Their Fight for Survival.
Neter, John & Wasserman, William. Applied Linear Regression Analysis.
Neth, R., ed. Modern Trends in Human Leukemia IV: Latest Results.
Neth, R., et al, eds. Modern Trends in Human Leukemia V: New Results in Clinical & Biological Research Including Pediatric Oncology; Proceedings, Wilsede, FRG, June 1982.
Nethery, Betty & Smith, Beverly B. Uniquely You.
Nethery, Susan. A Mother Shares: Meditations on Parenting.
Nethery, Wallace. Charles Lamb's Town & Country Revisited.
--Mr. H in America: Anonymus Redivivus.
--Random Notes on Men, Women & Books at USC.
Netschert, Bruce C., jt. auth. see Schurr, Sam.
Netter, Edith M., jt. ed. see Meck, Stuart.
Netter, Frank. Fad Diets Can Be Deadly: The Safe Sure, Way to Weight Loss & Good Nutrition.
Netter, J. Patrick. High-Tech Fitness.
Nettesheim, P., et al. Organ & Tissue Regeneration in Mammals I.
Nettl, J. P. Soviet Achievement.
Nettl, Paul. Beethoven Encyclopedia.
--Forgotten Musicians.
--Mozart & Masonry.
--The Other Casanova.
--The Story of Dance Music.
Nettleford, Rex. Dance Jamaica: Cultural Definition & Artistic Discovery, the National Dance Theatre Company of Jamaica 1962-1983.
Nettles, Tom, jt. auth. see Bush, Russ.
Nettleton, L. L. Gravity & Magnetics for Geologists & Seismologists.
Nettleton, M. A., et al. Coal: Current Advances in Coal Chemistry & Mining Techniques.
--Coal: Current Advances in Coal Chemistry & Mining Techniques.
Nettleton, T., jt. auth. see Harrison, H. R.
Netton, I. R. Muslim Neoplatonists.
Netushil, A., ed. Theory of Automatic Control.
Netzer, Aharon, jt. ed. see Rice, Rip G.
Netzer, Ahaton, jt. auth. see Rice, Rip G.
Netzer, Corinne T. The Low Salt Diet Counter.
Neubardt & Schulman, Harold. Techniques of Abortion.
Neubauer, Alfred. Chemistry Today: The Portrait of a Science.
Neubauer, Peter, et al. Early Child Day Care.
Neuberger, Beth. Good News!
Neuberger, Elsa, tr. see Neruda, Pablo & Frasconi, Antonio.
Neuberger, Thomas. Foundation: Building Sentence Skills.
Neubert, D., et al, eds. The Role of Pharmacokinetics in Prenatal & Perinatal Toxicology.
--Methods in Prenatal Toxicology.
Neubert, Diether & Merker, Hans J., eds. New Approaches to the Evaluation of Abnormal Embryonic Development.
Neubert, George. Wisconsin Biennial, 1984.
Neudert, Walter & Roepke, H. Atlas of Steroid Spectra. Leane, J. B., tr.
Neufeld, John. Family Fortunes.
--Freddy's Book.
--Sleep Two, Three, Four.
Neufeld, Vernon, ed. If We Can Love.
Neufert, Ernst. Architect's Data: The Handbook of Building Types, 2nd (International) English Edition.
Neugeboren, Jay. Before My Life Began.
--The Stolen Jew.
Neugroschel, Joachim, tr. see Schmidt, Matthias.
Neuhaus, Eugen, tr. see Doerner, Max.
Neuhaus, O. W. & Halver, J. E., eds. Fish in Research.

Neuhaus, Otto W., jt. auth. see Orten, James M.
Neuhaus, Richard J. Christian Faith & Public Policy: Thinking & Acting in the Courage of Uncertainty.
Neuhausel, Virginia. God's Cathedral.
Neuhauser, Duncan, jt. ed. see Kovner, Anthony R.
Neuhoff, V. Micromethods in Molecular Biology.
--Proceedings of the European Society for Neurochemistry.
Neuhold, E. J., ed. Gesellschaft Fur Informatik 6, Jahrestagung 29, September-1. Oktober 1976.
Neulinger, John. To Leisure: An Introduction.
Neuman, Jeffrey, jt. auth. see Pluto, Terry.
Neuman, Stephanie G. Defense Planning in Less-Industrialized States: The Middle East & South Asia.
Neuman, Stephanie G., jt. ed. see Harkavy, Robert E.
Neumann, B., ed. GWAI-83.
Neumann, G. C. Early American Antique Country Furnishings: Northeastern America, 1650-1800.
Neumann, H., jt. ed. see Hartkaemper, A.
Neumann, I. B., jt. ed. see Schneider, Otto.
Neumann, Joseph. Beschreibung der Bekanntesten Kupfermunzen.
Neumann, Sigmund. Modern Political Parties: Approaches to Comparative Politics.
Neumeister, Susan M. Passive Smoking: A Bibliography.
Neurath, H., ed. see International Symposium Held at the Battelle Seattle Research Center Seattle, WA, Nov. 4-6, 1974, et al.
Neuschel, Richard F. Management Systems for Profit & Growth.
Neusner, Jacob. Israel in America: A Too-Comfortable Exile?
--Israel in America: A Too-Comfortable Exile?
--Judaism: The Evidence of the Mishnah.
--Messiah in Context: Israel's History & Destiny in Formative Judaism.
--Midrash As Literature: The Primacy of Documentary Discourse.
--Midrash in Context.
--Torah: From Scroll to Symbol in Formative Judaism.
Neusner, Jacob, jt. ed. see Vermes, Geza.
Neustadt, L. W., jt. ed. see Balakrishnan, A. V.
Neustadt, Lucien W., jt. ed. see Balakrishna, A. V.
Neustatter, Lindesay. Psychological Disorder & Crime.
Neustatter, W. L. The Mind of the Murderer.
Neuweld, Mark, jt. ed. see Gruliow, Leo.
Neuwirth, Robert S. Hysteroscopy.
Neuwirth, Waltraud. Italian Glass, Nineteen Fifty to Nineteen Sixty.
--Josef Hoffmann's Bestecke Fur die Weiner Werkstatte: Josef Hoffmann's Flatware Designs for Wiener Werkstatte.
--Loetz Austria 1900 Glass-Glass-Verre-Vetri.
--Loetz Austria 1905-1918, Glass.
--Orientalisierende Glaser, Vol. 1: J. & L. Lobmeyr.
Nevakivi, Jukka. The Appeal That Was Never Made: The Allies, Scandinavia, & the Finnish Winter War, 1939-1940.
Nevanlinna, R. Analytic Functions. Emig, P., tr.
--Raum, Zeit und Relativitat.
Nevdeck, Gerold W., jt. auth. see Hayt, William H.
Neve, Lloyd R. Japan: God's Door to the Far East.
Nevett, Louise, illus. Masks & Puppets.
--Monsters & Dinosaurs.
Nevile, John, jt. ed. see Argy, Victor.
Neville, A. C. Biology of the Anthropod Cuticle.
Neville, Charles. The Biology of the Arthropod Cuticle. Head, J. J., ed.
Neville, Eric H. Elliptic Functions: A Primer. Langford, W. J., ed.
Neville, Joyce. How to Share Your Faith Without Being Offensive.
Neville, Kris, jt. auth. see Lee, Henry.
Neville, Robert C. Soldier, Sage, Saint.
Nevin, David. The American Touch in Micronesia.
Nevin, Jeanne, ed. see Hughes, K. Scott, et al.
Nevin, Jeanne, ed. see National Association of College & University Business Officers Staff, et al.
Nevins, Allan. Ordeal of the Union. Incl. Vol. 1. Ordeal of the Union: Fruits of Manifest Destiny, 1847-1852; Vol. 2. Ordeal of the Union: A House Dividing, 1852-1857; Vol. 3. The Emergence of Lincoln: Douglas, Buchanan, & Party Chaos, 1857-1859; Vol. 4. The Emergence of Lincoln: Prologue to Civil War, 1859-1861; Vol. 5. The War for the Union: The Improvised War, 1861-1862; Vol. 6. The War for the Union: War Becomes Revolution, 1862-1863; Vol. 7. The War for the Union: The Organized War, 1863-1864; Vol. 8. The War for the Union: The Organized War to Victory, 1864-1865. Scribner.
Nevins, Allan, ed. see Cooper, James Fenimore.
Nevins, Ann. Super Stitches: A Book of Superstitions.
Nevins, Francis M., Jr., ed. Nightwebs: A Collection of Stories by Cornell Woolrich.
Nevitt, Peter. Project Finance.
Nevitt, Peter K. & Fabozzi, Frank J, eds. Equipment Leasing.
Nevius, John L. Demon Possession.
New American Computer Dictionary Editors. The New American Computer Dictionary.
New American Webster Handy College Dictionary Editors. The New American Webster Handy College Dictionary.
New, Bill, jt. auth. see Wright, D. Franklin.
New Century Editors. New Century Velazquez Spanish-English Dictionary.
New, Christopher. Shanghai.
New, D. A. Techniques for Culture of Vertebrate Embryos.
New England Anti-Slavery Convention Staff. Proceedings: Proceedings of the New England Anti-Slavery Convention, 4th, Boston, 1837.
New England Bankruptcy Conference Staff & Massachusetts Continuing Legal Education, Inc. Staff. Bankruptcy Code Amendments - a Utility in Chapter 11: First Annual New England Bankruptcy Conference.
New England Historical Genealogical Society Staff. The Greenlaw Index of the New England Historic Genealogical Society.
New Jersey Conference of Social Work Staff. Negro in New Jersey.
New Jersey Institute for Continuing Legal Education Staff & Savage, Thomas J. Basic Labor Law.
New Jersey Institute for Continuing Legal Education Staff, et al. The Demise of the Professional Corporation? Seminar Materials.
New Jersey Institute for Continuing Legal Education Staff & Breitkopf, Herman L. Seminar Material for Settlement Techniques.
New, Melvyn, ed. see Sterne, Laurence.
New Orleans Academy of Ophthalmology Staff. Symposium on Cataract Surgery.
--Symposium on Medical & Surgical Diseases of the Retins & Vitreous.
New Pulps for the Paper Industry Symposium Staff. New Pulps for the Paper Industry: Proceedings of the Symposium, Brussels, Belgium, May 1979. Haas, Leonard E., ed.
New Riders Publishing Staff. Working Out with AutoCAD Curriculum Training Guide.
New World Records Staff, ed. Index of the Recorded Anthology of American Music.
New York Academy of Medicine Editors. New York Academy of Medicine, Illustration Catalog.
New York Academy of Medicine Staff. Author Catalog of the Library of the New York Academy of Medicine.
--Author Catalog of the Library of the New York Academy of Medicine, 1st Suppl.
--Portrait Catalog.
--Portrait Catalog: Third Supplement, 1971-1975.
--Subject Catalog of the Library of the New York Academy of Medicine.
--Subject Catalog of the Library of the New York Academy of Medicine, 1st Supplement.
New York Botanical Garden Library Staff. Biographical Notes Upon Botanists.
--Catalog of the Manuscript & Archival Collections & Index to the Correspondence of John Torrey.
New York Botanical Garden Staff. Wild Flowers of the Northeastern States.
New York City Graph Theory Conference Staff. Recent Trends in Graph Theory: Proceedings of the New York City Graph Theory Conference, 1st, 1970. Capobianco, M., et al, eds.
New York County Lawyers' Association Staff. Handbook on Patents, Trademarks & Copyrights.
New York Institute of Technology Staff. A Programmed Course in Basic Pulse Circuits.
New York-New Jersey Trail Conference Staff. The Long Path, A New York Hiking Trail.
New York Public Library, Office of Children's Services Staff. Children's Books, 1983.
New York Public Library, Office of Young Adult Services Staff. Easy-to-Read Books for the Teenage.
New York Public Library, Research Libraries Staff & Library of Congress, Research Libraries Staff. Bibliographic Guide to Soviet & East European Studies: 1979.
New York Public Library, Research Libraries Staff. Catalog of Government Publications, Economics Division.
--Catalog of the Theatre & Drama Collections: First Supplement to Pt. 1, Drama Collection.
--Catalog of the Theatre & Drama Collections.
--Dictionary Catalog & Shelf List of the Spencer Collection of Illustrated Books & Manuscripts & Fine Bindings.
--Dictionary Catalog of Jewish Collection.
--Dictionary Catalog of Materials on New York City.
--Dictionary Catalog of the Art & Architecture Division, Supplement 1974.
--Dictionary Catalog of the Art & Architecture Division, The Research Libraries of The New York Public Library.
--Dictionary Catalog of the Dance Collection, Performing Arts Research Center.
--Dictionary Catalog of the Henry W. & Albert A. Berg Collection of English & American Literature.
--Dictionary Catalog of the History of the Americas Collection.
--Dictionary Catalog of the History of the Americas Collection, First Supplement.
--Dictionary Catalog of the Jewish Collection, First Supplement.
--Dictionary Catalog of the Local History & Genealogy Division.
--Dictionary Catalog of the Manuscript Division.
--Dictionary Catalog of the Map Division.
--Dictionary Catalog of the Music Collection.
--Dictionary Catalog of the Music Collection.
--Dictionary Catalog of the Oriental Collection: First Supplement.
--Dictionary Catalog of the Oriental Collection.
--The Dictionary Catalog of the Prints Division.
--Dictionary Catalog of the Rare Book Division: First Supplement.
--Dictionary Catalog of the Rare Book Division.
--Dictionary Catalog of the Schomburg Collection of Negro Literature & History.
--Dictionary Catalog of the Slavonic Collection.
New York Public Library, Research Libraries, Rare Division Staff. The Imprint Catalog in the Rare Book Division.
New York Public Library, Research Libraries Staff. Music Subject Headings.
--Subject Catalog of the World War One Collection.
--Subject Headings.
--United States Local History Catalog.
New York Public Library Staff. Bibliographic Guide to Government Publications, Foreign 1987.
--Bibliographic Guide to Government Publications: U. S. 1987.
--Bibliographic Guide to Maps & Atlases 1987.
--Bibliographic Guide to North American History 1987.
--Bibliographic Guide to Soviet & East European Studies 1987.
--Bibliographic Guide to Technology: 1987.
--The Eno Collection of New York City Views. Weitenkampf, Frank, ed.
New York Public Library Staff & Library of Congress Staff. Guide to Festschriften.
New York Public Library Staff, ed. Bibliographical Guide to Dance, 1985.
--Bibliographical Guide to Education, 1985.
New York State Commission on Cultural Resources. Cultural Resource Development: A Planning Survey & Analysis.
New York State Department of Health, Birth Defects Institute Symposium Staff. Heredity & Society: Proceedings of the New York State Department of Health, Birth Defects Institute Symposium, 2nd, Oct. 1971. Porter, Ian H., et al, eds.
New York State Department of Health Staff. Inborn Errors of Specific Immunity: Proceedings of the New York State Department of Health on Birth Defects, 9th Symposium. Pollara, Bernard, et al, eds.
New York State Staff, ed. see Waren, Oscar & Heaton, Willis E.
New York Times Staff. The New York Times Everyday Dictionary. Paikeday, Thomas M., ed.
New York Times Staff, jt. auth. see Klott, Gary L.
New York University Editors. Library Catalog of the Conservation Center of the Institute of Fine Arts.
New Zealand Ministry of Agriculture & Fisheries Staff. Glasshouse Tomatoes.
Newall, Venetia. An Egg at Easter: A Folklore Study.
Newark, Peter. Sabre & Lance: An Illustrated History of Cavalry.
Newark, Tim. Celtic Warriors: 400 BC - AD 1600.
Newberg, Leslie A., jt. auth. see Lebowitz, Philip W.
Newberry Library, Chicago Staff. Bibliographical Inventory to the Early Music in the Newberry Library, Chicago, Illinois. Krummel, D. W., ed.
--Catalogue of the Greenlee Collection.
--Dictionary Catalog of the Edward E. Ayer Collection of Americana & American Indians, First Supplement.
--Dictionary Catalog of the Edward E. Ayer Collection of Americana & American Indians.
--Dictionary Catalogue of the History of Printing from the John M. Wing Foundation.
--Dictionary Catalogue of the History of Printing from the John M. Wing Foundation, First Supplement.
--Genealogical Index of the Newberry Library, Chicago.
Newbery, John. Little Pretty Pocket-Book.
Newbigging, Thomas. Fables & Fabulists, Ancient & Modern.
Newbold, H. L. The Psychiatric Programming of People: Neo-Behavioral Orthomolecular Psychiatry.
Newborn, Jud & Dumbach, Annette E. Shattering the German Night.
Newborn, Monroe, jt. auth. see Levy, David.
Newbould, Brian. Schubert & the Symphony.
Newbourne, Malcolm J. The Transportation & Distribution Manager's Guide to Time Sharing. Marshall, Kenneth, ed.
Newburger, Adele M., jt. auth. see Guertler, John T.
Newburgh, Charles, tr. see Geiger, Abraham.
Newburne, James W., jt. auth. see Fawcett, Don W.
Newbury, Josephine. Church Kindergarten Resource Book.
--More Kindergarten Resources.
Newbury, N. F. Teaching of Chemistry.
Newbury, P. A. R. A Geography of Agriculture.
Newby, Eric. On the Shores of the Mediterranean.
Newby, F. How to Find Out about Patents.
Newby, P. H. Saladin in His Time.
Newcomb, Duane. The Apartment Farmer.
--The Complete Vegetable Gardner's Sourcebook.
--The Owner-Built Adobe House.
Newcomb, Duane G. Fortune-Building Secrets of the Rich.
--Fortune-Building Secrets of the Rich.
Newcomb, Richard F. Pictorial History of the Vietnam War.
Newcomb, Robert D. & Jolley, Jerry L. Public Health & Community Optometry.
Newcomb, Robinson & Wherly, Max S. Mobile Home Parks: Part Two, An Analysis of Communities.
Newcombe, Jack. In Search of Billy Cole.
--Six Days to Saturday: Joe Paterno & Penn State.
Newcombe, Norman. Europe at School: A Study in Primary & Secondary Schools in France, West Germany, Italy, Portugal & Spain.
Newcomer, Phyllis L. Understanding & Teaching Emotionally Disturbed Children.
Newell, A. Donald. Gunstock Finishing & Care.
Newell, Allen, jt. auth. see Ernst, George W.
Newell, Charldean, jt. auth. see Kraemer, Richard.
Newell, Frank W. Strabismus & Amblyopia.
Newell, G. F. Approximate Stochastic Behavior of n-Server Service Systems with Large n.
Newell, Gilbert F., jt. auth. see Mead, Leon.
Newell, Jack E. Laboratory Management.
Newell, Nancy P. & Newell, Richard S. The Struggle for Afghanistan.
Newell, Richard S., jt. auth. see Newell, Nancy P.
Newell, Steven W. Dreams of Allon.
Newell, Sydney B. Chemistry: An Introduction.
Newell, W. C. The Casting of Steel.
Newell, William R. The Newell Commentaries.
--Studies in Joshua-Job.
Newfield, Marcia. A Book for Jodan.
Newhall, Beaumont. The Latent Image: The Discovery of Photography.
Newhall, Beaumont & Edkins, Diana E. William H. Jackson.
Newhall, Beaumont & Newhall, Nancy. T. H. O'Sullivan Photographer.
Newhall, Beaumont & Conger, Amy, eds. Edward Weston Omnibus.
Newhall, Beaumont, photos by. In Plain Sight: Photographs by Beaumont Newhall.
Newhall, Esther M. Sandy, the Talking Cat.
Newhall, Nancy. Ansel Adams the Eloquent Light.
--P. H. Emerson: The Fight for Photography As a Fine Art.
Newhall, Nancy, jt. auth. see Newhall, Beaumont.
Newhall, Nancy, ed. The Flame of Recognition.
Newhall, Sue M. Devil in God's Old Man.
Newhaus, Bo. It's Okay, God, We Can Take It.
Newhouse, Dave, jt. auth. see Plunkett, Jim.
Newhouse, Dora. The Encyclopedia of Homonyms 'Sound-Alikes'
Newhouse, John. Collision in Brussels: The Common Market Crisis of 30 June 1965.
Newhouse, Joseph P. The Economics of Medical Care.
Newhouse, Wade J. Constitutional Uniformity & Equality in State Taxation.
Newkirk, Lois G. Hudson: A Survey of Historic Structures.
Newland, Kathleen. Women, Men, & the Division of Labor.
Newland, Mary & Walklin, Carol. Printing & Embroidery.
Newlander, John. The Thousand Quotations: Olympic Edition.
Newlander, John A., jt. auth. see Atherton, Henry V.
Newlands, George. Theology of the Love of God.
Newlin, Claude. Philosophy & Religion in Colonial America.
Newlin, Dika. Bruckner-Mahler-Schoenberg.

Authors

Newman, A. A., ed. Photographic Techniques in Scientific Research.
--Photographic Techniques in Scientific Research.
Newman, Anne & Bowers, Cathy. Foreign Investment in South Africa & Namibia: A Directory of U. S., Canadian & British Corporations Operating in South Africa & Namibia. Mathiasen, Carolyn, ed.
Newman, Aryeh, tr. see Meiseles, Meir.
Newman, Barbara. The Nutcracker.
--Striking a Balance: Dancers Talk About Dancing.
Newman, Bernard. Epics of Espionage.
--Turkish Crossroads.
Newman, Cardinal see also Newman, John H.
Newman, Daisy. I Take Thee, Serenity.
--Indian Summer of the Heart.
Newman, Donald J. Conviction: The Determination of Guilt or Innocence Without Trial.
Newman, Dorothy K., et al. Protest, Politics & Prosperity: Black Americans & White Institutions.
Newman, Edwin. Sunday Punch.
Newman, Gerald. How to Write a Report.
Newman, Graeme R., ed. Crime & Justice in America: Seventeen Seventy-Six to Nineteen Seventy-Six.
Newman, Grant. Teaching Children Music: Fundamentals of Music & Method.
Newman, Harold. Your Child's Reading & What You Can Do about It.
Newman, James A. & Alexander, Roy. Climbing the Corporate Matterhorn.
Newman, John. Electrochemical Systems.
Newman, John H. see also Newman, Cardinal.
Newman, Judith Sternberg. In the Hell of Auschwitz.
Newman, L. B. Friction Materials: Recent Advances.
Newman, Larry J., et al. Developing Cost Volumes.
Newman, M. Haskell, et al, eds. Handbook of Ear, Nose & Throat Emergencies.
Newman, Margrit, jt. auth. see Falencki, Edye.
Newman, Martin, jt. auth. see Watt, Billie L.
Newman, Martin & Grey, Jerry, eds. Utilization of Alternative Fuels for Transportation, AAS2.
Newman, Michael & Goodman, Anthony, eds. Guide to Antibiotic Use in Dental Practice.
Newman, Mildred & Berkowitz, Bernard. How to Take Charge of Your Life.
Newman, Nancy, jt. auth. see Salisbury, Roger E.
Newman, Patti. As If by Magic.
Newman, Peter. King of the Castle, the Making of a Dynasty: Seagram's & the Bronfman Empire.
Newman, R. Fine-Line Lithography.
Newman, Ralph A., ed. see American Society for Legal History Staff.
Newman, Richard & Wright, R. Glenn. Index to Birthplaces of American Authors.
Newman, Richard, jt. ed. see Wills, David W.
Newman, Robert. The Boy Who Could Fly.
--The Case of the Etruscan Treasure.
--The Case of the Frightened Friend.
--Japanese: People of the Three Treasures.
--Night Spell.
--The Shattered Stone.
Newman, Sasha M. Arthur Dove & Duncan Phillips: Artist & Patron. Lynch, Kathleen A., et al, eds.
Newman, Sasha M., ed. Bonnard: The Late Paintings.
Newman, Shirlee. Tell Me Grandma, Tell Me Grandpa.
Newman, Shirlee P. Marian Anderson: Lady from Philadelphia.
Newman, Stanley, ed. Bull's-Eye Crosswords.
Newman, Stanley S. Yokuts Language of California.
Newman, Virginia H. Teaching an Infant to Swim.
--Teaching an Infant to Swim.
--Teaching an Infant to Swim.
--Teaching Young Children to Swim & Dive.
Newman, W. S., jt. auth. see King, J. W.
Newman, William M. Les Seigneurs De Nesle En Picardie (12e Siecle a 1286) Leurs Chartes et leur Histoire.
Newman, William S. Sonata in the Baroque Era.
--Sonata in the Classic Era.
--Sonata Since Beethoven.
--The Sonata since Beethoven.
Newmann, Fred M. Educational Reform & Social Studies: Implications of Six Reports.
Newmann, H. C., tr. see Hanack, Michael.
Newmans, Evans. The True Story of the Notorious Jesse James.
Newmarch, Rosa, tr. see Hoffmeister, Karel.
Newmark, Eileen. Women's Roles: A Cross-Cultural Perspective.
Newmark, Joseph. Statistics & Probability in Modern Life.
Newmark, Maxim. Dictionary of Science & Technology.
--Dictionary of Spanish Literature.
--Dictionary of Spanish Literature.
--Illustrated Technical Dictionary.
--Twentieth Century Modern Language Teaching.
Newmark, Maxim, tr. see Werfel, Franz.
Newmeyer, Frederick J. Linguistic Theory in America: The First Quarter Century of Transformational Generative Grammar.
--The Politics of Linguistics.
Newmeyer, William L. Primary Care of Hand Injuries.
Newmon, A. K. The Instant Chef: Shortcut Magic to Gourmet Cooking for the Working Person.
Newport, J. Herbert, jt. auth. see Steinwedel, Louis W.
Newport, John P. Paul Tillich.
Newport, M. Gene, jt. auth. see Trewatha, Robert L.
Newrock, Melody. Here Comes the Clones: A Guide to IBM-PC Compatible Computers & Software.
Newsholme, E. A. & Start, C. Regulation of Metabolism.
Newsletter Publications Center Staff. Genetic Engineering-Biotechnology Sourcebook. Pergolizzi, Robert, ed.
Newsom, Barbara, ed. The Art Museum As Educator.
Newsom, Doug & Scott, Alan. This Is PR: The Realities of Public Relations.
Newsome, Albert R., jt. auth. see Lefler, Hugh T.
Newsome, James D., Jr. By the Waters of Babylon: An Introduction to the History & Theology of the Exile.
Newsome, Walter L. Government Reference Books Eighty to Eighty-One: A Biennial Guide to U. S. Government Publications-7th Biennial Volume.
Newsome, Walter L., compiled by. Government Reference Books Seventy-Eight to Seventy-Nine: A Biennial Guide to U. S. Government Publications, 6th Biennial Volume.
Newson, Adele S. Zora Neale Hurston: A Reference Guide.
Newson, L. Aboriginal & Spanish Colonial Trinidad: A Study in Cultural Contact.
Newspaper Enterprise Association Editors. World Almanac & Book of Facts, 1986.
Newspaper Enterprise Association Staff. World Almanac Book of Facts 1983.
Newstead, P. E. Lectures on Introduction to Moduli Problems & Orbit Spaces.
Newstrom, John W., et al. Contingency Approach to Management Readings.
Newton, Astrid, jt. auth. see Castle, Coralie.
Newton, Charles. The People & Places of Constantinople.
Newton, Dennis W. Severe Weather Flying.
Newton, Donna J. Scottie Showcase: A Pictorial Introduction to Scottie Dog Collectibles.
Newton, Grant W. & Bloom, Gilbert D. Tax Planning for the Troubled Business 1987.
Newton, Harry. One Hundred One Saving Secrets Your Phone Company Won't Tell You.
Newton, Huey P. & Blake, Herman. Revolutionary Suicide.
Newton, Isaac. Opticks, or a Treatise of the Reflections, Refractions, Inflections & Colours of Light.
Newton, J. Electricity & Magnetism.
Newton, John, jt. ed. see Loudon, Nancy.
Newton, John R. Reading in Your School.
Newton, John R., jt. auth. see Clayton, Stanley.
Newton, Joseph F. The Builders: A Story & Study of Freemasonry.
Newton, Judith J. Guide on Data Entity Naming Conventions.
Newton, Linda. Therapy Made Fun! Set 2.
Newton, Mariana. Cerebral Palsy: Speech, Hearing, & Language Problems.
Newton, Marie W. Notes from Marie's Kitchen. Speir, Elizabeth, ed.
Newton, Miller, jt. auth. see Macdonald, Donald Ian.
Newton, Miller, jt. auth. see Polson, Beth.
Newton, Patricia M. The Five Sparrows: A Japanese Folktale.
--The Frog Who Drank the Waters of the World.
Newton, Peggy, jt. auth. see West, Michael A.
Newton, R., jt. auth. see Jenkins, G. Curtis.
Newton, R. C., et al, eds. Thermodynamics of Minerals & Melts.
Newton, Ramona R. Soliloquy & Other Poems.
Newton, Richard, ed. see Family Handyman Magazine Editors.
Newton, Stanley D. Mackinac Island & Saulte St. Marie.
Newton, Suzanne. Care of Arnold's Corners.
--What Are You up to, William Thomas?
Newton, William E., jt. ed. see Muller, Achim.
Newton, William R., ed. see Myers, M. Scott.
Newton, William R., ed. see Zand, Dale.
Newton-Smith, W. H. The Structure of Time.
Nexon, Phillip J. & Massachusetts Continuing Legal Education, Inc. Staff. Nexon on Commercial Real Estate Financing & Developments.
Ney, Philip G. & Mulvihill, Deanna L. Child Psychiatric Treatment: A Practical Guide.
Neyman, Jerzy, ed. see International Research Seminar - Berkeley - 1963.
NFL, ed. Official NFL Record & Fact Book 1984.
Ng, A. B., jt. auth. see Reagan, J. W.
Ng, David. Searching for the Real China.
--See It! Do It! Your Faith in Action.
Ng, E. W., ed. Symbolic & Algebraic Computation: EUROSAM Seventy-Nine: an International Symposium.
Ng, Lorenz K. & Davis, Devra, eds. Strategies for Public Health: Promoting Health & Preventing Disease.
Ng, Yew-Kwang. Welfare Economics: Introduction & Development of Basic Concepts.
Ngo, Bach & Zimmerman, Gloria. Classic Cuisine of Vietnam.
Ngongwikuo, Joseph A. Taboo Love.
Ngor Tharttse mKhanpo bSodnams rgyamtsho. Tibetan Mandalas: The Ngor Collection. Tachikawa, Musashi, ed.
Ngubane, Harriet. Body & Mind in Zulu Medicine: An Ethnography of Health & Disease in Nyuswa-Zulu Thought & Practice.
Ngugi. Writers in Politics.
Nguyen, An. Chinese Astrology.
Nguyen Dinh-Hoa. Colloquial Vietnamese.
Niaki, Shahzad & Broscious, John A. Underground Tank Leak Detection Methods: A State-of-the Art Review.
Niall, Ian. Portrait of a Country Artist: Charles Tunnicliffe R. A. 1901-1979.
Niatum, Duane, ed. Carriers of the Dream Wheel.
Niblett, C. A., et al. The Future for Ocean Technology.
Niblock, Tim & Lawless, Richard, eds. Prospects for the World Oil Industry.
Nicarthy, Ginny. Getting Free: A Handbook for Women in Abusive Relationships.
Nice, Richard. Crime & Insanity.
--Dictionary of Criminology.
--Handbook of Abnormal Psychology.
Niceron, Jean-Pierre. Memoires pour Servir a l'Histoire des Hommes Illustres.
Nichol, C. R. Baptist Answers Reviewed.
--A Study in Methodist Discipline.
Nichol, Todd. All These Lutherans: Three Paths Toward a New Lutheran Church.
Nicholas, Anna K. The Boxer.
Nicholas, Dudley, jt. auth. see Gassner, John.
Nicholas, Jean, jt. auth. see Sonnenschmidt, Fritz.
Nicholas, Ted. Management for Enterpreneurs.
Nicholas, Vera, ed. Catalog of California Grants Assistance 1987.
Nicholi, Armand M., Jr., ed. The Harvard Guide to Modern Psychiatry.
Nicholl, Charles. The Chemical Theatre.
--A Cup of News: The Life of Thomas Nashe.
Nicholl, Donald. Holiness.
Nicholls. Endodontics.
Nicholls, C. S., jt. auth. see Awdry, Philip.
Nicholls, D. The Chemistry of Iron, Cobalt & Nickel.
Nicholls, P., et al, eds. Membrane Proteins.
Nicholls, R. W., jt. auth. see Armstrong, B. H.
Nicholls, Richard E. The Plant Doctor: Growing & Healing Indoor Plants.
Nichols, Barbara, jt. auth. see Levin, Marvin T.
Nichols, Charles H., ed. Black Men in Chains: Narratives by Escaped Slaves.
Nichols, Dean. Islands of Experience.
Nichols, Donald R. Life Cycle Investing: Investing for the Time of Your Life.
--Starting Small, Investing Smart: What to Do with 5 to 5,000 Dollars.
Nichols, Dudley, jt. auth. see Gassner, John.
Nichols, Eleanor, ed. see Kolpas, Norman.
Nichols, Ellwyn. The People Pray.
Nichols, Eugene D., et al. Holt Algebra Two with Trigonometry.
--Holt Geometry.
Nichols, Frank. Theory & Practice of Body Massage.
Nichols, Frederick D; see O'Neal, William B.
Nichols, Frederick D. see O'Neal, William B.
Nichols, George & Wasserman, R. H., eds. Cellular Mechanism for Calcium Transfer & Homeostasis.
Nichols, J. Randall. Building the Word: The Dynamics of Communication & Preaching.
Nichols, James D. Bullwhacker.
Nichols, James H., jt. auth. see McNeill, John T.
Nichols, James W. Insinuation: The Tactics of English Satire.
Nichols, John. American Blood.
--A Fragile Beauty.
--A Ghost in the Music.
--The Last Beautiful Days of Autumn.
--The Nirvana Blues.
--On the Mesa.
--Sterile Cuckoo.
Nichols, John T. The Nirvana Blues.
Nichols, John Treadwell. The Magic Journey.
Nichols, Leigh. The House of Thunder.
Nichols, Lew, jt. auth. see Proulx, Annie.
Nichols, Marion. Encyclopedia of Embroidery Stitches, Including Crewel.
Nichols, Marion, ed. see Briggs, Wm. & Co.Staff.
Nichols, Nell B. The Farm Cook & Rule Book: The Golden Anniversary Edition.
--The Farm Cook & Rule Book: The Golden Anniversary Edition.
Nichols, Paul. Big Paul's School Bus.
Nichols, Peter. The National Health.
--Passion.
Nichols, R. & Stevens, L. A. Are You Listening?
Nichols, R. Eugene. Picture Yourself a Winner.
Nichols, Roger I. & Adams, George R. The American Indian: Past & Present.
Nichols, Roy F. Advance Agents of American Destiny.
Nichols, Ruth. The Marrow of the World.
--Walk Out of the World.
Nichols, Stuart & Ostrow, David G. Psychiatric Implications of Acquired Immune Deficiency Syndrome.
Nichols, William. Writing from Experience.
Nicholson. Nicholson's Visitors London.
Nicholson, C., jt. ed. see Kater, S. B.
Nicholson, James B. A Manual of the Art of Bookbinding Containing Full Instructions in the Different Branches of Forwarding, Gilding & Finishing. Bidwell, John, ed.
Nicholson, James R. Shetland.
Nicholson, Loren. Rails Across the Ranchos.
Nicholson, Louise. India: A Guide for the Quality-Conscious Traveler. Johnson, Joyce, ed.
Nicholson, Luree & Torbet, Laura. How to Fight Fair with Your Kids...& Win!
Nicholson, Michael. Across the Limpopo: A Family's Hazardous 4,000-mile Journey Through Africa.
--December Ultimatum.
Nicholson, Miklos. Corporate Secretary's Complete Forms Handbook.
Nicholson, Nigel, ed. see Woolf, Virginia.
Nicholson, Norm. Individual Investor's Microcomputer Resource Guide.
Nicholson, Normon. Selected Poems, Nineteen Forty to Nineteen Eighty-Two.
Nicholson Publications Staff. Nicholson's Guide to England & Wales.
--Nicholson's London Guide.
Nicholson, R. Steven. Chief Executive Officers: Contracts & Compensation 1981.
Nicholson, Reynold A., tr. Translations of Eastern Poetry & Prose.
Nicholson, Robert, Publications Staff. Nicholson's Complete London Guide.
Nicholson, Robert W. & Williams, Ralph R. The Language of National Defense in English.
Nicholson, W. L., jt. auth. see Dixon, W. J.
Nicholson, Walter. Intermediate Microeconomics & Its Applications.
Nicholson-Smith, Donald, tr. see Piaget, Jean.
Nickel, Helmut. Warriors & Worthies.
Nickel, K., ed. Interval Mathematics: Proceedings of the International Symposium, Karlsruhe, West Germany, May 20-24, 1975.
Nickel, Karl L. Interval Mathematics: 1980.
Nickelhoff, Andrew, compiled by. Extending Workplace Democracy - An Overview of Participatory Decisionmaking Plans for Unionists.
Nickell, Paulena, et al. Management in Family Living.
Nickels. Understanding Business.
Nickels, Sylvie. Scandinavia.
Nickelsburg, George W. & Stone, Michael E. Faith & Piety in Early Judaism: Texts & Documents.
Nickens, Christopher. Bette Davis: A Biography in Photographs.
--Natalie Wood: A Biography in Photographs.
Nickerson, G. Man's Cultural Dimension.
Nickerson, Jill, ed. Country Christmas Entertaining.
--Country Store Candy Cookbook.
Nickerson, Marina, jt. auth. see Farah, Cynthia.
Nickerson, Roy. Brother Whale: A Pacific Whalewatcher's Log.
--Sea Otters: A Natural History & Guide.
Nickerson, William. Nickerson's No-Risk Way to Real Estate Fortunes.
Nickey, J. M. Masonary Construction: The Trowel Worker's Bible.
Nickl, Peter. Crocodile, Crocodile. Cutler, M. E., tr. from Ger.
Nicklaus, Carol. Drawing Pets.
--Harry the Hider.
--Making Dolls.
--That's Not Chester!
Nicklaus, Carol, jt. auth. see Margolin, Harriet.
Nicklaus, Jack & Bowden, Ken. Golf My Way.
--Jack Nicklaus' the Full Swing.
Nickles, Herbert, jt. auth. see Culp, George.
Nickless, Graham, ed. Inorganic Sulphur Chemistry.
Nickol, Brent B., ed. Host-Parasite Interfaces.
Nicks, J E. BASIC Programming Solutions for Manufacturing.
Nicks, Roy S., ed. Community Colleges of Tennessee: The Founding & Early Years.
Nickson, Jack W., Jr. Economics & Social Choice.
Nickum, James, ed. A Research Guide to Jingji Yanjiu.

Authors

Nickum, James E., ed. Water Management Organization in China.
Nicol, A. W., ed. Physicochemical Methods of Mineral Analysis.
Nicol, C. W. Harpoon: A Novel.
Nicol, Dr. Davidson Foreword by see Kagwa, Benjamin N. H.
Nicol, E. Fiona, jt. ed. see Ford, Michael J.
Nicolai, Jurgen. Bird Keeping. Bleher, Petra, tr. from Ger.
Nicolais, Luigi, jt. ed. see Seferis, James C.
Nicolas, jt. auth. see Will.
Nicolas, Jean F. Elegant & Easy: Decorative Ideas for Food Presentations.
Nicolau, C. & Paraf, A., eds. Structural & Kinetic Approach to Plasma Membrane Functions: Proceedings,Grignon, September 6-9, 1976.
Nicolau, Claude, ed. Virus Transformed Cell Membranes.
Nicolaysen, Bruce. Beekman Place.
--From Distant Shores.
--Gracie Square.
--On Maiden Lane.
--The Pirate of Gramercy Park.
Nicoletti, Sally. Japanese Motifs for Needlepoint.
Nicolich, Lorraine, jt. auth. see Woolfolk, Anita E.
Nicolini, Claudio, ed. Cell Growth.
--Chemical Carcinogenesis.
Nicoll, A. R., tr. see German Society of Metallurgy Staff.
Nicoll, Bruce H. & Savery, Gilbert M., eds. Nebraska: A Pictorial History.
Nicoll, Helen & Pienkowski, Jan. Meg & Mog Birthday Book.
--Meg's Car.
--Mog at the Zoo.
Nicoll, Helens & Pienkowski, Jan. Meg's Castle.
Nicollier, Alain, ed. European Universities, Nineteen Seventy-Five to Eighty-Five: Proceedings of the 5th General Assembly of the Standing Conference of Rectors & Vice-Chancellors of the European Universities, Bologna, 1974.
Nicolson, Adam. Landscape of Britain.
Nicolson, Adam, et al. Long Walks in France.
Nicolson, Harold. King George V.
--Some People.
Nicolson, Harold G. Diaries & Letters of Harold Nicolson. Nicolson, Nigel, ed.
--Harold Nicolson: Diaries & Letters 1930-1939. Nicolson, N., ed.
Nicolson, I. Gravity: Black Holes & the Universe.
Nicolson, Iain. Simple Astronomy.
Nicolson, Marjorie & Rousseau, G. S. This Long Disease, My Life: Alexander Pope & the Sciences.
Nicolson, Marjorie H. Mountain Gloom & Mountain Glory.
Nicolson, N., ed. see Nicolson, Harold G.
Nicolson, Nigel, ed. Diaries & Letters of Harold Nicolson.
Nicolson, Nigel & Trautmann, Joanne, eds. The Letters of Virginia Woolf: 1888-1912.
--The Letters of Virginia Woolf: 1912-1922.
Nicolson, Nigel, ed. see Nicolson, Harold G.
Nicosia, Gerald. Memory Babe: A Critical Biography of Jack Kerouac. Jordan, Fred, ed.
--Memory Babe: A Critical Biography of Jack Kerouac.
Nicosia, Sal, jt. auth. see Pfaffle, A. E.
Nida, E. A. Toward a Science of Translating.
Nida, Eugene A. Customs & Cultures: Anthropology for Christian Missions.
Nida, Eugene A., jt. auth. see Waard, Jan de.
Nida, Patricia C. Managing the Mobile Employee.
Niddrie, David L. Tobago.
Nie, Norman H. & Hull, C. Hadlai. SPSS-Eleven: The SPSS Batch System for the DEC PDP-11.
Niedenthal, Morris & Lacocque, Andre. Pentecost 1.
Niedenzu, Kurt & Zimmer, Hans, eds. Annual Reports in Inorganic & General Syntheses.
Niederer, Frances J. Hollins College: An Illustrated History.
Niederhoffer, Arthur & Blumberg, Abraham S. The Ambivalent Force.
Niederman, Robert A., ed. Molecular Biology & Protein Synthesis.
Niedner, Frederick A., Jr., jt. auth. see Truemper, David G.
Niehaus, John F., jt. auth. see Thierauf, Robert J.
Niehaus, R., jt. ed. see Bryant, D.
Niehaus, Richard J., jt. ed. see Mensch, Gerhard O.
Niel, Fennand. The Mysteries of Stonehenge.
Nield, Jill S. & O'Connor, Ginger H. Fundamentals of Dental Hygiene Instrumentation.
Nielsen, Ernest D., ed. & tr. see Grundtvig, N. F.
Nielsen, Greg & Polansky, Joseph. Pendulum Power.
Nielsen, M. & Schmidt, E. M., eds. Automata, Languages, & Programming: Aarhus, Denmark 1982.
Nielsen, Peter. Black Man's Place in South Africa.
Nielsen, Ralph, jt. auth. see Sandrea, Rafael.
Nielsen, Sally E., ed. Investing in Old Buildings.
Nielsen, Swen C. General Organizational & Administrative Concepts for University Police.
Nielsen, Waldemar A. Africa.
Nieman, Charles. Leadership: You Can Have What It Takes.
Nieman, Linda, jt. auth. see Smith, Wm. Flint.
Nieman Reports Staff, ed. Reading, Writing & Newspapers: A Special Issue Devoted Wholly to a Discussion of the Conditions that Affect Newspaper Writing.
Niemann, Walter. Brahms. Phillips, Catherine A., tr.
Niemeier, Jean. Panama Story.
Niemi, Albert W., Jr. Understanding Economics.
--U. S. Economic History.
Niemoeller, Martin. God Is My Feurer.
--Of Guilt & Hope.
Nienaber, Jeanne, jt. auth. see Mazmanian, Daniel A.
Niepath, E. William. Leisure Leadership: Working with People in Recreation & Park Settings.
Niering, W. A. Life of the Marsh.
Nierlich, Donald P., et al, eds. Molecular Mechanisms in the Control of Gene Expression.
Nierman, Judith, ed. Edna St. Vincent Millay: A Reference Guide.
Nies, Richard C. The Security of Salvation.
Niessen, M. & Peschar, J., eds. Comparative Research on Education: Overview, Strategy & Applications in Eastern & Western Europe.
Niessen, M., et al. International Comparative Research: Social Structure & Public Institutions in Eastern & Western Europe.
Nieting, Lorenz. Lesser Festivals 4: Saints' Days & Special Occasions. Achtemeier, Elizabeth, et al, eds.
Nieting, Lorenz, tr. see Marxsen, Willi.
Nieto, M. The Titius-Bode Law of Planetary Distance.
Nietzel, Michael T., jt. auth. see Bernstein, Douglas A.
Nietzke, Ann. Windowlight: A Woman's Journal from the Edge of America.
Nietzsche, Friedrich. The Antichrist.
--Selected Letters of Freidrich Nietzsche. Middleton, Christopher, tr.
Nieuwenhuis, Paul, et al, eds. In Vivo Immunology: Histophysiology of the Lymphoid System.
Nieuwenhuysen, J. P. Competition in Australian Bookselling: Resale Price Maintenance & After.
Niewyk, Donald L. The Jews in Weimar Germany.
Nightingale, Demetra S. & Mitchell, John J. A Data Book for Welfare-Employment Programs.
Nigosian, Solomon. Islam: The Way of Submission.
Nigro, Nic, jt. auth. see Scott, Robert H.
Nihon Vogue Staff. Easy Lace.
--Fine Crochet Lace.
--Living with Beautiful Crochet.
--Summer Sweaters.
Nijssen, G. M., ed. Architecture & Models in Data Base Management: Proceedings of the IFIP-TC-2 Working Conference, 4th, Nice, January, 1977.
Niketic, S. R. The Consistent Force Field.
Nikhilananda, Swami, jt. auth. see Tapasyananda, Swami.
Nikitin, E. E. & Zuelicke, L. Selected Topics of the Theory of Chemical Elementary Processes.
Nikitine, S., jt. ed. see Haken, H.
Niklaus, Thelma, jt. auth. see Cotes, Peter.
Niklaus, Thelms, jt. auth. see Coates, Peter.
Nikol, Brent B., jt. ed. see Esch, Gerald W.
Nikolaeuskij, V. N. Mechanics of Porous & Fractured Media: W.S. Series in Theorical & Applied Mechanics.
Nikolaev, E. S., jt. auth. see Samarskii, A. A.
Nikolai, Loren A., et al. Intermediate Accounting.
--Principles of Accounting.
--Intermediate Accounting.
Nikolayev, F. A., jt. auth. see Bogdankevich, O. V.
Nikolayev, L. Afghanistan: Between the Past & the Future.
Nikol'skil, N. N. Practical Soil Science.
Nikolsky, S. M., jt. auth. see Bugrov, Y. S.
Nikolsky, S. M., jt. auth. see Bugrov, Ya S.
Nikora, Lise. European Desserts.
Niku-Lari, A., ed. Advances in Surface Treatments: Technology, Applications, Effects.
Niland, Deborah. ABC of Monsters.
Ni Laoghaire, Ida, jt. ed. see O'Brien, Michael.
Niles, Cornelia D., ed. see Smithsonian Institution, Washington, D. C. Staff.
Niles, Douglas. Escape from Castle Quarras.
Niles, John J. Singing Soldiers.
Niles, Nathan O. Plane Trigonometry.
Niles, Susan A. South American Indian Narrative Theoretical & Analytical Approaches: An Annotated Bibliography.
Nilles, Jack M., et al. The Telecommunications-Transportation Tradeoff: Options for Tomorrow.
Nilles, Nicolaus. Kalendarium Manuale Utriusque Ecclesiae Orientalis & Occidentalis.
Nilsen, Alleen, jt. auth. see Nilsen, Don L.
Nilsen, Alleen Pace & Donelson, Kenneth L. Literature for Today's Young Adults.
Nilsen, Don L. & Nilsen, Alleen. Language Play: An Introduction to Linguistics.
Nilsen, Mary Y. Tending the Family Tree: A Family-Centered, Bible-Based Experience for Church Groups.
Nilson, Bob. The Hanging Book.
Nilson, Peter. Uppsala General Catalogue of Twelve Thousand Nine Hundred & Twenty-One Galaxies.
Nilsson, Martin P. Greek Piety.
--History of Greek Religion.
Nilsson, Nils, jt. ed. see Nilsson, Sven.
Nilsson, Nils A. Art, Society, Revolution: Russia, 1917-1921.
Nilsson, Sven & Nilsson, Nils, eds. Super-Heavy Elements: Theoretical Predictions & Experimental Generation-(Proceedings of the 27th Nobel Symposium)
Nilsson, Ulf. Little Sister Rabbit. Kroupa, Melanie, ed.
Nimchuk, John, jt. ed. see Darnay, Brigitte T.
Nimkoff, Meyer, jt. auth. see Ogburn, William F.
Nimmo, W. S., jt. ed. see Prescott, L. F.
Nimoy, Leonard. You & I.
Nims, John F. The Kiss: A Jambalaya.
Nimse, Gordon. Once We Were Men.
Nin, Anais. Delta of Venus: Erotica.
--Delta of Venus: Erotica.
--The Diary of Anais Nin. Stuhlmann, Gunther, ed. Incl. Vol. 1. 1931-34; Vol. 2. 1934-39; Vol. 3. 1939-44; Vol. 4. 1944-47. HarBraceJ.
--Diary of Anais Nin.
--The Diary of Anais Nin, 1947-1955.
--The Diary of Anais Nin: 1955-1966. Stuhlmann, Gunther, ed.
--The Diary of Anais Nin: 1966-1974.
--The Early Diary of Anais Nin: Vol. IV, 1927-1931.
--The Early Diary of Anais Nin: 1920 to 1923.
--The Early Diary of Anais Nin: 1923-27.
--Linotte: The Early Diary of Anais Nin 1914-1920. Sherman, Jean, tr.
--Little Birds: Erotica.
--Little Birds: Erotica.
Nind, T. E. Principles of Oil Well Production.
Nineham, D. E. Saint Mark.
Nineham, D. E., ed. see Henderson, Ian.
Nineham, D. E., ed. see Thomas, J. Heywood.
Nineham, D. E., ed. see Towers, Bernard.
Nineham, Dennis. The Use & Abuse of the Bible.
Nineham, Dennis see McDonald, Durstan R., et al.
Nineham, Dennis E., ed. see Perkins, Robert L.
Nineham, Gillian, ed. Adventure Holidays 1984.
--Adventure Holidays 1985.
Ninemeier, Jack, jt. auth. see Zaccarelli, Herman.
Nineteenth-Century Fiction Staff. Narrative Endings: Narrative Endings.
Ninham, B. W., jt. ed. see Mahanty, J.
Ninkovich, Thomas & Vincent, Eleanor. Reunion Handbook: A Guide for Reunion Organizers.
Nipon, Pearl. Dining In - Philadelphia.
Nipp, Susan, jt. auth. see Beall, Pamela.
Nir, I., et al, eds. The Pineal Gland: Proceedings of the International Symposium, Jerusalem, Nov. 14-17, 1977.
Nirenberg, Helgard, jt. auth. see Gerlach, Wolfgang.
Nirenberg, J. How to Sell Your Ideas.
Nisbet, Brenda. Nutrition & Feeding Strategies in Protozoa.
Nisbet, Richard. Capacity of Negroes for Religious & Moral Improvement Considered.
Nisbet, Robert A., jt. ed. see Merton, Robert K.
Nisbett, Alec. Konrad Lorenz: A Bibliography.
Nisenson, Eric. Round about Midnight: A Portrait of Miles Davis.
Nisevich, N. I., jt. ed. see Marchuk, G. I.
Nish, I & Steeds, D. China, Japan, & Nineteenth Century Britain.
Nishi, Toshio. Unconditional Democracy: Education & Politics in Occupied Japan, 1945 to 1952.
Nishida, Kitaro. Art & Morality. Dilworth, D. A. & Viglielmo, V. H., trs. from Japanese.
Nishikawa, Kyotaro. Bugaku Masks. Bethe, Monica, tr.
Nishioka, Hayward. Foot Throws Karate, Judo & Self-Defense.
Nishizawa, Y., et al. Residue Reviews: Sumithion.
Niskanen, William A., et al. Tax & Expenditure Limitation by Constitutional Amendment: Four Perspectives on the California Initiative.
Nissanka, H. S. Sri Lanka's Foreign Policy: A Study in Non-Alignment.
Nissenson, Aaron. Song of Man.
Nissenson, Hugh. My Own Ground.
Nissim, Rina. Natural Healing in Gynecology: A Manual for Women.
Nissley, Julia. How to Probate an Estate: California.
Nister, Der. The Family Mashber. Wolf, Leonard, tr.
Nitchkey, Charles R. Gettysburg: Eighteen Sixty-Three & Today.
Nitecki, Joseph Z. OCLC in Retrospect.
Nitecki, Z. & Robinson, C., eds. Global Theory of Dynamical Systems: Proceedings.
Nitecki, Zbigniew H., jt. auth. see Guterman, Martin M.
Nitka, Louis. Ski with Nitka.
Nitko, Anthony J., jt. auth. see Lindvall, C. Mauritz.
Nitsch, Friedrich A. A General & Introductory View of Professor Kant's Principles. Wellek, Rene, ed.
Niven, David. Bring on the Empty Horses.
Niven, Larry. The Smoke Ring.
Niven, Larry & Pournelle, Jerry. Inferno.
--The Mote in God's Eye.
Nivens, Beatryce. Black Woman's Career Guide.
Niver, Kemp R. Motion Pictures from the Library of Congress Paper Print Collection, 1894-1912.
Nix, John, jt. auth. see Butterworth, Bill.
Nixon, jt. auth. see Spitz.
Nixon, Allan. Shadow of a Man.
Nixon, D. W., jt. ed. see Ross, N. W.
Nixon, George. People, Evaluation & Achievement.
Nixon, Gilbert. The World of Bees.
Nixon, Hershell H. & Lowery, Joan. Oil & Gas: From Fossils to Fuel.
Nixon, Hershell H. & Nixon, Joan L. Volcanoes: Nature's Fireworks.
Nixon, Joan L. The Boy Who Could Find Anything.
--The Boy Who Could Find Anything.
--Gloria Chipmunk, Star!
--The Kidnapping of Christina Lattimore.
--Muffie Mouse & the Busy Birthday.
--The Mysterious Prowler.
--The Mysterious Prowler.
--The Seance.
Nixon, Joan L., jt. auth. see Nixon, Hershell H.
Nixon, John & Jewett, Ann. Introduction to Physical Education.
Nixon, Mary & Taft, Ronald. Psychology in Australia.
Nixon, P. H. People & the Sea.
Nixon, R. E. Understanding the New Testament: John.
Nixon, Richard. No More Vietnams.
--No More Vietnams.
Nixon, Robert. Practical Business Communications.
Niyasi, S. At the Foot of Blue Mountains: Stories by Tajik Authors.
Nizami. Layla & Majnun. Gelpke, R., ed. & tr. from Persian.
Nizel, Abraham E. Nutrition in Preventive Dentistry: Science & Practice.
Nizza, Marco Da see Marco Da Nizza.
Njaa, L. Readings in Educational Psychology.
Njoku, B. C., jt. auth. see Ridge, G. R.
Njoku, John E. The Dawn of African Women.
Njus, Joel M., tr. see Wisloff, Hans E.
Nketia, J. H. Kwabena. African Music in Ghana.
Nkrumah, Kwame. Neo-Colonialism: The Last Stage of Imperialism.
NLG. Report on Nicaragua.
NLG Delegation. Democracy in Nicaragua: An Investigation of Political Pluralism.
No-Load Fund Investor Staff. The Handbook for No-Load Fund Investors.
Noack, Ferdinand & Lehmann-Hartleben, Karl. Baugeschichtliche Untersuchungen am Stadtrand von Pompeji.
Noad, Frederick M. The Guitar Songbook.
Noakes, David, tr. see Hodeir, Andre.
Noakes, J., jt. ed. see Pridham, G.
Noakes, Vivian. Edward Lear: Eighteen Twelve to Eighteen Eighty-Eight.
Noam, Eli M., ed. Telecommunications: Today & Tomorrow.
Noback, Charles R., ed. Sensory Systems of Primates.
Nobari, Nuchine. Books & Periodicals.
Nobay, A. R., jt. ed. see Artis, Michael J.
Nobel Foundation. Nobel Prize Lectures in Chemistry, 1901-1970. Incl. Vol. 1. 1901-1921; Vol. 2. 1922-1941; Vol. 3. 1942-1962; Vol. 4. 1963-1970. Elsevier.
Nobel, Marty, jt. auth. see Dykstra, Len.
Noble. The Cardiac Cycle.
Noble, A. Biophysics Progression: Some Physical, Mathematical & Logical Aspects.
Noble, Allen G., jt. ed. see Ma, Laurence J.
Noble, Andrew, ed. Edwin Muir: Uncollected Scottish Criticism.
Noble, Ben & Daniel, James W. Applied Linear Algebra.
Noble, Charles R., III, jt. auth. see Markowitz, Randi.
Noble, D. Progress in Biophysics & Molecular Biology.
--Progress in Biophysics & Molecular Biology.
Noble, D. & Blundell, T. L. Progress in Biophysics & Molecular Biology.
--Progress in Biophysics & Molecular Biology.
Noble, D. & Blundell, T. L., eds. Progress in Biophysics & Molecular Biology.
--Progress in Biophysics & Molecular Biology.

Authors

--Progress in Biophysics & Molecular Biology.
--Progress in Biophysics & Molecular Biology.
--Progress in Biophysics & Molecular Biology.
--Progress in Biophysics & Molecular Biology.
--Progress in Biophysics & Molecular Biology.
Noble, David, ed. see Que Corporation.
Noble, David W., et al. Twentieth Century Limited: A History of Recent America.
Noble, Elizabeth. Essential Exercises for the Childbearing Year: A Guide to Health & Comfort Before & After Your Baby Is Born.
Noble, Elmer R. & Noble, Glenn A. Parasitology: The Biology of Animal Parasites.
Noble, Glenn A., jt. auth. see Noble, Elmer R.
Noble, Ian, tr. see Pommaret-Imaeda, Francoise & Imaeda, Yoshiro.
Noble, Iris. Firebrand for Justice: A Biography of Louis Dembitz Brandeis.
--Interpol: International Crime Fighter.
Noble, John. Activities & Spaces: Dimensional Data for Housing Design.
Noble, John H., ed. see Adams, Robert Lang, & Associates Staff.
Noble, John H., et al, eds. Groping Through the Maze: Foreign Experience Applied to the U. S. Problem of Coordinating Development Controls.
Noble, June. Two Homes for Lynn.
Noble, M. E., jt. auth. see Coomaraswamy, A. K.
Noble, Richmond. Shakespeare's Biblical Knowledge & Use of the Book of Common Prayer.
Noble, Shlomo, tr. see Weinreich, Max.
Noble, Valerie. Hawaiian Prophet: Alexander Hume Ford.
Noble, Vicente N., ed. Readings & Applications in School Counseling.
Noble, W. G. The Assessment of Hearing Loss & Handicap in Adults.
Nochlin, Linda. Gustave Courbet: a Study of Style & Society.
Nock, O. S. GWR Stars Castle & Kings.
--The Last Years of British Railways Steam: Reflections Ten Years After.
--The Southern King Arthur Family.
--Tales of the Great Western.
Noe, jt. auth. see Mondy.
Noe, Robert M., jt. auth. see Mondy, R. Wayne.
Noel, ed. Knight's Modern Seamanship.
Noel, Atanielle A. The Duchess of Kneedeep.
--Murder on Usher's Planet.
Noel, Dix W. & Phillips, Jerry J. Products Liability in a Nutshell.
Noel, Dix W., et al. Cases & Materials on Torts & Related Law.
Noel, Frances. Echoes.
Noel, John V., Jr. & Bassett, Frank E. Knight's Modern Seamanship.
Noel, John V., Jr. & Beach, Edward L. Naval Terms Dictionary.
Noel, Lee, Jr., jt. auth. see Bateman, Selby.
Noel, Ruth S. Mythology of Middle Earth.
--The Mythology of Middle Earth.
Noel-Baker, Lord. The First World Disarmament: And Why It Failed.
Noel-Baker, Philip J. Arms Race: A Programme for World Disarmament.
Noel-Hume, Ivor. Historical Archaeology.
Noether, Gottfried E. Introduction to Statistics: A Nonparametric Approach.
Noethiger, R., jt. auth. see Ursprung, H.
Noffsinger, Ella M., jt. auth. see Allen, M. W.
Noga, H. Ayisha.
Nogas, G. D. & Bolitho, A. R. Start English for Science.
Nogee, Joseph L. & Donaldson, Robert H. Soviet Foreign Policy Since World War II.
--Soviet Foreign Policy since World War II.
Nogent, Guibert De see De Nogent, Guibert.
Noggle, Burl. Teapot Dome: Oil & Politics in the 1920's.
Noggle, Joseph H. Physical Chemistry.
Noggle, Joseph H. & Schirmer, Richard E. Nuclear Overhauser Effect: Chemical Applications.
Nogotov. Applications of Numerical Heat Transfer.
Nogotov, E. F. Applications of Numerical Methods to Heat Transfer.
Nogradi, M. Stereochemistry: Basic Concepts & Applications.
Noguchi, Thomas T. Coroner at Large.
Noguchi, Thomas T. & DiMona, Joseph. Coroner.
Nohl, Louis. Life of Liszt.
Nokes, M. C. Radioactivity Measuring Instruments.
Nolan, Christopher. Dam-Burst of Dreams.
Nolan, Daniel J. Radiological Atlas of Gastrointestinal Disease.
Nolan, David. Fifty Feet in Paradise: The Booming of Florida.
Nolan, Frederick, ed. Jay J. Armes: Investigator.
Nolan, John. Management Audit: Maximizing Your Company's Efficiency & Effectiveness.
Nolan, John T., et al. Used Oil: Disposal Options, Management Practices & Potential Liability.
Nolan, Michael, jt. auth. see Tucker, Ivan.
Nolan, Robert E., et al. Improving Productivity Through Advanced Office Controls.
Nolan, William F. The Black Mask Boys: Masters in the Hard-Boiled School of Detective Fiction.
Nolan, William F., ed. The Black Mask Boys.
--Max Brand's Best Western Short Stories.
Noland, Ronald G., et al. An Introduction to Elementary Reading: Selected Materials. Wright, Jone P. & Allen, Elizabeth, eds.
Noll, Edward M. Landmobile & Marine Radio Technology Handbook.
Noll, James W. Taking Sides: Clashing Views on Controversial Educational Issues.
--Taking Sides: Clashing Views on Controversial Educational Issues.
Noll, Paul & Murach, Mike. How to Evaluate & Improve Your COBOL Programming Methods. Taylor, Judy, ed.
Noll, Victor H., et al. Introduction to Educational Measurement.
Noll, Victor H., et al, eds. Introductory Readings in Educational Measurement.
Noll, W., et al. Continuum Theory of Inhomogeneities in Simple Bodies: A Reprint of Six Memoirs.
Nollau, Gunther. International Communism & World Revolution: History & Methods.
Nolle, Richard. Astrology Software Buyer's Guide.
Nollen, Stanley D. & Martin, Virginia H. Alternative Work Schedules, Pts. 2 & 3: Permanent Part-Time & the Compressed Workweek.
Nollen, Stanley D., et al. New Work Schedules in Practice.
Noller, Patricia, jt. auth. see Callan, Victor.
Nolling, Wilhelm, et al. Three Europeans Look at America: Welfare Policy, Social Trends & Foreign Affairs.
Nolte, Ernst. Marxism, Fascism, Cold War: Essays & Lectures 1974-1976. Krader, Lawrence, tr. from Ger.
Nolte, John. The Human Brain: An Introduction to Its Functional Anatomy.
Nolte, William A. Oral Microbiology: With Basic Microbiology & Immunology.
Nomizu, Katsumi. Fundamentals of Linear Algebra.
Non-Violent Revolution Committee. Alternative.
Nonet, Philippe, jt. auth. see Selznick, Philip.
Nonis, U. Mushrooms & Toadstools: A Colour Field Guide.
Nonken, Pam, et al. Milwaukee & More. McCoy, Sue W., ed.
Nonoyama, M., et al. Burkitt's Disease: Virology & Other Basic Studies.
Nonte, George C. Combat Handguns.
--Handgun Competition.
Nonweiler, Barry. That Other Realm of Freedom.
Noonan, Eileen. Books for Catholic Elementary Schools.
Noonan, Eileen F., compiled by. Books for Religious Education in Catholic Secondary Schools.
Noonan, Ellen. Counselling Young People.
Noonan, Gerald R. South American Species of the Subgenus Anistosarsus Chaudoir (Genus Notiobia Party: Carabidae: Coleoptera) Part II: Evolution & Biogeography.
--South American Species of the Subgenus "Anistosarsus" Chaudoir (Genus "Notiobia" Party-Carabidae-Coleoptera) Part I: Taxonomy & Natural History.
Noonan, John F. The Year Boston Won the Pennant.
Noonan, Karen A. Coping with Illness.
Noonan, Larry. The Basic BASIC-English Dictionary: For the Apple, IBM-PC, Commodore 64, VIC-20, Atari, TRS-80, TRS-80 Color Computer, TI 99-4A, PET & Timex-Sinclair.
Noonan, Michael. A Different Drummer: The Story of E. J. Banfield, the Beachcomber of Dunk Island.
Noor, A. K. & McComb, H. G., Jr. Trends in Computerized Structural Analysis & Synthesis.
Noor, A. K. & Housner, J. M., eds. Advances & Trends in Structural & Solid Mechanics: Proceedings of the Symposium, Washington D.C., October 4-7, 1982.
Noorbergen, Rene. Ellen G. White: Prophet of Destiny.
Noord, Glenn Van, jt. auth. see Hendricks, William C.
Noordewier, Helen C. Uncle Josh Stories.
Noose, Theodore. Hollywood Film Acting.
Nooteboom, S. G., ed. see Dynamic Aspects of Speech Perception Symposium Staff.
Nopany, Nandini & Lal, P., eds. Twenty-Four Stories by Premchand.
Nora, James J. The Whole Heart Book.
Nora, James J. & Fraser, F. Clark. Medical Genetics: Principles & Practice.
Nora, Paul F., ed. Operative Surgery: Principles & Techniques.
Norback, Craig, jt. auth. see Lachenbruch, David.
Norback, Craig T. The Puzzle King's Baffler.
Norback, Craig T. & Norback, Peter. The Must Words: The Six Thousand Most Important Words for a Successful & Profitable Vocabulary.
Norback, Craig T. & Asthma & Allergy Foundation of America Staff, eds. The Allergy Encyclopedia.
Norback, Judith, ed. Sourcebook of Aid for the Mentally & Physically Handicapped.
Norback, Judith & Weitz, Patricia, eds. Sourcebook of Sex & Sex Therapy.
Norback, Peter, jt. auth. see Norback, Craig T.
Norbert. Das Leben des Bischofs Benno der Zweiter von Osnabruck. Bd. with Ausfuehrliches Namenregister und Sachregister Mit Genauem Inhalsverzejchnis der Seither Erschienene Baende 1-90. Johnson Repr.
Norbu, Namkhai. The Crystal & the Way of Light: Meditation, Contemplation & Self Liberation. Shane, John, ed.
Norbu, Thubten Jigme, tr. see Kaufmann, Walter.
Norbu, Tsampa Yeshe. Rasa Tantra: Blood Marriage, The Sacred Initiation, A Marriage of the Faiths of East & West.
Norbury, James. Traditional Knitting Patterns from Scandinavia, the British Isles, France, Italy & Other European Countries.
Norby, J. G., jt. ed. see Skou, J. C.
Norbye, Jan. Automotive Fuel Injection Systems: A Technical Guide.
Norcross, Carl. Townhouses & Condominiums: Residents' Likes & Dislikes.
Norcross, John A. & Tracy, Joseph P. Doc Flighty.
Nordal, J. & Kristinsson, V., eds. Iceland, Eighteen Seventy Four to Nineteen Seventy-Four: A Handbook.
Nordanberg, T. Cataclysm as Catalyst: The Theme of War in William Faulkner's Fiction.
Nordberg, G. F. Effects & Dose Response Relationships of Toxic Metals.
Nordberg, Robert B. Coping with Changing Values.
Norden, Hugo. Foundation Studies in Fugue.
--Fundamental Harmony.
--Project Studies in Fugue.
Nordenfalk, Carl. The Life & Work of Vincent Van Gogh.
Nordhoff, Charles & Hall, James N. Men Against the Sea.
Nordin, Margareta C., jt. ed. see Ferrara, Peter L.
Nording, Carl & Osterman, Jonny. Physics Handbook: Elementary Constants & Units, Tables, Formulae & Diagrams & Mathematical Formulae.
Nordon, Hugo, tr. Chorale Harmonization in the Church Modes.
Nordqvist, Sven. Willie in the Big World: An Adventure with Numbers.
Nordstrom, Lois, ed. see Blake School Parent Association Cookbook Staff.
Nordstrom, O., ed. The Dynamics of Vehicles on Roads Tracks: Proceedings of the Ninth IAVSD Symposium Held at the Linkoping University, Linoping, Sweden, June 24-29, 1985.
Nordstrom, Richard D. Introduction to Selling. An Experiential Approach to Skill Development.
Nordtvedt, Matilda & Steinkuehler, Pearl. Showers of Blessing.
Nordyke, Cyndy, jt. auth. see Nordyke, Spencer.
Nordyke, Spencer. Tidal Wave.
Nordyke, Spencer & Nordyke, Cyndy. Essentials of Basic Youth Ministry.
--Youth WAV Curriculum.
Norenberg, W. & Weidenmuller, H. A. Introduction to the Theory of Heavy-Ion Collisions.
Norfolk, Donald. The Habits of Health.
Norgren, William, et al, eds. What Can We Share? A Lutheran-Episcopal Resource & Study Guide.
Norgren, William A., ed. Forum: Religious Faith Speaks to American Issues.
Noriega, L. A. De see De Noriega, L. A. & Leach, F.
Norkin, Israel. Mysterious Signs in the Sky.
Norlin, George. A Voice from Colorado's Past for the Present: Selected Writings of George Norlin. Ellsworth, Ralph, ed.
Norling, Richard. Using Macintosh BASIC.
Norlund, P. Viking Settlers in Greenland & Their Descendants During Five Hundred Years.
Norman, A. V. & Pottinger, Don. English Weapons & Warfare: 1449-1660.
Norman, Anthony W. Vitamin D: The Calcium Homeostatic Hormone.
Norman, Dorothy. Alfred Stieglitz: An American Seer.
--Encounters: A Memoir.
Norman, Dorothy & Stieglitz, Alfred, photos by. Beyond a Portrait. Holborn, Mark.
Norman, Elizabeth. Castle Cloud.
--If the Reaper Ride.
Norman, Geoffrey. Alabama Showdown: The Football Rivalry Between Auburn & Alabama.
--Midnight Water.
Norman, Geoffrey A., ed. Soybean Physiology, Agronomy, & Utilization.
Norman, George. Spatial Pricing & Differentiated Markets.
Norman, Gurney. Kinfolks: The Wilgus Stories.
Norman, Hilary. In Love & Friendship.
Norman, Howard. The Northern Lights.
Norman, Howard, tr. Where the Chill Came From: Cree Windigo Tales & Journeys.
Norman, Margaret, jt. auth. see Curran, Susan.
Norman, Michael, jt. auth. see Scott, Beth.
Norman, Philip. London Signs & Inscriptions.
--The Skater's Waltz: A Novel.
--Symphony for the Devil: The Rolling Stones Story.
Norman, Richard & Sayers, Sean. Hegel, Marx & Dialectic: A Debate.
Norman, Ruth. Future World.
--Lysistratha, Empress of the Planet Lustra.
--Preparation for the Landing.
--Science, Politics & the Great Deception, Religion.
Norman, Ruth & Spaegel, Charles. Scarpa, Planet of the Mindless Ones.
Norman, Theodore. An Outstretched Arm: The History of the Jewish Colonization Association.
Norman, Trevor R., jt. ed. see Burrows, Graham D.
Normanby, ed. National Art-Collections Fund Review 1985.
--National Art-Collections Fund Review 1984.
Norpoth, K. H. & Garner, R. C., eds. Short-Term Mutagenicity Test Systems for Detecting Carcinogens.
Norrie, D. H. & De Vries, G. An Introduction to Finite Element Analysis.
Norrie, Douglas H. & DeVries, Gerard, eds. The Finite Element Method: Fundamentals & Applications.
Norrie, Ian, ed. Mumby's Publishing & Bookselling in the 20th Century.
Norris, A. H., et al. The Central Nervous System & Aging.
Norris, Carolyn, et al. Jean's Christmas Stocking: Storybook for Young Deaf Children.
Norris, Carolyn B. Island of Silence.
Norris, D. E., et al. Microcomputers in Clinical Practice.
Norris, Docia W. Religious Science for Youth.
Norris, Frank. A Novelist in the Making: A Collection of Student Themes & the Novels Blix & Vandover & the Brute. Hart, James D., ed.
Norris, Geoffrey. Rakhmaninov.
Norris, Gunilla. Good Morrow.
Norris, Gunilla B. Take My Waking Slow.
Norris, H. Thomas, ed. Pathology of the Colon, Small Intestine, & Anus.
Norris, J. R. & Ribbons, D. W. Methods in Microbiology.
Norris, J. R. & Ribbons, D. W., eds. Methods in Microbiology.
Norris, James E. & Bair, Fred. A Practical Business & Tax Guide for the Craftsperson.
Norris, Jim. Los Olivos: California Crossroad.
Norris, Kenneth S., ed. Whales, Dolphins, & Porpoises.
Norris, Margot C. The Decentered Universe of Finnegans Wake: A Structuralist Analysis.
Norris, Marilyn W. Caring for Kids.
Norris, S. H. Complications of Hand Surgery.
Norris, Willa. The Career Information Service.
Norris, William. The Unsafe Sky.
--Willful Misconduct: The Story of the Crash of Pan American Flight 806 & of What Happened Afterward.
Norster, E. R. Combustion & Heat Transfer in Gas Turbine Systems.
Norsworthy, Kent & Robinson, William. David & Goliath: The U. S. War Against Nicaragua.
Nortex Press Staff, ed. see Sanders, Ottys & Sanders, Ruth.
North, A. M., jt. ed. see Ledwith, A.
North American Conference on Modernization of Land Data Systems, 2nd, Washington, DC, 1978. Land Data Systems Now: Proceedings of the North American Conference on Modernization of Land Data Systems, 2nd, Washington, D. C., 1978.
North American Symposium on Family Practice Staff. The Many Dimensions of Family Practice: Proceedings.
North, Barbara, tr. see Duverger, Maurice.
North Carolina State University, School of Design, Students & Wurman, Richard S. Cities: Comparisons of Form & Scale.
North, Carolyn. The Musicians & the Servants.
North Central Regional Center for Rural Development Staff. Communities Left Behind: Alternatives for Development.
--Rural Industrialization: Problems & Potentials.
North, Eric M. The Book of a Thousand Tongues.
North, Freddie. Aunt Agatha Plays Tournament Bridge.
North, Gary. Unconditional Surrender: God's Program for Victory.
North, Gary, ed. Tactics of Christian Resistance.
North, H., jt. ed. see Noth.
North, Hallie B. Commercial Food Patents, U. S. Nineteen Seventy-Nine.
North, Helen. From Myth to Icon: Reflections of Greek Ethical Doctrine in Literature & Art.

North, Helen F., ed. Interpretations of Plato: A Swarthmore Symposium.
North, Ira. Balance, A Tried & Tested Formula for Church Growth.
North, R. W. Easing into the Year Two Thousand: One-Liners for a Cartoonist's Pen.
North, Rachel. Flower of Love.
North, Robert, tr. see Duverger, Maurice.
North, Sterling. Captured by the Mohawks.
--Rascal.
North Texas State University Faculty of Computer Science Staff. Personal-Professional Computers: How Can They Help You?
North, W., ed. see Society of Manufacturing Engineers Staff.
Northall, G. F. English Folk-Rhymes: A Collection of Traditional Verses Relating to Places & Persons, Customs, Superstitions, Etc.
Northam, Ray M. Urban Geography.
Northcott, Cecil. Bible Encyclopedia for Children.
--People of the Bible.
Northcutt, Wayne. The French Socialist & Communist Party under the Fifth Republic, 1958-1981: From Opposition to Power.
Northeast Regional Agricultural Engineering Service Staff, jt. auth. see Midwest Plan Service Engineers Staff.
Northeast Regional Coastal Information Center Staff, jt. auth. see Marine Aquaculture Association Staff.
Northeastern University, Dodge Library, Boston Staff. Selective Bibliography in Science & Engineering.
Northouse, Cameron & Walsh, Thomas P. John Osborne: A Reference Guide.
Northouse, Cameron, jt. auth. see Walsh, Thomas P.
Northrop, Eugene P. Riddles in Mathematics: A Book of Paradoxes.
Northrop, Filmer S. The Complexity of Legal & Ethical Experience: Studies in the Method of Normative Subjects.
Northrop, Grace Emmert. Fantasy in Verse.
Northrup, Clyde J., Jr., et al, eds. Scientific Basis for Nuclear Waste Management.
Northrup, Herbert R. & Rowan, Richard L., eds. Employee Relations & Regulation in the 80's.
North Seymour, Whitney see Seymour, Whitney N., Jr.
Northup, George T., ed. Ten Spanish Farces of the Sixteenth, Seventeenth & Eighteenth Centuries.
Northwest Regional Educational Laboratory Staff. Introduction to Data Processing.
--Parents in Reading: Parents' Booklet Spanish-English Version.
Northwest Women's Law Center Staff, ed. Women & the Law in Washington State.
Northwestern University Staff. Catalog of the Melville J. Herskovits Library of African Studies, Northwestern University, & Africana in Selected Libraries, Evanston.
--Catalog of the Transportation Center Library, Northwestern University.
--Joint Acquisitions List of Africana: 1978.
Northwood, Thomas D., ed. Architectural Acoustics.
Norton, A. Hollis. How to Make It When You're Cash Poor.
Norton, Alice, ed. Public Relations Information Sources.
Norton, Aloysius A. Theodore Roosevelt.
Norton, Andre. Android at Arms.
--At Swords' Points.
--The Beast Master.
--Operation Time Search.
--Outside.
--Sea Siege.
--Shadow Hawk.
--Stand & Deliver.
--Stand to Horse.
--Star Guard.
--Star Rangers.
--Star Rangers.
--Ten Mile Treasure.
--Warlock of the Witch World.
--Witch World.
Norton, Andre & Madlee, Dorothy. Star Ka'ats & the Winged Warriors.
Norton, Andre & Miller, Phyllis. House of Shadows.
Norton, Andre, ed. Tales of the Witchworld.
Norton, Bruce F., ed. Inside Congress.
Norton, Bryan, ed. see AIME Staff.
Norton, C. McKim, jt. auth. see Jones, Russell K.
Norton, Charles A. Writing Tom Sawyer: The Adventures of a Classic.
Norton, D. Hospitals & the Long-Stay Patient.
Norton, D. F. & Capaldi, N., eds. McGill Hume Studies.
Norton, David F. David Hume: Common Sense Moralist, Sceptical Metaphysician.
Norton, L. A., jt. auth. see Schultz, D. O.
Norton, Lucy, tr. see Delacroix, Eugene.
Norton, M. Herter, tr. see Wiora, Walter.
Norton, Mary. Adventures of the Borrowers.
--Are All the Giants Dead?
--Bed-Knob & Broomstick.
Norton, Paul F. Latrobe, Jefferson, & the National Capitol.
Norton, Paul F. see O'Neal, William B.
Norton, Peter. The Peter Norton Programmer's Guide to the IBM PC: The Ultimate Reference Guide to the Entire Family of IBM Personal Computers.
Norton (R. W.) Art Gallery Staff. Loren D. Adams: A Retrospective Exhibition.
Norton Simon Museum Staff. Degas in Motion.
Norton, T. A. Synopsis of Biological Data on Saccorhiza Polyschides.
Norton, Thomas & Patterson, Jerry. Living It Up: A Guide to the Named Apartment Houses of New York.
Norton, Thomas A. Thieves.
Norton, Wesley. Religious Newspapers in the Old Northwest to 1861: A History, Bibliography, & Record of Opinion.
Norton, William, Jr. Annual Survey of Bankruptcy Law: 1979-1984.
Norton-Smith, Richard. Thomas E. Dewey & His Times.
Norusis, Marija, jt. auth. see SPSS, Inc. Staff.
Norusis, Marija J. The SPSS Guide to Data Analysis.
--SPSS-X Advanced Statistical Guide.
--SPSS-X Introducing Statistics Guide.
Norvell, M., ed. see Annual Hormone Research Symposium Staff.
Norvell, M. J., ed. see Annual Hormone Research Symposium Staff.
Norweb, Emery M. English Gold Coins: Ancient to Modern Times.
Norwegian Institute of Rock Schach Blasting Techniques Staff. Rock Bolting: A Practical Handbook Describing All Aspects of Rock Bolts & Their Application in Rock Engineering.
Norwick, Kenneth H. Molecular Dynamics in Biosystems.
Norwood, Christopher. How to Avoid a Cesarean Section.
--How to Avoid a Cesarean Section.
Norwood, Warren C. Final Command.
--Polar Fleet.
Nory, Jean-Loup, jt. auth. see Martinez, Alberto.
Noshiro, K., jt. auth. see Sario, L.
Nosow, Sigmund & Clark, Frederick R. Goals, Aims, Objectives: Duquesne University: a Case Study.
Nossal, G. J. & Ada, G. L. Antigens, Lymphoid Cells & the Immune Response.
Nossiter, Bernard. Britain, a Future That Works.
Nostlinger, Christine. Konrad. Bell, Anthea, tr.
--Luke & Angela. Bell, Anthea, tr.
--Marrying Off Mother. Bell, Anthea, tr.
Nostrand, A. D. Van see Van Nostrand, A. D., et al.
Notarianni, Frederick M. The Making of a Don.
Note, Gene Van see Van Note, Gene.
Notestein, Lucy L. Wooster of the Middle West.
--Wooster of the Middle West.
Noth & North, H., eds. Boron Chemistry-3.
Noth, Martin. The Deuteronomistic History.
--The Laws in the Pentateuch.
--Leviticus: A Commentary.
--Numbers: A Commentary. Martin, James D., tr.
Nothim, J. C. Mayflower.
Notkins, Abner L., ed. Viral Immunology & Immunopathology.
Notman, Larry. Advertising Layouts: Ad Kit 2.
Noton, A. R. Introduction to Variational Methods in Control Engineering.
Noton, Thomas A. Writers Inspirational Market News.
Nott, C. S., tr. see Attar, Farid Ud-Din.
Nott, S. C., ed. The Mahabharata.
Nott, Wanda L., jt. ed. see Hitchcock, Arthur A.
Nottebohm, Gustav. Beethoveniana: Aufsaetze und Mitteilungen.
Nottingham, Carolyn W. & Hannah, Evelyn. The Early History of Upson County, Georgia.
Nottingham, Elizabeth K. Religion: A Sociological View.
Not-Twain, Mark & Clark, Kent. Totally Outrageous Bumper-Snickers.
Noujaim, A. A., et al, eds. Liquid Scintillation: Science & Technology.
Nourse, Alan E. The Elk Hunt.
--Fractures, Dislocations & Sprains.
Nourse, Joan T. Quick & Easy Monarch Notes on Miller's Death of a Salesman.
Nova, Craig. The Geek.
--The Good Son.
--Turkey Hash.
Novack, George, et al. The First Three Internationals: Their History & Lessons.
Novak, Arne. Czech Literature. Harkins, W. E., ed.
Novak, Barbara. Lee Krasner, Solstice.
Novak, Elaine. Styles of Acting: A Scenebook for the Advanced Acting Student.
Novak, J. & Binder, R. Slovak-English, English-Slovak Concise Technical Dictionary.
Novak, J., ed. see General Topology & Its Relations to Modern Analysis & Algebra Symposium Staff.
Novak, J. Vladimir. Insect Hormones.
Novak, Jan. The Willys Dream Kit.
Novak, Joseph V. Reflections.
Novak, Michael. Confession of a Catholic.
--Freedom with Justice: Catholic Social Thought & Liberal Institutions.
--The Spirit of Democratic Capitalism.
Novak, Stephen R. Accounting Desk Book.
--Field Auditor's Manual & Guide.
Novak, T., jt. ed. see Humphreys, K. K.
Novak, W. J., jt. auth. see McPartland, Joseph F.
Novak, William, jt. auth. see Schmertz, Herbert.
Novakovic, L. The Pseudo-Spin Method in Magnetism & Ferroelectricity.
Novalis, pseud. Hymns to the Night. Higgins, Dick, tr. from Ger.
Novallo, Annette, jt. ed. see Lucas, Amy.
Novelli, Luca. My First Book About BASIC. Parma-Veigel, Laura, tr. from Ital.
--My First Book about Computers. Parma-Veigel, Laura, tr. from Ital.
--My First Computer Dictionary. Parma-Veigel, Laura, tr. from Ital.
Novellino, Peter. Automotive Shop Safety.
Novick, A., jt. auth. see Griffin, Donald R.
Novick, Marian. At Her Age.
--At Her Age.
Novick, Melvin R., jt. auth. see Lord, Frederic M.
Novicow, Jacques. Luttes entre les Societies Humaines et Leurs Phases Successives.
--War & Its Alleged Benefits.
Novik, I. Society & Nature.
Novik, Jack, jt. auth. see Hayden, Trudy.
Novik, Mary. Robert Creeley: An Inventory.
--Robert Creeley: An Inventory 1945-1970.
Novikoff, Harold, jt. auth. see Practising Law Institute Staff.
Novikov, V. Artistic Truth & Dialectics of Creative Work.
Novitch, Miriam, ed. Sobibor: Martyrdom & Revolt.
Novitski, Edward. Human Genetics.
Novoselov, S. P. Problems of the Communist Movement.
Novosti Press Editors. Soviet Almanac.
Novozhilov, Yuri V. Introduction to Elementary Particle Theory. Rosner, Jonathon L., tr.
Nowacki, E. K., jt. auth. see Waller, G. R.
Nowacki, W., ed. see CISM (International Center for Mechanical Sciences, Department of Mechanics of Solids Staff.
Nowak, C. M. Czechoslovak-Polish Relations 1918-1939: A Selected & Annotated Bibliography.
Nowak, Frank. Medieval Slavdom & the Rise of Russia.
Nowak, Jan. Courier from Warsaw.
Nowak, John & Rotunda, Ronald. Treatise on Constitutional Law, 1987: Substance & Procedure.
Nowak, John E., et al. Constitutional Law: 1982 Pocket Part.
Nowak, Stephen F. & Muswick, Gary J. Getting the Most from Your Pocket Computer.
Nowell, Charles E. The Great Discoveries & the First Colonial Empires.
Nowell, Henry F. Metaphysical Healing: Principles & Practice.
Nowicki, Alexander G. Ecuador: Development Problems & Prospects.
Nowikoff, Harold S. & Susko, A. Richard. ERISA & Bankruptcy.
Nowinski, W. W. & Goss, R. J., eds. Compensatory Renal Hypertrophy.
Nowinson, Marie. Winds of Change.
Nowlan, Kevin B. The Politics of Repeal.
Nowlan, Robert A. The College of Trivial Knowledge.
--The College of Trivial Knowledge.
Nowlis, Elizabeth A., jt. auth. see Ellis, Janice R.
Nowotny, A., ed. Cellular Antigens.
Nowotny, Robert A. The Way of All Flesh Tones: A History of Color Motion Picture Processes, 1895-1929. Jowett, Garth S., ed.
Noyce, Gaylord. The Art of Pastoral Conversation.
Noyce, Gaylord B. Survival & Mission for the City Church.
Noyelle, Thierry J. & Stanback, Thomas M., Jr. The Economic Transformation of American Cities.
Noyes, Ethel J. Women of the Mayflower & Women of Plymouth Colony.
Noyes, Florence, tr. see Krasinski, Zygmunt.
Noyes, George R., ed. see Dryden, John.
Noyes, George R., ed. see Krasinski, Zygmunt.
Noyes, George W., ed. John Humphrey Noyes: The Putney Community.
Noyes, Nell B. Your Future As a Secretary.
Noyes, Stanley. Faces & Spirits.
Noyle, Ken. Gone Tomorrow: Zen Inspired Poetry.
Nozaki, H., ed. Current Trends in Organic Synthesis: Proceedings of the Fourth International Conference on Organic Synthesis, Tokyo, Japan, August 22-27, 1982.
Nozick, Martin, ed. see Unamuno, M. De.
Ntiri, Daphne W., ed. One Is Not a Woman, One Becomes: The African Woman in a Transitional Society.
Nu-West Development Corporation Ltd. Ardrossan, County of Strathcona, Alberta, Canada.
Nuccio, Richard & McBride, Kelly A. What's Wrong, Who's Right in Central America: A Citizen's Guide.
Nuclear & Alternative Energy Systems Committee, Consumption, Location & Occupational Patterns Resource Group Synthesis Panel. Energy Choices in a Democratic Society.
Nuclear Safety Associates Staff. De Minimis Concentrations of Radionuclides in Solid Wastes (AIF-NESP-016)
Nuclear Safety Associates Staff & Impell Corporation Staff. Methodologies for Classification of Low-Level Radioactive Wastes from Nuclear Power Plants: AIF-NESP-027.
Nudel, Adele. For the Woman over Fifty.
--For the Woman over Fifty: A Practical Guide for a Full & Vital Life.
Nudelman, S. & Mitra, S. S., eds. Optical Properties of Solids.
Nuechterlein, Donald E. Iceland: Reluctant Ally.
Nueve, Milo M. Identifying American Furniture.
Nufer, Harold F. The Electoral College Abolition or Reform: Views of the U. S. Congress.
--Micronesia under American Rule: An Evaluation of the Strategic Trusteeship 1947-77.
Nuffield Foundation Staff. Nuffield Maths Four: Math Five-Eleven. Albany, Eric A., ed.
--Nuffield Maths Three: Maths Five to Eleven. Albany, Eric A., ed.
Nugent, Anne. Swan Lake.
Nugent, Elizabeth. Monarch Notes on Shakespeare's Richard Third.
Nugent, Jean. Prince Charles: England's Future King.
Nugent, Tom. Death at Buffalo Creek.
Nugent, Walter T. Money Question During Reconstruction.
Nukhovich, E. International Monopolies & the Developing Countries.
Null, Gary & Null, Steve. The Complete Handbook of Nutrition.
Null, Steve, jt. auth. see Null, Gary.
Nulte, James, jt. auth. see Beatty, Michael.
Num, Richard, jt. auth. see Hawthorne, Maurice.
Numerof, Rita E. The Practice of Management for Health Care Professionals.
Numeroff, Laura J. Beatrice Doesn't Want to.
Numrich, Charles H. For All Seasons.
Nunez, Ann R. & Russell, Jill F. As Others See Vocational Education.
Nunez, Emilio. Liberation Theology.
Nunez, J., jt. ed. see Dumont, J.
Nunez Del Prado, Oscar & Whyte, William F. Kuyo Chico: Applied Anthropology in an Indian Community.
Nunez-Harrell, Elizabeth. When Rocks Dance.
Nunis, Doyce B., Jr. Francis J. Weber: The Monsignor of the Archives.
Nunn, G. Raymond, ed. Asia - Reference Works: A Select Annotated Guide.
Nunn, G. Raymond, compiled by. Japanese Periodicals & Newspapers in Western Languages.
Nunn, H. V. Christian Inscriptions.
Nunn, John. Solving in Style.
Nunn, R. H., jt. auth. see Marto, P. J.
Nunn, Richard E. Popular Mechanics Complete Manual of Home Repair & Improvement.
Nunnally, Jim C. Educational Measurement & Evaluation.
Nunnally, Stephens W. Construction Methods & Management.
Nuno, Gaya A. Juan Gris.
Nurcombe, Valerie J. British Official Publications: Sources of Information.
--Contract in England: A Select Bibliography on the Forms of Contracts for Building Work Since 1980.
--James Stirling: A Select Bibliography.
--Norman Foster: RIBA Gold Medallist, 1983.
--Richard Rogers: RIBA Gold Medallist, 1985.
--Thomas Telford, 1757-1834: A Select Bibliography.
--Timber-Frame Housing in Britain.
Nurenberg, Phil, jt. auth. see Head, Robert G.
Nursery School Staff, jt. auth. see Buchenholz, Gretchen.
Nursten, Jean, ed. see Gore, Elizabeth.
NUS Corporation Staff. Alternatives for the On-Site Retention of Low-Level Radwaste at Nuclear Power Plants (AIF-NESP-015R)
--Nuclear Power Plant Demographic Siting Criteria.
--A Survey & Evaluation of Handling & Disposing of Solid Low-Level Nuclear Fuel Cycle Wastes (AIF-NESP-008)
--Technical Assessment of Specific Aspects of EPA Proposed Environmental Radiation Standard for the Uranium Fuel Cycle (40CFR 190) & Its Association Documentation (AIF-NESP-011)

Nussbaum, Annette, jt. auth. see Friedman, Roslyn.
Nussbaum, Bruce. The World After Oil: The Shifting Axis of Power & Wealth.
Nussbaum, Felicity A., jt. auth. see Backscheider, Paula R.
Nussbaumer. Away in a Manger.
Nustad, Harry L., jt. auth. see Wesner, Terry.
Nute, Grace L. Rainy River Country: A Brief History of the Region Bordering Minnesota & Ontario.
Nuti, Frances, ed. see Morgan, David H.
Nutsch, J. Readings in Contemporary Problems, Issues & Values.
Nutt, Grady. Agaperos.
Nutt, Merle C. Functional Plant Planning, Layout & Materials Handling.
--Meeting the Challenge of Supervision.
Nuttall, A. D. Overheard by God: Fiction & Prayer in Herbert, Milton, Dante & St. John.
Nuttall, Clayton L. The Conflict: The Separation of the Church & State.
Nuttall, Geoffrey F. & Chadwick, O., eds. From Uniformity to Unity, 1662-1962.
Nutter, T. Thomas, West Virginia, 1906.
Nuttin, Joseph & Greenwald, Anthony G. Reward & Punishment in Human Learning.
Nutting, Paul. Community-Oriented Primary Care: From Principle to Practice.
Nutting, Wallace. The Clock Book.
Nutzle, Futzie, illus. Modern Loafer.
Nuxoll, Elizabeth M. Congress & the Munitions Merchants: The Secret Committee of Trade During the American Revolution, 1775-1777. Bruchey, Stuart, ed.
Nyberg, Klas, jt. auth. see Eberson, Lennart.
Nyberg-Hansen, R. Functional Organization of Descending Supraspinal Fibre Systems to the Spinal Cord: Anatomical Observations & Physiological Correlations.
Nye, Adrian. XII Programming Manuals: Volumes 1 & 2 Sold As Set.
Nye, Bill see also Nye, Edgar W.
Nye, Edgar W. see also Nye, Bill.
Nye, Joseph S., jt. auth. see Keohane, Robert O.
Nye, Joseph S., Jr. Nuclear Ethics.
--Pan-Africanism & East African Integration.
Nye, Nelson. Triggers for Six.
--Wolftrap.
--Wolftrap.
Nye, Robert D. Three Psychologies: Perspectives from Freud, Skinner & Rogers.
Nye, Robert E. & Bergethon, Bjorner. Basic Music: Functional Musicianship for the Non-Music Major.
Nygren, Anders. Significance of the Bible for the Church. Reumann, John, ed. Rasmusen, Carl C., tr.
Nygren, Birgitta, jt. auth. see Anell, Lars.
Nygren, Gertrude L., jt. auth. see Wedin, Carol.
Nygren, William V. Business Forms Management.
Nyhart, J. D. & Carrow, Milton M., eds. Law & Science in Collaboration: Resolving Regulatory Issues of Science & Technology.
Nyhoff, Larry, jt. auth. see Leestma, Sanford.
Nyhoff, Larry R. & Leestma, Sanford. Seventy-Seven for Engineers & Scientists.
Nyhus, Lloyd. Surgery Annual, 1986.
Nyhus, Lloyd M., jt. auth. see Condon, Robert E.
Nyhus, Lloyd M., ed. Surgery Annual, 1985.
Nyhus, Paul L., tr. see Oberman, Heiko A.
Nykiel, Ronald A. Marketing in the Hospitality Industry.
Nykl, Thomas. Problem Solving & Mathematics for Physics.
Nylander, Jane C. Fabrics for Historic Buildings.
Nylander, W. Prodromus Lichenographiae Galliae et Algeriae.
Nyman, Michael. Experimental Music: Cage & Beyond.
Nyquist, Ewald B., et al. College Learning Anytime, Anywhere.
Nyrop, Richard F., ed. Iraq: A Country Study.
--Peru: A Country Study.
--Rwanda: A Country Study.
Nystrand, Raphael O., jt. auth. see Marks, Walter.
Nystrom, Carolyn. Before I Was Born.
--Characters & Kings: A Woman's Workshop on the History of Israel.
--Jesus Is No Secret.
--Who Is Jesus? A Woman's Workshop on Mark.
Nystrom, Fred & Nystrom, Mardi M. Special Places: For the Discerning Traveler in Oregon, Washington, Idaho, Montana, British Columbia & California Wine Country.
Nystrom, Mardi M., jt. auth. see Nystrom, Fred.
Nystuen, David W. & Lindeman, Carla G. The Excavation of Fort Renville: An Archaeological Report.
Nyszli. Mengeles Auschwitz.
Nyvall, Robert F. Field Crop Diseases Handbook.

O

O. Henry see Henry, O.
Oae, S., ed. Organic Chemistry of Sulfur.
Oakes, Annalee R, ed. see American Association of Critical Care Nurses Staff.
Oakes, Claudia M. United States Women in Aviation, 1930-1939.
Oakes, George & Chapman, Alexandra. Turn Right at the Fountain.
Oakes, George W. & Chapman, Alexandra. Turn Right at the Fountain.
Oakland, Thomas & Williams, Fern C. Auditory Perception: Diagnosis & Development for Language & Reading Abilities.
Oakland, William, jt. ed. see Mieszkowski, Peter.
Oaklander, Violet. Windows to Our Children.
Oakley, Allen. Marx's Critique of Political Economy: Intellectual Sources & Evolution.
--Marx's Critique of Political Economy: Intellectual Sources & Evolution, 1861-1863.
Oakley, Ann. The Captured Womb: A History of Medical Care of the Pregnant Woman.
--The Sociology of Housework.
Oakley, Barry. The Great God Mogadon & Other Plays.
--Marsupials & Politics: Two Comedies.
--Walking Through Tigerland.
Oakley, D. The Phenomenon of Architecture in Cultures in Change.
Oakley, David A. & Plotkin, H. C., eds. Brain, Behaviour, & Evolution.
Oakley, Giles. The Devil's Music: A History of the Blues.
Oakley, Graham. The Church Mice & the Moon.
Oakley, K. & Richmond, W. A Systematic Approach to Commercial & Clerical Training.
Oaks, Robert Q., Jr. & DuBar, Jules R., eds. Post-Miocene Stratigraphy Central & Southern Atlantic Coastal Plain.
Oaks, Sherry & Gruenfeld, Raymond. Up & down Vail Mountain.
Oandasan, William. A Branch of California Redwood.
--Round Valley Songs.
OAS, General Secretariat. Directorio Turisto-Tourist Directory.
--Informe Anual Del Secretario General 1980.
--Manual de Normas Vigentes en Materia de Direitos Humanos: Actualizado en Julho de 1980.
OAS, General Secretariat, ed. Anthology of Andres Bello. Huntley, Barbara D. & Liria, Pilar, trs. from Span.
OAS, General Secretariat, Department of Public Information Staff. The OAS & the Evolution of the Interamerican System.
OAS, General Secretariat, Inter-American Commission of Human Rights. Manual de Normas Vicentes en Materia de Derechos Humanos.
OAS, General Secretariat, Inter-American Nuclear Energy Staff. OAS Offical Documents Final Report: Twelfth Meeting of the Inter-American Nuclear Energy Commission, August 31 - September 4, 1981, La Paz, Bolivia.
OAS, General Secretariat, International Trade & Export Development Program Staff. Sistema Generalizado de Preferencial De Estados Unidos: Cobertura Y Procedimientos Administrativos Vignetes en 1980.
Oates, Gordon C. Aerothermodynamics of Gas Turbines & Rocket Propulsion.
Oates, Joyce Carol. The Seduction & Other Stories.
Oates, Joyce Carol & Ravenel, Shannon, eds. Best American Short Stories of Nineteen Seventy-Nine.
Oates, Leslie. Populist Nationalism in Pre-War Japan: A Biography of Nakano Seigo.
Oates, Stephen B. Portrait of America.
--Portrait of America: Vol. 1, from the Cliff Dwellers to the End of Reconstruction.
--Portrait of America: Vol. 2, from Reconstruction to the Present.
Oates, Wallace E. Fiscal Federalism.
Oates, Wayne E. The Christian Pastor.
--Pastoral Counseling.
--When Religion Gets Sick.
--When You Can't Find Time for Each Other.
Oatley, Keith. Selves in Relation: An Introduction to Psychotherapy & Groups. Herriot, Peter, ed.
Oats, William N. A Question of Survival: Quakers in Australia in the Nineteenth Century.
Obal, F. & Benedek, G., eds. Environmental Physiology: Proceedings of the 28th International Congress of Physiological Sciences, Budapest, 1980 (Including the Satellite Symposium on Sports Physiology)
O'Ballance, Edgar. The Kurdish Revolt, Nineteen Sixty-One to Nineteen Seventy.
--The Third Arab-Israeli War.
O'Banion, Terry. Organizing Staff Development: Programs That Work.
Obanyon, Constance. Savage Autumn.
O'Barr, Ann G. First Light.
Obel, Borge. Issues of Organizational Design: A Mathematical Programming View of Organizations.
Obelkevich, James, ed. Religion & the People, Eight Hundred to Seventeen Hundred.
Obeng, Ernest A. One Track Mind.
Ober, Josiah, jt. ed. see Eadie, John W.
Oberai, A. S. Changes in the Structure of Employment with Economic Development.
Oberdieck, Helmut, jt. auth. see Kruger, Arnd.
Oberg, Erik, et al. Machinery's Handbook. Schubert, Paul B., ed.
--Machinery's Handbook. Ryffel, Henry H., ed.
Oberhofer, M. & Scharmann, A., eds. Applied Thermoluminescence Dosimetry.
Oberhofer, Thomas R. Manual of Non-Fermenting Gram-Negative Bacteria.
--Manual of Practical Medical Microbiology & Parasitology.
Oberhoff, Kenneth E., jt. auth. see Murphy, Michael G.
Oberholtzer, Ellis P. Literary History of Philadelphia.
Oberman, Heiko A. Forerunners of the Reformation: The Shape of Late Medieval Thought. Nyhus, Paul L., tr.
--The Roots of Anti-Semitism: In the Age of Renaissance & Reformation. Porter, James I., tr. from Ger.
--The Virgin Mary in Evangelical Perspective.
Oberman, Heiko A., ed. see Tierney, Brian.
Oberman, Margaret & Steckler, Doug. I Could Have Been a Contender, or the Other Book of Lists.
Oberman, Phyllis, jt. auth. see Jay, Roma.
Oberman, R. M. Digital Circuits for Binary Arithmetic.
Oberrecht, Kenn. Plywood Projects Illustrated.
Obert, Edward F. & Young, Robert L. Elements of Thermodynamics & Heat Transfer.
Obert, John C., jt. auth. see McIntyre, Thomas J.
Oberti, Martha, tr. see Abel, Sally A.
Obeyesekere, Gananath. Medusa's Hair: An Essay on Personal Symbols & Religious Experiences.
Obler, Loraine K. & Albert, Martin L. Language & Communication in the Elderly: Clinical, Therapeutic, & Experimental Issues.
Obligado, Lilian, illus. The Three Little Kittens.
Obojski, Robert. Coin Collector's Price Guide.
Obrecht, F., jt. auth. see Shapiro, M.
O'Brein, Robert. Poor Mouth.
Obrentz, Bert N. & Woodard, Arthur F. ERISA: The Multiemployer Pension Plan Amendments Act 1980.
Obrentz, Bert N., jt. auth. see Milbauer, Barbara.
O'Brian, Charles, jt. auth. see Bruggen, Peter.
O'Brian, Paddy. Birth & Our Bodies: Exercises & Meditations for the Childbearing Year & Preparation for Active Birth.
O'Brian, Patrick, tr. see De Beauvoir, Simone.
O'Brien, B. P., ed. J. R. McCulloch (1789-1864) Treatise or Taxation?
O'Brien, Beatrice, jt. ed. see Seguin, Mary M.
O'Brien, Bonnie B. & Sample, Dorothy E. Life in the Fifth Dimension.
O'Brien, Bronterre, tr. see Buonarroti, Philippe.
O'Brien, Christian. The Genius of the Few: The Story of Those who Founded the Garden of Eden.
O'Brien, Conor C. The Siege: The Saga of Israel & Zionism.
O'Brien, Darcy. A Way of Life, Like Any Other.
O'Brien, David J. Neighborhood Organization & Interest-Group Processes.
--The Renewal of American Catholicism.
O'Brien, Edna. Mother Ireland.
--A Pagan Place: A Play.
O'Brien, Edward L. & Fisher, Margaret E. Practical Law for Correctional Personnel: A Resource Manual & a Training Curriculum (by the National Street Law Institute)
O'Brien, Eileen & Ratzlaff, Leslie. Education in the One Hundredth Congress: A Guide to Committees.
O'Brien, Flann. The Poor Mouth: A Bad Story about the Hard Life. Power, Patrick, tr. from Gaelic.
O'Brien, Frank J. Homebuilts: A Handbook for the First-Time Builder.
O'Brien, George D. God & the New Haven Railway.
O'Brien, Grace. Golden Age of Italian Music.
O'Brien, J., jt. auth. see Angel, M. V.
O'Brien, J., jt. ed. see Angel, M. V.
O'Brien, J. J., jt. ed. see Angel, M. V.
O'Brien, Jacqueline W., jt. ed. see Wasserman, Steven.
O'Brien, James. Construction Inspection Handbook.
O'Brien, James A. Computers & Information Processing.
O'Brien, James J. Value Analysis in Design & Construction.
O'Brien, John T., ed. Crime & Justice in America.
O'Brien, Joseph V. William O'Brien & the Course of Irish Politics, 1881-1918.
O'Brien, Justin. Portrait of Andre Gide.
O'Brien, Lynne W. Plains Indian Autobiographies.
O'Brien, Margaret, jt. ed. see McKee, Lorna.
O'Brien, Mary. The Politics of Reproduction.
O'Brien, Michael & Cargill, Burton F. Principles & Practices of Harvesting & Handling Fruits & Nuts.
O'Brien, Michael & Laoghaire, Ida N. Pictorial Ireland: 1987.
O'Brien, Michael & Ni Laoghaire, Ida, eds. Pictorial Ireland, 1989: Yearbook & Appointment Diary.
O'Brien, Michael, et al, eds. The Cannon Reservoir Human Ecology Project: An Archaeological Study of Cultural Adaptations in the Southern Prairie Peninsula.
O'Brien, Muriel. Merrie's Secret Wish.
O'Brien, P. T. & Peterson, D. G., eds. God Who Is Rich in Mercy.
O'Brien, R. D. & Yamamoto, Izuru, eds. Biochemical Toxicology of Insecticides.
O'Brien, Richard. American Premium Guide to Electric Trains: Identifications & Values.
--Collecting Toys: A Collectors Identification & Value Guide.
--Private Bank Lending to Developing Countries.
O'Brien, Richard & Dickinson, Alyce M., eds. Industrial Behavior Modification: A Management Handbook.
O'Brien, Robert C. Mrs. Frisby & the Rats of Nimh.
--Report from Group Seventeen.
O'Brien, Sally. A Negative Scream: A Story of Young People Who Took an Overdose.
Obrist, Jurg. They Do Things Right in Albern.
O'Bryant, James L. Give Us This Day - A Cautionary Tale.
Obudho, R. A. Urbanization in Kenya: A Bottom-Up Approach to Development Planning.
Obudhowski, jt. auth. see Kassakowski.
O'Byrne, John C. & Davenport, Charles. Farm Income Tax Manual.
O'Callaghan, Joseph F., tr. see St. Ignatius Loyola.
O'Callaghan, Sheila M. Cinderella of Europe.
Ocampo, Silvinia. Short Stories. Weiss, Jason, tr.
O'Carroll, Niall. The Forests of Ireland: History, Distribution & Silviculture.
Occhiogrosso, Peter. Inside Spinal Tap.
O'Cene, Sean. The Brier Patch.
Och, Armin, jt. ed. see Maeder, Herbert.
Ochberg, Richard L. Middle-Aged Sons & the Meaning of Work. Nathan, Peter, ed.
Ochiai, Hidy. Hidy Ochiai's Living Karate.
Ochs, Donovan J. & Winkler, Anthony C. A Brief Introduction to Speech.
Ochs, Elinor & Schieffelin, Bambi B. Acquiring Conversational Competence.
Ochs, Robert & Gray, James. Business Mathematics.
--Introduction to Business Mathematics.
Ockerman, Herbert W. Source Book for Food Scientists.
Ockham, William of see also William of Ockham.
OCLC Online Computer Library Center, Inc. Staff. U. S. Newspaper Program: National Union List.
O.C.L.C. Staff. On-Line Cataloging.
O'Collins, Gerald. The Calvary Christ.
O'Connell, April & Whitmore, Jacqueline. Choice & Change: The Psychology of Adjustment, Growth, & Creativity.
O'Connell, K. J. & Levy, David. Anatoly Karpov's Games As World Champion 1975-1977.
O'Connell, Marvin R. McElroy.
O'Connell, Mathew J., tr. see Gonzalez-Ruiz, Jose-Maria.
OConnell, Matthew J., tr. see Calvez, Jean-Yves.
O'Connell, Richard. Poems & Epigrams.
O'Connell, Vincent M. The Gambler, the Gunfighter & Other Poems & Ballads.
O'Connell, Walter E., ed. Psychotherapy: Theoretical & Technical Readings.
O'Conner, Daniel J. Airplanes & Income Tax.
O'Connor, Colin. Spanning Two Centuries: Historic Bridges of Australia.
O'Connor, D. J. Introduction to the Philosophy of Education.
O'Connor, Dagmar. How to Make Love to the Same Person for the Rest of Your Life: And Still Love It.
O'Connor, David, jt. auth. see Andruk, Susie.
O'Connor, Dick, jt. auth. see Owens, Jessie.
O'Connor, Elizabeth. The New Community.
O'Connor, Flannery. Good Man Is Hard to Find.
--Wise Blood. Bd. with The Violent Bear It Away; Everything That Rises Must Converge. NAL.
O'Connor, Francine & Boswell, Kathryn. ABC's of Faith.
O'Connor, Frank. A Lament for Art O'Leary.
--Lords & Commons.
--My Father's Son.
--An Only Child.
--The Wild Bird's Nest: Poems from the Irish.

O'Connor, Garry. The Pursuit of Perfection: A Life of Maggie Teyte.
--Ralph Richardson: An Actor's Life.
O'Connor, Ginger H., jt. auth. see Nield, Jill S.
O'Connor, John F. Sexual Compatibility: A Practical Approach to Solving Problems.
O'Connor, Leo F. Religion in the American Novel: The Search for Belief, 1860-1920.
O'Connor, Michael, ed. The Image Bank: Visual Ideas for the Creative Color Photographer.
O'Connor, N., jt. auth. see Hermelin, B.
O'Connor, N., ed. Present Day Russian Psychology.
O'Connor, Patricia W. & Pasquariello, Anthony M., eds. Contemporary Spanish Theatre: Seven One-Act Plays.
O'Connor, Patrick, compiled by. Buddhists Find Christ: The Spiritual Quest of Thirteen Men & Women in Burma, China, Japan, Korea, Sri Lanka, Thailand, Vietnam.
O'Connor, Philip F. Defending Civilization.
O'Connor, Robert. Choosing for Health.
O'Connor, Ulick. All The Olympians: A Biographical Portrait of the Irish Literary Renaissance.
--Brendan Behan.
O'Connor, William A. & Lubin, Bernard, eds. Ecological Approaches to Clinical & Community Psychology.
Ocran, Emanuel B. Ocran's Acronyms: A Dictionary of Abbreviations & Acronyms Used in Scientific & Technical Writing.
Ocran, Emanuel B., Jr. Transportation Costs & Costing, 1917-1973: A Select Annotated Chronological Bibliography.
Octopus, Conran. Children's Clothes.
--Embroidery.
--Fashion Knitting.
--Quilting, Patchwork, & Applique.
Oda, T. Lectures on Torus Embeddings & Applications.
Odabasi, Halis & Akyuz, O. Topics in Mathematical Physics.
Odabasi, Halis & Ulug, S. Erol, eds. Environmental Problems & Their International Implications.
Odabasi, Halis, jt. ed. see Brittin, Wesley E.
Odaka, Tadeshi, jt. ed. see Ikawa, Yoji.
O'Daly, John, ed. Laoithe Fiannuigheachta.
O'Day, Alan, ed. The Edwardian Age: Conflict & Stability, 1900-1914.
O'Day, Deirdre. Victorian Jewellery.
Oddy, Derek J. & Miller, Derek S., eds. Diet & Health in Modern Britain.
Oddy, Russell. For Sale by Owner.
Odell, Charles E., jt. auth. see Odell, Louise M.
O'Dell, Jerry W. Basic Statistics: An Introduction to Problem Solving with Your Personal Computer.
--TRS-80 As a Controller.
Odell, Louise M. & Odell, Charles E. You & the Senior Boom: New Challenges & Opportunities for All.
Odell, P. L., jt. ed. see Duran, B. S.
Odell, Peter R. Oil & World Power: Background to the Oil Crisis.
Odell, Peter R. & Rosing, Kenneth E. The Future of Oil: World Oil Resources & Use.
O'Dell, Scott. Child of Fire.
--The Hawk That Dare Not Hunt by Day.
--Journey to Jericho.
--The Treasure of Topo-el-Bampo.
O'Dell, T. H. The Electrodynamics of Magneto Electric Media.
--Ferromagnetodynamics: The Dynamics of Magnetic Bubbles Domains & Domain Walls.
--Magnetic Bubbles.
Odell, William, jt. auth. see McDonald, Perry.
Odell, William C. Josh Carter & the Old Stagecoach Mystery.
O'Dell, William F. How to Make Lifetime Friends with Peers & Parents.
Oden, J. T. & Becker, E. B. Computational Methods in Nonlinear Mechanics Structures.
Oden, J. T. & Reddy, J. N. Variational Methods in Theoretical Mechanics.
Oden, J. T., ed. Computational Mechanics: Lectures in Computational Methods in Nonlinear Mechanics.
Oden, J. T., ed. see International Conference on Computational Methods in Nonlinear Mechanics Staff.
Oden, John T. & Ripperger, Eugene A. Mechanics of Elastic Structures.
Oden, Thomas C. Agenda for Theology.
--Care of Souls in the Classic Tradition.
--The Intensive Group Experience: The New Pietism.
Oden, Thomas C., jt. auth. see John G. Finch Symposium on Psychology & Religion Staff.
Odent, Michael. Birth Reborn. Levin, Juliette & Pincus, Jane, trs.
Odets, Clifford, jt. auth. see Gibson, William.
Odier, Daniel see Delacorta, pseud.
Odier, Daniel see Delcorta, pseud.
Odiorne, George S. How Managers Make Things Happen.
Odiorne, George S., jt. auth. see Brooks, Earl.
Odle, Maurice A. Multinational Banks & Underdevelopment.
Odlum, Doris M. Psychology, the Nurse, & the Patient.
O'Doherty, Eamonn. The I. R. A. at War: An Illustrated History 1916 to the Present.
O'Donnell. Standard Handbook Modern Paper Money.
O'Donnell, Christopher. Life in the Spirit & Mary.
O'Donnell, James, ed. Ireland: A Dictionary for 1985.
--Ireland: A Directory 1985.
O'Donnell, James P. The Bunker.
O'Donnell, Mike & McNeill, Patrick. Age & Generation.
O'Donnell, Patrick. John Hawkes.
O'Donnell, Paul T. Dictionary Real Estate Terms.
O'Donnell, Paul T. & Maleady, Eugene L. Principles of Real Estate.
O'Donnell, Peter. Dragon's Claw.
O'Donnell, T. A. The Chemistry of Fluorine.
O'Donnell, Terence. Garden of the Brave in War: Recollections of Iran.
O'Donnell, William J. & Jones, David A. The Law of Marriage & Marital Alternatives.
O'Donoghue, David J. Poets of Ireland.
O'Donoghue, Denise, jt. ed. see McGrath, Rory.
O'Donovan, Thomas M. VisiCalc Made Simple.
Odor, Ruth. Bible Adventures.
--Bible Heroes.
--Jesus & His Friends.
--Moods & Emotions. Buerger, Jane, ed.
--Moods & Emotions: A Handbook About Feelings.
Odor, Ruth S. What's a Body to Do? A Handbook About Health.
O'Driscoll, Herbert. A Certain Life: Contemporary Meditations on the Way of Christ.
Odum, Howard. Southern Regions of the United States.
O'Dwyer, John J. College Physics.
Oe, Kenzaburo. A Personal Matter. Nathan, John, tr. from Japanese.
--Teach Us To Outgrow Our Madness. Nathan, John, tr. from Japanese. & intro. by.
OECD Staff. Bargain Price Offers & Similar Marketing Practices.
--Energy Balances of Developing Countries Nineteen Seventy-One tp Nineteen Eighty-Two.
--Energy Research, Development & Demonstration in the IEA Countries, 1983.
--European Conference of Ministers of Transport: (ECMT) 28th Annual Report-1981.
--Handbook of Information, Computer & Communications Activities of Major International Organizations.
--The Iron & Steel Industry in Nineteen Eighty-Three.
--Regulations Affecting International Banking Operations in Belgium-Luxembourg, France, Germany, the Netherlands, Sweden, Switzerland & the United Kingdom 1980-1981.
--Review of Fisheries in OECD Member Countries, 1983.
Oechsler, Ronald C. & Woods, Leyla. Statistical Abstract of East-West Trade & Finance: Staff Report.
Oechsner, Carl. Ossining New York: An Informal Bicentennial History.
Oehling, A., et al, eds. see International Congress of Allergology Staff.
Oehmichen, M. Mononuclear Phagocytes in the Central Nervous System: Origin, Mode of Distribution, & Function of Progressive Microglia, Perivascular Cells of Intracerebral Vessels, Free Subarachnoidal Cells, & Epiplexus Cells.
Oelahoyde, Melinda, jt. ed. see Horan, Dennis J.
Oeltjen, Jody, jt. auth. see Palmer, Elsie.
Oertel, Herbert, Jr., jt. ed. see Zierep, Juergen.
Oertzen, W. Von see Von Oertzen, W.
Oestreich, Alan E. Pediatric Radiology.
Oetting, Eugene R., jt. auth. see Drake, Lewis E.
Oettli, W. K. & Ritter, K. G., eds. Optimization & Operations Research.
O'Faolain, Sean. Selected Stories of Sean O'Faolain.
O'Faolain, Sean, ed. see Moore, Thomas.
O'Farrell, et al. Calculus Blackboard.
O'Ferrall, F. Catholic Emancipation: Daniel O'Connell & the Birth of Irish Democracy.
Off Off Broadway Alliance Staff & Levine, Mindy N. New York's Other Theatre: A Guide to Off Off Broadway.
Off the Wall Street Journal, Inc. Staff & Adelman, Bob. Reagan Report.
Offerman, Lynn, jt. auth. see Brown, Mik.
Office of Strategic Services Staff. OSS Sabotage & Demolition Manual.
Office of Technology Assessment, Congress of the United States Staff. Cancer Risk: Assessing & Reducing the Dangers in Our Society.
--Energy from Biological Processes.
--Information Technology Research & Development: Critical Trends & Issues.
Office of Technology Assessment Staff. Transportation of Hazardous Materials.
Office of Technology Assessment Task Force Staff, ed. Reproductive Health Hazards in the Workplace.
Office of Water Resources Research Staff, compiled by. Algae Abstracts: A Guide to the Literature. Incl. Vol. 1. To 1969; Vol. 2. 1970 to 1972; Vol. 3. 1972 to 1974. Plenum Pub.
Officer, Lawrence H. & Smith, Lawrence B. Issues in Canadian Economics.
Offir, Carole W., jt. auth. see Tavris, Carol.
Offner, Arnold A. American Appeasement: United States Foreign Policy & Germany 1933-1938.
Offord, R. E. Semisynthetic Proteins.
Offord, R. E. & Dibello, C., eds. Semisynthetic Peptides & Proteins.
Offord, Robin, jt. auth. see Yudkin, Michael.
O'Flaherty, Fred, et al, eds. The Chemistry & Technology of Leather.
O'Flaherty, Joseph S. An End & a Beginning: The South Coast & Los Angeles, 1850-1887.
--Those Powerful Years: The South Coast & Los Angeles 1887-1917.
O'Flaherty, Liam. The Wounded Cormorant & Other Stories.
O'Flaherty, Louise. Poppies in the Wind.
Ofori, Patrick E. Christianity in Tropical Africa: A Selective Annotated Bibliography.
--Islam in Africa South of the Sahara: A Select Bibliographic Guide.
--Land in Africa: Its Administration, Law, Tenure & Use: A Select Bibliography.
Ofuatey-Kodjoe, W., ed. Pan-Africanism: New Directions in Strategy.
Ogan, George, jt. auth. see Ogan, Margaret.
Ogan, Margaret & Ogan, George. Desert Road Racer.
--Donavan's Dusters.
--Grand National Racer.
--Raceway Charger.
--Tennis Bum.
Ogawa, Hiroshi, jt. auth. see Nakajima, Heitaro.
Ogawa, Tetsuro. Terraced Hell: A Japanese Memoir of Defeat & Death in Northern Luzon, Philippines.
Ogbourne, C. P., ed. Pathogenesis of Cyathostome (Trichonema) Infections of the Horse: A Review.
Ogburn, Floyd, Jr. Style As Structure & Meaning: William Bradford's "Of Plymouth Plantation"
Ogburn, William F. & Nimkoff, Meyer. Technology & the Changing Family.
Ogden, Charles K. Basic English: International Second Language. Graham, E. C., ed.
--Bentham's Theory of Fictions.
Ogden, Dunbar H. Wedding Bells.
Ogden, John A. Skeletal Injury in the Child.
Ogden, Melvin B. & Bowman, Arthur G. Ogden's Revised California Real Property Law.
Ogden, Richard W. Manage Your Plant for Profit & Your Promotion.
Ogden, Sheila J., jt. auth. see Radcliff, Ruth K.
Ogden, Suzanne. Global Studies: China, 1984.
Ogden, Suzanne, ed. World Politics 1988-89.
Ogden, Suzanne P. Annual Editions: World Politics, 1985-86.
Ogdin, Carol A. Microcomputer Design.
--Microcomputer System Design & Techniques.
Ogg, Frederic A. Opening of the Mississippi: A Struggle for Supremacy in the American Interior.
Oggel, Terry, ed. see Bibliographic Society of Northern Illinois Staff.
Ogilvie, Bruce & Waitley, Douglas. Rand McNally Children's Atlas of the World.
Ogilvie, C. Symptoms & Signs in Clinical Medicine.
Ogilvie, Charles. The King's Government & the Common Law, Fourteen Seventy-One to Sixteen Forty-One.
Ogilvie, Colin, ed. Birch's Emergencies in Medical Practice.
Ogilvie, Elisabeth. An Answer in the Tide.
--The Dreaming Swimmer.
--The Road to Nowhere.
--The Silent Ones.
--Strawberries in the Sea.
--There May Be Heaven.
--Weep & Know Why.
Ogilvie, Gordon. Jamie Reid.
Ogilvie, Lloyd. Congratulations - God Believes in You.
--Let God Love You.
Ogilvie, Lloyd J. The Bush Is Still Burning.
Ogilvie, Lloyd J., jt. auth. see Chafin, Kenneth L.
Ogilvy, C. Stanley. Win More Sailboat Races.
Ogilvy, David. Blood, Brains & Beer: An Autobiography.
--Confessions of an Advertising Man.
Ogilvy, James A. Self & World: Readings in Philosophy.
Ogino, Akihisa. Japanese Gothic.
Ogle, George E. Liberty to the Captives.
Ogle, Jane. The Stop Smoking Diet.
Ogle, Lucille. I Spy with My Little Eye.
Oglesby, Carole A., ed. Women & Sport: From Myth to Reality.
Oglesby, Stuart R. The Baby Is Baptized.
--Becoming a Member of the Presbyterian Church.
Oglesby, William B., Jr. With Wings As Eagles.
Ogletree, Earl J. & Hawkins, Maxine. Writing Instructional Objectives & Activities for the Modern Curriculum.
Ogletree, Earl J., ed. Issues in Urban Education.
--The Socially Disadvantaged.
Ogletree, Herbert H. Revelations: Forerunner of Christ.
Ogletree, Thomas W., jt. ed. see Lucas, George R., Jr.
Ognetov, I., jt. auth. see Divilkovsky, S.
Ognev, N. Kostya Ryabtsev's Diary.
O'Gorman, Denis. Scriptual Dramas for Children.
O'Gorman, Ned. Night of the Hammer.
Ogorodnikov, K. F. Dynamics of Stellar Systems.
O'Grady, James P., jt. auth. see Lynn, Robert A.
Ogrodowski, William. A Catholic Book of the Mass.
Ogston, D. Antifibrinolytic Drugs: Chemistry, Pharmacology & Clinical Usage.
Ogston, Derek. Venous Thrombosis: Causation & Prediction.
Ogus, H. D. Common Disorders of the Temporomandibular Joint.
Oh, Partick G. Sexual Imprisonment.
Ohanian, Hans C. Physics: Answers to Problems.
O'Hanlon, R. Joseph Conrad & Charles Darwin.
O'Hara, Albert. The Position of Woman in Early China.
O'Hara, D. M., jt. auth. see Chisolm, J. J.
O'Hara, Frank. Art Chronicles: 1954-1966.
--Meditations in an Emergency.
O'Hara, Gerald J. Malsum.
O'Hara, John. Selected Short Stories of John O'Hara. Trilling, Lionel, ed.
--Two by O'Hara. Bruccoli, Matthew J., ed.
O'Hara, Magdalen, ed. The Directory of Women Religious in the United States.
O'Hara, Mary. See-Sound Show: A Multimedia Kit.
--Sometimes Sad, Sometimes Glad.
O'Hara, Pat, jt. auth. see Manning, Harvey.
O'Hara, Tomie. A Woman Called En.
O'Hart, J. The Irish & Anglo-Irish Landed Gentry When Cromwell Came to Ireland.
Ohashi, Wataru & Hoover, Mary. Touch for Love.
Ohaver, M. E. Solving Cipher Secrets.
O'Hehir, Diana. I Wish This War Were Over.
O. Henry. The Gift of the Magi & Other Stories.
O. Henry, et al. Inspiration Three, Vol. 5: Three Famous Classics in One Book.
Ohio Department of Education Staff. Elementary Language Arts: Strategies for Teaching & Learning.
--Write On: Teaching Written Communication.
Ohio Genealogical Society, Ottawa County Chapter Staff. Cemetery Inscriptions of Ottawa County, Ohio.
Ohio Genealogical Society Staff. Ohio Cemeteries.
Ohio Judicial Conference Staff. Ohio Jury Instructions 1968-1985.
Ohio Psychology Publishing Co. Staff. Office Procedure Forms for the Professional Psychologist.
--Ohio Symposium on Stress Management: Proceedings of the First & Second Symposia.
Ohliger, John & Gueulette, David. Media & Adult Learning: A Bibliography.
Ohlin, Bertil. Interregional & International Trade.
Ohlsen, Merle M. Group Counseling.
--Guidance Services in the Modern School.
Ohlson, R., jt. ed. see Appelqvist, L. A.
Ohman, Jack. Back to the Eighties.
Ohno, S. Evolution by Gene Duplication.
--Sex Chromosomes & Sex-Linked Genes.
Ohnsorge, J. & Holm, R. Scanning Electron Microscopy.
Ohr, Judi, jt. auth. see Cadwallader, Sharon.
Ohrbach, Frank, jt. auth. see Hughes, Megan.
Ohri, Ashok, et al. Community Work & Racism.
Ohring, G. & Bolle, H. J., eds. Space Observations for Climate Studies: Proceedings of Symposium 4 of the COSPAR Twenty-Fifth Plenary Meeting Held in Graz Austria, 25 June-7 July 1984.
Ohrt, Cynthia L. Poor Little Star.
Ohsawa, George. Tea with George Ohsawa: Selected Writings by the Father of Modern Macrobiotics. Van Cauweberghe, Marc, tr.
Ohta, T., ed. Solar-Hydrogen Energy System: An Authoritative Review of Water-Splitting Systems by Solar Beam & Solar Heat; Hydrogen Production, Storage & Utilization.
Ohuche, R. O. & Otaala, B. The African Child & His Environment.
--The African Child & His Environment.
Oil & Gas Journal Staff, ed. International Petroleum Encyclopedia, 1988.
Oinas, Felix. Estonian General Reader.
Oizerman, T. I. & Bogomolov, A. S. Principles of the Theory of the Historical Process in Philosophy.
Oje, Oyediran, jt. auth. see Faniran, A.
Ojo, Oyediran. The Climates of West Africa.
Ojo, Sola, jt. ed. see Shaw, Timothy M.
Ojomo, Olatunde. Great Tortoise Stories.
Oka, Isaburo. Hiroshige. Imes, Stanleigh H., tr.
Oka, Isaburo, jt. auth. see Suzuki, Juzo.

Authors

Okada, Barbara T. Netsuke: Masterpieces from the Metropolitan Museum of Art. Howard, Kathleen, ed. Seki, Hozen & Cranston, Edwin A., trs.
Okada, Shigefumi see Altman, Kurt I.
Okada, Victor N., jt. ed. see Taylor, Halsey P.
Okamoto, K., ed. Spontaneous Hypertension: Its Pathogenesis & Complications.
Okamoto, Naomasa. Congenital Anomalies of the Heart.
Okamoto, S., jt. ed. see Copley, A.
Okantah, Mwatabu S. Afreeka Brass.
Oke, Janette. Love Comes Softly.
--My Favorite Verse.
Oke, T. R. Boundary Layer Climates.
O'Kearney, Nicholas, ed. The Battle of Gabhra.
--Feis Tighe Chonuin Chinn-Shleibhe.
O'Keefe, Bernard J. The Nuclear Hostages.
--Shooting Ourselves in the Foot.
O'Keefe, John. The Plays of John O'Keefe. Link, Frederick M., ed.
O'Keefe, Michael. The Adult, Education & Public Policy.
O'Keefe, Philip, ed. Regional Restructuring under Advanced Capitalism.
O'Keefe, T. J., ed. see World Symposium at the AIME Annual Meeting Staff.
O'Keefe, William & Elliott, Thomas C., eds. Solving Plant Problems: Design, Operation, Maintenance.
O'Keeffe, Timothy J. Milton & the Pauline Tradition: A Study of Theme & Symbolism.
O'Kelly De Galway, A. O. Tigran Petrosian - World Champion.
Okere, Theophilus. African Philosophy: A Historico-Hermeneutical Investigation of the Conditions of Its Possibility.
Okeson, Jeffrey P. The Fundamentals of Occlusion & Temporomandibular Disorders.
Oki, Masahiro. Practical Yoga: A Pictorial Approach.
--Zen Yoga Therapy.
Okikiolu, G. O. Aspects of the Theory of Bounded Integral Operators in LSRP-Spaces.
Okimoto, Daniel I. Pioneer & Pursuer: The Role of the State in the Evolution of the Japanese & American Semiconductor Industries.
Okin, Josee P. & Schmitt, Conrad J. Francais: Continuons.
Okladnikov, A. P. Yakutia: Before Its Incorporation into the Russian State. Michael, Henry N., ed.
Okner, Benjamin A., jt. auth. see Pechman, Joseph A.
Oko, Adolph S., compiled by see Columbia University Staff.
Okolo, Fr. Chukwudum Barnabas. Racism-a Philosophic Probe.
Okrent, ed. see Senzel, Howard.
Okrent, Daniel. Nine Innings.
--The Ultimate Baseball Book.
Okrent, Daniel, ed. see Alford, Terry.
Okrent, Daniel, ed. see Reeves, Richard.
Okrent, Daniel, ed. see Vadim, Roger.
Okrent, Hummel. Reactivity Coefficients in Large Fast Power Reactors.
Oksche, A. & Farner, D. S. Neurohistological Studies of the Hypothalamo-Hypophysial System of Zonotrichia Leucophrys Gambelii.
Oksenberg, Michel, jt. auth. see Lieberthal, Kenneth.
Oksenberg, Michel, et al. The Cultural Revolution: 1967 in Review.
Okte, Faik. The Tragedy of Capital Tax. Cox, Geoffrey, tr. from Turkish.
Okuguchi, J. Expectations & Stability in Oligopoly Models.
Okun, Arthur. Political Economy of Prosperity.
Okun, Daniel A., jt. auth. see Schulz, Christopher R.
Okun, L. B. Weak Interaction of Elementary Particles.
Okun, Milton. Neil Diamond: On the Way to the Sky. Fox, Dan, ed.
Okun, Milton, ed. Beatles Complete Easy Guitar.
--Pocket Beatles.
--Twenty Greatest Hits: The Beatles.
--World's Greatest Guitar Book: Blue Edition.
Okun, Milton & Fox, Dan, eds. Jim Henson's Muppets: Very Easy Piano Favorites.
--Neil Diamond: Heartlight.
--Pat Benatar: Get Nervous.
--World's Greatest Guitar Book.
Olafson, Frederick A. The Dialectic of Action: A Philosophical Interpretation of History & the Humanities.
Olander, Joseph, jt. auth. see Greenberg, Martin H.
Olander, Joseph D. & Greenberg, Martin H., eds. Arthur C. Clarke.
--Philip K. Dick.
--Ray Bradbury.
--Robert A. Heinlein.
--Robert Silverberg.
--Stanislaw Lem.
--Time of Passage: SF Stories About Death & Dying.
--Ursula K. LeGuin.
Olander, Joseph D., jt. ed. see Greenberg, Martin H.
Olanrewaju, S. A. & Falola, Toyin, eds. Transport Systems in Nigeria.
O'Laoghaire, D. T. Optimal Expansion of a Water Resources System.
Olausson, Eric & Cato, Ingemar. Chemistry & Biochemistry of Estuaries.
Olcott, Anthony, tr. see Olcott, Martha B., et al.
Olcott, Francis J. Good Stories for Great Holidays.
Olcott, Martha B., et al, eds. The Soviet Muntinational State. Vale, Michel & Olcott, Anthony, trs. from Rus.
Old Cars Editors. Best of Old Cars.
Old Cars Editors, ed. Best of Old Cars.
Old, David, jt. auth. see Sealey, Richard.
Old El Paso Staff. Old El Paso Sun Mexican Cookbook II.
Old-House Journal Staff. Old-House Journal Catalog, 1988 Edition: A Buyers Guide for the Pre-1939 House.
--The Old-House Journal Nineteen Seventy-Eight Yearbook: A One-Volume Compilation of All the Editorial Pages Printed in the Old-House Journal in 1978. Poore, Patricia & Labine, Clem, eds.
--The Old-House Journal Nineteen Seventy-Nine Yearbook: A One-Volume Compilation of All the Editorial Pages Printed in the Old-House Journal in 1979. Poore, Patricia & Labine, Clem, eds.
--The Old-House Journal Nineteen Seventy-Six Yearbook: A One-Volume Compilation of All the Editorial Pages Printed in the Old-House Journal in 1976. Poore, Patricia & Labine, Clem, eds.
--The Old-House Journal Nineteen Seventy-Seven Yearbook: A One-Volume Compilation of All the Editorial Pages Printed in the Old-House Journal in 1977. Poore, Patricia & Labine, Clem, eds.
--Old House Journal, 1985 Catalog: A Buyer's Guide for the Pre-1939 House.
--Old-House Journal, 1986 Catalog: A Buyer's Guide for the Pre-1939 House.
Old Slave Mart Museum & Library Staff. Catalog of the Old Slave Mart Museum & Library.
Old Sturbridge Village Staff. Small Town Sourcebook & Guide.
Olden, Kenneth & Paxent, James B., eds. Vertebrate Lectins: Recent Research.
Olden, Marc. Dai-Sho.
--Gaijin.
--Giri.
Oldenberg, Otto & Rasmussen, N. Modern Physics for Engineers.
Oldenburg, John, tr. see Schneider, Wolf.
Oldenquist, Andrew. Moral Philosophy: Text & Readings.
Older, Julia. Endometriosis: A Woman's Guide to a Common but Often Undetected Disease that Can Cause Infertility & Other Major Medical Problems.
Oldfather, William A., ed. see Aesopus.
Oldfield, Molly, jt. auth. see Meyer, Edwin W.
Oldfield, Pamela. Green Harvest.
--Summer Song.
Oldfield, Susan. The Counseling Relationship: A Study of the Client's Experience.
Oldham, Dale. The Sudden Land.
Oldham, Frank, Jr. Job Descriptions in Banking: The Complete Guide to Planning, Writing, & Using Job Descriptions. Seglin, Jeffrey L., ed.
Oldham, Joe. Supertuning Your Firebird Trans-Am.
--Supertuning Your Z-28 Camaro.
Oldham, John & Oldham, Ray. Gardens in Time.
Oldham, June. Grow up, Cupid.
Oldham, Kathleen I. The Annals of Flowerland.
Oldham, Ray, jt. auth. see Oldham, John.
Oldham, William G. & Schwartz, Steven E. An Introduction to Electronics.
Oldman, Oliver, et al. Financing Urban Development in Mexico City: A Case Study of Property Tax, Land Use, Housing, & Urban Planning. Herrmann, Lawrence M. & Lee, Laurence D., eds.
Oldring, Edward W. I Walk & Talk with Angels: A True Life Story.
Oldroyd, Harold. Natural History of Flies.
Olds, jt. auth. see Simon.
Olds, Clifton, et al. Durer's Cities: Nuremberg & Venice.
--Images of Love & Death in Late Medieval & Renaissance Art.
Olds, Sally W. & Eiger, Marvin S. The Complete Book of Breastfeeding.
Oldsen, A. C., jt. auth. see Kretzmann, O. P.
Oldsey, Bernard. Ernest Hemingway: The Papers of a Writer.
Oldshue, James Y. Fluid Mixing Technology.
O'Leary, J. Patrick & Woltering, Eugene A., eds. Techniques for Surgeons.
O'Leary, James P. Systems Theory & Regional Integration: The "Market Model" of International Politics.
O'Leary, M. Contemporary Organic Chemistry.
O'Leary, Michael. U. S. Sky Spies since World War I.
O'Leary, Michael K., jt. auth. see Coplin, William D.
O'Leary, T. J. & Williams, B. K. Computers & Information Processing with Business Applications.
O'Leary, Vincent, jt. auth. see Clear, Todd R.
Oleksy, Walter. Careers in the Animal Kingdom.
--It's Women's Work, Too!
--Quacky & the Crazy Curve Ball.
--Quacky & the Haunted Amusement Park.
--UFO: Teen Sightings.
Olenick, Arnold see Rousmaniere, Peter F., et al.
Olesen, Virginia see Lewin, Ellen.
Olesha, Yuri. Envy & Other Works. MacAndrew, Andrew R., tr.
Olesha, Yury. Yury Olesha: The Complete Short Stories & the Three Fat Men. Fisher, Aimee, tr. from Rus.
Olesky, Walter. Nature Gone Wild!
Olevnik, Peter. A Guide to Selected Microform Series & Their Indexes.
Olevnik, Peter P. Selected Medieval & Renaissance Manuscript Collections in Microform.
Olfe, Daniel B., jt. auth. see Penner, S. S.
Olfson, Lewy. Dramatized Classics for Radio-Style Reading.
Olien, Diana D. Morpeth: A Victorian Public Career.
Oliker, I., ed. Cogeneration District Heating Applications.
Olin, John C., ed. see Erasmus.
Olinekova, Gayle. Go for It!
--Legs! Super Legs in Six Weeks.
--The Sensuality of Strength.
Oliner, A. A. Acoustic Surface Waves.
Oliphant, David & Bellack, Alison. Solarman: The Beginning.
Oliphant, Eleana. The Haunting at Lost Lake.
Oliphant, Margaret W. Salem Chapel. Wolff, Robert L., ed.
Oliva, Peter F. Supervision for Today's Schools.
Oliva, Terence, jt. auth. see Peters, Michael.
Olivas, Michael A. Annotated Bibliography of John Updike Criticism 1967-73: & a Checklist of His Works.
Olive, Jane E., jt. auth. see Mori, Allen A.
Olive, Lindsay S. The Mycetozoans.
Olivecrona, H. & Ladenheim, J. Congenital Arteriovenous Aneurysms of the Carotid & Vertebral Arterial Systems.
Oliveira, E. De Arantes, ed. see CISM (International Center for Mechanical Sciences) Staff.
Oliveira, Fernandes E. de see De Oliveira, Fernandes E., et al.
Oliveira, Nuno. Reflections on Equestrian Art. Fields, Phyllis, tr. from Port.
Oliveira-Pinto, F. & Connolly, B. W., eds. Applicable Mathematics of Non-Physical Phenomena.
Olivella, Manuel Z. Chambacu: Black Slum. Tittler, Johnathan, tr.
Oliver, Alan C. Dampness in Buildings.
Oliver, Andrew, Jr. Ancient Glass: Ancient & Islamic Glass in the Carnegie Museum of Natural History.
Oliver, Anthony. Staffordshire Pottery: The Tribal Art of England.
--The Victorian Staffordshire Figure.
Oliver, Bernard M. & Cage, John M. Electronic Measurements & Instrumentation.
Oliver, Carl. Plane Talk: Aviators' & Astronauts' Own Stories.
Oliver, Chad. The Winds of Time.
Oliver, Donald, ed. The Greatest Revue Sketches.
Oliver, Eric & Wilson, John. Practical Security in Commerce & Industry.
--Security Manual.
Oliver, J. L. The Development & Structure of the Furniture Industry.
Oliver, James K., jt. auth. see Nathan, James A.
Oliver, Janie W., ed. see Jordan, William R., Sr.
Oliver, Jeff. Repairing Old China & Ceramic Tile.
Oliver, John W. see Ramsay, Allan.
Oliver, Joseph R. Big Tax Savings for Small Business.
Oliver, Judith, jt. ed. see Briggs, Anna.
Oliver, Keith. High Frontier.
Oliver, Lucille. Cry for the World.
Oliver, Paul. Aspects of the Blues Tradition.
Oliver, Ray. Principles of the Use of Radioisotope Tracers in Clinical & Research Investigations.
Oliver, Revilo, tr. see Sudraka, Kind.
Oliver, Robert. Cornucopia.
--Oliver's ADF Directory.
--Worlds Apart.
Oliver, Tyronne. One Hundred Fabulicious Drinks.
Olivier, Laurence. Confessions of an Actor: An Autobiography.
Olivieri, C., jt. auth. see Aziza, C.
Olivo, C. Thomas & Olivo, Thomas P. Fundamentals of Applied Physics.
Olivo, C. Thomas, et al. Basic Blueprint Reading & Sketching.
Olivo, Thomas P., jt. auth. see Olivo, C. Thomas.
Olken, Charles, et al. The Connoisseurs' Handbook of California Wines.
Ollard, Richard. The Image of the King: A Biography of Charles I & Charles II.
--Pepys.
--This War Without an Enemy.
Ollenburger, Ben C. Zion, the City of the Great King: A Theological Symbol of the Jerusalem Cult.
Ollendick, Thomas H., jt. ed. see Hersen, Michel.
Ollengren, A. Definition of Programming Languages.
Ollila, Lloyd O., ed. Handbook for Administrators & Teachers: Reading in the Kindergarten.
Olliver. Principles of Survey.
Ollivier, Jacqueline & Morran, Michelle. Appel: Initiation au Francais.
Olmstead, Albert T. History of Palestine & Syria to the Macedonian Conquest.
Olmstead, D. L. Ethnolinguistics So Far.
Olmsted, John C. George Meredith: An Annotated Bibliography 1925-1975.
--Thackeray & His Twentieth Century Critics: An Annotated Bibliography of British & American Criticism, 1900-1975.
Olmsted, John C. & Welch, Jeffrey. The Reputation of Trollope.
Olmsted, John M. Intermediate Analysis: An Introduction to Theory of Functions of One Real Variable.
Olmsted, Robert. The Diesel Years.
Olney, Judith. Comforting Food.
--Summer Food.
Olney, P. J., ed. International Zoo Yearbook, 1981.
Olney, Patricia J., jt. auth. see Olney, Ross R.
Olney, Richard. The French Menu Cookbook: A Revised & Updated Edition of a Culinary Classic.
Olney, Ross R. Farm Giants.
--Gymnastics.
--Keeping Our Cities Clean.
--Ocean-Going Giants.
--The Shell Auto Care Guide.
--Winners! Super-Champions of Ice Hockey.
Olney, Ross R. & Olney, Patricia J. How Long? To Go, To Grow, To Know.
O'Loughlin, C. National Economic Accounting.
Olowinski, R. Numerical Methods for Non-Linear Variational Problems.
Olsen & Ablon. Medical Dosage Calculations.
Olsen, Charles M. Cultivating Religious Growth Groups.
Olsen, Del. Made in God's Image.
Olsen, Frank H. Church Staff Support: Cultivating & Maintaining Staff Relationships.
Olsen, Henry, et al. Social Science Education: A Book of Readings.
Olsen, Jack. Missing Persons.
--Son: A Psychopath & His Victims.
Olsen, M., ed. Financial Management.
Olsen, M. Rolf. Family Therapy.
Olsen, Nancy. Starting a Mini-Business: A Guidebook for Seniors & Others Who Dream of Having Their Own Part-Time, Home-Based Business.
Olsen, O. Wilford, jt. auth. see Meyer, Marvin C.
Olsen, Roger E. American Business Encounters. Ryan, Gerry, ed.
Olsen, Roger E., jt. auth. see Lee, Lauri E.
Olsen, Roger E., ed. see Bassano, Sharron & Christison, Mary A.
Olsen, T. V. Keno.
--The Man From Nowhere.
Olsen, Tillie. Silences.
--Yonnondio.
Olsen, V. Norskov. John Foxe & the Elizabethan Church.
Olsen, Violet. Never Brought to Mind.
Olshaker, Bennett. What Shall We Tell the Kids?
--What Shall We Tell the Kids?
Olshakers, Thelma. Intimate Strangers.
Olshansky, Oscar. The Rise of the Western Philosophy: The Pre-Socratics.
Olshavsky, Richard W. No More Butts: A Psychologist's Approach to Quitting Cigarettes.
Olshen, Barry N. & Olshen, Toni A. John Fowles: A Reference Guide.
Olshen, Toni A., jt. auth. see Olshen, Barry N.
Ol'shevskii, V. V. Statistical Methods in Sonar.
Olson. Supervisors Resource Set.
Olson, Alan P., jt. auth. see Neely, James A.
Olson, Arnold T. This We Believe.
Olson, Bernadette M., et al. Managing Your Megabytes: Take Full Advantage of Hard Disks,the Streaming Tapes, Bernoulli Box, Hardboards & Optical Devices.
Olson, Bill & Linkert, Lo. Beat the Links.
Olson, Charles. Diagnosis & Management of Diabetes Mellitus: A Clinical Manual for Medical Students, Residents, & Primary Care Physicians.
Olson, Clarinda E. Basic Science for Dental Auxiliaries.
Olson, David O., et al. Solving Cash Flow Problems Using 1-2-3 & Symphony.

Olson, David R., ed. Media & Symbols: The Forms of Expression, Communication, & Education.
Olson, David V. Arab Republic of Egypt Military Decorations & Medals.
--Badges & Distinctive Insignia of the Multinational Force & Observers (MFO)
--Royal Kingdom of Egypt Military Decorations & Medals: Pre-1952 (French Version)
Olson, Donald. The Sky Children.
Olson, Evelyn F. The Months of the Year in Verse.
Olson, Gary L. How the World Works: A Critical Introduction to International Relations.
Olson, Gene. Bailey & the Bearcat.
--Drop into Hell.
--Most Beautiful Girl in the World.
--Pistons & Powderpuffs.
Olson, Harry E., Jr. Monday Morning Christianity.
Olson, Janice K., jt. ed. see Templin, Thomas J.
Olson, Joanne P., jt. auth. see Dillner, Martha H.
Olson, John. Olson's Encyclopedia of Small Arms.
Olson, Julius E. & Bourne, Edward G., eds. Northmen, Columbus & Cabot, Nine Eighty-Five to Fifteen Three.
Olson, Ken. Can You Wait 'til Friday: Psychology of Hope.
--Real Men Do.
Olson, Kenneth J. The Art of Hanging Loose in an Uptight World.
--I Hurt Too Much for a Band-Aid. Lovell, Helen, ed.
Olson, Kent D., et al. Account Book for Farm & Ranch Management.
Olson, Kiki. A Good Man's Not Hard to Find.
Olson, L. D., ed. Algebraic Geometry: Proceedings, Tromso Symposium, June 27-July 8,1977.
Olson, Lawrence. Costs of Children.
Olson, Margot, jt. auth. see Forrest, Mary.
Olson, Melfried, jt. auth. see Aichele, Douglas B.
Olson, Nancy B. A Manual of AACR 2 Examples for Microcomputer Software. Swanson, Edward, ed.
Olson, Nancy Z. Personal & Family Safety.
Olson, Paul. The Future of Being Human.
Olson, Richard P. Changing Male Roles in Today's World: A Christian Perspective for Men - & the Women Who Care about Them.
Olson, Robert G. Meaning & Argument: Elements of Logic.
--A Short Introduction to Philosophy.
Olson, Roberta J. M. Italian Drawings, 1780-1890.
Olson, Stanley. Harold Nicolson Diaries & Letters Nineteen Thirty to Nineteen Sixty-Four.
Olson, Toby. The Woman Who Escaped from Shame.
Olson, W. T., jt. ed. see Hawthorne, William R.
Olson, Wallace E. The Accounting Profession: Years of Trial, 1969-1980.
Olsson, Ake, ed. Adapting Work Sites for People with Disabilties: Ideas from Sweden.
Olsson, B., jt. ed. see Schlepper, M.
Olsson, David L., jt. auth. see Raphael, Harold J.
Olsson, G. Birds in Egg - Eggs in Bird.
Olsson, G., jt. ed. see Gould, P.
Olsson, Karl A. Find Your Self in the Bible: A Guide to Relational Bible Study for Small Groups.
--Meet Me on the Patio: New Relational Bible Studies for Individuals & Groups.
--When the Road Bends: A Book about the Pain & Joy Of Passage.
Olsson, Marie & Miller, Gerald. Parking Discounts & Carpool Formation in Seattle.
Olstad, Walter B., jt. auth. see Cohan, Christopher J.
Olstein, Judi & Buff, Sheila. New Mixer's Guide to Low-Alcohol & Non Alcoholic Drinks.
Olstreng, Willy. Politics in High Latitudes: The Svalbard Archipelago.
Olszak, W., ed. see CISM (International Center for Mechanical Sciences, Department of Mechanics of Solids Staff.
Oltmanns, Thomas F., jt. auth. see Neale, John M.
Olton, Roy, jt. auth. see Plano, Jack C.
Olvey, Lee D. & Leonard, Henry A. Industrial Capacity & Defense Planning: Sustained Conflict & Surge Capability in the 1980s.
Olweus, Dan. Aggression in the Schools: Bullies & Whipping Boys.
Olympic Mountain Rescue Staff. Climber's Guide to the Olympic Mountains.
Olzendam, Dorothy J. Book for a Friend.
Olzendam, Roderic M. & Keith, Gordon. Green Gold for America.
--It Came to Pass in the San Juan Islands.
--Liberty's Grandson: An Unconventional Autobiography.
O'Maille, T. Breacadh.
O'Malia, Thomas J. Banker's Guide to Financial Statements.
O'Malley, B. W. & Birnbaumer, L., eds. Receptors & Hormone Action.
O'Malley, B. W. & Birnbaumer, Lutz, eds. Receptors & Hormone Action.
O'Malley, Bert W., ed. Hormone Action.
O'Malley, Charles D., ed. see Vesalius, Andreas.
O'Malley, Padraig. Uncivil Wars: Ireland Today.
O'Malley, Pat. Law, Capitalism & Democracy: A Sociology of Australian Legal Order.
O'Malley, Susan G., ed. see Goffe, Thomas.
O'Malley, Timothy J. Twenty-Five Graphics Programs in MICROSOFT BASIC.
O'Malley, William J. The Living Word: Scripture & Myth.
Oman, C. The Civic Plate & Insignia of the City of Portsmouth.
Oman, Charles. Wellington's Army, Eighteen Hundred Nine to Eighteen Fourteen.
Oman, Julia T., jt. auth. see Strong, Roy.
Oman, Lela K. Eskimo Legends.
O'Mara, W. P., et al. Residential Development Handbook.
O'Marie, Carol A. A Novena for Murder.
Omark, Donald, et al. Dominance Relations: An Ethological View of Human Conflict & Social Interactions.
O'Meara, Carra F. The Iconography of the Facade of Saint-Gilles-Du-Gard.
O'Meara, Patrick, jt. ed. see Carter, Gwendolen M.
O'Meara, Patrick, jt. ed. see Martin, Phyllis M.
O'Meara, Walter. Sioux Are Coming.
Omenn, Gilbert S., jt. ed. see Ehrmann, Lee.
Omer, Akin. Psychology of Architectural Design.
Ominde, S. H., ed. Studies in East African Geography & Development.
Ominde, S. H. & Ejiogu, C. N., eds. Population Growth & Economic Development in Africa.
Omni Editors see Peary, Danny.
Omni Magazine Editors. Omni's Catalog of the Bizarre. Weintraub, Pamela, ed.
Omohundro, John T. Chinese Merchant Families of Iloilo: Commerce & Kin in a Central Philippine City.
Omond, Roger. The Apartheid Book.
O'Mongain, Eon & O'Toole, C. P., eds. Physics in Industry: Proceedings of an International Conference, Dublin, 1976.
Omori, H. Infinite Dimensional Lie Transformation Groups.
Omoyajowo, Akin. Diversity in Unity: The Development & Expansion of the Cherubim & Seraphim Church in Nigeria.
Omsby, John R., jt. auth. see Johnson, Thomas M.
Omura, George. Mastering AutoCAD.
--Mastering AutoCAD.
Omura, K., ed. C. G. in Japan.
Omura, Yoshiaki. A New Approach to Self-Diagnosis: Introducing Applied Kinesiology.
Omura, Ysohiaki. Acupuncture Therapy: Clinical Diagnosis & Treatment.
Onak, Thomas. Organoborane Chemistry.
O'Nan, Michael. Linear Algebra.
Onat, Etta S. & Orgel, Stephen, eds. The Witch of Edmonton by Thomas Dekker: A Critical Edition.
Ondaatje, Michael. The Collected Works of Billy the Kid.
--Running in the Family.
Ondori Publishing Company Staff. Beautiful Embroidery Designs.
--Crochet for the Home.
--Embroidery of Roses.
--Floral Embroidery.
--Handcraft for Baby: Cotton Wares up to Two Years Old.
--Huck Embroidery.
--Joyful Stuffed Dolls & Animals.
--One-Point Embroidery & Applique.
--Patchwork for Your Home.
--Romantic Lace Designs.
--Simple Embroidery Designs.
--Stitches & Samplers.
--A Treasury of Embroidery Samples.
One Club for Art & Copy Staff. The One Show, Vol. 6: Radio, T. V. & Print's Best Ads.
One Hundred & One Productions Editors. The Whole World Cookbook.
One Hundred Idees Staff. Decorative Home Embroidery.
O'Neal, F. Hodge. O'Neal's Oppression of Minority Shareholders.
O'Neal, James & Werner, G. A. American Communism: A Critical Analysis of Its Origins, Development & Programs.
O'Neal, Lawrence W., jt. auth. see Levin, Marvin E.
O'Neal, Robert, jt. ed. see Benson, Carl.
O'Neal, William see O'Neal, William B.
O'Neal, William B. see O'Neal, William B.
O'Neal, William B., ed. American Association of Architectural Bibliographers' Papers. Incl. Henry-Russell Hitchcock. Grady, James H; Walter Gropius. Shillaber, Carol; Philip C. Johnson. O'Neal, William; Early Architecture of Virginia. Nichols, Frederick D. U Pr of Va.
--American Association of Architectural Bibliographers' Papers. Incl. Sibyl Moholy-Nagy. Johnson, Philip C. & O'Neal, William B.; Holabird & Roche. Rudd, William; Early Architecture of Virginia. Nichols, Frederick D. U Pr of Va.
--American Association of Architectural Bibliographers' Papers. Incl. Walter Gropius. U Pr of Va.
--American Association of Architectural Bibliographers' Papers. Incl. Carroll L. V. Meeks. O'Neal, William B. & Nichols, Frederick D.; Charles-Louis Clerisseau. McCormick, Thomas J; Library at Biltmore. Gooch, Stapleton D; International Expositions, 1851-1900. Davis, Julia F. U Pr of Va.
--American Association of Architectural Bibliographers' Papers. Incl. Henry-Russell Hitchcock. Grady, James H; Architectural Comment in American Magazines, 1783-1815. Neil, J. Meredith; The Adam Style in America, 1770-1820. Boyd, Sterling M; Calvert Vaux. Sigle, John D; Alvar Aalto. Beal, Peter W. U Pr of Va.
--American Association of Architectural Bibliographers' Papers. Incl. Jefferson As an Architect. O'Neal, William B. U Pr of Va.
--American Association of Architectural Bibliographers' Papers. Incl. Sir Nikolaus Pevsner. Barr, John R. U Pr of Va.
--American Association of Architectural Bibliographers' Papers. Incl. A Supplement to the Bibliography of Walter Gropius. Gropius, Ise, ed; A Bibliography of Works About Sir Christopher Wren. Stringer, Gail G., ed; Benjamin Henry Latrobe. Norton, Paul F., ed; Frank Lloyd Wright in Print 1959-1970. Muggenberg, James, compiled by.. U Pr of Va.
--American Association of Architectural Bibliographers Papers. Incl. A Bibliography of Antonio Gaudi & the Catalan Movement, 1870-1930. Collins, George R. & Farinas, Maurice E., eds.. U Pr of Va.
--American Association of Architectural Bibliographers Papers, Vol. 11: Index to Papers 1-10.
O'Neil, Currey. Explore Australia: Touring for Leisure & Pleasure.
--Explore Australia: Touring for Leisure & Pleasure.
O'Neil, Isabel. Art of the Painted Finish for Furniture & Decoration.
O'Neil, Robert F. & Weinberg, Robert, eds. Learning Disabilities & Reading Difficulties.
O'Neil, Thomas. Towards the Life Divine: Sri Aurobindo's Vision.
O'Neil, W. M. A Century of Psychology in Australia.
--Early Astronomy from Babylonia to Copernicus.
--Fact & Theory.
--Time & the Calendars.
O'Neil, Will. The Libyan Kill.
O'Neill, Charles A., ed. see American Kennel Club Staff.
O'Neill, Cherry B. Dear Cherry: Questions & Answers on Eating Disorders.
O'Neill, Colman E. Meeting Christ in the Sacraments.
O'Neill, D. Colorado Accommodations Guide.
O'Neill, Dan. The Collective Unconscience of Odd Bodkins.
O'Neill, Eugene. The Calms of Capricorn. Gallup, Donald, ed.
O'Neill, Eugene see Weiss, Samuel A.
O'Neill, George, jt. auth. see O'Neill, Nana.
O'Neill, George, jt. auth. see O'Neill, Nena.
O'Neill, Gerard K. The Technology Edge: Opportunities for America in World Competition.
--Two Thousand & Eighty-one: A Hopeful View of the Human Future.
O'Neill, Hugh B. Companion to Chinese History.
O'Neill, James M. Early American Furniture.
O'Neill, John. Essaying Montaigne: A Study of the Renaissance Institution of Writing & Reading.
O'Neill, Joseph P. Corporate Tuition Aid Programs: A Directory of College Financial Aid for Employees at America's Largest Corporations.
O'Neill, Mary L. Ali.
O'Neill, Nana & O'Neill, George. Open Marriage: A New Lifestyle for Couples.
O'Neill, Nancy Chapel. The New American Stock Purchase Plan.
O'Neill, Nena & O'Neill, George. Shifting Gears.
O'Neill, Timothy R. The Individuated Hobbit: Jung, Tolkien & the Archetypes of Middle-Earth.
O'Neill, William L. A Better World-The Great Schism: Stalinism & the American Intellectuals.
O'Neill, William L., jt. auth. see Gardner, Lloyd C.
O'Neill, William L., ed. The American Sexual Dilemma.
O'Neill East, M., ed. Tioconazole: A New Antifungal in Dermatology.
Ong, Helen H. & Lewis, John C., eds. Hypertension: Physiological Basis & Treatment.
Ong, Walter J. Rhetoric, Romance & Technology: Studies in the Interaction of Expression & Culture.
Ongley, Edwin D. Introduction to the Physical Landscape: Watersheds & Fluvial Systems.
Onikov, E. Handbook of Cotton Weaving.
Onions, C. T., et al. The Fate of French-E in English: The Plural of Nouns Ending in-th. Commager, Steele, ed. Incl. Basic; Problems of Spelling Reform; Pure English of the Soil; Inflected English; The Critique of Pure English; Retrospect. Garland Pub.
Online Conference, Ltd., ed. Word Processing: Selection, Implementation & Uses.
Online Conference Staff. Micros in DP: Micro Monograph, Proceeding of the Online Conference, Interface, London, 1980.
--Viewdata '81: Proceedings of the Online Conference, London, 1981.
Online Conference, Toronto, 1981. Videotex: Papers.
Online Conferences Ltd., ed. Personal Computers in Business.
--Pragmatic Programming & Sensible Software.
--Word Processing: An Up-to-Date Assessment.
Onn, Gerald, tr. see Boudon, Philippe.
Ono, Hideichi. Everyday Expressions in Japanese.
Onoh, J. K., ed. The Foundations of Nigeria's Financial Infrastructure.
Onstott, Kyle. Mandingo.
Ontani, F. One Hundred Years of Health Progress in Japan: Progress in Japan.
Ontario Ministry of Treasury & Economics Library Staff. Budget & Expenditure Process & Reforms: A Bibliography with Emphasis on Canada.
Ontario Ministry of Treasury & Economics, Library Services Staff. Canadian & Provincial Industrial Policies - Strategy Debates since 1970: A Bibliography.
--Industrial Policies - Strategy Debate since 1970: General, International & United States, a Selected Bibliography.
--Public Sector Accountability: A Selected Bibliography with Emphasis on Canada.
Ontiveros, Suzanne R. Corporate Social Responsibility: Contemporary Viewpoints.
Ontiveros, Suzanne R., jt. ed. see Andrade, Kerry M.
Onuallain, Collin. The Presidency of the European Council of Ministers: Impact & Implications for National Government.
Ooi, Jin-Bee & Chiang, Hai D., eds. Modern Singapore.
Ooka, D. T., tr. see Nakano, Toru.
Oole, Eugenia M. Art Is for Children.
Oommen, T. K. Doctors & Nurses.
Ooms, Herman. Charismatic Bureaucrat: A Political Biography of Matsudaira Sadanobu, 1758-1829.
Oosawa, Fumio & Asakura, Sho. Thermodynamics of the Polymerization of Protein.
Oostdyk, Harv. Step One: The Gospel & the Ghetto.
Oosten, Jarich G. The War of the Gods: The Social Code in Indo-European Mythology.
Oosterbaan, John. Population Dispersal: A National Imperative.
Oosterveen, Karla, tr. see Mitterauer, Michael & Sieder, Reinhard.
Oosthuizen, Ann. Sometimes When It Rains: Short Stories by South African Women.
Oosthuizen, Ann, ed. Stepping Out: Short Stories on Friendships Between Women.
Oota, K. Histological Typing of Gastric & Oesophageal Tumors.
Oparin, A. I. The Origin of Life. Morgulis, Sergius, tr. & annotations by.
Opdyke, D. L., ed. Monographs on Fragrance Raw Materials.
OPEC Staff. Annual Statistical Bulletin, 1981.
Opeke, Lawrence K. Tropical Tree Crops.
Opella, S. J. & Lu, P. NMR & Biochemistry.
Open University Staff. Understanding the Twentieth Century: A Course Guide.
Opferkuch, W. & Rother, K., eds. Clinical Aspects of the Complement System.
Ophthalmic Microsurgery Study Group Symposium Staff. Microsurgery in Glaucoma: Proceedings of the Ophthalmic Microsurgery Study Group Symposium, 2nd, Buergenstock, 1968. Mackensen, G., ed.
Opie, L., jt. ed. see Harris, P.
Opie, Mrs. Adeline Mowbray: Or, The Mother & Daughter.
Opitz, H. A Classification System to Describe Workpieces, Classification System. Taylor, R. A., tr.
Opitz, Helmut & Strasser, Karl H., eds. Publisher's International Directory with ISBN Index, 1988.
Oplatka, Avraham & Balaban, Miriam, eds. Biological Structures & Coupled Flows.
Opoku, Khamal S. Fired.
Oppedahl, Carl. Advanced Programming for the Model 100.

Authors

Oppelt, Norman T. Guide to Prehistoric Ruins of the Southwest.
Oppeneer, Joan, jt. auth. see Vervoren, Thora.
Oppeneer, Joan E. & Vervoren, Thora M. Gerontological Pharmacology: A Resource for Health Practitioners.
Oppenheim, A. K. Impact of Aerospace Technology on Studies of the Earth's Atmosphere.
Oppenheim, A. K., ed. see CISM (International Center for Mechanical Sciences) Staff.
Oppenheim, A. Leo. Letters from Mesopotamia: Official, Business, & Private Letters on Clay Tablets from Two Millennia.
Oppenheim, David. Small Solar Buildings in Cool Northern Climates.
Oppenheim, Mary L. Aquatic Aide: A Guidebook for Water Safety Instruction.
Oppenheim, S. Chesterfield & Shields, Carrington. Newspapers & the Antitrust Laws.
Oppenheim, Shulamith. The Selchie's Seed.
Oppenheimer, Edna, jt. auth. see Stimson, Gerry V.
Oppenheimer, Joan F. Working on It.
Oppenheimer, Joan L. Stepsisters.
Oppenheimer, Joel. Houses.
Oppenheimer, Paul. Before a Battle & Other Poems.
Oppenheimer, Peter, ed. Issues in International Economics.
Oppenheimer, S. L. & Borchers. Direct & Alternating Currents.
Oppenheimer, Valerie K. The Female Labor Force in the United States: Demographic & Economic Factors Governing its Growth & Changing Composition.
Opperman, Hal N. Jean-Baptiste Oudry Sixteen Eighty-Six to Seventeen Fifty-Five.
Oppermann, Alfred. Dictionary of Modern Engineering.
--Dictionary of Modern Engineering.
Oppermann, Alfred, ed. Dictionary of Modern Engineering: English-German-German-English.
Oppermann, Edward B., jt. auth. see Plane, Donald R.
Oppert, J. Moving to Metrics in Home Economics.
Oppler, Ellen C. Fauvism Reexamined.
Opsahl, Paul D. The Holy Spirit in the Life of the Church: From Biblical Times to the Present.
Opsahl, Paul D. & Tanenbaum, Marc H., eds. Speaking of God Today: Jews & Lutherans in Conversation.
Optatus, Saint Optati Milevitani Libri Septum.
Optimization & Stability Problems in continuum Mechanics Symposium Staff. Proceedings of the Optimiztion & Stability Problems in Continuum Mechanics Symposium, Los Angeles, 1971. Wang, P. K., ed.
Optimization Symposium Staff. Proceedings of the Optimization Symposium, Nice, 1969. Balakrishna, A. V., et al, eds.
Opton, Gene & Hughes, Nancie. Honey Feast.
O'Quinn, J. Frank, ed. Jesus' Lost Gospels: The Discovery at Nag Hammadi.
O'Quinn, John, ed. see Lindsay, Jack.
O'Quinn, John, ed. see Ostrander, Sheila & Schroeder, Lynn.
O'Quinn, John F. Urine Therapy: Self-Healing Through Intrinsic Medicine.
O'Rahilly, Ronan, jt. auth. see Vidic, Branislav.
Oraker, James & Meredith, Char. Almost Grown: A Christian Guide for Parents of Teenagers.
Oram, Hiawyn. Angry Arthur.
Oram, Hugh. Where to Go in the West of Ireland.
Oram, R. B. Cargo Handling in a Modern Port.
Oram, R. B. & Baker, C. C. The Efficient Port.
Orange Book Co. Staff, jt. ed. see Graphic-Sha Staff.
Oravetz, Jules, Sr. Questions & Answers for Plumbers Examinations.
Orbach, Susie. Hunger Strike: The Anorectic's Struggle for Survival As a Metaphor for Our Age.
Orbis Editors. The Illustrated Who's Who of the Cinema.
Orchard, Edward G., ed. Soloviev - History of Russia.
Orchard, R. E. This Is Our Hope.
Orchard, Richard E. Look Who's Coming.
Orchard, W. E. Sancta Sanctorum.
Orchin, Milton M., jt. auth. see Jaffe, H. H.
Orcutt, Georgia. Soups, Chowders & Stews. Taylor, Sandra, ed.
Orcutt, Georgia & Taylor, Sandra, eds. Breads, Rolls, & Pastries.
--Poultry & Game Birds.
Orcutt, James D. Analyzing Deviance.
Ord, David. Handwriting Analysis.
Ord, H. W. & Livingstone, I. An Introduction to West African Economics.
Ord, H. W., jt. auth. see Livingstone, Ian.
Ord, J. K., jt. auth. see Cliff, A. D.
Ord, Margery G. & Stocken, Lloyd A. Cell & Tissue Regeneration: A Biochemical Approach.
Orde, Lewis. Eagles.
--Heritage.
--The Lion's Way.
--Munich Ten.
Orden, M. D. Van see Van Orden, M. D.
Ordish, George. The Living Garden: The 400-Year History of an English Garden.
Ordway, Nicholas, jt. auth. see Tosh, Dennis.
Oregon Association of Milk, Food, & Environment Sanitarians, Inc., Education & Training Committee. HTST Pasteurizer Operation Manual.
Oregon Competencies Program Northwest Regional Educ. Lab. Staff. Competency Based Education Sourcebook.
Oreilly, Emily. Country Inns Britain 86-87.
O'Reilly, J. Telecommunication Principles.
O'Reilly, J. J. Telecommunications Principles.
Orel, Harold, ed. Irish History & Culture: Aspects of a People's Heritage.
Orel, Harold, jt. ed. see Wiley, Paul L.
O'Relley, Z. Edward. Soviet-Type Economic Systems: A Guide to Information Sources.
Orentlicher, Herman, jt. auth. see Fryer, William T.
Orfanos, C. E., et al, eds. Hair Research: Status & Future Aspects.
Orfield, Gary. Congressional Power: Congress & Social Change.
Orford, Jim, jt. ed. see Feldman, Philip.
Organ, Dennis W. & Hamner, Clay. Organizational Behavior: An Applied Psychological Approach.
Organic Gardening Editors & Stoner, Carol H. Stocking Up.
Organick, E. I. & Hinds, J. A. Interpreting Machines: Architecture & Programming of the B1700-1800 Series.
Organization for Economic Cooperation & Development Staff. Company Tax Systems in OECD Member Countries.
--Meat Balances in OECD Countries, 1977-1983.
--Negative Income Tax: An Approach to the Co-Ordination of Taxation and Social Welfare Policies.
Organization of American States Editors. Index to Latin American Periodical Literature, 1929-1960.
--Index to Latin American Periodical Literature 1966-1970.
Organization of Peace Commission & Holcombe, Arthur N. Strengthening the United Nations.
Organization of the Petroleum Exporting Countries (OPEC) Staff, ed. Annual Statistical Bulletin, 1980.
Orgel, Stephen, ed. An Edition of Robert Wilson's Three Ladies of London & Three Lords & Three Ladies of London.
--Two Burlettas of Kane O'Hara, Midas & the Golden Pippin: An Edition with Commentary.
Orgel, Stephen, ed. see Bocchi, Achille.
Orgel, Stephen, ed. see Brome, Richard.
Orgel, Stephen, ed. see Clugston, George A.
Orgel, Stephen, ed. see Fletcher, John.
Orgel, Stephen, ed. see Goffe, Thomas.
Orgel, Stephen, ed. see Jones, Thomas.
Orgel, Stephen, ed. see Marmion, Shakerly.
Orgel, Stephen, jt. ed. see Onat, Etta S.
Orgel, Stephen, ed. see Shirley, James.
Orgel, Stephen, ed. see Tyson, Archie M.
Orgill, Michael, et al. Mind Angel & Other Stories. Elwood, Roger, ed.
Orhnial, Tony, ed. Limited Liability & the Corporation.
Orians, G. H., jt. ed. see Warfel, Harry R.
Orians, Gordon, jt. auth. see Purves, William.
Origo, Iris. Images & Shadows: Part of a Life.
--The Merchant of Prato: Francesco di Marco Datini.
--A Need to Testify.
Oringer, Maurice J. Electrosurgery in Dentistry.
Orion Research Corporation Staff. Orion Blue Book Audio 1988.
Orion Research Corporation Staff, ed. Audio Blue Book, 1987.
--Camera Blue Book, 1987.
--Computer Blue Book, 1987.
--Professional Sound Blue Book, 1987.
--Video Blue Book, 1987.
Orion Research Staff. Computer Buyer's Guide, 1985. Rohrs, Roger, ed.
O'Riordain, Sean P. Antiquities of the Irish Countryside.
O'Riordan, J. L. Recent Advances in Endocrinology & Metabolism.
O'Riordan, T. Perspectives on Resource Management.
O'Riordan, Timothy & Turner, R. Kerry, eds. Progress in Resource Management & Environmental Planning.
Oriti, Ronald, jt. auth. see Starbird, William.
Orkin, Harvey. Scuffler.
Orland, Frank J. Microbiology in Clinical Dentistry.
Orland, Henri, jt. auth. see Negele, John W.
Orland, Matthew J, jt. auth. see Cahill, Donald R.
Orlando, Ralph J., Sr. Talking with You.
Orlans, Harold. Contracting for Atoms.
Orlen, Steve. A Place at the Table.
Orlev, Uri. The Lead Soldiers. Halkin, Hillel, tr. from Hebrew.
Orlick, Gloria. The Ninth Reading Helper.
Orlick, Terry. The Cooperative Sports & Games Book: Challenge Without Competition.
Orlik, P. Seifert Manifolds.
Orlob, Helen. Wide World of Aaron Burr.
Orlosky, Donald E. & Smith, B. Othanel. Curriculm Development.
Orlov, Y. A., ed. Fundamentals of Paleontology: Mammals.
--Fundamentals of Paleontology: Porifera, Archaeocyatha, Coelentera, Vermes.
Orlova, Alexandra. Musorgsky's Days & Works: A Biography in Documents. Brown, Malcolm, ed. Guenther, Roy, tr.
Ormandy, P. G. An Introduction to Metallurgical Laboratory Techniques.
Orme, J. E. Abnormal & Clinical Psychology: An Introductory Text.
Orme, Michael. Micros: A Pervasive Force.
Orme, Nicholas. English Schools in the Middle Ages.
--Grammatical Miscellany of Fourteen Twenty-Seven to Fourteen Sixty-Five: From Bristol & Wiltshire.
Ormerod, Roger. Dead Ringer.
--Seeing Red.
--Still Life with Pistol.
Ormond, Brande. American Primitives in Needlepoint.
--Needlepoints to Go: Small Projects for Spare Moments.
Ormond, Brande & Muller, Marion. Museum Masterpieces in Needlepoint.
Ormond, Richard. Sir Edwin Landseer.
Ormondroyd, Edward. All in Good Time.
--Theodore's Rival.
--Time at the Top.
Ormston, B. J., et al. Current Studies on Thyrotropin, I.
Orna, Elizabeth & Stevens, Graham. The Presentation of Information.
Ornati, Oscar. Poverty Amid Affluence. Sweet, J. S., ed.
Orne, Peter, jt. auth. see Zbar, Paul B.
Orne, R., jt. auth. see Zbar, Paul B.
Ornish, Dean. Stress, Diet, & Your Heart.
Ornstein, Allan C. & Levine, Daniel U. An Introduction to the Foundations of Education.
Ornstein, Allan C. & Miller, Harry L. Looking into Teaching.
Ornstein, Robert E. Multimind.
--Psychology: The Study of Human Experience.
Ornstein, Robert E. & Thompson, Richard F. The Amazing Brain.
Ornston, L. Nicholas & Sligar, Steve, eds. Experiences in Biochemical Perception.
Orosius, Paulus. Historiarum Adversum Paganos Libri. Zangemeister, C., ed.
O'Rourke, Frank. A Texan Came Riding. Bd. with Desperate Rider. NAL.
O'Rourke, J., jt. auth. see Dale, Edgar.
O'Rourke, Janet & Wallat, Lee. Peter Pirate's Hospital Coloring Book.
O'Rourke, R. A., jt. auth. see Ross, J.
Orozco, R. Asepsis in Surgery: Its Special Application to Orthopedics. Garaza, E., tr. from Span.
Orpin, Alan, jt. auth. see Byfield, Brian.
Orr, A. P., jt. auth. see Marshall, S. M.
Orr, Alexandra. Handbook to the Works of Robert Browning.
Orr, Alexandra L. Life & Letters of Robert Browning.
Orr, Bill & Lutzer, Erwin. If I Could Change My Mom & Dad.
Orr, Clyde. Filtration.
Orr, D., ed. see Orr European Geophysical Symposium Staff.
Orr, Dan. A Common Sense Safety Guide to Applied Recreational Diving.
Orr, David W. & Soroos, Marvin S., eds. The Global Predicament: Ecological Perspectives on World Order.
Orr, Dick & Bartlett, David L. Bible Journeys.
Orr European Geophysical Symposium Staff. Geomagnetic Pulsations: Proceedings of the Orr European Geophysical Symposium, Budapest, August 1980. Orr, D., ed.
Orr, J. S., jt. ed. see Harland, W. A.
Orr, John H. Crime, Corruption, Conviction.
Orr, Larry L. Income, Employment & Urban Residential Location.
Orr, Larry L., et al. Income Maintenance: Interdiciplinary Approaches to Research.
Orr, Linda. A Certain X.
Orr, Sidney D., jt. auth. see Bates, Steven L.
Orr, Susan D. Baton Twirling Unlimited.
Orr, William I. Radio Handbook.
Orrall, Frank, ed. Solar Active Regions.
Orrey, Leslie. Bellini.
--Bellini.
Orsborn, Carol. Enough Is Enough: Exploding the Myth of Having It All.
Orsen, Dennis. Focus for Evangelism: The Evangelical Implications of Ministry.
Orser, Evelyn. On My Back, Looking Up! Coffen, Richard W., ed.
Orsini, Luigi. The Scuderia Ferrari.
Orso, Kathryn W. It's Great to Pray.
Orszagh, L. English-Hungarian Pocket Dictionary.
--Hungarian Deluxe Dictionary: English-Hungarian.
--Hungarian Deluxe Dictionary: Hungarian-English.
Orszagh, Laszlo. Hungarian Concise Dictionary: Hungarian-English.
--Hungarian-English-English-Hungarian Dictionary.
--Hungarian Pocket Dictionary: English-Hungarian.
--Hungarian Pocket Dictionary: Hungarian-English.
Ortali, Raymond. Aujourd'hui.
Ortano, Egidio, et al. The Problem of International Consultations.
Ortega, Carlos & Romera, Carlos. Communication Policies in Peru.
Ortega, Pedro R. La Conquistadora.
Ortega Y Gasset, Jose. Concord & Liberty.
--Dehumanization of Art, & Other Essays on Art, Culture & Literature.
--Idea of Principle in Leibnitz & the Evolution of Deductive Theory.
--An Interpretation of Universal History. Adams, Mildred, tr. from Span.
--Meditations on Quixote.
--Mission of the University.
--Phenomenology & Art. Silver, Philip W., tr. from Span.
--Velazquez Goya, the Dehumanization of Art & Other Essays. Brown, Alexis, tr.
Orten, James M. & Neuhaus, Otto W. Human Biochemistry.
Ortho Books Editorial Staff, jt. auth. see Williams, T. Jeff.
Ortho Books Editorial Staff, ed. Gardening with Color.
Ortho Books Editorial Staff, ed. see MacCaskey, Michael R.
Ortho Books Staff, ed. All about Roses.
Orthodox Eastern Church Staff. Prayers for the Dead.
Ortiz, Alfonso. Tewa World: Space, Time, Being, & Becoming in a Pueblo Society.
Ortiz, Simon J. A Good Journey.
Ortiz, Simon J. & Graves, Sharol. The People Shall Continue.
Ortiz-Griffin, Julia, jt. auth. see Sallese, Nicholas F.
Ortiz-Ortiz, Librado, et al, eds. Actinomycetes Biology.
Ortland, Anne. Disciplines of the Beautiful Woman.
Ortlund, Anne. The Acts of Joanna.
--Spiritual Disciplines.
--Up with Worship.
Ortlund, Raymond C. Lord, Make My Life Count.
Orton, Charles, ed. see IFSTA Committee.
Orton, D. H., et al. The Solid State Maser.
Orton, Harold, jt. auth. see Renwick, William L.
Orton, Joe. Up Against It.
Orton, Richard, compiled by. Records of California Men in the War of the Rebellion: 1861-1867.
Orton, Samuel T. Reading, Writing & Speech Problems in Children.
Orton, Vrest. The Homemade Beer Book.
Ortquist, Richard T. Depression Politics in Michigan, 1929-1933.
Ortzen, Len. Strange Stories of UFOs.
Orvell, Tamar, jt. auth. see Edelfelt, Roy A.
Orville-Thomas, W. J., jt. ed. see Barnes, A. J.
Orville-Thomas, W. J., jt. ed. see Ratajczak, H.
Orwell, George. Animal Farm. Dycko, Iryna, tr.
--The Collected Essays, Journalism, & Letters of George Orwell. Angus, Ian, ed. Incl. Vol. 1. An Age Like This: Nineteen Twenty to Nineteen Forty; Vol. II. My Country Right or Left: Nineteen Forty to Nineteen Forty-Three; Vol. III. As I Please: Nineteen Forty-Three to Nineteen Forty-Five; Vol. IV. In Front of Your Nose: Nineteen Forty-Five to Nineteen Fifty. HarBraceJ.
--Dickens, Dali, & Others.
--Nineteen Eighty-Four.
--Nineteen Eighty-Four & Animal Farm.
Orwell, George & Angus, Ian, eds. The Collected Essays, Journalism, & Letters of George Orwell.
Orwig, Sara. Heat Wave.
Oryx Press Staff. Directory of Biomedical & Health Care Grants.
Oryx Press Staff, ed. Directory of Research Grants 1986.
Osaba, David, jt. ed. see Lindahl.
Osadchy, Mykhaylo. Cataract. Carynnyk, Marco, tr. from Ukrainian.
--Cataract. Carynnyk, Marco, tr. from Ukrainian.
Osancova, K., tr. see Parizkova, Jana.
Osborn, A. D. Edmund Husserl & His Logical Investigations: Cambridge, Mass., 1949. Natanson, Maurice, ed.
Osborn, A. F., et al. The Social Life of Britain's Five-Year Olds: A Report on the Child Health & Education Study.

Authors

Osborn, D. Keith. Early Childhood Education in Historical Perspective.
Osborn, D. Keith & Osborn, Janie D. Discipline & Classroom Management.
Osborn, E. M. Short Visit to Ergon.
Osborn, Fairfield. Limits of the Earth.
Osborn, George C. & Martin, Don. The Role of the British Press in the 1976 American Presidential Election.
Osborn, H., jt. ed. see Cummings, J.
Osborn, Jack R. & Kornbluth, Jesse. Winning Croquet: From Backyard to Greensward.
Osborn, Janie D., jt. auth. see Osborn, D. Keith.
Osborn, John J., Jr. The Associates.
Osborn, Marijane & Longland, Stella. Rune Games.
Osborn, Richard N., et al. Organization Theory: An Integrated Approach.
Osborn, Robert. Osborn on Osborn.
Osborn, Robert & Benton, Fred W. Dying to Smoke.
Osborn, Roger. Tables of All Primitive Roots of Odd Primes Less Than 1,000.
Osborn, Susan. Free Things for Teachers.
Osborn, Susan & Weiss, Jeffrey, eds. The Book of Country Living.
Osborn, T. L. Faith Speaks.
--Miracles: Proof of God's Power.
--Soulwinning: Out Where the People Are.
Osborne, A., et al. Micro Systems in Business.
Osborne, A. K. Encyclopedia of Iron & Steel Industry.
Osborne, A. L. Dictionary of English Domestic Architecture.
Osborne, Adam. Running Wild: The Next Industrial Revolution.
Osborne, Adam, et al. The Osborne-McGraw-Hill Business System Buyer's Guide.
--CBM Professional Computer Guide.
Osborne, Alan, ed. An In-Service Handbook for Mathematics Education.
Osborne, B. W. Color Television: Reception & Decoding Techniques.
Osborne, C. W., ed. International Yearbook of Educational & Instructional Technology 1984-85.
Osborne, Cecil. Art of Understanding Your Mate: With Leader's Guide.
Osborne, Charles. The Complete Operas of Mozart.
--The Complete Operas of Puccini: A Critical Guide.
--The Dictionary of the Opera.
--The Dictionary of the Opera.
--The Life & Crimes of Agatha Cristie.
--Richard Wagner & His World.
--W. H. Auden: The Life of a Poet.
Osborne, Charles, ed. The Bram Stoker Bedside Companion: 10 Stories by the Author of Dracula.
--The Dictionary of Composers.
--The Opera House Album: A Collection of Turn-of-the-Century Postcards.
Osborne, Charles, ed. see Stoker, Bram.
Osborne, Chester G. The Memory String.
Osborne, Chris, ed. International Yearbook of Educational & Instructional Technology 1986-1987.
Osborne, E. Alfred. Funny Business: A Senile Executive's Guide to Power & Success.
Osborne, Elsie, jt. auth. see Dowling, Emilia.
Osborne, Gail B., jt. auth. see Brody, Jean.
Osborne, Grant R. The Resurrection Narratives: A Redactional Study.
Osborne, Harold. Aesthetics & Criticism.
--Theory of Beauty.
Osborne, Harrison. In Defense of Fascism: A New Critical Evaluation of the Fascist Experience in Modern History.
Osborne, Jerry. Fifty-Five Years of Recorded Country Western Music.
--A Guide to Record Collecting.
--Original Record Collectors Price Guide: Blues-Rhythm & Blues-Soul.
--Price Guide Popular & Rock Records 1948-1978: 45 & 78 R P M.
Osborne, Jerry & Hamilton, Bruce. Original Record Collectors Price Guide: Record Album Price Guide.
--Presleyana Price Guide.
Osborne, John. The Third Year of the Nixon Watch.
Osborne, John J., Jr. The Man Who Owned New York.
Osborne, June. Hampton Court Palace.
Osborne-McGraw-Hill Editors, ed. The Model 100 Companion: Business & Entertainment Programs for Portable Computing.
Osborne, Milton. Before Kampuchea: Preludes to Tragedy.
--River Road to China: The Mekong River Expedition, 1866-73.
--South East Asia.
Osborne, Neville N. Microchemical Analysis of Nervous Tissue.
Osborne, Neville N., ed. Biochemistry of Characterized Neurons.
Osborne, R. T., et al, eds. Human Variation: The Biopsychology of Age, Race, & Sex.
Osborne, R. Travis. Twins Black & White.
Osborne, Richard H. & De George, Frances V. Genetic Basis of Morphological Variation: An Evaluation & Application of the Twin Study Method.
Osborne, Robert. Sixty Years of the Oscar: The Official History of the Academy of Motion Picture Arts & Sciences.
Osborne, Samuel P. The Cross-Country Skier's Handbook: A Complete Guide to Technique, Equipment, Competition Clubs, & Trails.
Osborne, Thomas J. & Mabbutt, Fred R. Paths to the Present: Thoughts on the Contemporary Relevance of America's Past.
Osborne, W. C. Fans.
Osborne-Creigh, Richard. This Is Sailing.
Osbourne, Jerry & Hamilton, Bruce. Record Albums Price Guide.
Osbourne, Lloyd, jt. auth. see Stevenson, Robert Louis.
Osbourne, Pamela G. Regional Directory of Minority & Women-Owned Business Firms: Southeastern Region.
Osbourne, Pamela G., ed. National Directory of Minority-Owned Business Firms.
--National Directory of Women-Owned Business Firms.
--Regional Directory of Minority & Women-Owned Business Firms: North Central Region.
--Regional Directory of Minority & Women-Owned Business Firms: Western Region.
Osburn, Charlie & Lilly, Fred. The Charlie Osburn Story: You Gotta Give It All to Jesus.
Oschman, James L., jt. auth. see Berridge, Michael J.
Osdol, B. M. Von see Van Osdol, B. M., et al.
Osdol, Bob M. Van see Van Osdol, Bob M. & Perryman, Patricia.
Osdol, William R. Van see Van Osdol, William R.
Osee, Johan. Call of the Virgin at San Damiano.
Oser, H., et al, eds. Life Sciences & Space Research XXI (2) Proceedings of Workshops VII & XI & of the COSPAR Interdisciplinary Scientific Commission F (Meetings F1, F3, F5, F6, F7, & F9) of the COSPAR 25th Plenary Meeting Held in Graz, Austria, 25 June - 7 July 1984.
Oser, Jacob. The Evolution of Economic Thought.
Oser, Jacob & Blanchfield, William C. Evolution of Economic Thought.
Oser, Jacob, jt. auth. see Blanchfield, William C.
Osgood, Charles. Nothing Could Be Finer Than a Crisis That Is Minor in the Morning.
--There's Nothing That I Wouldn't Do If You Would Be My POSSLQ.
Osgood, Charles F., ed. Diophantine Approximation & Its Applications.
Osgood, Cornelius. Anthropology in Museums of Canada & the United States.
Osgood, Cornelius, ed. see Hoijer, Harry, et al.
Osgood, Don. Fatherbond.
Osgood, Lawrence see Corrigan, Robert W.
Osgood, W. Planning & Financing Your Business.
Osgood, William & Hurley, Leslie. The Snowshoe Book.
Osgood, William R. Basics of Successful Business Management.
--Planning & Financing Your Business: A Complete Working Guide.
O'Shaughnessy, Arthur. Music & Moonlight. Fletcher, Ian & Stokes, John, eds.
--Songs of a Worker. Fletcher, Ian & Stokes, John, eds.
Oshawa, George. You Are All Sanpaku.
O'Shea, John P. Scientific Principles & Methods of Strength Fitness.
O'Shea, Mary J. Chicago.
O'Shea, Peter V. Guide to Adirondack Trails: Northern Region. Burdick, Neal S., ed.
Osier, John. Covenant at Coldwater.
Osigweh, Chimezie A. Improving Problem-Solving Participation: The Case of Local Transnational Voluntary Organizations.
Osing, Gordon. From the Boundary Waters.
Osing, Gordon, ed. The Good People of Gomorrah.
Osing, Gordon T. A Town Down River. Easson, Roger R., ed.
Oski, Frank A. & Naiman, J. Lawrence. Hematologic Problems in the Newborn.
Osley, A. S., ed. Scribes & Sources.
Oslin, Dorothy. My Christmas Praise Book.
Osman, Betty B. Learning Disabilities: A Family Affair.
Osman, Tony. The Facts of Everyday Life.
Osman, William C. Evolutionary Biology of the Primates.
Osmond, D. S., tr. see Steiner, Rudolf.
Osmond, Humphry, jt. auth. see Hoffer, Abram.
Ossenbeck, Frederick J. & Kroeck, Patricia C., eds. Open Space & Peace.
Osseo-Asare, K. & Miller, J. D., eds. Hydrometallurgy-Research, Development & Plant Practice: Proceedings of the AIME Annual Meeting, Atlanta, 1983.
Osso, Nicholas. Statistics of Public School Library Media Centers, 1974 (LIBGIS I)
Ossowski, Stanislaw. Class Structure in the Social Consciousness. Patterson, Sheila, tr. from Pol.
Ost, Steve. How to Increase Your Faith.
Ostby, illus. Kittelsen Theodor.
O'Steen, Van & Bates, John R. Arizona No-Fault Divorce.
Osten-Sacken, Peter Von Der see Von Der Osten-Sacken, Peter.
Oster, Gerald, et al, eds. Physical Techniques in Biological Research. Incl. Vol. 1A. Optical Techniques. Oster, Gerald, ed; Vols. 2A-2B. Physical Chemical Techniques. Moore, Dan H., ed; Vol. 3. Cells & Tissues, 3 Pts. Pollister, Arthur W., ed; Vol. 4. Special Methods. Nastuk, William L., ed; Vol. 5. Electrophysiological Methods, Pt. A. Nastuk, William L., ed; Vol. 6. Electrophysiological Methods, Pt. B. Acad Pr.
Oster, Harry. Living Country Blues.
Oster, J. D., jt. auth. see Shainberg, I.
Oster, Jerry. Municipal Bonds.
Oster, Kenneth. Islam Reconsidered: A Brief Historical Background to the Religion & Thought of the Moslem World.
Oster, Maggie. Gifts & Crafts from the Garden.
Osterby, O. & Zlatev, Z. Direct Method for Sparse Matrices.
Ostergren, Jan. Rainmaker. Matthais, John & Printz-Pohlson, Goran, trs. from Swedish.
Osterheld, William, jt. auth. see Slurzberg, Morris.
Osterloh, Gunter. Applied Leica Technique. Fricke, Rolf, tr. from Ger.
Osterman, Jonny, jt. auth. see Nording, Carl.
Ostermeier, David M., jt. auth. see Sedjo, Roger A.
Osterrieth, P., et al. Improving Education for Disadvantaged Children: Some Belgian Studies.
Ostiguy, Jean-Rene. Modernism in Quebec Art, Nineteen Sixteen to Nineteen Forty-Six.
Ostler, Scott & Springer, Steve. Winnin' Times: The Rise & Rise of the Los Angeles Lakers.
Ostmann, Barbara G., jt. ed. see Baker, Jane.
Ostow, Mortimer, ed. The Psychodynamic Approach to Drug Therapy.
Ostrager, Barry R., jt. auth. see Practising Law Institute Staff.
Ostrander, Gilman M. Slavery in the Union.
Ostrander, Lee E. Proceedings of the Seventh New England (Northeast) Bioengineering Conference: Held March 22-23, 1979, at Rensselaer Polytechnic Institute, Troy, New York.
Ostrander, Linda, jt. auth. see Owyang, Lily.
Ostrander, Sheila & Schroeder, Lynn. Seventy-Six Psychic Techniques: A Primer in Parapsychology. O'Quinn, John, ed.
Ostriker, Alicia S. Stealing the Language: The Emergence of Women's Poetry in America.
--Stealing the Language: The Emergence of Women's Poetry in America.
Ostrin, S. L., jt. ed. see Ring, A. M.
Ostrin, Samuel & Ring, Alvin M. Review Questions In Clinical Pathology.
Ostrom, Charles W., jt. auth. see Starr, Harvey.
Ostrosky, Anthony L., Jr. & Koch, James V. Introduction to Mathematical Economics.
Ostrow, David G., jt. auth. see Nichols, Stuart.
Ostrow, Marshall. The T.F.H. Book of Gerbils.
Ostrowksi. Echo Time-Word His Te.
Ostrowsky, O. Engineering Drawing for Technicians.
--Engineering Drawing for Technicians.
Ostroy, Sanford E., jt. ed. see Abrahamson, Edwin.
Ostwalt, Adeline H. The Church Is for All People.
Osuagwu, Harold G. Investment Demand in a Developing Country: The Nigerian Case.
O'Sullivan, Bernard J., compiled by. Bloodstock Sales Analysis, 1962.
O'Sullivan, Eamon. Textbook of Occupational Therapy.
O'Sullivan, Joan, jt. auth. see Helmer, Howard.
O'Sullivan, John. From Voluntarism to Conscription: Congress & Selective Service, 1940-1945. Freidel, Frank, ed.
O'Sullivan, Patrick. Geographical Economics.
O'Sullivan, Patrick, et al. Transport Network Planning.
O'Sullivan, Susan B., et al. Physical Rehabilitation: Evaluation & Treatment Procedures.
Oswal, M. C. A Textbook of Soil Physics.
Oswald, jt. auth. see Krar, S. F.
Oswald, Adrian & Hildyard, R. J. English Brown Stoneware, Sixteen Seventy to Nineteen Hundred.
Oswald, Allan. History & Practice of Falconry.
Oswald, J. W., jt. auth. see Krar, S. F.
Oswald, John C. Benjamin Franklin, Printer.
Oswald, Kent, ed. see Atkinson, Hugh.
Oswald, Michael. Serious Stories for Children.
Oswalt, John. The Leisure Crisis.
Oswalt, Wendell H. This Land Was Theirs: A Study of the North American Indian.
Oswatitisch, K., ed. see Symposium Transsonicum Staff.
Otaala, B., jt. auth. see Ohuche, R. O.
Otcenasek, M. & Dvorak, J. Pictorial Dictionary of Medical Mycology: English-Russian-French-German-Latin.
Otero, George G. Teaching about New Mexico History & Culture.
Otero, George G. & Smith, Gary R. Teaching about Food & Hunger.
Otero, George G., Jr. Teaching about Perception: The Arabs.
Otero, Raymond B. Laboratory Exercises in Microbiology.
Otis, Alison T., et al. Forest Service & the Civilian Conservation Corps: 1933-42.
Otis, Charles E. Aircraft Gas Turbine Powerplants.
Otis, Jay L. & Leukart, R. H. Job Evaluation.
O'Toole, C. P., jt. ed. see O'Mongain, Eon.
O'Toole, G. J. The Spanish War: An American Epic 1898.
O'Toole, George. The Private Sector: Rent-a-Cops, Private Spies, & the Police-Industrial Complex.
O'Toole, James. Energy & Social Change. Center for Futures Research, ed.
--Guide to the Archives of the Archdiocese of Boston.
--Vanguard Management: Redesigning the Corporate Future.
O'Toole, R. Religion: Classic Sociological Approaches.
O'Toole, William A. Why America Will Survive: Some Thoughts on the Survival of Civilizations.
Ott, Gil. Maize.
Ott, H. & Fletcher, J. M. Mediaeval Statutes of the Faculty of Arts of the University of Freiburgh Im Breisgau.
Ott, Heinrich. God.
Ott, Henry W. Noise Reduction Techniques in Electronic Systems.
Ott, Joseph K. Rhode Island Furniture.
Ott, Karl O. & Bezella, Winfred A. Introductory Nuclear Reactor Statics.
Ott, L., jt. auth. see Lewis, C. L.
Ott, Lyman, jt. auth. see Mendenhall, William.
Ott, Patricia. Bitter Passion, Sweet Love.
Ott, Pierre, jt. auth. see Hill, Stuart.
Ott, Virginia, jt. auth. see Swanson, Gloria.
Ott, Wolfgang. Sharks & Little Fish.
Ottaway, David & Ottaway, Marina. Afrocommunism.
Ottaway, Hal N. & Edwards, Jim L. The Vanished Splendor: Postcard Views of Early Oklahoma City.
Ottaway, John R., jt. auth. see Baer, Charles J.
Ottaway, Marina, jt. auth. see Ottaway, David.
Otten, Anna, ed. Meistererzahlungen.
Otten, Terry. After Innocence: Visions of the Fall in Modern Literature.
Otterbeck, Lars, jt. auth. see Hedlund, Gunnar.
Otterbein, Keith. Comparative Cultural Analysis: An Introduction to Anthropology.
Otterstad, Robert L., jt. auth. see Beck, Hubert F.
Ottewell, Guy. Astronomical Calendar, 1988.
Ottewill, R. H., ed. Adsorption from Solution.
Ottewill, R. H., ed. see International Union of Pure & Applied Chemistry.
Ottley, John. Greenberg's Guide to LGB. Greenberg, Linda, ed.
Ottley, Reginald. Bates Family.
--Boy Alone.
--No More Tomorrow.
--Roan Colt.
Ottman, Robert W. Elementary Harmony.
Otto, Herbert A., jt. auth. see Loring, Rosalind K.
Otto, Luther B., jt. auth. see Call, Vaughn R.
Otto of Freising. Deeds of Frederick Barbarossa. Mierow, Christopher, tr.
Otto, Robert C. Publishing for the People: The Firm Posrednik, 1885-1905. McNeill, William H. & Jelavich, Barbara, eds.
Otto, Wayne & Smith, Richard J. Corrective & Remedial Teaching.
Otto, Wayne, et al. Corrective & Remedial Teaching.
Ottobre, Frances M., ed. see International Association for Educational Assessment Staff.
Ottoway, Richard N. Humanising the Workplace: New Proposals & Perspectives.
Otu, Ojaovo I. Bleeding Soul Ame.
Otwell, John, jt. auth. see Hordern, William.
Otwell, John H. And Sarah Laughed: The Status of Woman in the Old Testament.
Ouano, E. A., et al. Water Pollution Control in Developing Countries.
Ouden, Bernard D. Essays on Reason, Will, Creativity, & Time: Studies in the Philosophy of Friedrich Nietzsche.
--A Symposium on Ethics: The Role of Moral Values in Contemporary Thought.
Oudenhoven, van Nico J. see Van Oudenhoven, Nico J.
Ouellette, Fernand. Edgard Varese.
Ouellette, Robert P. & King, John A. Chemical Week Pesticides Register.
Ouellette, Sue E., ed. see University of Tennessee, 1979, Knoxville, Tenn. Staff.
Ough, C. S., jt. auth. see Amerine, M. A.

Oughton, Marguerita see Freeman, T. W., et al.
Ouida see also De La Ramee, Louise.
Ouimette, Helen E. Country Catalog of Memories: A Childhood on a German-American Farm in the Late 1920s & Early 1930s.
Oulton, J. E. & Chadwick, Henry, eds. Alexandrian Christianity.
Our Lady of Grace Montessori School of Manhasset Staff, compiled by. Specialties of the House.
Ousby, Ian. Literary Britain & Ireland.
Ousmane, Sembene. Xala. Wake, Clive, tr. from Fr.
Ouspensky, P. D. Conscience: The Search for Truth.
--Conscience: The Search for Truth.
--A Further Record.
--Letters from Russia, 1919.
--Strange Life of Ivan Osokin.
--Strange Life of Ivan Osokin.
--Talks with a Devil.
Outhwaite, William. Concept Formation in Social Science.
Outterson, Leslie A. This I Believe-Thank You, Billy Sunday, for the Goodness & Mercy Which I Know.
Ovchinniko, Yu A. & Ivanov, V. T. Conformational States & Biological Activity of Cyclic Peptides. Barton, Derek, ed.
Ovenden, Michael W. Looking at the Stars.
Overbeck, Cynthia. The Fruit Book.
--Splash the Dolphin. Hammarberg, Dyan, tr. from Fr.
Overbeck, Cynthia, jt. auth. see Thompson, Brenda.
Overbeck, Daniel B. Begin at the Beginning: Teaching Basic Response Patterns.
Overbeck, Wayne & Pullen, Rick D. Major Principles of Media Law.
Overdieck, D., et al, eds. Biometeorology: Ninth International Biometeorological Congress held in Osnabruck & Stuttgart-Hohenheim 1981.
Overduin, Daniel. Reflections Books.
--Reflections on the Creed.
--Reflections on the Lord's Prayer.
--Reflections on the Sacraments.
--Reflections on the Ten Commandments.
Overend, Tronn. Social Idealism & the Problem of Objectivity.
Overgard, William. Rudy in Hollywood.
Overholser, Grace M. God's Family in God's World.
Overholser, Grace M. & Beck, Madeline H. God Loves All People.
Overholser, Wayne D. The Best Western Stories of Wayne D. Overholser. Pronzini, Bill & Greenberg, Martin H., eds.
--Buckaroo's Code.
--Cast a Long Shadow.
--Fabulous Gunman.
Overholt, James. Dr. Jim's Elementary Math Prescriptions.
Overholtzer, Ruth. Song of the Shepherd.
--Wordless Book Visualized.
Overstad, Elizabeth, jt. ed. see Kysar, Ardis.
Overstake, Charles P. Stuttering: A New Look at an Old Problem Based on Neurophysiological Aspects.
Overstreet, Harry A. Mature Mind.
Overstreet, Helen-Mary F., jt. auth. see Kline, Draza.
Overstreet, Robert M. The Comic Book Price Guide.
--The Comic Book Price Guide.
--Comic Book Price Guide.
--The Comic Book Price Guide.
--The Comic Book Price Guide.
--The Comic Book Price Guide.
--The Comic Book Price Guide, No. 11.
Overton, Willis F. & Gallagher, J. M., eds. Knowledge & Development, Vol. 1: Advances in Research & Theory.
Ovesy, Regina, ed. see Fashion Group Inc., Members & Friends Staff.
Ovid. Metamorphoseon. Pontanus, Jacobus, ed.
--Metamorphoses. Garth, et al, trs.
Oviedo, Jose M. Escrito al Margen.
Ovies, Bob. New Lives: What Happened When Twenty-Two Ordinary People Encountered the Extraordinary Love of God.
Ovington, Ray. Tactics on Bass: How to Fish the 23 Most Common Bass "Hotspots"
Owen, Bill, jt. auth. see Buxton, Frank.
Owen, David. A Future That Will Work: Competitiveness & Compassion.
--Human Rights.
--None of the Above: Behind the Myth of Scholastic Aptitude.
Owen, David E. British Opium Policy in China & India.
Owen, David L. The Desert My Dwelling Place.
Owen, David M. Sounds of the Passion: Meditations on Jesus' Journey to the Cross.
Owen, Dilys. Leo Possessed.
Owen, Francis. The Germanic People.
Owen, G. E. Logic, Science, & Dialectic: Collected Papers in Greek Philosophy.
Owen, G. Frederick. Jerusalem.
Owen, Hugh. Gandhi.
Owen, J. B., ed. Performance Recording in Sheep.
Owen, J. I., ed. Brassey's Infantry Weapons of the World.
Owen, James J., jt. auth. see Byers, John R., Jr.
Owen, Jan. Guidebook to Adventure.
--Understanding Computer Information Networks.
Owen, John D. The Price of Leisure.
Owen, John E. Sociology: Readings.
Owen, Pat H. The Genesis Principle for Parents.
Owen, R. J. Trial of Faith.
Owen, Ray. Listening to Life. Penoi, Mary & Condit, Kay, eds.
--Probings in Prayer: Why the Closet?
Owen, Ray, jt. auth. see Woods, Sylvia.
Owen, Robert. New Moral World. Incl. Greenwood.
Owen, Robert & Bullock, John. Riding.
Owen, Roger. Middle East in the World Economy, 1800-1914.
Owen, Trefor, jt. auth. see Fenton, Alexander.
Owen, Trevor. The Manager & Industrial Relations.
Owen, Wendy. The Education of Winnie D.
Owens, Alfred W., II, jt. auth. see Hugenberg, Lawrence W., Sr.
Owens, Anne, ed. see Owens, Lawrence.
Owens, Charles E. Mental Health & Black Offenders.
Owens, Delia, jt. auth. see Owens, Mark.
Owens, Elisabeth A. International Aspects of U. S. Income Taxation: Cases & Materials.
Owens, Elisabeth A., jt. auth. see Gifford, William C.
Owens, Frank J., et al, eds. Magnetic Resonance of Phase Transitions.
Owens, Iris. Hope Diamond Refuses.
Owens, Iris see Daimler, Harriet, pseud.
Owens, Jessie & O'Connor, Dick. Track & Field.
Owens, Larry. How to Keep Your Subaru Alive: Easy Step by Step Repair & Maintenance Procedures.
Owens, Lawrence. Tax Havens Around the World. Owens, Rachel & Owens, Anne, eds.
Owens, Leroy. Memoirs of a Citizen-Politician.
Owens, Louis, jt. auth. see Colonnese, Tom.
Owens, Mark & Owens, Delia. Cry of the Kalahari.
--Cry of the Kalahari.
Owens, Mary B. A Caribou Alphabet.
Owens, Norma F., jt. auth. see Bouchard, Rosemary.
Owens, R. Glynn & Ashcroft, J. Barrie. Violence: A Guide for the Caring Professions.
Owens, Rachel, ed. see Owens, Lawrence.
Owens, Susan. Energy, Planning & Urban Form.
Owens, William, ed. Close-up Photography.
Ower, Ernest & Pankhurst, F. C. Measurement of Air Flow: In SI-Metric Units.
Owings, Donnell M. His Lordship's Patronage: Offices of Profit in Colonial Maryland.
Owings, Loren C., ed. Environmental Values, Eighteen Sixty to Nineteen Seventy-Two: A Guide to Information Sources.
Owman, Christer & Edvinsson, Lars, eds. Neurogenic Control of the Brain Circulation.
Owram, Doug. Promise of Eden: The Canadian Expansionist Movement & the Idea of the West, 1856-1900.
Owsley, Vicki B. Infant Temperament & Its Relationship to Child Abuse with the First Two Years of Life.
Owyang, Lily & Ostrander, Linda. Creative Piano: A Modular Approach for Adult Beginners.
Oxaal, Ivar, et al, eds. Beyond the Sociology of Development.
Oxenbury, Helen, jt. auth. see Maschler, Fay.
Oxenfeldt, Alfred R. Pricing Strategies.
Oxenfeldt, Alfred R., et al. A Basic Approach to Executive Decision Making.
--A Basic Approach to Executive Decision Making.
Oxenfelt, Alfred R. Pricing Strategies.
Oxenham, J., jt. ed. see Watson, K.
Oxenhandler, Neal. Change of Gods.
Oxford. Chemotherapy & Control of Influenza.
Oxford, Arnold. English Cookery Book to 1850.
Oxford Dietetic Group Staff & Mann, Jim. The Diabetics' Diet Book.
Oxford, J. S., et al, eds. Chemotherapy of Herpes Simplex Virus Infections.
Oxford Travel Guide Editors. Oxford Travel Guide.
Oxford University, British Commonwealth Group Staff. Germany's Colonial Demands. Bullock, A. L., ed.
Oxford University Press Editors. Dictionary of Chemistry.
Oxley, David, intro. by see French, Ray.
Oxley, David A. Three Decades to Doom.
Oxley, Dorothy. Summer Dreams.
--Winter Song.
Oxley, Mary B. Illustrated Guide to Individualized Kindergarten Instruction.
Oxley, R. & Poskitt, J. Management Techniques Applied to the Construction Industry.
Oxtoby & Sandison. Once upon a Christmas.
Oxtoby, L., tr. see Gruber, U. F.
Oyama, Masutatsu. The Kyokushin Way.
--This Is Karate.
--Vital Karate.
Oyen, Hendrik van see Van Oyen, Hendrik.
Oyer, J. S. Lutheran Reformers Against Anabaptists.
Oyeregui, Buenaventura de. Diccionario Vasco-Castellano, Castellano-Vasco De Voces Comunes a Dos O Mas Dialectos Del Euskera.
Oyler, William, tr. see Zink, Heidi & Zink, Jorg.
Oyono-Mbia, Guillaume. Three Suitors: One Husband & Until Further Notice.
Oz, Amos. Elsewhere Perhaps. De Lange, Nicholas, tr.
--The Hill of Evil Counsel.
--In the Land of Israel. Goldberg-Bartura, Maurie, tr.
--Touch the Water, Touch the Wind. DeLange, Nicholas, tr. from Hebrew.
--Unto Death: "Crusade" & "Late Love"
--Where the Jackals Howl & Other Stories. De Lange, Nicholas & Simpson, Philip, trs.
Ozaki, Robert S. The Japanese: A Cultural Portrait.
Ozanne, Charles G. The First Seven Thousand Years: A Study in Bible Chronology.
Ozanne, Larry, jt. auth. see Vanski, Jean.
Ozelton, E. C. & Baird, J. A. Timber Designer's Manual.
Ozenfant, A. Foundations of Modern Art. Rodker, John, tr.
Ozisik, M. Necati. Basic Heat Transfer.
Ozment, Robert V. Love Is the Answer.
Ozonoff, M. B. Pediatric Orthopedic Radiology.

P

P. S. Associates see Summerlin, Lee R.
Pabst, Robert, jt. auth. see Ingpen, Brian.
Paccard, Andre. Traditional Islamic Craft in Moroccan Architecture.
Pace, C. Robert. Measuring Outcomes of College: Fifty Years of Findings & Recommendations for the Future.
Pace Gallery Publications, ed. see Dine, Jim.
Pace Gallery Publications Staff, ed. Ad Reinhardt, Paintings & Watercolors.
--Lucas Samaras, Chair Transformations.
Pace Gallery Publications Staff, ed. see Bowman, Russell.
Pace Gallery Publications Staff, ed. see Hunter, Sam.
Pace Gallery Publications Staff, ed. see Ratcliff, Carter.
Pace, Mildred M. Pyramids: Tombs for Eternity.
Pace, Nicholas A. & Cross, Wilbur. Guidelines to Safe Drinking.
Pace, Patricia E. Kansas City: The Spirit, the People, the Promise.
Pacer Business Automation Staff & Duchesneau, David. Advanced Development Techniques for dBASE II & dBASE III.
Pacer Business Automation Staff, et al. Advanced Program Implementation for dBASE II & dBASE III.
Pacey, Arnold, ed. Water for the Thousand Millions.
Pacey, Desmond. Ten Canadian Poets: A Group of Biographical & Critical Essays.
Pachauri, R. K., ed. International Energy Studies.
Pachman, Ludek. Chess Endings for the Practical Player. Littlewood, John, ed. Hardy, Otto, tr.
--The Middle Game in Chess. Littlewood, John, tr.
--The Opening Game in Chess. Littlewood, John, tr.
Pachman, Ludek & Kuhnmund, Vas I. Computer Chess.
Pacholczyk, A. G. Radio Galaxies: Radiation Transfer, Dynamics, Stability & Evolution of a Synchroton Plasmon.
Pacholski, L., et al, eds. Model Theory of Algebra & Arithmetics.
Pachter, Josh, tr. see Luitjters, Guus & Timmer, Gerard.
Pacific Basin Conference Staff. American Nuclear Society Transactions: Nuclear Power Plant Construction, Operation, & Development, 2nd Conference.
Pacific Northwest Section Conference & Exhibit Staff. Instrumentation-82: Proceedings of the 1982 Pacific Northwest Section Conference & Exhibit.
Pacini, Kathy, ed. see Bartoli, Jennifer.
Pacini, Kathy, ed. see Hooker, Ruth & Smith, Carole.
Pacini, Kathy, ed. see Hopkins, Lee B.
Pacini, Kathy, ed. see Quackenbush, Robert.
Pacione, Michael, ed. Progress in Industrial Geography.
--Progress in Political Geography.
Paciorek, Karen M., jt. auth. see McKee, Judy S.
Paciorek, Karen M., jt. ed. see McKee, Judy S.
Pack, Alice C. Prepositions.
Pack, Greta, jt. auth. see Davis, Mary L.
Pack, Howard. Fostering the Capital-Goods Sector in LDCs: A Survey of Evidence & Requirements.
--Macroeconomic Implications of Factor Substitution in Industrial Processes.
Pack, Janet & Brehrens, Dietlinde. Dictionary Yakan-Filipino-English.
Pack, Melvyn, jt. auth. see Booth, Alan.
Pack, Robert, ed. see Alvarez, Julia.
Pack, Robert, ed. see Jackson, Richard.
Pack, Robert, ed. see Mariani, Paul.
Packard, Cindy. The Mother Load.
Packard, Edward. ESP McGee.
--Gorga, the Space Monster.
Packard, H. Jeremy. Battle Cry of Freedom: The United States 1848-1877.
Packard, Jerrold M. Peter's Kingdom: Inside the Papal City.
Packard, Karen L., jt. auth. see Hagerty, Bonnie K.
Packard, M. David, ed. Defense Management, Interim Report to the President.
Packard, Russell C. The Psych Wards.
Packard, Vance. Our Endangered Children: Growing up in a Changing World.
--The People Shapers.
Packard, William. Saturday Night at San Marcos.
Packard, Winthrop. Florida Trails: As Seen from Jacksonville to Key West & from November to April Inclusive.
Packe, Michael. Winged Stallion: Fighting & Training with the First Airborne.
Packer, Bernard. The Second Death of Samuel Auer.
--The Sons of Saintly Women.
Packer, Billy & Lazenby, Roland. Hoops! Confessions of a College Basketball Analyst.
Packer, David W. Resource Acquisition in Corporate Growth.
Packer, Lester. Biomembranes, Architecture, Biogenesis, Bioenergetics & Differentiation.
Packer, Lester, jt. ed. see Mukohata, Yusuo.
Packer, Lewis. Serpentine Futures.
Packer, Moira, jt. auth. see Leese, See.
Packer, William. Fashion Drawing in Vogue.
--Henry Moore: An Illustrated Biography.
Packie, Robert M. Storm Treasure.
Pactor, P. & Kargilis, G. Card-Punch Machine Operation.
--Card-Punch Machine Operation.
Padarathsingh, M., jt. auth. see Dean, J.
PADCO, Inc. Staff & World Bank Staff. The Bertaud Model: A Model for the Analysis of Alternatives for Low-Income Shelter in the Developing World.
Padday, J. F., ed. Wetting, Spreading & Adhesion.
Paddock, Elizabeth, jt. auth. see Paddock, William.
Paddock, William & Paddock, Elizabeth. We Don't Know How: An Independent Audit of What They Call Success in Foreign Assistance.
Pade, Victoria. Passion's Torment.
--Reckless Yearning.
--When Love Remains.
Paden, Ann, jt. ed. see Carter, Gwendolen M.
Paden, Grier L. Facts about Life All People Should Know.
Padfield, Peter. Rule Britannia: The Victorian & Edwardian Navy.
--Tide of Empires: Decisive Naval Campaigns in the Rise of the West.
--Tide of Empires: Decisive Naval Campaigns in the Rise of the West, 1654-1763.
Padgett, Ron. How to Be Modern Art.
Padgett, Ron, jt. ed. see Zavatsky, Bill.
Padgett, Vincent L. The Mexican Political System.
Padgett, W. J., jt. auth. see Tsokos, C. P.
Padgett, W. J., jt. auth. see Tsokos, Chris P.
Padgette, Paul, ed. see Van Vechten, Carl.
Padilla, George M., jt. ed. see Cameron, Ivan L.
Padilla, George M., et al. Cell Cycle Controls.
--Cell Cycle: Gene-Enzyme Interactions.
Padmanabham, K. A. & Davies, G. J. Superplasticity.
Padolecchia, Siro P. Marketing in the Developing World.
Padover, Saul K., ed. Karl Marx on Freedom of the Press & Censorship.
Padulo, Louis & Arbib, Michael A. System Theory: A Unified State-Space Approach to Continuous & Discrete Systems.
Padyluka, Helen A., ed. see International Society for Cell Biology Staff.
Padzensky, Herbert R. & Gibson, Jane. Goalguide: A Minicourse in Writing Goals & Behavioral Objectives for Special Education.
Paek, Min. Aekyung's Dream.
Paetro, Maxine. Manshare: A Novel.
Pagano, Alicia L., ed. Social Studies in Early Childhood: An Interactionist Point of View.
Pagano, Christian, jt. auth. see Fages, Jean B.
Page, A. A Dictionary of Photographic Terms.
Page, B. G. & Thomson, W. T. The Insecticide, Herbicide, Fungicide Quick Guide, 1988.
Page, Bill, jt. auth. see Pierce, Carol.
Page, Carole G. The Two Worlds of Tracy Corbett.

Page, Elizabeth. Tree of Liberty.
Page, Emma. Final Moments.
Page, Frank, ed. World of Sail & Power Nineteen Seventy-Eight to Nineteen Seventy-Nine.
Page, Harry R. Public Purchasing & Materials Management.
Page, J. H. Forgotten Railways: South Wales.
Page, Jake. Demon State.
Page, James A. & Roh, Jae M., eds. Selected Black American, African & Caribbean Authors: A Bio-Bibliography.
Page, Jesse. The Black Bishop: Samuel Adjai Crowther.
Page, John, Jr. Shadow Prices for Trade Strategy & Investment Planning in Egypt.
Page, John S. & Nation, Jim G. Estimator's Piping Man-Hour Manual.
Page, Jones. Practical Guide to Structured Systems Design.
Page, Joseph A. The Law of Premises Liability.
Page, Kirby. Now Is the Time to Prevent a Third World War.
Page, Kirby see Myers, Denys P.
Page, Kogan, jt. auth. see Cugy, Andre.
Page, Norman. Thomas Hardy.
--Thomas Hardy Annual.
--Wilkie Collins.
Page, P. K. The Sun & the Moon & Other Fictions.
Page, Paul F., ed. Gather 'Round.
--Gather 'Round Too!
Page, Robert M. Stigma.
Page, S. F., jt. auth. see Haynes, J. H.
Page, Spider. Legend in Blue Steel.
Page, T. Economics of Involuntary Transfers: A Unified Approach to Pollution & Congestion Externalities.
Page, Theresa. Lab Manual for Anatomy & Physiology.
Page, Tom, ed. The Upper Room Disciplines, 1986.
Page, Vicki. Partnership of Hearts.
Page, Victor W. Early V-Eight Ford Service Manual: 1932-1950. Clymer Publications, ed.
--Ford Model A Service Manual & Handbook of Repair & Maintenance. Clymer Publications, ed.
--Ford Owner's Handbook: Models T & a Nineteen Hundred & Eight to Nineteen Twenty-Eight. Clymer Publications, ed.
--Model A Ford: Care & Maintenance of Automobiles & Trucks.
Page, William. The Gatekeeper.
Page, William D. & Pinnell, Gay S. Teaching Reading Comprehension: Theory & Practice.
Page, William D., ed. Help for the Reading Teacher: New Directions in Research.
Pagels, Elaine H. The Gnostic Paul.
Pagels, Heinz. The Cosmic Code: Quantum Physics As the Law of Nature.
--Perfect Symmetry: The Search for the Beginning of Time.
Paget, Francis E. St. Antholin's; or, Old Churches & New: A Tale for the Times, 1841. Wolff, Robert L., ed. Bd. with Milford Malvoisin; or, Pews & Pew-Holders, 1842. Garland Pub.
Pagnol, Marcel. My Father's Glory & My Mother's Castle. Barisse, Rita, tr.
Pagnoni, A. & Rozenberg, G., eds. Applications & Theory of Petri Nets.
Pagtolun-an, Imelda, jt. auth. see Flieger, Wilhelm.
Paher, Stanley W. Nevada Towns & Tales: South.
Pahl, R. E., ed. Readings in Urban Sociology.
Pahl, T. Readings in Minnesota Government: Politics & Administration.
Pahler, Arnold J. & Mori, Joseph E. Advanced Accounting: Concepts & Practice.
--Advanced Accounting: Concepts & Practices.
Pahlow, M. Giftpflanzenkompass: Giftige Pflanzen und Ihre Fruechte Sicher Bestimmen.
Pai. Viscous Flow Theory: Laminar Flow.
Pai, Anna C. Foundations of Genetics: A Science for Society.
Pai, S. I., ed. see Dynamics of Fluids & Plasmas Symposium Staff.
Pai, Shi I., jt. auth. see Cramer, Kenneth R.
Pai, Young. Teaching, Learning, & the Mind.
Paidoussis, M. P., jt. ed. see Chen, S. S.
Paige, Barbara E. Your Future in a Dental Hygiene Career.
Paige, Connie. The Right to Lifers: Who They Are, How They Operate, Where They Get Their Money.
Paige, Donald D., jt. auth. see Willcutt, Robert E.
Paige, Glenn D. Korean People's Democratic Republic.
Paige, Nigel, jt. auth. see George, Susan.
Paige, Richard E. Little Inventions That Made Big Money: Children's Version.
Paikeday, Thomas M., ed. see New York Times Staff.
Pain, F. Practical Wood Turner.
Pain, James, ed. see Bulgakov, Sergius.
Paine, Albert B. Snowed-in Book. Roberts, Thom, ed.
Paine, Albert B., jt. ed. see Roberts, Thom.
Paine, David, jt. auth. see Buzby, Walter J.
Paine, Emmanuel & Paine, Wingate. The Book of Surrender.
Paine, Frank T. & Anderson, Carl R. Strategic Management.
Paine, Frank T. & Naumes, William. Organizational Strategy & Policy: Text & Cases.
Paine, Frank T., jt. auth. see Carroll, Stephen J., Jr.
Paine, Harriett, jt. auth. see McWilliams, Margaret.
Paine, Lauran. Assassins' World.
--The Medicine Bow.
Paine, Nigel, jt. auth. see Lewis, Roger.
Paine, Philbrook. Squarely Behind the Beavers.
Paine, R. & Soper, A. Art & Architecture of Japan.
Paine, Suzanne H., jt. auth. see Fforde, Adam.
Paine, Wingate, jt. auth. see Paine, Emmanuel.
Painter, Derek. The Future of the Word Processor. Hills, P. J., ed.
Painter, Genevieve. Teach Your Baby.
Painter, Helen W. Poetry & Children.
Painter, Martin. Steering the Modern State: Changes in Central Coordination in Three Australian State Governments.
Painter, Nell I. Exodusters: Black Migration to Kansas After Reconstruction.
Painter, Richard J. & Yantis, Richard C. Elementary Matrix Algebra with Applications.
Painter, Sidney. Mediaeval Society.
--The Rise of the Feudal Monarchies.
Painter, William H. Nineteen Eighty-Six Supplement to Corporate Tax Aspects of Closely Held Corporations.
Pai Shih-I. Radiation Gas Dynamics.
Paisner, Daniel, jt. auth. see Scott, Willard.
Paisner, Milton. One Word Leads to Another: A Light History of Words.
Pak, Charles Y. Calcium Urolithiasis: Pathogenesis, Diagnosis, & Management.
Pak, Pyong-ho, et al. Modernization & Its Impact upon Korean Law.
Pakula, Hannah. The Last Romantic: A Biography of Queen Marie of Roumania.
Pal, Anjali. Jataka Tales from the Ajanta Murals.
Pal, Pratapaditya. Tibetan Paintings: A Study of Tibetan Thankas, 11th-19th Centuries.
Pal, Pratapaditya, ed. Aspects of Indian Art.
Pal, Pratapaditya, et al. Light of Asia: Buddha Sakyamuni in Asian Art.
Palacios, Argentina, tr. see Bridwell, Norman.
Palacios, Jorge. Chile: An Attempt at "Historic Compromise" The Real Story of the Allende Years.
Palacios, Rafael, jt. ed. see Mora, Jaime.
Paladin Press Staff. Automatic & Concealable Firearms Design Book, III.
Paladino, Lawrence J. A Touch of Poetry.
Palaeontographical Society Staff. Directory of British Fossiliferous Localities.
Palandri, Angela J., tr. Modern Verse from Taiwan.
Palardy, J. Michael. Teaching Today: Tasks & Challenges.
Palau, Luis. My Response.
--So You Want to Grow.
--Time to Stop Pretending.
Palay, S. L. & Chan-Palay, V. Cerebellar Cortex: Cytology & Organization.
Palazzo, Tony. Animal Family Album.
--Animals of the Night.
Paleg, L. G. & Aspinall, D., eds. Physiology & Biochemistry of Drought Resistance in Plants.
Paleologue, Maurice. Three Critical Years, 1904-05-06.
Palestrina, Giovani Pierluigi da. Pope Marcellus Mass. Lockwood, Lewis, ed.
Paley, Norton, jt. auth. see Elam, Houston G.
Paley, Paula, tr. see Mririda.
Paley, Vivian G. Wally's Stories.
Paley, William. The Principles of Moral & Political Philosophy. Wellek, Rene, ed.
Palgrave, Robert H. Dictionary of Political Economy.
Paliano, Guido C. di see Di Paliano, Guido C., et al.
Palic, Vladimir M. Government Publications.
Palin, G. R. Chemistry for Technologists.
--Electrochemistry for Technologists.
Palin, Michael, jt. auth. see Jones, Terry.
Palinski, Christine O., jt. auth. see Pizer, Hank.
Paliouras, John D. Complex Variables for Scientists & Engineers.
Palisca, Claude, jt. auth. see Grout, Donald J.
Palisca, Claude V., tr. see Zarlino, Gioseffo.
Palit, D. K. Return to Sinai: The Arab Offensive 1973.
Palkovic, M. Hormones, Lipoproteins & Atherosclerosis: Proceedings of a Satelite Symposium of the 28th International Congress of Physiological Sciences, Bratislava, Czechoslovakia, 1980.
Palladian, Arthur. Careers in Soccer.
--Careers in the Air Force.
--Careers in the Army.
--Careers in the Navy.
Palladius. Spiritual Advice from the Early Christian Ascetics: Selections from the Lausaic History of Palladius.
Pallares, Eduardo. Dixcionario de Filosofia.
Pallasmaa, Juhani, ed. see Aalto, Alvar.
Palley, Marian L., jt. auth. see Gelb, Joyce.
Palliere, Aime. Unknown Sanctuary.
Palliser, Fanny M. Historic Devices, Badges, & War-Cries.
Pallister, Janis L., jt. auth. see Cormier, Ramona.
Pallos, Ferenc M. & Casida, John E., eds. Chemistry & Action of Herbicide Antidotes (Symposium) (MS-REPRO)
Pallotta, Jerry. The Bird Alphabet Book.
--The Icky Bug Alphabet Book.
--The Ocean Alphabet Book.
Palm, Franklin C. Calvinisim & the Religious Wars.
Palm, G. Neural Assemblies: An Alternative Approach to Artificial Intelligence.
Palm, Rick, ed. FCC Rule Book.
Palm, Thede. The Finnish-Soviet Armistice Negotiations of 1944.
Palma, Guiseppe Di see Di Palma, Giuseppe.
Palmer & Weinert. Where Is Bone?
Palmer, Adrian S. & Kimball, Margot C. Getting Along in English.
Palmer, Adrienne. Dealer's Choice.
Palmer, Alan. The Chancelleries of Europe.
Palmer, Alan, compiled by. Quotations in History: A Dictionary of Historical Quotations, c800 A. D. to the Present.
Palmer, Alan W. Dictionary of Modern History.
Palmer, Ann, jt. auth. see Cooper, Rosaleen.
Palmer, Arnold & Dobereiner, Peter. Arnold Palmer's Complete Book of Putting.
Palmer, Arnold & Furlong, Barry. Go for Broke.
Palmer, Bernard. Kid Breckenridge.
--The Mystery at Poor Boy's Folly.
--Shoot-Out at Buffalo Gulch.
Palmer, Bryan D. A Culture in Conflict: Skilled Workers & Industrial Capitalism in Hamilton, Ontario 1860-1914.
Palmer County Historical Society Staff. Parmer County History.
Palmer, Crystal S., ed. GeoRef Thesaurus & Guide to Indexing.
Palmer, David F., jt. auth. see Mariani, Michael P.
Palmer, David J., ed. Writers & Their Background: Alfred Tennyson.
Palmer, Donald F., jt. auth. see Allison, Ira S.
Palmer, Dorothy A., jt. auth. see Lee, Raymond L.
Palmer, E. Hoyt. Country Boy Grown Old: His Story of Earlier Days.
Palmer, Earl. In Search of a Faith That Works.
Palmer, Earl F. The Intimate Gospel: Studies in John.
Palmer, Edwin. History of Hollywood. Kupelnick, Bruce S., ed.
Palmer, Elsie & Oeltjen, Jody. Eating the Oregon Way.
Palmer, Frank. Grammar.
Palmer, Frederick. John J. Pershing, General of the Armies: A Biography.
Palmer, Friend. Early Days in Detroit: Papers Written by General Friend Palmer, of Detroit, Being His Personal Reminiscences of Important Events & Descriptions of the City for Over Eighty Years.
Palmer, Gene C., ed. Neuropharmacology of Cyclic Nucleotides: Role of CAMP in Affective Disorders, Epilepsy & Modified Behavioral States.
Palmer, George E. Nineteen Eighty-Four Supplement to Law of Restitution.
Palmer, Harold. Philosophy of Psychiatry: Psychiatric Prolegomena.
--Psychopathic Personalities.
Palmer, James A. & Feigenbaum, Edward D. Campaign Finance Law Eighty-Six: A Summary of State Campaign Finance Laws with Quick Reference Charts.
Palmer, Jim. Pitching. Cohan, Joel, ed.
Palmer, John D. An Introduction to Biological Rhythms.
Palmer, Kenneth T. & Horan, James F., eds. Studies in American Politics.
Palmer, King, jt. auth. see Rhys, Stephen.
Palmer, L. S. Man's Journey Through Time.
Palmer, Laura. Merry Mix-up: A Finder-Seeker Mystery.
--Ou Est Os?
Palmer, Lloyd. On This Rock.
Palmer, Lynne. Astrological Almanac for 1986.
--Astrological Almanac for 1987.
--Astrological Almanac, 1988: With 4 Months of 1987.
Palmer, Marjorie. God Helps David.
Palmer, Marjorie & Bowman, Ethel. The New Mother's Book of Baby Care.
--Young Mother's Book of Ideas.
Palmer, Martin, jt. auth. see Tang, Stephen.
Palmer, Martin, ed. & tr. T'ung Shu: The Ancient Chinese Almanac.
Palmer, Martin, tr. from Chinese. T'ung Shu.
Palmer, Monte. Dilemmas of Political Development.
Palmer, Nehemiah M. Understanding Yourself, Society & Marriage.
Palmer, Nigel. Sri Lanka.
Palmer, Norman D. The Irish Land League Crisis.
Palmer, Paige, ed. Guide to the Best Buys in Package Tours.
Palmer, R. B., jt. ed. see Fuerstenau, Maurice C.
Palmer, Robert. Baby, That Was Rock & Roll: The Legendary Leiber & Stoller.
Palmer, Rose A. The North American Indians: An Account of the American Indians North of Mexico.
Palmer, Sally L. The Gift of Life.
Palmer, Sue. Tales in Rhyme.
Palmer, Thomas. The Transfer.
Palmisano, A. International Distributor Locator.
Palmore, John S. Kentucky Instructions to Juries: 1975-86.
Palmquist, Peter E., jt. auth. see Amon Carter Museum Staff.
Palmquist, Roland E. House Wiring.
--Questions & Answers for Electricians Examinations.
Palms, Roger C. God Holds Your Tomorrows.
Palsson, L. Marriage & Divorce in Comparative Conflict of Laws.
Palter, Robert M. Whitehead's Philosophy of Science.
Paludan, Lis. Easy Embroidery.
Palumbo, Dennis & Taylor, George A., eds. Urban Policy: A Guide to Information Sources.
Palumbo, Michael. The Palestinian Catastrophe: The 1984 Expulsion of a People from Their Homeland.
Pama, R. P., jt. auth. see Cusens, A. R.
Pama, R. P., et al, eds. Low Income Housing: Technology & Policy: Proceedings of the International Conference, Bangkok, June 1977.
Pambrun, Andrew. Sixty Years on the Frontier in the Pacific Northwest.
Pampel, Fred C. Social Change & the Aged: Recent Trends in the United States.
Pamplin, B., ed. Inorganic Biological Crystal Growth.
--Progress in Crystal Growth & Characterization.
--Progress in Crystal Growth & Characterization.
--Progress in Crystal Growth & Characterization.
--Progress in Crystal Growth & Characterization.
--Progress in Crystal Growth & Characterization, Vol. 4.
Pamplin, B. R., et al, eds. Progress in Crystal Growth & Characterization, Vol. 10: Proceedings of the 6th International Conference on Ternary & Multinary Compounds, Car acas, Venezuela, 15-17 August 1984.
Pamplin, Brian. Crystal Growth.
Pamplin, Brian R. Crystal Growth.
--Molecular Beam Epitaxy.
Pamplin, Brian R., ed. Progress in Crystal Growth.
--Progress in Crystal Growth & Characterization.
--Progress in Crystal Growth & Characterization.
--Progress in Crystal Growth & Characterization.
--Progress in Crystal Growth & Characterization.
Pamplin, Robert B., Jr. Everything Is Just Great: A Story of Faith, Adventure, & Success.
Pan Am World Airways, Inc. Staff, ed. Pan Am's U. S. A. Guide.
Pan, Stephen, ed. see Yeh Ch'ing.
Panaccio, Tim, jt. auth. see Ibach, Bob.
Panagopoulos, E. P. Essays on the History & Meaning of Checks & Balances.
Panati, Charles. Breakthroughs: Astonishing Advances in Your Lifetime in Medicine, Science, & Technology.
--Links.
Pancake, John S. Samuel Smith & the Politics of Business, 1752-1839.
Panchapakesan, S., jt. auth. see Gupta, Shanti S.
Panchev, S. Random Functions & Turbulence.
Pandit, G. S. & Gupta, S. P. Structural Analysis: A Matrix Approach.
Pandit, Sri M. P., compiled by see Aurobindo, Sri.
Panek, Dennis. Matilda Hippo Has a Big Mouth.
Panel Publishers, Inc. Staff. The Closely Held Corporation Desk Book: Nineteen Eighty-Five Tax Planning Update.
--Executive Compensation Strategy.
--Multistate Corporate Tax Almanac.
--Pension & Profit Sharing: Sample Plans & Workbook.
--Pension & Retirement Plans: Issues & Strategies.
--Tax Audit Answer Book.
Panfilov, A. Broadcasting Pirates.
Pang, May & Edwards, Henry. Loving John: The Untold Story.
Pangborn, Edgar. The Judgement of Eve.
Panger, Daniel. Black Ulysses.
Pangle, Mary A., jt. auth. see Forte, Imogene.
Paniker, K. Ayyappa, ed. Malayalam Short Stories: An Anthology.
Panikkar, K. N., ed. National Left Movements in India.
Panin, Dimitri. The Notebooks of Sologdin.
Panin, George, ed. & tr. see Zetlin, Mikhael.
Panish, Anna B., jt. auth. see Panish, Paul.

--Ceremony.
--The Judas Goat.
--Parker on Writing.
--The Private Eye in Hammett & Chandler.
Parker, Robert B., jt. auth. see Parker, Joan H.
Parker, Robert M. L. A.
--L. A.
Parker, Ronald B. Inscrutable Earth: Explorations into the Science of Earth.
--The Sheep Book: A Handbook for the Modern Shepherd.
--The Tenth Muse: The Pursuit of Earth Science.
Parker, Rozsika & Pollack, Griselda, eds. Framing Feminism: Art & the Women's Movement, 1970-1985.
Parker, Stephen. A Lifetime of Happiness.
Parker, T. H. John Calvin: A Biography.
Parker, Tom. Small Business: A Novel.
Parker, Tony. Lighthouse.
Parker, W. B. Through Unexplores Texas.
Parker, W. H., ed. see Los Angeles Police Department Staff.
Parker, W. W. Restoring & Renovating Old Houses.
Parker, Warren W. Elfie Jingle: Santa's Right Hand Man.
Parker, William S. & Brown, William S. Comparative Ecology of Two Colubrid Snakes, Masticophis T. Taeniatus & Pituophis Melanolucus Deserticola in Northern Utah.
Parker, Xenia L. Mosaics in Needlepoint.
Parkes, E. W. Braced Frameworks: An Introduction to the Theory of Structures.
Parkes, G. D., jt. auth. see Mellor, J. W.
Parkes, James. God at Work.
Parkes, James W. Emergence of the Jewish Problem, 1878-1939.
Parkhouse & Pleuvry. Analgesic Drugs.
Parkhouse, Bonnie L., jt. auth. see Lapin, Jackie.
Parkhurst, Liz S. The Arkansas Traveller: Adapted for Today's Readers.
Parkhurst, Louis G., Jr. Francis Schaeffer: The Man & His Message.
Parkhurst, Louis G., Jr., jt. auth. see Bunyan, John.
Parkin, Andrew. COBOL for Students.
Parkin, B. R., jt. ed. see Morgan, W. B.
Parkin, Bernadette. Nate's Lady.
Parkin, Frank. Krippendorf's Tribe.
--The Mind & Body Shop.
Parkins, R. N., ed. Electrochemical Test Methods for Stress Corrosion Cracking: Selected Papers from the Conference on Electrochemical Test Methods for Stress Corrosion Cracking, Firminy, France, Sept. 1980.
Parkinson, C. Northcote. Dead Reckoning.
--Fireship.
--Parkinson: The Law 1980.
Parkinson, Cyril N. Touch & Go.
Parkinson, F. R. There is Music in the Street.
Parkinson, G. H., jt. auth. see Leibniz, Gottfried W.
Parkinson, G. H., ed. see Leibniz, Gottfried W.
Parkinson, G. H. R., et al. An Encyclopedia of Philosophy.
Parkinson, Lisa. Conciliation in Separation & Divorce: Finding Common Ground.
Parkinson, Norman. Would You Let Your Daughter?
Parkinson, Rebecca S., & Associates Staff. Managing Health Promotion in the Workplace: Guidelines for Implementation & Evaluation.
Parkison, Ralph F. Wooden Toys & Games.
Parkland Research Staff. Guide to National Practices in Western Europe.
Parkman, Francis. Montcalm & Wolfe.
Parkman, N., et al, eds. Properties of Amorphous Silicon.
Parkman, R. The Cybernetic Society.
Parks, A. Franklin, jt. auth. see Bielawski, Larry.
Parks, Alex L. Law of Tug, Tow, & Pilotage: Supplement.
Parks, Dennis. A Potter's Guide to Raw Glazing & Oil Firing.
Parks, Douglas R. A Grammar of Pawnee.
Parks, Duane J. A Woodpile Mouse & Other Stories.
Parks, Gordon. Flavio.
--The Learning Tree.
--To Smile in Autumn.
Parks, Janet B. Physical Education: The Profession.
Parks, Stephen. John Dunton & the English Book Trade: A Study of His Career with a Checklist of His Publications.
Parks, Sylvia F. Business Typewriting.
Parks, Tim. Tongues of Flame.
Parkus, H., ed. Random Excitation of Structures by Earthquakes & Atmospheric Turbulence.
Parkus, H., ed. see CISM (International Center for Mechanical Sciences), Department of Mechanics of Solids Staff.
Parkus, H., ed. see International Union of Theoretical & Applied Mechanics Symposium Vienna 1966.
Parlato, Salvatore J. Films Ex Libris: Literature in 16mm & Video.
Parlocha, Pamela Kees, jt. auth. see Hiraki, Akemi.
Parmalee, Alice. Introducing the Bible.
Parmar, H. A., jt. auth. see Taylor, S. E.
Parma-Veigel, Laura, tr. see Novelli, Luca.
Parmelee, Maurice. History of Modern Culture.
Parmenter, Thomas. The Peculiar Architecture of Turrets & Towers in Europe.
Parmington, Howard. Making Money with Your Microcomputer.
Parmley, Robert O. Standard Handbook of Fastening & Joining.
Parnell, A. C., jt. auth. see Butcher, D. G.
Parnell, A. C., jt. auth. see Butcher, E. G.
Parnell, Dale. A National Human Resource Development Policy: The Role of Postsecondary Vocational Education.
Parnell, Dale & Yarrington, Roger. Proven Partners: Business, Labor, & Community Colleges.
Parnell, Dale, intro. by. Thes Presidents & Chancellors.
Paro, JoAnn C. Inspirational & Other Poems.
Parr, Adolph H. Rendezvous with the Unknown.
Parr, Grace L. Justin.
Parr, Gwen, jt. auth. see Parr, Mike.
Parr, J. B., jt. ed. see Funck, R.
Parr, Jeanne. The Superwives.
Parr, Mike & Parr, Gwen. Restaurant Guide for Lake Tahoe & Vicinity.
Parramon, J. M., jt. auth. see Vendrell, C. S.
Parramore, Dock D. The Parramore Sketches.
Parravicini, Pastori, jt. auth. see Bassani, F.
Parrella, M. P. & Robb, K. L. Economically Important Members of the Genus Liriomyza Mik: A Selected Bibliography.
Parretta, Michael R. R: BASE System V: Techniques & Applications.
Parrillo, Vincent M. Strangers to These Shores: Race & Ethnic Relations in the United States.
Parrinder, Geoffrey. A Dictionary of Non-Christian Religions.
Parrinder, Geoffrey, tr. from Sanskrit. & intro. by. The Wisdom of the Forest: Selections from the Hindu Upanishads.
Parrinder, Patrick. H. G. Wells.
--Science Fiction: Its Criticism & Teaching.
Parrinder, Patrick, ed. see Gissing, George.
Parrington, Vernon L. Main Currents in American Thought, Vol. 1: The Colonial Mind, 1620-1800.
--Main Currents in American Thought, Vol. 2: The Romantic Revolution in America, 1800-1860.
--Main Currents in American Thought, Vol. 3: Beginnings of Critical Realism in America, 1860-1920.
Parriot, Sara. Futile: The Magazine for Adult Dating.
Parriott, Sara. Calories Don't Count When...
Parris, Carlo, et al. Neurophysiological Correlates of Normal Cognition & Psychopathology.
Parris, Henry. Crisis in the Nationalised Industries.
--Public Enterprise in Europe.
Parris, John. Retention of Title on the Sale of Goods.
Parris, Leslie, ed. The Preraphaelite Papers.
Parris, Leslie, ed. see Taite Gallery Staff.
Parris, Lloyd. Caves of Colorado.
Parrish, Alvin E. Kidney Disease Case Studies.
Parrish, Archie & Parrish, John. Best Friends.
Parrish, Carl, tr. see Keller, Hermann.
Parrish, G. The Influence of Microstructure on the Properties of Case: Carburized Components.
Parrish, John, jt. auth. see Parrish, Archie.
Parrish, John A. Dermatology & Skin Care.
Parrish, Louis. Cooking As Therapy.
--Cooking As Therapy.
Parrish, Lydia A. Slave Songs of the Georgia Sea Islands.
Parrish, Michael. Soviet Armed Forces: Books in English, 1950-1967.
Parrish, Michael E., jt. auth. see Kenny, David M.
Parrish, Robert. Growing up in Hollywood.
--Growing up in Hollywood.
Parrish, Stanley B., et al, eds. Exporter's Guide to Federal Resources for Small Business Exporters.
Parrish, William E. Missouri under Radical Rule, 1865-1870.
Parrot. Samaria.
Parrot, Andre. The Temple of Jerusalem.
Parrott, Andre. Babylon & the Old Testament.
--Flood & Noah's Ark.
--Golgotha & the Church of the Holy Sepulchre.
--Ninevah & the Old Testament.
--The Tower of Babel.
Parrott, J. E. & Stuckes, Audrey D. Thermal Conductivity of Solids.
Parrott, Jasper & Ashkenazy, Vladimir. Ashkenazy: Beyond Frontiers.
Parrott, Lora L. Come Over to My House.
Parry & Putnam. Birds of Prey.
Parry, Edward A. The Law & the Poor.
Parry, Geraint. John Locke.
Parry, James, tr. see Demers, Jocelyn.
Parry, M., jt. auth. see Miller, A. Austin.
Parry, Michel. Hounds of Hell: Stories of Canine Horror & Fantasy.
Parry, Michel, ed. The Devil's Children: Tales of Demons & Exorcists.
--Great Black Magic Stories.
--The Roots of Evil: Weird Stories of Supernatural Plants.
--Savage Heroes: Tales of Magical Fantasy.
--The Supernatural Solution: Chilling Stories of Spooks & Sleuths.
Parry, Robert W. & Kodama, Goji. Boron Chemistry Four: Fourth International Meeting on Boron Chemistry, Salt Lake City & Snowbird, Utah, 8-13 July 1979.
Parry, W. E., ed. Essays in Theoretical Physics: In Honor of Dirk ter Haar.
Parsey, J. M., Jr., jt. ed. see Kimerling, L. C.
Parshall, Phil. Bridges to Islam: A Christian Perspective on Folk Islam.
Parslow, R. D. & Green, R. Elliot, eds. Advanced Computer Graphics: Economics, Techniques & Applications.
Parslow, R. D., et al. Computer Graphics: Techniques & Applications.
Parson, Diane L. Lady of Light & Darkness.
Parson, Robinson H. Modern College Algebra.
Parson, Theodore. Achieving Classroom Communication Through Self Analysis.
Parsons, Chuck. The Capture of John Wesley Hardin.
Parsons, D. F., ed. Biological Techniques in Electron Microscopy.
Parsons, D. S. Roy Campbell: A Descriptive & Annotated Bibliography.
Parsons, D. W. The Political Economy of British Regional Policy.
Parsons, Eleanor C. Thachers: Island of the Twin Lights.
Parsons, Elizabeth. The Upside-Down Cat.
Parsons, Fred. Vision from God.
Parsons, Howard L. Man East & West: Essays in East-West Philosophy.
Parsons, Ian. Poetry for Pleasure: A Choice of Poetry & Verse on a Variety of Themes.
Parsons, Ian, jt. auth. see Spater, George.
Parsons, Jacqueline, ed. see Farley, Tom.
Parsons, Kenneth. No Message & No Song.
Parsons, Kitty. Up & down & Roundabout.
Parsons, Lee A. Pre-Columbian America: The Art & Archeology of South, Central & Middle America.
Parsons, M. L., et al. Handbook of Flame Spectroscopy.
Parsons, Mary E. The Wild Flowers of California.
--Wild Flowers of California. Ferris, Roxana S., ed.
Parsons, Nicholas. Letter Does Not Blush.
Parsons, S. A. How to Find Out about Economics.
Parsons, T. D., jt. auth. see Khoury, S. J.
Parsons, Talcott & Smelser, Neil J. Economy & Society: A Study in the Integration of Economic & Social Theory.
Parsons, Thomas, jt. ed. see Gans, Carl.
Parsons, Thomas S., jt. auth. see Romer, Alfred S.
Parsons, Virgil & Sanford, Nancy. Interpersonal Interaction in Nursing.
Parsons, W. Stuart, jt. auth. see Stanton, Thomas M.
Parsons, William B. An American Engineer in China.
Parston, Gregory. Planners, Politics & Health Services.
Partee, Barbara H. Subject & Object in Modern English. Hankamer, Jorge, ed.
Partee, Charles, ed. Calvin & Classical Philosophy 1977.
Partee, Morriss H. Plato's Poetics: The Authority of Beauty.
Parthasarathy, K. R. Multipliers on Locally Compact Groups.
Partington, David H., ed. The Middle East Annual: Issues & Events 1985.
Parton, V. Elastic-Plastic Fracture Mechanics.
Parton, V. Z. & Perlin, P. I. Mathematical Methods of the Theory of Elasticity.
Partridge, A. C. John Donne: Language & Style.
Partridge, Barbara. Bargain Hunting in Los Angeles.
Partridge, Cecily J. & Barnitt, Rosemary E. Research Guidelines: A Handbook for Therapists.
Partridge, Colin. Gissing.
Partridge, Eric. Concise Usage & Abusage.
--Origins: A Short Etymological Dictionary of Modern English.
--The Shaggy Dog Story.
--Slang Today & Yesterday: With a Short Historical Sketch & Vocabularies of English, American & Australian Slang.
--You Have a Point There: A New & Complete Guide to Punctuation.
Partridge, Eric & Clark, John W. British & American English since Nineteen Hundred.
Partridge, Frances. Everything to Lose: A Diary 1945 to 1962.
Partridge, Frances, jt. auth. see Strachey, Julia.
Partridge, Jenny. Colonel Grunt.
--Hopfellow.
--Mr. Squint.
--Peterkin Pollensnuff.
Partridge, P. H. Society, Schools & Progress in Australia.
Parun, Bernard B. The Perennial Rebel.
Parunak, H. van dyke see Van Dyke Parunak, H.
Parvan, Vasile. Dacia: An Outline of the Early Civilizations of the Carpatho-Danubian Countries. Evans, I. L. & Charlesworth, M. P., trs.
Parvey, Constance F. Come Lord Jesus! Come Quickly!
Parvey, Constance F., ed. The Community of Women & Men in the Church.
Parvin, Jack, jt. auth. see Cisin, Fred.
Pasachoff, Jay M. Astronomy: From the Earth to the Universe.
--Astronomy Now.
Pasachoff, Jay M., jt. auth. see Wolfson, Richard.
Pasadena Art Alliance Staff. All Things Wise & Wonderful.
--Let's Celebrate.
--To Talk of Many Things.
--Wish You Were Here.
--Wives' Tales.
Pasahow, Edward J. Digital Integrated Circuits for Electronics Technicians.
Pasantes-Morales, Herminia, jt. ed. see Huxtable, Ryan J.
Pascal, Blaise. Great Shorter Works of Pascal. Blankenagel, John C. & Cailliet, Emile, eds.
Pascal, Francine. Head over Heels.
--Wrong Kind of Girl.
Pascal, Gerald R. The Practical Art of Diagnostic Interviewing.
Pascal, Roy. German Sturm und Drang.
Pascale, Marc De see De Pascale, Marc.
Pascale, Richard T. & Althos, Anthony G. The Art of Japanese Management.
Paschal, Huston, ed. North Carolina Artists Exhibition 1984.
Paschal, Huston & Monbouquette, Jenny, eds. North Carolina Artists Exhibition, 1987.
Paschall, Eugene F., jt. ed. see Whistler, Roy L.
Paschall, Lee M. & Andriole, Stephen J., eds. Air & Satellite Communications.
Pascoe, D. & Edwards, R. W., eds. Freshwater Biological Monitoring: Proceedings of a Specialized Conference, Cardiff, U. K., Sept. 12-14, 1984.
Pascoe, K. J. Properties of Materials for Electrical Engineers.
Pascu, Stefan. A History of Transylvania. Ladd, D. Robert, tr.
Pasika, W. M., ed. Advances in Macromolecular Chemistry.
Pasini, Willy, jt. ed. see Forleo, Romano.
Pasko, W W., ed. American Dictionary of Printing & Bookmaking.
Paskoff, Benjamin. Linguet: Eighteenth-Century Intellectual Heretic of France.
Pasour, E. C. U. S. Agricultural Policies: A Market Process Approach.
Pasquali, Elaine A., et al. Mental Health Nursing: A Holistic Approach.
Pasqualini, J. R., ed. Recent Advances in Steroid Biochemistry.
Pasqualini, J. R., jt. ed. see James, V. H.
Pasquariello, Anthony M., jt. ed. see O'Connor, Patricia W.
Pasquier, Roger F. Watching Birds: An Introduction to Ornithology.
Pasquini, Bernardo. L'Idalma Overo Chi la Dura la Vince. Brown, Howard M., ed.
Pass, C. L., jt. auth. see Hawkins, K. H.
Pass, G. & Sutcliffe, H. Practical Inorganic Chemistry: Preparations, Reactions & Instrumental Methods.
Pass, Gail. Surviving Sisters.
Passage, Charles E., tr. see Horace.
Passatore, G., jt. ed. see Boffi, S.
Passel, Anne. Charlotte & Emily Bronte: An Annotated Bibliography.
Passell, Peter, jt. auth. see Cloverdale Press Staff.
Passett, Barry A. Leadership Development for Public Service.
Passin, Herbert, ed. The United States & Japan.
Passos, John Dos see Dos Passos, John.
Pastan, Linda. Aspects of Eve: Poems.
--Waiting for My Life: Poems.
Pasternack, Amos, jt. ed. see Wegelius, Otto.
Pasternak, Bill. The Practical Handbook of Amateur Radio FM & Repeaters.
--Video Cassette Recorders: Buying, Using & Maintaining.
Pasternak, Boris. My Sister, Life. Carlisle, Olga A., tr.
--The Voice of Prose: Early Prose & Autobiography. Barnes, Christopher, ed. & intro. by.
Pasternak, Ceel, ed. see Sawyer, Larry B.
Pastva, Loretta. Basic Grammar Guide: Advanced Practice for Competency & Proficiency Exams.
--Basic Grammar Guide: Intermediate Practice for Competency & Proficiency Exams.
Patai, Raphael. The Arab Mind.
--Society, Culture & Change in the Middle East.

Patai, Raphael, jt. auth. see Graves, Robert.
Patai, Saul. The Chemistry of the Amidines & Imidates.
Patai, Saul, ed. The Chemistry of Acid Derivatives, Supplement B.
--The Chemistry of Peroxides.
Pataki, L. & Zapp, E. Basic Analytical Chemistry.
Pataky-Brestyanszky, I. Mednyanszky. Horn, Zsuzanna, tr.
Patankar, S. V., et al, eds. Numerical Prediction of Flow, Heat Transfer Turbulence, & Combustion: Selected Works of Professor D. Brian Spalding.
Patankar, Suhas V. Numerical Heat Transfer & Fluid Flow.
Pate, Ellen & Spengler, Barbara. Handbook for Typists: Operation of the Selectric Typewriter, Technical Information, Format Illustrations & Procedures.
Pate, J. S., jt. ed. see Sutcliffe, J. F.
Patel. Multivariable System Theory & Design.
Patel, Dinker I. Exurbs: Urban Residential Developments in the Countryside.
Patel, J. K., et al. Handbook of Statistical Distributions.
Patel, S. J., ed. Pharmaceuticals in Developing Countries.
Patel, Surendra J., ed. Trademarks in Developing Countries.
Patenaude, Lionel V. Texans, Politics & the New Deal. Burke, Robert E. & Freidel, Frank, eds.
Patent, Dorothy H. Evolution Goes on Every Day.
--A Picture Book of Cows.
--The Quest for Artificial Intelligence.
--Raccoons, Coatimundis, & Their Family.
Pater, Walter. Cupid & Psyche.
Paternak, Boris. Adolescence of Zhenya Lyvers.
Paterno, Cynthia, jt. auth. see Lackner, Marie.
Paterson, A. R., jt. auth. see Henderson, J. Frank.
Paterson, Alan M. Land Water & Power: A History of the Turlock Irrigation District, 1887-1987.
Paterson, Alistair, ed. Fifteen Contemporary New Zealand Poets.
--Fifteen Contemporary New Zealand Poets.
Paterson, Antoinette M. The Infinite Worlds of Giordano Bruno.
Paterson, C. R. & MacLennan, W. J. Bone Disease in the Elderly.
Paterson, George. Helping Your Handicapped Child.
Paterson, George W. The Cardiac Patient.
Paterson, H. Wade & Thomas, Ralph H. Accelerator Health Physics.
Paterson, John. The Making of the Return of the Native.
Paterson, Judith. Be Somebody: A Biography of Marguerite Rawalt.
Paterson, Katherine. Angels & Other Strangers: Family Christmas Stories.
--Bridge to Terabithia.
--Great Gillis Hopkins.
--The Great Gilly Hopkins.
--Of Nightingales That Weep.
--The Sign of the Chrysanthemum.
Paterson, Kathy K., jt. auth. see Chappell, Williard R.
Paterson, Thomas G. & Clifford, J. G. American Foreign Policy: A History.
Paterson, W. F. see Latham, J. D.
Paterson, William. Glimpses of Colonial Society & Life at Princeton College, 1766-1773, by One of the Class of 1763. Mills, W. Jay, ed.
Patey, Pamela A. WordStar Made Easy: A Self-Pacing Manual.
Pathak, N. N., jt. auth. see Ranjhan, S. K.
Pathak, R. C., ed. Hindi-English, English-Hindi Standard Illustrated Dictionary.
Pathria, R. K. The Theory of Relativity.
Pathy, M. S. J. Principles & Practice of Geriatric Medicine.
Patience, J. Brindle Bear Telling the Time.
Patience, John. Adventures in Fern Hollow.
Patient Care Magazine Editors. Patient Care Flow Chart Manual.
Patil, Ramesh, ed. Artificial Intelligence in Medicine.
Paton, Alan. Ah, but Your Land Is Beautiful.
--Cry, the Beloved Country.
--Towards the Mountain.
Paton, David M., jt. auth. see Daniel, Edwin E.
Paton, David M., ed. The Release of Catecholamines from Adrenergic Neurons.
Paton, H. J. The Categorical Imperative: A Study in Kant's Moral Philosophy.
Paton, J. E., jt. ed. see Aitchison, Ian J.
Paton, John & Dell, Catherine. Nature Encyclopedia.
Paton, Kathi, ed. see Barkin, Carol & James, Elizabeth.
Paton, Kathi, ed. see Castle, Sue.
Paton, N. E. & Hamilton, C. H., eds. Superplastic Forming of Structural Alloys.
--Superplastic Forming: Proceedings. San Diego, 1982.
Paton Walsh, Jill. Children of the Fox.
Patriarca, P., jt. ed. see Rossi, F.
Patrick, Catharine. What is Creative Thinking?
Patrick, Dale. The Rendering of God in the Old Testament. Brueggemann, Walter & Donahue, John R., eds.
Patrick, Dale R. & Fardo, Stephen W. Energy Management & Conservation.
Patrick, Homer & Schaible, P. J. Poultry: Feeds & Nutrition.
Patrick, Hugh & Rosovsky, Henry, eds. Asia's New Giant: How the Japanese Economy Works.
Patrick, J. Max, ed. see Herrick, Robert.
Patrick, J. Max, et al. Attic & Baroque Prose Style: The Anti-Ciceronian Movement, Four Essays.
Patrick, James, ed. see Dunwell, Steve.
Patrick, James B., ed. see Dunwell, Steve.
Patrick, Lynn. Double or Nothing.
Patrick, Robert L. Application Design Handbook for Distributed Systems: For Distributed Systems.
Patrick, Ross. Horsewhip the Doctor: Tales from Our Medical Past.
Patrick, Ruth, ed. Diversity.
Patrick, Sam J. Presidents: Washington to Reagan.
Patrick, Vincent. Family Business.
Patsis, C. Greek-English, English-Greek Dictionary.
Patte, Aline, jt. auth. see Patte, Daniel.
Patte, Daniel. Paul's Faith & the Power of the Gospel: A Structural Introduction to the Pauline Letters.
--Preaching Paul.
--What Is Structural Exegesis? Via, Dan O., Jr., ed.
Patte, Daniel & Patte, Aline. Structural Exegesis - from Theory to Practice: Exegesis of Mark 15 & 16 Hermeneutical Implications.
Patte, Daniel, tr. see Calloud, Jean.
Pattee, Howard H., Jr., et al, eds. see International Symposium on X-Ray Optics & X-Ray Microanalysis Staff.
Pattee, Rowena. Moving with Change: A Women's Reintegration of the I Ching.
Patten, G. Z. You, Too, Can Stop Drinking.
Patten, Lewis B. The Angry Town of Pawnee Bluffs.
--Cheyenne Captives.
--Giant on Horseback.
Patten, Simon. The Social Basis of Religion.
Patter, Douglas M. Van see Marion, Jerry B. & Van Patter, Douglas M.
Pattersen, M. Divorce Guide for Washington: Step-by-Step Guide for Obtaining Your Own Divorce.
Patterson, B. D., jt. ed. see Heaney, L. R.
Patterson, Bob E. Reinhold Niebuhr.
Patterson, Bob E., ed. see Duncan, Elmer H.
Patterson, Bob E., ed. see Gragg, Alan.
Patterson, Bob E., ed. see Humphrey, J. Edward.
Patterson, Bob E., ed. see Mueller, David.
Patterson, Bob E., ed. see Panko, Stephen M.
Patterson, Bob E., ed. see Roark, Dallas M.
Patterson, C. W., jt. auth. see Harter, W. G.
Patterson, Charles, jt. auth. see Tippin, G. Lee.
Patterson, D. J., jt. ed. see Springer, G. S.
Patterson, David, ed. Pigments: An Introduction to Their Physical Chemistry.
Patterson, David W., ed. Crime & Criminal Justice.
Patterson, Douglas O., ed. Best Practices: How to Avoid Surprises in the World's Most Complicated Technical Process, the Transition from Development to Production.
Patterson, Elizabeth, ed. see Baba, Meher, et al.
Patterson, Elizabeth C., ed. see Baba, Meher, et al.
Patterson, Frances. Motion Picture Continuities. Kupelnick, Bruce S., ed.
Patterson, Francine & Linden, Eugene. The Education of Koko.
Patterson, Freeman. Photography & the Art of Seeing.
--Photography for the Joy of It.
Patterson, George. Church Planting Through Obedience Oriented Teaching.
Patterson, Gordon N. Message from Infinity: A Space-Age Correlation of Science & Religion.
Patterson, Grace. The Secret Visitor.
Patterson, J. G. Zola Dictionary.
Patterson, James. Black Market.
--Virgin.
Patterson, James T. America in the Twentieth-Century: A History.
--America in the Twentieth Century: A History.
--America in the Twentieth Century: A History.
--America's Struggle Against Poverty, 1900-1980.
Patterson, Jane & Madaras, Lynda. Woman-Doctor: The Education of Jane Patterson, M.D.
Patterson, Jerry, jt. auth. see Norton, Thomas.
Patterson, Jim. Greenberg's Price Guide to American Flyers S Gauge Trains 1945-1966. Greenberg, Linda, ed.
Patterson, Lachlan. The Three-Day Collision Course.
Patterson, M. Havill. My Morning Glory.
Patterson, M. K., jt. ed. see Kruse, Paul, Jr.
Patterson, Pat. C'mon Doc, You've Gotta Be Kiddin'
Patterson, R. F. The Story of English Literature.
Patterson, Rebecca. Emily Dickinson's Imagery. Freeman, Margaret H., ed.
Patterson, Richard N. Private Screening.
Patterson, Robert Leet. Adventures in the Philosophy of Religion.
--The Role of History in Religion.
Patterson, Sarah. The Distant Summer.
Patterson, Sheila, tr. see Ossowski, Stanislaw.
Patterson, Ward. Triumph over Temptation.
Patterson, William H. I Wish I Weres: Little Verses for Little Children.
Patterson, Yvonne. Happy Hannah.
Pattinson, James. The Courier Job.
--Homecoming.
--The Honeymoon Caper.
--Lethal Orders.
--The Stalking Horse.
Pattison, E. Mansell. Pastor & Parish: A Systems Approach. Clinebell, Howard J. & Stone, Howard W., eds.
Pattison, Harry A. The Handicapped & Their Rehabilitation.
Pattison, J. R., et al, eds. Quantitative Cytochemistry & Its Application.
Patton, Annie & Campbell, Pamela. Moving to Los Angeles: The Inside Scoop on Starting out, Settling in & Making It in the Big City.
Patton, Deborah. Bed & Breakfast Inns of New England. Corsey, Mark, ed.
Patton, Grant W. & Kistner, Robert W. Atlas of Infertility Surgery.
Patton, Harry D., jt. ed. see Ruch, Theodore C.
Patton, Michael J., jt. auth. see Pepinsky, Harold B.
Patton, Michael Q., ed. Culture & Evaluation.
Patton, Peter C. & Holoien, Renee A., eds. Computing in the Humanities.
Patton, Stuart & Jensen, Robert G. Biomedical Aspects of Lactation.
Patton, Temple C., ed. Pigment Handbook.
Patz, Nancy. Gina Farina & the Prince of Mintz.
Patzer, W., jt. auth. see Lenz, Karl.
Pau, F. L., ed. see Basar, T.
Pauk, Walter. How to Study in College.
Pauker, G. Y., ed. Energy Efficiency & Conservation in the Asia-Pacific Region: Proceedings of the Fouth Workshop, Honolulu, Hawaii, June 2-5, 1981.
Pauker, Guy J., et al. Diversity & Development in Southeast Asia.
Paul, A. Chemistry of Glasses.
Paul, Amy. The Grass Is Greener.
Paul, Anthony. The Tiger Who Lost His Stripes.
Paul, Arnold M., ed. Black Americans & the Supreme Court.
Paul, B., ed. Mechanics of Transportation Suspension Systems, AMD Vol. 15.
Paul, Barbara. But He Was Already Dead When I Got There.
--Cadenza for Caruso.
--Kill Fee.
--The Renewable Virgin.
Paul, Betty B., jt. auth. see Paul, Norman L.
Paul, Cecil & Lanham, Jan. Choices: In Pursuit of Wholeness.
Paul, Doris A., jt. auth. see Issari, Mohammed Ali.
Paul, Eddie. Skysurfing: A Guide to Hang Gliding.
Paul, Ellen F., ed. Liberty & Equality.
Paul, Ellen F., jt. ed. see Coleman, Jules.
Paul, I. H. The Form & Technique of Psychotherapy.
Paul, Igor, ed. Proceedings of the Eighth Northeast Conference.
Paul, John R. & White, Colin, eds. Serological Epidemology.
Paul, Korky, jt. auth. see Marshall, Ray.
Paul, Leslie A. Meaning of Human Existence.
Paul, Norman L. & Paul, Betty B. A Marital Puzzle.
Paul, Pauline C., et al, eds. Food Theory & Applications.
Paul, Richard S. & Shaevel, M. Leonard. Essentials of Technical Mathematics.
--Essentials of Technical Mathematics with Calculus.
Paul, Rodman, ed. see Foote, Mary H.
Paul, Samuel. Strategic Management of Development Programmes: Guidelines for Action. International Labour Office Staff, ed.
Paul, Sherman. Olson's Push: Origin, Black Mountain, & Recent American Poetry.
Paulaitis, Michael E. & Penninger, Johan M. L. Chemical Engineering at Supercritical Fluid Conditions.
Paul-David, Madeleine, et al. Musee Guimet, Paris.
Paulet, Michael. Shooting from Scratch.
Pauley, Steven E. Technical Report Writing Today.
--Technical Report Writing Today.
Pauli, Eugen. Classical Cooking the Modern Way.
Pauli, Hertha. Her Name Was Sojourner Truth.
Paulin, Mary Ann & Berlin, Susan T. Outstanding Books for the College Bound.
Paull, Rachel K. & Paull, Richard A. Geology of Wisconsin & Upper Michigan: Including Parts of Adjacent States.
Paull, Richard A., jt. auth. see Paull, Rachel K.
Paullin, Charles O. Atlas of the Historical Geography of the U. S. Wright, John K., ed.
Pauls, Michael, jt. auth. see Facaros, Dana.
Paulsell, William O. Taste & See.
Paulsen, Gary. Forehanding & Backhanding-If You're Lucky.
--Sailing: From Jibs to Jibing.
Paulsen, Russell. Short Term Skill Training: Alternative Approaches for Vocational Education.
Paulson, Arvid, tr. see Strindberg, August.
Paulson, Dennis, ed. Voices of Survival in the Nuclear Age.
Paulson, Ivar. Old Estonian Folk Religion.
Paulson, Michael G. The Fallen Crown: Three French Mary Stuart Plays of the Seventeenth Century.
Paulson, Paul L. Guide to Russian Silver Hallmarks.
Paulson, Ronald, jt. auth. see Bage, Robert.
Paulson, Ronald, ed. see Bage, Robert.
Paulson, Ronald, ed. see Fenelon & De Salignac De La Mothe, Francois.
Paulson, Ronald, ed. see Holcroft, Thomas.
Paulson, Ronald, ed. see Johnstone, Charles.
Paulson, Sig, jt. auth. see Loomis, Evarts G.
Paulson, Wayne. Parish Secretary's Handbook.
Paulsson, Bjorn K. Blind Landing. Toverud, Constance F., tr. from Norwegian.
Paulston, Christina B., et al. Developing Communicative Competence: RolePlays in English as a Second Language.
Paulston, Roland G. Society, Schools & Progress in Peru.
Paulus, Virginia, ed. Housing: A Bibliography 1960-1972.
Pauly, Bill. Wind the Clock by Bittersweet.
Pauly, Parakal. Secret Wars of CIA.
Pau On Lau, Estelle. Ellen C. Sabin: Proponent of Higher Education for Women.
Paust, Jordan L., et al. Business Law: Instructor's Manual with Test Bank.
Pautler, Albert J., jt. ed. see Lahren, James A.
Pauwels, Louis & Bergier, Jacques. Impossible Possibilities.
--Morning of the Magicians.
Pavelka, Ed, ed. see Matheny, Fred.
Pavia, Donald. Introduction to Organic Lab Techniques.
Pavillon, Fernand. The Stones of the Abbey.
Pavlenko, V. World Revolutionary Process.
Pavlic, Albert. Increible Historia de una Bella Joven.
--Misterioso Viaje a la Eternidad.
Pavlov, G. Soviet Political Posters.
Pavlov, I. Exprimental Psychology.
Pavolovsky, Michel N. Chinese Russian Relations.
Pavone-Macaluso, M. & Smith, P. H., eds. Cancer of the Prostate & Kidney.
Pavord, Tony & Fisher, Rod. The Equine Veterinary Manual.
Pawlak, Mark. The Buffalo Sequence & Other Poems.
Pawlikowski, John T. Christ in the Light of the Christian-Jewish Dialogue.
Pawlowski, L. Physiochemical Methods for Water & Wastewater Treatment.
Pawson, E. Transport & Economy: Turnpike Roads in Eighteenth Century Britain.
Paxent, James B., jt. ed. see Olden, Kenneth.
Paxinos, G. & Watson, C. The Rat Brain in Stereotoxic Coordinates.
Paxson, Frederic L. Last American Frontier.
Paxson, Margaret. Hearthsong: Rhyme & Reason.
Paxson, Ruth. Life on the Highest Plane.
--Rivers of Living Water.
--Wealth, Walk & Warfare of the Christian.
Paxson, William E., Jr. E. S. Paxson, Frontier Artist.
Paxton, J. H., tr. see Febvre, Lucien & Bataillon, Lionel.
Paxton, Paul, et al. The Heinemann New Family Medical Encyclopedia.
Paxton, Robert O. Europe in the Twentieth Century.
--Vichy France: Old Guard & New Order, 1940-1944.
Pay, Don. Thunder from Heaven: The Story of the 17th Airborne Division in WW II.
Paykel, Eugene S., jt. auth. see Weissman, Myrna M.
Paykin, Bentley H., jt. auth. see Gould, Jay M.
Payn, Graham & Morley, Sheridan, eds. The Noel Coward Diaries.
Payne & Hahn. Understanding Your Health.
Payne, Alma. The Baby Food Book.
Payne, Alma & Callahan, Dorothy. The Fat & Sodium Control Cookbook: A Handy & Authoritative Guide for Those on Sodium Restricted or Fat-Controlled Diets-Including Suggestions for Controlling Carbohydrate, Cholesterol & Saturated Fats.
Payne, Alma J. Louisa May Alcott: A Reference Guide.

Payne, Anthony. Frank Bridge: Radical & Conservative.
Payne, Bernal C., Jr. The Late Great Dick Hart.
Payne, Bruce L., jt. auth. see Fleishman, Joel L.
Payne, Christian & Cutts, Paddy. Creative Techniques in Animal Photography.
Payne, Christopher. Price Guide to Nineteenth Century European Furniture.
Payne, Darwin R. Materials & Craft of the Scenic Model.
Payne, E. M. F., jt. auth. see Godman, A.
Payne, Frank O. The Fun & Pleasure of Experimental Botany.
Payne, G. C., jt. ed. see Cuff, E. C.
Payne, Geoffrey K. Low-Income Housing in the Developing World: The Role of Sites & Services & Settlement Upgrading.
Payne, J. Barton. Hebrew Vocabularies.
Payne, J. P. & Bushman, J. A., eds. Artificial Ventilation: Technical, Biological & Clinical Aspects.
Payne, J. P., et al. The Medical & Biological Applications of Mass Spectroscopy.
Payne, J. W. Microorganisms & Nitrogen Sources: Transport & Utilization of Amino Acods, Peptides, Proteins & Related Substrates.
Payne, Karen. Between Ourselves: Letters Between Mothers & Daughters.
Payne, Laurence. Dead for a Ducat.
Payne, Leanne. Real Presence: The Holy Spirit in the Works of C. S. Lewis.
Payne, Michael. Precalculus Mathematics: New Impressions.
Payne, R., jt. ed. see Cooper, C. L.
Payne, Richard A. How to Get a Better Job Quicker.
Payne, Robert. Ancient Rome.
Payne, Stanley G. Spanish Revolution.
Payne, Suzzy C. & Murwin, Susan A. Creative American Quilting Inspired by the Bible.
Paynter, Raymond A., Jr. & Caperton, Alastair M. Ornithological Gazetteer of Paraguay.
Paynter, Will. British Trade Unions & the Problem of Change.
Paysan, Klaus. Aquarium Fish from Around the World.
--Wild Animals of Africa.
Payton, Colleen M. The Adventures of Wilbur H. Worm & His Friends.
Payton, Everett J. I Won't Be Crippled When I See Jesus.
Paz. Monkey Grammarian.
Paz, Alberto C. & Ferrari, Gustavo E. Argentina's Foreign Policy, 1930-62. Kennedy, J. J., tr.
Paz, Azaria. Introduction to Probabilistic Automata.
Paz, Azaria, jt. ed. see Kohavi, Zvi.
Paz, Octavio. Alternating Current.
--The Bow & the Lyre: The Poem, The Poetic Revelation, Poetry & History. Simms, Ruth L., tr. from Span.
--The Labyrinth of Solitude: Life & Thought in Mexico. Kemp, Lysander, tr. from Span.
--Labyrinth of Solitude, the Other Mexico, & Return to the Labyrinth of Solitude, Mexico & the U. S., & the Philanthropic Ogre. Kemp, Lysander, tr. from Span.
--Marcel Duchamp. Phillips, Rachel & Gardner, Donald, trs. from Span.
--One Word to the Other.
--Sor Juana Ines de la Cruz o las Trampas de la Fe.
Pazaurek, Gustav E. & Spiegl, Walter. Glas des 20. Jahrhunderts: Jugendstil--Art Deco.
PC World Editors, jt. auth. see Arnold, David.
Peabody, Helen. Lift up Your Face!
Peabody Museum of Archaeology & Ethnology Editors. Author & Subject Catalogues of the Library of the Peabody Museum of Archaeology & Ethnology: Fourth Supplement.
Peabody, Robert L. & Polsby, Nelson W. New Perspectives on the House of Representatives.
Peabody-DeShield, Angela. What Goes Around Comes Around.
Peace, A., jt. auth. see Mangham, E.
Peace Museum Staff. Give Peace a Chance: A Catalog of the Exhibition at the Peace Museum, Chicago. Philbin, Marianne, ed.
Peace, Nancy E., ed. Archival Choices: Managing the Historical Record in an Age of Abundance.
Peacemakers Staff. Handbook on Nonpayment of War Taxes.
Peacey, J. G. & Davenport, W. G. The Iron Blast Furnace: Theory & Practice.
Peacey, W. H. Pastoral Psychology & the Gospel.
Peach. Pilgrim Fathers.
Peachey, Paul, ed. Peace, Politics, & the People of Your Own.
Peachment, Brian. An Aeroplane or a Grave.
--Devil's Island.
--Down among the Dead Men.
--The Red Cross Story.
--Three Fighters for Freedom.
Peacock, A. D., jt. auth. see Uhlan, Edward.
Peacock, Carlos. Richard Parkes Bonington.
Peacock, D. P., ed. Pottery & Early Commerce: Characterization & Trade in Roman & Later Ceramics.
Peacock, Erle E. & Van Winkle, Walton. Wound Repair.
Peacock, Jane B., ed. see Mitchell, Margaret.
Peacock, R. see Kemmit, R.
Peacocke, A. R. The Sciences & Theology in the Twentiety Century.
Peacocke, Dennis. Liberator of the Nations: Biblical Blueprints on Political Action.
Peacocke, T. Atomic & Nuclear Chemistry: Atomic Theory & the Structure of the Atom.
Peakall, D. B. Residue Reviews.
Peake, Louis A. The U. S. in the Vietnam War, 1954-1975: A Selected, Annotated Bibliography.
Peake, Nigel. City at War: A Pictorial Memento of Portsmouth, Gosport, Fareham, Havant & Chichester During WWII.
Peaker, Gilbert F. An Empirical Study of Education in Twenty-One Countries.
Peale, Norman Vincent. Power of Positive Thinking.
--Power of the Plus Factor.
--Why Some Positive Thinkers Get Powerful Results.
Pear, Joseph, jt. auth. see Martin, Garry.
Pear, T. H., ed. Psychological Factors of Peace & War.
Pearce. Dementia: A Clinical Approach.
Pearce, Brian, tr. see Bettelheim, Charles.
Pearce, Brian, tr. see Claudin, Fernando.
Pearce, Brian, tr. see Emmanuel, Arghiri.
Pearce, Brian, tr. see Ladurie, Emmanuel L.
Pearce, Brian, tr. see Mandel, Ernest.
Pearce, C. Glenn, et al, eds. Guidelines for Research in Business Communication.
Pearce, Charles. Essentials of Auto Mechanics.
--Essentials of Drivers Education.
--Study Guide for California Drivers Handbook. Incl. Adapted N.Y. State Drivers Handbook. Hawkes Pub Inc.
Pearce, D. Public Sector Decision-Making.
Pearce, E. M. & Schaefgen, J. R., eds. Contemporary Topics in Polymer Science.
Pearce, Frank. Last Call for H.M.S. Edinburgh.
Pearce, I. F. International Trade.
Pearce, J. R., jt. ed. see Bachrach, A. L.
Pearce, J. Winston. Ten Good Things I Know about Retirement.
Pearce, Jenny, jt. ed. see Beeson, Trevor.
Pearce, Joan. The Common Agricultural Policy: Prospects for Change.
Pearce, Joan & Sutton, John. Protection & Industrial Policy in Europe.
Pearce, Mary E. Apple Tree, Lean Down.
--The Land Endures.
Pearce, Michael. John Drinkwater: A Comprehensive Bibliography of His Works.
Pearce, P. L. The Social Psychology of Tourist Behaviour.
Pearce, Peter & Pearce, Susan. Experiments in Form: A Foundation Course in Three-Dimensional Design.
Pearce, Richard. Critical Essays on Thomas Pynchon.
Pearce, Roy Harvey & Miller, J. Hillis, eds. A Study of the Indian & the American Mind.
Pearce, Susan, jt. auth. see Pearce, Peter.
Pearce, W. Barnett, jt. auth. see Rossiter, Charles M., Jr.
Pearce, Wesley. Intonation Studies for Band.
Pearl, H. World Peace.
Pearl, Jack. Time to Kill-A Time to Die.
Pearl, Judea & Shafer, Glenn. Uncertainty Management in AI Systems.
Pearl, Rueben. The Road to Peace.
Pearlman, Daniel D., et al. Guide to Rapid Revision.
Pearlman, Moshe. The Army of Israel.
--Zealots of Masada: Story of a Dig.
Pearlstein, Gloria S. Your Future As a Working Woman.
Pearlstein, Howard. Mandrake's Book.
Pearlstein, S., ed. Cross-Section Data for Nuclear Reactor Analyses.
Pears, D. F., tr. see Wittgenstein, Ludwig.
Pearsall, Derek, ed. Manuscripts & Readers in Fifteenth-Century England: The Literary Implications of Manuscript Study Essays from the Conference at the University of York.
Pearsall, Derek, jt. ed. see Edwards, A. S.
Pearsall, Margaret E., jt. auth. see Pearsall, Milo D.
Pearsall, Milo D. & Pearsall, Margaret E. Your Dog: Companion & Helper.
Pearsall, Nancy, jt. auth. see Nester, Eugene.
Pearsall, Ronald. Victorian Popular Music.
--Victorian Sheet Music Covers.
Pearse, John S., jt. ed. see Giese, Arthur C.
Pearse, R. O. Mountain Splendour.
Pearson, et al. On Your Own.
Pearson, Carl M. & Mostofi, F. K., eds. The Striated Muscle.
Pearson, Charles. What Is to Be Done with Our Criminals? A Letter to the Right Honorable the Lord Mayor.
Pearson, Craig & Marfuggi, Joseph. Creating & Using Learning Games.
Pearson, Drew. The President.
Pearson, E. A. & De Fraga Frangipane, E. Marine Pollution & Marine Waste Disposal.
Pearson, E. Norman. Space Time & Self.
Pearson, Frank A., jt. auth. see Warren, George F.
Pearson, Frederic S. & Rochester, J. Martin. An Introduction to International Relations: The Global Condition in the Late Twentieth Century.
Pearson, Hesketh. George Bernard Shaw: His Life & Personality.
Pearson, J. D. & Behn, Wolfgang, eds. Index Islamicus: First Supplement 1956-1960.
Pearson, John. Edward the Rake: An Unwholesome Biography of Edward the Seventh.
--James Bond: The Authorized Biography of 007.
--The Kindness of Dr. Avicenna.
--The Selling of the Royal Family: The Mystique of the British Monarchy.
--The Serpent & the Stag: The Saga of England's Powerful & Glamourous Cavendish Family from the Age of Henry the Eighth to the Present.
--The Sitwells: A Family's Biography.
Pearson, Karl G. & Litka, Michael P. Real Estate: Principles & Practices.
Pearson, Katherine, jt. auth. see Johnson, Mary E.
Pearson, Kent. Surfing Subcultures of Australia & New Zealand.
Pearson, Kevin. Character Jug Collector's Handbook.
--The Character Jug Collectors Handbook. Braithwrite, Catherine, ed.
Pearson, M. J. Ride the Red-Eyed Wind.
Pearson, M. N. Merchants & Rulers in Gujarat: The Response to the Portuguese in the Sixteenth Century.
Pearson, Richard, jt. auth. see Walsh, Kenneth.
Pearson, Roger, ed. Korea in the World Today.
Pearson, Ronald. Climate & Evolution.
Pearson, Ronald & Ball, John N. Lecture Notes on Vertebrate Zoology.
Pearson, Sidney A., Jr. The Constitutional Polity: Essays on the Founding Principles of American Politics.
Pearson, T. R. Off for the Sweet Hereafter.
--A Short History of a Small Place: A Novel.
Peary, Danny. Cult Movies: The Classics, the Sleepers, the Weird & the Wonderful.
Peary, Danny, ed. Omni's Screen Flights-Screen Fantasies: The Future According to Science Fiction Cinema. Omni Editors.
Pease, Allen & Richard, Wilfred, eds. Maine: Fifty Years of Change 1940-1990.
Pease, Daniel C. Histological Techniques for Electron Microscopy.
Pease, Donald E., jt. ed. see Michaels, Walter B.
Pease, Dudley A. Basic Fluid Power.
Pease, Jane & Pease, William H. They Who Would Be Free: The Blacks' Search for Freedom.
Pease, Otis, ed. Progressive Years: The Spirit & Achievement of American Reform.
Pease, R. S., ed. Pulsed Fusion Reactors: Proceedings of a Symposium, Erice-Trapani, Sicily, 1974.
Pease, Ralph W., jt. auth. see Johnson, Robert A.
Pease, William H., jt. auth. see Pease, Jane.
Peatman, John B. Digital Hardware Design.
Peattie, Donald C. Road of a Naturalist.
Peattie, Roderick. Mountain Geography: A Critique & Field Study.
Peavy, Charles D. Go Slow Now: Faulkner & the Race Question.
Peavy, William. Southern Gardener's Soil Handbook.
Pebay-Peyroula, J. C., jt. auth. see Cagnac, B.
Peberdy, J. F., et al, eds. Microbial & Plant Protoplasts.
Pebworth, Ted-Larry, jt. ed. see Summers, Claude.
Pe-Chin Chang. Chinese Opera & Painted Face.
Pechman, Joseph A. Federal Tax Policy.
Pechman, Joseph A. & Okner, Benjamin A. Who Bears the Tax Burden?
Pecht, I. & Rigler, R., eds. Chemical Relaxation in Molecular Biology.
Pecile, A., jt. ed. see Martini, L.
Peck, Abraham J., ed. Jews & Christians after the Holocaust.
Peck, Abraham J., jt. ed. see Marcus, Jacob R.
Peck, Alvin E. Love Is Better.
Peck, Dave & Day, Jerry. Dave Peck's World Championship Racquetball: Learning to Play by the Numbers.
Peck, David & Whitlow, David. Approaches to Personality Theory.
Peck, George. Pentecost 3.
Peck, George C. Techniques in Aesthetic Rhinoplasty.
Peck, George T. The Fool of God: Jacopone Da Todi.
Peck, Harold L. Stripping: The Assembly of Film Images.
Peck, Leigh. Pecos Bill & Lightning.
Peck, M. Scott. The Different Drum: Community Making & Peace.
--People of the Lie: The Hope for Healing Human Evil.
--The Road Less Traveled: A New Psychology of Love, Traditional Values & Spiritual Growth.
Peck, Mad. Mad Peck Studios: A Twenty Year Retrospective.
Peck, Paula. Art of Fine Baking.
Peck, Phyllis & Konkel, Gilbert. Exploring Careers in Word Processing. Rosen, R., ed.
--Your Future in Word Processing.
Peck, Phyllis & Konkel, Gilbert J. Aim for a Job in a Business Office.
Peck, Richard. Amanda-Miranda.
--Don't Look & It Won't Hurt.
--Jonathan Fisher & the Centerfold Caper.
--Pictures That Storm Inside My Head.
--Representing Superdoll.
--Through a Brief Darkness.
Peck, Robert N. Hamilton.
--Trig.
--Trig Goes Ape.
--Trig Sees Red.
--Wild Cat.
Peck, Theodore P. The Troubled Family: Sources of Information.
Peck, Theodore P., ed. Employee Counseling in Industry & Government: A Guide to Information Sources.
--Occupational Safety & Health: A Guide to Information Sources.
Peck, W. Bone & Mineral Research Annual.
Peckham, C. A., jt. ed. see Alberman, E. D.
Peckham, Elsie M. Sugarless Cookery for the Gourmet: Delectable Dietetic Dishes for Sugar-Restricted Diets.
Peckham, Morse. Romanticism & Behavior: Collected Essays.
Peckman, David A. Employee Stock Ownership Plans: A Decision Maker's Guide.
Pecsi, Kalman. The Future of Socialist Economic Integration. Marer, Paul, ed. Hajdu, George & Crane, Keith, trs. from Hungarian.
Pedagno, Antonio. Geometry's Oldest Challenges.
Pedder, Derek, ed. Microcomputing Systems in Business.
Pedder, I. J. & Wynne, E. G. Genetics: A Basic Guide.
Pedder, M., jt. auth. see Ryan, W.
Peddersen, Ray. Specs: The Comprehensive Foodservice Purchasing & Specification Manual.
Peddie, John. Whose Land? A Glimpse into the Middle East.
Peden, Margaret S., tr. see Fuentes, Carlos.
Peden, Margaret S., tr. see Quiroga, Horacio.
Peden, William. The American Short Story: Continuity & Change 1940-1975.
Pedersen, B. Martin, ed. Graphis Annual Reports 86-87.
Pedersen, Clemens, ed. The Danish Cooperative Movement.
Pedersen, Jean & Pedersen, Kent. Geometric Playthings.
Pedersen, Kent, jt. auth. see Pedersen, Jean.
Pederson, Cliff. Christians Alive: Leader's Guide.
Pederson, Cliff, ed. Christians Alive.
Pederson, E. O. Transportation in Cities.
Pederson, Phillip E., ed. What Does This Mean? Luther's Catechisms Today.
Pederson-Krag, Geraldine. The Lurking Keats.
Pedley, Timothy A. & Meldrum, Brian S., eds. Recent Advances in Epilepsy.
Pedneau, Dave. Presumption of Innocence.
Pedoe, Dan. Circles, A Mathematical View.
Pedretti, C. A Chronology of Leonardo Da Vinci's Architectural Studies after 1500.
Pedretti, Carlo. Leonardo: A Study in Chronology & Style.
--Leonardo, Architect.
Pedrick, Bob. The Confident Parent.
Pedrini, Duilio T. & Pedrini, Lura N. Pedrini Supplementary Aid to the Administration of the Stanford-Binet Intelligence Scale (Form L-M) A Handbook.
Pedrini, Lura N., jt. auth. see Pedrini, Duilio T.
Peduzzi, Anthony & Peduzzi, Judy. Making Action Toys in Wood.
Peduzzi, Judy, jt. auth. see Peduzzi, Anthony.
Peebles, P. J. Physical Cosmology.
Peecher, John P., ed. The Making of the Return of the Jedi.
Peed, Dorothy M. The Art of Communication: A Self-Help Course in Basics.
Peek, Peter & Standing, Guy, eds. State Policies & Migration: Studies in Latin America & the Caribbean.
Peek, Walter W., jt. auth. see Sanders, Thomas E.
Peel, E. A. Psychological Basis of Education.
Peel, J., jt. ed. see Chester, R.
Peel, J. D., ed. see Spencer, Herbert.
Peel, John, jt. ed. see Armytage, W. H.
Peel, Larry D. Simplified Apple Bookkeeping.
Peel, Robert. Mary Baker Eddy: The Years of Authority.

Authors

Peel, Roy V. & Sellin, Thorsten, eds. Ombudsman or Citizen's Defender: A Modern Institution.
Peele, David A., ed. Racket & Paddle Games: A Guide to Information Sources.
Peele, Stanton. The Science of Experience: A Direction for Psychology.
Peele, Stanton & Brodsky, Archie. Love & Addiction.
Peellaert, Guy & Herr, Michael. The Big Room: Forty-Eight Portraits from the Golden Age.
Peelle, Howard. Computer Metaphors: Approaches to Computer Literacy.
Peelman, Nancy. The Cross.
Peer Review Committee of the American Psychiatric Assn., et al, eds. Manual of Psychiatric Peer Review.
Peer, Willie van see Van Peer, Willie.
Peerman, Dean G., ed. Frontline Theology.
Peers, E. A. Mother of Carmel: A Portrait of St. Teresa of Jesus.
--Spirit of Flame: A Study of St. John of the Cross.
Peers, E. Allison, tr. see Lull, Ramon.
Peers, Frank W. The Public Eye: Television & the Politics of Canadian Broadcasting, 1952-68.
Peery, David J. Aircraft Structures.
Peet, Leslie J., et al. Household Equipment.
Peet, Louis H. Handy Book of American Authors.
Peeters, H. & Wright, P. H. Plasma Protein Pathology: A Workshop on Plasma Proteins, Their Availability, Assay & Therapeutic Uses--Proceedings of a Round Table Meeting, Seville, Spain, October-November 1977.
Peeters, H., ed. Phosphatidylcholine.
--Separation of Cells & Subcellular Elements.
Peeters, H. & Gresham, G. A., eds. Arterial Pollution: An Integrated View on Atherosclerosis.
Pegg, Brian F. & Stagg, William D. Plastering: A Craftsman's Encyclopedia.
Pegg, Mark. Broadcasting & Society, Nineteen Eighteen to Nineteen Thirty-Nine.
Pegington, John. Clinical Anatomy in Action: The Head & Neck.
Pegler, D. N. The Genus Lentinus: A World Monograph.
Pegler, Martin M., ed. Store Fronts & Facades.
Pegram, Don R. America: Christian or Pagan.
--Great Churches-Today's Essentials.
--Sheep among Wolves.
--Sinning Against the Holy Spirit.
--Why We Do Not Speak in Tongues.
Pegram, Samuel & Johnson, Joseph. Antibiotics in Clinical Medicine Case Studies.
Pegues, Guy. The Illustrated SuperCalc 3 Book.
Peguy, Charles. Le Mystere des Saints Innocents.
--Notre Patrie.
--Notre Seigneur.
--Pensees.
--Le Porche du Mystere de la Deuxieme Vertu.
Pehlke, Robert D. Unit Processes of Extractive Metallurgy.
Pehnt, Wolfgang. Der Anfang der Bescheidenheit.
--Lucien Kroll: Buildings & Projects.
Pei, Mario. The Sparrows of Paris.
Pei, Mario & Gaynor, Frank. Dictionary of Linguistics.
Peige, John, et al, eds. Fire Service First Aid Practices, IFSTA Committee.
Peiji, Zhang, tr. see Jingwen, Liao.
Peikari, Behrouz. Fundamentals of Network Analysis & Synthesis.
Peirce, Freddie. The Gourmet Woodburner.
Peirce, Neal R. The Border South States: People, Politics & Power in the Five States of the Border South.
--Megastates of America: People, Politics & Power in the Ten Great States.
Peirce, Neal R. & Keefe, John. The Great Lakes State of America.
Peixoto, M. M., ed. Dynamical Systems.
Pekar, P., jt. auth. see Ellis, D.
Pekar, Peter P., jt. auth. see Ellis, Darryl J.
Pekelis, V. Pequena Enciclopedia de la Gran Cibernetica.
--Realize Your Potential.
Pekic, Borislav. The Houses of Belgrade. Johnson, Bernard, tr.
--A Time of Miracles. Edwards, Lovett F., tr.
Peklenik, J. Advances in Manufacturing Systems - Research & Development.
Pel, Mario, tr. see Mazzolani, Lidia S.
Pelczar, Michael J., Jr., et al. Microbiology.
Peleg, Micha & Bagley, Edward B., eds. Physical Properties of Foods.
Pelfrey, William. The Big V.
--Hamburger Hill.
Pelikan, Jaroslav, et al. Mary.
Pelikan, Judy, jt. auth. see Levy, Judith.
Pelissero, John. Recruitment & Selection Practices in Oklahoma Police Departments.
Pelissero, John P. Citizen Evaluations of Community Services in Oklahoma.
Pell, Arthur & Sadek, George. Resumes for Engineers.
Pell, Arthur R. How to Sell Yourself on an Interview.
--The Part Time Job Book.
Pell, Derek. Doctor Bey's Bedside Bug Book.
Pell, Elsie. Francois Mauriac.
Pell, Erik M., ed. Proceedings: International Conference on Photoconductivity, 3rd, Stanford University, Aug. 12, 1969.
Pell, Eve. The Big Chill: How the Reagan Administration, Corporate America, & Religious Conservatives Are Subverting Free Speech & the Public's Right to Know.
Pellegrini, Angelo. Lean Years, Happy Years.
Pellegrino, Charles R. & Stoff, Jesse A. Darwin's Universe: Origins & Crises in the History of Life.
Pellegrino, Victor C. You Can Write! Practical Writing Skills for Hawaii.
Pellet, P. L. & Shadarevian, Sossy. Food Composition: Tables for Use in the Middle East.
Pelletier, Cathie. The Funeral Makers.
Pelletier, Kenneth R. Healthy People in Unhealthy Places: Stress & Fitness at Work.
--Healthy People in Unhealthy Places: Stress & Fitness at Work.
Pellettieri, L. Surgical Versus Conservative Treatment of Intracranial Arteriovenous Malformations.
Pelley, Lee. In One Barn: Efficient Livestock Housing & Management Under One Roof.
Pellicane, Patricia. Embers of Desire.
Pellicani, Luciano. Gramsci: An Alternative Communism? Watts, Mimi, tr. from Ital.
Pellicciotti, Joseph M. Handbook on Basic Trial Evidence.
Pelling, Henry. Modern Britain, Eighteen Eighty Five to Nineteen Fifty Five.
Pellissier & Smith. Bulletins: Primier Niveau.
Pelloux, R. & Stoloff, N., eds. Creep-Fatigue-Environment Interactions: Proceedings TMS-AIME Fall Meeting, Milwaukee, WI, 1979.
Pellowski, Michael J. Baseball Bear.
--Birthday Bear & the Runaway Skateboard.
--Ghost Toasties.
--Miss Kitty, the New Baby, & Me.
Pellowski, Michael J., adapted by. Howard the Duck--The Movie Storybook.
Pelmear, P. L., jt. ed. see Taylor, W.
Pelt, Nancy L. Van see Van Pelt, Nancy L.
Pelt, S. J. Van see Van Pelt, S. J.
Peltason, J. W. Corwin & Peltason's Understanding the Constitution.
--Understanding the Constitution.
Peltason, Jack W. Fifty-Eight Lonely Men: Southern Federal Judges & School Desegregation.
Pelto, Pertti J., jt. auth. see Bernard, H. Russell.
Pelton, Leroy H. The Psychology of Nonviolence.
Pelton, Ronald L. Out of Forever into Forever.
Peltu, Malcolm. Introducing Computers.
Peltz, Rosemonde. Dustman to Ashes.
Peltzer, Martin & Treumann, Walter. Produzentenhaftpflicht in U. S. A. und Deutschland: Product Liability in Germany & the U. S. A. German American Chamber of Commerce Staff, ed. Fischer-Theurer, Annette, tr.
Peluso, Emanuel see Hoffman, William M.
Pelz, Ruth. Our Region: The Pacific Northwest.
Pelzel, Thomas. Anton Raphael Mengs & Neoclassicism.
Pelzman, Fran & Thomases, Martha. Cute Guys.
Pemberton, Cindy. Getting in Shape: A Primer for Nutrition, Fitness & Weight Loss.
Pemberton, Doris H. Juneteenth at Comanche Crossing.
Pemberton, Henry. A View of Sir Isaac Newton's Philosophy.
Pemberton, J. E. British Official Publications.
--How to Find Out in Mathematics.
Pembrook, Linda. How to Beat Fatigue.
Pena, Alberto & Bliek, Ruth de. Cost Effectiveness in Training & Instruction.
Pena, Augustin de la see De la Pena, Augustin.
Pena, Carlos G. History of Mexican Literature. Nance, Gusta B. & Dunstan, Florene J., trs.
Pena, Carlos Gonzalez see Pena, Carlos G.
Pena, Sylvia C., ed. Kikiriki: Stories & Poems in English & Spanish for Children.
Penalver, M., jt. auth. see World Bank Staff.
Penberthy, John. To Bee or Not to Bee.
Pencak, William. America's Burke: The Mind of Thomas Hutchinson.
Penczek, S., ed. Polymerization of Heterocycles (Ring-Opening)
Pender, Nola. Health Promotion in Nursing Practice.
Pendergrast, Robin F. Where There's Smoke... How to Protect Yourself, Your Family, Your Property, Your Environment from Fire.
Penders, C. L. & Sundhaussen, Ulf. Abdul Haris Nasution: A Political Biography.
Pendleton, Charles E. At the Home Front in War & Life: Confessions of a Lawyer.
Pendleton, Jan see Kruse, Donald W.
Pendleton, Winston K. Five Hundred Five Jokes You Can Tell.
Pendola, Charles J. Hospital Budgeting: A Case Study Approach.
Pendorf, James G., jt. auth. see Lundquist, Helmer C.
Pendry, Eric. The Way to Go Home.
Penelhum, Terence. Survival & Disembodied Existence.
Penfield, Marjorie, jt. auth. see Campbell, Ada M.
Penfield, Paul, Jr., ed. see MIT Conference on Advanced Research in VLSI Staff.
Penfield, Wilder & Roberts, Lamar. Speech & Brain-Mechanisms.
Peng, Chin-Tzu, jt. ed. see Horrocks, Donald L.
Pengelley, Eric T. Circannual Clocks: Annual Biological Rhythms.
Penick, John, ed. Science as Inquiry.
Penick, John E., jt. ed. see Shymansky, James A.
Peniston, Silvina, jt. auth. see Gillman, Peter.
Penkovskiy, Oleg. The Penkovskiy Papers.
Penman, Kenneth A. & Adams, Samuel H. Assessing Athletics & Physical Education Programs: A Manual with Reproducible Forms.
Penman, Robyn. Communication Processes & Relationship.
Penman, Sharon K. Here Be Dragons.
--The Sunne in Splendour.
Penn, Bennett. The Path of Transcendence.
Penn, John. A Deadly Sickness.
--Mortal Term.
Penn, William. The Rise & Progress of the People Called Quakers.
Pennar, Jaan, et al. Modernization & Diversity in Soviet Education: With Special Reference to Nationality Groups.
Pennell, Arthur. An Edition of Anthony Munday's John a Kent & John a Cumber.
Pennell, C. R. A Country with a Government & a Flag: The Rif War in Morocco, 1921-1926.
Pennell, Joseph. Illustration of Books: A Manual for the Use of Students.
Pennell, Lucy. What Do These Things Mean?
Pennell, Lucy & Smith, Jackie M. Our Church at Work in the World.
Penner, Jonathan. Private Parties.
Penner, S. S. New Sources of Oil & Gas: Gases from Coal, Liquid Fuels from Coal, Shale, Tar Sands, & Heavy Oil Sources.
Penner, S. S. & Olfe, Daniel B. Radiation & Reentry.
Penney, David E., jt. auth. see Edwards, C. H.
Penney, G., ed. see National Computing Centre, Ltd. Staff.
Penney, Grace J. Moki.
Pennick, Nigel. Sacred Geometry.
Penning De Vries, Piet. Discernment of Spirits: According to the Life & Teachings of St. Ignatius Loyola van Heel.
--Prayer & Life.
Penninger, F. Elaine, ed. English Drama to Sixteen Sixty (Excluding Shakespeare): A Guide to Information Sources.
Penninger, Johan M. L., jt. auth. see Paulaitis, Michael E.
Pennington, Anne, tr. see Popa, Vasko.
Pennington, Basil. Challenges in Prayer.
Pennington, Campbell W. The Pima Bajo Nevome of Central Sonora, Mexico: Vol. 1, The Material Culture.
Pennington, Chester, jt. auth. see Kingsbury, Jack D.
Pennington, M. Basil. Monastery: Prayer, Work, & the Common Life.
Pennington, Malcom W. & Allio, Robert J. Corporate Planning: Techniques & Applications.
Pennington, Rod. Devon's Way: The Quicksilver Solution.
Pennington, T. H. & Ritchie, D. A. Molecular Virology.
Pennock, Michael, jt. auth. see Finley, James.
Pennsylvania Bar Institute & Pennsylvania Bar Institute Staff. Taxation in Common Transactions: Pennsylvania Legal Practice Course Materials.
Pennsylvania Bar Institute Staff. Attorney's Guide to Agricultural Real Estate Transactions.
--Basic Estate Planning & Administration.
--Buying & Selling a Business.
--Cable Television: Current Legal Issues.
--Civil Uses of RICO.
--Collection & Enforcement of Judgments.
--Computer Law: Buying & Selling Computer Hardware & Software.
--Counseling Small Businesses.
--Creditors' Remedies: Pennsylvania Legal Practice Course Materials.
--Criminal Law Symposium.
--Defending Traffic Cases.
--Drafting Wills & Trusts.
--Emerging Areas of Litigation Affecting Banks & Other Financial Institutions.
--Employee Benefits.
--Environmental Law: Groundwater Protection & Industrial Contamination.
--Equitable Distribution of Pensions.
--Estate Planning for Property Management & Health Care Financing for the Elderly.
--Estate Planning: Pennsylvania Legal Practice Course Materials.
--Export Trading Company Act of 1982.
--The Family Lawyer's Symposium.
--Fiduciary Income Taxes.
--Getting, Spending, Borrowing, Lending: What You Must Know about Government Regulation of Consumer Transactions.
--Handling Tax Disputes with the IRS 24th Annual Tax School.
--How to Draft Estate Documents.
--Insurance Practice & Litigation.
--Labor Law Colloquium.
--Labor Relations in Pennsylvania Construction Industry.
--Land Use Law & Litigation.
--Law Practice Management: Pennsylvania Legal Practice Course Materials.
--Marketing Your Law Firm's Services.
--Medical Malpractice Litigation.
--Medicare, Medicaid & the Law.
--Minority Shareholders.
--Patents, Trademarks, Copyrights & Trade Secrets: Pennsylvania Legal Practice Course Materials.
--Pennsylvania Appellate Practice.
--Pennsylvania Civil Practice & Procedure.
--Pennsylvania Legal Practice Manuals.
--Pennsylvania Workers' Compensation Practice & Procedure.
--Philadelphia Taxes on Business & Related Activities.
--Post-Mortem Estate Planning.
--Products Liability.
--Professional Corporations after TEFRA.
--Real Estate Practice.
--Real Estate Practice: Pennsylvania Legal Practice Course Materials.
--Real Estate Syndications.
--Representing Residential Landlords & Tenants.
--Residential Mortgage Foreclosures: Current Developments.
--The Securities Acts: Federal & Pennsylvania.
--Structured Settlements.
--Subchapter S Revisions of 1982.
--Tax-Exempt Industrial Development Financing.
--Transforming Ordinary Income into Capital Gain.
--Trial Techniques: A Young Lawyer's Guide to Civil Trial Advocacy.
--Valuation of a Closely Held Business.
--What Every Lawyer Needs to Know about Bankruptcy.
Pennsylvania Bar Institute Staff, jt. auth. see Pennsylvania Bar Institute.
Pennsylvania Department of Education, Social Studies Division Staff. A Conceptual Approach to Teaching about Pennsylvania.
Penny, James S., Jr. Archaeological Survey of Exchange Lands & Timber Sales in the Shawnee National Forest, Southern Illinois, 1982.
Penny, Julie. Narcissa.
--Narcissa.
Pennypincher, A., jt. auth. see Miser, A.
Penoi, Jon, ed. see Liliom, Tom C.
Penoi, Jon R. Tunnels: Journey into a Dark Universe.
Penoi, Lois, ed. see Liliom, Tom C.
Penoi, Mary, ed. see Dees, Mary R.
Penoi, Mary, ed. see Duncan, Juanita.
Penoi, Mary, ed. see Owen, Ray.
Penrose, Antony. The Lives of Lee Miller.
Penrose, Boies. Travel & Discovery in the Renaissance, 1420-1620.
Penrose, O. Foundations of Statistical Mechanics: A Deductive Treatment.
Pensler, Otto, et al. Detectionary.
Penson, John B., Jr. & Lins, David A. Agricultural Finance: An Introduction to Micro & Macro Concepts.
Pentecost, Hugh. Cannibal Who Overate.
--Remember to Kill Me.
Penton, M. James. Apocalypse Delayed: The Story of Jehovah's Witnesses.
Pentz, Lundy. The BioLab Book.
Penwarden, Thelma. Colourful Lady Lebanon.
Penzholz, H., ed. see Annual Meeting of the Deutsche Gesellschaft Fuer Neurochirurgie Staff, et al.
Penzler, Otto, jt. ed. see Steinbrunner, Chris.
People's Medical Publishing House Staff. The Chinese Way to a Long & Healthy Life.
People's Press Palestine Book Project Staff, et al. Our Roots Are Still Alive: The Story of the Palestinian People.
Pepe, Frank, et al, eds. Motility in Cell Function: Proceedings of the First John M. Marshall Symposium on Cell Biology.
Pepe, Phil. The Wit & Wisdom of Yogi Berra.
Pepe, Phil, jt. auth. see Martin, Billy.
Peper, Christian B., ed. An Historian's Conscience: The Correspondence of Arnold J. Toynbee & Columba Cary-Elwes, Monk of Ampleforth.
Peper, George. Golf's Supershots.
--Golf's Supershots: How the Pros Played Them - How You Can Play Them.
Pepinsky, Harold B. People & Information.
Pepinsky, Harold B. & Patton, Michael J. The Psychological Experiment: A Practical Accomplishment.
Pepinsky, Harold E. Crime & Conflict.
Peple, Edward. Night Out.

Authors

Peplow, Michael W. & Bravard, Robert S. Samuel R. Delany: A Primary & Secondary Bibliography, 1962-1979.
Peppe, Rodney. The Mice & the Flying Basket.
--Odd One Out.
Pepper, Claude. Ask Claude Pepper.
Pepper, Curtis B. We, the Victors.
Pepper, Stephen C. Concept & Quality: A World Hypothesis.
Pepper, Thomas, jt. auth. see Kahn, Herman.
Pepper, William F. & Kennedy, Florynce R. Sex Discrimination in Employment.
Peppercorn, Lisa M., ed. & tr. The Villa-Lobos Letters.
Pequegnat, Linda, jt. ed. see Bright, Thomas.
Pequegnat, Willis E. & Chace, Fenner A., Jr., eds. Contributions on the Biology of the Gulf of Mexico.
Peragallo, H. & Peragallo, M. Les Diatomees Marines de la France.
Peragallo, M., jt. auth. see Peragallo, H.
Perakh, Mark. Man in a Wire Cage.
Percival, Bob. The How-To-Do-It Encyclopedia of Painting & Wallcovering.
--Organic Vegetable Gardening.
Percival, Fred & Ellington, Henry. A Handbook of Educational Technology: A Practical Guide for Teachers.
Percival, James G. Uncollected Letters of James Gates Percival, Poet & Geologist, 1795-1856. Warfel, Harry R., ed.
Percival, Jan, et al. The Complete Guide to Total Fitness.
Percival, Julia & Burger, Pixie. The Stewardess.
Percivall, Julie, jt. auth. see Burger, Pixie.
Percus, J. K. Combinatorial Methods.
Percy, Ann, jt. ed. see Hiesinger, Ulrich W.
Percy, Christopher V. The Glass of Lalique: A Collector's Guide.
Percy, Eustace. John Knox.
Percy, Walker. Love in the Ruins.
--The Moviegoer.
Percy, William A. Sewanee.
Percy, William A., jt. auth. see Johnson, Jerah.
Perdue, Robert. The Negro in Savannah, Eighteen Sixty-Five to Nineteen Hundred.
Perea, Jose A., jt. auth. see Cabrera, Y. Arturo.
Perelman, Michael. Classical Political Economy: Primitive Accumulation & the Social Division of Labor.
Perelman, Michael, jt. auth. see Colman, Carol.
Perelman, S. J. The Last Laugh.
Perelman, Y. A. Fun with Maths & Physics.
Perelman, Ya. Problemas y Experimentos Recreativos.
Perepechko, I. I. Low-Temperature Properties of Polymers.
Perera, Ronald C., jt. ed. see Appleton, Jon H.
Peress, Gilles, photos by. Telex: Iran.
Peretti, Frank E. Tilly.
Perez, Carlos, ed. see Lobos, Amilcar & Mellot, Leland.
Perez, Joseph F. Family Roots of Adolescent Delinquency.
Perez, Juan A., ed. Spanish-English, English-Spanish Dictionary of Maritime & Shipbuilding Terms.
Perez-Bercoff, R., ed. Protein Biosynthesis In Eukaryotes.
Perez-Diaz, Victor M. State, Bureaucracy & Civil Society: A Critical Discussion of the Political Theory of Karl Marx.
Pérez Ponce, Jorge M., ed. Intercultural Education in the Two-Year College: A Handbook on Strategies for Change.
Perez Y Sabido, Jesus, jt. auth. see Howell, Grace.
Pergolizzi, Robert, ed. see Newsletter Publications Center Staff.
Perham, Richard, ed. Instrumentation in Amino Acid Sequence Analysis.
Perkins, Alice, jt. ed. see Carey, Katherine.
Perkins, Bradford. Prologue to War: England & the United States, 1805-1812.
Perkins, Carol M., jt. auth. see Perkins, Marlin.
Perkins, Clifford A. Border Patrol. Dickey, Nancy & Sonnichsen, C. L., eds.
Perkins, Dennis N., et al. Managing Creation: The Challenge of Building a New Organization.
Perkins, Dexter. American Approach to Foreign Policy.
Perkins, Ed see Consumer Report Book Editors.
Perkins, Elizabeth R. Education for Childbirth & Parenthood.
Perkins, Frances & St Sure, J. Paul. Two Views of American Labor.
Perkins, George W. The Bastard Child.
Perkins, Harold O. Espaliers & Vines for the Home Gardener.
Perkins, J. O. The Australian Financial System after the Campbell Report.
Perkins, James A. Billy the Kid, Chicken Gizzards & Other Tales.
Perkins, Jeff, ed. Shape Memory Effects in Alloys.
Perkins, John, jt. auth. see American Museum of Natural History Staff.
Perkins, Marlin & Perkins, Carol M. I Saw You from Afar: A Visit to the Bushmen of the Kalahari Desert.
Perkins, Maxwell E. Editor to Author: The Letters of Maxwell E. Perkins.
Perkins, Pheme. Reading the New Testament: An Introduction.
Perkins, Robert L. Soren Kierkegaard. Nineham, Dennis E. & Robertson, E. H., eds.
Perkins, Robert L., ed. Kierkegaard's Fear & Trembling: Critical Appraisals.
Perkins, Steve & Aiello, Greg. Dallas Cowboys Bluebook V.
Perko, Margaret. The Other Side of Silence.
Perkus, Cathy, ed. see Blackstock, Nelson, et al.
Perl, Lila. Annabelle Starr, E.S.P.
--Don't Ask Miranda.
--Pieface & Daphne.
--The Telltale Summer of Tina C.
--That Crazy April.
Perle, Ruth L. The Fisherman & His Wife with Benjy & Bubbles.
--Little Red Riding Hood with Benjy & Bubbles.
--Rumpelstilskin with Benjy & Bubbles.
--Sleeping Beauty with Benjy & Bubbles.
Perle, Ruth L., jt. auth. see Reinach, Jacquelyn.
Perle, Ruth L., ed. see Hefter, Richard, et al.
Perle, Ruth L., ed. see Reinach, J.
Perle, Ruth L., ed. see Reinach, Jacquelyn.
Perle, Ruth L., ed. see Reinach, Jacquelyn, et al.
Perle, Ruth L., ed. see Reinach, Jacquelyn.
Perley, Michael, jt. auth. see Howard, Ross.
Perlick, Walter W. & Lesikar, Raymond V. Introduction to Business: A Societal Approach.
Perlick, Walter W., jt. auth. see Alexander, David P.
Perlin, P. I., jt. auth. see Parton, V. Z.
Perlman, D., ed. Advances in Applied Microbiology.
--Fermentation Advances.
Perlman, Dorothy. The Magic of Honey.
Perlman, Ken. More Fingerstyle Guitar.
Perlman, Leonard, jt. auth. see Feingold, S. Norman.
Perlman, Richard, ed. Wage Determination: Market or Power Forces?
Perlman, Robert & Gurin, Arnold. Community Organization & Social Planning.
Perlmann, Moshe, ed. & tr. from Arabic. Ibn Kammuna's Examination of the Three Faiths: A Thirteenth-Century Essay in the Comparative Study of Religion.
Perlmutter, Amos. Israel: The Partitioned State.
Perlmutter, Arnold, ed. Field Theory in Elementary Particles.
Perlmutter, Arnold, jt. ed. see Kursunoglu, Behram.
Perlmutter, Judy. Kick It!
Perlmutter, Nathan & Perlmutter, Ruth A. The Real Anti-Semitism in America.
Perlmutter, Ruth A., jt. auth. see Perlmutter, Nathan.
Perlo, Ellen & Perlo, Victor. Dynamic Stability: The Soviet Economy Today.
Perlo, Victor, jt. auth. see Perlo, Ellen.
Perloe, Mark & Christie, Linda Gail. Miracle Babies & Other Happy Endings for Couples with Fertility Problems.
Perlson, Michael R. How to Understand & Influence People & Organizations: Practical Psychology for Goal Achievement.
Pern, Stephen. The Beach of Morning: A Walk in West Africa.
Pernichele, A. D., jt. ed. see Aplan, F. F.
Pernis, Benvenuto & Vogel, Henry J., eds. Cells of Immunoglobulin Synthesis.
--Regulatory T Lymphocytes.
Perovskaya, O. Kids & Cubs.
Perper, Menna, jt. auth. see Rausch, Erwin.
Perraton, Hilary, et al. Basic Education & Agricultural Extension: Costs, Effects & Alternatives.
Perrault, Charles, jt. auth. see Brown, Marcia.
Perrell, O. C., jt. auth. see Pride, William M.
Perren, S. M., jt. auth. see Allgower, M.
Perret, Gene. How to Write & Sell Your Sense of Humor.
Perret, Heli E. Using Communication Support in Projects: The World Bank's Experience.
Perret, R., ed. see IFAC Symposium Staff.
Perrett, Bryan. Allied Tanks Italy, World War II.
--Allied Tanks North Africa, World War II.
Perrett, Geoffrey. America in the Twenties: A History.
--America in the Twenties: A History.
Perrin, D. D. Dissociation Constants of Organic Bases in Aqueous Solution.
--Dissociation Constants of Organic Bases in Aqueous Solution.
Perrin, D. D., et al. Purification of Laboratory Chemicals.
Perrin, E. V. & Feingold, M. J. Pathobiology of Development.
Perrin, Gail, ed. see Murphy, Margaret D.
Perrin, James. Menlove.
Perrin, Noel. First Person Rural: Essays of a Sometime Farmer.
--Giving up the Gun: Japan's Reversion to the Sword, 1543-1879.
--Third Person Rural: Further Essays of a Sometime Farmer.
Perrin, Norman. Jesus & the Language of the Kingdom: Symbol & Metaphor in New Testament Interpretation.
--A Modern Pilgrimage in New Testament Christology.
--The Promise of Bultmann.
Perrin, Norman, jt. auth. see Abernathy, David.
Perrin, Norman, tr. see Jeremias, Joachim.
Perrin, Paul, jt. auth. see Francois, Bernard.
Perrin, Steve. Spawn of Dragonspear.
Perrin, Suzanne M. Comparable Worth & Public Policy: The Case of Pennsylvania.
Perrine, Laurence. Literature: Structure, Sound & Sense.
--Literature: Structure, Sound & Sense.
--Sound & Sense: An Introduction to Poetry.
--Sound & Sense: An Introduction to Poetry.
--Sound & Sense: An Introduction to Poetry.
--Story & Structure.
Perrine, Laurence & Arp, Thomas R. Literature: Structure, Sound & Sense.
--Story & Structure.
Perrine, Laurence, ed. Story & Structure.
Perrine, Mary. Salt Boy.
Perritt, G. W & Shannon, L. Kay. The Individual Investor's Guide to No-Load Mutual Funds.
Perritt, Henry H., Jr. Employee Dismissal Law & Practice.
Perrone, N. & Atluri, S. N., eds. Nonlinear & Dynamic Fracture Mechanics.
Perrone, N., jt. ed. see Herrmann, G.
Perrone, Nicholas & Pilkey, Walter D., eds. The Structural Mechanics Software Series.
Perrone, Nicholas, jt. ed. see Atluri, Satya.
Perrone, Nicholas, et al, eds. Fracture Mechanics.
Perrone, Philip & Male, Robert A. The Developmental Education & Guidance of Talented Learners.
Perrone, Vito. Open Education: Promise & Problems.
Perrot, Elizabeth. Microteaching in Higher Education.
Perrot, M. de. Energie et Societe.
--Energie Nucleaire et Societe.
Perrotta, Kevin. Taming the TV Habit.
Perrotta, Kevin, ed. see Colson, Charles, et al.
Perrow, Charles. The Radical Attack on Business: A Critical Analysis.
Perry, jt. auth. see Potter.
Perry, A. H., jt. auth. see Barry, R. G.
Perry, C. C. & Lissner, H. R. Strain Gage Primer.
Perry, Carmen, jt. auth. see Kendall, Dorothy S.
Perry, Dick. One Way to Write Your Novel.
Perry, Donald. Life above the Jungle Floor: A Biologist Explores a Strange & Hidden Tree Top World.
Perry, F. E. A Dictionary of Banking.
--The Elements of Banking.
Perry, George. The Great British Picture Show.
Perry, Hamilton D. Libby Holman: Body & Soul.
Perry, Helen S., ed. see Sullivan, Harry S.
Perry, J. C Illustrated, a Guide for Experienced Programmers.
Perry, J., jt. ed. see Domsky, I.
Perry, James T. A User's Guide to dBASE II.
Perry, James T. & McJunkins, Robert F. A User's Guide to dBASE II.
Perry, Jim, jt. ed. see Gibbs, Emily A.
Perry, Jim, ed. see Juge, Ed, et al.
Perry, John, jt. auth. see Barwise, Jon.
Perry, K. W. Accounting: An Introduction.
Perry, Marvin. Arnold Toynbee & the Crisis of the West.
Perry, Marvin, et al. Western Civilization: A Concise History.
Perry, Paul, jt. auth. see Phaigh, Rich.
Perry, Philip M. Successful Secrets to Smart Retailing.
Perry, Phillip M. Retailer's Complete Guide to Bigger Sales-Lower Costs-Higher Profits.
Perry, R., ed. see Institute of Criminology, University of Cambridge, England Staff.
Perry, Raymond E., jt. auth. see Bevis, Donald J.
Perry, Richard. Life at the Sea's Frontiers.
--Life in Forest & Jungle.
--Montgomery's Children.
--Watching Sea Birds.
--The World of the Jaguar.
Perry, Ritchie. One Good Death Deserves Another.
--Presumed Dead.
Perry, Robert H. & Chilton, C. H. Chemical Engineers' Handbook.
Perry, Roger & Young, Robert J., eds. Handbook of Air Pollution Analysis.
Perry, Ronald W. The Social Psychology of Civil Defense.
Perry, Ronald W., et al. Evacuation Planning in Emergency Management.
Perry, S. F. Reptilian Lungs: Functional Anatomy & Evolution.
Perry, S. G., et al. Practical Liquid Chromatography.
Perry, Samuel W. The Simon & Schuster Pocket Encyclopedia of Prescription & Nonprescription Drugs.
Perry, Stuart. The New Zealand Whiskey Book.
Perry, Susan. How Did We Get Clocks & Calendars?
Perry, Susan M. & Bellini, Lisa. Lean & Green Diet.
Perry, T. Anthony. Erotic Spirituality: The Integrative Tradition from Leone Ebreo to John Donne.
Perry, T. M. The Discovery of Australia: The Charts & Maps of the Navigators & Explorers.
Perry, Thomas. Big Fish.
--Island.
Perry, Thomas L & Foulks, James G., eds. End the Arms Race - Fund Human Needs: Proceedings of Vancouver Centennial Peaces & Disarmament Symposium, 1986.
Perry, Walter. The Open University: History & Evaluation of a Dynamic Innovation in Higher Education.
Perry, William, jt. auth. see Porter, W. Thomas, Jr.
Perry, William E. Cleaning up a Computer Mess.
--Effective Methods of EDP Quality Assurance.
--Ensuring Data Base Integrity.
--Evaluating the Costs-Benefits of Data Bases.
--The Micro-Mainframe Link: The Corporate Guide to Productive Use of the Microcomputer.
--Survival Guide to Computer Systems: A Primer for Executives.
Perry, William E., jt. auth. see Porter, W. Thomas, Jr.
Perry-Cowen, Frances. Chautauqua to Opera: An Autobiography of a Voice Teacher & Daughter of a Chautauqua Pioneer.
Perryman, James H., ed. Oral Physiology & Occlusion: An International Symposium.
Perryman, Jennifer. Where Are All the Kittens?
Perryman, Patricia, jt. ed. see Van Osdol, Bob M.
Persavich, Jon J., jt. ed. see Warmbrod, Catharine P.
Persavich, Jon J., jt. auth. see Warmbrod, Catherine P.
Perschke, Louis M. Helps & Hints at Bible Study.
Persell, Stuart M. The French Colonial Lobby, 1889-1938.
Persius. The Satires. Jenkinson, J. R., ed.
Persley, Garrielle J. & Fahy, Peter C., eds. Plant Bacterial Diseases: A Diagnostic Guide.
Person, Ron. Animation Magic with Your IBM PC & PCjr.
--Macintosh Game Animation.
--One-Two-Three Business Formula Handbook.
Person Wolinsky Associates Inc. How to Prepare for the Uniform Certified Public Accountant Examination.
Pertschuk, Michael. Giant Killers.
Pertzoff, V. A. Translation of Scientific Russian.
Perun, Pamela J., ed. The Undergraduate Woman: Issues in Educational Equity.
Pervier, Evelyn. Horsemanship: Basics for Intermediate Riders.
Pervin, Lawrence A. & Lewis, Michael, eds. Perspectives in Interactional Psychology.
Pervin, Lawrence A., et al, eds. The College Dropout & the Utilization of Talent.
Pervo, Richard I. & Carl, William J., III. Epiphany. Achtemeier, Elizabeth, et al, eds.
Pervozvanskii, A. A. Random Processes in Nonlinear Control Systems.
Pesce, B., ed. Electrolytes.
Pesce, Biagio, ed. Nuclear Magnetic Resonance in Chemistry: Proceedings.
Peschar, J., jt. ed. see Niessen, M.
Pesek, Ludek. Trap for Perseus. Bell, Anthea, tr.
Pesetsky, Bette. Author from a Savage People.
--Digs.
Pesez, M., jt. auth. see Bartos, J.
Peshkoff, Alexi M. see Gorky, Maxim.
Peskin, Dean B. A Job Loss Survival Manual.
Peskin, Henry M. & Seskin, Eugene P. Cost-Benefit Analysis & Water Pollution Policy.
Peskin, Sarah. Guiding Growth & Change: A Handbook for the Massachusetts Citizen.
Pesonen, M., jt. auth. see Hurme, R.
Pessemier, Edgar A. New Product Decisions.
Pestalozzi, Heinrich. Education of Man.
Pestemer, M. Correlation Tables for the Structural Determination of Organic Compounds by Ultraviolet Light Absorptiometry.
Pestka, Sidney, jt. ed. see Weissbach, Herbert.
Pestoff, Victor A. Voluntary Associations & Nordic Party Systems.
Petch, Simon. Art of Philip Larkin.
Peter & Donnelly. Marketing Management.
Peter Dickenson Book. The Poison Oracle.
Peter, J. Paul & Donnelly, James H., Jr. A Preface to Marketing Management.
Peter, Laurence J. Peter Pyramid.
Peter Peregrims, Ltd., jt. auth. see Institution of Electrical Engineers (UK) Staff.
Peter Peregrinus, Ltd., jt. auth. see Institution of Electrical Engineers (UK) Staff.
Peter Peregrinus, Ltd. Staff, jt. auth. see Institution of Electrical Engineers (UK) Staff.

Peter Perogrinus, Ltd., jt. auth. see Institute of Electrical Engineers (UK) Staff.
Peter, R., jt. ed. see Czihak, G.
Peter, Redgrove. The Black Goddess & the Unseen Real.
Peter, Roezsa. Recursive Functions in Computer Theory.
Peterenko, F. & Popov, V. Soviet Foreign Policy: Objectives & Principles.
Peterfi, William O., ed. Issues & Trends in Contemporary Politics.
Peterken, George. Woodland Conservation & Management.
Peterlik, Meindrad, jt. ed. see Bronner, Felix.
Peterman, Anthony E., ed. A Dramatic Portfolio of the Greatest Art Masterpieces of the Dutch Genius.
Peterman, Mary E. Healing: A Spiritual Adventure.
Peters. Design: Libraries for Schools & University.
Peters, et al. How to Prepare for High School Entrance Examinations: Including SSAT & CO-OP.
Peters, A. J. British Further Education.
Peters, A. T. Ferrous Production Metallurgy.
Peters, Aimee, ed. see Harper, Wilhemina.
Peters, B., ed. Cosmic Rays, Solar Particles & Space Research.
Peters, B. Guy. The Politics of Bureaucracy: A Comparative Analysis.
Peters, Barbara, ed. see Robinson, David F.
Peters, Charles & Nelson, Michael. The Culture of Bureaucracy.
Peters, Charlie. Paternity.
Peters, D. A. The Principles & Practice of Supervision.
Peters, D. K., jt. ed. see Jones, Norman F.
Peters, David B. A Betrayal of Innocence.
Peters, Delores, jt. auth. see Woodward, Delores M.
Peters, Dianne S. The Tree Burns Green & Other Stories.
Peters, Donald L., jt. ed. see Walcher, Dwain N.
Peters, Edward M. Europe & the Middle Ages: A Short History.
Peters, Elizabeth. The Copenhagen Connection.
--Lion in the Valley.
--Lion in the Valley: An Amelia Peabody Mystery.
--The Mummy Case.
--Silhouette in Scarlet.
--Trojan Gold.
Peters, Ellis. Dead Man's Ransom. Williams, Jennifer, ed.
--Never Pick up Hitch Hikers. Barzun, J. & Taylor, W. H., eds.
--St. Peter's Fair.
Peters, G., ed. see Gesellschaft Fuer Nephrologie, 5th Symposium, Switzerland, 1967.
Peters, George. A Theology of Church Growth.
Peters, H. F. My Sister, My Spouse: A Biography of Lou Andreas - Salome.
Peters, Hannah, et al. Mammalian Oogenesis.
Peters, Helen Hall. Physical Fitness & Mental Health Before & After Retirement.
Peters, J. Ross. Economics of the Canadian Corporate Bond Market.
Peters, Jens. The Philippines: A Travel Survival Kit.
Peters, Joseph P. A Strategic Planning Process for Hospitals.
Peters, M. C., jt. auth. see Francis, W.
Peters, Margaret. Spelling: Caught or Taught? A New Look.
Peters, Margaret W. What Good Is Your Religion Doing You?
Peters, Michael & Oliva, Terence. Operations & Production Management.
Peters, Mike. The Nixon Chronicles.
Peters, Mollie C., tr. see Von Staden, Wendelgard.
Peters, Nancy J., jt. auth. see Ferlinghetti, Lawrence.
Peters, R. S. Moral Development & Moral Education.
Peters, R. S., ed. The Concept of Education.
Peters, Richard, jt. auth. see Agazarian, Yvonne.
Peters, Robert. Byron Exhumed: A Verse Suite.
Peters, Robert A. ROI: Practical Theory & Innovative Application.
Peters, Robert L. Songs for a Son.
Peters, Roger. Dance of the Wolves.
Peters, Susan. Insects: A Selection.
Peters, T. R., Sr. The Education of Tom Webber.
Peters, Ted. Fear, Faith, & the Future: Affirming Christian Hope in the Face of Doomsday Prophecies.
--UFOs-God's Chariots? Flying Saucers in Politics, Science & Religion.
Petersdorf, Robert G., et al, eds. Update Five: Harrison's Principles of Internal Medicine.
--Update Seven: Harrison's Principles of Internal Medicine.
--Harrison's Principles of Internal Medicine: Update VI.
Petersen, Bill. Those Curious New Cults in the Eighties.
Petersen, Charles G., jt. auth. see Miller, Nancy E.
Petersen, Dan. Safety Management: A Human Approach.
--Safety Supervision.
Petersen, Daniel C. The O S H A Compliance Manual.
--Techniques of Safety Management.
Petersen, Daniel C. & Goodale, Jerry. Readings in Industrial Ancient Prevention.
Petersen, David M., ed. Police Work: Strategies & Outcomes in Law Enforcement.
Petersen, Eggert. A Reassessment of the Concept of Criminality: An Analysis of Criminal Behavior in Terms of Individual & Current Environment - the Application of a Stochastic Model.
Petersen, Evelyn & Petersen, J. Allan. For Women Only.
Petersen, J. Allan. The Art of Being a Man.
Petersen, J. Allan, jt. auth. see Petersen, Evelyn.
Petersen, J. L. Computer Programs for Spelling Correction.
Petersen, Jim. Evangelism As a Lifestyle.
--Evangelism for Our Generation.
Petersen, Johanna. Careers with a Fire Department.
--Careers with the Postal Service.
Petersen, Mark E. The Sons of Mosiah.
--Three Kings of Israel.
Petersen, Norman R. Literary Criticism for New Testament Critics. Via, Dan O., Jr., ed.
Petersen Publishing Co. Staff. How to Tune Your Car.
Petersen, Sheila. Successful Community Fundraising: A Complete How-to Guide.
Petersen, Stephen R. User's Guide to the Federal Building Life-Cycle Cost (FBLCC) Computer Program.
Petersen, W. P. & Fehr, Terry. Meditation Made Easy.
Petersen, William J. Catherine Marshall Had a Husband.
--Martin Luther Had a Wife.
Petersen, Wretha. An Educational Developmental Program, Kit 2: The Preacademic Instructional Program.
Peterson, B. E., ed. Cancer of the Lung.
Peterson, B. R. The Origial Roadkill Cookbook.
Peterson, Brenda, jt. auth. see Hafen, Brent Q.
Peterson, C. Hidden Assets.
Peterson, Clark C. The Great Hinckley Fire.
Peterson, Curt M. Plant Biology Laboratory Manual.
Peterson, D. G., jt. ed. see O'Brien, P. T.
Peterson, Dale. Big Things from Little Computers: A Layperson's Guide to Personal Computing.
Peterson, David M. & Thomas, Charles W. Corrections: Problems & Prospects.
Peterson, Dean F., jt. auth. see Crawford, A. Berry.
Peterson, Donald R., ed. Professional Psychology Review.
Peterson, Edward D. Cash Management: A Practical Guide to Increasing Profits.
Peterson, Eugene H. Growing up in Christ.
Peterson, F. & Carmi, S., eds. Three Dimensional Turbulent Shear Flows.
Peterson, G., jt. ed. see Mieszkowski, P.
Peterson, Gary. Et Al: A Collection of Short Stories.
Peterson, Geoffrey. Conscience & Caring.
Peterson, George, jt. auth. see Dickson, Elizabeth.
Peterson, George, ed. Property Tax Reform.
Peterson, George, et al. The Future of Boston's Capital Plant.
--The Future of Oakland's Capital Plant.
Peterson, George E. Tax-Exempt Financing of Housing Investment.
Peterson, Glen. Money is What Money Does: A Mini Book on the Macroeconomy.
Peterson, Glenda Y. How Come?
Peterson, Harold F. Argentina & the United States, 1810-1960.
Peterson, Jacqueline & Brown, Jennifer S., eds. The New Peoples: Being & Becoming Metis in North America.
Peterson, John. The Littles.
Peterson, John E. Oman in the Twentieth Century: Political Foundations of an Emerging State.
Peterson, John M. Basic Concepts of Elementary Mathematics.
Peterson, John M. & Smith, James E. Basic Concepts of Elementary Mathematics.
Peterson, Joseph L., jt. auth. see Jones, James H.
Peterson, Kathy, jt. auth. see Chappell, Willard.
Peterson, Leonard. The Grin on the Moon.
Peterson, Lorna. Absenteeism: A Selective Bibliography.
--Appraising the Boss: An Annotated Bibliography for Librarians.
--Assessment Centers for Supervisors & Managers in Public Administration: A Selective Checklist.
--Fringe Benefits for Librarians: A Selected Bibliography.
--Fund Raising for Libraries: A Selective Bibliography.
--In-Service Training & Staff Development for the Paraprofessional in Libraries: A Selective Bibliography.
--Insurance for Computers: A Checklist.
--Management of Employee Health Benefits: A Selective Bibliography.
--Participatory Management for Public Administrators: A Selective Bibliography.
--Planned Organizational Change & Its Evaluation: A Checklist.
--Professional Development for College & University Librarians: A Selective Bibliography.
--Risk Management for Librarians: A Bibliographical List.
--Strategic & Long-Range Planning for Public Administrators: A Selective Bibliography.
--Wage Determination & Comparable Worth for Librarians: A Checklist of Materials.
Peterson, Martin S. & Johnson, Arnold H. Encyclopedia of Food Science.
Peterson, Merrill D., jt. ed. see Levy, Leonard W.
Peterson, Michael L. Evil & the Christian God.
Peterson, R. Marketing & Society: Selected Readings.
Peterson, R. V., jt. auth. see Richardson, J. H.
Peterson, R. V., jt. ed. see Richardson, J. H.
Peterson, Renno L., jt. auth. see Esperti, Robert A.
Peterson, Richard. The Character Catalogue.
--Hemingway: Direct & Oblique.
Peterson, Richard L., jt. auth. see Kidwell, David S.
Peterson, Robert C. Understand Accounting-Fast.
Peterson, Robert M., jt. auth. see Kerin, Roger.
Peterson, Robert W. The Boy Scouts: An American Adventure.
Peterson, Robin T., jt. auth. see Gross, Charles W.
Peterson, Roger T. Field Guide to the Birds.
--Field Guide to the Birds.
Peterson, Russell. Technology: Its Promise & Its Problems.
Peterson, Shailer. Preparing to Enter Pharmacy School.
Peterson, Susan. The Living Tradition of Maria Martinez.
Peterson, Virgilia, tr. see Romanowicz, Zofia.
Peterson, Wallace C. Our Overloaded Economy: Inflation, Unemployment & the Crisis in American Capitalism.
Peterson, Warren S., ed. Light Metals 1979: Proceedings. AIME Annual Meeting, New Orleans, 1979.
Peterson, Wilfred A. The Art of Living Treasure Chest: The 75 Best & Most Inspiring Art of Living Essays.
Peterson, William S. Interrogating the Oracle: A History of the London Browning Society.
Peterson, Willis L. Principles of Economics.
Petersson, Robert T. Art of Ecstasy: Teresa, Bernini & Crashaw.
Peterzell, Jay. Nuclear Power & Political Surveillance.
Pethes, G. & Frenyo, V. L. Advances in Animal & Comparative Physiology: Proceedings of the 28th International Congress of Physiological Sciences, Budapest, 1980.
Pethes, G., et al, eds. Recent Advances of Avian Endocrinology: Proceedings of a Satellite Symposium of the 28th International Congress of Physiological Sciences, Budapest, Hungary, 1980.
Peticolas, W. L. & Hudson, B., eds. Proceedings of the Tenth International Conference on Raman Spectroscopy.
Peticolas, W. L., jt. ed. see Hudson, B.
Petievich, Gerald. Money Men & One Shot Deal.
--The Quality of the Informant.
--To Die in Beverly Hills.
--To Live & Die in L. A.
Petik, H., jt. ed. see Beranek, B. A.
Petit, Adrian M., tr. see Management Sciences for Health Staff, et al.
Petit, Herbert H., ed. Annuale Mediaevale.
Petkevich, John M. The Skater's Handbook.
Petkov, Boris. Afghanistan Today.
Petrakis, Peter L. Alcoholism: An Inherited Disease.
Petrarch, Francis. Songs & Sonnets from Laura's Lifetime. Kilmer, Nicholas, tr. from Ital.
Petras, James. Critical Perspectives on Imperialism & Social Class in the Third World.
Petras, John W., jt. auth. see Aho, Jennifer J.
Petrazhitskii, Lev I. Law & Morality. Babb, Hugh W., tr.
Petrelia, R., jt. ed. see Szalai, A.
Petre-Quadens, Olga & Schlag, John D., eds. Basic Sleep Mechanisms.
Petri, Darlene. The Hurt & Healing of Divorce.
Petrick, M., jt. auth. see Chaffee, S.
Petrides, Elfleida, jt. auth. see Petrides, Theodore.
Petrides, Heidrun. Hans & Peter.
Petrides, Theodore & Petrides, Elfleida. Folk Dances of the Greeks.
Petrie, jt. auth. see Murtha.
Petrie, Ferdinand, illus. The Watercolorist's Guide to Painting Water.
Petrie, Flinders. Syria & Egypt: From the Tell El Amarna Letters.
--Ten Years Digging in Egypt.
Petrie, Glen. The Fourth King.
Petrie, Graham. Hollywood Destinies: European Directors in America 1922-1931.
Petrie, J. C. & McIntyre, Neil, eds. The Problem-Orientated Medical Record in Clinical Practice.
Petrie, Sidney & Stone, Robert B. Fat Destroyer Foods: The Magic Metabolizer Diet.
Petronius Arbiter. Satyricon. Firebaugh, W. C., tr.
Petros, Sophie K. Sophie Kay's Microwave.
Petroski, Catherine. Beautiful My Mane in the Wind.
Petrosky, Anthony & Bartholomae, David, eds. The Teaching of Writing: The Eighty-Fifth Yearbook of the National Society for the Study of Education.
Petrosyan, M. Humanism: Its Philosophical, Ethical & Sociological Aspects.
Petrov, A. A. Einstein Spaces.
Petrov, M. P. Deserts of the World.
Petrov, Vladimir. June Twenty-Second, Nineteen Forty-One: Soviet Historians & the German Invasion. Nekrich, Aleksandr M., tr.
Petrovich, Michael B., tr. see Djilas, Milovan.
Petrovich, Michael B., tr. see Kusan, Ivan.
Petrovsky, V. Soviet Security Concept.
Petrucci, Ottaviano. Canti B Numero Cinquanta.
Petrucci, Ralph H. General Chemistry.
Petrucci, Ralph H. & Wismer, Robert K. Solutions Manual to Accompany Petrucci's General Chemistry.
Petrucci, S., ed. Ionic Interactions: From Dilute Solutions to Fused Salts.
Petrucelli, R. Joseph, jt. auth. see Lyons, Albert S.
Petruck, Peninah R. Y. American Art Criticism: 1910-1939.
Petry, Ray C., jt. ed. see Manschreck, Clyde L.
Pets Are Wonderful Council Editors. The Pets Are Wonderful Family Album.
Petsche, H., ed. see Austrian Academy of Sciences Symposium Staff.
Petska, Darrell E., jt. auth. see Baxa, Donald E.
Petsopoulos, Yanni. Kilims: Flat Woven Tapestry Rugs.
Petter, A. J. & Quentin, J. C., eds. CIH Keys to the Nematode Parasites of Vertebrates, No. 4: Keys to Genera of the Oxyuroidea.
Petterssen, Sverre. Introduction to Meteorology.
Pettersson, Alan R. Frankenstein's Aunt.
Petti, Michael A., jt. auth. see Poteet, G. Howard.
Pettifer, Julian & Turner, Nigel. Automania: Man & the Motor Car.
Pettigrew, T. F. Racially Separate or Together.
Pettijohn, F. J. & Potter, P. E. Atlas & Glossary of Primary Sedimentary Structures.
Pettijohn, Terry F. Psychology: A Concise Introduction.
Pettingill, Olin S., Jr. A Guide to Bird Finding East of the Mississippi.
Pettit, George R. Biosynthetic Products for Cancer Chemotherapy.
Pettit, George R. & Cragg, Gordon M., eds. Biosynthetic Products for Cancer Chemotherapy.
Pettit, Lawrence K., jt. auth. see Kirkpatrick, Samuel A.
Pettit, Paul. The Country Life Picture Book of Devon & Cornwall.
Pettit, Paul J. Compendium of Design Features to Reduce Occupational Radiaton Exposure at Nuclear Power Plants.
Pettit, Philip. Judging Justice: An Introduction to Contemporary Political Philosophy.
Pettitt, George A. Prisoners of Culture.
Pettman, Barrie O. Equal Pay for Women.
Pettman, Charles. Africanderisms.
Pettman, Ralph. Biopolitics & International Values: Investigating Liberal Norms.
Petts, Geoffrey E. Rivers.
Petty, Anne C. One Ring to Bind Them All: Tolkien's Mythology.
Petty, Charles S., et al. Scientific Death Investigation: Proceedings, 47th Annual Anatomic Pathology Slide Seminar.
Petty, Clayton. The Anesthesia Machine.
Petty, Jo, compiled by. Pathways.
Petty, Richard & Neely, William. King Richard I: The Autobiography of America's Greatest Auto Racer.
Petty, Thomas L., jt. auth. see Fenley, David C.
Petty, W. The Political Anatomy of Ireland.
Petty, Walter T. Curriculum for the Modern Elementary School.
Petty, Walter T., et al. Experiences in Language: Tools & Techniques for Language Arts.
Petushkova, E. My Life & My Dressage Horses.
Petz, Lawrence D. & Swisher, Scott N., eds. Clinical Practice of Blood Transfusion.
Petzinger, Thomas, Jr. Oil & Honor: The Texaco-Pennzoil Wars.
Petzold, Gertrud Von see Von Petzold, Gertrud.
Petzoldt, Paul. The Wilderness Handbook.
--The Wilderness Handbook.

Peurifoy, Robert L. Construction Planning, Equipment & Methods.
Peutherer, J. F., jt. auth. see Ross, P. W.
Pevoto, Charlotte W. Spanish Missions in Texas.
Pevsner, Nikolaus. Pioneers of Modern Design.
Pevsner, Y. State-Monopoly Capitalism & the Labour Theory of Value.
Pew, W. L., jt. auth. see Terner, Janet.
Pewe, Troy L., ed. The Periglacial Environment: Past & Present.
Peyerimhoff, A. Lectures on Summability.
Peynaud, Emile. The Taste of Wine: The Art & Science of Wine Appreciation. Schuster, Michael, tr. from Fr.
Peyre, Henri. French Literary Imagination & Dostovevsky & Other Essays.
--Victor Hugo: Philosophy & Poetry. Roberts, Roda P., tr. from Fr.
--What Is Romanticism? Roberts, Roda P., tr. from Fr.
--What Is Symbolism? Parker, Emmett, tr. from Fr.
Peyre, Henri, ed. see Vercors, Jean.
Peyre, Marguerite, ed. see Vercors, Jean.
Peyser, Joan. Boulez.
--Boulez.
Peyton, Mike. Out of Our Depth.
Peyton, Richard, ed. Deadlier Odds.
Pezet, A. W., jt. auth. see Abrahamson, E. M.
Pezzano, Chuck. Professional Bowlers Association Guide to Better Bowling: 25th Anniversary Edition.
Pezzini, Wilma. Fisher Guide to Italy.
Pfaffle, A. E. & Nicosia, Sal. Risk Analysis Guide to Insurance & Employee Benefits.
Pfaltz, John. Computer Data Structures.
Pfaltz, Marilyn, jt. auth. see Reed, Ann.
Pfaltzgraff, Robert L., Jr. & Ra'anan, Uri, eds. National Security Policy: The Decision-Making Process.
Pfalzer, T. New Trip.
Pfanner, Duff H. How to Travel & Stay Healthy.
Pfatteicher, Philip. The Lesser Festivals.
Pfeffer, Susan B. Fantasy Summer.
Pfeffer, Wilhelm. Osmotic Investigations.
Pfeifer, H; see Hilbers, C. W. & MacLean, C.
Pfeiffer, C. Boyd. Angler's Guide to Plug & Bait Casting: A Complete Manual of Revolving-Spool Tackle & How to Use It.
--Tackle Craft.
Pfeiffer, Carl J., et al. Gastro-Intestinal Ultrastructure: An Atlas of Scanning & Transmission Electron Micrographs.
Pfeiffer, Charles F. Book of Genesis.
--Ras Shamra & the Bible.
Pfeiffer, E. F., jt. ed. see Levine, R.
Pfeiffer, J. William, ed. Reference Guide to Handbooks & Annuals.
Pfeiffer, John. The Emergence of Society: A Prehistory of the Establishment.
Pfeiffer, Robert H. History of New Testament Times.
Pfeil, E., jt. ed. see Hoffman, E.
Pfeil, W. E., jt. ed. see Rollnik, H.
Pfister, Clara. A City Girl Sees, a City Girl Dreams.
Pfister, Marcus. The Sleepy Owl.
Pfister-Ammende, M., jt. ed. see Zwingmann, C.
Pfistermeister, Ursula, jt. auth. see Stille, Eva.
Pflatzgraff, Robert L., Jr., jt. ed. see Hahn, Walter F.
Pfommer, Marian. On the Range: Cooking Western Style.
Pfotzer, G. & Ehmert, A., eds. Measurements of High Energetic Auroral Radiations with Balloon-Borne Detectors in 1962 & 1963.
Pfotzer, G., et al. Time Pattern of Ionizing Radiation in Balloon Altitudes in High Latitudes.
Pfuhl, John J. Oil & Its Impact: A Case Study of Community Change.
Phaff, J. M., ed. Perinatal Health Services in Europe: Searching for Better Childbirth.
Phaidon Press Limited Staff. Austria: A Phaidon Cultural Guide.
--France: A Phaidon Cultural Guide.
--Germany: A Phaidon Cultural Guide.
--Great Britain & Ireland: A Phaidon Cultural Guide.
--Greece: A Phaidon Cultural Guide.
--Italyon Cultural Guide: A Phaidon Cultural Guide.
--Spain: A Phaidon Cultural Guide.
--Switzerland a Phaidon Cultural Guide.
Phaigh, Rich & Perry, Paul. Athletic Massage.
Pham, F. L., ed. see Symposium, Nice Staff.
Phares, E. Jerry. Introduction to Personality.
Phares, M. I., jt. auth. see Grubb, C. A.
Phares, Ross. Texas Tradition.
Pharmaceutical Society of Great Britain Staff, ed. British Pharmacopoeia.
Pharmaceutical Society of Great Britain Staff. British Pharmacopoeia: 1982 Addendum.
Phay, Robert E. The Law of Suspension & Expulsion: An Examination of the Substantive Issues in Controlling Student Conflict.
Phay, Robert E., ed. North Carolina Constitutional & Statutory Provisions with Respect to Higher Education.
Phelan, Thomas. The Hudson-Mohawk Gateway: An Illustrated History.
Phelan, Thomas P. Catholics in Colonial Days.
Phelon, Kenneth W., Jr., ed. Sheldon's Retail Directory, 1988.
Phelps & Lloyd. Radiology of the Ear.
Phelps, Edmund S. Inflation, Policy & Unemployment Theory.
Phelps, Edmund S., ed. Goal of Economic Growth.
--Problems of the Modern Economy.
Phelps, L. Allen & Batchelor, Laurie J. Individualized Education Programs (IEP's) A Handbook for Vocational Educators.
Phelps, Leland, jt. ed. see Loram, Ian.
Phelps, Lynn & Dewine, Sue. Interpersonal Communication Journal.
Phelps, M. F., jt. ed. see Heiss, W. D.
Phelps, Rose B., jt. auth. see Rodgers, Frank.
Phelps-Gunn, Trisha & Phelps-Terasaki, Diana. Written Language Instruction: Theory & Remediation.
Phelps-Terasaki, Diana, jt. auth. see Phelps-Gunn, Trisha.
Phelps-Terasaki, Diana, et al. Remediation & Instruction in Language: Oral Language, Reading & Writing.
Phenix, Philip H. Education & the Common Good: A Moral Philosophy of the Curriculum.
Phifer, Kenneth G. Tales of Human Frailty & the Gentleness of God.
Phifer, Marjorie, ed. see Cobb, Douglas, et al.
Phifer, Marjorie M., ed. see Cobb, Steven S., et al.
Philadelphia Daily News Staff. The Five Hundred Club.
Philadelphia Inquirer Staff. Movie Guide for VCR's, Nineteen Eighty-Nine.
--Movie Guide for VCRs 1988.
Philadelphia Macro-Analysis Collective of Movement for a New Society Staff. On Organizing Macro-Analysis Seminars: Study & Action for a New Society.
Philadelphia School Study Council Group C Staff. What Is Good Teaching.
Philadelphia Suburban School Study Council Staff. Developing a Respect for Work.
Philadelphia Suburban School Study Council, Group E Staff. The Educated Child.
Philadelphia Suburban School Study Council, Group A Staff. Improving Programs for the Gifted.
Philadelphia Suburban School Study Council Staff. Improving Today's Curriculum for Tomorrow's Challenges.
Philadelphia Suburban School Study Council, Group B Staff. The Junior High School Years.
Philadelphia Suburban School Study Council, Group C Staff. Science: Suggestions for Teaching.
Philbin, Marianne, ed. see Peace Museum Staff.
Philbrick, Charles. Voyages Down & Other Poems.
Philbrick, Helen, jt. auth. see Philbrick, John.
Philbrick, John & Philbrick, Helen. Gardening for Health & Nutrition: An Introduction to the Method of Bio-Dynamic Gardening Inaugurated by Rudolf Steiner.
Philcox, Phil. Computerized Bookkeeping & Tax Form Preparation: A Simple Guide to an Integrated Spreadsheet System.
Phildas, Ave. Photographic Composition.
Philip, A. E., jt. auth. see McCulloch, J. W.
Philip, Clifford. Desktop Publishing with WordPerfect Version 5.
Philip, David & Cohen, Joel. Table Tennis.
Philip, George, ed. Politics in Mexico.
Philip, Lotte B. The Ghent Altarpiece & the Art of Jan Van Eyck.
Philipp, Elliot. Overcoming Childlessness: Its Causes & What to Do About Them.
Philipp, Ernie & Day, Donald L. A Pathfinders Guide to Understanding Computers.
Philipp, Isidor, ed. French Piano Music: An Anthology, Forty-Four Pieces by Twenty-Eight Composers.
Philipp, Werner. Ansatze Zum Geschichtlichen und Politischen Denken Im Kiewer Russland.
Philippi, Donald, tr. from Ainu. Songs of Gods, Songs of Humans: The Epic Tradition of the Ainu.
Philippi, Herbert. Stagecraft & Scene Design.
Philippovich Von Philippsberg, Eugen. History of the Bank of England & Its Financial Services to the State. Meredith, Christabel, tr.
Philips, Ronald J., jt. ed. see Mercer, James L.
Philips, Sheldon W. & King, Brian L. GLAS: General Ledger Accounting System for SuperCalc.
--GLAS: Payroll for SuperCalc.
--GLAS: Payroll for VisiCalc.
--OSGLAS: General Ledger Accounting System for Osborne Computers.
--OSGLAS: Payroll for Osborne Computers.
Philipson, Morris. Secret Understandings.
Philipson, Morris, ed. see Huxley, Aldous.
Philipson, W. R. The Immaculate Forrest.
Phillimore, W. P. How to Write the History of a Family: A Guide for the Genealogist.
Phillimore, Walter G. Three Centuries of Peace Treaties & Their Teachings, 1582-1913.
Phillimore, William P. & Fry, E. A. Index to Changes of Name.
Phillip, Alban M. Prison-Breakers: A Book of Escapes from Captivity.
Phillipov, Vladimir, tr. see Levchev, Lyubomir.
Phillipps, D. Thomas. Phillipps Manuscripts: Catalogus Liberorum Maniscriptorum in Bibliotheca, 1837-71.
Phillipps, Lisle M. The Works of Man.
Phillips. Organic Electronics Spectral Data.
--Organic Electronics Spectral Data.
Phillips, et al, eds. Laboratory Methods in Antimicrobial Chemotherapy.
Phillips, Alan, pseud. Jazz Improvisation & Harmony.
Phillips, Angela. Your Body, Your Baby, Your Life.
Phillips, Aubrey. Landscape in Pastel.
--Sky & Water in Pastel.
Phillips, B. J., et al. Public Libraries: Legislation, Administration & Finance.
Phillips, Betty J. Manual of Echocardiographic Techniques.
Phillips, Bonnie D. Effective Business Communications.
Phillips, Bonnie D. & Storey, Dale A. Business Mathematics & Calculating Machines.
Phillips, Burt. The Ideal Horse: How to Train Him & Yourself.
Phillips, C., jt. auth. see Baxter, R. E.
Phillips, C. G., ed. Corticospinal Neurones: Their Role in Movement.
Phillips, Carole. Money Talk: The Last Taboo.
--The Money Workbook for Women: A Step-by-Step Guide to Managing Your Personal Finances.
Phillips, Carolyn. A Daddy, but No Mama.
Phillips, Carolyn E. Our Family Got a Divorce.
Phillips, Catherine A., tr. see Niemann, Walter.
Phillips, Celeste R. Family-Centered Maternity-Newborn Care: A Basic Text.
Phillips, Charles S. The Church in France, Seventeen Eighty-Seven to Eighteen Forty-Eight.
Phillips, Cheryl M., ed. see Lee, Laurel.
Phillips, Cheryl M., ed. see Stirrup Associates, Inc. Staff.
Phillips, Claire. Manila Espionage.
Phillips, D. L. Equality, Justice & Rectification: An Exploration in Normative Sociology.
Phillips, D. Z. Belief, Change & Forms of Life.
Phillips, D. Z., ed. see Anderson, John.
Phillips, David, jt. ed. see Rathwell, Tom.
Phillips, David, jt. auth. see Sainsbury, Eric.
Phillips, David A. Guidebook to Nutritional Factors in Foods.
--The Night Watch.
Phillips, David M. Spermiogenesis.
Phillips, Debora & Judd, Robert. How to Fall Out of Love.
Phillips, Dee. The Coconut Kiss: A Novel.
Phillips, Dezra D. Shadows over Nordmaar.
Phillips, E. Bryant. Nebraska Street & Interurban Railways.
Phillips, E. L., jt. auth. see Haring, Norris G.
Phillips, E. Lakin. Love, Poetry & Psychotherapy.
Phillips, E. Lee. Prayer for Our Day.
Phillips, Edward. Death Is Relative.
Phillips, Elwood. Florida Retirees' Handbook: Answers to Your Legal & Financial Questions.
Phillips, G., jt. auth. see Milner, G. W.
Phillips, G., et al, eds. Gums & Stabilisers for the Food Industry II: Application of Hydrocolloids; Proceedings of the International Conference, Clwyd, Wales, U. K., 11-15 July, 1983.
Phillips, G. O. & Wedlock, D. J., eds. Gums & Stabilizers for the Food Industry: Interactions of Hydrocolloids.
Phillips, Gary. IBM-PC Public Domain Software. Thomson, Monet, ed.
--IBM-PCjr Encyclopedia.
--Macintosh Expansion Guide.
Phillips, Gary & Phillips, Karen. The Reference Encyclopedia for the IBM Personal Computer.
Phillips, Gene D. The Movie Makers: Artists in an Industry.
Phillips, Gerald M. & Wood, Julia T. Communication & Human Relationships: The Study of Interpersonal Communication.
Phillips, Gerald M. & Zolten, J. Jerome. Structuring Speech: A How-to-Do-It Book About Public Speaking.
Phillips, Gerald M., et al. Group Discussion: A Practical Guide to Participation & Leadership.
Phillips, H. Faudel see Faudel-Phillips, H.
Phillips, Hosea, tr. see De Villiers du Terrage, Marc.
Phillips, I., et al, eds. Microbiological Hazards of Infusion Therapy.
Phillips, I. R. The Embryology of the Common Marmoset (Callithrix Jacchus) Brodal, A., et al, eds.
Phillips, J. A. Eve: The History of an Idea.
Phillips, J. P., et al, eds. Organic Electronic Spectral Data.
--Organic Electronic Spectral Data 1978.
Phillips, James. Bibliographic Essays on the Architecture of the Ancient City of Rome, No. 45: The City of Rome, No. 41: City Walls.
--Bibliographic Essays on the Architecture of the Ancient City of Rome, No. 44: The City of Rome, No. 40: City Gates: Porta Ostiensis - Porta Viminalis.
--Bibliographic Essays on the Architecture of the Ancient City of Rome, No. 43: The City of Rome, No. 39: City Gates: General Works - Porta Nomentana.
--Bibliographic Essays on the Architecture of the Ancient City of Rome, No. 42: The City of Rome, No. 38: Funerary Monuments: Sepulcrum Pomponii Hylae - Vatican Cemetery.
--Bibliographic Essays on the Architecture of the Ancient City of Rome, No. 41: The City of Rome, No. 37: Funerary Monuments: Sepulcretum-Sepulcrum Lucilii Paeti.
--Bibliographic Essays on the Architecture of the Ancient City of Rome, No. 40: The City of Rome, No. 36: Funerary Monuments: Ustrina, General Works on Tombs, Mausolea, & Pyramids.
Phillips, James M. From the Rising of the Sun: Christians & Society in Contemporary Japan.
Phillips, Janet & Phillips, Peter. Victorians at Home & Away.
Phillips, Jerry J., jt. auth. see Noel, Dix W.
Phillips, Joel & Wynne, Ronald D. Cocaine: The Mystique & the Reality.
Phillips, John. It Happened in Our Lifetime: A Memoir in Words & Pictures.
Phillips, John P. Automatic Titrators.
--Spectra-Structure Correlation.
Phillips, John P. & Thyagarajan, B. S. Organic Electronic Spectral Data.
Phillips, John P., et al. Organic Electronic Spectral Data.
--Organic Electronic Spectral Data: 1975.
Phillips, John P., et al, eds. Organic Electron Spectral Data.
Phillips, Karen, jt. auth. see Phillips, Gary.
Phillips, Kenneth F. & Teitz, Michael B. Housing Conservation in Older Urban Areas: A Mortgage Insurance Approach.
Phillips, Laughlin, intro. by. Duncan Phillips: Centennial Exhibition.
Phillips, Laura. Wembley's Egg.
Phillips, Lois. Lieder Line by Line.
Phillips, Louis. Baseball: Records, Stars, Feats, & Facts.
--The Brothers Wrong & Wrong Again.
--Freaky Facts.
--The Man Who Stole the Atlantic Ocean.
Phillips, Louis & Markoe, Arnie. Football: Records, Stars, Feats & Facts.
Phillips, Louis & Markoe, Karen. Fun Fact Fill-Ins.
--Travel Games.
--Women in Sports: Records, Stars, Feats, & Facts.
Phillips, Louis, jt. auth. see Markoe, Karen.
Phillips, Louise. The Bald Eagle's Flying Shadow: A Fourth of July Celebration.
Phillips, Marion. The Whale: Going...Going...Gone?
Phillips, Mark. Captain Mark Phillips on Riding: A Complete Guide for Beginners.
Phillips, Michael J. Selected Love Poems.
Phillips, N. V., jt. ed. see Smedema, C. H.
Phillips, Patricia. The Prehistory of Europe.
Phillips, Peter, jt. auth. see Phillips, Janet.
Phillips, Philip A. Paul De Lamerie, Citizen & Goldsmith of London 1688-1751.
Phillips, Phyllis P. Speech & Hearing Problems in the Classroom.
Phillips Publishing, Inc. Staff. The Local Area Networking Directory. Kimmel, Mark, ed.
Phillips, R. P., jt. auth. see Waterworth, K. G.
Phillips, Rachel, tr. see Paz, Octavio.
Phillips, Raymond E. The Cardiac Rhythms: A Kit for Instructors.
Phillips, Richard M., jt. auth. see Wolfson, Nicholas.
Phillips, Roger, jt. auth. see Rix, Martyn.
Phillips, Ronald L. & Burnham, Charles R. Cytogenetics.
Phillips, Rufus. Evolving Universe.
Phillips, Sheree. Mothers: At the Heart of Life.
Phillips, Sue. More Than Meets the Eye: New Look at Flower Arranging.
Phillips, Susan M. & Zecher, J. Richard. The SEC & the Public Interest.
Phillips, Susan M., jt. auth. see Practising Law Institute Staff.
Phillips, Terry. Gates of Death.
--The Soulforge: A Dragonlance Adventure.
Phillips, Uad & Yotey, H. L. Economic Analysis of Pressing Social Problems.
Phillips, W. Louis. Index to Franklin Co., Ohio Guardianships & Estates: 1803-1850.
--Jurisdictional Histories for Ohio's 88 Counties, 1788-1985.
Phillips, Walter. Defending "A Christian Country" Churchmen & Society in New South Wales in the 1880's & After.
Phillips, William, jt. ed. see Kurzweil, Edith.

Phillips-Birt, D. Naval Architecture of Small Craft.
Phillips-Birt, Douglas. The Building of Boats.
Phillips-Jones, Linda & Jones, Brian G. Developing Training Competencies for Career Guidance Personnel.
Phillis, J. W. The Pharmacology of Synapses.
Phillis, J. W., jt. ed. see Kerklit, G. A.
Phillis, J. W., jt. ed. see Kerkut, G. A.
Phillpotts, Beatrice. The Book of Fairies.
Phillpotts, Bertha. Kindred & Clan in the Middle Ages & After.
Phillps, Debora & Judd, Robert. Sexual Confidence.
Phillus, J. W., jt. ed. see Kerkut, G. A.
Philo, Harry, et al. Technical Sources for Conducting Personal Injury Action.
Philomusus, S. Mr. Law's Unlawfulness of the Stage Entertainment Examin'd. Bd. with The Entertainment of the Stage; Some Few Hints in Defence of Dramatical Entertainments. Ramsay, Allan. Garland Pub.
Philosophy Documentation Center Staff. The Philosopher's Index: A Retrospective Index to U. S. Publications from 1940. Lineback, Richard H., ed.
Philp, Richard & Whitney, Mary. Danseur: The Male in Ballet.
Philps, Caroline. Elizabeth Joy.
Phinney, John F., jt. auth. see Kemper, Robert V.
Phinny, Peter & Brainard, Jack. Training the Reined Horse.
Phippard, Martin, jt. auth. see Ingram, Arthur.
Phipps, David C. Cornelius.
Phipps, Lloyd J., jt. auth. see Cook, G. C.
Phipps, Marlynn, et al. Recipes for Self-Sufficient Living.
Phipps, William E. Influential Theologians on Wo-Man.
--Recovering Biblical Sensuousness.
Phipps, Wilma J., et al. Medical-Surgical Nursing: Concepts & Clinical Practice.
Phipson, Joan. The Cats.
--Family Conspiracy.
--The Family Conspiracy.
--Fly Free.
--Fly into Danger.
--Haunted Night.
--Horse with Eight Hands.
--Six & Silver.
--Threat to the Barkers.
--A Tide Flowing.
--The Way Home.
--When the City Stopped.
Phizacklea, Annie, ed. One Way Ticket: Migration & Female Labour.
Phlips, L. Applied Consumption Analysis.
Phoenix Art Museum Staff. Diego Rivera: The Cubist Years.
Phomvihane, K. Revolution in Laos.
Photoelectric Spectrometry Group, England Staff & Institut fuer Spektrochemie und Angewandte Spektroskopie, Germany Staff. U V Atlas of Organic Compounds.
Photographic Gelatin Symposium Staff. Photographic Gelatin: Proceedings of the Symposium, 2nd, Trinity College, Cambridge, 1970. Cox, R. J., ed.
PhotoGraphic Magazine Editors & Lahue, Kalton C. Creative Darkroom Techniques.
PhotoGraphic Magazine Editors & Yob, Parry C. Guide to Photo Equipment You Can Make.
PhotoGraphic Magazine Editors, et al. Blueprint Series.
Phy, Allene S., ed. The Bible & Popular Culture in America.
Phye, Gary D. & Reschly, Daniel J., eds. School Psychology: Perspectives & Issues.
Physick, John. Victorian Church Art.
Phytochemical Society. Aspects of Terpenoid Chemistry & Biochemistry: Proceedings. Goodwin, T. W., ed.
Phytochemical Society of North America Symposium Staff. Recent Advances in Phytochemistry: Structure, Biogenesis, Distribution. Runeckles, V. C. & Mabry, T. J., eds.
Phytochemical Society of North America Staff. Symposia. Runeckles, V. C. & Tso, T. C., eds. Incl. Vol. 5. Structural & Functional Aspects of Phytochemistry; Vol. 6. Terpenoids: Structure, Biogenesis, Distribution. Acad Pr.
Phytochemical Society Staff. Perspectives in Phytochemistry: Proceedings. Harborne, J. B. & Swain, T., eds.
--Phytochemical Phylogeny: Proceedings. Harborne, J. B., ed.
Phytochemical Society Symposium, No.11, University of Ghent, Belgium, Sept. 1973. The Chemistry & Biochemistry of Plant Proteins: Proceedings. Harborne, J. B. & Van Sumere, G. F., eds.
Pia, H. W. & Djindjian, R., eds. Spinal Angiomas: Advances in Diagnosis & Therapy.
Piachaud, David. The Distribution & Redistribution of Incomes.
Piaget, Jean. Behavior & Evolution. Nicholson-Smith, Donald, tr. from Fr.
--Biology & Knowledge. Walsh, Beatrix, tr. from Fr.
--Child's Conception of Number.
--Genetic Epistemology. Duckworth, Eleanor, tr.
--Moral Judgment of the Child. Gabain, Marjorie, tr.
--Principles of Genetic Epistemology.
Piaget, Jean & Garcia, R. Understanding Causality. Miles, Donald & Miles, Marguerite, trs. from Fr.
Piaggi, Anna. Lagerfeld's Sketchbook: Karl Lagerfeld's Illustrated Fashion Journal of Anna Piaggi.
Piatti, Celestino. Celestino Piatti's Animal ABC.
--Happy Owls.
Piazza, Gail. Farberware: World of Wok Cookery.
--World of Wok Cookery.
Pica, A. Italian Majolica Tile.
Picano, Felice. Eyes.
--Smart As the Devil.
Picard, C. F. Graphs & Questionnaires.
Picard, M. D. Grit & Clay.
Picasso, Pablo. Desire (A Play)
Picasso, Pablo, jt. auth. see Cesaire, Aime.
Piccinni, Niccolo. Catone in Utica. Brown, Howard M., ed.
Pichaske, David. A Generation in Motion: Popular Music & Culture in the 1960's.
Pichaske, David R. Beowulf to Beatles & Beyond.
Pichel, Mervyn & Curtis, Neal. Have Healthy Teeth & Gums.
Pick. Games for One Player.
Pick, Albert. Standard Catalog of World Paper Money: Specialized. Bruce, Colin & Shafer, Neil, eds.
Pick, Fred L. & Knight, G. Norman. Pocket History of Free Masonry.
Pick, Fred L. & Knight, Norman. Freemason's Pocket Reference Book.
Pick, H. L., et al, eds. From Research to Practice.
Pick, J. B. Dictionary of Games.
Pick, J. B., ed. & intro. by see Lindsay, David.
Pick, John. Arts Administration.
Pick, M., et al. Theory of the Earth's Gravity Field.
Pick, Michael, jt. auth. see Moore, Derry.
Pick, R. M., jt. ed. see Bratos, S.
Pickar, Gloria D. Dosage Calculations.
Pickar, Joanne, jt. ed. see Schiefelbusch, Richard L.
Pickard, Nancy. No Body: A Jenny Cain Mystery.
Pickard, Roy. Shirley Maclaine.
Picken, Stuart D. Shinto: Japan's Spiritual Roots.
Pickering, H. S. The Covalent Bond.
Pickering, James D., jt. ed. see Barnes, Robert D.
Pickering, James H. Fiction One Hundred.
Pickering, M. Village Song & Culture.
Pickering, Paul. Wild about Harry.
Pickering, Samuel F., Jr. A Continuing Education.
Pickering, W. J., jt. auth. see Mallows, D. F.
Pickering, W. S., ed. Durkheim: Essays on Morals & Education. Sutcliffe, H. L., tr. from Fr.
Pickersgill, J. W., ed. The Mackenzie King Record. Incl. Vol. 1. 1939-1944; Vol. 2. 1944-1945. Forster, D. F., ed; Vol. 3. 1945-1946. Forster, D. F., ed; Vol. 4. 1947-1948. Forster, D. F., ed. U of Toronto Pr.
Pickett, Hale. The Successful Activities of Hale Pickett.
Pickett, J. The Choice of Technology in Developing Countries.
Pickett, James M., jt. ed. see Levitt, Harry.
Pickett, John D. Expansion of Thought.
Pickett, Nell Ann, jt. ed. see Sparrow, W. Keats.
Pickhardt, Robert C., jt. auth. see McLaughlin, Frank S.
Pickles, Dorothy. Problems of Contemporary French Politics.
Pickles, J. O. An Introduction to the Physiology of Hearing.
Pickney, Patricia. Island Paradise.
Pickowicz, Paul. Marxist Literary Thought & China: A Conceptual Framework.
Pickthall, Barry. The Ultimate Challenge.
Pickup. Brittle Diabetes.
Picou, J. Steven. Vocational Education for Migrant Youth.
Picraux, S. T., et al, eds. Applications of Ion Beams to Metals.
Picton, John & Mack, John. African Textiles.
Pidal, Ramon Menendez see Menendez Pidal, Ramon.
Piddington, Ralph. The Psychology of Laughter.
Pieczenick, Steve R. The Mind Palace: A Novel.
Piediscalzi, Nicholas, jt. ed. see Barr, David L.
Piediscalzi, Nicolas & Thobaben, Robert G., eds. Three Worlds of Christian Marxist Encounters.
Piekalkiewicz, Janusz. Sea War 1939-1945.
--Tank War Nineteen Thirty-Nine to Nineten Forty-Five.
Pielou, E. C. Ecological Diversity.
Pienkowski, Jan. ABC.
--Colors.
--Home. Klimo, Kate, ed.
--I'm Cat.
--I'm Frog.
--I'm Mouse.
--I'm Panda.
--Numbers.
--Shapes.
--Sizes. Klimo, Kate, ed.
--Time. Klimo, Kate, ed.
--Weather. Klimo, Kate, ed.
Pienkowski, Jan, jt. auth. see Nicoll, Helen.
Pienkowski, Jan, jt. auth. see Nicoll, Helens.
Pieper, Josef. The End of Time: A Meditation on the Philosophy of History.
--Scholasticism.
Pieper, Josef, et al. Guide to Thomas Aquinas. Winston, Richard & Winston, Clara, trs. from Ger.
Piepkorn, Arthur Carl. The Survival of the Historic Vestments in the Lutheran Church after Fifteen Fifty-Five.
Pier, Tom. Elodea.
Pieraut-Le Bonniec, Gilbert. The Development of Modal Reasoning: Genesis of Necessity & Probability Notions.
Pierce, Allan D. Acoustics: An Introducton to Its Physical Principles & Applications.
Pierce, Arthur D. Iron in the Pines: The Story of New Jersey's Ghost Towns & Bog Iron.
Pierce, Carol & Page, Bill. A Male-Female Continuum: Paths to Colleagueship.
Pierce, Dale. Play Me the Song of Death.
Pierce, David, jt. auth. see Eagleton, Mary.
Pierce, F. F., ed. see Cervantes-Saavedra, Miguel De.
Pierce, Gregory F. Activism that Makes Sense: Congregations & Community Organization.
Pierce, James. From Abacus to Zeus: A Handbook of Art History.
Pierce, James S. Paul Klee & Primitive Art.
Pierce, Joe E. Languages & Linguistics: An Introduction.
Pierce, John G., ed. Proteins & Peptides Hormones.
Pierce, Johnnie B., Jr. The Observations of a Madman.
Pierce, Leona, jt. auth. see De Regniers, Beatrice S.
Pierce, Milton. The Financial Advisory: Hundreds of Ways to Save & Invest Your Money.
Pierce, Ovid. Old Man's Gold & Other Stories.
Pierce, Phyllis. The Dow Jones Investor's Handbook, 1984.
Pierce, Phyllis, ed. The Dow Jones Averages 1885-1985.
--The Dow Jones Investor's Handbook, 1987.
--The Dow Jones Investors Handbook, 1988.
Pierce, R. C., Jr., jt. auth. see Anderson, Chaney.
Pierce, Richard A., jt. auth. see Lantzeff, George V.
Pierce, Richard A., ed. Documents on the History of the Russian-American Company. Ramsay, Marina, tr.
Pierce, Richard A., ed. see Veniaminov, Ivan.
Pierce, Roy. French Politics & Political Institutions.
Pierce, Steven R. & Steane, Susan M., eds. Biochemistry for Blood Bankers.
Piercey, Jill. Brenda Chamberlain: Artist & Writer.
Piercy, B. & Jandrell, R. Coordinated Work Measurement.
Piercy, Marge. Braided Lives.
--Early Ripening: American Women's Poetry Now.
--Fly Away Home.
Piercy, Nigel & Evans, Martin J. Managing Marketing Information.
Pierhal, Jean. Albert Schweitzer: The Story of His Life.
Pierik, Robert. Rookfleas in the Cellar.
Pieroni, Robert E. Self-Assessment of Current Knowledge in Rheumatology.
Pierot, Suzanne W. What Can I Grow in the Shade?
Pierpoint, S., jt. auth. see Robb, D. A.
Pierre, Dominique la see La Pierre, Dominique.
Pierrot, Jean. The Decadent Imagination, Eighteen Eighty to Nineteen Hundred. Coltman, Derek, tr. from Fr.
Pierrot, Roger, jt. auth. see De Balzac, Honore.
Pierrot-Bults, A. C., jt. ed. see Van der Spoel, S.
Piers, Gerhart & Singer, Milton B. Shame & Guilt.
Piers, Maria W. Infanticide.
Piersol, Edna W. An Artist's Guide to Living by Your Brush Alone. Henning, Fritz, ed.
Pierson, Donald. Cruz das Almas, a Brazilian Village.
Pierson, Frank C. Community Manpower Services for the Disadvantaged.
Pierson, Jan. The Carson Kids & the Mystery of the Cove Point Stallion.
--The Carson Kids & the Shipwreck on Grizzly Island.
Pierson, K. Kendall. Principles of Prosecution: A Guide for the Anatomic Pathologist.
Pierson, Paul E. Themes from Acts.
Pierson, Robert H. Here Comes Adventure. Wheeler, Gerald, ed.
Pierson, Robert J. The Beach Towns - A Walker's Guide to L.A.'s Beach Communities: Detailed Walking Tours of Ten Beach Communities from Santa Monica to Long Beach.
Pierson, Stanley. British Socialists: The Journey from Fantasy to Politics.
Pierssens, Michel. Power of Babel: A Study of Logophilia. Lovitt, Carl R., tr. from Fr.
Pietrasinski, Z. The Art of Learning.
Pietro, Anthony San see San Pietro, Anthony, et al.
Pietro, Robert J. Di see Agard, Frederick B. & Di Pietro, Robert J.
Pietrofesa, John J., et al. Guidance: an Introduction.
--Counseling.
--The Authentic Counselor.
Pietsch, Paul. Shufflebrain.
Pietschmann, D., jt. ed. see Boeninger, Hildegard R.
Pifat, Greta & Herak, Janok N., eds. Supramolecular Structure & Function.
Pifer, George W. & Mutoh, Nancy W. Points of View.
Piff, Christine. Let's Face It.
Pigache, R. Anatomy of Paleocortex: A Critical Review.
Pigg, R. Morgan, Jr., jt. auth. see Rash, J. Keogh.
Piggott, John R., ed. Sensory Analysis of Food.
Piggott, Stuart. Ancient Europe: From the Beginnings of Agriculture to Classical Antiquity.
Pigman, Ward & Horton, Derek, eds. Advances in Carbohydrate Chemistry & Biochemistry.
Pigman, Ward, jt. ed. see Horowitz, Martin.
Pignatelli, Gaspare. The Christ Nobody Knows: A Sentimental Vision of His Life.
Pignatti, Terisio. The Golden Century of Venetian Painting. Donahue, Kenneth, ed. Baca, Murtha, tr. from Ital.
Pigou, Arthur C. Employment & Equilibrium: A Theoretical Discussion.
Pijl, L. Van Der see Van der Pijl, L.
Pijnenburg, Bert, jt. ed. see Mellors, Colin.
Pijoan, Michel. Game Fish of the Rocky Mountains: A Guide to Identification.
Pike, jt. auth. see Bartho.
Pike & Fischer, eds. Federal Rules Service Third: 1958-1959.
Pike & Fischer Staff, ed. Uniform Commercial Code Reporting: 1965-1983.
Pike, Andrew. Engineering Tenders, Sales & Contracts: Standard Forms & Procedures.
Pike, Arthur M., jt. auth. see Popkin, Gary S.
Pike, Christopher. Precious Ingredient.
Pike, Frederick B. Spanish America: Tradition & Social Innovation.
Pike, Joseph B., tr. see John Of Salisbury.
Pike, Robert E. Tall Trees, Tough Men.
Pike, Royston. Jehovah's Witnesses.
Pike, William H. Why Stocks Go up (& Down) A Guide to Sound Investing.
Pikelner, S. Soviet Science of Interstellar Space.
Pikulski, John J. & Shanahan, Timothy. Approaches to the Informal Evaluation of Reading.
Pikunas, Justin. Human Development: An Emergent Science.
Pilbeam, David. The Ascent of Man: An Introduction to Human Evolution.
Pilcer, Sonia. Teen Angels.
Pilcher, Donald. The Regency Style - Eighteen Hundred to Eighteen Thirty.
Pilcher, George W., jt. ed. see Davies, Samuel.
Pilcher, Mary T. Growing up on a Farm in Missouri.
Pilcher, Rosamunde. Voices in Summer.
Pile, John. Perspective for Interior Designers.
Pile, John, jt. auth. see Diekman, Norman.
Pile, John F. Design: Purpose, Form, & Meaning.
Pileggi, Anita P. On a Sacred Hill.
Pileggi, Nicholas. Wiseguy: The Rise & Fall of a Mobster.
Pilgrim, David. Psychology & Psychotherapy: Current Trends & Issues.
Pilgrim, Walter E. Good News to the Poor: Wealth & Poverty in Luke-Acts.
Pilinszky, Janos. Selected Poems. Hughes, Ted & Csokits, Janos, trs.
Piljac, Pamela A. The Bride to Bride Book: A Complete Wedding Planner for the Bride.
Pilkey, Walter D. & Pin Yu Chang. Modern Formulas for Statics & Dynamics: A Stress & Strain Approach.
Pilkey, Walter D., jt. ed. see Moyar, Gerald J.
Pilkey, Walter D., jt. ed. see Perrone, Nicholas.
Pilkington, John, jt. auth. see Bradt, Hilary.
Pillai, S. K. A First Course on Electrical Drives.
Pillai, Thakazhi S. Scavenger's Son. Asher, R. E., tr. from Malayalam.
Pilling, John. Autobiography & Imagination: Studies in Self-Scrutiny.
--Samuel Beckett.
Pilling, John, jt. auth. see Knowlson, James.
Pillo, G. di see Di Pillo, G.
Pillon, Nancy B. Reaching Young People Through Media.

Authors

Pillsbury Editors. Pillsbury Bake-Offs: Cookie Book.
Pillsbury, Parker. Acts of the Anti-Slavery Apostles.
Pilotta, Joseph J., ed. Interpersonal Communication: Essays in Phenomenology & Hermeneutics.
Pilpel, Robert H. Churchill in America: An Affectionate Portrait.
--To the Honor of the Fleet.
Piltch, Benjamin. Stories about Workers.
Pimentel, David. Food, Energy & Future of Society.
Pimm, S. L. Food Web.
Pimsleur, Beverly, jt. auth. see Pimsleur, Paul.
Pimsleur, Paul. C'est la Vie: Lectures d'aujourd'hui.
--Sol y Sombra: Lectures de Hoy.
Pimsleur, Paul & Berger, Donald. Encounters: A Basic Reader.
Pimsleur, Paul & Pimsleur, Beverly. C'est La Vie.
Pimsleur, Paul, et al. Encounters: A Basic Reader.
--Sol y Sombra.
Pincetl, Stanley J., ed. see Cru, Jean N.
Pinch, Steven. Cities & Services: The Geography of Collective Consumption.
Pinch, T. J., jt. auth. see Collins, H. M.
Pinchas, S. & Laulicht, I. Infrared Spectra of Labelled Compounds.
Pinchemel, Philippe see Freeman, T. W., et al.
Pinchera, A. & Doniach, D., eds. Autoimmune Aspects of Endocrine Disorders.
Pincherle, L. Worked Problems in Heat, Thermodynamics & Kinetic Theory.
Pincherle, Marc. Vivaldi: Genius of the Baroque.
--World of the Virtuoso.
Pinchot, Ann. Certain Rich Girls.
--Doctors & Wives.
--The Luck of the Linscotts: A Novel of Great New England Dynasty.
--A Moment in the Sun.
--Vanessa.
Pinchot, Gifford. To the South Seas: The Cruise of the Schooner Mary Pinchot to the Galapogos, the Marquesas, the Tuamotu Islands & Tahiti.
Pinchot Publications Staff. Computer Fitness.
--Computer Gardening.
--Computer Photography.
Pincoffs, Edmund L. Quandaries & Virtues: Against Reductivism in Ethics.
Pincus, Gregory, ed. Control of Fertility.
--Hormones & Atherosclerosis: Proceedings.
Pincus, Gregory & Vollmer, E., eds. Biological Activities of Steroids in Relation to Cancer: Proceedings.
Pincus, Harriet, ed. & illus. see Grimm, Jacob & Grimm, Wilhelm K.
Pincus, Jane, tr. see Odent, Michael.
Pincus, P., jt. auth. see Eisenreighler, E.
Pincus-Witten, Robert. Occult Symbolism in France: Josephin Peladan & the Salons De la Rose-Croix.
Pindar. The Olympian & Pthyian Odes. Gildersleeve, B. L., ed.
Pindborg, J. J. & Kramer, I. R. Histological Typing of Odontogenic Tumours, Jaw Cysts & Allied Lesions.
Pinder, John, ed. Fifty Years of Political & Economic Planning: Looking Forward 1931-1981.
Pinder, Polly. Decorating Cakes for Children's Parties.
Pindera, J. T., ed. New Physical Trends in Experimental Mechanics.
Pine, L. G. A Dictionary of Mottoes.
Pine, Nicholas. Goss China Arms, Decorations & Their Values.
--Goss China: 1986 Price Guide.
--The Price Guide to Goss China, 1984.
Pine, Nicholas, jt. auth. see Andrews, Sandy.
Pine, Tillie S. & Levine, Joseph. Africans Knew.
--Simple Machines & How We Use Them.
Pinella, Lou & Allen, Maury. Sweet Lou.
Pineo, Charles S., et al. Environmental Sanitation & Integrated Health Delivery Programs.
Pines, Burton Y. Back to Basics.
Pines, Harry. Evergreen Poems.
Pines, Helene J. Patent Law Handbook, 1986-87.
Pines, Malcolm, ed. The Evolution of Group Analysis.
Pines, Maya. The Brain Changers: Scientists & the New Mind Control.
--Inside the Cell.
Pines, Philip J. Fifty-Five Miles per Hour.
Pingree, Eleanor M., ed. see Twelve O'Clock Scholars Staff.
Ping-Ying, Hsieh. Autobiography of a Chinese Girl.
Pink, Annette. See Madeira & the Canaries.
Pink, George L. The Unity of One.
Pinka, Patricia G. This Dialogue of One: The Songs & Sonnets of John Donne.
Pinkard, Bruce. Indoor Photography.
Pinkert, Theodore, ed. Current Research on the Consequences of Maternal Drug Abuse.
Pinkerton, Kathrene. A Home in the Wilds.
Pinkerton, Kathrene S. Hidden Harbor.
--Steer North.
Pinkerton, Robert. The First Overland Mail.
Pinkerton, Susan S., et al. Behavioral Medicine: Clinical Applications.
Pinkerton, Todd. Breaking Communication Barriers with Roleplay.
Pinkham, Roger. Oliver Messel.
Pinkstaff, Dick & Pinkstaff, Marlene A. Personal Skill Building for the Emerging Manager.
Pinkstaff, Marlene A., jt. auth. see Pinkstaff, Dick.
Pinkster, J., ed. see CISM (International Center for Mechanical Sciences), Department of Experimental Methods in Mechanics Staff.
Pinkus, Charles E. & Dixson, Anne. Solving Local Government Problems: Practical Applications of Operations Research in Cities & Regions.
Pinkwater, Daniel. The Snarkout Boys & the Baconburg Horror.
Pinkwater, Daniel M. Attila the Pun: A Magic Moscow Book.
--Tooth-Gnasher Superflash.
--Yobgorgle: Mystery Monster of Lake Ontario.
Pinkwater, Manus. Three Big Hogs.
Pinnegar, Stefinee, jt. auth. see Thornburg, Hershel.
Pinnell, Gay S., jt. auth. see Page, William D.
Pinner, E. Curious Creatures.
Pinney, John J. Your Future in the Nursery Industry.
Pinney, Thomas, ed. see Macaulay, Thomas B.
Pinniger, Roger, ed. Jones' Animal Nursing.
Pinnock, Clark. Defense of Biblical Infallibility.
Pinnock, Clark H. Reason Enough: A Case for the Christian Faith.
Pino, David. The Clarinet & Clarinet Playing.
Pino-Saavedra, Yolando, ed. Folktales of Chile. Gray, Rockwell, tr.
Pinsky, A. A., jt. auth. see Yavorsky, B. M.
Pinsky, Mark, jt. ed. see Friedman, Avner.
Pinson, Koppel S. Modern Germany.
Pinson, Koppel S., ed. see Dubnow, Simon.
Pinson, Nancy, jt. auth. see Herr, Edward.
Pinson, William M. Applying the Gospel: Suggestions for Christian Social Action in the Local Church.
Pinstrup-Andersen, Per. Nutritional Consequences of Agricultural Projects: Conceptual Relationships & Assessment Approaches.
Pintauro, Joseph. Cold Hands.
Pintel, Gerald & Diamond, Jay. Basic Business Mathematics.
Pinter, Harold. Betrayal.
--Betrayal.
--The French Lieutenant's Woman: A Screenplay.
--The Hothouse.
--Landscape & Silence.
--Landscape & Silence.
--A Night Out, Night School, Revue Sketches: Early Plays.
--No Man's Land.
--One for the Road: A Play.
--Other Places: A Kind of Alaska; Victoria Station: Family Voices.
--Poems & Prose: 1949-1977.
--The Proust Screenplay.
Pinto & Rodway. The Common Muse.
Pinto, J. D. Behavior & Taxonomy of the Epicauta Maculata Group (Coleoptera: Meloidae)
Pinto, John A., jt. auth. see Lincoln, Eleanor T.
Pinto, Vivian D. The English Renaissance, Fifteen Ten to Sixteen Eighty-Eight.
Pintonelli, Deborah. Meat & Memory.
Pin Yu Chang, jt. auth. see Pilkey, Walter D.
Pinzino, Mary E. Come Children Sing!
Piorishkin, A. V. Fisica: Curso Introductorio.
Piotrowska, Irena. Art of Poland.
Piou, Nanie, ed. see Lefebvre, Claire.
Piper, Anson C. Asi Es la Vida.
Piper, Charlotte & Lewis, Dorothy, eds. Aquatics.
Piper, David. Companion Guide to London.
Piper, H. Beam. Lord Kalvan of Otherwhen. Del Rey, Lester, ed.
Piper, Joanne. Personal Shorthand Master Dictionary.
Piper, Roger. Story of Computers.
Piper, Vangie & Tickle, Phyllis, eds. On Beyond A-I-S.
Piper, Watty, ed. Mother Goose, a Treasury of Best Loved Rhymes.
Pipes. Nutrition in Infancy & Childhood.
Pipes, Richard. Formation of the Soviet Union: Communism & Nationalism 1917-1923.
--Survival Is Not Enough.
Pipkin, Francis M., jt. ed. see Kleppner, Daniel.
Pirandello, Luigi. Shoot! (Si Gura) The Notebook of Serafino Gubbio Cinematograph Operator. Kupelnick, Bruce S., ed.
Pirandello, Luigi see Weiss, Samuel A.
Piras, Horatio G., jt. ed. see Piras, Romano.
Piras, Romano & Piras, Horatio G., eds. Biochemistry of the Glycosidic Linkage: An Integrated View, Proceedings.
Piraux, Henry, ed. Dizionario Tecnico Inglese-Italiano: Elettronica, Elettrotecnica.
Pirhai, Imtiaz A., jt. auth. see Hatley, Derek J.
Pirie, David. A Heritage of Horror: The English Gothic Cinema, 1946-1972.
--William Wordsworth: The Poetry of Grandeur & of Tenderness.
Pirnicory, Vincent see Rousmaniere, Peter F., et al.
Pirone, Frank, jt. auth. see Favata, Benedict F.
Pir Vilayat Inayat Khan. The Call of the Dervish.
Pisan, Christine De see De Pisan, Christine.
Pisar, Samuel. Of Blood & Hope.
--Of Blood & Hope.
Piscator, Erwin. The Political Theatre: A History 1914-1929.
Pisciotta, John. Annual Editions: Macroeconomics, 1985-86.
Pisciotta, John & Vaughan, Mark. Macroeconomics, 1987-88.
Pisciotta, John, ed. Macroeconomics 1988-89.
Pisemskii, Aleksei F. One Thousand Souls. Litvinov, Ivy, tr.
Pishdad, A. Alan, ed. Hazardous Waste Sites in the U. S.
Pisk, Paul A., jt. auth. see Ulrich, Homer.
Pissiotis, C. A., et al. Vasopressin, II: Clinical Aspects.
Piston, Walter. Harmony. De Voto, Mark, ed.
--Harmony.
Pi-Sunyer, Oriol & Salzmann, Zdenek. Humanity & Culture: An Introduction to Anthropology.
Pitavy, Francois. William Faulkner's Light in August: A Critical Casebook.
Pitcher, Caroline. Party Time.
Pitcher, Carolyn. Games.
Pitcher, Tony J. & Hart, Paul J. Fisheries Ecology.
Pitfield, D., ed. Discrete Choice Models in Regional Science.
Pitfield, Ronald R. Business Organization.
Pitkin. Yearbook of Obstetrics & Gynecology, 1985.
Pitkin, Doree, ed. see Miles, Curtis & Rauton, Jane.
Pitkin, Harvey. Wintu Grammar.
Pitkin, Thomas M. & Cordasco, Francesco. The Black Hand: A Chapter in Ethnic Crime.
Pitman, E. J. Some Basic Theory for Statistical Inference.
Pitman, Isaac. Type Identification Chart.
Pitman, Liz. Transactional Analysis for Social Workers & Counsellors: An Introduction.
Pitrone, Jean M. & Elwart, Joan P. The Dodges: The Auto Family Fortune & Misfortune.
Pitt, Brice. Psychogeriatrics: An Introduction to the Psychiatry of Old Age.
Pitt, David. The Social Dynamics of Development.
Pitt, David, ed. Conservation for People: Alternatives for the Future.
Pitt, Douglas C. Telecommunications Function of the British Post Office.
Pitt, Leonard. We Americans.
--We Americans.
Pittenger, Norman. Catholic Faith in a Process Perspective.
Pittenger, Norman W. Passion & Perfection.
Pittiglio, D. Harmening. Modern Blood Banking & Transfusion Practices.
Pittman, Jeanne W. My Personal History Workbook.
Pittman, Rachel N. G. Washington Bear.
Pitts, Denis. The Predator.
Pitts, Dennis. Rogue Hercules.
Pitts, Gerald N., jt. auth. see Bateman, Barry L.
Pitts, James N., Jr., et al, eds. Advances in Photochemistry.
Pitts, Jesse R. The Tocqueville Review - La Revue Tocqueville, 1986-87.
Pitts, Jesse R. & Zunz, Olivier, eds. The Tocqueville Review - La Revue Tocqueville, 1985-86.
Pitts, John A. Human Factor: Biomedicine in the Manned Space Program to 1980.
Pitts, Joyce M. Managing Your Personal Finances.
Pitts, Robert F. Physiology of the Kidney & Body Fluids.
Pitts, William W. Commanding MultiMate Advantage II: A Comprehensive User's Guide.
Pitty, A. F. Geography & Soil Properties.
Pituitary Symposium Staff. Pituitary-A Current Review: Proceedings of the Symposium, Medical College of Georgia, Augusta, Georgia, May 20-22, 1976. Allen, Marshall B., Jr. & Mahesh, Vivenda B., eds.
Pitzer, Sara. Guide to the Recommended Country Inns of the South (North Carolina, South Carolina, Georgia, Florida, Alabama, Mississippi, Louisiana, Arkansas, Kentucky & Tennessee)
--The More Than Chicken Cookbook.
Pitzl, Gerald R. Annual Editions: Geography, 1986-87.
Pitzl, Gerald R., ed. Geography 1988-89.
Pival, Jean G., jt. auth. see Adelstein, Michael E.
Pivar, Stuart. Barye Bronzes, a Catalogue Raisonne.
Pivar, William H. Get Rich on Other People's Money: Real Estate Investment Secrets.
--Power Real Estate Listing.
--Power Real Estate Selling.
Piven, Frances, jt. auth. see Cloward, Richard.
Piver, M. Steven. Ovarian Malignancies: The Clinical Care of Adults & Adolescents.
Pix, Mary & Trotter, Catherine. The Plays of Mary Pix & Catherine Trotter. Steeves, Edna L. & Backscheider, P. R., eds.
Pixton, William H. Some Conventions of Standard Written English.
Pizam, Abraham, et al. The Practice of Hospitality Management I.
Pizan, Christine De see De Pizan, Christine.
Pizer, Donald, ed. see Garland, Hamlin.
Pizer, F. H., jt. auth. see Robinson, Susan.
Pizer, Hank & Palinski, Christine O. Coping with a Miscarriage.
Pizzarello, Donald J. & Witcofski, Richard L. Medical Radiation Biology.
Pizzi. Wood Adhesives: Chemistry & Technology.
Plaa, Gabriel L. & Duncan, W. A., eds. Proceedings of the First International Congress on Toxicology: Toxicology As a Predictive Science.
Place, Irene & Robertson, Leonard. Opportunities in Management Careers.
Place, Jonathan. How to Save a Million.
Place, Marian T. Comanches & Other Indians of Texas.
--First Astrowitches.
--The Resident Witch.
--The Witch Who Saved Halloween.
Place, Robin. Down to Earth.
--Finding Fossil Man.
Plachno, Larry & Wartenberg, Richard. The Bus Equipment Guide: Intercity Coaches 1955-1985.
Pladsen, Carol & Clifford, Denis. Your Family Records.
Plaidy, Jean. Caroline the Queen.
--The Heart of the Lion.
--The Lady in the Tower.
--The Princess of Celle.
--Spanish Inquisition: Its Rise.
Plain, Belva. The Golden Cup.
Plaisted, Elinor, jt. auth. see Neff, Robert.
Plakhotin, M. Manual of Veterinary Surgery.
Planche, James R. The Pursuivant of Arms; or, Heraldry Founded upon Facts.
Planck, Max. Scientific Autobiography.
Planck, Max, Society Staff, jt. ed. see Gottstein Research Unit Staff.
Plane, Donald R. & Oppermann, Edward B. Statistics for Management Decisions.
Plane, Robert A., jt. auth. see Sienko, Michell J.
Plank, John. Oh, the Anguish of English.
Plank, Tom M., jt. auth. see Blensly, Douglas L.
Plano, Jack C. & Greenberg, Milton. The American Political Dictionary.
Plano, Jack C. & Olton, Roy. The International Relations Dictionary.
Plansec Seminar De Re Metallica, Reutte, 4th, 1961. Powder Metallurgy in the Nuclear Atomic Energy. Benesovsky, F., ed.
Plansee Seminar De Re Metallica, Reutte, 4th, 1961. Powder Metallurgy in the Nuclear Age: Papers Presented at the Fourth Plansee Seminar. Benesovsky, F., ed.
Plansee Seminar De Re Metallica - 3rd - Reutte - 1958. Lectures Held at the Third Plansee Seminar. Benesovsky, F., ed.
Plansee Seminar De Re Metallica-5th-Reutte-1964. Metals for Space Travel: Lectures held at the Fifth Plansee Seminar. Benesovsky, F., ed.
--Metals for the Space Age: Papers Presented at the Fifth Plansee Seminar. Benesovsky, F., ed.
Plansee Seminar De Re Metallica - 6th - Reutte-1968. High Temperature Materials: Papers Presented at the Sixth Plansee Seminar. Benesovsky, F., ed.
Plant, L. Psychological Research: Selected Readings for Introductory Psychology.
Plant, Martin A. Drinking Careers: Occupations, Drinking Habits, & Drinking Problems.
Plant, Martin A., jt. ed. see Hore, Brian D.
Plant, Martin A., et al. Alcohol, Drugs & School-Leavers.
Plant, Richard, ed. see Boll, Heinrich.
Plant, Richard M., jt. auth. see James, Richard.
Plante, David. The Catholic.
--The Foreigner.
--Relatives.
Plantinga, Theodore. Historical Understanding in the Thought of Wilhelm Dilthey.
Plants, Helen & Venable, Wallace. Introduction to Statics.
Plas, E. H. Hueck-Van Der see Hueck-Van Der Plas, E. H.
Plas, Rob Van der see Van der Plas, Rob.
Plaskin, Glenn. Horowitz: A Biography of Vladimir Horowitz.
Plaster, C., et al, eds. Milling.
Plas Van Der, H. C. see Van Der Plas, H. C.
Plate, N. A., jt. ed. see Gordon, M.
Plater, William M. The Grim Phoenix: Reconstructing Thomas Pynchon.
Platnauer, Maurice. Life & Reign of the Emperor Lucius Septimius Severus.

Plato. The Dialogues of Plato. Greene, William C., ed. Jowett, B., tr.
--The Republic. Lindsay, A. D., tr.
--Trial & Death of Socrates. Warrington, John, tr.
Plato, jt. auth. see Socrates.
Platt & Munk Editors. More Easy Answers.
Platt, Arlene Quint see Quint Platt, Arlene.
Platt, Charles. Garbage World.
--More from Your Micro.
--Popular Superstitions.
--The Whole Truth Home Computer Handbook.
Platt, Colin. The Castle in Medieval England & Wales.
--Medieval Britain from the Air.
--Medieval England: A Social History & Archaeology from the Conquest to 1600 A. D.
Platt, D. C. Foreign Finance in Continental Europe & the U. S. A., 1815-1870: Quantities, Origins, Function & Distribution.
Platt, Jennifer. Realities of Social Research.
Platt, Jerome J. Heroin Addiction: Theory, Research & Treatment.
Platt, John. A Series of Elementary Exercises upon Geological Maps.
Platt, John & Challinor, John. Simple Geological Structures.
Platt, Kin. Pushbutton Butterfly.
Platt, Richard, jt. auth. see Kass, Edward H.
Platt, Rutherford. Wilderness, the Discovery of a Continent of Wonder.
Platt, Rutherford H. Land Use Control: Interface of Law & Geography. Natoli, Salvatore J., ed.
Platten, David. Outdoor Survival Handbook.
Plattner, Paul. Conflict & Understanding in Marriage.
Plaut, Thomas F. Children with Asthma: A Manual for Parents.
Plaut, W. Gunther. The Man in the Blue Vest: And Other Stories.
--The Toral: A Modern Commentary: Genesis.
Plautus. Plautus - Bacchides.
Players Magazine Staff. Sweet Lucy.
Playfair. Immunology at a Glance.
Playfair, Giles. Kean.
Playfair, Guy L. & Hill, Scott. The Cycles of Heaven.
Playfair, Guy L., jt. auth. see Geller, Uri.
Playgirl Editors, ed. The Playgirl Love & Sex Adviser.
--Zippers.
Playne, Caroline. Neuroses of the Nations.
Pleasance, Simon, tr. see Bologna, Gianfranco.
Pleasance, Simon, tr. see Tanara, Milli U.
Pleasants, Henry. The Great Singers.
Pleasants, Jeanne V. Pronunciation of French: Articulation & Intonation.
Pleck, Joseph H. & Sawyer, Jack, eds. Men & Masculinity.
Plemmons, Robert J., jt. auth. see Berman, Abraham.
Plender, R. International Migration Law.
Pleninger, Andrew. How to Survive & Market Yourself in Management.
--How to Survive & Market Yourself in Management.
Plescia, O. J., ed. see Symposium of the Institute of Microbiology, Rutgers University, 1967.
Plesser, Donna R. & Siegel, Mark A. Health: A Concern for Every American.
Plesser, Donna R., et al. Gambling: Crime or Recreation.
--Growing Old in America: Information Aids Ser.
Plesser, Donna R., et al, eds. Energy: An Issue of the Eighties.
Plessis, Menan du see Du Plessis, Menan.
Plesums, Guntis. Townframe: Environments for Adaptive Housing.
Pletcher, Barbara A. Travel Sense: A Guide for Business & Professional Women.
Pletcher, Derek. Industrial Electrochemistry.
Pleuvry, jt. auth. see Parkhouse.
Plewig, G. & Kligman, A. M. Acne: Morphogenesis & Treatment.
Plezbert, Michael J. A Dynamic Approach to Counseling.
Plimak, E. & Volodin, A. Como Se Desarrolla la Sociedad.
--Way Society Develops.
Plimpton, George. Curious Case of Sidd Finch.
--The Open Net.
--A Sports Bestiary.
Plitt, Bertha. Paul: A Son's Torment, a Mother's Anguish.
Plog, Stanley C. & Ahmed, Paul I., eds. The Principles & Techniques of Mental Health Consultation.
Ploghoft, Milton E. & Anderson, James A. Teaching Critical Television Viewing Skills: An Integrated Approach.
Plomer, William. Turbott Wolfe.
Plossu, Berenard. New Mexico Revisited.
Plotkin, Fred. The Authentic Pasta Book.
Plotkin, H. C., jt. ed. see Oakley, David A.
Plott, Doris F. Who's Who on TV Soaps, Mini Serials Movies & Lots More.
Plotts, J. N., ed. Poetical Tributes to the Memory of Abraham Lincoln.
Plourde, Gary Wayne, Sr. Visions in Depth.
Plowden, Alison. Lady Jane Grey & the House of Suffolk.
--Tudor Women.
Plowden, C. Chichely. A Manual of Plant Names.
Plowden, David. Industrial Landscape.
Plowden, G. F. C. Pope on Classic Ground.
Plowden, Gene. Plowden: Circus Press Agent.
Plowden, Judith. Afterglow.
Plowhead, Ruth G. Mile High Cabin.
Plowman, Judith, jt. auth. see Jackson, Constance.
Plowright, Piers see Milne, John.
Plumb, A., jt. ed. see Yeldham, R. F.
Plumb, G. R., ed. Nuclear Waste Reprocessing.
Plumb, J. H. Georgian Delights: The Pursuit of Happiness.
Plumb, J. H. & Wheldon, Huw. Royal Heritage: The Treasures of the Kings & Queens of England.
Plume, Ilse. The Story of Befana: An Italian Christmas Tale.
Plumme, Don E. The Wuzzles Book of Go-Togethers.
Plummer, Cameron & Plummer, Mary F. A Short View of Mobile's Ancient Money.
Plummer, Cameron, ed. see Staples, Alfred.
Plummer, Charles C. & McGeary, David. Physical Geology.
Plummer, D. Brian. The Complete Lurcher.
--Diary of a Hunter.
--The Fell Terrier.
--Merle: Start of a Dynasty.
--Modern Ferreting.
--Omega.
--Rogues & Running Dogs.
--Tales of a Rat-Hunting Man.
--The Working Terrier.
Plummer, John, intro. by. The Hours of Catherine of Cleves.
Plummer, John F., ed. Vox Feminae: Studies in Medieval Woman's Songs.
Plummer, Mary F., jt. auth. see Plummer, Cameron.
Plunkett, Horace. Ireland in the New Century.
Plunkett, Jim & Newhouse, Dave. The Jim Plunkett Story: The Saga of a Man Who Came Back.
Plunkett, W. Richard. Supervision: The Direction of People at Work.
Plunkett, Warren R. & Attner, Raymond F. Introduction to Management.
Pluta, Joseph E., et al. Texas Fact Book, 1982.
Pluth, Alphonsus, ed. see Smith, Thomas.
Pluth, James M., jt. auth. see Gosner, Robert W.
Pluto-Maspero Project Staff. World View 1982: An Economic & Geopolitical Yearbook. Camiller, Patrick, tr.
Pluto Press Staff, et al. State of the World Atlas.
Pluto, Terry & Neuman, Jeffrey. A Baseball Winter: The Off-Season Life of the Summer Game.
Plyushch, Leonid. History's Carnival: A Dissident's Autobiography.
Poag, C. Wylie. Ecologic Atlas of Benthic Foraminifera of the Gulf of Mexico.
Poatgieter, A. Hermina & Dunn, James T., eds. Gopher Reader I.
Poatgieter, Hermina. Indian Legacy: Native American Influences on World Life & Culture.
Pobee, John S. Persecution & Martyrdom: From Experience to Theology in Paul.
Pochan, Andre. The Mysteries of the Great Pyramids.
Pochedly, Carl. Neuroblastoma.
Pochedly, Carl, ed. Clinical Management of Cancer in Children.
Pochedly, Carl, jt. ed. see Schwartz, Elias.
Pochin-Mould, Daphne. The Aran Islands.
Pocock, J. G. Ancient Constitution & the Feudal Law: A Study of English Historical Thought in the 17th Century.
--Politics, Language & Time: Essays on Political Thought & History.
Pocock, J. G., ed. Three British Revolutions: 1641, 1688, 1776.
Pocock, Stuart J. Clinical Trials: A Practical Approach.
Pocs, Ollie. Annual Editions: Human Sexuality, 1985-86.
Pocs, Ollie & Walsh, Robert H. Annual Editions: Marriage & Family, 1985-86.
Pocs, Ollie, ed. Human Sexuality 1988-89.
Pocs, Ollie, jt. ed. see Walsh, Robert.
Podell, Joel, et al. Activity Guide for Salesmanship.
Podemski, Richard S., et al. Comprehensive Administration of Special Education.
Podesta. Membrane Physiology of Invertebrates.
Podgorecki, Adam, ed. Sociotechnics: A Trend Report & Bibliography.
Podgorecki, Adam, et al, eds. Legal Systems & Social Systems.
Podgorski, Frank R. Ego: Revealer-Concealer, a Key to Yoga.
Podhoretz, Norman. The Bloody Crossroads: Where Literature & Politics Meet.
--The Bloody Crossroads: Where Literature & Politics Meet.
--The Present Danger: Do We Have the Will to Reverse the Decline of American Power.
Podles, Mary S. & Porter, Vicki. A Guide to God's Minstrel: St. Francis of Assisi. Strohecker, Carol, ed.
Podmore, Frank. From Mesmer to Christian Science: A Short History of Mental Healing.
Podnos, Theodor H. Bagpipes & Tunings.
Podolsky, E. The Jealous Child.
Podolsky, Edward. Encyclopedia of Aberrations.
--Music Therapy.
--The Neuroses & Their Treatment.
Podolsky, Leo, ed. see Davison, June & Schaub, Ardella.
Podorhetz, Norman. Why We Were in Vietnam.
Podrazik, W. J., jt. auth. see Castleman, H.
Podrecca, Boris & Wang, Wilfried. Boris Podrecca.
Podsakoff, Phillip M., jt. auth. see Scott, William E.
Podszeck, H. K. Carrier Communication Over Power Lines.
Poduschka, Christl, jt. auth. see Poduschka, Walter.
Poduschka, Walter & Poduschka, Christl. Dearest Prickles: The Story of a Hedgehog Family.
Podvesko, M. L., compiled by. Ukrainian-English, English-Ukrainian Dictionary.
Poe, Edgar Allan. Great Works of Edgar Allan Poe: Tales.
--Narrative of Arthur Gordon Pym.
--The Other Poe: Comedies & Satires. Galloway, David, ed.
--Poems & Essays.
--Selected Writings. Galloway, David, ed.
--Tales.
--Tales of Suspense.
Poe, Jerry B. An Introduction to the American Business Enterprise.
Poe, Marian M. Family of Strangers.
Poe, Robert H. & Israel, Robert H., eds. Problems in Pulmonary Medicine for the Primary Physician.
Poe, Roy W. The McGraw-Hill Handbook of Business Letters.
Poe, Roy W. & Fruehling, Rosemary T. Business Communications: A Problem Solving Approach.
Poe, William D. & Holloway, Donald A. Drugs & the Aged.
Poehlman, John M. Breeding Field Crops.
Poel, Cornelius J. Van Der see Van Der Poel, Cornelius J.
Poen, Monte E. Strictly Personal & Confidential: The Letters That Harry Truman Never Mailed.
Poen, Monte M., jt. auth. see Truman, Harry S.
Pogany, G. O. Nineteenth Century Hungarian Painting.
Pogany, G. O., jt. auth. see Feher, Z. D.
Poggioli, Renato. Spirit of the Letter: Essays in European Literature.
Poggioli, Vicki. Tahiti: Complete Travel Guide to All of the Islands.
Poglazov, Boris F. Structure & Functions of Contractile Proteins.
Pogonowski, Iwo. Concise Polish-English, English-Polish Concise Dictionary.
--Practical Polish-English Dictionary: Polish-English; English-Polish.
Pogonowski, Iwo C. Poland: A Historical Atlas.
Pogrebin, Letty C. Getting Yours.
Pogson, C. I., jt. auth. see Denton, R. M.
Pogue, Joseph E. The Turquois: A Study in the History, Minerology, Geology, Ethnology, Archaeology, Mythology, Folklore & Technology.
Pogue, Thomas F. & Sgontz, Larry G. Government & Economic Choice: An Introduction to Public Finance.
Pohl, Fred. The Years of the City.
Pohl, Frederick, ed. Science Fiction of the Forties.
Pohl, Frederik. Beyond the Blue Event Horizon.
--The Black Star Rising.
Pohl, H., jt. ed. see Engels, W.
Pohlmann, Ken C. Principles of Digital Audio.
Pohlmann, Lillian. Love Can Say No.
--Sing Loose.
--Tall, Skinny, Towheaded & Miserable.
--The Unsuitable Behavior of America Martin.
Pohlmeyer, J., jt. ed. see Honerkamp, J.
Poindexter, J. Carl, Jr. Macroeconomics.
Poindexter, O. F., et al. Rocks & Minerals of Michigan.
Poiner, G. O., Jr., ed. CIH Key to the Groups & Genera of Nematode Parasites of Invertebrates.
Poinsett, Brenda. Understanding a Woman's Depression.
Poisson De Gomez, Madeleine Angelique. The Memoirs of the Baron Du Tan, to Which Is Added the Calabrian; or, the History of Charles Brachy, & the Hermit, 1744.
Poister, Theodore H. Performance Monitoring for Transportation Programs.
Poitras, Joseph A. Serenade: The Stories of Joseph A. L. Poitras.
Poitrass, Edward W., tr. see Hwang, Sun-won.
Pojman, Louis P. The Logic of Subjectivity: Kierkegaard's Philosophy of Religion.
Pokorny, Daniel H., ed. My Eyes Are My Ears.
Pokorny, George, et al. International Directory of Mountaineering Clubs & Organizations.
Pokras, Robert. Detailed Diagnosis & Procedures for Patients Discharged from Short-Stay Hospitals: United States, 1985.
--Utilization of Short-Stay Hospitals by Diagnosis-Related Groups: United States, 1980-1984.
Pokress, E. Profitable Thesis Typing.
Pokshishevsky, V. V. Geography of the Soviet Union.
Pokshishevsky, V. V., ed. Evaluation of the Soviet Population Census, 1970.
Pol, W. H. Van de see Van de Pol, W. H.
Polack, J. M. see Bloom, S. R.
Polak, Jeanne E. Food Service for Fitness.
Polak, Maralyn L. The Writer As Celebrity: Intimate Interviews.
Polakoff, Murray E. & Durkin, Thomas A. Financial Institutions & Markets.
Polakoff, Murray E., et al. Financial Institutions & Markets.
Polakoski, Kenneth, jt. ed. see Boyarsky, Saul.
Polan, Mary L. Second Seed.
Poland, D. & Scheraga, H. A. Theory of Helix Coil Transitions in Biopolymers.
Polano, H., tr. The Talmud of Jerusalem.
Polano, M. K., et al, eds. Advances in Topical Corticosteroid Therapy: Proceedings of the International Symposium, Amsterdam, Sept., 1975.
Polanski, Roman. Roman. Guarnaschelli, Maria D., ed.
--Roman by Polanski.
Polansky, Barbara F., jt. auth. see Weil, Ben H.
Polansky, Joseph, jt. auth. see Nielsen, Greg.
Polansky, Norman A. Ego Psychology & Communication: Theory for the Interview.
Polansky, Norman A., et al. Damaged Parents: An Anatomy of Child Neglect.
Polanyi, Thomas, jt. auth. see Andrews, Albert H., Jr.
Polchow, Michelle L. Nineteen Eighty-Five Health Care Cost Containment Legislation.
Poldauf, J. Czech-English-Czech Dictionary.
Pole, Kay, jt. ed. see Blake, Nigel.
Polebaum, Elliot E., jt. auth. see Brancato, Gilda.
Polednak, Anthony P. The Longevity of Athletes.
Polen, O. W. Editorially Speaking.
Polentz, Lloyd M. Engineering Fundamentals for Professional Engineers Exams.
Polenz, Joanna M. & Rosen, Marcia. Test Your Success I. Q.
Polenz, Joanna M., jt. auth. see Rosen, Marcia.
Poletti, Jacques & Lillard, Louise. L' Hexagone, C'Est la France.
Poley, Wayne, et al. Alcoholism: A Treatment Manual.
Polgar & Thomas. Introduction to Research in the Health Sciences.
Poliakoff, Stephen. American Days: A Play.
--Shout Across the River.
Polich, J. Michael & Armor, David J. The Course of Alcoholism: Four Years After Treatment. Braiker, Harriet B., ed.
Polikarpus, Viido & King, Tappan. Down Town.
Polimeni, Emmanuela. Leon Bloy: The Pauper Prophet.
Poling, David, compiled by. Inspiration Three, Vol. 3: Three Famous Classics in One Book - Wisdom of Luther, Calvin & Wesley.
Polish Scientific Publications Staff, jt. auth. see UNESCO Staff.
Polister, Peter E., jt. ed. see Price, Richards H.
Polite, Carlene H. Sister X & the Victims of Foul Play.
Politis, Jonathan, et al, eds. The Paramedic Review Manual.
Politzer, Georges. Elementary Principles of Philosophy.
Politzer, Heinz, jt. auth. see Kurtz, John W.
Polivanov, K. Theory of Electromagnetic Field.
Poliziano, Angelo. The "Stanze" of Angelo Poliziano. Quint, David, ed.
Polizzotti, R. S., jt. ed. see Luton, M. J.
Poljakoff-Mayber, A. & Gale, J., eds. Plants in Saline Environments.
Polk, Hiram C., Jr., ed. Infection & the Surgical Patient.
Polk, James. The Passion of Loreen Bright Weasel.
Polk, Noel. The Literary Manuscripts of Harold Frederic: A Catalogue.
Polk, Timothy. The Prophetic Persona: The Language of Self-Reference in Jeremiah.
Polk, William R. & Chambers, Richard L., eds. Beginnings of Modernization in the Middle East: The Nineteenth Century.
Polking, Fritz, ed. Nature Photography Yearbook, 1986-1987.
Polking, Kirk, ed. Freelance Jobs for Writers.
Polking, Kirk & Meranus, Leonard S., eds. Law & the Writer.
Polkinghorn, Harry, tr. River & Desert: A Bilingual Anthology of Mexican Literature, (Poetry)
Poll, Richard D. & Alexander, Thomas G., eds. Utah's History.

Pollack, Bruce. When the Music Mattered: Rock in the 1960s.
Pollack, Cecelia. My Own Reading Book.
--My Own Writing Book.
Pollack, Cecelia & Glasser, Diane. Blend-It.
Pollack, Emanual. Kronstadt Rebellion.
Pollack, Eva. Third Math Helper.
Pollack, George. Skywalking: The Life & Films of George Lucas.
Pollack, Griselda, jt. ed. see Parker, Rozsika.
Pollack, H. N. & Murthy, V. Rama, eds. Structure & Evolution of the Continental Lithosphere.
Pollack, Harriet & Smith, Alexander B. Civil Liberties & Civil Rights in the United States.
Pollack, Herman W. Manufacturing & Machine Tool Operations.
Pollack, Irving M., jt. ed. see Fabozzi, Frank J.
Pollack, Jack, jt. auth. see Sinclair, Lister.
Pollack, John. The Cambridge Seven.
--The Master: A Life of Jesus.
Pollack, Jonathan D. Security, Strategy, & the Logic of Chinese Foreign Policy.
Pollack, Kenneth & Gergen, Michael J. Energy Storage: Four Major Alternatives - Heat Storage, Cool Storage, Compressed Air Energy Storage & Underground Pumped Hydro Storage. Stryker, Perrin, ed.
Pollack, Sandra, jt. ed. see Bunch, Charlotte.
Pollack, Seymour V. Introducing Pascal.
--Programming the IBM Personal Computer: UCSD Pascal.
--UCSD Pascal Programming.
Pollack, Seymour V., jt. auth. see Sterling, Theodor D.
Pollack, Vera, jt. auth. see Weiner, Jack.
Pollak, Isaac G. The World of the Diamond.
Pollak, James. The Golden Egg. Kupelnick, Bruce S., ed.
Pollak, Patricia B. Aging-in-Place: Five Housing Alternatives for the Elderly.
Polland, Madelaine A. The Heart Speaks Many Ways.
Pollara, Bernard, et al, eds. see New York State Department of Health Staff.
Pollard, A. B. & Schofield, C. W. Basic Physical Science for Technicians.
Pollard, A. H. An Introduction to the Mathematics of Finance.
--Introductory Statistics: A Service Course.
Pollard, Albert F. History of England from the Accession of Edward Sixth to the Death of Elizabeth, 1547-1603.
Pollard, Albert J. Getting the Business: The Rewards & Hazards of Self-Employment.
Pollard, Arthur. Crabbe.
Pollard, David. The Poetry of Keats: Language & Experience.
Pollard, Edward A. Black Diamonds Gathered in Darkey Homes of the South.
--Echoes from the South.
Pollard, Francis E., et al. Democracy & the Quaker Method.
Pollard, Frank. Keeping Free.
Pollard, H. F. Sound Waves in Solids.
Pollard, Harold R. Trends in Management Thinking, 1960-1970.
Pollard, Hazel B., jt. auth. see Pollard, Richard.
Pollard, Morris. Virus Directed Host Response.
Pollard, Morris, ed. Antiviral Mechanisms.
--From Molecules to Man.
--Persistent Virus Infections.
--Virus-Induced Immunopathology.
Pollard, Richard & Pollard, Hazel B. From Human Sentience to Drama: Principles of Critical Analysis, Tragic & Comedic.
Pollen, Gerry, jt. auth. see Goodwin, Mary T.
Poller, L., ed. Recent Advances in Blood Coagulation.
Poller, Nidra. Eggs As Usual Breakfast...Etc.
Poller, R. C. Chemistry of Organotin Compounds.
Polleri, A. & Macleod, R. M., eds. Neuroendocrinology: Biological & Clinical Aspects.
Pollister, Arthur W. see Oster, Gerald, et al.
Pollitt, Christopher. Manipulating the Machine: Changing the Pattern of Ministerial Departments, 1960-83.
Pollnitz, Karl L. Les Amusemens De Spa; or, the Gallantries of the Spaw in Germany.
Pollo, Stefanaq & Puto, Arben. History of Albania: From Its Origins to the Present Day.
Pollock, Alex. British Watercolours: A Guide to Current Auction Prices up to 250 Pounds Sterling.
Pollock, Arthur. Ninety & Counting.
Pollock, Bruce. It's Only Rock & Roll.
--Me, Minsky, & Max.
--Playing for Change.
--When Rock Was Young: A Nostalgic Review of the Top Forty Era.
Pollock, Hugh M., ed. Reform of Industrial Relations.
Pollock, John. Amazing Grace: John Newton's Story.
--Apostle.
--The Apostle: A Life of Paul.
--Billy Graham-Evangelist to the World: An Authorized Biography.
--Pollock Personal Shorthand: A Primer.
Pollock, M., ed. Common Denominators in Art & Science.
Pollock, Marion B. & Middleton, Kathleen. Elementary School Health Instruction.
Pollock, Michael L. & Schmidt, Donald H., eds. Heart Disease & Rehabilitation.
Pollock, Morris & Geist, Harry. Structural COBOL Programming.
Pollock, P. Hamilton. Bell, Book & Scandal.
--Wings on the Cross.
Pollock, Penny. Stall Buddies.
Pollock, Ted. Managing Creatively.
Polmar, Norman. Guide to the Soviet Navy.
Polmar, Norman & Allen, Thomas. Ship of Gold.
Polmar, Norman & Allen, Thomas B. Rickover: Controversy & Genius - A Biography.
Polmar, Norman, jt. auth. see Mersky, Peter.
Polmer, Bunny & Yonkers, Ann. Capital Entertaining: Caterers to Call & Places to Party in & Around Washington, D. C.
Polner, Murray. Branch Rickey: A Biography.
Polo, Jose, ed. El Espanol Como Lengua Extranjera, Ensenanza de Idiomas y Traduccion tres calas Bibliograficas: Spanish as a Foreign Language.
Polos, N. C. Team Teaching & Flexible Scheduling for Tomorrow.
Pols, Edward. Recognition of Reason.
Polsby, Nelson W & Wildavsky, Aaron. Presidential Elections: Strategies of American Electoral Politics.
--Presidential Elections: Strategies of American Electoral Politics.
Polsby, Nelson W., jt. auth. see Peabody, Robert L.
Polsky, Milton. The Theatre Student: You Can Write a Play.
Polson, et al. Disposal of the Dead.
Polson, Beth & Newton, Miller. Not My Kid: A Parent's Guide to Kids & Drugs.
Polson, Jim G. Handbook of Farm & Ranch Estate Planning.
Polster, Diane, ed. see Edney, Margon & Grimm, Ede.
Poltrack, D. P. Television Marketing: Network, Local & Cable.
Poltroon, Milford S. The Worst of the Wretched Mess News.
Polunin, Miriam. The New Cookbook.
Polvani, Filippo, et al, eds. Meeting on Gas Chromatographic Determination of Hormonal Steroids.
Polya, G. & Szego, G. Problems & Theorems in Analysis, Vol. 2: Theory of Functions, Zeros, Polynomials, Determinants, Number Theory, Geometry. Billigheimer, C. E., tr. from Ger.
Polyak, Stephen. Vertebrate Visual System. Kluver, Heinrich, ed.
Polybius. The Histories of Polybius. Shuckburg, Evelyn S., tr.
Polzin, Robert M. Biblical Structuralism: Method & Subjectivity in the Study of Ancient Texts. Beardslee, William A., ed.
Polzin, Robert M. & Rothman, Eugene, eds. The Biblical Mosaic: Changing Perspectives.
Pomada, Elizabeth. Places to Go with Children in Northern California: More Than 350 Attractions Throughout Northern California to Delight Children & Parents.
--Places to Go with Children in Northern California.
Pomaine, Edouard de see De Pomaine, Edouard.
Pomasanoff, Alex. The Invisible World: Sights Too Fast, Too Slow, Too Far, Too Small for the Naked Eye to See.
Pomerance, Bernard. The Elephant Man.
Pomerance, Molly, jt. auth. see Greene, Amy.
Pomerance, Rocky & LeGrande, James L. Monarch's Preparation for the Police Officer Exam.
Pomerans, Arno, et al, trs. see Carotenuto, Aldo.
Pomerans, Arnold, tr. see Hillesum, Etty.
Pomerantz, Alfred. Of Man & God.
Pomeranz. Food Analysis Theory & Practice.
Pomeranz, Ruth. The Lady Apprentices.
Pomernacki, Charles, jt. auth. see Trost, Stanley R.
Pomeroy, Lawrence R., ed. Cycles of Essential Elements.
Pomeroy, W. J. Soviet Reality in the Seventies.
Pomeroy, Wardell B. Boys & Sex.
--Girls & Sex.
Pomeroy, William J. Beyond Barriers.
Pomian-Srzednicki, Maciej. Religious Changes in Contemporary Poland: Secularization & Politics.
Pommaret-Imaeda, Francoise & Imaeda, Yoshiro. Bhutan: A Kingdom of the Eastern Himalayas. Noble, Ian, tr.
Pommer, Henry F. Milton & Melville.
Pomper, Gerald M., et al. The Election of Nineteen Eighty-Four: Reports & Interpretations.
Pomraning, G. C. Radiation Hydrodynamics.
Ponce, Eliseo R. & Franchak, Stephen J. Evaluating Student Satisfaction: Measurement of Training & Job Satisfaction of Former Vocational Education.
Ponceau, Arthur De see De Ponceau, Arthur.
Ponce-Montoya, Juanita. Grief Work.
Pond, Mimi. Mimi Pond's Secrets of the Powder Room: What Every Man Should Know about Women.
Pond, W. G., jt. auth. see Church, D. C.
Pond, Wilson G. & Maner, Jerome H. Swine Production & Nutrition.
Ponder, Catherine. Dynamic Laws of Prosperity: Forces That Bring Riches to You.
Ponder, E. P. Red Cell Structure & Its Breakdown.
Ponge, Francis. Le Grand Recueil: Methodes.
--Le Grand Recueil: Pieces.
--Sun Placed in the Abyss & Other Texts. Gavronsky, Serge, tr. from Fr.
Ponnamperuma, Cyril, ed. Chemical Evolution of the Giant Planets.
--Comparative Planetology.
Ponnamperuma, Cyril & Cameron, A. G., eds. Interstellar Communication: Scientific Perspectives.
Ponomareov, B. N. El Socialismo Real y Su Significacion Internacional.
Ponomarev, B. Lenin & the World Revolutionary Process.
Ponomarov, B. N. Winning for Peace: The Great Victory - Its World Impact.
Ponomaryov, B. N., et al. A Short History of the CPSU.
Pons, Valdo & Francis, Ray, eds. Urban Social Research: Problems & Progress.
Ponsonby, Arthur. English Diaries: A Review of English Diaries from the Sixteenth to the Twentieth Century with an Introduction on Diary Writing.
Ponsot, Marie, tr. see Baudouy, Michel-Aime.
Ponsot, Marie, tr. see Clair, Andree.
Pont, Diana du see DuPont, Diana, et al.
Pontanus, Jacobus, ed. see Ovid.
Ponten, Jan. Spontaneous & Virus Induced Transformation in Cell Culture.
Pontier, Raymond J. On the Cutting Edge: Reflections of a Minister in Suburbia.
Pontiero, G. An Anthology of Brazilian Modernist Poetry.
Pontifical Council for the Family Staff. Family Hope for the World.
Pontifical Council for the Laity Staff. A Festival of Hope.
Pontifical Institute of Medieval Studies, Toronto Staff. Dictionary Catalog of the Library of the Pontifical Institute of Medieval Studies: First Supplement.
Pontifical Institute of Medieval Studies, Ontario Staff. Dictionary Catalogue of the Library of the Pontifical Institute of Medieval Studies.
Ponting, Clive. Whitehall: Tragedy & Farce.
Pontius-Woodward. Regional Geography: Global Patterns.
Pool, Elizabeth. Prologue to the Present: A Narrative World History.
Pool, Ithiel. Satellite Generals: A Study of Military Elites in the Soviet Sphere.
Pool, Ithiel de Sola. Technologies of Freedom.
Pool, Ithiel De Sola Sola de see Pool, Ithiel de Sola.
Pool, John. Lid off a Daffodil.
Pool, Thomas B., jt. ed. see Cameron, Ivan L.
Poole, A. Joe Foreword by see Machen, Elizabeth M.
Poole, Adrian, jt. auth. see Walsh, Dermot.
Poole, Charles P., et al. Relaxation in Magnetic Resonance: Dielectric & Mossbauer Applications.
Poole, David, ed. see Magon, Ricardo F.
Poole, Francis. Gestures.
Poole, Fred & Vanzi, Max. Revolution in the Phillipines: The U. S. in Hall of Cracked Mirrors.
Poole, J. C. Year of the Handicapped.
Poole, Keith & Zeigler, L. Harmon. Women Public Opinion, & Politics: The Changing Political Attitudes of American Women.
Poole, Lon. MacWork MacPlay: Creative Ideas for Fun & Profit on Your Apple Macintosh.
Poole, Lon & Davidson, Gregory. Practical Pascal Programs.
Poole, M. J., jt. auth. see Egelstaff, P. A.
Poole, Marshall S., jt. auth. see Folger, Joseph P.
Poole, Michael. Theories of Trade Unionism: A Sociology of Industrial Relations.
--Theories of Trade Unionism: A Sociology of Industrial Relations.
--Workers' Participation in Industry.
Poole, Michael, ed. Industrial Relations in the Future.
Poole, Millicent E. Youth: Expectations & Transitions.
Poole, Robert W., Jr., ed. Instead of Regulation: Alternatives to Federal Regulatory Agencies.
--Unnatural Monopolies: The Case for Deregulating Public Utilities.
Poole, Roger. The Unknown Virginia Woolf.
Poole, Shona C. The Christmas Cookbook.
--Iced Delights.
Poole, Susan. Ireland on Twenty-Five Dollars a Day.
--New Zealand on Twenty-Five Dollars a Day.
Poore, Henry R. Composition in Art.
Poore, Patricia, ed. see Old-House Journal Staff.
Poortvliet, Rien. He Was One of Us: The Life of Jesus of Nazareth.
Poortvliet, Rien & Huygen, Wil. Secrets of the Gnomes.
Poovey, W. A. Banquets & Beggers: Dramas & Meditations on Six Parables.
--Celebrate with Drama: Dramas & Meditations for Six Special Days.
--Cross Words: Sermons & Dramas for Lent.
--The Days Before Christmas: How Your Family Can Prepare for the Coming of Jesus.
--The Days Before Easter.
--The Days of Pentecost: Devotions, Customs, & Summertime Activities to Celebrate the Season of the Spirit.
--Faith Is the Password: Meditations on Romans.
--How to Talk to Christians about Money.
--Let Us Adore Him: Dramas & Meditations for Advent, Christmas, Epiphany.
--The Prayer He Taught: Seven Dramas & Meditations on the Lord's Prayer.
--Prodigals & Publicans: Dramas.
--Signs of His Coming: Dramas & Meditations for Advent, Christmas & Epiphany.
--Six Prophets for Today: Dramas on Jonah, Obadiah, Amos, Habakkuk, Hosea, Micah.
--That Wonderful Word Shalom: Dramas on the Biblical Concept of Peace.
--We Sing Your Praise, O Lord: Dramas & Meditations on Six Favorite Hymns.
Poovey, W. A., ed. Planning a Christian Funeral: A Minister's Guide.
Poovey, William A. Chancel Dramas for Lent.
--Lenten Chancel Dramas.
--Six Faces of Lent: Dramas.
--What Did Jesus Do.
Popa, Vasko. Vasko Popa: Selected Poems. Pennington, Anne, tr.
Pope, Alan & Goin, Kenneth L. High-Speed Wind Tunnel Testing.
Pope, Alexander. An Essay on Man by Alexander Pope. Mack, Maynard, ed.
--Pope & the Neo-Classicists.
Pope, Barbara H., ed. World Defense Forces: A Compendium of Current Military Information for All Countries of the World.
Pope, Benjamin & McGee, James P. Paraprofessionals in Mental Health.
Pope, Carl. Sahib: An American Misadventure in India.
Pope, David W. & Weiner, Norman L., eds. Modern Policing.
Pope, Dudley. Ramage & the Guillotine.
--Ramage & the Renegades.
Pope, Elizabeth M. Sherwood Ring.
Pope, Jerilyn D., jt. ed. see Hall, Elizabeth S.
Pope, John A., et al. The Freer Gallery of Art, Washington D. C.
Pope, K. S. & Singer, J. L., eds. The Stream of Consciousness: Scientific Investigations into the Flow of Human Experience.
Pope, Lillie. Psycho-Educational Battery.
--Tutor! A Handbook for Tutorial Programs.
Pope, Rex & Hoyle, Bernard, eds. British Economic Performance 1880-1980.
Pope, Rita. Cornwall.
Pope, Whitney. Durkheim's "Suicide" A Classic Analyzed.
Pope-Hennessy, John. Luca della Robbia.
Pope John Paul II. Family: Center of Love & Life.
--Light of Christ.
--The Things of the Spirit: Pope John Paul II. Spink, Kathryn, ed.
--The Way to Christ: Spiritual Exercises.
--The Word Made Flesh: The Meaning of the Christmas Season.
Pope John XXIII. Journal of a Soul. White, Dorothy, tr.
Popell, Charles. Bitter Water.
Pope Paul VI. Church: Light of All Mankind. Daughters of St. Paul Staff, ed.
Pope Pius Twelfth. Directives to Lay Apostles: Eighty-Six Pronouncements. Monks of Solesmes Staff, ed.
Popescu, J. Italian for Commerce.
Popescu, N. Abelian Categories with Applications to Rings & Modules.
Popham, Estelle L., jt. auth. see McCabe, Helen M.
Popham, G. T. Government in Britain.
Popham, Hugh. F. A. N. Y. The Story of the Women's Transport Service 1907-1984.
Popham, Janet, jt. auth. see Tedesco, Janis.
Popham, Peter. The Insider's Guide to Japan.
Popham, W. James. Educational Evaluation.
Popiel, W. J. Introduction to Colloid Science.
Popkin, Gary S. Advanced Structured COBOL.
--Comprehensive Structured COBOL.
--Introductory Structured COBOL Programming.
Popkin, Gary S. & Pike, Arthur M. Introduction to Data Processing.
Popkin, Henry, ed. see Chekhov, Anton.
Popkin, Henry, ed. see Gogol, Nikolai.
Popkin, Henry, ed. see Ibsen, Henrik.
Popkin, Henry, ed. see Synge, John Millington.
Popkin, Richard H. The High Road to Pyrrhonism. Watson, R. A. & Force, J. E., eds.

Authors

Popko, Edward. Transitions: A Photographic Documentary of Squatter Settlements.
Pople, J. A. & Beveridge, D. L. Approximate Molecular Orbital Theory.
Popouych. Tetraphenylborates.
Popov, V., jt. auth. see Peterenko, F.
Popovac, Gwynn. Wet Paint.
Popovic, ed. Nikola Tesla (1856-1943) Lectures, Patents, Articles.
Popovich, Dorothy. A Prescriptive Behavioral Checklist for the Severely & Profoundly Retarded.
Popovich, Dorothy & Laham, Sandra L., eds. The Adaptive Behavior Curriculum: Prescriptive Behavior Analyses for Moderately, Severely, & Profoundly Handicapped Students.
Popovics. Concrete Making Materials.
Popovics, Sandor. Concrete Making Materials.
Popovics, Sandor, ed. Fundamentals of Portland Cement Concrete - A Quantitative Approach: Fresh Concrete.
Popovych, Orest & Tomkins, Reginald P. Nonaqueous Solution Chemistry.
Popowski, Bert & Pyle, Wilf E. The Hunter's Book of the Pronghorn Antelope.
Poppel, Norman, ed. Parent-Child Relations: A Reader.
Popular Mechanics Co. Staff. How to Make Mission Style Lamps & Shades.
Popular Mechanics Editors. Home Security Handbook.
--Popular Mechanics Complete Car Repair.
Population Council Editors. Catalogue of the Population Council Library.
Poque, Paul. Start & Run a Profitable Beauty Salon: A Complete Step-by-Step Business Plan.
Poquelin, Jean-Baptiste see Moliere, pseud.
Porcella, Brewster. A Summary of Research on the Reading Interests & Habits of College Graduates.
Porch, Douglas. The Portuguese Armed Forces & the Revolution.
Pordes, Ilse, retold by. Favourite Stories from Japan.
Poretti, G., ed. see Symposium on High-Energy Electrons, Montreux, 1964.
Porges, F. The Design of Electrical Services for Buildings.
Porges, Irwin. Edgar Rice Burroughs: The Man Who Created Tarzan.
Porges, S. W. & Coles, G. H., eds. Psychophysiology.
Pories, Walter J., et al, eds. Clinical Applications of Zinc Metabolism.
Porricelli, Larry. The Art of Arranging Artificial Flowers.
Port, F. K., et al, eds. Advances in Internal Medicine & Pediatrics.
Porta, Ernesto, jt. ed. see Salvatore, Marco.
Porten, Ronald P. Von der see Goren, Charles H. & Von der Porten, Ronald P.
Porteous, Alexander. Forest Folklore, Mythology & Romance.
Porteous, J. Douglas. Canal Ports: The Urban Achievement of the Canal Age.
Porteous, Norman W. Daniel, a Commentary.
Porter. The Control of Human Fertility: A Text for Health Professionals.
Porter, A. R., et al. A Guidebook for Technology Assessment & Impact Analysis.
Porter, A. S. Lithographic Presswork.
Porter, Alyene. Papa Was a Preacher.
Porter, Andrew, jt. ed. see Rosen, David.
Porter, Arabel J., ed. see Rahv, Philip.
Porter, Bernard. Britain, Europe & the World, 1850-1986: Illusions of Grandeur.
Porter, Bernard H. Anything Book.
--H. L. Mencken: A Bibliography.
Porter, Burton F. Deity & Morality-with Regard to the Naturalistic Fallacy.
Porter, Cathy, tr. see Kollontai, Alexandra.
Porter, Charles E., ed. Statistical Theories of Spectra: Fluctuations.
Porter, Colin F. Environmental Impact Assessment: A Practical Guide.
Porter, Darwin. Dollarwise Guide to Austria & Hungary, 1985-1986.
--Dollarwise Guide to Bermuda & the Bahamas.
--Dollarwise Guide to England & Scotland.
--Dollarwise Guide to France.
--Dollarwise Guide to Italy.
--Dollarwise Guide to Portugal Including Madeira & the Azores.
--Dollarwise Guide to the Carribean.
--England on Thirty-Five Dollars a Day.
--Frommer's Dollarwise Guide to Austria & Hungary.
--Frommer's Dollarwise Guide to England & Scotland.
--Frommer's Dollarwise Guide to France.
--Frommer's Dollarwise Guide to Italy.
--Frommer's Guide to London.
--Frommer's Scandinavia on Forty Dollars a Day.
--Marika.
--Scandinavia on Thirty-Five Dollars a Day.
--Spain & Morocco (Plus the Canary Islands) on Twenty-Five Dollars a Day.
--Venus: A Novel Based on the Life of Anais Nin.
Porter, David. Children at Risk: The Growing Threat of Bizarre Toys, Fantasy Games, TV, Movies & Illegal Drugs.
--Fundamentals of Bonding: A Manual on Fidelity & Surety.
Porter, David L. Help! Let Me Out!
--Mine!
Porter, Donald C. The Sachem.
Porter, Douglas, jt. auth. see Valadian, Isabelle.
Porter, Eliot. In Wildness Is the Preservation of the World.
Porter, Eliot see Matthiessen, Peter.
Porter, Evelyn. The Story of Music.
Porter, Greg & Campbell, Roger. Adventure Pack, No. 1: Three Introductory Adventures for TimeLords.
Porter, Henry. The Two Angry Women of Abingdon: A Critical Edition. Evett, Marianne B., ed.
Porter, Ian H. & Hook, Ernest B., eds. Service & Education in Medical Genetics.
Porter, Ian H., jt. ed. see Vallet, H. Lawrence.
Porter, Ian H., et al, eds. see New York State Department of Health, Birth Defects Institute Symposium Staff.
Porter, J. F., jt. ed. see Manniche, P.
Porter, J. M., ed. Luther: Selected Political Writings.
Porter, Jack N. Conflict & Conflict Resolution.
Porter, Jack N., ed. Jewish Partisans: A Documentary of Jewish Resistance in the Soviet Union During World War II.
Porter, James I., tr. see Oberman, Heiko A.
Porter, Jill, jt. ed. see Coupe, Judith D.
Porter, K., jt. auth. see Ledbetter, M. C.
Porter, Katherine. Katherine Porter: Works on Paper 1969 to 1979.
Porter, Katherine A. Collected Stories of Katherine Anne Porter.
Porter, L. W., jt. ed. see Rosenzweig, M. R.
Porter, Larry. Illustrated Stories from Church History. Cheesman, Paul R., ed.
Porter, Lyman W., jt. auth. see Steers, Richard M.
Porter, Lyman W., ed. see Hall, Douglas T.
Porter, Lyman W., ed. see Schneider, Benjamin.
Porter, M. Gilbert. The Art of Grit: Ken Kesey's Fiction.
Porter, Margaret. Heiress of Ardara.
Porter, Martin. The Complete Guide to Making Home Video Movies.
Porter, Penny. Howard's Monster.
Porter Productions, ed. Up & down & in & Out.
Porter, Robert, ed. Guide to Corporate Giving in the Arts.
--United Arts Fundraising: 1985 Campaign Analysis.
--United Arts Fundraising: 1986 Campaign Analysis.
Porter, Robert A., ed. Guide to Corporate Giving in the Arts, Two.
Porter, Robert G. Preparation of Computerized Index to Nonfiction of Thomas Mann.
Porter, Robert J., jt. auth. see Wood, Oliver G.
Porter, Roger, jt. ed. see Johnson, Julian.
Porter Sargent Staff, ed. Directory for Exceptional Children.
--The Guide to Summer Camps & Summer Schools.
--Handbook for Private Schools.
--Handbook of Private Schools.
--Schools Abroad of Interest to Americans.
Porter, Stanley. Petroleum Accounting Practices.
Porter, Stephen R., jt. auth. see Cummings, P. Howard.
Porter, Sue. Daytime.
--My Body.
--My Clothes.
--Two.
Porter, Sylvia. Love & Money. Williams, Jennifer, ed.
--Sylvia Porter's Income Tax Book, 1982.
--Sylvia Porter's Income Tax Book, 1983.
--Sylvia Porter's Income Tax Book, 1984.
--Sylvia Porter's Income Tax Book, 1985.
--Sylvia Porter's Money Book.
--Sylvia Porter's Personel 1987 Income Tax Book.
--Sylvia Porter's Tax Book, 1981.
--Sylvia Porter's Tax Guide, 1986.
--Sylvia Porter's Three Hundred & Eighty Five Tax-Saving Tips: How to Profit from the New Tax Law.
--Sylvia Porter's Your Own Money.
Porter, Theodore. The Rise of Statistical Thinking, 1820-1900.
Porter, Tom. Architectural Color.
Porter, Vicki, jt. auth. see Podles, Mary S.
Porter, W. A., jt. ed. see Bedrosian, S. D.
Porter, W. Thomas. The Touche Ross Guide to Personal Financial Planning.
Porter, W. Thomas, Jr. & Perry, William E. EDP: Controls & Auditing.
Porter, W. Thomas, Jr. & Perry, William. EDP: Controls & Auditing.
Porter, William S. see Henry, O.
Porterfield, Christopher, jt. auth. see Cavett, Dick.
Porterfield, William M. Concepts of Chemistry.
Portnoi, Paul, ed. Jane's Airport & Handling Agents - Central & Latin America Including the Caribbean.
--Jane's Airports & Handling Agents - Far East, Asia, Australasia Region.
Portnoy, Howard. All the Fathers: The Fein Family Story.
Portugal, Franklin H. & Cohen, Jack S. A Century of DNA.
Portugali. Distribution, Allocation, Social Structure & Spatial Form: Elements of Planning Theory.
Portuges, Catherine, jt. ed. see Culley, Margo.
Portz, M. Susan. The Wedding Resource Directory.
--The Wedding Resource Directory: An Annual Directory of Wedding Services in the Denver-Boulder Area.
Porzecanski, Arturo C. Uruguay's Tupamaros: The Urban Guerilla.
Posch, Robert J. What Every Manager Needs to Know about Marketing & the Law.
Poschmann, Andrew W. Standards & Procedures for Systems Documentation.
Posell, Elsa Z. Russian Composers.
Posener, Jill. Louder Than Words.
--Spray It Loud.
Posey, Kayte Lee, jt. auth. see Arnold, Dovie.
Poskitt, J., jt. auth. see Oxley, R.
Posluns, Ronald J. Negotiate Your Way to Financial Success.
Posner, Barbara M., jt. auth. see McCool, Audrey C.
Posner, M. V. & Woolf, Stuart J. Italian Public Enterprises.
Posner, Mitchell J., jt. auth. see Goldberg, Philip.
Posokhin, M. Towns for People.
Possehl, G., jt. ed. see Kennedy, K.
Possinger, Callie, ed. The Official Directory of Industrial & Commercial Traffic Executives, 1983.
--The Official Directory of Industrial & Commercial Traffic Executives, 1984.
Post, Argie W. How to Get in Shape.
--Rape of Detroit.
Post, Chandler R. Mediaeval Spanish Allegory.
Post, Douglas E., jt. ed. see Joachain, Charles J.
Post, Laurens Van der see Van der Post, Laurens.
Post, Laurens Van Der see Van Der Post, Laurens.
Post, Marty, jt. auth. see Wischnia, Bob.
Post Office Research Dept. London, England Staff. Human Factors in Telecommunications International Symposium, 5th.
Post, Robert C., ed. Every Four Years: The American Presidency.
Post, Seymour C., ed. Moral Values & the Superego Concept in Psychoanalysis.
Post, Thomas R., jt. auth. see Reys, Robert E.
Post, W. Ellwood. The Complete Acolyte.
Postal, Bernard & Koppman, Lionel. Jewish Landmarks of New York: A Travel Guide & History.
Postan, Cynthia, tr. see Duby, Georges.
Posthuma, Fredrick E., ed. Energy & Education: Teaching Alternatives.
Postl, Anton. Laboratory Experiments in Physical Science.
Postlethwaite, N., jt. ed. see Choppin, B.
Postlethwaite, T. N. & Thomas, R. M., eds. Schooling in the Asean Region: Primary & Secondary Education in Indonesia, Malaysia, the Philippines, Singapore & Thailand.
Postlethwaite, T. N., jt. ed. see Choppin, B. H.
Postlethwaite, T. N., jt. ed. see Walberg, H. J.
Postlewaite, Jean, ed. Business Traveler's City Guide 1987.
Postman, Leo & Keppel, Geoffrey, eds. Norms of Word Association.
Postman, Neil, et al. Language in America: A Report on Our Deteriorating Semantic Environment.
Postnikova-Loseva, M., et al. Historical Museum, Moscow: Jewellery.
Poston, Carol H., ed. see Wollstonecraft, Mary.
Poston, J. W., jt. auth. see Eichholz, G. G.
Poston, T. & Woodcock, A. E. A Geometrical Study of the Elementary Catastrophes.
Postyn, Jo K., jt. auth. see Postyn, Sol.
Postyn, Sol & Postyn, Jo K. Raising Cash: A Guide to Financing & Controlling Your Business.
Posyniak, Henry. Guide to Accounting Principles, Practices & Systems for Nursing Homes.
Potapov, V. & Tatarindrick, S. Organic Chemistry.
Poteet, G. Howard. How to Treasure Hunt in the City. Nelson, Bettye, ed.
--Published Radio, Television & Film Scripts: A Bibliography.
Poteet, G. Howard & Petti, Michael A. Exploring Careers As a Chiropractor.
Potgieter, Herman. Aviation in South Africa.
Potgieter, P. J. Index to Literature on Race Relations in South Africa, 1910-1975.
Pothier, Patricia C. Psychiatric Nursing: A Basic Text.
Potholm, Christian P. The Theory & Practice of African Politics.
Poti, S. J. Quantitative Studies in Life Science.
Potier De Courcy, Pol. Continuation De L'Histoire Genealogique et Chronologique De la Maison Royale De France Du Pere Anselme.
Potocki, Patricia A. & Miller, Barbara L. Hands On: A Manipulative Curriculum for Teaching Multiple Handicapped Hearing Impaired Students.
Potok, Andrew. My Life with Goya.
Potok, Chaim. The Chosen.
--Davita's Harp.
--Theo Tobiasse: Artist in Exile.
--Wanderings.
Pottebaum, Gerard. Festival of Art.
Pottebaum, Gerard A. Ninety-Nine Plus One.
Potten, C. S., ed. Stem Cells: Their Identification & Characterization.
Pottenger, Francis M., et al. Fundamentals of Chemistry in the Laboratory.
Potter. Pocket Nurse Guide to Physical Assessment.
Potter & Perry. Fundamentals of Nursing: Concepts, Process & Practice.
Potter, B. Changing Performance on the Job.
Potter, Beatrix. Appley Dapply's Nursery Rhymes.
--Cecily Parsley's Nursery Rhymes.
--Ginger & Pickles.
--The History of the Writings of Beatrix Potter. Linder, Leslie, ed.
--New Adventures of Peter Rabbit.
--Pedrin, el Conejo Travieso: Peter Rabbit.
--Peter Rabbit.
--The Peter Rabbit Diary.
--Pie & the Patty Pan.
--Roly Poly Pudding.
--Story of a Fierce Bad Rabbit.
--Story of Miss Moppet.
--Tale of Benjamin Bunny.
--The Tale of Jeremy Fisher.
--Tale of Johnny Townmouse.
--Tale of Little Pig Robinson.
--Tale of Mr. Jeremy Fisher.
--Tale of Mister Tod.
--Tale of Mrs. Tiggy-Winkle.
--Tale of Mrs. Tittlemouse.
--Tale of Peter Rabbit.
--The Tale of Peter Rabbit.
--Tale of Peter Rabbit.
--Tale of Pigling Bland.
--Tale of the Flopsy Bunnies.
--Tale of Timmy Tiptoes.
--Tale of Tom Kitten.
--Tale of Two Bad Mice.
Potter, Betsy & Jarnow, Jill. Welcome Baby: Patchwork & Applique Projects for Infants & Toddlers.
Potter, Beverly. Beating Job Burnout.
Potter, Beverly A. From Conflict to Cooperation: A Manager's Guide to Mediation.
Potter, Bronson. Chibia, the Dhow Boy.
Potter, Clarkson N. Writers, Editors, & Moneymen: An Introduction to the Realities of Book Publishing.
Potter, David C., jt. ed. see Lewis, Paul G.
Potter, Dennis. Brimstone & Treacle.
--Singing Detective.
Potter, Jack & Lowell, Mark. Assessing the Effectiveness of Advertising.
Potter, Jay H. Turkey Shoot.
Potter, Jeremy. Good King Richard? An Account of Richard III & His Reputation.
Potter, Jonathan, et al. Social Texts & Contexts: Literature & Social Psychology.
Potter, Karl H., ed. The Encyclopedia of Indian Philosophies: Volume 1, Bibliography.
Potter, L. The Revels History of Drama in English: Medieval Drama.
Potter, Loren D. & Gosz, James R. Water Resources in the Southern Rockies & High Plains: Forest Recreation Use and Aquatic Life.
Potter, Loren D., jt. auth. see Barnard, Carolyn.
Potter, M., jt. ed. see Melchers, F.
Potter, Marian. A Chance Wild Apple.
Potter, Merle C. Mathematical Methods in the Physical Sciences.
Potter, Ned. Tracks on the Florida Trails.
Potter, P. E., jt. auth. see Pettijohn, F. J.
Potter, Ralph B. War & Moral Discourse.
Potter, Robert B. The Urban Retailing System: Location, Cognition & Behaviour.
Potter, Rosemary L. The Positive Use of Commercial Television with Children.
Potter, Shields. American Country.
Potter, T., et al. New Technology.
Pottiglio, Denise H. & Powers, Lawerence W. Clinical Hematology for Blood Bankers: A Case History Approach to Hemolytic Anemia. Ciesla, Betty, et al, eds.
Pottinger, Don, jt. auth. see Norman, A. V.
Pottinger, George. The Bubble Reputation.
Pottle, Frederick A., ed. see Boswell, James.
Potts, Abbie F. Shakespeare & the Faerie Queene.

Authors

Potts, D. C. & Charlton, D. G., eds. French Thought since Sixteen Hundred.
Potts, Eve, jt. auth. see Morra, Marion.
Potts, James B. Book of the Black Bass II: Ou Achigan Deux.
Potulny, Janice. You Think You Got Troubles.
Pouget, M. Manual of the Professional Cook.
Pouillon, Fernand. The Stones of the Abbey. Gillott, Edward, tr.
Poulin, A., Jr. Contemporary American Poetry.
--Contemporary American Poetry.
Poulos, George. Footsteps in the Sea: A Biography of Archbishop Athenagoras Cavadas.
Poulos, H. G. & Davis, E. H. Pile Foundation & Design.
Poulsen, Gunnar, tr. see Bodker, Cecil.
Poulsen, John L. The Plague: The Greatest Threat to the Civilized World.
Poulson, T., jt. auth. see Mohr, Charles E.
Poulton, Diane, ed. see Meyer, Ernst H.
Poulton, E. C. The Environment at Work.
Poulton, E. Christopher. Tracking Skill & Manual Control.
Pouncy, Mattie H. Reach a Little Deeper.
Pound, Ezra. Jefferson and-or Mussolini.
Pound, Ezra, ed. see Fenellosa, Ernest.
Pound, Ezra, ed. see Yeats, John B.
Pound, Ezra & Stock, Noel, trs. Love Poems of Ancient Egypt.
Pound, Louise. Nebraska Folklore.
Pound, Omar & Grover, Philip. Wyndham Lewis: A Descriptive Bibliography.
Pounder, C. C. Diesel Engine Principles & Practice.
Pounds, K., jt. ed. see Beer, P.
Pounds, Norman J. Political Geography.
Poundstone, William. Bigger Secrets: More Than 125 Things They Prayed You'd Never Find Out.
--The Recursive Universe: Cosmic Complexity & the Limits of Scientific Knowledge.
Pourjavady, N., jt. auth. see Wilson, P. L.
Pourkhesali, Mehrdad. Nine Thousand Miles to Freedom.
Pournelle, J. Twenty-Twenty Vision.
Pournelle, Jerry, jt. auth. see Niven, Larry.
Pournelle, Jerry & Carr, John F., eds. Nebula Award Stories Sixteen.
Pourtales, Guy De see De Pourtales, Guy.
Poussard, Wendy, jt. auth. see Eastman, Moira.
Povah, Nigel. Chess Training.
Powdermaker, Hortense. After Freedom: A Cultural Study in the Deep South.
--Life in Lesu.
--Stranger & Friend: The Way of an Anthropologist.
Powell. Stand Tough.
Powell, Adam. Notes of a Madman.
Powell, Alwyn V., jt. auth. see Winklevoss, Howard E.
Powell, Ann. The Origins of Western Art.
Powell, Anthony. O, How the Wheel Becomes It!
--The Strangers All Are Gone.
Powell, Arthur G. I Can Go Home Again.
Powell, Barbara. The Complete Guide to Your Child's Emotional Health: From Early Infancy to Early Adulthood.
Powell, Betty, jt. auth. see Powell, Thomas.
Powell, C. G. An Economic History of the British Building History: 1815-1979.
Powell, C Randall & Kirts, Donald K. Career Services Today: A Dynamic College Profession.
Powell, Charles G., jt. auth. see Zitron, Sherri.
Powell, Charles L. John James Wettstein, Sixteen Ninety-Three to Seventeen Fifty-Four: An Account of His Life, Work, & Some of His Contemporaries.
Powell, David, jt. auth. see Skrabanek, Petr.
Powell, Donalyn. Through a Child's Eyes.
Powell, Eric F. Biochemistry up-to-Date.
Powell, G. Bingham, Jr., jt. auth. see Almond, Gabriel A.
Powell, Gene. Semi-Quadratic Poetry Quaverly Quipped in Quatrain: The Q Volume.
Powell, Geoffrey. The Devil's Birthday: The Bridges to Arnhem 1944.
Powell, Graham E. Brain Function Therapy.
Powell, H. M. The Santa Fe Trail.
Powell, Hickman. Lucky Luciano: His Amazing Trial & Wild Witnesses.
Powell, Hollis C. The River Rat.
Powell, Howard B., jt. auth. see Shulz, William D.
Powell, J. W; see Boas, Franz.
Powell, James. Dow Jones-Irwin Guide to High Tech Investing: Picking Tomorrow's Winners Today.
Powell, James A. & Cooper, Ian, eds. Designing For Building Utilisation.
Powell, James A, jt. ed. see Brandon, Peter S.
Powell, James N. The Prentice-Hall Global Employment Guide: Information & Action Plans That Will Give You the Edge.
--The Tao of Symbols.
Powell, Jocelyn. Restoration Theatre Production.
Powell, Jody. The Other Side of the Story.
Powell, John, ed. Handbook of Architectural Practice & Management.
Powell, Judith A., ed. see Murray, Raymond L.
Powell, Karen H. & Sinwell, Joseph P., eds. Breaking Open the Word of God: Resources for Using the Lectionary for Catechists in the RCIA (Cycle C)
Powell, Lawrence C. An Orange Grove Boyhood: Growing up in Southern California 1910-1928.
--The River Between.
Powell, M. B., ed. see London Mathematical Society Instructional Conference Staff.
Powell, M. J., ed. Nonlinear Optimatization, 1981.
Powell, Michael. The Red Shoes.
Powell, Michael & Pressberger, Emeric. The Red Shoes.
Powell, Michael A., jt. auth. see Rosenthal, David W.
Powell, N. W. Handbook for Radiologic Technologists & Special Procedures Nurses in Radiology.
Powell, Painter E., jt. auth. see Marzano, Tony.
Powell, Patricia, jt. ed. see Kay, Peg.
Powell, Paul W. The Complete Disciple.
--Why Me, Lord?
Powell, Philip W. Mexico's Miguel Caldera: The Taming of America's First Frontier, 1548-1597.
Powell, Ralph A. Freely Chosen Reality.
Powell, Richard. I Take This Land.
Powell, Robert. Return to Meaningfulness.
Powell, Shirley. Running Wild.
Powell, Terry. Nobody's Perfect.
Powell, Thomas. Penet's Square.
Powell, Thomas & Powell, Betty. The Avant Gardener: A Handbook & Sourcebook of All That's New & Useful in Gardening.
Powell, Virgil S. Adeline, A Child of Yani.
--From the Slave Cabin of Yani.
--A Fury of Passions.
Powell, Wayne. Divorce Guide for British Columbia.
Powell-Smith, V. A Modern View of the Law for Builders & Surveyors.
Powell-Smith, Vincent, jt. auth. see Whyte, W. S.
Power, Crawford. Encounter.
Power, E. G. The Easter Rising & Irish Independence. Reeves, Marjorie, ed.
Power Editors. Plant Energy System: Energy Systems Engineering.
Power, Henry M. & Simpson, Robert J. Introduction to Dynamics & Control.
Power Instrumentation Symposium Staff. Instrumentation in the Power Industry, Vol. 24: Proceedings of the 24th Power Instrumentation Symposium.
--Instrumentation in the Power Industry, Vol. 26: Proceedings of the Power Instrumentation Symposium.
Power, J. M., jt. auth. see Low, N. P.
Power, Jonathan, et al. Migrant Workers in Western Europe & the United States.
Power, Patrick, tr. see O'Brien, Flann.
Power, Thomas C. DC-AC Laboratory Manual. Kosow, Irving L., ed.
Powers, Anne. Ride East, Ride West.
--The Thousand Fires.
Powers, Charles W. & Vogel, David. Ethics in the Education of Business Managers.
Powers, E. L., jt. ed. see Rodgers, M. A.
Powers, Edith, jt. auth. see Rodriguez, Gregorita.
Powers, Eileen E. Love on the Range.
Powers, Elizabeth. On Account of Murder.
Powers, G. Pat, jt. ed. see Baskin, Wade.
Powers, John R. The Unoriginal Sinner & the Ice-Cream God.
Powers, Lawerence W., jt. auth. see Pottiglio, Denise H.
Powers, Michael D. & Handleman, Jan S. Behavioral Assessment of Severe Developmental Disablities.
Powers, Pat, jt. auth. see Baskin, Wade.
Powers, Ron. White Town Drowsing: Journeys to Hannibal.
Powers, Stephanie & Quine, Judith B. Stefanie Powers: Superlife!
Powers, Thomas. Vietnam, the War at Home: The Antiwar Movement, 1964-1968.
Powers, Thomas F. Introduction to Management in the Hospitality Industry.
Powers, Tim. The Anubis Gates.
Powers, William E. Physical Geography.
Powers, William G., jt. auth. see Scott, Michael D.
Powicke, Frederick J. Cambridge Platonists, a Study.
Powicke, Hilda B. Barrier.
--No Certain Harbor.
Powicke, Michael. Military Obligation in Medieval England.
Powledge, Fred. Born on the Circus.
--Fat of the Land: What's Behind Your Shrinking Food Dollar, & What You Can Do about It.
--Mud Show: A Circus Season.
--The New Adoption Maze & How to Get Through It.
Pownall, Glen. Shell Craft.
Powys, John. The Inmates.
Powys, John C. In Spite Of.
--Porius.
--Rabelais.
Poyer, Dave, jt. auth. see Joynes, Monty.
Poyer, Joe. The Contract.
--Devoted Friends.
--Tunnel War.
--Vengeance Ten.
Poyner, James R. Towers to the Sky.
Poynter, Dan. Parachuting Manual for Square-Tandem Equipment.
--Parachuting: The Skydivers' Handbook.
Poynter, Margaret. Crazy Minnie.
--Frisbee Fun.
--The Racquetball Book.
--Search & Rescue: The Team & the Missions.
--Too Few Happy Endings: The Dilemma of the Humane Societies.
--The Zoo Lady: Belle Benchley & the San Diego Zoo.
Poynter, Margaret & Lane, Arthur L. Voyager: The Story of a Space Mission.
Poyser, J., ed. see GP-Info Symposium Staff.
Pozgar, George D. Legal Aspects of Health Care Administration.
Pozhela, J. Plasma & Current Instabilities in Semiconductors. Germogenova, O. A., tr.
Pozmantier, Frank. Tallest Tower.
Poznanin, L. P., ed. Ways & Means of Using Birds in Combating Noxious Insects.
Pozner, Andre, jt. auth. see Prevert, Jacques.
Pozo, Cal del see Del Pozo, Cal.
Pozoz, Robert S. & Born, David O. Hypothermia.
Pozzi-Johnson, David, jt. auth. see Goldman, Charlotte.
Pozzi-Johnson, David, ed. see Guynn, Denise Y.
Praag, Herman Meir van see Mendlewicz, Julien & Meir van Praag, Herman.
Prabhu, Barbara W. And Still in the Running: A Horse Called Port Conway Lane.
Prabhu, V. V. A Manager at Large.
Pracna, Charles F. Hobby Metalcraft.
Practchett, Terry. Dark Side of the Sun.
Practice, Dearle & Practice, Henderson. SMM6 Handbook: Guidelines for Architects, Quantity Surveyors, Estimators, Contractors.
Practice, Henderson, jt. auth. see Practice, Dearle.
Practice Law Institute Staff & Domcroft, Mark A. Aircraft Crash Litigation 1984.
Practicing Law Institute Staff & Alexander, Miles J. Trademark Litigation: Pragmatic Tactics & Techniques of Winning.
Practicing Law Institute Staff & Spiotto, James E. Current Municpal Defaults & Bankruptcy 1983.
Practicing Law Institute Staff & Tauber, Yale D. Executive Compensation•1983.
Practising Law Institute, jt. auth. see Fenwick, William A.
Practising Law Institute Staff. Advanced Antitrust Workshop: Fifteenth Annual Workshop.
--Antitrust Litigation.
--Banks, the SEC, & Regulatory Agencies: Enforcement & Civil Litigation Developments.
--Blue Sky Laws: State Regulation of Securities 1985.
--Business Information for Today's Practicing Lawyer.
--Comprehensive Crime Control Act of 1984.
--Congressional Oversight Investigations.
--Counseling Clients in the Entertainment Industry 1985.
--Creative Real Estate Financing 1986.
--Current Developments in Bankruptcy & Reorganization 1985: Vols. 344 & 345.
--Defaulted Bonds & Bankruptcy: The Problems of Indenture Trustees & Bondholders.
--Delaware Law for Corporate Lawyers: Recent Developments.
--Developments in Corporate Tax Accounting.
--Discovery in Medical Malpractice, Products Liability, & Personal Injury Cases.
--Hazardous Waste Litigation 1985.
--Hospitals in Today's Health Care Marketplace.
--Industrial Development Bond Financing 1985.
--The International Financial Markets Institute.
--International Taxation after the Tax Reform Act of 1984: Fifteenth Annual Institute on Internation Taxation.
--Investment Companies: Industry Responses to New Contexts & Concepts.
--Leveraged Acquisitions: Private & Public 1985.
--Mortgage-Backed Securities: Mortgage Pass-Throughs, CMOs, & Builder Bonds.
--Negative News.
--New & Extraordinary Relief in Intellectual Property Cases.
--New Banks & New Bankers, 1984.
--The New Era in CATV: The Cable Franchise Policy & Communications Act of 1984.
--The New Health Care Economy: Legal Responses to New Economic Forces.
--Nuclear Litigation Nineteen Eighty-Four.
--Planning & Administration of a Large Estate 1985.
--Practicing Before the International Trade Commission.
--Practising Before the U. S. Court of Appeals for the Federal Court.
--Preparation of Annual Disclosure Documents 1985.
--Preparation of the Fiduciary Income Tax Return 1985.
--Recent Developments in State Constitutional Law.
--Repurchase & Reverse Repurchase Agreements Revisited 1984.
--The Role of Outside Counsel in the Business Investigation.
--The Secured Creditor in Court 1985.
--Tax Aspects of Municipal Finance.
--Tax Reform Act of 1984.
--Tax Shelters: Advanced Planning Techniques.
--Unjust Dismissal 1984: Evaluating, Litigating, Setting, & Avoiding Claims.
--White Collar Criminal Practice 1985.
Practising Law Institute Staff & Barbash, Joseph. Employment Law: New Problems in the Workplace.
Practising Law Institute Staff & Beller, Alan L. International Financial Offerings.
Practising Law Institute Staff & Brown, Stanley J. Assessing Lawyer Evaluation & Partnership Decisions after Hishon V. King & Spaulding.
Practising Law Institute Staff & Clark, Roger A. Representing Trade Associations, 1985.
Practising Law Institute Staff & Cochrane, Luther P. Construction Claims Workshop, 1983.
Practising Law Institute Staff & Dayan, Rodney S. Structured Mortgage & Receivable Financing.
Practising Law Institute Staff & Dorsari, George R.. A Practical Guide to the Cable Communications Policy Act of 1984.
Practising Law Institute Staff & Dyk, Timothy B. Campaign Eighty-Four: Advertising & Programming Obligations of the Electronic Media.
Practising Law Institute Staff & Ferguson, M. Carr. Research & Development Limited Partnerships: Structuring, Financing, & Marketing.
Practising Law Institute Staff & Forrest, Herbert E. Implementing the AT&T Settlement: The New Telecommunications Era.
Practising Law Institute Staff & Garfinkel, Barry H. Current Problems in Federal Civil Practice, 1986.
Practising Law Institute Staff & Glascoff, Donald G. New Directions for the Thrift Industry.
Practising Law Institute Staff & Goldwasser, Dan L. Accountants' Liability: 1981.
Practising Law Institute Staff & Goldberg, Morton D. Software Proctection & Marketing: Computer Programs & Data Bases, Video Games & Motion Pictures 1983.
Practising Law Institute Staff & Heller, Fred I. Video Techniques in Trial & Pretrial.
Practising Law Institute Staff & Hillman, William C. Commercial Loan Documentation.
Practising Law Institute Staff & Hirschson, Linda B. Effective & Selective Use of the Marital Deduction.
Practising Law Institute Staff & Hinds, Richard D. OSHA, Toxic Substances in the Workplace.
Practising Law Institute Staff & Ingersoll, William B. The Legal Aspects of Real Estate Timesharing.
Practising Law Institute Staff & Katz, Melvin. Acquisitions & Mergers 1984: Tactics & Techniques, 1984.
Practising Law Institute Staff & Kaufman, David J. Franchising in New York.
Practising Law Institute Staff & Kraft, Melvin D. Remedies for Breach by Sellers & Buyers under the Uniform Commercial Code.
Practising Law Institute Staff & Lankenau, John C. Media Insurance & Risk Management, 1985.
Practising Law Institute Staff & Landenau, John C. Media Insurance: Protecting Against High Judgments, Punitive Damages, & Defense Costs.
Practising Law Institute Staff & Lobell, Carl D. Banks & Their Borrowers: New Opportunities in Financial Services.
Practising Law Institute Staff & McNaire, Robert M. Health Care: Legal Responses to New Economic Forces.
Practising Law Institute Staff & McCaffery, Carlyn S. Tax Planning for the Marital Dissolution.
Practising Law Institute Staff & Miller, David G. Depositions, Expert Witnesses & Demonstrative Evidence in Personal Injury Cases.
Practising Law Institute Staff & Mills, David W. Partnership Taxation: An Advanced Tax Program, 1984.
Practising Law Institute Staff & Miller, David G. Taking & Defending Depositions in Personal Injury Cases.
Practising Law Institute Staff & Novikoff, Harold. Chapter Eleven: Business Reorganizations.

Practising Law Institute Staff & Ostrager, Barry R. Insurance, Excess, & Reinsurance Coverage Disputes 1984.
Practising Law Institute Staff & Phillips, Susan M. The Commodity Futures Trading Commission: Current Issues.
Practising Law Institute Staff & Reisman, Albert F. Business Loan Workouts, 1983.
Practising Law Institute Staff & Ross, Kenneth. Consumer Products: Government Regulation & Product Liability.
Practising Law Institute Staff & Ryan, Reade H. Letters of Credit & Bankers' Acceptances 1984.
Practising Law Institute Staff & Sachs, Joel H. Environmental Compliance in a Changing Legal Environment.
Practising Law Institute Staff & Schwartz, Max J. Employee Benefits Legislation 1984.
--ERISA Litigation.
Practising Law Institute Staff & Selig, Stephen F. Commodity Futures: An Expanding Regulatory World.
Practising Law Institute Staff & Sederbaum, Arthur D. Income Taxation of Estates & Trusts, 1984.
Practising Law Institute Staff & Shenfield, John H. New Merger Guidelines.
Practising Law Institute Staff & Shapiro, George R. New Program Opportunities in the Electronic Media.
Practising Law Institute Staff & Sonsini, Larry W. Capital Formation 1984: Private & Public Financings.
Practising Law Institute Staff & Tondel, Lawrence C. Oil & Gas Financings: Current Practice & Anticipated Developments.
Practising Law Institute Staff & Vanyo, Bruce G. Recent Developments in Securitites Litigation.
Practising Law Institute Staff & Weiner, Paul I. Handling & Prevention of Fair Representation & Breach of Labor Contract Cases: Management & Union Viewpoints.
Practising Law Institute Staff & William C. Banking Problems under the UCC.
Practising Law Institute Staff & Yaeger, Dennis R. The Developing Law of Business Errors & Omissions Insurance.
Practising Law Institute Staff & Yaeger, Peter E. Securities Filings: Review & Update, 1983.
Practising Law Institute Staff & Zalaznick, Charles. Real Estate Development & Construction Financing, 1984.
Practising Law Institute Staff, jt. auth. see Securities & Exchange Commission, United States.
Practising Law Institute Staff, jt. auth. see Smith, Robert T.
Practising Law Institute Staff, ed. see Barbash, Joseph & Kauff, Jerome.
Practising Law Institute Staff, ed. see Strohofer, Jean & Wallce, Marie.
Practising Law Institute Staff, et al. International Exchange of Tax Information: Recent Developments.
--Condos & Co-Ops-Multi-Use Structures: Techniques.
--Construction Industry Labor Relations, 1982.
--Legal Aspects of Doing Business in Japan, 1983.
--Bankruptcy Practice for Bank Counsel, 1983.
--State Regulation of Capital Formation & Securities Transactions.
Prada Becares, Juan. Diccionario Terminologia Medica Explicada.
Prade, Ernstfried. Perfect Windsurfing.
Pradt, Mary A., jt. auth. see Slavin, Stephen L.
Praeder, Susan M. Miracle Stories in Christian Antiquity.
Prag, A. J. The Oresteia: Iconography & Narrative.
Prager, Dennis & Telushkin, Joseph. Nine Questions People Ask About Judaism.
--Why the Jews? The Reason for Anti-Semitism.
Prager, Frank D., ed. The Autobiography of John Fitch.
Prague, Cary N. Getting Great Graphics.
Prague, Cary N. & Hammitt, James E. Programming with dBASE MAC.
Prahl-Andersen, B. & Kowalski, Charles J., eds. A Mixed-Longitudinal, Interdisciplinary Study of Growth & Development.
Prak, Niels L. Architects: The Noted & the Ignored.
Prakash, N. Differential Geometry: An Integrated Approach.
Prall, Stuart E., jt. auth. see Willson, David H.
Pramoedya, Ananta T. Heap of Ashes.
Prange, Gordon W. At Dawn We Slept: The Untold Story of Pearl Harbor.
Prange, Gordon W. & Goldstein, Donald M. Pearl Harbor: The Verdict of History.
Prange, Gordon W., et al. Target Tokyo: The Story of the Sorge Spy Ring.
Prantera, Amanda. The Cabalist.
--Conversations with Lord Byron on Perversion, 163 Years after His Lordship's Death.
Prasad, Ananda S. Trace Elements & Iron in Human Metabolism.
Prasad, Benjamin S., jt. auth. see Negandhi, Anant R.
Prasad, Bimal, ed. India's Foreign Policy: Studies in Continuity & Change.
Prasad, Rajendra. At the Feet of Mahatma Gandhi.
--At the Feet of Mahtma Gandhi.
Prasanna, A. R., et al, eds. Gravitation, Quanta & the Universe: Proceedings of the Einstein Centenary Symposium Held at Ahmedabad, India 29 January to 3 February, 1979.
Prasow, Paul. Collective Bargaining & Civil Service in Public Employment: Conflict & Accommodation.
Prately, J. E. Principles of Field Crop Production.
Prater, Gene. Snowshoeing.
Prater, Pam. Letters to John.
Prather, Elizabeth M., jt. auth. see Kenney, Kathryn.
Pratima, Ma Yoga, ed. see Rajneesh, Bhagwan Shree.
Pratley, J. B. Study Notes for Technicians: Electrical & Electronic Principles.
Praton, Clifford H., ed. see Christophe, Henri.
Pratson, Fred. The Special World of the Artisan.
Pratson, Frederick. Consumer's Guide to Package Travel Around the World.
--Guide to Eastern Canada.
--Guide to Eastern Canada.
Pratt, A. M. Your Children, Their Teeth & Their Health.
Pratt, Alexander M. Illus. by see Pratt, A. M.
Pratt, Charles W. In the Orchard.
Pratt, David H. English Quakers & the First Industrial Revolution: A Study of the Quaker Community in Four Industrial Counties; York, Warwick, & Gloucester, 1750-1830.
Pratt, Edwin J., jt. auth. see Jordan, Donaldson.
Pratt, Elizabeth A., ed. see Townsend, Richard F.
Pratt, Fletcher, jt. auth. see De Camp, L. Sprague.
Pratt, Gerry. God Is Blue & Other Stories.
Pratt, J. Lowell. Currier & Ives Chronicles America.
Pratt, J. M. Inorganic Chemistry of Vitamin B1120.
Pratt, James, et al. Corporate, Partnership, Estate & Gift Taxation, 1989 Edition.
--Federal Taxation, 1989.
--Individual Income Tax, 1989.
Pratt, James N. The Tea Lover's Treasury.
--The Wine Bibber's Bible.
Pratt, James N. & De Caso, Jacques. The Wine Bibber's Bible.
Pratt, James W., et al. Corporate, Partnership, Estate & Gift Taxation, 1988.
--Federal Taxation, 1988.
--Individual Taxation, 1988.
Pratt, Lois. Family Structure & Effective Health Behavior: The Energized Family.
Pratt, Parley P. Voice of Warning.
Pratt, Paul W., ed. Feline Medicine.
Pratt, S. D., jt. auth. see Seavey, George R.
Pratt, Shannon. Valuing a Business: The Analysis & Appraisal of Closely Held Companies.
Pratt, Stanley, jt. auth. see Venture Capital Editors.
Pratt, William A., jt. auth. see Jennison, Keith.
Prausnitz, Frederick. Score & Podium: A Complete Guide to Conducting.
Prausnitz, John M., jt. auth. see Reid, Robert C.
Pray, Lawrence M. & Evans, Richard. The Journey of a Diabetic.
Pray, Lawrence M. & Evans, Richard, III. Journey of a Diabetic.
Praz, Manrio. Studies in Seventeenth Century Imagery.
Praz, Mario. Mnemosyne: The Parallel Between Literature & the Visual Arts.
--On Neoclassicism. Davidson, Angus, tr. from Ital.
Prazak, Milos. Language & Logic.
Pre Test Service, Inc. Pharmacology: Pretest Self-Assessment & Review.
Pre Test Services, Inc. & Tilton, Richard C. Microbiology: PreTest Self-Assessment & Review.
Prebble, John. John Prebble's Scotland.
Pree, Max De see De Pree, Max.
Preece, Ann. Manual for Histologic Technicians.
Preece, C. M., jt. ed. see Clayton, C. R.
Preece, Carolyn M., ed. see Annual Meeting of the Materials Research Society Staff.
Preece, Charles O. Teaching Without Tears: The Classroom Teachers Survival Book.
Pregeant, Russell. Christology Beyond Dogma: Matthew's Christ in Process Hermeneutic. Beardslee, William A. & Via, Dan O., Jr., eds.
Preger, Elfriede. Ancient Egypt: A Survey.
Pregosin, Ann. How Not to Kill Your Houseplants: The Foolproof Guide to Lush, Healthy Plants.
Pregosin, P. S., jt. auth. see Mullen, K.
Preiser, Wolfgang F., ed. Facility Programming.
Preiskel, Harold W. Precision Attachments in Prosthodontics: Overdentures & Telescopic Prostheses.
Preiss, Byron & Stout, William. The Little Blue Brontosaurus.
Prem, Hanns J., jt. ed. see Harvey, H. R.
Premack, Ann J., jt. auth. see Premack, David.
Premack, David & Premack, Ann J. The Mind of an Ape.
Premier Publishers, Inc. Staff. How to Prepare Your Own Mail Order Catalog (Without Merchandise & for Pennies)
Preminger, Erik L. Gypsy & Me: At Home & on the Road with Gypsy Rose Lee.
Prempeh, Albert K., jt. auth. see Courlander, Harold.
Prendergast, Alan. The Poison Tree: A True Story of Family Violence & Revenge.
Prendergast, Curtis & Colvin, Geoffrey. The World of Time Inc. Nineteen Sixty to Nineteen Eighty.
Prendergast, Maurice. Maurice Prendergast Water-Color Sketchbook: 1899.
Prendergast, Terrance, tr. see Leon-Dufour, Xavier.
Prendergast, Terrence, tr. see Leon-Dufour, Xavier.
Prendergast, William J. The Maqamat of Badi Al-Zaman Al-Hamadhani.
Prenter, Regin. Luther's Theology of the Cross. Anderson, Charles S., ed.
Prentice, C., jt. auth. see Serneri, Neri G. G.
Prentice-Hall Editorial Staff. Questions & Answers on the Pension & Profit Sharing Provisions of the New Tax Law: With an Explanation of the Retirement Plan Provisions of TEFRA.
Prentice-Hall Editorial Staff, ed. Legal Secretary's Encyclopedic Dictionary. DeVries, Mary A.
Prentice, Robin, compiled by. The National Trust for Scotland Guide.
Prentice, William E., jt. auth. see Bucher, Charles A.
Prentis, Malcolm D. The Scots in Australia: A Study of New South Wales, Victoria & Queensland, 1788-1900.
Prentiss, Joseph, jt. auth. see Donovan, Arthur.
Prentiss, Stan. Satellite Communications.
Preobrazhensky, V. & Krivosheyev, V. Recreational Geography of the U. S. S. R.
Presbie, Robert J. & Brown, Paul L. Physical Education: The Behavior Modification Approach.
Presbrey, Frank S. History & Development of Advertising.
Prescod, Horace J. The Hand of the Potter.
Prescott, Carol S. & Smith, Marion H. Our Needs.
Prescott, Carol S., jt. auth. see Smith, Marion H.
Prescott, Casey. The Asset in Black.
--Asset in Black.
Prescott, Ellen G., jt. auth. see Prescott, Lawrence M.
Prescott, H. F. The Man on a Donkey.
Prescott, J. R. Maritime Jurisdiction in Southeast Asia: A Commentary & Map.
Prescott, L. F. & Gibaldi, M., eds. Handbook of Clinical Pharmacokinetics.
Prescott, L. F. & Nimmo, W. S., eds. Rate Control in Drug Therapy.
Prescott, Lawrence M. & Prescott, Ellen G. Curry Every Sunday: An Asian Cookbook for Western Palates.
Prescott, Peter. Child Savers.
Prescott, Peter S. Never in Doubt: Critical Essays on American Books, 1972-1985.
Prescott, William H. History of the Conquest of Mexico. Gardiner, C. Harvey, ed.
President's Commission for a National Agenda: Panel on Policies & Prospects for Metropolitan & Nonmetropolitan America. Urban America in the Eighties: Perspectives & Prospects. Hicks, Donald, ed.
President's Commission on National Goals. Goals for Americans.
Presley, Bruce. Guide to Programming in Applesoft.
--Guide to Programming in Applesoft.
Presley, John & Dodd, William. Breakthrough: From Reading to Writing.
Press, Charles, jt. auth. see Adrian, Charles R.
Press, Gerald A. The Development of the Idea of History in Antiquity.
Press, Margaret L. Chemehuevi: A Grammar & Lexicon.
Pressat, Roland & Wilson, Christopher, eds. The Dictionary of Demography.
Pressberger, Emeric, jt. auth. see Powell, Michael.
Presseau, Jack R. Techniques: Creative Designs for Teaching.
Presseisen, Barbara Z. Thinking Skills: Research & Practice.
Presser, Harriet B. Sterilization & Fertility Decline in Puerto Rico.
Presser, Janice. Inspiring Parenthood.
Pressland, David. The Art of the Tin Toy.
Pressman, Abraham I. Switching & Linear Power Supply, Power Converter Design.
Pressman, Abraham I., jt. auth. see Raytheon Company Staff.
Pressman, David. Patent It Yourself. Elias, Stephen, ed.
Pressman, Hope H. A New Resource for Welfare Reform: The Poor Themselves.
Pressman, Maurice J. Workmen's Compensation in Maryland.
Pressman, Thelma. The Great Microwave Dessert Cookbook.
--Microwave Cooking: Meals in Minutes. Lawrence, Betsy, ed.
Presson, Hazel. Student Journalist & Interviewing.
--The Student Journalist & Layout.
--The Student Journalist & Twenty-One Keys to News Reporting.
Pressouyre, G. M., jt. ed. see Interrante, C. G.
Prest, A. R. & Barr, N. A. Public Finance: In Theory & Practice.
Prestayko, A. W., jt. ed. see Crooke, S. T.
Prestayko, A. W., et al, eds. Nitrosourea: Current Status & New Development.
Prestayko, Archie W., jt. auth. see Crooke, Stanley T.
Prestayko, Archie W., jt. ed. see Crooke, Stanley T.
Prestera, Hector, jt. auth. see Kurtz, Ron.
Presthus, Robert. Public Administration.
Preston, A., tr. see Chinal, J.
Preston, Antony. Warships of the World.
Preston, C. Iterates of Maps on an Interval.
--Random Fields.
--Trilogy of Christmas Plays for Children.
Preston, Charles. Acrostics for the Connoisseur.
--Dow Jones Crosswords for the Serious.
--Dow Jones-Irwin Crosswords for the Serious.
--Dow Jones-Irwin Crosswords for the Serious.
--Dow Jones-Irwin Crosswords for the Serious.
--Dow Jones-Irwin Crosswords for the Serious.
--Dow Jones-Irwin Crosswords for the Serious.
Preston, Charles, ed. Crosswords for the Connoisseur.
Preston, Daniel D. The Life & Work of the Minister.
Preston, George R., Jr. Thomas Wolfe: A Bibliography.
Preston, Hayter, jt. auth. see Brangwyn, Frank.
Preston, P. W. New Trends in Development Theory.
Preston, Paul. Communication for Managers.
--The Spanish Civil War: 1936-1939.
Preston, Ralph C., ed. Social Studies in the Elementary School.
Preston, Raymond. Chaucer.
Preston, Richard A. The Squat Pyramid: Canadian Studies in the United States.
Preston, Richard A., ed. For Friends at Home: A Scottish Emigrant's Letters from Canada, California, & the Cariboo, 1844-1864.
--Perspectives on Revolution & Evolution.
Preston, Richard J., Jr. Rocky Mountain Trees.
--Rocky Mountain Trees: A Handbook of the Native Species, with Plates & Distribution Maps.
Preston, Robert L. The Plot to Replace the Constitution.
--Wake-up America.
Preston, Seaton T., Jr. A Guide to the Analysis of Fatty Acids & Their Esters by Gas Chromatography.
--A Guide to the Analysis of Hydro-Carbons by Gas Chromatography.
Preston, Seaton T., Jr. & Pankratz, Ronald. A Guide to the Analysis of Alcohols by Gas Chromatography.
Preston, Seaton T., Jr. & Pankratz, Ronald E. A Guide to the Analysis of Ketones & Aldehydes by Gas Chromatography.
Preston, Seaton T., Jr. & Pankratz, Ronald. A Guide to the Analysis of Phenols by Gas Chromatography.
Preston, Thomas A. The Clay Pedestal: A Re-examination of the Doctor-Patient Relationship.
Preston-Dunlop, Valerie. Practical Kinetography Laban.
Prestopino, Chris J. Introduction to Estate Planning.
Prestressed Concrete Institute Staff. Factory Cast Prestressed Concrete: The Fire Fighter.
PreTest Editors. PreTest for Physicians Preparing for the American Board of Internal Medicine Certifying Examination.
Pretest Service Inc. Pathology: PreTest Self-Assessment & Review. Duray, Paul, ed.
PreTest Service Inc. & April, Ernest W. Anatomy: PreTest Self-Assessment & Review.
PreTest Service, Inc. & Chlapowski, F. Biochemistry: PreTest Self-Assessment & Review.
PreTest Service, Inc. Staff. Anatomy: PreTest Self-Assessment & Review.
--Biochemistry: PreTest Self-Assessment & Review.
--Harrison's Principles of Internal Medicine Patient Management Problems: PreTest Self-Assessment & Review. Bollet, A. J., ed.
--Microbiology: PreTest Self-Assessment & Review.
--Pediatrics: PreTest, Self-Assessment & Review.
--Physiology: PreTest Self-Assessment & Review. Dise, Craig A., ed.

--Psychiatry: PreTest Self-Assessment & Review. Nelson, J. Craig, ed.
PreTest Service, Inc. Staff & Dwyer, J. M. Medicine: Pre-Test Self-Assessment & Review.
PreTest Service, Inc. Staff & Greenfeld, D. Psychiatry: Pre-test Self-Assessment & Review.
PreTest Service, Inc. Staff, et al. Pharmacology: PreTest Self-Assessment & Review. Barbieri, Edward J. & DiGregorio, G. John, eds.
--Epidemiology & Public Health: PreTest Self-Assessment & Review.
Pretest Services Inc. & Evans, M. I. Obstetrics & Gynecology: PreTest Self-Assessment & Review.
Pretest Services, Inc., jt. auth. see Hurst, J. Willis.
Pretest Services, Inc. Staff, jt. auth. see Hurst, J. Willis.
PreTest Services, Inc Staff, et al. Surgery: PreTest Self-Assessment & Review.
Pretty, Ronald T., ed. Jane's Weapon System, 1982-1983.
--Jane's Weapon Systems, 1983-1984.
--Jane's Weapon Systems 1984-85.
--Jane's Weapon Systems, 1985-1986.
--Jane's Weapon Systems 1986-87.
Prettyman, Barrett, Jr. Death & the Supreme Court.
Preus, Christian, tr. see Von Hofmann, J. C.
Preus, David W. Go with the Gospel.
Preus, Herman A. A Theology to Live By.
Preus, Robert. Getting into the Theology of Concord.
Preusch, Deb, jt. auth. see Barry, Tom.
Preuss, Anne M., ed. see Harper, Prudence O. & Meyers, Pieter.
Preuss, Paul. Arthur C. Clarke's Venus Prime, Vol. 2: Maelstrom.
Preveden, Francis R. History of the Croatian People.
Prevention Magazine, ed. The Medical Care Yearbook.
Prevention Magazine Editors. The Complete Book of Vitamins. Gootlieb, William, ed.
Prevention Magazine Editors & Faelten, Sharon. Complete Book of Minerals for Health.
Prevert, Jacques. Choses et Autres.
--Fatras.
--Histoires.
--Paroles.
--La Pluie et le Beau Temps.
--Spectacle.
Prevert, Jacques & Pozner, Andre. Hebdromdaires.
Previts, Gary J. & Merino, Barabara D. A History of Accounting in America: An Historical Interpretation of the Cultural Significance of Accounting.
Prevo, Helen. Work for Everyone.
Prevo, Helen R. Family Life: Book One.
--Family Life: Book Two.
Prewit-Parker, Jolene. Forbidden Dreams.
Prez, Caroline S. De see De Prez, Caroline S. & De Prez, Richard J.
Prez, Richard J. De see De Prez, Caroline S. & De Prez, Richard J.
Pribble, Wayne I., jt. ed. see DuBois, J. Harry.
Pribram, Alfred F. Austria-Hungary & Great Britain, 1908-1914.
Pribram, Karl & Braodbent, Donald, eds. Biology of Memory.
Pribram, Karl H., jt. ed. see Isaacson, Robert L.
Price, A. Biological Hazards: The Hidden Threat.
Price, Alfred. Instruments of Darkness: The History of Electronic Warfare.
--Luftwaffe Handbook.
--The Spitfire Story.
Price, Alfred, jt. auth. see Ethell, Jeffrey.
Price, Anne, jt. auth. see Neifert, Marianne.
Price, Anthony. Other Paths to Glory.
Price, Brick. Sailboat Auxiliary Engine Maintenance: Atomic, Chrysler, Ford, Perkins, Pisces, Volvo-Penta, Westerbeke, Yanmar. Robinson, Jeff, ed.
Price, Carl E. Through Other Eyes: Vivid Narratives of Some of the Bible's Most Notable Characters.
--Writings in the Dust.
Price, Charles C., ed. Synthesis of Life.
Price, Charles P., jt. auth. see MacRae, George W.
Price, Cheryl A. Nineteenth Century Government Publications: An Historical Guide.
Price, D. & Williams, J. E. Time of Flight Mass Spectrometer.
Price, D. & Todd, J. F., eds. Dynamic Mass Spectrometry.
Price, D. & Williams, J. E., eds. Dynamic Mass Spectrometry.
Price, David. Introduction to Ada.
--Pascal: A Considerate Approach.
Price, E. M., jt. auth. see Buckingham, H.
Price, Edward R., ed. see White, Donald R.
Price, Eugenia. No Pat Answers.
--A Woman's Choice: Living Through Your Problems.
Price, George M. Evolutionary Geology & the New Catastrophism.
Price, Glanville, tr. see Leroy, Maurice.
Price, Hugh D. The Negro & Southern Politics: A Chapter of Florida History.
Price, J., jt. auth. see Flanders, H.
Price, James, jt. auth. see Price, William.
Price, James H., jt. auth. see Steen, Edwin B.
Price, James L., jt. auth. see Hall, Thor.
Price, Jane, ed. Teaching Handicapped Students in the English Classroom.
Price, John A. Native Studies: American & Canadian Indians.
Price, Jonathan. Thirty Days to More Powerful Writing.
--Thirty Days to More Powerful Writing.
Price, Julia S. The Off-Broadway Theater.
Price, Justin J., jt. auth. see Flanders, Harley.
Price, L. Sherley. Confucius & Christ.
Price, Mary L. Changing Stations: The Memoirs of an Air Force Wife.
Price, Mathew. My Daddy.
--My Mommy.
Price, Michael H., ed. The Development of the Secondary Curriculum.
Price, Michael P. The Amber Sword of World's End.
Price, Milburn, jt. auth. see Reynolds, William J.
Price, Molly. The Iris Book.
Price, Nancy. Sleeping with the Enemy.
Price, Nelson L. Called to Splendor.
--The Destruction of Death.
--Farewell to Fear.
Price, R. F. Reference Book of English Words & Phrases for Foreign Science Students.
Price, R. J. & Sugen, D. E., eds. Polar Geomorphology.
Price, Reynolds. Early Dark.
--A Generous Man.
--A Long & Happy Life.
--The Names & Faces of Heroes.
--A Palpable God.
--Permanent Errors.
--The Source of Light.
--Things Themselves: Essays & Scenes.
Price, Richard. Bloodbrothers.
--A Free Discussion of the Doctrine of Materialism and Philosophical Necessity, 1778. Wellek, Rene, ed.
--Ladies' Man.
--The Wanderers.
--The Wanderers.
Price, Richard H., et al. Principles of Psychology.
Price, Richard H., et al, eds. Prevention in Mental Health: Research, Policy, & Practice.
Price, Richard R. Abnormal Behavior: Perspectives in Conflict.
Price, Richards H. & Polister, Peter E., eds. Evaluation & Action in the Social Environment.
Price, Roger. The Economic Modernization of France Seventeen Thirty to Eighteen Eighty.
Price, Shirley S. Deviner et Appendre.
Price, Stephen & Shields, J. Webster. The Densa Quiz: The Official & Complete DQ Test of the International Densa Society.
Price, Susan. From Where I Stand.
Price, Susan M., jt. ed. see Dixon, W. M.
Price, Vincent Foreword by see King, Robert B.
Price, W. R., ed. see De Maupassant, Guy.
Price, Walter K. & Gillies, John. Antiochus: A Novel.
Price Waterhouse Staff. A Survey of Financial Reporting & Accounting Developments in the Hospital Industry.
Price, William & Price, James. Central Heating & Air Conditioning Repair Guide.
Price, William F., jt. auth. see Uren, John.
Price, William R., ed. see De Maupassant, Guy De.
Price, Wilson T. Data Processing: The Fundamentals.
--Elements of BASIC FORTRAN IV Programming.
--Elements of BASIC Plus Programming.
Price, Wilson T. & Miller, M. Elements of Data Processing Mathematics.
Prichard, H. A. Kant's Theory of Knowledge. Beck, Lewis W., ed.
Priddy, Frances. Challenge for Angel.
--Shell Beach Mystery.
Priddy, S., jt. auth. see Fiedorowicz, Z.
Pride, Kitty, jt. auth. see Pride, Leslie.
Pride, Leslie & Pride, Kitty. Vocabulario Chatino de Tataltepec.
Pride, William M. & Ferrell, O. C. Marketing: Basic Concepts & Decisions.
--Marketing: Basic Concepts & Decisions.
Pride, William M. & Perrell, O. C. Marketing: Basic Concepts & Decisions.
Pride, William M., jt. auth. see Robicheaux, Robert A.
Prideaux, John. The Irish Narrow Gauge Railway.
Pridham, Arthur. Notes on Romans.
Pridham, B. R., ed. Economy, Society & Culture in Contemporary Yemen.
Pridham, G. & Noakes, J., eds. Nazism 1919-1945: A Documentary Reader No. 3: Foreign Policy, War & Racial Extermination.
Pridham, G. J. Electronic Devices & Circuits.
--Solid State Circuits.
Pridham, G. J., jt. auth. see Abrahams, J. R.
Priebe, Duane A., tr. see Ebeling, Gerhard.
Priebe, Duane A., tr. see Pannenberg, Wolfhart.
Priesing, Elwood R. Music & the Dance.
Priest, Denis. Problems in Play: First Book of Bridge Problems.
--Problems in Play: Second Book of Bridge Problems.
Priest, R., ed. see Annual Conference for Psychosomatic Research Staff.
Priester, Gertrude. Who Are You, Lord?
Priester, Gertrude A. God Made Us a Good World.
--Let's Talk about God: Devotions for Families with Young Children.
Priestley, J. B. Charles Dickens & His World.
--Snoggle.
Priestley, Joseph. Disquisitions Relating Matter & Spirit. Wellek, Rene, ed. Bd. with The Doctrine of Philosophical Necessity Illustrated: Being an Appendix to the Disquestions Relating to Matter & Spirit. Garland Pub.
Priestley, Philip & McGuire, James. Learning to Help: Basic Skills Exercises.
Priestley, Philip, et al. Social Skills & Personal Problem Solving: A Handbook of Methods.
--Social Skills in Prison & the Community: Problem-Solving for Offenders.
Prieve, E. Arthur, ed. Survey of Arts Administration Training: 1985-86.
--Survey of Arts Administration Training: 1987-88.
Prigogine, I. & Rice, Stuart A. Advances in Chemical Physics.
Prigogine, I., et al, eds. Advances in Chemical Physics. Incl. Vol. 19; Vol. 20; Vol. 22; Vol. 23; Vol. 24; Vol. 25. Krieger.
--Advances in Chemical Physics.
--Advances in Chemical Physics.
Prigozy, Ruth, jt. auth. see Thune, Ensaf.
Priklonsky, Alexander. Blessed Athanasia.
Prilepko, A. I. Problems in High-School Mathematics.
Priletta, Mario. Vortex Universe.
Prilezhaeva, Maria. La Vida De Lenin.
Prillaman, Douglas & Abbott, John. Educational Diagnosis & Prescriptive Teaching: A Practical Approach to Special Education in the Least Restrictive Environment.
Primack, Martin L., jt. auth. see Willis, James F.
Primack, Robert B., ed. Issues in Foundations of Education.
Primm, James N. Lion of the Valley: Saint Louis, Missouri.
Primrose, S. B. & Dimmock, N. J. Introduction to Modern Virology.
Prince, Alison. The Red Jaguar.
--The Sinister Airfield.
Prince, David, jt. auth. see Hofmeister, Richard.
Prince, Derek. Eternal Judgment.
--Foundation for Faith.
--From Jordan to Pentecost.
--Laying on of Hands.
--Purposes of Pentecost.
--Repent & Believe.
--Resurrection of the Dead.
Prince, Francine. The Dieter's Gourmet Cookbook.
Prince, Francine & Prince, Harold. Feed Your Kids Bright.
Prince, Gary M. Vanya & the Clay Queen.
Prince, H. H. & D'Itri, F. M. Coastal Wetlands.
Prince, Harold, jt. auth. see Prince, Francine.
Prince, Howard T. Leadership in Organizations.
Prince, L. M. & Sears, D. F., eds. Biological Horizons in Surface Science.
Prince, Marjorie M. The Cheese Stands Alone.
--The Cheese Stands Alone.
Prince, Mary. The History of Mary Prince: Written by Herself.
Prince, Robert M. The Legacy of the Holocaust: Psychohistorical Themes in the Second Generation. Nathan, Peter E., ed.
Prince, S. D. The Software Marketplace: Where to Sell What You Program.
Prince, Vivien S. Kenya: The Years of Change.
Princeton University Art Museum Staff. Princeton Alumni Collections: Works on Paper.
Princeton University, Office of Population Research Staff. Population Index Bibliography: Cumulated 1969 to 1981.
Princeton University Office of Population Research Staff. Population Index Bibliography Cumulated 1935-1968 by Authors & Geographical Areas.
Princeton University Staff. Dictionary Catalog of the Princeton University Plasma Physics Laboratory Library.
--Dictionary Catalog of the Princeton University Plasma Physics Laboratory Library, First Supplement.
Princeton Water Resources Group Staff, jt. auth. see Wood, Eric F.
Principal, Victoria. The Beauty Principal: The Beauty Program for Life.
--The Body Principal: The Exercise Program for Life.
Prindle, David F. Petroleum Politics & the Texas Railroad Commission.
Pring, Martin J. The Conti Commodity Futures Handbook.
--How to Forecast Interest Rates: A Guide to Profits for Consumers, Managers & Investors.
--Technical Analysis Explained: An Illustrated Guide for the Investor.
Pring, Richard. Personal & Social Education in the Curriculum.
Pringle, Ian, jt. ed. see Freedman, Ariva.
Pringle, Laurence. The Controversial Coyote.
--Dinosaurs & People: Fossils, Facts & Fantasies.
--Dinosaurs & Their World.
--The Hidden World: Life under a Rock.
--Lives at Stake: The Science & Politics of Environmental Health.
--Only Earth We Have.
Pringle, Peter & Arkin, William. S. I. O. P.-The Secret U. S. Plan for Nuclear War.
Pringle, R., tr. see Steuber, U.
Pringle, Will. Look to the Harbour.
Prins, H. A. & Whyte, M. B. Social Work & Medical Practice.
Prins, Herschel. Criminal Behavior: An Introduction to Criminology & the Penal System.
Prins, Willy. Die Himmels Leiter.
Printz-Pahlson, Ulla, tr. from Swedish. A Dreamed Life.
Printz-Pohlson, Goran, tr. see Ostergren, Jan.
Prinz, Johannes. John Wilmot, Earl of Rochester: His Life & Writings.
Prinzhorn, H. Artistry of the Mentally Ill. Von Brockdorff, E., tr. from Ger.
Priolo, Pauline. Bravo Marco.
Prior, Allan. A Cast of Stars.
Prior, Richard. Deer Watch.
Prior, Robin. Churchill's "World Crisis" As History.
Prising, Robin. Manila Goodbye.
Pritam, Amrita. A Line in Water. Gorowara, Krishna, tr. from Punjabi.
Pritchard, A. J., jt. auth. see Curtain, R. F.
Pritchard, A. J., jt. ed. see Curtain, Ruth.
Pritchard, Alan. Alchemy: A Bibliography of English Language Writings.
Pritchard, Anthony. Racing Sports Car.
Pritchard, D. Brine. The Right Way to Play Chess.
Pritchard, David. Puzzles for Geniuses.
--Puzzles for Geniuses.
Pritchard, J. A., ed. see National Computing Centre, Ltd. Staff.
Pritchard, Jack. View from a Long Chair: The Memoirs of Jack Pritchard.
Pritchard, James B. Hebrew Inscriptions & Stamps from Gibeon.
Pritchard, John M. Africa: A Study Geography for Advanced Students.
Pritchard, M. E. A Short Dictionary of Weaving.
Pritchard, Robert E. & Hindelang, Thomas J. The Strategic Evaluation & Management of Capital Expenditures.
Pritchett, Elaine. Student Journalist & the Newsmagazine Format.
Pritchett, S. Travis & Stinton, John E. Individual Annuities As a Source of Retirement Income.
Pritchett, V. S. The Gentle Barbarian: The Life & Work of Turgenev.
--The Turn of the Years.
Pritikin, Nathan. The Pritikin Promise: Twenty-Eight Days to a Longer, Healthier Life.
Pritikin, Robert C. Christ Was an Ad Man: The Amazing New Testament in Advertising.
Pritsker, A. Alan. The Gasp IV Simulation Language.
Pritt, Ann F. How to Make an L.D.S. Quiet Book.
Pritulenko, P. V. Plane Figures & Sections: How to Construct Them Given Specific Conditions.
Private Eye Magazine Staff. Bumper Book of Covers.
--The Diaries of Auberon Waugh: A Turbulent Decade 1976-1985.
Private Eye "Pseud Corner" Column Staff. The Oxford Book of Pseuds.
Privorotskii, I. Thermodynamic Theory of Domain Structures.
Prizzi, Elaine & Hoffman, Jeanne. Diction Harry's Magical, Marvelous, Motivational Dictionary Kit.
--I. M. A. Booksnoop's Amazing, Astounding, Astonishing Library Kit.
Proano, Mario, tr. see Twitchell, Paul.
Proano, Mario, et al, trs. see Twitchell, Paul.
Probability Methods in Analysis Symposium Staff. Proceedings of the Probability Methods in Analysis Symposium, Loutraki, Greece, 1966.
Probert, H. A., intro. by. The Rise & Fall of the German Air Force 1933-1945.
Probert, S. D. & Hub, D. R. Thermal Insulation.
Probstein, R. F. & Hicks, R. E. Synthetic Fuels.
Probstein, Ronald F., ed. see Chernyi, G. G.
Proceedings of the International Conference, Los Angeles, 1972, et al. Few Particle Problems in the Nuclear Interaction. Moszkowski, Steven A. & Haddock, Roy P., eds.
Prochnow, Dave. One-Hundred One Experiments for the Young Scientist.
Prochnow, Dave, jt. auth. see Knott, Julie.

Prockter, Noel J. Simple Propagation.
Procter, William, jt. auth. see Gallup, George, Jr.
Proctor, jt. auth. see Thompson.
Proctor, George, jt. ed. see Clarke, Arthur C.
Proctor, Percy M. Star Myths & Stories: From Andromeda to Virgo.
Proctor, Raja. Waiting for Surabiel.
Proctor, Richard W. The Barber's Shop.
Proctor, William, jt. auth. see Burkett, Larry.
Proctor, William, jt. auth. see Robertson, Pat.
Proddow, Mary P., jt. auth. see Ferreira, T. Gomes.
Prodham, B. The Board & Financial Management.
Proehl, Stephen. Over New York: An Aerial View.
Proehl, Steven. Over Cape Cod & the Islands.
Proenneke, Richard, jt. auth. see Keith, Sam.
Professional Associates Staff, et al. Recruiting, Marketing, & Retention in Institutions of Higher Education.
Professional Education Systems Staff. Complying with Consumer Credit Regulations: A Creditor's Guide.
Professional Publications Staff. Handbook of Construction Resources & Support Services. MacDonald, Joseph A., ed.
Professional Rodeo Cowboys Association Staff. Official Professional Rodeo Guide, 1989.
Proffitt, Nicholas. Gardens of Stone.
Progoff, Ira. Depth Psychology & Modern Man.
Programa de Proyecto Frontera Staff. Ya Lo Leo. Quinones, Nathan, ed.
Programmed Instruction Staff. Self Study Books in Electrical & Semiconductor Engineering: PI-16 Three-Phase Power & Its Measurements.
Progressive Grocer Magazine Staff. Grocery Retailing in the Eighties.
Prohaska, Ray. A Basic Course in Design.
Project on Redefining the Meaning & Purpose of Baccalaureate Degrees Staff. A Search for Quality & Coherence in Baccalaureate Education.
Project SPAN Staff. The Current State of Social Studies: A Report of Project SPAN.
--The Future of Social Studies: A Report & Summary of Project SPAN.
--Working Papers from Project SPAN.
Prokes, J. Hydraulic Mechanisms in Automation.
Prokhorov, A. N. & Ursu, I., eds. Trends in Quantum Electronics.
Prokofiev, Sergei. Peter & the Wolf.
--Peter & the Wolf.
Prokofieva, S. I Won't Apologize.
--Raggity & the Cloud.
Prokop, Phyllis. The Sword & the Sundial.
Prokushev, Y. Sergei Yesenin: The Man, the Verse, the Age.
Prone, Terry. Write & Get Paid for It.
Pronin, Barbara. Syndrome.
Pronin, Monica, ed. Toxic Substance Sourcebook II.
Pronin, Monica, jt. ed. see Ross, Steven.
Pronko, Leonard C. Eugene Labiche & Georges Feydeau.
Pronzini, Bill. The Arbor House Necropolis -- Voodoo! Mummy! Ghoul!
--Creature! A Chrestomathy of "Monstery"
--Masques.
--Mummy! A Chrestomathy of Crypt-ology.
--Quincannon.
--Specter! A Chrestomathy of "Spookery"
--Voodoo!
--Werewolf!
Pronzini, Bill & Malzberg, Barry. Acts of Mercy.
Pronzini, Bill, jt. auth. see Muller, Marcia.
Pronzini, Bill, ed. The Arbor House Treasure of Detective & Mystery Stories from the Great Pulps.
--The Arbor House Treasury of Great Western Stories. Greenberg, Martin H.
--Midnight Specials.
Pronzini, Bill & Greenberg, Martin H., eds. The Best Western Stories of Lewis B. Patten.
--The Best Western Stories of Steve Frazee.
Pronzini, Bill & Malzberg, Barry, eds. Bug-Eyed Monsters.
Pronzini, Bill & Malzberg, Barry N., eds. The Arbor House Treasury of Mystery & Suspense.
Pronzini, Bill, jt. ed. see Muller, Marcia.
Pronzini, Bill, ed. see Overholser, Wayne D.
Pronzini, Bill, et al. Murder in the First Reel.
Pronzini, Bill, et al, eds. The Arbor House Treasury of Horror & the Supernatural.
--Mystery in the Mainstream: Suspense Stories by Classic Writers.
Prophet, Elizabeth, jt. auth. see Prophet, Mark.
Prophet, Elizabeth, ed. see Kuthumi, et al.
Prophet, Mark & Prophet, Elizabeth. My Soul Doth Magnify the Lord!
Prophet, Mark, ed. see Kuthumi, et al.
Proppe, Karl H., jt. auth. see Suit, Herman D.
Propper, Alice M. Prison Homosexuality: Myth & Reality.
Propst, Nell. Forgotten People: A History of the South Platte Trail.
ProQuest Staff, jt. auth. see Expert Systems Staff.
Prose, Francine. Household Saints.
--Judas the Pious.
Prose, Suzanne. The History of Education in Tolland, Connecticut.
Proshansky, H. M., et al. Environmental Psychology: People & Their Physical Settings.
Proskauer, Julien J. Spook Crooks: Exposing the Secrets of the Propheteers Who Conduct Our Wickedest Industry.
Proskine, Alec. Adirondack Canoe Waters: South & West Flow.
Prosser, Franklin P., jt. auth. see Winkel, David E.
Prosser, Lawrence. A Model for Planning & Managing National Parks.
Prosser, Michael H. The Cultural Dialogue: An Introduction to Intercultural Communication.
Prostano, Emanuel T. & Prostano, Joyce S. The School Library Media Center.
Prostano, Joyce S., jt. auth. see Prostano, Emanuel T.
Prothero, Mansell & Chapman, Murray, eds. Circulation in Third World Countries.
Protherough, Robert. Encouraging Writing.
Prothro, James W., jt. auth. see Matthews, Donald R.
Proud, Keith & Foyster, John. The Pheasant Book.
Proudfoot, A. T. Diagnosis & Management of Acute Poisoning.
Proudfoot, Alice B., ed. Patrick: Sixteen Centuries with Ireland's Patron Saint.
Proudhon, Pierre-Joseph. Guerre et la Paix.
Proudman, Robert & Rajala, Reuben. AMC Field Guide to Trail Building & Maintenance.
Proulx, Annie & Nichols, Lew. Sweet & Hard Cider: Making It, Using It, & Enjoying It.
Proulx, Earl. Yankee Magazine's Home Fix-It Book. Walz, Lila, ed.
Proulx, G. J. Dictionnaire d'Electronique et Tele-Communication: Anglais-Francais.
Proulx, Gerard J. Standard Dictionary of Meteorological Sciences: English-French - French-English.
Prouse, Derek, tr. see Ionesco, Eugene.
Prouse, G. & Amerio, L. Almost-Periodic Functions & Functional Equations.
Proust, Marcel. Contre Sainte-Beuve: Avec: Nouveaux Melanges 1954.
--Le Cote de Guermantes: A la Recherche Du Temps Perdu. Avec: Sodome et Gomorrhe.
--Lettre a la N. R. F.
--Oeuvres. Incl. Vols. 1-3. A la Recherche du Temps Perdu. Ferre & Clarac, eds.; Vol. 4. Jean Santeuil et Les Plaisirs et les Jours. Sandre & Clarac, eds.; Vol. 5. Contre Sainte-Beuve & Pastiches et Melanges. Sandre & Clarac, eds.. Schoenhof.
Prout, B. J. An Outline of Clinical Diagnosis.
Prout, Ebenezer. Double Counterpoint & Canon.
Prouty, R. W., jt. auth. see Rotor & Wing International Staff.
Provan, J. W., ed. see CISM (International Center for Mechanical Sciences), Department of Mechanics of Solids Staff.
Provence, Sally A., jt. ed. see Solnit, Albert J.
Providence Medical Center Staff. Manual for the Department of Social Service.
Provincial Archives Staff & Victoria, British Columbia. Dictionary Catalogue of the Library of the Provincial Archives of British Columbia.
Provine, William. Origins of Theoretical Population Genetics.
Provis, D. G., ed. Waves on Water of Variable Depth.
Provost, C. Antonio. The Sexual Revolution.
Provost, Gary. The Pork Chop War.
Provost, Rhonda, jt. auth. see Benyo, Richard.
Provost, Thomas T. & Farmer, Evan R. Current Therapy in Dermatology 1985-1986.
Prowse, Philip see Milne, John.
Proxmire, William. The Fleecing of America.
Prpic, G. J. A Century of World Communism: Selective Chronological Outline.
Prudden, Bonnie. Bonnie Prudden's after Fifty Fitness Guide.
--Pain Erasure: The Bonnie Prudden Way.
--Pain Erasure the Bonnie Prudden Way.
Prudden, Suzy. See How They Run: Suzy Prudden's Running Book for Kids.
Prudden, Suzy & Sussman, Jeffrey. Suzy Prudden's I Can Exercise Anywhere Book.
Prudential Insurance Company of America Staff. Health Insurance Fundamentals: To Prepare for the Health Insurance License Examination.
--Life Insurance Fundamentals: To Prepare for the Life Insurance Agents' License Examination.
Prue, J. E. Ionic Equilibria.
Pruett, Jakie L. & Cole, Everett B. Goliad Massacre: A Tragedy of Texas Revolution.
Pruitt, Basil A., jt. auth. see Salisbury, Roger E.
Pruitt, Bettye, ed. The Massachusetts Tax Valuation List of, 1171.
Pruitt, Fred. A Great Sacrifice.
Pruner, Francis, jt. auth. see Courteline, Georges.
Prunet, Antoine. The Ferrari Legend: Sports Cars & Prototypes.
Prunkl, Peter R. The Psychological Testing Workbook.
Prusek, Jaroslav. The Lyrical & the Epic: Studies of Modern Chinese Literature. Lee, Leo Ou-fan, ed.
Prusiner, Stanley & Stadtman, Earl R., eds. The Enzymes of Glutamine Metabolism.
Prusiner, Stanley B. & Hadlow, William J., eds. Slow Transmissible Diseases of the Nervous System: Clinical, Epidemiological, Genetic & Pathological Aspects of the Spongiform Encephalopathie.
--Slow Transmissible Diseases of the Nervous System: Pathogenesis, Immunology, Virology & Molecular Biology of the Spongiform Encephalopathies.
Prussner, Frederick, tr. see Barth, Markus.
Pruuden, Salme. A Catalogue of Books & Periodicals on Estonia in the British Library Reference Division.
Pruyser, Paul. Diagnosis & the Difference It Makes.
Pruzanski, W. & Keystone, E. C. Paraproteins in Disease: Investigation of Plasma Cell Dyscrasia.
Pryce-Jones, David. The Afternoon Sun.
--Cyril Connolly: Journal & Memoir.
--Paris in the Third Reich: A History of the German Occupation, 1940-1944.
Pryde, Lucy T., jt. auth. see Liska, Ken.
Pryde, Philip R. Nonconventional Energy Resources.
Pryor, Francis. Fengate.
Pryor, Karen. Don't Shoot the Dog!
--How to Teach Your Dog to Play Frisbee.
Pryor, T., ed. see Society of Manufacturing Engineers Staff.
Prytherch, R. J. Sources of Information in Librarianship & Information Science.
Prytherch, Ray. Harrod's Librarians' Glossary & Handbook. Harrod, L. M., ed.
--Sources of Information in Librarianship & Information Science: A Grafton Book.
Prywes, M., jt. ed. see Sela, M.
Przetak, Louis. Standard Details for Fire-Resistive Building Construction.
Ptacek, Paul H., et al. Index to Speech, Language & Hearing Journal Titles, 1954-1978.
Pual, Gerald, tr. see Mandel, Ernest, et al.
Public Archives Staff of Canada Ottawa. Catalogue of the National Map Collection.
--Catalogue of the Public Archives Library of Canada: Collection of Published Material with a Chronological List of Pamphlets.
Public Citizen Health Research Group Staff & Wolfe, Sidney M. Pills that Don't Work: A Consumer's & Doctor's Guide to 610 Prescription Drugs that Lack Evidence of Effectiveness.
Public Citizen Health Research Group Staff & Laws, Priscilla W. The X-Ray Information Book: A Consumers' Guide to Avoiding Unnecessary Medical & Dental X-Rays.
Public Management Institute Staff. Grants for the Child.
--Grantspro.
Public Securities Association Staff. Fundamentals of Municipal Bonds.
Public Service Satellite Consortium Staff. Teleguide: A Handbook for Video Teleconferencing.
Publications Committee, ASJA Staff, ed. Directory - American Society of Journalists & Authors, 1987.
Pucci, Pietro. The Violence of Pity in Euripides' Medea.
Pucciani, Oreste & Hamel, Jacqueline. Langue et Langue.
Puchala, Donald J., ed. see United Nations Association of the U. S. A. Staff.
Puck, Wolfgang. Wolfgang Puck's Modern French Cooking.
Puckett, Majorie. Shadow Quilting: A Leading Designer Introduces a Beautiful New Craft.
Puckett, Newbell N., compiled by. Popular Beliefs & Superstitions: A Compendium of American Folklore.
Pudovkin, V. I. Film Technique & Film Acting. Montagu, Ivor, ed. & tr.
--Mother.
Pugachev. Probability Theory & Mathematical Statistics. Sinitsyna, I. V., tr. Eykhoff, P., ed.
Pugachev, V. S. Theory of Random Functions.
Pugh, Emerson M. & Edgin, Ruth. Wyoming Scientist: Horses to Spaceships.
Pugh, G. J., jt. ed. see Dickinson, C. H.
Pugh, Griffith T. Guide to Research Writing.
Pugh, Kenneth. C Language for Programmers.
Pugh, Nathanael. Dating Tips. Wallace, Mary H., ed.
Pugh, Patricia. Educate, Agitate, Organize: One Hundred Years of Fabian Socialism.
Pugh, Thomas F., jt. auth. see Macmahon, Brian.
Pugh, Winfield S. War Medicine.
Pu Gill Gwon. The Dynamic Art of Breaking.
--Skill in Counterattacks.
Pugmire, M. C. Experiences in Music for Young Children.
Puhala, Bob. Guide to the Recommended Country Inns of the Midwest (Ohio, Indiana, Illinois, Missouri, Iowa, Minnesota, Wisconsin & Michigan)
Puig, Manuel. Betrayed by Rita Hayworth.
Puijk, Roel & Vaagland, Jorid. Notre Vin et Notre Patois.
Pujadas, Guillermo. Coronary Angiography.
Pujol, Juan & West, Nigel. Operation Garbo: The Personal Story of the Most Successful Double Agent of World War II.
Puleo, Nicole. Motorcycle Racing.
--Road Racing.
--Track Racing.
Pullan, Brian. The Jews of Europe & the Inquisition of Venice, 1550-1670.
Pullen, Rick D., jt. auth. see Overbeck, Wayne.
Pulleyn, Rob, ed. The Basketmaker's Art: Contemporary Baskets & Their Makers.
Pulliam, Tom & Carruth, Gorton, eds. The Complete Word Game Dictionary.
Pulliam, William E., et al. America Rediscovered. Incl. Its Economic Life; Its Foreign Affairs; Its People; Its Political Life. HM.
Pullias, Athens C. Sermons of Athens Clay Pullias. Thomas, J. D., ed.
Pulling, Edward. Challenge & the Fun of Teaching.
Pullman, B. & Bergman, E., eds. Quantum Aspects of Heterocyclic Compounds in Chemistry & Biochemistry: Proceedings.
Pullman, B., jt. ed. see Bergmann, E. D.
Pullman, B., ed. see Jerusalem Symposia on Quantum Chemistry & Biochemistry Staff.
Pullman, Bernard. Intermolecular Interactions: From Diatomics to Biopolymers.
Pullman, Bernard, ed. Electronic Aspects of Biochemistry: Proceedings.
--Frontiers in Physicochemical Biology.
--Molecular Associations in Biology.
Pullman, Bernard & Weissbluth, Mitchel, eds. Molecular Biophysics.
Pullman, Bernard, jt. ed. see Bergman, E. D.
Pulman, Jack. Collision.
Pulp & Paper Instrumentation Symposium Staff. Instrumentation in the Pulp & Paper Industry, Vol. 19: Proceedings of the Pulp & Paper Instrumentation Symposium.
--Instrumentation in the Pulp & Paper Industry, Vol. 18: Proceedings of the Pulp & Paper Instrumentation Symposium.
Pulparampil, John. Political Analysis: Shifting Trends & Questionable Assumptions.
Pultz, John. A Personal View: Photography in the Collection of Paul F. Walter.
Pulver, Jeffrey, ed. see Panum, Hortense.
Pun, L., et al. Integrated Automation Practice.
Punnett, R. M. British Government & Politics.
Punter, David. The Hidden Script: Writing & the Unconscious.
Punter, Ian. Projects & Designs in Woodwork.
Puntila, L. A. The Political History of Finland: 1809-1966.
Puotinen, C. J. Using the IBM-PC: WordStar.
Puppi, G., ed. Old & New Problems in Elementary Particles.
Purce, Jill. The Mystic Spiral: Journey of the Soul.
Purcell, Edwin J. Analytic Geometry.
Purcell, Edwin J. & Varberg, Dale E. Calculus with Analytic Geometry.
Purcell, Gary R. & Schlachter, Gail A. Reference Sources in Library & Information Services: A Guide to the Literature.
Purcell, H. J., jt. ed. see Rees, A. R.
Purcell, M. Papal Crusading Policy, Twelve Hundred Forty-Four to Twelve Hundred Ninety-One.
Purcell, W. R., Jr. Understanding a Company's Finances: A Graphic Approach.
Purcell, William L. An Introduction to Asian Music Nineteen Sixty Six: Asia Society Guides.
Purchase, Betty, jt. auth. see Purchase, Richard.
Purchase, Richard & Purchase, Betty. Let's Go Outdoors with Children: Administrative Guide for Grades 1-4.
Purdum, Jack. C Self-Study Guide.
Purdum, Jack & Leslie, Tim. C Standard Library.
Purdy, J. David. Dads Are Special, Too.
Purdy, James. The Candles of Your Eyes: Stories.
--In a Shallow Grave.
--In a Shallow Grave.
--In the Hollow of His Hand.
--The Mourners Below.
--Narrow Rooms.
--The Nephew.
Purdy, Strother B. The Hole in the Fabric: Science, Contemporary Literature, & Henry James.
Purdy, Virginia C., jt. ed. see Deutrich, Mabel E.
Puri, M. L., ed. Stochastic Processes & Related Topics: Proceedings, Vol. 1.
Puricelli, Luigi, jt. auth. see Cristini, Ermanno.
Purich, Donald J. Drinking & Driving: What to Do if Your'e Caught.
Purington, Chester H. I Walked Through the Valley of the Shadow of Alcoholism.
Puri Shashi, Lata. Legislative Elite in an Indian State: Rajasthan.
Purkis, Andrew, jt. auth. see Allen, Rosemary.
Purkis, H. J. Building Physics: Acoustics.
Purkiss, Gerri, jt. auth. see McNichols, Joan.

Authors

Purnell, Dick. Beating the Break-up Habit.
Purohit, R. K., jt. auth. see Sharma, B. L.
Purpel, David E. & Shapiro, Svi, eds. Schools & Meaning: Essays on the Moral Nature of Schooling.
Pursell, Garry G. Cost-Benefit Evaluation of LDC Industrial Sectors Which Have Foreign Ownership.
Pursell, John & Reese, N. Kayak Paddling Strokes.
Pursell, Margaret S. Boots the Kitten. Hammarberg, Dyan, tr. from Fr.
--A Look at Physical Handicaps.
--A Look at the Environment.
--Mandy the Monkey. Hammarberg, Dyan, tr. from Fr.
Pursell, Thomas F. The Burning Barn Mystery.
--The Mysterious Radio Code.
--The Mystery of Lost Beach.
--The Mystery of the Zebra Butterfly.
--The Prize Tomatoes Mystery.
Purser, B. H., ed. The Persian Gulf.
Purtscher, Nora. Rilke: Man & Poet.
Purucker, G. De see De Purucker, G.
Purver, et al. Business Law: Texts & Cases.
Purves, A. C., ed. Theodore Spencer: Selected Essays.
Purves, Alan, jt. auth. see National Council of Teachers of English Task Force on Measurement & Evaluation in the Study of English Staff.
Purves, William & Orians, Gordon. Life.
Puryear, Herbert B. Reflections on the Path.
--Sex & the Spiritual Path.
Pusch, Hans, tr. see Steiner, Rudolf.
Pusch, Ruth, tr. see Steiner, Rudolf.
Pushkarev, Boris S., et al. Urban Rail in America: An Exploration of Criteria for Fixed-Guideway Transit.
Pushkin, Aleksandr. Cuento de la Princesita Muerta y los Siete Paladines.
--Selections from Pushkin.
Pushkin, Aleksandr, et al. On Seashore Far, a Green Oak Tower.
Pushkin, Alexander. Captain's Daughter & Other Tales. Duddington, Natalie, tr.
Puterman, Martin L., ed. Dynamic Programming & Its Application.
Puth, Robert C. American Economic History.
Putman, Marc, jt. auth. see Engstrom, Robert E.
Putman, Robert. Early Sea Charts.
Putman, Stephen H. Integrated Urban Models.
Putnam, jt. auth. see Parry.
Putnam, Hilary. Meaning & the Moral Sciences.
--Meaning & the Moral Sciences.
Putnam, K Willis. O, Desert Dream!
Putnam, Katherine & Comiskey, Kate, eds. Encyclopedia for the TRS-80.
--Encyclopedia for the TRS-80.
--Encyclopedia for the TRS-80.
--Encyclopedia for the TRS-80.
Putnam, Katherine, ed. see Baird, Chuck, et al.
Putnam, Katherine, ed. see Blattner, John W., et al.
Putnam, Katherine, ed. see Blechman, Fred, et al.
Putnam, Katherine, ed. see Domuret, Allan J., et al.
Putnam, Lawrence H. Software Cost Estimating & Life-Cycle Control: Getting the Software Numbers.
Putnam, R. & Carlson, G. E. Architectural & Building Trades Dictionary.
Puto, Arben, jt. auth. see Pollo, Stefanaq.
Putt, A. Putt's Law & the Successful Technocrat.
Putte, S. C. Van Der see Van Der Putte, S. C.
Putterman, Jaydie & Lesur, Rosalynde. Police.
Putterman, Ron. To Find My Son.
Putyatin, E. V., jt. auth. see Vanikov, V. A.
Putz, George & Spectre, Peter, eds. Mariner's Catalog.
Putz, George & Spectre, Peter H., eds. The Mariner's Catalog.
Puyana De Palacios, Alicia. The Economic Integration among Unequal Partners: The Case of the Andean Group.
Puzo, Mario. The Godfather.
--The Sicilian.
Pye, David. Nature & Aesthetics of Design.
Pye, E. Kendall & Weetall, H. H., eds. Enzyme Engineering.
Pye, E. Kendall & Wingard, Lemuel B., eds. Enzyme Engineering.
Pye, Faye. Aspects of Jewish Prayer.
Pye, Lloyd. That Prosser Kid.
Pye, Michael, jt. ed. see Morgan, Robert.
Pyenson, Louis L. Fundamentals of Entomology & Plant Pathology.
--Plant Health Handbook.
Pyenson, Louis L. & Barke, Harvey E. Laboratory Manual for Entomology & Plant Pathology.
Pyfer, Jean, jt. auth. see Auxter, David.
Pyke, Magnus. Man & Food.
--Weird & Wonderful Science Facts.
Pyle, David W. Intelligence: An Introduction.
Pyle, Earl. How to Make a Million Dowsing & Drilling for Oil.
Pyle, H. Twilight Land.
Pyle, Ian. The Ada Programming Language.
Pyle, Robert M. Wintergreen: Rambles in a Ravaged Land.
Pyle, Vera. Current Medical Terminology.
Pyle, Wilf E., jt. auth. see Popowski, Bert.
Pyle, William W., et al. Initiation a la Compatibilite Financiere et Administrative.
Pyles, Thomas & Algeo, John. The Origins & Developments of the English Language.
Pym, Barbara. Crampton Hodnet.
--A Glass of Blessings.
--Jane & Prudence.
--Less Than Angels.
--No Fond Return of Love.
Pyman, Avril, ed. Alexander Blok: Selected Poems.
--Mikhail Bulgakov: Selected Works.
--Yevgeniy Shvarts: Three Plays.
Pyne, Stephen J. Dutton's Point.
Pynn, Ronald E. American Politics: Changing Expectations.
Pyron, Cherry & Silitch, Clarissa M., eds. The Forgotten Arts: Making Old-Fashioned Pickles, Relishes, Chutneys, Sauces & Catsups, Mincemeats, Beverages & Syrups.
Pyster, Arthur B. Compiler Design & Construction.
--Compiler Design & Construction.

Q

Qadir, Asghar, jt. ed. see Riazuddin.
QED Information Sciences, Inc. Staff. Multi-Vendor Data Communications Networks.
Qian, Wen-yuan. The Great Inertia: Scientific Stagnation in Traditional China.
Qifeng, Fu. Chinese Acrobatics Through the Ages. Caiwei, Ouyang & Stockwell, Rhoda, trs. from Chinese.
Qin, Zhong. Everydays Chinese: Selected Prose Readings.
Qing, Xia. Seven Clam Sisters.
Qingming, J., jt. ed. see Milliman, J. D.
Qi Wen. China: A General Survey.
Qizhong, Wang. The Golden Conch.
Quackenbush, Marcia & Sargent, Pamela. Teaching AIDS: A Resource Guide on Acquired Immune Deficiency Syndrome.
Quackenbush, Robert. Detective Mole.
--Don't You Dare Shoot That Bear! A Story of Theodore Roosevelt.
--Mark Twain? What Kind of a Name Is That? A Story of Samuel Langhorne Clemens.
--Piet Potter Returns.
--Piet Potter Strikes Again: Book 2.
--Piet Potter to the Rescue: Book 1.
--Piet Potter's First Case.
--Piet Potter's Hot Clue.
--Quit Pulling My Leg! A Story of Davy Crockett.
--Who Let Muddy Boots into the White House.
--Who Said There's No Man on the Moon? A Story of Jules Verne.
--Who Threw That Pie? The Birth of Movie Comedy. Pacini, Kathy, ed.
--Who's That Girl with the Gun? Story of Annie Oakley.
Quackenbush, Robert, ed. & illus. The Holiday Song Book.
Quaife, Milo M., ed. see Boller, Henry A.
Qualls, C. Brandon, et al, eds. The Prevention of Sexual Disorders: Issues & Approaches.
Quanbeck, Philip A. When God Speaks.
Quanbeck, Philip A., II, tr. see Gunkel, Hermann.
Quanbeck, Warren A. Search for Understanding: Lutheran Conversations with Reformed, Anglican, & Roman Catholic Churches.
Quandt, Ivan J. Teaching Reading.
Quant, Mary. Color by Quant: Your Complete Personal Guide to Beauty & Fashion.
Quantitative Micro Software Staff, ed. MicroTSP Version 5.0 (Software Package)
Quantrill, Malcolm. Reima Pietila: Architecture, Context & Modernism.
Quaresima, Donna, jt. auth. see Bruno, Susan.
Quarles, Benjamin. Frederick Douglass.
Quarles, John, Jr. Cleaning up America: An Insider's View of the Environmental Protection Agency.
Quarles, Susan B., ed. Guide to Federal Funding.
Quartermain, Peter, ed. American Poets, Eighteen Eighty to Nineteen Forty-Five: First Series.
Quarternary Stratigraphy Symposium Staff. Quarternary Stratigraphy of North America: Proceedings of the Symposium, 1975. Mahaney, W. C., ed.
Quarto Marketing, Ltd. Staff. Exerstyle.
Quarton, G. C., ed. The Neurosciences: A Study Program.
Quasney, James, jt. auth. see Maniotes, John.
Quastel, Michael R., ed. Cell Biology & Immunology of Leukocyte Function.
Quay, Richard H. In Pursuit of Equality of Educational Opportunity: A Selective Bibliography & Guide to the Research Literature.
Quayle, D. B. Tropical Oysters: Culture & Methods.
--Tropical Oysters: Culture & Methods.
Quaytman, Wilfred, ed. Holocaust Survivors: Psychological & Social Sequelae.
Quaytman, Wilfred, ed. & intro. by. The Vietnam Veteran - Studies in Post-Traumatic Shock Disorders: A Special Issue of the Journal of Contemporary Psychotherapy.
Que Corp, ed. IBM PC Expansion & Software Guide.
Que Corporation. IBM PC Expansion & Software Guide. Brown, Diane & Noble, David, eds.
Quebedeau, Denise B., pseud. Esoteric Substance of Voltarian Thought.
Queen, Ellery. Double, Double.
--Ellery Queen's Prime Crimes.
--Player on the Other Side.
Queen, Ellery, jt. auth. see Davis Publications Staff.
Queen, Ellery, ed. Ellery Queen's Champions of Mystery.
Queen, N. Methods of Applied Mathematics.
Queen, Stuart A. The American City.
Queen, William H., jt. auth. see Reimold, Robert J.
Queen Alexandra. Queen Alexandra's Christmas Gift Book. Battiscombe, Georgina, intro. by.
Queenan, Charles F. The Port of Los Angeles: From Wilderness to World Port.
Queenan, John T., ed. A New Life: Pregnancy, Birth, & Your Child's First Year.
Queiroz, Rachel de see De Queiroz, Rachel.
Quencer, R. M., jt. ed. see Naidich, T. P.
Queneau, Raymond. Le Dimanche de la Vie.
--Les Fleurs Bleues.
--Loin de Rueil.
--Pierrot Mon Ami.
--Zazie dans le Metro.
Quennell, Albert M., ed. Rift Valley: Afro-Arabian.
Quennell, Peter. The Wanton Chase.
Quenon, Paul. Carved in Stone.
Quenouille, M. H. Introductory Statistics.
Quentin, J. C., jt. ed. see Petter, A. J.
Quentin, Patrick. Puzzle for Fiends.
Quere, Ralph W. Evangelical Witness: The Message Medium, Mission, & Method of Evangleism.
Quere, Y., jt. auth. see Leteurtre, J.
Querin, Sandi H. I Shall Not Be Moved!
Quertermous, Russell & Quertermous, Steve. Modern Guns.
Quertermous, Steve, jt. auth. see Quertermous, Russell.
Quetsch, C. Numerical Record of University Attendance in Germany in the Last Fifty Years.
Quevedo. Lazarillo De Tormes, La Vida Del Buscon.
Quevedo, Francisco De & Ife, Barry. Francisco de Quevedo: La Vida del Buscon Llamado Don Pablos.
Quiasu, S., ed. see CISM (International Center for Mechanical Sciences), Department of Automation & Information Staff.
Quible, Zane K., et al. Introduction to Business Communication.
Quick, Dave, jt. auth. see Jenkins, Jim.
Quick, Jonathan D., ed. see Management Sciences for Health Staff, et al.
Quidam, R. D. Doctrine of Jehovah's Witnesses.
Quie, Gretchen & Hess, Karen M. In the Potter's Hand.
Quigg, P. J. Theory of Cataloguing.
Quigg, P. W. A Pole Apart: The Emerging Issues of Antarctica.
Quigley, Martin. The Original Colored House of David.
--Today's Game.
Quigly, Isabel, tr. see Parise, Goffredo.
Quillen, D. G. Homotopical Algebra.
Quiller-Couch, Arthur & Du Maurier, Daphne. Castle D'Or.
Quiller-Couch, Arthur, ed. The Oxford Book of Ballads.
Quilligan, E. J. & Kretchmer, Norman, eds. Fetal & Maternal Medicine.
Quillin, Roger T. Meeting Christ in Handel's Messiah: Lent & Easter Messages Based on Handel's Texts & Music.
Quilter, Chris, jt. auth. see Bayrd, Ned.
Quimby, Ian M., ed. American Furniture & Its Makers.
Quimby, Ian M. & Earl, Polly A., eds. Technological Innovation & the Decorative Arts.
Quinby, E. J. Wilkes-Barre & Hazelton RY.
Quine, Don. American Karate: A Complete Fitness Training & Self-Defense Program for Everyday Life.
Quine, Judith B., jt. auth. see Powers, Stephanie.
Quin-Harkin, Janet. Benjamin's Balloon.
--Helpful Hattie.
--Helpful Hattie.
--Septimus Bean & His Amazing Machine.
Quinlan, Mary, ed. The Best Fire Pictures of Nineteen Eighty-Five.
Quinlan, Michael, jt. auth. see Lever-Tracy, Constance.
Quinn, Arthur H., ed. Literature of the American People.
Quinn, Bernetta see Sr. Bernetta Quinn.
Quinn, David B., ed. see Cavendish, Thomas.
Quinn, Edward, tr. see Klein, Charlotte.
Quinn, Edward, tr. see Schnackenburg, Rudolf.
Quinn, F. M. The Principles & Practice of Nurse Education.
Quinn, Joan, et al. Coordinating Community Services for the Elderly: The Triage Experience.
Quinn, Phyllis, jt. ed. see Wills, Kendall.
Quinn, Robert E., jt. auth. see Kimberly, John R.
Quinn, Sally. Regrets Only.
Quinn, Terry, jt. auth. see Wei, Katherine.
Quinney, Douglas A. An Introduction to the Numerical Solutions of Differential Equations.
Quino. The World of Quino.
Quinones, Arcadio Diaz see Diaz Quinones, Arcadio.
Quinones, Nathan, ed. see Programa de Proyecto Frontera Staff.
Quinones, Nathan, ed. see Silverstein, Ruth, et al.
Quint, David, ed. The "Stanze" of Angelo Poliziano.
Quint, David, ed. see Poliziano, Angelo.
Quint, Howard H. & Cantor, Milton, eds. Men, Women, & Issues in American History.
Quint, Howard H., et al, eds. Main Problems in American History.
Quintana, Ricardo, ed. & intro. by see Swift, Jonathan.
Quintero, Angel G., et al. Puerto Rico: Identidad Nacional y Clases Sociales.
Quint Platt, Arlene. Cardinal Federico Borromeo As a Patron & a Critic of the Arts & His Museum of 1625. Freedberg, S. J., ed.
Quirk, Lawrence J. Films of Paul Newman.
--Jane Wyman - The Actress & the Woman: An Illustrated Biography.
--Jane Wyman: The Actress & the Woman.
Quirk, Randolph & Wrenn, C. L. An Old English Grammar.
Quirk, Robert E. The Mexican Revolution, Nineteen Fourteen to Nineteen Fifteen: The Convention of Aquascalientes.
--Mexican Revolution, 1914-1915.
Quirk, W. J., ed. Safety of Computer Control Systems 1985: Proceedings of the 4th IFAC Workshop, Como, Italy, 1-3 October 1985.
--Verification & Validation of Real-Time Software.
Quiroga, Horacio. The Decapitated Chicken & Other Stories. Peden, Margaret S., tr. from Span.
Quisling, Ronald G. & Lotz, Preston R. Correlative Neuroradiology: Intracranial Radiographic Analysis with Computed Tomography, Angiography & Magnetic Resonance Imaging.
Quistorp, Heinrich. Calvin's Doctrine of the Last Things.
Qun, Zhao C. An Illustrated English-Chinese Dictionary for Pupils.
Quo, F. Q., ed. Politics of the Pacific Nations.
Quoist, Michael. Prayers.
Qutb, Muhammad. Shubuhat Haul al-Islam.
Qutb, Sayyid. Al-Mustaqbal li-hadha ad-Din.
--Hadha ad-Din.
--Ma alim fi at-Tariq.

R

R. A. Ellis & Engineering Manpower Commission Staff. Engineering & Technology Degrees, Fall 1986.
R. S. Means Company, Inc. Staff. Building Construction Cost Data, 1988.
--Building Construction Cost Data, 1988: Western Edition. Mahoney, William D., ed.
--Means Assemblies Cost Data, 1988.
--Means Concrete Cost Data, 1988.
--Means Electrical Cost Data, 1988.
--Means Facilities Cost Data, 1988.
--Means Heavy Construction Cost Data, 1988.
--Means Historical Cost Indexes, 1988. Mahoney, William F., ed.
--Means Interior Cost Data, 1988.
--Means Labor Rates for the Construction Industry, 1988.
--Means Landscape Cost Data 1988. Mahoney, William, ed.
--Means Light Commercial Cost Data, 1988.
--Means Light Commerical Cost Data, 1988.
--Means Mechanical Cost Data, 1988.
--Means Open Shop Building Construction Cost Data, 1988.
--Means Repair & Remodeling Cost Data, 1988.
--Means Residential Cost Data, 1988.
--Means Site Work Cost Data, 1988.
--Means Square Foot Costs, 1988.
Raab, Carl. Budding Wonders: The Flowering Plants.
Raab, Thomas J., jt. auth. see Radcliffe, Robert A.

Raab, W. The Treatment of Mycosis with Imidazole Derivatives.
Raabe, Paul J. The Scientific & Humorous Revelations of God.
Raabe, Paul John. The Scientific Revelations of God.
Raalte, Susan D. Van see Van Raalte, Susan D.
Ra'anan, Uri, jt. ed. see Pfaltzgraff, Robert L., Jr.
Rabalivas, Andreas D., jt. ed. see Boulougouris, John C.
Raban, Avner, jt. auth. see Linder, Elisha.
Raban, Jonathan. Arabia: A Journey Through the Labyrinth.
Rabassa, Gregory, tr. see Aguilera-Malta, Demetrio.
Rabassa, Gregory, tr. see Amado, Jorge.
Rabat Seminar Staff. The Teaching of Sciences in African Universities: Report of the Rabat Seminar, 1962.
Rabb, Theodore K. & Rotberg, Robert I. The Family in History: Interdisciplinary Essays.
Rabb, Theodore K. & Rotberg, Robert I., eds. The New History, the 1980s & Beyond: Studies in Interdisciplinary History.
Rabbani, Ruhiyyih. Prescription for Living.
Rabbat, Guy. Hardware & Software Concepts in VLSI. Rabbat, Guy, ed.
Rabe, Claire. Sicily Enough.
Rabe, David. In the Boom Boom Room.
Rabe, Fred W. Introduction to Biology.
Raben, Joseph. Computer Assisted Research in the Humanities: A Directory of Scholars Active, 1966-1972.
Rabenau, A., ed. Problems of Nonstoichiometry.
Rabeneck, Malvern, jt. auth. see Ehrhardt, Roy.
Rabenhorst, G. Ludwig. Kryptogamenflora Von Deutschland Osterreich und der Schweiz.
Rabey, Steve. The Heart of Rock & Roll.
Rabil, Albert, Jr. Laura Cereta: Quattrocento Humanist.
Rabin. Jewish Lights: Substitute Teachers Kit.
Rabin, Carol P. Music Festivals in America.
Rabin, Chaim, tr. see Maimonides, Moses.
Rabin, Jennifer. Spell Bound.
Rabin, Lucy F. Ford Madox Brown & the Pre-Raphaelite History-Picture.
Rabiner, L. R., jt. ed. see Flanagan, J. L.
Rabinovitch, Sacha, tr. see Robert, Marthe.
Rabinow, Paul. Symbolic Domination: Cultural Symbols & Historical Change in Morocco.
Rabinow, Paul, ed. see Foucault, Michel.
Rabinowitch, E., jt. ed. see Rabinowitch, V.
Rabinowitch, V. & Rabinowitch, E., eds. Views on Science, Technology & Development.
Rabinowitz, David & Roth, Jesse, eds. Heterogeneity of Polypeptide Hormones.
Rabinowitz, Peter M., ed. Talking Medicine: America's Doctors Tell Their Stories.
Rabinowitz, Wilbur M. Almost Everywhere: Odysseys to Unusual Places.
Rabkin, Eric S. The Fantastic in Literature.
Rabkin, Jacob, jt. auth. see Rabkin, Richard.
Rabkin, Richard & Rabkin, Jacob. Nature in the West.
Rabone, David. Suzuki Owners Workshop Manual: Five Hundred Twins '68 Thru '76.
Rabotnov, Yu. Elements of Hereditary Solid Mechanics.
Raby, Simon. Rockliffe's Babies.
Raby, William L. & Tidwell, Victor H. Introduction to Federal Taxation: 1988 Edition.
Racah, G., ed. Nuclear Spectroscopy.
Racey, P. A., jt. ed. see Duckett, J. G.
Rachid, Sidna & Brown, Luanne. Egyptian Carpets.
Rachlin, Carl. Labor Law.
Rachlin, Nahid. Foreigner.
Rachlin, Robert, jt. auth. see Sweeny, H. W.
Rachman, David J. Marketing Today.
Rachman, David J. & Berman, Barry. Marketing Strategy & Structure: Study Guide.
Rachman, S. Critical Essays on Psychoanalysis.
--The Effects of Psychotherapy.
--Phobias: Their Nature & Control.
Rachman, S., ed. Advances in Behaviour Research & Therapy.
--Contributions to Medical Psychology.
Rachman, S. & Wilson, T., eds. Advances in Behavior Research & Therapy, Vol. 3.
--Advances in Behavior Research & Therapy.
--Advances in Behavior Research & Therapy.
--Advances in Behaviour Research & Therapy.
Rachman, S., jt. ed. see Eysenck, H. J.
Rachman, S. J. & Wilson, G. T. The Effects of Psychological Therapy.
Rachmaninoff, S. Second Concerto for Piano & Orchestra, Op. 18.
Rachowiecki, Rob. Ecuador & the Galapagos Islands-A Travel Survival Kit.
Rachowiecki, Robert. Climbing & Hiking in Ecuador.
Racine, jt. auth. see Wilbur, Richard.
Racine, Jean. Best Plays of Racine: Andromaque, Britannicus, Phaedre, Athalia. Lockert, Lacy, tr. from Fr.
--Phaedra. Wilbur, Richard, tr.
--Racine's Mid-Career Tragedies. Lockert, Lacy, tr.
Racine, Jean see Bentley, Eric.
Racine, Jean see Weiss, Samuel A.
Racker, Efraim. A New Look at Mechanisms in Bioenergetics.
Racker, Efriam. Science & the Cure of Diseases: Letters to Members of Congress.
Rackham, George W. Diving Complete.
Rackham, Jeff. From Sight to Insight: Steps in the Writing Process.
Rackley, R. Robert. Answers to the Study Guide for CFP 3.
Racquet & Tennis Club, New York Staff. Dictionary Catalogue of the Library of Sports in the Racquet & Tennis Club with Special Collections on Tennis, Lawn Tennis, & Early American Sports.
Rad, Gerhard von see Von Rad, Gerhard.
Rad, P. F. I A H S International Symposium on Housing Problems, 1976: Proceedings. Rad, P. F., et al, eds.
Radanovic, L., ed. Sensitivity Methods in Control Theory.
Radcliff, A., jt. auth. see Roberson, E. C.
Radcliff, Ruth K. & Ogden, Sheila J. Calculation of Drug Dosages: A Workbook.
Radcliffe College Editors. Catalog of the Arthur & Elizabeth Schlesinger Library on the History of Women in America: The Manuscript Inventories & the Catalogs of Manuscripts, Books, & Periodicals.
Radcliffe College, the Arthur & Elizabeth Schlesinger Library on the History of Women in America Staff. Manuscripts Inventory & the Catalogs of Manuscripts, Books & Pictures.
Radcliffe, Florence J. A Simple Matter of Justice: The Phyllis Wheatly YWCA Story.
Radcliffe, Philip. Mendelssohn.
Radcliffe, Robert A. & Raab, Thomas J. Data Handling Utilities in C.
Radcliffe, Talbot. Spaniels for Sport.
Radde, Paul O. Supervision Decision! Employee Guide to Choosing a Supervisory Position.
--Supervision Decision! Employee Workbook for Choosing a Supervisory Position.
Raddon, Rosemary. Planning Learning Resource Centres in Schools & Colleges.
Radel, J. Lucien. Roots of Totalitarianism: The Ideological Sources of Fascism, National Socialism, and Communism.
Radeloff, Deanna J. & Zechman, Roberta. Children in Your Life: A Guide to Child Care & Parenting.
Rademacher, H. Topics in Analytic Number Theory.
Rademacher, Hans & Toeplitz, Otto. Enjoyment of Mathematics: Selections from Mathematics for the Amateur.
Rademaker, O., et al. Dynamics & Control of Continuous Distillation Units.
Rader, Charles M., jt. auth. see Gold, Bernard.
Rader, Dotson. Tennessee: Cry of the Heart.
Rader, M., jt. auth. see Jessup, Bertram.
Rader, William. The Church & Racial Hostility: A History of Interpretation of Ephesians.
Radford, Bruce W., jt. auth. see Smart, Lucien E.
Radford, Edwin. Encyclopedia of Superstitions.
--Unusual Words.
Radford, Loren, jt. auth. see Haigh, Roger.
Radford, Loren E., jt. auth. see Haigh, Roger W.
Radford, Mary E. Parental Leave: Judicial & Legislative Trends: Current Practices in the Workplace.
Radhakrishna, S., ed. Science Technology & Global Problems-Views from the Developing World.
Radhakrishnan, S. Indian Religions.
Radhakrishnan, Sarvepalli. Recovery of Faith.
Radhakrishnan, T., jt. auth. see Rajaraman, V.
Radice, Judi. Menu Design.
Radiguet, Raymond. Le Bal du Comte d'Orgel.
Radin, Beryl. Implementation, Change, & the Federal Bureaucracy: School Desegregation Policy in HEW, 1964-1968.
Radin, Eric L., et al. Practical Biomechanics for the Orthopedic Surgeon.
Radin, Max. Law As Logic & Experience.
Radin, P., ed. see California State Library Sutro Branch San Francisco.
Radin, Paul. The Golden Mountain.
--Indians of South America.
--Road of Life & Death.
Radin, R. J. Full Potential: Your Career & Life Planning Workbook.
Radin, Stephen & Greenberg, Harold M. Computer Literacy for School Administrators.
Radiopress. China Directory, 1986.
Radji, Parviz C. In the Service of the Peacock Throne.
Radke, Barbara & Berger, Mike. Analysis of the 1977 University of California Union List of Serials.
Radl, Shirley L., jt. auth. see Zimbardo, Philip G.
Radlauer, Ed. Model Fighter Planes.
--Model Trucks.
--Model Warships.
Radlauer, Edward. CB Radio.
Radlauer, Ruth. Breakfast by Molly.
--Virgin Islands National Park.
Radlauer, Ruth, et al. Satellite Tech Talk.
Radler, K-H., jt. auth. see Krause, F.
Radley, Sheila. Death in the Morning.
--Fate Worse Than Death: A Novel of Suspense.
--The Quiet Road to Death.
--A Talent for Destruction.
Radloff, V. V. South-Siberian Oral Literature Turkic Texts.
Radlova, Lidia, jt. auth. see Levin, B.
Radlow, James. Finite Mathematics for Business, Economics, & Social Science.
Rado, P. An Introduction to the Technology of Pottery.
Rado, T. On the Problem of Plateau-Subharmonic Functions.
Radon, J. C. Fracture & Fatigue-Elasto-Plasticity, Thin Sheet & Micro-Mechanisms: Proceedings of the Third European Colloquium on Fracture, London, 8-10 September 1980.
Radosh, Ronald & Milton, Joyce. The Rosenberg File: A Search for the Truth.
Radouco-Thomas, C. & Garcin, F., eds. Progress in Neuropsychopharmacology.
Radovic, Igor D. Observations.
Radwan, Samir & Lee, Eddy. Agrarian Change in Egypt: An Anatomy of Rural Poverty.
Radwan, Samir, ed. see International Labour Office Staff.
Radwanski, George. Trudeau.
Radway, Robert J. Joint Ventures in Mexico.
Radzialowski. Hypertension Research: Methods & Models.
Rae, Alan N. Crop Management Economics.
Rae, Daphne. Love Until It Hurts: The Work of Mother Teresa & Her Missionaries of Charity.
Rae, Gwynedd. Mostly Mary.
Rae, Hugh C. The Travelling Soul.
Rae, John B. Nissan-Datsun: A History of Nissan Motor Corporation in the U. S. A. 1960-1980.
Rae, Patricia. The Touch.
Rae, Sharlotte. In Praise of God: Loving Thanks from a Grateful Daughter.
Raeburn, Anna. Joan Crawford: Legends.
Raedal, Margit. Timpetoo.
Raeder, J., ed. see Buende, R., et al.
Raff, Beverly, ed. see Friesner, Arlyne.
Raff, Ellison S., ed. Computers & Operations Research: Environmental Applications.
Raff, Joseph. Fielding's Economy Europe 1984.
--Fielding's Europe 1984.
--Fielding's Europe, 1985.
--Fielding's Europe, 1986.
--Fielding's Europe, 1987: Hotel Charts.
--Fielding's Europe, 1988.
Raff, Joseph & Raff, Judith. Fielding's Economy Europe, 1985.
--Fielding's Economy Europe, 1986.
--Fielding's Economy Europe, 1987.
--Fielding's Economy Europe 1988.
--Fielding's Selective Shopping Guide to Europe 1984.
--Fielding's Selective Shopping Guide to Europe, 1985.
--Fielding's Selective Shopping Guide to Europe, 1986.
--Fielding's Selective Shopping Guide to Europe, 1987.
Raff, Judith, jt. auth. see Raff, Joseph.
Raff, S. J. Microwave System Engineering Principles.
Raffat, Donne. The Caspian Circle.
Raffel, Burton & Burago, Alla, eds. Selected Works of Nikolai S. Gumilev.
Raffel, Marshall & Raffel, Norma K., eds. Perspectives on Health Policy: Australia, New Zealand, United States.
Raffel, Norma K., jt. ed. see Raffel, Marshall.
Raffio, Alexander W., jt. auth. see Goulden, Joseph C.
Rafoth, Richard. Bicycling Fuel: Nutrition for Bicyclists. Monk, Paddy, ed.
Rafroidi, Patrick. Irish Literature in English: The Romantic Period (1789-1850)
--Irish Literature in English: The Romantic Period, (1789-1850), Vol. 11, pt 4 Bibliography.
Ragan, David. Movie Stars of the Forties: A Complete Reference Guide for the Film Historian or Trivia Buff.
Ragan, Mark A. & Chapman, David J., eds. Biochemical Phylogeny of the Protists.
Ragan, Pauline K., ed. Aging Parents.
--Work & Retirement: Policy Issues.
Ragazzini, Giuseppe. Nuovissimo Dizionario Tecnico.
Ragel, M. E. Database Illustrated: A Professional Guide to Local Design.
Raggett, R. J., ed. Jane's Military Communications, 1986.
Raghavan, V. Experimental Embryognesis in Vascular Plants.
Ragin, Douglas H. Heartthrobs.
Ragnarsson, Ulf, ed. Peptides 1984: Proceedings of the Eighteenth European Peptide Symposium.
Rago, Michael & Bach, Joann. Zero Coupons: How to Make a Fortune & Secure Your Financial Future with Zero Coupon Bonds.
Ragsdell, K. M., jt. ed. see Mayne, R. W.
Ragusa, Isa & Green, Rosalie B., eds. Meditations on the Life of Christ: An Illustrated Manuscript of the Fourteenth Century.
Rahden, W. Van, jt. ed. see Hubig, Chr.
Rahe, Harves. Business Letters for Typing.
Rahim, Syed A., jt. auth. see Edgar, Patricia.
Rahman, Masihur. Political Economy of Income Distribution in Sri Lanka.
Rahmanoba. German-Russian Dictionary.
Rahmas, D. Steve, ed. see Salsini, Barbara.
Rahmato, Dessalegn. Agrarian Reform in Ethiopia.
Rahmlow, Lavina. Granny Glee & Sockabye Land.
--Granny Glee & Whoppity Sock.
Rahmy, Ali A. The Egyptian Policy in the Arab World: Intervention in Yemen, 1962-1967 Case Study.
Rahn, Joan E. Alfalfa, Beans & Clover.
--Eyes & Seeing.
--Grocery Store Botany.
--Grocery Store Zoology: Bones & Muscles.
--How Plants Are Pollinated.
--How Plants Travel.
--The Metric System.
--More About What Plants Do.
--Seeing What Plants Do.
--Traps & Lures in the Living World.
Rahn, K. A., ed. Arctic Air Chemistry: Proceedings of the Second Symposium, Graduate School of Oceanography, University of Rhode Island, 6-8 May 1980.
Rahner, Karl. Free Speech in the Church.
--Meditations on Freedom & the Spirit.
--Meditations on Hope & Love.
Rahula, Walpola. The Heritage of Bhikkhu.
--What the Buddha Taught.
--Zen & the Taming of the Bull: Towards the Definition of Buddhist Thought.
Rahv, Philip. Essays on Literature & Politics 1932-1972. Porter, Arabel J. & Dvosin, Andrew J., eds.
Rai, Krishna P., et al. Kulung-Nepali-English Glossary.
Rai, Raghu, jt. auth. see Singh, Khushwant.
Rai, Sudha. V. S. Naipaul: A Study in Expatriate Sensibility.
Raiborn, Mitchell H., jt. auth. see Anderson, Henry R.
Raichlen, Steven. Dining In - Boston.
Raiffa, Howard & Schlaifer, Robert. Applied Statistical Decision Theory.
Raim, Joan. Case Reports in Reading & Learning Disabilities: Psychoeducational Evaluation & Remedial Planning.
Raiman, Jennifer, jt. ed. see Wilson-Barnett, Jennifer.
Raimy, Victor. Misunderstandings of the Self: Cognitive Psychotherapy & the Misconception Hypothesis.
Rainbolt, Richard. Baseball's Home-Run Hitters.
--Hockey's Top Scorers.
Raine, David F. What to Expect If You Are...The Pregnant Father.
Raine, James W. Land of Saddle-Bags: A Study of the Mountain People of Appalachia.
Raine, Kathleen. Yeats the Initiate: Essays on Certain Themes in the Work of William Butler Yeats.
Rainer, John D., et al. Family & Mental Health Problems in a Deaf Population.
Raineri, A. & Kellerman, J. J., eds. Selected Topics in Preventive Cardiology.
Rainey, Lee, jt. auth. see Kyper, Frank.
Rainey, Sarita, ed. see Robinson, Sharon.
Rainey, Sarita R., ed. see Sheaks, Barclay.
Rainey, Sarita R., ed. see Wasserman, Burton.
Rainey, Thomas E., Jr. The Flute Manual: A Comprehensive Text & Resource Book for Both the Teacher & the Student.
Rainger, Philip. Movement Control in the Fabric of Buildings.
Rainoldes, John, et al. Th'overthrow of Stage-Players.
Rainsford, Christina. Spring Laughter.
Rainsford, K. D., et al, eds. Symposium on Aspirin & Related Drugs: Their Action & Uses.
Raintree, Lee. Dallas.
Rainville, E. D. & Bedient, P. E. Elementary Differential Equations.
Rainwater, Lee, ed. Black Experience: Soul.
--Social Problems & Public Policy: Inequality & Justice.
Rainwater, Lee, jt. ed. see Rein, Martin.
Raisanen, Heikki. Paul & the Law.
Raisin, J. S. Gentile Reactions to Jewish Ideals.
Raisin, Max. Great Jews I Have Known.
Raison, Laura, compiled by. Tuscany: An Anthology.
Raistrick, Arthur. Industrial Archaeology: An Historical Survey.
Raitt, Thomas M. A Theology of Exile: Judgment-Deliverance in Jeremiah & Ezekiel.
Raizen, Senta A., ed. see National Research Council.
Raizer, Y. P., ed. Laser-Induced Discharge Phenomena.
Raj, Rishi, ed. Flow & Fracture at Elevated Temperatures.

Authors

Rajagopal, R., ed. Environmental Mediation & Conflict Management: A Selection of Papers Presented at the 5th Annual Conference of the NAEP, Washington Dc, April 21-23 1980.
Rajagopalachari, Chakravarti, ed. & tr. see Valmiki.
Rajala, Reuben, jt. auth. see Proudman, Robert.
Rajan, K. T., jt. ed. see Richards, R. J.
Rajan, K. V. India's Religious Art: Ideas & Ideals.
--Invitation to Indian Architecture.
Rajaraman, V. & Radhakrishnan, T. An Introduction to Digital Computer Design.
Rajendra, Cecil. Bones & Feathers.
Rajgopal, P. R. Communal Violence in India.
Raj Gupta, Giri, ed. Religions in Modern India.
Rajneesh, Bhagwan S. Journey Toward the Heart: Discourses on the Sufi Way.
--The Mustard Seed: Discourses on the Sayings of Jesus from the Gospel According to Thomas.
--Roots & Wings: Talks on Zen.
--The Supreme Doctrine: Discourses on the Kenopanishad.
--Words Like Fire: Discourses on Jesus.
Rajneesh, Bhagwan Shree. Be Still & Know. Anurag, Ma Yoga, ed.
--Beware of Socialism. Sambuddha Swami Anand Maitreya, ed.
--Come Follow Me. Swami Deva Paritosh, ed.
--Far Beyond the Stars. Maneesha, Ma Prem, ed.
--Get Out of Your Own Way. Pratima, Ma Yoga, ed.
--Hammer on the Rock: A Darshan Diary.
--My Way: The Way of the White Clouds. Teertha, Swami Ananda, ed.
--The No Book: No Buddha, No Teaching, No Discipline. Maneesha, Ma Prem, ed.
--The Path of Love. Sudha, Ma Yoga, ed.
--The Sun Behind the Sun Behind the Sun. Maneesha, Ma Prem, ed.
--Tao: The Pathless Path. Asha, Ma Prem & Veena, Ma Prema, eds.
--This Very Body the Buddha. Vandana, Ma Ananda, ed.
--Unio Mystica. Vandana, Ma Ananda, ed.
--The Way of the White Clouds.
--The Wisdom of the Sands. Sudha, Ma Yoga, ed.
--Zen: Zest, Zip Zap & Zing. Asha, Ma Prem, ed.
Rajneesh, Bhagwan Shree & Sudha, Ma Yoga. The Wisdom of the Sands.
RAK Associates Staff & Kuehn, Dick. Interconnect: Why & How.
Rakauskas, Mary. Frommer's Dollarwise Guide to California & Las Vegas.
--Frommer's Guide to San Francisco.
Rakel, Robert F. Principles of Family Medicine.
Rakic, K., ed. Yugoslavia: Republics & Provinces.
Rakich, Jonathon, et al. Cases in Health Services Management.
Rakshit, M. K. The Labour Surplus Economy.
Ralbovsky, Edward. Automotive Diesels.
Raley, Nancy S., ed. Updating Your News Service.
Ralling, Christopher, ed. Shackleton: His Antarctic Writings Selected & Introduced by Christopher Ralling.
Rallison, Marvin L. Growth Disorders in Infants, Children & Adolescents.
Ralph, Diana. Work & Madness: The Rise of Community Psychiatry.
Ralph, Philip L., jt. auth. see Burns, Edward M.
Ralston, Mark A. Pierce Arrow.
Ralston, Peter. Integrity of Being.
Ram, Atma. Perspectives on R. K. Narayan.
Ram, Michael. Essential Mathematics for College Physics with Calculus: A Self Study Guide.
Ramachandran, L. & Dharmalingam, T. A Textbook of Health Education.
Ramachandran, Srinivasa, jt. auth. see Finch, Christopher.
Ramachandran, V. S. Calcium Chloride in Concrete: Science & Technology.
Ramacharaka, Yogi. The Hindu Yogi Science of Breath.
Ramage, C. S. Monsoon Meteorology.
Ramakrishna Math Staff, ed. Sadhanas for Spiritual Life.
Ramakrishnan, S., jt. ed. see Lin, Sein.
Ramamoorthy, C. V. see Vick, Charles R.
Raman, T. A. India.
Raman, T. A., et al. India & Southeast Asia.
Ramanadham, V. V., ed. Public Enterprise & the Developing World.
Ramanamurty, Y. V., jt. ed. see Rawer, K.
Ramanathan, R. Introduction to the Theory of Economic Growth.
Ramancese, Avan, jt. auth. see Burrows, Marjorie.
Ramani, R. V., ed. Application of Computers & Operations Research in the Mineral Industry (APCOM), 19th International Symposium.
Ramanujam, C. G. Indian Gymnosperms in Time & Space.
Ramanujan, A. K., tr. Fifteen Poems from a Classical Tamil Anthology.
Rama Rao, P. G. Ernest Hemingway: A Study in Narrative Technique.
Ramaswamy, P. New Delhi & Sri Lanka.
Ramaswamy, Saroja & Smith, Tony. Practical Contraception.
Ramati, Alexander. Barbed Wire on the Isle of Man.
Ramb, R., jt. auth. see Loose, S.
Rambeau, James, ed. see Shaw, George Bernard.
Rambo, A Terry. Conceptual Approaches to Human Ecology.
Rambo, William W. Work & Organizational Behavior.
Ramden, H. JCL & Advanced FORTRAN Programming.
Ramdin, Ron. Paul Robeson: The Man & His Mission.
Ramdohr, Freidrich W. B. Von see Von Ramdohr, Freidrich W. B.
Rame, Franca R., jt. auth. see Fo, Dario.
Ramella, Richard. Color Computer Fun House.
--Computer Carnival.
--Computer Carnival-Carnival Companion.
--Rainbow Quest.
--Rainbow Quest.
--Rainbow Quest: Color Computer Version.
--Rainbow Quest: Commodore 64.
Ramer, Ernest L. The Catholic Church of the Future.
--Religion Through Reason.
Ramer, Leonard V. Your Sexual Bill of Rights: An Analysis of the Harmful Effects of Sexual Prohibitions.
Ramfjord, Sigurd P., jt. auth. see Ash, Major M., Jr.
Ramirez, Bruce A., jt. ed. see Jordan, June B.
Ramirez, D. E., jt. auth. see Dunkl, C. F.
Ramirez, Francisco, jt. auth. see Slusher, Harold S.
Ramm, Agatha. Germany: Seventeen Eighty-Nine to Nineteen Nineteen.
Ramm, Carl. Operation Norfolk.
Rammairone, Raphael F. Concepts of Reality.
Rammuny, R. M., et al. The Arabic Reader I: An Introduction to Phonology & Script.
Ramon, Jose. The Triborough Plan.
Ramon, Shulamit. Psychiatry in Britain: Meaning & Policy.
Ramon-Moliner, E. Acetylthiocholinesterase Distribution in the Brain Stem of the Cat.
Ramon-Moliner, Enrique, tr. see Ramon y Cajal, Santiago.
Ramon Y Cajal, Santiago. The Structure of Ammon's Horn. Kraft, Lisbeth M., tr.
--The Structure of the Retina. Thorpe, Sylvia A. & Glickstein, Mitchell, trs.
--Studies on the Diencephalon. Ramon-Moliner, Enrique, tr.
Ramos, Gloria. Careers in Construction.
Ramos, Juan A. Papo Impala Esta Quitao.
Ramos, Manuel. Cuento de la Mujer del Mar.
Ramos-Otero, Manuel see Ramos, Manuel.
Ramot, Bracha, ed. Genetic Polymorphisms & Diseases in Man.
--Red Cell Structure & Metabolism: Proceedings.
Rampersad, Arnold. The Art & Imagination of W. E. B. Dubois.
Rampling, Anne, pseud. Belinda.
Rampling, Anne. Exit to Eden.
Rampp, Donald L. Auditory Processing & Learning Disabilities.
Ramprasad. Ramprasad: The Melodius Mystic. Buddhananda, tr.
Ramratnam, Malati. W. B. Yeats & the Craft of Verse.
Ramsay & Lasselle. Mac Multiplan.
Ramsay, Allan. Works of Allan Ramsay. Incl. Vols 1 & 2. Martin, Burns & Oliver, John W., eds.; Vol. 3. Kinghorn, Alexander M. & Law, Alexander, eds.. Johnson Repr.
Ramsay, Allan see Philomusus, S.
Ramsay, Bruce. Ghost Towns of British Columbia (1975)
Ramsay, Carol, jt. auth. see Lasselle, Joan.
Ramsay, DeVere. God's People Our Story: Bible Stories from the New Testament.
--The Old Testament: God's People-Our Story.
Ramsay, I. Synopsis of Endocrinology & Metabolism.
Ramsay, James O. Multiscale 2: Four Programs for Multidimensional Scaling by the Method of Maximum Likelihood.
Ramsay, Jim. Running.
Ramsay, John G. Folding & Fracturing of Rocks.
Ramsay, Marina, tr. see Pierce, Richard A.
Ramsay, Robert. Hawaiian Tramways.
Ramsay, William M. Historical Commentary on St. Paul's Epistle to the Galatians.
--Meaning of Jesus Christ.
Ramsay, William M. & Leith, John H. Church, a Believing Fellowship.
Ramsaye, Terry. Million & One Nights: A History of the Motion Picture through 1925.
Ramsdell, Charles W. Behind the Lines in the Southern Confederacy. Stephenson, Wendell H., ed.
Ramsden, E. & Green, R. N., eds. Microcomputers in Education: Commodore in the Classroom.
Ramsden, Evelyn, tr. see Hamre, Leif.
Ramsden, Evelyn, tr. see Senje, Sigurd.
Ramsden, Paul, jt. auth. see Entwhistle, Noel.
Ramsey, A. Michael, et al. Come Holy Spirit.
--The Charismatic Christ.
Ramsey, Brian G. Electronic Transitions in Organometalloids.
Ramsey, Dale E. Sing Praises! Management of Church Hymns.
Ramsey, Dan. Budget Flying.
--The Complete Book of Fences.
--How to Be a Disc Jockey.
--How to Forecast Weather.
--Paneling with Solid Lumber, Including Projects.
--Trouble-Free Swimming Pools.
Ramsey, Douglas K. The Corporate Warriors.
Ramsey, Ethel M. & Ramsey, William H., Jr., eds. State Emblems.
Ramsey, Evelyn. Show Me, Lord.
Ramsey, Frederic, Jr. & Smith, Charles E., eds. Jazzmen.
Ramsey, George W. Quest for the Historical Israel.
Ramsey, Georgia. My Psychic Experience.
Ramsey, Ian, ed. Prospect for Metaphysics.
Ramsey, Jackson E. Research & Development: Project Selection Criteria. Farmer, Richard, ed.
Ramsey, Judy, et al. The Complete Book of Bathrooms.
Ramsey, Lon W. Making Match Play Pay Off.
Ramsey, P. A., ed. Rome in the Renaissance: The City & the Myth.
Ramsey, Russell. A Lady, A Champion.
Ramsey, William H., Jr., jt. ed. see Ramsey, Ethel M.
Ramshaw, R. S. Power Electronics: Thyristor Controlled Power For Electric Motors.
Ramsower, Reagan M. Telecommuting: The Organizational & Behavioral Effects of Working at Home. Farmer, Richard, ed.
Ramsperger, Albert G., ed. see McGilvary, Evander B.
Rana, K. S., ed. see Hunter House Staff.
Ranadive, K. J., et al, eds. Gonadotrophins: Current Research.
Ranahan, Demerris C. Contributions of Women: Medicine.
Ranald, Margaret L. Monarch Notes on Shakespeare's Winter's Tale.
Ranald, Ralph. Monarch Notes on Hardy's Jude, the Obscure.
Rananujan, A. K., tr. from Tamil. Hymns for the Drowning: Poems for Vishnu by Nammalvar.
Ranchan, Som P. Sojourn in America: An Encounter & Reverbration.
Rancurello, Antos C. A Study of Franz Brentano.
Rand, Ann & Eksell, Olle. Edward & the Horse.
Rand, Ann & Rand, Paul. I Know a Lot of Things.
--Listen! Listen!
Rand, Ann & Snyder, Jerome. Umbrellas, Hats & Wheels.
Rand, Ann, jt. auth. see Rand, Paul.
Rand, Elizabeth, ed. see Edney, Margon & Grimm, Ede.
Rand, Elizabeth, ed. see Tucker, Joan C.
Rand McNally & Company Staff. The Atlas of Mankind.
--The Great Geographical Atlas.
--Rand McNally Handy Railroad Atlas of the United States.
--Rand McNally Road Atlas 1986.
--Rand McNally Zip Code Atlas.
Rand, Paul & Rand, Ann. I Know a Lot of Things.
Rand, Paul, jt. auth. see Rand, Ann.
Randa, James, jt. ed. see Mahanthappa, K. T.
Randall, Clay. The Killing of Billy Jowett.
--The Oceola Kid.
Randall, Clifford W. & Benefield, Larry D. Biological Processes Design for Wastewater Treatment.
Randall, D. J., jt. ed. see Hoar, W. S.
Randall, Dudley. A Litany of Friends: New & Selected Poems.
Randall, Florence E. All the Sky Together.
--Almost Year.
Randall, Lauren. To Love Is Not to Lose.
Randall, Lyman K. Your Future As an Airline Steward-Stewardess.
Randall, Margaret. Pueblo No Solo Es Testigo.
Randall, Marta. The Sword of Winter.
Randall, Marta, ed. The Nebula Awards.
Randall, Peter. The Products of Binns Road.
Randall, Rona. Glenrannoch.
--The Mating Dance.
Randall, Willard. A Little Revenge: Benjamin Franklin & His Son.
Randall-Maciver, David. The Iron Age in Italy.
Randisi, Robert J. Ham Reporter.
Randle & Swensen. Personal Financial Planning for Executives.
Randle, Gretchen R., ed. Electronic Industries Information Sources.
Randle, John. Understanding Britain: A History of the British People & Their Culture.
Randle, Kevin D. Death Before Dishonor.
Randle, Paul A. & Swenson, Philip R. Personal Financial Planning for Physicians & Dentists.
Randles, W. G. L' Ancien Royaume Du Congo Des Origines a la Fin Du XIXe Siecle.
Rando, Gaetano, tr. see Cappiello, Rose.
Randolph, Alan D. & Larson, Maurice A. Theory of Particulate Processes.
Randolph, Alan W. Understanding & Managing Organizational Behavior.
Randolph, David & Kingsbury, Jack D. Pentecost 1.
Randolph, Jeanne, jt. auth. see Friis-Hansen, Dana.
Randolph, John. Fishing Basics.
Randolph, Kenneth, jt. auth. see Giolas, Thomas G.
Randolph, Michael. Robland.
Randolph, Robert M. Thank God It's Monday: How to Turn Work into an Adventure.
Randolph, Vance. Ozark Magic & Folklore.
--Pissing in the Snow & Other Ozark Folktales.
Randolph, Vance, ed. Who Blowed up the Church House? & Other Ozark Folk Tales.
Randolph, Vel. Sean the Sea Gull.
Randow, R. Von see Von Randow, R.
Ranelagh, John. The Rise & Fall of the CIA: From Wild Bill Donovan to William Casey.
Ranft, Bryan & Till, Geoffrey. The Sea in Soviet Strategy.
Rang, Mercer. Anthology of Orthopaedics.
Ranganathan, D. Challenging Problems in Organic Reaction Mechanisms.
Ranganathan, N. Nuclear Holocaust or World Peace.
Range, Dale G., jt. auth. see Kohut, Sylvester, Jr.
Rangell, Leo. The Mind of Watergate: A Study of the Compromise of Integrity.
Ranger, Dan. Pacific Coast Shay.
Ranger, T. O. Revolt in Southern Rhodesia 1896-7.
Rani, Indi. Favorite Stories from Sri Lanka.
--More Favorite Stories from Sri Lanka.
Ranjhan, S. K. Animal Nutrition & Feeding Practices in India.
Ranjhan, S. K. & Pathak, N. N. Management & Feeding of Buffaloes.
Ranjhan, S. K., jt. auth. see Krishna, G.
Rank, Maureen, jt. auth. see Johnston, Russ.
Ranke, Friedrich. Sprache und Stil in Waelschen Gast Des Thomasin Von Circlaria.
Ranke, M. B. & Bierch, J. R. Growth Hormone Deficiency.
Rankin. Corporation Tax U. K.
Rankin, Chrissy. How Life Begins: A Look at Birth & Care in the Animal World.
Rankin, Dianne M. Financial Planning: A Home Study Course.
Rankin, Guy R. The Professional Handbook for Patrol & Security Guards.
Rankin, H. D. Sophists, Socratics & Cynics.
Rankin, Hugh F. Pirates of Colonial North Carolina.
Rankin, Ian. Knots & Crosses.
Rankin, Jake & Rankin, Marni. The Getaway Guide I: Short Vacations in the Pacific Northwest.
--The Getaway Guide IV: Short Vacations in Southern California.
Rankin, Jake, jt. auth. see Rankin, Marni.
Rankin, Marni & Rankin, Jake. The Getaway Guide III: Short Vacations in Northern California.
Rankin, Marni, jt. auth. see Rankin, Jake.
Ranney, Austin. Participation in American Presidential Nominations-1976.
Ransbury, Molly. How Can I Encourage My Primary Grade Child to Read?
Ransom, Bernard & Edwards, Owen D. James Connolly: Selected Political Writings.
Ransom, Bill. Last Call.
Ransom, Bill, jt. auth. see Herbert, Frank.
Ransom, Elizabeth, jt. auth. see Johnson, Daphne.
Ransom, John C. Selected Poems.
Ransom, P. J. The Archaeology of Canals.
Ransom, R. J. Computers & Embryos: Models in Developmental Biology.
Ransom, Roger L. Coping with Capitalism: The Economic Transformation of the United States 1776-1980.
Ransom, W. H. Building Failures: Diagnosis & Avoidance.
Ransom, W. M. Finding True North.
Ranson, Ann, ed. Academic American Encyclopedia.
Ranson, Ron & Chamberlain, Trevor. Oil Painting Pure & Simple.
Ranta, Donald E., ed. Applied Mining Geology: Ore Reserve Estimation.
Rantzen, M. J. Little Ship Astro-Navigation.
Ranum, Orest. Paris in the Age of Absolutism.
Ranum, Orest A. Richelieu & the Councillors of Louis XIII.
Ranwell, D. S. Ecology of Salt Marshes & Sand Dunes.
Rao, A. G. Madhava, ed. Modern Trends in Housing in Developing Countries.
Rao, C. N. & Rao, K. J. Phase Transition in Solids: An Approach to the Study of Chemistry & Physics of Solids.
Rao, C. R. Essays on Econometrics & Planning.
Rao, Chintamani N. Chemical Applications of Infrared Spectroscopy.

Rao, Dileep. The Handbook of Business Finance & Capital Sources.
Rao, Dittakavi N. Immigration, Aliens & Law: A Selected Bibliography.
--Publicity & Public Relations in Libraries: A Selected Bibliography.
--Sex Discrimination & Law: A Selected Bibliography.
Rao, Guthikonda V. Complex Digital Control Systems.
--Microprocessors & Microcomputer Systems.
Rao, Hanumantha, et al. Reflections on Economic Development & Social Change.
Rao, J. S. & Gupta, K. Introductory Course on Theory & Practice of Mechanical Vibrations.
Rao, J. S. & Gupta, K. N., eds. Proceedings of the Sixth World Congress on the Theory of Machines & Mechanisms: December 15-20, 1983.
Rao, J. S., ed. see Indian Society of Theoretical & Applied Mechanics, 20th Congress, India, 1975.
Rao, K. Bhaskara. Paul Scott.
Rao, K. J., jt. auth. see Rao, C. N.
Rao, K. L. Mahatma Gandhi & Comparative Religion.
Rao, K. N. Wavelength Standards in the Infrared.
Rao, K. R., jt. auth. see Ahmed, N.
Rao, K. Ramamohan & Srinivasan, Ram. Teleconferencing.
Rao, K. Ramamohan, ed. Discrete Transforms & Their Applications.
Rao, Krishna C., jt. auth. see Lee, Seungho H.
Rao, N. Narayana. Elements of Engineering Electromagnetics.
Rao, Nagaraja M. Madhu: Recent Researches in Indian Archaeology & Art History.
Rao, Nageswar E. Ernest Hemingway: A Study of His Rhetoric.
Rao, Ramachandra B. The American Fictional Hero.
Rao, S. M., et al. Industrial Applications of Radioisotopes & Radiation.
Rao, Shanto R. The Children's Mahabharata.
Rao, T. S. Power System Protection: Static Relays.
Rao, T. V., jt. auth. see Pareek, U.
Rao, V. G. The Corporation Income Tax in India.
Rao, V. P., et al, eds. A Review of the Biological Control of Insects & Other Pests in South-East Asia & the Pacific Region.
Rao, Y. K., jt. ed. see Kudryk, V.
Rao Lakshmana, N. S. & Kobus, H. E., eds. Characteristics of Self Aerated Free-Surface Flows.
Rapagnetta, Gabriele see D'Annunzio, Gabriele.
Rapaport, E. Cardiology Update, 1983: Reviews for Physicians.
Raper, Arthur F. Preface to Peasantry: A Tale of Two Black Belt Counties.
Raper, J. R., ed. see International Congress of Botany Staff.
Raphael. The Starseed Transmissions: An Extraterrestrial Report.
Raphael, Audrey M. Growing Pains.
Raphael, Bette-Jane. Can This Be Love? And Other Quandaries of Love in the Eighties.
Raphael, Chaim. Encounters with the Jewish People.
Raphael, Dana. Breast Feeding & Food Policy in a Hungry World.
Raphael, David D. Moral Judgment.
Raphael, Frederick. W. Somerset Maugham & His World.
Raphael, Fredrick. Richard's Things.
Raphael, Harold J. & Olsson, David L. Package Production Management.
Raphael, Lois A. Cape-To-Cairo Dream: A Study in British Imperialism.
Raphael, Marc L., ed. Jews & Judaism in the United States: A Documentary History.
Raphael, Phyllis, jt. auth. see Tabori, Paul.
Raphael, Rick. The President Must Die.
Raphael, Sally J. & Abadie, M. J. Finding Love: Practical Advice for Men & Women.
Rapkin, Richard H., ed. Practical Pediatrics.
Rapoport, David C. & Alexander, Yonah, eds. The Morality of Terrorism: Religious Origins & Ethical Implications.
Rapoport, Frank M., et al. Government Contracting & Subcontracting.
Rapp, Birger. Models for Optimal Investment & Maintenance Decisions.
Rapp, G. Color of Minerals.
Rapp, Hazel C. Bible Quiz: Five Hundred Questions & Answers with Bible References.
Rapp, J. Mother Earth's Hassle-Free Vegetable Cookbook.
Rapp, William F. The Postal History of Nebraska.
Rappaport, Armin & Traina, Richard. Source Problems in American History.
Rappaport, H., jt. auth. see Mathe, G.
Rappaport, Irwin. Textedit.
--Textedit: A Complete Word Processing System in Kit Form.
Rappaport, Jon, ed. see Donnelly, Mark & Fenton, Nina.
Rappaport, Julian, et al. Innovations in Helping Chronic Patients: College Students in a Mental Institution.
Rappaport, Stephen P., jt. auth. see Lamb, Robert.
Rappoport, Angelo S. Folklore of the Jews.
--Superstitions of Sailors.
Rappoport, Ken. The Nittany Lions: A Story of Penn State Football.
--The Trojans: A Story of Southern California Football.
Rapport, Jon, ed. see Williams, Thomas D.
Rapport, Paul. Opus Est: Six Composers from Northern Europe.
Rapport, Steve, jt. auth. see Waller, Johnny.
Rapson, Richard L. Fairly Lucky You Live Hawaii!
Raring, Richard H. Crib Death: Scourge of Infants, Shame of Society.
Rasdall, Mark, ed. Top Three Thousand Directories & Annuals 1986-1987.
--Top Three Thousand Directories & Annuals 1987-1988.
Rash, J. Keogh & Pigg, R. Morgan, Jr. The Health Education Curriculum.
Rashdall, Hastings. Philosophy & Religion: Six Lectures Delivered at Cambridge.
Rashed, Leon H. A Change-of-Name Guide for Bilalians.
Rashidov, S. Soviet Uzbekistan.
Rashiduzzaman, M. Rural Leadership & Population Control in Bangladesh.
Rashke, Richard. Escape from Sobibor.
--The Killing of Karen Silkwood.
Rashkind, William J., ed. Congenital Heart Disease.
Raskhodoff, Nicholas M. Electronic Drafting & Design.
Raskin, A. When Daddy Was a Little Boy.
Raskin, Bruce, ed. Mud Puddles, Rainbows & Asparagus Tips: Learning's Best Language Arts Ideas.
--The Whole Learning Catalog.
Raskin, Ellen. A & The or William T. C. Baumgarten Comes to Town.
--And It Rained.
--Franklin Stein.
--Moose, Goose & Little Nobody.
--Nothing Ever Happens on My Block.
--The Tattooed Potato & Other Clues.
--Twenty-Two, Twenty-Three.
--World's Greatest Freak Show.
Raskin, Herbert A., jt. auth. see Krystal, Henry.
Raskin, Jonah. My Search for B. Traven.
Raskova, H., ed. Pharmacology & Toxicology of Naturally Occurring Toxins.
Rasmusen, Carl C., tr. see Nygren, Anders.
Rasmussen, David W. & Struyk, Raymond J. A Housing Strategy for the City of Detroit: Policy Perspectives Based on Economic Analysis.
Rasmussen, Eileen C. Of Lost Loves & Other People.
Rasmussen, Henry. Ferraris for the Road.
--Mercedes for the Road.
--Porsches for the Road.
Rasmussen, Henry, ed. Corvettes for the Road.
Rasmussen, Knud. The People of the Polar North.
Rasmussen, Larry L. Economic Anxiety & Christian Faith.
Rasmussen, Larry L., jt. auth. see Birch, Bruce C.
Rasmussen, N., jt. auth. see Oldenberg, Otto.
Rasmussen, Richard M., jt. auth. see Rasmussen, Ronda.
Rasmussen, Ronda & Rasmussen, Richard M. Mr. Computer.
Raspa, Anthony, ed. John Donne: Devotions Upon Emergent Occasions.
Raspe, G., ed. Life Science Monograph. Long, J., et al, trs.
Rasper, Ludwig. The Bucket Wheel Excavator: Bulk Materials Handling Ser.
Rasponi, Lanfranco. The Last Prima Donnas.
Rassieur, Charles L. The Problem Clergymen Don't Talk About.
Rassinier, Paul. Debunking the Genocide Myth.
Rast, Walter E. Joshua, Judges, Samuel, Kings. McCurley, Foster R., ed.
Rastorfer, Darl, jt. ed. see Holod, Renata.
Rastyannikov, V. G. Agrarian Evolution in a Multiform Structure Society: Experience of Independent India. Kostrov, Konstantin A., tr. from Rus.
Raswan, Carl. Black Tents of Arabia.
Rat, Maurice, jt. auth. see Beaumarchais, Pierre de.
Ratajczak, H. & Orville-Thomas, W. J., eds. Molecular Interactions.
Ratcliff, Carter. Gilbert & George: The Complete Pictures, 1971-1985.
--Jean Dubuffet, Partitions 1980-1981; Psycho-Sites 1981.
--Lucas Samaras: Sittings. Pace Gallery Publications Staff, ed.
--Robert Longo.
--Willem De Kooning: The North Atlantic Light.
Ratcliff, Gerald L. Speech & Drama Club Activities.
Ratcliff, Richard U. Urban Land Economics.
Ratcliff, Rosemary. Dear Worried Brown Eyes.
Ratcliffe, Jennifer M. Lead in Man & the Environment.
Ratcliffe, N. A. & Llewellyn, P. J. Practical Illustrated Histology.
Ratcliffe, Thomas A. & Munter, Paul H. Complete Handbook of Inflation Accounting.
Ratensky, Alexander. Drawing & Modelmaking: A Primer for Students of Architecture & Design.
Rath, B. B., jt. ed. see Sadananda, K.
Rath, Patricia M. Succeeding on the Job: A Self-Study Guide for Students.
Rath, Patricia M, et al. Supervising on the Job: A Self-Study Guide for Students.
Rath, Sara & Smith, Rick. Easy Going: Madison & Dane County.
--Pioneer Photographer: Wisconsin's H. H. Bennet.
Rath, Sharada. Federalism Today: Approaches, Issues & Trends.
Rathbone, E., jt. auth. see Rathbone, R. S.
Rathbone, Julian. The Peron Tapes.
Rathbone, R. S. & Rathbone, E. Health & the Nature of Man.
Rathenau, Ernest G., compiled by. Oskar Kokoschka - Drawings 1906-1965.
Rathi, M., jt. ed. see Kumar, S.
Rathje, Linda. AppleWorks for Educators: A Beginners Workbook.
Rathjen, Diana P., jt. auth. see Foreyt, John P.
Rathjen, Frederick W. The Texas Panhandle Frontier.
Rathnam, P. V. Rathnam's Cost & Management Accounting: Problems & Solutions.
Rathus, Spencer A. Essentials of Psychology.
--Psychology.
Rathwell, Tom & Phillips, David, eds. Health, Race & Ethnicity.
Rathwick, Clyde W. God's Co-Workers: Your Importance to God.
Ratiu, T., jt. ed. see Bernard, P.
Ratliff, Bascom W. Leaving the Hospital: Discharge Planning for Total Patient Care.
Ratliff, Neil, intro. by. & intro. see Whistling, Carl F. & Hofmeister, Friedrich.
Ratliff, William F. Creaciones y Creadores: A Basic Literary Reader.
Ratner, A. M. Spectral, Spatial, & Temporal Properties of Lasers.
Ratner, David L. Securities Regulation in a Nutshell.
Ratner, Leonard G. Music: The Listener's Art.
Ratner, Michael, jt. auth. see Lobel, Jules.
Rattenbury, John M. Amino Acid Analysis.
Ratti, Jogindar & Manougian, Manoug. Introductory Calculus with Applications.
Rattigan, Terence. Plays: One.
Rattner, Naomi C., jt. auth. see Milan, Deanne K.
Ratz, G. A., jt. auth. see DeArdo, A. J.
Ratzlaff, Leslie, jt. auth. see O'Brien, Eileen.
Ratzlaff, Leslie A., ed. Education Directory 1987: A Guide to Decisionmakers in the Federal Government, the States & Education Associations.
Rau, M. Chalapathi. Journalism & Politics.
Rau, Santha R., jt. auth. see Devi, Gayatri.
Rauch, H. E., jt. auth. see IFAC Symposium Staff.
Rauch, Irmengard & Carr, Gerald F., eds. The Signifying Animal: The Grammar of Language & Experience.
Rauch, Leo. The Political Animal: Studies in Political Philosophy from Machiavelli to Marx.
--The Political Animal: Studies in Political Philosophy from Machiavelli to Marx.
Rauch, Paul. How to Be Your Own Contractor.
Rauch, William, jt. auth. see Koch, Edward I.
Raud, E. Bear's House.
Raudkivi, A. J. Hydrology.
Raudsepp, Eugene & Hough, George P. Creative Growth Games.
Raumer, Frederick Von see Von Raumer, Frederick.
Raumer, Rudolf H. Von see Von Raumer, Rudolf H.
Rauner, Judy, jt. auth. see Trost, Arty.
Raus, J., et al, eds. Cytotoxic Estrogens in Hormone Receptive Tumors.
Rausa, Rosario. The Blue Angels: An Illustrated History.
Rausch, D. O. & Mariacher, B. C., eds. Mining & Concentrating of Lead & Zinc.
Rausch, Edward N. Financial Keys to Small Business Profitability.
Rausch, Erwin & Perper, Menna. Resident Care Management System.
Rauschenbach, Hans S. Solar Cell Array Design Handbook: The Principles & Technology of Photovoltaic Energy Conversion.
Rauschenberg, Robert. Rauschenberg Photographs.
Rauson, Stewart & Tomlinson, John, eds. The Changing Government of Education.
Rauton, Jane, jt. auth. see Miles, Curtis.
Ravage, M. E. An American in the Making: The Life Story of an Immigrant.
Raveh, Yael-Anna, jt. auth. see Weinshall, Theodore D.
Raven, C. P. Outline of Developmental Physiology.
Raven, Charles E. War & the Christian.
Raven, Ronald W., ed. Principles of Surgical Oncology.
Ravenel, Mrs. St. Julien. Charleston, the Place & the People.
Ravenel, Shannon, jt. auth. see Tyler, Ann.
Ravenel, Shannon, jt. ed. see Calisher, Hortense.
Ravenel, Shannon, jt. ed. see Carver, Raymond.
Ravenel, Shannon, jt. ed. see Elkin, Stanley.
Ravenel, Shannon, jt. ed. see Oates, Joyce Carol.
Ravenel, Shannon, jt. ed. see Solotaroff, Theodore.
Ravenel, Shannon, jt. ed. see Updike, John.
Ravenette, A. T. Dimensions of Reading Difficulties.
Raverat, Gwen. Period Piece.
Ravetz, Alison. Remaking Cities: Contradictions of the Recent Urban Environment.
Raviart, P. A., jt. auth. see Girault, V.
Ravielli, Anthony. What Are Street Games?
--What Is Bowling?
--What Is Golf?
--What Is Tennis?
Ravila, Paavo. Finnish Literary Reader.
Ravin, A. W., jt. ed. see Caspari, E. W.
Ravin, Arnold W. Evolution of Genetics.
Ravindra, H, jt. ed. see Cropley, A. J.
Ravizza, jt. auth. see Ray.
Rawcliffe, Michael. The Roosevelt File.
Rawding, F. W. Gandhi & the Struggle for India's Independence.
Rawer, K. & Ramanamurty, Y. V., eds. International Reference Ionosphere - Status 1985-86: Proceedings of the URSI-COSPAR Workshop on the International Reference Ionosphere Held in Louvain-la-Neuve, Belgium, 25 October - 1st November.
Rawer, K., et al, eds. Models of the Atmosphere & Ionosphere: Proceedings of Workshops VIII & X of the COSPAR 25th Plenary Meeting held in Graz, Austria, 25 June-7 July 1984.
Rawitsch, Don, jt. auth. see Glenn, Allen.
Rawlings, Marjorie K. Cross Creek.
--The Yearling.
Rawlings, Meridel. Honor Thy Father. Keith, Bill, ed.
Rawlins, C. L., ed. see Barclay, William.
Rawlins, Clive. William Barclay: The Authorized Biography.
Rawlins, Ruth Parmelee, jt. auth. see Beck, Cornelia M.
Rawlinson, Arthur & Farnum, Dorothy. Jew Suss. Kupelnick, Bruce S., ed.
Rawls, George H. The Surgeon's Turn.
Rawls, Walter C., Jr., jt. auth. see Davis, Albert R.
Rawls, Walton. The Great Book of Currier & Ives' America.
Rawnsley, C. F. & Wright, Robert. Night Fighter.
Rawski, Evelyn S. Agricultural Change & the Peasant Economy of South China.
Rawson, Beryl. Politics of Friendship: Pompey & Cicero.
Rawson, D. W. & Wrightson, Sue. Australian Unions.
Rawson, Don & Fisher, Chris, eds. Changing Industrial Law.
Rawson, Geoffrey. Pandora's Last Voyage.
Rawson, Philip. The Art of Drawing.
Rawson, Raymond. The Way Home.
Ray & Ravizza. Methods Toward a Science of Behavior & Experience.
Ray, Ann. Journey into Light.
Ray, B. Two-Six Compounds.
Ray, Barbara J. Human Resource Dynamics Administration & Policy: A Bibliography.
Ray, Charles M. & Eison, Charles L. Supervision.
Ray, Cyril. Robert Mondavi of the Napa Valley.
Ray, Donald P. Trends in Social Science.
Ray, Edgar. Grand Huckster: Houston's Judge Roy Hofheintz, Genius of the Astrodome.
Ray, G. Precision Attachments.
Ray, G. Carleton & McCormick-Ray, M. G. Wildlife of the Polar Regions.
Ray, George E. Incorporating the Professional Practice.
--Incorporating the Professional Practice.
Ray, J. Methodus Plantarum Nova.
Ray, J. H. Randolph. My Little Church Around the Corner.
Ray, James L. Global Politics.
--Global Politics.
Ray, Jo A. Careers in Computers.
--Careers in Football.
--Careers in Hockey.
--Careers with a Police Department.
--Careers with a Television Station.
Ray, John. The First World War.
--The Wisdom of God Manifested in the Works of the Creation.
Ray, Keith, ed. see Architectural Record Magazine Editors.
Ray, Lawrence. The Dawning.
Ray, Mary. Spring Tide.
Ray, Oakley. Drugs, Society & Human Behavior.
Ray, Ruth. Inside Outside.
Ray, S. H; see Haddon, A. C.
Ray, Mrs. Sam. Postcards from Old Kansas City.

Ray, Sandy F. Journeying Through a Jungle.
Ray, Verne F. Cultural Relations in the Plateau of Northwestern America.
Ray, W. Harmon. Advanced Process Control.
Ray, Willis. Introduction to Manufacturing Careers.
Rayboy, David G., ed. Essays in Supply Side Economics.
Rayburn, L. G. Financial Tools for Marketing Administration.
Rayburn, L. Gayle. Principles of Cost Accounting with Managerial Implications.
Rayburn, William F. & Zuspan, Frederick P. Drug Therapy in Obstetrics & Gynecology.
Rayburn, William F. & Zuspan, Fredrick P. Every Woman's Pharmacy: A Guide to Safe Drug Use.
Raycraft, Carol, jt. auth. see Raycraft, Don.
Raycraft, Don & Raycraft, Carol. Wallace-Homestead Price Guide to American Country Antiques.
--Wallace-Homestead Price Guide to American Country Antiques.
Rayfield, Donald. The Confessions of Victor X.
--The Dream of Lhasa: The Life of Nikolay Przhevalsky (1839-88), Explorer of Central Asia.
Raygor, Alton L. & Wark, David M. Systems for Study.
Raygor, Alton L., ed. see Learning Technology, Inc. Staff.
Rayle, David & Wedberg, Hale. Botany: A Human Concern.
Raymo, Chet. The Soul of the Night: An Astronomical Pilgrimage.
Raymond, Alex. The Space Circus.
--The Time Trap of Ming the 13th.
--The Witch Queen of Mongo.
Raymond, Dick & Raymond, Jan. Home Gardening Wisdom.
Raymond, Irving W., jt. ed. see Lopez, Robert S.
Raymond, James C., ed. Literacy As a Human Problem.
Raymond, Jan, jt. auth. see Raymond, Dick.
Raymond, Janice G. A Passion for Friends: Toward a Philosophy of Female Affection.
Raymond, Jeanette. Implementing Pastoral Care in Schools.
Raymond, Jennifer. The Best of Jenny's Kitchen: Cooking Naturally with Vegetables.
Raymond, Steve. The Year of the Angler.
--The Year of the Trout.
Raymond of Cupua. The Life of Saint Catherine of Siena.
Raynal, Guillaume T. Philosophical & Political History of the Settlements & Trade of the Europeans in the East & West Indies. Justamond, J. O., tr.
Raynaud, C., ed. Nuclear Medicine & Biology Advances: Proceedings of the Third World Congress on Nuclear Medicine & Biology, August 29 - September 2, 1982, Paris, France.
Rayne, John & Crawford, G. Cullen. Development of the Muscles of Mastication in the Rat.
Rayner, E. G., jt. auth. see Dexter, N. C.
Rayner, William. The Day of Chaminuka.
--The Interface Assignment.
--Stag Boy.
Raynes, John. Painting Seascapes.
--Starting to Paint in Oils.
--Starting to Paint with Acrylics.
Raynor, Dorka. My Friends Live in Many Places. Tucker, Kathleen, ed.
Raynor, Eric. Human Development: An Introduction to the Psychodynamics of Growth, Maturity & Aging.
Raynor, Henry. A Social History of Music: From the Middle Ages to Beethoven & Music & Society since 1815.
Rayshich, Hale & McGuire. Blueprint Reading for Machine Technology.
Rayson, Steven. The Crows of War.
Raytheon Company Staff & Pressman, Abraham I. Switching & Linear Power Supply, Power Converter Design.
Rayward, W. Boyd. Systematic Bibliography in England, 1850-1895.
Razin, Andrew M, jt. auth. see Gurman, Alan S.
Raznjevic, Kuzman. Handbook of Thermodynamic Tables & Charts.
Razzi, Jim. Desert Flight.
RCC Pilotage Foundation Staff. The Atlantic Crossing Guide.
Re, Joseph M. Earn & Learn: Cooperative Education Opportunities Offered by the Federal Government, 1988-89.
Rea, jt. auth. see Lientz.
Rea, Frederick B. Alcoholism: It's Psychology & Cure.
Rea, Jesse R., jt. auth. see Kostiner, Edward.
Rea, Jesus G. see Rohmer, Harriet.
Rea, Jesus G., jt. auth. see Rohmer, Harriet.
Rea, Jesus G., jt. ed. see Rohmer, Harriet.
Rea, R. Sam. The Tax & Estate Planner's Complete Guide for Servicing the Professional Client.
Read. At Home in the Thrush Green.
--A Fortunate Grandchild.
Read, Ann K., jt. auth. see Garrison, Linda.
Read, Charles. Children's Categorization of Speech Sounds in English.
Read, Donald. Press & People, Seventeen Ninety to Eighteen Fifty.
Read, Donald A. & Greene, Walter H. Creative Teaching in Health.
Read, Elfreida. Brothers by Choice.
Read, Gardner. Contemporary Instrumental Techniques.
--Music Notation: A Manual of Modern Practice.
Read, Hadley. Morning Chores & Other Times Remembered: Poems.
Read, Herbert. Art of Sculpture.
Read, Herbert E., ed. Surrealism.
Read, Jan. The Wines of Spain.
Read, Keith. Aeromedicine for Aviators.
Read, M. D. & Wellby, D. A Practical Guide for the Obstetric Team.
Read, Michael D. & Mellor, Stuart. Obstetrics in Outline.
Read, Miss. Affairs at Thrush Green.
--Chronicles of Fairacre.
--Gossip from Thrush Green.
--No Holly for Miss Quinn.
--Return to Thrush Green.
--Summer at Fairacre.
--Village Affairs.
--Village Centenary.
Read, Peter G. Dictionary of Gemmology.
Read, Piers P. The Junkers.
--A Married Man.
--Monk Dawson.
--Polonaise.
--The Professor's Daughter.
--The Upstart.
--The Villa Golitsyn.
Read, R. B. The San Francisco Underground Gourmet.
Reade, Christopher B. Real Estate Guide to Microcomputers.
Reade, Davenport A. Lottie.
Readence, John E., jt. auth. see Searfoss, Lyndon W.
Readence, John E., jt. auth. see Moore, David W.
Reader, Aalitio. Finnish for Foreigners.
Reader, G. T. & Hooper, C. Stirling Engines.
Reader's Digest Association, Canada. Outdoors Canada.
Reader's Digest Association, London. Encyclopaedia of Garden Plants & Flowers.
Reader's Digest Editors. Consumer Adviser: An Action Guide to Your Rights.
--The Creative Kitchen Poultry Cookbook.
--Great Tales of the Sea.
--Marvels & Mysteries of the World Around Us.
--Our National Parks: America's Spectacular Wilderness Heritage.
--Reader's Digest Almanac & Yearbook, 1986.
--Reader's Digest Good Health Cookbooks 1-M Fish & Meat.
--Reader's Digest Good Health Cookbooks 1-M Vegetables & Desserts.
--Reader's Digest Great Biographies.
Reader's Digest Editors, jt. auth. see Hayakawa, S. I.
Reader's Digest Editors, ed. The Best of the West.
--Fireside Reader.
--Great Short Stories of the World.
--Great Stories of Mystery & Suspense.
--Great Stories of Mystery & Suspense.
--Reader's Digest Great Biographies.
--Reader's Digest Great Biographies.
--Reader's Digest Great Biographies.
--Reader's Digest 1981 Almanac & Yearbook.
--World's Best Short Stories.
Readett, Alan G., jt. auth. see Herbst, Robert.
Readett, Alan G., jt. ed. see Herbst, Robert.
Reading Catalog of the Library of the American Museum of Natural History Staff. Research Catalog of the Library of the American Museum of Natural History: Classed Catalog.
Reading, June A., ed. Consignments to El Dorado: A Record of the Voyage of the Sutton by Thomas Whaley.
Reading Laboratory Staff. Double Your Reading Speed.
Ready, Barbara C., ed. Clinical Pharmacology: A Guide to Training Programs.
Ready, Barbara C., jt. ed. see Conley, Diane.
Ready, Dolores. John's Magic: John Bosco.
--Wilfred's Hospital Ship: Wilfred Grenfell.
Ready, Kirk L. Custom Cars.
Reagan, Charlie. Charlie: The Story of a Baby in the Making.
Reagan, J. W. & Ng, A. B. The Cells of Uterine Adenocarcinoma.
Reagan, James, jt. auth. see Gerstein, Arnold.
Reage, Pauline. Story of O: Part Two, Return to the Chateau. D'Estree, Sabine, tr. from Fr.
Real Estate Education Company Staff. Illinois Supplement for Modern Real Estate Practice. Ballou, John D. & Bowman, Thomas H., Jr., eds.
Real Estate Education Company Staff & Grubb & Ellis Staff. Successful Industrial Real Estate Brokerage.
--Successful Leasing & Selling of Office Property.
--Successful Leasing & Selling of Retail Property.
Real Estate Institute of Canada Staff. Computer Product & Service Directory.
Realites Editors. Chateaux of France.
Reams, Bernard D., Jr. Tax Reform 1984: The Law, Reports, Hearings, Debates & Related Documents.
Reams, Bernard D., Jr., ed. Internal Revenue Acts of the United States: 1950-1951 Legislative Histories, Laws & Administrative Documents.
Reams, Bernard D., Jr., ed. see Burge, William.
Reaney, P. H. A Dictionary of British Surnames.
--The Origin of English Place-Names.
Reapsome, Martha. A Woman's Path to Godliness.
Reardon, Jean & Ebling, Ruth. Oysters: A Culinary Celebration.
Reaske, Christopher. How to Analyze Poetry.
Reaske, Christopher R. How to Analyze Drama.
--How to Analyze Poetry.
Reavey, George, tr. see Biely, Andrey.
Reavis, Charles. Home Sausage Making.
Reavis, Marshall W. Handbook of Insurance Terms & Concepts.
--Illinois Insurance Law: A License Preparation Manual for Life & Health, Property & Casualty.
Reay, D. A. & MacMichael, D. B. Heat Pumps.
Reay, D. A., jt. auth. see International Heat Pipe Conference Staff.
Reay, D. A., ed. Energy Economics & Management in Industry: Proceedings of the European Congress Held Algarve, Portugal, 2-5 April 1984.
Reay, David A. Heat Recovery Systems: A Directory of Equipment & Techniques.
--History of Man-Powered Flight.
Rebackoff, Zach. Tough Calls: An Illustrated Book of Official Baseball Rules.
Rebell, Arthur L., et al. Financial Futures & Investment Strategy.
Reber, Hort, jt. auth. see Meister, Peter W.
Reboullet, et al. Methode Orange 2.
Rebuck, John W., et al. The Reticuloendothelial System.
Receveur, Betty L. Molly Gallagher.
Rechenbach, Charles W. Swahili-English Dictionary.
Rechigl, M., Jr., ed. Nutrition & the World Food Problem.
Rechin, Bill & Wilder, Don. Crock Marches On.
Rechy, John. City of Night.
--City of Night-Access.
--The Fourth Angel.
--Numbers.
--Rushes.
--Rushes.
--The Vampires.
Reck, David. Music of the Whole Earth.
Reck, Vera T. Boris Pil'niak: A Soviet Writer in Conflict with the State.
Recondo, A. M. De see De Recondo, A. M.
Reconstruction of the Globe Playhouse Symposium Staff. The Third Globe: Symposium for the Reconstruction of the Globe Playhouse, Wayne State University. Hodges, C. Walter, et al, eds.
Record, Francis, jt. auth. see Eckholm, Erik P.
Record, Jeffrey, jt. auth. see Lawrence, Richard D.
Record, Wilson. Negro & the Communist Party.
Recreation Vehicle Industry Association (U.S.) Staff. RV Lawyers' Guide: Selected Franchise & Warranty Laws of the Fifty States Affecting the RV Manufacturer.
Rectanus, Mark, et al. Deutschland und Amerika: Unter der Lupe.
Rector, Margaret, ed. Cowboy Life on the Texas Plains: The Photographs of Ray Rector.
Rector, Robert E. & Zwick, Earl J. Finite Mathematics & Its Applications.
Recycling Consortium Staff. Apples: Uses for the Apple.
Reda, Jacques, jt. auth. see Aspinwall, Dorothy B.
Redd, Frank J., ed. Journal of Spacecraft & Rockets.
Redden, Charlotte A., jt. auth. see Switzer, Kenneth A.
Redden, Kenneth R. Federal Regulation of Family Law.
Redden, Kenneth R. & McClellan, James. Federal Regulation of Consumer-Creditor Relations.
Redden, Kenneth R., jt. auth. see University of Virginia School of Law Staff.
Redder, George. The Flight Instructor Murders.
Reddick, Bryan. Student Journalist & Effective Writing Style.
Reddick, John. Danzig Trilogy of Gunter Grass: A Study of The Tin Drum, Cat & Mouse, & Dog Years.
Reddick, Marshall E., jt. auth. see Cohen, William A.
Reddick, William J. Standard Musical Repertoire with Accurate Timings.
Reddin, W. J. Effective Management by Objectives: The 3-D Method of MBO.
--Managerial Effectiveness.
Redding, David. Amazed by Grace.
Redding, James L., jt. auth. see Doyle, Rodger P.
Redding, Saunders, jt. ed. see Davis, Arthur P.
Redding, W. Charles. The Corporate Manager's Guide to Better Communication.
Reddish, V. C. Stellar Formation.
Reddy, A. K. Technology, Development & the Environment: A Re-Appraisal.
Reddy, Francis. Halley's Comet!
Reddy, J. N., jt. auth. see Oden, J. T.
Reddy, J. N., ed. Penalty-Finite Elements Methods in Mechanics.
Redei, George P. Genetics.
Redei, L. Algebra.
--Foundation of Euclidean & Non-Euclidean Geometries According to F. Klein.
--The Theory of Finitely Generated Commutative Semigroups.
Redeker, James R. Discipline: Policies & Procedures.
Redeker, Martin. Schleiermacher: Life & Thought. Wallhausser, John, tr. from Ger.
Redelfs, Velma C. Transcendent Meditations.
Reder, Melvin W., jt. ed. see David, Paul A.
Redfarn, C. A. Guide to Plastics.
Redfearn, J. W. Can We Change?
Redfern. How Do We Talk?
Redfield, Bessie, ed. Capricorn Rhyming Dictionary.
Redfield, Margaret P., ed. see Redfield, Robert.
Redfield, Robert. The Little Community. Bd. with Peasant Society & Culture. U of Chicago Pr.
--Social Uses of Social Science. Redfield, Margaret P., ed.
Redfield, Sarah E. Vanishing Farmland: A Legal Solution for the States.
Redgrove, Peter. The Man Named East: And Other New Poems.
Redgrove, Peter, jt. auth. see Shuttle, Penelope.
Redies, Rainer, jt. auth. see Melle, Gerte.
Redinger, David H. The Story of Big Creek. Myers, Bill, ed.
Redish, Martin H. Federal Courts: Cases, Comments & Questions.
--Federal Courts, Cases, Comments & Questions: 1986 Supplement.
Redl, Fritz & Wattenberg, William. Mental Hygiene in Teaching.
Redleaf, Rhoda, ed. Field Trips: An Adventure in Learning.
Redlich, Hans F. Claudio Monteverdi: Life & Works. Dale, Kathleen, tr.
Redman, Barbara J. Consumer Behavior: Theory & Applications.
Redman, Barbara J., jt. auth. see Redman, John C.
Redman, Barbara K. The Process of Patient Teaching in Nursing.
Redman, John C. & Redman, Barbara J. Microeconomics: Resource Allocation & Price Theory.
Redman, S. & Standford, M. User Friendly Guide to Lap Portables: Featuring TRS Model 100 & Olivetti M-10.
Redman, W. C., jt. auth. see Davey, W. G.
Redmond, Howard A. Philosophy of the Second Advent.
Redmond, J., et al, eds. The Year's Work in English Studies: Vol. 57, 1976.
Redmond, Jeffrey R. Tales of the Vikings: Saga Translations & Their Histories.
Redmond, P. W. & Stevens, I. N. General Principles of English Law.
Redmore, Fred H. Fundamentals of Chemistry.
Redon, Odillon. Graphic Works: 209 Lithographs, Etchings Engravings.
Redpath, A. A. Why Do We Laugh?
Redpath, Ann, ed. see Frevert, Patricia D.
Redpath, Ann, ed. see Larson, Norita D.
Redshaw, L. C., ed. see Ilyushin, A. A. & Lenskii, V. S.
Redstone, Louis G. Masonry in Architecture.
--Public Art: New Directions.
Redtree Associates Staff. America's Meeting Places.
Redway, Maurine W., jt. auth. see Bracken, Dorothy K.
Redwood, John. Going for Broke: Gambling with Taxpayers' Money.
Ree, Gerry De La see De La Ree, Gerry.
Reece, Barry L. & Brandt, Rhonda. Effective Human Relations in Organizations.
Reece, Barry L. & Brandt, Rhonda O. Effective Human Relations in Business.
Reece, Colleen L. The Other Nine.
Reece, Collen L., jt. auth. see Furan Illustrators Staff.
Reece, James S., jt. auth. see Anthony, Robert N.
Reed, A. W. Myths & Legends of Australia.
Reed, Ann & Pfaltz, Marilyn. Your Secret Servant: Fix & Freeze Hors D'oeuvre for Easy Entertaining.
Reed, Bob & Reed, Pat. Sand Creatures & Castles: How to Build Them.
Reed, Dana. Deathbringer.
--Sister Satan.
Reed, Diane M. The "Oh, What a Wonderful Wedding" Book: How to Be a Beautiful Bride on a Budget.

Reed, Dolores M. Fight City Hall & Win.
Reed, Edward, ed. Readings for Democrats.
Reed, Edward W., et al. Casebook in Commercial Banking.
Reed, Eugene E. The Civilized vs. Civilization: Primitivism in the Literature of German Pre-Romanticism.
Reed, Eugene S., ed. see Callahan, Richard J.
Reed, Frank C., jt. auth. see Firestone, David B.
Reed, G. M., ed. Set-Theoretic Topology.
Reed, Graham. The Psychology of Anomalous Experience.
Reed, Gretchen M. & Sheppard, Vincent F. Regulation of Fluid & Electrolyte Balance: A Programmed Instruction in Clinical Physiology.
Reed, Gwendolyn, ed. Beginnings.
Reed, Ishmael. Flight to Canada.
--The Freelance Pallbearers.
--The Freelance Pallbearers.
--God Made Alaska for the Indians.
--The Last Days of Louisiana Red.
--Mumbo Jumbo.
Reed, Ishmael & Young, Al, eds. Yardbird Lives!
Reed, J. Diez Dias Que Estremecieron el Mundo.
Reed, James H., jt. auth. see McWaters, Marcus M.
Reed, James H., jt. auth. see Williams, Walter E.
Reed, Jeanne. Business English: A Gregg Text-Kit for Adult Education.
Reed, John. Schubert: The Master Musicians.
Reed, John & Lomas, Gillian, eds. Psychiatric Services in the Community: Developments & Innovations.
Reed, John R. Perception & Design in Tennyson's "Idylls of the King"
Reed, Luther D., ed. Lutheran Liturgy.
Reed, M. C. Abstract Non Linear Wave Equations.
Reed, Michael. The Age of Exuberance, Fifteen Hundred to Seventeen Hundred.
--The Georgian Triumph: Seventeen Hundred to Eighteen Thirty.
Reed, Michael, ed. Discovering Past Landscapes.
Reed, Mortimer P. Residential Carpentry.
Reed, Morton. Shadowed Lullabies.
Reed, Pat, jt. auth. see Reed, Bob.
Reed, Pat B. Nutrition: An Applied Science.
Reed, Philip & Muggeridge, Richard. Savate: Martial Art of France.
Reed, R. A., jt. auth. see Bennett, H.
Reed, R. P. & Clark, A. F., eds. Advances in Cryogenic Engineering.
Reed, R. P., jt. ed. see Clark, A. F.
Reed, Rex. Personal Effects: A Novel of Hollywood.
Reed, Robert. Old Washington, D. C. in Early Photographs Eighteen Forty-Six to Nineteen Thirty-Two.
Reed, Robert R. Colonial Manila: The Context of Hispanic Urbanism & Process of Morphogenesis.
Reed, Rufus M. The Valley of Vye-Vye: A Novel.
Reed, Stephen K. Cognition: Theory & Applications.
Reed, W. Maxwell. Earth for Sam. Brandwein, Paul F., ed.
--Stars for Sam. Brandwein, Paul F., ed.
Reed, W. Maxwell & Bronson, Wilfrid S. Sea for Sam. Brandwein, Paul F., ed.
Reed, Will L., ed. Second Treasury of Christmas Music.
Reeder, Harry P. Language & Experience: Descriptions of Living Language in Husserl & Wittgenstein.
Reeder, Rachel, ed. Liturgy: Celebrating with Children.
--Liturgy: Easter's Fifty Days.
Reeds, Brian, ed. see Seaby, H. A.
Reedstrom, Ernest L. Historic Dress of the Old West.
Reehl, W. F., jt. auth. see Lyman, W. J.
Reejhsinghani, Aroona. Indian Sweets & Desserts.
Reekie, Fraser. Draughtsmanship: Architectural & Building Graphics.
Reekie, W. D. Industry, Prices & Markets.
Reeman, Douglas. The Iron Pirate.
Rees, A. R. & Purcell, H. J., eds. Disease & the Environment: Proceedings of the Inaugural Conference of the Society for Environmental Therapy, Held in Oxford, 21-23March 1981.
Rees, Albert, jt. ed. see Watts, Harold W.
Rees, Claire. Matching the Gun to the Game.
Rees, D., jt. ed. see Warwick, K.
Rees, David M. Getting Publicity.
Rees, E. M. Thin Ice.
Rees, Goronwy. Chapter of Accidents.
Rees, Helen G. Shaniko: From Wool Capital to Ghost Town.
Rees, J., jt. auth. see Clark, T.
Rees, Judith. Natural Resources: Allocation, Economics & Policy.
Rees, Leighton & Lanning, Dave. Darts.
Rees, Lucy. Horse of Air.
Rees, Michael K. The Complete Family Guide to Living with High Blood Pressure.
Rees, Nigel. Nudge-Nudge Wink-Wink: A Quotebook of Love & Sex.
Rees, Paul K., et al. College Algebra.
Rees, Richard, tr. see Monnerot, Jules.
Rees, Samuel. David Jones: An Annotated Bibliography & Guide to Research.
Rees, Sian. Ancient Agricultural Implements.
Rees, Teresa L. & Atkinson, Paul. Youth Unemployment & State Intervention.
Rees, Thomas. Reminiscences of Literary London from 1779-1853.
Rees, Thomas & Simmons, Sylvia. More Than Just a Pretty Face: How Cosmetic Surgery Can Improve Your Looks & Your Life.
Rees, Vyvyan. South-West Wales: Pembrokeshire & Carmarthenshire.
Rees, W. David. The Skills of Management.
Reese, A. Principles of Pathology.
Reese, Colleen. Fourth Generation Preacher's Kid.
Reese, Francesca G., jt. ed. see Gardner, John W.
Reese, Hayne W. Basic Learning Processes in Childhood.
--Perception of Stimulus Relations: Discrimination Learning & Transposition.
Reese, John. Angel Range.
--The Sharpshooter.
--Springfield Forty-Five Seventy.
--Texas Gold.
Reese, Loretta. Fifty Craft Ideas with Patterns.
Reese, Lyn & Wilkinson, Jean. I'm on My Way Running: Women Speak on Coming of Age.
Reese, MacPhelan. Showdown & Other Poems.
Reese, Michael, II. Luger Tips.
Reese, N., jt. auth. see Pursell, John.
Reese, Terence, tr. see Sharif, Omar.
Reese, William G. Foreword by see Fields, Sidney Jacob.
Reese, William L. Dictionary of Philosophy & Religion: Eastern & Western Thought.
Reese, William L. & Freeman, Eugene, eds. Process & Divinity: The Hartshorne Festschrift.
Reesink, Marijke. The Princess Who Always Ran Away.
Reesink, Maryke & Apol, Georgette. Two Windmills.
Reeson, Margaret. Currency Lass.
Reetz, A., jt. ed. see Bleuler, K.
Reev. Susie in the Algrave or Susie the Tail-Wagger.
Reeve, F. D., ed. & tr. from Rus. Twentieth-Century Russian Plays: An Anthology.
Reeves, C. C., Jr., ed. Playa Lake Symposium.
Reeves, David S. & Geddes, A. M., eds. Recent Advances in Infection.
Reeves, Donald. Notes of a Processed Brother.
Reeves, Fionnuala. Deadly Inheritance.
Reeves, James, ed. see De France, Marie.
Reeves, John. Murder by Microphone.
Reeves, John & Maibach, Howard. Clinical Dermatology Illustrated.
Reeves, John P., ed. Microbial Permeability.
Reeves, John R. Questions & Answers about Acne.
Reeves, Lawrence. Mopeds: A Guide to Models, Maintenance, & Safety.
Reeves, Marjorie, jt. auth. see Addy, John.
Reeves, Marjorie, jt. auth. see Longmate, Elizabeth.
Reeves, Marjorie, ed. see Bolton, James.
Reeves, Marjorie, ed. see Bradbury, Jim.
Reeves, Marjorie, ed. see Clarke, Clorinda.
Reeves, Marjorie, ed. see Greenwood, Marjorie.
Reeves, Marjorie, ed. see Power, E. G.
Reeves, Marjorie, ed. see Ritchie, W. K.
Reeves, Marjorie, ed. see Sheppard, E. J.
Reeves, Marjorie, ed. see Speed, P. F.
Reeves, Marjorie, ed. see Sylvester, David.
Reeves, Marjorie, ed. see Tate, Nicholas.
Reeves, P. The Bacteriocins.
Reeves, R. A., jt. auth. see Dirksen, D. J.
Reeves, Richard. American Journey: Traveling with Tocqueville in Search of Democracy in America.
--Convention. Okrent, Daniel, ed.
--A Ford, Not a Lincoln.
--Passage fo Peshawar: Pakistan: Between the Hindu Kush & the Arabian Sea.
--Passage to Peshawar: Pakistan: Between the Hindu Kush & the Arabian Sea.
--The Reagan Detour: Conservative Revolutionary.
Reeves, Roxanne W., jt. auth. see Stampen, Jacob O.
Reeves, William J. Librarians As Professionals: The Occupation's Impact on Library Work Arrangements.
Reference International. Encyclopedia of Aviation.
Reference International Publishers Staff. Encyclopedia of Architectural Technology.
Reff, Theodore, ed. Impressionism.
--International Surveys: Exhibitions of Modern European Art.
--Post-Impressionist Group Exhibitions.
--Salons of the "Independants", 1884 to 1891.
--Salons of the "Independants", 1892 to 1895.
--Salons of the "Refuses"
--World's Fair of Eighteen Fifty-Five: Modern Art in Paris 1855-1900.
--World's Fair of Eighteen Sixty-Seven.
Refioglu, I. Electronic Displays.
Refsum, Helge & Mjos, Ole D., eds. Alpha-Andrenoceptor Blockers in Cardiovascular Disease.
Regalado, Antonio, et al, eds. Espana en el siglo XX.
Regamey, Pius R. Renewal in the Spirit.
Regamey, R. H., ed. Immunity to Infections of the Respiratory System in Man & Animals: Proceedings of the International Symposium.
Regamey, R. H., et al, eds. see International Congress of Microbiological Standardization Staff.
Regan, Robert M., ed. Hydraulic Engineering.
Regard, ed. see De Balzac, Honore.
Regardie, Israel. Ceremonial Magic: A Guide to the Mechanisms of Ritual.
--The Golden Dawn: An Account of the Teachings, Rites & Ceremonies of the Order of the Golden Dawn.
--Healing, Energy, Prayer & Relaxation.
--The Lazy Man's Guide to Relaxation.
--The Teachers of Fulfillment.
Regardie, Israel, ed. see Crowley, Aleister.
Regardie, Israel, et al. Mysticism, Psychology & Oedipus.
Regehr, Lydia, tr. Finist the Falcon Prince.
Regena, C. Programmer's Reference Guide to TI 99-4A.
Regena, C., jt. ed. see Compute! Magazine Staff.
Regens, James L., et al. An Analysis of Assaults on Police Officers in Forty-Six South Central Cities.
Reggio, Kathryn & Davidson, Josephine. Individualized Health Incentive Program Modules For Physically Disabled Students. Shooltz, Danna, ed. Incl. Vol. 1. Safety & Survival Education; Vol. 2. Environmental & Community Health; Vol. 3. Sociological Health Problems; Vol. 4. Mental Health & Family Life Education; Vol. 5. Physical Health. Human Res Ctr.
Reginald, R. & Lee, Billy, eds. The Stars Were Ours: The Best from Paperback Quarterly I.
Reginald, R. & Slusser, George, eds. Yesterday or Tomorrow? Aspects of the Work of Robert A. Heinlein.
Regional Conference on Relativity, Univ. of Pittsburgh, July 13-17, 1970. Methods of Local & Global Differential Geometry in General Relativity: Proceedings. Farnsworth, D., et al, eds.
Regis, Alice H. Cakes & Ale: The Ultimate Food Glossary: A Collection of Two Thousand Five Hundred Foods, Techniques, Tools & Cooking Terms.
--Kitchen ABC's: A Dictionary for Cooks.
Register, jt. auth. see Sharp.
Register, George. Basic Stamp Collecting for Pathfinders: A Youth Enrichment Skill.
Regnery, Henry. Memoirs of a Dissident Publisher.
Regnier, Susan. You & Me, Baby.
Regnier, Victor. Planning for the Elderly: Alternative Community Analysis Techniques.
Regniers, Beatrice S. De see De Regniers, Beatrice S.
Regniers, Beatrice S. De see De Regniers, Beatrice S. & Gordon, Isabel.
Regniers, Beatrice S. De see De Regniers, Beatrice S. & Haas, Irene.
Regniers, Beatrice S. De see De Regniers, Beatrice S. & Pierce, Leona.
Rego, Joseph. Avoidance of Baldness.
Regush, Nicholas M., ed. Frontiers of Healing: New Dimensions in Parapsychology.
Reh, J. G. Hands-on BASIC for Kids Using the Commodore 64.
Reh, Jane G. Commodore's Handbook of Simons' BASIC.
Rehbinder, Manfred. Internationale Bibliographie der rechtssoziologischen Literatur.
--Sociology of Law: A Trend Report & Bibliography Prepared for the International Sociological Assoc. Under the Auspices of the International Committee for Social Sciences Documentation.
Rehder, Jessie. The Young Writer at Work.
Rehder, Jessie & Kaufman, Wallace. The Act of Writing.
Rehfeld, J. F. & Amdrup, E., eds. Gastrin & the Vagus.
Rehfisch, Farnham, ed. Gypsies, Tinkers, & Other Travellers.
Rehmel, Judy. Key to a Fourth One Thousand Quilt Patterns.
--Key to a Second One Thousand Quilt Patterns.
--Key to a Third One Thousand Quilt Patterns.
Rehmus, Charles M., et al, eds. International Conference on Trends in Industrial & Labor Relations.
Rehn, James A. & Grant, Harold J., Jr. A Monograph of the Orthoptera of North America (North of Mexico)
Rehr, Helen, intro. by. Social Work Review: Approaches to Evaluation & Analysis of Patient Care, QRB Special Edition.
Rehrer, Ronald. Now What Do I Do?
Reiber, Beth. Frommer's Dollarwise Guide to Japan & Hong Kong.
Reibsamen, Gary G., jt. auth. see Christian, Jeffrey M.
Reich, Ali. The Care Bear Cousins Visit the Woods.
--The Wuzzle's Wishing Flower.
Reich, Bernard. Quest for Peace.
--The Quest for Peace: U. S. - Israeli Relations & the Arab-Israeli Conflict.
Reich, Cary. Financier: The Biography of Andre Meyer.
Reich, Deborah, jt. auth. see Gallup, Barbara.
Reich, Hanns, ed. Children & Their Fathers.
Reich, Jerome R. Colonial America.
Reich, Michael. Racial Inequality: A Political-Economic Analysis.
Reich, N. Consumer Legislation in the E. C. Countries.
--Consumer Legislation in the Federal Republic of Germany.
Reich, Naomi, et al. Essentials of Clothing Construction.
Reich, Pauline. Winning the Game.
Reich, Peter A., ed. see Linguistic Association of Canada & the U. S. Staff.
Reich, Robert C., jt. auth. see Magaziner, Ira C.
Reich, Steven D., jt. ed. see Crooke, Stanley T.
Reich, Tova. Mara.
Reich, Walter. A Stranger in My House: Jews & Arabs in the West Bank.
Reich, Wilhelm. Character Analysis.
Reichard, Joseph R., jt. auth. see Roseler, Robert O.
Reichardt, Christian. Solvent Effects in Organic Chemistry.
Reichardt, W., ed. Processing of Optical Data by Organisms & by Machines.
Reichelt, J., jt. auth. see Godfrey, T.
Reichelt, Karl L. Religion in Chinese Garment.
Reichenbach, Bruce. Is Man the Phoenix? A Study of Immortality.
Reichenbach, Hans. From Copernicus to Einstein.
--Modern Philosophy of Science: Selected Essays. Reichenbach, Maria, ed.
--The Theory of Probability: An Inquiry into the Logical & Mathematical Foundations of the Calculus of Probability.
Reichenbach, Karl Von see Von Reichenbach, Karl.
Reichenbach, Maria, ed. see Reichenbach, Hans.
Reichenbach-Klinke, H. H. Fish Pathology.
Reichert, Richard. Community of the Spirit.
--Confronting Christianity: Adults & Authority.
--Simulation Games for Religious Education.
Reichert, Richard J. A Learning Process for Religious Education.
Reichert, Victor E. Tower of David, 1964.
Reichl, L. E., jt. ed. see Horton, C. W., Jr.
Reichle, D. E., ed. Analysis of Temperate Forest Ecosystems.
Reichman, Louis C., jt. auth. see Wishart, Barry J.
Reichman, Warren N. Foreword by see McClernan, John B.
Reichmann, Edith, jt. auth. see Sparks, Kimberly.
Reicke, Bo. Gospel of Luke.
--The Roots of the Synoptic Gospels.
Reid, A. S., jt. auth. see Hazel, A. C.
Reid, Adrian. The Goddaughter.
Reid, Alastair, tr. see Neruda, Pablo.
Reid, Alexander J. Roots of Lomomba: Mongo Land.
Reid, B., jt. auth. see Coppleson, M.
Reid, C. N. Deformation Geometry for Material Scientists.
Reid, Charles. Portrait Painting in Watercolor.
Reid, Charlotte & Reid, John D. SOAR: A Program for the Gifted - Parent's Guidebook. Lovelady, Janet, ed.
--SOAR: A Program for the Gifted Using Bloom's Taxonomy - Teacher's Guidebook. Lovelady, Janet, ed.
Reid, Constance. Hilbert.
Reid, Dee & Herget, J. Barlow. Insiders' Guide to the Triangle of North Carolina: Raleigh, Cary, Durham, Chapel Hill.
Reid, Duncan E., et al. Principles & Management of Human Reproduction.
--Principles & Management of Human Reproduction.
Reid, E., ed. Trace-Organic Sample Handling.
Reid, E., et al. Cancer Cell Organelles: Biochemistry.
Reid, Fred. Keir Hardie: The Making of a Socialist.
Reid, Gilbert. A Christian's Appreciation of Other Faiths.
Reid, Howard, jt. auth. see Croucher, Michael.
Reid, Ian. The Short Story.
Reid, Ira D. In a Minor Key: Negro Youth in Story & Fact.
Reid, J. D. Atlas of Applied Human Histology: The Identification of Tissues by Light Microscopy for Students, Residents, & Pathologists.
Reid, J. H., jt. auth. see Boa, Elizabeth.
Reid, J. L. Total Geostrophic South Pacific: Flow Patterns, Tracers & Transports.
Reid, James. Peter, Peter, Pumpkin Eater.

Authors

Reid, James M., Company Staff. Business Writing for Bankers.
Reid, Janice. Body, Land & Spirit: Health & Healing in Aboriginal Society.
Reid, John C. The Grumpy Prophet & 22 other Bible Stories to Read & Tell.
--Marriage Covenant.
Reid, John D., jt. auth. see Reid, Charlotte.
Reid, John P. Man Without God: An Introduction to Unbelief.
Reid, Joseph L., jt. ed. see Capurro, L. R.
Reid, Karen K., jt. auth. see Brown, Harry M.
Reid, Ken. Disaffection from School.
Reid, Ken, jt. ed. see Hopkins, David.
Reid, Lawrence A. An Ivatan Syntax.
Reid, Lori. The Female Hand: Palmistry for Today's Woman.
Reid, Mado, jt. auth. see Cundiff, W. E.
Reid, Patrick R. The Colditz Story.
Reid, Peter. Affirmative Action Compliance Kit.
--Affirmative Action Compliance Kit: EEO Dictionary.
--Affirmative Action Compliance Kit: Reference Guide.
--Affirmative Action Compliance Kit: Working Manual.
Reid, R., ed. see Institute of Mathematics Staff.
Reid, Richard & Crum, Milton, Jr. Lesser Festivals 3: Saints' Days & Special Occasions. Achtemeier, Elizabeth, et al, eds.
Reid, Robert. Food Service & Restaurant Marketing.
--My Children, My Children.
Reid, Robert, ed. Country Inns of America Cookbook.
Reid, Robert, Associates Staff. Great Resorts of America.
Reid, Robert C. & Prausnitz, John M. Properties of Gases & Liquids.
Reid, Ron & Grand, Janet. Canoeing Ontario's Rivers: Great Canoe Trips in Canada's Northern Wilderness.
Reid, Samuel R. Merger, Managers & the Economy.
Reid, Stuart. The Verb Handbook.
--Verb Synonyms & Related Words.
--The Writer's Cue.
Reid, Sue T. Crime & Criminology.
--Crime & Criminology.
Reid, T. R. The Chip: How Two Americans Invented the Microchip & Launched a Revolution.
--The Chip: How Two Americans Invented the Microchip & Launched a Revolution.
Reid, Thomas. Essays on the Active Powers of Man. Wellek, Rene, ed.
Reid, Thomas F., et al. Seduction? A Biblical Response. Biros, Florence K. & Williams, Carole, eds.
Reid, Walter & Myddleton, D. R. The Meaning of Company Accounts.
Reid, William H. Basic Intensive Psychotherapy.
Reida, Bernice, jt. auth. see Irwin, Ann.
Reidt, Wilford H. & Lake, John G. Jesus God's Way of Healing & Power to Promote Health.
Reif, Arnold E., et al. Immunity & Cancer in Man: An Introduction.
Reiff, D. D., ed. Component Support Snubbers: Design, Application & Testing.
Reiff, Geoffrey, compiled by. Our American Heritage in Song.
Reiff, Robert F. A Stylistic Analysis of Arshile Gorky's Art from 1943-1948.
Reifsnyder, William E. Hut Hopping in the Austrian Alps.
Reiger, George. Wanderer on My Native Shore.
Reiger, George, jt. auth. see Line, Les.
Reigh, Mildred, et al. Brief Algebra Review Manual: A Program for Self-Instruction.
Reiland, Susan L. Statistics for Business & Economics.
Reiley, H. Edward & Shry, Carroll L., Jr. Introductory Horticulture.
--Introductory Horticulture.
Reiling, Henry B., et al. Business Law: Text & Cases.
Reilly, Frank K. Investments.
Reilly, Jill & Featherstone, Bonnie. College Comes Sooner Than You Think!
Reilly, Jim. Bonds Investments in the Eighties.
Reilly, John W. Language of Real Estate.
Reilly, Nancy & Doyle, Joan. Genitourinary Problems.
Reilly, Paul. An Introduction to Regency Architecture.
Reilly, Philip. Genetics, Law, & Social Policy.
Reilly, Robert. The God of Mirrors. Davison, Peter, ed.
Reilly, Robert T. Travel & Tourism Marketing Techniques: A Handbook of Travel Agency Advertising & Promotion.
Reilly, Robin. British Watercolours.
Reilly, Robin & Savage, George. The Dictionary of Wedgwood.
Reilly, Scott W., jt. auth. see Metropolitan Washington Council of Governments Staff.
Reim, jt. auth. see Long.
Reim, Terry & Long, Kim. Daily Planet Almanac, 1987.
Reim, Terry, ed. Daily Planet Almanac, 1985.
Reiman, Donald, ed. English Romantic Poetry, Eighteen Hundred to Eighteen Thirty-Five: A Guide to Information Sources.
Reiman, Donald H., ed. & intro. by. The Romantics Reviewed: A Collection in Depth of Periodical Reviews (1793-1830) Incl. Vols. I & II. Pt. A; Vols. I To V. Pt. B; Vols. I & II. Pt. C; Vols. I & II. Bibliography of Literary Reviews in British Periodicals 1798-1820. Ward, William S., ed. Garland Pub.
Reiman, Donald H., ed. see Hayley, William.
Reimold, Cheryl. Being a Boss.
--How to Write a Million Dollar Memo.
--The Woman's Guide to Staying Safe.
Reimold, Robert J. & Queen, William H. Ecology of Halophytes.
Rein, David M. Edgar Allan Poe: Inner Patterns.
Rein, Gerhard, ed. New Look at the Apostles Creed. LeFort, David, tr.
Rein, Martin & Rainwater, Lee, eds. Public-Private Interplay in Social Protection.
Reinach, J. Hippo Jogs for Health. Perle, Ruth L., ed.
Reinach, Jacquelyn. Fish & Flips. Perle, Ruth L., ed.
--Fixed by Camel.
--Goose Goofs Off.
--Me Too, Iguana.
--Nuts to Nightingale. Perle, Ruth L., ed.
--Octopus Protests. Perle, Ruth L., ed.
--Quail Can't Decide.
--Rest Rabbit Rest. Perle, Ruth L., ed.
--Who Stole Alligator's Shoe?
--Xerus Won't Allow It. Perle, Ruth L., ed.
Reinach, Jacquelyn & Perle, Ruth L. Elephant Eats the Profits.
--Turtle Throws a Tantrum.
Reinach, Jacquelyn, jt. auth. see Hefter, Richard.
Reinach, Jacquelyn, jt. auth. see Lewis, Shari.
Reinach, Jacquelyn, ed. see Hefter, Richard, et al.
Reinach, Jacquelyn, et al. Happy Birthday Unicorn. Reinach, Jacquelyn & Perle, Ruth L., eds.
Reinagle, Alexander. Four Sonatas; Andante, Theme & Variations; & Adagio for Piano.
Reinberg, A., et al, eds. Annual Review of Chronopharmacology.
Reinboth, R. Intersexuality in the Animal Kingdom.
Reinburg, J. H. Love Polynesian Flying: The Big Birds of Don Don Island-a Fantasy.
Reinecke, Robert, ed. Ophthalmology Annual, 1986.
Reiner, I. & Roggenkamp, K. W. Integral Representations.
Reiner, Irving, jt. auth. see Curtis, Charles W.
Reiner, Miriam, et al, eds. Standard Methods of Clinical Chemistry. Incl. Vol. 1. Reiner, Miriam, ed; Vol. 2. Seligson, David, ed; Vol. 3; Vol. 4; Vol. 5. Meites, S., ed; Vol. 6. MacDonald, R. P., ed; Vol. 7. Acad Pr.
Reinert, J. & Holtzer, H., eds. Cell Cycle & Cell Differentiation.
Reinert, J. & Ursprung, H., eds. Origin & Continuity of Cell Organelles.
Reinertsen, Lauren. Promotional & Program Artwork.
Reines, Frederick, ed. Cosmology, Fusion & Other Matters: A Memorial to George Gamow.
Reinfeld, Fred. Two Weeks to Winning Chess.
Reinfelds, Juris, jt. ed. see Klerer, Melvin.
Reingold, Carmel B. California Cuisine.
Reingold, Nathan, ed. The New American State Papers: Science & Technology Subject Set.
Reinhardt, Ed, jt. auth. see Rogers, Hal.
Reinhardt, Hans-Wolfgang, jt. ed. see Henneberg, Ulrich.
Reinhardt, William P., jt. ed. see Gustafson, Karl E.
Reinhart, C., et al, eds. Irritation Testing of Skin & Mucous Membranes: Proceedings of a Workshop Held at the Karthhaus-Ittingen, near Frauenfeld, Switzerland, April 1984.
Reinhart, Ken & Baker, Scott. Lake Powell in the Eighties.
Reinhart, Tanya. Anaphora & Semantic Interpretation.
Reinharz, Shulamit. On Becoming a Social Scientist: From Survey Research & Participant Observation to Experiential Analysis.
Reinheckel, Gunter. German & Austrian Ceramics. Charleston, Robert J., ed.
Reinhold, L., et al. Progress in Phytochemistry.
Reinhold, L., et al, eds. Progress in Phytochemistry.
--Progress in Phytochemistry.
Reinhold, O., et al. El Anticomunismo Moderno, Politica y Ideologica.
Reinicker, Juliette C., ed. Klondike Letters: The Correspondence of a Gold Seeker in 1898.
Reining, Priscilla & Tinker, Irene, eds. Population: Dynamics, Ethics & Policy.
Reinis, Z., ed. Adaptibility of the Vascular Wall: Proceedings.
Reinisch, Egon, et al. International Essays II.
Reinkraut-Freidjung, Pauline. Eine Deutsche Kulturgeschichte.
Reinl, Edda. The Little Snake.
Reinmuth, James, jt. auth. see Mendenhall, William.
Reinmuth, James E., jt. auth. see Mendenhall, William.
Reinsch, Lamar & Stano, Michael. Communications in Interviews.
Reinsmith, Richard. Somebody to Kill.
--Somebody to Kill.
Reinstedt, Randall A. Mysterious Sea Monsters of California's Central Coast.
Reis, Richard H. George MacDonald.
Reisberg, Gertrude T. Personal Inspirations & Reflections.
Reischauer, August K. Nature & Truth of the Great Religions: Toward a Philosophy of Religion.
Reisdorff, James J. North Platte Canteen.
--Static Steam: Locomotives on Display in Nebraska.
Reisdorff, James J., jt. auth. see Stagner, Lloyd E.
Reisdorff, James J., ed. see Kistler, Richard C.
Reisel, Jerome, jt. auth. see Weschler, Irving R.
Reiser, Bob, jt. auth. see Seeger, Pete.
Reiser, H. Joseph & Horowitz, Leonard, eds. Mechanisms & Treatment of Cardiac Arrhythmias: Relevance of Basic Studies to Clinical Management.
Reiser, Robert, jt. auth. see Balis, Andrea.
Reiser, Stanley J., et al, eds. Ethics in Medicine: Historical Perspectives & Contemporary Concerns.
Reiser, Walter A., Jr. Supplement to Wigmore on Evidence, 1985.
--Wigmore on Evidence: 1984 Supplement.
Reisfeld, Ralph A., jt. ed. see Kahan, Barry D.
Reisfeld, Ralph A., et al. Functional & Structural Nature of Biomembranes: II.
Reiskin, Allan B., ed. Advances in Oral Radiology.
Reis Krausz, Vera Van Der see Krausz, John & Van der Reis Krausz, Vera.
Reisman, Albert F., jt. auth. see Practising Law Institute Staff.
Reisman, Arnold. Phase Equilibria.
Reisman, Bernard. Traditional Values & Contemporary Federation Practices.
Reisman, Fredericka K. Teaching Mathematics: Methods & Content.
Reisman, Michael. Art of the Possible: Diplomatic Alternatives in the Middle East.
Reismann, Janos, jt. auth. see Illyes, Gy.
Reisner, K. & Gosepath, J. Craniotomography: An Atlas & Guide. Michaelis, L. S., tr. from Ger.
Reisner, W. & Rothe, M. Eisenhart. Bins & Bunkers for Handling Bulk Materials.
Reiss, Bob. The Casco Deception.
Reiss, David. The Family's Construction of Reality.
Reiss, Debra. Teamwork: A Prepared Approach to Childbirth.
Reiss, Ellen, jt. ed. see Baird, Martha.
Reiss, Ira L. Family Systems in America.
Reiss, Levi. Computer Literacy.
Reiss, Peter, jt. auth. see Bender's Editorial Staff.
Reiss, Rob. Divine Assassin.
Reiss, Samuel. Basis of Scientific Thinking.
--The Rise of Words & Their Meanings.
Reisser, Anne N. The Face of Love.
Reist, Benjamin A. Theology in Red, White & Black.
Reist, Jay R. Sonnets of Here & Now.
Reister, Floyd N., ed. Private Aviation: A Guide to Information Sources.
Reit, Seymour. Those Fabulous Flying Machines: A History of Flight in Three Dimensions with Punch-Out Plane Model.
Reiter, Sydney. Industrial & Commercial Heat Recovery Systems.
Reiter, Victoria, tr. see Delacorta.
Reiter, Victoria, tr. see Delcorta.
Reith, Edward J., et al. Textbook of Anatomy & Physiology.
Reith, Kimi. Poems for My Mother & the Women I Have Loved. Winans, A. D., ed.
Reithmaier, L. W. Instrument Pilot's Guide.
Reithmaier, L. W., jt. auth. see Gentle, E. J.
Reitman, Alan. The Pulse of Freedom: American Liberties 1920s-1970s.
Reitmeister, Louis A. A Philosophy of Time.
Reitsma, H. A. & Kleinpenning, J. M. The Third World in Perspective.
Reittinger, Merlin L. Odyssey to Omega.
Reitz, Conrad. South African Bibliography.
Reitz, D., et al. Philosophical Analysis & Educational Theory: Contemporary Readings.
Reitz, Victoria W. Map Workbook for Our United States.
Reizenstein, Elmer see Rice, Elmer.
Reizer, Aiala, et al. Dynamics of dBASE III.
Rejda, George E. Principles of Insurance.
Rejda, George E. & Ginsberg, Ralph B., eds. Risk & Its Treatment: Changing Societal Consequences.
Rejnis, Ruth. The Single Parent Housing Guide.
Rekers, George A. & Swihart, Judson J. Making Up the Difference: Help for Single Parents with Teenagers.
Relais et Chateaux Staff. The International Guide to the Relais et Chateaux, 1985.
Relative Value Studies, Inc. Staff. Relative Values for Physicians.
Reliability Analysis Center. Hybrid Microcircuit Reliability Data Compiled by IIT Research Institute, Chicago.
Relier, J. P., ed. Eighteenth Journees Nationales de Neonatologie, 1988.
Rellstab, Ludwig, jt. auth. see Brinkman, Alfred.
Relph, E. Place & Placelessness.
--Place & Placelessness.
Remak, Joachim. The Origins of the Second World War.
Remarque, Erich M. All Quiet on the Western Front.
--Full Circle.
--Full Circle.
--Night in Lisbon. Manheim, Ralph, tr.
--Shadows in Paradise.
Rembar, Charles. The Law of the Land: The Evolution of Our Legal System.
--Perspective.
Remer, C. F. Readings in Economics for China.
Remer, Daniel. Legal Care for Your Software.
--Legal Care for Your Software.
Remer, J. Changing Schools Through the Arts.
Remers, William A. Antineoplastic Agents.
Remes, jt. ed. see Mrazkova.
Remes, Vladimir, jt. auth. see Mrazkova, Daniela.
Remington, Robin A., ed. The International Relations of Eastern Europe: A Guide to Information Sources.
Remini, Robert V. Martin Van Buren & the Making of the Democratic Party.
Remizov, Aleksei. On a Field Azure. Scott, Beatrice, tr. from Rus.
Remmer, Karen L. & Merkx, Gilbert W., eds. New Perspectives on Latin America: Political Conflict & Social Change.
Remmers, H. Lee, jt. auth. see Brooke, Michael Z.
Remond, A., ed. EEG Informatics: A Didactic Review of Methods & Applications of EEG Data Processing.
Remson, Susan T. & Ackermann, Philip G. Calculations for the Medical Laboratory.
Renault, Mary. Funeral Games.
--The Middle Mist.
--The Praise Singer.
Rendall, F. Geoffrey. The Clarinet.
Rendel, James M. Canalisation & Gene Control.
Rendell, D. A., jt. auth. see Hill, R. R.
Rendell, R. International Financial Law.
Rendell, Ruth. Death Notes.
--The Killing Doll.
--The Killing Doll.
--Master of the Moor.
--A New Lease of Death. Barzun, J. & Taqylor, W. H., eds.
--Speaker of Mandarin.
Rendel-Short, John. Man: Ape or Image.
Render & Stair. Quantitative Analysis for Management.
Rendleman, Ron. You Can't Fly Home Again.
Rendle-Short & Gray. Synopsis of Children's Diseases.
Rendtorff, Rolf. Das Uberlieferungsgeschichtliche Problem des Pentateuch.
Renfrew, C. E. Speech Disorders in Children.
Renfrew, Colin. The Emergence of Civilisation, the Cyclades & the Aegaen in the Third Millennium.
Renfrew, Colin, ed. The Explanation of Culture Change: Models in Prehistory.
Renfrew, Colin, et al. Theory & Explanation in Archaeology: The Southampton Conference.
Renfroe, Cornelia M. Kitchen Communion.
Renier, F. G., tr. see Dourlein, Peter.
Reninger, H. W., jt. auth. see Knickerbocker, K. L.
Renken, Aleda. Adventure on Padre Island.
--Donnie's Dangers.
--Grandma Haley.
--Jeff & the Bad Guy.
--Mystery of Cottage Cove.
--Never the Same Again.
--Picked on Pat.
Renko, Hal & Edwards, Sam. Crazy Games for Your Commodore 64.
Renneker, Mark & Leib, Steven. Understanding Cancer.
Rennell, Francis J. British Military Administration of Occupied Territories in Africa During the Years of 1941-1947.
Renner, B. Current Algebras & Their Applications.
Renner, Frederic G. Charles M. Russell: Paintings, Drawings & Sculpture in the Amon G. Carter Collection.
--Charles M. Russell: Paintings, Drawings & Sculpture in the Amon G. Carter Museum.
Renner, Ginger. A Limitless Sky: The Work of Charles M. Russell.
Renner, Harry D. Raven's Ghosts.
Renner, Peter F. Basic Hotel Front Office Procedures.
Renner, Robert P., jt. auth. see Boucher, Louis J.

Authors

Renner, Ruediger & Tooth, Jeffery. Legal Terminology English & German.
Rennert, Jack & Terry, Walter. One Hundred Years of Dance Posters.
Rennert, Jack & Weill, Alain. Alphonse Mucha: The Complete Posters & Panels.
Rennie, Ysabel. The Search for Criminal Man.
Renninger, John P. Multinational Cooperation for Development in West Africa.
Reno, Robert C. A Physics Review for the MCAT.
Renoir, Jean. My Life & My Films. Denny, Norman, tr. from Fr.
Renold, Edward, jt. auth. see Fuller, John.
Renoud, W. E. Criminal Investigation Digest.
Renouf, Alan. Let Justice Be Done: The Foreign Policy of Dr. H. V. Evatt.
Rensch, Roslyn. The Harp.
Rense, Paige, ed. Architectural Digest California Interiors.
--Architectural Digest, Celebrity Homes.
--Architectural Digest Historic Interiors.
--Architectural Digest New York Interiors.
--Architectural Digest Traditional Interiors.
Rense, Paige, intro. by. Chateaux & Villas.
--The Collectors.
Rense, Paige, ed. & intro. by. Contemporary Apartments.
Rense, Paige, intro. by. Country Homes.
Renshaw, Betty, jt. auth. see Hacker, Diana.
Renshaw, Domeena C. The Hyperactive Child.
Rensin, Joseph K. & Goldstein, Larry J. BASICally Kaypro: Programming the 2, 4 & 10.
Rensin, Joseph K., jt. auth. see Goldstein, Larry J.
Rensselaer, John K. Van see Van Rensselaer, Mrs. John K.
Rensselaer, Mariana G. Van. Henry Hobson Richardson & His Works.
Renton, W. J., jt. ed. see Wang, S. S.
Rentschler, Bill, ed. The Paper Sword of Bill Rentschler.
Renty, Ivan de. Lexique de L'Anglais des Affaires.
Rentz, D. C. & Weissman, David B. Faunal Affinities, Systematics & Bionomics of the Orthoptera of the California Channel Islands.
Rentz, Tom W. Low Cost Solar Heaters for Your Home.
Renvoizie, Jean. Web of Violence: A Study of Violence in the Family.
Renwick, Andrew G., jt. auth. see George, Charles F.
Renwick, Fred B., ed. Financing & Investing in Hi-Tech.
Renwick, William L. & Orton, Harold. The Beginnings of English Literature to Skelton, Fifteen Nine.
Renyi, A. Briefe uber die Wahrscheinlichkeit.
Renz, Loren, ed. Foundations Today: Facts & Figures on Private Foundations.
Renz, Loren, ed. see Foundation Center Staff.
Renzi, Ennio De see De Renzi, Ennio.
Repak, T. A., jt. auth. see Levin, Murray B.
Repetto, Robert, ėt al, eds. The Global Possible: Resources Development & the New Century.
Rephotographic Survey Project Staff. Second View.
Repka, Kathleen, jt. auth. see Repka, William.
Repka, William & Repka, Kathleen. Dangerous Patriots: Canada's Unknown Prisoners of War.
Replansky, Dennis H., et al. Truth in Lending Simplification: A Compliance Manual for Creditors & Attorneys on Regulation E.
Report of the Goodman Committee. Charity Law & Voluntary Organizations.
Repp, Gloria. Dave Durant & the Mystery of the Stone House.
Repp, Stan. Super Chief: Train of the Stars.
Repp, William. Complete Handbook of Business English.
Reppy, Judith, jt. ed. see Long, Franklin A.
Reps, John W. Monumental Washington: The Planning & Development of the Capital Center.
Repton, Humphry. Observations on the Theory & Practice of Landscape Gardening.
Requa, Barbara & Holroyd, Sam V. Applied Pharmacology for the Dental Hygienist.
ReQua, Eloise & Statham, Jane, eds. Developing Nations: A Guide to Information Sources.
Reque, John. The Student Journalist & Staff Management.
Reschenthaler, G. B. & Roberts, B. Perspectives on Canadian Airline Regulation.
Rescher, N. & Urquhart, A. J. Temporal Logic.
Rescher, Nicholas. A Theory of Possibility: A Constructivistic & Conceptualistic Account of Possible Individuals & Possible Worlds.
Rescher, Nicholas & Brandom, Robert. The Logic of Inconsistency: A Study in Nonstandard Possible-World Semantics & Ontology.
Reschke, R. C., jt. auth. see Lytle, R. J.
Reschly, Daniel J., jt. ed. see Phye, Gary D.
Resciniti, Angelo. Vanessa's First Love.
Resciniti, Angelo G. Racing Dragsters.
Research & Education Association Staff, ed. Advanced Methods for Solving Differential Equations.
Research & Education Association Staff. College Board Achievement Test Biology.
--Complex Variables Problem Solver.
--The English Handbook of Grammar, Style, & Composition.
--The Essentials in Economics: Quick Access to the Important Facts & Concepts.
--The Essentials in Electronic Communications: Quick Access to the Important Facts & Concepts.
--The Essentials in Statistics: Quick Access to the Important Facts & Concepts.
--The Essentials in Vector Analysis: Quick Access to the Important Facts & Concepts.
--Essentials of Electronic Communications II: Quick Access to the Important Facts & Concepts.
--GRE Literature in English.
--Handbook & Guide for Selecting a Career & Preparing for the Future.
--Handbook of Computers & Data Processing.
--Handbook of Museum Technology.
--Handbook of Psychiatric Rating Scales.
--Machine Design Problem Solver.
--Mathematical Modeling.
--Operations Research Problem Solver.
--Pre-Calculus Problem Solver.
--Thermodynamics Problem Solver.
--Transport Phenomena Problem Solver.
--Vector Analysis Problem Solver.
Research Institute for Mathematical Sciences Staff. Kuramochi Boundaries of Riemann Surfaces: Proceedings of the Research Institute for Mathematical Sciences Symposium, Kyoto, 1965.
Research Institute of America Staff. The RIA Federal Tax Course: Individual Income Tax.
Research Publications, Inc. Staff, ed. Hickcox's Monthly Catalog of U. S. Government Publications, 1885-1894 with Superintendent of Documents Classification Numbers Added.
--Meed Index: Le Monde Index.
Research Symposium on Complexes of Biologically Active Substances with Nucleic Acids & Their Modes of Action Staff. Proceedings of the Research Symposium on Complexes of Biologically Active Substances with Nucleic Acids & Their Modes of Action. Hahn, F. E., et al, eds.
Reseck, John, Jr. Scuba Safe & Simple.
Resetarits, Paul J. & Bertoline, Gary R. Using CADKEY.
Resh, Howard M. Hydroponic Food Production: A Definitive Guide to Soilless Culture.
Residential Real Estate Law & Practice Symposium Staff, et al. Seminar Materials for ICLE's Second Annual Symposium on Residential Real Estate Law & Practice.
Resnick, Elizabeth. Graphic Design: A Problem Solving Approach to Visual Communication.
Resnick, Matthew C., jt. auth. see Seidel, Beverly L.
Resnick, Melvyn C. Interact in Spanish.
Resnick, W. Process Analysis & Design for Chemical Engineers.
Resnicow, Herb, jt. auth. see Tarkenton, Fran.
Resnicow, Herbert. The Gold Deadline.
--Gold Frame.
--The Gold Solutions.
Resnik, Hank, jt. auth. see Schimmels, Cliff.
Resnik, Hank, ed. see Collins, Gary R., et al.
Resnik, Robert, jt. auth. see Creasy, Robert K.
Resnikoff, H. L. & Wells, R. O., Jr., eds. Complex Analysis.
--Complex Analysis, 1969.
--Complex Analysis, 1972, Vol. 1: Geometry of Singularities.
--Complex Analysis, 1972, Vol. 2: Analysis on Singularities.
Resource Publications, Inc. Staff. MusiCatalog. Cunningham, W. P., ed.
Resource Systems International Staff. Applied Math: I.
--Applied Math: II.
--Applied Math: III.
--Applied Math: IV.
--Applied Math: V.
--Applied Metric Math.
--Arc Welding: Equipment.
--Arc Welding: Gas Metal (Mig)
--Arc Welding: Gas Tungsten (Tig)
--Arc Welding: Other Processes.
--Arc Welding: Shielded Metal I.
--Arc Welding: Shielded Metal II.
--Blueprint Reading: Boilermaker.
--Blueprint Reading: Tanks & Vessels.
--Boiler: Installation.
--Boiler: Repair & Maintenance.
--Boiler Systems & Components I.
--Boiler Systems & Components II.
--Boilermaker Hand Tools.
--Boilermaker Power Tools.
--Construction Materials II.
--Cutting: Arc.
--Cutting: Oxyfuel I.
--Cutting: Oxyfuel II.
--Dictionary of Boilermaker Items.
--Layout Procedures & Techniques.
--Mechanical Drawing: Dimensioning.
--Mechanical Drawing: Field Sketching.
--Mechanical Drawing: Isometric & Obilique.
--Mechanical Drawing: Orthographic.
--Mechanical Drawing: Tools & Lettering.
--Metallurgy: Weldability of Metals.
--Metallurgy: Welding.
--Nuclear Power.
--Rigging & Boilermaker Safety.
--Rigging: Basic Principles.
--Rigging: Cranes & Other Lifting Equipment.
--Rigging: Equalizing & Distributing Loads.
--Rigging: Ropes.
--Rigging: Tools.
--Special Applications & Techniques: Applications & Techniques.
--Welding & Cutting Safety.
--Welding: Blueprint Reading.
--Welding: Design, Testing, & Inspection.
--Welding: Performance Qualifications.
Resseh, Hugh W. Van see Van Resseh, Hugh W.
Ressner, Ulla & Gunnarson, Evy. Organised Work: A Female Perspective.
Restany, Pierre. Yves Klein.
Retail Reporting Association Staff, ed. Shopping Centers & Malls.
Retherford, Robert D. Migration & Unemployment in Hawaii.
Rettich, Margret. The Voyage of the Jolly Boat. Jones, Olive, tr. from Ger.
Rettig, Richard P., et al. Manny: A Criminal-Addict's Story.
Rettig, T., jt. auth. see Castro, L.
Reuben, Bryan G., jt. auth. see Wittcoff, Harold.
Reuben, Bryan G., jt. auth. see Wittcoff, Harold A.
Reuland, R., jt. ed. see Cassee, E.
Reulen, H. J., jt. ed. see Schuermann, K.
Reumann, John. Righteousness in the New Testament: Justification in Lutheran-Catholic Dialogue.
Reumann, John, ed. The Church Emerging: A U. S. Lutheran Case Study.
Reumann, John, ed. see Barrett, C. K.
Reumann, John, ed. see Brown, Raymond E.
Reumann, John, ed. see Ellis, E. Earle.
Reumann, John, ed. see Gartner, Bertil.
Reumann, John, ed. see Gunkel, Hermann.
Reumann, John, ed. see Hahn, Ferdinand.
Reumann, John, ed. see Harner, Philip B.
Reumann, John, ed. see Hengel, Martin.
Reumann, John, ed. & tr. see Jeremias, Joachim.
Reumann, John, ed. see Jeremias, Joachim.
Reumann, John, ed. see Lewis, C. S.
Reumann, John, ed. see Manson, T. W.
Reumann, John, ed. see Marxsen, Willi.
Reumann, John, ed. see Moule, C. F.
Reumann, John, ed. see Nygren, Anders.
Reumann, John, ed. see Westermann, Claus.
Reumann, John, ed. see Windisch, Hans.
Reumann, John, ed. see Wolff, Hans W.
Reumann, John, et al. Holy Communion: The Lord's Supper in Changing Times.
Reumann, John, et al, eds. Studies in Lutheran Hermeneutics.
Reunion de Historiadores Mexicanos y Norteamericanos Staff. Contemporary Studies in Mexican History (Investigaciones contemporaneas sobre historia de Mexico)
Reuse, Patricia A. Our World of Things.
Reuss, Carl F. Profiles of Lutherans in the U. S. A.
Reuss, Carol, jt. auth. see Hiebert, Ray.
Reute, H., jt. auth. see Baker, P. F.
Reuterswaerd, C. W., ed. see International Astronautical Congress, 11th, Stockholm, 1960.
Reuterswaerd, C. W. see International Astronautical Congress, 11th, Stockholm, 1960.
Reuther, David & Thorn, John, eds. The Armchair Mountaineer: The Triumphs & Tragedies of Ascent, from Fact & Fiction.
Reuther, Victor G. Brothers Reuther & the Story of the U.A.W. A Memoir.
--The Brothers Reuther & the Story of the U.A.W. A Memoir.
Reutov, O. A., et al. CH-Acids.
Reveen, Peter. The Superconscious World.
ReVelle, Charles S. & ReVelle, Penelope L. Sourcebook on the Environment: The Scientific Perspective.
ReVelle, Penelope L., jt. auth. see ReVelle, Charles S.
Revelli, George. Commander Amanda.
Reventlow, Henning G. The Authority of the Bible & the Rise of the Modern World. Bowden, John, tr. from Ger.
--Problems of Biblical Theology in the 20th Century.
Revere, Paul. Do Your Own Car Body Repairs.
Revesz, G. The Origins & Prehistory of Language.
Revesz, P., jt. ed. see Ganssler, P.
Revie, R. W., et al, eds. Proceedings of the International Conference on Pipeline Inspection.
Revlon. Revlon Art of Beauty.
Rew, Alan. Social Images & Process in Urban New Guinea: A Study of Port Moresby.
Rewa, Michael P. Reborn As Meaning: Panegyrical Biography from Isocrates to Walton.
Rewald, John. Cezanne, the Steins & Their Circle.
--Pissarro.
Rewald, Sabine. Balthus. Howard, Kathleen, ed.
Rex, Barbara. I Want to Be in Love Again.
Rex, John, et al. Colonial Immigrants in a British City: A Class Analysis.
Rex, Walter, jt. auth. see Schwab, Richard.
Rexford, Kenneth. Electrical Control for Machines.
Rexine, John E. Religion in Plato & Cicero.
Rexroth, Kenneth. Classics Revisited.
Rey, H. A. Cecily G. & the Nine Monkeys.
Rey, J. J. Robust Statistical Methods.
Rey, Judy-Lynn Del see Del Rey, Judy-Lynn.
Rey, Lester del see Farmer, Philip Jose.
Rey, Lester del see Fort, Charles.
Rey, Lester del see Piper, H. Beam.
Rey, Lester del see Smith, Edward E.
Rey, Lester del see Smith, Edward E. & Garby, Lee H.
Rey, Robert. Daumier.
Reyes, Benito F. Dialogues with God: Sonnet Psalms on the Significance of Being Human.
--Education for World Peace.
--Moments Without Self.
--Scientific Evidence of the Existence of the Soul.
Reyes, G., jt. auth. see Makkai, M.
Reyes, Miguel A. Soft Drink, Hard Labor: Coca-Cola Workers in Guatemala.
Reymann, Joseph. Understanding FORTH.
Reyment, R. A., jt. auth. see Blackith, R. E.
Reymond, Robert. The Justification of Knowledge.
Reyna, Rudy de see De Reyna, Rudy.
Reynell, Joan. Language Development & Assessment.
Reyner, J. H. Encyclopedia of Radio & Television.
Reyner, J. H., et al. Psionic Medicine: The Study & Treatment of the Causative Factors in Illness.
Reynolds. Social Work & Social Living.
Reynolds, Alan, jt. auth. see Meltzer, Allan.
Reynolds, Beatrice, tr. see Bodin, Jean.
Reynolds, Ben, et al. Writing Instruction for Verbally Talented Youth: The Johns Hopkins Model.
Reynolds, Blair. Manner & Method: A Translation of the French Reformed Church's Liturgy.
Reynolds, Bruford S. Money Saving Recipes Through Sprouting & Gardening.
Reynolds, Charles E. & Steedman, James C. Examples of the Design of Buildings to CP 110 & Allied Codes.
--Reinforced Concrete Designer's Handbook.
Reynolds, Clark G. The Fast Carriers: The Forging of an Air Navy.
Reynolds, Denise A. Sensitive Thoughts for the New Wave Soul.
Reynolds, Donald M. Hiram Powers & His Ideal Sculpture.
Reynolds, Earle L. The Forbidden Voyage.
Reynolds, Evangelist Charlotte. The Devil's Imp.
Reynolds, Fiona. War in the Far East.
Reynolds, Frank E., et al. Guide to Buddhist Religion.
Reynolds, Fred D. & Wells, William D. Consumer Behavior.
Reynolds, G. F., tr. see Galus, Z.
Reynolds, G. J. Measurement of Civil Engineering Work.
Reynolds, Graham. Constable's England.
--Constable's England. Laing, Mary, ed.
Reynolds, Helen. Cops & Dollars: The Economics of Criminal Law & Justice.
Reynolds, Isaac N., et al. Principles of Accounting.
Reynolds, J. & Tampion, J. Double Flowers: A Scientific Study.
Reynolds, J. A., jt. auth. see Steinhardt, J.
Reynolds, James F. & Wentworth, Thomas R. Introduction to Ecology Laboratory Manual.
Reynolds, Jan. Williams Family of Painters.
Reynolds, Jean, ed. New Book of Knowledge.
Reynolds, John. Case Method in Management Development: Guide for Effective Use.
--Media Matter: A Practical Guide to New Zealand Media.
Reynolds, John L. Yankee Lover.
Reynolds, Kirk. The Peoples of the Arctic.
Reynolds, Lillian R. No Retirement: Devotions on Christian Discipleship for Older People.
--Paul, Apostle of Jesus Christ.
Reynolds, Lily, jt. auth. see Jones, Mary G.
Reynolds, Linda & Barret, Stephen. Sign & Guiding for Libraries: A Practical Guide to Design & Production.
Reynolds, Lloyd G., et al. Evolution of Wage Structure.
Reynolds, Lloyd J. My Dear Runemeister: A Voyage Through the Alphabet.
Reynolds, Mack. The Fracas Factor.
--Space Search.

Reynolds, Mark. Honda CB350 & CB500 Fours '73 - '75.

Reynolds, Mark & Shoemark, P. Yamaha 200 Twins '71 - '79.

Reynolds, Mary T. Joyce & Dante: The Shaping Imagination.

Reynolds, Max, jt. auth. see Ilfrey, Jack.

Reynolds, Michael. The Young Hemingway.

Reynolds, Michele. Critters' Kitchen.

Reynolds, Moira D. Aim for a Job in a Medical Laboratory.

Reynolds, Moira S. The Outstretched Hand: Advances in Modern Medicine.

Reynolds, Osborne M., jt. auth. see Kutner, Peter B.

Reynolds, Pamela. Horseshoe Hill.

Reynolds, R. Gene. Assurance.

Reynolds, Rebecca, jt. auth. see Hanson, Richard.

Reynolds, Rebecca, jt. auth. see Strong, Bryan.

Reynolds, Reginald. Beards.

--Cleanliness & Godliness.

Reynolds, Robert, photos by. Texas.

Reynolds, Robert D., jt. ed. see Leklem, James E.

Reynolds, Roger. Mind Models: New Forms of Musical Experience.

Reynolds, S. H. The Pleistocene Mustelidae.

Reynolds, William H., jt. auth. see Myers, James H.

Reynolds, William J. & Price, Milburn. A Joyful Sound: Christian Hymnody.

Reys, Robert E. & Post, Thomas R. The Mathematics Laboratory: Theory to Practice.

Reys, Robert E., jt. auth. see Aichele, Douglas B.

Reys, Robert E., jt. auth. see Bestgen, Barbara J.

Rezak, Richard & Henry, Vernon J., eds. Contributions on the Geological & Geophysical Oceanography of the Gulf of Mexico.

Rezak, Richard, et al. Reefs & Banks of the North Western Gulf of Mexico: Their Geological, Physical & Biological Dynamics.

Rezanov, I. A. Catastrophes in the Earth's History. Creishton, H. Campbell, tr.

Rezk, A. M., ed. Heat & Fluid Flow in Power System Components.

Rezneck, Samuel. The Saga of an American Jewish Family since the Revolution: A History of the Family of Jonas Phillips.

Reznikoff, S. C. Specifications for Commercial Interiors: Professional Liabilities, Regulations, & Performance Criteria.

Reznikov, A. Comintern & the East: Strategy & Tactics.

Rhee, Jhoon. Chung-Gun & Toi Gye of Tae Kwon Do Hyung.

--Hwa-Rang & Chung-Mu of Tae Kwon Do Hyung.

Rhee, Taek-Hyung. United States, Republic of Korea Combined Operations: A Korean Perspective.

Rhein, Phillip H. Albert Camus.

Rheinboldt, W. C., tr. see Stiefel, E. L.

Rheingold, Howard & Levine, Howard. Talking Tech: A Conversational Guide to Science & Technology.

Rhind, D. The Census Users Handbook.

Rhine & Brier. Parapsychology Today.

Rhoades, John. Linguistic Diversity & Language Belief in Kenya: The Special Position of Swahili.

Rhoades, Stephen A. Power, Empire Building, & Mergers.

Rhoads, David M. Israel in Revolution, 6-74 C.E. A Political History Based on the Writings of Josephus.

Rhoads, J. W. The Contract.

--The Contract.

Rhoda, Franklin. Summits to Reach: Report on the Topography of the San Juan Country. Foster, Mike, ed.

Rhode, Irma. Cool Entertaining.

--Practical Entertaining.

Rhodes, A. & Fletcher, D. L. Principles of Industrial Microbiology.

Rhodes, Alexandra M. Hat Pin & Tie Pins. Riley, Noel, ed.

Rhodes, D. N., jt. ed. see Morton, I.

Rhodes, Donald. Introduction to Monopulse.

Rhodes, Evan H. Bless This House: American Palace No. 1.

Rhodes, Helen C. Place of Shine & Shadow.

Rhodes, Irma G. In Quest of Treasure: New Poems for Young People with Study Guides.

Rhodes, Jerry L. Basic Accounting & Budgeting for Long Term Care Facilities.

Rhodes, John S., et al, eds. Advances in X-Ray Analysis.

Rhodes, Lucien, jt. auth. see Little, Jeffrey B.

Rhodes, Neil. Elizabeth Grotesque.

Rhodes, Neil S., jt. auth. see Lieberman, Jethro K.

Rhodes, Nicholas, jt. auth. see Bruce, Colin R., II.

Rhodes, Philip. Letters to a Young Doctor.

Rhodes, R. A. Public Administration & Policy Analysis.

Rhodes, Robert E. & Janik, Del Ivan, eds. Studies in Ruskin: Essays in Honor of Van Akin Burd.

Rhodes, Royal W., jt. auth. see Baly, Denis.

Rhodes, S. A. Gerard de Nerval, Eighteen Hundred Eight to Eighteen Fifty-Five.

Rhodes, Tonya S. Color Related Decorating Textiles.

Rhodes, Vivian. Groomed for Murder.

Rhodin, Eric. The Good Greenwood.

--The Sinister Affair.

Rhodin, Victoria, tr. see Zink, Jorg.

Rhoer, Edward Van Der see Van Der Rhoer, Edward.

Rholes, Julia M., et al. Rural Energy & Developing Countries: A Bibliography.

Rhone. A Wage & Salary Program Based on Position Evaluation for Administrative & Supervisory Staff.

Rhoodie, N. J., ed. South African Dialogue: Contrasts in South African Thinking on Basic Race Issues.

Rhymer, John D. IDA: Independent Democratic, Amalgamated.

Rhymes, Douglas A. Through Prayer to Reality.

Rhyne, Nancy. Coastal Ghosts: Haunted Places from Wilmington to Savannah.

Rhyne, V. Thomas. Fundamentals of Digital Systems Design.

Rhys, Ernest, ed. Prelude to Poetry.

Rhys, Jean. Jean Rhys: The Complete Novels.

Rhys, John & Jones, David B. Welsh People: Chapters on Their Origin, History, Laws, Language, Literature & Characteristics.

Rhys, Stephen & Palmer, King. ABC of Church Music.

Rhys-Thomas, Deirdre. Letters for My Children: One Mother's Quest for Answers about the Nuclear Threat.

Riain, Noirin N., et al. Irish Women: Image & Achievement. Chuilleanain, Eilean N., ed. & intro. by.

Riazuddin & Qadir, Asghar, eds. Physics & Contemporary Needs.

Ribalow, Harld V. & Ribalow, Meir. The Jewish Baseball Stars.

Ribalow, Harold U. & Ribalow, Meir Z. The Jew in American Sports.

Ribalow, Meir, jt. auth. see Ribalow, Harld V.

Ribalow, Meir Z., jt. auth. see Harold U.

Ribalow, Meir Z., jt. auth. see Ribalow, Harold U.

Ribalta, Marta. Habitat: Areas of Communication.

--Habitat: The Living Room.

Ribaudo, Mary I. Love Poems by Invadelle.

Ribbens, William B. & Mansour, Norman. Understanding Automotive Electronics.

Ribbens, William B. & Mansour, Norman P. Understanding Automotive Electronics. Luecke, Gerald, et al, eds.

Ribbons, D. W., jt. auth. see Norris, J. R.

Ribbons, D. W., jt. ed. see Norris, J. R.

Ribbons, D. W., jt. ed. see Smith, E. E.

Ribeiro, Aileen. Visual History of Costume: The Eighteenth Century.

Ribeiro, Joao U. Sergeant Getulio.

Ribes-Inesta, Emilio, jt. ed. see Bijou, Sidney W.

Ribes-Inesta, Emilio, jt. ed. see Keller, Fred S.

Ribi, W. A. The Neurons of the First Optic Ganglion on the Bee (Apis Mellifera)

Ribman, Ronald. Five Plays by Ronald Ribman.

Ribner, Irving, ed. Doctor Faustus: Text & Major Criticism, Marlowe.

Riccardo, Martin V. Vampires Unearthed: The Vampire & Dracula Bibliography of Books, Articles, Movies, Records, & Other Material.

Ricchini, John A. Construction & Documentation.

Ricci, J. Elsevier's Banking Dictionary.

Ricci, M., et al, eds. Developments in Clinical Immunology.

Ricciardi, Antonio. St. Maximilian Kolbe.

Riccio, Dolores, jt. auth. see Bingham, Joan.

Ricciuti, Ed. Fish of the Atlantic.

Ricciuti, Edward R. Wildlife of the Mountains.

Ricciuti, Henry, jt. auth. see Willis, Anne.

Riccobono, John A. Use of Electronic Information Technologies for Non-School Learning in American Households: Report of Findings from the 1985 Home Information Technology Study (HITS), Contractor Report.

Rice. The Adolescent.

Rice, Anne. The Feast of All Saints.

Rice, Anne see Rampling, Anne, pseud.

Rice, B. J. & Strange, Jerry D. Applied Analysis for Physicists & Engineers.

Rice, Bernard J. & Strange, Jerry D. Algebra & Trigonometry.

--College Algebra.

Rice, C. B., jt. auth. see Stock, R.

Rice, Charles & Martyn, J. Louis. Easter.

Rice, Charles, jt. auth. see Collins, Adela Y.

Rice, Clyde. A Heaven in the Eye.

Rice, Craig S. Your Team of Tigers: Getting Good People & Keeping Them.

Rice, David, jt. ed. see Botein, Michael.

Rice, David A. Consumer Transactions: Cases & Materials.

Rice, Dorothy. Gypsy Laddie.

Rice, Edward. American Saints & Seers: American-Born Religions & the Genius Behind Them.

--Mother India's Children.

Rice, Eugene F., Jr. Saint Jerome in the Renaissance.

Rice, F. Philip. Morality & Youth: A Guide for Christian Parents.

Rice, Geoffrey. Black November: The Nineteen Eighteen Influenza Epidemic in New Zealand.

Rice, Helen S. Heart Gifts from Helen Steiner Rice.

--Lovingly: Poems for All Seasons.

--Prayerfully.

--Remembering with Love.

Rice, John A., jt. auth. see Lynch, Robert E.

Rice, John R. Introduction to Computing with BASIC.

--When a Christian Sins.

Rice, Joyce G. Love Never Ends.

Rice, Karen, jt. auth. see Rice, Timothy.

Rice, Keith A. Out of Canaan.

Rice, Laura N., jt. auth. see Wexler, David A.

Rice, Laura W., jt. auth. see Rice, Robert P.

Rice, Lawrence D. Negro in Texas, 1874-1900.

Rice, Linda. Using Professional File on the PC.

--Using Professional Write on the PC.

Rice, Linda L. PFS on the IBM PC, Using.

Rice, M. S., ed. see Curtiss Aeroplane & Motor Corp.

Rice, Marion J. & Cobb, Russell L. What Can Children Learn in Geography? A Review of Research.

Rice, Marion J., et al, eds. Anthropological Resources & Teaching.

Rice, Myron A., jt. auth. see Muenscher, Walter C.

Rice, Otis K. Charleston & the Kanawha Valley (West Virginia)

Rice, Patty C. Amber: The Golden Gem of the Ages.

Rice, Philip B. On the Knowledge of Good & Evil.

Rice, Rex. VLSI--the Coming Revolution in Applications & Design.

Rice, Rip G. & Netzer, Ahaton. Handbook of Ozone Technology & Applications.

Rice, Rip G. & Netzer, Aharon, eds. Handbook of Ozone Technology & Applications.

Rice, Robert P. & Rice, Laura W. Practical Horticulture.

Rice, Russ. The Wildcats: Kentucky Football.

Rice, Russell. Kentucky Basketball: Big Blue Machine.

Rice, Sgt. Gregory L. Dress Blues & Tears.

Rice, Stanley. Tell Time.

Rice, Stuart A. Polyelectrolyte Solutions: A Theoretical Introduction.

Rice, Stuart A., jt. auth. see Prigogine, I.

Rice, Tim & Webber, Andrew L. Joseph & the Amazing Technicolor Dreamcoat.

Rice, Tim, jt. auth. see Webber, Andrew Lloyd.

Rice, Timothy & Rice, Karen. Mastering ProDOS.

Rice, Wayne. Junior High Ministry: A Guidebook for the Leading & Teaching of Early Adolescents.

Rich & Hager. Understanding Breast Cancer.

Rich, Adrienne. Of Woman Born: Motherhood As Experience & Institution.

--Of Woman Born: Motherhood As Experience & Institution.

--Poems: Selected & New, 1950-1974.

--Poems: Selected & New, 1950-1974.

Rich, Alan. The Lincoln Center Story.

Rich, Daniel, jt. ed. see Byrne, John.

Rich, Daniel C. Seurat & the Evolution of the La Grande Jatte.

Rich, Elizabeth, jt. auth. see Greenwald, Harold.

Rich, Irene, ed. see Byrd, Anne.

Rich, Irene, ed. see Yueh, Jean.

Rich, John M. Innovations in Education: Reformers & Their Critics.

Rich, Kathleen. The Lucifer Mask.

Rich, Mark. Custom Vans.

--Earth Movers.

Rich, Meredith. Little Sins.

Rich, Norman. Hitler's War Aims: Ideology, the Nazi State, & the Course of Expansion.

--Hitler's War Aims: The Establishment of the New Order.

Rich, Richard C., ed. Analyzing Urban Service Distributions: New Concepts & New Measures.

Rich, Robert M. Essays on the Theory & Practice of Criminal Justice.

Rich, Stephen. Rendering Standards in Architecture & Design.

Rich, Stephen W. Rendering Standards.

Richard, A. J., ed. The Pollination of Flowers by Insects.

Richard, C. & Granger, P. Chemically Induced Dynamic Nuclear & Electron Polarizations-Cidnp & Cidep.

Richard, Cole. Dealer Take All.

Richard, E. Johnson, et al. Calculus with Analytic Geometry.

Richard, Frederick S. Hispanoamerica Moderna.

Richard, J. F. Posterior & Predictive Densities for Simultaneous Equation Models.

Richard, Lucien J. The Spirituality of John Calvin.

Richard, Marie Helene, jt. auth. see De Balzac, Honore.

Richard, P., et al. Oxytocin: Current Research.

Richard, Stephen. Directory of British Official Publications: A Guide to Sources.

Richard, Timothy, tr. see Ashvagosha.

Richard, W. Our Market System of Capitalism Close-Up.

--Readings in Political Economy.

Richard, Wilfred, jt. ed. see Pease, Allen.

Richards, Arlene K. & Willis, Irene. Leaving Home.

Richards, Carl, jt. auth. see Swisher, Doug.

Richards, Carl, et al. Stoneflies.

Richards, Caroline. Sweet Country.

--Sweet Country.

Richards, Colin, ed. New Directions in Primary Education.

Richards, Dennis L., ed. Montana's Genealogical Records.

Richards, Dorothy F. Abe Lincoln, Make It Right!

--Pray in This Way.

Richards, Dusty. Winter Camp Kid & Will.

Richards, E. J., tr. see De Pizan, Christine.

Richards, Elton P., Jr. Outreach Preaching: The Role of Preaching in Evangelism.

Richards, Eric. History of the Highland Clearances: Vol. I, Agrarian Transformation & the Evictions 1746-1886.

--A History of the Highland Clearances: Vol. 2: Emigration, Protest, Reasons.

Richards, Ernest, jt. auth. see Hodgson, John.

Richards, Eugene & Lynch, Dorothea. Fifty Hours.

Richards, Francis A., ed. Coastal Upwelling Ecosystems Analysis Program.

Richards, Harold. Earthquake.

Richards, Hubert. Reading Paul Today: A New Introduction to the Man & His Letters.

Richards, I. A. Beyond.

--Tomorrow Morning, Faustus.

Richards, J. M. The National Trust Book of English Architecture.

Richards, Jack C., ed. Understanding Second & Foreign Language Learning.

Richards, James. Pascal.

Richards, Jean H. Jesus Went about Doing Good.

Richards, Jeffrey. The Age of the Dream Palace: Cinema & Society in Britain 1930-1939.

--Consul of God.

--Thorold Dickinson: The Man & His Films.

Richards, Jeffrey, jt. auth. see Aldgate, Anthony.

Richards, Joan M., ed. American Firms Importing from the People's Republic of China.

Richards, John B., jt. auth. see Magoon, Paul M.

Richards, Judith. Triple Indemnity.

Richards, K., et al, eds. Geomorphology & Soils.

Richards, Katharine L. How Christmas Came to the Sunday-Schools: The Observance of Christmas in the Protestant Church Schools of the United States.

Richards, Kent D. Isaac I. Stevens: Young Man in a Hurry.

Richards, Larry. Pass It on.

--Years of Darkness, Days of Glory.

Richards, Lawrence & Martin, Gib. Theology of Personal Ministry.

Richards, Lawrence O. The Dictionary of Basic Bible Truths.

--Love Your Neighbour: A Woman's Workshop on Fellowship.

--A Theology of Christian Education.

--The Word Bible Handbook.

--The Word Parents Handbook.

Richards, Lawrence O. & Hoeldtke, Clyde. A Theology of Church Leadership.

Richards, Mary. Public School & the Whole Person.

Richards, Mary C. Centering in Pottery, Poetry, & the Person.

Richards, Mary C., tr. see Artaud, Antonin.

Richards, Mildred. Paraside Then, & Again.

Richards, Norman V. Heart to Heart: The Cleveland Clinic Guide to Understanding Heart Disease & Open-Heart Surgery.

Richards, O. W. The Social Insects.

Richards, O. W. & Davies, R. G. Imm's Outline of Entomology.

Richards, P. & Leonor, M. Education & Income Distribution in Asia: A Study Prepared for the International Labour Office Within the Framework of the World Employment Programme.

Richards, R. J. An Introduction to Dynamics & Control.

Richards, R. J. & Rajan, K. T., eds. Tissue Culture in Medical Research (II) Second International Symposium on Tissue Culture in Medical Research, 1-3 April 1980, Cardiff, Wales.

Richards, R. J., tr. see Bree, Germaine.

Richards, R. Michael, jt. auth. see Lawson, David H.

Richards, Stanley, ed. Best Mystery & Suspense Plays of the Modern Theatre.

Richards, Steve. Luck, Chance, & Coincidence.
Richards, Wyn. The Lingering Summer.
Richardson, jt. auth. see Fitter.
Richardson, A. E. & Corfiato, Hector O. Art of Architecture.
--Design in Civil Architecture.
Richardson, Alan. Creeds in the Making: A Short Introduction to the History of Christian Doctrine.
--Experiential Definition of Psychology.
--The Experimental Dimension of Psychology.
Richardson, Alan, ed. Dictionary of Christian Theology.
Richardson, Alan, et al. Our Secular Cathedrals: Change & Continuity in the University. Littleton, Taylor, ed.
Richardson, Albert E. An Introduction to Georgian Architecture.
Richardson, Ann. Participation.
Richardson, Ann, ed. see Texas Homes Editors.
Richardson, Anthony, jt. auth. see Bernstein, Levitt.
Richardson, Arleta. Angelina's Adventure.
--Passport South America.
Richardson, Bessie E. Old Age among the Ancient Greeks: The Greek Portrayal of Old Age in Literature, Art & Inscriptions.
Richardson, Carol. Bible Programs & Dramas for Children.
Richardson, Curtis J., ed. Pocosin Wetlands: An Integrated Analysis of Coastal Plain Freshwater Bogs in North Carolina.
Richardson, D. H. The Biology of Mosses.
Richardson, David, jt. auth. see Hapgood, David.
Richardson, Donald W. The Revelation of Jesus Christ.
Richardson, Doug. Naval Armament.
Richardson, Edward A. Collect Canada Covers.
Richardson, Edward W. Standards & Colors of the American Revolution.
Richardson, Glenn E. Educational Imagery: Strategies to Personalize Classroom Instruction.
Richardson, H. Edward. Jesse: The Biography of an American Writer-Jesse Hilton Stuart.
Richardson, H. Edward, intro. by see Stewart, Jesse.
Richardson, H. L. What Makes You Think We Read the Bills?
Richardson, H. W. The New Urban Economics, & Alternatives.
Richardson, Hugh E. Tibet & Its History.
Richardson, I. M., retold by. The Fisherman & His Wife.
Richardson, Ilona E. Before the World Was.
Richardson, J. Memoir of a Gambler.
Richardson, J. A., jt. auth. see Rodger, I. A.
Richardson, J. F. A Selection of European Folk Dances.
Richardson, J. G., ed. Practical Formwork & Mould Construction.
Richardson, J. H. & Peterson, R. V. Systematic Materials Analysis.
Richardson, J. H. & Peterson, R. V., eds. Systematic Materials Analysis.
--Systematic Materials Analysis.
Richardson, Jean, tr. see De Carli, Franco.
Richardson, Jeanne M., jt. auth. see Malinowsky, H. Robert.
Richardson, Jerry & Margulis, Joel. The Magic of Rapport: How You Can Increase Your Communication Skills to Gain Personal Power in Any Situation.
--The Magic of Rapport: The Business of Negotiation.
Richardson, John E., ed. Marketing 1988-89.
Richardson, K. I. The Gyroscope Applied.
Richardson, L., Jr. Pompeii: The Casa dei Dioscuri & Its Painters.
Richardson, Lloyd I., et al. A Mathematics Activity Curriculum for Early Childhood & Special Education.
Richardson, M. D., jt. ed. see Warnock, D. W.
Richardson, Margaret. The Craft Architects.
Richardson, Marian K. & Stover, Mary B. Songs for the Space Age Child.
Richardson, Marilyn. Black Women & Religion.
Richardson, Mike & Richardson, Sue. Dinky Toys & Modelled Miniatures.
Richardson, Otis D. God in the High Country.
--Start Point: Six Studies in Violence.
Richardson, Otis Dunbar. The Hoods of Manor Grove.
--The Phantom Homestead: A Circuit of Our People.
--Says Who?--Authority & Old Adam.
Richardson, P. N. Introduction to Extrusion. Mendoza, Luis E., tr.
Richardson, Peter. Paul's Ethic of Freedom.
Richardson, Peter N. German-Romance Contact: Name-Giving in Walser Settlements.
Richardson, Ralph W. The Hudson River Basin.
--The Hudson River Basin: Environmental Problems & Instititional Response.
Richardson, Richard E. & Barton, Roger E. The Dental Assistant.
Richardson, Richard W. Family Ties That Bind: A Self-Help Guide to Change Through Family of Origin Therapy.
Richardson, Rupert N. The Comanche Barrier to South Plains Settlement.
Richardson, Samuel. Pamela.
Richardson, Selma K., ed. Children's Services of Public Libraries.
Richardson, Sue, jt. auth. see Richardson, Mike.
Richberg, Donald R. & Britt, Albert. Only the Brave Are Free.
Richens, Alan, jt. auth. see Laidlaw, John P.
Richert, H. E., jt. auth. see Halberstam, H.
Riches, Anne. Victorian Church Building & Restoration in Suffolk.
Riches, Colin. Developing Interviewing Skills in Education.
Riches, John, ed. see Theissen, Gerd.
Riches, Phyllis M., ed. Analytical Bibliography of Universal Collected Biography.
Richet, Diana, ed. Sciences de L'education-Sciences of Education: Catalogues et Inventaires.
Richey, C. B., et al. Agricultural Engineers' Handbook.
Richey, Charles R. Manual on Employment Discrimination & Civil Rights Actions in the Federal Courts, Attorneys' ed.
--Manual on Employment Discrimination & Civil Rights Actions in the Federal Courts: Attorney's Edition.
Richey, Robert W. Preparing for a Career in Education: Challenges, Changes, & Issues.
Richie, Donald & Maeda, Mana. Ji: Signs & Symbols of Japan.
Richie, Margaret B., jt. auth. see Bye, Ranulph.
Richie, Mary. Loving Upward.
Richler, Mordecai. The Best of Modern Humor.
--Images of Spain.
Richman, Carol. Lekachmacher Family.
Richman, Irwin. Historical Manuscript Depositories in Pennsylvania.
Richman, Phyllis C. Best Restaurants & Others: Washington, D. C.
--Best Restaurants Washington D. C. & Environs.
--Best Restaurants: Washington D.C. & Environs.
Richmond, Anthony H. Readings in Race & Ethnic Relations.
Richmond, Doug. Mexico-A Travel Survival Kit.
Richmond, Gail L. Federal Tax Research: Guide to Materials & Techniques.
Richmond, Hugh M. Shakespeare's Sexual Comedy: A Mirror for Lovers.
Richmond, J. Erskine. Bread & Freedom, Man.
Richmond, James, jt. ed. see Bowden, John.
Richmond, Jerry. Denver: America's Mile High Center of Enterprise.
Richmond, Kenneth. Education in the U. S. A.
Richmond, Lee. High on Gold.
Richmond, Robert. Kansas a Land of Contrast.
Richmond, Roe. Lashtrow: Nevada Queen High.
Richmond, W., jt. auth. see Oakley, K.
Richmond, W. H. & Sharma, P. C., eds. Mining & Australia.
Richmond, W. Kenneth. Education & Schooling.
Richter, ed. The Making of a Pilot.
Richter, Alan A. Direct Payment for Services.
Richter, Anton H., tr. see Eisenberg, C. G.
Richter, Catherine, jt. auth. see Dial, Hertha.
Richter, D., ed. Biochemical Factors Concerned in the Functional Activity of the Nervous System.
Richter, Derek. The Challenge of Violence.
Richter, Dietmar, jt. auth. see Koch, Gebhard.
Richter, Dietmar, jt. auth. see Koch, Gerhard.
Richter, Dietmar, jt. ed. see Koch, Gerhard.
Richter, F. K. A New Economy: An Argument for Economic Reform.
Richter, Gustav. Studien Zur Geschichte der Alteren Arabischen Furstenspiegel.
Richter, Herbert P. & Schwan, W. Creighton. Practical Electrical Wiring.
--Practical Electrical Wiring: Residential, Farm & Industrial.
Richter, Joan, jt. auth. see Gelman, Rita.
Richter, P., jt. auth. see La Fauci, H. M.
Richter, Paul W. Corporate Anti-Takeover Defenses: The Posion Pill Device.
Richter, Peyton E., jt. auth. see Fogg, Walter L.
Richter-Dyn, Nira, jt. auth. see Goel, Narendra.
Richthofen, Manfred Von see Von Richthofen, Manfred.
Richtmyer, R. D., ed. see International Conference on Numerical Methods in Fluid Dynamics Staff.
Rickard, David, ed. see Royal Swedish Academy of Sciences Staff.
Rickard, Henry C. & Dinoff, Michael. Behavior Modification in Children: Case Studies & Illustrations from a Summer Camp.
Rickard, Henry C., ed. Behavioral Intervention in Human Problems.
Rickard, Marvin G. Let It Grow: Your Church Can Chart a New Course.
Rickard, Robert J., jt. auth. see Michell, John.
Rickards, Barrie. Angling: Fundamental Principles.
Rickards, Barrie & Whitehead, Ken. Spinning & Plug Fishing: An Illustrated Textbook.
Rickards, Maurice. Where They Lived in London: A Guide to Famous Doorsteps.
Rickell, Walter. The Misunderstood Male.
Ricken, Robert. Love Me When I'm Most Unlovable: Guide to the Middle School Years.
Ricker, George M. The Faith Once Given: The Apostle's Creed Interpreted for Today.
Rickerson, Wayne. Christian Family Activities for Families with Children.
--Christian Family Activities for Families with Preschoolers.
--Christian Family Activities for Families with Teens.
Rickert, Edith, ed. Babees' Book: Medieval Manners for the Young.
Rickett, Francis. An Affair of Doctors.
Rickett, R. M. W. see Wilson, J. R., et al.
Ricketts, Mac L., tr. see Eliade, Mircea.
Rickham, P. P. & Hecker, W. C. Management of the Burned Child.
Rickham, P. P., ed. Endocrine Disorders & Tumors in Children: Pathology of Sexual Development.
--Pediatric Surgery in Tropical Countries.
Rickham, P. P., et al. Genito-Urinary Problems in Childhood.
Rickman, Gregg. Philip K. Dick: In His Own Words.
Rickman, John, ed. see Freud, Sigmund.
Ricks, Chip. Carol's Story.
Ricks, Christopher, ed. see Tennyson, Alfred.
Ricks, David A., ed. see Kujawa, Duane.
Ricks, Delthia T., et al. Hysterectomy & You.
Ricks, Truett A., jt. auth. see Gaines, Larry K.
Rico, Armando B. Three Coffins for Nino Lencho.
Rico, Ul De see De Rico, Ul.
Ricoeur, Paul. Essays on Biblical Interpretation. Mudge, Lewis S., ed.
Riddell, Frederick R., ed. Hypersonic Flow Research, PAAS7.
Riddell, Peter. The Thatcher Government.
Riddle, Janet T. Anatomy & Physiology Applied to Nursing.
--Objective Tests for Nurses.
--Objective Tests for Nurses: The Digestive System & the Urinary System.
Riddle, Janet T. & Dinner, Joan. Objective Tests for Nurses.
Riddle, Maxwell. The Complete Brittany Spaniel.
Riddle, Peter. Time-Lapse Cinemicroscopy.
Riddle, Roz. The City Cat: How to Live Healthily & Happily with Your Indoor Pet.
Riddle, W. E. & Fairley, R. E. Software Development Tools.
Riddle, William E. & Wileden, Jack C. Tutorial on Software System Design: Description & Analysis.
Riddy, F. & Bawcutt, P., eds. An Anthology of Longer Scottish Poems.
Ridenhour, Thomas E., jt. auth. see Micks, Marianne H.
Ridenour, Fritz. Faith It or Fake It?
--How to Be a Christian in an Unchristian World.
Ridenour, Nina & Johnson, Isabel. Some Special Problems of Children Aged 2-5.
Rider, David F., ed. Jane's Airport Equipment 1986-87.
Rider, John R. Student Journalist & Broadcasting.
--Your Future in Broadcasting.
Rider, R., jt. auth. see Rose, T.
Rider, Warrick W. Dyed for Death.
Ridge, G. R. & Njoku, B. C. The Christian Tragic Hero in French & English Literature.
Ridge, J. D. Annotated Bibliographies of Mineral Deposits in Africa Asia (Exclusive of the U. S. S. R.) & Australasia.
Ridge, Martin, et al. Liberty & Union.
Ridgeway, James, jt. auth. see Cockburn, Alexander.
Ridgeway, Rick. The Boldest Dream: The Story of Twelve Who Climbed Mount Everest.
Ridgway, Arlene M., ed. Chicken Foot Soup & Other Recipes from the Pine Barrens.
Ridgway, Athol J. The Love Birds: A Book of Poems.
Ridgway, R. S. Voltaire & Sensibility.
Ridho, Abu. Museum Pusat, Jakarta.
Riding, Laura. Selected Poems: In Five Sets.
Ridley, Charles P., et al. The Making of a Model Citizen in Communist China.
Ridley, F. F., ed. Policies & Politics in Western Europe: The Impact of Recession.
Ridley, Jasper. The History of England.
Ridley, Joanne. Michelle, la Chienne Francais.
Ridlon, G. T. Coolbroth Family.
Ridout, Samuel. Judges & Ruth.
Ridpath, Ian. Discovering Space & Astronomy.
Ried, Glenda E., jt. auth. see Gaylord, Gloria L.
Riedel, Johannes. Lutheran Chorale - Its Basic Traditions.
Riedel, W. R. & Saito, T., eds. Marine Plankton & Sediments: Kiel Symposium.
Rieder, Thomas J. The George A. Meyers Papers: An Inventory to the Microfilm Edition.
Riedl, Frederick. History of Hungarian Literature. Ginever, C. A., tr.
Riedler, W. & Friedrich, M., eds. Scientific Ballooning-II.
Riedler, W. & Torkar, K., eds. Scientific Ballooning: Proceedings of Symposium 7 of the COSPAR Twenty-Fifth Plenary Meeting Held in Graz, Austria, 25 June -7 July 1984.
Riedman, Sarah R. Trees Alive.
Riedy, James L. Chicago Sculpture: Text & Photographs.
Riegel, Klaus F. Psychology, Mon Amour: A Countertext.
--Psychology of Development & History.
Rieger, Eliezer. Modern Hebrew.
Rieger, James & Mathews, Boots. Dining In - Kansas City.
Riegert, Eduard & Hiers, Richard H. Pentecost 2.
Riegert, Ray. Hidden Hawaii: The Adventurer's Guide. Young, Sayre V. & Henriques, Leslie, eds.
--Hidden San Francisco & Northern California: The Adventurer's Guide.
Riehl, H. Climate & Weather in the Tropics.
Rieke, Richard D., jt. auth. see Willbrand, M. L.
Riekehof, Lottie L. The Joy of Signing: The New Illustrated Guide for Mastering Sign Language & the Manual Alphabet.
Rieker. The Secret of Meditation.
Riekkinen, Paavo, et al. The Nature of Multiple Sclerosis.
Rielly & Savage. Dictionary of Wedgwood.
Riely, Marianne G. The Whore of Babylon.
Rieman, W. & Walton, H. Ion Exchange in Analytical Chemistry.
Riemer, A. Reading of Shakespeare's "Antony & Cleopatra"
Riemer, A. P., ed. Macbeth.
Riemer, Edwin & Leibling, Louis. Barron's How to Prepare for Civil Service Examinations: Clerks, Stenographers, Typists.
Riemer, Neal. Political Science: An Introduction to Politics.
Rienhardt, Mona. Programmer's Desk Reference for Commodore 64 BASIC.
Riera, Russell. Two Hundred Good Restaurants: A Guide to Good Eating in the San Francisco Bay Area.
Ries, Al & Trout, Jack. Positioning: The Battle for Your Mind.
Ries, Estelle H. Elias Ries, Inventor.
Ries, Peter W. Current Estimates from the National Health Interview Survey, United States 1984.
Riese, Randall & Hitchens, Neal. The Unabridged Marilyn: Her Life from A to Z.
Riesen, Austin H. Developmental Neuropsychology of Sensory Deprivation.
Riesenberg, Felix, Jr. Sea War: The Story of the United States Merchant Marine in World War II.
Riesman, David & Riesman, Evelyn T. Conversations in Japan: Modernization, Politics, & Culture.
Riesman, Evelyn T., jt. auth. see Riesman, David.
Riesner, Dietner, jt. auth. see Schweik, R. C.
Riess, Ludwig. The History of English Electoral Law in the Middle Ages.
Riess, W. Teen-Ager, the Bible Speaks to You.
Riess, Walter. Teen-Ager You're Dating.
Riethmaier, jt. auth. see Gentle.
Riethmuller, Gert, et al, eds. Natural & Induced Cell-Mediated Cytotoxicity: Effector & Regulatory Mechanisms.
Rietstap, Johannes B. Armorial General Precede d'un Dictionnaire des Termes du Blason.
Rif, Andrea Da see Da Rif, Andrea.
Rifkin, Bernard. American Labor Sourcebook.
Rifkin, Jeremy & Howard, Ted. The Emerging Order: God in the Age of Scarcity.
--Who Should Play God?
Rifkin, Natalie, ed. U. S. S. R.-Land of the Russian Bear.
Rifkin, Robert W., ed. ATLA Masters at Work, I.
Rifkin, Susan B. Health Planning & Community Participation: Case Studies in Southeast Asia.
Rigal. Shortcut to the Italian Language.
Rigg, A. G., ed. Editing Medieval Texts: English, French & Latin Written in England. Papers Given at the 12th Annual Conference on Editorial Problems, University of Toronto, 5-6 November 1976.
Rigg, Douglas. Keelhauled: Unsportsmanlike Conduct & the America's Cup.
Riggan, Rob. Free Fire Zone.
Riggs, David. Shakespeare's Heroical Histories: Henry Six & Its Literary Tradition.
Riggs, Jack R. Hosea's Heartbreak.
Riggs, James L. Engineering Economics.
--Production Systems: Planning, Analysis & Control.
Riggs, Ralph M. Living in Christ.
--So Send I You.
Riggs, Rollin. The Rites of Spring: A Student's Guide to Spring Break in Florida.
Riggs, Rollin & Jacobsen, Bruce. Europe: Where the Fun Is.
Riggs, Rollin, jt. auth. see Jacobsen, Bruce.
Riggs, Timothy A. Hieronymus Cock: Printmaker & Publisher.
Riggs, W. F., jt. ed. see Malhortra, D.
Riggs, William G. The Christian Poet in Paradise Lost.

Rigler, R., jt. ed. see Pecht, I.
Rigsby, Mike. Verbal Control with Microcomputers.
Riha, I., jt. ed. see Sterzl, J.
RIIA Staff, ed. The Chatham House Affairs: International Economic & Monetary Issues.
Riis, Jacob A. The Children of the Poor.
--The Children of the Poor.
Rijk, Lambertus M. De see De Rijk, Lambertus M.
Rijnsdorp, J. E., ed. see IFAC-IFIP-IEA-IFORS Symposium Staff & Johannsen, G.
Rijnsdorp, J. E., ed. see IFAC Symposium Staff.
Rikal, Rudolf. How to Drive & Survive.
Rikon, Irving. Peace as It Can Be.
Rikuyo-Sha Staff, ed. Advertising Design in Japan.
--Display & Commercial Space Design.
Rikuyo-sha, ed. Advertising Design in Japan.
--Display & Commercial Space Design.
Riland, George. New Steinerbooks Dictionary of the Paranormal.
Riley, Clayton, jt. auth. see King, Martin Luther, Sr.
Riley, Daniel P. Strength Training for Football: The Penn State Way.
Riley, Donald P., jt. auth. see Apgar, Kathryn.
Riley, Isaac W. American Thought from Puritanism to Pragmatism & Beyond: A Greenwood Archival Edition.
Riley, Jocelyn. Crazy Quilt.
Riley, Joseph E., jt. auth. see Mitchell, Charles W.
Riley, Mary F., jt. auth. see Bechtle, Thomas C.
Riley, Matilda W. & Merton, Robert K., eds. Sociological Research.
Riley, Noel, ed. see Agius, Pauline.
Riley, Noel, ed. see Kevill-Davies, Sally.
Riley, Noel, ed. see Rhodes, Alexandra M.
Riley, Philip & Candlin, C. N., eds. Discourse & Learning.
Riley, Sharon J., ed. GeoRef Thesaurus & Guide to Indexing.
Riley, Tom. The Price of a Life: One Woman's Death from Toxic Shock.
Rilke, Rainer M. Letters to Benvenuta.
--The Life of the Virgin Mary.
--Visions of Christ: A Posthumous Cycle of Poems. Mandel, Siegfried, ed. Kramer, Aaron, tr. from Ger.
Rilling, John W. A Table Before Me.
Rima, I. H. Development of Economic Analysis.
Rimanoczy, Richard S., jt. auth. see Wilkie, Leighton A.
Rimbaud, Arthur. Poesies Completes.
Rimbeaux, B. C., jt. auth. see Cassidy, John.
Rimell, Raymond L. The Royal Air Force Between the Wars.
--Royal Flying Corps in World War I.
Rimer, J. Thomas. Toward a Modern Japanese Theatre: Kishida Kunio.
Rimer, Thomas J., ed. Multiple Meanings: The Written Word in Japan, Past, Present & Future.
Rimington, Critchell, ed. The Sea Chest: A Yachtsman's Reader.
Rimland, Ingrid. The Furies & the Flame.
--Psyching Out Sex.
Rimm, David C. & Somervill, John W. Abnormal Psychology.
Rimm, Sylvia, jt. auth. see Davis, Gary A.
Rimmer, J. G., jt. auth. see Titherington, D.
Rimoin, David L., jt. ed. see Emery, Alan E.
Rimon, S. G. Fluids & Applied Mathematics.
Rimsky-Korsakov, Nikolay. Principles of Orchestration: With Musical Examples Drawn from His Own Works. Steinberg, Maximilian, ed.
Rinald, Ann. But in the Fall I'm Leaving.
Rinaldi, Peter M. I Saw the Holy Shroud.
Rinaldi, S., ed. Topics in Combinatorial Optimization.
Rinder, Robert M. A Practical Guide to Small Computers for Business & Professional Use.
Rindfuss, R. R. & Sweet, James, eds. Postwar Fertility Trends & Differentials in the United States.
Rindos, David. The Origins of Agriculture: An Evolutionary Perspective (Monograph)
Rinehart, Kenneth L, Jr. & Suami, Tetsuo, eds. Aminocyclitol Antibiotics.
Rinehart, Stacy P., jt. auth. see Christian Character Library Staff.
Rinella, R. & Robbins, C. Career Power.
Ring, A. M. & Ostrin, S. L., eds. Review Questions in Anatomic Pathology.
Ring, Alvin M., jt. auth. see Ostrin, Samuel.
Ring, Arthur. Planning & Producing Handmade Slides & Filmstrips for the Classroom.
Ring, Kenneth. Heading Toward Omega: In Search of the Meaning of the Near-Death Experience.
Ring, Lawrence J., et al. Decisions in Marketing.
Ring, Leonard. Facts on Backs. Clarke, Doug, ed.
Ringel, C. M., ed. see Tachikawa, H.
Ringel, Martin, ed. see Lanzano, Susan & Abreu, Rosendo.
Ringel, William E. Identification & Police Line-Ups.
--Obscenity Law Today.
Ringer, Robert J. Winning Through Intimidation.
Ringertz, N. R. & Savage, R. E. Cell Hybrids.
Ringertz, Nils, jt. auth. see Sidebottom, Eric.
Ringgren, Helmer. Israelite Religion. Green, David E., tr. from Ger.
--Religions of the Ancient Near East. Sturdy, John, tr.
Ringleb, Al H., jt. auth. see Meiners, Roger E.
Ringsdorf, W. M., Jr., jt. auth. see Cheraskin, E., Jr.
Ringstad, Muriel. Claiming a Right.
Ringwalt, J. Luther & Bidwell, John, eds. American Encyclopaedia of Printing.
Rinhart, Floyd & Rinhart, Marion. Victorian Florida: America's Last Frontier.
Rinhart, Marion, jt. auth. see Rinhart, Floyd.
Rink, Henrik. Tales & Traditions of the Eskimo.
Rink, Henry W., jt. auth. see Gallo, Joseph D.
Rinkel, Max. Insulin Treatment in Psychiatry.
--Specific & Non-Specific Factors in Psychopharmacology.
Rinker, Harry L., ed. Warman's Americana & Collectibles.
--Warman's Americana & Collectibles.
--Warman's Antiques & Their Prices.
--Warman's Antiques & Their Prices.
--Warman's Antiques & Their Prices.
--Warman's Antiques & Their Prices.
--Warman's Antiques & Their Prices.
Rinpoche, Dudjom. The Nyingma School of Tibetan Buddhism. Dorje, Gyurme & Kapstein, Matthew, eds.
Rinsky, Lee-Ann. Teaching Word Attack Skills.
Rinzler, Carol. Your Adolescent: An Owner's Manual.
Rinzler, Carol E. The Girl Who Got All the Breaks.
Rinzler, Carol E. & Gelman, Joan. How to Set up for a Mah-Jongg Game & Other Lost Arts.
Rio, Angel Del see Del Rio, Angel.
Rio, Michel & Carlson, William. Dreaming Jungles.
Riolo, Al. How to Convert Your Favorite Hobby, Sport, Pastime or Idea to Cash.
Riordan, James, jt. auth. see Monaco, Bob.
Riordan, John. Combinatorial Identities.
Riordan, John J. & Cotliar, William. How to Develop Your GMP QC Manual.
Riordan, Mary, et al, eds. Michigan's Masterpieces: Art from Public Collections.
Riordan, Pauline. World Weather Extremes.
Riordan, William. On the Take.
Rios, Eliezer. Seashells of Brazil.
Riotton, C. & Christopherson, William. Cytology of Female Genital Tract Tumours.
Riotton, G. & Christopherson, W. M. Cytology of Non-Gynaecological Sites.
Ripa, Cesare. Iconologia.
Ripa, Louis & Barenie, James, eds. Management of Dental Behavior in Children.
Ripley, Alexandra. New Orleans Legacy.
--The Time Returns.
--The Time Returns: A Novel of Friends & Mortal Enemies in Fifteenth Century Florence.
Ripley, Randall B. Congress.
Ripp, R., jt. auth. see Kalmus, I.
Ripp, Victor. Moscow to Main Street: Among the Russian Emigres.
Rippa, Alexander S. Education in a Free Society: An American History.
Rippe, James, jt. auth. see Southmayd, William.
Ripperger, Eugene A., jt. auth. see Oden, John T.
Rippin, D. W. & Hughes, R. R., eds. Computer Applications in Chemical Engineering: Proceedings of the 12th Symposium of the European Federation of Chemical Engineering, Montreaux, April 1979.
Rippon, Sadhya. The Bristol Recipe Book: Over 150 Recipes from the Cancer Help Kitchen.
Risbeth, Henry & Garriott, O. K. Introduction to Ionospheric Physics.
Risch, Erna. Supplying Washington's Army.
Riser, Wayne H. Your Future in Veterinary Medicine.
Rishbeth, H., ed. EISCAT Science: Results from the First Year's Operation of the European Incoherent Scatter Radar: Papers from the EISCAT Workshop, Aussois, France, 5-8 September 1983.
Rishbeth, H., jt. ed. see Thomas, L.
Risk, Paul H. Outdoor Safety & Survival.
Riss, W., ed. Do Renshaw Cells Exist?
Riss, W., et al, eds. see Downstate Medical Center Conference, Brooklyn, 1971.
Riss-Carstensen, Erik. North Light.
Rist, Ray C., ed. Confronting Youth Unemployment in the Nineteen Eighties: Rhetoric Versus Reality.
Ristic, Miodrag, jt. auth. see Weinman, David.
Rita, G., ed. The Interferons.
Ritch, Robert & Shields, M. Bruce. The Secondary Glaucomas.
Ritcheson, Charles R. Aftermath of Revolution: British Policy Toward the United States, 1783-1795.
Ritchey, John A., jt. auth. see Amrine, Harold T.
Ritchie, Alice. Treasure of Li-Po.
Ritchie, Antonia F., jt. auth. see Sirna, Anne L.
Ritchie, C. Monty. Cops & Kidnappers.
Ritchie, D. A., jt. auth. see Pennington, T. H.
Ritchie, D. A., jt. auth. see Smith, K. M.
Ritchie, David. The Binary Brain: Artificial Intelligence in the Age of Electronics.
--The Computer Pioneers: The Making of the Modern Computer.
--The Ring of Fire.
Ritchie, Dennis M., jt. auth. see Kernighan, Brian W.
Ritchie, Marilynne K. Ramon Makes a Trade.
Ritchie, Peter, Jr. In Search of God.
Ritchie, R. O. & Lankford, J., eds. Small Fatigue Cracks.
Ritchie, Simon. The Hollow Woman.
Ritchie, W. K. The France of Louis XIV. Reeves, Marjorie, ed.
Ritschl, Albrecht. Three Essays. Hefner, Philip, tr. from Ger.
Ritson, Joseph. Ancient Songs & Ballads, from the Reign of King Henry Second to the Revolution.
Ritsos, Yannis. Eighteen Short Songs of the Bitter Motherland. Stavrou, Theofanis G., ed. Mims, Amy, tr. from Gr.
--Ritsos in Parentheses. Keeley, Edmund, tr. from Gr.
--Subterranean Horses. Savvas, Minas, tr. from Gr.
Ritt, Lawrence, jt. ed. see Bauer, Carol.
Rittenberg, Larry E. Auditor Independence & Systems Design.
Ritter, Alan, ed. see Rousseau, Jean-Jacques.
Ritter, John N., tr. Novalis Spiritual Saturnalia: Fragments of Existence by Friedrich von Hardenberg.
Ritter, K. G., jt. ed. see Oettli, W. K.
Ritter, Margaret. Women in the Wind.
Ritter, P. Concrete Fit for People.
Ritter, Paul. Educreation: Education for Creation, Growth & Change.
--Planning for Man & Motor.
Ritter, William. The T.F.H. Book of Guinea Pigs.
Rittershausen, Wilma, ed. An Illustrated Guide to Growing Your Own Orchids.
Ritti, Richard R., jt. auth. see Klein, Stuart M.
Rittmayer, Jane F. Life-Time.
Ritvo, et al, eds. Autism: Diagnosis, Current Research & Management.
Ritz, David. Divided Soul.
--Divided Soul: The Life of Marvin Gaye.
Ritzer, George. Contemporary Sociological Theory.
--Sociological Theory.
Rivabella, Omar. Requiem for a Woman's Soul.
Rivas, Rafael Alberto. Survival: My Life in Love & War.
Rivenes, Richard, et al. Foundations of Physical Education.
Rivera, jt. auth. see Tapia, Alejandro.
Rivera, Richard J., jt. auth. see Lowery, Andrew.
Rivera, Susana. El Piojo y la Liendre.
Rivera, W. M. & Schram, Susan G., eds. Agricultural Extension Worldwide: Issues, Practices & Emerging Priorities.
Rivera, William M. Planning Adult Learning: Issues, Practices & Directions.
Rivers, Caryl & Barnett, Rosalind. Beyond Sugar & Spice: How Women Learn, Grow.
Rivers, E. L. Thirty-Six Spanish Poems.
Rivers, Wilga M. Teaching Foreign Language Skills.
Rivers, William J. A Sketch of the History of South Carolina to the Close of the Proprietary Government by the Revolution of 1719.
Rivers, William L. Finding Facts: Interviewing, Observing, Using Reference Sources.
Riviere, Bill, jt. auth. see Lyman, Tom.
Riviere, Peter, ed. see McLennan, John F.
Rivkin, Robert S. The Rights of Servicemen.
Rivkin, S. Technology Unbound.
Rivlin, H. Encyclopedia of Modern Education.
Rivlin, Robert & Gravelle, Karen. Deciphering the Senses: The Expanding World of Human Perception.
Rix, Martyn & Phillips, Roger. The Bulb Book: A Photographic Guide to over Eight Hundred Hardy Bulbs.
Rizal, Jose. Subversive. Guerrero, Leon M., tr.
Rizer, Arden, Jr. Healing Gardens. American Spiritualist Assembly Staff, ed.
Rizzi, Luigi. Issues in Italian Syntax.
Rizzo, Betty & Mahoney, Robert. Christopher Smart: An Annotated Bibliography.
Rizzo, John R., jt. ed. see Nasri, William Z.
Rizzoli International Staff, ed. see Waldman, Diane.
Rizzuto, James J. Barron's How to Prepare for the College Board Achievement Tests - Mathematics Level I.
Roach, Eloise, tr. see Jimenez, Juan R.
Roach, Marilynne K. Down to Earth at Walden.
--Presto: Or the Adventures of a Turnspit Dog.
Roach, Marion. Another Name for Madness.
Roach, Megan, jt. auth. see Copeland, Tom.
Road, Sinclair, tr. see Cocteau, Jean.
Roadarmel, Gordon, ed. & tr. A Death in Delhi: Modern Hindi Short Stories.
Roadarmel, Gordon C. A Bibliography of English Source Materials for the Study of Modern Hindi Literature.
Roaf, Robert. Posture.
Roalman, Arthur R. Investor Relations that Work.
Roalson, Louise. On Iowa: A University & Its People.
Roark, Dallas M. Dietrich Bonhoeffer. Patterson, Bob E., ed.
Roark, Raymond J. & Young, Warren C. Formulas for Stress & Strain.
Roback & Kiernan. Pictorial History of Psychology & Psychiatry.
Roback, A. A. History of Psychology & Psychiatry.
--Present-Day Psychology.
Robards, A. W., jt. ed. see Gunning, B. E.
Robards, Karen. Forbidden Love.
--Island Flame.
--Seafire.
Robards, Terry. California Wine Label Album.
Robat, N. J., ed. see Erades, P. A.
Robat, Nico J., jt. auth. see Van Ek, Jan A.
Robb, Carol S., intro. by see Harrison, Beverly W.
Robb, D. A. & Pierpoint, S. Metals & Micronutrients: Uptake & Utilization by Plants.
Robb, Dale. Love & Living Together.
Robb, K. L., jt. auth. see Parrella, M. P.
Robbat, Richard J. Computers & Indivdualized Instruction Moving to Alternative Learning Environments.
Robbe-Grillet, Alain. Djinn. Lenard, Yvonne & Wells, Walter, trs. from Fr.
--Djinn: Text Edition.
--For a New Novel: Essays on Fiction. Howard, Richard, tr. from Fr.
--In the Labyrinth. Howard, Richard, tr. from Fr.
--Jalousie. Bree, Germaine & Schoenfeld, Eric, eds.
--Jealousy. Howard, Richard, tr. from Fr.
--Last Year at Marienbad: Text for the Film by Alain Resnais. Howard, Richard, tr. from Fr.
--La Maison de Rendez-vous. Howard, Richard, tr. from Fr.
--Recollections of the Golden Triangle: A Novel. Underwood, J. A., tr.
--The Recurring Mirror.
--Topology of a Phantom City. Underwood, J. A., tr. from Fr.
--Topology of a Phantom City. Underwood, J. A., tr. from Fr.
--Voyeur. Howard, Richard, tr. from Fr.
Robbe-Grillet, Alain, jt. auth. see Hamilton, David.
Robbie, Malcolm, et al. Lending Packages for Small & Medium-Sized Enterprises.
Robbin, Alice. Strategies for Increasing the Use of Statistical Data.
Robbins, Anthony. Unlimited Power: The New Science of Personal Achievement.
Robbins, C., jt. auth. see Rinella, R.
Robbins, Clarence R. The Chemical & Physical Behavior of Human Hair.
Robbins, D. Christopher, jt. ed. see Caskey, C. Thomas.
Robbins, David. The Wereling.
Robbins, Dennis A. Legal & Ethical Issues in Cancer Care in the United States.
Robbins, Edwin, et al. Management of Behavioral & Psychiatric Emergencies.
Robbins, Franklyn A., jt. auth. see Mancini, Janet K.
Robbins, G. E. Partridges.
Robbins, Harold. Descent from Xanadu.
--The Storyteller: A Novel.
Robbins, Ira A. The Rolling Stone Review 1985: The Year In Rock Music.
Robbins, Jacob J. Asthma Is Curable.
--None Need Suffer from Asthma: Nor in All Probability Develop Emphysema.
Robbins, Judd. Essential OS-2.
Robbins, Judy & Thomas, Gretchen. Hands All Around: Making Cooperative Quilts.
Robbins, Ken. The Hamptons: America's East End.
Robbins, Marjorie H. Feed My Sheep: Questions & Answers for the Christian & the Potential Christian.
Robbins, Patricia. No More Loving.
Robbins, R. Robert, jt. auth. see Jefferys, William H.
Robbins, Ray F. The Revelation of Jesus Christ.
Robbins, Richard S. Bible Stories in Action for Children.
Robbins, Ruth. Baboushka & the Three Kings.
--Taliesin & King Arthur.
Robbins, Sara. Crushed for Better Wine.
Robbins, Stephen P. Essentials of Organizational Behavior.
--Management: Concepts & Practices.
Robbins, Tom. Even Cowgirls Get the Blues.
Roberson, E. C. & Radcliff, A. Atomic Energy.
Roberson, John A. & Crowe, Clayton T. Engineering Fluid Mechanics.
--Engineering Fluid Mechanics.
Roberson, R., et al, eds. see CISM (International Center for Mechanical Sciences), Department for General Mechanics Staff.

Authors

Roberson, R. E. & Farrior, J. S., eds. Guidance & Control, PAAS8.
Roberson, Rick, jt. auth. see Engdahl, Sylvia L.
Roberson, William H. Louis Simpson: A Reference Guide.
Robert. Dictionnaire Alphabetique et Analogique de la Langue Francaise.
Robert Bentley, Inc. Volkswagen GTI Golf Jetta Official Service Manual: 1985-1988.
Robert, Henry F., Jr., intro. by see Montgomery Museum of Fine Arts Staff.
Robert, Marthe. Origins of the Novel. Rabinovitch, Sacha, tr.
Robert, R., ed. Materials & Fabrication.
Roberton, Mary Ann & Halverson, Lolas E. Developing Children - Their Changing Movement: A Guide for Teachers.
Roberton, N. R., ed. Textbook of Neonatology.
Roberts, A. Wayne & Varberg, Dale E. Convex Function.
Roberts, Alan P., jt. auth. see Allen, T. O.
Roberts, Albert F. Geotechnology: An Introductory Text for Students & Engineers.
Roberts, Albert R. Runaways & Non-Runaways in an American Suburb: An Exploratory Study of Adolescent & Parental Coping.
Roberts, Allen E. The Craft & Its Symbols.
Roberts, Augustine. Centered on Christ.
Roberts, B., jt. auth. see Reschenthaler, G. B.
Roberts, B. C., ed. Industrial Relations in Europe: The Imperatives of Change.
Roberts, Benjamin C., ed. Towards Industrial Democracy: Europe, Japan & the United States.
Roberts, Bob. Last of the Sailormen.
Roberts, Bobby, II, ed. see Williams, Hobie L.
Roberts, Bobby, III, ed. see Williams, Hobie L.
Roberts, Brian & Furneaux, Barbara, eds. Autistic Children: Teaching, Community & Research Approaches.
Roberts, Bruce, jt. auth. see Roberts, Nancy.
Roberts, Chalmers M. The Washington Post: The First Hundred Years.
Roberts, Charles G. Red Fox.
Roberts, D. & Sowray. Local Analgesia in Dentistry.
Roberts, D. F. & Chester, R., eds. Changing Patterns of Conception & Fertility.
Roberts, D. H. & Sowray, J. H. Local Analgesia in Dentistry.
Roberts, Dennis. Student Leadership Programs in Higher Education.
Roberts, E., et al, eds. GABA in Nervous System Function.
Roberts, E. Wilson. How, When, & Where to Go Public with a Small Company.
Roberts, Edith T., tr. see Erhard, Ludwig.
Roberts, Elizabeth. A Woman's Place: An Oral History of Working Class Women, 1890-1940.
--A Woman's Place: An Oral History of Working-Class Women 1890-1940.
Roberts, Eric B. From Football to Finance: The Story of Brady Keys Jr.
Roberts, Estelle. Fifty Years a Medium.
Roberts, Evelyn. Heaven Has a Floor.
Roberts, Fitzmahan & Associates Staff, jt. auth. see Developmental Research & Programs, Inc. Staff.
Roberts, Geoffrey K. West German Politics.
Roberts, Gillian. Caught Dead in Philadelphia: A Mystery Introducing Amanda Pepper.
Roberts, Harry V. & Ling, Robert F. Conversational Statistics with IDA.
Roberts, Harry V., jt. auth. see Ling, Robert F.
Roberts, Hayden. Alternative Adult Education.
--Community Development: Learning & Action.
Roberts, Helen. The Patient Patients: Women & Their Doctors.
Roberts, Helen M. Mission Tales: Stories of the Historic California Missions: Missions San Gabriel, San Fernando Rey, San Buenaventura.
--Mission Tales: Stories of the Historic California Missions: Missions Santa Barbara, Santa Ines, Purisima.
Roberts, Howard W. The Lasting Words of Jesus.
Roberts, I. F., jt. auth. see Cantor, Leonard.
Roberts, Irose A. Faith, Hope & Love.
Roberts, J. Walter Benjamin.
Roberts, J. Deotis. Roots of a Black Future: Family & Church.
Roberts, J. Deotis, jt. ed. see Gardiner, James J.
Roberts, J. Deotis, Sr. A Black Political Theology.
Roberts, J. Gordon. Cancer: How & Why It May Be Wiped Out.
Roberts, J. T., jt. auth. see Brumfit, C. J.
Roberts, Jack & Gunther, Dick. Who Needs Midlife at Your Age? A Survival Guide for Men over 30.
Roberts, Jane. Dreams, "Evolution," & Value Fulfillment: A Seth Book.
--Dreams, "Evolution" & Value Fulfillment.
--How to Develop Your ESP Power.
--Oversoul Seven & the Museum of Time.
--The Unknown Reality: Vol. One of a Seth Book.
--Unknown Reality: Vol. 1 of a Seth Book.
Roberts, Jane, jt. auth. see Keele, Kenneth.
Roberts, Janet L. The Dancing Doll.
Roberts, Jesse D. Bears, Bibles & a Boy.
Roberts, Jo. Internal Gravity Waves in the Ocean.
Roberts, John. A String of Pearls: An Abbreviated Poetic Version of Holy Scripture.
Roberts, John, ed. Warship.
Roberts, John S. Black Music of Two Worlds.
Roberts, Karlene H. & Burstein, Leigh, eds. Issues in Aggregation.
Roberts, Keith. Kiteworld.
Roberts, Kenneth. Leisure.
--Northwest Passage.
--Youth & Leisure.
Roberts, Kenneth B. Manual of Clinical Problems in Pediatrics.
Roberts, Kenneth D. Contributions of Joseph Ives to Connecticut Clock Technology, 1810-1862.
Roberts, Kenneth G. & Shackleton, Philip. The Canoe: A History of the Craft from Panama to the Arctic.
Roberts, Lamar, jt. auth. see Penfield, Wilder.
Roberts, Larry S., jt. auth. see Schmidt, Gerald D.
Roberts, Larry S., jt. auth. see Hickman, Cleveland P.
Roberts, Lathrop E., ed. see Roberts, Sarah E.
Roberts, Leslie. Cancer Today: Origins, Prevention, & Treatment.
Roberts, Lois W., ed. Anacapa Island.
Roberts, Lucille. Computercise: Your 21-Day Personalized Body Shaping Program.
Roberts, M. J., jt. ed. see Carson, T. R.
Roberts, Mary S., ed. see Sparkman, Ervin L.
Roberts, Melissa, ed. see Fannin, Angela & Fannin, Jerry.
Roberts, Mervin F. The T.F.H. Book of Hamsters.
Roberts, Nancy. David.
Roberts, Nancy & Roberts, Bruce. Ghosts of the Carolinas.
Roberts, Neal A. & Brown, H. James, eds. Property Tax Preferences for Agricultural Land.
Roberts, Neil. George Eliot: Her Beliefs & Her Art.
Roberts, Neil & Gifford, Terry. Ted Hughes: A Critical Study.
Roberts, Neil, jt. auth. see Gifford, Terry.
Roberts, Nora. From This Day.
--Island of Flowers.
Roberts, Norma, ed. see Baur, John I. & Wootten, Richard.
Roberts, O. Fixed Bridge Prosthesis.
Roberts, Oral. The Call.
Roberts, P. H. & Soward, A. M., eds. Rotating Fluids in Geophysics.
Roberts, Patricia. Tender Prey.
Roberts, Paul. English Syntax.
--Modern Grammar.
Roberts, Paul M. Review Text in United States History.
Roberts, Paula. Come Home to Love.
Roberts, Peg. Mr. Rumpletop's Gift.
Roberts, Penfield. The Quest for Security, 1715-1740.
Roberts, Peter. In Search of Early Christian Unity.
--Plays & Players: Thirty Years of British Theatre 1953-1983 Vol. Two 1969-1983.
Roberts, Peter, ed. Plays & Players: Thirty Years of British Theatre 1953-1983, Vol. One-1953-1968.
Roberts, Peter C. Modelling Large Systems: Limits to Growth Revisited.
Roberts, R., ed. Pressure Vessel & Piping: Design & Analysis - A Decade of Progress: Materials & Fabrication.
Roberts, R. D. & Roberts, T. M., eds. Planning & Ecology.
Roberts, Ralph. The Word Processor Buyer's Survival Manual.
Roberts, Randy. Jack Dempsey: The Manassa Mauler.
Roberts, Rich. Eric Dickerson: Record-Breaking Rusher.
Roberts, Robert C. Spirituality & Human Emotion.
Roberts, Roda P., tr. see Peyre, Henri.
Roberts, Roger. Holiness: Every Christian's Calling.
Roberts, S. M. & Scheinmann, F., eds. Chemistry, Biochemistry & Pharmacology of Prostanoids.
Roberts, Sanford M. Dynamic Programming in Chemical Engineering & Process Control.
Roberts, Sarah E. Alberta Homestead: Chronicle of a Pioneer Family. Roberts, Lathrop E., ed.
Roberts, Sharon. Behavioral Concepts & the Critically Ill Patient.
Roberts, Sharon L. Behavioral Concepts & Nursing Throughout the Lifespan.
Roberts, Sheila. Johannesburg Requiem.
Roberts, T. M., jt. ed. see Roberts, R. D.
Roberts, Ted. Failing Forward.
Roberts, Thom. A Born Carpenter.
Roberts, Thom & Paine, Albert B., eds. The Hollow Tree.
Roberts, Thom, ed. see Paine, Albert B.
Roberts, W. Dayton, ed. Africa: A Season for Hope.
Roberts, William. Earlier History of English Bookselling.
Roberts, William, jt. auth. see Johnson, Ivan C.
Roberts, William P. Touchstones for Prayer.
Roberts, Willo D. A Long Time to Hate.
--The Minden Curse.
Roberts-Goodson, R. B. Illustrated Custom Boat Building.
Robertson. Group Accounts.
--Speak, Angele.
Robertson, A. H., ed. European Yearbook.
Robertson, A. H., jt. ed. see Landheer, B.
Robertson, A. J. Catalysis of Gas Reactions by Metals.
Robertson, A. T., jt. auth. see Monser, Harold E.
Robertson, Alan. Architectural Antiques.
Robertson, Alec. Dvorak.
--Interpretation of Plainchant: A Preliminary Study.
Robertson, Audrey. Health, Safety & First Aid: A Guide for Training Child Care Workers.
Robertson, Audrey, ed. Infant-Toddler Growth & Development: A Guide for Training Child Care Workers.
Robertson, Auguste V. Europe: It's Choice: Soviet Invasion with the Death of the Empires.
Robertson, B., ed. see Hengener, Henri.
Robertson, C. Alton. Is God Still Here: Q-Book No. 15.
Robertson, Claire C. Sharing the Same Bowl: A Socioeconomic History of Women & Class in Accra, Ghana.
Robertson, Colin & Little, Keith, eds. A Manual of Accident & Emergency Resuscitation.
Robertson, D., jt. auth. see Corbet, H.
Robertson, David. The Old Testament & the Literary Critic. Tucker, Gene M., ed.
--Sir Charles Eastlake & the Victorian Art World.
Robertson, Dede. The New You.
Robertson, Dougal. Survive the Savage Sea.
Robertson, E. H., ed. see Henderson, Ian.
Robertson, E. H., ed. see Perkins, Robert L.
Robertson, E. H., ed. see Thomas, J. Heywood.
Robertson, E. H., ed. see Towers, Bernard.
Robertson, Edwin H. Dietrich Bonhoeffer.
Robertson, Edwin H., tr. see Hampe, Johann C.
Robertson, Edwin H., tr. see Lienhard, Marc.
Robertson, Edwin H., tr. see Lochman, Jan M.
Robertson, Elizabeth C. & Wood, Margaret I. Today's Child: A Modern Guide to Baby Care & Child Training.
Robertson, George. Port.
Robertson, Ian. Ireland.
--Loire Valley, Normandy, Brittany.
--Paris & Environs.
--Paris & Environs.
--Portugal.
--Portugal.
--Spain: The Mainland.
Robertson, J. A. Irradiation Effects in Nuclear Fuels.
Robertson, J. Douglas, jt. auth. see Grillo, John P.
Robertson, J. M., jt. ed. see Dummer, Geoffrey W.
Robertson, Jack C. & Davis, Frederick G., eds. Auditing.
Robertson, James. Any Fool Can Be a Pig Farmer.
--Connoisseur's Guide to Beer.
--Connoisseur's Guide to Beer: 1984.
--Young Children in Hospital.
Robertson, James C. The British Board of Film Censors: Film Censorship in Britain, 1896-1950.
Robertson, Jenny. Circle of Shadows.
--Fior, Son of the King.
Robertson, John. Effective Classroom Control.
--Mechanising Vegetable Production.
Robertson, John M. Comfort: Prayers & Promises for Times of Sorrow.
Robertson, Leonard, jt. auth. see Place, Irene.
Robertson, Mary E. Jemimalee.
--Speak, Angel.
Robertson, Mary Elsie. The Clearing.
Robertson, Pat & Proctor, William. Beyond Reason: How Miracles Can Change Your Life.
Robertson, Pat & Slosser, Bob. The Secret Kingdom.
Robertson, R. Build Your Own Database in a Basic.
Robertson, Raymond. Build Your Own Database in Basic.
Robertson, Richard T., ed. Neuroanatomical Research Technique.
Robertson, Ross M. History of the American Economy.
Robertson, Ross M. & Walton, Gary M. History of the American Economy.
Robertson, Roy. The Timothy Principle.
Robertson, Shirley. Traveling a Half-Century: A Selection of Poems.
Robertson, Stephen J., jt. auth. see Slusher, Harold S.
Robertson, Stuart M. Media Law Handbook.
Robertson, Thomas, jt. auth. see Kassarjian, Harold.
Robertson, William. Progress of Society in Europe: A Historical Outline from the Subversion of the Roman Empire to the Beginning of the 16th Century. Gilbert, Felix & Krieger, Leonard, eds.
Robertson, William S. Iturbide of Mexico.
Robeson, Paul. Here I Stand.
Robey, Cora L., et al. Workbook of Basic Writing Skills.
--Handbook of Basic Writing Skills.
Robey, Harriet. An Ordinary Marriage.
Robey, Sidney J., jt. auth. see Bruyere, Toni M.
Robichaud, Beryl, et al. Introduction to Data Processing.
Robicheaux, Robert A. Marketing: Contemporary Dimensions.
Robicheaux, Robert A. & Pride, William M. Marketing: Contemporary Dimensions.
Robicheaux, Robert A., et al. Marketing: Contemporary Dimensions.
Robichon, Clement & Varille, Alesandre. Eternal Egypt.
Robillard, Mark J. Hero One: Advanced Programming & Interfacing.
Robin, Gordon, ed. Scoliosis.
Robin, Patrick & Haddad, Remy. Time Capsule: The Year 1983 in Photographs.
Robin, Robert. Something in Common.
Robin, Stanley S., jt. auth. see Bosco, James J.
Robinet, B., ed. see Colloque Sur la Programmation, Paris, 9-11 April, 1974.
Robinette, Danny R., jt. auth. see Scrivner, Louise M.
Robinette, Gary O., ed. Energy-Efficient Site Design.
--Evergreen Form Studies: Design Characteristics of Conifers.
Robinette, Gary O., ed. see Environmental Design Press Staff.
Robins, Betty D., jt. auth. see Bussabarger, Robert F.
Robins, Denise. Bittersweet.
--Dance in the Dust.
--The Feast Is Finished.
--The Long Shadow.
--Love Me No More.
--Love, Vol. I.
--Love, Vol. IV.
--More Than Love.
--My True Love.
--Only My Dreams.
--Second Marriage.
--Something to Love.
--The Uncertain Heart.
Robins, Eric. Ebony Ark: Black Africa's Battle to Save Its Wild Life.
Robins, Lynton. Political Institutions in Britain.
--Politics & Policy Making in Britain.
Robins, Madeleine. The Spanish Marriage.
Robins, Natalie & Aronson, Steven M. Savage Grace.
Robins, Patricia. Play Fair with Love.
Robinson, Anthony. RAF Fighter Squadrons in the Battle of Britain.
Robinson, Arthur, jt. ed. see Kaplan, Nathan O.
Robinson, B. W. Persian Paintings.
Robinson, Barbara. The Best Christmas Pageant Ever.
--The Best Christmas Pageant Ever.
--Temporary Times, Temporary Places.
Robinson, Barbara, ed. Where Atlantans Dine.
Robinson, Barry & Dain, Martin J. On the Beat: Policemen at Work.
Robinson, Benjamin W. Life of Paul.
Robinson, Bill. Cruising: The Boats & the Places.
--Islands.
--South to the Caribbean: How to Carry Out the Dream of Sailing Your Own Boat to the Caribbean.
Robinson, C., jt. ed. see Nitecki, Z.
Robinson, Carline S. The Blacks in These Sea Islands.
Robinson, Charles. New Kid in Town.
Robinson, Charlotte, ed. The Artist & the Quilt.
Robinson, Christine, ed. International Writers' & Artists' Yearbook, 1988.
Robinson, Clark Z. Top Dollars for Technical Scholars: A Guide to Engineering, Math, Computer Science & Science Scholarships.
Robinson, D. J. & James, S. E., eds. Anodes for Electrowinning: Proceedings, AIME Annual Meeting, Los Angeles, 1984.
Robinson, D. W., ed. Occupational Hearing Loss.
Robinson, Daniel N. & Utall, William R. Foundations of Psychobiology.
Robinson, Daniel S., ed. see Gomperz, Heinrich.
Robinson, Darline, jt. auth. see Robison, James.
Robinson, Darrell W. Total Church Life.
Robinson, David. Chaplin: His Life & Art.
--From Drinking to Alcoholism: A Sociological Commentary.
--Hollywood in the Twenties.
Robinson, David F. Living Wild: The Secrets of Animal Survival. MacConomy, Alma D., ed.
--A Wildlife Family Album. MacConomy, Alma D. & Peters, Barbara, eds.
Robinson, David G. Plant Membranes: Endo- & Plasma Membranes.
Robinson, Dennis M., jt. auth. see Robinson, Jacqueline.

Authors

Robinson, Derek. The Eldorado Network.
Robinson, Donald L. To the Best of My Ability: The President & the Constitution.
Robinson, Dow F. Aztec Studies II: Sierra Nahuat Word Structure.
Robinson, Edward H., jt. auth. see Rotter, Joseph C.
Robinson, Eleanor. The Silverleaf Syndrome.
Robinson, Ellis. A Commentary on Catulus, Oxford, Eighteen Eighty-Nine. Commager, Steele, ed.
Robinson, Eric H. & Musson, James, eds. James Watt & the Steam Revolution, a Documentary History.
Robinson, F. A. The Vitamin Co-Factors of Enzyme Systems.
Robinson, F. M. Macroscopic Electromagnetism.
Robinson, F. N., ed. see Chaucer, Geoffrey.
Robinson, Floyd A. This Is Home Now.
Robinson, Frank E., jt. auth. see Gerbracht, Carl.
Robinson, Frank S. Children of the Dragon.
Robinson, Frank T. Living New England Artists: Biographical Sketches. Weinberg, H. Barbara, ed.
Robinson, Frederick W. High Church. Wolff, Robert L., ed.
Robinson, H. Alan, jt. auth. see Thomas, Ellen L.
Robinson, H. Wheeler. Corporate Personality in Ancient Israel.
Robinson, Helen M. Sequential Development of Reading Abilities.
Robinson, Helen M., ed. Innovation & Change in Reading Instruction.
Robinson, Henry H. Negotiability in the Federal Sector.
Robinson, Horace. Bloomfield.
Robinson, J. Highways & Our Environment.
Robinson, J. Grall. Criminal Law Defenses: 1986 Pocket Parts.
Robinson, J. Lewis, ed. British Columbia.
Robinson, J. P. The Effects of Weapons on Ecosystems.
Robinson, Jacqueline & Robinson, Dennis M. Complete Preparation for High School Entrance Examination for Special Private & Parochial High Schools.
Robinson, James M. A New Quest of the Historical Jesus & Other Essays.
--The Problem of History in Mark & Other Markan Studies.
Robinson, James M. & Koester, Helmut. Trajectories Through Early Christianity.
Robinson, James W. Atomic Absorption Spectroscopy.
Robinson, Janice S. H. D. The Life & Work of an American Poet.
Robinson, Jay L., jt. auth. see Bailey, Richard W.
Robinson, Jean. Nursing Photobook Annual, Nineteen Eighty-Seven.
--Strange but Wonderful Cosmic Awareness of Duffy Moon.
Robinson, Jean & McVan, Barbara, eds. Assessing Your Patients.
--Caring for Surgical Patients.
--Controlling Infection.
--Coping with Neurologic Disorders.
--Dealing with Emergencies.
--Ensuring Intensive Care.
--Hypertension.
--Implementing Urologic Procedures.
--Nursing Pediatric Patients.
--Performing G. I. Procedures.
--Providing Early Mobility.
--Providing Respiratory Care.
--Using Monitors.
--Working with Orthopedic Patients.
Robinson, Jean & McVann, Barbara, eds. Helping Geriatric Patients.
Robinson, Jeff. AMC Service-Repair Handbook: Pacer, Gremlin, Hornet-1971-1980. Robinson, Jeff, ed.
Robinson, Jeff, ed. Audi Service-Repair Handbook: 100 LS Series, 1970-1977.
--British Seagull Outboards Service-Repair 2-6 hp Handbook.
--Chevrolet Car Tune-up: All Models, 1966-1980.
--CZ Service-Repair Handbook: Single Exhaust Models-Through 1978.
--Dodge Car Tune-up & Maintenance, 1968-1982.
--Husqvarna Service - Repair Handbook: 125-450cc Singles, 1966-1975.
--Jaguar Service - Repair Handbook: All 3.8 & 4.2 E-Types.
--Mercury Capri Service Repair Handbook All Models, 1970-1976.
--Ossa Service - Repair Handbook: 125-250cc Singles, 1971-1978.
--Plymouth Tune-Up-Maintenance, 1967-1978 Models.
--Porsche: 914 Series, 1970-1976-Service, Repair Handbook.
--Powerboat Maintenance.
--Ride, & Stay Alive.
--Saab Service Repair Handbook 95, 96, 99, & Sonett 1967-1979.
--Sailboat Maintenance.
--Sprite--MG Midget Service--Repair Handbook: All Models, 1958-1979.
--Volkswagen Performance Tuning: 1200-2000cc Air-Cooled Engines, All Years.
--Volkswagen Service--Repair Handbook: Dasher, 1974-1980.
--Volkswagen Service--Repair Handbook: Rabbit, Scirocco-1975-1981.
--Volkswagen Service-Repair Handbook: Type 3, 1962-1973.
Robinson, Jeff, ed. see Ahlstrand, Alan.
Robinson, Jeff, ed. see Lockwood, Tim.
Robinson, Jeff, ed. see Price, Brick.
Robinson, Jo, jt. auth. see Anderson, Karen.
Robinson, John A. Christian Freedom in a Permissive Society.
--The Difference in Being a Christian Today.
--New Reformation.
--Redating the New Testament.
--Truth Is Two-Eyed.
Robinson, John J. Of Suchness: Glimpses of the Anatomy & Pathology of God.
Robinson, John L. Bartolome Mitre: Historian of the Americas.
Robinson, Jonathan. Duty & Hypocrisy in Hegel's Phenomenology of Mind.
Robinson, Joseph A., jt. auth. see McGregor, Georgette F.
Robinson, Joseph R., ed. Ophthalmic Drug Delivery Systems.
Robinson, Judith, jt. auth. see Aluri, Rao.
Robinson, Julian. The Golden Age of Style.
Robinson, Katherine. The Clothing Care Handbook.
Robinson, Ken, ed. Exploring Theatre & Education.
Robinson, Laura. A Life Partially Relived in Vignettes.
Robinson, Leigh. Landlording: A Handymanual for Scrupulous Landlords & Landladies Who Do It Themselves.
Robinson, Lennox, compiled by. A Little Anthology of Modern Irish Verse.
Robinson, Lennox, ed. see Yeats, John B.
Robinson, Logan. Evil Star.
Robinson, Louie, ed. see Ashe, Arthur.
Robinson, Lytle W. Is It True What They Say About Edgar Cayce?
Robinson, M. J., ed. Practical Paediatrics.
Robinson, Mairi, ed. Scots Concise Dictionary.
Robinson, Mary E. Jemimalee.
Robinson, Paul W., et al. Manipulating Parents: Tactics Used by Children of All Ages & Ways Parents Can Turn the Tables.
Robinson, Pauline C. ESP (English for Specific Purposes) The Present Position.
Robinson, Phillip R. CD-ROMs: The New Generation in Data Storage.
--Using Turbo Prolog.
Robinson, Phyllis, jt. auth. see Heckscher, August.
Robinson, R. Gene Mapping in Laboratory Animals. Incl. Pt. A; Pt. B. Plenum Pub.
Robinson, Randall N. Chemical Engineering Practice Exam Set.
Robinson, Ray. Housing Economics & Public Policy.
Robinson, Raymond. The Growing of America: Seventeen Eighty-Nine to Eighteen Forty-Eight.
Robinson, Rebecca. City on the Bluff.
Robinson, Rich. How to Save Tax Dollars When You Sell Your House.
Robinson, Richard D. Internationalization of Business: An Introduction.
Robinson, Robert. Shellfish Heritage Cookbook.
Robinson, Roy. Lepidoptera Genetics.
Robinson, Russell D. Group Dynamics for Student Activities.
Robinson, Sandra K., jt. ed. see Mertens, Thomas.
Robinson, Sharon. Contemporary Basketry. Horn, George & Rainey, Sarita, eds.
--Contemporary Quilting.
Robinson, Solon. Wisdom of the Land.
Robinson, Spider. Mindkiller.
Robinson, Susan & Pizer, F. H. Having a Baby Without a Man.
Robinson, T. J., jt. auth. see Manning, D. J.
Robinson, Terry. Star Guide (Nineteen Eighty-Eight to Nineteen Eighty-Nine) Where to Reach Movie Stars, TV Stars, Rock Stars, Sports Stars, & Other Famous Celebrities.
Robinson, Tim. In Worlds Apart-Professionals & Their Clients in the Welfare State.
Robinson, Virgil. James White.
Robinson, William, jt. auth. see Norsworthy, Kent.
Robinson, William A. Return to the Sea.
Robinson, William C. The Utility of Retail Site Selection for the Public Library.
Robinson, William H. Phillis Wheatley: A Bio-Bibliography.
Robinson, William L. & Bolen, Eric G. Wildlife Ecology & Management.
Robisnon, Jeff, ed. Volvo Service Repair Handbook: 140 Series, 1967-1974.
Robison, G. Alan. Cyclic AMP.
Robison, Georgia. Revelliere-Lepeaux, Citizen Director, 1753-1824.
Robison, J. Vincent. Modern Algebra & Trigonometry.
Robison, James. Rumor & Other Stories.
Robison, James & Robinson, Darline. Children's Travel Guide.
Robitscher, Jonas. The Powers of Psychiatry.
Robitzek, Klara C. Peter in the Land of Musical Instruments.
--Peter in the Land of Musical Theory.
Roblee, Charles L. & McKechnie, Al. Investigation of Fires.
Robles, Al. Looking for Ifugao Mountain: Bilingual, Pilipino & English.
Robles de Medina, E. D., ed. New Coding System for Electrocardiography.
Robock, Stefan H., et al. International Business & Multinational Enterprises.
Robotic Industries Association Staff. Robots East Seminar: Proceedings.
Robots Eight, Detroit, Mich., June 1984. Robots Eight Conference Proceedings, Detroit, Michigan, June, 1984. Incl. Vol. I. Applications for Today; Vol. II. Future Considerations. Robot Inst Am.
Robots Institute of America Staff, jt. auth. see International Symposium on Industrial Robots Staff.
Robottom, John. Modern China.
--Modern Russia.
Roboz, Steven, ed. see Steiner, Rudolf.
Robson, Ann P. On Higher Than Commercial Grounds: The Factory Controversy, 1830-1853.
Robson, Brian. The Road to Kabul: The Second Afghan War, 1878-1881.
Robson, D. & Fox, J. D., eds. Nuclear Analogue States.
Robson, David, jt. auth. see Goldberg, Adele.
Robson, Eric. American Revolution, in Its Political & Military Aspects: 1763-1783.
Robson, Graham. Lamborghini Countach.
--The Mighty MG's: The Twin-Cam, MGC & MGB GT V8 Stories.
Robson, John M., ed. Editing Nineteenth-Century Texts.
Robson, John M., ed. see Mill, John Stuart.
Robson, Mike. Journey to Excellence.
Robson, P. D., jt. auth. see Harris, D. J.
Robyns, Gwen. Barbara Cartland: An Authorized Biography.
Rocco, C. Di see Di Rocco, C.
Rocco, Sha see Sha Rocco.
Rocha, Roberto, jt. auth. see Hanson, James A.
Rocha E Silva, M. & Leme, J. Garcia. Chemical Mediators in the Acute Inflammatory Reaction.
Rochat, Jean-Claude. Mathematiques pour la Question de l'Environment.
Roche, Cecil. The Great Barzhoon.
Roche, Daniel. Le Siecle des Lumieres en Province: Academies et Academiciens Provincieaux, 1680-1789.
Roche, Edward B., ed. Design of Biopharmaceutical Properties Through Prodrugs & Analogs.
Roche, Henri-Pierre. Jules & Jim.
Roche Institute of Molecular Biology Symposium Staff. Teratomas & Differentiation: Proceedings of the Roche Institute of Molecular Biology Symposium, Nutley, NJ, May 1975. Sherman, Michael I. & Solter, Davor, eds.
Roche, James. Biorhythms at Your Fingertips.
Roche, Joseph de see De Roche, Joseph.
Roche, Ruth. The Child & Science: Wondering, Exploring, Growing. Baron, Bonnie D., ed.
Rochelle, Jay C. I'm Not the Same Person I Was Yesterday.
Rochester, Earl of see Wilmot, John.
Rochester, J. Martin, jt. auth. see Pearson, Frederic S.
Rochester, Jack B., jt. auth. see Benson, Ramsey J.
Rochette, Edward C. Making Money: Rogues & Rascals Who Made Their Own.
--The Other Side of the Coin.
Rochkind, Marc J. Advanced UNIX Programming.
Rochlin, Doris. Frobisch's Angel: A Novel.
Rochlin, Harriet. Pioneer Jews: A New Life in the Far West.
Rochlin, Margy, jt. auth. see Rowland, Mark.
Rochow, E. G. The Chemistry of Silicon.
Rochow, E. G. & Abel, E. W. The Chemistry of Germanium, Tin & Lead.
Rochow, Eugene G., jt. auth. see Rochow, Theodore G.
Rochow, Theodore G. & Rochow, Eugene G. Resinography: An Introduction to the Definition, Identification, & Recognition of Resins, Polymers, Plastics, & Fibers.
Roch-Ramel, F., ed. see Gesellschaft Fuer Nephrologie, 5th Symposium, Switzerland, 1967.
Rock, Barbara, ed. Oil & Gas Journal DataBook, 1987.
Rock, Irvin. Orientation & Form.
Rock, Maxine. The Fiction Writer's Help Book.
--The Marriage Map: Understanding & Surviving the Stages of Marriage.
Rockcastle, Madeline T. Where to Start: An Annotated Career-Planning Bibliography 1983-85.
Rockcastle, Verne N., jt. auth. see Schmidt, Victor E.
Rockefeller, John D. Interview, Nineteen Seventeen - Nineteen Twenty, Conducted by William O. Inglis. Hawke, David F., ed.
Rockefeller, Nelson A. Future of Federalism.
--Future of Federalism.
Rockefeller University Staff, et al. The Future of Biology: Proceedings of the Rockefeller University & State Univesity of New York Conference on the Future of Biology, Nov. 26-27, 1965. Bronk, Detlev W., ed.
Rockley, Alicia A. History of Gardening in England.
Rockley, L. E. Finance for the Purchasing Executive.
Rockowitz, et al. Basic Tips on the GED.
--How to Prepare for the High School Equivalency Exam (GED)
Rocks, Lawrence. Developing Your Chemistry Fundamentals.
Rockstein. Physiology of the Insecta.
Rockstein, Morris & Baker, George T., eds. Molecular Genetic Mechanisms in Aging & Development.
Rockstein, Morris & Sussman, Marvin L., eds. Development & Aging in the Nervous System.
Rockstroh, et al. Slow Brain Potentials & Behavior.
Rockwell, Ann. Befana: A Christmas Story.
Rockwell, Anne. A Bear, a Bobcat & Three Ghosts.
--The Boy Who Drew Sheep.
--Temple on a Hill.
Rockwell, Anne & Rockwell, Harlow. My Barber.
--The Night We Slept Outside.
--When I Go Visiting.
Rockwell, David L., et al. Fundamentals of Idaho Real Estate.
--Fundamentals of Montana Reál Estate.
--Fundamentals of Utah Real Estate.
--Fundamentals of Washington Real Estate.
--Principles of California Real Estate.
Rockwell, George L. History of Ridgefield, Connecticut.
Rockwell, Harlow, jt. auth. see Rockwell, Anne.
Rockwell, Hays H., jt. auth. see Clifford, Richard J.
Rockwell, Jane. Dogs & Puppies.
Rockwell, Joan. Fact in Fiction: The Use of Literature in the Systematic Study of Society.
Rockwell, Kenneth G. Megalomania & Mediocrity in the Leadership of Nations: The Meaning for the World.
Rockwell, Margaret. Stepping Out, Sharing Christ in Everyday Circumstances.
Rockwell, Molly, ed. Norman Rockwell's Christmas Book.
Rockwell, Norman. Norman Rockwell: Special Days Come to Life.
Rockwell, Thomas. Oatmeal Is Not for Mustaches.
Rockwood, Charles E. National Incomes Policy for Inflation Control.
Rockwood, Irving, ed. see Elder, Charles D. & Cobb, Roger W.
Rockwood, Joyce. To Spoil the Sun.
Rockwood, Linn. Public Parks & Recreation Administration: Behavior & Dynamics.
Rocky Flats Wind Energy Research Center Staff, ed. Small Wind Turbines Systems Conference, 1981.
Rodabaugh, Barbara J. & Austin, Melanie. Sexual Assault: A Guide for Community Action.
Rodahl, Kaare. Akiviak.
Rodale Food Center Staff & Hurley, Judith. Garden Fresh Cooking: Hundreds of Wonderful Ways to Cook, Serve, & Store Your Favorite Vegetables & Fruits. Halpin, Anne & Gerras, Charlie, eds.
Rodale Press, Inc. Editors. The Organic Gardeners Complete Guide to Vegetables & Fruits. Halpin, Anne, ed.
Rodale, Robert. The Best Health Ideas I Know: My Personal Plan for Living.
Roddy, D. Radio & Line Transmission.
Roddy, Lee. Love's Far Horizon.
--The Mystery of Aloha House.
Roddy, Lee, jt. auth. see Douglass, Stephen B.
Rodee, Carlton C., et al. Introduction to Political Science.
Roden, Donald. Monarch Notes on Buck's the Good Earth.
Rodenberger, Lou H., ed. Her Work: Stories by Texas Women.
Rodenbery, C., tr. see Eugippius.
Roderick, G. W. & Stephens, M. D. Post-School Education: Educational Values in America & England in the Nineteenth Century.
Roderick, G. W., jt. ed. see Stephens, M. D.
Roderigue, F. Laurier. The Pursuit of Wisdom.
Roderus, Frank. Billy Ray & the Good News.
--Stillwater Smith.
Rodes, Basil C. The Hellenes.
Rodger, Frederick C., ed. Onchocerciasis in Zaire.
Rodger, I. A. & Richardson, J. A. Self-Evaluation for Primary Schools.

Rodgers, Barbara N. The Careers of Social Studies Students.
Rodgers, Bill & Concannon, Joe. Marathoning.
Rodgers, C. Leland. Essentials of Biology: A Basic Text of Current Biological Thought.
Rodgers, Charles A., jt. auth. see Juszli, Frank L.
Rodgers, D. & Rodgers, I. A. J. R. R. Tolkien.
Rodgers, Dorothy. House in My Head.
Rodgers, Eamon J., ed. Benito Perez Galdos: Tormento.
Rodgers, Frank & Phelps, Rose B. A Guide to British Parliamentary Papers.
Rodgers, Frederick A. Curriculum & Instruction in the Elementary School.
Rodgers, Harrell R. & Bullock, Charles S. Law & Social Change: Civil Rights Laws & Their Consequences.
Rodgers, I. A., jt. auth. see Rodgers, D.
Rodgers, Jesse. ESP McGee & the Dolphin's Message.
Rodgers, John F., jt. auth. see Crawford, H. Warren.
Rodgers, Leroy A., jt. ed. see Mayhew, Harry E.
Rodgers, M. A. & Powers, E. L., eds. Oxygen & Oxy-Radicals in Chemistry & Biology.
Rodgers, Pepper. Fourth & Long Gone.
Rodgers, Steve. Creating a Database: Undersea Adventure.
Rodgers, William, ed. Socialism & Affluence.
Rodgers, William P. Introduction to System Safety Engineering.
Rodi, Stephen. Complete Solutions Manual to Accompany Swokowski's Calculus: Alternate Ed.
Rodick, Burleigh C. American Constitutional Custom.
--Appomatox.
Rodiger. Larry's Number One.
Rodiger, Ann L. Blues a la Gauche.
--Scrabble.
Rodin, Auguste. On Arts & Artists.
Rodin, Burton. Basic Calculus with Applications.
Rodin, E. Y. Computers & Mathematics with Applications: A Memorial Dedicated to Cornelius Lanczos.
Rodin, R. & Sario, L. Principal Functions.
Rodinelli, Dennis A. Planning Development Projects.
Rodinson, Maxime. Marxism & the Muslim World.
Roditi, Edouard. Emperor of Midnight.
Roditi, Edouard, tr. see Suares, Carlo.
Rodker, John, tr. see De Lautreamont, Comte & Ducasse, Isidore.
Rodker, John, tr. see Ozenfant, A.
Rodkiewicz, C. M. Arteries & Arterial Blood Flow.
Rodman, George, jt. auth. see Adler, Ronald B.
Rodman, Julius S. The Kahuna Sorcerers of Hawaii, Past & Present: With a Glossary of Ancient Religious Terms & the Books of the Hawaiian Royal Dead.
Rodney, Janet. Crystals.
Rodney, Morgan R. see Downie, Don.
Rodney, Morgan R., jt. ed. see Downie, Don.
Rodolphe-Piccard, Jean. Dream Cars.
Rodoreda, Merce. Time of the Doves. Rosenthall, David, tr.
Rodriguez, Barbara & Miller, Tom. Interstate Gourmet: Texas & the Southwest.
Rodriguez, Barbara, ed. Last of a Breed: Portrait of Working Cowboys.
Rodriguez, Barbara, ed. see Ashby, Lynn.
Rodriguez, Barbara, ed. see Foster, Nancy H. & Fairbank, Ben.
Rodriguez, Barbara, ed. see Willoughby, Larry.
Rodriguez, Cookie. Please Make Me Cry!
Rodriguez, Elmer A., jt. auth. see Labarca, Angela.
Rodriguez, F. Principles of Polymer Systems.
Rodriguez, Gregorita & Powers, Edith. Singing for My Echo: Memories of a Native Healer of Santa Fe.
Rodriguez, Mario B. Cuentistas de Hoy.
Rodriguez, Richard. Hunger of Memory: The Education of Richard Rodriguez, An Autobiography.
Rodriquez, jt. auth. see Bodey.
Rodriquez, Barbara, ed. see Butler, Ron.
Rodriquez, Barbara, ed. see Finstad, Suzanne.
Rodriquez, Barbara, ed. see Smith, Griffin, Jr. & Bradshaw, Reagan.
Rodriquez, Eugenio C. Latinoamerica: Su Civilizacion y Su Cultura.
Rodriquez-Julia, Edgardo. La Noche Oscura del Nino Aviles.
Rodway, jt. auth. see Pinto.
Rodway, James. In the Guiana Forest: Studies of Nature in Relations to the Struggle for Life.
Rodwell, Jenny. Flower Painting.
Rodwell, Jenny & Short, George. The Complete Guide to Framing.
Roe. Military Memoir of Colonel John Birch. Webb, ed.
Roe, Alan R., jt. auth. see Bhatt, Vinayak V.
Roe, Albert S. Blake's Illustrations to the Divine Comedy.
Roe, Benson B. Perioperative Management in Cardiothoracic Surgery.
Roe, Betty D., jt. auth. see Burns, Paul C.
Roe, Betty D., et al. Reading Instruction in the Secondary School.
--Secondary School Reading Instruction: The Content Areas.
Roe, Daphne A. Geriatric Nutrition.
--Interactions of Selected Drugs & Nutrients in Patients: Handbook.
Roe, Derek. Prehistory: An Introduction.
Roe, Earl, ed. see Augsburger, David.
Roe, Earl O., ed. see Dowley, Tim.
Roe, Ernest, et al. Reviewing Academic Performance Approaches to the Evaluation of Departments & Individuals.
Roe, F. J., jt. auth. see Ambrose, E. J.
Roe, Francis J., ed. Metabolic Aspects of Food Safety.
Roe, Frederick. Old England & the Destruction of Its Prehistoric Remains.
Roe, H. S. Progress in Oceanography.
Roe, Kathy G. Goodbye, Secret Place.
Roe, Kenn S. Moonblood.
Roe, Michael. Nine Australian Progressives: Vitalism in Bourgeois Social Thought.
Roeber, A. G., ed. A New England Woman's Perspective on Norfolk, Virginia, 1801-1802: Excerpts from the Diary of Ruth Henshaw Bascom.
Roeber, Joe. Social Change at Work: The ICI Weekly Staff Agreement.
Roebuck, Graham. Clarendon & Cultural Continuity: A Bibliographical Study.
Roebuck, Janet. Making of Modern English Society.
Roebuck, Julian B. & Hickson, Mark L., III. The Southern Redneck: A Phenomenological Class Study.
Roeder, D. & Gilbert, O. E. Evolution & Macroscopic Structure of Valley & Ridge Thrust Belt: Tennessee & Virginia.
Roeder, Martin. Land Plants: Origins, Sex & Making a Living.
Roeder, William S. Dictionary of European History.
Roederer, J. G. Dynamics of Geomagnetically Trapped Radiation.
Roederer, Scott. The Compleat Angler's Catalog: A Sourcebook for Fly Fishermen.
Roediger, Henry, III, jt. auth. see Kantowitz, Barry.
Roediger, Henry L., III, jt. auth. see Kantowitz, Barry H.
Roehrborn, G., jt. ed. see Vogel, F.
Roehrig, Terry D. Bus Ride.
Roelker, Jack R. Mathu of Kenya: A Political Study.
Roelofs, H. M. & Houseman, Gerald L. The American Political System.
Roemer, Kenneth M. Build Your Own Utopia: An Interdisciplinary Course in Utopian Speculation.
Roemer, Ruth, jt. auth. see Shonick, William.
Roepke, H., jt. auth. see Neudert, Walter.
Roesch, Eugene J. The Totalitarian Threat.
Roesch, John. Historic White Plains.
Roeseler, W. G. Successful American Urban Plans.
Roessel, Robert A. Coyote Stories of the Navajo People.
Roessel, Robert, Jr. Pictorial History of the Navajo from 1860-1910.
Roessler, Carl. Mastering Underwater Photography.
Roethke, Theodore. Selected Poems.
Roethlisberger, Fritz J. Management & Morale.
Roets, Lois. How to Write & Market Your Own Educational Materials.
Roets, Lois S. Famous People: Grades Five to Thirteen.
--Public Speaking.
--Survey & Public Opinion Research: Grades Five to Twelve.
Roetzel, Calvin J. The Letters of Paul: Conversations in Context.
Rofes, Eric E., jt. auth. see Fayerweather Street School Staff.
Roffman, Etomar Ben. The Great Christ Debate: A Quest for the Theological Reconciliation of Judaism, Christianity, & Islam.
Rogal, Samuel J. Sisters of Sacred Song: Selected Listing of Women Hymnodists in Great Britain & America.
Rogan, Helen. Mixed Company: Women in the Modern Army.
Rogatti, W., jt. ed. see Sinzinger, H.
Rogbinson, Jeff. Audi Service-Repair Handbook: Fox--1973-1979.
Roger, Colin. A Social Psychology of Schooling.
Rogers & Thatcher. The Home Stretch.
Rogers, A. Statistical Analysis of Spatial Dispersion.
Rogers, A. Robert. The Humanities: A Selective Guide to Information Sources.
Rogers, Alan. Landscapes & Documents.
Rogers, Alan, jt. auth. see Buni, Andrew.
Rogers, Alva. Requiem for Astounding.
Rogers, Annie, jt. ed. see Shibles, Loana.
Rogers, Barbara. In the Center: The Story of a Retreat.
Rogers, Carl R. Counseling & Psychotherapy.
--A Way of Being.
Rogers, Chris. Kawasaki AE-AR 50 & 80 '81-'84.
--Suzuki 100, 125, 185, & 250 Trail Bikes '79-'81.
Rogers, Chris, jt. auth. see Clew, Jeff.
Rogers, Cornwell B. Spirit of Revolution in Seventeen Eighty-Nine: A Study of Public Opinion As Revealed in the Political Songs & Other Popular Literature.
Rogers, Cyril, ed. see Rutgers, A.
Rogers, Cyril H. Parrot Guide.
Rogers, D., ed. Gabriel Tellez: El Condenado por Desconfiado.
Rogers, D. F., ed. Computer Applications in the Automation of Shipyard Operation & Ship Design.
--Computer Graphics in Engineering Education.
Rogers, Dale E. Angel Unaware.
--Dearest Debbie.
--Let Us Love.
Rogers, E. L. The World's Best Fishing Holes: Over Seventy Great Destinations Where the Joy of Fishing Is Worth a Special Trip.
Rogers, E. M. Teaching Physics for the Inquiring Mind.
Rogers, G. L. Noncoherent Optical Processing.
Rogers, George C., Jr. History of Georgetown County, South Carolina.
Rogers, H., ed. see Cambridge Summer School in Mathematical Logic Staff.
Rogers, H. C. Steam from Waterloo.
Rogers, Hal & Reinhardt, Ed. How to Make Your Own Picture Frames.
Rogers, Isabel. Christian & World Affairs.
--In Response to God: How Christians Make Ethical Decisions.
Rogers, Jack. Confessions of a Conservative Evangelical.
Rogers, Jacquelyn. You Can Stop.
Rogers, Jean. Introduction to Computing: Content for a High School Course.
Rogers, Jean, ed. Topics: Computer Education for Colleges of Education.
Rogers, Jerry, ed. Global Risk Assessments: Issues, Concepts & Applications.
Rogers, Jim. Tunnelling into Colditz: A Mining Engineer in Captivity.
Rogers, John B., Jr. Pentecost Three: Proclamation 3B.
Rogers, Kenny. Kenny Roger's America.
Rogers, Mary. Women, Divorce, & Money.
Rogers, May. Waverly Dictionary.
Rogers, Michael. Silicon Valley.
Rogers, Michael A. Living with Paraplegia.
Rogers, Norma. How Can I Help My Child Get Ready to Read?
Rogers, Pat. Defoe.
--Hacks & Dunces: Pope, Swift & Grub Street.
Rogers, Pat, ed. Defoe: The Critical Heritage.
Rogers, Pat, jt. ed. see Harbert, Wally.
Rogers, Paul, jt. auth. see Skellern, Claire.
Rogers, Robert S. & Chamberlain, V. B., 3rd, eds. National Account Marketing Handbook.
Rogers, Rolf E. The Political Process in Modern Organization.
Rogers, Rosemary. Lost Love, Last Love.
--Love Play.
--The Wanton.
Rogers, Roy & Wojahn, Karen A. Growing up with Roy & Dale.
Rogers, Steve & Rosa, Tina. Twenty-Two Days in Mexico.
Rogers, Thomas. Greek Word Roots: A Practical List with Greek & English Derivatives.
Rogers, Vivian, et al, eds. Developing Through Relationships: A Reader.
Rogers, W. G. Mightier Than the Sword: Cartoon, Caricature, Social Comment.
Rogers, W. W., jt. auth. see Ward, R. D.
Rogers, Warren, jt. auth. see Watson, Paul.
Rogers, Will. Autobiography of Will Rogers. Day, Donald, ed.
--The Illiterate Digest.
Rogers, William F. Ye Shall Be Comforted.
Rogers-Lafferty, Sarah. Brent Riley Drawings: Segments I.
--Segments I: Brent Riley Drawings.
Rogerson, J. W. Anthropology & the Old Testament.
Rogerson, John, jt. auth. see Kaye, Bruce.
Rogerson, John W. Old Testament Criticism in the Nineteenth Century.
Rogge, Benjamin A., ed. see Velasco, Gustavo R.
Roggenkamp. Stave Churches in Norway.
Roggenkamp, K. W., jt. auth. see Reiner, I.
Rogin, Gilbert. Preparations for the Ascent.
Rogliatti, Gianni. Leica, the First Sixty Years.
Rogness, Alvin N. Bridges to Hope.
--Forgiveness & Confession: Keys to Renewal.
--The Jesus Life: A Guide for Young Christians.
--The Land of Jesus.
--The Story of the American Lutheran Church.
--Table of the Lord: Holy Communion in the Life of the Church.
--Touch of His Love: Devotions for Every Season.
Rogness, Michael. The Hand That Holds Me.
Rogo, D. Scott. Mind over Matter: The Case for Psychokinesis.
--Miracles: A Parascientific Inquiry into Wonderous Phenomena.
--Welcoming Silence.
Rogoff, Abraham M. Formative Years of the Jewish Labor Movement in the United States: (1890-1900)
Rogoff, Mortimer. Calculator Navigation.
Rogosin, Donn. Invisible Men: Life in Baseball's Negro Leagues.
Rogovin, Z. A., et al, eds. Advances in Polymer Science.
Rogowsky, Edward T., jt. auth. see Abbot, David W.
Roh, Jae M., jt. ed. see Page, James A.
Rohan Barondes, R. de see De Rohan Barondes, R.
Rohatgi, V. K., jt. ed. see Gani, J.
Rohde, Eleanour S. Herbs & Herb Gardening.
Rohde, S., ed. Energy Conservation Through Fluid Film Lubrication Technology: Frontiers in Research & Design.
Rohde, S. M. & Cheng, H. S., eds. Surface Roughness Effects in Hydrodymanic & Mixed Lubrication.
Rohde, S. M., et al, eds. Fundamentals of the Design of Fluid Film Bearings.
Rohde, Ulrich L. Digital PLL Frequency Synthesizers: Theory & Design.
Rohermer, Harriet, adapted by. The Mighty God Viracocha: El Dios Poderoso Viracocha.
Rohlfs, K. Lectures on Density Wave Theory.
Rohmer, Harriet. Atariba & Niguayona.
--The Invisible Hunters.
--Land of the Icy Death: Tierra De la Muerte Glacial.
--Read-Along with "The Legend of Food Mountain"
Rohmer, Harriet & De Lopez, Graciela C. How We Came to the Fifth World: Como Vinimos al Quinto Mundo.
Rohmer, Harriet & Rea, Jesus G. Read-Along with "Atariba & Niguayona"
Rohmer, Harriet, adapted by. Cuna Song: Cancion de los Cunas. Rea, Jesus G.
Rohmer, Harriet & Rea, Jesus G., eds. The Treasure of Guatavita: El Tesoro De Guatavita.
Rohn, Arthur H. see Smith, Watson & Breternitz, David A.
Rohn, Jim. Seven Strategies for Wealth & Happiness: Power Ideas from America's Foremost Business Philosopher.
Rohr, D. G., ed. Commentaries on European Affairs, 1870-1914.
Rohr, Donald G., jt. auth. see Ergang, Robert.
Rohrbaugh, Richard L. The Biblical Interpreter: An Agrarian Bible in an Industrial Age.
Rohrer, jt. auth. see Morris.
Rohrer, Norman B. Mom LeTourneau. Throop, Isabel A., ed.
Rohrer, Norman B. & Sutherland, S. Philip. Why Am I Shy? Turning Shyness into Confidence.
Rohrer, R. A., ed. see Motil, John M.
Rohrlich, George F., jt. auth. see Yung-Ping Chen.
Rohrs, Roger, ed. see Orion Research Staff.
Rohsenow, Warren M. & Hartnett, James P. Handbook of Heat Transfer.
Rohwer, Jurgen. Superpower Confrontation on the Seas: Naval Development & Strategy Since 1945.
Roisen, Fred J. & Hsu, Linda. Histology Review.
Roitt, et al. Immunology.
--Slide Atlas of Immunology.
Rojas-Lombardi, Felipe. Soup, Beautiful Soup.
Rokem, Freddie. Theatrical Space in Ibsen, Chekhov & Strindberg: Public Forms of Privacy. Brockett, Oscar, ed.
Rokkan, Stein, jt. auth. see European Consortium for Political Research Staff.
Rokkan, Stein, et al. Nation-Building: A Review of Recent Comparative Research & a Select Bibliography of Analytical Studies.
Rokossovsky, K. A Soldier's Duty.
Rola, Klossowski K. De see De Rola, Klossowski.
Roland, Alex. Spacefaring People: Perspectives on Early Spaceflight.
Roland, Donna. Grandfather's Stories.
Rolander-Chilo, Brita, ed. Nutritional Research: An International Approach.
Rolde, Neil. Lord Lobster.
Roleder, George. Marriage Means Encounter.
Rolfe, E. J., jt. ed. see Hawthorne, J.
Rolfe, Frederick C. Nicholas Crabbe: Or, The One & the Many, a Romance.
Rolfe, John C. Cicero & His Influence.
Rolfe, R. E. Steel for the User.
Rolfe, Sidney E. & Burtle, James L. The Great Wheel: The World, Monetary System; a Reinterpretation.
Rolfe, Stanley T. & Barson, John M. Fracture & Fatigue Control in Structures: Applications of Fracture Mechanics.
Rolfsen, Dale. Knots & Links.
Rolin, Jean. Police Drugs.
Rolland, Romain. Essays on Music.
--Journey Within.
--Richard Strauss & Romain Rolland: Correspondence.
--Tolstoy.

Roller, Duane & Goodman, Marcia M. Catalogue of the History of Science: Collections of the University of Oklahoma Libraries.
Rolleston, Humphrey. Minor Surgery.
Rollin, Betty. Last Wish.
--Last Wish.
Rollin, H. The Mentally Abnormal Offender & the Law.
Rolling Stone Press Staff & Cott, Jonathan. Dylan.
--Dylan.
Rollins, Jack, jt. auth. see Nelson, Steve.
Rollins, Joan H., ed. Hidden Minorities: The Persistence of Ethnicity in American Life.
Rollins, Richard M., intro. by. The Autobiographies of Noah Webster: From the Letters & Essays, Memoir & Diary.
Rollinson, C. L. The Chemistry of Chromium, Molybdenum & Tungsten.
Rollnick, H., ed. see Theoretical Physics International Summer Institute, Bonn, 1974.
Rollnik, H. & Pfeil, W. E., eds. Electron & Photon Interactions at High Energies.
Rollock, Barbara. Black Experience in Children's Books.
Rolloff, John A., jt. auth. see De Vore, Jack B., Jr.
Rollow, Cooper. Cooper Rollow's Chicago Bears Football Book.
Rolls, Maurice J., jt. ed. see Jones, Gwyn E.
Rolnick, Michael & Kane, James C. Infectious Diseases in Emergency Medicine.
Rol'nik, V. V. Suitability of Hen Eggs for Incubation in the Fresh State & After Storage.
Roloff, Joan G. Encounter: Readings for Thinking, Talking, Writing.
Roloff, Leland H. The Perception & Evocation of Literature.
Roloff, Michael, ed. Contemporary German Theater.
Roloff, Michael, tr. see Hesse, Hermann.
Roloff-Stoddard, Joan, et al. Vocabulary: The Words Used to Express Ideas & Feelings.
Rolph, Elizabeth S. Nuclear Power & the Public Safety: A Study in Regulation.
Rolph, John, jt. auth. see Morris, Carl.
Rolston, Holmes. The Apostle Peter Speaks to Us Today.
--Stewardship in the New Testament Church.
Rolston, Holmes, III. John Calvin vs. the Westminster Confession.
Rolston, Holmes, 3rd. Cosmic Christ.
Rolt, L. T. Red for Danger.
Romagnoli, G. Franco, jt. auth. see Romagnoli, Margaret.
Romagnoli, Margaret & Romagnoli, G. Franco. The New Italian Cooking.
Romain, Mark. Escrima Self Defence: Stick, Empty Hand, Knife.
Romains, Jules. Copains.
--Europe.
--Les Hommes De Bonne Volonte.
--Knock; or, the Triumph of Medicine: A Comedy in Three Acts. Sacks, Betty S., tr.
--Knock ou le Triomphe de la Medecine.
Romalis, Shelly, ed. Childbirth: Alternatives to Medical Control.
Roman, I., jt. auth. see Baum.
Roman, Murray. Telephone Marketing Techniques.
Romand, J., jt. auth. see Vodar, Boris.
Romanne-James, Constance. Herb-Lore for Housewives.
Romano, Joseph A. & Wiener, Matthew B. Mill's Pharmacy State Board Review.
Romano, Louis G., et al. The Management of Educational Personnel.
Romanowicz, Zofia. Passage Through the Red Sea. Peterson, Virgilia, tr.
Romans, Robert C. & McCann, Patricia S. Bibliography of Ohio Paleobotany.
Romans, Robert C., ed. Geobotany I.
--Geobotany II.
Romantik Hotel & Restaurants Association Staff, ed. Romantik Hotels & Restaurants: Charming Historic Hotels in Europe & the United States.
Romanucci-Ross, Lola, et al, eds. The Anthropology of Medicine: From Culture to Method.
Romanyshyn, John M., ed. Social Science & Social Welfare.
Romashko, Sandra. The Savory Shellfish of North America.
Romberg, Rosemary. Circumcision: The Painful Dilemma.
Romberger, J. A. Meristems, Growth & Development in Woody Plants: An Analytical Review of Anatomical, Physiological & Morphogenic Aspects.
Romberger, J. A. & Mikola, P., eds. International Review of Forestry Research.
Romen, A. S. Self-Suggestion & Its Influence on the Human Organism. Lewis, A. S. & Forsky, V., eds.
Romer, Alfred S. Osteology of the Reptiles.
Romer, Alfred S. & Parsons, Thomas S. The Vertebrate Body: Shorter Version.
Romer, John. Ancient Lives: Daily Life in Egypt of the Pharaohs.
Romer, Terry L. Complete Kindergarten Handbook.
Romera, Carlos, jt. auth. see Ortega, Carlos.
Romero, Fred. Chicano Workers: Their Utilization & Development.
Romero, R., jt. auth. see Jeanty, P.
Romero, Sidney J. Religion in the Rebel Ranks.
Romesburg, H. Charles. Cluster Analysis for Researchers.
Romeuf, Jean & Guinot, Jean P. Diccionario del Jefe de Empresa.
Romey, W. D. Field Guide to Plutonic & Metamorphic Rocks.
Romey, William D. Teaching the Gifted & Talented in the Science Classroom.
Romig, David W. Celebrate the Future.
Romilly, Samuel. Memoirs of the Life of Sir Samuel Romilly: With a Selection from His Correspondence.
Romine, Aden F., jt. auth. see Romine, Mary C.
Romine, Mary C. & Romine, Aden F. The Fellowship.
Romiti, A., ed. see CISM (International Center for Mechanical Sciences), Department of Hydro & Gasdynamics Staff.
Romm. Basic Suturing.
Romm, J. Leonard. The Swastika on the Synagogue Door.
Rommel, Kurt. The Best Is Yet to Be. Scheidt, David L., tr. from Ger.
--Our Father Who Art in Heaven. Cooperrider, Edward A., tr. from Ger.
Romney, Arnold B., jt. auth. see Burbank, Nelson L.
Romney, Ronna & Harrison, Beppie. Giving Time a Chance: The Secret of a Lasting Marriage.
Romney, Seymour, et al, eds. Gynecology & Obstetrics: The Health Care of Women.
Rompuy, P. Van, jt. ed. see Chatterji, M.
Ron, Judith S., jt. auth. see Costa, Barbara C.
Rona, P. A. & Lowell, R. P. Seafloor Spreading Centers: Hydrothermal Systems.
Rona, Peter A. The Central North Atlantic Ocean Basin & Continental Margins: Geology, Geophysics, Geochemistry, & Resources, Including the Trans-Atlantic Geotraverse (TAG)
Rona, Thomas P.. Our Changing Geopolitical Premises.
Ronaldson, Dolores, ed. see Witter, Evelyn.
Ronay, Egon. Egon Ronay's Lucas Guide to Hotels, Restaurants & Inns in Great Britain & Ireland, 1983.
Roncaglia, Alessandro. International Oil Market. Kregel, J. A., ed.
Ronen, Avraham. Introducing Prehistory.
Ronen, Joshua. Entrepreneurship.
Ronen, Simcha. The Flexible Work Schedule: An Innovation in the Quality of Work Life.
Ron-Feder, Galila. To Myself: The Story of a Foster Child. Arad, Miriam, tr. from Hebrew.
Ronnberg, Erik A., Jr. Gloucester Clipper Fishing Schooners. Gentle, Ernest J., ed.
Roo, Ann De see De Roo, Ann.
Rood, David S. Wichita Grammar.
Rood, Robert T. & Trefil, James S. Are We Alone?
Rood, Ronald. It's Going to Sting Me: A Coward's Guide to the Great Outdoors.
--Laska: Adventures with a Wolfdog.
--Who Wakes the Groundhog?
Roodkowsky, Mary, jt. auth. see Leghorn, Lisa.
Roody, Peter, et al. Medical Abbreviations & Acronyms.
Roof, Wade C. & Ginsberg, Ralph B., eds. Race & Residence in American Cities.
Rooijmans, C. J., ed. Crystals for Magnetic Applications.
Rooke. Gerontology.
Rooker, C. Keith, jt. auth. see Hill, Marvin S.
Rooks, Brian, ed. Developments in Robotics.
Rooks, George. Conversations sans Fin.
--Non-Stop Discussion Workbook! Problems for Intermediate & Advanced Students of English.
Rooks, George, et al. Conversar Sin Parar.
Rooks, Nancy, jt. auth. see Gutter, Mae.
Room, Adrian. Dictionary of Cryptic Crossword Clues.
--Dictionary of Cryptic Crossword Clues.
--A Dictionary of True Etymologies.
--Room's Dictionary of Confusibles.
--Room's Dictionary of Distinguishables.
--Room's Dictionary of Distinguishables & Confusibles.
Rooney. Valedictory.
Rooney, Andrew A. And More by Andy Rooney.
--A Few Minutes with Andy Rooney.
--Pieces of My Mind.
--Pieces of My Mind.
--Word for Word.
Rooney, David. Sir Charles Arden-Clarke.
Rooney, John F., Jr., et al, eds. This Remarkable Continent: An Atlas of U. S. & Canadian Society & Cultures.
Roorbach, Rosemary K., ed. Discovery: A Resource Book for Use with Persons Who Have Learning Difficulties.
Roos, Stephen. Fairweather Friends.
Roose-Evans, James. Experimental Theater.
Roosevelt, Caleb. I Know Some Spinners Weave My End.
Roosevelt, Eleanor. The Autobiography of Eleanor Roosevelt.
Roosevelt, Elliott. As He Saw It.
--The Conservators.
--The Hyde Park Murder.
--Murder & the First Lady.
Roosevelt, James & Shalett, Sidney. Affectionately, F. D. R.
Roosevelt, Kermit. Countercoup: The Struggle for the Control of Iran.
Roosevelt, Michele C. Animals in the Woods.
Roosevelt, Theodore. Hunting Trips of a Ranchman: Sketches of Sport on the Northern Cattle Plains.
--Ranch Life in the Far West.
Root, A. I. ABC & XYZ of Bee Culture.
--ABC & XYZ of Bee Culture.
Root, A. W., jt. auth. see La Cuaza, C.
Root, Franklin R. Entry Strategies for Foreign Markets: From Domestic to International Business.
--Foreign Market Entry Strategies.
Root, Jane. Pictures of Women: Sexuality.
Root, Jane, jt. auth. see Colvin, Ruth J.
Root, Judith. Weaving the Sheets: Poems.
Root, Oren. Persons & Persuasions.
Root, W. S. & Hoffman, F. G., eds. Physiological Pharmacology: A Comprehensive Treatise. Incl. Vol. 1. The Nervous System, Part A; Vol. 2. The Nervous System, Part B; Vol. 3. The Nervous System, Part C; Vol. 4. The Nervous System, Part D; Vol. 5. The Nervous System, Part E. Acad Pr.
Root, Waverley. Paris Dining Guide.
Root, William P. Storm & Other Poems.
Rootes, Nina, tr. see Apollinaire, Guillaume.
Rootman, Irving & Moser, Joy. Community Response to Alcohol-Related Problems: World Health Organization Project Monograph.
Roots, B., jt. auth. see Johnston, P.
Roper, jt. auth. see Trevor.
Roper, Nancy. New American Pocket Medical Dictionary.
Roper, Paul M. & Loertscher, David V. Modular Computer Lesson Design.
Roper, R. G., ed. Interim Results of the Middle Atmosphere Program: A Selection of Invited Papers from the Symposium Jointly Sponsored by the IAGA & IAMAP at the XVIII General Assembly of the IUGG, Hamburg, Federal Republic of Germany, August 1985.
Roper, Steve & Steck, Allen, eds. Ascent, 1984: The Mountaineering Experience in Word & Image.
Roper-Hall, M. J. Eye Surgery (Stallard)
Ropiequet, Suzanne, jt. ed. see Lambert, Steve.
Ropp, Steve C. & Morris, James A., eds. Central America: Crisis & Adaptation.
Rorabaugh, Britt. Data Communications & Local Area Networking Handbook.
Rorem, Ned. Setting the Tone: Essays & a Diary.
Rorex, Robert A. & Wen Fong, trs. Eighteen Songs of a Nomad Flute: The Story of Lady Wen-Chi.
Rorimer, Anne, jt. auth. see Speyer, A. James.
Rorke, M. Christmas Could-be Tales & Other Verses.
Rorty, Richard, ed. Linguistic Turn: Recent Essays in Philosophical Method.
Rorvik, David. Good Housekeeping Woman's Medical Guide.
Rosa, Jose A. & Altman, Nathaniel. Power Spots.
Rosa, Tina, jt. auth. see Rogers, Steve.
Rosa, Veronica di see Feuer, Janice.
Rosa Angeles de, la see De La Rosa, Angeles & Fernandez, C. Gandia.
Rosage, David. Abide in Me: A Pocket Guide to Daily Scriptural Prayer.
--Climbing Higher: Reflections on Our Spiritual Journey.
--Follow Me: A Pocket Guide to Daily Scriptual Prayer.
Rosage, David E. The Bread of Life.
Rosato, Frank. Jogging for Health & Fitness.
Rosberg, Robert, ed. see Mosler Anti-Crime Bureau Staff.
Rosborough, Pearl M. Physical Fitness & the Child's Reading Problem.
Roscoe, Theodore. A Grave Must Be Deep.
--Z Is for Zombie.
Roscow, Judith, jt. auth. see Klein, Barbara.
Rosdahl, Caroline B., jt. auth. see Story, Donna K.
Rosdail, J. Hart. Biking Alone Around the World.
Rose. Money & Capital Markets.
Rose, Angie. Love Notes: A Compleat Parenting Kit.
Rose, Ann. The Power Of: Step-by-Step Through LOGO Turtle Graphics.
Rose, Anne. Hamid & the Sultan's Son.
Rose, Anthony H. Chemical Microbiology: An Introduction to Microbial Physiology.
Rose, Anthony H., ed. Thermobiology.
Rose, Barbara. Unspoken Feelings.
Rose, Barbara, jt. auth. see Kalil, Susie.
Rose, Bernice. Jackson Pollock: Drawing into Painting.
Rose, Bernice, jt. auth. see Monnier, Genevieve.
Rose, Burton D. Pathophysiology of Renal Disease.
Rose, C. J. Crop Protection.
Rose, C. W. Agricultural Physics.
Rose, Carol M. Some Emerging Issues in Legal Liability of Children's Agencies.
Rose, Charles L., jt. auth. see Bosse, Raymond.
Rose, D. J., ed. Nuclear-Electric Power in the Asia-Pacific Region: Proceedings of the Workshop Held in Honolulu, Hawaii, 23-28 January 1983.
Rose, Darrell E. Audiological Assessment.
Rose, Dorothy. Farm Animals.
--Heads & Tails.
--Mother Goose.
--Numbers.
Rose, Dorothy, jt. auth. see Jarrette, Peter.
Rose, Elizabeth. Grand Jury.
Rose, Elizabeth & Rose, Gerald. Wolf! Wolf!
Rose, Evelyn & Rose, Judi. The First-Time Cookbook.
Rose, George G., ed. Atlas of Vertebrate Cells in Tissue Culture.
--Cinemicrography in Cell Biology.
Rose, Gerald. The Bag of Wind.
--Rabbit Pie.
--The Tiger-Skin Rug.
Rose, Gerald, jt. auth. see Rose, Elizabeth.
Rose, H. C., jt. auth. see Miller, W. R.
Rose, Hilary. Doctors, Patients & Pathology.
Rose, J. W. & Cooper, J. R., eds. Technical Data on Fuel: S. I. Units.
Rose, James M. & Brown, Barbara, eds. Black Roots in Southeastern Connecticut 1650-1900: A Guide to Information Sources.
Rose, James M., jt. ed. see Eichholz, Alice.
Rose, Jerome G. Legal Foundations of Land Use Planning.
Rose, Jerry D. Introduction to Sociology.
--Peoples: The Ethnic Dimension in Human Relations.
Rose, John E., Jr. Big Words for Big Shooters.
Rose, John H. Mediterranean in the Ancient World.
Rose, Joseph B., jt. ed. see Chaison, Gary N.
Rose, Joseph H. & Miller, Harry, eds. Scott Standard U. S. Coin Catalogue 1984.
Rose, Joseph L. & Goldberg, B. B. Basic Physics in Diagnostic Ultrasound.
Rose, Judi, jt. auth. see Rose, Evelyn.
Rose, Karen. In the Land of the Mind.
Rose, Karen & Halfyard, Lynda. Kristin & Boone.
Rose, Kenneth. King George V.
Rose, Larry L. & Hadaway, C. Kirk, eds. The Urban Challenge.
Rose, Leo E. The Politics of Bhutan.
Rose, Louis F., jt. auth. see Kaye, Donald.
Rose, Michael. Servants of Post-Industrial Power: Sociologie Du Travail in Modern France.
Rose, Michael D., ed. Selected Federal Taxation, Statutes & Regulations, 1988.
--Selected Federal Taxation Statutes & Regulations: 1987 Edition.
Rose, Mike. Writer's Block: The Cognitive Dimension.
Rose, Minnie & Hamilton, Kellen. NRL Yearbook Eighty-Six.
Rose, Minnie B., jt. ed. see Hamilton, Helen.
Rose, Nikolas. The Psychological Complex: Social Relation & the Psychology of the Individual.
Rose, Noel R., jt. ed. see Thompson, R. A.
Rose, Peter I., ed. Nation of Nations: The Ethnic Experience & the Racial Crisis.
Rose, Peter R. Money & Capital Markets.
Rose, Peter S. & Fraser, Donald R. Financial Institutions.
--Financial Institutions.
Rose, Peter S., jt. auth. see Fraser, Donald R.
Rose, Peter S., jt. ed. see Fraser, Donald R.
Rose, Richard. Appleworks User's Handbook.
--Politics in England.
Rose, Richard M. The Satyr Candidate.
Rose, Ronald. Ngari the Hunter.
Rose, Seraphim & Abbot Herman. Blessed John the Wonderworker.
Rose, Seraphim, tr. see Maximovitch, John.
Rose, T. & Rider, R. Corrosion of Metals in Concrete.
Rosebault, Charles J. When Dana Was the Sun: A Story of Personal Journalism.
Roseberry, Eric. Ludwig Van Beethoven.
Roseberry, William. Coffee & Capitalism in the Venezuelan Andes.
Roseboom, E. H. & Weisenberger, F. P. A History of Ohio.
Roseboro, John & Libby, Bill. Glory Days with the Dodgers: And Other Days with Others.
Rosefielde, Steven. False Science: Underestimating the Soviet Threat.
Rosefsky, Bob. Money Talks: Bob Rosefsky's Complete Program for Financial Success.
Rosegger, Gerhard. The Economics of Production & Innovation: An Industrial Perspective.
Rose-Hancock, Marga, jt. ed. see McCrone, Carole N.
Rosel, Paul. Silent Night, Holy Night.
Roseler, Robert & Duckert, Audrey, eds. Moderne Deutsche Erzaehler.
Roseler, Robert O. German in Review.

Roseler, Robert O. & Reichard, Joseph R. German Grammar Workbook.
Roseliep, Raymond. Listen to Light: Haiku.
--Sun in His Belly.
--Walk in Love.
Roselle, Daniel. Samuel Griswold Goodrich, Creator of Peter Parley.
Roseman, Curtis C. Multiple Residence & Cyclical Migration in Western Societies: A Bibliography.
Roseman, Edward. Confronting Nonpromotability: How to Manage a Stalled Career.
--Managing Employee Turnover: A Positive Approach.
--Managing the Problem Employee.
Roseman, Mill. Detectionary. Fenzler, Otto, et al, eds.
Rosemond, John. Parent Power: A Common Sense Approach to Raising Your Children in the Eighties.
Rosen & Haining. Intraocular Lens Implantation.
Rosen, jt. auth. see Barkin.
Rosen, Benson & Jerdee, Thomas H. Older Employees: New Roles for Valued Resources.
Rosen, Bernard. Strategies of Ethics.
Rosen, Charles. Have Jump Shot Will Travel.
--Mile Above the Rim.
--Players & Pretenders: The Basketball Team That Couldn't Shoot Straight.
--Sonata Forms.
Rosen, Charles, ed. see Meyerbeer, Giacomo.
Rosen, Charles, ed. see Rossini, Gioachino.
Rosen, David, ed. Megatoons: Cartoonists Against Nuclear War.
Rosen, David & Porter, Andrew, eds. Verdi's Macbeth: A Source Book.
Rosen, Gerald. The Carmen Miranda Memorial Flagpole.
--Zen in the Art of J. D. Salinger.
Rosen, Harvey S. Public Finance.
Rosen, Howard F., jt. auth. see Hufbauer, Gary C.
Rosen, Ira, jt. auth. see Gray, Mike.
Rosen, Kenneth, frwd. by. Voices of the Rainbow.
Rosen, L; see Wenner, H. A., et al.
Rosen, Lawrence. Investing in Zero's Coupon Bonds: All About Cats, Strips, Tigers, Lions, TR & TBRs.
Rosen, Lawrence R. The Dow Jones-Irwin Guide to Interest.
Rosen, Leonard, jt. auth. see Behrens, Laurence.
Rosen, Linda R., jt. auth. see Rosen, Raymond.
Rosen, M. J. Introduction to Photography: A Self Directing Approach.
Rosen, Marcia & Harris, Henry. Test Your Baby's I. Q.
Rosen, Marcia & Polenz, Joanna M. Test Your Marriage I. Q.
Rosen, Marcia, jt. auth. see Polenz, Joanna M.
Rosen, Michael. Smelly Jelly Smelly Fish.
Rosen, Nathan A. Real Estate Syndication: A Selected Bibliography of Articles, Books & Serials.
Rosen, Norma G. At the Center.
Rosen, Paul P., jt. auth. see Sommers, Sheldon C.
Rosen, Paul Peter, jt. auth. see Sommers, Shedlon C.
Rosen, Peter, et al. Emergency Medicine: Concepts & Clinical Practice.
Rosen, R., ed. see Anderson, Lynne.
Rosen, R., ed. see Peck, Phyllis & Konkel, Gilbert.
Rosen, R. D. Psychobabble.
--Psychobabble.
Rosen, Raymond & Rosen, Linda R. Human Sexuality.
Rosen, Robert, ed. Foundations of Mathematical Biology. Incl. Vol. 1. Subcellular Systems; Vol. 2. Cellular Systems; Vol. 3. Acad Pr.
--Progress in Theoretical Biology.
--Progress in Theoretical Biology.
Rosen, Ruth, ed. see Collins, Robert F.
Rosen, Ruth, ed. see Jones, Marilyn.
Rosen, Ruth C., ed. see Garven, Charles.
Rosen, Ruth C., ed. see Ward, William G.
Rosen, Ruth C., ed. see Wright, Glen.
Rosen, Sherry. Mei Foo Sun Chuen, Middle Class Chinese Families in Transition.
Rosenau, Fred S. & Chase, Leslie, eds. Business Realities in the Information Industry.
Rosenau, Fred S. & Chase, Leslie R., eds. Increasing Your Sales Through Customer Services: A Critical Function in Transition.
Rosenau, James N., jt. ed. see Knorr, Klaus.
Rosenau, Milton D. & Lewin, Marsha D. Software Project Management: Step-by-Step.
Rosenbach, Joseph B., et al. College Algebra.
Rosenbauer, Tom. The Orvis Fly-Fishing Guide.
Rosenbaum, Daniel J., jt. auth. see Stewart, Charles O., III.
Rosenbaum, Ernest H. Can You Prevent Cancer? Realistic Guidelines for Developing Cancer-Preventive Life Habits.
Rosenbaum, H. J., jt. auth. see Hellman, R. G.
Rosenbaum, Lawrence & Linden, Jonathan, eds. The PC CAD-CAM-CAE Software & Systems Directory.
Rosenbaum, Patricia, jt. auth. see Schoenberg, Sandra.
Rosenbaum, Robert A., et al, eds. The Concord Desk Encyclopedia.
Rosenbaum, Robert J. Mexicano Resistance in the Southwest: "The Sacred Right of Self-Preservation"
Rosenbaum, Sidonia C. Modern Women Poets of Spanish America: The Precursors, Delmira Agustine, Gabriela Mistral, Alfonsina Storni, Juana de Ibarbourou.
Rosenberg, Alfred. The Myth of the Twentieth Century. Whisker, James B., tr. from Ger.
Rosenberg, Amye, illus. My Cash Register Book.
--My Clock Book.
--My Telephone Book.
Rosenberg, Andrew. Tax Planner: User's Guide & Documentation to Accompany Hoffman & Willis West's Federal Taxation.
Rosenberg, Arnold. The Social Studies Student Investigates Modern Wars.
Rosenberg, Bernard, jt. auth. see Coser, Lewis A.
Rosenberg, Charles E. Cholera Years: The United States in 1832, 1849, & 1866.
--Trial of the Assassin Guiteau: Psychiatry & the Law in the Gilded Age.
--Trial of the Assassin Guiteau: Psychiatry & the Law in the Gilded Age.
Rosenberg, David. Blues of the Sky: Interpreted from the Original Hebrew Book of Psalms.
--Lightworks: Interpreted from the Original Hebrew Book of Isaiah.
Rosenberg, Emily S., jt. auth. see Rosenberg, Norman L.
Rosenberg, Harold. Barnett Newman.
Rosenberg, Israel. The World of Words.
Rosenberg, J., ed. International Conference on Laboratory Astrophysics.
Rosenberg, Jakob. Great Draughtsmen from Pisanello to Picasso.
Rosenberg, James L; see Corrigan, Robert W.
Rosenberg, Jane E. & Sullivan, Maureen. Resource Notebook on Staff Development.
Rosenberg, Jerry M. Dictionary of Computers, Data Processing & Telecommunications.
Rosenberg, John. Dorothy Richardson: The Genius They Forgot.
Rosenberg, L., jt. auth. see Mandell, Maurice I.
Rosenberg, Mark L. Patients: The Experience of Illness.
Rosenberg, Marvin & Schiff, Martin. Educational Law.
Rosenberg, Maurice, et al. Elements of Civil Procedure, Cases & Materials: 1982 Suplement.
Rosenberg, Max. The Building of Perry's Fleet on Lake Erie: 1812-1813.
--Introduction to Philosophy.
Rosenberg, Naomi R. & Sekulow, Marianne W. Inside Outlets: The Best Bargain Shopping in New England.
Rosenberg, Norman L. & Rosenberg, Emily S. In Our Times.
Rosenberg, Philip. Contract on Cherry Street.
--The Spivey Assignment.
Rosenberg, Philip, jt. auth. see Grosso, Sonny.
Rosenberg, Philip, ed. Toxins: Animal, Plant & Microbial.
Rosenberg, Pierre, jt. auth. see Rubin, James H.
Rosenberg, R. Robert, et al. College Business Law. Byers, Edward E., ed.
Rosenberg, Richard. Lovejoy's Math Review for the SAT.
Rosenberg, Richard & Kelly, John D. Lovejoy's Preparation for the PSAT.
Rosenberg, Robert. Electric Motor Repair.
Rosenberg, Steven A., ed. Serologic Analysis of Human Cancer Antigens.
Rosenberg, Stuart E. New Jewish Identity in America.
Rosenberger, Francis C., ed. Records of the Columbia Historical Society of Washington D.C. 1957-1974. Incl. 1957-1959; 1960-1962; 1963-1965; 1966-1968; 1969-1970; 1971-1972; 1973-74. U Pr of Va.
Rosenberger, Joseph. Escape from Gulag Taria.
Rosenberry, Edward H. Melville.
--Melville & the Comic Spirit.
Rosenblatt, G. M., ed. Progress in Solid State Chemistry.
Rosenblatt, G. M. & Worrell, W. L., eds. Progress in Solid State Chemistry.
--Progress in Solid State Chemistry.
--Progress in Solid State Chemistry.
Rosenblatt, S. Bernard, et al. Modern Business: A Systems Approach.
Rosenblatt, Samuel. Hear, Oh Israel.
Rosenbloom, Bert. Marketing Channels.
Rosenbloom, Jerry S., jt. auth. see Hallman, G. Victor.
Rosenbloom, Jonathan. Blue Jeans.
Rosenbloom, Joseph. Deputy Dan & the Bank Robbers.
--The Looniest Limerick Book in the World.
--Mad Scientist: Riddle-Jokes-Fun.
--Wild West Riddles & Jokes.
Rosenblueth, E., jt. auth. see Lomnitz, C.
Rosenblum, Joseph, ed. see Holcroft, Thomas.
Rosenblum, Leonard A., ed. Primate Behavior: Developments in Field & Laboratory Research.
Rosenblum, Marc. Economics of the Consumer.
--How a Market Economy Works.
--Stock Market.
Rosenblum, Martin J. & Nelson-Raney, Steve. Brite Shade.
Rosenblum, Mort. Mission to Civilize: The French Way.
Rosenblum, Mort & Williamson, Doug. Squandering Eden: Africa at the Edge.
Rosenblum, Richard. My Bar Mitzvah.
--Wings: The Early Years of Aviation.
Rosenblum, Robert & Ingres, Jean A. Ingres.
Rosenblum, Robert & Marshall, Richard. Alex Katz.
Rosenblum, Robert, intro. by. Mark Rothko: The Surrealist Years.
Rosenblum Cale, Karen. Teaching Thinking Skills: Social Studies.
Rosenbluth, Lewis, jt. auth. see Mancuso, Anthony.
Rosenbluth, M. N., ed. Advanced Plasma Theory.
Rosenbluth, Sally. A Feast of Ashes.
Rosenbrock, H. H. Computer-Aided Control System Design.
Rosenburg, Louis, jt. auth. see Grigsby, William G.
Rosencraig, Allan. Photoacoustics & Photoacoustic Spectroscopy.
Rose-Neil, Sidney. Acupuncture & the Life Energies.
Rosenfeld, A. The Quintescence of Irving Langmuir.
Rosenfeld, A., ed. Digital Picture Analysis.
Rosenfeld, Al, ed. Mind & Supermind.
Rosenfeld, Albert. Prolongevity II: An Updated Report on the Scientific Prospects for Adding Good Years to Life. Elliott, Charles, ed.
Rosenfeld, Albert, jt. auth. see Kilman, Gilbert M.
Rosenfeld, Albert, jt. auth. see Kliman, Gilbert W.
Rosenfeld, C., jt. auth. see Serrou, B.
Rosenfeld, Daniel, commentary by. Nineteen-Hundred to Now: Art from Rhode Island Collections.
Rosenfeld, Daniel, text by. The Spirit of Barbizon: France & America.
Rosenfeld, Geller. Afro-Asian Culture Studies.
Rosenfeld, Herbert A. Psychotic States: A Psychoanalytic Approach.
Rosenfeld, I. Complete Medical Examination.
Rosenfeld, Irene & Beath, O. A. Selenium.
Rosenfeld, Isadore. Modern Prevention: The New Medicine.
Rosenfeld, Israel. Freud: Character & Consciousness.
Rosenfeld, Rachel A. Farm Women: Work, Farm & Family in the United States.
Rosenfeld, Robert, jt. auth. see Zirkel, G.
Rosenfeld, Stephen S. & Sidney, Rosary. Time of Their Dying.
Rosenfeldt, Diane. Ken Russell: A Guide to Reference & Resources.
--Richard Lester: A Guide to References & Resources.
Rosenfels, Paul. Homosexuality: The Psychology of the Creative Process.
Rosengart, Oliver & Weinheimer, Gail. The Rights of Suspects.
Rosengrant, Judson, tr. see Limonov, Edward.
Rosenheim, Edward W., Jr. Swift & the Satirist's Art.
Rosenheim, Richard. Eternal Drama.
Rosenman, Mervin. Forgery, Perjury, & an Enormous Fortune: 2303 Claimants to the Ella Wendell Estate (1931)
Rosenmuller, J. Extreme Games & Their Solutions.
Rosenoer, Victor, et al, eds. Albumin: Structure, Function & Uses.
Rosenow, Frank. The Ditty Bag Book.
--Manual Art: A Practical Guide to Drawing & Painting.
Rosenqvist, Terkel. Principles of Extractive Metallurgy.
Rosenstein, E., ed. Diccionario de Especialidades Farmaceuticas.
--Diccionario de Especialidades Farmaceuticas.
Rosenstein, Solomon N. Dentistry in Cerebral Palsy & Related Handicapping Conditions.
Rosenstiel, Annette. Education & Anthropology: An Annotated Bibliography.
Rosenstock, Janet, jt. auth. see Adair, Dennis.
Rosenstrauch, Henrietta. Essays on Rhythm, Music, Movement.
Rosental, M. Diccionario de Philosofia.
Rosenthal, jt. auth. see Butler.
Rosenthal, A. M. & Gelb, Arthur, eds. The New York Times of New York: An Uncommon Guide to the City of Fantasies.
Rosenthal, A. M., et al, eds. The Sophisticated Traveler: Winter: Love It or Leave It.
Rosenthal, Alan S., ed. see Leukocyte Culture Conference Staff.
Rosenthal, Alan S., jt. ed. see Unanue, Emil R.
Rosenthal, Bernard. Critical Essays on Charles Brockden Brown.
Rosenthal, Bernard G. & Mayer, John E. Crowding Behavior & the Future.
Rosenthal, Bernice, jt. auth. see Chomiak, Martha.
Rosenthal, Bert. Marques Johnson: Nobody Does it Better.
Rosenthal, Chuck. Loop's Progress.
Rosenthal, Daniel. Resistance & Deformation of Solid Media.
Rosenthal, David. Materialism & the Mind-Body Problem.
Rosenthal, David W. & Powell, Michael A. Careers in Marketing.
Rosenthal, Ed & Frank, Mel. Marijuana Techniques & Politics.
Rosenthal, Ed, jt. auth. see Frank, Mel.
Rosenthal, G., jt. auth. see Butler, R.
Rosenthal, Gary. The Spalding Guide to Fitness for the Weekend Athlete.
Rosenthal, Harold. Fifty Faces of Football: The American Game & What has Made it Great.
Rosenthal, Lucy. The Ticket Out.
Rosenthal, Lynne S. Integrated Software for Microcomputer Systems.
Rosenthal, Lynne S., jt. auth. see Barkley, John.
Rosenthal, Lynne S., ed. Guidance on Requirements Analysis for Office Automation Systems.
Rosenthal, M. L., tr. see Collodi, C.
Rosenthal, Mitchell, et al. Rehabilitation of the Head Injured Adult.
Rosenthal, Peggy & Dardess, George. Every Cliche in the Book. Guarnaschelli, Maria D., ed.
Rosenthal, Raymond, tr. see Busi, Aldo.
Rosenthal, Renate. Jewelry of the Ancient World.
Rosenthal, S., et al, eds. Gene Function: Proceedings of the 12th FEBS Meeting, Dresden, 1978.
Rosenthal, Sol R. BCG Vaccine: Tuberculosis-Cancer.
Rosenthal, Stuart & Kass, Judith M. The Hollywood Professionals, Vol. 4: Browning & Siegel.
Rosenthal, Susan, jt. auth. see Borg, Seth A.
Rosenthal, Sylvia, jt. auth. see Hovis, Gene.
Rosenthall, David, tr. see Rodoreda, Merce.
Rosenthal-Schneider, Ilse. Reality & Scientific Truth: Discussions with Einstein, von Laue, & Planck. Braun, Thomas, ed.
Rosenzweig. Book of Poverbs.
Rosenzweig, Ed & Harrison, Harland. Programming the Sixty-Eight Thousand: An Apple Press Book.
Rosenzweig, James, jt. auth. see Kast, Fremont.
Rosenzweig, M. R. & Porter, L. W., eds. Annual Review of Psychology.
--Annual Review of Psychology.
Rosenzweig, Mark R. & Leiman, Arnold L. Physiological Psychology.
Rosenzweig, Mark R. & Bennett, Edward L., eds. Neural Mechanisms of Learning & Memory.
Rosevear, Ray W. People Without Names.
Rosholt, Malcolm & Rosholt, Margaret. The Story of Old Abe.
Rosholt, Margaret, jt. auth. see Rosholt, Malcolm.
Rosier, James L. & Marckwardt, Albert. Old English Language & Literature.
Rosin, Carol, jt. auth. see Sheffield, Charles.
Rosing, Kenneth E., jt. auth. see Odell, Peter R.
Roskamm, Csapo. Disorders of Cardiac Function.
Roskill, Stephen. Admiral of the Fleet, Earl Beatty: The Last Naval Hero.
Roskin, Alexander. The Life of Maxim Gorky.
Roskin, Michael G. Countries & Concepts: An Introduction to Comparative Politics.
Roskind, Robert. The Do-It-Yourself Show Book of Home Improvements.
Roslin-Williams, Anne. The Border Terrier.
Rosman, Abraham, jt. auth. see Rubel, Paula G.
Rosman, Doreen. Evangelicals & Culture.
Rosner, Bernard & Beckerman, Jay. Inside the World of Miniatures & Dollhouses: A Comprehensive Guide to Collecting & Creating.
Rosner, Jerome. Pediatric Optometry.
Rosner, Jonathon L., tr. see Novozhilov, Yuri V.
Rosner, Stanley & Abt, Lawrence E. The Creative Expression.
Rosner, Stanley & Hobe, Laura. The Marriage Gap.
Rosoff, David. Growing up: A Bar Mitzvah Story.
Rosovsky, Henry, ed. Discord in the Pacific: Challenges to the Japanese-American Alliance.
Rosovsky, Henry, jt. ed. see Patrick, Hugh.
Rosow, Jerome, ed. Made in America: A Consumer's Guide to More Than 12000 Products Made in America, for Americans & 100 Per Cent by Americans.
Rosow, Jerome M., ed. Productivity: Prospects for Growth.
Rosowsky. Advances in Cancer Chemotherapy.
Ross & Westerfield. Corporate Finance.
Ross, Aileen. Student Unrest in India: A Comparative Approach.
Ross, Alan O. Learning Disability: The Unrealized Potential.
Ross, Alec. The Men Who Loved Miss Greto Garbo.
--Words for Work: Writing Fundamentals for Vocational-Technical Students.

Ross, Alec, jt. auth. see Kocher, Helen R.
Ross, Andrea. Chester the Little Black Earth Ant.
Ross, Ann. The Murder Cure.
--The Pilgrimage: Being the Narrative of Emma Louise Heath with Excerpts from the Private Journal of Jessie Elizabeth Heath.
Ross, B., ed. see International Conference, New Haven Staff.
Ross, B. Joyce. J. E. Spingarn & the Rise of the NAACP.
Ross, Betty. A Museum Guide to Washington D. C.
Ross, Betty, tr. see Schoeck, Helmut.
Ross, Bob, jt. auth. see Fisher, Bob.
Ross, Bob, jt. auth. see Fletcher, Mike.
Ross, Bow. Cooking Amid Chaos.
Ross, C. A., ed. Paleobiogeography.
Ross, C. T. & Johns, T. Computer Analysis of Skeletal Structures.
Ross, Charles. The Inner Sanctuary.
Ross, Clarissa. Evil of Dark Harbor.
--A Hearse for Dark Harbor.
--Terror at Dark Harbor.
Ross, Corinne M. The Mid-Atlantic Bed & Breakfast Book.
--The New England Bed & Breakfast Book.
--The Southern Bed & Breakfast Book.
Ross, D. A. Opportunities & Uses of the Ocean.
Ross, D. B. & Guder, W. G., eds. Biochemical Aspects of Renal Function: Proceedings of a Symposium Held in Honour of Professor Sir Hans Krebs FRS, at Merton College, Oxford, 16-19 September 1979.
Ross, Dana F. Louisiana!
--Missouri.
--Oregon!
Ross, David A. Introduction to Oceanography.
Ross, Donald A., ed. Reader's Guide to the Everyman's Library.
Ross, Dorothea M. & Ross, Shella A. Hyperactivity: Current Issues, Research & Theory.
Ross, E. Denison. This English Language.
Ross, Euan, ed. Paediatric Perspectives on Epilepsy: A Symposium Held at the Grand Hotel, Eastbourne, December 1984.
Ross, Euan, et al, eds. Epilepsy in Young People: Symposium Held at the Holiday Inn, Portsmouth, June 1986.
Ross, Eulalie S., ed. Lost Half-Hour: A Collection of Stories.
Ross, Frank. Dead Runner.
--The Shining Day.
--The Sixty Fifth Tape.
--Sleeping Dogs.
Ross, Frank A. Conspiracy of Angels.
Ross, Frank, Jr. The Space Shuttle: Its Story & How to Make a Flying Paper Model.
Ross, George, jt. auth. see Lange, Peter.
Ross, Harriet, compiled by. Great Stories about Animals.
Ross, Harriet K., ed. Great English Story Poems: Collections.
Ross, Heather C. The Art of Bedouin Jewelery: A Saudi Arabian Profile.
Ross, Helen S. & Mico, Paul. Theory & Practice in Health Education.
Ross, J. & O'Rourke, R. A. Understanding the Heart & Its Disease.
Ross, Jacquelene, jt. auth. see Cook, A. J.
Ross, James F. Philosophical Theology.
Ross, James F., jt. auth. see Fear, Richard A.
Ross, James O. The Heart Machine: A Personal Account of Open-Heart Surgery.
Ross, Jim. Treachery at Cimarron.
Ross, Joel E. Modern Management & Information Systems.
Ross, Jonathan. A Rattling of Old Bones.
Ross, K. A., jt. auth. see Hewitt, E.
Ross, Kenneth, jt. auth. see Practising Law Institute Staff.
Ross, Lanson. A Kid's Goal-Setting Guide: (For Parents)
Ross, Lena. Bed Airobics for Seniors & Lazy Juniors.
Ross, Leona C. Resurrexit.
Ross, Leonard Q. Education of Hyman Kaplan.
Ross, Leonard Q. see also Rosten, Leo.
Ross, Lillian. Reporting.
Ross, M. Aesthetic Impulse.
--The Development of Aesthetic Experience.
Ross, M., ed. The Arts: A Way of Knowing.
Ross, Maggie. Fire of Your Life: A Solitude Shared.
Ross, Marc H. & Williams, Robert H. Our Energy-Regaining Control.
Ross, Margaret L., jt. auth. see Chaney, Margaret S.
Ross, Marilyn, jt. auth. see Ross, Tom.
Ross, Mark. Hard of Hearing Children in Regular Schools.
Ross, Mark & Giolas, Thomas G. Auditory Management of Hearing-Impaired Children.
Ross, Marvin. Economic Opportunity & Crime.
Ross, Max. Double-Agent Fugitive.
Ross, Michael J. California: Its Government & Politics.
Ross, Monique, jt. auth. see Gody, Dale.
Ross, Murray G. The University: The Anatomy of Academe.
Ross, N. W. & Nixon, D. W., eds. Boat & Marine Equipment Theft: Summary Report of a 1979 National Workshop.
Ross, P. W. Clinical Bacteriology.
Ross, P. W. & Peutherer, J. F. Clinical Microbiology.
Ross, Patricia. Trouble in School.
Ross, Patricia F. Mexico.
Ross, Peter, ed. see Conference of the British Educational Research Association 1980.
Ross, Ralph. Symbols & Civilization: Science, Religion, Morals, Art.
Ross, Ramon R. Prune.
Ross, Richard D., jt. auth. see Conway, Richard A.
Ross, Robert. Cape of Torments: Slavery & Resistance in South Africa.
Ross, Robert S. American National Government.
Ross, Ronald G. Data Dictionaries & Data Administration: Concepts & Practices for Data Resource Management.
Ross, Sally & Johnson, Linda. Historic Texas Hotels & Country Inns I.
Ross, Sheldon. A First Course in Probability.
Ross, Shella A., jt. auth. see Ross, Dorothea M.
Ross, Shirley. First Aid for House Plants.
--The Seafood Cookbook.
--The World Almanac Guide to Natural Foods.
Ross, Sidney, et al. Anodic Oxidation.
Ross, Skip & Carlson, Carole C. Say Yes to Your Potential.
Ross, Stan. World of Drafting.
Ross, Stephen D. Literature & Philosophy: An Analysis of the Philosophical Novel.
Ross, Steven & Pronin, Monica, eds. Toxic Substances Sourcebook: The Professional's Guide to the Information Sources, Key Literature & Laws of a Critical New Field.
Ross, Steven S., ed. Toxic Substances Sourcebook: The Professional's Guide to Information Sources, Key Literature, & Laws.
Ross, Susan D. Rights of Women.
Ross, Terrence. Bitter Graces.
Ross, Tom & Ross, Marilyn. The Complete Guide to Self-Publishing: Everything You Need to Know to Write, Publish, Promote & Sell Your Own Book.
Ross, Tony. Jack the Giantkiller.
--Naughty Nicky.
Ross, W. D. Aristotle's Prior & Posterior Analytics: A Revised Text with Introduction & Commentary.
Ross, W. E. The House on Mount Vernon Street.
Ross, W. Gillies, ed. An Arctic Whaling Diary: The Journal of Captain George Comer in Hudson Bay 1903-1905.
Rossabi, Morris. China & Inner Asia: From 1368 to the Present Day.
Rossage, David. Rejoice in Me: A Pocket Guide to Daily Spritual Prayer.
Rossant, Colette. New Kosher Cooking.
Rossel, Seymour. The Holocaust.
Rossel, Seymour, ed. see Langer, Jiri.
Rossen, Don Van see Van Rossen, Don & Woodrich, Barbara.
Rosser, C. & George, A. S. The Banksias.
Rosser, Colin & Harris, C. C. The Family & Social Change: A Study of Family & Kinship in a South Wales Town.
Rosser, J. Barkley & Turquette, Atwell R. Many-Valued Logics.
Rosser, John B. Logic for Mathematicians.
Rosset, Barney, ed. Evergreen Review Reader.
--Evergreen Review Reader: Vol. 1. 1957-1961.
Rosset, Barney & Jordan, Fred, eds. Evergreen Review.
Rosset, Hannelore, ed. see Batchelor, Stephen.
Rosset, Peter, jt. auth. see Vandermeer, John.
Rosset, Peter & Vandermeer, John, eds. Nicaragua: Unfinished Revolution.
Rossi, Alice S., et al, eds. The Family.
Rossi, B., ed. Space Exploration & the Solar System.
Rossi, B. E., ed. Experimental Mechanics: Proceedings, International Congress on Experimental Mechanics - 1st.
Rossi, Ernest, jt. ed. see Erickson, Milton H.
Rossi, Ernest L. Dreams & the Growth of Personality: Expanding Awareness in Psychotherapy.
Rossi, Ethel J. Draw a Dozen with Basic Shapes.
Rossi, F. & Patriarca, P., eds. Biochemistry & Function of Phagocytes.
Rossi, Ino, et al. Anthropology Full Circle.
Rossi, Lee D. The Politics of Fantasy: C. S. Lewis & J. R. R. Tolkien. Scholes, Robert, ed.
Rossi, Lee D. & Gasser, Michael. Academic English.
Rossi, Luigi. Il Palazzo Incantato overo la Guerriera Amante. Brown, Howard M., ed.
Rossi, Nick & Choate, Robert. Music of Our Time.
Rossi, Peter H., jt. auth. see Wright, James D.
Rossi, Peter H. & Williams, Walter, eds. Evaluating Social Programs: Theory, Practice, & Politics.
Rossi, Peter H., et al, eds. Handbook of Survey Research.
Rossides, Daniel W. The American Class System: An Introduction to Social Stratification.
--The History & Nature of Sociological Theory.
Rossides, Eugene T. Foreign Unfair Competition: Practice & Procedure.
Rossier, jt. auth. see Hardy.
Rossini, F. P. Atlas of Coloscopy.
Rossini, Gioachino. Guillaume Tell. Gossett, Phillip & Rosen, Charles, eds.
--Mose in Egitto. Gossett, Phillip & Rosen, Charles, eds.
Rossiter, Bryant W. & Weissberger, A. Chemical Experimentation under Extreme Conditions.
Rossiter, Charles M., Jr. & Pearce, W. Barnett. Communicating Personality: A Theory of Interpersonal Communication & Human Relationships.
Rossiter, Clinton. Alexander Hamilton & the Constitution.
--American Presidency.
--American Quest.
--Marxism: The View from America.
--The Political Thought of the American Revolution.
--Seedtime of the Republic.
--Six Characters in Search of a Republic: Studies in the Political Thought of the American Colonies.
Rossiter, Elizabeth. Some Pleasure There to Find.
Rossiter, Frank. Charles Ives & His America.
Rossiter, John. Dark Flight.
--The Man Who Came Back.
Rossiter, Stuart. England.
--Greece.
--London.
Rossiter, V. Electromagnetism.
Rossman, Vern. Drum, Hammer & Cross.
Rossner, John. Toward Recovery of the Primordial Tradition: Ancient Insights & Modern Discoveries. Incl. Bk. 1. From Ancient Magic to Future Technology; Bk. 2. Toward a Parapsychology of Religion: from Ancient Religion to Future Science. U Pr of Amer.
Rossner, Judith. Attachments.
--Emmeline.
--Looking for Mr. Goodbar.
Rosso, Julee. The Silver Palate Gift Set.
Rost, J. L. Die Unglueckselige Atalanta.
Rost, Thomas L. & Gifford, Ernest M., eds. Mechanisms & Control of Cell Division.
Rostal, Max. Beethoven: The Sonatas for Piano & Violin.
Rosten, Leo. Infinite Riches.
--Joys of Yiddish.
--Passions & Prejudices.
--The Power of Positive Nonsense.
Rosten, Leo see also Ross, Leonard Q.
Rosten, Norman. Love in All Its Disguises.
Rostovtsev, Mikhail. History of the Ancient World. Duff, J. D., tr. from Rus.
Rostow, W. W. Eisenhower, Kennedy, & Foreign Aid.
Rostow, Walt W. Getting There from Here.
Roszkowski, Mark. Commercial Law for the CPA Candidate.
Roszkowski, Mark E. Business Law: Principles, Cases & Policy.
Rota, Gian-Carlo, ed. Studies in Analysis.
Rotberg, Robert I. Imperialism, Colonialism, & Hunger: East & Central Africa.
Rotberg, Robert I., jt. auth. see Rabb, Theodore K.
Rotberg, Robert I., ed. Namibia: Political & Economic Prospects.
Rotberg, Robert I., jt. ed. see Rabb, Theodore K.
Rotella, Alexis. After the Affair.
--On a White Bud.
--The Power of Affirmations: You Can Heal Your Life with Words & Thoughts.
Rotella, Guy L. E. E. Cummings: A Reference Guide.
Roth, A. Vacuum Sealing Techniques.
Roth, A. E. Axiomatic Models of Bargaining.
Roth, Arnold. Two for Survival.
Roth, Audrey J. The Research Paper: Process, Form, & Content.
Roth, B., jt. auth. see Bottema, O.
Roth, Cecil. Benjamin Disraeli, Earl of Beaconsfield.
--Historical Background of the Dead Sea Scrolls.
--Soncino Haggadah.
Roth, Charles E. The Plant Observer's Guidebook: A Field Botany Manual for the Amateur Naturalist.
Roth, David. Best of Friends.
--River Runaways.
Roth, David & Wilson, Frank L. The Comparative Study of Politics.
--The Comparative Study of Politics.
Roth, Hal. The Longest Race.
--Two Against Cape Horn.
Roth, Henry. Call It Sleep.
Roth, J. Paul. Computer Logic, Testing & Verification.
Roth, Jesse, jt. ed. see Rabinowitz, David.
Roth, John, jt. ed. see Medcof, John.
Roth, John K. A Consuming Fire: Encounters with Elie Wiesel & the Holocaust.
Roth, Karl, jt. auth. see Cohn, Robert M.
Roth, Lane. Film Semiotics, Metz, & Leone's Trilogy. Jowett, Garth S., ed.
Roth, Lazlo. Package Design: An Introduction to the Art of Packaging.
Roth, Lloyd J. & Stumpf, Walter, eds. Autoradiography of Diffusible Substances.
Roth, M., jt. ed. see Hansen, H. H.
Roth, Philip. Goodbye, Columbus.
--The Great American Novel.
Roth, R. The Parameters of Personality.
Roth, Richard. Your Future in Architecture.
Roth, Robert J., ed. Person & Community: A Philosophical Exploration.
Roth, Robert P. The Theater of God: Story in Christian Doctrine.
Roth, S. H., et al, eds. Rheumatic Therapeutics.
Roth, Stephanie, jt. auth. see Weidlein, Marianne.
Roth, Susan A., jt. auth. see Howard, Elliot J.
Roth, Theodore W. Is There a Fortune Waiting for You?
Roth, Walton T., jt. auth. see Insel, Paul M.
Roth, Willard E. No More the Round Mud Hut: Voices of Young Africa.
Roth, William, jt. auth. see Gliedman, John.
Roth, Wolfgang & Ruether, Rosemary R. The Liberating Bond: Covenants Biblical & Contemporary.
Roth, Wolfgang, jt. auth. see Hoyer, George W.
Rotha, Paul. Rotha on the Film. Kupelnick, Bruce S., ed.
Rothaus, et al. Earl Campbell.
--Robin Yount.
--Wayne Gretzky.
Rothaus, James. The Atlanta Falcons.
--The Buffalo Bills.
Rothaus, James R. The Chicago Bears.
--The Cleveland Browns.
--The Detroit Lions.
--The Green Bay Packers.
--The New England Patriots.
--The New Orlean Saints.
--Pittsburgh Steelers.
--Tampa Bay Buccanners.
Rothaus, Jim. Houston Oilers.
Rothbard, Murray N., ed. The Review of Austrian Economics.
Rothbart, Linda, et al. Sources of Information in Transportation: Part 5, Trucking.
Rothblat, George H. & Christofalo, Vincent J., eds. Growth, Nutrition & Metabolism of Cells in Culture.
Rothchild, Sylvia. A Special Legacy: An Oral History of Soviet Jewish Emigres in the United States.
--A Special Legacy: An Oral History of Soviet Jewish Emigres in the United States.
Rothe, M. Eisenhart, jt. auth. see Reisner, W.
Rothenberg, Albert. The Emerging Goddess: The Creative Process in Art, Science, & other Fields.
Rothenberg, Gunther. Military Border in Croatia, Seventeen Forty-Eighteen Eighty One: A Study of an Imperial Institution.
Rothenberg, Gunther E. The Army of Francis Joseph.
Rothenberg, Jerome, jt. auth. see Edel, Matthew.
Rothenberg, Marie & White, Mel. David.
--David.
Rothenberg, Michael B., jt. auth. see Spock, Benjamin.
Rothenberg, Randall. The Neoliberals: Creating the New American Politics.
Rothengatter, T. Traffic-Safety Education of Young Children.
Rothenstein, J. Moderns & Their World.
Rother, K., jt. ed. see Opferkuch, W.
Rotheroe, J. Discovering Suffolk.
Rothfeder, Jack. Home Computer Basics: An Introduction for Young People.
Rothfels, Hans. The German Opposition to Hitler: An Appraisal. Wilson, Lawrence, tr.
Rothfield, Lawrence I., ed. Structure & Function of Biological Membranes.
Rothko, compiled by. Toward a New Strategy for Development.
Rothmaler, Audrey, jt. auth. see Fuelling, Daniel.
Rothman, David. XyWrite Made Easier: Revised & Expanded to Include Version XyWrite III Plus.
Rothman, David J., jt. ed. see Rothman, Sheila M.
Rothman, Eugene, jt. ed. see Polzin, Robert M.
Rothman, Joel. Adultery Can Be Funny.
--Antique Humour.
--Booze Who: Intoxicating Humour.
--The Cannibal Cookbook.
--Politics Is a Funny Business.
--Smokers' Humour.
Rothman, Sheila M. & Rothman, David J., eds. The Origins of Day Care: Selections from the Conferences on Day Nurseries, 1893-1925.
Rothschild, Joan, ed. Women, Technology & Innovation.
Rothschild, M. A., et al, eds. Alcohol & Abnormal Protein Biosynthesis, Biochemical & Clinical.
Rothschild, Marcus A. & Waldmann, Thomas, eds. Plasma Protein Metabolism: Regulation of Synthesis, Distribution & Degradation.

Rothschild, Michael L. An Incomplete Bibliography of Works Relating to Marketing for Public Sector & Nonprofit Organizations.
Rothschild, Miriam & Clay, Theresa. Fleas, Flukes, & Cuckoos.
Rothschild, William E. Putting It All Together: A Guide to Strategic Thinking.
--Putting It All Together: A Guide to Strategic Thinking.
--Strategic Alternatives: Selection, Development & Implementation.
Rothschild, Zeev. Knowing Your Tefilen & Mezuzos: A Layman's Guide to Understanding & Appreciating Tefilin & Mezuzos.
Rothstein, A. The Enzymology of the Cell Surface. Bd. with Tension at the Cell Surface. Harvey, E. N. Springer-Verlag.
Rothstein, Arthur. The American West in the Thirties.
--The Depression Years: As Photographed by Arthur Rothstein.
Rothstein, Eric. Restoration & Eighteenth-Century Poetry 1660-1780.
Rothstein, Halina, jt. auth. see Rothstein, Robert.
Rothstein, Mark A. Occupational Safety & Health Law, Nineteen Eighty-Five Pocket Part.
Rothstein, Robert & Rothstein, Halina. Polish Scholarly Prose: A Humanities & Social Sciences Reader.
Rothstein, Robert, jt. auth. see Lamberg, Stanley L.
Rothstein, Robert, jt. auth. see Scimone, John.
Rothstein, Robert J., ed. see American College of Emergency Physicians Staff.
Rothwell, Nancy, jt. auth. see Stock, Michael.
Rotisserie League Staff. Rotisserie League Baseball. Waggoner, Glen, ed.
Rotor & Wing International Staff & Prouty, R. W. Helicopter Aerodynamics.
RotoVision. Jan Saudek-Photographs.
RotoVision Staff, ed. A. D. France Two.
--Art Directors' Index to Illustrators.
--Creative Advertising of France Three.
--Dossier Agences '87.
--Omnibook Three.
Rotsler, William. The Love Boat: Voyage of Love. Barish, Wendy, ed.
--Magnum, P. I. Number One: Maui Mystery. Barish, Wendy, ed.
--Mr. Merlin: Episode No. 2.
--Plot-Your-Own-Adventure: Distress Call. Barish, Wendy, ed.
--Staying Alive. Barish, Wendy, ed.
Rottensteiner, Franz, ed. The Slaying of the Dragon: Modern Tales of the Playful Imagination.
Rottensteiner, Franz, ed. see Lem, Stanislaw.
Rotter, Jerome I., et al, eds. The Genetics & Heterogeneity of Common Gastrointestinal Disorders.
Rotter, Joseph C. & Robinson, Edward H. Parent Teacher Conferencing.
Rottmamn, Meg, jt. auth. see Liu, Aimee.
Rotunda, Ronald, jt. auth. see Nowak, John.
Rotunda, Ronald D. Modern Constitutional Law, Cases & Notes: 1986 Supplement.
--Professional Responsibility.
Rotwein, Eugene, ed. David Hume: Writings on Economics.
Rouart, Denis & Wildenstein, Daniel. Manet's Complete Paintings.
Roucek, J. S. The Slow Learner.
Roucek, Joseph. Difficult Child.
Roucek, Joseph S. Challenge of Science Education.
--Contemporary Sociology.
--Juvenile Delinquency Today.
--Slavonic Encyclopedia.
--Social Control.
--Twentieth Century Political Thought.
Roucek, Joseph S., ed. Sociology of Crime.
Rouder, Susan. American Politics: Playing the Game.
Roueche, Berton. Black Weather.
--Feral.
Roueche, Helda. Business Mathematics: A Collegiate Approach.
Rouge Et Noir Staff. Gambling World.
Rougemont, Denis de see De Rougemont, Denis.
Rough, Worth S. Synopsis: Past-Present-Future.
Rouif, Denis Fauvel, et al. Anarchism.
Rouiller, C., ed. The Liver: Morphology, Biochemistry, Physiology.
Roulac, Stephen E., jt. auth. see Maisel, Sherman J.
Round Table Conference, Rome, Oct. 30-31, 1974. Platelet Aggregation in the Pathogenesis of Cerebrovascular Disorders. Agnoli, A. & Fazio, C., eds.
Rounds, Glen. The Day the Circus Came to Lone Tree.
--Mr. Yowder & the Windwagon.
--Whitey & the Colt-Killers.
--Whitey Takes a Trip.
--Whitey's First Roundup.
--Whitey's New Saddle.
Rounds, Susan. Teaching the Young Child: A Handbook of Open Classroom Practice.
Rouner, Arthur A., Jr. Receiving the Spirit at Old First Church.
--Struggling with Sex: Serious Call to Marriage-Centered Sexual Life.
Rountree, Owen. Cord, Hunt the Man Down.
--Cord, the Nevada War.
--Gunsmoke River.
Rouquerol, J. & Sabbah, R., eds. Chemical Thermodynamics - 4: Proceedings.
Rourke, C. P. & Sanderson, B. J. Introduction to Piecewise-Linear Topology.
Rourke, Constance. American Humor: A Study of the National Character.
--Davy Crockett.
Rourke, Francis E. & Brooks, Glenn E. The Managerial Revolution in Higher Education.
Rourke, John T. Taking Sides: Clashing Views on Controversial Issues in World Politics.
Rourke, Margaret V. & Gentry, Christine A. So You Want a Successful HERO Program. Simpson, Elizabeth, ed.
Rouse, Beatrice A., ed. Self-Report Methods of Estimating Drug Use: Meeting Current Challenges of Validity.
Rouse, Beatrice A., jt. ed. see Ewing, John A.
Rouse, John E., Jr., ed. Urban Housing--Public & Private: A Guide to Information Sources.
Rouse, Robert S. & Smith, Robert O. Energy: Resource, Slave, Pollutant; a Physical Science Text.
Rouse, Rose. The Thompson Twins: The Official Biography.
Rouse, Ruth & Neill, Stephen C., eds. History of the Ecumenical Movement: 1517 to 1948.
Roush, Ann. Tacoma: The City of Destiny, 1884-1984.
Roush, Barbara. Labor of Love.
Roush, Marvin L., jt. auth. see Marion, Jerry B.
Rousmaniere, John. The Sailing Lifestyle: A Guide to Sailing & Cruising for Pleasure.
Rousmaniere, John, jt. auth. see Time-Life Books Editors.
Rousmaniere, Peter F., et al, eds. Local Government Auditing: A Manual for Public Officials. Olenick, Arnold & Pirnicory, Vincent.
Rousseas, Stephen. The Political Economy of Reaganomics: A Critique.
Rousseau, G. S. Goldsmith: The Critical Heritage.
Rousseau, G. S., jt. auth. see Nicolson, Marjorie.
Rousseau, Jean-Jacques. Dictionnaire De Musique.
--On the Social Contract & Discourse on the Origin of Inequality & Discourse on Political Economy & Rousseau's Notes to Discourse on the Origin of Inequality. Cress, Donald A., tr. from Fr.
--Rousseau's Political Writings. Ritter, Alan, ed. Bondanella, Julia, tr.
Rousseau, Patricia A. Window Goes On.
Rousseau, Richard W., ed. Interreligious Dialogue: Facing the Next Frontier.
Roussel, Raymond. How I Wrote Certain of My Books. Winkfield, Trevor & Koch, Kenneth, trs. from Fr.
Roussev, M., jt. auth. see Athanassova, T.
Roussy De Sales, Raoul De see Hitler, Adolph.
Routh, Donald K., jt. ed. see Frazier, James R.
Routh, Francis. Stravinsky.
Routh, Joseph I. Introduction to Biochemistry.
Routh, Joseph I., et al. Introduction to Biochemistry.
Routisie, Albert de. Irene.
Routley, Eric. Hymns & Human Life.
Routley, Erik. Conversion.
Routtenberg, Aryeh, ed. Biology of Reinforcement: Facet of Brain Stimulation Reward.
Rouverol, Jean. Writing for the Soaps.
Roux, Albert & Roux, Michel. New Classic Cuisine.
Roux, J. H. Le see Coetzer, P. W. & Le Roux, J. H.
Roux, J. P. Cape Peninsula Ferns.
Roux, Michel, jt. auth. see Roux, Albert.
Roux, William C. What's Cooking Down in Maine.
Roveda, C., ed. see IFAC Symposium Staff.
Rovelstad, James M., jt. auth. see Goodwin, John R.
Rovenger, Judith, ed. & intro. by. Libraries Serving Youth: Directions for Service in the 1990's.
Rovere. Senator Joe McCarthy.
Rovin, Jeff. Stallone!
Rovinsky, Robert T., jt. ed. see Weinstock, John M.
Rovit, Earl H. The Player King.
Row, T. S. Geometric Exercises in Paper Folding. Berman, W. W. & Smith, D. E., eds.
Rowan, John. The Reality Game: A Guide to Humanistic Counselling & Therapy.
Rowan, Richard L., jt. ed. see Northrup, Herbert R.
Rowan, Richard L., et al. Multinational Union Organizations in the Manufacturing Industries.
Rowan, Roy. The Four Days of Mayaguez.
--The Intuitive Manager.
Rowan-Robinson, Michael, ed. Vistas in Astronomy, Supplement: Far Infrared Astronomy.
Rowat, R. Trained Manpower for Agricultural & Rural Development.
Rowbotham, Fred. The Severn Bore.
Rowe. Accounting Reports Today U. K.
Rowe, Anne E. The Enchanted Country: Northern Writers in the South, 1865-1910.
Rowe, Brenda J. The Minority Administrator: Blacks & Women in Public Sector Management.
Rowe, D. J. Lead Manufacturing in Britain: A History.
Rowe, David N. Informal "Diplomatic Relations" The Case of Japan & the Republic of China, 1972-1974.
Rowe, Francis W., jt. auth. see Clark, Ailsa M.
Rowe, Frederick A. I Launch at Paradise: A Consideration of John Donne, Poet & Preacher.
Rowe, G. S. Thomas McKean: The Shaping of an American Republicanism.
Rowe, G. W. Principles of Industrial Metalworking Processes.
Rowe, Jack. Inyo-Sierra Passage.
Rowe, Jane. Yours by Choice: A Guide for Adoptive Parents.
Rowe, John S., jt. auth. see Morrison, Samuel L.
Rowe, Lois. On Call.
Rowe, Marguerite M. A Fork in the Road.
Rowe, Mary B. Teaching Science As Continuous Inquiry: A Basic 2-E.
Rowe, Nicholas. The Fair Penitent. Goldstein, Malcolm, ed.
Rowe, Patricia L. Shorthand Fashion Sketching.
Rowe, Peter, jt. auth. see Aiken, Miles.
Rowe, Peter G., ed. see Bosch, Vanden, et al.
Rowe, Richard D., et al. The Neonate with Congenital Heart Disease.
Rowe, W. D., jt. ed. see Goodman, G. T.
Rowe, William. Clapp's Rock.
Rowe, William, ed. Jose M. Arguedas: Los Rios profundos.
Rowe, William L. & Wainwright, William J., eds. Philosophy of Religion: Selected Readings.
Rowell, Galen. High & Wild: A Mountaineer's World.
--In the Throne Room of the Mountain Gods.
Rowell, R. M. & Youngs, R. Modified Cellulosics.
Rowen, Betty. The Children We See: An Observational Approach to Child Study.
--Learning Through Movement: Activities for the Preschool & Elementary Grades.
Rowen, Herbert H., ed. From Absolutism to Revolution: 1648-1848.
Rowen, Herbert H., jt. auth. see Lyon, Bruce.
Rowes, Barbara, jt. auth. see Klinger, Georgette.
Rowland, Beryl. Animals with Human Faces: A Guide to Animal Symbolism.
Rowland, Christopher. The Open Heaven: The Study of Apocalyptic in Judaism & Early Christianity.
Rowland, Don. British Railway Wagons.
Rowland, Eron. Varina Howell: Wife of Jefferson Davis.
Rowland, John. Ernest Rutherford: Atom Pioneer.
Rowland, Kurt. A History of the Modern Movement: Art, Architecture, Design.
Rowland, Lewis P., ed. Merritt's Textbook of Neurology.
Rowland, Mark & Rochlin, Margy. Prince.
Rowland, T. J., jt. ed. see Machlin, E. S.
Rowlands, Gerald. How to Know the Fullness of the Spirit.
Rowlands, John. Spotlight Heroes: Two Decades of Rock & Roll Superstars As Seen Through the Camera of John Rowlands.
Rowlands, John J. Cache Lake Country: Life in the North Woods.
Rowledge, J. W. GWR Locomotive Allocations, 1922-67.
Rowles, Catharine B. Tomahawks to Hatpins.
Rowlett, Martha G. In Spirit & in Truth: A Guide to Praying.
Rowley, Charles K. Readings in Industrial Economics.
Rowley, J. C. & Trivedi, P. K. Econometrics of Investment.
Rowley, Trevor. The High Middle Ages.
--The Norman Heritage Ten Sixty-Six to Twelve Hundred.
Rowlinson, J. S. The Perfect Gas.
Rowney, J. M., et al, eds. Thick Plate Working.
Rowntree, Derek. Do You Really Need a Home Computer? The Book to Read Before You Byte.
Rowse, A. L. Milton the Puritan: Portrait of a Mind.
--The Poet Auden: A Personal Memoir. Strachan, Bill, ed.
Rowse, Alfred L. Appeasement: A Study in Political Decline, 1933-34.
Rowson, Susanna. Charlotte's Daughter: Or the Three Orphans.
--Charlotte's Temple, a Tale of Truth.
Roxas, Sixto K. Money & Capital Markets in an Asian Setting.
Roxe, Linda A. Personnel Management for the Smaller Company: A Hands-on Manual.
Roy, Ashim K. & Gidwani, N. W. Indus Valley Civilization: A Bibliographic Essay.
Roy, Beth. Bullock Carts & Motor Bikes: Ancient India on a New Road.
Roy, C. C., jt. ed. see Fisher, M. M.
Roy, Cal. The Legend & the Storm.
Roy, Cristina. Sunshine Country.
Roy, Dilip K. Tunnelling & Negative Resistance Phenomena in P-N Junctions.
Roy, Dilip K., jt. auth. see Devi, Indira.
Roy, Ewell P. Contract Farming & Economic Integration.
Roy, Ewell P., et al. Economics: Applications to Agriculture & Agribusiness.
Roy, Jules. The War in Algeria. Howard, Richard, ed.
Roy, M., ed. see De Pisan, Christine.
Roy, Maria, ed. Battered Women: A Psychosociological Study of Domestic Violence.
Roy, Mary L. Sources of Information in Transportation: Part 6, Inland Water Transportation.
Roy, R., jt. auth. see Henisch, H. K.
Roy, R., jt. auth. see Muller, O.
Roy, Ron. Breakfast with My Father.
Roy, Rustrum. Experimenting with Truth: The Fusion of Religion with Technology Needed for Humanity's Survival.
Roy, S. N., et al. Analysis & Design of Certain Quantitative Multiresponse Experiments.
Roy, Walter. The New Examinations System.
--Teaching under Attack.
Royal Academy of Arts Staff. The Exhibition of the Royal Academy of Arts.
Royal Aircraft Establishment Staff. Table of Earth Satellites, Nineteen Fifty-Seven to Nineteen Eighty.
Royal Barry Wills Associates. More Houses for Good Living.
Royal Borough staff. Urban Conservation & Historic Buildings.
Royal Botanic Gardens Library Staff, Kew, England. Author & Classified Catalogues of the Royal Botanic Gardens Library.
Royal, Brian J. Enemies.
Royal College of Psychiatrists Staff. Alcohol: Our Favorite Drug.
Royal Entomological Society of London Staff. Catalog of the Library of the Royal Entomological Society of London.
Royal Historical Society Staff, ed. The Papers of George Wyatt.
--Records of the Trial of Walter Langeton, 1307-12.
Royal Institute of British Architects Staff, ed. Sixty Six Portland Place: The London Headquarters of the Royal Institute of British Architects.
Royal Institute of International Affairs Staff. Britain in Western Europe: WEU & the Atlantic Alliance.
--British Foreign Policy: Some Relevant Documents, January, 1950 - April, 1955.
Royal Institute of International Affairs, London Staff, ed. Index to Periodical Articles, 1950-1964.
Royal Institute of International Affairs Staff. International Gold Problem.
Royal Ministry of Foreign Affairs Staff, ed. see Aftenposten.
Royal Society of London Staff. Risk Assessment: A Study Group Report.
Royal Society Staff. Selected Lectures.
Royal Swedish Academy of Sciences Staff. Chemistry & Geochemistry of Solutions at High Temperatures & Pressures: Proceedings of the Royal Swedish Academy of Sciences, Nobel Symposium, Bjorkborns Herrgard, Karlskoga, Sweden, Sept., 1979. Rickard, David & Wickman, Frans E., eds.
Royal United Services Institute for Defense Studies Staff, ed. Rusi & Brassey's Defence Yearbook, 1977-78.
Royal United Services Institute for Defence Studies (RUSI), London Staff. Rusi & Brassey's Defence Yearbook 1985.
Royal Yatching Association Staff. Navigation: An RYA Manual.
Royall, Vanessa. Flames of Desire.
Royce, Anya P. The Anthropology of Dance.
Royce, Helane. Sportshape: Body Conditioning for Women & Men-from the Daily Jogger to the Weekend Athlete.
Royce, Joseph R., ed. Multivariate Analysis & Psychological Theory.
Royce, Josiah. Conception of Immortality.
--Principles of Logic.
Royce, Kenneth. The Concrete Boot.
--The Masterpiece Affair.
--The Miniatures Frame.
--The XYY Man.
Royce, Kenneth, ed. The Third Arm.
Royce, Michael. Studies for Student Pilots.
Royce, Patrick M. Trailerboating Illustrated.
Royce, William F. Introduction to Fishery Sciences.
Royds, T. S., tr. see Virgil.

Royer, Garfield P., jt. ed. see Weetall, Howard H.
Roysdon, Christine M. & Khatri, Linda A. American Engineers of the Nineteenth Century: A Biographical Index.
Rozee, K. R., jt. ed. see Stuttard, Colins.
Rozel, Nicholas J. & Adams, Edgar H. Cocaine Use in America: Epidemiological & Clinical Perspectives.
Rozenberg, G. & Salomaa, A., eds. L Systems.
Rozenberg, G., jt. ed. see Pagnoni, A.
Rozendal, Nancy & Fallon, Patricia. Psychiatric Nursing: PreTest Self-Assessment & Review.
Rozental, D. E. Modern Russian Usage. James, C. V., ed.
Rozentals, Janis. Promise of Eternal Life: Biblical Witness to Christian Hope.
Rozman, Gilbert. Urban Networks in Ch'ing China & Tokugawa Japan.
Rozsa, K. S., ed. Neurotransmitters in Invertebrates: Proceedings of a Satellite Symposium of the 28th International Congress of Physiological Sciences, Veszprem, Hungary, 1980.
Rozsa, Miklos. A Double Life: The Autobiography of Miklos Rozsa.
Rozvany, G. I. Optimal Design of Flexural Systems.
Rozzelle, Robert W. & McCoy, Vivian, eds. Life-Career Manual for Leaders.
--Life-Career Manual for Participants.
Rozzoli, R., ed. see Stringer, T.
Ruane, Pat, jt. auth. see Hyman, Jane.
Ruark, Robert. Old Man & the Boy.
Ruas, Charles. Conversations with American Writers.
Rubbra, Benedict. Draw Portraits.
--Painting Children.
Rubel, Evelyn, jt. auth. see Stiggins, Richard J.
Rubel, M., jt. auth. see Hession, W.
Rubel, Nicole. Bruno Brontosaurus.
--Bruno le Brontosaure.
--Le Noel de Sam et Violet.
--Sam & Violet Are Twins.
--Sam & Violet Go Camping.
--Sam & Violet's Bedtime Mystery.
--Sam & Violet's Birthday Book.
--Sam & Violet's Christmas Story.
--Sam Et Violet Sont Jumeaux.
Rubel, Paula G. & Rosman, Abraham. Your Own Pigs You May Not Eat.
Ruben, Ann G. Our Teachers Are Crying: A Positive Approach to Solving Classroom Problems.
Ruben, Brent D., ed. Communication Yearbook.
Ruben, Brent D., jt. ed. see Budd, Richard W.
Ruben, David. Marxism & Materialism.
Ruben, Harvey L. Supermarriage: Overcoming the Predictable Crises of Married Life.
Ruben, Marilyn, jt. auth. see Hagelthorn, Joyce.
Ruben, Samuel. The Founders of Electrochemistry.
Rubens. Rubens: The Antwerp Altarpieces. Martin, John R., ed.
Rubens, Bernice. Birds of Passage. Silberman, J., ed.
--Mate in Three.
--Set on Edge.
Rubenstein. Great Tradition in English Literature.
Rubenstein, et al, eds. Molecular Genetic Modification of Eucaryotes.
Rubenstein, Bob. Best Restaurants of the Pacific Northwest: Pacific Northwest.
Rubenstein, Bonnie, jt. auth. see Greer, Mary.
Rubenstein, D. & Wayne, D. Lecture Notes on Clinical Medicine.
Rubenstein, E. A., et al, eds. New Directions in Sex Research.
Rubenstein, Harold F., tr. see Jaques-Dalcroze, Emile.
Rubenstein, Irwin, et al, eds. The Plant Seed: Development, Preservation & Germination.
Rubenstein, Ken see Hoffman, William M.
Rubenstein, Mark, jt. auth. see Cirillo, Dennis P.
Rubenstein, Richard. The Cunning of History: The Holocaust & the American Future.
Ruberti, A., jt. auth. see Mohler, R. R.
Ruberti, A., ed. Modelling & Identification of Distributed Parameter Systems: IFIP Working Conference, Rome Italy, June 21-24,1976.
--Realization Theory.
Ruberti, A., ed. see Conference on Optimization Techniques, 5th.
Rubiao, Murilo. The Ex-Magician & Other Stories. Colchie, Thomas, tr.
Rubicon Consulting Staff. AIDS.
--Computers & Executives.
--Electronic Warfare & the U. S. S. R.
--Electronic Warfare: 1985.
--Management & Computers: 1985.
Rubin. Biomaterials in Reconstructive Surgery.
--Travel Library.
Rubin, Al, ed. Prentice-Hall Federal Tax Course, 1987, Student Edition.
Rubin, Arnold P. Evil That Men Do: The Story of the Nazis.
Rubin, Audrey S., ed. Gregg Typing for Colleges: Complete Course.
Rubin, Augusta. J. S. Bach: The Modern Composer.
Rubin, Barry, tr. see Brodsky, Joseph.
Rubin, Bernard, ed. Small Voices & Great Trumpets: Minorities & the Media.
Rubin, Berthold. Theoderich Und Iustinian.
Rubin, Caroline, ed. see Bishop, Ann.
Rubin, Caroline, ed. see Fleishman, Seymour.
Rubin, Caroline, ed. see Schlein, Miriam.
Rubin, Charles. AppleWorks: Boosting Your Business with Integrated Software.
--Command Performance: AppleWorks.
Rubin, Diane. Caring: A Daughter's Story.
Rubin, Dorothy. Diagnosis & Correction in Reading Instruction.
--A Practical Approach to Teaching Reading.
Rubin, Ira L., jt. auth. see Frieden, Julian.
Rubin, Irene S. Shrinking the Federal Government.
Rubin, James H. & Rosenberg, Pierre. Eighteenth-Century French Life-Drawing.
Rubin, Jonathan. The Barking Deer.
Rubin, Joseph J. The Historic Whitman.
Rubin, Laurie. Food First Curriculum Sampler.
Rubin, Leona R. Your Nineteen Eighty-Seven to Eighty-Eight Guide to Social Security Benefits.
Rubin, Louis D., Jr. The Even-Tempered Angler.
--Surfaces of a Diamond, Novel.
Rubin, Louis D., Jr. & Harmon, William. Uneeda Review.
Rubin, Louis D., Jr. & Holman, C. Hugh, eds. Southern Literary Study: Problems & Possibilities.
Rubin, Michael, ed. Defending the Galaxy: The Complete Handbook of VideoGaming.
Rubin, Phillip & Casarett, George W. Clinical Radiation Pathology.
Rubin, Richard L. Press, Party, & Presidency.
Rubin, Rick, jt. auth. see Byerly, Greg.
Rubin, S. G., ed. see Computers in Aerodynamics Symposium Staff.
Rubin, Seymour J. & Graham, Thomas R., eds. Environment & Trade: The Relation of International Trade & Environmental Policy.
Rubin, Steven J. Combat Films: American Realism.
Rubin, Susan, jt. auth. see Ilyin, Donna.
Rubin, Theodore I. Compassion & Self-Hate.
--Dr. Rubin, Please Make Me Happy.
Rubin, William. Anthony Caro.
Rubincam. Genealogical Research, Vol. 1: Methods & Sources.
Rubinfeld, Daniel, ed. Essays on the Law & Economics of Local Governments.
Rubinow, S. I. Introduction to Mathematical Biology.
Rubinsky, Elizabeth W., jt. auth. see Clarke, Stevens H.
Robinson & Alles. Health Education: Foundations for the Future.
Rubinstein, Alvin Z. Soviet Foreign Policy since World War II: Imperial & Global.
Rubinstein, Beryl. Outline of Piano Pedagogy.
Rubinstein, Charlotte S. American Women Artists: From Early Indian Times to the Present.
--American Women Artists from Early Indian Times to the Present.
Rubinstein, Hilary. Europe's Wonderful Little Hotels & Inns.
Rubinstein, Hilary, ed. Europe's Wonderful Little Hotels & Inns: 1985.
Rubinstein, Joseph. The Study of Psychology.
Rubinstein, Joseph & Slife, Brent D. Taking Sides: Clashing Views on Controversial Psychological Issues.
Rubinstein, Mark & Cirillo, Dennis P. New Choices: The Latest Options in Treating Breast Cancer.
Rubinstein, W. D. The Left, the Right & the Jews.
--Wealth & Inequality in Britain.
Rubio, Antonio, jt. auth. see Jackson, Eugene.
Rubio, J. E. Theory of Linear Systems.
Rubio, J. M., ed. see International Symposium on Fosfomycin Staff.
Rubira, Jose C. Encyclopedia of French Period Furniture Designs.
--Encyclopedia of Spanish Period Furniture Designs.
Rubissow, Helen. Art of Asia.
--Art of Russia.
Rubsamen, Walter A., ed. Court Intrigue & Scandal, Two: With the Fox Uncased, the Court Legacy, the Court Medley, the Fortunate Prince, the Wedding.
Rubsamen, Walter H., ed. American Ballad Operas.
--Classical Subjects 2: Pastoral & Comedy.
--Country Operas, One: Romantic Intrigue & Deception with Southwark Fair, the Village Opera, the Chamber Maid, the Gentleman Gardiner, the Country Coquet, an Opera Called Westmeon Village.
--Country Operas, Three: Sentimental & Moral Comedies with Sylvia, the Jovial Crew, Lucinda, the Reapers.
--Country Operas, Two: Farcial Humor & Stratagem With Country Wedding, the Wedding (Hawker), Flora, a Sequel to Flora, the Livery Rake, the Whim, the Deceit, the Country-Wedding.
--Court Intrigue & Scandal, One: With Calista, Vanelia, the Humours of the Court, the Intriguing Courtiers.
--Farce: Amorous Intrigue & Deception 1.
--Farce: Amorous Intrigue & Deception 2.
--Farce, Broad or Satirical.
--Farce: Magical Transformation & Necromancy.
--Harlots, Rakes, & Bawds.
--Historical & Patriotic Subjects.
--The Medical & Legal Professions.
--Political Operas 1: Satire & Allegory.
--Political Operas 2: Attack upon Excise.
--Satire, Burlesque, Protest & Ridicule 1.
--Satire, Burlesque, Protest, & Ridicule 2.
--Scottish Ballad Operas, One: Pastoral Comedies.
--Scottish Ballad Operas, Three: Farce & Satire.
--Scottish Ballad Operas, Two: History & Politics.
--Topical & Nautical Operas.
--York Ballad Operas & Yorkshiremen.
Ruby, Doris & Ruby, Grant. Bulletin Boards for the Middle Grades.
Ruby, Grant, jt. auth. see Ruby, Doris.
Ruby, Michael G., jt. auth. see Halvorsen, Robert.
Ruccio, David, jt. ed. see Kim, Kwan.
Ruch, Floyd L., jt. auth. see Zimbardo, Philip G.
Ruch, John C. Psychology: The Personal Science.
Ruch, Theodore C. & Patton, Harry D., eds. Physiology & Biophysics. Incl. Vol. 1. The Brain & Neural Function; Vol. 2. Circulation, Respiration & Fluid Balance; Vol. 3. Digestion, Metabolism, Endocrine Function & Reproduction; Vol. 4. Excitable Tissues & Reflex Control of Muscle. Saunders.
Ruchlis, Hy. Bathtub Physics.
--Science Projects Ser. Mirrors.
Ruchlis, Hy, jt. auth. see Brandwein, Paul F.
Ruck, George T., et al. Radar Cross Section Handbook.
Ruck, H. C., ed. Deciduous Fruit Tree Cultivars for Tropical & Sub-Tropical Regions.
Ruckebusch, et al. Veterinary Pharmacology & Toxicology.
Ruckebusch, Y. & Thivend, P. Digestive Physiology & Metabolism in Ruminants.
Rucker, Allen, jt. auth. see Mull, Martin.
Rucker, John. Melancholy Bay: An Odyssey.
Rucker, Marion E., jt. ed. see Rucker, William B.
Rucker, Rudy. The Fourth Dimension: Toward a Geometry of Higher Reality.
--Mind Tools: The Five Levels of Mathematical Reality.
Rucker, William B. & Rucker, Marion E., eds. Drugs, Society & Behavior 1988-89.
Ruckman, Ivy. In a Class By Herself.
--Melba the Brain.
Ruck-Pauquet, Gina. Oh That Kaola.
Ruckstuhl, William J., et al. Context of Public Policy.
Ruda, Jeffrey. Filipo Lippi Studies: Naturalism Style Andiconography in Early Renaissance Art.
Ruda, M. C., ed. International Conference on Nonimaging Concentrators.
Rudd. A Treatise on Angel Magic, Being a Complete Transcription of Ms. Harley 6482 in the British Library. Mclean, Adam, ed.
Rudd, Andrew, jt. auth. see Jarrow, Robert.
Rudd, Donnie. The Everything Book on Condominiums.
Rudd, Robert L. Environmental Toxicology: A Guide to Information Sources.
Rudd, Steele. The Steele Rudd Selection.
Rudd, William see O'Neal, William B.
Rudd, William J., jt. auth. see Merkel, Jayne.
Ruddel, JoAnna, jt. auth. see Donaghey, Robert.
Ruddick, William, ed. John Gibson Lockhart: Petter's Letters to His Kinfolk.
Ruddle, Kenneth. The Yukpa Cultivation System: A Study of Shifting Cultivation in Columbia & Venezuela.
Rudduck, Jean. Learning Through Small Group Discussion.
Rude, Brian D. Tactics & Strategies of Classroom Discipline.
Rudegeair, Jean, illus. The Puppy's New Adventures: A B C.
--The Puppy's New Adventures: The Puppy Who Wanted a Boy.
Rudelius, William. Introduction to Contemporary Business.
Rudelius, William, et al. An Introduction to Contemporary Business.
Ruder, Kenneth F. Developmental Language Intervention: Psycholinguistic Application. Smith, Michael D., ed.
Ruderman, Harry D., ed. NYSML-ARML Contests 1973-1985.
Ruderman, Jack. Ninety Plus & Swinging: One Man's Love Affair with Life.
Rudhyar, Dane. Astrology & the Modern Psyche: An Astrologer Looks at Depth Psychology.
--The Magic of Tone & the Art of Music.
--Modern Man's Conflicts.
--The Practice of Astrology.
Rudhyar, Leyla Rael. The Lunation Process.
Rudiak, Il'ia, ed. Moisei Nappelbaum Our Age: Photographs.
Rudin, A. James. Israel for Christians.
Rudin, Donald O., et al. The Omega-Three Phenomenon.
Rudin, Harry R. Armistice 1918.
Rudin, Walter. Real & Complex Analysis.
Rudinger, Joel. Firelands Art Review 1977.
--The Human Condition.
Rudinger, Joel, ed. Firelands Art Review 1978.
--Firelands Review 1979.
Rudkin, A. M., ed. Electronic Test Equipment: Operation & Applications.
Rudkin, David. Hippolytus.
Rudman, Jack. Five Days to a High School Diploma.
--Head Accountant-Audit Clerk.
--Home Study Course.
--How to Get a Summer Job.
--Motor Vehicle Program Manager I.
--Motor Vehicle Program Manager II.
--Numerical & Aphabetical Progressions & Abstract Reasoning.
--Promotion Course.
--Senior Examiner-Social Services.
--Senior Personnel Examiner.
--Senior Principal Supervising Cashier-TA.
--Six Hundred School.
--Supervisor 2 (Child Welfare)
Rudman, Jeffrey B., jt. auth. see Garahan, James C.
Rudman, Stanley, tr. see Franke, Wolfgang.
Rudnick, Lois P. Mabel Dodge Luhan: New Woman, New Worlds.
Rudnick, Milton L. Christian Ethics for Today: An Evangelical Approach.
Rudnik, Raphael. Frank Two Hundred Seven Poems.
Rudnik, Ray. Monarch Notes on a Survey of Pre-Twentieth Century American Poets.
Rudofsky, Bernard. The Prodigious Builders.
--The Prodigious Builders.
Rudolf, Max. Grammar of Conducting.
Rudolph, James D., ed. Argentina: A Country Study.
Rudolph, L. C. People of the Church.
--Story of the Church.
Rudolph, Mary B. Church Teaching Children Grades One Through Six.
--Living in Covenant with God.
Rudolph, Richard C., ed. Chinese Archaeological Abstracts.
Rudolph, Valerie C. The Plays of Eliza Haywood.
Rudolph, Valerie C., ed. see Johnson, Samuel.
Rudorf, E. Hugh, jt. auth. see Hodges, R. E.
Rudorff, D. W. Modern Marine Engineering.
Rudorff, Raymond. The Dracula Archives.
--House of the Brandersons.
Rudovsky, David, et al. The Rights of Prisoners.
Rudowski, Peter. The Gospel in Madison Avenue.
Rudoy, Dean W. Armed & Alone: The American Security Dilemma.
Rudrud, Eric H., et al. Proactive Vocational Habilitation.
Rudrum, Alan & Dixon, Peter, eds. Selected Poems of Samuel Johnson & Oliver Goldsmith.
Rudwick, Elliot. Race Riot at East St. Louis, July 2, 1917.
Rudwick, Elliott M., jt. ed. see Meier, August.
Rudy, Peter, et al. Russian: A Complete Elementary Course.
Rue, Leslie W. & Byars, Lloyd L. Management: Theory & Application.
Rue, Nancy N., jt. auth. see Wayne, David J.
Ruediger, Horst. Kleines Literarisches Lexikon.
--Kleines Literarisches Lexikon: Autoren 1, Von Den Anfaengen Bis Zum 19. Jahrhundert.
--Kleines Literarisches Lexikon: Sachbegriffe.
Rueger, Christoph. Musical Instruments & Their Decoration.
Ruelas, Miguel, ed. see Altamirano, Ignacio M.
Ruesch, Jurgen. Disturbed Communication.
--Knowledge in Action.
--Therapeutic Communication.
Ruesch, Jurgen & Bateson, Gregory. Communication: The Social Matrix of Psychiatry.
Ruesink, Albert & Slovin, Malcolm. Biological Science for Elementary Teachers: Laboratory Manual.
Ruether, Rosemary R. Religion & Sexism.
Ruether, Rosemary R., jt. auth. see Roth, Wolfgang.
Ruff, Howard. How to Prosper During the Coming Bad Years.
--Making Money.
--Making Money: Winning the Battle for Middle-Class Financial Success.
Ruff, Julius R. Crime, Justice & Public Order in Old Regime France: The Senechaussee of Libourne, 1696-1789.
Ruff, Richard & Shylo, Bruce. Vocational Education: A Look into the Future.
Ruffin, Roy & Gregory, Paul. Principles of Economics.

Authors

--Principles of Macroeconomics.
--Principles of Microeconomics.
Ruffner, James, jt. ed. see Bair, Frank E.
Ruffo-Fiore, Silvia. Niccolo Machiavelli.
Rufinius, Tyrannius. Opera Pars 1. Orationum Gregorii Nazianzeni Novem Interpretation. Engelbrecht, A., ed.
Rugg, Donald D. & Hale, Norman B. The Dow Jones-Irwin Guide to Mutual Funds.
Rugg, Tom. Thirty Two Basic Programs for the IBM-PC Jr.
Rugg, Tom & Feldman, Phil. Turbo Pascal Program Library.
--Turbo Pascal Tips, Tricks and Traps.
Ruggeberg, Rand. Songwriter's Market, 1985.
--Summer Employment Directory of the U. S. 1985.
Ruggeberg, Rand, ed. Songwriter's Market '86.
--Summer Employment Directory of the U. S., 1986.
Ruggiero, G., et al. Radiological Exploration of the Ventricles & Subarachnoid Space.
Rugh, Thomas F. & Silva, Erin R., eds. History As a Tool in Critical Interpretation: A Symposium.
Rugh, William A. The Arab Press: News Media & Political Process in the Arab World.
Ruhe, Benjamin & Darnell, Eric. Boomerang: How to Throw, Catch, & Make It.
Ruhe, Robert. Geomorphology: Geomorphic Processor & Surficial Geology.
Ruhl, Werner, ed. Field Theoretical Methods in Particle Physics.
Rui An, et al, trs. see Wang Meng.
Ruitenbeek, Hendrik. Psychotherapy: What It's All about.
Ruitenbeek, Hendrik M. New Group Therapies.
Ruitenbeek, Luisa G., et al. Spanish-English, English-Spanish Dictionary of Banking Accounting & Related Fields.
Ruiz, Juan. Libro de Buen Amor.
Ruiz, Stacey, jt. ed. see Anderson, Kenneth.
Ruiz, Stacey L., jt. ed. see Anderson, Kenneth R.
Ruiz Torres, F. Spanish-English & English-Spanish Medical Dictionary.
Ruiz Torres, Francisco. Diccionario Aleman-Espanol, Espanol-Aleman de Medicina.
Rukeyser, Louis. What's Ahead for the Economy.
--What's Ahead for the Economy: The Challenge & the Chance.
Rukeyser, Muriel. Bubbles.
--The Collected Poems of Muriel Rukeyser.
--Gates.
Rule, Ann. Beautiful Seattle.
--Possession: A Novel.
--The Stranger Beside Me.
Rule, Jane. Contract with the World.
Rule, John, ed. British Trade Unionism, 1750-1850: The Formative Years.
Rule, Paul. Mao Zedong.
Rule, Warren R. Lifestyle Counseling for Adjustment to Disability.
Rule, Wilfred P. FORTRAN IV Programming.
Ruley, M. J. Practical Metal Projects.
Rulfo, Juan. Pedro Paramo: A Novel of Mexico. Kemp, Lysander, tr. from Span.
Rullo, Thomas A. Advances in Data Communications Management.
Rullo, Thomas A., ed. Advances in Data Processing Management.
Rumble, III, ed. Oxide Minerals.
Rumelhart, David E., jt. ed. see Hinton, Geoffrey E.
Rummel, W., jt. ed. see Forth, W.
Rummo, Carmen P. Functional Piano.
Rumney, Jay & Murphy, Joseph P. Probation & Social Adjustment.
Rumney, Thomas A. The Historical Geography of Canada: A Selected Bibliography.
--A Selected Bibliography on the Economic Geography of Canada: Agriculture, Land Use, Resources, Energy, Development, Recreation & Tourism.
--A Selected Bibliography on the Economic Geography of Canada: Industry, Transportation, Urban, & Tertiary Systems.
Rumpf, Dieter. South Korea.
Rumshiskii, L. Z. Elements of Probability Theory.
Rumyantsev, A. M. Political Economy.
Rumyantsev, V. V., jt. auth. see Moiseyev, N. N.
Runco, Patti. A Creative Woman's Guide to Success in Real Estate.
Runcorn, S. K., ed. Continental Drift.
Runcorn, S. K., jt. ed. see Tarling, D. H.
Runeckles, V. C., ed. see Phytochemical Society of North America Staff.
Runeckles, V. C., ed. see Phytochemical Society of North America Symposium Staff.
Runes. Spinoza Dictionary.
--Twentieth Century Philosophy.
Runes, D. D. The War Against the Jew.
--Who's Who in Philosophy.
--The Wisdom of the Torah.
Runes, Dagobert D. Art of Thinking.
--Book of Contemplation.
--Crosscuts Through History.
--Despotism.
--Diccionario De Filosofia.
--Dictionary of Thought.
--Encyclopedia of Arts.
--Hebrew Impact on Western Civilization.
--Letters to My Daughter.
--Letters to My Son.
--Pictorial History of Philosophy.
--Selected Writings of Benjamin Rush.
--Treasury of Philosophy.
--Treasury of World Science.
--Treasury of World Science.
Runes, Dagobert D., ed. Spinoza: Dictionary.
Runes, Dagobert D., ed. see Spinoza, Baruch.
Runge, Senta M. Face Lifting by Exercise.
Runkel, Philip J., jt. auth. see Schmuck, Richard A.
Runkel, Philip J., et al. Transforming the School's Capacity for Problem Solving.
--Organizational Renewal in a School District: Self-Help Through a Cadre of Organizational Specialists.
Runkle, Gerald. Theory & Practice: An Introduction to Philosophy.
Runner, Meredith N. & Runner, Meredith N., eds. Changing Syntheses in Development.
Runner's World Magazine Editors. The Complete Runner.
Running Press Staff. Fatherhood: A Personal Journal with Quotes.
--The Sailing Journal: An Illustrated Notebook with Quotes.
Running, Thrope. Borges' Ultraist Movement & Its Poets.
Runnymede Trust Staff. Britain's Black Population.
Runstein, Robert E. Modern Recording Techniques.
Runyon, Charles W. Soulmate.
Runyon, Damon. Romance in the Roaring Forties & Other Stories.
Runyon, Richard P. Fundamentals of Statistics in the Biological, Medical, & Health Sciences.
Ruocco, Frances. True Love Will Never Die.
Ruoff, Norman D., ed. Writings of President Frederick M. Smith.
--The Writings of President Frederick M. Smith.
--The Writings of President Frederick M. Smith, Vol. III: The Zionic Enterprise.
Ruotolo, Lucio P., ed. see Woolf, Virginia.
Rupley, William H. & Blair, Timothy R. Reading Diagnosis & Direct Instruction: A Guide for the Classroom.
--Reading Diagnosis & Remediation.
--Reading Diagnosis & Remediation: Classroom & Clinic.
Ruppe, Harry O. Introduction to Astronautics.
Rusch, Harley G. Dudley's Dog Days: Joining Faith to Life.
Rusch, William G. Ecumenism: A Movement Toward Church Unity.
--Reception: An Ecumenical Opportunity.
Ruse, Michael. Taking Darwin Seriously: A Naturalistic Approach to Philosophy.
Rush, Beverly. Stitch with Style.
Rush, Peter. Papier Mache: An Introduction to the Art of Modeling in Paper.
Rush, Richard H. Investing in Classic Automobiles for Profit & Capital Gain.
Rushford, Pat. Kristen's Choice.
Rushford, Patricia H. Caring for Your Sick Child.
Rushing, Jane G. Against the Moon.
--The Raincrow.
--Walnut Grove.
Rushing, T. Benny. Topological Embeddings.
Rushmer, Robert F. Medical Engineering: Projections for Health Care Delivery.
Rushmore, Helen. Cowboy Joe of the Circle S.
Rushmore, Stephen, jt. auth. see American Institute of Real Estate Appraisers Staff.
Ruskin, Ariane. Nineteenth-Century Art.
Ruskin, Ariane, ed. Prehistoric Art & Ancient Art of the Near East.
Ruskin, R. S. Evaluation of an Undergraduate Course Involving Student Placement in Institutional Settings.
Ruskin, Robert S., ed. Selected Readings in Behavior Modification.
Rusmore, Jean & Spangle, Frances. Peninsula Trails.
Russ, C. A., ed. see Lenz, Siegfried.
Russ, Frederick A. & Kirkpatrick, Charles A. Marketing.
Russ, Joanna. Magic Mommas, Trembling Sisters, Puritans & Perverts: Feminist Essays.
Russ, Joel & Lynn, Lou. Contemporary Stained Glass.
Russ, John C. & Barrett, Charles S., eds. Advances in X-Ray Analysis.
Russ, Lavinia. The April Age.
--Over the Hills & Far Away.
Russ-Eft, Darlene F., et al. Issues in Adult Basic Education & Other Adult Education: An Annotated Bibliography & Guide to Research.
Russel, Alan & Boehm, David A., eds. Guinness Book of World Records, 1988.
Russel, J. Stuart. Parousia.
Russel, Lauren. Advances on the AIDS Horizon.
Russel, P. see Huth, F., et al.
Russell, A. D. Pharmaceutical Microbiology. Hugo, W. B., ed.
Russell, A. D. & Fuller, R., eds. Cold Tolerant Microbes in Spoilage & the Environment.
Russell, A. Lewis. Corporate & Industrial Security.
Russell, Alan, et al, eds. Guinness Book of World Records 1987.
Russell, Barry. Building Systems: Industrialization & Architecture.
Russell, Bertrand. The Art of Philosophizing & Other Essays.
--Authority & the Individual.
--Education & the Good Life.
--Essays in Skepticism.
--Freedom Versus Organization: 1814-1914.
--Future of Science.
--Good Citizens Alphabet.
--Human Society in Ethics & Politics.
--Introduction to Mathematical Philosophy.
--Logic & Knowledge: 1901-1950. Marsh, Robert C., ed.
--An Outline of Philosophy.
--Philosophical Essays.
--The Philosophy of Logical Atomism & Other Essays, 1914-1919. Slater, John G., ed.
--Power.
--Understanding History.
Russell, Brenda P. Smoky Mountain Dreams: The Life Story of Edith Wilson Heston.
Russell, C. Allyn. Voices of American Fundamentalism: Seven Biographical Studies.
Russell, C. R. Reactor Safeguards.
Russell, C. T., ed. Active Experiments in Space Plasmas.
Russell, C. V. Post O-Level Studies in Modern Languages.
Russell, Charles M. Long Live the Spy.
Russell, D. S. Apocalyptic: Ancient & Modern.
Russell, Deter L., et al. Quantitative Obstetrical Ultrasonography.
Russell, Diane. Claude Lorrain: Sixteen Hundred to Sixteen Eighty-Two.
Russell, Don. The Wild West: A History of the Wild West Shows.
Russell, Dora. The Dora Russell Reader: Fifty Seven Years of Writing & Journalism, 1925-1982.
--The Religion of the Machine Age.
--The Tamarisk Tree: My Quest for Liberty & Love.
Russell, E. John. Science & Modern Life.
Russell, E. W. Soil Conditions & Plant Growth.
Russell, Ellen. Last Fix: Dan Russell & the World That Lost Him.
Russell, Ethan A. Dear Mr. Fantasy: Diary of a Decade.
--Dear Mr. Fantasy: Diary of a Decade, Our Time & Rock & Roll.
Russell, Frank. A Century of Chair Design.
Russell, G. K. Marihuana Today: A Compilation of Medical Findings for the Layman.
Russell, G. W. The National Being: Some Thoughts on An Irish Polity.
Russell, George B. J. Bracken Lee: The Taxpayer's Champion.
Russell, George K. Laboratory Investigations in Human Physiology.
Russell, George W. E. Sydney Smith.
Russell, Gordon W., ed. Violence in Intimate Relationships.
Russell, Graeme. The Changing Role of Fathers.
Russell, Harold. Foozles & Frauds.
Russell, James A., jt. ed. see Suedfeld, Peter.
Russell, Jeffrey B. A History of Witchcraft: Sorcerers, Heretics & Pagans.
Russell, Jill F., jt. auth. see Nunez, Ann R.
Russell, Joan. The Woman's Day Book of Soft Toys & Dolls.
Russell, John M. Giving & Taking: Across the Foundation Desk.
Russell, K. C. Phase Stability under Irradiation.
Russell, K. C., ed. see TMS-AIME Fall Meeting, Niagara Falls,1976.
Russell, Kate. Billy Idol.
Russell, Keith C. The Duck-Huntingest Gentleman.
--Fly Fishingest Gentlemen.
--For Whom the Ducks Toll: A Select Gathering of Memorable Waterfowling Tales.
Russell, Keith C., et al. For Whom the Duck Tolls.
Russell, Keith P. Eastman's Expectant Motherhood Seventh Edition Revisied.
Russell, Kirk. The Conservative Mind.
Russell, Larry. Arizona's Red Rock Country: Seasons in Oak Creek Canyon & Sedona.
Russell, Lee, jt. auth. see Meisner, Arnold.
Russell, Letty M., ed. Changing Contexts of Our Faith.
Russell, Marjorie. The Arcadia Story.
Russell, Martin. Prime Target.
--The Search for Sara: A Novel.
Russell, R. C. & MacMillan, D. H. Waves & Tides.
Russell, R. C., ed. Recent Advances in Surgery.
Russell, Ray. The Bishop's Daughter: A Chronicle of Certain Personal Events Written by Miss Mellissa Worthing of Hans Town, London to Mollify Her Mind & Chasten Her Spirit in a Time of Great Tribulation.
Russell, Ray, ed. Princess Pamela.
Russell, Robert. Valentin Kataev.
Russell, Robert D. Education in the Eighties: Health Education.
Russell, Roger W., ed. Frontiers in Physiological Psychology.
Russell, Ross R. W. Vascular Disease of the Central Nervous System.
Russell, S. P. Animales Que Ayudan.
Russell, Sandy, et al, eds. Naval Aviation 1911-1986: A Pictorial Study.
Russell, Stanley. The Stapeley Book of Water Gardens.
Russell, Thomas R., et al, eds. From Gene to Protein: Information Transfer in Normal & Abnormal Cells.
Russell, Wrio, jt. auth. see Fukushima, Sho.
Russell, Yvonne. My First Bible Word Book.
Russell-Manning, Betsy. Home Remedies for Candida.
Russell-Manning, Betsy, ed. Wheatgrass Juice-Gift of Nature.
Russo, Raymond M., jt. auth. see Laude, Theresita.
Russo, Ronald A. Plant Galls of the California Region.
Russo, Susan. Joe's Junk.
Russo, Susan, ed. & illus. The Ice Cream Ocean: & Other Delectable Poems of the Sea.
Russo-Alesi, Anthony I. Martyrology Pronouncing Dictionary.
Russon, A. & Russon, L. J. Advanced German.
Russon, L. J., jt. auth. see Russon, A.
Rust, William J. Kennedy in Vietnam: American Vietnam Policy 1960-1963. U. S. News Books Staff, ed.
Rustagi, Jagdish S., ed. Optimizing Methods in Statistics: Proceedings of an International Conference.
Rustam, Phillis A. Cloth Dolls: A Guide for Collectors.
Rustgi, Vinod K. & Cooper, James N. Gastrointestinal & Hepatic Complications in Pregnancy.
Rustow, Dankwart A. Oil & Turmoil: America Faces OPEC & the Middle East.
Ruszkiewicz, John J. Well-Bound Words: A Rhetoric.
Ruszkiewicz, John J., jt. auth. see Corder, Jim W.
Rutenberg, David. Multinational Management.
Rutenberg, Michael E. Edward Albee: A Playwright in Protest.
Rutford, Robert H., jt. auth. see Zumberge, James H.
Rutgers, A. Budgerigars in Color: Their Care & Breeding. Rogers, Cyril, ed.
Rutherford, Anna & Hannah, Donald, eds. Commonwealth Short Stories.
Rutherford, Mark see also White, W. Hale.
Rutherford, Mark see also White, William H.
Rutherford, Richard. The Death of a Christian: The Rite of Funerals.
Rutherford, Ward. John Stainier.
--Pythagoras: Lover of Wisdom.
Rutishauser, H. Automatische Rechenplanfertigung Bei Programmgesteuerten Rechenmaschinen.
--Handbook for Automatic Computation: Vol. 1. Pt. A. Description of ALGOL 60. Bauer, F. L., et al, eds.
--Der Quotienten-Diferenzen-Algorithmus.
Rutishauser, H., et al. Programmgesteuerte Digitale Rechengerate.
Rutkoff, Peter M. Revanche & Revision: The Ligue des Patriotes & the Origins of the Radical Right in France, 1882-1900.
Rutkowski, Anthony M., jt. auth. see Codding, George, Jr.
Rutland, Jonathan. Exploring the Violent Earth.
--See Inside a Submarine. Warwick Press, ed.
--See Inside an Airport. JV-Warwick Press Staff, ed.
--See Inside an Oil Rig & Tanker. JV-Warwick Press Staff, ed.
Rutledge, A. J. Anatomy of a Park Plan: The Essentials of Recreation Area Design.
Rutledge, Archibald. The Heart's Citadel & Other Poems.
Rutman, Darrett B. American Puritanism: Faith & Practice.
--Morning of America: 1603-1789.
Rutstrum, Calvin. Hiking.
--Wilderness Cabin.
Rutt, August. Coxarthrosis: Surgical & Conservative Treatment.
Ruttan, V. W. Agricultural Research Policy & Development.
Ruttan, Vernon W. Agricultural Research Policy.
Ruttan, Vernon W., et al, eds. Agricultural Policy in an Affluent Society.
Rutten, Felix. Die Victorverehrung Im Christlichen Altertum.
Rutter, E. A., ed. see Conference on Commutative Algebra.
Rutter, Michael & Jones, Robin R. Lead Versus Health: Sources & Effects of Low Level Lead Exposure.
Rutter, William J., jt. ed. see Papaconstantinou, John.
Ruttinger, Friedrich W. Leica Advertising 1925-1950.

Rutz, Peter. Zweiwertige und Mehrwertige Logik: Ein Beitrag Zur Geschichte und Einheit der Logik.
Ruud, Charles A. Fighting Words: Imperial Censorship & the Russian Press, 1804-1906.
Ruud, Erling. God Makes Old Age Young. Moe, J. Melvin, tr. from Norwegian.
Ruvalds, J., jt. ed. see Dash, J. G.
Ruxin, Robert H. An Athlete's Guide to Agents.
Ruys, J. H., ed. see Boerhaave Course, Univ of Leiden, Netherlands, 1969.
Ruzicka, J. & Stary, J. Substoichiometry in Radiochemical Analysis.
Ruzicka, Jaromir & Hansen, Elo H. Flow Injection Analysis.
Ruzicka, Rudolph. Studies in Type Design: Alphabets with Random Quotations.
Ryall, A. Lloyd & Lipton, Werner J. Handling, Transportation & Storage of Fruits & Vegetables: Vegetables & Melons.
Ryals, Clyde L., ed. see Ward, Mrs. Humphrey.
Ryan, Alan. Bones Wizard.
--Property & Political Theory.
--Quadriphobia.
--Vampires: Two Centuries of Great Vampire Stories.
Ryan, Allan A. Quiet Neighbors: Prosecuting Nazi War Criminals in America.
Ryan, Alvan, ed. Newman & Gladstone: The Vatican Decrees.
Ryan, Anne, jt. auth. see Sluzas, Raymond.
Ryan, Betsy, jt. auth. see Binswanger, Barbara.
Ryan, C., jt. auth. see Turney, C.
Ryan, Cathleen, jt. auth. see Blair, Margot C.
Ryan, Colleen. The Job Search Workshop for Disabled, Dislocated & Discouraged Workers: Participant Manual.
--The Job Search Workshop for Disabled, Dislocated & Discouraged Workers: Trainer Manual.
Ryan, Colleen & Nalbandian, Carol, eds. Planning Your Career Pathways: Supervisor's Manual.
Ryan, Colleen, jt. ed. see Nalbandian, Carol.
Ryan, Cornelius. A Bridge Too Far.
Ryan, Cornelius & Ryan, Kathryn M. A Private Battle.
Ryan, Desmond. Video Capsule Reviews.
Ryan, Desmond & Shurkin, Joel. Helix.
Ryan, Elizabeth B. & Eakins, William J. The Lord Peter Wimsey Cookbook.
Ryan, Frank L. The Immediate Critical Reception of Ernest Hemingway.
Ryan, Frank L. & Clark, James I. Windows on Japan.
Ryan, Gerry, ed. see Olsen, Roger E.
Ryan, James, jt. auth. see Carisella, P. J.
Ryan, Juanita. Standing By.
Ryan, Judith. The Uncompleted Past: Postwar German Novels & the Third Reich.
Ryan, Kathryn M., jt. auth. see Ryan, Cornelius.
Ryan, Kevin & Cooper, James M. Kaleidoscope: A Book of Readings.
--Kaleidoscope: Readings in Education.
--Those Who Can, Teach.
--Those Who Can, Teach.
Ryan, Kevin, ed. Don't Smile Until Christmas: Accounts of the First Year of Teaching.
--Teacher Education.
Ryan, Lee F. & Townsend, Andrew. The KAYPRO Connection-Selecting, Installing & Using Peripherals.
Ryan, Michael, ed. see Cimino, Louis.
Ryan, Michael, tr. see Negri, Antonio.
Ryan, Michael K. In Winter.
Ryan, Nigel, tr. see Simenon, Georges.
Ryan, Reade H., jt. auth. see Practising Law Institute Staff.
Ryan, Roderick T., ed. Principles of Color Sensitometry.
Ryan, Thomas. Fasting Rediscovered: A Guide to Health & Wholeness for Your Body-Spirit.
Ryan, Tom K. Tumbleweeds.
Ryan, W. & Pedder, M. Basic Science for Nurses.
Ryan, William, jt. auth. see Wiles, Cheryl.
Ryans, John K., Jr. & Shanklin, William L. Strategic Planning: Concepts & Implementation Text, Readings & Cases.
Rybak, B. Principles of Zoophysiology.
Rybalka, Michel, ed. see Sartre, Jean-Paul.
Ryberg, J., jt. ed. see Choppin, G.
Rychlak, Joseph F. Introduction to Personality & Psychotherapy.
Ryckman, W. G. What Do You Mean by That?
Rycroft, Charles. Imagination & Reality.
Rycroft, P. V., ed. Corneo-Plastic Surgery.
Ryden, Elihu D. Federal Fertility in the Stream of Commerce.
Ryden, Mats. Shakespearean Plant Names: Identifications & Interpretations.
Rydenfelt, Sven. A Pattern for Failure: Socialist Economies in Crisis.
Ryder, Ambrose. Science of Coexistence.
Ryder, Arthur W., tr. Panchatantra.
Ryder, Edward J. Leafy Salad Vegetables.
Ryder, Frank G. & McCormick, E. Allen. Lebendige Literatur: Deutsches Lesebuch Fur Anfanger.
Ryder, G. H., ed. Gates' Jigs, Fixtures, Tools & Gauges.
Ryder, Michael L. & Stephenson, Stuart K. Wool Growth.
Rydin, Y. Residential Development & the Planning System: A Study of the Housing Land System at the Local Level.
Rydin, Yvonne. Housing Land Policy: A Study of the Housebuilding Industry & the Planning System.
Ryding, William, jt. auth. see Sareil, Jean.
Rydjord, John. Heading for the Holocaust: A History of War.
Rydzewski, Pamela. Art & Human Experience.
Ryen, Dag, tr. see Hamre, Leif.
Ryffel, Henry H., ed. see Amiss, John M. & Jones, Franklin D.
Ryffel, Henry H., ed. see Oberg, Erik, et al.
Ryken, Leland, ed. The Christian Imagination: Essays on Literature & the Arts.
Rykwert, Anne, jt. auth. see Rykwert, Joseph.
Rykwert, Joseph & Rykwert, Anne. Robert & James Adams: Birth of Style.
Ryland, Frederick. Chronological Outlines of English Literature.
Rylander, Paul N. Catalytic Hydrogenation over Platinum Metals.
Rylands, Leanne, jt. auth. see Taylor, Don.
Ryley, Thomas W., jt. auth. see Karfunkel, Thomas.
Rymalov, V. V. World Capitalist Economy.
Ryman. Warrior Who Carried Life.
Ryn, Claes G. Democracy & the Ethical Life: A Philosophy of Politics & Community.
Rynberg, Elbert. Lithuania Calling Collect: An Exploration of the Roads to Love.
--Quests Beyond the Mirror: A Trio of Tales.
Ryndina, M. N., et al. Fundamentals of Political Economy.
Rynin, David, ed. see Johnson, Alexander B.
Ryrie, Charles. Ryrie's Concise Guide to the Bible.
--We Believe in Creation.
Ryshik, I. M., jt. auth. see Gradshteyn, I. S.
Ryuichi, Tamura. Dead Languages: Selected Poems, 1946-1984. Drake, Christopher, tr. from Japanese.
Ryuzo, Nagao. Chinese Folklore: Belief & Marriage.
Rywell, Martin, ed. see Scott, H. L.
Rywerant, Yochanan. The Feldenkrais Method: Teaching by Handling, A Technique for Individuals.
Rywick, T. Experimentation on Interpersonal Behavior: The Social Psychological Approach.
Rywkin, Michael. Moscow's Muslim Challenge: Soviet Central Asia.
Rywkin, Michael, ed. Russian Colonial Expansion to 1917.
Ryzin, Lani Van see Van Ryzin, Lani.
Rzheshevsky, O. World War II: Myths & Realities.
Rzhevsky, Leonid. Zvezdopad.
Rzhevsky, Leonid D. Solzhenitsyn: Creator & Heroic Deed. Miller, Sonja, tr. from Rus.

S

S C & A Inc. Staff, jt. auth. see Faucett, Jack, Associates Staff.
Saad, M. N., jt. auth. see Barron, J.
Saad, M. N., ed. see Barron, J.
Saagpakk, Paul F. Estonian-English Dictionary.
Saakyan, Gurgen S. Equilibrium Configurations of Degenerate Gaseous Masses. Hall, C. F., tr. from Rus.
Saalbach, Robert Palmer. Dialectic.
Saalbach, Robert Palmer, ed. see Dreiser, Theodore.
Saalman, Howard. Filipo Brunelleschi: The Cupola of Santa Maria Del Fiore.
Saarinen, Thomas. Environmental Planning: Perception & Behavior.
Saaty, T. L. Analytical Planning: The Organization of Systems.
Saavedra, Dane, jt. auth. see Madaras, Lynda.
Sabarsky, Serge, ed. Egon Schiele.
--Egon Schiele.
Sabatier, P. C., jt. auth. see Chadan, K.
Sabatier, Robert. Diccionario Ilustrado de la Muerte.
Sabatini, Rafael. Scaramouche.
Sabatino, David & Mann, Lester. Discipline & Behavioral Management: A Handbook of Tactics, Strategies & Programs.
--Handbook of Diagnostic & Prescriptive Teaching.
Sabatino, David, et al. Learning Disabilities: Systemizing Teaching & Service Delivery.
Sabatino, David A., jt. auth. see Mann, Lester.
Sabato, Larry. Goodbye to Goodtime Charlie: American Governorship Transformed.
Sabato, Larry, jt. ed. see Thomas, Morris R.
Sabbag, Robert. Snowblind.
Sabbagha, Rudy E. Ultrasound in High-Risk Obstetrics.
Sabbah, R., jt. ed. see Rouquerol, J.
Sabbata, Venzo De see Bergmann, Peter G. & De Sabbath, Venzo.
Sabbe, H., ed. The Composer Between Man & Music.
--Composer Society: Le Compositeur dans la Societe - Komponist und Gesellschaft.
Sabbe, Herman, et al, eds. Report on the International Conference on New Musical Notation Organized by the Index of New Musical Notation (New York) & the Seminar of Musicology (Ghent)
Sabel, W. Basic Techniques of Preparative Organic Chemistry.
Saberhagen, Fred. The Berserker Throne.
--The Berserker Throne.
Saberi, Reza. The Labyrinth.
Sabet, Huschmand. The Heavens Are Cleft Asunder. Coburn, Oliver, tr. from Ger.
Sabin, Sharon, jt. auth. see Zizmor, Jonathan.
Sabine, Paul. Atoms, Men, & God.
Sabol, Blair. The Body of America: An Insider's Journey Through the Bumps & Pumps, Groans & Moans, Pecs & Wrecks, Sweat & Sex of the Fitness Explosion.
Sabol, C. Ruth & Bender, Todd K. A Concordance to Ford Madox Ford's The Good Soldier.
Sacchet, Uli, tr. see Twitchell, Paul.
Sacco, Luigi. Manual of Cryptography.
Saccone, C., jt. ed. see Kroon, A. M.
Sacharoff, Shanta N. The Ethnic Vegetarian Kitchen.
--The Flavors of India.
Sacharow, Stanley. Packaging Regulations.
Sacharow, Stanley & Griffin, Roger C., Jr. Basic Guide to Plastics in Packaging.
Sachen, William. Bridge: A Reference Guide.
Sachs, Bessie, jt. auth. see Jefferys, Margot.
Sachs, Curt. History of Musical Instruments.
--Real Lexikon der Musikinstrumente Zugleich ein Polyglossar fur das Gesamte Instrumentengebiet.
--Rhythm & Tempo: A Study in Music History.
--Rise of Music in the Ancient World.
Sachs, Elizabeth-Ann. Just Like Always.
--Where Are You, Cow Patty?
Sachs, Emil S. The Choice Before South Africa.
Sachs, George, ed. see Gastric Secretion Symposium Staff.
Sachs, Jeffrey D., ed. Foreign Debt & Economic Performance: Special Topics.
Sachs, Joel H., jt. auth. see Practising Law Institute Staff.
Sachs, Jonathan. The Osborne-McGraw Hill CP-M-86 User's Guide.
Sachs, Kurt. World History of the Dance. Schonberg, Bessie, tr.
--World History of the Dance.
Sachs, Leroy, ed. Student Merit Awards: High School.
--Student Merit Awards: Middle School.
Sachs, Lewis B., jt. auth. see Jacobs, Alfred.
Sachs, Marilyn. Beach Towels.
Sachs, P. Wind Forces in Engineering.
--Wind Forces in Engineering.
Sachs, William S. Advertising Management.
Sachs, William S. & Benson, George. Product Planning & Management.
Sachse, William L., jt. auth. see Green, Eugene.
Sack, John. M.
Sack, S. M. Don't Get Taken! A Preventive Legal Guide to Protect Your Home, Money, Family & Job.
Sacke, Georg. Die Gesetzgebende Kommission Katharinas Second.
Sacker, R. J., tr. see Lavrentiev, M. M.
Sackett, Russell. Edge of the Sea.
Sackett, S. J N, tr. see Daisne, Johan.
Sackett, Susan. Passion's Gold.
Sackheim, Eric, compiled by. The Blues Line: A Collection of Blues Lyrics.
Sackheim, George I. Chemical Calculations.
--Chemical Calculations.
Sackmary, A., et al. Understanding & Teaching the Slower Student.
Sackrey, Charles. The Political Economy of Urban Poverty.
Sacks, Betty S., tr. see Romains, Jules.
Sacks, David H. Trade, Society & Politics in Bristol: 1500-1640. Mathias, Peter & Bruchey, Stuart, eds.
Sacks, Frank, et al. The New IRA Handbook: Everyone's Guide to Successful Investing after Tax Reform.
Sacks, Herbert S., ed. Hurdles: The Admissions Dilemma in American Education.
Sacks, Oliver. A Leg to Stand On.
--The Man Who Mistook His Wife for a Hat & Other Clinical Tales.
Sacks, Peter. In These Mountains.
Sacks, Richard S., jt. auth. see Brown, William E.
Sackson, Sid. Playing Cards Around the World.
Sackville-West, Vita. The Edwardians.
--Saint Joan of Arc.
Sacred Congregation of the Clergy Staff. General Catechetical Directory: Proceedings of the Sacred Congregation of the Clergy on the Official English Translation of the Latin Document, April 11, 1971.
Sadamoto, Kuni, ed. see Kato, Ichiro.
Sadananda, K. & Rath, B. B., eds. Micro & Macro Mechanics of Crack Growth: Proceedings. TMS-AIME Fall Meeting, Louisville, 1981.
Sadek, George, jt. auth. see Pell, Arthur.
Sadek, Konrad E. KEANAS.
Sadha, Mouni. Samadhi: The Superconsciousness of the Future.
Sadka, Tova. No Way Back.
Sadler, M. T. The Law of Population: A Treatise in Six Books.
Sadler, Marilyn. Alistair in Outer Space.
--Alistair's Elephant.
Sadlier, Heather, jt. auth. see Sadlier, Hugh.
Sadlier, Hugh & Sadlier, Heather. Short Walks on Cape Cod & the Vineyard.
Sadlier, Paul, jt. auth. see Sadlier, Ruth.
Sadlier, Ruth & Sadlier, Paul. Fifty Hikes in Vermont: Walks, Day Hikes & Backpacking Trips in the Green Mountain State.
Sadoff, Ira. Palm Reading in Winter.
--Settling Down.
--Uncoupling.
Sadovsky, A. D., ed. see ISSS Working Group Staff.
Sa'edi, Gholam-Hossein. Fear & Trembling. Southgate, Minoo, tr. from Farsi.
Saeger, W. see Huth, F., et al.
Saenger, ed. see Sevcik, Otakar.
Saenger, G., ed. see Mazas, F.
Saenger, Gustav, ed. see Sitt, Hans.
Saenz, Pilar. The Life & Works of Eugenio D'Ors.
Saettler, Paul. Instructional Technology & Programmed Instruction.
Saez, Richard, jt. ed. see Wilhelm, James J.
SAF National Convention Staff. Increasing Forest Productivity: Proceedings of the SAF National Convention, 1981.
Safar, P., ed. see European Congress of Anaesthesiology of the World Federation of Societies of Anaesthesiologists, 1st, Vienna, 1962.
Safdie, Moshe. Form & Purpose: Is The Emperor Naked.
Saferstein, Richard. Criminalistics: An Introduction to Forensic Science.
Saff, E. B. & Varga, R. S., eds. Pade & Rational Approximation: Theory & Applications.
Saffady, William. Introduction to Automation for Librarians.
Saffar, Ruth E. Critical Essays on Cervantes.
Saffell, David C. & Gilbreth, Terry. Subnational Politics: Readings in State & Local Government.
Saffen, Wayne. The First Season: Advent, Christmas, Epiphany.
--The Second Season: Lent, Easter, Ascension.
Saffon, Joe & Fancisco, Charles. Complete Skin & Hair Care Program for the Active Man.
Safford, Edward L., Jr. The Complete Microcomputer Systems Handbook.
--The Fiberoptics & Laser Handbook.
Safford, Florence. Caring for the Mentally Impaired Elderly: A Family Guide.
Safir, Leonard, jt. auth. see Safire, William.
Safire, William. Full Disclosure.
--I Stand Corrected.
--On Language.
Safire, William & Safir, Leonard. Good Advice.
Safranski, Scott R. Managing God's Organization: The Catholic Church in Society. Farmer, Richard, ed.
Safrit, Margaret J. Evaluation in Physical Education.
Saga, Junichi. Memories of Silk & Straw: A Self-Portrait of Small-Town Japan.
Sagafi-Nejad. Technology Transfer.
Sagafi-nejad, Tagi & Belfield, Robert. Transnational Corporations, Technology Transfer & Development: A Bibliographic Sourcebook.
Sagafi-Nejad, Tagi & Contractor, Farok J. International Technology & Transfer: Major Issues & Policy Responses.
Sagalyn, Lynee B., jt. ed. see Sternlieb, George.
Sagalyn, Lynne B. & Sternlieb, George. Zoning & Housing Costs: The Impact of the Land-Use Controls on Housing Price.
Sagamore Computer Conference, Aug. 20-23, 1974. Parallel Processing: Proceedings. Tse-Yun Feng, ed.
Sagan, Carl. Contact.
Sagan, Hans. Advanced Calculus.
Sagar, Keith M. The Life of D. H. Lawrence.
Sagarin, Edward. Deviants & Deviance.
Sagarin, Edward E. Sociology: The Basic Concepts.
Sagasti, F. Science et Technologie pour le Developpement: Rapport Comparatif Principal du Project "Instruments de Politique Scientifique et Technique"
Sagdeev, R. Z., jt. ed. see Stiller, H.
Sage, A. P., ed. Control Frontiers in Knowledge Based & Man-Machine Systems.
Sage, Andrew P., ed. Systems Engineering: Methodology & Applications.
Sage, Anne, ed. Meeting & Event Planning Guide: Northeast Meeting Sites & Services Directory - Spring, 1989.

Authors

--Meeting & Event Planning Guide: Southern Meeting Sites & Services Directory - Fall, 1988.
Sage, Bruce H., jt. auth. see Lacey, William N.
Sage, G. Arthur. The Completely Civil Servant.
Sage, Lorna. Doris Lessing.
Sage, M., et al, eds. Simulators.
Sager, Carole B. Extravagant Gestures.
Sager, Clifford J. & Hunt, Bernice. Intimate Partners: Hidden Patterns in Love Relationships.
Sager, Floyd C. & Toby, Milton C. Colonel Sager, Practitioner.
Sager, Gordon. Hawaii.
Sager, Lawrence. Wisconsin Supplement for Modern Real Estate Practice.
Sager, Robert J., jt. auth. see Gabler, Robert E.
Sager, Ruth. Cytoplasmic Genes & Organelles.
Sagerman, Robert H. & Abramson, David H. Eye & Ocular Adnexae.
Saginario, John A. The Deadly Dilemma.
Sagirow, P. Stochastic Methods in the Dynamics of Satellites.
Sagnier, Thierry J. The IFO Report.
Sagues, Paul, jt. auth. see Auslander, David.
Saha, J., jt. ed. see Salkin, H. M.
Saha, P., ed. Scaling in Two-Phase Flow.
Saha, Suranjit K. & Barrow, Christopher J. River Basin Planning: Theory & Practice.
Sahakian, Mabel L., jt. auth. see Sahakian, William S.
Sahakian, William. Systems of Ethics & Value Theory.
Sahakian, William S. Learning.
--Psychology of Personality.
--Psychotherapy & Counseling.
Sahakian, William S. & Sahakian, Mabel L. Plato.
--Realms of Philosophy.
Sahgal, Nayantara. The Day in Shadow.
--Plans for Departure.
Sahi, Jyoti. The Child & the Serpent: Reflections on Popular Indian Symbols.
Sahl, Mort. Heartland.
Sahlins, Marshall. Culture & Practical Reason.
--Islands of History.
Sahm, Lawrence A., jt. auth. see Goldhor, Herbert.
Sahn, David J. & Anderson, Fred. Two Dimensional Anatomy of the Heart: An Atlas for Echocardiographers.
Sahn, Seung. Bone of Space.
--Dropping Ashes on the Buddha: The Teaching of Zen Master Seung Sahn. Mitchell, Stephen, tr.
Sahney, Badri N., jt. ed. see Law, Alan G.
Sahni, Bhisham. Kites Will Fly: A Novel.
Sahni, Kalpana, ed. Reminiscences of Tolstoy.
Sahs, Adolph L., et al. Aneurysmal Subarachnoid Hemorrhage: Report of the Cooperative Study.
Sahukar, Mani. Sai Baba, the Saint of Shirdi.
Sahula-Dycke, Ignatz. Nebe.
SAI Services, Inc. Compilation & Analysis of Data on Occupational Radiation Exposure Experienced at Operating Nuclear Power Plants (AIF NESP-005)
Saiady, C. & Stokes, A. V., eds. What to Read in Microcomputing.
Said, Abdul A. & Lerche, Charles. Concepts of International Politics: A Global Perspective.
Said, Abdul A. & Simmons, Luiz R., eds. Ethnicity in an International Context.
Said, Edward W. Joseph Conrad & the Fiction of Autobiography.
Said, Laila. A Bridge Through Time: A Memoir.
Saidin, Ahmad, jt. auth. see Gladwin, Thomas.
Saidis, Frank. One Hundred One Uses for an Unused Home Computer.
Saikowski, Charlotte, et al, eds. Current Soviet Policies: The Documentary Record of the Twenty-Second Congress of the Communist Party of the Soviet Union. Current Digest of the Soviet Press Staff, tr. from Rus.
Sail Magazine, ed. The Best of Sail Magazine.
--More Sail Trim: An Anthology from Sail Magazine.
Saila, Saul B., ed. Coastal & Offshore Environmental Inventory: Cape Hatteras to Nantucket Shoals.
Saindon, Gary. The Off Season Angler.
Sainer, Arthur. The Radical Theater Notebook.
Sainer, Elliot A., ed. Who's Who in Health Care.
Sainsbury, David. Poultry Health & Management.
Sainsbury, Diana, jt. auth. see Singleton, Paul.
Sainsbury, Eric & Phillips, David. Social Work in Focus: Clients' & Social Workers' Perception in Long Term Social Work.
Sainsbury, Geoffrey, tr. see Beucler, Andre.
Sainsbury, Geoffrey, tr. see Simenon, Georges.
Sainsbury, Isobel S. The Milk Free & Milk & Egg Free Cookbook.
Sainsbury, M. J. Key to Psychiatry: A Textbook for Students.
Sainsbury, Sally. Measuring Disability.
--Registered As Disabled.
St. Ama, Johnny W. Elkaz Kazan's Dilemma. Hill, Renais, ed.
St. Aubyn, Giles. The Art of Argument.
--Edward Seventh, Prince & King.
--The Year of Three Kings: 1483.
St. Clair, David. Mine to Kill.
St. Claire, Jessica. Cerissa.
St. Cyprian of Carthage. The Lord's Prayer. Bonin, Edmond, ed.
Saint, Harry. Memoirs of an Invisible Man.
St. Ignatius. Spiritual Exercises of St. Ignatius of Loyola. Delmage, Lewis, tr.
St. Ignatius Loyola. The Autobiography of St. Ignatius Loyola, with Related Documents. O'Callaghan, Joseph F., tr.
St. James, Ian. Balfour Conspiracy.
--The Money Stones.
St. James, Warren. NAACP: Triumphs of a Pressure Group 1909-1980.
St. Jaques, Raymond. Book of Numbers.
St. Jeor, Sachiko, et al. Meal Planning for People with Kidney Disease.
St. John-Stevas, Norman. The Two Cities.
St. John. Air Traffic Control Specialist Employment Guide.
--Airline Pilot Employment Test Guide.
St. John, Bob. Man Inside... Landry,
St. John, C. Boeing-727: Flight Engineer Written Test Guide.
St. John, Clark. Airline Pilot Employment Interview.
--Airline Pilot Employment Test Guide.
St. John, David. Hush.
St. John, Glory. What I Did Last Summer.
St. John, Jeffrey. Day of the Cobra.
St. John, Primus. Skins on the Earth.
St. John, Thomas. Forgotten Dreams: Rituals in American Popular Art.
St. John, Wylly F. Mystery Book Mystery.
--The Mystery of the Gingerbread House.
--The Mystery of the Other Girl.
--The Secret of the Seven Crows.
--The Secrets of Hidden Creek.
--Uncle Robert's Secret.
St. John de Crevecoeur, J. Hector. Letters from Nantucket & Martha's Vineyard.
St. John's Episcopal Church Staff & Deloache, Michel. Little Bit Different.
St. Johns Hospital Staff. The Administrative Manual of Saint Johns Hospital: Springfield, Illinois.
St. Joseph Hospital Staff. Patient-Centered Care Manual for the Nursing Department.
St. Joseph Medical Center Staff. Obstetrical Procedure Manual: Delivery Suite, Nursery, Post Partum.
St. Louis Public Library Staff. Heraldry Index of the St. Louis Public Library.
St. Mary's Memorial Hospital, Knoxville, Tennessee Staff. Guidelines to Orthopedic Nursing.
St. Paul's Greek Orthodox Church Women Staff. Art of Greek Cookery.
--The Regional Cuisines of Greece.
St. Philastrius Bishop of Brescia. Sancti Filastrii Episcopi Brixiensis Diversarum Hereseon Liber.
St. Pierre, Brian. John Steinbeck: The California Years.
St. Pierre, Kent E. Auditor Risk & Legal Liability. Farmer, Richard N., ed.
St. Tamara. Chickaree: A Red Squirrel.
Saint-Aubin, Charles G. Art of the Embroiderer: Charles Germain de Saint-Aubin, Designer to King Louis XV. Scheuer, Nikki, tr. from Fr.
Saint-Beuve. Port Royal.
St. Clair, Mae G., jt. auth. see Turner, Gladys D.
Saint-Exupery, Antoine de. Airman's Odyssey.
--Wind, Sand & Stars. Galantiere, Lewis, tr.
Saint-Exupery, Antoine De see De Saint-Exupery, Antoine.
Saint-George, Henry. The Bow: Its History, Manufacture & Use.
Saint-James, D., et al. Type Two Superconductivity.
Saint John-Perse. Oeuvre Poetique. Incl. Eloges; La Gloire des Rois; Anabase; Exil. Schoenhof.
--Oeuvre Poetique. Incl. Vents; Amers; Chronique. Schoenhof.
Saint-John Perse, pseud. Pour Dante.
St. Jorre, John de see De St. Jorre, John.
Saint-Leger, Alexis see Saint-John Perse, pseud.
Saint-Mery, Mederic L. Moreau De see Moreau De Saint-Mery, Mederic L.
St. Onge, Richard A., jt. auth. see Luby, Sue.
Saintsbury, George. East India Slavery.
Saintsbury, George E. Dryden.
Saint-Simon, Fernand de, jt. auth. see Sereville, Etienne de.
Sainz, Gustavo. The Princess of the Iron Palace. Hurley, Andrew, tr.
Saisselin, Remy G. The Literary Enterprise in Eighteenth Century France.
Saito, Gen. All About Selected American Restaurants.
Saito, T., jt. ed. see Riedel, W. R.
Sakagami, Ryusho & Sakagami, Setsumei. Nunchaku & Sai: Ancient Okinawan Martial Arts.
Sakagami, Setsumei, jt. auth. see Sakagami, Ryusho.
Sakai, Hikoichi & Mohri, Hideo, eds. Biological Functions of Microtubules & Related Structure: Proceedings, 13th Oji International Seminar, Tokyo, Japan, December, 1981.
Sakai, S. C-Algebras & W-Algebras.
Sakala, Carol. Women of South Asia: A Guide to Resources.
Sakamoto, Yoshikazu & Falk, Richard A. World Demilitarized.
Sakanishi, Shio, tr. see Ishikawa, Takuboku.
Sakatani, Baron Y. Manchuria: A Survey of Its Economic Development.
Sakel, Manfred. The Management of Epilepsy.
--Schizophrenia.
Sakharov, Andrei, et al. The Politics of Human Rights.
Sakharov, Andrei D. Progress, Coexistence & Intellectual Freedom.
--Progress, Coexistence & Intellectual Freedom.
Saki see also Munro, H. H.
Sakiya, Tetsuo. Honda Motor: The Men, the Management, the Machines.
Saks, Sol. The Craft of Comedy Writing.
Sakurai, Atsushi. Salmon.
Sala, Harold. My Favorite Verse.
Sala, Harold J. Guidelines for Living.
Salacrou, Armand. Les Nuits de la Colere: Avec: Poof.
--Poof: Avec: L'Achipel Lenoir.
Saladino, Salvatore. Italy from Unification to 1919: Growth & Decay of a Liberal Regime.
Salaff, Janet W., jt. ed. see Sheridan, Mary.
Salak, John S. Dictionary of Gambling.
Salaman, Graeme. Working.
Salaman, Malcolm C. British Book Illustration Yesterday & Today, with Commentary. Holme, Geoffrey, ed.
Salaman, Nicholas. Falling Apart.
Salaman, R. A. Dictionary of Tools Used in the Woodworking & Allied Trades c. 1700-1970.
Salamander Books. Harmony Illustrated Encyclopedia of Rock.
Salamini, Leonardo. The Sociology of Political Praxis: An Introduction to Gramsci's Theory.
Salamon, Lester, ed. see Musselwhite, James C., Jr. & Saunders, Lauren K.
Salamon, Lester M. & Abramson, Alan J. The Federal Budget & the Nonprofit Sector.
Salancik, Gerald R., jt. auth. see Staw, Barry M.
Salanki, J., ed. Neurobiology Invertebrates: Proceedings of a Satellite Symposium of the 28th International Congress of Physiological Sciences, Tihany, Hungary, 1980.
Salanki, J., et al, eds. Physiology of Non-Excitable Cells: Proceedings of the 28th International Congress of Physiological Sciences, Budapest, 1980.
--Physiology of Excitable Membranes: Proceedings of the 28th International Congress of Physiological Sciences, Budapest, 1980.
Salas, Rafael M. International Population Assistance: the First Decade.
--People: An International Choice, the Multilateral Approach to Population.
--Population: un choix international: Approche multilaterale au probleme demographique.
Salasin, Susan E., ed. Evaluating Victim Services.
Salazar, Omar M., et al. Bronchogenic Carcinoma.
Salcedo-Bastardo, J. L. Bolivar: A Continent & Its Destiny. McDermott, Annella, ed. & tr. from Span.
Sale, Florentia. The First Afghan War. Macrory, Patrick, ed.
Sale, J. Russell. Filipino Lippi's Strozzi Chapel in Santa Maria Novella. Freedberg, Sydney J., ed.
Sale, Richard. The Cotswolds.
Sale, Teel, jt. auth. see Betti, Claudia W.
Saleeb, Atef F., jt. auth. see Chen, Wai-Fah.
Saleh, Dennis. Science Fiction Gold: Classic Films of the 50's.
Salem, H. & Aviado, D. M. Anti-Tussive Agents.
Salem, M. J. & Busrewil, M. T., eds. The Geology of Libya.
Salem, M. Ramez. Pediatric Anesthesia: Current Practice.
Salem, Norma. Habib Bourguiba, Islam & the Creation of Tunisia.
Salemson, Harold J., tr. see Beauvais, Robert.
Salemson, Harold J., tr. see Fesquet, Henri.
Salerno, Elizabeth M., jt. auth. see Blair, Carole L.
Salerno, Lynn M. Computer Briefing: Using the Trends for Better Managerial Decisions.
Salerno, M. Constance, jt. auth. see Ingalls, A. Joy.
Salerno, Thomas J., ed. Advanced Chapter 11 Bankruptcy Practice.
--Advanced Chapter 11 Bankruptcy Practice.
--Advanced Chapter 11 Bankruptcy Practice.
--Advanced Chapter 11 Bankruptcy Practice.
Salerno, Tony. The Amazing Book.
Sales, Bruce D., ed. The Criminal Justice System.
Sales, Bruce D., jt. ed. see Lipsitt, Paul D.
Sales, David. John Deere Snowmobile Service-Repair: 1972-1977. Jorgenson, Eric, ed.
Sales, Francois De see De Sales, Saint Francoise.
Sales, Grover. Jazz: America's Classical Music.
--John Maher of Delancey Street: A Guide for Peaceful Revolution in America.
Sales, Raoul De Roussy De see Hitler, Adolph.
Saletore, R. N. Encyclopaedia of Indian Culture.
--Indian Witchcraft.
Saletu, B., et al, eds. Neuro-Psychopharmacology: Proceedings of the Collegium Internationale Neuro-Psychopharmacologium 11th Congress, Vienna, 1979.
Salevouris, Michael J., jt. auth. see Furay, Conal.
Saliba, David R. A Psychology of Fear: The Nightmare Formula of Edgar Allan Poe.
Saliers, Don E., jt. auth. see Brown, Schuyler.
Salignac De La Mothe, Francois De see Fenelon & De Salignac De La Mothe, Francois.
Salih, K., jt. ed. see Lo Fu-Chen.
Salinger, J. D. The Catcher in the Rye.
Salinger, Margaretta, jt. auth. see Sterling, Charles.
Salinger, Nicole, jt. auth. see Galbraith, John Kenneth.
Salisbury, Dallas L., ed. America in Transition: Implications for Employee Benefits.
Salisbury, Gregorius. The Essence of the Supply-Side Economics for the Benefit of Politicians & Businessmen.
Salisbury, Harrison. Nine Hundred Days: The Siege of Leningrad.
Salisbury, Harrison E. China: One Hundred Years of Revolution.
--Russia.
--War Between Russia & China.
Salisbury, Harrison E., ed. Soviet Union: The Fifty Years.
Salisbury, John. The Baby Sitters.
Salisbury, John W. & Glaser, Peter E., eds. Lunar Surface Layer: Materials & Characteristics: Proceedings.
Salisbury, Roger E. & Newman, Nancy. Manual of Burn Therapeutics: An Interdisciplinary Approach.
Salisbury, Roger E. & Pruitt, Basil A. Burns of the Upper Extremity.
Salisbury, Stephan, jt. auth. see Westin, Ala F.
Salit, C. R. Man in Search of Immortality.
Saliwanchik, R. Legal Protection for Microbiology & Genetic Engineering Inventions. Davies, J. E., ed.
Salk, Lee. What Every Child Would Like His Parents to Know to Help Him with the Emotional Problems of Everyday Life.
Salkeld, Audrey, jt. auth. see Holzel, Tom.
Salkeld, Robert & Davidson, Frank P., eds. Macro-Engineering: The Rich Potential.
Salkey, Andrew, ed. West Indian Stories.
Salkey, Andrew, ed. see Naipaul, V. S., et al.
Salkin, H. M. & Saha, J., eds. Studies in Linear Programming.
Salkind, Neil J., jt. auth. see Ambron, Sueann R.
Salle, Jacques. Larousse Book of Cocktails.
Sallee, Susan, tr. see Farrokhzad, Forugh.
Sallese, Nicholas F. & Ortiz-Griffin, Julia. Espanol Practico para los Negoclos.
Salley, Alexander S., Jr., ed. Narratives of Early Carolina, Sixteen Fifty to Seventeen Eight.
Salley, Christopher & Behm, Ronald. What Color Is Your God? Black Consciousness & the Christian Faith.
Salling, A. Danish: Laer at Talk.
Sallis, Joan. Schools, Parents & Governors: A New Approach to Accountability.
Sallis, John. Research in Phenomenology.
--Research in Phenomenology.
--Research in Phenomenology.
Sallis, John & Maly, Kenneth. Heraclitean Fragments: A Companion Volume to the Heidegger-Fink Seminar on Heraclitus.
Sallis, John, ed. Merleau-Ponty: Perception, Structure, Language: a Collection of Essays.
--Philosophy & Archaic Experience.
--Research in Phenomenology.
--Research in Phenomenology, 1980.
--Research in Phenomenology, 1985.
Sallis, John, et al. Research in Phenomenology: 1975.
--Research in Phenomenology: 1976.
Sallis, John, et al, eds. Research in Phenomenology.
Salmi, Mario, intro. by. The Grimani Breviary.
Salmon, Alice W. & Dunn-Meynell, Hugo. The Wine & Food Society Menu Book: Recipes for Celebration.
Salmon, Charles S. Caribbean Confederation: A Plan for the Union of the Fifteen British West Indian Colonies.
Salmon, J. Warren, ed. Alternative Medicines: Popular & Policy Perspectives.
Salmon, James F., jt. ed. see King, Thomas M.
Salmon, Patricia. Japanese Antiques: With a Guide to Shops.
Salmon, Phillida & Claire, Hilary. Classroom Collaboration.
Salmon, Tim, jt. auth. see Baillie, Kate.
Salmon, W. H., tr. see Iyas, Ibn.
Salmona, M., et al, eds. Insolubilized Enzymes.
Salmond, S. D. Biblical Doctrine of Immortality.
Salmonson, R. F., et al. Survey of Basic Accounting.
Salomaa, A., jt. ed. see Rozenberg, G.
Salomon, G., jt. ed. see Caille, J. M.
Salomon, M. Silver Azide, Cyanide, Cyanamides, Cyanate, Selenocyanate & Thiocyanate: Solubilities of Solids.
Salomon, M., jt. ed. see Siekierski, S.
Salomonovich, A. E., jt. auth. see Kuzmin, A. D.

Salomonsky, Verna C. Masterpieces of Furniture.
Salone, M. J. How to Copyright Software.
Salop, L. J. Precambrian of the Northern Hemisphere.
Salpeter, E. E., jt. auth. see Bethe, Hans A.
Salpointe, J. B. Soldiers of the Cross: Notes on the Ecclesiastical History of New Mexico, Arizona, & Colorado.
Salsbury, Stephen. State, the Investor, & the Railroad: The Boston & Albany, 1825-1867.
Salsini, Barbara. Irving Berlin: Master Composer of Twentieth Century Songs. Rahmas, D. Steve, ed.
Salt, B. Programmes for Animation Fifty-Seven: Handbook for Animation Technicians.
Salt, Brian G. Basic Animation Stand Techniques.
--Movements in Animation.
Salt, George W., ed. Ecology & Evolutionary Biology: A Round Table on Research.
Saltarelli, Mario. Basque.
Salten, Felix. Fairy Tales Near & Far.
Salter. Common Gastroenterological Problems.
Salter, Charlie J. Biology Laboratory Manual.
Salter, James. Light Years.
Salter, Lionel. Going to the Opera.
Salter, P. J. & Goode, J. E., eds. Crop Responses to Water at Different Stages of Growth.
Salter, R. H. Synopsis of Gastroenterology.
Saltonstall, Maxine. Dining In - Hawaii.
Saltonstall, William G. Lewis Perry of Exeter.
Saltsburg, Howard, et al, eds. Fundamentals of Gas-Surface Interactions: Proceedings.
Saltykov, Mikhail E. Fables. Volkhovsky, Vera, tr. from Rus.
Saltz, Daniel, jt. auth. see Bryant, Steven.
Saltzberg, Barney. Utter Nonsense.
--What to Say to Clara.
Saltzburg, Stephen A. American Criminal Procedure, Cases & Commentary: 1986 Supplement.
--American Criminal Procedure Cases & Commentary: 1987 Supplement.
--American Criminal Procedure, Cases & Commentary.
Saltzman, Barbara F., ed. see Saltzman, Kathryn M. & Saltzman, Marvin L.
Saltzman, Barbara F., ed. see Turpin, Kathryn S. & Saltzman, Marvin L.
Saltzman, Kathryn M. & Saltzman, Marvin L. Eurail Guide: How to Travel Europe & All the World by Train, 1983. Saltzman, Barbara F., ed.
Saltzman, Marvin L., jt. auth. see Saltzman, Kathryn M.
Saltzman, Marvin L., jt. auth. see Turpin, Kathryn S.
Salunkhe, D. K., jt. auth. see Haard, Norman F.
Salus, Peter H. Linguistics.
Salusinszky, Imre. Criticism in Society.
Salvador, Mari L. Yer Dailege! Kuna Women's Art.
Salvadori, B., ed. see International Symposium on Feto-Placental Insufficiency, 1st, Italy, 1974.
Salvadori, Mario. Why Buildings Stand Up: The Strength of Architecture.
Salvatore, Dominick. Theory & Problems of International Economics.
Salvatore, Dominick, jt. auth. see Berliner, Herman.
Salvatore, Gayle E. Sinfully Good Cookbook.
Salvatore, Marco & Porta, Ernesto, eds. Radioisotopes in Cardiology.
Salvemini, Gaetano. French Revolution.
Salvia, John & Ysseldyke, James E. Assessment in Special & Remedial Education.
--Assessment in Special & Remedial Education.
Salvin, Marina, jt. auth. see Shotwell, James T.
Salwak, Dale. A. J. Cronin: A Reference Guide.
Salwak, Dale, ed. see Stovel, Nora.
Salzburg, Joseph S. The Right Time, the Right Place.
--Vietnam, Beyond the War.
Salzer, F. & Schacheter, C. Counterpoint in Composition: The Study of Voice Leading.
Salzinger, Kurt & Feldman, Richard S. Studies in Verbal Behavior: An Empirical Approach.
Salzinger, Kurt & Salzinger, Suzanne, eds. Research in Verbal Behavior & Some Neuro-Physiological Implications.
Salzinger, Suzanne, jt. ed. see Salzinger, Kurt.
Salzinger, Suzanne, et al, eds. The Ecosystem of the "Sick" Child: Implications for Classification & Intervention for Disturbed & Mentally Retarded Children.
Salzman, Jack, ed. Theodore Dreiser: Sister Carrie.
Salzman, Jack & Wallenstein, Barry, eds. Years of Protest: A Collection of American Writings of the 1930's.
Salzman, N. P., jt. ed. see Habel, K.
Salzman, Philip C., ed. When Nomads Settle: Processes of Sedentarization As Adaptation & Response.
Salzman, Regina A. Catholic Press Directory.
Salzman, Stanley A., jt. auth. see Miller, Charles D.
Salzmann, Laurence, jt. auth. see Gursan-Salzmann, Ayse.
Salzmann, Regina A. Catholic Press Directory, 1986.
Salzmann, Zdenek, jt. auth. see Pi-Sunyer, Oriol.
Sama devi dasi, jt. ed. see Krsna devi dasi.
Samagalski, Alan, jt. auth. see Buckley, Michael.
Samaha, M. A., et al, eds. see Training Workshop on Water Management for Arid Regions, Ministry of Irrigation, Government of Egypt, in Cooperation with the United Nations Environment Programme, Cairo, Egypt.
Samama, Jean-Claude. Ore Fields & Continental Weathering.
Samarskii, A. A. & Nikolaev, E. S. Numerical Methods for Grid Equations.
Samartha, S. J. Courage for Dialogue: Ecumenical Issues in Inter-Religious Relationships.
Samborski, Jeffrey, jt. auth. see Lambert, Jacklyn.
Sambuddha Swami Anand Maitreya, ed. see Rajneesh, Bhagwan Shree.
Sambul, Nathan J. The Handbook of Private Television: A Complete Guide for Video Facilities & Networks Within Corporations, Nonprofit Institutions & Government Agencies.
Sametz, Arnold, ed. Securities Activities of Commercial Banks.
Samkange, Stanlake. Origins of Rhodesia.
Sammes, P. G. Photo-Enolisation.
--Topics in Antibiotic Chemistry: Aminoglyosides & Ansamycins.
Sammet, Ingeborg, tr. see Schneider, Wolf.
Sammon, Rick. Minolta XG's.
Sammons, Donna, jt. auth. see Wiltsee, Joseph L.
Sammons, Jeffrey L. Heinrich Heine: A Selected Critical Bibliography of Secondary Literature, 1956-1980.
Samoilenko, A. M., et al. Methods of Accelerated Convergence in Nonlinear Mechanics. Kumar, V., tr. from Rus.
Samouilidis, J. E. Management Science for Energy Policy.
Samperi, Frank. Branches.
--Of Light.
--Quadrifariam.
Sampford, Charles & Galligan, D. J., eds. Law, Rights & the Welfare State.
Sample, Dorothy E., jt. auth. see O'Brien, Bonnie B.
Sample, R. G., et al. Psychopharmacologic Drugs: A Pocket Reference.
Sampley, J. Paul. Pauline Partnership in Christ: Christian Community & Commitment in Light of Roman Law.
Sampley, J. Paul, jt. ed. see Francis, Fred O.
Sampley, J. Paul, et al. Ephesians, II Colossians, Thessalonians: Pastoral Epistles.
Sampson, Anthony. The Changing Anatomy of Britain.
Sampson, C. Garth. The Stone Age Archaeology of Southern Africa.
Sampson, Elois S. The Tall Stance.
Sampson, J. R. Adaptive Information Processing: An Introductory Survey.
Sampson, Karen G., jt. ed. see Stern, Duke N.
Sampson, Ronald, tr. see Tolstoy, Leo.
Sampson, Roy J. & Calmus, Thomas W. Economics: Concepts, Applications, Analysis.
Sampson, Roy J. & Farris, Martin T. Domestic Transportation: Practice, Theory, & Policy.
Sampson, Roy, J., jt. auth. see Farris, Martin T.
Sampson, Timothy J. Welfare: A Handbook for Friend & Foe.
Sams, Conway W. The Conquest of Virginia. Incl. The Forest Primeval; The First Attempt, 1584-1602; The Second Attempt, 1606-1610; The Third Attempt, 1610-1624. Reprint.
Samson, Jack. Successful Outdoor Writing.
Samson, Jim. Music in Transition: A Study of Tonal Expansion & Atonality, 1900-1920.
--The Music of Szymanowski.
Samson, Joan. The Auctioneer.
--Watching the New Baby.
Samsonov, G. V., ed. Refractory Transition Metal Compounds: High Temperature Cermets.
Samuda, Ronald J. & Woods, Sandra L., eds. Perspectives in Immigrant & Minority Education.
Samuel, Ben. see Stuart.
Samuel, Ben. Bomber.
Samuel, Maurice, tr. see Bein, Alex.
Samuel, Millard A. How to Get Your Share of Business Insurance.
Samuel, Otto. Foundations of Ontology.
Samuel, Raphael, ed. Village Life & Labour.
Samuels. Management of Company Finance.
Samuels, Barbara. Copycat.
Samuels, Clifford L., jt. auth. see Brejcha, Mathias F.
Samuels, Edward. Biotutorial: A Modular Program for Introductory Biology. Student Laboratory Guide.
Samuels, J. & Wilkes, F. Management of Commercial Finance.
Samuels, Jayne, jt. auth. see Strachey, Barbara.
Samuels, Linda B., jt. auth. see Coffinberger, Richard L.
Samuels, M., jt. auth. see Ley, David.
Samuels, Marwyn S. Contest for the South China Sea.
Samuels, Michael A., ed. The Horn of Africa.
Samuelson, Arnold. With Hemingway: A Year in Key West & Cuba.
Samuelson, Larry, jt. auth. see Baer, Werner.
Samuelson, Paul A. Economics.
--Foundations of Economic Analysis.
Samuelsson, G., jt. auth. see Grubb, R.
San Diego Zoological Society Staff, ed. Friends.
--Spots & Stripes.
San Francisco Opera Staff. Adler Years, 1954-1981.
San Giorgio Staff & Skinner Hersey Staff. Pasta Cookbook.
Sana, Josephine M. & Judge, Richard P. Physical Assessment Skills for Nursing Practice.
Sanabria, Edgardo. Delfia cada tarde.
Sanadi, D. Rao, ed. Current Topics in Bioenergetics.
Sanakoyev, Sh. P. & Kapachenko, N. E. Socialism: Foreign Policy in Theory & Practice.
Sanasarian, Eliz. Women's Rights Movement in Iran: Mutiny, Appeasement, & Repression from 1900 to Khomeini.
Sanborn, Franklin B. Recollections of Seventy Years.
Sanborn, Margaret. Yosemite: Its Discovery, Its Wonders & Its People.
Sanborn, Robin. Mohammed Wong Spouts: Being an Eyewitness Account of the Antediluvian Sex Life of Atlantis & Other Things.
San Casciani, Paul. The Technique of Decorative Stained Glass.
Sanceau, Elaine. The Reign of the Fortunate King: Manuel First of Portugal.
Sances, Anthony, Jr. & Larson, Sanford J. Electroanesthesia: Biomedical & Biophysical Studies.
Sanchez, Carmen C. Nurse's Aide Handbook.
Sanchez, E. Fuzzy Information, Knowledge Representation & Decision Analysis: Proceedings of the IFAC-IFIP-IFORS Symposium, Marseille, France, July 1983. Gupta, M. M., ed.
Sanchez, John. Flexible Weapons.
Sanchez, Pedro C., jt. auth. see Carano, Paul.
Sanchez, Ricardo. Canto y Grito mi Liberacion: The Liberation of A Chicano Mind.
Sanchez, Rosaura. Chicano Discourse: Socio-Historic Perspectives.
Sanchez, Rosaura & Cruz, Rosa M., eds. Essays on la Mujer.
Sanchez-Palencia, E. Non-Homogeneous Media & Vibration Theory.
Sanchez-Perez, J. M. Babelism: Social Problems of the Watergate Era.
--Beliefs & Their Engrammes: Revised & Tested on the QE-2 World Cruise.
--A Doctor's Odyssey.
--Engrammes of the Universe: Extra-Cerebral Memory, Reincarnation & Demonic Possession.
--The Hispanico.
--Oppression, Violence & Repression.
--Our Sixth Sense: An Organic Theory of the Unknown.
Sanchez Salazar, Gustavo A., jt. auth. see Gonzales, Luis J.
Sanctuary, Anthony. Rope, Twine & Net Making.
Sand, Georges. Indiana.
Sandage, Allan & Sandage, Mary, eds. Galaxies & the Universe.
Sandage, Mary, jt. ed. see Sandage, Allan.
Sandak, Cass R. Football.
Sandbach, F. H. The Stoics. Finley, M. I., ed.
Sandberg, Alvin, jt. auth. see Fawcett, Susan E.
Sandberg, E. W., jt. auth. see Fowler, F. Parker, Jr.
Sandberg, Janet, jt. ed. see Cox, Evelyn.
Sandberg, L. B., et al, eds. Elastin & Elastic Tissue.
Sandberg, Peter L. Stubb's Run.
Sandborn, E. B. Cells & Tissues by Light & Electron Microscopy.
--Light & Electron Microscopy of Cells & Tissues: An Atlas for Students in Biology & Medicine.
Sandburg, Carl. Abraham Lincoln: The Prairie Years.
--Abraham Lincoln: The Prairie Years & the War Years.
--Abraham Lincoln: The Prairie Years & the War Years.
--Abraham Lincoln: The War Years.
--Breathing Tokens.
--Early Moon.
--Prairie-Town Boy.
--Selected Poems. West, Rebecca, ed.
--Wedding Procession of the Rag Doll & the Broom Handle & Who Was in It.
--Wind Song.
--Wind Song.
Sandburg, Carl, ed. American Songbag.
Sandburg, Helga. A Great & Glorious Romance: The Story of Carl Sandburg & Lilian Steichen.
Sande, Arlene F. Oh Mountains Be My Refuge.
Sandeen, Ernest R., ed. The Bible & Social Reform.
Sandeen, Ernest R. & Hale, Frederick, eds. American Religion & Philosophy: A Guide to Information Sources.
Sandell, Rolph. Linguistic Style & Persuasion.
Sandeman, J. C. The Blood-Line: A Translation of Gustav Wied's Slaegten.
Sanden, John H. Painting the Head in Oil.
Sanden, Richard. Advent.
Sander, August, illus. August Sander.
Sander, B. An Introduction to the Study of Fabrics of Geological Bodies.
Sander, Gunther, ed. August Sander: Citizens of the Twentieth Century, Portrait Photographs, 1892-1952. Keller, Linda, tr. from Ger.
Sander, U., et al, eds. Sulphur, Sulphur Dioxide, Sulphuric Acid. More, A. I., tr.
Sandercock, Leonie. Cities for Sale.
Sanders, Daniel S. & Estes, Richard J. International Social Welfare: A Selected Bibliography.
Sanders, Donald H. More about BASIC: Supplement.
Sanders, Donald H., et al. Statistics: A Fresh Approach.
Sanders, E. P., ed. Jewish & Christian Self-Definition, Vol. 1: The Shaping of Christianity in the Second & Third Centuries.
Sanders, E. P., jt. ed. see Meyer, Ben F.
Sanders, E. P., et al, eds. Jewish & Christian Self-Definition, Vol. 2: Aspects of Judaism in the Greco-Roman Period.
Sanders, Ed. The Family.
Sanders, F. David, jt. auth. see Kirkland, James W.
Sanders, F. Kingsley. Viruses. Head, J. J., ed.
Sanders, Henry A. New Testament Manuscripts in the Freer Collection.
Sanders, Herbert H. & Tomimoto, Kenkichi. The World of Japanese Ceramics.
Sanders, Howard J., jt. auth. see Josephs, Melvin J.
Sanders, Irwin T. & Bisselle, Walter C. East European Peasantries: Social Relations: An Annotated Bibliography of Periodical Articles.
Sanders, Irwin T. & Whittaker, Roger. East European Peasantries: Social Relations; an Annotated Index of Periodical Articles.
Sanders, Ivan, tr. see Konrad, George.
Sanders, J. M. The Velocity of Light.
Sanders, J. O. Paul the Leader.
Sanders, J. Oswald. Certainties of Christ's Coming.
--Promised-Land Living.
Sanders, J. Oswald & Gould, Dana. Spiritual Leadership: Leader's Guide.
Sanders, Jack T. Ethics in the New Testament: Change & Development.
Sanders, James A. God Has a Story Too: Biblical Sermons in Context.
Sanders, James B., ed. see L'Hote, Jean.
Sanders, Joan. Other Lips & Other Hearts.
Sanders, Joseph, jt. auth. see Lempert, Richard O.
Sanders, Kamala. Strange Tunes.
--Tempestuous Heights.
Sanders, Lawrence. Anderson Tapes.
--The Eighth Commandment.
--Fourth Deadly Sin.
Sanders, Lloyd C. Celebrities of the Century: Being a Dictionary of Men & Women of the Nineteenth Century.
Sanders, Lois J. Procedure Guides for Evaluation of Speech & Language Disorders in Children.
Sanders, Marion K. The Lady & the Vote.
Sanders, Murray, jt. auth. see Neasom, Mike.
Sanders, Norman. A Manager's Guide to Profitable Computers.
Sanders, Ottys & Sanders, Ruth. Interlude & Other Poems. Nortex Press Staff, ed.
Sanders, Ronald. The Days Grow Short: The Life & Music of Kurt Weill.
--The High Walls of Jerusalem: A History of the Balfour Declaration & the Birth of the British Mandate for Palestine.
Sanders, Ruth, jt. auth. see Sanders, Ottys.
Sanders, Ruth A. Child Support & Alimony: 1983: Supplemental Report.
Sanders, Scott R. Wilderness Plots: Tales about the Settlement of the American Land.
Sanders, Steve & Williams, Donnie. Championship Kenpo.
Sanders, T. H., Jr. & Starke, E. A., Jr., eds. Aluminum-Lithium Alloys: Proceedings. Stone Mountain, Georgia, 1980.
Sanders, T. H., Jr., jt. ed. see Starke, E. A., Jr.
Sanders, Thomas E. & Peek, Walter W. Literature of the American Indian.
--Literature of the American Indian.
Sanders, William B. Juvenile Delinquency: Causes, Patterns, & Reactions.
--Rape & Woman's Identity.
Sanderson, B. J., jt. auth. see Rourke, C. P.
Sanderson, Glen C. & Schultz, Helen C., eds. Wild Turkey Management: Current Problems & Programs.
Sanderson, Ivan T. Invisible Residents.
Sanderson, J. B., tr. see Hegel, Georg W.

Sanderson, J. D. How to Stop Worrying about Your Kids.
Sanderson, Jean. The Million Dollar Contest Cookbook.
Sanderson, Joy L., jt. auth. see Thomas, Lowell J.
Sanderson, Liz. How to Make Your Own Herbal Cosmetics.
Sanderson, P. C. Computer Languages.
Sanderson, P. J. Antibiotics for Surgical Infections.
Sandford, Cedric. Taxation & Social Policy.
Sandifer, Kevin W. Accessioning: Registration, Documentation, & Filing. Gill, Rowland P., ed.
Sandifer, Linda P. Heart of the Hunter.
--Pride's Passion.
--Tylers Woman.
Sandige, Richard. Digital Concepts Using Standard Integrated Circuits.
Sandison, jt. auth. see Oxtoby.
Sandkowsky, Suzanne H., jt. auth. see Live, Anna H.
Sandle, Marjorie, tr. see D'Epinay, Christian L.
Sandler, Corey. How to Telecommunicate: A Personal Computer User's Guide.
--The IBM PC-AT: A Guide for Users & Managers.
Sandler, M. & Gessa, G., eds. Sexual Behavior: Pharmacology & Biochemistry.
Sandler, Maurice & Bourne, Geoffrey H., eds. Atherosclerosis & Its Origin.
Sandler, P. L., jt. auth. see Bolitho, A. R.
Sandler, S. Gerald & Silvergleid, Arthur J., eds. Autologous Transfusion.
Sandler, Stanley R. & Karo, Wolf. Organic Functional Group Preparations.
Sandlin, Tim. Sex & Sunsets.
Sandmel, Samuel. Anti-Semitism in the New Testament?
--The Genius of Paul: A Study in History.
--When a Jew & Christian Marry.
Sandner, Donald. Navaho Symbols of Healing.
Sandon, Henry. Flight & Barr Worcester: Seventeen Eighty-Three to Eighteen Forty.
--Illustrated Guide to Worcester Porcelain, 1751-1793.
--Royal Worcester Porcelain.
Sandor, Bela I. & Schlack, A. L. Learning & Review Aid for Statics: To Go with Engineering Mechanics.
Sandow, Stuart. Durations: The Encyclopedia of How Long Things Take.
Sandoz, Ltd. Staff, ed. Psychopathology & Pictorial Expression.
Sandoz, Mari. Old Jules Country.
--Winter Thunder.
Sandpiper Studios Staff, ed. Creeds to Love & Live by.
Sandqvist, Karin. Fathers & Family Work in Two Cultures: Antecedents & Concomitants of Fathers' Participation in Child Care & Household Work in Germany, Israel, Sweden, United States & Wales.
Sandre see Proust, Marcel.
Sandrea, Rafael & Nielsen, Ralph. Dynamics of Petroleum Reservoirs Under Gas Injection.
Sandritter, W. see Huth, F., et al.
Sandro, Paul. Diversions of Pleasure: Luis Bunuel & the Crises of Desire.
Sands, Harry & Minters, Frances C. The Epilepsy Fact Book.
Sandum, Howard E., ed. see Goodman, Eugene B.
Sandvik, Glenn N. Duluth: An Illustrated History of the Zenith City.
Sandzen, S. C., Jr. Atlas of Acute Hand Injuries.
--Atlas of Wrist & Hand Fractures.
Sanecki, Kay N. Old Garden Tools.
San'ei Shobo Publishing Co. Staff, ed. Luigi Colani Design Series.
Sanford, John A. The Man Who Wrestled with God: Light from the Old Testament on the Psychology of Individuation.
Sanford, Jon A. & Taylor, J. Scott. The Design of Exhibition Facilities: A Focus on Architecture Contributions to Visitor Experience in Zoos, Aquariums, & Related Facilities.
Sanford, Linda T. & Donovan, Mary E. Women & Self Esteem: Understanding & Improving the Way We Think & Feel About Ourselves.
Sanford, Nancy, jt. auth. see Parsons, Virgil.
Sanford, Ruth. The First Years Together.
Sanger, D. J., jt. ed. see Blackman, D. E.
Sanger, Margaret. Works. Incl. Vol. 1. Margaret Sanger, an Autobiography. Guttmacher, A., intro. by.; Vol. 2. Happiness in Marriage; Vol. 3. Motherhood in Bondage: Motherhood in Bondage; Vol. 4. My Fight for Birth Control; Vol. 5. The New Motherhood; Vol. 6. The Pivot of Civilization; Vol. 7. What Every Boy & Girl Should Know; Vol. 8. Woman & the New Race. Pergamon.
Sanger, Mary B. Welfare of the Poor.
Sanger, Sirgay & Kelly, John. The Woman Who Works, the Parent Who Cares: A Revolutionary Program for Raising Your Child.
Sangster, Jimmy. Snowball.
Sangster, P. E. Speech in the Pulpit.
Sangster, Paul. A History of the Free Churches.
Sankalia, H. D. Prehistory of India.
San Lazzaro, G. Di see Di San Lazzaro, G.
Sano, Keiji, jt. auth. see Takakura, Kintomo.
Sano, Roy see McDonald, Durstan R., et al.
San Pietro, Anthony, et al, eds. Harvesting the Sun: Photosynthesis in Plant Life.
--Regulatory Mechanisms for Protein Synthesis in Mammalian Cells.
San Pletro, Anthony, ed. see Symposium, Bloomington Staff.
Sans, John C., Jr. The Complete Communications Handbook.
Sansan. Eighth Moon. Lord, Bette B., as told to.
Sansom, R. G. Language of the Navy in English.
Sansom, William. The Icicle & the Sun.
Sansone, V. Siberia: Epic of the Century.
San Souci, Daniel, illus. The Mother Goose Book.
SanSouci, Robert. Blood Offerings.
Sant, M. E. Industrial Movement & Regional Development: The British Case.
Santa Barbara Museum of Natural History Staff. California's Chumash Indians.
Santa Fe Opera Guild Staff. Cooking with the Santa Fe Opera.
Santa Maria, Jack. Greek Vegetarian Cookery.
Santamore, William P. & Bove, Alfred A., eds. Coronary Artery Disease: Etiology, Hemodynamic Consequences, Drug Therapy & Clinical Implications.
Santana, Isabel. Love Song.
Santa Pinter, Jose J. Curso Basico de Ciencias Sociales: Con especial interes para Puerto Rico.
Santayana, George. Atoms of Thought.
--Character & Opinion in the United States.
--Ideas & Concepts.
--Reason in Common Sense.
--Scepticism & Animal Faith.
Santee, Frederick L. The Devil's Wager: A Faustian Drama of the Second Fall & a Second Redemption.
Santeusanio, Richard P. Developing Reading Skills for Business & Industry.
Santholzer, R. W. Five Language Dictionary of Surface Coatings, Platings, Product Finishing, Plastics & Rubber.
Santiago, Danny. Famous All over Town.
Santiago, Jose R. Pakistan: A Travel Survival Kit.
Santiago, Paul J. An Audio-Tutorial Introduction to Chemistry. Incl. Metric System; Signed Numbers & Solving Simple Linear Equations; Definition of Chemistry; Chemical Classification of Matter; Sub-Atomic Structures of the Isotopes; Periodic Table; Bonding of Atoms; Writing Formulas for Ionic Compounds; Calculating Formula Weights & Percentage Compositions; The Mole Concept; Balancing a Chemical Equation; Calculation of the Simplest Formula for a Compound; Weight-Weight Problems; Kinetic Molecular Theory of Matter & the Gas Laws; General Gas Law Equation; Volume-Volume & Weight-Volume Problems; Density of Gas at S.T.P.; Solutions; Definition of Electrolites, Acids, Bases, & Salts; Single Replacement Reactions; Double Replacement Reactions; Neutralization. HM.
Santilli, Nicolas R., jt. ed. see Meacham, John A.
Santini, Rosemarie. The Secret Fire: How Women Live Their Sexual Fantasies.
Santis, Marie De see De Santis, Marie.
Santis, Marie de see De Santis, Marie.
Santmire, H. Paul. The Travail of Nature: The Ambiguous Ecological Promise of Christian Theology.
Santmire, H. Paul, jt. auth. see Lutz, Paul E.
Santora, Dolores. Conceptual Frameworks Used in Baccalaureate & Master's Degree Curricula.
Santora, Joseph C. Collective Bargaining in the Public Sector: A Selected Periodical Guide, 1974-1984.
--Employee Stock Ownership Plans: A Selected Bibliography, 1974-1984.
Santos, Miguel A., ed. Readings in Biology & Man.
Santos, Milton. The Shared Space: The Two Circuits of the Urban Economy in Underdeveloped Countries.
Santrock, John W. Psychology: The Science of Mind & Behavior.
Sanusi, I. Daniel, jt. auth. see Misra, Raghunath P.
Sanyal, B. C. University Education & the Labour Market in the Arab Republic of Egypt.
Sanyal, Bishwapriya, jt. auth. see Bamberger, Michael.
Sanzotta, D., et al. Exploring the Basics: Readings in Psychology.
Sapan, Joshua. Making It in Cable TV: Career Opportunities in Today's Fastest-Growing Media Industry.
Saperstein, Alan. Camp.
Saperstein, Albert H. Musings of a Mild Manic-Depressive.
Saphier, M. Planning the New Office.
Sapir. Language: An Introduction to the Study of Speech.
Sapir, Andre, jt. ed. see Baldwin, Robert E.
Sapolsky, Harvey M., jt. ed. see Altman, Stuart.
Sapori, Armando. Italian Merchant in the Middle Ages.
Sapp, Gary L., ed. Perspectives in Educational Psychology: Old Wine in New Bottles.
Sapp, Stephen. Sexuality, the Bible & Science.
Sarabyanov, Dmitry & Arbuzo, Grigory. Valentin Serov: Paintings, Graphic Works, Stage Designs.
Saraf, D. N. Indian Crafts.
Sarant, Elizabeth. Heritage of Deceit.
Sarason, Barbara R., jt. auth. see Sarason, Irwin G.
Sarason, Barbara R., jt. auth. see Sarason, Irwin J.
Sarason, I. G., ed. see Morris, Larry W.
Sarason, I. G., jt. ed. see Spielberger, C. D.
Sarason, Irwin G. & Sarason, Barbara R. Abnormal Psychology.
Sarason, Irwin G. & Spielberger, Charles D. Stress & Anxiety.
Sarason, Irwin G. & Spielberger, Charles D., eds. Stress & Anxiety.
Sarason, Irwin J. & Sarason, Barbara R. Abnormal Psychology: The Problem of Maladaptive Behavior.
Sarbaugh, L. E. Intercultural Communication.
Sarbhoy, A. K. Advanced Mycology.
Sarbin, Theodore R. & Mancuso, James C. Schizophrenia: Medical Diagnosis or Moral Verdict?
Sarch, Ray. Basic Guide to Data Communications.
--Data Network Design Strategies.
Sarch, Ray, jt. auth. see Held, Gilbert.
Sardar, Ziauddin. The Future of Muslim Civilisation.
--Science, Technology & Development in the Muslim World.
Sarde, Michele. Colette: A Biography. Miller, Richard, tr. from Fr.
Sareil, Jacqueline, jt. ed. see Sareil, Jean.
Sareil, Jean & Ryding, William. Au Jour le Jour: A French Review.
Sareil, Jean & Sareil, Jacqueline, eds. Pas a pas.
Sargant, William & Slater, Eliot, eds. Introduction to Physical Methods of Treatment in Psychiatry.
Sargent, Bargi. The Story of Poppyseed.
Sargent, Bill. Shallow Waters: A Year on Cape Cod's Pleasant Bay.
Sargent, J. Society, Schools & Progress in India.
Sargent, J. L., ed. Amador County (CA) History.
Sargent, J. R., jt. ed. see Matthews, R. C.
Sargent, Jean V. An Easier Way: Handbook for the Elderly & Handicapped.
Sargent, Jim. American Premium Guide to Pocket Knives.
Sargent, Marion. All About the Birds & Bees & Other Stinging Satire.
Sargent, Michael. Mycenae. McLeish, Kenneth & McLeish, Valerie, eds.
Sargent, Murray, III & Shoemaker, Richard. The IBM-PC from the Inside Out.
Sargent, Pamela, jt. auth. see Quackenbush, Marcia.
Sargent, Robert. Now Is Always the Miraculous Time.
Sargent, S. Stansfeld. Nontraditional Therapy & Counseling with the Aging.
Sargent, S. Stansfeld & Smith, Marion, eds. Culture & Personality.
Sargent, Shirley, ed. see Hutchings, James M.
Sargent, Thomas. Macroeconomic Theory.
Sargent, William. Shallow Waters: A Year on Cape Cod's Pleasant Bay.
Saric, Zinka. The Essence of Living.
Sario, L. & Noshiro, K. Value Distribution Theory.
Sario, L., jt. auth. see Rodin, R.
Sario, L., et al. Classification Theory of Riemannian Manifolds.
Sarkar, A. D. Mould & Core Material for the Steel Industry.
--Wear of Metals.
Sarkesian, Sam C. Beyond the Battlefield: American Military Professionalism.
Sarkissian, Adele, ed. High-Interest Books for Teens: A Guide to Book Reviews & Bibliographic Sources.
--Writers for Young Adults: Biographies Master Index.
Sarlo, Carmine R. De see De Sarlo, Carmine R.
Sarma, P. S., et al. Current Topics in Microbiology & Immunology.
Sarma, Ramaswamy H. Stereodynamics of Molecular Systems.
Sarma, Y. S. & Khan. Algal Taxonomy in India.
Sarmiento. Facundo: Civilizacion y Barbarie.
Sarnat, Marshall. Capital Investment & Financial Decisions.
Sarno, Robert C., jt. auth. see Griffiths, Harry J.
Sarnoff. Society with Tears.
Sarnoff, Dorothy. Make the Most of Your Best.
Sarosi, B. Gypsy Music.
Saroyan, Aram. Last Rites: The Death of William Saroyan.
--Trio: Portrait of an Intimate Friendship.
--William Saroyan.
--William Saroyan.
Saroyan, William. Chance Meetings.
--The Human Comedy.
Sarpkaya, Turgut & Isaacson, Michael. Mechanics of Wave Forces on Offshore Structures.
Sarraute, Nathalie. Disent les Imbeciles.
--Entre la Vie et la Mort: Roman.
--Ere de Soupcon: Essais sur le roman.
--Les Fruits d'Or.
--Martereau.
--Le Planetarium.
--Portrait d'un Inconnu.
--Vous les Entendez?
Sarrazin, Johan, jt. auth. see AISLIN Staff.
Sarrel, Lorna J. & Sarrel, Philip M. Sexual Unfolding: Sexual Development & Sex Therapies in Late Adolescence.
Sarrel, Philip M., jt. auth. see Sarrel, Lorna J.
Sarris, Andrew. The American Cinema: Directors & Directions, 1929-1968.
--The John Ford Movie Mystery.
Sarris, Andrew, ed. Interviews with Film Directors.
Sartakov, S. Siberian Stories.
Sartarelli, Stephen, tr. see Duranti, Francesca.
Sarti, Dennis A. Atlas of Obstetric & Gynecologic Ultrasound.
Sarti, Roland. Fascism & the Industrial Leadership in Italy, 1919-1940: A Study in the Expansion of Private Power Under Fascism.
Sarton, George. History of Science, One: Ancient Science Through the Golden Age of Greece.
--History of Science, Two: Hellenistic Science & Culture in the Last Three Centuries B.C.
Sarton, May. At Seventy: A Journal.
--Bridge of Years.
--The Bridge of Years.
--Crucial Conversations.
--Faithful Are the Wounds.
--The House by the Sea: A Journal.
--Joanna & Ulysses.
--Kinds of Love.
--The Magnificent Spinster.
--Plant Dreaming Deep.
--Poet & the Donkey.
Sarton, May A. Private Mythology.
Sartorelli, Stephen, tr. see Granzotto, Gianni.
Sartori, Mario. The Bow Tie Book: Learn to Tie It, Wear It, Love It.
Sartoris, Alberto. Metafisica Della Architettura.
Sartre, Jean-Paul. L' Age de Raison.
--Being & Nothingness.
--Les Chemins de la liberte. Incl. Tome I. L' Age de Raison; Tome II. La Mort dans l'Ame; Tome III. Le Sursis. Schoenhof.
--The Condemned of Altona. Leeson, Sylvia & Leeson, George, trs. from Fr.
--Critiques Litteraires.
--Diable et le Bon Dieu.
--Le Diable et le Bon Dieu.
--The Emotions: Outline of a Theory.
--Essays in Aesthetics.
--Existential Psychoanalysis.
--Existentialism.
--Freedom Condemned.
--Les Mains Sales: Piece en 7 Tableaux.
--La Mort dans l'ame.
--Mots.
--Le Mur.
--Nausee.
--Of Human Freedom.
--Philosophy of Existentialism.
--Psychology of Imagination.
--Sartre on Theater. Contat, Michel & Rybalka, Michel, eds. Jellinek, Frank, tr. from Fr.
--Sequestres d'Altona.
--The War Diaries of Jean-Paul Sartre: November 1939 to March 1940.
--What is Literature?
Sarup, Madan. Education, State & Crisis: A Marxist Perspective.
Sarver, jt. auth. see Souviney, Randall.
Sarvetnick, Harold A. Polyvinyl Chloride.
S. A. S. Don't Be Afraid...Recovery from Alcoholism.
SAS Institute Inc. SAS Companion for the VSE Operating System, 1983.
--SAS Technical Report: Changes & Enhancements to Base SAS Software for Personal Computers, Release 6.03.
SAS Institute, Inc. Staff. Eine Einfuehrung in das SAS.
--Guia Introductory al SAS, Edicion Revisada.
--SAS Applications Guide, 1980 Edition.
--SAS Basic Video Course: Coordinator's Guide.
--SAS-ETS User's Guide, 1982 Edition.
--SAS-FSP User's Guide, 1982 Edition.
--SAS-GRAPH User's Guide, 1980 Edition.
SAS Institute Inc. Staff. SAS Language Guide for Personal Computers, Version 6.
SAS Institute, Inc. Staff. SAS-OR User's Guide, 1983 Edition.
SAS Institute Inc. Staff. SAS Procedures Guide for Personal Computers, Version 6.
SAS Institute, Inc. Staff. SAS User's Guide: Basics, 1982 Edition.
--SAS User's Guide: Statistics, 1982 Edition.
--SAS Video Training Basics 100-Series Instructional Guide, 1981.

--SAS Views: Introduction to SAS, 1982 Edition.
--SAS Views: Procedure Writing, 1981 Edition.
--SAS Views: Regression & ANOVA, 1981.
--SAS Views: SAS Color Graphics, 1983 Edition.
--SUGI Supplemental Library User's Guide, 1983 Edition.
SAS Institute, Inc. Staff, ed. SAS-GRAPH User's Guide, 1981 Edition.
Sasaki, Clarence T. & Jafek, Bruce W. Head & Neck Surgery.
Sasaki, Genjun H. Linguistic Approach to Buddhist Thought.
Sasazuki, Takehiko & Tada, Tomio, eds. Immunogenetics: Its Application to Clinical Medicine.
Sashkin, Marshall. Assessing Performance Appraisal.
Sasnett, Martena & Sepmeyer, Inez. Educational Systems of Africa.
Saso, Michael R. Taoism & the Rite of Cosmic Renewal.
Sasowsky, Norman. The Prints of Reginald Marsh.
Sass, C. Joseph. A Structured Approach to FORTRAN 77 Programming: With WATFIV.
Sass, Lorna J. Christmas Feasts from History. Atcheson, Jean, ed.
Sasse, H. Rainer. Adhesion Between Polymers & Concrete.
Sasse, Kathryn H. My Favorite Place.
Sasser, W. Earl, jt. auth. see Wyckoff, D. Daryl.
Sastry, N. S. & Thomas, C. K. Farm Animal Management & Poultry Production.
Sastry, S. S. Introductory Methods of Numerical Analysis.
Sasuly, Max. Trend Analysis of Statistics: Theory & Technique.
Sasuly, Richard. Bookies & Bettors: Two Hundred Years of Gambling.
Satake, I. Classification Theory of Semi-Simple Algebraic Groups.
Satas, Donastas, ed. Handbook of Pressure-Sensitive Adhesive Technology.
Sateren, Leland B. New Song.
Saterstrom, Mary H., ed. Educators Guide to Free Guidance Materials.
Sathe, Vijay. Controller Involvement in Management.
Sathe, Vijay V. Culture & Related Corporate Realities.
Satinoff, E., ed. Thermoregulation.
Satir, P. Structure & Function in Cilia & Flagella. Alfert, M., et al, eds. Bd. with Trichocystoides. Corps Trichocytoides. Cnidocystes & Colloblastes. Horvasse, R. Springer-Verlag.
Satir, Virginia M. Peoplemaking.
Sato, Hiroaki & Watson, Burton, eds. From the Country of Eight Islands: An Anthology of Japanese Poetry.
Sato, Hiroaki, tr. see Miyazawa, Kenji.
Sato, Nobuyuki, jt. auth. see Inokuma, Isao.
Sato, Osamu, jt. auth. see Isozaki, Arata.
Sato, P. Pater Sato-Portfolio.
--Pater Sato Portfolio.
Sato, Pater. Fashion Illustration in New York.
Satran, Paul R. Balancing Act.
Satre, Elizabeth D. The Story of Ellen: How Love Transforms a Troubled Child.
Satta, Salvatore. Day of Judgment.
Sattelmeyer, Robert, ed. see Thoreau, Henry David.
Satter, Ellyn. Child of Mine: Feeding with Love & Good Sense.
Satterthwaite, C. B., jt. ed. see Jena, P.
Sattilaro, Anthony J. & Monte, Tom. Living Well Naturally.
Sattinger, D. H. Group Theoretic Methods in Bifurcation Theory.
Sattler, Fred P., et al, eds. Veterinary Critical Care.
Sattler, Helen. Bible Puzzle Trails.
Sattler, Henry V. All about Love.
Saturday Evening Post Editors. The Saturday Evening Post Norman Rockwell Book.
--The Saturday Evening Post Vegetable Primer.
Satyanarayanan, Mahadev. Modelling Storage Systems. Stone, Harold, ed.
Satz, Ronald N. American Indian Policy in the Jacksonian Era.
Sau, R. Underdeveloped Capitalism & the General Law of Value.
Sauchelli, Vincent. Phosphates in Agriculture.
--Trace Elements in Agriculture.
Saudek, Jan. The World of Jan Saudek.
Sauer, B. W., ed. Biomedical Engineering IV: Recent Developments: Proceedings of the Fourth Southern Biomedical Engineering Conference, Jackson, MS, U. S. A. October 11-12, 1985.
Sauer, Barbara. Walk the Dinosaur Trial.
Sauer, Carl O. Land & Life: A Selection from the Writings of Carl Ortwin Sauer. Leighly, John, ed.
Sauer, Gordon C. John Gould, the Bird Man: A Chronology & Bibliography.
Sauer, I. Eve's Little Friends.
Sauer, Val J., Jr. The Eschatology Handbook: The Bible Speaks to Us about Endtimes.
Sauerberg, Lars O., et al. The Practice of Literary Criticism.
Sauerman, Thomas H. & Schomaker, Linda, eds. Starting a Church-Sponsored Weekday Preschool Program: A Manual of Guidance.
Sauermann, Heinz. Bargaining Behavior: Beitraege zur Experimentellen Wirtschaftsordnung.
Saul, A. J., jt. auth. see Lomax, W. R.
Saul, John. Brainchild.
--Nathaniel.
Saul, John R. The Next Best Thing.
Saul, Leon J. Childhood Emotional Pattern: Human Hostility.
--Childhood Emotional Pattern: Psycho Therapy.
Saul, Lou E. The North Pacific Cretaceous Trigoniid Genus Yaadia.
Saul, Norman E. Russia & the Mediterranean 1797-1807.
Saul, S. B. The Myth of the Great Depression 1873-1896.
--The Myth of the Great Depression 1873-1896.
Saunder, Stephen. Breastfeeding: A Problem-Solving Manual.
Saunders, B. John Evelyn & His Times.
Saunders, Beatrice. Tchekov the Man.
--Tchekov the Man.
Saunders, Brigitte, et al, eds. Scholastic Aptitude Test (SAT) Preparation for the College Entrance Examination.
Saunders, Bruce T., ed. Approaches with Emotionally Disturbed Children.
Saunders, C. T., ed. Industrial Policies & Technology Transfers Between East & West.
Saunders, Cicely & Summers, Dorothy. Hospice: The Living Idea.
Saunders, Dan. Alaska: Memoir of a Vanishing Frontier.
Saunders, Diana. Tana Maguire.
Saunders, E. Dale, tr. see Abe, Kobo.
Saunders, Ernest W. & Craddock, Fred B. Epiphany. Achtemeier, Elizabeth, et al, eds.
Saunders, Frank & Southwood, James. Torn Lace Curtains.
Saunders, Hal M., jt. auth. see Carman, Robert A.
Saunders, Harvey R. Fires of Hell.
Saunders, J. B., ed. see Vesalius, Andreas.
Saunders, J. H. Careers in Industrial Research & Development.
Saunders, J. V. Differential Fertility in Brazil.
Saunders, John W. Developmental Biology: Patterns, Problems & Principles.
Saunders, K. J. Organic Polymer Chemistry.
Saunders, Kay. Workers in Bondage: The Origins & Bases of Unfree Labour in Queensland 1824-1916.
Saunders, Kay, ed. Indentured Labour in the British Empire, 1840 to 1920.
Saunders, Lauren K., jt. auth. see Musselwhite, James C., Jr.
Saunders, M. Health Visiting Practice.
--Multicultural Teaching: A Guide for the Classroom.
Saunders, M., tr. see Vercel, Roger.
Saunders, Michael F., et al. Research Needs Associated with Toxic Substances. Water Pollution Control Federation Staff, ed.
Saunders, Peter. Social Theory & the Urban Question.
Saunders, Robert J., et al. Telecommunications & Economic Development.
Saunders, Rubie. Baby-Sitting: A Concise Guide.
--The Beauty Book. Barish, Wendy, ed.
--The Beauty Book.
Saunders, Susan. A Sniff in Time.
Saunders, Thomas J. The Sign of the Crescent Moon.
Saunders, Vivien. The Golfing Mind.
Saunders, William H., jt. auth. see DeWeese, David F.
Sauneron, Serge. The Priests of Ancient Egypt.
Saunier, Charles. Auguste Lepere: Peintre et Graveur.
Sauppe, Eberhard, ed. Standard Dictionary of Librarianship: Standardworterbuch fur das Bibliothekswen.
Saurat, J. Retinoids: New Trends in Research & Therapy.
Sauro, Regina. Too-Long Trunk.
Saushkin, Y. G. Economic Geography: Theory & Methods.
Saussine, Renee De see De Saussine, Renee.
Saussure, Ferdinand de see De Saussure, Ferdinand.
Saussy, George S. The Oxter English Dictionary: Uncommon Words Used by Uncommonly Good Writers.
Sauter, Eric. Hunter.
Sautter, M. G. Employment in Michigan: A Guide to Employment Practices & Regulations.
Sauvain, Philip. Man & Environment.
Sauvant, Karl P., ed. Changing Priorities on the International Agenda: The New International Economic Order.
Sauveur, Albert. Metallurgical Reminiscences & Dialogue.
Savage. Art & Antique Restorers Handbook.
Savage, jt. auth. see Rielly.
Savage, Barbara. Miles from Nowhere: Round-the-World Bicycle Adventure.
Savage, Beth, jt. auth. see Marzollo, Jean.
Savage, Christina. Dawn Wind.
Savage, Cindy. Just Between Sisters.
Savage, Donald T., et al. Economics of Environmental Improvement.
Savage, Ernest. Pastels for Beginners.
--Two If by Sea.
Savage, Ernest A. Old English Libraries.
Savage, Gail, et al. Three New England Watercolor Painters.
Savage, George, jt. auth. see Reilly, Robin.
Savage, Helen, ed. Library of Congress Classification Schedules: A Cumulation of Additions & Changes Through 1985.
--Library of Congress Classification Schedules: A Cumulation of Additions & Changes Through 1986.
--Library of Congress Classification Schedules: Complete Schedule plus Additions & Changes Through 1986.
Savage, Ian. The Deregulation of Bus Services.
Savage, Jay M. Evolution.
Savage, Jim, jt. auth. see Elliott, Roth.
Savage, John. High Touch Selling.
Savage, Jon. The Kinks: The Official Biography.
Savage, Mary. Addicted to Suicide: A Woman Struggling to Live.
Savage, Michael. Good News, Bad News.
Savage, P. E. Disasters: Hospital Planning.
Savage, R., jt. ed. see Leakey, L.
Savage, R. D., et al. Personality & Adjustment in the Aged.
Savage, R. E., jt. auth. see Ringertz, N. R.
Savage, Thomas. For Mary, with Love.
Savage, Thomas G. And Now a Word from Our Creator.
Savage, Thomas J., jt. auth. see New Jersey Institute for Continuing Legal Education Staff.
Savageau, David, jt. auth. see Boyer, Richard.
Savary, Louis M. & Berne, Patricia H. Prayerways: For Those Who Feel Discouraged or Distraught, Frightened or Frustrated, Angry or Anxious, Powerless or Purposeless, Over-Extended or Under-Appreciated, Burned Out or Just Plain Worn Out.
Savary, Louis M., jt. auth. see Berne, Patricia H.
Savas, E. S. Privatizing the Public Sector: How to Shrink Government.
Savas, E. S., jt. auth. see Savas, Stephen D.
Savas, Stephen D. & Savas, E. S. BASIC Programming for Kids--& Grown-ups, Too!
Savelle, Jerry. Man's Crown of Glory.
--A Right Mental Attitude.
Savelle, Max. Seeds of Liberty: The Genesis of the American Mind.
Saverio, Mercadante. La Vestale.
Savery, Gilbert M., jt. ed. see Nicoll, Bruce H.
Savich, Richard S. Internal Audit of the Budget Process.
Savigny, Friedrich K. The History of the Roman Law During the Middle Ages. Cathcart, E., tr.
Saville, Diana. Walled Gardens: Their Planting & Design.
Saville, J., jt. ed. see Milliband, Ralph.
Savino, Margaret M. Community Development Paraprofessionals in Bolivia: NCDS Promoters in the Field.
Savitch, H. V. Urban Policy & the Exterior City: Federal, State & Corporate Policies.
Savitch, W. J. Pascal: An Introduction to the Art & Science of Programming.
Savitt, Sam. Draw Horses with Sam Savitt.
Savitz, Leonard D. & Johnston, Norman, eds. Crime in Society.
Savold, David, jt. ed. see Klein-Helmuth, Barbara C.
Savoldi, Gloria R. Tennessee Boy.
Savona, Jeannette L. Jean Genet.
--Jean Genet.
Savory, T. H. Introduction to Zoology.
Savory, Teo. Dragons of Mist & Torrent.
Savory, Teo, ed. Unicorn Journal.
Savoy, Louis G. Savoy Heritage: Sixteen Twenty-One to the Present.
Savoy, Susanne. More Than Forever.
Savvas, Minas, tr. see Ritsos, Yannis.
Sawai, Y., ed. Animal Plant & Microbial Toxins.
Sawaragi, Yoshikazu, et al. Statistical Decision Theory in Adaptive Control Systems.
Sawczuk, A. Plasticity Today: New Solutions & Trends in Plasticity: Special Memorial Issue in Honor of Prof. Waclaw Olszak. Proceedings of the Plasticity Today Symposium, Udine, Italy, 27-30 June 1983.
Sawer, Marian & Sims, Marian. A Woman's Place: Women & Politics in Australia.
Sawer, Marian, ed. Program for Change: Affirmative Action in Australia.
Sawhill, Isabel V., jt. ed. see Anderson, Bernard E.
Sawicki, Carole R., jt. auth. see Sawicki, Eugene.
Sawicki, Eugene & Sawicki, Carole R. Aldehydes-Photometric Analysis.
Sawin, Lewis. A Concordance to the Poetry of George Meredith.
Sawin, Lewis, jt. auth. see McCullen, Maurice.
Sawin, Lewis, ed. see Meredith, George & Sutro, Alfred.
Sawislak, Arnold. Dwarf Rapes Nun, Flees in UFO.
Sawkins, F. J., et al. Evolving Earth.
Sawko, F., jt. auth. see Cope, R.
Sawmill Clinic Staff. Modern Sawmill Techniques Vol. 5: Proceedings of the Sawmill Clinic, 5th, Portland, Oregon, March, 1975. White, Vernon S., ed.
Sawusch, Mark. One Thousand One Things to Do with Your Personal Computer.
Sawusch, Mark R. The One-hundred Best IBM Utilities.
Sawusch, Mark R. & Summers, Tan A. One Thousand & One Things to Do with Your Commodore 64.
Sawyer, Ann L., jt. auth. see University of North Carolina, Institute of Government, Chapel Hill Staff.
Sawyer, Ann L., ed. North Carolina Legislation, 1981: A Summary of Legislation in the 1981 General Assembly of Interest to North Carolina Public Officials.
Sawyer, Brian. The IBM-PCjr Entertainer.
Sawyer, Constance, et al. Solar Flare Prediction.
Sawyer, George. Business & Society: Managing Corporate & Social Impact.
Sawyer, Jack, jt. ed. see Pleck, Joseph H.
Sawyer, Jesse C. Faces of Communication: A New Approach to Interpersonal Development.
Sawyer, Kieran. Developing Faith: Lesson Plans for Senior High Religion Classes.
Sawyer, Larry B. The Practice of Modern Internal Auditing. Pasternak, Ceel, ed.
Sawyer, Lawrence B. The Manager & the Modern Internal Auditor.
Sawyer, Marcia J., compiled by see Association of American Veterinary Medical Colleges.
Sawyer, Mark. Early Days: Photographer George A. Grant & the Western National Parks.
--Forman Hanna, Pictorial Photographer of the Southwest.
Sawyer, Roger. Casement: The Flawed Hero.
Sax. Hazardous Chemicals Information Annual, No. 1.
Sax, Gilbert. Principles of Educational & Psychological Measurement & Evaluation.
Sax, Irene. Cook's Marketplace New York: A Culinary Sourcebook.
Sax, N. Irving & Feiner, Benjamin. Dangerous Properties of Industrial Materials.
Sax, Richard. Old-Fashioned Desserts. Atcheson, Jean, ed.
Sax, Richard, ed. see Bon Appetit Magazine Editors.
Sax, Sidney. A Strife of Interests: Politics & Policies in Australian Health Services.
Saxe, A. A. Notes on Academic Disciplines.
Saxe, Barry, jt. auth. see Carroll, David.
Saxe, Leonard, jt. auth. see Bar-Tal, Daniel.
Saxe, Leonard, ed. Making Evaluations Useful to Congress.
Saxena, H. M. Geography of Marketing: Concepts & Methodology.
Saxena, M. C. & Singh, K. B., eds. Chickpea.
Saxl, Fritz. Rembrandt's Sacrifice of Manoah.
Saxon, Burt, jt. auth. see Kellman, Peter.
Saxon, J. & Englander, W. ANSI COBOL Programming.
Saxon, Nancy. Panky & William.
--Panky in the Saddle.
Saxon, Richard. Atrium Buildings.
Saxon, Sable. The Christmas Angel.
Saxon, Sue V. & Etten, Mary J. Physical Change & Aging: A Guide for the Helping Professions.
Saxton. Mosby's Assesstest (Secured), 86: A Practice Exam for RN Licensure.
--Mosby's Assesstest 86: A Practice Exam for RN Licensure.
Saxton, Dolores F., et al. Mosby's Comprehensive Review of Nursing.
--Mosby's Assesstest: A Practice Exam for RN Licensure (Unsecured Version.
Saxton, Dolores F., et al, eds. Mosby's Comprehensive Review of Nursing.
Saxton, John A., ed. Advances in Radio Research.
Saxton, Josephine. Little Tours of Hell: Tall Tails of Food & Holidays.
Saxton, Mark. Havoc in Islandia.
--The Two Kingdoms.
Saxton, Martha. Louisa May.
--Louisa May: A Modern Biography of Louisa May Alcott.
Saye, Albert B. New Viewpoints in Georgia History.
Saye, Nan Dobson. Glimpses of Glory: Scripture Poems.
Sayegh, Fayez & Soukkary, Sohair. Palestine: Concordance of United Nations Resolutions 1967-71.
Sayer, Ian & Botting, Douglas. Nazi Gold.
--Nazi Gold.
Sayer, John & Jones, Neville, eds. Teacher Training & Special Educational Needs.
Sayer, M. S., tr. see Hausen, Helmuth.
Sayers, Dorothy L. Busman's Honeymoon.
--Clouds of Witness.
--Documents in the Case.

Authors

--Five Red Herrings.
--Gaudy Night.
--Hangman's Holiday.
--Have His Carcase.
--In the Teeth of the Evidence.
--Lord Peter.
--Lord Peter Views the Body.
--The Man Born to Be King.
--The Mind of the Maker.
--Murder Must Advertise.
--Strong Poison.
--Unnatural Death.
--Unpleasantness at the Bellona Club.
--Whose Body?
Sayers, Frances C. Anne Carroll Moore: A Biography.
--Oscar Lincoln Busby Stokes.
Sayers, Gayle & Griese, Bob. Offensive Football. Bonderunt, Bill, ed.
Sayers, Julie, ed. see Sayers, Scott.
Sayers, Richard S. Bank of England Operations Eighteen Ninety to Nineteen Fourteen.
Sayers, Scott. Texas State Directory. Sayers, Julie, ed.
Sayers, Sean, jt. auth. see Norman, Richard.
Sayers, Stanley E. Bridging the Generation Gap.
--Drink from the Deeper Wells.
Sayler, Mary H. Downhill Flats.
--Hand Me Down the Dawn.
Sayles, Leonard, jt. auth. see Wegner, Robert.
Sayles, Leonard R. Managerial Behavior: Administration in Complex Organizations.
Saylor, James. Real Estate Exchange Desk Book.
Saypol, Judyth R. & Wikler, Madeline. My Very Own Chanukah Book.
Saypol, Judyth R., jt. auth. see Brinn, Ruth E.
Sayre, Joan M. Teaching Language Through Sight & Sound - Set 1.
Sayre, Kenneth M. Plato's Analytic Method.
Sayre, Nora. Sixties Going on Seventies.
Sayre, Robert, jt. auth. see Erickson, Jonathan.
Sayre, Wallace S. & Kaufman, Herbert. Governing New York City.
Scaer, David. Getting into the Story of Concord.
Scagel, R. F., et al. Nonvascular Plants: An Evolutionary Survey.
Scaglione, Aldo, tr. see McCrickard, Eleanor F.
Scaglione, Aldo D. Nature & Love in the Middle Ages.
Scagnetti, Jack. The Life & Loves of Gable.
--The Life & Loves of Gable.
Scahill, Edward M. The Effect of Research & Development on U. S. Market Structure. Bateman, Fred, ed.
Scaife, A., ed. Plant Nutrition, 1982.
Scaife, B. K. Studies in Numerical Analysis.
Scaife, Charles W., jt. auth. see Baum, Stuart J.
Scalapino, Robert A. & Yu, George T. The Chinese Anarchist Movement.
Scalapino, Robert A. & Sung-joo, Han, eds. United States- Korea Relations.
Scales, Pat R., jt. ed. see Aaron, Shirley L.
Scaletta, jt. auth. see Cameron.
Scalf, Cherie & Waters, Kenneth. Dating & Relating.
Scalia, Toni. Bitches & Abdicators. Katz, Herb, ed.
Scally, Kevin. How to Wake a Sleeping Beauty.
Scandizzo, Pasquale L., jt. auth. see Knudsen, Odin K.
Scanlin, Margery, jt. auth. see Kraus, Richard.
Scanlon, Leo. The Sixty-Eight Thousand: Principles & Programming.
Scanlon, Leo J. The WordPerfect Book (Covering Versions 4.0 & 4.1)
Scanlon, Mark, jt. auth. see Grill, Tom.
Scanlon, Noel. Apparitions.
Scanlon, William, jt. auth. see Holahan, John.
Scanlon, William, et al. Long-Term Care: Current Experience & a Framework for Analysis.
Scannell, David. The Hood.
Scannell, Vernon. Ring of Truth.
Scaravelli, Paola & Cohen, Jon. Cooking from an Italian Garden: Classic Meatless Recipes from Antipasti to Dessert.
Scarborough, Dorothy. Supernatural in Modern Fiction.
--The Wind.
Scarborough, Elizabeth A. The Unicorn Creed.
Scarborough, John. Facets of Hellenic Life.
Scarborough, Stan & Warren, William E. Option Football: Concepts & Techniques for Winning.
Scardina, Phillip. Aris, the Christmas Wolf.
Scarff, R. W. & Torloni, H. Histological Typing of Breast Tumours.
Scarlatti, Alessandro. Telemaco. Brown, Howard M., ed.
Scarne, John. Scarne's Complete Guide to Gambling.
--Scarne's Guide to Casino Gambling.
--Scarne's Guide to Modern Poker.
Scarr, Sandra, ed. Psychology & Children: Current Research & Practice.
Scarrett, D. Property Management.
Scarry, John, jt. auth. see Kirby, Lee.
Scarry, Richard. Pig Will & Pig Won't.
--Richard Scarry's Busy Houses.
--Richard Scarry's Great Big Air Book.
--Richard Scarry's Lowly Worm Car & Truck Book.
--Richard Scarry's Peasant Pig & the Terrible Dragon.
--Richard Scarry's Stories to Color: With Lowly Worm & Mr. Paint Pig.
--Richard Scarry's Toy Book.
Scarzella, Patrizia. Steel & Style: The Story of Alessi Household Ware.
Scase, Richard & Goffee, Robert. The Entrepreneurial Middle Class.
Scase, Richard, ed. Readings in the Swedish Class Structure.
Scattergood, John, ed. see Skelton, John.
Scavo, Janet. The Condominium Home: A Special Marketing Challenge. Allen, Patricia, ed.
Schaad, Esther C. & Wiese, Edna E. Reflections - Nineteen Hundred to Nineteen Fifty.
Schaad, Hans P. Rhine Pirates. Crawford, Elizabeth D., tr.
Schaaf, James L., tr. see Aland, Kurt.
Schaap, A. P., ed. Singlet Molecular Oxygen.
Schaap, Dick. Sport.
--Steinbrenner!
Schaap, James C. Home Free.
Schaar, John H. Legitimacy in the Modern State.
Schabert, Kyrill, tr. see Winterfeld, Henry.
Schacheter, C., jt. auth. see Salzer, F.
Schachman, Howard K. Ultracentrifugation in Biochemistry.
Schacht, Hjalmar H. Confessions of the Old Wizard.
Schachtel, Hyman J. How to Meet the Challenge of Life & Death.
Schachter, et al. Employment Practices for the Professional Firm.
Schachter, Albert, jt. auth. see Ellis, C. Douglas.
Schachter, Bruce J., jt. auth. see Ahuja, Narendra.
Schachter, Carl, jt. auth. see Aldwell, Edward.
Schachter, Julius & Dawson, Chandler. Human Chlamydial Infections.
Schachter, Victor, et al. AIDS: A Manager's Guide.
Schachter, Zalman M. & Hoffman, Edward. Sparks of Light: Counseling in the Hasidic Tradition.
Schackleton, V. J., jt. auth. see Davies, D. R.
Schade, Charlene. Move with Me from A to Z.
Schade, D., jt. auth. see Busch, G.
Schade, J. see Wiener, Norbert & Schade, J. P.
Schade, J. P., jt. auth. see Wiener, Norbert.
Schadewald, Robert J. & Dickey, William. The DBASE II Guide for Small Business.
Schadlich, Hans J. Approximation. Winston, Richard & Winston, Clara, trs.
Schaeck, Elisabeth, jt. auth. see Koch, Walter A.
Schaefer, Charles E., et al. Therapies for Psychosomatic Disorders in Children.
Schaefer, G. & Klingenberg, M., eds. Energy Conservation in Biological Membranes: April 6-8, 1978, Mosbach, Germany.
Schaefer, Henry F., ed. Methods of Electronic Structure Theory.
Schaefer, Jack. The Canyon.
--The Collected Stories of Jack Schaefer.
--Mavericks.
--Old Ramon.
--Old Ramon.
--Short Novels of Jack Schaefer.
Schaefer, Johanna. A Walk Toward Peace.
Schaefer, Ludwig F., et al. The Shaping of Western Civilization.
Schaefer, Richard T. Racial & Ethnic Groups.
Schaefer, Rudolph J. J. E. Buttersworth, 19th-Century Marine Painter.
Schaefer, Vernon J. We Ate Gooseberries: Growing up on a Minnesota Farm During the Depression.
Schaeffer, Dirk L., tr. see Cohen, Rudolf.
Schaeffer, Edith. Everybody Can Know.
--Lifelines: The Ten Commandments for Today.
--The Tapestry.
Schaeffer, Elizabeth, jt. auth. see Albright, John.
Schaeffer, Howard. Data Center Operations: A Guide to Effective Planning, Processing & Performance.
Schaeffer, O. A. & Zaehringer, J., eds. Potassium Argon Dating.
Schaeffer, S. Allyn. The Oil Painter's Guide to Painting Skies.
--The Oil Painter's Guide to Painting Trees.
Schaeffer, Susan F. Falling.
--Mainland: A Novel.
Schaefgen, J. R., jt. ed. see Pearce, E. M.
Schaerf, C., ed. see International School on Electro & Photonuclear Reactions Staff.
Schafer, Dan, ed. see Waite Group Staff.
Schafer, Eldon L., jt. auth. see Decoster, Don T.
Schafer, Eldon L., et al. Practical Financial Management for Dental Practice Administration. Center for Research in Ambulatory Health Care Administration Staff, ed.
Schafer, Harald. Chemical Transport Reactions. Frankfort, Hans, tr.
Schafer, Mike & McKinney, Kevin. Passenger Train Annual, 1987.
Schafer, R. W. & Markel, J. D., eds. Speech Analysis.
Schaff, A. Structuralism & Marxism.
Schaff, Adam. History & Truth.
--Language & Cognition. Cohen, Robert S., ed. Wojtasiewicz, Olgierd, tr. from Pol.
Schaff, M. E. & Siebring, B. R. Basic Chemistry: Problems Book.
Schaff, M. E., jt. auth. see Siebring, B. R.
Schaffer, Evelyn B. Community Policing.
Schaffer, Francis A., et al. Who Is For Life?
Schaffer, H. R. Child Care & the Family.
Schaffer, H. R., ed. see Centre for Advanced Study in the Developmental Sciences Study Group Staff.
Schaffer, James & Todd, Colleen. Christian Wives: Women Behind the Evangelists.
Schaffer, Jeffery P., et al. The Pacific Crest Trail: Vol. 1, California.
Schaffer, Ulrich. Greater Than Our Hearts: Prayers & Reflections.
--A Growing Love: Meditations on Marriage & Commitment.
--Searching for You.
--Surprised by Light.
Schaffner, Kenneth F. Nineteenth Century Aether Theories.
--Three-Acylcyclopentenes & Five-Acylbiyclo (2.1.0) Pentanes: Photochemical & Thermal Isomerizations.
Schaffner, Nicholas. The Boys from Liverpool.
Schaffter, Dorothy. War & Military Courts: Judicial Interpretation of Its Meaning.
Schaible, P. J., jt. auth. see Patrick, Homer.
Schaie, K. Warner, jt. ed. see Baltes, Paul B.
Schaie, Warner K. & Geiwitz, James. Readings in Adult Development & Aging.
Schaill, William S., jt. auth. see Judson, Horace.
Schain, George M. Saving Time & Taxes in Planning & Preparing Estate, Gift, & Fiduciary Returns.
Schain, Martin A., jt. ed. see Cerny, Philip G.
Schajowicz, F., et al. Histological Typing of Bone Tumours.
Schaldach, M. & Furman, S., eds. Advances in Pacemaker Technology.
Schaldach, M. & Hohmann, D., eds. Advances in Artificial Hip & Knee Joint Technology.
Schalet, Lilian L. Reality: Glimpses of Life.
Schalit, M. Guide to the Literature of the Sugar Industry.
Schalkwijk, Bob & Lincoln, Nina. Ninos, Children of Mexico.
Schall, James V. Liberation Theology in Latin America.
Schall, Keith L., ed. Stony the Road: Essays from the Hampton Institute Archives.
Schall, Lawrence D. & Haley, Charles W. Introduction to Financial Management.
Schall, Lawrence D., jt. auth. see Haley, Charles W.
Schall, William E. Activity-Oriented Mathematics.
Schaller, D. A., jt. auth. see Lornell, R.
Schaller, Frank, tr. see Marmont, Auguste F.
Schaller, George B. Deer & the Tiger: A Study of Wildlife in India.
--The Mountain Gorilla: Ecology & Behavior.
Scham, Alan. Lyautey in Morocco: Protectorate Administration, 1912-1925.
Schampers, Karel & Van Colmjon, Godert. The Rodin Museum.
Schanda, E., ed. Remote Sensing for Environmental Sciences.
Schandel, Terry K. Tax Tactics for Salespersons.
--Tax Tactics for Teachers.
--Tax Tactics for the Retired.
--Tax Tactics for the Singled & Divorced.
Schang, F. C. Visiting Cards of Painters.
Schank, Kenneth, jt. ed. see Arnold, Joseph.
Schantz, Daniel. Upside Down Eddie.
Schantz, William T. & Jackson, Janice E. Review Outlines & Materials for Business Law & CPA Law Review.
Schanz, Holly L. Greek Sculptural Groups: Archaic & Classical.
Schanz, Johannes. Mitteilungen Ueber Die Besiedelung Des Kilimandscharo.
Schanzer, Stephan N., jt. auth. see Brown, Herbert P.
Schaper, Jo. W.A.M.T.
Schapiro. Guernica: Studies - Postscripts.
Schapiro, Leonard see Hayward, Max.
Schapiro, Meyer. Modern Art-19th & 20th Century: Selected Papers.
Schara, August W. All the Presidents Plus: An Insight into Moments of History Through Biorhythms.
Scharf, Bella. Illustrated Patchwork Crochet: Contemporary Granny Squares for Clothing & Home Decorating.
Scharf, Peter L., jt. auth. see Hickey, Joseph E.
Scharff, B. Basics of Electric Appliance Servicing.
Scharff, Robert. The Complete Book of Home Remodeling.
--Complete Book of Wood Finishing.
Scharffenberg, John A. Problems with Meat As Human Food.
Scharkemann, Martin N. Stephen: A Singular Saint.
Scharlemann, Martin H. Qumran & Corinth.
Scharmann, A., jt. ed. see Oberhofer, M.
Scharp, Hal. Freshwater Angler's Clinic.
Scharper, Philip J., jt. ed. see Eagleson, John.
Scharrer, B., ed. see International Symposium on Neurosecretion, Kiel, 1969.
Schary, Dore. Case History of a Movie. Kupelnick, Bruce S., ed.
Schat, Stan. Business & Home Applications for the Macintosh Using Microsoft BASIC.
Schatt, Stan. Multiplan on the Macintosh: Including Word, File & Chart.
Schatten, Robert. Theory of Cross-Spaces.
Schatz, K. W., jt. auth. see Heimenz, U.
Schatzberg, Alan F. Common Treatment Problems in Depression.
Schatzman, E. L. Structure of the Universe.
Schaub, Ardella, jt. auth. see Davison, June.
Schauber, Ellen. The Syntax & Semantics of Questions in Navajo. Hankamer, Jorge, ed.
Schauder, P., jt. ed. see Creutzfeldt, W.
Schauenstein, E., et al. Aldehydes in Biological Systems: Their Natural Occurence & Biological Activities.
Schauer, Fred, jt. auth. see Gunther, Gerald.
Schaufelberger, W., ed. see IFAC-FIP International Conference Staff.
Schauffler, Robert H. Florestan: The Life & Work of Robert Schumann.
Schaum, Konrad, ed. Deutsche Lyrik.
Schaumann, B. & Alter, M. Dermatoglyphics in Medical Disorders.
Scheader, Catherine. Contributions of Women: Music.
Scheaffer, R. L. & Mendenhall, Wm. Introduction to Probability: Theory & Applications.
Scheaffer, Richard & McClave, James. Statistics for Engineers.
Scheaffer, Richard L., jt. auth. see Mendenhall, William.
Schebitz, H. & Wilkens, H. Atlas of Radiographic Anatomy of the Dog & Cat.
--Atlas of Radiographic Anatomy of the Horse.
Schechner, Richard. Public Domain.
Schechter, Alan N. & Dean, Ann. The Impact of Protein Chemistry on the Biomedical Sciences.
Schechter, Alan N., jt. ed. see Anfinsen, C. B.
Schechter, Betty. Dreyfus Affair: A National Scandal.
Schechter, Gil. Learn BASIC Programming in Fourteen Days on Your Commodore 64.
Schechter, Lucille H., jt. auth. see Marks, Betty.
Schechter, Roger E. Unfair Trade Practices & Intellectual Property.
Schechter, Solomon. Studies in Judaism.
Schechtman, Joseph B. The Arab Refugee Problem.
Scheck, Jennifer, jt. auth. see Duffy, Gloria C.
Scheck, Joann. Bible Pop-O-Rama Books. Incl. God Loves His People; When Jesus Was a Baby; Jesus Tells a Story; Jesus Does Great Things. Augsburg Fortress.
Scheckels, Theodore F., Jr. Debating: Applied Rhetorical Theory.
Schecter, Arnold J., ed. Drug Dependence & Alcoholism, Vol. 1: Biomedical Issues.
--Drug Dependence & Alcoholism, Vol. 2: Social & Behavioral Issues.
Schede, Martin, jt. auth. see Krencker, Daniel.
Scheduin, C. B. & McCarty, J. W. Urbanization in Australia.
Schedvin, C. B., jt. auth. see McCarty, J. W.
Scheel, H. J., jt. auth. see Elwell, D.
Scheele, Matt. Art Boggs, Private Investigator.
Scheer, David. PG: A Parental Guide to Rock.
Scheer, Richard K., jt. auth. see Carney, James D.
Scheer, Robert. With Enough Shovels: Reagan, Bush, & Nuclear War.
Scheerenberger, R. C. Deinstitutionalization & Institutional Reform.
Scheffer, V., tr. see Sinai, Y. G.
Scheffer, Victor B. Natural History of Marine Mammals.
Scheffler, Israel. Reason & Teaching.
Scheffler, Linda. Help Thy Neighbor: How Counseling Works & When It Doesn't.
--Help Thy Neighbor: How Counseling Works & When It Doesn't.
Scheffler, Wolfgang. Goldsmiths: An Main und Neckar Daten - Werke -Zeichen.
--Goldsmiths: Des Ostallgaus Daten - Werke - Zeichen.
Scheflen, Albert. How Behavior Means.
Schehr, Lawrence R., tr. see Serres, Michel.
Scheib, W., jt. auth. see Knop, A.
Scheibe, E. The Logical Analysis of Quantum Mechanics.
Scheick, William J. Critical Essays on Jonathan Edwards.
Scheick, William J. & Doggett, Joella. Guide to Seventeenth-Century American Poetry: A Reference Guide.
Scheid, Ann. Pasadena: Crown of the Valley.
Scheidel, Thomas M. Speech Communication & Human Interaction.
Scheidell, John M. Advertising, Prices & Consumer Reaction: A Dynamic Analysis.
Scheidler, Joseph M. Closed: Ninety-Nine Ways to Stop Abortion.
Scheidt, David L., tr. see Lubkoll, Hans-Georg & Wiesnet, Eugen.
Scheidt, David L., tr. see Rommel, Kurt.

Authors

Scheidt, David L., tr. see Soelle, Dorothee.
Scheidt, David L., tr. see Westermann, Claus.
Scheidt, David L., tr. see Zickgraf, Cordula.
Scheie, Harold G. & Alert, Daniel M. Textbook of Ophthalmology.
Scheifele, G., jt. auth. see Stiefel, E. L.
Scheimann, Eugene & Neimark, Paul. Doctor's Sensible Approach to Dieting & Weight Control.
Schein, Bruce E. Following the Way: The Setting of John's Gospel.
Schein, Edgar H., et al. Coercive Persuasion.
Schein, Martin, jt. ed. see Goodman, Irving.
Schein, Martin W., ed. Social Hierarchy & Dominance.
Scheinberg, I. Herbert & Sternlieb, Irmin. Wilson's Disease.
Scheiner, Irwin, jt. ed. see Najita, Tetsuo.
Scheingold, Stuart A., jt. ed. see Lindberg, Leon N.
Scheinkman, Jose A., jt. ed. see Green, Jerry.
Scheinmann, F. An Introduction to Spectroscopic Methods for the Identification of Organic Compounds.
Scheinmann, F., jt. ed. see Roberts, S. M.
Scheler, Max. Man's Place in Nature. Meyerhoff, Hans, tr. from Ger.
Scheline, R. R. Mammalian Metabolism of Plant Xenobiotics.
Schell, Catherine, jt. auth. see Kunz, Marilyn.
Schell, Frank R. Practical Problems in Mathematics--Metric System.
Schell, Frank R. & Matlock, Bill J. Practical Problems in Mathematics for Welders.
Schell, Jessie. Sudina.
Schell, Leo, ed. Diagnostic & Criterion Referenced Reading Tests: Review & Evaluation.
Schell, Mildred. Look, Listen & Learn: A Primary Class Activity Packet on the Americas.
Schell, Mildred, ed. Points of Entry.
Schell, Orville. To Get Rich Is Glorious: China in the Eighties.
--Watch Out for the Foreign Guests! China Encounters the West.
Schellenberg, Kathryn. Computer Studies: Computers in Society.
Scheller, Klaus. The Larval Serum Proteins of Insects.
Scheller, Mary D. Power of 3: A New Model for Hospital and Nursing Home Care.
Scheller, William G. Country Walks Near New York.
--Train Trips.
Schellinger, Mary A., ed. FYI... Resources on Local Government, 1983-1986.
Schemenaur, P. J., ed. Writer's Market, 1983.
Schemering, Christopher. The Soap Opera Encyclopedia.
Schenck, H. V., jt. auth. see Cichy, F. C.
Schenck, P. A. Advances in Organic Geochemistry, 1968: Proceedings.
Schenk, Erich. Mozart & His Times.
Schenk, Fredrick J. & Anderson, James V. Aging Together, Serving Together: A Guide to Congregational Planning for the Aging.
Schenk, G. H. Organic Functional Group Analysis, Theory & Development.
Schenk, George. The Complete Shade Gardener.
Schenkein, James N., ed. Studies in the Organization of Conversational Interaction.
Schenkel, Chris. How to Watch Football on TV.
Schenkel, S. Giving Away Success: How Women Get Stuck & What to Do About It.
Schenkkan, Robert, tr. see Ibsen, Henrik.
Schepp, Brad & Hastie, Stephen M. The Complete Passive Solar Home Book.
Scheppach, Raymond C. & Ehrlich, Everett M. Energy-Policy Analysis & Congressional Action.
Scher, Bob. The Fear of Cooking: The Absolute Foolproof Cookbook for Beginners (& Everyone Else)
Scheraga, H. A., jt. auth. see Poland, D.
Scheraga, Harold A. Protein Structure.
Scheraga, Mona, jt. auth. see Maculaitis, Jean D.
Scherer, Donald, et al. Introduction to Philosophy: From Wonder to World View.
Scherer, Felicia. For the Shape of Your Life.
Scherer, Jacqueline & Shepherd, Gary. Victimization of the Weak: Contemporary Social Reactions.
Scherer, James A. Global Living Here & Now.
Scherer, John L., ed. China Facts & Figures Annual.
--China Facts & Figures Annual, 1978-1984.
Scheret, J. L. China Facts Figures Annual 1987.
Scherfig, Hans. Stolen Spring. Brondum, Jack, tr. from Danish.
Scherman, Katharine. Daughter of Fire: A Portrait of Iceland.
Schermer, Judith. Mouse in House.
Schermerhorn, John R., Jr., et al. Managing Organizational Behavior.
Schermers, H. G., jt. auth. see Brinkhorst, L. J.
Scherr, Raquel L., jt. auth. see Lakoff, Robin T.
Scherrei, Rita A., jt. auth. see Astin, Alexander W.
Scherrer, Robert A. & Whitehouse, Michael W., eds. Anti-Inflamatory Agents: Chemistry & Pharmacology.
Schertel, Lothar, et al. Atlas of Xeroradiography.
Schertle, Alice. Hob Goblin & the Skeleton.
--Hob Goblin & the Skeleton.
--My Two Feet.
Schettler, G., ed. Lipids & Lipidoses.
Schettler, G., ed. see International Symposium on Atherosclerosis Staff.
Schettler, Margret & Schettler, Rolf. Kashmir, Ladakh & Zanskar: A Travel Survival Kit.
Schettler, Rolf, jt. auth. see Schettler, Margret.
Schetzen, Martin. The Volterra & Weiner Theories of Nonlinear Systems.
Scheuer, Nikki, tr. see Saint-Aubin, Charles G.
Scheuer, P. Liver Biopsy Interpretation.
Scheuer, Paul J. Chemistry of Marine Natural Products.
Scheuer, Sidney H. The Ethics of International Economics: An Innovative Approach to World Affairs.
Scheunert, M. S. The Theory of Lie Superalgebras: An Introduction.
Scheurleer, Lunsingh & Charleston, Robert J. English & Dutch Ceramics.
Scheurmann, Ines. Water Plants in the Aquarium.
Scheve, Larry G. Elements of Biochemistry.
Scheven, Yvette, ed. Bibliographies for African Studies 1980-1983.
Schevill, James. The Mayan Poems.
Schevill, Margot B. Evolution in Textile Design from the Highlands of Guatemala.
Schey, John A. Metal Deformation Processes: Friction & Lubrication.
Schiani, Alfred. A Former Marine Tells It Like It Was, & Is.
Schick, Allen. Congress & Money: Budgeting, Spending & Taxing.
Schick, Allen, ed. Perspective on Budgeting (Par Classics)
Schick, Edwin A. Revelation-The Last Book of the Bible.
Schick, Kurt. Principios of Electricidad.
Schickel, Richard. D. W. Griffith: An American Life.
--Disney Version.
--Gary Cooper: Legends.
--James Cagney: A Celebration.
Schieber, Sylvester J. & George, Patricia M. Retirement Income Opportunities in an Aging America: Vol. 1: Coverage & Benefit Entitlement.
Schiebler, T. H., et al, eds. see International Congress of Histochemistry & Cytochemistry, 2nd, Frankfurt Am Main, 1964.
Schiefelbusch, Richard L. & Bricker, Dianne D., eds. Early Language: Acquisition & Intervention.
Schiefelbusch, Richard L. & Pickar, Joanne, eds. Acquisition of Communicative Competence.
Schiefer, W., et al. Clinical Echo-Encephalography. Klinger, M., tr.
Schieffelin, Bambi B., jt. auth. see Ochs, Elinor.
Schierlova, M., tr. see Stembera, Z., et al.
Schiff, Eric, tr. see Ikle, Max.
Schiff, Gert & Waetzoldt, Stephen. German Masters of the Nineteenth Century: Paintings & Drawings from the Federal Republic of Germany.
Schiff, Marilyn, jt. auth. see Flato, Anne.
Schiff, Martin, jt. auth. see Rosenberg, Marvin.
Schiff, Michael. Business Experience with Value Added Taxation.
Schiff, Roselyn L., et al. Communication Strategy: A Guide to Speech Preparation.
Schiff, Stuart D., ed. Whispers VI.
Schiff, William. Perception: An Applied Approach.
Schiff, Ze'ev & Ya'ari, Ehud. Israel's Lebanon War. Friedman, Ina, tr.
Schiffer, Don & Duroska, Lud. Football Rules in Pictures.
Schiffer, M. B. & Gumerman, G. J., eds. Conservation Archaeology: A Guide for Cultural Resources Management Studies.
Schiffer, Mortimer, jt. auth. see Slavson, S. R.
Schiffman, Leon G. & Kanuk, Leslie L. Consumer Behavior.
Schiffman, Ted, jt. auth. see Lariviere, Susan.
Schiffman, Yale M. & D'Alessio, Gregory J. Limits to Solar & Biomass Energy Growth.
Schifrin, Ben. High Sierra Hiking Guide to Pinecrest.
Schilcher, Florian Von & Tennant, Neil. Philosophy, Evolution & Human Nature.
Schild, Erich, et al. Environmental Physics in Construction: Its Application in Architectural Design.
Schilder, Klass. The Trilogy.
Schildt, Herbert. Advanced Turbo Pascal: Programming & Techniques.
--Advanced Turbo Prolog.
Schildt, John, ed. The Lincoln Calendar.
Schildt, John W. Roads to Gettysburg.
--September Echoes: A Study of the Maryland Campaign of 1862.
Schileo, jt. auth. see Weissert.
Schill, Gottfried. Catenanes, Rotaxanes & Knots. Boeckmann, J., tr. from Ger.
Schiller, Bradley R. The Economics of Poverty & Discrimination.
Schiller, Eric. Catalan.
--Gruenfeld Defense, Russian Variations.
Schiller, Ferdinand C. Humanism: Philosophical Essays.
Schiller, Friedrich Von see Von Schiller, Friedrich.
Schiller, John A., ed. The American Poor.
Schiller, Siegfried, et al. Electron Beam Technology.
Schilling, Betty. Two Kittens Are Born: From Birth to Two Months.
Schilling, K., jt. ed. see Mutter, K. H.
Schilling, Patricia M. Designsource Nineteen Eighty-Six.
Schillinger, Joseph. Mathematical Basis of the Arts.
Schilpp, Paul A. Kant's Pre-Critical Ethics. Beck, Lewis W., ed.
Schilt, A. A. Analytical Applications of 1, 10-Phen'-antroline & Related Compounds.
Schimanke, Dieter, jt. auth. see Von Loelhoeffel, Dieter.
Schimke, Robert T. & Katunuma, Nobuhiko, eds. Intracellular Protein Turnover.
Schimmel, jt. auth. see Lieberman.
Schimmel, Herbert D. & Cate, Phillip D. The Henri de Toulouse-Lautrec: W. H. B. Sands Correspondence.
Schimmels, Cliff. I Was a High School Drop-In.
--Rites of Autumn.
--Rivals of Spring.
--Summer Winds.
--When Junior Highs Invade Your Home.
--Winter Hunger.
Schimmels, Cliff & Resnik, Hank. The Surprising Years: Understanding Your Changing Adolescent.
Schinazi, R. F. & Nahmias, A. J., eds. AIDS in Children, Adolescents & Heterosexual Adults: An Interdisciplinary Approach.
Schinder, James, jt. auth. see Davidson, Sidney.
Schindler, Anton. Life of Beethoven. Moscheles, Ignace, tr.
Schindler, Anton F. Beethoven As I Knew Him. MacArdle, Donald W., ed. Jolly, Constance S., tr.
Schindler, George. Ventriloquism: Magic with Your Voice.
Schindler, Marian, jt. auth. see Schindler, Robert.
Schindler, Robert & Schindler, Marian. Mission Possible.
Schiotz, Fredrik A. One Man's Story.
Schipkowensky, Nikola. Psychotherapy Versus Iatrogeny: A Confrontation for Physicians.
Schirmer, Richard E., jt. auth. see Noggle, Joseph H.
Schirmer, Roger E. Modern Methods of Pharmaceutical Analysis.
Schirokauer, Conrad. A Brief History of Chinese & Japanese Civilizations.
Schirra, Walter M. & Billings, Richard N. Schirra's Space.
Schirren, C. Praktische Andrologie.
Schittkowski, K. Nonlinear Programming Codes.
Schittkowski, K., jt. auth. see Hock, W.
Schlachter, Gail & Thomison, Dennis. Library Science Dissertations, Nineteen Seventy-Three to Nineteen Eighty-One: An Annotated Bibliography.
Schlachter, Gail A., jt. auth. see Purcell, Gary R.
Schlachter, Gail A., ed. The Service Imperative for Libraries: Essays in Honor of Margaret E. Monroe.
Schlack, A. L., jt. auth. see Sandor, Bela I.
Schlag, John D., jt. ed. see Petre-Quadens, Olga.
Schlagenhauff, Reinhold E., jt. auth. see Warfel, John H.
Schlaifer, R. & Heron, S. D. Development of Aircraft Engines & Fuels.
Schlaifer, Robert. Computer Programs for Elementary Decision Analysis.
Schlaifer, Robert, jt. auth. see Raiffa, Howard.
Schlant, Ernestine, jt. auth. see Feix, Irmgard.
Schlee, Ann. The Consul's Daughter.
--Guns of Darkness.
--The Proprietor.
--Rhine Journey.
Schlee, Ernst. German Folk Art.
Schlegel, Dorothy. Gem Stones of the United States.
Schlegel, H. G. Microbial Energy Conversion.
Schleh, Edward C. The Management Tactician: Executive Tactics for Getting Results.
Schleher, D. C., ed. MTI Radar.
Schleiden, Hans W. Tabellenbuch zur Umrechnung metrischer Masse in englische Masse; Tables for the Conversion Metric System of Measurement to the British System.
Schleier, Curt. You'd Better Not Tell.
Schleiermacher, Friedrich. Brief Outline on the Study of Theology. Tice, Terrence N., tr.
--The Christian Faith. Mackintosh, H. R. & Stewart, J. S., eds.
--The Life of Jesus. Verheyden, Jack C. & Keck, Leander E., eds. MacLean, Gilmour, tr. from Ger.
Schleifer, James T. The Making of Tocqueville's "Democracy in America"
Schlein, Miriam. The Girl Who Would Rather Climb Trees.
--I Hate It. Rubin, Caroline, ed.
--Metric: The Modern Way to Measure.
--Metric: The Modern Way to Measure.
Schlein, Miriam R. & Ito, Susuu. A Color Atlas of Insect Tissues Via the Flea.
Schleisman, Jessie B. Golden Blue of the Sunset.
Schleker, Peggy J., ed. see Weisbrod, Harry, et al.
Schlensker, K. H. Atlas of Ultrasonic Diagnosis in Obstetrics & Gynecology.
Schlepper, M. & Olsson, B., eds. Cardiac Arrythmias: Diagnosis, Prognosis, Therapy-Proceedings.
Schlerath, B. Sanskrit Vocabulary Arranged According to Word Families with Meanings in English, German & Spanish.
Schlesinger, Arthur M. In Retrospect: The History of a Historian.
Schlesinger, Arthur M., Jr. Age of Roosevelt: The Crisis of the Old Order.
--American As Reformer.
--Imperial Presidency.
--Nothing Stands Still: Essays by Arthur M. Schlesinger Jr.
--The Politics of Upheaval (The Age of Roosevelt)
--Prelude to Independence: The Newspaper War on Britain, 1764-1776.
--Thousand Days: John F. Kennedy in the White House.
Schlesinger, Arthur M., Jr., ed. & intro. by. The Dynamics of World Power. Incl. Vol. 1. Western Europe; Vol. 2. Eastern Europe & the Soviet Union; Vol. 3. Latin America; Vol. 4. Far East; Vol. 5. United Nations, Middle East, Subsaharan Africa. McGraw.
Schlesinger, Arthur M., Jr., ed. The Equal Employment Opportunities Commission.
Schlesinger, Arthur M., Sr. Critical Period in American Religion 1875-1900. Wolf, Richard C., ed.
Schlesinger, B. The Upper Brainstem in the Human: Its Nuclear Configuration & Vascular Supply.
Schlesinger, Benjamin. Sexual Behaviour in Canada: Patterns & Problems.
Schlesinger, Eric, jt. auth. see Settle, Wendy.
Schlesinger, Kurt, jt. auth. see Groves, Philip M.
Schlesinger, Rudolf. Federalism in Central & Eastern Europe.
--History of Communist Party of the U. S. S. R., Past & Present.
Schlesselman, R. & Ahrens, L. Dear Father in Heaven.
Schlicht, Adolf, jt. auth. see Angolia, John R.
Schlier, C., ed. Molecular Beams & Reaction Kinetics.
Schlieve, Paul & Berghauser, Tom W. The Illustrated AutoCAD Book (2.18)
Schlieve, Paul L. Illustrated Turbo Pascal 3.01.
Schlink, Basilea. Behold His Love.
--A Matter of Life & Death.
--Mirror of Conscience.
Schlipf, Frederick L., ed. Collective Bargaining in Libraries.
Schlitt, W. J. & Larson, W. C., eds. Gold & Silver Leaching, Recovery & Economics.
Schlitt, W. Joseph, ed. Salts & Brines Nineteen Eighty-Five.
Schlittler, Emil, ed. Antihypertensive Agents.
Schlitzer, Albert L., ed. Spirit & Power of Christian Secularity.
Schlobin, Roger C. Andre Norton: A Primary & Secondary Bibliography.
--The Literature of Fantasy: An Annotated Bibliography of Modern Fantasy Fiction.
Schlobin, Roger C., jt. auth. see Tymn, Marshall B.
Schlobin, Roger C., ed. see Clark, Beverly L.
Schlobin, Roger C., ed. see Davis, J. Madison.
Schlobin, Roger C., ed. see Elliot, Jeffrey M.
Schlobin, Roger C., ed. see Hassler, Donald M.
Schlobin, Roger C., ed. see Touponce, William F.
Schloegl, Irmgard, tr. from Chinese. The Zen Teaching of Rinzai (Rinzai Roku)
Schlomann, A. Illustrierte Technische Woerterbucher: Maschinenelemente.
Schloss, Patrick J. Social Development of Handicapped Children & Adolescents.
Schloss, Patrick J., jt. auth. see Miller, Sidney R.
Schlossberg, Dan. The Baseball Catalog.
--The Baseball Catalog.
--The Baseball Catalogue.
Schlossberg, David. Megillon on Sefer Rus - in Hebrew.
Schlossberg, Nancy K., et al. Perspectives on Counseling Adults.
Schlossstein, Steven. Kensei.
Schlote, Werner. British Overseas Trade from 1700 to the 1930's.
Schlozman, Kay L. & Verba, Sidney. Injury to Insult: Unemployment, Class, & Political Response.
Schlueter, David A., jt. auth. see Wendorf, Hulen D.

Authors

Schlueter, Paul. Shirley Ann Grau.
Schlueter, R. A., et al. Wind Turbine Arrays & Power Systems Operation.
Schluger, Paul R., jt. ed. see Scholle, Peter A.
Schlumpf, Lester, ed. Barron's Three-Year Sequence for High School Mathematics.
Schlumph, Margret & Lichtensteiger, Walter, eds. Drugs & Hormones in Brain Development.
Schlunder, E. U., jt. auth. see Afgan, N. H.
Schlunegger, U. P. Advanced Mass Spectrometry: Applications in Organic & Analytical Chemistry.
Schluter, Hans, et al. Index Libycus: Supplement I, Nineteen Seventy to Nineteen Seventy-five.
Schmaehl, D., et al. Iatrogenic Carcinogenesis.
Schmalensee, Richard. The Control of Natural Monopolies.
Schmalhausen, Ivan I. Origin of Terrestrial Vertebrates. Kelso, Leon, tr.
Schmalleger, Frank & Gustafson, Robert. The Social Basis of Criminal Justice: Ethical Issues for the Eighty's.
Schmeckebier, Laurence E. The Art of A. Henry Nordhausen.
Schmeidek, P., ed. Microsurgery for Stroke.
Schmer, Gottfried & Strandjord, Paul E., eds. Current Topics in Coagulation.
Schmerling, E. R., et al, eds. Magneto & Iono Plas: ASR Vo514 Proceedings of Symposium Nine & the COSPAR Interdisciplinary Scientific Commission D of the COSPAR Twenty-fifth Plenary Meeting Held in Graz, Austria, 25 June-7 July 1984.
Schmertz, Herbert. Corporations & the First Amendment.
Schmertz, Herbert & Novak, William. Goodbye to the Low Profile: The Art of Creative Confrontation.
Schmid, Alex P. Political Terrorism: A Research Guide To Concepts, Theories, Data Bases, & Literature.
Schmid, Alex P. & Jongman, A. J. Political Terrorism: A New Guide to Actors & Authors, Databases, & Literature.
Schmid, E., ed. see CISM (International Center for Mechanical Sciences), Department for Mechanics of Defamable Bodies Staff.
Schmid, E. W. & Ziegelmann, H. The Quantum Mechanical Three-Body Problem.
Schmid, Franz. Cell Therapy: A New Dimension in Medicine.
Schmid, George H. The Chemical Basis of Life: General, Organic, & Biological Chemistry for the Health Sciences.
Schmid, Heinrich. Doctrinal Theology of the Evangelical Lutheran Church.
Schmid, Rex E., et al. Contemporary Issues in Special Education.
Schmidman, John. Unions in Post-Industrial Society.
Schmidt, Allan. Computer Graphics in Energy Exploration & Production.
Schmidt, Alvin J. Oligarchy in Fraternal Organizations: A Study in Organizational Leadership.
Schmidt, Arno. Evening Edged in Gold.
Schmidt, Arno B. The Banquet Business.
Schmidt, B. GPSS FORTRAN.
Schmidt, Carol Von see Gerlock, Larry & Von Schmidt, Carol.
Schmidt, Dennis. Kensho.
Schmidt, Donald H., jt. ed. see Pollock, Michael L.
Schmidt, E. M., jt. ed. see Nielsen, M.
Schmidt, Emerson P. Union Power & the Public Interest.
Schmidt, Erich F. Alishar Huyuk, Seasons of 1928-1929.
Schmidt, Frank W. & Willmott, A. John. Thermal Energy Storage & Regeneration.
Schmidt, Garfield C. Basic Linear Algebra with Applications.
Schmidt, Gerald D. & Roberts, Larry S. Foundations of Parasitology.
Schmidt, Gerard F. Hoer Gut Zu: A Beginning German Audio-Lingual Reader.
Schmidt, H. J., jt. ed. see Hartkamper, A.
Schmidt, Harvey & Jones, Tom. Fantasticks.
Schmidt, Helmut & Von Stackelberg, Mark. Modern Polarographic Methods. Maddison, R. E., tr.
Schmidt, Henry J., ed. see Buchner, Georg.
Schmidt, J. E. Analyzer of Medical-Biological Words: A Clarifying Dissection of Medical Terminology, Showing How It Works, for Medics, Paramedics, Students, & Visitors from Foreign Countries.
--English Idioms & Americanisms for Foreign Students, Professionals & Physicians.
--Index of Paramedical Vocabulary.
Schmidt, Jeremy, jt. auth. see Fuller, Steven.
Schmidt, M., et al. The Chemistry of Sulphur, Selenium, Tellurium & Polonium.
Schmidt, Maarten, jt. ed. see Blaauw, Adriaan.
Schmidt, Magdalena. Die Komposition Von Vergils Georgica, Mit Vier Beilagen.
Schmidt, Matthias. Albert Speer: The End of a Myth. Neugroschel, Joachim, tr.
Schmidt, Maurice. How to Achieve Mastery in Painting & Drawing: An Illustrated Guide to the Fundamental Principles & Techniques of Art.
Schmidt, Michael. A Reader's Guide to Fifty British Poets: 1300-1900.
Schmidt, Michelle, jt. auth. see Almond Growers Exchange Staff.
Schmidt, Mike & Walder, Barbara. Always on the Offense.
Schmidt, Nathalie J., jt. ed. see Lennette, Edwin H.
Schmidt, Peggy. Making It Big in the City: A Woman's Guide to Living, Loving, & Working There.
Schmidt, Peggy J. Making It on Your First Job: When You're Young, Inexperienced & Ambitious.
Schmidt, R. A. Coal in America: Reserves, Production & Use.
Schmidt, R. Marilyn. Gardening on the Eastern Seashore.
Schmidt, R. R., jt. auth. see Lemmerz, A. H.
Schmidt, Robert G. Geology, Earthquake Hazards & Land Use in the Helena Area, Montana: A Review.
Schmidt, Steffen W., et al. American Government & Politics Today.
Schmidt, Stephen. Master Recipes.
Schmidt, Steven. Creating the Technical Report.
Schmidt, U., jt. ed. see Dubach, U. C.
Schmidt, Victor E. & Rockcastle, Verne N. Teaching Science with Everyday Things.
Schmidt, W. J. & Keil, A. Polarization Microscopy of Dental Tissues. Middle, P., tr.
Schmidt, W. M. Equations over Finite Fields: An Elementary Approach.
Schmidt, Walt. Spice for Life.
Schmidt, Walter A. Recruiting Evangelism Callers: Enlisting & Coordinating Workers.
Schmidt, Warren H. & Beckhand, Richard. The Fact-Finding Conference.
Schmidtke, G. & Champion, K. S. W. The Mesosphere & Thermosphere.
Schmidt-Koenig, K. Avian Orientation & Navigation.
Schmithals, Walter. Introduction to the Theology of Rudolf Bultmann. Bowden, John, tr.
Schmitt, Barton D., ed. The Child Protection Team Handbook.
Schmitt, Carl. The Crisis of Parliamentary Democracy. Kennedy, Ellen, tr. from Ger.
Schmitt, Conrad J., jt. auth. see Okin, Josee P.
Schmitt, Conrad J., et al. Espanol: A Descubrirlo, Learning Spanish the Modern Way.
Schmitt, Friedrich. Getting along with Difficult People. Schultz, Erich R., tr. from Ger.
Schmitt, Gladys. The Godforgotten.
--Sonnets for an Analyst.
Schmitt, Jack, tr. see Machado de Assis, Joaquim M.
Schmitt, Karl M. Communism in Mexico.
Schmitt, Klaus, ed. Delay & Functional Differential Equations & Their Applications.
Schmitt, Paul, jt. auth. see Industrial Design Magazine Editors.
Schmitt, Peter J. & Massie, Larrie B. Battle Creek: The Place Behind the Products: An Illustrated History.
Schmittroth, John, Jr., ed. Online Database Search Services Directory.
Schmitz, Hubert. Technology & Employment Practices in Developing Countries.
Schmitz, Joseph W. Texan Statecraft, Eighteen Thirty-Six to Eighteen Forty-Five.
Schmitz, Kurt. Langfristplanung in der Energiewirtschaft.
Schmitz, W., ed. Convertibility, Multilateralism & Freedom: World Economic Policy in the Seventies. Essays in Honour of Reinhard Kamitz.
Schmokel, Wolfe W., jt. auth. see Andrea, Alfred J.
Schmookler, Jacob. Invention & Economic Growth.
Schmuck, Patricia A., jt. auth. see Schmuck, Richard A.
Schmuck, Richard A. & Runkel, Philip J. Organizational Training for a School Faculty.
Schmuck, Richard A. & Schmuck, Patricia A. Group Processes in the Classroom.
Schmuck, Richard A., jt. auth. see Schwartz, Mitchell.
Schmudde, Theodore H., jt. auth. see Harper, Robert A.
Schmuhl, Robert, ed. The Responsibilities of Journalism.
Schnabel, Artur. My Life & Music & Reflections on Music.
Schnabel, Ernst. Anne Frank: A Portrait in Courage.
--Anne Frank: A Portrait in Courage.
Schnabel, Tom. Stolen Moments: Conversations with Contemporary Musicians.
Schnackenburg, Rudolf. Christ--Present & Coming. Quinn, Edward, tr. from Ger.
--Present & Future: Modern Aspects of New Testament Theology.
Schneck, Stephen. The Nightclerk.
Schneebaum, Tobias. Keep the River on Your Right.
Schneede, Uwe M., et al. George Grosz: His Life & Work. Flatauer, Susanne, tr.
Schneer, C. J., ed. Crystal Form & Structure.
Schneeweiss, H. & Strecker, H., eds. Contributions to Econometrics & Statistics Today.
Schneider, Benjamin. Staffing Organizations. Porter, Lyman W., ed.
Schneider, Benjamin, jt. auth. see Hall, Douglas T.
Schneider, Carl & Vinovskis, Maris A., eds. The Law & Politics of Abortion.
Schneider, Catherine, ed. More Wife Savers.
Schneider, Daniel E. Od Infinitum.
Schneider, David. The San Francisco Symphony: Music, Maestros & Musicians.
Schneider, David, jt. auth. see Goldstein, Larry J.
Schneider, David I. Handbook of BASIC for the IBM PC.
Schneider, Dennis M., et al. Linear Algebra: A Concrete Approach.
Schneider, Dick. The Harness Horse & Strategic Win Betting.
Schneider, E. L., ed. The Genetics of Aging.
Schneider, Edward D., ed. Questions about the Beginning of Life.
Schneider, Elisabeth. Coleridge, Opium & Kubla Khan.
Schneider, F. Qualitative Organic Microanalysis: Cognition & Recognition of Carbon Compounds.
Schneider, Frank L. Qualitative Organic Microanalysis.
Schneider, Fred W. & Carlson, Stephen P. PCC-From Coast to Coast.
Schneider, G. M., et al, eds. Extraction with Supercritical Gases.
Schneider, G. Michael & Bruell, Steven C. Advanced Programming & Problem Solving with PASCAL.
Schneider, Gertrude. Journey into Terror: The Story of the Riga Ghetto.
Schneider, H. R. The Off-Key Angel.
Schneider, Hans J. Timely & Profitable Help for Troubled Americans.
Schneider, Harold K. Livestock & Equality in East Africa: The Economic Basis for Social Structure.
Schneider, Ilya I. Isadora Duncan: The Russian Years. Magarshack, David, tr.
Schneider, Ira & Korot, Beryl. Video Art.
Schneider, Isidore, tr. see Gorky, Maxim.
Schneider, Joyce A. Stryker's Children.
Schneider, Leo. Lifeline: The Story of Your Circulatory System.
--Long Life to You: Modern Medicine at Work.
--Microbes in Your Life.
--You & Your Cells.
--You & Your Senses.
Schneider, Leo & Ames, Maurice U. Wings in Your Future: Aviation for Young People.
Schneider, Madelin, jt. auth. see Tucker, Georgina.
Schneider, Meg, ed. see Arneson, D. J.
Schneider, Meg, ed. see Milton, Hilary.
Schneider, Meg, ed. see Nash, Bruce.
Schneider, Meg F. Pregnant; With Style!
Schneider, Meir. Self Healing.
Schneider, Mitchell, tr. see Trifonov, Yuri.
Schneider, Nina. The Woman Who Lived in a Prologue.
Schneider, Otto & Neumann, I. B., eds. Der Anbrunch.
Schneider, Peter. The Wall Jumper. Hafrey, Leigh, tr.
Schneider, Peter, jt. auth. see Lieverman, Theodore.
Schneider, Pierre. Louvre Dialogues. Southgate, Patsy, tr. from Fr.
Schneider, Raymond K. HVAC Control Systems.
Schneider, Richard C. Head & Neck Injuries in Football: Mechanisms, Treatment & Prevention.
Schneider, Richard H. Freedom's Holy Light: Like the Country She Symbolizes, She Stands Tall & Proud, Upholding...
Schneider, Steven J. & Bacon, Paul. The International Album of Wine: Your Personal Record of Wine Labels & Tastes.
Schneider, Stuart, jt. auth. see Etter, Roberta.
Schneider, Susan W. Jewish & Female: Choices & Changes in Our Lives Today.
Schneider, Toni, jt. ed. see Bernasconi, J.
Schneider, W., Jr., jt. ed. see Holst, J. J.
Schneider, Wolf. Babylon Is Everywhere: The City As Man's Fate. Sammet, Ingeborg & Oldenburg, John, trs.
Schneiderman, Beth K., ed. By & about Women: An Anthology of Short Fiction.
Schneiderman, Leo, jt. ed. see Kornfeld, Alfred D.
Schneiderman, Richard S. A Catalogue Raisonne of the Prints of Sir Francis Seymour Haden.
Schnell, J. D. Zytologie und Mikrobiologie der Vagina.
Schnell, Judith, ed. see Thomas, Martha.
Schnell, William J. How to Witness to a Jehovah's Witness.
Schnepper, Jeff A. How to Pay Zero Taxes: Over One Hundred Fifty Ways to Reduce Your Taxes- to Nothing!
Schneyer, Charlotte A., ed. see International Conference on Mechanisms of Salivary Secretion & Their Regulation-2nd-Birmingham-Ala.-1966.
Schneyer, Leon H., ed. see International Conference on Mechanisms of Salivary Secretion & Their Regulation-2nd-Birmingham-Ala.-1966.
Schnidler, Ruben, jt. auth. see Brawley, Edward A.
Schnidman, Frank & Baker, R. Lisle. Planning for Platted Lands: Land Use Remedies for Lot Sale Subdivisions.
Schnirring, Melissa. The Well-Being Guide to Health Spas in North America.
Schnitzer, Eduard. Emin Pasha, His Life & Work. Schweitzer, George, ed.
Schnitzer, J. G. & Schnitzer, Mechthilde. Schnitzer-Intensive Nutrition, Schnitzer-Normal Nutrition: 14 Day Menu Plan for Both Nutrition Forms.
Schnitzer, Martin. Contemporary Government & Business Relations.
--Contemporary Government & Business Relations.
Schnitzer, Mechthilde, jt. auth. see Schnitzer, J. G.
Schnitzer, Robert J. & Grunberg, Emanuel. Drug Resistance of Microorganisms.
Schnitzlein, H. Norman, et al. Computed Tomography of the Head & Spine: A Photographic Atlas of CT, Gross & Microscopic Anatomy.
Schnitzler, H. & Lieth, H., eds. The Twenty-Five Years International Journal of Biometeorology Index.
Schnotzelhorst, Englebert D. They Came to Praise I. C. C.
Schnurnberger, Lynn. Let There Be Clothes.
--Let There Be Clothes: Forty Thousand Years of Fashion Unveiled.
Schnurr, Constance B. Crazy Lady.
Schock, Al. Schock's Abc's of Telling & Remembering Stories.
--Schock's Emceeing & Unrelated Items.
Schock, T. A. Pratfall.
Schoder, Judith. The Blood Suckers.
Schoder, Stewart A. Project Finance: The Credit Perspective.
Schoderbek, Peter P., et al. Management Systems: Conceptual Considerations.
Schoeck, Helmut. Envy: A Theory of Social Behaviour. Glenny, Michael & Ross, Betty, trs.
Schoeck, R. J., ed. Editing Sixteenth-Century Texts.
Schoell. Marketing: Contemporary Concepts & Practices.
Schoell, William. Spawn of Hell.
Schoen, Carol, et al. The Writing Experience.
Schoen, Elin. Tales of an All-Night Town.
Schoen, Linda, ed. The AMA Book of Skin & Hair Care.
Schoen, Max. Enjoyment of the Arts.
--Thinking about Religion.
Schoen, Sterling H. & Hilgert, Raymond L. Cases in Collective Bargaining & Industrial Relations: A Decisional Approach.
Schoenauer, Norbert, jt. auth. see Bland, John.
Schoenbaum, David. Zabern Nineteen Hundred Thirteen: Consensus Politics in Imperial Germany.
Schoenbaum, Thomas J. Environmental Policy Law: Cases, Readings & Text.
--Islands, Capes, & Sounds: The North Carolina Coast.
Schoenberg, A. Preparative Organic Photochemistry.
Schoenberg, Arnold. Style & Idea.
Schoenberg, H. H., tr. from Ger. Stuckenschmid.
Schoenberg, Harold C. The Great Pianists.
Schoenberg, Robert J. Geneen.
Schoenberg, Sandra & Rosenbaum, Patricia. Neighborhoods That Work: Sources for Viability in the Inner City.
Schoenbrun, David. America Inside Out: At Home & Abroad from Roosevelt to Reagan.
--As France Goes.
--Vietnam: How We Got in, How to Get Out.
Schoenebaum, Eleanora W. Profiles of an Era: The Nixon-Ford Years.
Schoener, Allon. The American Jewish Album: From Sixteen Fifty-Four to the Present.
Schoenfeld, A. Clay & Diegmueller, Karen S. Effective Feature Writing.
Schoenfeld, Charles. God & Country.
Schoenfeld, Eric, ed. see Robbe-Grillet, Alain.
Schoenfeld, H., ed. Epidemiologie, Diagnose, Klinik und Therapie Systemischer Pilzerkrankungen: Ancotil Roche 5-Fluorocytosin.
Schoenfeld, Norman, jt. auth. see Parker, Frank J.
Schoenfeld, Robert. The Chemist's English.
Schoenfeld, Stuart, et al. Bar Mitzvah.
Schoenhofer, Peggy J. Fiddlin' Around.

Schoeninger, Margaret J. Dietary Reconstruction at Chalcatzingo, a Formative Period Site in Morelos, Mexico.
Schoenl, William J. The Intellectual Crisis in English Catholicism: Liberal Catholics, Modernists, & the Vatican in the Late Nineteenth & Early Twentieth Centuries. Stanmsky, Peter & Hume, Leslie, eds.
Schoenman, Helen B., tr. see Schoenman, Theodore.
Schoenman, Theodore, ed. Journey in North America by Alexander Boloni Farkas (Kolozsvar, 1834) Schoenman, Helen B., tr.
Schoenstadt, A. L., et al, eds. Information Linkage Between Applied Mathematics & Industry II.
Schoenstein, Ralph. Every Day Is Sunday.
Schoeny, Donna H. & Decker, Larry E., eds. Community, Educational & Social Impact Perspectives.
Schoeps, Hans J. Paul: The Theology of the Apostle in the Light of Jewish Religious History. Knight, Harold, tr.
Schoffeniels, E., et al, eds. Dynamic Properties of Glia Cells: An Interdisciplinary Approach to Their Study in the Central & Peripheral Nervous System.
Schoffeniels, Ernest, jt. auth. see Florkin, Marcel.
Schofield, C. W. Basic Mathematics for Technicians.
Schofield, C. W. & Smethurst, D. Mathematics for Level-Two Technicians.
Schofield, C. W., jt. auth. see Pollard, A. B.
Schofield, Janet W. Black & White in School: Trust, Tension, or Tolerance.
Schofield, Norman, ed. Crisis in Economic Relations between North & South.
Schofield, Toy T. Tricks of the Trade.
Schoggen, Phil, jt. auth. see Barker, Roger G.
Scholander, P. F., jt. auth. see Hammel, H. T.
Scholar, Nancy. Anais Nin.
Scholberg, Diana E., jt. auth. see Scholberg, Kenneth R.
Scholberg, Kenneth R. & Scholberg, Diana E. Aqui Mismo.
Scholes, Percy A. Great Dr. Burney: His Life, His Travels, His Works, His Family & His Friends.
Scholes, Robert. Fabulation & Metafiction.
Scholes, Robert, ed. see Rossi, Lee D.
Scholes, Walter V., ed. United States Diplomatic History: Readings for the Twentieth-Century.
Scholey, Arthur. Baboushka.
Scholl, Geraldine T., jt. auth. see Kroth, Roger L.
Scholle, Peter A. & Schluger, Paul R., eds. Aspects of Diagenesis.
Scholtissek, C., et al. Chemistry & Cytochemistry of Nucleic Acids & Nuclear Proteins.
Schomaker, Linda, jt. ed. see Sauerman, Thomas H.
Schonbaum, jt. auth. see Lomax.
Schonberg, Arnold. Letters.
--Style & Idea.
Schonberg, Bessie, tr. see Sachs, Kurt.
Schonberg, Harold C. Facing the Music.
--Grandmasters of Chess.
--Lives of the Great Composers.
Schonberg, James. The Grain Trade, How It Works.
Schonberger, Richard J. Operations Management: Planning & Control of Operations & Operating Resources.
--Operations Management: Productivity & Quality.
Schoneberger, William A. & Sonnenburg, Paul. California Wings: A History of Aviation in the Golden State.
Schonell, F. Eleanor. Educating Spastic Children.
Schonert, H., jt. auth. see Haase, T.
Schonfeld-Brand, Rebecca, tr. see Meiseles, Meir.
Schonfeldt, N. Surface Active Ethylene Oxide Adducts.
Schonfield, Hugh J. The Suez Canal in World Affairs.
Schongut, Emanuel. Look Kitten. Klimo, Kate, ed.
--Play Kitten. Klimo, Kate, ed.
--Wake Kitten. Klimo, Kate, ed.
School of Philosophy Editorial Committee. The Physical & Transcendental Analysis of the Soul.
--The Theory of the Innate Ideas & Their Correlation with the Eternity of the Being.
School of Salerno Staff. Cooking Bibliography.
School Tech News Staff, ed. Only the Best: The Discriminating Software Guide for Preschool-Grade 12, 1986 Edition.
Schoolbred, C. F., jt. auth. see Vick, R. W.
Schoolcraft, Henry. Algic Researches: Comprising Inquiries Respecting the Mental Characteristics of the North American Indians.
Schoolcraft, Victoria, ed. Nursing in the Community.
Schoolland, Marian, tr. see Murray, Andrew.
Schools Council History 13-16 Project Staff. Arab-Israeli Conflict.
--The Irish Question.
--The Rise of Communist China.
Schoonover, Shirley. Mountain of Winter.
--A Season of Hard Desires.
--Winter Dream.
Schoor, Gene. Young John Kennedy.
Schopler, Eric, et al. The Childhood Autism Rating Scale (CARS) For Diagnostic Screening & Classification of Autism.
Schopler, John, jt. auth. see Insko, Chester A.
Schopper, H., ed. see International School of Nuclear Physics, Sept 23-30, 1974.
Schora, Frank J., et al. Fuel Gases from Coal.
Schorah, C. J., jt. auth. see Basu, T. K.
Schorer, Mark, et al. Harbrace College Reader. Durham, Philip & Jones, Everett L., eds.
Schorer, Mark, et al, eds. Harbrace College Reader.
Schories, Pat, illus. Bubble Trouble.
Schorsch, Alexander P. & Schorsch, M. Delores. Our Lord & Our Lady.
Sehorsch, Anita. Pastoral Dreams.
Schorsch, M. Delores, jt. auth. see Schorsch, Alexander P.
Schostak, John F. & Logan, Tom. Pupil Experience.
Schott, Richard L., jt. auth. see Dodd, Lawrence C.
Schott, Sally E. & Land, Lois B. Something to Sing about, for Young Voices.
Schottenfeld, David, ed. Cancer Epidemiology & Prevention: Current Concepts.
Schottroff, Luise, et al. Essays on the Love Commandment. Fuller, Reginald H., ed. & tr. from Ger.
Schou, M. Lithium Treatment of Manic-Depressive Illness.
Schou, M. & Stromgren, E., eds. Origin, Prevention & Treatment of Affective Disorders.
Schouls, Peter A, ed. see MacLean, Kenneth.
Schoultz, Bonnie, jt. auth. see Williams, Paul.
Schouten, Peter, jt. auth. see Selkin, James.
Schover, Leslie R. Prime Time: Sexual Health for Men over Fifty.
Schowalter, William R. Mechanics of Non-Newtonian Fluids.
Schrader, J. L. Gifts of the Magi.
Schrader, Robert F. The Indian Arts & Crafts Board: An Aspect of New Deal Indian Policy.
Schrader, William B., ed. Measurement, Guidance, & Program Improvement.
Schraff, Francis, et al. Learning about Jesus.
Schram, Joseph E., Jr., et al. Financing Residential Real Estate.
Schram, Susan G., jt. ed. see Rivera, W. M.
Schramm, David N. & Arnett, W. David, eds. Explosive Nucleosynthesis: Proceedings of the Conference on Explosive Nucleosynthesis Held in Austin, Texas, on April 2-3, 1973.
Schramm, Gunther, jt. auth. see Munasinghe, Mohan.
Schramm, Henry W. The New York State Fair: An Empire Showcase.
Schramm, John & Schramm, Mary. Things That Make for Peace: A Personal Search for a New Way of Life.
Schramm, Mary, jt. auth. see Schramm, John.
Schramm, Wilbur, et al. Handbook of Communication.
Schraufnagel, Noel. From Apology to Protest: The Black American Novel.
Schrauzer, G. N. Transition Metals in Homogeneous Catalysis.
Schreck, Alan. What Do Catholics Believe about Mary?
Schrecker, John E. Imperialism & Chinese Nationalism: Germany in Shantung.
Schreiber, Arthur F., et al. Economics of Urban Problems.
Schreiber, B. C. Meditations for Mature Christians.
Schreiber, Carol T. Changing Places: Men & Women in Transitional Occupations.
Schreiber, Flora R. The Shoemaker: The Anatomy of a Psychopath.
Schreiber, Irving, ed. The Closely Held Corporation: Tax, Financial & Estate Planning. Skiba, Jonathan.
Schreiber, Irving & Sullivan, Joseph P., eds. How to Use Tax Shelters Today.
Schreiber, Joan E. Using Children's Books in Social Studies: Early Childhood Through Primary Grades.
Schreiber, K. & Luckner, M., eds. Regulation of Secondary Product & Plant Hormone Metabolism: Proceedings of the 12th FEBS Meeting, Dresden, 1978.
Schreiber, Linda & Stang, JoAnne. Marathon Mom: The Wife & Mother Running Book.
Schreiber, Linda M. ATARI Programming... with Fifty-Five Programs.
Schreiber, Louis A. Dangerous Games.
Schreiber, Martin H. Last of a Breed: Portraits of Working Cowboys.
Schreiber, P. Anesthesia Equipment: Performance, Classification & Safety.
Schreiber, Vernon R. Wrestling with God: Messages for Lent & Easter on the Life of Jacob.
Schreiber-Jacoby, Beverly. Francois Boucher's Early Development As a Draughtsman: 1720-1734. Freedberg, S. J., ed.
Schreibner, Vernon. My Servant Job: A Devotional Guide to the Book of Job.
Schreibner, Vernon R. My Redeemer Lives: Messages from the Book of Job for Lent & Easter.
Schreiner, Samuel A., Jr. Angelica.
--A Place Called Princeton.
--Pleasant Places.
--The Possessors & the Possessed.
--Thine Is the Glory.
--The Van Alens: First Family of a Nation's First City.
Schreivogel, Paul. Small Prayers for Small Children About Big & Little Things.
Schrieber, Peter, ed. see Shugart, Cooksey.
Schriebman, Robert S. When You Can't Pay Your Taxes! How to Deal with the IRS.
Schrier, Allan M., et al, eds. Behavior of Non-Human Primates: Modern Research Trends.
Schrire, Robert, jt. auth. see Weinstein, Warren.
Schrock, Miriam M. Holistic Assessment of the Healthy Aged.
Schroder, Eberhard. Durer - Kunst und Geometrie.
Schroder, Eberhard & Lubke, Kraus, eds. The Peptides. Incl. Vol. 1. Methods of Peptide Synthesis; Vol. 2. Synthesis, Occurrence & Action of Biologically Active Polypeptides. Acad Pr.
Schroder, Johannes H. Genetics for Aquarists.
Schrody, Marjorie F. The T.F.H. Book of Kittens.
Schroedel, John G. Attitudes Toward Persons with Disabilities: A Compendium of Related Literature.
Schroeder, Albert H. Apache Indians: A Study of the Apache Indians.
Schroeder, Charles R. Astrowheeling: Space-Age Twirling.
Schroeder, Donald & Lombardo, Frank. How to Prepare for the Police Officer Entrance Examination.
Schroeder, Donald J. & Lombardo, Frank A. How to Prepare for the Police Officer Examination (Including Transit & Housing Officer)
Schroeder, Edward H., tr. see Elert, Werner.
Schroeder, Fred E. Joining the Human Race: How to Teach the Humanities.
Schroeder, Frederick & Meyers, Craig. The Potential for Spiritual Direction in the New Rite of Penance.
Schroeder, Howard, ed. see Furan Illustrators Staff & Reece, Collen L.
Schroeder, J. W., jt. ed. see Berman, I.
Schroeder, Lynn, jt. auth. see Ostrander, Sheila.
Schroeder, Oliver C., Jr., ed. Dental Jurisprudence: A Handbook of Practical Law.
Schroeder, Peter. Contact at Sea.
Schroeder, Theodore W. Pastor's Counseling Manual for Ministry to Those Who Must Sustain a Loved One in Crisis.
Schroeder, W. Practical Astronomy.
Schroeter, L. C. Ingredient X.
Schroeter, Louis C. Self-Discipline.
Schroyer, Helen Q. A Guide to a Course in Government Documents.
Schubel, Jerry R. & Marcy, Barton C., Jr., eds. Power Plant Entrainment: A Biological Assessment.
Schubert, D., jt. auth. see Schubert, I.
Schubert, Delwyn G. A Dictionary of Terms & Concepts in Reading.
Schubert, E., ed. Models & Measurements of the Cardiac Electric Field.
Schubert, Franz. Complete Song Cycles: From the Breitkopf & Hartel Complete Works Edition. Drinker, Henry S., tr.
Schubert, I. & Schubert, D. There's a Crocodile under My Bed.
Schubert, Paul B., ed. see Oberg, Erik, et al.
Schubert, Walter J. Lignin Biochemistry.
Schuck, Peter H. Agent Orange on Trial: Mass Toxic Disasters in the Courts.
Schuck, Victoria, jt. ed. see Milburn, Josephine.
Schuckit, Marc A. Drug & Alcohol Abuse: A Clinical Guide to Diagnosis & Treatment.
Schuckman, Terry. Aging Is Not for Sissies.
Schuclein, Werner & Eulenberger, Peter. Anwendung des Simulationsmodells BAYMO 70 auf die Stadtentwicklungsplanung.
Schuder, Charles B. Energy Engineering Fundamentals: With Residential & Commercial Applications.
Schudson, Michael, jt. ed. see Manoff, Robert K.
Schuefftan, Kim, tr. see Yoneda, Soei.
Schuell, Hildred. Aphasia Theory & Therapy: Selected Lectures & Papers of Hildred Schuell. Sies, Luther F., ed.
Schuermann, et al, eds. see Annual Meeting on Brain Edema Staff.
Schuermann, K. & Reulen, H. J., eds. Steroids & Brain Edema.
Schuett, F. Die Peridineen der Plankton-Expedition der Humboldt-Stiftung I: Allgemeiner Teil.
Schuettinger, Robert. Lord Acton: Historian of Liberty.
--Saving Social Security.
Schuetz, Robert D., jt. auth. see Hart, Harold.
Schuh, Russell G. A Dictionary of Ngizim.
Schuiling, Walter C. San Bernardino County: Land of Contrasts.
Schuitema, Paul. Syst-O-Color, Vier-Kleurensysteem.
Schulein, Werner. Anwendung des Simulationsmodells BAYMO 70 auf die Stadtentwicklungsplanung.
Schulenberg, David. The Instrumental Music of Carl Philipp Emanuel Bach. Buelow, George, ed.
Schuler, Charles A., ed. see Tokheim, Roger L.
Schuler, Max & Gebelein, H. Five Place Tables of Elliptical Functions. Larsen, L. S., tr.
Schuler, Randall S. Personnel & Human Resource Management (International Edition)
Schuler, Robert M. English Magical & Scientific Poems to 1700: An Annotated Bibliography.
Schulkind, Jeanne, ed. & intro. by see Woolf, Virginia.
Schull, W. J. & Chakraborty, R., eds. Human Genetics: A Selection of Insights.
Schuller, Carol. In the Shadow of His Wings.
Schuller, Gunther & Williams, Martin, eds. Big Band Jazz: From the Beginnings to the Fifties.
Schuller, Robert. Daily Power Thoughts.
Schuller, Robert A. Getting Through the Going Through Stage.
Schuller, Robert H. Be Happy - You Are Loved!
--Discover Self-Love.
--Move Ahead with Possibility Thinking.
--Possibility Thinkers Bible: The New King James Version.
--Power Ideas for a Happy Family.
--Self-Esteem: The New Reformation.
--Self-Love.
--Tough Minded Faith for Tender Hearted People.
--Tough Times Never Last but Tough People Do!
--Turning Your Stress into Strength.
--Turning Your Stress into Strength.
--Your Church Has a Fantastic Future! A Possibility Thinker's Guide to a Successful Church.
Schullery, Paul. Mountain Time.
Schullery, Paul, ed. The Grand Canyon: Early Impressions.
Schulman, Elayne E. Data Bases for Beginners.
Schulman, Estella F. Now Listen Good! A Collection of Authentic West Indian Recipes.
Schulman, Grace, ed. Ezra Pound.
Schulman, Harold, jt. auth. see Neubardt.
Schulman, J. Neil. Alongside Night.
--The Ranibow Cadenza.
Schulman, Janet, ed. see Sesame Street Staff.
Schulman, Margaret B. The Dow Jones-Irwin Guide to Property Ownership: How to Understand, Control & Protect Your Assets.
Schulman, Neil J. The Rainbow Cadenza: A Novel in Logosta Form.
Schulman, Stephen, jt. auth. see Siegel, Stanley.
Schult, Joachim. Curious Boating Inventions.
--Curious Yachting Inventions.
Schulte. Reporting Public Affairs.
Schulte, Elaine L. Song of Joy.
--Whither the Wind Bloweth.
Schulte, Joachim, tr. see Waismann, Friedrich.
Schulte, Rainer, ed. Contemporary Writing from the Continents.
Schulteis & Sumner. Management Information Systems.
Schultheisz, E., ed. History of Physiology: Proceedings of the 28th International Congress of Physiological Sciences, Budapest 1980.
Schulthess, Emil. Antarctica.
Schultz, Arlo, tr. see Zankov, L. V., et al.
Schultz, Barbara, jt. ed. see Schultz, Mark.
Schultz, Christine S., compiled by. Formulary 1987: Veterinary Hospital Pharmacy, Washington State University.
Schultz, Clara P. Because of the Wind in the Wheat.
Schultz, D. O. & Norton, L. A. Police Operational Intelligence.
Schultz, Don A., jt. auth. see Springer, Marilyn.
Schultz, Don A., jt. auth. see Springer, Marylyn.
Schultz, Donald. Principles of Physical Security.
Schultz, Donald & Melsa, J. State Functions & Linear Control Systems.
Schultz, Donald O. Criminal Investigation Techniques.
--Police Pursuit Driving Handbook.
Schultz, Donald O., ed. Modern Police Administration.
Schultz, Duane P. Psychology & Industry Today.
Schultz, Erich R., tr. see Schmitt, Friedrich.
Schultz, F. A. Scales & Chords for Piano.
Schultz, Fred. Annual Editions: Education, 1985-86.
Schultz, Fred, ed. Education 1988-89.
Schultz, G. & Moss, T. S., eds. High-Resolution Infrared & Submillimetre Spectroscopy: A Selection of Papers Presented at a Workshop Held in Bonn, 1977.

Schultz, George P., jt. auth. see Myers, Charles A.

Schultz, Gordon W., jt. auth. see Jensen, Clayne R.

Schultz, Hans J., ed. Jesus in His Time. Watchorn, Brian, tr. from Ger.

Schultz, Harold W. Food Law Handbook.

Schultz, Helen C., jt. ed. see Sanderson, Glen C.

Schultz, J. & Gratzner, H. G., eds. The Role of Cyclic Nucleotides in Carsinogenesis.

Schultz, J. & Whelan, W. J., eds. Genetic Manipulation As It Affects the Cancer Problem.

Schultz, J. S. Comparative Statutory Sources.

Schultz, Judithm. & Dark, Sheila L. Manual of Psychiatric Nursing Care Plans.

Schultz, Julius & Black, Ronald E., eds. Membrane Transformation in Neoplasia.

Schultz, Julius, ed. see Miami Winter Symposium Staff.

Schultz, Julius, jt. ed. see Mozes, Lee.

Schultz, Ken. Bass Fishing Fundamentals.

Schultz, Lawrence. How to Repair CB Radios. Haas, Mark, ed.

Schultz, Linford. From Continent to Continent: In Search of a New Life.

Schultz, Margaret A., ed. Lawyer's Register by Specialties & Fields of Law.

Schultz, Mark & Schultz, Barbara, eds. Bicycles & Bicycling: A Guide to Information Sources.

Schultz, Morton J. How to Fix It.

Schultz, Robert C., tr. see Vischer, Lukas.

Schultz, Russel R. Blueprint Reading for the Machine Trades.

Schultz, Russell E. A Milwaukee Transport Era: The Trackless Trolley Years. Sebree, Mac, ed.

Schultz, T. P., jt. auth. see Nelson, Richard R.

Schultz, Theodore W., ed. Investment in Education: The Equity-Efficiency Quandary.

Schultz, Thom, ed. The Best of Try This One.

--More...Try This One.

--Youth Group Travel Directory: 1981-82 Edition.

Schultz, V., jt. ed. see Klement, A. W.

Schultz, V., et al. A Bibliography of Quantitative Ecology.

Schultz, Wallace W. & Navratil, James D., eds. Science & Technology of Tributyl Phosphate: Selected Technical & Industrial Uses.

Schulz, Anne. The Sculpture of Giovanni & Bartolomeo Bon & Their Workshop.

Schulz, Charles M. Un Beagle qui a du Chien.

--Don't Give up, Charlie Brown: Selected from Vol. 2 of "You've Had It, Charlie Brown"

--Here Comes Charlie Brown: Selected Cartoons from "Good Ol' Charlie Brown"

--I Never Promised You an Apple Orchard.

--Incredible Charlie Brown.

--Je ne T'ai Jamais Promis un Verger de Pommiers.

--Peanuts Double.

--Peanuts Double.

--Peanuts Jubilee.

--Peanuts Treasury.

--Race for Your Life, Charlie Brown.

--Sandlot Peanuts.

--Snoopy on Wheels.

Schulz, Charles M. & Kiliper, R. Smith. Charlie Brown, Snoopy & Me.

Schulz, Christopher R. & Okun, Daniel A. Surface Water Treatment for Communities in Developing Countries.

Schulz, David A. The Changing Family: Its Function & Future.

--Human Sexuality.

Schulz, Esther D. & Williams, Sally R. Family Life & Sex Education: Curriculum & Instruction.

Schulz, Florence. Nobody Else Is Just Like Me.

Schulz, James H. & Leavitt, Thomas D. Pension Integration: Concepts, Issues & Proposals. Moore, Patricia G. & Johnson, Lynn Ann, eds.

Schulz, Phillip S., jt. auth. see Greene, Bert.

Schulz, Richard. Psychology of Death: Dying & Bereavement.

Schulz, Warren E. Ilion-The Town Remington Made.

Schulze, Fred. The U. S. S. R. Today. Current Digest of the Soviet Press Staff, tr. from Rus.

Schumach, Murray. The Diamond People.

Schumacher, Claire. Alto & Tango.

--King of the Zoo.

--Nutty's Christmas.

Schumacher, Claude. Alfred Jarry & Guillaume Apollinaire.

--Alfred Jarry & Guillaume Apollinaire.

Schumacher, F. Carl & Wilson, George C. Bridge of No Return: The Ordeal of the U. S. S. Pueblo.

Schumacher, Nancy C. Epilepsy: A Personal Approach.

Schumacher, Sally, jt. auth. see McMillan, James H.

Schuman, Frederick L. The Commonwealth of Man: An Inquiry into Power Politics & World Government.

Schuman, Joseph. The Draft: Gay Question, Serious Answers.

Schuman, Michael. Favorite Daytrips in New England.

Schumann, Elisabeth. German Song.

Schumann, Marguerite. Tar Heel Sights: Guide to North Carolina's Heritage.

Schumann, Marguerite, ed. Grand Old Ladies: North Carolina Architecture During the Victorian Era.

Schumann, Robert A. The Musical World of Robert Schumann: A Selection from His Own Writings.

Schumer, Fran, jt. auth. see Cunningham, Mary.

Schumm, Stanley A., ed. Drainage Basin Morphology.

--River Morphology.

Schumm, Stanley A. & Mosley, M. Paul, eds. Slope Morphology.

Schumpeter, Joseph A. Business Cycles: A Theoretical, Historical & Statistical Analysis of the Capitalist Process.

Schunk, Carol. Bowling.

Schuppli, R. Immunbiologie: Einfuehrung in die allergologischen und immunologischen Grundlagen der klinischen Medizin.

Schur, Edwin M. The Awareness Trap: Self-Absorption Instead of Social Change.

--Narcotic Addiction in Britain & America: The Impact of Public Policy.

Schur, Norman W., ed. English English.

Schur, Sylvia. The Sweet Touch in Family Cooking.

Schur, Sylvia, jt. auth. see Baker, Samm S.

Schurman, Dewey. Athletic Fitness: The Athlete's Guide to Training & Conditioning.

--Volleyball.

Schurman, Paul G. Money Problems & Pastoral Care.

Schurr. Poetry Pack Rat.

Schurr, G. Le Guidargus de la Peinture du XIX Siecle a Nos Jours.

Schurr, Gerald. Guidargus de la Peinture de XIXe Siecle a Nos Jours.

--Les Petits Maitres de la Peinture Valeur de Demain, 1820-1920.

--Les Petits Maitres de la Peinture Valeur de Demain, 1820-1920.

--Les Petits Maitres de la Peinture Valeur de Demain, 1820-1920.

--Les Petits Maitres de la Peinture Valeur de Demain, 1820-1920.

--Les Petits Maitres de la Peinture Valeur de Demain, 1820-1920.

Schurr, Sam & Netschert, Bruce C. Energy in the American Economy, 1850-1975: An Economic Study of Its History & Prospects.

Schurr, Sam H., ed. Energy, Economic Growth, & the Environment.

Schusky, Ernest L. & Culbert, T. Patrick. Introducing Culture.

Schussler, Theodore. Federal Courts, Jurisdiction & Practice.

Schuster, Edgar H., jt. auth. see Guth, Hans P.

Schuster, H., ed. see Wissenschaftliche Konferenz der Gesellschaft Deutscher Naturforscher und Aerzte, 4th, Berlin, 1967.

Schuster, H. G., ed. see GPS Summer School, Saarbruecken, F. R. Germany, Jul 10-12, 1974.

Schuster, Michael, tr. see Peynaud, Emile.

Schuster, P., jt. auth. see Eigen, M.

Schuster, Robert O., jt. auth. see Grigarick, Albert A.

Schuter, Hans. Index Libycus: A Cumlative Index to Bibliography of Libya, 1915-1975.

Schutte, J. Everything You Always Wanted to Know about Elementary Statistics: But Were Afraid to Ask.

Schutte, William M. & Steinberg, Erwin R. Communication in Business & Industry.

Schutte, William M. & Steinberg, Erwin R., eds. Personal Integrity.

Schutz, Alexander H., jt. auth. see Holmes, Urban T.

Schutz, Benjamin M. A Tax in Blood.

Schutz, J. W. Foundations of Special Relativity: Kinematic Axioms for Minkowski Space-Time.

Schutz, Susan P., ed. A Mother's Love.

Schutz, Will. Profound Simplicity.

Schutz, William C. Joy: Expanding Human Awareness.

Schutze, Martin, ed. Goethe Centenary Papers.

Schuyler, George. Hunger in a Land of Plenty.

Schuyler, George W. Saint John: Two Hundred Years Proud.

Schuyler, V., et al. Parent-Infant Communication: A Program of Clinical & Home Training for Parents & Hearing Impaired Infants.

Schvey, Henry I. Oskar Kokoschka: The Painter As Playwright.

Schwab, Arnold. A Matter of Life & Death: Vital Biographical Facts About Selected American Artists.

Schwab, George. Soviet Foreign-Policy Aims: Neutralism & Finlandism.

Schwab, Inke, jt. auth. see Schwab, Michael.

Schwab, Michael & Schwab, Inke. Start Well! A Guide to Healthy Eating for You & Your Baby.

Schwab, Peter. Ethiopia: Politics, Economics & Society. Szajkowski, Bogdan, ed.

Schwab, Richard & Rex, Walter. Preliminary Discourse to the Encyclopedia of Diderot D'Alembert.

Schwab, Simon. These & Those.

Schwalb, Ann W., ed. see Champlin, Connie.

Schwalb, Marvin N. & Miles, Philip G., eds. Genetics & Morphogenesis in the Basidiomycetes.

Schwaller, John F. The Origins of Church Wealth in Mexico: Ecclesiastical Revenues & Church Finances, 1523-1600.

Schwan, Karsten. Tailoring Software for Multiple Processor Systems. Stone, Harold, ed.

Schwan, W. Creighton, jt. auth. see Richter, Herbert P.

Schwark, Mary B., illus. The Flea Trainer.

--The Four-Foot Forks.

--The Worst Peanuts in Town.

Schwarta, M. M. Source Book on Innovative Welding Processes.

Schwartlbaum, Avraham. The Bamboo Cradle.

Schwartz. Compendium of Immunology.

--Compendium of Immunology.

Schwartz, A., jt. auth. see Archer, Jerome W.

Schwartz, Alan U., jt. auth. see Ernst, Morris L.

Schwartz, Arleen G. & Jabarin, Dorothy. The Book of BASIC.

Schwartz, Arthur P., jt. auth. see Frishman, Austin M.

Schwartz, B. Clinical Venereology.

Schwartz, Barry. Psychology of Learning & Behavior.

Schwartz, Barry, ed. The Changing Face of the Suburbs.

Schwartz, Benjamin I. Communism & China: Ideology in Flux.

Schwartz, Bernard, jt. auth. see Wood, Paul E.

Schwartz, Betty, jt. auth. see Shea, George.

Schwartz, Betty, ed. Great Ghost Stories.

Schwartz, Betty, ed. see DePasquale, Michael, Jr.

Schwartz, Betty, ed. see Milton, Hilary.

Schwartz, Betty, ed. see Shea, George.

Schwartz, Betty, et al, eds. see Milton, Hilary.

Schwartz, Bill & McCormick, Mike. Seattle Celebrity Chefs.

Schwartz, Brian B., jt. ed. see Foner, Simon.

Schwartz, David. Hanukkah Latkes & Rothschild's Millions.

--Introduction to Management: Principles, Practices, & Processes.

Schwartz, David, jt. auth. see Weiner, Neil.

Schwartz, David J. Marketing Today: A Basic Approach.

--Marketing Today: A Basic Approach.

--Marketing Today: A Basic Approach.

Schwartz, David J., jt. auth. see Mauser, Ferdinand F.

Schwartz, David M., jt. auth. see Weiner, Neal O.

Schwartz, Edwin J., ed. see Zagat, Eugene H., Jr. & Zagat, Nina S.

Schwartz, Elias & Pochedly, Carl, eds. Hemoglobinopathies in Children.

Schwartz, Elliot S. The Symphonies of Ralph Vaughan Williams.

Schwartz, Florence S., ed. Voluntarism & Social Work Practice: A Growing Collaboration.

Schwartz, Gail G. & Choate, Pat. Being Number One: Rebuilding the U. S. Economy.

Schwartz, George. Food Power.

Schwartz, H. G., Jr., et al. Joint Treatment of Industrial & Municipal Wastewaters. Water Pollution Control Federation Staff, ed.

Schwartz, Harold L., jt. ed. see Erickson, Gerald.

Schwartz, Harry. China.

Schwartz, Harvey. The March Inland: Origins of the ILWU Warehouse Division, 1934-1938.

Schwartz, Henry. Kit Carson's Long Walk & Other True Tales of Old San Diego.

Schwartz, Howard. Vessels.

Schwartz, Jacob T., jt. auth. see Dunford, Nelson.

Schwartz, Janet, et al. Nutrition Care in Family Planning: A Guide for Administrators.

--Connections: Nutrition, Contraception, Women, Eating.

--Connections: Nutrition, Contraception, Women, Eating.

Schwartz, Jean-Michael. Mysteries of Easter Island.

Schwartz, Jonathan. Distant Stations.

Schwartz, Joseph. Don't Ever Retire but Do It Early & Often.

--Hart Crane: A Reference Guide.

Schwartz, Jules J. Corporate Policy: A Casebook.

Schwartz, Julius. Earthwatch: Space-Time Investigations with a Globe.

Schwartz, L. Complex Analytic Manifolds.

Schwartz, Lauren R. Computer Law Forms Handbook: A Legal Guide to Drafting & Negotiating.

Schwartz, Lazar M. Compendium of Immunology.

Schwartz, Lazar M., ed. Compendium of Immunology.

Schwartz, Leonard. Heavyhands: The Ultimate Exercise System.

Schwartz, Lester & Brechner, Irv. The Career Finder: Pathways to over 1500 Entry-Level Jobs.

Schwartz, M., ed. Prescription Drugs in Short Supply: Case Histories.

Schwartz, M. L., ed. Spits & Bars.

Schwartz, M. M. Source Book on Brazing & Brazing Technology.

--Source Book on Electron Beam & Laser Welding.

Schwartz, Malcolm, jt. auth. see Maher, Tom.

Schwartz, Martin. Commercial Radio Operator's Question & Answer License Guide.

--Gadgets.

Schwartz, Marvin D. American Furniture of the Colonial Period.

Schwartz, Max J., jt. auth. see Practising Law Institute Staff.

Schwartz, Michael. Radical Protest & Social Structure: The Southern Farmer's Alliance & Cotton Tenancy, 1880-1890.

Schwartz, Mitchell & Schmuck, Richard A. The Development of Educational Teams.

Schwartz, Morris S. & Shockley, Emmy L. The Nurse & the Mental Patient: A Study in Interpersonal Relations.

Schwartz, Mortimer. Environmental Law: A Guide to Information Sources.

Schwartz, Mortimer D. & Wydick, Richard C. Legal Ethics Problems.

Schwartz, Mortimer O. & Wydick, Richard C. Legal Ethics Problems.

Schwartz, Murray. Designing & Building Your Own Professional Office.

Schwartz, Murray L., ed. Law & the American Future.

Schwartz, Peter, et al. Fabric Forming Systems.

Schwartz, Pushpa N., ed. Confrontation of Co-Operation? Twelfth World Conference of the Society for International Development Proceedings.

Schwartz, Rachel, jt. auth. see Aikman, Ralph.

Schwartz, Randall. Carnivorous Plants.

Schwartz, Richard H. Judaism & Vegetarianism.

Schwartz, Robert M., ed. see MassCOSH Legal Committee.

Schwartz, Sam. Co-Op City: A Fantastic Cartoon History.

Schwartz, Seymour & Goodman, Sidney. Plastics Materials & Processes.

Schwartz, Seymour I., et al, eds. Principles of Surgery.

--Principles of Surgery.

Schwartz, Sheila. One Day You'll Go.

Schwartz, Stephen, jt. auth. see Hirson, Roger O.

Schwartz, Stephen E. Trace Atmospheric Constituents: Properties, Transformations & Fates.

Schwartz, Steven E., jt. auth. see Oldham, William G.

Schwartz, Toby D. Mercy Lord, My Husband's in the Kitchen & Other Equal Opportunity Conversations with God.

Schwartz, Wendy C., ed. see CEP Staff & Simich, Tina L.

Schwartzman, Helen B., ed. Transformations: The Anthropology of Children's Play.

Schwartz-Nobel, L. Starving in the Shadow of Plenty.

Schwarz & Goldberg. New York State in Story.

Schwarz, jt. auth. see Berthold.

Schwarz, Berthold E. UFO-Dynamics: Psychiatric & Psychic Aspects of the UFO Syndrome.

Schwarz, Boris. Great Masters of the Violin.

--Music & Musical Life in Soviet Russia: 1917-1970.

Schwarz, F. Charles. Sidelights on Christology: Did Jesus Die on the Cross?

Schwarz, H. J., et al, eds. Laser Interaction & Related Plasma Phenomena.

Schwarz, Hans. Beyond the Gates of Death: A Biblical Examination of Evidence for Life After Death.

--The Christian Church: Biblical Origin, Historical Transformation, & Potential for the Future.

--Colour for the Artist.

--Divine Communication: Word & Sacrament in Biblical, Historical & Contemporary Perspective.

--Draw Buildings & Cityscapes.

--Draw in Pencil, Charcoal, Crayon & Other Media.

--Figure Painting.

--On the Way to the Future: A Christian View of Eschatology in the Light of Current Trends in Religion, Philosophy & Science.

--On the Way to the Future: A Christian View of Eschatology in the Light of Current Trends in Religion, Philosophy, & Science.

--Our Cosmic Journey: Christian Anthropology in the Light of Current Trends in the Sciences, Philosophy, & Theology.

--Painting in Towns & Cities.

--Responsible Faith: Christian Theology in the Light of 20th-Century Questions.

--The Search for God.

Schwarz, Helmut J. & Hora, Heinrich, eds. Laser Interaction & Related Plasma Phenomena. Incl. Vol. 1; Vol. 2; Vol. 3A; Vol. 3B; Vol. 4A; Vol. 4B. Plenum Pub.
Schwarz, Jordan A. Ordeal of Twentieth-Century America: Interpretive Readings.
Schwarz, Karl. Jewish Artists of the Nineteenth & Twentieth Centuries.
Schwarz, M. Roy, ed. see Leukocyte Culture Conference Staff.
Schwarz, Marian, tr. see Chomiak, Martha & Rosenthal, Bernice.
Schwarz, Osias L. Average Man Against Superior Man.
Schwarz, Ralph & Friedland, B. Linear Systems.
Schwarz, Rosalie. Lawless Liberators.
Schwarz, Stephen, jt. auth. see Hutton, William T.
Schwarz, Stephen C. & Brunner, Calvin R. Energy & Resource Recovery from Waste.
Schwarz, Ted. How to Make Money with Your Camera.
Schwarz, Ted, jt. auth. see Green, Bernard.
Schwarz, Urs & Hadik, Laszlo. Strategic Terminology.
Schwarz, V. Leningrad-Art & Architecture.
Schwarz, Werner & Haringer, Monica. Guitar Bibliography: An International Listing of Literature on Classical Guitar from the Beginning to the Present.
Schwarz-Bart, Andre. A Woman Named Solitude. Manheim, Ralph, tr. from Fr.
Schwarzenberger, Georg. The Dynamics of International Law.
Schwarzenberger, Georg & Brown, E. D. A Manual of International Law.
Schwarzenberger, R. L. Elementary Differential Equations.
Schwarzenegger, Arnold. Arnold's Bodyshaping for Women.
Schwarzenegger, Arnold & Dobbins, Bill. Arnold's Bodybuilding for Men.
Schwarzenegger, Arnold & Hall, Douglas K. Arnold: The Education of a Body Builder.
Schwarzkopf, A. B., et al, eds. Optimal Control & Differential Equation.
Schwarzkopf, Elisabeth. On & off the Record: A Memoir of Walter Legge.
Schwarzkopf, LeRoy C. Government Reference Books, 1982-1983: A Biennial Guide to U. S. Government Publications.
Schwarzkopf, P. Living Metals.
Schwarzlose, Harald, jt. auth. see Das, Robert.
Schwarzrock, Shirley & Wrenn, C. Gilbert. Alcohol As a Crutch.
--Can You Talk with Someone Else?
--Changing Roles of Men & Women.
--Coping with Cliques.
--Do I Know the "Me" Others See?
--Easing the Scene.
--Facts & Fantasies about Drugs.
--Facts & Fantasies about Smoking.
--Food As a Crutch.
--Grades, What's So Important about Them, Anyway?
--I'd Rather Do It Myself, If You Don't Mind.
--In Front of the Table & Behind It.
--Living with Differences.
--The Mind Benders.
--Some Common Crutches.
--Understanding the Law of Our Land.
--You Always Communicate Something.
Schwebel, Andrew, et al. Rewriting Your Family Drama.
Schwebel, Milton. Who Can Be Educated?
Schwebel, Milton, ed. Behavioral Science & Human Survival.
Schwed, Peter. Hanging in There: How to Resist Retirement from Life & Avoid Being Put Out to Pasture.
Schwefel, Hans-Paul. Numerical Optimization of Computer Models.
Schwegler, Robert. Patterns in Action.
Schwegler, Robert A., jt. auth. see Decker, Randall E.
Schweibcl, H. Mental Health Implications of Life in the Nuclear Age.
Schweik, R. C. & Riesner, Dietner. English & American Literature: A Guide to Reference Materials.
Schweiker, Roioli. Canoe Camping Vermont & New Hampshire Rivers. Baker, Catherine J., ed.
Schweiker, Roioli, ed. see AMC River Guide Committee.
Schweiss, Josef. M. S. Nurnberg: Memoirs of a Danube River Boatman During the Second World War.
Schweitzer, Albert. Essence of Faith.
--Reverence of Life.
Schweitzer, Avraham. Israel: The Changing National Agenda.
Schweitzer, Byrd B. Amigo.
Schweitzer, Christoph E., ed. see Goes, Albrecht.
Schweitzer, David, jt. ed. see Geyer, Felix R.
Schweitzer, George, ed. see Schnitzer, Eduard.
Schweitzer, James A. Protecting Information on Local Area Networks.
Schweitzer, John C., jt. auth. see Dillenback, Marsden.
Schweitzer, Philip A. Handbook of Separation Techniques for Chemical Engineers.
Schweizer, Eduard. Church As the Body of Christ.
--The Holy Spirit.
Schweizer, Edward. The Letter to the Colossians: A Commentary. Chester, Andrew, tr.
Schweizerische Gesellschaft fuer Gynaekologie Staff. Aesthetisch-Plastische Operationen in der Gynaekologie: Proceedings of the Schweizerische Gesellschaft fuer Gynakologie, Bericht Ueber die Jahresversammlung, Lugano, June 30 - July 2, 1977. Dreher, E., ed.
--Praeventivmassnahmen in der Gynaekologie und ihre oekonomischen Aspekte: Proceedings of the Schweizerische Gesellschaft fuer Gynakologie, Bericht Ueber die Jahresversammlung, Lugano, June 30 - July 2, 1977. Dreher, E., ed.
Schwemm, Robert G. Housing Discrimination Law.
--Housing Discrimination Law: 1986 Supplement.
Schwendinger, Robert J. International Port of Call: An Illustrated Maritime History of the Golden Gate.
Schwendowius, B. & Domling, W., eds. Johann Sebastian Bach: Life, Times, Influence.
Schwenger, Peter. Phallic Critiques: Masculinity & Twentieth Century Literature.
Schwenker, Robert F., Jr. & Garn, Paul. Thermal Analysis.
Schwerdtfeger, Friedrich W. Traditional Housing in African Cities: A Comparative Study of Houses in Zaria, Ibadan & Marrakech.
Schwerin, Doris. Rainbow Walkers.
--The Tree That Cried.
Schweyer, Ruth A. Family Financial Planning: A Handbook for Family Stewardship.
Schwicker, jt. auth. see Gagnacci-Schwicker, A.
Schwieger, Robert G., ed. Fluidized Bed Combustion & Applied Technology.
Schwimmer, Erik, ed. Yearbook of Symbolic Anthropology.
Schwimmer, Sigmund. Source Book of Food Enzymology.
Schwindt, Richard, jt. ed. see Dean, James W.
Schwinger, Julian. Einstein's Legacy.
Schwinn, Monika & Diehl, Bernhard. We Came to Help.
Schwizer, Eduard. Luke: A Challenge to Present Theology.
Schwolsky, Rick & Hayes, John, eds. Solar Business Experience.
Sciacca, Carl. How to Get the Most Out of Your Social Security & Monthly Benefits.
Sciarra, D. J., jt. auth. see Milgram, J. I.
Sciarra, Dorothy J. & Dorsey, Anne G. Developing & Administering a Child Care Center.
Sciascia, Leonardo. Candido or, Dream Dreamed in Sicily. Wolff, Helen, ed. Foulke, Adrienne, tr.
Science & Mechanics Magazine Staff, ed. Treasury of Woodworking Projects.
Science Applications, Inc. Staff. Evaluation of an Environs Exposure Rate Monitoring System for Post-Accident Assessment: AIF-NESP 023.
--A Generic Assessment of Barge Transportation of Spent Nuclear Fuel (AIF-NESP-014)
Science Council of Japan Staff, ed. see International Seaweed Symposium Staff.
Science Fiction Writers of America Staff, ed. Writing & Selling Science Fiction.
Science for the People. China: Science Walks on Two Legs.
Science Press Staff. China-U.S. Bilateral Symposium of Polymer Chemistry & Physics: Proceedings.
--English-Chinese Dictionary of Metals & Their Heat Treatment.
--Guangzhou Conference, 1980: Proceedings.
--Irreversible Thermodynamics.
--Modern Fluid Mechanics.
--Nucleic Acids & Proteins: The Proceedings of China-West Germany Symposium on Nucleic Acids & Proteins.
--The Role of RNA in Development & Reproduction: Proceedings of the Second International Symposium April 25-30, 1980.
Science Research Associates, Data Processing & Curriculum Group Staff. Case Study in Business System Design.
Scientific American Editors. The Dynamic Earth.
--Volcanoes & the Earth's Interior: Readings from Scientific American.
Scientific American, Inc. Staff. Scientific American Cumulative Index 1948-1978.
Scientific Research Staff, ed. Drugs Studies in CVD & PVD: Proceedings of the International Symposium, Geneva, May 25-26, 1981.
Sciglimpaglia, Donald. Applied Marketing.
Sciglimpaglia, Donald & Zikmund, William G. Applied Marketing Research.
Scimecca, Joseph. Education & Society.
Scimone, John & Rothstein, Robert. Clinical Chemistry: Functional Medical Laboratory Manual.
Scimone, John, ed. Clinical Bacteriology.
Sclar, D. Auto Repairs for Dummies.
Sclater, Neil. Introduction to Electronic Speech Synthesis.
Sclove, Stanley L., jt. auth. see Anderson, Theodore W.
Scobey, Joan, ed. see Field, Michael.
Scobie, Grant M. Investment in International Agricultural Research: Some Economic Dimensions.
Scobie, W. I., jt. auth. see Foley, Charles.
Scoble, John. The Complete Book of Budgerigars.
Scofield, Michael L., jt. auth. see Harris, J. Mel.
Scoggan, Nita. Pentagon Tidbits.
Scoggins, Bruce, jt. ed. see Stanley, Philip E.
Scolari, Massimo, et al. Hypnos: Massimo Scolari Works 1980-1986.
Scoles, Eugene F. & Halbach, Edward C. Problems & Materials on Decedents' Estates & Trusts.
Scollon, Ronald & Scollon, Suzanne B. Linguistic Convergence: An Ethnography of Speaking at Fort Chipewyan, Alberta.
Scollon, Suzanne B., jt. auth. see Scollon, Ronald.
Scorer, R. S. Air Pollution.
--Air Pollution.
Scorseby, Lynn A. Marriage Dialogue.
Scot, Donald C. The IBM Displaywriter Simplified.
--Reportpack Simplified.
Scott. Computer Law 1986: Cumulative Supplement.
--Scott U. S. Coin Catalog.
Scott, A., jt. auth. see Scott, T.
Scott, A. F. The Early Hanoverian Age 1714-1760: Commentaries of an Era.
--What Fires Kindle Genius?
Scott, A. I. Concerning the Biosynthesis of Vitamin B12.
Scott, A. J. The Urban Land Nexus & the State.
Scott, Alan, jt. auth. see Newsom, Doug.
Scott, Alexander. Poems. Cranstoon, James, ed.
Scott, Alexander, ed. see MacDiarmid, Hugh.
Scott, Amy H. Storms.
Scott, Andrew. The Anatomy of Communism.
Scott, Ann H. Census, U. S. A. Fact Finding for the American People, 1790-1970.
Scott, Anne F. Women in American Life.
Scott, Araby. Heart of the Flame.
--Wild Sweet Witch.
Scott, Arthur F., ed. Survey of Progress in Chemistry. Incl. Vol. 1; Vol. 2; Vol. 3; Vol. 4; Vol. 5; Vol. 6; Vol. 7; Vol. 8; Vol. 9; Vol. 10. Acad Pr.
Scott, Austin, jt. auth. see LaFave, Wayne R.
Scott, Beatrice, tr. see Remizov, Aleksei.
Scott, Bernard B. Jesus, Symbol-Maker for the Kingdom.
--The Word of God in Words: Reading & Preaching the Gospels.
Scott, Beth & Norman, Michael. Haunted Heartland.
--Haunted Wisconsin.
Scott, Charles R., Jr. & Strickland, Alonzo J., III. Tempomatic IV: A Management Simulation.
Scott, Christopher, et al. Conducting Surveys in Developing Countries: Practical Problems & Experiences in Brazil, Malaysia & the Philippines.
Scott, Claudia D. Forecasting Local Government Spending.
Scott, Curt. The Complete Guide to Specialty Cars. Scott, Judy, ed.
--The Complete Guide to Specialty Cars. Scott, Judy, ed.
--The Complete Guide to Specialty Cars. Scott, Judy, ed.
--Kit Car Catalog, 1985. Scott, Judy, ed.
Scott, D. S., jt. ed. see Mueller, G. H.
Scott, David & Inwood, Kristiaan. A Taste of Thailand.
Scott, David L., jt. auth. see Ferretti, Val S.
Scott, Dorothea H. Chinese Popular Literature & the Child.
Scott, Doug, tr. see Zimmerli, Walther.
Scott, Douglas. Shadows.
Scott, Douglas M., ed. International Who's Who In Music & Musicans Directory.
Scott, Ed. Batavus Moped Owner Service-Repair: 1976-1978.
--Garelli Moped Owner Service-Repair: 1976-1978.
--Peugeot Moped Owners Service-Repair, 1976-1978.
--Yamaha XS1100 Fours: 1978-1981 Service-Repair-Performance.
Scott, Eugene. Ivan Lendl's Power Tennis.
Scott, F. S. English Grammar: A Linguistic Study of Its Classes & Structures.
Scott, Fela D. Shadow of Desire.
Scott, Genevieve. The Water Horse.
Scott, George & Stone, Llma. The Mosses of Southern Australia.
Scott, Gregory J. Marketing Bhutan's Potatoes.
Scott, H. L. Civil War Military Dictionary. Rywell, Martin, ed.
Scott, Helen G., jt. auth. see Truffaut, Francois.
Scott, Herbert. Groceries.
Scott, Hilda. Working Your Way to the Bottom: The Feminization of Poverty.
Scott, Hilda, jt. ed. see Eichler, Margrit.
Scott, Hugh A. The Blue & White Devils: A Personal Memoir & History of the Third Infantry Division in World War II.
Scott, Ian, ed. & tr. see Luscher, Max.
Scott, J. P., ed. Critical Periods.
Scott, Jack. A Knife Between the Ribs.
--Plunderbund & Proletariat: A History of the IWW in B. C.
Scott, Jack D. Discovering the American Stork.
--Discovering the Mysterious Egret.
--The Survivors: Enduring Animals of North America.
Scott, Jack S. An Uprush of Mayhem.
--The View from Deacon Hill.
Scott, James. Film: The Medium & the Maker.
--Palaeontology: An Introduction.
Scott, James D., et al. Introduction to Marketing Management.
Scott, James H. & Symons, Norman. Introduction to Dental Anatomy.
Scott, Jane. Cross Fox.
Scott, Joan E. Introduction to Interactive Computer Graphics.
Scott, Joanna. Fading, My Parmacheene Belle.
Scott, John. Basic Computer Logic.
Scott, John & Fisher, Eric. Approaches to Clay Modelling.
Scott, John, tr. see Sima Qian.
Scott, John A. St. Clair: Three Narratives.
Scott, John D. Pretty Penny.
Scott, John P. & Fuller, John L., eds. Dog Behavior: The Genetic Basis.
Scott, Judy, ed. see Scott, Curt.
Scott, Justin. Normandie Triangle.
--A Pride of Royals.
--Rampage.
Scott, Kenneth J., ed. see Tyson, Joseph B.
Scott, Latayne C. To Love Each Other: A Woman's Workshop on First Corinthians.
Scott, M. L. Homeopathy: Nature's Healing Law.
Scott, Margaret. The History of Dress: Late Gothic Europe, 1400-1500.
Scott, Michael. The Craft Business Encyclopedia.
--The Record of Singing.
Scott, Michael D. & Powers, William G. Interpersonal Communication: A Question of Needs.
Scott, Natalie. Wherever We Step the Land Is Mined.
Scott, Nathan A., Jr. The Poetry of Civic Virtue: Eliot, Malraux, Auden.
Scott, Nathan A., Jr., ed. Adversity & Grace: Studies in Recent American Literature.
Scott, Neville W. Today & Tomorrow.
Scott, Niki. The Balancing Act: A Handbook for Working Mothers.
Scott, Otto J. The Creative Ordeal: The Story of Raytheon.
--The Professional.
Scott, P. A Coloured Key to the Wildfowl of the World.
Scott, Patrick, ed. see Clough, Arthur H.
Scott, Patrick B., jt. auth. see Howell, Richard D.
Scott, Patrick G. The Early Editions of Arthur Hugh Clough.
Scott, Paul. Raj Quartet.
Scott, Peter. The Crisis of the University.
Scott, Peter G. Strategies for Postsecondary Education.
Scott Publishing Company Staff, ed. Scott Nineteen Eighty-One Stamp Catalogue: United States-United Nations-Canada.
Scott, Quinta. Eads Bridge: Photographic Essay.
Scott, R. H. Jean-Baptiste Lully, the Founder of French Opera.
Scott, R. W. Handy Medical Guide for Seafarers: Fishermen, Trawlermen & Yachtsmen.
Scott, Rachel. In the Dead of the Night.
--Stalk a Stranger.
Scott, Randolph. The Barn.
Scott, Ray G. How to Build Your Own Underground Home.
--How to Build Your Own Underground Home.
Scott, Richard. A Game of Chess.
Scott, Robert. Office at Home.
--Office at Home: Everything You Need to Know to Work Efficiently & Happily from Home.
Scott, Robert F. Shooter's Bible: 1984 Edition.
Scott, Robert G. Design Fundamentals.
Scott, Robert H. & Nigro, Nic. Principles of Economics.
--Principles of Macroeconomics.
Scott, Robert S. The Physicians & Sportsmedicine Guide to Raquetball & Squash.
Scott, Sir Robert. Limuria: The Lesser Dependencies of Maritius.
Scott, Ronald. Chemical Hazards in the Workplace.
Scott, Ronald B. & Fraser, James. The Medical Annual 1981-82.
--The Medical Annual 1982-83.
Scott, Ruth K. & Hrebenar, Ronald J. Parties in Crisis: Party Politics in America.
Scott, Sally. Brand New Kitten.
--Judy's Summer Adventure.

Authors

--What Susan Wanted.
Scott, Shirley. The Thoughts of Giants & Other Poems.
Scott, Stanley & Davis, Levi. A Giant in Texas o.p.
Scott, Stanley, jt. auth. see Squire, Peverill.
Scott, Stanley, ed. Coastal Conservation: Essays on Experiments in Governance.
Scott, Stanley & Nathan, Harriet, eds. Adapting Government to Regional Needs: Report of the Conference on Bay Area Regional Organization, April 18, 1970.
Scott, T. & Scott, A. British Parasitic Copepoda.
Scott, Thomas & Brewer, Mary, eds. Concise Encyclopedia of Biochemistry.
Scott, Timothy Van see Van Scott, Timothy & Weiss, Sidney J.
Scott, Tom. Ten Years Inside.
Scott, Tom, ed. Plant Regulation & World Agriculture.
Scott, Toni. The Complete Book of Stuffedwork.
Scott, Virginia M. Belonging.
Scott, W. A. & Werner, R., eds. Molecular Cloning of Recombinant DNA.
Scott, Walter. The Abbot.
--The Fortunes of Nigel. Link, Frederick M., ed.
--Ivanhoe.
--Rob Roy.
--Waverley.
Scott, Walter, ed. & tr. Hermetica: The Ancient Greek & Latin Writings Which Contain Religious or Philosophic Teachings Ascribed to Hermes Trismegistus.
Scott, Walter A., et al, eds. Mobilization & Reassembly of Genetic Information: Vol. 17 of the Miami Winter Symposia.
Scott, Willard & Paisner, Daniel. America Is My Neighborhood.
Scott, William E. & Podsakoff, Phillip M. Behavioral Principles in the Practice of Management.
Scott, William G. & Hart, David K. Organizational America.
--Organizational America.
Scott, William L. Investing at the Race Track.
Scott, William R. & Gross, Fletcher, eds. Proceedings of the Conference on Finite Groups.
Scott, Winfield T. A Dirty Hand: The Literary Notebooks of Winfield Townley Scott.
Scott-Drennan, Lynn. Sweet Thunder.
Scott-Giles, C. W. Wimsey Family.
Scotti, Paul C. Police Divers.
Scottish Classics Group Staff, ed. Cicero: Pro Lege Manilia.
--Ecce Romani: Versiculi: A Companion in Verse.
Scottish Tourist Board Publication Staff. Scotland: Self Catering Accommodation.
Scott-Moncrieff, C. K., tr. see Stendhal.
Scott-Morgan, John. The Colonel Stephens Railways.
Scotto, Robert M. Three Contemporary Novelists: An Annotated Bibliography of Works by & About John Hawkes, Joseph Heller & Thomas Pynchon.
Scott-Washburn, Mildred. The Charm of Your Children.
Scott-Whiting, John. Return to God & His Gift of Healing.
Scourse, Nicolette. The Victorians & Their Flowers.
Scouten, Arthur H., intro. by. Restoration & Eighteenth Century Drama.
Scovel, Myra. In Clover.
Scoville, Joseph A. Old Merchants of New York City.
Scragg, Walter R. Directions: A Look at the Paths of Life.
Screen, Robert M. With My Face to the Rising Sun.
Scriabine, Alexander, et al. Nitrendipine.
Scribner, Charles, ed. see Hemingway, Ernest.
Scribner, Jay, ed. The Politics of Education: 76th Yearbook, Part 2.
Scribner, Kimball. Your Future in Aviation Careers in the Air.
--Your Future in Aviation Careers on the Ground.
Scribner, Toni. The Best Place in the World: A Wrinkles Storybook.
Scribner's, Charles, & Sons Staff. Historic Buildings of Massachusetts.
Scrimgeour, K. G. Chemistry & Control of Enzyme Reactions.
Scrimshaw & Vogel. Commodore 64 Music Master.
Scrimshaw, Susan C. & Hurtado, Elena. Rapid Assessement Procedures for Nutrition & Primary Health Care: Anthropological Approaches to Improving Programme Effectiveness.
Scripps, Edward W. Damned Old Crank: A Self-Portrait of E. W. Scripps Drawn from His Unpublished Writings. McCabe, Charles R., ed.
Scripta Technica, tr. see Bass, Jean.
Scripta Technica, tr. see Turov, E. A.
Scriven, Carl & Stevens, James. Food Equipment Facts: A Handbook for the Food Service Industry.
Scriven, Michael. Primary Philosophy.
Scrivner, Louise M. & Robinette, Danny R. Guide to Oral Interpretation: Solo & Group Performance.
Scrocco, Jean L., ed. A Christmas Treasury: Featuring Twas the Night Before Christmas.
Scrocco, Joseph D., Jr., jt. ed. see McGuire, William J.
Scroggie, M. G. Foundations of Radio.
Scroggie, W. Graham. Know Your Bible.
--Tested by Temptation.
Scroggins, Clara J. Silver Christmas Ornaments: A Collector's Guide.
Scrosati & Vincent, Colin A., eds. Alkali Metal, Alkaline-Earth Metal & Ammonium Halides in Amide Solvents.
Scruggs, jt. auth. see Flatt.
Scull, Andrew, ed. Madhouses, Mad-Doctors, & Madmen: The Social History of Psychiatry in the Victorian Era.
Scull, Theodore W. The Carefree Getaway Guide for New Yorkers: Day & Weekend Trips Without a Car.
Scullard, H. H. History of the Roman World: 753-146 BC.
Scullin, C. Michael. Excavation & Grading Code Administration, Inspection & Enforcement.
Scullion, John J., tr. see Westermann, Claus.
Scullion, John J., tr. see Zimmerli, Walther.
Scully, C. & Cawson, R. A. Medical Problems in Dentistry.
Scully, Diane H. Men Who Control Women's Health.
Scully, J. C., ed. Env-Sens Crack Prob in Nuc.
--Ion Implantation & Ion Beam Analysis Techniques in Corrosion Studies.
--Ion Implementation & Ion Beam Analysis Techniques in Corrosion: Selected Papers Presented at the Conference at the Corrosion & Protection Centre, UMIST, Manchester, 28-30 June 1978.
Scully, J. S. Electrochemical Techniques in Corrosion Testing & Research.
Scully, Muriel, jt. auth. see Scully, Peter.
Scully, Peter & Scully, Muriel. Modern Gym Fitness: The Complete Course.
Scully, R. F., jt. auth. see Serov, S. F.
Scully, V. J., Jr., jt. auth. see Downing, A. F.
Scully, Vincent. Shingle Style & the Stick Style: Architectural Theory & Design from Richardson to the Origins of Wright.
Scuro, jt. auth. see Lavine.
Scuro, Vincent. Wonders of Cattle.
Scurra, John, ed. see Kong, Bucksam & Ho, Eugene H.
Scutts, Jerry. Lion in the Sky.
Sea World, Inc. Staff. Shamu, Sea World Star.
Sea World Press Staff & Alan Sloan, Inc. The Sea World Alphabet Book.
Seabaugh, Jan. The Wings of Adrian.
Seaborg, G. T. & Loveland, W., eds. Nuclear Chemistry.
Seabrook, Jeremy, jt. auth. see Blackwell, Trevor.
Seabrooke, W., jt. auth. see Miles, C. W.
Seabury, David. Art of Selfishness: How to Deal with the Tyrants & Tyrannies in Your Life.
Seabury, Paul. The Wilhelmstrasse: A Study of German Diplomats under the Nazi Regime.
Seaby, H. A. Standard Catalogue of British Coins, Vol. One: Coins of England & the United Kingdom. Mitchell, Stephen & Reeds, Brian, eds.
Seagle, Janet, jt. ed. see Murdoch, Joseph S.
Seagle, John P., jt. auth. see Holstein, William K.
Seagraves, Margaret C. Move to Learn: Lessons Plans for Elementary Physical Education.
Seah, P., jt. auth. see Fry, L.
Seal, Hilary L. Survival Probabilities: The Goal of Risk Theory.
Seal, Robert A. & Martin, Sarah S. A Bibliography of Astronomy 1970 to 1979.
Seale, M. S. Qur'an & Bible: Studies in Interpretation & Dialogue.
Seale, Roland. Practical Designs for Wood Turning.
Seale, William. A Tasteful Interlude: American Interiors Through the Camera's Eye, 1860 to 1917.
Seale, William, jt. auth. see Hitchcock, Henry-Russell.
Sealey, Richard & Old, David. How to Keep Your Honda ATC Alive: A Manual of Step by Step Procedures Anyone Can Understand.
Sealy, Shirley. The Celebrity Sex Register: The Private Loves of Public People.
--I Have Chosen You.
Seaman, Donald. The Committee.
--Rogue Bear.
Seaman, Janet & Depauw, Karen. The New Adapted Physical Education: A Developmental Approach.
Seaman, Julian. Showing-Off: The Lighter Side of Show-Jumping.
Seaman, L. C. Post-Victorian Britain: 1902-1951.
Seaman, William, Jr., ed. Florida Aquatic Habitat & Fishery Resources.
Seaquist, V. G., jt. auth. see Carter, E. A.
Searcy, Margaret Z. The Charm of the Bear Claw Necklace: A Story of Stone Age Southeastern Indians.
Seare, Nicholas. Thirteen Thirty-Nine or So: Being an Apology for a Pedlar.
Searfoss, Lyndon W. & Jacobs, H. Donald. Decoding Inventory.
Searfoss, Lyndon W. & Readence, John E. Helping Children Learn to Read.
Searight, Mary. The Second Step: Baccalaureate Education for Registered Nurses.
Searight, Roland, jt. auth. see Hill, Frank W.
Searle, G. R., ed. see White, Arnold.
Searle, H., tr. see Stuckenschmidt, Hans H.
Searle, Ronald. The Big Fat Cat Book.
--Ronald Searle in Perspective: The Best of His Work 1938-1985. Brady, Upton & Evans, Harold, eds.
--To the Kwai -& Back: War Drawings, 1939 - 1945.
Searle, Ronald, jt. auth. see Shaw, Irwin.
Searle, W. & Jones, D. Smart BASIC for the Adam.
Searle-Chatterjee, Mary. Reversible Sex Roles: The Special Case of Benares Sweepers.
Searles, Baird. A Reader's Guide to Science Fiction.
Searles, Leon R. Captain Whistler.
Searls, Hank. Overboard.
Sears, Brenda. Which Way Are You Headed?
Sears, Cecil & Buckwalter, Jane. Dollars & Percents of Development Finance, 3rd Quarter to the 4th Quarter 1985.
Sears, D. F., jt. ed. see Prince, L. M.
Sears, David O. & McConahay, John B. Politics of Violence: The New Urban Blacks & the Watts Riot.
Sears, Donald A. Harbrace Guide to the Library & the Research Paper.
Sears, Lloyd C. Eyes of Jehovah: Life of James A. Harding.
Sears, Mary, compiled by. Oceanographic Index: Author Cumulation, 1946-1970: Woods Hole Oceanographic Institution, Mass.
Sears, Richard D. The Day of Small Things: Abolitionism in the Midst of Slavery, Berea, Kentucky, 1854-1864.
Sears, Robert R. & Feldman, S. Shirley, eds. The Seven Ages of Man: A Survey of Human Development.
Seashore, Carl E. Psychology of Music.
Seaton, Lionel. The International Arms Review, Vol. I.
Seaton, Lionel, tr. The International Arms Review.
Seaton, Shirley, jt. auth. see Brown, Malcolm.
Seattle Art Museum Staff. Earthworks: Land Reclamation as Sculpture.
Seaver. Jeannette's Secret.
Seaver, Richard, tr. see Duras, Marguerite.
Seaver, Richard, tr. see Ionesco, Eugene.
Seaver, Tom & Appel, Martin. Tom Seaver's All-Time Baseball Greats. Barish, Wendy, ed.
Seaver, Tom & Seigel, Alice. Tom Seaver's Baseball Card Book.
Seavey, George R. & Pratt, S. D. Disposal of Dredged Material in Rhode Island: An Evaluation of Past Practices & Future Options.
Seavey, Warren A., et al. Cases on Agency & Partnership.
Seawell, L. Hospital Financial Accounting Theory & Practice.
Seay, Bill M. & Gottfried, Nathan. The Development of Behavior: A Synthesis of Developmental & Comparative Psychology.
Seay, Davin & Neely, Mary. Stairway to Heaven: Religion in Rock.
Seay, Maurice F. Community School.
Sebald, A. V., ed. Mathematical Models & Simulation in Solar Energy Research for Buildings.
Sebald, William J. & Brines, Russell. With MacArthur in Japan.
Sebba, Anne. Samplers: Four Centuries of a Gentle Craft.
Sebba, G. Bibliographia Cartesiana: A Critical Guide to the Descartes Literature (1800-1960)
Sebeok, T. A., jt. ed. see Umiker-Sebeok, D. J.
Sebeok, Thomas A., ed. Native Languages of the Americas, Vol. 1.
--Native Languages of the Americas, Vol. 2.
--Sight, Sound, & Sense.
Sebree, Mac, ed. see Hamm, Edward, Jr.
Sebree, Mac, ed. see Johnston, Hank.
Sebree, Mac, ed. see Schultz, Russell E.
Sebree, Mac, ed. see Youngblood, Peter.
Sechi, Stephan M. The Talislantan Handbook.
Sechi, Stephan M. & Keith, J. Andrew. The Bestiary.
Sechi, Stephen M., et al. The Lexicon.
Sechrest, Lee, ed. Training Program Evaluators.
Seckler, David. Thorstein Veblen & the Institutionalists: A Study in the Philosophy of Economics.
Seckler, David, jt. auth. see Barkley, Paul W.
Seckler, David, ed. California Water: A Study in Resource Management.
Seckler, Dorothy G. Provincetown Painters. Kuchta, Ronald A., ed.
Secor, Marie & Fahnestock, Jeanne. A Rhetoric for Argument.
Secrest, Meryle. Being Bernard Berenson.
--Kenneth Clark.
Securities & Exchange Commission, United States & Practising Law Institute Staff. SEC Enforcement Issues: An Advanced Seminar.
Seddon, Edmund. Modern Economic History.
Seddon, George. The Pocket Guide to Indoor Plants.
Seddon, Leigh. Your Window Greenhouse.
Seddon, R. G., ed. see Steiner, Rudolf.
Sedej, Ivan. Lackovic.
Seder, John & Burrell, Berkeley G. Getting It Together: Black Businessmen in America.
Sederbaum, Arthur D., jt. auth. see Practising Law Institute Staff.
Sederberg, Peter C. Interpreting Politics: An Introduction to Political Science.
Sedgwick, Catherine M. Hope Leslie: Or, Early Times in the Massachuetts.
Sedjo, Roger A. & Ostermeier, David M. Policy Alternatives for Nonindustrial Private Forests.
Sedlack, Elaine. The Nordic Skier's Guide to Montana.
Sedlar, Jean W. India in the Mind of Germany: Schelling, Schopenhauer & Their Times.
Sedov, L. I., ed. see International Union of Theoretical & Applied Mechanics Symposium Vienna 1966.
Sedra, Adele S. & Smith, Kenneth C. Microelectronic Circuits.
Sedugin, P. I., jt. auth. see Gureyev, P. P.
Sedwick, Frank. Conversation in Spanish: Points of Departure.
Sedwick, Frank, jt. auth. see Bonnel, Peter.
Sedwick, Frank, jt. auth. see Bonnell, Peter.
See, Carolyn. Golden Days.
See, Ruth D. Make the Bible Your Own.
See, Ruth D., jt. auth. see Hageman, Howard G.
See, Thomas, jt. auth. see Wheatley, Paul.
Seebeck, jt. auth. see Hummel.
Seeber, Gerd C. The Abduction.
Seeberg, Erling & Kleppe, Kjell, eds. Chromosome Damage & Repair.
Seeburg Company Staff. Seeburg Jukebox Service Manual, Brochure & Trouble-Shooting Guide for 1957 Models KS200, KD200 & L100. Adams, Frank, ed.
Seeds, Harice L. Structured FORTRAN 77 for Business & General Applications.
Seeds, Michael A. Horizons: Exploring the Universe.
Seeds, Nicholas M., et al, eds. Cell Aggregation & Adhesion.
Seeger, Pete & Reiser, Bob. Carry It On: A History in Song of Working Men & Women.
Seeger, Raymond J. Benjamin Franklin.
--Galileo Galilei, His Life & Work.
--Josiah Willard Gibbs - American Physicist Par Excellance.
See-Lasley, Kay & Ignoffo, Robert. Manual of Oncology Therapeutics.
Seele, Hermann. The Cypress & Other Writings of a German Pioneer in Texas. Breitenkamp, Edward C., tr. from Ger.
Seele, Keith C. Tomb of Tjanefer at Thebes.
Seele, Keith C., ed. see Hayes, William C.
Seeler, Edgar, jt. auth. see Seeler, Katherine.
Seeler, Katherine & Seeler, Edgar. Nantucket Lightship Baskets.
Seeley, Colleen, jt. auth. see Seeley, Mildred.
Seeley, John R. The Expansion of England. Gross, John, ed.
Seeley, Mildred & Seeley, Colleen. Doll Collecting for Fun & Profit.
--Doll Costuming.
Seeley, R. R., jt. ed. see Lawton, C. W.
Seeley, Vernon D. & Thompson, Robert L. Activities in Ceramics.
Seelig, Mildred S., jt. ed. see Cantin, Marc.
Seely, Clinton, tr. see Sen, Ramprasad.
Seely, G. R., jt. auth. see Vernon, Leo P.
Seely, James. Great Wines of Bordeaux.
Seely, Margaret. A Handbook for Citizenship.
Seely, Norma. Dream Chaser.
Seely, Samuel. Introduction to Engineering Systems.
Seelye, John. Dirty Tricks: Or Nick Noxin's Natural Nobility.
Seese, William S. & Daub, Guida H. Basic Chemistry.
Seesholtz, Anne. Saint Elizabeth.
Seetzen, Jurgen V., et al, eds. Makrookonomische Input-Output Analysen und Dynamische Modelle zur Erfassung Technischer Entwicklung.
Seferis, James C. & Nicolais, Luigi, eds. The Role of the Polymeric Matrix in the Processing & Structural Properties Composite Materials.
Sefton, Catherine. Blue Misty Monsters.
--The Emma's Dilemma.
--Ghost & Bertie Boggin.
Segal. Be My Friend.
--Immigrating to Canada.
Segal, Arthur. City Planning in Ancient Times: Digging up the Past.

Authors

Segal, Edith. Come with Me: Poems for the Young.
Segal, Erich. The Class.
--Love Story.
--Love Story.
--Oliver's Story.
Segal, Harold & Doyle, Darrell J., eds. Protein Turnover & Lysosome Function.
Segal, Hillel & Burst, Jess. How to Select Your Small Computer Without Frustration.
Segal, Jeanne. Feeling Great.
--Living Beyond Fear: A Tool for Transformation.
Segal, Julius & Segal, Zelda. Growing up Smart & Happy: What Every Parent Should Know.
Segal, Julius & Yahraes, Herbert. A Child's Journey: Forces That Shape the Lives of Our Young.
Segal, Marilyn. From Birth to One Year. Bardige, Betty, ed.
Segal, Marilyn & Adcock, Don. From One to Two Years. Spiegel, Ruth, ed.
--From Two to Three Years Old-Play & Learning. Talpins, Susan, ed.
Segal, Marilyn, jt. auth. see Adcock, Don.
Segal, Ronald, jt. auth. see Kidron, Michael.
Segal, S. J. & Winikoff, B., eds. Health & Population in Developing Countries: Selected Papers from the 5th Bellagio Populaion Conference, Rockefeller Foundation, Bellagio, 1979.
Segal, S. S. No Child Is Ineducable.
Segal, Sheldon J., jt. ed. see Channing, Cornelia C.
Segal, Sydney J., ed. see Center for Research in Cognition & Effect Staff.
Segal, Zelda, jt. auth. see Segal, Julius.
Segall, J. Peter. Deduct This Book: How Not to Pay Taxes While Ronald Reagan Is President.
Segall, Marshall, jt. ed. see Ulin, Priscilla.
Segall, Marshall H., jt. auth. see Brislin, Richard W.
Segall, Marshall H., et al. Political Identity: A Case Study from Uganda.
Segallis, William. Guide to Electronic Components.
Segalowitz, Sid J. Two Sides of the Brain.
Segel, Harold B., ed. Polish Romantic Drama: Three Plays in English Translation.
Seger, Doris. Obedience to Authority.
Seger, Gerhart H. Germany.
Segerstedt, T., ed. Ethics for Science Policy: Proceedings.
Segerstedt, Torgny, ed. The Frontiers of Human Knowledge: Lectures Held at the Quincentenary Celebrations of Uppsala University 1977.
Segi, Shinichi. Yoshitoshi-the Splendid Decadent: The Last Master of Ukiyo-e. Birnbaum, Alfred, tr.
Seglin, Jeffrey L., ed. see Oldham, Frank, Jr.
Segovia, Fernando F., ed. Discipleship in the New Testament.
Segraves, Judy. Come on into My House. Wallace, Mary, ed.
Seguin, Mary M. & O'Brien, Beatrice, eds. Releasing the Potential of the Older Volunteer.
Segundo, Juan L. The Community Called Church. Drury, John, tr. from Span.
--Our Idea of God. Drury, John, tr. from Span.
Segura, Robert, jt. auth. see Hanson, Marilyn.
Seguy, E. A. Exotic Floral Patterns in Color.
Sehgal, V. N. Clinical Leprosy.
--A Textbook of Venereal Diseases.
Sehlinger, Bob. The Unofficial Guide to Disneyland.
Sehlinger, Bob & Finley, John. The Unofficial Guide to Walt Disney & Epcot.
Sehnert, Keith W. & Eisenberg, Howard. How to Be Your Own Doctor (Sometimes)
Sehnert, Keith W., jt. auth. see Eisenberg, Howard.
Seibel, Hugo & Guyer, Kenneth E. Barron's How to Prepare for the New Medical College Admission Test (MCAT)
Seiber, Marilyn J. International Borrowing by Developing Countries.
Seiber, Marilyn J., jt. auth. see Franko, Lawrence G.
Seiberling, Grace. Monet's Series.
Seibert, Charles H., tr. see Heidegger, Martin & Fink, Eugen.
Seidel, Beverly L. & Resnick, Matthew C. Physical Education: An Overview.
Seidel, Beverly L., et al. Sports Skills: A Conceptual Approach to Meaningful Movement.
Seidel, G. E., et al. Gonadotrophins: Current Research.
Seidel, Hans, ed. Geldwertstabilitat und Wirtschaftswachstum.
Seidel, Linda. Romanesque Sculpture from the Cathedral of Saint-Etienne, Toulouse.
Seiden, Art, illus. My ABC Book.
Seiden, Donald, jt. auth. see Meilach, Dona Z.
Seiden, Eric A. DARAD Plus. DAR Systems International Staff, ed.
Seiden, Lewis S. & Dykstra, Linda A. Psychopharmacology: A Behavioral & Biochemical Approach.
--Psychopharmacology: A Biochemical & Behavioral Approach.
Seiden, Othniel J. Coping with Diabetes.
Seiden, Rudolph. Livestock Health Encyclopedia. Gough, W. James, ed.
Seidenberg, Dana A. Uhuru & the Kenya Indians: The Role of a Minority Community in Kenya-1939-1963-Politics.
Seidenberg, Margaret M. Click's Cookie Cornucopia.
Seidenberg, Robert. Corporate Wives Corporate Casualties: Why Women are Challenging American Business.
Seidenberg, Robert & DeCrow, Karen. Women Who Marry Houses: Panic & Protest in Agoraphobia.
Seidensticker, Edward G. Genji Days.
Seidensticker, John. Managing Elephant Depredation in Agricultural & Forestry Projects.
Seidl, Frederick, et al. Delivering In-Home Services to the Aged & Disabled: The Wisconsin Experiment.
Seidler, Armond. Defend Yourself: Scientific Personal Defense.
Seidler, Barbara. Queen Wanda & the Wawel Dragon. Kedron, Jane, tr.
Seidler, G. L. The Emergence of the Eastern World.
Seidman, Ann. The Roots of Crisis in Southern Africa.
Seidman, Ann & Makgetla, Neva S. Outposts of Monopoly Capitalism: Southern Africa in the Changing Global Economy.
Seidman, Ann & Seidman, Neva. South Africa & U. S. Multinational Corporations.
Seidman, Arthur H., jt. auth. see Kaufman, Milton.
Seidman, Hugh. Blood Lord.
Seidman, Neva, jt. auth. see Seidman, Ann.
Seifert, Hans T., ed. see Duvernoy, J. B.
Seifert, Hans T., ed. see Streabbog, L.
Seifert, Harvey. New Power for the Church.
Seifert, Harvey, jt. auth. see Bennett, John C.
Seifert, Ralph T., jt. auth. see Gucker, Frank T.
Seiffert, G. Virus Diseases in Man, Plant, & Animal.
Seifritz, W., ed. see World Hydrogen Energy Conference Staff.
Seigel, Alice, jt. auth. see Seaver, Tom.
Seigfried, Charlene H. Chaos & Context: A Study in William James.
Seiichiro, Takahashi, ed. see Lane, Richard.
Seiler, Beth. Phonics Fun Crossword Puzzles.
Seiler, Farrell S. Wind Energy Abstracts, 1983.
--Wind Energy Abstracts: 1984.
--Wind Energy Abstracts: 1985.
Seiler, Farrell S., ed. Wind Energy Abstracts, 1983.
--Wind Energy Abstracts, 1984.
--Windmills & Windpumps.
Seiler, Sabine, ed. see Steiner, Rudolf.
Seilhamer, Frank H. Prophets & Prophecy: Seven Key Messengers.
Seims, Charles. Mount Lowe: Railway in the Clouds.
Sein, Kenneth & Withey, J. A. The Great Po Sein: A Chronicle of the Burmese Theater.
Seinfeld, John H., jt. auth. see Lapidus, Leon.
Seipel, L., jt. ed. see Loogen, F.
Seireg, Ali, ed. Advances in Computer Technology. Incl. Vol. I. Industry; Energy; Robots & Manipulators; Mini & Micro Software; Application & Design; Vol. II. Microprocessor; Automotive Development; Systems; Data Base; Finite Elements; Graphics; Education; Manufacturing; Management; Language Standards; Personal Computing. ASME.
Seiss, Joseph. Gospel in Leviticus.
Seitelberger, F., ed. see Brain Edema Symposium Staff.
Seitelberger, F., ed. see International Symposium on Malignant Lymphomas of the Nervous System.
Seitelberger, F., ed. see Symposium on Pathology of Axons & Axonal Flow, Vienna, 1970.
Seitelberger, F., ed. see Symposium on Presenile Spongy Encephalopathies, Vienna, 1965.
Seiter, Charles, jt. auth. see Weiss, Robert.
Seitz, Don C. Under the Black Flag.
Seitz, F. Students Concerto No. 4 in D Major for Violin & Piano, Op..15.
Seiver, Daniel A. Outperforming Wall Street: Stock Market Profits Through Patience.
Seixas, Vic, Jr. & Cohen, Joel. Prime Time Tennis.
--Prime Time Tennis.
Seizo, Hayashiya. Chanoyu: Japanese Tea Ceremony.
Sekhar, Uday. Industrial Location Policy: The Indian Experience.
Seki, Hozen, tr. see Okada, Barbara T.
Sekiguchi, Sueo, ed. ASEAN-Japan Relations: Investment.
Sekler, Mary P. The Early Drawings of Charles Edouard Jeanneret le Corbusier 1902-1908.
Sekowsky, Jo Anne, ed. see Wood, George.
Sekulow, Marianne W., jt. auth. see Rosenberg, Naomi R.
Sekura, Ronald & Moss, Joel, eds. Pertussis Toxin.
Sela, M. & Prywes, M., eds. Topics in Basic Immunology.
Selbourne, David, ed. The Making of a Midsummer Night's Dream: An Eye-Witness Account of Peter Brook's Production from First Rehearsal to First Night.
Selby, Bettina. Riding to Jerusalem.
Selby, George. Migraine & Its Variants.
Selby, Henry A., jt. auth. see Johnston, Francis E.
Selby, Hubert, Jr. Last Exit to Brooklyn.
--Last Exit to Brooklyn: A Novel.
Selby, John B. & Frey, Donald G. Self-Assessment of Current Knowledge in Nuclear Medicine.
Selby, P., ed. Influenza: Virus Vaccines & Strategy.
Selby, Peter. Look for the Living: The Corporate Nature of Resurrection Faith.
Selby-Bigge, L. A., ed. British Moralists.
Selden, George. Irma & Jerry.
--Oscar Lobster's Fair Exchange.
--Tucker's Countryside.
Selden, Mark, ed. People's Republic of China: A Documentary History of Revolutionary Change.
Seldes, Marian. The Bright Lights: A Theatre Life.
--Time Together.
Seldin, Tim. Geography & History for the Young Child: The Montessori Approach.
Seldon, Anthony & Pappworth, Joanna, eds. By Word of Mouth.
Selecky, Paul A. Pulmonary Disease.
Seley, John E. The Politics of Public-Facility Planning.
Self, Charles R. The Complete Handbook of Woodworking Tools & Hardware.
Self, Huber. Environment & Man in Kansas: A Geographical Analysis.
Self, Tim, jt. auth. see Srnka, Q. M.
Selfe, Lorna. Nadia: A Case of Extraordinary Drawing Ability in an Autistic Child.
Selig, Stephen F., jt. auth. see Practising Law Institute Staff.
Seliger, Howard H. & McElroy, W. D. Light: Physical & Biological Action.
Seligman, Gerald. Business Spelling.
Seligman, Joel. The High Citadel.
--The Transformation of Wall Street.
Seligman, Lester G. & Cornwell, Elmer E., Jr., eds. New Deal Mosaic: Roosevelt Confers with His National Emergency Council 1933-1936.
Seligman, Martin E., jt. ed. see Garber, Judy.
Seligman, Paul. The Apeiron of Anaximander.
Seligson, David see Reiner, Miriam, et al.
Seligson, Harry & Bardwell, George. Labor-Management Relations in Colorado.
Seligson, Marcia. Cosmopolitan's Super Diets & Exercise Guide.
Seligson, Mitchell A. & Williams, Edward J. Maquiladoras & Migration: Workers in the Mexico-U.S. Border Program.
Selin, Iuan. Detection Theory.
Selincourt, Basil De see De Selincourt, Basil.
Selinker, Larry & Gass, Susan. Workbook in Second Language Acquisition.
--Workbook in Second Language Aquisition.
Selinker, Larry, jt. ed. see Gass, Susan.
Selkin, James & Schouten, Peter. The Child Sexual Abuse Case in the Courtroom: A Source Book.
Selkirk, Elisabeth O. Phonology & Syntax: The Relation Between Sound & Structure.
Selkowe, Valrie M. Spring Green.
Sell, Betty, jt. ed. see Sell, Kenneth D.
Sell, Kenneth D. & Sell, Betty, eds. Divorce in the United States, Canada & Great Britain: A Guide to Information Sources.
Sell, Nancy J. Industrial Pollution Control: Issues & Techniques.
Sell, Stewart, jt. ed. see Fishman, William H.
Sell, Stewart, jt. ed. see Milman, Harry A.
Sellars, Dot. Computerizing Your Medical Office: A Guide for Physicians & Their Staffs.
Sellars, Wilfrid. Science & Metaphysics: Variations on Kantian Themes.
Sellars, Wilfrid, jt. ed. see Freeman, Eugene.
Selle, Robert, jt. auth. see Worswick, Marilyn.
Seller, Maxine S. To Seek America: A History of Ethnic Life in the United States.
Sellers, Charles, et al. A Synopsis of American History: Complete Volume.
Sellers, Charles C., ed. see Belknap, Waldron P., Jr.
Sellers, Con. Those Frightened Years.
Sellers, Gene, jt. auth. see Groza, Vivian S.
Sellers, K. C., jt. ed. see Lloyd, D. H.
Sellers, L. The Simple Subs Book.
Sellers, Larry G., et al. Explorations in Zoology.
Sellers, Robert V. Two Ancient Christologies: A Study in the Christological Thought of the Schools of Alexandria & Antioch in the Early History of Christian Doctrine.
Sellers, Steve. Terror on Highway Fifty-Nine.
Sellers, Terence. The Correct Sadist.
Sellery, J'nan M., jt. ed. see Vickery, John B.
Selley, R. C. Introduction to Sedimentology.
Sellin, Don & Birch, Jack. Educating Gifted & Talented Learners.
--Psychoeducational Development of Gifted & Talented Learners.
Sellin, Donald F. Mental Retardation: Nature, Needs, & Advocacy.
Sellin, Thorsten & Young, Donald, eds. China, the Annals of the American Academy of Political & Social Science.
Sellin, Thorsten, ed. see American Academy of Political & Social Science, Philadelphia Staff.
Sellin, Thorsten, jt. ed. see Peel, Roy V.
Sellman, Hunton D. & Lessley, Merrill J. Essentials of Stage Lighting.
Sellon, Emily B., jt. ed. see Laszlo, Ervin.
Sells, jt. auth. see Haskins.
Sells, jt. auth. see Weidner.
Sells, A. Lytton, tr. see James Second King of Great Britain.
Sellstedt, B., jt. auth. see Naeslund, B.
Selma, Jose U., adapted by. Don Quijote De la Mancha.
Selman, Edythea G., jt. auth. see Lindenauerer, Nancy.
Selsam, Millicent E. & Goor, Ronald. Backyard Insects.
Seltz, David. How to Get Started in Your Own Franchise Business.
Seltz, David D. Branchising: Proven Techniques for Rapid Company Expansion.
Seltz, David D. & Leslie, Mary. New Businesses Women Can Start & Successfully Operate.
Seltzer, Albert P., et al, eds. Pulmonary Pathology & Aging.
Seltzer, George. Music Making.
Seltzer, Sanford & Stackhouse, Max L. Death of Dialogue & Beyond.
Selub, Morton & Bramson, Morris. How to Prepare for the High School Competency & Proficiency Tests.
Seluca, Tom. The Power of the TRS-80 Color Computer.
Selvey, Nancy, jt. ed. see White, Philip.
Selwood, Pierce W. Adsorption & Collective Paramagnetism.
Selwyn, Edward G. The First Epistle of St. Peter.
Selz, Jean. Foujita.
Selz, Nina. Teaching of Employability Skills: Who's Responsible?
Selz, Nina & Ashley, William L. Teaching for Transfer: A Perspective.
Selz, Nina, et al. Functional Competencies for Adapting to the World of Work.
Selz, Peter. Sam Francis. Einstein, Susan & Butterfiled, Jan, eds.
Selzer, Arthur. The Heart: Its Function in Health & Disease.
Selzer, Richard. Mortal Lessons, Notes in the Art of Surgery.
--Mortal Lessons: Notes on the Art of Surgery.
--Rituals of Surgery.
Selznick, Philip & Nonet, Philippe. Law, Society, & Industrial Justice.
Semat, Henry & Baumel, Philip. Fundamentals of Physics.
Sembach, Klaus-Jurgen. Marlene Dietrich: Portraits 1926-1960. Wensinger, Arthur S. & Wood, Richard H., trs.
Semchyshen, M. Advanced Materials for Pressure Vessel Service with Hydrogen at High Temperature & Pressures.
Semel, Ann. Monarch Notes: Introduction to American Minority Literature.
Semendyayev, K. A., jt. auth. see Bronshtein, I. N.
Semenenko, L., et al. La Revolucion Debe Saber Defenderse.
Semenza, G. Of Oxygen, Fuels & Living Matter.
Semere, Mario G. A Guide to Hand Lettering.
Seminar on Differential Equations & Dynamical Systems, 2nd, 1969. Proceedings. Yorke, J. A., ed.
Seminar on Engineering Equipment for Foundries & Advanced Methods of Producing Such Equipment, Geneva, 1977. Engineering Equipment for Foundries: Proceedings. United Nations Economic Commission for Europe, Geneva, ed.
Seminar on Petroleum Legislation Staff. Offshore Operation: Proceedings.
SEMINEX Staff. Semiconductor & Microprocesor Technology 1979: Proceedings of the Seminex Technical Seminar & Exhibition, London, England, March 26-30, 1979. Dummer, G. W. A., ed.
Semm, K., ed. see World Conference on Embryo Transfer in Vitro Fertilization & Instrumental Insemination Staff.
Semmler, Clement. The Banjo of the Bush: The Life & Times of A. B. "Banjo" Paterson.
Semper, Edward & Coggin, Philip, eds. Hidden Factors in Technological Change.
Semprun, Jorge. What a Beautiful Sunday! Sheridan, Alan, tr. from Fr.
Semyonov, V. Nations & Internationalism.
Sen, Anupam. The State, Industrialization & Class Formations in India: A Neo-Marxist Perspective on Colonialism, Underdevelopment & Development.

Authors

Sen, K. D. Atomic & Molecular Polarizability.
Sen, P. K. Logic, Induction & Ontology.
Sen, Ramprasad. Grace & Mercy in Her Wild Hair. Nathan, Leonard & Seely, Clinton, trs. from Bengali.
Senay, Edward C. Substance Abuse Disorders in Clinical Practice.
Sendak, Jack. The King of the Hermits & Other Stories.
Sendak, Maurice. Chicken Soup with Rice: A Book of Months.
Sendaydiego, Henry, jt. ed. see Slaatte, Howard A.
Sender, Florence H., ed. see Sender, Ramon.
Sender, Ramon. Jubileo en el Zocalo. Sender, Florence H., ed.
Sendov, B. & Stanchev, I., eds. Children in an Information Age: Tomorrow's Problems Today: Selected Papers from the International Conference, Varna, Bulgaria, 6-9 May 1985.
Sendry, Alfred. Music in Ancient Israel.
Senefelder, Alois. A Complete Course of Lithography.
Senelick, Laurence. Anton Chekhov. King, Bruce & King, Adele, eds.
--Anton Chekhov. King, Bruce & King, Adele, eds.
Senelick, Laurence, jt. auth. see Haskell, Patricia.
Seng, Peter J. The Vocal Songs in the Plays of Shakespeare: A Critical History.
Senghor, L. S. Nocturnes.
Sen Gupta, Bhabani. The Afghan Syndrome: How to Live with Soviet Power.
Sengupta, Jati K., jt. auth. see Tintner, Gerhard.
Sengupta, S. P. Some Aspects of Shakespeare's Sonnets.
Senhouse, Roger, tr. see Colette.
Senior, Bernard M. Jamaica, As It Was, As It Is, & As It May Be.
Senior, Donald. God the Son.
Senior, John. Way down & Out: The Occult in Symbolist Literature.
Senior, Michael, ed. see Malory, Thomas.
Senje, Sigurd. Escape! Ramsden, Evelyn, tr.
Senn, Alfred. Lithuanian Dialectology.
Senn, Alfred E. The Emergence of Modern Lithuania.
Senn, Frank C. Christian Worship & Its Cultural Setting.
--The Pastor As Worship Leader: A Manual for Corporate Worship.
Senn, Steve. Circle in the Sea.
--In the Castle of the Bear.
--Ralph Fozbek & the Amazing Black Hole Patrol.
Senna, Joseph J. & Siegel, Larry J. Introduction to Criminal Justice.
Senna, Joseph J., jt. auth. see Siegel, Larry J.
Sennett, Mack. King of Comedy.
Sennett, Richard. Families Against the City: Middle Class Homes of Industrial Chicago, 1872-1890.
Sennett, Ted. Great Hollywood Movies.
--Great Movie Directors.
Sennett, Ted, ed. The Movie Buff's Book.
Sennholz, Lyn M. & Sennholz, Robert F. Future Broker Home Study Course.
Sennholz, Robert F., jt. auth. see Sennholz, Lyn M.
Seno, S., jt. auth. see Cowdry, E. V.
Sensoir, Jean-Jacques. The Ninth Decade: Secret Plans for the Coming Communist Takeovers.
Senter, Mark, III. The Art of Recruiting Volunteers.
Senter, Sylvia, et al. Women at Work.
Senterfitt, Arnold D. Airports of Baja California & North Western Mexico.
Sentlowitz, Michael, jt. auth. see Brett, William.
Senzaki, Nyogen, jt. auth. see McCandless, Ruth S.
Senzel, Howard. Baseball & the Cold War: Being a Soliloquy on the Necessity of Baseball. Okrent, ed.
Seo, Hiroshi. Boeing 747.
--Civil Aircraft in Colour.
--Military Aircraft in Colour.
--Military Aircraft of the World.
Sepetys, Jonas. Critique of Relativity.
--The Revelation of Humanity.
Seplaki, Les. Antitrust & the Economics of the Market: Text, Readings, Cases.
Sepmeyer, Inez, jt. auth. see Sasnett, Martena.
Seppala, M., jt. ed. see Grudzinskas, J. B.
Ser-Vol-Tel Institute Staff. Fry Cooking.
Serafini, Aldo, ed. Nuclear Cardiology: Principles & Methods.
Serafini, P. Mathematics of Multi Objective Optimization.
Seranne, Ann, jt. auth. see Hettich, Arthur.
Seraphin, B. O., ed. Solar Energy Conversion: Solid-State Physics Aspects.
Serapiao, Luis B. & El-Khawas, Mohamed A. Mozambique in the Twentieth Century: From Colonialism to Independence.
Serban, George, ed. Nutrition & Mental Functions.
Sercarz, Eli, ed. Regulatory Genetics of the Immune System.
Sercarz, Eli, et al, eds. The Immune System: Genes, Receptors, Signals.
Sercarz, Eli E. & Cunningham, Alastair J., eds. Strategies of Immune Regulation.
Serebriakoff, Victor. How Intelligent Are You?
Sereville, Etienne de & Saint-Simon, Fernand de. Supplement au Dictionnaire de la Noblesse Francaise.
Sergeant, Howard. Poems from the Medical World.
Sergeant, Howard, ed. African Voices.
Sergeant, Philip W. Witches & Warlocks.
Sergel, David. Macrobiotic Shiatsu.
Sergent, Bernard. Homosexuality in Greek Myth. Goldhammer, Arthur, tr. from Fr.
Sergeyev, F. Chile, CIA, Big Business.
Sergrovanni, Thomas J., et al. Educational Governance & Administration.
Serig, Joseph A., jt. ed. see Hughes, Richard.
Serjeant, R. B. & Bidwell, R. L., eds. Arabian Studies.
Serling, Rod. Stories from the Twilight Zone.
Serneri, Neri G. G. & Prentice, C. Haemostasis & Thrombosis.
Seroff, Victor. Common Sense in Piano Study.
--Sergei Prokofiev: A Soviet Tragedy.
Serota, Nicholas, jt. auth. see Nairne, Sandy.
Serov, S. F. & Scully, R. F. Histological Typing of Ovarian Tumours.
Serpell, Christopher & Serpell, Jean. The Travellers' Guide to Elba & the Tuscan Archipelago.
Serpell, Jean, jt. auth. see Serpell, Christopher.
Serpico, Tom. Tom, the Poet & Gadgetmaker.
Serra, Pere A. Miro & Mallorca.
Serrano, Miguel. NOS: Book of Resurrection.
Serrano Mesa, Eleesbaan. Diccionario Ingles-Espanol, Espanol-Ingles Forja.
Serre, J. P. & Zagier, D. B., eds. Modular Functions of One Variable: Proceedings of the International Conference, Sonderforsch-ungsbereich Theoretische Mathmatik, University of Bonn, July, 1976.
--Modular Functions of One Variable 5: Proceedings.
Serres, Frederick J. de see De Serres, Frederick J., et al.
Serres, Michel. The Parasite. Schehr, Lawrence R., tr. from Fr.
Serri, F., ed. International Conference on Five per Cent Fluorouracil Ointment in Dermatology.
Serrou, B. & Rosenfeld, C. Human Lymphocyte Differentiation: Its Application to Cancer.
Sertima, Ivan Van see Van Sertima, Ivan.
Serullaz, Maurice. Velazquez.
Servan-Schreiber, Jean-J. The American Challenge. Steel, Ronald, tr. from Fr.
Servan-Schreiber, Jean-Jacques. Spirit of May.
Ser Vass, Cory & Turgeon, Charlotte. The High Lysine & Fiber Cancer Prevention Cookbook.
Serventy, Vincent. Desert Walkabout.
Service, Elman R. Origins of the State & Civilization: The Process of Cultural Evolution.
--Spanish-Guarani Relations in Early Colonial Paraguay.
Servin, Manuel P. Mexican Americans.
Servodidio, Mirella & Welles, Marcia L., eds. From Fiction to Metafiction: Essays in Honor of Carmen Martin Gaite.
Serway, Raymond. Physics for Scientists & Engineers.
Serwer, Jacquelyn D., jt. auth. see Calingaert, Efrem F.
Sesame Street Staff. Bathtime on Sesame Street. Schulman, Janet, ed.
--The Sesame Street Mother Goose.
--Sesame Street Pop-up Riddle Book.
Sesay, Amadu, ed. Africa & Europe: From Partition to Interdependence or Dependence?
Seskin, Eugene P., jt. auth. see Peskin, Henry M.
Sesser, Stan, jt. auth. see Unterman, Patricia.
Sessions, Ken, ed. Master Handbook of One Thousand & One Practical Electronic Circuits.
Sessions, Roger. Harmonic Practice.
Sessions, Thelma S. Country Folk Ain't So Bad: Recollections of the Old South.
Sessions, William A. Henry Howard, Earl of Surrey.
Sessle, B., jt. ed. see Klineberg, I.
Sessle, Barry J. & Hannam, Alan G., eds. Mastication & Swallowing: Biological & Clinical Correlates.
Sessoms, Douglas H. & Stevenson, Jack L. Leadership & Group Dynamics in Recreation Services.
Setchell, Brian P., ed. Male Reproduction.
Seth, Andrew. The Development from Kant to Hegel, with Chapters on the Philosophy of Religion. Beck, Lewis W., ed.
Seth, B. R., ed. see CISM (International Center for Mechanical Sciences), Department for Mechanics of Deformable Bodies Staff.
Seth, R. The Undaunted.
Seth, Ronald. Art of Spying.
Seth, Vikram. The Golden Gate.
Sethares, George C., jt. auth. see Bent, Robert J.
Sethi, G. S. & Kakkar, K. C. Workshop Calculations.
Sethuraman, S. V., ed. see International Labour Office Staff.
Setidisho, N. O. University Education in Botswana.
Setlowe, Richard. The Haunting of Suzanna Blackwell.
Seton, Anya. Avalon.
--Dragonwyck.
--Green Darkness.
--Hearth & the Eagle.
--Katherine.
--My Theodosia.
--Winthrop Woman.
Seton, Cynthia P. A Glorious Third.
--A Glorious Third.
--A Private Life.
Seton, Julia. Fasting for Regeneration: The Short Cut.
Seton-Sears, Julia. Key to Health, Wealth, & Love.
Seton-Watson, R. W. Racial Problems in Hungary.
Settin, Joan. Gerontologic Human Resources: The Role of the Paraprofessional.
Settle, Elizabeth A. & Settle, Thomas A. Ishmael Reed: A Primary & Secondary Bibliography.
Settle, Elkanah. A Defence of Dramatick Poetry. Incl. A Farther Defence of Dramatick Poetry. Garland Pub.
Settle, Mary L. Blood Tie.
--The Kiss of Kin: A Novel.
--Prisons.
--The Scapegoat.
Settle, Mary Lee. Blood Tie.
Settle, T. G., ed. see Hook, Thom.
Settle, Thomas A., jt. auth. see Settle, Elizabeth A.
Settle, Wendy & Schlesinger, Eric. A Leader's Guide to the Successful Job Search in Student Development.
Settlemire, Mary Ann. Energy Education Programs: Perspectives for Community, Junior, & Technical Colleges.
Seufert, C. D., jt. ed. see Soling, H. D.
Seuling, Barbara. How to Write a Children's Book & Get It Published.
--Just Me.
--Just Me.
--The Triplets.
Seurat, Silvere. Technology Transfer: A Realistic Approach.
Seuss, Dr. see Dr. Seuss.
Sevareid, Eric. Not So Wild a Dream.
Sevastyanov, V. The Universe & Civilization.
Sevcik. Preparatory Trill Studies for Violin.
Sevcik, O. School of Technic for Violin.
--School of Technic for Violin, Op. 1, Pt. 4: Exercises in Double Stops.
Sevcik, Otakar. Preparatory Studies in Double Stopping for Violin. Saenger, ed.
--School of Bowing for Violin.
Sevelius, Pritz, et al. Keeping Your Horse Healthy: The Prevention & Cure of Illness.
Seven Who Hear Staff. Listen the Lord.
Several Complex Variables Symposium Staff. Proceedings of the Several Complex Variables Symposium, Park City, Utah, 1970. Brooks, R. M., ed.
Severin, Inge. See Malta & Gozo.
Severin, Tim. The Jason Voyage: The Quest of the Golden Fleece.
--Tracking Marco Polo.
Severinghaus, Leslie R. Religions & History: A Textbook for the Enlightenment of 12th Graders in our Tax-Supported Public High Schools.
Severinghaus, Lucia L., tr. see Severinghaus, Sheldon & Blackshaw, Kenneth.
Severinghaus, Sheldon & Blackshaw, Kenneth. A New Guide to the Birds of Taiwan. Severinghaus, Lucia L., tr.
Severinghaus, Sheldon R., et al. A New Guide to the Birds of Taiwan.
Severn, Bill. Bill Severn's Impromptu Magic.
Severy, Larry, ed. Crowding: Theoretical & Research Implications for Population - Environment Psychology.
Sevin, Dieter, et al. Wie Geht's: An Introductory German Course.
Sevitt, Simon. Bone Repair & Fracture Healing in Man.
Sevrok, V., ed. How Wars End.
Sevruk, V. Password 'Victory' The 1941-1945 Great Patriotic War.
Sewall, Marcia. The Little Wee Tyke.
--The World Turned Upside Down.
Seward, Alice. This Is Cape Breton.
Seward, Charles & Mattingly, David. Bedside Diagnosis.
Seward, G., jt. auth. see Killey, H.
Seward, Harold A. The Murders on Fraternity Row.
Seward, Jack. More about the Japanese.
Seward, R. W., ed. NBS Standard Reference Materials Catalog, 1986-87.
Sewell, A. J. Dog's Medical Dictionary.
Sewell, Anna. Black Beauty.
Sewell, Darrel. Thomas Eakins: Artist of Philadelphia.
Sewell, Doug. A Way in the Desert.
Sewell, Geof. Coping with Special Needs: A Guide for New Teachers.
--Reshaping Remedial Education.
Sewell, James P. UNESCO & World Politics: Engaging in International Relations.
Sewell, Robert T. A Forgotten Empire-Vijayanagar: A Contribution to the History of India.
Sewell, Rupert J. Forecasting Your Future: How to Prepare Your Own Astrological Time-Scan.
Sewell, W. D., jt. auth. see Coppock, J. T.
Sewell, William. Hawkstone: A Tale of & for England in 1840, 1845. Wolff, Robert L., ed.
Sewter, A. C. Baroque & Rococo.
Sexton, Anne. All My Pretty Ones.
--The Awful Rowing Toward God.
--The Book of Folly.
--The Death Notebooks.
--Forty-Five Mercy Street. Sexton, Linda G., ed.
--Live or Die.
--Love Poems.
--To Bedlam & Part Way Back.
Sexton, Linda G., ed. Words for Dr. Y: Uncollected Poems of Anne Sexton with Three Stories.
Sexton, Linda G. & Ames, Lois, eds. Anne Sexton: A Self-Portrait in Letters.
--Anne Sexton: A Self-Portrait in Letters.
Sexton, Linda G., ed. see Sexton, Anne.
Seybold, P. B. & Marshak, R. T. Integrated Desk-Top Environments: Symphony, Framework, Visi-On & DesQ.
--Word Processing Software for the IBM PC.
Seybolt, Peter J., ed. The Rustication of Urban Youth in China: A Social Experiment.
Seyler, H. L., jt. ed. see Lonsdale, Richard E.
Seymore, Peter. Colors.
Seymour, Arabella. Dangerous Deceptions.
Seymour, Charles. American Diplomacy During the World War.
Seymour, Charles, Jr. Michelangelo's David: A Search for Identity.
Seymour, Claire. Precipice: Learning to Live with Alzheimer's Disease.
Seymour, Elizabeth. Hobble-de-hoy: The Word Game for Geniuses.
Seymour, Eugene, ed. Psychosocial Needs of the Aged: A Health Care Perspective.
Seymour, Flora W. Indian Agents of the Old Frontier.
Seymour, Gabriel N. Concord Hymn.
Seymour, Gerald. Field of Blood.
--In Honor Bound: A Novel.
Seymour, Harold J. Designs for Fund-Raising: Principles, Patterns, Techniques.
Seymour, Jan P., jt. auth. see Laffer, Arthur B.
Seymour, Jeanette. Emmie.
Seymour, Malcolm. Puritan Migration to Connecticut: The Saga of the Seymour Family, 1129-1746.
Seymour, Mary. Draw Flowers & Plants.
Seymour, Peter. Frontier Town.
--Numbers.
--Opposites.
--Pendragon Castle. Moseley, Keith, designed by.
--Peter Spier's Little Bible Storybooks.
--Playtime, Worktime.
Seymour, Peter, compiled by. Moments Bright & Shining: Three Hundred & Sixty-Five Thoughts to Enjoy Day by Day.
Seymour, Whitney N., Jr. Making a Difference: There's a Lot More to Living Than Money & Success.
Seymour, William K. Burns into English.
Seymour-Smith, Martin. Robert Graves: His Life & Work.
SF. Jailhouse Lawyers Manual.
Sgontz, Larry G., jt. auth. see Pogue, Thomas F.
Sgro, Joseph A., ed. Virginia Tech Symposium on Applied Behavioral Science.
Sgroi, Peter P. Why the United States Purchased Alaska.
Sgroi, Suzanne M. VD: A Doctor's Answers.
Shaaber, M. A. Check-List of Works of British Authors Printed Abroad, in Languages Other Than English to 1641.
Shaara, Michael. The Broken Place.
--The Herald.
Shabalin, E. P. Fast Pulsed & Burst Reactors: A Comprehensive Account of the Physics of Both Single Burst & Repetitively Pulsed Reactors.
Shabhazi, Shapur, tr. see Andreae, Bernard.
Shachtman, Tom. The Birdman of St. Petersburg.
--Decade of Shocks: From Dallas to Watergate, 1963-1974.
Shackel. Man-Computer Communication.
Shackelford, George T. Degas: The Dancers.
Shackelford, Jean A., ed. Urban & Regional Economics: A Guide to Information Sources.
Shackleton, Elizabeth, jt. auth. see Shackleton, Robert.
Shackleton, Philip, jt. auth. see Roberts, Kenneth G.
Shackleton, Robert & Shackleton, Elizabeth. Quest of the Colonial.

Authors

Shackleton, V. J. & Fletcher, C. A. Individual Differences.
Shackley, Myra. Environmental Archaeology.
--Still Living? Yeti, Sasquatch & the Neanderthal Enigma.
Shacklock, Floyd. Man of Two Revolutions: The Story of Justo Gonzales.
Shadarevian, Sossy, jt. auth. see Pellet, P. L.
Shade, Gary A. Advanced Data Communications.
Shader, Richard, jt. ed. see DiMascio, Alberto.
Shadily, Hassan, jt. auth. see Echols, John M.
Shaevel, M. Leonard, jt. auth. see Paul, Richard S.
Shaevitz, Marjorie, jt. auth. see Lenz, Marjorie.
Shaevitz, Marjorie H., jt. auth. see Shaevitz, Morton H.
Shaevitz, Morton H. Sexual Static: How Men Are Confusing the Women They Love.
Shaevitz, Morton H. & Shaevitz, Marjorie H. Making It Together: As a Career Couple.
Shafarevich, I. R., jt. auth. see Borevich, Z. I.
Shafer, Boyd C. Faces of Nationalism.
Shafer, Dan. Turbo Prolog Primer.
Shafer, Glenn, jt. auth. see Pearl, Judea.
Shafer, Neil, ed. see Pick, Albert.
Shafer, Wade H., ed. Master Theses in the Pure & Applied Sciences--Accepted by Colleges & Universities of the United States & Canada.
Shaff, Jo. Fencing.
Shaffer, David R. Social & Personality Development.
Shaffer, John R., ed. Current Issues in Secondary Education.
Shaffer, Kenneth, jt. auth. see Snyder, Graydon.
Shaffer, Peter. Equus.
--Equus & Shrivings.
Shaffer, Wilma. Fourteen Women's Programs: Making Your House a Home.
Shaffer, Wm. D. & Wheelwright, Richard, eds. Creating Original Programming for Cable TV.
Shafir, M. Los Soviets, Organos Del Poder Popular.
Shafiroff, Ira L. Internal Revenue Service Practice & Procedure Deskbook.
Shafrir, E., ed. Contemporary Topics in the Study of Diabetes & Metabolic Endocrinology.
--Impact of Insulin on Metabolic Pathways.
Shagass, Charles. Evoked Brain Potentials in Psychiatry.
Shah, Adries. Seeker after Truth: A Handbook of Sufi Tales & Teachings.
Shah, D. O., ed. Surface Phenomena in Enhanced Oil Recovery.
Shah, Nasra M. & Smith, Peter C. Nonfamilial Roles of Women & Fertility: Pakistan & the Philippines Compared.
Shah, Pravin. Cost Control & Information Systems: A Complete Guide to Effective Design & Implementation.
Shah, Pravin M., et al. Doppler Echocardiography: A Practical Manual.
Shah, R. Yeats & Eliot: Perspectives on India.
Shah, R, ed. Compact Heat Exchangers: HTD-Vol. 10.
Shah, Ramesh & London, A. L. Laminar Flow Forced Convection in Ducts: Supplement 1 to Advances in Heat Transfer.
Shah, Sayed I. Oriental Magic.
Shaham, Milton A. Religious Unbeliever.
Shahan, Sherry. One Sister Too Many.
Shahandeh, Behrouz, jt. auth. see International Labour Office Staff.
Shahane, V. A., ed. Focus on Forster's "A Passage to India" Indian Essays in Criticism.
Shahani, Ranjee. The Indian Way.
Shahar, David. His Majesty's Agent. Bilu, Dalya, tr.
Shaher, Reda M. Complete Transposition of the Great Arteries.
Shaiken, Harley. Work Transformed: Automation & Labor in the Computer Age.
Shain, Michael, jt. ed. see Longley, Dennis.
Shainberg, I. & Oster, J. D. Quality of Irrigation Water.
Shair Management Services Staff, ed. Business Laws & Practices of Bahrain.
--Business Laws & Practices of Jordan.
Shairo, Chava, compiled by. Learn While You Play.
Shakal, Charles L. Profile Survey 8-B: Arts Programs, Finances & Attendance.
Shaked, Israel, jt. auth. see Michel, Allen.
Shakely, Lauren, tr. see Apollinaire, Guillaume.
Shaker, Fouad E. Pillars of Atonia: A Journey Through Time & Space.
Shakespeare, William. Antony & Cleopatra.
--As You Like It.
--As You Like It: An Old-Spelling & Old-Meaning Edition. Trauvetter, Christiane, ed.
--A Choice of Shakespeare's Verse. Hughes, Ted, ed.
--The Comedy of Errors. Wright, Louis B. & LaMar, Virginia, eds.
--Coriolanus. Wright, Louis B. & LaMar, Virginia A., eds.
--Courtly Cats.
--Globe Illustrated Shakespeare.
--Hamlet. Harrison, George B., ed.
--Hamlet. Wilkes, G. A., ed.
--Henry Eighth. Wright, Louis B. & LaMar, Virginia A., eds.
--Henry IV, Pt. 1.
--Julius Caesar. Walter, J. H., ed.
--Julius Caesar.
--King Lear: Text, Sources, Criticism. Harrison, George B. & McDonnell, Robert F., eds.
--King Lear: TV Edition. Harbage, Alfred, ed.
--Macbeth. Harrison, George B., ed.
--Macbeth.
--Measure for Measure. Wright, Louis B. & LaMar, Virginia A., eds.
--Measure for Measure: An Old-Spelling & Old-Meaning Edition. Leisi, Ernst, ed.
--Merchant of Venice. Walter, J. H., ed.
--The Merchant of Venice.
--Midsummer Nights' Dream.
--Midsummer Night's Dream. Walter, J. H., ed.
--A Midsummer Night's Dream.
--Much Ado about Nothing. Wright, Louis B. & LaMar, Virginia A., eds.
--Othello. Walter, J. H., ed.
--Othello.
--Romeo & Juliet.
--Soliloquies.
--Twelfth Night. Walter, J. H., ed.
Shakespeare, William. Comedies see Individual Plays.
Shakespeare, William. Histories see Individual Plays.
Shakespeare, William. Tragedies see Individual Plays.
Shakhbazyana, M. & Ivanova, O. Embroidery of Ourha.
Shakhnazarov, G. The Destiny of the World: The Socialist Shape of Things to Come.
Shakir, Mahomodali H. The Holy Qur'an.
Shakum, Melvin F., jt. ed. see Lewin, Arie Y.
Shalala, Donna E., et al. Readings in American Politics & Education.
Shalamov, Varlam. Kolyma Tales. Glad, John, tr.
Shaldach, Herbert Von see Von Schaldach, Herbert.
Shalett, Sidney, jt. auth. see Roosevelt, James.
Shalhevet, J., et al, eds. Irrigation of Field & Orchard Crops Under Semi-Arid Conditions.
Shallenberger, Robert S. Advanced Sugar Chemistry.
Shaltiel, S., ed. Metabolic Interconversion of Enzymes 1975: Fourth International Symposium Held in Arab, April 27th-May 2nd, 1975.
Shaltry, Paul, jt. ed. see Campbell, Robert E.
Shamai, Ruth, tr. see Muir, John.
Shambaugh, George & Shea, John J. Proceedings of the Shambaugh Fifth International Workshop on Middle Ear Microsurgery & Fluctant Hearing Loss.
Shames, Irving H. Introduction to Solid Mechanics.
Shames, Irving H. & Dym, Clive L. Energy & Finite Element Methods in Structural Mechanics.
Shamma, M. & Hindenlang, D. M. Carbon-13 NMR Shift Assignments of Amines & Alkaloids.
Shamma, Maurice. The Isoquinoline Alkaloids: Chemistry & Pharmacology.
Shampine, Lawrence F. & Allen, Richard C. Numerical Computing: An Introduction.
Shanahan, P. The Atiyah-Singer Index Theorem: An Introduction.
Shanahan, Timothy, jt. auth. see Pikulski, John J.
Shanahan, William F. Essential Math, Science, & Computer Terms for College Freshmen.
Shand, David G., jt. ed. see Turner, Paul.
Shandong Medical College Staff. Anatomical Atlas of Chinese Acupuncture Points.
Shandruk, Pavlo. Arms of Valor.
Shane, Harold G., ed. United States & International Education.
Shane, Harold G. & Goodlad, John I., eds. The Elementary School in the United States.
Shane, Harold G., jt. ed. see Anderson, Robert H.
Shane, John, ed. see Norbu, Namkhai.
Shangle, Robert D., ed. see Foster, Lee.
Shangle, Robert D., ed. see Waesche, James F.
Shani, Uri. Understanding Three-Dimensional Images: Recognition of Abdominal Anatomy from CAT Scans. Stone, Harold, ed.
Shanin, Sandra J. Songs for Language Learning.
Shank, C. V., et al, eds. Picosecond Phenomena: Proceedings of the First International Conference on Picosecond Phenomena, Hilton Head, SC, U. S. A., May 24-26, 1978.
Shank, John, jt. auth. see Dearden, John.
Shank, John K. Contemporary Managerial Accounting: A Casebook.
Shankar, Hari, ed. Mathematical Essays Dedicated to A. J. MacIntyre.
Shankara. Laghu-Vakya-Vritti.
Shanken, Marvin. Impact Yearbook.
Shanken, Marvin, ed. The Wine Spectator Guide to Selected Wines, 1985.
Shanken, Marvin R. Beverage Trends in America, 1960-2000.
--The Impact American Beer Market Review & Forecast: 1983.
--The Impact American Beer Market Review & Forecast: 1982 Edition.
--The IMPACT American Beer Market Review & Forecast: 1986 Edition.
--The IMPACT American Beer Market Review & Forecast: 1987 Edition.
--The Impact American Beer Market Review & Forecast.
--The Impact American Beer Market Review & Forecast.
--The Impact American Beer Market Review & Forecast.
--The IMPACT American Beer Market Review & Forecast.
--The Impact American Distilled Spirits Market Review & Forecast.
--The Impact American Distilled Spirits Market Review & Forecast.
--The Impact American Distilled Spirits Market Review & Forecast.
--The Impact American Distilled Spirits Market Review & Forecast.
--The IMPACT American Distilled Spirits Market Review & Forecast.
--The Impact American Distilled Spirits Market Review & Forecast.
--The IMPACT American Distilled Spirits Market Review & Forecast.
--The IMPACT American Distilled Spirits Market Review & Forecast.
--The IMPACT American Distilled Spirits Market Review & Forecast.
--The Impact American Distilled Spirits Review & Forecast.
--The IMPACT American Wine Market Review & Forecast: 1983.
--The Impact American Wine Market Review & Forecast.
--The Impact American Wine Market Review & Forecast.
--The Impact American Wine Market Review & Forecast.
--The Impact American Wine Market Review & Forecast.
--The Impact American Wine Market Review & Forecast.
--The IMPACT American Wine Market Review & Forecast.
--The IMPACT American Wine Market Review & Forecast.
--The IMPACT American Wine Market Review & Forecast.
--The IMPACT American Wine Market Review & Forecast.
--The IMPACT Beverage Trends in America Review & Forecast.
--The IMPACT Beverage Trends in America Review & Forecast.
--The IMPACT Beverage Trends in American Review & Forecast.
--Impact Yearbook: 1985 Edition.
--IMPACT Yearbook, 1986.
--IMPACT Yearbook, 1987.
--Leaders 87.
--Market Watch Creative Adbook.
--The Wine Spectator Wine Maps: The Complete Guide to Wineries, Restaurants & Lodging in California Wine Country.
--The Wine Spectator Wine Maps: The Complete Guide to Wineries, Restaurants & Lodging in California Wine Country, 1985.
--The Wine Spectator Wine Maps, 1986: The Complete Guide to Wineries, Restaurants & Lodging in California Wine Country.
Shanken, Marvin R., ed. The Impact American Distilled Spirits Market Review & Forecast.
--The Impact American Distilled Spirits Market Review & Forecast.
--The Impact American Wine Market Review & Forecast.
--The Impact American Wine Market Review & Forecast.
Shanker, S. G., jt. ed. see Shanker, V. A.
Shanker, V. A. & Shanker, S. G., eds. A Wittgenstein Bibliography.
Shankland, Craig, et al. The Golfer's Stroke Saving Handbook.
Shanklin, Eugenia, jt. ed. see Berleant-Schiller, Riva.
Shanklin, Imelda O. What Are You?
Shanklin, William L., jt. auth. see Ryans, John K., Jr.
Shankman, Florence. Games & Activities to Reinforce Reading Skills.
--Specialized Methods of Teaching Reading.
Shankman, Florence, ed. Methods of Teaching Reading.
Shankman, Sam. Molding Forces.
Shanks, Bernard. Wilderness Survival.
Shanks, Bob. The Cool Fire: How to Make It in Television.
--Love Is Not Enough.
Shanks, Michael. European Social Policy, Today & Tomorrow.
Shanks, Ralph C., Jr. Lighthouses & Lifeboats on the Redwood Coast.
Shanks, Thomas, compiled by. The International Atlas: World Latitudes, Longitudes, & Time Changes.
Shanmugaratnam, K. Histological Typing of Upper Respiratory Tract Tumors.
Shann, C. D. Pipeline Glossary & Directory.
Shann, Renee. Forecast for Love.
--A Young Wife's Tale.
Shannon, Elizabeth. Up in the Park: The Diary of the Wife of the American Ambassador to Ireland, 1977-1981.
Shannon, Fred A. The Organization & Administration of the Union Army 1861-1865.
Shannon, J. Michael, jt. auth. see Shannon, Robert.
Shannon, Jacqueline. Too Much T. J.
Shannon, John. Courage.
Shannon, John K., ed. see Trollope, Anthony.
Shannon, Kristin, jt. auth. see Cohen, Dian.
Shannon, L. Kay, jt. auth. see Perritt, G. W.
Shannon, Richard. Gladstone: Volume I, Eighteen Hundred Nine to Eighteen Sixty-Five.
Shannon, Robert & Shannon, J. Michael. Expository Preaching.
Shannon, Robert C., jt. auth. see Eubanks, David L.
Shannon, Samuel H., jt. auth. see Davis, George L.
Shannon, Thomas. Bioethics.
--Urban Problems in Sociological Perspective.
Shannon, William H. Thomas Merton's Dark Path.
--Thomas Merton's Dark Path: The Inner Experience of a Contemplative.
Shanskii, N. M. Russian Lexicology.
Shantar, Stan, jt. auth. see Smith, Philip K.
Shapcott, D. & Hubert, J. Chromium in Nutrition & Metabolism: Proceedings of a Symposium Held in Sherbrooke, Canada, June, 1979.
Shapcott, Thomas. Welcome!
Shapcott, Thomas, ed. Consolidation: The Second Poets Anthology.
--Contemporary American & Australian Poetry.
Shapira, Jacob, et al. Biology of Turbellaria.
Shapiro, jt. auth. see Boericke.
Shapiro, Alan C. Foreign Exchange Risk Management.
Shapiro, Andrew O., jt. auth. see Striker, John M.
Shapiro, Andy, jt. auth. see Alward, Ron.
Shapiro, Arnold, jt. auth. see Kolman, Bernard.
Shapiro, B. L., ed. Heterogeneous Catalysis: Proceedings of the Annual Symposia of the Industry-University Chemistry Program (IUCCP) of Tex A&M Univ Chemistry Department.
--Organometallic Compounds-Synthesis, Stucture, & Theory: Proceedings of the Annual Symposia of the Industry-University Cooperative Chemistry Program (IUCCP) of the Texas A&M University Department of Chemistry.
Shapiro, Barbara J. Probability & Certainty in Seventeenth Century England: A Study of the Relationships Between National Science, Religion, History, Law & Literature.
Shapiro, Benson P. Lotus Data Matrix.
Shapiro, Bernard L., ed. New Directions in Chemical Analysis: Proceedings of the Annual Symposia of the Industry University Cooperative Chemistry Program (IUCCP) of the Texas A&M Univ. Chemistry Department.
Shapiro, Charles. Theodore Dreiser: Our Bitter Patriot.
Shapiro, Charles, ed. Twelve Original Essays on Great American Novels.
Shapiro, Deborah, jt. auth. see Grow, Lucille J.
Shapiro, Diane R. Foundations for Sociology.
Shapiro, Edward. Macroeconomic Analysis.
--Macroeconomic Analysis.
--Understanding Money.
Shapiro, Elliot, jt. auth. see Dichter, Harry.
Shapiro, George R., jt. auth. see Practising Law Institute Staff.
Shapiro, H. S. Topics in Approximation Theory.
Shapiro, Harvey. Assembly Language Programming for the PDP-11.
Shapiro, Howard I. The Birth Control Book.
Shapiro, Ira, ed. American Illustration Showcase, 8.
--American Photography Showcase, 8.
Shapiro, Jean. A Child: Your Choice.
Shapiro, Jeremy, tr. see Mannheim, Karl.
Shapiro, Jeremy F. Mathematical Programming: Structures & Algorithms.
Shapiro, Keith J. & James, Bruce A. Searching for the Core.
Shapiro, Lawrence E. The New Short-Term Therapies for Children: A Guide for Parents & the Helping Professions.
Shapiro, Linda G., jt. auth. see Baron, Robert J.
Shapiro, M. & Obrecht, F. How to Prepare for the American College Testing Program (ACT)
Shapiro, Mary J. The Dover New York Walking Guide: Greenwich Village.
--A Picture History of the Brooklyn Bridge.
Shapiro, Max S., ed. see Hendricks, Rhoda A.
Shapiro, Milton. Ranger Battalion: American Rangers in World War II.
Shapiro, Milton J. Behind Enemy Lines: America Spies & Saboteurs in World War II.

Shapiro, Murray, et al. Barron's How to Prepare for the American College Testing Program (ACT)
Shapiro, Nat & Hentoff, N. Hear Me Talkin' to Ya.
Shapiro, Nat, ed. Whatever It Is, I'm Against It.
Shapiro, Neal & Lehrman, Steve. The World of Horseback Riding.
Shapiro, P., jt. auth. see Anderson, B.
Shapiro, Pamela J, jt. auth. see Anderson, Barbara.
Shapiro, R. Gary. Exhaustive Concordance of the Book of Mormon, Doctrine & Covenants & Pearl of Great Peace.
Shapiro, Robert. Origins: A Skeptic's Guide to the Genesis of Life on Earth.
Shapiro, Robert H. & Depuy, Charles H., eds. Exercises in Organic Spectroscopy.
Shapiro, Roy D. Optimization Models for Planning & Allocation: Text & Cases in Mathematical Programming.
Shapiro, Roy D., jt. auth. see Dyer, James S.
Shapiro, S. L., ed. Ultrashort Light Pulses: Picosecond Techniques & Applications.
Shapiro, Samuel. Cultural Factors in Inter-American Relations.
Shapiro, Sidney, tr. see She, Lao.
Shapiro, Sidney, tr. see Shi, Nai'an & Luo Guanzhong.
Shapiro, Stanley J., jt. auth. see McCarthy, J. E.
Shapiro, Svi, jt. ed. see Purpel, David E.
Shapland, C. R. The Letters of Saint Athanasius.
Shapland, Joanna. Between Conviction & Sentence: The Process of Mitigation.
Shapley, ed. see Intersociety Working Group Staff.
Shapley, et al, eds. see Intersociety Working Group Staff.
Shapley, Harlow. Galaxies.
Shapot, V. S. Biochemical Aspects of Tumour Growth.
Sharamanyan, H., ed. Armenian Jewelry Art.
Sharbrough, David. American Premium Guide to Olde Cameras.
Sharer, Robert J. Quirigua: A Classic Maya Center & Its Sculptures.
Sharer, Robert J., ed. The Prehistory of Chalchuapa, El Salvador.
Shargava, A. K., ed. see Kumar, Dharmenora & Jain, S. K.
Sharif, Omar. Omar Sharif's Life in Bridge. Reese, Terence, tr. from Fr.
Sharif, Walid I. Oil & Development in the Arab Gulf States: A Selected Annotated Bibliography.
Sharkansky, Ira. Public Administration.
Sharkansky, Ira & Van Meter, Donald. Policy & Politics in American Governments.
Sharkey, Jacqueline, ed. see Honter, John, et al.
Sharkey, John. Celtic Mysteries: The Ancient Religion.
Sharlin, Judith. The Romantic Vegetarian: A Seasonal Cookbook.
Sharlot, M. Michael, jt. auth. see Dix, George E.
Sharma & Sharma. Chromosome Techniques.
Sharma, B. L. & Purohit, R. K. Semiconductor Heterojunctions.
Sharma, Basudeo. The Victorian Novel: Problems & Portraits of the Child.
Sharma, J. N. The International Fiction of Henry James.
Sharma, J. P., jt. auth. see Tiwari, R. D.
Sharma, K. K. Joyce Cary: His Theme & Technique.
--Modern Fictional Theorists.
--Perspectives on Raja Rao.
Sharma, K. K., ed. Indo-English Literature: A Collection of Critical Essays on Indian Creative Writers in English.
Sharma, P. C., jt. ed. see Richmond, W. H.
Sharma, P. D. The New Caribbean Man.
Sharma, Partap. The Surangini Tales.
Sharma, R. K. Isolation & Protest.
Sharma, R. S. Anita Desai.
Sharma, Ravinder N. Indian Librarianship.
Sharma, Roshan L., et al. Network Systems.
Sharma, Ursula. Woman, Work & Property in North-West India.
Sharma, V. K., ed. see All India Symposium Staff.
Sharmat, Majorie W. Say Hello, Vanessa.
Sharmat, Marjorie W. Burton & Dudley.
--Griselda's New Year.
--Nate the Great Stalks Stupidweed.
--Rich Mitch.
--Sasha the Silly.
--Sophie & Gussie.
--Thornton the Worrier.
--Twitchell the Wishful.
Sharmat, Mitchell. Come Home, Wilma. Tucker, Kathleen, ed.
--The Seven Sloppy Days of Phineas Pig.
Sharmon, Fay & Boehm, Klaus. The Taste of France.
Sharnik, John. Remembrance of Games Past: On Tour with the Tennis Grand Masters.
Sha Rocco. The Masculine Cross & Ancient Sex Worship.
Sharp & Register. Economics of Social Issues.
Sharp & Sliger. Public Finance.
Sharp, Ansel M., jt. auth. see Leftwich, Richard H.
Sharp, C. The Economics of Time.
Sharp, Cecil J., jt. ed. see Karpeles, Maud.
Sharp, D. H., jt. ed. see Wightman, A. S.
Sharp, D. R. Concrete in Highway Engineering.
Sharp, Evelyn. Thinking Is Child's Play.
Sharp, Harry. Fifty Thousand Words Divided & Spelled.
Sharp, Henry. Devil at the Reins.
Sharp, J. D. Elements of Steelmaking Practice.
Sharp, Jim, jt. auth. see Garland, Joe.
Sharp, John K. Old Priest Remembers, Eighteen Ninety-Two to Nineteen Seventy-Eight.
Sharp, Mitchell, et al. Security & Disarmament.
Sharp, P. E., jt. auth. see Brichta, A.
Sharp, Pamela. Turtlesteps: An Introduction to Apple LOGO & Terrapin LOGO.
Sharp, R. Farquharson, ed. Dictionary of English Authors: Biographical & Bibliographical.
Sharp, Robert, ed. Pocketguide to the Art Institute of Chicago.
Sharp, Robert M. Calculated Risk: A Master Plan for Common Stocks.
Sharp, Shirley I., jt. auth. see Cattell, Nancy G.
Sharp, Stanley L. The Real Reason Why Johnnie Still Can't Read.
Sharpe, Charles K. Historical Account of the Belief in Witchcraft in Scotland.
Sharpe, D. Mollusca of the Chalk.
Sharpe, Don. The New Woman Driver: All a Woman Needs to Know about Cars to Buy One, Drive It, Have It Maintained.
Sharpe, Eric J. Fifty Key Words: Comparative Religion.
Sharpe, Fred, jt. auth. see Atkinson, Scott.
Sharpe, Kenneth H., jt. auth. see Clidero, Robert K.
Sharpe, Kevin, ed. Faction & Parliament: Essays on Early Stuart History.
Sharpe, Mitchell R. Yuri Gagarin: First Man in Space.
Sharpe, Pamela J. Barron's How to Prepare for the Test of English as a Foreign Language--TOEFL.
--Barron's How to Prepare for the TOEFL: Test of English As a Foreign Language.
Sharpe, Peter. Lost Goods & Stray Beasts.
Sharpe, S. M., jt. ed. see Burgess, R. L.
Sharpe, Sally, ed. see Grubb, Jan.
Sharples, Antony. The Scorpion's Tail.
Sharpley, J. Miles & Kaplan, Arthur M., eds. Proceedings of the Third International Biodegradation Symposium.
Sharpton, Robert. Designing Pictures with String.
Sharratt, Bernard. Reading Relations - Structures of Literary Production: A Dialectical Text-Book.
Sharrock, J. T., ed. Birds New to Britain & Ireland.
Sharron, W. Harvey, Jr., ed. The Community College Foundation.
Shartar, Martin, jt. auth. see Shavin, Norman.
Sharygin, I. F. Problems in Solid Geometry.
Shashua, Leon & Goldschmidt, Yaaqov. Tools for Financial Management: Emphasis on Inflation.
Shastry, P. S. Studies in Elizabethan Literature.
Shatalin, Stanislav S., jt. auth. see Cao-Pinna, Vera.
Shatrov, M., et al. Nine Modern Soviet Plays.
Shatsky, S. Teacher's Experience.
Shattock, Joanne & Wolff, Michael, eds. The Victorian Periodical Press: Samplings & Soundings.
Shattock, Michael, ed. The Structure & Governance of Higher Education.
Shattuck, Roger. Marcel Proust.
Shaughnessey, Marlene, jt. auth. see Bickner, Mei L.
Shaughnessy, Phyllis. I Am Who I Am.
Shaull, Richard, jt. auth. see Gutierrez, Gustavo.
Shaum, John H., Jr. & Flayhart, William H., III. Majesty at Sea: The Four-Stackers.
Shavelson, Melvin. Lualda.
Shavelson, Richard J. Statistical Reasoning in the Behavioral Sciences.
Shaver, James K. & Curtis, Charles K. Handicapism & Equal Opportunity: Teaching about the Disabled in Social Studies.
Shaver, Jess. Tributaries of Learning.
Shaver, Jess, ed. Candidates for Maturity.
Shaver, Kelley G. Principles of Social Psychology.
Shaver, Kelly G. An Introduction to Attribution Processes.
Shavin, Norman. The Antebellum Plantation at Stone Mountain Park.
--Underground Atlanta.
Shavin, Norman & Galphin, Bruce. Atlanta: Triumph of a People.
Shavin, Norman & Mcdermott, Austin. Strange Tales of 'Gone with the Wind'
Shavin, Norman & Shartar, Martin. The Wonderful World of Coca-Cola.
Shaw. California Angels.
--Chicago White Sox.
--Montreal Expos.
--Texas Rangers.
--Toronto Blue Jays.
Shaw, Alan C. Logical Design of Operating Systems.
Shaw, B. L. Inorganic Hydrides.
Shaw, B. L. & Tucker, N. I. Organo-Transition Metal Compounds & Related Aspects of Homogenous Catalysis.
Shaw, Barry, jt. auth. see Gartenberg, Michael.
Shaw, Bill & Wolfe, Arthur D. The Structure of the Legal Environment: Law, Ethics & Business.
Shaw, Bradley, jt. ed. see Vera, Nora.
Shaw, Bruce, jt. auth. see Tree, Christina.
Shaw, Clifford R. & McKay, Henry D. Juvenile Delinquency & Urban Areas.
Shaw, D. J., jt. auth. see Avery, H. E.
Shaw, D. L., ed. Eduardo Mallea: Todo verdor perecera.
Shaw, E. N. Europe's Nuclear Power Experiment: History of the OECD Dragon Project.
Shaw, E. W. Heating & Hot-Water Services: Selected Subjects with Worked Examples in SI Units.
Shaw, Elizabeth M. Hydrology in Practice.
Shaw, Evelyn & Darling, Joan. Female Strategies.
Shaw, G., jt. auth. see Brooks, J.
Shaw, G., jt. ed. see Donnachie, A.
Shaw, G. B. Crime of Imprisonment.
Shaw, Gareth & Wheeler, Dennis. Statistical Techniques in Geographical Analysis.
Shaw, George Bernard. Agitations: Letters to the Press, 1875-1950. Laurence, Dan H. & Rambeau, James, eds.
--Back to Methuselah.
--Collected Letters Eighteen Seventy-Four to Eighteen Ninety-Seven.
--Collected Plays with Their Prefaces: Definitive Edition in Seven Volumes.
--Complete Plays with Prefaces.
--Four Plays by Bernard Shaw. Incl. Candida; Caesar & Cleopatra; Pygmalion; Heartbreak House. Modern Lib.
--Heartbreak House. Weintraub, Stanley & Wright, Anne, eds.
--On Language. Tauber, A., ed.
--The Quintessence of Ibsenism.
--The Rationalization of Russia. Geduld, Harry M., ed.
--Saint Joan. Weintraub, Stanley, ed.
--Saint Joan.
--Shaw's Dramatic Criticism from the Saturday Review 1895-1898. Matthews, John F., ed.
Shaw, George Bernard & Douglas, Alfred. Bernard Shaw & Alfred Douglas: A Correspondence. Hyde, Mary, ed.
Shaw, George Bernard see Weiss, Samuel A.
Shaw, George Bernard, ed. Fabian Essays in Socialism.
Shaw, Graham. The Cost of Authority: Manipulation & Freedom in the New Testament.
Shaw, Harry. Dictionary of Literary Terms.
Shaw, Idries. World Tales.
Shaw, Irwin. Acceptable Losses.
--God Was Here but He Left Early.
--God Was Here but He Left Early.
--God Was There but He Left Early.
--Two Weeks in Another Town.
Shaw, Irwin & Searle, Ronald. Paris! Paris!
Shaw, J. The Audit Report.
Shaw, Jackie. Tole Technique & Decorative Arts.
Shaw, James H., et al. Textbook of Oral Biology.
Shaw, Jean M. & Cliatt, Mary Jo P. Mental Gymnastics.
Shaw, Jean M., jt. auth. see Cliatt, Mary J.
Shaw, John, ed. Australian Encyclopedia.
Shaw, John C. The Quality-Productivity Connection in Service-Sector Management.
Shaw, John H., et al. Selected Team Sports for Men.
Shaw, John M. Christian Doctrine.
Shaw, John M., ed. Childhood in Poetry: A Catalogue, with Biographical & Critical Annotations, of the Books of English & American Poets Comprising the Shaw Childhood in Poetry Collection in the Library of the Florida State University.
--Childhood in Poetry: First Supplement.
--Childhood in Poetry: Second Supplement--a Catalogue with Biographical & Critical Annotations, of the Books of English & American Poets Comprising the Shaw Childhood in Poetry Collection in the Library of the Fla. St. U.
Shaw, Joseph M., et al, eds. Readings in Christian Humanism.
Shaw, Josephine. Secretarial Management.
Shaw, K. E., jt. auth. see Bloomer, M.
Shaw, Leslie, jt. ed. see Demers, Laurence.
Shaw, Lloyd. The Round Dance Book.
Shaw, Lois B., ed. Unplanned Careers: The Working Lives of Middle-Aged Women.
Shaw, Lois M. The Abode of an Unknown God: A Study of Ancient Egypt & the Significance of the Great Pyramid.
Shaw, Luci. The Secret Trees.
Shaw, M. P., et al. The Gunn-Hilsum Effect.
Shaw, Malcolm E., et al. Role Playing: A Practical Manual for Group Facilitators.
Shaw, Merville C. School Guidance Systems: Objectives, Functions, Evaluation, & Change.
Shaw, Michael. The Modern Lurcher.
--The Modern Working Terrier.
Shaw, Michael, tr. see Bauer, Wolfgang.
Shaw, Myril C. & Shaw, Susan S. Essential PC-DOS.
Shaw, N. H. & Bryan, W. W., eds. Tropical Pasture Research: Principles & Methods.
Shaw, Nancy S. Forced Labor: Maternity Care in the United States.
Shaw, Patricia A. Theoretical Issues in Dakota Phonology & Morphology. Hankamer, Jorge, ed.
Shaw, Patrick W. Literature: A College Anthology.
Shaw, Richard. Lamprey's Legacy.
Shaw, Richard J. Field Guide to the Vascular Plants of Grand Teton National Park & Teton County, Wyoming.
Shaw, Richard P., ed. Computing Methods in Geophysical Mechanics-AMD.
Shaw, Robbie. NATO Aircraft in Colour.
--U. S. Air Power in Colour 1.
Shaw, Robin. The Climber's Bible: A Complete Basic Guide to Rock & Ice Climbing & an Introduction to Mountaineering.
Shaw, Rodney, ed. Selected Readings in Image Evaluation.
Shaw, Russell, jt. auth. see Grisez, Germain.
Shaw, Susan S., jt. auth. see Shaw, Myril C.
Shaw, Sydney, jt. auth. see Brewin, Bob.
Shaw, Terry, ed. Handicapped Students in the Social Studies Classroom: Teaching.
Shaw, Thomas W. Roughshod.
Shaw, Timothy M. & Anglin, Douglas G. Alternative Sources of Event Data on Zambian Foreign Policy.
Shaw, Timothy M. & Tandon, Yash. Regional Development at the International Level, Vol. II: African & Canadian Perspectives.
Shaw, Timothy M. & Ojo, Sola, eds. Africa & the International Political System.
Shaw, Timothy M. & Tandon, Yash, eds. Regional Development at the International Level, Vol. I: Canadian & African Perspectives.
Shawcross, William. The Quality of Mercy: Cambodia, Holocaust, & Modern Conscience.
--The Quality of Mercy: Cambodia, Holocaust & Modern Conscience.
Shawhan, Narcissa T. Parliamentary Law Textbook.
Shawn, Bernard. Foundations of Citizenship.
Shawn, Wallace. Marie & Bruce.
Shawn, Wallace & Gregory, Andre. My Dinner with Andre.
Shawn, William, ed. see Flanner, Janet.
Shay, Frank, ed. A Treasury of Plays for Women.
Shay, Griff, jt. auth. see National Research Council, Board on Science & Technology for International Development.
Shay, J. L. & Wernick, J. H. Ternary Chalcopyrite Semiconductors: Growth, Electronic Properties & Applications.
Shayne, Neil. Advanced Techniques in Automobile Accident Litigation.
Shchastlivyi, J., jt. auth. see Chizhikov, T.
Shchastlivyi, T., jt. auth. see Chizhikov, V.
She, Lao. Crescent Moon & Other Stories. Cohn, Don J & Shapiro, Sidney, trs. from Chinese.
Shea, George. ESP McGee to the Rescue.
--Manage Your Own Baseball Team: Make the Playoffs! Blues vs. Sharks. Schwartz, Betty, ed.
--Nightmare Nina.
Shea, George & Schwartz, Betty. Coach Your Own Football Team: Make It to the Superbowl! Panthers vs. Grizzlies.
Shea, John. The Hour of the Unexpected.
Shea, John J., jt. auth. see Shambaugh, George.
Shea, Margaret, ed. see Chase, Virginia.
Shea, Michael. Polyphemus.
Shea, Richard. Shea Lectures: Solving General Chemistry Problems.
Sheaffer, Billie C. A Manual for the Care of Wild Birds.
Sheaffer, Louis. O'Neill, Son & Playwright.
Sheahan, Richard, ed. Evaluating the FBC Option, 1985.
Sheahan, Richard T. Evaluating the FBC Option.
--Fluidized Bed Combustion: Technical, Financial & Regulatory Issues.
Sheahan, Richard T., ed. Evaluating the FBC Option: 1984.
Sheaks, Barclay. Painting with Oils. Horn, George F. & Rainey, Sarita R., eds.
Shealy, Ann. The Ravaged Garden: A Critical Study of Shelley's Epipsychidion.
Shealy, Julian B. The Destiny of Our Monetary & Economic World.
--The Future Position of the English-Speaking Peoples in World Prophecy & Events.
--The Heavens Speak in Astrology Marvelous Things.
--Unmasking Hidden Money: The Periodic Currency Replacement Plan.
Shean, Glenn D. Dimensions in Abnormal Psychology.
Shear, Jack, photos by. Four Marines & Other Portraits.
Sheard, Geraldine B. Say it, Spirit.
Sheard, James L. & Stalley, Rodney E. Opening Doors to the Job Market.

Authors

Shearer, Ann. Handicapped Children in Residential Care: A Study of Policy Failure.
Shearer, William. The Illustrated Notebook for Anatomy Students.
Shearman, David J. & Finlayson, Niall D., eds. Diseases of the Gastrointestinal Tract & Liver.
Shears, Barbara & Wood, Susan. Teaching Children with Severe Difficulties: A Radical Reappraisal. Barton, Len, ed.
Shears, Judith, jt. auth. see Hotchkiss, Bill.
Shears, Loyda M. & Bower, Eli M. Games in Education & Development.
Shearston, Trevor. White Lies.
Sheats, John, jt. ed. see Carraher, Charles E.
Sheban, Joseph, ed. see Gibran, Kahlil.
Shebar, Jonathan M. & Shebar, Sharon S. Animal Dads Take Over.
Shebar, Sharon S. Whaling for Glory.
Shebar, Sharon S., jt. auth. see Shebar, Jonathan M.
Sheckley, Robert. Dramocles: An Intergalactic Soap Opera.
--Is That What People Do?
--Is That What People Do?
Shecter, Ben. The Discontented Mother.
Shecter, Howard L. Acquiring or Selling the Privately Held Company '87.
Shedd, Charlie. Celebration in the Bedroom.
--Devotions for Dieters.
--If I Can Write, You Can Write.
Shedd, Charlie & Shedd, Martha. Praying Together: Making Marriage Last.
Shedd, Charlie W. The Best Dad Is a Good Lover.
--The Fat Is in Your Head.
--The Pastoral Ministry of Church Officers.
--Smart Dads I Know.
--The Stork Is Dead.
--You Can Be a Great Parent.
Shedd, Charlie W. & Shedd, Martha. Tell Me a Story: Stories for Your Grandchildren & the Art of Telling Them.
Shedd, Jeanne H. Serials in Selected European Languages: The Language Problem.
Shedd, Martha, jt. auth. see Shedd, Charlie.
Shedd, Martha, jt. auth. see Shedd, Charlie W.
Shedd, William G. Commentary on Romans: A Classic Commentary from the Reformed Perspective.
Sheed, F. J. The Holy Spirit in Action.
--To Know Christ Jesus.
Sheed, F. J., tr. & frwd. by. The Confessions of St. Augustine.
Sheed, Frank J. Christ in Eclipse: A Clinical Study of the Good Christian.
Sheed, Rosemary, tr. see De Surgy, Paul.
Sheed, Wilfred. Frank & Maisie: A Memoir with Parents.
Sheed, Wilfrid. Frank & Maisie: A Memoir with Parents.
--Max Jamison.
--People Will Always Be Kind.
Sheehan, David V. The Anxiety Disease & How to Overcome It.
Sheehan, Denza C. & Hrapchak, Barbara B. Theory & Practice of Histotechnology.
Sheehan, George A. Dr. Sheehan on Fitness.
--Running & Being.
--This Running Life.
Sheehan, H. Marxism & the Philosophy of Science- A Critical History: Vol. 1: The First Hundred Years.
Sheehan, Larry, jt. auth. see Kramer, Jack.
Sheehan, Larry, jt. auth. see Snead, Sam.
Sheehan, Larry, ed. The Whole Golf Catalog.
Sheehan, Larry, ed. see Smith, Stan, et al.
Sheehan, Larry, ed. see Smith, Stan.
Sheehan, Patrick A. The Triumph of Failure. Bd. with A Flower of Asia. Dennehy, Henry E. Garland Pub.
Sheehan, Susan. Kate Quinton's Days.
--A Prison & a Prisoner.
--A Welfare Mother.
Sheehan, Thomas J., jt. auth. see Watkins, John V.
Sheehy. Emergency Nursing: Principles & Practice.
Sheehy, Ann D., jt. auth. see McCarthy, Constance F.
Sheehy, Emma D. Children Discover Music & Dance.
Sheeler, Philip. Centrifugation in Biology & Medical Science.
Sheen, Fulton J. The World's Great Love: The Prayer of the Rosary.
Sheen, Jack H. Aesthetic Rhinoplasty.
Sheen, Rachel. Diary of an Artist.
Sheer. Basic Mathematic Skills.
Sheets, Herman E. & Boatwright, Victor T., eds. Hydronautics.
Sheffield, Berthold. Planning for a Successful Retirement: A Home Study Course.
Sheffield, Charles & Rosin, Carol. Space Careers.
Shefner, Jeremy M., jt. auth. see Levine, Michael W.
Shefter, Harry, et al, eds. see Thackeray, William Makepeace.
Shehadeh, Raja. Occupiers' Law. International Commission of Jurists (Geneva, Switzerland) Staff, ed.
Sheidley, William E. see Butler, Francelia, et al.
Sheiman, Bruce, jt. auth. see Glotzer, Arline.
Sheiman, Bruce S. Monarch's Complete Guide to Getting into Graduate Business School.
Sheinkopf, Kenneth, jt. auth. see Grasty, William K.
Sheinwold, Alfred. Short Cut to Winning Bridge.
Sheinwold, Patricia F. Husbands & Other Men I've Played with.
Shekleton, Maureen E., jt. auth. see Groer, Maureen W.
Shelah, S. Proper Forcing.
Shelby, Kermit. Covered Wagon Boy.
Sheldon, Alan. Managing Doctors.
Sheldon, Alan & Windham, Susan R. Competitive Strategy for Health Care Organizations.
Sheldon, Charles. In His Steps.
Sheldon, Charles H., jt. auth. see Baker, Donald G.
Sheldon, Charles M. Bible Stories.
--In His Steps.
Sheldon, Esther. Thomas Sheridan of Smock-Alley, 1719-1788.
Sheldon, G. W. Hours with Art & Artists. Weinberg, H. Barbara, ed.
Sheldon, George W. Recent Ideals of American Art.
Sheldon, Huntington. Boyd's Introduction to the Study of Disease.
Sheldon, Huntington & Braun, Simon. Cases for Diagnosis.
Sheldon, Peter. Guide to Greece.
Sheldon, Randall G. Criminal Justice in America: A Sociological Approach.
Sheldon, Sidney. The Other Side of Midnight.
Sheline, Glenn E., et al. Pituitary Adenomas.
Shell, Karl, jt. auth. see Fisher, Franklin M.
Shell, Karl, jt. ed. see Cass, David.
Shell, Olive, jt. ed. see Estrella, Gregorio.
Shellard, Alan. Growing & Showing Geraniums.
Shellenberger, T., ed. see Annual Hormone Research Symposium Staff.
Shellenberger, T. E., ed. see Annual Hormone Research Symposium Staff.
Shelley, Bruce L. Christian Theology in Plain Language.
Shelley, John, tr. see Soelle, Dorothee.
Shelley, Marshall, jt. auth. see Hunter, Jim.
Shelley, Mary Wollstonecraft. Frankenstein.
Shelley, Percy Bysshe. Shelley.
--Shelley's Critical Prose. McElderry, B. R., Jr., ed.
Shelley, Susanne. Modern Intermediate Algebra for College Students.
Shelley, Violet M. Symbols & the Self.
Shellow, Jill R. Grant Seekers Guide National Network of Grantmakers.
Shelly, Judith A. Not Just a Job: Serving Christ in Your Work.
Shelly, Maynard W., ed. Analyses of Satisfaction.
--Analyses of Satisfaction, Vol. 1.
--Analyses of Satisfaction, Vol. 2.
Shelly, Maynard W. & Adelberg, Tina Z., eds. Recent Readings in Reinforcement & Satisfaction.
Shelon Electric Co. Staff. The Natural Way to Health, Vigor & Beauty.
Shelp, Earl E. & Sunderland, Ronald H., eds. A Biblical Basis for Ministry. Achtmeier, Paul J., et al.
Shelston, Alan. Biography.
Shelton, Gene. Track of the Snake.
Shelton, Jay W. Wood Heat Safety.
Shelton, John L. Behavior Modification for Counseling Centers: A Guide to Program Development.
Shelton, Robert M. Use of Things.
Shem, Samuel. Fine.
Shemel, Sidney & Krasilovsky, M. William. This Business of Music.
Shemel, Sidney & Krislovsky, M. William. More about This Business of Music. Zhito, Lee, ed.
Shen, C. N., jt. auth. see Mohler, R. R.
Shen, Mitchell, ed. Contemporary Topics in Polymer Science.
Shenayev, V. N. Western Europe Today.
Shenfield, John H., jt. auth. see Practising Law Institute Staff.
Shen Fu. From Concept to Context: Approaches to Asian & Islamic Calligraphy.
Sheng, P. Scattering & Localization of Classical Wave in Random Media.
Shenk, Al. Calculus & Analytic Geometry.
Shenkel, William M. Modern Real Estate Management.
--Modern Real Estate Principles.
--Real Estate Finance.
Shenker, I. R., ed. Adolescent Medicine: Selected Topics.
Shenker, Israel. In the Footsteps of Boswell & Johnson.
Shenstone, William, jt. auth. see Attiret, Jean D.
Shentao, Ye. How Mr. Pan Weathered the Storm. Wenxue & Johnstone, Simen, trs. from Chinese.
Shenton, Alan & Shenton, Rita. The Price Guide to Clocks, 1840-1940.
Shenton, Edward H. Diving for Science: The Story of the Deep Submersible.
--Exploring the Ocean Depths.
Shenton, Rita, jt. auth. see Shenton, Alan.
Shep, Robert L. Cleaning & Caring for Books.
--Cleaning & Caring for Books.
Shepard, Andrea J. Sing a New Song.
Shepard, Francis P. Earth Beneath the Sea.
Shepard, Jack, jt. auth. see Glover, Bob.
Shepard, Jon M. & Voss, Harwin L. Social Problems.
Shepard, Leslie A. Encyclopedia of Occultism & Parapsychology: Vols. 1 & 2.
Shepard, Merle & Lawn, R. J. Insects on Grain Legumes in Northern Australia: A Survey of Potential Pests & Their Enemies.
Shepard, Odell. Thy Rod & Thy Creel.
Shepard, Paul & McKinley, Daniel, eds. Subversive Science: Essays Toward an Ecology of Man.
Shepard, Priscilla, compiled by. Fields of Gold.
Shepard, Sheldon R. Let's Have Music.
Shepard, Thomas H. Catalog of Teratogenic Agents.
Shepard's Citation, Inc. Staff. The New York Court of Appeals Case Names Citator.
--The New York Supreme Court Appellate Division Case Names Citator.
--Professional & Judicial Conduct Citations.
--Restatement Citations.
--Shepard's Atlantic Reporter Citations: A Compilation of Citations to all Cases Reported in the Atlantic Reporter. The Citations...Include Affirmances, Reversals & Dismissals by Higher State Courts & by the United States Supreme Court.
--Shepard's Bankruptcy Citations: Cases & Statutes, a Compilation of Citations to United States Supreme Court Decisions.
--Shepard's Indiana Citations Cases: A Compilation of Citations Which Include Affirmances, Reversals, & Dismissals by the Indian Courts & the United States Supreme Court..,
--Shepard's Missouri Citations, Statutes.
--Shepard's Nevada Citations, Cases & Statutes: A Compilation of Citations to Nevada Cases Reported in the Nevada Reports & in the Pacific Reporter, the United States Constitution & Statutes, & the Nevada Constitution, Codes, Statutes, Ordinances, & Court Rules.
--Shepard's New Mexico Citations, Cases & Statutes: A Compilation of Citations to New Mexico Cases Reported in the New Mexico Reports & in the Pacific Reporter, to the United States Constitution & Statutes, New Mexico Constitution, Statutes, Laws, Charters, Ordinances, Court Rules, & Jury Instructions.
--Shepard's North Carolina Citations, Cases.
--Shepard's Ohio Citations, Cases.
--Shepard's Oklahoma Citations: A Compilation of Citations to Oklahoma Cases Reported in the Various Seriers of Oklahoma Reports & Southwestern Reporter.
--Shepard's South Carolina Citations Cases: A Compilation of Citations Which Include Affirmances, Reversals, & Dismissals by the South Carolina Courts & the United States Supreme Court.
--Shepard's Texas Case Names Citator: A Compilation of Case Names & Citations of Texas Cases Decided from 1940 to the Present.
--Shepard's Vermont Citations: Cases & Statutes.
--Shepard's Washington Case Names Citator: A Compilation of Case Names & Citations of Washington Cases Decided from 1940 to the Present.
Shepard's Citation, Inc. Staff & American Law Institute Staff. Shepard's Restatement of the Law Citations: A Compilation of Citations to the American Law Institute's Restatement of the Law.
Shepard's Citation, Inc. Staff, et al. Small Business Financing.
Shepard's McGraw-Hill Staff. Shepard's California Citations.
--Shepard's Connecticut Case Names Citator: A Compilation of Case Names & Citations of Connecticut Cases Decided From 1935 to the Present.
Shephard, Roy J. Physiology & Biochemistry of Exercise.
Shepher, Joseph. Incest: A Biosocial View.
Shepher, Joseph, jt. auth. see Tiger, Lionel.
Shepherd & Monaghan. Clinical Gynaecological Oncology.
Shepherd, Gary, jt. auth. see Scherer, Jacqueline.
Shepherd, J. Barrie. A Diary of Prayer: Daily Meditations on the Parables of Jesus.
Shepherd, Jack. The Adams Chronicles: Four Generations of Greatness.
Shepherd, James F. A Balance of Payments for the Thirteen Colonies 1768-1772. Bruchey, Stuart, ed.
--College Study Skills.
--College Study Skills.
--College Vocabulary Skills.
--College Vocabulary Skills.
--Reading Skills for College Study.
--RSVP: The Houghton Mifflin Reading, Study, & Vocabulary Program.
Shepherd, John. Tin Pan Alley.
Shepherd, John, et al. Whose Music? A Sociology of Musical Language.
Shepherd, M. The Psycho-Social Matrix of Psychiatry.
Shepherd, Margaret. Capitals for Calligraphy: A Sourcebook of Decorated Letters.
Shepherd, Massey H., Jr. The Psalms in Christian Worship: A Practical Guide.
Shepherd, Michael. Sherlock Holmes & the Case of Doctor Freud.
Shepherd, Michael, et al, eds. Mental Health in Primary Care Settings.
Shepherd, Naomi. A Refuge from Darkness: Wilfrid Israel & the Rescue of the Jews.
Shepherd, P. J., ed. & tr. see Sitenko, A. G.
Shepherd, R. B. Physiotherapy in Paediatrics.
Shepherd, Rebecca A., ed. Peterson's Annual Guide to Independent Secondary Schools, 1983-84.
Shepherd, Rebecca A. & Hunter, Joan H., eds. Guide to Independent Secondary Schools 1984-85.
Shepherd, Roberta, jt. auth. see Carr, Janet.
Shepherd, Roberta B., jt. auth. see Carr, Janet H.
Shepherd, Stella. Like a Mantle, the Sea.
Shepherd, Walter. Outline of History of Science.
Shepherd, William G., ed. Public Policies Toward Business: Readings & Cases.
Shepherd-Moore, Marie. To Strive to Search, to Find.
Sheppard, Charles L. Guide for Selecting Microcomputer Data Management Software.
Sheppard, E. J. Ancient Athens. Reeves, Marjorie, ed.
Sheppard, Eric W. A Short History of the British Army.
Sheppard, Georgie M., jt. auth. see Liebers, Arthur.
Sheppard, Harold. New Perspectives on Older Workers.
Sheppard, Harold & Striner, Herbert. Civil Rights, Employment, & the Social Status of American Negroes.
Sheppard, Helen E., jt. ed. see Towell, Julie E.
Sheppard, J. T. Aeschylus & Sophocles: Their Work & Influence.
Sheppard, Mubin. Taman Budiman: Memoirs of an Unorthodox Civil Servant.
Sheppard, P. M. Natural Selection & Heredity.
Sheppard Press, Ltd. Bookdealers' & Collectors' Year-Book & Diary, 1984.
Sheppard Press, Ltd., Staff, compiled by. Bookdealers in India, Pakistan, Etc.
Sheppard Press, Ltd. Staff, compiled by. Bookdealers in North America: A Directory of Dealers in Secondhand & Antiquarian Books in Canada & the United States of America, 1983-1985.
--Dealers in Books: A Directory of Dealers in Secondhand & Antiquarian Books in the British Isles, 1984-1986.
Sheppard, Stephen. Monte Carlo.
Sheppard, Vincent F., jt. auth. see Reed, Gretchen M.
Sheppard, William C. & Willoughby, Robert H. Child Behavior.
Sheppard, William E. Fund Raising Letter Collection.
Sheppard-Jones, Elisabeth. Stories of Wales: Told for Children.
Shepperson, Bob. The Sandman.
Shepperson, W., et al. Questions from the Past.
Shepro, David & Fulton, George P. Microcirculation As Related to Shock.
Sher, R., jt. ed. see Williams, M. M.
Sheras, Peter L. & Worchel, Stephen. Clinical Psychology: A Social Psychological Approach.
Sheraton, Mimi, jt. auth. see King, Alan.
Sheraton, Thomas. The Cabinet-Maker & Upholsterer's Drawing Book.
Sherburne, James. Death's Clenched Fist.
--Death's Gray Angel.
--Death's Pale Horse.
--Poor Boy & a Long Way from Home.
Shercliff, J. A. A Textbook of Magnetohydrodynamics.
Shere, Waris. Miracles of Survival: Canada & French Canada.
Shere, Waris, ed. In Search of Peace.
Sherer, Michael L. Stories for Special Days: Messages for Children on the Lesser Festivals.
Sherer, Robert G. Subordination or Liberation? The Development & Conflicting Theories of Black Education in Nineteenth Century Alabama.
Sherer, Robert V. Industrial Golden Egg Goose: One Man's Struggle Against Pollution & Unethical Practices.
Sheridan, Alan, tr. see Foucault, Michel.
Sheridan, Alan, tr. see Ghanem, Ali.
Sheridan, Alan, tr. see Japrisot, Sebastien.
Sheridan, Alan, tr. see Semprun, Jorge.
Sheridan, Alan, tr. see Tournier, Michel.
Sheridan, Eleanor, et al. Falconer's the Drug, the Nurse, the Patient.
Sheridan, Frances. The Memoirs of Miss Sidney Bidulph.

Authors

Sheridan, James F., Jr. Once More from the Middle: A Philosophical Anthropology.
Sheridan, Mary & Salaff, Janet W., eds. Lives: Chinese Working Women.
Sheridan, Michael. The Fifth Season.
Sheridan, P. J., ed. see Engineering Manpower Commission.
Sheridan, T. B. & Johannsen, G., eds. Monitoring Behavior & Supervisory Control.
Sherif, Carolyn W., jt. auth. see Sherif, Muzafer.
Sherif, Carolyn W. & Sherif, Muzafer, eds. Attitude, Ego-Involvement & Change.
Sherif, Muzafer & Sherif, Carolyn W. Groups in Harmony & Tension.
Sherif, Muzafer, jt. ed. see Sherif, Carolyn W.
Sheriff, John K. The Good-Natured Man: The Evolution of a Moral Ideal, 1660-1800.
Sheriff, Margaret L. Saints' Craftbook. Margolis, Bette S., tr.
Sherlock. J. B.'s Daughter.
Sherman, Alan, et al. Basic Concepts of Chemistry.
--Basic Concepts of Chemistry.
Sherman, Charles E. How to Do Your Own Divorce in California.
Sherman, Charles E. & Simons, Jim. How to Do Your Own Divorce in Texas.
Sherman, Charles E., ed. see Johnson, R. Charles.
Sherman, Chris, jt. auth. see Holder, Steven L.
Sherman, Dan. Dynasty of Spies.
--King Jaguar.
--The Man Who Loved Mata Hari.
--The Mole.
--The Prince of Berlin.
--Riddle.
--Swann.
--The White Mandarin.
--The White Mandarin.
Sherman, Ed. Up & Running: Adventures of a Software Entrepreneurs.
Sherman, Emalene. Student Journalist & Free-Lance Writing.
Sherman, Frank A., III. Pancakes at Four.
Sherman, Franklin, ed. see Elert, Werner.
Sherman, Franklin, ed. see Milford, T. R.
Sherman, Franklin, ed. see Moberly, Walter.
Sherman, Franklin, ed. see Temple, William.
Sherman, Franklin, ed. see Tillich, Paul.
Sherman, Franklin, ed. see Van Oyen, Hendrik.
Sherman, Harvey. It All Depends: A Pragmatic Approach to Organization.
Sherman, Howard D., jt. auth. see Heard, James E.
Sherman, Howard J. Macrodynamic Economics: Growth, Employment & Prices.
Sherman, Ivan. I Am a Giant.
--I Do Not Like It When My Friend Comes to Visit.
--Robert & the Magic String.
--Walking, Talking Words.
Sherman, James R. Get Set... Go!
--How to Overcome a Bad Back.
--Stop Procrastinating--Do It!
Sherman, Jean, tr. see Nin, Anais.
Sherman, Jory. Song of the Cheyenne.
Sherman, Josepha. The Invisibility Factor.
--Song of the Dark Druid.
Sherman, Margaret M. Pastor to the Outports: The Story of William & Emma McKirdy.
Sherman, Martin. Bent.
Sherman, Marty, ed. Alaska Angling Guide.
--Alaska Angling Guide 1987.
Sherman, Michael I., ed. see Roche Institute of Molecular Biology Symposium Staff.
Sherman, R. J. Pastor of the Range.
Sherman, Richard B. The Republican Party & Black America: From McKinley to Hoover, 1896-1933.
Sherman, T. D. O & M in Local Government.
Sheron, Carole. The Rise & Fall of Superwoman.
Sherratt, A. F., ed. Air Conditioning & Energy Conservation.
--Applications of Ambient Energy in Buildings.
--Integrated Environment in Building Design.
Sherratt, A. F., jt. ed. see Croome, D. J.
Sherrer, Arthur, jt. auth. see Nadel, Max.
Sherrerd, Henry D., Jr. The Onawa Bestiary: An Opinionated Survey with Digressions.
Sherrick, Joseph C., jt. auth. see Elias, H.
Sherrill, Culver. Crimes Without Punishment & Other Tales.
--Have You Heard This One? A Lifetime of Jokes Compiled with an Elastic Memory, Somewhat Depraved Sense of Humor, & a Pair of Scissors.
Sherrill, Helen H. Christian Parenthood.
Sherrill, Helen H., jt. auth. see Sherrill, Lewis J.
Sherrill, John, jt. auth. see Blair, Charles.
Sherrill, Lewis J. & Sherrill, Helen H. Becoming a Christian.
Sherrill, Robert. Why They Call It Politics: A Guide to America's Government.
--Why They Call It Politics: A Guide to America's Government.
Sherrill, Robert, et al. Governing America: An Introduction.
Sherrill, Rowland A. The Prophetic Melville: Experience, Transcendence, & Tragedy.
Sherrill, W. A. & Chu, W. K. An Anthology of I Ching.
Sherring. Law & Accounts for Executives.
Sherrod, Philip L. Mr. Wigley Cums.
--Purple Shit! Onspot - On Location in the Street.
--SEX-I-CON! Poetry.
--Sixty-Nine Images...Below the Belt! Poetry.
Sherron, R. H. & Lumsden, D. B., eds. Introduction to Educational Gerontology.
Sherry, Norman, ed. Conrad: The Critical Heritage.
Sherry, Norman, ed. see Conrad, Joseph.
Sherry, S., jt. auth. see Paoletti, R.
Shertzer, Bruce E. Career Planning: Freedom to Choose.
--Career Planning: Freedom to Choose.
Shertzer, Bruce E. & Stone, Shelley C. Fundamentals of Counseling.
--Fundamentals of Guidance.
--Fundamentals of Guidance.
Shertzer, Bruce E., jt. auth. see Stone, Shelley C.
Sherwen, Douglas S. Hitler's Master Plan: The Secret Conquest Strategy.
--The Persian Corridor: The Little-Known Story of the Signal Corps in the Middle East During World War II.
Sherwin, Byron L. The Golem Legend: Origins & Implications.
Sherwin, E. & Weston, G. J. Chemistry of the Non-Metallic Elements.
Sherwin-White, Nicholas. Ancient Rome.
Sherwood & Talner. Uroradiology.
Sherwood, Andrew. Breakpoints: Making Career Stages Work for You.
Sherwood, David, jt. auth. see Levinson, David.
Sherwood, David R. & Whistance, Dennis J. Piping Guide: A Compact Reference for the Design & Drafting of Industrial Piping Systems.
--The Piping Guide: A Compact Reference for the Design & Drafting of Industrial Piping Systems.
Sherwood, Hugh C. How to Invest in Bonds.
Sherwood, John. A Botanist at Bay.
--The Mantrap Garden: A Celia Grant Mystery.
Sherwood, Rae. The Psychodynamics of Race: Vicious & Benign Spirals.
Sherwood, T., jt. ed. see Steiner, R. E.
Sherwood, Terry G. Fulfilling the Circle: A Study of John Donne's Thought.
Sherwood, Valerie. This Loving Torment.
Shetter, W. Z. An Introduction to Dutch.
--The Pillars of Society: Six Centuries of Civilization in the Netherlands.
Shetter, W. Z., jt. auth. see Bird, R. B.
Shetterly, Anya. Romewalks.
Shetty, C. M., jt. auth. see Bazaraa, M. S.
Shevell, Richard S. Fundamentals of Flight.
Shevelov, George Y. Teasers & Appeasers: Essay & Studies on Themes of Slavic Philology.
Shevett, Anita & Shevett, Steve. Red, Yellow, Blue: A Wrinkles Book of Colors.
Shevett, Anita, photos by. Good Night, Little Wrinkle.
Shevett, Anita & Shevett, Steve, photos by. Big & Little: A Wrinkles Book of Opposites.
--One Red Wagon: A Wrinkles Book of Numbers.
Shevett, Steve, jt. auth. see Shevett, Anita.
Shevky, Eshref & Bell, Wendell. Social Area Analysis.
Shevtsov, V. S. State & Nations in the U. S. S. R.
Shewbridge, Edythe A. Portraits of Poverty.
Shewell, Lauri J. One Day at a Time.
Shewey, Don. Sam Shepard.
Shewmon, Paul G. Transformations in Metals.
Shi, Nai'an & Luo Guanzhong. Outlaws of the Marsh. Shapiro, Sidney, tr.
Shibata, H. & Ariman, T., eds. Recent Advances in Lifeline Earthquake Engineering in Japan.
Shibata, Hirofumi, jt. ed. see Drysdale, Peter.
Shibata, Shoji & Bailey, Leslie E., eds. Recent Developments in Cardiac Muscle Pharmacology.
Shiber, Etta, et al. Classics of World War Two - The Shadow War: Paris-Underground.
Shibles, Loana & Rogers, Annie, eds. All Maine All Poultry Cookbook.
Shichor, David, jt. auth. see Decker, David L.
Shideler, Ross, tr. Staffan.
Shideler, Ross, tr. see Enquist, Per Olov.
Shidell, Doug, jt. auth. see Van Valkenberg, Philip.
Shiel, D. J. Ben Hall Bushranger.
Shield, Renee R. Making Babies in the 80's: The New Parents Baby Book.
Shieldrop, E. B. The Air.
Shields, C. Boilers.
Shields, Carol. Small Ceremonies.
Shields, Carrington, jt. auth. see Oppenheim, S. Chesterfield.
Shields, David. Heroes.
Shields, Edward D. see Melnick, Michael.
Shields, J. Webster, jt. auth. see Price, Stephen.
Shields, Jerry. The Invisible Billionaire, Daniel Ludwig.
Shields, Laurie. Displaced Homemakers: Organizing for a New Life.
Shields, M. Bruce, jt. auth. see Ritch, Robert.
Shields, Mike. A Taste of Rabbit Tracks: Expedition into a Frozen Wilderness.
Shields, Paul. Theory of Bernouilli Shifts.
Shields, Pete. Guns Don't Die -- People Do: The Pros, the Cons, the Facts.
Shields, Roger E., jt. auth. see Jefferson, Thomas, Center Foundation Staff.
Shields, Sue. The Edwardians: Costume Cut-out Book.
--The Elizabethans: Costume Cut-out Book.
Shields, Thomas W., ed. General Thoracic Surgery.
Shiels, Frederick L., ed. Ethnic Separatism & World Politics.
Shiels, William E. Gonzalo De Tapia, 1561-1594: Founder of the First Permanent Jesuit Mission in North America.
Shiers, George. Electronic Drafting Techniques & Exercises.
Shifrin, Adah F. The Flower of Contemplation.
Shigley, Joseph E. Applied Mechanics of Materials.
Shigo, Alex L. Tree Defects: A Photo Guide.
Shih, C. Y., jt. auth. see Kessel, R. G.
Shih, Kitty M., jt. auth. see Klemperer, Katharina.
Shih, Vivian E. Laboratory Techniques for the Detection of Hereditary Metabolic Disorders.
Shih Kuo-Heng & Fei Hsiao-T'Ung, eds. China Enters the Machine Age: A Study of Labor in Chinese War Industry.
Shih-Tsai Chen, Samuel. Basic Documents of International Organization.
Shikes, R. H. Rocky Mountain Medicine: Doctors, Drugs & Disease in Early Colorado.
Shikes, Ralph E. The Indignant Eye: The Artist As a Social Critic in Prints & Drawings from the 15th Century to Picasso.
Shiki, et al. Thistle Brilliant Morning. Higginson, William J., tr. from Japanese.
Shillaber, Carol see O'Neal, William B.
Shiller, Robert E. Methods of Knowledge & Values.
Shilling, A. G. & Sokoloff, Kiril. Is Inflation Ending? Are You Ready?
Shilo, Moshe, ed. Strategies of Microbial Life in Extreme Environments.
Shiloh, Ailon, ed. Studies in Human Sexual Behavior: The American Scene.
Shilov, G. Y. Mathematical Analysis: A Special Course.
Shilova, I., jt. auth. see Dulmatovskaya, G.
Shils, Edward. The Intellectuals & the Powers: And Other Essays.
Shim, E. The Boy in the Forest.
Shim, Jae K. & Geller, Louis. Readings in Cost & Managerial Accounting.
Shiman, Alexander, jt. auth. see Shimanovskaya, K.
Shimanovskaya, K. & Shiman, Alexander. Radiation Injury of Bone: Bone Injuries Following Radiation Therapy of Tumors. Haigh, Basil, tr.
Shimazu, Koichi, jt. auth. see White, Robert.
Shimek, William J. The Liter.
Shimidzu, T., et al. Reactivities.
Shimizu, Akinao & Aoki, Katsutada. Application of Invariant Imbedding to Reactor Physics.
Shimizu, F., jt. ed. see Thun, Matteo.
Shimizu, Fumio, et al. The Italian Interior.
Shimizu, Kay. Asian Flavors.
Shimm, Melvin G. European Regional Communities: A New Era on the Old Continent.
Shimmin, Sylvia, jt. auth. see Blacker, Frank.
Shimoda, K., ed. High-Resolution Laser Spectroscopy.
Shimoji, Mitsuo. Liquid Metals: An Introduction to the Physics & Chemistry of Metals in the Liquid State.
Shimshak, Robert H., jt. auth. see Johnson, Robert F.
Shin, Kyung Sun, jt. auth. see Kim, Daeshik.
Shindler, Colin. Hollywood Goes to War.
Shindler, Merrill, ed. see Zagat, Eugene H., Jr. & Zagat, Nina S.
Shin Duk Kung. One-Step Sparring.
Shine, I. Serendipity in St. Helena.
Shinebourne, Elliot A., jt. ed. see Anderson, Robert H.
Shiner, Joyce J. Thoughts of Mine.
Shingle, Frank. Room with No Number: A Novel.
Shingles, Carol R., jt. auth. see Boillot, Michel H.
Shinkokai, Kokusai B., compiled by. Current Contents of Academic Journals in Japan, 1970.
Shinn. Evaluations of Drug Interactions EDI.
--Evaluations of Drug Interactions EDI-Student Version.
Shinn, Arthur F., et al, eds. Evaluations of Drug Interactions.
Shinn, Charles H. The Story of the Mine.
Shinn, Duane. How to Play Piano from Chord Symbols: A Guide to Playing More Notes Without Reading More Notes.
--Piano Breakthrough: How to Revolutionize Your Playing Through Chords & Broken Chords.
Shinn, Julie A. & Douglas, Marilyn K. Advances in Cardiovascular Nursing.
Shinn, Rinn-Sup, jt. ed. see Bunge, Frederica M.
Shinn, Roger L. New Directions in Theology Today: Man: the New Humanism, Vol. 6.
Shinn, Roger L., ed. Faith & Science in an Unjust World, Vol. 1: Plenary Presentations.
Shinskey, F. Gregg. Process Control Systems.
Shiplett, Gary R. Every Pastor's Worship Planning Book. Meyer, Sheila, ed.
Shipley, Joseph T. Dictionary of Early English.
--Dictionary of World Literature.
--Encyclopedia of Literature.
--Trends in Literature.
Shipley, Kenneth G. & Banis, Carolyn S. Teaching Morphology Developmentally: Methods & Materials for Teaching Bound Morphology.
Shipley, Reginald A. & Clark, Richard E. Tracer Methods for in Vitro Kinetics: Theory & Applications.
Shipley, Robert H. QuitSmart: A Guide to Freedom from Cigarettes.
Shipley, T., ed. The Beginnings of Visual Photochemistry: Translations & Biographies in Honor of F. Boll & F. W. Kuhne.
Shipley, Thorne. Classics in Psychology.
Shipman, Carl. Canon SLR Cameras.
--Pentax SLR Cameras.
--SLR Photographer's Handbook.
Shipman, Gordon. Handbook for Family Analysis.
Shipman, Harry L. Black Holes, Quasars, & the Universe.
--Black Holes, Quasars, & the Universe.
--The Restless Universe: An Introduction to Astronomy.
Shipp, Bob. Dr. Bob Shipp's Guide to the Fishes of the Gulf of Mexico.
Shipp, G. P. Modern Greek Evidence for the Ancient Greek Vocabulary.
Shipp, Horace. Dutch Masters.
--English Masters.
Shipp, Ralph D., Jr. Retail Merchandising: Principles & Applications.
Shippy, Beverly B. Common Knowledge: Controlling Your Destiny.
Shipton, Clifford K. New England Life in the Eighteenth Century: Representative Biographies from Sibley's Harvard Graduates.
Shipway, George. Free Lance.
--The Paladin.
Shirani Kali, Natari. Passions, Realms & Visions.
Shirer, William. Gāndhi: A Memoir.
Shirer, William L. The Challenge of Scandinavia: Norway, Sweden, Denmark, & Finland in Our Time.
--Rise & Fall of the Third Reich: A History of Nazi Germany.
Shires, David B. & Hennen, Brian K. Family Medicine: A Guidebook for Practitioners of the Art.
Shires, Henry M. Finding the Old Testament in the New.
Shirley, James. The Lady of Pleasure. Thorensen, Marilyn J. & Orgel, Stephen, eds.
--Love's Cruelty: Edited from the Quarto of 1640 with Introduction & Notes. Orgel, Stephen, ed.
Shirley, R. W. Bibliotheca Vinaria.
--Early Printed Maps of the British Isles, 1477-1650.
Shirreffs, Gordon D. Enemy Seas.
--Torpedoes Away.
Shirts, Morris. Warm up for Little League Baseball.
Shirts, Morris A. Warm up for Little League Baseball.
Shisha, Oved, ed. Inequalities: Proceedings.
Shivanandan, Mary. When Your Wife Wants to Work.
Shively, Norman B. Index to S. T. Wiley's History of Monongalia County (1883)
Shivers, Louise. Here to Get My Baby.
Shkaratan, O., jt. auth. see Blyakhman, L.
Shklovski, I. S. Universo, Vida, Intelecto.
Shlain, Bruce, jt. auth. see Lee, Martin A.
Shles, Larry. Moths & Mothers, Feathers & Fathers: A Story About a Tiny Owl Named Squib.
Shmelev, G. Personal Subsidiary Farming under Socialism.
Shneiderman, Ben, jt. auth. see Kreitzberg, Charles B.
Shneidman, Edwin S. Suicide Thoughts & Reflections: 1960-1980.
Shneidman, Edwin S. & Farberow, Norman L., eds. Clues to Suicide.
Shobe, John & Kelley, Kate. Divers Guide to Underwater America.
Shoben, Edward J., Jr., jt. ed. see Milton, Ohmer.
Shockley, Ann A. Loving Her.
Shockley, Emmy L., jt. auth. see Schwartz, Morris S.
Shockley, James E. Calculus & Analytic Geometry.

Authors

Shockley, Robert & Cutlip, Glen W. Excelling: Raising Your Grades with High Tech.
Shockman, Gerald & Wicken, Anthony, eds. Chemistry & Biological Activities of Bacterial Surface Amphiphiles.
Shoden, Rebecca & Griffin, Sue. Fundamentals of Clinical Nutrition.
Shoecraft, Paul. Math Games & Activities.
Shoemaker. Mosby's Med-Tech Assess Test.
Shoemaker, Dennis E. The Global Connection: Local Action for World Justice.
Shoemaker, Helen S. I Stand by the Door.
--The Secret of Effective Prayer.
Shoemaker, James S. Small Fruit Culture.
Shoemaker, Richard, jt. auth. see Sargent, Murray, III.
Shoemaker, Robbin. Effects of Changes in United States Agricultural Production on Demand for Farm Inputs.
Shoemaker, Robert S., jt. auth. see McQuiston, Frank W., Jr.
Shoemaker, Sydney. Self-Knowledge & Self-Identity.
Shoemaker, Terry. Performance Activities in Mathematics. Incl. Bk. 1; Bk. 2; Bk. 3; Bk. 4; Bk. 5; Bk. 6. Pawnee Pub.
Shoemaker, Thomas M., jt. auth. see Kurtz, Edwin B.
Shoemark, P., jt. auth. see Reynolds, Mark.
Shoemark, Pete. CZ 250 Twins '74-'78.
--Honda XL-XR 250 & 500: '78-'81.
--NVT BSA Easy Rider Mopeds Seventy-Six to Seventy-Nine.
--Puch MS, MV, M2, M3, & VS Mopeds '68-'76.
--Suzuki RM Series '79-'80.
--Triumph Tiger Cub & Terrier '52 - '66.
--Vespa Ciao & Bravo Mopeds '68 on.
--Yamaha RS100 & 125 Singles '74-'79.
Shoemyen, Anne, ed. Nineteen Eighty-Seven Florida Statistical Abstract.
Shoenfelt, Joseph F. Designing & Making Handwrought Jewelry.
Shoff, Janet see Corrigan, L. Luan.
Shoham, S. Giora. Rebellion, Creativity & Revelation. Cherns, Albert, intro. by.
--Sex As Bait: Eve, Casanova & Don Juan.
Shoham, S. Giora, ed. Youth Unrest.
Shoham, Shlomo G. The Myth of Tantalus: A Scaffolding for an Ontological Personality Theory.
Shoham, Yoav, jt. auth. see Dean, Thomas.
Shohet, J. L. Plasma State.
Shohet, Robin. Dream Sharing.
Shokeid, Moshe. The Dual Heritage: Immigrants from the Atlas Mountains in an Israeli Village.
Sholiton, Robert D. & Van Campen, Joseph A. Pattern Drills for Introductory Russian.
Sholokhov, M. Virgin Soil Upturned.
Sholokhov, Mikhail. Mikhail Sholokhov, Collected Works.
--Mikhail Sholokhov, Collected Works.
--Mikhail Sholokhov, Collected Works.
--Mikhail Sholokhov, Collected Works.
--Mikhail Sholokhov, Collected Works.
--Mikhail Sholokhov, Collected Works.
--Mikhail Sholokhov, Collected Works.
Shone, Ronald. Autohypnosis: A Step-by-Step Guide to Self-Hypnosis.
Shonick, William & Roemer, Ruth. Public Hospitals under Private Management: The California Experience.
Shonk, James H. Working in Teams: A Practical Manual for Improving Work Groups.
Shontz, F. C. Perceptual & Cognitive Aspects of Body Experience.
Shontz, Franklin C. The Psychological Aspects of Physical Illness & Disability.
Shook, C. H. Muskies & Muskie Fishing: How to Catch the King of Freshwater Game Fish.
Shook, Georg & Witt, Gary. Sharp Focus Watercolor Painting: Techniques for Hot-Pressed Surfaces.
Shook, Robert L. The Book of Why.
Shoolbred, C. F. A Guide to Recent Criminal Legislation.
Shooltz, Danna, ed. see Reggio, Kathryn & Davidson, Josephine.
Shope, David F. Interpersonal Sexuality.
Shopland, A. J. Refer to Occupational Therapy.
Shore, Dinah. Dinah Shore Cookbook.
Shore, Leslie, ed. see Haverkamp-Begemann, Egbert, et al.
Shore, R. W., jt. auth. see Holt, C. A.
Shores, Christopher. Duel for the Sky.
Shores, David L. & Hines, Carole P., eds. Papers in Language Variation: Samla-Ads Collection.
Shorey, Paul. Selected Papers.
Shorris, Earl. Power Sits at Another Table & Other Observations on the Business of Power.
Short, Ann. Seeking Change: Early Childhood Education for the Disadvantaged in South Africa.
Short, Anne, et al, eds. see AAUW, Wisconsin State Division Staff.
Short, Byron, et al. Pressure Enthalpy Charts.
Short, Douglas D., jt. auth. see Burton, Sarah K.
Short, Edmund C., ed. Competence: Inquiries into Its Meaning & Acquisition in Educational Settings.
Short, Ernest. Fifty Years of Vaudeville.
Short, Francis H. & Zabinsky, Michael P. IBM-PC for Kids from Eight to Eighty.
Short, George, jt. auth. see Rodwell, Jenny.
Short, J. A. Drilling.
Short, John, et al. The Social Psychology of Telecommunications.
--Housebuilding, Planning & Community Action: The Production & Negotiation of the Built Environment.
Short, John Rendel see Rendel-Short, John.
Short, K. Microprocessors & Programmed Logic.
Short, Katharine. A Book for Mom.
Short, Luke. Bounty Guns.
--The Branded Man.
--Luke Short's Best of the West.
--The Stalkers.
Short, Michael & Holst, Imogen. Your Book of Music.
Short, N. M., jt. ed. see Green, J.
Short, Pat & Davidson, Billee. Totalaction: Ideas & Activities for Teaching Children Ages 5 to 8.
Short, Patricia, jt. auth. see Kane, Paula.
Short, Raymond W. & DeMaria, Robert, eds. Subjects & Sources for Research Writing, Second Ser.
Short, Robert L. Parables of Peanuts.
Short, William A. A Generation of Motion Pictures. Kupelnick, Bruce S., ed.
Shortell, Stephen M. & Kaluzny, Arnold D. Health Care Management: A Text in Organization Theory & Behavior.
Shorter, Aylward, ed. African Christian Spirituality.
Shorter, Edward. Bedside Manners: The Troubled History of Doctors & Patients.
--Bedside Manners: The Troubled History of Doctors & Patients.
--The Historian & the Computer: A Practical Guide.
Shorter, Frank & Bloom, Marc. Olympic Gold: A Runner's Life & Times.
Shorter, J., jt. ed. see Chapman, N. B.
Shorthill, R. W., ed. Progress in Planetary Exploration.
--Venus, Mars & Satellites of the Outer Planets: Proceedings of Symposium 3 of the COSPAR Twenty-Fifth Plenary Meeting Held in Graz, Austria, 25 June-7 July 1984.
Shortridge, James R. Kaw Valley Landscapes: A Guide to Eastern Kansas.
Shortt, James G. British Special Forces, Nineteen Forty-Five to the Present.
--The Paras: The British Parachute Regiment.
Shortt, Terence. Wild Birds of the Americas.
Shortz, Will. Brain Games.
--Brain Games, No. 2.
--World Class Championship Crosswords.
Shortz, Will, ed. Games Magazine Book of Crossword Puzzles.
Shostak, Jerome. How to Prepare for the College Board Achievement Test - English.
Shostakovich, Dmitri. Russian Symphony.
Shosteck, Robert. Weekender's Guide to the Four Seasons.
Shotter, John. Images of Man in Psychological Research.
Shotwell, James T. & Salvin, Marina. Lessons on Security & Disarmament from the History of the League of Nations.
Shotwell, R. The Ethernet Sourcebook.
Shoubao, Huang. Ethnic Costume from Guizhou: Clothing Designs & Decorations from Minority Ethnic Groups in Southwest China. Bingwen, Liu, tr. from Chinese.
Shoumatoff, Alex. In Southern Light: Treks Through Brazil & Africa.
--The Mountain of Names: A History of the Human Family.
--The Mountain of Names: An Informal History of Kinship.
Shoup, Cynthia A. Laboratory Exercises in Respiratory Therapy.
Shoup, T., et al. Introduction to Engineering Design with Graphics & Design Projects.
Shourd, Melvin L., jt. auth. see Winter, H. Frank.
Shourie, Arun. Hinduism: Essence & Consequence.
--Mrs. Gandhi's Second Reign.
Shourie, V. Black American Literature.
Shouse, Sarah, jt. auth. see Stephens, Elise H.
Showalter, Elaine. Women's Liberation & Literature.
Showalter, Elaine, ed. These Modern Women: Autobiographical Essays from the Twenties.
Showalter, Michael J., jt. auth. see Mabert, Vincent A.
Showalter, R. E., jt. auth. see Carroll, R. W.
Showalter, Ray, jt. auth. see Dvorak, Eileen M.
Showers, Renald E. What on Earth Is God Doing? Satan's Conflict with God: Study Guide.
Shrader, Robert L. Electronic Fundamentals for Technicians.
Shragge, Eric. Pensions' Policy in Britain: Socialist Analysis.
Shragin, V. Chile Corvalan Struggle.
Shrake, Edwin, jt. auth. see Jenkins, Dan.
Shrake, H. L. Let's Worship God Alone.
Shreck, Peter K. First Letters.
--First Sentences.
--First Story.
--First Words.
--Macmillan Learning Window Books: First Letters, First Sentences, First Story, & First Words.
Shreeve, Carolyn. Depression: Its Causes & How to Overcome Them.
Shreve, R. Norris & Brink, Joseph. Chemical Process Industries.
Shreve, Susan. The Bad Dreams of a Good Girl.
--How I Saved the World on Purpose.
--The Nightmares of Geranium Street.
--The Revolution of Mary Leary.
--A Woman Like That.
Shrew, Scheherazade. Tickling Tails.
Shreyder, E. Y., jt. auth. see Bochkova, O. P.
Shriner, Charles A. Wit, Wisdom & Foibles of the Great.
Shriner, R. L. Organic Syntheses: Collective Volumes, 1-49.
Shriver, Donald W., Jr. How Do You Do- & Why?
--The Lord's Prayer: A Way of Life.
--Rich Man, Poor Man.
Shroff, Homai J. The Eighteenth Century Novel: The Idea of the Gentleman.
Shrope, Wayne A. Experiences in Communication.
--Speaking & Listening: A Contemporary Approach.
Shroyer, Edgar H., jt. ed. see Tweedie, David.
Shrubb, Lee, jt. ed. see Coleman, Peter.
Shry, Carroll L., Jr., jt. auth. see Reiley, H. Edward.
Shtern, V. Y. The Gas-Phase Oxidation of Hydrocarbons. Mullins, B. P., ed.
Shub, Anatole. New Russian Tragedy.
Shubnikov, A. V. & Belov, N. V. Colored Symmetry.
Shuckburg, Evelyn S., tr. see Polybius.
Shuckburgh, Evelyn. Descent to Suez: Foreign Office Diaries 1951-1956. Charmley, John, ed.
Shufang, Xiao, jt. auth. see Zuoren, Wu.
Shufen, Li. Why Tomorrow?
Shufunmoto Company, Ltd. Staff. The Ikebana & Bonsai, 1989.
Shufunotomo Editorial Staff & Tetsuzo Tanikawa, eds. Gendai Chato Taikan: A General View of Contemporary Tea Ceremony & Ceramic Ware.
Shugaev, V., et al. Ferryboat Across the Kirenga.
Shugar, D., jt. auth. see McLaren, A. D.
Shugar, D., ed. Enzymes & Isoenzymes: Structure, Properties & Function.
Shugart, Cecil G., ed. see Einstein Centennial Celebration Staff.
Shugart, Cooksey. The Complete Guide to American Pocket Watches: Pocket Watches from 1809-1950. Schrieber, Peter, ed.
Shugart, Grace, et al. Food for Fifty.
Shugrue, Michael F. The Essay.
Shugrue, Michael F., ed. Adventures of a Cork-Screw, Seventeen Seventy-Five.
--Adventures of a Jesuit, Seventeen Seventy-One.
--The Adventures of an Author: Written by Himself and a Friend.
--Fatal Friendship: A Novel; by a Lady, 1771.
--The History of the Human Heart; or, the Adventures of a Young Gentleman, 1749.
Shugrue, Michael F., ed. see Graffigny, Francoise.
Shugrue, Michael F., ed. see Hawkesworth, John.
Shugrue, Michael F., ed. see Woodfin, Mrs. A.
Shuhan, Zhao, ed. see Xinglian, Zhang.
Shuhan, Zhao, tr. see Er Si, et al.
Shukhat, M. Moldavia: A Guide.
Shukla, A. C. & Misra, S. P. Essentials of Paleobotany.
Shukla, P. D. Toward New Patterns of Education in India.
Shuler, K. E. & Fenn, J. B., eds. Ionization in High-Temperature Gases, PAAS12.
Shuler, Philip L. A Genre for the Gospels: The Biographical Character of Matthew.
Shull, Barbara. How to Become a Skilled Intercessor.
Shull, L. R., jt. auth. see Cheeke, Peter R.
Shulman, Abraham. The Adventures of a Yiddish Lecturer.
Shulman, Albert M. The Religious Heritage of America.
Shulman, Bernard, ed. see Adler, Alfred.
Shulman, Colette, jt. auth. see Clements, Barbara.
Shulman, David. An Annotated Bibliography of Cryptography.
Shulman, Irving. The Amboy Dukes.
--Cry Tough.
Shulman, Julius. Cataracts: The Complete Guide from Diagnosis to Recovery for Patients & Families.
Shulman, Lawrence. A Casebook of Social Work with Groups: The Mediating Model.
Shulman, Neil. Finally...I'm a Doctor.
Shulman, Robert. Social Criticism & Nineteenth-Century American Fictions.
Shulman, Susan. Real Estate Mathematics Simplified.
Shultz, Ellen, ed. see Baetjer, Katharine.
Shultz, Ellen, ed. see Crosby, Sumner M., et al.
Shultz, George P. & Dam, Kenneth W. Economic Policy Beyond the Headlines.
Shultz, James H. The Economics of Aging.
Shultz, John F. Facing Life: A Scientist's View of How Things Work.
Shultz, Richard H., Jr. & Sloan, Stephen, eds. Responding to the Terrorist Threat: Security & Crisis Management.
Shultz, Richard H., Jr., jt. ed. see Hunt, Richard A.
Shulz, William D. & Powell, Howard B. Laboratory Manual for Schnid's the Chemical Basis of Life.
Shumacher, Harold V. Atlanta Restaurant Guide.
Shumake, Gisele. Etude Simplifiee de Classiques.
Shumaker, Wayne. Elements of Critical Theory.
Shuman, Bernard, jt. auth. see Gross, Barbara.
Shuman, R. Baird. Education in the Eighties: English.
--Elements of Early Reading Instruction.
--Robert E. Sherwood.
Shuman, R. Baird, jt. auth. see Krajewski, Robert J.
Shumway, jt. auth. see Jamieson.
Shumway, Nicholas & Forbes, David. Espanol en Espanol: La Lengua del Mundo Hispano.
Shupe, Anson D., Jr., jt. auth. see Bromley, David G.
Shupp, Robert P., jt. auth. see Bragger, Jeanette D.
Shupp, Robert P., jt. auth. see Bragger, Jeannette.
Shur, Janet L., et al. Where Do You Look? Whom Do You Ask? How Do You Know? An Information Resource for Child Advocates.
Shura, Mary F. Pornada.
--A Season of Silence.
Shurden, Walter B., ed. The Life of Baptists in the Life of the World.
Shurina, Mary A. Speech & Lipreading Instructional Program.
Shurkin, Joel, jt. auth. see Ryan, Desmond.
Shurkin, Joel N. Update: Report on the Planet Earth.
Shurlock, Barry. The Winchester Story.
Shurter, Robert L. Effective Letters in Business.
Shurtleff, William & Aoyagi, Akiko. Bibliography of Soymilk, from 1500 to 1988.
--Bibliography of Tempeh, from 1815 to 1988.
Shurtleff, William & Aoyagi, Akiko, eds. Bibliography of Tofu & Tofu Products, from A.D. 950 to 1988.
Shusaku Endo. When I Whistle. Gessel, Van C., tr. from Japanese.
Shuster, George. On the Side of Truth: An Evaluation with Readings. Lannie, Vincent P., ed.
Shuster, William M. Strangling of Persia: Story of the European Diplomacy & Oriental Intrigue That Resulted in the Denationalization of Twelve Million Mohammedans, a Personal Narrative.
Shute, Nevil. Stephen Morris.
Shuter-Dyson, Rosamund & Gabriel, Clive. The Psychology of Musical Ability.
Shutt, R. P., ed. Bubble & Spark Chambers: Principles & Use.
Shutt, V. Gladys. Food for Thought from God's Kettle.
--Hey Traveler! Wanna Ride?
Shuttle, Penelope & Redgrove, Peter. The Wise Wound: Myths, Realities, & Meanings of Menstruation.
Shuttlesworth, Dorothy. Exploring Nature with Your Child.
Shuttleworth, Charles, jt. auth. see Comber, Leon.
Shuval, J. T. Entering Medicine: the Dynamics of Transition: A Seven Year Study of Medical Education in Israel.
Shvarts, K. K., jt. ed. see Tuchkevich, V. M.
Shvets, I. & Yudin, I. CPSU: Ideological, Political & Organizational Principles.
Shvyrkov, V. S. Legend in Applied Probability & Statistics.
--Statistical Methods: (New Quality Philosophy)
Shvyrkov, V. V. S. Legend in Applied Probability & Statistics.
--Statistical Science in Economic Forecasting.
Shwartz, Susan. Queensblade.
Shy, DeWitt M. Live Smart, Die Smarter.
Shy, John, compiled by. The American Revolution.
Shyer, Marlene F. Blood in the Snow.
Shyh-Yuan, David L. How to Make over Eighty Thousand Dollars a Year on CICS Command Level Programming.
Shykind, Maury. Resumes for Job Hunters.
Shylo, Bruce, jt. auth. see Ruff, Richard.
Shymansky, James A. & Penick, John E., eds. Journal of Research in Science Teaching.
Sias, Twila. You Can Teach Children Successfully.
Siberell, Anne. Houses: Shelters from Prehistoric Times to Today.
Sibert, Edgar H. Railfan's Guide to Colorado.

Authors

Sibley, Agnes. Exchange Teacher.
Sibley, Celestine, jt. auth. see Middleton, Sallie.
Sibley, Susan. Woodsmoke.
Sibley, William G. The French Five Hundred.
Sibson, R. B., jt. auth. see Falla, R. A.
Sibson, Robert E. Compensation.
Sichel, Marion. Costume of the Classical World.
--Costume Reference, No. 1: Roman Britain & the Middle Ages.
--Costume Reference, No. 4: The Eighteenth Century.
--Costume Reference, No. 6: The Victorians.
Sichel, Werner & Eckstein, Peter. Basic Economic Concepts: Macroeconomics.
Sick, H., jt. auth. see Korite, J. G.
Sickle, Dirck Van see Van Sickle, Dirck.
Siddiqi, I. W., jt. auth. see Johnson, R. M.
Siddiqui, M. A., et al, eds. Molecular Approaches to Gene Expression & Protein Structure.
Siddiqui, M. I. What Agitates the Mind of the East.
Siddiqui, M. S. Call to Islam.
Siddons, Anne R. The House Next Door.
--The House Next Door.
Sidebotham, R. Accounting for Industrial Management.
--Introduction to the Theory & Context of Accounting.
Sidebottom, Eric & Ringertz, Nils. Experimental Cell Fusion. Head, J. J., ed.
Sidel, Ruth & Sidel, Victor W. The Health of China.
Sidel, Victor W., jt. auth. see Sidel, Ruth.
Sideman, Samuel, ed. see Meeting on Hemoperfusion, Kidney & Liver Supports & Detoxification Staff.
Sider, Ronald J. Rich Christians in an Age of Hunger: A Biblical Study.
Sider, Ronald J., ed. Karlstadt's Battle with Luther: Documents in a Liberal-Radical Debate.
Sider, Ronald J. & Brubaker, Darrel J., eds. Preaching on Peace.
Sideri, S. & Johns, S., eds. Mining for Development in the Third World: Multinationals, State Enterprises & the International Economy.
Sidgwick. Introductory Astronomy.
Sidhu, C. D. The Pattern of Tragicomedy in Bernard Shaw.
Sidlaukas, Susan. Intimate Architecture: Contemporary Clothing Design.
Sidley, John. River Piking.
Sidnell, Michael. Dances of Death.
Sidney, C. Standard Teachers Guide for Beauty Culture.
Sidney, Joan S. Deep Between the Rocks.
Sidney, Margaret. Five Little Peppers & How They Grew.
Sidney, Philip. Sir Philip Sidney's Defense of Poesy. Soens, Lewis, ed.
Sidney, Rosary, jt. auth. see Rosenfeld, Stephen S.
Sidorova, Vera F. The Postnatal Growth & Restoration of Internal Organs in Vertebrates. Carlson, Bruce M., ed. & intro. by.
Siebel, Hans D. The Dynamics of Achievement.
Siebenmann, R. E., jt. auth. see Williams, E. D.
Siebenschuh, William R., jt. auth. see Mundhenk, Robert T.
Sieber, Roy. African Furniture & Household Objects.
Siebert, Donald T., ed. see Hoole, John.
Siebert, H. & Eichberger, J. Trade & Environment: A Theoretical Enquiry.
Siebert, Rudolf J. Horkheimer's Critical Sociology of Religion: The Relative & the Transcendent.
Siebert, Wilbur H. Vermont's Anti-Slavery & Underground Railroad Record.
Siebring, B. R. & Schaff, M. E. Chemistry: A Basic Approach.
Siebring, B. R., jt. auth. see Schaff, M. E.
Sieburg, H. Introduction to Mathematical Modelling: A Summer School at Stanford 1985.
Siedel, George J., jt. auth. see Lieberman, Jethro K.
Siedentop, Daryl. Developing Teaching Skills in Physical Education.
Siedentopf, Heinrich, jt. auth. see Caiden, Gerald E.
Sieder, Reinhard, jt. auth. see Mitterauer, Michael.
Siedler, G., et al. GATE: Containing Results from the GARP Atlantic Tropical Experiment (GATE) Including the Proceedings of the GATE Symposium on Oceanography & Surface Layer Meteorology, Kiel May 1978.
Siefkes, D. Decidable Theories: Buechi's Monadic Second Order Successor Arithmetic.
Sieg, Edward Chan. Eden on the Marsh: An Illustrated History of Savannah.
Siegal, Barbara, jt. auth. see Siegal, Scott.
Siegal, Barry S. & Gillespie, Alan R. Remote Sensing in Geology.
Siegal, Frederick P. & Siegal, Marta. AIDS: The Medical Mystery.
--AIDS: The Medical Mystery.
Siegal, Harvey A., jt. auth. see Inciardi, James A.
Siegal, Marjorie, jt. auth. see Thomas, Sharon K.
Siegal, Marta, jt. auth. see Siegal, Frederick P.
Siegal, Mordecai. The Good Cat Book.
Siegal, Mordecai, jt. auth. see Margolis, Matthew.
Siegal, Scott & Siegal, Barbara. The Champ of T. V. Wrestling.
Siegel, A. Politics & the Media in Canada.
Siegel, A. & Fawcett, B. Transformation el Utilisation des Legumineuses Alimentaires (Application Particuliere aux Pays en Development)
Siegel, Alice & McLoone, Margo. It's a Girl's Game Too.
Siegel, Alice & McLoone-Basta, Margo. The Kids' World Almanac of Records & Facts.
Siegel, Alice, jt. auth. see McLoone, Margo.
Siegel, Alice, jt. auth. see McLoone-Basta, Margo.
Siegel, B. Psychology of Childhood.
Siegel, Barbara & Siegel, Scott. Battle Drive.
--Death Race.
--How to Date with Confidence.
--Scarlet Shield of Shalimar.
--The Warrior Women of Weymouth: Wizards, Warriors & You Ser.
Siegel, Barbara, jt. auth. see Siegel, Scott.
Siegel, David N. The Success Book for Landlords: A Money-Making Guide for Property Owners, Managers & Investors.
Siegel, Dorothy S. Winners: Eight Special Young People.
Siegel, Eli. Aesthetic Realism Acting Lesson.
--Feminine Mind Is Magnificent & Exacting: An Aesthetic Realism Lesson of Two College Girls.
Siegel, Ernest & Gold, Ruth. Educating the Learning Disabled.
Siegel, Howard J. Interconnection Networks for Large-Scale Parallel Processing: Theory & Case Studies.
Siegel, Irving H. Aggregation & Averaging.
Siegel, Joel, et al, eds. Grammar & the Teaching of English.
Siegel, Julia. Glory Road: Josh White.
Siegel, Larry J. Criminology.
Siegel, Larry J. & Senna, Joseph J. Juvenile Delinquency: Theory, Law & Practice.
Siegel, Larry J., jt. auth. see Senna, Joseph J.
Siegel, Linda S., ed. Alternatives to Piaget: Critical Essays on the Theory.
Siegel, Marcia B. The Shapes of Change.
--The Shapes of Change: Images of American Dance.
Siegel, Marjorie, jt. auth. see Thomas, Sharon K.
Siegel, Mark, et al, eds. Immigration & Illegal Aliens-Burden or Blessing?
Siegel, Mark A., jt. auth. see Plesser, Donna R.
Siegel, Mark A. & Jacobs, Nancy R., eds. Capital Punishment-Cruel & Unusual?
--Consumer Regulation Needed Protection or Too Much Bureaucracy?
--Education: Reflecting Our Society.
--Energy: An Issue of the Eighty's.
--Health: A Concern for Every American.
--Into the Third Century: Where Do We Stand?
Siegel, Mark A. & Siegel, Nancy R., eds. The Women's Changing Role.
Siegel, Mark A., et al, eds. Domestic Violence: No Longer Behind the Curtains.
--The American Judiciary: Will a Uniform System Help?
--Gambling-Crime or Recreation?
--Illegal Drugs & Alcohol: An Injury to America?
--Abortion: An Eternal Social & Moral Issue.
Siegel, Mary-Ellen, jt. auth. see Sweet, O. Robin.
Siegel, Mayer & Buckmann, Carol I. Executive's & Professional's Guide to Pension & Retirement Benefits.
Siegel, Michael E., jt. ed. see Nelsen, William C.
Siegel, Nancy R., jt. ed. see Siegel, Mark A.
Siegel, Patricia J. Alfred de Musset: A Reference Guide.
Siegel, R. Modern American Graphic Designers: Thirty Years of Design Imagery.
Siegel, Robert. Alpha Centauri.
--Whalesong.
Siegel, Robert & Howell, John R. Thermal Radiation Heat Transfer.
Siegel, Scott. Revenge of the Falcon Knight.
Siegel, Scott & Siegel, Barbara. Doug Flutie.
Siegel, Scott, jt. auth. see Siegel, Barbara.
Siegel, Stanley & Schulman, Stephen. Michigan Business Corporations: 1979.
Siegelman, Jim, jt. auth. see Conway, Flo.
Siegener, Ray. Staying in the Game: How to Keep Young & Active.
Siegener, Ray, ed. see Gogolak, Pete.
Siegener, Ray, ed. see Monroe, Earl & Unseld, Wes.
Siegert, R., jt. ed. see Martini, G. A.
Siegfried, Andre. Routes of Contagion.
Siegfried, Linda, jt. auth. see Chenel, Laura.
Siegl, Theodor. The Thomas Eakins Collection.
Siegla, Donald C. & Smith, George W., eds. Particulate Carbon: Formation During Combustion.
Siegman, Gita, ed. Awards, Honors & Prizes--Supplement.
--Awards, Honors & Prizes, Vol. 1: United States & Canada.
--Awards, Honors & Prizes, Vol. 2: International & Foreign.
Siegman, Gita, jt. ed. see Wasserman, Paul.
Siegner, Otto. Oberammergau: The Passion-Play-Village & Its Text in German-English-French.
Siek, Marguerite. More Favorite Stories from Indonesia.
Siek, Marguerite, retold by. Favourite Stories from Burma.
--Favourite Stories from India.
--Favourite Stories from Indonesia.
Siekierski, S. & Salomon, M., eds. Scandium, Yttrium, Lanthanum & Lanthanide Nitrates.
Sieller, William L. Returning to a Dream.
Sieller, William V. Gather Back the Dream.
--Green Water for a Granite Valley.
Siemens Staff. Handbook of Electromedicine: Basic Principles, Applications, Equipment.
Siemers, J. P., ed. European Integration: Select International Bibliography of Theses & Disserations 1957-1977.
Siemon, Michael, jt. auth. see Green, Sharon.
Sien, Chia Lin, jt. ed. see MacAndrews, Colin.
Sienkiewicz, Magdalen, jt. auth. see Hunter, Lea A.
Sienko, M. J., jt. ed. see Lagowski, J. J.
Sienko, Michael J. Chemistry Problems.
Sienko, Michell J. & Plane, Robert A. Experimental Chemistry.
Sierles, Frederick S. Behavioral Science for the Boreds.
Sierra Club International Earthcare Center Staff, ed. Directory of U. S. College & University Programs in Environmental Studies & Natural Resources Management.
Sierra, Gregorio M. Mama.
Sierra, Gregorio Martinez see Martinez Sierra, Gregorio.
Sies, H., ed. see Gesellschaft Fuer Biologische Chemie, 20th Colloquium, Mossbach-Baden, 1969.
Sies, Leora M., ed. see Buchenholz, Gretchen & Nursery School Staff.
Sies, Luther F., ed. see Schuell, Hildred.
Siesjo, B. K., ed. see Benzon, Alfred, Symposium, et al.
Siesjo, Bo. K. Brain Energy Metabolism.
Siest, G., et al, eds. Interpretation des Examens de Laboratoire.
--Interpretation of Clinical Laboratory Tests.
Sieveling, E. New York Cuisine.
Sieverding, C. H., jt. auth. see Moore, M. J.
Sieverling, Helen, compiled by. The Teddy Bear & Friends Price Guide.
Sievers, Robert E. Nuclear Magnetic Resonance Shift Reagents.
Siewert, Carol H., et al. Basic Textiles: A Learning Package.
Sifu Jim Fung, jt. auth. see Armstrong, Karen.
Sigafoos, Robert A. Absolutely, Positively Overnight.
Sigal, Clancy. Weekend in Dinlock.
Sigal, Phillip. New Dimensions in Judaism: A Creative Analysis of Rabbinic Concepts.
Sigalov, E., jt. auth. see Baikov, V.
Sigband, Norman B. & Bateman, David N. Communicating in Business.
Sigband, Norman B. & Bell, Arthur H. Communication for Management & Business.
Sigband, Norman B., et al. Successful Business English.
Sigel. Metal Ions in Biological Systems: Nucleotides & Derivatives--Their Ligating Ambivalency.
Sigel, Bernard. Operative Ultrasonography.
Sigel, Helmut, ed. Metal Ions in Biological Systems: High Molecular Complexes.
Sigel, Lois S. Exploring Careers in Community & Public Health.
Sigelman, Jesse, jt. auth. see Jakobiec, Frederick A.
Sigerist, Henry E. Civilization & Disease.
Siggia, Sidney & Hanna, J. Gordon. Quantitative Organic Analysis Via Functional Groups.
Siggins, Ian. Luther & His Mother.
Sigh, Nirbhan N. & Wilton, Keri M., eds. Mental Retardation in New Zealand.
Sigl, Rupert. In the Claws of the KGB: Memoirs of a Double Agent.
Sigle, John D; see O'Neal, William B.
Sigleo, Anne C. & Hattori, Akihiko, eds. Marine & Estuarine Geochemistry.
Sigman, David S. & Brazier, Mary, eds. The Evolution of Protein Structure & Function: A Symposium in Honor of Prof. Emil L. Smith.
Sigman, Harry C., jt. auth. see California Continuing Education of the Bar Staff.
Sigmon, Buster. The Twelfth Chapter: Interpretation of God's Mystery.
Sigmon, Scott B. Radical Socioeducational Analysis.
Sigmund, Diane & Steiner, Erwin. Protecting Your Rights As Creditors in Bankruptcy.
Signoret, Simone. Adieu Volodia. Hochman, Stanley, tr. from Fr.
Signs of the Times Magazine Editors. Sign Design.
Signs of the Times Staff, ed. Crane Safety & Operation.
Sigurdson, Jon, jt. ed. see Granstrand, Ove.
Sigurdsson, A. Icelandic-English Dictionary.
Sih, G. C. & Francois, D., eds. Progress in Fracture Mechanics: Fracture Mechanics Research & Technological Activities of Nations Around the World.
Sih, Paul K., ed. Nationalist China During the Sino-Japanese War, 1937-1945.
Siikala, K. Finlandia: Pictures of Finland.
Sikarskie, D. L., ed. Rock Mechanics Symposium: AMD.
--Rock Mechanics Symposium: Proceedings.
Sikat, Dorian. To Where Streets Are Made of Gold: The Story of a Filipino Immigrant.
Sikes, H. M., ed. see Hazlitt, William.
Siklua, Andrew F. & McKenna, John F. The Management of Human Resources: Personnel Text & Current Issues.
Sikorowa, Ludwika, et al, eds. Salivary Gland Tumors.
Silber, Sherman J. The Male: From Infancy to Old Age.
--The Male: From Infancy to Old Age.
Silberger, A. J. PGL-2, Over the P-Adics: Its Representations, Spherical Functions, & Fourier Analysis.
Silberman, J., ed. see Rubens, Bernice.
Silberman, Mary. The Eleventh Commandment & Other Short Stories.
Silberman, Stephen L. & Tryon, Ames F. Community Dentistry: A Problem-Oriented Approach.
Silbermann, Alphons. La Sociologie Des Communications De Masse: Tendences Actuelles De la Recherche et Bibliographie.
Silberschmidt, Max. The United States & Europe: Rivals & Partners.
Silberstang, Edwin. Playboy's Guide to Casino Gambling: Craps, Blackjack, Roulette, & Baccarat.
--The Winner's Guide to Casino Gambling.
Silberstein, Warren P. & Galton, Lawrence. Helping Your Child Grow Slim.
Silberstein-Storfer, Muriel & Jones, Mablen. Doing Art Together: The Remarkable Parent-Child Workshop of the Metropolitan Museum of Art.
Silberston, A., et al. British Manufacturing Investment Overseas: Causes & Consequences.
Silbey, Joel H. A Respectable Minority: The Democratic Party in the Civil War Era, 1860-1868.
Silcock, Arnold. Verse & Worse: A Private Collection.
Silcox, Claris E. Catholics, Jews, & Protestants: A Study of Relationships in the United States & Canada.
Silfen, Paul H. The Volkisch Ideology & the Roots of Nazism: The Early Writings of Arthur Moeller van den Bruck.
Silfen, Paul Harrison. Essays in English History: World History in Six Dimensions.
--Essays in French & German History: World History in Six Dimensions.
--Essays in Greek & Roman History: World History in Six Dimensions.
--Essays in Russian History: World History in Six Dimensions.
--Essays in World History from Antiquity to the Present.
--The Influence of the Mongols of Russia: A Dimensional History.
--New Jersey: Some Dimensions of Local History.
Silitch, Clarissa, ed. Old Farmer's Almanac Colonial Cookbook.
--The Old Farmer's Almanac Heritage Cookbook.
Silitch, Clarissa M., ed. Danger, Disaster, & Horrid Deeds.
--Good Neighbors U. S. A. Cookbook.
--The Old Farmer's Almanac Book of Old-Fashioned Puzzles.
--Yankee's Book of Whatsits.
Silitch, Clarissa M., jt. ed. see Pyron, Cherry.
Silj, Alessandro. Europe's Political Puzzle: A Study of the Fouchet Negotiations & the 1963 Veto.
Silk, Leonard. Economics in the Real World: How Political Decisions Affect the Economy.
--The Economists.
Silkin, Jon. Selected Poems.
Sill, Sterling W. Christmas Sermons.
--Great Literature & the Good Life. Syndergaard, Iris, ed.
--The Law of the Harvest.
--Lessons from Great Lives.
--Meditations on Death & Life.
--The Nine Lives of Sterling W. Sill: An Autobiography.
--The Power of Poetry.
Silliman, Ron. B A R T.

Authors

Silliphant, Leigh & Silliphant, Sureleigh. Making Seventy-Thousand Dollars a Year As a Self-Employed Manufacturer's Representative.
Silliphant, Sureleigh, jt. auth. see Silliphant, Leigh.
Sillitoe, Alan. The Lost Flying Boat.
--Saturday Night & Sunday Morning.
Sillitoe, Allan. Her Victory.
Sills, Beverly & Linderman, Larry. Beverly: An Autobiography.
Silman, Roberta. Boundaries.
Silton, Lawrence C. Taking Cash Out of the Closely-Held Corporation.
--Taking Cash Out of the Closely-Held Corporation.
Siluk, Dennis L. The Other Door: Poetic Exhortations!
Silva, Erin R., jt. ed. see Rugh, Thomas F.
Silva, J. R. Da see Williams, R. J. & Da Silva, J. R.
Silva, John W., ed. An Introduction to Crime & Justice.
Silva, Jose & Miele, Philip. The Silva Mind Control Method.
Silva, Julian. The Gunnysack Castle.
Silva, Sharon, jt. auth. see Killeen, Jacqueline.
Silvaroli, Nicholas J. & Kear, Dennis J. A Classroom Guide to Reading Assessment & Instruction.
Silveira, Theodore. The McGraw-Hill Guide for Preparing Students for the New High School Equivalency Examination (GED)
Silvennoinen, P. Reactor Core Fuel Management.
Silver, A. David. Entrepreneurial Megabucks: The One-Hundred Greatest Entrepreneurs of the Last Twenty-Five Years.
--Who's Who in Venture Capital.
Silver, A. I. The French-Canadian Idea of Confederation, Eighteen Sixty-Four to Nineteen Hundred.
Silver, Abba H. History of Messianic Speculation in Israel from the First Through the Seventeenth Centuries.
Silver, Alain & Ward, Elizabeth. Robert Aldrich: A Guide to References & Resources.
Silver, Alfred. Good Time Charlie's Back in Town.
Silver, C. G., jt. auth. see Neaman, J. S.
Silver, Carole G., ed. The Golden Chain.
Silver, Caroline. Classic Lives: The Education of a Racehorse.
Silver, Gerald A. Simplified FORTRAN IV Programming.
--The Social Impact of Computers.
Silver, Gerald A. & Silver, Joan B. Data Processing for Business.
--Data Processing for Business.
--Data Processing for Business.
--Simplified ANSI FORTRAN IV Programming.
Silver, Harold. Education & the Social Condition.
Silver, Harold, ed. Equal Opportunity in Education.
Silver, Herbert, et al, eds. Problem Solving in Immunohematology.
Silver, I., intro. by. Challenge of Crime in a Free Society.
Silver, Isidore. Law & Economics.
Silver, Joan B., jt. auth. see Silver, Gerald A.
Silver, Joan M. & Boyd, Julianne. A... My Name Is Alice.
Silver, Larry B. The Misunderstood Child: A Guide for Parents of Learning-Disabled Children.
Silver, Maxwell. The Way to God.
Silver, Milton, jt. auth. see Garrett, Leonard J.
Silver, Philip, tr. see Ferrater Mora, Jose.
Silver, Philip W., tr. see Cebrian, Juan L.
Silver, Philip W., tr. see Ortega y Gasset, Jose.
Silver, Rae, ed. Parental Behavior in Birds.
Silver, Rollo G. Aprons Instead of Uniforms: The Practice of Printing, 1776-1787.
--Publishing in Boston, 1726-1757.
Silver, Warren A. The Green Rose.
Silverberg, Robert. The Conglomeroid Cocktail Party.
--Gilgamesh the King.
--Lord of Darkness.
--Majipoor Chronicles.
--Man in the Maze.
--Nightwings.
--Valentine Pontifex.
--World of a Thousand Colors.
Silverberg, Robert, ed. The Nebula Awards.
Silverberg, Robert & Greenberg, Martin H., eds. The Arbor House Treasury of Great Science Fiction Short Novels.
--The Arbor House Treasury of Science Fiction Masterpieces.
--Fantasy Hall of Fame.
Silverberg, Robert, jt. ed. see Greenberg, Martin H.
Silverberg, Robert, ed. see Milan, Victor.
Silverberg, Robert, ed. see Sterling, Bruce.
Silverberg, Steven G., ed. Principles & Practice of Surgical Pathology.
Silvergleid, Arthur J., jt. ed. see Sandler, S. Gerald.
Silverman, Al. Foster & Laurie.
Silverman, Bertram, ed. Man & Socialism in Cuba: The Great Debate.
Silverman, David, tr. see Boudon, Raymond.
Silverman, H. Out of Yesterday & Into Tomorrow: Selected Poems 1935-1970.
Silverman, Harold M. The Consumer's Guide to Poison Protection.
--Travel Healthy: The Traveler's Complete Medical Kit.
--The Women's Drug Store.
Silverman, Harold M., et al. The Pill Book.
Silverman, Herb. Complex Variables.
Silverman, Hirsch L. Humanism, Psychology & Education.
Silverman, Hugh. Piaget, Philosophy & the Human Sciences.
Silverman, Irving, et al. Psychotherapy & Drug Addiction, II.
Silverman, Irwin, ed. Generalizing from Laboratory to Life.
Silverman, J., ed. Trends in Radiation Processing: Transactions of the Third International Meeting on Radiation Processing, Held in Tokyo, Japan, October 1980.
Silverman, Joseph, ed. Advances in Radiation Processing: Transactions of the Second International Meeting on Radiation Processing Held at Miami, Florida 22-26 Oct. 1978.
Silverman, Judith, compiled by. Index to Collective Biographies for Young Readers.
Silverman, Julian. Health Care & Consciousness: Think of Yourself Now & Then.
Silverman, Leslie. Particle Size Analysis in Industrial Hygiene.
Silverman, Louis. The Determination of Impurities in Nuclear Grade Sodium Metal & Related Sodium Compounds.
Silverman, Melvin. The Art of Managing Technical Project.
Silverman, S. Richard, tr. Stuttering: Integrating Theory & Practice.
Silverman, Samuel. I, Sami: Or Sixty-Five Years on the Road.
Silvers, Arthur L., jt. auth. see Krueckeberg, Donald A.
Silverstein, Alvin & Silverstein, Virginia. Animal Invaders.
--Code of Life.
--Guinea Pigs, All About Them.
--Metamorphosis.
--World in a Drop of Water.
Silverstein, Alvin & Silverstein, Virginia B. The World of Bionics.
Silverstein, Charles. Man to Man: Gay Couples in America.
Silverstein, Judith. Sexual Enhancement for Women.
Silverstein, M. L. Boundary Theory for Symmetric Markov Processes.
Silverstein, Mira. Fun with Bargello.
--International Needlework Designs.
Silverstein, Ruth, et al. Spanish Now! Quinones, Nathan, ed.
Silverstein, Samuel. The Child Is Superior to the Man: Children's Experiences with God in the Public School Classroom.
Silverstein, Theodore, ed. English Lyrics Before Fifteen Hundred.
Silverstein, Virginia, jt. auth. see Silverstein, Alvin.
Silverstein, Virginia B., jt. auth. see Silverstein, Alvin.
Silverstone, Barbara & Hyman, Helen K. You & Your Aging Parent: The Modern Family's Guide to Emotional, Physical & Financial Problems.
Silverstone, Paul H. Directory of the World's Capital Ships.
Silverstone, Rosalie & Ward, Audrey, eds. Careers of Professional Women.
Silverstone, Trevor. Obesity: Its Pathogenesis & Management.
Silverstone, Trevor & Turner, Paul. Drug Treatment in Psychiatry.
Silverthorne, Elizabeth. Marjorie Kinnan Rawlings: Sojourner at Cross Creek.
Silverthorne, Jeanne, et al. Projects: Made in Philadelphia Four.
Silvestre, Lucio B. The End of the World, A.D. 2133.
Silvis, Craig. Rat Stew.
Silvis, Randall. The Luckiest Man in the World.
Silvius, G. Harold & Bohn, Ralph C. Planning & Organizing Instruction.
Silvius, George H. & Curry, Estell H. Managing Multiple Activities in Industrial Education.
Simader, C. G. On Dirichlet's Boundary Value Problem.
Simak, Clifford. City.
Simak, Clifford D. Time Is the Simplest Thing.
--The Visitors.
Sima Qian. Selections from Records of the Historian.
--War Lords. Dolby, William & Scott, John, trs.
Simard, R. L., jt. ed. see Zebroski, E. L.
Simcox, Carroll E. Learning to Believe: A Meditation on the Christian Creed.
Simcox, George A. A History of Latin Literature.
Sime, Mary. Read Your Child's Thoughts: Pre-School Learning Piaget's Way.
Simels, Steven. Gender Chameleons: Androgeny in Rock 'n Roll.
Simenaver, Jacqueline & Carroll, David. Singles: The New Americans.
Simenon, Georges. The Accomplices. Frechtman, Bernard, tr.
--African Trio: Talatala, Tropic Moon, Aboard the Aquitaine.
--Aunt Jeanne. Sainsbury, Geoffrey, tr. from Fr.
--Big Bob. Lowe, Eileen M., tr.
--The Delivery. Ellenbogen, Eileen, ed.
--The Disappearance of Odile.
--The Family Lie. Hillier, Caroline, tr.
--Girl with a Squint.
--The Glass Cage.
--The Grandmother. Stewart, Jean, tr.
--The Hatter's Phantoms. Trask, Willard R., tr.
--The House on the Quai Notre-Dame. Hamilton, Alastair, tr.
--The Innocents.
--Letter to My Mother. Manheim, Ralph, tr.
--The Little Doctor. Stewart, Jean, tr. from Fr.
--Maigret Afraid. Duff, Margaret, tr. from Fr.
--Maigret & the Apparition. Ellenbogen, Eileen, tr.
--Maigret & the Black Sheep. Thompson, Helen, tr.
--Maigret & the Informer.
--Maigret & the Man on the Bench. Ellenbogen, Eileen, tr.
--Maigret & the Millionaires. Stewart, Jean, tr. from Fr.
--Maigret & the Nahour Case.
--Maigret & the Spinster. Ellenbogen, Eileen, tr.
--Maigret & the Toy Village. Ellenbogen, Eileen, tr.
--Maigret at the Coroner's. Keene, Frances, tr.
--Maigret at the Coroner's. Keene, Frances, tr.
--Maigret Bides His Time. Hamilton, Alastair, tr. from Fr.
--Maigret et les braves gens: Student Edition. Daudon, Rene, ed.
--Maigret Has Doubts. Moir, Lyn, tr.
--Maigret in Court. Brain, Robert, tr.
--Maigret in Exile. Ellenbogen, Eileen, tr.
--Maigret on the Defensive. Hamilton, Alastair, tr.
--Maigret's Boyhood Friend.
--Maigret's Christmas: Nine Short Stories.
--Maigret's Pipe. Stewart, Jean, tr.
--Maigret's Rival. Thomson, Helen, tr.
--Maigret's Rival.
--Maigret's War of Nerves. Sainsbury, Geoffrey, tr.
--The Man on the Bench in the Barn. Budberg, Moura, tr.
--Monsieur Monde Vanishes. Stewart, Jean, tr.
--The Nightclub. Stewart, Jean, tr.
--November. Stewart, Jean, tr. from Fr.
--Rich Man.
--Sunday. Ryan, Nigel, tr.
--The Survivors. Gilbert, Stuart, tr. from Fr.
--The Venice Train. Hamilton, Alastair, tr. from Fr.
--When I Was Old.
--The White Horse Inn. Denny, Norman, tr.
--The Widower. Baldick, Robert, tr. from Fr.
Simeone, Joseph F. Complete Spanish-English Reference Guide.
Simerly, David K. Advanced Excel Solutions.
--Practical Applework Uses.
Simic, Andrei. The Peasant Urbanites: A Study of Rural-Urban Mobility in Serbia.
Simich, Tina L., jt. auth. see CEP Staff.
Simini, Joseph P. Cost Accounting Concepts for Nonfinancial Executives.
--Cost Accounting Concepts for Nonfinancial Executives & Managers.
Simkin, Diana. The Complete Pregnancy Exercise Program.
Simkin, Mark G., jt. auth. see Moscove, Stephen A.
Simkin, Tom, et al. Volcanoes of the World: A Regional Gazetteer & Chronology of Volcanism During the Last 10,000 Years.
Simko, Patricia A. The Insider's Guide to Owning Land in Subdivisions: How to Buy, Appraise & Get Rid of Your Lot.
Simko, Patricia A., et al. Promised Lands 3: Subdivisions & the Law.
Simkovich, Marcellus. The Approaching Maximal Leadership Conflict for Domination of the World.
Simmel, George. Sociology of Religion.
Simmins, Bob. Nobody Does It Better.
Simmonds, Ian D. Goannas & Goblins: Whimsey & Satire for Older Children.
Simmonite, W. J. The Arcana of Astrology.
Simmons & Luck. General Surgery in Gynaecological Practice.
Simmons, Adele S. Modern Mauritius: The Politics of Decolonization.
Simmons, Diane. Let the Bastards Freeze in the Dark.
Simmons, Ernest J. Outline of Modern Russian Literature: 1880-1940.
Simmons, Garner. Peckinpah: A Portrait in Montage.
Simmons, Geoffrey. Adam Experiment.
--Murdock.
--Pandemic.
Simmons, Geoffrey S. The Z-Papers.
Simmons, James. Sean O'Casey.
--Sean O'Casey.
Simmons, Luiz R., jt. ed. see Said, Abdul A.
Simmons, Mary Ann, jt. ed. see Knight, Allen W.
Simmons, Mary K. A Fire in the Blood.
Simmons, Otis D. Teaching Music in Urban Schools.
Simmons, Ozzie G. Development Perspectives & Population Change.
Simmons, Paula. Raising Sheep the Modern Way. Griffith, Roger, ed.
--Zucchini Cookbook.
Simmons, Richard J. Employee Handbook & Personnel Policies Manual.
Simmons, Seymour & Winer, Marc S. Drawing: The Creative Process.
Simmons, Sylvia, jt. auth. see Rees, Thomas.
Simmons, Sylvia H. How to Be the Life of the Podium.
Simmons, William Richard. Roll, Justice, Roll! A Salute to Israel.
Simmons, William S. Kasimir Malevich's Black Square & the Gensis of Suprematism 1907-1915.
Simms, D. J. Lectures on Geometric Quantization. Ehlers, J., et al, eds.
Simms, George. In My Understanding.
Simms, Jacqueline. Unsolicited Gift.
Simms, Ruth L., tr. see Paz, Octavio.
Simms, William G. Voltmeier: Or, the Mountain Men. Guilds, John C., ed.
Simnad, Massoud. Fuel Element Experience in Nuclear Power Reactors.
Simo, Connie, et al. Sandtiquity.
Simoes, Antonio, Jr., ed. The Bilingual Child: Research & Analysis of Existing Educational Themes.
Simon. IBM Graphics from the Ground Up.
Simon & Olds. Helping Your Child Learn Right from Wrong.
Simon, Alfred E., jt. auth. see Kimball, Robert E.
Simon, Andre. Bibliotheca Bacchica Wine & Cooking Bibliography.
--Bibliotheca Gastronomica.
Simon, Andrew L. Energy Resources.
Simon, Anita, jt. auth. see Bramnick, Lea.
Simon, Ann, ed. Heads Bowed Together.
Simon, Arthur. Breaking Bread with the Hungry.
Simon, Brian. Politics of Educational Reform 1920-1940.
Simon, Claude. Conducting Bodies.
Simon, David E. IBM BASIC from the Ground Up.
Simon, Ericka. The Ancient Theatre.
Simon, Gary. Choosing Accounting Software for Your Micro.
Simon, George T. Feeling of Jazz.
Simon, Gil & Cohen, Marcia. The Parent's Pediatric Companion.
Simon, H. A., jt. auth. see Ijiri, Y.
Simon, H. A., jt. ed. see Bugliarello, George.
Simon, Hansjorg & Bloomfield, Dennis A. Cardioactive Drugs: A Pharmacologic Basis for Practice.
Simon, Harvey B., jt. auth. see Levisohn, Steven R.
Simon, Heather. The Fox & the Hound.
Simon, Henry W. New Victor Book of the Opera.
Simon, Herbert. Introduction to Printing: The Craft of Letterpress.
Simon, Iris Illus. by see Burkart, Betty Lou.
Simon, Iris Illus. by see Millett, Esther Lee.
Simon, J. Pattern & Operators: The Foundation of Data Representation.
Simon, James, et al. Herbs: An Indexed Bibliography, 1971-1980.
Simon, Jim. The Bionic Joke Book.
--The King Kong Joke Book.
Simon, Jo A. Hold Fast to Love.
--Love Once Again.
Simon, Jo Ann. Beloved Captain.
Simon, John. Ingmar Bergman Directs: A Visual Analysis by Halcyon.
Simon, John, frwd. by see Young, Dennis R.
Simon, John B. To Become Somebody: Growing up Against the Grain of Society.
Simon, Julian L. How to Start & Operate a Mail Order Business.
Simon, Kate. Fifth Avenue: A Very Special History.
Simon, Leon, ed. Selected Essays of Ahad Ha-'Am.
Simon, Leonard. Irving Solution.
--The Irving Solution.
--Reborn.
Simon, Linda. The Biography of Alice B. Toklas.
--Of Virtue Rare: Margaret Beaufort, Matriarch of the House of Tudor.
Simon, Linda, ed. Gertrude Stein: A Composite Portrait.
Simon, Lucinda. A Guide to Legislative Leadership.
Simon, Marc. Samuel Greenberg, Hart Crane & the Lost Manuscripts.
Simon, Marcel. Jewish Sects at the Time of Jesus. Farley, James H., tr. from Fr.
Simon, Marica L. A Special Gift.
Simon, Michael & Moore, Dennis. First Lessons in Black & White Photography.
Simon, Morris. Jaguar.

Simon, Nanette. The Green Stone.
Simon, Neil. The Comedy of Neil Simon.
Simon, Norma. Elly the Elephant. Tucker, Kathleen, ed.
--Go Away, Warts! Tucker, Kathleen, ed.
--Where Does My Cat Sleep? Tucker, Kathy, ed.
Simon, P. A., ed. Solar Maximum Analysis: Proceedings of Symposium 2 of the COSPAR 25th Plenary Meeting, Graz, Austria, 25 June-7 1984.
Simon, P. C., jt. ed. see Ebel, A.
Simon, Peter & Lang, Jack. The New York Mets: 25 Years of Baseball Magic.
Simon, Peter, jt. auth. see Davis, Stephen.
Simon, Rita J. Public Opinion & the Immigrant: Mass Media Coverage, 1880 to 1980.
Simon, Rita J. & Altstein, Howard. Transracial Adoption: A Follow-Up.
Simon, Rita J., jt. auth. see Adler, Freda.
Simon, Robert. Percy Grainger: The Pictorial Biography.
Simon, Roger. Simon Says: The Best of Roger Simon.
Simon, Roger L. California Roll. Gethers, Peter, ed.
Simon, Samuel A. & Whalen, Michael. Teleconsumers & the Future: A Manual on the AT&T Divestiture.
Simon, Seymour. Animal Fact: Animal Fable.
--Discovering What Gerbils Do.
Simon, Seymour & Kendrick, Dennis. About Your Brain.
Simon, Sidney. Vulture.
Simon, Ulrich. A Theology of Auschwitz: The Christian Faith & the Problem of Evil.
Simon, William E. A Time for Truth.
Simon, Yves. Tradition of Natural Law: A Philosopher's Reflections. Kuic, Vukan, ed.
Simonds, John O. Earthscape.
Simonds, Nina. Classic Chinese Cuisine.
Simonds, Peter. The White Silk Dress.
Simonds, Rollin H., jt. auth. see Grimaldi, John V.
Simone, C. B. Cancer & Nutrition: A Ten-Point Plan to Reduce Your Chances of Getting Cancer.
--Cancer & Nutrition: A Ten-Point Plan to Reduce Your Chances of Getting Cancer.
Simone, Daniel R. Forest Firefighting.
Simone, Diane de see Durden-Smith, Jo & DeSimone, Diane.
Simone, Emily. The Human Side of the Game: Lives in Bowling.
Simonet, Andre. Apostles for Our Time: Thoughts on Apostolic Spirituality. Bouchard, M. Angeline, tr. from Fr.
Simonhoff, Harry. Under Strange Skies.
Simonian, Charles. Basic Foil Fencing.
--Fundamentals of Sports Biomechanics.
Simonov, Konstantin M. Living & the Dead. Ainsztein, R., tr.
Simons, Elwyn L. Primate Evolution: An Introduction to Man's Place in Nature.
Simons, G. L., ed. see National Computing Centre, Ltd. Staff.
Simons, Gene M. Early Childhood Musical Development: A Bibliography of Research Abstracts, 1960-1975.
Simons, Herbert W. Persuasion: Understanding, Practice & Analysis.
Simons, J. H., ed. Fluorine Chemistry.
Simons, Jeff. Whisper's Mysterious Adventure.
Simons, Jim, jt. auth. see Sherman, Charles E.
Simons, John D. Friedrich Schiller.
Simons, R. H., jt. auth. see Bean, A. R.
Simons, Robin. Recyclopedia.
Simonson, Lee, ed. Theatre Art.
Simonton, Wesley & McClaskey, Marilyn J. AACR Two & the Catalog: Theory-Structure-Changes.
Simon-Vandenbergen, A. M. The Grammar of Headlines in the Times: 1870-1970.
Simon Yang & L. K. Tao. A Study of the Standard of Living of Working Families in Shanghai. Myers, Ramon H., ed.
Simonyi, K. Foundations of Electrical Engineering.
Simpas, Santiago S., et al. Local Government & Rural Development in the Philippines.
Simper, Robert. Beach Boats of Britain.
Simpkin, R. E. Human Factors in Mechanized Warfare.
Simpkins, Gary, et al. Bridge: A Cross Culture Reading Program.
Simpson, A. B. Life of Prayer.
--Spirit Filled Church in Action.
Simpson, Alan. Advanced Techniques in dBASE II.
--Advanced Techniques in dBASE III.
--Advanced Techniques in Framework.
--The Best Book of Framework.
--The Best Book of Symphony.
--Data File Programming on Your IBM PC.
--DBASE III Plus Programmer's Reference Guide.
--Focus on Symphony Macros.
--Mastering Paradox.
--Mastering Paradox.
--Simpson's dBASE III Library.
--Understanding R: BASE System V.
--Understanding R: Base 5000.
Simpson, Alan, jt. auth. see Galton, Ray.
Simpson, Alan, ed. New Developments in Office Technology.
--Planning for Information Handling.
--Planning for Office Microcomputers.
--Planning for Telecommunications.
--Planning for the Electronic Mail.
--Planning for the Office of the Future.
--Planning for the Word Processing.
Simpson, Albert B. In Heavenly Places.
--When the Comforter Came.
Simpson, B. Rocks & Minerals.
Simpson, C. F., et al. Lead Poisoning in Animal Models.
Simpson, Catherine, jt. auth. see Simpson, Claude C.
Simpson, Claude. Panhandle Personalities.
Simpson, Claude C. & Simpson, Catherine. North of the Narrows: Men & Women of the Upper Priest Lake Country Idaho.
Simpson, D. H. First Supplement to the Subject Catalogue of the Royal Commonwealth Society.
Simpson, Dorothy. Dead on Arrival: An Inspector Luker Thanet Mystery.
--Last Seen Alive.
--The Night She Died.
--A Puppet for a Corpse: A Luke Thanet Mystery.
Simpson, Edwin L. How to Get Rich with Your Microcomputer.
Simpson, Eileen. Orphans: Real & Imaginary.
--Reversals: A Personal Account of Victory over Dyslexia.
Simpson, Elizabeth, jt. ed. see Gomez, Thelma J.
Simpson, Elizabeth, ed. see Rourke, Margaret V. & Gentry, Christine A.
Simpson, Elizabeth J. Educating for the Future in Family Life.
Simpson, Elizabeth L. Notes on an Emergency.
Simpson, F. Dale. Leading the First Century Church in the Space Age.
Simpson, Frank, tr. see Lem, Stanislaw.
Simpson, George E. Melville J. Herskovitz.
Simpson, George E. & Burger, Neal R. Fair Warning.
--Ghostboat.
--Severed Ties.
Simpson, George G. Biology & Man.
--A Catalogue of Mesozoic Mammalia in the Geological Department of the British Museum.
--This View of Life: The World of an Evolutionist.
Simpson, George G. & Beck, William S. Life: An Introduction to Biology.
Simpson, Henry. Serious Programming in BASIC.
--True BASIC: A Complete Manual.
Simpson, Henry K. Design of User-Friendly Programs for Small Computers.
Simpson, Howard R. Gathering of Gunmen.
--Junior Year Abroad.
Simpson, J. Ernest, et al. An Outline of Organic Chemistry.
Simpson, June A. Prisoner's Plaint.
Simpson, Kieran, ed. Canadian Who's Who 1988.
Simpson, L. A., ed. Fracture Problems & Solutions in the Energy Industry: Proceedings of the 5th Canadian Fracture Conference (CFC5), Winnipeg, Canada, September 3-4, 1981.
Simpson, L. E. & Weir, M. The Weaver's Craft.
Simpson, Lucie. The Greek Spirit in Renaissance Art.
Simpson, Mayling, jt. ed. see Hull, Valerie.
Simpson, Norman T. Bed & Breakfast, American Style.
--Country Inns & Back Roads: North America.
Simpson, Norman T., ed. Bed & Breakfast, American Style.
--Country Inns & Back Roads Cookbook.
Simpson, P. G., jt. auth. see Davies, E. J.
Simpson, Patti. Hello Friend: Reflections for the New Student.
--Paulji: A Memoir.
Simpson, Peter & Levitt, Ruth. Going Home.
Simpson, Philip, tr. see Oz, Amos.
Simpson, R. A. Selected Poems.
Simpson, R. W., jt. auth. see Adams, Harry.
Simpson, Richard L. Conferencing Parents of Exceptional Children.
Simpson, Robert. Carl Nielsen: Symphonist.
--Essence of Bruckner.
Simpson, Robert J., jt. auth. see Power, Henry M.
Simpson, William. Buddhist Praying Wheel.
--The Jonah Legend: A Suggestion of Interpretation.
Simpson, William J. St. Augustine's Conversation: An Outline of His Development to the Time of His Ordination.
--A Study of Bossuet.
Simrin, Steven. MS-DOS Bible.
Sims, Chester T. & Hagel, William C., eds. The Superalloys.
Sims, Dorothea F. Diabetes: Reach for Health & Freedom.
Sims, Graeme. Painting & Drawing Animals: Practical & Colorful Lessons on Painting Mammals, Fish, Birds, & Insects.
Sims, Marian, jt. auth. see Sawer, Marian.
Sims, Phillip L., jt. ed. see Vallentine, John F.
Sims, Roberta S., jt. auth. see Blowers, Margaret G.
Simson, Otto Von see Von Simson, Otto.
Simundson, Daniel J. The Message of Job: A Theological Commentary.
Simundson, Danile J. Faith under Fire: Biblical Interpretations of Suffering.
Sinaer, George, jt. auth. see Campbell, Frank.
Sinai, Y. G. Introduction to Ergodic Theory. Scheffer, V., tr. from Rus.
Sinaiko, H. W., jt. ed. see Gerver, D.
Sinanoglu, Oktay, ed. Modern Quantum Chemistry.
Sinanoglu, Paula A., jt. ed. see Maluccio, Anthony N.
Sinatra, Richard. Visual Literacy Connections to Thinking, Reading & Writing.
Sinberg, Janet. Divorce Is a Grown up Problem.
--We Got This New Baby at Our House: How a Child Feels When a Brother or Sister Is Born.
Sinclair, Andrew. The Facts in the Case of E. A. Poe.
--The Red & the Blue: A Study in Treason & Intelligence.
Sinclair, Andrew, jt. auth. see Farago, Ladislas.
Sinclair, Bruce A. Philadelphia's Philosopher Mechanics: A History of the Franklin Institute, 1824-1865.
Sinclair, Catherine. Beatrice; or, the Unknown Relatives, 1852. Wolff, Robert L., ed.
Sinclair, D. J., jt. auth. see Jones, E.
Sinclair, H. M. Progress in Food & Nutrition Science.
Sinclair, Ian. Disk Systems for the BBC Micro.
Sinclair, Ian R. Inside Your Computer.
Sinclair, John A. God vs We the People.
Sinclair, John H., ed. Protestantism in Latin America: A Bibliographical Guide.
Sinclair, Kevin. The Yellow River: A Five Thousand Year Journey Through China.
Sinclair, Lister & Pollack, Jack. The Art of Norval Morrisseau.
Sinclair, M. E. & Lillis, Kevin. School & Community in the Third World.
Sinclair, May. Mary Olivier: A Life.
Sinclair, Michael. The Dollar Covenant.
--A Long Time Sleeping.
--The Masterplayers.
Sinclair, Peter. Unemployment Theories, Policies & Evidence.
Sinclair, Robert A. Winds over Lake Huron: Chronicles in the Life of a Great Lakes Mariner.
Sinclair, Stuart W., jt. auth. see Hallwood, C. Paul.
Sinclair, Upton. Affectionately Eve.
--The Jungle.
--Upton Sinclair's "The Jungle" The Lost First Edition. DeGruson, Gene, ed. & intro. by.
Sinclair, William A. Socialism & the Individual: Notes on Joining the Labour Party.
Sindell, Gerald S., ed. see Venus, Brenda & Miller, Henry.
Sinden, Donald. Laughter in the Second Act.
Sinden, F. W. An Oscillation Theorem for Algebraic Eigenvalue Problems & Its Applications.
Sinding, Franey, tr. see Bernhardsen, Christian.
Sindoni, E., jt. ed. see Eubank, H.
Sindoni, E., jt. ed. see Wharton, C.
Sindwani, M. L. Understanding Children.
Sine. The French Cat.
Sine, Richard L. & Cummings, William W., eds. Scott Specialized Catalogue of United States 1988.
--Scott Specialized Catalogue of United States Stamps, 1987.
--Scott Standard Postage Stamp Catalogue Nineteen Eighty Eight: United States, Canada, Great Britain & the Commonwealth United Nations.
--Scott Standard Postage Stamp Catalogue, 1988: Countries of the World A-F.
--Scott Standard Postage Stamp Catalogue, 1987, Vol. 1: U. S. Canada, G.B., & the Commonwealth, U. N.
--Scott Standard Postage Stamp Catalogue 1988, Vol. 1-4.
--Scott Standard Postage Stamp Catalogue 1987, Vol. 3: Countries of the World G-O.
--Scott Standard Postage Stamp Catalogue 1988, Vol. 3: Countries of the World G-O.
--Scott Standard Postage Stamp Catalogue 1988, Vol. 4: Countries of the World P-Z.
Sine, Robert D., et al. Basic Rehabilitation Techniques: A Self-Instructional Guide.
Siner, H. Sports Classics: American Writers Choose Their Best.
Siner, Helen B. Series in Mathematics Modules: Practical Mathematics. Ablon, Leon J., ed.
Sinetar, Marsha. Do What You Love, the Money Will Follow: Discovering Your Right Livelihood.
Sinfield, Alan. Literature in Protestant England: 1560-1660.
Sing, Phia. Traditional Recipes of Laos.
Singe, John. The Torres Strait: People & History.
Singell, Larry D., ed. The Collected Papers of Kenneth E. Boulding: Towards the Twenty First Century.
Singell, Larry D., ed. see Boulding, Kenneth E.
Singer, Aaron, jt. auth. see Heilbroner, Robert L.
Singer, Albert, jt. auth. see Lees, David.
Singer, Albert, jt. auth. see Lees, David H.
Singer, Andre. Lords of the Khyber: The Story of the North West Frontier.
Singer, Barry, jt. ed. see Abell, George O.
Singer, Bernard M. Programming in BASIC, with Applications.
Singer, Bertrand B. Mathematics at Work: Algebra.
--Mathematics at Work: Decimals.
--Mathematics at Work: Fractions.
Singer, Charles. Short History of Anatomy & Physiology: From the Greeks to Harvey.
Singer, Daniel. The Road to Gdansk: Poland & the U. S. S. R.
Singer, Eric. Graphologists Alphabet.
Singer, F. Industrial Ceramics. Singer, S., ed.
Singer, Frederick, ed. Paget's Disease of Bone.
Singer, G. & Wallace, M. The Administrative Waltz or Ten Commandments for the Administrator.
Singer, G., jt. auth. see Campbell, F.
Singer, I. J. The Brothers Ashkenazi.
Singer, I. M., ed. see Conference on K-Theory & Operator Algebras, University of Georgia, Athens, Ga., Apr. 21-25, 1975.
Singer, Irving. Santayana's Aesthetics: A Critical Introduction.
Singer, Isaac Bashevis. Elijah the Slave.
--Enemies: A Love Story.
--The Family Moskat.
--The Fearsome Inn.
--The Image & Other Stories.
--The Image & Other Stories.
--Joseph & Koza, or the Sacrifice to the Vistula.
--Lost in America.
--Lost in America.
--Love & Exile: A Memoir.
--Love & Exile: A Memoir.
--The Magician of Lublin. Gottlieb, Elaine & Singer, Joseph, trs.
--The Manor.
--The Manor incl. the Estate.
--The Penitent.
--Shosha.
--The Spinoza of Market Street.
--When Shlemiel Went to Warsaw & Other Stories.
--A Young Man in Search of Love.
Singer, Isaac Bashevis & Burgin, Richard. Conversations with Isaac Bashevis Singer.
Singer, J. L., jt. ed. see Pope, K. S.
Singer, Jerome E., jt. auth. see Glass, David C.
Singer, Jerome L., ed. Control of Aggression & Violence.
Singer, Joe, jt. auth. see Adams, Norman.
Singer, Joseph, tr. see Singer, Isaac Bashevis.
Singer, Jules & Deckinger, Larry. Exploring Careers in Advertising.
Singer, Julia. Impressions: A Trip to the German Democratic Republic.
--We All Come from Puerto Rico Too.
--We All Come from Someplace: Children of Puerto Rico.
Singer, June F. The Debutantes.
--The Markoff Women: A Novel.
--President's Women.
--Star Dreams.
Singer, Loren. The Parallax View.
Singer, Marcus G. Generalization in Ethics: An Essay in the Logic of Ethics, with the Rudiments of a System of Moral Philosophy.
Singer, Marilyn. Archer Armadillo's Secret Room.
Singer, Martin. Canadian Academic Relations with the People's Republic of China Since 1970: China Profiles of Canadian Universities-Supplementary Materials.
Singer, Michael. Introduction to the DEC System Ten Assembler Language Programming.
Singer, Milton B., jt. auth. see Piers, Gerhart.
Singer, Norman M., ed. see Dede, Christopher J., et al.
Singer, Peter. The Expanding Circle: Ethics & Sociobiology.
Singer, Peter & Wells, Deane. Making Babies: The New Science & Ethics of Conception.
Singer, Peter, ed. In Defense of Animals.
Singer, R. The Neotropical Species of Campanella & Aphyllotus with Notes on some Species of Marasmiellus.
Singer, Robert. The Bad Guys' Quote Book.
Singer, Robert, ed. How to Pick up Two Girls.
Singer, Robert M. & Dick, Walter. Teaching Physical Education: A Systems Approach.
Singer, Robert N. Motor Learning & Human Performance: An Application to Motor & Movement Behaviors.
Singer, Robert N. & Dick, Walter. Teaching Physical Education: A Systems Approach.
Singer, Rolf. Boletes & Related Groups in South America.
Singer, S., ed. see Singer, F.
Singer, S. Fred, ed. Torques & Attitude Sensing in Earth Satellites.

Authors

Singer, Samuel L. The Student Journalist & Reviewing the Performing Arts.
Singer, T. E., ed. Searching the Chemical Literature.
Singer, Thomas P., et al, eds. Monoamine Oxidase: Structure, Function & Altered Functions.
--Mechanism of Drug Action: Symposium.
Singerman, Robert. Jewish & Hebrew Onomastics: A Bibliography.
--The Jews in Spain & Portugal: A Bibliography.
Singewald, Frank D. Amos R. Anderson: The Lone Wolf of Boston Post Road.
--To Succeed in Business, Get There, Honestly If You Can, but Get There.
Singh, jt. auth. see Bajaj.
Singh, A. & Bernstein, M. D., eds. Testing & Analysis of Safety-Relief Value Performance.
Singh, A. K., et al, eds. Economic Policy & Planning in India.
Singh, Ajit. Formation & Role of Excited States in Radiolysis: Special Issue of International Journal for Radiation Physics & Chemistry.
Singh, Amrik. Asking for Trouble: What It Means to Be a Vice-Chancellor Today.
Singh, B. The Philosophy of Upanishads.
Singh, Balbir. Hindu Metaphysics.
Singh, Bawa S. The Jammu Fox: A Biography of Maharaja Gulab Singh of Kashmir, 1792-1857.
Singh, Brijraj. Milton: An Introduction.
Singh, Darshan. Soviet Family of Nations: A Latvian Journey.
Singh, Diwakar P. American Attitude Towards Indian Nationalist Movement.
Singh, G. Poetry As Metaconsciousness: Readings in William Blake.
Singh, Gurdit. The Visions of James Thomson ("B.V.") An Exploration.
Singh, Jacquelin. Fat Gopal.
Singh, Jagjit. Great Ideas in Information Theory, Language & Cibernetics.
--Memoirs of a Mathematician Manque.
Singh, Jarnail. Sikh Symposium 1985.
Singh, Joseph A. & Zingg, Robert M. Wolf-Children & Feral Man.
Singh, K. B., jt. ed. see Saxena, M. C.
Singh, Khushwant. A Bride for the Sahib & Other Stories.
--Gurus, Godman & Good People.
Singh, Khushwant & Rai, Raghu. Sikhs.
Singh, Lachhman. Indian Sword Strikes in East Pakistan.
Singh, N. Iqbal. Amrita Sher-Gil.
Singh, Narinder, jt. auth. see Ginsberg, Matthew.
Singh, Patwant & Malik, Harji, eds. Punjab: The Fatal Miscalculation.
Singh, R. John. French Diplomacy in the Caribbean & the American Revolution.
Singh, Raghubir. Banares: The Sacred City of India.
Singh, Raghubir, ed. Rajasthan: India's Enchanted Land.
Singh, S. R., et al, eds. Pests of Grain Legumes: Ecology & Control.
Singh, Sarva D. Polyandry in Ancient India.
Singh, Sushila. Jane Austen: Her Concept of Social Life.
Singh, Tajindar. The Literary Criticism of D. H. Lawrence.
Singh, Tara. How to Learn from a Course in Miracles.
Singh, Y. An Illustrated Guide to the Design of Computer Programs.
Singhal, Radhey L. see Thomas, John A.
Singhal, Radhey L. & Thomas, John A., eds. Lead Toxicity.
Singhal, S. C., ed. High Temperature Protective Coatings: Proceedings of the AIME Annual Meeting, Atlanta, 1983.
Singhal, Subhash C., ed. High-Temperature Protective Coating.
Singham, A. W., ed. The Nonaligned Movement in World Politics.
Singhvi, A. K., et al, eds. Theory & Practice of Thermally Stimulated Luminescence & Related Phenomena: Proceedings of the National Symposium Held in Ahmedabad, India, 8-10 February 1984.
Singler, Robert E. & Byrne, Catherine A., eds. Elastomers & Rubber Technology: Proceedings of the 32nd Sagamore Conference held July 22-26, 1985, Lake Luzerne, New York.
Singleton, E. Winifred. For Humans & Angels.
Singleton, Esther. The Shakespeare Garden: With Numerous Illustrations from Photographs & Reproductions of Old Wood Cuts.
Singleton, F. B. Background to Eastern Europe.
Singleton, Paul & Sainsbury, Diana. Dictionary of Microbiology.
Singleton, Rebecca. Jersey Blue: An Irreverent Saga of the Making of the New World.
Singleton, W. T., ed. The Human Operator in Complex Systems.
Singley, Grover. Tracing Minnesota's Old Government Roads.
Singmaster, David. Notes on Rubik's Magic Cube.
Sinha, Mridula. Sobs That Bloom: A Novel.
Sinha, R. Social Change in Indian Society.
Sinha, R., et al. Income Distribution, Growth & Basic Needs in India.
Sinha, R. K., jt. auth. see Mirsha, Jagannath.
Sinha, Radha & Drabek, Gordon, eds. The World Food Problem: Consensus & Conflict.
Sinha, S. Europium.
Siniavskii, Andrei D. On Trial: The Soviet State vs. "Abram Tertz" & "Nikolai Arzhak" Hayward, Max, ed.
Sinios, Alexander, jt. auth. see Bernbeck, Rupprecht.
Sinise, Dorothy, jt. auth. see Sinise, Jerry.
Sinise, Jerry. George Washington Arrington: Civil War Spy, Texas Ranger, Sheriff & Rancher.
Sinise, Jerry & Sinise, Dorothy. Texas Show Caves.
Sinitsyna, I. V., tr. see Pugachev.
Sinkler, Lorainne, ed. see Goldsmith, Joel S.
Sinkler, Lorraine. The Spiritual Journey of Joel S. Goldsmith.
Sinkler, Lorraine, ed. see Goldsmith, Joel S.
Sinn, Paul, jt. auth. see Layne, Lisa.
Sinnema, William. Electronic Transmission Technology: Lines, Waves & Antennas.
Sinner, Howard. Baseball's Top Teams since 1920.
Sinnes, A. Cort, jt. auth. see Doty, Walter.
Sinnigen, W. G. The Officium of the Urban Prefecture During the Later Roman Empire.
Sinning, Wayne E. Experiments & Demonstrations in Exercise Physiology.
Sinnott, Edmund W. Matter, Mind & Man: The Biology of Human Nature.
Sinnott, Loraine T., jt. auth. see Cline, Hugh F.
Sinor, John. Small Escapes under the Sun.
Sintetos, L. H. Housemates: How to Find Them, Screen Them, & Live with Them.
Sin The & Hiang The. Karate.
Sinwell, Joseph P., jt. ed. see Powell, Karen H.
Sinzinger, H. & Rogatti, W., eds. Prostaglandin E-1 in Atherosclerosis.
Sioussat, Annie L. Old Manors in the Colony of Maryland.
Sipe, Frederic C., jt. auth. see Bobbitt, Arch N.
Sipe, Lynn F. Western Sahara: A Comprehensive Bibliography.
Sipley, Richard M. Understanding Divine Healing.
Siposs, Allan J. Exporting: Practical Guide for Entrepreneurs & Managers.
Sippel, Curtis L., jt. auth. see Meriwether, Crystal K.
Sippl, Charles. Data Communications Dictionary.
Sippl, Charles J. Computer Dictionary.
Sipress, David. Is It Really Only Monday? PlanBook.
Siragusa, Chris. Introduction to BASIC: A Structured Approach.
Siragusa, Chris R. Introduction to Programming BASIC: A Structured Approach.
Siri, Gabriel. El Salvador & Economic Integration in Central America: An Econometric Study.
Siri Amir Singh Khalsa, ed. see Harbhajan Singh Khalsa.
Sirianni, Carmen, jt. ed. see Fischer, Frank.
Sirica, John J. To Set the Record Straight: The Break-in, the Tapes, the Conspirators, the Pardon.
Siriwardenc, Reggie, jt. auth. see De Silva, M. A.
Sirken, Irving A. Education Programs & Projects: Analytical Techniques, Case Studies, & Exercises.
Sirley, Glenn. Red Yesterdays.
Sirlin, J. L. Biology of RNA.
Sirna, Anne L. & Ritchie, Antonia F. Chapwoman's Guide: Shemanship & Pilot Handling.
Sirof, Harriet. The Junior Encyclopedia of Israel.
Siropolis, Nicholas C. Small Business Management.
--Small Business Management: A Guide to Entrepreneurship.
Sirota, David. Essentials of Real Estate Investment.
Sirotnak, F. M., et al. Folate Antagonisms As Therapeutics Agents: Vol. 2: Pharmacology, Experimental & Clinical Therapeutics.
Sirotnak, F. M., et al, eds. Folate Antagonists As Therapeutics Agents: Biochemistry, Molecular Actions, & Synthetic Design.
Sirovich, Lawrence. Techniques of Asymptotic Analysis.
Sisay, Hassan B. Big Powers & Small Nations: A Case Study of United States-Liberian Relations.
Sisco, Joseph J. & Avineri, Shlomo. The Trilateral Countries & the Middle East.
Sisemore, John T. The Ministry of Visitation.
Sisk, Jonathan & Van Arsdale, Steven. Exploring the PICK Operating System.
Sisler, Harry H. Of Outer & Inner Space.
Sisley, Nick. Grouse & Woodcock: An Upland Hunter's Book.
Sisskind, Mitch. Visitations. Wieder, Laurance, ed.
Sisson, A. F. Unabridged Crossword Puzzle Dictionary.
Sisson, C. H. English Poetry, Nineteen Hundred to Nineteen Fifty: An Assessment.
Sisson, Edith. Nature with Children of All Ages: Adventures for Exploring, Learning, & Enjoying the World Around Us.
Sisson, James E. & Martens, Robert W. Jack London First Editions.
Sisson, R. D., Jr., ed. Coatings & Bimetallics for Aggressive Environments.
Sisson, Roger L., jt. auth. see Emshoff, James R.
Sissons, Michael & French, Philip, eds. Age of Austerity.
Sitenko, A. G. Fluctuations & Non-Linear Wave Interactions in Plasmas. Kocherga, O. D., tr.
--Lectures in Scattering Theory. Shepherd, P. J., ed. & tr.
Sites, George L. Boater's Guide to Biscayne Bay: Miami to Jewfish Creek.
Sitkoff, Harvard, ed. Fifty Years Later: The New Deal Evaluated.
Sitt, H. Scale Studies for Violin: Appendix to H. Schradieck's Scales.
Sitt, Hans. Studies for Violin, Op. 32. Saenger, Gustav, ed.
Sitt, Hans, ed. see Wohlfahrt, Franz.
Sitte, P., ed. Problems of Reduplication in Biology.
Sitterson, J. Carlyle. Sugar Country.
Sittig, M. Particulates & Fine Dust Removal: Processes & Equipment.
Sittig, Marshall. Metal & Inorganic Waste Reclaiming Encyclopedia.
--Polyacetal Resins.
--Veterinary Drug Manufacturing Encyclopedia.
Sittler, Joseph. Ecology of Faith.
--Essays on Nature & Grace.
Sittler, Joseph A. Care of the Earth.
--Grace Notes & Other Fragments. Herhold, Robert M. & Delloff, Linda M., eds.
Sitton, Marie L. Workbook for Papier-Mache Dolls & Furniture.
Sitton, Thad & King, Lincoln. The Loblolly Book: Omnibus Edition.
Sitwell, Edith. Bath.
--I Live under a Black Sun: A Novel.
Sitwell, Sacheverell. Liszt.
--Mozart.
Siudy. Worship.
Siudzinski, Paul. Japanese Brush Painting Techniques: Sumi-e - A Meditation in Ink.
Siuru, William D., Jr., jt. auth. see Holder, William G.
Sivaramamurti, C. Rishis in Indian Art & Literature.
Sive, Helen. Music's Connecticut Yankee: An Introduction to the Life & Music of Charles Ives.
Siverd, Bonnie. Count Your Change: A Woman's Guide to Sudden Financial Change.
Sivin, Nathan. Chinese Alchemy: Preliminary Studies.
Siviter, R. E. A Handbook of Railway Photography.
Siweck, Paul. Enigma of the Hereafter.
Siy, L., jt. auth. see Bennett, A. E.
Sizaire, P. Dictionnaire Technique De la Construction Electrique.
Sizemore, Michael, et al. Energy Planning for Buildings.
Sizer, Nancy F. Making Decisions: Cases for Moral Discussion.
Sizer, Theodore R. Horace's Compromise: The Dilemma of the American High School.
Sizov, E. S. Treasures from the Kremlin: E. S. Sizov, Chief Curator of the State Museums of the Moscow Kremlin. Bowlt, John E., tr.
Sjoberg, Leif, tr. see Lundkvist, Artur.
Sjoden, Per-Olow & Bates, Sandra, eds. Trends in Behavior Therapy.
Sjodin, R. A. Transport in Skeletal Muscle.
Sjogren, Per-Olof. The Jesus Prayer. Linton, Sydney, tr. from Swedish.
Sjoman, Vilgot. I Am Curious (Yellow)
Skachinsky. Makro & Mikro.
Skachinsky, Alexander. Sudba Faini: A Novel.
Skagen-Munshi, Kiki, jt. auth. see Kaushall, Phillip.
Skal, David J., ed. Graphic Communications for the Performing Arts.
Skamene, Emil, ed. Genetic Control of Natural Resistance to Infection & Malignancy.
Skandalakis, Mimi. The Little Bulldog.
Skarin, Annalee. Celestial Song of Creation.
--Ye Are Gods.
Skarmeta, Antonio. Sone Que la Nieve Ardia.
Skaupy, Franz. Principles of Powder Metallurgy.
Skees, William D., jt. auth. see Fell, Peter J.
Skeet, Ian. Oman Before Nineteen Seventy: The End of an Era.
Skeet, Muriel & Elliott, Katherine, eds. Health Auxiliaries & the Health Team.
Skehan, Everett M. A Bullet for Georgie.
Skelcher, Derek. Word Processing Equipment Survey.
Skellern, Claire & Rogers, Paul. Basic Botany.
Skelley, Esther. Medications & Mathematics for the Nurse.
--Medications & Mathematics for the Nurse.
Skelley, Esther G., jt. auth. see Ferris, Elvira.
Skelley, Esther G., jt. auth. see Ferris, Elvira B.
Skelly, James R., jt. auth. see Zim, Herbert S.
Skelly, M., ed. American Indian Gestural Code Based on Universal American Indian Hand Talk.
Skelsey, Alice. Cucumbers in a Flowerpot.
Skelton, Geoffrey. Paul Hindemith: The Man Behind the Music.
--Richard & Cosima Wagner: Biography of a Marriage.
--Wagner at Bayreuth.
--Wieland Wagner: The Positive Sceptic.
Skelton, Geoffrey, tr. see Frisch, Max.
Skelton, Geoffrey, tr. see Wagner, Cosima.
Skelton, John. Ballade of the Scottysshe Kynge.
--John Skelton: The Complete English Poems. Scattergood, John, ed.
Skelton, Mollie. You & Your Poodle.
Skelton, Teressa, jt. auth. see Byrne, Robert.
Skene, Felicia. Use & Abuse. Wolff, Robert L., ed. Bd. with Hidden Depths. Garland Pub.
Skene Smith, N. Introductory Atlas: Economics, Commerce & Administration, a Visual Analysis.
Skerman, P. J. Tropical Forage Legumes.
Sketchley, Rose E. English Book-Illustration of To-Day: Appreciations of the Work of Living English Illustrators with Lists of Their Books.
Skiathos, Greece, jt. auth. see NATO Advanced Study Institute Staff.
Skiba, Jonathan see Schreiber, Irving.
Skiba, Jonathan W. & Sullivan, Joseph P. The Tax Shelter Answer Book.
Skidmore, David, jt. auth. see Butterworth, Charles A.
Skidmore, Ian. Lifeboat: The Story of Coxwain Dick Evans & His Many Rescues.
Skidmore, Linda, jt. auth. see Jaffe, Marie.
Skidmore, Rex A. & Thackeray, Milton G. Introduction to Social Work.
Skidmore-Roth, Linda C. Medication Cards for Clinical Use, 1986.
Skier, Kenneth. Top-Down Assembly Language for Your VIC-20 & Commmodore 64.
--Top-Down Assembly Language Programming for Your VIC-20 & Commodore-64.
Skiff, F. J., jt. auth. see Dawson, Thomas.
Skilbeck, Malcolm. Evaluating the Curriculum in the 80's.
Skiles, J. D., tr. see Fernandes, Florestan.
Skillcorn, David B., jt. auth. see Barnard, David T.
Skillen, Anthony. Ruling Illusions: Philosophy & the Social Order.
Skillen, Ennis. Navajo Neverland.
Skillen, James, ed. Nineteen Eighty-Eight Candidate Profiles: A Look at the Leading Presidential Contenders.
Skilleter, Paul. The Jaguar XK: Collectors Guide.
Skillicorn, jt. auth. see Barnard.
Skillman, William. Radar Calculations Using the TI-59 Programmable Calculator.
Skillman, William. A. Radar Calculations Using Personal Computers.
Skilton, David & Dennis, Barbara. Reform & Intellectual Debate in Victorian England, 1830-1880.
Skilton, M. Deutsche Texte und Wortschatzuebungen.
Skimin, E. & McMurtrie, P. Gregg Shorthand Structured Learning Method.
Skinner, Andrew, jt. auth. see Taylor, George.
Skinner, B. F. Contingencies of Reinforcement: A Theoretical Analysis.
Skinner, Brian J., jt. auth. see Emery, K. O.
Skinner, Brian J., ed. Paleontology & Paleoenvironments.
--The Solar System & Its Strange Objects.
--Use & Misuse of Earth's Surface.
Skinner, Charles M. American Myths & Legends.
--Myths & Legends of Our New Possessions & Protectorate.
Skinner, Cornelia Otis. Life with Lindsay & Crouse.
--Madam Sarah.
Skinner, Cornelia Otis & Kimbrough, Emily. Our Hearts Were Young & Gay.
Skinner, Craig. Lamplighter & Son.
Skinner, David E. Thomas George Lawson: African Historian & Administrator in Sierra Leone.
Skinner, Donna. Games & Gadgets for the Church School.
Skinner, F. A. & Lovelock, D. W. Identification Methods for Microbiologists.
Skinner, F. A. & Hugo, W. B., eds. Inhibition & Inactivation of Vegetative Microbes.
Skinner, F. A., jt. ed. see Sykes, G.
Skinner, F. A., et al, eds. Gonorrhoea: Epidemiology & Pathogenesis.
Skinner, Gordon S., jt. auth. see Heisel, W. D.
Skinner Hersey Staff, jt. auth. see San Giorgio Staff.
Skinner, John V., tr. see Eckhart, Meister, et al.
Skinner, Michael. Red Flag.
Skinner, Renate, jt. auth. see Iversen, Edwin S.
Skinner, Stephen. The Living Earth Manual of Peng-Shui: Chinese Geomancy.
--Terrestrial Astrology: Divination by Geomancy.
Skipper, Harold, Jr., jt. auth. see Black, Kenneth, Jr.

Authors

Skira-Rizzoli Staff & Leymarie, Jean. Balthus.
Skira-Rizzoli Staff & Milman, Miriam. Tromp-L'oeil Painting: The Illusion of Reality.
Skirakawa, Yoshikazu. The Himalayas.
Skitok, J. & Marshall, Roger G. Electromagnetic Concepts & Applications.
Skivington, James. Managing to Survive: How to Outsmart the One-Minute Manager.
Skjei, Eric, jt. auth. see Howard, Robert.
Sklar, Maurice. How Children Learn to Speak.
Sklarew, Myra. Like a Field Riddled.
Skobel & McDonald. Semka, The Sammy Skobel Story.
Skoda, J. & Langen, P., eds. Antimetabolites in Biochemistry, Biology & Medicine: Proceedings, Prague, 1978.
Skodol, Andrew E., jt. auth. see Spitzer, Robert L.
Skogerboe, G. V. Water & Energy Development in an Arid Environment: The Colorado River Basin.
Skoglund, Elizabeth. Growing through Rejection.
Skold, Betty W. I'm Glad You're Open Weekdays: Everyday Prayers to the God Who Works Between Sundays.
--The Kids Are Gone, Lord, but I'm Still Here: Prayers for Mothers.
Skolnick, Arlene S. & Skolnick, Jerome H. Family in Transition: Rethinking Marriage, Sexuality, Child Rearing, & Family Organizations.
--Intimacy, Family, & Society.
Skolnick, Jerome H. & Currie, Elliott. Crisis in American Institutions.
Skolnick, Jerome H., jt. auth. see Kaplan, John.
Skolnick, Jerome H., jt. auth. see Skolnick, Arlene S.
Skolnik, Richard. Money Talks: An Irreverent Guide for the Curious, Penurious, Pennywise & Pound Foolish.
Skomal, Edward N. Automatic Vehicle Locating System.
--Man-Made Radio Noise.
Skoog, Douglas A. & West, Donald M. Fundamentals of Analytical Chemistry.
Skorohod, A. V., jt. auth. see Gihman, I. I.
Skorohod, A. V., jt. auth. see Gihman, L. I.
Skoryna, S. C., et al. Intestinal Absorption of Metal Ions, Trace Elements & Radionuclides.
Skou, J. C. & Norby, J. G., eds. NA, K-Atpase: Structure & Kinetics.
Skousen, Mark. Mark Skousen's Guide to Financial Privacy.
Skovholt, Thomas M., et al. Counseling Men.
Skrabanek, Petr & Powell, David. Substance P. Horrobin, D. F., ed.
Skrade, Carl. God & the Grotesque.
Skram, Amalie. Betrayed. Hennes, Aileen, tr.
Skrine, Peter N., jt. auth. see Furst, Lillian R.
Skripov, B. P. Metastable Liquids.
Skrjabina, Elena. After Leningrad: A Diary of Survival During World War Two.
Skrotzki, Bernhardt G. & Vopat, W. A. Power Station Engineering & Economy.
Skuce, Doug & Sowa, John. Knowledge Representation: Design Issues.
Skujins, J., jt. ed. see West, N. E.
Skujins, Z. A Man in His Prime.
Skurka, Margaret F. Organization of Medical Record Departments in Hospitals. Converse, Mary E., ed.
Skurnik, W. A., ed. Sub-Saharan Africa: A Guide to Information Sources.
Skurzynski, Gloria. Caught in the Moving Mountains.
--Honest Andrew.
--Honest Andrew.
--Martin by Himself.
--Safeguarding the Land.
--Safeguarding the Land.
--Swept in the Wave of Terror.
Sky & Telescope Editors. Mr. Halley's Comet.
Sky Prints Corp. Staff. Sky Prints Aviation Enroute Atlas.
Skybova, Anna, jt. auth. see Hroch, Miroslav.
Skydell, Barbara & Crowder, Anne S. Diagnostic Procedures: A Reference for Health Practitioners & a Guide for Patient Counseling.
Skydell, Ruth H., jt. auth. see Belkin, Gary S.
Skynner, Robin & Cleese, John. Families & How to Survive Them.
SLA, Social Science Group, Washington DC Chapter Staff. A Sampler of Forms for Special Libraries.
Slaatte, Howard A. Fire in the Brand: An Introduction to the Creative Work & Theology of John Wesley.
Slaatte, Howard A. & Sendaydiego, Henry, eds. The Philosophy of Martin Heidegger.
Slabaugh, Dennis, tr. see Bethge, Eberhard & Bethge, Renate.
Slack. Poverty & Policy in Tudor Stuart England.
Slack, Anne & Mueller, Marlies. A Propos! Communication et Culture: Un Debut.
Slack, Kathleen M. Old People & London Government.
Slack, Kenneth. The United Reformed Church.
Slack, Robert C. & Cottrell, Beekman W. Writing: A Preparation for College Composition.
Slack, Robert C., ed. see Hardy, Thomas.
Slade, Afton, jt. auth. see Lande, Nathaniel.
Slade, B. A. Complete Course in Short-Cut Mathematics.
Slade, Jack. Blood Knife.
--Honcho.
--Renegade & the Comancheros.
--Wolverine.
Slade, Michael. Headhunter.
Slade, N. & Gillespie, W. A. The Urinary Tract & the Catheter.
Slade, Peter. Child Drama.
Slade, Roger, jt. auth. see Feder, Gershon.
Sladek, John. Using XyWrite III.
Sladen, Douglas. Queer Things about Japan, to Which Is Added a Life of the Emperor of Japan.
Sladkovsky, M. I. Long Road: Sino-Russian Economic Contacts from Ancient Times to 1917.
Slaff, Betrand. What Happens in Therapy.
Slaikeu, Karl & Lawhead, Steve. The Phoenix Factor: Surviving & Growing Through Personal Crisis.
Slama, Anton. Sixty-Six Etudes in All the Major & Minor Keys.
Slama, K., et al. Insect Hormones & Bioanalogues.
Slamecka, V. & Borka, H., eds. Planning & Organisation of National Research Programs in Information Science.
Slaney, Brenda, ed. Occupational Health Nursing.
Slania, Kasimir B. The Parable of a Siamese Cat That Kept Purring among Thorns.
Slappey, G. Sterling, ed. see Center for Strategic & International Studies, Georgetown University Staff.
Slappey, Mary M. Exploring Military Service for Women.
Slater, jt. auth. see Curwin.
Slater, Beverly. A Positive Approach to Head Injury: Guidelines for Professionals & Families.
--Stranger in My Bed.
Slater, Carl D., et al. Infrared Spectroscopy.
Slater, Eliot, jt. ed. see Sargant, William.
Slater, Eve E., jt. auth. see Doroghazi, Robert M.
Slater, Harry & Smith, Lee. Basic Plumbing.
Slater, James M. Precision Radiotherapy Planning.
Slater, John G., ed. see Russell, Bertrand.
Slater, John H. Illustrated Sporting Books.
Slater, K. The Thermal Behaviour of Textiles.
Slater, Martin & Lecomber, Richard. Income Distribution: The Limits to Redistribution. Collard, David, ed.
Slater, Michael, ed. see Dickens, Charles.
Slater, Miriam. Family Life in the Seventeenth Century: The Verneys of Claydon.
Slater, Niall W. Plautus in Performance: The Theatre of the Mind.
Slater, Nigel. Crossfire.
--Falcon.
Slater, Peter. The Dynamics of Religion: Meaning & Change in Religious Traditions.
--Field Guide to Australian Birds: The Passerines.
--Field Guide to Australian Birds, Vol. 1: The Non-Passerines.
Slater, Phil. Origin & Significance of the Frankfurt School, a Marxist Perspective.
Slater, Philip. How I Saved the World.
Slater, Ray. Texas Night Riders.
Slater, T. F., ed. Biochemical Mechanisms of Liver Injury.
Slatin, Rudolf C. Fire & Sword in the Sudan. Wingate, Francis R., tr.
Slatkes, Leonard J. Rembrandt & Persia.
Slatoff, Walter J. With Respect to Readers: Dimensions of Literary Response.
Slatt, Bernard J., jt. auth. see Stein, Harold A.
Slattery, Kathryn, jt. auth. see Blackwood, Cheryl P.
Slattery, Matthew T. Felipe Angeles & the Mexican Revolution.
Slaughter, Bob H. & Walton, Dan W., eds. About Bats: A Chiropteran Symposium.
Slaughter, Carolyn. The Banquet.
--Dreams of the Kalahari.
--The Innocents.
Slaven, A & Checkland, S. G., eds. Dictionary of Scottish Business Bioghraphy.
Slavens. The Retrieval of Information in the Humanities & Social Science.
Slavens, Thomas P., jt. auth. see Tice, Terrence N.
Slavin, Albert, et al. Financial Accounting: A Basic Approach.
Slavin, Arthur J., ed. Tudor Men & Institutions: Studies in English Law & Government.
Slavin, Morris. Atomic Absorption Spectroscopy.
Slavin, Neal. When Two or More Are Gathered Together.
Slavin, Robert E. Cooperative Learning: Student Teams.
--Educational Psychology: Theory into Practice.
--Student Team Learning: An Overview & Practical Guide.
Slavin, Simon, ed. Social Administration: The Management of the Social Services.
Slavin, Stephen L. & Pradt, Mary A. The Einstein Syndrome: Corporate Anti-Semitism in America Today.
Slavin, W., ed. Graphite Furnace Technology & Atomic Absorption Spectroscopy: Commemorating the 25th Anniversary of the Publication of the First Paper by B. V. L'vov.
Slavitt, David. King of Hearts.
Slavitt, David R. Physicians Observed.
Slavitt, David R., jt. auth. see Adler, Bill.
Slavkin, Harold C. & Bavetta, Lucien A., eds. Developmental Aspects of Oral Biology.
Slavkin, Harold C. & Grevlich, Richard C., eds. Extracellular Matrix Influences on Gene Expression.
Slavkin, Harold C., et al, eds. Cellular Induction.
Slavson, S. R. & Schiffer, Mortimer. Dynamics of Group Psychotherapy.
--Group Psychotherapies for Children: A Textbook.
Slawecki, Leon M. French Policy Towards the Chinese in Madagascar.
Sleasar, Henry. Acrostic Mysteries.
Sleath, J. F. Sea Bed Mechanics.
Sleator, William. Blackbriar.
--Run.
Slebsager, Astrid. Cooking with the Danes.
Sleeman, B. D., jt. ed. see Everitt, W. N.
Sleep, Wayne. Variations on Wayne Sleep.
Sleeth, Ronald E. & Donahue, John R. Pentecost 1.
Sleigh, M. A., ed. Cilia & Flagella.
Sleightholme, Des. Better Boat Handling.
Sleightholme, J. D. Cruising: A Manual for the Small Sailing Boat Owner.
Slepian, Jan. Lester's Turn.
Slesar, Henry. Murders Most Macabre.
Slesinger, Reuben & Beeson, Glen. Annual Editions: Economics, 1985-86.
Slesser, Malcolm & Lewis, Chris. Biological Energy Resources.
Slichter, Sumner H., et al. The Impact of Collective Bargaining on Management.
Slide, Anthony. Early American Cinema.
Slife, Brent D., jt. auth. see Rubinstein, Joseph.
Sligar, Steve, jt. ed. see Ornston, L. Nicholas.
Sliger, jt. auth. see Sharp.
Slim, Field-Marshall W. Unofficial History.
Slim, Iceberg. Death Wish.
Slimmon, Robert F. Successful Pension Design for the Small to Medium Size Business.
Slinkman, John & Navy Times Editors, eds. Duel to the Death: Eyewitness Accounts of Great Battles at Sea.
Sliwa, Curtis, jt. auth. see Alliance of Guardian Angels, Inc. Staff.
Sloan, A. Elizabeth, jt. auth. see Labuza, Theodore P.
Sloan, Allan. Three Plus One Equals Billions: The Bendix-Martin Marietta War.
Sloan, David L. Johnny Takes a Reigncheck.
Sloan, Frank A., et al, eds. Uncompensated Hospital Care: Rights & Responsibilities.
Sloan, Irving J. Environment & the Law.
--Youth: The Law, Rights, Privileges & Obligations.
Sloan, James P. The Last Cold-War Cowboy.
--War Games.
Sloan, John. New York Etchings: Nineteen Five to Nineteen Forty-Nine.
Sloan, John, ed. see Christian, Sharon & Johnson, Margaret.
Sloan, Joyce. A for Effort.
Sloan, Liz & Kramer, Ann. Running: The Women's Handbook.
Sloan, Stephen, jt. ed. see Shultz, Richard H., Jr.
Sloan, Thomas J. International Interactions: Events-Data Analysis Applied to the Middle East.
Sloan, Timothy, jt. auth. see Lee, Alfred.
Sloan, W. W. A Survey of the New Testament.
Sloane, Arthur A. & Witney, Fred. Labor Relations.
Sloane, Bruce. Cavers, Caves, & Caving.
Sloane, David E. Mark Twain As a Literary Comedian.
Sloane, Eric. The Do's & Don'ts of Yesterday.
--Eighty: An American Souvenir.
Sloane, Eugene A. The All New Complete Book of Bicycling.
--The All New Complete Book of Bicycling.
Sloane, Irving. Classic Guitar Construction.
--Guitar Repair: A Manual of Repair for Guitars & Fretted Instruments.
Sloane, J. Biopsy Pathology of the Breast.
Sloane, Julia, ed. see Sloane, William.
Sloane, Mary. The Visual in Metaphysical Poetry.
Sloane, N. J. A Short Course on Error Correcting Codes.
Sloane, William. The Craft of Writing. Sloane, Julia, ed
Sloan-White, Barbara & Woods, Charles R. Blonds.
Slobodek, Mitchell. A Selective Bibliography of California Labor History.
Slobodkin, Lawrence B. Growth & Regulation of Animal Populations.
Slocum, Milton J. Manhattan Country Doctor: A Memoir.
Slocum, Olive D. Pioneer Homesteaders in Union County New Mexico.
Sloggett, Gordon & Dickason, Clifford. Ground-Water Mining in the United States.
Sloma, Richard S. No-Nonsense Management.
Sloman, Larry. Reefer Madness: Marijuana in America.
Slonaker, Larry. Voice of the Visitor.
Slonczewski, Joan. A Door into Ocean.
Slonim, N. Balfour. Respiratory Physiology.
Slonimsky, Juris. Soviet Ballet.
Slonimsky, Nicolas. Music Since 1900.
--Thesaurus of Scales & Melodic Patterns.
Slonneger, J. C. Dynagraph Analysis of Sucker Rod Pumping.
Sloper, Patricia, jt. auth. see Cunningham, Cliff.
Slosberg, Paul S. Neurology.
Sloshberg, Willard & Nessmith, William C. Contemporary American Society: An Introduction to Social Science.
Slosser, Bob, jt. auth. see Kinchlow, Ben.
Slosser, Bob, jt. auth. see Robertson, Pat.
Slote, Al. The Devil Rides with Me, Six Fantastic Stories.
Slote, Alfred. The Biggest Victory.
--C.O.L.A.R.
--Hang Tough, Paul Mather.
--Matt Gargan's Boy.
--My Father, the Coach.
--My Robot Buddy.
--My Trip to Alpha I.
--Tony & Me.
Slote, Bernice, ed. see Cather, Willa.
Slote, Stanley J. Weeding Library Collections II.
Slotkin, Richard. The Crater.
--The Fatal Environment: The Myth of the Frontier in the Age of Industrialization 1800-1890.
Slottman, William B., jt. ed. see Janos, Andrew C.
Slovenko, Ralph. Psychiatry & Law.
Slovin, Malcolm, jt. auth. see Ruesink, Albert.
Slovo, Gillian. Death by Analysis.
Slowinski, Emil, jt. auth. see Masterton, William.
Sloyan, Gerard S. Advent-Christmas.
--Jesus on Trial.
--Worshipful Preaching.
Sloyan, Gerard S. & Kee, Howard C. Pentecost 3.
Sloyan, Virginia, ed. Signs, Songs & Stories.
Sloyan, Virginia, jt. ed. see Huck, Gabe.
Sloyer, Clifford, jt. auth. see Crouse, Richard.
Sluckin, Andy. Growing up in the Playground: The Social Development of Children.
Sluckin, W. Fear in Animals & Man.
Sluder, Troy B., jt. auth. see Murray, Henry V.
Slung, Michele. Women's Wiles.
Slupecki, J. & Borkowski, L. Elements of Mathematical Logic & Set Theory.
Slurzberg, Morris & Osterheld, William. Essentials of Communication Electronics.
Slusher, Harold S. Age of the Cosmos.
--Critique of Radiometric Dating.
--The Origin of the Universe.
Slusher, Harold S. & Gamwell, Thomas P. Age of the Earth.
Slusher, Harold S. & Ramirez, Francisco. The Motion of Mercury's Perihelion.
Slusher, Harold S. & Robertson, Stephen J. The Age of the Solar System.
Slusky. Cases in Database Design.
Slusser, D. M. & Slusser, Gerald H. Technology: The God That Failed.
Slusser, George, jt. ed. see Reginald, R.
Slusser, Gerald H. A Christian Look at Secular Society.
Slusser, Gerald H., jt. auth. see Slusser, D. M.
Slutzky, Gerald M., ed. Biochemistry of Parasites: Proceedings of Satellite Conference of the 13th Annual Meeting of the Federation of European Biochemical Societies (FEBS), Jerusalem, August 1980.
Sluyter, Peter, jt. auth. see Danckaerts, Jasper.
Sluzalis, L. I. & Dempsey, P. E., eds. Performance of Pressure Vessels with Clad & Overlayed Stainless Steel Linings.
Sluzas, Raymond & Ryan, Anne. A Graphic Guide to Industrialized Building Elements.
Sluzis, Robert C. Free Like a Dream.
Slyke, Helen van see Van Slyke, Helen.
S. M. Die Kluge & Narrische Welt.
Smakov, Gennady. Baryshnikov: From Russia to the West.
Smales, Lindsay M. & Goodey, Brian. The Essex Design Guide for Residential Areas: A Bibliography.
Small, Albion & Vincent, George. An Introduction to the Study of Society.
Small, Bertrice. Skye O'Malley.
Small Computers in Business Seminar, London. Small Computers in Business.
Small, David. Almost Famous.
Small, Dwight H. After You've Said I Do.
--How Should I Love You?

Authors

Small, J. The PH of Plant Cells. Bd. with The PH of Animal Cells. Wiercinski, F. J. Springer-Verlag.
Small, John, jt. auth. see Nadell, Bonnie.
Small, Lawrence F. A Century of Politics on the Yellowstone.
--Journey with the Law.
Small, Lawrence F. & Henderson, Harley. Montana Passage.
Small, Miriam R. Oliver Wendell Holmes.
Small, P. A., et al. Advances in Polymer Science: Macro-Conformation of Polymers.
Small, Robert Van Dyke. Darkness Where Light Fails to Shine: Open Fields Where the Wisdom of Men Seldom Probes.
Small, W. Emmett, ed. see De Purucker, G.
Small, William J. Political Power & the Press.
Smalley, Barbara. George Eliot & Flaubert: Pioneers of the Modern Novel.
Smalley, Donald. Anthony Trollope.
Smalley, Gary. The Key to Your Child's Heart.
--Language of Love.
Smalley, I. J., ed. Loess: Lithology & Genesis.
Smalley, Mary B., jt. ed. see Legg, Alicia.
Smalley, Mary R. Writing English As a Second Language.
Smalley, Peter. Trove.
Smalley, Regina L. & Hank, Mary K. Refining Composition Skills.
Smalley, William A. Manual of Articulatory Phonetics.
Smallman, Basil. The Background of Passion Music.
Smallman, R. E. & Ashbee, K. H. Modern Metallography.
Smallwood, Carol. Exceptional Free Library-Resource Materials.
Smal-Stocki, Roman, jt. auth. see Manning, Clarence A.
Smart, Alastair. The Dawn of Italian Painting, 1250-1400.
Smart, Barry, jt. auth. see Smart, Carol.
Smart, Carol. Women, Crime, & Criminology: A Feminist Critique.
Smart, Carol & Smart, Barry. Women, Sexuality & Social Control.
Smart, Carol, jt. ed. see Brophy, Julia.
Smart, Charles A. Viva Juarez! A Biography.
Smart, Christopher. For I Will Consider My Cat Jeoffry.
Smart, J. D., tr. see Barth, Karl & Thurneysen, Eduard.
Smart, James D. ABC's of Christian Faith.
--The Cultural Subversion of the Biblical Faith: Life in the 20th Century under the Sign of the Cross.
--Doorway to a New Age: A Study of Paul's Letter to the Romans.
--History & Theology in Second Isaiah: A Commentary on Isaiah 35, 40-66.
--The Rebirth of Ministry: A Study of the Biblical Character of the Church's Ministry.
Smart, K. F., ed. Malnutrition & Endemic Diseases: Their Effects on Education in the Developing Countries.
Smart, Lucien E. & Radford, Bruce W. Public Utilities Reports Digest: Supplements A & B, 1983-1986.
Smart, Ninian. Beyond Ideology: Religion & the Future of Western Civilization.
--The Religious Experience of Mankind.
--The Science of Religion & the Sociology of Knowledge: Some Methodological Questions.
--Worldviews: Crosscultural Explorations in Human Beliefs.
Smart, Orval. Christ of the Antichrist?
Smart, Patricia, jt. auth. see Brownhill, Robert.
Smart, Richard. The Snow Papers: A Memoir of Illusion, Power-Lust & Cocaine. Johnson, Joyce, ed.
Smart, Robert A. The Nonfiction Novel.
Smath, Jerry. Leon's Prize.
Smeaton, R. W. Motor Application & Maintenance Handbook.
--Switchgear & Control Handbook.
Smedema, C. H. & Phillips, N. V., eds. Real Time Programming, 1977: Proceedings of the IFAC-IFIP Workshop, Eindhoven, The Netherlands, June 1977.
Smedley, Agnes. China Correspondent.
--Portraits of Chinese Women in Revolution. MacKinnon, Jan & MacKinnon, Steve, eds.
Smedley, Dan. Programming the PL-1 Way.
Smedley, Don. Teaching the Basic Skills in English: The Role of Spelling, Punctuation & Grammar in Secondary English.
Smee, Nicola, illus. Rex Q. C.
Smeets, G. P., jt. ed. see Hunter, W. J.
Smejkalova, J., et al. Pocket Dictionary: English-Slovak-English.
Smellie, Alexander. Men of the Covenant: The Story of the Scottish Church in the Years of the Persecution.
Smellie, R. M., ed. see Biochemical Society Symposium, 31st.
Smellie, R. M., ed. see Biochemical Society Symposium, 34th.
Smellie, R. M., jt. ed. see Ganguly, J.
Smelser, George K., ed. Structure of the Eye.
Smelser, Neil J. Comparative Methods in the Social Science.
Smelser, Neil J., jt. auth. see Parsons, Talcott.
Smeltzer, Donald. Man & Number.
Smerk, George M. Urban Mass Transportation: A Dozen Years of Federal Policy.
Smetana, Karel, jt. ed. see Busch, Harris.
Smethurst, D., jt. auth. see Schofield, C. W.
Smethurst, David. Mathematics for Level-Three Technicians.
Smethurst, George. Basic Water Treatment for Application Worldwide.
Smethurst, Wood. Teaching Young Children to Read at Home.
Smets, G., ed. Photochemical Processes in High Polymers: Proceedings of the Second International Symposium on Photochemical Processes in Polymer Chemistry, Leuven, Belgium, 1976.
Smets, G. & De Schryver, F. C., eds. Photochemical Processes in Polymer Chemistry: Proceedings of the First International Symposium, on Photochemical Processes in Polymer Chemistry, Leuven, Belgium, 1972.
Smidt, Kristian. Uncomformities in Shakespeare's History Plays.
Smidt, Ollie. Engineering Economics.
Smil, Vaclav. The Bad Earth: Enviromental Degradation in China.
Smiles, Samuel. Josiah Wedgewood.
Smiley, Larry L., jt. auth. see Franchak, Stephen J.
Smiley, Virginia. Return to Love.
Smirnov, B. M. Negative Ions.
Smirnov, L. N., ed. Legislative Acts of the U. S. S. R., 1977-1979.
Smirnov, V., ed. Studies of Mineral Deposits.
Smirnova, M. A. The Hausa Language: A Descriptive Grammar.
Smiroldo, Paul A. Simply Italian.
Smit, Kornelis, ed. see Means, R. S., Company, Inc. Staff.
Smith. All Trivia.
--Statistical Reasoning.
Smith, jt. auth. see Pellissier.
Smith, jt. auth. see Williams.
Smith, A. C. Labyrinth: A Novel.
--Lady Jane.
Smith, A. D., et al. Commentaries in the Neurosciences.
Smith, A. G., et al. Community Influence on Local Planning Policy.
Smith, A. H. Chinese Characteristics.
Smith, A. J., ed. John Donne: The Critical Heritage.
Smith, Abbot E. Colonists in Bondage: White Servitude & Convict Labor in America, 1607-1776.
Smith, Adeline M. Free Magazines for Libraries.
Smith, Alan. Woodframe Furniture Restoration.
Smith, Alan G. Science & Society in the Sixteenth & Seventeenth Centuries.
Smith, Alan G., ed. Government of Elizabethan England.
Smith, Alexander B. & Harriet, Pollack. Criminal Justice: An Overview.
Smith, Alexander B., jt. auth. see Pollack, Harriet.
Smith, Alexander, Jr. Frank O'Hara: A Comprehensive Bibliography.
Smith, Alice L. Microbiology & Pathology.
Smith, Alison. Someone Else's Grave.
Smith, Allan B. & Smith, Helen B. Individual Open Salts Illustrated: The 1976 Annual.
--Individual Open Salts Illustrated: The 1978 Annual.
--Six Hundred Fifth More Individual Open Salts Illustrated.
--The Third Book of Individual Open Salts Illustrated.
Smith, Allan B., et al. Eleven Hundred Open Salts.
Smith, Andrew C. Schizophrenia & Madness.
Smith, Andrew C. & Stafford-Clark, David. Psychiatry for Students.
Smith, Annette. Terror in Cairo.
Smith, Anthony. The Human Pedigree.
--The Shadow in the Cave: The Broadcaster, His Audience, & the State.
Smith, Anthony, jt. ed. see Curran, James.
Smith, Anthony D. Nationalism: A Trend Report & Bibliography Prepared for the International Sociological Association Under the Auspices of the International Committee for Social Sciences Documentation.
Smith, Arthur A. Rachel.
Smith, Arthur H. China in Convulsion.
Smith, August W. Management Systems.
Smith, B. Babington, ed. Training in Small Groups: A Study of Five Methods. Farrell, B. A.
Smith, B. H. Bridged Aromatic Compounds.
Smith, B. J. & Harrell, Irene B. Divorced.
Smith, B. L. What Is Man?
Smith, B. Othanel, jt. auth. see Orlosky, Donald E.
Smith, B. R., jt. auth. see Cummings, Catherine M.
Smith, Barbara. After the Revolution: The Smithsonian History of Everyday Life in the 18th Century.
--How to Teach Junior Highs.
--Young People's Bible Dictionary.
Smith, Barbara L., jt. ed. see Jones, Richard M.
Smith, Barbara L., et al. Political Research Methods: Foundations & Techniques.
Smith, Barry, tr. see Bretano, Franz.
Smith, Barry, et al. Recurrent Education: A Revived Agenda. Duke, Chris, ed.
Smith, Barry J. & Delahaye, Brian L. How to Be an Effective Trainer: Skills for Managers & New Trainers.
Smith, Beatrice S. The Ghost in the Park.
Smith, Bede. The Lancashire Watch Company, Prescott, Lancashire, England 1889-1910.
Smith, Bernard, jt. auth. see Joppien, Rudiger.
Smith, Bernard H. Differential Diagnosis in Neurology.
Smith, Bernice D. Shellbby Rumford: The Story of a Happy Rabbit.
Smith, Bert K. The Pursuit of Dignity: New Living Alternatives for the Elderly.
Smith, Beverly B. & De Vorss, Patricia. Caught in the Middle.
Smith, Beverly B., jt. auth. see Nethery, Betty.
Smith, Billy E. Managing the Information Systems Audit: A Case Study-Policies, Procedures, & Guidelines.
Smith, Bonnie S. If You Love Me, Call Me Dorrie.
Smith, Bradley F. The War's Long Shadow: China, Russia, Britain, America.
Smith, Brenda D. Bridging the Gap: College Reading.
Smith, Brian J., jt. auth. see Lewis, Theodore G.
Smith, Brian J., ed. National Radio Publicity Directory: 1978.
--National Radio Publicity Directory 1978-79.
Smith, Bruce. The BBC Micro Machine Code Portfolio.
Smith, Bruce, jt. auth. see Balakian, Peter.
Smith, Bruce A., ed. A Perspective on Energy Modeling.
Smith, Bryan C. Community Health: An Epidemiological Approach.
Smith, Bud E. DAC Easy Made Easy.
Smith, Buford D. Design of Equilibrium Stage Processes.
Smith, C. Anson. Understanding.
Smith, C. B., jt. ed. see Fazzolare, Rocco.
Smith, C. Jay, Jr. The Russian Struggle for Power.
Smith, C. W. The Thin Men of Haddam.
--The Vestal Virgin Room.
--Will They Love Me When I Leave? A Weekend Father's Struggle to Stay Close to His Kids.
Smith, Carlton G. Serial Dissections of the Human Brain.
Smith, Carole. Danger at the Golden Dragon. Fay, Ann, ed.
Smith, Carole, jt. auth. see Hooker, Ruth.
Smith, Carole S. The End.
Smith, Carter, ed. Country Antiques & Collectibles: How to Find Them--Where to Buy Them--How to Decorate with Them.
Smith, Catharine P. From Mama's Honey Jar. Kuse, James & Luedtke, D. Ralph, eds.
Smith, Catriona, jt. auth. see Smith, Ray.
Smith, Cecil. Worlds of Music.
Smith Center for the History of Cartography Staff & Long, John H. Historical Atlas & Chronology of County Boundaries, 1788-1980.
Smith, Charles A. Promoting the Social Development of Young Children.
Smith, Charles E. Innocent Three, Church Defender.
Smith, Charles E., jt. ed. see Ramsey, Frederic, Jr.
Smith, Charles M. Reverend Randollph & the Avenging Angel.
--Reverend Randollph & the Fall from Grace, Inc.
--Reverend Randollph & the Unholy Bible.
--Reverend Randollph & the Wages of Sin.
--Reverend Randolph & the Holy Terror.
Smith, Charles Page. James Wilson, Founding Father: 1742-1798.
Smith, Charles W. & Koester, Helmut. Lent.
Smith, Charlie. Canaan.
--Canaan.
Smith, Charlotte. The Old Manor House.
Smith, Chester M., Jr. American Philatelic Periodicals.
Smith, Christine. The Baptistery of Pisa.
Smith, Christopher, ed. Exploring Biology with Microcomputers.
Smith, Clarence J. Russian Struggle for Power, Nineteen Fourteen to Nineteen Seventeen: A Study of Russian Foreign Policy During the First World War.
Smith, Clement. The Children's Hospital of Boston: "Built Better Than They Knew"
Smith, Clifford N. British Deportees to America, Pt. 1: 1760-1763.
--A Calendar of Archival Materials on the Land Patents Issued by the United States Government with Subject, Tract & Name Indexes.
Smith, Clyde, photos by. Appalachian Mountains.
Smith, Clyde H., photos by. New England Coast.
Smith College, Sophia Smith Collection Staff. The Author, Subject & Manuscript Catalogs of the Sophia Smith Collection (Women's History Archive)
--Picture Catalog of the Sophia Smith Collection.
Smith, Cordwainer. You Will Never Be the Same. Del Ray, Lester, ed.
Smith, Craig B. Energy Management Principles: Applications, Benefits, Savings.
Smith, Curt. America's Dizzy Dean.
Smith, Cynthia J., jt. auth. see Frazer, Joan M.
Smith, D. Rhodesia, the Problem.
Smith, D. C. & Tiffon, Y., eds. Nutrition in the Lower Metazoa: Proceedings.
Smith, D. E., ed. see Row, T. S.
Smith, D. G., jt. auth. see Dunlop, J.
Smith, D. I., ed. Editing Eighteenth-Century Texts.
--Editing Seventeenth-Century Prose.
Smith, D. J. Amateur Acting & Stage Encyclopedia.
--Discovering Country Crafts.
--Discovering Horse-Drawn Transport of the British Army.
Smith, D. K. Cementing.
Smith, D. K., et al, eds. Advances in X-Ray Analysis.
Smith, D. M., tr. see Barrett, C. K.
Smith, D. Moody. Interpreting the Gospels for Preaching.
Smith, D. N. A Forgotten Sector: The Training of Ancillary Staff in Hospitals.
Smith, Dan. The Defence of the Realm in the 1980's.
Smith, Dan, jt. ed. see Thompson, E. P.
Smith, Dana P. An Old Creed for a New Day.
Smith, Dave. Cumberland Station: Poems.
Smith, David. Mathematics.
--Socialist Propaganda in the Twentieth-Century British Novel.
Smith, David A. Interface: Calculus & the Computer.
Smith, David B., jt. auth. see Zimmermann, Barbara.
Smith, David C. A History of Lumbering in Maine, 1861-1960.
Smith, David C. & Tierney, Richard L. Red Sonja, No. 4: Endithor's Daughter.
Smith, David H. & Hokelman, Robert A. Controversies in Child Health & Pediatrics.
Smith, David H. & Til, John Van, eds. International Perspectives on Voluntary Action Research.
Smith, David J. & Gray, Jeremy. Police & People in London.
Smith, David S. Muscle.
Smith, David W. Helvetius: A Study in Persecution.
Smith, Delia. A Feast for Lent.
Smith, Dennie L. & Smith, Lana J. Seeing Through Stone: A Teacher's Guide to Lessons in Studio Poetry.
Smith, Dennis. Barrington Moore Jr. A Critical Appraisal.
--Conflict & Compromise: Class Formation in English Society, 1830-1914, with Particular Reference to Education, Industry & Politics in Birmingham & Sheffield.
--Steely Blue.
Smith, Dennis & Judd, John, eds. Blood Banking in a Changing Environment.
Smith, Dian G. Careers in the Visual Arts: Talking with Professionals.
Smith, Dick. Fun Way into Electronics.
Smith, Don & Smith, Jo-An. The Housebuying Checklist.
Smith, Don I. By the River of No Return.
Smith, Donald E. & Gomon, Audrey. Prescribing for Deficits in Reading & Writing.
Smith, Donald E., jt. auth. see Geake, R. Robert.
Smith, Donald E., ed. see Smith, Judith M.
Smith, Donald G. And They Also Kick You When You're Down: An Irreverent Guide to the Way the Real World Works.
Smith, Doris B. Salted Lemons.
Smith, Doris D. A Limb of Your Tree: The Story of an Adopted Twin's Search for Her Roots.
Smith, Doris S. The Country Life of J. B. Rabbit.
Smith, Douglas. Hotel & Restaurant Design.
Smith, Duane A. Horace Tabor: His Life & the Legend.
--A Taste of the West: Essays in Honor of Robert G. Athearn. Smith, Duane A., ed.
Smith, Dwight L., ed. The History of Canada: An Annotated Bibliography.
Smith, E. Village Children.
Smith, E. Brooks & Meredith, Robert. The Coming of the Pilgrims.
--Pilgrim Courage.
Smith, E. E. & Ribbons, D. W., eds. Molecular Approaches to Immunology.
Smith, E. L., jt. ed. see Cool, J.
Smith, Ed D., jt. ed. see Wu, Yeun C.

Smith, Edward E. Skylark Three. Del Rey, Lester, ed.
Smith, Edward E. & Garby, Lee H. The Skylark of Space. Del Rey, Lester, ed.
Smith, Edward J. There Is No Happiness Without a Feeling.
Smith, Edward L., jt. auth. see Gross, Stephen H.
Smith, Edward L. see Lucie-Smith, Edward.
Smith, Edwin, photos by. The Romantic Eye.
Smith, Edwin W. & Dale, A. M. Ila-Speaking Peoples of Northern Rhodesia.
Smith, Elinor. Aviatrix.
Smith, Elisabeth E., jt. auth. see Whitall, Hannah.
Smith, Elizabeth S., jt. auth. see Corbett, J. Elliott.
Smith, Elsdon C. Personal Names: A Bibliography.
Smith, Elske P. & Jacobs, Kenneth C. Introductory Astronomy & Astrophysics.
Smith, Elwyn A. Religious Liberty in the United States: The Development of Church-State Thought Since the Revolutionary Era.
--A Spiritual Exercise for New Parents.
Smith, Elwyn A., ed. Religion of the Republic: Is There an American Religion.
Smith, Emma. No Way of Telling.
Smith, Eric. Some Versions of the Fall: The Myth of the Fall of Man in English Literature.
Smith, Euclid O. Social Plays in Primates.
Smith, Eugene H. & Baron, Marvin J. Faculty Member's Guide to the U. S. Immigration Law.
Smith, Eugenie. One More Time for Rhyme.
Smith, Eugenie B. Mix 'n Match.
Smith, F., et al. Teaching Mathematics in the Elementary School: Selected Readings.
Smith, F. B., jt. auth. see Eastwood, J. J.
Smith, F. G. Prophetic Lectures on Daniel & Revelations.
Smith, Frank. Comprehension & Learning: A Conceptual Framework for Teachers.
--Tron Computer Age Activities. Klimo, Kate, ed.
--Understanding Reading.
--Writing & the Writer.
Smith, Frank J. & Dunham, Randall. Organizational Surveys: An Internal Assessment of Organizational Health.
Smith, Frank K. Flying the Bahamas: The Weekend Pilot's Guide.
--How to Take Great Photos from Airplanes.
Smith, Franklin H. Beneath the Eagle's Eye.
Smith, Fred. You & Your Network.
Smith, Fred H. The Meanarthal Remains from Krapina.
Smith, Frederick R. The Minder: The Story of the Courtship, Call & Conflicts of John Ledger, Minder & Minister, 1900. Wolff, Robert L., ed. Bd. with The Coming of the Preachers: A Tale of the Rise of Methodism, 1901. Garland Pub.
Smith, G. Dallas. Outline of Bible Study.
Smith, G. Dallas, ed. Outlines of Bible Study: An Easy-to-Follow Guide to Greater Bible Knowledge.
Smith, G. E. Architecture in America: A Pictorial History. Davidson, Marshal B., intro. by.
Smith, G. Geoffrey. Gas Turbines & Jet Propulsion.
Smith, G. N. Elements of Soil Mechanics for Civil & Mining Engineers.
--Elements of Soil Mechanics for Civil & Mining Engineers.
Smith, G. V. Cast Metals for Structural & Pressure Containment Application: MPC-11.
Smith, G. V., ed. Characterization of Materials for Service at Elevated Temperatures, MPC-7.
--Ductility & Toughness Considerations in Elevated Temperature Service: MPC-8.
--Effects of Melting & Processing Variables on Mechanical Properties of Steels, Series MPC-6.
--Properties of Steel Weldments for Elevated Temperature Pressure Containment Applications: MPC-9.
Smith, Gaddis. Dean Acheson. Ferrel, Robert H., ed.
Smith, Garry & Smith, Vesta. Poco.
Smith, Gary R. Teaching about Colorado & Community History.
Smith, Gary R., jt. auth. see Otero, George G.
Smith, Gene. The Shattered Dream: Herbert Hoover & the Great Depression.
Smith, Genevieve L. & Davis, Phyllis E. Medical Terminology: A Programmed Text.
Smith, Geoffrey & Brown, Paul B. Sweat Equity: What it Really Takes to Build America's Best Small Companies - By the Guys Who Did It.
Smith, George F. & Vidyasagar, Dharmapuri. Historical Reviews & Recent Advances in Perinatal Medicine.
Smith, George V., ed. Material-Environment Interactions in Structural & Pressure Containment Devices.
Smith, George W., jt. ed. see Siegla, Donald C.
Smith, Gerald, ed. see Tozer, W.
Smith, Gerald B., jt. ed. see Mathews, Shailer.
Smith, Gerard V., ed. Catalysis in Organic Synthesis, 1977.
Smith, Gerry, tr. see Galich, Alexander.
Smith, Glen C. Evangelizing Adults.
Smith, Glenn, jt. auth. see Cooper, Jerry.
Smith, Glenn C. Evangelizing Youth.
Smith, Glenn H. Langer of North Dakota: A Study in Isolationism 1940-1959. Freidel, Frank, ed.
Smith, Gordon B., et al, eds. Soviet & East European Law & the Scientific-Technical Revolution.
Smith, Gregory W., jt. auth. see Naifeh, Steven.
Smith, Griffin, Jr. & Bradshaw, Reagan. Forgotten Texas. Rodriquez, Barbara, ed.
Smith, Gus, jt. auth. see Hickey, Des.
Smith, H. Commentaries in the Neurosciences: International Student Edition.
Smith, H., ed. Commentaries in Plant Science.
Smith, H. Allen. Larks in the Popcorn.
Smith, H. Daniel. Reading the Ramayana: A Bibliographic Guide for Students & College Teachers. Indian Variants on the Rama Theme in English Translations.
--The Smith Agama Collection: Sanskrit Books & Manuscripts Relating to Pancaratra Studies- a Descriptive Catalog.
Smith, H. J. & Williams, H. Introduction to the Principles of Drug Design.
Smith, H. R., jt. auth. see Dickson, G. W.
Smith, Hallett, jt. ed. see Lamson, Roy.
Smith, Hannah W. Daily He Leads Me: Inspirational Devotions for Every Day of the Year. Spangler, Ann, ed.
Smith, Harry, ed. Commentaries in Plant Science.
Smith, Hattie. Let's Talk it Over God!
Smith, Helen B., jt. auth. see Smith, Allan B.
Smith, Henry. The Master Dictionary of Food & Cookery & Menu Translator.
Smith, Henry C. & Wakeley, John H. Psychology of Industrial Behavior.
Smith, Henry N. Mark Twain: The Development of a Writer.
Smith, Henry N., ed. see Clemens, Samuel L.
Smith, Henry P. Glossary of Terms & Phrases.
Smith, Herb, ed. see Architectural Record Magazine Editors.
Smith, Herbert F. The Popular American Novel, 1865-1920.
--Sexual Inversion: The Questions-with Catholic Answers.
Smith, Herschel. Aircraft Piston Engines: From the Manly Baltzer to the Continental Tiara.
Smith, Howard E., Jr. From Under the Earth: America's Metals, Fuels, & Minerals.
Smith, Howard R. The Capitalistic Imperative: The New Biology & the Old Bureaucracy.
Smith, Hugh J., et al. Management: Making Organizations Perform.
--Readings in Management: Making Organization Peform.
Smith, Huston. Beyond the Post-Modern Mind.
--Beyond the Post-Modern Mind.
--The Purposes of Higher Education.
Smith, I. E. Combustion in Advanced Gas Turbine Systems.
Smith, I. M. Programming the Finite Element Method with Application to Geomechanics.
Smith, Iain C. On the Island.
Smith, J. C. Jacoby's First Case.
Smith, J. D. The Chemistry of Arsenic, Antimony & Bismuth.
Smith, J. D., jt. ed. see Celis, J. E.
Smith, J. David. Minds Made Feeble: The Myth & Legacy of the Kallikaks.
Smith, J. E., ed. Integrated Injection Logic.
Smith, J. F., jt. auth. see Chang, Y. A.
Smith, J. F., ed. see TMS Staff & AIME Staff.
Smith, J. M. A History of Australian Vegetation.
Smith, J. P. Body & Soul.
Smith, J. Richard & Creek, Eddie J. Dornier 335.
--Messerschmitt 262 A-1.
Smith, J. Richard, et al. Focke-Wulf 190 D. Hitchcock, Thomas H., ed.
Smith, J. T., jt. ed. see Hamilton-Miller, J. M.
Smith, J. V. Feldspar Minerals, Vol. 2: Chemical & Textural Properties.
Smith, Jack. Jack Smith's L.A.
Smith, Jackie M. Face to Face.
--Is God Cruel?
Smith, Jackie M., jt. auth. see Pennell, Lucy.
Smith, Jackson A. Up Your Spirits: Everything You Wanted to Know About Alcohol but Were Not Quite Sober Enough (or Too Scared) to Ask.
Smith, Jaclyn. The American Look.
--Jaclyn Smith Beauty Book.
Smith, James, ed. see Leffler, John F.
Smith, James E. What the Bible Says about the Promised Messiah.
Smith, James E., jt. auth. see Peterson, John M.
Smith, James H. History of Dutchess County, New York: 1683-1882.
Smith, James R. Hard-Core: A Study of the Unemployables in Contemporary American Society.
Smith, Jamesetta. How Strong Is Strong.
Smith, Jane S. & Carlson, Betty. A Gift of Music.
Smith, Jean L. Good News Anyone.
Smith, Jean R. Hyacinth from Limbo & Other Stories.
Smith, Jean R., jt. auth. see McGill, Shirley L.
Smith, Jeffery M. Preventing Legal Malpractice.
Smith, Jerome & Miroff, Franklin I. You're Our Child: A Social-Psychological Approach to Adoption.
Smith, Jewell E. Great Jehoshaphat & Gully Dirt!
Smith, Jim. Abnormal Behaviors: Outlined Reference.
--The Frog Band & the Onion Seller.
Smith, Jo-An, jt. auth. see Smith, Don.
Smith, Jo L., jt. auth. see Stein, Marshall D.
Smith, Joan. Babe.
Smith, Joan F. & Nachazel, Delbert P. Ophthalmologic Nursing.
Smith, Joan M., ed. State Legislative Summary 1985: Children & Youth Issues.
Smith, Joanmarie, jt. auth. see Durka, Gloria.
Smith, John. Skytrap: An Adventure Novel.
Smith, John F., compiled by. A Critical Bibliography of Building Conservation: Historic Towns, Buildings, Their Furnishings & Fittings.
Smith, John M. The Complete Bible: An American Translation. Goodspeed, Edgar J., ed.
--Prophets & Their Times. Irwin, William A., ed.
Smith, Jon, jt. auth. see Jenkins, John.
Smith, Jon M. Mathematical Modeling & Digital Simulation for Engineers & Scientists.
Smith, Jonathan C. Relaxation Dynamics: Nine World Approaches to Self-Relaxation.
Smith, Joseph B. The Plot to Steal Florida: James Madison's Phony War.
Smith, Joseph C. This Was My Life.
Smith, Joseph H. & Kerrigan, William, eds. Interpreting Lacan.
Smith, Joyce M. Art History: A Study Guide. Masters, Janet F., tr.
--Growing When You Don't Feel Like It.
--A Listening Heart.
--A Rejoicing Heart.
--Young Disciples.
Smith, Joyce Marie. The Significance of Jesus.
Smith, Judith M. Letter Mastery. Smith, Donald E., ed.
Smith, K. C., ed. The Science of Photobiology.
Smith, K. M. & Holroyd, P. Engineering Principles for Electrical Technicians.
Smith, K. M. & Ritchie, D. A. Introduction to Virology.
Smith, K. M; see Luria, S. E.
Smith, Karl J. The Nature of Mathematics.
--Trigonometry for College Students.
Smith, Kat. The Informed Performer's Directory of Instruction for the Performing Arts.
Smith, Kathy & Jones, Judy. Katy Smith's Winning Workout.
Smith, Keith V. Readings on the Management of Working Capital.
Smith, Kendric C. & Hanawalt, Philip C. Molecular Photobiology: Inactivation & Recovery.
Smith, Kenn. Flower of Gold.
Smith, Kenneth A., jt. auth. see Francisco, Albert K.
Smith, Kenneth C., jt. auth. see Sedra, Adele S.
Smith, Kenneth H. American Economic History.
--International Trade.
--Money & Banking.
--Taxes.
Smith, Kennwyn K., jt. auth. see Berg, David N.
Smith, Kent D. Faith: Reflections on Experience, Theology & Fiction.
Smith, L. L. Ice Is Also Great.
Smith, L. Neil. Lando Calrissian & the Flamewind of Oseon.
--Lando Calrissian & the Starcave of Thonboka.
Smith, L. T., ed. see Kyngeston, Richard.
Smith, Lacey B. A History of England, Vol. I: The Making of England 55 B. C. to 1399. Hollister, C. W., ed.
Smith, Lana J., jt. auth. see Smith, Dennie L.
Smith, Lawrence, et al. The British Museum, London.
Smith, Lawrence B., jt. auth. see Officer, Lawrence H.
Smith, Lee, jt. auth. see Slater, Harry.
Smith, Len Y., et al. Business Law.
Smith, Lendon. Dr. Lendon Smith's Diet Plan for Teenagers.
--Dr. Lendon Smith's Low-Stress Diet.
--Feed Your Kids Right: Dr. Smith's Program for Your Child's Total Health.
--Feed Yourself Right.
Smith, Leta May. The End of the Trail.
Smith, Lillian. Our Faces, Our Words.
--The Winner Names the Age: A Collection of Writings. Cliff, Michelle, ed.
Smith, Lillian V. English Reserve - Italian Fire.
Smith, Linda C., ed. New Information Technologies-New Opportunities: Proceedings of the Clinic on Library Applications of Data Processing, 1981.
Smith, Lloyd H. & Wyngaarden, James B. Cecil Review of General Internal Medicine.
Smith, Lloyd M. The Manager's Digest: A Handbook for Decision-Making.
Smith, Logan P. All Trivia.
--A Chime of Words: The Letters of Logan Pearsall Smith. Tribble, Edwin, ed.
--Words & Idioms.
Smith, Logan P., et al. Needed Words. Commager, Steele, ed. Incl. The B.B.L.'s Recommendations for Pronouncing Doubtful Words; The Bull's Bellow; The Possibility of a Universal Language; Robert Bridges Recollections; Colloquial Language in Literature; Oxford English; Arabic Words in English; The Best English; Index to Tracts XXI-XXIX. Garland Pub.
Smith, Louis A. & Barndt, Joseph R. Beyond Brokenness.
Smith, Lucia B. My Mom Got a Job.
Smith, Lydia A. Activity & Experience: Sources of English Informal Education.
Smith, Lynn S., jt. auth. see Brown, Clara D.
Smith, M. B. The Single Woman of Today.
Smith, M. Daniel. Educational Psychology & Its Classroom Applications.
Smith, M. Pamela, Sr. Waymakers: Eyewitnesses to the Christ.
Smith, Marcelle d'Argy, ed. International Art & Antiques Yearbook Nineteen Seventy-Nine to Nineteen Eighty.
Smith, Margaret F. Articulation Worksheets: For Remediation & Carryover of Speech & Language Skills.
--Speech, Language & Reading Worksheets: Fun with Language.
Smith, Marilyn Z., jt. auth. see Cooper, Laura G.
Smith, Marilyn Z., jt. auth. see Lewis, Theodore G.
Smith, Marion, jt. ed. see Sargent, S. Stansfeld.
Smith, Marion C., jt. auth. see Mulcahy, Charles C.
Smith, Marion H. & Prescott, Carol S. Families Around the World.
--Our Earth.
Smith, Marion H., jt. auth. see Jennings, Jerry E.
Smith, Marion H., jt. auth. see Prescott, Carol S.
Smith, Mark. The Death of the Detective.
Smith, Mark & Black, Naomi. The American Mail-Order Gourmet: The Catalog of Hundreds of Hard-to-Find Delectable Delights.
Smith, Martin. Maxims of Management: Working Smart to Increase Profits.
Smith, Martin B. Five-Line Frolics: Two Hundred Ten Original Limericks.
Smith, Martin C. Canto for a Gypsy.
--Gypsy in Amber.
--Nightwing: A Novel.
Smith, Martin R. Manufacturing Controls: How the Manufacturing Manager Can Improve Profitability.
Smith, Marvin B. Handbook of Ocular Pharmacology.
--Handbook of Ocular Toxicity.
Smith, Mary. Baba of Karo.
Smith, Mary, tr. see Buhlmann, Walbert.
Smith, Mary-Ann T. Book of Phoebe.
Smith, Mary C. Mothers.
Smith, Maury, jt. auth. see Hall, Brian.
Smith, Mavis, jt. auth. see Ziefert, Harriet.
Smith, May. Handbook of Industrial Psychology.
Smith, Michael see Hoffman, William M.
Smith, Michael, jt. auth. see Harri-Augstein, Sheila.
Smith, Michael A. Legacy of the Lake.
Smith, Michael D., ed. see Ruder, Kenneth F.
Smith, Michael L., jt. auth. see Bertin, John J.
Smith, Michael P., & Associates Staff. Politics in America: Studies in Policy Analysis.
Smith, Mickey C., ed. Principles of Pharmaceutical Marketing.
Smith, Moody D. Johannine Christianity: Essays on Its Setting, Sources, & Theology.
Smith, Morton. The Secret Gospel: The Discovery & Interpretation of the Secret Gospel According to Mark.
Smith, Nancy A. Old Furniture: Understanding the Craftsman's Art.
Smith, Nathan J. Food for Sport.
Smith, Neil. Uneven Development: Nature, Capital & the Production of Space.
Smith, Nick, ed. Federal Efforts for Developing New Evaluative Methods.
Smith, Nick L., ed. Field Assessments of Innovative Evaluation Methods.
Smith, Nila B. Be a Better Reader, Canadian Ed. Jenkinson, M., et al, eds.
Smith, Norman, jt. ed. see Hall, A. Rupert.
Smith, Norman B., jt. auth. see Follin, Marion G., III.
Smith, Norman F. Energy Isn't Easy.
--Inside Story of Metal.
Smith, O. C., Jr. The First Collected Insights of the Prophet O. C.
Smith, Oscar E., Jr. Yankee Diplomacy: U. S. Intervention in Argentina.

Smith, P. & Morrison, W. I. Simulating the Urban Economy.
Smith, P. A. Derivatives of Hydrazine & Other Hydronitogens Having N-N Bonds.
Smith, P. H., jt. ed. see Pavone-Macaluso, M.
Smith, P. R. Advances in Computer-Assited Learning: Selected Proceedings from the CAL 85 Symposium.
--Air Portfolios No. 1: Boeing 737.
--Air Portfolios No. 2: Shorts 330 & 360.
--Air Portfolios No. 3: Douglas DC-9 & McDonnell Douglas MD-80.
--Air Portfolios No. 4: Airbus A300 & 310.
--Air Portfolios, No. 5: Boeing 727.
--Air Portfolios, No. 6: DeHavilland Canada DHC-6, DHC-7, & DHC-8.
Smith, P. R., ed. Instructional Technology: Selected Proceedings of the Fourth Canadian Symposium, Winnipeg, Canada, October 1983.
Smith, Page. Reflections on the Nature of Leadership.
--Shaping of America: A People's History of the Young Republic.
--Trial by Fire: A People's History of the Civil War & Reconstruction.
Smith, Page & Daniel, Charles. The Chicken Book.
--The Chicken Book.
Smith, Patricia H. Illiteracy in America: Extent, Causes & Suggested Solutions.
Smith, Patricia J. The Golf Widow's Revenge.
Smith, Patrick D. Forever Island: A Novel.
Smith, Patti. Witt: A Book of Poems.
Smith, Paul. The Book of Nasty Legends.
--The Complete Book of Office Mispractice.
--Pound Revised.
--Reader's Guide to the Short Stories of Ernest Hemingway.
Smith, Paul, jt. auth. see Foulke, Robert.
Smith, Paul H. Loyalists & Redcoats: A Study in British Revolutionary Policy.
Smith, Paul. J. & Lucie-Smith, Edward. American Craft Today.
Smith, Paula W., et al. A Point in Time...Readings in Early Childhood Education.
Smith, Perry, et al. Creating Strategic Vision: Long-Range Planning for National Security.
Smith, Peter C. Stuka at War.
Smith, Peter C. & Karim, Mehtab S. Urbanization, Education, & Marriage Patterns: Four Cases from Asia.
Smith, Peter C., jt. auth. see Shah, Nasra M.
Smith, Peter J. Highlights of the Off-Season.
Smith, Philip. Total Breathing.
Smith, Philip D., jt. auth. see Smith, Robert M.
Smith, Philip K. & Shantar, Stan. Greenberg's Enjoying Lionel- Fundimensions Trains. Greenberg, Linda, ed.
Smith, Phyllis. A Look at Boulder: From Settlement to City.
Smith, R., jt. auth. see Aaronovitch, S.
Smith, R., ed. see Migraine Symposium, 2nd, London, 1967.
Smith, R. A., ed. Fatigue Crack Growth: Proceedings of a Conference on Fatigue Crack Growth, Cambridge, U. K. 09-20-1984.
--Fracture Mechanics, Current Status, Future Prospects: Proceedings of a Conference Held at Cambridge University, March 16, 1979.
Smith, R. B. Setting up Shop: The Do's & Dont's of Starting a Small Business.
Smith, R. Craig. Enjoy Golf & Win: Mental Golf--Its Impact on Scoring & Enjoyment.
Smith, R. Douglas, et al. Multiple Personality: Theory, Diagnosis & Treatment.
Smith, R. E. Sheet Metalwork.
Smith, R. F., jt. auth. see Miller, K. J.
Smith, R. H. Harbors, Anchorages & Marinas.
Smith, R. Michael. Coaching Junior High & Youth League Football.
Smith, R. Stafford. Local Income Taxes: Economic Effects & Equity.
Smith, Randall, jt. auth. see Means, Robin.
Smith, Ray & Smith, Catriona. The Long Dive.
--The Long Slide.
Smith, Ray F., jt. ed. see Apple, J. Lawrence.
Smith, Red. To Absent Friends.
Smith, Red, ed. Press Box: Red Smith's Favorite Sport Stories.
--Press Box: Red Smith's Favorite Sports Stories.
Smith, Reva A. Battle for Barbie. Wheeler, Gerald, ed.
Smith, Richard. The Dieter's Guide to Weight Loss after Sex.
--The Dieter's Stress Guide: A Weight-Loss Guide for Professional Eaters.
Smith, Richard & Van Der Meer, Ron. The Good Health Kit.
Smith, Richard D. & Dick, Ginger. Getting Sales: A Practical Guide to Getting More Sales for Your Business.
Smith, Richard H., photos by. Minnesota II.
Smith, Richard J., jt. auth. see Otto, Wayne.
Smith, Richard J., et al. The School Reading Program: A Handbook for Teachers, Supervisors, & Specialists.
Smith, Richard N. The Harvard Century: The Making of a University to a Nation.
--Thomas E. Dewey & His Times.
--An Uncommon Man: The Triumph of Herbert Hoover.
Smith, Richard P. Hunting Rabbits & Hares: The Complete Guide to North America's Favorite Small Game.
Smith, Richard T. Electrical Machine Analysis.
Smith, Richard T. & Landy, Maurice, eds. Immune Surveillance.
--Immunobiology of the Tumor-Host Relationship: Proceedings.
Smith, Rick, jt. auth. see Rath, Sara.
Smith, Robert. Hiking Kauai: The Garden Isle.
--Hiking Maui: The Valley Isle.
Smith, Robert, jt. auth. see Mullin, Raymond.
Smith, Robert, ed. Tarikh: Historical Method.
Smith, Robert & Kidd, J. Roby, eds. Handbook of Adult Education 1970.
Smith, Robert A., ed. Semiconductors.
Smith, Robert A., et al. Clinical Applications of Ribavirin.
Smith, Robert C. The Noble Savage.
Smith, Robert C. & Lounibos, John, eds. Pagan & Christian Anxiety: A Response to E. R. Dodds.
Smith, Robert E. Discovering BASIC: A Problem Solving Approach.
--Forging & Welding.
--Machine Woodworking.
--Patternmaking & Founding.
Smith, Robert F., Jr. Organic Gardening in the West: Raising Vegetables in a Short, Dry Growing Season.
Smith, Robert H. Association Meetings & Conventions in the 1990s.
--Bob Smith's Complete Guide to Harbors, Anchorages & Marinas.
--Bob Smith's Complete Guide to Harbors, Anchorages & Marinas.
--Easter Gospels: The Resurrection of Jesus According to the Four Evangelists.
Smith, Robert K. Chocolate Fever.
Smith, Robert L. Electrical Wiring: Industrial.
--Electrical Wiring-Industrial.
--Electrical Wiring-Industrial.
--A Tutorial for Using the TERAK-RT-11.
Smith, Robert L., jt. auth. see Marcus, Genevieve G.
Smith, Robert L., jt. auth. see Mullin, Ray C.
Smith, Robert M. Introduction to Mental Retardation.
Smith, Robert M. & Smith, Philip D. With Chennault in China: A Flying Tiger's Diary.
Smith, Robert M., jt. auth. see Neisworth, John T.
Smith, Robert O., jt. auth. see Rouse, Robert S.
Smith, Robert P. Where Did You Go? Out - What Did You Do? Nothing.
Smith, Robert R. Field Guide to the Vegetation of San Salvador Island, Bahamas.
--United States Army in World War 2: War in the Pacific, Triumph in the Philippines.
Smith, Robert S. The Lagos Consulate, 1851-1861.
Smith, Robert S., jt. auth. see Ehrenberg, Ronald G.
Smith, Robert T. How to Fly Lightplanes.
Smith, Robert T. & Practising Law Institute Staff. Project Financing 1986: Power Generation, Waste Recovery, & Other Industrial Facilities.
Smith, Robert W. Dictionary of English Word-Roots.
--Dictionary of English Word-Roots: English-Roots & Roots-English with Examples & Exercises.
Smith, Rodney. In the Land of Light: Israel, a Portrait of Its People.
Smith, Ronald. Alkan, the Enigma.
--Alkan: The Music.
Smith, Ronald G. Martin Buber.
Smith, Ronald G., tr. see Ebeling, Gerhard.
Smith, Ronald L. Let Peas Be with You: Food Poems.
Smith, Rowland. Lyric & Polemic: The Literary Personality of Roy Campbell.
Smith, Russell E. Electricity for Refrigeration, Heating, & Air Conditioning.
Smith, Ruth E. & Feltner, Hellen A. Price Guide to Miniature Lamps Combining Book I & II.
Smith, Samuel S. Lewis Morris, Anglo-American Statesman, ca 1613-1691.
Smith, Sandra F. NCLEX Review Questions.
--Sandra Smith's Review for NCLEX-RN.
Smith, Sandra F. & Duell, Donna. Clinical Nursing Skills.
Smith, Sandra F., ed. Review of Practical Nursing for State Board Examinations.
--Sandra Smith's Review of Nursing for State Board Examinations.
Smith, Scottie F., et al, eds. see Fitzgerald, F. Scott.
Smith, Seba. Way down East, or Portraitures of Yankee Life.
Smith, Sharon, ed. Handcraft Centers of New England.
Smith, Sharon, ed. see Janericco, Terence.
Smith, Sharon, ed. see Welsch, Ulrike.
Smith, Shirley J. Worklife Estimates: Effects of Race & Education.
Smith, Stan. Artist's Manual.
--Stan Smith's Six Tennis Basics. Sheehan, Larry, ed.
Smith, Stan, et al. Modern Tennis Doubles. Sheehan, Larry, ed.
Smith, Stephen P. An Officer & a Gentleman.
Smith, Steve, jt. auth. see Fox, Mike.
Smith, Steve, jt. auth. see Lazell, Barry.
Smith, Steven. Meister Eckhart.
Smith, Steven, jt. auth. see Gengle, Dean.
Smith, Steven P. The Long Riders.
Smith, Susan. Made in America.
Smith, Susan, jt. ed. see Jackson, Peter.
Smith, Susan, jt. ed. see Morad, Martin.
Smith, Susan H., jt. auth. see Georgia Hospitality & Travel Association Staff.
Smith, Susan H., jt. auth. see Louisiana Restaurant Association Staff.
Smith, Susan H., ed. see Young, Dale.
Smith, Syndey B. Sherca.
Smith, T., jt. ed. see Barker, J.
Smith, T. E. Elections in Developing Countries.
Smith, T. J., jt. ed. see Steinhart, J. S.
Smith, Terrence L. The Money War.
Smith, Theodore A. Dynamic Business Strategy: The Art of Planning for Success.
Smith, Thomas. De Republica Anglorum: A Discourse on the Commonwealth of England.
--The Good News about Jesus As Told by Mark. Pluth, Alphonsus, ed.
Smith, Thomas A. The Birds & Bee of Education.
Smith, Thomas H., ed. Ohio in the American Revolution.
Smith, Thomas J. Good News About Jesus As Told by Mark.
Smith, Thomas L. Brazil, Portrait of Half a Continent.
Smith, Thomas V., ed. Philosophers Speak for Themselves: From Aristotle to Plotinus.
Smith, Tilman R. Boards: Purposes, Organization, Procedures.
Smith, Tim D., jt. auth. see Fowler, Charles W.
Smith, Toby. Kid Blackie: The Colorado Days of Jack Dempsey.
--Romantic Inns of Mexico: A Selective Guide to Charming Accommodations South of the Border.
Smith, Tony, jt. auth. see Ramaswamy, Saroja.
Smith, Trevor. Homeopathic Medicine: A Doctor's Guide to Remedies for Common Ailments.
--The Homeopathic Treatment of Emotional Illness.
Smith, Vesta, jt. auth. see Smith, Garry.
Smith, Virginia. Alphagraphics.
Smith, Virginia C. & Alberger, Patricia L., eds. Involving Volunteers in Your Advancement Programs.
Smith, Virginia C. & Stubbs, Weslie S., eds. Case Currents Index, 1975-1984.
Smith, Vivian. The Poetry of Robert Lowell.
Smith, W. B. Birth of the Gospel.
Smith, W. H. Small Arms of the World: A Basic Manual of Small Arms.
Smith, W. H., jt. auth. see Ezelle, Edward C.
Smith, W. J., et al, eds. Optical Specifications: Components & Systems.
Smith, W. L., jt. auth. see Cox, D. R.
Smith, W. L. & Culbertson, J. M., eds. Public Finance & Stabilization Policy.
Smith, Wanda V. Love Knots.
Smith, Watson & Breternitz, David A., eds. Prehistoric Ceramics of the Mesa Verde Region. Rohn, Arthur H. & Morris, Elizabeth A.
Smith, Wendell, jt. auth. see Branch, Houston.
Smith, Wendy & Cohn, Stanton H. Osteoporosis: How to Prevent the Brittle-Bone Disease.
Smith, Whitney, ed. see Talocci, Mauro.
Smith, Wilbur. Cry Wolf.
--Eagle in the Sky.
--The Eye of the Tiger.
Smith, Wilfred C. Faith & Belief.
Smith, William. Ancient Education.
Smith, William, tr. see Fichte, Johann G.
Smith, William A., Jr. & Wechsler, Ben L. Planning Guide for Information System Evaluation Studies.
Smith, William C. Was It Murder (Centralia Massacre)
Smith, William D. Multitude of Men.
Smith, William E., et al. Design of Organizations for Rural Development Projects: A Progress Report.
Smith, William F. Noticiario: Primer Nivel.
--The Shaping of the Earth.
Smith, William F. & Liedlich, Raymond D. From Thought to Theme.
--From Thought to Theme: A Rhetoric & Reader for College English.
--From Thought to Theme: A Rhetoric & Reader for College English.
--Rhetoric for Today.
--Rhetoric for Today.
--Rhetoric for Today.
Smith, William H. Tree Pathology.
Smith, William J., ed. Granger's Index to Poetry.
Smith, William Jay, tr. see Lundkvist, Artur.
Smith, William K. Handbook of Strategic Growth Through Mergers & Acquisitions.
Smith, William R. The Prophets of Israel.
Smith, Wm. Flint & Medley, Frank. Noticiario: Segundo Nivel.
Smith, Wm. Flint & Nieman, Linda. Noticiario: Tercer Nivel.
Smitherman, Geneva. Talkin' & Testifyin' The Language of Black America.
Smithers, David. Dicken's Doctors.
Smithers, Jack. Combined Forces.
Smithfield, Leonard S., Jr. From Hell to Heaven.
Smithson, Alison & Smithson, Peter. Without Rhetoric: An Architectural Aesthetic 1955-1972.
Smithson, Peter, jt. auth. see Smithson, Alison.
Smithsonian Institution, Washington, D. C. Staff. Catalog to Manuscripts at the National Anthropological Archives.
--Dictionary Catalog of the Library of the Freer Gallery of Art.
--Index to Grass Species. Chase, Agnes & Niles, Cornelia D., eds.
Smithsonian Magazine Editors. Best of Smithsonian.
Smithsonian Science Information Exchange Inc. Energy Research & Development Activity 1974-1976.
Smithy-Willis, Deborrah, et al. How to Use SuperCalc.
Smithy-Willis, Debra & Willis, Jerry. How to Use SuperCalc.
Smits, Myrtle H. Compiled by see Howard, Rev. Fielding T.
Smitten, Richard. Twice Killed.
Smoak, Dona V. & Isaacsen-Bright. Crazy Town.
--Crazy Town.
Smock, David R. Conflict & Control in an African Trade Union: A Study of the Nigerian Coal Miner's Union.
Smock, Winston. Technical Writing for Beginners.
Smoke & Isaacsen-Bright. Crazy Town. Holland, Margaret, ed.
Smoke, Jim. Turning Points.
Smoke, Jim & Guest, Lisa. Growing Through Divorce: Working Guide.
Smolan, Rick & Cohen, David. A Day in the Life of Hawaii.
Smolensky, Eugene, jt. ed. see Moon, M. L.
Smoler, Roberta W., tr. see Troisgros, Jean & Troisgros, Pierre.
Smoler, Roberta W., tr. see Verge, Roger.
Smolin, Pauline & Clayton, Philip T. Words: Form & Function.
Smolin, Ronald P., ed. Directory of Public High Technology & Medical Corporations, 1988.
Smolinski, Leon, intro. by. Kantorovich: Essays in Optimal Planning.
Smolka, Gerry, jt. auth. see Leat, Diana.
Smollar, Jacqueline, jt. auth. see Youniss, James.
Smollett, Tobias G. Roderick Random.
Smolowe, John, jt. auth. see Deliman, Tracy.
Smoodin, Roberta. Inventing Ivanov.
--Presto!
Smorodinsky, M. Ergodic Theory, Entropy.
Smrtic, James D. Abnormal Psychology, A Perspectives Approach.
Smullyan, R. M. First-Order Logic.
Smullyan, Raymond. The Chess Mysteries of Sherlock Holmes.
Smuskiewicz, Ted. Creative Painting of Everyday Subjects.
Smykatz-Kloss, W. Differential Thermal Analysis: Application & Results in Mineralogy.
Smykla, John O. Community Based Corrections.
--Probation & Parole: Crime Control in the Community.
Smyth, Bernard T. Paul: Mystic & Missionary.
Smyth, Charles H. Cranmer & the Reformation under Edward VI.
Smyth, D. G., et al. Oxytocin: Current Research.
Smyth, Michael P. Linear Engineering Systems: Tools & Techniques.
Smyth, Peter R. A Guide to Marine Photography.
Smyth, Thomas. More Wandering Thoughts.
--Still More Wandering Thoughts.
--Wandering Thoughts.
--Wandering Thoughts Again Wander.
--Wandering Thoughts Doze.
--Wandering Thoughts Sleep.
--Wandering Thoughts Still Come.
--Yet More Wandering Thoughts.
Smyth, W. Franklin, ed. Polarography of Molecules of Biological Significance.
Smyth, William. Lessons of History.
Smythe, John. The Game's the Same.
Smythe, Kathleen. Seashells of the Arabian Gulf.
Smythe, Lewis. The Christian in Today's World: Inner City to World Community.
Smythe, Reginald. Andy Capp: Man of the Hour.
--Andy Capp: This Is War.
--Hard at Work, Andy Capp.
--In Your Eye, Andy Capp.
--Let's Salute Andy Capp.
--Like Your Style, Andy Capp.
--Live It up Andy Capp.
--Meet Andy Capp.
--Nice to See You, Andy Capp!
--Right on Cue, Andy Capp.
--Right on Time Andy Capp.
--Take a Bow, Andy Capp.
--The Undisputed Andy Capp.

--You Were Saying, Andy Capp.
--You're a Right Hero, Andy Capp.
--You're All Heart, Andy Capp.
--You're the Boss, Andy Capp.
Smythe, Seymour. Culture & Immorality As Forces Capable to Create & Destroy Nations & the Position of the United States in the Conflict.
Smythies, J. R. Brain Mechanisms & Behaviour.
Smythies, John R. & Bradley, Ronald J., eds. Receptors in Pharmacology.
Snaffles, jt. auth. see Keane, Molly.
Snape, W. H. How to Find Out about Local Government.
Snead, Sam & Sheehan, Larry. Sam Snead: Teaches You His Simple "Key Approach" to Golf.
Snead, Sam & Stump, Al. Education of a Golfer.
Sneck, William J. Charismatic Spiritual Gifts: A Phenomenological Analysis.
Snedaker, Samuel C., jt. ed. see Hamilton, Lawrence S.
Sneddon, I. N. Applications of Integral Transforms in the Theory of Elasticity.
Sneddon, I. N., ed. Encyclopedic Dictionary of Mathematics for Engineers.
Sneeden, R. P. Organochromium Compounds.
Sneen, David. Visions of Hope: Apocalyptic Themes from Biblical Times.
Snegirev, V., jt. auth. see Tretyak, Vladislav.
Snell, E. E., et al, eds. Chemical & Biological Aspects of Pyridoxal Catalysis.
Snell, Foster D., et al. Colorimetric Methods of Analysis: Inorganic Determinations Including Photometric Methods. Incl. Krieger.
Snell, Frank M., ed. Progress in Theoretical Biology.
Snell, George D. & Hildemann, W. H. Cell Surface Antigens: Studies in Mammals Other Than Man.
Snell, K. S. & Morgan, J. B. Elementary Analysis.
Snell, Nigel. David's First Day at School.
--Peter Gets a Hearing Aid.
Sneller, Anne G. Vanished World.
Snellgrove, David. Buddhist Himalaya.
--Himalayan Pilgrimage: A Study of Tibetan Religion.
Snellgrove, L. E. Franco & the Spanish Civil War.
Snelling, George N. Born into Eternity.
Snelling, Laurence. Long Shadows.
--The Temptation of Archer Watson.
Snetselaar, Linda G. Nutrition Counseling Skills: Assessment, Treatment & Evaluation.
Snider. Economics: Principles & Issues.
Snider, Arthur J. & Adatto, I. J. A Doctor Discusses Learning to Live with Heart Trouble.
Snider, H. Wayne. Life Insurance Investment in Commercial Real Estate.
Snider, Harold. That Amazing Book-Genesis!
Snitzer, Herb, jt. auth. see Cohen, Joel.
SnO Publications Staff, ed. The Norman Rockwell Bicycle Tour of Stockbridge.
Sno, William. Carnival of Demons.
Snodgrass, Melinda. The Tears of the Singers.
Snodin, David. A Mighty Ferment: Britain in the Age of Revolution, 1750-1850.
Snodin, Michael. English Silver Spoons.
Snodrass, Jon, jt. auth. see Jack-Roller.
Snodsmith, Ralph. Tips from the Garden Hotline.
Snook, Barbara. Puppets.
Snook, Harry J., jt. auth. see Johnson, Myrtle E.
Snook, Lee E. The Anonymous Christ: Jesus As Savior in Modern Theology.
Snopek, Albert M. Fundamentals of Special Radiographic Procedures.
Snow, C. P. In Their Wisdom.
--The Physicists.
--Strangers & Brothers: Omnibus Edition.
Snow, Edgar. Red Star over China.
Snow, Edward R. Boston Bay Mysteries & Other Tales.
--Marine Mysteries & Dramatic Disasters of New England.
Snow, G. A., jt. ed. see Franklin, T. J.
Snow, Helen F. My China Years: A Memoir.
Snow, John H. & Furnish, Victor P. Easter.
Snow, Joseph T. Celestina by Fernando de Rojas: An Annotated Bibliography of World Interest 1930-1985.
Snow, Leo. Southern Dreams & Trojan Women.
--Southern Dreams & Trojan Women.
Snow, Peter G. Argentine Radicalism.
Snow, Philip. Stranger & Brother: A Portrait of C. P. Snow.
Snow, Richard F. Freelon Starbird.
Snow, Theodore P., Jr. The Dynamic Universe: An Introduction to Astronomy.
Snowden, R. & Mitchell, G. D. The Artificial Family: A Consideration of Artificial Insemination by Donor.
Snowdon. Israel: A First View.
Snowdon, Sondra. The Global Edge: How Your Company Can Win in the International Marketplace.
Snowman, Daniel. The World of Placido Domingo.
Snowman, Daniel, ed. If I Had Been... Ten Historical Fantasies.
Snowran, Jack, jt. auth. see Biehler, Robert F.
Snuggs, Henry L., tr. see Giraldi, Cinthio.
Snyder, A. W. & Menzel, R., eds. Photoreceptor Optics.
Snyder, Bernadette M. Everyday Prayers for Everyday People.
--Hoorays & Hosannas.
Snyder, Bernhart R., rev. by see Keir, Jack & Lundy, Carl P.
Snyder, Chuck. Other Than That I Have No Opinion.
Snyder, Don. Aquarian Odyssey: A Nineteen Sixties Album.
Snyder, Eugene F. From a Doctor's Heart.
Snyder, Fred, ed. Lipid Metabolism in Mammals. Incl. Vol. 1; Vol. 2. Plenum Pub.
Snyder, Fred L., ed. Ether Lipids: Chemistry & Biology.
Snyder, Graydon & Shaffer, Kenneth. Texts in Transit.
Snyder, H. A., jt. ed. see Timmerhaus, K. D.
Snyder, James C., ed. Architectural Research.
Snyder, James P., ed. Nonbenzenoid Aromatics.
Snyder, Jerome, jt. auth. see Rand, Ann.
Snyder, Joel. American Frontiers: The Photographs of Timothy H. O'Sullivan 1867-1874.
Snyder, Leslie. Gold & Black Gold: Basic Value Investing for the New Economic Era.
--Why Gold? The One Sure Cure for Inflation & Economic Tyranny.
Snyder, Llewellyn R. Computational Arithmetic.
Snyder, Louis L. War: A Concise History, 1939-1945.
Snyder, Louis L., ed. Documents of German History.
Snyder, Mariah, ed. A Guide to Neurological & Neurosurgical Nursing.
Snyder, Mary E. Crackle Weave.
Snyder, Paul. Health & Human Nature.
Snyder, Richard V. Color Creations in Buttercream.
--Decorating Cakes for Fun & Profit.
--Sixty-Five Buttercream Flowers.
--Twenty Eight More Floral Creations for Cake Decorators.
--Twenty-Nine New Floral Creations for Cake Decorators.
--Twenty-Seven Special Creations for Cake Decorators.
Snyder, Solomon, jt. ed. see Usdin, Earl.
Snyder, Solomon H. Madness & the Brain.
Snyder, Thomas D. Digest of Education Statistics, 1987.
Snyder, Thomas L. & Bauer, Jeffrey C. Personalized Guide to Establishing Associateships & Partnerships.
Snyder, Thomas L. & Berning, Randall K. Personalized Guide to Legal Issues.
Snyder, Thomas L. & Domer, Larry R. Personalized Guide to Practice Evaluation.
Snyder, Thomas L. & Felimeister, Charles J., eds. Personalized Guide to Stress Evaluation.
Snyder, Thomas L. & Felmeister, Charles J., eds. Personalized Guide to Computers & Your Dental Practice.
--Personalized Guide to Marketing Strategy.
Snyder, Thomas L., et al, eds. Personalized Guide to Financial Planning.
Snyder, W. S., et al, eds. Radiation Protection: Proceedings of the First International Congress.
Snyder, William. Tory's.
Snyder, Zilpha K. The Birds of Summer.
--Black & Blue Magic.
--A Fabulous Creature.
--Heirs of Darkness.
--Today Is Saturday.
Snyderman, M., et al. Mediators of the Allergic State: Recent Investigations I.
Snypp, Wilbur & Hunter, Bob. The Buckeyes: A Story of Ohio State Football.
So, Frank, intro. by. Planning Nineteen Eighty-One.
Soal, Samuel G. & Bateman, F. Modern Experiments in Telepathy.
Soames, Mary. Clementine Churchill: The Biography of a Marriage.
--Family Album: A Personal Selection from Four Generations of Churchills.
Soames, Nicolas, jt. auth. see Fromm, Alan.
Soards, Marion L. The Passion According to Luke: The Special Material of Luke 22.
Soare, M. Application of Finite Difference Equations to Shell Analysis.
Soares, Robert, et al. Applications of GaAs MESFETs.
Sobczak, Joan, ed. Wife Savers III.
Sobeck, Joan, jt. auth. see Cyr, John.
Sobejano, Gonzalo & Keller, Gary D., eds. Cuentos Espanoles Concertados.
Sobek's International Explorers Society Staff, ed. Sobek Adventure Vacations.
Sobel, David S. Ways of Health: Holistic Approaches to Ancient & Contemporary Medicine.
Sobel, David S., ed. Ways of Health: Holistic Approaches to Ancient & Contemporary Medicine.
Sobel, Joseph J., jt. auth. see Bayer, Barry D.
Sobel, Lester. Peacemaking in the Middle East.
Sobel, Max, jt. auth. see Meserve, Bruce E.
Sobel, Max A. & Banks, J. Houston. Algebra: Its Elements & Structure.
Sobel, Max A. & Lerner, Norbert. Algebra & Trigonometry: A Pre-Calculus Approach.
Sobel, Max A., jt. auth. see Meserve, Bruce E.
Sobel, Robert. Inside Wall Street: Continuity & Change in the Financial District.
--The Last Bull Market.
Sobel, Robert S. Quit for Life: The Sensational New Program for Smokers.
Sobel, Rochelle S. Mi Ani? (Who Am I?)
Sobel, Ruth. Gogol's Forgotten Book: Selected Passages & Its Contemporary Readers.
Sobel'man, I. I. Introduction to the Theory of Atomic Spectra.
Soberman, Richard M. Transport Technology for Developing Regions: A Study of Road Transportation in Venezuela.
Sobieszek, Robert A., ed. The Architectural Photography of Hedrich-Blessing.
Sobin, Anthony. The Sunday Naturalist.
Sobin, L. H., jt. auth. see Zimmerman, L. E.
Sobol, Dorothy M. Europe Confronts the Dollar: The Creation of the SDR, 1963-69.
Sobol, Harriet L. My Other-Mother, My Other-Father.
Sobol, I. M. The Monte Carlo Method. Fortini, Peter, et al, trs. from Rus.
--Monte Carlo Method.
Sobol, Ken. A Cosmic Christmas.
--The Devil & Daniel Mouse.
Sobolev, V. S. Metamorphic Map of Asia.
Sobolev, V. S., et al, eds. Metamorphic Complexes of Asia.
Sobolev, V. V. Light Scattering in Planetary Atmospheres. Irvine, W. M., tr.
Sobotta, Johannes. Atlas of Human Anatomy. Figge, Frank H. & Hild, Walter J., eds. Incl. Vol. 1. Regions, Bones, Ligaments & Muscles; Vol. 2. Visceral Anatomy (Cardiovascular, Lymphatic, Digestive, Respiratory & Urogenital Systems; Vol. 3. Central Nervous System, Autonomic Nervous System, Sense Organs & Skin, Peripheral Nerves & Vessels. Urban & S.
Sobrero, Acquiles, ed. see Stone, Hannah & Stone, Abraham.
Socha, John. Assembly Language Safari on the IBM PC: First Explorations.
Sochanski, Wanda Illus. by see Sluzis, Robert C.
Socialist Workers Party. International Socialist Review. Incl. Greenwood.
--International Socialist Review. Incl. Greenwood.
--New International. Incl. Greenwood.
Socialist Workers Party Staff. Labor Power.
--New York Communist.
--Party Builder.
Societe Francaise des Sciences et Techniques Pharmaceutiques Working Group Staff & Hirtz, J. L., eds. The Fate of Drugs in the Organism: A Bibliographic Survey.
Society for Academic Gaming & Simulation in Education & Training Staff. Perspectives on Academic Gaming & Simulations: Games & Simulations - the Real & the Ideal. Hollinshead, Betty & Yorke, Mantz, eds.
Society for Developmental Biology Symposium Staff. The Cell Surface: Mediator of Developmental Processes. Subtelny, Stephen & Wessels, Norman K., eds.
Society for International Development Staff. International Development 1964 Motivations: Methods in Development: Foreign Aid.
Society for Psychical Research, London, England Staff. Catalogue of the Library of the Society for Psychical Research, London, England.
Society for Psychosomatic Research Staff. Psychosomatics in War & Peace: Proceedings of the Society for Psychosomatic Research, 22nd, Royal College of Physicians, London, Nov. 27-28, 1978. Williams, P., ed.
Society for the Advancement of Material & Process Engineering Staff. Materials Sciences for the Future.
Society for the Right to Die Staff. Handbook of 1985 Living Will Laws.
Society for the Study of Developmental Biology Staff. Communication in Development: Proceedings of the Society for the Study of Developmental Biology, 28th Symposium, 1969. Lang, Anton, ed.
--Current Status of Some Major Problems in Developmental Biology: Proceedings of the Soceity for the Study of Developmental Biology, 25th Symposium. Locke, Michael, ed.
--Cytodifferentiation & Macromolecular Synthesis: Proceedings. Locke, Michael, ed.
--Emergence of Order in Developing Systems: Proceedings of the Society for the Study of Developmental Biology, 27th Symposium. Locke, Michael, ed.
--Reproduction: Proceedings of the Society for the Study of Developmental Biology, 24th Symposium. Locke, Michael, ed.
--The Role of Chromosomes in Development: Proceedings of the Society for the Study of Developmental Biology, 23rd Symposium. Locke, Michael, ed.
Society of American Foresters. Society of American Foresters Ethics Guide.
Society of American Foresters Staff. Land Use Allocation: Processes, People, Politics, Professionals. Evans, H. H., ed.
--SAF Forest Policies & Positions, 1985.
Society of Automotive Engineers Staff. Accident Causation.
--Automotive Aerodynamics.
--Automotive Application of Sensors: Proceedings of the Automotive Engineering Congress, 1978.
--Cumulative Index of SAE Technical Papers, 1965-1985.
--Electric Vehicle Development: Proceedings of the International Electric Vehicle Development Group Conference, 1st, London, 1977.
--Energy Saving Ideas for Mobile Equipment Designers.
--Topics on Contamination in Hydraulic Systems.
Society of Friends of Eastern Art Staff, ed. Index of Japanese Painters.
Society of Industrial Realtors Staff, et al. Industrial Real Estate.
Society of Manufacturing Engineers Staff. Applying Automated Inspection. Pryor, T. & North, W., eds.
--AUTOFACT Europe: Proceedings.
--AUTOFACT Europe '84: Proceedings.
--AUTOFACT Six: Proceedings.
--Automach Australia 1985: Proceedings.
--FABTECH International Conference Proceedings. Fabricating Manufacturers Association Staff, ed.
--Gear Processing & Manufacturing.
--Group Technology at Work. Hyer, Nancy, ed.
--Inspection, Gaging & Testing.
--NAMRC 1985 XIII: Proceedings.
--Proceedings of the Manufacturing Productivity Solutions Conference, 2nd, Washington D. C., Oct. 2-3, 1979.
--A Program Guide for CIM Implementation.
--RADCURE '84 Conference Proceedings.
--Superabrasives 1985: Proceedings.
Society of Manufacturing Engineers Staff & Murphy, J. A. Surface Preparation & Finishes for Metals.
Society of Manufacturing Engineers Staff. Turning & Boring: Angles & Applications. Wood, D., ed.
--User's Guide to Powder Coating.
Society of Mexican Architects, ed. Four Thousand Years of Mexican Architecture.
Society of Mining Engineers of AIME, 1973. Hydrometallurgy: Proceedings.
Society of Naval Architects & Marine Engineers Staff. Historical Transactions, 1893 to 1943.
Society of Photo-Optical Instrumentation Engineers Staff. Acquisition & Analysis of Pictorial Data: Proceedings.
Society of Photo-Optical Instrumentation Engineers, Staff. Application of Optical Instrumentation in Medicine I: Proceedings.
Society of Photo-Optical Instrumentation Engineers Staff. Application of Optical Instrumentation: Proceedings.
--Effective Systems Integration & Optical Design I: Proceedings.
--Engineering Applications of Holography: Proceeding of the SPIE Seminar, Los Angeles, 1972.
--Fiber Optics Comes of Age: Proceedings of the SPIE Seminar, San Mateo, 1972.
--Human in the Photo-Optical System: Proceedings.
--Image Information Recovery: Proceedings.
--Medical X-Ray Photo-Optical Systems Evaluation: Proceedings.
--Optical Instrumentation: A Problem-Solving Tool in Automotive Safety Engineering & Bio-Mechanics, Proceedings.
--Optical Instrumentation: A Tool for Solving Problems in Security, Surveillance & Law Enforcement, Proceedings.
--Photo-Optical Data Reduction: Proceedings of the SPIE Seminar, St. Louis, 1964.
--Photo-Optical Techniques in Simulators I: Proceedings of the SPIE Seminar, New York, 1969.
--Proceedings of the Society of Photo-Optical Instrumentation Engineers, 13th Annual Technical Symposium, Washington D. C. Proceedings.
--Proceedings of the Society of Photo-Optical Instrumentation Engineers, 14th Annual Technical Symposium, San Francisco: Proceedings.
--Quantitative Imagery in the Bio-Medical Sciences, 2: Proceedings. Herron, R. E., ed.

--Remote Sensing of Earth Resources & the Environment: Proceedings of the SPIE Seminar, Palo Alto, 1971.
--Scanners & Imagery Systems for Earth Observation: Proceedings.
--Underwater Photo-Optical Instrumentation Applications, 1968: Proceedings.
Society of Professional Journalists Staff. Leading Journalists Tell What a Free Press Means to America.
Society of Publication Designers Staff. Twentieth Publication Design Annual.
Socolich, Sally. Bargain Hunting in the Bay Area.
--Bargain Hunting in the Bay Area.
Socolow, Elizabeth A. Laughing at Gravity: Conversations with Isaac Newton.
Socrates & Plato. The Psychology of Fate & of Free Will.
Soderback, Martin. Elementary Spoken Swedish.
Soderberg, George A. Finishing Technology.
Soderlund, Sven. The Greek Text of Jeremiah: A Revised Hypothesis.
Soderstrand, Michael A. Applications of Computers Laboratory Manual.
Soderstrom, Elisabeth. In My Own Key.
Sodha, M. S. & Ghatak, A. K. Inhomogeneous Optical Waveguides.
Sodha, Mahendra S., et al. Solar Crop Drying.
Sodhi, Ranbir S. Decimation.
Soe, Christian, ed. Comparative Politics 1988-89.
Soeharjo, Mintari, jt. auth. see Marks, Copeland.
Soelle, Dorothee. The Arms Race Kills Even Without War.
--Choosing Life. Kohl, Margaret, tr. from Ger.
--Death by Bread Alone: Texts & Reflections on Religious Experience. Scheidt, David L., tr. from Ger.
--Political Theology. Shelley, John, tr. from Ger.
Soelle, Dorothee & Steffensky, Fulbert. Not Just Yes & Amen: Christians with a Cause.
Soen, D., ed. New Trends in Urban Planning: Studies in Housing, Urban Design & Planning--Papers Presented at the Symposium Held in Tel Aviv, Israel, December 1977.
Soens, Lewis, ed. see Sidney, Philip.
Soffer, Eliezer Z. Yalkut Eliezer.
Sofr, Ota, tr. see Weisser, Otto & Landa, S.
Softky, Sheldon D. The ABC's of Developing Software: A Primer on Essentials of Software Development.
Softsync, Inc. Staff, et al. Brain Games for Kids & Adults Using the Apple II, IIe, & IIc.
Software Lab East Staff. Computer Workout.
Sogen, Omori & Katsujo, Terayama. Zen & the Art of Calligraphy. Stevens, John, tr. from Japanese.
Soghoian, Richard J. The Ethics of G. E. Moore & David Hume: The Treatise as a Response to Moore's Refutation of Ethical Naturalism.
Sohm, Philio L. The Scuola Grande di San Marco, Nineteen Thirty-Seven to Fifteen Fifty: The Architecture of a Venetial Lay Confraternity.
Sohm, Rudolph. Institutes.
Sohn-Rethel, Alfred. Intellectual & Manual Labour: A Critique of Epistemology.
Soil Chemistry, Soil Fertility & Soil Clay Mineralogy Commissions of the International Society of Soil Science, 13-18 July 1976, Jerusalem. Agrochemicals in Soils: Selected Papers. Banin, A. & Kafkafi, U., eds.
Soil Survey Staff. Taxonomia de Suelos. Leighton, Walter L., tr. from Eng.
Soilacher, A., jt. ed. see Einsele, G.
Soja, E. W. The Political Organization of Space.
Sokatch, John R. Bacterial Physiology.
Sokolinsky, Martin, tr. see Paris, Alain.
Sokoloff, Boris. The Mad Philosopher, Auguste Comte.
Sokoloff, Kiril. The Paine Webber Handbook to Stock & Bond Analysis.
--The Thinking Investor's Guide to the Stock Market.
Sokoloff, Kiril, jt. auth. see Clairmont, George B.
Sokoloff, Kiril, jt. auth. see Shilling, A. G.
Sokoloff, L. The Joints & Synovial Fluid. Sokoloff, Leon, ed.
Sokoloff, Leon, ed. see Sokoloff, L.
Sokolov, A. Quantum Mechanics.
Sokolov, A. A. Synchrotron Radiation.
Sokolov, A. N. Inner Speech & Thought.
--Inner Speech & Thought.
Sokolov, Sasha. Mezhdu Sobakoi I Volkom.
Sokolov, V., jt. auth. see Gligoric, S.
Sokolovskill. Statics of Granular Media.
Sokolow, Leonid. A Dual Ether Universe: Introducing a New Unified Field Theory.
Sokolowski, M., ed. see CISM (International Center for Mechanical Sciences), Department for Mechanics of Deformable Bodies Staff.
Sokolyszyn, Aleksander & Wertsman, Vladimir, eds. Ukrainians in Canada & the United States: A Guide to Information Sources.
Sola, Carla De see De Sola, Carla.
Sola, Ralph de see De Sola, Ralph.
Sola, Ralph De see De Sola, Ralph.
Sola de Pool, Ithiel De Sola see Pool, Ithiel de Sola.
Solano, Frances, et al, eds. see American Instructors of the Deaf Staff.
Solar Cooling & Heating Forum Staff. Solar Cooling & Heating: Proceedings of the Solar Cooling & Heating Forum, Miami Beach, Dec. 13-15, 1976. Veziroglu, T. N., ed.
Solar Energy Conversion Course, 5th, University of Waterloo, Ontario, August 6-19, 1978. Solar Energy Conversion: An Introductory Course. Dixon, A. E. & Leslie, J. D., eds.
Solar Energy Research Institute Staff, ed. The Design of Energy-Responsive Commercial Buildings.
Solberg. Intermediate Microeconomics.
Solberg, Patrice. North Carolina Dog Law Manual.
--North Carolina Law & the Health Department.
--Public Health Nursing & the Law.
Solberg, Patricia, compiled by. North Carolina Dog Law Manual: 1979 Supplement.
Solberg, Richard W. Lutheran Higher Education in North America.
Solberg, Richard W. & Strommen, Merton P. How Church-Related Are Church-Related Colleges? Answers Based on a Comprehensive Survey of Supporting Constituencies of 18 LCA Colleges.
Solberg, Thorvald, ed. see U. S. Copyright Office.
Solberg, William K. & Clark, Glenn T. Temporomandibular Joint Problems: Biologic Diagnosis & Treatment.
Soldati, Mario. The Emerald. Weaver, William, tr.
Soled, Alex J., ed. The Essentials Guides to Wills, Estates, Trusts, & Death Taxes.
Soleil, Rinaja. The Essential Santa Fe.
Soleri, Paolo. Fragments: A Selection from the Notebooks of Paolo Soleri.
Solesbury, William. Policy in Urban Planning: Structure Plans, Local Plans, & Urban Development.
Sole Tura, Jorge. Diccionario del Comunismo.
Solie, Gordon & Forbes, Dee. Gordon Solie: Master of the Ring.
Soligo, Ronald, ed. see Bender, Stephen O., et al.
Soling, H. D. & Seufert, C. D., eds. Biochemical & Clinical Aspects of Ketone Body Metabolism.
Soling, H. D. & Willms, B., eds. Regulation of Gluconeogenesis.
Solis, Leopoldo. Economic Policy Reform in Mexico: A Case Study for Developing Countries.
Solkoff, Joel. Learning to Live Again: My Triumph over Cancer.
Soll, Robert W. & Grenoble, Penelope B. MS: Something Can Be Done & You Can Do It.
Sollertinsky, Dmitri & Sollertinsky, Ludmilla. Pages from the Life of Dmitri Shostakovich. Hobbs, Graham & Midgely, Charles, trs.
Sollertinsky, Ludmilla, jt. auth. see Sollertinsky, Dmitri.
Sollitt, Edna R. Dufay to Sweelinck, Netherlands Masters of Music.
Sollitto, Sharmon & Veatch, Robert M. Bibliography of Society, Ethics & the Life Sciences, Nineteen Seventy-Six to Seventy-Seven. Taylor, Nancy, rev. by.
Solman, Paul & Friedman, Thomas. Life & Death on the Corporate Battlefield.
Solmsen, Friedrich. Intellectual Experiments of the Greek Enlightenment.
Solmssen, Arthur R. A Princess in Berlin.
--Takeover Time.
Solnit, Albert J. & Provence, Sally A., eds. Modern Perspectives in Child Development.
Solodkoff, Alexander Von see Von Solodkoff, Alexander, et al.
Solodovnikov, A. S. Systems of Linear Inequalities.
Solodovnikov, V. & Bogoslovski, V. La Experiencia Historica De Desarollo No Capitalista.
Soloman, Richard, ed. The China Factor: Sino-American Relations & the Global Scene.
Solomon, Brad. The Gone Man.
--Jake & Katie.
Solomon, Bruce & Uslan, Michael. The Gossip Trivia Quiz Book.
--TV Commercial Trivia Quiz Book.
Solomon, Charmaine. Mastering the Art of Chinese Cooking.
Solomon, Cynthia. Computer Environments for Children: A Reflection of Theories of Learning & Education.
Solomon, Denise, ed. see Longman, Lester D. & Maurice, Bloch.
Solomon, E. P., jt. auth. see Davis, P. William.
Solomon, Flora & Litvinoff, Barry. A Woman's Way: The Memoirs of Flora Solomon.
Solomon, Henry A. The Exercise Myth.
--The Exercise Myth.
Solomon, J. B., ed. Aspects of Developmental & Comparative Immunology I: First Congress of Developmental & Comparative Immunology, 27 July-1 August 1980, Aberdeen.
Solomon, Jerome. Financial & Accounting Handbook for the Service Industries.
Solomon, Joan. The Atomic Bomb.
--Bobbi's New Year.
--Energy: The Power to Work.
--Evolution & the Human Population.
--Health, Food & Population.
--How Can We Be Sure?
--Technology, Invention & Industry.
--Ways of Living.
--Wedding Day.
Solomon, Joel & Keeley, Kim. Perspective in Alcohol & Drug Abuse: Similarities & Differences.
Solomon, Lawrence & Bramson, Morris. Medical College Admission Test (MCAT)
Solomon, Lawrence M., et al. Adolescent Dermatology.
Solomon, Lewis D., et al. Corporations Law & Policy.
--Corporations-Law & Policy Materials & Problems 1984: Supplement to Solomon, Stevenson & Schwartz's.
--Supplement to Corporations 1986: Law & Policy, Materials & Problems, 1982.
Solomon, Miriam L., ed. Art Directors Annual, 64th.
Solomon, Morton B., et al, eds. KMG Main Hurdman Guide To Preparing Financial Reports.
Solomon, Nathan A. Medical Examination Review: Nuclear Medicine.
Solomon, Neil & Lipton, Mark. Sick & Tired of Being Sick & Tired.
Solomon, P. M. & Edmunds, M. G. Giant Molecular Clouds in the Galaxy.
Solomon, Richard, jt. auth. see Biller, Henry.
Solomon, Robert C. The Big Questions: A Short Introduction to Philosophy.
--History & Human Nature: A Philosophical Review of European History & Culture, 1750-1850.
--Introducing Philosophy: A Text with Readings.
--Introducing Philosophy: Problems & Perspectives.
--Introducing Philosophy: Problems & Perspectives.
Solomon, Rowena, jt. auth. see Ferguson, Jean.
Solomon, S., jt. ed. see Bernstein, Seymour.
Solomon, Samuel. The Fall of Hitler; or, Where Is Thy Peace.
--Hawaii & Other Poems.
Solomon, Stanley J. The Film Idea.
Solomon, Stanley J., ed. The Classic Cinema: Essays in Criticism.
Solomons, David. Divisional Performance.
Solomons, T. W., jt. auth. see Truitt, Willis H.
Solon, Gidada. The Other Side of Darkness. Fairman, Marion, ed.
Solotaroff, Theodore & Ravenel, Shannon, eds. The Best American Short Stories 1978.
Soloveitchik, Aaron. The Fire of Sinai.
Soloviev, V. G. Theory of Complex Nuclei.
Solovyov, A. A., ed. Against Trotskyism.
Solovyov, B. Turning Point of World War II.
Solso, Robert L. Cognitive Psychology.
Solter, Davor, ed. see Roche Institute of Molecular Biology Symposium Staff.
Soltow, Willow A. Kids Very Own Quilt Book.
Soltzberg, Leonard, et al. BASIC & Chemistry.
Soltzberg, Leonard J. Sing a Song of Software: Verse & Images for the Computer-Literate.
Solvay American Corporation, tr. see Lefevre, M. J.
Solyom, Bronwen, jt. ed. see Solyom, Garrett.
Solyom, Garrett & Solyom, Bronwen, eds. Rites of Passage.
Solzhenitsyn, Aleksandr. Detente: Prospects for Democracy & Dictatorship.
Solzhenitsyn, Alexander. Lenin in Zurich. Willetts, H. T., tr. from Rus.
--The Love-Girl & the Innocent. Bethell, Nicholas & Burg, David, trs. from Rus.
Soma, Hiroaki, ed. The Biology & Management of Capricornis & Related Mountain Antelopes.
Somasundaran, P., intro. by. Advances in Mineral Processing.
Somasundaran, P. & Arbiter, N., eds. Beneficiation of Mineral Fines.
Sombart, Werner. Jews & Modern Capitalism.
Somers, Jane. If the Old Could.
Somers, John. Security of Englishmen's Lives, or the Trust Power & Duty of Grand Juries.
Somers, Lucy. How to Crochet a High Fashion Wardrobe.
Somers, Paul, Jr. Johnson J. Hooper.
Somers, Ronald, ed. Road User Protection: Selected Papers from the 8th International Conference on Accident & Traffic Medicine, Aarhus, Denmark, 10-13 June 1980.
Somers, Suzanne. Touch Me.
Somerscales, Euan F. & Knudsen, James G., eds. Fouling of Heat Transfer Equipment.
Somerset, Anne. Ladies-in-Waiting: From the Tudors to the Present Day.
Somervell, D. C. Classics in Western Civilization.
Somervell, D. C., abridged by see Toynbee, Arnold.
Somervill, John W., jt. auth. see Rimm, David C.
Somerville, John. Soviet Philosophy.
Somerville, Neil. Your Chinese Horoscope for Nineteen Eighty-Nine.
Somerville, W. M., jt. auth. see Beattie, D. H.
Somerville-Large, Peter. Dublin.
Somit, Albert & Tanenhaus, Joseph. Development of American Political Science: From Burgess to Behavioralism.
Somiya, S. & Kanai, E., eds. Ceramic Components for Engines: Proceedings, First International Symposium, Hakone, Japan, October 17-19, 1983.
Sommer, Doris. One Master for Another: Populism As Patriarchal Rhetoric in Dominican Novels.
Sommer, Elyse. How to Make Money in the Antiques-&-Collectibles Business.
--Perfect Writer Made Perfectly Clear.
Sommer, H., jt. auth. see Lesobre, J.
Sommer, Scott. Nearing's Grace.
Sommerfeld, Ray M. Federal Taxes & Management Decisions, 1987-88.
Sommerfeld, Ray M. & Anderson, Hershel M. An Introduction to Taxation.
--An Introduction to Taxation Advanced Topics.
Sommerfeld, Ray M., et al. An Introduction to Taxation: Advanced Topics.
--Introduction to Taxation: 1983 Edition.
--Harcourt Brace Jovanovich Federal Tax Course, 1986.
--HBJ Federal Tax Course 1985.
--HBJ Federal Tax Course 1987.
--An Introduction to Taxation.
--Introduction to Taxation: 1983-1984 Supplement.
--An Introduction to Taxation, 1989.
Sommers, Albert T. The U. S. Economy Demystified: What Their Major Economic Statistics Mean & Their Significance for Business.
Sommers, Anita A., ed. Productivity Measurement in Education.
Sommers, Christina H. Vice & Virtue in Everyday Life.
Sommers, Jeanne. Comanche Revenge.
Sommers, Shedlon C. & Rosen, Paul Peter. Pathology Annual, 1982, Vol. 17.
Sommers, Sheldon C. & Rosen, Paul P. Pathology Annual, 1982.
Sommers, Sheldon C., et al, eds. Pathology Annual, 1985.
Sommerville, George. Ideology for Survival.
Sommerville, R. G. Essential Clinical Virology.
Somogyi, A. J., ed. Cosmic Rays in the Heliosphere.
Somogyi, J. C. & Haenel, H. Nutrition in Early Childhood & Its Effects in Later Years.
Somogyi, J. C. & Varela, G., eds. Nutritional Deficiencies in Industrialized Countries.
Somogyi, J. C., et al. Worldwide Problems of Nutrition.
Somorjai, G. A. & Van Hove, M. A. Absorbed Monolayers on Solid Surfaces.
Somwaru, Agapi. Disaggregated Farm Income by Type of Farm, 1959-82.
Sondak, Norman, et al. The Complete Guide to Success with the IBM PCjr.
Sondashi, Ludwig S. Marriage is Not for Weaklings.
Sondeno, Stanley R. Small Business Management Principles.
Sondergard, Sid. The Smile of Blazing Wings & Other Plays.
Sondheim, Stephen & Furth, George. Merrily We Roll along.
Sondrup, Steven P. & Inglis, Craig M. Konkordanz zu den Gedichten: Hugo von Hofmannsthals.
Song, Choan-Seng. The Tears of Lady Meng: A Parable of People's Political Theology.
Songling, Pu. Selected Tales of Laiozhai.
Song Pill-Soon, ed. Symposium on Photomorphogenesis.
Songying, Lin. The Kitten Visits the Park.
Sonino, Michael, ed. see Vasari, Giorgio.
Sonkin, Daniel J. & Durphy, Michael. Learning to Live Without Violence: A Handbook for Men.
Sonnaillon, Bernard. King of Instruments: A History of the Organ. Spencer, Stewart, tr.
Sonneck, Oscar G. Beethoven: Impressions by His Contemporaries.
Sonnenberg, Ben, ed. A Grand Street Reader.
Sonnenberg, Janet. Race for Life: The Joel Sonnenberg Story.
Sonnenburg, David & Birnbaum, Michael. Understanding Pacemakers.
Sonnenburg, Paul, jt. auth. see Schoneberger, William A.
Sonnenfeld, Albert, ed. Thirty-Six French Poems.
Sonnenfeld, Peter, ed. Tethys: The Ancestral Mediterranean.
Sonnenschein, William S. Best Books.
Sonnenschmidt, Fritz & Nicholas, Jean. The Professional Chef's Art of Garde Manger.
Sonnershein, Richard, ed. see Marmion, Shakerly.
Sonnery, Jean-Louis, jt. ed. see Berjonneau, Gerald.
Sonnichsen, C. L., ed. see Perkins, Clifford A.
Sonnier, Austin M., Jr. Willie Geary "Bunk" Johnson: The New Iberia Years.
Sonnier, Isadore L. Cajun Boy: The Story of Acadiana.

Authors

Sonntag, Wendy W. A Working Approach to Chemistry.
Sons, Ray, jt. auth. see Meyer, Ray.
Sonsini, Larry W., jt. auth. see Practising Law Institute Staff.
Sontag, E. D. Polynomial Response Maps.
Sontag, Frederick. Existentialist Prolegomena: To a Future Metaphysics.
--A Kierkegaard Handbook.
Sontag, Raymond J. & Beddie, James S., eds. Nazi-Soviet Relations, 1939-1941: Documents from Archives of German Foreign Office.
Sontag, Susan. The Benefactor.
--The Benefactor.
--Brother Carl.
--Illness As Metaphor.
--Illness As Metaphor.
--On Photography.
Sontag, Susan, ed. On Photography.
Sontag, Susan, ed. see Artaud, Antonin.
Soo, Chee. Taoist Yoga: The Chinese Art of K'ai Men.
Sood, James H. Situations in Marketing: A Collection of Marketing Cases & Questions.
Sood, Mohan K. Modern Igneous Petrology.
Soong, Maling. Art of Chinese Paper Folding: For Young & Old.
Soong, T. T. Probabilistic Modeling & Analysis in Science & Engineering.
Soon Man Rhim. Women of Asia: Yesterday & Today.
Sooter, Wilburn L. Eye: A Light Receiver.
Soothill, et al. Paediatric Immunology.
Soothill, William E. The Hall of Light.
Sopa, Geshe L. & Hopkins, Jeffrey. The Practice & Theory of Tibetan Buddhism.
Soper, A., jt. auth. see Paine, R.
Soper, Edward D. Racism, a World Issue.
Soper, Gill, jt. auth. see Stuart, Monica.
Soper, M. F. Birds of New Zealand & Outlying Islands.
Soper, Robert T., jt. auth. see Liechty, Richard D.
Soper, Tony. The Shell Book of Beachcombing.
Soper, Tony & Sparks, John. Penguins.
Soper, Tony, jt. auth. see Arbib, Robert.
Soper, Tony, jt. auth. see Sparks, John.
Sophocles see Weiss, Samuel A.
Sopikov, V. S. An Attempt at a Russian Bibliography or a Complete Dictionary of Works Printed in Church Slavonic & Russian from the Introduction of Printing in 1813.
Sopp, LaVerne. Personal Name Index to the Eighteen Fifty-Six City Directories of Iowa.
Soppeland, Mark, ed. Words.
Soraas, H., jt. ed. see Bjerke, L.
Sorani, Robert P. Circuit Training.
Sorass, jt. ed. see Byerke.
Sorauf, Frank J. Party Politics in America.
Sorayama, Hajime. Pin-Up.
Sorbom, Dag, jt. auth. see Joreskog, Karl G.
Sorcar, Prafulla C. Energy Saving Lighting Systems.
--Rapid Lighting Design & Cost Estimating.
Sorden, L. G., jt. auth. see Gard, Robert E.
Sorel, Edward, jt. auth. see Miller, Warren.
Sorel, Julia. Rocky.
Sorelle, Rupert P., et al. Mecanografia: Metodo Racional.
Sorensen, Chris & Flying Magazine Editors. Antique Airplanes.
Sorensen, Eric. Using WordStar 2000.
Sorensen, Grethe. Needlepoint Designs from Oriental Rugs.
--Needlepoint Designs from Oriental Rugs.
Sorensen, James L., jt. auth. see Bernal, Guillermo.
Sorensen, K. E., jt. auth. see Davis, Calvin V.
Sorensen, Robert J. Design for Accessibility.
Sorensen, Robert M. Basic Coastal Engineering.
Sorensen, S. C., ed. see Benzon, Alfred, Symposium, et al.
Sorensen, Virginia. Around the Corner.
--Curious Missie.
--Friends of the Road.
--Lotte's Locket.
--Miracles on Maple Hill.
--Plain Girl.
Sorenson, Dolf. James Joyce's Aesthetic Theory: Its Development & Application.
Sorenson, Don L., ed. see Christian, Esther.
Sorenson, Don L., ed. see Loesch, Larry C. & Wheeler, Paul T.
Sorenson, J. A., jt. auth. see DeBlanc, H. J.
Sorenson, Jacki & Bruns, Bill. Jacki Sorenson's Aerobic Lifestyle Book.
--Jacki Sorenson's Aerobic Lifestyle Book.
Sorenson, Jane. Boy Friend.
--In Another Land.
--Once upon a Friendship.
--Out with the In Crowd.
Sorenson, Jim, ed. Sons & Daughters of Mystical Creatures Coloring Book.
Sorenson, Lewell L. Beyond Charted Space: A Search for Stolen Treasure.
Sorgenfrey, Robert H., jt. auth. see Dolciani, Mary P.
Sorin, Martin D. Data Entry Without Keypunching: Improved Preparation for Social-Data Analysis.
Sorkin, Alan. The Economics of the Postal System: Alternatives & Reform.
--Health Care & the Changing Economic Environment.
Sorkin, Alan L. Economic Aspects of Natural Hazards.
Sorlien, Sandra. Keeping Christmas: Activities & Devotions for the Twelve Days of Christmas.
Sorlier, Charles. Chagall Lithographs V: 1974-1979.
Sormo, Maitland C. De see Stoddard, Seneca R.
Sorokin, P. A. Forms & Techniques of Altruistic & Spiritual Growth: A Symposium.
--Reconstruction of Humanity.
Soroos, Marvin S., jt. ed. see Orr, David W.
Sorrell, Alan, jt. auth. see Hamilton, John.
Sorrels, William W. The Maroon Bulldogs: Mississippi State Football.
Sorrentino. Moby's Textbook for Nursing Assistants.
Sorrentino, Gilbert. Mulligan Stew.
--Mulligan Stew.
--Perfect Fiction.
Sors, Andrew I. & Coleman, David, eds. Pollution Research Index: A Guide to World Research in Environmental Pollution.
Sors, L. Fatigue Design of Machine Components.
Sorvisto, Edwin M. Roughing It with Charlie, "C" Co., 2nd. Ranger Btn.
Sosin, Mark & Kreh, Lefty. Fishing the Flats.
Sosin, Mark, jt. auth. see Kreh, Lefty.
Sosnowski, Kiryl. The Tragedy of Children under Nazi Rule.
Sotatsu, Tawaraya. Library of Japanese Art: Sotatsu. Tanaka, Ichimatsu, ed.
Sotiriou, Peter E. Integrating College Study Skills: Reasoning in Reading, Listening, & Writing.
Soto, Osvaldo N. Repaso De Gramatica.
Soubiran, Andre. Diary of a Woman in White.
Souchal, Francois. French Sculptors of the Seventeenth & Eighteenth Centuries: The Region of Louis XIV.
Soucie, Gary. Hook, Line, & Sinker: The Complete Angler's Guide to Terminal Tackle.
--Soucie's Fishing Databook.
Souder, William E. Management Decision Methods: For Managers of Engineering & Research.
--Project Selection & Economic Appraisal.
Soukkary, Sohair, jt. auth. see Sayegh, Fayez.
Soukup, James R., et al. Party & Factional Division in Texas.
Soule, Charles E. Disability Income Insurance: The Unique Risks.
Soulen, Richard N. Care for the Dying.
Soulen, Robert J., Jr., jt. auth. see Wise, Jacqueline A.
Soulsby, Basil H. A Catalogue of the Works of Linnaeus Preserved in the Libraries of the British Museum (Natural History)
Sourdel, Dominique. Medieval Islam.
Sourek, Otaker. Antonin Dvorak.
Sours, Keith J. SCSS Short Guide: An Introduction to the SCSS Conversational System.
Souryal, Sam S. Police Organization & Administration.
Sousa, Maria S. De see De Sousa, Maria S., et al.
Sousa-Pinto, A. Cortical Projections of the Medial Geniculate Body in the Cat.
Souter, John, ed. Future.
Souter, John C. Communicate.
--The Word.
Souter, John C., ed. Relate.
South Africa, Commissioner on Native Grievances Inquiry. Report of the Native Grievances Inquiry, 1913-1914.
South Carolina Department of Archives & History Staff. A Guide to the Local Records in the South Carolina Archives.
Southall, Thomas W., ed. Diane Arbus: Magazine Work Essay.
Southard, Edna C. The Frescoes in Siena's Palazzo Pubblico, Twelve Eighty-Nine to Fifteen Thirty-Nine: Studies in Imagery & Relations to Other Communal Palaces in Tuscany.
Southard, Samuel. Anger in Love.
--Like the One You Love: Intimacy & Equality in Modern Marriage.
--Pastoral Evangelism.
Southard, W. W. Bitter Pecos.
--Reckoning at Arrowhead.
Southeast Resource Center for Children & Youth Services Staff, ed. Media Resources Catalog.
Southerland, Ellease. Let the Lion Eat Straw.
Southern, Eileen. Music of Black Americans: A History.
Southern, Eileen, ed. Readings in Black American Music.
Southern, Karen. The Nelson Island Story. Brown, Diane, ed.
Southern Living Magazine Food Editors. Southern Living Annual Recipes, 1980.
--Southern Living 1984 Annual Recipes.
Southern Living Magazine Gardening Editors & Floyd, John A., Jr. Southern Living Garden Guide.
Southern, R. W. Medieval Humanism: And Other Stories.
--Medieval Humanism: And Other Studies.
Southern Society for the Promotion of the Study of Race Conditions & Problems in the South Staff. Race Problems of the South.
Southern Sociological Congress Staff. Call of the New South: Addresses Delivered at the Southern Sociological Congress. McCulloch, James E., ed.
Southern, Terry. Flash & Filigree.
Southey, Robert. Essays, Moral & Political.
Southgate, Minoo, tr. see Sa'edi, Gholam-Hossein.
Southgate, Patsy, tr. see De Berg, Jean.
Southgate, Patsy, tr. see Schneider, Pierre.
Southmayd, William & Rippe, James. The Sports Performance Factors.
Southward, John. Practical Printing: A Handbook of the Art of Typography.
Southwell, Robert. An Epistle of Comfort. Waugh, Margaret, ed.
Southwestern Law Enforcement Institute Staff. Criminal Investigation.
--Homicide Investigation Techniques: Personal Experience Accounts of Professionals & Experts.
--Traffic Law Enforcement: A Guide for Patrolmen.
Southwick, Albert P. Quizzism & Its Key.
--Wisps of Wit & Wisdom, or Knowledge in a Nutshell.
Southwick, Lawrence, compiled by. Yankee Verse by Nathan Marshall Southwick (1872-1963) The Wit & Wisdom of a New England Philosopher.
Southwick, P. D., ed. Accelerated Cooling of Steel.
Southwood, James, jt. auth. see Saunders, Frank.
Southworth, R. & De Leeuw, S. Digital Computation & Numerical Methods.
Souviney, Randall & Sarver. Mathmatters.
Souza, F. Refugees: Viewpoints, Case Studies & Theoretical Considerations on the Care & Management of Refugees.
Sova, Margaret, jt. auth. see Kreitner, Robert.
Sovenson, Lois B. What Does It Mean to Believe in Jesus.
Sovey, George D. Arykosia.
Sovik, Edward A. Architecture for Worship.
Sovold, Pamela, et al. Market Notebook.
Sowa, John, jt. auth. see Skuce, Doug.
Soward, A. M., jt. ed. see Roberts, P. H.
Sowell, Thomas, ed. American Ethnic Groups.
Sowerby, L. M. Dictionary of Photography.
Sowers, J. R., ed. Hypothalmic Hormones.
Sowers, Robert. The Language of Stained Glass.
Sowray, jt. auth. see Roberts, D.
Sowray, J. H., jt. auth. see Roberts, D. H.
Sox, Harold C., Jr., et al, eds. Carbohydrate Moieties of Immunoglobulin.
Soyinka, Wole. Death & the King's Horseman: A Play.
Soyinka, Wole, ed. Poems of Black Africa.
Sozzi, G. L., jt. ed. see Hochreiter, L. E.
Spacek, Tim. Fathers: There at the Birth.
Spacks, Patricia M. The Female Imagination.
Spada, Simonetta, jt. auth. see Mejetta, Mirko.
Spadaccini, Victor M. Minnesota Data Book: 1985-1986.
Spadijer, M. Montenegro.
Spady, Richard H. Econometric Estimation of Cost Functions for the Regulated Transportation Industries.
Spaegel, Charles, jt. auth. see Norman, Ruth.
Spaeth, David. Ludwig Karl Hilberseimer: An Annotated Bibliography & Chronology.
Spaeth, David, ed. see Dearstyne, Howard.
Spaeth, Joe L. American College Faculty Members: Nineteen Sixty-Three.
Spaeth, Sigmund. Fifty Years with Music.
Spaeth, Steven. National Directory of ZIP Codes & Post Offices, 1986.
Spaggiari, Albert. Fric-Frac: The Great Riviers Train Robbery.
Spahr, Frederick T. & Kawana, Alfred K., eds. ASHA Membership Directory, 1986-87.
Spain, Daphne, jt. auth. see Bianchi, Suzanne M.
Spalding, Baird T. Life & Teaching of the Masters of the Far East.
Spalding, D. B. Combustion & Mass Transfer.
Spalding, Dudley B., ed. GENMIX: A General Computer Program for Two-Dimensional Parabolic Flow.
--Progress in Heat & Mass Transfer, Vol. 19, No. 10: Alan Ede Memorial Issue: Developments in Heat & Mass Transfer.
Spalding, Henry D. Encyclopedia of Black Folklore & Humor.
--The Lilt of the Irish-An Encyclopedia of Irish Humor & Lore.
--The Nixon Nobody Knows.
--A Treasure-Trove of American Jewish Humor.
Spalding, Jack. Santi Di Tito.
Spalding, K. H. The Philosophy of Shakespeare.
Spalding, Phinizy. Oglethorpe in America.
Spallholz, J. E., et al. Selenium in Biology & Medicine: Second International Symposium.
Spaltenholz, Hans, tr. see Stauffer, Ethelbert.
Spangenburg & Moser. The Survival Kit Series: Educational Software.
Spangenburg, Ray & Moser, Dian. The Survival Kit for Apple Computer Games.
Spangenburg, Raymond & Moser, Diane. The Kilobyte Kid's Book of Personal Computers.
Spangle, Frances, jt. auth. see Rusmore, Jean.
Spangler, Ann. Bright Legacy: Portraits of Ten Outstanding Christian Women.
Spangler, Ann, ed. Bright Legacy: Portraits of Ten Outstanding Christian Women.
Spangler, Ann, ed. see Smith, Hannah W.
Spangler, David. Links with Space.
--Reflections on the Christ.
Spangler, Mary M. Principles of Education: A Study of Aristotelian Thomism Contrasted with Other Philosophies.
Spangler, Richard J., jt. auth. see International Computer Programs, Inc. Staff.
Spangler, Richard J., ed. see International Computer Programs, Inc. Staff.
Spangler, Sharon. On Foot in the Grand Canyon.
Spanier, Graham B., jt. auth. see Lerner, Richard M.
Spanier, John. American Foreign Policy since World War II.
--Foreign Policy Making.
Spanier, John & Uslaner, Eric M. Foreign Policy & the Democratic Dilemmas.
Spano, Rick. The Rank & File Movement in Social Work.
Sparagna, Aniceto. Personal Evangelism among Roman Catholics.
Spargo, John. Early American Pottery & China.
Sparke, Archibald, ed. see Corns, Albert R.
Sparke, Penny. Consultant Design: The History & Practice of the Designer in Industry.
--An Introduction to Design & Culture in the Twentieth Century.
Sparkes, Ivan G., ed. Dictionary of Collective Nouns & Group Terms.
Sparkes, J. J. Transistor Switching & Sequential Circuits.
Sparkes, Robert S., et al, eds. see ICN-UCLA Symposia Staff.
Sparkman, Ervin L. The People's History of Live Oak County, Texas. Roberts, Mary S., ed.
Sparkman, Ivo. Journeys with the Senator.
Sparks, A. Gilchrist, III, jt. auth. see Drexler, David A.
Sparks, Albert K. Invertebrate Pathology: Noncommunicable Diseases.
Sparks, B. W. & West, R. G. The Ice Age in Britain.
Sparks, Donald B. Administrative Improvement Methods.
Sparks, Esther. Ernst Damitz: 1805-1883.
Sparks, H. F. Formation of the New Testament.
Sparks, Jennifer, ed. see Beranbaum, Rose L.
Sparks, John. The Discovery of Animal Behavior.
--The Sexual Connection.
Sparks, John & Soper, Tony. Owls: Their Natural & Unnatural History.
--Owls: Their Natural & Unnatural History.
Sparks, John, jt. auth. see Soper, Tony.
Sparks, Judy, ed. Christmas Programs for the Church.
Sparks, Ken & Bjorkland, Gary. Long Distance Runner's Guide to Training & Racing: Build Your Endurance, Strength & Efficiency.
Sparks, Kimberly & Reichmann, Edith. So ist es! A Contemporary Reader.
Sparks, Kimberly & Vail, Van H. German in Review.
Sparks, Kimberly, jt. auth. see Vail, Van Horn.
Sparks, Lee, ed. Try This One... Too.
--The Youth Group How-To Book.
--Youth Group Travel Directory.
Sparks, Richard, jt. auth. see Hood, Roger.
Sparks, Shirley N. Birth Defects & Speech-Language Disorders.
Sparks-Forrester, Viktoria, jt. auth. see Goff, Victoria.
Sparling, Joyce. Wedlocked.
Sparnaay, M. J. The Electrical Double Layer.
Sparrow, E. M. & Cess, R. D. Radiation Heat Transfer: Augmented Edition.
Sparrow, John. Half Lines & Repetitions in Virgil. Commager, Steele, ed.
Sparrow, W. Keats & Pickett, Nell Ann, eds. Technical & Business Communication in Two-Year Programs.
Spartano, Philip J. Giacomo Zanella: Poet, Essayist, & Critic of the "Risorgimento"
Spasowski, Romuald. The Liberation of One: The Autobiography of Romuald Spasowski, Polish Ambassador to the Unites States. Lourie, Richard, tr.
Spataro, Francis C. Charles Mason Remey & the Baha'i Faith.
Spate, O. H. Paradise Found & Lost.
Spater, George & Parsons, Ian. A Marriage of True Minds: An Intimate Portrait of Leonard & Virginia Woolf.
--A Marriage of True Minds: An Intimate Portrait of Leonard & Virginia Woolf.
Spath, Helmuth. Cluster Dissection & Analysis Theory FORTRAN Programs Examples.
Spatola, Anthony L. Mastering Medical Language.

Spatz, Jacob W. Coping With the Corporate Jungle: Ten Keys to Success.
--The Speaker's Bible.
Spatz, M., et al, eds. Circulatory & Developmental Aspects of Brain Metabolism.
Spaulding, M. L., jt. auth. see Gordon, R.
Spaulding, Malcolm, jt. auth. see Gordon, Robert.
Speaks, R. L. The Prelude to Pentecost.
Spear, Barbara. MultiMate User's Guide.
--Word Processing with Your ADAM.
Spear, Elizabeth, ed. see Young, Dale.
Spear, George E., jt. auth. see Mocker, Donald W.
Spear, Roberta. Silks.
--Taking to Water.
Spearing, G. W. The Craft of the Gunsmith.
Spears, Harold. Principles of Teaching.
Spears, Ross & Cassidy, Jude, eds. Agee: His Life Remembered.
Spears, W. Eugene Jr. The Church on Assignment.
Speas, Jan C. Bride of the Machugh.
--The Growing Season.
--My Lord Monleigh.
Speas, Sam & Coel, Margeret. Goin' Railroading.
Specht, R. L., jt. auth. see Clifford, H. T.
Specht, Riva & Craig, Grace J. Human Development: A Social Work Perspective.
Special Commission on Social Security Disability. Investigation, Findings & Recommendations: Special Commission on Social Security Disability in the Commonwealth of Massachusetts.
Special Libraries Association Staff. SLA Triennial Salary Survey.
--Who's Who in Special Libraries, 1987-88.
Specialists Meeting on Transient Two-Phase Flow Staff. Transient Two-Phase Flow: Proceedings of the Specialists Meeting, Toronto, Canada, Aug. 3-4, 1979. Banerjee, S. & Weaver, K., eds.
Specialized Systems Consultants, Inc. Staff. MS-DOS Command Summary.
Specialized Systems Consultants Inc., Staff. UNIX--XENIX Text Processing Reference.
Specialized Systems Consultants, Inc. Staff. UNIX Command Summary (BSD 4.2)
Specialty Travel Index Publishers Staff. The Adventure Vacation Catalog.
Speck, Vicky H., ed. Wisconsin Misdemeanors & Moving Traffic Violations.
Speck, W. A. Butcher: The Duke of Cumberland & the Suppression of the Forty-Five.
Speckels, Milton J. Complete Guide to Micromounts.
Speckman, E. J. & Caspers, H. Origin of Cerebral Field Potentials.
Speckmann, E. J. & Elger, C. E., eds. Epilepsy & Motor System.
Spector, Deborach C., jt. auth. see Jensen, Rosalie S.
Spector, Ivar. The Golden Age of Russian Literature.
Spector, Margaret. The American Department of the British Government, 1768-1782.
Spector, Norman B., tr. The Romance of Tristan & Isolt.
Spector, R., et al. Psychiatry: Common Drug Treatments.
Spector, Ronald H. United States Marines in Grenada, 1983.
Spector, V. G. Introduction to General Pathology.
Spectre, Peter, jt. ed. see Putz, George.
Spectre, Peter H., jt. ed. see Putz, George.
Spedding, A., jt. ed. see Chiddick, D.
Spedding, C. R. The Biology of Agricultural Systems.
Spedding, J., et al, eds. see Bacon, Francis.
Speed, P. F. The Potato Famine & the Irish Emigrants. Reeves, Marjorie, ed.
Speedwriting Institute. Mastering Typing.
Speedwriting Institute Staff. Typing for Beginners.
Speer, Betty J. Jenny Saw.
Speer, Frederic. Food Allergy.
Speer, James A. Affirming the Family in an Urban World.
Speer, Michael L. A Complete Guide to the Christian's Budget.
Speh, Thomas W., jt. auth. see Hutt, Michael D.
Speicher, John. Didman.
Speidel, Richard E., et al. Commercial & Consumer Law Teaching Materials.
Speight, Charlotte F. Hands in Clay: An Introduction to Ceramics.
Speir, Elizabeth, ed. see Newton, Marie W.
Speirs. Self-Assessment in Dentistry.
Speirs, E. B., tr. see Hegel, Georg W.
Speirs, R. L., ed. Self-Assessment in Basic Sciences for Dentists.
Speiser, P., jt. ed. see Breimer, D. D.
Speitel, H. H., jt. ed. see Mather, J. Y.
Speke, John H. Journal of the Discovery of the Source of the Nile.
Spelder, Charles De see De Spelder, Charles.
Speller, Benjamin F., Jr. Zero Based Budgeting for Libraries & Information Centers: A Continuing Education Manual.
Spellman, Cathy C. An Excess of Love.
Spellman, Norman W. Growing a Soul: The Story of A. Frank Smith.
Spellman, Peter W., jt. auth. see Askew, Thomas A., Jr.
Spence & Windsor. Microcomputers in Business: Wordstar, Lotus, Base II & II.
--Using Microcomputers: Applications for Business.
Spence, Alastair A., jt. auth. see Campbell, Donald.
Spence, Alastair A., ed. Respiratory Monitoring in Intensive Care.
Spence, Gerry L. Trial by Fire: The True Story of a Woman's Ordeal at the Hands of Justice.
Spence, Joseph. Anecdotes, Observations & Characters of Books & Men: Collected from the Conversation of Mr. Pope & Other Eminent Persons of His Time.
--Letters from the Grand Tour. Klima, Slava, ed.
--Polymetis.
Spence, Mary L., ed. see Fremont, John C.
Spence, N., et al, eds. British Cities: An Analysis of Urban Change.
Spence, R. & Brayton, R. Sensitivity & Optimization.
Spence, Robin & Cook, David. Building Materials in Developing Countries.
Spence, Sharon. Collage of Dreams: The Writings of Anais Nin.
Spence, William P. Drafting: Technology & Practice.
Spence, William P. & Vequist, David G. Graphic Reproduction.
Spencer, A. G., ed. Milling.
Spencer, Anita L. Crises & Growth: Making the Most of Hard Times.
Spencer, Anne. On the Edge of the Organization: The Role of the Outside Director.
Spencer, Brian. Lake District.
Spencer, Chris. Starforce Red Alert.
Spencer, Colin. Cordon Vert: Fifty-Two Vegetarian Gourmet Dinner Party Menus.
Spencer, Dean & Nelson, Dean. God Never Said We'd Be Leading at the Half.
Spencer, Donald D. BASIC Programming.
--Computer Dictionary.
--Computer Dictionary for Everyone.
--Computer Dictionary for Everyone.
--Computers: An Introduction.
--Microcomputers at a Glance.
--What Computers Can Do.
Spencer, Elizabeth. Fire in the Morning.
--The Voice at the Back Door.
Spencer, Herbert. The Evolution of Society: Selections from Herbert Spencer's "Principles of Sociology" Carniero, Robert L., ed.
--Herbert Spencer on Social Evolution. Peel, J. D., ed.
--Literary Style & Music.
--The Principles of Sociology.
Spencer, Ivor D., abridged by. & t see Moreau De Saint-Mery, Mederic L.
Spencer, Kenneth A. & Steyskal, George C. Manual of the Agromyzidae (Diptera) of the United States.
Spencer, LaVyrle. The Endearment.
Spencer, M., jt. auth. see Clark, Harold B.
Spencer, Metta & Inkeles, Alex. Foundations of Modern Sociology.
Spencer, Pat. Birds of a Feather.
Spencer, Randolph E. A West Virginian's View of Musical Life Yesterday & Today with Successful Techniques for Teaching Band Instruments.
Spencer, Scott. Endless Love.
--Preservation Hall.
Spencer, Stewart, tr. see Sonnaillon, Bernard.
Spencer, T. J., ed. Shakespeare: A Celebration Fifteen Sixty-Four to Nineteen Sixty-Four.
Spencer, Zane & Leech, Jay. Branded Runaway.
--Cry of the Wolf.
Spender, D. & Spender, L., eds. Gatekeeping: The Denial, Dismissal & Distortion of Women.
Spender, Dale. Invisible Women: The Schooling Scandal.
--Man Made Language.
--Mothers of the Novel.
--Mothers of the Novel: One Hundred Good Women Writers Before Jane Austen.
--There's Always Been a Women's Movement This Century.
--Women of Ideas: And What Men Have Done to Them.
Spender, Dale, ed. Time & Tide Wait for No Man.
Spender, L., jt. ed. see Spender, D.
Spender, Stephen. European Witness.
--Mary Stuart.
--Selected Poems.
Speneer, Earl. Japan & the East.
Spengler, Barbara, jt. auth. see Pate, Ellen.
Spengler, Carol, jt. auth. see Grissum, Marlene.
Spengler, Oswald. The Decline of the West. Werner, Helmut, ed.
--The Decline of the West.
--Man & Technics.
Spenser, Edmund. Edmund Spenser's Poetry. Maclean, Hugh, ed.
Spera, David, ed. Wind Turbine Technology: Horizontal Axis Megawatt Wind Energy Systems.
Spergel, Irving. Community Problem Solving: The Delinquency Example.
Spering, Don, jt. auth. see Linn, Don.
Sperling, Joann, jt. auth. see Wortman, Max.
Sperling, L. H., jt. ed. see Carraher, Charles E., Jr.
Sperling, Veronica & Mills, Sonya, eds. Cook Ahead.
Sperlinger, David. Animals in Research: New Perspectives in Animal Experimentation.
Spero, Abby. In America & in Need: Immigrant, Refugee & Entrant Women.
Spero, Moshe H., jt. auth. see Bulka, Reuven P.
Spero, Simon. Worcester Porcelain: From the Klepser Collection.
Spero, Sterling D. & Harris, Abram L. Black Worker.
Speroni, Charles & Golino, Carlo L. Basic Italian.
Sperry, Armstrong. All Sail Set: A Romance of the Flying Cloud.
Sperry, Kip. Index to Genealogical Periodical Literature, 1960-1977.
Sperry, Kip, ed. Survey of American Genealogical Periodicals & Periodical Indexes.
Speyer, A. James & Benezra, Neal. Seventy-Fifth American Exhibition.
Speyer, A. James & Rorimer, Anne. Seventy-Fourth American Exhibition.
--Seventy-Third American Exhibition: The Art Institute of Chicago.
Speyer, N., et al, eds. see International Congress on Suicide Prevention 7th.
Spezio, E. Aniello. Aspects of Love.
Spezzano, Charles. Using Enable.
Spice, J. E. Chemical Binding & Structure.
Spicer, David, ed. Artworks.
Spicer, Dorothy. The Tower Room.
Spicer, Dorothy G. Folk Festivals & the Foreign Community.
Spicer, Edward D. Automotive Collision Work.
Spicer, Stephen, jt. auth. see Kenny, James.
Spickard, Anderson & Thompson, Barbara R. Dying for a Drink: What You Should Know about Alcoholism.
Spidchenko, Konstantin. U. S. S. R. Geography of the Eleventh Five-Year Plan.
Spidle, Jake W., Jr. The Lovelace Medical Center: Pioneer in American Health Care.
SPIE - International Society for Optical Engineering Staff. Sensor Design Using Computer Tools: Proceedings of SPIE Seminar on Sensor Design Using Computer Tools, Los Angeles, California, Jan., 1982. Jamieson, John A., ed.
Spiegal, Richard, jt. ed. see Fisher, Barbara.
Spiegel, Allen D. Home Healthcare.
Spiegel, Barbara, ed. see Kutner, Lynn.
Spiegel, Lawrence. A Question of Innocence. McGuire, William, ed.
Spiegel, R., jt. ed. see Koeberle, S.
Spiegel, Rene & Aebi, Hans-J. Psychopharmacology: An Introduction. Kerr, Kathleen, tr. from Ger.
Spiegel, Ruth, ed. see Segal, Marilyn & Adcock, Don.
Spiegel, Shalom. The Last Trial: On the Legend & Lore of the Command to Abraham to Offer Isaac As a Sacrifice - the Akedah.
Spiegel, Steven, jt. auth. see Drop, Mark.
Spiegel, Steven, jt. ed. see Center for International & Strategic Affairs, Univ. of California, Los Angeles Staff.
Spiegelman, Judith M. & UNICEF Staff. We Are the Children. Weis, Jennifer, ed.
Spiegl, Fritz. Music Through the Looking Glass.
Spiegl, Walter, jt. auth. see Pazaurek, Gustav E.
Spiekerman, Joseph A., tr. see Hermans, Hubert J.
Spielberg, Franklin. Transportation Improvements in Madison, Wisconsin: Preliminary Analysis of Pricing Programs for Roads & Parking in Conjunction with Transit Changes.
Spielberger, C. D., ed. Current Topics in Clinical & Community Psychology.
Spielberger, C. D. & Sarason, I. G., eds. Stress & Anxiety.
Spielberger, C. D., ed. see Morris, Larry W.
Spielberger, Charles D., jt. auth. see Sarason, Irwin G.
Spielberger, Charles D., jt. ed. see Sarason, Irwin G.
Spielberger, Charles D., et al, eds. Stress & Anxiety.
Spielmann, M. H. History of Punch.
Spier, Margaret, ed. The Bowker Annual, 1987.
Spier, Peter. The Legend of New Amsterdam.
--The Pet Store.
--The Toy Store.
Spiers, Barbara, jt. auth. see Jewell, Peter.
Spiers, Richard P., jt. auth. see Anderson, William J.
Spies, Joseph R. Big Cats & Other Animals: Their Beauty, Dignity & Survival. Leth, Kathy, ed.
Spies, Werner. Max Ernst Loplop: The Artist in the Third Person. Gabriel, J. W., tr. from Ger.
Spiess, H. W. & Steigel, A. Dynamic NMR Spectroscopy.
Spiess, Lincoln B. Historical Musicology: A Reference Manual for Research in Music.
Spilhaus, Athelstan. Satellite of the Sun: The Science of the Earth & Its Surroundings.
Spilker, John & Strudwick, Karen, eds. Pocket Publisher: A Business Communication & Desktop Publishing Style Guide.
Spillane, John. TV Field & Bench Servicer's Handbook.
Spiller, Gene A., ed. Topics in Dietary Fiber Research.
Spiller, Sam. Confession of a Prime Minister.
--Stories of Men & Rats.
Spillers, W. R. Automated Structural Analysis: An Introduction.
Spillman, Pat. Hastening Time.
Spillman, Ron. The Complete Photobook.
Spina, John F., jt. auth. see Weiner, Donald D.
Spinard, Norman. Songs from the Stars.
Spindler, George, ed. see Harris, Clement.
Spindler, George, ed. see Trigger, Bruce G.
Spindler, George D. Doing the Ethnography of Schooling: Educational Anthropology in Action.
--Education & the Cultural Process: Toward an Anthropology or Education.
Spindler, Louise, ed. see Harris, Clement.
Spindler, Louise, ed. see Trigger, Bruce G.
Spindler, Susan, jt. auth. see Van Den Brul, Caroline.
Spinell, Michael R. A Clinical Guide to Soft Contact Lenses.
Spinelli, Jerry. Night of the Whale.
Spingarn, Joel E. History of Literary Criticism in the Renaissance.
Spink, Frank H., Jr., ed. see Lochmoeller, Donald C.
Spink, Ian. English Song: Dowland to Purcell.
Spink, Kathryn. The Miracle of Love: Mother Teresa of Calcutta, Her Missionaries of Charity, & Her Co-Workers.
Spink, Kathryn, ed. see Pope John Paul II.
Spink, Kathryn, tr. see La Pierre, Dominique.
Spinner, Morton. Injuries to the Major Branches of the Peripheral Nerves of the Forearm.
Spinner, Stephanie, ed. see Martin, Lee.
Spinner, Stephanie, ed. see Stine, Megan & Stine, H. William.
Spino, Dyveke. New Age Training for Fitness & Health.
Spinoza, Baruch. Book of God.
--Hebrew Grammar.
--Reflections & Maxims. Runes, Dagobert D., ed.
--The Road to Inner Freedom.
Spinrad, Norman. The Iron Dream.
--The Men in the Jungle.
Spiotto, James E., jt. auth. see Practicing Law Institute Staff.
Spirer, Herbert F. & Dueker, Marilynn. Vazsonyi's Introduction to Data Processing: Study Guide.
Spirer, Janet E. The Case Study Method: Guidelines, Practices & Applications for Vocational Education.
--Performance Testing: Issues Facing Vocational Education.
Spirer, Janet E., jt. auth. see Franchak, Stephen J.
Spires, Elizabeth. Swan's Island.
Spiro, Jack D. Time to Mourn: Judaism & the Psychology of Bereavement.
Spiro, Peter. Electroforming.
Spiro, Thomas G. Iron-Sulfur Proteins.
--Zinc Enzymes.
Spiro, Thomas G. & Stigliani, William M. Environmental Issues in Chemical Perspective.
Spiro, Thomas G., ed. Metal Ion Activation of Dioxygen.
Spisak, John F. & Jergensen, Gerald V., II, eds. Frontier Technology in Mineral Processing.
Spitler, Sue. Twice As Fast: Food Processor-Microwave Cooking.
Spitsyn, V. I. & Katz, J. J., eds. Moscow Symposium on the Chemistry of Transuranium Elements: Proceedings.
Spitz & Nixon. Rob & Smith's Operative Surgery: Paediatric Surgery.
Spitz, A. Dictionary of Astronomy & Astronautics.
Spitz, Bruce & Weeks, Jane. Medicaid Nursing Home Reimbursement in Illinois.
--Medicaid Nursing Home Reimbursement in Minnesota.
Spitz, Edna H., jt. ed. see Herrmann, Elizabeth R.
Spitz, John. Building Your Management Team: A Framework for Public Sector Labor Relations.
Spitz, Lewis W. & Lohff, Wenzel, eds. Discord, Dialogue, & Concord: Studies in the Lutheran Reformation's Formula of Concord.
Spitz, Robert S. The Making of Superstars: The Artists & Executives of the Rock Music World.
Spitzer, Doreen C. By One & One.
Spitzer, John J., ed. Myocardial Injury.
Spitzer, Manon L., jt. ed. see Miller, Norman N.

Authors

Spitzer, Robert L. & Skodol, Andrew E. A Psychiatrist's Casebook (The DSM Case Book)
Spitzer, Robert L., et al. DSM III Case Book: A Learning Companion to the Diagnostic & Statistical Manual of Mental Disorders.
Spitzer, S. P. & Denzin, Norman K. Mental Patient: Studies in the Sociology of Deviance.
Spitzer-Resnick, Jeffrey. Your Real Medicare Handbook.
Spitznagel, J. A., jt. ed. see Wiffen, F. W.
Spitznas, M., ed. Current Research in Ophthalmic Electron Microscopy.
--Current Research in Ophthalmic Electron Microscopy: Transactions of the 5th Annual Meeting of the European Club for Opthalmic Fine Structure in Zuerich, March 25 & 26, 1977.
Spiva, Ulysses V. How to Get a Grant for Your Own Special Project.
Spivak, Burton. Jefferson's English Crisis, 1803-1809: Commerce, Embargo, & the Republican Revolution.
Spivak, Jennie see Charsky, Jennie, pseud.
Splaver, Sarah. Paraprofessions: Careers of the Future & the Present.
Spletter, Mary. A Woman's Choice: New Options in the Treatment of Breast Cancer.
Splettstoesser, John F., ed. Ice-Core Drilling.
Splitter, Randolph. Proust's "Recherche" A Psychoanalytic Interpretation.
Spock, Benjamin & Rothenberg, Michael B. Baby & Child Care.
Spock, Marjorie. Teaching As a Lively Art.
Spodek, Bernard. Early Childhood Education.
Spoehr, Alexander, ed. Maritime Adaptations: Essays on Contemporary Fishing Communities.
Spoel, S. Van der see Van der Spoel, S. & Pierrot-Bults, A. C.
Spohn, Eric E., et al. Operative Dentistry Procedures for Dental Auxiliaries.
Sponar, J., ed. see FEBS Symposium on DNA, Liblice, 24-29 September, 1979.
Spong, John S. This Hebrew Lord.
Sponheim, Paul R. Faith & Process: The Significance of Process Thought for Christian Faith.
--God: The Question & the Quest.
Spooner, John D. Sex & Money.
Spooner, M. F., ed. The Amoco Cadiz Oil Spill.
Spooner, William A., ed. Simplified LRP for Faster Business Growth & Profit.
Spores, Ronald, jt. ed. see Bricker, Victoria R.
Sporing, Eileen, jt. auth. see Hayman, Laura L.
Sporing, Eileen M., et al. Pediatric Nursing Policies, Procedures, & Personnel.
Sporleder, Frank, ed. see Unger, Hans-Georg.
Sporn, Philip. Energy in an Age of Limited Availability & Delimited Applicability.
Sporting News Editors. Cooperstown: Where Baseball Legends Live Forever.
Spoto, Donald. Falling in Love Again: Marlene Dietrich.
Spove, Steen H., ed. see Brome, Richard.
Sprackling, M. T. The Plastic Deformation of Simple Ionic Crystals.
Spradley, James P. & McCurdy, David W. Anthropology: A Cultural Perspective.
Spradley, James P. & Spradley, Thomas S. Deaf Like Me.
Spradley, James P., jt. auth. see Veninga, Robert L.
Spradley, James P., jt. ed. see McCurdy, David W.
Spradley, Thomas S., jt. auth. see Spradley, James P.
Spradlin, William H., Jr. The Building Estimator's Reference Book.
Spragg, S. P. The Physical Behavior of Macromolecules with Biological Functions.
Sprague, Arthur C. & Trewin, J. C. Shakespeare's Plays Today: Some Customs & Conventions of the Stage.
Sprague, Elmer & Taylor, Paul W., eds. Knowledge & Value: Introductory Readings in Philosophy.
Sprague, Gretchen A. Question of Harmony.
Sprague, Janet, jt. auth. see Austin-Lett, Genelle.
Sprague, Jo & Stuart, Douglas. The Speaker's Handbook.
Sprague, Roderick & Krantz, Grover S., eds. The Scientist Looks at the Sasquatch II.
Sprandel, U. & Stark, F. Kompendium der Inneren Medizin.
Spratt, Barnett. Tom & the Redcoats.
Spratt, John S. Neoplasms of the Colon, Rectum & Anus: Mucosal & Epithelial.
Spratt, John S., Jr., jt. auth. see Donegan, William L.
Spreafico, F. & Arnon, R., eds. Tumor Associated Antigens & Their Specific Immune Responses.
Sprecher, C. Ronald. Essentials of Investments.
--Introduction to Investment Management.
Spreiregen, Paul D. Design Competitions.
Sprenger, Christine, et al. KC's Deals on Wheels.
--Teresa Tendon, Podiatrist: Computerized Accounting Practice Set.
--Lite Flight.
Sprengling, Martin & Graham, William C., eds. Barhebraeus' Scholia on the Old Testament Pt. 1: Genesis 2nd Samuel.
Spretnak, Charlene. Lost Goddesses of Early Greece: A Collection of Pre-Hellenic Mythology.
Spring, Gerald M. The Return from Babel.
Spring, Harry M. Boiler Operator's Guide.
Spring, Ira & Manning, Harvey. One Hundred Hikes in the North Cascades.
Spring, Kenneth H., ed. Direct Generation of Electricity.
Spring, Vicky & King, Gordon. Ninety-Five Hikes in the Canadian Rockies: Banff, Kootenay, & Assiniboine Parks.
Spring, Vicky & Urbick, Dee. Ninety-Four Hikes in the Canadian Rockies: Yoho, Jasper, Mt. Robson & Willmore Wilderness Parks.
Spring, Vicky, jt. auth. see Kirkendall, Tom.
Springborg, Robert. Family, Power, & Politics in Egypt: Sayed Bey Marei-His Clan, Clients & Cohorts.
Springer, G. S. & Patterson, D. J., eds. Engine Emissions: Pollutant Formation & Measurement.
Springer, George S., ed. Environmental Effects on Composite Materials.
Springer, Haskell S. Washington Irving: A Reference Guide.
Springer, Marilyn. Dollarwise Guide to Florida.
Springer, Marilyn & Schultz, Don A. Frommer's Dollarwise Guide to the Northwest.
Springer, Marylyn. Arthur Frommer's Guide to Orlando, Disney World & EPCOT.
Springer, Marylyn & Schultz, Don A. Dollarwise Guide to Cruises from the United States, 1985-1986.
--Dollarwise Guide to the Northwest.
--Frommer's Dollarwise Guide to Cruises: Including Alaska, Canada, the Carribean, Hawaii, Mexico, Panama & the U. S.
Springer, Steve, jt. auth. see Ostler, Scott.
Springer, T. A. Invariant Theory.
Springer, T. A., ed. see Conference on Local Fields - NUFFIC Summer School - Driebergen - 1966.
Springstubb, Tricia. The Blueberry Troll.
--Give & Take.
--The Moon on a String.
Sprinkle, Patricia H. Hunger: Understanding the Crisis Through Games, Dramas, & Songs.
Sprintzen, David A. The Drama of Thought: An Inquiry into the Place of Philosophy in Human Experience.
Sproat, Iain. Wodehouse at War.
Sproat, Kezia V., et al. The National Longitudinal Surveys of Labor Market Experience: An Annotated Bibliography of Research.
Spronk, N., jt. ed. see Addink, A. D.
Sprott, Richard L., ed. Age, Learning Ability & Intelligence.
Sproul, R. C. One Holy Passion: The Consuming Thirst to Know God.
--Stronger Than Steel: The Wayne Alderson Story.
Sproull, Wayne T. Air Pollution & Its Control.
Sprouse, Mary L. Sprouse's Income Tax Handbook, 1986.
--Sprouse's Income Tax Handbook, 1987.
Spruch, Grace M., jt. auth. see Spruch, Larry.
Spruch, Larry & Spruch, Grace M. The Ubiquitous Atom.
Sprudzs, Adolf, jt. auth. see Kavass, Igor I.
Sprung, Mervyn, et al, trs. from Sanskrit. Lucid Exposition of the Middle Way: The Essential Chapters from the Prasannapada of Candrakirti.
Sprunt, James, et al. From Bondage to Freedom.
Spruth, W. C., jt. ed. see Hasselmeier, H.
SPSS, Inc. Staff. SPSS-PCplus Tables.
--SPSS-X Graphics.
--SPSS-X Tables.
--SPSS-X User's Guide.
--SPSS-X User's Guide.
SPSS, Inc. Staff & Norusis, Marija. SPSS-PCplus.
--SPSS-PCplus Advanced Statistics.
Spuhler, Friedrich. Islamic Carpets & Textiles. Wingfield Digby, George & Wingfield Digby, Cornelia, trs.
Spulber, Nicolas. Soviet Economy.
Spulber, Nicolas & Horowitz, Ira. Quantitative Economic Policy & Planning: Theory & Models of Economic Control.
Spurdens, Dave. BMX Freestyle.
Spurgeon, C. H. Gleanings among the Sheaves.
--Metropolitan Tabernacle Pulpit.
--Types & Emblems.
Spurgeon, Charles H. Daily Help.
Spurling, John. Graham Greene.
Spurling, T. H., jt. auth. see Mason, E. A.
Spurlock, Julia. Pass Thy Hand for the Finishing Touch: The Homemaker's Guide to Refinishing & Restoring Antiques.
Spurrier, Robert L., Jr., et al. Oklahoma State University Supplement to Governing the Nation: American National Government.
Spurrier, William A. Natural Law & the Ethics of Love: A New Synthesis.
Spyker, John H. Little Lives.
Spykman, Elizabeth C. Edie on the Warpath.
--Lemon & a Star.
--Terrible, Horrible Edie.
--Terrible, Horrible Edie.
--Wild Angel.
Spyri, Johanna. Heidi. Barish, Wendy, ed.
--Heidi.
Squier, Elizabeth. Guide to Recommended Country Inns of New England.
--Guide to the Recommended Country Inns of New England, (Connecticut, Rhode Island, Massachusetts, Vermont, New Hampshire & Maine)
Squier, Elizbeth. Guide to the Recommended Country Inns of New England.
Squiers, Granville. Secret Hiding-Places: The Origins, Histories & Descriptions of English Secret Hiding-Places Used by Priests, Cavaliers, Jacobites, & Smugglers.
Squire, et al, eds. Baldwin's Ohio School Law Handbook.
Squire, Aelred. Asking the Fathers.
Squire, James R. Responses of Adolescents While Reading Four Short Stories.
Squire, James R. & Applebee, Roger K. High School English Instruction Today: The National Study of High School English Programs.
Squire, Lucy F., jt. auth. see Heller, Richard M.
Squire, Lucy F., et al. Exercises in Diagnostic Radiology, Vol. 3: Bone.
Squire, Peverill & Scott, Stanley. The Politics of California Coastal Legislation: The Crucial Year, 1976.
Squire, W. B., ed. see Byrd, William, et al.
Squires, Dick. Complete Book of Platform Tennis.
--How to Play Platform Tennis.
--The Other Racquet Sports.
Squires, Geoffrey. The Curriculum Beyond School.
Squires, Geoffrey, ed. Innovation Through Recession: SRHE Annual Conference, 1982.
Squires, P., ed. see National Center for Atmospheric Research Staff.
Squires, Terence L. Beginners Guide to Electronics.
Squires, V., ed. Livestock Management in the Arid Zone.
Sr. Bernetta Quinn. Randall Jarrell.
Srebrny, M., jt. ed. see Marek, W.
Sreebny, L. M. & Meyer, J., eds. Salivary Glands & Their Secretions.
Srere, Paul A. & Estabrook, Ronald W., eds. Microenvironments & Metabolic Compartmentation.
Sri Chinmoy Centre Staff, ed. Sri Chinmoy Family Cookbook.
Sri Aurobindo. Bases of Yoga.
--Essays on the Gita.
--The Life Divine.
Sri Chinmoy. Matsyendranath & Gorakshanath: Two Spiritual Lions.
Srinivasan, B. Representations of Finite Chevalley Groups.
Srinivasan, R. Biomolecular Structure, Conformation, Function & Evolution. Incl. Vol. 1. Diffraction & Related Studies; Vol. 2. Physico-Chemical & Theoretical Studies. Pergamon.
Srinivasan, Ram, jt. auth. see Rao, K. Ramamohan.
Srivastava, A. L. Life in Sanchi Sculptures.
Srivastava, H. M. & Karlsson, P. W. Multiple Gaussian Hypergeometric Series.
Srivastava, H. M. & Manocha, H. L. A Treatise on Generating Functions.
Srivastava, Rajeshwar. Punjab Painting.
Srivastava, U. K., et al. Quantitative Techniques for Managerial Decision Making: Concepts, Illustrations, & Problems.
Sr. Louis Passero. Hands for Others.
Srnka, Q. M. & Self, Tim. Systematic Medication Profile Review.
Sroge, Maxwell H. All about Mail Order: Facts, Trends, Key Data.
Sroge, Maxwell H., Staff, ed. Catalog Marketer Suppliers Guide, 1983.
Sryodoyev, N. Soviet Land Legislation.
Staal, Gert & Wolters, Hester, eds. Dutch Design Nineteen Fourty-Five to Nineteen Eighty-Seven.
Staar, Richard F. Communist Regimes in Eastern Europe.
Staar, Richard F., ed. see Kovrig, Bennett.
Staats, Arthur W. Learning, Language, & Cognition: Theory, Research, & Method for the Study of Human Behavior & Its Development.
Stabile, Toni. Everything You Want to Know about Cosmetics or What Your Friendly Clerk Didn't Tell You.
Stabler, Arthur P., ed. Four French Renaissance Plays.
Stabler, Ken & Stainback, Berry. Snake: The Candid Autobiography of Football's Most Outrageous Renegade.
Stabley, Don H. Assembler Language for Application Programming.
Stabley, Fred. W. The Spartans: A Story of Michigan State Football.
Stace, C. A., ed. Hybridization & the Flora of the British Isles.
Stacey, Allan. The Art of Egg Decorating.
--The Art of Egg Decorating.
Stacey, Barrie. Psychology & Social Structure.
Stacey, G. Dental Elevators: Principles for Safe Usage.
Stacey, Nicholas A. & Aubrey, Wilson. The Changing Pattern of Distribution.
Stacey, W. H., Jr. Space-Time Nuclear Reactor Kinetics.
Stacey, Weston M., Jr. Variational Methods in Nuclear Reactor Physics.
Stachowiak, Herbert, ed. Pragmatic Thought from Its Origins to the Eighteenth Century.
Stachowitz, Rolf A. & Chan, Chin-Liang. Verification & Validation of Expert Systems.
Stack, E. M. Reading French in the Arts & Sciences.
Stack, John. Policy Choices: Critical Issues in American Foreign Policy.
Stack, Stephen M., et al. The Meiotic Process, II: Pairing, Recombination, & Chromosome Movements.
Stackelberg, Mark Von see Schmidt, Helmut & Von Stackelberg, Mark.
Stackhouse, Max L., jt. auth. see Seltzer, Sanford.
Stackpole Books, Inc. Staff, ed. Taking Care of Outdoor Gear.
Stackpole, Edouard A. The Sea-Hunters.
Stack-Staikidis, William, jt. auth. see LaLonde, William S.
Stacy, Ralph W. & Waxman, Bruce. Computers in Biomedical Research.
Stacy, William H. Let's Live.
Staddor, J., jt. ed. see Honig, Werner K.
Stade, George. Confessions of a Ladykiller.
Stade, George, ed. see Cummings, e. e.
Stadelmann, Rudolph. The Social & Political History of the German 1848 Revolution. Chastain, James G., tr. from Ger.
Staden, Wendelgard von see Von Staden, Wendelgard.
Stadler, John. Animal Cafe.
--Hector, the Accordion-Nosed Dog.
Stadler, Jozef, tr. see Lange, Oskar.
Stadnichenko, A. La Crisis Del Sistema Monetario Del Capitalismo.
Stadt, Ronald W., jt. auth. see Bailey, Larry J.
Stadt und Universitatsbucherei & Frankfurt am Main, eds. Subject Catalogue Film, Vol. 1: Individual Holding as of July 1981.
Stadter, Philip A. Plutarch's Historical Methods: An Analysis of the Mulierum Virtutes.
Stadtman, Earl R., jt. ed. see Prusiner, Stanley.
Staehle, R. W., jt. ed. see Fontana, M. G.
Staemmler, ed. see Kaufmann, E.
Staff & Viewers of The Eyes of Texas. The Eyes of Texas CookBook.
Staffman, Daniel, tr. see Kopacsi, Sandor.
Staffman, Judy, tr. see Kopacsi, Sandor.
Stafford, Bill. The Adventure of Giving. Griffin, Ted, ed.
Stafford, Carolyn, jt. auth. see Stafford, Robert.
Stafford, Clifford T. Starlight Furnace: An Historical Novel.
Stafford, D. C. The Economics of Housing Policy.
Stafford, Jean. Boston Adventure.
Stafford, Robert & Stafford, Carolyn. The Parent Child Fun Kit.
Stafford, Tim. Knowing the Face of God.
--Knowing the Face of God: The Search for a Personal Relationship with God.
Stafford-Clark, David, jt. auth. see Smith, Andrew C.
Stafford-Deitsch, Jeremy. Shark: A Photographer's Story.
Stafleu, Frans A., ed. International Code of Botanical Nomenclature.
Stage, Sarah. Female Complaints: Lydia Pinkham & the Business of Women's Medicine.
--Female Complaints: Lydia Pinkham & the Business of Women's Medicine.
Stageberg, Norman C., jt. ed. see Anderson, W. L.
Stagg, Frank. Polarities of Man's Existence in Biblical Perspective.
Stagg, Louis C. The Figurative Language of the Tragedies of Shakespeare's Chief Sixteen-Century Contemporaries: An Index.
Stagg, William D., jt. auth. see Pegg, Brian F.
Stagner, Lloyd E. & Reisdorff, James J. North American Hudsons: The 4-6-4 Steam Locomotive.
Stagner, Ross, jt. ed. see Meltzer, H.
Stagnitto, Joseph. Schizoid.
Stahl, Barbara J. & McQuaid, Patrick. How to Get into an Ivy League School.
Stahl, Ben. Blackbeard's Ghost.
Stahl, Frederick A. Guide to the Maintenance Repair & Alteration of Historic Buildings.
Stahl, Hilda. Elizabeth Gail & Double Trouble.
--Elizabeth Gail & the Frightened Runaways.
--Elizabeth Gail & the Holiday Mystery.
--Elizabeth Gail & the Missing Love Letters.
--Elizabeth Gail & the Music Camp Romance.

--Elizabeth Gail & the Mystery at the Johnson Farm.
--Elizabeth Gail & the Secret Box.
--Elizabeth Gail & the Strange Birthday Party.
--Elizabeth Gail & the Time for Love.
--Elizabeth Gail & Trouble from the Past.
--Teddy Jo & the Stolen Ring.
--Teddy Jo & the Strange Medallion.
--Tina's Eighteenth Summer.
--Tina's Reluctant Friend.
--Tina's Secret Rival.
Stahl, I., ed. Operational Gaming: An International Approach.
Stahl, Konrad & Struyk, Raymond J. U. S. & West German Housing Markets.
Stahl, Norman & Horan, D. The Buried Man.
Stahl, O. Glenn. The Personnel Job of Government Managers.
Stahl, P. W., ed. KG Two Hundred.
Stahle, J. Vestibular Function on Earth & in Space.
Stahler, Charles, jt. auth. see Wasserman, Debra.
Stahnke, A. A., jt. auth. see Ellsworth, J. W.
Stainback, Berry, jt. auth. see Stabler, Ken.
Stainback, Berry, jt. auth. see Weaver, Earl.
Stainer, F. W., jt. auth. see Garland, D. J.
Staines, P. J., jt. auth. see Bell, P. B.
Stainforth, Diana. Mara's Way.
Stainton, Audrey. Sweet Rome.
Stainton, Lindsay. Turner's Venice.
Stair. Computers in Today's World: Microcomputer Study Guide.
Stair, jt. auth. see Render.
Stair, Ralph M. Principles of Data Processing: Concepts, Cases & Applications.
Stair, Ralph M., Jr. Programming in BASIC: Structured Programming, Cases, Applications & Modules. Fetter, Robert B. & McMillan, Claude, eds.
Stair, Rolland. Be Reconciled.
Stakeova, V., jt. ed. see Kloudova, B.
Stakes, Mary E. Controlling Public Pensions.
Stakgold, I., et al, eds. see Battelle Summer Institute, Seattle, Jul. 3-28, 1972.
Stakman, E. C., et al. Campaigns Against Hunger.
Stalberg, Roberta & Nesi, Ruth. China's Crafts: The Story of How They're Made & What They Mean.
Staley, Thomas F. & Benstock, Bernard, eds. Approaches to Ulysses: Ten Essays.
Stalick, Wayne M., jt. auth. see Hines, Herman.
Stalin, Iosif. Selected Writings.
Stalin, Joseph. Foundations of Leninism.
--Leninism: Selected Writings.
Stalker, G. M., jt. auth. see Burns, Tom.
Stalker, James M. The Stalker Trilogy.
Stallard, John. Four in a Wild Place.
Stallard, John J. & Terry, George R. Office Systems Management.
Stallard, John J., et al. The Electronic Office: A Guide for Managers.
Stallard, Mary G. Appalachian Andy.
Stalley, Rodney E., jt. auth. see Sheard, James L.
Stallings & Hutchinson. Computers: The User Perspective.
Stallings, Penny. Rock 'n' Roll Confidential.
Stallings, William. Integrated Services Digital Networks (ISDN)
--ISDN: Technology, Applications & Standards.
Stallings, William, ed. Computer Communications: Architectures, Protocols, & Standards.
Stallknecht, Newton P. & Frenz, Horst, eds. Comparative Literature: Method & Perspective.
Stallman, Robert. The Captive.
Stallybrass, Gunnvor, tr. see Hamsun, Knut.
Stallybrass, Oliver, tr. see Hamsun, Knut.
Stallybrass, Oliver, tr. see Jensen, Niels.
Stalvey, Lois M. The Education of an Ordinary Woman.
Stam, Paul J. Thirty Degrees North, One Sixty Fifth East.
Stamaty, Mark A. More Washingtoons.
Stamberg, Susan, jt. auth. see National Public Radio Staff.
Stambler, Moses, ed. A Systems Approach to Social Foundation of American Education.
Stambolian, George & Marks, Elaine, eds. Homosexualities & French Literature: Cultural Contexts, Critical Texts.
Stamler, Jeremiah, jt. auth. see Kaplan, Norman M.
Stamm, Marta, jt. auth. see Stanforth, Deidre.
Stamm, T. T. Foot Troubles.
Stammbach, U. Homology in Group Theory.
Stammers, M. K. Discovering Maritime Museums & Historic Ships.
Stamp, Dudley, ed. Land Use & Resources: Studies in Applied Geography.
Stamp, L. Dudley. Asia: A Regional & Economic Geography.
Stampe, David. A Dissertation on Natural Phonology. Hankamer, Jorge, ed.
Stampen, Jacob O. & Reeves, Roxanne W. Student Aid & Public Higher Education: A Progress Report.
Stamper, Jamie. Kitty the Raccoon.
Stamper, Judith B. Autobot Alert!
--Deception Poison.
Stampfli, K., ed. see International Society of Blood Transfusion Staff.
Stampp, Kenneth M. Indiana Politics during the Civil War.
Stamps, Jeffrey, jt. auth. see Lipnack, Jessica.
Stamps, Judy A., et al. A Zoology Lab Manual.
Stan, Anisoara. Romanian Cook Book.
Stanard, Mary N. Colonial Virginia: Its People & Customs.
Stanback, Thomas M., Jr., jt. auth. see Noyelle, Thierry J.
Stanberry, D. Elaine. Love's Perplexing Obsession, Experienced by Two Geniuses: Heinrich Heine & Percy Bysshe Shelley.
Stanbery, James. California Two-Thousand Campaign: The Populist Movement with a Meaning for All America.
Stanbrook, C., jt. ed. see Lew, J.
Stanbury, W. T. Government Regulation: Scope, Growth, Process.
Stanbury, W. T., jt. auth. see Gorecki, P. K.
Stanchev, I., jt. ed. see Sendov, B.
Stancil, Ryburn T. Spiritual Nuggets: A Devotional Book.
Stancl, Donald L. & Stancl, Mildred L. Applications of College Mathematics: Management, Life, & Social Sciences.
Stancl, Mildred L., jt. auth. see Stancl, Donald L.
Standage, Blaine D., et al. Compute's Data File Handler for the Commodore 64. Compute! Magazine Staff, ed.
Standard & Poor's Research Dept. Staff. Standard & Poor's Rating Guide. Incl. Corporate Bonds; Commercial Paper; Municipal Bonds; International Securities. McGraw.
Standard Educational Corporation Staff. New Standard Encyclopedia. Downey, Douglas W., et al, eds.
--New Standard Encyclopedia. Downey, Douglas W., et al, eds.
Standard, Paul, tr. from Ital. Arrighi's Running Hand.
Standard's & Poor's Staff. Options Handbook.
--OTC Handbook.
--Stockmarket Encyclopedia of the Fortune.
Standen, O. D., jt. auth. see Way, W. Dennis.
Standford, M., jt. auth. see Redman, S.
Standhardt, Robert T. Journey to the Magical City: A Quadriplegic Person's Reflections on Suffering & Love.
Standiford, Sally N., et al. Computers in the English Classroom: A Primer for Teachers.
Standing Conference on Library Materials on Africa Staff. Periodicals from Africa: A Bibliography & Union List of Periodicals Published in Africa. Travis, Carole, ed.
Standing, Guy. Labour Force Participation & Development.
Standing, Guy, ed. Labour Circulation & the Labour Process.
Standing, Guy, jt. ed. see Peek, Peter.
Stanek, Jaroslav, et al. Oligosaccharides. Mayer, Karel, tr.
Stanek, Muriel. Left, Right, Left, Right.
Stanesby, Derek. Science, Reason & Religion.
Stanfill, Francesca. Shadows & Light.
Stanford, A. L. Exercises & Solutions Manual for Foundations in Biophysics.
Stanford Cade Memorial Symposium Staff. Interaction of Radiation & Anti-Tumor Drugs: Proceedings of the Stanford Code Memorial Symposium, Royal Institute, London, Sept., 1976. Hellmann, Kurt, ed.
Stanford, Charles V. Musical Composition.
Stanford, Derek, ed. Pre-Raphaelite Writing.
Stanford, Gene, ed. Classroom Practices in Teaching English 1978-1979: Activating the Passive Student.
Stanford, Gene, jt. ed. see National Council of Teachers of English Staff.
Stanford, Jay G., jt. auth. see Tees, David W.
Stanford, Melvin J. Management Policy.
Stanford, Neal. I Do Windows.
--Open Windows.
--The Windowless View.
Stanford Research Institute Staff. Gas Tracer Study of Roof-Vent Effluent Diffusion at Millstone Nuclear Power Station AIF-NESP-007B.
--General Field Test Plan for Evaluation of Roof-Vent Effluent Diffusion from Reactor & Turbine Buildings (AIF-NESP-007A)
Stanford University, Hoover Institution on War, Revolution & Peace Staff. Catalog of the Chinese Collection.
--Catalog of the Chinese Collection First Supplement.
--The Catalog of the Chinese Collection: Second Supplement.
--Catalog of the Japanese Collection.
--Catalog of the Japanese Collection, First Supplement.
--Catalog of the Japanese Collection: Second Supplement.
--Catalog of the Western Language Collections.
--Catalogs of the Western Language Serials & Newspaper Collection.
Stanford, W. B. Enemies of Poetry.
--Greek Tragedy & the Emotions.
--Ireland & the Classical Tradition.
Stanford, W. Bedell. Enemies of Poetry.
Stanforth, Deidre & Stamm, Marta. Buying & Renovating a House in the City: A Practical Guide.
Stanforth, Deirdre. The New Orleans Restaurant Cookbook.
Stang, JoAnne, jt. auth. see Schreiber, Linda.
Stang, N. Edward Munch.
Stang, Peter J., et al. Vinyl Cations.
Stang, Ragna. Vigeland: The Sculptor & His Works.
Stanga, Keith G., jt. auth. see Williams, Jan R.
Stanger, Frank B. Gifts of the Spirit.
Stanger, Margaret A. That Quail Robert.
Stanhope, et al. Home Health Care: Current Practice.
Stanhope, Marcia & Lancaster, Jeannette. Community Health Nursing: Process & Practice for Promoting Health.
Stanier, Roger & Doudoroff, M. The Microbial World.
Stanish, Bob. Creativity for Kids Through Word Play.
Stanislavsky, Konstantin. Stanislavsky on the Art of the Stage. Magarshack, David, tr. & intro. by.
Stanislawski, Dan. Landscapes of Bacchus: The Vine in Portugal.
Stanislawski, J. Polish-English, English-Polish Dictionary (The Great) 1975.
--Polish-English, English-Polish Practical Dictionary.
Stanistreet, Grace M., ed. Recitations for Children.
Staniszewski, Amy G., ed. see Callahan, Richard J.
Stankard, Martin F., Jr. Successful Management of Large Clerical Operations: A Guide to Improving Service Transaction Systems.
Stankiewicz, W. J. Politics & Religion in Seventeenth-Century France.
Stankovsky, Jan, jt. auth. see Levcik, Friedrich.
Stanley. Public School & Public Policy.
Stanley, Autumn. The Enchanted Quill.
--Mainder the Buttercup.
Stanley, Carol. For Keeps?
Stanley, D. J. & Kelling, G., eds. Sedimentation in Submarine Canyons, Fans & Trenches.
Stanley, Dave, jt. auth. see Hill, Ronald C.
Stanley, David. Alaska-Yukon Handbook: A Gypsy Guide to the Inside Passage & Beyond. Castleman, Deke & Hume, Diane, eds.
--Life with Elvis.
--South Pacific Handbook.
Stanley, David M. Apostolic Church in the New Testament.
Stanley, David T., et al. Bankruptcy: Problem, Process, Reform.
Stanley, Delmar S., jt. auth. see Black, John G.
Stanley, Gary. The Garimus File.
Stanley, George E. Crime Lab.
--The Mexican Tamale Mystery.
Stanley, Harold W. Senate vs. Governor, Alabama 1971: Referents for Opposition in a One-Party Legislature.
Stanley, Jackson, jt. auth. see Kantar, Edwin B.
Stanley, James C., et al. Renovascular Hypertension.
Stanley, John. The Essence of Biometry.
--Viva Knievel.
--World War III.
Stanley, L., jt. ed. see Wise, S.
Stanley, Liz & Wise, Sue. Breaking Out: Feminist Consciousness & Feminist Research.
Stanley, Lloyd H., ed. Guide to Evaluation of Training.
--Guide to Training Needs Assessment.
Stanley, Melissa & Andrykovitch, George. Living: An Interpretive Approach to Biology.
Stanley, Michael. The Boomerang Conspiracy.
--The Swiss Conspiracy.
Stanley, Philip E. & Scoggins, Bruce, eds. Liquid Scintillation Counting: Recent Developments.
Stanley, R. G. & Linskens, H. F. Pollen: Biology, Biochemistry, & Management.
Stanley, Roy M., II. Prelude to Pearl Harbor: War in China, 1937-41; Japan's Rehearsal for World War II.
Stanley, William B., ed. Review of Research in Social Studies Education: 1976-1983.
Stanmsky, Peter, ed. see Schoenl, William J.
Stannage, Tom. Baldwin Thwarts the Opposition: The British General Election of 1935.
Stannard, Bruce. Ben Lexcen: The Man, the Keel & the Cup.
Stannard, Neville. The Beatles: The Long & Winding Road, a History of the Beatles on Record.
Stannard, Neville & Tobler, John. The Beatles: Working Class Heroes.
Stannett, V. T., jt. ed. see Jenkins, A. D.
Stano, Michael, jt. auth. see Reinsch, Lamar.
Stanovich, Betty Jo. Hedgehog Surprises.
Stansfield, Richard H. The Best Ever How-to-Get-a-Job Book.
Stansfield, William D. Genetics.
Stansky, Peter & Abrahams, William. Journey to the Frontier: Two Roads to the Spanish Civil War.
--Orwell: The Transformation.
--The Unknown Orwell.
Stansky, Peter, ed. see Kinzer, Bruce L.
Stansky, Peter, ed. see Kruppa, Patricia S.
Stanton, Erwin S. Reality-Centered People Management: Keys to Improved Productivity.
Stanton, Graham, ed. The Interpretation of Matthew.
Stanton, Jeffery, et al, eds. The Addison-Wesley Book of Atari Software 1983.
Stanton, Jeffrey & Dickey, John, eds. The Addison-Wesley Book of Apple Software 1983.
Stanton, John R. Theory & Practice of Propellers for Auxiliary Sailboats.
Stanton, Marjorie, jt. auth. see Torres, Gertrude.
Stanton, Martin. Outside the Dream: Lacan & French Styles of Psychoanalysis.
Stanton, Maura. Cries of Swimmers.
--Molly Companion.
--Snow on Snow.
Stanton, Reggie. Drawing & Painting Buildings: Reggie Stanton's Guide to Architectural Rendering.
Stanton, Robert J. Gore Vidal: A Primary & Secondary Bibliography.
Stanton, Sybil. The Twenty-Five Hour Woman.
Stanton, Thomas M. & Parsons, W. Stuart. Decision Analysis in Litigation.
Stanway, Andrew. Infertility: A Common-Sense Guide for the Childless.
--Infertility: A Common-Sense Guide for the Childless.
Stanwood, Brooks. The Glow.
Stanwood, Donald. The Seventh Royale.
Stanworth, John, et al. The Survival of the Small Firm.
Stanyon, J. Sandys, tr. see Herrmann, Wilhelm.
Staple, Peter H., ed. Advances in Oral Biology.
Staples, Alfred. Mobile Carnival: Mardi Gras History 1947. Plummer, Cameron, ed.
Staples, I. Ezra, et al. Impact of Decentralization on Curriculum: Selected Viewpoints.
Staples, R. Introduction to Black Sociology.
Staples, Richard C., jt. auth. see Mussell, Harry.
Staples, Robert. The Black Woman in America: Sex, Marriage & the Family.
Stapleton, Gerald. Beginner's Guide to Computer Logic.
Stapleton, John. How to Prepare a Marketing Plan.
Stapleton, John F., jt. auth. see Sussex, Margie.
Stapleton, Katie. Denver Delicious.
Stapleton, Marjorie. Make Things Sailors Made.
Stapleton, Michael. The Concise Dictionary of Greek & Roman Mythology.
Stapleton, Peter. New Directions for a Musical Church.
Stapp, William B. & Liston, Mary D., eds. Environmental Education: A Guide to Information Sources.
Star, Steven H., jt. auth. see Corey, E. Raymond.
Starbird, Irving R., et al. United States Cotton Industry.
Starbird, William & Oriti, Ronald. Introduction to Astronomy.
Starbuck, Alma J. Complete Irish Wolfhound.
Starchild, Adam. Building Wealth: A Layman's Guide to Trust Planning.
--Tax Havens for Corporations.
Starcke, Walter. The Ultimate Revolution.
Stare, Fredrick J., jt. auth. see Whelan, Elizabeth.
Stare, Fredrick J., jt. auth. see Whelan, Elizabeth M.
Starhawk. Dreaming the Dark: Magic, Sex, & Politics.
Stark. Spina Bifida: Problems & Management.
Stark, Arlene, jt. auth. see Kudler, Jacqueline.
Stark, E., et al, eds. Endocrinology, Neuroendocrinology, Neuropeptides-Part II: Proceedings of the 28th International Congress of Physiological Sciences, Budapest, 1980.
--Endocrinology, Neuroendocrinology, Neuropeptides-Part 1: Proceedings of the 28th International Congress of Physiological Sciences, Budapest, 1980.
Stark, Edward. Intimacy.
Stark, F., jt. auth. see Sprandel, U.
Stark, G., ed. see Deutsche Gesellschaft Fur Biophysik, Annual Meeting, Konstanz, October 1979.
Stark, George R., ed. Biochemical Aspects of Reactions on Solid Supports.
Stark, John E., et al. Manual of Chest Medicine.
Stark, Lawrence. Neurological Control Systems: Studies in Bioengineering.
Stark, M., jt. auth. see Mostowski, J.
Stark, Norman. The Formula Book.
Stark, Peter, jt. auth. see Young, George.
Stark, Richard. The Hunter.
--The Man With the Getaway Face.
--The Outfit.
--The Score.
--The Seventh.

Authors

Stark, Robert M. & Mayer, Robert H. Quantitative Construction Management: Uses of Linear Optimization.
Stark, Robin & Leitner, Stuart. Maximum Performance with Lotus 1-2-3, Versions 1.0 & 2.0.
Stark, Rodney. Sociology.
Starke, E. A., Jr. & Sanders, T. H., Jr., eds. Aluminum-Lithium Alloys II: Proceedings, Monterey, California, 1983.
Starke, E. A., Jr., jt. ed. see Sanders, T. H., Jr.
Starkey. Laplace Transform for Electrical Engineers.
Starkey, Frank L., jt. auth. see Nelson, Steven M.
Starkey, Otis P., et al. The Anglo-American Realm.
Starkie, Walter, tr. see Menendez Pidal, Ramon.
Starks, Charles. Free Radical Telomerization.
Starks, Michael. Fabulous Illustrated Story of Psychoactive Plants.
--Marijuana Potency.
Starling, Grover. The Changing Environment of Business.
Starling, Kenneth E. Fluid Thermodynamic Properties for Light Petroleum Systems.
Starlinger, P., jt. ed. see Hofschneider, P. H.
Starmark Publishing. The No-Nonsense Guide to Starting Your Own Business.
Starokadomskiy, L. M. Charting the Russian Northern Sea Route: The Arctic Ocean Hydrographic Expedition, 1910-1915. Barr, William, tr.
Starr, jt. auth. see Lafleur.
Starr, Bill. The Treasure of Wonderwhat: A Farstar & Son Novel.
Starr, C. Current Issues in Energy.
Starr, Cecie & Taggart, Ralph. Biology: The Unity & Diversity of Life.
Starr, Chester G. Civilization & the Caesars.
Starr, Fern. Ordeal: One Family's Experience with Stroke.
Starr, George R., Jr. Decoys of the Atlantic Flyway.
--How to Make Working Decoys.
Starr, Harold & Merz, Harold. Conditions Affecting Vocational Education Planning: Implications for Administration & Research.
Starr, Harold, et al. Coordination in Vocational Education Planning: Barriers & Facilitators.
--Selecting, Analyzing, & Displaying Planning Information.
--Using Labor Market Information in Vocational Planning.
Starr, Harvey & Ostrom, Charles W. A Collective Goods Approach to Understanding Transnational Action.
Starr, Hill. The George Eliot Calender: Diary 1986.
Starr, Irina. The Sound of Light.
Starr, John B. & Dyer, Nancy A. Post-Liberation Works of Mao Zedong: A Bibliography & Index.
Starr, Kevin. Land's End.
Starr, Marvin M., jt. auth. see Miller, Harry B.
Starr, Richard F., ed. Yearbook on International Communist Affairs: 1975.
Starr, Ruth. Wonders from the Heavens.
Starr, S. Frederick. Decentralization & Self-Government in Russia, 1830-1870.
Starr, V. Hale & McCormick, Mark. Jury Selection: An Attorney's Guide to Jury Law & Selection.
Starr, William J., jt. auth. see Bockmon, Guy A.
Starsinic, Donald E. Patterns of Metropolitan Area & County Population Growth: 1980-1984.
Start, C., jt. auth. see Newsholme, E. A.
Start, Clarissa. The Happy Gardener. Franzwa, Gregory M., ed.
Startt, James D. Journalism's Unofficial Ambassador: A Biography of Edward Price Bell 1869-1943.
Startzman, Paul. Tutankhamon: A Novel of Ancient Egypt.
Stary, J., jt. auth. see Ruzicka, J.
Staryos, Michelle M. & Winig, Laura. Collaborations for Literacy: Tutor's Handbook.
Starzhinskii, V. M. Applied Methods in the Theory of Nonlinear Oscillations.
Starzyk, Lawrence J. & Jewell, John B. Effective Business Writing.
Staschewski, F. Die Banjangi.
Stasheff, Christopher. Escape Velocity.
--King Kobold Revived.
--The Warlock Enraged.
--The Warlock in Spite of Himself. Del Ray, Lester, ed.
--The Warlock Is Missing.
--The Warlock Unlocked.
Stashower, Daniel. The Adventure of the Ecoplasmic Man.
Stasi, Lawrence Di see Di Stasi, Lawrence.
Stasinska, Joanna, tr. see Krall, Hanna.
Stasio, D. L. Fate Stepped In.
Stasny, Charles & Tyrnauer, Gabrielle. Who Rules the Joint? A Study of the Changing Political Culture of Maximum-Security Prisons in America.
Stassinopoulos, Arianna. Maria Callas: The Woman Behind the Legend.
Stassinopoulos, Arianna & Beny, Roloff. The Gods of Greece.
State Bar of California, Committee on Continuing Education of the Bar. California Commercial Law.
State Bar of Nevada. Nevada Civil Practice Manual.
State Bar of Texas, Pattern Jury Charges Committee, ed. Texas Pattern Jury Charges: 1973 Cumulative Supplement.
State Bar of Texas, Professional Efficiency & Economic Research Committee. Texas Collections Manual. Hickey, Firmin A., Jr., ed.
State Labs Staff, jt. ed. see EPA Staff.
State Statistical Bureau Staff. China: A Statistics Survey in 1985.
Statham, Daphne. Radicals in Social Work.
Statham, I. C. Coal Mining.
Statham, Ian & Finlayson, Brian. Hillslope Analysis.
Statham, Jane, jt. ed. see ReQua, Eloise.
Statham, June, jt. ed. see Booth, Tony.
Stathas, Thalia, ed. see Centlivre, Susannah.
Stather, J. W., jt. auth. see Nenot, J. C.
Statistics Canada Staff. Canada Handbook: The 48th Annual Handbook of Present Conditions & Recent Progress.
Statler, Oliver. All Japan: The Catalogue of Everything Japanese.
Staton, Knofel. Bible Keys for Today's Family.
--Check Your Commitment: Student.
--Check Your Discipleship.
--Check Your Homelife.
--Check Your Life in Christ.
--Check Your Lifestyle.
--Check Your Morality.
--Grow, Christian, Grow: Student.
--Struggle for Freedom.
--What to Do till Jesus Comes.
Staton-Bevan, Tony. The Care & Repair of Glassfibre Yachts: Includes the Detection, Prevention & Treatment of Osmosis.
Stauber, Alvin & Young, E. Neil. Business Law-Florida Edition, Cases & Materials.
Staubesand, Jochen, jt. auth. see Zuleger, Susanna.
St Aubyn, Fiona, jt. auth. see Ager, Stanley.
Stauffer, Ethelbert. Jesus & the Wilderness Community at Qumran. Spaltenholz, Hans, tr.
Stauffer, Francis H. Queer, the Quaint, the Quizzical.
Stauffer, M. R., ed. Fabric of Ducile Strain.
Stauffer, S. Anita. The Altar Guild: A Guide for the Ministry of Liturgical Preparations.
Staugaard, Andrew C., Jr. Microcomputer Programming & Interfacing, 6801, 68701 & 6803.
Staunton, Howard. Chess Player's Handbook.
Stauter, Jay. Let's Go Visiting.
--The World & I: Memoirs of a Nobody.
--The World I Knew: What Was So Good about the Good Old Days?
Stave, Albert D. Mr. Humanity.
Stave, Uwe, ed. Perinatal Physiology.
Stavenhagen, Lee, ed. & tr. see Morienus.
Stavrakas, Nick & Allen, Keith, eds. Studies in Topology.
Stavrou, P. Cyprus, the Sweet Land.
Stavrou, Theofanis G., ed. Russia under the Last Tsar.
Stavrou, Theofanis G., ed. see Ritsos, Yannis.
Stavroulakis, Peter, ed. Distributed Parameter Systems Theory. Incl. Pt. 1. Control; Pt. 2. Estimation. Van Nos Reinhold.
Staw, Barry M. & Salancik, Gerald R. New Directions in Organizational Behavior.
Stayman, Harold W., Jr. & Stayman, Norma H. Insider's Guide to Florida Restaurants.
Stayman, Norma H., jt. auth. see Stayman, Harold W., Jr.
Stead, Christina. For Love Alone.
--Letty Fox: Her Luck.
--The Little Hotel.
--Man Who Loved Children.
--The Man Who Loved Children.
--Miss Herbert: The Suburban Wife.
Steadman. Inspector Mouse.
Steadman, David W. The Fine Art of Food.
Steadman, David W., ed. Selections from the Norton Simon Museum of Art.
Steadman, Henry J., et al. Developing Jail Mental Health Services: Practices & Principles.
Steadman, Mimi E., jt. auth. see Tree, Christina.
Steadman, Ralph. Between the Eyes.
Steamer, Robert J. The Supreme Court in Crisis: A History of Conflict.
Steane, Susan M., jt. ed. see Pierce, Steven R.
Steans, D. J. Backward Glance.
Stearn, Jess. A Matter of Immortality.
Stearn, Jess, jt. auth. see Caldwell, Taylor.
Stearn, W. T. Three Prefaces on Linnaeus & Robert Brown.
Stearns, Bill. Filling Up Your Think Tank.
Stearns, F. & Montag, T., eds. The Urban Ecosystem: A Holistic Approach.
Stearns, Kathleen D. Eager Reader.
Stearns, Louis W. Sea Urchin Development: Cellular & Molecular Aspects.
Stearns, Pamela. Into the Painted Bear Lair.
--The Mechanical Doll.
Stearns, Peter N. European Experience Since Eighteen Fifteen.
Stearns, Peter N., ed. The Other Side of Western Civilization-Readings in Everyday Life: The Sixteenth Century to the Present.
Stearns, Peter N. & Walkowitz, Daniel J., eds. Workers in the Industrial Revolution: Recent Studies of Labor in the United States & Europe.
Stearns, Robert. From Performance.
Stearns, Sam D. Digital Signal Analysis.
Steaton, Albert. The Battle of Moscow.
Stebbins, Robert C., et al. Teaching & Research in the California Desert.
Stebbins, William C., jt. auth. see Geis, George L.
Steben, Ralph & Bell, Sam. Track & Field Coaching.
Stecher, Miriam B. Daddy & Ben Together.
Stechow, Wolfgang, et al. Studies in the History of Art, 1973.
Steck, Allen, jt. ed. see Roper, Steve.
Steckler, Doug, jt. auth. see Oberman, Margaret.
Stedman, John G. Narrative of an Expedition Against the Revolted Negroes of Surinam. Van Lier, R. A., ed.
Stedman, Ray. Acts Trilogy: Birth of the Body; Growth of the Body; Triumph of the Body.
Stedmond, John M. Comic Art of Laurence Sterne: Convention & Innovation in "Tristram Shandy" & "A Sentimental Journey"
Stedwell, Paki. Vaulting: Gymnastics on Horseback.
Steedman, Carolyn. Policing the Victorian Community: The Formation of English Provincial Police Forces, 1856-1880.
Steedman, James C., jt. auth. see Reynolds, Charles E.
Steedman, Julie. Emergency Room: An ABC Tour.
Steeds, D., jt. auth. see Nish, I.
Steeg, Clarence L. Ver see Ver Steeg, Clarence L.
Steegman, John. Victorian Taste: A Study of the Arts & Architecture from 1830 to 1870.
Steel, B. Translation from Spanish: An Introductory Course.
Steel, Danielle. Changes.
--Family Album.
--Fine Things.
--Full Circle.
--Loving.
--Now & Forever.
--Secrets.
--Thurston House.
Steel, David. Preaching Through the Year.
Steel, Donald. Golf Records, Facts & Champions.
Steel, R. J., jt. auth. see McWilliams, J.
Steel, Ronald, tr. see Servan-Schreiber, Jean-J.
Steel Structures Painting Council Staff, et al. Color Photographic Standards for Surface Preparation (SSPC-Vis 1)
Steele, A. O. The Questing Christ.
Steele, Algernon O. Bible & the Human Quest.
Steele, Danielle. Thurston House.
Steele, F. & Bourne, A., eds. The Man-Food Equation.
Steele, Gerald L. Exploring the World of Plastics.
--Fiber Glass.
Steele, Guy L., Jr., jt. auth. see Harbison, Samuel P.
Steele, James B., jt. auth. see Barlett, Donald L.
Steele, James W. Paying for Performance & Position: Dilemmas in Salary Compression & Merit Pay.
Steele, Jonathan. Soviet Power: The Kremlin's Foreign Policy-Brezhnev to Andropov.
--Soviet Power: The Kremlin's Foreign Policy-Brezhnev to Andropov.
Steele, Kathleen C. How to Be a Legal Secretary Without a Computer: Shortcuts to Ignorance.
Steele, Kurt D. Electronic Information Publishing: Old Issues in a New Industry.
Steele, Melba. Cowboy, Game Warden & Longhorns.
Steele, Nancy. Tracking.
Steele, Pauline F., ed. Dental Specialties for the Dental Hygienist.
Steele, R., ed. see Bartholomaeus, Anglicus.
Steele, Sara. Cost-Benefit Analysis & the Adult Educator: A Literature Review.
Steele, Vera. Princess Zettie & the Teeny Weeny People.
Steele, William A. The Interaction of Gases with Solid Surfaces.
Steele, William O. Andy Jackson's Water Well.
--The Buffalo Knife.
--Daniel Boone's Echo.
--Davy Crockett's Earthquake.
--Far Frontier.
--Flaming Arrows.
--Flaming Arrows.
--Lone Hunt.
--The Lone Hunt.
--The Magic Amulet.
--The Man with the Silver Eyes.
--No-Name Man of the Mountain.
--Old Wilderness Road: An American Journey.
--Perilous Road.
--The Perilous Road.
--Tomahawks & Trouble.
--Trail Through Danger.
--The War Party.
--The War Party.
--Westward Adventure: The True Stories of Six Pioneers.
--Wilderness Journey.
--Wilderness Tattoo: A Narrative of Juan Ortiz.
--Winter Danger.
--Year of the Bloody Sevens.
Steeley, G. C., jt. auth. see Cowling, T. M.
Steelman, Robert. Border Riders.
Steelman, Robert J. The Fox Dancer.
Steen, Edwin B. & Price, James H. Human Sex & Sexuality.
Steen, Frederick H. Elements of Probability & Mathematical Statistics.
Steen, Peter, jt. auth. see Lonnroth, Mans.
Steene, Sara J. Thomas Middleton: A Reference Guide.
Steenson, Gary P. Karl Kautsky, Eighteen Fifty-Four to Nineteen Thirty-Eight: Marxism in the Classical Years.
Steenson, Michael K. Minnesota No-Fault Automobile Insurance.
Steenwyk, Elizabeth Van see Van Steenwyk, Elizabeth.
Steer, Donald R., et al, eds. The Emerging Adolescent: Characteristics & Educational Implications. Eichhorn & Epstein.
Steers, Richard M. Introduction to Organizational Behavior.
Steers, Richard M. & Porter, Lyman W. Motivation & Work Behavior.
Steeves, Edna L., ed. see Pix, Mary & Trotter, Catherine.
Steeves, Paul D., ed. Modern Encyclopedia Religions in Russia & Soviet Union.
Stefanini, A., ed. Miniaturization of High-Energy Physics Detectors.
Stefanis, C. N. Recent Advances In Depression.
Stefanovic, Slavoljub. Put Ka Ostravenju Demokratije.
Stefanovich, V. Animal Models & Hypoxia: Proceedings of an International Symposium on Animal Models & Hypoxia, Held at Weisbaden, FRG, on 19 November 1979.
Stefansoon, Vilhialmur. Adventures in Error.
Stefansson, Vilhjalmur. Arctic Manual.
Steffe, Leslie P., ed. Research on Mathematical Thinking of Young Children.
Steffen, John J., jt. auth. see Karoly, Paul.
Steffen, John J. & Karoly, Paul, eds. Autism & Severe Psychopathology: Advances in Child Behavioral Analysis Therapy.
Steffen, John J., jt. ed. see Karoly, Paul.
Steffenhagen, R. A., ed. Hypnotic Techniques for Increasing Self Esteem.
Steffens, Lincoln. Autobiography of Lincoln Steffens.
--Boy on Horseback.
Steffensen, Arnold R. & Johnson, L. Murphy. Algebra & Trigonometry.
Steffensen, Arnold R., jt. auth. see Johnson, L. Murphy.
Steffensky, Fulbert, jt. auth. see Soelle, Dorothee.
Stefferud, Alfred. Wonders of Seeds.
Steffy, Wilbert. Economics of Machine Tool Procurement.
Steffy, Wilbert & Darby, Daniel R. Computer-Generated Time Standards: A Methodology.
--Performance Evaluation Systems.
Steffy, Wilbert & Hawley, Leonard. The Industrial Engineering Plant Audit.
Steffy, Wilbert, jt. auth. see Gray, Steven.
Steffy, Wilbert, et al. Production Control for the Small & Medium Sized Firms.
--Computer Ratio Analysis: An Aid to Decision Making.
--Management Control Systems for Small & Medium-Sized Firms.
--Industrial Purchasing Controls for the Small & Medium Sized Firm.
--Economic Guidelines for Justifying Capital Purchases: With Numerical Control Emphasis.
Stegeman, John F. These Men She Gave: Civil War Diary of Athens, Georgia.
Stegemann, Wolfgang. The Gospel & the Poor. Elliott, Dietlinde, tr. from Ger.
Steger, Wilber A., jt. auth. see House, Peter A.
Stegman, Michael A., ed. Housing in New York: Study of a City.
Stegmuller, Camille Mirepoix. Glory for Fanchon: Five Years in Fascinating Mexico.
Stegner, Page. Islands of the West: From Baja to Vancouver.
Stegner, Wallace. Beyond the Hundredth Meridian.
--One Way to Spell Man.
Stegner, Wallace E. The Writer's Art, A Collection of Short Stories.
Stehmann, Wilhelm. Die Mittelhochdeutsche Vovelle Vom Studentenabrnteuer.
Steichen, Edward. Family of Man.

Authors

Steichen, Edward, ed. Sandburg: Photographers View Carl Sandburg.
Steichen, James B., jt. auth. see Strickland, James W.
Steig, William. C D B.
--Sylvester & the Magic Pebble.
Steigel, A., jt. auth. see Spiess, H. W.
Steiger, Brad. Atlantis Rising.
--Gods of Aquarius: UFO's & the Transformation of Man.
--In Meiner Seele Bin Ich Frei.
--In My Soul I Am Free.
--Monsters Among Us.
--The Reality Game & How to Win It: Making the Mysteries of Time & Space Work for You.
Steiger, H. W. Christian Science & Philosophy.
Steigert, Hermann, jt. auth. see Bickel, Margot.
Steigerwald, Robert. Anti-Communist Myths in Left Disguise.
Steil, Lyman K., et al. Listening: It Can Change Your Life.
Steiman, Harvey, jt. auth. see Hom, Ken.
Steimle, Edmund A. Are You Looking for God?
--From Death to Birth.
--God the Stranger: Reflections about Resurrection.
Steimle, Edmund A., et al. Preaching the Story.
Stein, Ben. Bunkhouse Logic.
Stein, Ben & Stein, Herbert. Moneypower: How to Make Inflation Make You Rich.
Stein, Ben, jt. auth. see Tavoulereas, William.
Stein, Benjamin. The Croesus Conspiracy.
Stein, Charles, ed. Critical Materials Problems in Energy Production.
Stein, Donald G., et al, eds. Plasticity & Recovery of Function in the Central Nervous System.
Stein, E. P. Flight of the Vin Fiz.
Stein, Edward V. Guilt: Theory & Therapy.
Stein, Elly, tr. see De Chambrun, Rene.
Stein, Emanuel, jt. auth. see Fox, William.
Stein, Gary S., ed. see Symposium, University of Florida, Gainsville Staff.
Stein, Gertrude. The Autobiography of Alice B. Toklas.
--Fernhurst, Q. E. D., & Other Early Writings.
--Gertrude Stein on Picasso. Burns, Edward, ed.
--How to Write.
--Narration: Four Lectures.
--The World Is Round.
Stein, Gordon. Robert G. Ingersoll: A Checklist.
Stein, Harold, ed. American Civil-Military Decisions.
Stein, Harold A. & Slatt, Bernard J. Ophthalmic Assistant: Fundamentals & Clinical Practice.
Stein, Harold A., et al. Manual of Ophthalmic Terminology.
Stein, Harry. How to Interpret Visual Resources.
Stein, Herbert. Presidential Economics: The Making of Economic Policy from Roosevelt to Reagan & Beyond.
Stein, Herbert, jt. auth. see Stein, Ben.
Stein, Howard & Zalkind, Ronald. Promoting Rock Concerts: A Practical Guide.
Stein, J. F. An Introduction to Neurophysiology.
Stein, Jane J. Making Medical Choices: Ethics & Medicine in a Technological Age.
Stein, Jay H. Internal Medicine.
Stein, Jean. Jazz-Five Easy Pieces.
Stein, Jess, ed. Student's Webster Dictionary.
Stein, Joan. Freethinkers Handbook.
Stein, Judith, jt. auth. see Holcombe, Marya.
Stein, Kevin, jt. auth. see Marsh, Dave.
Stein, L. I. & Test, M. A., eds. Alternatives to Mental Hospital Treatment.
Stein, Leon. The Racial Thinking of Richard Wagner.
Stein, Leslie. Growth of East African Exports & Their Effect on Economic Development.
Stein, M. R., ed. Algebraic K-Theory.
Stein, Margery, ed. see Arum, Nancy.
Stein, Marshall D. & Smith, Jo L. Instructions for Authors: Biomedical Journals.
Stein, Michele, jt. auth. see Masie, Elliott.
Stein, Norman, jt. auth. see Goldstein, Arnold P.
Stein, P., jt. auth. see Krug, S.
Stein, R. Conrad. Me & Dirty Arnie.
Stein, Robert. Media Power: Who Is Shaping Your Picture of the World?
Stein, Sara B. Cat.
--Mouse.
Stein, Sara B., jt. auth. see Children's Television Workshop Staff.
Stein, Sherman & Crabill, Calvin. Elementary Algebra: A Guided Inquiry.
Stein, Sherman K. Calculus & Analytic Geometry.
--Calculus: In the First Three Dimensions.
Stein, Sol. The Childkeeper.
--Living Room.
--Other People.
Stein, Stanley J. Vassouras: A Brazilian Coffee County, 1850-1900.
Stein, Steven J. Trade Secret Litigation: A Course Handbook.
Stein, Toby. Getting Together.
--Only the Best: A Love Story.
Stein, Walter J. Gold in History & Modern Times & Labour in History & in Modern Times.
Stein, Walter M., et al. Increasing Guidance Effectiveness Through School-Community Cooperation: A Guide to Developing Cooperative Relationships Between Schools & Business, Industry & Labor in Rural Communities.
Stein, William I. & Danielson, Rodger. Users Guide for Seeds of Western Trees & Shrubs.
Stein, William W. Hualcan: Life in the Highlands of Peru.
Stein, Zane B. Essence & Application: A View from Chiron.
Steinauer, Dennis D. Security of Personal Computer Systems: A Management Guide.
Steinbach, A., jt. auth. see Alexander, R.
Steinbach, Marten. Medical Palmistry: Health & Character in the Hand.
Steinbach, Valeri. Six Hundred & Thirty-Eight Olympic Champions. Kopytkin, Y. & Timofeyev, A., trs.
Steinberg, Carl P. & Cohen, Alan B. Nuclear Magnetic Resonance Imaging Technology: A Clinical, Industrial, & Policy Analysis.
Steinberg, David. Anemia: Facts about Low Blood.
Steinberg, E. P. Practice for Air Force Placement Tests.
--Practice for Army Placement Tests.
--Scoring High on the Armed Forces Test.
Steinberg, Erwin R., jt. auth. see Schutte, William M.
Steinberg, Erwin R., ed. Rule of Force: Readings on the Totalitarian Challenge to Democracy.
Steinberg, Erwin R., jt. ed. see Schutte, William M.
Steinberg, Eve. American College Testing Program (ACT)
Steinberg, Eve P. Post Office Clerk-Carrier.
Steinberg, Franz U., ed. Cowdry's Care of the Geriatric Patient.
Steinberg, H. & McCloskey, A. L., eds. Progress in Boron Chemistry.
Steinberg, J. Leonard, ed. Counselor As an Applied Behavioral Scientist.
Steinberg, Jeff & Hefley, James C. Masterpiece in Progress.
Steinberg, Jill A. Climbing the Ladder of Success in High Heels: Backgrounds of Professional Women. Nathan, Peter, ed.
Steinberg, Leo. Borromini's San Carlo Alle Quattro Fontane: A Study in Multiple Form & Architectural Symbolism.
Steinberg, Louis & Tong, Christopher. Artificial Intelligence & Design.
Steinberg, Margery A. Mickey's Practice Workbook: Division & Fractions.
--Mickey's Practice Workbook: Math Puzzles & Games.
Steinberg, Maximilian, ed. see Rimsky-Korsakov, Nikolay.
Steinberg, Milton. Basic Judaism.
--A Partisan Guide to the Jewish Problem.
Steinberg, Phil. You & Your Pet: Aquarium Pets.
--You & Your Pet: Birds.
Steinberg, Rafael, jt. auth. see Javits, Jacob K.
Steinberg, Richard M. & Danker, Harold. Pensions: An ERISA Accounting & Management Guide.
Steinberg, Ronald. Fra Girolamo Savonarola, Florentine Art & Renaissance Historiography.
Steinberg, Sigfrid H. Thirty Years' War.
Steinberg, Stephen. The Ethnic Myth: Race, Ethnicity & Class in America.
--The Ethnic Myth: Race, Ethnicity, & Class in America.
Steinberger, E., jt. ed. see Fabbrini, A.
Steinberger, J., ed. Selected Topics in Particle Physics.
Steinbergh, Judith, jt. auth. see Cockburn, Victor.
Steinbicker, Earl. Daytrips in Germany: Fifty One Day Adventures by Rail or Car.
Steinbrunner, Chris & Penzler, Otto, eds. Encyclopedia of Mystery & Detection.
Steindl, J. Random Processes & the Growth of Firms: A Study of the Pareto Law.
Steindler, Geraldine. Game Cookbook.
Steindler, R. A. Steindler's New Firearms Dictionary.
Steinel, Daniel V., compiled by. Music & Music Education: Data & Information.
Steinem, Gloria. Marilyn.
--Outrageous Acts & Everyday Rebellions.
Steiner. Essential Paediatric Radiology.
Steiner, Bernard C. Life of Roger Brooke Taney, Chief Justice of the United States Supreme Court.
Steiner, Bradley J. Below the Belt: Unarmed Combat for Women.
--Manuals on Mayhem: An Annotated Bibliography of Books on Combat Martial Arts & Self-Defense.
Steiner, Claude M. Healing Alcoholism.
--The Other Side of Power.
--Scripts People Live.
--When a Man Loves a Woman: How to Love a Woman of the Eighties.
Steiner, Erwin, jt. auth. see Sigmund, Diane.
Steiner, Franz B. Taboo.
Steiner, Frederick. The Politics of New Town Planning: The Newfields, Ohio, Story.
Steiner, Gary A., jt. auth. see Berelson, Bernard.
Steiner, George. Death of Tragedy.
--The Portage to San Cristobel of A.H.
Steiner, Hillel. An Essay on Rights.
Steiner, James B., jt. auth. see Lord, Kenniston W., Jr.
Steiner, Jorg. Rabbit Island. Lammers, Ann C., tr.
Steiner, Karl-Heinz. Interactions Between Electromagnetic Fields & Matter.
Steiner, Kurt von see Von Steiner, Kurt.
Steiner, Mary M., jt. auth. see Levin, Jane W.
Steiner, Merrilee. Bareback.
--Pirate Moon.
Steiner, Moses J. Satan in the Woods.
Steiner, R. E. & Sherwood, T., eds. Recent Advances in Radiology & Medical Imaging.
Steiner, Raymond J. The Vessel of Splendor: A Return to the One.
Steiner, Richard. Individualized Student Teaching: A Systematic Approach.
Steiner, Robert F. The Chemical Foundations of Molecular Biology.
Steiner, Robert L., jt. auth. see Masson, Alison.
Steiner, Rudolf. At the Gates of Spiritual Science.
--The Calendar of the Soul. Pusch, Ruth & Pusch, Hans, trs. from Ger.
--The Christmas Foundation Meeting of the Anthroposophical Society. Seddon, R. G., ed.
--The Holy Grail: From the Works of Rudolf Steiner. Roboz, Steven, ed.
--Occult Science & Occult Development: Christ at the Time of the Mystery of Golgotha & Christ in the Twentieth Century. Osmond, D. S., tr.
--Proceedings of the Christmas Foundation Meeting of the General Anthroposophical Society. Seiler, Sabine, ed. Dawson, Frances, tr. from Ger.
--Road to Self Knowledge.
Steiner, Rudolf, et al. Education as an Art. Allen, Paul M., intro. by.
Steiner, Stan. Dark & Dashing Horsemen.
--Spirit Woman.
Steinfeld, Jake & Miller, Melissa. Body by Jake.
Steinfield, M. Cracks in the Melting Pot.
Steingass, F. Arabic-English Dictionary.
Steinhardt, H., ed. see International Conference on Noise Control Engineering Staff.
Steinhardt, J. & Reynolds, J. A. Multiple Equilibria in Proteins.
Steinhart, J. S. & Smith, T. J., eds. The Earth Beneath the Continents.
Steinhart, Lawrence M. Beauty Through Health: From the Edgar Cayce Readings.
--Beauty Through Health: From the Edgar Cayce Readings.
Steinhauer, Harry. Kulturlesebuch Fur Anfanger.
Steinhauer, Harry, ed. Das Deutsche Drama.
--Die Deutsche Novelle, 1880-1950.
Steinhausen, M. & Tanner, G. A. Microcirculation & Tubular Urine Flow in the Mammalian Kidney Cortex: In Vivo Microscopy.
Steinhauser, F., ed. Problems of Weather Forecasting.
Steinhoff, Ernst A., ed. Organizing Space Activities for World Needs.
Steinhoff, Patricia G., jt. auth. see Chung, Chin S.
Steinhoff, Richard. Basic Mathematics.
Steinike, Otto A. Blueprint Reading, Checking & Testing.
Steinitz, Paul. Bach's Passions.
Steinke, Peter L. Preaching the Theology of the Cross: Sermons & Worship Ideas for Lent & Easter.
Steinkoler, Ronnie. A Jewish Cookbook for Children.
Steinkraus, William C. Riding & Jumping.
Steinkuehler, Pearl, jt. auth. see Nordtvedt, Matilda.
Steinman, G. D., jt. auth. see Kenyon, D.
Steinmann, Martin, Jr. Words in Action: A Rhetoric Reader.
Steinmann, O. Perturbation Expansions in Axiomatic Field Theory.
Steinmetz, David C. Reformers in the Wings.
Steinmetz, H. Farm Implements & Machinery: Multilingual Illustrated Dictionary.
Steinmetz, Lawrence L. & Todd, H. Ralph, Jr. First-Line Management: Approaching Supervision Effectively.
Steinmetzer, Franz X. Die Babylonischen Kudurru Als Urkundenform.
Steinmiller, Oswald M. The Approaching Seven Major Political Revolutions Which Will Transform Radically the World.
Steinor, Bradley. Close Shaves: The Complete Book of Razor Fighting.
Steinwede, Dietrich. Reformation: A Picture Story of Martin Luther. Cooperrider, Edward A., tr. from Ger.
Steinwedel, Louis W. & Newport, J. Herbert. The Duesenberg.
Steiss, Alan W. Management Control in Government.
Stejneger, Leonard. Poisonous Snakes of North America.
Stekel, Wilhelm. Autobiography of Wilhelm Stekel.
--Peculiarities of Behavior.
Stele, F., jt. auth. see Bratko, I.
Stelmack, R. M., ed. New Directions in the Psychophysiology of Individual Differences: A Symposium of Papers from the 22nd Annual Meeting of the Society for Psychophysiological Research, Minneapolis, 21-24 October 1982.
Stelter. Lawyers & Creditors Service Directory.
Steltz, W. E. & Donaldson, A. M., eds. Aero-Thermodynamics of Steam Turbines.
Steltz, W. G., jt. ed. see Herring, H. J.
Stelzer, Leigh & Banthin, Joanna. Teachers Have Rights, Too: What Educators Should Know About School Law.
Stemach, Jerry, jt. auth. see Venable, Gail P.
Stembera, Z., et al, eds. High Risk Pregnancy & Child. Schierlova, M., tr. from Czech.
Stembera, Z. K., et al, eds. Perinatal Medicine: Fourth European Congress.
Stemp, Robin. Guy & the Flowering Plum Tree.
Stenbock, Evelyn. Teach Yourself To Write.
Stendahl, Brita. The Force of Tradition: A Case Study of Women Priests in Sweden.
--Sabbatical Reflections: The Ten Commandments in a New Day.
Stendahl, Krister. Holy Week.
--Holy Week Preaching.
Stendenbach, F. J. Learning & Behavior.
Stendhal. Armance. Martineau, ed.
--Best Restaurants New York.
--Best Restaurants New York.
Stendhal, pseud. Red & the Black. Scott-Moncrieff, C. K., tr.
Stendler, Faith, jt. auth. see Lavatelli, Celia S.
Stengel, Gretchen, ed. see Chirich, Nancy.
Stenhagen, Einar, et al. Computer Tape Atlas of Mass Spectral Data.
Stenholm, S., jt. auth. see Moss, T. S.
Stenhouse, Lawrence & Gajendra, Verna K. Teaching About Race Relations: Problems & Effects.
Stenner, R. W., jt. auth. see Hall, A. Y.
Stensio, E. Anatomic Studies on the Arthrodiran Head.
Stensio, Erik A. The Cephalaspids of Great Britain.
Stenson, Janet S. Now I Have a Step-Parent, & It's Kind of Confusing.
Stenson, Patrick. The Odyssey of C. H. Lightoller.
Stenstroem, B. Rings & Modules of Quotients.
Stensvold, Mike, ed. Available Light.
--Blueprint Series.
Stensvold, Mike, ed. see Jacobs, Lou, Jr.
Stepanenko, I. P. Fundamentals of Microelectronics.
Stepanoff, Alexely. Gravity Flow & Transportation of Solids in Suspension.
Stephans, Mark, jt. auth. see Kafrissen, Edward.
Stephen. Solubilities on Inorganic & Organic Compounds.
Stephen, E. Residential Care for the Mentally Retarded.
Stephen Greene Press (Illus.) Staff & Viherjuvri, H. J. Sauna: The Finnish Bath.
Stephen, James. Crisis of the Sugar Colonies: Or, an Enquiry into the Objects & Probable Effects of the French Expedition to the West Indies.
Stephen, Martin, ed. Never Such Innocence: A New Anthology of Great War Verse.
Stephen, Russell J. Allegoresis: The Craft of Allegory in Medieval Literature.
Stephens. Smooth Muscle Contractions.
Stephens, Anne C. Signpost-Middle East.
Stephens, Don. Trial by Trial: Destiny of a Believer.
Stephens, Elise H. & Shouse, Sarah. Historic Huntsville: A City of New Beginnings.
Stephens, Evan. Eight Favorite Anthems.
Stephens, Gertrude. Gertrude Stephens' Crossword Dictionary.
Stephens, James. The Insurrection in Dublin.
Stephens, Jennifer. Vengeance of the Cat Goddess.
Stephens, M. B. The Detection of New Adverse Drug Reactions.
Stephens, M. D., jt. auth. see Roderick, G. W.
Stephens, M. D. & Roderick, G. W., eds. Universities for a Changing World: The Role of the University in the Later Twentieth Century.
Stephens, Martha, ed. The Pig & Other True Stories.
Stephens, Mary Jo. Witch of the Cumberlands.
--Zoe's Zodiac.
--Zoe's Zodiac.
Stephens, Mitchell. Broadcast News: Radio Journalism & an Introduction to Television.
Stephens, R. C. Strength of Materials: Theory & Examples.
Stephens, R. W., ed. Sound: In Eight Languages.
Stephens, Rory D. Sequence: A Basic Writing Course.
Stephens, S. D., ed. Disorders of Auditory Function, II.
Stephens, Simon. Death Comes Home.

Stephens, Trent D. Atlas of Human Embryology.
Stephenson, A. M. Unbirthday.
Stephenson, A P. Discovering BBC Micro Machine: How to Get More Speed & Power.
Stephenson, A. P. & Stephenson, D. J. Advanced Machine Code Techniques for the BBC Micro.
--Filing Systems & Database for the BBC Micro.
Stephenson, Bette, ed. see Findlay, James V.
Stephenson, Colin. Merrily on High.
Stephenson, D. J., jt. auth. see Stephenson, A. P.
Stephenson, Dianna. Bookshops of London.
Stephenson, E. T., jt. ed. see Marder, A. R.
Stephenson, F. R., jt. ed. see Clark, D. H.
Stephenson, F. W., jt. auth. see Bowron, P.
Stephenson, G. R., jt. auth. see McEwen, F. L.
Stephenson, Gilbert T. Race Distinctions in American Law.
Stephenson, J., jt. auth. see Wilson, T. D.
Stephenson, J. W., et al, eds. Incinerator & Solid Waste Technology, 1962-1975.
Stephenson, John G. & Cahill, Bob. How to Maintain & Service Your Small Computer.
Stephenson, John R., ed. Molecular Biology of RNA Tumor Viruses.
Stephenson, June. Humanity's Search for the Meaning of Life: A Brief Survey of History, Philosophy, Religion, Art, Music, & Architecture.
Stephenson, Lynda R. Starlife!
Stephenson, Marylee. Canada's National Parks: A Visitor's Guide.
Stephenson, Ralph. The Animated Film.
Stephenson, Reginald J. Exploring in Physics: A New Outlook on Problems in Physics.
Stephenson, Stuart K., jt. auth. see Ryder, Michael L.
Stephenson, Wendell H., ed. see Ramsdell, Charles W.
Stephenson, William, jt. auth. see Doherty, Joseph F.
Stepka, Joseph A. Poems Now.
Stepney, Rob. Tobacco.
Steptoe, A., ed. Problems of Pain & Stress: Twenty-Sixth Annual Conference of the Society for Psychosomatic Research.
Sterin, K. E., et al. Raman Spectra of Hydrocarbons: A Data Handbook.
Sterling, Bruce. Schismatrix. Silverberg, Robert, ed.
Sterling, Carlos M. & Sterling, Manuel M. Historia de la Isla de Cuba.
Sterling, Charles & Salinger, Margaretta. A Catalogue of French Paintings: Nineteenth & Twentieth Centuries.
--A Catalogue of French Paintings: Nineteenth Century.
Sterling, Charles R., jt. auth. see Aikawa, Masamichi.
Sterling, Christopher H. & Kittross, John M. Stay Tuned: A Concise History of American Broadcasting.
Sterling, Claire. The Time of the Assassins.
--The Time of the Assassins: Anatomy of an Investigation.
Sterling, Dorothy. Black Foremothers: Three Lives.
--We Are Your Sisters: Black Women in the Nineteenth Century.
Sterling, Leon, jt. auth. see Hardy, Steven.
Sterling, Manuel M., jt. auth. see Sterling, Carlos M.
Sterling, Richard W. Ethics in a World of Power: The Political Ideas of Friedrich Meinecke.
Sterling, T., et al, eds. Visual Prosthesis: The Interdisciplinary Dialogue, Proceedings.
Sterling, Theodor D. & Pollack, Seymour V. Computers & the Life Sciences.
Sterman, M. B., et al. Brain Development & Behavior.
Stermer, Dugald, jt. auth. see Kortum, Jeanie.
Stern, Alfred. Mail Order Dealer's Advertising Rate Manual.
Stern, Bert & Golbitz, Pat. The Last Sitting.
Stern, Carol E., ed. see Stern, Jean.
Stern, Chaim. Gates of Freedom: A Passover Haggadah.
Stern, Daniel. The Suicide Academy.
Stern, Duke N. & Sampson, Karen G., eds. West Virginia Practice Handbook.
Stern, E. Mark, ed. The Other Side of the Couch: What Therapists Believe.
Stern, Ellen & Michaels, Jonathan. The Good Heart Diet Cookbook.
Stern, Fred. Word Processing & Beyond: The Introductory Computer Book.
Stern, Gai. International Whole Meals: International Cuisines-the Wholefood Way.
Stern, Gary H., jt. auth. see DeRosa, Paul.
Stern, Gerald. Lucky Life.
--The Red Coal.
Stern, Henry B., ed. Resume Writing Guide.
Stern, J. Comparative Religious Scripture.
Stern, Jean. Alson Skinner Clark.
--The Paintings of Franz A. Bischoff (1864-1929) Stern, Carol E., ed.
--Western Masters.
Stern, Jean & Westphal, Ruth. The Paintings of Sam Hyde Harris (1889-1977)
Stern, Jean, ed. see Dominik, Janet B.
Stern, Jeffrey A. How to Become Financially Independent Before You're 35.
Stern, Joel, tr. see Lem, Stanislaw.
Stern, Joel, tr. see Zoshchenko, Mikhail.
Stern, Joseph J. & Lewis, Jeffrey D. Employment Patterns & Income Growth.
Stern, Joyce D. & Chandler, Marjorie O., eds. Condition of Education, 1987: A Statistical Report.
Stern, Joyce D. & Williams, Mary F., eds. Condition of Education, 1986: A Statistical Report.
Stern, Kingsley. Introductory Plant Biology.
Stern, Leo. Drug Use in Pregnancy.
Stern, Lillian V., jt. auth. see Stern, Philip V.
Stern, Loraine & McKay, Kathleen. Off to a Great Start: How to Relax & Enjoy Your Baby.
Stern, Louis W. & El-Ansary, Adel I. Marketing Channels.
Stern, Louis W., ed. Distribution Channels: Behavioral Dimensions.
Stern, Mark. It's a Dog's Life.
Stern, Milton R. Critical Essays on F. Scott Fitzgerald's Tender is the Night.
Stern, Milton R. & Gross, Seymour L., eds. American Literature Survey. Incl. Vol. 1. Colonial & Federal to 1800; Vol. 2. The American Romantics 1800-1860. Brooks, Van W., pref. by.; Vol. 3. Nation & Region 1860-1900. Jones, Howard M., pref. by.; Vol. 4. The Twentieth Century. Cowley, Malcolm, pref. by.. Penguin.
Stern, Nancy & Stern, Robert A. Structured COBOL Programming.
Stern, Nicholas, jt. auth. see Carr-Hill, Roy.
Stern, Philip V. & Stern, Lillian V. Prehistoric Europe.
Stern, Philip V., ed. see Thoreau, Henry David.
Stern, Richard. A Father's Words.
--Natural Shocks.
--Other Men's Daughters.
--Stitch.
Stern, Richard M. Wildfire.
Stern, Robert A., jt. auth. see Stern, Nancy.
Stern, Robert C. Airwar over the Pacific.
--F-4 Phantom II.
--U-Boats of World War Two.
--U. S. Marines in World War II.
Stern, Robert L. Appellate Practice in the United States.
Stern, Robert M. & Davis, Christopher M., eds. Gastric Motility: A Selectively Annotated Bibliography.
Stern, Robert W. Process of Opposition in India: Two Case Studies of How Policy Shapes Politics.
Stern, Roger. Spider-Man: The Secret Story of Marvel's World Famous Wall Crawler.
Stern, S. M., ed. see Israeli, Isaac.
Stern, Steven B. Guide to Great Resorts of the World.
--Guide to the Cruise Vacation.
Stern, W. T., jt. ed. see Asberg, M.
Sternberg, David. Fishing with Artificial Lures.
Sternberg, David J. Radical Sociology: A Critical Introduction to American Behavioral Science.
Sternberg, Dick. Fishing with Live Bait.
Sternberg, Dick & Ignizio, Bill. Panfish.
Sternberg, Patricia. Be My Friend: The Art of Good Relationships.
Sternberg, Robert J. Barron's How to Prepare for the Miller Analogies Test (MAT)
Sternberg, Robert J., ed. Mechanisms of Cognitive Development.
Sternberger, Ludwig A. Immunocytochemistry.
Sternburg, Janet, ed. The Writer on Her Work.
Sterne, George, jt. auth. see Von Hoelscher, Russ.
Sterne, Laurence. The Life & Opinions of Tristram Shandy, Gentleman. New, Melvyn, ed.
Sternglass, Ernest. Secret Fallout: Low-Level Radiation from Hiroshima to Three-Mile Island.
Sternheim, Morton M., jt. auth. see Kane, Joseph W.
Sternhell, S., jt. auth. see Jackman, L. M.
Sternlieb, George, jt. auth. see Sagalyn, Lynne B.
Sternlieb, George, ed. Housing: An Anthology.
Sternlieb, George & Hughes, James W., eds. America's Housing: Prospects & Problems.
Sternlieb, George & Sagalyn, Lynee B., eds. Housing 1970-1971: An Anthology.
Sternlieb, George, et al, eds. Housing 1973-1974: An Anthology.
Sternlieb, Irmin, jt. auth. see Scheinberg, I. Herbert.
Sternloff, Robert E. & Warren, Roger. Park & Recreation Management.
Sterns, Indrikis, ed. The Greater Medieval Historians: A Reader.
Stertz, Eda. The Mystery of the Buried Gold.
Sterzl, J. & Riha, I., eds. Developmental Aspects of Antibody Formation & Structure: Proceedings.
Stetler, Cheryl B., et al, eds. see Massachusetts General Hospital Department of Nursing Staff.
Stetler, Susan L., ed. Biography Almanac.
Stetser, David. Physics Modeling Using Lotus 1-2-3 Release 2. Thomas, Kim, ed.
Stetson, Fred, ed. see Graves, Will.
Stetsovky, Y. Right of the Accused to Defence in the U. S. S. R.
Stettner, N. Productivity, Bargaining & Industrial Change.
Steuart, James. Works, Political, Metaphysical, Chronological.
Steuber, U. International Banking: The Foreign Activities of the Banks of Principal Industrial Countries (1976) Pringle, R. & Pringle, R., trs. from Ger.
Steubing, Jan. More of the Best of Bon Apetit.
Steuck, Jeanine. Good Morning Judy!
Steuer, Ralph E. Multiple Criteria Optimization: Theory, Computation & Application.
Steurer, Stephen. Wheels Teacher's Guide.
--Wheels Workbook.
Stevens. Artificial Intelligence.
--Comprehensive Review for the Radiologic Technologist.
Stevens, Albert C. Cyclopaedia of Fraternities.
Stevens, Ann, tr. see Eca de Queiroz.
Stevens, Anthony. Archetypes: A Natural History of the Self.
Stevens, Barbara J. Handbook of Municipal Waste Management Systems: Planning & Practice.
Stevens, C. Claxton. Eighteenth Century English Furniture: The Norman Adams Collection, Whittington.
Stevens, Carla. Hooray for Pig!
--How to Make Possum's Honey Bread.
--Pig & the Blue Flag.
--Sara & the Pinch.
--Stories from a Snowy Meadow.
--Your First Pet: & How to Take Care of It.
Stevens, Charles E. Anthony Burns, a History.
Stevens, Cindy. Public Assistance in France.
Stevens, Clifford. The Blessed Virgin.
--Man of Galilee.
Stevens, David, ed. Adventure Holidays Nineteen Eighty-Eight.
--Adventure Holidays, Nineteen Eighty-Seven.
Stevens, David W. Assisted Job Search for the Insured Unemployed.
Stevens, Dennis W. A History of Song.
Stevens, E. A., jt. auth. see Brede, H. D.
Stevens, E. Jackson. Scale Model Electric Tramways & How to Model Them.
Stevens, Edward. Business Ethics.
--The Religion Game, American Style.
Stevens, Edward B. The History of Medical Group Management Association Nineteen Twenty-six to Nineteen Seventy-six.
Stevens, Edward F. Ocean Carriage.
Stevens, Edwards B. The History of MGMA, Nineteen Twenty-Six to Nineteen Seventy-Six.
Stevens, F. S. Racism, the Australian Experience, Volume Two: Black Versus White.
--Racism, the Australian Experience, Volume Three: Colonialism.
Stevens, Florence. Strategies for Second Language Acquisition.
Stevens, Frank S., ed. Racism, the Australian Experience, Volume One: Prejudice & Xenophobia.
Stevens, Franklin. Dance As Life.
Stevens, G. T., Jr. Economic & Financial Analysis of Capital Investments.
Stevens, George De see De Stevens, George.
Stevens, George E., jt. ed. see Glueck, William F.
Stevens, Graham, jt. auth. see Orna, Elizabeth.
Stevens, I. N., jt. auth. see Redmond, P. W.
Stevens, Isaac I. Treaty Between the U. S. & the Indians of the Willamette Valley.
--Treaty Between the U. S. & the Nisqually & Other Bands of Indians.
--Treaty Between the U. S. & the Yakima Nation of Indians.
Stevens, Jack G., et al, eds. Persistent Viruses.
Stevens, James, jt. auth. see Scriven, Carl.
Stevens, Jan, ed. see Mishkoff, Henry C.
Stevens, Jim, jt. auth. see Jenson, Ron.
Stevens, John. Medieval Romance: Themes & Approaches.
--Sacred Calligraphy of the East.
--The Sword of No-Sword: Life of the Master Warrior Tesshu.
Stevens, John, tr. see Sogen, Omori & Katsujo, Terayama.
Stevens, John D. & Garcia, Hazel D. Communication History.
Stevens, Kenneth. Charleston Antebellum Architecture & Civic Destiny.
Stevens, L. A., jt. auth. see Nichols, R.
Stevens, Laurence. Guide to Buying, Selling & Starting a Travel Agency.
--Guide to Starting & Operating a Successful Travel Agency.
--Your Career in Travel & Tourism.
--Your Career in Travel & Tourism.
Stevens, Mark. The Big Eight: Inside America's Largest Accounting Firms.
--The Insiders: The Truth Behind the Scandal Rocking Wall Street.
--Land Rush: The Secret World of Real Estate's Super Brokers & Developers.
--Leveraged Finance: How to Raise & Invest Cash.
--Power of Attorney: The Rise of the Big Ten Law Firms.
Stevens, Mick & Monagram, Charles. Poodles from Hell.
Stevens, Nola. God & You Unlimited.
Stevens, Paul C., jt. auth. see Clapp, Joy.
Stevens, Peter S. A Handbook of Regular Patterns: An Introduction to Symmetry in Two Dimensions.
--Patterns in Nature.
Stevens, Rebecca A. Old Traditions-New Traditions.
Stevens, Robert V. Studies on the Synthesis of Corrins and Related Ligands.
Stevens, Robert W. & Swisher, Ted, eds. Community Self-Help Housing Manual: Partnership in Action.
Stevens, Roger. The Land of the Great Sophy.
Stevens, Rolland E. & Walton, Joan M. Reference Work in the Public Library.
Stevens, Rolland E., ed. Research Methods in Librarianship: Historical & Bibliographical Methods in Library Research.
--Supervision of Employees in Libraries.
Stevens, Scott, jt. auth. see Fuller, Robert.
Stevens, W. A. Virology of Flowering Plants.
Stevens, W. R. Building Physics: Lighting.
Stevens, Wallace. The Necessary Angel.
Stevens-Arroyo, Antonio, ed. Prophets Denied Honor: An Anthology on the Hispanic Church in the U. S.
Stevens-Long, Judith. Adult Life: Developmental Processes.
Stevens-Long, Judith & Cobb, Nancy J. Adolescence & Early Adulthood.
Stevenson. Fraggle Rock.
Stevenson, Adlai E. Call to Greatness.
Stevenson, Burton. The Home Book of Quotations: Classical & Modern.
Stevenson, Burton E. The Home Book of Verse.
Stevenson, C. E., et al. Process Chemistryar Energy.
Stevenson, D. E. Listening Valley.
--Rochester's Wife.
--Still Glides the Stream.
Stevenson, George H. Roman Provincial Administration till the Age of the Antonines.
Stevenson, Gordon. Andreas Schleiermacher's Bibliographic Classification & Its Relationship to the Dewey Decimal & Library of Congress Classifications.
--Rudolph Focke & the Theory of the Classified Catalog.
Stevenson, Harold W., et al, eds. Early Behavior: Comparative & Developmental Approach.
--Child Psychology.
Stevenson, Herbert F. Three Prophetic Voices: Studies in Joel, Amos & Hosea.
Stevenson, Howard H., et al. New Business Ventures & the Entrepreneur.
Stevenson, Jack L., jt. auth. see Sessoms, Douglas H.
Stevenson, James. The Catacombs: Life & Death in Early Christianity.
Stevenson, Janet. Departure.
Stevenson, Jocelyn. Red & the Pumpkins.
Stevenson, John C. & Chahal, Pritpal. Aids to Endocrinology.
Stevenson, June & Jones, Catherine. Yearbook of Social Policy in Britain 1982.
Stevenson, June, jt. auth. see Jones, Catherine.
Stevenson, June, jt. ed. see Jones, Catherine.
Stevenson, Kenneth & Habermas, Gary B. Verdict on the Shroud: Evidence for the Death & Resurrection of Jesus Christ.
Stevenson, Michael. Developing High Technology Industries: The Case of Massachusetts.
--Sweden in the Nineteen Eighty's.
--The U. S. Debate on Industrial Policy: A Bibliography, 1980-1985.
Stevenson, Nancy. The Natural Way to Reading: A How-to Method for Parents of Slow Learners, Dyslexic, & Learning Disabled Children.
Stevenson, Noel. Successful Cross-Examination.
Stevenson, Noel C. Genealogical Evidence: A Guide to the Standard of Proof Relating to Pedigrees, Ancestry, Heirship & Family History.
--Search & Research.
Stevenson, R. Scott. In Search of Spanish Painting.
Stevenson, Richard A. Fundamentals of Investments. Jennings, Edward H., ed.
Stevenson, Robert. Music Before the Classic Era: An Introductory Guide.
--Protestant Church Music in America: A Short Survey of Men & Movements from 1564 to the Present.
Stevenson, Robert Louis. The Cevennes Journal.
--A Child's Garden of Verses.
--A Child's Garden of Verses.
--A Child's Garden of Verses to Color.
--Kidnapped.
--Kidnapped.
--The New Arabian Nights.
--Prayers Written at Vailima.

--Selected Poetry & Prose of Robert Louis Stevenson. Booth, Bradford A., ed.
--Treasure Island.
Stevenson, Robert Louis & Osbourne, Lloyd. The Wrecker.
Stevenson, Ronald, ed. see Ziehn, Bernhard.
Stevenson, William. Bushbabies.
--Eclipse.
--The Ghosts of Africa.
--The Ghosts of Africa.
--A Man Called Intrepid: The Secret War. Moore, John, tr.
Stevenson, William W. Vocational Education Evaluation: Problems, Alternatives, Recommendations.
Steves, Rick. Europe in Twenty-Two Days.
--Europe in Twenty-Two Days.
--Europe Through the Back Door.
--Europe Through the Back Door.
--Europe 101: History, Art & Culture for the Traveler.
--Germany, Austria & Switzerland in Twenty-Two Days.
--Great Britain in Twenty-Two Days.
--Spain & Portugal in Twenty-Two Days.
--Spain & Portugal in Twenty-Two Days.
Steves, Rick & Gottberg, John. Asia Through the Back Door.
Stevick, Daniel B. & Johnson, Ben. Holy Week.
Stevick, E. W. & Aremu, Odaleye. Spoken Yoruba.
Stevick, Robert D. Beowulf: An Edition with Manuscript Spacing Notation & Graphotactic Analyses.
Steward, D. E. Contact Inhibition.
Steward, Fred M. Century.
Steward, J. W. Tailed Amphibians of Europe.
Stewart. Ideal Managers Library.
Stewart, A., jt. auth. see Stewart, V.
Stewart, A. C. Silas & Con.
Stewart, A. M., tr. see Wilckens, Ulrich.
Stewart, Alice, et al. Burkitt's Disease: Immunological Aspects.
Stewart, Alistair D. & Hunt, David M. Genetic Basis of Development.
Stewart, Allan. Dangerous Hideaway Assignment.
--Rick Shannon & the Case of the Missing Pilot.
--Rick Shannon & the Secret of the Blue Dragon.
Stewart, Alva W. Child Welfare & Social Services: A Bibliograhic Review.
--The European Common Market: Problems & Prospects.
--The First Amendment in the Federal Courts: Freedom of Speech & the Press.
--State Executive Reorganization since 1940: A Selected Bibliography.
--Teacher Strikes: Boon or Bane? A Bibliographic Review.
--The U. S. Postal Service: Problems & Prospects.
--Wilderness Protection: A Bibliographic Review.
Stewart, Alva W., jt. auth. see Chisholm, Clarence E.
Stewart, Andrew. Skopas in Malibu.
Stewart, Angus, ed. Contemporary Britain.
Stewart, C. S. Journal of a Residence in the Sandwich Islands, 1823-1825.
Stewart, Charles J. Interviewing Principles & Practices: A Project Text.
--Interviewing Principles & Practices: A Project Text.
Stewart, Charles J. & Cash, William B., Jr. Interviewing: Principles & Practices.
Stewart, Charles O., III & Rosenbaum, Daniel J. WordPerfect Tips, Tricks & Traps.
Stewart, Charles W. When a Caring Family Faces Crises.
Stewart, Christina D. The Taylors of Ongar: An Analytical Bio-Bibliography.
Stewart Conference on Research in Nursing Staff. Perspectives on Nursing Leadership: Proceedings of the Conference on Research in Nursing, Sixteenth Conference. Ketefian, Shake, ed.
Stewart, David A. Preface to Empathy.
Stewart, David H., jt. auth. see Eckhardt, Caroline D.
Stewart, David O., ed. Representing Small Businesses.
Stewart, Desmond. The Vampire of Mons.
Stewart, Don. Ninety-Five Questions People Ask Most about the Holy Spirit.
--Ninety-Nine Questions People Ask Most about the Bible.
Stewart, Donald H. Prayers: Disturbance & Transfiguration.
Stewart, Dugald. Elements of the Philosophy of the Human Mind.
--Outlines of the Moral Philosophy.
Stewart, Ed. Here Comes Jesus.
Stewart, Elbert W. & Glynn, James A. Introduction to Sociology.
Stewart, Elwin L., et al. Deuteromycotina & Selected Ascomycotina from Wood & Wood Products.
Stewart, Fred M. Ellis Island.
--Lady Darlington.
--Lady Darlington.
--The Mannings.
--The Methusaleh Enzyme.
--Six Weeks.
--Star Child.
--The Titan.
Stewart, G. B. A New Mythos: The Novel of the Artist As Heroine, 1877-1977.
Stewart, George. The C-64 Program Factory.
--The Macintosh Program Factory.
Stewart, George, ed. see Arme, C., et al.
Stewart, George R. Earth Abides.
Stewart, Grace. A New Mythos: The Novel of the Artist As Heroine 1877-1977.
Stewart, Hugh B. Transitional Energy Policy 1980-2030: Alternative Nuclear Technologies.
Stewart, I. N. Lie Algebras.
Stewart, I. N. & Tall, D. O. Algebraic Number Theory.
Stewart, Ian, jt. auth. see Jones, Robin.
Stewart, J. & Hennessey, E. F. Orchids of America.
Stewart, J. D. & Hallett, J. P. Traction & Orthopaedic Appliances.
Stewart, J. E. Infrared Spectroscopy: Experimental Methods & Techniques.
Stewart, J. I. Andrew & Tobias.
--The Bridge at Arta: And Other Stories.
--The Naylors.
--Naylors.
--An Open Prison.
--Parlour Four & Other Stories.
Stewart, J. I. M. Full Term.
Stewart, J. M. Non-Equilibrium Relativistic Kinetic Theory.
Stewart, J. S., ed. see Schleiermacher, Friedrich.
Stewart, James A. The Partners: Inside America's Most Powerful Law Firms.
Stewart, James C. & Stewart, Shirley L. Easy Going: A Comprehensive Guide to Grant, Iowa & Lafayette Counties.
Stewart, James H., jt. auth. see Harper, Dennis O.
Stewart, James W. & Zitlow, David R. The Law & the Citizen-Student in Wisconsin: A Handbook for Secondary Students.
Stewart, Jan, ed. Exploring Primary Science & Technology with Microconputers.
Stewart, Jean, tr. see Guiguet, Jean.
Stewart, Jean, tr. see Simenon, Georges.
Stewart, Jesse. Best Loved Short Stories of Jesse Stewart. Richardson, H. Edward, intro. by.
Stewart, Joanna. Waiting Works.
Stewart, John. The Canadian House of Commons: Procedure & Reform.
--Secret of the Bats: The Exploration of Carlsbad Caverns.
--Winds in the Woods: The Story of John Muir.
Stewart, John & D'Angelo, Gary A. Together: Communicating Interpersonally.
Stewart, John, jt. auth. see Alvarado, Manuel.
Stewart, John, jt. auth. see Jones, George.
Stewart, John J. How to Gain a Testimony of the Gospel of Jesus Christ.
Stewart, Ken. Practical Christian Living.
Stewart, Kenneth L., et al. Clinical Removable Partial Prosthodontics.
Stewart, Marie M., et al. College English & Communication.
Stewart, Marjabelle Y. Your Complete Wedding Planner.
Stewart, Mary. This Rough Magic.
--A Walk in Wolf Wood.
--A Walk in Wolf Wood.
Stewart, Michael. Far Cry.
Stewart, O. Danger in the Air.
Stewart, P. C., jt. auth. see Bugg, J. L., Jr.
Stewart, Patrick, ed. Lone Star Regionalism: The Dallas Nine & Their Circle.
Stewart, Philip D. Political Power in the Soviet Union: A Study of Decision Making in Stalingrad.
Stewart, R. J. The Mystic Life of Merlin.
--The Prophetic Vision of Merlin: Prediction, Psychic Transformation, & the Foundation of the Grail Legends in an Ancient Set of Visionary Verses.
Stewart, R. J., ed. The Book of Merlin: Insight from the Merlin Conference.
Stewart, Ramona. Seasons of the Heart.
Stewart, Roderick. The Mind of Norman Bethune.
Stewart, Rosemary. Continuously Under Review.
Stewart, Shirley L., jt. auth. see Stewart, James C.
Stewart, Stanley. Air Disasters.
Stewart, V. & Stewart, A. Business Applications of Repertory Grid.
Stewart, Warren E., et al, eds. Dynamics & Modeling of Reactive Systems.
Stewart, William. Counselling in Rehabilitation.
Stewart, William C. Mathematics: With Applications.
Stewart, William H., Jr. The Alabama Constitutional Commission: A Pragmatic Approach to Constitutional Revision.
Stewart-David, David. Theory & Practice of Transport.
Stewart-Green, Miriam. Women Composers: A Checklist of Works for the Solo Voice.
Stewig, John W. Exploring Language Arts in the Elementary Classroom.
--Read to Write: Using Children's Literature As a Springboard for Teaching Writing.
--Sending Messages.
Steyaert, Thomas A. Biology: A Contemporary View.
Steyermark, Al. Quantitative Organic Microanalysis.
Steyert, Richard D., jt. ed. see American Society of Civil Engineers Staff.
Steyskal, George C., jt. auth. see Spencer, Kenneth A.
Steyskal, George C., et al. Insects & Mites: Techniques for Collection & Preservation.
Stibbs, Andrew. Assessing Children's Language: Guidelines for Teachers.
Stichting ILRA International Research Association Staff. Lactic Acid: Properties & Chemistry of Lactic Acid & Derivatives.
Stickel, D. L. The Brain Death Criterion of Human Death.
Stickle, Warren E., jt. ed. see Brownell, Blaine A.
Stickney, Clyde P., jt. auth. see Belcher, Finley E.
Stieb, Ernst, jt. auth. see Griffenhagen, George.
Stiefel, E. L. Introduction to Numerical Mathematics. Rheinboldt, W. C., tr.
Stiefel, E. L. & Scheifele, G. Linear & Regular Celestial Mechanics: Perturbed Two-Body Motion, Numerical Methods, Canonical Theory.
Stiehl, Ulrich, ed. Dictionary of Book Publishing: German-English.
Stiehm, E. Richard & Fulginiti, Vincent A. Immunologic Disorders in Infants & Children.
Stiehm, E. Richard, et al. Immunotherapy: Cellular Transplants & Immunostimulation.
Stiehm, J., ed. Women's & Men's Wars.
Stierlin, Henri. Encyclopedia of World Architecture.
--The Pre-Colombian Civilizations: The World of the Maya, Aztecs & Incas.
Stiernotte, Alfred P. God & Space Time.
Stifel, Laurence D. Textile Industry: A Case Study of Industrial Development in the Philippines.
Stifel, Laurence D., et al, eds. Social Sciences & Public Policy in the Developing World.
Stifle, J. M. ABC Bible Characters.
--ABC Bible Stories.
--ABC Book about Jesus.
Stigger, Judith A. Coping with Infertility.
Stiggins, Richard J. & Rubel, Evelyn. Measuring Thinking Skills in the Classroom.
Stigler, George J. Essays in the History of Economics.
--Production & Distribution Theories: The Formative Period.
Stigliani, William M., jt. auth. see Spiro, Thomas G.
Stigum, Marcia. Money Market Calculations.
Stijgeren, E. Van see Van Stijgeren, E.
Stiles, David. Easy-to-Make Children's Furniture.
--Huts & Hideaways.
--The Kids' Fort Book.
--The Tree House Book.
Stiles, Henry R. Bundling: Its Origin, Progress & Decline in America.
Stiles, Karen, et al. Kirby Koala Happy Day Rhymes.
Stiles, Karl A. Handbook of Histology.
Stiles, Karl A., jt. auth. see Burns, Robert D.
Stiles, W. An Introduction to the Principles of Plant Physiology.
Stiles, W. S. Mechanisms of Color Vision.
Still, Alfred. Borderlands of Science.
Still, Bayrd. Mirror for Gotham: New York As Seen by Contemporaries from Dutch Days to the Present.
Still, Steven. Herbaceous Plants.
Still, William G. William Grant Still & the Fusion of Cultures in American Music. Haas, Robert B., ed.
Stille, Eva & Pfistermeister, Ursula. Christbaumschmuck.
Stiller, H. & Sagdeev, R. Z., eds. Planetary Interiors.
Stiller, Richard. The White Minority: Pioneers for Racial Equality.
--Your Body Is Trying to Tell You Something: How to Understand Its Signals & Respond to Its Needs.
Stillinger, Elizabeth, jt. auth. see Davidson, Marshall B.
Stillion, Judith M. Innovative Therapies in the Care of the Terminally Ill & Bereaved.
Stillman, Beatrice, ed. & tr. see Dostoyevsky, Anna.
Stillman, Beatrice, tr. see Chukofky, Kornei.
Stillman, Beatrice, tr. see Dostoevesky, Anna.
Stillman, David M. & Gordon, Ronni L. Comunicando: A First Course in Spanish.
Stillman, Irwin M. & Baker, Samm S. The Doctor's Quick Inches-off Diet.
--The Doctor's Quick Weight Loss Diet.
Stillman, R. C. & Willette, R. E., eds. The Psychopharmacology of Hallucinogens.
Stillman, Richard & Mosher, Frederick C., eds. Professions in Government.
Stillman, Richard J. Dow Jones Industrial Average: History & Role in an Investment Strategy.
--Public Administration: Concepts & Cases.
Stillman, Richard J., II. Public Administration: Concepts & Cases.
Stillwell, Lyda, jt. auth. see Heinig, Ruth B.
Stillwell, Margaret B. The Awakening Interest in Science During the First Century of Printing, 1450-1550.
--The Beginning of the World of Books: 1450-1470.
Stillwell, Paul, ed. Naval Review 1986.
Stilson, David C., et al, eds. Holistic Education: A Wellness Manual.
Stilz, Carol C. Kirsty's Kite.
Stimely, Keith, ed. see Institute for Historical Review Staff.
Stimmann, M. W. Pesticide Application & Safety Training.
Stimpson, George W. Nuggets of Knowledge.
Stimpson, Kate. Class Notes.
Stimson, Gerry V. Heroin & Behavior.
Stimson, Gerry V. & Oppenheimer, Edna. Heroin Addiction.
Stimson, Harriet R. Alphabet of Beauty & Other Poems.
Stimson, Henry L., jt. auth. see U. S. War Department Staff.
Stimson, John, et al. Social Problems: Impact, Process & Solution.
Stimson, William. A View of the Falls: An Illustrated History of Spokane.
Stinchcombe, Arthur L. Constructing Social Theories.
--Theoretical Methods in Social History.
Stinchcombe, Arthur L., et al. Crime & Punishment: Changing Attitudes in America.
Stinchcombe, Arthur W. Creating Efficient Industrial Management.
Stine, Deborah D. Exploring Careers in Engineering.
Stine, G. Harry. Handbook for Space Colonists.
--On the Frontiers of Science: Strange Machines You Can Build.
--The Untold Story of the Computer Revolution: Bits, Bytes, Bauds & Brains.
Stine, H. William, jt. auth. see Stine, M.
Stine, H. William, jt. auth. see Stine, Megan.
Stine, Hank, ed. see Bradley, Marion Zimmer.
Stine, Julie A. Dear Friend: Heart-to-Heart Talks with God.
Stine, M. & Stine, H. William. Conquest of the Barbarians.
Stine, M., jt. auth. see William, H.
Stine, Megan & Stine, H. William. A Chipmunk Christmas.
--The Spear of Azzurra. Spinner, Stephanie, ed.
--The Thundercats & the Ghost Warrior: A Find Your Fate Fantasy.
--The Thundercats & the Snowmen of Hook Mountain: A Find Your Fate Fantasy.
--Who Kidnapped Princess Saralinda.
Stine, R. L. Cavern of the Phantoms.
--Challenge of the Wolf Knight.
--Conquest of the Time Master.
--Mystery of the Imposter.
--Through the Forest of Twisted Dreams.
Stine, William B. & Harrigan, Raymond W. Solar Energy Fundamentals & Design: With Computer Applications.
Stinebricker, Bruce, ed. Annual Editions: American Government 1988-1989.
Stinebrickner, Bruce. Annual Editions: American Government, 1985-86.
--Annual Editions: State & Local Government, 1985-1986.
--State & Local Government.
Stineman, Esther & Loeb, Catherine. Women's Studies: A Recommended Core Bibliography.
Stiner, Frederic M., Jr., jt. auth. see Charles, Thomas W.
Stinneford, Carol, jt. auth. see Whittenburg, Clarice.
Stinnett, Nick & DeFrain, John. Secrets of Strong Families.
Stinson, Jim. Double Exposure.
--Low Angles: A Stoney Winston Mystery.
Stinto, Judith. Tom's Tale.
Stinton, Darrol. The Anatomy of the Aeroplane.
Stinton, John E., jt. auth. see Pritchett, S. Travis.
Stipe, Robert E., ed. see Dale, Anthony.
Stirk, John L., jt. auth. see Balaskas, Arthur S.
Stirling, James H. What Is Thought?
Stirling, Jocelyn. Venture to Love.
Stirling, Leader. Tanzanian Doctor.
Stirling, Monica. A Screen of Time: A Study of Luchino Visconti.
Stirling, Norman. Introduction to Technical Drawing: Metric Edition.
Stirner, Max. Ego & Its Own. Byington, Steven, tr. from Ger.
Stirrup Associates, Inc. Staff. All about Love. Phillips, Cheryl M. & Harvey, Bonnie C., eds.
Stiscak, Donna. Lollipops & Parachutes: One Hundred & Twenty Stimulating Learning Activities for Children of Active, Caring Adults.
Stitt, Milan. The Runner Stumbles.

Stitzel, Thomas E., jt. auth. see Widicus, Wilbur W.
Stivers, Robert L. Hunger, Technology & Limits to Growth: Christian Responsibility for Three Ethical Issues.
--The Sustainable Society: Ethics & Economic Growth.
Stivison, Douglas S. Introduction to Turbo Pascal.
--Introduction to Turbo Pascal.
--Turbo Pascal Library.
Stix, Hugh, et al. The Shell: Gift of the Sea.
Stjernsward, J., et al. Tumor Immunology.
St. John De Crevecoeur, J. Hector see De Crevecoeur, J. Hector.
Stobaugh, Beverly P. Women in Parliament Nineteen Eighteen to Nineteen Seventy.
Stobaugh, Robert, jt. auth. see Ghadar, Fariborz.
Stobaugh, Robert B., Jr. Petrochemical Manufacturing & Marketing Guide. Incl. Vol. 1. Aromatics & Derivatives; Vol. 2. Olefins, Diolefins & Acetylene. Gulf Pub.
Stobbs, William. Motor Museums of Europe.
Stock, Augustine. Call to Discipleship: A Literary Study of Mark's Gospel.
Stock, Barbara R. Handbook of Avoiding Probate (With Legal Forms)
--How to Survive Probate & Minimize the Attorney's Fee.
--Joint Living Trust Forms Kit (Married)
--Living Trust Forms Kit (Individual--Married)
--Living Trust Forms Kit (Single)
Stock, Dennis. Flower Show.
Stock, J. R. Die Mathematische Grundlagen Fur Die Organisation der Elektronishen Rechenmaschine der Eidgenossis Chen Technischen Hochschule.
Stock, Michael & Rothwell, Nancy. Obesity & Leanness: Basic Aspects.
Stock, Noel, ed. Ezra Pound Perspectives: Essays in Honor of His Eightieth Birthday.
Stock, Noel, jt. tr. see Pound, Ezra.
Stock, R. & Rice, C. B. Chromatographic Methods.
Stockard, James G. Rethinking People Management: A New Look at the Human Resources Function.
Stockbridge, Grant. Corpse Cargo.
--The Prince of Evil.
--Satan's Death Blast.
Stocken, Lloyd A., jt. auth. see Ord, Margery G.
Stockhammer, M., ed. Thomas Aquinas Dictionary.
Stockholm International Peace Research Institute (SIPRI) Staff. The Arms Trade Registers.
Stockholm International Peace Research Institute Staff. Problem of Chemical & Biological Warfare: A Study of the Historical, Technical, Military, Legal & Political Aspects of CBW, & Possible Disarmament Measures, Vol. 6, Technical Aspects of Early Warning & Verification 1975.
Stockholm International Peace Research Institute (SIPRI) Staff. World Armaments & Disarmament: SIPRI Yearbook 1976.
Stocking, George W. & Watkins, Myron W. Cartels in Action: Case Studies in International Business Diplomacy.
Stocking, George W., ed. see Boas, Franz.
Stockinger, L., ed. see Austrian Society for Electron Microscopy Staff.
Stockkigt, J. R., et al, eds. Thyroid Research III: Eighth International Thyroid Congress 3-5 February 1980, Sydney, Australia.
Stockley, David. Drug Warning: Illustrated Guide for Parents & Teachers.
Stockman, Harry E. The Network Theorem Book.
Stockton, Doris S. Essential Algebra & Trigonometry.
--Essential College Algebra.
--Essential Trigonometry.
Stockton, Elizabeth L. PBX Switchboard Workbook.
Stockton, Frank. The Lady or the Tiger? & Other Stories.
Stockton, Richard B. Capital Management for Financial Executives.
--ROI: Planning for Profitable Growth.
Stockum, Hilda Van see Van Stockum, Hilda.
Stockwell, Felicity. The Nursing Process in Psychiatric Nursing.
--The Unpopular Patient.
Stockwell, Foster & Bowen, Tang, eds. Recent Discoveries in Chinese Archaeology. Boyang, Zuo, tr. from Chinese.
Stockwell, John. In Search of Enemies: A CIA Story.
Stockwell, P. B., jt. ed. see Foreman, J. K.
Stockwell, Rhoda, tr. see Qifeng, Fu.
Stoddard, Sandol. God's Little House.
Stoddard, Seneca R. Old Times in the Adirondacks. De Sormo, Maitland C., ed.
Stoddard, T. Lothrop. The French Revolution in San Domingo.
Stoddard, Whitney S. Sculptors of the West Portals of Chartres Cathedral.
Stoddart, D. M. The Ecology of Vertebrate Olfaction.
Stoddart, D. M., ed. Ecology of Small Mammals.
Stoecker, Barbara J. & Montgomery, Evelyn T., eds. Developing Nations: Challenges Involving Women.
Stoecker, W. F. Refrigeration & Air Conditioning.
--Using SI Units (Standard International Metric) in Heating, Air Conditioning, & Refrigeration.
Stoekel, Horst. Quantitation, Modeling & Control in Aneasthesia.
Stoelting, Robert K. & Miller, Ronald D. Basics of Anesthesia.
Stoer, J., ed. Optimization Techniques, Part 2: Proceedings of the 8th IFIP Conference & Optimization Techniques, Wuerzburg, Sept. 5-9, 1977.
--Optimization Techniques: Proceedings of the 8th IFIP Conference on Optimization Techniques, Wuerzburg, Sept 5-9, 1977.
Stoessinger, John G. Crusaders & Pragmatists: Movers of Modern American Foreign Policy.
--Henry Kissinger: The Anguish of Power.
Stoever, William A. Renegotiations in International Business Transactions: The Process of Dispute-Resolution Between Multinational Investors & Host Societies.
Stoewer, H. & Bainum, P. M., eds. From Spacelab to Space Station: Fifth DGLR-AAS Symposium, Oct. 3-5, 1984, Hamburg, Gemany.
Stofen, D. & Walsren, H. A. Sub-Clinical Lead Poisoning.
Stoff, Jesse A., jt. auth. see Pellegrino, Charles R.
Stoffel, Ernest L. The Dragon Bound: Revelation Speaks to Our Times.
Stoffel, Ernest Lee. Believing the Impossible Before Breakfast.
Stoffel, R. & Lavalla, Patrick. Survival Sense for Pilot & Passengers.
Stohlman, Martha L. John Witherspoon: Parson, Politician, Patriot.
Stoikov, Vladimir. The Economics of Recurrent Education & Training.
Stojadinovic, N. D., ed. Advances in Microelectronics: Review Papers from the 12th Yugoslav Conference on Microelectronics, Yugoslavia, 7-9 May 1984.
Stojanovic, R., ed. see CISM (International Center for Mechanical Sciences Staff.
Stojanovic, Radmila, ed. Functioning of the Yugoslav Economy.
Stok. Notes on Medicine for Occupational Health Nurses.
Stoken, Dick. Cycles: What They Are, What They Mean, How to Profit by Them.
Stoker, Bram. The Bram Stoker Bedside Companion: Ten Stories by the Author of Dracula. Osborne, Charles, ed.
--Dracula.
--The Jewel of Seven Stars.
--Under the Sunset.
Stoker, J. J. Nonlinear Vibrations in Mechanical & Electrical Systems Pure & Aplied Mechanics.
Stokes & Lukenbill. Using the Apple Computer.
Stokes, A. V., jt. ed. see Saiady, C.
Stokes, Adrian. Michaelangelo - A Study in the Nature of Art.
Stokes, Adrian D. Art & Science: A Study of Alberti, Pierodella Francesca & Giorgione.
Stokes, Allen W., ed. Territory.
Stokes, Arch. The Equal Opportunity Handbook for Hotels, Restaurants & Institutions.
Stokes, Curtis. The Evolution of Trotsky's Theory of Revolution.
Stokes, Doris. Whispering Voices.
Stokes, Durward T. Company Shops: The Town Built by a Railroad.
Stokes, Edward. Hawthorne's Influence on Dickens & George Eliot.
Stokes, Francis G. A Dictionary of the Characters & Proper Names in the Works of Shakespeare.
Stokes, Gordon. Cleared for Takeoff: Flying for Beginners.
Stokes, Jack. Monster Madness Outrageous Jokes about Weird Folks.
Stokes, John, ed. see Allen, Grant.
Stokes, John, ed. see Egerton, George.
Stokes, John, ed. see Harland, Henry.
Stokes, John, ed. see O'Shaughnessy, Arthur.
Stokes, Lillian G., jt. auth. see Billings, Diane M.
Stokes, Lynette & Duchaine, Fawn, eds. Unsportsmanlike Conduct.
Stokes, M. Conquering Government Regulation: A Business Guide.
Stokes, Myra J. Organizational Barriers & Their Impact on Women in Higher Education.
Stokes, R. H., jt. auth. see Guggenheim, E. A.
Stokes, Stewart L., Jr. It's about Time: A Practical Guide to Managing Your Most Important Resource.
Stokesbury, James L. Navy & Empire.
--A Short History of Air Power.
Stokinger, Herbert E., ed. Beryllium.
Stokke, Allan H., jt. auth. see Ferguson, Robert W.
Stokoe, James. Decorative & Ornamental Brickwork.
Stokols, Daniel, ed. Perspectives on Environment & Behavior: Theory, Research & Applications.
Stolbov, Bruce. Last Fall.
Stoler, P., ed. Photopion Nuclear Physics.
Stoler, Peter. Decline & Fail: The Ailing Nuclear Power Industry.
Stoljar, Margaret M. Poetry & Song in Late Eighteenth Century Germany: A Study in the Musical Sturm und Drang.
Stoll, B. A. Cancer Treatment: End-Point Evaluation.
Stoll, Basil A., ed. New Horizons in Oncology: Screening & Monitoring of Cancer.
--Risk Factors & Multiple Cancers.
Stoll, Frances A. Dental Health Education.
Stoll, Gaby. Natural Crop Protection Based on Local Farm Resources in the Tropics & Subtropics. Coates, John, tr. from Ger.
Stoll, John E. The Great Deluge: A Yeats Bibliography.
Stollak, Gary E. & Lieberman, Michael, eds. Child Custody Disputes: A Source Book.
Stoloff, Carolyn. Stepping Out.
--Swiftly Now.
Stoloff, N., jt. ed. see Pelloux, R.
Stoltz, Donald & Stoltz, Marshall. The Advertising World of Norman Rockwell.
Stoltz, Marshall, jt. auth. see Stoltz, Donald.
Stolyarenko, A. Psychology of Management of Labor Collectives.
Stolz, Benjamin A., jt. ed. see Matejka, Ladislav.
Stolzenberg, Jacob. Psychosomatics & Suggestion Therapy in Dentistry.
Stolzenberg, Mark. Clown: For Circus & Stage.
Stominger, J. S., jt. ed. see Parham, B.
Stonberg, Selma F. From Start to Finish.
Stone, A. Harris. Last Free Bird.
Stone, Abraham, jt. auth. see Stone, Hannah.
Stone, Alan, jt. auth. see Knight, Kenneth L.
Stone, Albert E. The Innocent Eye: Childhood in Mark Twain's Imagination.
Stone, Alfred R. & Deluca, Stuart M. Investigating Crimes: An Introduction.
Stone & Webster Engineering Corporation Staff. Analysis of Nuclear Power Reactor, Decommissioning Costs.
Stone, Bernard. A Day to Remember.
--The Tale of Admiral Mouse.
Stone, Carl & Brown, Aggrey, eds. Essays on Power & Change in Jamaica.
Stone, Christopher. Where the Law Ends, the Social Control of Corporate Behavior.
Stone, Christopher D. Should Trees Have Standing? Toward Legal Rights for Natural Objects.
Stone, Clifford. The Great Sunflower.
Stone, Dave. New Home Sales.
Stone, David. How to Sell New Homes & Condominiums.
Stone, Deborah L. The Illustrated RM-COBOL Book.
Stone, Donald B., et al. Elementary School Health Education: Ecological Perspectives.
Stone, Doris M. The Great Public Gardens of the Eastern United States: A Guide to Their Beauty & Botany.
Stone, Doris Z., jt. ed. see Lange, Frederick W.
Stone, Eddie. Donald Writes No More.
--Jesse Jackson.
Stone, Edmund, tr. see Bion, M.
Stone, Erika. Pro Techniques of Photographing Children.
Stone, Frederick H. & Koupernik, Cyrille. Child Psychiatry for Students.
Stone, Gayle, jt. auth. see Crowther, C. Edward.
Stone, Gerald W., jt. auth. see Byrns, Ralph T.
Stone, Gerald W. Jr., jt. auth. see Byrns, Ralph T.
Stone, Gerald W., Jr., jt. auth. see Byrns, Ralph T.
Stone, Gregory P. Games, Sport & Power.
Stone, Hannah & Stone, Abraham. Marriage Manual. Aitken, Gloria S. & Sobrero, Acquiles, eds.
Stone, Harold. Introduction to Computer Organization & Data Structures.
Stone, Harold, ed. see Betteridge, Terry.
Stone, Harold, ed. see Carr, Richard W.
Stone, Harold, ed. see Chansler, Robert J., Jr.
Stone, Harold, ed. see Cohoon, James P.
Stone, Harold, ed. see Drongowski, Paul J.
Stone, Harold, ed. see French, James C.
Stone, Harold, ed. see Georgiou, Vassilios J.
Stone, Harold, ed. see Goldman, Ron.
Stone, Harold, ed. see Hsu, Chi-Ping.
Stone, Harold, ed. see Johnson, Scott D.
Stone, Harold, ed. see Karp, Richard A.
Stone, Harold, ed. see Mueller, Robert A.
Stone, Harold, ed. see Satyanarayanan, Mahadev.
Stone, Harold, ed. see Schwan, Karsten.
Stone, Harold, ed. see Shani, Uri.
Stone, Harold, ed. see Trimberger, Stephen.
Stone, Harold S., ed. see Carlbom, Ingrid.
Stone, Harriet M. see Sidney, Margaret.
Stone, Harry, ed. see Dickens, Charles.
Stone, Howard. Short Bike Rides in Rhode Island.
Stone, Howard E., ed. see Stone, Howard W.
Stone, Howard W. Suicide & Grief.
--Using Behavioral Methods in Pastoral Counseling. Clinebell, Howard J. & Stone, Howard E., eds.
Stone, Howard W., ed. see Augsburger, David W.
Stone, Howard W., ed. see Clements, William M.
Stone, Howard W., ed. see Clinebell, Charlotte H.
Stone, Howard W., ed. see Clinebell, Howard J.
Stone, Howard W., ed. see Cobb, John B., Jr.
Stone, Howard W., ed. see Colston, Lowell G.
Stone, Howard W., ed. see Irwin, Paul B.
Stone, Howard W., ed. see Leas, Speed & Kittlaus, Paul.
Stone, Howard W., ed. see Pattison, E. Mansell.
Stone, Hoyt E. Dare to Live Free.
Stone, James. How to Have Powerful Daily Devotions.
Stone, Josephine R. Green Is for Galanx.
--The Mudhead.
--Praise All the Moons of Morning.
--Those Who Fall from the Sun.
Stone, Julius. Legal Controls of International Conflict.
Stone, Justin F. The Metaphysics of Wall Street.
Stone, K. M., jt. auth. see Kirschner, E.
Stone, Lawrence. The Past & the Present.
Stone, Lawrence M. Federal Income Taxation: 1983 Supplement.
Stone, Leroy O. & Marceau, Claude. Canadian Population Trends & Public Policy Through the 1980s.
Stone, Llma, jt. auth. see Scott, George.
Stone, Marie K., jt. auth. see Kahan, Jane.
Stone, Merlin. Ancient Mirrors of Womanhood: A Treasury of Goddess & Heroine Lore from Around the World.
Stone, Michael E. Scriptures, Sects & Visions: A Profile of Judaism from Ezra to the Jewish Revolts.
Stone, Michael E., jt. auth. see Nickelsburg, George W.
Stone, Morris. Benefit Plans Disputes: Arbitration Case Stories.
--Employee Discipline & Arbitration.
--Labor-Management Contracts at Work: Analysis of Awards Reported by the American Arbitration Association.
Stone, Nancy. Dune Shadow.
Stone, Natalie. Summer Fling: Candlelight Ecstasy 288.
Stone, P. A. Building Design Evaluation.
Stone, Paula S. The Illustrated MultiMate Book.
Stone, Peter. Charade.
Stone, Ralph. The Irreconcilables: The Fight Against the League of Nations.
Stone, Robert. Dog Soldiers.
--A Hall of Mirrors.
Stone, Robert & Stone, Webster. Zit Wars: The Battle for Great Skin.
Stone, Robert B., jt. auth. see Petrie, Sidney.
Stone, Robert H. Spilt Emotions.
--A Stone Collection: The Origins, Migrations & Growth of an Illustrious Family.
Stone, Robert L., ed. Essays on the Closing of the American Mind.
Stone, Ron. The Book of Texas Days.
Stone, Ronald H. Paul Tillich's Radical Social Thought.
Stone, Ruth. Cheap: New Poems & Ballads.
--Cheap: New Poems & Ballads.
--Topography & Other Poems.
Stone, Scott C. Song of the Wolf.
Stone, Shelley C. & Shertzer, Bruce E. Careers in Counseling & Guidance.
Stone, Shelley C., jt. auth. see Shertzer, Bruce E.
Stone, Thomas H. Understanding Personnel Management.
Stone, Webster, jt. auth. see Stone, Robert.
Stone, Wilfred & Bell, Jess G. Prose Style.
Stone, Wilfred & Hoopes, Robert, eds. Form & Thought in Prose.
Stonecipher, Judy. Creation: For Kids & Other People Too.
Stonecypher, D. D., Jr. Getting Older & Staying Young.
Stonehouse, Bernard. Penguins.
Stonely, Jack. Jenny's War.
Stoner, Carol H. Stocking Up.
Stoner, Carol H., jt. auth. see Organic Gardening Editors.
Stoner, I. B. Always April.
Stones, Christopher. Buildings & Towns in Pastel.
Stonesong Press Staff & Tarrant, John J. Stalking the Headhunter: The Smart Job-Hunter's Guide to Executive Recruiters.
Stonham, Peter, jt. ed. see Bushell, Chris.
Stonham, T. J. Digital Logic Techniques.
Stonier, T., jt. auth. see Braun, A. C.
Stoodley, R. J. Rearrangements of Pencillanic Acid Derivatives.
Stoodt, Barbara D. Reading Instruction.
Stoops, John D. The Kingdom of Jesus.
Stopes, Marie G. Sleep.
Stopher, Peter, jt. ed. see Hensher, David.
Stopher, Peter R., et al, eds. New Horizons in Travel-Behavior Research.
Stoppard, Miriam. Being a Well Woman.
--Dr. Miriam Stoppard's Book of Baby Care.
Stoppard, Tom. Enter a Free Man.

--Every Good Boy Deserves Favor & Professional Foul.
--The Real Thing.
--Rosencrantz & Guildenstern Are Dead.
--Rosencrantz & Guildenstern Are Dead.
--Travesties.
Storace, Patricia. Heredity.
Storch, J. Patient's Rights: Ethical & Legal Issues in Health Case & Nursing.
Storen, Helen F. Disadvantaged Early Adolescent.
Storer, Charles Russell. Beautiful Biblical Beams.
Storer, T., ed. see Interdisciplinary Conference, Ann Arbor, March 1973.
Storey, Dale A., jt. auth. see Phillips, Bonnie D.
Storey, David. The Changing Room. Incl. Home; The Contractor. Avon.
--Pasmore.
--Radcliffe.
--A Temporary Life.
--This Sporting Life.
Storey, Edward. A Right to Song: The Life of John Clare.
Storey, John. Managerial Prerogative & the Question of Control.
Storey, Mark, ed. Clare: The Critical Heritage.
Storey, Robert F. Pierrot: A Critical History of a Mask.
Storm, Hyemyohsts. The Song of Heyoehkah.
Storms, C. Samuel. The Grandeur of God.
Storms, Ray E. Myths & Realities of the Energy Shortage: Contrivance by the Companies or Bungling by the Government.
Stornetta, Ruth R. David's Real World.
Storr, Anthony. The Dynamics of Creation.
Storr, Catherine. The Chinese Egg.
--Clever Polly & the Stupid Wolf.
--Vicky.
Storrer, Carol M. & Hesterman, Vicki. Walking Home.
Storrer, Philip & Williams, Brian. Tax Fighters Guide, 1982.
Stortz, Diane. God Cares for Me.
Story, Donna K. & Rosdahl, Caroline B. Principles & Practices of Nursing Care.
Storzer, Gerald H., jt. auth. see Gerber, Barbara L.
Stotland, Ezra, et al. Empathy & Birth Order: Some Experimental Explorations.
Stotler, R. E. The Genus Frullania Subgenus Frullania in Latin America.
Stott, David, ed. see Thinley, Karma.
Stott, Deborah A. Jacques Lipschitz & Cubism.
Stott, Doug, tr. see Van Der Geest, Bans.
Stott, F. D., ed. ISAM Nineteen Seventy-Seven.
Stott, F. D., et al, eds. ISAM-GENT Nineteen Eighty-One.
Stott, John R. One People.
Stott, John R. & Coote, Robert. Down to Earth: Studies in Christianity & Culture.
Stott, P. E., et al, eds. Diagnostics for Fusion Reactor Conditions: Proceedings of the Course & Workshop, Varenna, 6-17 September 1982.
Stott, Philip. Historical Plant Geography.
Stough, Evelyn. They, Too, Were Flesh & Blood.
Stoughton, Cecil & Clifton, Chester V. The Memories-JFK Nineteen Sixty-one to Nineteen Sixty-three of Cecil Stoughton & Major General Chester V. Clifton.
Stouriotis, S. D. Practical Modern Greek for English Speaking People.
Stout, Joseph A., Jr., jt. ed. see Faulk, Odie B.
Stout, Rex. Champagne for One.
--Fer-de-Dance.
--Too Many Cooks.
--Too Many Cooks.
--Where There's a Will: Nero Wolfe.
Stout, Ruth. As We Remember Mother.
--I've Always Done It My Way.
Stout, William, jt. auth. see Preiss, Byron.
Stoutenbergh, John L., Jr. Dictionary of the American Indian.
Stovall, Floyd, ed. The Development of American Literary Criticism.
Stovall, Sidney T., et al. Composition: Skills & Models.
Stove, David. Popper & After: Four Modern Irrationalists.
Stovel, Edith. Salt-Free Herb Cookery.
Stovel, Nora. Margaret Drabble. Salwak, Dale, ed.
Stover, Edgar M., jt. auth. see Kitson, Harry D.
Stover, Marjorie F. Chad & the Elephant Engine.
Stover, Mary B., jt. auth. see Richardson, Marian K.
Stover, William J. Military Politics in Finland: The Development of Governmental Control Over the Armed Forces.
Stovin, Jean, ed. Journals of a Methodist Farmer, 1871 to 1875.
Stow, John. Survey of London.
Stow, Randolph. The Girl Green As Elderflower.
--The Merry-Go-Round in the Sea.
--The Suburbs of Hell.
--To the Islands.
--Tourmaline: A Novel.
--Visitants.
--Visitants: A Novel.
Stowe, Harriet Beecher. Uncle Tom's Cabin.
Stowe, William W., jt. ed. see Most, Glenn W.
Stowell, Alan M., ed. U. S. International Trade Laws.
Stowell, Gordon, jt. auth. see Groves, Sheila.
Stowell, Jerald P. The Beginner's Guide to American Bonsai.
Stowell, Joseph M. Kingdom Conflict.
Stower, Caleb. The Printer's Manual, an Abridgement of Stower's Grammar, Comprising All the Plans in That Work for Imposing Forms, Several Tables & Other Useful Articles.
Stowers, John M., jt. ed. see Sutherland, Hamish W.
Stowitschek, Joseph J., et al. Instructional Materials for Exceptional Children: Selection, Management & Adaptation.
--Direct Teaching Tactics for Exceptional Children: A Practice & Supervision Guide.
Stoye, John W. English Travellers Abroad, 1604-1667.
Strachan. The Petroleum Refinery Engineer's Handbook.
Strachan, Bill, ed. see Rowse, A. L.
Strachan, C. The Theory of Beta-Decay.
Strachan, J. G. Alcoholism: Treatable Illness.
--Practical Alcoholism Programming: An Honorable Approach to Man's Alcoholism Problem.
Strachan, W. J. Modern Italian Stories.
Strachey, Barbara & Samuels, Jayne. Mary Berenson: A Self Portrait from Her Letters & Diaries.
Strachey, C., jt. auth. see Milne, R.
Strachey, Giles L. Characters & Commentaries.
Strachey, James, ed. & tr. see Freud, Sigmund.
Strachey, James, tr. see Freud, Sigmund.
Strachey, John. Socialism Looks Forward.
Strachey, Julia & Partridge, Frances. Julia: A Portrait of Julia Strachey.
Stradella, Alessandro. Corispero. Brown, Howard M., ed.
--Moro per Amore. Brown, Howard M., ed.
Stradling, Leslie E. Praying the Psalms.
Stradling, R. A. Europe & the Decline of Spain.
Strage, Mark. Women of Power: The Life & Times of Catherine de Medici.
Strahan, Bradley R. Love Songs for an Age of Anxiety.
Strahan, David. Middle School Research Studies, 1985.
Strahan, Edward. The Art Treasures of America.
Strain, Samuel F. From the Nolichucky to Memphis: Reminiscences of a Tennessee Doctor.
Strakhovsky, Leonid I. Alexander I of Russia, the Man Who Defeated Napoleon.
--Craftsmen of the Word: Three Poets of Modern Russia Gumilyov, Akhmatova, Mandelstam.
Stralen, D. Van & Cole, Robert. Boiling Phenomena.
Stramesi, Annette. The Inside Story: Creative Home Decorating.
Stranahan, Patricia. Yan'an Women & the Communist Party.
Strand, Elenora. Ideas to Make Your Days Easier: A Potpourri of Helpful Hints.
Strand, Helen R. An Illustrated Guide to Medical Terminology.
Strand, Mark. The Late Hour.
--Selected Poems.
Strand, Stanley. Marketing Dictionary.
Strand, Stanley & Gruber, Edward C. Resumes for Better Jobs.
Strandberg, Bror, jt. ed. see Engstrom, Arne.
Strandholt, S. Norman. The Adventures of Dan & Mark.
Strandjord, P. E., jt. ed. see Benson, E. S.
Strandjord, Paul E., jt. ed. see Schmer, Gottfried.
Strang, Harold R., ed. Intrinsic Bases of Adaptation: A Collection of Readings.
Strang, John. Readings & Writing Termcap Entries. Dougherty, Dale, ed.
Strang, Ruth. Education in Rural Communities.
--Juvenile Delinquency & the Schools.
Strang, Ruth, et al. Improvement of Reading.
Strange, Edward F. Hiroshige's Woodblock Prints.
Strange, Howard. How to Save Lots of Money on Your Phone Bill.
Strange, Ian J. Guide to the Falkland Islands & Their Natural History.
Strange, Jerry D., jt. auth. see Rice, B. J.
Strange, Jerry D., jt. auth. see Rice, Bernard J.
Strange, Julie M. Gastrointestinal Problems.
Strange, Marliss G. & Bennett, Jack W. Applying to Graduate School: A Student's Guide.
Strange, Michele, jt. auth. see Nakata, Yuri.
Strange, Philip G., ed. Cell Surface Receptors.
Strange, Susan & Tooze, Roger, eds. The International Politics of Surplus Capacity: Competition for Market Shares in the World Recession.
Stranger, Robert A., & Co., Staff. Stanger's Partnership Performance Yearbook: Oil & Gas, 1985.
--Stanger's Tax Shelter Yearbook, 1984.
Stransky, Thomas, jt. ed. see Anderson, Gerald.
Stransky, Thomas F., jt. auth. see Henry, Patrick.
Stranz, Walter. George Cadbury.
Strasinger, Susan K. Urinalysis & Body Fluids.
Strassels, Paul N. Paul Strassels' Quick & Easy Guide to Tax Management for 1985-1986.
Strassels, Paul N. & Mead, William B. Money Matters: The Hassle-Free-Month-by-Month Guide to Money Management.
Strasser, Karl H., jt. ed. see Opitz, Helmut.
Strassfeld, Michael, jt. ed. see Strassfeld, Sharon.
Strassfeld, Sharon & Strassfeld, Michael, eds. Third Jewish Catalog: Creating Community.
Straszak, A. & Tuch, R., eds. The Shinkansen High-Speed Rail Network of Japan: Proceedings of a IIASA Conference, June 27-30 1977.
Strategic Operations Group Staff & Davies, W. X. Countdown WW III, No. 4: Operation Persian Gulf.
--Countdown WW III: Operation North Africa.
Strath, Bo. The Politics of De-Industrialisation: The Contraction of the West European Shipbuilding Industry.
Stratila, S. V. & Voiculescu, D. V. Representations of AF-Algebras & of the Group U (Infinity)
Stratton, Clarence. Handbook of English.
Stratton, Craig. The Bio-Imagery Method of Breast Enlargement & Waist Reduction.
--Winning at Weight Loss.
Stratton, Joanne. Pioneer Women: Voices from the Kansas Frontier.
Stratton, John R., jt. auth. see Leger, Robert G.
Stratton, Stephen S. Nicolo Paganini: His Life & Work.
Straub, Davis. SUNDAY Documentation & User's Manual.
Straub, Joseph T. Managing: An Introduction.
Straub, Joseph T. & Kossen, Stan. Introduction to Business.
Straub, P. A., jt. auth. see Heilbronner, E.
Straub, Peter. Leeson Park & Belsize Square.
Straudinger, H., ed. see Gesellschaft Fuer Biologische Chemie, 19th Colloquium, Mossbach-Baden, 1968.
Strauer, B. E., ed. Heart in Hypertension: Symposium.
Straughan, Robert P. The Salt-Water Aquarium in the Home.
Straughn, Charles T. & Colby, Marvelle S. Lovejoy's Guide for the Learning Disabled.
Straus, E. W., et al. Psychiatry & Philosophy. Natanson, M., ed. Eng, E. & Kennedy, S. C., trs.
Straus, Franklin. Destructive David.
Strause, Glynis H. & Ambrester, Marcus L. Games: Games Activities Measures Exercises in Speech.
Strauss, Allan R., Jr. A Critical Study of Freud's Concept of Unconscious Mental Processes with Special Reference to Gestalt Psychology.
Strauss, Anselm, ed. see Mead, George H.
Strauss, Anselm L., ed. Where Medicine Fails.
--Where Medicine Fails.
Strauss, Botho. Big & Little. Cattaneo, Anne, tr. from Ger.
Strauss, David F. The Christ of Faith & the Jesus of History: A Critique of Schleiermacher's The Life of Jesus. Keck, Leander E., tr. & intro. by.
--The Life of Jesus Critically Examined. Hodgson, Peter C. & Keck, Leander E., eds.
Strauss, David P. & Worth, Fred L. Hollywood Trivia.
Strauss, E. G. & Strauss, J. H. Current Topics in Microbiology & Immunology.
Strauss, George, et al. Organizational Behavior.
Strauss, J. H., jt. auth. see Strauss, E. G.
Strauss, John S., et al, eds. The Origins & Course of Psychopathology: Methods of Longitudinal Research.
Strauss, K. Applied Science in the Casting of Metals.
Strauss, Lehman. First Person.
--Second Person.
--Third Person.
Strauss, Leo. Persecution & the Art of Writing.
--Xenophon's Socratic Discourse.
Strauss, Leo & Cropsey, Joseph. History of Political Philosophy.
Strauss, Melvin J. Computer Capacity: A Production Control Approach.
Strauss, Richard. A Working Friendship: The Correspondence between Richard Strauss & Hugo Von Hofmannsthal.
Strauss, Richard L. How to Raise Confident Children.
Strauss, Ruby G., ed. If Grandma Had Wheels: Jewish Folk Sayings.
Strauss, Stephen. Copyright: Practical Guide to Microcomputer Licenses.
Strauss, Werner. Industrial Gas Cleaning.
Strausz, Otto P. & Lown, Elizabeth M., eds. Oil Sand & Oil Shale Chemistry.
Strautberg, Susan. Pregnancy Nine to Five.
Stravinsky, Igor F. Conversations with Igor Stravinsky.
Straw, Allan & Clayton, Keith. Eastern & Central England.
Straw Dog. Improvising Rock Guitar.
Strawson, P. F. Freedom & Resentment & Other Essays.
--Logico-Linguistic Papers.
Strax, Philip. Control of Breast Cancer Through Mass Screening.
Strayer, Joseph R. Mainstream of Civilization.
--The Reign of Philip the Fair.
Strayer, Joseph R. & Gatzke, Hans W. The Mainstream of Civilization.
--The Mainstream of Civilization: Since 1500.
Strayer, Joseph R., ed. The Interpretation of History.
Strayer, Joseph R., et al. The Mainsteam of Civilization: Since 1500.
Streabbog, L. Twelve Melodious Studies for Piano, Op. 63. Seifert, Hans T., ed.
Streater, R. F., ed. Mathematics of Contemporary Physics.
Streatfeild, Noel. Gemma.
Streatfeild, Richard A. Handel.
Streb, Judith. Holiday Parties.
Strebeck, Mary. Single But Not Alone.
Strecker, H., jt. ed. see Schneeweiss, H.
Strecker, Matthias. Rock Art of East Mexico & Central America: An Annotated Bibliography.
Street & Burch. Essential Primary Care.
Street, Bradford. For Pete's Sake.
Street, Donald J., Jr. Street's Cruising Guide to the Eastern Caribbean.
Street, Donald M. A Cruising Guide to the Lesser Antilles.
Street, Donald M., Jr. Seawise.
Street, Donald M., Jr., ed. Street's Cruising Guide to the Eastern Caribbean.
Street, G. S. Autobiography of a Boy.
Street, H. E. & Cockburn, W. Plant Metabolism.
Street, H. E., ed. Essays in Plant Taxonomy.
Street, Philip. Animal Migration & Navigation.
--Animal Weapons.
--Between the Tides.
Street, T. Watson. The Church & the Churches.
Streeter, Donald. Professional Smithing.
Streeter, Tal. Japanese Kites.
Streeter, Victor L. Handbook of Fluid Dynamics.
Streetly, Martin. Airborne Electronic Warfare: History, Weapons & Tactics.
--Confound & Destroy: One Hundred Group & the Bomber Support Campaign.
--World Electronic Warfare Aircraft.
Strege, John, jt. auth. see Bavasi, Buzzie.
Streib, Dan. The Mind Breakers.
Streips, Uldis N., et al, eds. Genetic Exchange: A Celebration & a New Generation.
Streitenberg, H., ed. Kontaktlinsenvademekum, 1987.
Streitwieser, A. & Taft, R. W., eds. Progress in Physical Organic Chemistry.
Streitwieser, A., Jr. & Brauman, J. I. Supplemental Tables of Molecular Orbital Calculations.
Strelkov, S. Mechanics.
Strete, Craig K. Death Chants.
Strewart, Don. You Be the Judge.
Striano, Judi. Harmful Psychotherapy.
Stribling, Catherine. Getting the Most from Your Bank.
Strich, Christian, ed. Fellini's Faces.
Strick, Ivy. The Home Makers.
--Scot Free.
Strick, Peter L., jt. ed. see Morrison, Adrian R.
Strick, Philip, ed. Antigrav: Cosmic Comedies by SF Masters.
Strickberger, Monroe W., Jr. Genetics.
Stricker, Louis. Devils-Jewish Style.
Strickland & Thompson. Cases in Strategy & Policy.
Strickland & Thompson, eds. Strategy Formulation & Implementation.
Strickland, A. J. & Thompson, Arthur A., Jr. Cases in Strategic Management.
Strickland, A. J., III, jt. auth. see Thompson, Arthur A., Jr.
Strickland, A. J., 3rd, jt. auth. see Thompson, Arthur A., Jr.
Strickland, A. W. & Ackerman, Forrest J. A Collection of Great Science Fiction Films.
--Reference Guide to American Science Fiction Films: Vol. I, 1897-1929.
Strickland, Alison. Why Can't He Be Mine?
Strickland, Allyn D. Government Regulation & Business.
Strickland, Alonzo J., III, jt. auth. see Scott, Charles R., Jr.
Strickland, James W. & Steichen, James B. Difficult Problems in Hand Surgery.
Strickland, L. H., ed. Soviet & Western Perspectives in Social Psychology.
Strickland, Mark, jt. auth. see Umen, Samuel.
Strickland, Ron. Vermonters: Lively Oral Histories from Down Country to the Northeast Kingdom.
Strickland, Stephen P., jt. auth. see Kryder, Christian.
Strickland, Walter G. Dictionary of Irish Artists.
Strickler, George M., Jr., jt. auth. see Friedman, Joel W.
Strickler, Nancy E., ed. Marketing Life & Health Insurance.

Authors

Striebel, C. Optimal Control of Discrete Time Stochastic Systems.
Strieber, Whitley. The Night Church.
Strieber, Whitley & Kunetka, James W. Warday: And the Journey Onward.
Strieder, Peter. Albrecht Durer: Paintings, Prints, Drawings.
Striedieck, Werner F. Energie: Von der Tretmuhle zum Kernreaktor.
Striefel, Sebastian & Cadez, Mary J. Serving Children & Adolescents with Developmental Disabilities in the Special Education Classroom: Proven Methods.
Striggles, Theodore W., ed. see Volunteer Lawyers for the Arts.
Striker, John M. & Shapiro, Andrew O. Super Tenant: New York City Tenant Handbook.
Striker, Susan. The Anti-Coloring Book of Red-Letter Days.
Strinati, Dominic. Capitalism, the State & Industrial Relations.
Strindberg, August. A Dream Play. Chwat, Jacques, ed.
--Miss Julie.
--The Natives of Hemso. Paulson, Arvid, tr. from Swedish.
Strindberg, August see Weiss, Samuel A.
Striner, Herbert. Continuing Education as a National Capital Investment.
Striner, Herbert, jt. auth. see Sheppard, Harold.
Stringer, Arthur J. Red Wine of Youth: A Life of Rupert Brooke.
Stringer, Bruce. Earlihee the Turtle.
Stringer, Gail G. see O'Neal, William B.
Stringer, J. Hydraulic Systems Analysis.
--An Introduction to the Electron Theory of Solids.
Stringer, P. & Bannister, D., eds. Constructs of Sociability & Individuality.
Stringer, T. Plasma Transport Heat & MHD Theory: Proceedings of a Workshop at Varenna, Italy, 12-16 Sept. 1977. Rozzoli, R., ed.
Stringfellow, William. Instead of Death: New & Expanded Edition.
Strippel, Dick. Amelia Earhart: The Myth & the Reality.
Stritch, Elaine. Am I Blue? Living with Diabetes & Dammit, Having Fun!
Strobe, Wolfgang, jt. ed. see Eiser, J. R.
Strobel, Henry A. Useful Measurements for Violin Makers: A Reference for Shop Use.
Strobridge, Idah M. In Miners' Mirage Land.
Strock, O. J. Telemetry Computer Systems: An Introduction.
Strode, Hudson. Now in Mexico.
--Ultimates in the Far East: Travels in the Orient & India.
Strode Publishers Staff, ed. How to Get a Manuscript Published.
Stroebel, Leslie, et al. Visual Concepts for Photographers.
Strogonov, B. P., et al. Structure & Function of Plant Cells in Saline Habitats. Gollak, B., ed. Mercado, A., tr. from Rus.
Stroh, C. M. Vigilance: The Problem of Sustained Attention.
Stroh, Robert C., ed. see National Association of Home Builders Staff.
Stroh, Thomas F. Managing the Sales Function.
Strohecker, Carol, ed. see Podles, Mary S. & Porter, Vicki.
Strohecker, Rolf & Henning, Heinz M. Vitamin Assay: Tested Methods.
Strohmeier, W. Variable Stars.
Strohofer, Jean & Wallce, Marie. The Private Law Library in the High-Tech Era. Practising Law Institute Staff, ed.
Strolsahl, J. Patrick, et al. A Manual of Cloisonne & Champleve Enameling.
Strolz, Walter. Human Existence: Contradiction & Hope.
Strom, David, jt. auth. see Edelhart, Mike.
Strom, Deborah, compiled by. Birdwatching with American Women: A Selection of Nature Writings.
Strom, Frederic A. Land Use & Environment Law Review: 1984. Incl. 1984; 1976; 1977; 1978; 1979. Clark Boardman.
Strom, Gabriele W. Development & Dependence in Lesotho the Enclave of South Africa.
Stromberg, Ann H. & Harkess, Shirley, eds. Women Working: Theories & Facts in Perspective.
Stromberg, Mark S., jt. auth. see Clark, Tim W.
Stromberg, Roland N. Europe in the Twentieth Century.
Stromgren, E., jt. ed. see Schou, M.
Strommen, Merton P. Bridging the Gap: Youth & Adults in the Church.
Strommen, Merton P., jt. auth. see Solberg, Richard W.
Stronach, Rena. How to Take the Hassle Out of Homemaking.
Strong, Arline. Glowing in the Dark.
--Veterinarian, Doctor for Your Pet.
Strong, Bryan & Reynolds, Rebecca. Understanding Our Sexuality.
Strong, D. E. Greek & Roman Gold & Silver Plate.
Strong, D. E., ed. Archeological Theory & Practice.
Strong, Donald S. Issue Voting & Party Realignment.
Strong, Eugenia. Apotheosis & after Life.
Strong, Jean W., jt. auth. see Barclay, Morgan J.
Strong, John W., jt. auth. see Cleary, Edward W.
Strong, June. Where Are We Running?
Strong, Kathy. The California Bed & Breakfast Book.
--The California Bed & Breakfast Book.
--The Caribbean Bed & Breakfast Book.
Strong, Mary S. see Horowitz, Irving L.
Strong, P. M. The Ceremonial Order of the Clinic: Parents, Children & Medical Bureaucracies.
Strong, Roy. Artists of the Tudor Court: The Portrait Miniature Rediscovered, 1520-1620.
Strong, Roy & Oman, Julia T. The English Year.
Strong, Roy, intro. by. Vienna in the Age of Schubert: The Biedermeirer Interior, 1815-1848.
Strong, S. J. & Corney, G. The Placenta in Twin Pregnancy.
Strong, William S. The Copyright Book: A Practical Guide.
Stronge, Susan. Bidri Ware.
Strongman, K. T. Psychology for the Paramedical Professions.
Stroop, Jurgen. The Stroop Report: The Jewish Quarter of Warsaw Is No More!
Strother, Edward S. & Huckleberry, Alan W. Effective Speaker.
Strother, G. K. & Weber, Robert L. Physics with Applications in Life Sciences.
Strotman, Paul. The Log of Baker Abel.
Stroud, A. H. Numerical Quadrature & Solution of Ordinary Differential Equations: A Textbook for a Beginning Course in Numerical Analysis.
Stroud, Dorothy. Sir John Soane, Architect.
Stroud, George M. A Sketch of the Laws Relating to Slavery in the Several States of the United States of America.
Stroud, Marion. Celebrate Friendship.
--Celebrate the Golden Years.
Stroud, Oxford S. Writing Prose That Makes a Difference, & the Grammar Minimum.
Stroud, Parry. Stephen Vincent Benet.
Stroud, T. Services for Children & Their Families.
Stroup, George W. The Promise of Narrative Theology: Recovering the Gospel in the Church.
Stroup, Herbert W., Jr. & Wood, Norma S. Sexuality & the Counseling Pastor.
Stroup, Richard, jt. auth. see Gwartney, James D.
Stroup, Richard L. & Baden, John A. Natural Resources: Bureaucratic Myths & Environmental Management.
Strouse, Jean. Alice James: A Biography.
Strouse, Jean, ed. Women & Analysis: Dialogues on Psychoamalytic Views of Femininity.
Strozier, Robert M. Selected Speeches of Robert M. Strozier.
Strub, A. S. & Ehringer, H., eds. Energy Conservation in Industry.
Struble, Mitch. Stretching a Point.
--The Web of Space-Time: A Step by Step Exploration of Relativity.
Struchen, Jeanette. This Is the Puzzle of Poverty.
Structural Optimization Symposium Staff. AMD: Proceedings.
Strudwick, Karen, jt. ed. see Spilker, John.
Strudwick, Peter. Come Run with Me.
Struening, Elmer L. & Guttentag, Marcia, eds. Handbook of Evaluation Research.
Struhl, Karsten J. & Struhl, Paula R. Philosophy Now.
Struhl, Paula R., jt. auth. see Struhl, Karsten J.
Struik, Dirk J. A Concise History of Mathematics.
Strum, Jay, tr. see Kowalsky, Hans J.
Struminger, Laura S. Women & the Making of the Working Class: Lyon 1830-1870.
Strunk, Oliver. Essays on Music in the Western World.
Strupp, H. Psychotherapy & the Modification of Abnormal Behavior.
Strute, Karl & Doelken, Dr. Theodor, eds. Who's Who in the Arts & Literature. Incl. Vol. 1, Pt. 1. The Fine Arts (A-O; Vol. 1, Pt. 2. The Fine Arts (P-Z; Vol. 2. Applied Arts and Music; Vol. 3. Literature. UNIPUB.
Struther, Jan. Mrs. Miniver.
Strutt, Malcolm. Wholistic Health & Living Yoga.
Struve, Walter. Elites Against Democracy: Leadership Ideals in Bourgeois Political Thought in Germany, 1890-1933.
Struyk, Raymond, jt. ed. see Follain, James.
Struyk, Raymond J. A New System for Public Housing: Salvaging a National Resource.
--Saving the Housing Assistance Plan: Improving Incentives to Local Governments.
--Should Government Encourage Homeownership?
Struyk, Raymond J., jt. auth. see Rasmussen, David W.
Struyk, Raymond J., jt. auth. see Stahl, Konrad.
Struyk, Raymond J. & Bendick, Marc, Jr., eds. Housing Vouchers for the Poor: Lessons from a National Experiment.
Struyk, Raymond J., et al. Housing Policies for the Urban Poor.
Stryk, Lucien. World of the Buddha: An Introduction to Buddhist Literature.
Stryk, Lucien, et al, trs. from Chinese & Japanese. The Crane's Bill: Zen Poems of China & Japan.
Stryker, Perrin, ed. see Pollack, Kenneth & Gergen, Michael J.
Stryker, Ruth, jt. auth. see Gordon, George K.
Stryker, Steven C. Guide to Successful Consulting with Forms, Letters, & Checklists.
Strzelecki, Z. Contemporary Polish Stage Design. Baldyga, Jerzy A., tr. from Pol.
St Sure, J. Paul, jt. auth. see Perkins, Frances.
Stuart & Samuel. Applied Surgical Pathology.
Stuart, Anthony. Force Play.
--The London Affair.
--Midwinter Madness.
--Russian Leave.
--Vicious Circles.
Stuart, Bruce. State Regulation of Health Service Utilization: Lessons from Michigan.
Stuart, Douglas, jt. auth. see Sprague, Jo.
Stuart, Fredric. Introduction to Standard COBOL Programming.
Stuart, Gail W. & Sundeen, Sandra J. Principles & Practice of Psychiatric Nursing.
Stuart, George. Clues to America's Past. Crump, Donald J., ed.
Stuart, Ian. Sandscreen.
Stuart, Irving & Abt, Lawrence. Children of Separation & Divorce.
Stuart, Irving R. & Wells, Carl F. Pregnancy in Adolescence: Needs, Problems & Management.
Stuart, Irving R., jt. auth. see Abt, Lawrence E.
Stuart, Micheline. The Tarot Path to Self-Development.
Stuart, Micheline, tr. see Suares, Carlo.
Stuart, Monica & Soper, Gill. The Bazaar Stall.
Stuart, Reginald. Bailout: America's Billion Dollar Gamble on the "New" Chrysler Corporation.
Stuart, Richard B. Act Thin, Stay Thin: New Ways to Lose Weight & Keep It off.
Stuart, Richard B. & Davis, Barbara. Slim Chance in a Fat World: Behavioral Control of Obesity.
Stuart, Robert & Johnson, Richard, eds. New Horizons for Academic Libraries.
Stuart, Robert C., jt. auth. see Gregory, Paul R.
Stuart, Roderick W. Royalty for Commoners: The Complete Known Ancestry of John of Gaunt, Son of Edward III, King of England, & Queen Phillippa.
Stuart, Simon. Say: An Experiment in Learning.
Stuart, Vincent, tr. see Suares, Carlo.
Stuart, Vincent, et al, trs. see Diel, Paul.
Stuart, W. J. Forbidden Planet.
Stuart, Whitey. Recommunion: A True Story.
Stuart-Fox, David, jt. ed. see Levine, Suarti.
Stuart-Harris, Charles H. Influenza: The Viruses & the Disease.
Stubbe, John, jt. auth. see Gore, Marvin.
Stubbe, John W., jt. auth. see Gore, Marvin R.
Stubbings, G. W. Dictionary of Church Music.
Stubbs, Adrian, ed. see Biko, Stephen.
Stubbs, Burns A., compiled by. Paintings, Pastels, Drawings, Prints & Copper Plates by & Attributed to American & European Artists.
Stubbs, Donald W., jt. ed. see Brown, Arthur M.
Stubbs, F., jt. auth. see Havers, J.
Stubbs, George. The Anatomy of the Horse.
Stubbs, Joanna. With Cat's Eyes You'll Never Be Afraid of the Dark.
Stubbs, Marcia, jt. auth. see Barnet, Sylvan.
Stubbs, Marcia & Barnet, Sylvan, eds. The Little, Brown Reader.
Stubbs, Margaret L., jt. ed. see Amabile, Teresa M.
Stubbs, Roy C. Environmental Administration in Thailand.
Stubbs, Weslie S., jt. ed. see Smith, Virginia C.
Stubenhaus, Joanne Illus. by see Barton, Amsel.
Stuckenschmidt, Hans H. Arnold Schoenberg. Searle, H., tr. from Ger.
--Maurice Ravel Variations on His Life & Work.
Stuckert, Frank H. August Nineteen Ninety-Nine.
Stuckes, Audrey D., jt. auth. see Parrott, J. E.
Stuckey, D. C., ed. Management of Industrial Wastewater in Developing Countries: Proceedings of the International Symposium Held in Alexandria, Egypt, March 28-31, 1981.
Stuckey, Debra. God Made Everything.
--God Made Me.
Stuckey, Debra K. God Made Families.
--God Made Prayer.
Stuckey, Ronald L. Bibliography of Aquatic Flowering Plants of Ohio.
Studd, John & Gibb, D. M. MCQs in Obstetrics & Gynaecology.
Studd, John, ed. Progress in Obstetrics & Gynaecology.
Studdert, Richard de C. Selection: The Stress Theory of Evolution.
Studenikin, M. Por la Salud de Nuestros Ninos.
Student Buyers' Association Staff. Steward's Manual.
Studio D Staff. Crazy Creature Number Puzzles.
--Crazy Creature Picture Puzzles.
Studio Magazine Staff. Graphic Excellence.
Study Group of New York Staff. Children & Sex: The Parents Speak.
Stuempfle, Herman G., Jr. Preaching Law & Gospel.
Stuempfle, Herman G., Jr. & Kearney, Peter J. Lent.
Stuempfle, Herman G., Jr., ed. Preaching in the Witnessing Community.
Stuenkel, Omar. Marriage is for Two: How to Build a Marriage That Lasts & Works.
--We Are One in the Spirit: How to Receive & Use the Holy Spirit's Gifts.
Stuermann, Walter E., jt. auth. see Hill, Johnson D.
Stuhlmacher, Peter. Historical Criticism & Theological Interpretation of Scripture: Towards a Hermeneutic of Consent. Harrisville, Roy A., tr. from Ger. & intro. by.
--Reconciliation, Law & Righteousness: Essays in Biblical Theology. Kalin, Everett R., tr.
Stuhlman, Daniel D. Library of Congress Subject Headings for Judaica.
Stuhlmann, Gunther, ed. see Nin, Anais.
Stukane, Eileen, jt. auth. see Lauersen, Niels.
Stuligross, Katherine, ed. see League of Women Voters of New York State Staff.
Stull, Karl, ed. see Beimer, Martin E.
Stultz, Russell A. The Illustrated dBASE III Book.
--The Illustrated MS-PC-DOS Book (3.2) Berliner, Thomas H., ed.
Stulz, Roland. Appropriate Building Materials: A Catalogue of Potential Solutions.
Stum, Stephen B. Beyond Inspiration.
Stumm, David A. Advanced Industrial Selling.
Stumm, Werner, ed. Global Chemical Cycles & Their Alterations by Man.
Stumme, Wayne. Christians & the Many Faces of Marxism.
Stummer, Friedrich. Summerisch-Akkadische Parallelen Zum Aufbau Alttestamentlicher Psalmen.
Stump, Al, jt. auth. see Snead, Sam.
Stump, Gladys S. About People for a Special Time.
Stump, Jane B. What's the Difference? How Men & Women Compare.
Stumpf, Samuel E. Elements of Philosophy: An Introduction.
--Socrates to Sartre.
Stumpf, Walter, jt. ed. see Roth, Lloyd J.
Stumpp, Jane B. What's the Difference: How Men & Women Compare.
Stunard, E. Arthur, jt. auth. see Wagner, Betty J.
Stunkard, Albert J. Obesity.
Stuntz, Hugh C. Gringo Yanqui.
Stupka, Arthur, jt. auth. see Huheey, James E.
Stupochenko, Y. V., et al. Relaxation in Shock Waves. Lee, R. Shao-Lin, tr.
Sturdy, John, tr. see Kaiser, Otto.
Sturdy, John, tr. see Moltmann, Jurgen.
Sturdy, John, tr. see Ringgren, Helmer.
Sturgeon, R. E see Chakrabarti, C. L.
Sturgeon, R. E., jt. ed. see Chakrabarti, C. L.
Sturges, Lena, ed. Our Best Recipes: Vol. 1.
Sturges, Patricia P. The Endless Chain of Nature: Experiment at Hubbard Brook.
Sturgis, Alice F. Sturgis Standard Code of Parliamentary Procedure.
Sturgis, Margie. Let the Record Show: Memoirs of a Parole Board Member.
Sturgis, Yoshiko C. Oh, My Son, Forgive Me.
Sturm, Dorothy. Cobalt: A Retrospective of the Life & Art of Dorothy Sturm. Carrier, Karen B. & Leatherman, Donna, eds.
Sturm, Harlan, jt. ed. see Walsh, Donald D.
Sturma, Michael. Vice in a Vicious Society: Crime & Convicts in Mid-Nineteenth Century New South Wales.
Sturmer, Marie. The Stenciled Quilt. Baskin, Cathryn, ed.
Sturrock, P. A., ed. Plasma Astrophysics.
Sturrock, Peter, ed. Solar Flares.
Sturz, Harry A. The Byzantine Text-Type & New Testament Textual Criticism.
Sturzo, Luigi. Church & State, Two Vols.
Stuteville, John R. Marketing in a Consumer-Oriented Society.
Stutinsky, F., ed. see International Symposium on Neurosecretion, 4th, Strasbourg, 1966.
Stutley, Margaret. Ancient Indian Magic & Folklore: An Introduction.
--Hinduism: An Introduction.
Stutman, Suzanne, jt. auth. see Epstein, David.
Stuttard, Colins & Rozee, K. R., eds. Plasmids & Transposons: Environmental Efforts & Maintenance Mechanisms.
Stutz, Frederick P. Using the Keypunch & Other Punched Card Equipment.
Stuyt, Alexander M. Survey of International Arbitrations, 1794-1970.
Styan, John L. The State of Drama Study.
Stych, F. S. How to Find Out about Italy.

Styles, B. T., jt. ed. see Burley, J.
Su, Kendall L. Fundamentals of Circuits, Electronics, & Signal Analysis.
Suami, Tetsuo, jt. ed. see Rinehart, Kenneth L, Jr.
Suanders, Norah & Kelly, A. A. Joseph Campbell: A Critical Biography.
Suares, jt. auth. see Timothy.
Suares, Carlo. Genesis Rejuvenated. Roditi, Edouard, tr.
--The Qabala Trilogy. Stuart, Micheline & Stuart, Vincent, trs. from Fr.
Suares, J. C. The Snoopy Collection.
Suares, Jean-Claude, ed. Art of the Times.
Suarez & Castroleal. Aprende en Espanol y en Ingles: Readiness Level.
Suarez, Diamantina V., jt. auth. see Castroleal, Alicia.
Suarez, E. M., et al. Sanity, Insanity & Common Sense.
Suarez-Murias, Marguerite C. Essays on Hispanic Literature - Ensayos de Literatura Hispana: A Bilingual Anthology.
Suassure, Eric de see De Suassure, Eric.
Subak-Sharpe, Genell J. Overcoming Breast Cancer.
Subak-Sharpe, Genell J., jt. auth. see Warren, James V.
Subblefield, LaVerne. Animal Crackers in My Soup.
Subotnick, Steven I. Podiatric Sports Medicine of the Lower Extremity.
Subrahmanyam, Marti G., jt. auth. see Altman, Edward.
Subrahmanyam, Marti G., jt. auth. see Altman, Edward I.
Subramaniam, C. The New Strategy in Indian Agriculture.
Subramanian, Gopal, ed. Radiopharmaceuticals.
Subramanyam, Ka N., ed. Contemporary Indian Short Stories.
Subtelny, Stephen & Konigsberg, Irwin R., eds. Determinants of Spatial Organization: Symposium of the Society for Developmental Biology, 37th.
Subtelny, Stephen & Sussex, Ian M., eds. The Clonal Basis of Development.
Subtelny, Stephen, ed. see Society for Developmental Biology Symposium Staff.
Subtle, Susan, jt. auth. see Lester, Michael.
Sucher, Harry V. Simplified Boatbuilding: Flat Bottom.
--Simplified Boatbuilding: The V-Bottom Boat.
Sucheston, Martha E. & Cannon, M. Samuel. Congenital Malformations: Case Studies in Developmental Anatomy.
Suchet, J. P. Crystal Chemistry & Semiconduction in Transition Metal Binary Compounds.
--Electrical Conduction in Solid Materials: Physico-Chemical Bases & Possible Applications.
Suchoff, B., jt. auth. see Bartok, B.
Suchoff, Benjamin, jt. auth. see Bartok, Bela.
Suchoff, Benjamin, ed. see Bartok, Bela.
Suckling, Norman. Paul Valery & the Civilized Mind.
Sucksdorff, Astrid B. Chendru: The Boy & the Tiger.
--The Roe Deer. Tapsell, Alan, tr. from Swedish.
--Tooni, the Elephant Boy.
Suda, Zdenek L. Zealots & Rebels: A History of the Communist Party of Czechoslovakia.
Suddick, Tom. A Few Good Men.
Suderman. Batter & Breading.
Suderman, Darrel R. & Cunningham, Frank E. Batter & Breading Technology.
Sudha, Ma Yoga, jt. auth. see Rajneesh, Bhagwan Shree.
Sudha, Ma Yoga, ed. see Rajneesh, Bhagwan Shree.
Sudhalter, Richard M. & Evans, Philip R. Bix: Man & Legend.
Sudhoff, K. Kurzes Handbuch der Geschichte der Medizin.
Sudjic, Deyan. Norman Foster, Richard Rogers, James Stirling: New Directions in British Architecture.
Sudjic, Deyan, ed. The House Style Book: New Directions in Design & Decorating for Every Room in the House.
Sudol, Ronald A., ed. Revising: New Essays for Teachers of Writing.
Sudraka, Kind. Mrcchakatika, the Little Clay Cart. Oliver, Revilo, tr. from Sanskrit.
Sudworth, George B. Forest Trees of the Pacific Slope.
Sue, David, et al. Understanding Abnormal Behavior.
Suechting, A. G., ed. Thine Forever.
Suedfeld, Peter & Russell, James A., eds. The Behavioral Basis of Design: Selected Papers.
Suemitsu, Sanzen, tr. Between Life & Death: The Letters of Krystyna Wituskiej.
Suendermann, J. & Holz, K. P., eds. Mathematical Modelling of Estuarine Physics: Proceedings.
Suendermann, J., jt. ed. see Brosche, P.
Suenens, Leon J. A New Pentecost?
Sueno, Akira. Entrepreneur & Gentleman: The Case History of a Japanese Business. Donner, Neal, tr.
Suess, M. J. Examination of Water for Pollution Control: Handbook for Management & Analysts.
Suess, M. J. see Klug, W., et al.
Suess, M. J., ed. Examination of Water for Pollution Control, Vol. 1: Sampling, Data Analysis & Laboratory Equipment: A Reference Handbook.
--Examination of Water for Pollution Control, Vol. 2: Physical Chemical & Radiological Examination: A Reference Handbook.
--Examination of Water for Pollution Control, Vol. 3: Biological, Bacteriological & Virological Examination: A Reference Handbook.
Sueyeshi, Akiko. Ladybird on a Bicycle.
Suffern, Richard K. Logical Answers to Difficult Questions.
Sugandhi, Krishna K. & Sughandi, Rajendra K. Thyristors: Theory & Applications.
Sugar, A. T., tr. see Von Frisch, Karl.
Sugar, Bert, ed. The Ring Record Book & Boxing Encyclopedia.
Sugden, T. M. & West, T. F., eds. Chlorofluorocarbons in the Environment: The Aerosol Controversy.
Sugen, D. E., jt. ed. see Price, R. J.
Sugerman, Shirley. Sin & Madness: Studies in Narcissism.
Sugg, Richard P. Appreciating Poetry.
Sughandi, Rajendra K., jt. auth. see Sugandhi, Krishna K.
Sugiyama, Koich, et al, eds. The Collector's Guide to Japanese Cameras.
Sugiyama, S. Embryology of the Human Thyroid Gland Including the Ultimobranchial & Other Related Organs.
--Histological Studies of the Human Thyroid Gland.
Suh. Elements of the Mechanical Behavior of Solids.
Suh, N. P., ed. Manufacturing Science & Technology of the Future.
Suhadolnik, Robert J. Nucleosides As Biological Probes.
Suhl, Yuri. On the Other Side of the Gate.
Suhr, Elmer G. The Ancient Mind & Its Heritage. Incl. Vol. 1. Exploring the Primitive, Egyptian & Mesopotamian Cultures; Vol. 2. Exploring the Hebrew, Hindu, Greek & Chinese Cultures. Exposition-Phoenix.
Suid, Murray, jt. auth. see Morrow, James.
Suinian, Liu, ed. China's Socialist Economy: An Outline History, 1949-1984.
Suit, Herman D. & Proppe, Karl H. Soft Tissue Sarcomas.
Sukdeo, Iris D. The Emergence of a Multiracial Society: The Sociology of Multiracism with Reference to Guyana.
Sukhanov, V. Petroleum Processing.
Sulc, Lawrence B. The KBG & the United Nations. Hale, Nathan, Institute Staff, ed.
Suld, Henry. Cry from The Abyss.
Sullerot, Evelyne. Woman, Society & Change. Archer, Margaret S., tr. from Fr.
Sullins, Z. R., ed. see Donne, John.
Sullivan, Barbara. Page a Day for Lent 1987.
Sullivan, Barry J. Industrialization in the Building Industry.
Sullivan, D. T., jt. auth. see Dickinson, W. J.
Sullivan, David R., et al. Computing Today: Microcomputer Concepts & Applications.
Sullivan, Eleanor, ed. Alfred Hitchcock's Tales to Be Read with Caution.
--Alfred Hitchcock's Tales to Fill You with Fear & Trembling.
--Alfred Hitchcock's Tales to Scare You Stiff.
--Alfred Hitchcock's Tales to Send Chills Down Your Spine.
Sullivan, Faith. Repent, Lanny Merkel.
--Watchdog.
Sullivan, Francis A. Charisms & Charismatic Renewal: A Biblical & Theological Study.
Sullivan, George. All about Baseball.
--Cross-Country Skiing: The Complete Beginner's Book.
--How Do They Build It?
--How Do They Find It?
--More How Do They Make It?
Sullivan, Harry R. Frederic Harrison.
Sullivan, Harry S. Fusion of Psychiatry & Social Science. Perry, Helen S., ed.
--Personal Psychopathology: Early Formulations.
Sullivan, Herbert. Sir Arthur Sullivan His Life Letters & Diaries.
Sullivan, J. Readings in the Physical, Social & Psychological Dimensions of Education.
Sullivan, Jo. Global Studies: Africa.
Sullivan, John. Carmelite Studies II: Carmel & Psychology.
--God & the Interior Life.
--How to Beat the Stock Market Rip-off.
Sullivan, John & Victor, Joseph, eds. Criminal Justice 1988-89.
Sullivan, John J. & Victor, Joseph L. Annual Editions: Criminal Justice, 1985-86.
Sullivan, John J., ed. Explorations in Urban Land Economics.
Sullivan, John J., tr. The Autobiography of Venerable Marie of the Incarnation.
Sullivan, John L. Biomedical Psychiatric Therapeutics.
Sullivan, John W. Aim for a Job in the Iron & Steel Industry.
Sullivan, Joseph P., jt. auth. see Skiba, Jonathan W.
Sullivan, Joseph P., jt. ed. see Schreiber, Irving.
Sullivan, Kate. Women of the Plains.
Sullivan, Kathleen E. Paragraph Practice: Writing the Paragraph & the Short Composition.
Sullivan, Lawrence P. & Grantham, Jared J. Physiology of the Kidney.
Sullivan, Louis H. Kindergarten Chats.
--Kindergarten Chats & Other Writings.
Sullivan, Lydia G. Lou Gehrig's Disease.
Sullivan, Margaret. The New Carbohydrate Gram Counter.
Sullivan, Mary Ann. Child of War.
Sullivan, Maureen, jt. auth. see Rosenberg, Jane E.
Sullivan, Michael. The Arts of China.
Sullivan, Michael, jt. auth. see Mizrahi, Abe.
Sullivan, Michael P. International Relations: Theories & Evidence.
Sullivan, Monique, jt. auth. see Hammett, Theodore M.
Sullivan, Nancy, intro. by. The Treasury of American Poetry: A Collection of the Finest by America's Poets.
Sullivan, Peggy A. Desirable Characteristics of Student Library Media Personnel & The Concept of the Future As It Is Presented in Children's Books Today.
Sullivan, Peter. Christ the Answer.
Sullivan, Robert J., jt. auth. see Wright, Marion I.
Sullivan, Ruth, ed. Fine Lines: The Best of Ms. Fiction.
Sullivan, Sheila. The Calling of Bara.
Sullivan, Thomas F. TSCA Inspection Manual Part I.
Sullivan, Thomas J., et al. Social Problems: Divergent Perspectives.
Sullivan, Tony. In the Palm House.
Sullivan, Walter. Black Holes.
Sullivan, William C. & Brown, Bill. The Bureau: My Thirty Years in Hoover's FBI.
Sullivan & Sullivan. Programmed Astronomy: The Night Sky.
Sulman, F. G. Hypothalamic Control of Lactation.
Sultan, C., et al. Manual of Hematology.
Sultan, William J. Practical Baking Manual.
Sultan, William J., jt. auth. see Fabbricante, Thomas.
Sulzberger, C. L. The Coldest War: Russia's Game in China.
--The Coldest War: The Russian Game in China.
--How I Committed Suicide: A Reverie.
--The Test: De Gaulle & Algeria.
--Unconquered Souls: The Resistentialists.
Sulzer, Elmer G. Electric Railroads of Kentucky & Tennessee.
Sulzer-Azaroff, Beth. Applying Behavior Analysis Procedures with Children & Youth. Mayer, G. Roy, ed.
Sulzer-Azaroff, Beth & Mayer, G. Roy. Behavior Modification: Procedures for School Personnel.
Sumich, James L. An Introduction to the Biology of Marine Life.
Summer, Bob, jt. auth. see Coe, Boyer.
Summer, Charles E. Strategic Behavior in Business & Government.
Summer, Claire & Levy, Walter A. The Affordable Computer: Microcomputer Applications in Business & Industry.
--Microcomputers for Business.
Summer School in Logic, Leeds, 1967. Proceedings. Loeb, M. H., ed.
Summer Workshop on Invariant Imbedding - University of Southern California - Jun-Aug, 1970. Proceedings.
Summerall, Charles P. Lessons in EKG Interpretation: A Basic Self-Instructional Guide.
Summerfield, Joanne, jt. auth. see Demare, G.
Summerfield, Marc. Unit Dose Primer.
Summerfield, Maurice. The Classical Guitar.
Summerhays, R. S. & Walker, Stella A. The Controversial Horse.
Summerlin, Lee R. Chemistry for the Life Sciences. Incl. P. S. Associates; Hendrickson, William & Healy, Juanita.. Random.
Summers, Anthony. Goddess: The Secret Lives of Marilyn Monroe.
Summers, Claude & Pebworth, Ted-Larry, eds. The Eagle & the Dove: Reassessing John Donne.
Summers, Dorothy, jt. auth. see Saunders, Cicely.
Summers, Essie. Autumn in April.
--A Lamp for Jonathan.
Summers, Harry G., Jr. Vietnam War Almanac.
Summers, James L. The Long Ride Home.
--Senior Dropout.
--You Can't Make It by Bus.
Summers, Montague. History of Witchcraft & Demonology.
--Vampire in Europe.
--Werewolf.
Summers, Robert S., jt. auth. see White, James J.
Summers, Tan A., jt. auth. see Sawusch, Mark R.
Summers, True. Poppy.
Summersell, Charles G., ed. see Hamilton, Peter J.
Summerson, John. The Life & Work of John Nash, Architect.
--Victorian Architecture in England: Four Studies in Evaluation.
Summerson, John N. John Nash: Architect to King George the Fourth.
--Sir John Sloane: Seventeen Fifty-Three to Eighteen Thirty-Seven.
Summerville, Margaret. Rogue's Masquerade.
Sumner, jt. auth. see Schulteis.
Sumner, Austin J. The Physiology of Peripheral Nerve Disease.
Sumner, Benedict H. A Short History of Russia.
Sumner, Edward D. Handbook of Geriatric Drug Therapy for Health Care Professionals.
Sumner, Lee E., Jr., jt. auth. see Gehman, Walt.
Sumner, Mary. Computers: Concepts & Uses.
Sumner, William G. Essays of William Graham Sumner. Keller, Albert G. & Davie, Maurice R., eds.
--Forgotten Man's Almanac: Rations of Common Sense from William Graham Sumner. Keller, A. G., ed.
--Sumner Today. Davie, Maurice, ed.
Sumner, William L. The Organ: Its Evolution, Principles, Construction & Use.
Sumner-Boyd, H. & Freely, J. Istanbul: Strolling Through Istanbul.
Sumprer, Gerry, jt. auth. see Walfish, Steven.
Sumption, Lois L. & Ashbrook, Marguerite L. Breads from Many Lands.
Sumrall, Lester. Alien Entities.
--Faith to Change the World.
--Victory & Dominion Over Fear.
Sun, K. H., et al, eds. Thermal-Hydraulics in Nuclear Power Technology.
Sunar, D. G. The Expert Witness Handbook-A Guide for Engineers.
Sunbeam Staff. The Cook & Serve Book. Kostick, Marilyn, ed.
Sund, Robert. Ish River.
Sundar, Shyam. The Cosmic Society: Essays on the Social Concepts of Prout.
Sundaram, P. S. R. K. Narayan.
Sundaram, P. V. & Eckstein, F., eds. Theory & Practice in Affinity Techniques.
Sundberg, A. C., Jr. Old Testament of the Early Church: A Study of Canon.
Sundburg, M. & Goldkuhl, G. Information Systems Developement: A Systematic Approach.
Sundeen, Sandra, et al. Nurse-Client Interaction: Implementing the Nursing Process.
Sundeen, Sandra J., jt. auth. see Stuart, Gail W.
Sundel, Martin & Sundel, Sandra S. Behavior Modification in the Human Services: A Systematic Introduction to Concepts & Applications.
Sundel, Sandra S., jt. auth. see Sundel, Martin.
Sunderland, Eric. Elements of Human & Social Geography (Some Anthropological Perspectives)
Sunderland, Luther. Darwin's Enigma.
Sunderland, Ronald H., jt. ed. see Shelp, Earl E.
Sundhaussen, Ulf, jt. auth. see Penders, C. L.
Sundquist, Eric J. Faulkner: The House Divided.
Sundquist, Ralph R., Jr. Whom God Chooses: The Child in the Church.
Sundsfjord, J. A., et al. Progesterone Physiology.
Suner, Pi. Classics of Biology.
Sung-Ho Lin. Factory Workers in Tangku. Myers, Ramon H., ed.
Sung-joo, Han, jt. ed. see Scalapino, Robert A.
Sunkara, Prasad, ed. Novel Approaches to Cancer Chemotherapy.
Sunset Editors. Arizona: Travel Guide.
--Barbecue Cook Book.
--Basic Carpentry Illustrated.
--Bathrooms.
--Cheese.
--Favorite Recipes.
--Fireplaces: How to Build.
--Garden Pools, Fountains & Waterfalls.
--Gardening in Containers.
--Hawaii: Travel Guide.
--Hot Tubs, Spas & Home Saunas.
--House Plants: How to Grow.
--Kitchens: Planning & Remodeling.
--New Zealand.
--Woodworking Projects I.
Sunset Magazine & Books Editors. Alaska: Travel Guide.
--Back Roads of California.
--Bedroom & Bath Storage.
--Bookshelves & Cabinets.
--California Coast.
--Children's Rooms & Play Yards.
--Decorating with Plants.
--Energy-Saving Projects.
--Entertaining for All Seasons.
--Europe: Discovery Trips.
--Family Rooms, Dens & Studios.

--Gardener's Answer Book.
--Home Lighting.
--Hot Tubs, Spas & Home Saunas.
--International Vegetarian Cook Book.
--Mexico: Travel Guide.
--New Western Garden Book.
--Orient Travel Guide.
--Patio Roofs: How to Build.
--Remodeling Your Home.
--Roses.
--Tile: Remodeling with.
--Wine Country: California.
--Wok Cook Book.
Sunshine, Jonathan H. & Dicker, Marvin. Family Out-of-Pocket Expenditures for Health Care: United States, 1980.
Sunshine, Tina. Dating Games.
Suntag, Beu, jt. auth. see Keogh, James E.
Suntharalingam, R. Indian Nationalism: An Historical Analysis.
Super, Terri, illus. Toys on Wheels.
Superka, Douglas P. & Hawke, Sharryl. Social Roles: A Focus for Social Studies in the Nineteen Eighty's.
Superka, Douglas P., jt. auth. see Greenwald, G. Dale.
Supervielle, Jules. L' Enfant de la Haute Mer.
--L' Enfant de la Haute Mer.
--Le Voleur d'Enfants.
Supka, Magdolna B. Genre Painting in the Hungarian National Gallery.
Suppes, Patrick & Morningstar, Mona. Computer-Assisted Instruction at Stanford, 1966-68.
Suppes, Patrick C., et al. Computer-Assisted Instruction: Stanford's 1965-66 Arithmetic Program.
Supraner, Robyn. Would You Rather Be a Tiger?
Supreme Court Committee on Civil Jury Instructions. Colorado Jury Instructions: Civil.
Suprunenko, Dmitri A. & Tyshkevich, R. I. Commutative Matrices.
Suratgar, D. Default & Rescheduling: Corporate & Sovereign Borrowers, 1984.
Surge, Frank. Western Lawmen.
Surgy, Paul De see De Surgy, Paul.
Surpateanu, J. P., et al. Structure & Reactivity of Cycloimmonium Ylides.
Surplus, Robert W. Story of Musical Organizations.
Surrency, Erwin C., et al. Guide to Legal Research with 1966 Supplement.
Surrey, Stanley S., et al. Federal Income Taxation, Cases & Materials: 1985 Legislative Supplement.
Surtees, R. S. Mr. Sponge's Sporting Tour. Blain, Virginia, ed.
Surtees, Virginia. The Ludovisi Goddess: The Life of Louisa Lady Ashburton.
Survey & Cultivation of Edible Mushrooms in India, National Symposium Staff. Indian Mushroom Science I: Proceedings of the Survey & Cultivation of Edible Mushrooms in India National Symposium, 1st, Srinagar, 1976. Atal, C. K., et al, eds.
Survey Magazine Staff & Labedz, Leopold, eds. Poland Under Jaruzelski: A Comprehensive Sourcebook on Poland During & after Martial Law.
Survey Research Group Staff. The Markets of Asia-Pacific. Incl. Singapore; Malaysia; Thailand; Indonesia; Hong Kong & Macau; Philippines; Taiwan; South Korea; Australia; Japan; China. Facts on File.
Surwit, Richard S. & Williams, Redford B., Jr., eds. Behavioral Treatment of Disease.
Susan, ed. see Doty, Walter & Sinnes, A. Cort.
Susans, Wendy. Duet.
Suski, Wojciech, jt. ed. see Guertin, Robert P.
Suskin, Harold, jt. auth. see Lawton, Esther C.
Suskis, Henry. Forgotten Writings of Mark Twain.
Susko, A. Richard, jt. auth. see Nowikoff, Harold S.
Susman, Warren, ed. Culture & Commitment (1929-1945)
Susnjara, Ken. A Manager's Guide to Industrial Robots.
Suss, Elaine. Money Marriage: A Novel.
Sussex, Ian M., jt. auth. see Ebert, James D.
Sussex, Ian M., jt. ed. see Subtelny, Stephen.
Sussex, Margie & Stapleton, John F. The Complete Real Estate Math Book.
Sussman, Alan. The Rights of Young People.
Sussman, Carl, ed. Planning the Fourth Migration: The Neglected Vision of the Regional Planning Association of America.
Sussman, Jeffrey. How To Sleep Without Drugs.
Sussman, Jeffrey, jt. auth. see Prudden, Suzy.
Sussman, Jodyt. United States Information Service Libraries.
Sussman, Leonard R., jt. auth. see Media Institute Staff.
Sussman, Marvin B., ed. Sourcebook in Marriage & the Family.
Sussman, Marvin B., jt. ed. see Lewis, Robert A.
Sussman, Marvin L., jt. ed. see Rockstein, Morris.
Sussman, Robert W. Primate Ecology: Problem Oriented Field Studies.
Susswein, Donald B. How to Understand & Survive the Coming Tax Reforms.
Sustendal, Pat, illus. The Care Bear Bath Book.
Sutch, Virginia, ed. A Son Is Given.
Sutcliffe, Anthony. The Autumn of Central Paris: The Defeat of Town Planning, 1850-1970.
Sutcliffe, B. T., jt. auth. see McWeeny, R.
Sutcliffe, H., jt. auth. see Pass, G.
Sutcliffe, H. L., tr. see Pickering, W. S.
Sutcliffe, J. F. & Pate, J. S., eds. The Physiology of the Garden Pea.
Sutcliffe, J. P. Conceptual Analysis & Method in Psychology: Essays in Honour of W. M. O'Neil.
Sutcliffe, Justin. Holes.
Sutcliffe, Katherine. Desire & Surrender.
Sutcliffe, L. H., jt. ed. see Emsley, J. W.
Sutcliffe, Serena. Andre Simon's Wines of the World.
--The Wine Handbook.
Suter, Antoinette B., jt. auth. see Geismer, Barbara P.
Suter, Ronald. Six Answers to the Problem of Taste.
Sutherland. Hannah Hereafter.
Sutherland, Allan T. Disabled We Stand.
Sutherland, Arthur E. Law at Harvard: A History of Ideas & Men, 1817-1967.
Sutherland, C. Bruce, jt. auth. see Jost, Lee F.
Sutherland, C. H. Art in Coinage.
Sutherland, Edwin H., ed. Professional Thief.
Sutherland, Efua. Playtime in Africa.
Sutherland, Gillian R., et al, eds. Education in Nineteenth-Century Britain.
Sutherland, Hamish W. & Stowers, John M., eds. Carbohydrate Metabolism in Pregnancy & the Newborn.
Sutherland, I. W., jt. auth. see Dawes, I. W.
Sutherland, James. Daniel Defoe: A Critical Study.
Sutherland, John. Best Sellers: Popular Fiction of the 1970s.
Sutherland, John M. & Eadie, Mervyn. The Epilepsies.
Sutherland, Martha. Lettering for Architects & Designers.
Sutherland, N. S. & MacKintosh, N. J. Mechanisms of Animal Discrimination & Learning.
Sutherland, N. S., jt. ed. see Gilbert, R. M.
Sutherland, Neil. Children in English-Canadian Society 1880-1920: Framing the 20th-Century Consensus.
Sutherland, R. L. & Jordan, V. C., eds. Non-Steroidal Antioestrogens: Molecular Pharmacology & Antitumor Activity.
Sutherland, Robert F. & Gilman. This Is VIC: 20 BASIC.
Sutherland, S. Philip, jt. auth. see Rohrer, Norman B.
Sutphen, Dick. Poet: Anthology Nineteen Seventy to Nineteen Eighty-Five. Abbey, Dawn, ed.
Sutphen, Richard. Rattlesnake Karma.
Sutro, Alfred, jt. auth. see Meredith, George.
Sutryn, Barbara M. The Sign Painter.
Suttles, Gerald D. Social Construction of Communities.
Sutton, Albert A. Design & Makeup of the Newspaper.
Sutton, Andrew, jt. ed. see Cottam, Philippa J.
Sutton, Andrew, jt. ed. see McPherson, Ian.
Sutton, Ann & Carr, Richard. Tartans: Their Art & History.
Sutton, Ann, et al. The Craft of the Weaver.
Sutton, Audrey L. Bedside Nursing Techniques in Medicine & Surgery.
Sutton, Christine. The Particle Connection: The Most Exciting Scientific Chase since DNA & the Double Helix.
Sutton, Clay, jt. auth. see Dunne, Pete.
Sutton, David. Radiology & Imaging for Medical Students.
Sutton, Denys. Kimura: Paintings & Works on Paper 1968-1984. Lyon, Judith & Lancaster, Jan, eds.
Sutton, Felix. The Big Book of Wild Animals.
Sutton, George W., ed. AIAA Journal.
Sutton, H. Eldon. An Introduction to Human Genetics.
--Mutagenic Effects of Environmental Contaminants.
Sutton, H. Eldon & Wagner, Robert P. Genetics: A Human Concern.
Sutton, Hilton. He's Coming!
Sutton, Imre, et al, eds. Irredeemable America: The Indians' Estate & Land Claims.
Sutton, Jane. Me & the Weirdos.
--What Should a Hippo Wear?
Sutton, John, jt. auth. see Pearce, Joan.
Sutton, John R. & Houston, Charles S., eds. Hypoxia: Man at Altitude.
Sutton, Ken. Travels with an Angle.
Sutton, Larry. The Case of the Trick Note.
--Ghost Plane Over Hartley Field.
--The Mystery of the Blue Champ.
Sutton, Marilyn, jt. ed. see Galdieri-Wilcox, Sandra.
Sutton, Michael & Mandelberg, Cynthia. Looking Glass.
Sutton, Michael, jt. auth. see Brough, Walter.
Sutton, R. J. Stamp Collector's Encyclopedia.
--Stamp Curiosities.
--Stamps Are Money.
Sutton, Remar. Don't Get Taken Every Time: The Insider's Guide to Buying Your Next Car.
Sutton, Robert M. What You Should Know to Make Money from Your Investments.
Sutton, Sharon E. Learning Through the Built Environment: An Ecological Approach to Child Development.
Suvorov, Viktor. The Liberators: My Life in the Soviet Army.
Suyin, Han. Birdless Summer.
--The Crippled Tree.
--The Enchantress.
--A Mortal Flower.
--My House Has Two Doors.
--Phoenix Harvest.
Suzuki. Studies in Zen.
Suzuki, D. T. Introduction to Zen Buddhism.
--Introduction to Zen Buddhism.
Suzuki, Daisetz T. Studies in the Lankavatara Sutra: An Elucidation & Analysis of One of the Most Important Texts of Mahayana Buddhism, in Which Almost All Its Principal Tenets Are Presented Including the Teaching of Zen.
--Zen Buddhism: Selected Writings of D. T. Suzuki.
Suzuki, H. Electronic Absorption Spectra & Geometry of Organic Molecules.
Suzuki, H., jt. ed. see McKoy, Vincent.
Suzuki, Juzo & Oka, Isaburo. The Decadents. Bester, John, tr.
Suzuki, Peter T. Vernacular Taxicabs: Jitneys & Gypsies in Urban America.
Suzuki, Shinichi. Nurtured by Love: The Classic Approach to Talent Education. Suzuki, Waltraud, tr.
Suzuki, Shuetu, et al. Recent Studies on Preimplantation Mammalian Embryos In Vitro.
Suzuki, Takao. Japanese & the Japanese: Words in Culture. Miura, Akira, tr.
Suzuki, Waltraud, tr. see Suzuki, Shinichi.
Suzuki, Yoko. Pretty Lace.
Svaren, Jacqueline. Written Letters: Twenty-Nine Alphabets for Calligraphers.
Svec, J. J. & Jeffers, P. E. Modern Masonry Panel Construction Systems.
Svehla, G. & Wilson, C., eds. Comprehensive Analytical Chemistry: Analysis of Complex Hydrocarbon Mixtures.
Svehla, Gyula. Automatic Potentiometric Titrations.
Sveics, V. V. Small Nation Survival.
Svejnar, Jan, jt. ed. see Jones, Derek C.
Svelto, Orazio. Principles of Lasers. Hanna, David C., tr. from Ital.
Sven B. Lundstedt, Ohio State University & E. William, JFK School of Government, Harvard University, eds. Managing Innovation: The Social Dimensions of Creativity, Invention & Technology.
Svennas, Elsie. Advanced Quilting.
Svensen, C. L., jt. auth. see French, Thomas E.
Svenssons, A. Swedish Arbetshafte.
Sverdlova, K. Yakov Sverdlov.
Sves, J. J., et al, eds. Electronic & Newer Ceramics.
Svinicki, Marilla D. Teaching Methods for the Bibliographic Instruction Librarian.
Svirezhev, Y. Stability of Biological Communities.
Sviridov, G. Discovery of the Century.
Swabb, Barbara S. & Thomason, Mary E. Mathematics Bulletin Boards.
Swabey, Marie C. The Judgment of History.
Swados, Harvey. Celebration.
--A Radical's America.
Swados, Harvey, ed. American Writer & the Great Depression.
Swails, L. F., Jr. The Genus Porella in Latin America.
Swaim, John, jt. auth. see Needham, Richard, & Associates Staff.
Swaiman, Kenneth F. & Ashwal, Stephen. Pediatric Neurology Case Studies.
Swain, Barbara. Cookery for One or Two.
Swain, Dwight V. Film Scriptwriting.
Swain, James J., jt. auth. see Biles, William E.
Swain, Joseph R. What Does God Do All Day?
Swain, Margaret. Ayshire & Other Whitework.
Swain, Peter, tr. see Bianco, Enzo.
Swain, Roger B. Earthly Pleasures: Tales from a Biologist's Garden.
--Field Days: Journal of an Itinerant Biologist.
Swain, T., ed. Chemistry in Evolution & Systematics: Proceedings of an International Symposium, Strasbourg, 1972.
Swain, T., ed. see Phytochemical Society Staff.
Swaine, D. J., ed. The Trace-Element Content of Soils.
Swainson, Charles. A Handbook of Weather Folk-Lore: Being a Collection of Proverbial Sayings in Various Languages Relating to the Weather.
Swajeski, Donna, jt. auth. see Jones, Jane.
Swajeski, Donna, jt. auth. see Jones, Jeanne.
Swallow, jt. auth. see Thompson.
Swallow, J. N., jt. auth. see Holloway, P. J.
Swalls, Fred, et al, eds. Legal Rights & Responsibilities of Indiana Teachers.
Swami, Bhakivedanta. Srimad Bhagavatam: Eleventh Canto.
Swami Akhikananda. Hindu View of Christ.
Swami Deva Paritosh, ed. see Rajneesh, Bhagwan Shree.
Swami Muktananda. Paramartha Katha Prasang: Spiritual Conversations with Swami Muktananda.
Swami Muktananda, ed. Where Are You Going? A Guide to the Spiritual Journey.
Swaminathan, S., ed. Fixed Point Theory & Its Applications.
Swami Sivananda Radha. Gods Who Walk the Rainbow.
Swamy, P. A. Statistical Inference in Random Coefficient Regression Models.
Swamy, Subramanian. Economic Growth in China & India, 1952-70.
Swan. Pascal Programs for Business.
Swan, D. K., ed. New Method Supplementary Readers: Bestseller Pack. Incl. Alice in Wonderland; Black Beauty; Dracula; Frankenstein; King Arthur & the Knights of the Round Table; The Secret Garden; Oliver Twist; Robin Hood; Seven Detective Stories; Three Adventures of Sherlock Holmes. Longman.
Swan, Earl M. Don Quixote Rides Again: Or the Truth of the Story as Told by Sancho Panza.
Swan, Helena. Girls' Christian Names: Their History, Meaning & Association.
Swan, Henry, jt. auth. see Broster, W. H.
Swan, James G. Haidah Indians of Queen Charlotte Islands.
--Indians of Cape Flattery.
Swan, L. Alex. The Politics of Riot Behavior.
Swan, Sara K. Home-Made Baby Toys.
Swanberg, Alfred V. Mission at Rangorwich.
Swanberg, Christine. Tonight on This Late Road.
Swanberg, K., jt. auth. see Zanstra, H.
Swanberg, W. A. First Blood: The Story of Fort Sumter.
--Luce & His Empire: A Biography.
Swanborough, Gordon, jt. auth. see Taylor, John W.
Swancara, Frank. Thomas Jefferson Versus Religious Oppression.
Swanger, David J. The Poem As Process.
Swank, Jerold & Gibbs, Emily, eds. The Magic of Ham Radio.
Swank, Patsy, jt. auth. see Beck, Toni.
Swann. Electrical Safety.
Swann, Brian. The Fox & the Buffalo. Green Tiger Press Staff, ed.
Swann, Dennis. Competition & Industrial Policy in the European Economic Community.
Swann, Donald, jt. auth. see Tolkien, J. R. R.
Swann, Lois. The Mists of Manittoo.
Swann, Philip D., et al. Extraction of Useful Chemical Derivatives from Coal.
Swansea, Charleen & Campbell, Barbara, eds. Love Stories by New Women.
Swanson, Andrew P. The Determinative Team.
Swanson, B. Marion & Willis, Diane J. Understanding Exceptional Children & Youth.
Swanson, Barbara M. Careers in Health Care.
Swanson, Barbara M., jt. auth. see Swanson, Robert E.
Swanson, Bessie R. Music in the Education of Children.
Swanson, Burton E., ed. Agricultural Extension: A Reference Manual.
Swanson, Carl P. & Webster, Peter L. The Cell.
Swanson, Cheryl & Hale, Charles D. A Question of Height Revisited: Assaults on Police.
Swanson, Don R., ed. Intellectual Foundations of Library Education.
Swanson, Dorothy T. Guide to the Manuscript Collection of the Tamiment Library.
Swanson, Edward, ed. see Olson, Nancy B.
Swanson, Elizabeth E. & Eller, Clyde H. American Menus-Winter.
Swanson, Glen. Oil & Water.
Swanson, Gloria & Ott, Viginia. Dr. Anne.
Swanson, Jack & Karsh, Jeff. Rail Ventures.
Swanson, Marilyn A., jt. auth. see Cinnamon, Pamela A.
Swanson, Peter W., jt. auth. see Fetters, Thomas T.
Swanson, Richard W. & Marquardt, Charles E. On Communications: A Fundamental Approach to Reading, Writing, Speaking & Listening.
Swanson, Robert E. & Swanson, Barbara M. Tax Shelters: A Guide for Investors & Their Advisors.
Swanson, Stephen O. The Double Cross: Messages on the Seven Deadly Sins & the Seven "Deadly" Virtues.
--Stewardship Preaching.
Swanson, Steve. For Every Body: Exercise, Nutrition & Health for Young Christians.
Swanson, Susan C. & Fuller, Elizabeth G. Westchester County, a Pictorial History.
Swanton, Donald E. Maximizing Tax Benefits in Business Construction.

Authors

Swanwick, Keith & Taylor, Dorothy. Discovering Music: Developing Music Curriculum in Secondary Schools.
Sward, Keith. Legend of Henry Ford.
Swarthmore College Staff. Catalog of the Peace Collection.
Swartout, Robert R., Jr. An American Adviser in Late Yi Korea: The Letters of Owen Nickerson Denny.
Swarts, William, 3rd. Treehouse of the Mind.
Swartz, H., jt. auth. see Franks, R.
Swartz, Thomas R. & Bonello, Frank J. Taking Sides: Clashing Views on Controversial Economic Issues.
Swartzlander, Earl E. Computer Design Development: Principal Papers.
Swarup, Ram. Understanding Islam Through Hadis: Religious Faith or Fanaticism?
Swaszek, Peter F., ed. Quantization.
Swaton, J. Norman. Personal Finance: Getting Along & Getting Ahead.
Swaybill, Roger E. Final Witness.
Swazey, Judith P. Reflexes & Motor Integration: Sherrington's Concept of Integrative Action.
Swearer, Donald K. Buddhism in Transition.
Swearer, Harvey F. & Carr, Joseph J. Commercial FCC License Handbook.
Swearingen, Phyllis van see Van Swearingen, Phyllis.
Sweazey, George E. The Church As Evangelist.
Swedberg, Harriett, jt. auth. see Swedberg, Robert W.
Swedberg, Richard. Sociology as Disenchantment: The Evolution of the Work of George Gurvitch.
Swedberg, Robert W. & Swedberg, Harriett. American Oak Furniture Styles & Prices.
Swedenborg, Emanuel. Charity.
--Emanuel Swedenborg's Journal of Dreams.
--The Mechanical Inventions of Emanuel Swedenborg. Acton, Alfred, ed. & tr. from Lat. & Swedish.
--Psychologica: Being Notes & Observations on Christian Wolf's Psychologica Empirica. Acton, Alfred, tr. & pref. by.
Swedenborg, Emmanuel. The Infinite & Final Cause of Creation. Wilkinson, J. J., tr. from Lat.
Sweder, Gerri L., jt. auth. see Grollman, Earl A.
Swedish Institute of International Affairs. European Neutrals & the Soviet Union. Huldt, Bo & Lejins, Atis, eds.
Swedish Telecommunications Administration Staff & LM Ericson Telephone Company Staff. Human Factors in Telecommunications International Symposium, 6th.
Swedish Trade Council Staff, ed. Swedish Export Directory, 1982.
Swedlin, Rosalie. A World of Salads.
Swedlow, J. L., ed. Solid Earth Geophysics & Geotechnology.
Sweedler, M. E., jt. auth. see Chase, U.
Sweeney, Charles. Naturalist in the Sudan.
Sweeney, Dennis M. & Lyko, James J. Practice Manual for Social Security Claims: Plus 1983 Supplement.
--Practice Manual for Social Security Claims: 1983 Supplement.
Sweeney, Gerard M. Melville's Use of Classical Mythology.
Sweeney, James B. True Spy Stories.
Sweeney, James S., Jr. Seasonal Star Charts.
Sweeney, John J. Love Be Our Light.
Sweeney, Neil R. For Those Who Would Be President: Sixteen Management Skills for the Top Job.
Sweeney, Stephen B., et al. Education for Administrative Careers in Government Service.
Sweeney, Veronica G. The Emancipist: A Saga of the Early Days of Australia.
Sweeny, Allen. Accounting Fundamentals for Non-Financial Executives.
Sweeny, Allen & Wisener, John N., Jr. Budgeting Fundamentals for Nonfinancial Executives.
Sweeny, H. W. & Rachlin, Robert. Handbook of Budgeting.
Sweeny, Z. T. Spirit & the Word.
Sweet, Doris, jt. ed. see Lewis, Richard L.
Sweet, Dovie D. Red Light, Green Light: The Life of Garrett Morgan & His Invention of the Stoplight.
Sweet, Frank. Building Database Application.
Sweet, Frederick A. Ivan Albright: A Retrospective Exhibition.
Sweet, George E. Shake-Speare: The Mystery.
Sweet, J. S., ed. see Ornati, Oscar.
Sweet, James, jt. ed. see Rindfuss, R. R.
Sweet, Jeffrey. Something Wonderful Right Away.
Sweet, Leonard I. Black Images of America, 1784-1870.
Sweet, Muriel. Common Edible & Useful Plants of the East & Midwest.
Sweet, O. Robin & Siegel, Mary-Ellen. The Nanny Connection: How to Find & Keep a Perfect Nanny.
Sweet, Ralph, jt. auth. see Keller, Kate V.
Sweet, Waldo E. & Knudsvig, Glenn M. A Course on Words.
Sweeting, M. M., ed. Karst Geomorphology.
Sweetman, John. Operation Chastise: The True Story of the Famous Dams Raid.
Sweetser, Wesley D. Ralph Hodgson: A Bibliography.
Sweezy, Paul M. Four Lectures on Marxism.
--Monopoly & Competition in the English Coal Trade: 1550-1850.
Swendsen, Louise A. & Barnett, Vivian E. Kandinsky Watercolors: A Selection from the Solomon R. Guggenheim Museum & the Hilla von Rebay Foundation.
Swengle, Nicole. Britain.
Swensen, jt. auth. see Randle.
Swenson, Christine. Charles Hullmandel & James Duffield Harding: The English Art of Drawing on Stone 1800-1850.
Swenson, David, tr. see Kierkegaard, Soren.
Swenson, Philip R., jt. auth. see Randle, Paul A.
Swenson, Pina, jt. auth. see Bartoli, Cecilia.
Swerdlow, Amy, et al. Household & Kin.
Swete, H. B., jt. auth. see Maclaren, Alexander.
Swets, Johns A., jt. ed. see Druckman, Daniel.
Swett, Ira L. Cars of Pacific Electric: Locomotives, Combination Cars, Etc. Walker, Jim, ed.
Swick, John C. The Luscombe Story.
Swidan, Eleanor A., jt. auth. see Bell, Marion V.
Swidler, Arlene, ed. Sister Celebrations: Nine Worship Experiences.
Swidler, Leonard, tr. see Lapide, Pinchas & Moltmann, Jurgen.
Swidler, Leonard, tr. see Mussner, Franz.
Swiecicka-Ziemianek, Maria, tr. see Lem, Stanislaw.
Swierczewski, G., jt. auth. see Felkin, H.
Swierenga, Robert P., ed. Quantification in American History: Theory & Research.
Swieringa, Robert, jt. auth. see Dykman, Thomas.
Swift, Graham. Learning to Swim & Other Stories.
--Waterland.
Swift, Hildegarde H. Railroad to Freedom.
Swift, Jonathan. Gulliver's Travels.
--Gulliver's Travels. Greenberg, Robert A., ed.
--Gulliver's Travels.
--Gulliver's Travels.
--Gulliver's Travels & Other Writings. Quintana, Ricardo, ed. & intro. by.
--A Tale of a Tub & Other Satires. Williams, Kathleen, ed.
Swift, L. H. Botanical Bibliographies: Guide to Bibliographic Materials Applicable to Botany.
Swift, Rebecca. Project Noroz.
Swift, Roger & Gilley, Sheridan, eds. The Irish in the Victorian City.
Swift-Hook, D. T., jt. ed. see Barak, M.
Swigart, Rob. A.K.A. A Cosmic Fable.
--Little America.
--Still Lives.
--The Time Trip.
Swiggett, Hal. Hal Swiggett on North American Deer.
Swihart, Judson J., jt. auth. see Rekers, George A.
Swihart, Thomas L. Journey Through the Universe: An Introduction to Astronomy.
Swillens, Stephane & Dumont, Jacques E., eds. Cell Regulation by Intracellular Signal Molecules.
Swinburne. The Language of Publishing in English.
Swinburne, Algernon C., jt. auth. see Gordon, Mary.
Swinburne, Herbert. Design Cost Analysis for Architects & Engineers.
Swindell, William, ed. Polarized Light.
Swindells, Philip. Waterlilies.
Swindells, Robert. Norah & the Whale.
Swindells, Robert E. The Moonpath & Other Tales of the Bizarre.
Swindle. Fundamentals of Modern Business.
Swindle, Elizabeth M., jt. auth. see Swindle, Robert E.
Swindle, Robert E. Business Math Basics.
--Business Math Basics.
Swindle, Robert E. & Swindle, Elizabeth M. The Business Communicator.
Swindler, Daris. Dentition of Living Primates.
Swindler, Lorraine B. Poems from the Heart.
Swindoll, Charles A. Dropping Your Guard.
Swindoll, Charles R. Standing Out: Being Real in an Unreal World.
--Strengthening Your Grip.
Swindoll, Chuck. Compassion: Life Maps.
--Improving Your Serve.
--Victory: Life Maps.
Swindoll, Luci. My Favorite Verse.
--You Bring the Confetti.
Swineford, A., ed. National Conference on Clays & Minerals, 8th: Proceedings.
--National Conference on Clays & Minerals, 9th: Proceedings.
Swinfen, Ann. In Defence of Fantasy: A Study of the Genre in English & American Literature since 1945.
Swinfen, Averil. The Irish Donkey.
Swinford, Betty. Dark Is the Forest.
Swinton, W. E. Dinosaurs.
Swire, Margaret R., jt. auth. see Kavaler, Florence.
Swirsky, Jessica, jt. auth. see Vandergoot, David.
Swisher, Doug & Richards, Carl. Fly Fishing Strategy.
--Selective Trout.
Swisher, Doug, et al. Stoneflies.
Swisher, James H., jt. ed. see Carlson, Claire L.
Swisher, Scott N., jt. ed. see Petz, Lawrence D.
Swisher, Ted, jt. ed. see Stevens, Robert W.
Swiss Association of Bank Employees Staff, ed. Banking Dictionary.
Swiss Office for the Development of Trade, Geneva Staff. Swiss Export Products & Services Directory, 1983-85.
Swit, Loretta & Appel, Ellen. Needlepoint Scrapbook.
Switzer, Ellen. How Democracy Failed.
--There Ought to Be a Law: How Laws Are Made & Work.
Switzer, Ellen A. Dancers! Horizons in American Dance.
--Our Urban Planet.
Switzer, Kenneth A. & Mulloy, Paul. Global Issues: Activities & Resources for the High School Teacher.
Switzer, Kenneth A. & Redden, Charlotte A. Teaching about Diversity: Latin America.
Switzer, Lorne. The Financing of Technological Change. Bateman, Fred, ed.
Switzer, R. M. Algebraic Topology-Homotopy & Homology.
Switzer, Richard & Gochberg, Herbert S., eds. New Century Vest Pocket French Dictionary.
Switzer, Robert, ed. World-Wide French Dictionary.
Swoboda, A. K., ed. Europe & the Evolution of the International Monetary System.
Swoboda, Alexander K., jt. auth. see Johnson, Harry G.
Sword, Randall S. & Keller, Janet. Trauma Center: Three Days in the Life of an Emergency Room Doctor.
Sworder, David D. Optimal Adaptive Control Systems.
Swycaffer, Jefferson P. The Praesidium of Archive.
Swyhart, Barbara Ann D. Bioethical Decision Making: Releasing Religion from the Spiritual.
Sybex Staff & Zaks, Rodnay. The SYBEX Personal Computer Dictionary.
Sycamore, Roger. Out of Order.
Sychev, Y. The Individual & the Microenvironment.
Sydenham, M. J. The First French Republic, Seventeen Ninety-Two to Eighteen Four.
Sydenham, Peter H. Basic Electronics for Instrumentation. Davidovici, Sorin, ed.
Sydney, Clare. Flower Painting.
Sydney Labour History Group Staff. What Rough Beast?
Sydnor, William. Real Prayer Book, Fifteen Forty-Nine to the Present.
Sydow, A., et al, eds. Systems Analysis & Simulation, 1985: Proceedings of the 2nd International Symposium on Systems Analysis & Simulation, Berlin, GDR, 26-31 August, 1985.
Sydsaeter, Knut. Topics in Mathematical Analysis for Economists.
Syer, John. Team Spirit.
Syka, Josef & Aitkin, Lindsay, eds. Neuronal Mechanisms of Hearing.
Sykes, A. G. Kinetics of Inorganic Reactions.
Sykes, Arlene, ed. Three Political Plays.
Sykes, Egerton. Everyman's Dictionary of Non-Classical Mythology.
Sykes, G. & Skinner, F. A., eds. Actinomycetales: Characteristics & Practical Importance.
Sykes, John P. Slaves Uprooted & the Mau Mau Massacre.
Sykes, Pamela. Mirror of Danger.
Sykes, Reverend William G. Visions of Faith: An Anthology of Reflections.
Sykes, Roberta B. Incentive, Achievement & Community: An Analysis of Black Viewpoints on Issues Relating to Black Australian Education.
Sykes, S. C. U. S. S. A.
Sykes, Stephen. Friedrich Schleiermacher.
--The Identity of Christianity.
--An Introduction to Christian Theology Today.
Sykoutres, Ioannes. Die Briefe des Sokrates und der Sokratiker.
Sykova, Eva, et al, eds. Ion-Selective Microelectrodes & Their Use in Excitable Tissues.
Sylvester, David. Interviews with Francis Bacon.
--Napoleon & the French Empire. Reeves, Marjorie, ed.
Sylvester, David & McEwen, John. Howard Hodgkin: Forty Paintings.
Sylvester, Edward J. & Klotz, Lynn C. The Gene Age: Genetic Engineering & the Industrial Revolution.
Sylvia, J. Jerry. Pardon My Convicts: Memoirs of a Prison Warden.
Symes, Kenneth M. Two Voices: Writing about Literature.
Symmers, W. St. C. Systemic Pathology.
--Systemic Pathology.
Symmes, Daniel, jt. auth. see Morgan, Hal.
Symmons, Sarah. Flaxman & Europe: The Outline Illustrations & Their Influence.
Symonds, Arthur, ed. The Savoy.
Symonds, Curtis W. Basic Financial Management.
--Basic Financial Management.
Symonds, Henry E. The Church Universal & the See of Rome: A Study of the Relations Between the Episcopate & the Papacy up to the Schism Between East & West.
Symonds, John & Grant, Kenneth, eds. The Confessions of Aleister Crowley: An Autobiography.
Symonds, John A. Sir Philip Sidney.
Symonds, P. S., jt. ed. see Lee, E. H.
Symonds, Percival M. & Jensen, Arthur R. From Adolescent to Adult.
Symonds, R. W. English Furniture from Charles II to George II.
Symons, Julian. Critical Observations.
--The Detling Secret.
Symons, Julian, ed. see Collins, Wilkie.
Symons, Norman, jt. auth. see Scott, James H.
Symposium at University of Florence, Italy Staff. The Endocrine Function of the Human Testis: Proceedings. James, V. H., et al, eds.
Symposium, Bloomington Staff. Horizons of Bioenergetics: Proceedings of the Symposium, Bloomington, Oct. 1970. San Pletro, Anthony & Gest, Howard, eds.
Symposium, Dundee Staff. Spectral Theory & Differential Equations: Proceedings of the Symposium, Dundee, 1974. Everitt, W. N., ed.
Symposium Held in Honor of David B. Dill Staff. Physiological Adaptations: Proceedings of the Symposium Held in Honor of David B. Dill, April 1971. Yousef, Mohamed K., et al, eds.
Symposium, Kingston, Jamaica Staff. Hypoglycin: Proceedings. Kean, Eccleston A., ed.
Symposium, Muenchen Staff. Zucker und Zuckeraustauschstoffe: Proceedings of the Symposium, Muenchen, 1974. Zoellner, N. & Heuckenkamp, P., eds.
Symposium, Nice Staff. Hyperfunctions & Theoretical Physics: Proceedings of the Symposium, Nice, 1973. Pham, F. L., ed.
Symposium of the Entymological Society of America - Atlantic City - 1960. Biological Transmission of Disease Agents: Proceedings. Maramorosch, K., ed.
Symposium of the Institute of Microbiology, Rutgers University, 1967. Nucleic Acids in Immunology: Proceedings. Plescia, O. J. & Braun, W., eds.
Symposium on Antibiotics Resistance, 2nd, Smolenice Castle, Czechoslovakia, Jun 5-8, 1974. Drug-Inactivating Enzymes & Other Problems of Resistance to Antibacterial Drugs: Proceedings. Mitsuhashi, S., et al, eds.
Symposium on Biophysics & Physiology of Biological Transport, Frascati, 1965. Proceedings. Bolis, L., et al, eds.
Symposium on Computer Applications in the Mineral Industry, 10th, South Africa, 1972. Proceedings.
Symposium on Energy Metabolism, Troon Scotland, 3d, 1964. Energy Metabolism: Proceedings. Blaxter, K. L., ed.
Symposium on Filament Winding, Pasedena, Ca. Mar. 28-30, 1961. Proceedings.
Symposium on Germinal Centers in Immune Responses - University Of Bern-Switzerland - 1966. Proceedings. Cottier, H., et al, eds.
Symposium on High-Energy Electrons, Montreux, 1964. Proceedings. Zuppinger, A. & Poretti, G., eds.
Symposium on Mechanical Behavior of Materials Under Dynamic Loads, San Antonio, 1967. Proceedings. Lindholm, U. S., ed.
Symposium on Modern Anesthetic Agents, 1st, Hamburg, Nov. 9-10, 1973. Ethrane: Proceedings.
Symposium on Neuroglia, 12th Meeting, Berlin, 1966. Proceedings. Erbsloeh, F., et al, eds.
Symposium on Pathology of Axons & Axonal Flow, Vienna, 1970. Proceedings. Friede, R. L. & Seitelberger, F., eds.
Symposium on Presenile Spongy Encephalopathies, Vienna, 1965. Proceedings. Guazzi, G. L. & Seitelberger, F., eds.
Symposium On Relaxation Methods In Relation To Molecular Structure - Aberystwyth - 1965. Molecular Relaxation Processes: Proceedings. Cross, R. C., ed.
Symposium on the Biochemistry of Sensory Functions, Colloquium Mosbach, Apr. 1974. Proceedings. Jaenicke, L., ed.
Symposium on the Impact of Science on Society, Brussels, 1971. Scientists in Search of Their Conscience: Proceedings. Michaelis, A. & Harvey, H., eds.
Symposium on the Theory of Scheduling & Its Applications. Proceedings. Elmaghraby, S. E., ed.
Symposium Transsonicum Staff. Proceedings of the Symposium Trnassonicum, Aachen, 1962. Oswatitisch, K., ed.

Authors

Symposium, University of California, Santa Barbara Staff. Subject & Topic: Proceedings of the Symposium, University of California, Santa Barbara, Mar. 1975. Li, Charles N., ed.
Symposium, University of Florida, Gainsville Staff. Chromosomal Proteins & Their Role in the Regulation of Gene Expression: Proceedings of the Symposium, University of Florida, Gainsville, March 1975. Stein, Gary S. & Kleinsmith, Lewis J., eds.
Symposium, Vienna, Sept. 4-6, 1974. Drug Receptor Interactions in Antimicrobial Chemotherapy: Proceedings. Drews, J. & Hahn, F. E., eds.
Symposuim on Bicentennial of Materials Progress, los Angeles, California, April 26-28, 1976. Proceedings.
Synder, Karl E. The Faire Maide of the Exchange.
Syndergaard, Iris, ed. see Sill, Sterling W.
Syndor, William. Sunday's Scriptures: An Interpretation.
Synge, Hugh, ed. Biological Aspects of Rare Plant Conservation.
Synge, John Millington. Deidre of the Sorrows: And the Tinker's Wedding & the Shadow of the Glen.
--Playboy of the Western World. Popkin, Henry, ed.
--Tinker's Wedding.
Sypher, Lucy. Cousins & Circuses.
Sypher, Lucy J. The Edge of Nowhere.
--The Spell of the Northern Lights.
--The Turnabout Year.
Sypher, Wylie, ed. Enlightened England.
Syrdal, Rolf A. Go Make Disciples.
Syrokomsky, V. International Terrorism & the CIA.
Syrop, Konrad. Spring in October: The Story of the Polish Revolution 1956.
Syrop, Konrad, tr. see Andrzejewski, Jerzy.
Syski. Random Processes: A First Look.
Systech Corporation Staff. Emergency Medical Services Communications Design Manual.
Systems & Procedures Exchange Center Staff. Corporate Use of Research Libraries.
--Fund Raising.
--Interlibrary Loan.
Systems Symposium Staff. Systems Theory & Biology: Proceedings of the Systems Symposium 3rd, Case Western Reserve University, Institute of Technology. Mesavoric, M. D., ed.
Systems Symposium - 4th - Case Western Reserve University, Institute of Technology. Theoretical Approaches to Non-Numerical Problem Solving: Proceedings. Banerji, R. B. & Mesarovic, M. D., eds.
Syverud, Genevieve W. This Is My Song of Songs.
Syvrud, Donald E. Foundations of Brazilian Economic Growth.
Szabo & Floris-Soltesz, Elizabeth. The Book of Hours of Pannonhalma.
Szabo, Ervin. Socialism & Social Science: Selected Writings of Ervin Szabo. Litvan, Gyorgy & Bak, Janos, eds.
Szabo, Marc. Drawing File for Architects, Illustrators, & Designers.
Szabo, T. & Czeh, C., eds. Sensory Physiology of Aquatic Lower Vertebrates: Proceedings of a Satellite Symposium of the 28th International Congress of Physiological Sciences, Budapest, Hungary, 1980.
Szabo, Zoltan. Zoltan Szabo Paints Landscapes: Advanced Techniques in Watercolor.
Szabolcsi, Bence. A History of Melody.
Szabo-Pelsoczi, Miklos. Bicentennial Papers: Toward Economic Reconstruction.
Szajkowski, Bogdan, ed. see Schwab, Peter.
Szalai, A. & Petrelia, R., eds. Cross-National Comparative Survey Research: Theory & Practice - Papers & Proceedings of a Round Table Conference, Budapest, 1972.
Szalay, Lorand B. & Deese, James. Subjective Meaning & Culture: An Assessment Through Word Associations.
Szanto, Gregory. Astrotherapy: Astrology & the Realization of the Self.
--The Marriage of Heaven & Earth: The Philosophy of Astrology.
Szanton, Peter, ed. Federal Reorganization: What Have We Learned?
Szarek, Walter A., jt. ed. see Horton, Derek.
Szarkowski, John. American Landscapes.
--E. J. Bellocq: Storyville Portraits.
--Mirrors & Windows: American Photography Since 1960.
--William Eggleston's Guide, with an Essay by John Szarkowski.
Szarkowski, John, ed. From the Picture Press.
Szasz, Margaret C. Education & the American Indian: The Road to Self-Determination since 1928.
Szasz, Suzanne. The Body Language of Children.
Szasz, Suzanne & Taleporos, Elizabeth. Sisters, Brothers, & Others.
Szasz, Thomas. Karl Kraus & the Soul-Doctors: A Pioneer Critic & His Criticism of Psychiatry & Psychoanalysis.
Szathmary, Louis. The Bakery Restaurant Cookbook.
Szczawinski, Adam F., jt. auth. see Turner, Nancy J.
Szczesniak, Lenny, tr. see Zanzucchi, Anne M.
Szebehely, V., ed. see CISM (International Center for Mechanical Sciences), Department for General Mechanics Staff.
Szebehely, Victor G., ed. Celestial Mechanics & Astrodynamics.
Szecske, Tibor, jt. auth. see Cadiou, Yves L.
Szego, G., jt. auth. see Polya, G.
Szego, G. C. & Taylor, J. E., eds. Space Power Systems Engineering. PAAS16.
Szegoe, G. P., jt. auth. see Bhatia, N. P.
Szegoe, G. P., ed. see International Summer School on Mathematical Systems Theory & Economics, Varenna, Italy, 1967.
Szekely, Beatrice B., ed. see Zankov, L. V., et al.
Szekely, David. Unicode, ein Verfahren Zur Optimierung der Begrifflichen Gehirnleistung.
Szekely, Gy., et al, eds. Neural Communication & Control: Satellite Symposium of the 28th International Congress of Physiological Sciences, Debrechen, Hungary, 1980.
Szekely, J. & Apelian, D., eds. Plasma Processing & Synthesis of Materials: Proceedings of Symposium, 1983, Boston, MA, Materials Research Society.
Szekely, M., jt. auth. see Szelenyi, Z.
Szekely, Maria. From DNA to Protein: The Transfer of Genetic Information.
--From DNA to Protein: The Transfer of Genetic Information.
Szekeres, Cyndy. Long Ago.
Szelenyi, Ivan, jt. auth. see Konrad, George.
Szelenyi, Z & Szekely, M. Contributions to Thermal Physiology: Proceedings of a Satellite Symposium of the 28th International Congress of Physiological Sciences, Budapest, 1980.
Szenasy, Susan S. Light: The Complete Handbook of Lighting Design.
Szendrey, Thomas, tr. see Malyusz, Edith C.
Szentagothai, J., et al. Regulatory Functions of the CNS - Motion & Organization Principles: Proceedings of the 28th International Congress of Physiological Sciences, Budapest, 1980.
--Regulatory Functions of the CNS Subsystems: Proceedings of the 28th International Congress of Physiological Sciences, Budapest, 1980.
Szent-Gyorgyi, Albert. Bioelectronics.
--The Living State with Remarks on Cancer.
Szentivanyi, M. & Juhasz-Nagy, A., eds. Factors Influencing Adrenergic Mechanisms in the Heart: Proceedings of a Satellite Symposium of the 28th International Congress of Physiological Sciences, Visegrad, Hungary, 1980.
Szeplaki, Joseph. The Hungarians in America 1583-1974: A Chronology & Fact Book.
Szeri. Tribology: Friction, Lubrication & Wear.
Szidarovszky, F. & Yakowitz, S., eds. Principles & Procedures of Numerical Analysis.
Szilagyi, Andrew D., Jr. Management & Performance.
Szilard, J, ed. Ultrasonic Testing: Non-Conventional Testing Techniques.
Szilard, Leo. The Voice of the Dolphins.
Szklarski, L. Underground Electric Haulage.
Szmukler, G. I., et al, eds. Anorexia Nervosa & Bulimic Disorders: Current Perspectives: Proceedings of the Conference on Anorexia Nervosa & Related Disorders Held at University College, Swansea, Wales, on 3-7 September 1984.
Szoka, Kathryn, jt. auth. see Filley, Richard D.
Szokolay, Steve, jt. auth. see Greenland, Jack.
Szokolay, Steven V. Environmental Science Handbook for Architects & Builders.
Szollosi-Nagy, A., jt. ed. see Wood, E. F.
Sztankay, Zoltan. Christianity, Democracy, & Technology.
Sztompka, Piotr. System & Function: Toward a Theory of Society.
Sztorc, Mary V. Student's Values in Drugs & Drug Abuse.
Szulc, Tad. Latin America.
Szweda, Ralph A. Information Processing Management.
Szwengrub, L. M., jt. ed. see Durand-Drouhin, J. L.
Szwengrub, Lili-Marie, jt. ed. see Durand-Drouhin, Jean-Louis.
Szwilski, A. B. & Brawner, C. O., eds. Stability in Underground Mining II.

T

T., Ginny. A Hair of the Dog.
Taaffe, William, jt. auth. see Wolf, Warner.
Taam, C. T., ed. see Dudley, R. M.
Taam, C. T., ed. see Glimm, J., et al.
Tab-Aero Staff. AIM-FAR, 1987: Complete Combined Edition.
--Airman's Information Manual, 1987.
--Federal Aviation Regulations for 1987.
TAB Editorial Staff. The Master Semiconductor Replacement Handbook: Listed by Industry Standard Number.
Taba, Hilda. Curriculum Development: Theory & Practice.
Taback, Simms, illus. From the Smithsonian: More Science Activities.
Tabarly, Eric. Ocean Racing.
Tabata, Y. Three Thirty-One Last Processes in Radiation Chemistry: International Symposium on Fast Processes in Radiation Chemistry.
Tabataba'i, Allamah S. The Qur'an in Islam: Its Impact & Influence on the Life of Muslims.
Tabataba'i, Allamah. A Shi'ite Anthology. Chittick, William C., ed.
Taber, Gladys. Amber, a Very Personal Cat.
--The Book of Stillmeadow.
Tabler, D. N., et al. IBM OS Assembler Language-Arithmetic Operations.
Tabler, Donna & Ashley, Ruth. IBM OS Assembler Language: Language Basics.
Tabler, Donna N., et al. IBM OS Assembler Language - Subroutines Macros & Tables.
Tabler, Judith. The New Puppy.
Tabori, Paul. Companions of the Unseen.
Tabori, Paul & Raphael, Phyllis. Beyond the Senses: A Report on Psychical Research in the Sixties.
Taborko, V., jt. auth. see Kondratyeva, M.
Taborsky, Edward. President Edvard Benes, Between East & West: 1938-1948.
Tabucanon, M. T. & Abdulbhan, P., eds. Industrial Systems Engineering & Management in Developing Countries: Proceedings of the International Conference, 3-6 November 1980, Asian Institute of Technology, Bangkok, Thailand. Incl. Fracture & Society, Vol. 4: Fracture & Society. Pergamon.
Tabucanon, M. T., jt. ed. see Adulbhan, P.
Tachau, Frank, ed. Political Elites & Political Development in the Middle East.
Tachikawa, H. QF-Three & QF-One Rings. Ringel, C. M., ed.
Tachikawa, Musashi, ed. see Ngor Tharttse mKhanpo bSodnams rgyamtsho.
Tacker, W. A., Jr., intro. by. Cardiac Defibrillation & Cardiopulmonary Resuscitation, Abstracts & Published Papers: Proceedings, 4th Conference.
Tackett, T. Priest & Parish in Eighteenth-Century France.
Tackler, Elizabeth. Arson.
Tackwood, Louis, jt. auth. see Citizens Research & Investigation Committee Staff.
Tada, Joni E. Choices...Changes.
--Joni Nineteen Eighty-Nine Planner.
--Secret Strength... for Those Who Search.
Tada, Tomio, jt. ed. see Sasazuki, Takehiko.
Tadayoshi, Onuma, tr. see Minoru, Yoshioka.
Tadej, Lorine. Strict Vegetarian Cookbook.
Tadgell, Christopher. Ange-Jacques Gabriel.
Tadokoro, Hiroyuki. Structure of Crystalline Polymers.
Taetzsch, Lyn, jt. auth. see Kirsner, Laura T.
Taeuber, Alma F., jt. auth. see Taeuber, Karl E.
Taeuber, Karl E. & Taeuber, Alma F. Negroes in Cities: Residential Segregation & Neighborhood Change.
Taevernier, Aug. Ensor's Complete Graphic Work.
Taff, Charles A. Management of Physical Distribution & Transportation.
Taffee, Stephen. Computer Studies: Computers in Education.
Taft, Barbara, ed. Absolute Liberty: A Selection from the Articles & Papers of Caroline Robbins.
Taft, Edna. Puritan in Voodoo-Land.
Taft, R. W., jt. ed. see Streitwieser, A.
Taft, Ronald, jt. auth. see Nixon, Mary.
Tager, A. Physical Chemistry of Polymers.
Tager, Mark J., jt. auth. see Ardell, Donald.
Taggart, Karen. No Sugar Cooking.
Taggart, Laura. Carol Visits Cloud land.
Taggart, Ralph, jt. auth. see Starr, Cecie.
Taggart, Ralph E. New Weather Satellite Handbook.
Taggart, Robert. Marine Propulsion: Principles & Evolution.
Tagliabue, John. Buddha Uproar.
--The Doorless Door.
Tagliacozzo, Giorgio, ed. Vico & Marx.
Tagore, Rabindranath. A Bunch of Tagore Poems. Varma, Monika, tr.
--Love Poems of Tagore. Choudhury, Rabindra N., tr. from Bengali.
Tagore, Rabindranath. Sheaves: Poems & Songs.
--A Tagore Testament. Dutt, Indu, tr.
Taha Jabir al Alwani. Al Muslimun Wa al Badil al Hadari: "Muslims & the Civilizational Alternative"
Taherzadeh, Habib, tr. see Baha'u'llah.
Tahlequah Indian Writer's Group Staff. Echoes of Our Being. Conley, Robert J., ed.
Tahori, A. S., ed. Pesticide Terminal Residues (Additional Publication) Proceedings of an International Symposium.
Tai, Dwan L. Chiang Ch'ing: The Emergence of a Revolutionary Political Leader.
Taibi, John, jt. auth. see Mulhearn, Daniel.
Taine, Hippolyte A. The Ancient Regime.
Taine, John, pseud. The Time Stream. Del Ray, Lester, ed.
Taintor, Charles M., intro. by see Taintor, Michaell.
Taintor, Michaell. Extracts from the Records of Colchester with Some Transcripts from the Recording of Michaell Taintor of "Brainford", Conn. Taintor, Charles M., intro. by.
Taintor, Zebulen, jt. ed. see Cancro, Robert.
Tait, Colin C. & LaPlante, Joseph A. Handbook of Connecticut Evidence: 1986 Supplement.
Tait, E. V. Elements of Marine Ecology.
Tait, Elaine. Best Restaurants: Philadelphia.
--Best Restaurants Philadelphia & Environs.
--Best Restaurants Philadelphia & Environs.
Taite Gallery Staff. The Pre-Raphaelite Papers. Parris, Leslie, ed.
--The Pre-Raphaelites. Parris, Leslie, ed.
Taitz, Emily, jt. auth. see Henry, Sondra.
Tajeri, Teymoor. Diary of a Mad Iranian.
Tajgman, David. Lovejoy's Shortcuts & Strategies for the LSAT Revised.
Takacs, L., ed. Advances in Physiological Sciences: Kidney & Body Fluids.
Takada, Koin. Spirit of Buddhism Today. Yampolsky, Philip, tr.
Takagi, Haruo. The Flaw in Japanese Management. Farmer, Richard, ed.
Takahama, Toshie, jt. auth. see Temko, Florence.
Takahara, Y., jt. auth. see Mesarovic, M. D.
Takahashi, K. & Kondo, T., eds. Physics in Collision: Proceedings of the Seventh International Conference.
Takahashi, Mutsumasa. Atlas of Carotid Angiography.
Takahashi, Rumiko. Lum: Urusei Yatsura. Horibuchi, Seiji, ed. Jones, Gerard & Fujii, Satoru, trs.
--Lum: Urusei Yatsura. Horibuchi, Seiji, ed. Jones, Gerard & Fujii, Satoru, trs.
--Lum: Urusei Yatsura. Horibuchi, Seiji, ed. Jones, Gerard & Fujii, Satoru, trs.
--Lum: Urusei Yatsura. Horibuchi, Seiji, ed. Jones, Gerard & Fujii, Satoru, trs.
--Lum: Urusei Yatsura. Horibuchi, Seiji, ed. Jones, Gerard & Fujii, Satoru, trs.
--Lum: Urusei Yatsura. Horibuchi, Seiji, ed. Jones, Gerard & Fujii, Satoru, trs.
--Lum: Urusei Yatsura. Horibuchi, Seiji, ed. Jones, Gerard & Fujii, Satoru, trs.
--Lum: Urusei Yatsura. Horibuchi, Seiji, ed. Jones, Gerard & Fujii, Satoru, trs.
Takahashi, Y. An Introduction to Field Quantization.
Takakura, Kintomo & Sano, Keiji. Metastatic Tumors of the Central Nervous System.
Takama, Shinji. Bamboo of Japan: Splendor in Four Seasons.
Takashi, Takako. Fairy Tale Land: Art Doll Illustration.
Takeda, Tsuneo. Kano Eitoku. Horton, H. Mack & Kaputa, Catherine, trs. from Japanese.
Takekoshi, Yosaburo. Japanese Rule in Formosa. Braithwaite, George, tr.
Takeuchi, Kei, et al. The Foundations of Multivariate Analysis: A Unified Approach by Means of Projection onto Linear Subspaces.
Takeuchi, Kenji. Tropical Hardwood Trade in the Asia-Pacific Region.
Takeuti, G. & Zaring, W. Axiomatic Set Theory.
Takpo Tashi Namgyal. Mahamudra: The Quintessance of Mind & Meditation. Lhalungpa, Lobsang P., tr. from Tibetan.
Talal, N., ed. Autoimmunity: Genetic, Immunologic, Virologic & Clinical Aspects.
Talarzyk, W. Wayne, jt. auth. see Engel, James P.
Talbert, Charles H. What Is a Gospel? The Genre of the Canonical Gospels.
Talbert, Charles H. & Keck, Leander E., eds. Reimarus: Fragments. Fraser, Ralph S., tr. from Ger.
Talbot, A. Approximation Theory.
Talbot, Charlene J. The Great Rat Island Adventure.
--A Home with Aunt Florry.
--An Orphan for Nebraska.
Talbot, Charles, jt. auth. see Andersson, Christiane.
Talbot, John A., ed. see American Psychiatric Association Conference Staff.
Talbot, Michael. The Delicate Dependency: A Novel of Vampire Life.
--Vivaldi.
Talbot, Percy A. In the Shadow of the Bush.
Talbot, William S. Jasper F. Cropsey, Eighteen Twenty-Three to Nineteen Hundred.
Talbot-Booth, E. C. Talbot-Booth's Merchant Ships.
--Talbot-Booth's Merchant Ships.
Talbot-Booth, E. C., jt. auth. see Greenman, David.
Talbott, John. A Practical Tax Guide for the Horse Owner, 1986 Edition.
Talbott, Ran, jt. auth. see Heilborn, John.
Talbott, Toby, tr. see Costantini, Humberto.
Talcott Mountain Science Center Staff. Discovering Science on Your ADAM, with 25 Programs.

Taleb, Mirza. Hannibal, Man of Destiny.
Taleporos, Elizabeth, jt. auth. see Szasz, Suzanne.
Taliaferro, W. H. & Humphrey, J. H., eds. Advances in Immunology. Incl. Vol. 1; Vol. 2; Vol. 3. Dixon, F. J., Jr. & Humphrey, J. H., eds.; Vol. 4; Vol. 5; Vol. 6; Vol. 7. Dixon, F. J., Jr. & Kunkel, Henry G., eds.; Vol. 8; Vol. 9; Vol. 10; Vol. 11; Vol. 12; Vol. 13; Vol. 14; Vol. 15; Vol. 16; Vol. 17; Vol. 18; Vol. 19; Vol. 20; Vol. 21; Vol. 22; Vol. 23; Vol. 24; Vol. 25; Vol. 26. Kunkel, Henry G. & Dixon, E. J., eds.; Vol. 27; Vol. 28; Vol. 29. Acad Pr.
Taliaferro, William H., et al. Radiation & Immune Mechanisms.
Talkington, Sylvia. ECG: A Pocket Guide.
Tall, D. O., jt. auth. see Stewart, I. N.
Tallan, N. M., ed. Electrical Conductivity in Ceramics & Glass.
Talland, George A. Deranged Memory: A Psychonomic Study of the Amnesic Syndrome.
Tallarico, Anthony. Mystery Picture Puzzles.
Tallarico, Tony, illus. Colors.
Tallarieo, Tony. Search A Picture Puzzles.
Tallemant Des Reaux. Historiettes.
Tallet, Jorge. Absolute Being.
Talley, David. Basic Carrier Telephony.
--Basic Carrier Telephony.
--Basic Electronic Switching for Telephone Systems.
--Basic Telephone Switching Systems.
Tallis, Thomas see Buck, P. C. & Fellowes, E. H.
Tallis, Thomas, et al. Thomas Tallis. Buck, P. C., ed.
Tallman, Marjorie. Dictionary of American Folklore.
Tallon, Robert. The Alligator's Song.
--Flea Story.
--Worm Story.
Talmage, Frank E. David Kimhi: The Man & the Commentaries.
Talmon, J. L. Origins of Totalitarian Democracy.
Talmor, E., ed. Europe in a Changing World.
Talmor, S. The Rhetoric of Criticism: From Hobbes to Coleridge.
Talmor, Sascha. Glanville: Scepticism.
Talner, jt. auth. see Sherwood.
Talocci, Mauro. Guide to the Flags of the World. Smith, Whitney, ed.
Talpe, J. Theory of Experiments in Paramagnetic Resonance.
Talpins, Susan, ed. see Segal, Marilyn & Adcock, Don.
Tamamushi, R. Kinetic Parameters of Electrode Reactions of Metallic Compounds.
Tamarin, R. H., ed. Population Regulation.
Tamberg, Andreas, ed. see Merkin, Victor.
Tamchina, Jurgen. Dominique & the Dragon.
Tames, Richard. Growing up in the Nineteen Sixties.
--Makers of Modern Britain.
--William Morris.
Tamiazzo, John. Love & Be Loved: A How-To Book.
Taminiaux, J. Dialectic & Difference. Decker, J. & Crease, R., trs.
Tamir, Pinchas, ed. The Role of Evaluators in Curriculum Development.
Tamir, Vicki. Bulgaria & Her Jews: The History of a Dubious Symbiosis.
Tamiya, M. Military Illustration.
Tamm, I. E. Fundamentals of the Theory of Electricity.
Tammelo, Ilmar. Outlines of Modern Legal Logic.
Tammsaare, A. Misadventure of the New Satan.
Tammuz, Benjamin. The Orchard. Flantz, Richard, tr. from Hebrew.
Tampion, J., jt. auth. see Reynolds, J.
Tamura, Kyoko, jt. auth. see Goldstein, Bernice.
Tan, Chester C. Boxer Catastrophe.
Tan, K. S. Eye on the World.
Tan, K. T. Chinese-English Dictionary: Taiwan Dialect.
Tan, Kim H. Andosols.
Tan, Paul L. Jesus Is Coming.
--Literal Interpretation of the Bible.
Tanabe, Y., et al, eds. Biological Rhythms in Birds: Neural & Endocrine Aspects.
Tanahashi, Kazuaki. Enku: Sculptor of a Hundred Thousand Buddhas.
Tanaka, Ichimatsu, jt. auth. see Ishizawa, Masao.
Tanaka, Ichimatsu, ed. see Sotatsu, Tawaraya.
Tanaka, Ichimatsu, jt. auth. see Ishizawa, Masao.
Tanaka, Richard K. America on Trial.
Tanaka, Sen'o. The Tea Ceremony.
Tanaka, Y., jt. ed. see May, C.
Tanara, Milli U. The World of Amphibians & Reptiles. Pleasance, Simon, tr.
Tancer, Jack. Our Reader.
Tancock, John L. Multiples: The First Decade.
--Rodin Museum Handbook.
Tancredi, Laurence, ed. see Institute of Medicine Staff.
Tanczer, T., ed. First FGGE Results from Satellites.
Tandler, Bernard & Hoppel, Charles L. Mitochandria.
Tandon, Yash, jt. auth. see Shaw, Timothy M.
Tandon, Yash, jt. ed. see Shaw, Timothy M.
Tandy, Clifford. The Landscape of Industry.
Taneja, Nawal K. Airline Planning: Corporate, Financial, & Marketing.
--U. S. Airfreight Industry.
Tanenbaum, Andrew S. Computer Networks.
Tanenbaum, Marc H. & Wilson, Marvin R., eds. Evangelicals & Jews in an Age of Pluralism.
Tanenbaum, Marc H., jt. ed. see Opsahl, Paul D.
Tanenhaus, Joseph, jt. auth. see Somit, Albert.
Taney, Retta M. Restoration Revivals on the British Stage, 1944-1979: A Critical Survey.
Tang, Chi-Yu. An Economic Study of Chinese Agriculture.
Tang, Stephen & Palmer, Martin. Chinese Herbal Prescriptions: A Practical & Authoritative Self-Help Guide.
Tang, Truong N., et al. A Vietcong Memoir.
Tangerman, E. J. The Modern Book of Whittling & Woodcarving.
Tangerman, Elmer J. Whittling & Woodcarving.
Tang Guang You & Li Wei, eds. Wildlife of China.
Tanham, George K. Trial in Thailand.
Tan Huay Peng. Fun with Chinese Characters.
Taniguchi, Kazuko. Monster Mary, Mischief Maker.
Tanikawa, Kyuichi. Ultrastructural Aspects of the Liver & Its Disorders.
Tanitch, Robert. Olivier: The Complete Career.
Taniuti, T., jt. ed. see Jeffrey, Alan.
Tannahill, Neal & Bedichek, Wendell M. American Government: Policy & Politics.
Tannahill, Neal, jt. auth. see Bedichek, Wendell M.
Tannehill, Robert C. The Sword of His Mouth. Beardslee, William A., ed.
Tannen, Deborah. Lilika Nakos.
Tannen, Mary. The Lost Legend of Finn.
--The Wizard Children of Finn.
Tannenbaum, D. Leb. Baby Talk.
Tannenhauser, Carol & Moch, Cheryl. In Celebration of Babies.
Tanner, B. K. X-Ray Diffraction Topography.
Tanner, Beverly, et al. Shelter What You Make; Minimize the Take: Tax Shelters for Financial Planning.
Tanner, Clay. Chance, No. 10: Bayou Bluff.
--Chance, No. 3: Dead Man's Hand.
--Chance, No. 4: Gambler's Revenge.
--Chance, No. 5: Delta Raiders.
--Chance, No. 7: Dakota Showdown.
--Chance, No. 8: Missouri Massacre.
--Chance, No. 9: Deadly Deal.
--Chance: Riverboat Rampage.
Tanner, Dennis F. The TRS-80 Graphics Handbook.
Tanner, G. A., jt. auth. see Steinhausen, M.
Tanner, Ira J. Healing the Pain of Everyday Loss.
Tanner, J. The Junior Confirmation Book.
Tanner, J. F. & Vann, J. Don. Samuel Beckett: A Checklist.
Tanner, J. M. & Whitehouse, R. H., eds. Atlas of Children's Growth: Normal Variation & Growth Disorders.
Tanner, J. M., et al. Assessment of Skeletal Maturity & Prediction of Adult Height: TW 2 Method.
Tanner, L. N. Classroom Discipline for Effective Teaching & Learning.
Tanner, Ogden. Garden Rooms: Greenhouses, Sunrooms & Solariums.
Tanner, Paul & Gerow, Maurice. Study of Jazz.
Tanner, Paul O., et al. Jazz.
Tanner, Terence A. Frank Waters: A Bibliography.
Tanner, William R., jt. ed. see Krog, Carl E.
Tansey, Richard G., jt. auth. see De La Croix, Horst.
Tansey, Richard G., jt. auth. see De la Croix, Horst.
Tansill, Charles C., ed. see U. S. Library of Congress, Legislative Reference Service Staff.
Tansley, David. The Raiment of Light: A Study of the Human Aura.
Tantzos, G. Nicholas. The Inheritors of Alexander the Great.
Tanz, Ralph D., et al, eds. Factors Influencing Myocardial Contractility.
Tanzer, Milt. Commercial Real Estate Desk Book.
--Converter's Guide to High Profits from Condo & Time Sharing Conversion.
--Real Estate Investments & How to Make Them: The Only Guide You'll Ever Need.
Tanzi, Vito, ed. The Underground Economy in the United States & Abroad.
Tanzik, David A. & Elliott, James F. Managing Police Organizations.
Tapasyananda, Swami & Nikhilananda, Swami. Sarada Devi, the Holy Mother: Her Life & Conversations.
Tape, Rollo. Rollo Tape's Secret Techniques in Tape Reading & Stock Market Tactics.
Taphouse, Kate, jt. auth. see Townsend, Kevin.
Tapia, Alejandro & Rivera. Enardo & Rosael.
Tapia, R. & Cotman, C. W., eds. Regulatory Mechanisms of Synaptic Transmission.
Tapia, Richard A. & Thompson, James R. Nonparametric Probability Density Estimation.
Tapio, Pat D. The Lady Who Saw the Good Side of Everything.
Tapley, Caroline. John Come Down the Backstay.
Tapley, Norah, jt. ed. see Levitt, Seymour H.
Taplin, ed. see Dance in Canada Annual Conference, 7th, Waterloo, Ontario, June 27-July 2, 1979.
Taplin, D. M. Advances in Research on the Strength & Fracture of Materials. Incl. Vol. 1. An Overview; Vol. 2a. Physical Metallurgy of Fracture; Vol. 2b. Fatigue; Vol. 3a; Vol. 3b. Applications & Non-Metals. Pergamon.
Tapp, Jack, ed. Reinforcement.
Tapp, Robert B. Religion among the Unitarian Universalists: Converts in the Step Father's House.
Tappan, Frances. Healing Massage Techniques: A Study of Eastern & Western Methods.
Tappan, William T. The Real Estate Acquisition Handbook: Money-Making Techniques for the Serious Investor.
Tappen, Ruth M. Nursing Leadership: Concepts & Practice.
Tapper, Richard. Pasture & Politics: Economics, Conflict & Ritual among Shahsevan Nomads of Northwestern Iran.
Tappert, Theodore G., tr. Augsburg Confession: Anniversary Edition.
Tapply, William G. Dead Meat: A Brady Coyne Mystery.
--The Dutch Blue Error.
--Follow the Sharks.
Tapsell, Alan, tr. see Sucksdorff, Astrid B.
Taqylor, W. H., ed. see Rendell, Ruth.
Tara, William. A Challenge to Medicine: Macrobiotics & the Biological Revolution.
Tarabilda, James. Black Sun.
Taraboi, V. Organization, Functioning & Activities of National Documentary Information Systems in the Scientific, Technical & Economic Fields.
Tarabrin, E. A., et al. U. S. S. R. & Countries of Africa.
Tarachow, Michael. In Place & Out.
--The Turning Point.
Taraman, K. S., ed. CAD-CAM: Meeting Today's Productivity Challenge.
Taran, Leonardo. Academica: Plato, Philip of Opus, & the Pseudo-Platonic Epinomis.
Taran, Leonardo, ed. see Apelt, Otto.
Taran, Leonardo, ed. see Heidel, William A.
Taran, Leonardo, ed. see Jones, Roger M.
Taran, Leonardo, ed. see Wilson, John C.
Taranow, Gerda. Sarah Bernhardt: The Art Within the Legend.
Taras, David, jt. auth. see Mandel, Eli.
Tarasov, K., jt. auth. see Zubenko, V.
Tarasov, L. V. Laser Physics.
Tarasov, Nikolai I. Ballet Techniques for the Male Dancer.
Tarassuk, Leonid. Italian Armor for Princely Courts.
Tarbell, Ida M. All in the Day's Work.
Tarbert, Gary C. & Beach, Barbara, eds. Book Review Index: Annual Cumulation, 1985.
Tarbert, Gary C., jt. ed. see Beach, Barbara.
Tarbox, Charles H. Five Ages of the Cinema.
Tarbuck, Edward J., jt. auth. see Lutgens, Frederick K.
Tarbuck, Kenneth J., ed. see Luxemburg, Rosa & Bukharin, Nikolai.
Tarbush, Mohammad. Reflections of a Palestinian.
Tardiff, Olive. Molly Stark: Woman of the Revolution.
--They Paved the Way: A History of N. H. Women.
Tardivel, Jules-Paul. For My Country. Fischman, Sheila, tr.
Tardy. French Clocks the World Over: Part 1-From Their Beginnings to the Louis XV-Louis XVI Transition Period. Ballantyne, Alexander, tr.
--French Clocks the World Over: Part 2-From Louis XVI Style to Louis XVIII-Charles X Period. Ballantyne, Alexander, tr.
--French Clocks, the World Over: Part 3. Ballantyne, Alexander, tr.
--International Hallmarks on Silver Collected by Tardy.
--Les Poincons de Garantie Internationaux pour L'or, Le Platine et Le Palladium.
--Les Porcelaines Francaises.
--Les Poteries-Faiences Porcelaines, Europeennes: Characteristiques Marques.
--Les Poteries-Faiences Porcelaines, Europeennes: Characteristiques Marques.
Tardy & Bidault, M. L'Abbe. Les Ivoires.
Tardy & Brateau, Paul. Dictionnaire Des Horlogers Francais (Dictionary of Clock & Watchmakers in France)
Tardy, et al. Poincons d'Etain.
Target, C. M. The Nun in the Concentration Camp.
Tari, Mel & Dudley, Cliff. Like a Mighty Wind.
Tari, Mel & Tari, Noni. Gentle Breeze of Jesus.
Tari, Noni, jt. auth. see Tari, Mel.
Tarkenton, Fran & Resnicow, Herb. Murder at the Super Bowl: A Memory of Love.
Tarkington, Booth. The Magnificent Ambersons.
Tarle, Eugene. Napoleon's Invasion of Russia in 1812.
Tarleton, Frank L. Some Strike It Rich: Memoirs & Tales of a Native Son of California.
Tarling, D. H., ed. Economic Geology & Geotectonics.
Tarling, D. H. & Runcorn, S. K., eds. Implications of Continental Drift to the Earth Sciences.
Tarlow, Carol, jt. auth. see Yanker, Gary.
Tarlow, David M. Allied Health Professions Admission Test (AHPAT) Practice Examination Number 4 - Annotated Answers.
Tarlton, Leigh G. The Two Worlds of Coral Harper.
Tarn, W. Greeks in Bactria & India.
Tarnoi, Laszlo. Wingless Victory.
Tarnopol, Lester, ed. Learning Disorders in Children: Diagnosis, Medication, Education.
Tarnowski, Knut, tr. see Adorno, Theodor W.
Tarnowski, S. Chopin: As Revealed by Extracts from His Diary. Doscher, David, ed.
Tarpy, Roger & Mayer, Richard. Readings in Learning & Memory.
Tarr, Judith. The Lady of Han-Gilen.
Tarr, Rodger L. Thomas Carlyle: A Bibliography of English-Language Criticism, 1824-1974.
Tarraborrelli, J. Randy & Wilson, Reggie. Diana.
Tarrant, Graham. Rabbits.
Tarrant, John. The Clauberg Trigger.
--Perks & Parachutes: How to Get the Ideal Employment Package.
Tarrant, John J., jt. auth. see Stonesong Press Staff.
Tarrant, John R. Agricultural Geography: Problems in Modern Geography.
--The Food Policies.
Tarrant, Naomi. Collecting Costume: The Care & Display of Clothes & Accessories.
Tarrants, William E. The Measurement of Safety Performance.
Tarrants, William E., ed. Dictionary of Terms Used in the Safety Profession.
Tarrh, John M., jt. auth. see Thome, Richard J.
Tarschys, Daniel. The Soviet Political Agenda: Problems & Priorities, 1950-1970.
Tarshis, Barry. The Average American Book: An up-to-the Minute Look at the Traits, Habits, Tastes, Life Styles & Attitudes of the American People.
--Tennis & the Mind.
Tarsky, Sue. Apple & Pear.
--Cup & Bowl.
--Doll & Drum.
--Playtime.
--The Potted Plant Book.
--Shopping.
--Table & Chair.
Tart, Charles T. Waking Up.
Tartakow, I. Jackson & Vorperian, John H. Foodborne & Waterborne Diseases: Their Epidemiological Characteristics.
Tarter, Ralph E. Principles of Solid State Power Conversion.
Taryam, Abdulah O. The Establishment of the United Arab Emirates.
Tasch, Paul. Paleobiology of the Invertebrates: Data Retrieval from the Fossil Record.
Tasch, Peter A., ed. see Bickerstaff, Issac.
Tasch, Peter A., ed. see Colman, George the Younger.
Tasher, Steven A., et al. Environmental Laws & Real Estate Handbook.
Tashman, Leonard J. & Lamborn, Kathleen R. The Ways & Means of Statistics.
Tasie, G. O. Christian Missionary Enterprise in the Niger Delta, 1864-1918.
Task Committee on Wind Forces. Wind Forces on Structures.
Task Force on Institutional Evaluation Staff. Evaluation of Archival Institutions: Services, Principles, & Guide to Self-Study.
Task Force on World Hunger Staff. And He Had Compassion on Them: The Christian & World Hunger.
Task Force, 1974 Staff. The Adolescent, Other Citizens, & Their High Schools.
Tassel, Katrina Van see Van Tassel, Katrina.
Tatalovich, Raymond & Daynes, Byron W. Presidential Power in the United States.
Tatalovich, Raymond, jt. auth. see Daynes, Byron W.
Tatarindrick, S., jt. auth. see Potapov, V.
Tatarinov, V. G. Anatomia y Fisiologia Humanas.
Tatchell, Peter. AIDS: A Guide to Survival.
--Democratic Defence.
Tate, A. Jefferson Davis: His Rise & Fall.
Tate, A., jt. auth. see Billington, E. W.
Tate, Curtis E., Jr., et al. Successful Small Business Management.
Tate, Donald. Bravo Burning.
Tate, Donald R. & Tate, Leora B. The Mystic Poet: Biography-Poetry-Lyrics of a Mysterious Man.
Tate Gallery, London Staff & Walker Art Gallery Staff. Patrick Caulfield.
Tate Gallery, London Staff, ed. George Stubbs: Seventeen Twenty-Four to Eighteen Six.
Tate, Leora B., jt. auth. see Tate, Donald R.
Tate, Michael L. The American West.

Tate, Nicholas. Pizarro & the Incas. Reeves, Marjorie, ed.
Tate, Robert G., Jr. Company Wide Quality Control: Questions & Answers.
Tate, Thad W. & Ammerman, David L., eds. The Chesapeake in the Seventeenth Century: Essays on Anglo-American Society.
Tatford, Frederick A. Revelation.
Tatham, Julie C. The Old Testament Made Easy.
Tatlow, Peter, et al. The World of Gymnastics.
Tatman, Sandra L. & Moss, Roger W. Biographical Dictionary of Philadelphia Architects & Master Builders: 1760-1930.
Taton. Reason & Chance in Scientific Discovery.
Tatreau, Bobbe, jt. auth. see Tatreau, Doug.
Tatreau, Doug & Tatreau, Bobbe. Parks of the Pacific Coast: The Complete Guide to the National & Historic Parks, California, Oregon, Washington.
Tattersall, M. H. & Fox, R. M., eds. Nucleosides in Cancer Treatment: Rational Approaches to Antimetabolite Selectivity & Modulation.
Tattersfield, D. Projects & Demonstrations in Astronomy.
Tattersfield, Donald. Halley's Comet.
Tattum, Delwyn P., ed. Management of Disruptive Pupil Behavior in Schools.
Tatum, Howard J., jt. auth. see Connell, Elizabeth B.
Tatum, Howard J., jt. auth. see Connell-Tatum, Elizabeth.
Taub, Doris L., jt. auth. see Taub, Richard P.
Taub, Richard P. & Taub, Doris L. Entrepreneurship in India's Small-Scale Industries: An Exploration of Social Contexts.
Taubenfeld, Howard J., jt. auth. see Lay, S. Houston.
Tauber. Last Best Hope.
Tauber, A., ed. see Shaw, George Bernard.
Tauber, P. F., jt. ed. see Ludwig, H.
Tauber, Yale D., jt. auth. see Practicing Law Institute Staff.
Taubes, Frederic. Oil Painting for the Beginner.
Taubman, Joseph. The Business & Law of Music.
--Copyright & Antitrust.
Taubner, Jennifer. Prince Junior Gorg.
--Red Fraggle's Birthday.
Taubr, Paul, jt. auth. see Alyeshmerni, Mansoor.
Tauc, J. Photo & Thermoelectric Effects in Semiconductors.
Tauc, J., ed. Optical Properties of Solids.
Tauriac, Michel. La Louisiane Au Jourd' Hui.
Tausky, Margaret, tr. see Janacek, Leos.
Tausky, Vilem, tr. see Janacek, Leos.
Taussig, Hal, tr. see Meves, Christa.
Tautu, P., jt. auth. see Iosifescu, M.
Tavakolian, Susan, ed. Language Acquisition & Linguistic Theory.
Tavard, George H., jt. auth. see Edwards, Mark.
Tavel, Charles. The Third Industrial Age: Strategy for Business Survival.
Tavistock Joint Library, London Staff. Catalogue of the Tavistock Joint Library.
Tavolga, W. N., ed. Sound Reception in Fishes.
Tavolga, William N., ed. Sound Production in Fishes.
Tavoulereas, William & Stein, Ben. Fighting Back.
Tavris, Carol. Anger: The Misunderstood Emotion.
Tavris, Carol & Offir, Carole W. The Longest War: Sex Differences in Perspective.
Tavuchis, Nicholas & Goode, William J. The Family Through Literature.
Tawes, Roy L., jt. auth. see Brown, William H.
Tawil, Natalie & Hyson, Athena. Selected Agricultural Statistics on Spain, 1970-82.
Tawney, R. H. Land & Labor in China.
Tawney, Richard H. The Acquisitive Society.
Tawshunsky, Ben. Effective Remedies for Common Ailments.
Tax Reduction Institute, Washington D. C. Staff. The Prentice-Hall Business Tax Deduction Master Guide.
Tax, Sol & Freeman, Leslie G., eds. Horizons of Anthropology.
Tax, Sol, ed. see Americanists Staff.
Taylo, Don H. Trade Union Financial Administration.
Taylor. English & Japanese in Contrast.
Taylor & Douglas. Mountain Wild Flowers of the Pacific Northwest.
Taylor, jt. auth. see Hewett.
Taylor, A., ed. see International Association of Universities Staff.
Taylor, A., tr. see Baernreither, Joseph M.
Taylor, A. J. How Wars Begin.
--An Old Man's Diary.
--Origins of the Second World War.
--Revolutions & Revolutionaries.
--The War Lords.
Taylor, A. Robert. How to Select & Use an Executive Search Firm.
Taylor, Alan C. Aerial Banner Towing.
Taylor, Albert J. How to Teach Flying.
Taylor, Alexander S. Bibliografa Californica: Supplement. Basso, Dave, ed.
Taylor, Alison. Off Stage & On: An Introduction to Youth Drama.
Taylor, Allen G. R: Base System V User's Guide.
Taylor & Francis Inc Europa Staff. The Far East & Australasia 1987.
Taylor & Francis Inc. Staff. The Middle East & North Africa 1987.
Taylor, Andrew. The Politics of the Yorkshire Miners.
--Selected Poems Nineteen Sixty to Nineteen Eighty.
--The Trade Unions & the Labour Party.
--Travelling.
Taylor, Angela & Baker, John, eds. Methods of Cultivating Parasites in Vitro.
Taylor, Angela E. & Muller, Ralph, eds. The Relevance of Parasitology to Human Welfare Today.
Taylor, Anita, et al. Communicating.
Taylor, Archer. Comparative Studies in Folklore: Asia, Europe, America.
Taylor, Arthur. Discovering Military Traditions.
Taylor, B., ed. Long Range Planning Cumulative Index.
Taylor, B. N., et al. Fundamental Constants & Quantum Electrodynamics.
Taylor, Barbara J. Dear Mom & Dad: Parents & the Preschooler.
Taylor, Benjamin J. & Whitney, Fred. Labor Relations Law.
Taylor, Bernard, jt. ed. see Farmer, David H.
Taylor, Bernard W., III. Introduction to Management Science.
Taylor, Bernie. Practical Football Coaching Techniques.
Taylor, Beverly. Case Studies in Child Development.
Taylor, Bob L., jt. auth. see Lunstrum, John P.
Taylor, Brian B. Geoffrey Bawa.
Taylor, C. Barr, jt. auth. see Ferguson, James M.
Taylor, C. W., ed. Climate for Creativity.
Taylor, Charles D. Show of Force.
Taylor, Christopher. The Archaeology of Gardens.
Taylor, Christopher & Muir, Richard. Visions of the Past.
Taylor, Clarence R. How to Be a Successful Inventor: Patenting, Protecting, Marketing & Selling Your Invention.
Taylor, Cliff & Emerson, David. Rural Post Offices.
Taylor, Colin. Great Rail Non-Journeys of Australia.
Taylor, Conan J. Lichens of Ohio, Pt. II: Fruticose & Cladoniform.
Taylor, Constance G. Four Stories.
Taylor, D. R. Education & Training in Contemporary Cartography.
--Graphic Communication & Design in Contemporary Cartography.
Taylor, David, ed. see National Computing Centre, Ltd. Staff.
Taylor, Day. The Magnificent Dream.
Taylor, Decoury, jt. auth. see Eisenberg, Lee.
Taylor, Delores A. & Alpert, Stuart W. Continuity & Support Following Residential Treatment.
Taylor, Derek. The Making of Raiders of the Lost Ark.
Taylor, Dick. Guns from the East.
Taylor, Domini. Gemini.
--Teacher's Pet.
Taylor, Don. Mastering Rubik's Cube.
Taylor, Don & Rylands, Leanne. Cube Games.
Taylor, Donald E. Allied Health Professions Admissions Test.
Taylor, Donald S. Thomas Chatterton's Art: Experiments in Imagined History.
Taylor, Dorothy, jt. auth. see Swanwick, Keith.
Taylor, Dorothy E. Fleur de Lis.
Taylor, E. Openshaw. Nuclear Power Plant.
Taylor, Ed S., ed. The History of Playing Cards, with Anecdotes of Their Use in Conjuring, Fortune-Telling, & Card-Sharking.
Taylor, Edith C. Money: The Root of All Evil.
Taylor, Elizabeth. Angel.
Taylor, Eric. Be Fit Through Your Forties.
Taylor, F., jt. auth. see Kingsley, D.
Taylor, Florance W. Plane Ride.
Taylor, Frank S. Conquest of a Bacteria.
Taylor, Fred. The Shooting Time Guide to Ferretting.
Taylor, Fred M., jt. auth. see Lange, Oskar.
Taylor, G. F. Second Coming of Jesus.
Taylor, Gardner C., jt. auth. see Edwards, O. C., Jr.
Taylor, George. The American High School Band.
--The High School Stage Band.
Taylor, George & Skinner, Andrew. Maps of the Roads of Ireland.
Taylor, George, et al. Spiralian Embryology.
Taylor, George A., jt. ed. see Palumbo, Dennis.
Taylor, George E. The Livestock of China.
Taylor, George J., jt. auth. see Moses, H. Weston.
Taylor, Gordon. Place of the Dawn.
Taylor, Gordon R., ed. & intro. by see Briffault, Robert.
Taylor, Griffith. Twentieth Century Geography.
Taylor, H. F., ed. Chemistry of Cements.
Taylor, Halsey P. Reading for Meaning.
Taylor, Halsey P. & Taylor, Sheila F. Read to Write.
Taylor, Halsey P. & Okada, Victor N., eds. The Craft of the Essay.
Taylor, Harold. The Pianist's Talent.
Taylor, Heather, ed. Information Technology: Practice, Potential, Limitations & Effects on the Profession: Proceedings of the 55th Aslib Annual Conference.
Taylor, Henry F., ed. Fiber Optics Communications.
Taylor, Henry O. Greek Biology & Greek Medicine.
Taylor, Herman, Jr., et al. Current Research in Petroleum Fuels, II.
Taylor, Howard E., jt. auth. see Wade, Thomas L.
Taylor, Hugh. The Arrangement & Description of Archival Materials.
Taylor, Ina. An Edwardian Lady.
Taylor, Isaac. Words & Places, or Etymological Illustrations of History, Ethnology, & Geography.
Taylor, J., jt. auth. see Dobson, R. B.
Taylor, J. A. Climatic Resources & Economic Activity.
Taylor, J. B., jt. ed. see Veziroglu, T. N.
Taylor, J. E. The New Tolkien Companion.
Taylor, J. E., jt. ed. see Szego, G. C.
Taylor, J. Golden, ed. Literature of the American West.
Taylor, J. H., ed. Molecular Genetics: An Advanced Treatise.
Taylor, J. Scott, jt. auth. see Sanford, Jon A.
Taylor, J. W. Aircraft Today.
Taylor, Jack A., jt. auth. see Balkin, Alfred B.
Taylor, James. The Andrew Project.
--An Everyday God.
Taylor, James W. Competitive Marketing Strategies: An Alexander Hamilton Book.
--Planning Profitable New Product Strategies.
Taylor, Janelle. Savage Conquest.
Taylor, Jared. Shadows of the Rising Sun: A Critical View of the Japanese Miracle.
Taylor, Jayne. Whirlwind Courtship.
Taylor, Jean. Creative Flower Arrangement.
Taylor, Jenny. Notebooks-Memoirs-Archives: Readings & Re-readings Doris Lessing.
Taylor, Jenny, ed. Notebooks, Memoirs, Archives: Reading & Rereading Doris Lessing.
Taylor, Jim, jt. auth. see Gretzky, Wayne.
Taylor, John. Black Holes: The End of the Universe?
Taylor, John C., jt. ed. see George, David B.
Taylor, John R. The Art Nouveau Book in Britain.
--Orson Welles: A Celebration.
--Strangers in Paradise: The Hollywood Emigres, 1933-1950.
Taylor, John S. Commonsense Architecture.
Taylor, John V. Enough Is Enough: A Biblical Call for Moderation in a Consumer Oriented Societed.
--Weep Not for Me.
Taylor, John W. & Monday, David. Spies in the Sky.
Taylor, John W. & Swanborough, Gordon. Civil Aircraft of the World.
Taylor, John W., ed. Jane's All the World's Aircraft 1986-87.
Taylor, Joshua C. Learning to Look: A Handbook for the Visual Arts.
Taylor, Joyce. Horses in Suburbia.
Taylor, Judy. Dudley & the Monster.
--Dudley & the Strawberry Shake.
--Dudley Goes Flying.
--Dudley in a Jam.
Taylor, Judy, ed. see Noll, Paul & Murach, Mike.
Taylor, K. Stages in Writing.
Taylor, Kenneth N. Almost Twelve.
--Devotions for the Children's Hour.
--Stories for the Children's Hour.
Taylor, Kenneth N., tr. Soul Food.
Taylor, L. B., Jr. Haunted Houses.
--Spotlight on Scott Baio, Clark Brandon, Leif Garret & John Schneider. Barish, Wendy, ed.
Taylor, L. J., jt. auth. see Ayliffe, G. A.
Taylor, Lance, et al. Trade Patterns in Developing Countries, 1970-1981.
Taylor, Lauriston S. Radiation Protection Standards.
Taylor, Leslie A., ed. Auto Racing U. S. A., 1986: The Year in Review.
Taylor, Lester D., jt. auth. see Ingbar, Mary L.
Taylor, Lillian. Clean up the Blood Stream & Live.
Taylor, Lily Ross. The Divinity of the Roman Emperor, Middletown, 1931.
Taylor, Lisa, ed. Urban Open Spaces.
Taylor, Lonn W., ed. A Common Agenda for History Museums: Conference Proceedings.
Taylor, Lynda, jt. auth. see Worthington, Bonnie.
Taylor, M. Pseudo Differential Equations.
Taylor, Malcolm. Health Insurance & Canadian Public Policy: The Seven Decisions That Created the Canadian Health Insurance System.
Taylor, Mark. The Case of the Purloined Compass.
--Henry Explores the Jungle.
--The Winds' Child.
Taylor, Maxwell D. Precarious Security.
Taylor, Michael. The Geography of Australian Corporate Power.
--Naval Air Power.
Taylor, Michael J. Missiles of the World.
--Planemakers Four: Shorts.
--Strategic Bombers, 1945-1985.
--Warplanes of the World, Nineteen Eighteen to Nineteen Thirty-Nine.
--World Fighters, Nineteen Forty-Five to Nineteen Eighty-Five.
Taylor, Michael J., jt. auth. see Mondey, David.
Taylor, Michael J., ed. Jane's Aviation Review.
--Jane's Aviation Review.
--Planemakers: Boeing.
Taylor, Nancy, rev. by see Sollitto, Sharmon & Veatch, Robert M.
Taylor, Norman, ed. Encyclopedia of Gardening.
--Guide to Garden Shrubs & Trees.
Taylor, O. Nuclear Reactors for Power Generation.
Taylor, P. J., jt. ed. see Johnston, R. J.
Taylor, P. R., et al, eds. Recycle & Secondary Recovery of Metals.
Taylor, Pat E. Afoot in the Field of Men.
--The God Chaser.
Taylor, Paul A. & Gibbs, Ronald K. How Ought Science Be Taught.
Taylor, Paul W., jt. ed. see Sprague, Elmer.
Taylor, Peter. Old Forest & Other Stories.
--The Smoke Ring: Tobacco, Money & Multinational Politics.
Taylor, Peter J. Quantitative Methods in Geography: An Introduction to Spatial Analysis.
Taylor, Peter J., jt. auth. see Gudgin, Graham.
Taylor, Peter J., jt. ed. see Burnett, Alan D.
Taylor, Philip A. A New Dictionary of Economics.
Taylor, Phoebe A. Sandbar Sinister.
--Three Plots for Asey Mayo.
Taylor, R. A., tr. see Opitz, H.
Taylor, R. J. Galaxies: Structure & Evolution.
Taylor, R. W. Stored Data Description & Data Translation: A Model & Language.
Taylor, Renee. My Life on a Diet: Confessions of a Hollywood Diet Junkie.
Taylor, Richard. R. Taylor's Wrong Bag.
Taylor, Robert. Saranac: America's Magic Mountain.
Taylor, Robert B., et al, eds. Family Medicine: Principles & Practice.
Taylor, Robert J., ed. Massachusetts, Colony to Commonwealth: Documents on the Formation of Its Constitution, 1775-1780.
Taylor, Robert L. Mind or Body: Distinguishing Psychological from Organic Disorders.
Taylor, Robert R., Jr. A Review of "Shall We Splinter?"
Taylor, Roger C. The Fourth Book of Good Boats.
Taylor, Ronald. Richard Wagner: His Life, Art & Thought.
Taylor, Ronald, tr. see Hoffmann, E. T.
Taylor, Ronald, tr. see Lorenz, Konrad.
Taylor, Ronald B. The Kid Business: How it Exploits the Children it Should Help.
Taylor, Ross, jt. auth. see Levinson, A. A.
Taylor, S. E. & Parmar, H. A. Aviation Law for Pilots.
--Ground Studies for Pilots. Incl. Vol. I. Radio Aids; Vol. II. Plotting & Flight Planning; Vol. III. Navigation General. Gower Pub Co.
Taylor, S. Martin, jt. auth. see Dear, Michael J.
Taylor, S. S. B., ed. The Theatre of the French & German Enlightenment: Five Essays.
Taylor, Samuel W. Nightfall at Nauvoo.
Taylor, Sandra, ed. Yankee Magazine's Great New England Recipes: And the Cooks Who Made Them Famous.
Taylor, Sandra, ed. see Gorman, Judy.
Taylor, Sandra, jt. ed. see Orcutt, Georgia.
Taylor, Sandra, ed. see Orcutt, Georgia.
Taylor, Sandra, jt. ed. see Orcutt, Georgia.
Taylor, Sandra B. Faulkner: Jimmy, That Is.
Taylor, Sandra J., ed. The Famous New Englanders Cookbook.
Taylor, Sandra J., ed. see Gorman, Judy.
Taylor, Sharon A. The Book: That Which Has Been & That Which Shall Be.
Taylor, Sheila F., jt. auth. see Taylor, Halsey P.
Taylor, Suzanne. Cooking from a Country Kitchen. Atcheson, Jean, ed.
Taylor, T. N., jt. ed. see Dilcher, D. L.
Taylor, Talbot J. Linguistic Theory & Structural Stylistics.
Taylor, Telford. Munich: The Price of Peace.
Taylor, Theodore. H. M. S. Hood vs. Bismarck: The Battleship Battle.
--Rocket Island.
--Teetoncey.
Taylor, Theodore, jt. auth. see Hedren, Tippi.
Taylor, Thomas A. Reclaiming the Bar-V.
Taylor, Thomas J. Get Rich on the Obvious: How to Turn Your Everyday Observations into Stock Market Profits.
Taylor, Vic & Babb, Harold. Making & Repairing Wooden Clock Cases.
Taylor, W., ed. The Vibration Syndrome.

Taylor, W. & Pelmear, P. L., eds. Vibration White Finger in Industry.
Taylor, W. D. Symbiotic Imperative: A Blueprint for Living Together Campatibly.
Taylor, W. H., ed. see Cross, Amanda.
Taylor, W. H., ed. see Francis, Dick.
Taylor, W. H., ed. see Hillerman, Tony.
Taylor, W. H., ed. see James, P. D.
Taylor, W. H., ed. see MacDonald, John D.
Taylor, W. H., ed. see Peters, Ellis.
Taylor, W. J. & Watling, T. F. Successful Project Management.
Taylor, Welford D., ed. see Anderson, Sherwood.
Taylor, Wendell H., ed. see Crispin, Edmund.
Taylor, Wendell H., ed. see MacDonald, Ross.
Taylor, William. The Military Roads in Scotland.
Taylor, William E. A Short Guide to Reading & Writing Poetry.
Taylor, William E., Jr., ed. see Bruemmer, Fred, et al.
Taylor, William J., jt. auth. see Jordan, Amos A.
Taylor, William N. Marathon Running: A Medical Science Handbook.
Taylor, Zack. Successful Waterfowling.
Taylor-Gooby, Peter & Dale, Jennifer. Social Theory & Social Welfare.
Taylor-Robinson, D. & Caunt, A. E. Varicella Virus.
Tazawa, Yutaka, ed. Biographical Dictionary of Japanese Art.
Tazewell, Charles. Deluxe Littlest Angel.
Tchekov see Chekhov, Anton.
Tcherikower, Elias, ed. Geshikhte Fun der Yidisher Arbeterbavegung.
Tchudi, Stephen. The Green Machine & the Frog Crusade.
Tchudi, Stephen N. Teaching Writing in the Content Areas: College.
Tchudi, Stephen N. & Huerts, Margie C. Teaching Writing in the Content Areas: Middle School-Junior High.
Tchudi, Stephen N. & Tchudi, Susan J. Teaching Writing in the Content Areas: Elementary.
Tchudi, Stephen N. & Yates, Joanne. Teaching Writing in the Content Areas: Senior High School.
Tchudi, Susan J., jt. auth. see Tchudi, Stephen N.
Teachers & Writers Collaborative Staff. The Whole Word Catalogue.
Teaching of the Twelve Apostles Staff. Die Lateinische Ubersetzung der Didache.
Teaford, Jon C. City & Suburb: The Political Fragmentation of Metropolitan Areas, 1850-1970.
Teague, Edward H. Architecture Librarianship: A Selective Bibliography.
--The Architecture of Tibet: An Introductory Bibliography.
--The Demolition of Buildings: A Bibliography.
--Fallout Shelter Architecture: A Bibliography.
--Floors & Floorcoverings: A Bibliography.
--Frei Otto: A Bibliography & Building List.
--Fritz Schumacher: A Bibliography.
--John Lautner: Bibliography & Building List.
--Leon Krier: Bibliography & Building List.
--Rudolf Schwarz: Bibliography & Building List.
--Sculpture Gardens: A Bibliography of Periodical Literature.
--William Morgan: Bibliography & Building List.
Teale, A. E. Kantian Ethics.
Teale, Edwin W. The Golden Throng: A Book about Bees.
Teasdale, Sara. Mirror of the Heart. Drake, William, ed.
Tech Tran Consultants Staff. A Tech Tran Special Report: Machine Vision Systems.
Tech Tran Corporation Staff. Industrial Robots: A Summary & Forecast.
--Lasers in Metalworking: A Summary & Forecast.
Te-Chen Wang, Elizabeth. Ladies of the T'ang: 22 Classical Chinese Stories.
Technical Insights, Inc. Staff. Advanced Materials Research: A Guide to R&D Centers.
--Advances in Bioprocess Technology: Industrial-Specialty Chemicals via Biological Sources-Routes.
--Advances in Enzyme Technology: Artificial & Semisynthetic Designed Enzymes.
--Drug Delivery Systems: A Technology Survey.
--Genetic Technology: A Guide to Key R & D Projects.
--Monoclonal Antibodies: Technical Opportunities.
--Robots in Industry: Applications for the Electronics Industry.
--Robots in Industry: General Applications.
--Three-D Machine Vision.
Technische Hochschule, Darmstadt Staff, et al. Travelling Wave Solid State Devices: A Special Issue of International Journal of Electronics.
Technology Assessment & Utilization Committee. A National Strategy for Improving Productivity in Building & Construction.
Tecklin, jt. auth. see Irwin.
Tedder, Clarence L. The Spiritual Rock.
Tedeschi, Cesare G., et al, eds. Forensic Medicine.
Tedeschi, Frank P. & Kueck, Gary. One Hundred One Microprocessor Software & Hardware Projects.
Tedeschi, Henry. Cell Physiology.
--Cell Physiology: Molecular Dynamics.
Tedesco, Janis & Popham, Janet. Introduction to the Raj Quartet.
Tedlock, Barbara, jt. ed. see Tedlock, Dennis.
Tedlock, Dennis & Tedlock, Barbara, eds. Teachings from the American Earth: Perspectives on the Religion, Philosophy, & Spirituality of the American Indian.
Tedrow, John C., jt. auth. see Murray, R. C.
Teece, David J., jt. ed. see Griffin, James M.
Teegarden, Kenneth L. We Call Ourselves Disciples.
Teeguarden, Ron. The Complete Guide to Oriental Manual Therapy.
Teertha, Swami Ananda, ed. see Rajneesh, Bhagwan Shree.
Tees, David W. & Stanford, Jay G. A Code Enforcement Handbook for Municipal Officials.
Teets, Bob, jt. auth. see Young, Shelby.
Tefft, Benjamin F., ed. see Elliott, Charles.
Tefler, William. The Treasure of Sao Roque.
Tega, Vasile G., ed. Management & Economics Journals: An International Selection.
Teglovic, Steve & Lynch, Robert, eds. Topics in Management Information Systems.
Tegnaeus, Harry. Blood Brothers.
Tegner, Bruce. Judo: Sport Techniques for Physical Fitness & Tournament.
Teharanian, Majid, et al, eds. Communications Policy for National Development: A Comparative Perspective.
Teich, ed. see Intersociety Working Group Staff.
Teich, Albert, et al. Congressional Action on R & D in FY 1987 Budget.
Teicher, Morton I., et al, eds. Reaching the Aged: Social Services in Forty-Four Countries.
Teichman, Jenny. Pacifism & the Just War: A Study in Applied Philosophy.
Teideman, David B., et al. The Cross Sectional Story of Early Career Development.
Teikmanis, Arthur L. Preaching & Pastoral Care.
Teilhard De Chardin, Pierre. Activation of Energy.
--Building the Earth.
--Christianity & Evolution. Hague, Rene, tr.
--The Heart of the Matter. Hague, Rene, tr.
--Human Energy.
--Human Energy.
--Toward the Future. Hague, Rene, tr. from Fr.
Teilhet-Fisk, Jehanne. Paradise Reviewed: An Interpretation of Gauguin's Polynesian Symbolism. Foster, Stephen C., ed.
Teiser, Ruth & Harroun, Catherine. Winemaking in California.
Teitel, Maurice, et al. Breastfeeding: The Art of Mothering.
Teitelbaum, Michael. Santa Claus the Movie: The Boy Who Didn't Believe in Christmas.
Teitz, Michael B., jt. auth. see Phillips, Kenneth F.
Teixeira, Bernardo. Flowers for the Executioner.
Teja, Edward R. Teaching Your Computer to Talk: A Manual of Command & Response.
Tejima, Keizaburo. The Bear's Autumn.
Tej Vir Singh, et al. Studies in Tourism, Wildlife Parks & Conservation.
Tek, M. Rasin, jt. auth. see Yellig, William F., Jr.
Tekippe, Terry J., ed. Papal Infallibility: An Application of Lonergan's Theological Method.
Tel Aviv University Conference on Erythropoiesis Staff. Erythropoiesis: Regulatory Mechanisms & Developmental Aspects, Proceedings of the Tel Aviv University Conference, Petah Tikva, July 1970. Matoth, Yehuda, ed.
Tele-Record Productions Staff. Great Chefs of Chicago.
--The Great Chefs of New Orleans II.
--The Great Chefs of San Francisco.
Telecom Library Research Group Staff. Telecom Library Guide to Key Systems & Mini-PBXs.
Telek, Lehel & Graham, Horace D. Leaf Protein Concentrates.
Television History Workshop Staff. Making Cars: A History of Car-Making at Cowley by the People Who Make the Cars.
Telfer, Elizabeth, jt. auth. see Downie, R. S.
Telfer, Judie. Training Minority Journalists: A Case Study of the San Francisco Examiner Intern Program.
Telford, Lawrence S. From Helgoland to Hollywood.
--Wild Life in Alaska.
Telford, William R., ed. The Interpretation of Mark.
Teller, Edward. Energy from Heaven & Earth.
--Reluctant Revolutionary.
Teller, Walter M. Joshua Slocum.
Telles, Lygia F. The Girl in the Photograph.
--Marble Dance.
Tellez, Gabriel Medina see Medina Tellez, Gabriel.
Telser, Lester G. Economic Theory & the Core.
Teluk, John, jt. auth. see Katsaros, Thomas.
Telushkin, Joseph, jt. auth. see Prager, Dennis.
Temam, R., ed. see International Conference on Numerical Methods in Fluid Mechanics, 3rd.
Temam, R. M., ed. see Conference Held at the Univ. of Paris-Sud, Orsay, 12-13 June 1975.
Temes, Gabor C. & Mitra, Sanjit K., eds. Modern Filter Theory & Design.
Temes, Lloyd. Electronic Circuits for Technicians.
Temes, Terry L. The Inner I.
Temianka, Henri. Facing the Music: An Inside View of the Real Concert World.
Temin, Howard M. The Biology of RNA-Tumor Viruses.
Temin, Peter. Causal Factors in American Economic Growth in the Nineteenth Century.
Temkine, Raymond. Grotowski.
Temko, Florence. Come to My House. Lawrence, Leslie & Weingartner, Ronald, eds.
Temko, Florence & Takahama, Toshie. The Magic of Kirigami: Happenings with Paper & Scissors.
Temko, Phillip, jt. ed. see Moravcsik, Julius.
Temm, Peter N., jt. auth. see Cathie, Bruce L.
Temperley, H. N. Graph Theory & Applications.
Temperley, Harold, ed. see Great Britain, Foreign Office Staff.
Temperley, Howard. British Antislavery Eighteen Thirty-Three to Eighteen Seventy.
Temperley, Howard, jt. ed. see Bradbury, Malcolm.
Temple, Barker & Sloane, Inc. Staff. Transportation Strategies for the Eighties.
Temple, Charles. The Beginnings of Writing.
Temple, Charles & Gillet, Jean W. Language Arts: Learning Processes & Teaching Practices.
Temple, Cliff. The Marathon Made Easier.
Temple, Lynn G. Wyoma.
Temple, William. What Christians Stand For in the Secular World. Sherman, Franklin, ed.
Templer, Otis W. Social Science Research in the Dry Lands.
Templeton, Harley M. From BASIC to C.
Templeton, J. G., jt. auth. see Bagchi, T. P.
Templeton, Janet. Reluctant Heiress.
--Suitor to Spare.
Templeton, Lee. Columbus' Cabin Boy.
--Little Girl Lost.
--The Mountain Boy.
--Silver Tip, My Crippled Coyote.
Templin, Thomas J. & Olson, Janice K., eds. Teaching in Physical Education.
Tempsky, Alexa Von see Von Tempsky, Alexa.
Ten Cate, A. Richard. Oral Histology: Development, Structure & Function.
Tendler, Moshe. Pardes Rimonim.
Tenenbaum, Aaron M., jt. auth. see Augenstein, Moshe.
Tenenbaum, Frances. Gardening with Wildflowers.
--Over Fifty-Five Is Not Illegal.
Tenenbaum, Frances, jt. auth. see Martin, Alice A.
Tenenbaum, Frances, jt. auth. see Meras, Phyllis.
Tenenbaum, J. Martin & Witken, Andrew, eds. Physical & Biological Approaches to Computational Vision.
Tenenbaum, Joseph F. Underground, the Story of a People.
Teng, Ssu-Yu. Protest & Crime in China: A Bibliography.
Tengbom, Luverne, jt. auth. see Tengbom, Mildred.
Tengbom, Mildred. The Bonus Years.
--Is Your God Big Enough?
--Why Waste Your Illness: Let God Use It for Growth.
Tengbom, Mildred & Tengbom, Luverne. Fill My Cup, Lord: Meditations on Word Pictures in the New Testament.
Tenn, William. The Seven Sexes.
Tennant, Emma. The Bad Sisters.
--The Half-Mother.
--Wild Nights.
Tennant, Eugenia L. American Christmases: From the Puritans to the Victorians.
Tennant, Neil, jt. auth. see Schilcher, Florian Von.
Tennant, Roger. Joseph Conrad.
Tennenhouse, Leonard, ed. The Practice of Psychoanalytic Criticism.
Tennessee Nurses' Association Staff. An Apple a Day. Burd, Shirley & White, Linda S., eds.
Tennessee. Supreme Court Staff & Michie Company Staff, eds. Tennessee Court Rules Annotated. Walter, Richard W. & Cole, Bonnie C.
Tennyson, Alfred. Poems.
--Poems of Tennyson. Ricks, Christopher, ed.
--Tennyson.
--Works of Tennyson. Tennyson, Hallam, ed. Incl. Vol. 1; Vol. 2; Vol. 3; Vol. 4; Vol. 5; Vol. 6; Vol. 7; Vol. 8; Vol. 9. Greenwood.
Tennyson, Hallam, ed. see Tennyson, Alfred.
Tennyson, W. Wesley & Hansen, L. Sunny. Career Development Education: A Program Approach for Teachers & Counselors.
Tenpas, Margaret L. Bridge to Blue Hill.
Ten Seldam, R. E. & Helwig, E. B. Histological Typing of Skin Tumours.
Tentler, T. Sin & Confession on the Eve of the Reformation.
Teodorescu, E. C., et al, trs. see Bartok, Bela & Suchoff, Benjamin.
Teodosiu, C., jt. auth. see Dinca, F.
Teplov, L., jt. auth. see Vladmirov, S.
Tepper, Albert. Speech Communication: Theory & Practice.
Teranishi, Roy. Agricultural & Food Chemistry: Past, Present, Future.
Terblanche, H. J. Teach Yourself Afrikaans.
Tercentenary of Scientific Hydrology Staff. Three Centuries of Scientific Hydrology, 1674-1974: Papers, Paris, 1974.
Terebilov, V. The Soviet Court.
Terence. The Comedies of Terence. Copley, Frank O., ed.
Terenius, L. Y., jt. ed. see Kosterlitz, H. W.
Tereshchenko, Nicholas. A Look at Fourth Way Work: A System of Esoteric Exercises Based on the Work of Gurdjieff.
Teresi, Dick, jt. auth. see Hecht, Jeff.
Ter Haar, D. L. D. Landau.
--The Old Quantum Theory.
Ter-Haar, D. & Henin, F. Lectures on Selected Topics in Equilibrium & Non-Equilibrium Statistical Mechanics.
Ter Haar, D., ed. Problems in Quantum Mechanics.
Ter Haar, D., ed. see Kapitza, P. L.
Ter Harr, D., ed. see Elgaroy, O.
Terhune, Frances W., ed. Census Handbook, 1980: Florida Counties.
Terjeson, Thomas. Ellis Island & Me.
Terkel, Studs. Division Street: America.
--Working.
--Working.
Terlouw, Jan. Winter in Wartime.
Terman, Douglas. First Strike.
--Shell Game.
Terman, Douglas C. Free Flight.
Terminello, Joanne, ed. The Energy Directory 1983.
--The New Biotechnology Marketplace: Japan.
--The New Biotechnology Marketplace: U. S. & Canada.
Terner, Janet & Pew, W. L. The Courage to Be Imperfect: The Life & Work of Rudolf Dreikurs.
Ternon, Yves. Armenian Cause.
Terpstra, P. & Codd, L. W. Crystallometry.
Terpstra, Vern. International Marketing.
Terrace, Herbert S., jt. ed. see Bever, Thomas G.
Terrace, Vincent. Television Nineteen Seventy to Nineteen Eighty.
Terraine, John. The Life & Times of Lord Mountbatten.
Terrell, James C., jt. auth. see Daniel, Wayne W.
Terrien, James S., tr. Prophecies & Revelations about the Jesuits.
Terrien, Samuel. Holy Week.
Terrill, Ross. The White-Boned Demon: A Biography of Madame Mao Zedong. Golbitz, Pat, ed.
Terrill, Tom E. & Hirsch, Jerrold, eds. Such As Us: Southern Voices of the Thirties.
--Such As Us: Southern Voices of the Thirties.
Terris, Susan. No Scarlet Ribbons.
Terry, Ann. Secret of the Diamond Fireside.
Terry, Ann, jt. auth. see Terry, Keith.
Terry, Ann, et al. Mormons & Women.
Terry, Charles, tr. see Higuchi, Tadahiko.
Terry, Charles, tr. see Matsushita, Konosuke.
Terry, Charles S., tr. see Itoh, Teiji.
Terry, Charles S., tr. see Naito, Akira.
Terry, George R., jt. auth. see Stallard, John J.
Terry, Janice J. Mistaken Identity: Arab Stereotypes In Popular Writing.
Terry, John R. America's Revolutionary Spirit: The Evangelical Religious Heritage of the Nation.
Terry, Keith & Terry, Ann. To Love Again.
Terry, Mitchell. The Science of Teaching Art.
Terry, R. C. Victorian Popular Fiction, 1860-80.
Terry, W. Richard Cragun.
Terry, Walter, jt. auth. see Rennert, Jack.
Tertullianus, Quintus S. Opera.
Terwiel, B. J. A History of Modern Thailand.
Terwillegar, Jane, jt. auth. see Miller, Rosalind.
Terwilliger, Robert E. Christian Believing.
Terzakis, Angelos. Homage to the Tragic Muse. Anagnostopoulos, Athan, tr. from Gr.
Terzani, Tiziano. Behind the Forbidden Door: Travels in Unknown China.
--Behind the Forbidden Door: Travels in Unknown China.
Terzis, Julia K. Microreconstruction of Nerve Injuries.
--Peripheral Nerve Surgery.
Tesch, F. W. The Eel: Biology & Management of Anguillid Eels. Greenwood, Jennifer, tr.
Teschner, Richard V. Spanish Orthography, Morphology & Syntax for Bilingual Educators.
Tesconi, Charles A. Schooling in America: A Social Philosophical Perspective.
TeSelle, Eugene. Christ in Context: Divine Purpose & Human Possibility.
Teski, Marea, et al. A City Revitalized: The Elderly Lose at Monopoly.
Tesla Museaum Staff. Nikola Tesla: Tribute.

Authors

Tesla Museum Staff. Nikola Tesla: Colorado Spring Notes 1899-1900.
Tesla, Nikola. My Inventions: Moji Pronalasci.
TESOL Professional Standards Committee. Profiles of Selected ESL Programs & Their Staff Employment Conditions: ESL in Higher Education.
--Profiles of Selected ESL Programs & Their Staff Employment Conditons: ESOL Programs Outside the U. S.
Tessier, Thomas. Finishing Touches.
--The Nightwalker.
--Phantom.
Tessitore, John, ed. Issues Before the 41st General Assembly of the United Nations.
Test, M. A., jt. ed. see Stein, L. I.
Testa, Fulvio. The Ideal Home.
Testa, R. B., ed. Aerostructures, Selected Papers of Nicholas J. Hoff.
Testrake, John & Wimbish, Dave. Triumph over Terror on Flight 847.
Teter, Don. Goin' Up Gandy.
Teternikov, Fedor. The Old House & Other Tales.
Tether, Graham. Skunk & Possum.
Tetley, R. M. Small Cruiser Navigation.
Tetsuzo Tanikawa, jt. ed. see Shufunotomo Editorial Staff.
Tetzlff, Judith & Nama, Prabharathie G. How to Examine Your Breasts: A Guide to Breast Health Care.
Teubner, Christian & Wolter, Annette. Best of Cooking for All Occasions.
Teunissen, John J., ed. see Williams, Roger.
Teutsch, Gotthard M. & Von Loeper, Eisenhart, eds. Intensivhaltung von Nutztieren aus ethischer, rechtlicher und ethologischer Sicht.
Tevis, Walter. The Hustler.
--The Man Who Fell to Earth.
Tevoedjre, Albert. Poverty: Wealth of Mankind.
Tewary, V. K. Mechanics of Fibre Composites.
Teweles, Richard J. & Bradley, Edward S. The Stock Market.
Teweles, Richard J., et al. The Commodity Futures Game: Who Wins? Who Loses? Why?
--The Commodity Futures Game: Who Wins? Who Loses? Why?
Texas A & M University Library Staff. Energy Bibliography & Index.
Texas Critic Editors. Best Restaurants of Texas.
Texas Homes Editors. The Grand Homes of Texas. Richardson, Ann, ed.
Texas Instruments Engineering Staff. High Speed CMOS Logic Circuits Data Book.
--Optoelectronic Data Book.
Texas Instruments Engineering Staff, ed. Telecommunications Circuits Data Book.
Texas Instruments Engineering Staff. TTL Data Book.
--TTL Data Book.
--TTL Data Book.
Texas Instruments Inc. M O S, Special-Purpose Bipolar Integrated-Circuits & R-F Power Transistor Circuit Design.
Texas Instruments, Inc., Engineering Staff. MOS Memory Data Book, Nineteen Eighty-Six.
Texas Instruments, Inc. Staff. Designing with TTL Integrated Circuits.
--Transistor Circuit Design.
Texas Instruments Staff. Sourcebook for Programmable Calculators.
Texas Press Women's Assn. Texas Press Women's Cookbook.
Textile Institute Staff. International Textile Directory.
Textile Museum, Washington D. C. Rug & Textile Arts: A Periodical Index, 1890-1982.
Tey, Josephine. The Franchise Affair.
--A Shilling for Candles.
Teyler. Brain, Mind, & Behavior. Chaput, Linda & Mauer, Jim, eds.
Teynac, Francoise, et al. Wallpaper: A History.
Tezenas du Montcel, Henri. Dictionnaire des Science de la Gestion.
TFP Sullivan Staff, ed. Environmental Statutes.
--U. S. Environmental Protection Agency Guidebook, 1984-1985.
Thacker, Cathy G. The Wildfire Trace.
Thacker, Jada. Finally the Pawn.
Thacker, Ronald. Accounting Principles-Working Papers: Group B.
Thacker, Tony, jt. auth. see Key, Mike.
Thackeray, Alec. You'll Need a Guardian Angel.
Thackeray, Milton G., jt. auth. see Skidmore, Rex A.
Thackeray, William Makepeace. Vanity Fair.
--Vanity Fair.
--Vanity Fair. Shefter, Harry, et al, eds.
Thain, Richard J. Think Twice Before You Accept That Job.
Thain, William. Monitoring Toxic Gases in the Atmosphere.
Thakkur, Chandrasehekhar. Introduction to Ayurveda: The Science of Life.
Thakur, Shrinivas Y. Indian Economic Development: Retrospect & Prospect.
Thal, Helen M. Your Family & Its Money.
Thaler, Mike. Chocolate Marshmelephant Sundae.
--Un Hippopotame a Mange la Maitresse.
--Stuffed Feet.
--What's up Duck?
Thaler, Mike, jt. auth. see Cole, William.
Thalhammer, O., et al, eds. see European Congress on Perinatal Medicine, Sixth, Vienna, 1978.
Thalheimer, Alvin. Existential Metaphysics.
Thaman, Mary P. Manners & Morals of the Nineteen Twenties: A Survey of the Religious Press.
Thambipillai, Pushpa, ed. Southeast Asian Affairs, 1984.
Thames, J. L., jt. ed. see Kunkle, S. H.
Thane, Elswyth. Potomac Squire.
Thapa, Shyam, jt. auth. see Banister, Judith.
Thapar, Romila. Ancient India.
--Medieval India.
Thaqi, Nexhat. The Stroke.
Tharp, Roland & Wetzel, Ralph. Behavior Modification in the Natural Environment.
Tharpe, Jac L., ed. Walker Percy: Art & Ethics.
Tharu, S. Sense of Performance in the Post-Art Theatre.
Thass-Thienemann, Theodore. The Interpretation of Language. Incl. Vol. 1. Understanding the Symbolic Meaning of Language; Vol. 2. Understanding the Unconscious Meaning of Language. Aronson.
Thatcher, jt. auth. see Rogers.
Thatcher, David S., jt. auth. see Gooch, Bryan N.
Thatcher, Floyd & Thatcher, Harriett. Long Term Marriage.
Thatcher, Harriett, jt. auth. see Thatcher, Floyd.
Thatcher, James. Teaching Reading to Mentally Handicapped Children.
Thatcher, Martha. The Freedom of Obedience.
Thaves, Bob. Frank & Ernest.
Thaxton, Nolan A., jt. ed. see Bucher, Charles A.
Thayer, D. W., ed. Microbial Interaction with the Physical Environment.
Thayer, Lee, ed. Communication: Concepts & Perspectives.
Thayer, Louis, ed. Fifty Strategies for Experiential Learning: Book One.
--Fifty Strategies for Experiential Learning: Book Two.
Thayer, Nelson S. Spirituality & Pastoral Care.
Thayer, Tiffany. Thirty-Three Sardonics.
Thayer, William R. The Life & Times of Cavour.
Thayse, Harris. Professional Bar Service Management.
Theal, George M. History of the Boers in South Africa.
Thear, Katie. Practical Rabbit-Keeping.
Theden, G., jt. ed. see Becker, G.
Theilman, K. Dictionary of Biochemistry.
Theimer, Francois. Le Guidargus des Poupees de Collection.
Theisen, R. Quantitative Electron Microprobe Analysis.
Theismann, Joe & Kindred, Dave. Theismann.
Theissen, Gerd. A Critical Faith: A Case for Religion. Bowden, John, tr. from Ger.
--The Miracle Stories of the Early Christian Tradition. Riches, John, ed. McDonagh, Francis, tr.
Thelen, Herbert A. The Classroom Society: The Construction of Educational Experience.
Thelwell, Michael. The Harder They Come.
Thenebe, Carl. Touching Closeness.
Thenius, E. Fossils & the Life of the Past. Crook, B. M., tr. from Ger.
Theocaris, P. S. Moire Fringes in Strain Analysis.
Theodore, Chris A. Managerial Statistics: A Unified Approach.
Theodore, Louis. Air Pollution Control for Hospitals & Other Medical Facilities.
Theodore, Louis & Buonicore, Anthony J., eds. Air Pollution Control Equipment: Selection, Design, Operation & Maintenance.
Theodoresco, Rado, jt. auth. see Hengartner, Walter.
Theoharis, Athan. The Yalta Myths: An Issue in U. S. Politics, 1945-1955.
Theoharis, Athan G., ed. Beyond the Hiss Case: The FBI, Congress, & the Cold War.
Theoretical Physics International Summer Institute, Bonn, 1974. Trends in Elementary Particle Theory: Proceedings. Rollnick, H. & Dietz, K., eds.
Theory Conference Staff. Theoretical Developments in Marketing: Proceedings of the Theory Conference, Phoenix, Arizona, February, 1980. Lamb, Charles W., Jr. & Dunne, Patrick M., eds.
Theosophical Research Centre, London Staff. Psychism & the Unconscious Mind.
Theran, Susan. Leonard's Annual Price Index of Art Auctions: 1985-1986 Auction Season.
--Leonard's Annual Price Index of Art Auctions, 1986-1987 Auction Seasons.
Theriault, Jean Y. & Jennings, Joseph. Full-Contact Karate.
Theriot, Nancy M., ed. New America: The Child in Contemporary America.
Thermophysical Properties Symposium Staff. Thermophysical Properties of Fluids: Proceedings of the Symposium, 8th.
Thernstrom, Stephan. Poverty & Progress: Social Mobility in a Nineteenth Century City.
Theroux, Alexander. The Great Wheadle Tragedy.
Theroux, Gary, jt. auth. see Gilbert, Bob.
Theroux, Paul. The Black House.
--The Kingdom by the Sea.
--London Snow.
--O-Zone.
--The Old Patagonian Express: By Train Through the Americas.
--Sunrise with Seamonsters: Travels & Discoveries 84.
--World's End & Other Stories.
Theroux, Paul, jt. auth. see Chatwin, Bruce.
Therrien, Vincent. Reaching Out: Together, Through the Holy Spirit.
Thesen, Arne. Winter Simulation Conference Proceedings, (Atlanta)
Thesleff, S., ed. Motor Innervation of Muscle.
Thesman, Jean. Running Scared.
Thew, Carol L., jt. ed. see Johnson, Carolyn E.
Thewlis, J., ed. Concise Dictionary of Physics.
Thews, G. E., et al. Human Anatomy, Physiology & Pathophysiology.
Thibault, Jacques A. see France, Anatole.
Thibaut, John & Walker, Laurens. Procedural Justice: A Psychological Analysis.
Thibodeau, jt. auth. see Booher.
Thibodeau, Gary A., jt. auth. see Anthony, Catherine P.
Thibodeau, Janice A., jt. auth. see Hawkins, Joellen B.
Thie, John F., et al. Touch for Health.
Thie, Paul R. An Introduction to Linear Programming & Game Theory.
Thiel, E. & Thierfelder, S., eds. Leukemia: Recent Developments in Diagnosis & Therapy.
Thiel, Y. Greer. Artists & People.
Thiele, Thom. Computerized Knitting.
Thiele, Victoria. Clinical Nutrition.
Thielen, Thomas W. The Complete Guide to Gun Shows.
Thielicke, Helmut. Being a Christian When the Chips Are Down. Anderson, H. George, tr. from Ger.
--The Doctor as Judge of Who Shall Live & Who Shall Die. Cooperrider, Edward A., tr. from Ger.
--Faith the Great Adventure.
--How Modern Should Theology Be? Anderson, H. George, tr. from Ger.
--How the World Began: Man in the First Chapters of the Bible. Doberstein, John W., tr. from Ger.
--How to Believe Again. Anderson, H. George, tr. from Ger.
--I Believe: The Christian's Creed. Anderson, H. George & Doberstein, John W., trs. from Ger.
--Life Can Begin Again: Sermons on the Sermon on the Mount. Doberstein, John W., tr. from Ger.
Thien Binh, Vu see Binh, Vu T.
Thienell, G. M. My Battle with Low Blood Sugar.
Thierauf, Robert J. & Niehaus, John F. Study Guide to Accompany an Introduction to Data Processing for business & Management.
Thierfelder, S., jt. ed. see Thiel, E.
Thiery, Herman see Daisne, Johan, pseud.
Thiess, Susan, jt. auth. see Carver, Robert C.
Thiessen, Diane, et al. Elementary Mathematical Methods.
Thiffault, Mark. The Complete Survival Guide.
--Fishermen's Digest.
Thigpen, Janet. Power Volleyball for Girls & Women.
Thigpen, M. Elton & Maw-Cheng Yang. International Cotton Market Prospects.
Thigpen, Paul. Stories in the Sky.
Thijn, C. J. Arthrography of the Knee Joint.
Thijssen, H. O., ed. Liber Amicorum Presented to Prof. Dr. Wm. Penn.
Thimann, I. C. Montmorillon: Portrait of a Provincial Town.
--A Short History of French Literature.
Thimm, B. M. Brucellosis: Distribution in Man, Domestic & Wild Animals.
Thimme, Diether, jt. ed. see Bowie, Theodore.
Thimme, Jurgen, ed. Art & Culture of the Cyclades in the Third Millennium B. C. Cornford, A. & Getz-Preziosi, P., trs. from Ger.
Thinley, Karma. The History of the Sixteen Karmapas of Tibet. Stott, David, ed.
Thio, Alex. Deviant Behavior.
--Deviant Behavior.
Third European Congress. Prenatal Diagnosis. Murken, J. D., et al, eds.
Thirring, W., ed. see Boltzmann Equation Symposium Staff.
Thirsk, H. R. & Harrison, J. A. A Guide to the Study of Electrode Kinetics.
Thirsk, H. R., ed. Electrochemistry.
Thirsk, Joan. English Peasant Farming: The Agrarian History of Lincolnshire from Tudor to Recent Times.
Thiselton-Dyer, Thomas F. British Popular Customs, Present & Past.
--Folk-Lore of Plants.
Thistlewood, David. Herbert Read-Formlessness & Form: An Introduction to His Aesthetics.
Thivend, P., jt. auth. see Ruckebusch, Y.
Thobaben, Robert G., jt. ed. see Piediscalzi, Nicolas.
Thoburn, John T. Primary Commodity Exports & Economic Development: Theory, Evidence, & a Study of Malaysia.
Thoburn, Robert, jt. auth. see Haines, Helen S.
Thody, A. J., ed. The MSH Peptides.
Thody, Philip & Evans, Howard. Mistakable French: A Dictionary of Words & Phrases Easily Confused.
Thoelke, Shay, jt. auth. see Neilson, Stefan.
Thom, Randy, et al. AudioCraft: An Introduction to the Tools & Techniques of Audio Production.
Thoma, Henry F. The American Prospect: Insights into Our Next One Hundred Years.
Thoma, M., ed. see Egardt, B.
Thoma, Marta. Graphic Illustration: Tools & Techniques for Beginning Illustrators.
Thoma, R. W., ed. Industrial Microbiology.
Thomae, H. Beobachtung und Beurteilung von Kindern und Jugendlichen.
Thoman, Evelyn B., ed. Origins of the Infant's Social Responsiveness.
Thoman, Richard S. & Corbin, Peter. The Geography of Economic Activity.
Thomas. Natural Washington.
Thomas, jt. auth. see Polgar.
Thomas, ed. Teen-Age Underwater Adventure.
Thomas, A. D. Planning in Residential Conservation Areas.
Thomas, A. F. & Abbey, F. Calculational Methods of Interacting Arrays of Fissile Material.
Thomas, A. J., Jr., jt. auth. see Thomas, Ann V.
Thomas, A. J., Jr., jt. auth. see Thomas, Ann Van Wynen.
Thomas, A. R. B. Chess Techniques.
Thomas, Aaron J. & Thomas, Ann. Dominican Republic Crisis, 1965. Carey, John, ed.
Thomas, Alastair H., jt. auth. see Elder, Neil.
Thomas & Leeds Staff. Skiers Directory & Almanac: 1983.
Thomas, Ann, jt. auth. see Thomas, Aaron J.
Thomas, Ann V. & Thomas, A. J., Jr. Legal Limits on the Use of Chemical & Biological Weapons.
--Non-Intervention: The Law & Its Import in the Americas.
Thomas, Ann Van Wynen & Thomas, A. J., Jr. Organization of American States.
--A World Rule of Law: Prospects & Problems.
Thomas, Art. Backpacking Is for Me.
Thomas, Arthur L. Financial Accounting: The Main Ideas.
Thomas, Benjamin E., et al. Africa.
Thomas, Benjamin P., ed. see Cadawallader, Sylvanus.
Thomas, Bill. American Rivers: A Natural History.
--The Island: A Native History of America's Coastal Islands.
Thomas, Bill & Thomas, Phyllis. Indiana: Off the Beaten Path, A Guide to Unique Places.
--Natural New York.
--Natural Washington.
Thomas, Bill, jt. auth. see Thomas, Phyllis.
Thomas, Brinley. International Migration & Economic Development.
Thomas Bros. Maps. Orange County Street Atlas, 1985.
--Riverside County Street Atlas, 1985.
--San Bernardino County Street Atlas, 1985.
--San Bernardino-Riverside Counties Street Atlas, 1985.
Thomas Bros. Maps Staff. Alameda - Santa Clara Counties Street Guide & Directory 1988.
--Alameda-Contra Costa Counties Street Atlas Combination 1985.
--Alameda-Contra Costa Counties Street Atlas Combination: 1987.
--Alameda-Contra Costa Counties Street Guide & Directory, 1988.
--Alameda County Street Atlas 1985.
--Alameda County Street Atlas: 1987.
--Alameda County Street Guide & Directory, 1988.
--Alameda-Santa Clara Counties Street Atlas & Directory, 1987.
--Alameda-Santa Clara Counties Street Atlas 1985.
--California Road Atlas & Driver's Guide, 1988.
--California Road Atlas 1986.
--Contra Costa County Street Atlas 1985.
--Contra Costa County Street Atlas: 1987.
--Contra Costa County Street Guide & Directory, 1988.
--Contra Costa-Solano Counties Street Atlas & Directory, 1988.
--Contra Costa-Solano Counties Street Guide & Directory, 1988.
--Contra Costa Street Guide & Directory, 1988.
--Golden Gate Counties Street Atlas 1986.
--Golden Gate: Marin, San Francisco, San Mateo & Santa Clara Counties Street Guide & Directory, 1987.
--Golden Gate Street Atlas & Directory, 1987.
--Golden Gate Street Guide & Directory 1988.
--King & Pierce Counties Street Guide & Directory, 1989.
--King-Pierce Counties Street Atlas & Directory, 1989.
--King-Pierce Counties Street Atlas, 1986.

--King-Pierce-Snohomish Counties Street Atlas & Directory, 1987.
--King-Pierce-Snohomish Counties Street Atlas, 1986.
--King-Snohomish Counties Street Atlas, 1986.
--King-Snohomish Counties Street Atlas & Directory, 1987.
--Los Angeles & Ventura Counties Thomas Guide, 1988.
--Los Angeles County Street Atlas, 1986.
Thomas Bros Maps, Staff. Los Angeles County Street Atlas 1987.
Thomas Bros. Maps Staff. Los Angeles County Street Guide & Directory Zip Code Edition 1988.
--Los Angeles-Orange Counties Street Atlas, 1986.
Thomas Bros Maps, Staff. Los Angeles-Orange Counties Street Atlas 1987.
Thomas Bros. Maps Staff. Los Angeles-Orange Counties Zip Code Street Atlas, 1986.
Thomas Bros Maps, Staff. Los Angeles-Orange Counties Zip Code Street Atlas 1987.
--Los Angeles-Ventura Counties Street Atlas 1987.
Thomas Bros. Maps Staff. Los Angeles Zip Code Street Atlas, 1986.
Thomas Bros Maps, Staff. Los Angeles Zip Code Street Atlas 1987.
Thomas Bros. Maps Staff. Marin County Street Atlas & Directory, 1986.
--Marin County Street Atlas, 1985.
--Marin County Street Guide & Directory 1988.
--Monterey County Street Atlas 1985.
--Nineteen Eighty-Six San Francisco County Street Atlas & Directory.
--Orange County Street Atlas, 1986.
Thomas Bros Maps, Staff. Orange County Street Atlas 1987.
Thomas Bros. Maps Staff. Orange County Zip Code Street Atlas, 1986.
--Orange-Los Angeles Counties Street Atlas, 1986.
Thomas Bros Maps, Staff. Orange-Los Angeles Counties Street Atlas 1987.
Thomas Bros. Maps Staff. Phoenix & Vicinity Street Atlas, 1986.
--Phoenix Metropolitan Area Street Atlas & Directory, 1986.
--Pierce County Street Atlas & Directory, 1989.
--Pierce County Street Atlas, 1987.
--Portland & Vicinity Street Atlas & Directory, 1987.
--Portland Metropolitan Street Atlas 1989.
--Riverside County Street Atlas, 1987.
--Riverside County Thomas Guide, 1988.
--Sacramento County Including Portions of Placer County Street Guide & Directory, 1988.
--Sacramento County Street Atlas 1985: Including Placer & El Dorado.
--Sacramento County Street Atlas: 1987.
--Sacramento-Solano Counties Street Atlas & Directory, 1980.
--San Bernadino County Street Guide & Directory, 1988.
--San Bernardino County Street Atlas, 1987.
--San Bernardino-Riverside Counties Census Tract.
--San Bernardino-Riverside Counties Street Atlas & Directory with Zip Codes, 1987.
--San Bernardino-Riverside Counties Street Atlas & Directory, 1987.
--San Bernardino-Riverside Counties Street Atlas, 1986.
--San Bernardino-Riverside Counties Street Guide & Directory 1989.
--San Bernardino-Riverside Zip Code Atlas: 1987.
--San Diego - Street Guide & Directory Including Imperial County, 1988.
--San Diego County Street Atlas & Directory, 1987.
--San Diego County Street Atlas, 1987: Including Imperial County.
--San Diego County Zip Code Atlas 1986.
--San Diego County Zip Code Street Atlas & Directory, 1987.
--San Diego-Orange Counties Combination Street Atlas, 1986.
Thomas Bros Maps, Staff. San Diego-Orange Counties Combination Street Atlas 1987.
Thomas Bros. Maps Staff. San Francisco County Street Atlas 1987.
--San Francisco County Street Guide & Directory 1988.
--San Francisco: Marin Counties Street Guide & Directory Census Tract Edition, 1987.
--San Mateo County Street Atlas & Directory, 1986.
--San Mateo County Street Atlas 1987.
--San Mateo County Street Guide & Directory 1988.
--Santa Barbara County, Including Portions of San Luis Obispo County Thomas Guide 1988.
--Santa Barbara County, Including Portions of San Luis Obispo County & Ventura County Thomas Guide 1988.
--Santa Barbara County Street Atlas 1985: Including San Luis Obispo.
--Santa Barbara County Street Atlas: 1987 (Including San Luis Obispo)
--Santa Barbara-Ventura Counties Street Atlas 1985, Including San Luis Obispo County.
--Santa Barbara-Ventura Counties Street Atlas: 1987 (Including San Luis Obispo County)
--Santa Clara - San Mateo Counties Street Guide & Directory 1988.
--Santa Clara County Street Atlas & Directory, 1986.
--Santa Clara County Street Atlas 1987.
--Santa Clara County Street Guide & Directory 1988.
--Santa Clara-San Mateo Counties Street Atlas & Directory 1987.
--Santa Clara-San Mateo Counties Street Atlas 1985.
--Snohomish County Street Atlas & Directory, 1987.
--Snohomish County Street Atlas, 1986.
--Solano County Street Atlas: 1988 (Plus the Cities of Woodland, Davis & Napa)
--Solano-Sonoma Counties Street Atlas & Directory, 1988.
--Sonoma County Street Atlas, 1988.
--Sonoma-Marin Counties Street Atlas, 1984.
--Ventura County Street Atlas 1985.
--Ventura County Street Atlas: 1986.
--Ventura County Street Atlas 1987.
--Ventura County Thomas Guide 1988.
--Ventura-Los Angeles Counties Street Atlas 1985.
--Ventura-Los Angeles Counties Street Atlas: 1988.
Thomas Bros.Maps. Los Angeles County Street Atlas, 1985.
Thomas Brothers Maps. California Road Atlas & Travel Guide.
--Los Angeles County Street Atlas, 1984.
--Los Angeles-Orange Counties Street Atlas, 1984.
--Los Angeles-Orange Counties Street Atlas, 1985.
--Riverside County Street Atlas 1984.
--San Bernardino County Street Atlas 1984.
--San Bernardino-Riverside Counties Street Atlas 1984.
--San Diego County Street Atlas 1984.
Thomas Brothers Maps Staff. Monterey County Street Guide & Directory, 1987.
--Orange County Street Atlas 1984.
--Sonoma-Marin Counties Street Atlas 1988.
Thomas, Bruce. Men for Boot Hill.
Thomas, C. K., jt. auth. see Sastry, N. S.
Thomas, C. William & Henke, Emerson O. Auditing: Theory & Practice.
Thomas, Cal. Book Burning.
Thomas, Champ. How to Create a Super Boxer.
Thomas, Charles, ed. see International Fire Service Training Association Staff.
Thomas, Charles E., ed. see International Fire Services Training Association Committee.
Thomas, Charles L. Catalytic Processes & Proven Catalysts.
Thomas, Charles W., jt. auth. see Peterson, David M.
Thomas, Clayton L., ed. Taber's Cyclopedic Medical Dictionary.
--Taber's Cyclopedic Medical Dictionary.
Thomas, Colin J., jt. auth. see Herbert, David T.
Thomas, Craig. Wolfbane.
Thomas, D. M., tr. see Akhmatova, Anna.
Thomas, D. T. Engineering Electromagnetics.
Thomas, David. Henrik Ibsen.
--Henrik Ibsen.
--Reporting from Moscow: Soviet Successions. Laquer, Walter & Ledeen, Michael, eds.
Thomas, David & Morgan, Prys. Wales: The Shaping of a Nation.
Thomas, David A. Crete Nineteen Forty-One: The Battle at Sea.
--Principles of Sentencing: The Sentencing Policy of the Court of Appeal, Criminal Division.
--Utah Civil Procedure.
Thomas, David M. When God Is at Home with Your Family.
Thomas, David S. & Whitehouse, P. B. The Great Western Railway: One Hundred Fifty Glorious Years.
Thomas, David S., jt. auth. see Whitehouse, Patrick.
Thomas, Dennis, jt. auth. see Williams, Karel.
Thomas, Donald G. Silencer Patents, Vol. III: European Patents 1901-1978.
Thomas, Dorothy. Wigmore on Evidence: Indexes.
Thomas, E. J., tr. from Sanskrit. The Perfection of Wisdom: The Career of the Predestined Buddhas.
Thomas, Earl W. Syntax of Spoken Brazilian Portuguese.
--The Syntax of Spoken Brazilian Portuguese.
Thomas, Edward. Collected Poems.
--For the Birds & Other Stories.
--A Language Not to Be Betrayed: Selected Prose. Longley, Edna, ed.
Thomas, Ellen L. & Robinson, H. Alan. Improving Reading in Every Class: A Sourcebook for Teachers.
Thomas, Estelle W. Gift of Laughter.
Thomas, Evan, jt. auth. see Isaacson, Walter.
Thomas, Frank & Johnston, Ollie. Disney Animation: The Illusion of Life.
Thomas, Franklin F. The Luncheon Guest: Talks with College Men & Women about a Search for God.
Thomas, George B. Young Black Adults: Liberation & Family Attitudes.
Thomas, Gilbert. Collected Poems.
Thomas, Gordon. Desire & Denial: Celibacy & the Church.
Thomas, Gordon & Morgan-Witts, Max. Averting Armageddon.
Thomas, Gretchen, jt. auth. see Robbins, Judy.
Thomas, H. Randoph, jt. auth. see Willenbrock, Jack H.
Thomas, Howard C. & Jones, E. Anthony, eds. Recent Advances in Hepatology.
Thomas, Ianthe. Eliza's Daddy.
Thomas, J. A. An Introduction to Geological Maps.
Thomas, J. Andre, ed. Organ Culture.
Thomas, J. B. Shop Boy: An Autobiography.
Thomas, J. B., jt. ed. see Kassam, S. A.
Thomas, J. D. Facts & Faith: Reason, Science & Faith.
--Ion-Selective Electrode Reviews.
Thomas, J. D., ed. Ion-Selective Electrode Reviews.
--Ion-Selective Electrode Reviews.
--Ion-Selective Electrode Reviews.
--Ion-Selective Electrode Reviews.
--Ion-Selective Electrode Reviews.
--Sermons of Jim Bill McInteer.
--Sermons of M. Norvel Young.
--Sermons of Willard Collins.
Thomas, J. D., ed. see Abilene Christian University Lectureship Staff.
Thomas, J. D., ed. see Black, V. P.
Thomas, J. D., ed. see Cosofret, V. V.
Thomas, J. D., ed. see Goodpasture, B. C.
Thomas, J. D., ed. see Pullias, Athens C.
Thomas, J. D., et al. Sorrow & Joy.
Thomas, J. D. R. Ion-Selective Electrode Reviews.
Thomas, J. Heywood. Paul Tillich. Nineham, D. E. & Robertson, E. H., eds.
Thomas, J. Moulton. The Great Beyond: A Pastoral Approach to Death.
Thomas, James L., ed. Nonprint in the Elementary Curriculum: Readings for Reference.
Thomas, Jane R. Elizabeth Catches a Fish.
Thomas, Jean. Modern Oil-Hydraulic Engineering.
Thomas, John. The West Highland Railway.
Thomas, John A., ed. Advances in Sex Hormone Research. Singhal, Radhey L.
Thomas, John A., jt. ed. see Singhal, Radhey L.
Thomas, John I. Education for Communism: School & State in the People's Republic of Albania.
Thomas, Kas. Personal Aircraft Maintenance.
Thomas, Kas & Lambie, Jack. The Complete Guide to Homebuilt Rotorcraft.
Thomas, Kim, ed. see Stetser, David.
Thomas, Kurt & Hannon. Kurt Thomas on Gymnastics.
Thomas, L. & Rishbeth, H., eds. Photochemical & Transport Processes in the Upper Atmosphere.
Thomas, L. C. Game Theory & Its Application.
--The Identification of Functional Groups in Organophosphorus Compounds.
Thomas, L. R. European Trade Fairs: A Guide for Exporters.
Thomas, Lawrence G., ed. Philosophical Redirection of Educational Research.
Thomas, Leslie. Ormerod's Landing.
Thomas, Leslie G. Truth, the Millennium, & the Battle of Armageddon.
Thomas, Lewis. Late Night Thoughts on Listening to Mahler's Ninth Symphony.
Thomas, Lindon. Fundamentals of Heat Transfer.
Thomas, Louise. The Myth of Evolution.
Thomas, Lowell J. & Sanderson, Joy L. First Aid for Backpackers & Campers.
Thomas, Lyn, jt. ed. see Meredith, Philip.
Thomas, Lynda K. For All It May, or May Not Mean!
Thomas, M. Plant Physiology.
Thomas, M. Angele, ed. Education of the Gifted - A Challenge & a Promise: Special Issue of Exceptional Children, October 1981.
--Microcomputers in Special Education: Special Issue of Exceptional Children, October 1982.
--The Yet to Be Served: Special Issue of Exceptional Children.
Thomas, M. M. Christian Response to the Asian Revolution.
Thomas, M. Thomas, ed. Special Education & Pediatrics: A New Relationship. Special Issue of Exceptional Children.
Thomas, Margaret R., jt. auth. see Winger, Alan R.
Thomas, Maria. Come to Africa & Save Your Marriage: And Other Stories.
Thomas, Marlo, et al. Free to Be... You & Me.
Thomas, Martha. No Job for a Lady. Schnell, Judith, ed.
Thomas, Mary L. The Elves' Secret.
Thomas, Meirion & Belstead, John S. Aids to Postgraduate Surgery.
Thomas, Michael. Green Monday.
Thomas, Morris R. & Sabato, Larry, eds. Virginia Goverment & Politics: Readings & Comments.
Thomas, Neil. Playing Popular Piano.
Thomas, Nestina, ed. see Meltzer, Ida S.
Thomas, Norman. Great Dissenters.
--Is Conscience a Crime? Bd. with War's Heretics: A Plan for the Conscientious Objector. Thomas, Norman; Individual & the State. Baldwin, Roger. Garland Pub.
Thomas, Norman C. Rule Nine: Politics, Administration & Civil Rights.
Thomas, Norman L. Modern Logic: An Introduction.
Thomas, Northcote W. Anthropological Report on the Edo-Speaking Peoples of Nigeria.
Thomas, Owen P., jt. ed. see Levine, George.
Thomas, Phyllis & Thomas, Bill. Natural Chicago.
Thomas, Phyllis, jt. auth. see Thomas, Bill.
Thomas, R. & Yates, J. User Guide to the Unix Systems.
Thomas, R. C. Ion-Sensitive Intracellular Micro-Electrodes: How to Make & Use Them.
Thomas, R. Hinton. Liberalism, Nationalism & the German Intellectuals, 1822-1847.
Thomas, R. M., jt. ed. see Postlethwaite, T. N.
Thomas, R. W., ed. see Jones, C. E.
Thomas, Raju G., ed. The Great Power Triangle & Asian Security.
Thomas, Ralph H. Ultrasonics in Packaging & Plastics Fabrication.
Thomas, Ralph H., jt. auth. see Paterson, H. Wade.
Thomas, Rebecca, jt. auth. see Yates, Jean.
Thomas, Richard. Poems by Richard Thomas.
Thomas, Robert B. The Old Farmer's Almanac, 1986.
Thomas, Robert M. Advanced Techniques in AutoCAD.
Thomas, Roger. The Country Life Picture Book of Wales.
Thomas, Rosie. Love's Choice.
--Strangers.
Thomas, Ross. Briarpatch.
--Briarpatch.
--Chinaman's Chance.
--Eighth Dwarf.
--The Fools in Town Are on Our Side.
--The Fools in Town Are on Our Side.
--If You Can't Be Good.
--Missionary Stew.
--Missionary Stew.
--The Singapore Wink.
--Yellow-Dog Contract.
Thomas, Roy, ed. Insurance Information Sources.
Thomas, S. Bernard. Proletarian Hegemony in the Chinese Revolution & the Canton Commune of 1927.
Thomas, Sewell. Silhouettes of Charles S. Thomas, Colorado Governor & United States Senator.
Thomas, Sharon K. & Siegal, Marjorie. No Baths for Tabitha. Holland, Margaret, ed.
Thomas, Sharon K. & Siegel, Marjorie. No Baths for Tabitha.
Thomas, Stephen D. The Last Navigator.
Thomas, Susan, jt. auth. see Kater, David A.
Thomas, Timoux. Think Thin Today.
Thomas, Tony, et al. The Hollywood Professionals, Vol. 2: Wood, King & Milestone.
Thomas, Tracy Y. Plastic Flow & Fracture in Solids.
Thomas, Vinod. Differences in Income, Nutrition, & Poverty Within Brazil.
Thomas, Violet, et al. Records Management Applications.
Thomas, W. A. The Finance of British Industry, Nineteen Eighteen to Nineteen Twenty-Six.
Thomas, W. T., jt. auth. see Harvey, Lori.
Thomas, Walter, jt. auth. see Langer, Victor.
Thomas, Wilbur. General George H. Thomas, the Indomitable Warrior.
Thomas, Wilbur D. General James "Pete" Longstreet.
Thomas, William A., ed. Indicators of Environmental Quality.
Thomas, William E. So You Want to Be a Dancer.
Thomas, William I. W. I. Thomas on Social Organization & Social Personality. Janowitz, Morris, ed.
Thomas, William L., jt. auth. see Barham, Jerry N.
Thomas, William W., III, jt. auth. see National Underwriter Co. Staff.
Thomas, Wolfgang H. Economic Development in Namibia: Toward Acceptable Development Strategies for Independent Namibia.
Thomas a Kempis. The Imitation of Christ.
--Imitation of Christ.
Thomases, Martha, jt. auth. see Pelzman, Fran.
Thomasma, David, jt. auth. see Bergsma, Jurrit.
Thomason, Mary E., jt. auth. see Swabb, Barbara S.
Thomassen, Cora E., ed. Cooperation Between Types of Libraries: The Beginnings of a State Plan for Library Services in Illinois.

Authors

Thomasson, Henri. The Pursuit of the Present: Journal of Twenty Years in the Gurdjieff Work. Hands, Rina, tr.

Thome, Richard J. & Tarrh, John M. MHD & Fusion Magnets: Field & Force Design Concepts.

Thomee, V. Galerkin Finite Element Methods for Parabolic Problems.

Thome-Kozmiensky, K. J., ed. Recycling Berlin Seventy-Nine.

Thomis, Malcolm I. A Place of Light & Learning: The University of Queensland's First Seventy-Five Years.

Thomison, Dennis, jt. auth. see Schlachter, Gail.

Thomlinson, Ralph. Sociological Concepts & Research: Acquisition, Analysis, & Interpretation of Social Information.

Thomopoulos, N. Applied Forecasting Methods.

Thompsom. Manual of Structural Kinesiology.

Thompson. The Hitchhikers.

Thompson & Proctor. A Concise Textbook of Hematology.

Thompson & Swallow. Animals Around Us.

Thompson, jt. auth. see Strickland.

Thompson, ed. Canadian Minerals Year Book, 1983-84.

Thompson, jt. ed. see Strickland.

Thompson, et al. Adult Health Management: Guidelines for Nurse Practitioners.

Thompson, Andrew D. When Your Child Learns to Choose.

Thompson, Ann M. & Wood, Marcia D. Management Strategies for Women: Self-Tests, Helpful Hints, Wit & Wisdom & Superb Management Strategies for Woman.

Thompson, Anthony, ed. National Library Buildings.

Thompson, Anthony W. & Bernstein, I. M., eds. Effect of Hydrogen on Behavior of Materials: Proceedings of Symposium, Jackson Lake, Wyoming, 1975.

Thompson, Anthony W., jt. ed. see Bernstein, I. M.

Thompson, Anthony W., ed. see TMS Staff & AIME Staff.

Thompson, Arthur A., Jr. Economics of the Firm: Theory & Practice.

Thompson, Arthur A., Jr. & Strickland, A. J., III. Strategy & Policy.

Thompson, Arthur A., Jr. & Strickland, A. J., 3rd. Strategy Formulation & Implementation: Tasks of the General Manager.

Thompson, Arthur A., Jr., jt. auth. see Strickland, A. J.

Thompson, Barbara R., jt. auth. see Spickard, Anderson.

Thompson, Ben. A History of the Lumber Business at Davis, West Virginia.

Thompson, Betty. A Chance to Change: Women & Men in the Church.

Thompson, Bob. Guide to California.

Thompson, Brenda & Giesen, Rosemary. Bones & Skeletons.

--Flags.

--Gold & Jewels.

--The Story of Steel.

Thompson, Brenda & Overbeck, Cynthia. The Children's Crusade.

Thompson, Bruce. Black Walnut for Profit: A Guide to Risks & Rewards.

Thompson, C. J. Hand of Destiny: The Folk-Lore & Superstition of Everyday Life.

--Love, Marriage & Romance in Old London.

--The Lure & Romance of Alchemy.

--Magic & Healing.

--Mysteries & Secrets of Magic.

--Mysteries of History, with Accounts of Some Remarkable Characters & Charlatans.

--Mystery & Art of the Apothecary.

--The Mystery & Lore of Apparitions, with Some Account of Ghosts, Spectres, Phantoms & Boggarts in Early Times.

--Mystery & Lure of Perfume.

--The Mystic Mandrake.

--Quacks of Old London.

Thompson, Carey C., ed. Institutional Adjustment: A Challenge to a Changing Economy.

Thompson, Carol L., et al, eds. The Current History Encyclopedia of Developing Nations.

Thompson, Carolyn H. Human Organ Transplantation & Public Policy.

Thompson, Charles. Wild Notes from the Lyre of a Native Minstrel.

Thompson, Charles L. & Bell, Johnny F. Language Arts Bulletin Boards.

Thompson, Chris. Care & Repair of Small Marine Diesels.

Thompson, Christine E. Decision Support Systems: A Bibliography, 1980-1894.

--Management Information Systems Bibliography.

--The Works of Zbigniew Kazimierz Brzezinski.

Thompson, Conrad M. Mender of Broken Hearts: How Christ Gives Us Courage to Live.

Thompson, Craig R., tr. see Erasmus, Desiderius.

Thompson, D. E. God's Abundant Supply.

Thompson, D. V., Jr., tr. see Cennini, C. D'Andrea.

Thompson, David. David Thompson's Narrative of His Explorations in Western America, 1784-1812. Tyrrell, J. B., ed.

Thompson, David A. Five Steps Toward a Better Marriage.

Thompson, David L. Unfinished Heartbeats: Poems.

Thompson, David M., ed. Nonconformity in the Nineteenth Century.

Thompson, Debbie. Guide to London Keep-Fit Clubs & Dance Centres.

Thompson, Denise. Flaws in the Social Fabric: Homosexuals & Society in Sydney.

Thompson, Doris V. Chart Your Own Stars.

Thompson, Dorothy L. Plenty.

Thompson, E. Yoga Cookbook.

Thompson, E. Brad & Papaconstantinou, John, eds. DNA: Protein Interactions & Gene Regulation.

Thompson, E. Margaret. The Carthusian Order in England.

Thompson, E. P. & Smith, Dan, eds. Protest & Survive.

Thompson, E. Seymer. The Meno of Plato.

Thompson, E. V. Republic! A Novel of Texas.

Thompson, Edgar T. The Plantation: An International Bibliography.

Thompson, Eleanor S. The Little Angel Who Would Not Obey.

Thompson, Eric. T. S. Eliot: The Metaphysical Perspective.

Thompson, Ernest T. Presbyterians in the South. Incl. Vol. 1. 1607-1861; Vol. 2. 1861-1890; Vol. 3. 1890-1972. Westminster John Knox.

--Through the Ages: A History of the Christian Church.

Thompson, F. & Hayward, G. G. Structural Analysis Using Virtual Work.

Thompson, Frances. Mountain Relics.

Thompson, Frank J. Health Policy & the Bureaucracy: Politics & Implementation.

Thompson, Fred, ed. Regulatory Regimes in Conflict: Problems of Regulation in a Continental Perspective.

Thompson, George. Prison Life & Reflections.

Thompson, George C. & Brady, Gerald P. Essential CPA Law Review.

--Shortened CPA Law Review.

--Shortened CPA Law Review.

Thompson, Gerald. Edward F. Beale & the American West.

Thompson, Gordon B. Memo from Mercury: Information Technology Is Different.

Thompson, Grahame. Conservative Economic Policy: 1979-1984.

Thompson, Helen, tr. see Simenon, Georges.

Thompson, Homer B. California Juvenile Court Deskbook.

Thompson, Howard A. Great Writing in Marketing.

Thompson, Hunter S. Hell's Angels: The Motor Cycle Gangs.

Thompson, Ian E. & Melia, Kath M. Nursing Ethics.

Thompson, J. Foundations of Vocational Education: Social & Philosophical Concepts.

Thompson, J., jt. auth. see Vane, H.

Thompson, J. A., tr. see Laxness, Halldor.

Thompson, J. E. Algebra for the Practical Worker.

--Arithmetic for the Practical Worker.

--Calculus for the Practical Worker.

--Geometry for the Practical Worker.

--Mathematics Library for the Practical Worker.

Thompson, J. Eric. Thomas Gage's Travels in the New World.

Thompson, Jacqueline & Image Industry Publications Staff, eds. Directory of Personal Image Consultants 1986-1987.

Thompson, James A., Jr., jt. auth. see Zimmer, Michael J.

Thompson, James C., ed. Gastrointestinal Hormones: A Symposium.

Thompson, James M. Louis Napoleon & the Second Empire.

Thompson, James R., jt. auth. see Tapia, Richard A.

Thompson, Jane. Learning Liberation: Women's Response to Men's Education.

Thompson, Jean. My Wisdom.

Thompson, Jim. The Kill-Off.

Thompson, John. Trailer Life's Secrets of Successful RVing: Detailed Tips & Hints for Successful RV Trips.

Thompson, John O., ed. Monty Python: Complete & Utter Theory of the Grotesque.

Thompson, John S. The Mechanism of the Linotype. Bidwell, John, ed. Bd. with History of Composing Machines. Garland Pub.

Thompson, Joseph W. Selling: A Managerial & Behavioral Science Analysis.

Thompson, Joyce. The Blue Chair.

--Thirty Five-Cent Thrills.

--Willie & Phil.

Thompson, Julian. No Picnic.

Thompson, Julian F. Simon Pure.

Thompson, June. No Flowers by Request.

Thompson, June M., jt. auth. see Bowers, Arden C.

Thompson, Keith. Introducing the Macintosh Office.

Thompson, Kenneth, jt. ed. see Tunstall, Jeremy.

Thompson, Kenneth W., ed. see Kertesz, Stephen.

Thompson, L., ed. Robert Frost: The Early Years, 1894-1915.

--Robert Frost: The Years of Triumph, 1915-1938.

Thompson, L., ed. see Frost, Robert.

Thompson, L., ed. see Garcia, Ronda.

Thompson, Larry W., jt. ed. see Gallagher, Dolores.

Thompson, Leonard, et al. Southern African History Before 1900: A Select Bibliography of Articles.

Thompson, Leroy. Elite Unit Insignia of the Vietnam War: An Illustrated Reference Guide for Collectors.

--Uniforms of the Indo-China & Vietnam Wars.

--Uniforms of the Soldiers of Fortune.

--United States Airborne Forces, 1940-1986.

Thompson, Linda J. & Johnson, Marlys C. Dollars for Scholars Student Aid Catalog: New Hampshire Edition. Citizen's Scholarship Foundation of America Staff, ed.

Thompson, Linda J., jt. auth. see Johnson, Marlys C.

Thompson, Linda L. Consumer Mathematics.

Thompson, Liz. Bringing Up a Mentally Handicapped Child.

Thompson, Louis M. & Troeh, Frederick. Soils & Soil Fertility.

Thompson, M. Keith. Caring for an Elderly Relative.

Thompson, Marilou B., ed. Poets of the River City.

Thompson, Melvin R. Why Should I Hire You? How to Get the Job You Really Want!

Thompson, Michael & Walsh, J. N. Handbook of Inductively-Coupled Plasma Spectrometry.

Thompson, Mollie. Of Caesar's Household. Clanton, Charles, ed.

--When You're in You're Out.

Thompson, Morris M. Maps for America: Cartographic Products of the United States Geological Survey & Others.

Thompson, Olive R. Devil & I.

Thompson, Orin D. Even If I'm Bad: Sermons for Children.

Thompson, Paul. Our Common History.

Thompson, Paul E. & Werbel, Leslie M. Antimalarial Agents: Chemistry & Pharmacology.

Thompson, Philip C. Quality Circles.

Thompson, R. A. Techniques in Clinical Immunology.

Thompson, R. A., ed. Recent Advances in Clinical Immunology.

Thompson, R. A. & Rose, Noel R., eds. Recent Advances in Clinical Immunology.

Thompson, R. G., jt. auth. see Kim, Y. Y.

Thompson, R. Motson. Nietzsche & Christian Ethics.

Thompson, Ralph B., ed. Florida Statistical Abstract, 1973.

--Florida Statistical Abstract, 1974.

Thompson, Ray. After Eighteen Eighty Three: One Hundred Years of Organized Veterinary Medicine in Pennsylvania.

Thompson, Richard. An Introduction to Physical Signs.

Thompson, Richard B. College Algebra.

--Intermediate Algebra: An Individual Learning System.

Thompson, Richard E. Helping Hospital Trustees Understand Physicians.

Thompson, Richard F., jt. auth. see Ornstein, Robert E.

Thompson, Robert. The Pocket Encyclopedia of California Wines.

Thompson, Robert L., jt. auth. see Seeley, Vernon D.

Thompson, Robert W., ed. The Machinability of Engineering Materials.

Thompson, Roger, jt. ed. see Allen, H. C.

Thompson, Russell G., et al, eds. The Cost of Energy & a Clean Environment.

Thompson, Ruth P. The Giant Horse of Oz.

Thompson, S. & Kahn, J. H. The Group Process As a Helping Technique.

Thompson, Sandra. Wild Bananas. Johnson, Joyce, ed.

Thompson, Silvanus P. Calculus Made Easy.

Thompson, Theodore R. Intensive Care of Newborn Infants: A Practical Manual.

Thompson, Thomas. Lost.

--Outlaw Valley.

Thompson, Thomas, Jr. Games & Graphics for the TI 99-4A.

Thompson, Tommy. Script Letter: Its Form, Construction & Application.

Thompson, Travis & Dockens, William S., eds. Application of Behaviour Modification.

Thompson, Vernon. Reading Imaginative Literature.

Thompson, W. Scott, ed. The Third World: Premises of U. S. Policy.

Thompson, Wayne, ed. Air Leadership: Proceedings of a Conference at Bolling Air Force Base, Apr. 13-14, 1986.

Thompson, Wayne N. Responsible & Effective Communication.

Thompson, William A. A Change of Air: Climate & Health.

--Herbs That Heal.

Thompson, William B. Introduction to Plasma Physics.

Thompson, William I. Islands Out of Time: A Memoir of the Last Days of Atlantis.

Thompson, Zadock. Natural History of Vermont.

Thompson-Awiakta, Marilou B. Abiding Appalachia: Where Mountain & Atom Meet.

Thoms, William J., ed. Anecdotes & Traditions, Illustrative of Early English History & Literature.

Thomsen, Charles B. CM: Developing, Marketing & Delivering Construction Management Services.

Thomsen, Gregory & McInerny, Paul M. An Accent Guide: One Hundred Fifty-One Tax Deductions You Can Take.

Thomsen, Helen, jt. auth. see Thomsen, John.

Thomsen, Helen S. This Was the Son of God.

Thomsen, Ian. Flutie! The Story of Boston College Quaterback Doug Flutie, Winner of the 1984 Heisman Trophy.

Thomsen, John & Thomsen, Helen. Teacher's Manual for the Man for All Time.

Thomsen, Moritz. Farm on the River of Emeralds.

Thomsen, Russel J. Atlas of Intrauterine Contraception.

Thomsen, Vilhelm. On the Influence of Germanic Languages on Finnish & Lapp.

Thomson. Dictionary of Medical Ethics & Practice.

--Occlusion.

Thomson, Betty F. The Changing Face of New England.

--The Shaping of America's Heartland: The Landscape of the Middle West.

Thomson, Chilton. Old Timbers.

Thomson, D. M., ed. Assessment of Immune Status by the Leukocyte Adherence Inhibition Test.

Thomson, David. The Babeuf Plot: The Making of a Republican Legend.

Thomson, Dorothy Lampen. Adam Smith's Daughters.

Thomson, F. P. Money in the Computer Age.

Thomson, George. The Butterflies of Scotland: A Natural History.

--The First Philosophers.

Thomson, George H., ed. see Forster, E. M.

Thomson, George L. New Better Handwriting.

Thomson, Helen, tr. see Simenon, Georges.

Thomson, J. S., ed. International Youth in Achievement.

Thomson, James. The Plays of James Thomson. Backscheider, Paula R., ed.

Thomson, John, photos by. China: The Land & Its People.

Thomson, June. Sound Evidence.

Thomson, Malcolm M. The Beginning of the Long Dash: A History of Timekeeping in Canada.

Thomson, Monet, ed. see Phillips, Gary.

Thomson, Norman, jt. auth. see Easton, Brian.

Thomson, Pat. Rhymes Around the Day.

Thomson, Patricia, ed. Wyatt: The Critical Heritage.

Thomson, Peter. Shakespeare's Theatre.

Thomson, Philip. The Grotesque.

Thomson, R. H., ed. Marine Natural Products.

Thomson, R. L., ed. Adtimchiolan Chreidimh.

Thomson, Robert W., et al, trs. see Gregory.

Thomson, Ruth. Making a Book.

Thomson, S. J., jt. ed. see Lenihan, J. M.

Thomson, Scott, jt. auth. see McCleary, Lloyd.

Thomson, Selina. Birds on a Banana Tree or How Not to Retire & Move to Florida.

Thomson, Susan O. American Book Design & William Morris.

Thomson, Virgil. A Virgil Thomson Reader.

Thomson, W. T. Agricultural Chemicals, Bk. One, 1985-86: Insecticides, Acaracides, & Ovicides.

--Agricultural Chemicals, Bk. Two, 1986-87: Herbicides.

--Agricultural Chemicals, Book I: Insecticides.

--Agricultural Chemicals, Book III: Fumigants, Growth Regulators, Repellents, Rodenticides.

Thomson, W. T., jt. auth. see Page, B. G.

Thondup, Tulko. Buddhist Civilization in Tibet.

Thooft, et al, eds. Recent Developments in Gauge Theories.

Thorburn, David, ed. Initiation: Stories & Short Novels on Three Themes.

Thoreau, David. City at Bay.

--Dynasty of Power.

--The Santanic Condition.

Thoreau, Henry David. The Annotated Walden. Stern, Philip V., ed.

--Cape Cod. Lunt, Dudley C., ed.

--Clear Sky, Pure Light: Encounters with Henry David Thoreau. Childs, Christopher, ed.

--Henry David Thoreau: Essays, Journals & Poems. Flower, Dean S., ed.

--The Illustrated World of Thoreau. Chapnick, Howard, ed.
--In the Woods & Fields of Concord: Selections from the Journals of Henry David Thoreau. Harding, Walter, ed.
--The Maine Woods. Lunt, Dudley C., ed.
--The Natural History Essays. Sattelmeyer, Robert, ed.
--On Man & Nature.
--Thoreau: People, Principles, & Politics. Meltzer, Milton, ed.
--Thoreau: People, Principles & Politics. Meltzer, Milton, ed.
--The Variorum Civil Disobedience. Harding, Walter, ed.
--The Variorum Walden. Harding, Walter, ed.
--The Variorum Walden. Harding, Walter, ed. Bd. with The Variorum Disobedience. WSP.
--Walden. Lunt, Dudley C., ed.
--Walden.
--Walden: A Writer's Edition. Ziff, Larzer, ed.
--Walden: Down the River with Henry Thoreau.
Thorensen, Marilyn J., ed. see Shirley, James.
Thoresen, Carl E. The Behavior Therapist.
Thorington, Richard, Jr., ed. see Institute for Laboratory Animal Resources Staff.
Thorkelson, Willmar. Lutherans in the U. S. A.
Thorman, Carolyn. Fifty Years of Eternal Vigilance.
Thorman, Richard. Bachman's Law.
Thorn, John. The Armchair Aviator.
Thorn, John, jt. ed. see Reuther, David.
Thorn, N. A., ed. Secretary Mechanisms of Exocrine Glands.
Thorn, Richard S. The Rising Yen.
Thorn, Richard S., jt. ed. see Malloy, James M.
Thornburg, Hershel & Pinnegar, Stefinee. Middle School Research Studies, 1984.
Thornburg, Newton. Dreamland.
--Dreamland.
--Knockover.
Thornbury, Robert. The Changing Urban School.
Thorndike, Ashley H., jt. auth. see Neilson, William A.
Thorndike, Edward L. & Lorge, Irving. Teachers' Word Book of Thirty Thousand Words.
Thorndike, Lynn, tr. University Records & Life in the Middle Ages.
Thorndike, Ruth M. God's Everlasting Arms of Love.
Thorne. Introductory Statistics for Psychology.
Thorne, Anne P. Spectrophysics.
Thorne, Barrie. Language & Sex. Henley, Nancy, ed.
Thorne, D. Wynne, jt. auth. see Thorne, Marlowe D.
Thorne, Florence C. Samuel Gompers: American Statesman.
Thorne, Frank. Ghita of Alizarr.
--Ghita Two: The Thousand Wizards of Urd.
Thorne, Jerry. My Uncle.
Thorne, Marlowe D. & Thorne, D. Wynne. Soil, Water & Crop Production.
Thorne, Oakleigh H. see Lochmoeller, Donald C.
Thorne, Robert, ed. Fugitive Facts.
Thorne, Samuel E., jt. ed. see Berkowitz, David S.
Thornely, Arthur, ed. see Means, R. S., Company, Inc. Staff.
Thorner, Marvin E. & Herzberg, R. J. Non-Alcoholic Food Service Beverage Handbook.
Thornes, John & Brunsden, Denys. Geomorphology & Time.
Thornhill, Ira M., ed. see Dick, Philip K.
Thornhill, William T. Complete Handbook of Operational & Management Auditing.
Thornley, Jenny. Workers Co-Operatives: Jobs & Dreams.
Thornton, C. S. & Bromley, S. C., eds. Vertebrate Regeneration.
Thornton, Carol A., jt. auth. see Bley, Nancy S.
Thornton, J. L. & Tully, R. I. Scientific Books, Libraries, & Collectors: Supplement to the Third Edition.
Thornton, John L. Medical Librarianship.
Thornton, Lynne. Les Orientalistes, Peintres Voyageurs 1828-1908.
--The Orientalists, Painter-Travellers 1828-1908.
Thornton, M. J. Nazism Nineteen Eighteen to Nineteen Forty-Five.
Thornton, Mary C. The Church & Freemasonry in Brazil, 1872-1875.
Thornton, Michael. Royal Feud: The Dark Side of the Love Story of the Century.
Thornton, Susan M., jt. ed. see Frankeburg, William K.
Thoroughbred Owners & Breeders Association Staff. The Breeder's Guide for 1980.
--Sires of Runners of 1978: Supplement.
Thorp, John. Free Will: A Defence Against Neuro-Physiological Determinism.
Thorp, Raymond. Viper.
Thorp, Robert L., jt. auth. see Bower, Virginia.
Thorp, Roderick. Nothing Lasts Forever.
--Rainbow Drive.
Thorpe, Clarence D., ed. Complete Poems & Selected Letters: Keats.
Thorpe, J. A. & Kumpel, P. G. Elementary Linear Algebra.
Thorpe, J. E., ed. Rhythmic Activity of Fishes.
Thorpe, Marion, ed. Peter Pears: A Tribute on His 75th Birthday.
Thorpe, Neal O. Cell Biology.
Thorpe, Robert T. Tramp & I.
Thorpe, Sylvia A., tr. see Ramon Y Cajal, Santiago.
Thorpe, W. A. History of English & Irish Glass to 1969.
Thorpe, William H. Science, Man, & Morals.
Thorsby, E., et al. Genetics of Human Histocompatibility Antigens & Their Relation to Disease.
Thorson, Esther, ed. Simulation in Higher Education: Papers from the Denison Simulation Center, Denison University, Granville, Ohio.
Thorson, Gunner. Life in the Sea.
Thorson, John, jt. auth. see White, D. C.
Thorstenson, Clark T., jt. auth. see Heaton, Israel C.
Thorton, Don. The Eggbeater Book: The First & Last Word about Man's Greatest Invention.
Thorwald, Jurgen. Century of the Detective.
--Crime & Science: The New Frontier in Criminology.
--The Illusion: Soviet Soldiers in Hitler's Armies. Winston, Richard & Winston, Clara, trs.
--Science & Secrets of Early Medicine: Egypt-Babylonia-India-China-Mexico-Peru.
Thota, Anand R. Emily Dickinson & Metaphysical Tradition.
Thrainsson, Hoskuldur. On Complementation in Icelandic.
Thrall, Robert M., jt. ed. see Tsokos, Chris P.
Thrasher, Crystal. The Dark Didn't Catch Me.
--End of a Dark Road.
Thrasher, Jack D., jt. ed. see Cameron, Ivan L.
Thrasher, Max B. Tuskegee: Its Story & Its Work.
Threadgold, L. T. The Ultrastructure of the Animal Cell. Kerkut, G. A., ed.
Threlfall, Robert, jt. auth. see Carley, Lionel.
Thring, Meredith W. Robots & Telechirs.
Thro, Ellen. Making Friends with AppleWriter II.
Throop, Isabel A., ed. see Rohrer, Norman B.
Throop, John R. Shape up from the Inside Out.
Throop, Thomas. Computer Bridge.
Throughbred Owners & Breeders Association Staff. Stakes Winners of 1978: Supplement.
Throwe, Anita N., jt. auth. see Fought, Sharon G.
Thrower, Norman J. & Bradbury, D. E., eds. Chile-California Mediterranean Scrub Atlas.
Thubron, Colin. A Cruel Madness. Johnson, Joyce, ed.
--The God in the Mountain.
Thucydides. Pylos Four Hundred Twenty-Five B. C. Wilson, J., ed.
Thuesen, Gerald J., jt. auth. see Fabrycky, Walter J.
Thuillier. Lexique Anglais-Francais des Termes Appartenant Aux Technques En Usage I.G.N.
Thulin, Richard L. The Lesser Festivals 1: Saints' Days & Special Occasions. Achtemeier, Elizabeth, et al, eds.
Thulin, Richard L., jt. auth. see Furnish, Victor P.
Thum, Gladys & Thum, Marcella. The Persuaders: Propaganda in War & Peace.
Thum, Marcella. Exploring Black America.
Thum, Marcella, jt. auth. see Thum, Gladys.
Thumann, Albert, jt. auth. see Fairmount Press, Inc. Staff.
Thumboo, Edwin. Gods Can Die.
Thumboo, Edwin, ed. The Second Tongue: An Anthology of Poetry from Malaysia & Singapore.
Thun, Matteo & Shimizu, F., eds. The Italian Design: Descendants of Leonardo da Vinci.
Thune, Ensaf & Prigozy, Ruth. Short Stories: A Critical Anthology. English, D. Anthony, ed.
Thurau, K., ed. see International Symposium on Renal Transport, West Germany, 1968.
Thurber, Donald N. D'Nealian Manuscript: A Continuous Stroke Approach to Handwriting.
Thurber, James. The Great Quillow.
Thurber, Kenneth J. Distributed Processor Communication Architecture.
--A Pragmatic View of Distributed Processing Systems.
Thurber, Kenneth J. & Masson, G. M. Distributed Processor Communication Architecture.
Thurber, Kenneth L. Computer Systems Requirements.
Thurian, Max. Our Faith: Basic Christian Belief. Chisholm, Emily, tr. from Fr.
Thurley, Geoffrey. The Turbulent Dream: Passion & Politics in the Poetry of W. B. Yeats.
Thurman, Anne S., ed. see Thurman, Howard.
Thurman, Howard. For the Inward Journey: The Writings of Howard Thurman. Harding, Vincent & Thurman, Anne S., eds.
--With Head & Heart: The Story of Howard Thurman.
Thurman, Judith. Flashlight & Other Poems.
--I Became Alone.
--I'd Like to Try a Monster' S Eye.
--Lost & Found.
Thurman, Judith see Moore, Lilian.
Thurman, Mark, jt. auth. see Bodger, Joan.
Thurman, Ronald G., et al, eds. Alcohol & Aldehyde Metabolizing Systems.
Thurneysen, Eduard. Sermon on the Mount.
Thurneysen, Eduard, jt. auth. see Barth, Karl.
Thurn-Taxis, Mary. The Tea Party of Miss Moon: From GrandMama's Tales.
Thurow, L., jt. auth. see Heilbroner, Robert L.
Thurow, Lester. The Zero-Sum Solution: Building a World Class American Economy.
Thurow, Lester, jt. auth. see Heilbroner, Robert L.
Thurow, Lester C., jt. auth. see Heilbroner, Robert L.
Thurston, David B. Design for Flying.
--Home Built Aircraft.
Thurston, Mark. How to Change Attitudes & Emotions.
Thwaite, Ann. Edmund Gosse: A Literary Landscape, 1849-1928.
Thwaite, Ann, ed. My Oxford, My Cambridge. Hayman, Ronald.
Thwaite, Anthony. Beyond the Inhabited World: Roman Britain.
--Larkin at Sixty.
Thwaite, Daniel. Seething African Pot, a Study of Black Nationalism, 1882-1935.
Thwaite, Mary K. From Primer to Pleasure in Reading.
Thwaites, Jeanne C. Starting & Succeeding in Your Own Photography Business.
Thwaites, Lyndsay. Rosie's Wonderful Dances.
Thwing, Annie H. Crooked & Narrow Streets of the Town of Boston, 1630-1822.
Thyagarajan, B. S., jt. auth. see Phillips, John P.
Thygerson, Alton L. Disaster Survival Handbook.
--The First Aid Book.
Thygesen-Blecher, Lone, tr. see Lagercrantz, Rose.
Thyne, James M. Psychology of Learning & Technique of Teaching.
Thys, J., et al, eds. see Aerobic Gram-Negative Bronchopneumonia Symposium Staff.
Tiao, George C., ed. see Box, George E.
Tibbetts, A. M. & Tibbetts, Charlene. What's Happening to American English?
Tibbetts, A. M., jt. auth. see Tibbetts, Charlene.
Tibbetts, Charlene & Tibbetts, A. M. Strategies: A Rhetoric & Reader.
Tibbetts, Charlene, jt. auth. see Tibbetts, A. M.
Tibbits, Donald F. Language Disorders in Adolescents.
Tibbles, Thomas H. Buckskin & Blanket Days: Memoirs of a Friend of the Indians.
--The Ponca Chiefs: An Account of the Trial of Standing Bear. Graber, Kay, ed.
Tibell, G., ed. High Energy Physics & Nuclear Structure: Proceedings of the 5th International Conference, Uppsala, Sweden-1973.
Tiber, Elliott, jt. auth. see Ernotte, Andre.
Tiberghien, Jacques. The Pascal Handbook.
Tice, Terrence N. & Slavens, Thomas P. Research Guide to Philosophy.
Tice, Terrence N., tr. see Schleiermacher, Friedrich.
Ticer, James W. Radiographic Technique in Veterinary Practice.
Tickell, C. Climatic Change & World Affairs.
Tickell, James. American Express Pocket Guides to Mexico.
Tickle, John. Un Estudio de la Biblia. Diaz, Olimpia, Sr., tr. from Eng.
--Un Estudio de la Biblia. Diaz, Olimpia, tr.
Tickle, Phyllis. Figs & Fury.
--The Story of Two Johns.
Tickle, Phyllis, jt. ed. see Piper, Vangie.
Tickle, Phyllis A. The City Essays.
--On Beyond Koch.
Tickton, S. G., et al. Idea Handbook for Colleges & Universities, 1981: Educational Opportunities for Handicapped Students.
Tickton, Sidney G. Idea Handbook, 1982: Attracting & Retaining Highly Qualified Young Faculty Members at Colleges & Universities.
Tidball, Derek. The Social Context of the New Testament: A Sociological Analysis.
Tideman, jt. ed. see Ladd.
Tidman, D. A. Shock Waves in Collisionless Plasmas. Krali, N. A., ed.
Tidwell, Samuel M., jt. auth. see Herrington, Robert W., Jr.
Tidwell, Victor H., jt. auth. see Raby, William L.
Tidyman, Ernest. Big Bucks.
--Big Bucks: The True, Outrageous Story of the Plymouth Mail Robbery... & How They Got Away With It.
Tieck, Ludwig & Brentano. Der Blonde Eckbert. Atkinson, Margaret E., ed.
Tiede, David L. Prophecy & History in Luke-Acts.
Tiede, David L. & Kavanagh, Aidan. Pentecost 1. Achtemeier, Elizabeth, et al, eds.
Tiede, Tom & Findleton, Jack. The Great Whale Rescue: An American Folk Epic.
Tiedemann, K. The Mesonephros of Cat & Sheep.
Tiedjens, V. A. More Food from Soil Science: The Natural Chemistry of Lime in Agriculture.
Tiedt, Iris M. Exploring Books with Children.
Tiegs, Cheryl. The Way to Natural Beauty.
Tiemeyer, Raymond. Ordination of Women.
Tien, John K. & Elliot, John F., eds. Metallurgical Treatises.
Tien, John K., et al, eds. Alloy & Microstructural Design.
Tien, Mary A. The Yellow Thread Cat.
Tierney, Alison, ed. Clinical Nursing Practice.
Tierney, B. Origins of Papal Infallibility 1150-1350.
Tierney, Brian. Ockham, the Conciliar Theory, & the Canonists. Oberman, Heiko A., ed.
Tierney, Richard L., jt. auth. see Smith, David C.
Tierney, William F. Modern Upholstering Methods.
Tietenberg, Thomas H. Environmental Economics.
Tietjen, Sari B. The Dog Judge's Handbook.
Tietze, Christopher, et al. Birth Control & Abortion.
Tietze, W., ed. Cities & Urbanism.
--The European North Calotte.
--Man-Made Landscape.
--Northern Frontier Problems.
--Settlement: The Most Important Productive Medium of Economic Man.
Tieu, Chang L. & Lienhard, John H. Statistical Thermodynamics.
Tiffany, J. M., jt. auth. see Blough, H. A.
Tiffany, J. M., jt. ed. see Blough, H. A.
Tiffany, Robert, ed. Cancer Nursing.
Tiffon, Y., jt. ed. see Smith, D. C.
Tiger, Edith, ed. In Re Alger Hiss.
Tiger, Lionel & Shepher, Joseph. Women in the Kibbutz.
Tiger, Miller R., jt. auth. see Minugh, Carol J.
Tighe, Mary Ann & Lang, Elizabeth E. Art America.
Tight, Malcolm, ed. Adult Learning & Education.
--Opportunities for Adult Education.
Tignor, R. Colonial Transformation of Kenya: The Kamba, Kikuyu, & Maasai from 1900-1939.
Tijerina, Andres A. History of Mexican Americans in Lubbock County, Texas.
Tiktin, Carl. The Hourglass Man.
--Ron.
Til, Cornelius Van see Van Til, Cornelius.
Til, John Van, jt. ed. see Smith, David H.
Til, William Van see Van Til, William.
Tilak, B. V., jt. ed. see Weissberger, N. L.
Tilberg, Cedric W. Revolution Underway: An Aging Church in an Aging Society.
Tilbury, Fred & Edward, Derek. Casework in Context: A Basis for Practice.
Tilden, J. W., jt. auth. see Garth, John S.
Tiley, Nancy A. Discovering DNA.
Tilgner, Linda. Let's Grow! Children's Gardening Fun Kit.
Tilke, M., jt. auth. see Bruhn, W.
Tilke, Max. Costume Patterns & Designs.
Tilkian, Sarko M., et al. Clinical Implications of Laboratory Tests.
Till, Geoffrey, jt. auth. see Ranft, Bryan.
Tillet, Gregory. The Elder Brother: A Bibliography of Charles Webster Leadheater.
Tillich, Paul. My Search for Absolutes: A Credo Perspective. Anshen, Ruth N., ed.
--World Situation. Sherman, Franklin, ed.
Tilling, Thomas, jt. auth. see Toney, Albert.
Tillinghast, Richard. Sewanee in Ruins.
Tillion, Germaine. The Republic of Cousins: Women's Oppression in Mediterranean Society.
Tillman, Albert A. Skin & Scuba Diving.
Tillman, K. The Rheumatoid Foot: Diagnosis, Pathomechanics, & Treatment. Goldie, Ian F., tr. from Ger.
Tillmann, Bernhard. A Contribution to the Functional Morphology of Articular Surfaces. Bargmann, Wolfgang & Doerr, Wilhelm, eds. Konorza, G., tr. from Ger.
Tillotson, Delight M., jt. auth. see Butnarescu, Glenda F.
Tillotson, Kathleen, jt. auth. see Butt, John.
Tillotson, Kathleen, ed. see Collins, Wilkie.
Tillson, Benjamin F. Mine Plant.
Tillstrom, Burr. The Dragon Who Lived Downstairs.
Tillyard, Eustace M. The Epic Strain in the English Novel.
--Five Poems, Fourteen Seventy-Eighteen Seventy: An Elementary Essay on the Background of English Literature.
Tilson, Marie & Law, Jane. Sources of Information in Transportation: Part 7, Pipelines.
Tilton, Eleanor M., intro. by see Holmes, Oliver W.
Tilton, Rafael. The Immortal Dragon of Sylene & Other Faith Tales.
Tilton, Richard C., jt. auth. see Pre Test Services, Inc.
Tim, O'Reilly & Todins, Grace. Managing UUCP & USENET. Dougherty, Dale, ed.
Timashkova, O. K. Scandinavian Social-Democracy Today.
Timber Engineering Company staff. Timber Design & Construction Handbook.
Timber Research & Development Association Staff. Timber in Excavations.
Timberg, Bernard, jt. ed. see Lawrence, John S.

Authors

Timberg, Thomas A. The Federal Executive: The President & the Bureaucracy.
--The Marwaris: From Traders to Industrialists.
Timberlake, Bob. The World of Bob Timberlake.
Timberlake, James H. Prohibition & the Progressive Movement, 1900-1920.
Timberlake, Richard H., Jr. The Origins of Central Banking in the United States.
Timbs, John. Clubs & Club Life in London with Anecdotes of Its Famous Coffee-Houses, Hostelries, & Taverns from the Seventeenth Century to the Present Time.
--Curiosities of London.
--English Eccentrics & Eccentricities.
--Historic Ninepins.
--Romance of London.
--Things Not Generally Known. Wells, David A., ed.
Time-Life Book Editors. Computer Basics.
Time-Life Books Editors. Arabian Peninsula.
--Artificial Intelligence.
--Australia.
--Brazil.
--Canada.
--China.
--The Commonsense Guide to Birth & Babies.
--Commonsense Guide to Birth & Babies.
--Computer Images.
--Computers Security.
--East Africa.
--Eastern Europe.
--Fabled Lands.
--The Fall of Camelot.
--France.
--Fresh Ways with Fish & Shellfish.
--Germany.
--Giants & Ogres.
--How Things Work in Your Home (and What to Do When They Don't)
--India.
--Israel.
--Italy.
--Japan.
--Major Appliances.
--Mexico.
--Psychic Powers.
--Puzzle Master.
--Scandinavia.
--Seekers & Saviors.
--Southeast Asia.
--Soviet Union.
--Spain.
--Spells & Bindings.
--Teaching Good Behavior.
Time-Life Books Editors & Gruppe, Henry. The Frigates.
Time-Life Books Editors & Lehane, Brendan. The Northwest Passage.
Time-Life Books Editors & Miller, Russell. The East Indiamen.
Time-Life Books Editors & Rousmaniere, John. Luxury Yachts.
Time-Life Books Editors, jt. auth. see Crocket, James U.
Time-Life Books Editors, jt. auth. see Maddocks, Melvin.
Time-Life Books Editors, jt. auth. see Walker, Bryce.
Time-Life Books Editors, jt. auth. see Wernick, Robert.
Time-Life Books Editors, jt. auth. see Whipple, A.
Time-Life Books Editors, jt. auth. see Whipple, A. B.
Time-Life Books Editors, jt. auth. see Wood, Peter.
Time-Life Books Editors, ed. International Great Meals in Minutes.
--Recreational Areas.
Time-Life Books Staff, ed. Decorative Techniques.
--Novel Materials.
Time Life Books Staff, ed. Restyling Your Wardrobe.
Time Magazine Staff. Present Status & Future Role of Risk Managers: A Survey of U. S. Risk Managers.
Timm, Carey. My Little Pony: A Book of Favorite Things to Touch & Feel.
Timm, Paul R. & Jones, Christopher G. Business Communication: Getting Results.
Timman, R., jt. auth. see Kuipers, L.
Timmer, Gerard, jt. auth. see Luitjters, Guus.
Timmerhaus, K. D. & Snyder, H. A., eds. Advances in Cryogenic Engineering.
Timmerman, John. A Layman Looks at the Names of Jesus.
Timmis, Gerald & Westveer, Douglas, eds. Cardiovascular Review 1982.
Timmis, Gerald C., et al. Cardiovascular Review: 1984.
Timmis, Gerald C., et al, eds. Cardiovascular Review 1983.
Timmons, Tim. Loneliness Is Not a Disease.
Timmons, Tim & Arterburn, Stephen. Growing up Addicted: Why Our Children Abuse Alcohol & Drugs & What We Can Do about It.
Timms, Kathleen. One Eyed Merchants.
Timms, Noel. Social Work Values: An Inquiry.
Timofeyev, A., tr. see Steinbach, Valeri.
Timofeyev, T. Workers in Society.
Timofeyev, T., jt. auth. see Fedoseyev, P.
Timoney, John F., jt. auth. see Gillespie, James H.
Timothy & Suares. Suddenly Poor: A Guide for the Downwardly Mobile.
Timothy, Christopher. Vet Behind the Ears.
Timothy, Mary. Jury Woman.
Timpe, A. Dale, ed. Corporate TrendTrac: Issues 7-88 Through 6-89.
Tims, Frank M. & Leukefeld, Carl G., eds. Relapse & Recovery in Drug Abuse.
Tindall, B. Allan, jt. ed. see Lancy, David F.
Tindall, David S. This Can't Be Me.
Tindall, Gillian. The Born Exile: George Gissing.
--Looking Forward.
Tindall, William N., et al, eds. Communication in Pharmacy Practice: A Practical Guide for Students & Practitioners.
Tindall, William Y. A Reader's Guide to James Joyce.
Tiner, John H. When Science Fails.
Tinervia, Joseph, ed. see Fruehling, Rosemary T. & Bouchard, Sharon.
Ting, Irwin, ed. Man in the Natural World.
Ting, Mei, ed. Echo.
Tingle, Donald A. & Fordyce, Richard A. Phases & Faces of the Moon: A Critical Evaluation of the Unification Church & Its Principles.
Tingley, Donald F., ed. Social History of the United States: A Guide to Information Sources.
Tingquan, Zhang, tr. see Mei'E, Ren, et al.
Tinker, Ben. Mexican Wilderness & Wildlife.
Tinker, Edward L. Gombo Comes to Philadelphia.
--Lafcadio Hearn's American Days.
Tinker, Edward L., ed. Odyssey of a Santo Domingan Creole.
Tinker, Irene, jt. ed. see Reining, Priscilla.
Tinkham, Sandra S. & Hardcastle, Bruce B., eds. National Inventory of Documentary Sources in the United States, Manuscript Division, Library of Congress Index 1983.
Tinkle, Lon. Texas.
Tinkle, Lon, intro. by. Texas: A Picture Tour.
Tinnell, Richard W. Television Symptom Diagnosis.
Tint, Herbert. France since Nineteen Eighteen.
Tinterow, Gary, jt. auth. see Cooper, Douglas.
Tintner, Gerhard & Sengupta, Jati K. Stochastic Economics: With Applications of Stochastic Processes, Control & Programming.
Tipler, Frank J., ed. Essays in General Relativity.
Tippens, Paul E. Applied Physics.
Tippin, G. Lee. The Arab.
Tippin, G. Lee & Patterson, Charles. The Heroes Who Fell from Grace.
Tipping, Richard K. Nearer by Far.
Tipps, Steve, et al. Nudges: IBM Logo Projects for Children.
Tipson, R. Stuart, jt. ed. see Zorbach, W. Werner.
Tipton, Keith & Dostert, P., eds. Mondamine Oxidase & Disease.
Tirabassi, Becky. My Daily Partner.
--Quietimes.
Tirapegui, Enrique, jt. ed. see Antoine, Jean-Pierre.
Tiruchelvan, Nellan, jt. ed. see Gunatilleke, Godfrey.
Tischler, Henry L., jt. auth. see Berry, Brewton.
Tischler, Henry L., et al. Introduction to Sociology.
--Introduction to Sociology.
Tischler, Nancy. Legacy of Eve: Women of the Bible.
Tischler, Nancy M. Dorothy L. Sayers: A Pilgrim Soul.
Tischner, Joseph. The Spirit of Solidarity. Zaleski, Marek B. & Fiori, Benjamin, trs.
Tisdale, Betsy. Guide to Adirondack Trails: Eastern Region. Burdick, Neal S., ed.
Tisdall, Archie, jt. auth. see Tisdall, Mary.
Tisdall, Mary & Tisdall, Archie. Grand Canaria & Eastern Canary Islands.
--Tenerife & Western Canary Islands.
Tisdall, Patricia. Agents of Change: The Development & Practice of Management Consultancy.
Tisdell, C. A. & McDonald, P. W. Economics of Fibre Markets: Interdependence Between Man-Made Fibres, Wool, & Cotton.
Tisdell, F. Science & Technology Policy: Priorities of Governments.
Tishler, William H. A Working Bibliography on Norwegian Vernacular Architecture.
Tiso, Francis, jt. auth. see Catholic Heritage Press Staff.
Tiso, Francis, et al, eds. Aging: Spiritual Perspectives.
Titard, Pierre L. Managerial Accounting: An Introduction.
Titchener, Edward B. Experimental Psychology: A Manual of Laboratory Practice.
Titchmarsh, Alan. The Step-By-Step Guide to Gardening Techniques.
Tite, M. S. Methods of Physical Examination in Archaeology.
Titherington, D. & Rimmer, J. G. Applied Mechanics.
Titlow, Richard E. Americans Import Merit: Origins of the United States Civil Service System & the Influence of the British Model.
Titmuss, F. H. Concise Encyclopedia of World Timbers.
Tittel, Josef, jt. ed. see Wengler, Wilhelm.
Tittler, Johnathan, tr. see Olivella, Manuel Z.
Tittler, Robert. Nicholas Bacon: The Making of a Tudor Statesman.
Tittler, Robert & Loach, Jennifer, eds. The Mid-Tudor Polity, c. Fifteen Forty to Fifteen Sixty.
Titunik, I. R., tr. see Ejxenbaum, B. M.
Titus, Christopher A., et al. STD Bus Interfacing.
Titus, Eve & Galdone, Paul. Anatole & the Pied Piper.
Titus, Jonathan A., et al. Commodore 64 Starter Book.
Titus, Jonathan S., et al. Apple II Interfacing.
Titus, William A. Wisconsin Writers.
Tiurikov, V. Bukhara: A Guide.
Tiusanen, Timo. Durrenmatt: A Study in Plays, Prose, Theory.
Tiwari, R. D. & Sharma, J. P. The Determination of Carboxylic Functional Groups.
Tiwarni, Kapil, ed. Indians in New Zealand: Studies in a Sub-Culture.
Tixier-Vidal, A. & Farquhar, Marilyn G., eds. The Anterior Pituitary.
Tizard, Ian R. Immunology: An Introduction.
Tjalsma, William, tr. see Erofeev, Venedikt.
Tjosvold, Dean & Johnson, David W. Productive Conflict Management: Perspectives for Organizations.
Tjur, Tue. Probability Based on Radon Measures.
Tkacz, Yuri, tr. see Luckyj, George.
Tlusty, J., jt. auth. see Koenigsberger, F.
TMI Kemeny Commission. Tech. Staff Anal.
TMS-AIME Fall Meeting, Niagara Falls,1976. Precipitation Processes in Solids: Proceedings of the TMS-AIME Fall Meeting, Niagara Falls, NY, 1976. Russell, K. C. & Aaronson, H. I., eds.
TMS-AIME Fall Meeting Symposium Staff. Boron in Steel: Proceedings of the TMS-AIME Fall Meeting Symposium, Milwaukee, WI, Sept. 16-20, 1979. Morral, J. E. & Banerji, S. K., eds.
TMS Staff & AIME Staff. Calculation of Phase Diagrams & Thermochemistry of Alloy Phases: Proceedings of the TMS-AIME Fall Meeting, Milwaukee, 1979. Chang, Y. A. & Smith, J. F., eds.
--Failure Modes in Composites II: Proceedings of the TMS-AIME Spring Meeting, Pittsburgh, 1976. Fleck, James N. & Mehan, Richard L., eds.
--Formability: Analysis, Modeling & Experimentation: Proceedings of the TMS-AIME Fall Meeting, Chicago, IL, 1977. Hecker, S. S., et al, eds.
--Formable HSLA & Dual-Phase Steels: Proceedings of the TMS-AIME Fall Meeting, Chicago, IL, 1977. Davenport, A. T., ed.
--Hardenability Concepts with Applications to Steels: Proceedings of the TMS-AIME Fall Meeting, Chicago, IL, 1977. Doane, D. V. & Kirkaldy, J. S., eds.
--New Developments & Applications in Composites: Proceedings of the TMS-AIME Fall Meeting, St. Louis, 1978. Kuhlmann - Wilsdorf, Doris & Harrigan, W. C., eds.
--Thermomechanical Processing of Aluminum Alloys: Proceedings of the TMS-AIME Fall Meeting, St. Louis, 1978. Morris, James G., ed.
--Work Hardening in Tension & Fatigue: Proceedings of the TMS-AIME Fall Meeting, Cincinnati, 1975. Thompson, Anthony W., ed.
Toai, Doan Van see Chanoff, David & Van Toai, Doan.
Toai, Doan van see Van Toai, Doan & Chanoff, David.
Toal, James E. Visions of Yesterday.
Tobach, Ethel, et al. Biopsychology of Development.
Tobey, Kathrene M. Church & Children Under Two.
--Learning & Teaching Through the Senses.
Tobias, Andrew. The Invisible Bankers: Everything the Insurance Industry Never Wanted You to Know.
--The Invisible Bankers: Everything You Always Wanted to Know About Insurance But Were Afraid to Ask.
--Money Angles.
--The Only Investment Guide You'll Ever Need.
Tobias, Cornelius A. & Todd, Paul, eds. Space Radiation Biology & Related Topics.
Tobias, Doris & Merris, Mary. The Golden Lemon: A Collection of Special Recipes.
Tobias, Henry. Music in My Heart, Borscht in My Blood.
Tobias, Joyce. Beyond Mindstorms: Teaching with IBM Logo.
Tobias, Richard C. The Art of James Thurber.
Tobias, S. The Effect of Creativity, Response Mode & Subject Matter Familiarity on Achievement from Programmed Instruction.
Tobias, S. A. & Koenigsberger, F., eds. Proceedings of the Thirteenth International Machine Tool Design & Research Conference.
Tobias, S. A. & Koenigsberger, T., eds. Proceedings of the Seventeenth International Machine Tool Design & Research Conference.
Tobias, S. A., ed. see Machine Tool Design & Research International Conference Staff, et al.
Tobias, Sheila. Succeed with Math: Every Student's Guide to Conquering Math Anxiety.
Tobias, Tobi. How Your Mother & Father Met.
Tobin, J. J. Shakespeare's Favorite Novel: A Study of the Golden Asse As Prime Source.
Tobin, Terence. Plays by Scots 1660-1800.
Tobin, Wallace E., III. Mariner's Pocket Companion, 1986.
--Mariner's Pocket Companion 1987.
--The Mariner's Pocket Companion 1988.
Tobler, John, jt. auth. see Stannard, Neville.
Toboldt, Bill. Fix Your Chevrolet.
Toboldt, William K. & Johnson, Larry. Automotive Encyclopedia.
Toby, Milton C., jt. auth. see Sager, Floyd C.
Tocci, Ronald J. Digital Systems: Principles & Applications.
Tocci, Ronald J. & Laskowski, Lester P. Microprocessors & Microcomputers: Hardware & Software.
Toch, Hans. Agents of Change: A Study in Police Reform.
--Violent Men.
Toch, Henry. Economics for Professional Studies.
Tocqueville, Alexis De see De Tocqueville, Alexis.
Tod, Osma G. & Del Deo, Josephine C. Designing & Making Handwoven Rugs: Techniques for Creating European, Oriental & American Rugs & Household Fabrics.
Toda, Kenji. Japanese Scroll Painting.
Todaro, George J., et al. Investigation of Oncogenic Viruses.
Todaro, Michael P. Economic Development in the Third World.
Today's Transport International Staff. Today's Fleet Maintainance: A Reader for Fleet Executives.
Todd, Charles B. In Olde Connecticut.
--In Olde Massachusetts: Sketches of Old Times & Places During the Early Days of the Commonwealth.
Todd, Colleen, jt. auth. see Schaffer, James.
Todd, Dale R. Willow's End.
Todd, Dallas. Cathouse Showdown.
Todd, Frank S. Waterfowl: Ducks, Geese & Swans of the World.
Todd, Frankie. Planning Continuing Professional Development. Hills, P. J., ed.
Todd, Gary Price. The Eternal Triangle (You, Your Neighbour & God)
Todd, H. Ralph, Jr., jt. auth. see Steinmetz, Lawrence L.
Todd, Helen, ed. see De Purucker, G.
Todd, Ian P. & Fielding, L. P. Alimentary Tract & Abdominal Wall (Colon, Rectum, & Anus)
Todd, J. F., jt. ed. see Price, D.
Todd, Janet M. Mary Wollstonecraft: An Annotated Bibliography of Her Works & Criticism.
Todd, John. Basic Numerical Mathematics, Vol. 2: Numerical Algebra.
--Luther: A Life.
Todd, John R., jt. auth. see Yeric, Jerry L.
Todd, Karen R., jt. auth. see Todd, Ronald.
Todd, Loreto. Tortoise the Trickster: And Other Folktales from Cameroon.
Todd, M. J. The Computation of Fixed Points & Applications.
Todd, Michael, Jr. & Todd, Susan M. A Valuable Property: The Life Story of Michael Todd.
Todd, Paul, jt. ed. see Tobias, Cornelius A.
Todd, Richard. Iris Murdoch.
Todd, Richard G. From Flowchart to Program.
Todd, Ronald & Todd, Karen R. Aim for a Job Working with Your Hands.
Todd, Ruthven, ed. see Gilchrist, Alexander.
Todd, Susan, jt. auth. see Edgar, David.
Todd, Susan M., jt. auth. see Todd, Michael, Jr.
Todd, Vivian E. & Heffernan, H. Years Before School: Guiding Preschool Children.
Todhunter, Hazel. Make It in Denim.
Todins, Grace, jt. auth. see Tim, O'Reilly.
Toepfer, Caroline T., et al. Environmental Psychology: Selected Readings.
Toeplitz, Otto, jt. auth. see Rademacher, Hans.
Toeppe, William F., jt. auth. see Leonard, William L.
Toesca, Maurice. Dictionnaire de la Contradiction.
Toff, Nancy. The Flute Book: A Complete Guide for Students & Performers.
Toffel, Neile M. My Husband, My Friend.
Toft, A. D., et al. Diagnosis & Management of Endocrine Diseases Including Diabetes Mellitus.
Toft, P., jt. ed. see Huck, P. M.
Togawa, Yukio. African Animals.
Tognoni, G., jt. ed. see Garattini, S.
Tohei, Koichi. Kiatsu.
Tokaev, G. A. Soviet Imperialism.

Tokheim, Roger L. Digital Electronics. Schuler, Charles A., ed.
Tokheim, Russell. Get the Message Out: Communication Techniques for Congregations.
Tokmakoff, George. P. A. Stolypin & the Third Duma: An Appraisal of the Three Major Issues.
Tokson, Elliot. Harem Games.
--When Dragons Dance.
Toland, John. A Collection of Several Pieces. Wellek, Rene, ed.
--Pantheisticon. Wellek, Rene, ed.
Tolbert, E. L., ed. An Introduction to Guidance: The Professional Counselor.
Tolbert, Emory J. UNIA & Black Los Angeles: Ideology & Community in the American Garvey Movement. Hill, Robert A., ed.
Tolbert, Mary Ann. Perspectives on the Parables: An Approach to Multiple Interpretations.
Tolbert, William R., jt. ed. see Feder, Joseph.
Tolchin, Martin, jt. auth. see Tolchin, Susan J.
Tolchin, Susan J. & Tolchin, Martin. Dismantling America: The Rush to Deregulate.
Toldi, Julius. American Kaleidoscope.
Toledo, Romeo T. Fundamentals of Food Process Engineering.
Toledo-Pereyra, Luis H., ed. The Pancreas: Principles of Medical & Surgical Practice.
Tolf, Robert. Country Inns of the Old South.
--Florida Restaurant Guide: Broward - Palm Beach Edition.
--How to Survive Your First Six Months in Florida.
Tolf, Robert W. Best Restaurants Florida's Gold Coast.
--Country Inns of the Old South.
--Country Inns of the Old South.
Tolgyessy, J., et al. Isotope Dilution Analysis.
Tolins, Stephen, jt. auth. see Brand, Janet.
Tolivar, Robin. In Love's Fury.
Tolkien, Baille, ed. see Tolkien, J. R. R.
Tolkien, Christopher, jt. ed. see Carpenter, Humphrey.
Tolkien, Christopher, ed. see Tolkien, J. R. R.
Tolkien, J. R. R. The Book of Lost Tales. Tolkien, Christopher, ed.
--The Father Christmas Letters.
--The Father Christmas Letters. Tolkien, Baille, ed.
--The Hobbit.
--Mr. Bliss.
--The Pictures of J. R. R. Tolkien.
Tolkien, J. R. R. & Swann, Donald. The Road Goes Ever on.
Tolle, Gordon J. Human Nature under Fire: The Political Philosophy of Hannah Arendt.
Tollefson, James W. The Language Situation & Language Policy in Slovenia.
Tolley, George S., et al. Agricultural Price Policies & the Developing Countries.
Tollison, Robert D., jt. auth. see Ekelund, Robert B.
Tolmacheva, V. O., et al. Mosaic: Russian for Children.
Tolman, Edward C. Behavior & Psychological Man: Essays in Motivation & Learning.
Tolmazin, D. Changing Coastal Oceanography of the Black Sea.
Tolor, Alexander & Deignan, Margaret C. Adjustment Problems in Children.
Tolson, Billy J. The Golden Book of Theology.
Tolstoi, A. Ordeal.
Tolstoi, D. M., ed. English-Russian Physics Dictionary.
Tolstoy, A. Nikita's Childhood.
--Peter the Great.
Tolstoy, Ivan. James Clerk Maxwell: A Biography.
Tolstoy, Leo. Fables, Tales, Stories.
--The Fruits of Enlightenment. Frayn, Michael, tr. from Rus.
--The Inevitable Revolution. Sampson, Ronald, tr.
--War & Peace.
Tolstoy, Nikolai. The Quest for Merlin.
--Stalin's Secret War.
--The Tolstoys: Twenty Generations of Russian History 1353 to 1983.
Tolve, Arthur. Standardizing Foodservice for Quality & Efficiency.
Tom, Baldwin H. & Allison, James P., eds. Hybridomas & Cellular Immortality.
Tom, Clara T. Clara Tom's Old Fashioned Method of Cantonese Chinese Cooking.
Tomain, Joseph P. Energy Law in a Nutshell.
Tomain, Joseph P. & Hollis, Shelia S. Energy Decision Making: The Interaction of Law & Policy.
Tomal, Daniel R. & Gedeon, David V. Principles & Practice of Electrical & Electronics Troubleshooting.
Tomalin, Claire. The Life & Death of Mary Wollstonecraft.
Tomalin, Ruth. Little Nasty.
--A Summer Ghost.
--W. H. Hudson: A Biography.
Toman, J., jt. ed. see Kuenzel, W.
Toman, W. An Introduction to Psychoanalytic Theory of Motivation.
Tomas, Andrew. Mirage of the Ages: A Critique of Christianity.
Tomasch, E. J. & Larmer, Oscar. A Foundation for Expressive Drawing.
Tomashevskii, Boris V. Teoriia Literatury Poetika.
Tomasino, Joseph, jt. auth. see Vasi, Susanne.
Tomaskovic-Devey, Donald, jt. auth. see Miller, S. M.
Tomboulian, Sherryl J., jt. auth. see Bowyer, Kevin W.
Tomczak, M., jt. ed. see Boje, R.
Tom Dieck, T. Transformation Groups & Representation Theory.
Tomek, Ivan. The First Book of Josef: An Introduction to Computer Programming.
Tomes, John. Belgium & Luxembourg.
--Holland.
--Scotland.
Tomimoto, Kenkichi, jt. auth. see Sanders, Herbert H.
Tomita, Jun & Tomita, Noriko. Japanese IKAT Weaving.
Tomita, K., jt. auth. see Joly, H. L.
Tomita, Kumasaku, jt. auth. see Joly, Henri L.
Tomita, Noriko, jt. auth. see Tomita, Jun.
Tomizuka, Carl & Emrick, Roy, eds. Physics of Solids at High Pressures.
Tomkies, Mike. Golden Eagle Years.
Tomkins, D. Michael. Trial & Error.
Tomkins, Jasper. The Catalog.
--Nimby.
--The Sky Jumps Into Your Shoes at Night.
Tomkins, Reginald P., jt. auth. see Popovych, Orest.
Tomkins, Thomas. Services. Buck, P. C., ed.
Tomlin, E. W. Psyche, Culture & the New Science: The Role of PN.
Tomlin, Gwynne, jt. auth. see Cherry, Joetta.
Tomlinson, Dorothy, ed. Walk in Dread: Twelve Classic Eerie Tales.
Tomlinson, Jill. Hilda, the Hen Who Wouldn't Give up.
Tomlinson, Jim. British Macroeconomic Policy Since 1940.
--Problems of British Economic Policy, 1870-1945.
Tomlinson, John, jt. ed. see Rauson, Stewart.
Tomlinson, M. An Introduction to the Chemistry of Benzenoid Components.
Tomlinson, Richard. Disability, Theatre & Education.
Tomonaya, S. Spin the Spin.
Tompkins, B. & Laney, D. H. Leica Pocket Book.
Tompkins, B. A. The Carpenter's Wife.
Tompkins, Barbara H., ed. see Tompkins, Walker A.
Tompkins, Dorothy C. Court Organization & Administration: A Bibliography.
--Local Public Schools: How to Pay for Them?
--Power from the Earth: Geothermal Energy.
--The Prison & the Prisoner.
--Research & Service: A Fifty Year Record.
--Selection of the Vice President.
--Strip Mining for Coal.
Tompkins, E. Berkeley, ed. Peaceful Change in Modern Society.
Tompkins, P., ed. see Lawrence, Sidney & Foy, George.
Tompkins, R. P. T., jt. auth. see Janz, George J.
Tompkins, Stuart R. The Triumph of Bolshevism: Revolution or Reaction?
Tompkins, Walker A. Santa Barbara History Makers. Tompkins, Barbara H., ed.
Ton, Mary E. For the Love of My Daughter.
Tondel, Lawrence C., jt. auth. see Practising Law Institute Staff.
Tondo, Clovis L. & Gimpel, Scott E. The C Answer Book.
Toner, Amy, jt. auth. see Baylin, Frank.
Toney, Albert & Tilling, Thomas. High Tech: How to Find & Profit from Today's New Super Stock.
Tong, Christopher, jt. auth. see Steinberg, Louis.
Tong, P., jt. ed. see Geers, T. L.
Tong, S. Y., jt. ed. see Vanselow, Ralf.
Tongg, Richard C., jt. auth. see Kuck, Loraine E.
Tongren, Sally. What's for Lunch: Animal Feeding at the Zoo.
Tongue, Ruth L. The Chime Child: Or, Somerset Singers - Being an Account of Some of Their Songs Collected over Sixty Years.
Tonks, Doris B. For Parents Only: Are Your Children Flowers or Weeds?
Tonndorf, Juergen, ed. Physiological Acoustics.
Tonomura, Yuji, jt. auth. see Fleischer, Sidney.
Tonsor, Stephen. Tradition & Reform in Education.
Tooke, Andrew. The Pantheon.
Tooker, Dan & Hofheins, Roger. Fiction! Interviews with Northern California Novelists.
Tooker, Dan & Hofheins, Roger, eds. Fiction! Interviwes with Northern California Novelist.
Toole, John K. A Confederacy of Dunces.
Toole, K. Ross, jt. auth. see Farr, William.
Toole, Vera A. The Realm of Feelings.
Tooley, R. V. Mapping of Australia.
Tooley, Ronald V. Some English Books with Coloured Plates.
Toolsie, Harold T. Repent, O Graduate.
Toomay, John C. Radar Principles for the Non-Specialist.
Toomay, Pat. The Crunch.
Toombs, Jane. Arapaho Spirit.
--The Scots.
Toomer, Clarence, jt. auth. see Chrisholm, Clarence E.
Toomer, Jean see Harrison, Paul C.
Toon, Peter. Protestants & Catholics: A Guide to Understanding the Differences.
Toon, Peter & Martin, Peter, eds. Evangelical Theology, Eighteen Thirty-Three to Eighteen Fifty-Six: A Response to Tractarianism.
Toon, Peter, ed. see Avis, Paul D.
Toon, Peter, jt. ed. see Martin, Ralph.
Toone, Lavern. Toone, Tune & Toon of America: A Family History.
Toong, Hoo-min D. & Gupta, Amar. Personal Computers.
Tootell, Betty. All Four Engines Have Failed: Flight BA 009 & the "Jakarta Incident"
Tooth, Jeffery, jt. auth. see Renner, Ruediger.
Tootill, Elizabeth, ed. The Facts on File Dictionary of Biology.
Tooze, Roger, jt. ed. see Strange, Susan.
Tope, Wallace. The Mormon Documents Behind the Zion Curtain.
Topiol, Jack. Principles of Accounting.
Topkis, Gladys, ed. see Kafka, Barbara.
Topkis, Gladys, ed. see Kump, Peter.
Toplin, Robert B. Abolition of Slavery in Brazil: 1880-1888.
Topor, Tom. Bloodstar.
Toporov, Vladimir N. Akhmatova i Blok.
Topper, Suzanne. Astaire & Rogers.
--The Fruit Cookbook.
Topping, Frank. Lord of the Morning.
Topping, J. Errors of Observation & Their Treatment: SI Edition.
Torbet, Laura, jt. auth. see Nicholson, Luree.
Torby, Bruce J. Advanced Dynamics for Engineers.
Torchia, Joseph. As If after Sex.
--The Kryptonite Kid.
--The Kryptonite Kid.
Torda, Florence, jt. auth. see Burack, Elmer H.
Torg, Joseph S., ed. Athletic Injuries to the Head, Neck, & Face.
Torgersen, Don. Elephant Herds & Rhino Horns.
--Giraffe Hooves & Antelope Horns.
Torgersen, Don A. The Angry Giants of Troll Mountain.
--The Wicked Witch of Troll Cave.
Torgeson, Dewayne C., ed. Fungicides: An Advanced Treatise.
Torghele, Mark. Atlanta Job Atlas & Business Directory.
--Atlanta Job Atlas & Business Directory.
--Atlanta Job Atlas & Business Directory.
Tori, Barbara. Affair at Santa Marguerita.
--The Cinderella Factor.
Torkar, K., jt. ed. see Riedler, W.
Torkildsen, G. Leisure & Recreation Management.
Torloni, H., jt. auth. see Scarff, R. W.
Tormey, John. To Love & Be Loved.
Tornatzky, Louis G., jt. auth. see Fairweather, George W.
Toro, Gelson & Ackermann, Philip G. Practical Clinical Chemistry.
Torquato, John. Why Winners Win!
Torrance, K. E. Environmental Effects of Atmospheric Heat-Moisture Releases: Cooling Towers, Cooling Ponds & Area Sources. Watts, R. G., ed.
Torrance, K. E., jt. ed. see Catton, I.
Torrend, J. Specimens of Bantu Folk-Lore from Northern Rhodesia.
Torrens, Ian M. Interatomic Potentials.
Torrens, Paul R., jt. ed. see Williams, Stephen J.
Torrens, Robert W., ed. see L'Hote, Jean.
Torres, Edwin. After Hours.
--Carlito's Way.
--Q & A.
Torres, George J. Space Shuttle: A Quantum Leap.
Torres, Gertrude & Stanton, Marjorie. Curriculum Process in Nursing: A Guide to Curriculum Development.
Torres, Joan, jt. auth. see Forward, Susan.
Torres, Louis. Tuckahoe Marble: The Rise & Fall of an Industry in Eastchester, N. Y., 1822-1930.
Torres, Sergio, jt. ed. see Appiah-Kubi, Kofi.
Torrey, Charles C. Hebb's Textbook of Psychology: Study Guide.
Torrey, E. F. The Roots of Treason: Ezra Pound & the Secret of St. Elizabeth's.
Torrey, E. Fuller. The Roots of Treason: Ezra Pound & the Secret of St. Elizabeths.
Torrey, John G. Development in Flowering Plants.
Torrey, Lee. Stretching the Limits: Breakthroughs in Sports Science That Create Super Athletes.
Torrey, R. A. How to Bring Men to Christ.
--Power & Peace in Prayer.
Torrey, S., ed. Edible Oils & Fats: Developments since 1978.
--Enzyme Technology: Preparation, Purification, Stabilization, Immobilization-Recent Advances.
Torriente, Donna D. de la see De La Torriente, Donna D.
Tors, Ivan. My Life in the Wild.
Tortora, Gerard J., et al. Microbiology: An Introduction.
Tortorici, Marianne R. Fundamentals of Angiography.
Torvik, P. J., ed. Damping Applications for Vibration Control.
Tosches, Nick. Country: Living Legends & Dying Metaphors in America's Biggest Music.
--Unsung Heroes of Rock 'n' Roll.
Tosh, Dennis & Ordway, Nicholas. Real Estate Principles for License Preparation.
Tosi, Henry L. & Hamner, W. Clay. Organizational Behavior & Management.
Tosi, Henry L. & Hamner, W. Clay, eds. Organizational Behavior & Management: A Contingency Approach.
Toski, Bob. Complete Guide to Better Golf.
--Twelve Shortcuts to Better Golf. Aultman, Dick, ed.
Toski, Bob, et al. How to Become a Complete Golfer.
Totah. Dynamite in the Middle East.
Total Environmental Action, Inc. Staff. The Energy-Efficient Church. Hoffman, Douglas, ed.
Toth, Gabor. Harmonic & Minimal Maps: With Applications in Geometry & Physics.
Tothill, J. C. & Hacker, J. B. The Grasses of Southern Queensland.
Tothill, J. C. & Mott, J. J., eds. Ecology & Management of the World's Savannas.
Tottle, John. Benjamin Franklin.
Tottress, Richard E. Truth Speaks.
Totty, P. & Crystal, M. Corporate Insolvency.
Tou, Julius. Software Engineering.
Tou, Julius, ed. Optimum Design of Digital Control Systems Via Dynamic Programming.
Tou, Julius T., ed. Applied Automata Theory.
Touche Ross & Co. Staff. Controlling Assets & Transactions in Hospitals: How to Improve Internal Accounting Control.
Tougas, Gerard. History of French-Canadian Literature. Cook, Alta L., tr. from Fr.
Tough, Joan. Talk Two: Children Using English as a Second Language.
Touliatos, John, ed. Family & Human Development.
Toulmin, Stephen. Human Understanding, Vol. 1: The Collective Use & Evolution of Concepts.
--Knowing & Acting: An Invitation to Philosophy.
Touloukian, Y. S. & Ho, C. Y. Physical Properties of Rocks & Minerals.
--Properties of Nonmetallic Fluid Elements.
--Thermal Accommodation & Adsorption Coefficients of Gases.
Touponce, William F. Ray Bradbury. Schlobin, Roger C., ed.
Tourangeau, Kevin. Strategy Management: How to Plan, Execute & Control Strategic Plans for Your Business.
Tourette, Amelie la see La Tourette, Amelie.
Tourette, Jacqueline La see La Tourette, Jacqueline.
Tourn, Giorgio, et al. The Waldensians.
Tournier, Michel. Gilles & Jeanne. Sheridan, Alan, tr. from Fr.
Tournier, Paul. Are You Nobody?
--Creative Suffering.
--A Doctor's Casebook in the Light of the Bible.
--Escape from Loneliness.
--Guilt & Grace.
--The Meaning of Gifts.
--Reflections: A Personal Guide for Life's Most Crucial Questions.
--Seasons of Life. Gilmour, John S., tr.
--Secrets.
--To Resist or Surrender.
--To Understand Each Other.
--The Violence Within.
Tourville, Robert E. The Acts of the Apostles.
Touschek, B., ed. Physics with Intersecting Storage Rings.
Tousignaut, Dwight R., ed. IPA Thesaurus & Frequency List.
Tousley, Clare M. Letter to Jeanie: Highlights of Sixty Years with Social Work Professionals & Volunteers.
Tousley, Pershing. The Master Sculptor.
Toussaint, Charmian E. The Trusteeship System of the United Nations.
Toussaint, Stanley D. & Dyer, Charles, eds. Essays in Honor of J. Dwight Pentecost.
Toussoun, T. A., et al, eds. Root Diseases & Soil-Borne Pathogens.
Touster, Oscar, tr. see Hollmann, Siegfried.
Tovar & Encinas, Lydia P. Tovar's Classic Beauty Book.
Tovatt, Anthony see Carlsen, G. Robert, et al.
Toverud, Constance F., tr. see Paulsson, Bjorn K.
Tovey, Doreen. Double Trouble.
Tovey, John. Feast of Vegetables.
Towell, David & Harries, Clive, eds. Innovations in Patient Care: An Action Research Study of Change in a Psychiatric Hospital.
Towell, Julie E., ed. Reverse Acronyms, Initialisms & Abbreviations Dictionary, Vol. 3.

Authors

Towell, Julie E. & Sheppard, Helen E., eds. Acronyms, Initialisms, & Abbreviations Dictionary.

--New Acronyms, Initialisms & Abbreviations Dictionary.

Tower, Cynthia C. Child Abuse & Neglect: How Schools Can Help Combat.

Tower, Edward. Effective Protection, Domestic Resource Costs & Shadow Prices: A General Equilibrium Perspective.

Tower, Edward, compiled by. Development Economics Reading Lists.

--Industrial Organization & Regulation Exams, Puzzles & Problems.

--Industrial Organization & Regulation Reading Lists.

--International Economics Exams, Puzzles & Problems.

--International Economics Reading Lists.

--Macro & Monetary Economics Exams, Puzzles & Problems.

Tower Publishing Company Staff, ed. Maine Bar Directory, 1987.

--Portland City Directory, 1987.

Tower Staff, ed. Maine Bar Directory, 1988.

Towers, Bernard. Teilhard de Chardin. Nineham, D. E. & Robertson, E. H., eds.

Towers, Brian, jt. auth. see Kniveton, Bromley.

Towers, J. Role Playing for Managers.

Towers, J. Maxwell. Role-Playing for Supervisors.

Towers, T. D. Towers' International Digital IC Selector.

Towey, Veronica P. The Adventures of Tumbletin the Robot.

Towle, Faith M. The Magic Cooking Pot.

Towle, Laird & Brown, Ann A. New Hampshire Genealogical Research Guide.

Towler, Robert. The Need for Certainty: A Sociological Study of Conventional Religion.

Town, H. C. Hydraulic & Pneumatic Operation of Machines.

Town, H. C. & Colebourne, R. Engineering Inspection, Measurement & Testing.

Towne, Bonnie. Hollywood Jr. High.

--A Summer to Remember.

Towne, Mary. First Serve.

--Goldenrod.

Towne, Robert. Chinatown, the Last Detail, Shampoo: Screenplays.

Townes, C. H. & Miles, P. A., eds. Quantum Electronics & Coherent Light.

Townes, Henry, et al. Catalogue & Reclassification of the Eastern Palearctic Ichneumonidae.

Townley, Roderick. Safe & Sound: A Parent's Guide to Child Protection.

--Safe & Sound: A Parent's Guide to Child Protection.

Towns, Elmer L. Say-It-Faith.

Townsend, Alan R. The Impact of Recession: On Industry, Employment & the Regions, 1976-1981.

Townsend, Andrew, jt. auth. see Ryan, Lee F.

Townsend, Carl. Introduction to Turbo Prolog.

--Mastering Excel.

Townsend, Colin R. & Calow, Peter, eds. Physiological Ecology: An Evolutionary Approach to Resource Use.

Townsend, Doris M. Cheese Cookery.

Townsend, Duane E., jt. auth. see Morrow, C. Paul.

Townsend, Elsie D. None to Give Away.

Townsend, George. Everything You Wanted to Know about American Watches & Didn't Know Who to Ask: 1983 Price Guide.

Townsend, Guy, et al. Rex Stout: A Primary & Secondary Bibliography.

Townsend, H. Scale, Innovation, Merger & Monopoly.

Townsend, Harvey G., ed. see Edwards, Jonathan.

Townsend, John R. Written for Children: An Outline of English-Language Children's Literature.

Townsend, Kevin & Taphouse, Kate. Word Processing for Solicitors.

Townsend, Peter. The Girl in the White Ship.

Townsend, Peter, ed. The Fifth Social Service: A Critical Analysis of the Seebohn Proposal.

--Social Service for All?

Townsend, Peter & Bosanquet, Nicholas, eds. Labor & Inequality.

Townsend, Richard F. The Art of Tribes & Early Kingdoms. Pratt, Elizabeth A., ed.

Townsend, Sue. The Adrian Mole Diaries: A Novel.

Townsend, Zella. Whisperings in the Silence.

Townsend-Coles, Edwin. Adult Education in Developing Countries.

Townshend, A., jt. auth. see Burns, D. T.

Townshend, George. The Heart of the Gospel.

Townshend, J. R., ed. Terrain Analysis & Remote Sensing.

Townshend, Pete. Horse's Neck.

Townsley, David & Bjork, Russell. Scripture Index to the New International Dictionary of New Testament Theology: And Index to Selected Extrabiblical Literature. Brown & Colin, eds.

Townson, Duncan. Muslim Spain.

Towse, Raymond J. Industrial Parks: A Bibliography & Geographical Introduction.

Toxicology & Nutrition Symposium Staff. Toxicology & Nutrition: Proceedings of the Symposium, Paris, November, 1976. Ferrando, R. & Truhaut, R., eds.

Toy, A. D. The Chemistry of Phosphorous.

Toye, Randall & Gaffney, Judith H. The Agatha Christie Crossword Puzzle Book.

Toynbee. Patients.

Toynbee, et al. Crescent & Green.

Toynbee, Arnold. A Study of History. Somervell, D. C., abridged by.

Toynbee, Arnold J., ed. The Toynbee-Ikeda Dialogue: Man Himself Must Choose. Ikeda, Daisaku & Gage, Richard, trs.

Toyne, B., et al. The Global Textile Industry.

Toys 'n Things Press Staff. Basic Guide to Record Keeping & Taxes. Copeland, Tom, ed.

--Calendar-Keeper 1987: A Record Keeping System for Child Care Providers Large Edition. Glander, Deb, ed.

--Calendar-Keeper 1988: A Record Keeping System for Child Care Providers. Hix, Jill, ed.

Tozer, A. W. The Knowledge of the Holy.

Tozer, Mary. The King's Beard.

Tozer, W. Tragedy in the Church. Smith, Gerald, ed.

Traba, Marta. Las Ceremonias del Verano.

Trabert, Tony & Hook, Jim. The Serve: Key to Winning Tennis.

Tracey, Patrick A., Jr. How to Open a Small Sophisticated Restaurant & What Everyone Should Know about Dining Out.

--How to Open a Small Sophisticated Restaurant & What Everyone Should Know about Dining Out.

Tracey, Steve, jt. auth. see Carr, Pat.

Tracht, Myron E. & Ali, Majid, eds. Pathology Specialty Board Review.

Trachtenberg, Inge. An Arranged Marriage.

Tractenberg, Alan. America & Lewis Hine.

Tractenberg, Paul, ed. Selection of Teachers & Supervisors in Urban School Systems: A Transcript of the Public Hearings Held before the New York City Commission on Human Rights, January 25-29, 1971.

Tracton, Ken. The Most Popular Subroutines in BASIC.

--Twenty-Four Tested Ready-to-Run Game Programs in BASIC.

Tracy, A. Destutt De see Destutt De Tracy, A.

Tracy, David. Celebrating the Medieval Heritage: A Colloquy on the Thought of Aquinas & Bonaventura.

Tracy, David & Cobb, John B., Jr. Talking about God: Doing Theology in the Context of Modern Pluralism.

Tracy, David, jt. auth. see Happel, Stephen.

Tracy, Jack W., ed. see Doyle, Arthur Conan.

Tracy, Joseph P., jt. auth. see Norcross, John A.

Tracy, Lisa. The Gradual Vegetarian: For Everyone Finally Ready to Make the Change.

Tracy, Michael. Agriculture in Western Europe: Challenge & Response, 1880-1980.

Tracy, Noel. The Origins of the Social Democratic Party.

Tracy, Robert & DeLano, Sharon. Balanchine's Ballerinas: Conversations with the Muses.

Tracy, Wesley. When Adam Clarke Preached, People Listened.

Tracz, Richard F., jt. auth. see Howard, C. Jeriel.

Trade & Technical Press Editors. Handbook of Industrial Materials.

--Handbook of Instruments & Instrumentation.

--Handbook of Mechanical Power Drives.

--Handbook of Noise & Vibration Control.

--Pneumatic Data.

--Pneumatic Power Glossary.

--Pumping Data.

Trade & Technical Press Ltd, ed. Pneumatic Handbook.

Trade & Technical Press, Ltd. Staff, ed. Handbook of Industrial Fire Protection & Security.

--Industrial Fasteners Handbook.

Traetta, Tommaso. Ifigenia in Tauride. Brown, Howard M., ed.

Trafalgar House Publishing, Inc. Staff. The Complete Pre-GED Basic Skills Program. Dembofsky, Thomas J., ed.

Traffic World Editors. Traffic World's Question & Answer Book.

Trager, G. I. The Field of Linguistics.

Trager, James. Letters from Sachiko.

Traguth, Fred. Modern Jazz Dance.

Trahair, N. S. The Behaviour & Design of Steel Structures.

Trahey, Jane. Taste of Texas.

--Thursdays 'til Nine.

Trail, Ronald, ed. Patterns in Clause, Sentence & Discourse in Selected Languages in India & Nepal.

Trailer Life Editors & Wright, Don. Trailer Life's Guide to Fulltime RVing: Everything You Need to Know to Enjoy the Total Freedom & Adventure of Life on the Road.

Trailer Life Staff, ed. Trailer Life Campground & RV Services Directory.

Traill, Henry D. Coleridge.

Traill, John S. The Political Organization of Attica.

Traina, Richard, jt. auth. see Rappaport, Armin.

Traina, Robert A. Methodical Bible Study.

Trainer, Jennifer, jt. ed. see Kaku, Michio.

Trainer, M. Ann. A Beginner's Workbook to Safe & Profitable Investing.

Training Workshop on Water Management for Arid Regions, Ministry of Irrigation, Government of Egypt, in Cooperation with the United Nations Environment Programme, Cairo, Egypt. Water Management for Arid Lands: Proceedings. Samaha, M. A., et al, eds.

Traister, John, ed. see Wahl, Paul.

Traister, John E. Automotive Air Conditioning Handbook: Installation, Maintenance & Repair.

--Basic Blueprint Reading for Practical Applications.

--Handbook of Power Generation: Transformers & Generators.

--The Second Book of Electronics Projects.

Traister, John E., jt. auth. see Chapman, C. Keeler.

Traister, Robert J. Build a Personal Earth Station for Worldwide Satellite TV Reception.

--The Five Hundred Fifty-Five IC Project Book.

--The Joy of Flying.

--Music & Speech Programs for the IBM PC.

--The Quadram Connection.

--Thirty-Three Games of Skill & Chance for the IBM PC.

Traister, Robert J. & Harris, Susan E. Astronomy & Telescopes: A Beginner's Handbook.

Trambouze, P., jt. ed. see Villermaux, J.

Tran Duy Ly. Clocks: A Guide to Identification & Prices.

--Clocks: A Guide to Identification & Prices.

--Cuckoo Clocks, a Guide to Repair, Identification & Prices.

--Electric Clocks: A Guide to Repair, Identification & Prices.

Tran-Khanh-Tuyet & Hom, Nancy. The Little Weaver of Thai-Yen Village: Bilingual in Vietnamese & English.

Transemantics, Inc., tr. see Blechschmidt, E.

Transportation Consulting Division, Booz, Allen & Hamilton Inc. Staff, et al. Impacts of Federal Grant Requirements on Transit Agencies: National Cooperative Transit Research & Development Program Report 2.

Transportation Research Board Staff. Highway Capacity, Traffic Flow, & Traffic Control Devices.

Transtromer, Tomas. Tomas Transtromer: Selected Poems. Hass, Robert, ed. Fulton, Robin, et al, trs. from Swedish.

Tranter, Nigel. Tales & Traditions of Scottish Castles.

Tranter, William, jt. auth. see Ziemer, Rodger E.

Trapeznikov, S. P. Leninism & the Agrarian & Peasant Question.

Trapido, Barbara. Noah's Ark: A Novel.

Trapp, J., ed. see Yates, Frances A.

Trapp, Johnnie. How & Why? Ask You & I: The Communities Business.

Trapp, Juli S. Gifts of the Earth: Fifty-Five Authentic Indian American Recipes from Fifteen Tribes.

Trapp, Maria von see Von Trapp, Maria.

Trappl, Robert, ed. Progress in Cybernetics & Systems Research.

Traquair, R. H. The Fishes of the Old Red Sandstone.

--Ganoid Fishes of British Carboniferous Formations.

Trask, Roger R. Secretaries of Defense: A Brief History, 1947-1985.

Trask, Samuel, et al. Forestry Education in America Today & Tomorrow.

Trask, Willard R., tr. see Casanova, Giacomo.

Trask, Willard R., tr. see Corbin, Henry.

Trask, Willard R., tr. see Mann, Thomas.

Trask, Willard R., tr. see Simenon, Georges.

Trattler, Ross. Better Health Through Natural Healing: How to Get Well Without Drugs or Surgery.

Traub, Charles, ed. The New Vision: Forty Years of Photography at the Institute of Design.

Traub, Hamilton P. The Genera of Amaryllidaceae.

Traub, Joseph F., ed. Cohabiting with Computers: A Computer Science Convocation at Columbia University.

Trauger, Wilmer K. Language Arts in Elementary Schools.

Trausch, Susan. It Came from the Swamp: Your Federal Government at Work.

Trauth, Mary P. Italo-American Diplomatic Relations, Eighteen Sixty-One to Eighteen Eighty-Two: The Mission of George Perkins Marsh, First American Minister to the Kingdom of Italy.

Trautmann, Joanne, jt. ed. see Nicolson, Nigel.

Trautmann, Joanne, ed. see Woolf, Virginia.

Trauvetter, Christiane, ed. see Shakespeare, William.

Travel & Living Costs Worldwide, Inc. Staff. Guide to Travel & Residence Expenses for the Multinational Executive, 1979.

Traven, B. The Creation of the Sun & the Moon.

--Macario. Wilson, S. R., ed.

Traver, Hope. Love Is for Tomorrow.

Traver, Lela Mawdsky. Gifts of the Spirit.

Travers, A. A. Transcription of DNA. Head, J. J., ed.

Travers, Bill, jt. auth. see McKenna, Virginia.

Travers, Edwina Lindsay. The Caul.

--The Dolls.

Travers, Jeanette. Starting from Scratch: Our Island for Ocelots.

Travers, Jeffrey & Goodson, Barbara D. Research Results of the National Day Care Study.

Travers, P. L. The Complete Mary Poppins.

--Mary Poppins.

Travers, P. L. & Moore-Betty, Maurice. Mary Poppins in the Kitchen: A Cookery Book with a Story.

Travers, Pamela L. Maria Poppina AB ad ZA. Lyne, G. M., tr.

--Mary Poppins & Mary Poppins Comes Back.

--Mary Poppins in Cherry Tree Lane.

Travers, Will. Rogue Rancher.

Traversi, Derek. T. S. Eliot: The Longer Poems.

Traversi, Derek, intro. by. Renaissance Drama.

Traversi, Derek T. T. S. Eliot: The Longer Poems.

Travis, Alphonzo. Too Young to Die.

Travis, Carole, ed. see Standing Conference on Library Materials on Africa Staff.

Travis, Dave L., photos by. A Bit of a Star, Media Women...Their Fine Points & Phobias.

Travis, Doris C. Pardon Me While I Be Myself.

Travis, E. L. Primer of Medical Radiobiology.

Travis, Martin B., Jr., jt. ed. see Buck, Philip W.

Travis, Neal. Castles.

--Island.

--Mansions.

--Palaces.

--Wings.

Travis, Stephen H. Christ & the Judgment of God: Divine Retribution in the New Testament.

Travisono, Diana N., ed. Juvenile & Adult Correctional Departments, Institutions, Agencies & Paroling Authorities Directory 1987.

Travolta, John. John Travolta: Staying Fit!

Traylor, Ellen G. Jonah.

Traynor, Carol, jt. auth. see McKay, Robert.

Treadgold, Donald W. Twentieth Century Russia.

Treadwell, Harry, ed. see Walsh, James P.

Treagus, S. H., ed. Strain Patterns in Rocks.

Trebek, Elaine C., jt. auth. see Borgnine, Tova.

Trecker, Jerry. The Magic of Soccer.

Tree, Christina. Maine: An Explorer's Guide.

Tree, Christina & Jennison, Peter. Vermont: An Explorer's Guide.

Tree, Christina & Jennison, Peter S. Vermont: An Explorer's Guide.

Tree, Christina & Shaw, Bruce. The Best Places to Stay in New England.

Tree, Christina & Steadman, Mimi E. Maine: An Explorer's Guide.

Treece. Communication for Business & the Professions.

Treece, Patricia. A Man for Others: Maximilian Kolbe in the Words of Those Who Knew Him.

Trees, H. L. Van see Van Trees, Harry L.

Trefil, James. Meditations at Ten Thousand Feet: A Scientist in the Mountains.

Trefil, James S. From Atoms to Quarks.

--Physics As a Liberal Art.

--A Scientist at the Seashore.

--The Unexpected Vista: A Physicist's View of Nature.

Trefil, James S., jt. auth. see Rood, Robert T.

Trefusis, Violet. Broderie Anglaise. Bray, Barbara, tr.

Tregear, Mary. Song Ceramics.

Tregear, P., jt. auth. see Burley, T.

Tregear, Thomas R. China: A Geographical Survey.

Trehan, G. L. College Library Management.

Treichler, Paula A., jt. auth. see Kramarae, Cheris.

Treiman, Sam B. & Jackiw, Roman. Lectures on Current Algebra & Its Applications.

Trejo, Arnulfo D., ed. Bibliografia Chicana: A Guide to Information Sources.

Trejo, Joel. The Earth Song.

Trela, James E., ed. Social Rehabilitation & Poverty: The Cleveland Inner-City Project.

Trelease, Richard N., et al. Biology One Hundred One Laboratory Manual.

Trelford, Donald. Snookered.

Tremain, Rose. The Swimming Pool Season.

Tremaine. Indian & Pioner Settlement in the Nooksack Lowland to 1890.

Tremaine, Jennie. Maggie.

Tremblay, Bill. Second Sun.

--Second Sun.

Tremblay, Edward. When You Go to Tonga.

Tremblay, Ernest. The Italians.

Trembley, Edward L., jt. auth. see Malnati, Richard J.

Trembly, Cynthia. Morning News.

Tremillon, B., jt. auth. see Charlot, G.
Tremlett, George, jt. auth. see Caitlin, Thomas.
Tremolieres, J., ed. Alcohols & Derivatives.
Trenaman, Joseph. Out of Step.
Trench. Dictionary of Obsolete English.
Trench, Charles C. The Road to Khartoum: A Life of General Charles Gordon.
Trengove, Alan. The Story of the Davis Cup.
Trent, John. Growing Together.
Trent, Robert, ed. Pilgrim Century Furniture: An Historical Survey.
Trentin, H. George, jt. auth. see Jones, Reginald.
Trepelkov, V. General Crisis of Capitalism.
Tresch, Richard W. Public Finance: A Normative Theory.
Tresemer, David. Transplants in Soil Blocks.
Treshow, Michael. The Human Environment.
Tresillian, Richard. Bloodheart Royal.
Tress, Arthur. Shadow.
Tress, Arthur & Minahan, John. The Dream Collector.
Tressler, Donald K., jt. auth. see Desrosier, Norman W.
Tretyak, Vladislav & Snegirev, V. The Hockey I Love. Konstantin, Anatole, tr. from Rus.
Treumann, Walter, jt. auth. see Peltzer, Martin.
Trevallion, B. A. Metropolitan Kano.
Trevanian. The Loo Sanction.
--The Main.
Trevelyan, George M. Garibaldi's Defence of the Roman Republic, 1848-9.
Trevern, Dawes & Dawes, Anna. Natural Wonders of New Zealand.
Treverton, Gregory F. The "Dollar Drain" & American Forces in Germany: Managing the Political Economics of Alliance.
Trevino, Elizabeth B. De. Casilda of the Rising Moon.
--Juarez, Man of Law.
--Nacar, the White Deer.
Trevino, Lee & Aultman, Dick. Groove Your Golf Swing My Way.
Trevino, Lee & Blair, Sam. The Snake in the Sandtrap: And Other Misadventures on the Pro Golf Tour.
Trevor & Roper. Lecture Notes on Opthalmology.
Trevor, H. Moulden. Fundamentals of Transonic Flow.
Trevor-Roper, Hugh. Rise of Christian Europe.
Trevor-Roper, Hugh, ed. Final Entries 1945: The Diaries of Joseph Goebbels.
Trewartha, G. T., ed. The More Developed Realm: A Population Geography.
Trewatha, Robert L. & Newport, M. Gene. Management.
Trewin, J. C. The Journal of William Charles Macready, 1832-1851.
--The Simon & Schuster Pocket Companion to Shakespeares' Plays.
Trewin, J. C., jt. auth. see Sprague, Arthur C.
Trexler, Edgar R. Mission in a New World.
Trexler, Pat. Pat's Pointers: The Needlepoint Handbook.
Trexler, Richard C. Public Life in Renaissance Florence.
Trezza, Alphonse F., ed. Library Buildings, Innovation for Changing Needs: Proceedings.
Tribble, Edwin, ed. A President in Love: The Courtship Letters of Woodrow Wilson & Edith Bolling Galt.
Tribble, Edwin, ed. see Smith, Logan P.
Tribe, K., jt. ed. see Hussain, A.
Trice, J. E., jt. auth. see Medjati, Z. M.
Triche, Charles W. & Triche, Diane S. The Sickle Cell Hemoglobinopathies: A Comprehensive Bibliography 1910-1972.
Triche, Diane S., jt. auth. see Triche, Charles W.
Tricker, R. A. Contributions of Faraday & Maxwell to Electrical Science.
--Early Electrodynamics.
Tricker, R. I. Effective Information Management.
Tricker, R. I., ed. The Individual, the Enterprise & the State.
Trickey, Geoffrey. The Presentation & Settlement of Contractors' Claims.
Triebel, H. Interpolation Theory: Function Spaces, Differential Operators.
Trifiletti, Don. The Wind in the Willows: A Musical Adaptation.
Trifonov, Yuri. Another Life: The House on the Embankment. Glenny, Michael, tr. from Rus.
--Another Life-the House on the Embankment: Novellas. Glenny, Michael, tr.
--The Old Man. Edwards, Jacqueline & Schneider, Mitchell, trs.
Trigg, Elwood B. Gypsy Demons & Divinities: The Magic & Religion of the Gypsies.
Trigger, Bruce G. Beyond History: The Methods of Prehistory. Spindler, George & Spindler, Louise, eds.
--The Children of Aataentsic: A History of the Huron People to 1660.
Triggle, C. R., jt. auth. see Triggle, D. J.
Triggle, D. J. & Triggle, C. R. Chemical Pharmacology of the Synapse.
Triggle, D. J., et al, eds. Cholinergic Ligand Interactions.
Trillin, Calvin. Alice, Let's Eat: Further Adventures of a Happy Eater.
--Floater.
--Killings.
--Third Helpings.
--Uncivil Liberties.
Trilling, Diana. Reviewing the Forties.
--We Must March, My Darlings.
Trilling, James. The Medallion Style: A Study in the Origins of Byzantine Taste. Freedberg, S. J., ed.
Trilling, Lionel. Beyond Culture.
--The Middle of the Journey.
Trilling, Lionel, ed. see O'Hara, John.
Trillo, Richard. The Rough Guide to Kenya.
Trillo, Robert L., ed. Jane's High Speed Marine Craft & Air Cushion Vehicles, 1986.
Trimberger, George W. & Etgen, William M. Dairy Cattle Judging Techniques.
Trimberger, Stephen. Automated Performance Optimization of Custom Integrated Circuits. Stone, Harold, ed.
Trimble, M. R., ed. Benzodiazepines Divided: A Multidisciplinary Review.
Trimble, Michael. Neuropharmacology of Epilepsy.
Trimble, Michael R. see Bolwig, Tom G.
Trimble, Michael R., ed. Between Neurology & Psychiatry.
Trimmer, Joseph F. The National Book Awards for Fiction: An Index to the First Twenty-Five Years.
Trimmer, Joseph F. & Jennings, C. Wade. Fictions.
Trimmer, Joseph F. & Kettler, Robert. American Oblique: Writing about the American Experience.
Trindade, M, jt. ed. see Barbier, E.
Trine, Ralph W. In Tune with the Infinite.
Trinet, Inc. Staff, ed. see Gould, Jay M. & Paykin, Bentley H.
Triola, Mario F. Elementary Statistics.
Trip, Maggie, ed. Woman in the Year Two Thousand.
Tripathy, R. N. Federal Finance & Economic Development in India.
Tripitaka Master Hua. Listen to Yourself; Think Everything Over. Buddhist Text Translation Society Staff, tr. from Chinese.
--The Ten Dharma Realms Are Not Beyond a Single Thought. Buddhist Text Translation Society, tr. from Chinese.
Tripitaka Master Hua, commentary by. Dharani Sutra. Buddhist Text Translation Society Staff, tr. from Chinese.
Triplett, William. Flowering of the Bamboo: A Bizarre International Mystery.
Tripp, C. A. Homosexual Matrix.
Tripp, Eleanor B. To America.
Tripp, Miles. A Charmed Death.
Tripp, Raymond P. With Pen of Truth: A Reading of Walden.
Trirogoff, K. N., tr. see Vakman, D. E.
Trisco, Robert, jt. auth. see Ellis, John T.
Triska, Jan F., ed. Constitutions of the Communist Party-States.
Trismegistos, Hermes. The Hymns of Hermes. Mead, G. R. S., tr. from Gr.
Trissel, Lawrence A. Handbook on Injectable Drugs.
--Pocket Guide to Injectable Drugs.
Triston, H. U. Men in Cages.
Tritton, D. J. Physical Fluid Dynamics.
Tritton, S. M. Tritton's Guide to Better Wine & Beer Making for Beginners.
Trivedi, P. K., jt. auth. see Rowley, J. C.
Trivelpiece, Laurel. In Love & in Trouble.
Trivers, James. Hamburger Heaven.
Trivieri, Lawrence. Basic Arithmetic with Applications.
Trjapitzin, V., jt. auth. see Gordh, Gordon.
Trobisch, Ingrid. On Our Way Rejoicing.
Trobisch, Walter. Spiritual Dryness.
Trocchi, Alexander. Cain's Book.
Trocme, Etienne. The Formation of the Gospel According to Mark. Gaughan, Pamela, tr.
Troeger, Thomas H. Are You Saved? Answers to the Awkward Question.
--Meditation: Escape to Reality.
Troeh, Frederick, jt. auth. see Thompson, Louis M.
Troelstra, A. S. Metamathematical Investigations of Intuitionistic Arithmetic & Analysis.
Troeltsch, Ernst. Absoluteness of Christianity & the History of Religions.
Troise, Joe. Cherries & Lemons: The Used-Car Buyer's Handbook.
--Drive It Till It Drops: Keep Your Car Running Forever.
Troisgros, Jean & Troisgros, Pierre. The Nouvelle Cuisine of Jean & Pierre Troisgros. Smoler, Roberta W., tr. from Fr.
Troisgros, Pierre, jt. auth. see Troisgros, Jean.
Troitsky, M. S. Cable-Stayed Bridges: Theory & Design.
--Cable-Stayed Bridges: Theory & Design.
Trojan, Paul K., jt. auth. see Flinn, Richard A.
Trojanowicz, Robert C. & Morash, Merry. Juvenile Delinquency: Concepts & Controls.
Trollope, Anthony. Framley Parsonage.
--Thackeray.
--Two Heroines of Plumplington. Shannon, John K., ed.
Tromba, Anthony, jt. auth. see McAloon, Kenneth.
Trombley, D. J. Off the Cuff.
Tromp, S. W. & Bouma, J. J., eds. Biometeorological Survey: Human Biometeorology, 1973-1978.
Tromp, S. W. & Weihe, W. H., eds. Biometerology-2: Proceedings, International Bioclimatological Congress - 3rd.
Trooboff, Peter D., ed. Law & Responsibility in Warfare: The Vietnam Experience.
Trope, Mike & Delsohn, Steve. Necessary Roughness: The Other Game of Football Revealed by Its Most Controversial Agent.
Tropman, John E., et al, eds. Strategic Perspectives on Social Policy.
Tropp, Jack. Cancer-A Healing Crisis: The Whole-Body Approach to Cancer Therapy.
Tropp, Martin. Mary Shelley's Monster: The Story of Frankenstein.
Troppmann, Bob. Football's New Master Defense Guide.
Trost, Arty & Rauner, Judy. Gaining Momentum for Board Action.
Trost, Barry M. & Melvin, Lawrence S., Jr. Sulfer Ylides: Emerging Synthetic Intermediates.
Trost, Barry M. & Hutchinson, C. R., eds. Organic Synthesis--Today & Tomorrow: Third IUPAC Symposium on Organic Synthesis, Madison, Wisconsin, U. S. A., 15-20 June 1980.
Trost, Stanley R. Advanced Business Models with 1- 2- 3.
--Atari BASIC Programs in Minutes.
Trost, Stanley R. & Pomernacki, Charles. VisiCalc for Scientists & Engineering.
Trost, Stanley R., jt. auth. see King, Richard A.
Trotman-Dickenson, A. F. & Parfitt, G. D. Chemical Kinetics & Surface & Colloid Chemistry.
Trotman-Dickenson, D. I. Economic Workbooks & Data.
Trott, A. R. Refrigeration & Air Conditioning.
Trotter, Catherine, jt. auth. see Pix, Mary.
Trotter, Elizabeth M. Yesterday, Today & Tomorrow.
Trotter, Gwendolyn, jt. auth. see Kahn, Jane.
Trotter, Mark. Grace All the Way Home.
Trotter, W., jt. auth. see Anderson, Thomas J.
Trotter, W. P. & Burt, R. A. Battleships of the Grand Fleet: A Pictorial Review of British Battleships & Battlecruisers, 1906-1921.
Trotter, Wilfred. Instincts of the Herd in Peace & War.
Trotter, William R., jt. auth. see Anderson, Thomas J.
Trotti, John B. The Lesser Festivals 2: Saints' Days & Special Occasions. Achtemeier, Elizabeth, et al, eds.
Troupe, Quincy. Skulls along the River.
Trout, Jack, jt. auth. see Ries, Al.
Troutman, Andria P. & Lichtenberg, Betty K. Mathematics: A Good Beginning.
Trouton, Ruth. Peasant Renaissance in Yugoslavia, 1900-1950.
Trow, M. A., jt. auth. see Halsey, A. H.
Trowbridge, Keith. Resort Timesharing.
Trowbridge, Keith W., jt. auth. see Lynge, Richard.
Trowbridge, Rob & Hale, Judson, eds. The Old Farmer's Almanac, 1984.
Trowbridge, Rob & Hale, Judson D., eds. The Old Farmer's Almanac, 1985.
Trowbridge, Rob, jt. ed. see Hale, Judson.
Trowbridge, W. A Detailed Account of the Major Famous Audacities Associated with Leading Characters of History.
Trowell, H. C. Kwashiokor.
Trower, Peter, ed. Radical Approaches to Social Skills Training.
Trower, W. Peter & Bellini, Gianpaolo, eds. Physics in Collision: High-Energy ee-ep-pp Interactions.
Trower, W. Peter, jt. ed. see Carlson, Per.
Trower, W. Peter, jt. ed. see Carrigan, Richard A.
Troxler, L. William, ed. Along Wit's Trail: The Humor & Wisdom of Ronald Reagan.
Troy, George. Native to the Grain.
Troy, William. The Rabbits Are Eating Mrs. Koster's Marigolds.
Troyat, Henri. Baroness.
--Kisling Eighteen Ninety One to Nineteen Fifty-Three. Feinberg, Michael, tr. from Fr.
Troyer, Henry. Principles & Techniques of Histochemistry.
Troyer, Warner. Divorced Kids: Children of Divorce Speak Out & Give Advice to Mothers, Fathers, Lovers, Stepparents, Brothers & Sisters, Boyfriends & Girlfriends, Each Other.
Troyes, Chretien de see De Troyes, Chretien.
Troyna, Barry & Willams, Jenny. Racism, Education & the State: The Racialisation of Education Policy.
Truax, Carol. The Woman's Day Book of Thin Italian Cooking.
Trubo, Richard. The Consumer Book of Hints & Tips.
Trubo, Richard, jt. auth. see Bresler, David E.
Truby, J. David. Quiet Killers.
--Quiet Killers II: Silencer Update.
Truby, John O., Jr. The Science & Strategy of Squash.
Truch, Stephen. TM Technique & the Art of Learning.
Trudeau, G. B. The Doonesbury Desk Diary 1988.
--Stalking the Perfect Tan.
Trudeau, Garry. Adjectives Will Cost You Extra.
--Gotta Run, My Government Is Collapsing.
Trudeau, Margaret. Beyond Reason.
Trudell, Clyde F., jt. auth. see Briggs, Carl.
Trudgill, Peter. Coping with America.
True, June A. Finding Out: Conducting & Evaluating Social Research.
Trueb, E., jt. ed. see Urbistondo, R.
Trueb, Linda. Cranial Osteology of the Hylid Frog: Smilisca Baudini.
Trueblood, Carol & Fenn, Donna, eds. The Hazards of Walking & other Memos from Your Bureaucrats.
Trueblood, D. Elton. Essays in Gratitude.
Trueblood, E. J. Dawn of the Post-Modern Era.
Trueblood, Elton. The Incendiary Fellowship.
Trueman, Richard E. Quantitative Methods for Decision Making in Business.
Truemper, David G. & Niedner, Frederick A., Jr. Keeping the Faith: A Guide to the Christian Message.
Truemper, John J., Jr. A Century of Service Eighteen Eighty-Five to Nineteen Eighty-Five at the Firm of Cromwell Truemper Levy Parker & Woodsmall Inc.
Truesdell, C. & Bharatha, S. The Concept & Logic of Classical Thermodynamics As a Theory of Heat Engines. Rigorously Constructed Upon Foundations Laid by S. Carnot & F. Reech.
Truesdell, C., ed. Mechanics of Solids, Vol. 2: Linear Theories of Elasticity & Thermoelasticity, Linear & Nonlinear Theories of Rods, Plates, & Shells.
Truesdell, C. A. Essays in the History of Mechanics.
Truesdell, Clifford A. Unified Theory of Special Functions.
Truett. Macroeconomics.
--Microeconomics.
--Principles of Economics.
Truett, Dale B., jt. auth. see Truett, Lila F.
Truett, Lila F. & Truett, Dale B. Economics.
--Macroeconomics.
--Microeconomics.
Truffaut, Francois. Hitchcock.
--Small Change.
--The Story of Adele H.
Truffaut, Francois & Scott, Helen G. Hitchcock.
Truffer, Michael, ed. see Howeski, Dave.
Truhaut, R., ed. Potential Carcinogenic Hazards from Drugs: Evaluation of Risks.
Truhaut, R., ed. see Toxicology & Nutrition Symposium Staff.
Truhlar, D. G., ed. Potential Energy Surfaces & Dynamics Calculations for Chemical Reactions & Molecular Energy Transfer.
Truitt, A. D., tr. see Bree, Germaine.
Truitt, Anne. Daybook: The Journal of an Artist.
Truitt, Deborah, ed. Dolphins & Porpoises: A Comprehensive, Annotated Bibliography of the Smaller Cetacea.
Truitt, Gloria. Foods. Mahany, Patricia, ed.
Truitt, John. Dynamics of Police Administration.
Truitt, Willis H. & Solomons, T. W. Science, Technology, & Freedom.
Trukhanovsky, V. Winston Churchill: A Political Biography.
Truman, Charles. Sevres Egyptian Service: 1810-12.
Truman, D. E., jt. ed. see Clayton, R. M.
Truman, Harry S. The Free World & Free Trade.
Truman, Harry S. & Poen, Monte M. Letters Home.
Truman, Margaret. Bess W. Truman.
--Letters from Father: The Truman Family's Personal Correspondence.
--Murder at the FBI.
--Murder in the Smithsonian.
--Murder in the Supreme Court.
--Murder in the White House.
--Murder on Capitol Hill.
--Murder on Embassy Row.
--Murder on Embassy Row.
Trumble, Alfred. Representative Works of Contemporary American Artists. Weinberg, H. Barbara, ed.
Trump, B. F. & Jones, R. T. Diagnostic Electron Microscopy.
--Diagnostic Electron Microscopy.
--Diagnostic Electron Microscopy.
Trump, Benjamin F. & Arstila, A. U., eds. Pathobiology of Cell Membranes.
--Pathobiology of Cell Membranes.
Trump, Benjamin F. & Arstila, Antti U., eds. Pathobiology of Cell Membranes.
Trump, Benjamin F. & Jones, Raymond T., eds. Diagnostic Electron Microscopy.
Trump, Sandra. Two Grains of Sand.

Authors

Trumpower, Bernard L., ed. Function of Quinones in Energy Conserving Systems.
Trumpy, J. H. Transneuronal Degeneration in the Pontine Nuclei on the Cat.
Trungpa, Chogyam. Cutting Through Spiritual Material.
--Myth of Freedom.
--The Rain of Wisdom. Nalanda Translation Committee, tr. from Tibetan.
Trungpa, Chogyam, ed. Empowerment.
Trunkey, Donald D. & Lewis, Frank R., Jr., eds. Current Therapy of Trauma.
Truscott, Alan. The Great Bridge Scandal.
Truscott, Harold. The Music of Franz Schmidt, Vol. 1: The Orchestral Music.
Truscott, T. G., jt. auth. see Bensasson, R. V.
Trusky, A. Thomas. Thomas Hornsby Ferril.
Trusler, Ivan & Ehret, Walter. Functional Lessons in Singing.
Trusler, John, jt. auth. see Morris, Robert.
Truss Fabricators in the United States Staff. Factors Affecting the Use of Lumber.
Truss, Jan. Jasmin.
Trussell, Ruth C., ed. U. S. Labor & Employment Laws, 1987 Edition.
Trustees of the British Museum (Natural History) Report on the British Museum (Natural History) 1978-1980.
Trutko, John, et al. A Comparison of the Experimental Housing Allowance Program & Great Britain's Rent Allowance Program.
Truxal, John G., ed. see Motil, John M.
Truzzi, Marcello, ed. Chess in Literature.
Truzzi, Marcello, jt. ed. see Chamelin, Neil C.
Trylinski, W. Fine Mechanisms & Precision Instruments, Principles of Design.
Tryon, Ames F., jt. auth. see Silberman, Stephen L.
Tryon, Thomas. Other.
Tsaloumas, Dimitris. The Book of Epigrams. Grundy, Philip, tr. from Gr.
Tsang, Chiu-Sam. Society, Schools & Progress in China.
Tsang, Wing-Sum & Griffin, Gary W. Metabolic Activation of Polynuclear Aromatic Hydrocarbons.
Tschan, Francis J., tr. see Helmold Priest Of Bosau.
Tschumi, Raymond. Philosophy of Literature.
Tselikov, A. I. Theory of Lengthwise Rolling.
Tseng, Vincent. Microprocessor Development & Development Systems.
Tserpes, N. A., jt. auth. see Mukherjea, A.
Tsetlin, M. L. Automata Theory & Modeling of Biological Systems.
Tse-Yun Feng, ed. see Sagamore Computer Conference, Aug. 20-23, 1974.
T'Shaka, Obu. Political Legacy of Malcolm X.
Tsidil'Kovskii, I. M. Thermomagnetic Effects in Semiconductors. Goldsmid, H. J., et al, eds. Tybulewicz, A., tr.
Tsipis, Kosta. Arsenal: Understanding Weapons in the Nuclear Age.
Tsirakis, Jack K. The Art of Jeet-Kung-Tao.
Tsirpanlis, Constance N. The Anthropology of Saint John of Damascus.
--Greek Patristic Theolgy, Vol. 1: Eleven Studies in Eastern Orthodox Doctrine Spirituality.
--The Liturgical & Mystical Theology of Nicolas Cabasilas.
--Make Eugenicus & the Council of Florence: A Historical Re-evaluation of His Personality.
--Studies in Byzantine History & Modern Greek Folklore.
Ts'o. Basic Principles of Nucleic Chemistry.
Ts'o, P. O., ed. Chemical Carcinogenesis. Di Paolo, J. A.
--Chemical Carcinogenesis. Di Paolo, J. A.
Tso, T. C., ed. see Phytochemical Society of North America Staff.
Tsokos, C. P. & Padgett, W. J. Random Integral Equations with Applications to Stochastic Systems.
Tsokos, Chris P. & Padgett, W. J. Random Integral Equations with Applications to Life Sciences & Engineering.
Tsokos, Chris P. & Thrall, Robert M., eds. Decision Information.
Tsomin, Wang. The American Kaleidoscope. Liancheng, Duan, ed. & tr. from Chinese.
Tsongas, Paul. Heading Home.
Tsoukalis, Loukas. The European Community & Its Mediterranean Enlargement.
Tsoulfanidis, Nicholas. Measurement & Detection of Radiation.
Tsoumis, G. Wood As a Raw Material.
TSR Inc. Staff. Invisible Rival.
Tsuan, T. H., tr. see Yeh Ch'ing.
Tsuboi, T. Primary Generalized Epilepsy with Sporadic Myoclonias of Myoclonic Petit Mal Type: A Clinical, Electroencephlographic, Statistical & Genetic Study of 399 Probands. Becker, Peter E., et al, eds.
Tsuboi, T. & Christian, W. Epilepsy: A Clinical, Electroencephalographic, & Statistical Study 466 Patients.
Tsuchida, E., et al. Molecular Properties.
Tsuda, Satoru, jt. auth. see Green, Suzanne.
Tsui, Kitty. The Words of a Woman Who Breathes Fire.
Tsuji, Kaichi. Kaiseki: Zen Tastes in Japanese Cooking.
Tsujimoto, Satochiro. Architectural Presentation by Rendering.
Tsumura, Akira. Banjos: The Tsumura Collection.
--Guitars: The Tsumura Collection.
Tsuneyomo, Yamamoto. Hagakure: The Book of the Samurai. Wilson, William S., tr.
Tsunoda, S., et al, eds. Brassica Crops & Wild Allies.
Tsurumi, Kazuko. Social Change & the Individual: Japan Before & After Defeat in World War II.
Tsurumi, Y. Sogoshosha: Engines of Export-Based Growth.
Tsuruta, Teiji, jt. ed. see Bailey, William J.
Tsutsui, M., ed. Fundamental Research in Homogeneous Catalysis.
Tsutsui, M. & Ugo, R., eds. Fundamental Research in Homogeneous Catalysis.
Tsutsui, M., jt. ed. see Ishii, Y.
Tsutsui, Minoru & Ishii, Yoshio, eds. Fundamental Research in Organometallic Chemistry.
Tsvetkov, Aleksei. Sbornik P'es Dlia Zhizni Solo: Stikhi.
Tsvetkov, Alexei. Sostoianie Sna.
Tsytovich, V. N. An Introduction to the Theory of Plasma Turbulence.
Tsytovich, V. N., jt. auth. see Kaplan, S. A.
Tu, Anthony T., ed. Survey of Contemporary Toxicology.
--Survey of Contemporary Toxicology.
Tuama, Sean O., ed. An Duanaire Sixteen Hundred to Nineteen Hundred: Poems of the Dispossessed. Kinsella, Thomas, tr. from Irish.
Tuan, Francis C. China's Livestock Sector.
Tubbs, D. B. Zeiss Ikon Cameras, 1926-1939.
Tubbs, E. J. Visual Arabic Grammar-Lexicon.
Tubbs, Gabi. Knitting Now!
Tubbs, N. & London, P. S. Topical Reviews in Accident Surgery.
Tubbs, Stewart L. & Moss, Sylvia. Interpersonal Communication.
Tubesing, Richard. Architectural Preservation in the United States, 1941-1975: A Bibliography of Federal, State, & Local Government Publications.
Tubiana, J., ed. Modern Ethiopia: From the Accession of Menilek II to the Present, Proceedings of the International Conference of the Ethiopian Studies, Nice, 5th, 19-22 December 1977.
Tuccillo, John. Housing & Investment in an Inflationary World: Theory & Evidence.
Tuccillo, John & Villani, Kevin, eds. House Prices & Inflation.
Tuch, R., jt. ed. see Straszak, A.
Tucher, Andrea J. Agriculture in America, Sixteen Twenty-Two-Eighteen Sixty: Printed Works in the Collections of the American Philosophical Society, the Historical Society of Pennsylvania, the Library Company of Philadelphia.
Tucher, Andrea J., ed. Natural History in America, 1609-1860: Printed Works in the Collections of the American Philosophical Society, the Historical Society of Pennsylvania, & the Library Company of Philadelphia.
Tuchkevich, V. M. & Shvarts, K. K., eds. Defects in Insulating Crystals: Riga 1981: Proceedings.
Tuchman, Barbara W. The March of Folly: From Troy to Vietnam.
Tuck, Bob. Hauling Heavyweights: Moving Extra Large Loads by Road.
Tuck, James A. Maritime Provinces Prehistory.
Tucker, A. W., ed. see Kuhn, Harold W.
Tucker, Alvin. The Role of Education in National Defense.
Tucker, Bruce, jt. auth. see Brown, James.
Tucker, Charles O., jt. auth. see Hess, Herbert J.
Tucker, Cynthia G. A Woman's Ministry: Mary Collson's Search for Reform as a Unitarian Minister, Hull House Social Worker, & a Christian Science Practioner.
Tucker, D. G. & Gazey, B. K. Applied Underwater Acoustics.
Tucker, Don H., ed. Vector & Operator-Valued Measures & Applications.
Tucker, Edwin W. CPA Examination Review: Business Law.
Tucker, Gabe, jt. auth. see Crumbaker, Marge.
Tucker, Gardiner. Toward Rationalizing Allied Weapons Production.
Tucker, Gene M., ed. see Klein, Ralph W.
Tucker, Gene M., ed. see Robertson, David.
Tucker, Georgina & Schneider, Madelin. The Professional Housekeeper.
Tucker, Howard. Automatic Transmissions Workbook on Service & Repair.
Tucker, Ivan & Nolan, Michael. Educational Audiology.
Tucker, Joan C. San Diego & the Southland: Just the Facts. Rand, Elizabeth, ed.
Tucker, John M. Articles on Library Instruction in Colleges & Universities, 1876-1932.
Tucker, John M., jt. ed. see Gleaves, Edwin S.
Tucker, John R. The Bicentennial Tragedy: An Indictment of the Law.
Tucker, Jonathan B. Ellie: A Child's Fight Against Leukemia.
Tucker, Kathleen, ed. see Bates, Betty.
Tucker, Kathleen, ed. see Bunting, Eve.
Tucker, Kathleen, ed. see Guzzo, Sandra E.
Tucker, Kathleen, ed. see Raynor, Dorka.
Tucker, Kathleen, ed. see Sharmat, Mitchell.
Tucker, Kathleen, ed. see Simon, Norma.
Tucker, Kathleen, ed. see Van Woerkom, Dorothy.
Tucker, Kathy, ed. see Chevalier, Christa.
Tucker, Kathy, ed. see Simon, Norma.
Tucker, Kenneth. John Marston: A Reference Guide.
Tucker, Lewis R., jt. auth. see Jain, Subhash C.
Tucker, Mitchell. It's Your Time - Use It or Lose It.
Tucker, N. I., jt. auth. see Shaw, B. L.
Tucker, Nita. Beyond Cinderella: The Modern Woman's Guide to Finding a Prince.
Tucker, Richard P. Ranade & the Roots of Indian Nationalism.
Tucker, Robert C. Political Culture & Leadership in Soviet Russia: From Lenin to Gorbachev.
Tucker, Robert C., ed. Marx-Engels Reader.
Tucker, Ronald D. & Hufton, Richard A. Foundations for Christian Growth.
--God's Plan for Christian Service.
Tucker, Spencer A. Handbook of Business Formulas & Controls.
--Pricing for Higher Profit.
--Profit Planning Decisions with the Break-Even System.
Tucker, Susan M., et al. Patient Care Standards.
Tucker, Vincent, jt. auth. see Linehan, Mary.
Tuckerman, Bayard. William Jay & the Constitutional Movement for the Abolition of Slavery.
Tuckerman, Bryant. Planetary, Lunar & Solar Positions Six Hundred-One B. C to A. D One at Five-Day & Ten-Day Intervals.
Tuckett, Christopher, ed. The Messianic Secret.
Tuckett, David & Kaufert, Joseph M., eds. Basic Readings in Medical Sociology.
Tuckett, David, et al. Meetings Between Experts: An Approach to Sharing Ideas in Medical Consultations.
Tuckman, Bruce W. Conducting Educational Research.
--Conducting Educational Research.
--Measuring Educational Outcomes: Fundamentals of Testing.
Tudor, Andrew. Beyond Empiricism: Philosophy of Science in Sociology.
Tudor, Bethany. Drawn from New England: A Portrait in Words & Pictures.
Tudor, Tasha, illus. First Poems of Childhood.
Tuer, Andrew W. One Thousand Quaint Cuts from Books of Other Days.
--Pages & Pictures from Forgotten Children's Books.
--Stories from Old-Fashioned Children's Books, Brought Together & Introduced to the Reader.
Tuffrau, jt. auth. see Lanson.
Tufnell, Robert. Prototype Locomotives.
Tufts, Susan E., jt. ed. see Gill, Kay.
Tufty, Barbara. One Thousand & One Questions Answered about Earthquakes, Avalanches, Floods, & Other Natural Disasters.
Tuggle, Robert. The Golden Age of Opera.
Tuglas, F. Riders in the Sky.
Tugwell, Rexford G. Battle for Democracy.
--A Chronicle of Jeopardy: Nineteen Forty-Five to Nineteen Fifty-Five.
Tulane University, New Orleans Staff. Catalog of the Latin American Library of the Tulane University Library: Third Supplement.
--Catalog of the Latin American Library of the Tulane University Library.
--Catalog of the Latin American Library of the Tulane University Library, First Supplement.
--Catalog of the Latin American Library of the Tulane University Library, Second Supplement.
Tuleja, Thaddeus. Land of Precious Snow.
Tuleja, Thaddeus V. Twilight of the Sea Gods.
Tulku, Tarthang, ed. Crystal Mirror.
Tulley & Campbell. Manual of Practical Orthodontics.
Tullius, John. The Science Digest Book of Halley's Comet.
Tullius, John, jt. auth. see Burwash, Peter.
Tullo, Frank Di see Di Tullo, Frank.
Tulloch, Patricia. Poor Policies: Australian Income Security Nineteen Seventy-Two to Nineteen Seventy-Seven.
Tullock, Gordon & McKenzie, Richard B. The New World of Economics: Explorations into the Human Experience.
Tulloh, Bruce see Milne, John.
Tully, Andrew. Berlin: Story of a Battle.
Tully, J. R., jt. ed. see Bollinger, L. L.
Tully, Mary J. A Family Book of Praise.
Tully, Mary J., jt. auth. see Fearon, Mary.
Tully, Mary Jo. Church: A Faith Filled People.
Tully, Paul. The Jehovah's Jailbreak.
Tully, R. I., jt. auth. see Thornton, J. L.
Tuma, Elias H. Twenty-Six Centuries of Agrarian Reform: A Comparative Analysis.
Tuma, Jan J. Handbook of Physical Calculations.
--Technology Mathematics Handbook.
Tumblin, Charles R. Construction Cost Estimates.
Tumins, Valerie A. Tsar Ivan Fourth's Reply to Jan Roktya.
Tumlir, Jan, jt. auth. see Blackhurst, Richard.
Tung, Fei H. Chinese Village Close-Up.
Tung, Fei H., et al. Small Towns in China.
Tung, P. P., et al. Fracture & Failure: Analyses, Mechanisms & Applications.
Tung, Rosalie L. Business Negotiations with the Japanese.
--Key to Japan's Economic Strength: Human Power.
Tunis, Barbara L. In Caps & Gowns: The Story of the McGill School for Graduate Nurses, 1920-1964.
Tunis, John R. City for Lincoln.
--Duke Decides.
--Iron Duke.
--Kid from Tomkinsville.
--The Kid from Tomkinsville.
--World Series.
--Yea, Wildcats.
Tunkin, Gregory, jt. auth. see Dupuy, Rene J.
Tunley, Malcolm. Library Structures & Staffing Systems.
Tunnicliffe, Charles. A Sketchbook of Birds.
Tunnicliffe, S. Poetry Experience: Teaching & Writing Poetry in Secondary Schools.
Tunstall, Jeremy & Thompson, Kenneth, eds. Sociological Perspectives.
Tunyogi, Andrew C. Divine Struggle for Human Salvation: Biblical Convictions in Their Historical Settings.
Tuohy, Frank. The Collected Stories.
--Live Bait.
Tuohy, James, jt. auth. see McComas, Tom.
Tuoming, Wang, ed. Sea Sailing.
Tupholme, G. Twentieth Century Engineering.
Tuplin, W. A. The Steam Locomotive.
--The Steam Locomotive.
Tupper, E. Frank. Theology of Wolfhart Pannenberg.
Turbak, Gary. The Traveler's Guide to Montana.
Turban & Loomba. Cases & Readings in Management Science.
Turban & Meredith. Fundamentals of Management Science.
Turban, jt. auth. see Meredith.
Turban, Efraim & Meredith, Jack. Fundamentals of Management Science.
Turban, Efraim & Loomba, N. Paul, eds. Readings in Management Science.
Turberville, Arthur S. House of Lords in the Eighteenth Century.
--The House of Lords in the Reign of William Third.
Turbett, Pam. Cut & Sew: Working with Machine Knitted Fabrics.
Turbeville. The Electric Railway Era in Northwest Washington, 1890-1930.
Turbott, E. G., ed. Buller's Birds of New Zealand.
Turco, Emanuele. The Bilateral Treaties in Force Between the U. S. A. & Italy.
Turell Baldovi, Fausto. Diccionario Auxiliar del Crucigramista.
Turgenev, Ivan S. Turgenev's Letters. Knowles, A. V., ed. & tr.
--Virgin Soil. Garnett, Constance, tr. from Rus.
Turgeon, Charlotte, jt. auth. see Ser Vass, Cory.
Turgeon, Charlotte, ed. The Creative Cooking Course.
Turgeon, Charlotte, ed. see Montagne, Prosper.
Turin, Alan C. No More Headaches!
Turk, Amos, jt. auth. see Green, Michael E.
Turk, Amos, jt. auth. see Turk, Jonathan.
Turk, Amos & Johnston, James, Jr., eds. Human Responses to Environmental Odors.
Turk, Amos, et al. Ecology, Pollution & Environment.
Turk, Christopher & Kirkman, John. Effective Writing.
Turk, Frederick J. & Gallo, Robert P. Financial Management Strategies for Arts Organizations.
Turk, Jonathan. Introduction to Environmental Studies.
Turk, Jonathan & Turk, Amos. Environmental Science.
Turk, V. & Vitale, L. J. Proteinases & Their Inhibitors: Structure, Function & Applied Aspects.
Turkevich, Julianna, jt. auth. see Meras, Phyllis.
Turkle, Sherry. Psychoanalytic Politics: Freud's French Revolution.
--Second Self: Computers & the Human Spirit.
Turleau, Catherine, jt. auth. see De Grouchy, Jean.
Turley, Peter T. Peirce's Cosmology.
Turn, Rein, ed. Advances in Computer System Security.
Turnage, Anne, jt. auth. see Turnage, Mac.
Turnage, Anne S., jt. auth. see Turnage, Mac N.
Turnage, Mac & Turnage, Anne. People, Families & God.
Turnage, Mac N. & Turnage, Anne S. More Than You Dare Ask: The First Year of Living with Cancer.
--Mystery of Prayer.
Turnage, Sheila. Trout the Magnificent.
Turnbull, et al. Selecting a Preschool.

Turnbull, Agnes S. The Flowering.
--Golden Journey.
--The Golden Journey.
--King's Orchard.
--Many a Green Isle.
Turnbull, Ann. The Frightened Forest.
--The Wolf King.
Turnbull, Colin M. Forest People.
--Lonely African.
Turnbull, George. A Treatise on Ancient Painting.
Turnbull, H. Rutherford. The Law & the Mentally Handicapped in North Carolina.
--Legal Aspects of Educating the Developmentally Disabled.
Turnbull, H. Rutherford, 3rd. Primary & General Election Law & Procedure.
Turnbull, Ralph G., jt. ed. see Moody, Dwight L.
Turnbull, S. R. The Samurai: A Military History.
Turner. Essays in American History Dedicated to Frederick Jackson Turner.
--Language of the Army in English.
Turner, Bryan S. For Weber: Essays in the Sociology of Fate.
Turner, Bryan S. & Hepworth, Mike. Confession: Studies in Deviance & Religion.
Turner, Charles, ed. see Blamires, Harry, et al.
Turner, D. C., tr. see Hadorn, E.
Turner, David R. Catholic High School Entrance Examinations.
--Complete Guide to U. S. Civil Service Jobs.
--Preliminary Scholastic Aptitude Test: National Merit Scholarship Qualifying Test (PSAT-NMSQT)
Turner, Dean. Lonely God, Lonely Man.
Turner, Denise. Scuff Marks on the Ceiling: Surviving & Enjoying Your Child's Early Years.
Turner, Dennis C. A Field Study in Behavior & Ecology: A Field Study in Behavior & Ecology.
Turner, Elizabeth S. Be Ye Transformed.
--Your Hope of Glory.
Turner, Francis J. Metamorphic Petrology.
Turner, Frederick J. U. S. Eighteen Thirty to Eighteen Fifty.
--The United States: 1830-1850.
Turner, G. Alan. Heat & Concentration Waves: Analysis & Applications.
Turner, Gladys D. & St. Clair, Mae G. One Hundred Twenty-Three Questions & Answers: From the Edgar Cayce Readings.
Turner, Gladys T. Papa Babe's Stamp Collection.
Turner, Gregg M. & Jacobus, Melancthon W. Connecticut Railroads: An Illustrated History. Jensen, Oliver O., ed. & frwd. by.
Turner, Gwenda. New Zealand ABC Frieze.
Turner, H. A. Collector's Guide to Staffordshire Pottery Figures.
Turner, H. A. & Zoeteweij, H. Prices, Wages & Incomes Policies in Industrialised Market Economies.
Turner, Henry & Vieg, J. Government & Politics of California.
Turner, Herbert H. Astronomical Discovery.
Turner, Howard. Africa South of the Sahara.
Turner, Ian, ed. Cinderella Dressed in Yella: The First Attempt at a Definitive Study of Australian Children's Play Rhymes.
Turner, J. A. Cotton Planter's Manual.
Turner, James E., et al. Regeneration in Lower Vertebrates & Invertebrates.
Turner, Jeffrey S. & Helms, Donald B. Contemporary Adulthood.
--Contemporary Adulthood.
Turner, Jessie. Silhouettes of Thought.
Turner, Johanna. Cognitive Development & Education. Herriot, Peter, ed.
Turner, Jonathan E. & Beeghley, Leonard. The Emergence of Sociological Theory.
Turner, June, jt. auth. see Arbit, Naomi.
Turner, Louis. Coal's Contribution to U. K. Self-Sufficiency.
--Invisible Empires: Multinational Companies & the Modern World.
Turner, Martha A. The World of Col. John W. Thomason, USMC.
Turner, Michael, jt. auth. see Battie, David.
Turner, Nancy J. & Szczawinski, Adam F. Wild Coffee & Tea Substitutes of Canada.
Turner, Nigel, jt. auth. see Pettifer, Julian.
Turner, Noel D. American Silver Flatware.
Turner, P. P. The Cardiovascular System.
Turner, P. W., jt. auth. see Haigh, R. H.
Turner, Paul, jt. auth. see Silverstone, Trevor.
Turner, Paul & Shand, David G., eds. Recent Advances in Clinical Pharmacology.
Turner, Paul V. The Education of le Corbusier.
Turner, Peter. Films Stars Don't Die in Liverpool.
Turner, R. Kerry, jt. ed. see O'Riordan, Timothy.
Turner, Ralph H. & Killian, Lewis. Collective Behavior.
Turner, Raymond W. Solution Manual for Operating Systems: Design & Implementation.
Turner, Richard A. The Vision of Landscape in Renaissance Italy.
Turner, Robert. The Heptarchia Mystica of John Dee.
--Vancouver Island Railroads.
Turner, Roger & Green, Al. Body Culture.
Turner, Rufus. Practical Oscilloscope Handbook.
Turner, Rufus P. & Gibilisco, Stan. The Illustrated Dictionary of Electronics.
Turner, Silvie. Screen Printing Techniques.
Turner, Simon, jt. auth. see Milne, Dennis W.
Turner, Stansfield. Secrecy & Democracy: The CIA in Transition.
Turner, Stephen & Factor, Regis. Max Weber & the Dispute over Reason & Value: A Study of Philosophy, Ethics & Politics.
Turner, W. D., ed. Solar Engineering, 1982.
Turner, Walter J. Wagner.
Turner, Wayne C., et al. Introduction to Industrial & Systems Engineering.
Turner, William C. & Malloy, John F. Handbook of Thermal Insulation Design Economics for Pipes & Equipment.
--Thermal Insulation Handbook.
Turner Ettlinger, D. M., ed. Natural History Photography.
Turney, C. Pioneers of Australian Education.
Turney, C. & Cairns, L. C. Sydney Micro Skills, Series 3 Handbook: Classroom Management & Discipline.
Turney, C. & Cairns, L. G. The Practicum in Teacher Education: Research, Practice & Supervision.
--Supervisor Development Programmes: Role Handbook.
Turney, C. & Ryan, C. Inner City Teaching.
Turney, C., ed. Innovation in Teacher Education.
--Pioneers of Australian Education: Studies of the Development of Education in Australia, 1900-50.
Turney, C., et al. Sydney Micro Skills, Series 4 Handbook: Guiding Small Group Discussion, Small Group Teaching & Individualized Instruction.
--Sydney Micro Skills Series 5 Handbook: Guiding Discovery Learning & Fostering Creativity.
--Microteaching.
--Inner-City Schools: Children, Teachers & Parents.
--Isolated Schools.
Turney, Catherine. Byron's Daughter.
Turney, Cliff, ed. Sydney Micro Skills Redeveloped: Series One Handbook.
--Sydney Micro Skills Redeveloped: Series Two Handbook.
Turnill, Reginald, ed. Jane's Spaceflight Directory, 1986.
Turnquist, C. H., jt. auth. see Althouse, Andrew.
Turnquist, Jeanette, jt. auth. see Birkey, Verna.
Turov, E. A. Physical Properties of Magnetically Ordered Crystals. Scripta Technica, tr.
Turow, Joseph. Media Industries: The Production of News & Entertainment.
Turpin, John. John Hogan: Irish Neoclassical Sculptor in Rome 1800-1858: A Biography & Catalogue Raisonne.
Turpin, Kathryn S. & Saltzman, Marvin L. Eurail Guide: How to Travel Europe & All the World by Train, 1984. Saltzman, Barbara F., ed.
--Eurail Guide: How to Travel Europe & All the World by Train 1985. Saltzman, Barbara F., ed.
--Eurail Guide: How to Travel Europe & All the World by Train 1987.
--Eurail Guide: How to Travel Europe & All the World by Train, 1988.
Turquette, Atwell R., jt. auth. see Rosser, J. Barkley.
Turrell, G. Infrared & Raman Spectra of Crystals.
Turrentine, Parnell, Jr. Black Reality.
Tursky, B., jt. ed. see Weisenberg, M.
Turtledove, Harry. Agent of Byzantium.
Turton, R. K. Principles of Turbomachinery.
Turvey, Valerie. Bean Feast: An International Legumes Cookbook.
Turvey, Vincent N. Beginning of Seership: Astral Projection, Clairvoyance & Prophecy.
Turyn, Anne. Volunteer: A Photo Novel.
Tusenius, Micheline, jt. auth. see Cooper, Alison.
Tuska, Jon. The Vanishing Legion: A History of Mascot Pictures, 1927-1935.
Tuten, Frederic. Adventures of Mao on the Long March.
Tuten, Rich & Moore, Clancy. A Football Strength & Conditioning Program for all Seasons.
Tuthill, Marge. Art for Children's Liturgy: What You Need & How To Do It.
Tutoo, D. N., jt. auth. see Kundu, C. L.
Tutt, J. F., ed. see Hayes, Horace M.
Tutt, Norman. Care or Custody: Community Homes & the Treatment of Delinquency.
Tuttle, Frederick B., Jr. Composition: A Media Approach.
Tuttle, Frederick B., Jr. & Becker, Laurence A. Characteristics & Identification of Gifted & Talented Students.
--Program Design & Development for Gifted & Talented Students.
Tuttle, Patti, jt. ed. see Chase, Leslie R.
Tuttle, Robert G. Help Is on the Way: Overcoming Barriers to Spirit-Assisted Prayer.
Tuttleton, James W., ed. see Irving, Washington.
Tutuola, Amos. My Life in the Bush of Ghosts.
--The Palm-Wine Drinkard.
Tver, David F. & Berry, Richard W. Petroleum Dictionary.
Tver, David F., compiled by. Dictionary of Business & Science.
Twain, Mark. Adventures of Huckleberry Finn.
--Adventures of Tom Sawyer.
--The Adventures of Tom Sawyer. Barish, Wendy, ed.
--The Adventures of Tom Sawyer.
--The Adventures of Tom Sawyer & Huckleberry Finn.
--A Connecticut Yankee in King Arthur's Court.
--Life on the Mississippi.
--The Prince & the Pauper.
Tweedie, David & Shroyer, Edgar H., eds. The Multihandicapped Hearing Impaired: Identification & Instruction.
Tweedie, Jill. Letters from a Faint-Hearted Feminist.
Tweedle, D. E. F. Metabolic Care.
Tweedsmuir, Lord. The Country Life Picture Book: Scotland.
Twelve O'Clock Scholars Staff. A Cape Cod Sampler: A Second Anthology. Kelly, Margaret M. & Pingree, Eleanor M., eds.
Twelvetrees, A. C. Community Associations & Centres: A Comparative Study.
Twentieth Century Fund Staff. Report on the Greeks: Findings of a Twentieth Century Fund Team Which Surveyed Conditions in Greece in 1947.
Twentieth Century Fund, Task Force on Labor Disputes in Public Employment Staff. Pickets at City Hall.
Twiford, Rainer. Managing Children's Behavior: A Guide for Parents, Teachers, Counselors, Coaches & All Others Who Work with Children.
Twigg, Bernard A., jt. auth. see Kramer, Amihud.
Twigg, Blanche. Penance: God's Gift for Forgiveness.
Twin, Stephanie L., ed. Out of the Bleachers: Writings on Women & Sport.
Twiname, Eric. Start to Win.
Twing, J. W., jt. auth. see Morrison, Phyllis C.
Twiss, Ruth M. Morning, Noon & Night: A Teacher's Diary.
Twiss, Sumner B., Jr., jt. auth. see Little, David.
Twitchel, Paul. Spirituelle Aufzeichnungen. Institutue Lanfranco, et al, trs. from Ger.
Twitchell, Hanford. Summer Pioneers: Memories of Old Field.
Twitchell, Paul. Anitya.
--Briefe an Gail. Eckankar Studiengruppe Munchen, tr.
--Le Carnet De Notes Spiritual.
--Coins of Gold.
--El Colmillo Del Tigre. Gilpatrick, Lottie, et al, trs.
--El Cuaderno Espiritual. Proano, Mario & De Mercado, Maria A., trs.
--Dialoge Mit Dem Meister. DeWitt, Steve, et al, trs.
--Drums of ECK.
--Le Eck-Vidya: Ancienne Science de Prophetie. Marchand, L., et al, trs. from Fr.
--Die Eck Vidya, die Uralte Wissenschaft der Propheseiuns.
--Eckankar: Der Schlussel Zu Geheim Welten.
--Eckankar: La Clave de los Mondos Secretos.
--Eckankar: La Cle des Mondes Secrets.
--En Mi Alma Soy Libre.
--En Mon Ame Je Suis Libre. Martin, Yves, tr.
--L' Etranger au Bord de La Riviere.
--La Flauta de Dios. Proano, Mario, et al, trs. from Span.
--Die Flote Gottes. Eckankar Studiengruppe Munchen, tr.
--La Flute De Dieu.
--Der Fremde Am Fluss.
--La Griffe de Tigre.
--The Key to Eckankar.
--Krauter: Die Magischen Heiler.
--Les Plantes: Guerisseuses Magiques. Lasnier, Denis R., et al, trs.
--Das Shariyat-Ki-Sugmad: Buch Eins. DeWitt, Steve, et al, trs. from Ger.
--Das Shariyat Ki Sugmad: Buch Zwei. Dewitt, Steve & Sacchet, Uli, trs. from Eng.
--Le Shariyat-Ki-Sugmad: Premier Livre. Martin, Yves D., tr. from Fr.
--The Three Masks of Gaba.
--Way of Dharma.
Twitchett, John. Derby Porcelain.
Twombly, Gerald H. An Analytical Survey of the Bible.
Twombly, Robert C., ed. Blacks in White America Since 1865: Issues & Interpretations.
Twombly, Wells. Blanda, Alive & Kicking.
Twomey, J. J. & Good, R. A., eds. Immunopathology of Lymphoreticular Neoplasms.
Twomey, Jeremiah J. The Pathophysiology of Human Immunologic Disorders.
Twycross, R. G. & Ventafridda, V. The Continuing Care of Terminal Cancer Patients: Proceedings of an International Seminar on Continuing Care of Terminal Cancer Patients, 19-20 October 1979, Milan, Italy.
Tyagunenko, V. L. Industrialization of Developing Countries.
Tyayanov, V. His Nameless Love.
Tybulewicz, A., tr. see Tsidil'Kovskii, I. M.
Tydeman, William. English Medieval Theatre Fourteen Hundred to Fifteen Hundred.
Tye, R. P., ed. Thermal Conductivity.
Tyebjee, Faraz. Sojourn on This Sable Earth.
Tyers, Rodney, jt. ed. see Chisholm, Anthony H.
Tygier, C. Basic Handbook of Foreign Exchange: A Guide to Foreign Exchange Dealing.
Tyldesley, W. R. Oral Diagnosis.
Tylecote, Andrew. The Causes of the Present Inflation: An Interdisciplinary Explanation of Inflation in Britain, Germany & the United States.
Tyler. Book of Puzzles.
Tyler, jt. auth. see Warender.
Tyler, Ann & Ravenel, Shannon. The Best American Short Stories 1983.
Tyler, Anne. The Accidental Tourist.
--A Slipping Down Life.
Tyler, David M. The Bomb in the Bible: An Incredible Look at the Prophecies Concerning Nuclear War.
Tyler, Fred T. Individualizing Instruction.
Tyler, J. E. Tolkien Companion.
Tyler, Michael J., ed. The Gastric Brooding Frog.
Tyler, O. Z., Jr. Sweet Land of Liberty.
Tyler, O. Z., Jr., ed. see Cohen, M. M.
Tyler, Parker. Classics of the Foreign Film.
Tyler, R. W. Changing Concepts of Educational Evaluation.
Tyler, Ralph W. Social Forces Influencing American Education.
Tyler, Ralph W., ed. Educational Evaluation: New Roles, New Means.
Tyler, Ralph W., ed. see National Society for the Study of Education Staff.
Tyler, Richard W. & Elizondo, Sergio D. The Characters, Plots & Settings of Calderon's Comedias.
Tyler, Ron, et al. American Frontier Life: Early Western Painting & Prints.
Tyler, W. T. The Shadow Cabinet.
Tyler, William R., tr. see Janssen, Pierre.
Tylor, Edward. The Origins of Culture.
Tymes, Elna. Mastering AppleWorks.
Tymes, Elna & Antoniak, Peter. Multiplan: Home & Office Companion.
--SuperCalc: Home & Office Companion.
Tymes, Elna & Dowden, Tony. One-Two-Three from A to Z: 59 Complete Templates.
Tymn, Marshall. The Year's Scholarship in Science Fiction, Fantasy, & Horror Literature, 1982.
Tymn, Marshall B. & Schlobin, Roger C. The Year's Scholarship in Science Fiction & Fantasy, 1976-1979.
Tymn, Marshall B., et al. A Research Guide to Science Fiction Studies.
Tyne, Claude H. Van see Van Tyne, Claude H.
Tyner, Thomas E. College Writing Basics: A Progressive Approach.
Type Directors Club Staff. Typography Three: The Annual of the Type Director's Club.
Tyran, Michael R. Computerized Accounting Methods & Controls.
--Computerized Financial Forecasting & Performance Reporting.
Tyras, G. Radiation & Propagation of Electromagnetic Waves.
Tyrell, R., rev. by see Laws, W.
Tyrer & Lee. Synopsis of Occupational Medicine.
Tyrer, Polly, jt. auth. see Leith, Prue.
Tyres. Firebird.
Tyrnauer, Gabrielle, jt. auth. see Stasny, Charles.
Tyrone, Alfred J. & Cannon-Alfred, C. Medical Handbook for the Layman.
Tyror, J. G. & Vaughan, R. I. Introduction to Neutron Kinetics of Nuclear Power Reactors.
Tyrrell, G. N. Homo Faber: A Study of Man's Mental Evolution.
Tyrrell, J. B., ed. see Thompson, David.
Tyrrell, John & Wise, Rosemary. A Guide to International Congress Reports in Musicology, 1900-1975.
Tyrrell, R. Emmett, Jr. The Liberal Crackup.
Tyrrell, William B. Medical Terminology for Medical Students.
Tyshkevich, R. I., jt. auth. see Suprunenko, Dmitri A.
Tysoe, B. A. Construction Costs & Price Indices: Description & Use.
Tyson, Alan, ed. & pref. by. Beethoven Studies.
Tyson, Archie M. Every Woman in Her Humor: A Critical Edition. Orgel, Stephen, ed.
Tyson, James L. Target America: The Influence of Communist Propaganda on U. S. Media.
Tyson, Joseph B. A Study of Early Christianity. Scott, Kenneth J., ed.
Tyson, Joseph B. & Longstaff, Thomas R. W. Synoptic Abstract. Baird, J. Arthur & Freedman, David Noel, eds.
Tyson, Laura, jt. ed. see Zysman, John.
Tytell, John. Naked Angels: The Lives & Literature of the Beat Generation.
Tyurikov, V. Tashkent: A Guide.

Tzanetakis, John. Develop Your Potential: How to Use Applied Psychology to Accomplish Your Purpose.
Tzannes, Nicolaos, ed. see International Conference on Information Sciences & Systems Staff.
Tzedakis, Y., jt. auth. see Georgiou, Hara.

U

U. N. see United Nations.
U-Bild Enterprises Staff. Patterns for Better Living.
U. K. Association of Investment Trust Cos. Staff. Investment Trust Yearbook & Who's Who 1986.
U. S. A. Today Editors. The U. S. A. Today Travel Tips.
U. S. S. R. Ministry of Defense Staff. Desarme: Quien esta en Contra.
--Star Wars: Delusions & Dangers.
--Whence the Threat to Peace.
U. S. S. R. Minutes of Defense Staff. Las Guerras de las Estrellas: Illusiones y Peligros.
U. S. see United States.
Ubarov, Chapman. Diccionario de Ciencias.
Ubbelohde, Carl, et al. A Colorado History.
Ubbelohde, Carl, et al, eds. A Colorado Reader.
Ubell, Earl. How to Save Your Life.
Uberall, Herbert. Electron Scattering from Complex Nuclei Pts. A & B.
Uberstine, Gary A. Covering All the Bases: A Comprehensive Research Guide to Sports Law.
Ubu Repertory Theater Publications Staff. UBU Repertory Theater Publications.
--UBU Repertory Theater Publications.
Ucelay, Margarita, jt. auth. see DaCal, Ernesto G.
Uchida, Yoshiko. Magic Listening Cap: More Folk Tales from Japan.
--The Magic Listening Cap: More Folk Tales from Japan.
--Promised Year.
Uchiyama, Akira. Sri Lanka.
Uchiyama, Yuri. Ribbon Flowers, Paper Flowers.
Ucko, David. Living Chemistry.
UCLA-CEB Estate Planning Institute Staff. Estate Planning: Proceedings of the UCLA CEB Estate Planning Institute, Los Angeles, April, 1982.
Udall, Stewart, et al. The Energy Balloon.
Udall, Stewart L. Quiet Crisis.
Ud Din Attar, Farid see Attar, Farid Ud-Din.
Ude, Wayne. Buffalo & Other Stories.
Udell, William L., jt. auth. see Franke, Lois.
Uden, G. Understanding Book-Collecting.
Udhari, Abdullah al- see Al-Udhari, Abdullah.
Udintsev, G. B., ed. Geological-Geophysical Atlas of the Indian Ocean.
Udintsev, G. B., jt. ed. see Vinogradov, A. P.
Udo, Reuben K., ed. Population Education Sourcebook for Sub-Saharan Africa.
Udolf, Roy. Handbook of Hypnosis for Professionals.
Udolf, Roy, jt. auth. see Cohn, Alfred.
Ueda, R., ed. see International Spring School on Crystal Growth Staff.
Uehling, Carl T. Prayers for Lay Ministry.
--Prayers for Public Worship.
Ufliand, Vladimir. Teksty, Nineteen Fifty-Five to Nineteen Seventy-Seven.
Ugeux, Georges. Floating Rate Notes.
Ugo, R., jt. ed. see Tsutsui, M.
Uhl, Harold J. Good News from John: Visual Messages for Children.
Uhl, J., et al. An Attribute Grammar for the Semantic Analysis of Ada.
Uhlan, Edward. Dynamo Jim Stiles, Pioneer of Progress.
Uhlan, Edward & Peacock, A. D. To Save a Boy: The Story of Boys Home, North Carolina.
Uhlan, Edward, et al. What Every Writer Should Know about Publishing His Own Book.
Uhlan, Edward Foreword by see Lee, J. D.
Uhlendorf, Bernhard A., tr. see Dippel, Horst.
Uhles, E. N. How to Become an Effective Supervisor: A Survival Manual for the Man in the Middle.
Uhlig, H., ed. System & Theory of Geosciences.
Uhlir, Ludvik & Miklos, Frantisek, eds. Czechoslovakia.
Uhlman, Fred. Reunion.
Uhlmann, John & Heinrich, Peggy. Soul of Fire.
Uhnak, Dorothy. Victims.
Uhr, Carl G. Economic Doctrines of Knut Wicksell.
Uhr, Jonathan W. & Landy, Maurice, eds. Immunologic Intervention.
Uhran, Mark. Solar Energy for the Northeast.
Uitti, Karl D. Linguistics & Literary Theory.
--Story, Myth & Celebration in Old French Narrative Poetry 1050-1200.
Ulam, Adam. Fall of the American University.
Ulam, Adam B. The Rivals: America & Russia Since World War II.
Ulam, S. M. Adventures of a Mathematician.
Ulanoff, Stanley. Fighter Pilot: Aerial Combat Aces from Nineteen-Fourteen to the Present Day.
Ulanoff, Stanley M., ed. see Von Richthofen, Manfred.
Ulanov, Ann & Ulanov, Barry. Religion & the Unconscious.
Ulanov, Barry, jt. auth. see Ulanov, Ann.
Ulbrich, H. & Yandle, Bruce. Managing Personal Finance.
Uldall. Renal Nursing.
Ulehla, Ivan, et al. Optical Model of the Atomic Nucleus. Alter, G., tr.
Ulich, Robert. Education in Western Culture.
Ulick, Terry. Personal Publishing with the Macintosh.
Ulin, Priscilla & Segall, Marshall, eds. Traditional Health Care Delivery in Contemporary Africa.
Ulin, Richard O. Teaching & Learning about Aging.
Ullman, Agnes, jt. ed. see Lwoff, Andre.
Ullman, David, jt. auth. see Caswell, Christopher.
Ullman, James R. Banner in the Sky.
--Banner in the Sky.
--The Day on Fire.
Ullman, Jeffrey. The Single's Almanac.
Ullman, John, jt. auth. see Zilbergeld, Bernie.
Ullmann, L. P., jt. auth. see Krasner, L.
Ullmann, Stephen. Words & Their Use.
Ullmann, Walter. Law & Politics in the Middle Ages: An Introduction to the Sources of Medieval Political Ideas.
--A Short History of the Papacy in the Middle Ages.
Ullrich, Robert A. The Robotics Primer: The What, Why & How of Robots in the Workplace.
Ulmer, L. The Bible That Wouldn't Burn.
Ulrich, Celeste, ed. Physical Education.
Ulrich, Christine & Carolan, Milou. Software Reference Guide.
Ulrich, Dolph E., jt. auth. see Gustason, William.
Ulrich, F. Short Term Transit Policies & Downtown Revitalization.
Ulrich, Henri. Cycloaddition Reactions of Heterocumulenses.
Ulrich, Homer. Music: A Design for Listening.
Ulrich, Homer & Pisk, Paul A. History of Music & Musical Style.
Ulrich, R. D., ed. Contemporary Topics in Polymer Science, Vol. 1: Macromolecular Science - Retrospect & Prospect.
Ulrich, Tom J. Birds of the Northern Rockies.
Ultmann, J. E., et al, eds. Current Concepts in the Management of Lymphoma & Leukemia.
Ulug, S. Erol, jt. ed. see Odabasi, Halis.
Ulyanova, A. I. Lenin's Boyhood & Adolescence.
Ulyanovsky, R. Present-Day Problems in Asia & Africa.
Ulyanovsky, R. A. Socialism & the Newly Independent Nations.
Umbral, Francisco. A Mortal Spring. Lane, Helen R., tr. from Span.
Umbral Perez, Francisco. Diccionario Para Pobres.
Ume, Kalu E. The Rise of British Colonialism in Southern Nigeria, 1700-1900: A Study of the Bights of Benin and Bonny.
Umen, Samuel. Links Between Judaism & Christianity.
Umen, Samuel & Strickland, Mark. Pathway to the Bible.
Umiker. Effective Laboratory Supervisor.
Umiker-Sebeok, D. J. & Sebeok, T. A., eds. Aboriginal Sign Languages of the Americas & Australia. Incl. Vol. 1. North America - Classic Comparative Perspectives; Vol. 2. The Americas & Australia. Plenum Pub.
Umphred. Neurological Rehabilitation.
Umphrey, Don. The Meanest Man in Texas.
Umstot, Denis D. Understanding Organizational Behavior.
UN see United Nations.
Unamuno, M. De. Ficciones: Four Stories & a Play. Kerrigan, Anthony, tr. from Span. Nozick, Martin, ed.
Unamuno, Migual. Perplexities & Paradoxes.
Unanue, Emil R. & Rosenthal, Alan S., eds. Macrophage Regulation of Immunity.
Unbehauen, H., ed. Methods in Adaptive Control: Proceedings.
UNCTAD, Secretariat. Operation & Effects of the Generalized System of Preferences.
Underground Space Center Staff. Earth Sheltered Community Design: Energy-Efficient Residential Development.
--Earth Sheltered Housing: Code, Zoning, & Financing Issues.
Underground Space Center Staff, et al. Underground Building Design: Commercial & Institutional Structures.
Underhill, Edward B. West Indies: Their Social & Religious Condition.
Underhill, Evelyn. Light of Christ.
Underhill, Janet, jt. auth. see Faulhaber, Martha.
Underhill, Raymond A. Laboratory Anatomy of the Frog.
Underhill, Ruth. First Penthouse Dwellers of America.
Underhill, Ruth M. Red Man's America: A History of the Indians in the United States.
Underhill, Stefan, jt. auth. see Darbyshire, Tom.
Underhill, Tim & Miller, Chuck, eds. Jack Vance.
Underhill, W. Vance. Introduction to Analysis.
Underkoffler, Milton. Introduction to Structured Programming with Pascal.
--Introduction to Structured Programming with PL-1 & PL-C.
Underwager, Ralph C. I Hurt Inside: A Christian Psychologist Helps You Understand & Overcome Feelings of Fear, Frustration, & Failure.
Underwood, Betty. The Forge & the Forest.
--Tamarack Tree.
Underwood, C. H. Texas Six Man Football.
Underwood, Francis. The Colonial House Then & Now: A Picture Study of the Early American House Adapted to Modern Living.
Underwood, J. A., tr. see Robbe-Grillet, Alain.
Underwood, Jane H. Human Variation & Human Microevolution.
Underwood, John. Madcaps, Millionaires & Mose.
--Spoiled Sport: A Fan's Notes on the Troubles of Spectator Sports.
Underwood, John, jt. auth. see Williams, Ted.
Underwood, Lorraine A. Women in Federal Employment Programs.
Underwood, Michael. Death in Camera.
--The Silent Liars.
Underwood, Peter. Jack the Ripper: One Hundred Years of Mystery.
Underwood, Ralph L. Empathy & Confrontation in Pastoral Care.
Underwood, Tim & Miller, Chuck, eds. Kingdom of Fear.
Underwood, Trevor, ed. Foreign Exchange Yearbook, 1980.
Undy, Roger, jt. auth. see Martin, Roderick.
UNECE Staff. Economic Bulletin for Europe.
--Energy Modelling Studies & Conservation: Proceedings of a Seminar of the United Nations Economic Commission for Europe, Washington, D. C. 24-28 March 1980.
UNESCO General Conference Staff. From Concertation to Consensus: Proceedings of the UNESCO General Conference, 20th Session, 1978. M'Bow, Amadou-Mahtar, ed.
UNESCO, Regional Office for Education in Asia & the Pacific Staff. Directory of National Institutions of Educational Planning & Administration in Asia & the Pacific.
--Population Education in Non-Formal Education & Development Programmes: A Manual for Field Workers.
UNESCO Staff. Copyright Laws & Treaties of the World.
--Diccionario de Ciencias Sociales.
--Implementing Curriculum Change: Proceedings.
--Paris Cumulative Index to English Translations, 1948-1968.
--Race, Science, & Society.
--Records of the UNESCO General Conference, Nineteenth, 1976: Vol. 1, Resolutions.
--Records of the UNESCO General Conference, Third Extraordinary Session, Paris, 1973: Resolutions & Proceedings.
--World Conference on Cultural Policies: Final Report-Mexico City, July 26-August 6,1982.
UNESCO Staff & Polish Scientific Publications Staff. International Review of Sport Sociology: A Quarterly Edited by the Committee for Sociology of Sport of the International Council of Sport & Physical Education (UNESCO) & of the International Sociological Association.
UNESCO Staff, ed. Scientific Forecasting & Human Needs: Trends, Methods & Message.
UNESCO-United Nations Educational, Scientific & Cultural Organization (Paris) Staff. Statistical Yearbook (UNESCO) 1981.
Ungar, S. G. The Earth's Surface Studied from Space: Proceedings of Workshop II of the COSPAR Twenty-Fifth Plenary Meeting Held in Graz, Austria, 25 June-7 July 1984.
Ungar, Sanford J. Africa.
--Africa: The People & Politics of an Emerging Continent.
Ungaro, Dan & Borba, Michele. The Inner World of Reading.
Unger, F., ed. Assisted Circulation.
Unger, H. G. Introduction to Quantum Electronics.
Unger, Hans-Georg. Waveguide Tapers, Transitions & Couplers. Sporleder, Frank, ed.
Unger, Maurice A. How to Invest in Real Estate.
Unger, Merrill F. Unger's Bible Dictionary.
--Unger's Concise Bible Dictionary.
Ungerer, Tomi. Far Out Isn't Far Enough.
--The Joy of Frogs.
--Three Robbers.
Unger-Hamilton, Clive, jt. auth. see Kurtz, Irma.
Ungerson, Bernard, ed. Recruitment Handbook.
Ungerson, Clare. Moving Home.
Ungerson, Clare, jt. ed. see Evans, Mary.
Uniglobe Travel International Incorporated Staff. World Business Travel Guide.
Union of Concerned Scientists, jt. auth. see National Education Association Staff.
Union of Concerned Scientists Staff, et al. Beyond the Freeze: The Road to Nuclear Sanity.
Union of International Associations, Brussels Editors, ed. Yearbook of International Organizations 1986-87.
Union of International Associations, Brussels Editors. Yearbook of International Organizations 1986-87, Vol. 2: International Organization Participation Country Directory of Secretariats & Membership (Geographic Volume)
--Yearbook of International Organizations 1986-87, Vol. 3: Global Networks Classified Directory by Subject & Region.
Union of International Organizations Staff, ed. Yearbook of International Organizations, 1987-88: Global Networks: Classified Directory by Subject & Region (Subject Volume)
--Yearbook of International Organizations, 1987-88: International Organization Participation: Country Directory of Secretariats & Membership (Geographic Volume)
--Yearbook of International Organizations, 1987-88: Organizations Descriptions & Index.
Union of Soviet Socialist Republics see U.S.S.R.
Union Theological Seminar Library Staff. Alphabetical Arrangement of Main Entries from the Shelf List of the Union Theological Seminary Library.
--Shelf List of the Union Theological Seminary Library (New York))
United Airlines Friendship Guild Staff. Private-Stock Cookbook.
United Business Service Staff, ed. Successful Investing.
United Features Syndicate Staff. Wordy Gurdy.
United Libertarian Organization Staff. Spanish Revolution.
United Media Syndicate Staff. Star Hawks.
United Nations. Yearbook of Industrial Statistics 1981. Incl. Vol. I-General Industry Statistics, 1971-80; Vol. II-Commodity Production Data, 1971-1980. UN.
United Nations, ed. World Economic Survey, 1981-82.
United Nations Association of the U. S. A. Staff. Issues Before the Thirty-Seventh General Assembly of the United Nations. Puchala, Donald J., ed.
United Nations Association Staff. Issues Before the 38th General Assembly of the United Nations.
United Nations Centre for Natural Resources, Energy & Transport Staff. Register of International Rivers.
United Nations Centre on Transnational Corporations Staff. Transnational Corporations & International Trade: Selected Issues.
United Nations Conference on Science & Technology for Development Staff. Technology, Employment & Basic Needs - ILO Overview Paper: United Nations Conference on Science & Technology for Development.
United Nations Conference on Trade & Development Staff, produced by. Crop Insurance for Developing Countries.
United Nations Conference on Trade & Development Staff. Sixth International Tin Agreement.
United Nations Congress on the Prevention of Crime & the Treatment of Offenders Staff & Nelson, Alvar. Crime & Responses to Crime: Discussion Paper, Topic 1.
United Nations Decade for Women World Conference Staff. Equality, Development & Peace: Report.
United Nations, Department of International Economic & Social Affairs Staff. World Population Trends & Policies: 1981 Monitoring Report.
United Nations, Department of Public Information Staff. United Nations, Image & Reality.
United Nations, Department of Technical Cooperation for Development Staff. Workshop on Public Accounting & Auditing: Report-UN Headquarters March 2-10, 1981.
United Nations Development Fund for Women Staff. Development Co-operation with Women: The Experience & Future Directions of the Fund: Summary Findings, Conclusions & Future Operational Features of the Fund.
United Nations Economic & Social Council Staff. Transport of Dangerous Goods.
United Nations Economic Commission for Europe, Geneva, ed. see Seminar on Engineering Equipment for Foundries & Advanced Methods of Producing Such Equipment, Geneva, 1977.
United Nations Economic Commission for Europe, ed. see Load-Curve Coverage in Future Electrical Power Generating Systems Symposium Staff.

United Nations Economic Commission for Europe. Building Research Policies.
--Coal: Nineteen Eighty-Five & Beyond - A Perspective Study.
--Combined Production of Electric Power & Heat: Proceedings of a Seminar Organized by the Committee on Electric Power of the United Nations Economic Commission for Europe, Hamburg, FR Germany, 6-9 November 1978.
United Nations Economic Commission for Europe, Geneva, Switzerland. Energy Aspects of the Forest Industries: Proceedings of a Seminar Organized by the Timber Committee of the United Nations Economic Commission for Europe, Udine, Italy 13-17 Nov. 1978.
--Environment & Energy: Environmental Aspects of Energy Production & Use with Particular Reference to New Technologies.
United Nations Economic Commission for Europe. Environmental Impact Assessment: Proceedings of a Seminar of the United Nations Economic Commission for Europe, Villach, Austria.
--Factors of Growth & Investment Policies: An International Approach.
--Fine Particulate Pollution.
United Nations Economic Commission for Europe, Commission on Gas. The Gas Industry & the Environment: Proceedings of the United Nations Economic Commission for Europe, Commission on Gas, Minsk, U. S. S. R., 1977.
United Nations Economic Commission for Europe. Gas Situation in the EEC Region Around the Year 1990.
--Housing for Special Groups: Proceedings.
United Nations Economic Commission for Europe, Geneva, Switzerland. Hydroelectricity Prospects in the New Energy Situation: Proceedings of a Symposium of the Committee on Electric Power of the United Nations Commission for Europe, Athens, Greece, Nov. 5-9, 1979.
United Nations Economic Commission for Europe. Non-Waste Technology & Production: Proceedings of an International Seminar Held in Paris, Nov.-Dec. 1976.
United Nations Economic Commission for Europe, Geneva, Switzerland. Oils & Gases from Coal: A Review of the State-of-the-Art in Europe & North America Based on the Work of the Symposium on the Gasification & Liquefaction of Coal Held Under the Auspices of the UNECE, Katowice, Poland. 23-27 April 1979.
United Nations Economic Commission for Europe. Problems of the Agricultural Development of Less-Favoured Areas.
United Nations Economic Commission for Europe, Committee on Water Problems. Selected Water Problems in Islands & Coastal Waters: Proceedings, Malta, 1978.
United Nations Economic Commission for Asia & the Pacific. Statistical Indicators for Asia & the Pacific: September 1984.
United Nations Economic Commission for Western Asia, Natural Resources, Science & Technology Division. Technology Transfer & Change in the Arab World: Proceedings of a Seminar, Beirut, Oct. 1977. Zahlan, A. B., ed.
United Nations Economic Commission for Latin America. Water Management & Environment in Latin America: Analysis & Case Studies of Water Management, Including New Approaches Through Simulation Modelling & the Environmental Consequences of Past & Potential Trends in Water Use.
United Nations Educational, Scientific, Cultural Organization see UNESCO.
United Nations Environment Programme Staff & Moo-Young, M. Biotechnology & Waste Treatment: Proceedings of a Workshop Sponsored by the United Nations Environment Programme Held at the University of Waterloo, Canada, July 27-31, 1981.
United Nations Environment Programme Staff. Directory of Institutions & Individuals Active in Environmentally-Sound & Appropriate Technologies.
--Environmental Law: An In-Depth Review.
United Nations Fund for Population Activities Staff. Population Policy Compendium.
UN High Commission for Refugees, jt. auth. see International Labour Office Staff.
United Nations Industrial Development Organization Staff. Changing Patterns of Trade in World Industry: An Empirical Study on Revealed Comparative Advantage.
United Nations Institute for Disarmament Research Staff. Repertory of Disarmament Research: 1982.
United Nations Institute for Training & Research Staff. Assessing the United Nations Sale of Assessments: Is It Fair? Is It Equitable?
--International Conference on the Future Supply of Nature-Made Petroleum & Gas: Proceedings.
--New International Development Strategy: A Systems Analysis Approach.
United Nations Publications Staff. World Economic Survey 1984: Current Trends in the World Economy.
United Nations Scientific Committee on the Effects of Atomic Radiation. Ionizing Radiation Sources & Biological Effects: 1982 Report of the General Assembly, with Annexes.
United Nations, Secretariat. Conference on Desertification, Nairobi 1977. Desertification: Its Causes & Consequences.
United Nations Staff. Demographic Year Book.
--Demographic Year Book 1980.
--Demographic Yearbook: General Tables, 1978.
--Demographic Yearbook, 1980.
--Disarmament: A Periodic Review by the United Nations.
--Economic & Social Survey of Asia & the Pacific.
--Economic & Social Survey of Asia & the Pacific.
--Economic & Social Survey of Asia & the Pacific, 1976.
--Economic & Social Survey of Asia & the Pacific, 1977.
--Economic & Social Survey of Asia & the Pacific, 1978.
--Economic & Social Survey of Asia & the Pacific, 1980.
--Economic & Social Survey of Chamber of Commerce Japan, Asia & Pacific.
--Economic Bulletin for Africa.
--Economic Bulletin for Asia & the Pacific.
--Economic Survey of Europe.
--Economic Survey of Europe.
--Economic Survey of Europe in 1979.
--Economic Survey of Europe in 1980.
--Economic Survey of Latin America 1977.
--Economic Survey of Latin America 1979.
--Economic Survey of Latin America, 1980.
--International Immigration Policies & Programmes: World Survey.
--Statistical Yearbook for Latin America, 1979.
--Statistical Yearbook for Latin America, 1980.
--Statistical Yearbook 1978.
--Statistical Yearbook, 1979-1980.
--Statistical Yearbook, 1979-80.
--United Nations Disarmament Yearbook.
--World Economic Survey, 1980-1981.
--Yearbook National Accounts Statistics, 1980.
--Yearbook of Industrial Statistics, 1979: Vol. 1-General Industrial Statistics.
--Yearbook of International Trade Statistics-Annuaire Statistique du Commerce International, 1980: Vol. 1-Trade by Country; Vol. 2-Trade by Commodity.
--Yearbook of National Accounts Statistics, 1981.
--Yearbook of the United Nations.
--Yearbook of the United Nations, Vol. 32: Nineteen Seventy-Eight.
United Nations Staff, ed. Yearbook of the United Nations.
United Nations Statistical Office Staff, compiled by. A Global Review of Human Settlements & Statistical Annex.
UNICEF Staff, jt. auth. see Spiegelman, Judith M.
United States Advisory Commission on Intergovernmental Relations. State Constitutional & Statutory Restrictions upon the Structural, Functional, & Personnel Powers of Local Government.
United States Army, Continental Army Staff. General Orders of George Washington: Commander-in-Chief of the Army of Revolution Issued at Newburgh on the Hudson, 1782-1783. Boynton, Edward C., ed.
U. S. Army, Natick Labs. Staff. Glossary of Environmental Terms (Terrestrial)
U. S. Army, Security Agency, Historical Section Staff. Origin & Development of the Army Security Agency, 1917-1947.
U. S. Army Staff. Border Security - Anti-Infiltration Operations FM 31-55.
--Prisoner of War Resistance.
United States Attorney General's National Committee to Study the Antitrust Laws. Report of the United States Attorney General's National Committee to Study the Antitrust Laws.
U. S. Bureau of Labor Staff. Slums of Baltimore, Chicago, New York & Philadelphia.
United States Bureau of Labor Statistics Staff. The Gift of Freedom: A Study of the Economic & Social Status of Wage Earners in the United States.
--History of Wages in the United States from Colonial Times to 1928 with Supplement, 1929-1933.
--Subject Index of Bulletins Published by the Bureau of Labor Statistics: Consisting of "Subject Index of the Publications of the United States Bureau of Labor Statistics up to May 1, 1915" (Issued in 1915) & "Subject Index of Bulletins Published by the Bureau of Labor Statistics, 1915-1959" (Issued in 1960)
U. S. Bureau of the Census Staff. Heads of Families, First Census of the United States, 1790: Connecticut.
--Heads of Families, First Census of the United States, 1790: Maine.
--Heads of Families, First Census of the United States, 1790: Rhode Island.
--Heads of Families, First Census of the United States, 1790: Vermont.
--Marriage & Divorce, Nineteen Sixteen, Nineteen Twenty-Two to Thirty-Two.
U. S. Bureau of the Census Staff & Hall, Charles E. Negroes in the United States, 1920-1932.
U. S. Catholic Bishops Staff. The Challenge of Peace: God's Promise & Our Response.
U. S. Children's Bureau Staff. Handbook for Recreation.
United States Children's Bureau Staff. Rural Children in Selected Counties of North Carolina. Bradley, Francis S. & Williamson, Margaretta A., eds.
U. S. Commission on Civil Rights. Civil Rights U. S. A. Public Schools, Southern States, 1962, Staff Reports.
U. S. Congress, House Committee on Agriculture. Food Costs-Farm Prices: A Compilation or Information Relating to Agriculture.
U. S. Congress, House Committee on Banking & Currency. Money Trust Investigation of Financial & Monetary Conditions in the United States.
U. S. Congress, Senate Staff. Presidential Vetoes.
U. S. Copyright Office. Copyright in Congress, Seventeen Hundred Eighty-Nine to Nineteen Hundred Four. Solberg, Thorvald, ed.
U. S. Copyright Office Staff. Dramatic Compositions Copyrighted in the United States, 1870-1916.
U. S. Department of Agriculture, Agricultural Research Service Staff. Common Weeds of the United States.
United States Department of Agriculture, Bureau of Agricultural Economics Staff. Culture of Contemporary Rural Communities.
U. S. Department of Agriculture Staff. Handbook of Nutritional Contents of Foods.
U. S. Department of Agriculture, Soil Conservation Service Staff. Keys to Soil Taxonomy.
U. S. Department of Agriculture Staff. Plant Science Catalog: Botany Subject Index.
U. S. Department of Commerce Staff. Foreign Business Practices: Materials on Practical Aspects of Exporting, International Licensing & Investing.
U. S. Department of Commerce, Special Advisory Committee on Employment Statistics. The Measurement of Employment & Unemployment by the Bureau of the Census in Its Current Population Survey.
U. S. Department of Commerce Staff & Hopkins, R. A. NBS Metric Practice Guide & Style Manual.
U. S. Department of Commerce, National Technical Information Service Staff. Patent Profiles: Robots.
U. S. Department of Commerce Staff. Technical Digest-Symposium on Optical Fiber Measurements.
U. S. Department of Forestry Staff. Encyclopedia of Wood.
U. S. Department of Health, Education & Welfare, Washington, D. C. Staff. Author-Title Catalog of the Department Library: First Supplement. Incl. Author-Title Catalog. G K Hall.
U. S. Department of Health, Education & Welfare, Washington, D. C. Staff, ed. Author-Title Catalog of the Department Library.
--Subject Catalog of the Department Library.
--Subject Catalog of the Department Library: First Supplement.
U. S. Department of Housing & Urban Development, Washington, D. C. Staff, ed. Dictionary Catalog of the United States Department of Housing & Urban Development Library & Information Division.
--Dictionary Catalog of the United States Department of Housing & Urban Development Library & Information Division, First Supplement.
U. S. Department of Housing & Urban Development Staff. How to Insulate Your Home & Save Fuel.
United States Department of Housing & Urban Development Staff. How to Insulate Your Home & Save Fuel.
U. S. Department of Justice Staff. Police Handgun Ammunition: Incapacitation Effects.
U. S. Department of Justice Staff & Clark, Tom C. Prejudice & Property: An Historic Brief Against Racial Coveneants, Submitted to the Supreme Court.
U. S. Department of Labor. OSHA Field Operations Manual.
U. S. Department of the Interior, Washington, D. C. Staff, ed. Biographical & Historical Index of American Indians & Persons Involved in Indian Affairs.
U. S. Department of the Interior, U. S. Geological Survey, Washington, D. C. Staff, ed. Catalog of the United States Geological Survey Library.
--Catalog of the United States Geological Survey Library: Supplement 1.
--Catalog of the United States Geological Survey Library: 2nd Suppl.
--Catalog of the United States Geological Survey 3rd Suppl.
U. S. Department of the Interior, Washington, D. C. Staff, ed. Dictionary Catalog of the Department Library.
--Dictionary Catalog of the Department Library, Fourth Suppl.
U. S. Department of the Interior, Federal Water Pollution Control Administration, Committtee on Water Quality Criteria, et al. Health Information Systems Evaluation: Fish, Other Aquatic Life, & Wildlife - Report, 1968. Hurst, Leanard L. & Giebink, Gerald A., eds.
U. S. Department of the Interior Staff. Manual of Instructions for the Survey of the Public Lands of the United States.
U. S. Department of War Staff. Dog Team Transportation: Basic Field Manual.
U. S. Environmental Protection Agency Staff. Multi-Media Compliance Inspection Manual.
United States Federal Board for Vocational Education Staff. Study of Home-Economics Education in Teacher-Training Institutions for Negroes.
U. S. Federal Works Agency Staff. Final Report on the WPA Program, 1935-1943.
United States Geographic Board Staff. Sixth Report of the United States Geographic Board: 1890-1932.
U. S. Geological Survey Staff. Geology of Washington.
United States Immigration Commission. Dictionary of Races or Peoples.
United States Library of Congress, Census Library Project Staff. General Censuses & Vital Statistics in the Americas: An Annotated Bibliography of the Historical Censuses & Current Vital Statistics of the 21 American Republics.
U. S. Library of Congress, General Reference & Bibliography Division Staff. Current National Bibliographies.
--Sixty American Poets, Eighteen Ninety-Six to Nineteen Forty-Four.
U. S. Library of Congress, Legislative Reference Service Staff. Proposed Amendments to the Constitution of the United States Introduced in Congress from Dec. 4, 1889 to July 2, 1926. Tansill, Charles C., ed.
U. S. Library of Congress Staff. Guide to the Official Publications of Other American Republics: Washington, 1945-48.
U. S. National Archives Staff. Handbook of Federal World War Agencies & Their Records, 1917-1921.
--Lincoln Papers: The Story of the Collection with Selections to July 4, 1861.
U. S. Naval Academy, Class of 1934 Staff. The Golden Lucky Bag. Gralla, Arthur R., ed.
U. S. News Books Staff, ed. see Rust, William J.
United States Office of Adviser on Negro Affairs Staff. Urban Negro Worker in the United States, 1925-1936.
United States Office of Education, Division of Higher Education Staff. College Presidency Nineteen Hundred to Nineteen Sixty: An Annotated Bibliography. Eells, Walter C., ed.
United States Office of Education Staff. Negro Education: A Study of the Private & Higher Schools for Colored People in the United States.
--Survey of Negro Colleges & Universities.
U. S. Olympic Water Polo Team Staff & Hale, Ralph W., eds. The Complete Book of Water Polo.
U. S. Pharmacopeial Convention, Incorporated Staff. Drug Information for the Consumer, 1988 Edition.
United States Pharmacopoeial Convention Staff. The Physicians' & Pharmacists' Guide to Your Medicines.
U. S. Policy Toward Southern Africa Study Commission. South Africa: Time Running Out.
U. S. Post Office Department Staff. Street Directory of the Principal Cities of the United States: Embracing Letter-Carrier Offices Established to April 30, 1908.
U. S. President's Commission on the Status of Women. American Women: The Report. Mead, Margaret & Kaplan, Frances B., eds.
U. S. Public Health Service. Air Pollution in Donora: An Analysis of the Extreme Effects of Smog.
United States Securities & Exchange Commission & Federal Bar Association, Securities Law Committee. Regulation D Offerings of Limited Partnerships & Corporate Capital Raising: At the Commission & in Practice: ALI-ABA Course of Study Materials.
U. S. Specialty Group on Infrared Detectors. Infrared Detectors. Moss, T. S. & Wolfe, W. L., eds.

U. S. Strategic Bombing Survey Staff. Campaigns of the Pacific War.
United States Superintendent of Documents. Decennial Cumulative Index 1941-1950 to United States Government Publications Monthly Catalog.
United States Supreme Court Staff, jt. auth. see Judicial Conference of the United States, Committee on Rules of Practice & Procedure.
U. S. Synchronized Swimming Staff. U. S. Synchronized Swimming Rulebook, 1985.
United States Task Force on the Administration of Justice. Task Force Report: The Courts.
U. S. Tennis Association, Education & Research Center Staff. Financing Public Tennis Courts.
United States Trademark Association Staff. Trademark Law Handbook 1985-86.
U. S. Travel Data Center Staff, jt. auth. see Business Research Division Staff.
U. S. War Department Staff & Stimson, Henry L. Prelude to Invasion.
Unity School of Christianity Staff, ed. Works & Wonders.
Universal City Studios, Inc. Staff. Talking E. T. Wordbook.
Universal Races Congress Staff. Papers on Inter-Racial Problems.
Universite Laval, Centre d'Etudes Nordiques, Quebec Staff. Bibliographie de la Peninsule du Quebec-Labrador. Cooke, Alan & Caron, Fabien, eds.
University Books, ed. Study & Practice of Yoga.
University Film Centers Consortium Staff. Motion Picture Film Maintenance Manual, 16MM.
University of Akron, School of Law Staff & American Law Institute-American Bar Association Committee on Continuing Professional Education. Tax Planning for Closely Held Businesses: University of Akron School of Law Institute Symposium III: ALI-ABA Course of Study Materials.
University of Arizona Library Staff, ed. The Arizona Index: A Subject Index to Periodical Articles About the State.
University of California, Berkeley Staff, ed. Bancroft Library, Catalog of Printed Books.
--Dictionary Catalog of the Giannini Foundation of Agricultural Economics Library.
--Dictionary Catalog of the Water Resources Center Archives.
--Dictionary Catalog of the Water Resources Center Archives, Fourth Suppl.
--Dictionary Catalog of the Water Resources Center Archives: Sixth Supplement.
University of California - Berkeley Staff. East Asiatic Library. Incl. Pt. 1. Author-Title Catalog; Pt. 2. Subject Catalog. G K Hall.
University of California, Berkeley Staff. East Asiatic Library. Incl. Author Catalog, First Supplement; Subject Catalog, First Supplement. G K Hall.
University of California, Department of Nursing Service Staff. Mosby's Manual of Clinical Nursing Procedures.
University of California, Heller Committee for Research in Social Economics. Cost of Living Studies.
University of California, San Diego Staff, ed. Catalogs of the Scripps Institution of Oceanography Library, First Supplement to Pt. 1: Author-Title Catalog.
University of California Staff. Publications in Economics.
--Publications in International Relations.
--Publications in Mathematical & Physical Sciences.
University of Chicago Staff. Catalog of the Oriental Institute Library, Supplement I.
--Catalogs of the Far Eastern Library.
University of Colorado, Boulder School of Law Staff & American Law Institute-American Bar Association Committee on Continuing Professional Education. The Bankruptcy Code Reexamined & Updated.
University of Connecticut, Center for Real Estate & Urban Economic Studies Staff & Galonska, Michael L. Connecticut Supplement for Modern Real Estate Practice.
University of Denver, College of Law Staff & Motor Carriers Lawyers Association Staff. Transportation Law: Institute 81 (A Practice Primer for the Eighties - 14th Annual)
University of Florida, Gainesville, Baldwin Library of Childrens Literature Editors. Index to Children's Literature in English Before 1900: Catalog of the Baldwin Library of the University of Florida at Gainesville.
University of Florida Staff. Another Step Forward.
University of Geneva Staff. Archives Jean Piaget: Catalog of the Jean Piaget Archives.
University of Glasgow Staff & Abbott, George. Sugar.
University of Hawaii, Environmental Center Staff, jt. auth. see Hawaii, Office of Environmental Quality Control Staff.
University of Hawaii, Honolulu Staff. Sinclair Library: Dictionary Catalog of the Hawaiian Collection.
University of Illinois at Urbana, University Library, Champaign Staff, ed. Catalog of the Rare Book Room.
--Mereness Calendar: Federal Documents on the Upper Mississippi Valley, 1780-1890.
University of Illinois, Communications Library Staff, ed. Catalog of the Communications Library.
University of Kansas Academic Computing Services Staff. Learning Z-BASIC on the Heath-Zenith Z-100.
University of London, Institute of Education Staff. Catalogue of the Comparative Education Library, 1st Suppl.
--Catalogue of the Comparative Education Library.
University of London, Institute of Historical Research Staff. Corrections & Additions to the Dictionary of National Biography Cumulated from the Bulletin of the Institute of Historical Research Covering the Years 1923-1963.
University of London Library Staff. Palaeography Collection.
University of London - School of Oriental & African Studies Staff. Library Catalogue of the School of Oriental & African Studies.
University of London, School of Oriental & African Studies Staff. Library Catalogue of the School of Oriental & African Studies: Third Supplement.
University of London - School of Oriental & African Studies Staff. Library Catalogue of the School of Oriental & African Studies: 2nd Supplement.
University of London - Warburg Institute Staff. Catalog of the Warburg Institute Library.
University of Michigan, Ann Arbor, Clements, William L., Library Staff. Author-Title & Chronological Catalogs of Americana, 1493-1860, in the William L. Clements Library.
University of Michigan Staff. Catalogs of the Asia Library, the University of Michigan.
University of Missouri-Kansas City School of Law Staff, et al. Growing Companies: Tax & Business Planning for the '80s (ALI-ABA Course of Study Materials)
University of Natal - Pietermaritzburg - Department of Sociology & Social Work Staff. Small Towns of Natal, a Socioeconomic Sample Survey.
University of Nebraska Medical School Symposium Staff. The Role of Membranes in Metabolic Regulation: Proceedings of the University of Nebraska Medical School Symposium, Omaha, Neb, May 1972. Mehlman, Myron A. & Hanson, Richard W., eds.
University of North Carolina at Chapel Hill Institute of Government & Drennan, James C. The Safe Roads Act of Nineteen Eighty-Three: A Summary & Compilation of Statutes Amended or Affected by the Act.
University of North Carolina, Institute of Government, Chapel Hill Staff & Sawyer, Ann L. Liquor Offenses: Arrest Warrant Forms.
University of Pennsylvania Staff. Catalog of the Edgar Fahs Smith Memorial Collection in the History of Chemistry.
University of Pittsburgh Staff, jt. auth. see Instrument Society of America Staff.
University of Sheffield Conference Staff. Hydraulic Cement Pastes, Their Structure & Properties: Proceedings of the University of Sheffield Conference, April 8-9, 1976.
University of Singapore Library Staff. Catalogue of the Singapore-Malaysia Collection.
University of Southern California, Los Angeles Staff. Catalog of the Hoose Library of Philosophy.
University of Southern California Staff. Author-Title & Subject Catalogs of the Ethel Percy Andrus Gerontology Center.
University of Tennessee, 1979, Knoxville, Tenn. Staff. Independent Living Skills for the Severely Handicapped Deaf Person Preparing to Enter Gainful Employment. Ouellette, Sue E. & Lloyd, Glenn T., eds.
University of Texas at Austin Staff. Catalog of the Latin American Collection of the University of Texas Library.
--Catalog of the Latin American Collection of the University of Texas Library: Second Supplement.
--Catalog of the Latin American Collection of the University of Texas Library, Third Supplement.
University of Texas, Austin Staff. Catalog of the Texas Collection in the Barker Texas History Center.
University of Texas Library, Austin Staff. Catalog of the Latin American Collection of the University of Texas Library, First Supplement.
--Catalog of the Latin American Collection of the University of Texas Library.
University of the State of New York, Foreign Area Materials Center Staff. Africa South of the Sahara: A Bibliography for Undergraduate Libraries. Duignan, Peter, ed.
--Middle East & North Africa: A Bibliography for Undergraduate Libraries. Howard, Harry N., ed.
--Southeast Asia: A Bibliography for Undergraduate Libraries. Johnson, Donald C., ed.
University of the West Indies, Imperial College of Tropical Agriculture, Trinidad Staff. Catalogue of the Imperial College of Tropical Agriculture.
University of Virginia School of Law Staff & Redden, Kenneth R. Federal Special Court Litigation.
University of Washington Staff. Manual of Freshman English.
University of Wisconsin, Madison, Land Tenure Center Staff. The Land Tenure Center: Its First Three Years: a Cooperative Program of the American Nations, the Agency for International Development, & the University of Wisconsin.
University of Wyoming Staff. Packing & Outfiting Field Manual.
Unopolus, James J. Scriptural Signs of the Second Coming.
Unruh, Adolph & Willier, Robert A. Public Relations for Schools.
Unseld, D. W. German-English, English-German Medical Dictionary.
Unseld, Wes, jt. auth. see Monroe, Earl.
Unsworth, Barry. The Rage of the Vulture.
--Stone Virgin.
Unsworth, Richard P., jt. auth. see Kenseth, Arnold.
Unsworth, Walt. Everest: A Mountaineering History.
Unterecker, John. Voyager: A Life of Hart Crane.
Unterman, Alan. The Jews.
Unterman, Isaac. Pirke Aboth.
Unterman, Patricia & Sesser, Stan. Restaurants of San Francisco: The Definitive Guide to the Bay Area's Best.
Untermeyer, Louis. Long Feud: Selected Poems.
Untermeyer, Louis, ed. The Forms of Poetry: A Pocket Dictionary of Verse.
--Magic Circle: Stories & People in Poetry.
--A Miscellany of American Poetry, 1920.
--Modern American & Modern British Poetry.
--Modern American Poetry.
--Modern British Poetry.
--Rainbow in the Sky.
--This Singing World: Junior Edition.
--Treasury of Great Poems. Incl. Vol. 1. Chaucer to Burns; Vol. 2. Wordsworth to Dylan Thomas. S&S.
Untersteiner. The Sophists.
Unwin, David. Fifty Years with Father.
--Introductory Spatial Analysis.
Unwin, J. C. The Hungry Forties: Life Under the Bread Tax.
Unwin, James O. The Future of Religion.
Unwin, Philip. The Printing Unwins.
Upadhyaya, K. N. A Textbook of Inorganic Chemistry: General Principles.
--A Textbook of Inorganic Chemistry: The Representative Elements.
--A Textbook of Inorganic Chemistry: The Transition Elements.
Updike, David. A Winter's Journey.
Updike, John. Centaur.
--The Witches of Eastwick.
Updike, John & Ravenel, Shannon, eds. The Best American Short Stories 1984.
Updite, Evelyn F. Tambia Bourri.
Upfield, Arthur. The Bone Is Pointed.
Upfield, Arthur W. The House of Cain. Farmer, Philip Jose, intro. by.
Upham, Charles W. Salem Witchcraft.
Upham, N. E. Anchors.
Uphoff, Norman. Analyzing Options for Local Institutional Development.
Uphoff, Norman T. & Ilchman, Warren F., eds. The Political Economy of Development: Theoretical & Empirical Contributions.
Uphoff, Robert W. That the Door May Open.
UPI Staff & American Heritage Magazine Staff. Four Days: The Historical Record of the Death of President Kennedy.
Upper Room Staff. Journeying Through the Days, 1988.
Upson, Norma S. When Someone You Love Is Dying.
Upton, Arvin. Lorenzino.
Upton, Barbara L. & Upton, John. Photography.
Upton, John, jt. auth. see Upton, Barbara L.
Uraguchi, Kenji & Yamazaki, Mikio, eds. Toxicology: Biochemistry & Pathology of Mycotoxins.
Ural, Oktay, ed. Energy Resources & Conservation Related to Built Environment: Proceedings of the International Conference, Dec. 7-12, 1980, Miami Beach, Florida.
Urang, Gunnar. Shadows of Heaven: Religion & Fantasy in the Writing of C. S. Lewis, Charles Williams & J. R. R. Tolkien.
Urban & Regional Planning Advisory Committee, ed. see Hart, Douglas.
Urban, G. R., ed. Detente.
Urban, George. Hazards of Learning: An International Symposium on the Crisis of the University.
Urban Innovations Group, Inc. Staff. The Arts in the Economic Life of the City.
Urban, Julia M. The Smile & the Cry: Memoirs of a Lithuanian Woman.
Urban Land Institute, Panel Advisory Service Staff. Cleveland, Ohio: An Evaluation of the Target Area Investment Program for the City of Cleveland, June 5-10, 1983; a Panel Advisory Service Report.
Urban, Mark. Soviet Land Power.
Urban, P. Topics in Applied Quantum Electrodynamics.
Urban, P., ed. Contacts Between High Energy Physics & Other Fields of Physics: Proceedings.
--Current Problems in Elementary Particle & Mathematical Physics.
Urban, P., ed. see International Universitaetswochen Fuer Kernph Staff.
Urban, P., ed. see International University Courses on Nuclear Physics Staff.
Urban, P., ed. see International University Courses on Nuclear Physics, 3rd, Schladming, Austria, 1964.
Urban, P., ed. see International University Courses on Nuclear Physics, 5th, Schladming, Austria, 1966.
Urban, P., ed. see International University Courses on Nuclear Physics, 6th, Schladming, Austria, 1967.
Urban, P., ed. see International University Courses on Nuclear Physics, 7th, Schladming, Austria, 1968.
Urban, P., ed. see International University Courses on Nuclear Physics, 8th, Schladming, Austria, 1969.
Urban, Wayne J. Why Teachers Organized.
Urban, Wilbur M. The Intelligible World: Metaphysics & Value.
Urban Wildlife Research Center, Inc. Staff, et al. Planning for Wildlife in Cities & Suburbs.
Urbana Conference on Phonology Staff. Issues in Phonological Theory: Proceedings of the Urbana Conference on Phonology, University of Illinois, 1971. Kenstowicz, Michael J. & Kisseberth, Charles W., eds.
Urbanska, Wanda. Singular Generation.
Urbaschek, B. & Urbaschek, R., eds. Gram-Negative Bacterial Infections & Mode of Endotoxin Actions - Pathophysiologic, Immunologic, & Clinical Aspects.
Urbaschek, R., jt. ed. see Urbaschek, B.
Urbick, Dee, jt. auth. see Spring, Vicky.
Urbistondo, R., ed. Contamination of Groundwater & Groundwater Treatment: Part of the Proceedings of the Specialized Conference of the IWSA Held in Berlin, FRG, 22-28 April 1985.
Urbistondo, R. & Bays, L. R., eds. Groundwater Management: Part of the Proceedings of the Specialized Conference of the IWSA Held in Berlin, FRG, 22-28 April 1985.
--Water Quality & Treatment.
--Water Supply: Second Atlantic Workshop: Prooceedings of the Specialised Workshop of the ISWA Held in Nice, France, 3-7 March 1984.
Urbistondo, R. & Trueb, E., eds. World Water Supply: Proceedings of the Fourteenth World Congress of the International Water Supply Association held in Zurich, Switzerland, 6-10 September, 1982.
Urdahl, Richard. Last Night I Dreamed: Twenty One Short Plays.
--Plays for Clowns in Christ: Four Short Plays for the Fun of Playing!!
Urdang, Constance. The Lone Woman & Others.
Urdang, Elliott B., tr. see Caraion, Ion.
Urdang, Laurance, ed. Allusions Cultural, Literary, Biblical, & Historical: A Thematic Dictionary.
Urdang, Laurence. Lives of the Georgian Age: 1714-1837. Gould, William & Hanks, Patrick, eds.
Urdang, Laurence, ed. Verbatim: A Language Quarterly.
Urdang, Stephanie. A Revolution within a Revolution: Women in Guinea-Bissau.
Ure, Andrew. Cotton Manufacture of Great Britain Systematically Investigated.
Ure, Jean. Supermouse.
--The You-Two.
Uren, John & Price, William F. Calculations for Engineering Surveys.
Uren, Philip E., jt. auth. see Fischer, Lewis A.
Urena, Rafael A. The Travels of the Golden Fish & Other Bilingual Children's Stories.
Urguhart, N. Scott, jt. auth. see Clow, Duane J.
Uri, Pierre. Development Without Dependence.
Uribe, M. Tecnicas Modernas De Archivo.
Urie, Paul M., jt. auth. see Anstall, Harold B.

Authors

Urinary Tract Infection Symposium Staff. Urinary Tract Infection: Proceedings of the Symposium, London, England, Sept. 23-24, 1974. Asscher, A. W. & Brumfit, W., eds.
Uris, Auren. The Executive Deskbook.
--Executive Dissent: How to Say No & Win.
--Realworld Management Deskbook.
Uris, Jill. Ireland Revisited.
Uris, Leon. The Haj.
--QB Seven.
Uroff, Margaret D. Becoming a City: From Fishing Village to Manufacturing Center.
--Sylvia Plath & Ted Hughes.
Urosevich, Patricia R. & McVan, Barbara, eds. Attending Ob-Gyn Patients.
--Carrying Out Special Procedures.
Urosevich, Patti & McVan, Barbara, eds. Aiding Ambulatory Patients.
--Giving Cardiovascular Drugs Safely.
Urosevich, Patti & McVann, Barbara, eds. Managing Diabetes Properly.
Urquhart, jt. auth. see Grist.
Urquhart, A. J., jt. auth. see Rescher, N.
Urquhart, Jane M., jt. auth. see Engeln, Oscar Dedrich Von.
Urquhart, R. M. Scottish Burgh & County Heraldry.
Urry, John, jt. auth. see Abercrombie, Nicholas.
Ursin, H. & Murison, R., eds. Biological & Physical Basis of Psychosomatic Disease: Based on Papers Presented at a Conference on Psychological Load & Stress in the Work Environment, Bergen, Norway, 1980.
Ursin, Holger, et al, eds. Psychobiology of Stress: A Study of Coping Men.
Ursprung, H. & Noethiger, R. The Biology of Imaginal Disks.
Ursprung, H., ed. Nucleic Acid Hybridization in the Study of Cell Differentiation.
--Stability of the Differentiated State.
Ursprung, H., jt. ed. see Reinert, J.
URSS, Ministerio de Defensa Staff. Quienes Amenazan a la Paz.
Ursu, I., jt. ed. see Prokhorov, A. N.
Urton, Gary. At the Crossroads of the Earth & the Sky: An Andean Cosmology.
Urvater, Michele. Fine Fresh Food-Fast. Atcheson, Richard, ed.
Urvater, Michele & Liedermann, David. Cooking the Nouvelle Cuisine in America.
Urwick, L. & Wolf, W. The Golden Book of Management.
Urwick, Lydall, jt. ed. see Gulick, Luther H.
Uscinski, Barry J. The Elements of Wave Propagation in Random Media.
Usda, et al. Soil Taxonomy: A Basic System of Soil Classification for Making & Interpreting Soil Surveys.
Usdin, E. & Hanin, I., eds. Biological Markers in Psychiatry & Neurology: Symposium on Biological Markers in Psychiatry & Neurology, Ochsner Clinic, New Orleans, U. S. A., 8-10 May 1981.
Usdin, Earl & Efron, Daniel H. Psychotropic Drugs & Related Compounds.
Usdin, Earl & Snyder, Solomon, eds. Frontiers in Catecholamine Research: Proceedings, International Catecholamine Symposium, 3rd, Strasbourg, France, May, 1973.
Usdin, Earl, ed. see Barchas, Jack.
Usdin, Earl, et al, eds. Catecholamines: Basic & Clinical Frontiers: Proceedings of the Fourth International Catecholamine Symposium; Asilomar Conference Center, Pacific Grove, California; September 17-22, 1978.
--Catecholamines & Stress.
Usdin, Gene & Lewis, Jerry M., eds. Psychiatry in General Medical Practice.
Useem, Michael. Protest Movements in America.
Uselding, Paul, jt. ed. see Cain, Louis.
Usherwood, P. N. Insect Muscle.
Ushiba, Nobuhiko & Curtis, Gerald L. Japan: A Partnership in Progress.
Ushinsky, K. Selected Works.
Uslan, Michael, jt. auth. see Solomon, Bruce.
Uslander, Arlene & Weiss, Lee D. A Doctor Discusses Talking with Your Child About Sex.
Uslander, Arlene, jt. auth. see Weiss, Caroline.
Uslaner, Eric M., jt. auth. see Spanier, John.
Uslenghi, Piergiorgio L., ed. Electromagnetic Scattering.
U.S.S. Will Rogers Wive's Staff. Chuckwagon Cookbook. Bremer, Kathy A., ed.
Ussing, H. H., et al, eds. see Benzon, Alfred, Symposium.
Ussovsky, B. N. & Linnard, W. Comprehensive Russian-English Agricultural Dictionary.
Ustinov, Peter. My Russia.
Usui, Masao, illus. Form & Function: Japanese Brushes.
--Form & Function: Japanese Knives.
--Form & Function: Japanese Spoons & Ladles.
Usvatov, A., et al. Kampuchea: From Tragedy to Rebirth.
Utah Governor's Commission on the Status of Women, compiled by. Utah Women & the Law: A Resource Handbook.
Utall, William R., jt. auth. see Robinson, Daniel N.
Utke, Allen R. Bio-Babel: Can We Survive the New Biology?
Utley, Robert M. & Washburn, Wilcomb E. The American Heritage History of the Indian Wars.
Utrecht, William. Be Your Own Doctor.
Utterback, James M., jt. ed. see Hill, Christopher T.
Uttley, A. M. Information Transmission in the Nervous System.
Uttley, Alison. Foxglove Tales. Meredith, Lucy, selected by.
--A Traveller in Time.
Utz, Fred. Collision Course: How to Handle Your Own Automobile Damage Claim Without Getting Ripped Off.
Utz, Peter. Video User's Handbook.
Uvarov, E. B., et al. Dictionary of Science.
Uvezian, Sonia. The Best Foods of Russia: Culinary Classics from the Caucasus.
--The Book of Salads.
--Cooking from the Caucasus.
Uviller, H. Richard. Processes of Criminal Justice: Investigation.
Uwechue, Ralph. Know Africa. Incl. Vol. 1. Africa Today; Vol. 3. Makers of Modern Africa; Vol. 3. Africa Who's Who. Gale.
Uys, Errol L. Brazil.
Uzgiris, I. C. & Weizman, F., eds. The Structuring of Experience.
Uzkan, T., ed. Flows in Internal Combustion Engines.

V

Vaage, S. Segmentation of the Primitive Neural Tube in Chick Embryos: A Morphological, Histochemical & Autoradiographical Investigation.
Vaagland, Jorid, jt. auth. see Puijk, Roel.
Vacc, Nicholas & Wittmer, Joseph. Let Me Be Me.
Vaccara, Beatrice N. Employment & Output in Protected Manufacturing Industries.
Vaccara, Beatrice N., jt. ed. see Kendrick, John W.
Vaden, Frank S., jt. auth. see Arnold, Tom.
Vadim, Roger. Bardot, Deneuve, Fonda: An Autobiography.
--The Hungry Angel. Attwood, William, tr.
--Memoirs of the Devil. Okrent, Daniel, ed. Beglan, Peter, tr.
Vaes, Alain. The Wild Hamster.
Vagg, John & Maguire, Mike, eds. Accountability & Prisons: Opening up a Closed World.
Vagner, R., jt. ed. see Bowen, A.
Vago, Bela, jt. ed. see Mosse, George.
Vago, C. Invertebrate Tissue Culture.
Vago, Steven. Law & Society.
--Social Change.
Vagtborg, Harold. Research & American Industrial Development.
Vahanian, Gabriel. The Death of God.
Vaid, Sudesh. The Divided Mind: Studies in Defoe & Richardson.
Vaihinger, H. The Philosophy of As If: A System of the Theoretical, Practical & Religious Fictions of Mankind.
Vaihinger, Hans. Commentar Zu Kants Kritik der Reinen Vernunft. Beck, Lewis W., ed. Incl. Vol. 1. Stuttgart 1881; Vol. 2. Stuttgart & Berlin 1892. Garland Pub.
Vail, David J. Technology for Ujamaa Village Development in Tanzania.
Vail, Linda. Choices & Chances.
Vail, Peter, jt. auth. see Genis, Alexandr.
Vail, Van H., jt. auth. see Sparks, Kimberly.
Vail, Van Horn & Sparks, Kimberly. Modern German.
--Der Weg Zum Lesen.
Vaill, Peter B. Managing As a Performing Art: New Ideas for a World of Chaotic Change.
Vaillant, George C. Indian Arts in North America.
Vainberg, M., ed. Electrical Shocks-Safety & Related Criteria: Symposium on Safety-Related Criteria for Electrical Shocks, Toronto, Canada, Sept. 7-9, 1983.
Vainio, Harri, et al, eds. Occupational Cancer & Carcinogenesis.
Vainshtein, B. K. Structure Analysis by Electron Diffraction.
Vaish, M. C. Money Banking & International Trade.
Vaitses, Allan H. Boatbuilding One-Off in Fiberglass.
Vaizey, Marina. The Artist As Photographer.
--Peter Blake.
Vajda, S. Linear Programming: Algorithms & Applications.
--Mathematics of Manpower Planning.
Vajta, Vilmos, ed. The Gospel & the Ambiquity of the Church.
--The Gospel As History.
--The Lutheran Church: Past & Present.
Vakman, D. E. Sophisticated Signals & the Uncertainty Principle in Radar. Jacobs, Ernest, ed. Trirogoff, K. N., tr.
Valadian, Isabelle & Porter, Douglas. Physical Growth & Development: From Conception to Maturity.
Valanis, K. C., ed. Constitutive Equations in Viscoplasticity: Phenomenological & Physical Aspects AMD.
Valatx, J., jt. ed. see Borbely, A.
Valcour, Gary. The Color of Greed.
Valdene, Guy de la see De la Valdene, Guy.
Valdez, Pamela. Complete Guide to Bed & Breakfast Inns.
Valdman, Albert & Barnett, Marva A. Instructor's Manual for en Route: Introduction au Francais: Et au Monde Francophone.
Valdre, U., ed. see Centre for Scientific Culture Ettore Majorana, International School of Electron Microscopy Staff.
Vale, Michel, tr. see Fernandes, Florestan.
Vale, Michel, tr. see Komarov, Boris.
Vale, Michel, tr. see Olcott, Martha B., et al.
Valencia, Pablo & Merlonghi, Franca. En Contacto: A First Course in Spanish.
Valenti, Jack. A Very Human President.
Valentine, Alan & Valentine, Lucia. The American Academy in Rome, 1894-1969.
Valentine, C. W. Psychology & Its Bearing on Education.
Valentine, Douglas. The Hotel Tacloban.
Valentine, E. R. Conceptual Issues in Psychology.
Valentine, Ferdinand. Art & Technique of Prayer.
Valentine, James. Florida, Images of the Landscape.
Valentine, James, photos by. Georgia.
Valentine, Lucia, jt. auth. see Valentine, Alan.
Valentine, Mary H. Saints for Contemporary Women.
Valentine, P. F. The American College.
Valentine, P. F., ed. Twentieth Century Education.
Valenza, Joseph J. Program Housing Standards in the Experimental Housing Allowance Program: Analyzing Differences in the Demand & Supply Experiments.
Valenza, Samuel W., Jr., ed. The Lottery Players Magazine Official Traveler's Guide to Lotteries 1983.
Valenzuela, Arturo & Valenzuela, J. Samuel, eds. Chile: Politics & Society.
Valenzuela, J. Samuel, jt. ed. see Valenzuela, Arturo.
Valenzuela, Luisa. Clara: Thirteen Short Stories & a Novel. Carpentier, Hortense & Castello, Jorge, trs.
--Strange Things Happen Here: Twenty-Six Short Stories & a Novel.
Valeri, Maria. The Alphabet Book of Feelings.
Valeriani, Richard. Travels with Henry.
Valerio, D. A., et al. Macaca Mulatta: Management of a Laboratory Breeding Colony.
Valerius, Sandra. Rumbeard.
Valery, Paul. Les Bucoliques de Virgile. Bd. with Variations sur les Bucoliques. French & Eur.
--Les Cahiers.
--Cahiers.
--Le Cimetiere Marin. Martin, Graham D., ed. & tr. from Fr.
--L' Idee Fixe ou Deux Hommes a la Mer.
--Introduction a la Methode de Leonardo da Vinci.
--Mon Faust.
--Poesies. Bd. with Album de Vers Anciens; La Jeune Parque; Charmes; Pieces Diverses; Cantate du Narcisse; Amphion; Semiramis. Schoenhof.
--Regards sur le Monde Actuel.
Valeton, E. M. Dutch Costumes.
Valette, Jean P., jt. auth. see Valette, Rebecca M.
Valette, Jean-Paul & Valette, Rebecca. Contacts: Langue et Culture Francaises.
--Contacts: Langue et Culture Francaises.
Valette, Jean-Paul, et al. Con Mucho Gusto: Lengua y Cultura del Mundo Hispanico.
Valette, Rebecca, jt. auth. see Valette, Jean-Paul.
Valette, Rebecca M. Lectures libres.
Valette, Rebecca M. & Disick, Renee S. Modern Language Performance Objectives & Individualization: A Handbook.
Valette, Rebecca M. & Morgenroth, Robert L. C'est de la Prose.
Valette, Rebecca M. & Valette, Jean P. France: A Cultural Review Grammar.
Valette, Rebecca M., jt. auth. see Allen, Edward D.
Valin, Jonathan. Life's Work: A Harry Stoner Novel.
--Natural Causes.
Valkenberg, Phil Van see Van Valkenberg, Phil.
Valkenberg, Philip Van see Van Valkenberg, Philip.
Valkenberg, Philip Van see Van Valkenberg, Philip & Shidell, Doug.
Valkenburg, M. E. Van see Van Valkenburg, M. E.
Valkenburgh, Van see Van Valkenburgh, et al.
Vall, Stephen Du see Du Vall, Stephen.
Vallance, H. A. The Highland Railway: The History of the Railways of the Scottish Highlands.
Vallbona, Rima. Mujeres y Agonias.
Valle, Victor, tr. see De Carvalho-Neto, Paulo.
Vallee, Lillian, tr. see Mur, Jan.
Valle-Inclan, Ramon. The Pleasant Memoirs of the Marquis De Bradomin. Heywood Broun, May & Walsh, Thomas, trs. from Span.
Vallejo, Antonio Buero see Buero Vallejo, Antonio.
Vallentin, Antonina. This I Saw: The Life & Times of Goya. Woods, Katherine W., tr. from Fr.
Vallentine, John F. Range Development & Improvements.
Vallentine, John F. & Sims, Phillip L., eds. Range Science: A Guide to Information Sources.
Vallet, H. Lawrence & Porter, Ian H., eds. Genetic Mechanisms of Sexual Development.
Vall-Spinosa, Arthur, et al. Rifomycin: Chemotherapy.
Valman, H. Bernard. ABC of One to Seven.
Valmiki. Ramayana. Rajagopalachari, Chakravarti, ed. & tr. from Tamil.
Valois, Robert F., et al. Wellness R.S.V.P.
Valone, James J. The Ethics & Existentialism of Kierkegaard: Outlines for a Philosophy of Life.
Valverde, Carlos M., jt. ed. see Mena, Flavio.
Vampilov, A., et al. Farewell in June: Four Russian Plays. Windle, Kevin & Metcalf, Amanda, trs. from Rus.
Van, Cornelius S. van see Winkle, Cornelius S. van.
Van Valkenburgh, Nooger & Neville, Inc. Staff. Basic Solid-State Electronics: Information Reception.
--Basic Solid-State Electronics: Information System Building Blocks.
--Basic Television 1972, British Edition.
Van Aarle, Thomas see Aarle, Thomas Van.
Van Allen, Edward. Your Future As a Shorthand Repcrter.
Van Allen, Rodger, ed. American Religious Values & the Future of America.
Van Amerongen, Jerry. Business As Usual: Business Cartoons for Business People from the Nationally Syndicated Comic "The Neighborhood"
--The Neighborhood.
Van Andel, Tjeerd. Tales of An Old Ocean.
Van Arsdale, Steven, jt. auth. see Sisk, Jonathan.
Van Atta, Robert E. Instrumental Techniques for Food Analysis.
Van Atta, Winfred. The Adam Sleep.
Van Auken, Robert C. Courtroom Jungle.
Van Ausdle, Stephen. Comprehensive Institutional Planning in Two-Year Colleges: A Planning Process & Case Study.
Van Ausdle, Steven. Comprehensive Institutional Planning in Two-Year Colleges: An Overview & Conceptual Framework.
Van Beeck, Frans J. Christ Proclaimed: Christology As Rhetoric.
--Grounded in Love: Sacramental Theology in an Ecumenical Perspective.
Van Beek, Steve. Guide to Pattaya & Southern Thailand.
Van Bekkum, O. & De Vries, H. Radiation Chimeras.
Van Benthem, Johan. A Manual of Intensional Logic.
Van Blankenstein, M. see Blankenstein, M. Van & Welbergen, U. R.
Van Blerkom, Jonathan see Blerkom, Jonathan Van & Motta, Pietro.
Van Briessen, Fritz. Way of the Brush: Painting Techniques of China & Japan.
Van Buitenen, J. A., tr. see Dimmitt, Cornelia.
Van Buren, David P. Crime, Delinquency, & Criminal Justice Within the Rural Context: A Bibliography.
Van Buren, J. M. & Borke, R. C. Variations & Connections of the Human Thalamus. Incl. Pt. 1. The Nuclei & Cerebral Connections of the Human Thalamus; Pt. 2. Variations of the Human Diencephalon. Springer-Verlag.
Van Buren, Martin. Metrics for Architects, Designers & Builders.
Van Campen, Joseph A., jt. auth. see Sholiton, Robert D.
Van Campen, Shirley. Hawaii: A Woman's Guide.
VanCaspel, Venita. Energizing Your Investments.
--The Power of Money Dynamics.
--The Real Rewards of Real Estate.
--To Win the Money Game.
Van Cauweberghe, Marc, tr. see Ohsawa, George.
Van Cauwenberge, H. & Franchimont, P. Assay of Protein & Polypeptide Hormones.
Vance, B. Dwain. General Botany.
Vance Bibliographies Staff. Index to Architecture Series: Bibliography A 637-A 876 (January 1982-December 1982)
--Index to Architecture Series: Bibliography No. A-877 to A-1296 (January 1983-December 1984)
--Index to Public Administration Series: Bibliography No. P-1117 to P 1596 (January 1983-December-1984)

Authors

--Index to Public Administration Series: Bibliography P 877- P 1116 (January 1982-December 1982)
Vance, Carole, ed. Pleasure & Danger: Exploring Female Sexuality.
Vance, Charles C. Dragon Robe.
--A Grave for a Russian.
Vance, Cyrus R. Hard Choices: Four Critical Years in Managing America's Foreign Policy.
Vance, Cyrus R., et al. Education & the World View.
Vance, Jack. The Complete Magnus Ridolph.
--Cugel's Saga.
--Dirdir.
--The Gray Prince.
--The Man in the Cage.
--Pnume.
--Space Opera.
Vance, Jene & Weaver, Charles. A Preliminary Assessment of the Potential Impacts on Operating Nuclear Power Plants of a Five Hundred MREM-Year Occupational Exposure Limit.
Vance, John T. The Background of Hispanic-American Law: Legal Sources & Juridical Literature of Spain.
Vance, Mary. Adobe Building: A Revision of A-76.
--Aggregates-Building Materials: Monographs.
--Ahrends, Burton & Koralek, Architects: A Bibliography.
--Aluminum Construction.
--Architect-Client Relationship.
--Architects' Contracts: A Bibliography.
--Architects, Legal Status, Laws, Etc.
--Architectural Design: Monographs.
--Architecture of Mexico & Central America: Monographs Published 1970-1984.
--Architecture of South America: Monographs Published 1970-1984.
--Art Deco: Monographs.
--Automation in Buildings.
--Bibliographical Exhibitions: Monographs.
--Building Contracts: A Bibliography.
--Building Estimates & Costs: A Bibliography.
--Building Laws: A Bibliography.
--Business & Politics: Monographs.
--Chinoiseries: A Bibliography.
--Church Portals: A Bibliography.
--Citizen Participation: Material Published 1980-1984.
--City Planning & Redevelopment Law: Monographs.
--Coastal Zone Management: Monographs.
--Concrete Construction Standards.
--Concrete Placing: A Bibliography.
--Construction Equipment: Monographs.
--Crime Prevention: Monographs.
--Domes: A Bibliography.
--Earthquakes & Buildings: A Revision of A-521.
--Facades: A Bibliography.
--Flood Damage Prevention: Monographs.
--Foreign Loans: Material Published 1980-1984.
--Foundations & Piling: A Revision of A-71.
--Furniture Making, Repairing & Finishing: Monographs.
--Gardens: Monographs Published 1970-1984.
--Gothic Revival in Architecture, Art & Literature.
--Historic Buildings: Monographs Published since 1970.
--Historic Preservation: Monographs.
--Historical Farms & Agricultural Museum: A Bibliography.
--The History of Architecture: Selected List of Books Published in Great Britain from 1974-1984.
--Housing for the Aged: A Bibliography.
--The Interior Design of Stores: A Bibliography.
--Land Subdivision: Monographs.
--Landscape Architecture: Monographs Published 1970-1984.
--Louis Comfort Tiffany, 1848-1933.
--Management in the Construction Industry: A Bibliography.
--Marine Pollution: Monographs.
--Mechanical Equipment for Buildings: A Bibliography.
--New Business Enterprises: Monographs.
--New Publications for Architecture Libraries: (April, 1985)
--New Publications for Architecture Libraries: (August 1985)
--New Publications for Architecture Libraries: (December, 1985)
--New Publications for Architecture Libraries (February 1985)
--New Publications for Architecture Libraries: (July, 1985)
--New Publications for Architecture Libraries: (June, 1985)
--New Publications for Architecture Libraries: (January, 1985)
--New Publications for Architecture Libraries (March 1985)
--New Publications for Architecture Libraries: (May, 1985)
--New Publications for Architecture Libraries: (November, 1985)
--New Publications for Architecture Libraries: (October 1985)
--New Publications for Architecture Libraries: (September 1985)
--New Towns: Monographs Published 1970-1984.
--Office Design & Decoration: A Bibliography.
--Office Furniture: A Bibliography.
--Office Layout: A Bibliography.
--Office Lighting: A Bibliography.
--Open Spaces: Monographs Published since 1970.
--Pesticides & the Environment: Monographs.
--Planning in Brazil: Monographs Published since 1950.
--Planning in France: Monographs Published since 1950.
--Planning in Germany: Monographs Published since 1950.
--Planning in India: Monographs Published since 1950.
--Planning in Italy: Monographs Published since 1950.
--Planning in the Netherlands: Monographs.
--The Planning of London: Monographs & Journal Articles Published since 1950.
--Prefabrication: An Update of A-80 & A-292.
--Press & Politics: Monographs.
--Public Buildings: A Bibliography for Architects, Planners & Administrators.
--Public Relations & Advertising for Architects.
--Public Welfare in the U. S. Monographs.
--Race Relations in the United States: Material Published 1980-1984.
--Radioactive Waste Disposal: A Bibliography.
--Rapid Construction: A Bibliography.
--Real Property Tax: Monographs.
--Roofs & Roofing: A Revision of A-557.
--Selected Architecture Books Published in Canada 1974-1984.
--Skylights: A Revision of A-621.
--Skyscrapers: A Revision of A-577.
--Social Conditions in the United States: Materials Published 1980-1984.
--Solar Collectors: A Revision of A-560.
--Solar Houses: A Bibliography.
--Special Services in Hospitals: Monographs.
--Squatter Settlements: Monographs.
--Steel Construction: A Bibliography.
--Tapestry: Monographs.
--Technology & State: Monographs.
--Thomas Chippendale, 1718-1779: A Bibliography.
--Tiles: Monographs.
--Trade Unions in the Construction Industry.
--Underground Construction: A Bibliography.
--Urban Economics: Monographs.
--Urban Planning in Stockholm: Journal Articles & Monographs Published since 1950.
--Urban Policy: A Bibliography of Material Published 1980-1984.
--Zoning & Zoning Law: A Revision of A-481.
Vance, Mary A. Civil Rights in the U. S. Material Published 1980-1984.
Vance, Samuel. Courageous & the Proud.
Vancil, Chris. College Algebra & College Algebra Trigonometry.
Van Cleave, William R., jt. auth. see Cohen, S. T.
Van Cleef, E. Cities in Action.
Van Clief, Sylvia, jt. auth. see Heide, Florence P.
Van Colmjon, Godert, jt. auth. see Schampers, Karel.
Van Cortlandt, Philip. The Revolutionary War Memoir & Selected Correspondence of Philip Van Cortlandt. Judd, Jacob, ed.
Van Dalen, D. & Lascar, D., eds. Logic Colloquium 1980: Papers Intended for the European Meeting of the Association for Symbolic Logic.
Van Damme, E. Refinements of the Nash Equilibrium Concept.
Vandamme, Jacques, ed. Employee Consultation & Information in Multinational Corporations.
--New Dimensions in European Social Policy.
Vandana, Ma Ananda, ed. see Rajneesh, Bhagwan Shree.
Van De Graaff, Kent M. Human Anatomy.
Van Delft, Pieter & Botermans, Jack. Creative Puzzles of the World.
Vandeman, G. Showdown in the Middle East.
Van DeMeer. Monster Island.
Van Den Bercken, J. H., et al, eds. Achievement & Task Motivation.
Van Den Berg, C. J., jt. ed. see Hommes, E. A.
Vandenberg, Philipp. The Curse of the Pharoahs.
Van Den Bergh, T. Trade Unions: What Are They?
Van Den Berghe, P. L. Human Family Systems: An Evolutionary View.
VandenBos, Gary R., et al, eds. Human Resources in Psychology.
Van Den Bossche, ed. Comparative Biochemistry of Parasites.
Van Den Brul, Caroline & Spindler, Susan. Tomorrow's World: Food.
Van Den Dreissche, P., ed. see Victoria Conference on Mathematical Problems in Biology Staff.
Van de Pol, W. H. The Christian Dilemma.
Van Der, H. C. Plas see Van Der Plas, H. C.
Vander, Karen D. Ven see Vander Ven, Karen D.
Van Der Aart, Dick. Aerial Espionage: Secret Intelligence Flights by East & West.
VanDerBeets, Richard, ed. Held Captive by Indians: Selected Narratives, 1642-1836.
Van Der Beets, Richard, jt. ed. see Bowen, James K.
Vanderbilt, Arthur T., II. Treasure Wreck: The Fortunes & Fate of the Pirate Ship Whydah.
Vanderbilt, Kermit. Charles Eliot Norton: Apostle of Culture in a Democracy.
Vanderburg, William. Mines of Churchill Country.
Vandereycken, W. & Vanderlinden, J., eds. The Family Approach to Eating Disorders: Assessment & Treatment of Anorexia Nervosa & Bulimia.
Van Der Geest, Bans. Presence in the Pulpit: The Impact of Personality in Preaching. Stott, Doug, tr.
Vandergoot, David & Avellani, Pamela B. A Compendium of Placement-Related Literature.
Vandergoot, David & Swirsky, Jessica. A Review of Placement Services Within a Comprehensive Rehabilitation Framework: Technical Report.
Vandergraft, James S. Introduction to Numerical Computations.
Vandergrift, Kay E. & Hannigan, Jane A., eds. Child & Story: The Literary Connection.
Van Der Haak, Kees, et al. Broadcasting in the Netherlands.
Vanderhaeghe, Guy. Man Descending.
Van Der Heijden, A. H. Short-Term Visual Information Forgetting.
Van Der Hoeven, Johan, jt. ed. see Hart, Hendrik.
VanderKaay, Dorothy. Women's World Handbook.
Van der Klift, Tellegen. Knitting from the Netherlands.
Van Der Kloot, William G. Behavior.
Van der Knapp, G. A. & Wever, E., eds. New Technology & Regional Development.
Van Der Kolk, Bessel A. Post-Traumatic Stress Disorder: Psychological & Biological Sequelae.
Vander Kolk, Justin. To Set Things Right: The Bible Speaks on Faith & Justice.
Vanderlinden, J., jt. ed. see Vandereycken, W.
Vander Linden, Peter J. & Farrar, Donald R. Forest & Shade Trees of Iowa.
Vanderlip, D. George. Christianity According to John.
Van Der Loos, H., jt. auth. see Molliver, M. E.
Vanderman, Robert E. Mutiny on the Enterprise.
Van der Meer, Antonia. Kisses That Miss & Other Awkward Moments.
Vander Meer, Charles. Quickie Quizzes from the Bible.
Van Der Meer, Frederick. Apocalypse: Visions from the Book of Revelations in Western Art.
Vandermeer, John & Rosset, Peter. The Nicaragua Reader: Documents of a Revolution under Fire.
--The Nicaragua Reader: Documents of a Revolution under Fire.
Vandermeer, John, jt. ed. see Rosset, Peter.
Van der Meer, Ron. Majesty in Flight: Nature's Birds of Prey in Three Dimensions.
Van Der Meer, Ron, jt. auth. see Smith, Richard.
Van Der Meid, Louise B. Siamese Cats.
Van Der Meulen, Henk, jt. ed. see Baudet, Henri.
Vandermeulen, J. H. & Hrudey, S. E., eds. Oil in Freshwater: Chemistry, Biology, Countermeasure: Proceedings of the Symposium on Oil Pollution in Freshwater, Edmonton, Alberta, Canada, 15-19 October 1984.
Van Der Meulen, Jan, et al. Chartres Cathedral: Sources & Literary Interpretation, a Critical Bibliography.
Vandermey, Mary A. Love Is Like the Sunlight.
Vanderniet, Deborah. How Do We Eat It?
Van der Pijl, L. Principles of Dispersal in Higher Plants.
Van Der Plas, H. C. Ring Transformation of Heterocycles.
Van der Plas, Rob. The Mountain Bike Book: Choosing, Riding, & Maintaining the Off-Road Bicycle.
--The Mountain Bike Book: Choosing, Riding & Maintaining the Off-Road Bicycle. Monk, Paddy, ed.
Van Der Poel, Cornelius J. The Search for Human Values.
Vanderpoel, Sally. The Care & Feeding of Your Diabetic Child.
Van der Post, Laurens. Venture to the Interior.
--Venture to the Interior.
Van Der Putte, S. C. The Development of the Lymphatic System in Man.
Van der Reis Krausz, Vera, jt. auth. see Krausz, John.
Van der Rhoer, Edward. The Shadow Network: Espionage Ss an Instrument of Soviet Policy.
Van der Spoel, S. & Pierrot-Bults, A. C., eds. Zoogeography & Diversity in Plankton.
Vanderstappen, Harrie A., ed. The T. L. Yuan Bibliography of Western Writings on Chinese Art & Archaeology.
Van Der Vat, Dan. The Last Corsair.
--The Ship That Changed the World: The Escape of the Goeben to the Dardenelles in 1914.
Van Der Veer, Judy. Higher Than the Arrow.
Vandervelde, G. Original Sin: Two Major Trends in Contemporary Roman Catholic Reinterpretation.
Vandervelde, Maryanne. The Changing Life of the Corporate Wife.
Vander Ven, Karen D. Home & Community Influences on Young Children.
Vandervoort, Tom. Sailing Is for Me.
Vanderwaert, Lois. Affirmative Action in Higher Education: A Sourcebook.
Van der Waij, Dirk. Antibiotic Choice: The Importance of Colonisation Resistance.
Van Der Wal, John, jt. auth. see Dorland, Gilbert N.
Van der Zee, John. Bound over: Indentured Servitude & American Conscience.
--The Gate: The True Story of the Design & Construction of the Golden Gate Bridge.
--The Greatest Men's Party on Earth: Inside the Bohemian Grove.
--Stateline.
Van der Zeeuw, Gijsbert. Miracles or Law: Lessons by & Experiences with the Masters of Mystery. Volume I-The Yellow Robe. Zonneveld, L. W. C., tr.
Vanderzwaag, Harold J. Sport Management in Schools & Colleges.
Vande Velde, Vivian. Once upon a Test: Three Light Tales of Love. Fay, Ann, ed.
Van De Ven, A. A., jt. auth. see Hutter, K.
Van De Ven, Andrew H. Group Decision Making & Effectiveness: An Experimental Study.
Van de Wetering, Janwillem. Bliss & Bluster.
--The Blond Baboon.
--The Butterfly Hunter.
--The Corpse on the Dike.
--Death of a Hawker.
--The Empty Mirror: Experiences in a Japanese Zen Monastery.
--The Empty Mirror: Experiences in a Japanese Zen Monastery.
--A Glimpse of Nothingness: Experiences in an American Zen Commune.
--The Japanese Corpse.
--Little Owl: An Eightfold Buddhist Admonition.
--The Maine Massacre.
--The Mind-Murders.
--Outsider in Amsterdam.
--The Rattle-Rat.
--Tumbleweed.
Van de Wetering, Janwillem, tr. see David-Neel, Alexandra & Yongden, Lama.
Vande Woude, G. F., et al, eds. Cancer Cells 2: Oncogenes & Viral Genes.
Vandier-Nicolas, Nicole. Chinese Painting: An Expression of a Civilization.
Van Dijk, J. Rubella Handicapped Children: The Effects of Bi-Lateral Cataract & Or Hearing Impairment on Behavior & Learning.
Van Dine, S. S. The Canary Murder Case.
--The Kennel Murder Case.
--The Kennel Murder Case: A Philo Vance Mystery.
Vandiveer, Clarence A. Fur-Trade & Early Western Exploration.
Vandiver, Frank E. The Southwest: South or West?
Van Dixhoorn, J. & Karnopp, D., eds. Physical Structure in Modelling: Proceedings of the Bond Graph Workshop Held at the Twente University of Technology, Enschede, The Netherlands, 1983.
Van Dixhoorn, J. J. & Evans, F. J., eds. Physical Structure in Systems Theory: Network Approaches Engineering & Economics.
Van Dolson, Bobbie J., ed. see Dewees, Eleanor.
Van Dolson, Bobbie J., ed. see Hills, Desmond B.
Van Dolson, Bobbie J., ed. see Irland, Nancy B.
Van Dolson, Leo R. Taming Tension Through Total Health. Coffen, Richard W., ed.
Van Dongen, R. J. Photographic Atlas of Reconstructive Arterial Surgery.
Van Dongen, R. J. A. M., jt. ed. see Loose, K. E.
Van Doornik, N. Francis of Assisi: A Prophet for Our Time.
Van Doren, Carl C. Benjamin Franklin.
Van Doren, Mark, ed. see Bartram, William.
Van Doren, V. E., jt. ed. see Devreese, J. T.
Van Druten, John. I Remember Mama: A Play in Two Acts.
Van Duyn, Janet. The Greeks.
Van Duyn, Julia. Developing a Data Dictionary System.
Van Duyn, Mona. To See, to Take.
Van Duyneveldt, A. J., jt. auth. see Carlin, R. L.
Van Dyke, Jon M., ed. Consensus & Confrontation: The United States & the Law of the Sea Convention, W7, Law of the Sea Workshop, No. 7.

Van Dyke Parunak, H., ed. Computer Tools for Ancient Texts: Proceedings of the 1980 Ann Arbor Symposium on Biblical Studies & the Computer.
Van Dyne, Susan, ed. Woman's Voices in American Poetry: "The Beauty of Inflections or the Beauty of Innuendoes.
Vane, H. & Thompson, J. An Introduction to Macroeconomic Policy.
Vane, Lenchen De see De Vane, Lenchen Coleman.
Vane, William C. De see DeVane, William C.
Vanecko, James J., et al. Community Organization Efforts, Political & Institutional Change, & Diffusion of Change Produced by Community Action Programs.
VanEgmond-Pannell, Dorothy. School Foodservice.
Van Eijk Van Voorthuijsen, M. E., ed. World Collectors Annuary, 1983-84.
Van Eijndhover, J., intro. by. Deaf-Blind Children & Their Education: Proceedings of the International Conference, St. Michielsgstel, The Netherlands, Aug. 25-29, 1968.
Van Ek, Jan A. & Robat, Nico J. The Student's Grammar of English.
Vanek, Zdenko & Hostalek, Z., eds. Biogenesis of Antibiotic Substances: Proceedings.
Van Erk, Rien. Oscilloscopes: Functional Operation & Measuring Examples.
Vaness-Ann Collection Staff. A Little French Pantry. Marti, Margaret, ed.
Van Ess, Donald H. Heritage of Musical Style.
Vanessa-Ann Collection Staff. Garden Song. Marti, Margaret, ed.
--A Grand Celebration. Marti, Margaret, ed.
--Holidays in Cross-stitch, 1987.
Van Every, Dale. Disinherited: The Lost Birthright of the American Indian.
Vanevery, Edward. Sins of New York As "Exposed" by the Police Gazette.
Van Fleet, David D., jt. auth. see Albanse, Robert.
Van Gieson, Susan & Kurtz, Regina. Interior Planting Design File.
Van Ginneken, J. K. & Muller, A. S., eds. Maternal & Child Health in Rural Kenya.
Van Ginneken, Jaap. The Rise & Fall of Lin Piao.
Van Ginneken, Wouter & Garzuel, Michel. Unemployment in France, the Federal Republic of Germany & the Netherlands: A Survey of Trends, Causes & Policy Options.
Van Gorder, Barbara & Ellis, Ann, eds. Information Sources 1988.
Van Greenaway, Peter. The Killing Cup.
Van Gulik, R. H. Hsi K'ang & His Poetical Essay on the Lute.
Van Gulik, Robert. The Emperor's Pearl: A Judge Dee Mystery.
--The Phantom of the Temple.
Van Gulik, Robert H. Sexual Life in Ancient China.
Van Gundy, Arthur B. Techniques of Structured Problem Solving.
Van Haaften, Julia. From Talbot to Stieglitz: Masterpieces of Early Photography from the New York Public Library.
Van Halsema, Thea. Three Men Came to Heidelberg.
Van Heel, W. Dudok Translated by see Penning De Vries, Piet.
Van Heemst, H. D., jt. auth. see Makkink, G. F.
Van Heerikhuizen, F. W. Rainer Maria Rilke: His Life & Work.
Van Heijenoort, Jean. Frege & Godel: Two Fundamental Texts in Mathematical Logic.
Van Helden, Albert. Measuring the Universe: Cosmic Dimensions from Aristarchus to Halley.
Van Hoek, Kees. Pope Pius XII.
Van Holk, A. G., ed. Dutch Contributions to the Sixth International Congress of Slavicists, Prague, 1968.
Van Hoof, F., jt. ed. see Hers, H. G.
Van Hook, John E. Systematic Philosophy: An Overview of Metaphysics Showing the Development from the Greeks to the Contemporaries with Specified Directions & Projections.
Van Hoose, William H., et al, eds. Elementary School Guidance & Counseling: A Composite View.
Van Horn, Bill. Strangers.
Van Horn, William. Harry Hoyle's Giant Jumping Bean.
--Twitchtoe the Beastfinder.
--The Very Special Birthday Present.
Van Horne, James C. Financial Management & Policy.
--Function & Analysis of Capital Market Rates.
Van Hove, M. A., jt. auth. see Somorjai, G. A.
Van Hulzen, J. A., ed. Computer Algebra.
Van Iherbeek, A., ed. see International Institute of Refrigeration.
Van Iken, ed. Australian Science Fiction.
Vanikov, V. A. & Putyatin, E. V. Introduction to Energy Technology.
Van Iwaarden, John L. Elementary Numerical Techniques for Ordinary Differential Equations.
Van Kaam, Adrian. Mystery of Transforming Love.
Van Kamm, Adrian & Healy, Kathleen. The Demon & the Dove: Personality Growth Through Literature.
Van Keep, P. A. & Lauritzen, C., eds. Aging & Estrogens.
Van Keep, P. A., ed. see Estrogen Therapy Workshop Staff.
Van Kleek, Peter. Cooking with Pride.
Van Kleek, Peter E. Beverage Management & Bartending.
Van Kospoth, Sylvia-Monica, tr. see Von Duerckheim, Karlfried.
Vanlandingham, Hugh F. Solutions Manual for Introduction to Digital Control Systems.
Van Lawick, Hugo. Solo: The Story of the African Wild Dog.
Van Lawick-Goodall, Hugo, jt. auth. see Van Lawick-Goodall, Jane.
Van Lawick-Goodall, Jane. In the Shadow of Man.
Van Lawick-Goodall, Jane & Van Lawick-Goodall, Hugo. Innocent Killers.
Van Leeuwenhoek, Anthony see Leeuwenhoek, Anthony Van.
Van Lemmen, Hans. Tiles: A Collector's Guide.
Van Leuven, Hendrick. UCLA Football: Touchdown UCLA.
Van Lier, R. A., ed. see Stedman, John G.
Van Lint, J. H. Coding Theory.
Van Lint, J. H., ed. see Combinational Theory Seminar Staff.
Van Loon, Hendrik W. Story of America.
--The Story of Mankind.
--Wilbur the Hat.
Van Loon, J. C., jt. auth. see Beamish, F. E.
Van Lustbader, Eric. Beneath an Opal Moon.
--The Black Heart.
--Shan.
--Sirens.
Van Maanen, Marj, jt. auth. see Van Maanen, Paul.
Van Maanen, Paul & Van Maanen, Marj. The Final Turning Point.
Van Matre, Joseph G. & Gilbreath, Glenn H. Statistics for Business & Economics.
Van Matre, Steve. Acclimatization.
--Acclimatizing.
Van Meter, Donald, jt. auth. see Sharkansky, Ira.
Van Meter, Margaret, ed. Managing the Critically Ill Effectively.
Van Meter, Margaret, ed. see Yacone, Linda A.
Vann, Howard. Never Say Can't.
Vann, J. Don, jt. auth. see Tanner, J. F.
Van Nagell, John R., Jr. & Barber, Hugh R., eds. Modern Concepts of Gynecological Oncology.
Van Ness, Christine M., jt. ed. see Van Ness, John R.
Van Ness, John R., jt. auth. see Kutsche, Paul.
Van Ness, John R. & Van Ness, Christine M., eds. Spanish & Mexican Land Grants in New Mexico & Colorado.
Van Nest, Dean G. Developing Global New Products: Challenges to U.S. Competitiveness. Farmer, Richard, ed.
Vannier, Maryhelen & Gallahue, David L. Teaching Physical Education in Elementary Schools.
Van Nieuwenhuijze, C. A. Aspects of Islam in Post-Colonial Indonesia: Five Essays.
Van Noord, Glenn see Hendricks, William C. & Noord, Glenn Van.
Vannorsdall, John W. Dimly Burning Wicks: Reflections on the Gospel after a Time Away.
Van Nostran, William. The Nonbroadcast Television Writer's Handbook.
Van Nostrand, A. D., et al. Functional Writing.
Van Note, Gene. Ministering to Single Adults.
Vanorden, Bianca. Water Music.
Van Orden, M. D. The Book of United States Navy Ships.
Van Orden, Phyllis J. The Collection Program in Elementary & Middle Schools: Concepts, Practices, & Information Sources.
Van Orman, Ward T. & Hull, Robert. The Wizard of the Winds.
Van Osdol, B. M., et al. Teaching Phonetic Skills through Body Movement.
Van Osdol, Bob M. & Perryman, Patricia, eds. Special Education: A New Look.
Van Osdol, William R. Parents, Teachers, Kids.
Van Oudenhoven, Nico J. Common Afghan Street Games.
Van Oyen, Hendrik. Affluence & the Christian. Sherman, Franklin, ed. Clarke, Frank, tr.
Van Patter, Douglas M., jt. ed. see Marion, Jerry B.
Van Peer, Willie. Stylistics & Psychology: Investigations of Foregrounding.
Van Pelt, Nancy L. How to Turn Minuses into Pluses. Coffen, Richard W., ed.
Van Pelt, S. J. Hypnotic Suggestion.
Vanpeperstraete, F. The Cartilaginous Skeleton of the Bronchial Tree.
Van Raalte, Susan D. Apply Yourself: Writing College Applications That Get Results.
Van Rensselaer, Mrs. John K. Prophetical, Educational & Playing Cards.
Van Rensselaer, Mariana G. Book of American Figure Painters. Weinberg, H. Barbara, ed.
Van Rensselaer, Mariana G. see Rensselaer, Mariana G. Van.
Van Resseh, Hugh W. Open Your Eyes, Your Heart, & Your Soul: A Philosophy of Life for Every Individual.
Van Riper, Charles. A Career in Speech Pathology.
Van Rompuy, P. see Chatterji, M. & Rompuy, P. Van.
Van Rossen, Don & Woodrich, Barbara. Competitive Swimming for New Champions.
Van Ryckeghem, W., jt. auth. see Maynard, Geoffrey.
Van Ryzin, Lani. A Patch of Earth.
Van Scott, Timothy & Weiss, Sidney J. Self-Assessment of Current Knowledge in Ophthalmology.
Vanselow, Ralf & Tong, S. Y., eds. Chemistry & Physics of Solid Surfaces.
Van Sertima, Ivan, ed. The African Presence in Early Asia.
Van Servellen, Gwen M. Group & Family Therapy: A Model for Psychotherapeutic Nursing Practice.
Van Sickle, Dirck. Montana Gothic.
Van Siclen, Charles C., III. The Chapel of Sesostris III at Uronarti.
Vansittart, Jane, ed. Lifelines: The Stacey Letters, 1836-1858.
Vansittart, Peter. Voices Eighteen Seventy to Nineteen Fourteen.
--Voices from the Great War.
Vansittart, Peter, ed. John Masefield's Letters from the Front 1915-1917.
Vanski, Jean & Ozanne, Larry. Simulating the Housing Allowance Program in Green Bay & South Bend: A Comparison of the Urban Institute Housing Model with the Supply Experiment.
Van Slyke, Helen. The Heart Listens.
--No Love Lost.
Van Steenwyk, Elizabeth. Cameo of a Champion.
Van Stijgeren, E., ed. Computer Aided Design of Pipe & Pipe Supports.
--Recent Advances in Pipe Support Design.
Van Stijgeren, E. & Krawzya, L., eds. Practical Considerations in Piping Analysis.
Van Stockum, Hilda. Winged Watchman.
Vanstone, S. A., jt. auth. see Jackson, D. M.
Van Sumere, G. F., ed. see Phytochemical Society Symposium, No.11, University of Ghent, Belgium, Sept. 1973.
Van Swearingen, Phyllis. Bits of Americana: Whirly-Girlys to Country Gossip.
Van Tassel, Katrina. Trundlewheel.
Van Til, Cornelius. Christian Theistic Ethics.
--Christian Theory of Knowledge.
--Common Grace & the Gospel.
--The Doctrine of Scripture.
Van Til, John see Smith, David H. & Til, John Van.
Van Til, William. Curriculum: Quest for Relevance.
--Education: A Beginning.
--Secondary Education: School & Community.
Van Toai, Doan & Chanoff, David. Vietnamese Gulag.
Van Toai, Doan, jt. auth. see Chanoff, David.
Van Trees, Harry L., ed. Satellite Communications.
Van Turnhout, J., jt. ed. see Fillard, J. P.
Van Tyne, Claude H. The Loyalists in the American Revolution.
Van Valkenberg, Phil. More Wisconsin Bike Trips.
Van Valkenberg, Philip. Wisconsin Bike Trips: Twenty Tours for Young & Old.
Van Valkenberg, Philip & Shidell, Doug. Bicycle Escape Routes.
Van Valkenburg, M. E., ed. Circuit Theory: Foundations & Classical Contributions.
Van Valkenburgh, et al. Basic Electricity.
--Basic Electronics.
Van Vechten, B. D. The First Year of Forever.
Van Vechten, Carl. The Dance Writings of Carl Van Vechten. Padgette, Paul, ed.
Van Velzen, T. Rozenburg: Monographie Einer Manufaktur 1883-1917.
Van Vleck, David. How & Why Not to Have That Baby.
Van Vooren, Monique. Night Sanctuary.
Van Voorhis, Kenneth R. Entrepreneurship & Small Business Management.
Van Voorthuijesn, M. E. Van Eijk see Van Eijk Van Voorthuijsen, M. E.
Van Voorthuijsen, A. M. World Collectors Annuary.
Van Voorthuijsen, J. J. World Collectors Index, 1946-1972, with Supplements 1978-81: An Alphabetical Index to Volumes 1-33 of World Collectors Annuary.
Van Voris, Jacqueline. College: A Smith Mosaic.
--The Look of Paradise: A Pictorial History of Northampton, Mass.
Van Vors, B. L. End of the River.
Van Vorst, W. D., et al, eds. see World Hydrogen Energy Conference Staff & Veziroglu, T. N.
Van Vuuren, Nancy. The Subversion of Women As Practiced by Churches, Witch-Hunters, & Other Sexists.
Van Wert, Diane. Meditations for Children.
Van Wert, William F. The Film Career of Alain Robbe-Grillet.
Van Winkle, Walton, jt. auth. see Peacock, Erle E.
Van Woerkom, Dorothy. Something to Crow About. Tucker, Kathleen, ed.
Van Wormer, Laura. Dallas.
Van Wynen, Donald & Van Wynen, Mabel. Fonemas Tacana Vy Modelos de Acentuacion.
Van Wynen, Mabel, jt. auth. see Van Wynen, Donald.
Vanyo, Bruce G., jt. auth. see Practising Law Institute Staff.
Van Zeist, W. & Casarie, W. A., eds. Plants & Ancient Man - Studies in Palaeoethnobotany: Proceedings of the 6th Symposium of the International Work Group for Palaeoethnobotany, Groningen, 30 May - 3 June 1983.
Van Zeller, Hubert. Ideas for Prayer.
Vanzi, Max, jt. auth. see Poole, Fred.
Van Zomeren, A. H. see Zomeren, A. H.
Vaporis, Nomikos M., ed. Mikron Euchologion: An Orthodox Prayer Book. Gelsinger, Michael, tr. from Gr. & pref. by.
Varadhan, S. R. Diffusion Problems & Partial Differential Equations.
Varadpande, M. L. Religion & Theatre.
Varberg, Dale E., jt. auth. see Fleming, Walter.
Varberg, Dale E., jt. auth. see Purcell, Edwin J.
Varberg, Dale E., jt. auth. see Roberts, A. Wayne.
Varco, Richard L., jt. ed. see Delaney, John P.
Vardaman, George T. Making Successful Presentations.
Vardar, Yusuf, jt. auth. see Kaldewey, Harald.
Vardeman, Robert E. Crystal Clouds.
--Frozen Waves.
--The Klingon Gambit.
--The Quaking Lands.
--The White Fire.
Vardeman, Robert E. & Milan, Victor. Destiny Stone.
--The War of Powers: In the Shadow of Omizatrim.
Varela, G., jt. ed. see Somogyi, J. C.
Varela, Robert, ed. see Haberek, Judy.
Varese, Louise, tr. see Gracq, Julien.
Varga, R. S., jt. ed. see Saff, E. B.
Vargas, Jose J. Articulos y Ensayos. Vargas-Baron, Anibal, ed.
Vargas-Baron, Anibal, ed. see Vargas, Jose J.
Vargo, Richard J. Readings in Government & Non-Profit Accounting.
Varian, Hal R. Microeconomic Analysis.
Variety Staff. Variety Film Reviews; 1983-1984.
Varille, Alesandre, jt. auth. see Robichon, Clement.
Varketta, Ralph. Gourmet Cooking Confidential.
Varkey, Alexander. Comparative Cranial Myology of North American Natricine Snakes.
Varley, Helen, jt. auth. see Graham, Ian.
Varma, Baidya N. The Sociology & Politics of Development: A Theoretical Study.
Varma, Monika, tr. see Tagore, Rabindranath.
Varma, Ravi & Hrubesh, Lawrence W. Chemical Analysis by Microwave Rotational Spectroscopy.
Varmuza, K. Pattern Recognition in Chemistry.
Varner, Joseph, jt. ed. see Bonner, James.
Varney. Nurse - Midwifery.
--Varney's Nurse-Midwifery.
Varney, Allen. The Vanishing City.
Varnon, Bevon. On the Banks of the Blanco.
Varo, P., ed. Pesticide Chemistry-Three: Proceedings, Helsinki, 1974.
Varon, Benison, ed. see Carman, John S.
Varon, Bension. Zaire: Current Economic Situation & Constraints.
Vartanian, Aram. Diderot & Descartes: A Study of Scientific Naturalism in the Enlightment.
Varvasovszky, Laszlo. Henry in Shadowland.
Vary, Colin. The Victims.
Vasari, Giorgio. The Great Masters. Sonino, Michael, ed. De Vere, Gaston Du C., tr.
--Vasari on Technique. Brown, B. Baldwin, ed.
Vasconcellos, Muriel, tr. see Meyer, Lorenzo.
Vasconelos, E. Modern Methods of Amputation.
Vasek, Karel. The International Dimensions of Human Rights. Alston, Philip, ed.
Vash, Carolyn L. The Burnt-out Administrator.
Vasi, Susanne & Tomasino, Joseph. Auditory, Reading & Dialogue Comprehension Exercises in Spanish.
Vasil, Indra, ed. Biotechnology: Perspectives, Policies, & Issues.
Vasile, Albert J. & Mintz, Harold K. Speak with Confidence.
Vasiliev, Y. M. General & Historical Geology.
Vasquez, Richard. Another Land.
Vass, I. Epee Fencing.
--Epee Fencing.
Vass, Winifred K. Thirty-One Banana Leaves.
Vassal, Jacques. Electric Children: Roots & Branches of Modern Folkrock. Barnett, Paul, tr. from Fr.

Vassale, Mario, ed. Cardiac Physiology for the Clinician.
Vasseur, J. P. Properties & Applications of Transistors.
Vassil, Thomas V., jt. auth. see Balgopal, Pallassana R.
Vassilyev, B. The Dawns Are Quiet Here.
--His Name Was Not Listed.
Vassilyeva, Larissa. Lara in London. Franklin, Olga, tr.
Vassos, John H. Manna: True Stories of Life in the United States, 1900 to 1940 & the Utopia of Manna.
Vasta, Joseph A. Understanding Data Base Management Systems.
Vasta, Ross F., jt. auth. see Whitehurst, Grover J.
Vasudev, Aruna A. & Lenglet, Philippe, eds. Indian Cinema Superbazaar.
Vaswig, William L. At Your Word, Lord.
--I Prayed, He Answered.
Vat, Dan van Der see Van der Vat, Dan.
Vatai, Frank L. Intellectuals in Politics in the Greek World: From Early Times to the Hellenistic Age.
Vatai, Laszlo. Man & His Tragic Life. Keskemethy, Laszlo, tr.
Vathes, Christine Le see Fashion Group Inc., Friends & Staff.
Vatja, Vilmos & Kantzenback, Friedrich W., eds. Oecumenica 1966 Yearbook for Ecumenical Studies.
--Oecumenica 1967 Yearbook for Ecumenical Studies.
--Oecumenica 1968 Yearbook for Ecumenical Studies.
--Oecumenica 1969 Yearbook for Ecumenical Studies.
--Oecumenica 1971 & 72 Yearbook for Ecumenical Studies.
Vatja, Vilmos, jt. ed. see Gassmann, Gunther.
Vatsyayan, K. The Square & the Circle of the Indian Arts.
Vatsyayan, Kapila. Traditional Indian Theatre: Multiple Streams.
Vatter, Harold G., jt. ed. see Will, Robert E.
VauDell, W. W. The Power of God Within You.
Vaughan, Curtis, jt. ed. see Drumwright, Huber L.
Vaughan, Cynthia, jt. auth. see Gordan, Gilbert S.
Vaughan, Floyd L. The United States Patent System: Legal & Economic Conflicts in AMerican Patent History.
Vaughan, Frank, jt. auth. see Cook, Rick.
Vaughan, George B. The Community College in America: A Short History.
Vaughan, Henry H. Welsh Proverbs with English Translations.
Vaughan, J., et al, eds. Maintenance of Factory Services: Part Two.
--Maintenance of Factory Services: Part 0ne.
--Mechanical Maintenance (& Installation) II.
Vaughan, Mark, jt. auth. see Pisciotta, John.
Vaughan, Mary A., jt. auth. see Land, Lois R.
Vaughan, R. I., jt. auth. see Tyror, J. G.
Vaughan, Richard. Valois Burgundy.
Vaughan, Robert. The Age of Great Cities.
--The Age of Great Cities.
Vaughan, Rodney. Urban Spatial Traffic Patterns.
Vaughan, Roger. Herbert Von Karajan: A Biographical Portrait.
Vaughan, Rubye C. The New Breed: Getting to Know You.
Vaughan, Samuel S., intro. by. Book Publishing Career Directory, 1986: 20 Top Book Publishing Professionals.
Vaughan, Thomas, et al. A Sense of Grace: Celebrating the Life of the Honorable Grace Olivier Peck.
Vaughan, William. Antiarrhythmic Action: The Puzzle of Perhexiline.
Vaughan Williams, Ralph. The Making of Music.
Vaughn, Donald E., Jr., jt. auth. see Aby, Carroll D.
Vaughn, Emmett. Agency Management Manual: Continuing Manual (Looseleaf) Merrit Company Staff, ed.
Vaughn, Jack A. Drama A to Z: A Handbook.
Vaughter, Carolyn. West Wind Wild.
Vautour, Chris. Prime-Time Soap Opera Trivia.
Vaux, Calvert. Villas & Cottages: A Series of Designs Prepared for Execution in the United States.
Vaux, Kenneth L. Will to Live-Will to Die: Ethics & the Search for a Good Death.
Vaux, Kenneth L., jt. auth. see Marty, Martin E.
Vavra, Michael H. Aero-Thermodynamics & Flow in Turbomachines.
Vavra, Robert. All Those Girls in Love with Horses.
--Anna & Dula.
--Equus: The Creation of a Horse.
--Felipe the Bullfighter.
Vavra, Robert & Cowles, Fleur. To Be a Unicorn.
Vawter, Bruce. Advent-Christmas.
--Biblical Inspiration.
Vawter, Bruce & Carl, William J., III. Easter.
Vawter, Bruce & Elliott, John H. Pentecost 3.
Vayhinger, John M. Before Divorce. Hulme, William E., ed.
Vaz, Kevin S. Memory Training for Students & Executives.
Vazquez, Josefina Z. & Meyer, Lorenzo. The U. S. & Mexico.
VDE Berlin Staff. Human Factors in Telecommunications International Symposium, 4th.
Veatch, H. C. Pulse & Switching Circuit Action.
Veatch, Robert M. Death, Dying, & the Biological Revolution: Our Last Quest for Responsibility.
Veatch, Robert M., jt. auth. see Sollitto, Sharmon.
Veatch, Robert M., ed. Life Span: The Hastings Center Report on Values & Life-Extending Technologies.
Veblen, Thorstein. The Theory of Business Enterprise.
Vecchi, Orazio. Amfiparnasso. Eitner, Robert, ed.
Vecchia, Giorgio de see De Vecchia, Giorgio.
Vecellius, Anthony de see De Vecellius, Anthony.
Vechten, Carl van see Van Vechten, Carl.
Vecsei, Paul, jt. auth. see Glaz, Edith.
Vecsey, George, jt. auth. see Welch, Bob.
Veena, Ma Prema, ed. see Rajneesh, Bhagwan Shree.
Veer, Judy Van Der see Van Der Veer, Judy.
Vega, Ana L. Encancaranublado.
Vega, Garcilasco De La see De La Vega, Garcilasco.
Vega, Lope De see Lope de Vega.
Vega, Pablo A. The Apparitions of Our Blessed Mother in Cuapa, Nicaragua.
Vega, S., jt. ed. see Heras, F. G. de las.
Vega, Vincente. Diccionario Ilustrado De Frases Celebres y Citas Literarias.
Vegas, Federico. Venezuelan Vernacular.
Vegetarian Times Editors. Vegetarian Times Cookbook.
Veglahn, Nancy. The Vandals of Treason House.
Vego, Milan. Soviet Navy Today.
Veistman, E. A., jt. ed. see Milovanov, E. L.
Veitch, Douglas W. Lawrence, Greene & Lowry: The Fictional Landscape of Mexico.
Veith, Richard H. Multinational Computer Nets: The Case of International Banking.
Vekua, I. N. Generalized Analytic Functions.
Velasco, Dorothy. Lane County: An Illustrated History of the Emerald Empire.
Velasco, Gustavo R. Labor Legislation from an Economic Point of View. Rogge, Benjamin A., ed.
Velasco, Jesus-Augustin. Impacts of Mexican Oil Policy on Economic & Political Development.
Velasquez, Manuel G. Business Ethics: Concepts & Cases.
Velazquez, Clara V. English As a Second Language.
--English As a Second Language: An Interdisciplinary Approach.
Velco, G. Textile Dictionary.
Veldhuis, Michael J. DOA: I Came Back.
Velikhov, E. P., et al, eds. Science, Technology & the Future: Soviet Scientists Analysis of the Problems of & Prospects for the Development of Science & Technology & Their Role in Society.
Velo, G. & Wightman, A. S., eds. Rigorous Atomic & Molecular Physics.
Velo, G., ed. see International School of Mathematical Physics Staff.
Velo-News, ed. see Burke, Ed, et al.
Velo-News Staff, ed. see Burke, Ed, et al.
Velz, Clarence J. Applied Stream Sanitation.
Velzen, T. van see Van Velzen, T.
Ven, A. A. Van De see Hutter, K. & Van De Ven, A. A.
Venable, Gail P. & Stemach, Jerry. The Easy-to-Read California Driver's Handbook.
Venable, Wallace, jt. auth. see Plants, Helen.
Venables, E. Leaving School & Starting Work.
Venables, J. A. Developments in Electron Microscopy & Analysis.
Venables, J. A., jt. ed. see Klein, M. L.
Venderheiden, Gregg C. & Grilley, Kate. Non-Vocal Communication Techniques & Aids for the Severely Physically Handicapped.
Vendler, Zeno. Linguistics in Philosophy.
Vendrell, C. S. & Parramon, J. M. Winter.
Veneziale, Carlo M. Control of Cell Growth & Proliferation.
Veniaminov, Ivan. Notes on the Islands of the Unalashka District. Pierce, Richard A., ed. Geoghegan, Richard, tr.
Veniard, John. Fly Tying Problems.
Veninga, Robert L. A Gift of Hope: How We Survive Our Tragedies.
--A Gift of Hope: How We Survive Our Tragedies.
Veninga, Robert L. & Spradley, James P. The Work-Stress Connection: How to Cope with Job Burnout.
Venit, S., jt. auth. see Burns, Diane.
Venit, Sharyn & Burns, Diane. Jazz at Work.
Venkataraman, K. Power Development in India.
Venkataramani, M. S. Bengal Famine of Nineteen Forty-Three: The American Response.
--The Sunny Side of F.D.R.
Venkatarayudu, T., jt. auth. see Bhagavantam, S.
Venkatesan, K., jt. auth. see Mathews, P. M.
Vennard, Edwin. Electric Power Business.
--Management of the Electric Energy Business.
Vennen, Mark V., tr. see Goudzwaard, Bob.
Vennewitz, Leila, tr. see Becker, Jurek.
Vennewitz, Leila, tr. see Boll, Heinrich.
Vennewitz, Leila, tr. see Matsubara, Hisako.
Vennewitz, Leila, tr. see Walser, Martin.
Vennewitz, Lelia, tr. see Walser, Martin.
Venning, Muriel & Frith, Owen. The Craftsman in Engineering.
Veno, K. Classification Theory of Algebraic Varieties & Compact Complex Spaces.
Venolia, Jan. Write Right!
Ventafridda, V., jt. auth. see Twycross, R. G.
Venti, Pamela R. Why Should I?
Venture Capital Editors & Pratt, Stanley. How to Raise Venture Capital.
Venturi, Rauch & Scott Brown Staff. Venturi, Rauch & Scott Brown.
Venugopal, B. & Luckey, T. D. Metal Toxicity in Mammals. Incl. Vol. 1, Physiologic & Chemical Basis for Metal Toxicity; Vol. 2, Chemical Toxicity of Metals & Metalloids. Plenum Pub.
Venus, Brenda & Miller, Henry. Dear, Dear Brenda: The Love Letters of Henry Miller to Brenda Venus. Sindell, Gerald S., ed.
Venuti, Lawrence, tr. see Alberti, Barbara.
Venzi. Little Angel with the Pink Wings.
Vepa, Ram K. Mao's China: A Nation in Transition.
--Small Industry in the Eighties.
Vequist, David G., jt. auth. see Spence, William P.
Vera, Nora & Shaw, Bradley, eds. Critical Perspectives on Gabriel Garcia Marquez.
Verba, Sidney, jt. auth. see Schlozman, Kay L.
Vercel, Roger. Bertrand of Brittany: Biography of Messire du Guesclin. Saunders, M., tr.
Vercelli, Book. The Poetry of the Codex Vercellensis, with an English Translation.
Vercors, Jean. Silence de la Mer. Peyre, Henri & Peyre, Marguerite, eds.
Verderber, Kathleen S. & Verderber, Rudolph F. Inter-Act: Using Interpersonal Communication Skills.
Verderber, Rudolph F., jt. auth. see Verderber, Kathleen S.
Verdery, John. Partial Recall.
Verdesi, Elizabeth H. In But Still Out: Women in the Church.
Verdet, Andre. Chagall's World: Reflections from the Mediterranean.
Verdi, Giuseppes. La Traviata.
Verdier, Paul A. Brainwashing & the Cults: An Expose on Capturing the Human Mind.
Verdier, Philippe. Russian Art, Icons & Decorative Arts from the Origin to the 20th Century.
Verdon, Thomas A., Jr. Nuclear Medicine for the General Physician.
Verduin, John R., jt. auth. see Miller, Harry G.
Verduin, John R., Jr., et al. Adults Teaching Adults: Principles & Strategies.
Vere, Gaston Du C. de see Vasari, Giorgio.
Vereketi, C. Anna.
Verey, Rosemary. The Herb Growing Book.
Verga, Giovanni. Cavalleria Rusticana, & Other Stories. Lawrence, D. H., tr. from Ital.
--Little Novels of Sicily. Lawrence, D. H., tr.
Vergara, Fausto, et al. Aqui, Alla y Aculia: Conversacion y Composicion.
Vergara, William C. Electronics in Everyday Life.
Verge, Roger. Roger Verge's Cuisine of the South of France. Smoler, Roberta W., tr. from Fr.
Vergers, Charles A. Network Synthesis.
Vergil see Virgil.
Vergilius Maro, Publius. L' Eneide de Virgile, Prince des Poetes Latines.
Vergo, Peter, ed. see Kandinsky, Wassily.
Verheijen, J. A. Het Hoogste Wezen Bij De Manggaraiers.
Verheyden, Jack C., ed. see Schleiermacher, Friedrich.
Verheyen, Egon. The Paintings in the Studiolo of Isabella d'Este at Mantua.
Verhonick, Phyllis J., ed. Nursing Research I.
Verkamp, Bernard J. The Indifferent Mean: Adiaphorism in the English Reformation to 1554. Walton, Robert C. & Bebb, Philip N., eds.
Verlag, Alban. Guide Rouge Swiss 1986-87.
Verlag Vereinigung Staff. German Books in Print: Author-Title-Catchword Catalogue 1985-86.
--German Books in Print: ISBN Index to Spring Supplement 1985-86.
--German Books in Print: ISBN Index 1985-86.
--German Books in Print: Spring Supplement, 1985-86.
--German Books in Print: Subject Guide to German Books in Print 1985-86.
Verlaine, Paul. La Bonne Chanson. Bd. with Romances sans Paroles; Sagesse. Schoenhof.
--Confessions of a Poet.
Verleyson, Alfred. The Astrological Foundation of Stock Market Price Movements.
Verloop, N., jt. ed. see Creemers, B.
Verma, A., jt. auth. see Verma, H. N.
Verma, Amrit, jt. auth. see Verma, H. N.
Verma, H. N. & Verma, A. Hundred Great Indians Through the Ages.
Verma, H. N. & Verma, Amrit. Indian Women Through the Ages (1976)
Verma, Kiran, ed. see Dickey, John W.
Verma, S. N. Frank Norris: A Literary Legend.
Verma, S. P. International System & the Third World.
Verma, Som P. Art & Material Culture in the Paintings of Akbar's Court.
Vermeer, Jackie & Frew, Marian L. Making Decorative Planters: From Practically Anything.
Vermeer, Jackie & Lariviere, Marian. The Little Kid's Craft Book.
Vermeij-Keers, C. Transformations in the Facial Region of the Human Embryo.
Vermes, Geza. Jesus & the World of Judaism.
--Scripture & Tradition in Judaism.
Vermes, Geza & Neusner, Jacob, eds. Essays in Honour of Yigael Yadin.
Vermeule, C. C., jt. auth. see Comstock, M. B.
Vermeule, Cornelius. Numismatic Art in America: Aesthetics & the United States Coinage.
Vermeule, Cornelius C. Roman Imperial Art in Greece & Asia Minor.
Vermiglio, Maria & Henkin, Bill. The Plant Book.
Vernadsky, George. The Origins of Russia.
Vernan, Ivan R., jt. auth. see Berkman, Harold W.
Vernazza, Marcelle. Complete Handbook of Kindergarten Music Lesson Plans & Activities.
Vernberg, F. J., jt. auth. see Vernberg, W. B.
Vernberg, W. B. & Vernberg, F. J. Environmental Physiology of Marine Animals.
Verney, Michael. Care & Repair of Hulls.
Vernon, Arthur. The History & Romance of the Horse.
Vernon, Betty D. Ellen Wilkinson, Eighteen Ninety-One to Nineteen Forty-Seven.
--Margaret Cole, 1893-1980: A Political Biography.
Vernon, Claire. The Doctor Was a Guest.
Vernon, Edward. Practice Makes Perfect.
Vernon, Frances. A Desirable Husband.
Vernon, Graham D., ed. Soviet Perceptions of War & Peace.
Vernon, Grenville. Yankee Doodle-Doo: A Collection of Songs of the Early American Stage.
Vernon, Ivan R., ed. First-Line Management: The Foreman's Role in Manufacturing.
--Modern Aspects of Manufacturing Management: Selected Readings.
--Organization for Manufacturing.
Vernon, J. Peter & Fram, Eugene H., eds. Readings in Consumer Behavior: A Student's Choice.
Vernon, Jack. Macroeconomics.
Vernon, Leo P. & Seely, G. R. Chlorophylls: Physical, Chemical & Biological Properties.
Vernon, Louise A. Doctor in Rags.
--The King's Book.
Vernon, Philip E. Personality Assessment.
Vernon, Raymond. Dilemma of Mexico's Development: The Roles of the Private & Public Sectors.
Vernon, Raymond, jt. auth. see Wells, Louis T.
Vernon, Raymond, ed. The Oil Crisis.
Vernon, Robert G. The Acquisition of Noncompetitive Federal Oil & Gas Leases on the Public Domain.
Vernon, Steven K. Antique Fishing Reels: Your Illustrated Guide to Identifying & Understanding U. S. Patented Models Through 1920.
Vernon, Thomas S. A Philosophy of Language Primer.
Vernon, Walter M. Introductory Psychology.
Vernon, Walter N. Forever Building: The Life & Ministry of Paul E. Martin.
Vernon, William. Cleaning the Bones.
Verny, Thomas & Kelly, John. The Secret Life of the Unborn Child.
Veronesi, U. & Bonadonna, G., eds. Clinical Trials in Cancer Medicine: Past Achievement & Future Prospects.
Verrall, Harold E. & Bird, Gail B. California Community Property Cases & Materials.
Verrier, Anthony. Through the Looking Glass.
Verschuur, G. L. The Invisible Universe: The Story of Radio Astronomy.
Versluis, Arthur. The Egyptian Mysteries.
--The Philosophy of Magic.
Verstappen, H. T., ed. Aerospace Observation Techniques.
Ver Steeg, Clarence L. Robert Morris: Revolutionary Financier.
Versteeg, Jennie G., intro. by. Lake Champlain: Reflections on Our Past.
Vervoren, Thora & Oppeneer, Joan. Workbook of Solutions & Dosages of Drugs, Including Arithmetic.
Vervoren, Thora M., jt. auth. see Oppeneer, Joan E.
Verwey, Gerlof. Economist's Handbook: A Manual of Statistical Sources.

Verwilghen, R., jt. auth. see Lewis, S. M.
Very, Donald & Keefe, Eugene F. The Legal Guide for the Family.
Veryan, Patricia. Love's Duet.
--Sanguinet's Crown.
Verzariu, Pompiliu. International Countertrade: A Guide for Managers & Executives.
Vesalius, Andreas. The Illustrations from the Works of Andreas Vesalius of Brussels. Saunders, J. B. & O'Malley, Charles D., eds.
Vesell, Elliot S., jt. auth. see Goth, Andres.
Vesely, Anton. Kawasaki KDX 80-420 Singles 1979-1981. Jorgensen, Eric, ed.
Vesely, Anton & Wauson, Sydnie. Kawasaki Jet Ski 1976-1983 Service-Repair-Maintenance.
Veseth, Michael. Introductory Microeconomics.
Veseth, Michael, ed. Introductory Economics.
Vesey, Constance, ed. see Montgelas, Maximilian.
Vesey, Godfrey, ed. Human Values.
Vesey, Mollie. An Unnecessary Woman.
Vesilind, P. Aarne. Environmental Engineering.
Vesley, Anton. Kawasaki KZ, Z, & ZX750: 1980-1985 Service Repair Performance. Wauson, Sydnie A., ed.
Vesper, Carl H. Engineers at Work: A Casebook.
Vessels, J. E. More Deadly Than the Male (The Secrets of Women Exposed)
Vessey, Stephen H., jt. auth. see Drickamer, Lee C.
Vestal, Katherine W. Pediatric Critical Care Nursing.
Vestal, R. E., ed. Drug Therapy in the Elderly.
Vestal, Stanley. The Missouri.
Vested, I. M. The Confidential Memos of I. M. Vested: An Expose of Corporate Mismanagement by a Senior Executive of a Major American Company.
Vestermark, Mary, jt. auth. see Channels, Vera.
Vestermark, Mary J., jt. auth. see Johnson, Dorothy E.
Veterinary Medicine Publishing Co. Staff, ed. Starting Your Own Veterinary Practice.
Vetrov, Boris. Poems.
Vetrova, N. & Lipkin, R. El Crecimiento Del Militarismo y la Explotacion Fiscal De los Trabajadores En EE. UU.
Vetter, Klaus J. Electrochemical Kinetics Theoretical Aspects.
Vetter, Louise, et al. Sex Equity Strategies.
Vettorazzi, G. International Regulatory Aspects for Pesticide Chemicals.
Veubeke, B. F. De see De Veubeke, B. F.
Vevers, Gwynne. Blood & Lungs.
--Feeding & Digestion.
--Muscles & Movement.
--Skin & Bone.
Veziroglu, T. N., jt. auth. see World Hydrogen Energy Conference Staff.
Veziroglu, T. N. & Taylor, J. B., eds. Hydrogen Energy Progress V: Proceedings of the 5th World Hydrogen Energy Conference, Toronto, Canada, 15-20 July 1984.
Veziroglu, T. N., ed. see Solar Cooling & Heating Forum Staff.
Veziroglu, T. N., ed. see World Hydrogen Energy Conference Staff.
Veziroglu, T. N., et al, eds. Hydrogen Systems: Proceedings of the Beijing International Symposium on Hydrogen Systems, Beijing, China, 7-11 May 1985.
Veziroglu, T. N., et al, eds. see World Hydrogen Energy Conference Staff, et al.
Veziroglu, T. Nejat, ed. Energy Conservation: Proceedings of the Energy Research & Development Administration Conference Held at the University of Miami, Dec. 1975.
--Proceedings of the Clean Energy Research Institute, 1st, Miami Beach, 1976.
--Remote Sensing: Energy Related Studies.
--Solar Energy, International Progress: Proceedings of the International Symposium-Workshop on Solar Energy, 16-22 June 1978, Cairo, Egypt.
Via, Dan O., Jr. Kerygma & Comedy in the New Testament: A Structuralist Approach to Hermeneutic.
--The Parables: Their Literary & Existential Dimension.
Via, Dan O., Jr., ed. see Beardslee, William A.
Via, Dan O., Jr., ed. see Boers, Hendrikus.
Via, Dan O., Jr., ed. see Patte, Daniel.
Via, Dan O., Jr., ed. see Petersen, Norman R.
Via, Dan O., Jr., ed. see Pregeant, Russell.
Viano, D. C., ed. Nineteen Eighty-One Advances in Bioengineering.
Viano, Emilio & Cohn, Alvin W. Social Problems & Criminal Justice.
Viau, Monnette C. Understanding & Resolving Grief.
Viaud, Louis M. see Loti, Pierre.
Vicente-Gella, Pilar De see De Vicente-Gella, Pilar.
Vichenevetsky, Robert. Computer Methods for Partial Differential Equations: Elliptical Equations & the Finite Element Method.
Vicinus, Martha, ed. A Widening Sphere: Changing Roles of Victorian Women.
Vick, Bill, et al. Encyclopedia for the TRS-80. McCarthy, Nan & Crocker, Chris, eds.
Vick, Charles R., ed. Handbook of Software Engineering. Ramamoorthy, C. V.
Vick, Edward W. H. Jesus: The Man.
Vick, R. W. & Schoolbred, C. F. The Administration of Civil Justice in England & Wales.
Vicker, Ray. The Dow Jones-Irwin Guide to Retirement Planning.
Vickers, Brain. Laboratory Work in Soil Mechanics.
Vickers, Brian. The Artistry of Shakespeare's Prose.
Vickers, D. Decision Processes in Visual Perception.
Vickers, Douglas. A Christian Approach to Economics & the Cultural Condition.
--Now That You Have Believed: An Exploration of the Life & Walk of Faith.
Vickers, Edward D., ed. The Reach of Song.
Vickery, John B. & Sellery, J'nan M., eds. Scapegoat: Ritual & Literature.
Vickery, Olga W., jt. auth. see Hoffman, Frederick J.
Vickery, Walter N., jt. ed. see McLean, Hugh.
Vickman, Thomas. Financial Officer's Manual & Guide.
Victor, A. Paul, jt. auth. see Applebaum, Harvey M.
Victor, Christina R. Old Age in Modern Society.
Victor, Joseph, jt. ed. see Sullivan, John.
Victor, Joseph L., jt. auth. see Sullivan, John J.
Victor, Thomas. The Making of a Dance.
Victoria & Albert Museum National Art Library, London Staff. Catalogue of Exhibition Catalogues.
Victoria, British Columbia, jt. auth. see Provincial Archives Staff.
Victoria Conference on Mathematical Problems in Biology Staff. Proceedings of the Victoria Conference on Mathematical Problems in Biology. Van Den Dreissche, P., ed.
Victoria, Pablo E. Foundations of Economic Development: Intelligence vs. Capital.
Victorica, Ricardo. Nueva Epanortosis al Diccionario de Anonimos Seudonimos de J. T. Medina.
Victoroff, Victor. The Suicidal Patient: Recognition, Intervention, Management.
Victory, Kathleen M., ed. The Merger Directory.
Vida, Julius A. Chemistry & Pharmacology of Androgens & Anabolic Agents.
Vida, Marco G. The Christiad: Latin-English Edition. Drake, Gertrude C. & Forbes, Clarence A., eds.
Vidal, Gore. Vidal in Venice.
Vidal, Gore, et al. Great American Families.
Vidal, Harriette, jt. auth. see Kelleher, Ed.
Vidali, Vittorio. Diary of the Twentieth Congress of the Communist Party of the Soviet Union. Cattonar, Nell A. & Elliot, A. M., trs. from Ital.
Vidic, Branislav & O'Rahilly, Ronan. Atlas of the Anatomy of the Ear.
Vidler, Anthony, jt. auth. see Durand, J. N.
Vidler, Virginia. Niagara Falls: One Hundred Years of Souvenirs.
Vidor, King. A Tree Is a Tree. Kupelnick, Bruce S., ed.
Vidyarthi, L. P. The Rise of Anthropology in India: A Social Science Orientation. Incl. Vol. I. The Tribal Dimensions; Vol. II. The Rural Urban & Other Dimensions. Humanities.
Vidyasagar, Dharmapuri, jt. auth. see Smith, George F.
Vieg, J., jt. auth. see Turner, Henry.
Viehboeck, F. P., ed. see International Symposium on Electromagnetic Separation of Radioactive Isotopes, Vienna, 1960.
Vieira, Anthony G. An Outline of Weather Control.
Vieira, Luandino. The Real Life of Domingos Xavier.
Viel, Lyndon C. Antique Ethnic Furniture with Prices.
Viele, Egbert L. Hand-Book for Active Service.
Vienna. Banners & Mobiles & Odds & Ends.
Viera, jt. auth. see Xavier.
Viereck, Peter R. The First Morning: New Poems.
--Strike Through the Mask: New Lyrical Poems.
Viertel, Jack, jt. auth. see Jaffe, Sandra S.
Viertel, Peter. American Skin.
Vieth, David M. Swift's Poetry 1900-1980: An Annotated Bibliography of Studies.
Vigar, Penelope. The Novels of Thomas Hardy: Illusion & Reality.
Vigeland, Carl. Great Good Fortune: How Harvard Makes Its Money.
Vigeveno, Guido. The Bomb & European Security.
Vigh, B., jt. auth. see Vigh-Teichmann, I.
Vigh-Teichmann, I. & Vigh, B. The Infundibular Cerebrospinal-Fluid Contacting Neurons.
Vigil, Evangelina. The Computer Is Down.
Vigilante, Mary. Worship the Night.
Viglielmo, V. H., tr. see Nishida, Kitaro.
Vigna, Judith. The Hiding House. Fay, Ann, ed.
--The Little Boy Who Loved Dirt & Almost Became a Superslob.
Vigny, Alfred De see De Vigny, Alfred.
Vigyikan, Paul. Triangles.
Viherjuvri, H. J., jt. auth. see Stephen Greene Press (Illus.) Staff.
Viidik, A., ed. Lectures on Gerontology.
Viirmaa, V. Contemporary Rural Architecture of Soviet Estonia.
Vijnananda. At the Feet of Ski Ramakrishna.
Vikhert, Anatolii M. & Zhdanov, Valentin S. The Effects of Various Diseases on the Development of Atherosclerosis. Muller, James E., ed.
Viking Seven Seas, Ltd. Staff, ed. Maori Songs of New Zealand.
Vilar, Pierre. Spain: A Brief History.
Villa, Jaime. Biology of a Neotropical Glass Frog, Centrolenella Fleischmanni (Boettger), with Special Reference to its Frogfly Associates.
--Synopsis of the Biology of the Middle American Highland Frog Rana Maculata Brocchi.
Villa, Vicente D., et al. Biological Science: Demonstration - Recitation Guide.
Villani, Kevin, jt. ed. see Tuccillo, John.
Villanucci, Robert S. & Avtgis, Alexander W. Electronic Shop Fabrication: A Basic Course.
Villars, Elizabeth. The Very Best People.
Villas, James. American Taste.
--American Taste: The American Palate Coast-to-Coast.
Villaverde, Manuel M. Internal Medicine: Medical Examination Manual.
Villaverde, Manuel M. & Macmillan, C. Wright. Ailments of Aging: From Symptom to Treatment.
Villee, C. A., ed. Control of Ovulation.
Villee, Claude A. & Walker, Warren F., Jr. Introduction to Animal Biology.
Villee, Claude A., et al, eds. Respiratory Distress Syndrome: Based on a Conference at Dedham, Mass., May, 1973.
Villegas, Daniel Cosio see Cosio Villegas, Daniel.
Villella, Joseph A. The Hospitality Industry-the World of Food Service.
Villeneuve, Anselm Z. The Problem with Management: Is It a Science or a Lot of Nonsense Taken Seriously?
Villermaux, J. & Trambouze, P., eds. Chemical Reaction Engineering: International Symposium on Chemical Reaction Engineering, Nice, France, March 25-27, 1980.
--Chemical Reaction Engineering: Sixth International Symposium on Chemical Reaction Engineering--Plenary Lectures.
Villez, Randy De see DeVillez, Randy.
Villiers du Terrage, Marc de see De Villiers du Terrage, Marc.
Villines, William M., Jr., jt. auth. see Hickey, Henry V.
Vilquin, Jean-Claude, jt. ed. see Issacharoff, Michael.
Vinacke, W. Edger. Myths, Fables, & Legends for the Young & Old.
Vinaver, Martin. La Vida De los Novios: The Life of Two Sweethearts.
Vince, John. Wells & Water Supply.
Vincent, Alex, et al. Studies in New Guinea Linguistics.
Vincent, Carol. Lettering & Design: A Practical Approach Through Handwriting.
Vincent, Carole. Teach Yourself Painting & Drawing.
Vincent, Colin A., jt. ed. see Scrosati.
Vincent, Eleanor, jt. auth. see Ninkovich, Thomas.
Vincent, George, jt. auth. see Small, Albion.
Vincent, J. L., ed. Intensive Care & Emergency Medicine: Proceedings of the Fourth International Symposium.
Vincent, Jack E. International Relations: Vol. 1, Law.
Vincent, Larry M. The Dancer's Book of Health.
Vincent, M. O. God, Sex & You.
Vincent, Marvin. Word Studies in the New Testament.
Vincent, Nigel & Harris, Martin. Studies in the Romance Verb.
Vinci, John. The Art Institute of Chicago: The Stock Exchange Trading Room.
Vinci, Leo. The Book of Practical Candle Magic.
Vinci, Leonardo da see Da Vinci, Leonardo.
Vine, Louis L. Behavior & Training of Dogs & Puppies.
Vine, P. A. London's Lost Route to the Sea: An Historical Account of the Inland Navigations Which Linked the Thames to the English Channel.
Vine, Paul A. London's Lost Route to Basing-Stoke: The Story of the Basinstoke Canal.
Vine, Victor T. Le see Le Vine, Victor T.
Vine, W. E. Expository Dictionary of New Testament Words.
--Expository Dictionary of New Testament Words.
Vineberg, Arthur M. Myocardial Revascularization by Arterial-Ventricular Implants.
Viner, Jacob. The Customs Union Issue.
Vines, Robert F., jt. ed. see Carter, William C.
Vineyard, Ben S., jt. auth. see Kimbrell, Grady.
Vinge, Joan D. The Snow Queen.
Vinitsky, Barbara B. & Benjamin, Janice Y. How to Become Happily Employed: A Simple Guide to the Nitty Gritty of Finding the Job That Is Right for You.
Vinkovetsky, Diana. Iljushiny Razgovory.
Vinnikov, Y. A. Sensory Reception: Cytology, Molecular Mechanisms & Evolution.
Vinogradoff, Paul. Self Government in Russia.
Vinogradov, A. Differential Diagnosis of Internal Diseases.
Vinogradov, A. P. & Udintsev, G. B., eds. The Rift Zones of the World Ocean. Kaner, N., tr.
Vinogradov, I. Fundamentos de la Teoria de los Numeros.
Vinogradov, V. V. Russkii Iazyk: Grammaticheskoe Uchenie O Slove.
Vinokur, Grigory. A Grain of Salt.
Vinokurov, E. Selected Poems.
Vinovskis, Maris A. Fertility in Massachusetts from the Revolution to the Civil War.
Vinovskis, Maris A., jt. ed. see Schneider, Carl.
Vinson, Carl, Institute of Government Staff, et al. Handbook for Georgia Legislators.
Vinson, J. R., ed. Emerging Technologies in Aerospace Structures, Design, Structural Dynamics & Materials.
--Modern Developments in Composite Materials & Structures.
Vinson, James, ed. The Novel to Nineteen Hundred.
--Renaissance Drama.
--Twentieth Century American Literature.
Vinson, Kathryn. Run with the Ring.
Viollet-le-Duc, Eugene. An Essay on the Military Architecture of the Middle Ages.
Viollet-Le-Duc, Eugene E. Habitations of Man in All Ages. Bucknall, Benjamin, tr.
Viorst, Judith. Alexander & the Terrible, Horrible, No Good, Very Bad Day.
--I'll Fix Anthony.
Viorst, Milton, ed. Making a Difference: The Peace Corps at Twenty-Five.
Vipont, Elfrida. The Story of Quakerism.
Vipont, Elfrida, ed. Bless This Day: A Book of Prayer for Children.
Vipperman, Carl J. Rise of Rawlins Lowndes, 1721-1800.
Viragh, S., jt. ed. see Challice, C. E.
Virbila, Sherry. Cooks' Marketplace: San Francisco Bay Area Sourcebook.
Virdell, Paul. The Initiates.
--Mirror Man.
Virgil. Eclogues & Georgics. Royds, T. S., tr.
Virginia Genealogical Society Staff. Index to Hayden's Virginia Genealogies.
--Marriages of Middlesex County, Virginia, 1740-1852.
Virginia. Laws, Statutes Staff. Code of Virginia.
Virginia Municipal League Staf. Tax Rates in Virginia's Cities, Counties, & Selected Towns: 1983.
Virmani, Arvind. Government Policy & Development of Financial Markets: The Case of Korea.
Virtue, Noel. The Redemption of Elsdon Bird.
Viscardi, Henry, Jr. & Friedman, Irving M. A Study of Workmen's Compensation In Relation To Sheltered Workshops.
Vischer, Lukas. Tithing in the Early Church. Lee, Clarence L., ed. Schultz, Robert C., tr. from Ger.
Viscione, Jerry A. & Aragon, George A. Cases in Financial Management.
--Cases in Financial Management.
Visco, Louis J. The Manager As an Editor: Reviewing Memos, Letters & Reports.
Visconti, A. Quantum Field Theory.
Viscott, David. Dorchester Boy.
--How to Live with Another Person.
--Making of a Psychiatrist.
--The Making of a Psychiatrist.
--The Making of a Psychiatrist.
Viscott, David S. How to Live with Another Person.
Visentin, Charles. A Message to an Aborted Baby Killed by the Cowardice of His Mother & the Venal Complicity of the Attending Physician.
Vishneva-Sarafanova, N. Privileged Generation: Children in the Soviet Union. Glasgoleva, Galina, tr.
--Soviet Women: A Portrait.
Vishnevskaya, Galina. Galina: A Russian Story. Daniels, Guy, tr. from Rus.
Vishniak, Mark. Gody Emigratsii (Years of Emigration)
Visiak, E. H. The Mirror of Conrad.
Viskochil, Larry A. Chicago at the Turn of the Century in Photographs.
Visscher, Martha O. The Ideas of Chemistry.
Visser, H. The Quantity of Money.
Visson, Lynn, tr. see Grekova, I.
Vitale, Edmund. Building Regulations: A Self Help Guide for the Owner-Builder.
Vitale, Joseph J., ed. Advances in Human Clinical Nutrition.
Vitale, L. J., jt. auth. see Turk, V.
Vitek, Donna K. Passion's Price.
Vitelli, James R. Van Wyck Brooks: A Reference Guide.

Authors

Vitetta, Ellen S., ed. B & T Cell Tumors: Symposium.
Vitkauskas, Arejas. An Immigrant's Story.
Vitriano, Dorothy B. Legends of the Earth.
Vitro, F., et al. The Self-Concept in Education: Selected Readings for Educational Psychology.
Vittenberg, E. Working Class & Trade Unions in the U. S. S. R. The Period of Developed Socialism.
Vittorini. The Age of Dante.
Vivaldi, Antonio. La Griselda. Brown, Howard M., ed.
Vivante, Arturo. Run to the Waterfall.
Vivian, Daisy. Fair Game.
Vivona, Charles M., ed. The Meanings of Deviance.
Vizinczey, Stephen. An Innocent Millionaire.
Vizzini, Joseph J. Beauty Is My Business: The ABC's of Successful Salon Management.
Vizzini, Sal, et al. Vizzini: The Secret Lives of Americas' Most Successful Undercover Agent.
Vlach, John M. The Afro-American Tradition in Decorative Arts.
Vladimir, Andy & Vladimir, Ute. Miami, Orlando & the Gold Coast.
Vladimir, Ute, jt. auth. see Vladimir, Andy.
Vladmirov, S. & Teplov, L. NATO: A Bleak Picture.
Vlangas, Alex W. & Williams, Richard J. Learning Centers & Individualized Reading in Behavioral Terms.
Vlasic, Ivan A., ed. Explorations in Aerospace Law: Selected Essays by John Cobb Cooper, 1946-1966.
Vlasopolos, Anca. The Symbolic Method of Coleridge, Baudelaire, & Yeats.
Vlastos, Gregory. Platonic Studies.
Vleck, David Van see Van Vleck, David.
Vleeskens, Cornelis. The Day the River.
Vles, Joseph M. Computer Basics: A Guide for Business Application.
--Computer Fundamentals for Nonspecialists.
Vliet, R. G. Solitudes.
Vlk, Ronald G. Cram Course for the GRE.
--Cram Course for the LSAT.
Vlk, Suzee. Interviews That Get Results.
Vlk, Suzee J., jt. auth. see Cardoza, Anne.
Vlodaver, Zeev, et al. Coronary Arterial Variations in the Normal Heart & in Congenital Heart Disease.
Vocational Evaluation & Work Adjustment Association Staff. Vocational Evaluation & Work Adjustment Bulletin, Special Edition: Final Report. Nadolsky, Julien M., ed.
Vocations for Social Change Staff & Brandow, Karen. No Bosses Here: A Manual on Working Collectively & Cooperatively.
Vocations for Social Change Staff, et al. No Bosses Here: A Manual on Working Collectively & Cooperatively.
Vochko, Lee E., ed. Manipulative Activities & Games in the Mathematics Classroom.
Vodar, B., ed. see International AIRAPT Conference Staff.
Vodar, Boris & Romand, J. Some Aspects of Vacuum Ultraviolet Radiation Physics.
Vodopich, Darrell & Moore, Randy. Deserts.
Voe, Thomas F De see De Voe, Thomas F.
Voelckers, Ellen. Girls' Guide to Menstruation.
Voelkel, A. H. Fields, Particles & Currents.
Voelkel, Robert T., ed. see Herrmann, Wilhelm.
Voelker, Francis H. & Voelker, Ludmila A. Mass Media: Forces in Our Society.
Voelker, Francis H. & Voelker, Ludmila A., eds. Mass Media: Forces in Our Society.
Voelker, Ludmila A., jt. auth. see Voelker, Francis H.
Voelker, Ludmila A., jt. ed. see Voelker, Francis H.
Voelkl, J., jt. ed. see Alefeld, G.
Voelter, Wolfgang & Doves, Doyle C. Biologically Active Principles of Natural Products.
Voelter, Wolfgang, jt. auth. see Gupta, Derek.
Voeltz, Luanna M., jt. auth. see Wuerch, Bonnie B.
Voge, J., jt. auth. see David, P.
Vogel, jt. auth. see Scrimshaw.
Vogel, Amos. Film As a Subversive Art.
Vogel, Arthur A. The Jesus Prayer for Today.
Vogel, Arthur A., jt. auth. see Krentz, Edgar.
Vogel, Azra. Comeback: Capturing the Future for America.
Vogel, David, jt. auth. see Powers, Charles W.
Vogel, Ezra. Comeback: Building the Resurgence of American Business.
Vogel, F. & Roehrborn, G., eds. Chemical Mutagenesis in Mammals & Man: Proceedings.
Vogel, H. J., ed. Nucleic Acid-Protein Recognition.
Vogel, Henry J., jt. ed. see Bryson, Vernon.
Vogel, Henry J., jt. ed. see Pernis, Benvenuto.
Vogel, Henry J., et al, eds. Organizational Biosynthesis.
Vogel, Henry J., et al, eds. see Informational Macromolecules Symposium Staff.
Vogel, Isle-Margret. Don't Be Scared Book: Scares, Remedies & Pictures.
Vogel, John J. Study & Like It.
Vogel, Linda J. Helping a Child Understand Death.
Vogel, Mark A. Divorce Taxation Guide.
Vogel, Robert, ed. A Breviate of British Diplomatic Blue Books, 1919-1939.
Vogel, Rosemarie, et al. Natural Proteinase Inhibitors.
Vogel, Steven J., intro. by. Auto-Carto Seven: International Syposium on Computer Assisted Cartography.
Vogel, Susan, ed. For Spirits & Kings: African Art from the Paul & Ruth Tishman Collection.
Vogel, Ted. The Muskie Murders.
Vogel, W. Structure & Crystallization of Glasses.
Vogel, W., jt. ed. see Kohlman, M.
Vogel-Jorgensen, T. Rasputin: Prophet, Libertine, Plotter. Harvey, William F., tr. from Danish.
Vogelman, Joyce. Getting It Right.
Vogels, Walter. Reading & Preaching the Bible: A New Approach.
Vogelsang, Arthur. A Planet.
Voget, Fred W. Osage Indians, Vol. One: Osage Research Project.
Vogler, Daniel E., jt. auth. see Asche, F. Marion.
Vogt, Christian. Christian Vogt: In Camera.
Vogt, Evon Z. & Albert, Ethel M., eds. People of Rimrock: A Study of Values in Five Cultures.
Vogt, Evon Z. & Leventhal, Richard M., eds. Prehistoric Settlement Patterns: Essays in Honor of Gordon R. Willey.
Vogt, Howard. Flagstad: Singer of the Century.
Vogt, John. Capital Improvement Programming: A Handbook for Local Government Officials.
Vogt, P. K. & Koprowski, H., eds. Retroviruses, Vol. I.
Vogt, R. M., jt. auth. see Boardman, J. M.
Vogt, Richard J. Altering Course.
Vohn, Rick. Getting Control of Your Inner Self.
Vohra, Ranbir. The Chinese Revolution: 1900-1950.
Vohs, John L. & Mohrmann, Gerald P. Audiences, Messages, Speakers: An Introduction to Human Communication.
Voiculescu, D. V., jt. auth. see Stratila, S. V.
Voight, Johan C. Fifty Years of the History of the Republic in South Africa, 1795-1845.
Voigt, Cynthia. Dicey's Song.
Voigt, Ellen B. The Lotus Flowers: Poems.
Voisin, Andre. Grass Productivity.
--Soil Grass & Cancer.
Voitle, Robert B., Jr. Samuel Johnson the Moralist.
Vokes, Frederick E. The Riddle of the Didache: Fact or Fiction, Heresy or Catholicism?
Volant, F. & Warren, J. R., eds. Memoirs of Alexis Soyer: With Unpublished Receipts & Odds & Ends of Gastronomy.
Volborth, Carl-Alexander von see Von Volborth, Carl-Alexander.
Volguine, Alexander. Lunar Astrology.
Volguine, Alexandre. Technique of Solar Returns. Broglio, John, tr. from Fr.
Volgyes, Ivan, ed. The Peasantry of Eastern Europe: Roots of Rural Transformation.
Volgyes, Ivan, jt. ed. see Enyedi, Gyorgy.
Volk, B. W., jt. ed. see Aronson, S. M.
Volk, Patricia. White Light.
Volkenshtein, M. V. Biophysics.
Volkhovsky, Vera, tr. see Saltykov, Mikhail E.
Volkoff, Vladimir. The Set-Up: A Novel of Disinformation.
--Tchaikovsky: A Self-Portrait.
Volkomer, Walter E. American Government.
--American Government.
Volkov, Solomon. Balanchine's Tchaikovsky: Interviews with George Balanchine. Bouis, Antonina W., tr. from Rus.
--Balanchine's Tchaikovsky: Interviews With George Balanchine.
Volkswagen of America, Inc. Audi 5000s Official Factory Repair Manual: 1984-1985: Gasoline Models including Wagon & Turbo.
--Volkswagen GTI, Golf, Jetta Official Factory Repair Manual including GLI, Gasoline, Diesel & Turbo Diesel Models: 1985.
--Volkswagen Quantum Official Factory Repair Manual: 1982-1985, Including Gasoline & Turbo Diesel.
Volkswagen United States Inc. Volkswagen Fox Official Factory Repair Manual: 1987-1988.
Volkswagen United States, Inc. Volkswagen, GTI, Golf, & Jetta Official Factory Repair Manual: 1985, 1986 & 1987 Gasoline, Diesel & Turbo Diesel Including Golf, GT, Jetta, GLI, & 16V Models.
Volkswagen United States Inc. Volkswagen Vanagon Official Factory Repair Manual: 1980-1987.
Voll, Sarah P. A Plough in Field Arable: Western Agribusiness in Third World Agriculture.
Vollman, Rudolf F. Menstrual Cycle.
Vollman, Thomas E. & Whybark, D. Clay. Manufacturing Planning & Control Systems.
Vollmar, Jorg. Reconstructive Surgery of the Arteries.
Vollmer, E., jt. ed. see Pincus, Gregory.
Vollmer, Howard M. Employee Rights & the Employment Relationship.
Vollmer, Jurgen. Rock 'n' Roll Times: The Style & Spirit of the Early Beatles & Their First Fans.
Vollmert, B. Polymer Chemistry. Immergut, E. H., tr.
Vollstedt, Maryana. Pacific Fresh: A Seafood Cookbook.
--What's for Dinner in the Northwest?
Volodin, A., jt. auth. see Plimak, E.
Volokhonsky, Henri. Stikhotvoreniya.
Volpe, R. Auto-Immunity in the Endocrine System.
Volpi, Alexander De see De Volpi, Alexander.
Volta, Alessandro G. Opere.
Voltaire. Age of Louis Fourteenth.
--Philosophical Dictionary. Gay, Peter, tr.
Voltaire see Johnson, Samuel.
Voltz, Jeanne, ed. see Ham, Marion N.
Volunteer Lawyers for the Arts. Fear of Filing: A Beginner's Guide to Tax Preparation & Record Keeping for Artists, Performers, Writers & Freelance Professionals. Striggles, Theodore W., ed.
Von Abrams, Karin, tr. see Von Weizsacker, Richard.
Von Aulock, Wilhelm H., ed. Handbook of Microwave Ferrite Materials.
Von Bally, G., ed. Holography in Medicine & Biology.
Von Balthasar, Hans U. Life out of Death: Meditations on the Easter Mystery.
Von Bayros, Franz. The Amorous Drawings of the Marquis Von Bayros.
Von Bertalanffy, Ludwig. Robots, Men & Minds.
Von Blum, Paul. The Critical Vision: A History of Social & Political Art in the U. S.
Von Bonsdorff, Bertel. Diphyllobothriasis in Man.
Von Bothmer, Dietrich. The Amasis Painter & His World: Vase Painting in Sixth-Century B. C. Athens.
Von Bothmer, Dietrich & Mertens, Joan R. Greek Art of the Aegean Islands.
Von Brandt, A. Fish Catching Methods of the World.
Von Brockdorff, E., tr. see Prinzhorn, H.
Von Bulow, Hans, ed. see Cramer, J. B.
Von Campenhausen, Hans. The Formation of the Christian Bible. Baker, J. A., tr. from Ger.
Von Campenhausen, Hans & Chadwick, Henry. Jerusalem & Rome: The Problem of Authority in the Early Church: Luetkeholter, G. W., tr. from Ger.
Von Cleef, Monique & Waterman, William. The House of Pain.
Von der Mehden, Fred R., ed. see Bender, Stephen O., et al.
Von der Osten, Hans H. Explorations in Hittite Asia Minor, Nineteen Twenty-Nine.
Von Der Osten-Sacken, Peter. Christian-Jewish Dialogue: Theological Foundations. Kohl, Margaret, tr. from Ger.
Von der Porten, Ronald P., jt. auth. see Goren, Charles H.
Von Duerckheim, Karlfried. Hara: The Vital Centre of Man. Van Kospoth, Sylvia-Monica & Healey, Estelle R., trs. from Ger.
Von Einsiedel, Heinrich, intro. by. The Onslaught: The German Drive to Stalingrad.
Von Elbe, Guenther, jt. auth. see Lewis, Bernard.
Von Engeln, Oscar Dedrich see Engeln, Oscar Dedrich Von & Urquhart, Jane M.
Von Euler, C. & Lagercrantz, H., eds. Central Nervous Control Mechanisms in Breathing--Physiological & Clinical Aspects of Regular, Periodic & Irregular Breathing in Adults & in the Perinatal Period: Proceedings of the International Symposium Held at the Wenner-Gren Center, Stockholm, Sweden, Sept. 4-6, 1978.
Von Euler, U. S., et al, eds. Mechanisms of Release of Biogenic Amines.
--Structure & Function of Inhibitory Neuronal Mechanisms.
Von Euler, Ulf S. & Eliasson, Rune, eds. Prostaglandins.
Von Fieandt, Kai & Mousgaard, I. K. The Perceptual World.
Von Franz, Marie-Louise. C. G. Jung: His Myth in Our Time. Kennedy, William H., tr.
Von Freytag, Bruno B. & General Loringhoff. Philsophical Problems of Mathematics.
Von Frisch, Karl. The Dancing Bees: An Account of the Life & Senses of the Honey Bee. Ilse, Dora, tr.
--Man & the Living World. Lowenstein, Elsa B., tr.
--Twelve Little Housemates. Sugar, A. T., tr.
Von Frisch, Karl see Frisch, Karl Von.
Von Frisch, Otto, jt. auth. see Folsom, Anne.
Von Furer Haimendorf, Christoph. The Gonds of Andhra Pradesh: Tradition & Change in an Indian Tribe.
Von Furer-Haimendorf, Christoph. Highlanders of Arunachal Pradesh.
Von Furer-Haimendorf, Christoph, ed. Asian Highland Societies: An Anthropological Perspective.
Von Furstenberg, Egon & Duhe, Camille. The Power Look.
Von Gaertner, H. R. & Wehner, H. Advances in Organic Geochemistry, 1971.
Von Gloeden, Wilhelm. Taormina.
Von Gloeden, Wilhelm, photos by. Taormina.
Von Graz, William. Swiss Bank Accounts: Investments Through Swiss Banks.
Von Grimmelshausen, Hans J. C. Simplicius Simplicissimus. Weissenborn, Lesley & Weissenborn, Helmut, trs. from Ger.
Von Gustorf, Ernest A., ed. The Organic Chemistry of Iron.
Von Hardenburg, Georg F. see Novalis, pseud.
Von Hattingberg, M. Rainer Maria Rilke: Letters to Benvenuta.
Von Hehn, Jurgen. Lettland Zwischen Demokratie und Diktatur.
Von Heinecken, Karl H. Dictionnaire Des Artistes, Dont Nous Avons Des Estampes, Avec une Notice Detailee De Leurs Ouvrages Graves.
Von Hildebrand, Alice J. Introduction to a Philosophy of Religion.
Von Hoelscher, Russ & Sterne, George. Dynamics of Personal Financial Planning.
--New Investment Opportunities for the Mid-1980's.
Von Hofmann, J. C. Interpreting the Bible. Preus, Christian, tr.
Vonk, Hubertus J. & Western, Richard H., eds. Comparative Biochemistry & Physiology of Enzymatic Digestion.
Von Kleist, Friedrich see Weiss, Samuel A.
Von Krzywoblocki, M. Z. Bergmann's Linear Integral Operator Method in the Theory of Compressible Fluid Flows.
Von Laue, Max. Theory of Superconductivity.
Von Laue, Theodore. Sergei Witte & the Industrialization of Russia.
Von Leyden, Rudolph. Ganjifa, Playing Cards India.
Von Leyden, Wolfgang. Growing up under the Weimar Republic, 1918-1933.
Von Lichem, Heinz. Leica R-3 & R-3 MOT Reflex Manual.
Von Lilienfeld, Christian. Christanus Campoliliensis. Dreves, G. M., ed.
Von Loelhoeffel, Dieter & Schimanke, Dieter. Kommunalplanung Von Neuen Herausfurderungen.
Von Loeper, Eisenhart, jt. ed. see Teutsch, Gotthard M.
Von Loewenich, Walter. Luther's Theology of the Cross. Bouman, Herbert J., tr.
Von Louth, Andrew L. If the Shoe Fits.
Von Magyary-Kossa, Ilona see Magyary-Kossa, Ilona von.
Von Maltitz, F. Living & Learning in Two Languages: Bilingual-Bicultural Education in the U. S.
Von Mauntz, Alfred. Heraldik in Diensten der Shakespeare-Forschung.
Von Mehren, Arthur T., ed. Law in Japan: The Legal Order in a Changing Society.
Von Mises, Richard. Theory of Flight.
Von Muench, I. see Muench, I. Von.
Von Muralt, A., ed. see Nestle Foundation Symposium Staff.
Vonnegut, Kurt, Jr. Bluebeard.
--Galapagos.
--Welcome to the Monkey House.
Von Oertzen, W., ed. Deep Inelastic & Fusion Reactions with Heavy Ions.
Von Petzold, Gertrud. Harriet Martineau und Ihre Sittlich Religiose Weltschau.
Von Philippsberg, Eugen Philippovich see Philippovich Von Philippsberg, Eugen.
Von Rad, Gerhard. The Problem of the Hexateuch & Other Essays.
Von Ramdohr, Friedrich W. B. Ueber Mahlerei & Bildhauerarbeit in Rom fur Liebhaber des Schonen in der Kunst.
Von Randow, R. Introduction to the Theory of Matroids.
Von Raumer, Frederick. England in Eighteen Thirty- Five.
Von Raumer, Rudolf H. Geschichte der Germanischen Philologie Vorzugsweise in Deutschland.
Von Reichenbach, Karl. Researches on Magnetism, Electricity, Heat, Light, Crystallization & Chemical Attraction in Relation to the Vital Force. Gregory, William, tr.
Von Reinken, Liselotte, ed. see Modersohn-Becker, Paula.
Von Richthofen, Manfred. The Red Baron. Ulanoff, Stanley M., ed. Kilduff, Peter, tr. from Ger.
Von Rosenstein, Nicholas R. The Diseases of Children & Their Remedies.
Von Schaldach, Herbert. DTV Woerterbuch der Medizin.
Von Schiller, Friedrich. Mary Stuart. Wilkins, Sophie, tr. from Ger.
Von Schleyer, P. R., jt. auth. see Bingham, R. C.
Von Schmidt, Carol, jt. auth. see Gerlock, Larry.
Von Schmidt, W. A. & Hinrichs, H. Blick & Einsicht: Intermediate German.
Von Simson, Otto. The Gothic Cathedral: Origins of Gothic Architecture & the Medieval Concept of Order.
Von Solodkoff, Alexander, et al. Masterpieces from the House of Faberge. Forbes, Christopher, ed.

Von Stackelberg, Mark, jt. auth. see Schmidt, Helmut.
Von Staden, Wendelgard. Darkness over the Valley. Peters, Mollie C., tr. from Ger.
Von Steiner, Kurt. Resistance Fighter: Anti-Nazi Terror Tactics of the Austrian Underground.
Von Tempsky, Alexa. Seascapes by Alexa.
Von Trapp, Maria. Maria.
Von Troyes, Christian see Chretian De Troyes.
Von Volborth, Carl-Alexander. The Art of Heraldry.
Von Wartburg, Ursula. The Workshop Book of Knitting.
Von Weizsacker, Richard. A Voice from Germany: Speeches by Richard von Weizsacker. Von Abrams, Karin, tr. from Ger.
Von Welanetz, Diana & Von Welanetz, Paul. The Pleasure of Your Company.
Von Welanetz, Paul, jt. auth. see Von Welanetz, Diana.
Von Wellnitz, Marcus. Christ & the Patriarchs: New Light from Apocryphal Literature & Tradition.
Von Werder, Klaus, jt. ed. see Fahlbusch, Rudolf.
Von Willisen, F. K., jt. ed. see Kmetz, A. R.
Von Zittel, K. A. Geschichte der Geologie und Paleontologie.
Vooren, Monique van see Van Vooren, Monique.
Voorhes, Meg. Black South African Views on Disinvestment.
Voorhis, Kenneth R. Van see Van Voorhis, Kenneth R.
Voorthuijesn, M. E. Van Eijk Van see Van Eijk Van Voorthuijsen, M. E.
Voorthuijsen, A. M. Van see Van Voorthuijsen, A. M.
Vopat, W. A., jt. auth. see Skrotzki, Bernhardt G.
Vore, Jack B. De see De Vore, Jack B., Jr. & Rolloff, John A.
Vore, M. Susan De see De Vore, M. Susan.
Vorenberg, James. Criminal Law & Procedure, Cases & Materials: 1985 Supplement.
Vorherr, Helmuth. Breast Cancer: Epidemiology, Endocrinology, Biochemistry & Pathobiology.
--The Breast: Morphology & Lactation.
Voris, Jacqueline van see Van Voris, Jacqueline.
Vorndran, B. J., jt. auth. see Winn, Charles S.
Vorohin, S. Nine White Swans.
Voronov, A. A. Basic Principles of Automatic Control Theory: Special Linear & Nonlinear Systems.
Voronov, A. A., ed. Management & Control in Large Systems.
Voronov, N. The Crest of the Summer.
Voros, Gerald J. & Alvarez, Paul, eds. What Happens in Public Relations.
Vorpahl, Ben M. Frederic Remington & the West: With the Eye of the Mind.
Vorperian, John H., jt. auth. see Tartakow, I. Jackson.
Vors, B. L. Van see Van Vors, B. L.
Vorss, Patricia De see Smith, Beverly B. & De Vorss, Patricia.
Vorster, Willem, jt. auth. see Lategan, Bernard.
Vorster, Willem S., jt. auth. see Lategan, Bernard C.
Vos, Cor, illus. Cyclist Training Diary.
Vos, Geerhardus. Redemptive History & Biblical Interpretation. Gaffin, Richard B., Jr., ed.
Vos, Howard F. Effective Bible Study.
Vosburgh, Paul N. Commercial Applications of Wind Power.
Vose, Allen D., jt. auth. see Kane, Robert M.
Vose, Ruth H. Agoraphobia.
Voshell, Dorothy. Whom Shall I Marry?
Voskoboinokov, V. Masha Nikiforova's Days.
Voskrenskaya, Z. Surprise.
Vosper, Robert. The Farmington Plan Survey: A Summary of the Seperate Studies of 1957-1961.
Vosresentskaya, Z., et al. Stories about Lenin & the Revolution.
Voss, Carl, jt. auth. see Huebner, Theodore.
Voss, Harwin L., jt. auth. see Shepard, Jon M.
Voss, Jacqueline & Gale, Jay. A Young Woman's Guide to Sex.
Votaw, Clyde W. Gospels & Contemporary Biographies in the Greco-Roman World.
Voth, Alden H. Moscow Abandons Israel for the Arabs: Ten Crucial Years in the Middle East.
Voth, Anne. Women in the New Eden.
Voth, D., ed. Tumors of the Central Nervous System in Infancy & Childhood.
Voto, Bernard De see De Voto, Bernard.
Voute, Peter. Only a Free Man: War Memories of Two Dutch Doctors (1940-1945)
Vowles, K. Surgical Problems in the Aged.
Voyce, Arthur. Russian Architecture.
--Russian Architecture, Trends in Nationalism & Modernism.
Voyutsky, S. Colloid Chemistry.
Vozdvizhensky, B. Exploratory Drilling.
Voznesensky, Andrei. Dogalypse.
Vranicar, John, et al. Streamlining Land Use Regulation: A Guidebook for Local Governments.
Vrba, Rudolf & Bestic, Alan. Escape from Auschwitz.
--Escape from Auschwitz: I Cannot Forgive.
Vrbova, G., et al. Nerve-Muscle Interaction.
Vreeland, Diana, intro. by. The Vogue Poster Book: A Collection of Magazine Covers from Vogue (1911-1927)
Vreeland, Helen K., ed. see Austin, Mary S.
Vrettos, Theodore. Birds of Winter.
--Lord Elgin's Lady.
Vreuls, Diane. Are We There Yet?
--Instructions.
Vries, A. De see De Vries, A.
Vries, Barend A. de. Export Promotion Policies.
Vries, Barend A. de see De Vries, Barend A. & Brakel, Willem.
Vries, Dawn De see De Vries, Dawn.
Vries, G. A. Amsterdam: Where to Go.
Vries, G. de see Norrie, D. H. & De Vries, G.
Vries, H. De see Van Bekkum, O. & De Vries, H.
Vries, Mary De see De Vries, Mary.
Vries, Tom De see De Vries, Tom.
Vrieze, K., jt. auth. see Kepert, D. L.
Vrooman, Alan. Good Writing: An Informal Manual of Style.
Vrooman, Dik. Architecture: Perspective Shadows & Reflections.
Vsesoiuznaia Konferentsiia Po Voprosam Psikhoterapil Staff. Psychotherapy in the Soviet Union. Winn, Ralph B., tr.
Vu, My T. World Population Projections 1984: Short & Long Term Estimates by Age & Sex with Related Demographic Statistics.
Vu, Theresa. Short Stories.
Vuilleumier, Marion, jt. auth. see Buddington, Anita.
Vuke, Susan. Processes of the Earth's Surface.
Vulcanescu, Neagu. Serene Thoughts of a Poet.
Vulliamy, Graham. Jazz & Blues.
Vulliamy, Graham & Lee, Edward. Popular Music: A Teacher's Guide.
Vuuren, Nancy Van see Van Vuuren, Nancy.
Vvedenskii, Aleksandr. Polnoe Sobranie Sochinenii. Meilakh, M., ed.

W

W H O see World Health Organization.
Waack, William L., ed. Careers & Career Education in the Performing Arts: An Annotated Bibliography.
Waagenaar, Sam. The Pope's Jews.
Waal, Ronald B. De see De Waal, Ronald B.
Waard, Jan de & Nida, Eugene A. From One Language to Another: Functional Equivalence in Bible Translation.
Waard, Romke De see De Waard, Romke.
Wabbes, Marie. Goodnight, Little Rabbit.
--Little Rabbit's Garden.
Waber, Bernard. Cheese.
--Dear Hildegarde.
--Firefly Named Torchy.
--Goodbye, Funny Dumpy-Lumpy.
--Just Like Abraham Lincoln.
--Mice on My Mind.
--Nobody Is Perfick.
Wace, Robert & Layamon. Arthurian Chronicles: A Paraphrase of Wace's "Roman De Brut" Mason, Eugene, tr.
Wach, Joachim. Sociology of Religion.
Wachman, Barbara. The Woman's Book of Non-trivial Trivia.
Wachman, Harold Y., jt. auth. see Goodman, Frank O.
Wachorst, Wyn. Thomas Alva Edison: An American Myth.
Wachspress, Eugene L., jt. ed. see McLeod, Robin J.
Wachtel, Henry. Security for All & Free Enterprise.
Wachtel, S. Eric. How to Hold on to Your Job.
Wachter, Kenneth W., et al. Statistical Studies of Historical Social Structure.
Wackenheim, A. & Babin, E. The Narrow Lumbar Canal: Radiologic Signs & Surgery.
Wackenheim, A. & Braun, J. P. Angiography of the Mesencephalon: Normal & Pathological Findings.
Wacker, Hansjorg, ed. Continuation Methods.
Waddell, Austine. Buddhism & Lamaism of Tibet.
Waddell, Bernard. I Am Somebody: The True Story of a Black U. S. Navy Frogman.
Waddell, Charles. Faith, Hope & Luck: A Sociological Study of Children Growing up with a Life-Threatening Illness.
Waddell, Helen, tr. Mediaeval Latin Lyrics.
Waddell, J. P. The Waddell System of Nutritional Analysis.
Waddell, Joseph J., ed. Concrete Construction Handbook.
Waddell, L. A. The Makers of Civilization.
Waddell, Roberta, ed. The Art Nouveau Style in Jewelry, Metalwork, Glass, Ceramics, Textiles, Architecture & Furniture.
Waddell, Thomas E., ed. The Off-Site Costs of Soil Erosion.
Waddell, William C. Overcoming Murphy's Law.
Wadden, Paul. Stork Tracks.
Waddington, Lawrence C. Arrest, Search & Seizure.
Waddington, P., ed. I. S. Turgenev: Dvoryanskoye Gnezdo.
Waddington, P. A. Training of Prison Governors: Role Ambiguity & Socialization.
Waddington, Richard. Catching Salmon.
Waddy, Lawrence. Faith of the Fathers.
Waddy, Lawrence H. Faith of Our Fathers.
Wade, Carlson. Encyclopedia of Power Foods for Health & Longer Life.
Wade, Charles, ed. Fishing with the Experts.
Wade, David. Pattern in Islamic Art.
Wade, Elbert. All Signs Rising.
Wade, Horrace. A Boy's Life.
Wade, J. E. & Hewson, E. W. Wind Power Prospecting: A Guide to Biological Indicators.
Wade, J. E., jt. ed. Wind Power Potential: A Prospector's Handbook of Remote Sensing Techniques.
Wade, John. The Extraordinary Black Book.
Wade, John W. God's Word B. C.
Wade, Kevin. Key Exchange.
Wade, Lord. Europe & the British Health Service.
Wade, Mary. To the Miner Born: Life in a Mining Village 1918-1945, from a Woman's Point of View.
Wade, N. A., jt. auth. see Wallace, J. E.
Wade, Nicholas, jt. auth. see Broad, William.
Wade, R. G., ed. Soviet Chess.
Wade, Richard C., ed. Cities in American Life.
Wade, Richard C. & Anderson, Howard R., eds. Negro in American Life.
Wade, Stuart. Vocal Sight Reading Tests for Treble Voices.
Wade, Thomas L. & Taylor, Howard E. Contemporary Analytic Geometry.
Wade, Virginia. Ladies of the Court: A Century of Women at Wimbledon.
Wadley, Susan S., ed. The Powers of Tamil Women.
Wadlington, Walter. Domestic Relations, Cases & Other Materials: Successor Edition, 1985 Supplement.
Wadstrom, T., ed. see Eaker, D.
Wadsworth, Barry J. Piaget's Theory of Cognitive & Affective Development.
Wadsworth, Bruce. An Adirondack Sampler: Day Hikes for All Seasons.
--Guide to Adirondack Trails: Central Region. Burdick, Neal S., ed.
--Guide to Adirondack Trails: The Northville-Placid Trail. Burdick, Neal S., ed.
Wadsworth, Olive A. Over in the Meadow.
Waegell, B., jt. auth. see Brun, P.
Waehrer, Helen Y., jt. auth. see Glazer, Nona Y.
Waelbroeck, L. Topological Vector Spaces & Algebras.
Waelti-Walters, Jennifer. Fairy Tales & the Female Imagination.
Waelty, Mathilde. The Horseshoe: A Romance in Four Acts.
Waesche, James F. Beautiful Maryland. Shangle, Robert D., ed.
Waesche, R. H., ed. Journal of Propulsion & Power.
Waetzoldt, Stephan, et al. German Masters of the Nineteenth Century: Paintings & Drawings from the Federal Republic of Germany. Walter, Emily, ed.
Waetzoldt, Stephen, jt. auth. see Schiff, Gert.
Wafer, James W. Drippings from a Cracked Churn: The Foibles & Follies of Our Educational Bureaucracy.
Wagel, Srinvas. Finance in China.
Wageman, Virginia, ed. Selections from the Collection of Marion & Gustave Ring.
Wagenhaar, Theodore C. High School Diploma As a Terminal Degree: Contractor Report.
Wagenknecht, David. Blake's Night: William Blake & the Idea of Pastoral.
Wagenknecht, Edward, ed. see Whittier, John Greenleaf.
Wagenseil, Joh. Chr. Tela Ignea Satanae.
Wagenvoord, James. Computerspace: Home Office Strategies That Work for Computers.
--Personal Style.
Wagenvoord, James, ed. Man's Book.
--Men: A Book for Women.
--Women: A Book for Men.
Wagenvoort, Hendrik. Roman Dynamism: Studies in Ancient Roman Thought Language & Custom.
--Studies in Roman Literature, Culture & Religion. Commager, Steele, ed.
Wager, Walter. Blue Leader.
--Blue Moon.
--Blue Murder.
--Designated Hitter.
Wages, Jack D. Seventy-Five Writers of the Colonial South: A Reference Guide.
Waggener, Florence E. Story of the Old Testament Simply Told.
Waggoner, Diane. The Hills of Faraway: A Guide to Fantasy.
Waggoner, Glen, ed. see Rotisserie League Staff.
Waggoner, Hyatt H. Hawthorne: A Critical Study.
Waggoner, Susan, jt. auth. see Dietrich, John.
Wagle, N. K., ed. Images of Maharashtra: A Regional Profile in India.
Wagman, Richard, ed. The New Complete Medical & Health Encyclopedia.
Wagner, Anthony. Pedigree & Progress: Essays in the Genealogical Interpretation of History.
Wagner, Augusta. Labor Legislation in China.
Wagner, Betty J. & Stunard, E. Arthur. Making & Using Inexpensive Classroom Media.
Wagner, C. Peter. Church Growth & the Whole Gospel: A Biblical Mandate.
--Our Kind of People: The Ethical Dimensions of Church Growth in America.
--The Protestant Movement in Bolivia.
Wagner, C. Peter & Dayton, Edward. Unreached Peoples '79.
Wagner, C. Peter, jt. auth. see Dayton, Edward.
Wagner, C. Peter, et al. Unreached Peoples, Eighty-One.
Wagner, Catherine. American Classrooms. Wagner, Catherine.
Wagner, Cosima. Cosima Wagner's Diaries: 1869 to 1877. Gregor-Dellin, Martin & Mack, Dietrich, eds. Skelton, Geoffrey, tr.
--Cosima Wagner's Diaries: 1878 to 1883. Skelton, Geoffrey, tr.
Wagner, D. Introduction to the Theory of Magnetism.
Wagner, H. K., ed. see International Congress on Medicinal Plant Research, Section A Staff.
Wagner, James K., jt. auth. see Day, Albert E.
Wagner, Johannes, ed. Adult Baptism & the Catechumenate.
Wagner, Leopold. More about Names.
Wagner, Leslie, ed. Agenda for Institutional Change.
Wagner, Linda, ed. see Williams, William Carlos.
Wagner, Linda W., ed. Ernest Hemingway: Five Decades of Criticism.
Wagner, Matthew. Grendel: Devil by the Deed.
Wagner, Norman E., ed. see Westermann, Claus.
Wagner, P. J., et al. Triplet States: No. 3.
Wagner, Peter C. Effective Body Building: Biblical Steps to Spiritual Growth.
Wagner, Petti. Murdered Heiress, Living Witness.
Wagner, Ray. American Combat Planes.
Wagner, Richard. Actors & Singers.
--Art & Politics.
Wagner, Richard H. Environment & Man.
--Environment & Man.
Wagner, Richard M. & Wright, Roy J. Streamliners & War Horses.
Wagner, Robert P., jt. auth. see Sutton, H. Eldon.
Wagner, Robert P., ed. Genes & Proteins.
Wagner, Robert R., jt. ed. see Fraenkel-Conrat, Heinz.
Wagner, Sharon B. Legacy of Loneliness.
Wagner, V. Russian for English-Speaking Learners.
Wagner, Walter F., Jr., jt. auth. see Architectural Record Magazine Editors.
Wagner, Wilhelm. Die Chinesische Landwirtschaft.
Wagner, William. Lightning Bugs & Other Reconnaissance Drones.
Wagner, Willis H. Modern Carpentry.
Wagoner, David. In Broken Country.
--Who Shall Be the Sun?: Poems Based on the Lore, Legends, & Myths of Northwest Coast & Plateau Indians.
Wagoner, R. H., ed. Novel Techniques in Metal Deformation Testing: Proceedings. TMS-AIME Fall Meeting, St. Louis, 1982.
Wagoner, R. H., et al. Societal Crises & Educational Response: A Book of Readings.
Wagschal, Peter H., ed. see Fuller, R. Buckminster, et al.
Wagstaffe & Fidler. The Preservation of Natural History Specimens.
Wagstaffe, Reginald & Fidler, J. Havelock. Preservation of Natural History Specimens. Incl. Vol. 1. Invertebrates; Vol. 2. Vertebrates, Geology, & Botany. Beekman Pubs.
Wah-Be-Gwo-Nese, pseud. Ojibwa Indian Legends.
Wahi, Pradeep & Gupta, K. C. Fiber Optics for Communication & Sensors.
Wahl, Jan. How the Children Stopped the Wars.
--Jamie's Tiger.
--Old Hippo's Easter Egg.
--Old Hippo's Easter Egg.
--So Many Raccoons.
--Tiger Watch.
Wahl, Jean. A Short History of Existentialism.
Wahl, John & Wahl, Stacey. I Can Count the Petals of a Flower.
Wahl, Paul. Gun Trader's Guide. Traister, John, ed.
--Gun Trader's Guide.
--Gun Trader's Guide.
Wahl, Stacey, jt. auth. see Wahl, John.
Wahler, Robert G., et al. Ecological Assessment of Child Problem Behavior.
Wahlfeldt, Bette G. Successful Sandy Soil Gardening.
Wahlquist, Wayne L., et al, eds. Atlas of Utah.
Wahlster, W., ed. Artificial Intelligence, Bad Honnef, FRG 1982: Proceedings.
Wahlstrom, Eric H., tr. see Aulen, Gustaf.

Wahlstrom, Eric H., tr. see Aulen, Gustaf E.
Wahlstrom, Eric H., tr. see Lindblom, J.
Wahnert, John. America's Priceless Heritage, the King James Version of the Bible.
Waid, John S., ed. PCBs & the Environment: Differences Between Yusho & Other Kinds of Poisoning Involving Only PCBs.
--PCBs & the Environment: Polychlorinated Biphenyls: Accumulation & Effects upon Plants.
Wain. Mathematical & Education.
Wain, John. Samuel Johnson.
Wainapel, David. From Death Row to Freedom.
Wainerdi, R. E. Analytical Chemistry in Space.
Wainhouse, Austryn, tr. see Klossowski, Pierre.
Wainhouse, Austryn, tr. see Marquis de Sade.
Wainio, Walter W. Mammalian Mitochondrial Respiratory Chain.
Wainwright. The Problem of the Picts.
Wainwright, Abbott, ed. see Woodrow, Raymond J.
Wainwright, Arthur. Beyond Biblical Criticism: Encountering Jesus Christ in the Scripture.
Wainwright, David. Broadwood by Appointment: A History.
Wainwright, Don. Existentialist Essays.
Wainwright, John. Clouds of Guilt.
--The Ride.
Wainwright, R. N. Radio & Television Servicing.
Wainwright, William J. Philosophy of Religion: An Annotated Bibliography of Twentieth-Century Writings in English.
Wainwright, William J., jt. ed. see Rowe, William L.
Wairawen, Michael, ed. see Fitzgerald, Hiram E.
Waisbard, Simone. The Mysteries of Machu Picchu.
Waisel, Yoav. Biology of Halophytes.
Waismann, Friedrich. Ludwig Wittgenstein & the Vienna Circle: Conversations Recorded by Friedrich Waismann. McGuinness, Brian, ed. Schulte, Joachim & McGuiness, B., trs.
Wait, J. R., et al, eds. Integrated Optics: Related Conference Proceedings.
Wait, William A. Reverence for Life.
Waitakin, Howard & Waterman, Barbara. The Exploitation of Illness in Capitalist Society.
Waite, A. E. The Book of Ceremonial Magic.
Waite, Arthur E. Alchemists Through the Ages.
--Brotherhood of the Rosy Cross.
--Occult Sciences.
Waite, David H., jt. auth. see Neher, William W.
Waite, Frederick C. The Story of a Country Medical College: A History of the Clinical School of Medicine & the Vermont Medical College, Woodstock, Vermont, 1827-1856.
Waite Group. Microsoft C Programming for the PC.
Waite Group, jt. auth. see Berry, John.
Waite Group Staff. Orchestrating Symphony. Schafer, Dan, ed.
Waite Group Staff & Waite, Mitchell. Microsoft Macinations: An Introduction to Microsoft BASIC for the Apple Macintosh.
Waite Group Staff, et al. C Primer Plus.
--Macintosh Midnight Madness: Games, Utilities & Other Diversions In Microsoft BASIC for the Apple Macintosh.
Waite, H. H., ed. Quality Assurance-Applications-Components.
Waite, Mitchell, jt. auth. see Fox, David.
Waite, Mitchell, jt. auth. see Murtha, Stephen M.
Waite, Mitchell, jt. auth. see Waite Group Staff.
Waite, Mitchell, et al. UNIX System V Primer.
Waite, Robert G. Vanguard of Nazism: The Free Corps Movement in Postwar Germany, 1918-23.
Waitley, Denis. Being the Best.
Waitley, Douglas, jt. auth. see Ogilvie, Bruce.
Waitt, Ian, jt. ed. see Gray, Lynton.
Wajenberg, Earl, jt. auth. see Emery, Clayton.
Wakat, Diane, jt. auth. see Armstrong, Nell.
Wake, Clive, tr. see Ousmane, Sembene.
Wake Forest University, Continuing Legal Education Staff. North Carolina Trial Book Criminal: Master Case.
Wake Forest University School of Law Staff. Current Employment Law Issues.
--North Carolina Collection & Enforcement of Judgments.
--North Carolina Fifth Annual Review.
--North Carolina Professional Malpractice.
--North Carolina Wills & Probate Handbook.
--Personnel Law Handbook.
Wakefield, B. J. The Chemistry of Organolithium Compounds.
Wakefield, Dan. Selling Out.
Wakefield, Eva I. The Letters of Robert G. Ingersoll.
Wakefield, Norman. Listening.
Wakefield, Walter L. Heresy, Crusade, & Inquisition in Southern France, 1100-1250.
Wakeford, Jacqueline. Fly Tying Techniques.
Wakeham, Duane A. Mendelowitz's Guide to Drawing.
Wakeley, John H., jt. auth. see Smith, Henry C.
Wakeman, Geoffrey. Victorian Book Illustration.
Wakerly, J. F. Error-Detecting Codes, Self-Checking Circuits & Applications.
Wakil, Salih J., ed. Lipid Metabolism.
Wakoski, Diane. Waiting for the King of Spain.
Walberg, H. J., ed. Evaluation in Education.
Walberg, H. J. & Postlethwaite, T. N., eds. Evaluation in Education.
Walcher, D. N., et al, eds. Food, Man, & Society.
Walcher, Dwain N. & Peters, Donald L., eds. Early Childhood: The Development of Self-Regulatory Mechanisms.
Walcott, Derek. Another Life.
Waldberg, Michael. Gurdjieff: An Approach to His Ideas. Cox, Steve, tr.
Waldecki, Michael. The Book of Dreams.
Waldemar, Carla. Dining In - Minneapolis-St. Paul.
Walden. IBM Business Set.
Walden, Amelia. Case of the Diamond Eye.
--Escape on Skis.
--Go, Phillips, Go!
--Heartbreak Tennis.
--Play Ball, McGill!
--A Spy Case Built for Two.
--The Spy on Danger Island.
--To Catch a Spy.
--Valerie Valentine Is Missing.
--Where Is My Heart?
--Where Was Everyone When Sabrina Screamed?
Walden, Hilary. Ice Cream.
Walden, Jeffrey B. The IBM-PC in Your Corporation.
Walden, W. Charles, jt. auth. see Levins, Richard A.
Waldenfels, Hans. Absolute Nothingness: Foundations for a Buddhist-Christian Dialogue. Heisig, James W., tr. from Ger.
Walder, Barbara, jt. auth. see Schmidt, Mike.
Walder, Dennis. Athol Fugard.
--Athol Fugard.
Waldersee, Alfred H. A Field-Marshal's Memoirs: From the Diary, Correspondence, & Reminiscences of Alfred Count Von Waldersee.
Waldersee, James. Catholic Society in New South Wales 1788-1860.
Waldhart, jt. auth. see Applegate.
Waldhart-Applegate. Introduction to Communication Studies.
Waldie, Jerome & Frobish, Nestle J. Fair Play for Frogs: The Waldie-Frobish Papers.
Waldinger, Robert. Fundamentals of Psychiatry.
Waldman, Anne. Countries.
--Makeup on Empty Space.
Waldman, Diane. Enzo Cucchi. Rizzoli International Staff, ed.
--Kenneth Noland: A Retrospective.
Waldman, Guido, tr. see Allain, Marie-Francoise.
Waldman, Michael, jt. auth. see Green, Mark.
Waldman, Stuart, jt. auth. see Goldstein, Marty.
Waldmann, Thomas, jt. ed. see Rothschild, Marcus A.
Waldo, Dwight. Democracy, Bureaucracy & Hypocrisy.
Waldo, Gordon P., jt. auth. see American Society of Criminology Staff.
Waldo, Myra. Myra Waldo's Chinese Cooking.
Waldorf, Mary. Jake McGee & His Feet.
--Thousand Camps.
Waldowski, Therese F., jt. auth. see Gregorich, Barbara.
Waldrip, Donald R., jt. ed. see Estes, Nolan.
Waldron, Ann. Close Connections: Caroline Gordon & the Southern Renaissance.
Waldron, B. A. Management of Epidural Analgesia in Childbirth.
Waldron, Maggie. Barbeque & Smoke Cookery.
--Strawberries.
Waldron, Peter. The Price Guide to Antique Silver.
Waldron, Ronald J., et al. The Criminal Justice System: An Introduction.
--The Criminal Justice System: An Introduction.
--The Criminal Justice System: An Introduction.
Waldron, Sidney R., jt. auth. see Koehn, Peter.
Waldron, T. P. Principles of Language & Mind: An Evolutionary Theory of Meaning.
Waldron, Tom, jt. auth. see Gleeson, James.
Waldrop, Frank C. McCormick of Chicago.
Waldstein, Baron. The Diary of Baron Waldstein: A Traveller in Elizabethan England. Groos, G. W., tr.
Waldstein, Steve. How to Choose the Diet That's Right for You.
Wales, N. Y. Fables & Parables.
Wales Tourist Board Staff. Castles & Historic Places in Wales.
Waley, A. A Half of Two Lives.
Waley, Arthur. The Way & Its Power: A Study of the Tao Te Ching & Its Place in Chinese Thought.
Waley, Arthur, tr. The Book of Songs.
Waley, Arthur, tr. from Chine see Wu Ch'Eng-En.
Walfish, Paul G., et al, eds. Autoimmunity & the Thyroid.
Walfish, Steven & Sumprer, Gerry. Clinical Counseling & Community Psychology: A Student Guide to Graduate Training & Professional Practice.
Walford, A. J. Guide to Reference Material: Science & Technology.
Walford, Geoffrey, ed. Schooling in Turmoil.
Walford, Roy. The One Hundred & Twenty Year Diet: How to Double Your Vital Years.
Walford, Roy L. The One Twenty Year Diet: How to Double Your Vital Years.
Walgenbach, Paul H., et al. Financial Accounting: An Introduction.
--Principles of Accounting.
--Principles of Accounting.
--Principles of Accounting.
--Principles of Accounting.
Walgrave, Jan H. Unfolding Revelation: The Nature of Doctrinal Development.
Wali, Mohan K., ed. see International Congress for Energy & the Ecosystem Staff.
Waliszewski, Kazimierz. Peter the Great. Loyd, Mary, tr.
Walk, Richard D. Perceptual Development.
Walke, Jerry L. & Whitt, Angela Y. Get Your Head Out of the Fridge: How to Stop Being a Foodaholiç.
Walkenstein, Eileen. Don't Shrink to Fit! A Confrontation with Dehumanization in Psychiatry & Psychology.
Walker. American Politics & the Constitution.
Walker & Cooper. Experimental & Clinical Interventions in Aging.
Walker, jt. auth. see Boyd.
Walker, A. M. A New Look at the Commonwealth.
Walker, Aidan. Wood Polishing & Finishing Techniques.
Walker, Alexander. Bette Davis: A Celebration.
--The Once & Future Film: British Cinema in the 70's & 80's.
--Stanley Kubrick Directs.
--Vivien: The Life of Vivien Leigh.
Walker, Alfred J. HRIS Development: A Project Team Guide to Building an Effective Information System.
Walker, Alicė. In Love & Trouble: Stories of Black Women.
--The Third Life of Grange Copeland.
--The Third Life of Grange Copeland.
--You Can't Keep a Good Woman Down: Stories.
Walker Art Gallery Staff, jt. auth. see Tate Gallery, London Staff.
Walker, Arthur L., et al. How to Use Adding & Calculating Machines.
Walker, B. J. & Blake, Ian F. Computer Security & Protection Structures.
Walker, Barbara. A Good Fish Dinner.
Walker, Barbara G. Knitting from the Top.
--Treasury of Knitting Patterns.
Walker, Benjamin. Beyond the Body: The Human Double & the Astral Planes.
Walker Books Staff. Mealtime.
Walker, Bryce & Time-Life Books Editors. The Armada.
Walker, C. T. Geochemistry of Boron.
Walker, Charls E., jt. ed. see Baughn, William H.
Walker, Craig, jt. auth. see Laube, Ed.
Walker, D., jt. auth. see McRae, R.
Walker, D. P. Spiritual & Demonic Magic from Ficino to Campanella.
Walker, David. Big Ben.
Walker, David F. Canada's Industrial Space-Economy.
Walker, David F., ed. Planning Industrial Development.
Walker, E. & Williams, G. ABC of Healthy Travel.
Walker, Edward D. Transparent Watercolor.
Walker, Elinor, compiled by. Book Bait: Detailed Notes on Adult Books Popular with Young People.
Walker, Elizabeth N. The Loving Seasons.
Walker, Evelyn & Young, Perry D. A Killing Cure.
Walker, Flora K. Bibliography & Index of U. S. Geological Survey Publications Relating to Coal: January 1971 Through June 1978.
Walker, Frances S. Puppets, Creative Ideas & Other Neat Things.
Walker, Frank. Hugo Wolf: A Biography.
Walker, Franklin. Jack London & the Klondike: The Genesis of an American Writer.
--The Two F's of Modern Living.
Walker, Fred M. Song of the Clyde: A History of Clyde Shipbuilding.
Walker, Fred M., jt. auth. see Johnson, Glen R.
Walker, G. B. Coloured Type & Song Canaries.
Walker, G. S., ed. see National Computing Centre, Ltd. Staff.
Walker, Gary C. The War in Southwest Virginia 1861-65.
Walker, George L. The Chronicles of Doodah.
Walker, Glen. Credit Where Credit Is Due.
Walker, Glynnis. Solomon's Children: Exploding the Myths of Divorce.
Walker, Grace. Living Together.
Walker, Irma. Custody.
--Enduring Passion.
--Inherit the Earth.
Walker, J., et al. Combined Textbook of Obstetrics & Gynecology.
Walker, J. H., jt. auth. see Mayer, R. J.
Walker, J. Ingram. Everybody's Guide to Emotional Well-Being: Helping Yourself Get Help.
Walker, Jacilyn G. & DeHaven, Martha L. Texas Conservation Guide for Municipal Services.
Walker, James W. & Gutteridge, Thomas G. Career Planning Practices.
Walker, Jeremy. To Will One Thing: Reflections on Kierkegaard's Purity of Heart.
Walker, Jerry, jt. auth. see Adams, Kay Angana.
Walker, Jerry P., jt. auth. see Mc Caslin, N. L.
Walker, Jim, ed. see Bradley, Bill.
Walker, Jim, ed. see Long, Raphael.
Walker, Jim, ed. see Myrick, David F.
Walker, Jim, ed. see Swett, Ira L.
Walker, John. The National Gallery of Art: Washington, D.C.
Walker, John C. Plant Pathology.
Walker, John M. Pharmacology of Naturally Occurring Polypeptides & Lipid Soluble Acids.
Walker, John M., jt. auth. see Farmeer, Peter B.
Walker, John M., Jr., intro. by. Crime Scene & Evidence Collection Handbook.
Walker, John R. Modern Metalworking.
Walker, Katherine S. De Basil's Ballets Russes.
Walker, Katherine S., ed. see Chandler, Raymond.
Walker, Kenneth. The Making of Man.
--The Story of Blood.
Walker, L. E., jt. auth. see Ballentyne, D. W.
Walker, Larry. State Legislative Control of Federal Aid Funds: The Case of Oklahoma.
Walker, Laurens, jt. auth. see Thibaut, John.
Walker, Leslie J., tr. see Machiavelli, Niccolo.
Walker, Lucye. Daystar.
Walker, Lyn. Visions & Revisions--a Guide for Creative Writing.
Walker, Margaret. Jubilee.
Walker, Mary A. Maggot.
Walker, Mary Lu, jt. auth. see Marbach, Ethel.
Walker, Melissa. Writing Research Papers: A Norton Guide.
Walker, Michael. The Cocktail Book.
Walker, Mildred. A Piece of the World.
--Winter Wheat.
Walker, N., et al. Legal Pitfalls in Architecture, Engineering & Building Construction.
Walker, N. W. Discover Your Fountain of Health.
Walker, Nicolette M. Introduction to Dinghy Sailing.
Walker, Nigel. Morale in the Civil Service: A Study of the Desk Worker.
Walker, Peter. Moral Choices: Memory, Desire, & Imagination in Nineteenth-Century American Abolition.
Walker, Philip. Zola.
Walker, Pinkney C., ed. Essays in Monetary Policy in Honor of Elmer Wood.
Walker, R. & Knowles, M. E., eds. International Symposium on Food Toxiology: A Special Issue of Food Addictives & Contaminants.
Walker, R. B. The Newspaper Press in New South Wales 1803-1920.
--Yesterday's News.
Walker, Ralph C. Kant.
Walker, Richard C., ed. An Introduction to Accounting: Selected Readings.
Walker, Rikki. A Guide to Post-Cranial Bones of East African Animals: Mrs. Walker's Bone Book.
Walker, Robert. Exploring Photography.
Walker, Robert & Adelman, Clem. A Guide to Classroom Observation.
Walker, Robert W; see Kruse, Donald W.
Walker, Sharon. Circle of Hope: A Child Rescued by Love from a Medical Death Sentence.
Walker, Stella A., jt. auth. see Summerhays, R. S.
Walker, Stephen. Animal Thought.
--Learning Theory & Behavior Modification. Herriot, Peter, ed.
Walker, Stephen, jt. ed. see Barton, Len.
Walker, Stuart. Winning: The Psychology of Competition.
Walker, Stuart H. Advanced Racing Tactics.
--Performance Advances in Small Boat Racing.
Walker, Stuart H., ed. Techniques of Small Boat Racing.
Walker, Sydney, 3rd. Help for the Hyperactive Child.
Walker, T. Understanding Management Accounting.
--Understanding Standard Costing.
Walker, W. F. Fundamentals of Press Tool Design.
Walker, W. G., ed. see Cowen, Zelman.
Walker, Warren F., Jr., jt. auth. see Villee, Claude A.
Walker, Warren S., ed. see Cooper, James Fenimore.
Walker, Wilbert L. The Pride of Our Hearts.
Walker, Wilfred, ed. Metallogeny & Global Tectonics.
Walker, William & Lonnroth, Mans. Nuclear Power Struggles: Industrial Competition & Proliferation Control.
Walker, William, jt. auth. see Leocha, Charles.

Walker, Winifred. Valley of Vision: Discovering God Around the World.
Walker's Manual Incorporated Staff. Walker's Manual of Western Corporations.
--Walker's Manual of Western Corporations.
--Walker's Manual of Western Corporations.
--Walker's Manual of Western Corporations.
Walkes, Joseph A., Jr. Black Square & Compass: 200 Years of Prince Hall Freemasonry.
Walklin, Carol, jt. auth. see Newland, Mary.
Walkowitz, Daniel J., jt. ed. see Stearns, Peter N.
Wall, Alexander C., jt. auth. see Wall, Elizabeth S.
Wall, Andrew, jt. auth. see Levitt, Ruth.
Wall, Ann, ed. Mindscapes: Poems by Dale Zieroth, Paulette Jiles, Susan Musgrave, Tom Wayman.
Wall, Elizabeth S. The Computer Alphabet Book.
Wall, Elizabeth S. & Wall, Alexander C. The Beginner's Computer Dictionary.
Wall, Fred J. This Mess We're In!
Wall, H. S. Creative Mathematics.
Wall, James D., ed. Environmental Management Handbook for the Hydrocarbon Processing Industries.
Wall, Jerry A., jt. auth. see Glueck, William F.
Wall, Jesse D. Introductory Physics: A Problem-Solving Approach.
Wall, John E., jt. auth. see Evans, James E.
Wall, Leo A. Fluoropolymers.
Wall, Maggie. Creative Needlepoint Borders.
Wall, Norbert, jt. auth. see Creedy, Judith.
Wall, Patrick D. & Melzack, Ronald, eds. Textbook of Pain.
Wall, Rosalind S. When the Coast Was Wild & Lonely: Early Settlers of The Sur.
Wall, Wendell. Laboratory Manual for Introductory Biology.
Wallace, Alfred R., jt. auth. see Darwin, Charles.
Wallace, Andrew. Differential Topology: First Steps.
Wallace, Barbara B. Miss Switch to the Rescue.
Wallace, C. Treasury of Games & Puzzles.
Wallace, Carlton. Dictionary of Civil Defense.
Wallace, Carol M., et al. Dance: A Very Social History.
Wallace, Chick. Husbands, Lovers & Other Perishables.
Wallace, Daisy, ed. Giant Poems.
Wallace, Doris. Lamp unto My Feet.
Wallace, Edgar. The Brigand.
Wallace, Edwin R. Dynamic Psychiatry in Theory & Practice.
Wallace, Frank R. Eric Flame.
--Man's Choice.
--Neo-Tech & Business.
--Neo-Tech I, the Pre-Discovery.
--Three Neo-Tech Papers.
--We the Creators of Heavens & Earths.
Wallace, George J. My World of Birds: Memoirs of an Ornithologist.
Wallace, Hal & Heberle, Dave. The Winning Edge: A Foreman's Guide to Supervision.
Wallace, Helen, et al. Policy-Making in the European Community.
Wallace-Homestead Co. Staff. Oak Furniture, Styles & Prices.
Wallace, Hugh. Vertebrate Limb Regeneration.
Wallace, Hugh A. & Martin, J. R. Asphalt Pavement Engineering.
Wallace, Iain. The Transportation Impact of the Canadian Mining Industry.
Wallace, Irving. The Celestial Bed.
--The Seventh Secret.
--Writing of One Novel.
Wallace, J. E. & Wade, N. A. Review Questions in Analytical Toxicology.
Wallace, J. F., jt. auth. see Klahr, David.
Wallace, Joanne. The Confident Woman.
--Dress with Style.
--The Working Woman.
Wallace, Judith. Memories of a Country Childhood.
Wallace, M., jt. auth. see Singer, G.
Wallace, Marjorie. The Silent Twins.
Wallace, Martin. A Short History of Ireland.
Wallace, Mary, ed. see Adams, Jennifer K.
Wallace, Mary, ed. see Haney, Joy.
Wallace, Mary, ed. see Segraves, Judy.
Wallace, Mary E., ed. see Edwards, Rosemary W.
Wallace, Mary H. It's Real.
--My Name Is Christian Woman.
--Pioneer Pentecostal Women.
--Pioneer Pentecostal Women.
Wallace, Mary H., jt. auth. see Cagle, Paul R., Jr.
Wallace, Mary H., ed. Harvestime Pulpit Library: Let Them Know.
Wallace, Mary H., ed. see Freeman, Nona.
Wallace, Mary H., ed. see Jackson, Sue B.
Wallace, Mary H., ed. see Moore, Gary.
Wallace, Mary H., ed. see Pugh, Nathanael.
Wallace, Mary H., ed. see Westberg, Barbara.
Wallace, Melanie, jt. auth. see Manheim, Jarol B.
Wallace, Mike & Gates, Gary P. Close Encounters.
Wallace, Patricia, jt. auth. see Brown, Thomas S.
Wallace, Paul A. W. Indian Paths of Pennsylvania.
Wallace, R. R., jt. ed. see Healey, M. C.
Wallace, Ralph G., jt. auth. see Houghton, Diane.
Wallace, Robert. How They Do It.
Wallace, Robert A., et al. Biosphere: The Realm of Life.
Wallace, S. C. Federal Departmentalization: A Critique of Theories of Organization.
Wallace, Stephen, et al. Navajo Changes.
Wallace, W. E. Rare Earth Intermetallics.
Wallace, William. Britain's Bilateral Links with Western Europe.
Wallace, William A. Galileo's Early Notebooks.
Wallace, William J., jt. auth. see Ingmanson, Dale E.
Wallace, William S. Dictionary of North American Authors Deceased Before 1950.
Wallace-Brodeur, Ruth. One April Vacation.
Wallace-Crabbe, Chris, ed. The Golden Apples of the Sun.
Wallach, Carla. Gardening in the City: Backyards, Balconies, Terraces & Penthouses.
Wallach, D. F. The Plasma Membrane: Dynamic Perspectives, Genetics & Pathology.
Wallach, D. F. & Winzler, R. J. Evolving Strategies & Tactics in Membrane Research.
Wallach, D. F., ed. see Gesellschaft Fuer Biologische Chemie, 22nd Colloquium, Mossbach Baden, 1971.
Wallach, Donald. Plasma Membranes & Diseases.
Wallach, Donald P., et al. Prostaglandins I: Basic Physiology.
Wallach, Geraldine P., jt. auth. see Butler, Katherine G.
Wallach, Paul. Metric Drafting.
--Paul Wallach's Guide to Restaurants of Los Angeles & Southern California.
--Paul Wallach's Guide to the Restaurants of Northern California.
Wallack, L. R. American Pistol & Revolver Design & Performance.
--American Shotgun Design & Performance.
Wallack, Stanley S. & Kretz, Sandra E. Rural Medicine: Obstacles & Solutions for Self-Sufficiency.
Wallack, Stanley S., jt. ed. see Callahan, James J., Jr.
Wallant, Edward L. The Human Season.
Wallanu, Larry B., jt. auth. see Gravetter, Frederick J.
Wallat, Lee, jt. auth. see O'Rourke, Janet.
Wallbank, T. W. Contemporary Africa: Continent in Transition.
Wallbank, T. Walter, et al. Civilization Past & Present: Special Printing.
Wallce, Marie, jt. auth. see Strohofer, Jean.
Wallen, Saul. Urban Problems & the Private Sector.
Wallendorf, Melanie & Zaltman, Gerald. Readings in Consumer Behavior: Individuals, Groups, & Organizations.
Wallenkampf, Arnold V. Salvation Comes from the Lord. Wheeler, Gerald, ed.
Wallenstein, Barry, jt. ed. see Salzman, Jack.
Waller, Adrian. Theatre on a Shoestring.
Waller, Don. The Motown Story.
Waller, G. R. & Nowacki, E. K. Alkaloid Biology & Metabolism in Plants.
Waller, George R. & Dermer, Otis C. Biochemical Applications of Mass Spectrometry: First Supplementary Volume.
Waller, Gregory A. The Stage-Screen Debate: A Study in Popular Aesthetics. Jowett, Garth S., ed.
Waller, Irene. Textile Sculptures.
Waller, John L. Colossal Hamilton of Texas.
Waller, Johnny. The Phil Collins Story.
Waller, Johnny & Rapport, Steve. Eurythmics: Sweet Dreams-The Definitive Biography.
Waller, P. J., jt. ed. see Anderson, N.
Waller, R. A. Building on Springs.
Waller, Robert J. The Atlas of British Politics.
Waller, T. Gary. Think First, Read Later! Piagetian Prerequisites for Reading. Murray, Frank B., ed.
Wallerstein, Edward. Circumcision: An American Health Fallacy.
Walley, B. H. Office Administration Handbook.
Wallfesh, Henry M. The Effects of Extending the Mandatory Retirement Age.
Wallgren, Mark. The Beatles on Record.
Wallhausser, John, tr. see Redeker, Martin.
Wallich, Christine. India: Studies in State Finances.
--Revenue Sharing in India.
Wallich, Henry C. Monetary Policy & Practice: A View from the Federal Reserve Board.
Wallihan, Jim. Union Government & Organization.
Wallin, Barbara J., jt. auth. see DeGraw, Linda.
Walling, D. E., jt. auth. see Gregory, K. J.
Walling, R., ed. see Bright, J.
Walling, Regis. When Pregnancy Is a Problem.
Wallis. Differential & Integral Calculus U. K.
Wallis, Arthur. Revival: The Rain from Heaven.
Wallis, Charles L. The Minister's Manual for 1981.
Wallis, Charles L., compiled by. Holy Holy Land.
Wallis, Charles L., ed. The Ministers Manual, 1983.
Wallis, Jim. Agenda for Biblical People.
Wallis, John. Thinking about Retirement.
Wallis, John E. A History of the Church of Blackburnshire.
Wallis, Kenneth F., jt. ed. see Hendry, David F.
Wallis, Louis. Young People's Hebrew History.
Wallis, Reginald. New Boy.
Wallis, Robert. Time: Fourth Dimension of the Mind.
Wallis, Roy. The Elementary Forms of the New Religious Life.
Wallis, Roy, jt. ed. see Morley, Peter.
Wallis, W. D., et al. Combinatorics: Room Squares, Sum-Free Sets, Hadamard Matrices.
Walliser, Blair. Competitive Fitness: Featuring the Officially Licensed Fitness Program of the XIV Olympic Winter Games.
Wallman, Jeffrey M. Clean Sweep.
--Judas Cross.
Wallmann, Jeffrey M. Brand of the Damned.
--The Manipulator.
Wallo, Olav. The New Complete Norwegian Elkhound.
Wallop, Douglas. Regatta.
Wallop, Douglass. The Other Side of the River: A Novel.
Walls & Martin. In Malaysia.
Walls, D. F. & Harvey, J. D, eds. Laser Physics: Proceedings on the 2nd New Zealand Summer School in Laser Physics.
Walls, Dwayne E. The Chickenbone Special.
Walls, H. J. Scotland Yard Scientist: My Thirty Years in Forensic Science.
Walls, Ian. Making the Most of Your Greenhouse.
Walls, Jerry G. Shell Collecting.
Walmsley, Leo. Approaches to Painting.
Walne, Peter. Dictionary of Archival Terminology: With Equivalents in Dutch, German, Italian, Russian & Spanish.
Walpole, Horace. The History of the Modern Taste in Gardening with Journals of Visits to Country Seats. Hunt, John D., ed.
Walpole, Margaret. Walking into the Morning.
Walpole, Ronald E. & Myers, Raymond H. Probability & Statistics for Engineers & Scientists.
Walpole, Ronald E., jt. auth. see Freund, John E.
Walpot, Peter. True Surrender & Christian Community of Goods, 1521-1578.
Walraven, Michael, jt. auth. see Fitzgerald, Hiram E.
Walraven, Michael G. & Fitzgerald, Hiram, eds. Human Development 1988-89.
Walraven, Michael G., jt. ed. see Fitzgerald, Hiram.
Walser, Martin. The Inner Man. Vennewitz, Leila, tr. from Ger.
--Letter to Lord Liszt. Vennewitz, Lelia, tr.
--Runaway Horse. Vennewitz, Leila, tr. from Ger.
Walser, Richard. Black Poet.
--Thomas Wolfe Undergraduate.
Walsh, Anne B. A Gardening Book: Indoors & Outdoors.
Walsh, Beatrix, tr. see Piaget, Jean.
Walsh, Bob. The Pilot's Quiz Book: Flying Logic Made Easy.
Walsh, Chad. Early Christians of the Twenty-First Century.
--The Literary Legacy of C. S. Lewis.
Walsh, Charles V. The Fire Problem & Its Solution.
Walsh, Chris. The Bowerman System.
Walsh, D. C. & Egdahl, R. H., eds. Women, Work, & Health: Challenge to Corporate Policy.
Walsh, Dermot & Poole, Adrian. A Dictionary of Criminology.
Walsh, Don & Cappellari, Marjorie, eds. Energy & Sea Power - Challenge for the Decade.
Walsh, Donald, ed. see Martinez Sierra, Gregorio.
Walsh, Donald, tr. see Crow, Mary.
Walsh, Donald D. Introductory Spanish.
Walsh, Donald D. & Sturm, Harlan, eds. Repaso.
Walsh, Donald D., tr. see Cabestrero, Teofilo.
Walsh, Doris M. Gifts from above.
Walsh, E. G. Lurchers & Longdogs.
--The Poacher's Companion.
Walsh, E. G. & Lowe, Mary. The English Whippet.
Walsh, Frances. A Bibliography of Nursing Literature: Holdings of the Royal College of Nursing, London.
Walsh, George. Public Enemies: The Mayor, the Mob, & the Crime That Was.
Walsh, Gerard P. Federal Food, Drug, & Cosmetic Act as Amended & Related Laws.
Walsh, Graham. The Roof of Queensland.
Walsh, Grahame L. Didane the Koala.
--The Goori Goori Bird.
Walsh, Huber M. Introducing the Young Child to the Social World.
Walsh, J. N., jt. auth. see Thompson, Michael.
Walsh, Jackie, ed. see Mayer, Paul.
Walsh, James J. Cures: The Story of Cures That Failed.
Walsh, James P. The First Rotarian: The Life & Times of Percy Paul Harris, Founder of Rotary. Treadwell, Harry, ed.
Walsh, Jill P. Fireweed.
--Goldengrove.
--The Island Sunrise: Prehistoric Culture in the British Isles.
--Unleaving.
Walsh, Joan, jt. auth. see Anglund, Joan W.
Walsh, John, ed. Inside Football.
Walsh, John, jt. ed. see Massillon Society Staff.
Walsh, Joy, ed. see Fried, Emanuel.
Walsh, Kenneth & Pearson, Richard. U. K. Labor Market Guide.
Walsh, Lawrence A., jt. auth. see Winn, Charles S.
Walsh, Patricia L. Forever Sad the Hearts.
Walsh, Richard. Charleston's Sons of Liberty: A Study of the Artisans, 1763-1789.
Walsh, Richard, ed. Mind & Spirit of Early America: Sources in American History, 1607-1789.
Walsh, Richard & Fox, William L., eds. Maryland: A History.
Walsh, Robert & Pocs, Ollie, eds. Marriage & Family, 1988-89.
Walsh, Robert H., jt. auth. see Pocs, Ollie.
Walsh, Thomas, tr. see Valle-Inclan, Ramon.
Walsh, Thomas P. & Northouse, Cameron. John Barth, Jerzy Kosinski & Thomas Pynchon.
Walsh, Thomas P., jt. auth. see Northouse, Cameron.
Walsh, Warren B., ed. Readings in Russian History: From Ancient Times to the Eighteenth Century.
Walsh, William. F. R. Leavis.
Walsh, William H. Metaphysics.
Walshe, Maurice O. Buddhism for Today.
Walshe, Robert. Wales' Work.
Walsren, H. A., jt. auth. see Stofen, D.
Walston, Betty J. & Walston, Keith E. The Nurse Assistant in Long Term Care: A New Era.
Walston, Keith E., jt. auth. see Walston, Betty J.
Walt Disney Productions. Walt Disney's Donald Duck: Fifty Years of Happy Frustration.
Waltenspiel, Moe E. Quick & Friendly: Book One: Working on Pomo Valley Ranch.
--Working in the Redwood in California.
Walter, Bruno. Of Music & Music-Making.
Walter, Carl. China's Banking System: Structure & Reform.
Walter, Claire. The Book of Winners.
Walter, E. V., et al, eds. Civilizations East & West: A Memorial Volume for Benjamin Nelson.
Walter, Emily, ed. see Waetzoldt, Stephan, et al.
Walter, Eugen. The First Epistle to the Corinthians. McKenzie, John L., ed.
Walter, George W. Sinners & Saints.
Walter, H. & Harnickell, E. Climate-Diagram Maps: Of the Individual Continents & the Ecological Climatic Regions of the Earth.
Walter, H., ed. Laser Spectroscopy of Atoms & Molecules.
Walter, Ingo. Deregulating Wall Street: Commercial Bank Penetration of the Corporate Securities Market.
Walter, J. H., ed. see Shakespeare, William.
Walter, James. Come Through Dayton.
--The Leader: A Political Biography of Gough Whitlam.
Walter, John. The Airgun Book.
Walter, John B. An Introduction to the Principles of Disease.
Walter, Mildred P. Because We Are.
--The Girl on the Outside.
Walter, Richard W. see Tennessee. Supreme Court Staff & Michie Company Staff.
Walter, W. Grey. Living Brain.
Walters, A. A. Costs & Scale of Bus Services.
--Introduction to Econometrics.
Walters, Anna, ed. Elizabeth Gaskell: Four Short Stories.
Walters, Carl, Jr. I, Mark: A Personal Encounter.
Walters, David R. Physical & Sexual Abuse of Children: Causes & Treatment.
Walters, David W. The Intelligent Investor's Guide to Real Estate.
Walters, Derek. The Alternative I Ching.
Walters, Dorothy, ed. The Synergists.
Walters, Douglas & Jameson, C. W. Health & Safety for Toxicity Testing.
Walters, Douglas B., jt. auth. see Jameson, C. W.
Walters, Eva M. Three Strikes, but Not Out: Perspectives on Modern Education.
Walters, Fred H., jt. auth. see Braun, Robert D.
Walters, Garry R. The San Agustin Acasaguastlan Archaeological Project: Report on the 1979 Field Season.
Walters, Garry R., jt. ed. see Feldman, Lawrence H.
Walters, Henry B. London Churches at the Reformation: With an Account of Their Contents.
Walters, Kenneth C. I, the President.
Walters, LeRoy, jt. ed. see Beauchamp, Tom L.
Walters, Michael. The Complete Birds of the World.

Walters, P. Ergodic Theory: Introductory Lectures.
Walters, Richard F., et al, eds. A MUMPS Primer. Bowie, J. & Wilcox, J. C.
Walters, Richard P. Forgive & Be Free: Healing the Wounds of Past & Present.
Walters, Rita T., jt. auth. see Walters, Thomas P.
Walters, Susan, ed. Canadian Almanac & Directory, 1981.
Walters, Thomas P & Walters, Rita T. Making a Difference: A Catechist's Guide to Successful Classroom Management.
Walters, Vivienne. Class Inequality & Health Care: The Origins & Impact of the National Health Service.
Walthall, Joe E. & Love, Harold D. Habilitation of the Mentally Retarded Individual.
Walthall, Melvin. Lightning Forward: A History of the 25th Infantry Division (Tropic Lightning) 1941-1978.
Walthall, Melvin Curtis. We Can't All Be Heroes: A History of the Separate Infantry Regiments in World War II.
Walther, Herbert, ed. Hitler.
Walther, Ingo F. Picasso: Genius of the Century.
--Vincent Van Gogh: Vision & Reality.
Walther, Rudolph. Technical Dictionary of Production Engineering.
Waltke, Bruce K. Introduction to Biblical Hebrew Syntax.
Waltmann, Henry, et al. The American Search: Readings in American History.
Walton, A. G. Recombinant DNA: Proceedings of the Third Symposium on Macromolecules, Cleveland, June 1981.
Walton, Alan G. & Blackwell, John. Biopolymers.
Walton, Alan H., ed. see Ashvagosha.
Walton, Clarence C., ed. The Ethics of Corporate Conduct.
Walton, Craig & Anton, John P., eds. Philosophy & the Civilizing Arts: Essays Presented to Herbert W. Schneider.
Walton, Dan W., jt. ed. see Slaughter, Bob H.
Walton, E. W. Two Years in the Antarctic.
Walton, Evangeline. The Sword Is Forged.
Walton, F. A. From Death Unto Life.
--Keys to the Kingdom.
Walton, Gary M. & Wykoff, Frank C. Understanding Economics Today.
Walton, Gary M., jt. auth. see Robertson, Ross M.
Walton, Gary M., ed. Regulatory Change in an Atmosphere of Crisis: Current Implications of the Roosevelt Years.
Walton, H., jt. auth. see Rieman, W.
Walton, H. F., ed. Ion-Exchange Chromatography.
Walton, Harry, ed. Wordless Workshop.
Walton, Isaak. The Compleat Angler.
Walton, Jeremy. Escort MK 1, 2, & 3: The Development & Competition History.
Walton, Jill P. Never Give Up.
Walton, Joan M., jt. auth. see Stevens, Rolland E.
Walton, John, jt. auth. see Mastaglia, F. L.
Walton, Lewis E. A Poetaster's Scrapbook.
Walton, Mary. Deming Management Method.
Walton, R. G. & Elliott, D., eds. Residential Care: A Reader in Current Theory & Practice.
Walton, Richard J. The Power of Oil: Economic, Social, Political.
--The United States & Latin America.
--The United States & the Far East.
Walton, Robert C., ed. Bible Study Source Book: New Testament.
--Bible Study Source Book: Old Testament.
Walton, Robert C., ed. see Verkamp, Bernard J.
Walton, Rus. One Nation under God.
Walton, W. H., ed. Carbon Monoxide, Industry & Performance.
Waltraud, Neuwirth. Bottgersteinzeug, Yixing, Und Andere Rote Ware.
Walty, Arthur A. Solving the Riddle of the Universe.
Waltz, jt. auth. see Kaplan.
Waltz, Jon R., jt. auth. see Kaplan, John.
Walvin, James, jt. ed. see Emsley, Clive.
Walvoord, John F. Nations in Prophecy.
Walvoord, John F. & Zuck, Roy B. The Bib Sac Reader.
Walworth, Arthur. America's Moment: Nineteen Eighteen.
Walz, Garry, et al, eds. A Comprehensive View of Career Development.
Walz, Jay. Middle East.
Walz, Lila, ed. see Proulx, Earl.
Walz-Chojnacki, Greg. Comet! The Story Behind Halley's Comet. Mack, Nancy, ed.
Walzer, Stuart B. California Marital Termination Settlements.
Wambaugh, Joseph. Lines & Shadows.
--The Secrets of Harry Bright.
Wampler, Dee. The Missouri Criminal Law Handbook.
Wanamaker, Dix. Just Cleo & Me.
Wanat. Introduction to Budgeting.
Wandersman, Abraham, et al. Humanism & Behaviorism: Dialogue & Growth.
Wandke, Richard D. Vietnam Remembered.
Wandor, Michelene. Understudies: Theatre & Sexual Politics.
Wandor, Michelene, ed. On Gender & Writing.
Wandycz, Piotr S. Soviet-Polish Relations, 1917-1921.
Wanefsky, David. The Prophets Speak to Us Anew.
Wanefsky, Joseph. From the Shadow of Insight.
Wanefsty, Joseph. From the Shadow of the Insight.
Wang, C. C., ed. see CISM (International Center for Mechanical Sciences), Department of Mechanics of Solids Staff.
Wang, C. C., jt. ed. see Cullen, G. W.
Wang, Charles P., ed. Lasers in Fluid Mechanics & Plasmdynamics, 1983.
Wang, Chi-Chen, tr. see Chou Shu-Jen.
Wang, F. F. Introduction to Solid State Electronics.
Wang, H. P. Modeling an Ocean Pond.
Wang, Hao. Popular Lectures on Mathematical Logic.
Wang, James C. Contemporary Chinese Politics: An Introduction.
--The Cultural Revolution in China: An Annotated Bibliography.
Wang, Lawrence & Hudson, Jack W., eds. Strategies in Cold: Natural Torpidity & Thermogenesis.
Wang, N. T. China's Modernization & Transnational Corporations.
Wang, P. K., ed. see Optimization & Stability Problems in continuum Mechanics Symposium Staff.
Wang, Peter C., ed. see Automation Technology Symposium Staff.
Wang, Peter C., et al, eds. Information Linkage Between Applied Mathematics & Industry.
Wang, Ping-Chun. Numerical & Matrix Methods in Structural Mechanics, with Applications to Computers.
Wang, S. S. & Renton, W. J., eds. Nineteen Eighty-One Advances in Aerospace Structures & Materials (AD-01)
Wang, Shih Y., ed. Photochemistry & Photobiology of Nucleic Acids.
Wang, Wilfried, jt. auth. see Podrecca, Boris.
Wang, Y. C., jt. auth. see Hsia, Linda.
Wangerin, Walter, Jr. My First Book about Jesus.
Wangermann, Ernst. The Austrian Achievement: 1700-1800.
Wang Kung-Hsing. Chinese Mind.
Wang Meng. The Butterfly & Other Stories. Rui An, et al, trs. from Chinese.
Waniek, Marilyn, jt. auth. see Espeland, Pamela.
Wanless, R. M. Finance for Mine Management.
Wann, K. T., jt. auth. see Macdonald, A. G.
Wannall, W. Raymond. Who Is Tracking the Terrorists? Hale, Nathan, Institute Staff, ed.
Wannamaker, Bruce. Fixing Fences.
--God's Care Is Everywhere.
--The Kindness Weapon.
Wanninen, Erkki, ed. Essays on Analytical Chemistry: In Memory of Professor Anders Ringbom.
Wanniski, Jude. The Way the World Works: How Economics Fail & Succeed.
Wanous, S. J., et al. Advanced Typewriting.
Wansart, William L., jt. auth. see DeRuiter, James A.
Wanscher, J. H., jt. auth. see Kornup, A.
Want, Mary, jt. auth. see Hawthorne, Rosemary.
Wantz, Molly, jt. auth. see Engs, Ruth.
Wantz, Richard, jt. auth. see Hollis, Joseph W.
Waples, Jude. P.E.T. Pierre Elliott Trudeau & His Unearthly Adventures.
Wapner, Seymour, et al, eds. Experiencing the Environment.
Wapnick, Simon & Carnevale, Nino. Surgery Examination Review.
War, P. B., jt. ed. see Dearnaley, E. J.
Warbick-Cerone, Ann & Johnston, Linda G., eds. Quality Assurance of Pharmaceuticals Manufactured in the Hospital: Proceedings of the International Symposium on Drug Quality Assurance in the Hospital, Toronto, Ontario, Canada, June 10-14, 1984.
Warburg, Sandol S. Hooray for Us.
--On the Way Home.
Warburton, ed. Works with English Texts.
Warburton, David M., jt. ed. see Hamilton, Vernon.
Warburton, Geoffrey B., ed. Dynamical Behaviour of Structures.
Warburton, Thomas. Josquin Des Prez's "Missa Pange Lingua" An Edition, with Notes for Performance & Commentary.
Warburton-Brown, D. Induction Heating Practice.
Ward. New York Yankees.
--Super Bowl II: Green Bay Packers vs. Oakland Raiders.
Ward, Alfred C. Illustrated History of English Literature.
Ward, Allen M. Marcus Crassus & the Late Roman Republic.
Ward, Alton. My Birthday Praise Book.
--My Sunday Praise Book.
--My Thanksgiving Praise Book.
--Ten Pennies for Jesus.
Ward, Arthur S. see Rohmer, Sax.
Ward, Audrey, jt. ed. see Silverstone, Rosalie.
Ward, Barbara. Lopsided World.
--Nationalism & Ideology.
Ward, Bill. Student Journalist & Creative Photography.
--The Student Journalist & Photographing Sports.
Ward, Bill G. Student Journalist & Depth Reporting.
Ward, C. H., et al, eds. Offshore Ecology Investigation.
Ward, C. M. The Playboy Comes Home.
Ward, Carol. The Christian Sourcebook.
Ward, Darrell L., jt. auth. see Irby, Thomas C.
Ward, Don. Seattle Supersonics.
Ward, E. P. The Dynamics of Planning.
Ward, Ed. Michael Bloomfield: The Rise & Fall of an American Guitar Hero.
Ward, Elaine. After My House Burned Down.
Ward, Elizabeth. Father-Daughter Rape.
Ward, Elizabeth, jt. auth. see Silver, Alain.
Ward, Gray, ed. Integrated Optics & Optical Communications.
Ward, Greg. The Rough Guide to Brittany & Normandy.
Ward, Harry M. The Department of War, Seventeen Eighty-One to Seventeen Ninety-Five.
Ward, Herbert, ed. New Library Buildings 1973-74.
Ward, Mrs. Humphrey. Robert Elsmere. Ryals, Clyde L., ed.
Ward, J. Kingsley. Mark My Words: Letters of a Businessman to His Son.
Ward, James. A Study of Kant. Beck, Lewis W., ed. Bd. with Immanual Kant (Seventeen Twenty-Four to Eighteen Hundred Four) The British Academy Annual Philosophical Lecture. Garland Pub.
Ward, James M. Daredevil & Kingpin in the King Takes a Dare.
--The Doomsday Device.
--Dragonsword of Lankhmar.
Ward, James M., jt. auth. see Blashfield, Jean.
Ward, James M., jt. ed. see Mentzer, Frank.
Ward, John M. James MacArthur: Colonial Conservative 1798-1867.
Ward, Leslie. Forty Years of Spy.
Ward, Lynd, jt. auth. see Commager, Henry Steele.
Ward, M. L. Readers & Library Users: A Study of Reading Habits & Public Library Use.
Ward, Michael J., et al. Everybody Counts! A Workshop Manual to Increase Awareness of Handicapped People.
Ward, Nancy J. Central Coast Women's Yellow Pages.
Ward, Natasha, tr. see Aitmatov, Chinghiz.
Ward, Nathaniel. Simple Cobler of Aggawam in America. Zall, Paul M., ed.
Ward, Patricia A., jt. auth. see Farm Journal Editors.
Ward, Peter A., jt. auth. see Lepow, Irwin H.
Ward, R. D. & Rogers, W. W. Labor Revolt in Alabama: The Great Strike of 1894.
Ward, Richard H. & McCormack, Robert. An Anti-Corruption Manual for Administrators in Law Enforcement.
Ward, Robert. Debugging C.
Ward, Robert E. Japan's Political System.
Ward, Sandra E., ed. see Bulatao, Rodolfo A. & Fawcett, James T.
Ward, Sol A. & Litchfield, Thorndike. Cost Control in Design & Construction.
Ward, W. Peter. White Canada Forever: Popular Attitudes & Public Policy toward Orientals in British Columbia.
Ward, William. Egypt & the East Mediterranean World: 2200-1900 B.C.
Ward, William A., ed. The Role of Phoenicians in the Interaction of Mediterranean Civilizations.
Ward, William B. After Death, What?
--Toward Responsible Discipleship.
--When You're Married.
Ward, William G. Student Journalist & Designing the Opinion Pages.
--Student Journalist & Editorial Leadership.
--Student Journalist & Thinking Editorials. Rosen, Ruth C., ed.
Ward, William S. see Reiman, Donald H.
Ward, Winifred. Stories to Dramatize.
Warden, Carol D., jt. auth. see Lewis, Marcia.
Warder, A. K. Pali Metre: A Contribution to the History of Indian Literature.
Warders, Donald F., jt. auth. see Willingham, John R.
Wardlaw, Don M. Takestock: Worship.
Wardle, Lynn D. & Wood, Mary A. A Lawyer Looks at Abortion.
Wardle, William L. The History & Religion of Israel.
Ware. Dictionary of Architecture.
Ware, Caroline F. Greenwich Village, 1920-1930: A Comment on American Civilization in the Post-War Years.
Ware, Dora M. This Is My Story.
Ware, Leon. Delta Mystery.
Ware, W. R., jt. ed. see Gordon, M.
Ware, William R., ed. Creation & Detection of the Excited State.
--Creation & Detection of the Excited State.
--Creation & Detection of the Excited State.
Wareham, John. Secrets of a Corporate Headhunter.
Waren, Oscar & Heaton, Willis E. Warren's Heaton Pamphlet Edition, New York SCPA-EPTL, Anatomical Gifts Act (Public Health Law) As Ammended Through the July 2, 1982 Recess of the Regular Legislative Session of 1982. New York State Staff & Matthew Bender Publishers Staff, eds.
Warender & Tyler. The Instant Answer Book of Countries.
Warenski, Marilyn. Patriarchs & Politics.
Warfel, Harry R. & Orians, G. H., eds. American Local Color Stories.
Warfel, Harry R., ed. see Percival, James G.
Warfel, John H. & Schlagenhauff, Reinhold E. Understanding Neurologic Disease: A Textbook for Therapists.
Warfel, William B. Handbook of Stage Lighting Graphics.
Warfield, R. B., Jr. Nilpotent Groups.
Warford, Malcolm L. The Education of the Public.
Warga, Richard G. Personal Awareness: A Psychology of Adjustment.
Warga, Wayne. Hardcover.
Wargo, Stephanie. Soft Crafts for Special Occasions: A Wrights Idea Book.
Warhol, Andy. The Philosophy of Andy Warhol: From A to B & Back Again.
Warhol, Andy & Hackett, Pat. POPism: The Warhol Sixties.
Warhurst, John. Jobs or Dogma: The Industrial Assistance Commission & Australian Politics.
Waring, A. G. Russian Science Grammar.
Waring, Janet. Early American Stencils on Walls & Furniture.
Waring, William W. & Jeansonne, Louis O. Practical Manual of Pediatrics: A Pocket Reference for Those Who Treat Children.
Warisila, Robert, jt. auth. see Habibi, Mohamad.
Wark, David M., jt. auth. see Raygor, Alton L.
Wark, Robert R. Ten British Pictures, 1740-1840.
Warkov, Seymour, et al. Graduate Student Finances, 1963: A Survey of Thirty-Seven Fields of Study.
Warlick, Jennifer L., et al. Retirement Policy: Planning for Change. Anderson, Kathryn H., ed.
Warlow, Peter. The Reversing Earth.
Warmbrod, Catharine P. & Persavich, Jon J., eds. Postsecondary Program Evaluation.
Warmbrod, Catharine P., et al. Business, Industry & Labor Input in Vocational Education Personnel Development.
Warmbrod, Catharine P. & Persavich, Jon J. Sharing Resources: Post Secondary Education & Industry Cooperation.
Warme, Paul. BASEX.
Warmington, B. H. Nero: Reality & Legend.
Warne, Colston. Yearbook of American Labor.
Warne, E. J. Russian Scientific Reader.
Warnecke, Steven J. Uranium, Nonproliferation & Energy Security.
Warner, et al. California Marriage & Divorce Law.
Warner, Ann. Dialectic of Illusion.
Warner, Carmen G. Emergency Care: Assessment & Intervention.
Warner, Eldridge. Reminiscing with Horace: A Delightful Conversation Between a Man & the Cat Who "Owns" Him.
Warner, F. L. Microwave Attenuation Measurement.
Warner, Gilmore Foreword by see Hess, David.
Warner, Ken. Gun Digest, 1985.
--Knives 1984.
Warner, Ken, ed. Gun Digest 1986.
--Gun Digest, 1987.
--Gun Digest, 1988.
--Handloader's Digest.
--Knives Eighty Five.
--Knives '88.
Warner, L. J. Mammal Photography & Observation: A Practical Guide.
Warner, Langdon. The Enduring Art of Japan.
Warner, Margery. The Secret of the Disappearing Sultan.
Warner, Marina. The Crack in the Teacup: Britain in the Twentieth Century.
--The Skating Party.
Warner, Mignon. Illusion.
Warner, Oliver. Captain Marryat: A Rediscovery.
Warner, Penny. Healthy Snacks for Kids.
Warner, Philip. Horrocks: The General Who Lead from the Front.
--The Soldier: His Daily Life Through the Ages.
Warner, R. M. & Grung, B. L. Transistors: Fundamentals for the Integrated-Circuit Engineer.
Warner, Ralph. Everybody's Guide to Small Claims Court, California Edition.
--Everybody's Guide to Small Claims Court, California Edition.
--Everybody's Guide to Small Claims Court.
Warner, Ralph & Ihara, Toni. Homestead Your House: California Edition.
--Treasure of Lost Dragon Castle.

Authors

--Twenty-Nine Reasons Not to Go to Law School.
--Ups & Downs.
Warner, Ralph, jt. auth. see Clifford, Denis.
Warner, Ralph, jt. auth. see Ihara, Toni.
Warner, Ralph, jt. auth. see Moskovitz, Myron.
Warner, Ralph, ed. see Clifford, Denis & Curry, Hayden.
Warner, Ralph, ed. see Kosel, Janice.
Warner, Ralph, ed. see Mancuso, Anthony.
Warner, Rex. The Stories of the Greeks.
Warner, Richard. Antiquitates Culinariae: Or, Curious Tracts Relating to the Culinary Affairs of the Old English.
Warner, Roger. Invisible Hand: The Marijuana Business.
Warner, Ronald, jt. ed. see Lechene, Claude P.
Warner, Ross. Fulfillment of Book of Mormon Prophecies.
Warner, Ruth, tr. see Erdozain, Placido.
Warner, Susan. The Wide, Wide World.
Warner, W. Lloyd & Abegglen, James. Big Business Leaders in America.
Warner, William L. Color & Human Nature: Negro Personality Development in a Northern City.
--The Family of God: A Sympolic Study of Christian Life in America.
--Social Life of a Modern Community.
Warner, William L., et al. The American Federal Executive.
Warner, William W. Distant Water: The Fate of the North Atlantic Fisherman.
Warnke, Frank J., jt. auth. see Witherspoon, Alexander M.
Warnock, D. W. & Richardson, M. D., eds. Fungal Infection in the Compromised Patient.
Warnock, G. J. Object of Morality.
Warnock, Robert. Representative Modern Plays: Ibsen to Tennessee Williams.
Warr, Gene. The Godly Man.
Warr, Irma. The Godly Woman.
Warren, Alan M. Rescued from Barry: Locomotive Restoration.
Warren, Beverly C. Stars over Texas.
--The Wild Vines.
Warren, Carl D. The MC6809 Cookbook.
Warren, Cathy. Fred's First Day.
Warren, Charles, et al. California Perspectives: Four Leaders Look at the State of the State.
Warren, Dorothy M., ed. Anthology of Bells: The Bell Collectors' Treasury of Verses.
Warren, Elizabeth V., jt. auth. see Barbaer, Lynda G.
Warren, Elizabeth V., jt. auth. see Lipman, Jean.
Warren, Geoffrey. Kitchen Bygones: A Collector's Guide.
--A Stitch in Time: Victorian & Edwardian Needlecraft.
Warren, George F. & Pearson, Frank A. Gold & Prices.
Warren, Harris G. Herbert Hoover & the Great Depression.
Warren, Ines. Little Al's Beautiful Dream.
Warren, J. R., jt. ed. see Volant, F.
Warren, Jack D., jt. auth. see Lutz, Donald S.
Warren, James R. Where Mountains Meet the Sea: An Illustrated History of Puget Sound.
Warren, James V. & Subak-Sharpe, Genell J. Managing Hypertension: The Complete Program Developed by the Cleveland Clinic.
Warren, James V., ed. Cardiovascular Physiology.
Warren, Janet. A Feast of Scotland.
Warren, Joyce W. A Mouse to Be Free.
Warren, Katherine B., ed. see International Society for Cell Biology Staff.
Warren, Kenneth F. Administrative Law in the American Political System.
Warren, Kenneth S. & Hoffman, Donald B. Schistomiasis III: Abstracts of the Complete Literature 1963-1974.
Warren, Kenneth S., ed. Tropical & Geographical Medicine. Mahmoud, Adel A.
Warren, Kenneth S., jt. ed. see Hoffman, Donald B., Jr.
Warren, Louis A. Lincoln's Youth: Indiana Years, Seven to Twenty-One, 1816-1830.
Warren, M. L. Prairie Vengeance.
Warren, Margaret J., jt. auth. see Comaromi, John P.
Warren, Mary P. Ghost Town for Sale.
--The Land of Christmas.
--On Our Way to Christmas: A Family Activity Book for Advent.
--Walk in My Moccasins.
Warren, Mervyn A. God Made Known. Wheeler, Gerald, ed.
Warren, Michael. Shorelines: Birds at the Water's Edge.
Warren, Michael, photos by. Appalachian Trail.
--Appalachian Trail.
Warren, Neil, ed. Studies in Cross-Cultural Psychology.
Warren, Nigel. The Outboard Book.
Warren, Phelps. Irish Glass: Waterford, Cork, Belfast in the Age of Exuberance.
Warren, Richard, compiled by. Charles E. Ives: Discography.
Warren, Robert Penn, jt. auth. see Brooks, Cleanth.
Warren, Roger, jt. auth. see Sternloff, Robert E.
Warren, Roland L. The Community in America.
--New Perspectives on the American Community.
Warren, Sanford, Jr., et al, eds. Nephrology.
Warren, Thomas B. & Elkins, Garland, eds. Some Modern Cults, Sects, Movements & World Religions.
Warren, William D., jt. auth. see Jordan, Robert L.
Warren, William E. The Headless Ghost: True Tales of the Unexplained.
Warren, William E., jt. auth. see Scarborough, Stan.
Warren, Willis D. Mid-Century Appraisal of Civilization.
Warrick, Bill & McLellan, Dave. The Lake Shore & Michigan Southern.
Warrick, Patricia, jt. auth. see Katz, Harvey A.
Warriner, Doreen. Land Reform & Development in the Middle East.
Warriner, Hope R. Sights & Sounds of the City: Vistas y Sonidos de la Ciudad.
Warring, R. H. Filters & Filtration.
--Filters & Filtration.
--Fluids for Power Systems.
--Robots & Robotology.
--Seals & Sealing.
Warring, R. H. & Horn, Delton T. One Hundred Seventeen Practical IC Projects You Can Build.
Warrington, A. R. Protective Relays: Their Theory & Practice. Incl. Vol. 1, 2nd ed; Vol. 2, 3rd ed. Routledge Chapman & Hall.
Warrington, John, tr. see Aristotle.
Warrington, John, tr. see Plato.
Warschaw, Tessa A. Rich Is Better: How Women Can Bridge the Gap Between Wanting & Having It All.
Warshaw, Tessa A. Winning by Negotiation.
Warshow, Robert. Immediate Experience: Movies, Comics, Theatre & Other Aspects of Popular Culture.
Wartburg, Ursula Von see Von Wartburg, Ursula.
Wartell, Michael & Cummins, Jack. Fundamentals of Chemistry.
Wartenberg, Richard, jt. auth. see Plachno, Larry.
Wartick, Wallace. Lessons on New Testament Evidences.
--Twenty-Six Lessons on the Four Gospels.
Warusfel, Andre. Dictionnaire Raisonne De Mathematiques.
Warwick, Donald P. The Teaching of Ethics & the Social Sciences.
Warwick, Helen. Complete Labrador Retriever.
Warwick, Jack. Long Journey: Literary Themes of French Canada.
Warwick, James. Designing Jewelery.
Warwick, K. & Rees, D., eds. Industrial Digital Control Systems.
Warwick Press, ed. see Kerrod, Robin.
Warwick Press, ed. see Rutland, Jonathan.
Warwick, R., ed. Nomina Anatomica.
Warwick, Robert J., jt. auth. see Benjamin, Ludy T., Jr.
Warwick, Ronald, compiled by. Commonwealth Literature Periodicals: A Bibliography, Including Periodicals of Former Commonwealth Countries, with Locations in the United Kingdom.
Wasco, James E. Not for Doctors Only: Breakthrough Reports from the Medical Front.
Wasendorf, Russell R. Commodities Trading: The Essential Primer.
Washburn, Deric see Corrigan, Robert W.
Washburn, Mark. Distant Encounters: The Exploration of Jupiter & Saturn.
--Distant Encounters: The Exploration of Jupiter & Saturn.
--In the Light of the Sun: From Sunspots to Solar Energy.
Washburn, Stan. A Moral Alphabet of Vice & Folly.
Washburn, Susan. Partners.
Washburn, W-Ilcomb E. & Aubrey, John. The North American Indian Captivity.
Washburn, Wilcomb E., jt. auth. see Utley, Robert M.
Washburne, Randel. Kayak Trips in Puget Sound & the San Juan Islands.
Washington, Allyn J. Arithmetic & Beginning Algebra.
Washington, Booker T. The Booker T. Washington Papers, Vol. 13: 1914-15. Harlan, Louis R, et al, eds.
--Story of the Negro: The Rise of the Race from Slavery.
Washington Center Staff. Directory of Undergraduate Internships in the Humanities.
Washington Post Book World Editors, ed. The Book Bag Treasury of Literary Quizzes.
Washington Post Writers Group. The Editorial Page.
--Of the Press, by the Press, for the Press (& Others, Too)
--Writing in Style.
Washington Researchers, Limited Staff. Who Knows: A Guide to Washington Experts.
Washington Researchers Publishing Staff. Federal Fast Finder.
--How to Find Company Intelligence in Federal Documents.
--How to Find Company Intelligence in Libraries.
--How to Find Company Intelligence in State Documents.
--How to Find Company Intelligence in State Documents.
--How to Find Company Intelligence On-Line.
--How to Find Information about Acquisition Candidates.
--How to Find Information about Executives.
--How to Find Information about Foreign Firms.
--How to Find Information about Private Companies.
--How to Find Information about Service Companies.
--Who Knows: A Guide to Washington Experts.
--Who Knows about Foreign Industries & Markets: Country Experts in the Federal Government.
--Who Knows about Industries & Markets: Industry Analysts in the Federal Government.
--Who Knows about Industries & Markets.
Washington Researchers Staff. Federal Fast Finder.
--How to Find Company Intelligence in Federal Documents.
--How to Find Company Intelligence in Libraries.
--How to Find Company Intelligence in State Documents.
--How to Find Company Intelligence On-line.
--How to Find Information about Companies: The Corporate Intelligence Source Book.
--How to Use the Freedom of Information Act.
--Who Knows about Foreign Industries & Markets.
--Who Knows about Industries & Markets.
Washington, Rosemary G. Softball Is for Me.
Washington State Bar Association, Continuing Legal Education Committee. Washington Commercial Law Deskbook.
Wasiolek, Edward, ed. & tr. see Dostoyevsky, Fyodor.
Waskow, Arthur I. Seasons of Our Joy: A Handbook of Jewish Festivals.
--These Holy Sparks: The Rebirth of the Jewish People.
Waskow, Howard J. Whitman: Explorations in Form.
Wason, Roly. Rebel Scotland: A History of Democracy in Scotland.
Wass. Dying.
Wass, Alonzo. Construction Management & Contracting.
--Estimating Residential Construction.
Wass, Douglas. Government & the Governed.
Wass, Hannelore, et al. Death Education: An Annotated Resource Guide.
Wass, Hennelore. Dying: Facing the Facts.
Wassall, Gregory H. Tax-Exempt Property: A Case Study of Hartford, Connecticut.
Wassall, Gregory H., jt. auth. see Birkelbach, Aubrey W., Jr.
Wassell. Group Psychoanalysis.
Wassenberger, Robert, ed. Vienna in the Biedermeier Era 1815-1848.
Wassenbergh, H. A. Public International Air Transportation Law in a New Era: Economic Regulation of International Air Carrier Operations.
Wasser, Edna. Creative Approaches in Casework with the Aging.
Wasserman, Anthony I. Programming Language Design.
Wasserman, Burton. Exploring the Visual Arts. Horn, George F. & Rainey, Sarita R., eds.
Wasserman, Debra & Stahler, Charles. Healthy Holidays: No-Cholesterol Vegetarian Recipes.
Wasserman, Edward & Gromisch, Donald S. Survey of Clinical Pediatrics.
Wasserman, Gary. The Basics of American Politics.
Wasserman, Harry, jt. auth. see Bubis, Gerald B.
Wasserman, Harry H. & Murray, Robert W., eds. Singlet Oxygen.
Wasserman, Harvey. Energy War: Reports from the Front.
Wasserman, Jack. Leonardo Da Vinci.
Wasserman, Mark, jt. auth. see Keen, Benjamin.
Wasserman, Paul. Librarian & the Machine.
Wasserman, Paul, ed. Training & Development Organizations Directory.
Wasserman, Paul & Herman, Esther, eds. Library Bibliographies & Indexes: A Subject Guide to Resource Material Available from Libraries, Information Centers, Library Schools, & Library Associations in the U. S. & Canada.
Wasserman, Paul & Siegman, Gita, eds. Consumer Sourcebook: Supplement.
Wasserman, Pauline, jt. auth. see Wasserman, Sheldon.
Wasserman, R. H., jt. ed. see Nichols, George.
Wasserman, Rosanne, ed. see Watts, Edith.
Wasserman, Sheldon & Wasserman, Pauline. Sparkling Wine.
Wasserman, Steven & O'Brien, Jacqueline W., eds. Law & Legal Information Directory.
--Statistics Sources.
Wasserman, William, jt. auth. see Neter, John.
Wassermann, G., ed. see International Symposium Clausthal - Zellerfeld, 1968.
Wassermann, G. D. Molecular Control of Cell Differentiation & Morphogenesis: A Systematic Theory.
Wassermann, Steven A. The Complete Book of Manufacturing Management.
Wasserstein, Bruce. Corporate Finance Law: A Guide for the Executive.
Wasserstein, Wendy. Uncommon Women & Others.
Wassil-Grimm, C., ed. see Hunter House Staff.
Wasson, Chester R. Managerial Economics: Text & Cases.
Wasson, Chester R., et al. Competition & Human Behavior.
Wasson, Gordon. The Road to Eleusis: Unveiling the Secret of the Mysteries.
Wasson, John, et al. The Common Symptom Guide.
Wasson, Louise E. & Miguel, Richard J. Collaboration in Experiential Education: A Profile of Participant Expectations.
Wasson, R. Gordon. Soma: Divine Mushroom of Immortality.
Wasson, R. Gordon, et al. Maria Sabina & Her Mazatec Mushroom Velada.
Waste Isolation Systems Panel, Board on Radioactive Waste Management, National Research Council Staff. A Study of the Isolation System for Geologic Disposal of Radioactive Wastes.
Watabe, Masakazu & Gilbert, Kent S. Japanese: A Graded Approach to Reading, Writing & Vocabulary Building.
Watabe, Norimitsu & Wilbur, Karl M., eds. The Mechanisms of Mineralization in the Invertebrates & Plants.
Watanabe, Masahiro & Nagashima, Kei. Instant Japanese.
Watanabe, S. Lectures on Stochastic Differential Equations & Malliavin Calculus.
Watanabe, S., jt. auth. see Ikeda, N.
Watanabe, S., ed. Frontiers of Pattern Recognition: Proceedings of the International Conference on Frontiers of Pattern Recognition, Jan. 1971.
--Methodologies of Pattern Recognition.
Watanabe, Sadao. Biblical Prints.
Watanabe, Shigeo. What a Good Lunch!
Watanabe, Takeshi, et al. North & South: After Cancun - Where to?
Watchel, Howard. The New Gnomes: A Multinational Banks in the Third World.
Watchorn, Brian, tr. see Schultz, Hans J.
Water Pollution Control Federation Staff, ed. see Saunders, Michael F., et al.
Water Pollution Control Federation Staff, ed. see Schwartz, H. G., Jr., et al.
Water Pollution Control Federation Staff. Aeration in Wastewater Treatment ('71)
--Financing & Charges for Wastewater Systems ('73)
--Odor Control for Wastewater Facilities.
Water Research Enter. Water Purification in the EEC.
Waterbridge, Edmund. Hinterland.
Waterbury, John. Egypt: Burdens of the Past, Options for the Future.
Waterford, Van. The Complete Guide to Car Stereo Systems.
--Microcomputer-Controlled Toys & Games & How They Work.
Waterhouse, Marian. Practical Mathematics in Allied Health: A Textbook for the Medical Disciplines.
Waterhouse, Philip. Managing the Learning Process.
--Supported Self-Study in Secondary Education.
Waterhouse, R. B. Fretting Corrosion.
Watering, Janwillem van de see Van de Wetering, Janwillem.
Waterlow. The Conveyancer's Guide to Local & Public Authorities: A Desk-Top Companion.
Waterlow Publishers, Ltd. Staff, ed. The Solicitors' & Barristers' Directory & Diary 1985.
Waterlows Publishers Staff, ed. The Solicitors' & Barristers' Directory & Diary: 1984 Edition.
Waterman, Barbara, jt. auth. see Waitakin, Howard.
Waterman, Leroy. Forerunners of Jesus.
--The Religion of Jesus: Christianity's Unclaimed Heritage of Prophetic Religion.
Waterman, Leroy, ed. Royal Correspondence of the Assyrian Empire.
Waterman, T. T. Notes on the Ethnology of the Indians of Puget Sound.
Waterman, William, jt. auth. see Von Cleef, Monique.
Watermulder, David B. & Krodel, Gerhard. Advent-Christmas.
Waters, Delta. Littlest Pine Cone.
Waters, Elinor, ed. Resocializing Sex Roles: A Guide for Educators.
Waters, Farl J. ABC's of Electronics.

Waters, Harold. The Handbook of Cancer Immunology, Vol. 1: Basic Cancer-Related Immunology.
--Handbook of Cancer Immunology, Vol. 2: Cellular Escape from Immune Destruction.
--Handbook of Cancer Immunology, Vol. 3: Immune Status in Cancer Treatment & Prognosis, Pt. A.
--Handbook of Cancer Immunology, Vol. 4: Immune Status in Cancer Treatment & Prognosis, Pt. B.
--Handbook of Cancer Immunology, Vol. 5: Immunotherapy.
Waters, John. Crackpot: The Obsessions of John Waters.
Waters, John J., Jr. The Otis Family in Provincial & Revolutionary Massachusetts.
Waters, Kenneth, jt. auth. see Scalf, Cherie.
Waters, Margaret, jt. auth. see Yale Daily News Staff.
Waters, Michael D., et al, eds. Short-Term Bioassays in the Analysis of Complex Environmental Mixtures, Pt. 1.
--Short-Term Bioassays In the Analysis of Complex Environmental Mixtures, Pt. 2.
Waters, Peter. Color Your Hair.
Waters, R. S., jt. ed. see Brown, E. H.
Waters, Richard D. Dangerfield Newby Moves Uptown.
Waters, Roger. Pink Floyd: The Wall.
Waters, Thomas A. The Lost Victim.
Waters, W. E. & Cliff, K. S. Community Medicine: A Textbook for Nurses & Health Visitors.
Waterson, A. P., ed. Recent Advances in Clinical Virology.
Waterson, D. Squatter, Selector, & Storekeeper.
Waterson, Merlin. The Country House Remembered: Recollections of Life Between the Wars.
Watersworth, G. Electrical Principles for Technicians.
Waterton, Betty. A Salmon for Simon.
Waterton, Charles. Wanderings in South America, the Northwest of the United States, & the Antilles in the Years Eighteen Twelve, Eighteen Sixteen, Eighteen Twenty, & Eighteen Twenty-Four.
Waterworth, K. G. & Phillips, R. P. Electrical Principles for Technicians.
Wa Thiong O, Ngugi. Secret Lives: And Other Stories.
Watkin, Bruce. Buckinghamshire: A Shell Guide.
Watkins, A. J. Electrical Installation Calculations.
--Electrical Installation Calculations.
--Electrical Installation Calculations.
Watkins, Arthur M. The New Complete Book of Home Remodeling, Improvement, & Repair.
Watkins, Bruce O., jt. auth. see Jensen, Randall W.
Watkins, Charmian. Charmian Watkins' Clothes Book.
Watkins, Chris, et al. Shelley Potteries: The History & Production of a Staffordshire Family of Potters.
Watkins, Floyd C. & Dillingham, William B. Practical English Handbook.
--Practical English Handbook.
Watkins, Floyd C., jt. auth. see Cullen, John B.
Watkins, Floyd C., et al. Practical English Workbook.
--Practical English Workbook.
--Practical English Workbook Form B.
Watkins, George A., ed. A New Generation of Environmental Essays.
Watkins, Harold. Time Counts.
Watkins, Harold C. Voyage Through Interplanetary Space.
Watkins, John V. & Sheehan, Thomas J. Florida Landscape Plants: Native & Exotic.
Watkins, John V. & Wolfe, Herbert S. Your Florida Garden.
Watkins, Leslie. The Killing of Idi Amin.
Watkins, Mary M., ed. Research Centers Directory, Nineteen Eighty-Seven.
Watkins, Myron W., jt. auth. see Stocking, George W.
Watkins, Paul. See Cyprus.
--See Sicily.
Watkins, Ralph J., ed. Directory of Selected Scientific Institutions in Mainland China.
Watkins, T. F., et al. Chemical Warfare, Pyrotechnics & the Fireworks Industry.
Watkins, Thomas W., jt. auth. see Hilder, Frazer F.
Watkins, Wesley W. The Entrepreneurs of Entrepreneurship.
Watkins, Williams D., jt. auth. see Geisler, Norman L.
Watling, T. F., jt. auth. see Taylor, W. J.
Watney, John. The Royal Marines Commandos Fitness & Survival Skills.
Watson. Words to Read.
Watson, et al. Hazardous Waste Handbook.
--Modular Study Guide to Fundamentals of Nursing.
Watson, A. H., jt. auth. see Munby, Denys.
Watson, Alan. The Evolution of Law.
--The Law of the Ancient Romans.
Watson, Alan D. Society in Colonial North Carolina.
Watson, Annita & Mayers, Marlene. How to Write Nursing Care Plans.
Watson, Barbara B. Shavian Guide to the Intelligent Woman.
Watson, Burton, jt. ed. see Sato, Hiroaki.
Watson, Burton, tr. Su Tung-P'o: Selections from a Sung Dynasty Poet.
Watson, Burton, tr. see Ikeda, Daisaku.
Watson, Burton, tr. see Iwao, Seiichi.
Watson, C., jt. auth. see Paxinos, G.
Watson, Charles S. Antebellum Charleston Dramatists.
Watson, Clarissa. The Bishop in the Back Seat.
--Runaway.
Watson, D. Richard Wagner: A Biography.
Watson, David. My God Is Real.
Watson, Deryn, ed. Exploring Geography with Microcomputers.
Watson, Diane. Magazine.
Watson, Donald. Designing & Building a Solar House.
--Designing & Building a Solar House: Your Place in the Sun.
--The Hen Harrier.
Watson, Donald, tr. see Ionesco, Eugene.
Watson, Donald A. Energy Conservation Through Building Design.
Watson, Donald S. & Getz, Malcolm. Price Theory in Action.
Watson, Donald S. & Holman, Mary A. Price Theory & Its Uses.
Watson, Donald S., ed. Price Theory in Action: A Book of Readings.
Watson, Dorothy J., jt. ed. see Allen, P. David.
Watson, Douglas S. West Wind: The Life Story of Joseph Reddeford Walker.
Watson, E. LaPlace Transforms & Applications.
Watson, Edward W. The Church of England.
Watson, Elbert. Alabama United States Senators.
Watson, Elizabeth, jt. auth. see Lamb, Warren.
Watson, Elizabeth E. All About Hands.
--God Made the Sea, the Sand & Me.
Watson, Elizabeth W. Gift Wrap, Please.
Watson, Ellen, tr. see De Loyola Brandao, Ignacio.
Watson, Francis. Louis XVI Furniture.
Watson, G. A., ed. Numerical Analysis.
Watson, G. O. Marine Electrical Practice.
Watson, Geoffrey S. Statistics on Spheres.
Watson, George. Memorable Memoirs.
--Writing a Thesis: A Guide to Long Essays & Dissertations.
Watson, Georgia B. Life in the Retirement Bed of Roses.
Watson, Graham. Book Society.
Watson, H. J. Modern Gear Production.
Watson, Harold M. Claudel's Immortal Heroes: A Choice of Deaths.
Watson, Hugh H. & Carroll, Archie B. Computers for Business: A Book of Readings.
Watson, Hugh J. & Carroll, Archie B. Computers for Business: A Managerial Emphasis.
Watson, Hugh J., jt. auth. see Kroeber, Donald W.
Watson, Hugh J. & Carroll, Archie B., eds. Computers for Business: A Book of Readings.
Watson, Ian. Evil Water.
Watson, J. Semiconductor Circuit Design: For A.C. & D.C. Amplification Switching.
Watson, J. D. Molecular Biology of the Gene.
Watson, James, et al. Effects of Hormones on Immunity, Vol. 1.
Watson, James G. William Faulkner, Letters & Fictions.
Watson, Jean, retold by see Bunyan, John.
Watson, Jeffrey A. Looking Beyond.
Watson, Jenny, jt. auth. see Watson, Tom.
Watson, Jenny, retold by. Favourite Stories from Thailand.
Watson, John L. English IV: Franco, Slav & Flank Defence.
Watson, K. & Oxenham, J., eds. Research, Co-Operation & Evaluation of Educational Programmes in the Third World: Workshops Held by the Development Studies Association-Education in Developing Countries Study Group, University of Leeds, U. K., March 30, 1984 & IDS, University of Sussex, U. K., April 9-13, 1984.
Watson, Keith, ed. Dependence & Interdependence in Education: International Perspectives.
--Education in the Third World.
--Key Issues in Education: Comparative Perspectives.
Watson, Keith & Wilson, Raymond, eds. Contemporary Issues in Comparative Education.
Watson, Ken. Paddle Steamers: An Illustrated History of Steamboats on the Mississippi & Its Tributaries.
Watson, L. S., Jr. Child Behavior Modification: A Manual for Teachers, Nurses & Parents.
Watson, Lillian E. Light from Many Lamps.
Watson, Marjorie. Coshiri.
--Mainstreaming the Educable Mentally Retarded.
Watson, Miles W. Ma 'n Me 'n Hockey.
Watson, N. & Janota, M. S. Turbocharging the Internal Combustion Engine.
Watson, Nancy R. Taking off with BASIC on the IBM PCjr.
Watson, P. S., tr. see Luther, Martin.
Watson, Patty J., jt. auth. see Watson, Richard A.
Watson, Paul & Rogers, Warren. Sea Shepherd: One Man's Crusade for Whales & Seals.
Watson, Pauline. Curley Cat Baby-Sits.
--Curley Cat Baby-Sits.
--Wriggles: The Little Wishing Pig.
Watson, Philip S., ed. The Message of the Wesleys: A Reader of Instruction & Devotion.
Watson, Philippa, ed. Social Security Law of the European Communities.
Watson, R. A., ed. see Popkin, Richard H.
Watson, R. T., jt. ed. see Ghazi, A.
Watson, Richard. The Philosopher's Diet.
Watson, Richard A. Downfall of Cartesianism, Sixteen Seventy-Three to Seventeen Twelve.
--The Runner.
Watson, Richard A. & Watson, Patty J. Man & Nature: An Anthropological Essay in Human Ecology.
Watson, Robert. Christmas in Las Vegas.
--Night-Blooming Cactus.
Watson, S. R., ed. The Practice of Decision Making.
Watson, Sterling. The Calling.
Watson, T. J. & Chapman. Judy: Portrait of an American Legend.
Watson, Tom & Hannigan, Frank. The New Rules of Golf: The 1988-1991 Edition.
Watson, Tom & Watson, Jenny. Breakfast.
--Evening Meal.
--Midday Meal.
Watson, Tom, Jr. How to Be Happy No Matter What.
Watson, Tony. Sociology, Work & Industry.
Watson, W. E. Cell Biology of Brain.
Watson, W. Scott. Fifty-Five Advanced Computer Programs in BASIC.
Watson, Wayne T. An Introduction to Structured BASIC for the Cromemco C-10.
Watson, William C. Physiological Psychology: An Introduction.
Watt, Alexander. The Art of Papermaking, 1890.
Watt, Billie L. & Newman, Martin. Phillis.
Watt, Daniel. Learning with Commodore LOGO.
--Learning with TI LOGO.
Watt, Donald, ed. Aldous Huxley: The Critical Heritage.
Watt, George W., et al. Chemistry in the Laboratory.
Watt, Gordon. Cross in Faith & Conduct.
Watt, Hugh. John Knox in Controversy.
Watt, James & Wead, Doug. The Courage of a Conservative.
Watt, Kenneth E. Understanding the Environment.
Watt, Robert. Bibliography of Robert Watt.
Watt, Simon, compiled by. Chinese Chain & Washer Pumps: Twenty-One Chain & Washer Pumps from the 1958 Peking Agricultural Exhibition.
Wattenberg, Ben J. The Good News Is the Bad News Is Wrong.
--The Good News Is the Bad News Is Wrong.
Wattenberg, William, jt. auth. see Redl, Fritz.
Wattenberg, William W. Adolescent Years.
Wattenberg, William W., ed. Social Deviancy among Youth.
Watters, Barbara. An Horary Astrology & Judgment of Events.
Watters, Mary. Illinois in the Second World War: Vol. 1, Operation Home Front.
--Illinois in the Second World War: Vol. 2, The Production Front.
Watters, Pat & Cleghorn, Reese. Climbing Jacob's Ladder: The Arrival of Negroes in Southern Politics.
Watters, Ron. Ski Trails & Old Timers' Tales in Idaho & Montana.
Watterson, Joseph. Architecture: A Short History.
Watt-Evans, Lawrence. The Book of Silence.
--The Chromosomal Code.
Watton, W. G., jt. auth. see Cole, G. H.
Watts, A. G. Counselling at Work.
Watts, Alan W. The Spirit of Zen: A Way of Life, Work & Art in the Far East.
Watts, B. K. Elements of Finance for Managers.
Watts, Don. A Catalog of Operational Transfer Functions.
Watts, Edith. A Young Person's Guide to European Arms & Armor in the Metropolitan Museum of Art. Wasserman, Rosanne, ed.
Watts, Etheldra M., jt. auth. see Watts, Walter N.
Watts, Harold W. & Rees, Albert, eds. The New Jersey Income Maintenance Experiment.
Watts, Harris. The Programme-Maker's Handbook or Goodbye Totter TV.
Watts, Henry E. Life of Miguel De Cervantes.
Watts, Isaac. Logic: Or, the Right Use of Reason in the Enquiry after Truth, with a Variety of Rules to Guard Against Error, in the Affairs of Religion & Human Life as Well as the Sciences.
Watts, J. McK., et al. Infection in Surgery: Basic & Clinical Aspects.
Watts, Mabel. Yin Sun & the Lucky Dragon.
Watts, Melvin, jt. ed. see Doty, Robert.
Watts, Meredith W., ed. Biopolitics: Ethological & Physiological Approaches.
Watts, Mimi, tr. see Pellicani, Luciano.
Watts, Nelson B. & Keffer, Joseph H. Practical Endocrine Diagnosis.
Watts, Oswald M., ed. Reed's Nautical Almanac & Coast Pilot: East Coast.
--Reed's Nautical Almanac & Coast Pilot: West Coast.
Watts, R. G., ed. see Torrance, K. E.
Watts, R. W. E., et al. Gout II: Recent Studies.
Watts, Richard G. Straight Talk About Death with Young People.
Watts, Thomas M., jt. auth. see Dickey, John W.
Watts, Walter N. Liberation & Freedom in an Urban Learning Community.
Watts, Walter N. & Watts, Etheldra M. Learning to Read the Language of Americans: Sounds & Symbols.
Watts, William. The United States & Asia: Changing Attitudes & Policies.
Wauchope, Robert, ed. Handbook of Middle American Indians: Ethnology.
Waud, Clarice & Hutchings, Mark. The Papillon Butterfly Dog.
Waugh, Auberon. Brideshead Benighted.
Waugh, Carol & LaBelle, Judith. Quilter's Precise Yardage Guide.
Waugh, Carol, jt. auth. see LaBelle, Judith.
Waugh, Carol-Lynn R. My Friend Bear.
Waugh, Carol-Lynn R. & Greenberg, Martin H., eds. Thirteen Horrors of Halloween.
Waugh, Carol-Lynn R., et al. Show Business Is Murder.
Waugh, Carol-Lynn R., et al, eds. Murder on the Menu.
Waugh, Charles, jt. ed. see Greenberg, Martin H.
Waugh, Charles G., jt. ed. see Greenberg, Martin H.
Waugh, Evelyn. The Letters of Evelyn Waugh. Amory, Mark, ed.
--Scoop.
--A Tourist in Africa.
Waugh, Hillary. Madman at My Door.
Waugh, Margaret, ed. see Southwell, Robert.
Waugh, Teresa. An Intolerable Burden.
Waughfield, Claire, jt. auth. see Kalman, Natalie.
Wauson, Sydnie, jt. auth. see Vesely, Anton.
Wauson, Sydnie A., ed. see Ahlstrand, Alan.
Wauson, Sydnie A., ed. see Vesley, Anton.
Wauson, Sydnie A., ed. see Wright, Ron.
Wavada, James. Yup the Organization.
Waverley, Root. Food.
Waverman, Lucy. The Penny Pincher's Wine Guide.
Wax, Murray L., ed. When Schools Are Desegregated: Problems & Possibilities for Students, Educators, Parents & the Community.
Waxman, Bruce, jt. auth. see Stacy, Ralph W.
Way, Douglas S. Terrain Analysis: A Guide to Site Selection Using Aerial Photographic Interpretation.
Way, E. Leong, ed. Endogenous & Exogenous Opiate Agonists & Antagonists: Proceedings of the International Narcotic Club Conference, 11-15 June 1979, North Falmouth, Massachusetts, U. S. A.
Way, Peter. Icarus.
Way, Stanley. Malignant Disease of the Vulva.
Way, W. Dennis & Standen, O. D. Zoology in Postage Stamps.
Wayembergh, Josse, jt. auth. see Bring, Mitchell.
Wayman, Joe. Colors of My Rainbow Activity Book.
Wayman, Joe & Mitchell, Don. Imagination & Me Book.
Waymire, Stuart D. The Gambling Professional's Textbook: Winning Statistics for Las Vegas.
--The Starlord: The Conquest of Earth.
Wayne, D., jt. auth. see Rubenstein, D.
Wayne, David J. & Rue, Nancy N. Home: Love It or Leave It.
Wayne, Frank. Worried Money: A Guide to Swiss Banking.
Wayne Green Books Editors. Encyclopedia for the TRS-80.
--The Rest of Eighty. Hutchinson, Sandra, ed.
Wayne, Jane E. Stanwyck.
Wayne, Jennifer. Sprout & the Helicopter.
Wayne, Les. Warpaint.
--West of Omaha.
Waynman, Richard, ed. Medical & Health Encyclopedia.
Wayre, Philip. The River People: Adventuring with Otters.
Wayrich, Becky L. Tainted Lilies.
Waznak, Robert. Sunday after Sunday: Preaching the Homily as a Story.
Wead, Doug. Where Is the Lost Ark?
Wead, Doug, jt. auth. see Watt, James.
Weagant, Warren. How to Buy U. S. Government Surplus.
Weakley, Brenda. Beginner's Handbook in Biological Transmission Electron Microscopy.

Authors

Weale, Margaret. The Slimmer's Microwave Cookbook.
Weale, R. A. The Vertebrate Eye. Head, J. J., ed.
Weales, Gerald, ed. see Wycherley, William.
Weales, Gerald C. Religion in Modern English Drama.
Weaner, Frank A. Ships that Pass.
Wearing, Betsy. The Ideology of Motherhood: A Study of Sydney Suburban Mothers.
Wearing-King, R. The English Sixth Form College: An Educational Concept.
Wearne, S. H. Principles of Engineering Organization.
Wearne, S. H., ed. Control of Engineering Projects.
Weast, Robert C. HB Chemistry & Physics.
Weast, Robert C., ed. CRC Handbook of Chemistry & Physics.
Weatherford, Jack M. Porn Row: An Inside Look at the Sex-for-Sale District of a Major American City.
Weatherford, Richard, ed. Stephen Crane: The Critical Heritage.
Weatherford, Richard M., ed. Stephen Crane: The Critical Heritage.
Weatherhead, A. Kingsley. The British Dissonance: Essays on Ten Contemporary Poets.
Weatheritt, Mollie. Innovations in Policing.
Weathers, Thomas & Hunter, Claud. Fundamentals of Electricity & Automotive Electrical Systems.
Weaver. Bovine Surgery: The Library of Veterinary Practice.
Weaver, Alice, jt. auth. see Weaver, Janet.
Weaver, Ann A. & Hudson, Margaret W. On the Job.
Weaver, Charles, jt. auth. see Vance, Jene.
Weaver, Earl & Stainback, Berry. It's What You Learn After You Know It All That Counts: The Autobiography of Earl Weaver.
Weaver, Francine L., jt. auth. see Fox, C. Lynn.
Weaver, Glenn. Hartford: An Illustrated History of Connecticut's Capital.
Weaver, Gordon. Getting Serious, Stories.
Weaver, Gordon, ed. see Mauzey, Merritt.
Weaver, Helen, tr. see Artaud, Antonin.
Weaver, Janet & Weaver, Alice. Huggables: How to Make Large Stuffed Animals.
Weaver, John D. Brownsville Raid.
--Brownsville Raid.
Weaver, K., ed. see Specialists Meeting on Transient Two-Phase Flow Staff.
Weaver, L. E., jt. ed. see Karam, R. A.
Weaver, Lawrence, ed. Small Country Houses of Today.
Weaver, Paul. Charlie Dye: One Helluva Western Painter.
Weaver, Paul H. The Twilight of the Corporate State: How Big Business Hurts the Economy, & What to Do about It.
Weaver, Raymond, ed. see Melville, Herman.
Weaver, Robert C. Dilemmas of Urban America.
Weaver, Sally M. Medicine & Politics Among the Grand River Iroquois: A Study of the Non-Conservatives.
Weaver, W. Timothy. The Contest for Educational Resources: Equity & Reform in a Meritocratic Society.
Weaver, Will. Red Earth, White Earth.
Weaver, William. The Golden Century of Italian Opera: From Rossini to Puccini.
Weaver, William, tr. Seven Puccini Librettos.
Weaver, William, tr. see Calvino, Italo.
Weaver, William, tr. see Cespedes, Alba de.
Weaver, William, tr. see De Carlo, Andrea.
Weaver, William, tr. see Eco, Umberto.
Weaver, William, tr. see Elkann, Alain.
Weaver, William, tr. see Fruttero, Carlo & Lucentini, Franco.
Weaver, William, tr. see Levi, Primo.
Weaver, William, tr. see Soldati, Mario.
Weaver, William, et al, trs. see Calvino, Italo.
Webb, ed. see Roe.
Webb, Adrian L. Income Redistribution & the Welfare State.
Webb, Barbara O. In Christ, My Lord.
Webb, Brian & Duncan, John. AC Electric Locomotives of the British Rail.
Webb, Byron H., et al, eds. Fundamentals of Dairy Chemistry.
Webb, David, jt. auth. see Harris, Robert.
Webb, Eugene J. & Campbell, Donald T. Nonreactive Measures in the Social Science.
Webb, Forrest. Caviar Cruise.
Webb, G. A., jt. ed. see Witanowski, M.
Webb, George D., jt. auth. see Moore, Richard D.
Webb, Godfrey E. Gypsies: The Secret People.
Webb, James. A Country Such as This.
Webb, Kaye, ed. Lilliput Goes to War.
Webb, M. J., et al. Oxytocin: Current Research.
Webb, Margaret. An Underwater Tour.
Webb, Mary. Precious Bane.
Webb, Mary, jt. auth. see Webb, William.
Webb, Ned. From Last to First (Neil Bonnett Auto Racing)
Webb, Paul A., jt. auth. see Bender, Marilyn J.
Webb, Raymond E., jt. auth. see Cantelo, William W.
Webb, Richard D., ed. Life & Letters of Captain John Brown.
Webb, S. David, ed. Pleistocene Mammals of Florida.
Webb, Samuel C. Managerial Economics.
Webb, Stanley G. Marketing & Strategic Planning for Professional Service Firms.
Webb, Sterling K. America Hxatal: Two Books of a Poem.
Webb, Sylvia P. Creating an Information Service.
Webb, Val J. Cameo Proofs.
Webb, Vincent J., jt. auth. see Fairchild, Erika.
Webb, W. L., ed. Stratospheric Circulation, PAAS22.
Webb, Willard. Crucial Moments of the Civil War.
Webb, William & Webb, Mary. Exploring Hawaii. Incl. Bk. I. Ohau; Bk. II. Maui. Island Heritage.
Webb, Willis L. Structure of the Stratosphere & Mesosphere.
Webb, Willis L., ed. Stratospheric Circulation.
Webbe, G., jt. auth. see Jordan, P.
Webber, Andrew L., jt. auth. see Rice, Tim.
Webber, Andrew Lloyd & Rice, Tim. Evita: The Legend of Eva Peron, 1919-1952.
Webber, Bert. Kita Taiheiyo ni Hyoryushita Nihon Nanpasen. Adachi, Sakyo, tr. from Japanese.
--Silent Siege: Japanese Attacks Against North America in World War II.
Webber, Bonnie L., jt. auth. see Allen, James F.
Webber, Carolyn & Wildavsky, Aaron. A History of Taxation & Expenditure in the Western World.
Webber, Julian L. Song of the Birds: Sayings, Stories & Impressions of Pablo Casals.
Webber, M. J. Explanation, Prediction & Planning: The Lowry Model.
Webber, Margaret S. Communication Skills for Exceptional Learners.
Webber, Max. Basic Concepts in Sociology.
Webber, N. B. Fluid Mechanics for Civil Engineers.
Webber, Robert E. The Book of Family Prayer.
--Evangelicals on the Canterbury Trail: Why Evangelicals Are Attracted to the Liturgical Church.
--I Believe: A Woman's Workshop on Relational Doctrine.
--In Heart & Home: A Woman's Workshop on Worship.
--Worship Is a Verb.
Webber, Robert P. Business Mathematics: A Consumer's Approach.
Webber, Roger. Evolution of Belief.
Webber, Toni. First Pony.
Weber, Alfred. Farewell to European History: or, the Conquest of Nihilism. Hull, R. F., ed.
Weber, Andrew M. Profiles in Exploration.
Weber, Bill. Conquering the Kill-Joys: Positive Living in a Negative World.
Weber, Bruce. Magic Johnson Larry Bird.
Weber, Catherine. Blackfoot Ambush.
Weber, Christa. Before the Moon Dies.
Weber, David R., ed. Civil Disobedience in America: A Documentary History.
Weber, E., jt. ed. see Hirsch, R.
Weber, E. H., tr. The Sense of Touch.
Weber, Eric. The Divorced Woman's Guide to Meeting New Men: Where to Go & What to Do to Find Your Man. Golbitz, Pat, ed.
--Separate Vacations.
Weber, Erwin. Jenny Lind Chapel: Pioneer Church at Andover.
Weber, Eugen. Europe since Seventeen Fifteen: A Modern History.
Weber, Evelyn. Kindergarten: Its Encounter with Educational Thought in America.
Weber, Francis J. Minibibliophilia.
--Up Sixty-Five Years to Larchmont.
Weber, Hans-Ruedi. Experiments with Bible Study.
--Jesus & the Children: Biblical Resources for Study & Preaching.
Weber, Hans-Ruedi, jt. ed. see Neill, Stephen C.
Weber, Jeffrey R. Camera Repair Simplified.
--IBM PC & XT User's Handbook.
--User's Guide to PET-CBM Computers.
--User's Handbook to the IBM Personal Computer.
Weber, Jon N., ed. Geochemistry of Germanium.
Weber, Judith. I Dedicate This Song to You.
Weber, Judith E. Lights, Camera, Cats!
Weber, Loraine J. & Covino, William A. GED Writing Skills Test Preparation Guide: High School Equivalency Examination.
Weber, Marcea. Sweet Life! Macrobiotic Desserts.
Weber, Max. Basic Concepts of Sociology.
Weber, Neal A. Gardening Ants, the Attines.
Weber, Renee K., jt. ed. see Fraser, James R.
Weber, Robert L., jt. auth. see Strother, G. K.
Weber, Samuel, jt. auth. see Electronics Magazine Editors.
Weber, Shierry, tr. see Mannheim, Karl.
Weber, Sophie. How OSHA Enforces the Law.
Weber Systems, Inc. Staff. Apple IIc User's Handbook.
--Apple Macintosh User's Handbook.
--Atari ST User's Handbook.
--Coleco Adam User's Handbook.
Weber Systems Inc. Staff. Commodore 64 User's Handbook.
Weber Systems, Inc. Staff. Compaq User's Handbook.
--IBM-PCjr User's Handbook.
--Symphony User's Handbook.
--UNIX: User's Handbook.
--User's Handbook to the Atari 400-800.
Weber, Theodore R. Foreign Policy Is Your Business.
Weber, W. P. & Gokel, G. W. Phase Transfer Catalysis in Organic Synthesis.
Weber, Walter. Fleas, Ticks & Cockroaches: Disease Transmitters.
Weber, William A. Theodore D. A. Cockerell: Letters from West Cliff, Colorado, 1887-1889.
Weber, William J. Wild Orphan Babies: Mammals & Birds Caring for Them & Setting Them Free.
--Wild Orphan Friends.
Weber, William P. Silicon Reagents for Organic Synthesis.
Webster. FS-CS Set European G.
--FS Earth Science SRS.
--People Pat Cos CS.
Webster, Alec & Ellwood, John. The Hearing-Impaired Child in the Ordinary School.
Webster, Bob. The South Texas Garden Book.
Webster, Bryce. The Insider's Guide to Franchising.
Webster, Christopher D., jt. ed. see Krueger, Mark A.
Webster, Duane E. Resource Notebook on Organization.
Webster, Fran. Basketball's Amoeba Defense: A Complete Multiple System.
Webster, Harriet. Coastal Daytrips in New England.
--Trips with Children in New England.
Webster, Harriet, jt. auth. see Webster, Jonathan.
Webster, Hutton. Rest Days, the Christian Sunday, the Jewish Sabbath & Their Historical & Anthropological Prototypes.
Webster, Irene B. Guilford County, North Carolina, Will Abstracts, 1771-1841.
Webster, J. Automotive Power Trains Systems.
Webster, James K., ed. Bibliographic Utilities: A Guide for the Special Librarian.
Webster, Jan. Muckle Annie.
Webster, Jay. Auto Mechanics.
Webster, John see Harrier, Richard C.
Webster, Jonathan & Webster, Harriet. The Underground Marketplace: A Guide to New England & the Middle Atlantic States.
Webster, Ned, ed. Penny Crossword Puzzles No. 39.
--Penny Puzzles No. 44.
Webster, Noah. Flight from Paris.
Webster, Paula, jt. auth. see Gilbert, Lucy.
Webster, Peter L., jt. auth. see Swanson, Carl P.
Webster, Tony. Microcomputer Buyer's Guide.
--Microcomputer Buyer's Guide.
--Office Automation & Word Processing Buyer's Guide.
--Portable Computer Buyer's Guide.
--Software Buyer's Guide.
--Terminals & Printers Buyer's Guide.
Webster, Trevor. Where to Go in Greece.
Wechsler, Ben L., jt. auth. see Smith, William A., Jr.
Wechsler, Herman J; see Delteil, Loys.
Wechsler, James & Lavine, Harold. War Propoganda & the United States.
Wechsler, James A. Labor Baron: A Portrait of John L. Lewis.
Weck, Alain L. De see De Weck, Alain L., et al.
Wecker, E. & Horack, I., eds. Retrovirus Genes in Lymphocyte Function & Growth.
Wedberg, Hale, jt. auth. see Rayle, David.
Wedde, H. F., ed. Innovative Computer Developments & Their Impact on Organizations.
Wedding, Dan & Corsini, Raymond J., eds. Great Cases in Psychotherapy.
Weddington, Doris C. Patterns for Practical Communications: Combined Sentence & Composition Packages.
Weddle, Robert S. Plow-Horse Cavalry: The Carey Creek Boys of the Thirty-Fourth Texas.
Wedeck, H. Pictorial History of Morals.
Wedeck, Harry. Concise Dictionary of Medieval History.
--Treasury of Witchcraft.
Wedeck, Harry E. Dictionary of Erotic Literature.
--Dictionary of Magic.
--Love Potions.
--Short Dictionary of Classical Word Origins.
--The Triumph of Satan.
Wedeck, Harry E., tr. see Gabriol, Solomon I.
Wedge, George A. The Gist of Music.
--Keyboard Harmony.
Wedge, Jeff. Stole Patterns.
Wedgewood. Meditation for Beginners.
Wedgwood, Cicely V. William the Silent: William of Nassau, Prince of Orange, 1533-1584.
Wedin, Carol & Nygren, Gertrude L. Housing Perspectives: Individuals & Families.
Wedlock, D. J., jt. ed. see Phillips, G. O.
Weed, Katherine K. & Bond, Richmond P. Studies of British Newspapers & Periodicals from Their Beginning to 1800.
Weeden, Robert B. Alaska: Promises to Keep.
Weeden, Theodore J., Sr. Mark-Traditions in Conflict.
Weedon, Basil, et al, eds. Carotenoids-Four: Proceedings.
Weedy, B. M. Electric Power Systems.
Weegmann, Edna P. The Tree House.
Weekley, James. Recycled Hallelujahs.
Weeks, jt. auth. see Forman.
Weeks, Edward, ed. see Household, Geoffrey.
Weeks, Edwards. My Green Age: A Memoir.
Weeks, Jane, jt. auth. see Spitz, Bruce.
Weeks, John. The Airborne Soldier.
--The Pyramids.
Weeks, John, jt. auth. see Hogg, Ian.
Weeks, John R. Population: An Introduction to Concepts & Issues.
Weeks, Kent R., jt. auth. see Harris, James E.
Weeks, Morris. The Last Wild Horse.
Weeks, Philip E. After You Receive Power.
Weeks, Robert P., ed. Machines & the Man: A Sourcebook on Automation.
Weeks, Thomas M., ed. Journal of Aircraft.
Weemhoff, Harold, jt. auth. see Henshaw, Paul.
Weems, Katherine L. Odds Were Against Me.
Weerman, F., jt. ed. see Zonneveld, W.
Weese, Samuel H. Non-Admitted Insurance in the United States.
Weesner, Theodore. The True Detective.
Weetall, H. H., jt. ed. see Pye, E. Kendall.
Weetall, Howard H. & Royer, Garfield P., eds. Enzyme Engineering.
Weete, John D. Fungal Lipid Biochemistry.
Wegelin, Christof. Image of Europe in Henry James.
Wegelin, Oscar. Early American Plays, 1714-1830.
Wegelius, Otto & Pasternack, Amos, eds. Amyloidosis.
Wegener, William E., ed. Prayers for Protestants.
Wegman, David H., jt. ed. see Levy, Barry S.
Wegman, William. Everyday Problems. Wieder, Laurance, ed.
Wegmann, Brenda. Ocho Mundos: A Cultural Reader.
Wegmann, Brenda, jt. auth. see Kiddle, Mary E.
Wegmann, Robert & Johnson, Miriam. Looking for Work in the New Economy.
Wegner, Hans G. Theodor Fontane und der Roman Vom Markischen Junker.
Wegner, Robert & Sayles, Leonard. Cases in Organizational & Administrative Behavior.
Wegner, Robert E. The Poetry & Prose of E. E. Cummings.
Wehberg, Hans. Die Internationale Beschrankung der Rustungen.
Wehman, Paul. Competitive Employment: New Horizons for Severely Disabled Individuals.
Wehner, H., jt. auth. see Von Gaertner, H. R.
Wehner, R., ed. Information Processing in the Visual Systems of Arthropods.
Wehr, Demaris S. Jung & Feminism: Liberating the Archetypes.
Wehrli, K. Division.
Wehrli, Kitty. Math Readiness Workbook: Math Readiness Pretest Manual.
--Numbers & Numerals.
--Overview of All Programs.
--Subtraction 20-10.
--A Teachers' Script A: Numbers & Numerals, Addition 0-10, Addition 10-20, Multiplication 1&2.
--Teachers' Script B: Subtraction 10-0, Subtraction 20-10, Division.
--Visual & Transfer Skill Mastery.
Wehrly, Max. Mobile Homes.
Wei, Katherine & Quinn, Terry. Second Daughter: Growing up in China 1930-1949.
--Second Daughter: Growing up in China, 1930 to 1949.
Weibel, Kathleen. The Evolution of Library Outreach 1960-75 & Its Effect on Reader Services.
Weick, Carl. Applied Electronics.
Weidenbach, Gretchen, ed. see Jacobs, Alexandra.
Weidenbach, Gretchen, ed. see Kelley, Clarence.
Weidenbaum, Murray L. Business, Government, & the Public.
Weidenhan, Joseph L. Baptismal Names.
Weidenmuller, H. A., jt. auth. see Norenberg, W.
Weider, Betty, jt. auth. see Weider, Joe.
Weider, Charles, ed. Complete Humorous Sketches & Tales of Mark Twain.
--Complete Short Stories of Mark Twain.
Weider, Joe & Weider, Betty. The Best of Joe Weider's Muscle & Fitness Women's Weight Training & Bodybuilding Training Tips & Routines.
Weidhaas, Ernest R. Architectural Drafting & Construction.
--Architectural Drafting & Design.
--Reading Architectural Plans for Residential & Commercial Construction.

Weidlein, Marianne & Roth, Stephanie. Empowering Vision: For Your Service Business.
Weidman, Jerome. I Can Get It for You Wholesale.
Weidmann, J., jt. auth. see Joergens, K.
Weidner & Sells. Physics: Elementary.
Weidner, Elizabeth F. Along the Shore.
Weigand, James E., ed. Developing Teacher Competencies.
Weigert, Andrew J. Life & Society: A Meditation on the Social Thought of Jose Ortega y Gassett.
Weightman, John. Concept of the Avant-Garde.
Weigle, Oscar. Jokes & Riddles.
Weigle, Oscar, ed. Great Big Joke & Riddle Book.
Weihe, W. H., jt. ed. see Tromp, S. W.
Weihrauch. Esophageal Manometry: Methods & Clinical Practice.
Weijnen, J., ed. Brainstem Organization of Interacting Behavioral Systems.
Weijnen, J. A. & Mendelson, J., eds. Drinking Behavior: Oral Stimulation, Reinforcement, & Preference.
Weik, Martin H. Communications Standard Dictionary.
Weik, Mary H. A House on Liberty Street.
--Jazz Man.
--Scarlet Thread.
Weiker, Walter F. The Turkish Revolution, Nineteen Sixty to Nineteen Sixty-One: Aspects of Military Politics.
Weil, Andrew. Health & Healing: Understanding Conventional & Alternative Medicine.
--The Natural Mind: A New Way of Looking at Drugs & the Higher Consciousness.
Weil, Ben H. & Polansky, Barbara F. Modern Copyright Fundamentals.
Weil, C., ed. Medical Geographic Research in Latin America.
Weil, Carrol S., jt. auth. see Gad, Shayne.
Weil, G. L. Trade Policy in the 70's: A New Round.
Weil, Grete. My Sister, My Antigone. Winston, Krishna, tr.
Weil, Lisl. Donkey Head.
--Gillie & the Flattering Fox.
--The Riddle Monster.
--The Story of the Wise Men & the Child.
--To Sail a Ship of Treasures.
Weil, Martin. A Pretty Good Club: The Founding Fathers of the U. S. Foreign Services.
Weil, Mildred & Hartley, Duncan, eds. The Sociology of the Arts.
Weil, Mildred W. Marriage, the Family, & Society: Toward a Sociology of Marriage & the Family.
Weil, Simone. Intimations of Christianity Among the Ancient Greeks.
--The Notebooks. Wills, Simone, tr. from Fr.
--Oppression & Liberty.
Weil, Thomas E. Haiti: A Country Study.
Weiland, J. C. & Wilhelmsson, H. Coherent Non-Linear Interaction of Waves in Plasmas.
Weiler, Joseph. Israel & the Creation of a Palestinian State: A European Perspective.
Weiler, Kathi M., jt. auth. see Kernicki, Jeanette G.
Weiler, R., jt. ed. see Zettler, F.
Weilgart, W. John. Communication: Logic & Command.
Weill. Ultrasonography of Digestive Diseases.
Weill, Alain, jt. auth. see Rennert, Jack.
Weill, Gus. Paradiddle.
Weill, Herman N. European Diplomatic History 1815-1914: Documents & Interpretations.
Weiller, Sharinne S. Madam President.
Weill-Raynal, Jean, jt. auth. see Mathieu, Jean.
Weiman, Eiveen. It Takes Brains.
--Which Way Courage.
Weimar, Karl S., ed. Thirty-Six German Poems.
Weimer, Walter B., ed. Notes on the Methodology of Scientific Research.
Weinbach, Sheindel. Avi Names His Price.
Weinbaum, Paul. Statue of Liberty: Heritage of America.
Weinberg. History of Plene Spelling.
Weinberg, Amy S., jt. auth. see Berwick, Robert C.
Weinberg, Arthur & Douglas, William O., eds. Attorney for the Damned.
Weinberg, Eve. Community Surveys with Local Talent: A Handbook.
Weinberg, George. Self Creation.
--Society & the Healthy Homosexual.
Weinberg, Gerald M. Psychology of Computer Programming.
--Rethinking Systems Analysis & Design.
Weinberg, Gerald M., jt. auth. see Gause, Don C.
Weinberg, H. Barbara. The American Pupils of Jean-Leon Gerome.
--The Decorative Work of John la Farge.
Weinberg, H. Barbara, ed. see Benjamin, S. G.
Weinberg, H. Barbara, ed. see Cook, Clarence.
Weinberg, H. Barbara, ed. see Jarves, James J.
Weinberg, H. Barbara, ed. see Koehler, S. R.
Weinberg, H. Barbara, ed. see Robinson, Frank T.
Weinberg, H. Barbara, ed. see Sheldon, G. W.
Weinberg, H. Barbara, ed. see Trumble, Alfred.
Weinberg, H. Barbara, ed. see Van Rensselaer, Mariana G.
Weinberg, Jeffrey, ed. Water Row Review.
Weinberg, Julia. The Big Beautiful Book of Hors D'Oeuvres. Wyler, S., ed.
--Hors d'Oeuvres Artistry.
Weinberg, Kurt. On Gide's Promethee: Private Myth & Public Mystification.
Weinberg, Larry. Tron: The Story Book.
Weinberg, Lawrence. The Forgetful Bears.
Weinberg, Paul N. & Groff, James R. Understanding UNIX: A Conceptual Guide.
--Understanding XENIX: A Conceptual Guide.
Weinberg, Robert, jt. ed. see O'Neil, Robert F.
Weinberg, Sharon L. & Goldberg, Kenneth P. Basic Statistics for Education & the Behavioral Sciences.
Weinberger, Jane. Wee Peter Puffin.
Weinberger, Michael J. Estate & Gift Tax after ERTA.
Weinberger, P. E. Perspectives on Social Welfare: An Introductory Anthology.
Weinbert, R., jt. auth. see Lerman, F.
Weinburg, Larry. Guess a Rhyme: Poems to Complete! Riddles to Solve!
Weindling, Paul, ed. The Social History of Occupational Health.
Weine, Franklin S. Endodontic Therapy.
Weiner, jt. auth. see Brownstein.
Weiner, Andrew. Station Gehenna.
Weiner, Annette B. Women of Value, Men of Renown: New Perspectives in Trobriand Exchange.
Weiner, Bernard. Theories of Motivation.
Weiner, Donald D. & Spina, John F. The Sinusoidal Analysis & Modeling of Weakly Nonlinear Circuits: With Application to Nonlinear Interference Effects.
Weiner, Elizabeth H., ed. Sex Role Stereotyping in the Schools.
Weiner, Herbert. Wild Goats of Ein Gedi.
Weiner, Jack & Pollack, Vera. Structure, Extractives, & Utilization of Bark.
Weiner, Jack B. Drinking.
Weiner, Linda, jt. auth. see Dziech, Billie W.
Weiner, M. L. Personality: The Human Potential.
Weiner, Michael. Vital Signs.
Weiner, Michael A. & Gross, Kathleen. Maximum Immunity.
Weiner, Mitchel. Barron's Verbal Aptitude Workbook for College Entrance Examinations.
Weiner, Mitchel, jt. auth. see Brownstein, Samuel C.
Weiner, Myron E. Human Services Management: Analysis & Applications.
Weiner, Neal O. & Schwartz, David M. Interstate Gourmet: California & Pacific Northwest.
--The Interstate Gourmet: California & the Pacific Northwest.
--Interstate Gourmet: Mid Atlantic.
--The Interstate Gourmet: Mid-Atlantic States.
--The Interstate Gourmet: New England.
--The Interstate Gourmet: Routes 91 & 89.
Weiner, Neil & Schwartz, David. The Interstate Gourmet: Southeast.
Weiner, Norbert. Human Use of Human Beings: Cybernetics & Society.
Weiner, Norman L., jt. ed. see Pope, David W.
Weiner, Paul I., jt. auth. see Practising Law Institute Staff.
Weiner, Roy S., et al, eds. Bone Marrow Transplantation.
Weiner, Stewart, jt. auth. see Jewell, Geri.
Weiner, Sue & Howard, Lisa. The Rolling Stones A to Z.
Weiner, Walter. So Call It a Mitzvah.
Weinert, jt. auth. see Palmer.
Weinert, H. L., ed. Reproducing Kernel Hilbert Spaces: Applications in Statistical Signal Processing.
Weinfeld, Barbara A., jt. ed. see Cummings, William W.
Weinfield, Barbara A., jt. ed. see Cummings, William W.
Weingarten, Henry. A Modern Introduction to Astrology.
Weingarten, Kathy, jt. auth. see Daniels, Pamela.
Weingartner, C., compiled by. Machinists' Ready Reference.
Weingartner, Ronald, ed. see Temko, Florence.
Weingold, Allan B., jt. ed. see Kase, Nathan G.
Weingram, S., jt. auth. see Lundell, A. T.
Weinheimer, Gail, jt. auth. see Rosengart, Oliver.
Weinheimer, Peter. Characterization of Erythrocyte-Reactive Factors of Panulirus Argus: A Contribution to Immunophylogeny.
Weinhouse, Sidney, jt. ed. see Klein, George.
Weinlander, Albertina A. Barron's How to Prepare for the National Teachers Examinations-Common Exam: Education in the Elementary School.
Weinman, David & Ristic, Miodrag. Infectious Blood Diseases of Man & Animals.
Weinman, J. An Outline of Psychology As Applied to Medicine.
Weinman, Paul. Adam's at Bat.
--He Swings a Straight Stick.
Weinmann, Ronald, jt. auth. see Frommer, Harvey.
Weinrach, Stephen G., ed. Counseling for Careers.
Weinreb, Lloyd L. Criminal Justice, Leading Constitutional Cases.
--Criminal Law: Cases, Comment & Questions.
--Criminal Process: Cases, Comments, Questions, 1985 Supplement to.
Weinreich, Max. History of the Yiddish Language. Noble, Shlomo & Fishman, Joshua A., trs. from Yiddish.
--History of the Yiddish Language. Noble, Shlomo & Fishman, Joshua A., trs.
Weinreich, Uriel. Modern English-Yiddish, Yiddish-English Dictionary.
--Yidish Launiversitah: Hebrew Edition of "College Yiddish" Bahat, S. & Goldwasser, M., trs.
Weinreich-Haste, Helen & Locke, Don. Morality in the Making: Thought, Action & the Social Context.
Weinrich, Peter H. Social Protest from the Left in Canada Eighteen Seventy to Nineteen Seventy.
Weinshall, Theodore D. & Raveh, Yael-Anna. Managing Growing Organizations: A New Approach.
Weinsheimer, Joel. Imitation.
Weinsier, Roland L. & Butterworth, C. E., Jr. Handbook of Clinical Nutrition: Clinician's Manual for the Diagnosis & Management of Nutritional Problems.
Weinstein, Alan J., jt. auth. see Gibbs, Ronald S.
Weinstein, Amy, ed. Public Welfare Directory, 1981-1982.
--Public Welfare Directory, 1982-83.
--Public Welfare Directory, 1983-84.
--Public Welfare Directory, 1984-85.
--Public Welfare Directory, 1985-86.
--Public Welfare Directory 1986-87.
Weinstein, Bob. How to Switch Careers.
Weinstein, Boris, ed. Chemistry & Biochemistry of Amino Acids, Peptides & Proteins.
Weinstein, Frida. A Hidden Childhood: A Jewish Girl's Sanctuary in a French Convent, 1942-1945.
Weinstein, Grace. Life Plans: Looking Forward to Retirement.
Weinstein, Howard. The Covenant of the Crown.
Weinstein, Howard, jt. auth. see Crispin, A. C.
Weinstein, Jack B., et al. Evidence, Rules, & Statute Supplement, 1984.
Weinstein, Jay. Sociology-Technology: The Foundations of Postacademic Social Science.
Weinstein, Malcolm S. Health in the City: Environmental & Behavioral Influences.
Weinstein, Martin. Android Design.
Weinstein, Martin, jt. ed. see Muchnick, David M.
Weinstein, Robert A. & Booth, Larry. Collection, Use, & Care of Historical Photographs.
Weinstein, Robin, ed. Photographer's Market 1986.
Weinstein, Warren & Schrire, Robert. Political Conflict & Ethnic Strategies: A Case Study of Burundi.
Weinstock, Comilda, jt. auth. see Whitbourne, Susan K.
Weinstock, H. R. Essays in Relating Theory to Practice in Education.
Weinstock, Herbert. Handel.
--Rossini a Biography.
Weinstock, John M. & Rovinsky, Robert T., eds. The Hero in Scandinavian Literature: From Peer Gynt to the Present.
Weintraub, A. Psychorheumatologie.
Weintraub, Dov, et al. Agrarian Development & Modernization in the Philippines.
Weintraub, Karl J. Visions of Culture: Voltaire, Guizot, Burckhardt, Lamprecht, Huizinga, Ortega Y Gasset.
Weintraub, Pamela, ed. The Omni Interviews.
Weintraub, Pamela, ed. see Omni Magazine Editors.
Weintraub, Sam, et al, eds. Annual Summary of Investigations Relating to Reading: July 1, 1982 to June 30, 1983.
Weintraub, Stanley. The London Yankees: Portraits of American Writers & Artists in England, 1894-1914. Ellenbogen, Eileen, tr.
Weintraub, Stanley, ed. see Shaw, George Bernard.
Weir, C. I. Introduction to Injection Molding. Mendoza, Luis E., tr.
Weir, Gregory, jt. auth. see Weir, Walter J.
Weir, Jean, tr. from Ital. Armed Struggle in Italy: A Chronology.
Weir, Lavada. Grass Skiing: A Complete Beginner's Book.
--The Roller Skating Book.
--Skateboards & Skateboarding: The Complete Beginner's Guide.
Weir, M., jt. auth. see Simpson, L. E.
Weir, Walter J. & Weir, Gregory. Fundamentals of Mathematics: Outline & Review Problems for Electronic Circuit Fundamentals.
Weis, Charles M., ed. see Boswell, James.
Weis, Jennifer, ed. see Spiegelman, Judith M. & UNICEF Staff.
Weisbart, Melvin, et al. Isolation & Purification of Hormones.
Weisberg, Gabriel P. Traditions & Revisions: Themes from the History of Sculpture.
Weisberg, Joseph S. Meteorology.
--Meteorology: The Earth & Its Weather.
Weisberg, Richard C. The Politics of Crude Oil Pricing in the Middle East, 1970 to 1975: A Study in International Bargaining.
Weisberger, Bernard A. The American Newspaperman.
--Cold War, Cold Peace: The United States & Russia since 1945.
--The Statue of Liberty: The First Hundred Years.
Weisbrod, Harry, et al. Wage-Hour & Employment Practices Manual for the Multihousing Industry. Schleker, Peggy J., ed.
Weisbrot, Robert. Father Divine.
Weischedel, Randall. The Joy of Ascension.
Weisenberg, M. & Tursky, B., eds. Pain: New Perspectives In Therapy & Research.
Weisenberger, F. P., jt. auth. see Roseboom, E. H.
Weisenburger, F. P. Ordeal of Faith.
Weiser, Carol, et al. Mix Me a Person.
Weiser, Conrad. Dancing All the Dances, Singing All the Songs.
--I Don't Need to Know Your Name to Be Your Friend.
--Promises of Steel, Covenants of Glass.
Weiser, Francis X. Handbook of Christian Feasts & Customs.
Weiser, Marjorie P. & Arbeiter, Jean S. Womanlist.
Weiser, Peter B., jt. auth. see Burdick, John.
Weiser, Theresa. Music for God.
Weisgal. Entertaining in Jerusalem.
Weisgard, Leonard. Treasures to See: A Museum Picture-Book.
Weisgard, Leonard, jt. auth. see Joslin, Sesyle.
Weisgerber, Robert A., ed. Vocational Education: Teaching the Handicapped in Regular Classes.
Weishaar, Tom & Kersey, Burt. The DOStalk Scrapbook.
Weisheit, Eldon. God's Word in a Child's World: Messages & Guidelines for Sharing the Gospel with Children.
--Should I Have an Abortion?
--The Zeal of His House.
Weisinger, Nina L. A Guide to Studies in Spanish American Literature.
Weiskopf, Donald. Recreation & Leisure: Improving the Quality of Life.
Weisman, Alan. La Frontera: The United States Border with Mexico.
Weisman, Carlos S., jt. auth. see Crain, Robert L.
Weisman, Herman M. Technical Correspondence: A Handbook & Reference Source for the Technical Professional.
Weisman, Thomas. Drug Abuse & Drug Counseling.
Weisman, Willi, et al, eds. Children's Picture Books in German: A Checklist of Titles 1945 - 1975.
Weisner, Ira. Trader Ike & Our Home in the North.
Weiss, Allen. The Organization Guerrilla: Playing the Game to Win.
--Write What You Mean: A Handbook of Business Communication.
--Write What You Mean: A Handbook of Business Communications.
Weiss, Ann E. The Nuclear Question.
--What's That You Said.
--What's That You Said? How Words Change.
Weiss, Caroline & Uslander, Arlene. Doctor Talks to Nine to Twelve Year Olds.
Weiss, Caroline, et al. Creative Cooking Sugar Free.
--Gourmet Cookbook for Those Interested in Weight Control.
Weiss, D. W., ed. Immunological Parameters of Host - Tumor Relationships.
Weiss, David, ed. Immunological Parameters of Host-Tumor Relationship.
Weiss, David W., jt. ed. see Zuckerman, Avivah.
Weiss, Edwin. Algebraic Number Theory.
Weiss, Ellen. Millicent Maybe.
--Things to Make & Do for Christmas.
Weiss, G. B., ed. Calcium in Drug Action.
Weiss, H. Structure & Application of Galvanomagnetic Devices.
Weiss, Harold & McGrath, J. B. Technically Speaking: Oral Communication for Engineers, Scientists & Technical Personnel.
Weiss, Harvey R., jt. ed. see Merrill, Gary F.
Weiss, Herman. The Sound of Dreams.
Weiss, Jason, tr. see Ocampo, Silvinia.
Weiss, Jeffrey. Rugs.
Weiss, Jeffrey, jt. ed. see Osborn, Susan.
Weiss, Jess E. The Adam & Eve Fantasy.
Weiss, Joan S. Raising a Son: The Essential Guide to a Healthy Mother-Son Relationship.
Weiss, Joan T. Home for a Stranger.
Weiss, Johannes. Jesus' Proclamation of the Kingdom of God. Keck, Leander E., ed. Hiers, Richard H. & Holland, David L., trs. from Ger.

Authors

Weiss, John. Trail Cooking.
Weiss, K. M. & Ballonoff, P. A., eds. Demographic Genetics.
Weiss, L. & Wolfowitz, J. Maximum Probability Estimators & Related Topics.
Weiss, Leatie. Heather's Feathers.
--My Teacher Sleeps in School.
Weiss, Lee D., jt. auth. see Uslander, Arlene.
Weiss, Leinhauser. Quilting: An Annotated Bibliography.
Weiss, Leon & Lansing, Lambert, eds. Histology: Cell & Tissue Biology.
Weiss, Leonard A., jt. auth. see Cavender, Nancy M.
Weiss, Malcolm E. Seeing Through the Dark: Blind & Sighted, Vision Shared.
--Why Glass Breaks, Rubber Bends, & Glue Sticks: How Everyday Materials Work.
Weiss, Marian, ed. Early Therapeutic, Social, & Vocational Problems in the Rehabilitation of Persons with Spinal Cord Injuries.
Weiss, Marie. Who Says It Can't Be Done?
Weiss, Mike. No Go on Jackson Street: A Mystery Introducing Ben Henry.
Weiss, Nicki. Hank & Oogie.
Weiss, Paul A. Dynamics of Development: Experiments & Inferences.
Weiss, Piero. Letters of Composers Through Six Centuries.
Weiss, Richard A. Relativistic Thermodynamics.
--Relativistic Thermodynamics.
Weiss, Rita, ed. see Dunlap, William.
Weiss, Robert & Seiter, Charles. Pascal for FORTRAN Programmers.
Weiss, Samuel A., ed. Drama in the Western World, Fifteen Plays with Essays. Incl. Oedipus the King. Sophocles; The Bacchae. Euripides; Lysistrata. Aristophanes; The Misanthrope. Moliere; Phaedra. Racine, Jean; The Prince of Homburg. Von Kleist, Friedrich; Ghosts. Ibsen, Henrik; A Dream Play. Strindberg, August; Caesar & Cleopatra. Shaw, George Bernard; Uncle Vanya. Chekhov, Anton; Six Characters in Search of an Author. Pirandello, Luigi; Desire Under the Elms. O'Neill, Eugene; The Caucasian Chalk Circle. Brecht, Bertolt; The Glass Menagerie. Williams, Tennessee; All That Fall. Beckett, Samuel. Heath.
Weiss, Sharon W., jt. auth. see Enzinger, Franz M.
Weiss, Shirley F., jt. ed. see Chapin, F. Stuart, Jr.
Weiss, Sidney J., jt. auth. see Van Scott, Timothy.
Weiss, Sol. Elementary College Mathematics.
--Elementary Mathematics: Teaching Suggestions & Strategies.
Weiss, T. G., jt. ed. see Jennings, A.
Weiss, Theodore. Breath of Clowns & Kings: Shakespeare's Early Comedies & Histories.
Weiss, Theodore J. Foods Oils & Their Uses.
Weiss, Ulrich & Edwards, J. Michael. Biosynthesis of Aromatic Compounds.
Weiss, Volker, jt. ed. see Burke, John J.
Weiss, Volker, jt. ed. see Kula, Eric.
Weiss, W. H. The Supervisor's Problem Solver.
Weiss, Walter A. The Best I've Read.
Weiss, William. Home Maintenance: A Guide to Taking Better Care of Your House.
Weissbach, Herbert & Kunz, Robert. Dimension in Health Research: Search for the Medicines of Tomorrow.
Weissbach, Herbert & Pestka, Sidney, eds. Protein Biosynthesis.
Weissberg, Michael. Dangerous Secrets: Maladaptive Responses to Stress.
Weissberg, Robert, jt. auth. see Jacob, Herbert.
Weissberger, A., jt. auth. see Rossiter, Bryant W.
Weissberger, N. L. & Tilak, B. V., eds. Technique of Electroorganic Synthesis: Scale-up & Engineering Aspects.
Weissbluth, Marc. Crybabies: Coping with Colic, What to Do When Baby Won't Stop Crying.
Weissbluth, Mitchel, jt. ed. see Pullman, Bernard.
Weissbort, Daniel & Hughes, Ted, eds. Modern Poetry in Translation 1983.
Weissbort, Daniel, tr. see Dore, Gustave.
Weissbourd, Katherine. Growing up in the James Family: Henry James, Sr. As Son & Father. Nathan, Peter E., ed.
Weissenborn, Helmut, tr. see Von Grimmelshausen, Hans J. C.
Weissenborn, Lesley, tr. see Von Grimmelshausen, Hans J. C.
Weisser, Otto & Landa, S. Sulphide Catalysts, Their Properties & Applications. Sofr, Ota, tr.
Weissert & Schileo. Fabrication of Thorium Fuel Elements.
Weisskopf, V. F., jt. auth. see Blatt, J.
Weisskopf, Victor. Science & Other Matters.
Weisskopf, Victor F., ed. Nuclear Physics.
Weissman, David. Dispositional Properties.
Weissman, David B., jt. auth. see Rentz, D. C.
Weissman, G. Cell Biology of Inflammation.
Weissman, Irving, compiled by. Annual Reviews Reprints: Immunology, 1977-1979.
Weissman, Irving, et al. Essential Concepts in Immunology.
Weissman, Myrna M. & Paykel, Eugene S. The Depressed Woman: A Study of Social Relationships.
Weissman, Steve, ed. Big Brother & the Holding Company: The World Behind Watergate.
Weissmann, Adolf. The Problems of Modern Music.
Weissmann, Gerald. The Woods Hole Cantata: Essays on Science & Society.
Weissmann, John S. Goffredo Petrassi.
Weiss-Rosmarin, Trude. Jerusalem.
--Jewish Survival.
Weisstein, Ulrich, ed. Essence of Opera.
Weisstub, David N., ed. Law & Psychiatry III: Selected Papers Presented at the Fourth International Congress on Law & Psychiatry, Pembroke College, Oxford England, 19-22 July 1979.
Weisz, Frank B. An Estate Planner's Guide to Business Agreements & Estate Documents.
Weisz, H. Microanalysis by the Ring Oven Technique.
Weisz, P. B. & Marshall, J. F., eds. Fuels from Biomass.
Weisz, Paul B. & Keogh, Richard N. Elements of Biology.
Weitenkampf, Frank. American Graphic Art.
Weitenkampf, Frank, ed. see New York Public Library Staff.
Weithaus, J. C. Dear Mr. President.
Weitz, Patricia, jt. ed. see Norback, Judith.
Weitzman, David. Traces: A Field Guide to the History on Your Doorstep.
--Traces of the Past.
Weitzmann, Kurt. The Miniatures of the Sacra Parallela: Parsinius Graecus 923.
Weixlmann, Joseph. John Barth: An Annotated Bibliography.
Weizel, A., ed. see International Symposium on Atherosclerosis Staff.
Weizman, F., jt. ed. see Uzgiris, I. C.
Weizman Institute of Science Conference Staff & Littauer, U. Z. Neurotransmitters-Receptor Interactions: Proceedings of the Weizman Institute of Science Conference, Rehovot, Israel, Feb. 1980.
Weizsacker, Richard von see Von Weizsacker, Richard.
Wekker, Herman & Haegeman, Liliane. A Modern Course in English Syntax.
Weksler, Marc E. see Exton-Smith, A. Norman.
Welanetz, Diana Von see Von Welanetz, Diana & Von Welanetz, Paul.
Welanetz, Paul Von see Von Welanetz, Diana & Von Welanetz, Paul.
Welbergen, U. R., jt. auth. see Blankenstein, M. Van.
Welbers, Thomas. Banquet of the Word: Bible Study Based on the Sunday Readings.
Welborn, Andrea, ed. see Moore, Sandra S.
Welborn, Don. On the Subject of Tongues: From the New Testament.
Welbourne, Michael. The Community of Knowledge.
Welch, Adam C. Kings & Prophets of Israel.
Welch, Bob & Vecsey, George. Five O'Clock Comes Early: A Ballplayer's Battle with Alcoholism.
--Five O'Clock Comes Early: A Young Man's Battle with Alcoholism.
Welch, Chris. Hendrix: A Biography.
Welch, D. Don. Law & Morality.
Welch, Don. Law & Morality.
Welch, Gerry F., jt. auth. see Welch, Patrick J.
Welch, James, ed. see Hugo, Richard.
Welch, Jeffrey, jt. auth. see Olmsted, John C.
Welch, Jeffrey E. Elizabeth Gaskell: An Annotated Bibliography, 1929-1975.
Welch, Joe L. Marketing Law.
Welch, John F., ed. Van Sickle's Modern Airmanship.
Welch, Mary S. Networking: The Great New Way for Women to Get Ahead.
Welch, Micaela, jt. auth. see La Monte, Francesca.
Welch, Michael J., ed. Radiopharmaceuticals & Other Compounds Labelled with Short-Lived Radionuclides.
Welch, Pat, jt. auth. see Dowdall, Mike.
Welch, Patrick J. & Welch, Gerry F. Economics: Theory & Practice.
Welch, Raquel. Raquel: The Raquel Welch Total Beauty & Fitness Program.
Welch, Richard E., Jr. George F. Hoar & the Half-Breed Republicans.
Welch, Robert. Things That Go Bump in the Flight: A Reassuring Guide to Air Travel.
Welch, Rosa P. & Myers, Oma L. Rosa's Song: The Life & Ministry of Rosa Page Welch.
Welch, Stuart C. India: Art & Culture, 1300-1900.
--King's Book of Kings: The Shah-nameh of Shah Tahmasp.
Welch, William A. Lightplane Propeller Design, Selection, Maintenance & Repair.
Welcher, Frank J., et al, eds. Standard Methods of Chemical Analysis: Vol. IIIA, Instrumental Methods.
Welchman, Gordon. The Hut Six Story: The Story of Breaking the Enigma Codes.
Welcome, John. Bellary Bay.
--Grand National.
Weld, John. Young Man in Paris: 1927-1932.
Weld, Philip S. Moxie: The American Challenge.
Welder, G. Chemisorption: An Experimental Approach. Klemperer, D., tr.
Welding Institute of Canada, ed. Advances in Thermal Spraying: Proceedings of the International Thermal Spraying Conference, 11th, September 8-12, 1986, Montreal, Canada.
--Welding in Energy-Related Projects: Proceedings of the International Conference on Welding in Energy-Related Projects; Toronto, Canada, September 20-21, 1983.
Weldon, Chichester P. The New Departure Classics.
Weldon, Fay. Letters to Alice: On First Reading Jane Austen.
--Letters to Alice: On First Reading Jane Austen.
Weldon, John. Nineteen Eighties, Decade of Shock.
Weldy, Norma J. Body Fluids & Electrolytes: A Programmed Presentation.
Welford, jt. auth. see McLeod.
Welin, G., jt. auth. see Welin, S.
Welin, S. & Welin, G. The Double Contrast Examination of the Colon: Experiences with the Welin Modification.
Welker, Robert H. Birds & Men: American Birds in Science, Art, Literature, & Conservation, 1800-1900.
Welkowitz, Walter, ed. Bioengineering: Proceedings of the Ninth Northeast Conference, March, 1981, Rutgers University, Piscataway, New Jersey.
Well, Rosemary. Fog Comes on Little Pig Feet.
Welland, Dennis. Miller: The Playwright.
Wellbank, J. H., jt. auth. see Mason, David T.
Wellborn, Starnes R. The Age of Trust: How to Prevent Future War.
Wellby, D., jt. auth. see Read, M. D.
Wellek, Nonna, jt. auth. see Wellek, Rene.
Wellek, Rene & Wellek, Nonna. Chekhov: New Perspectives.
Wellek, Rene, ed. see Beattie, James.
Wellek, Rene, ed. see Bentley, Richard.
Wellek, Rene, ed. see Blaguy, John.
Wellek, Rene, ed. see Browne, Peter.
Wellek, Rene, ed. see Collins, Anthony.
Wellek, Rene, ed. see Cudworth, Ralph.
Wellek, Rene, ed. see Edward, Herbert.
Wellek, Rene, ed. see Gildon, Charles.
Wellek, Rene, ed. see Glanville, Joseph.
Wellek, Rene, ed. see Law, Edmund.
Wellek, Rene, ed. see Nitsch, Friedrich A.
Wellek, Rene, ed. see Paley, William.
Wellek, Rene, ed. see Price, Richard.
Wellek, Rene, ed. see Priestley, Joseph.
Wellek, Rene, ed. see Reid, Thomas.
Wellek, Rene, ed. see Toland, John.
Wellens, Hein J. J., jt. ed. see Josephson, Mark E.
Weller, M. Protein Phosphorylation.
Welles, Edwin S. Some Notes on Wampum.
Welles, Marcia L., jt. ed. see Servodidio, Mirella.
Welles, Patricia. Members Only.
Welles, Sigourney & Darbey, Jill. The Best Bed & Breakfast in the World.
--The Best Bed & Breakfast in the World: England, Scotland & Wales.
--The Best Bed & Breakfast in the World: United Kingdom, 1987 Edition.
--The Best Bed & Breakfast in the World 1986: The United Kingdom & Ireland.
--Historic Country House Hotels 1987: Great Britain & Ireland.
Welle-Strand. Norway Motoring.
--Norway: Tourist in. Lundevall, E., ed.
Welle-Strand, E., ed. Norway, Tourist In.
Wellingham-Jones, Patricia. Evaluation of Adolescent Self-Esteem Through the Coopersmith Self-Esteem Inventory & Graphometric Analysis of Handwriting.
Wellington, Dorothy G., et al. Cancer Mortality: Environmental & Ethnic Factor.
Wellington, Herbert, ed. see Delacroix, Eugene.
Wellisch, Hans H. Indexing & Abstracting: An International Bibliography.
--Indexing & Abstracting, 1977-1981: An International Bibliography.
Welliver, W. Character, Plot & Thought in Plato's Timaeus-Critias.
Wellman, Alice. The Wilderness Has Ears.
Wellman, James & Zierold, Norman. Chart Your Own Way to Career Happiness.
Wellman, Manly W. Valley So Low.
Wellman, Paul I. Greatest Cattle Drive.
Wellner, Marcel. Essentials of Physics.
Wellnitz, Marcus Von see Von Wellnitz, Marcus.
Wells, Alan. Criminal Law.
Wells, Alexander T. Air Transportation: A Management Perspective.
Wells, Andy J. Building Stereo Speakers.
Wells, Anna M. Miss Marks & Miss Wooley.
Wells, C. Cleft Palate & Its Associated Speech Disorders.
Wells, C. H. J., jt. auth. see Davis, R.
Wells, Carl F., jt. auth. see Stuart, Irving R.
Wells, Carolyn. Carolyn Wells' Book of American Limericks.
--Parody Anthology.
--A Whimsey Anthology.
Wells, Carolyn, ed. Nonsense Anthology.
Wells, David A., ed. see Timbs, John.
Wells, Deane, jt. auth. see Singer, Peter.
Wells, Dee. Jane.
Wells, E. H. Up & down the Yukon.
Wells, Ellen B., ed. Horsemanship: A Guide to Information Sources.
Wells, Floyd. In the Life of Floyd Wells.
Wells, G. A. Did Jesus Exist?
--The Plays of Grillparzer.
Wells, G. P., ed. H. G. Wells in Love: Postscript to an Experiment in Autobiography.
Wells, Gordon, jt. ed. see Kroll, Barry M.
Wells, Gwenn E. The Pen Renderings of Elmer Rising: New England in Black & White.
Wells, H. G. Experiment in Autobiography: Discoveries & Conclusions in a Very Ordinary Brain (since 1866)
--Outline of History.
--Twenty-Eight Science Fiction Stories.
Wells, Henry & Gowda, H. H. Style & Structure in Shakespeare.
Wells, J. Gipson. Current Issues in Marriage & the Family.
Wells, Jill. The Construction Industry in Developing Countries: Alternative Strategies for Development.
Wells, Joseph M. & Buck, Otto, eds. Ultrasonic Fatigue: Proceedings. Champion, Pennsylvania, 1981.
Wells, Kenneth M., jt. auth. see Weston, Paul B.
Wells, Lawrence. Let the Band Play Dixie.
Wells, Lee F. Tarnished Star.
Wells, Louis T. & Vernon, Raymond. Manager in the International Economy.
Wells, Louis T., Jr., ed. The Product Life Cycle & International Trade.
Wells, M. G. H. & Lherbier, L. W., eds. Processing & Properties of High School Tool Steels: Proceedings. AIME Annual Meeting, Las Vegas, 1980.
Wells, M. K., ed. Advances in Bioengineering: 1979.
Wells, Malcolm. Gentle Architecture.
Wells, Malvern, jt. ed. see Dummer, G. W.
Wells, Martin. Lower Animals.
Wells, Merle. Boise: An Illustrated History.
Wells, Merle & Hart, Arthur A. Idaho: Gem of the Mountains.
Wells, Merle W. Anti-Mormonism in Idaho, Eighteen Seventy-Two to Ninety-Two.
Wells, P. N., ed. Scientific Basis of Medical Imaging.
Wells, Patricia. The Food Lover's Guide to Paris.
Wells, Peter N., jt. auth. see Goldberg, Barry.
Wells, Phil, jt. auth. see Brooner, E. G.
Wells, R. Anarchist Handbook: The Materials & Production of Improvised Weapons.
--Solid State Power Rectifiers.
Wells, R. O., Jr., jt. ed. see Resnikoff, H. L.
Wells, Roe, ed. The Microcirculation in Medicine.
Wells, Rosemary. Leave Well Enough Alone.
--None of the Above.
--Through the Hidden Door.
Wells, Susan, ed. see McDonald, Archie P.
Wells, Susan, ed. see McLaughlin, Kenneth.
Wells, Susan, ed. see Williams, C. Fred.
Wells, Theodore W., jt. ed. see Cleary, Vincent J.
Wells, Tobias. Of Graves, Worms & Epitaphs.
Wells, Tom H. Commodore Moore & the Texas Navy.
Wells, Walter. Communications in Business.
--Tycoons & Locusts: A Regional Look at Hollywood Fiction of the 1930s.
Wells, Walter, tr. see Robbe-Grillet, Alain.
Wells, William D., jt. auth. see Reynolds, Fred D.
Wells, William W. & Eisenberg, Frank, Jr., eds. Cyclitols & Phosphoinositides.
Welmers, William E. Grammar of Vai.
Wels, Byron G. The Medicine Cabinet. Brady, Frank, ed.
Welsch, Delane E., et al. The Account Book for Farm & Ranch Management.
Welsch, Glenn A., et al. Intermediate Accounting.
--Intermediate Accounting.
Welsch, Ulrike. Faces of New England. Smith, Sharon, ed.
--World I Love to See.
Welsh, A. N. The Skills of Management.
Welsh, Alexander. Hero of the Waverley Novels.
Welsh Arts Council Staff, ed. Photographs from Welsh Collections.
Welsh, Evan. A Touch of Heaven Here.
Welsh, James R. Fundamentals of Plant Genetics & Breeding.
Welsh, Ken. Hitchhiker's Guide to Europe: The 1986 Guidebook for People on a Hitchhiking Budget.
Welsh, Robert P. Piet Mondrian's Early Career: The Naturalistic Periods.
Welsh, William, ed. Survey Research & Public Attitudes in Eastern Europe & the Soviet Union.

Welsingford, Horace H. How to Use the Sixteen Charts which Helped Jesse Livermore Make Three Times a Fortune in the Stock Market.
Welt, Leo G. ETCs, New Methods for U. S. Exporting.
Weltmer, S. A. Regeneration.
Weltner, W. Magnetic Atoms & Molecules.
Welton, David A. Realms of Teaching.
Welton, Harry. The Third World War.
Welty, Carl. The Life of Birds.
Welty, Eudora. Curtain of Green & Other Stories.
--Delta Wedding.
--The Golden Apples.
--One Writer's Beginnings.
--Ponder Heart.
--Robber Bridegroom.
--Robber Bridegroom.
--The Wide Net & Other Stories.
Welty, Joe. Welty's Book of Procedures for Meetings, Boards, Committees & Officers.
Wemp, C. Sumner. Guide to Practical Pastoring.
Wen, Cheng, jt. auth. see Zhiyan, Li.
Wen, Qi. China: An Introduction. Yicheng, Zhou, tr. from Chinese.
Wen, Zhang, ed. The Yellow Robe Monster.
Wenberg, Donald C. Blue Ridge Mountain Pleasures: An A-Z Guide to North Georgia, Western North Carolina & the Upcountry of South Carolina.
Wenckheim, Nicholas. Image & Likeness: A Play in Three Acts.
--Twelve Hundred Hostages: A Play in Seven Scenes. Lipp, Sylvia E., tr.
Wende, S., ed. Proceedings of the Eleventh Symposium Neuroradiologicum: Wiesbaden, June 4-10, 1978.
Wende, S., et al. Cerebral Magnification Angiography: Physical Basis & Clinical Results.
Wendel, Tim. Going for the Gold.
Wendelken, Claire. Children in & Out of Care. Davies, Martin, ed.
Wender, Paul H. & Klein, Donald F. Mind, Mood & Medicine: A Guide to the New Biopsychiatry.
Wender, Theodora. Knight Must Fall.
--Murder Gets a Degree.
Wendland, W., jt. auth. see Haack, W.
Wendling, Becky & Kirschner, Becky. Discovery to Discourse: The Composing Process.
Wendorf, Fred, ed. Contributions to the Prehistory of Nubia.
--The Prehistory of Nubia.
Wendorf, Fred & Close, Angela E., eds. Advances in World Archaeology.
Wendorf, Hulen D. & Schlueter, David A. Texas Rules of Evidence Manual.
Wendorf, Richard, ed. Articulate Images: The Sister Arts from Hogarth to Tennyson.
Wendt, F. W., et al, eds. Mechanics of Composite Materials: International Conference on the Mechanics & Chemistry & Solid Propellants.
Wendt, H. & Frosch, P. J. Clinico-Pharmacological Models for the Assay of Topical Corticoids.
Wendt, Herbert. Sex Life of the Animals.
Wendt, Ingrid, jt. ed. see Hedges, Elaine.
Wendt, Jo Ann. Beyond Surrender.
Wen Fong, jt. tr. see Rorex, Robert A.
Weng, Will. The Crosswords Club, The Third Year.
Wenger, Nanette K. & Hellerstein, Herman K. Rehabilitation of the Coronary Patient.
Wengert, Norman. The Political Allocation of Benefits & Burdens.
Wengler, Wilhelm & Tittel, Josef, eds. Documents of the Arab-Israel Conflict: The Resolutions of the United Nations Organization.
Wengrov, Charles. Jewish Symbols.
Wengrov, Charles, jt. auth. see Zaretsky, David.
Wengrow, C., tr. The Hafetz Hayyim on the Siddur.
Wenham, David. The Jesus Tradition Outside the Gospels.
--The Rediscovery of Jesus' Eschatological Discourse: Studies in the History of Gospel Traditions.
Wenham, David & Blomberg, Craig. The Miracles of Jesus.
Wenham, John. Easter Enigma: Are the Resurrection Accounts in Conflict?
Wenig, A., jt. ed. see Gaertner, W.
Wenk, H. R., et al, eds. Electron Microscopy in Mineralogy.
Wenk, Richard. Indiana Jones & the Eye of the Fates.
Wenk, Robert B. Coaching Youth Softball.
Wenkam, Robert. Kauai: Hawaii's Garden Island.
Wenming, Su, ed. China's Patent Law.
Wenner, H. A., et al. Echo Viruses. Bd. with Reoviruses. Rosen, L. Springer-Verlag.
Wennerstrom, Mary H. Anthology of Twentieth Century Music.
Wensel, Louise. Acupuncture in Medical Practice.
Wensinger, Arthur S., tr. see Modersohn-Becker, Paula.
Wensinger, Arthur S., tr. see Sembach, Klaus-Jurgen.
Wensley, G. F., jt. auth. see Keay, F.
Went, H. A. The Behaviour of Centrioles & the Structure & Formation of the Achromatic Figure.
Went, R. W., et al. Phytohormones.
Wentworth, Berttina B. & Judson, Franklyn N., eds. Laboratory Methods for the Diagnosis of Sexually Transmitted Diseases.
Wentworth, Thomas R., jt. auth. see Reynolds, James F.
Wentworth, Wayne, jt. auth. see Becker, Ralph S.
Wentworth, Wayne E., jt. auth. see Becker, Ralph S.
Wentzel, E. Operations Research: A Methodological Approach.
Wenxue, tr. see Shentao, Ye.
Wenzel, E. & Leipnitz, eds. Plasminogen: Function Assay & Clinical Significance.
Wenzel, George L. Motivation Training Manual.
Wenzel, Gertrude. Broken Star-the Warburgs of Altona: Their Life in Germany & Their Death in the Holocaust.
Wenzel, William J. Motivation Training Manual.
Wenzl, Michael, jt. auth. see Harrington, John.
Weores, Sandor & Juhasz, Fernec. Selected Poems. Wevill, Davis & Morgan, Edward, trs.
Werbach, Melvyn R. Third Line Medicine: Modern Treatment for Persistent Systems.
Werbel, Leslie M., jt. auth. see Thompson, Paul E.
Werbell, Frederick E. & Clarke, Thurston. Lost Hero: The Mystery of Raoul Wallenberg.
Werble, Beatrice, jt. auth. see Grinker, Roy R., Sr.
Werbner, R. P. Regional Cults.
Werdet, Edmond. Histoire du Livre en France depuis les Temps les Plus Recules Jusqu'en, 1789.
Werfel, Franz. Between Heaven & Earth. Newmark, Maxim, tr.
--Gedichte Aus Den Jahren 1908-1945.
Werkman, Sidney L. Role of Psychiatry in Medical Education: An Appraisal & a Forecast.
Werkman, Sidney L., intro. by see Casewit, Curtis.
Werkmeister, William H. A History of Philosophical Ideas in America.
Werley, Harriet, et al, eds. Health Research: The Systems Approach.
Werlich, David P. Research Tools for Latin American Historians: A Select, Annotated Bibliography.
Wermer, J. Potential Theory.
--Potential Theory.
Wernecke, Herbert H., ed. Celebrating Christmas Around the World.
Werner, Dennis. The Amazon Journey: An Anthropologist's Year Among Brazil's Mekranoti Indians.
--Anthropology: Study Guide & Workbook.
--Cultural Anthropology: Study Guide & Workbook.
Werner, Emmy E. Child Care: Kith, Kin & Hired Hands.
Werner, Floyd G. Common Names of Insects & Related Organisms.
Werner, Forman, jt. auth. see Bancroft-Hunt, Norman.
Werner, G. A., jt. auth. see O'Neal, James.
Werner, G. H. & Floc'h, F., eds. The Pharmacology of Immunoregulation: Present Concepts As a Basis for the Development of Immunopharmacological Agents.
Werner, Helmut, ed. see Spengler, Oswald.
Werner, R., jt. ed. see Scott, W. A.
Werner, Raymond J. Real Estate Closings.
Werner, William E., Jr., jt. auth. see Benton, Allen H.
Wernham, R. B. Before the Armada: The Emergence of the English Nation, 1485-1588.
Wernick, J. H., jt. auth. see Shay, J. L.
Wernick, Robert & Time-Life Books Editors. The Vikings.
Werning, Waldo J. Vision & Strategy for Church Growth.
Wersba, Barbara. The Country of the Heart.
--The Dream Watcher.
--Let Me Fall before I Fly.
--Run Softly, Go Fast.
Wersell, Thomas W. Spiritual Thoughts & Prayers.
Werstein, Irving. Eighteen Ninety-Eight: The Story of the Spanish American War & the Philippine Insurrection Told with Pictures.
--Eighteen Sixty-One to Eighteen Sixty-Five: The Adventure of the Civil War Told with Pictures.
Wert, Diane van see Van Wert, Diane.
Wert, William F. Van see Van Wert, William F.
Wertenbaker, Lael T. Death of a Man.
Wertenbaker, Thomas J. Father Knickerbocker Rebels: New York City During the Revolution.
--Middle Colonies.
Wertenschlag, Eva, ed. see Birkhauser, Kaspar.
Werth, Paul. Focus, Coherence & Emphasis.
Wertheim, Arthur F., ed. American Popular Culture: A Historical Bibliography.
Wertheim, Bill & Gonzalez, Irma, eds. Talkin' about Us: Writing by Students in the Upward Bound Program.
Wertheimer, Michael. A Brief History of Psychology.
Werther, William B. & Lockhart, Carol A. Labor Relations in the Health Professions.
Werthmann, Barbara U. Medical Malpractice Law: How Medicine Is Changing the Law.
Wertsman, Vladimir, ed. The Romanians in America & Canada: A Guide to Information Sources.
Wertsman, Vladimir, jt. ed. see Sokolyszyn, Aleksander.
Wertz, Dorothy C., jt. auth. see Miller, David M.
Weschcke, Carl L., jt. ed. see Buske, Terry.
Weschcke, Carl L., ed. see Godwin, David.
Weschler, Irving R. & Reisel, Jerome. Inside a Sensitivity Training Group.
Weschler, Lawrence, tr. see Krall, Hanna.
Weschler, Mary. Marriage & Family Law in Washington.
Wescombe, Christabel, jt. auth. see Cleverly, John F.
Wescott. Strength Fitness: Physiological Principles Training Techniques.
Wescott, Glenway. Grandmothers.
--The Grandmothers.
Wescott, Lynanne & Degen, Paula, eds. Wind & Sand: The Story of the Wright Brothers at Kitty Hawk.
Wescott, Patsy & Black, Leyardia. Alternative Health Care for Women.
Wescott, Steven D. Comprehensive Bibliography of Music for Film & Television.
Weske, Dorothy B. Convocation of the Clergy: A Study of Antecedents & Its Rise, with Special Emphasis upon Its Growth & Activities in the Thirteenth & Fourteenth Centuries.
Wesley, Mary. The Camomile Lawn.
--Harnessing Peacocks.
Wesley, Ralph E., ed. Techniques in Opthalmic Plastic Surgery.
Wesley-Hosford, Zia. Skin Care for Men Only: A Complete Guide.
Wesner, George M., jt. auth. see Culp, Russell L.
Wesner, Maralene & Miles, E. You Are What You Choose.
Wesner, Terry & Nustad, Harry L. Intermediate Algebra with Applications.
Wesp, Beverly M. Versatile Verse for a Rainy Afternoon.
Wessel, Helen. Natural Childbirth & the Christian Family.
Wessell, Leonard P. Karl Marx, Romantic Irony & the Proletariat: Studies in the Mythopoetic Origins of Marxism.
Wessells, Norman K. Tissue Interactions & Development.
Wessels, Norman K., ed. see Society for Developmental Biology Symposium Staff.
Wessels, Wolfgang, jt. auth. see Bulmer, Simon.
Wessler, Daniel B. & Wessler, M. Jenelyn. The Gifts of Silence.
Wessler, M. Jenelyn, jt. auth. see Wessler, Daniel B.
Wessman, A. E., jt. ed. see Gorman, B. S.
Wessman, James W. Anthropology & Marxism.
Wesson, Robert, ed. see Anderson, Thomas P.
Wesson, Robert G. Foreign Policy for a New Age.
West. To See the Dream.
--Witch Diggers.
West, Bonnie. An Airport Adventure.
--Mystery under the Big Top.
West, Bruce. Outrageously Yours: The Explosive West Letters.
West, Bruce J., jt. auth. see Lindenburg, Katja.
West, C. T., jt. ed. see Doyle, M. P.
West, Carl, jt. auth. see MacLean, Katherine.
West, Carolyn & West, Jack. Cruising the Pacific Coast: Acapulco to Skyway.
West, David & Wood, Glenn. Personal Financial Management.
West, Donald M., jt. auth. see Skoog, Douglas A.
West, E. G. Copper & Its Alloys.
West, Earl I. Search for the Ancient Order.
West, Elmer H. How to Sell a Dealership.
West, Emory. Housing Policy for the Nineteen Eighties.
West, G. F., jt. auth. see Grant, F. S.
West, Gary & Mills, William R. DAC-Easy Accounting & Payroll Made Easy.
West, George A. Copper: Its Mining & Use by the Aborigines of the Lake Superior Region.
West, J., ed. Alternatives in Development: Is Europe Responding to Third World Needs?
West, Jack, jt. auth. see West, Carolyn.
West, Jackie, ed. Work, Women, & the Labour Market.
West, James L., ed. Gyascutus: Studies in Antebellum Southern Humorous & Sporting Writings.
West, James L., III, jt. ed. see Casclato, Arthur D.
West, Jessamyn. Crimson Ramblers of the World, Farewell.
--Double Discovery.
--Except for Me & Thee.
--Except for Me & Thee.
--Hide & Seek.
--Leafy Rivers.
--The Life I Really Lived. Muller, Julian P., ed.
--Love, Death & the Ladies' Drill Team.
--The Massacre at Fall Creek.
--The Secret Look: Poems.
--To See the Dream.
--The Woman Said Yes: Encounters with Life & Death.
West, Joan B. Elvis: His Life & Times in Poetry & Lines.
West, John B. Everest: The Testing Place.
West, John F. Faroe: The Emergence of a Nation.
West, Karen. The Best of Polish Cooking: Recipes for Entertaining & Special Occasions.
West, Leonard J. Modern College Typewriting: A Basic Course.
--Modern College Typewriting: An Advanced Course.
West, Michael A. & Newton, Peggy. The Transition from School to Work.
West, Morris. Cassidy.
West, N. E. & Skujins, J., eds. Nitrogen in Desert Ecosystems.
West, Nigel, jt. auth. see Pujol, Juan.
West Publishing Co. Editorial Staff. Federal Rules of Civil Appellate & Supreme Court.
--Federal Rules of Criminal Procedure: 1986 Law School Edition.
--Selected Environmental Law Statutes.
West Publishing Company Staff. Bankruptcy Code, Rules & Official Forms: Law School & C.L.E. Edition, 1984 Edition Revision As Amended to July 10, 1984.
--Federal Rules of Civil-Appellate-Criminal Procedure: Law School Edition, 1982.
West, R. G., jt. auth. see Sparks, B. W.
West, R. G., jt. ed. see Birks, H. J.
West, Raeto. Programming the VIC-20.
West, Ranyard. Conscience & Society: A Study of the Psychological Prerequisites of Law & Order.
West, Rebecca. Black Lamb & Grey Falcon.
--Rebecca West: A Celebration.
--Strange Necessity: Essays.
West, Rebecca, ed. see Sandburg, Carl.
West, Richard & McVan, Barbara, eds. Giving Cardiac Care.
--Managing IV Therapy.
West, Robert. The Oxocarbons.
West, Robert C. Cultural Geography of the Modern Tarascan Area.
West, Robin. Paper Circus: How to Create Your Own Circus.
West, T. F., jt. auth. see Green, Maurice B.
West, T. F., jt. ed. see Sugden, T. M.
West, T. S., jt. ed. see Egan, H.
West, Thomas. Ted Hughes.
West, Trudy. Timber-Frame House in England.
West, Uta. If Love Is the Answer, What Is the Question?
--Women in a Changing World.
Westacott. Roger Bacon.
Westberg, Barbara. Christmas Plays. Wallace, Mary H., ed.
Westbrook, Bert W. Career Development Needs of Adults.
Westbrook, Perry. Mary Wilkins Freeman.
Westbury, Lord. Handlist of Italian Cookery Books.
Westcott, Edward N. David Harum.
Westcott, Jeanette. Paper Flower Sculpture.
Westcott, Ray D., jt. auth. see Fessler, George R.
Westerfield, jt. auth. see Ross.
Westerfield, H. Bradford. The Instruments of America's Foreign Policy.
Westerholm, Stephen, tr. see Gerhardsson, Birger.
Westerlin, Dan. Empty Hand, Loaded Gun: The Ultimate System for Close Combat.
Westerman, Claus. Old Testament & Jesus Christ. Kaste, Omar, tr.
--What Does the Old Testament Say About God? Golka, F. W., ed.
Westermann, Claus. Beginning & End in the Bible. Reumann, John, ed. Crim, Keith, tr. from Ger.
--Blessing: In the Bible & the Life of the Church. Brueggeman, Walter & Donahue, John R., eds. Crim, Keith, tr. from Ger.
--Creation. Scullion, John J., tr. from Ger.
--Genesis Accounts of Creation. Wagner, Norman E., ed.
--God's Angels Need No Wings. Scheidt, David L., tr.
--The Promises to the Fathers: Studies on the Patriarchal Narratives. Green, David E., tr. from Ger.
--The Structure of the Book of Job: A Form-Critical Analysis. Muenchow, Charles A., tr. from Ger.
--A Thousand Years & a Day.
Westermann, Claus, ed. Essays on Old Testament Hermeneutics.
Westermann, Claus & Mays, James L., eds. Essays on Old Testament Hermeneutics.
Western, J. S. & Hughes, Colin A. The Mass Media in Australia: Second Edition.

Authors

Western, John S., jt. ed. see Gross, Edward.
Western, Richard H., jt. ed. see Vonk, Hubertus J.
Western Writers of America. Water Trails West.
Western Writers of America Staff. The Women Who Made the West.
--The Women Who Made the West.
Westerveld, A. & Marin, G. Mammalian Cell Hybridization I.
Westervelt, A. B. & Westervelt, W. T. American Antique Weather Vanes.
Westervelt, W. T., jt. auth. see Westervelt, A. B.
Westfall, Gloria. French Official Publications.
Westheimer, Ruth. Doctor Ruth's Guide to Good Sex.
Westin, Ala F. & Salisbury, Stephan. Individual Rights in the Corporation: A Reader on Employee Rights.
Westin, Alan F., jt. auth. see Harris, Louis, & Associates Staff.
Westin, Alan F., ed. Information Technology in a Democracy.
Westin, Av. Newswatch: How TV Decides the News.
Westin, Jeane. Love & Glory: A Novel.
Westin, Jeane E. Finding Your Roots.
Westin, Richard A. & Neff, Alan H. Tax, Attacks, & Counterattacks: Your Indispensable Guide to Long-Range Tax Strategy.
Westing, Arthur, ed. The Environmental Modification Convention of 1977: A Technical, Legal & Policy Appraisal.
Westing, Harold J. Evaluate & Grow.
Westlake, Donald E. The Busy Body.
--God Save the Mark.
--The Spy in the Ointment.
Westlake, Ray, jt. auth. see Churchill, Colin.
Westland, Gordon. Current Crises of Psychology.
Westley, Bruce H. News Editing.
Westley, Margaret W., jt. auth. see Westley, William A.
Westley, William A. & Westley, Margaret W. The Emerging Worker: Equality & Conflict in the Mass Consumption Society.
Westmaas Research Group on New Tillage Systems Staff. Experiences with Three Tillage Systems on a Marine Loam Soil I: 1972-1975.
Westmacott, Mary. Absent in the Spring.
--The Burden.
Westmacott, Mary, pseud. The Burden.
Westmacott, Mary. A Daughter's a Daughter.
--A Daughter's a Daughter.
Westmacott, Mary, pseud. A Daughter's a Daughter.
Westmacott, Mary. Giants Bread.
Westmacott, Mary, pseud. Giant's Bread.
--Giants' Bread.
Westmacott, Mary. The Rose & the Yew Tree.
--The Rose & the Yew Tree.
--Unfinished Portrait.
--Unfinished Portrait.
Westmacott, Mary see Christie, Agatha, pseud.
Westman, Barbara. Anna's Magic Broom.
--The Bean & the Scene.
Westman, Barbara & Kenny, Herbert. A Boston Picture Book.
Westman, Paul. Andrew Young: Champion of the Poor.
--Jesse Jackson: I Am Somebody.
--John Young: Space Shuttle Commander.
--Thor Heyerdahl: Across the Seas of Time.
Westmeyer, Nancy. Parish Life: Manual for Spiritual Leadership Formation.
Weston, Drake. Guidebook for Alcoholics.
Weston, G. J., jt. auth. see Sherwin, E.
Weston, J. Fred & Brigham, Eugene F. Essentials of Managerial Finance.
--Managerial Finance.
Weston, Lee. Body Rhythm: The Circadian Rhythms Within You.
Weston, Paul B. The New Handbook of Handgunning.
--Supervision in the Administration of Justice: Police, Corrections, Courts.
Weston, Paul B. & Wells, Kenneth M. The Administration of Justice.
Weston, Wallace. The Manfred Selig Collection of European Drawings & Prints.
Westover, Madeline, et al. Home Cooking... On Your Own: Recipes for Students, Newlyweds, & Those Who Live Alone.
Westphal, jt. ed. see McLaughlin.
Westphal, Merold. History & Truth in Hegel's Phenomenology.
Westphal, Ruth, jt. auth. see Stern, Jean.
Westphal, U. Steroid-Protein Interactions.
Westrup, J. A. & Harrison, F. L. The New College Encyclopedia of Music.
Westrup, J. A. & Harrison, F. L., eds. New College Encyclopedia of Music.
Westrup, Jack A. Purcell.
--Purcell.
West's Editorial Staff. Bankruptcy Code, Rules & Forms, Including: Federal Rules of Civil Procedure & Federal Rules of Evidence, 1987 Edition.
--Bankruptcy Code, Rules & Official Forms, 1987.
Westveer, Douglas, jt. ed. see Timmis, Gerald.
Wetering, Janwillem van De see David-Neel, Alexandra & Yongden, Lama.
Wetering, Janwillem Van de see Van de Wetering, Janwillem.
Wetering, Janwillem Van De see Van De Wetering, Janwillem.
Wetering, Janwillem Van De see Van de Wetering, Janwillem.
Wetering, Janwillem Van De see Van De Wetering, Janwillem.
Wetering, Janwillem van de see Van de Wetering, Janwillem.
Wetering, Janwillem Van de see Van De Wetering, Janwillem.
Wetherbe, James C. Cases in Structured Systems Design.
--Systems Analysis & Design: Traditional Structured & Advanced Concepts & Techniques.
Wethered, H. H. Curious Art of Autobiography.
Wetherell, Charles, intro. by. For These or Such Like Reasons: John Holt's Attack on Benjamin Franklin.
Wetherell, W. D. Vermont River.
Wetherill, G. B., jt. auth. see Hine, J.
Wetherill, G. Barrie. Intermediate Statistical Methods.
--Intermediate Statistical Methods: Worked Solutions.
--Sequential Methods in Statistics.
Wetherill, Louisa W., jt. auth. see Gillmor, Frances.
Wetherill, Louisa Wade see Gillmor, Frances & Wetherill, Louisa W.
Wetmore, Donna, ed. Guidebook.
Wetmore, Ruth Y. First on the Land: The North Carolina Indians.
Wettereau, James O. Statistical Records of the First Bank of the United States. Bruchey, Stuart, ed.
Wetterer, Margaret K. Patrick & the Fairy Thief.
Wettlin, Margaret, tr. see Mossman, Elliot.
Wetzel. Lost Skiff.
Wetzel, Elizabeth. A Is for Aggravation: Alphabet Book.
Wetzel, Guy F. Automotive Diagnosis & Tune-up.
Wetzel, Ralph, jt. auth. see Tharp, Roland.
Wetzel, Robert G. & Likens, Gene E. Limnological Analyses.
Wever, E., jt. ed. see Van der Knapp, G. A.
Wever, Egbert, jt. ed. see Keeble, David.
Wevill, Davis, tr. see Weores, Sandor & Juhasz, Fernec.
Wewitt, Nancy A. Women's Activism & Social Change: Rochester, New York, 1822-1872.
Wexler, David A. & Rice, Laura N. Innovations in Client-Centered Therapy.
Wexler, Elizabeth, jt. auth. see Levine, Erwin L.
Wexler, Joyce. Laura Riding: A Bibliography.
Wexler, Philip. Critical Social Psychology.
Wexman, Virginia W. & Bisplinghoff, Gretchen. Roman Polanski: A Guide to References & Resources.
Weydemeyer, Winton. A Grange Master's America: In Defense of Freedom.
--Picture Taking in Glacier Park.
Weydenthal, Jan B. De see De Weydenthal, Jan B.
Weydenthal, Jan B. de see De Weydenthal, Jan B., et al.
Weygandt, Cornelius. Irish Plays & Playwrights.
Weygoldt, Peter. Biology of Pseudoscorpions.
Weyl, Adolph, ed. Die Jules Fonrobert'che Sammlung Mittel & Sudamerikanischer Munzen & Medaillen.
Weyl, Hermann. Philosophy of Mathematics & Natural Science.
Weyler, Rex. Blood of the Land.
Weyna, Kathy, jt. auth. see LeFever, Marlene.
WGBH Educational Foundation, Office of Radio & Television for Learning Staff. Working on Working.
Whalen, Carol K. & Henker, Barbara, eds. Hyperactive Children: The Social Ecology of Identification & Treatment.
Whalen, Doris H. Secretary's Handbook.
--The Secretary's Handbook: A Manual for Office Personnel.
--The Secretary's Handbook: A Manual for Office Personnel.
Whalen, George J., jt. auth. see Graf, Rudolf F.
Whalen, Michael, jt. auth. see Simon, Samuel A.
Whalen, Philip. On Bear's Head.
--On Bear's Head: Poems 1950-1967.
Whalen, Richard E., jt. ed. see Gorski, Roger A.
Whalen, Richard E., et al, eds. Neural Control of Behavior.
Whalen, William J. Minority Religions in America.
Whalen, William J., jt. auth. see Arden, Kelvin J.
Whaley, Bo. How to Love Yankees with a Clear Conscious.
Whaley, Douglas J. Warranties & the Practitioner.
Whaley, Julie, ed. Songwriter's Market '87.
--Songwriter's Market 88.
--Summer Employment Directory of the U. S. 1987.
Whaley, Keith, ed. Methods in Complement for Clinical Immunologists.
Whaley, Lucille F. & Wong, Donna L. Nursing Care of Infants & Children.
Whaling, Frank, ed. The World's Religious Traditions.
Whalley, Joyce. Historia Naturalis of Pliny.
Whalley, Joyce I. The Student's Guide to Western Calligraphy: An Illustrated Survey.
Wharton, C. & Sindoni, E., eds. Course in Diagnostics for Fusion Experiments: Proceedings of the Commission of the European Communities, Varenna, Italy, 1978.
Wharton, C. B., jt. auth. see Heald, M. A.
Wharton, Carolyn A. Rising Thunder.
Wharton, Edith. The Edith Wharton Omnibus.
--Ethan Frome.
--Ethan Frome.
--Fast & Loose: A Novelette by David Olivieri.
Wharton, James. Easter.
Wharton School Staff. The Wharton Annual: 1984.
Wharton, William. Pride.
Whatcom Museum of History & Art Staff. Arts of a Vanished Era.
--Green Gold Harvest: A History of Logging & Its Products.
--Whatcom Seascapes: The Influence of the Sea on Whatcom County.
Whatley, H. A., ed. British Librarianship & Information Science 1971-1975.
Whatley, Robert L. Honestly, I Love You, Douglas County.
Whatley, Thomas. Observations on Modern Gardening. Hunt, John D., ed.
Whatmore, D. E. H. Rider Haggard: A Bibliography.
Wheat, J. Maps & Charts Published in America Before 1800.
Wheat, Joe B. The Gift of the Spiderwoman: Southwestern Textiles.
Wheatcroft, Andrew. The World Atlas of Revolution.
Wheatcroft, Anita L. Promises.
Wheatcroft, Geoffrey. The Randlords: The Exploits & Exploitations of South Africa's Mining Magnates.
Wheatcroft, Harry, jt. auth. see Hessayon, D. G.
Wheatley, George. The Young Rider's Companion.
Wheatley, Henry B. Dedication of Books to Patron & Friend.
--Literary Blunders.
Wheatley, Paul & See, Thomas. From Court to Capital: A Tentative Interpretation of the Origins of the Japanese Urban Tradition.
Wheatly, Meg & Hirsch, Marcie S. Managing Your Maternity Leave.
Wheaton, Chistopher S. Primary Cinema Resources: An Index of Screen Plays, Interviews & Special Collections at the University of Southern California.
Wheaton, Margo. Sing a Song for Me.
Wheaton, Philip D. The Best is Yet to Be.
Wheaton, William C., ed. Interregional Movements & Regional Growth.
Whedon, Peggy. Always on Sunday.
Wheeler, Barry C. Modern Fighters & Attack Aircraft.
Wheeler, Bonnie. Challenged Parenting: A Practical Handbook for Parents of Children with Handicaps.
Wheeler, Brandon W., jt. auth. see Crowdis, David G.
Wheeler, C. C., jt. ed. see Gemme, Robert.
Wheeler, Cindy. Marmalade's Picnic.
Wheeler, Cork. First Book of Animal Life: First Nature Book.
Wheeler, Dennis, jt. auth. see Shaw, Gareth.
Wheeler, Diana S., jt. auth. see Levick, Myra.
Wheeler, Gerald, ed. see Behrman, Carol H.
Wheeler, Gerald, ed. see Byers, Carolyn.
Wheeler, Gerald, ed. see Davy, Yvonne.
Wheeler, Gerald, ed. see Doherty, Ivy D.
Wheeler, Gerald, ed. see Dudley, Roger L. & Cummings, Des, Jr.
Wheeler, Gerald, ed. see Kistler, Robert.
Wheeler, Gerald, ed. see Parker, Lois.
Wheeler, Gerald, ed. see Parker, Lois M.
Wheeler, Gerald, ed. see Pierson, Robert H.
Wheeler, Gerald, ed. see Smith, Reva A.
Wheeler, Gerald, ed. see Wallenkampf, Arnold V.
Wheeler, Gerald, ed. see Warren, Mervyn A.
Wheeler, Jacob D. Practical Treatise on the Law of Slavery.
Wheeler, John. Touched with Fire: The Future of the Vietnam Generation.
Wheeler, John, jt. auth. see Kuhaulua, Jesse.
Wheeler, Jon D. Tax Desk Book for Farming & Ranching.
Wheeler, Kenneth W. To Wear a City's Crown: The Beginnings of Urban Growth in Texas, 1836-1865.
Wheeler, Lynde P. Josiah Willard Gibbs: The History of a Great Mind.
Wheeler, Margariete M., ed. Mathematics Library: Elementary & Junior High School.
Wheeler, Michael. Divided Children: A Legal Guide for Divorcing Parents.
Wheeler, Michael, jt. auth. see Mayer, Andre.
Wheeler, Paul. Bodyline.
Wheeler, Paul T., jt. auth. see Loesch, Larry C.
Wheeler, Penny E. The Appearing.
Wheeler, R. Man, Nature & Art.
Wheeler, Robert C., et al. Voices from the Rapids: An Underwater Search for Fur Trade Artifacts, 1960-73.
Wheeler, Robert G., et al, eds. Intrauterine Devices: Development, Evaluation, & Program Implementation.
Wheeler, Russell R., jt. ed. see Levin, Leo A.
Wheeler, Ruth E. Ivory Palaces.
Wheeler, Stanton, jt. auth. see Brim, Orville G., Jr.
Wheeler, Susan. An Old Fashioned Country Christmas.
Wheeler, Tony. Australia: A Travel Survival Kit.
--Burma: A Travel Survival Kit.
--New Zealand-A Travel Survival Kit.
--Papua New Guinea: A Travel Survival Kit.
--South-East Asia on a Shoestring.
--Sri Lanka: A Travel Survival Kit.
--Sri Lanka Travel Survival Kit.
Wheeler, Tony, jt. auth. see Crowther, Geoff.
Wheeler, W. H., jt. auth. see Hirschfeld, J.
Wheeler, William A. Familiar Allusions: A Hand-Book of Miscellaneous Information.
Wheelis, Allen. The Doctor of Desire: A Novel.
--The Scheme of Things.
Wheelock, Arthur K., Jr. Perspecture, Optics, & Delft Artists Around Sixteen Fifty.
--Vermeer.
Wheelock, John H. By Daylight & in Dream: New & Collected Poems, 1904-1970.
--This Blessed Earth: New & Selected Poems 1927-1977.
Wheelwright, Richard, jt. ed. see Shaffer, Wm. D.
Wheelwright, S. C., ed. see Makridakis, S.
Whelan, A. & Brydson, J. A., eds. Developments with Thermosetting Plastics.
Whelan, Donald J., ed. Handbook for Development Officers at Independent Schools.
Whelan, Elizabeth. A Smoking Gun: How the American Tobacco Industry Gets Away with Murder.
Whelan, Elizabeth & Stare, Fredrick J. Panic in the Pantry.
Whelan, Elizabeth M. The Pregnancy Experience: The Psychology of Expectant Parenthood.
--Preventing Cancer.
--Preventing Cancer.
Whelan, Elizabeth M. & Stare, Fredrick J. The One Hundred Percent Natural, Purely Organic, Cholesterol-Free, Megavitamin, Low Carbohydrate Nutrition Hoax.
Whelan, James R. & Bozell, Patricia. Catastrophe in the Caribbean: The Failure of America's Human Rights Policy in Central America.
Whelan, John, ed. Oman: A Middle East Economic Digest Guide.
Whelan, John, ed. see Middle East Economic Digest Staff.
Whelan, John W., jt. auth. see York, Kenneth H.
Whelan, Michael. Michael Whelan's Works of Wonder.
Whelan, W. J., ed. see Conference on Recombinant DNA, Committee on Genetic Experimentation (COGENE) & the Royal Society of London, Wye College, Kent, UK, April, 1979.
Whelan, W. J., jt. ed. see Schultz, J.
Whelchel, L. H., Jr. My Chains Fell Off: William Wells Brown, Fugitive Abolitionist.
Wheldon, David. The Viaduct.
Wheldon, Huw, jt. auth. see Plumb, J. H.
Whelpton, Barbara. Getting to Know Pictures.
Whelton, Clark. CB Baby.
Whempner, R. J. Corporate Aviation.
Whendall, Kevin & Merrett, Frank, eds. Behaviour Analysis in Educational Psychology.
Wherly, Max S., jt. auth. see Newcomb, Robinson.
Wherry, Joseph H. MG: Sports Car Supreme.
Whetmore, Edward J. Mediamerica: Form, Content, & Consequence of Mass Communication.
Whetten, L. L. The Canal War: Four-Power Conflict in the Middle East.
Whetten, Lawrence L. New International Communism: The Foreign & Defense Policies of the Latin European Communist Parties.
Whetten, Lawrence L., ed. The Present State of Communist Internationalism.
Whichcote, Benjamin. The Works.
Whicher, Olive, jt. auth. see Adams, George.
Whiddington, R., jt. auth. see Crowther, J. G.
Whiffen, D. H., ed. Expression of Results in Quantum Chemistry.
Whincup, Michael. Consumer Legislation in U. K. & Ireland.
Whinney, jt. auth. see Ernst.
Whinney, Bob. The U-Boat Peril: An Anti-Submarine Commander's Story.
Whinston, Andrew B., jt. ed. see Ijiri, Yuji.
Whipple, A. & Time-Life Books Editors. The Racing Yachts.
Whipple, A. B. Storm.
Whipple, A. B. & Time-Life Books Editors. The Clipper Ships.

Authors

--Fighting Sail.
--The Whalers.
Whipple, Alan L. Research & the Library: A Student Guide to Basic Techniques.
Whipple, Beverly, jt. auth. see Ladas, Alice K.
Whipple, Chandler. The Indian & the White Man in New England.
Whipple, Thomas W., jt. auth. see Courtney, Alice E.
Whisenand, P. The Effective Police Manager.
Whisker, James B., tr. see Rosenberg, Alfred.
Whistance, Dennis J., jt. auth. see Sherwood, David R.
Whistler, Rex. AHA.
Whistler, Rex, jt. auth. see Larn, Richard.
Whistler, Roy L. & Paschall, Eugene F., eds. Starch: Chemistry & Technology. Incl. Vol. 1. Fundamental Aspects; Vol. 2. Industrial Aspects. Acad Pr.
Whistler, Roy L., et al, eds. Methods in Carbohydrate Chemistry, Vol. 9: Lipopolysaccharide Methods, General Methods.
Whistling, Carl F. & Hofmeister, Friedrich. Handbuch der Musikalischen Litteratur (the 1817 Edition & the Ten Supplements, 1818-27) Ratliff, Neil, intro. by. & intro. by.
Whitaker, Arthur P. Huancavelica Mercury Mine: A Contribution to the History of the Bourbon Renaissance in the Spanish Empire.
--Spain & Defense of the West: Ally & Liability.
--U. S. & the Independence of Latin America, 1800-1830.
Whitaker, Arthur P., ed. The U. S. & the Southern Cone: Argentina, Chile, Uruguay.
--The Western Hemisphere Idea: Its Rise & Decline.
Whitaker, Carl A. & Malone, Thomas P. The Roots of Psychotherapy.
Whitaker, Dorothy. Using Groups to Help People.
Whitaker, Dorothy S. & Lieberman, Morton A. Psychotherapy Through the Group Process.
Whitaker, E. A., et al. The Rectified Lunar Atlas.
Whitaker, George O. & Meyers, Joan. Dinosaur Hunt.
Whitaker, J. & Sons Ltd., ed. Cumulative Book List: Annual Volume, 1986.
--Whitaker's Children's Books in Print, 1987.
--Whitaker's Religious Books in Print, 1987.
Whitaker, John O., Jr., jt. auth. see Hamilton, William J., Jr.
Whitaker, Muriel. Arthur's Kingdom of Adventures: The World of Malory's Morte Darthur.
Whitaker, O'Kelly. Sister Death: Leader's Guide.
Whitaker, S. Fundamental Principles of Heat Transfer.
Whitaker, Thomas. Design of Piled Foundations.
--Tom Stoppard.
--Tom Stoppard.
Whitall, Hannah & Smith, Elisabeth E. The Christian's Secret of a Happy Life: Proven Word.
Whitbourne, Susan K. & Weinstock, Comilda. Adult Development: The Differentiation of Experience.
Whitburn, Joel. The Billboard Book of Top Forty Hits: 1955 to Present.
--The Billboard Book of Top Forty Hits: 1955 to Present.
--Billboard's Top One Thousand, 1955-1986.
--Billboard's Top Two Thousand: 1955-1985.
--Pop Annual, Nineteen Fifty-Five to Nineteen Seventy-Seven.
--Pop Annual 1955-1982.
--Top Country & Western Records, 1976.
Whitburn, Joel, compiled by. Top Country & Western Records Nineteen Forty-Nine to Nineteen Seventy-One.
Whitby, Martin, jt. auth. see Hodge, Ian.
Whitby, Max. Tomorrow's World: Space Technology.
Whitby, Sharon. The Savage Web.
Whitcomb, Edward A. Napoleon's Diplomatic Service.
Whitcomb, Esther K. About Bolton.
Whitcomb, Helen & Cochran, L. The Modern Ms.
Whitcomb, Helen & Lang, Rosalind. Charm: The Career Girls Guide to Business & Personal Success.
Whitcomb, John C. Origin of the Solar System.
--World That Perished.
Whitcomb, Joyce S. Dakota Skies.
--Magic Moments.
--Prairie Poet: This Land Called South Dakota & Other Poems.
--Sing Me a Song.
Whitcomb, Michael E. Normal Lung: Its Diseases.
Whitcoullls Publishers Staff, ed. The Birthday Party Book.
White. Index to American Jewish Archives I-XXIV.
White, tr. see Eikhenbaum, Boris.
White, Ada. Emergency Health Help: A Modern Grandma's Natural Guide to Health.
White, Agustus A., ed. see American Academy of Orthopedic Surgeons Staff.
White, Alan. The Long Fuse.
--The Long Midnight.
--Ravenswyke.
White, Albert B. Self-Government at the King's Command.
White, Alice. The Complete Nutrition Guide for You & Your Baby: From Pregnancy Through the First Three Years.
White, Alice P. The Dominant Firm: A Study of Market Power. Bateman, Fred, ed.
White, Allon. The Uses of Obscurity: The Fiction of Early Modernism.
White, Andrew D. Fiat Money Inflation in France.
White, Ann T. Eugene Debs: American Socialist.
White, Anne S. Healing Devotions.
White, Anthony G. American Architectural Iron: A Selected Bibliography.
--Architectural Daylighting: A Recent Bibliography.
--Architectural Drawings-Collections: A Selected Bibliography.
--Comparable Work & Equal Pay: A Bibliography.
--Energy Auditing for Commercial Buildings: A Selected Bibliography.
--Enterprise Zones: A Bibliographic Update.
--European Architectural Iron: A Selected Bibliography.
--Industrial Energy Conservation: A Selected Bibliography.
--Mayan Architecture: A Selected Bibliography.
--Municipal Bonding & Taxation.
--New Zealand Architecture: A Selected Bibliography.
--Primitive Architecture: A Selected Bibliography.
--Confidentiality Privacy Issues: A Bibliographic Update.
--Reforming Metropolitan Governments: A Bibliography.
--Swiss Architecture: A General Sourcelist.
White, Arnold. Efficiency & Empire. Searle, G. R., ed.
White, Arthur. Palaces of the People: A Social History of Commercial Hospitality.
White, Arthur H. Back School & Other Conservative Approaches to Low Back Pain.
White, Arthur H., jt. auth. see Mulry, Ray C.
White, B. Kirke, compiled by. Pittsylvania County Inventory: Circuit Court Clerk.
White, Barnetta M. On Becoming a Leader: Leadership Training for Women in Higher Education.
White, Beatrice. Essays & Studies, 1983.
White, Ben B. Falling Arches: The Case Against Federal Intervention in the Practice of Medicine.
White, Benjamin. Silver: Its History & Romance.
White, Bernard, et al. Cases in Organizations: Behavior, Structure, Processes.
White, Bessie F., tr. Nine One Act Plays from the Yiddish.
White, Betty. Betty White in Person.
White, Bettye, jt. auth. see Michels, Barbara.
White, Beverly. Bean Cuisine: A Culinary Guide for the Ecogourmet.
White, Burton L. The First Three Years of Life: A Guide to Physical, Emotional, & Intellectual Growth of Your Baby.
White, Burton L., et al. The Origins of Human Competence: The Final Report of the Harvard Preschool Project.
White, C. J. Consistency in Cognitive Social Behavior: An Introduction to Social Psychology.
White, C. M. Bases of Modern Librarianship.
White, Colin, jt. ed. see Paul, John R.
White, Collis H. Win or Lose? What You Should Know About the ERA.
White, D. How to Find Out about Iron & Steel.
White, D. C. & Thorson, John. The Kinetics of Muscle Contraction.
White, David M. The Affirmation of God: A World Treasury of Quotations about the Meaning of the Divine.
--The Search for God.
White, David O., jt. auth. see Fenner, Frank J.
White, Deborah G. Ar'n't I a Woman? Female Slaves in the Plantation South.
White, Donald D. Contemporary Perspectives in Organizational Behavior.
White, Donald H., jt. auth. see White, Harvey E.
White, Donald R. Electrical Noise & EMI Specifications.
--EMI Control Methodology & Procedures. Price, Edward R., ed.
--EMI Control Methods & Techniques.
--EMI Specifications, Standards & Regulations.
--EMI Test Methods & Procedures.
White, Donald R. & Duff, William G. EMI Prediction & Analysis Techniques.
White, Donald R., ed. see Carstensen, Russell V.
White, Donald R., ed. see Feher, Kamilo.
White, Donald R., ed. see Gard, Michael F.
White, Donald R., ed. see Herman, John R.
White, Donald R., ed. see Jansky, Donald M.
White, Donald R., ed. see Keiser, Bernhard E.
White, Dorothy, tr. see Pope John XXIII.
White, Douglas M. The Excellence of Exposition: Practical Procedure in Expository Preaching.
White, E. B. Charlotte's Web.
White, Eddie. Yesterday's Cake.
White, Edward J. Commentaries on the Law in Shakespeare.
White, Edward M. Writer's Control of Tone.
White, Elijah. Exorcism As a Christian Ministry.
White, Ellen. Passions.
White, Ellen G. Day of Benediction.
White, Elsberry V. The First Iron-Clad Naval Engagement in the World: The Merrimac & the Monitor.
White, Eric W. A History of English Opera.
--The Rise of English Opera.
--Stravinsky: His Life & Work.
White, Ernest G. Science & Singing.
White, Gail. The Last Eve.
White, George E. To Stand Alone.
White, Gifford. Eighteen-Forty Citizens of Texas: Land Grants.
--Eighteen Thirty Citizens of Texas.
White, Gilbert. Natural History of Selbourne.
--The Portrait of a Tortoise.
White, Gilbert F., jt. ed. see Holdgate, Martin W.
White, Gloria W. Personnel Program Appraisal Workbook.
White, H. P. Forgotten Railways: South-East England.
White, Harry A. Riding Bareback to Las Vegas.
White, Harvey E. & White, Donald H. Physics & Music.
White, Howard. Data File Handling for the IBM PC & XT.
White, J. Anthropology.
White, J. H. A Reference Book of Chemistry.
White, J. Lee. For Whom You Search.
White, Jack. Beach Hotels of the World. Hogan, David, ed.
White, James. Deadly Litter.
White, James G. The Nomad Queen.
White, James J. & Summers, Robert S. Handbook of the Law under the Uniform Commercial Code.
--Uniform Commercial Code.
White, James R. Successful Supervision.
White, Jay C. Pilots & Aircraft Owners Legal Guide.
White, Jeffrey R., ed. Products Liability: The First 25 Years.
--The Trial Lawyer & the Federal Rules of Evidence.
White, Jeremy J. Central Administration in Nigeria, Nineteen Fourteen to Nineteen Forty-Eight: The Problem of Polarity.
White, Jerry. The Power of Commitment.
--The Worst Street in North London: A Social History of Campbell, Bunk, Islington, Between the Wars.
White, Joe. Who's Number One.
White, John. The Aims of Education Restated.
White, John, et al. Tables for Statisticians.
White, John A. Siberian Intervention.
White, John S. Renaissance Cavalier.
White, John W. Re-Entry II.
White, John, Warren, Nineteen Thirty-Nine. Everything You Want to Know About TM Including How to Do It.
White, Julie E., ed. A Sociology Sampler.
White, K., jt. auth. see Bray, H. G.
White, Karol. What To Do When You Think You Can't Have a Baby.
White, Ken. Bookstore Planning & Design.
White, Kenneth S. Einstein & Modern French Drama: An Analogy.
White, Lawrence J. The Public Library in the Nineteen Eighties: The Problems of Choice.
White, Lawrence J., jt. ed. see Keenan, Michael.
White, Leonard D. The Federalists: A Study in Administrative History.
White, Leslie A. Evolution of Culture.
White, Linda S., ed. see Tennessee Nurses' Association Staff.
White, Lucia, jt. auth. see White, Morton.
White, Lynn K., jt. auth. see Brinkerhoff, David B.
White, M. Paul. Dead Man's Cache.
White, Margaret B. Portrait of Myself: Margaret Bourke-White.
White, Marjorie. Cordial Cookery.
White, Mark. You Must Remember This: Popular Songwriters, 1900-1980.
White, Mary. How to Make Baskets.
White, Mel, jt. auth. see Rothenberg, Marie.
White, Michael. Payment Systems in Britain.
White, Michael, jt. auth. see Golembiewski, Robert T.
White, Michelle J., ed. Nonprofit Firms in a Three-Sector Economy.
White, Minor. Mirrors-Messages-Manifestations.
White, Morgan, Jr. Las Vegas Trivia.
White, Morton & White, Lucia. The Intellectual Versus the City: From Thomas Jefferson to Frank Lloyd Wright.
White, Mosezelle, ed. see Williams, Hobie L.
White Mountain Guide Book Committee. AMC Guide to Mt. Washington & the Presidential Range.
White, Ned. Taking on Tomorrow.
White, Norman A. Financing the International Petroleum Industry.
White, O. R., et al, eds. The Solar Output & Its Variation.
White, Patricia. Beyond Domination: An Essay in the Political Philosophy of Education.
White, Paul. The Cool Pool.
--Donkey Wisdom.
--Famous Monkey Last Words.
--Jungle Doctor Meets Mongoose.
--Jungle Doctor's Fables.
--Jungle Doctor's Hippo Happenings.
--Jungle Doctor's Monkey Tales.
--Jungle Doctor's Rhino Rumblings.
--Jungle Doctor's Tug-of-War.
--Monkey Crosses the Equator.
--Monkey in a Lion's Skin.
--The Monkeys & the Eggs.
--Reflections of Hippo.
--Sweet & Sour Hippo.
White, Peter. The Past Is Human: Ancient Mysteries Explained.
White, Philip & Selvey, Nancy, eds. Let's Talk About Food.
White, Philip L. & Nagy, Margarita E., eds. Total Parenteral Nutrition.
White, R. E. The Answer Is the Spirit.
--The Mind of Matthew.
White, R. V., jt. auth. see Lackstrom, J. E.
White, Randall. Dark Caves, Bright Visions: Life in Ice Age Europe.
White, Ray L. Index to Best American Short Stories & O. Henry Prize Stories.
White, Richard, jt. auth. see Fidler, Isiah.
White, Richard N., et al. Structural Engineering.
White, Robert & Shimazu, Koichi. One World, One People: A Collection of Photographs & Essays on the Power of the Human Experience.
White, Robert G. Handbook of Industrial Infrared Analysis.
White, Robert S., jt. ed. see McGregor, Graham.
White, Rodney A. & Grundfest, Warren, eds. Lasers in Cardiovascular Disease.
White, Roger & Brockington, Dave. Tales Out of School.
White, Roger, tr. see Frege, Gottlob.
White, Rosemary, ed. Political Issues in Nursing: Past, Present & Future.
White, Ruth, jt. auth. see Ewan, Christine.
White, Ruthe. Today's Woman in Search of Freedom.
--Touch Me Again, Lord.
White, S. & Williamson, K. RN Medication Tips.
White, Samuel V. Here I Am: Forty-Five & Still Going.
White, Stewart E. Unobstructed Universe.
White, Stuart C., jt. auth. see Goaz, Paul W.
White, T. D., jt. auth. see Harris, J. M.
White, T. H. The Book of Merlyn.
--The Book of Merlyn: The Unpublished Conclusion to "The Once & Future King"
White, Theodore. Breach of Faith: Fall of Richard Nixon.
White, Theodore H. Breach of Faith: The Fall of Richard Nixon.
--Making of the President Nineteen Sixty.
--Making of the President Nineteen Sixty-Eight.
White, Tony. Animator's Workbook.
White, Trentwell M. & Elhmann, Paul W. Writers of Colonial New England.
White, Vernon S., ed. see Sawmill Clinic Staff.
White, W. Hale see also Rutherford, Mark.
White, Warren, ed. Plumes & Visibility.
White, William. Nathanael West: A Comprehensive Bibliography.
--Wilfred Owen, 1893-1918: A Bibliography.
White, William C., Jr., jt. auth. see Boskind-White, Marlene.
White, William F. Psychosocial Principles Applied to Classroom Teaching.
White, William G., jt. auth. see Cummins, D. Duane.
White, William H. The Revolution in Tanner's Lane, 1887. Wolff, Robert L., ed. Bd. with Miriam's Schooling, Eighteen Ninety. Garland Pub.
White, William H. see also Rutherford, Mark.
White, William L. Lost Boundaries.
--Lost Boundaries.
--They Were Expendable.
Whitebird, J., ed. see Bright, Susan.
White-Bowden, Susan. Everything to Live For.
Whitebread, Charles H. Criminal Procedure: An Analysis of Constitutional Cases & Concepts.
--Criminal Procedure, 1984 Supplement.
Whitebread, Charles H., 2nd, ed. Mass Production Justice & the Constitutional Ideal.
Whitehand, J., ed. The Urban Landscape: Historical Development & Management.
Whitehead. Quality Assurance in Clinical Chemistry.
Whitehead, Alfred N. An Enquiry Concerning the Principles of Natural Knowledge.
Whitehead, Alfred North. An Enquiry Concerning the Principles of Natural Knowledge.
Whitehead, Charles, et al. Reimos en Serio.

Whitehead, Evelyn E. & Whitehead, James D. Christian Life Patterns: The Psychological Challenges & Religious Invitations of Adult Life.
--Seasons of Strength: New Visions of Adult Christian Maturing.
Whitehead, James. Joiner.
Whitehead, James D., jt. auth. see Whitehead, Evelyn E.
Whitehead, John. Implementing the Electronic Office.
--Maugham: A Reappraisal.
--Planning the Electronic Office.
Whitehead, Ken, jt. auth. see Rickards, Barrie.
Whitehead, Laurence, jt. ed. see Foxley, Alejandro.
Whitehead, R. W., jt. auth. see Bell, E. C.
Whitehead, Raymond. Love & Struggle in Mao's Thought.
Whitehead, Ted. The Man Who Fell in Love with His Wife.
Whitehill, Robert, tr. see Megged, Aharon.
Whitehill, Walter M. & Kotker, Norman. Massachusetts: A Pictorial History.
--Massachusetts: A Pictorial History.
Whitehill, Walter M., jt. auth. see Electa-Rizzoli Staff.
Whitehill, Walter M., et al, eds. Boston Furniture of the Eighteenth Century.
Whitehous, Gary, ed. Microsoftware: Statistical Analysis.
Whitehouse, jt. auth. see Mendelson.
Whitehouse, Gary, ed. Microsoftware: Operations Research IBM.
Whitehouse, Gary, et al. IIE Microsoftware: Economic Analysis.
--IIE Microsoftware: Work Measurement.
Whitehouse, Michael, jt. auth. see Williams, Christopher J.
Whitehouse, Michael W., jt. ed. see Scherrer, Robert A.
Whitehouse, N. D., jt. auth. see Benson, Rowland S.
Whitehouse, P. B., jt. auth. see Thomas, David S.
Whitehouse, Patrick & Thomas, David S. The Great Western Railway: One Hundred Fifty Glorious Years.
Whitehouse, R. H., jt. ed. see Tanner, J. M.
Whitehouse, Robert A. & Beaudoin, Cathleen C. Port of Dover: Two Centuries of Shipping on the Cochecho.
Whitehouse, Roger. A London Album: 1840-1915.
Whitehouse, W. A. Christian Faith & the Scientific Attitude.
Whitehurst, Grover J. & Vasta, Ross F. Child Behavior.
Whitelaw, jt. auth. see Jackson.
Whitelaw, R. R. Marketing & Economics.
Whitelaw, Ralph T. Virginia's Eastern Shore: A History of Northampton & Accomack Counties.
Whiteley, George. Northern Seas, Hardy Sailors.
Whiteley, John M. Counseling Psychology: A Historical Perspective.
--The History of Counseling Psychology.
Whiteley, John M. & Flowers, John V. Approaches to Assertion Training.
Whiteley, John M. & Fretz, Bruce R. The Present & Future of Counseling Psychology.
Whiteley, John M., jt. auth. see Ellis, Albert.
Whiteley, John M., jt. auth. see Erickson, V. Lois.
Whiteley, John M., jt. auth. see Loxley, Janet C.
Whiteley, John M., et al. The Coming Decade in Counseling Psychology.
Whiteley, Sandy, ed. ACRL University Library Statistics 1983-84.
--Reference Books Bulletin, 1985-1986.
Whitely, Rocky. Crazy Charlie's Crew.
Whiteman, Gloria. The Tree You Can Never Climb.
Whiten, Faith & Whiten, Geoff. The Chelsea Flower Show.
--Creating a New Garden.
Whiten, Geoff, jt. auth. see Whiten, Faith.
Whiteside, I. W. Sharon's UFO Code for Outer Space.
Whiteside, R., ed. Major Companies of Scandinavia 1985.
--Major Energy Companies of Western Europe 1985.
--Major Financial Institutions of Continental Europe 1985.
Whiteside, R. M., ed. Major Companies of Europe 1986: Austria, Finland, Liechtenstein, Norway, Sweden, Switzerland.
--Major Companies of Europe 1986: Belgium, Denmark, Erie, France, Germany, Greece, Italy, Luxembourg, the Netherlands, Portugal, Spain.
--Major Companies of Europe 1986: United Kingdom.
Whiteside, Thomas. An Agent in Place: The Wennerstrom Affair.
--The Investigation of Ralph Nader.
--Selling Death: Cigarette Smoking & Advertising.
Whitfield, Clovis & Martineau, Jane, eds. Painting in Naples: From Caravaggio to Giordano.
Whitfield, I. C. Electrical Installations Technology.
Whitfield, Philip. The Animal Family: The Fascinating Variety of Parenthood, from the Courtship Displays to the Day the Children Leave Home.
Whitfield, Phillip. The Hunters.
Whitfield, Raoul. Death in a Bowl.
Whitfield, Roderick. The Art of Central Asia: The Stein Collection in the British Museum, Textiles, Sculpture & Other Arts.
--In Pursuit of Antiquity.
Whitford & Foster. Concise Dictionary of American Grammar & Usage.
Whitford, Frank. Arts & Crafts of Turkestan: Bauhaus.
--Oskar Kokoschka: A Life.
Whiting, Charles E. Nathaniel Lord Crewe, Bishop of Durham, 1674-1712, & His Diocese.
--Studies in English Puritanism from the Restoration to the Revolution, 1660-1688.
Whiting, D. P. Finance of International Trade.
Whiting, F. B. Grit, Grief & Gold.
Whiting, H. T. Acquiring Ball Skill.
Whiting, John. A Penny for a Song: A Comedy.
Whiting, John & Bottomley, Tom. Chapman's Log & Owner's Manual.
Whiting, Oliver K. Open Your Eyes to Opportunity.
Whiting, Robert. The Chrysanthemum & the Bat: Baseball Samurai Style.
Whiting, Robert B. Estey Reed Organs on Parade: A Pictorial Review of the Many Parlour, Boudoir, Philharmonic, & Other Types of Reed Organs Made Over a 100-Year Period by the Famous Estey Organ Company, Together with a Brief Corporate History.
Whitley, Dianna, jt. ed. see Zeman, Jacklyn.
Whitley, Richard, ed. Social Processes of Scientific Development.
Whitley, Richard, et al. Masters of Business.
Whitlock, Brand. J. Hardin & Son. Miller, Paul W., ed.
Whitlock, Dave. Dave Whitlock's Guide to Aquatic Trout Foods.
--L. L. Bean Fly-Fishing Handbook.
Whitlock, Francis A., et al. Amphetamines: Medical & Psychological Studies.
Whitlow, David, jt. auth. see Peck, David.
Whitman, Alfred. Print Collector's Handbook.
Whitman, C. I., jt. ed. see Aqua, E. N.
Whitman, Cedric H. Abelard.
--Homer & the Heroic Tradition.
Whitman, Dale, jt. auth. see Nelson, Grant.
Whitman, David, et al. A Place Apart: Canaveral National Seashore.
Whitman, G. B. Lectures on Wave Propagation.
Whitman, Gweneth G., jt. ed. see Hall, Elizabeth S.
Whitman, H. S., tr. see Mendax, F.
Whitman, J. Russ. Loco the Burro & Ali the Jungle Beasts: A Story Poem for Children.
Whitman, John. The Best European Travel Tips.
Whitman, Malcolm D. Tennis Origins & Mysteries.
Whitman, Marina v. N. International Trade & Investment: Two Perspectives.
Whitman, Richard F. & Boase, Paul H. Speech Communication: Principles & Contexts.
Whitman, Robert V., jt. auth. see Lambe, T. William.
Whitman, Walt. Illustrated Leaves of Grass. Chapnick, Howard, ed.
--Leaves of Grass.
--Leaves of Grass: Comprehensive Reader's Edition. Bradley, Sculley, et al, eds.
Whitman, William & Johnson, William. Refrigeration & Air Conditioning Technology: Concepts, Procedures & Troubleshooting Techniques.
Whitmarsh, Katherine. A Concordance to the Gospel of Sri Ramakrishna.
Whitmarsh, W. F. Cours Superieur.
Whitmore, Charles. Winter's Daughter.
Whitmore, D. A. & Ibbetson, J. The Management of Motivation & Remuneration.
Whitmore, George. Nebraska.
--Someone Was Here: Profiles in the AIDS Epidemic.
Whitmore, Jacqueline, jt. auth. see O'Connell, April.
Whitmore, Joanne R. & Maker, C. June. Intellectual Giftedness in Disabled Persons.
Whitmore, R. L. Coal in Queensland: The First Fifty Years.
--Coal in Queensland: The Late Nineteenth Century.
--Rheology of the Circulation.
Whitmoyer, C. W., Sr. Your Health Is What You Make It: A Guide for Diet, Vitamin Supplementation, Cholesterol Control, Exercise, Mental Health, and Longevity.
Whitnah, Dorothy L. Outdoor Guide to the San Francisco Bay Area.
Whitnall, Ernest S. The Anatomy of the Human Orbit & Accessory Organs of Vision.
Whitney, Arthur H. Colloquial Hungarian.
Whitney, C. E. Discovering Cinque Ports.
Whitney, Charles A. Whitney's Star Finder: Revised for 1982 Through 1985.
Whitney, David C. American Presidents.
Whitney, Eleanor N. & Cataldo, Corrine. Understanding Normal & Clinical Nutrition.
Whitney, Fred, jt. auth. see Taylor, Benjamin J.
Whitney, Frederick C., jt. auth. see Black, Jay.
Whitney, George D., jt. auth. see Whitney, Leon F.
Whitney, Gleaves. Colorado Front Range: A Landscape Divided.
Whitney, Henry J. Foreword by see Smith, Leta May.
Whitney, James P. Reformation Essays.
Whitney, John. Digital Harmony: On the Complementarity of Music & Visual Art.
Whitney, John R. & Howe, Susan W. Religious Literature of the West.
Whitney, Leon F. & Whitney, George D. Complete Book of Cat Care.
Whitney, Mary, jt. auth. see Philp, Richard.
Whitney, Maurice. Backgrounds in Music Theory.
--One Hundred Fifty Progressive Exercises for Melodic Dictation.
Whitney Museum of American Art Staff. Catalog of the Library of the Whitney Museum of American Art.
--Selections from the Permanent Collection.
Whitney, Norman see Milne, John.
Whitney, Phyllis A. Dream of Orchids.
--The Fire & the Gold.
--Flaming Tree.
--Flaming Tree.
--The Golden Unicorn.
--Mystery of the Crimson Ghost.
--Mystery of the Golden Horn.
--Mystery of the Green Cat.
--Mystery of the Haunted Pool.
--Mystery of the Scowling Boy.
--Secret of Haunted Mesa.
--Secret of the Emerald Star.
--Secret of the Stone Face.
--Vanishing Scarecrow.
Whitsett, Dan D. Does Prayer Make a Difference?
Whitsett, David A. & Yorks, Lyle. From Management Theory to Business Sense: The Myths & Realities of People at Work.
Whitsitt, Robert E., II & Bryan, Lana K. Illustrated Microsoft Windows 1.03.
Whitsitt, William T. The Last Prophet.
Whitson, Skip, compiled by. Old Long Island.
Whitt, Angela Y., jt. auth. see Walke, Jerry L.
Whitt, Don, ed. Basic Automotive Troubleshooting.
Whittaker. History of the Theories of Aether & Electricity.
Whittaker, James K. Social Treatment: An Approach to Interpersonal Helping.
Whittaker, James O. Introduction to Psychology: Student's Workbook.
Whittaker, Robert H. & Levin, Simon A., eds. Niche: Theory & Application.
Whittaker, Roger, jt. auth. see Sanders, Irwin T.
Whittaker, W., jt. auth. see McLachlan, K. S.
Whittemore, Adrian C. The Discoveries of Christ & the Destinies of Mankind.
Whittemore, Edward. Jericho Mosaic.
--Jerusalem Poker.
--Nile Shadows.
--Sinai Tapestry.
--Sinai Tapestry.
Whitten & Bentley. Systems Analysis & Design Methods.
--Systems Analysis & Design Methods: International Edition.
--Using Excelerator for System Analysis & Design.
Whitten, et al. Systems Analysis & Design Methods.
Whitten, Anthony J., et al. The Ecology of Sumatra.
Whitten, Kenneth W. & Gailey, Kenneth D. General Chemistry with Qualitative Analysis.
--Problem Solving in General Chemistry.
Whitten, Les. A Day Without Sunshine.
Whitten, Mary E. Creative Pattern Practice: A New Approach to Writing.
--Decisions, Decisions: Style in Writing.
Whitten, Mary E., jt. auth. see Hodges, John C.
Whitten, Tony. The Gibbons of Siberut.
Whittenburg, Clarice & Stinneford, Carol. Wyoming's People.
Whittenburg, Ruth S. Time for Everything Under the Sun.
Whittick. European Architecture in the Twentieth Century, 1924-33.
Whittier, John Greenleaf. The Supernaturalism of New England. Wagenknecht, Edward, ed.
Whittingham, C. P. Chemistry of Plant Processes.
--Photosynthesis. Head, J. J., ed.
Whittingham, M. S., jt. ed. see Libowitz, G. G.
Whittingham, Richard. Sports Places Rated.
--The White Sox: A Pictorial History.
Whittington, Dorothy, jt. ed. see Ellis, Roger.
Whittington, Herschel & Whittington, Ray. Step-by-Step Guide: Carburetor Tuneup & Overhaul.
Whittington, Ray, jt. auth. see Whittington, Herschel.
Whittington, Stephen N. The Psychology of Murder & of Murderers.
Whittle, Frank. Jet.
Whittle, John G. Readings in Human Behavior.
Whittlesey, Marietta. Killer Salt.
Whittlesey, Marjorie T. Ilma Ruth Aho: Worker in His Field.
Whittmore, Charles. Winter's Daughter: The Saying of Signe Ragnhilds-Datter, A Novel.
Whittow, G. Causey, ed. Comparative Physiology of Thermoregulation.
Whitwell, David. A New History of Wind Music.
Whitworth, J. A., jt. ed. see Kincaid-Smith, P. S.
WHO Staff. Fish & Shellfish Hygiene.
Wholey, Dennis. Are You Happy? Some Answers to the Most Important Question in Your Life.
--The Courage to Change: Hope & Help for Alcoholics & Their Families.
--The Courage to Change: Personal Conversations about Alcoholism.
Wholey, Joseph S., et al. Federal Evaluation Policy: Analyzing the Effects of Public Programs.
Whordley, Derek, jt. auth. see Caballero, Jane A.
Whorlow, R. W. Rheological Techniques.
Whorton, Joseph W., Jr. & Morgan, David R. Measuring Community Performance: A Handbook of Indicators.
Whyard, Florence. Canadian Bush Pilot: Ernie Boffa.
Whybark, D. Clay, jt. auth. see Vollman, Thomas E.
Whyburn, G. & Duda, E. Dynamic Topology.
Whyld, Ken. Chess: The Records.
Whymper, Edward. Scrambles Amongst the Alps.
--Travels Amongst the Great Andes of the Equator.
Whynes, David, jt. ed. see Bean, Philip.
Whyte, Arthur J. Evolution of Modern Italy.
--The Political Life & Letters of Cavour, 1848-1861.
Whyte, Frederic. Life of W. T. Stead.
Whyte, M. B., jt. auth. see Prins, H. A.
Whyte, Malcolm, ed. Gorey Cats Paper Dolls.
Whyte, W. S. & Powell-Smith, Vincent. The Building Regulations Explained & Illustrated.
Whyte, William F., jt. auth. see Nunez Del Prado, Oscar.
Wiarda, Howard & Kline, Harvey F. Latin American Politics & Development.
Wibbelsman, Charles, jt. auth. see McCoy, Kathy.
Wibberley, Leonard. Guarneri: Story of a Genius.
Wibberley, Mary. The Whispering Gate.
Wiberg, Hugh. Backyard Vegetable Gardening for the Beginner.
Wichern, Dean W., jt. auth. see Johnson, Richard A.
Wichmann, B. ALGOL Sixty Compilation & Assessment.
Wichmann, Rudolf, tr. see Luxemburg, Rosa & Bukharin, Nikolai.
Wick, Alexander, jt. auth. see Dolphin, David.
Wick, Esther E. River in Winter & Other Poems.
Wicke, D. Lucinda. Thekla.
Wicken, Anthony, jt. ed. see Shockman, Gerald.
Wickens, James F. Colorado in the Great Depression. Freidel, Frank, ed.
Wicker, Brian. Toward a Contemporary Christianity.
Wicker, Tom. Kennedy Without Tears: The Man Beneath the Myth.
Wickesberg, Albert K. Management Organization.
Wickett, Ann, jt. auth. see Humphry, Derek.
Wickham, T. F. Seamanship.
Wickler, Wolfgang. Mimicry in Plants & Animals.
Wicklund, Robert A., jt. auth. see Duval, Shelley.
Wickman, Frans E., ed. see Royal Swedish Academy of Sciences Staff.
Wickman, Peter M. & Dailey, Timothy E. White Collar & Economic Crime: Multidisciplinary & Cross-National Perspectives.
Wickner, Reed B., ed. DNA Replication & Biosynthesis.
Wickramasinghe, Chandra, jt. auth. see Hoyle, Fred.
Wickremasinghe, Walter, ed. Scholarships & Grants for Study or Research in U. S. A. A Scholarship Handbook for Foreign Nationals.
Wicks, A. A. Tools & Techniques for Electronics.
Wicks, Robert J. Guard! Society's Professional Prisoner.
Wickstrom, Jean. Our Best Recipes.
Wickstrom, Ralph L. Fundamental Motor Patterns.
Wicomb, Zoe. You Can't Get Lost in Capetown.
Widder, D. V. Transform Theory.
Widder, Keith R. Mackinac National Park, 1875-1895. Armour, David A., ed.
Widdop, B., ed. Therapeutic Drug Monitoring.
Wideman, John E. Brothers & Keepers.
--The Homewood Trilogy.
Widgery, Alban G. Interpretations of History: Confucius to Toynbee.
Widicus, Wilbur W. & Stitzel, Thomas E. Personal Investing.
Widmark, E. M. Principles & Applications of Medicolegal Alcohol Determination.

Authors

Widmer, Patricia P. Pat Widmer's Cat Book: Straight Talk for City & Suburban Cat Owners.
Widner, Ellis & Carter, Walter. The Oak Ridge Boys: Our Story.
Wiebe, Dallas. The Transparent Eyeball & Other Stories.
Wiebe, Robert H. The Segmented Society: An Introduction to the Meaning of America.
Wieckert, Jeanne E. & Bell, Irene W. Media-Classroom Skills: Games for the Middle School.
Wieczynski, J. L., ed. Modern Encyclopedia Russia & Soviet History.
Wied, George. Introduction to Quantitative Cytochemistry.
Wied, George & Bahr, Gunter F. Introduction to Quantitative Cytochemistry, 2.
Wiedemann, Hans G. Thermal Analysis. Vol. I: Theory Instrumentation-Applied Sciences Industrial-Applications.
Wiedemann, Thomas. Greek & Roman Slavery: A Source Book.
Wiedenhoeft, Ronald V. Cities for People.
Wieder, H. H. Intermetallic Semiconducting Films.
--Laboratory Notes on Electrical & Galvano-Magnetic Measurements.
Wieder, Laurance, ed. see Sisskind, Mitch.
Wieder, Laurance, ed. see Wegman, William.
Wieder, Sol. The Foundations of Quantum Theory.
Wiederhold, Gio. Database Design.
Wiederhold, Richard. Electrocardiography: The Monitoring Lead.
Wiederholt, J. Lee, et al. The Resource Teacher: A Guide to Effective Practices.
Wiederholt, Wigbert C., ed. Neurology for Non-Neurologists.
Wiedmann, August. Romantic Art Theories.
Wiedmann, August K. Romantic Roots in Modern Art.
Wiegert, Richard G., ed. Ecological Energetics.
Wiegner, Kathleen. Encounters.
Wieland, O., et al, eds. see Konferenz der Gesellschaft Deutscher Naturforscher und Aerzte Staff.
Wielgolaski, F. E., et al, eds. Fennoscandian Tundra Ecosystems, Pt. 2: Animals & Systems Analysis.
Wieman, Henry N. Religious Experience & Scientific Method.
Wien, Barbara J., ed. Peace & World Order Studies: A Curriculum Guide.
--Peace & World Order Studies: A Curriculum Guide.
Wiencke, Gustav K., ed. Christian Education in a Secular Society.
Wiener, A. Patterns of Control in Post-Industrial Society: Magnificent Myth.
Wiener, Harvey & Bazerman, Charles. Reading Skills Handbook.
Wiener, Harvey S. Any Child Can Write: How to Improve Your Child's Writing Skills.
--Creating Compositions. Butcher, Phillip A., ed.
Wiener, Harvey S. & Bazerman, Charles. English Skills Handbook: Reading & Writing.
--Reading Skills Handbook.
Wiener, Howard J., jt. auth. see Hardy, C. Colburn.
Wiener, Leigh. Leigh Wiener: Memoir of a Master Photojournalist.
Wiener, Matthew B., jt. auth. see Romano, Joseph A.
Wiener, N. see Wiener, Norbert & Schade, J. P.
Wiener, Norbert. Time Series.
Wiener, Norbert & Schade, J. P. Progress in Biocybernetics. Incl. Vol. 1; Vol. 2. Progress in Biocybernetics. Wiener, N. & Schade, J., eds.; Vol. 3. Elsevier.
Wiener, R. & Christian, R. Insolvency Accounting.
Wiener, Solomon. The High School Graduate Guide for Scoring High on Civil Service Tests.
--How to Take & Pass Simple Tests for Civil Service Jobs.
--Officer Candidate Tests.
--Questions & Answers on American Citizenship.
Wieniewska, Celina, tr. see Kusniewicz, Andrezej.
Wiens, Grace. Unto You & to Your Children.
Wiens, Thomas B. The Microeconomics of Peasant Economy: China 1920-1940. Myers, Ramon H., ed.
Wier, Allen. Departing As Air.
Wiercinski, F. J; see Small, J.
Wiersbe, Warren. Five Secrets of Living.
--My Favorite Verse.
--Thoughts for Men on the Move.
Wiersbe, Warren W. A Basic Library for Bible Students.
--Listen! Jesus Is Praying.
--Windows on the Parables.
Wiersbe, Warren W., ed. Giant Steps.
Wiersbe, Warren W., ed. see Marchant, James.
Wiersma, C. A., ed. Invertebrate Neurons & Behavior.
Wiersma, William, jt. auth. see Lemke, Elmer.
Wiersum, Beverly. The Story of Easter for Children. Kuse, James A., ed.
Wierwille, Victor P. Power for Abundant Living.
Wiese, Edna E., jt. auth. see Schaad, Esther C.
Wiesel, Elie. The Accident. Borchardt, Ann, tr.
--Dawn.
--Five Biblical Portraits.
--Gates of the Forest.
--Legends of Our Time.
--Night.
Wiesel, Elie, ed. The Golem: The Story of a Legend. Borchardt, Anne, tr.
Wieseltier, Leon. Nuclear War, Nuclear Peace.
Wiesendanger, M. Pathophysiology of Muscle Tone.
Wiesner, E. & Willer, S. Lexikon der Genetik der Hundekrankheiten.
Wiesner, William. Hansel & Gretel.
--Turnabout.
Wiesner, William, compiled by. How Silly Can You Be? A Book of Jokes.
Wiesnet, Eugen, jt. auth. see Lubkoll, Hans-Georg.
Wietzke, Walter E., tr. see Holl, Karl.
Wietzke, Walter R. Believers Incorporated: The Message of Ephesians for Evangelical Outreach.
Wietzke, Walter R., tr. see Holl, Karl.
Wiffen, F. W. & Spitznagel, J. A., eds. Advanced Techniques for Characterizing Microstructures.
Wigander, K., et al. Structured Analysis & Design of Information Systems.
Wigfield, Jack. First Steps in Reading & Writing.
Wiggert, Djimitri. Error-Control Coding & Applications.
Wiggin, Kate D. The Birds' Christmas Carol.
--Rebecca of Sunnybrook Farm.
Wiggins, Arthur W. Physical Science with Environmental Applications.
Wiggins, Gary. English Language Sources for Reference Questions Related to Soviet Science (with an Emphasis on Chemistry)
Wiggins, James. Tested Practices: Organizing a School Counseling Program - the Priority: Career Counseling Program.
Wiggins, Marianne. Babe.
Wigginton, Eliot. Foxfire.
Wigginton, Eliott. Foxfire Books.
Wigglesworth, jt. auth. see Pape.
Wight, Denman B. Androscoggin River Valley: Gateway to the White Mountains.
Wight, Martin. Power Politics. Bull, Hedley, ed.
Wight, Oliver W. Production & Inventory Management in the Computer Age.
Wightman, A. S. & Sharp, D. H., eds. Local Currents & Their Applications.
Wightman, A. S., ed. see International School of Mathematical Physics Staff.
Wightman, A. S., jt. ed. see Velo, G.
Wiginton, John C., jt. auth. see Neave, Edwin H.
Wigley, C. B., jt. ed. see Franks, L. M.
Wigner, Eugene P., ed. Dispersion Relations & Their Connection with Causality.
Wijdeveld, Paul. The House Wittgenstein Built.
Wijesinha, Rajiva. The Androgynous Trollope: Attitudes to Women Amongst Early Victorian Novelists.
Wijeyewardene, Gehan, tr. see Khammaan, Khonkhai.
Wijkmark, Carl H. The Hunters of Karinhall.
Wijngaards, J. N. Did Christ Rule Out Women Priests?
Wijngaards, John. Handbook to the Gospels: A Guide to the Gospel Writings & the Life & Times of Jesus.
Wikan, Unni. Behind the Veil in Arabia: Women in Oman.
Wikler, Madeline, jt. auth. see Groner, Judye.
Wikler, Madeline, jt. auth. see Saypol, Judyth R.
Wilansky, Albert. Modern Methods in Topological Vector Spaces.
Wilber, C. K. & Jameson, K. P., eds. Socialist Models of Development.
Wilber, Donald N. Persepolis - The Archaeology of Persa, Seat of the Persian Kings.
--Riza Shah Pahlavi: The Resurrection & Reconstruction of Iran 1878-1944.
Wilber, Ken, et al. Transformations of Consciousness: Conventional & Contemplative Developmental Approaches.
Wilberforce, William. Journey to the Lake District from Cambridge: A Summer Diary, 1779. Wrangham, C. E., ed.
Wilbert, Johannes. Folk Literature of the Chamacoco Indians.
Wilbraham, Antony & Matta, Michael. Introduction to Organic & Biological Chemistry.
Wilbur, Charles J., ed. see Gross, Rosalind L.
Wilbur, Karl M., jt. ed. see Watabe, Norimitsu.
Wilbur, M. E., tr. see Dumas, Alexandre.
Wilbur, Marguerite E. Thomas Jefferson: The Apostle of Liberty.
Wilbur, Richard. The Mind-Reader.
--Opposites.
--Opposites: Poems & Drawings.
--Responses: Prose Pieces, 1948-1976.
--Walking to Sleep: New Poems & Translations.
--Walking to Sleep: New Poems & Translations.
Wilbur, Richard & Racine. Andromache.
Wilbur, Richard, tr. The Learned Ladies.
--Moliere: Four Comedies.
Wilbur, Richard, tr. see Racine, Jean.
Wilbur, William H. Russian Communism.
Wilburn, Kathy, illus. The Gingerbread Boy.
Wilburn, Michael D. & Gladstone, Robert M. Optimizing Development Profits in Large Scale Real Estate Projects.
Wilby, C. B. Design Graphs for Brick-Block Double Skin Panel Walls.
Wilby, Kevin, ed. The Lemegetton: A Medieval Manual of Solomonic Magic.
Wilckens, Ulrich. Resurrection. Stewart, A. M., tr. from Ger.
Wilcox, Brian, et al. The Preparation for Life Curriculum.
Wilcox, Clair, et al. Economies of the World Today: Their Organization, Development & Performance.
Wilcox, D. & Masse, W. B., eds. The Protohistoric Period in the North American Southwest, A. D. 1470-1700.
Wilcox, Donald J. In Search of God & Self: Renaissance & Reformation Thought.
Wilcox, Francis O. & Marcy, Carl M. Proposals for Changes in the United Nations.
Wilcox, Gary, et al, eds. see ICN-UCLA Symposia Staff.
Wilcox, J. C. see Walters, Richard F., et al.
Wilcox, John A. Leaf Beetle Host Plants in Northeastern North America: Coleoptera: Chrysomelidae.
Wilcox, John A. & Arnett, Ross H., Jr. Checklist of the Beetles of North & Central America & the West Indies: The Leaf Beetles & the Bean Weevils.
Wilcox, Larry. The Constitution Will Hang by a Thread.
Wilcox, Michael. To See His Face.
Wilcox, R. Paul, jt. auth. see Knight, C. Gregory.
Wilcox, Robert V. Weight Training & Conditioning for Basketball.
--Weight Training for Baseball.
--Weight Training for Football.
Wilcox, Roger. Communication at Work: Writing & Speaking.
Wilcox, Ronald. The Rig.
Wilcox, W. R., ed. Chemical Vapor Transport Secondary Nucleation & Mass Transfer in Crystal Growth.
Wilcoxon, George D. Athens Ascendant.
Wilcoxson, Georgeann. Baldicer: A Simulation Game on Feeding the World's People.
Wilczak, Paul F. When a Family Loses a Loved One.
Wild, David. The Movies of Woody Allen: A Short, Neurotic Quiz Book.
Wild, Peter. The Saguaro Forest.
Wild, Rolf H. Management by Compulsion: The Corporate Urge to Grow.
Wild, U. P., et al. Triplet States Two.
Wildavsky, Aaron, jt. auth. see Polsby, Nelson W.
Wildavsky, Aaron, jt. auth. see Webber, Carolyn.
Wildavsky, Aaron B., jt. ed. see May, Judith V.
Wildbur, Peter. International Trademark Design: A Handbook of Marks of Identity.
Wilde, Alan. Critical Essays on E. M. Forster.
--Horizons of Assent: Modernism, Postmodernism, & the Ironic Imagination.
Wilde, Carroll O., ed. Functional Analysis: Proceedings.
Wilde, Jennifer. Love Me, Marietta.
--Love's Tender Fury.
Wilde, Larry. The Great Comedians.
Wilde, Oscar. The Birthday of the Infanta & Other Stories by Oscar Wilde.
--De Profundis.
--De Profundis.
--Happy Prince & Other Stories.
--The Plays of Oscar Wilde.
--Plays, Prose Writings, & Poems.
--Selfish Giant.
Wilden, Theodore. To Die Elsewhere.
Wildenstein, Daniel, jt. auth. see Rouart, Denis.
Wilder. Athletes: The Paintings of Joe Wilder, M. D.
Wilder, Amos N. Jesus' Parables & the War of Myths: Essays on Imagination in the Scriptures.
--Theopoetic: Theology & the Religious Imagination.
--Thornton Wilder & His Public.
Wilder, Anne. Fair & Wilder.
Wilder, Charles. Another Side of the Blues: Seven Stories.
Wilder, Cherry. The Luck of Brin's Five.
--The Nearest Fire.
--The Tapestry Warriors.
Wilder, Don, jt. auth. see Rechin, Bill.
Wilder, Franklin. Father of the Wesleys.
--Martha Wesley.
--The Remarkable World of John Wesley: Pioneer in Mental Health.
Wilder, Joan. Jewel of the Nile.
--The Jewel of the Nile.
--Romancing the Stone.
Wilder, Louise B. The Fragrant Garden: A Book About Sweet Scented Flowers & Leaves.
Wilder, Mary A. The Silent Epidemic: We Can Stop Teenage Suicide.
Wilder, Thornton. The Bridge of San Luis Rey.
--The Eighth Day.
--Heaven's My Destination.
--The Long Christmas Dinner & Other Plays in One Act.
--Our Town.
--Theophilus North.
--Three Plays by Thornton Wilder.
--The Woman of Andros.
Wilder, Warren F., jt. auth. see Giese, Frank S.
Wilder-Smith, Beate. The Day Nazi Germany Died.
Wilding, M. Milton's Paradise Lost.
Wilding, Michael. Aspects of the Dying Process.
--Political Fictions.
Wilding, Michael, ed. see Miller, John.
Wilding, Paul. Professional Power & Social Welfare.
Wilding, Paul, jt. auth. see George, Vic.
Wilding, Philip. Shadow over the Earth.
--Spaceflight-Venus.
Wildlife Society Staff, jt. auth. see American Forestry Association Staff.
Wildman, Eugene. Montezuma's Ball.
--Nuclear Love.
Wildon, Lester N., ed. Helping Special Student Groups.
Wildridge, Thomas T. Grotesque in Church Art.
Wildy, P., ed. see International Committee on Taxonomy of Viruses.
Wileden, Jack C., jt. auth. see Riddle, William E.
Wilensky, R. H. An Outline of English Painting.
Wiles, Cheryl & Ryan, William. Communication for Dental Auxilliaries.
Wiles, Maurice. Faith & the Mystery of God.
--The Remaking of Christian Doctrine.
Wiley, B. I. Plain People of the Confederacy.
Wiley, Basil. The Seventeenth Century Background Studies in the Thought of the Age in Relation to Poetry & Religion.
Wiley, Bell I., ed. see National Historical Society Staff.
Wiley, David & Crofts, Marylee. The Third World: Africa.
Wiley, Don W. Introduction by see Bohannan, Jean E.
Wiley, E. O. The Phylogeny & Biogeography of Fossil & Recent Gars (Actincopterygii: Lepisosteidae)
Wiley, E. O., jt. auth. see Brooks, Daniel R.
Wiley, Howard A. Night Thoughts of an Aging Orphan.
Wiley, Jack. The Kite Building & Kite Flying Handbook, with 42 Kite Plans.
--The Tumbling Book.
--Woodcarving, with Projects.
Wiley, Paul L. & Orel, Harold, eds. British Poetry, Eighteen Eighty to Nineteen Twenty: Edwardian Voices.
Wiley, Robert J. How to Evaluate Your Net Worth: Making Financial Statements Work for You.
Wiley, William L. Gentleman of Renaissance France.
Wilgus, A. Curtis. Historical Atlas of Latin America: Political, Geographic, Economic, Cultural.
Wilhelm, Hans. Your Chinese Horoscope.
Wilhelm, Homer. San Juan Islands.
Wilhelm, J. Objectives & Multi-Objective Decision Making Under Uncertainty.
Wilhelm, James J. & Saez, Richard, eds. Joyce's Debt to Rabelais.
Wilhelm, John. John Wilhelm's Guide to Mexico.
Wilhelm, Kate. Listen, Listen.
--Oh, Susannah!
--A Sense of Shadow.
Wilhelm, Louis A. Criticism, Cynicism, & a Bit of Witticism.
Wilhelm, Richard. Chinese Economic Psychology. Myers, Ramon H., ed.
Wilhelm, Richard, tr. see Lao Tsu.
Wilhelmsen, Inga, jt. auth. see Allwood, Martin S.
Wilhelmsson, H., jt. auth. see Weiland, J. C.
Wilhite, Bob, ed. see Lemke, Robert & Krause, Cheste.
Wilhoit, Francis M. The Politics of Massive Resistance.
Wilk, Janet. Chinese Cookbook.
--Holiday Cooking for Kids.
--Holiday Cooking for Kids.
Wilk, Max. Every Day's a Matinee: Memoirs Scribbled on a Dressing Room Door.
--The Kissinger Noodles... or Westward, Mr. Ho: A Novel.
--My Masterpiece.
--They're Playing Our Song.
--A Tough Act to Follow: A Novel.
Wilk, Sarah B. The Sculpture of Tullio Lombardo: Studies in Sources & Meaning.
Wilk, Valerie A., jt. auth. see Farmworker Justice Fund Staff.
Wilken-Jensen, K. Lexikon Allergologicum.
Wilkens, H., jt. auth. see Schebitz, H.
Wilkens, Herbert. The Two German Economies.
Wilkerson, Cynthia. The Fast Life.
Wilkerson, David. Personal Pocket Promise Book.
--Promesas de Jesus.
--Racing Toward Judgment.
--The Vision.

Wilkerson, James A., ed. Medicine for Mountaineering.
Wilkerson, Rich. Carnal Christians: And Other Words That Don't Go Together.
--Peer Pressure.
Wilkes, F., jt. auth. see Samuels, J.
Wilkes, G. A. A Dictionary of Australian Colloquialisms.
--Studying Literature.
Wilkes, G. A., ed. The Tempest.
Wilkes, G. A., ed. see Shakespeare, William.
Wilkes, John. Hernan Cortes: Conquistador in Mexico.
--The London Police in the Nineteenth Century.
Wilkes, John, ed. Exploring History with Microcomputers.
Wilkes, Lyall. South & North & Other Poems.
Wilkes, Mary & Crosswait, C. Bruce. Professional Development: The Dynamics of Success.
--Professional Development: The Dynamics of Success.
Wilkes, Wall. The Aesthetic Obsession: A Portrait of Sir William Eden.
Wilkie, Leighton A. & Rimanoczy, Richard S. Principles of American Prosperity.
Wilkin, David. Caring for the Mentally Handicapped Child.
Wilkin, Eloise. Baby's Playground.
Wilkins, Alan L. Developing Corporate Character: How to Successfully Change an Organization Without Destroying It.
Wilkins, Amy, jt. auth. see Blank, Helen.
Wilkins, Barratt. Survey of State Library Agencies, 1977: For the National Center for Educational Statistics.
Wilkins, Barry. The Internal Auditor's Information Security Handbook.
Wilkins, Charles L., jt. ed. see Klopfenstein, Charles E.
Wilkins, Charles L., et al. Digital Electronics & Laboratory Computer Experiments.
Wilkins, David G. Maso Di Banco, A Florentine Artist of the Early Trecentine. Freedberg, S. J., ed.
Wilkins, Ernest H. Studies in the Life & Works of Petrarch.
Wilkins, Esther M. Clinical Practice of the Dental Hygienist.
Wilkins, Frances. Growing up During the Norman Conquest.
--Transport & Travel from Nineteen Thirty to the Nineteen Eighty's.
Wilkins, Frank. Woodwork - for Student, Apprentice & Handyman.
Wilkins, Gregory L. African Influence in the United Nations, 1967-1975: The Politics & Techniques of Gaining Compliance to U. N. Principles & Resolutions.
Wilkins, Kirby L. King Season.
Wilkins, Lewis L., tr. see Pannenberg, Wolfhart.
Wilkins, Mary E. see Freeman, Mary E.
Wilkins, N. P. & Gosling, E. M., eds. Genetics in Aquaculture.
Wilkins, Roger. A Man's Life: An Autobiography.
--A Man's Life: An Autobiography.
Wilkins, Sophie, tr. see Von Schiller, Friedrich.
Wilkins, Stewart. Honda CB250 & 350 Twins '68 - '70.
--MZ 150 & 250 '69 - '79.
--Suzuki B100 P, B120 Student '66 - '77.
Wilkinson, Barry. Diverting Adventures of Tom Thumb.
Wilkinson, Burke. Uncommon Clay: The Life & Works of Augustus Saint Gaudens.
Wilkinson, Charles F., jt. auth. see Coggins, George C.
Wilkinson, Charles K. & McNab, Jessie. Chess: East & West, Past & Present.
Wilkinson, D., ed. Proceedings of the International School of Nuclear Physics, Erice, 2-14 Sept. 1976.
Wilkinson, Denys, ed. Progress in Particle & Nuclear Physics: Mesons, Isobars, Quarks & Nuclear Excitations.
--Progress in Particle & Nuclear Physics.
--Progress in Particle & Nuclear Physics.
--Progress in Particle & Nuclear Physics.
--Progress in Particle & Nuclear Physics.
--Progress in Particle & Nuclear Physics.
--Progress in Particle & Nuclear Physics.
--Progressive in Particle & Nuclear Physics: Collective Bands in Nuclei.
Wilkinson, Dorcas, jt. auth. see Wilkinson, Larry.
Wilkinson, E. M., tr. see LaTouche, Robert.
Wilkinson, Ellen. The Division Bell Mystery.
Wilkinson, F. Chemical Kinetics & Reaction Mechanisms.
Wilkinson, Fred. Badges of the British Army: Eighteen-Twenty to the Present.
Wilkinson, Geoffrey, jt. auth. see Cotton, F. Albert.
Wilkinson, Gerald. Woodland Walks in Britain.
Wilkinson, Graham N., jt. ed. see Launer, Robert L.
Wilkinson, Greg, ed. Mental Health Practices in Primary Care Settings: An Annotated Bibliography.
Wilkinson, Henrietta T. God Is at Work.
--Living As Disciples.
--Mystery of Missions.
Wilkinson, J. J., tr. see Swedenborg, Emmanuel.
Wilkinson, Jean, jt. auth. see Reese, Lyn.
Wilkinson, John, jt. auth. see Chichester, Michael.
Wilkinson, John, et al. The Dynamic Programming of Human Systems: A Social & Historical Analysis.
Wilkinson, John P., jt. auth. see Levy, Samuel.
Wilkinson, Jule. Complete Book of Cooking Equipment.
Wilkinson, Jule, ed. The Anatomy of Food Service Design 1.
--Making the Most of Fruit on Foodservice Menus.
Wilkinson, L. P., ed. & tr. see Cicero, Marcus T.
Wilkinson, Larry & Wilkinson, Dorcas. Gifts from Korea.
Wilkinson, Norman B. Bibliography of Pennsylvania History.
Wilkinson, O. N. Old Glass: Its Manufacture Styles Uses.
Wilkinson, Peter, ed. Photography Year Book 1985.
--Photography Yearbook, 1986-1987.
Wilkinson, Peter C. Chemotaxis & Inflammation.
Wilkinson, Richard. Class & Health: Health & Social Mobility.
Wilkinson, Sandra. Death On Call.
--Death on Call.
Wilkinson, Stephan. Return of the Dinosaurs. Dupuy, Ernest, ed.
Wilkinson, Sylvia. Endurance Racing.
--Shadow of the Mountain.
--Sprint Cars.
--Stock Cars.
Wilkinson, Theodore S. Churches at the Testing Point: A Study in Rural Michigan.
Wilkinson, Walter D. Fabrication of Refractory Metals.
--Properties of Refractory Metals.
Wilkomirsky, I., jt. auth. see Coudurier, L.
Wilks, Brian. The Brontes.
Wilks, M. The Weather Works.
Wilks, Mike. The Weather Works.
Wilks, Samuel S. Elementary Statistical Analysis.
Will & Nicolas. The Boy & the Forest.
--Chaga.
--Four-Leaf Clover.
Will, Frederic. The Fact of Literature: Three Essays on Public Material.
Will, Frederick, tr. see Adorno, Theodor W.
Will, George F. The New Season: A Spectator's Guide to the 1988 Election.
--Statecraft As Soulcraft: What Government Does.
--Statecraft As Soulcraft: What Government Does.
Will, Lawrence E. Okeechobee Hurricane.
Will, Robert E. & Vatter, Harold G., eds. Poverty in Affluence: The Social, Political & Economic Dimensions of Poverty in the United States.
Will, Robert J. How to Beat Workers' Compensation Before It Beats You.
Will, Robin. Beautiful Yosemite National Park.
Willadeene. Denim, Lace, & Bandanas.
Willadeene & Joan. Sounds of My Soul.
Willams, Jenny, jt. auth. see Troyna, Barry.
Willand, Lois. Use-It-Up Cookbook.
Willard. Instrumental Methods Analysis.
Willard, Barbara. The Gardener's Grandchildren.
--Lark & the Laurel.
--Richleighs of Tantamount.
--Spell Me a Witch.
--Storm from the West.
Willard, Nancy. Angel in the Parlor: Five Stories & Eight Essays.
--Carpenter of the Sun.
--Childhood of the Magician.
--Sailing to Cythera: And Other Anatole Stories.
--Simple Pictures Are Best.
--Stranger's Bread.
--The Well-Mannered Balloon.
Willard, Stephen. Calculus & Its Applications.
Willbrand, M. L. & Rieke, Richard D. Teaching Oral Communication in Elementary Schools.
Willbrand, Mary L., jt. auth. see Mecham, Merlin J.
Willcocks, John, jt. ed. see Galton, Maurice.
Willcox & Willcox. Venereological Medicine Pocket Consultant.
Willcox, Alfred B., jt. auth. see Buck, R. Creighton.
Willcox, Alfred B., et al. Introduction to Calculus One & Two.
Willcox, James L. Poems by James Lyndon Willcox.
Willcutt, Robert E. & Paige, Donald D. Elementary Mathematics.
Wille, Beatrice B. Sunny-side Up.
Willeford, Charles. Cockfighter.
Willems, Jos L., et al, eds. Cardiac Function & Aging.
Willems-Treeman, Elizabeth, tr. see Haak, Bob.
Willen, D., ed. see Chiaromonte, Nicola.
Willen, David C. IBM-PCjr Assembler Language.
Willen, David C. & Krantz, Jeffrey I. Eighty Eighty-Eight Assembler Language Programming: The IBM-PC.
Willen, Drenka, tr. see Kusan, Ivan.
Willenbrock, Jack H. & Thomas, H. Randoph. Planning, Engineering & Construction of Electric Power Generation Facilities.
Willens, Harold. The Trimtab Factor: How Business Executives Can Help Solve the Nuclear Weapons Crisis.
Willer, S., jt. auth. see Wiesner, E.
Willerding, Margaret. The Business of Mathematics.
--First Course in College Mathematics.
--Numbers Game.
Willerman, Lee. The Psychology of Individual & Group Differences.
Willes, Burlington. Games & Ideas for Teaching Spanish.
Willes, Mary J. Children into Pupils: A Study of Language in Early Schooling.
Willes, P. Competence: A Continuum.
Willet, C. S. Gas Lasers.
Willett, John. Art & Politics in the Weimar Republic: The New Sobriety, 1917-1933.
--Brecht in Context.
--The Singer in the Stone.
Willett, John, ed. see Brecht, Bertolt.
Willett, Robert F. A Primer for Christian Meditation.
Willette, R. E., jt. ed. see Stillman, R. C.
Willetts, H. J., jt. auth. see Byrde, R. J.
Willetts, H. T., tr. see Solzhenitsyn, Alexander.
Willetts, R. F. Argo: Poems.
Willey, David. Rome.
Willey, Fay, jt. ed. see Lautz, Terry E.
Willey, Gordon R. Introduction to American Archaeology, Vol. 1: North & Middle America.
Willey, Ray. Working with Youth.
Willgoose, Carl. Health Teaching in Secondary Schools.
Willhoite, Fred H., Jr. Beyond Nihilism: Albert Camus's Contribution to Political Thought.
William C., jt. auth. see Practising Law Institute Staff.
William, H. & Stine, M. Tournament for Terror.
William, Linda. Words from My Mind.
William, Lindsey & Wilson, Clifford. Energy Non-Crisis.
William of Ockham see also Ockham, William of.
William, Thomas. Game Playing with Digital Computer.
Williams. Arithmetic the Easy Way.
--Finite Element Methods in Radiation Physics: Proceedings of the International Seminar, Imperial College of Science Technology, UK. Goddard, A. J., ed.
--Nutrition & Diet Therapy.
--Pocket Nurse Guide to Nutrition.
Williams & Smith. Trauma of the Chest.
Williams, jt. auth. see Haughton.
Williams, jt. auth. see Isaacson.
Williams, et al. Textbook of Uncommon Cancer.
Williams, Adele. Gracious Living: How to Enjoy Being a Woman.
--Thrift Shop Decorating.
Williams, Alan. Gentleman Traitor.
Williams, Alfred. Folksongs of the Upper Thames.
Williams, Alice C. Thru' the Turnstile: Tales of My Two Centuries.
Williams, Anne Roslin see Roslin-Williams, Anne.
Williams, Arthur. Managing Your Investment Manager: The Complete Guide to Selection, Measurement, & Control.
Williams, Arthur B. Electronic Filter Design Handbook.
Williams, B., ed. Film Preparation & Etching Using Vacuum or Plasma Technology: Proceedings of the SIRA International Seminar, Brighton, U. K., 22-24 March 1983.
Williams, B. K., jt. auth. see O'Leary, T. J.
Williams, Barbara. Brigham Young & Me, Clarissa.
--The Horrible, Impossible, Bad Witch Child.
--The Secret Name.
--So What If I'm a Sore Loser?
--La Villiane Petite Sorciere: The Horrible Impossible Bad Witch Child.
--Whatever Happened to Beverly Bigler's Birthday.
--Whatever Happened to Beverly Bigler's Birthday.
--Where Are You, Angela Von Hauptmann, Now That I Need You?
Williams, Barbara & Grundmann, Carol. Twenty-Six Lively Letters-Making an ABC Quiet Book.
Williams, Barbara & Williams, Rosemary. Cookie Craft: No-Bake Designs for Edible Party Decorations.
Williams, Barbara L. Ideal Book for Children: Freddie & the Ten Commandments.
Williams, Basil. Stanhope: A Study in Eighteenth-Century War & Diplomacy.
Williams, Becky, ed. Writer's Market '87.
Williams, Ben A. House Divided.
Williams, Ben A., Jr. Bank of Boston Two Hundred: A History of New England's Leading Bank, Seventeen Eighty-Four - Nineteen Eighty-Four.
Williams, Benjamin, ed. Remodelers Handbook: A Manual of Professional Practice for Home Improvement Contractors.
Williams, Brad. Tumulto.
Williams, Brian, jt. auth. see Fenton, Pat.
Williams, Brian, jt. auth. see Kuipers, Benjamin.
Williams, Brian, jt. auth. see Storrer, Philip.
Williams, Brian G. Compton Scattering: A Tool for the Investigation of Electron Momentum Distribution.
Williams, Brian K., jt. auth. see Hales, Dianne R.
Williams, C. Abdy. Story of Notation.
--Story of Organ Music.
Williams, C. F. The Story of the Organ.
Williams, C. Fred. Arkansas: An Illustrated History of the Land of Opportunity. Wells, Susan, ed.
Williams, C. H. see Bissett, D. E., et al.
Williams, C. K. Flesh & Blood.
--With Ignorance.
Williams, Calvin. The Encounter Between Two Worlds.
Williams, Carole, ed. see Reid, Thomas F., et al.
Williams, Cecil. I'm Alive: An Autobiography.
Williams, Charles W. Descent of the Dove.
Williams, Christopher. Canticle Majesty.
Williams, Christopher J. & Whitehouse, Michael. Cancer of the Female Reproductive System.
Williams, Colin W. New Directions in Theology Today: The Church, Vol. 4.
Williams, Connie E., ed. see International Fire Service Training Association Staff.
Williams, D. Agriculture in the Australian Economy.
Williams, D., ed. Stochastic Process: Proceedings.
Williams, D. A. & Jones, G. Liquid Fuels.
Williams, D. A., jt. auth. see Dyson, J. E.
Williams, D. B. Agriculture in the Australian Economy.
Williams, D. H. & Fleming, I. Spectroscopic Methods in Organic Chemistry.
Williams, Dakin & Mead, Shepherd. Tennessee Williams: An Intimate Biography.
Williams, Daniel D. The Minister & the Care of Souls.
Williams, David. Murder in Advent.
--Treasure Preserved.
--Wedding Treasure.
Williams, David, jt. auth. see Fritz, Paul.
Williams, David, jt. auth. see Hughes, Peter.
Williams, David B. Practical Analytical Electron Microscopy in Materials Science.
Williams, David J. Acts: A Good News Commentary.
Williams, David R. Faith Beyond Humanism.
Williams, Dayle Z., jt. auth. see Needles, Belverd E., Jr.
Williams, Dick. Prayers for Today's Church.
Williams, Donald R. Labor Force Participation of Black & White Youth. Bateman, Fred, ed.
Williams, Donnie, jt. auth. see Sanders, Steve.
Williams, Doyle Z., jt. auth. see Needles, Belverd E.
Williams, Duncan. To Be or Not to Be: A Question of Survival.
Williams, E. D. & Siebenmann, R. E. Histological Typing of Endocrine Tumours.
Williams, E. W. Modern Law Enforcement & Police Science.
Williams, E. W. & Hall, R. Luminescence & the Light Emitting Diode.
Williams, Earl P., Jr. What You Should Know about the American Flag.
Williams, Edward B. One Man's Freedom.
Williams, Edward E. & Manzo, Salvatore E. Business Planning for the Enterpreneur.
Williams, Edward J., jt. auth. see Seligson, Mitchell A.
Williams, Elizabeth. Halo.
Williams, Ernest W., Jr., jt. auth. see Fair, Marvin L.
Williams, Ethel W. Know Your Ancestors: A Guide to Genealogical Research.
Williams, Fern C., jt. auth. see Oakland, Thomas.
Williams, Francis. Twilight of Empire: Memoirs of Prime Minister Clement Attlee.
Williams, Francis L. A Founding Family: The Pickneys of South Carolina.
Williams, Frank J., jt. auth. see Freund, John E.
Williams, Frederick. Framework for II Writers.
--The New Communications.
Williams, Frederick C. & Deese, David A., eds. Nuclear Nonproliferation: The Spent Fuel Problem.
Williams, Frederick D., jt. ed. see Brown, Harry J.
Williams, G. Atlas des Maladies Renales. Levy, Micheline, tr.
Williams, G., jt. auth. see Walker, E.
Williams, G. E., ed. Megacycles: Long-Term Episodity in Earth & Planetary History.
Williams, G. H., ed. Advances in Free Radical Chemistry.

Authors

Williams, Gareth & Blackstone, Tessa. Response to Adversity: Higher Education in a Harsh Climate.
Williams, Gareth, jt. auth. see Cannon, Ray.
Williams, Gene B. How to Repair & Maintain Your IBM Computer.
Williams, George H. Radical Reformation.
Williams, George J., III. Gold Trails of Big Bear Valley.
--How to Make a Professional Demo Tape.
--The Rape of Owens Valley & Mono Lake.
Williams, Gillian, jt. ed. see Hutter, Bridget.
Williams, Gordon. Big Morning Blues.
--No Risk: Gordon Williams' Step-by-Step Program to Safeguard Your Financial Future.
--Pomeroy.
Williams, Grace. The Very Last Virgin at Hobeck High.
Williams, Gurney, III, jt. auth. see Glazer, Joan.
Williams, Guy. The Royal Parks of London.
Williams, Gwyn A. Artisans & Sans-Culottes.
--The Welsh in Their History.
Williams, Gwyneth & Hackland, Brian. Dictionary of Contemporary Politics of Southern Africa.
Williams, H., jt. auth. see Smith, H. J.
Williams, H. A. The Simplicity of Prayer: A Discussion of the Methods & Results of Christian Prayer.
--Tensions: Necessary Conflicts in Life & Love.
Williams, H. Bruce. Symposium on Vascular Malformations & Melanotic Lesions.
Williams, Hank, Jr. Living Proof.
Williams, Harold H. Book Clubs & Printing Societies of Great Britain & Ireland.
Williams, Heathcote. The Immortalist.
Williams, Henry H. Logic for Living. Hammer, Mary J., ed.
Williams, Hiram. Notes for a Young Painter: Revised & Expanded Edition of a Classic Handbook for Beginning Artists.
Williams, Hobie L. The American Artists Today in Black. White, Mosezelle & Roberts, Bobby, II, eds.
--The American Artists Today in Black & White. White, Mosezelle & Roberts, Bobby, III, eds.
Williams, Howard. Giving up for Good.
Williams, Howel, et al. Petrography: An Introduction to the Study of Rocks in Thin Sections.
Williams, I., jt. auth. see Baxter, R.
Williams, Ida J. Starting Anew after Seventy: The Story of Ida Ella Jones, Primitive Artist.
Williams, Ioan. Meredith.
Williams, Ivy. Swiss Civil Code: English Version, with Vocabularies & Notes.
Williams, J., ed. Carbon Dioxide, Climate & Society: Proceedings of an IIASA Workshop, Feb. 1978.
Williams, J., et al. Readings in Multiple Regression & Intermediate Educational Statistics.
--Aperture.
Williams, J. C. & Belov, A. F., eds. Titanium & Titanium Alloys: Scientific & Technological Aspects.
Williams, J. E., jt. auth. see Price, D.
Williams, J. E., jt. ed. see Price, D.
Williams, J. F. see Francis-Williams, Jesse.
Williams, J. L. The Fire Inside.
Williams, J. Richard. Passive Solar Heating.
Williams, J. W. Ultracentrifugation of Macromolecules: Modern Topics.
Williams, Jack & Yung Teng Chia-Yee. Readings in Chinese Geography: Vol. 1, Chinese Text, Vol. 2, Vocabulary, Notes & Translations.
Williams, James. Letters on Slavery from the Old World.
Williams, James G. Women Recounted: Narrative Thinking & the God of Israel.
Williams, Jan R. & Stanga, Keith G. Intermediate Accounting.
Williams, Jane A. How to Stock a Quality Home Library Inexpensively.
Williams, Jay & Abrashkin, Raymond. Danny Dunn & the Universal Glue.
--Danny Dunn & the Universal Glue.
--Danny Dunn & the Voice from Space.
--Danny Dunn, Scientific Detective.
Williams, Jean, jt. auth. see Bryant, Beverley.
Williams, Jeanne. The Cave Dreamers.
--The Heaven Sword.
--A Lady Bought with Rifles.
--So Many Kingdoms.
--Texas Pride.
Williams, Jennifer, ed. see Cadell, Elizabeth.
Williams, Jennifer, ed. see Peters, Ellis.
Williams, Jennifer, ed. see Porter, Sylvia.
Williams, Jerry. And Yet They Come: Portuguese Immigration from the Azores to the United States (1820-1978)
Williams, Jerry J. Contemporary Astrology.
Williams, Jill, jt. auth. see Williams, Pat.
Williams, Joan. Pariah & Other Stories.
--The Wintering.
Williams, John. The Holy Spirit, Lord & Life-Giver: A Biblical Introduction to the Doctrine of the Holy Spirit.
--An Introduction to Hunting.
Williams, John & Dunning, Eric. Hooligans Abroad: The Behaviour & Control of English Fans at Continental Football Matches.
Williams, John, ed. English Renaissance Poetry: A Collection of Shorter Poems from Skelton to Jonson.
Williams, John A. Click Song.
Williams, John D. Compleat Strategyst.
Williams, John-Michael. Kenny Duncan Is Dead: Reflections on a Teenage Suicide.
Williams, Joseph M. Style: Ten Lessons in Clarity & Grace.
Williams, Joy. Florida Keys: A History & Guide.
--State of Grace.
Williams, Juanita H. Psychology of Women.
--Psychology of Women: Behavior in a Biosocial Context.
Williams, Juanita H., ed. Psychology of Women: Selected Readings.
Williams, Julia & Hamilton, Lawrence S. Watershed Forest Influences in the Tropics & Subtropics: A Selected, Annotated Bibliography.
Williams, Karel & Thomas, Dennis. Why Are the British Bad at Manufacturing?
Williams, Kathleen, ed. see Swift, Jonathan.
Williams, Kim. Kim Williams' Cookbook & Commentary.
Williams, Laurie, jt. auth. see Gilbert, Chris.
Williams, Lawrence. Fiery Furnace.
Williams, Leigh. The Saga of Silent Sue.
Williams, Leslie. What's Behind That Tree?
Williams, Linda. Figures of Desire: A Theory & Analysis of Surrealist Film.
Williams, Linda V. Teaching for the Two-Sided Mind: A Guide to Right Brain-Left Brain Education.
Williams, Lois, jt. auth. see Wink, Richard L.
Williams, M. Climatic Change in Deserts.
--Essentials of Pulmonary Medicine.
--The Making of the South Australian Landscape: A Study in the Historical Geography of South Australia.
Williams, M. M. Nuclear Safety.
--Progress in Nuclear Energy: The Role of the Boltzmann Transport Equation in Radiation Damage Calculations.
--Random Processes in Nuclear Reactors.
Williams, M. M., ed. Fast Reactor Physics. McCormick, N. J.
--Progress in Nuclear Energy.
--Progress in Nuclear Energy.
--Progress in Nuclear Energy.
--Progress in Nuclear Energy.
--Reactor Noise - Smorn II: Proceedings of the 2nd Specialists' Meeting on Reactor Noise 1977.
--Reactor Noise - Smorn III: Proceedings of the Third Specialists Meeting on Reactor Noise at Tokyo, Japan, October 26-30, 1981.
--Reactor Noise: An International Symposium: Special Multi Issue of Journal of Annals of Nuclear Energy.
Williams, M. M. & McCormick, N. J., eds. Progress in Nuclear Energy.
--Progress in Nuclear Energy.
--Progress in Nuclear Energy.
--Progress in Nuclear Energy.
--Progress in Nuclear Energy.
--Progress in Nuclear Energy.
--Progress in Nuclear Energy.
--Progress in Nuclear Energy.
--Progress in Nuclear Energy: Selected Staff Reports to the President's Commission on the Accident at Three Mile Island.
--Reactor Noise - Smorn IV.
Williams, M. M. & Sher, R., eds. Progress in Nuclear Energy New Series.
--Progress in Nuclear Energy: New Series.
Williams, M. R. & McCormick, N. J., eds. Progress in Nuclear Energy.
Williams, Mansfield W. Inventory & Production Decisions. Bateman, Fred, ed.
Williams, Marianne M. A Grammar of Tuscarora.
Williams, Mark, ed. Virgin Guide to London.
Williams, Martha E., ed. Annual Review of Information Science & Technology.
--Annual Review of Information Science & Technology, 1978.
--Annual Review of Information Science & Technology, 1980.
--Annual Review of Information Science & Technology, 1981.
--Annual Review of Information Science & Techology, 1979.
--Annual Review of Information Science & Technology, 1977.
--Annual Review of Information Science & Technology, 1982.
--The Annual Review of Information Science & Technology, 1983.
--Annual Review of Information Science & Technology, 1984.
Williams, Martin, ed. The Smithsonian Collection of Classic Jazz.
Williams, Martin, jt. ed. see Schuller, Gunther.
Williams, Mary F. The Public School & Finances.
Williams, Mary F., jt. ed. see Stern, Joyce D.
Williams, Max H. History of Union Parish, Louisiana: A Genealogical Profile of Its Pioneer Men & Women, Slaves & Ex-Slaves, & Immigrants.
Williams, Maxine. Eyes Have It.
Williams, Melvin H. Nutrition for Fitness & Sport.
Williams, Michael L. F.T.L. Further Than Life.
Williams, Michael Z., jt. auth. see Filippone, Samuel R.
Williams, Miller, ed. Ozark, Ozark: A Hillside Reader.
--Ozark, Ozark: A Hillside Reader.
Williams, Moyra. Breed of Horses.
Williams, Murial B. Marriage: Fielding's Mirror of Morality.
Williams, N. H. Combinatorial Set Theory.
Williams, Norman, Jr. American Land Planning Law.
Williams, P., ed. see Society for Psychosomatic Research Staff.
Williams, Pat & Jenkins, Jerry. The Power Within You.
Williams, Pat & Williams, Jill. Keep the Fire Glowing: How a Loving Marriage Builds a Loving Family.
Williams, Patti. Hurting & Healing: How to Cope with Hurt Feelings.
Williams, Paul. Das Energi.
Williams, Paul & Schoultz, Bonnie. We Can Speak for Ourselves.
Williams, Peggy R. Holli & Pandi's Hospital Adventure.
Williams, Peter H. Teaching Craft, Design & Technology Five to Thirteen.
Williams, Philip L. The Heart of a Distant Forest: A Novel.
Williams, Philip M. Hugh Gaitskell: A Political Biography.
Williams, Philip W. When Death Draws Near: Meditations for All Who Walk in the Valley of the Shadow.
Williams, R. & Elliott, J. Basic & Applied Dental Biochemistry.
Williams, R. A. & Kruk, Z. L. Biochemistry & Pharmacology of Antibacterial Agents.
Williams, R. C. Bibliography of the Seventeenth Century Novel in France.
Williams, R. H., ed. To Live & to Die: When, Why, & How.
Williams, R. H., et al, eds. Interdisciplinary Surface Science: Proceedings of the 5th Interdisciplinary Surface Science Conference, (ISSC), April 6-9, 1981, University of Liverpool, U. K.
Williams, R. J. & Da Silva, J. R., eds. New Trends in Bio-Inorganic Chemistry.
Williams, R. J., et al see Dunitz, J. D., et al.
Williams, Ralph R., jt. auth. see Nicholson, Robert W.
Williams, Raymond. Culture & Revolution.
Williams, Raymond W. Techniques & Components of Analogue Computation.
Williams, Redford B., Jr., jt. ed. see Surwit, Richard S.
Williams, Reese. Figure-Eight.
Williams, Richard J., jt. auth. see Vlangas, Alex W.
Williams, Robert E. & King, Brian. The Power of VisiCalc.
Williams, Robert H., jt. auth. see Ross, Marc H.
Williams, Robert L. & Long, James D. Toward a Self-Managed Life Style.
Williams, Robert R. Schleiermacher the Theologian: The Construction of the Doctrine of God.
Williams, Roger. A Key into the Language of America. Teunissen, John J. & Hinz, Evelyn J., eds.
--The Nuclear Power Decisions: British Policies, 1953-1978.
Williams, Roger J. Biochemical Individuality: The Basis for the Genetotrophic Concept.
Williams, Roger J. & Kalita, Dwight K., eds. A Physician's Handbook on Orthomolecular Medicine.
Williams, Roger L. Aven Nelson of Wyoming.
--French Revolution of 1870-1871.
--The Horror of Life.
Williams, Rosemary, jt. auth. see Williams, Barbara.
Williams, Rowan. Christian Spirituality: A Theological History from the New Testament to Luther & St. John of the Cross.
Williams, Rudolph L. Pamela Deck.
Williams, Ruth, jt. auth. see Chung, K. L.
Williams, S. Voodoo & the Art of Haiti.
Williams, Sallie Y. The Art of Presenting Food: Everyone's Perfect Cooking Companion.
Williams, Sally R., jt. auth. see Schulz, Esther D.
Williams, Sandy. Victorian Doll Family.
Williams, Sandy, designed by. Colonial Doll Family.
Williams, Selma R. Demeter's Daughters: The Women Who Founded America (1587-1792)
--Divine Rebel: The Life of Anne Marbury Hutchinson.
--Kings, Commoners & Colonists.
--Riding the Nightmare.
Williams, Stephen J. & Torrens, Paul R., eds. Introduction to Health Services.
Williams, Stephen W., jt. auth. see Beaumont, John R.
Williams, Sue R. Mowry's Basic Nutrition & Diet Therapy.
Williams, Susan & McVan, Barbara, eds. Assessing Vital Functions Accurately.
--Coping with Neurologic Problems Proficiently.
--Giving Emergency Care Competently.
--Nursing Critically Ill Patients Confidently.
Williams, Susan R. & McVan, Barbara, eds. Combatting Cardiovascular Diseases Skilfully.
--Drug Interactions.
Williams, T. I. Elements of Chromatography.
Williams, T. Jeff & Ortho Books Editorial Staff. Basic Home Repairs.
Williams, Tannis M. Infant Care: Abstracts of the Literature--Supplement.
Williams, Ted. The Science of Hitting.
Williams, Ted & Underwood, John. The Science of Hitting.
Williams, Tennessee. The Glass Menagerie & a Streetcar Named Desire.
--Tennessee Williams' Letters to Donald Windham: 1940-1965. Winham, Donald, ed.
--Tennessee Williams: Memoirs.
--Tennessee Williams: Memoirs.
Williams, Tennessee see Weiss, Samuel A.
Williams, Theodore J., jt. auth. see Lu, Yong-Zai.
Williams, Thomas. Moon Pinnace.
Williams, Thomas D. The Dissection of a Principal. Rapport, Jon, ed.
Williams, Thomas E. Silverstreet.
Williams, W. E. The State Against Blacks.
--The State Against Blacks.
Williams, W. H. H. L. Mencken.
Williams, W. S. Introduction to Elementary Particles.
Williams, Walter & Elmore, Richard F., eds. Social Program Implementation.
Williams, Walter, jt. ed. see Rossi, Peter H.
Williams, Walter E. & Reed, James H. Fundamentals of Business Mathematics.
Williams, Walter L. The Spirit & the Flesh: Sexual Diversity in American Indian Culture.
Williams, William Carlos. Collected Earlier Poems: Before Nineteen Forty.
--Interviews W. C. Williams: Speaking Straight Ahead. Wagner, Linda, ed.
--Kora in Hell: Improvisations.
--Motoring Mascots of the World.
--Selected Poems.
Williams, William J. A Heritage of American Paintings.
Williams, William P. Jeremy Taylor, Seventeen Hundred to Nineteen Seventy-Six: An Annotated Checklist.
Williams, William P. & Abbott, Craig S. An Introduction to Bibliographical & Textual Studies.
Williams, William W. Coastal Changes.
Williams Boyd, Patricia. How Schools Can Help Combat Student Suicide.
Williamsen, Marvin & Morehouse, Cynthia T., eds. International-Intercultural Education in the Four-Year College: A Handbook on Strategies for Change.
Williamson, Adolph A. Moses, Who First Saw the Pyramid of Life.
Williamson, Arlene E. The Mayor of Prairieville.
Williamson, Bill. Class, Culture & Community: A Biological Study of Social Change in Mining.
Williamson, C. Letters from the Saints.
Williamson, Chip. Saltbound: A Winter on Block Island.
Williamson, Craig. African Wings: Poems.
Williamson, David, Jr. R & D for National Strength.
Williamson, Doug, jt. auth. see Rosenblum, Mort.
Williamson, G. C. English Conversation Pictures of the 18th & Early 19th Centuries.
Williamson, G. I. Westminster Confession of Faith.
Williamson, Geoffrey. Inside Buchmanism.
Williamson, George. Milton & Others.
Williamson, J. N. Ghost.
--Playmates.
--Premonition.
--The Ritual.
--The Tulpa.
Williamson, Jack. The Humanoid Touch.
Williamson, James A. Sir Francis Drake.
Williamson, John B., jt. auth. see Johnson, Elizabeth S.
Williamson, K., jt. auth. see White, S.
Williamson, Lamar, Jr. God's Work of Art: Images of the Church in Ephesians.
Williamson, Lamar, Jr., jt. auth. see Beck, Madeline H.
Williamson, M. F., jt. auth. see Evans, R. G.
Williamson, Margaretta A., ed. see United States Children's Bureau Staff.
Williamson, Peter S., ed. see Colson, Charles, et al.
Williamson, Ray A. Living the Sky: The Cosmos of the American Indian.
Williamson, Roger. The Cheesemaker Mice & the Giant.

Williamson, Tony. The Samson Strike.
--Technicians of Death.
Williamson, William B. A Handbook for Episcopalians.
Williamson, Yvonne M. Research Methodology & Its Application to Nursing.
Williams-Thompson, M. How to Run a Public Relations Campaign.
Willie, Charles V. Church Action in the World.
--The Ivory & Ebony Towers: Race Relations & Higher Education.
Willier, Robert A., jt. auth. see Unruh, Adolph.
Williford, Jacklyn M. Word Processing Handbook: Wang OIS 142 System.
Willig. Good Manufacturing Practices for Pharmaceuticals.
Willig, P. Lichtstreifen.
Willig, Paul M., jt. auth. see Anastasia, Salvatore.
Willig, Robert D. Welfare Analysis of Policies Affecting Prices & Products.
Willing, Jules Z. The Reality of Retirement: The Inner Experience of Becoming a Retired Person.
Willingham, John R. & Warders, Donald F. A Handbook for Student Writers.
Willingham, Lauvenia. Adultery.
Willis, Anne & Ricciuti, Henry. A Good Beginning for Babies: Guidelines for Group Care.
Willis, Arthur & Willis, Christopher. Elements of Quantity Surveying.
Willis, Arthur J. & George, W. N. The Architect in Practice.
Willis, Arthur J. & Willis, Christopher J. Elements of Quantity Surveying.
--Practice & Procedure for the Quantity Surveyor.
--Specification Writing for Architects & Surveyors.
Willis, Charles D. End of Days, Nineteen Seventy-One to Two Thousand One: An Eschatological Study.
Willis, Christopher. Problem-Solving in General Chemistry.
Willis, Christopher, jt. auth. see Willis, Arthur.
Willis, Christopher J., jt. auth. see Willis, Arthur J.
Willis, Cleve E., jt. ed. see Field, Barry C.
Willis, David. Daring Prayer.
Willis, Diane J., jt. auth. see Swanson, B. Marion.
Willis, E. David, jt. ed. see McKelway, Alexander J.
Willis, E. H., jt. ed. see Millhone, J. P.
Willis, Hulon. A Brief Handbook of English.
--A Brief Handbook of English: With Research Paper.
--Content & Structure: Readings for College Writers.
--Writing Term Papers: The Research Paper - the Critical Paper.
--Writing Term Papers: The Research Paper-the Critical Paper.
Willis, Hulon & Klammer, Enno. A Brief Handbook of English.
Willis, Irene, jt. auth. see Richards, Arlene K.
Willis, Irene C. England's Holy War: A Study of English Liberal Idealism During the Great War.
Willis, J. H. A Handbook to Plants in Victoria, Vol. 2: Dicotyledons.
Willis, James, tr. see Frankel, Hermann.
Willis, James F. & Primack, Martin L. Explorations in Economics.
Willis, Jane. Teaching English Through English.
Willis, Jeanne. The Tale of Fearsome Fritz.
--The Tale of Georgie Grub.
Willis, Jerry. Desktop Publishing with Your IBM PC & Compatible.
--The Essential Commodore 128 User's Guide.
--How to Use the Macintosh.
Willis, Jerry & Manning, William. How to Use the IBM PC.
Willis, Jerry & Miller, Merl. Computers for Everybody.
Willis, Jerry, jt. auth. see Smithy-Willis, Debra.
Willis, John R. A History of Christian Thought: From Apostolic Times to Saint Augustine.
Willis, K. G. The Economics of Town & Country Planning.
Willis, Larryann C. The Horse-Breeding Farm.
Willis, Meredith S. Higher Ground.
--Only Great Changes.
Willis, Paul E. Learning to Labour: How Working Class Kids Get Working Class Jobs.
Willis, Peter. Charles Bridgeman: And the English Landscape Garden. Harris, John & Laing, Alastair, eds.
Willis, Peter, ed. see Kent, William.
Willis, Roy. A State in the Making: Myth, History, & Social Transformation in Pre-Colonial Ufipa.
Willis, Ted. The Buckingham Palace Connection.
Willis, Tom, tr. see Altimiras, J.
Willis, W. D. & Coggeshall, R. E., eds. Sensory Mechanisms of the Spinal Cord.
Willis, Wesley R. Colossians, Philippians & Philemon.
Willis, William D., Jr. & Grossman, Robert G. Medical Neurobiology: Neuroanatomical & Neurophysiological Principles Basic to Clinical Neuroscience.
Willisen, F. K. Von see Kmetz, A. R. & Von Willisen, F. K.
Willison, Anita M. Always a Rainbow.
Willison, George F. Here They Dug the Gold: Colorado's Gold Rush, 1859-1869.
Williston, Glenn & Johnstone, Judith. Soul Search: Spiritual Growth Through a Knowledge of Past Lifetimes.
Williston, Hamlin L. Managing the Family Forest in the South.
Willliams, George, III. Rosa May: The Search for a Mining Camp Legend. Dalton, Bill, ed.
Willman, Andrew. You, Still, Can Become a Millionaire by 1984! Investments Perspectives Through the Mid-1980s & Applicable Investment Strategy.
--You, Still, Can Become a Millionaire by 1984: Investment Perspectives Through the Mid-1980's & Applicable Investment Strategy.
Willmer, E. N. Cells & Tissues in Culture: Methods, Biology, & Physiology.
Willmer, John E. The National Political Boundary.
Willmington, H. L. Signs of the Times.
Willmott, A. John, jt. auth. see Schmidt, Frank W.
Willms, B., jt. ed. see Soling, H. D.
Willmuth, Sidney. Mass Society, Social Organizations, & Democracy.
Willocks, James. Essentials of Obstetrics & Gynaecology.
Willoughby, A. F, jt. ed. see Landsberg, P. T.
Willoughby, Charles C., jt. auth. see Hamilton, Henry W.
Willoughby, David. What Time Is It? Clanton, Arthur L., ed.
Willoughby, Geoff. Ferrari 308, 328, Mondial Autohistory.
Willoughby, Kenneth W. Secrets of Ego Power & Control.
Willoughby, Larry. Texas Rhythm, Texas Rhyme. Rodriguez, Barbara, ed.
Willoughby, Michael L. Paediatric Haematology.
Willoughby, Robert H., jt. auth. see Sheppard, William C.
Willoughby, Robin K. The Zodiac Poems.
Willoughby, Vic. Back to Basics.
Willoughby, Westal W. China at the Conference: A Report.
Willow Creek Press Editors. Wingshooter's Autumn.
Wills, B. A. Mineral Processing Technology: An Introduction to the Practical Aspects of Ore Treatment & Mineral Recovery.
Wills, David W. & Newman, Richard, eds. Black Apostles at Home & Abroad: Afro-Americans & the Christian Mission from the Revolution to Reconstruction.
Wills, G. Marketing Through Research.
Wills, Garry. Lead Time.
Wills, George. Alice in Bibleland.
Wills, Kendall & Quinn, Phyllis, eds. The Pulitzer Prizes 1987.
Wills, Simone, tr. see Weil, Simone.
Wills, Walter J. An Introduction to Grain Marketing.
Willsher, Betty & Hunter, Doreen. Stones: Eighteenth Century Scottish Gravestones.
Willsky, Alan S. Digital Signal Processing & Control & Estimation Theory: Points of Tangency, Areas of Intersection, & Parallel Directions.
Willson. A Textbook for Ward Clerks & Unit Secretaries.
Willson, A. Leslie, ed. A Gunter Grass Symposium.
Willson, A. Leslie, tr. see Grass, Gunter.
Willson, Alan N., Jr., ed. Nonlinear Networks: Theory & Analysis.
Willson, David H. & Prall, Stuart E. A History of England.
Willson, J. Robert & Carrington, Elsie R. Obstetrics & Gynecology.
Willson, K. C., jt. ed. see Clifford, M. N.
Willson, Moya. Occupational Therapy in Long-Term Psychiatry.
Willson, Robert F., Jr. Writing: Analysis & Application.
Willson, Robina B. The Voice of Music.
Wilmer, C. C. Utrecht in Drawings-Utrecht Getekend.
Wilmington Section Symposium Staff. Microprocessor Control Systems, the Concept - The Reality: Proceedings of the Wilmington Section Symposium.
Wilmore. Training for Sport & Activity: The Physiological Basis of the Conditioning Process.
Wilmore, Gayraud S. Secular Relevance of the Church.
Wilmore, Sylvia B. Swans of the World.
--Swans of the World.
Wilmot, R., ed. Who's Who in Insurance.
Wilmoth, D. Structure & Agency in the Formation of National Urban Policy in the U. S. A., 1976-1980.
Wilner, Daniel. Radiology of Bone Tumors & Allied Disorders.
Wilner, Daniel M., et al. Introduction to Public Health.
Wilpert, Bernhard, jt. auth. see Negandhi, Anant R.
Wilpert, Bernhard, et al, eds. Workers' Participation in an Internationalized Economy.
Wilson & Edington. First Child, Second Child: Your Birth Order Profile.
Wilson, jt. auth. see Harrington.
Wilson, A., ed. Major Companies of U. S. A. 1986.
Wilson, A. Bennet, Jr. Limb Prosthetics.
Wilson, A. G., et al. Optimization in Locational & Transport Analysis.
Wilson, A. N. Hilaire Belloc.
--How Can We Know? An Essay on the Christian Religion.
Wilson, Adrian. Family. McNeill, Patrick, ed.
Wilson, Alan G. Papers in Urban & Regional Analysis.
Wilson, Alex & Glennie, W., eds. Proceedings: Tenth National Passive Solar Conference, Raleigh.
Wilson, Alex, jt. ed. see Hayes, John.
Wilson, Andrew. Solar System Log.
--Space Shuttle Story.
Wilson, Arnold. Dictionary of British Marine Painters.
Wilson, Aubrey. Practice Development for Professional Firms.
Wilson, B., et al, eds. Efficiency of Manufacturing Systems.
Wilson, B. F. The Growing Tree.
Wilson, Bennie J., ed. Guard & Reserve in the Total Force: The First Decade, 1973-1983.
Wilson, Bernard E., compiled by. The Newberry Library Catalog of Early American Printed Sheet Music.
Wilson, Beth, ed. Wage Restraint & the Control of Inflation: An International Survey.
Wilson, Beth P. Giants for Justice: Bethune, Randolph & King.
Wilson, Brent. Art Education, Civilization & the 21st Century: A Researcher's Reflections on the National Endowment for the Arts' Report to Congress.
Wilson, Bruce. Can God Survive in Australia.
Wilson, Bruce L. & Corcoran, Thomas B. Places Where Children Succeed: A Profile of Outstanding Public Elementary Schools.
Wilson, C. Applied Statistics for Engineers.
Wilson, C., jt. ed. see Svehla, G.
Wilson, C. Chrisman, jt. auth. see Haynes, Stephen N.
Wilson, C. W. World Nuclear Directory.
Wilson, Carolyn F. Violence Against Women: An Annotated Bibliography.
Wilson, Charles. The Transformation of Europe, 1558-1648.
Wilson, Charles & Parker, Geoffrey, eds. Introduction to the Sources of European Economic History, 1500-1800.
Wilson, Charles B. & Hoff, Julian T. Current Surgical Management of Neurologic Disease.
Wilson, Charles L. The World of Terrariums.
Wilson, Christine, ed. see Mohamed, Ethel W.
Wilson, Christopher. Jokes: Context Use & Function.
Wilson, Christopher & Hall, Deborah. Preventing Burnout in Education: A Self-Help Approach to Managing Stress.
Wilson, Christopher, jt. ed. see Pressat, Roland.
Wilson, Clifford. Crash Go the Chariots.
Wilson, Clifford, jt. auth. see William, Lindsey.
Wilson, Clive G., et al, eds. Radionuclide Imaging in Drug Research.
Wilson, Colin. Afterlife.
--Ritual in the Dark.
--The Strength to Dream: Literature & the Imagination.
Wilson, D. Broadcasting-Vision & Sound.
--The Communicators & Society.
Wilson, D. R. Modern Practice in Servo Design.
Wilson, Daniel J. Arthur O. Lovejoy: An Annotated Bibliography.
Wilson, Dave & Wilson, Jeanne. Mr. Terwillger's Secret.
Wilson, David. The Colder, the Better.
--The Vikings & Their Origins.
Wilson, David A. VisiCalc Disk Guide.
Wilson, David G. The Treatment & Management of Urban Solid Waste.
Wilson, Derek. The Tower: The Tumultuous History of the Tower of London from 1078.
--A Tudor Tapestry: Men, Women & Society in Reformation England.
Wilson, Derek & Ayerst, Peter. White Gold: The Story of African Ivory.
Wilson, Donald T. International Business Transactions in Nutshell.
Wilson, Dorothy C. Dr. Ida: Passing on the Torch of Life.
--Queen Dolley: The Life & Times of Dolly Madison.
Wilson, Doug, jt. auth. see Mitcalfe, Ann.
Wilson, E. N., jt. auth. see Michalos, James.
Wilson, Earl J. The Mexican Caribbean: Twenty Years of Underwater Exploration.
Wilson, Edgar. The Mental As Physical.
Wilson, Edgar B. Introduction to Scientific Research.
Wilson, Edmund. The American Earthquake: A Documentary of the Twenties & Thirties.
--The Devils & Canon Barham: Essays on Poets, Novelists & Monsters.
--The Fifties: From Notebooks & Diaries of the Period. Edel, Leon, ed. & intro. by.
--Israel & the Dead Sea Scrolls.
--Stories of Light.
--The Thirties: From Notebooks & Diaries of the Period. Edel, Leon, ed.
Wilson, Edmund & Mitchell, Joseph. Apologies to the Iroquois: With a Study of the Mohawks in High Street.
Wilson, Edwin. The Theater Experience.
Wilson, Eliane, ed. Images of Christmas.
Wilson, Elizabeth, et al. Television Mythologies: Stars, Shows & Signs. Masterman, Len, ed.
Wilson, Ellen. Margaret Fuller: Bluestocking, Romantic, Revolutionary.
Wilson, Emily S. Inhabitants of New Hampshire: 1776.
Wilson, Erica. Ask Erica.
--Craft of Crewel Embroidery.
--Needlepoint Designs from the Metropolitan Museum of Art.
Wilson, Ernest H. Aristocrats of the Trees.
--Aristocrats of the Trees.
Wilson, Ernest T. The Farewell Ministry of Christ: John 13-17.
Wilson, Eugene S. & Bucher, Charles A. College Ahead! A Guide for High School Students & Their Parents.
Wilson, F. Design Calculations in Wastewater Treatment.
--Emerging Form in Architecture.
Wilson, F., jt. auth. see Barnes, D.
Wilson, Faye D., jt. auth. see Mihalyka, Jean M.
Wilson, Forbes. The Conquest of Copper Mountain.
Wilson, Frank A. Art As Revelation: The Role of Art in Human Existence.
Wilson, Frank C. Managing Costs & Improving Cash Flow.
Wilson, Frank E. Outline of Christian Symbolism.
--Outline of the Old Testament & Apocrypha.
Wilson, Frank E. & Morehouse, Clifford P. Outline Life of Christ.
Wilson, Frank L., jt. auth. see Roth, David.
Wilson, Franklin D. Residential Consumption, Economic Opportunity & Race.
Wilson, Fred M. So You Have a Retinal Detachment: A Guide for Patients.
Wilson, G. T., jt. auth. see Rachman, S. J.
Wilson, Gahan. Gahan Wilson's America.
--Gahan Wilson's America.
--I Paint What I See.
Wilson, George & Moss, Joyce. Dictionary of World Cultures.
Wilson, George C., jt. auth. see Schumacher, F. Carl.
Wilson, George W. Inflation: Causes, Consequences, & Cures.
Wilson, Gina. All Ends Up.
--Cora Ravenwing.
--The Whisper.
Wilson, Glenn D., jt. auth. see Eysenck, Hans J.
Wilson, Grady. Count It All Joy.
Wilson, Graeme, tr. see Natsume, Soseki.
Wilson, H. E., jt. auth. see Basgoz, Ilhan.
Wilson, H. T. Tradition & Innovation: The Idea of Civilization As Culture & Its Significance.
Wilson, Harold. The Chariot of Israel: Britain, America & the State of Israel.
Wilson, Harold K. & Hickman, Ronald D. The World of Business Game.
Wilson, Henry. Benares.
--Silverwork & Jewelery.
Wilson, Howard A. Invasion from the East.
Wilson, Ian. The Mysterious Shroud.
Wilson, J. Moral Education & the Curriculum.
Wilson, J., ed. see Thucydides.
Wilson, J. A. & Kaufman, Milton. Learning Electricity & Electronics Through Experiments.
Wilson, J. Christy. Flaming Prophet: The Story of Samuel Zwemer.
Wilson, J. Douglas. Practical House Carpentry: Simplified Methods for Building.
Wilson, J. P. Inflation, Deflation, Reflation: Managemnent & Accounting in Economic Uncertainty.
Wilson, J. R., jt. auth. see Johnson, G. I.
Wilson, J. R., et al. Experiments in Physical Chemistry.
Wilson, J. R., et al, eds. Experiments in Physical Chemistry. Rickett, R. M. W.
Wilson, J. S., ed. Multinational Enterprises.
Wilson, Jacques M. The Development of Education in Ecuador.
Wilson, James A. Principles of Animal Physiology.
Wilson, James B. SSB..the Misunderstood Mode.
Wilson, James F., ed. Dynamics of Offshore Structures.
Wilson, James G. Environmental & Birth Defects.
Wilson, James Q. & Herrnstein, Richard J. Crime & Human Nature.

Wilson, James R. No Ordinary Crime.
Wilson, Jane B. Children's Writings: A Bibliography of Works in English.
Wilson, Jane W. Eating Well! Living Well! The Over-50 Cookbook.
Wilson, Jeanne, jt. auth. see Wilson, Dave.
Wilson, Jerry, jt. auth. see Fuqua, Paul.
Wilson, Jerry B. Death by Decision: The Medical, Moral, & Legal Dilemmas of Euthanasia.
Wilson, Jerry D. Practical Physics.
Wilson, Jim, jt. auth. see Wilson, Lynn.
Wilson, Joan H. Ideology & Economics: U. S. Relations with the Soviet Union, 1918-1933.
Wilson, John, jt. auth. see Oliver, Eric.
Wilson, John, ed. Working Posture: Case Studies in Ergonomic Practice.
Wilson, John C. On the Interpretation of Plato's Timaeus. Taran, Leonardo, ed. Bd. with On the Platonist Doctrine of the Classical Review XVIII. Garland Pub.
Wilson, John D. The Elizabethan Shakespeare.
Wilson, John H., ed. Genetic Recombination & Rearrangement.
Wilson, John H., Jr. Glory in the Flower.
Wilson, John M. The Painting of the Passions in Theory, Practice & Criticsm in Later Eighteen Century France.
Wilson, John O. The Power Economy: Building an Economy That Works.
Wilson, Jose & Leaman, Arthur. The Collectors Catalogue.
--The Second Complete Home Decorating Catalogue.
Wilson, Jose, jt. auth. see Groff, Betty.
Wilson, Justin & Jacobs, Howard. More Cajun Humor.
Wilson, Keith. Homestead.
Wilson, Keith M., ed. Imperialism & Nationalism in the Middle East: The Anglo-Egyptian Experience 1882-1982.
Wilson, Ken. God First: What It Means to Love God Above All Things.
--How to Repair the Wrong You've Done.
--Sons & Daughters of God: Our New Identity in Christ.
Wilson, Lanford. The Gingham Dog.
Wilson, Laurie. Louise Nevelson: Iconography & Sources.
Wilson, Lawrence, tr. see Rothfels, Hans.
Wilson, Leslie A., tr. see Grass, Gunter.
Wilson, Loring D. Encyclopedia of Fishing Lures.
Wilson, Lynn & Wilson, Jim. Sierra Sunrise. Leon, Vicki, ed.
Wilson, M. J., jt. auth. see Miller, P. M.
Wilson, McClure. The Anatomic Foundation of Neuroradiology of the Brain.
Wilson, Mae. Wake up, Poor American People.
Wilson, Mamie T. A Teachers Guide for Teaching Educable Mental Retardates How to Read.
Wilson, Marjorie K., tr. see Lorenz, Konrad.
Wilson, Marvin R., jt. ed. see Tanenbaum, Marc H.
Wilson, May. Smoke Away!
Wilson, Mercedes. The Ovulation Method of Birth Regulation.
Wilson, Mercedes A. The Ovulation Method of Birth Regulation: The Latest Advances for Achieving or Postponing Pregnancy--Naturally.
Wilson, Michael. History for Pupils with Learning Difficulties.
Wilson, Michael, jt. auth. see Wuerl, Donald.
Wilson, Milton T. Shelley's Later Poetry.
Wilson, Nadine C. Guide to Decoration in the Early American Manner.
Wilson, Nancy O. Parents' Guide to "Teacherese" A Glossary of Special Education Terms.
Wilson, P. L. & Pourjavady, N. Kings of Love: The Poetry & History of the Ni'matullahi Sufi Order of Iran.
Wilson, P. N. & Brigstocke, T. D. Improved Feeding of Cattle & Sheep.
Wilson, Patricia P. Household Equipment: Selection & Management.
Wilson, Paul. Turning Islands.
Wilson, Paul R. The Other Side of Rape.
Wilson, Peter, jt. auth. see Gibbons, Bob.
Wilson, Peter H., et al. Behavioral Interviewing for Adult Disorders.
Wilson, Peter L., tr. see Nasr, Seyyed H.
Wilson, Peter M. Simplified Swahili.
Wilson, R. A. The Miraculous Birth of Language.
Wilson, R. A., tr. see Ebeling, Gerhard.
Wilson, R. A., tr. see Franke, Wolfgang.
Wilson, R. A., tr. see Hollenwager, Walter J.
Wilson, R. B. Henry James's Ultimate Narrative: The Golden Bowl.
Wilson, R. D, jt. auth. see McLean, Eric.
Wilson, R. M. The Lost Literature of Medieval England.
Wilson, Raymond, jt. ed. see Watson, Keith.
Wilson, Reggie, jt. auth. see Tarraborrelli, J. Randy.
Wilson, Richard F., ed. Designing Academic Program Reviews.
Wilson, Robert, jt. auth. see Carroll, Jackson.
Wilson, Robert E. The Modern School Superintendent: His Principles & Practices.
Wilson, Robert W., et al. Innovation, Competition & Government Policy in the Semiconductor Industry.
Wilson, Ruth. Here is Haiti.
Wilson, S. E., et al. Intra-Abdominal Infection.
Wilson, S. R., ed. see Traven, B.
Wilson, Sandi. Be the Boss: Start & Run Your Own Service Business.
Wilson, Sherrian, ed. see Jordan, William R., Sr.
Wilson, Sherrian P., ed. see Jordan, William R., Sr.
Wilson, Sloan. The Greatest Crime.
--Ice Brothers.
--The Man in the Gray Flannel Suit.
--Pacific Interlude.
--Small Town.
--What Shall We Wear to This Party? The Man in the Gray Flannel Suit Twenty Years Before & after.
Wilson, Snoo. Pleasure Principle.
Wilson, Stephen. Harvey Couch: An Entrepreneur Brings Electricity to Arkansas.
Wilson, T., jt. ed. see Rachman, S.
Wilson, T. D. & Stephenson, J. Dissemination of Information.
Wilson, Tom. Ziggy in the Rough.
Wilson, Verity. Chinese Dress.
Wilson, Vivian, compiled by. Bibliography of Published Works by Kenneth E. Boulding.
Wilson, W. D., jt. auth. see Cunningham, Joyce I.
Wilson, W. K., jt. ed. see Aitken, F. C.
Wilson, Wesley R., jt. auth. see Hale, Charles D.
Wilson, William E., jt. auth. see Garcia-Prada, Carlos.
Wilson, William S., tr. see Tsuneyomo, Yamamoto.
Wilson-Barnett, Jennifer & Raiman, Jennifer, eds. Nursing Issues & Research in Terminal Care.
Wilson-Heaney, Katherine, illus. Benji & Zax: A Maze Story Book.
Wilson-Kastner, Patricia. Faith, Feminism & the Christ.
Wilt, J. Encyclopedia of Architecture. Papworth, W., ed.
Wilt, Judith. The Readable People of George Meredith.
Wilterdink, Garret. Tyrant or Father? A Study of Calvin's Doctrine of God.
Wilton, George W. Fingerprints: History, Law & Romance.
Wilton, Keri M., jt. ed. see Sigh, Nirbhan N.
Wilton, McKinley & Wilton, Norman. Pictorial Encyclopedia of Modern Cake Decorating.
Wilton, Norman, jt. auth. see Wilton, McKinley.
Wilton-Ely, John. The Mind & Art of Giovanni Battista Piranesi.
Wiltsee, Joseph L. & Sammons, Donna. You Can Profit from the New Tax Law.
Wiltsher, Anne. Most Dangerous Women: Feminist Peace Campaigners of the Great War.
Wiltz, John E. & Cridland, Nancy C. Books in American History: A Basic List for High Schools & Junior Colleges.
Wilvert, Ruth B. Georgia Psychic: Ellen Evans.
Wimbish, Dave, jt. auth. see Testrake, John.
Wimmer, Joseph F. Fasting in the New Testament.
Wimperis, Arthur, jt. auth. see Biro, Lajos.
Wimsatt, James I. Allegory & Mirror: Tradition & Structure in Middle English Literature.
Wimsatt, William K., Jr. The Prose Style of Samuel Johnson.
Winans, A. D., ed. see Reith, Kimi.
Winberg, G. G. Methods for the Estimation of Production of Aquatic Animals.
Winblad, ed. see International Symposium on Yersinia, Pasteurella & Francisella Staff.
Winbolt, Samuel E. Latin Hexametre Verse. Commager, Steele, ed.
Winburne, Frank. Elevations of Love-to Women (Real & Imagined)
Winch, Peter. Ethics & Action.
Winchester, A. M. Genetics: A Survey of the Principles of Heredity.
Winchester, Mark B., ed. The International Essays for Business Decision Makers.
--The International Essays for Business Decision Makers.
--The International Essays for Business Decision Makers 1977.
Winckelmann, J. J. Versuch einer Allegorie. Bd. with De L'Allegorie. Winckelmann, J. J. Garland Pub.
Wincor, Richard. Rights Contracts in the Communictions Media.
Wind, Herbert W. Following Through: Herbert Warren Wind on Golf.
Windass, Stan. Politics Thro' the Looking Glass.
Windeknect, Thomas G. General Dynamical Processes: A Mathematical Introduction.
Windell, John T., et al. Ecological Characteristics of Rocky Mountain Montane & Subalpine Wetlands.
Winders, P. Understanding Hamlet.
Windham, Kathryn T. Jeffrey's Latest Thirteen: More Alabama Ghosts.
--Southern Cooking to Remember.
--Thirteen Georgia Ghosts & Jeffrey.
--Thirteen Mississippi Ghosts & Jeffrey.
--Treasured Alabama Recipes.
--Treasured Georgia Recipes.
--Treasured Tennessee Recipes.
Windham, Kathryn T. & Figh, Margaret G. Thirteen Alabama Ghosts & Jeffrey.
Windham, Susan R., jt. auth. see Sheldon, Alan.
Windisch, Hans. Spirit-Paraclete in the Fourth Gospel. Reumann, John, ed. Cox, James W., tr. from Ger.
Windle, Kevin, tr. see Vampilov, A., et al.
Windle, William F. The Pioneering Role of Clarence Luther Herrick in American Neuroscience.
Windmuller, John P., ed. Collective Bargaining in Industrialised Market Economies: A Comparative Study of Methods & Practices.
Windsor, jt. auth. see Spence.
Windsor, Colin G. Pulsed Neutron Scattering.
Windsor, Patricia. How a Weirdo & a Ghost Can Change Your Entire Life.
Windsor, Rudolphf R. The Valley of the Dry Bones.
Windt, Gaye de. Mystical Poems.
Windt, Gaye de see De Windt, Gaye.
Windt, Gaye de see Windt, Gaye de.
Windt, Theodore. Presidential Rhetoric, Nineteen Sixty-One to the Present.
Windt, Theodore O. & Ingold, Beth. Essays in Presidential Rhetoric.
Wine Museum of San Francisco Staff, ed. Wine & the Artist: One Hundred & Four Prints & Drawings from the Christian Brothers Collection at the Wine Museum of San Francisco.
Winebrenner, Rosemary. How Can I Get My Teenager to Read?
Winer, Gershon. The Founding Fathers of Israel.
Winer, Marc S., jt. auth. see Simmons, Seymour.
Winfree, Arthur T. The Timing of Biological Clocks.
Wing. What Is a Case?
Wing, Charles. From the Walls In.
--House Warming.
Wing, Herbert. Tests of Musical Ability & Appreciation.
Wing, John, jt. auth. see Leech, John.
Wingard, Lemual B., et al, eds. Enzyme Engineering: Future Directions.
Wingard, Lemuel B., jt. ed. see Pye, E. Kendall.
Wingate, Francis R., tr. see Slatin, Rudolf C.
Wingate, Isabel B., et al. Know Your Merchandise: For Retailers & Consumers.
Winger, Alan R. & Thomas, Margaret R. Financing Real Estate: Analysis & Application.
Winger, Howard W., ed. American Library History: 1876-1976.
Wingert, Norm, jt. auth. see Miller, Al.
Wingfield, Sheila. Collected Poems, 1938-1983.
Wingfield Digby, Cornelia, tr. see Spuhler, Friedrich.
Wingfield Digby, George, tr. see Spuhler, Friedrich.
Wingfield-Stratford, Esme C. Before the Lamps Went Out.
Wingo, Nancy J., jt. auth. see Wingo, Robert M.
Wingo, Robert M. & Wingo, Nancy J. Charley Potata's.
Wingren, Gustaf. Credo: The Christian View of Faith & Life. Carlson, Edgar M., tr.
Wingrove, Janet M. see Boswell, David M.
Winham, Donald, ed. see Williams, Tennessee.
Winick, Charles. Dictionary of Anthropology.
Winick, Mariann P. The Progressive Education Movement: An Annotated Bibliography.
--The Teacher in Fiction, Non-Fiction, Films & Drama: An Annotated Bibliography.
Winick, Myron, ed. see Institute of Human Nutrition, Columbia University College of Physicians & Surgeons.
Winig, Laura, jt. auth. see Staryos, Michelle M.
Winikoff, B., jt. ed. see Segal, S. J.
Wink, Richard. Fundamentals of Music.
Wink, Richard L. & Williams, Lois. Invitation to Listening.
Winkel, David E. & Prosser, Franklin P. The Art of Digital Design: An Introduction to Top-Down Design.
Winkel, Zum, et al, eds. Radionuclides in Nephrology.
Winkelmann, Richard K., et al, eds. Systemic Sclerosis: Current Research.
Winkfield, Patricia W., et al. Bridges to Employment: Recruitment & Counseling Practices for Disadvantaged, Unemployed, Out-of-School Youth in Vocational Programs.
Winkfield, Trevor, tr. see Roussel, Raymond.
Winkle, Cornelius S. van. The Printer's Guide: Or, an Introduction to the Art of Printing Including an Essay on Punctuation & Remarks on Orthography.
Winkle, Gary M., jt. auth. see Cook, John W.
Winkler, Anthony C. & McCuen, Jo R. Rhetoric Made Plain.
Winkler, Anthony C. & McCuen, Jo Ray. Rhetoric Made Plain.
--Writing the Research Paper: A Handbook.
Winkler, Anthony C., jt. auth. see McCuen, Jo R.
Winkler, Anthony C., jt. auth. see McCuen, Jo Ray.
Winkler, Anthony C., jt. auth. see McCuen, JoRay.
Winkler, Anthony C., jt. auth. see Ochs, Donovan J.
Winkler, Carl A., jt. auth. see Wright, A. Nelson.
Winkler, Charles, jt. auth. see Figueroa, Oscar.
Winkler, E. M. Stone, Properties, Durability in Man's Environment.
Winkler, John K. Farm Animal Health & Disease Control.
Winkler, Paul W., jt. ed. see Gorman, Michael.
Winkless, Nelson B., III. If I Had a Robot... What to Expect from the Personal Robot.
Winklevoss, Howard E. Pension Mathematics: With Numerical Illustrations.
Winklevoss, Howard E. & Powell, Alwyn V. Continuing Care Retirement Communities: An Empirical, Financial, & Legal Analysis.
Winks, Robin W. An American's Guide to Britain.
--An American's Guide to Britain.
Winks, Robin W., ed. Colloquium on Crime: Eleven Reowned Mystery Writers Discuss Their Work.
Winn, Albert C. A Sense of Mission: Guidance from the Gospel of John.
--Worry & Wonder of Being Human.
Winn, Albert C., jt. auth. see Burgess, Joseph A.
Winn, Charles S. Careers in Focus Program Guide.
Winn, Charles S. & Baker, M. C. Exploring Occupations in Food Service & Home Economics.
Winn, Charles S. & Davis, L. M. Exploring Occupations in Science, Fine Arts & Humanities.
Winn, Charles S. & Healy, C. Discovering You.
Winn, Charles S. & Heath, L. Exploring Occupations in Electricity & Electronics.
Winn, Charles S. & Vorndran, B. J. Exploring Occupations in Personal Services, Hospitality & Recreation.
Winn, Charles S. & Walsh, Lawrence A. Exploring Transportation Occupations.
Winn, Charles S., et al. Exploring Health Occupations.
--Exploring Occupations in Agribusiness & Natural Resources.
--Exploring Occupations in Communication & Graphic Arts.
--Exploring Occupations in Engineering & Manufacturing.
--Exploring Occupations in Public & Social Services.
--Exploring Marketing Occupations.
--Exploring Construction Occupations.
Winn, Chris. My Day.
Winn, Dilys. Murder Ink: Revived, Revised, Still Unrepentant.
Winn, Janet, jt. auth. see Boehm, Bruce.
Winn, Joshua N., III. Muscle Shoals Canal...Life with the Canalers.
Winn, Lela P. The Marsh: A Century of Cranberries.
Winn, Paul R., jt. auth. see Johnson, Ross H.
Winn, Ralph B. Dictionary of Existentialism.
--Dictionary of Hypnosis.
--Encyclopedia of Child Guidance.
Winn, Ralph B., tr. see Vsesoiuznaia Konferentsiia Po Voprosam Psikhoterapil Staff.
Winner, Walter P., ed. see Federal Aviation Administration Staff.
Winnie, Richard E., et al. Jobs & Earnings for State Citizens: Monitoring the Outcomes of State Economic Development & Employment & Training Programs.
Winokur, Robert P., jt. auth. see DeByle, Norbert V.
Winpenny, Thomas R. Industrial Progress & Human Welfare: The Rise of the Factory System in 19th Century Lancaster.
Winsberg, Fred & Cooperberg, Peter L., eds. Real-Time Ultrasonography.
Winsbury, Rex, et al. Viewdata in Action: A Comparative Study of Prestel.
Winship, Elizabeth. Ask Beth: You Can't Ask Your Mother.
Winslow, Anna G. Diary of Anna Green Winslow, a Boston Schoolgirl of 1771. Earle, Allic M., ed.
Winslow, Edward, jt. auth. see Bradford, William.
Winslow, Laurel. Captured Images.
--Heart Songs.
Winslow, R. C. Butterflies: If You Throw It.
Winslow, Robert W. & Dallin, Leon. Music Skills for Classroom Teacher.
Winslow, Ron. Hard Aground: The Story of the Argo Merchant Oil Spill.
Winspear, Violet. The Awakening of Alice.
--The Burning Sands.
--The Valdez Marriage.
Winstead, Verna S. Lines from Beyond.
Winstedt, Richard. Indian Art.
--Malay Proverbs. Kwang, Tan C., ed.
--The Malays.
Winston. Logos.

Winston, Clara, tr. see Arendt, Hannah.
Winston, Clara, tr. see Benary-Isbert, Margot.
Winston, Clara, tr. see Fest, Joachim.
Winston, Clara, tr. see George, Uwe.
Winston, Clara, tr. see Gisevius, Hans B.
Winston, Clara, tr. see Hochhuth, Rolf.
Winston, Clara, tr. see Pieper, Josef, et al.
Winston, Clara, tr. see Schadlich, Hans J.
Winston, Clara, tr. see Thorwald, Jurgen.
Winston, Daoma. Emerald Station.
--Mira.
--Moorhaven.
--A Sweet Familiarity.
Winston, Krishna, tr. see Weil, Grete.
Winston, Mary & Eshleman, Ruthe, eds. American Heart Association Cookbook.
Winston, Patrick, jt. auth. see Davis, Randall.
Winston, Richard, tr. see Arendt, Hannah.
Winston, Richard, tr. see Benary-Isbert, Margot.
Winston, Richard, tr. see Fest, Joachim.
Winston, Richard, tr. see George, Uwe.
Winston, Richard, tr. see Gisevius, Hans B.
Winston, Richard, tr. see Hochhuth, Rolf.
Winston, Richard, tr. see Pieper, Josef, et al.
Winston, Richard, tr. see Schadlich, Hans J.
Winston, Richard, tr. see Thorwald, Jurgen.
Winston, Stephanie. Getting Organized: Time & Paperwork.
--The Organized Executive: New Ways to Manage Time, Paper, & People.
Winstone, Harold, jt. ed. see Jasper, Ronald.
Winter, Alice. The Velvet Bubble.
Winter, D., ed. see Interdisciplinary Conference, Ann Arbor, March 1973.
Winter, E. R., et al. Recent Developments in Boiling & Condensation: Reprotext.
Winter, Ella. And Not to Yield: An Autobiography.
Winter, George D., et al, eds. Biomaterials, 1980.
Winter, Gordon. Country Camera, Eighteen Forty-Four to Nineteen Fourteen: Rural Life As Depicted in Photographs from the Early Days of Photography to the Outbreak of the First World War.
--The Country Life Picture Book of Britain.
--The Country Life Picture Book of Royal London.
--The Country Life Picture Book of the Thames.
Winter, H. Frank & Shourd, Melvin L. Review of Human Physiology.
Winter, John V. & Conner, David A. Power Plant Siting.
Winter, Michael E. Basic Clinical Pharmacokinetics.
Winter, Michael F. The Professionalization of Librarianship.
Winter, Ralph K., Jr. The Consumer Advocate Versus the Consumer.
Winter, Robert H., et al, eds. A Guide to Shark Repellant & Golden Parachute Clauses.
Winter, Robin M., et al. The Malformed Fetus & Stillbirth: A Diagnostic Approach.
Winter, Ruth. The Consumer's Dictionary of Cosmetic Ingredients.
--A Consumer's Dictionary of Food Additives.
Winter School on Probability Staff, et al. Probability Winter School: Proceedings of the Winter School on Probability, 4th, Karpacz, Poland, Jan., 1975.
Wintercross, Paul W. The Absolutely Definite Philosophy for the Intelligence of Contemporary Man.
Winterfeld, Henry. Castaways in Lilliput. Schabert, Kyrill, tr.
--Detectives in Togas.
--Mystery of the Roman Ransom. McCormick, Edith, tr.
--Mystery of the Roman Ransom. McCormick, Edith, tr. from Ger.
Winterfeldt, E., jt. ed. see Mutschler, E.
Winterfield, Henry. Star Girl.
Winterich, John T. Early American Books & Printing.
Winterkorn, Hans F. & Fang, F. Y., eds. Foundation Engineering Handbook.
Winternitz, Emanuel. Musical Autographs from Monteverdi to Hindemith.
Winters, J. C. Berlin Fugle.
Winters, Jon. The Catenary Exchange.
--The Drakov Memoranda.
Winters, Margaret K., jt. ed. see Higbee, Homer.
Winters, Raymond J. It's Different When You Manage.
Winters, Robert W., ed. The Body Fluids in Pediatrics: Medical, Surgical, & Neonatal Disorders of Acid-Base Status, Hydration & Oxygenation.
Winters, Ted & Janssen, Al. Lifer.
Winterspoon, Jeanette. Fit for the Future: The Guide for Women Who Want to Live Well.
Winterspoon, Jeannette, ed. Passion Fruit.
Winther, Aage, jt. ed. see Alder, Kurt.
Winther, Trygve. Trygve.
Winthrop, Elizabeth. Potbellied Possums.
--Sloppy Kisses.
Winthrop, H. Psychological Aspects of Community: Alienation, Identity & Social Breakdown.
Winthrop, Henry. The Humanistic Viewpoint in the Social Sciences.
--Marginal Aspects of Contemporary American Culture.
Winthrop, Robert D., jt. auth. see Munch, Theodore W.
Wintle, Justin. Mortadella.
Wintle, Justin, ed. Dictionary of Modern Culture.
Winton, R. C., jt. auth. see Dummer, Geoffrey W.
Winton, Tim. Shallows.
Wintrobe, Maxwell M., et al. Clinical Hematology.
Winward, Walter. Fives Wild.
Winzler, R. J., jt. auth. see Wallach, D. F.
Wionczek, M. S., jt. auth. see World Hydrocarbon Markets Staff.
Wionczek, Miguel S. Some Key Issues for the World Periphery: Selected Essays.
Wiora, Walter. Four Ages of Music. Norton, M. Herter, tr.
Wipke, W. Todd, et al, eds. Computer Representation & Manipulation of Chemical Information.
Wire, Elinor de see De Wire, Elinor.
Wireman, Peggy. Urban Neighborhoods, Networks & Families.
Wiren, Gary. Golf.
Wirsen, Claes, et al. A Child Is Born: The Drama of Life Before Birth.
Wirt, George, jt. auth. see Dawkins, Darryl.
Wirt, Sherwood. Go Tell It.
Wirt, Sherwood E. The Confessions of Augustine in Modern English.
--The Making of a Writer: A Christian Writer's Guide.
Wirt, Sherwood E. & McKinney, Ruth. You Can Tell the World: New Directions for Christian Writers.
Wirtenberg, Patricia Z. The All-Around-the-House Art & Craft Book.
--All-Around-The-House Art & Craft Book.
Wirth, Beverly. Margie & Me.
Wirthmuller, K., jt. auth. see Gibson, C. G.
Wirths, Wallace R. Democracy: Panacea or Pandemonium?
Wischnia, Bob & Post, Marty. Running: A Guide to the Literature.
Wischnitzer, Saul. Barron's Guide to Medical & Dental Schools.
Wisdom, John. The Socratic: Comtemporary Philosophy & Christian Faith.
Wisdom, Linda R. For Better or Worse.
--Guardian Angel.
--Island Rogue.
Wise. Academic Achievement Job.
Wise, A., jt. auth. see Monie, J.
Wise, David, jt. auth. see Cummings, Milton C., Jr.
Wise, E. M. & Mueller, G. O. Studies in Comparative Criminal Law.
Wise, George S. & Issawi, Charles, eds. Middle East Perspectives: The Next Twenty Years.
Wise, J. C. Philosophic History of Civilizations.
Wise, Jacqueline A. & Soulen, Robert J., Jr. Thermometer Calibration: A Model for State Calibration Laboratories.
Wise, Katherine, ed. see Fisher Broadcasting Staff.
Wise, M. The Common Fisheries Policy of the European Community.
Wise, Robert. The Pastors' Barracks.
Wise, Robert E., jt. auth. see Hatfield, Philip M.
Wise, Robert L. The Scrolls of Edessa.
Wise, Rosemary, jt. auth. see Tyrrell, John.
Wise, S. & Stanley, L., eds. Men & Sex: A Case Study in "Sexual Politics"
Wise, Sue, jt. auth. see Stanley, Liz.
Wise, Thomas J. Introduction to the Ashley Library Catalog 1922-30.
Wiselogle, Anndy & Church, Virginia. Best Bike Rides Around Portland.
Wiseman, A. J., jt. auth. see Lockhart, J. A.
Wiseman, Alan, ed. Principles of Biotechnology.
Wiseman, Ann. Making Things.
Wiseman, Anne, tr. see Caesar, Julius.
Wiseman, Bernard. Don't Make Fun!
--Handy Hound.
Wiseman, D. J., ed. see Wiseman, P. J.
Wiseman, Lawrence. Discipling for Jesus.
Wiseman, Nicholas P. Fabiola; or, the Church of the Catacombs, 1854. Wolff, Robert L., ed.
Wiseman, P. J. Ancient Records & the Structure of Genesis. Wiseman, D. J., ed.
Wiseman, Peter, tr. see Caesar, Julius.
Wiseman, Rex. The Okara Mask.
Wiseman, Thomas. Children of the Ruins.
Wisener, John N., Jr., jt. auth. see Sweeny, Allen.
Wisenthal, J. L. Shaw & Ibsen: Bernard Shaw's 'The Quintessence of Ibsenism' & Related Writings.
Wiser, Guy B. Wolf Not Native France.
Wiser, William. Ballads, Blues & Swan Songs.
--The Crazy Years: Paris in the Twenties.
--Disappearances.
Wish, Harvey. The American Historian: A Social-Intellectual History of the Writing of the American Past.
Wishard, Laurie & Wishard, William R. Adoption: The Grafted Tree.
Wishard, Roy H., jt. auth. see Brown, Robert H.
Wishard, William R., jt. auth. see Wishard, Laurie.
Wishart, Arthur A. Foreword by see Zimmerman, Adam C.
Wishart, Barry J. & Reichman, Louis C. Modern Sociological Issues.
Wishman, Seymour. Anatomy of a Jury: The System on Trial.
Wiskemann, Elizabeth. Europe of the Dictators, 1919-1945.
Wiskemann, Elizabeth, tr. see Leonhard, Wolfgang.
Wisland, Milton V. Psychoeducational Diagnosis of Exceptional Children.
Wisler, G. Clifton. The Trident Brand.
Wisloff, Fredrik. On Our Father's Knee: Devotions for Times of Illness.
Wisloff, Hans E. Safe in His Arms. Njus, Joel M., tr.
Wismer. Introduction to Nonlinear Optimization.
Wismer, Don. The Islamic Jesus: An Annotated Bibliography of Sources in English & French.
Wismer, Robert K., jt. auth. see Petrucci, Ralph H.
Wisner, D. E. A Robber of a Tither?
Wissenschaftliche Konferenz der Gesellschaft Deutscher Naturforscher und Aerzte, 4th, Berlin, 1967. Molecular Genetics: Proceedings. Wittmann, H. G. & Schuster, H., eds.
Wissler, Robert W. & Geer, J. C., eds. The Pathogenesis of Arteriosclerosis.
Wissman. Wealth of the Mind.
Wister, Owen. The Virginian.
Wister, Sarah. Sally Wister's Journal.
Wistrand, Erik. Caesar & Contemporary Roman Society.
Wistrand, Magnus. Cicero Imperator: Studies in Cicero's Correspondence 51 to 47 B. C.
Witanowski, M. & Webb, G. A., eds. Nitrogen NMR.
Witbeck, Pete, jt. auth. see Allsen, Philip E.
Witcher, William K. How To Solve Your Small Business Advertising Problems: The All Media Guide To Effective Advertising.
Witcofski, Richard L., jt. auth. see Pizzarello, Donald J.
Witcomb, John, jt. auth. see Collett, George.
Witherell, Warren. How the Racers Ski.
Witheridge, Elizabeth. Just One Indian Boy.
Withers, Carl A. Rocket in My Pocket: Rhymes & Chants of Young Americans.
Withers, Lyndsey A. & Alderson, P. G. Plant Tissue Culture & Its Agricultural Applications.
Withers, William. Politics & Economics Policy: From Hoover to Reagan.
Witherspoon, Alexander M. & Warnke, Frank J. Seventeenth Century Prose & Poetry.
Witherspoon, Alexander M., ed. College Survey of English Literature.
Witherspoon, Gary, jt. auth. see Carlson, Vada.
Witherspoon, June N. Lazy Jack & Other Children's Stories.
Withey, Elsie R., jt. auth. see Withey, Henry F.
Withey, Henry F. & Withey, Elsie R. Biographical Dictionary of American Architects Deceased.
Withey, J. A., jt. auth. see Sein, Kenneth.
Witken, Andrew, jt. ed. see Tenenbaum, J. Martin.
Witkin, B. E. California Crimes & Criminal Procedure.
Witkin, Joel P., photos by. Joel Peter Witkin: Photographs.
Witkin, Joel-Peter, ed. Masterpieces of Medical Photography.
Witkin, Ruth K. Managing Your Business with Multiplan: How to Use Microsoft's Award-Winning Electronic Spreadsheet on Your IBM PC.
Witkowski, Isidor see Harden, Maximilian.
Witlig, Monique. Les Guerilleres.
Witmer, Dallas. El Reino de las Tinieblos.
Witney, Fred, jt. auth. see Sloane, Arthur A.
Witt, Gary, jt. auth. see Shook, Georg.
Witt, Peter A., jt. ed. see Goodale, Thomas.
Witt, Peter N., et al. Spider's Web: Problems in Regulatory Biology.
Witt, Robert E. Another Autumn & Other Poems.
--Indian Summer & More.
Witt, Ted R. Responsible with Creation.
Witt, Twylla. Bosoms & Bras & Me.
Wittcoff, Harold & Reuben, Bryan G. Industrial Organic Chemicals in Perspective, Part 2: Technology, Formulation & Use.
Wittcoff, Harold A. & Reuben, Bryan G. Industrial Organic Chemicals in Perspective.
Witte, Michael C. Claus!
Witte, Robert S. Statistics.
Witte, Stephen P., jt. auth. see Faigley, Lester.
Wittek, P. Turkish Reader.
Wittels, Fritz. Freud & His Time.
Wittels, Herbert G. Blood Sun in Jerusalem.
Wittemore, Edward. Quin's Shanghai Circus.
Witter, Evelyn. How to Make Sunday School Fun for Everyone. Ronaldson, Dolores, ed.
Witter, Evelyn, jt. auth. see Collins, David.
Witters, Weldon, jt. auth. see Witters-Jones, Patricia.
Witters-Jones, Patricia & Witters, Weldon. Drugs & Society: A Biological Perspective.
Wittes, Robert E., ed. Head & Neck Cancer.
Wittgenstein, Ludwig. Last Writings, Preliminary Studies for Part Two Philosophical Investigations. Luckhardt, C. G. & Aue, Maximilian A. E., trs.
--Tractatus Logico-Philosophicus. Pears, D. F. & McGuinness, B. F., trs. from Ger.
--Wittgenstein's Lectures, Cambridge 1932-1935. Macdonald, Margaret & Ambrose, Alice, eds.
Wittich, John. Discovering London's Villages.
Wittig, Arno F. Schaum's Outline of Psychology of Learning.
Wittig, Monique & Zeig, Sande. Lesbian Peoples.
Wittington, Vi. Special Occasion Cake Decorating.
Wittke, Carl. The First Fifty Years: The Cleveland Museum of Art 1916-1966.
Wittman, A. & Klos, J. Dictionary of Data Processing, Including Applications in Industry.
Wittmann, H. G., ed. see Wissenschaftliche Konferenz der Gesellschaft Deutscher Naturforscher und Aerzte, 4th, Berlin, 1967.
Wittmer, Joseph, jt. auth. see Vacc, Nicholas.
Wittram, Reinhard. Russia & Europe.
Witty, Paul A., ed. Development in & Through Reading.
--Mental Health in Modern Education.
Witzel, S. A. Log Buildings.
Witzmann, Rupert F. Steroids: The Keys to Life.
Wixom, William D. Renaissance Bronzes: From Ohio Collections.
Wizenberg, Larry, jt. ed. see Bobrow, Edwin E.
Wizig, Jerry. Eat 'Em up, Cougars, Houston Football.
Wiznitzer, Martine R. Power Skills in Mathematics.
Wobbe, R. A. Graham Greene: A Bibliography & Guide to Research.
Wobschall, Darold C. Circuit Design for Electronic Instrumentation: Analog & Digital Devices from Sensor to Display.
Wodarski, John S. Introduction to Human Behavior.
Wodehouse, Lawrence, ed. American Architects from the Civil War to the First World War: A Guide to Information Sources.
--British Architects, Eighteen Forty to Nineteen Seventy-Six: A Guide to Information Sources.
--Indigenous Architecture Worldwide: A Guide to Information Sources.
Wodehouse, P. G. Bachelors Anonymous.
--Fore! The Best of Wodehouse on Golf. Bensen, D. R., ed.
--Jeeves, Jeeves, Jeeves.
--A Wodehouse Bestiary. Bensen, D. R., ed.
--Wodehouse on Crime. Bensen, D. R., ed.
--The World of Mr. Mulliner.
Wodsedalek, J. E. & Lytle, Charles F. General Zoology Laboratory Guide: Complete Version.
Woehr, Richard, et al. Espanol Esencial: Un Repaso.
Woelck, Wolfgang, ed. see Linguistic Association of Canada & the U. S. Staff.
Woelcken, Fritz. Der Literarische Mord. Bleiler, E. F., ed.
Woelfel, Julian B., ed. Dental Anatomy: Its Correlation with Dental Health Service.
Woelfl, Paul. Politics & Jurisprudence.
Woellner, Elizabeth H. Requirements for Certification of Teachers, Counselors, Librarians, Administrators for Elementary Schools, Secondary Schools, Junior Colleges, 1981-82.
--Requirements for Certification of Teachers, Counselors, Librarians, Administrators for Secondary Schools, Junior Colleges, 1983.
--Requirements for Certification of Teachers, Counselors, Librarians, Administrators: 1980-81.
Woerdeman, M. W., jt. auth. see Langman, Jan.
Woerdeman, M. W., jt. auth. see Longman, Jan.
Woerdman, M. W., jt. auth. see Langman, Jan.
Woerkom, Dorothy Van see Van Woerkom, Dorothy.
Woessner, J. F., Jr., ed. see Miami Winter Symposium Staff.
Woff, Richard. Soviet High Command.
Woffinden, Bob. Miscarriages of Justice.
Wofford, Harris. Of Kennedys & Kings: Making Sense of the Sixties.
Wofford, J. C. Organizational Behavior: Foundation for Organizational Effectiveness.
Wofsy, Samuel A., ed. see Buero Vallejo, Antonio.
Wogaman, J. P. Economics & Ethics: A Christian Inquiry.
Wogaman, J. Philip. A Christian Method of Moral Judgment.
--Faith & Fragmentation: Christianity for a New Age.
Wohl, Anthony S. The Eternal Slum: Housing & Social Policy in Victorian London.
Wohl, G., jt. auth. see Edwards, A.
Wohl, Martin & Hendrickson, Chris. Transportation Investment & Pricing Principles: An Introduction for Engineers & Planners.

Wohl, Milton. Techniques for Writing: Composition.
Wohlbier, H., et al, eds. Worldwide Directory of Mineral Industries Education & Research.
Wohlers, Ronald W. Lumped & Distributed Passive Networks: A Generalized & Advanced Viewpoint.
Wohlfahrt, Franz. Forty Elementary Exercises for Violin. Sitt, Hans, ed.
Wohlfarth, Hannsdieter. Johann Sebastian Bach. Blackwell, Albert L., tr.
Wohlgemuth, M. Song of Zion.
Wohlwill, J. F., jt. ed. see Altman, Irwin.
Woiwode, Larry. Beyond the Bedroom Wall.
Wojahn, Karen A., jt. auth. see Rogers, Roy.
Wojciechowska, Maia. The Life & Death of a Brave Bull.
--Through the Broken Mirror with Alice.
--Till the Break of Day.
Wojtasiewicz, Olgierd, tr. see Schaff, Adam.
Wojtyla, Karol see Pope John Paul II.
Wolansky, William D., et al. Fundamentals of Fluid Power.
Wolberg, Arlene R. The Borderline Patient.
Wolberg, Barbara J. Zooming in: Photographic Discoveries Under the Microscope.
Wolberg, John R. Conversion of Computer Software.
Wolchonok, Louis. Art of Three-Dimensional Design: How to Create Space Figures.
Wolcott, Carolyn, jt. auth. see Wolcott, Leonard.
Wolcott, Harry F. Teachers Versus Technocrats: An Educational Innovation in Anthropological Perspective.
Wolcott, Leonard & Wolcott, Carolyn. Through the Moongate.
Wold, Allen. The Pursuit of Diana.
Wold, Erling & Wold, Marge. Thanks for the Mountain.
--What Do I Have to Do---Break My Neck?
--Who's Running Your Life?
Wold, Margaret. The Critical Moment: How Personal Crisis Can Enrich a Woman's Life.
--The Shalom Woman.
Wold, Marge, jt. auth. see Wold, Erling.
Wolde, Gunilla. Betsy & Peter Are Different.
--Betsy & the Vacuum Cleaner.
--Tommy Builds a House.
--Tommy Cleans His Room.
--Tommy Goes Out.
--Tommy Takes a Bath.
Wolenik, Robert. MacWrite Made Easy.
Wolf, Barbara. Living with Pain.
Wolf, Carolyn & Wolf, Richard. Basic Library Skills: A Short Course.
Wolf, Charles P., jt. ed. see Finsterbusch, Kurt.
Wolf, Clarence, Jr. Seven Letters: The Securities Market & You.
Wolf, D., ed. Noise in Physical Systems: Proceedings of the Fifth International Conference on Noise, Bad Nauheim, March 13-16, 1978.
Wolf, Duquesne A. The Infantry Brigade in Combat: First Brigade, 25th Infantry Division ("Tropic Lightning") in the Third Viet Cong-North Vietnamese Army Offensive, August 1968.
Wolf, E., jt. ed. see Mandel, L.
Wolf, E. J. Separation Methods in Organic Chemistry & Biochemistry.
Wolf, Elliott. Dining In: Restaurant Guide. Hosner, Sheila, ed.
Wolf, Eric R., jt. auth. see Cole, John W.
Wolf, Fred A. The Body Quantum: The New Physics of Body, Mind, & Health.
--Star Wave: Mind, Consciousness, & Quantum Physics.
Wolf, H. F. Silicon Semiconductor Data.
Wolf, Harold A. Personal Finance.
Wolf, Heinrich F. Philosophy for the Common Man.
Wolf, Jill. Felice: God's Little Lamb in Making Friends.
--Hulk Hogan: Battle of the Bands.
--I Know God Loves Me.
Wolf, Jill, adapted by. The Bride Movie Storybook.
Wolf, Jill, ed. More Cute & Crazy Cats.
Wolf, John B. The Barbary Coast: Algeria Under the Turks.
--The Emergence of the Great Powers. Langer, William L., ed.
--Louis the Fourteenth of France:
Wolf, John K. Practical Clinical Neurology.
Wolf, Larry L., jt. auth. see McNaughton, S. J.
Wolf, Leo. Der Groteske und Hyperbolische Stil Des Mittelhochdeutschen Volksepos.
Wolf, Leonard. False Messiah.
Wolf, Leonard, tr. see Nister, Der.
Wolf, Lillian K., jt. auth. see Wolf, William.
Wolf, Martin L. Dictionary of the Arts.
Wolf, Paul P. De see De Wolf, Paul P.
Wolf, Paul R. Elements of Photogrammetry.
Wolf, Reinhart. New York.
Wolf, Reinhart, photos by. Japan: The Beauty of Food.
Wolf, Richard, jt. auth. see Wolf, Carolyn.
Wolf, Richard C., ed. see Brauer, Jerald C.
Wolf, Richard C., ed. see Carter, Paul A.
Wolf, Richard C., ed. see Clebsch, William A.
Wolf, Richard C., ed. see Handy, Robert T.
Wolf, Richard C., ed. see Loetscher, Lefferts A.
Wolf, Richard C., ed. see Loewenberg, Bert J.
Wolf, Richard C., ed. see McAvoy, Thomas T.
Wolf, Richard C., ed. see Schlesinger, Arthur M., Sr.
Wolf, Robert C. Fossils of Iowa: Field Guide to Paleozoic Deposits.
Wolf, Robert E., tr. see Honisch, Dieter.
Wolf, Stanley. New Ways to Enjoy Chicken.
Wolf, Stanley M., jt. ed. see Buck, Otto.
Wolf, Stewart, jt. ed. see Epstein, Henry F.
Wolf, W., jt. auth. see Urwick, L.
Wolf, Warner. Gimme a Break! Warner Wolf on Sports.
Wolf, Warner & Taaffe, William. Gimme a Break!
Wolf, William & Wolf, Lillian K. Landmark Films: The Cinema & Our Century.
Wolf, William J. Lincoln's Religion.
Wolfe, Art, photos by. The Imagery of Art Wolfe. Mauzy, Charles, ed.
Wolfe, Arthur D., jt. auth. see Shaw, Bill.
Wolfe, Bill & Wolfe, Janita. Yearbook: Untold Stories.
Wolfe, Bill & Wolfe, Martha. Leaders Guide for Yearbook: Untold Stories.
Wolfe, Bob & Wolfe, Diane. Emergency Room.
Wolfe, Charles K. Tennessee Strings: The Story of Country Music in Tennessee.
Wolfe, Clara M. God, Country & Family Stuff.
Wolfe, Diane, jt. auth. see Wolfe, Bob.
Wolfe, Don M. Milton in the Puritan Revolution.
Wolfe, Douglas A., ed. Fate & Effects of Petroleum Hydrocarbons in Marine Organisms & Ecosystems.
Wolfe, Elizabeth. Ice Castle.
Wolfe, Gene. The Citadel of the Autarch.
--The Wolfe Archipelago.
Wolfe, George H., ed. Faulkner: Fifty Years after "The Marble Faun"
Wolfe, Herbert S., jt. auth. see Watkins, John V.
Wolfe, Janita, jt. auth. see Wolfe, Bill.
Wolfe, John. Sell Like an Ace...Live Like a King.
Wolfe, Kenneth C. Cooking the Professional Way.
Wolfe, Linda. The Cosmo Report: An In-Depth Landmark Work Revealing "the Sexual Behavior of 106,000 'Cosmopolitan' Readers"
Wolfe, Louis. Disaster Detectives.
Wolfe, Martha, jt. auth. see Wolfe, Bill.
Wolfe, Michael. The Panama Paradox.
Wolfe, Richard D. Knee Arthrography: A Practical Approach.
Wolfe, Richard J. Secular Music in America Eighteen One to Eighteen Twenty-Five: A Bibliography.
Wolfe, Ron, jt. auth. see Wooley, John.
Wolfe, S. Key to Dooyeweerd.
Wolfe, Sidney M., jt. ed. see Public Citizen Health Research Group Staff.
Wolfe, Stephen L. Biology of the Cell.
Wolfe, Thomas W., jt. auth. see Hosmer, Steven T.
Wolfe, Tom. The Right Stuff.
Wolfe, W. L., ed. see U. S. Specialty Group on Infrared Detectors.
Wolfe, Winifred. Josie's Way.
Wolfenbarger, D. O. Factors Affecting Dispersal Distances of Small Organisms.
Wolfendale, Arnold W. Cosmic Rays.
Wolfenden, Samuel. A Treatise on the Art of Pianoforte Construction.
Wolfenstein, E. Victor. Revolutionary Personality: Lenin, Trotsky, Gandhi.
Wolfenstein, Martha & Leites, Nathan. Movies: A Psychological Study.
Wolfers, Arnold. Britain & France Between Two Wars: Conflicting Strategies of Peace from Versailles to World War Two.
Wolfers, Michael. Poems from Angola.
Wolfert, Helen. Music.
Wolfert, Paula. The Cooking of South-West France: A Collection of Traditional & New Recipes.
Wolff, Benjamin. Hyde & Seek.
--Hyde in Deep Cover.
Wolff, Charlotte. The Hand in Psychological Diagnosis.
Wolff, Craig T. Wayne Gretzky: Portrait of a Hockey Player.
Wolff, Diane. Chinese Writing: An Introduction.
Wolff, Edward A., ed. Urban Alternatives: Proceedings of the USERC Environmental Resources & Urban Development Workshop.
Wolff, George T. & Klimisch, Richard L., eds. Particulate Carbon: Atmospheric Life Cycle.
Wolff, Hans W. Amos the Prophet: The Man & His Background. Reumann, John, ed. McCurley, Foster, tr. from Ger.
--Anthropology of the Old Testament. Kohl, Margaret, tr. from Ger.
--Confrontations with Prophets.
--Micah the Prophet. Gehrke, Ralph D., tr. from Ger.
--The Old Testament: A Guide to Its Writings. Crim, Keith R., tr. from Gr.
Wolff, Hans W., jt. auth. see Brueggemann, Walter.
Wolff, Helen, ed. see Becker, Jurek.
Wolff, Helen, ed. see Blythe, Ronald.
Wolff, Helen, ed. see Lem, Stanislaw.
Wolff, Helen, ed. see Lorenz, Konrad.
Wolff, Helen, ed. see Sciascia, Leonardo.
Wolff, Janet. Aesthetics & the Sociology of Art.
Wolff, John U. Beginning Indonesian.
Wolff, John U., et al. Beginning Indonesian Through Self-Instruction.
Wolff, Joseph L. Readings in Educational Psychology.
Wolff, Kurt H. The Sociology of Knowledge in the United States of America.
Wolff, Lise, jt. auth. see Geissler, E. A.
Wolff, Luther H. Forward Surgeon.
Wolff, Michael, jt. auth. see Dyos, H. J.
Wolff, Michael, jt. ed. see Dyos, H. J.
Wolff, Michael, jt. ed. see Shattock, Joanne.
Wolff, Michael, et al, eds. The Waterloo Directory of Victorian Periodicals.
Wolff, Nancy. Income Redistribution & the Social Security Program. Bateman, Fred, ed.
Wolff, P. M., ed. see International Congress on Medicinal Plant Research, Section A Staff.
Wolff, Robert L. The Balkans in Our Time.
Wolff, Robert L., ed. Aurora Floyd.
Wolff, Robert L., ed. see Arnold, William D.
Wolff, Robert L., ed. see Barry, William F.
Wolff, Robert L., ed. see Bayley, Ada E.
Wolff, Robert L., ed. see Besant, Walter.
Wolff, Robert L., ed. see Buchanan, Robert.
Wolff, Robert L., ed. see Butler, Samuel.
Wolff, Robert L., ed. see Corelli, Marie.
Wolff, Robert L., ed. see Davies, Charles M.
Wolff, Robert L., ed. see Dering, Edward H.
Wolff, Robert L., ed. see Douglas, Gertrude.
Wolff, Robert L., ed. see Edgar, A. H.
Wolff, Robert L., ed. see Fullerton, Georgiana.
Wolff, Robert L., ed. see Kennedy, Grace.
Wolff, Robert L., ed. see Kingsley, Charles.
Wolff, Robert L., ed. see Linton, Eliza L.
Wolff, Robert L., ed. see Longueville, Thomas de.
Wolff, Robert L., ed. see Oliphant, Margaret W.
Wolff, Robert L., ed. see Paget, Francis E.
Wolff, Robert L., ed. see Robinson, Frederick W.
Wolff, Robert L., ed. see Sewell, William.
Wolff, Robert L., ed. see Sinclair, Catherine.
Wolff, Robert L., ed. see Skene, Felicia.
Wolff, Robert L., ed. see Smith, Frederick R.
Wolff, Robert L., ed. see White, William H.
Wolff, Robert L., ed. see Wiseman, Nicholas P.
Wolff, Toni. Christianity Within.
Wolff, W. J., jt. ed. see Jones, N. V.
Wolffe, Lenard L. New Zoning Landmarks in Planned Unit Developments.
Wolfgang, Aaron, ed. Nonverbal Behavior: Applications & Cultural Implications.
Wolfgang, Marvin E., et al. National Survey of Crime Severity.
Wolfgang, Michael. England under George I: The Beginnings of the Hanoverian Dynasty.
Wolfgram, Frederick, ed. Multiple Sclerosis.
Wolfhard, H. G., jt. auth. see Gaydon, A. G.
Wolfort, Francis G., ed. Acute Hand Injuries: A Multispecialty Approach.
Wolfowitz, J., jt. auth. see Weiss, L.
Wolfowitz, Jacob. Coding Theorems of Information Theory.
Wolfram, Sybil & Hall, Margaret. In-Laws & Outlaws: Kingship & Marriage in England, 1800-1980.
Wolfson, Harry A. Crescas' Critique of Aristotle: Problems of Aristotle's Physics in Jewish & Arabic Philosophy.
--Religious Philosophy: A Group of Essays.
--Religious Philosophy: A Group of Essays.
Wolfson, Jay & Levin, Peter J. Managing Employee Health Benefits: A Guide to Cost Control.
Wolfson, Joseph. The Social Studies Student Investigates Business in the American Economy.
Wolfson, Marcia. Silk & Satin.
Wolfson, Murray. A Textbook of Economics.
Wolfson, Nicholas & Phillips, Richard M. Regulation of Brokers, Dealers & Securities Markets.
Wolfson, Randy, jt. auth. see DeLuca, Virginia.
Wolfson, Richard & Pasachoff, Jay M. Physics: Extended Version.
Wolitzer, Meg. Sleepwalking.
Wolke, Robert L. Chemistry Explained.
Wolken, Jerome J. Invertebrate Photoreceptors: A Comparative Analysis.
--Photoprocesses, Photoreceptors, & Evolution.
Wolkin, Paul A., frwd. by. Partnerships, UPA, ULPA, Taxation, Securities, & Bankruptcy.
Woll, B., et al, eds. Perspectives on British Sign Language & Deafness.
Woll, Bencie, jt. ed. see Kyle, Jim G.
Woll, Peter. Administrative Law: The Formal Process.
--American Bureaucracy.
--Behind the Scenes in American Government.
--Debating American Government.
Wollaston, Nicholas. The Stones of Bau.
Wollenburg, David W. Campus Symbolism: Devotions for New Students.
Wolley, Charles. A Two Year's Journal in New York & Part of Its Territories in America.
Wollheim, Richard. On Art & the Mind.
Wollman, E., jt. auth. see Jacob, Francois.
Wollman, Harry, et al, eds. Health Care Delivery in Anesthesia.
Wollrab, James E. Rotational Spectra & Molecular Structure.
Wollstonecraft, Mary. A Vindication of the Rights of Woman. Poston, Carol H., ed.
--Vindication of the Rights of Woman. Hagelman, Charles W., Jr., ed.
Wolman, Benjamin B. Interactional Psychotherapy.
--Psychological Aspects of Obesity: A Handbook.
Wolman, Benjamin B., ed. Clinical Diagnosis of Mental Disorders: A Handbook.
--Handbook of Dreams: Research, Theories & Applications.
--Manual of Child Psychopathology.
Wolman, Moshe, ed. Pigments in Pathology.
Wolman, William, jt. auth. see Klein, Roger.
Woloch, Isser. The Peasantry in the Old Regime: Conditions & Protests.
Woloch, Nancy. Preliminary Practice for the High School Equivalency Diploma Test.
Woloshyn, Richard M., jt. ed. see Boal, David H.
Wolovich, W. A. Linear Multivariable Systems.
Wolpe, David, jt. auth. see Wolpe, Joseph.
Wolpe, Joseph. Theme & Variations: A Behavior Therapy Casebook.
Wolpe, Joseph & Wolpe, David. Our Useless Fears.
Wolpert, Joyce F., jt. auth. see Wolpert, Samuel A.
Wolpert, Samuel A. & Wolpert, Joyce F. Economics of Information.
Wolstenholme, E. E. Elementary Vectors.
Woltenholme, G. E., ed. see CIBA Foundation.
Wolter, Annette, jt. auth. see Teubner, Christian.
Wolter, Daniel, jt. auth. see Markel, Geraldine.
Wolter, Kurt. Mathematic Refresher.
Woltering, Eugene A., jt. ed. see O'Leary, J. Patrick.
Wolters, Hester, jt. ed. see Staal, Gert.
Wolters, Richard A. Art & Technique of Soaring.
Wolverton, Mike. And Now... the News.
Wolverton, Van. Quick Reference Guide to MS-DOS Commands.
--Quick Reference Guide to MS-DOS Commands.
--Running MS-DOS.
--Running MS-DOS.
--Running MS-DOS: The Microsoft Guide to Getting the Most Out of the Standard Operating System for the IBM PC & 50 Other Personal Computers.
--Supercharging MS-DOS (Software Version)
--Supercharging MS-DOS: The Microsoft Guide to High Performance Computing for the Experienced PC User.
Wolvin, Andrew D. & Coakley, Carolyn G. Listening.
Wolvin, Andrew D., jt. auth. see Berko, Roy M.
Wolvovitz, Barbara, jt. auth. see Lobel, Jules.
Wolz, Carl. Aubade.
Womack, Jack. Ambient.
Woman's Day Editors. The Best Vegetable Recipes from Woman's Day.
--The Woman's Day Book of Weekend Crafts: More Than 100 Quick-to-Finish Projects.
Women on Words & Images Staff. Guidelines for Sex-Fair Vocational Education Materials.
Women's Action Alliance Staff. Women Helping Women: A State by State Directory of Services.
Womens Anglow Staff. The Ministry of Prayer.
Women's Club of Havana Staff. Flowering Plants from Cuban Gardens.
Women's Co-operative Guild & Martin, Anna. Working Women & Divorce: An Account of Evidence Given on Behalf of the Women's Co-operative Guild Before the Royal Commission on Divorce, London, 1911. Bd. with The Married Working Woman: A Study, London, 1911. Garland Pub.
Women's Legal Defense Fund Staff. The Custody Handbook: A Woman's Guide to Child Custody Disputes.
--It Pays to Be a Man: Pay Equity Information Packet.
--Legal Remedies for Sexual Harassment.
--Your Pension Rights at Divorce: What Women Need to Know.
Wong, Benita M. The Culinary Art of Modern Taiwan.
Wong, C. S. A Cycle of Chinese Festivities.
Wong, Donna L., jt. auth. see Whaley, Lucille F.
Wong, Frederick. The Complete Calligrapher.
Wong, Hon Sun. How I Overcame Inoperable Cancer.
Wong, Jeanyee, illus. The Cherry Tree Carol.
Wong, Martin R., jt. ed. see Bart, William M.
Wong, Mary G. Nun: A Memoir.
Wong, May. Superstitions.
Wong, Peter, jt. auth. see Hush, Joanne.
Wong, Richard W. Prayers from an Island.
--Prayers from an Island.
Wong, Sau-Ling, jt. auth. see McKay, Sandra.
Wong, Siu-Lun. Sociology & Socialism in Contemporary China.

Authors

Wong, Stanley. The Foundations of Paul Samuelson's Revealed Preference Theory: A Study by the Method of Rational Reconstruction.

Wong, Swee H. The Phoenix & Other Stories.

Wong, T. Y. My "Y" Shaped Travels in China.

Wong, William. A Management Overview of Software Reuse.

Wonnacott, Paul & Wonnacott, Ron. Introduction to Macroeconomics.

Wonnacott, Ron, jt. auth. see Wonnacott, Paul.

Woo, Nancy E., jt. auth. see McKee, David.

Wood. Gynaecology Pocket Consultant.

--Mind & Memory Training.

Wood, Alexander, ed. The Physics of Music.

Wood, Allen. Karl Marx.

Wood, Audrey. Tickleoctopus.

Wood, B. A. Human Evolution.

Wood, Barry. Questions Christians Ask about Prayer & Intercession.

Wood, Brenda & Jones, Clara. Light 'N Easy Cooking: Recipes for a Trimmer Slimmer Lifestyle.

Wood, Bruce, jt. auth. see Burch, Martin.

Wood, Carl P. Gun Digest Book of Sporting Dogs.

Wood, Charles. Dingo.

Wood, Charles M. The Formation of Christian Understanding: An Essay in Theological Hermeneutics.

Wood, Chris. The SuperCalc Program Made Easy.

Wood, Christina. Safari South America: The Saki Monkeys of Guyana & Other Wildlife.

Wood, Christopher. James Bond & Moonraker.

--Kago.

--North to Rabaul.

Wood, D., ed. see Society of Manufacturing Engineers Staff.

Wood, D. F., jt. auth. see Elwell, W. T.

Wood, David, et al. Working with under Fives.

Wood, David E. & Gillis, James C. Adventure Education.

Wood, Derek. Jane's World Aircraft Recognition Handbook.

--Project Cancelled: The Disaster of Britain's Abandoned Aircraft Projects.

--This Modern World.

Wood, Donald F. & Johnson, James C. Contemporary Transportation.

--Readings in Contemporary Transportation.

Wood, Donna, ed. New Trade Names.

Wood, Dorothy, jt. auth. see Mosenkis, Robert.

Wood, Dorothy, jt. ed. see Mosenkis, Robert.

Wood, E. F. & Szollosi-Nagy, A., eds. Real-Time Forecasting Control of Water Resource Systems: Proceedings of a IIASA Workshop, October, 1979.

Wood, E. G. Costing Matters for Managers.

Wood, Edward J. Curiosities of Clocks & Watches from the Earliest Times.

Wood, Eileen C. Pure Thoughts.

Wood, Elizabeth. Mothers & Lovers.

Wood, Elmer. Monetary Control.

Wood, Eric F. & Princeton Water Resources Group Staff. Groundwater Contamination from Hazardous Wastes.

Wood, Ernest. Great Systems of Yoga.

--Vedanta Dictionary.

--Yoga Dictionary.

Wood, Ethel M., jt. auth. see Elles, Gertrude L.

Wood, F., jt. ed. see Droop, M.

Wood, Forrest G. Era of Reconstruction: 1863-1877.

Wood, Frank H. & Lakin, K. Charlie, eds. Disturbing, Disordered, or Disturbed? Perspectives on the Definition of Problem Behavior in Educational Settings.

Wood, Fred M. The Dilemma of Daniel.

Wood, George. The Successful Life. Sekowsky, Jo Anne, ed.

Wood, Glenn, jt. auth. see West, David.

Wood, Gordon S., ed. The Rising Glory of America, 1760-1820.

Wood, Henry, jt. auth. see Adams, Herbert B.

Wood, J. B. Gun Digest Book of Gun Care, Cleaning & Refinishing, Book 1: Handguns.

--Gun Digest Book of Gun Care, Cleaning & Refinishing, Book 2: Long Guns.

Wood, Jacqueline & Gilchrist, Joelyn S. The Campus Survival Cookbook.

Wood, James P. Poetry Is.

Wood, John A. & Chang, Sherwood. Cosmic History of the Biogenic Elements & Compounds.

Wood, John B., tr. see Erhard, Ludwig.

Wood, John C., ed. Alfred Marshall: Critical Assessments.

--John Maynard Keynes: Critical Assessments.

--John Stuart Mill: Critical Assessments.

--Thomas Robert Malthus: Critical Assessments.

Wood, Jonathan S. Your Future in the Science of Oceanography.

Wood, Julia T. Human Communication: A Symbolic Interactionist Perspective.

Wood, Julia T., jt. auth. see Phillips, Gerald M.

Wood, Kenneth. Shining Armour.

Wood, L. J., jt. auth. see Lee.

Wood, Lana. Natalie: A Memoir by Her Sister.

Wood, Leon J. Elijah: Prophet of God.

Wood, Manfri F. In the Life of a Romany Gypsy. Brune, J. A., ed.

Wood, Marcia D., jt. auth. see Thompson, Ann M.

Wood, Margaret I., jt. auth. see Robertson, Elizabeth C.

Wood, Marilyn. Marilyn Wood's Wonderful Weekends.

Wood, Marilynn T., jt. auth. see Brink, Pamela J.

Wood, Mary A., jt. auth. see Wardle, Lynn D.

Wood, Mary M. Developmental Therapy Sourcebook.

--Developmental Therapy Sourcebook.

Wood, Matthew, ed. see Llewellyn Publications Staff.

Wood, Miriam. Those Happy Golden Years.

Wood, Mitt, ed. Llewellyn's Sun Sign Book, 1984.

Wood, Morrison. More Recipes with a Jug of Wine.

Wood, Nancy. Many Winters.

Wood, Norma S., jt. auth. see Stroup, Herbert W., Jr.

Wood, Norman K. Reviews of Diagnosis: Oral Medicine, Radiology & Treatment Planning.

Wood, Oliver G. & Porter, Robert J. Analysis of Bank Financial Statements.

Wood, Oliver G., Jr. Commercial Banking.

--Introduction to Money & Banking.

Wood, Oliver G., Jr. & Barksdale, William C. How to Borrow Money.

Wood, P. J. Reflector Antenna Analysis & Design.

Wood, Pamela. You & Aunt Arie: A Guide to Cultural Journalism.

Wood, Paul E. & Schwartz, Bernard. How to Get Children to Do What You Want Them to Do.

Wood, Peter & Time-Life Books Editors. The Spanish Main.

Wood, Phyllis A. Andy.

--I Think This Is Where We Came in.

Wood, Ralph L. Modern Handbook of Humor.

Wood, Richard H. Wood Notes: A Companion & Guide for Birdwatchers.

Wood, Richard H., tr. see Sembach, Klaus-Jurgen.

Wood, Robert. A Thirty-Day Experiment in Prayer.

--Thirty Days Are Not Enough: More Images for Meditative Journaling.

Wood, Robert C. The MSX Standard - The New Computers.

Wood, Robin. Howard Hawks.

Wood, S. V. Crag Mollusca.

Wood, Steve. Using Turbo Pascal.

Wood, Stuart, Jr. Heavy Construction: Equipment & Methods.

Wood, Susan. Bazaar.

Wood, Susan, jt. auth. see Shears, Barbara.

Wood, Ted. Corkscrew.

--Fool's Gold.

Wood, W. Raymond & McMillan, R. Bruce, eds. Prehistoric Man & His Environment: A Case Study in the Ozark Highland.

Wood, W. Raymond, ed. see Calabrese, F. A., et al.

Woodall, Irene R. Legal, Ethical & Management Aspects of the Dental Care System.

Woodall, Irene R., et al. Comprehensive Dental Hygiene Care.

Woodall, John. The Surgeon's Mate, Sixteen Hundred Seventeen.

Woodall's Staff, ed. Woodall's Tenting Directory, 1986: Eastern Edn.

Woodard & Bischoff. Storehouses of the Snow.

Woodard, Arthur F., jt. auth. see Obrentz, Bert N.

Woodard, Eleanor M. Black Satin.

Woodard, W. P. The Allied Occupation of Japan 1945-1952 & Japanese Religions.

Woodbine, Paul. Revisor.

Woodbine, Paul, ed. Primal Printing.

Woodbridge, Barry A. A Guidebook for Spiritual Friends.

Woodbridge, John & Woodbridge, Sally. Architecture, San Francisco: The Guide.

Woodbridge, Sally, jt. auth. see Woodbridge, John.

Woodburn, James. Causes of the American Revolution.

Woodburne, Michael & Clemens, William A., eds. Revisions of the Ektopodonitdae (Mammalia, Marsupialia, Phalangeroidea) of the Australian Neogene.

Woodcock, A. E., jt. auth. see Poston, T.

Woodcock, Alexander & Davis, Monte. Catastrophe Theory.

Woodcock, C., jt. auth. see Henley, W.

Woodcock, C. L., ed. Progress in Acetabularia Research.

Woodcock, George. Notes on Visitations: Poems 1936-1975.

--To the City of the Dead: An Account of Travels in Mexico.

Woodcock, George, tr. see Giraud, Marcel.

Woodcock, John, ed. Wisden Cricketers' Almanack 1985.

--Wisden Cricketers' Almanack 1986.

Woodcock, Mike & Francis, Dave. The Unblocked Boss: Activities for Self-Development.

--Unblocking Your Organization.

Woodcock, Mike, jt. auth. see Francis, Dave.

Wooden, Kenneth, ed. The Children of Jonestown.

Wooden, Warren W. John Foxe.

Woodfield, Denis B. Surreptitious Printing in England, 1550-1640.

Woodfin, Mrs. A. The Auction: A Modern Novel, 1760. Shugrue, Michael F., ed.

Woodford, Mona. Conquering Your Agoraphobia.

Woodforde, John. The Story of the Bicycle.

--The Strange Story of False Teeth.

--The Truth about Cottages.

Wood-Gush, D. G. Elements of Ethology: A Textbook of Agricultural & Veterinary Students.

Woodhams, Wilbur, ed. see Bayne, Stephen.

Woodham-Smith, Cecil. Florence Nightingale.

--The Reason Why.

Woodhead, Caroline, jt. auth. see Franklin, Peter J.

Woodhead, H. G., et al. Extraterritoriality in China: The Case Against Abolition.

Woodhead, Leslie. Boxful of Spirits: Adventures of a Film-Maker in Africa.

Woodhouse, Barbara. Barbara's World of Horses & Ponies.

--Walkies.

Woodhouse, Jennifer, tr. see Bykov, Vasil.

Woodhouse, Robert, tr. see Bykov, Vasil.

Woodhouse, Sarah. India Widow.

Woodin, J. C. & Hayes, Louis. Home & Building Maintenance.

Woodman, A. J. Rhetoric in Classical Historiography.

Woodman, D. The Republic of Indonesia.

Woodman, Francis. The Architectural History of Canterbury Cathedral.

--The Architectural History of King's College Chapel.

Woodman, Leonora & Adler, Thomas P. The Writer's Choices.

Woodman, M. J., jt. ed. see Holdgate, M. W.

Woodrell, Daniel. Under the Bright Lights.

--Woe to Live On.

Woodress, Fred A. Public Relations for Community & Junior Colleges.

Woodress, James, et al, eds. Eight American Authors.

Woodrich, Barbara, jt. auth. see Van Rossen, Don.

Woodring, June M. Malevolent Force.

Woodroffe, Paul, jt. auth. see Moorat, Joseph.

Woodroof, J. G. Coconuts: Production, Processing, Products.

--Tree Nuts: Production, Processing, Products.

Woodroof, J. G., jt. auth. see Luh, B. S.

Woodrow, Raymond J. Management for Research in U. S. Universities. Wainwright, Abbott, ed.

Woodruff, A. M., jt. ed. see Brown, James R.

Woodruff, A. M., et al, eds. International Seminar on Land Taxation, Land Tenure & Land Reform in Developing Countries.

Woodruff, Leroy L. Cooking the Dutch Oven Way.

Woods. Argument: The Logic of the Fallacies.

Woods, jt. auth. see Moxley.

Woods, B. W. Christians in Pain: Perspectives on Suffering.

Woods, Bill, jt. auth. see Woods, Erin.

Woods, Bonnie. Words of Wisdom in Counted Cross-Stitch.

Woods, Carolyn. The Comprehensive Employment & Training Act of 1973: A Selected & Annotated Bibliography.

Woods, Charles G. Natural Architecture: 40 Earth Sheltered House Designs.

Woods, Charles R., jt. auth. see Sloan-White, Barbara.

Woods, Charles R., ed. see Junor, Penny.

Woods, Diane, jt. ed. see Duncan, Barbara.

Woods, Donald. Asking for Trouble.

Woods, Eleanor. High Stakes.

Woods, Erin & Woods, Bill. Bicycling the Backroads Around Puget Sound.

Woods, Guy N. How to Read the Greek New Testament.

Woods, H. Macrurous Crustacea.

Woods Hole Oceanographic Institution, Woods Hole, Massachusetts Staff, jt. auth. see Marine Biological Laboratory Staff.

Woods, John B., et al. Student Teaching: The Entrance to Professional Physical Education.

Woods, John E., tr. see Bihalji-Merin, Oto.

Woods, Katherine W., tr. see Vallentin, Antonina.

Woods, Kenneth B. Highway Engineering Handbook.

Woods, L. Milton. Sometimes the Books Froze: Wyoming's Economy & Its Banks.

Woods, Leyla, jt. auth. see Oechsler, Ronald C.

Woods, Linda K. Mac Multiplan. Lenfest, ed.

Woods, Marjorie B. It's Your Wedding: How to Plan & Enjoy it.

Woods, Mia, illus. My Little Pony Sea Ponies Water Fun.

Woods, Michael. Perspective in Art.

Woods, Pamela. Making Floral Designs.

Woods, Peter. Sociology & the School: An Interactionist Viewpoint.

--Teacher Strategies: Explorations in the Sociology of the School.

Woods, Peter, ed. Pupil Strategies: Explorations in the Sociology of the School.

Woods, R. G. & Barrow, R. St. Introduction to Philosophy of Education.

Woods, Richard D., jt. ed. see Graham, Ann H.

Woods, Sandra L., jt. ed. see Samuda, Ronald J.

Woods, Sara. Let's Choose Executors.

--Nor Live So Long.

Woods, Sherryl. Jamaican Midnight.

Woods, Shirley E. The Money Labyrinth.

Woods, Stuart. Blue Water, Green Skipper.

--Deep Lie: A Novel.

--Run Before the Wind: A Novel.

Woods, Sylvia & Owen, Ray. Old English Sheepdogs.

Woodside, Alexander B. Community & Revolution in Modern Vietnam.

--Vietnam & the Chinese Model: A Comparative Study of Nguyen & Ch'ing Civil Government in the First Half of the Nineteenth Century.

Woodside, Arch G., jt. auth. see Etzel, Michael J.

Woodside, B. Brush up Your Math.

Woodsmall, Annabel W., et al. Contemporary Appliqued Beadwork. Harvey, Virginia I. & Adams, Vicki, eds.

Woodson, Carter G. Negro Professional Man & the Community, with Special Emphasis on the Physician & the Lawyer.

Woodson, Carter G., ed. Mind of the Negro As Reflected in Letters Written During the Crisis 1800-1860.

Woodson, William. Standing for Their Faith.

Woodstock Artists Association Staff, ed. Woodstock Art Heritage.

Woodsworth, David E. Social Security & National Policy: Sweden, Yugoslavia, Japan.

Woodward, jt. auth. see Jones.

Woodward, A. Smith. The Fishes of the English Chalk.

Woodward, Addison E., Jr., jt. auth. see Hilligoss, Pamela J.

Woodward, Anthony. Ezra Pound & the Pisan Cantos.

Woodward, Bob. Wired: The Short Life & Fast Times of John Belushi.

Woodward, Bob & Bernstein. Final Days.

Woodward, Bob & Bernstein, Carl. All the President's Men.

Woodward, Bronte. Meet Me at the Melba.

Woodward, C. Vann. American Counterpoint: Slavery & Racism in the North & South.

Woodward, David. Five Centuries of Map Printing.

Woodward, Delores M. & Peters, Delores. The Learning Disabled Adolescent: Learning Success in Content Areas.

Woodward, Dolores M. Mainstreaming the Learning Disabled Adolescent: A Manual of Strategies & Materials.

Woodward, George Henry. Sea of Thought.

Woodward, John B. Low Speed Marine Diesel Engines.

Woodward, Kathleen, ed. The Myths of Information: Technology & Post-Industrial Culture.

Woodward, N. B., et al. An Outline of Balanced Cross-Sections.

Woodward, R. B. & Hoffmann, R. The Conservation of Orbital Symmetry.

Woodward, Ralph L., Jr. Belize.

Woodward, Richard, tr. see Mitterand, Francois.

Woodward, Richard S., tr. see Lange, Monique.

Woodward, W. E. George Washington: The Image & the Man.

Woodwell, Donald R. Managing Personal Computer Workstations: A Corporate Resource.

Woodwell, George M., ed. The Role of Terrestrial Vegetation in the Global Carbon Cycle: Measurement by Remote Sensing.

Woodworth, David, ed. Directory of Overseas Summer Jobs 1985.

--Directory of Overseas Summer Jobs 1987.

--Directory of Overseas Summer Jobs 1988.

Woodworth, David P. International Yearbook of Serials Librarianship.

Woody, Charles D. Memory, Learning & Higher Function: A Cellular View.

Woody, Charles D., ed. Conditioning: Representation of Involved Neural Functions.

Woody, Regina J. Second Sight for Tommy.

Woody, Robert H. Bodymind Liberation: Achieving Holistic Health.

Woody, Robert H., ed. Encyclopedia of Clinical Assessment.

Wookey, Celia. Myalgic Encephalomyelitis: Post-Viral Fatigue Syndrome & How to Cope with It.

Wool, John D. How to Write Yourself Up.

--Useful Arithmetic.

Wool, Robert, jt. auth. see Cohen, Stanley J.

Woolcock, Stephen. Western Policies on East-West Trade.

Woolcott, T. W. Liquified Petroleum Gas Tanker Practice.
Wooldridge, Dean E. Machinery of the Brain.
Wooldridge, Powhatan, et al. Behavioral Science & Nursing Theory.
Wooldridge, Rhoda. Fort Osage.
Wooldridge, Ronald J., ed. Evaluation of Complex Systems.
Woolery, Arlo. Transcript of the Money Market Symposium Relating to Appraisal of Railroad & Utility Properties.
Wooley, John & Wolfe, Ron. Old Fears.
Wooley, Reginald M. Exorcism & the Healing of the Sick.
Woolf, A. L., ed. see International Symposium On Classification Of Brain Tumors - Cologne - 1961.
Woolf, Bob. Behind Closed Doors.
Woolf, David. The Art of Verga.
Woolf, Eugene T. Theodore Winthrop: Portrait of an American Author.
Woolf, Leonard. In Savage Times: Leonard Woolf on Peace & War. Incl. Fear & Politics: a Debate at the Zoo; The Way of Peace; The League & Abyssinia; The International Postwar Settlement. Garland Pub.
Woolf, Leonard, ed. Intelligent Man's Way to Prevent War.
Woolf, S. J., ed. Fascism in Europe.
Woolf, Stuart. A History of Italy Seventeen Hundred to Eighteen Sixty: The Social Constraints of Political Change.
--A History of Italy, Seventeen Hundred to Eighteen Sixty: The Social Constraints of Political Change.
Woolf, Stuart J., jt. auth. see Posner, M. V.
Woolf, Virginia. Books & Portraits: Some Further Selections from the Literary & Biographical Writings of Virginia Woolf.
--Collected Essays.
--The Common Reader: First Series.
--The Diary of Virginia Woolf, Vol. 2: 1920-1924. Bell, Anne O., ed. & pref. by.
--The Diary of Virginia Woolf: Vol. 3, 1925-1930. Bell, Anne O. & McNeillie, Andrew, eds.
--Diary of Virginia Woolf, Vol. 4: 1931-1935. Bell, Anne O., ed.
--Freshwater: A Comedy.
--Freshwater: A Comedy. Ruotolo, Lucio P., ed.
--The Letters of Virginia Woolf.
--The Letters of Virginia Woolf, 1929-1931.
--The Letters of Virginia Woolf: 1936-1941. Nicholson, Nigel & Trautmann, Joanne, eds.
--Moments of Being: Unpublished Autobiographical Writings. Ferrone, J., ed.
--Moments of Being: Unpublished Autobiographical Writings. Schulkind, Jeanne, ed. & intro. by.
--Mrs. Dalloway.
--Mrs. Dalloway.
--The Pargiters: The Novel Essay Portion of the Years.
--A Room of One's Own.
--The Second Common Reader.
--To the Lighthouse.
Woolfolk, Anita E. & Nicolich, Lorraine. Educational Psychology for Teachers.
Woolford, Don. Papua New Guinea: Initiation & Independence.
Woolham, Frank. The Handbook of Aviculture.
Woollacott, Robert M. & Zimmer, Russell L., eds. The Biology of Bryozoans.
Woollerton, Henry & McLean, Colleen J. Acupuncture Energy in Health & Disease: A Practical Guide for Advanced Students.
Woolley. Dead Towns & Living Men.
--Key to the Stars.
Woolley, A. E. Photography: A Practical & Creative Introduction.
Woolley, Bryan. Some Sweet Day.
Woolley, C. Leonard. Forgotten Kingdom.
Woolley, Catherine. Libby Shadows a Lady.
Woolley, Diana. Advertising Law Handbook.
Woolley, Ivan. Off to Mt. Hood: An Autobiography of the Old Road.
Woolley, Leonard. Ur 'of the Chaldees' A Revised & Updated Edition of Sir Leonard Woolley's Excavations at Ur by P. R. S. Moorey.
Woolley, R. G., ed. Quantum Dynamics of Molecules: The New Experimental Challenge to Theorists.
Woolner, Frank & Lyman, Henry. Bottom Fishing.
Woolner, Lionel R., ed. The Hunting of the Hare.
Woolrich, Cornell. Black Alibi.
--The Black Angel.
--The Black Curtain.
--Deadline at Dawn.
--Night Has a Thousand Eyes.
--Phantom Lady.
Woolsey, G. A., jt. ed. see Emelus, K. G.
Woolsey, Raymond, ed. see Jordan, Jeanne.
Woolsey, Raymond H. & Anderson, Ruth. Harry Anderson: The Man Behind the Paintings.
Woolsey, Raymond H., ed. see Earnhardt, Crystal.
Woolsey, Raymond H., ed. see Muir, Wellesley.
Wooster, Claire, jt. auth. see Meyners, Robert.
Wooten, Dudley G. A Comprehensive History of Texas.
Wooton, Barbara. Freedom under Planning.
Wooton, William, jt. auth. see Drooyan, Irving.
Wootten, Morgan & Gilbert, Bill. From Orphans to Champions: The Story of Dematha's Morgan Wootten.
Wootten, Richard, jt. auth. see Baur, John I.
Wootters, John. A Guide to Hunting in Texas.
Wootton, Anthony. Animal Folklore, Myth & Legend.
Worboys, Anne. Run Sara Run.
Worcester, Thomas K., ed. see Lowe, Don & Lowe, Roberta.
Worchel, Stephen & Goethals, George R. Adjustment: Pathways to Personal Growth.
Worchel, Stephen, jt. auth. see Sheras, Peter L.
Worden, A. B., ed. see Ludlow, Edmund.
Wordsworth, Mary. Letters of Mary Wordsworth, Eighteen Hundred to Eighteen Fifty-Five. Burton, Mary E., ed.
Wordsworth, William. Concerning Relations of Great Britain, Spain, & Portugal, to Each Other, & to the Common Enemy, at This Crisis; & Specifically as Affected by the Convention of Cintra: The Whole Brought to the Test of Those Principles, by Which Alone the Independence & Freedom of Nations Can Be Preserved or Recovered.
--Wordsworth.
Work for Hire Staff. Mechanical Working & Steel Processing Proceedings.
Workbench Magazine Staff. The Workbench Treasury of Chair Projects.
--The Workbench Treasury of Occasional & End Table Projects.
Workers Educational Institute Staff. Marxist.
Worker's League for a Revolutionary Party. Bulletin.
Worker's Party of Marxist Unification, U.S.A. Staff. New Militant.
--Spanish Revolution.
Workers Party of the United States. Labor Action. Incl. Greenwood.
Working Woman Editors, jt. auth. see Bryant, Gay.
Working Woman Magazine Staff, ed. The Working Woman's Success Book.
Workman, Brooke. Writing Seminars in the Content Area: In Search of Hemingway, Salinger, & Steinbeck.
Workman, Robert, et al. The Eden of America: Rhode Island Landscapes, 1820-1920.
Workshop for Biological Chemistry Staff. The Immune System: Proceedings of the Colloquium of the Workshop for Biological Chemistry, Mosbach, Baden, Germany, April 29 - May 1, 1976. Melchers, F., ed.
Worland, Peter B. Introduction to BASIC Programming: A Structured Approach.
Worland, Stephen T. Scholasticism & Welfare Economics.
World Almanac Editors, ed. The Greatest Hits of the World Almanac.
World Association of Girl Guides & Girl Scouts Staff. The Story of the Four World Centres: For Girls & Leaders.
World Association of Societies of Pathology Staff & Levy, E. Advances in Pathology (Anatomic & Clinical) Laboratory Medicine: Proceedings of the Triennial World Congress of the World Association of Societies of Pathology, 11th, Jerusalem, Israel, Sept. 20-25, 1981.
World Bank Staff. Philippines: A Framework for Economic Recovery.
World Bank Staff & Penalver, M. Brazil, Industrial Policies & Manufactured Exports.
World Bank Staff, jt. auth. see PADCO, Inc. Staff.
World Bank Staff, et al. Domestic Resource Mobilization in Pakistan: Selected Issues.
World Book Editors, ed. Childcraft: 1988 Edition.
--The World Book Encyclopedia: 1988 Edition.
World Book Editors Staff. Christmas in Washington, D. C.
World Book, Inc. Staff, ed. Best-Loved Bible Stories: Old Testament & New Testament.
--Childcraft: The How & Why Library.
--Christmas in Denmark.
--Christmas in Ireland.
--Conquest of the Sky: Childcraft Annual, 1985.
--Great Myths & Legends.
--Mysteries & Fantasies.
--Science Year: The World Book Science Annual.
--Today Nineteen Eighty-Six: A Personal Record & Reference Book.
--Today 1988: A Personal Record & Reference Book.
--Winning with Words.
--The World Book Atlas of the United States & Canada.
--The World Book Desk Reference Set.
--The World Book Encyclopedia: 1988 Edition.
--The World Book Illustrated Home Medical Encyclopedia.
--The World Book of America's Presidents.
--The World Book Student Handbook: Information Finder.
--The World Book Student Handbook: Student Guide.
--The World Book Year Book.
--The World Book Year Book.
World Book Staff. The World Book Desk Reference Set. Incl. Grammar & Style Guide; Instant Facts; Book of Nations; Tables & Formulas. World Bk.
World Book Staff, ed. The World Book Health & Medical Annual.
--The World Book Health & Medical Annual.
--World Book Year, 1987.
World Conference of the United Nations Decade for Women Staff. Report of World Conference of the United Nations Decade for Women: Proceedings of the World Conference on Equality, Development & Peace, Copenhagen, July 14-30, 1988.
World Conference on Embryo Transfer in Vitro Fertilization & Instrumental Insemination Staff. In Vitro Fertilization & Embryo Transfer: Proceedings of the World Conference, Kiel, West Germany, September 24-27, 1980. Hafez, E. S. & Semm, K., eds.
World Conference on Transport Research Staff. Transport Research for Social & Economic Progress: Proceedings of the World Conference, London, 1980. Yerrell, J. Stuart, ed.
--Transport Research for Social & Economic Progress: Proceedings of the World Conference, London, 1980. Yerrell, J. Stuart, ed.
--Transport Research for Social & Economic Progress: Proceedings of the World Conference, London, 1980. Yerrell, J. Stuart, ed.
--Transport Research for Social & Economic Progress: Proceedings of the World Conference, London, 1980. Yerrell, J. Stuart, ed.
--Transport Research for Social & Economic Progress: Proceedings of the World Conference, London, 1980. Yerrell, J. Stuart, ed.
World Congress of Anaesthesiology, 3rd, Sao Paulo, 1964. Proceedings of the World Congress of Anaesthesiology, 3rd, Sao Paulo, 1964. Frey, R., et al, eds.
World Council of Churches, Geneva, Switzerland Staff. Classified Catalog of the Ecumenical Movement.
--Classified Catalog of the Ecumenical Movement: First Supplement.
World Employment Program Study. Basic Needs, Poverty & Government Policies in Sri Lanka.
World Energy Conference Staff. Standard Terms of Energy Economy: Ruttley.
World Energy Conference Staff, ed. Energy Terminology: A Multi-Lingual Glossary.
World Health Organization. Waste Discharge into the Marine Environment: Principles & Guidelines for a Mediterranean Action Plan.
World Hydrocarbon Markets Staff & Wionczek, M. S. World Hydrocarbon Markets-Current Status, Projected Prospects & Future Trends: Proceedings of the International Workshop, Mexico City, April 1982.
World Hydrogen Energy Conference Staff & Veziroglu, T. N. Hydrogen Energy Process IV: Proceedings of the World Hydrogen Energy Conference, 4th, Pasadena, CA, June 13-17, 1982. Van Vorst, W. D., et al, eds.
World Hydrogen Energy Conference Staff, et al. Hydrogen Energy Progress: Proceedings of the World Conference, 3rd, Tokyo, Japan, June 23-26, 1980. Veziroglu, T. N., et al, eds.
World Hydrogen Energy Conference Staff. Hydrogen Energy System: Proceedings of the World Conference, 2nd, Zurich, Aug. 1978. Veziroglu, T. N. & Seifritz, W., eds.
World Hydrogen Energy Conference Staff & Veziroglu, T. N. Hydrogen: Proceedings of the World Hydrogen Energy Conference Papers on Today, Tomorrow & Beyond, 4th, CA, June 13-17, 1982.
World of Information Editorial Staff. Pacific Business Guide, 1987.
World Religions Delvelopment Center. The Jewish Tradition.
World Religions Development Center. The Buddhist Tradition.
--The Christian Tradition.
--The Christian Tradition, Guide.
--The Hindu Tradition.
--The Islamic Tradition.
--The Jewish Tradition, Guide.
--Religious Expression.
World Religious Development Center. Religious Expression, Guide.
World Symposium at the AIME Annual Meeting Staff. Lead-Zinc-Tin '80: Proceedings of the World Symposium at the AIME Annual Meeting, Las Vegas, 1980. Cigan, T. S. & O'Keefe, T. J., eds.
Worley, Robert C. Change in the Church: A Source of Hope.
--A Gathering of Strangers: Understanding the Life of Your Church.
Wormald, B. H. Clarendon: Politics, History, & Religion 1640-1660.
Wormell, Jeremy J. The Gilt-Edged Market.
Wormer, Laura van see Van Wormer, Laura.
Wormhoudt, Arthur. Hamlet's Mousetrap.
Wormhoudt, Arthur, tr. from Arabic. Al Ganna wa'l Mugana I (Songs & Singers)
--Al Ganna wa'l Muganna II (Songs & Singers)
Wormhoudt, Arthur, tr. Diwan Abu Tammam.
Wormhoudt, Arthur, tr. from Arabic. Diwan Al Sanaubari.
--Diwan Ibn Al Rumi,'Ali Ibn Al' Abbas.
Wormhoudt, Arthur, tr. Diwan Imru Al Qais.
Wormhoudt, Arthur, tr. from Arabic. Diwan Ka'b ibn Zuhair & Akhbar Majnun.
--Diwan 'Umar Ibn Abu Rabi'a Al Makhzumi.
Wormhoudt, Arthur, tr. Diwan Zuhair Ibn Abu Sulma & Diwan Al Hallaj.
Wormhoudt, Arthur, tr. see Ma'Arri, Abu Ala Al.
Wormser, Gary P., et al, eds. AIDS-Acquired Immune Deficiency Syndrome-& Other Manifestations of HIV Infection: Epidemiology, Etiology, Immunology, Clinical Manifestations, Pathology, Control, Treatment & Prevention.
Wormser, I. Maurice. Disregard of the Corporate Fiction & Allied Corporation Problems.
Wormser, Rene A. The Story of the Law.
Wormuth, Francis D. & Firmage, Edwin B. To Chain the Dog of War: The War Power of Congress in History & Law.
Worrall, A. & Worrall, O. The Gift of Healing.
Worrall, Ambrose A. & Worrall, Olga N. Explore Your Psychic World.
Worrall, Nick. Nikolai Gogol & Ivan Turgenev.
Worrall, O., jt. auth. see Worrall, A.
Worrall, Olga N., jt. auth. see Worrall, Ambrose A.
Worrel, J. W. Directory of Music Companies: United States & Foreign.
Worrell, A. C. Principles of Forest Policy.
Worrell, Estelle A. Make Your Own Miniature Rooms. Blau, Clare, ed.
Worrell, W. L., jt. ed. see Rosenblatt, G. M.
Worsdall, Vivien. Special English for Hotel Personnel, Bk. 1: Office Managers, Clerks, Cashiers, Telephone Operators.
Worsley, Dale & Mayer, Bernadette. The Art of Science Writing.
--The Art of Science Writing: A Guide for Teachers & Students.
Worsley, F. A. Shackleton's Boat Journey.
Worsley, John C., ed. see Marlowe, Lynn G., et al.
Worsley, Peter, et al, eds. Introducing Sociology.
Worsley, T. C. Fellow Travellers.
Worst, Edward F. Weaving with Foot-Power Looms.
Worster, Donald. Nature's Economy: The Roots of Ecology.
--Rivers of Empire: Water, Aridity, & the Growth of the American West.
Worswick, Clark. The Last Empire: Photography in British India 1855-1911.
Worswick, Marilyn & Selle, Robert. Thank You Davey; Thank You, God.
Worth, B. J. Income Tax Law for Ministers & Religious Workers: 1988 Edition.
--Professional Tax Record Book.
Worth, Courtia. The Bed & Breakfast Guide: West Coast.
Worth, Courtia & Berger, Terry. The West Coast Bed & Breakfast Guide: California-Oregon-Washington.
Worth, Fred L., jt. auth. see Strauss, David P.
Worth, Katharine. Oscar Wilde.
--Oscar Wilde.
Worth, Katharine, ed. Beckett the Shape Changer.
Worth, Leslie. Laying a Watercolour Wash.
--Sea & Sky in Watercolour.
--Working with Watercolour.
Worth, Leslie, et al. Painting in Watercolors.
Worth, Thomas. BASIC for Everyone.
--COBOL for Beginners.
Worthen, Helena. Perimeters.
Worthen, Helena H. Damages.
Worthing, Michelle G. Elements of Music: A Programmed Approach.
Worthington, Bonnie & Taylor, Lynda. A Doctor Discusses Nutrition During Pregnancy & Breast Feeding.
Worthington, E. Barton, ed. Arid Land Irrigation in Developing Countries: Environmental Problems & Effects.
Worthington, Hazel L. Nannie Mama.
Worthington, Phoebe & Worthington, Selby. Teddy Bear Postman.
Worthington, Rudolph H. The Twelve Signs of the Zodiac & Their Irresistible Effect upon the Stock Market.
Worthington, Selby, jt. auth. see Worthington, Phoebe.
Worthington, Vivian. A History of Yoga.
Worthington-Roberts, Bonnie S., et al. Nutrition in Pregnancy & Lactation.
Worthley, Jean R. The Complete Family Nature Guide.
Worthley, William J. Sourcebook of Articulation Learning Activities.

Wortley, Ben A. The United Nations: The First Ten Years.
Wortman, Leon A. A Deskbook of Business Management Terms.
--Successful Small Business Management.
Wortman, Max & Sperling, Joann. Defining the Manager's Job.
Wortmen, Max S., Jr. & Luthans, Fred. Emerging Concepts in Management.
Worvill, Roy. Stars & Telescopes for the Beginner.
Worwood, M., jt. ed. see Jacobs, A.
Woshinsky, Oliver H., jt. auth. see Coogan, William H.
Wosmek, Frances. Mystery of the Eagle's Claw.
Wotruba, jt. auth. see Haas.
Wotten, W. J. Quest.
Woude, G. F. Vande see Vande Woude, G. F., et al.
Wouk, Arthur. A Course of Applied Functional Analysis.
Woy, James, ed. Encyclopedia of Business Information Sources.
--Encyclopedia of Business Information Sources: Supplement.
Woy, James B., ed. Business Trends & Forecasting Information Sources.
Woyde, Horst, tr. see Crump, Fred, Jr.
Woytinsky, Wladimir S. Three Aspects of Labor Dynamics.
Wozniak, John S. Contact, Negotiation, & Conflict: An Ethnohistory of the Eastern Dakota, 1819-1839.
Wrage, Karl H. Man & Woman: The Basics of Sex & Marriage. Gilder, Stanley S., tr.
Wragg, E. C., ed. Classroom Teaching Skills.
Wraith, G. C., jt. ed. see Maurer, C.
Wrangel, P. N. Always with Honour.
Wrangham, C. E., ed. see Wilberforce, William.
Wraxall, tr. see Houden, Robert.
Wray, William C., jt. auth. see Greenfield, Joseph D.
Wrede, Stuart. The Architecture of Erik Gunnar Asplund.
Wreh, Tuan. The Love of Liberty: The Rule of President William V. S. Tubman in Liberia 1944-1971.
Wren, Carol T., et al, eds. Language Learning Disabilities: Diagnosis & Remediation.
Wren, Christopher G. & Wren, Jill R. The Legal Research Manual: A Game Plan for Legal Research & Analysis.
Wren, Jill R., jt. auth. see Wren, Christopher G.
Wrench, David. Readings in Psychology: Foundations & Applications.
Wrenn, C. Gilbert. The World of the Contemporary Counselor.
Wrenn, C. Gilbert, jt. auth. see Schwarzrock, Shirley.
Wrenn, C. L., jt. auth. see Quirk, Randolph.
Wrenn, Charles L. Study of Old English Literature.
Wretlind, A., ed. see European Nutritionists Staff.
Wright. General Microbiology: Study Guide.
--General Mirobiology: Laboratory Manual.
Wright & Andrejko. Passive Solar Architecture: 35 Outstanding Houses Across the United States.
Wright, A. D. Workshoes for Christ.
Wright, A. Nelson & Winkler, Carl A. Active Nitrogen.
Wright, Anne, ed. see Shaw, George Bernard.
Wright, Arlene A., ed. see Hall, Woodie.
Wright, Arthur. Color Me White: The Autobiography of a Black Dancer Who Turned White.
Wright, Arthur F., ed. Studies in Chinese Thought.
Wright, Barbara, tr. see Benmussa, Simone.
Wright, Barton. Kachinas: A Hopi Artist's Documentary. Bd. with Kachinas of the Zuni. Northland.
Wright, Becky A. Apprenticeship Fund Institutes: Proceedings, Nov. 21-24, 1982, Holliwood Fl.
--Collection of Employer Contributions: Institute Proceedings, May 10-13, 1982, Las Vegas.
--Handbook for Benefit Plan Professionals, 1983.
Wright, Becky A., ed. Annual Educational Conference Proceedings: 1982 Focus on Education.
--Benefit Plan Professionals Institute: Proceedings, June 20-23, 1982, Lake Tahoe, Nev.
--Communications Institute Proceedings, July 11-14, 1982, Hershey, Pa.
--EDP: Applications for Employee Benefit Plans, 1983.
--EDP Institute, Dec. 1-4, 1982, Miami, Florida: Proceedings.
--Effective Collection of Employer Contributions 1983.
--Food Industry Institute Proceedings April 18-21, 1982.
--Health Care Cost Containment Seminar November 7-10, 1982, Hollywood, Florida.
--Health Care Cost Containment, 1983.
--International Benefits, 1983.
--Nineteen Eighty-Three Annual Educational Conference Proceeding: Design for the Future.
Wright, Blanche F., illus. Animal Rhymes.
--Bedtime Rhymes.
--Cat & the Fiddle.
--Jack & Jill & Other Favorite Rhymes.
--Playtime Rhymes.
--The Real Mother Goose Piano Book.
--Rhymes of Boys & Girls.
Wright, Burton & Fox, Vernon. Criminal Justice & the Social Sciences.
Wright, C. A., ed. Biochemical & Immunological Taxonomy of Animals.
Wright, C. A., jt. ed. see Canning, E. V.
Wright, Charles. Constructions of Deviance in Sociological Theory: The Problem of Commensurability.
Wright, Charles & Neil, Charles, eds. The Protestant Dictionary: Containing Articles on the History, Doctrines, & Practices of the Christian Church.
Wright, Charles H. Studies in Daniel's Prophecies.
Wright, Christopher. The Art of the Forger.
Wright, Conrad. Religion in American Life.
Wright, D., jt. auth. see Janowitz, Morris.
Wright, D., ed. The French Revolution: Introductory Documents.
Wright, D. Franklin & New, Bill. Introductory Algebra.
Wright, David. The Harley-Davidson Motor Company.
Wright, David H. Co-Operatives & Community.
Wright, Dick. Hardball Job Hunting Tactics.
--Hardball Job Hunting Tactics.
Wright, Don. Mantle of Christ: A History of the Sydney Central Methodist Mission.
Wright, Don, jt. auth. see Trailer Life Editors.
Wright, Donald N., jt. auth. see Jensen, Marcus M.
Wright, Doris M. A Yankee in Mexican California, Abel Stearns, 1798-1948.
--Yankee in Mexican California: Abel Stearns, 1798-1848.
Wright, Edmund, ed. Scott Specialized Catalogue of Canadian Stamps & Covers, 1984.
Wright, Edmund H., et al, eds. Scott Specialized Catalogue of Canadian Stamps & Covers: 1985 Edition.
Wright, Elizabeth. Independence in All Things, Neutrality in Nothing.
--Miller Freeman, Man of Action.
Wright, Elizabeth M. Rustic Speech & Folklore.
Wright, Eric. A Body Surrounded by Water.
--The Man Who Changed His Name.
--The Man Who Changed His Name: An Inspector Charlie Salter Mystery.
--Smoke Detector.
--Smoke Detector: An Inspector Charlie Salter Mystery.
Wright, Erik O. Class Structure & Income Determination.
Wright, F. F., jt. auth. see Council on Education in the Geological Sciences Staff.
Wright, Frank Lloyd. The Plan for Restoration & Adaptive Use of the Frank Lloyd Wright Home & Studio.
Wright, Fred B., ed. see Ergodic Theory Symposium Staff.
Wright, Freire, illus. Beauty & the Beast.
Wright, G. Ernest. Biblical Archaeology.
--Biblical Archaeology.
Wright, G. Ernest & Filson, Floyd V., eds. Westminster Historical Atlas to the Bible.
Wright, Gene Foreword by see Foresi, Joseph, Jr.
Wright, Geoffrey. Discovering Epitaphs.
--The Stone Villages of Britain.
Wright, George B., jt. auth. see Feldman, Edwin B.
Wright, Gerald Z. Behavior Management in Dentistry for Children.
Wright, Glen. Fascinating Tales of the Pacific. Murphy, Carol, ed.
--Gold of the Gods. Murphy, Carol, ed.
--The Land Divers of Pentecost. Murphy, Carol, ed.
--A Mountain Blows Its Top. Murphy, Carol, ed.
--The Pigeon with Nine Heads. Murphy, Carol, ed.
--Snatched by a Killer Wave. Murphy, Carol, ed.
--Student Journalist & Making Advertising Pay for the School Publication. Rosen, Ruth C., ed.
--Unfriendly Natives of the Pacific. Murphy, Carol, ed.
Wright, Glover. The Hound of Heaven.
Wright, Gordon, ed. see Michelet, Jules.
Wright, H. Curtis. Ancient Burials of Metallic Foundation: Documents in Stone Boxes.
Wright, H. Norman. Communication: Key to Your Marriage, Manual.
--Making Peace with Your Past.
Wright, Irene A. Early History of Cuba, 1492-1586.
Wright, J. S., jt. auth. see Burrell, M. C.
Wright, J. V. Quebec Prehistory.
Wright, Jack & Lewis, Peter. Modern Criminal Justice.
Wright, Jackson W., Jr., jt. auth. see Farr, James F.
Wright, James. Historia Histrionica: An Historical Account of the English Stage. Bd. with Roscius Anglicanus: An Historical Review of the Stage. Downes, John. Garland Pub.
Wright, James D. & Rossi, Peter H. Armed Criminal in America: A Survey of Incarcerated Felons.
Wright, Jean. Learning to Learn in Higher Education.
Wright, Jenifer. Count Your Calories Cookbook.
Wright, Joanne, jt. auth. see Ames-Lewis, Francis.
Wright, John K., ed. see Paullin, Charles O.
Wright, Jonathan V. & Baldwin, Carol, eds. Dr. Wright's Guide to Healing with Nutrition.
Wright, Jone P., ed. see Noland, Ronald G., et al.
Wright, Judith. The Double Tree: Selected Poems 1942-1976.
Wright, Larry. Celebrity Cats.
Wright, Lawrence. Clean & Decent: The History of the Bathroom & the W. C.
--Perspectives in Perspective.
Wright, Leonard M. The Winchester Press Fish Finding Guide.
Wright, Leonard M., Jr. Fly-Fishing Heresies.
Wright, Linda R. A Cord of Three Strands.
--Staying on Top When Things Go Wrong.
Wright, Linda R., jt. auth. see Wright, Rusty.
Wright, Louis B. Barefoot in Arcadia: Memories of a More Innocent Era.
--Of Books & Men.
Wright, Louis B., ed. see Shakespeare, William.
Wright, Margaret. Practical Optimization.
Wright, Margaret, jt. auth. see Morgan, Brian.
Wright, Margaret H. The Sisters.
Wright, Marion I. & Sullivan, Robert J. The Rhode Island Atlas.
Wright, Martha R., ed. The Bay Boy or the Autobiography of a Youth of Massachusetts Bay by Royall Tyler.
Wright, Mike, jt. auth. see Coyne, John.
Wright, Moorhead, et al. Essay Collections in International Relations: A Classified Bibliography.
Wright, Nadean E. Central Supply Procedure Manual.
Wright, Nancy M. Make Your Own Change.
Wright, Nathalia, ed. The Complete Works of Washington Irving, Journals & Notebooks: 1803-1806.
Wright, Nicholas. The Red Baron.
Wright, Norman. Answer to Divorce.
--An Answer to Submission & Decision Making.
--Help I'm a Camp Counselor!
--How to Have a Creative Crisis.
Wright, P. H., jt. auth. see Peeters, H.
Wright, Patricia. Shadow of the Rock.
Wright, Paul & Gardner, Robert W. Ethnicity, Birthplace, & Achievement: The Changing Hawaiian Mosaic.
Wright, Paul S. Duties of the Ruling Elder.
Wright, Quincy. Problems of Stability & Progress in International Relations.
Wright, R. C. Simple Plant Propagation.
Wright, R. Glenn, jt. auth. see Harris, Mark.
Wright, R. Glenn, jt. auth. see Newman, Richard.
Wright, Richard. Farthing's Fortunes.
--Savage Holiday.
--Twelve Million Black Voices: A Folk History of the Negro in the U. S.
Wright, Richard O., ed. Whose FBI?
Wright, Robert, jt. auth. see Rawnsley, C. F.
Wright, Robin. Sacred Rage: The Crusade of Modern Islam.
Wright, Ron. Pontiac: Phoenix 1980 Shop Manual. Wauson, Sydnie A., ed.
Wright, Roy J., jt. auth. see Wagner, Richard M.
Wright, Russell. The Makings of an Olympic Champion: A New Approach to Weight Training & Weight Lifting.
Wright, Rusty & Wright, Linda R. Secrets of Successful Humor.
Wright, S. A Bibliography of the Writings of Walter H. Pater.
Wright, Sandra L. Country Handcrafts Christmas Collection.
--Country Handcrafts Doll & Toy Collection.
Wright, Sandra R. Planning & Development of Quality Services in the Schools.
Wright, Sara M. Brief Survey of the Bible.
Wright, Stanley. Kiangsi Native Trade & Its Taxation.
Wright, Thomas. Biographia Britannica Literaria.
Wright, Tom. Large Gardens & Parks: Maintenance, Management & Design.
Wright, Vernon. David Lange: Prime Minister.
Wright, Vincent. The Government & Politics of France.
Wright, Wilbur. Carter's Castle.
Wright, Willard H. see Van Dine, S. S.
Wright, William. Lillian Hellman: The Woman Who Made the Legend.
Wright, Winthrop R. British-Owned Railways in Argentina: Their Effect on the Growth of Economic Nationalism, 1854-1948.
Wrightsman, Lawrence C., jt. auth. see Deaux, Kay.
Wrightson, Patricia. Feather Star.
--The Ice Is Coming.
--The Nargun & the Stars.
--An Older Kind of Magic.
--Racecourse for Andy.
Wrightson, Sue, jt. auth. see Rawson, D. W.
Wrigley, E. A. Population & History.
Wrigley, N. Statistical Applications in the Spatial Sciences.
Wrigley, Neil & Bennett, Robert J., eds. Quantitative Geography in Britain: Retrospect & Prospect.
Wrigley, Robert. The Sinking of Clay City.
Wrigley, W., ed. Space Relativity: Selected Papers Presented at the 4th, 5th & 6th International Sympodia on Space Relativity.
Wringe, Colin A. Children's Rights: A Philosophical Study.
--Children's Rights: A Philosophical Study.
Wriothesley, Charles W. A Chronicle of England During the Reigns of the Tudors.
Wriston, Henry M. Diplomacy in a Democracy.
Wrixon, Fred. Moonstalker.
Wrobleski, Henry M., ed. see Hess, Karen M.
Wrottesley, A. J. The Midland & Great Northern Joint Railway.
Wroughton, John, jt. auth. see Cook, Chris.
Wu, C. S., jt. ed. see Hughes, Vernon.
Wu, Chien-Shiung, jt. ed. see Yuan, Luke C.
Wu, Chun-hsi. Dollars, Dependents, & Dogma: Overseas Chinese Remittances to Communist China.
Wu, Eugene, jt. auth. see Berton, Peter.
Wu, Jack A., jt. auth. see Wu, Nesa L.
Wu, John C. Beyond East & West.
--Fountain of Justice: A Study of the Natural Law.
Wu, Margaret S. An Introduction to Computer Data Processing.
--Introduction to Computer Data Processing.
--Introduction to Computer Data Processing with BASIC.
Wu, Nesa L. & Wu, Jack A. Introduction to Management Science.
Wu, S. Cooking with Madame Wu & Yang Recipes for Health & Longevity.
Wu, Silas H. Communication & Imperial Control in China: Evolution of the Palace Memorial System, 1693-1735.
Wu, Tai T. New Methodologies in Studies of Protein Configuration.
Wu, Yeun C. & Smith, Ed D., eds. Fixed-Film Biological Processes for Wastewater Treatment.
Wu, Yuan-li. Economic Development & the Use of Energy Resources in Communist China.
Wu Cheng'en. Journey to the West. Jenner, W. J., tr. from Chinese.
Wu Ch'Eng-En. Monkey. Waley, Arthur, tr. from Chinese. & pref. by.
Wu-chi Liu. Confucius, His Life & Time.
Wuehrmann, Arthur H. & Manson-Hing, Lincoln R. Dental Radiology.
Wuellenweber, R., et al, eds. Advances in Neurosurgery.
Wuerch, Bonnie B. & Voeltz, Luanna M. Longitudinal Leisure Skills for Severely Handicapped Learners: The Ho'onanea Curriculum Component.
Wuerl, Donald & Wilson, Michael. A Visit to the Vatican for Young People.
Wuertenberger, T., ed. see International Congress on Criminology, 6th, Madrid, 1970.
Wuertz-Schaefer, Karin. Hiking Virginia's National Forests.
Wuest, Kenneth S. Word Studies in the Greek New Testament, for the English Reader. Incl. Bk. 1. Golden Nuggets; Bk. 2. Bypaths; Bk. 3. Treasures; Bk. 4. Untranslatable Riches; Bk. 5. Studies in Vocabulary; Bk. 6. Great Truths to Live by; Bk. 7. Mark; Bk. 8. Romans; Bk. 9. Galatians; Bk. 10. Ephesians & Colossians; Bk. 11. Philippians; Bk. 12. The Pastoral Epistles; Bk. 13. Hebrews; Bk. 14. First Peter; Bk. 15. In These Last Days; Bk. 16. Prophetic Light in the Present Darkness. Eerdmans.
Wulf, Dick. Find Yourself, Give Yourself.
Wulf, Kathleen. I'm Glad I'm Little.
Wulf, W. A., et al. HYDRA-C.mmp: An Experimental Computer System.
Wulff. Philosophy of Medicine: An Introduction.
Wulff, Kurt & Bruns, Bill. How to Profit from the Coming Oil Crisis.
Wullenweber, Ernst W., Jr. Greenberg's American Flyer Numerical Parts List.
Wunderlich, Berhard. Macromolecular Physics: Crystals, Structure, Morphology & Defects.
Wunderlick, Ray C., jt. auth. see Gegan, R. A.
Wunsch, William F. Marriage: Ideals & Realizations.
Wuolle, A. Finnish-English, English-Finnish Dictionary.
Wurm, Stephen A., jt. ed. see McCormack, William C.
Wurman, Richard S. Access.
--Baseball-Access.
--Las Vegas-Access.
--The Los Angeles-Access.
--Medical-Access.
--MOMA-Access.
--New Orleans-Access.

Authors

--NYC Access.
--San Francisco Access.
--Tokyo-Access.
--Tokyo-Access.
--Washington, D. C.
--What Will Be Has Always Been: The Words of Louis I. Kahn.
Wurman, Richard S., jt. auth. see North Carolina State University, School of Design, Students.
Wurman, Richard S., ed. Football-Access.
--Hawaii-Access.
--NYC Access.
--San Francisco-Access.
Wurman, Richard S., created by. Summer Games Access, 1988: A Viewer's Guide to the Sports, Athletes, Records & Sites.
Wurtman, Judith J. The Carbohydrate Craver's Diet.
Wurtman, Judith J. & Leibenstein, Margaret. The Carbohydrate Craver's Diet Cookbook.
Wurtman, Richard J., et al. Pineal.
Wurtzel, David. Thomas Lyster.
Wuthnow, Robert, et al. Cultural Analysis: The Work of Peter L. Berger, Mary Douglas, Michel Foucault, & Jurgen Habermas.
Wuttke, W. & Horowski, R., eds. Gonadal Steroids & Brain Function: IUPS-Satellite Symposium 1980.
Wyandt, Christine R. A Librarian's Hints for Students.
Wyatt. Financial Planning under the New Rules.
Wyatt, A. J. Old English Riddles.
Wyatt, Allen L. Basic Tricks for the Apple.
--Basic Tricks for the IBM.
Wyatt, Barb. The Greasy Thumb Automechanics Manual for Women.
Wyatt, Donald. Aldous Huxley.
Wyatt, Thomas. Poetry of Sir Thomas Wyatt: A Selection & Study by E. M. W. Tillyard.
Wyatt, Wyatt. Deep in the Heart.
Wyatt-Brown, Bertram. Lewis Tappan & the Evangelical War Against Slavery.
Wybrow, Robert J., jt. ed. see Heald, Gordon.
Wycech-Los, M., et al, eds. Warsaw Fall Seminars in Mathematical Economics 1975.
Wycherley, William. Complete Plays of William Wycherley. Weales, Gerald, ed.
Wyckoff, D. Daryl. Truck Drivers in America.
Wyckoff, D. Daryl & Sasser, W. Earl. The U. S. Lodging Industry.
Wyckoff, Hogie. Solving Problems Together.
Wyckoff, Hogie, ed. Love, Therapy & Politics: Issues in Radical Therapy - The First Year.
Wyckoff, R. W. Crystal Structures: The Structure of Benzene Derivatives.
Wyckoff, Richard D. Wall Street Ventures & Adventures Through Forty Years.
Wyden, Peter. Day One: Before Hiroshima & After.
--The Passionate War: A Narrative History of the Spanish Civil War, 1936-1939.
Wydick, Richard C., jt. auth. see Schwartz, Mortimer D.
Wydick, Richard C., jt. auth. see Schwartz, Mortimer O.
Wye, Deborah. Louise Bourgeois.
Wyer, John. The Certain Sound: Thirty Years of Motor Racing.
Wyeth, Andrew & Wyeth, Betsy J. Christina's World & Wyeth at Kuerners.
Wyeth, Betsy J. Christina's World: Paintings & Prestudies of Andrew Wyeth.
--Wyeth at Kuerners.
Wyeth, Betsy J., jt. auth. see Wyeth, Andrew.
Wyeth, Jamie. Jamie Wyeth.
Wyker, Bertha P. Spanning the Decades: A Spiritual Pilgrimage.
Wykes-Joyce, M. Seven Thousand Years of Pottery & Porcelain.
Wykoff, Frank C. Macroeconomics: Theory, Evidence & Policy.
Wykoff, Frank C., jt. auth. see Walton, Gary M.
Wyland, Johanna L. Your Paths in Ink: Graphoanalysis & the Personality.
Wyld, Henry C. Historical Study of the Mother Tongue.
Wyld, Lionel. Boaters & Broomsticks.
Wylde, Augustus B. Eighty-Three to Eighty-Seven in the Saudan, with an Account of Sir William Hewett's Mission to King John of Abyssinia.
Wyler, Rose, jt. auth. see Elting, Mary.
Wyler, S., ed. see Weinberg, Julia.
Wylie, Betty J. Beginnings.
Wylie, Betty J. & MacFarlane, Lynne. Everywoman's Money Book.
Wylie, C. Ray. The World of Eric Lim.
Wylie, James. The Homestead Grays.
Wylie, Jonathan & Margolin, David. The Ring of Dancers: Images of Faroese Culture.
Wylie, Laura. The Night Visitor.
Wylie, Samuel & McKenzie, John L. Advent-Christmas.
Wyllie, M. R. Fundamentals of Well-Log Interpretation.
Wyman. Lure for Feeling.
Wyman, Dorothy. Bruce.
Wyman, Joe. If You Promise Not to Tell Activity Book.
Wyman, Leland C. Southwestern Indian Drypainting.
Wymore, jt. auth. see Buzzacott.
Wynar, Bohdan S., ed. Best Reference Books 1981-1985.
--Recommended Reference Books for Small & Medium-Sized Libraries & Media Centers 1986.
Wynd, Oswald. The Blazing Air.
Wynder, Ernest L. & Hoffman, Dietrich, eds. Tobacco & Tobacco Smoke.
Wyndham, Joan. Love Lessons: A Wartime Diary.
Wyndham, Lee & Madison, Arnold. Writing for Children & Teenagers.
Wyndham, Robert. Chinese Mother Goose Rhymes.
Wynen, Donald van see Van Wynen, Donald & Van Wynen, Mabel.
Wynen, Mabel van see Van Wynen, Donald & Van Wynen, Mabel.
Wynes, C. E., ed. Negro in the South Since Eighteen Sixty-Five.
Wyngaarden, James B., jt. auth. see Smith, Lloyd H.
Wynkoop, Shari H., jt. auth. see Kime, Helen R.
Wynmalen, Henry. Equitation.
Wynn, Daniel W. Timeless Issues.
Wynn, Martin. Planning Games: Case Study Simulations in Land Management & Development.
Wynn, R. M., tr. see Kern, Guenther & Kern-Bontke, E.
Wynn, Tommy E. Biology in the Modern World.
Wynne, E. G., jt. auth. see Pedder, I. J.
Wynne, Edward A. Looking at Schools: Good, Bad, & Indifferent.
Wynne, Edward A., ed. Character Policy: An Emerging Issue.
Wynne, James D. Learning Statistics: A Common-Sense Approach.
Wynne, Ronald D., jt. auth. see Phillips, Joel.
Wynne-Morgan, John. Nude & the Portrait: How to Pose & Paint Them.
Wynn-Parry, C. B. Rehabilitation of the Hand.
Wynter, Andrew. Curiosities of Civilization.
--Our Social Bees.
--Subtle Brains & Lissom Fingers.
Wyon, Olive. Prayer.
Wyrick, Jean. Steps to Writing Well: A Concise Guide to Composition.
Wyrick, Jean, ed. Discovering Ideas: An Anthology for Writers.
Wyse, Bonita W., jt. auth. see Hansen, R. Gaurth.
Wyse, Lois. Company Manners: An Insider Tells How to Succeed in the Real World of Corporate Protocol & Power Politics.
--The Six Figure Woman.
Wyss, Johann. Swiss Family Robinson.
Wyszynski, Stefan. A Freedom Within: The Prison Notes of Stefan Cardinal Wyszynski. Krzywick-Herburt, Barbara & Ziemba, Walter, trs.

X

Xanthos, Paul, jt. auth. see Johnson, Joan D.
Xavier & Viera. World of the Spirit.
Xenakis, John. Structured PL-1 Programming: An Introduction.
Xhng, M. K. & Hirono, R., eds. ASEAN-Japan Industrial Co-operation: An Overview.
Xianliang, Zhang, et al. Contemporary Chinese Short Stories.
Xianyi, Yang & Yang, Gladys. Excerpts from Three Classical Chinese Novels.
Xianyi, Yang, tr. see Ling, Ding.
Xiaoying, Le. Le Xiaoying's Cartoons for Children.
Xin, Deng, tr. see Yunlei, Zhang, et al.
Xinglian, Zhang. A Glossary of Chinese Archaeology. Shuhan, Zhao, ed.
Xinhua News Agency, Beijing, China, Staff. People's Republic of China Year-Book 1983.
Xiyang, Tang. Living Treasures: An Odyssey Through China's Extraordinary Nature Reserves.
Xueyuan, Tian, et al. An English Chinese Dictionary of Demography.

Y

Ya'ari, Ehud, jt. auth. see Schiff, Ze'ev.
Yablon, Isadore G., et al. Ankle Injuries.
Yablonsky, Lewis. Fathers & Sons.
--Fathers & Sons.
Yablonsky, Lewis, jt. auth. see Haskell, Martin R.
Yabrov, Alexander. Interferon & Nonspecific Resistance.
Yaciuk, Gordon. Food Drying: Proceedings of a Workshop Held at Edmonton, Alberta, 6-9 July 1981.
Yackel, James, jt. ed. see Gupta, Shanti S.
Yackel, James W., jt. auth. see Moore, David S.
Yacone, Linda A. Cardiovascular Problems. Van Meter, Margaret, ed.
Yacorznski, G. K. Frontiers of Psychology.
Yaeger, Dennis R., jt. auth. see Practising Law Institute Staff.
Yaeger, Peter E., jt. auth. see Practising Law Institute Staff.
Yaffe, James. Saul & Morris, Worlds Apart.
Yaffe, L., ed. Nuclear Chemistry.
Yager, Jan. Women & Friendship: Modern Responses to Changing Roles.
Yager, Ronald R., ed. Fuzzy Set & Possibility Theory: Recent Developments.
Yaglom, I., jt. auth. see Golovina, L.
Yagodin, B. A., ed. Agricultural Chemistry in Two Vols.
Yahraes, Herbert, jt. auth. see Segal, Julius.
Yahya, S. M. Fundamentals of Compressible Flow.
Yakhnin, L. Cardboard Clock Square.
Yakimenko, L. Sholokhov: A Critical Appreciation.
Yakovlev, A. M. Fundamentals of Political Science.
Yakowicz, Joseph V. Poland's Postwar Recovery: Economic Reconstruction, Nationalization & Agrarian Reform in Poland after World War II.
Yakowitz, S., jt. ed. see Szidarovszky, F.
Yakushenkov, Y. Electro-Optical Devices.
Yaldwyn, John C., jt. auth. see Healy, Anthony.
Yale Daily News Staff & Waters, Margaret. The Insider's Guide to the Colleges: 1984-85.
Yale Daily News Staff, ed. The Insider's Guide to the Colleges.
Yale University - Henry S. Graves Memorial Library Staff. Dictionary Catalogue of the Yale Forestry Library.
Yale University Library Staff. A Guide to the Romanization of Standard Chinese.
Yale University Staff. Catalog of the Yale Collection of Western Americana.
--Southeast Asia Collection: Checklist of Southeast Asian Serials.
Yalin, Mehmet S. Mechanics of Sediment Transport.
Yalisove, I. L. & Dietz, J. B., Jr. Telescopic Prosthetic Therapy: Peridontal Prosthesis - Fixed & Removable.
Yalow, jt. auth. see Luft.
Yalow, Rosalyn S., ed. Radioimmunoassay.
Yamada, Abbot S., jt. auth. see Covell, Jon Carter.
Yamada, Hiroshi. Strength of Biological Materials.
Yamagiwa, Joseph K., tr. The Okagami: A Japanese Historical Tale.
Yamamoto, Izuru, jt. ed. see O'Brien, R. D.
Yamamoto, Kaoru, ed. Child & His Image: Self Concept in the Early Years.
Yamamura, Kozo. A Study of Samurai Income & Entrepreneurship.
Yamamura, Kozo, jt. auth. see Hanley, Susan B.
Yamamura, Sakae. Theory of Linear Induction Motors.
Yamamura, Y., et al, eds. Humoral Factors in Host Defense: Symposium.
Yamamura, Yuichi. Immunomodulation by Microbial Products & Related Synthetic Compounds.
Yamamuro, S. Differential Calculus in Topological Linear Spaces.
Yaman, Peter, jt. auth. see Carter, Loretta M.
Yamanobe, Tomoyuki, ed. see Kubota, Itchiku.
Yamashita, Tadashi. Kusarigama. Lee, Mike, ed.
Yamauchi, E. Jesus, Zoroaster, Buddha, Socrates, Muhammad.
Yamauchi, Edwin. Stones & the Scriptures.
Yamazaki, Mikio, jt. ed. see Uraguchi, Kenji.
Yamori, Yukio, jt. ed. see Lovenberg, Walter.
Yampolsky, Philip, tr. see Takada, Koin.
Yan, Stephen. The Stephen Yan Seafood Wokbook.
Yanagihara, H. Theory of Hopf Algebras Attached to Group Schemes.
Yanaihara, Tadao. Pacific Islands under Japanese Mandate.
Yanda, Bill & Fisher, Rick. The Food & Heat Producing Solar Greenhouse.
Yandian, Bob. End Time Prophecy.
--How to Become Great in the Kingdom of God.
--Joel: The Outpouring of God's Glory.
--Oil & Wine.
Yandle, Bruce, jt. auth. see Ulbrich, H.
Yanenko, N. N. Method of Fractional Steps: The Solution of Problems of Mathematical Physics in Several Variables. Holt, M., ed.
Yang, Ch'ing-k'un. The Chinese Family in the Communist Revolution.
Yang, Edward S. Fundamentals of Semiconductor Devices.
Yang, Gladys. Seven Contemporary Chinese Women Writers.
Yang, Gladys, jt. auth. see Xianyi, Yang.
Yang, Gladys, tr. see Hua, Gu.
Yang, Gladys, tr. see Ling, Ding.
Yang, Gladys, tr. see Youmei, Deng, et al.
Yang Han, et al. Chinese Painting & Calligraphy (Chinese-English)
Yang Jiang. A Cadre School Life: Six Chapters. Barme, Geremie & Lee, Bennett, trs. from Chinese.
Yanick, Paul, Jr., jt. auth. see Clark, John G.
Yankelovich, Skelly & White, Inc. Staff. Consumer Research Study on Reading & Book Purchasing, 1978.
Yanker, Gary. Gary Yanker's Sportwalking.
Yanker, Gary & Tarlow, Carol. America's Greatest Walks: A Traveler's Guide to One Hundred Scenic Adventures.
Yankowitz, Susan see Hoffman, William M.
Yanowitch, Murray & Fisher, Wesley A., eds. Social Stratification & Mobility in the U. S. S. R.
Yanrong, Wang. Bird Neighbour.
Yantis, Richard C., jt. auth. see Painter, Richard J.
Yao, Andrew. Probabilistic Algorithms.
Yao, S. B. & Kunii, T. L., eds. Data Base Design Techniques II: Physical Structures & Applications Tokyo 1979: Proceedings.
Yao, S. B., et al, eds. Data Base Design Technique I: Requirements & Logical Structures New York 1978: Proceedings.
Yao, Wang. Tales from Tibetan Opera.
Yap, Elsa P., jt. auth. see Bunye, Maria V.
Yapko, Michael D. Trancework: An Introduction to Clinical Hypnosis.
Yapp, Kathleen. Master of Mackenzie Station.
--Romance at Redhaven.
Yapp, Peter, compiled by. The Travellers' Dictionary of Quotation.
Yaqub, Adil. Elementary Functions.
Yarber, Robert E. Writing for College: A Practical Approach.
Yarbrough, Mary, jt. auth. see Axnick, Karen.
Yard, Sally. Willem De Kooning: The First Twenty-Six Years in New York. Freedberg, S. J., ed.
Yardley, Herbert O. American Black Chamber.
--Chinese Black Chamber: An Adventure in Espionage.
Yarian, Rick, ed. Health 1988-89.
Yarington, David J. Surviving in College.
Yariv, Amnon. Introduction to Optical Electronics.
Yarker, K. A. International Marketing.
Yarmolinsky, Adam & Lambert, Richard D., eds. The Military & American Society.
Yarmolinsky, Avraham, ed. see Babel, Issac.
Yarmolinsky, Avrahm, ed. Soviet Short Stories.
Yarmolinsky, Avrham, ed. see Dostoyevsky, Fyodor.
Yarmosky, Michael. I'm Gonna Hit Myself a Homerun Today.
Yarn, David H. The Four Gospels As One.
Yaron, B., et al, eds. Arid Zone Irrigation.
Yaroslarisev & Kreshkov. A Course in Analytical Chemistry.
Yarrington, Roger, jt. auth. see Parnell, Dale.
Yarrington, Roger, ed. Strengthening Humanities in Community Colleges.
Yarshater, Ehsan, jt. ed. see Ettinghausen, Richard.
Yarwood, J. Vacuum Devices: Proceedings of the Conference, University of Cambridge, 25-27 March 1980.
Yarwood, J., jt. auth. see Close, K. J.
Yarwood, J., ed. Israeli Vacuum Congress, Fourth: Proceedings.
--Vacuum & Thin Film Technology.
--Vacuum Seventy-Eight: Selected Proceedings of the Conference on Medium High & Ultra-High Vacuum Technology, Oxford, England, 1978. Grossart, G. S.
Yarwood, J., ed. see Israeli Vacuum Congress Staff.
Yasen, Behdan, ed. A Ukrainian Priest's Appeals from a Soviet Labor Camp.
Yasko, Joyce. Care of the Client Receiving External Radiation Therapy.
Yasko, Joyce & Lauffer, Barbara. Care of the Client Receiving Chemotherapy.
Yasuda, Mac. The Vintage Guitar.
Yates, Alfred G., Jr. The Pocket Income Tax Calculator.
Yates, B. How to Find Out about the United Kingdom Cotton Industry.
Yates, Brock. Sunday Driver.
Yates, D. A., et al. Tres Cuentistas Hispanoamericanos.
Yates, Elizabeth. Skeezer: Dog with a Mission.
--Sound Friendships: The Story of Willa & Her Hearing Ear Dog.
--Your Prayers & Mine.
Yates, Frances A. The French Academies of the Sixteenth Century.
--Renaissance & Reform: The Italian Contribution. Trapp, J., ed.
Yates, H. & Hasler, A. F., eds. Weather Satellites, Stereoscopy & Sounding: Proceedings of the Topical Meeting of the COSPAR Interdisciplinary Scientific Commission A (Meetings A3 & A4) of the COSPAR 24th Plenary Meeting held in Ottawa, Canada, 16 May-2 June, 1982.
Yates, J., jt. auth. see Thomas, R.
Yates, Jean & Thomas, Rebecca. User Guide to the UNIX System.

Yates, Jere E. Managing Stress: A Businessperson's Guide.
Yates, Joanne, jt. auth. see Tchudi, Stephen N.
Yates, Joanne M. Writing in the Content Areas: Research Implications.
Yates, Keith D. The Complete Book of Taekwon Do Forms.
Yates, Madelein, jt. auth. see Miklowitz, Gloria D.
Yates, Richard. Cold Spring Harbor.
--Disturbing the Peace.
--The Easter Parade.
--A Good School.
--Liars in Love.
--Revolutionary Road.
--Young Hearts Crying.
Yates, Richard E. The Hardscrabble Letters.
Yates, Steve A., ed. The Essential Landscape: The New Mexico Photographic Survey.
Yatron, Michael. America's Literary Revolt.
Yatsimirskii, K. B. Kinetic Methods of Analysis. Harvey, P. J., tr.
Yau, John. Corpse & Mirror.
Yavorski, B. M. & Detlaf, A. A. Manual De Fisica Para Ingenieros y Estudiantes.
Yavorsky, B. & Detlaf, A. Handbook of Physics.
Yavorsky, B. M. & Pinsky, A. A. Fundamentals of Physics.
Yaw, Yvonne. Sky.
Yawitz, Jess B., jt. auth. see Hempel, George.
Yaxley, Mike. Soccer.
Yazdani, Masoud, ed. New Horizons in Educational Computing.
Yazkova, V. Socialist Life Style & the Family.
Yazzie, Alfred. Navajo Police.
Yeadon, David. Secluded Islands of the Atlantic Coast.
Yeager, Trisha. The California Beauty Book: A Total Guide to Health & Beauty.
Yeagle, Dean. Summer Fun with the Fraggles.
Yeakley, Flavil. Church Leadership & Organization.
Yearley, Clifton K., Jr. Britons in American Labor.
Yearsley, Macleod. Folklore of Fairy-Tale.
Yeates, Maurice, ed. see Igu Commission on Quantitative Geography, Meeting, 1972.
Yeates, N. T., et al. Animal Science: Reproduction, Climate, Meat & Wool.
Yeates, Sybil. Development of Hearing.
Yeatman, Linda. Treasury of Animal Stories. Klimo, Kate, ed.
Yeats, George, jt. auth. see Yeats, William Butler.
Yeats, Jack B. La la Noo.
--Verses.
Yeats, John B. Further Letters of John Butler Yeats. Robinson, Lennox, ed.
--Passages from the Letter of John Butler Yeats. Pound, Ezra, ed.
Yeats, William B., ed. Representative Irish Tales.
Yeats, William Butler & Yeats, George. Ballylee: The Tower Poems with Letter by George Yeats.
Yee, Min S. & Layton, Thomas N. In My Father's House.
Yefimov, N. V. Quadratic Forms & Matrices: An Introductory Approach.
Yeh Ch'ing. Inside Mao Tse-Tung's Thought: An Analytical Blueprint of His Actions by a Former Top Chinese Communist Leader. Pan, Stephen, ed. Tsuan, T. H. & Mortensen, Ralph, trs. from Chinese.
Yekovlev, E. Of Time & People.
Yektai, Niki. Sun Rain.
Yeldham, R. F. & Plumb, A., eds. The Practitioners' Probate Manual.
Yelland, Jones E. Handbook of Literary Terms.
Yellig, William F., Jr. & Tek, M. Rasin. Prospects for Oil & Gas from Silurian-Niagaran Trend Areas in Michigan.
Yellin, Stanley J., jt. auth. see Brunetti, Frank L.
Yemel'yanov, V. S. & Yevstyukin, A. I. Metallurgy of Nuclear Fuels.
Yenne, Bill. Space Shuttle.
Yeo, Don. Bangladesh: A Traveller's Guide.
Yeoman, John, jt. auth. see Blake, Quentin.
Yep, Laurence. Liar, Liar.
--Liar, Liar.
--The Tom Sawyer Fires.
Yeranian, Arthur S. The Civilized.
Yerby, Frank. The Foxes of Harrow.
Yerby, Lorees see Corrigan, Robert W.
Yergin, Daniel H. & Hillenbrand, Martin, eds. Global Insecurity: A World Plan for Energy & Econonic Upheaval.
Yeric, Jerry L. & Todd, John R. Public Opinion: The Visible Politics.
Yerman, Ron. Religion: Innocent or Guilty.
Yerrell, J. Stuart, ed. see World Conference on Transport Research Staff.
Yershov, P. The Little Humpbacked Horse.
Yetiv, Jack & Bianchine, Joseph, eds. Recent Advances in Clinical Therapeutics, Vol. 1: Selected Topics: Hypertension, Cardiovascular Disease, Analgesics & Endocrine Disorders.
Yette, Frederick W., jt. auth. see Yette, Samuel F.
Yette, Samuel F. & Yette, Frederick W. Washington & Two Marches.
Yevstyukin, A. I., jt. auth. see Yemel'yanov, V. S.
Yevteyev, M. & Kirin, V. A. New Soviet Legislation to Combat Crime.
Yezierska, Anzia. Red Ribbon on a White Horse.
Yglesias, Helen. The Saviors.
Yglesias, Jose. Double Double.
Yi, Zhou, et al. Ancient Architecture in Beijing.
Yicheng, Zhou, tr. see Wen, Qi.
Yin, John. Government of Socialist China.
Yin, Khin. Using Turbo Prolog.
Ying, jt. auth. see He.
Ying, Mei. Kindhearted Xiawudong.
--Zhen Zhen's Dream.
Ying, Mei & Ying, Mei, illus. Magic Deer.
Yinger, J. Milton. Scientific Study of Religion.
Yinger, Winthrop. Cesar Chavez: The Rhetoric of Nonviolence.
Yip, Sidney, jt. auth. see Boon, Jean P.
Yipp Wai-Lim. Ezra Pound's Cathay.
Yiqun, Fang. Two Little Kittens.
Yllo, Kersti, jt. auth. see Finkelhor, David.
Ylvisaker, Donald, jt. auth. see Gangolli, R. A.
YMCA of the U. S. A. Staff. Examining Our Faith.
--National YMCA Progressive Gymnastics Program for Youth.
--The New Y-Indian Guide Program.
--Physical Fitness Through Water Exercise.
--YMCA Camping Centennial: No. 3, Promotion.
--YMCA Camping Centennial Series.
--YMCA Cardiac Therapy Participant's Handbook.
--YMCA Directory, 1985.
YMCA of the U. S. A. Staff & Monaco, Anthony L., Jr. Youth Employment Series.
Yob, Parry. Photo Equipment You Can Make.
Yob, Parry C., jt. auth. see PhotoGraphic Magazine Editors.
Yockey, Ross. New Orleans Scrapbook.
Yocom, Charles, et al. Wildlife & Plants of the Southern Rocky Mountains.
Yoder, Claude H., et al. Chemistry.
--Chemistry.
Yoder, Dale & Heneman, Herbert G., Jr., eds. Professional PAIR.
Yoder, Dale, Jr. & Heneman, Herbert G., Jr., eds. ASPA Handbook of Personnel & Industrial Relations: Employee & Labor Relations.
Yoder, Elizabeth, jt. auth. see Yoder, Perry.
Yoder, John H. Christian & Capital Punishment.
Yoder, John H., ed. see Arnold, Eberhard.
Yoder, Perry & Yoder, Elizabeth. New Men-New Roles.
Yoell, John. Nordic Sound.
Yoffe, Emily, jt. auth. see King, Larry.
Yoffey, J. M. & Coortice, F. C. Lymphatics, Lymph & the Lymphomyelard Complex.
Yogananda, P. Autobiography of a Yogi.
Yogerst, Joe. East Africa with Malawi & Zambia.
Yohalem, Alice M., jt. auth. see Ginzberg, Eli.
Yohn, Richard V. Explore the Bible Yourself: Firsthand Joy.
Yohn, Rick. Overcoming.
--What Every Christian Should Know about God: A Study Manual.
Yolen, Jane. Dragon Night & Other Lullabies.
--The Girl Who Cried Flowers: And Other Tales.
--The Hundredth Dove.
--Tales of Wonder.
Yolen, Jane H. Friend: The Story of George Fox & the Quakers.
--The Giants' Farm.
--The Giants Go Camping.
--The Little Spotted Fish.
--Ring Out! A Book of Bells.
--Zoo Two Thousand: Twelve Stories of Science Fiction & Fantasy Beasts.
Yolen, Jane H., compiled by. Shape Shifters: Fantasy & Science Fiction Tales About Humans Who Can Change Their Shapes.
Yolton, Jean S., jt. auth. see Yolton, John W.
Yolton, John W. Thinking & Perceiving.
Yolton, John W. & Yolton, Jean S. John Locke: A Reference Guide.
Yoneda, Soei. Good Food from a Japanese Temple. Schuefftan, Kim, tr. from Japanese.
Yonemasu, Kunio, et al, eds. Resolution, Properties, & Genetic Aspects of Complement.
Yonezawa, Yoshio, et al. Arts of China, Vol. 3: Paintings in Chinese Museums.
Yongden, Lama, jt. auth. see David-Neel, Alexandra.
Yonkers, Ann, jt. auth. see Polmer, Bunny.
Yoors, Jan. The Gypsies.
Yorgason, Blaine M. & Eaton, Carl J. The Shadow Taker.
York, D. Planet Earth.
York, Kenneth H. & Whelan, John W. General Practice Insurance Law, Cases, Materials & Problems, 1985.
--Insurance Law Cases, Materials & Problems.
York, Phyllis, et al. Toughlove Solutions.
York, R. A. The Poem As Utterance.
York, Richard L., jt. auth. see Brown, John P.
York, Thomas. Trapper.
Yorke, J. A., ed. see Seminar on Differential Equations & Dynamical Systems, 2nd, 1969.
Yorke, Malcolm. Eric Gill: Man of Flesh & Spirit.
Yorke, Mantz, ed. see Society for Academic Gaming & Simulation in Education & Training Staff.
Yorke, Margaret. The Apricot Bed.
--China Doll.
--No Fury.
Yorke, R. Electric Circuit Theory.
Yorke, Ritchie. The History of Rock 'n Roll.
Yorke-Long, Alan. Music at Court: Four Eighteenth Century Studies.
Yorks, Lyle, jt. auth. see Morin, William J.
Yorks, Lyle, jt. auth. see Whitsett, David A.
Yoseph. The Gilgal Theophany.
Yoshida, H. & Gigihara, Y., eds. Advances in Pharmacology & Therapeutics: Proceedings of the Eighth International Congress of Pharmacology, Tokyo, Japan, 19-24 July, 1981.
Yoshida, H., et al, eds. Advances in Pharmacology & Therapeutics: Proceedings of the Eighth International Congress of Pharmacology, Tokyo, Japan, July 19-24, 1981.
--Advances in Pharmacology & Therapeutics: Proceedings of 8th International Congress of Pharmacology, Tokyo, Japan, July 19-24, 1981.
--CNS Pharmacology - Neuropeptides: Proceedings of the Eighth International Congress of Pharmacology, Tokyo, Japan,19-24 July, 1981.
--Neurotransmitters-Receptors: Proceedings of 8th International Congress of Pharmacology, Tokyo, Japan, July 19-24, 1981.
--Advances in Pharmacology & Therapeutics: Proceedings of Eighth International Congress of Pharmacology, Tokyo, Japan, 19-24 July 1981.
Yoshida, Kenichi. Japan Is a Circle.
Yoshikura, H., et al. Mouse Sarcoma Virus.
Yoshino, M. Y. Japanese Marketing System: Adaptations & Innovations.
Yoshizawa, T. Stability Theory & Existence of Periodic Solutions & Almost Periodic Solutions.
Yost, Charles W. History & Memory: A Statesman's Perceptions of the Twentieth Century.
Yost, Gaylord. Bow & Finger Magic.
--Exercises for Change of Position.
--Studies in Pizzicato & Harmonics.
--Twelve Daily Exercises.
--Yost Violin Method.
Yost, George, jt. auth. see Cawley, Robert.
Yost, Nellie S. A Man As Big As the West: The Ralph Hubbard Story.
Yotey, H. L., jt. auth. see Phillips, Uad.
You, P. S. & Lim, C. Y. Singapore Economy.
Youd, Samuel. Messages of Love.
Youden, W. J. Experimentation & Measurement.
Youdes, Pamela. China.
Youell, Tessa & Kimball, George. The Pocket Guide to French Food & Wine.
Youldon, Gillian. Numbers.
Youmei, Deng, et al. Snuff Bottles & Other Stories. Yang, Gladys, tr. from Chinese.
Young. Hydrogen & Deuterium.
--Oxides of Nitrogen, Sulfur & Chlorine: Gas Solubilities.
Young, A. D., ed. Progress in Aerospace Sciences.
--Progress in Aerospace Sciences.
Young, A. S. Black Champions of the Gridiron: O. J. Simpson & Leroy Keyes.
--Mets from Mobile: Cleon Jones & Tommie Agee.
--Sulfur Dioxide, Chlorine, Fluorine & Chlorine Oxides.
Young, Agatha. Dr. Moore's Legacy.
--I Swear by Apollo.
--The Town & Dr. Moore.
Young, Al, jt. ed. see Reed, Ishmael.
Young, Albert D., Jr., jt. auth. see Kane, Raymond W.
Young, Alida E. Is Chelsea Going Blind?
--Too Young to Die.
--What's Wrong with Daddy?
Young, Allen, pref. by. Orange Illustrated, Nineteen Hundred Four: A Pictorial of a Massachusetts Town.
Young, Anthony & Dent, David. Soil Survey & Land Evaluation.
Young, Arthur C., ed. see Gissing, George R.
Young, Axel. Blood Rubies.
--Wicked Stepmother.
Young, Bob & Young, Jan. Liberators of Latin America.
Young, C. L., jt. ed. see Clever, H. L.
Young, Callie B. Your Mule Is Crowing.
Young, Corbin. San Francisco Works Out.
Young, Cyril, jt. auth. see Cowper, Ann.
Young, Dale. Marmac Guide to Houston. Smith, Susan H., ed.
--A Marmac Guide to Houston. Spear, Elizabeth, ed.
Young, Daniel. The Daily News Fifteen Dollars Restaurant Guide.
Young, Darrell D. Wild Plants You Can Eat.
Young, Darroch F., jt. auth. see Carter, Juanita E.
Young, David. Marooned in Fraggle Rock.
Young, David, jt. auth. see Anthony, Robert.
Young, David P. The Names of a Hare in English.
Young, David W. Financial Control in Health Care.
Young, Dennis R. Casebook of Management for Nonprofit Organizations: Entrepreneurship & Organizational Change in the Human Services.
--How Shall We Collect the Garbage? A Study in Economic Organization.
--If Not for Profit, for What? A Behavioral Theory of the Nonprofit Sector Based on Entrepreneurship. Simon, John, frwd. by.
Young, Donald, jt. ed. see Sellin, Thorsten.
Young, Donald F., et al. Essentials of Mechanics: A Unified First Course.
Young, E. Neil, jt. auth. see Stauber, Alvin.
Young, Edna C. Language Approach to Open Syllables.
Young, Edward J. My Servants the Prophets.
Young, Eli. Hillbilly.
Young, Elizabeth. Blandford Family Quiz Book 2.
Young, F. M., ed. see Beyers, Coralie M.
Young, Fay. The Awakening.
Young, Frances M. From Nicaea to Chalcedon: A Guide to the Literature & Its Background.
--Sacrifice & the Death of Christ.
Young, Francis A., jt. auth. see McCann, Phillip.
Young, George. Digital Electronics: A Hands-on Learning Approach.
--Selectric Interface. McCarthy, Nan, ed.
Young, George & Henkin, Bill. San Francisco by Cable Car.
Young, George & Stark, Peter. Kilobaud Klassroom: A Course in Digital Electronics. Crocker, Chris, et al, eds.
Young, Gordon D., ed. Mari at Fifty: Studies in Honor of the 50th Anniversary of the Discovery of Tell Hariri-Mari.
Young, Graham, ed. China: Dilemmas of Modernisation.
Young, Gregory G. Your Personality & How to Live with It.
Young, H. Edwin. A Winning Walk.
Young, Harben B. & Ferguson, Lucy R. Puberty to Manhood in Italy & America.
Young, Harold C. Planning, Programming, Budgeting Systems in Academic Libraries: An Exploratory Study of PPBS in University Libraries Having Membership in the Association of Research Libraries.
Young, Henry J., ed. Preaching on Suffering & a God of Love.
--Preaching the Gospel.
Young, Hugh D. Fundamentals of Waves, Optics & Modern Physics.
Young, I. S. Uncle Herschel, Doctor Padilsky, & the Evil Eye: A Novel of Old Brooklyn.
Young, Isobel I. The Glory of the Journey.
Young, J., et al, eds. Centerary Book of the University of Sydney Faculty of Medicine.
Young, J. Francis, ed. see American Ceramic Society, Inc. Staff.
Young, J. W. Projective Geometry.
Young, James J. When You're Divorced & Catholic.
Young, James L. Workers' Compensation Law of Ohio.
Young, James R. & Mondy, Robert W. Personal Selling: Function, Theory, & Practice.
Young, James S. Washington Community: 1800-1828.
Young, James S., ed. Problems & Prospects of Presidential Leadership in the Nineteen-Eighties.
Young, Jan, jt. auth. see Young, Bob.
Young, Jean A., ed. Tales of a Hoosier Village: A History of Bristol, Indiana.
Young, Jeffrey M., jt. auth. see Herman, William.
Young, Joanne B., jt. auth. see Lewis, Taylor B., Jr.
Young, John. Adventurous Spirits: Australian Migrant Society in Pre-Cession Fiji.
Young, John A. Business & Sentiment in a Chinese Market Town.
Young, John D. Microelectronics: A Standard Manual & Guide.
Young, John R. The French Foreign Legion: The Inside Story of the World Famous Fighting Force.
Young, John V. The State Parks of Arizona.
Young, Keith. Geology: The Paradox of Earth & Man.
Young, Kenneth B. Impulse.
Young, Kevin, et al. Malaysia: Growth & Equity in a Multiracial Society.
Young, Leontine. Wednesday's Children.
Young, Lincoln B. Poet's Handbook, One Thousand Two Hundred Ninety-Nine Places to Send Poems.
Young, Lloyd Y., jt. ed. see Katcher, Brian S.
Young, Louise B. The Unfinished Universe.
--The Unfinished Universe.
Young, M. Optics & Lasers: Including Fibers & Integrated Optics.
Young, Marquerite. Miss Macintosh, My Darling.

Young, Michael, ed. Society, State & Schooling.
Young, Michael J. Performance Programming Under MS-DOS.
--Programmer's Guide to OS-2.
Young, Miriam. The Secret of Stone House Farm.
--A Witch's Garden.
Young, Norman. Creator, Creation, & Faith.
Young, P. Great Ideas in Music.
Young People's Socialist League Staff. Challenge.
Young, Percy M. Choral Tradition.
--Messiah, a Study in Interpretation.
--Sir Arthur Sullivan.
Young, Perry D. God's Bullies: Power Politics & Religious Tyranny.
Young, Perry D., jt. auth. see Kopay, David.
Young, Perry D., jt. auth. see Walker, Evelyn.
Young, Peter, ed. The World Almanac Book of World War II.
Young, Philip K. Y., jt. ed. see Kim, W. Chan.
Young, R. E., jt. auth. see King, R. J.
Young, Richard A., jt. auth. see Cheremisinoff, Paul N.
Young, Richard M., jt. ed. see Klein, Lawrence R.
Young, Robert. Young's Analytical Concordance to the Bible.
Young, Robert & Klohn, LaVonne. Swatting Flies.
Young, Robert F. Eridahn.
Young, Robert J., jt. ed. see Perry, Roger.
Young, Robert L., jt. auth. see Obert, Edward F.
Young, Robert T. Holy Moments.
Young, Rodney. Five-Minute Lessons in Successful Selling: Increase Your Sales Skills Without Going Back to School.
Young, Roland. Cobalt in Biology & Biochemistry.
Young, S. J. Real Time Language Design & Development.
Young, Sayre V., ed. see Riegert, Ray.
Young, Sharon, jt. auth. see Barnett, Carne S.
Young, Shelby & Teets, Bob. Killing Waters.
Young, Stark, tr. see Chekhov, Anton.
Young, Stephen. Privatisation & Planning in Declining Areas.
Young, T. R. New Sources of Self.
Young, Theodore A. Completing Berkeley's Project: Classical vs. Modern Philosophy.
Young, Thomas. Linear Integrated Circuits.
Young, Thomas D. Tennessee Writers.
Young, Vernon. Cinema Borealis: The Art of Ingmar Bergman.
Young, Virgil. The Story of Idaho.
Young, Walter J. Stamp Collecting A-Z.
Young, Warren C., jt. auth. see Roark, Raymond J.
Young, William. Hegel's Dialectical Method.
Young, William C. Higher Education Opportunities for Minorities & Women: Annotated Selections, 1985-86.
Young, William E. Shark Hunter.
Young, Willias. Peace in the Valley.
Young Bear, Ray. The Winter of the Salamander: The Keeper of Importance.
Youngblood, Dorothy F. I Hurried, I Waited: A Belgian Odyssey.
Youngblood, Ila D. Bitter Promise.
Youngblood, Joan E. Merry-Go-Round: A Treasury of Poems.
Youngblood, Peter. Modeling Cajon. Sebree, Mac, ed.
Youngblood, Ronald. Themes from Isaiah.
Youngblood, Ronald, ed. The Genesis Debate: Persistent Questions about Creation & the Flood.
Youngblood, Ronald & Kaiser, Walter C., Jr., eds. A Tribute to Gleason Archer.
Younger, Edward & Moore, James T., eds. The Governors of Virginia, Eighteen Sixty to Nineteen Seventy-Eight.
Younger, MarySue. First Course in Linear Regression.
Youngjohns, B. A. Co-operative Organisation: An Introduction.
Youngs, R., jt. auth. see Rowell, R. M.
Youngson, A J. The Prince & the Pretender: A Study in the Writing of History.
Youngson, R. M. Stroke: A Self-Help Manual for Stroke Sufferers & Their Relatives.
Youniss, James & Smollar, Jacqueline. Adolescent Relations with Mothers, Fathers, & Friends.
Yourcenar, Marguerite. Oriental Tales. Manguel, Alberto, tr.
--With Open Eyes: Conversations with Matthieu Galey. Goldhammer, Arthur, tr.
--With Open Eyes: Conversations with Matthieu Galey. Goldhammer, Arthur, tr. from Fr.
Yourdon, Edward. How to Manage Structured Programming.
--Structured Walkthroughs.
Youree, Gary. The Girl in the White Coat on the Delta Eagle.
Yourgrau, Barry. A Man Jumps Out of An Airplane.
Yourgrau, Wolfgang, jt. ed. see Breck, Allan D.
Youse, Bevan K., jt. auth. see Hardy, F. Lane.
Youse, Bevan K., jt. auth. see Hardy, Lane F.
Yousef, Mohamed K., et al, eds. see Symposium Held in Honor of David B. Dill Staff.
Youth with a Mission Staff. The Singing Word: Youth with a Mission Songbook.
Youtsey. Mosby's Respiratory Therapy Assess Test.
Yowell, J. B., ed. The Municipal Yearbook, 1987.
Yram. Practical Astral Projection.
Ysseldyke, James E., jt. auth. see Salvia, John.
Yu, Eui-Young, jt. auth. see Koo, Hagen.
Yu, Francis T. Optics & Information Theory.
Yu, George T., jt. auth. see Scalapino, Robert A.
Yu, Paul N. & Goodwin, John F., eds. Progress in Cardiology.
--Progress in Cardiology.
Yuan, Luke C. & Wu, Chien-Shiung, eds. Elementary Particles: Science, Technology & Society.
Yuan, Robert T. Biotechnology in Western Europe.
Yuan, Shao. Foundations of Fluid Mechanics.
Yuan, Tian. Ancient Chinese Toys & Ornaments. Li, Liu, tr. from Chinese.
Yuasa, Nobuyuki, tr. from Japanese. The Zen Poems of Ryokan.
Yuceoglu, U., jt. ed. see Laurenson, R. M.
Yucheng Lo, Irving, jt. ed. see Liu, Wu-Chi.
Yudin, I., jt. auth. see Shvets, I.
Yudkin, Michael & Offord, Robin. Biochemistry.
Yudovich, Mikhail. Spanish...Without A6.
Yue, David. Perspective Drawings by Programmable Calculator: A Method with Graphic Arts.
Yueh, Jean. Dim Sum & Chinese One Dish Meals. Becker, Anne & Rich, Irene, eds.
Yuen, Kam. Three Sectional Staff.
Yuengling, David G. Letters to an Unknown Generation.
Yukl, Gary. Leadership in Organizations.
Yule, John-David, ed. Concise Encyclopedia of the Sciences.
Yule, William, ed. Behavior Modification for People with Mental Handicaps. Carr, Janet.
Yules, Richard B., et al. Speech-Hearing Pathology & Surgery.
Yulsman, Jerry. Color Photography Simplified.
Yunck, John A. Lineage of Lady Meed: The Development of Mediaeval Venality-Satire.
Yung-Ping Chen & Rohrlich, George F. Checks & Balances in Social Security: Symposium in Honor of Robert J. Myers.
Yung Teng Chia-Yee, jt. auth. see Williams, Jack.
Yunis, Edmond, jt. ed. see Makinodan, T.
Yunis, Edmond J., et al. Tissue Typing & Organ Transplantation.
Yunis, Jorge, ed. Biochemical Methods in Red Cell Genetics.
Yunlei, Zhang, et al, eds. Across China-China Pictorial Photos over 35 Years. Xin, Deng, tr. from Chinese.
Yunlu, Ke, et al. Prize-Winning Stories from China, 1980-1981. Chau, W. C., et al, trs. from Chinese.
Yura, Helen & Friesner, Arlyne. Curriculum Process for Developing or Revising Baccalaureate Nursing Programs.
Yurick, Sol. The Big Green-Out.
--Richard A.
Yurka, Blanche. Bohemian Girl: Blanche Yurka's Theatrical Life.
Yurova, T. Levitan.
Yutang, Lin. Chinatown Family.
Yu-T'Ang Lin. Little Critics: Essays, Satires & Sketches on China.
--Little Critics: Essays, Satires, Sketches on China.
Yuvacharya Shri Mahaprajna. Mind Beyond Mind: Perceptive Meditation, Form & Function.
Yuzhen, Ding. The Long Haired Maiden.
Yuzheng, Ding. Battle in the River of Heaven.
Yuzher, Ding. Hedgehog's New House.
Yvon, J. Correlations & Entropy in Classical Statistical Mechanics.

Z

Zabarenko, Lucy M., jt. auth. see Zabarenko, Ralph N.
Zabarenko, Ralph N. & Zabarenko, Lucy M. The Doctor Tree: Developmental Stages in the Growth of Physicians.
Zabeeh, Farhang, et al, eds. Readings in Semantics.
Zabinski & Mazzola. Apple II for Kids from Eight to Eighty.
Zabinski, Michael P. TRS-80 for Kids from Eight to Eighty.
Zabinsky, Michael P., jt. auth. see Short, Francis H.
Zabka, John R., Associates Inc. Staff. Compensation Report on Hospital-Based Physicians, 1984-85.
--Hospital Salary Survey Report 1984-85.
Zablocki, Benjamin. The Joyful Community: An Account of the Bruderhof, a Communal Movement Now in Its Third Generation.
Zabriskie, Allison P., ed. Public Utilities Law Anthology Index (1987)
Zabriskie, Edward H. American-Russian Rivalry in the Far East.
Zabriskie, George A. Summerdog Comes Home: The Previous Adventures of Hobo.
Zabriskie, John B., et al, eds. Clinical Immunology of the Kidney. Becker, E. Lovell.
Zabrodsky, A. Hopf Spaces.
Zabusky, N. J., ed. see International School Of Nonlinear Mathematics & Physics-Munich-1966.
Zaccarelli, Herman & Ninemeier, Jack. Cost Effective Contract Food Service: An Institutional Guide.
Zaccaria, Joseph S. Facing Change: Strategies for Problem Solving in the Congregation.
Zach, Cheryl. Growing Pains.
Zacharia, Theodore P., ed. Immune Response at the Cellular Level.
Zacharia, Theodore P. & Breese, S., Jr., eds. Immunopathology: Methods & Techniques.
Zachariah, K. C., jt. auth. see Cochrane, Susan H.
Zacharias, Lee. Lessons.
Zacharias, Paul B. Insights into the Beyond.
Zacharis, John. Exploring Careers in Communications & Telecommunications.
Zachary, Bill. The Contest Cookbook.
Zachary, Hugh. Murder in White.
Zacher, H. H., jt. auth. see Burfeindt-Moral.
Zacherl, M. K., jt. ed. see Grasserbauer, M.
Zachmann, H. G., jt. ed. see Kausch, H. H.
Zachry, Juanita D. Abilene: The Key City.
Zack, Arnold M. & Bloch, Ricard I. Alcohol, Drugs, & Arbitrition: Concepts & Questions.
Zacklin, Ralph, ed. Changing Law of the Sea.
Zackon, Fred, et al. Addict Aftercare: Recovery Training & Self-Help.
Zadeh & Fu, King-Sun, eds. Fuzzy Sets & Their Applications to Cognitive & Decision Processes.
Zadeh, L. A., et al, eds. Computing Methods in Optimization Problems Two.
Zadra, Dan. Boston Celtics.
--Warming Up.
Zadra, Dan, jt. auth. see Klingel, Cynthia.
Zadra, Dan, et al. Kansas City Kings.
Zadrazil, S., ed. see FEBS Symposium on DNA, Liblice, 24-29 September, 1979.
Zaehringer, J., jt. ed. see Schaeffer, O. A.
Zaferatos, Olga. Painting the Still Life.
Zagat, Eugene H., Jr. & Zagat, Nina S. Zagat 1987 Chicago Restaurant Survey. McGuire, Carolyn, ed.
--Zagat 1987 Los Angeles Restaurant Survey. Shindler, Merrill & Berk, Karen, eds.
--Zagat 1987 New York City Restaurant Survey.
--Zagat 1987 San Francisco Restaurant Survey. Blue, Anthony D. & Schwartz, Edwin J., eds.
--Zagat 1987 Washington D.C. Restaurant Survey. Boikess, Olga, ed.
Zagat, I. R., ed. see Zagat, S.
Zagat, Nina S., jt. auth. see Zagat, Eugene H., Jr.
Zagat, S. Jewish Life on New York's Lower East Side: Drawings & Paintings, 1912-1962. Zagat, I. R., ed.
Zagel, James. Confessions & Interrogations after Miranda: A Comprehensive Guideline of the Law-1982 Supplement.
Zager, Masha & Chase, Claire. Using Microsoft Word.
Zagier, D. B. Equivariant Pontrjagin Classes & Applications to Orbit Spaces.
Zagier, D. B., jt. ed. see Serre, J. P.
Zagladin, V. Socialism: Its Role in History.
Zagladin, V., ed. Europa y los Comunistas.
Zagladin, V. V. The Working Class: The Leading Force of the World Revolutionary Process.
Zagladin, V. V., ed. World Communist Movement.
Zagona, H. G. The Legend of Salome.
Zagona, Salvatore V., ed. Studies & Issues in Smoking Behavior.
Zagorin, Perez. Court & the Country: The Beginning of the English Revolution.
Zahlan, A. B., ed. see United Nations Economic Commission for Western Asia, Natural Resources, Science & Technology Division.
Zahn, Douglas A., jt. auth. see Boen, James R.
Zahorski, Kenneth J., jt. auth. see Boyer, Robert H.
Zahradnik, R. & Hartmann, H. New Concepts Three.
Zaikov, G. E., jt. auth. see Bochkov, A. E.
Zais, James P., et al. Modifying Section Eight: Implications from Experiments with Housing Allowances.
Zaitsev, N. America Latina: Cooperacion Regional y Problemas del Desarrollo.
Zaitsev, V., et al. Elementary Mathematics.
Zajda, Joseph I. Education in the U. S. S. R.
Zajic, J. E. Water Pollution: Disposal & Reuse.
Zaks, Rodnay. The CP-M Handbook with MP-M.
--Don't (or How to Care for Your Computer)
--Don't (or How to Care for Your New Computer)
--From Chips to Systems: An Introduction to Microprocessors.
--Introduction to Pascal: Including Turbo Pascal.
--A Microprogrammed APL Implementation.
--Programming the 6502.
--Six Thousand Five Hundred & Two Applications.
--Your First Apple II Program.
--Your First Atari Program.
--Your First BASIC Program.
--Your First Computer.
--Your First Computer: A Guide to Business & Personal Computing.
Zaks, Rodnay, jt. auth. see Sybex Staff.
Zakus, Sharron. Clinical Skills & Assisting Techniques for the Medical Assistant.
Zakusov, V. V. Pharmacology of Central Synapses.
Zakydalsky, Taras, ed. Three Philosophers: Political Prisoners in the Soviet Union.
Zalaznick, Charles, jt. auth. see Practising Law Institute Staff.
Zalben, Jane B. Will You Count the Stars Without Me?
Zalcman, L., jt. ed. see Kirwan, W. E.
Zaleski, Marek B., tr. see Tischner, Joseph.
Zaleznick, Abraham & Kets De Vries, Manfred E. Power & the Corporate Mind.
Zalis, Paul. Who Is the River.
Zalk, Sue R., jt. auth. see Bittman, Sam.
Zalkind, Ronald, jt. auth. see Lambert, Dennis.
Zalkind, Ronald, jt. auth. see Stein, Howard.
Zall, P. M., selected by. Peter Pindar's Poems.
Zall, Paul M., ed. see Ward, Nathaniel.
Zallinger, Peter. Dinosaurs.
Zalmanova, T. S., jt. auth. see Kologrivova, S. V.
Zaloga, Steven J. Israeli Tanks & Combat Vehicles.
--Patton's Tanks.
--Soviet Army Uniforms in World War II.
--U. S. Halftracks of World War Two.
--U. S. Tank Destroyers of World War II.
Zaloga, Steven J. & Grandsen, James. Operation Barbarossa.
Zaloga, Steven J. & Green, Michael. U. S. Infantry Combat Vehicles Today.
Zaltman, Gerald, jt. auth. see Bonoma, Thomas V.
Zaltman, Gerald, jt. auth. see Wallendorf, Melanie.
Zaltman, Gerald, et al. Innovations & Organizations.
Zamagni, Jim. Building Successful Quality Circles: A Corporate Facilitator's Guide to Perfectly Operating Quality Circles.
Zaman, V. Handbook of Medical Parasitology.
Zamansky, H., jt. ed. see Frankel, F. H.
Zambito, Raymond F. Hospital Dental Practice: A Manual.
Zamir, Meir. The Formation of Modern Lebanon.
Zamir, Yaron. A Testament Perhaps. Altshuler, David, ed. Leon, Dan, tr. from Hebrew.
Zamm, Alfred. Why Your House May Endanger Your Health.
Zamonski, John A. An Annotated Bibliography of John Dryden: Text & Studies, 1949-1973.
Zamoyski, Adam. Paderewski.
Zamyatnin, A. A., jt. auth. see Gorbachev, V. M.
Zand, Dale. Information-Organization-Power: Management in a Knowledge Society. Newton, William R., ed.
Zanden, James V. Social Psychology.
Zander, Maximilian. Phosphorimetry: The Application of Phosphoresence to the Analysis of Organic Compounds. Goodwin, Thomas H., tr.
Zander, Michael. Cases & Materials on the English Legal System.
Zander, Michael, ed. What's Wrong with the Law?
Zandi, I., ed. Advances in Solid-Liquid Flow in Pipes & Its Application.
Zandvoort, R. W. Wartime English.
Zane, Christine, jt. auth. see Zane, Frank.
Zane, Christine, jt. auth. see Zane, Frank C.
Zane, Eva. Greek Cooking for the Gods.
--Middle Eastern Cookery.
Zane, Frank & Zane, Christine. Frank & Christine Zane's Super Bodies in 12 Weeks.
--The Zane Way to a Beautiful Body Through Weight Training for Men & Women.
Zane, Frank C. & Zane, Christine. Zane Nutrition: Sensible Way of Eating.
Zanetti, Adriano. The World of Insects. Atthill, Catherine, tr.
Zangemeister, C., ed. see Orosius, Paulus.
Zanger, Virginia V. Exploracion Intercultural: Una Guia para el Estudiante.
Zangwill, O., jt. ed. see Lebrun, Yvan.
Zangwill, O. L. Introduction to Modern Psychology.
Zankov, L. V., et al. Teaching & Development: A Soviet Investigation. Szekely, Beatrice B., ed. Schultz, Arlo, tr.
Zann, Leon P. Living Together in the Sea.
Zannas, Eliky. Khajuraho.
Zannie, William Illus. by see Forrester, Glenn C.
Zanozinski, J. Contemporary Polish Paintings.
Zanstra, H. & Swanberg, K. Caqueza: Living Rural Development.
Zant, James H., jt. auth. see Keller, Marion W.
Zanuso, Billa. The Young Freud: The Origins of Psychoanalysis in Late Nineteenth-Century Viennese Culture.

Authors

Zanzig, Thomas. Understanding Your Faith: An Introduction to Catholic Christianity for Freshmen.
Zanzucchi, Anne M. The Difficult Role of a Mother. Bartram, Gerry, ed. Szczesniak, Lenny, tr. from Ital.
Zapel, Arthur L., ed. see Gladman, Donna.
Zapel, Arthur L., ed. see Maschke, Ruby.
Zapletal, B. Open Messencephalotomy & Thalamotomy for Intractable Pain.
Zapoleon, Marguerite W. Everyone Needs a Mountain: Or Skylife at Eidolon.
Zapp, E., jt. auth. see Pataki, L.
Zappalorti, Robert. Drawing Sharp Focus Still Lifes.
Zarantonello, Eduardo H., ed. see MRC Symposium Staff.
Zarate, Stella G. Woman of the Maya.
Zarb, Frank G., jt. auth. see Fabozzi, Frank J.
Zarca, Albert, jt. auth. see Brogan, Patrick.
Zarco, Cyn & Hofler, Robert. Wild Style: The Next Wave.
Zaremba, Joseph, ed. Mathematical Economics & Operations Research: A Guide to Information Sources.
--Statistics & Econometrics: A Guide to Information Sources.
Zaremba, M., ed. see IFAC Symposium Staff.
Zaremba, S. K., ed. see Centre for Research in Mathematics, University of Montreal Symposium Staff.
Zaretsky, David & Wengrov, Charles. The Stories & Parables of the Hafetz Hayyim.
Zaric, Z., ed. Heat & Mass Transfers in Flows with Separated Regions.
Zaring, Jane. The Return of the Dragon.
Zaring, W., jt. auth. see Takeuti, G.
Zarlino, Gioseffo. The Art of Counterpoint. Marco, Guy A. & Palisca, Claude V., trs.
Zarnecki, George. English Romanesque Lead Sculpture.
--The Monastic Achievement.
Zarodov, K. The Political Economy of Revolution.
Zaslavsky, Robert. Platonic Myth & Platonic Writing.
Zassenhaus, Hans. Number Theory & Algebra: Collected Papers Dedicated to Henry B. Mann, Arnold E. Ross & Olga Taussky-Todd.
Zastrow, Charles. The Practice of Social Work.
Zaum, Marjorie. All about Cats As Pets.
Zavatsky, Bill & Padgett, Ron, eds. Whole Word Catalogue 2.
Zavodskaya, I. S., et al. Neurogenic Heart Lesions.
Zavos, Spiro. Faith of Our Fathers.
Zawacki, Frank R. Famous Faces: Price Guide & Catalog for Magazine Collectors.
Zawacki, Robert A., jt. auth. see Dittrich, John E.
Zawadzki, Sandra M. Art Adventures: Shapes.
--Art Adventures: Textures.
Zax, Melvin & Cowen, Emory L. Abnormal Psychology: Changing Concepts.
Zayas-Bazan, Eduardo, tr. see Montaner, Carlos A.
Zbar, Paul B. Basic Electronics: A Text-Lab Manual.
Zbar, Paul B. & Orne, Peter. Industrial Electronics: A Text-Lab Manual.
Zbar, Paul B. & Orne, R. Electronics Instruments & Measurement.
Zbar, Paul B., jt. auth. see Electronic Industries Association Staff.
Zbinden, G. Progress in Toxicology, Volume 2: Special Topics.
Zbinden, G., ed. Fine Needle Aspiration Biopsy of the Rat Liver - Cytological, Cytochemical & Biochemical Methods: Proceedings of a Workshop on Technique & Application of Fine Needle Aspiration Biology in Experimental Toxicology, Zurich, 1979.
Zbinden, Rudolph. Infrared Spectroscopy of High Polymers.
Zbozny, Frank, ed. Annuale Mediaevale.
Zbozny, Frank, et al, eds. Annuale Mediaevale.
Zbozny, Frank T., ed. Annuale Mediaevale.
Zdanys, Jonas, tr. see Martin, Brone.
Zearfoss, Dr. Robert Foreword by see Baylis, Fred S.
Zears, Russell, jt. auth. see Maloff, Chalda.
Zebas-Thomas. Scientific Exercise Training.
Zebroski, E. L. & Simard, R. L., eds. Information Management in the Nuclear Industry.
Zebrowski, George, et al. Adrift in Space & Other Stories. Elwood, Roger, ed.
Zech, Lore, jt. ed. see Caspersson, Torbjorn.
Zecher, J. Richard, jt. auth. see Phillips, Susan M.
Zechman, Roberta, jt. auth. see Radeloff, Deanna J.
Zechmeister, L. Cis-Trans Isometric Carotenoids. Vitamins A, - Arylpolyenes.
Zechmeister, Laszlo. CIS-Trans Isomeric Carotenoids, Vitamins A & Arylpolyenes.
Zee, John Van der see Van der Zee, John.
Zee, John van Der see Van der Zee, John.
Zee, John Van der see Van der Zee, John.
Zeevaert, Leonardo. Foundation Engineering for Difficult Subsoil Conditions.
Zeeveld, William G. Foundations of Tudor Policy.
Zeff, Stephen A., jt. auth. see Keller, Thomas F.
Zeffirelli, Franco. Zeffirelli: An Autobiography.
Zegura, S. L., jt. ed. see Jamison, P. L.
Zeidler, Frank. Management's Rights under Public Sector Collective Bargaining.
Zeidner, Janie, jt. auth. see Zeidner, Ron.
Zeidner, Ron & Zeidner, Janie. Exaltation One Step at a Time.
Zeig, Sande, jt. auth. see Wittig, Monique.
Zeigler, A. Billing & Collections.
Zeigler, L. Harmon, jt. auth. see Poole, Keith.
Zeisler, R. & Ardizzone, G. D. The Inland Waters of Latin America.
Zeist, W. van see Van Zeist, W. & Casarie, W. A.
Zeitler, E., ed. Percutaneous Vascular Recanalization: Technique - Application - Clinical Results.
Zeitlin, Irving M. Ideology & the Development of Sociological Theory.
Zeitlin, Maurica. American Society, Inc.
Zeitlin, Steven J. & Kotkin, Amy J. A Celebration of American Family Folklore: Tales & Traditions from the Smithsonian Collection.
Zeitner, June C. Midwest Gem Trails Field Guide.
Zeitz, James V. Spirituality & Analogia Entis According to Erich Przywara, S. J. Metaphysics & Religious Experience, the Ignation Exercises, the Balance in 'Similarity' & 'Greater Dissimilarity' According to Lateran IV.
Zelade, Richard. Austin: The Texas Monthly Guidebook. Lubeck, Scott, ed.
Zelayeta, Elena. Elena's Secrets of Mexican Cooking.
Zelazny, Roger. Blood of Amber.
--Eye of Cat.
--To Spin Is Miracle Cat.
--Unicorn Variations.
Zeldin, Jesse, jt. ed. see Debreczeny, Paul.
Zeldin, Theodore. Political System of Napoleon 3rd.
Zeleny, M. Linear Multiobjective Programming.
Zeleny, M., ed. Multiple Criteria Decision Making, Kyoto, 1975.
Zelis, Robert F., jt. ed. see Flaim, Stephen.
Zell, Hans & Bundy, Carol, eds. African Book World & Press: A Directory.
Zeller, George W. God's Gift of Tongues: The Nature, Purpose, & Duration of Tongues As Taught in the Bible.
Zeller, Hubert Van see Van Zeller, Hubert.
Zeller, Richard A. & Carmines, Edward G. Statistical Analysis of Social Data.
Zellers, Margaret. Fielding's Caribbean 1984.
--Fielding's Caribbean, 1985.
--Fielding's Caribbean, 1986.
--Fielding's Caribbean, 1987.
--Fielding's Caribbean, 1988.
--Fielding's Discover Europe: Off the Beaten Path, 1986.
--Fielding's Discover Europe off the Beaten Path 1987.
--Fielding's Economy Caribbean 1984.
--Fielding's Economy Caribbean, 1985.
--Fielding's Economy Caribbean, 1986.
--Fielding's Economy Caribbean, 1987.
Zelles, T., ed. Saliva & Salivation: Proceedings of a Satellite Symposium to the 28th International Congress of Physiological Held at Szekesfehervar, Hungary, 1980.
Zellner, Arnold. Basic Issues in Econometrics.
Zellner, Miriam, jt. auth. see Maccoby, Eleanor E.
Zelver, Patricia. A Man of Middle Age.
Zeman, Jacklyn & Whitley, Dianna. Jackie Zeman's Beauty on the Go.
Zeman, Z. & Zoubek, J., eds. East-West Trade 1975: International Yearbook.
Zeman, Zavis. Men with the Yen.
Zembrosky-Barkin, Patti & Nave, Gary. Interactive Video in Special & General Education: A Development Manual.
Zemel, Z. & Hyslop, N. St. G., eds. Biometeorology Seven: Proceedings of the Eighth International Biometeorological Congress 9-15 September 1979, Supplement to Volume 24 of the International Journal of Biometeorology.
Zemel, Z., ed. see Biometerological Congress Staff.
Zemel, Z., ed. see International Biometeorological Congress Staff.
Zender, Bob & Cleveland, Charles. Winning Golf the Professional Way.
Zendex Corporation Staff & Effron, Joel. Data Communications Techniques & Technology.
Zenker, W. Juxtaoral Organ: Morphology & Clinical Aspects.
Zenkovsky, Serge A. Pan-Turkism & Islam in Russia.
Zeno. The Four Sergeants.
Zenoff, David B. Management Principle for Finance in the Multinational.
Zerbe, Jerome & Connolly, Cyril. Les Pavillons of the Eighteenth Century.
--Les Pavillons of the Eighteenth Century.
Zeri, Federico & Gardner, Elizabeth E. A Catalogue of Italian Paintings: Venetian School.
Zernich, Theodore, jt. ed. see Hardiman, George W.
Zernicke, Ronald F., jt. auth. see Broer, Marion R.
Zernov, Nicolas, ed. see Bulgakov, Sergius.
Zetlin, Mikhael. The Five: The Evolution of the Russian School of Music. Panin, George, ed. & tr. from Rus.
Zetterling, Mai. All Those Tomorrows: An Autobiography.
Zettler, F. & Weiler, R., eds. Neural Principles in Vision.
Zeuner, Milton L. Universal Majesty.
Zeuthen, Peter, jt. auth. see Jul, Mogens.
Zevin, Robert B. A Greater Good: Potentials for an Intelligent Economy.
Zey, Michael G. The Mentor Connection.
Zeyadi, Sham. The Lavandar.
Zeydel, Edwin. A First Course in Written & Spoken German: A Review & Exercise Book.
Zhdanov, G. S. Crystal Physics.
Zhdanov, Valentin S., jt. auth. see Vikhert, Anatolii M.
Zheleznova, I. Northern Lights.
Zheleznova, I., tr. Little Round Bun.
Zheleznyakov, V. V. Radio Emission of the Sun & Planets.
Zherebstov, I. P. Fundamentos de la Electronica.
Zhijuan, Ru. Lilies & Other Stories.
Zhito, Lee, ed. see Shemel, Sidney & Krislovsky, M. William.
Zhivkov, T. Todor Zhivkov: Statesman & Builder of New Bulgaria.
Zhivkova, L., ed. Ludmila Zhivkova: Her Many Worlds-New Culture & Beauty-Concepts & Action.
Zhiyan, Li & Wen, Cheng. Chinese Pottery & Porcelain. Caiwei, Ouyang, tr. from Chinese.
Zhizhong, Bian. Daoist Health Preservation Exercise. Zongren, Liu, tr. from Chinese.
Zhongmin, Xu & Daguang, Zhou, eds. Selected Paintings by Fan Zeng. Ling, Miao, tr. from Chinese.
Zhordania, Noah. Moya Zhizn (My Life)
Zhukovitsky, L. Astride a Dolphin.
Zhukovskaya, Vera. Charlas Sobre la Educacion.
Zi, Ju. Birds' Homes.
Ziadeh, Farhat J. Lawyers, the Rule of Law & Liberalism in Modern Egypt.
Ziadeh, Farhat J. & Freiji, I. History of the American People.
Ziai, Mohsen. Bedside Pediatrics: Diagnostic Evaluation of the Child.
Zichella, L., jt. ed. see Carenza, L.
Zichichi, A., ed. Elementary Processes at High Energy, Pts. A-B.
--Hadrons & Their Interactions: Current - Field Algebra, Soft Pions, Supermultiplets, & Related Topics.
--Strong & Weak Interactions.
--Subnuclear Phenomena.
--Symmetries in Elementary Particle Physics.
--Theory & Phenomenology in Particle Physics.
Zichichi, Antonino, ed. The Unity of the Fundamental Interactions.
Zichichi, Antonio, ed. Pointlike Structures Inside & Outside Hadrons.
Zichlichi, A., ed. Recent Developments in Particle Symmetries.
Zickgraf, Cordula. I Am Learning to Live Because You Must Die: A Hospital Diary. Scheidt, David L., tr. from Ger.
Zickler, Joyce K., jt. auth. see Levitan, Sar A.
Zidonis, Frank, jt. auth. see Bateman, Donald.
Ziedonis, I. Thoughtfully I Read the Smoke.
Ziefert, Harriet. Baby Ben Gets Dressed.
--Let's Go! Piggety Pig.
--Lewis Said, Lewis Did.
--Listen! Piggety Pig: A Book of Animal Noises.
--No More! Piggety Pig.
--Piggety Pig from Morning 'til Night.
--So Big!
--So Busy!
--So Clean!
--Suppertime for Baby Ben.
--What Do I Hear?
--What Do I See?
--What Do I Smell?
--What Do I Taste?
--What Do I Touch?
Ziefert, Harriet & Smith, Mavis. So Little!
Ziegelmann, H., jt. auth. see Schmid, E. W.
Ziegenfuss, James T., Jr. Patient's Rights & Professional Practice.
Ziegenfuss, James T., Jr., ed. see Byron, Leo C.
Ziegenfuss, Mary Lou. Christmas in Those Days. Feeling, Durbin, tr.
Ziegert, Beate. The Debschitz School: A Selectively Annotated Bibliography.
Ziegler, A. Patient Records Control.
--Supplies & Office Maintenance.
Ziegler, Avis. Doctors' Administrative Program. Incl. Dap 1. Patient Contact & Public Relations; Dap 2. Bookkeeping & Tax Reports; Dap 3. Insurance & Third-Party-Payable Claims; Dap 4. Correspondence; Dap 5. Billing & Collections; Dap 7. Clinical Assisting. Med Economics.
Ziegler, B., jt. auth. see Jochim, H.
Ziegler, Frederick J., et al. Vasectomy: Current Research in Male Sterilization.
Ziegler, Hans, ed. Gyrodynamics.
Ziegler, J. F., ed. The Stopping & Range of Ions in Matter, Volumes 1-4.
Ziegler, Jack. Hamburger Madness.
--Hamburger Madness.
Ziegler, James F., ed. Ion Implantation: Science & Technology.
--New Uses of Ion Accelerators.
Ziegler, Philip. Melbourne.
Ziegler, Ronald, ed. Wilderness Waterways: A Guide to Information Sources.
Ziegler, Sandra. Friends: A Handbook about Getting Along Together.
Ziehn, Bernhard. Canonic Studies. Stevenson, Ronald, ed.
Ziel, Ron. Long Island Heritage.
Zielhuis, R. L., ed. see Commission of the European Communities.
Ziemba, Walter, tr. see Wyszynski, Stefan.
Ziemba, William T. & Hausch, Donald B. Beat the Racetrack.
Ziemer, Rodger E. & Tranter, William. Principles of Communciations: Systems Modulation & Noise.
Ziemian, Joseph. The Cigarette Sellers of Three Crosses Square.
Zierep, Juergen & Oertel, Herbert, Jr., eds. Convective Transport & Instability Phenomena.
Zierold, Norman, jt. auth. see Wellman, James.
Zieschang, H., et al. Surfaces & Planar Discontinuous Groups: Revised & Expanded Translation.
Ziff, Larzer, ed. see Thoreau, Henry David.
Ziff, Norman D. Paul Delaroche: A Study in 19th Century French History Painting.
Zigan, Li. Left & Right.
Zigerell, James, ed. Catalog of Mass Media College Courses.
Zigerell, James J., et al. Television in Community & Junior Colleges: An Overview & Guidelines.
Ziglar, Zig. Cry in Echo Canyon.
--The Genius Nobody Knew.
--Two-Horse Cadillac.
Zijderveld, Anton. Reality in a Looking Glass: Rationality Through an Analysis of Traditional Folly.
Zikas, Philotheos. Love Never Fails: The Autobiography of Philotheos Zikas, a Christian Pastor in Northern Greece.
Zikmund, Barbara B., jt. ed. see Manschreck, Clyde L.
Zikmund, Joseph & Dennis, Deborah E., eds. Suburbia: A Guide to Information Sources.
Zikmund, William G. Business Research Methods.
--A Corporate Bestiary.
Zikmund, William G. & D'Amico, Michael. Transparencies to Accompany Marketing.
Zikmund, William G., jt. auth. see Sciglimpaglia, Donald.
Zilbergeld, Bernie. The Shrinking of America: Myths of Psychological Change.
Zilbergeld, Bernie & Ullman, John. Male Sexuality: A Guide to Sexual Fulfillment.
Zilboorg, Gregory. A History of Medical Psychology.
Zilboorg, Gregory & Henry, George W. History of Medical Psychology.
Zilboorg, Gregory, tr. see Korolenko, Vladimir.
Zilinsky, Ursula. A Happy English Child.
Zill, Dennis G. A First Course in Differential Equations with Applications.
Ziller, R. C. The Social Self.
Zilversmit, Arthur. First Emancipation: The Abolition of Slavery in the North.
Zim, Herbert S. Mice, Men & Elephants.
--Plants: A Guide to Plant Hobbies.
--What's Inside of Animals.
Zim, Herbert S. & Skelly, James R. Hoists, Cranes, & Derricks.
Zimansky, Curtis A. English Literature, Sixteen Sixty to Eighteen Hundred: A Bibliography of Modern Studies.
Zimbardo, Philip & Maslach, Christina. Psychology for Our Times.
Zimbardo, Philip G. Psychology & Life.
Zimbardo, Philip G. & Radl, Shirley L. The Shy Child: A Parent's Guide to Preventing & Overcoming Shyness from Infancy to Adulthood.
Zimbardo, Philip G. & Ruch, Floyd L. Psychology & Life.
Zimbardo, Philip G., jt. auth. see Dempsey, David.
Zimelman, Nathan. Cats of Kilkenny.
Zimelman, Nathan see McClelland, Herbert L.
Zimmer, A. B. Employing the Handicapped: A Practical Compliance Manual.

Authors

Zimmer, H. G. Computational Problems, Methods, & Results in Algebraic Number Theory.
Zimmer, Hans, ed. Annual Reports in Inorganic & General Syntheses.
Zimmer, Hans, jt. ed. see Niedenzu, Kurt.
Zimmer, Joseph. The History of the Forty-Third Infantry Division.
Zimmer, Kenneth. High School Typewriting.
Zimmer, Michael, ed. Cogeneration: Current Prospects & Future Opportunities.
Zimmer, Michael J. & Thompson, James A., Jr. Acid Rain: Planning for the Eighties.
Zimmer, Michael J., ed. Cogeneration & Resource Recovery: Current Prospects & Future Opportunities.
--Cogeneration: Current Prospects & Future Opportunities.
Zimmer, Michael J. & Heavner, Martin L., eds. Cogeneration in California.
Zimmer, Russell L., jt. ed. see Woollacott, Robert M.
Zimmer, Ruth K. James Shirley: A Reference Guide.
Zimmer, William, ed. Brice Marden, Marbles, Paintings & Drawings Text.
Zimmerli, Walther. I Am Yahweh. Brueggemann, Walter, ed. Scott, Doug, tr. from Ger.
--The Old Testament & the World. Scullion, John J., tr. from Ger.
--Old Testament Theology in Outline. Green, David E., tr.
Zimmerman, A. M., et al, eds. Drugs & the Cell Cycle.
Zimmerman, Adam C. Gypsy in My Verse.
Zimmerman, Alex H., et al. Basic Piano for the College Student.
Zimmerman, Andrea. Yetta the Trickster.
Zimmerman, Arthur M. High Pressure Effects on Cellular Processes.
Zimmerman, Catherine S. The Bride's Book.
Zimmerman, David R., jt. auth. see Gorbach, Sherwood L.
Zimmerman, Donald A., jt. auth. see Golden, Lawrence G.
Zimmerman, Ernest O. The Blue Brotherhood.
Zimmerman, Gloria, jt. auth. see Ngo, Bach.
Zimmerman, Gordon I. Public Speaking Today.
Zimmerman, Irene. Guide to Current Latin American Periodicals: Humanities & Social Sciences.
Zimmerman, Jan. Once upon the Future: A Woman's Guide to Tomorrow's Technology.
Zimmerman, L. E. & Sobin, L. H. Histological Typing of Tumours of the Eye & its Adnexa.
Zimmerman, Larry & Hart, Glen. Value Engineering: A Practical Approach for Owners, Designers, & Contractors.
Zimmerman, Marc, ed. & tr. see Cardenal, Ernesto.
Zimmerman, Paul. The New Thinking Man's Guide to Pro Football.
Zimmerman, S. Mort. Business: Unsafe at Any Level.
Zimmerman, Sherwood E. & Miller, Harold D., eds. Corrections at the Crossroads: Designing Policy.
Zimmerman, Stephen W., jt. auth. see Harrington, Avery R.
Zimmerman, Steven & Conrad, Leo. Business Applications for the IBM Personal Computer.
Zimmerman, Steven, et al. Business Applications for the Apple II & IIe under CP-M.
Zimmerman, Steven M. & Conrad, Leo M. Understanding & Using Microcomputers in Business.
Zimmerman, William. Soviet Perspectives on International Relations, 1956-1967.
Zimmermann, Barbara & Smith, David B. Careers in Health: The Professionals Give You the Inside Picture about Their Jobs.
Zimmermann, Erich W. Conservation in the Production of Petroleum.
Zimmermann, George. Ohio: Off the Beaten Path.
Zimmermann, Georges D. Songs of Irish Rebellion: Political Street Ballads & Rebel Songs, 1780-1900.
Zimmermann, R., jt. auth. see Bestmann, H.
Zimmermann, U. & Dainty, J., eds. Membrane Transport in Plants.
Zimmerman-Stidham, Susan, jt. auth. see Gandy, Charles D.
Zimmern, Alice, tr. The Letter of Porphyry the Neo-Platonist.
Zimpfer, David G. Paraprofessionals in Counseling, Guidance & Personnel Services.
Zinchella, L., ed. see International Congress of Psychosomatic Obstetrics & Gynecology Staff.
Ziner, Feenie. Within This Wilderness.
Zingg, Robert M., jt. auth. see Singh, Joseph A.
Zingmark, Richard G. An Annotated Checklist of the Biota of the Coastal Zone of South Carolina.
Zink, Harold. The United States in Germany 1944-1955.
Zink, Heidi & Zink, Jorg. Will My Dog Go to Heaven? Oyler, William, tr.
Zink, Jorg. Turn Toward Life: The Bible & Peacemaking. Rhodin, Victoria, tr. from Ger.
Zink, Jorg, jt. auth. see Zink, Heidi.
Zink, Lydia P. Helps for Identifying & Teaching the Problem Reader.
Zinkus, J. Lithuania: Encyclopedic Survey.
Zinman, Joseph Aaron. Secrets of Health That Many Doctors & Dentists May Not Know.
Zinn, Howard, ed. New Deal Thought.
Zinn, Jack. R. E. Lee's Cheat Mountain Campaign.
Zinner, Stephen. STD: Sexually Transmitted Diseases.
Zinns, Ken, et al. Licensed Architect: Building Design Examination Primer.
Zinoviev, Alexander. Homo Sovieticus.
Zinsser, William, intro. by see Caro, Robert A., et al.
Ziolkowski, Theodore. Novels of Hermann Hesse: A Study in Theme & Structure.
Ziomek, Joseph S., jt. auth. see Ferraro, John R.
Zion, Sidney. Read All About It! The Collected Adventures of a Maverick Reporter.
Zipes, Jack. Fairy Tales & the Art of Subversion: The Classical Genre of Children & the Process of Civilization.
Zipkin, M A. & Edwards, R. N., eds. Power Systems for Space Flight, PAAS11.
Ziran, Goland. The Counselor.
Ziring, Lawrence. The Middle East Political Dictionary.
Zirkel, G. & Rosenfeld, Robert. Beginning Statistics.
Zirker, Jack B., ed. Coronal Holes & High Speed Wind Streams.
Zis, A. Foundations of Marxist Aesthetics.
--Fundamentos de la Estetica Marxista.
Zisi, Mohsen, et al. Assessment of the Newborn: A Guide for the Practitioner.
Zisman, M., jt. auth. see Gabriel, Pierre.
Ziswiler, V. Extinct & Vanishing Animals: A Biology of Extinction & Survival. Bunnell, F. & Bunnell, P., trs.
Zitlow, David R., jt. auth. see Stewart, James W.
Zitner, Rosalind & Miller, Shelby M. Our Youngest Parents: A Study of the Use of Support Services by Adolescent Mothers.
Zitron, Sherri & Powell, Charles G. Contemporary Cooking: Lessons & Recipes from the School of Contemporary Cooking.
Zittel, K. A. Von see Von Zittel, K. A.
Ziv, Frederic W., ed. The Valiant Muse: An Anthology of Poems by Poets Killed in the (First) World War.
Zivojinovic, Dragan. The United States & Vatican Policies, 1914-1918.
Ziyang, Zhao, et al. The Fourth Session of the Sixth National People's Congress.
Zizmor, Jonathan & Foreman, John. Dr. Zizmor's Skin Care Book.
Zizmor, Jonathan & Sabin, Sharon. Younger Skin: How to Get It, How to Keep It.
Zlatev, Z., jt. auth. see Osterby, O.
Zlatkis, A., jt. auth. see Ettre, L. S.
Zlatkis, Albert, et al. A Concise Introduction to Organic Chemistry.
Zlotin, R. I. & Khodashova, K. S., eds. The Role of Animals in Biological Cycling of Forest-Steppe Ecosystems. Lewus, William & Grant, W. E., trs. from Rus.
Zlotnickiego, Boleslaw. Lexicon Medicum.
Zmud, Robert W., jt. auth. see Athey, Thomas H.
Znaniecki, Florian. Modern Nationalities.
Zochert, Donald. The Man of Glass.
Zodikoff, David. Readings in Social Studies Education.
Zoellner, N., ed. see Symposium, Muenchen Staff.
Zoeteweij, H., jt. auth. see Turner, H. A.
Zografakis, Stephen. I, Too, Have Heard the Wind.
Zohar, David, jt. auth. see Beck, Yoram.
Zohn, David A. & Mennell, John M. Musculoskeletal Pain: Principles of Physical Diagnosis & Physical Treatment.
Zokeisha. Animal Friends.
--Baby Animals.
--Bedtime Stories.
--Fun with the Alphabet.
--Goodnight, Good Day.
--Little Nursery Rhymes.
--My Garden.
--My House.
--Playtime.
--Tasty Treats.
--Three Little Kittens.
Zola, Elemire, et al. Archetypes: The Persistence of Unifying Patterns.
Zola, Emile. L' Argent.
--Au Bonheur des Dames.
--J'accuse.
Zola, Jaye, jt. auth. see Zola, John.
Zola, John & Zola, Jaye. Teaching about Peace & Nuclear War: A Balanced Approach.
Zola, Paul. Sales Laws (N. Y.)
Zolberg, Aristide R. Creating Political Order: The Party-States of West Africa.
Zollar, Ann C. A Member of the Family: Strategies for Black Family Continuity.
Zollers, Frances E. & Foreman, Gail H. Practical Business Law.
Zollinger, Heinrich. Chemie und Hochschule.
Zollinger, Norman. Corey Lane.
Zolotow, Nina, jt. auth. see Goldman, Joshua.
Zolten, J. Jerome, jt. auth. see Phillips, Gerald M.
Zomeren, A. H. Reaction Time & Attention after Closed Head Injury.
Zongren, Liu. Two Years in the Melting Pot: China Books & Periodicals.
Zongren, Liu, tr. see Zhizhong, Bian.
Zonneveld, L. W. C., tr. see Van der Zeeuw, Gijsbert.
Zonneveld, W. & Weerman, F., eds. Linguistics in the Netherlands 1977-1979.
Zook, Ardith. Captain Gaius Sees a Miracle.
Zook, Elvin G., ed. The Primary Care of Facial Injuries.
Zook, Wayne H. Constructing & Manufacturing Wood Products.
Zoological Society of London Symposium Staff. Comparative Physiology of Desert Animals: Proceedings of the Zoological Society of London Symposium, 31st. Maloiy, C. M. O. & MacFarlane, W. V., eds.
--Diseases in Free Living Wild Animals: Proceedings of the Zoological Society of London Symposium, 24th. McDiarmid, ed.
--Diseases of Fish: Proceedings of the Zoological Society of London Symposium, 30th. Mawdesley-Thomas, Lionel E., ed.
--Echinoderm Biology: Proceedings of the Zoological Society of London Symposium, 20th. Millot, N., ed.
Zorab, P. A., ed. General Medical Aspects of Scoliosis.
Zorbach, W. Werner & Tipson, R. Stuart, eds. Synthetic Procedures in Nucleic Acid Chemistry: Vol. 1.
Zorn. Illustrated Yoga.
Zorn, Jay & Hanshumaker, James. Fundamentals Learning Through Making Music. Feldstein, Sandy, ed.
Zoshchenko, Mikhail. Youth Restored. Stern, Joel, tr.
Zotov, V. Lenin's Doctrine on National Liberation Revolutions & the Modern World.
Zotterman, Yngve, jt. auth. see Emmelin, N.
Zotterman, Yngve, ed. Olfaction & Taste.
--Sensory Functions of the Skin with Special Reference to Man.
Zoubek, Charles E. Gregg Expert Speed Building.
Zoubek, Charles E., jt. auth. see Leslie, Louis A.
Zoubek, J., jt. ed. see Zeman, Z.
Zraly, Kevin. Windows on the World: Complete Wine Course.
--Windows on the World Complete Wine Course.
Zrenner, E. & Meissl, H., eds. Ocular & Extraocular Processing of Visual Information: Journal: Ophthalmic Research.
Zschoche. Mosby's Comprehensive Review of Critical Care.
Zschock, Dieter K. Health Care Financing in Developing Countries.
Zsoldos, L., jt. auth. see Kovacs, T.
Zuanich, Margaret A., jt. auth. see Lipscomb, Susan D.
Zubatsky, David S. The History of American Colleges & Their Libraries in the Seventeenth & Eighteenth Centuries: A Bibliographical Essay.
Zubek, John P., ed. Sensory Deprivation: Fifteen Years of Research.
Zubenko, V. & Tarasov, K. La CIA Contra America Latina.
Zuber, Rene. Who Are You Monsieur Gurdjieff? Koralek, Jenny, tr.
Zuberbuhler, J. R. Clinical Diagnosis in Pediatric Cardiology.
Zuber-Skerrit, Ortrun, ed. Video in Higher Education.
Zubrick, James W. The Organic Chemistry Laboratory Survival Manual: A Student's Guide to Techniques.
Zubrowski, Bernie. A Children's Museum Activity Book: Ball-Point Pens.
Zuck, Roy B., jt. auth. see Walvoord, John F.
Zucker, Jeff & Hogfoss, Bob. Oregon Indians: Culture, History & Current Affairs; an Atlas & Introduction.
Zucker, Paul. New Architecture.
Zuckerman. Classics in Biology.
Zuckerman, A., ed. Dynamic Aspects of Host-Parasite Relationships.
Zuckerman, A. J., et al, eds. Principles & Practice of Clinical Virology.
Zuckerman, Arie & Howard, Colin. Hepatitis Viruses of Man.
Zuckerman, Avivah & Weiss, David W., eds. Dynamic Aspects of Host Parasite Relationships.
Zuckerman, Barry S. & Zuckerman, Pamela M., eds. Child Health: A Pediatrician's Guide.
Zuckerman, Beverly. The Broom & Ashes.
Zuckerman, J. J., jt. auth. see Christian, S. D.
Zuckerman, J. J., ed. see Atkinson, G.
Zuckerman, Jim. Image Magic.
Zuckerman, Martin M. Elementary Algebra: A Straightforward Approach.
--Intermediate Algebra.
--Intermediate Algebra: Alternate Edition.
Zuckerman, Michael. Peaceable Kingdoms: New England Towns in the Eighteenth Century.
Zuckerman, Pamela M., jt. ed. see Zuckerman, Barry S.
Zuckerman, S. The Social Life of Monkeys & Apes.
Zuckerman, Solly, ed. Ovary. Incl. Vol. 1. General Aspects; Vol. 2. Physiology; Vol. 3. Regulation of Oogenesis & Sleriodogenesis. Acad Pr.
Zuckman, Harvey L. & Gaynes, Martin J. Mass Communications Law in a Nutshell.
Zuehlke, Wilmer M. Spiritual Breakthrough.
Zuelch, K. J., ed. Cerebral Circulation & Stroke.
Zuelch, K. J., ed. see International Symposium On Classification Of Brain Tumors - Cologne - 1961.
Zuelch, K. J., et al, eds. Cerebral Localization: An Otfried Foerster Symposium.
Zuelicke, L., jt. auth. see Nikitin, E. E.
Zuelzer, Wolf. The Nicolai Case: A Biography.
Zuesse, Evan M. Ritual Cosmos: The Sanctification of Life in African Religions.
Zufelt, David L., jt. ed. see Gonzalez, Joe R.
Zugibe, Frederick T. The Cross & the Shroud: A Medical Examiner Investigates the Crucifixion.
--Fourteen Days to a Healthy Heart.
--Fourteen Days to a Healthy Heart.
Zuidema, George D., jt. auth. see Judge, Richard D.
Zukas, Harriet, jt. auth. see De Broglie, Marie-Blanche.
Zuker, Joel S. Arthur Penn: A Guide to Reference & Resources.
--Francis Ford Coppola: A Guide to References & Resources.
Zuker, R. Fred & Hegener, Karen C. Peterson's Guide to College Admissions: Getting into the College of Your Choice.
Zukofsky, Louis. All: The Collected Short Poems, 1923-1958.
Zukowsky, John. Walter Burley Griffin, Marion Mahoney Griffin: Architectural Drawings in the Burnham Library of Architecture.
Zulch, K. J. Histological Typing of Tumors of the Central Nervous System.
Zuleger, Susanna & Staubesand, Jochen. Atlas of the Central Nervous System in Sectional Planes: Selected Myelin Stained Sections of the Human Brain & Spinal Cord.
Zuman, P. Elucidation of Organic Electrode Processes.
Zuman, Petr, jt. auth. see Meites, Louis.
Zumberge, James H. & Nelson, Clemens A. Elements of Physical Geology.
Zumberge, James H. & Rutford, Robert H. Laboratory Manual for Physical Geology.
Zumbo, Jim & Zumbo, Lois. The Venison Cookbook: More Than 200 Tested Recipes for Deer, Elk, Moose & Other Game.
Zumbo, Lois, jt. auth. see Zumbo, Jim.
Zumbro, Ralph. Tank Sergeant.
Zumdahl, Steven S. General Chemistry Problem Solving II.
Zumeta, William. Extending the Educational Ladder: The Quality & the Postdoctoral Study.
Zumwalt, Elmo, et al. My Father, My Son.
Zumwalt, Eva. The Unforgiving.
Zundell, George. Hydration & Intermolecular Interaction: Infrared Investigations with Polyelectrolyte Membranes.
Zunkel, A. D., et al, eds. Complex Sulfides: Processing of Ores, Concentrates & By-Products.
Zunz, Olivier, jt. ed. see Pitts, Jesse R.
Zuoren, Wu & Shufang, Xiao. Selected Paintings of Wu Zuoren & Xiao Shufang.
Zuppinger, A., ed. see Symposium on High-Energy Electrons, Montreux, 1964.
Zuppinger, A., et al, eds. High Energy Electrons in Radiation Therapy.
Zurbuchen, Mary S. Introduction to Old Javanese Language & Literature: A Kawi Prose Anthology.
Zurier, Rebecca. The American Firehouse: An Architectural & Social History.
--Art for the Masses 1911-1917: A Radical Magazine & its Artists.
Zuromskis, Diane, illus. Farmer in the Dell.
Zuspan, Frederick P., jt. auth. see Rayburn, William F.
Zuspan, Fredrick P., jt. auth. see Rayburn, William F.
Zussman, J., ed. Physical Methods in Determinative Mineralogy.
Zussman, John & Cortesi, David E. Executive Computing: The IBM Personal Computer.
Zutter, Marguerite. Lady Nobody.
Zutz, Don. Handloading for Hunters.
Zuverink, Mary & Haskin, Georgettecompiled by. Listen to a Shadow.
Zuyev, Yu. S., jt. auth. see Bartenev, G. M.
Zvidadze, Givi. A Dictionary of Contemporary English.
Zweifach, Benjamin W., et al, eds. The Inflammatory Process.
Zweifel, P. F., jt. ed. see Inonu, E.
Zweig, Phillip L., ed. The Asset Securitization Handbook.

Authors

Zwerdling, Daniel. Workplace Democracy.
Zwick, Earl J., jt. auth. see Rector, Robert E.
Zwick, George. Beginner's Guide to TV Repair.
Zwicky, Fritz. Morphological Astronomy.
Zwier, Robert. Born-Again Politics: The New Christian Right in America.
Zwingmann, C. & Pfister-Ammende, M., eds. Uprooting & After.
Zwirn, Jerrold. Congressional Publications: A Research Guide to Legislation, Budgets & Treaties.
Zwirz, Bob. The Illustrated Guide to Better Fishing.
--The Illustrated Guide to Better Fishing.
Zylstra, Henry, tr. see Bavinck, Herman.
Zysman, John & Tyson, Laura, eds. American Industry in International Competition: Government Policies & Corporate Strategies.
Zytaruk, George J., ed. The Quest for Rananim: D.H. Lawrence's Letters to S.S. Koteliansky, 1914-1930.

Authors

O.P-O.S.I. RETAILERS

ALASKA

KENAI — 1324. Area code 907

THE BOOK CACHE — General
Kenai Mall, Box 267, 99611. Tel 907-283-7497
Owner, Karluk Corp Buys through hq
Types: Hb, juvenile, out of print, papbk
Subj: Alaskana, art, rel-c,j,p, sci-tech

SITKA — 7803. Area code 907

ALASKAN HERITAGE BOOKSHOP — Antiquarian
PO Box 22165, 99802. Tel 907-479-2819
Mgr, Richard Alan Wood
Estab 1983. 7000 Titles. 7500 Vols
Types: Illus bk, old & rare, out of print, remainders
Subj: Alaskana, birds, polar

BIG CITY BOOKS LTD — General
100 N Franklin, 99801. Tel 907-586-2130
Mgr & Buyer, Christine McQuitty
14,000 Titles. 22,000 Vols. 4000 sq ft
Types: Hb, juvenile, out of print, papbk, imp UK
Subj: Cooking, Alaskana, hist, nature & environ, aviation, fiction, boating, nautical charts

THE OBSERVATORY — Antiquarian-Alaskana
202 Katlian St, 99835. Tel 907-747-3033, 747-3457. Cable address: Polarlook
Estab 1977. 10,000 Vols. 450 sq ft
Types: Fine bnd, 1st ed, hb, illus bk, imp, juvenile, ltd ed, old & rare, out of print, used
Subj: Arctic, Can, polar regions

OLD HARBOR BOOKS INC — General
201 Lincoln St, 99835. Tel 907-747-8808
Estab 1976. 10,000 Vols. 1500 sq ft
Types: Hb, juvenile, out of print, papbk
Subj: Alaskana, how-to

UNALASKA — 1322. Area code 907

NICKY'S PLACE — Antiquarian
Box 225, 99685. Tel 907-581-1570
Estab 1980. 1000 Vols
Types: Pvt presses, out of print, hb, papbk
Subj: Alaskana, anthrop, hist, WW II in the Aleutians, diaries of Russian & American visitors to the Aleutians

BISBEE — 7154. Area code 602

ATALANTA RECORDS & BOOKS — Paperback
32 Main St (Mail add: PO Box 317, 85603-0317). Tel 602-432-9976
Estab 1975. 4500 Vols. 480 sq ft
Types: Hb, juvenile, mass mkt papbk, out of print, remainders, Sp lang, used, comics
Subj: Arts & crafts, astrol, cooking, energy, fiction, medicine, metaphys & occult, psychol, Western Amer, ecology

CAREFREE — Area code 602

READEX BOOK EXCHANGE — Antiquarian-Art
PO Box 1125, 85377-1125. Tel 602-488-3304
Estab 1937. 4500 Titles. 2500 Vols. Cat
Types: 1st ed, facsimile editions, hb, imp, new & used, out of print, papbk, remainders, old & rare
Subj: Indust & labor, sci-tech

CAVE CREEK — Area code 602

RUSS TODD BOOKS — Antiquarian
Star Rte Two, Box 872F, 85331. Tel 602-585-0070
5000 Vols. Cat 2x ann
Types: 1st ed, old & rare, out of print
Subj: Am Indian studies, Arizonana, New Mexicana, Western Amer

DOUGLAS — 13,058. Area code 602

CHIRICAHUA BOOK COMPANY — General
1015 G Ave, PO Box 672, 85608. Tel 602-364-3177
Estab 1986. 2500 Titles. 3500 Vols. 500 sq ft. Cat 8x ann
Types: Sp lang, hb, juvenile, out of print, papbk, high priced papbk, remainders, used, best sellers, facsimile editions, fine bnd, 1st ed, illus bk, imp Mex, new, old & rare
Subj: Cooking, reference, Southwestern Amer, Mex

FLAGSTAFF — 34,641. Area code 602

DUCK'S BOOKS — General
1800 S Milton, 86001. Tel 602-779-5365
Estab 1981. 20,000 Vols. 1260 sq ft
Types: Out of print, papbk, remainders, new
Subj: Southwestern Amer

GRAND CANON BOOK SEARCH — Mail Order-Antiquarian
PO Box G, 86002-0958. Tel 602-779-2797
Estab 1986. 200 Titles. 300 Vols
Types: Hb, out of print, used, 1st ed, papbk
Subj: Southwestern Amer, Grand Canyon, Colorado River

GREEN VALLEY — Area code 602

SADDLE HORN SALES — Mail Order-Western Americana
PO Box 82, 85622-0082. Tel 602-625-8645
Estab 1953. 1400 Titles. 2500 Vols
Types: 1st ed, hb, new & used, out of print, papbk, old & rare, remainders

KINGMAN — 9257. Area code 602

WONDERLAND — General
708 E Beale St, 86401. Tel 602-753-4568
Mgr, Marian E Darton
Types: Hb, papbk, juvenile, remainders, used, out of print

LITCHFIELD PARK — 1664. Area code 602

BONITA PORTER BOOKS — Antiquarian
506 E Indian Sch, PO Box 1765, Litchfield Park, 85340-1765. Tel 602-935-3643
Estab 1965. 4000 Vols. 450 sq ft. Cat 2x ann
Types: 1st ed, hb, illus bk, ltd ed, out of print
Subj: Arizonana, Southwestern Amer, cowboy art bk

MESA — 152,453. Area code 602

CYCLO DAP ARCHIVES — Asian Studies
1462 W University, 85201. Tel 602-962-4347
Merch Mgr, John Laurie
Estab 1981. 500 Titles. 5000 Vols. 550 sq ft. Cat 2x ann
Types: Used, col & el-hi text, remainders, hb, imp Fr, out of print, papbk, high priced papbk, imp Australia
Subj: Military, polit sci, sociol, hist, class studies, fiction, nonfiction, Vietnam & South East Asia

MESA TEMPLE VIEW BOOK & SUPPLY INC — Religious-C
409 E First Ave, 85204. Tel 602-969-7962, 834-0073. WATS 800-528-8275
Estab 1965. 10,000 Titles. 80,000 Vols. 4600 sq ft. Cat 12x ann
Types: For lang, hb, imp, juvenile, out of print, papbk
Subj: Genealogy, archaeol

PHOENIX — 764,911. Area code 602

ALPHA BOOK CENTER — Metaphysics & Occult
1928 E McDowell Rd, 85006. Tel 602-237-3213, 253-1223. Info: 602-957-7381
Owner, New Age Community Church
Estab 1967. 1500 Titles. 7000 Vols. 1200 sq ft. Cat ann
Types: Hb, out of print, papbk
Subj: Astrol, self-develop, magic & conjuring, psychic, spiritualism

DISCOUNT BOOK LTD — General
8044 North 27th Ave, 85051. Tel 602-995-9060
Mgr, Tina S Howze
Estab 1988. 50,000 Titles. 50,000 Vols. 4000 sq ft
Types: Used, juvenile, out of print, high priced papbk, mass mkt papbk only
Subj: Southwestern Amer, sci fiction & fantasy

NORTH MOUNTAIN BOOKS — Science-Technology
9226-C N Seventh St, 85020. Tel 602-997-1643
Estab 1981. 5500 Titles. 5500 Vols. 700 sq ft
Types: Hb, new & used, out of print, remainders
Subj: Bus & mgt, scholarly lit

PHOENIX ART MUSEUM BOOKSTORE — Museum
1625 N Central Ave, 85004. Tel 602-257-1880
Mgr, Marsha Weiss
Estab 1950. 500 Vols
Types: Juvenile, out of print
Subj: Art, costuming, Diego Rivera: The Cubist Years, The Elegant Brush

PRESCOTT — 20,055. Area code 602

JUST PAPERBACKS — General
Iron Springs Plaza, 1201 Iron Springs Rd, 86301. Tel 602-445-6385
Estab 1981. 21,000 Vols. 1000 sq ft
Types: Juvenile, out of print, used, papbk, hb

SCOTTSDALE — 88,364. Area code 602

GUIDON BOOKS — Antiquarian-Western Americana
7117 Main St, 85251. Tel 602-945-8811
Estab 1964
Types: 1st ed, hb, imp, new, out of print, papbk, remainders, old & rare
Subj: Civil War

WILLIAM R HECHT — Mail Order-Antiquarian
Box 67, 85252. Tel 602-948-2536
Owner, William R Hecht
Estab 1950. 5000 Vols. Cat 4x ann
Types: Imp, new & used, out of print, old & rare
Subj: Amer, natural hist, falconry

TEMPE — 106,743. Area code 602

RUBY D KAUFMAN BOOKS — Mail Order-Antiquarian
518 E Loma Vista Dr, 85282-2333. Tel 602-968-9517
Estab 1980
Types: Juvenile, out of print, illus bk, used

OLD TOWN BOOKS — Southwestern Americana
518 S Mill Ave, 85281. Tel 602-968-9881
Mgr, Greg Johnson
Estab 1984. 5000 Titles. 800 sq ft
Types: Used, juvenile, out of print, hb, old & rare, 1st ed, illus bk
Subj: Arizonana, fly fishing, Grand Canyon

THOSE WERE THE DAYS! — Antiquarian
516 S Mill Ave, 85281. Tel 602-967-4729
Estab 1973. 3500 Titles. 15,000 Vols
Types: Hb, new, out of print, used, remainders, old & rare
Subj: Antq, collecting, furniture

TUCSON — 330,537. Area code 602

A BOOKLOVER'S SHOP — Mail Order-Antiquarian
PO Box 43607, 85733. Tel 602-881-8192
Estab 1977. 14,000 Vols
Types: 1st ed, hb, out of print
Subj: Arizonana, Southwestern Amer, bibliog, New Mexicana, Bisbee, AZ, Catholica, Thomas Merton, rel art & archit

BASEBALL BOOKS ONLY — Mail Order-Sports
5672 E Scarlett St, 85711. Tel 602-747-5394
2400 Titles. 6000 Vols
Types: Hb, juvenile, out of print, used
Subj: Baseball

BEACHCOMBER BOOKSHOP — Military
5763 W Potvin Rd (Mail add: PO Box 197, Cortaro, 85230). Tel 602-744-0487
Estab 1959. 80,000 Vols. 3000 sq ft. Cat
Types: Hb, used, imp, out of print, Jap lang, Fr lang, Ger lang, Pol lang
Subj: Aviation

BOOKMAN'S — General
1930 E Grant Rd, 85719. Tel 602-325-5767, 5055
Owner, Intergalactic Inc; Mgrs, Mara Lynn Monrey & Robert Schlesinger
Estab 1973. 500,000 Vols. 16,500 sq ft
Types: Juvenile, out of print, papbk, 1st ed, new & used, hb, for lang, for lang per
Subj: Amer, art, auto, literary criticism, sci-tech, fiction, Southwestern Amer, mystery & detective, computer sci

THE BOOK STOP INC — Used
2504 N Campbell Ave, 85719. Tel 602-326-6661
Estab 1967. 100,000 Titles. 100,000 Vols. 3600 sq ft
Types: Out of print, old & rare
Subj: Arizonana, biog, hist, scholarly lit, Southwest

CLASSIC AUTOMOBILE RESEARCH SERVICE — General
PO Box 7866, 85725-7866. Tel 602-578-0585
Estab 1985. 10,000 Titles. 10,000 Vols. Cat
Types: Hb, out of print, old & rare, new & used
Subj: Auto

PAUL GAUDETTE BOOKS — Military
2050 E 17th St, 85719. Tel 602-791-3868
Mgr, Sharon Pappas
10,000 Titles. 15,000 Vols. 2500 sq ft. Cat 12x ann
Types: Imp Gr, imp Australia, imp UK, imp Pol, out of print, remainders, used, hb, new, old & rare
Subj: Aviation, naval

GOODBOOKS — Used
431 N Fourth Ave, 85705. Tel 602-792-9551
Estab 1984. 65,000 Vols. 1250 sq ft
Types: Hb, papbk, new, old & rare, 1st ed, illus bk, out of print
Subj: Art, cooking, Southwestern Amer, espionage

KERBER'S BOOKSTORE — General
1015 W Prince Rd, 85705. Tel 602-887-6082
25,000 Vols
Types: 1st ed, hb, out of print, papbk
Subj: Cooking

TRUEPENNY BOOKS — Antiquarian
2509 N Campbell, Box 117, 85719. Tel 602-881-4822
Estab 1984. 10,000 Titles. 10,000 Vols. 1200 sq ft. Cat 8x ann
Types: Hb, out of print, fine bnd, old & rare, 1st ed, facsimile editions, incunab, illus bk, imp EEur, ltd ed, remainders, new, used, fine presses
Subj: Art, hist, philos, bks on bks, scholarly lit, fine printing

GENE VINIK BOOKS — Mail Order-Antiquarian
2213 E Copper St, 85719-3215. Tel 602-323-7188
Estab 1984. 4000 Titles. 4000 Vols. Cat
Types: Used, old & rare, out of print

YUMA — 42,433. Area code 602

THE RAVENSTREE CO — Mail Order-Antiquarian
PO Box 10552, 85366-8552. Tel 602-785-4003
Estab 1964. 3000 Titles. 4000 Vols. Cat 14x ann
Types: 1st ed, fine bnd, hb, illus bk, imp, incunab, juvenile, ltd ed, old & rare, out of print, used
Subj: Amer, bibliog, drama, Eng hist & lit, class lit

EL DORADO — 26,685. Area code 501

BOOKS & BYTES — General
403 N Newton, 71730. Tel 501-862-0972
Estab 1976. 2500 Titles. 35,000 Vols. 1600 sq ft. Cat
Types: Hb, new, out of print, papbk, used
Subj: Mystery & detective, sci fiction & fantasy

EUREKA SPRINGS — 1989. Area code 501

JACK BAILES - BOOKS — Search Service
PO Box 150, 72632. Tel 501-253-9131
Estab 1937. 10,000 Vols. Cat
Types: Illus bk, out of print
Subj: Arkansiana, hunting & fishing, caves, Harrison Fisher, Maud Humphrey, Kay Nielsen, Maxfield Parrish, A Rackham

FAYETTEVILLE — 36,604. Area code 501

RICHARD BYNUM — Antiquarian-Metaphys & Occult
927 Applebury Dr, 72701. Tel 501-443-4563
16,000 Titles. 16,000 Vols. Cat 2x ann
Types: Old & rare, out of print, used
Subj: Metaphys & occult, astrol, ancient hist & lit, self-develop, health, psychol, alchemy,growth directed healing

DICKSON STREET BOOKSHOP — General
325 W Dickson, 72701. Tel 501-442-8182
Estab 1978. 40,000 Vols. 1200 sq ft
Types: 1st ed, facsimile editions, hb, illus bk, old & rare, out of print, papbk, used
Subj: Hist, Irish hist & lit, Ozarkiana, poetry, Ozarks

FORT SMITH — 71,384. Area code 501

MARTIN HOUSE BOOKS — Antiquarian
2212 South T St, 72901. Tel 501-783-0145
Estab 1980. 4000 Titles. 4000 Vols
Types: 1st ed, hb, illus bk, out of print, used
Subj: Biog, gardening, natural hist, photog

PAPERBACKS PLUS — Antiquarian
2207 Rogers, 72901. Tel 501-785-5642
Estab 1982. 30,000 Titles. 50,000 Vols. 2500 sq ft
Types: 1st ed, fine bnd, hb, illus bk, juvenile, ltd ed, old & rare, out of print, papbk, remainders, used, comics

SNOOPER'S BARN USED BOOKS — Used
208 Towson, 72901. Tel 501-783-7100
Estab 1970. 90,000 Vols. 6000 sq ft
Types: Col & el-hi text, for lang, hb, juvenile, out of print, papbk
Subj: Medicine, sci fiction & fantasy

HARDY — 643. Area code 501

APPLETREE BOOKS — Mail Order-Antiquarian
Rte 1, Box 69, 72542. Tel 501-856-2755
Estab 1970. 1500 Titles. 1500 Vols. Cat
Types: Hb, imp, out of print, used, 1st ed
Subj: Gardening, arts & crafts, hist, biog, watercolors, knitting

HOT SPRINGS — 36,166. Area code 501

YESTERDAY'S BOOKS ETC — Antiquarian
767 Park Ave, PO Box 1728, 71902. Tel 501-624-6300
Estab 1974. Cat 3-4x ann
Types: Hb, old & rare, out of print, used
Subj: Amer, Arkansiana

JONESBORO — 31,530. Area code 501

BOOKS PLUS — Antiquarian
2314 E Matthews, 72401. Tel 501-935-6672
Estab 1982. 60,000 Titles. 60,000 Vols. 2300 sq ft
Types: For lang, hb, out of print, mass mkt papbk, used, fine bnd, new, old & rare, 1st ed
See Also: Blytheville; Gosnell

LITTLE ROCK — 158,461. Area code 501

FOX ORCHIDS INC — Horticulture
6615 W Markham, 72205. Tel 501-663-4246
Mgr & Buyer, John M Fox
Estab 1948. 350 Vols. 160 sq ft. Cat 2x ann
Types: Hb, out of print, high priced papbk, remainders
Subj: Bromeliads, carnivorous plants, cactus, ferns, orchids, water plants

TROLLEY LINE BOOKSHOP — Used
2701 Kavanaugh Blvd, Suite 101 (Mail add: PO Box 5005, 72225). Tel 501-663-6006
Estab 1986. 15,000 Titles. 20,000 Vols. 700 sq ft. Cat 2x ann
Types: Facsimile editions, fine bnd, 1st ed, hb, illus bk, imp Eng, Jap, Fr, juvenile, new & used, old & rare, out of print, papbk, remainders
Subj: Southern Arkansas region

WORDSWORTH BOOKS & CO — General
5823 Kavanaugh Blvd, 72207-4478. Tel 501-663-9198
Owner, Kari Whisenhunt
Estab 1975. 25,000 Vols. 1780 sq ft. Cat 4x ann
Types: Hb, out of print, papbk, small presses, univ presses
Subj: Literary

RUSSELLVILLE — 14,000. Area code 501

EMPORIUM BOOKS — Remainder
214 W Main, PO Box 771, 72801-0771. Tel 501-968-1110
Buyer, E Jones
Estab 1973. 2100 Titles. 6500 Vols. 1900 sq ft. Cat ann
Types: Facsimile editions, 1st ed, hb, incunab, illus bk, juvenile, old & rare, out of print, papbk, used
Subj: Amer, Eng hist & lit, hist, metaphys & occult, survival, back-to-the-earth

ALAMEDA — 63,852. Area code 415

KEVIN PATRICK BOOKS — General
2170 Encinal Ave, 94501. Tel 415-865-3880
Types: Romance lang, hb, imp, papbk, out of print, juvenile, used

ALBANY — 15,130. Area code 415

BEST BOOK LTD — Mail Order-Antiquarian
1005 Clay St, 94706. Tel 415-527-7707
1000 Titles. 1000 Vols. Cat 3x ann
Types: Hb, imp, out of print, fine bnd, illus bk
Subj: East Asia, Philippines, Japan

ROSS VALLEY BOOK CO, INC — Western Americana
1407 Solano Ave, 94706. Tel 415-526-6400
Estab 1978. 4500 Titles. 5000 Vols. 1800 sq ft. Cat 3-4x ann
Types: Facsimile editions, fine bnd, 1st ed, hb, illus bk, new & used, old & rare, out of print, papbk, remainders
Subj: Am Indian studies, Californiana, Southwestern Amer

ALPINE — 1570. Area code 714

AMS COLLEGE BOOKSTORE — College
2605 W Alpine Blvd, 92001. Tel 619-445-0303
Mgr & Buyer, Kenneth Nguyen
Estab 1977. 600 Titles. 10,000 Vols. 2500 sq ft. Cat 2x ann
Types: Hb, papbk, out of print

ANAHEIM — 221,847. Area code 714

THE BOOK BARON — Antiquarian
1236 S Magnolia Ave, 92804. Tel 714-527-7022
Estab 1980. 250,000 Titles. 250,000 Vols. 13,000 sq ft. Cat 2x ann
Types: 1st ed, facsimile editions, fine bnd, hb, illus bk, juvenile, ltd ed, new, old & rare, out of print, papbk, remainders, used
Subj: Fiction, mystery & detective, sci fiction & fantasy

APPLE VALLEY — 6702. Area code 714

GAIL KLEMM - BOOKS — Antiquarian
PO Box 518, 92307. Tel 619-242-5921
Estab 1969. 10,000 Titles. 10,000 Vols. Cat
Types: Out of print, hb, juvenile, fine bnd, 1st ed, illus bk, imp, ltd ed, old & rare, juv (16th-20th century), printing, papermaking
Subj: Antq

ARCATA — 12,338. Area code 707

ARCATA BOOKS LTD — Antiquarian
931 I St, 95521. Tel 707-822-1024. WATS: 800-537-4355 (outside CA)
Estab 1975. 12,000 Titles. 15,000 Vols. Cat 4x ann
Types: Imp, old & rare, out of print, new
Subj: Natural hist, hist of printing, invertebrates, mollusks

ATHERTON — 7797. Area code 415

DIANE PETERSON BOOKLADY — Antiquarian
PO Box 2544, 94026. Tel 415-324-1201
Cat
Types: Fine bnd, 1st ed, hb, illus bk, juvenile, ltd ed, old & rare, out of print, papbk, used
Subj: Mod lit, sci fiction & fantasy, miniature bks, Steinbeckiana

BAKERSFIELD — 105,611. Area code 805

THE BOOK EXCHANGE — Paperback
2007 H St, 93301. Tel 805-327-1041
40,000 Titles. 70,000 Vols
Types: Juvenile, out of print, used
Subj: Biog, comedy, mystery & detective, romance, sci fiction & fantasy, warfare

W R SLATER BOOKS — Used
509 Malibu Ct, 93309-1752. Tel 805-322-9492
Estab 1976. 10,000 Vols. Cat
Types: Out of print
Subj: Sci fiction & fantasy, children's series

BELLFLOWER — 53,441. Area code 213

BELL ROSE USED BOOKSTORE — Used
14224 Bellflower Blvd, 90706. Tel 213-925-8634
Estab 1981. 55,000 Vols. 1000 sq ft
Types: Juvenile, papbk, hb, out of print

GREEN DOOR BOOKS & ANTIQUES — Antiquarian
17824 S Clark Ave, 90706. Tel 213-925-0630
Estab 1959
Types: Out of print, used
Subj: Amer, antq

BERKELEY — 103,328. Area code 415

ADAMS ANGLING BOOKS & PARAPHERNALIA — Antiquarian
1170 Keeler Ave, 94708. Tel 415-849-1324
Estab 1978. 3500 Titles. 5000 Vols. 400 sq ft. Cat 2x ann
Types: Facsimile editions, fine bnd, 1st ed, hb, illus bk, imp, ltd ed, old & rare, out of print, used
Subj: Natural hist, nature & environ, hunting & fishing

BERKELEY BOOK CONSORTIUM — Used
1700 Shattuck Ave, 94609. Tel 415-486-0166
Buyer, Victor Prada
Estab 1984. 50,000 Titles. 60,000 Vols. 2000 sq ft
Types: For lang, hb, juvenile, out of print
Subj: Philos, military, women's studies, black studies, educ, poetry, hist, mystery & detective

BIBLIOFILE BOOK SEARCH — Mail Order-Antiquarian
1912 Blake St, 94704. Tel 415-540-8223
Estab 1984. 1000 Titles. 1000 Vols. Cat 2x ann
Types: Out of print, old & rare, fine bnd, 1st ed, hb, illus bk, ltd ed
Subj: Archit, poetry, mod lit, photog, rare art

BLACK OAK BOOKS — Scholarly Lit
1491 Shattuck Ave, 94709. Tel 415-486-0698, 486-0699
Papbk Buyer, Donald Pretari
Estab 1983. 60,000 Titles. 100,000 Vols. 5500 sq ft
Types: For lang, hb, papbk, imp, out of print, remainders, new & used, 1st ed, illus bk, old & rare
Subj: Art, food, women's studies, sci-tech, Greek & Latin classics

ROY BLEIWEISS FINE BOOKS — Antiquarian
92 Northgate Ave, 94708. Tel 415-654-8886
Estab 1972. 3500 Vols. 800 sq ft. Cat 4x ann
Types: Fine bnd, 1st ed, hb, illus bk, ltd ed, old & rare, out of print, fine press
Subj: Amer, law, scholarly lit, art, archit

CARTESIAN BOOKSTORE — Used
2445 Dwight Way, 94704. Tel 415-549-3973
Estab 1977. 3000 Vols. 500 sq ft
Types: Gr lang, hb, out of print, papbk, Rom lang
Subj: Archaeol, church hist, philos, rel, class studies

PETER R FELTUS — Antiquarian
PO Box 5339, 94705-5339. Tel 415-658-9627
Estab 1975. 3 Titles. 500 Vols. Cat books & stamps cat
Types: Out of print, new
Subj: Philately, hist, geog, mod Egypt & Sudan, Baedeker, Cook & Murry travel guides 1840-1940

DONALD L FOLEY - BOOKS — Antiquarian-Scholarly Lit
1050 Mariposa Ave, 94707. Tel 415-525-6983
Estab 1982. 7000 Vols
Types: Univ presses, hb, papbk, old & rare, out of print, used
Subj: Univ of California Press bks

HALF PRICE BOOKS, RECORDS & MAGAZINES — General
2525 Telegraph Ave, 94704. Tel 415-843-6412
Estab 1982. 75,000 Vols. 4000 sq ft
Types: For lang, hb, papbk, col & el-hi text, juvenile, out of print, imp, fine bnd, 1st ed, new & used, old & rare

HOUSEHOLD WORDS — Mail Order-Used
284 Purdue Ave (Mail add: PO Box 7231, 94707). Tel 415-524-8859
Estab 1977. 5000 Titles. 5000 Vols. 360 sq ft. Cat 1-2x ann
Types: Out of print
Subj: Cooking, wines

THE INVISIBLE BOOKMAN — Mail Order-Antiquarian
97 Franciscan Way, 94707. Tel 415-524-7823
Estab 1963. 7500 Vols
Types: 1st ed, out of print, old & rare, used
Subj: Drama, fiction, humanities, literary criticism, poetry

IAN JACKSON — Mail Order-Antiquarian
PO Box 9075, 94709. Tel 415-548-1431
Estab 1978. 3000 Titles. 3000 Vols. Cat 8x ann
Types: 1st ed, hb, illus bk, ltd ed, old & rare, out of print, used, imp, scholarly bks
Subj: Botany, gardening, lit

MOE'S BOOKS INC — Used
2476 Telegraph Ave, 94704-2392. Tel 415-849-2087
, Robert Baldock, et al
Estab 1959. 300,000 Vols
Types: Hb, illus bk, imp, juvenile, new, out of print, papbk, old & rare, remainders
Subj: Art, philos, photog, poetry, scholarly lit

J B MUNS FINE ARTS BOOKSELLER — Antiquarian
1162 Shattuck Ave, 94707-2698. Tel 415-525-2420
Estab 1964. 2000 Titles. 2500 Vols. Cat ann
Types: Hb, imp, old & rare, out of print, remainders, used
Subj: Art, music, archit, photog, mus autographs

PEGASUS FINE BOOKS — Used
1855 Solano Ave, 94707. Tel 415-525-6888. WATS 800-825-0100
Merch Mgr, J Armbruster & B Ruhland; Mgr, Susan Forster; Retail Supvr, Amy Thomas
Estab 1970. 80,000 Titles. 100,000 Vols. 3500 sq ft Buys indep & through hq
Types: 1st ed, hb, illus bk, juvenile, ltd ed, new, out of print, old & rare, papbk, remainders, Fr, Ger & Sp lang
Subj: Art, hist, metaphysics, sci fiction & fantasy, mystery & detective, cooking

REGENT PRESS — Mail Order-Antiquarian
2747 Regent St, 94705. Tel 415-547-7602
Estab 1978. 1000 Vols. 140 sq ft. Cat ann
Types: Old & rare, out of print
Subj: Design, graphic arts, psychol, yoga

SCATTERGOOD BOOKS — Mail Order-Antiquarian
Landscape Sta, PO Box 7043, 94707. Tel 415-525-5454
Estab 1968. 6400 Titles. 7000 Vols. Cat
Types: Old & rare, out of print
Subj: Communism, socialism, radical polit, Jewish question, Russia

SHAKESPEARE & COMPANY BOOKS — Used
2499 Telegraph Ave, 94704. Tel 415-841-8916
Estab 1965. 2000 sq ft
Types: Hb, papbk, for lang, juvenile, out of print, remainders
Subj: Art, photog

SARKIS SHMAVONIAN RARE BOOKS — Antiquarian
1796 Shattuck Ave, 94709. Tel 415-845-0548
Estab 1975. 2000 Vols. 1500 sq ft
Types: Out of print, hb, imp, old & rare, 1st ed, incunab, scholarly bks
Subj: Discovery & explor, bks on bks, bibliog, 17th & 19th century lit, hist of sci

SUNRISE BOOKSHOP & METAPHYSICAL CENTER — Metaphysics & Occult
3054 Telegraph Ave, 94705. Tel 415-841-6372
Mgr, Richard C Cook
Estab 1974. Cat
Types: Hb, juvenile, out of print, papbk, used
Subj: Astrol, health & phys educ, inspirational, self-develop, Eastern & Western spiritual traditions, hermetica

TOAD HALL — Mail Order-Antiquarian
PO Box 902, 94701. Tel 415-843-0383
Estab 1976. Cat
Types: Fine bnd, 1st ed, hb, juvenile, old & rare, out of print, used
Subj: Children's, garden design & hist

WHALING RESEARCH — Mail Order-Antiquarian
PO Box 5034, 94705-5034
Estab 1963. 3000 Vols
Types: 1st ed, hb, imp, out of print, old & rare, used
Subj: Whales & whaling

BEVERLY HILLS — 32,367. Area code 213

ERIC CHAIM KLINE BOOKSELLER — Antiquarian
2221 Benedict Canyon Dr, 90210. Tel 213-395-4745
Estab 1985. 10,000 Titles. 401 Vols. 1000 sq ft. Cat 4x ann
Types: Used, Fr lang, Ger lang, Hebr lang, hb, out of print, facsimile editions, fine bnd, 1st ed, illus bk, imp Isr, imp Isr, ltd ed, old & rare
Subj: Judaica, philos, archaeol, Egyptology, rel-j
See Also: wholesale section; Morrison & Kline Books, Santa Monica

PROFESSIONAL BOOKS SERVICE — Law
9016 Wilshire Blvd, Suite 105, 90211. Tel 213-256-0833
Mgr, Gene Mayl
Types: Imp, out of print, used
Subj: Law, medicine, bus & mgt, tech

BIG BEAR CITY — Area code 714

JONES BOOKSTORE — Used Paperback
PO Box 3331, 92315. Tel 714-866-3669
Estab 1979. 12000 Titles. 35000 Vols. 800 sq ft
Types: Juvenile, out of print

BISHOP — 3333. Area code 619

THE WORN BOOKWORM — Used
177A Short St, 93514. Tel 619-873-6074
Estab 1983. 21,000 Titles. 32,000 Vols. 1200 sq ft
Types: For lang, hb, juvenile, out of print, mass mkt papbk, papbk, 1st ed, illus bk
Subj: Fiction, hist, Western Amer, romance, sci fiction & fantasy

BURBANK — 84,625. Area code 818

BOOK CITY OF BURBANK — General
308 N Golden Mall, 91502. Tel 818-848-4417
Asst Mgr, Richard Bellamy
Estab 1981. 200,000 Titles. 500,000 Vols. 10,000 sq ft
Types: Out of print, hb
Subj: Art, biog, films & filmmaking, metaphys & occult, photog, cooking, military, hist, mod lit

HAROLD B DIAMOND BOOKSELLER — Mail Order-Antiquarian
Box 1193, 91507-1193. Tel 818-846-0342
Estab 1964. Cat 6x ann
Types: 1st ed, illus bk, ltd ed, out of print, old & rare, imp EEur
Subj: Art, bks on bks, econ, Latin Am, polit sci, reference, sci-tech, scholarly lit, soc sci, archit, performing arts, sci fiction & fantasy, class studies, Judaica, natural hist, medicine, Am hist & lit, Eng hist & lit, Fr hist & lit, Ger hist & lit, Sp hist & lit, law, Western Amer, Dickensiana, Mark Twain, World War I, Shakespeariana, Napolean, French revolution

DUTTON'S BOOKS — Antiquarian
3806 W Magnolia Blvd, 91505. Tel 818-840-8003
Mgr, Katherine Gill
Types: For lang, used, papbk, juvenile, out of print, imp UK, old & rare, illus bk, fine bnd
Subj: Art, hist, music, class

GARVIN'S BOOK SHOP AND ROCK SHOP — Used
321 N Golden Mall, 91502. Tel 818-848-2132
Estab 1966. 15,000 Titles. 17,000 Vols. 1500 sq ft. Cat 2x ann
Types: Hb, out of print, hb, facsimile editions, fine bnd, 1st ed
Subj: Mineralogy, mining, geol, gemology, Amer, paleontology, earth sci, fossils, U S Geological Survey

BURLINGAME — 26,173. Area code 415

VERNON HOWARD BOOKS — Antiquarian
733 Plymouth Way, 94010. Tel 415-347-5620
5000 Titles. 5000 Vols. 200 sq ft. Cat
Types: Hb, imp, out of print, old & rare, used, remainders
Subj: Hist, travel, Western Amer, mountains, mountaineering

PENINSULA BOOKSEARCH — Mail Order-Antiquarian
PO Box 1305, 94011-1305
Estab 1978
Types: 1st ed, illus bk, ltd ed, out of print, pvt presses
Subj: Fiction, mod lit, Oz bks

CAMBRIA — 1716. Area code 805

TAYLOR COFFMAN BOOKSELLER — Mail Order-Antiquarian
1441 Astor Ave, 93428. Tel 805-927-4343
Estab 1980. 500 Vols. Cat
Types: Hb, out of print, remainders
Subj: Archit, art, hist, humanities

CAMPBELL — 27,067. Area code 408

BOOKS — Used
116 San Tomas Aquino Rd, 95008. Tel 408-374-0933
Estab 1979. 20,000 Titles. 25,000 Vols. 1700 sq ft
Types: Hb, out of print
Subj: Fiction

CAPITOLA — 9095. Area code 408

CAPITOLA BOOK CAFE — General
1475 41st Ave, 95010. Tel 408-462-4415
Juv Buyer, Kathy Kitsose
Estab 1980. 27,000 Titles. 40,000 Vols. 4000 sq ft. Cat
Types: For lang, hb, juvenile, out of print, papbk, remainders

CARDIFF — 5724. Area code 714

BOOKPOST — Mail Order-Antiquarian
962 Greenlake Ct, PO Box 666, 92007-0666. Tel 619-753-3392
Estab 1954. 1200 Vols. 360 sq ft
Types: Hb, new & used, out of print
Subj: Metaphys & occult, parapsychol, Eastern philos, yoga, bot med, new age philos, unorthodox healing, psychic res

CARLSBAD — 35,490. Area code 714

JAMES HANSEN BOOKS — Mail Order-Antiquarian
3514 Highland, 92008. Tel 619-729-3383
Estab 1979. 15,000 Vols. 1200 sq ft. Cat ann
Types: 1st ed, fine bnd, hb, illus bk, juvenile, ltd ed, old & rare, out of print, papbk, remainders, used
Subj: Californiana, Southwestern Amer, Amer & British literary 1st editions

CASTRO VALLEY — 44,760. Area code 415

DON DISCHER BOOK SCOUT — Mail Order-Antiquarian
4830 Audrey Dr, 94546. Tel 415-537-5218
Estab 1973. 700 Vols. Cat 12x ann
Types: 1st ed, hb, out of print, used
Subj: Sci fiction & fantasy, mystery & detective

CHICO — 26,601. Area code 916

ASSOCIATED STUDENTS BOOKSTORE — College
California State Univ at Chico, 95929-0761. Tel 916-895-6044. Telex 37-7313
Mgr, Richard Blankenship; Buyer, Lou Bentley; Text Buyer, Bob Paolone
Estab 1942. 20,000 Vols. 3000 sq ft
Types: Hb, juvenile, out of print, papbk, remainders

MCLAUGHLIN'S BOOKS — General
929 W Eight Ave, 95926. Tel 916-891-0951
Estab 1946. 1000 Titles. 1500 Vols. Cat 2x ann
Types: Hb, old & rare, out of print
Subj: Alaskana, Arctic, Can, Western Amer, local hist, big game & hunting

CLAREMONT — 30,950. Area code 714

CHAPTER ONE BOOKS — Antiquarian
147 Yale Ave, 91711-4723. Tel 714-621-9972
Estab 1984. 25,000 Titles. Cat 2x ann
Types: Hb, papbk, used, 1st ed, incunab, illus bk, ltd ed, old & rare, out of print

COMPTON — 81,286. Area code 213

AVIATION BOOKMOBILE - MIL-AIR PHOTOS & BOOKS — Mail Order-Antiquarian
901 W Alondra Blvd Compton Airport, Hangars D-10, M-9, Q-5, 90220. Tel 213-632-8081
Estab 1960. 10,000 Vols Buys indep & through hq
Types: 1st ed, hb, imp, new & used, old & rare, out of print, papbk, remainders
Subj: Aviation, hunting & fishing, military, nature & environ, photog, radio, sci-tech, tv, Western Amer, guns, lighter-than-air flight tech

CONCORD — 103,251. Area code 415

BAY BOOKS — Used
1830 Salvio, 94520. Tel 415-671-2245
Estab 1988. 50,000 Titles. 50,000 Vols. 1800 sq ft
Types: 1st ed, hb, illus bk, juvenile, ltd ed, out of print, old & rare, remainders, papbk

BROOKS BOOKS — Mail Order
1343 New Hampshire Dr (Mail add: PO Box 21473, 94521-3804). Tel 415-672-4566
Estab 1986. 1500 Titles. 1750 Vols. Cat 3x ann
Types: Hb, out of print, remainders, used, new, Imp Australia, South Africa & Eng
Subj: Botany, hort, gardening

LIBERTY QUILL ARTS — Mail Order-Used
3636 Sanford St (Mail add: PO Box 272, 94522). Tel 415-685-2484
Estab 1983. 8000 Titles. 10,000 Vols
Types: Out of print, 1st ed, used

COSTA MESA — 82,291. Area code 714

APOLLO BOOK SHOP* — Antiquarian
545 W 18th St, 92627. Tel 714-646-7045
Estab 1961. 25,000 Vols
Types: Out of print, used
Subj: Alaskana, Arctic, humor, nautical, South Seas, Western Amer

VISIONS & DREAMS A METAPHYSICAL FIVE & DIME — Religious
1804 Newport Blvd, 92627. Tel 714-650-6929
Mgr & Merch Mgr, Linda Blair
Estab 1983. 1250 sq ft
Types: Hb, out of print, papbk, used, 1st ed, new, old & rare
Subj: Metaphysics, self-develop, astrol, philos, psychol, New Age, Holistic, spiritual, E & W Indian

COVINA — 33,751. Area code 818

PATHFINDER — Religious-Christian
1010 E Arrow Hwy, 91724. Tel 818-967-2893
Owner & Mgr, Ed Bowling
Types: Out of print, papbk, juvenile, used, remainders, hb, imp, col text, bibles
Subj: Music

CRESTLINE — 3509. Area code 714

GEORGE FREDERICK KOLBE FINE NUMISMATIC BOOKS — Antiquarian
PO Drawer 3100, 92325. Tel 714-338-6527
Estab 1967. 10,000 Titles. 25,000 Vols. 1100 sq ft. Cat 4x ann
Types: New, old & rare, out of print, Fr lang, Ger lang
Subj: Numismatics

CULVER CITY — 38,139. Area code 213

DENNIS B MARQUAND — Mail Order-Used
3536 Centinela (Mail add: P O Box 1187, 90232-1187). Tel 213-313-0177
Estab 1980. 200 Titles. 800 Vols. Cat 2x ann
Types: Ger lang, hb, imp Ger, imp Ital, out of print, remainders, used
Subj: Art, Oriental rugs & textiles

CYPRESS — 40,391. Area code 714

BLIND MOTH BOOKS & DRINKS — Mail Order
4822 Ashbury Ave (Mail add: PO Box 1531, 90630-1531). Tel 714-821-1527
Estab 1987. Cat 6x ann
Types: Hb, juvenile, papbk, out of print, Fr lang, Sp lang, imp UK

DALY CITY — 78,519. Area code 415

BEAVER BOOKS — Mail Order-Antiquarian
Box 974, 94017. Tel 415-584-1302
2500 Vols. Cat 1-2x ann
Types: Facsimile editions, 1st ed, hb, ltd ed, new & used, old & rare, out of print, imp Can & Eng
Subj: North Am fur trade & related exploration, Lewis & Clark, Hudson's Bay Co

DANVILLE — Area code 415

DANVILLE BOOKS — Antiquarian
176 S Hartz Ave, 94526. Tel 415-837-4200
Estab 1977. 8000 Titles. 8500 Vols. 350 sq ft. Cat
Types: Fine bnd, 1st ed, hb, illus bk, juvenile, ltd ed, old & rare, out of print, used
Subj: Belles lettres, Chinese-Am studies, Civil War, hist, Calif auth, Eugene O'Neill, Mark Twain, J Muir, Steinbeck

DAVIS — 36,640. Area code 916

BERRY'S USED BOOKS — General
620 G St, 95616. Tel 916-758-4576
Estab 1985. 20,000 Vols. 1000 sq ft
Types: For lang, hb, papbk, used, out of print

DEL MAR — 5017. Area code 619

AVIATION PUBLICATIONS SERVICE — Mail Order-Aviation
1327 Maiden Lane (Mail add: Box 400, 92014). Tel 619-755-1199. WATS 800-621-5640 (add 335627 after tone)
Owner, Aviation Designers & Consultants; Mgr, Rebecca A Dennis; Merch Mgr & Text Buyer, David C Weiss; Buyer, Sally Rice
Estab 1953. 9180 Titles. 15,200 Vols. 2700 sq ft. Cat 3x ann
Types: Col text, Fr, Ger & Sp lang, hb, out of print, high priced papbk, used, imp Fr, imp Ger, imp UK
Subj: Engineering, aviation, flight training, aviation maintenance, operation & management, aviation history

DOMINGUEZ — area code 213

PIC N SAVE — Remainder
2430 E Del Amo Blvd, 90220-6306. Tel 213-537-9220
Mgr, Mas Egawa; Buyer, Neil Johnsky
Types: Hb, papbk, mass mkt papbk, juvenile, out of print

DUTCH FLAT — Area code 916

TOWN & GOWN BOOK CO — Mail Order-Antiquarian
PO Box 190, 95714-0190. Tel 916-389-2363 (by appt)
Estab 1960. 100,000 Vols. Cat
Types: Old & rare, out of print, used
Subj: Soc sci, hist, law, women's studies

EL CAJON — 73,892. Area code 619

LINDA VISTA BAPTIST BIBLE COLLEGE & SEMINARY BOOKSTORE — College
2075 E Madison Ave, 92021. Tel 619-442-9841
Mgr, Dr Otto Reese
Estab 1946. 600 Vols
Types: For lang, hb, out of print, papbk
Subj: Hist, sociol, lang arts, theol, rel-c

THE VALLEY BOOKSTORE — General
120 W Main St, 92020. Tel 619-447-9068
Estab 1973. 20,000 Vols. 900 sq ft
Types: Hb, juvenile, out of print, papbk, used
Subj: Antq, sci fiction & fantasy, mystery & detective, comedy

EL CERRITO — 22,731. Area code 415

GRAEME VANDERSTOEL — Mail Order-Antiquarian
Box 599, 94530-0599. Tel 415-527-2882
Estab 1962. 4000 Vols. Cat 4x ann
Types: New, old & rare, out of print
Subj: Africa, art, Asian studies, Australia, Orientalia, Pacific, performing arts, jazz

EL GRANADA — Area code 501

MONTARA MOUNTAIN BOOKS — Mail Order-Search Service
PO Box 553, 94018. Tel 408-479-0280
Estab 1984
Types: Out of print

EL JARDIN — area code 805

KATIE BOOKS — General
461 E Main St, Suite C, 93001. Tel 805-653-5534
Mgr, J A Miller
Types: Juvenile, out of print
Subj: Sci fiction & fantasy

ELKGROVE — 17,327. Area code 916

P & P CHRISTIAN BOOKSTORE — Religious
9219 Camden Lake St, 165 Western Ave N, 95624. Tel 916-686-4498
Mgr, Robert Porter
Estab 1984
Types: Hb, papbk, juvenile, out of print

TEN O'CLOCK BOOKS — Mail Order
8786 Cling Ct, 95624-1837. Tel 916-685-8219
Estab 1973. Cat ann
Types: Out of print, Sp lang, Sp & Latin Am lit in translation
Subj: Humanities

ISABEL VOGT - BOOK SCOUT — Mail Order
8568 Diamond Oak Way, 95624. Tel 916-685-7802
Estab 1978. 4500 Vols
Types: Out of print, hb, used
Subj: Californiana, natural hist, political thought, Western Amer, fiction

EL SEGUNDO — 13,752. Area code 213

UPTON & SONS BOOKSELLERS & PUBLISHERS — Mail Order-Americana
917 Hillcrest St, 90245. Tel 213-322-7202 (by appt only)
Mgr, Frances Upton; Merch Mgr, Kip Upton
Estab 1975. 8000 Vols. Cat 4x ann
Types: Out of print, hb
Subj: Western Amer, Am Indian studies, military

ENCINITAS — 5375. Area code 619

RAIR LITERATURE — Antiquarian-Aviation
PO Box 2488, Leucadia, 92024-0960
Mgr, Burton Gerard
Estab 1960. 3500 Vols. Cat
Types: Hb, papbk, old & rare, out of print, used
Subj: Military

ENCINO — Area code 818

BOOKS & THE COLLECTOR ARTS — Mail Order-Antiquarian
PO Box 589, 91316. Tel 818-343-1946
Estab 1971. 5000 Vols. 1000 sq ft. Cat
Types: Facsimile editions, fine bnd, 1st ed, hb, imp, incunab, ltd ed, new & used, out of print, old & rare, remainders, fine press
Subj: Art, printing & bookmaking

THE WAVERLY SHOP — General
PO Box 437, 91316. Tel 818-784-8494
Estab 1964
Types: Col & el-hi text, hb, juvenile, out of print, papbk, remainders, imp Fr & Sp

ESCONDIDO — 62,480. Area code 619

AMERICAN FRAGMENTS — Antiquarian
1327 Alita Lane, 92027. Tel 619-747-8327
Estab 1976. 3000 Vols. 600 sq ft. Cat 2x ann
Types: Fine bnd, 1st ed, hb, illus bk, imp, juvenile, ltd ed, new & used, old & rare, out of print

BOOK NOOK — Used
845 S Escondido Blvd, 92025. Tel 619-746-9797
Estab 1960. 90,000 Vols
Types: Hb, out of print, papbk, juvenile
Subj: Metaphys & occult, class, turn of the century

HERITAGE BOOKS — General
410 C West Felicita Ave, 92025. Tel 619-746-6601
Mgr, Jennifer Nikuls
Estab 1966. 35,000 Vols. 2000 sq ft
Types: Col & el-hi text, hb, juvenile, out of print, remainders, for lang
Subj: Antq, art, cooking, rel

EUREKA — 24,153. Area code 707

EUREKA BOOKS — General
415 Fifth St, 95501. Tel 707-444-9593
Mgr, J B Bowden
Estab 1988. 75,000 Titles
Types: 1st ed, old & rare, out of print
Subj: Californiana

RARE BOOK CO — Mail Order
2035 Everding St, 95501. Tel 707-445-0507
Estab 1947. Cat weekly
Types: Used, out of print, papbk, hb, old & rare

ROSEBUD BOOKS & BOOKBINDINGS — General
1695 Myrtle Ave, PO Box 4862, 95501. Tel 707-445-8508
Estab 1970. 1000 sq ft
Types: Hb, juvenile, papbk, used, remainders, imp, out of print
Subj: Cooking, math, gardening

FAIRFAX — 7391. Area code 415

NEW ALBION BOOKSHOP — Used
1820 Sir Francis Drake Blvd, PO Box 521, 94930. Tel 415-456-1464
Mgr, William Bertram
Estab 1965. 20,000 Vols. 1500 sq ft
Types: Hb, juvenile, out of print, papbk
Subj: Drama, fiction, military, mystery & detective, soc sci, sci fiction & fantasy, Western Amer

FAIR OAKS — 11,256. Area code 916

BOOK ATTIC — General
10239 Fair Oaks Blvd, 95628. Tel 916-961-3703
Estab 1976. 20000 Titles. 20,000 Vols. 1200 sq ft
Types: Facsimile editions, fine bnd, 1st ed, hb, illus bk, juvenile, ltd ed, old & rare, out of print, used

FERNDALE — 1367. Area code 707

FERNDALE BOOKS — General
405 Main St, PO Box 1034, 95536-1034. Tel 707-786-9135
Estab 1980. 5000 Titles. 10,000 Vols. 3500 sq ft. Cat 4x ann
Types: 1st ed, old & rare, out of print, imp Latin Am
Subj: Californiana, Latin Am
See Also: Eureka Books, Eureka

FOLSOM — 11,003. Area code 916

PACIFIC WESTERN TRADERS — American Indian Studies
305 Wool St (Mail add: PO Box 95, 95630). Tel 916-985-3851
Mgr & Buyer, Herbert C Puffer
Estab 1971. 1500 Titles. 2500 Vols. 675 sq ft. Cat American Indians, 2x ann
Types: Hb, imp Can, juvenile, out of print, papbk, remainders, col & el-hi text
Subj: Art, hist, arts & crafts, music, anthrop, archery, lang arts, wildlife, food, hort

FORT BRAGG — 5019. Area code 707

FIDDLERS GREEN — General
140 E Laurel St, 95437. Tel 707-964-7168
Estab 1983. 30,000 Titles. 30,000 Vols. Cat
Types: Facsimile editions, imp, ltd ed, old & rare, used, for lang, hb, juvenile, out of print, papbk, mass mkt papbk
Subj: Military

FREMONT — 131,945. Area code 415

ROBERT MITCHELL - BOOKS — Mail Order
PO Box 3121, 94539. Tel 415-656-5418
Estab 1979. 2000 Vols. 400 sq ft. Cat
Types: Hb, out of print, used
Subj: Californiana, Western Amer

FRESNO — 218,202. Area code 209

AMERICAN BOOKSTORE — Antiquarian
608 E Olive, 93728. Tel 209-264-2648
Estab 1972. 35,000 Titles. 35,000 Vols. 1600 sq ft
Types: Out of print, old & rare, used
Subj: Amer, fiction, nonfiction, rel, sports, biog, natural hist, hist

BOOK STALL* — Used
931 N Blackstone Ave, 93701. Tel 209-266-1344
Estab 1970. 100,000 Vols. 2200 sq ft
Types: For lang, hb, juvenile, out of print, old & rare, papbk
Subj: Reference

MONROE BOOKS — Antiquarian-General
809 E Olive, 93728. Tel 209-441-1282
Mgr, Jack M Perz
35,000 Titles. 45,000 Vols. Cat ann
Types: 1st ed, hb, new & used, out of print, remainders, pamphlets
Subj: Archaeol, art, travel, Western Amer, Californiana, mystery & detective, William Saroyan, modern first eds, juvenile

R SORSKY BOOKSELLER — Mail Order
3845 N Blackstone, 93726. Tel 209-227-2901. WATS 800-345-4447
Estab 1977. 1000 Vols. 500 sq ft. Cat 5x ann
Types: Hb, out of print, remainders, used, imp Fr, imp India, imp Jap, imp UK
Subj: Blacksmithing, carving, timber, woodworking

STORY TIME CHILDREN'S USED BOOKS* — Used
1440 N Van Ness Ave, 93728. Tel 209-237-5481
Estab 1984. 5000 Vols
Types: For lang, hb, juvenile, out of print, mass mkt papbk, high priced papbk

VALLEY BOOK CENTER — General
1141 N Fulton, 93728. Tel 209-268-3788
Estab 1970. 100,000 Vols. 4500 sq ft
Types: Hb, papbk, out of print, new & used
Subj: Metaphys & occult
Branches:
— 838 E Olive, 93728
Types: Hb, out of print, papbk, new & used

FULLERTON — 102,034. Area code 714

ALADDIN BOOKS — Antiquarian
122 W Commonwealth Ave, PO Box 152, 92632. Tel 714-738-6115
Estab 1982. 20,000 Titles. 20,000 Vols. 1300 sq ft
Types: Hb, new, out of print, papbk
Subj: Mod lit, mystery & detective, sci fiction & fantasy, performing arts, films & filmmaking

BOOK CELLAR — Antiquarian
124 Orangefair Mall, 92632. Tel 714-879-9420. CABLE: "RAREBOOKS"
Mgr, Steve Askins
Estab 1975. 100,000 Titles. 126,000 Vols. 3100 sq ft. Cat 2x ann
Types: Bibles, facsimile editions, fine bnd, 1st ed, hb, illus bk, ltd ed, old & rare, out of print, used, papbk, manuscripts, influential, scholarly
Subj: Archit, art, biog, bks on bks, literary criticism, philos, photog, utopias, cooking, wines, discovery & explor, hist of ideas, alt life styles, Amer, belles lettres, Henry Miller, curiosa, iconoclastic works, lit, erotica, Yosemite, heritage Pres, Franklin Library, women

THE BOOK HARBOR — Antiquarian
201 N Harbor Blvd, 92632. Tel 714-738-1941
Estab 1978. 65,000 Vols. 3000 sq ft
Types: Facsimile editions, fine bnd, 1st ed, hb, illus bk, imp, juvenile, ltd ed, new & used, old & rare, out of print, papbk, remainders
Subj: Art, cooking, fiction, metaphys & occult, philos, photog, transp, Eastern philos, military, literature in translation

RALSTON POPULAR FICTION — Mail Order-Antiquarian
PO Box 4174, 92634. Tel 714-990-0432
Estab 1976. 7500 Vols. Cat 3x ann
Types: 1st ed, hb, imp, juvenile, old & rare, out of print, used
Subj: Drama, fiction, mystery & detective, poetry, sci fiction & fantasy, westerns

GARBERVILLE — 8265. Area code 707

BRANNAN BOOKS — Antiquarian-Art
879 Sunnybank Lane, PO Box 475, 95440. Tel 707-923-3552 (by appt only)
Estab 1980. 9000 Vols. Cat 10x ann
Types: Out of print, old & rare

GARDENA — 45,165. Area code 213

SECONDHAND PROSE — Used
16010 Crenshaw Blvd, 90249. Tel 213-538-3194
Estab 1979. 25,000 Titles. 1800 sq ft
Types: For lang, hb, imp, juvenile, out of print, papbk, remainders, 1st ed, illus bk, ltd ed
Subj: Hist, biog, how-to, art, psychol, poetry, philos, rel, class lit, natural sci

GEORGETOWN — Area code 916

TALISMAN PRESS, BOOKSELLERS & PUBLISHERS* — Mail Order-Antiquarian
Box 455, 95634. Tel 916-333-4486
Estab 1954. 12,000 Vols. Cat 5x ann
Types: 1st ed, hb, new & used, out of print, old & rare, remainders
Subj: Amer, bibliog, reference, photographica

GLENDALE — 139,060. Area code 818

ARTHUR H CLARK CO — Antiquarian
PO Box 230, 91209. Tel 818-241-2858
Mgr, Cecila L Clark; Buyer, Robert A Clark
Estab 1902. 15,000 Titles. 50,000 Vols. 2500 sq ft. Cat 5x ann
Types: 1st ed, hb, new & used, out of print, old & rare,

O.P. Resources

fine print
Subj: Amer, Western Amer

MYSTERY & IMAGINATION BOOKSHOP — Mail Order-Antiquarian
515 1/2 E Broadway (Mail add: PO Box 75686, Los Angeles, 90005). Tel 213-389-4768 (by appt only)
Mgr, Christine Francis
Estab 1978. 25,000 Vols. Cat 2x ann
Types: Imp UK, 1st ed, old & rare, out of print, fine bks
Subj: Fiction, poetry, mystery & detective, sci fiction & fantasy, Amer & Eng lit, plays a theatre

XANADU GALLERIES CO — Antiquarian
4527 San Fernando Rd, 91204-1933. Tel 818-244-0828
Estab 1950. 10,000 Vols. Cat
Types: 1st ed, hb, imp, new & used, out of print, old & rare, remainders
Subj: Civil War, drama, hist, natural hist, Western Amer, 19th & 20th Century Am art

GLENDORA — 38,654. Area code 818

WAYNE G KOSTMAN BOOKS — Mail Order-Antiquarian
Box 393, 91740. Tel 818-963-1755
Estab 1975. 4000 Titles. 5000 Vols. 1000 sq ft. Cat
Types: Hb, old & rare, out of print, travel guides
Subj: Travel, ref & facsimiles on mss illumination, color imprints, Murray & Baedeker guides

GLEN ELLEN — Area code 707

JACK LONDON BOOKSTORE — Antiquarian
14300 Arnold Dr (Mail add: PO Box 337, 95442). Tel 707-996-2888
Estab 1971. 12,000 Vols. 4000 sq ft
Types: Fine bnd, 1st ed, hb, illus bk, juvenile, ltd ed, new, old & rare, out of print, remainders, used
Subj: Alaskana, Californiana, Hawaiiana, Western Amer, Jack London

GRASS VALLEY — 6697. Area code 916

AMES BOOKSTORE — Used
309 Neal St, 95949. Tel 916-273-9261
Estab 1968. 150,000 Titles. 200,000 Vols. 2882 sq ft. Cat
Types: Papbk, out of print, old & rare, hb, juvenile
Subj: Art, biog, drama, sci fiction & fantasy, cooking, health & phys educ, mystery & detective, nature & environ, sci-tech, aviation, World War I & II, animals

THREE R'S BOOKSTORE — Used
302-A W Main St, 95945. Tel 916-273-9874, 273-4648
Estab 1962. 75,000 Vols. 5600 sq ft
Types: Hb, out of print, papbk
Subj: Fiction, natural hist, Western Amer, art

HAWTHORNE — 56,447. Area code 213

SOUTH BAY TECHNICAL BOOKS — Education
13887 S Hawthorne Blvd, 90250. Tel 213-973-6495
Types: Hb, out of print, papbk

HAYWARD — 94,167. Area code 415

THE BOOKSHOP — General
982 B St, 94541. Tel 415-538-3943
Estab 1961. 2500 Titles. 10,000 Vols. 1500 sq ft. Cat ann
Types: Hb, out of print, papbk, remainders, juvenile, new & used
Subj: Medicine, self-develop, class studies

MOUNT EDEN BOOKS & BINDERY — Mail Order-Antiquarian
2315 Bermuda Lane (Mail add: PO Box 421, Mount Eden, 94557-0421). Tel 415-782-7723
Estab 1980. 3500 Vols. Cat 2x ann
Types: Old & rare, out of print, used
Subj: Anthrop, geol, mining, geography, paleontology

HERMOSA BEACH — 18,070. Area code 213

THE SILVER DOOR — Antiquarian-Mystery & Detective
1546 Silver St (Mail add: PO Box 3208, Redondo Beach, 90277). Tel 213-379-6005
Estab 1980. 12,000 Vols. 2000 sq ft. Cat 3x ann
Types: 1st ed, hb, illus bk, imp, old & rare, out of print, papbk, used
Subj: Fiction, nonfiction

HOLLYWOOD — Area code 213

CINEMA COLLECTORS POSTERS, PHOTOS & BOOKS — Antiquarian-Films & Filmmaking
1507 N Wilcox Ave (Mail add: 7057 Lexington Ave, Suite 103, Los Angeles, 90038). Tel 213-461-6516
Mgr, T J Wong; Merch Mgr, Carlos Batres
Estab 1984. 2000 Vols. 1350 sq ft
Types: Hb, papbk, remainders, new & used, 1st ed, illus bk, old & rare, out of print
Subj: Biog, hist, photoplay editions

LARRY EDMUNDS CINEMA & THEATRE BOOKSHOPINC — Performing Arts
6658 Hollywood Blvd, 90028. Tel 213-463-3273
Estab 1948. 40,000 Vols. Cat
Types: Hb, old & rare, out of print, papbk, remainders, new
Subj: Motion pictures, theatre & television
See Also: Studio City

SUN DANCE BOOKS — Antiquarian
1520 N Crescent Heights, 90046. Tel 213-654-2383
Estab 1967. 3000 Titles. 6000 Vols
Types: Hb, out of print, old & rare, used
Subj: Southwestern Amer, utopias, gambling, Pacific Ocean voyages, imaginary voyages, foreign sci fict, cryptography

HUNTINGTON BEACH — 170,505. Area code 714

DONALD J WEINSTOCK BOOKS — Mail Order-Antiquarian
Box 2051, 92647-0051. Tel 714-848-1128
Estab 1971. 20,000 Titles. 25,000 Vols. 1000 sq ft. Cat
Types: Out of print, used
Subj: Fiction, hist, literary criticism, philos, rel studies, soc sci

JOSHUA TREE — Area code 619

NEW AGE WORLD SERVICES & BOOKS — Mail Order-Metaphys & Occult
62091 Valley View Circle, 92252-2548. Tel 619-366-2833
Estab 1957. 12,000 Vols. Cat ann
Types: Hb, imp, new & used, old & rare, out of print, papbk
Subj: Metaphysics, mysticism, astrol, hypnosis, yoga, UFOs, health, new age related, lost continents

KENSINGTON — 4823. Area code 415

WILLIAM RILEY - BOOKS* — Antiquarian
86 Arlington, 94707. Tel 415-526-2300
Estab 1972. 7000 Titles. 8500 Vols. Cat 4x ann
Types: 1st ed, ltd ed, out of print, remainders
Subj: Fiction, poetry, 20th century lit

LAFAYETTE — 20,879. Area code 415

CAROL DOCHEFF BOOKSELLER — Antiquarian
1390 Reliez Valley Rd, 94549. Tel 415-935-9595
Estab 1979. 12,500 Titles. 15,000 Vols. 2000 sq ft. Cat monthly
Types: 1st ed, illus bk, juvenile, out of print, young adult
Subj: Folklore, sci fiction & fantasy, black studies, Newberry & Caldecott authors, animal titles, xmas titles, bks about juv bks, fairy tales, award bks

DOWAGER BOOKS — Mail Order-Used
PO Box 1836, 94549. Tel 415-283-0201
Cat 6x ann
Types: Hb, out of print, old & rare
Subj: Maritime

FRANK MIKESH SPORTING BOOKS & ART — Mail Order-Antiquarian
3694 Sundale Rd, 94549. Tel 415-283-1895
Estab 1973. 500 Titles. 500 Vols. Cat 6x ann
Types: Hb, high priced papbk, used, out of print, fine bnd, 1st ed, ltd ed, old & rare
Subj: Hunting & fishing, natural hist, outdoor adventure, sporting & wildlife art

LAGUNA BEACH — 17,860. Area code 714

JEANNE KUWALSKY BOOKS — Mail Order-Antiquarian
518 Flora St, 92651. Tel 714-494-8927
Estab 1972. 9000 Titles. 9050 Vols
Types: Hb, 1st ed, illus bk, old & rare, out of print, signed mat & press bks

LA JOLLA — Area code 619

LAURENCE MCGILVERY — Antiquarian-Art
PO Box 852, 92038-0852. Tel 619-454-4443
Estab 1960. 105,000 Vols. Cat
Types: Old & rare, out of print

D G WILLS BOOKS — Used
7527 La Jolla Blvd, 92037. Tel 619-456-1800
Estab 1979. 20,000 Vols. 1000 sq ft
Types: For lang, hb, out of print, remainders, papbk
Subj: Military, philos, sci-tech

LA PALMA — 151,663. Area code 714

NORMAN A GONSALVES — Hawaiiana
5600 Orangethorpe, No 301, 90623. Tel 714-522-8692
Cat ann
Types: Fine bnd, 1st ed, hb, audio visual mat, imp, juvenile, ltd ed, old & rare, out of print, used

LEMON GROVE — 20,780. Area code 714

LEMON GROVE BOOKSTORE — Antiquarian
7904-7908 Broadway, 92045. Tel 619-463-2503
Estab 1980. 60,000 Vols. 1600 sq ft
Types: Hb, out of print, papbk, remainders, used

LODI — 35,221. Area code 209

THE BOOK LADY — Used
440 E Kettleman Lane, 95240. Tel 209-368-8018
Types: Out of print, papbk

LOMPOC — 26,267. Area code 805

E LOUIS HINRICHS BOOKS — General
313 A North K St (Mail add: PO Box 1090, 93438). Tel 805-735-4761
Types: Hb, imp, juvenile, out of print, high priced papbk, remainders, text bks, new & used, facsimile editions, fine bnd, 1st ed, illus bk, ltd ed, old & rare, Ger, Sp & Russ lang
Branches:
— PO Box 1090, 93438-1090. Tel 805-735-4761
Estab 1967. 5000 Titles. Cat
Types: Ger lang, Sp lang, Russ lang, juvenile, out of print, high priced papbk, remainders, col text, used, new, facsimile editions, 1st ed, fine bnd, hb, illus bk, imp, ltd ed, old & rare
Subj: Astron, physics, computer sci, hist, sci-tech
See Also: wholesale section

MERLIN'S BOOKSHOP — Antiquarian
PO Box 1747, 93438. Tel 805-736-2234
Estab 1975. 4500 Titles. 5000 Vols. 350 sq ft. Cat 6x ann
Types: 1st ed, hb, papbk, ltd ed, old & rare, out of print, used, signed ed
Subj: Sci fiction & fantasy, physics, higher math, recreational math, hist & phil of sci

LONG BEACH — 361,334. Area code 213

ACRES OF BOOKS INC — Used
240 Long Beach Blvd, 90802. Tel 213-437-6980
Mgr, Jacqueline Smith
Estab 1933. 1,000,000 Vols. 13,000 sq ft
Types: Hb, out of print, papbk, remainders

ASSOCIATED BOOK SERVICE — Antiquarian-Western Americana
910 E Artesia Blvd (Mail add: PO Box 7764, 90807). Tel 213-422-0059
Estab 1972. 1000 sq ft. Cat 4x ann
Types: Used, 1st ed, hb, ltd ed, old & rare, out of print
Subj: Bks on bks

BARGAIN BOOKSHOP — Used
3325 South St, 90805. Tel 213-531-6909
Estab 1967. 30,000 Titles
Types: Hb, juvenile, out of print, papbk
Subj: World Wars I & II, biblical studies, Amer, metaphys & occult, biog, antq, auto, movies, cookbks

THE BEAUTIFUL & THE UNUSUAL — Antiquarian
PO Box 15676, 90815. Tel 213-421-1382
Estab 1977
Types: 1st ed, hb, illus bk, juvenile, new, old & rare, out of print, used, old primers
Subj: Cooking, medicine, warfare, occult

THE BOOK STOP — General
4420 E Village Rd, 90808. Tel 213-445-8661
Estab 1987. 15,000 Titles. 15,000 Vols. 1400 sq ft
Types: Juvenile, out of print, mass mkt papbk, text bks, used

EYE OF THE CAT — Mail Order-Used
3314 E Broadway, 90803. Tel 213-438-3569, 433-6049. 636-9058
Estab 1974. 1000 Titles. 12,000 Vols. 1200 sq ft. Cat ann
Types: Out of print, papbk, hb, illus bk, ltd ed, new, old & rare
Subj: Metaphys & occult, astrol, nature & environ, mythology

LONG BEACH MUSEUM OF ART BOOKSHOP & GALLERY — Museum
2300 E Ocean Blvd, 90803. Tel 213-439-2119
Mgr, James Nelson
Estab 1970. 3000 Vols. 80 sq ft
Types: Hb, juvenile, high priced papbk, out of print, remainders, master prints & drawings
Subj: Art

LOS ALAMITOS — 11,529. Area code 213

GEORGE S DEEDS BOOK SEARCHER — Mail Order-Antiquarian
11312 Reagan St, 90720. Tel 213-430-2310
Estab 1970. 2000 Titles
Types: Used, fine bnd, 1st ed, hb, incunab, illus bk, imp, juvenile, ltd ed, new, old & rare, out of print
Subj: Civil War, Amer, 20th century illustrators

LOS ALTOS — 25,769. Area code 415

THE BOOK NEST — Antiquarian
366 Second St, 94022. Tel 415-948-4724
Estab 1978. 10,000 Vols. 1200 sq ft
Types: Fine bnd, 1st ed, hb, juvenile, ltd ed, old & rare, out of print, used
Subj: John Steinbeck

LOS ALTOS HILLS — 7421. Area code 415

FIRST STREET BOOKS & ANTIQUES — Mail Order-Used
14510 Manuela Rd, 94022. Tel 415-948-8903
Estab 1981. 1500 Titles. 2000 Vols
Types: Hb, juvenile, out of print, fine bnd, 1st ed, illus bk, ltd ed, high priced papbk, old & rare, modern 1st
Subj: Illus

LOS ANGELES — 2,966,763. Area code 213

ABBEY BOOKSHOP — Mail Order-Antiquarian
Box 64384, 90064. Tel 213-470-2296
Estab 1937. 10,000 Vols. Cat 6x ann
Types: Hb, old & rare, out of print, used
Subj: Hist, econ, Amer, Mex, Latin Am, travel, Asian studies, Africa, hunting & fishing, discovery & explor, military, Palestine

ART CATALOGUES — Art
625 N Almont Dr, 90069. Tel 213-274-0160
Estab 1977. 4000 Titles. 5000 Vols. 1000 sq ft. Cat 3x ann
Types: For lang, imp, out of print, papbk, 20th century art cat
Subj: Fine arts, graphic arts, photog

ATENEO BOOKSELLERS — Spanish Lang
745 Crane Blvd, 90065-4038. Tel 213-227-1794
Mgr, Philip Gillette
Estab 1984. 6000 Titles. 6000 Vols. Cat bimonthly
Types: Hb, juvenile, out of print, papbk, used, imp Latin Am
Subj: Port lang

AUDUBON SOCIETY OF LOS ANGELES BOOKSTORE — Nature & Environment
7377 Santa Monica Blvd, 90046. Tel 213-876-0202
Mgr, Olga Clarke
Estab 1919. 300 sq ft. Cat 2x ann
Types: Hb, juvenile, out of print, papbk
Subj: Ornith, natural hist

BAROQUE BOOKSTORE — Used
1643 N Las Palmas Ave, 90028. Tel 213-466-1880
Estab 1972. 6000 Vols
Types: 1st ed, out of print
Subj: Eng hist & lit, poetry

IRWIN BELSKY — Mail Order-Antiquarian
Box 48585, 90048. Tel 619-946-0367
Estab 1970. 4000 Titles. 5000 Vols. Cat
Types: Facsimile editions, 1st ed, hb, old & rare, out of print, used
Subj: Humanities, ancient hist & lit, archaeol, metaphys & occult, psychol, anthrop, philos, sci-tech, early rel

DAVID BERMAN BOOKS — Mail Order-Antiquarian
PO Box 64574, 90064. Tel 213-470-2296
20,000 Titles. Cat 4x ann
Types: Hb, out of print, mass mkt papbk only
Subj: Hist, military, art, Asian studies, Africa, arms & armor, Pacific, sports, natural hist, golf, archery, big game hunting

CARAVAN BOOKSTORE — Antiquarian
550 S Grand Ave, 90071. Tel 213-626-9944
Mgr, Leonard Bernstein
Estab 1954. 45,000 Vols. 1700 sq ft
Types: 1st ed, hb, imp, incunab, new & used, old & rare, out of print
Subj: Art, discovery & explor, nautical, railroadiana, Western Amer, cooking

CHAPMAN & BERRYMAN BOOKSELLERS — Mail Order-Antiquarian
2377 Teviot St, 90039. Tel 213-667-2430
Estab 1977. 3000 Vols. Cat 6x ann
Types: Hb, old & rare, out of print, used
Subj: Hawaiiana, health, bodybuilding

GRAYSON D COOK BOOKSELLER — Mail Order
367 W Ave 42, 90065. Tel 213-227-8899
Estab 1971. 6000 Titles. 6000 Vols. 250 sq ft
Types: Hb, illus bk, used, out of print, 1st ed
Subj: Sci fiction & fantasy, Western Amer, mystery & detective, illus, cinema

COSMOPOLITAN BOOKSHOP — Used
7007 Melrose Ave, 90038. Tel 213-938-7119
Estab 1958. 500,000 Vols
Types: 1st ed, hb, out of print, papbk
Subj: Films & filmmaking, psychol

COUNTERPOINT BOOKS & RECORDS — Used
5911 Franklin Ave, 90028. Tel 213-469-4465
Estab 1979. 20,000 Vols. 1200 sq ft
Types: Hb, used, out of print, papbk
Subj: Sci fiction & fantasy, metaphys & occult, performing arts, lang arts, biog, cooking, poetry, rel studies, philos, art, music, sci-tech, hist

DAWSON'S BOOKSHOP — Antiquarian
535 N Larchmont Blvd, 90004. Tel 213-469-2186
Mgr, Michael Dawson
Estab 1905. 25,000 Vols. 3233 sq ft. Cat 6x ann
Types: 1st ed, new, old & rare, out of print, ltd ed, miniature
Subj: Hist, Western Amer, photog, hist of bks & printing, moutaineering

GENE DECHENE - BOOKSELLERS — General
11556 Santa Monica Blvd, 90025. Tel 213-477-8734
Mgr, Diana Dechene
Estab 1968. 40,000 Vols. 950 sq ft
Types: Hb, out of print, papbk, used
Subj: Psychiat, psychol, sexuality

A DIFFERENT LIGHT — Homosexuality
4014 Santa Monica Blvd, 90029. Tel 213-668-0629
Owner, Androgyny Books, Inc; Mgr, Jim Morrow
Estab 1979. 6000 Titles. 8000 Vols. 1300 sq ft. Cat 7x ann
Types: Col & el-hi text, Ger lang, hb, imp Australia, juvenile, out of print, papbk, remainders, Can, Eng & Neth
Subj: Gay & lesbian lit

KAREN ENDE BOOKS — Mystery & Detective
1112 Alvira St, 90035. Tel 213-934-4269
Cat 2x ann
Types: 1st ed, old & rare, out of print, hb, used
Subj: Mystery & detective

FRONTIER PIONEER BOOKS — Mail Order-Search Service
6014 Burwood Ave, 90042-1206. Tel 213-256-2321
Estab 1979. 4000 Vols. Cat 2x ann
Types: 1st ed, hb, juvenile, old & rare, out of print, papbk, used
Subj: Alaskana, camping & hiking, hunting & fishing, auto, Can

GEORGES GENERAL STORES — General
4806 Fountain Ave, 90029. Tel 213-660-7381
Mgr, Richard C Rivera
Estab 1980. 200 Titles. 800 Vols. 300 sq ft
Types: Out of print
Subj: Reference, sci fiction & fantasy

GOLDEN LEGEND INC — Antiquarian
7615 Sunset Blvd, 90046. Tel 213-850-5520
Estab 1981. 2000 Titles. 2000 Vols. 900 sq ft. Cat 6x ann
Types: Out of print, illus bk, old & rare
Subj: Performing arts

HOLLYWOOD BOOK CITY — General
6625-31 Hollywood Blvd, Hollywood, 90028. Tel 213-466-2525, 466-1049
200,000 Titles. 500,000 Vols. 10,000 sq ft
Types: Facsimile editions, fine bnd, 1st ed, hb, imp, illus bk, juvenile, ltd ed, old & rare, out of print, new & used
Subj: Art, aviation, biog, films & filmmaking, metaphys & occult, photog, World Wars I & II
See Also: Book City of Burbank, Burbank

GEORGE HOULE - RARE BOOKS & AUTOGRAPHS — Antiquarian
7260 Beverly Blvd, 90036-2537. Tel 213-937-5858, 937-5859
Estab 1976. 15,000 Vols. Cat 8x ann
Types: 1st ed, facsimile editions, fine bnd, hb, illus bk, imp, ltd ed, old & rare, out of print, remainders, used
Subj: Antq, art

HYMAN & SONS RARE BOOKS — Antiquarian-Egyptology
2341 Westwood Blvd, Suite No 2-3, 90064-2118. Tel 213-474-8023
Dirs, V Lee Blackburn & Paul S Hyman
Estab 1978. 20,000 Titles. 20,000 Vols. 3000 sq ft. Cat
Types: Facsimile editions, fine bnd, 1st ed, for lang, hb, incunab, illus bk, imp, old & rare, out of print
Subj: Middle East, archaeol, for lang, Arab studies, Hieroglyphics, Babylonian, Assyrian & Coptic lang, Sumerian, Egyptology in Ger, Fr, Swed & Ital langs

INVESTMENT CENTRE BOOKSTORE — Investing
2124 Sepulveda Blvd, 90025. Tel 213-478-5263
Estab 1977. 5000 Titles. 25,000 Vols. 2500 sq ft. Cat 4x ann
Types: Hb, used, new, old & rare, out of print
Subj: Wall st, stock market, commodity trading

ELLIOT M KATT BOOKSELLER — Performing Arts
8568 Melrose Ave (Mail add: PO Box 1455, Studio City, 91604). Tel 213-652-5178
Estab 1983. 15,000 Titles. 20,000 Vols. 800 sq ft. Cat 8x ann
Types: 1st ed, hb, illus bk, ltd ed, old & rare, out of print, new & used
Subj: Drama, music, opera, circus, ballet, acting, cinema, nostalgia

JAY KIEFFER BOOKS — Mail Order-Antiquarian
430 S Burnside, Apt 12L, 90036. Tel 213-938-4627
Estab 1940. 10,000 Vols
Types: Hb, out of print, old & rare

ALFRED KRONFELD BOOKSELLER — Mail Order-Antiquarian
1621 Golden Gate Ave, 90026. Tel 213-661-3658
Estab 1980. 20,000 Vols
Types: 1st ed, hb, juvenile, ltd ed, old & rare, out of print
Subj: Soc sci, Amer, Western Amer, Californiana, films & filmmaking, fiction, drama

MESSRS BERKELOUW INC — Antiquarian
830 N Highland Ave, 90038. Tel 213-466-3321
Dir, Isidoor Berkelouw
Estab 1985. 100,000 Titles. 100,000 Vols. Cat 12x ann
Types: Used, out of print, fine bnd, out of print
Subj: Africa, Australia, South Seas, Antarctic

METROPOLIS BOOKS — Architecture
634A N Robertson Blvd, 90069. Tel 213-659-5436
Estab 1987. 4500 Titles
Types: 1st ed, out of print, first printings
Subj: Art, archit, design, contemporary lit

NEEDHAM BOOK FINDERS — Antiquarian
PO Box 491040, 90049. Tel 213-410-0035
Estab 1954. 5000 Vols. Cat
Types: Out of print, used
Subj: Judaica, cooking

PETTLER & LIEBERMAN BOOKSELLERS — Antiquarian
2345 Westwood Blvd, No 3, 90064-2427. Tel 213-474-2479
Estab 1978. 8000 Vols. 800 sq ft. Cat 3-5x ann
Types: 1st ed, hb, imp, ltd ed, old & rare, out of print, papbk, used
Subj: Poetry, drama, fiction, films & filmmaking, humor, mystery & detective

PEARL ELLIS ROSE BOOKSELLER — Mail Order
337 N Kilkea Dr, 90048. Tel 213-655-0032
Estab 1937. 6000 Titles. 6000 Vols
Types: Used, juvenile, hb, out of print, fine bnd, 1st ed, illus bk, ltd ed, old & rare
Subj: Amer, Californiana, Civil War

J ROTH BOOKSELLER, INC — Religious-J
9427 W Pico Blvd, 90035-1288. Tel 213-557-1848
Mgr, Laurie Cohen
Estab 1942. 2500 Titles. 20,000 Vols. 3000 sq ft. Cat ann
Types: Imp UK, imp Isr, juvenile, out of print, papbk, remainders, hb
Subj: Judaica

SAM: JOHNSON'S BOOKSHOP — Scholarly Lit
12310 Venice Blvd, 90066. Tel 213-391-5047
Estab 1977. 25,000 Titles. 25,000 Vols. 1400 sq ft
Types: Out of print, used
Subj: Belles lettres, sci fiction & fantasy, mystery & detective, G K Chesterton, Dr Johnson

THE SCHOLARLY BOOKFINDERS — Mail Order-Antiquarian
415 W Ave 42, 90065. Tel 213-223-8257
Estab 1981. Cat 2x ann
Types: Fine bnd, old & rare, out of print, used
Subj: Travel, mod foreign fict

SYLVESTER & ORPHANOS — Mail Order-Antiquarian
2484 Cheremoya Ave (Mail add: Box 2567, 90078-2567). Tel 213-461-1194
Estab 1973. 30,000 Vols. 770 sq ft. Cat 4x ann
Types: Hb, 1st ed, ltd ed, old & rare, out of print
Subj: Contemporary literature

THIRD WORLD ETHNIC BOOKS — Antiquarian
3617 Montclair St (Mail add: PO Box 38237, 90038). Tel 213-737-3292
Estab 1972. 25,000 Titles. 12,000 Vols
Types: New & used, out of print, old & rare
Subj: Black studies, Mex, Asian Am, Black cinema

MICHAEL R THOMPSON RARE BOOKS — Antiquarian-Philosophy
1001 North Fairfax, 90046. Tel 213-650-4887
Estab 1972. 20,000 Vols. 11,000 sq ft. Cat
Types: New & used, hb, papbk, for lang, 1st ed, old & rare, out of print, used
Subj: Hist, soc sci, sci-tech, art, Western philos, lit

TOLLIVER'S BOOKS — Antiquarian-Natural History
1634 Stearns Dr, 90035-4516. Tel 213-939-6054
Buyer, Rachel Tolliver
Estab 1969. 12,000 Vols. 5000 sq ft. Cat 6x ann
Types: 1st ed, hb, new & used, out of print, papbk, old & rare, remainders, for lang
Subj: Anthrop, archaeol, biol, geol, ichthyol, math, natural hist, oceanog, ornith, physics, Mex, elec engineering, mesoamer, Baja Calif

VAGABOND BOOKS — Antiquarian
2076 Westwood Blvd, 90025. Tel 213-475-2700
Estab 1978. 100,000 Vols. 1000 sq ft. Cat monthly
Types: 1st ed, fine bnd, hb, illus bk, juvenile, ltd ed, old & rare, out of print, new & used
Subj: Art, mystery & detective, fiction, hist, cinema, hist

WALL STREET BOOKS — Mail Order-Antiquarian
PO Box 24A06, 90024. Tel 213-476-6732
Estab 1983. 1500 Titles. 5000 Vols. Cat 2x ann
Types: Old & rare, out of print
Subj: Stock market, commodities market, hist of Wall Street

WEST LOS ANGELES BOOK CENTER — Antiquarian
1650 Sawtelle Blvd, 90025. Tel 213-473-4442
Estab 1959. 50,000 Vols. 1000 sq ft
Types: Facsimile editions, fine bnd, 1st ed, hb, illus bk, juvenile, ltd ed, old & rare, out of print, papbk, remainders, used
Subj: Art, drama, Eng hist & lit, Eur studies, films & filmmaking, humor, mystery & detective, poetry, sci fiction & fantasy

LOS GATOS — 26,593. Area code 408

CURIOUS BOOK SHOPPE — Antiquarian
198 W Main St, 95030. Tel 408-354-5560
Estab 1973. 70,000 Vols
Types: Fine bnd, 1st ed, hb, illus bk, juvenile, ltd ed, out of print, remainders, used

LOS OSOS — 10,726. Area code 805

VOICES MILITARY BOOKS — Military
2149 Tenth St (Mail add: PO Box 6397, 93402). Tel 805-528-1614
Estab 1980. 4000 Titles. Cat
Types: Hb, used, out of print
Subj: Nonfiction, World War II, mil manuals

MALIBU — Area code 213

PEPPERDINE UNIVERSITY -MALIBU BOOKSTORE — College
Malibu Campus, 24255 Pacific Coast Hwy, 90265. Tel 213-456-4291
Mgr, Masood Mahmood
Estab 1983. 25,000 Vols
Types: Hb, out of print, papbk, remainders

MANHATTAN BEACH — 31,542. Area code 213

G F HOLLINGSWORTH BOOKS — Mail Order-Antiquarian
PO Box 3725, 90266. Tel 213-374-1641
Estab 1953. 5000 Titles. 30,000 Vols. Cat 8x ann
Types: 1st ed, facsimile editions, out of print, old & rare, remainders, used
Subj: Western Amer

MENDOCINO — 9979. Area code 707

R L SHEP — Mail Order-Antiquarian
Box 668, 95460. Tel 707-937-1436
Estab 1963. 1000 Vols. Cat 2x ann
Types: Hb, illus bk, imp, old & rare, out of print, used
Subj: Costuming, fashion, textiles, weaving, needlecrafts, sewing

MENLO PARK — 25,673. Area code 415

EAST WEST BOOKSHOP — Metaphysics
1170 El Camino Real, 94025-4358. Tel 415-325-5709
Owner, Fellowship of Inner Communion; Mgr & Juv Buyer, Jacqueline Snitkin; Merch Mgr & Buyer, Norman Snitkin
Estab 1965. 17,000 Titles. 24,000 Vols. 1600 sq ft. Cat ann
Types: Hb, imp, used, juvenile, out of print, mass mkt papbk, high priced papbk
Subj: Astrol, psychol, yoga, rel, consciousness expansion, healing

WESSEX BOOKS & RECORDS — Used
558 Santa Cruz Ave, 94025. Tel 415-321-1333
Estab 1975. 70,000 Vols. 2000 sq ft. Cat
Types: 1st ed, hb, imp, ltd ed, out of print, remainders, univ presses
Subj: Fiction, hist, philos, music, scholarly lit

MILL VALLEY — 12,967. Area code 415

ETHNOGRAPHIC ARTS PUBLICATIONS — Mail Order
1040 Erica Rd, 94941. Tel 415-383-2998, 332-1646
Estab 1978. 12,000 Titles. 125,000 Vols. Cat 3x ann
Types: 1st ed, for lang, hb, high priced papbk, ltd ed, out of print, old & rare, used, facsimile editions, imp
Subj: Anthrop, Africa, Am Indian studies, primitive, tribal & ethnographic art, pre-Columbian, Latin Am, Southeast Asian, Oceanic

MILPITAS — 37,820. Area code 408

RIK THOMPSON BOOKS — Mail Order-Antiquarian
PO Box 361420, 95035. Tel 408-946-0698
Estab 1972. 3500 Titles. 5000 Vols. Cat 1-4x ann
Types: 1st ed, hb, juvenile, ltd ed, new, old & rare, out of print, papbk, remainders, used
Subj: Mystery & detective, nonfiction, sci fiction & fantasy

MODESTO — 106,105. Area code 209

GEORGE TAYLOR BOOKSELLER — Used
305 Poplar Ave, 95354. Tel 209-521-2596
Estab 1984. 5000 Titles. 5000 Vols. 400 sq ft. Cat 2x ann
Types: Hb, juvenile, out of print, 1st ed, new, old & rare, remainders
Subj: Scotland, Scottish authors

YESTERDAY'S BOOKS — Used
Western Plaza, 2717 Coffee Rd, Suite E, 95355-1750. Tel 209-521-9623
Estab 1980. 70,000 Vols
Types: Hb, papbk, juvenile, out of print
Subj: Protestant theology

MONTCLAIR — 22,628. Area code 714

THIS OLD HOUSE BOOKSHOP — General
5399 W Holt Blvd, 91763. Tel 714-624-5144
Estab 1956. 20,000 Vols. 1760 sq ft
Types: Juvenile, out of print, papbk, used, 1st ed
Subj: Arts & crafts, fiction, for lang, nonfiction, rel, cooking, drama

MONTEREY — 27,558. Area code 408

THE BOOK END — General
245 Pearl St, 93940. Tel 408-373-4046
Estab 1976. 15,000 Vols
Types: Hb, papbk, used, 1st ed, out of print, juvenile, for lang, cookbooks

OLD CAPITOL BOOKS — Used
639-A Lighthouse Ave, 93940. Tel 408-375-2665
Estab 1983. 30,000 Titles. 40,000 Vols. 2500 sq ft
Types: Out of print, used, fine bnd, juvenile, ltd ed, old & rare, remainders
Subj: Hist, sci-tech, art, philos, rel, fiction, cooking, nautical

OLD MONTEREY BOOK CO — Antiquarian
136 Bonifacio Pl, 93940. Tel 408-372-3111
Estab 1960. 10,000 Vols
Types: Old & rare, out of print, used

MONTROSE — Area code 818

BOOKSVILLE — General
2626 Honolulu Ave, 91020. Tel 818-248-9149
Mgr & Merch Mgr, Shirley McCormick
Estab 1983. 15,000 Titles. 25,000 Vols. 800 sq ft
Types: Juvenile, out of print, mass mkt papbk, used

MORAGA — 15,014. Area code 415

SLEEPY HOLLOW BOOKS — Mail Order-Antiquarian
1455 Camino Pearl, 94556. Tel 415-376-9235
Estab 1980. 8000 Titles. 8000 Vols. Cat 2-3x ann
Types: Hb, imp, juvenile, out of print, high priced papbk, facsimile editions, fine bnd, 1st ed, illus bk, ltd ed, imp UK, fine presses
Subj: Bks on bks, Am hist & lit, Eng hist & lit, Western Amer, Californiana, mystery & detective, printing, typography, LEC, Sherlockania

MORRO BAY — 9064. Area code 805

THE BOOK PEDDLER — Antiquarian
842 Main St, 93442-9998. Tel 805-772-3810
Estab 1980. 15,000 Vols. 800 sq ft
Types: 1st ed, hb, facsimile editions, illus bk, juvenile, ltd ed, papbk, remainders, old & rare, out of print, imp UK
Subj: Hearst Castle, William R Hearst, Marion Davies

MOUNTAIN VIEW — 58,655. Area code 415

FLORIAN J SHASKY -BOOKS — Antiquarian
970 Terra Bella, Suite 1, 94043. Tel 415-967-5330
Estab 1981. 10,000 Titles. 15,000 Vols. 1000 sq ft. Cat 2-3x ann
Types: 1st ed, hb, illus bk, ltd ed, old & rare, out of print, used
Subj: Hist, Amer, lit

MURPHYS — 950. Area code 209

MURPHYS STAGE STOP — General
416 Main St (Mail add: PO Box 867, 95247). Tel 209-728-2200
Estab 1977. 5873 Titles. 7000 Vols
Types: Hb, out of print, papbk, used
Subj: Californiana

NATIONAL CITY — 48,772. Area code 619

BOOKS UNLIMITED — General
1127 Highland Ave, 92050. Tel 619-477-1717
Estab 1955. 1600 sq ft
Types: Hb, papbk, juvenile, out of print
Subj: Civil serv, medicine, sci-tech, computer sci

MAGICK BOOKSTORE — Metaphysics & Occult
2306 Highland Ave, 92050. Tel 619-477-5260
Estab 1975. 2000 Titles. 10000 Vols. Cat
Types: Hb, out of print, used, bibles, juvenile, best sellers
Subj: Mysticism, Orientalia, yoga, Indianiana, psychol, graphic arts, women's studies, positive thinking, divinations, reincarnation

NEVADA CITY — 2431. Area code 916

MOUNTAIN HOUSE BOOKS — General
418 Broad St, 95959. Tel 916-265-2647
8000 Vols. Cat 6x ann
Types: Fine bnd, 1st ed, hb, ltd ed, old & rare, out of print, used, small presses
Subj: Californiana, Western Amer

NORTH HOLLYWOOD — Area code 818

DUTTON'S BOOKS — General
5146 Laurel Canyon Blvd, 91607. Tel 818-769-3866
Mgr, Steve Daly
Estab 1960. 200,000 Vols. Cat
Types: Hb, papbk, juvenile, imp, out of print, remainders, old & rare, for lang, imp UK, illus bk, fine bnd, new
Subj: Art, humanities, hist, music
See Also: Burbank, Los Angeles

RUDOLPH WILLIAM SABBOT NATURAL HISTORY BOOKS — Antiquarian-Natural History
6821 Babcock Ave, 91605. Tel 818-982-4911
Estab 1965. 8000 Vols. Cat 6x ann
Types: 1st ed, hb, incunab, old & rare, out of print, used, imp
Subj: Scholarly lit

VALLEY BOOK CITY — Antiquarian-General
5249 Lankershim Blvd, 91601-3192. Tel 818-985-6911
Owner, Mark Marlow; Mgr, Harry Brenton
Estab 1975. 100,000 Titles. 100,000 Vols. 4500 sq ft
Types: Fine bnd, 1st ed, hb, illus bk, juvenile, ltd ed, new & used, old & rare, out of print
Subj: Art, circus, drama, magic & conjuring, photog, sci fiction & fantasy, Western Amer, fiction, military

VALLEY PLAZA HOBBY SHOP — Military
12160 Hamlin St, 91606. Tel 818-762-1927
1000 Vols
Types: Hb, papbk, imp, new & used, out of print, old & rare
Subj: Reference

NORWALK — 85,232. Area code 213

H N MILLER — Mail Order-Aviation
PO Box U, 90651-5023. Tel 213-863-5028, 632-8081
Estab 1960. 10,000 Titles. 10,000 Vols. Cat
Types: 1st ed, hb, imp, new & used, old & rare, out of print, papbk, remainders
Subj: Aviation, military, photog, radio, sci-tech, tv, Naval, Marine Corps, guns
See Also: Aviation Bookmobile - Mil-Air Photos & Books, Compton

MIND SNACK* — Mail Order-Antiquarian
14317 Ibex, 90650. Tel 213-864-8974
Estab 1981. 5000 Vols
Types: Out of print
Subj: Biog, class studies, health, parenting, psychol, sci fiction & fantasy, women's studies

NOVATO — 43,916. Area code 415

CRUM'S BOOKMARK — Parenting
866 Grant Ave, 94945. Tel 415-897-1183
Estab 1985. 7500 Titles. 7500 Vols. 500 sq ft
Types: Used, hb, juvenile, out of print, fine bnd, 1st ed, illus bk
Subj: Art, cooking, biog, Californiana, hist, nautical, Western Amer

OAKLAND — 339,288. Area code 415

ARCHAEOLOGIA — Antiquarian-Archaeology
707 Carlston Ave, 94610. Tel 415-832-1405
Dir, Andrew H Gordon
Estab 1983. 5000 Vols. 2500 sq ft. Cat 3x ann
Types: Incunab, ltd ed, old & rare, out of print, used
Subj: Archaeol, Egypt, ancient Gr, ancient Rome, Mesopotamia, Central Am

THE HOLMES BOOK CO, INC — Antiquarian-General
274 14th St (Mail add: PO Box 858, 94604). Tel 415-893-6860
Vpres & Gen Mgr, Craig H Keyston; Mgr Used Bks, Frederick Moore; Mgr Rare Bks, David A Lemmo; Mgr New Bks, David N Hurlbut
Estab 1894. 500,000 Vols. Cat
Types: Hb, out of print, old & rare, papbk, remainders, used
Subj: Western Amer

LIBERTY TREE NETWORK — Mail Order
354 98th Ave, 94104. Tel 415-981-1326
Estab 1986
Types: Hb, imp UK, juvenile, out of print, mass mkt papbk, mass mkt papbk only, remainders
Subj: Hist, philos, polit sci, econ, educ, self-develop, bus & mgt, pub policy, self defense, freedom vs govt, personal investment
See Also: Wholesale section, San Francisco

MAMA BEARS — General
6536 Telegraph Ave, 94609. Tel 415-428-9684
Mgr, Alice Malloy
Types: Hb, papbk, used, out of print, juvenile
Subj: Women's studies

NIGHTMARES & NOTIONS — Comics
5904 Foothill Blvd, 94605-1523. Tel 415-562-0956
Estab 1986. 5000 Titles. 100,000 Vols. 1200 sq ft
Types: Hb, out of print, papbk, mass mkt papbk, high priced papbk, used, ltd ed
Subj: Sci fiction & fantasy, tv, radio, horror

PENDRAGON FINE BOOKS — General
5560 College Ave, 94618. Tel 415-652-6259
Mgr, Kenneth Damacion
Estab 1974. 60,000 Titles. 60,000 Vols. 1600 sq ft Buys indep
Types: 1st ed, hb, illus bk, juvenile, ltd ed, new, out of print, old & rare, papbk, remainders, used

Subj: Art, hist, metaphysics, sci fiction & fantasy, mystery & detective, lit, minorities

MARVIN STANLEY BOOKSELLERS — Antiquarian
2809 38th Ave, 94619. Tel 415-536-4071
Estab 1975. 30,000 Vols. 1350 sq ft
Types: Fine bnd, 1st ed, hb, illus bk, juvenile, old & rare, out of print, used
Subj: Rel studies, theol, hist

TOWNSEND BOOKSELLERS — Antiquarian-General
4033 Maple Ave, 94602. Tel 415-530-9065
Estab 1984. 6000 Titles. 6000 Vols. 300 sq ft. Cat 2x ann
Types: Fine bnd, 1st ed, hb, illus bk, juvenile, ltd ed, old & rare, out of print, used
Subj: Humanities, fiction, Amer, scholarly lit, soc sci

OCEANSIDE — 76,698. Area code 619

REINE PARR BOOKS — Antiquarian-General
169 Raymar Rd (Mail add: 4375 Adams Ave, San Diego, 92116). Tel 619-283-0913
Estab 1984. 10,000 Titles. Cat 2x ann
Types: Used, 1st ed, hb, illus bk, juvenile, old & rare, out of print
Subj: Fiction, medieval studies, nonfiction, World Wars I & II, adventure, Oz

OJAI — 6816. Area code 805

TIME PORTAL — Antiquarian
212 E Ojai Ave, 93023. Tel 805-646-7729
Estab 1986. 70,000 Titles. 80,000 Vols. 1900 sq ft
Types: Out of print, imp, old & rare, used British imp
Subj: Sci fiction & fantasy, metaphys & occult, rel, hist, art, archaeol, travel, discovery & explor, Egyptology, British Isles, Elizabethan studies, Shakespeare, geol & mining

ORANGE — 91,788. Area code 714

BOOK CARNIVAL — Antiquarian
870 N Tustin, 92667. Tel 714-538-3210
Owner, What Books Inc
Estab 1981. 12,000 Vols. 1100 sq ft
Types: 1st ed, hb, ltd ed, new & used, out of print, papbk
Subj: Mystery & detective, sci fiction & fantasy

MILITARY HOBBIES — Aviation
138 E Taft Ave, 92667. Tel 714-637-1211
Estab 1971. 3000 Titles. 5000 Vols. 1600 sq ft
Types: Hb, imp UK, out of print, remainders
Subj: Military, warfare, World Wars I & II, Vietnam

21ST CENTURY COMICS & TOYS — Comics
169 N Glassell, 92666. Tel 714-633-3440
Mgr, Barry Short
Estab 1981. 400 Titles. 1600 sq ft
Types: Juvenile, out of print, mass mkt papbk, papbk
Subj: Collecting, animation & comic art, Disneyana

ORINDA — 6790. Area code 415

DANIEL HOLMES BOOKSELLER — Mail Order-Antiquarian
Six Via San Inigo, 94563. Tel 415-254-3360
Estab 1978. 1200 Titles. 1600 Vols. Cat 2x ann
Types: Old & rare, out of print, used
Subj: Geol, Western Amer

OROVILLE — 8683. Area code 916

WAYNE PIERCE - BOOKS — General
4400 Pine Cluster Lane, 95965. Tel 916-533-0105
Mgr, Gum P Dog
Estab 1968. 20,000 Vols. 5000 sq ft. Cat 2-3x ann
Types: Hb, imp Cuba, juvenile, out of print, used
Subj: Natural hist, post-Victorian women's fiction

PACIFICA — 38,866. Area code 415

DIANE PYKE - BOOKS — Mail Order-Foreign Lang
1107 Glacier Ave, 94044. Tel 415-355-7611
Estab 1987
Types: Fr lang, new & used, imp Fr, imp Switz, out of print, hb, old & rare, papbk

PACIFIC PALISADES — Area code 213

INTERNATIONAL BOOKFINDERS INC — Mail Order-Antiquarian
PO Box 1, 90272-0001
Estab 1950
Types: 1st ed, ltd ed, out of print, old & rare

PALO ALTO — 55,255. Area code 415

BELL'S BOOKSTORE — Used
536 Emerson St, 94301. Tel 415-323-7822
Estab 1936. 100,000 Titles. 100,000 Vols. Cat
Types: Hb, juvenile, out of print
Subj: Hist, hort, scholarly lit

THE BOOK PLACE — General
2710 Middlefield Rd, 94306. Tel 415-324-1471
Estab 1984. 35,000 Titles. 35,000 Vols. 1500 sq ft
Types: Juvenile, out of print, high priced papbk, used
Subj: Fiction, Judaica, mystery & detective, sci fiction & fantasy, cookbks

BUCKABEST BOOKS & BINDERY — Antiquarian
247 Fulton St, 94301. Tel 415-325-2965
Estab 1973. 2000 Vols. 110 sq ft. Cat
Types: Fine bnd, 1st ed, hb, imp, old & rare, out of print, used
Subj: Biog, drama, ballet, Wales, unicorns, theatre

CHIMERA BOOKS — Antiquarian
405 Kipling, 94301. Tel 415-329-9217
Estab 1970. 100,000 Vols. 2500 sq ft
Types: New, for lang, hb, juvenile, out of print, papbk, used, imp UK
Subj: Art, fiction, poetry, class studies, scholarly lit

CLARK'S — General
2625 Middlefield Rd, 94306
Mgr, Jan Starratt
Estab 1988.
Types: Hb, juvenile, out of print, mass mkt papbk, remainders, text bks, used
Subj: Cooking, psychol

MEGA BOOKS — Used
444 University Ave, 94301. Tel 415-326-4730
Mgr, Lee Marsullo
Estab 1968
Types: Col text, hb, juvenile, out of print, papbk, remainders
Subj: Art, psychol, sci-tech, cooking, philos, rel studies, sports

MINERVA BOOKS — Metaphysics & Occult
1027 Alma St, 94301. Tel 415-326-2006
Mgr & Buyer, Robert Clark
Estab 1979. 10,000 Vols. 1200 sq ft. Cat 2x ann
Types: Hb, imp, out of print, remainders
Subj: Metaphysics, philos

THE PRINTERS' SHOP — Graphic Arts
4047 Transport St, 94303. Tel 415-494-6802
Estab 1974. 1000 Vols. 500 sq ft. Cat
Types: Hb, high priced papbk, imp UK, old & rare, out of print, used, fine press
Subj: Printing, bnd, paper making & typography

RECYCLE BOOKSTORE — Used
230 Hamilton Ave, 94301. Tel 415-321-2846
Mgr, Patricia Sobrero
Estab 1977. 40,000 Vols Buys through hq
Types: 1st ed, hb, new & used, out of print
Subj: Mystery & detective, sci fiction & fantasy

STARRATT ENTERPRISES — Mail Order
3669 Middlefield Rd, 94303. Tel 415-493-3185
Estab 1983. 7000 Titles. 10,000 Vols
Types: Hb, used, out of print, juvenile
Subj: Folklore, poetry, fairy tales

WILLIAM P WREDEN BOOKS & MANUSCRIPTS — Antiquarian
206 Hamilton Ave, PO Box 56, 94302-0056. Tel 415-325-6851
Mgr, William P Wreden Jr
Estab 1938. 12,000 Vols. 1500 sq ft. Cat 2x ann
Types: 1st ed, hb, incunab, ltd ed, out of print, old & rare
Subj: Western Amer, Eng & Am lit, fine printing

PASADENA — 119,374. Area code 818

BOOK COMPANY — General
1328 N Lake Ave, 91104. Tel 818-798-4630
Estab 1983. 7000 Vols. 900 sq ft. Cat 17x ann
Types: Fine bnd, hb, out of print, papbk, remainders, used, 1st ed, old & rare

BOOK VILLAGE — General
1766 E Colorado Blvd, 91106. Tel 818-793-7780
Estab 1976. 140,000 Vols. 1680 sq ft. Cat ann
Types: For lang, hb, imp, juvenile, out of print, papbk, remainders, col & el-hi text, used, 1st ed, facsimile editions, ltd ed, incunab
Subj: Californiana, philos, poetry
See Also: Monrovia

DANIEL H DEUTSCH BOOKS — Mail Order-Antiquarian
141 Kenworthy Dr, 91105. Tel 213-681-9638
Types: Hb, old & rare, papbk, used, out of print
Subj: Astron, chem, physics, thermodynamics

M GORDON BOOKS — Mail Order
1185 N Michillinda, 91107. Tel 818-351-8525
Estab 1979. 12,000 Titles
Types: Juvenile, out of print, hb, used
Subj: Biog, performing arts, fiction, sci fiction & fantasy

G F GUSTIN JR BOOKS — Antiquarian
56 E Colorado Blvd, 91105. Tel 818-795-8528
Estab 1974. 10,000 Vols
Types: Fine bnd, 1st ed, hb, juvenile, ltd ed, old & rare, out of print, used
Subj: Literary criticism, local hist, Western Amer

THE MAGICK CIRCLE — Metaphysics & Occult
956 N Lake Ave, PO Box 93124, 91109. Tel 818-794-6013
Owner, Light of Truth Church, Inc
Estab 1972. 1000 Titles. 2000 Vols. 400 sq ft. Cat 2x ann
Types: Hb, imp, out of print, papbk, used
Subj: Rel, philos

MITCHELL BOOKS — Mystery & Detective
1395 E Washington Blvd, 91104. Tel 818-798-4438
Estab 1978. 13,000 Vols. 1350 sq ft. Cat 3x ann
Types: Hb, used, 1st ed, out of print
Subj: Steinbeckiana

PRUFROCK BOOKS & ETC — Antiquarian
531 S Marengo Ave, 91101. Tel 818-795-3558
Estab 1979. 5000 Vols. Cat
Types: Fine bnd, out of print
Subj: Fiction, Californiana, archit, mod film editions

NORTON SIMON MUSEUM BOOKSHOP — Museum
411 W Colorado Blvd, 91105. Tel 818-449-6840
Marketing Dir, Philip Juwig
Estab 1975. 2500 Titles. 3500 Vols. 1400 sq ft
Types: Hb, imp, out of print, high priced papbk, remainders
Subj: Art, archit, sculpture

PETALUMA — 33,834. Area code 707

CROSSROAD BOOKS & SKILLS FOR GROWTH & CHANGE — General
115 Liberty St, 94952. Tel 707-763-3674
Types: Juvenile, out of print, text bks, used

WEST WIND BOOK — Used
17A Fourth St, 94952. Tel 707-762-6909
Estab 1986. 4500 Titles. 5000 Vols. 300 sq ft
Types: Hb, juvenile, out of print, mass mkt papbk, high priced papbk, remainders, facsimile editions, fine bnd, illus bk, imp UK, ltd ed
Subj: Anthrop, hist, natural hist

PISMO BEACH — 5364. Area code 805

PAT HOLDEN'S BIGFOOT HOBBIES — Hobbies
1020 Price St, PO Box 762, 93449. Tel 805-773-0779
Estab 1976. 1000 Vols. 500 sq ft
Types: Ger lang, hb, Jap lang, out of print, papbk, imp Eng, Ger & Jap
Subj: Biol, railroadiana, aviation, hist, railroadiana

QUINCY — 6529. Area code 916

DAY'S PAST — Used
2163 E Main St, PO Box 1846, 95971. Tel 916-283-1899
Estab 1979. 10,000 Vols. 1200 sq ft
Types: Fine bnd, 1st ed, illus bk, ltd ed, hb, papbk, juvenile, old & rare, out of print

RANCHO CORDOVA — 30,451. Area code 916

JOANNA TAYLOR BOOKS — Antiquarian-Women's Studies
2461 El Pavo Way, 95670. Tel 916-362-6963 (for appt)
Estab 1976. 3 Titles. 7000 Vols. Cat 8x ann
Types: Out of print
Subj: Reference, bibliog

RANCHO MIRAGE — 6281. Area code 714

SNEIDER ANTIQUARIAN BOOK CO — Antiquarian-Natural History
72081 Palm Haven Dr, 92270. Tel 619-346-5687
Estab 1979. 1500 Titles. 2000 Vols. 800 sq ft. Cat ann
Types: 1st ed, old & rare, out of print
Subj: Medicine, sci-tech

RANCHO SANTA FE — Area code 619

RANCH BOOKS & OFFICE SUPPLIES — General
6030 La Flecha (Mail add: PO Box K, 92067). Tel 619-756-2265
Estab 1962. 4000 Vols
Types: Hb, juvenile, papbk, out of print
Subj: Local hist

REDLANDS — 43,619. Area code 714

THE BOOK CASE — Antiquarian
101 S Sixth St, 92373. Tel 714-798-1681
Estab 1981. 5000 Titles. 7000 Vols
Types: Out of print, 1st ed
Subj: Western Amer, Hemingway, Zane Grey, Faulkner

PAUL MELZER FINE BOOKS — Mail Order
612 E Central Ave (Mail add: PO Box 1143, 92373)
Estab 1986. 2000 Titles. 3000 Vols
Types: Out of print, used, facsimile editions, fine bnd, 1st ed, hb, incunab, illus bk, juvenile, old & rare, ltd ed
Subj: Western Amer, mod iit, voyages, sci & med

REDONDO BEACH — 57,102. Area code 213

BAILEY SEARCH SERVICE — Mail Order-Antiquarian
PO Box 326, 90277
Estab 1959. 5000 Vols
Types: Hb, imp, new & used, out of print, old & rare
Subj: Metaphys & occult, sci fiction & fantasy, Edgar Rice Burroughs, Aleister Crowley, pulps of the 1930s & 1940s

RESEDA — Area code 818

THE BOOKIE JOINT — Antiquarian
7246 Reseda Blvd, 91335. Tel 818-343-1055, 345-2983
Estab 1975. 100,000 Vols. 2200 sq ft
Types: Facsimile editions, fine bnd, 1st ed, hb, illus bk, juvenile, ltd ed, old & rare, out of print, papbk, used
Subj: Anthrop, archaeol, comedy, cooking, Judaica, Middle East, sci fiction & fantasy, sociol, Bible research, Islamic, scholarly

SACRAMENTO — 275,471. Area code 916

ACADEMIC LIBRARY SERVICE — Mail Order-Antiquarian
6489 South Land Park Dr, 95831. Tel 916-428-2863
4000 Titles. 6000 Vols. Cat 6x ann
Types: Juvenile, out of print, used, 1st ed, illus bk, ltd ed, old & rare

ARGUS BOOKS & GRAPHICS — Antiquarian
1714 Capitol Ave, 95814. Tel 916-443-2223
Estab 1971. 10,000 Vols. Cat
Types: Facsimile editions, fine bnd, hb, illus bk, ltd ed, old & rare, out of print, used
Subj: Californiana, local hist, mining, Western Amer, archaic skills

BLACK SWAN BOOKS — Antiquarian
PO Box 22028, 95822. Tel 916-441-2156
Estab 1979. 2500 Vols. Cat 3x ann
Types: Old & rare, out of print
Subj: Natural hist, gardening, hort

BOOK CHEK — Used Paperback
2800 Marconi Ave, 95821. Tel 916-487-3723
50,000 Vols
Types: Hb, juvenile, out of print, papbk, mass mkt papbk
Subj: Comedy, romance, sci fiction & fantasy

BOOKMINE — Antiquarian
1015 Second St, 95814. Tel 916-441-4609
Estab 1985. 10,000 Titles. 10,000 Vols
Types: Hb, out of print, fine bnd, 1st ed, illus bk, imp, ltd ed, old & rare, juvenile
Subj: Western Amer, railroadiana, medicine, travel

THE BOOK REVIEW — General
3233 Riverside Blvd, 95818. Tel 916-443-7984
Mgr, Genevieve Flett
Estab 1979. 31,000 Vols. 1100 sq ft
Types: Juvenile, papbk, old & rare, out of print, 1st ed, used, for lang, fine bnd
Subj: Rel studies

CHLOE'S BOOKSTORE — Mail Order-Antiquarian
PO Box 255673, 95865. Tel 916-488-3892
Estab 1973. Cat 6x ann
Types: 1st ed, ltd ed, out of print, used
Subj: Mod lit, poetry

THE CHURCHILLIANA CO — Mail Order
4629 Sunset Dr, 95822. Tel 916-448-7053
Estab 1970. 12,000 Vols
Types: Hb, papbk, out of print
Subj: World Wars I & II, Sir Winston S Churchill, Marlborough, Mountbatten, Eisenhower

HAMMON'S ARCHIVES & ARTIFACTS — Antiquarian-Californiana
1115 Front St, 95814. Tel 916-446-1782
Estab 1975. 4000 Vols. 542 sq ft. Cat 2x ann
Types: Hb, out of print, old & rare, used
Subj: Amer, geol, mining, Nevadiana, railroadiana, Japan

MILEPOST 1 — Railroadiana
115 I St, 95814. Tel 916-447-9665
Owner, Railway & Locomotive Historical Society - Pacific Coast Chapter; Mgr, Bruce Kleinschmidt
Estab 1981. 1700 Titles. 7500 Vols. Cat 3x ann
Types: New & used, out of print

RICHARD L PRESS FINE & SCHOLARLY BOOKS — Antiquarian
1727 1/2 I St, 95814. Tel 916-447-3413
Estab 1980. 4500 Vols. 800 sq ft. Cat 2x ann
Types: Fine bnd, 1st ed, hb, illus bk, juvenile, ltd ed, new, out of print, old & rare, remainders
Subj: Archit, art, fine arts, graphic arts, Middle East, Judaica

TIME-TESTED BOOKS — Western Americana
1114 21st Street, 95814. Tel 916-447-5696
Estab 1980. 25,000 Vols. 1500 sq ft
Types: 1st ed, juvenile, new & used, out of print, papbk
Subj: Am hist & lit, polit sci, illus, Californiana

SAN ANSELMO — 11,927. Area code 415

CREEKSIDE BOOKS — Search Service
Nine Sunview Ave, 94960. Tel 415-453-1806
Estab 1977. 20,000 Vols
Types: Out of print, papbk

SAN BERNARDINO — 118,057. Area code 714

HAPPY BOOKER — Used
4096 N Sierra Way, 92407. Tel 714-883-6110
Estab 1973. 40,000 Vols. 2000 sq ft
Types: Fine bnd, 1st ed, hb, juvenile, new, old & rare, out of print

ST FRANCIS BOOK STORE — Religious-C
462 W Highland Ave, 92405. Tel 714-886-8371
Mgr, Joel A Reyes
Estab 1987. 1000 Titles. 3000 Vols
Types: New, out of print, papbk, used

THE UNICORN, BOOK DEPT — Antiquarian
393 W Athol St, No 4 (Mail add: 4040 E Piedmont, Suite 110, 92346). Tel 714-862-5373, 885-4905
Mgr, Curt Norman
Estab 1975. 15000 Titles. 15,000 Vols. 800 sq ft
Types: 1st ed, illus bk, old & rare, out of print, used

SAN CARLOS — 24,710. Area code 415

CARLOS CANTERBURY BOOKSTORE — General
1121 Laurel St, 94070. Tel 415-593-3392
Estab 1951. 45,000 Titles. 45,000 Vols
Types: Fine bnd, 1st ed, hb, illus bk, juvenile, ltd ed, old & rare, out of print, papbk, used
Subj: Californiana

SAN CARLOS AVIATION — Aviation
620 Airport Dr, 94070. Tel 415-592-2322
Estab 1967. 700 Vols. 1000 sq ft. Cat 6x ann
Types: Hb, papbk, out of print, remainders
Subj: Aviation, WW II hist

SAN CLEMENTE — 27,325. Area code 714

OUT-OF-STATE BOOK SERVICE — Mail Order-Antiquarian
PO Box 3253 D, 92672-1053. Tel 714-492-2976
Estab 1958. 5000 Vols
Types: Out of print, new
Subj: Fiction, nonfiction

SAN DIEGO — 875,504. Area code 619

ADAMS AVENUE BOOKSTORE — Antiquarian
3502 Adams, 92116. Tel 619-281-3330
Estab 1965. 80,000 Vols
Types: Hb, papbk, out of print, juvenile, used
Subj: Amer, mystery & detective, cooking, technical

BARGAIN BOOKSTORE — Used
1053 Eight Ave, 92101. Tel 619-234-5380
Estab 1952. 100,000 Titles. 125,000 Vols
Types: Out of print, small presses
Subj: Archit, art, fiction, Southwestern Amer

BLUE LANTERN BOOKS — Mail Order
PO Box 8009, 92102. Tel 619-235-6751
Estab 1986. 1000 sq ft. Cat 6x ann
Types: Juvenile, out of print, used, illus bk, old & rare, new & used
Subj: Art, mystery & detective, botany, cinema

COMMAND POST LTD, INC — Hobbies
4690 Convoy St, 92111. Tel 619-277-4533
Gen Mgr & Buyer, M R Baulch
Estab 1973. 2200 Vols. 1560 sq ft
Types: Imp, out of print, remainders, hb, papbk,
Subj: Aviation, hist, military, hobbies, military ref bks

GROUNDS FOR MURDER, A MYSTERY BOOK STORE — Mystery & Detective
Old Town Mercado, 2707 Congress St, 92110. Tel 619-294-9497
Estab 1981. 20,000 Titles. 50,000 Vols. 1058 sq ft. Cat 4x ann
Types: Hb, juvenile, out of print, papbk, remainders, used, 1st ed, imp
Subj: Mystery & detective, class "whodunits", espionage, police procedural, romantic suspense, true crime

J & J HOUSE BOOKSELLERS — Antiquarian
632 Broadway, 92101. Tel 619-232-8331
Estab 1978. 35,000 Titles. 45,000 Vols. Cat 4x ann
Types: 1st ed, facsimile editions, fine bnd, illus bk, ltd ed, old & rare, out of print, pvt presses, color plate bks, view bks
Subj: Am Indian studies, Californiana, Orientalia, natural hist, Western Amer, philos, sci-tech, voyages

OLINGHOUSE & TYSON BOOKSELLERS & LA QUERENCIA PRESS — Mail Order-Natural History
Box 3120, 92103. Tel 619-233-4881
Estab 1979. 3000 Vols. Cat
Types: Old & rare, out of print, used
Subj: Amer, anthrop, natural hist

OTENTO BOOKS — Used
3817 Fifth Ave, 92103. Tel 619-296-1424
Estab 1963. 35,000 Titles. 40,000 Vols. 1500 sq ft. Cat
Types: Out of print, fine bnd
Subj: Hist, nautical, sci fiction & fantasy, travel, arts & crafts, cooking, Ger, Fr, Ital, Russ & Hungarian langs

PACIFIC BEACH BOOKSTORE — Used
1972 Garnet Ave, 92109. Tel 619-273-9082
10,000 Vols
Types: Hb, juvenile, out of print, papbk, remainders

J PARMER BOOKSELLERS — Mail Order-Antiquarian
7644 Forrestal Rd, 92120. Tel 619-287-0693
Estab 1984. 7000 Titles. 7500 Vols. Cat 6x ann
Types: Hb, remainders, used, new, old & rare, out of print
Subj: Travel, Amer, exploration-polar & Africa

PERI LITHON BOOKS — Mail Order-Geoscience
5372 Van Nuys Court (Mail add: PO Box 9996, 92109-0340). Tel 619-488-6904
Estab 1971. 7500 Vols. Cat 6x ann
Types: Col text, hb, imp, new & used, old & rare, out of print, papbk
Subj: Chem, gemology, geol, jewelry, metallurgy, mineralogy, mining

JOHN ROBY — Mail Order-Antiquarian
3703 Nassau Dr, 92115. Tel 619-583-4264
Estab 1960. 8000 Titles. 10,000 Vols. Cat
Types: 1st ed, papbk, remainders, out of print, new & used
Subj: Nautical, sci-tech, aviation technology

SILVERGATE BOOKS — Mail Order-Railroadiana
6156 Camino Largo, 92120. Tel 619-582-6737
Estab 1972. 4000 Vols. 2000 sq ft
Types: Hb, high priced papbk, remainders, used, 1st ed, ltd ed, out of print, old & rare
Subj: Transp

JOSEPH TABLER -BOOKS — Antiquarian
5650 Riley St, 92110. Tel 619-291-6399
Estab 1982. 5000 Titles. 5000 Vols. Cat 2x ann
Types: Hb, out of print, old & rare, used
Subj: Archit, surfing, decorative art, model making, alcoholics anonymous

N ASHTON TITLOW BOOKSELLER — Mail Order-Used
4683 Point Loma Ave (Mail add: PO Box 7276-0276, 92107-0276). Tel 619-223-1685
Estab 1980. 25,000 Titles. 25,000 Vols. Cat
Types: Hb, illus bk, out of print
Subj: Autg, travel, cooking, music, World War II & U S Marine Corps

VAN NORMAN BOOKSELLERS — Mail Order-Antiquarian
4047 Bay View Ct, 92103. Tel 619-296-6451
Estab 1979. 19,000 Titles. 16,000 Vols. 1000 sq ft. Cat
Types: Out of print, used, juvenile, Amer
Subj: Amer, biog, dance, art, illus, tech

WAHRENBROCK'S BOOK HOUSE — General
726 Broadway, 92101. Tel 619-232-0132
Mgr & Buyer, Jan Tonnesen
Estab 1935. 250,000 Titles. 300,000 Vols. Cat 4x ann
Types: 1st ed, incunab, new & used, out of print, remainders, papbk, old & rare, imp Sp, UK & Scotland
Subj: Western Amer, travel

YESTERDAY'S BOOKS — Used
2861 University Ave, 92104. Tel 619-298-4503
Estab 1976. 35,000 Vols. 2500 sq ft
Types: Hb, out of print, papbk
Subj: Amer, art, philos, aviation, photog, metaphysics, sea & ships

SAN FERNANDO — 17,731. Area code 818

SAN FERNANDO BOOK CO — General
PO Box 447, 91341-0447. Tel 818-362-2173
Estab 1969. 3000 Titles. 8000 Vols. Cat
Types: Hb, out of print, used, new
Subj: Numismatics, treasure hunting, antq, money & banking hist, silver & gold mining, collectibles

SAN FRANCISCO — 678,974. Area code 415

AARDVARK BOOKS — Used
237 Church St, 94114. Tel 415-552-6733
Merch Mgr, D Lugn; Inventory Control, R Lipp; Research, B Leigh; Papbk Buyer, B Ghoreyshi
Estab 1978. 25,000 Titles. 35,000 Vols. 1700 sq ft
Types: 1st ed, illus bk, hb, new & used, papbk, old & rare, out of print

ABOUT MUSIC — Music
PO Box 31415, 94131. Tel 415-647-3343
Estab 1979. 3000 Titles. 6000 Vols. Cat ann
Types: Out of print, imp Eng
Subj: Dance, musicians

ACORN BOOKS — Antiquarian
740 Polk St, 94109. Tel 415-563-1736
Estab 1980. 100,000 Vols. 4000 sq ft. Cat
Types: Fine bnd, 1st ed, hb, illus bk, juvenile, ltd ed, old & rare, out of print, papbk, used

THE ALBATROSS BOOK CO — Antiquarian
166 Eddy St, 94102. Tel 415-885-6501
Estab 1961. 400,000 Vols. 3300 sq ft. Cat
Types: 1st ed, illus bk, juvenile, out of print, remainders, used, old & rare, hb, press bks
Subj: Art, aviation, biog, metaphys & occult, mystery & detective, sci fiction & fantasy, Western Amer, poetry, maritime, technical, winemaking

ANTIQUUS BIBLIOPOLE — Antiquarian
4147 24th St, 94114. Tel 415-285-2322
Estab 1973. 20,000 Vols. 3000 sq ft
Types: 1st ed, out of print, old & rare, signed
Subj: Bibliog, philos, Western Amer, literary criticism

ARGONAUT BOOKSHOP — Antiquarian-Western Americana
786-792 Sutter St, 94109. Tel 415-474-9067
Assoc, Beverly A Haines
Estab 1941. 20,000 Titles. 1500 sq ft. Cat 6x ann
Types: 1st ed, hb, illus bk, ltd ed, old & rare, out of print, used
Subj: Californiana, art, cartography, illus, 19th century lit

ALAN S BAMBERGER — Mail Order-Antiquarian
2510 Bush St, 94115. Tel 415-931-7875
Cat 2-4x ann
Types: Hb, ltd ed, old & rare, out of print
Subj: Art, archit, photog, design, decorative arts, California art & artists

BOOKS AMERICA — Mail Order-Antiquarian
PO Box 4006, 94101. Tel 415-566-5525
Estab 1980. 1500 Titles. 10,000 Vols. 500 sq ft
Types: Hb, out of print, col text, new
Subj: Jap-Am studies

BOOKS & RECORDS — General
2222 Polk St, 94109. Tel 415-771-0758
Estab 1974. 20,000 Vols. 2000 sq ft
Types: Hb, out of print, papbk, remainders, used
Subj: Ventriloquism

BOOKSEARCH OF SAN FRANCISCO — Mail Order-Search Service
170 26th Ave, PO Box 210265, 94121. Tel 415-221-5575
Estab 1981. 5000 Vols
Types: Hb, out of print, used, 1st ed, old & rare

BOOKS ETC — Used
538 Castro St, 94114. Tel 415-621-8631
Mgr, Damien S DiPace
1200 sq ft
Types: For lang, hb, imp UK, facsimile editions, fine bnd, 1st ed, new & used, old & rare, out of print, papbk, remainders
Subj: Art, metaphys & occult, homosexuality

THE BOOKSTALL — Antiquarian
708 Sutter St, 94109. Tel 415-673-5446
Estab 1975. 10,000 Titles. 10,000 Vols. 1200 sq ft. Cat 2x ann
Types: Fine bnd, 1st ed, hb, juvenile, ltd ed, out of print, old & rare, used, illus bk
Subj: Californiana, gardening, math, physics, aviation, children's collectables, cooking, hist of science, mountain climbing

MEYER BOSWELL BOOKS, INC — Antiquarian
982 Hayes St, 94117. Tel 415-346-1839
Estab 1976. 3000 Vols. 500 sq ft. Cat 2x ann
Types: Facsimile editions, fine bnd, hb, incunab, imp, new, old & rare, out of print, used
Subj: Law, legal & constitutional hist, trials, international law

THE BRICK ROW BOOK SHOP — Antiquarian
278 Post St, Suite 303, 94108-5071. Tel 415-398-0414
Estab 1915. 10,000 Vols. 1200 sq ft. Cat 4x ann
Types: 1st ed, old & rare, out of print, imp
Subj: Am hist & lit, bibliog, Eng hist & lit, fine printing

LOUIS COLLINS BOOKS — Mail Order-Antiquarian
1083 Mission St, 98103. Tel 415-431-5134
Estab 1970. 10,000 Vols. 700 sq ft. Cat 3x ann
Types: 1st ed, hb, old & rare, out of print
Subj: Am Indian studies, anthrop
See Also: Collins Rare Books, Seattle, WA

THE COMPASS BOOKSTORE — Antiquarian
689 Clay St, 94111. Tel 415-397-0663
Types: Out of print, used
Subj: Discovery & explor, Orientalia

COOKBOOK CORNER — Cooking & Nutrition
620 Sutter St, 94102. Tel 415-673-6281
Estab 1977. 2000 Vols. 400 sq ft
Types: Hb, imp, out of print, papbk, remainders, new & used, old & rare

A DIFFERENT LIGHT — Homosexuality
489 Castro St, 94114. Tel 415-431-0891
Mgr, Richard LaBonte
Types: Fr, Ger & Sp lang, imp Australia, imp Neth, imp Fr, imp Ital, imp UK, imp Can, juvenile, out of print, papbk, remainders, text bks, col text
Subj: Gay & lesbian lit

DRAMA BOOKS — Performing Arts
134 Ninth St, 94103. Tel 415-255-0604
Estab 1975. 10,000 Titles. Cat
Types: Hb, out of print, papbk, remainders, col text, used
Subj: Dance, design, films & filmmaking, theatre, dramatic lit

871 FINE ARTS — Art
871 Folsom St, 94107. Tel 415-543-5155
Estab 1987. 600 sq ft. Cat ann
Types: New, out of print, papbk, used
Subj: 20th century art

ELDORADO BOOKS* — Mail Order-Antiquarian
PO Box 14036, 94114. Tel 415-552-8122
Estab 1962. 6000 Vols
Types: Hb, out of print, old & rare, used
Subj: Am hist & lit, Californiana, Eng hist & lit, fine arts

EVEREST-ASPIRATION BOOKSTORE — Metaphysics
1393 Eighth Ave, 94122. Tel 415-753-3798
Mgr, Nachiketa Acebo
Estab 1984. 2000 Titles. 3000 Vols. 600 sq ft. Cat ann
Types: Sp lang, imp India, imp UK, juvenile, papbk, mass mkt papbk, used, hb, illus bk, imp, ltd ed, new, out of print, remainders
Subj: Rel, sports, art, poetry, psychol, self-develop, music, cooking, health, alternative medicine

FANTASY ETC — Science Fiction & Fantasy
808 Larkin St, 94109. Tel 415-441-7617
Estab 1976. 500 sq ft
Types: Hb, juvenile, out of print, papbk, remainders, used
Subj: Mystery & detective, horror, espionage & adventure

FIELDS BOOKSTORE — Metaphysics & Occult
1419 Polk St, 94109. Tel 415-673-2027
Estab 1932. 25,000 Titles. 30,000 Vols. Cat semi-ann
Types: Hb, out of print, new & used, papbk
Subj: Health, magic & conjuring, parapsychol, philos, psychol, rel-Eastern, mythology, folklore, hermetics, Egypt, Ancient Near East, A E Waite, Aleister Crowley, mnemonics, Gurdjieff & Ouspensky

FONG-PLUMMER ASSOCIATES — Used
Box 14821, 94114. Tel 415-647-2651
Estab 1987. 10,000 Titles. 10,000 Vols. 1000 sq ft
Types: Remainders, out of print, high priced papbk, imp, hb, trade
Subj: Asian studies

FOREVER AFTER BOOKS — General
1475 Haight St, 94117. Tel 415-431-8299
Estab 1985. 30,000 Titles. 30,000 Vols. 1300 sq ft
Types: Used, hb, juvenile, out of print, papbk, mass mkt papbk, high priced papbk
Subj: Health, criminology, hist, mystery & detective, psychol, nonfiction, sci fiction & fantasy, spirituality, borderland of sci

GOURMET GUIDES — Cooking & Nutrition
1767 Stockton St, 94133. Tel 415-391-5903
Estab 1974. 20,000 Vols. 1000 sq ft. Cat 12x ann
Types: Hb, out of print, mass mkt papbk, remainders, imp European
Subj: Travel, gourmet

GREEN APPLE BOOKS — General
506 Clement St, 94118. Tel 415-387-2272
Estab 1967. 130,000 Titles. 150,000 Vols. 5000 sq ft
Types: New & used, out of print, papbk, remainders, old & rare
Subj: Art, hist, metaphys & occult, rel-Eastern

HAIGHT-FILLMORE BIBLIOMANTIC BOOK GALLERY — General
518 Haight St, 94117. Tel 415-861-2989
Estab 1982. 30,000 Vols. 2000 sq ft. Cat 2x ann
Types: Hb, papbk, juvenile, out of print, remainders, new & used, facsimile editions, fine bnd, 1st ed, old & rare, imp Eng, India
Subj: Art, health, philos, metaphys & occult, rel studies, hist

RICHARD HILKERT BOOKSELLER LTD — Interior Design
333 Hayes St, 94102. Tel 415-863-3339
Estab 1981. 7000 Vols. 700 sq ft
Types: Hb, out of print, used, 1st ed, old & rare, fine bnd
Subj: Biog, travel, interior design

LIBRERIA LA LATINA BOOKSTORE — Spanish Lang
2548 Mission St, 94110. Tel 415-824-0327
Mgr, J E Zelaya
Estab 1973. 10,000 Vols. 4640 sq ft. Cat 12x ann
Types: Hb, juvenile, out of print, mass mkt papbk, col text, imp Mex, Sp, & Argentina

THE LIMELIGHT BOOKSTORE — Films & Filmmaking
1803 Market St, 94103. Tel 415-864-2265
Estab 1976. 5000 Titles. 15,000 Vols. 1500 sq ft
Types: Hb, old & rare, out of print, papbk, remainders, new & used
Subj: Film & theatre

MAELSTROM — Used
572 Valencia, 94110. Tel 415-863-9933
12000 Titles. 1000 sq ft
Types: 1st ed, hb, illus bk, imp, juvenile, ltd ed, out of print, old & rare, papbk, remainders
Subj: Art, metaphys & occult, European fict in translation

RONALD W MAYER — Antiquarian-General
30 Lopez Ave, 94116. Tel 415-661-4279
Estab 1977. 6700 Titles. 6750 Vols. 250 sq ft. Cat 3x ann
Types: Hb, out of print, remainders, used
Subj: Biog, hist, medicine, philos, psychol, hist of sci

MCDONALD'S BOOKSHOP — Antiquarian
48 Turk St, 94102. Tel 415-673-2235
Mgr, Itzhak Volansky
Estab 1926. 1,000,000 Vols
Types: Out of print, used

MEDICI GALLERIES — Used
PO Box 3141, 94119. Tel 415-397-6319
Mgr, Carlos Grider
Estab 1984. 3000 Titles. 4500 Vols. Cat semi-ann
Types: New, out of print
Subj: Antq, fine arts, archit, archaeol, decorative arts

JEREMY NORMAN & CO, INC — Antiquarian
442 Post St, 94102-1579. Tel 415-781-6402. Telex 26-5816
Estab 1970. 5000 Vols. Cat 2x ann
Types: Facsimile editions, 1st ed, illus bk, incunab, old & rare, out of print
Subj: Hist of ideas, sci-tech, travel, Norman Publ

TODD PRATUM BOOKS — Metaphysics
843 37th Ave, 94121-3407. Tel 415-221-8348
Estab 1981. 4000 Titles. 4000 Vols. 1000 sq ft. Cat 4x ann
Types: Ger lang, Fr lang, hb, out of print, remainders, imp Fr, imp Ger, facsimile editions, fine bnd, 1st ed
Subj: Metaphys & occult, philos, psychol

SAN FRANCISCO CONSERVATORY OF MUSIC BOOKSTORE — College
1201 Ortega St, 94122. Tel 415-564-8086
Mgr, Patricia B Reardon
Estab 1971. 540 sq ft
Types: Hb, imp, juvenile, out of print, papbk, remainders, used
Subj: Music

SECOND FRONT BOOKSTORE — Used
4079 19th Ave, 94132. Tel 415-584-1692
Estab 1973. 30,000 Vols. 1800 sq ft
Types: Hb, out of print, papbk
Subj: Medicine, nature & environ, psychol, sociol, math, anthrop, linguistics

SEVEN ROADS — Mail Order-Antiquarian
2611 Lake St, 94121. Tel 415-751-7427
Estab 1984. Cat ann
Types: 1st ed, hb, old & rare, out of print, used
Subj: Class studies, music, psychol, philos, class lit

SUNSET BOOKSTORE — Used
2161 Irving St, 94122. Tel 415-664-3644
Estab 1974. 25,000 Vols
Types: Hb, out of print, papbk, remainders
Subj: Art, how-to, fiction, psychol

TILLMAN PLACE BOOKSHOP — General
Eight Tillman Pl, 94108. Tel 415-392-4668
Estab 1956. 20,000 Vols
Types: Hb, imp, out of print, papbk, remainders, used

TRANSITION BOOKS — Antiquarian
209 Post St, Suite 614, 94108. Tel 415-391-5161, 346-2619
Mgr, Roger Wicker
Estab 1979. 4000 Titles. 4000 Vols. 500 sq ft. Cat 3x ann
Types: 1st ed, imp Fr, illus bk, ltd ed, old & rare, out of print
Subj: Mod lit, photog, illus, literary criticism, archit, Dada, surrealism, French artists bks, Am lit, Eng lit

ALAN WOFSY FINE ARTS — Antiquarian-Art
401 China Basin St (Mail add: PO Box 2210, 94126). Tel 415-986-3030
Estab 1969. 2000 Titles. 4000 Vols. Cat 3x ann
Types: Imp, out of print, old & rare
Subj: Art, bibliog, reference, 15th-20th century illus

YERBA BUENA BOOKS — Used
882 Bush St, 94108. Tel 415-474-2788
Estab 1984. 2500 Vols. 200 sq ft. Cat ann
Types: Hb, out of print, facsimile editions, fine bnd, 1st ed, illus bk, old & rare
Subj: Californiana, bks on bks, California authors

SAN GABRIEL — 30,072. Area code 818

GARY'S CORNER BOOKSTORE — Comics
1051 San Gabriel Blvd, 91776. Tel 818-285-7575
Estab 1977. 75,000 Vols. 1000 sq ft
Types: Out of print, papbk, new & used
Subj: Fiction, mystery & detective, nonfiction, romance, sci fiction & fantasy, Western Amer, comic collecting aids

MARIAN L GORE BOOKSELLER — Antiquarian
PO Box 433, 91778-0433. Tel 818-287-2946
Estab 1965. 5000 Vols. Cat 2x ann
Types: Out of print, old & rare, for lang
Subj: Food, wines, beverages, cookery, hotels & inns, history of food, menus in English & other lang

SAN JOSE — 636,550. Area code 408

BOOK WORLD — Antiquarian
1165A S Saratoga, Sunnyvale Rd, 95129. Tel 408-996-2384
Estab 1982. 1200 sq ft
Types: Hb, juvenile, out of print, papbk, used, new, old & rare
Subj: Railroadiana, Western Amer

SAN JOSE, CALIFORNIA

BREAD & ROSES BOOKSHOP — General
950 S First St, 95110. Tel 408-294-2930
Estab 1972. 10,000 Vols. 2000 sq ft
Types: Hb, juvenile, out of print, papbk, remainders, used
Subj: Am Indian studies, black studies, Chicano studies, feminism, Latin Am, labor & trade-unionism, Marxism

PERRY'S BOOKS — Antiquarian
1863 W San Carlos, 95128. Tel 408-286-0426
Estab 1949. 180,000 Vols
Types: 1st ed, hb, juvenile, ltd ed, out of print, old & rare, illus bk
Subj: Western Amer, Edgar Rice Burroughs, Jack London, 20th century lit, L F Baum, H R Haggard

RECYCLE BOOKSTORE — Antiquarian-General
138 E Santa Clara St, 95113. Tel 408-286-6275, 249-8208
Mgr, Jerry Goldstein; Buyer, Joe Avila
Estab 1973. 40,000 Titles. 120,000 Vols
Types: For lang, hb, imp, imp UK, juvenile, out of print, papbk, fine bnd
Subj: Metaphys & occult, psychol, sci fiction & fantasy, mystery & detective, fiction, art, films & filmmaking
See Also: Palo Alto

SAN LEANDRO — 63,952. Area code 415

ROSKIE & WALLACE BOOKSTORE — Antiquarian
14595 E 14th St, 94578. Tel 415-483-4163
Estab 1940. 500,000 Vols
Types: Used, out of print
Subj: Auto

SAN LUIS OBISPO — 34,252. Area code 805

WILLIAM H HESSEL BOOKS — Antiquarian-General
533 Pismo St, No 7, 93401. Tel 805-546-0947
5000 Titles
Types: Out of print, old & rare

THE NOVEL EXPERIENCE — Used
778 Marsh St, 93401. Tel 805-544-1549
Estab 1976. 7500 Titles. 7500 Vols. 300 sq ft
Types: Fine bnd, 1st ed, hb, illus bk, juvenile, old & rare, out of print, new
Subj: Belles lettres

PHOENIX BOOKS — Antiquarian-General
990 Monterey St, 93401. Tel 805-543-3591
Estab 1981. 31,000 Titles. 40,000 Vols. 1500 sq ft
Types: Hb, papbk, mass mkt papbk, remainders, fine bnd, 1st ed, old & rare, out of print, used
Subj: Sci fiction & fantasy, art, fine arts

SAN MATEO — 77,561. Area code 415

THE BOOKSTORE — General
132 E Third Ave, 94401. Tel 415-343-2751
Estab 1958. 50,000 Vols
Types: Hb, juvenile, out of print, papbk, remainders
Subj: Art, rel-c,j,p

BOOKS UNLIMITED — Antiquarian-General
22 E 25th Ave, 94403. Tel 415-574-5377
Estab 1978. 36,000 Vols. 700 sq ft
Types: Hb, papbk, juvenile, used, old & rare, out of print
Subj: Sci fiction & fantasy, Western Amer, fiction, nonfiction

GRAPEVINE ANTIQUES & BOOKS — Mail Order-Antiquarian
PO Box 1134, 94403. Tel 415-341-7009
Estab 1972. 6000 Vols
Types: Fine bnd, 1st ed, hb, illus bk, juvenile, ltd ed, out of print, used

SAN RAFAEL — 44,700. Area code 415

CARL BLOMGREN BOOKS — Antiquarian
138 Woodland Ave (Mail add: PO Box 3597, 94912-3597). Tel 415-456-1471
Cat 3x ann
Types: 1st ed, hb, illus bk, old & rare, out of print
Subj: Californiana, photog, art

MANDRAKE BOOKSHOP — General
910 Lincoln Ave, 94901. Tel 415-453-3484
Mgr, Virginia Berry
Estab 1968. 100,000 Vols. 4000 sq ft
Types: Hb, juvenile, new & used, out of print, illus bk
Subj: Soc sci, sci-tech, mod lit, hist, drama, mystery & detective, sci fiction & fantasy, Western Amer, mil hist
See Also: New Albion Bookshop, Fairfax

JOHN YATES BOOKSELLER — Mail Order-Antiquarian
810 Pine Lane, 94903-2336. Tel 415-479-2582
Estab 1985. 4000 Titles. 4000 Vols. Cat 2x ann
Types: Imp, fine bnd, 1st ed, hb, ltd ed, used, out of print
Subj: Hist, travel, 19th & 20th century Eng lit, naval & military hist, oriental hist

SAN RAMON — 4084. Area code 415

LIGHT FOR YOUR LIFE BOOKSTORE — Religious-C, J, P
20801 San Ramon Valley Blvd, 94583. Tel 415-828-8011
Mgr, Dianne Allender
Estab 1977
Types: Col & el-hi text, hb, juvenile, out of print, papbk

SANTA ANA — 203,713. Area code 714

BOOK CENTER, DAVE HENSON, BOOKS — Mail Order-Antiquarian
PO Box 11402, 92711-1402. Tel 714-542-8839
Estab 1959. Cat 10x ann
Types: Hb, out of print, old & rare, remainders, used
Subj: Californiana, the West

PACIFIC LAW BOOKS INC — Law
1903 S. Main St, 92707. Tel 714-549-1187
Pres, Robert Thompson
Estab 1969. 70,000 Vols
Types: Hb, out of print, new & used
Subj: Nursing, travel

SANTA BARBARA — 74,542. Area code 805

ANDROMEDA BOOKSHOP — Science Fiction & Fantasy
741 De La Guerra Plaza, 93101. Tel 805-965-2400
Mgr, Lisa McNary
Estab 1979. 5000 Titles. 15000 Vols. 1100 sq ft
Types: Hb, imp, out of print, used, papbk
Subj: Horror
See Also: Goleta

AVALON BOOKS — Used
733 Chapala St, 93101. Tel 805-966-5612
Estab 1972. 5000 Vols
Types: Illus bk, fine bnd, 1st ed, hb, juvenile, ltd ed, new, old & rare, out of print, illus bk
Subj: Art

THE BOOK DEN — Used
15 E Anapamu St (Mail add: PO Box 733, 93102-0733). Tel 805-962-3321
Estab 1902. 25,000 Titles. 30,000 Vols. Cat 4x ann
Types: Out of print, juvenile, 1st ed
Subj: Mod lit, archit of California, Sp & Mex

DREW'S BOOKSHOP — Antiquarian
31 E Canon Perdido (Mail add: PO Box 163, 93102). Tel 805-966-3311
Estab 1957. 15,000 Vols. 1100 sq ft. Cat 3-4x ann
Types: 1st ed, hb, illus bk, juvenile, old & rare, out of print
Subj: Amer, Am hist & lit, Eng hist & lit, literary criticism

RICHARD GILBO - BOOKS — Mail Order-Antiquarian
3204 State St (Mail add: PO Box 12, 93013). Tel 805-687-7990
Estab 1987. 4000 Vols. Cat 6x ann
Types: Out of print, used
Subj: Black studies, hunting & fishing, black lit, fine printing, gastronomy, mod 1st ed, mountaineering, SW hist & lit, exotic travel

LOST HORIZON BOOKSTORE — Used
703 Anacapa St, 93101. Tel 805-962-4606
Estab 1983. 9000 Titles. 9000 Vols. 700 sq ft. Cat 1-2x ann
Types: Fine bnd, 1st ed, hb, illus bk, ltd ed, out of print, papbk, remainders, antiquarian
Subj: Art, Californiana, anthrop

NORTHWOODS BOOKS* — Mail Order-Juvenile
PO Box 23435, 93121. Tel 805-563-2433
1900 Titles. 2000 Vols. Cat 3x ann
Types: Hb, illus bk, out of print

RUDD'S CHRISTIAN SUPPLY* — General
3333 State St, 93105. Tel 805-682-8063
Mgr, Ruth Ann Roberts; Buyer, Debbie Lawson; Merch Mgr, Tony Quicke
Estab 1954. 12,000 Titles. 26,000 Vols. Cat ann
Types: For lang, hb, bibles, juvenile, out of print, papbk, remainders, col text
Subj: Inspirational, biog, reference, family studies, health, India, prospecting, Bible study

MARTIN A SILVER MUSICAL LITERATURE — Mail Order-Antiquarian
643 Willowglen Rd, 93105-2437. Tel 805-687-4198
Estab 1970. 5000 Vols. Cat
Types: Facsimile editions, 1st ed, hb, imp, old & rare, out of print, papbk, remainders, used

SANTA CRUZ — 41,483. Area code 408

CHIMNEY SWEEP BOOKS — Antiquarian
419 Cedar St, 95060-4304. Tel 408-458-1044
Estab 1972. 25,000 Vols. 1200 sq ft. Cat 4x ann
Types: Old & rare, out of print
Subj: Gardening, Irish hist & lit, rel studies

LOGOS BOOKS & RECORDS — Used
1117 Pacific Ave, 95060. Tel 408-426-2106
Owner, Gemini Sales Inc; Mgr, John Livingston
Estab 1969
Types: Col text, for lang, hb, juvenile, new, old & rare, out of print, papbk, remainders

SANTA MARIA — 39,685. Area code 805

BROADWAY BOOKS — General
115 N Broadway, 93454. Tel 805-925-1090
Estab 1983. 15,000 Titles. 20,000 Vols. 1500 sq ft
Types: Used, remainders, juvenile, hb, for lang, out of print, mass mkt papbk, high priced papbk, old & rare
See Also: Broadway Books at That Olde House, Los Alamos

KENNETH L WOLF - BOOKS — Mail Order-Antiquarian
PO Box 5673, 93456. Tel 805-928-8024
2000 Titles. 2500 Vols. Cat ann
Types: Old & rare, out of print, papbk, used
Subj: Aubrey Beardsley

SANTA MONICA — 88,314. Area code 213

A CHANGE OF HOBBIT — Science Fiction & Fantasy
1853 Lincoln Blvd, 90404. Tel 213-473-2873
Mgr, Bill Glass
Estab 1972. 50,000 Titles. 200,000 Vols. 4800 sq ft
Types: 1st ed, hb, imp UK, mass mkt papbk, old & rare, out of print, papbk, remainders, used
Subj: Horror

CHEROKEE BOOKSHOP INC — Antiquarian
1212 Santa Monica Mall, 90401. Tel 213-458-9176
Estab 1950. 80,000 Vols
Types: Illus bk, fine bnd, out of print, old & rare, used, 1st ed, color plated
Subj: Amer, art, hist, metaphys & occult

FOWLER-MILLS GALLERIES — Art Gallery
3005 Main St, Suite 519, 90405. Tel 213-392-3313
Estab 1978. 5000 Titles. 8000 Vols
Types: For lang, hb, imp, out of print, old & rare, used
Subj: Anthrop, art, Asian studies, Indonesia, Oceania, primitive cultures

HENNESSEY & INGALLS INC — Art
1254 Third St Promenade, 90401. Tel 213-458-9074
Mgr & Buyer, Mark P Hennessey
Estab 1968. 75,000 Vols. 6000 sq ft. Cat
Types: Hb, out of print, papbk, remainders, used
Subj: Art, archit, gardening, graphic design

HI DE HO COMICS & FANTASY — Science Fiction & Fantasy
525 Santa Monica, 90401. Tel 213-394-2820, 451-0463
Estab 1977. 500,000 Vols. 2000 sq ft
Types: 1st ed, illus bk, juvenile, ltd ed, new & used, old & rare, out of print, papbk, remainders

KENNETH KARMIOLE BOOKSELLER, INC — Antiquarian
1225 Santa Monica Mall, 90401. Tel 213-451-4342
Estab 1976. 20,000 Vols. 3000 sq ft. Cat 15x ann
Types: 1st ed, incunab, illus bk, ltd ed, old & rare, out of print
Subj: Art, bks on bks, hist of printing

HOWARD KARNO BOOKS & GALLERY — Antiquarian-Latin America
1229 Santa Monica Blvd (Mail add: PO Box 431, 90406). Tel 213-458-1619
Estab 1978. 15,000 Vols. Cat 20x ann
Types: Facsimile editions, 1st ed, hb, illus bk, imp, old & rare, out of print, papbk, used, Port lang, Sp lang
Subj: Archaeol, Mex, art, Judaica, genealogy, hist, music, natural hist, opera, scholarly lit, performing arts, art, food, wines, Arctic art

KROWN & SPELLMAN BOOKSELLERS — Mail Order-Antiquarian
1243 Santa Monica Mall, 90401. Tel 213-395-0300
Estab 1977. 10,000 Vols. Cat 3x ann
Types: Facsimile editions, 1st ed, hb, imp, incunab, out of print, old & rare, remainders
Subj: Ancient hist & lit, Egyptology, medieval studies, Renaissance hist & lit, theol, class lang

BARRY R LEVIN SCIENCE FICTION & FANTASY LITERATURE — Psychiatry
726 Santa Monica Blvd, Suite 201, 90401. Tel 213-458-6111
Estab 1973
Types: Fine bnd, 1st ed, hb, imp UK, new & used, old & rare, ltd ed, out of print, proofs & review copies

MORRISON AND KLINE BOOKS — Antiquarian
309 Arizona Ave, 90401. Tel 213-395-4747
Estab 1985. 20,000 Titles. 25,000 Vols. 1200 sq ft. Cat 2x ann
Types: Hb, imp Isr, imp Ger, imp Fr, Fr lang, Ger lang, Hebr lang, facsimile editions, fine bnd, 1st ed, illus bk, juvenile, ltd ed, old & rare, out of print, remainders, used
Subj: Judaica, metaphysics, scholarly lit, humanities, hist of religions

TWELFTH STREET BOOKSELLERS — Antiquarian
827 12th St (Mail add: PO Box 3103, 90403). Tel 213-393-1891
Estab 1984. 1800 Titles. 1800 Vols. Cat 3-4x ann
Types: 1st ed, hb, illus bk, old & rare, out of print, remainders, used, fine bnd
Subj: Gemology, jewelry, Antartica

SANTA PAULA — 20,552. Area code 805

MR NICHOLS — Paperback
910 E Main St, 93060. Tel 805-525-7804
Estab 1986. 5000 Titles. 5000 Vols. 2400 sq ft
Types: Juvenile, out of print, new & used

SANTA ROSA — 83,205. Area code 707

VIRGINIA BURGMAN — Mail Order-Antiquarian
3198 Hidden Valley Dr, 95404-1832. Tel 707-526-2482
Estab 1959. 3000 Vols. Cat 2x ann
Types: 1st ed, hb, old & rare, out of print
Subj: Art, Californiana, mystery & detective

TREEHORN BOOKS — Antiquarian
625 Fourth St, 95404. Tel 707-525-1782
Estab 1979. 40,000 Vols. 4000 sq ft
Types: Illus bk, out of print

SEBASTOPOL — 5500. Area code 707

BETSY HOOK BOOKFINDER — Mail Order-Antiquarian
321 S Main St, 95472. Tel 707-829-0916
Types: Out of print
Subj: Luther Burbank

SEPULVEDA — Area code 818

B LYNCH BOOK FINDER — Search Service
8840 Debra Ave, 91343. Tel 818-892-8491
Types: Out of print, used, 1st ed, hb, old & rare

SHERMAN OAKS — Area code 818

DANGEROUS VISIONS — Science Fiction & Fantasy
13563 Ventura Blvd, 91423. Tel 818-986-6963
Estab 1981. 19,000 Titles. 40,000 Vols. 1500 sq ft
Types: Out of print, 1st ed, ltd ed, new & used, imp UK, juvenile, old & rare, papbk, remainders
Subj: Philos, poetry, mod lit, Latin Am, horror

SCENE OF THE CRIME — Mystery & Detective
13636 Ventura Blvd, 91423-3798. Tel 818-981-2583
Estab 1975. 50,000 Titles. 75,000 Vols. 2600 sq ft. Cat 4x ann
Types: Hb, imp, new & used, out of print, papbk, remainders

SHINGLE SPRINGS — Area code 916

BARNSTORMER BOOKS — Antiquarian-Aviation
P O Box 147, 95682-0147. Tel 916-677-8823
Estab 1984. 3000 Titles. 3100 Vols. Cat 6x ann
Types: 1st ed, hb, old & rare, out of print, used
Subj: Jazz

SIERRA MADRE — 10,837. Area code 818

SULLIVAN-GOSS GALLERY — Art
27 N Baldwin Ave, 91024. Tel 818-355-2338
Estab 1984. 8000 Titles. 4 Vols. Cat 6x ann
Types: Out of print, used, fine bnd, 1st ed, illus bk, new & used, old & rare, juvenile
Subj: Illus, catalog raisonnes

SIMI VALLEY — 77,500. Area code 805

BILL'S OLD BOOKS & MAGAZINES — Mail Order
2035 N Brower, 93065. Tel 805-526-3285
Estab 1965. 21,000 Titles. 5000 Vols. 875 sq ft
Types: Hb, for lang, out of print, papbk, col text, used
Subj: Rel, fiction, nonfiction, mags from 1850-1980

SOLVANG — 2004. Area code 805

HOROLOGICAL RESTORATION SERVICES-RENAISSANCE BOOK DEPT — Antiques
1656 Mission Dr, 93463-2633. Tel 805-688-4774, 688-6222. FAX: 805-686-4044
Estab 1974. 300 Titles. 400 Vols. 200 sq ft
Types: Hb, imp, out of print, papbk
Subj: Horological & automatic musical instruments lit

SONOMA — 6054. Area code 707

THE BROWN STUDY BOOKSHOP — General
752 Broadway, 95476. Tel 707-996-6888
Estab 1984. 15,000 Titles. 15,000 Vols. 750 sq ft
Types: Hb, imp, juvenile, out of print, papbk, remainders, used, imp UK
Subj: Gardening, hist

SONOMA BOOKENDS BOOKSTORE — General
201 W Napa St, 95476. Tel 707-938-5926
Estab 1979. 14,000 Titles. 65,000 Vols. Cat 3x ann
Types: Hb, juvenile, out of print, papbk, remainders

SONORA — 3239. Area code 209

ALTA'S — General
20418 Green Acres Rd, 95370
Estab 1983. 10,000 Titles. 10,000 Vols
Types: Hb, illus bk, juvenile, old & rare, out of print, papbk, used

STANFORD — 8691. Area code 415

QUEST RARE BOOKS — General
774 Santa Ynez, 94305. Tel 415-324-3119
Estab 1986. 9000 Titles. 10,000 Vols. 4000 sq ft. Cat 2x ann
Types: Imp UK, out of print, fine bnd, 1st ed, hb, illus bk, old & rare
Subj: Econ, landscape archit, garden hist & design, polit economy

STANFORD BOOKSTORE — College
515 Lasuen St, 94305-3079. Tel 415-329-1217
Gen Mgr, Eldon Speed
Estab 1897. 125,000 Titles. 500,000 Vols
Types: Hb, juvenile, out of print, papbk, remainders, used
Subj: Medicine
See Also: Palo Alto

THULASI BOOK IMPORTS — Importer
Box 7850, 94305-0186. Tel 415-968-6345
Mgr, Francis Assisi; Merch Mgr, Aruna Yasmeen; Juv Buyer, Shashi Khalil
Estab 1976. 1600 sq ft. Cat 4x ann
Types: Out of print, Sanskrit lang
Subj: India, rel-Hindu

STOCKTON — 149,779. Area code 209

THE BOOK SELLER — Antiquarian
1415 Belvedere Ave, 95205. Tel 209-466-0445
Estab 1963. 100,000 Vols. 4000 sq ft. Cat
Types: Col & el-hi text, 1st ed, hb, juvenile, out of print, papbk, used
Subj: Am hist & lit, art, biog, fiction, literary criticism, metaphys & occult, warfare, world hist, cooking, archit, drama, engineering, law, music, poetry, sci fiction & fantasy

HARVARD BOOK STORE — Used
336 E Market, 95202. Tel 209-464-6571
Mgr, Fred Heil
Estab 1920. 25,000 Titles. 25,000 Vols
Types: Hb, juvenile, out of print, mass mkt papbk, used, 1st ed, illus bk

MAXWELL'S BOOKMARK — General
2103 Pacific Ave, 95204-5380. Tel 209-466-0194
Estab 1939. 10,000 Vols. Cat ann
Types: Hb, juvenile, out of print, old & rare, papbk, remainders, small presses, new, antiquarian
Subj: Art, Californiana, cooking, mod lit, Western Amer, golf

STUDIO CITY — Area code 818

LARRY EDMUNDS CINEMA & THEATRE BOOKSHOP — Performing Arts
11969 Ventura Blvd, 91604. Tel 818-508-7511
Types: Hb, out of print, papbk, remainders

SUNNYVALE — 106,618. Area code 408

NORMAN HOPPER BOOKS — Mail Order
1142 Plymouth Dr, 94087. Tel 408-736-8714
Estab 1979. 7000 Titles. 8000 Vols. 600 sq ft
Types: Hb, juvenile, out of print, used

SUN VALLEY — Area code 818

EXPENDABLE SUPPLY STORE INC — Variety Store
7848 N San Fernando Rd, 91352. Tel 818-767-5065
Types: Out of print, papbk, col text, el-hi text, used

THOUSAND OAKS — 77,797. Area code 805

SCIENCE FICTION BOOKS — Science Fiction & Fantasy
783 Thousand Oaks Blvd (Mail add: PO Box 1038, 91301). Tel 805-495-0299
Mgr, Ray Ellingsen
Estab 1965. 60,000 Vols. Cat 4x ann
Types: Hb, out of print, used

TOPANGA — Area code 213

BOULEVARD BOOKS — Mail Order-Used
PO Box 89, 90290. Tel 213-455-1036
Estab 1958. 30,000 Vols. Cat 3x ann
Types: Hb, out of print
Subj: Mystery & detective, plays & screenplays

TORRANCE — 131,497. Area code 213

BOOK BUDDY — General
1328 Sartori Ave, 90501. Tel 213-328-1134
Assistant Mgr, Bill Wilson
Estab 1977. 30,000 Vols. 1500 sq ft
Types: Hb, papbk, old & rare, out of print, used

TORRANCE BOOKSTORE — Used
1338 El Prado, 90501. Tel 213-212-7712
Estab 1985. 50,000 Vols
Types: Hb, out of print, papbk, new

TURLOCK — 26,291. Area code 209

BOOKS IN TRANSIT — Arts & Crafts
2830 Case Way, 95380. Tel 209-632-6984
Estab 1975. 1500 Titles. 1600 Vols. Cat 3x ann
Types: Used, out of print

GARCIA-GARST, BOOKSELLER — Antiquarian-General
334 North Center, 95380. Tel 209-632-5054
Mgr, Beverly A Garst
Estab 1978. 70,000 Vols. 2000 sq ft
Types: 1st ed, hb, juvenile, old & rare, out of print, papbk, new & used, illus bk
Subj: Amer, Californiana, Gene Stratton-Porter, Stephen King, Jessie Willcox Smith, Oz bks, Maxfield Parrish, Nielson

TWIN PEAKS — Area code 714

UPPER ROOM BOOKSTORE — Religious
PO Drawer A, 26409 Hwy 189, 92391. Tel 714-337-6116
Owner, Calvary Chapel of Costa Mesa; Admin Richard Goswiller
Estab 1974
Types: High priced papbk, hb, juvenile, mass mkt papbk, out of print

VAN NUYS — Area code 818

DAVIS & SCHORR ART BOOKS — Antiquarian-Art
6131 Atoll Ave, 91401. Tel 818-787-1322
Estab 1972. 11,250 Titles. 12,000 Vols. 1200 sq ft. Cat 3x ann
Types: Facsimile editions, hb, illus bk, imp, ltd ed, new, old & rare, out of print, papbk, used
Subj: Archit, fine arts, photog, artists monographs, art hist

THEODORE FRONT MUSICAL LITERATURE, INC — Music Store
16122 Cohasset St, 91406. Tel 818-994-1902
Mgr & Buyer, Christine Dimidgian-Clark
Estab 1961. 32,000 Vols. Cat 2x ann
Types: Hb, imp, out of print, old & rare, remainders, new & used, audio visual mat, for lang
Subj: Dance

JOHN MAKAREWICH, BOOKS — Mail Order-Antiquarian
PO Box 7032, 91409
20,000 Vols. Cat
Types: Ltd ed, 1st ed, hb, out of print, used, illus bk, fine press
Subj: Martial arts, performing arts, scholarly lit, art, bks on bks, Western Amer, Eng & Am 20th century lit

VENICE — Area code 213

SMALL WORLD BOOKS — Paperback
1407 Ocean Front Walk, 90291. Tel 213-399-2360
Estab 1974. 65,000 Vols. 2500 sq ft
Types: Hb, juvenile, small presses, new & used, out of print
Subj: Poetry

VENTURA — 55,797. Area code 805

CALICO CAT BOOKSHOP — Antiquarian
495 E Main St, 93001-2696. Tel 805-643-7849
Owner, Robinson's Books & Creative Arts Inc; Vpres, Richard Cormack
Estab 1975. 15,000 Vols. 1500 sq ft
Types: Facsimile editions, fine bnd, 1st ed, hb, illus bk, juvenile, ltd ed, new, old & rare, out of print, papbk, used
Subj: Art, cooking, gardening, Western Amer

SECOND TIME AROUND BOOKSHOP — Antiquarian
391 E Main St, 93001. Tel 805-643-3154
Mgr, James Staley
Estab 1971. 40,000 Titles. 40,000 Vols
Types: Hb, juvenile, papbk, used, old & rare, 1st ed, out of print
Subj: Metaphys & occult, sci fiction & fantasy, mysticism, mod 1st ed

VISTA — 35,834. Area code 619

THE BOOK DELI — General
206 S Santa Fe, 92084. Tel 619-758-9000
Estab 1980. 42,000 Titles. 45,000 Vols. 1300 sq ft. Cat 2x ann
Types: Out of print, juvenile, hb, papbk, used
Subj: Cooking, hist, rel studies

RAINBOW GARDENS BOOKSHOP — Mail Order-Horticulture
1444 E Taylor St, 92084. Tel 619-758-4290

Estab 1980. 225 Titles. 2000 Vols. Cat ann
Types: Jap lang, Sp lang, hb, imp, facsimile editions, 1st ed, illus bk, old & rare, out of print, papbk, remainders, new & used
Subj: Cactus & succulent bks only

CHARLES E WYATT BOOKSELLER — Mail Order-Antiquarian
PO Box 2883, 92083. Tel 619-726-7442
Estab 1984. 2000 Titles. Cat 5x ann
Types: Used, 1st ed, fine bnd, illus bk, ltd ed, old & rare, out of print
Subj: Sci fiction & fantasy, illus, Arthurian, Celtic hist

WALNUT — 9978. Area code 714

GRAND AVENUE BOOKSHOP — General
1249 N Grand Ave, 91789. Tel 714-595-8992
Estab 1987. 35,000 Titles. 40,000 Vols. 1500 sq ft
Types: Used, juvenile, out of print, high priced papbk, mass mkt papbk, remainders
Subj: Literary criticism, antq, jazz

WALNUT CREEK — 53,643. Area code 415

THE BOOK SHOP — Used
2687 Cherry Lane, 94596. Tel 415-937-5040
Estab 1979. 4000 Vols. 500 sq ft. Cat 2x ann
Types: 1st ed, hb, illus bk, ltd ed, out of print

HOOKED ON BOOKS — Used
1854 Tice Valley Blvd, 94595. Tel 415-933-1025
Estab 1975. 60,000 Vols
Types: Hb, out of print, papbk, new & used, comics
Subj: Fiction, romance, sci fiction & fantasy

GEORGE HUBERT BOOKS — Mail Order-Antiquarian
2173-2 Ptarmigan Dr, 94595. Tel 415-937-6652
Estab 1976. 400 sq ft. Cat
Types: Out of print, used, old & rare
Subj: Metaphys & occult, freemasonry, alchemy, hermetics, kabala

BEA SIEGEL BOOKS — Antiquarian
333 Shady Glen Rd, 94596. Tel 415-945-7031
Estab 1981. 5000 Titles. 5000 Vols. Cat 4x ann
Types: Hb, 1st ed, out of print, old & rare
Subj: Amer, Western Amer, Californiana

WEAVERVILLE — 5950. Area code 916

BLITZ BOOKS — Mail Order-Antiquarian
PO Box 1076, 96093. Tel 916-623-5430
Estab 1957. 5000 Vols. Cat 8x ann
Types: Old & rare, out of print
Subj: Californiana, Western Amer

WEST COVINA — 80,094. Area code 818

REDEEMERS — Religious
551 Francisquito, Suite D, 91791. Tel 818-917-7618
Mgr, Sharon Dew
2100 sq ft
Types: Hb, papbk, juvenile, Sp lang, out of print
Subj: Educ, multi-denominational

WEST HOLLYWOOD — Area code 213

EFFORTLESS BOOKS — General
1215 N Genesee Ave, 90048. Tel 213-656-6948
Types: Hb, out of print, papbk, used

FRONT ROW CENTER — Performing Arts
8127 W Third, 90048. Tel 213-852-0149
Estab 1976
Types: Hb, out of print, papbk, used, 1st ed, old & rare
Subj: Drama, opera, circus, ballet, play scripts

WESTLAKE VILLAGE — Area code 818

221 BOOKS — Mail Order-Antiquarian
760 Carlisle Canyon Rd, 91361. Tel 818-889-2640
Estab 1978. 4500 Vols. 250 sq ft. Cat
Types: 1st ed, old & rare, out of print, used
Subj: Literary criticism, A Conan Doyle, H Rider Haggard, Sherlock Holmes, H G Wells

WHITTIER — 68,872. Area code 213

FAMILY BOOKSTORE — Antiquarian
6725 Comstock Ave, 90601. Tel 213-696-2683
Estab 1956. 65,000 Vols
Types: Facsimile editions, hb, imp, out of print, papbk, old & rare, used
Subj: Alaskana, Arctic, Can, hunting & fishing, stock market

R VALDEZ BOOKSELLER & BOOKBINDER — Antiquarian
7022 Milton Ave (Mail add: PO Box 607, 90608). Tel 213-693-6684
Mgr, Timothy Rodriguez
Estab 1981. 60,000 Vols. 4000 sq ft
Types: Fine bnd, 1st ed, hb, illus bk, juvenile, ltd ed, old & rare, out of print, papbk, used
Subj: Californiana, Western Amer, 19th century British lit

WOODLAND HILLS — Area code 818

ROBERT ROSS & CO — Mail Order-Antiquarian
6101 El Escorpion Rd, 91367. Tel 818-346-6152
Cat
Types: Illus bk, old & rare, out of print, used
Subj: Hist, travel, cartography, geography

LEN UNGER RARE BOOKS — Antiquarian-Mystery & Detective
23133 Ventura Blvd, Suite 101, 91364. Tel 805-497-7281. Also 818-883-2437
Estab 1981. 3000 Vols. Cat 2x ann
Types: 1st ed, hb, ltd ed, old & rare, out of print, imp Eng
Subj: Fiction

BEULAH — Area code 719

BARRIE D WATSON BOOKSELLER — Antiquarian
PO Box 38, 8760 Grand, 81023. Tel 719-485-3136
Estab 1969. 20,000 Vols. Cat 4x ann
Types: Facsimile editions, 1st ed, hb, incunab, out of print, old & rare, used
Subj: Am hist & lit, law, natural hist, falconry

BOULDER — 76,685. Area code 303

COLORADO BOOKSTORE — College
1111 Broadway, 80302. Tel 303-442-5051. Telex 45-902
Mgr, Steve Falke
Types: Hb, juvenile, out of print, papbk

THE KING'S MARKET, BOOKS & PRINTS — Antiquarian
PO Box 709, 80306. Tel 303-449-8999
Estab 1981. 10,000 Vols. 1000 sq ft. Cat 2x ann
Types: Fine bnd, 1st ed, hb, old & rare, out of print, used
Subj: Coloradiana, geol, natural hist, psychol, sci-tech, Western Amer, mining, mountaineering, Govt docs

CASTLE ROCK — 3921. Area code 303

HOOKED ON BOOKS — General
112 S Wilcox St, 80104. Tel 303-688-1186
Estab 1986. 5000 Titles. 2200 sq ft
Types: Hb, juvenile, out of print, mass mkt papbk, high priced papbk, used, books-on-tape, young readers
Subj: Coloradiana, Western Amer, fiction, nonfiction, women's studies, western art

COLORADO SPRINGS — 215,150. Area code 719

ALLBOOKS — Antiquarian
1331 Imperial Rd, 80918. Tel 719-548-1273
Estab 1979. 3,000 Titles. 3000 Vols. 150 sq ft. Cat
Types: Hb, out of print, old & rare, papbk, used
Subj: Geol, Am Indian studies, Lin Yutang

THE BOOK HOME INC — Antiquarian-General
119 E Dale (Mail add: PO Box 825, 80901). Tel 719-632-0555
Merch Mgr, Charles Thomas
Estab 1942. 60,000 Vols. Cat
Types: Hb, out of print, high priced papbk, used, Ger lang
Subj: Sci-tech

THE CHINOOK BOOKSHOP INC — General
210 N Tejon St, 80903. Tel 719-635-1195
Estab 1959. 60,000 Vols. 5000 sq ft
Types: Hb, juvenile, out of print, papbk, remainders
Subj: Bus & mgt, medicine, sci-tech, Western Amer, Fr, Ger & Sp lang

HENRY A CLAUSEN BOOKSHOP — Used
224 1/2 N Tejon St, 80903. Tel 719-634-1193
Estab 1946. 50,000 Vols
Types: Facsimile editions, 1st ed, hb, out of print, old & rare, remainders
Subj: Class studies, Coloradiana, hist, theol

BERNARD A MARGOLIS - BOOKS — Mail Order-Antiquarian
10640 Hungate Rd, 80908. Tel 313-243-5213
Estab 1975. 5000 Titles. 5000 Vols. Cat
Types: Fine bnd, 1st ed, hb, illus bk, juvenile, ltd ed, old & rare, out of print, papbk, used
Subj: Beats, Jack Kerouac, Shakers, United Soc of Believers, Eric Sloane

CORTEZ — 7095. Area code 303

DON WOODARD'S INDIAN TRADING POST MUSEUM — Museum
27688 E Hwy 160, 81321-9366. Tel 303-565-3986
Estab 1952. 500 Titles. 3000 Vols. 4400 sq ft. Cat ann
Types: Col text, hb, juvenile, out of print, high priced papbk, remainders, used
Subj: Am Indian studies

DENVER — 491,396. Area code 303

ASTORIA BOOKS & PRINTS — Antiquarian
1801 Lawrence St, 80202. Tel 303-292-4122
Estab 1979. 25,000 Vols. 1700 sq ft. Cat 4x ann
Types: Out of print, juvenile, mod 1st editions
Subj: Mod lit, art

BOOK FORUM — General
709 E Sixth, 80203. Tel 303-837-9069
Estab 1980. 20,000 Vols. 1500 sq ft
Types: Hb, old & rare, out of print
Subj: Hist

THE BOOK PROSPECTOR — Antiquarian
1738 E Evans, 80210. Tel 303-777-0649
Estab 1974. 12,000 Titles. 12,000 Vols
Types: High priced papbk, out of print
Subj: Scholarly lit, Western Amer, hist, antq

CITY SPIRIT BOOKS — Art
1434 Blake St, 80202. Tel 303-595-0434
Owner, City Spirit, Inc; Mgr, Michael Fagan
Estab 1983. 10,000 Titles. 12,000 Vols. Cat 4x ann
Types: Hb, papbk, col text, old & rare, out of print, folios
Subj: Art, design

CULPIN'S ANTIQUARIAN BOOKSHOP — Antiquarian
3827 W 32nd Ave, 80211-3192. Tel 303-455-0317. WATS 800-545-BOOK
Estab 1976. 85,000 Titles. 90,000 Vols. 3200 sq ft. Cat
Types: Hb, imp UK, juvenile, out of print, remainders, facsimile editions, fine bnd, 1st ed, incunab, illus bk, ltd ed, new, old & rare
Subj: Western Amer, fiction, military, geol, Amer, railroadiana, sci-tech, art

DENVER BOOK FAIR — Used Paperback
44 S Broadway, 80209. Tel 303-777-9946
Estab 1968. 100,000 Vols. 3000 sq ft
Types: Hb, out of print, papbk, juvenile, nostalgic mag

THE HERMITAGE ANTIQUARIAN BOOKSHOP — Antiquarian
2817 E Third Ave, 80206. Tel 303-388-6811
Mgr, Glenn Finley
25,000 Vols. Cat
Types: 1st ed, hb, out of print, old & rare
Subj: Hist, philos, scholarly lit, Western Amer, western hist

MURDER BY THE BOOK — Mystery & Detective
1574 South Pearl St, 80210. Tel 303-871-9401
Estab 1980. 20,000 Vols. 1000 sq ft
Types: Hb, juvenile, out of print, papbk, used, imp Eng, Jap, Fr
Subj: Fiction, Sherlockiana

MUSEUM OF WESTERN ART BOOKSHOP — Museum
1727 Tremont Pl, 80202. Tel 303-292-0500
Estab 1983. 100 Titles. 6500 Vols. 3000 sq ft. Cat 2x ann
Types: 1st ed, hb, illus bk, remainders, papbk, out of print, ltd ed, new
Subj: Western artists, Am Indian studies, photog, Western Amer

ROSENSTOCK ARTS BOOK DEPT — Americana
1228 E Colfax Ave, 80218. Tel 303-832-7190
Mgr, Linda M Lebsack
Estab 1928. 10,000 Vols
Types: New, out of print
Subj: Art, fine arts

DURANGO — 11,426. Area code 303

SOUTHWEST BOOK TRADER — Antiquarian-General
175 E Fifth St, 81301. Tel 303-247-8479
Estab 1983. 20,000 Titles. 20,000 Vols
Types: Used, fine bnd, 1st ed, hb, illus bk, juvenile, ltd ed, new, old & rare, out of print, papbk
Subj: Photog, railroadiana

ENGLEWOOD — 30,021. Area code 303

COLORADO PIONEER BOOKS — Antiquarian-Western Americana
4755 S Broadway, 80110. Tel 303-789-0379
Estab 1982. 7500 Vols. 600 sq ft
Types: Old & rare, out of print

FORT COLLINS — 64,632. Area code 303

OLD CORNER BOOKSHOP — Antiquarian
216 Linden St, 80524. Tel 303-484-6186
Estab 1970. 50,000 Vols
Types: Hb, juvenile, for lang, 1st ed, old & rare, out of print, papbk, new & used, fine bnd
Subj: Coloradiana, Western Amer

GREELEY — 53,006. Area code 303

MOUNT FALCON BOOKS INC — Antiquarian
926 Ninth Ave, 80631. Tel 303-356-9211
Estab 1979. 12,000 Vols. 1700 sq ft
Types: Facsimile editions, 1st ed, hb, mass mkt papbk, old & rare, out of print, used
Subj: Western Amer, military

GUNNISON — 5785. Area code 303

BOOK WORM — General
21 N Main, 81230. Tel 303-641-3693
Mgr, Jim Houston; Asst Mgr Ann Atchley
Estab 1987. 4000 Titles. 5000 Vols. 1200 sq ft
Types: Hb, papbk, juvenile, out of print, used, 1st ed, new, old & rare
Subj: Natural hist, railroadiana, regional

LAKEWOOD — 112,848. Area code 303

COLORADO CHRISTIAN COLLEGE BOOKSTORE — College
180 S Garrison St, 80226. Tel 303-238-5386
Mgr, Jo Lewis
Estab 1985
Types: Hb, out of print, papbk
Subj: Rel studies

LOVELAND — 30,244. Area code 303

THE CACHE — Antiquarian
7157 W US 34, 80537. Tel 303-667-1081
Estab 1973. 20,000 Vols. 400 sq ft. Cat
Types: 1st ed, hb, juvenile, new, out of print, old & rare, papbk, used
Subj: Coloradiana, Zane Grey

MONTROSE — 8722. Area code 303

MOUNTAIN VALLEY BOOKSELLERS — General
328 Main, 81401. Tel 303-249-1841
Estab 1984. 12,000 Titles. 18,000 Vols. 2000 sq ft
Types: Hb, juvenile, out of print, mass mkt papbk, papbk
Subj: Western Amer

PUEBLO — 101,686. Area code 719

MILLET & SIMPSON ANTIQUARIAN BOOKSELLERS — Antiquarian
224 S Union Ave, 81003. Tel 719-542-4462
Estab 1975. 6500 Vols. Cat 3x ann
Types: 1st ed, hb, illus bk, juvenile, ltd ed, out of print, old & rare
Subj: Western Amer

RIDGEWAY — area code 303

COLORADO BOOKMAN — Antiquarian-Western Americana
PO Box 346, 81432. Tel 303-327-4616
Estab 1974. 3000 Titles. 3000 Vols
Types: Out of print
Subj: Coloradiana, photog, Am Indian studies

BETHANY — 4330. Area code 203

WHITLOCK FARM BOOKSELLERS — Antiquarian
20 Sperry Rd, 06525. Tel 203-468-4730
Mgr, Everett Whitlock
Estab 1948. 50,000 Vols. 6500 sq ft. Cat 24x ann
Types: Fine bnd, 1st ed, hb, illus bk, incunab, imp, juvenile, ltd ed, new & used, old & rare, out of print, papbk
Subj: Agr, Amer, art, natural hist, country living

BRIDGEPORT — 142,546. Area code 203

BOB COWELL BOOKSELLER — Antiquarian
15 Pearsall Way, 06605. Tel 203-334-3025
5000 Titles. 5000 Vols. Cat ann
Types: Old & rare, out of print, used
Subj: Dogs

MURRAY'S BOOKFINDING SERVICE — Mail Order-Antiquarian
292 Jackson Ave, 06606. Tel 203-335-5598
Estab 1953. 45,000 Vols
Types: Old & rare, out of print, used
Subj: Fiction

CANTERBURY — 3426. Area code 203

STONE OF SCONE ANTIQUES & BOOKS — Antiquarian-Connecticutana
19 Water St, 06331. Tel 203-546-9917
Mgr, Jan Stratton
Estab 1976. 3500 Vols. 432 sq ft. Cat 2x ann
Types: 1st ed, hb, illus bk, juvenile, old & rare, out of print, used
Subj: New England, Western Amer, Amer, firearms ref

COLEBROOK — 1221. Area code 203

COLEBROOK BOOK BARN — Antiquarian
Rte 183, Box 108, 06021. Tel 203-379-3185
Estab 1955. 10,000 Vols. Cat
Types: Hb, used, 1st ed, out of print, old & rare, leather bound bks
Subj: Amer

COLUMBIA — 3386. Area code 203

HOP RIVER BOOKS — Mail Order
PO Box 261, 06237. Tel 203-228-3070
Estab 1968. 5000 Titles. 5000 Vols. Cat 2-3x ann
Types: Out of print, used
Subj: Military, natural hist

COVENTRY — 8895. Area code 203

ALLINSON GALLERY INC — Antiquarian-Art
46 Fieldstone Lane, 06238. Tel 203-742-8990
Estab 1977. 300 Vols. Cat ann
Types: Out of print
Subj: Fine prints & drawings, paintings

COVENTRY BOOKSHOP — Antiquarian
1159 Main St, PO Box 36, 06238. Tel 203-742-9875
Estab 1981. 15,000 Vols. 750 sq ft
Types: Fine bnd, 1st ed, hb, incunab, illus bk, juvenile, ltd ed, new, old & rare, out of print, papbk, remainders, used

DANBURY — 60,470. Area code 203

DEER PARK BOOKS — Mail Order-Used
27 Deer Park Rd, 06811. Tel 203-743-2246
Cat 12x ann
Types: Out of print, used, 1st ed, hb, illus bk, old & rare

LAURIAT'S L-320 — General
Danbury Fair, 7 Backus Ave, 06810. Tel 203-791-1134
Mgr, Pat Tiffany
Types: Hb, out of print

BARBARA WEINDLING BOOKSELLER — Mail Order
69 Ball Pond Rd, 06811. Tel 203-746-2514
Estab 1972. 5000 Titles. 7000 Vols. Cat 2x ann
Types: Juvenile, out of print, used
Subj: Cooking

DANIELSON — 4553. Area code 203

EXTENSIVE SEARCH SERVICE — Antiquarian
51 Squaw Rock Rd, 06239. Tel 203-774-1203
Estab 1981. Cat 3x ann
Types: Juvenile, out of print, high priced papbk, used
Subj: Connecticutana, local hist, Walt Disney titles, cartoon and comic character titles, Tv Guide mag

DERBY — 12,346. Area code 203

BOOKS BY THE FALLS — Antiquarian-General
253 Roosevelt Dr, Rt 34, 06418. Tel 203-734-6112
Mgr, Mark Maciag
Estab 1982. 40,000 Titles. 40,000 Vols. 3000 sq ft. Cat ann
Types: Used, for lang, out of print, fine bnd, 1st ed, hb, juvenile, ltd ed, old & rare, papbk, cookbks
Subj: Class studies, poetry, philos, metaphys & occult, art, esoteric

EAST HADDAM — 5621. Area code 203

CONNECTICUT RIVER BOOKSHOP — Antiquarian
PO Box 461, Goodspeed Landing, 06423. Tel 203-873-8881
Estab 1986. 15,000 Titles. 40,000 Vols. 1000 sq ft
Types: Out of print, juvenile
Subj: Nautical, hunting & fishing, art, archery, New England, travel, Amer

MAGIC HORN LTD — Used
95 Ray Hill Rd, 06423. Tel 203-873-1346
Mgr, Frederick H Miller
Estab 1983. 3000 Titles. 3000 Vols. 200 sq ft
Types: Hb, imp, juvenile, out of print, papbk, illus bk, old & rare, fine bnd, 1st ed, comics

EAST HAMPTON — 8572. Area code 203

BIBLIOLATREE — Antiquarian
Country Store Rte 66 (Mail add: Box 151, 06424). Tel 203-267-8222
Estab 1976. 25,000 Titles. 30,000 Vols. 1250 sq ft
Types: 1st ed, hb, illus bk, juvenile, old & rare, out of print, used
Subj: Art, nature & environ, hist, Amer, Eng hist & lit

ENFIELD — 42,695. Area code 203

JAN'S PAPERBACKS — Used Paperback
551 Hazard Ave, 06082. Tel 203-749-4228
Estab 1985. 8000 Titles. 20,000 Vols. 1000 sq ft
Types: Mass mkt papbk, high priced papbk, out of print, juvenile, used, best sellers, new
Subj: Metaphys & occult, mystery & detective, romance, adventure, horror, espionage, hist romance

FAIRFIELD — 54,849. Area code 203

A LUCAS BOOKS — Used
89 Round Hill Rd, 06430. Tel 203-259-2572
Estab 1972. 15,000 Titles. 15,000 Vols. 625 sq ft
Types: For lang, hb, juvenile, out of print, 1st ed

THE MUSEUM GALLERY BOOKSHOP — Antiquarian
360 Mine Hill Rd, 06430. Tel 203-259-7114
Estab 1976. 16,000 Vols. 610 sq ft. Cat
Types: Out of print, old & rare
Subj: Archaeol, archit, art, graphic arts, dec arts

JOHN M SKUTEL RARE BOOKS — Antiquarian
251 Carroll Rd, 06430
Cat 4x ann
Types: Out of print, old & rare
Subj: Am Indian studies, Amer, aviation, illus, medicine

GOSHEN — 1706. Area code 203

ANGLER'S & SHOOTER'S BOOKSHELF — Mail Order-Antiquarian
06756. Tel 203-491-2500
Estab 1967. 30,000 Vols. Cat 2x ann
Types: Facsimile editions, 1st ed, hb, imp, incunab, new & used, out of print, old & rare

HAMDEN — 51,071. Area code 203

AMERICAN WORLDS BOOKS — Mail Order
PO Box 6305 Whitneyville Sta, 06517-6305. Tel 203-776-3558
Estab 1975. 8000 Vols. Cat 8x ann
Types: Hb, old & rare, out of print, papbk, remainders, used
Subj: Am auth, Am hist & lit, biog, literary criticism

ANTIQUE BOOKS — Antiquarian
3651 Whitney Ave, 06518. Tel 203-281-6606
Estab 1972. 15,000 Titles. 25,000 Vols. 1950 sq ft. Cat 11x ann
Types: 1st ed, hb, juvenile, old & rare, out of print, used
Subj: Agr, hist, sci-tech, Amer, medicine, 19th century bks

FOLKWAYS SCHOLARLY BOOKS — Mail Order-Antiquarian
188 Armory St, 06517. Tel 301-320-5672
Estab 1978. 3500 Vols. Cat 1-2x ann
Types: Hb, old & rare, out of print, used
Subj: Soc sci, psychol, medicine, philos

DAVID LADNER BOOKS — Mail Order-Antiquarian
34 Wakefield St (Mail add: PO Box 6179, Whitneyville, 06517). Tel 203-288-6575
9500 Titles. 10,000 Vols. Cat 2-3x ann
Types: Facsimile editions, fine bnd, hb, illus bk, imp, ltd ed, old & rare, out of print, remainders, used, Hebr, Grk, Slavic, Latin, Ger, Polish & Eng langs
Subj: Art, bibliog, bks on bks, hist, literary criticism, early printing

MCBLAIN BOOKS — Antiquarian
PO Box 5062, 06518. Tel 203-281-0400 (by appt)
Estab 1970. 6000 Vols. Cat 6-10x ann
Types: Old & rare, out of print
Subj: Africa, Asian studies, black studies, Latin Am, Middle East, Pacific, West Indies, East Eur studies

HARTFORD — 136,392. Area code 203

WALTER E HALLBERG - BOOKSELLER — Antiquarian
16 Hawthorn St, 06105. Tel 203-524-1618
Estab 1935. 5000 Vols
Types: Old & rare, out of print
Subj: Connecticutana

THE JUMPING FROG — Antiquarian
161 South Whitney St, 06105. Tel 203-523-1622
Mgrs, William M & Deidre K W McBride
Estab 1978. 17,000 Vols. Cat 6x ann
Types: 1st ed, hb, old & rare, out of print, used, juvenile
Subj: Drama, fiction, humor, poetry, biog, nature & environ, art, Amer, mystery & detective, sci fiction & fantasy, travel, performing arts, warfare
Branches:
— MCBRIDE FIRST EDITIONS
157-B Sisson Ave, 06105. Tel 203-523-1622
Estab 1983. 2200 Titles. 2000 Vols. 725 sq ft. Cat 6 x ann
Types: 1st ed, hb, used, old & rare, out of print, remainders
Subj: Fiction, poetry, drama, humor, sci fiction & fantasy, mystery & detective, literary criticism

THE READER'S FEAST — General
529 Farmington Ave, 06105. Tel 203-232-3710
Asst Mgr, Tollie Miller
Estab 1975. 8000 Vols. 700 sq ft
Types: Hb, juvenile, out of print, papbk, remainders
Subj: Feminism, homosexuality, fiction, Social Studies

KENSINGTON — Area code 203

JULIAN J NADOLNY & CO — Mail Order
121 Hickory Hill Rd, 06037. Tel 203-225-5353
Estab 1967. Cat
Types: New, out of print, old & rare
Subj: Botany, geol, natural hist, zool, paleontology, hist of sci

LITCHFIELD — 7605. Area code 203

COBBLE COURT BOOKSHOP — General
PO Box 154, 06759. Tel 203-567-0084
Estab 1964. 5000 Vols
Types: Hb, imp, juvenile, out of print, papbk, remainders, used

STEELE BOOKSHOP — General
15 South St, 06759-1091. Tel 203-567-0748
Estab 1983. 25,000 Titles. 26,000 Vols. 1000 sq ft
Types: Juvenile, out of print, high priced papbk, mass mkt papbk only, remainders, used, hb, for lang
Subj: Hist, fiction, sci-tech

MANCHESTER — 49,761. Area code 203

BURIED UNDER BOOKS — Used
188 W Middle Tpke, 06040-4025. Tel 203-643-7295
Mgr, S Eldridge; Merch Mgr, Marc Patten
Estab 1980. 28,000 Titles. 50,000 Vols. 1550 sq ft
Types: Out of print, mass mkt papbk, remainders, comics, papbk, first ed papbk

MONROE — 14,010. Area code 203

THE BOOK SHOP — Used Paperback
146 Main St, 06468. Tel 203-261-6745
Estab 1982. 50,000 Titles. 1400 sq ft. Cat ann
Types: Out of print, juvenile, remainders, used
Subj: Fiction, mystery & detective, romance, sci fiction & fantasy

MYSTIC — 2568. Area code 203

MYSTIC SEAPORT MUSEUM STORES INC — Nautical
39 Greenmanville Ave, 06355. Tel 203-572-8551
Mgr & Buyer, Anne McNiel
Estab 1955. 10,000 Titles. 18,000 Vols. 1700 sq ft. Cat ann
Types: Hb, imp UK, juvenile, out of print, papbk, remainders
Subj: Antq, arts & crafts, whales & whaling, New England

TRADE WINDS GALLERY — Art Gallery
20 W Main St, 06355. Tel 203-536-0119
Estab 1974. 1200 sq ft
Types: Out of print, used
Subj: Cartography, hist of exploration & voyages

NEW HAVEN — 126,109. Area code 203

BRYN MAWR BOOKSHOP — Used
56 1/2 Whitney Ave, 06510. Tel 203-562-4217
Owner, Bryn Mawr Scholarship Fund; Mgrs, J W Meigs, et al
Estab 1970. 40,000 Vols
Types: For lang, hb, imp, out of print, papbk, juvenile
Subj: Fiction, biog, sci-tech, rel, philos, soc sci

O'CONNELL COMMUNICATIONS CONSULTING & SERVICES — Used
828 Orange St, 06511. Tel 203-777-3786
Estab 1976. 5000 Titles. 5000 Vols
Types: For lang, hb, imp, juvenile, out of print, papbk, high priced papbk
Subj: Am hist & lit, Brit hist & lit

OLD BOOK & PHOTO — Mail Order-Antiquarian
PO Box 1070, 06504-1070. Tel 203-562-7800
Estab 1974
Types: New, old & rare, out of print
Subj: Hist of photog

THE PAPERBACK TRADER — Used
1181 Chapel St, 06511. Tel 203-787-1727
Estab 1975. 40,000 Vols
Types: Fr, Ger & Sp lang, juvenile, out of print, papbk, new & back issue comics
Subj: Biog, class studies, fiction, psychol, sci-tech, mystery & detective, sci fiction & fantasy, romance, lit

PHAROS BOOKS — Antiquarian
248 View St (Mail add: P O Box 17, Fair Haven Sta, 06513). Tel 203-562-0085
Estab 1976. 65,000 Titles. 65,000 Vols. Cat 24x ann
Types: Fine bnd, 1st ed, hb, illus bk, imp Gr, juvenile, ltd ed, old & rare, out of print
Subj: Poetry, Ezra Pound, Greek Lit

R W SMITH BOOKSELLER — Antiquarian
51 Trumbull St, 06510. Tel 203-776-5564
Estab 1975. 15,000 Titles. 15,000 Vols. 200 sq ft. Cat 2x ann
Types: Out of print
Subj: Antq, archit, photog, Am art

WHITLOCK'S INC — Antiquarian
17 Broadway, 06511. Tel 203-562-9841
Estab 1900
Types: Hb, imp UK, old & rare, out of print, papbk
Subj: Connecticutana

NEW MILFORD — 19,420. Area code 203

F & S COMICS & FANTASY SHOP — Comics
54 Bank St, 06776. Tel 203-355-3426
Estab 1979. 20,000 Vols
Types: 1st ed, illus bk, imp UK, juvenile, new, old & rare, out of print, remainders, used
Subj: Fiction, sci fiction & fantasy, dungeon & dragons

SCARLET LETTER BOOKS & PRINTS — Mail Order-Antiquarian
155 Candlewood Mountain Rd, 06776. Tel 203-354-4181
Estab 1971. 3000 Vols. 200 sq ft. Cat ann
Types: 1st ed, illus bk, old & rare, out of print, hb, young adult
Subj: Antq, fore-edge
See Also: Kathleen & Michael Lazare, Saint Andrews, NB

NEW PRESTON — Area code 203

BRITANNIA BOOKSHOP — Antiquarian
At The Waterfall (Mail add: PO Box 295, 06777). Tel 203-868-0368
Mgrs, Sarah Stock & Barbara Corey Tippin
Estab 1984. 8000 Vols. 2500 sq ft. CatBuys indep
Types: Hb, imp, old & rare, juvenile, out of print, imp UK
Subj: Art, archit, auto, biog, drama, fiction, hunting & fishing, gardening, hist, music, natural hist, poetry, reference, rel studies, travel, animals, birds, theatre, royalty, British & Irish: 1850-1945

TIMOTHY MAWSON BOOKS — Mail Order-Antiquarian
Main St, 06777. Tel 203-868-0732
Estab 1979. 5000 Vols. Cat 4x ann
Types: Illus bk, out of print, old & rare, imp Eng
Subj: Gardening, wines, food, decorative arts

NEWTOWN — 19,107. Area code 203

BANCROFT BOOK MEWS — Mail Order-Antiquarian
86 Sugar Lane, 06470. Tel 203-426-6338
Estab 1982. 3500 Titles. 3500 Vols. Cat ann
Types: 1st ed, old & rare, out of print
Subj: Music, dance, films & filmmaking, theatre

THE PAGES OF YESTERYEAR — Antiquarian
9 Old Hawleyville Rd, 06470. Tel 203-426-0864 (by appt)
Estab 1964. 2000 Vols. Cat
Types: Fine bnd, old & rare, out of print
Subj: Hist, travel, art, illus, sci-tech, music, dance, gardening, agr

NORTHFORD — Area code 203

CARRIAGE-HOUSE BOOKS — Mail Order
726 Totoket Rd, 06472. Tel 203-484-9724
Estab 1981. 5000 Titles. 5,000 Vols. 1500 sq ft
Types: 1st ed, hb, illus bk, juvenile, old & rare, out of print, used

ELLIOT'S BOOKS OUT OF PRINT SPECIALISTS — Antiquarian-Scholarly Lit
Forest Rd, Box 6, 06472. Tel 203-484-2184
Estab 1957. 500,000 Vols. 10,000 sq ft
Types: 1st ed, illus bk, incunab, imp, ltd ed, old & rare, out of print, papbk
Subj: Art, humanities, soc sci, scholarly lit, sci-tech

NORTH HAVEN — 22,080. Area code 203

GREATER NEW HAVEN STATE TECHNICAL COLLEGE BOOKSTORE — College-Sci-Tech
88 Bassett Rd, 06473. Tel 203-239-3049
Mgr, Barbara Monca
Estab 1981
Types: Out of print, papbk, used
Subj: Computer sci, chem, math

ORANGE — 13,237. Area code 203

KEN NESHEIM — General
881 Indian Hill Rd, 06477
Estab 1985. Cat ann
Types: Facsimile editions, fine bnd, 1st ed, hb, illus bk, imp, ltd ed, old & rare, out of print, used, incunab

PLAINVILLE — 16,401. Area code 203

TREE OF LIFE BOOKSTORE — Religious-Christian
90 Whiting St, 06062. Tel 203-747-3732
Mgrs, William Lester & Edward Adamowich
Types: Hb, papbk, juvenile, out of print, bibles

POMFRET — 2775. Area code 203

ROGER BLACK — Antiquarian
Route 44 & 169, PO Box 214, 06259. Tel 203-928-2862
Mgr, Judith A Black
Estab 1975. 6000 Vols. Cat 2x ann
Types: Old & rare, out of print, used
Subj: Connecticutana

PUTNAM — 6855. Area code 203

BLUE STAR BOOKSTORE — Antiquarian-Science Fiction & Fantasy
355 1/2 Kennedy Dr (Mail add: 355 Kennedy Dr, 06260). Tel 203-928-4832
Mgr, Susannah Bates
Estab 1976. 24,000 Vols. Cat 6x ann
Types: 1st ed, hb, illus bk, imp, juvenile, ltd ed, new, out of print, old & rare, papbk, used
Subj: Mystery & detective, Western Amer, Britian

RIDGEFIELD — 20,120. Area code 203

SPORTS PRODUCTS INC — Mail Order
412 Main St, PO Box 392, 06877. Tel 203-438-3055
1400 Vols. Cat 4x ann
Types: Hb, papbk, out of print, remainders
Subj: Sports

SALISBURY — 3896. Area code 203

LION'S HEAD BOOKS — General
Academy St, 06068. Tel 203-435-9328
Estab 1974. 10,000 Titles. 600 sq ft. Cat
Types: 1st ed, hb, imp, juvenile, out of print, old & rare, papbk, used, new
Subj: Natural hist, gardening

SOUTHINGTON — 36,879. Area code 203

OMNI BOOKS — Paperback
102 Center St, 06489. Tel 203-276-8767
Estab 1987. 80,000 Titles. 80,000 Vols. 1500 sq ft
Types: Out of print, mass mkt papbk, remainders, used, comics
Subj: Mystery & detective, sci fiction & fantasy, new age

SOUTH NORWALK — Area code 203

WASHINGTON STREET BOOK STORE — General
119 Washington St, 06854. Tel 203-866-9204
Estab 1984. 18,000 Titles. 15,000 Vols. 1200 sq ft
Types: Hb, juvenile, out of print, mass mkt papbk, papbk, used
Subj: Nonfiction, arts & crafts, antq, cooking

SOUTH WINDSOR — 17,198. Area code 203

JOHN WOODS BOOKS — Antiquarian
347 Main St, 06074. Tel 203-289-3927, 236-5614
Estab 1976. 8000 Vols. Cat
Types: Fine bnd, ltd ed, out of print
Subj: Medicine

STONINGTON — 16,220. Area code 203

THE BOOK MART — General
17 High St, 06378. Tel 203-535-0401
50,000 Vols
Types: Hb, imp UK, juvenile, out of print, papbk, remainders

STRATFORD — 50,541. Area code 203

PRESTON C BEYER FINE LITERARY PROPERTY — Antiquarian
752A Pontiac Lane, 06497-8330. Tel 203-375-9073
Estab 1975. 3000 Vols. Cat 4-5x ann
Types: Facsimile editions, fine bnd, 1st ed, hb, illus bk, ltd ed, old & rare, out of print, used
Subj: Bks on bks, American expatriate writers

TORRINGTON — 30,987. Area code 203

ATTIC BOOKS & RECORDS — Mail Order
60 Northside Dr, 06790. Tel 203-496-9260
Estab 1969. 10,000 Titles. 10,000 Vols. Cat
Types: Papbk, out of print
Subj: Amer, fiction, art

JOHN S CRAIG PHOTOGRAPHIC HISTORIAN — Mail Order-Antiquarian
PO Box 1637, 06790. Tel 203-496-9791
Estab 1970. 1000 Titles. 5000 Vols. 1600 sq ft. Cat
Types: Facsimile editions, 1st ed, illus bk, old & rare, out of print, remainders, new & used

NUTMEG BOOKS — Antiquarian
354 New Litchfield St, 06790. Tel 203-482-9696
Estab 1977. 20,000 Vols. 800 sq ft. Cat 6x ann
Types: Out of print, old & rare

TRUMBULL — 32,989. Area code 203

WARREN BLAKE -BOOKS — Antiquarian-Astronomy
308 Hadley Dr, 06611
Estab 1972. 1200 Titles. 1500 Vols. 300 sq ft. Cat quarterly
Types: Old & rare, out of print
Subj: Astron

UNION — Area code 203

TRAVELER RESTAURANT — General
741 Buckley Hwy, Rte 84 Exit 74, 06076. Tel 203-684-4920
Mgr, Kathy Lisiewski; Clerk Victoria Walmus
Estab 1984. 25,000 Titles. 35,000 Vols. 2000 sq ft
Types: For lang, hb, imp, juvenile, out of print, mass mkt papbk, used

WALLINGFORD — 37,274. Area code 203

LIBRARY HOURS BOOKSHOP — General
40 N Main, 06492. Tel 203-284-1818
Mgr, Patricia B Kenyon
Types: Hb, papbk, juvenile, out of print

WASHINGTON — 3657. Area code 203

CROFTERS BOOK — Mail Order-Antiquarian
Old Litchfield Rd, PO Box 236, 06793
2000 Titles. 4000 Vols. 2000 sq ft
Types: Old & rare, out of print, remainders, used
Subj: Aviation, films & filmmaking, indust & labor

WASHINGTON DEPOT — Area code 203

HICKORY STICK BOOKSHOP — General
06794. Tel 203-868-0525
Mgr, Joanna Lawrence
Estab 1955. 14,000 Titles. 20,000 Vols Buys through hq
Types: Hb, juvenile, papbk, remainders, used, out of print, books-on-tape

WEST CORNWALL — Area code 203

DEBORAH BENSON BOOKSELLER — Antiquarian
River Rd, 06796. Tel 203-672-6614
Estab 1956. 13,000 Vols
Types: Fine bnd, 1st ed, illus bk, ltd ed, old & rare, out of print
Subj: Am hist & lit, Eng hist & lit, bks on bks, early scientific & med, diabetes, Alice in Wonderland variants

BARBARA FARNSWORTH BOOKSELLER — Antiquarian
Rte 128, 06796. Tel 203-672-6571
Estab 1968. 45,000 Vols. 3600 sq ft. Cat
Types: 1st ed, fine bnd, hb, illus bk, juvenile, ltd ed, old & rare, out of print, used, fine printing
Subj: Am hist & lit, art, Eng hist & lit, hort, gastronomy

POOR FARM — Mail Order-Antiquarian
River Road (Mail add: PO Box 193, 06796). Tel 203-672-6567
Estab 1977. 2000 Titles. 2000 Vols. Cat
Types: 1st ed, hb, old & rare, out of print, used
Subj: Auto

WEST HARTFORD — 61,301. Area code 203

WEST HARTFORD BOOKSHOP — Used
322 Park Rd, 06119. Tel 203-232-2028
Estab 1984. 10,000 Titles. 10,000 Vols
Types: Juvenile, out of print, facsimile editions, fine bnd, 1st ed, illus bk, ltd ed, new, old & rare
Subj: Art, Amer, natural hist, cooking

WESTON — 8284. Area code 203

KETTLE CREEK BOOKS — Mail Order-Antiquarian
51 Kettle Creek Rd, 06883. Tel 203-227-0660
Mgr, Gail Hirsch
Estab 1980. 20,000 Titles. 20,000 Vols. Cat 2x ann
Types: Fine bnd, 1st ed, hb, illus bk, imp, juvenile, old & rare, out of print, used, univ presses
Subj: Math, medicine, mystery & detective, fiction, scholarly lit, hist of sci, 20th cent lit, learning & teaching

WESTPORT — 25,290. Area code 203

BANKSIDE BOOKS — Mail Order-Antiquarian
372 Greens Farms Rd, 06880. Tel 203-255-5379
Estab 1966. Cat
Types: 1st ed, hb, ltd ed, new & used, out of print, old & rare, remainders
Subj: World Wars I & II, Lincoln Steffens, Mark Twain, John Sloan, Normandie, Ocealiners, battle field art

MICHAEL S SACHS INC — Mail Order-Art
PO Box 2837, 06880-0837. Tel 203-227-1058
Estab 1968
Types: Illus bk, out of print, imp UK, Fr, Ger, & Neth

TURKEY HILL BOOKS — Antiquarian
46 Turkey Hill Rd S, 06880. Tel 203-255-0041
Mgr, Jack L Grogins
Estab 1977. 15,000 Titles. 15,000 Vols. Cat ann
Types: Fine bnd, 1st ed, hb, illus bk, juvenile, ltd ed, old & rare, out of print, used, signed edition
Subj: Amer, fiction, poetry

WEST REDDING — Area code 203

PAULA STERNE - BOOKS — Mail Order-Antiquarian
40 Huckleberry Rd, 06896. Tel 203-938-2756
Types: Old & rare, out of print
Subj: Amer, dogs, guns, sports

WETHERSFIELD — 26,013. Area code 203

E TATRO - BOOKSELLER — Mail Order-Antiquarian
60 Goff Rd, 06109. Tel 203-563-7884
Cat 10x ann
Types: Out of print, old & rare, used
Subj: Health & phys educ, sports, olympics

WILLIMANTIC — 14,652. Area code 203

MARK ZIESING BOOKSELLER — Science Fiction & Fantasy
762 Main St, PO Box 806, 06226. Tel 203-423-5836
Estab 1984. 30,000 Vols. 750 sq ft. Cat 8x ann
Types: Hb, out of print, papbk, used, small presses
Subj: Horror & mystery

WILTON — 15,351. Area code 203

WOLFGANG SCHIEFER BOOKS ABOUT BRAZIL — Mail Order-Antiquarian
23 Church St, 06897-9998. Tel 203-544-9046
Estab 1979. 3000 Titles. 3000 Vols. 400 sq ft. Cat
Types: Out of print, old & rare, imp Brazil
Subj: Brazil

WINDSOR — 25,204. Area code 203

CEDRIC L ROBINSON BOOKSELLER — Antiquarian
597 Palisado Ave, 06095. Tel 203-688-2582
Estab 1946. 20,000 Vols. Cat 3x ann
Types: Out of print, hb
Subj: Art, archit, Am hist & lit, Am Indian studies, oceanog, Western Amer

WOODBURY — 6942. Area code 203

BOOKS ABOUT ANTIQUES — Antiques
139 Main St N, 06798. Tel 203-263-0241
Estab 1988. 4000 Titles. 2800 Vols. 950 sq ft. Cat ann
Types: Hb, out of print, remainders
Subj: Antq, art, interior design, arts & crafts, archit

DELAWARE

BETHANY BEACH —330. Area code 302

ECHO BOOKS ETC — General
778 Garfield Pkwy, PO Box 1407, 19930. Tel 302-537-1675
Estab 1987. 10,000 Titles. 10,000 Vols. 360 sq ft
Types: Used, 1st ed, hb, juvenile, new, old & rare, out of print, papbk
Subj: Fiction

GREENVILLE — Area code 302

BOOKS INC — General
3826 Kennett Pike (Mail add: PO Box 3798, 19807-0798). Tel 302-652-3209
Mgr, Sally Knox
Estab 1964. 2300 sq ft. Cat
Types: Hb, juvenile, out of print, papbk
Subj: Art, gardening, health, nature & environ, fiction, nonfiction

MILFORD — 5356. Area code 302

KEN BESSINGER — Mail Order-Antiquarian
916 S Dupont Blvd, 19963. Tel 302-422-5483
Estab 1966. 2500 Vols
Types: Hb, juvenile, out of print, used
Subj: Discovery & explor, mystery & detective

MILLSBORO — 1233. Area code 302

VILLAGE GREEN PAPERBACK EXCHANGE — Paperback
Village Green Complex, Rte 24, PO Box 703, 19966. Tel 302-934-9540
Estab 1986. 10,000 Titles. 660 sq ft
Types: Juvenile, out of print, high priced papbk, mass mkt papbk
Subj: Fiction, mystery & detective, romance, sci fiction & fantasy, nonfiction, biog, cooking, women's studies, warfare, arts & crafts, Delawariana, hist fict, horror, regional, craft, suspense, western

NEW CASTLE — 4907. Area code 302

OAK KNOLL BOOKS — Antiquarian-Books On Books
414 Delaware St, 19720. Tel 302-328-7232
Owner, Cedar Lane Inc
Estab 1976. 9000 Titles. 20,000 Vols. 3000 sq ft. Cat monthly
Types: Facsimile editions, 1st ed, hb, imp, old & rare, out of print
Subj: Bibliog

REHOBOTH BEACH — 1730. Area code 302

GINGERBREAD SQUARE BOOKS — General
167 Rehoboth Ave (Mail add: PO Drawer O, 19971-0816). Tel 302-227-3573, 227-7400
Estab 1941. 10,000 Vols. 1400 sq ft. Cat
Types: Hb, juvenile, out of print, papbk, remainders, used
Subj: Antq, circus, oceanog, films & filmmaking, mystery & detective

WILMINGTON — 70,195. Area code 302

PALMA BOOK SERVICE — Mail Order-Antiquarian
PO Box 602, 19899. Tel 302-656-8629
Mgr, Harry M Stuart
4000 Vols
Types: Hb, out of print, used
Subj: Amer, biog, hist

WASHINGTON — 637,651. Area code 202

ABERDEEN BOOKSHOP — Used
3236 P St NW, 20007. Tel 202-338-2747
Estab 1985. 15,000 Titles. 18,000 Vols. 2200 sq ft
Types: Hb, out of print, papbk
Subj: Art, hist, fiction, reference, cooking, travel, philos

BACKSTAGE BOOKS & COSTUMES — Mail Order-Drama
2101 P St NW (Mail add: PO Box 53383, 20009). Tel 202-775-1488
Mgr, Harold Rosenthal
Estab 1981. 10,000 Titles. 20,000 Vols. Cat 4x ann
Types: Hb, out of print, papbk, imp UK, theatre scripts
Subj: Drama, dance, opera, movies, acting, theatre

BICKERSTAFF & BARCLAY — Mail Order-Antiquarian
PO Box 46259, 20050-6259
Estab 1979. 10,000 Titles. Cat 1-2x ann
Types: Used, out of print, old & rare
Subj: Photog

ESTATE BOOK SALES — Antiquarian
2914 M St NW, 20007. Tel 202-965-4274
Estab 1985. 30,000 Vols. 2000 sq ft
Types: Used, out of print
Subj: Am hist & lit, art, biog, Eng hist & lit, music, philos, psychol

FULLER & SAUNDERS BOOKS — Antiquarian-Americana
3238 P St NW, 20007. Tel 202-337-3235
Estab 1985. 4000 Titles
Types: 1st ed, hb, old & rare, out of print, used
Subj: Amer, local hist

THE LANTERN BRYN MAWR BOOKSTORE OF WASHINGTON — Used
3222 O St NW, 20007. Tel 202-333-3222
Owner, The Lantern Bryn Mawr Bookshop Inc; Mgr, Nancy E Madeira
Estab 1977. 10,000 Titles. 10,000 Vols
Types: For lang, hb, imp, juvenile, out of print, papbk

THE PRESIDENT'S BOX BOOKSHOP — Mail Order-Antiquarian
PO Box 1255, 20013. Tel 202-751-5813
Estab 1984. 2000 Titles. Cat 2x ann
Types: Facsimile editions, fine bnd, 1st ed, hb, illus bk, ltd ed, old & rare, out of print, papbk, remainders, used
Subj: Assassination of American Presidents, Lincoln, Garfield, J F Kennedy & McKinley, assasins John Wilkes Booth, Charles J Guiteau, Lee Harvey Oswald & Leon Czolglsz

THE RAMPANT LION — Used
PO Box 5887, 20016. Tel 202-364-2431
Estab 1983. 350 Titles. 750 Vols
Types: For lang, hb, imp, out of print, papbk, remainders, new, old & rare
Subj: Silver

OSCAR SHAPIRO — Mail Order-Antiquarian
3726 Connecticut Ave, NW, 20008. Tel 202-244-4446
Estab 1961. 5000 Vols. Cat
Types: Out of print, old & rare
Subj: Chess, music, violin

TEXTILE MUSEUM SHOP — Museum
2320 S St NW. 20008. Tel 202-667-0441
Mgr, Sandy Borchetta
Estab 1971. 500 Titles
Types: New, out of print
Subj: Textiles, related arts, rugs

WAYWARD BOOKS — Antiquarian-General
325 Seventh St SE, 20003. Tel 202-546-2719
10,000 Vols. 1000 sq ft
Types: 1st ed, illus bk, out of print, pvt presses, used
Subj: Mod lit, Afro-Amer fict, civil liberties

ATLANTIC BEACH — 7847. Area code 904

TAPPIN BOOK MINE INC — Antiquarian
705 Atlantic Blvd, 32233. Tel 904-246-1388
Estab 1975. 30,000 Vols. 1600 sq ft
Types: 1st ed, hb, illus bk, juvenile, old & rare, out of print, papbk, used
Subj: Military, nautical, sci-tech

BRADENTON — 30,170. Area code 813

ONE BOOKS — Metaphysics
PO Box 2010, 34208. Tel 813-747-1066
Estab 1975. 10,000 Titles. 50,000 Vols. Cat
Types: Fine bnd, facsimile editions, illus bk, 1st ed, imp, ltd ed, old & rare, papbk, out of print
Subj: Southern Amer, Floridiana

SOCOLOF ENTERPRISES BOOK DEPT — Antiquarian-Natural History
PO Box 1987, 34206. Tel 813-355-8995
Estab 1973. 5000 Titles. 5000 Vols. Cat ann
Types: 1st ed, hb, illus bk, out of print, imp, used
Subj: Ichthyol, natural hist, herpetology

CAPE CORAL — 32,103. Area code 813

DAVE MATTSON NAUTICAL BOOKS — Mail Order
2514 SE 26th Ave (Mail add: PO Box 803, 33910-0803). Tel 813-722-5723
Estab 1983. 2500 Titles. 2500 Vols. 300 sq ft. Cat 6x ann
Types: Hb, remainders, used, out of print, nautical, shipwreck

CASSELBERRY — 15,247. Area code 407

HARBAR BOOK EXCHANGE — Used
916 E Semoran Blvd, 32707-5633. Tel 407-834-0153
Estab 1980. 24,000 Titles. 33,000 Vols. 1050 sq ft
Types: Hb, juvenile, new & used, out of print, old & rare, papbk, collectibles
Subj: Fiction, nonfiction, old prints, ephemera bk preservation, restoration products, library sup

CHULUOTA — Area code 407

MICKLER'S ANTIQUARIAN BOOKS — Antiquarian-Floridiana
154 Lake Dr, PO Box 38, 32766. Tel 407-365-3636
Owner, Florida Breezes, Inc; Pres, Georgine J Mickler; VPres & Secy Thomas Mickler
Estab 1960. 40,000 Vols. 1700 sq ft. Cat
Types: Out of print, hb, old & rare, memorabilia
Subj: Doc, ephemera

CLEARWATER — 85,450. Area code 813

A BLUE MOON BOOKS & RECORDS — Antiquarian
1415 Cleveland St, 34615. Tel 813-443-7444
Mgr, Jane Jorgensen
Estab 1979. 50,000 Vols. 1500 sq ft. Cat
Types: 1st ed, fine bnd, illus bk, ltd ed, old & rare, out of print
Subj: Art, Civil War, fiction, Floridiana, photog, rel, Southern Amer
Branches:
— LAURIAT'S INC
Shoppers World, Rte 9, 01701. Tel 617-879-0303
Types: Hb, out of print, papbk, remainders

THE BOOKCASE — General
4900 E Bay Dr, Unit A, 34624. Tel 813-536-3443
Estab 1979. 25,000 Titles. 75,000 Vols
Types: Hb, juvenile, out of print, papbk, used, new, comics
Subj: Fiction, romance, sci fiction & fantasy

FLIGHTSHOPS — Aviation
St Petersburg-Clearwater Airport, 34622. Tel 813-530-1415
Mgr, James Swan
Estab 1971. 15,000 Vols. 2000 sq ft. Cat
Types: Hb, out of print, papbk, remainders, col text
See Also: Fort Lauderdale

THE MIDNIGHT BOOKMAN — Antiquarian
1908 Seagull Dr, 34624. Tel 813-536-4029 (by appt)
Estab 1981. 5000 Vols. Cat
Types: Old & rare, out of print
Subj: Aviation, fine arts

CORAL GABLES — 43,241. Area code 305

AMERICANA BOOKSHOP & GALLERY INC — Antiquarian
1719 Ponce De Leon Blvd, 33134. Tel 305-442-1776
Estab 1983. 5000 Vols. 500 sq ft
Types: Fine bnd, 1st ed, hb, illus bk, imp, juvenile, ltd ed, old & rare, out of print, remainders, used
Subj: Floridiana, treasure hunting, military, Napoleonic wars, Cuba, pirates, Sp-Amer War

GABLES BOOKSELLERS — Antiquarian
222 Andalusia Ave, 33134. Tel 305-446-7215
Estab 1986. 12,000 Titles. 12,000 Vols. 900 sq ft
Types: Fr & Sp lang, juvenile, hb, imp, out of print, remainders, high priced papbk
Subj: Hist, art, local hist, lit

DAYTONA BEACH — 54,176. Area code 904

MANDALA BOOKS — Antiquarian-General
204 Volusia Ave, 32014. Tel 904-255-6728
Mgr, Victor Newman
Estab 1981. 65,000 Titles. 85,000 Vols. 3000 sq ft
Types: Fine bnd, 1st ed, hb, illus bk, old & rare, out of print, papbk, remainders, used
Subj: Art, biog, fiction, metaphys & occult, travel, black studies, photog, hist, spiritual

DE LAND — 15,354. Area code 904

FAMILY BOOK SHOP — Used Paperback
1301 N Woodland Blvd, 32720. Tel 904-736-6501
Estab 1976. 50,000 Titles. 100,000 Vols. 4000 sq ft
Types: Hb, papbk, out of print

DESTIN — 1536. Area code 904

ARMCHAIR SAILOR BOOKSTORE — Nautical
546 Hwy 98 East, 32541-0698. Tel 904-837-1577. WATS 800-451-4185
Mgr, Jay Ogle
Estab 1985. 6000 Titles. 10,000 Vols. Cat 3x ann
Types: Hb, papbk, out of print, new & used, juvenile
Subj: Navigation

EUSTIS — 9453. Area code 904

JEFFERSON DAVIS AUCTION GALLERIES — Antiquarian
432 N Eustis St, 32726-9998. Tel 904-357-7145
Estab 1962. Cat ann
Types: New & used, out of print, remainders, old & rare

RAINTREE BOOKS — Paperback
432 N Eustis St, 32726-9998. Tel 904-357-7145
Estab 1962. 2400 Titles. 250,000 Vols. 6000 sq ft. Cat ann
Types: New & used, out of print, remainders, old & rare

FORT LAUDERDALE — 153,256. Area code 305

ALL BOOKS & RECORDS — General
917 N Federal Hwy, 33304. Tel 305-537-4899
Mgr, JoAnne Cronk; Merch Mgr, Louis Ludivico
Estab 1975. 100,000 Vols. 1500 sq ft
Types: Hb, juvenile, out of print, papbk, remainders, col text, new & used, Fr, Ger, Sp & Gr
Subj: Hist, art, biog, psychol, nonfiction, reference, children's poetry, plays, encyclopedias, adventure

ROBERT A HITTEL - BOOKSELLER — Antiquarian
3020 N Federal Hwy, Bldg 6, 33306. Tel 305-563-1752
Estab 1974. 80,000 Vols. 2600 sq ft. Cat 2-3X ann
Types: Fine bnd, 1st ed, hb, illus bk, juvenile, ltd ed, new & used, old & rare, out of print, mass mkt papbk, remainders
Subj: Am Indian studies, Amer, cooking

WAKE-BROOK HOUSE BOOKS — Antiquarian
PO Box 11072, 33339. Tel 305-563-9301
Estab 1947. 2000 Vols. Cat
Types: 1st ed, hb, out of print, papbk, old & rare
Subj: Boats, rum running, Seminole Indians, S Fla hist
See Also: Hyannis, MA

FORT MYERS — 36,638. Area code 813

THE BOOK DEN SOUTH — General
2249 First St, 33901. Tel 813-332-2333
Estab 1985. 12,000 Titles. 12,000 Vols. 1500 sq ft
Types: Fine bnd, 1st ed, hb, illus bk, juvenile, used, old & rare, out of print, papbk
Subj: Edison, SW Florida

GAINESVILLE — 81,371. Area code 904

FLORA & FAUNA BOOKS — Mail Order-Natural History
738 NE Seventh Ave (Mail add: PO Box 15718, 32604). Tel 904-373-5630
Mgr, M Rojas
Estab 1987. 3200 Titles. 400 Vols. Cat 4x ann
Types: For lang, hb, imp, out of print, papbk, high priced papbk, remainders, col text, used, new, facsimile editions
Subj: Biol, medicine, vet med, sci-tech, hist, travel, nature & environ, pets

HOBE SOUND — 70,734. Area code 407

FLORIDA CLASSIC LIBRARY BOOKSTORE — General
11950 SE Dixie Hway (Mail add: PO Box 1657, Port Salerno, 34992-1657). Tel 407-546-9380
Estab 1984. 2500 Titles. 5000 Vols. 1050 sq ft. Cat
Types: Hb, juvenile, out of print, mass mkt papbk, papbk
Subj: Floridiana

HOLLYWOOD — 117,188. Area code 305

BOOK FAIR — General
5650 Stirling Rd, 33021. Tel 305-987-6695
Estab 1968. 3000 Titles. 15,000 Vols. 1000 sq ft
Types: Hb, juvenile, out of print, mass mkt papbk, facsimile editions, 1st ed, illus bk, new, old & rare, papbk, remainders, used

JACKSONVILLE — 540,898. Area code 904

EPISCOPAL HIGH SCHOOL BOOKSTORE — El Hi Text
4455 Atlantic Blvd, 32207. Tel 904-396-5751, ext 17
Mgr, Judy M Miller
Types: Out of print, papbk, col text, el-hi text

MCQUERRY ORCHID BOOKS — Mail Order-Antiquarian
5700 W Salerno Rd, 32244. Tel 904-387-5044
Estab 1954. Cat ann
Types: Facsimile editions, fine bnd, 1st ed, hb, illus bk, imp, ltd ed, old & rare, out of print, used, antiquarian color plate bks
Subj: Orchid bks & per

THE OLD BOOKSHOP — General
3142 Beach Blvd, 32207. Tel 904-398-6163
Estab 1970. 100,000 Vols. 4000 sq ft
Types: 1st ed, hb, out of print, papbk, used, comics

SAN MARCO BOOKSTORE — Antiquarian
1971 San Marco Blvd, 32207. Tel 904-396-7597
Estab 1978. 8000 Titles. 8000 Vols
Types: Hb, out of print, old & rare, used
Subj: Floridiana, hist, nonfiction

KEY WEST — 24,292. Area code 305

LAY WITNESS CHRISTIAN BOOKSTORE — Religious-C, J, P
3708 N Roosevelt Blvd, Perry's Plaza (Mail add: PO Box 2682, 33045). Tel 305-294-7212
Estab 1974. Cat ann
Types: Juvenile, mass mkt papbk, high priced papbk, hb, illus bk, new, out of print, used

LAKELAND — 47,406. Area code 813

ABACUS HOBBIES — Used
2088 Edgewood Dr, 33803. Tel 813-665-8586
Estab 1966. 200,000 Vols. 1000 sq ft. Cat
Types: New, papbk, remainders, hb, old & rare, out of print, comics
Subj: Films & filmmaking, sports, super heroes

LAKE WORTH — 27,048. Area code 407

ALLA T FORD RARE BOOKS — Mail Order-Antiquarian
114 S Palmway Ave, 33460. Tel 407-585-1442
Estab 1956. 7000 Vols. Cat
Types: 1st ed, hb, juvenile, out of print, old & rare, miniatures
Subj: Sci fiction & fantasy, Edgar Burroughs, L Frank Baum, Sherlock Holmes

MIAMI — 346,931. Area code 305

AFRO-IN BOOKS & THINGS — Black Studies
5575 NW Seventh Ave, 33127. Tel 305-756-6107
Mgr, Eursla A Wells
Estab 1979. 5000 Vols. 1675 sq ft. Cat ann
Types: Hb, papbk, juvenile, remainders, used, out of print, Sp, Fr, Latin lang, imp Afr, Haiti, Bahamas

BOOKS & ART PRINTS STORE — Antiquarian
4329 SW Eight St, 33134-2654. Tel 305-444-5001
Estab 1949. 100,000 Vols. 2200 sq ft
Types: 1st ed, papbk, used, out of print, comics
Subj: Art, fiction, hist, metaphys & occult, nonfiction, poetry, rel studies

FLORIDA INTERNATIONAL UNIVERSITY BOOKSTORE — College

11000 SW Eighth St, 33174. Tel 305-554-2370. Telex 51-8720
Mgr, Richard Lindsay
Types: Hb, juvenile, out of print, papbk

GORDON'S BOOK STORE — Used
1815 Ponce De Leon Blvd, 33138. Tel 305-441-1120
Mgr, Jose Horta
Estab 1984. 20,000 Titles. 17,000 Vols. 1400 sq ft
Types: For lang, hb, out of print, papbk, mass mkt papbk, high priced papbk, remainders, 1st ed, illus bk, new, old & rare, out of print

LIBRERIA & DISTRIBUIDORA UNIVERSAL — Spanish Lang
3090 SW Eighth St (Mail add: PO Box 450353, Shenandoah Sta, 33145-0450). Tel 305-642-3234. Telex 68-11258
Gen Mgr, Marta Salvat-Golik
Estab 1965. 15,000 Titles. 500,000 Vols. 6000 sq ft. Cat 5x ann
Types: Col & el-hi text, hb, juvenile, old & rare, out of print, papbk, imp Sp, imp Latin Am
Subj: Art, black studies, rel-c, Cuba

NAPLES — 17,581. Area code 813

THE BOOK TRADER — General
170 Tenth St N, 33940. Tel 813-262-7562, 263-3683
Estab 1976. 200,000 Vols. 8000 sq ft. Cat Christmas
Types: Juvenile, out of print, mass mkt papbk, remainders, used, new, hb
Subj: Fiction, nonfiction, sci fiction & fantasy, mystery & detective, romance, antq
See Also: Fort Myers, South Fort Myers

MYCOPHILE BOOKS — Mail Order-Antiquarian
1800 Tiller Terrace, 33940. Tel 813-262-3363
2000 Vols. Cat 2x ann
Types: Out of print, old & rare, new
Subj: Pharmacy, drug culture, mushrooms

OCALA — 37,170. Area code 904

RAY THE TRADERS' THREE FOR $1 BOOKSTORE — Used
739 E Silver Springs Blvd, Esquire S/Ctr, 32670-6759. Tel 904-629-0903
Owner, Cates Enterprises, Inc
Estab 1969. 100,000 Vols
Types: Hb, out of print, papbk, old & rare, new & collectors comic bks
Subj: Medicine, military, sci fiction & fantasy
See Also: Gainesville; Uncle Ray's 3 For $1 Bookstore, Daytona Beach

ORANGE CITY — 2795. Area code 407

BUNKER BOOKS — Mail Order
770 Briarwood Ct (Mail add: Box 0119, 32763). Tel 407-774-9210
Estab 1972. 30,000 Vols. 800 sq ft
Types: Out of print, papbk, used
Subj: Mystery & detective, sci fiction & fantasy, Western Amer, vintage 1939-1959, "TV Guides" 1953-1987

PANAMA CITY — 33,346. Area code 904

AGELESS BOOK SHOPPE — General
1090 Florida Ave (Mail add: PO Box 2501, 32401). Tel 904-763-5264
Estab 1984. 30,000 Titles. 1730 sq ft
Types: For lang, hb, juvenile, used, col text, col & el-hi text, fine bnd, 1st ed, illus bk, ltd ed, new, old & rare, out of print

PENSACOLA — 57,619. Area code 904

FARLEY'S OLD & RARE BOOKS — Antiquarian
5855 Tippen Ave, 32504. Tel 904-477-8282
8000 Titles. 12,000 Vols. 700 sq ft
Types: Fine bnd, 1st ed, hb, illus bk, imp UK, juvenile, ltd ed, old & rare, out of print, used
Subj: Hist, military, theol

KING & QUEEN BOOKS — Mail Order-Antiquarian
PO Box 15062, 32514-0062. Tel 904-477-6811
Estab 1975. 5000 Titles. Cat 3x ann
Types: Hb, out of print, used, old & rare
Subj: Floridiana, The South

PINELLAS PARK — 32,811. Area code 813

QUILL & CLEF BOOKS — Performing Arts
7301 55th St N, 34665. Tel 813-545-2270
Estab 1987. 4000 Titles. 10,000 Vols. 960 sq ft. Cat 4x ann
Types: Hb, 1st ed, out of print, papbk, used
Subj: Photog, dance, lit, jazz, rock & roll

PLANTATION — 48,501. Area code 305

HISTORICAL BOOKSHELF LTD — Mail Order-Antiquarian
4210 SW Third St, 33317. Tel 305-583-2378
Mgr, Jim Wilkinson
Estab 1978. 8000 Vols. 733 sq ft. Cat
Types: 1st ed, hb, imp, old & rare, out of print, used
Subj: Aviation, hist, hunting & fishing, military, political thought, railroadiana

POMONA PARK —791. Area code 904

CARLING'S OF FLORIDA — Mail Order-Numismatics
116 W Main St (Mail add: PO Drawer 580, 32081-0580). Tel 904-649-9730
Estab 1982. 2500 Titles. 3000 Vols. 800 sq ft. Cat 2x ann
Types: Sp lang, hb, out of print, old & rare, used, imp Latin Amer
Subj: Floridiana, world hist, pirates

SAINT AUGUSTINE — 11,985. Area code 904

WOLF'S HEAD BOOKS — Antiquarian
48 San Marco, PO Box 3705, 32085-3705. Tel 904-824-9357
Mgr, Barbara E Nailer
Estab 1988. 20,000 Vols. 14,000 sq ft. Cat 5x ann
Types: 1st ed, hb, juvenile, old & rare, out of print, papbk, used
Subj: Amer, Appalachia, archit, art, fiction, military, mysticism, West Virginiana

SAINT PETERSBURG — 236,893. Area code 813

HASLAM'S BOOKSTORE INC — General
2025 Central Ave, 33713-8896. Tel 813-822-8616
Estab 1933. 325,000 Vols. 31,000 sq ft
Types: Hb, juvenile, new & used, out of print, papbk, juvenile
Subj: Floridiana, rel, metaphys

LIGHTHOUSE BOOKS — Antiquarian
1735 First Ave N, 33713. Tel 813-822-3278
Estab 1977. 10,000 Titles. 15,000 Vols. 1200 sq ft. Cat 3x ann
Types: Facsimile editions, fine bnd, 1st ed, hb, illus bk, incunab, ltd ed, old & rare, out of print, remainders
Subj: Floridiana, Southern Amer, Am hist & lit, Latin Am, Caribbean hist

SALVADOR DALI FOUNDATION INC — Museum
1000 Third St S, 33701. Tel 813-823-3767
Mgr, Kathleen White
Estab 1982. 92 Titles. 100 Vols. Cat ann
Types: Hb, out of print, papbk, imp Sp, imp Den, imp Jap, imp EEur
Subj: Fine arts, Salvador Dali, surrealism

SARASOTA — 48,868. Area code 813

PARKER'S BOOKS INC — Antiquarian
1488 Main St, 34236. Tel 813-366-2898
Mgr, Alan Corey
Estab 1976. 100,000 Vols. Cat
Types: Old & rare, out of print, used, 1st ed
Subj: Cooking, art, photog, railroadiana, Amer, hist

WILLIAM H PETTIBON — Antiquarian-Floridiana
1911 Oak St, 33577. Tel 813-365-6871
Types: Hb, old & rare, out of print

SEMINOLE — 4586. Area code 813

BRASSER'S BOOKS — Antiquarian
8701 Seminole Blvd, 34642. Tel 813-393-6707
Estab 1972. 60,000 Titles. 65,000 Vols. 4000 sq ft. Cat 2x ann
Types: 1st ed, hb, out of print, old & rare, papbk
Subj: Biog, Civil War, World Wars I & II, cooking, Floridiana, sports, sailing, Sp-Am War, Cuba

SOUTH MIAMI — area code 305

A & M COMICS & BOOKS — Used
6650 SW 40th St, 33155. Tel 305-665-4167
Mgr, George Perez
Estab 1977. 1000 sq ft
Types: Out of print
Subj: Comedy, metaphys & occult, mystery & detective, sci fiction & fantasy

DAVID HOLLOWAY BOOKSELLER — Mail Order-Antiquarian
6760 SW 76th Terr, 33143. Tel 305-665-5567
Mgr, Valerie Eastwood
Estab 1984. 4000 Titles. 4500 Vols. 1000 sq ft. Cat
Types: Remainders, used, hb, 1st ed, illus bk, out of print
Subj: Fiction, poetry, art

TALLAHASSEE — 81,548. Area code 904

BILL'S BOOKSTORE INC — College
107 S Copeland St, 32304-4398. Tel 904-224-3178
Mgr & Buyer, M C McNeil; Papbk Buyer & Text Buyer, John Reynolds
Estab 1950
Types: Hb, out of print, papbk, used, Fr, Ger, It & Sp lang

TAMPA — 271,523. Area code 813

HYDE PARK BOOKSHOP — General
1109 Swann Ave, 33606. Tel 813-259-1432
Estab 1980. 10,000 Vols. 1000 sq ft. Cat 1-2x ann
Types: Facsimile editions, 1st ed, hb, illus bk, juvenile, ltd ed, new & used, old & rare, out of print, papbk, remainders, mod 1st ed
Subj: Floridiana

RED HORSE AT YBOR SQUARE — Antiquarian
1901 N 13th St, 33605-3627. Tel 813-248-8859
Estab 1965. 8000 Titles. 3000 Vols
Types: Hb, out of print
Subj: Amer, archit, art, fiction, Floridiana, for lang, hist, military, trades

JIM SHELTON - BOOKSELLER — Antiquarian
105 B South Fielding, 33606. Tel 813-254-4935
Estab 1986. 3000 Titles. 3000 Vols. 500 sq ft. Cat 10x ann
Types: Hb, out of print, 1st ed, papbk, fine bnd
Subj: Civil War, Floridiana, fiction

TAMPA ANTIQUARIAN BOOK CO — Antiquarian
6310 Armenia Ave (Mail add: 6402 Felice Ave, 33614). Tel 813-871-3919
Estab 1984. 12,000 Titles. 1000 sq ft
Types: Hb, out of print, used, 1st ed, incunab, illus bk, old & rare
Subj: Floridiana, military, biog, Amer, cooking, sports, poetry, arts & crafts, philos, auto, railroadiana, medicine, rel, metaphys & occult, fiction, gardening, bus & mgt, nautical, circus, travel, animals, famous people, show people, organizations, children

WESTVILLE —343. Area code 904

ALEC R ALLENSON INC — Antiquarian
PO Box 133, 32464
Pres, Robert D Allenson
Estab 1924. 50,000 Titles. 200,000 Vols. 3500 sq ft. Cat
Types: Old & rare, out of print
Subj: Philos, hist, bibliog, rel

WINTER HAVEN — 21,119. Area code 813

THE BOOKTRADERS INC — Used
301 W Central, 33884. Tel 813-299-4904. WATS 800-626-8102
Vpres, Sue Ujlaki
Estab 1977. 350,000 Vols. 23,000 sq ft
Types: Hb, juvenile, out of print, papbk, col text, fine bnd, 1st ed, illus bk, ltd ed, old & rare
Subj: Medicine, sci-tech
See Also: Book Traders Exchange, Bartow; Las Vegas, NV

WINTER PARK — 22,314. Area code 407

BRANDYWINE BOOKS — Antiquarian
114 Park Ave S, Suite E, 32789-3214. Tel 407-644-1711
Estab 1984. 5000 Titles. 5000 Vols
Types: Ltd ed, 1st ed, hb, juvenile, out of print
Subj: Floridiana, music, photog, antq, world hist, cooking, gardening, mystery & detective, art, Amer, poetry, warfare, Sherlock Holmes, lit

ATHENS — 42,549. Area code 404

ABALON BOOKS — General
Homewood S/Ctr, 2463 Jefferson Rd, 30607. Tel 404-549-4002
Mgr & Buyer, Robert B Kinzey
Estab 1977. 15,000 Vols. 1500 sq ft
Types: Hb, juvenile, out of print, papbk, remainders

JACKSON STREET BOOKS — Used
260 N Jackson St, 30601. Tel 404-546-0245
Estab 1984. 20,000 Vols
Types: Hb, juvenile, papbk, mass mkt papbk, high priced papbk, remainders, imp, for lang, fine bnd, 1st ed, illus bk, ltd ed, old & rare, out of print
Subj: Hist, philos, fine arts, lit

UNIVERSITY OF GEORGIA COLLEGE BOOKSTORE — College
PO Box 2217, 30602. Tel 404-542-3171. Telex 54-2163
Mgr, W R Powell
Estab 1900. 30,000 Vols. 57,000 sq ft
Types: Hb, juvenile, mass mkt papbk, out of print, remainders
Subj: Art, black studies, law, pharmacy, sci-tech

ATLANTA — 425,022. Area code 404

ATLANTA BOOK EXCHANGE — General
1000 N Highland Ave NE, 30306. Tel 404-872-2665
Estab 1976. 40,000 Titles
Types: Hb, papbk, used, out of print, trade pbk
Subj: Hist, literary criticism, philos, art

THE BOOK DISPENSARY INC - ADMINISTRATIVE OFFICES — Antiquarian
2922 Marlin Dr, 30341. Tel 404-451-2063
Estab 1975. 100,000 Titles
Types: Old & rare, out of print, collectibles
See Also: Columbia, SC

JULIAN BURNETT BOOKS — Mail Order-Antiquarian
PO Box 229, 30301. Tel 404-252-5812
Estab 1979. 1500 Titles. 1500 Vols. Cat ann
Types: 1st ed, facsimile editions, fine bnd, hb, illus bk, incunab, imp, ltd ed, out of print, old & rare
Subj: Maritime, naval, Panama Canal, nautical documents & autographs

COLLECTOR'S WORLD — Antiquarian-Comics
5351-1 Buford Hwy, 30340. Tel 404-452-7102
Estab 1980. 7500 Vols. 1400 sq ft
Types: Hb, illus bk, out of print, old & rare, papbk, used
Subj: Military

C DICKENS OUT OF PRINT & COLLECTIBLE BOOKS — Antiquarian
Lenox Sq, 3393 Peachtree Rd, 30326. Tel 404-231-3825
Estab 1984. 10,000 Titles. 2260 sq ft
Types: Fine bnd, 1st ed, hb, incunab, ltd ed, old & rare, out of print, illus bk, juvenile, collectible 1st ed
Subj: Gone with the Wind

EPONA BOOKS — Mail Order-Horses
1093 Atlantic Dr, 30318. Tel 404-873-1148
Estab 1982. 2000 Titles. 2500 Vols. Cat 4x ann
Types: Hb, used, out of print, old & rare
Subj: Dogs, horses

THE MILITARY SHOPPE — Military
5000 Buford Hwy, 30341. Tel 404-634-9801
Estab 1969. 7000 Titles. 8000 Vols
Types: Hb, out of print, papbk
Subj: Hist, biog, Civil War, Nazis, World War II

OLD NEW YORK BOOKSHOP — Antiquarian
1069 Juniper St NE, 30309. Tel 404-881-1285
Estab 1971. 50,000 Titles. 50,000 Vols. Cat
Types: 1st ed, ltd ed, out of print, used, hb, signed ed
Subj: Amer

SMALL PRESS BOOKSHOP — Scholarly Lit
804 N Highland Ave, 30306. Tel 404-872-4354
Mgr, Robert Cheatham
Estab 1980. 14,000 Titles. 15,000 Vols. 1500 sq ft. Cat ann
Types: Hb, imp, out of print, papbk, small presses, univ presses, new & used
Subj: Philos, art, polit

SOUTHERN HIGHLANDS BOOKSTORE INC — Antiquarian
3325 Buford Hwy NE, 30329. Tel 404-321-3369. FAX 404-261-4476
Mgr, Mary Adamson
Estab 1982. 150,000 Titles. 200,000 Vols. Cat 2x ann
Types: New, old & rare, out of print
Subj: Civil War, Southern Amer, World Wars I & II, children's

SYMMES SYSTEMS — Mail Order
PO Box 8101, 468 Armour Dr, 30306. Tel 404-876-7260
Estab 1970. 5000 Vols. Cat
Types: Hb, high priced papbk, out of print, imp China, imp Jap, imp UK
Subj: Gardening, photog, bonsai

TROLLEY STOP INC — Antiquarian
780 N Highland Ave, 30308. Tel 404-873-3495
Estab 1978. 6000 Titles. 6000 Vols. 1000 sq ft. Cat 4x ann
Types: Facsimile editions, fine bnd, 1st ed, hb, illus bk, juvenile, ltd ed, old & rare, out of print, used
Subj: Amer, black studies, Latin Am, photog, West Indies, Am Indian

YESTERYEAR BOOKSHOP INC — Antiquarian
3201 Maple Drive NE, 30305. Tel 404-237-0163
Owner & Vpres, Polly G Fraser
Estab 1971. 22,000 Vols. 1700 sq ft. Cat ann
Types: 1st ed, hb, out of print, old & rare, used, fine bnd, mod 1st ed
Subj: Am hist & lit, archit, biog, Georgiana, Southern Amer, Civil War, autg, bks on bks, early newspapers, decorative arts

DANIELSVILLE —Area code 404

THE OLD BOOK SCOUT - JIM MCMEANS — Antiquarian
Rte 3, Box 3181, 30633. Tel 404-789-3206
3000 Vols. Cat 4x ann
Types: 1st ed, hb, old & rare, out of print
Subj: Fiction, Georgiana, hist, Southern Amer, military

DECATUR — 18,404. Area code 404

BROCK'S SURPLUS INC — Military
640 Valley Brook Rd (Mail add: PO Box 33242, 30033). Tel 404-294-9500
Estab 1972. 1000 Vols. 2500 sq ft. Cat 3x ann
Types: Hb, imp Ger, out of print, used, imp Jap
Subj: Hist, firearms

GAINESVILLE — 15,280. Area code 404

SOUTHERN BOOKCASE — Mail Order
4712 Highland Circle (Mail add: PO Box 907155 NLP, 30501). Tel 404-983-3684. WATS 800-456-7716
Types: Hb, papbk, out of print, remainders
Subj: Computer sci, class studies

KENNESAW — 5095. Area code 404

WILDMAN'S CIVIL WAR SURPLUS — Museum
2879 Main St NW, 30144. Tel 404-422-1785
Estab 1971. 2000 Titles. 2000 Vols. Cat
Types: Hb, out of print, used, facsimile editions, 1st ed, ltd ed, old & rare, papbk
Subj: Metaphys & occult, World Wars I & II, warfare, Civil War

MACON — 116,860. Area code 912

DANIEL METTS ANTIQUARIAN BOOKS — Antiquarian
2452 Vineville Ave, PO Box 7353, 31209. Tel 912-746-0968
Estab 1985. 5000 Titles. 5000 Vols
Types: Out of print, fine bnd, 1st ed, old & rare, used, imp
Subj: Georgiana, Civil War

MARIETTA — 30,805. Area code 404

ROBERT MURPHY BOOKSELLER — Antiquarian-Americana
3113 Bunker Hill Rd, 30062. Tel 404-973-1523
Estab 1971. 1000 Titles. 1000 Vols
Types: Hb, old & rare, out of print
Subj: Regional Americana

ROSSVILLE — 3749. Area code 404

WHISTLES IN THE WOODS — Antiquarian-Natural History
Rte 1, Box 265-A, 30741. Tel 404-375-4326
Estab 1954. 4500 Vols. 1200 sq ft. Cat 3-4x ann
Types: Hb, imp, new & used, out of print, papbk, old & rare, remainders
Subj: Antq, collecting, natural hist, railroadiana, steam engines, water wheels, machinery of 19th century, indust archaeol, hist of tech, goats & sheep, ruminant animals

SAVANNAH — 141,634. Area code 912

LONNIE E EVANS - BOOKS, USED RARE & OUT-OF-PRINT — Mail Order-Antiquarian
PO Box 10445, 31412-0645. Tel 912-236-3364
5000 Vols. Cat 3x ann
Types: 1st ed, hb, illus bk, juvenile, old & rare, out of print, used
Subj: Georgiana, mystery & detective, Kay Boyle, Paris in the 1920s, Gertrude Stein, Boys & Girls Series, Sherlock Holmes, Gene Stratton-Porter
Branches:
— THE BOOK LADY
17 W York St, 31401-3703. Tel 912-233-3628
Mgr, Lonnie Evans
Estab 1979. 5000 Titles. 5000 Vols
Types: Juvenile, papbk, 1st ed, old & rare, out of print
Subj: Amer, art, music, philos, cooking, films & filmmaking, polit sci, women's studies, poetry, journalism, regional, fict

JACQUELINE LEVINE ABAA — Antiquarian
107 E Oglethorpe Ave, 31401. Tel 912-233-8519
Estab 1938. 10,000 Vols. Cat 2x ann
Types: Ltd ed, out of print, fore-edge paintings
Subj: Bks on bks, Amer, nautical

E SHAVER BOOKSELLER — General
326 Bull St, 31401. Tel 912-234-7257
Estab 1975. 30,000 Vols. 5000 sq ft
Types: Hb, juvenile, out of print, papbk, remainders, used
Subj: Art, archit, Amer, regional

STONE MOUNTAIN — 4867. Area code 404

ARCTURUS BOOK SERVICE — General
PO Box 831383, 30083-0023. Tel 518-374-2115
Estab 1980. 300 Titles. 3000 Vols. 500 sq ft. Cat monthly
Types: Hb, imp, out of print, mass mkt papbk
Subj: Unidentified flying objects, crytozoology, hollow earth, natural & Phenomena

ASPEN BOOKSHOP — General
5986 Memorial Dr, 30083. Tel 404-296-5933
Estab 1976. 75,000 Vols. 1500 sq ft
Types: Col text, for lang, hb, juvenile, old & rare, out of print, papbk, remainders, used
Subj: Hist, medicine, sci-tech, rel

MEMORABLE BOOKS — Antiquarian
5380 Manor Dr, 30083. Tel 404-469-5911
Mgr, Ella J Hoak
Estab 1979. 25,000 Vols. 1000 sq ft
Types: Fine bnd, 1st ed, hb, illus bk, juvenile, old & rare, out of print, used
Subj: Anthrop, archaeol, arts & crafts, biog, hist, mod lit, Amer, military

WARNER ROBINS — 39,893. Area code 912

THE BOOKSHOP — General
Miller Hills S/Ctr, 31088. Tel 912-922-7231
Estab 1970. 30,000 Vols
Types: Bibles, hb, juvenile, papbk, remainders, used, out of print
Subj: Georgiana

HAWAII

HILO — 26,353. Area code 808

BOOKFINDERS OF HAWAII — Antiquarian-Hawaiiana
160 Haili St, 96720. Tel 808-961-5055
Estab 1970. 200 Vols. Cat 2x ann
Types: Out of print
Subj: Hawaiiana, whales & whaling, tropical flora & fauna, volcanoes

HONOLULU — 324,871. Area code 808

BOOK PEOPLE — Used
762 Kapahulu Ave, 96816. Tel 808-735-8566
Mgr, Dennis Grannen
Estab 1983. 30,000 Titles. 70,000 Vols
Types: Hb, juvenile, out of print, mass mkt papbk, high priced papbk, facsimile editions, fine bnd, 1st ed, illus bk, ltd ed, new, old & rare, remainders
Subj: Hawaiiana, sci fiction & fantasy, women's studies

HAWAII CONFERENCE OF THE UNITED CHURCH OF CHRIST BOOK ROOM — Religious-C, J, P
15 Craigside Pl, 96817. Tel 808-537-9516
Mgr, Carolyn Feletcher
Estab 1863. 4000 Vols
Types: Bibles, for lang, hb, juvenile, out of print, papbk
Subj: Feminism, Hawaiiana, rel-ecumenical, theol

PACIFIC BOOK HOUSE — Antiquarian-Hawaiiana
637 Sheridan St, 96814. Tel 808-942-2242
Estab 1963. 6000 Vols. Cat 5x ann
Types: 1st ed, out of print, old & rare, used
Subj: Pacific, humanities, Eng & Am lit

KAILUA — 33,783. Area code 808

TUSITALA BOOKSHOP — General
116 Hekili St, 96734. Tel 808-262-6343
Mgr, Nancy Abe
Estab 1976. 40,000 Titles. 45,000 Vols. 1750 sq ft. Cat
Types: Fine bnd, 1st ed, hb, illus bk, juvenile, ltd ed, out of print, old & rare, papbk, used
Subj: Hawaiiana, Pacific, Robert Louis Stevenson

WAILUKU — 7979. Area code 808.

COMPLEAT COMICS COMPANY — Comics
1728 Kaahumanu Ave, 96793. Tel 808-242-5875
Estab 1983. 1000 Titles. 25,000 Vols. 1000 sq ft
Types: Hb, papbk, mass mkt papbk, used, trade, ltd ed, out of print

BOISE — 102,451. Area code 208

BOISE BOOKS & SEARCH — Used
4212 Emerald St (Mail add: Box 6638, 83707). Tel 208-345-8670
Mgr, Beryl Mary
Estab 1986. 20,000 Titles. 20,000 Vols. 1500 sq ft. Cat 3x ann
Types: Juvenile, out of print, hb, new & used, illus bk, ltd ed, facsimile editions, 1st ed, incunab
Subj: Western Amer, hunting & fishing, photog, Judaica, political thought, military, rel

THE BOOKSHOP INC — General
908 Main St, 83702. Tel 208-342-2659
Estab 1900. 60,000 Titles
Types: Hb, juvenile, out of print, papbk, remainders, used
Subj: Western Amer

HYDE PARK BOOK STORE — General
1507 N 13th St, 83702
Estab 1982. 50,000 Titles
Types: Juvenile, out of print, 1st ed, hb, old & rare
Subj: Local hist

KING'S KOMIX KASTLE — Comics
1706 N 18th St, 83702. Tel 208-343-7142
Estab 1973. 400 sq ft
Types: 1st ed, hb, out of print, old & rare, papbk, remainders, used

10TH STREET BOOKS-GALLERY — General
109 N Tenth St, 83702. Tel 208-342-4928
Mgr, Nan Rick
Types: Hb, juvenile, papbk, out of print

CALDWELL — 17,699. Area code 208

FOOD FOR THOUGHT BOOKSHOP — General
307 S Kimball Ave, Shoppers Plaza, 83605. Tel 208-459-8298
Estab 1984. 6000 Titles. 6166 Vols. 1060 sq ft
Types: Hb, juvenile, out of print, mass mkt papbk, high priced papbk, remainders, used, antq bks

COEUR D'ALENE — 20,054. Area code 208

BROWSERS BOOKS — Used
N 1030 4th, 83814. Tel 208-667-3964
Estab 1986. 10,000 Titles. 10,000 Vols. 1000 sq ft
Types: Fr lang, hb, out of print, mass mkt papbk, high priced papbk, used, remainders, juvenile
Subj: Rel, metaphys & occult, sci fiction & fantasy, Amer, mil hist, self-help, lit class

GEORGE NOLAN BOOKS — Antiquarian
118 N Second St, 83814. Tel 208-667-2222
Estab 1984. 12,000 Titles. 12,000 Vols. 600 sq ft
Types: Fine bnd, 1st ed, hb, illus bk, imp, juvenile, ltd ed, old & rare, out of print, used
Subj: Nonfiction

MOSCOW — 16,513. Area code 208

TWICE SOLD TALES — Used
220 W Third St, 83843. Tel 208-882-8781
Estab 1977. 40,000 Titles. 75,000 Vols. 1700 sq ft
Types: Hb, juvenile, out of print, papbk, mag
Subj: Fiction, nonfiction, romance, sci fiction & fantasy, comedy

NAMPA — 25,112. Area code 208

THE YESTERYEAR SHOPPE — Antiquarian-Idahoana
1211 First St S, P O Box 797, 83653-0797. Tel 208-467-3581
Asst Mgr, Stephen Gonzales
Estab 1974. 95,000 Titles. 100,000 Vols. 4000 sq ft
Types: Illus bk, juvenile, ltd ed, old & rare, out of print, papbk
Subj: Amer

POCATELLO — 46,340. Area code 208

IDAHO STATE UNIVERSITY BOOKSTORE — College
Box 8013, 83209-0009. Tel 208-236-3237. Telex 15-0050
Mgr, Leland R Hill
Estab 1941. 15,000 Titles. 13,000 sq ft
Types: Hb, juvenile, out of print, papbk, remainders, used
Subj: Reference, computer sci, professional, technical

SANDPOINT — 4460. Area code 208

BOOKS AT FOSTER'S CROSSING — General
504 Oak St, 83864
Mgr, Gene Brown; Merch Mgr, Carla Brown
Estab 1985. 20,000 Titles. 20,000 Vols. 1240 sq ft
Types: Used, Fr lang, hb, imp, juvenile, out of print, mass mkt papbk, high priced papbk
Subj: Guns, Amer, how-to, Northwest, hunting

BOOKTRADER II — Used
216 N First Ave, 83864. Tel 208-263-1041
Estab 1981. 20,000 Titles. 760 sq ft
Types: Hb, used, new, juvenile, out of print, old & rare, remainders
Subj: Metaphysics

SUN VALLEY — 545. Area code 208

EX LIBRIS — General
PO Box 225, 83353-0225. Tel 208-622-8174
Estab 1968. 800 sq ft
Types: Hb, juvenile, papbk, out of print

TWIN FALLS — 26,209. Area code 208

BOYLAN'S BOOKS — Used
570 Addison West, 83301
Estab 1986. 40,000 Titles. 60,000 Vols
Types: Hb, new & used, old & rare, out of print, papbk, comics, antiquarian
Subj: Northwest Amer

ILLINOIS

ALSIP — 17,134. Area code 312

FRIENDLY FRANK'S COMICS INC — Comics
11941 S Cicero, 60658. Tel 312-371-6760
Estab 1983. 1000 Titles. 100,000 Vols
Types: Papbk, new & used, out of print, imp UK
See Also: Hobart, IN; Lansing, MI; Friendly Frank's Distribution, Inc, Gary, IN, wholesale & retail sections

ARLINGTON HEIGHTS — 66,116. Area code 312

CONSERVATIVE BOOKS — Mail Order-Used
PO Box 1653, 60006. Tel 312-359-4923
250 Titles. 400 Vols. Cat ann
Types: Out of print, used, hb, papbk, new
Subj: Conservative polit

DRUMMER & THUMBS BOOKSTORE — Used
One East Campbell St, 60005. Tel 312-398-8968
Estab 1987. 15,000 Titles. 15,000 Vols. 1000 sq ft
Types: Hb, papbk, new, out of print

PLAIN TALES BOOKS — Mail Order-Antiquarian
Box 1691, 60006. Tel 312-253-1472
2000 Vols
Types: 1st ed, out of print, used, old & rare, mod 1st eds
Subj: Literary criticism, India, travel

AURORA — 81,293. Area code 312

KROCH'S & BRENTANO'S INC — General
2284 Fox Valley Mall, 60504. Tel 312-851-7773
Mgr, Jeff Talley
Estab 1975. 35,000 Titles Buys through hq
Types: Hb, imp, juvenile, out of print, papbk, remainders, for lang
Subj: Art, music, psychol, rel, sci-tech

BERKELEY — 5467. Area code 312

ESTATE BOOKS — Mail Order-Antiquarian
5827 Burr Oak, 60163. Tel 312-547-6239
2000 Titles. 2000 Vols. Cat 2x ann
Types: 1st ed, hb, illus bk, juvenile, old & rare, out of print, used
Subj: Civil War, Abraham Lincoln, Chicago, Jesse Stuart

BLOOMINGTON — 44,189. Area code 309

ROLLY'S USED & RARE BOOKS — General
212 N Center, 61701. Tel 309-827-3693
Estab 1988. 2500 Titles. 2500 Vols. 168 sq ft
Types: 1st ed, old & rare, out of print, used
Subj: Civil War, hist, mystery & detective, poetry, sports

CALUMET CITY — 39,673. Area code 312

KROCH'S & BRENTANO'S INC — General
18 River Oaks Ctr, 60409. Tel 312-868-1666
Mgr, Caryn Reinholtz
Estab 1966. 35,000 Titles Buys through hq
Types: Hb, imp, juvenile, out of print, papbk, remainders, for lang
Subj: Art, music, psychol, rel, sci-tech

CHAMPAIGN — 58,133. Area code 217

JANE ADDAMS BOOK SHOP — Antiquarian
208 N Neil St, 61820. Tel 217-356-2555
Estab 1984. 40,000 Vols
Types: Hb, juvenile, old & rare, out of print, papbk, illus bk, used
Subj: Biog, fiction, hist, mystery & detective, poetry, women's studies

STONEHILL'S BOOKS & SOFTWARE — Antiquarian-Americana
806 Richards Ln, 61820. Tel 217-359-5289
Estab 1976. 15,000 Vols. 1000 sq ft. Cat
Types: Fine bnd, 1st ed, hb, illus bk, ltd ed, old & rare, out of print, used
Subj: Amer, graphic arts, Illinoisiana

CHARLESTON — 19,355. Area code 217

MADIGAN'S BOOKS — Mail Order
846 Tenth, 61920. Tel 217-345-3657
Estab 1986. 1000 Titles. 350 Vols. Cat 2x ann
Types: Out of print, old & rare
Subj: Genealogy, regional Am & family hist

CHICAGO — 3,005,072. Area code 312

ABRAHAM LINCOLN BOOKSHOP — American Hist & Lit
18 E Chestnut St, 60611. Tel 312-944-3085
Estab 1933. Cat 2x ann
Types: 1st ed, facsimile editions, hb, imp, new, out of print, old & rare, used
Subj: Civil War, presidents & presidency, Lincolniana, Frontier & Indian wars

ACT I BOOKSTORE — Drama
2632 N Lincoln, 60614. Tel 312-348-6757
Estab 1987. 4000 Titles. 7000 Vols
Types: Hb, out of print, papbk, remainders, col & el-hi text, used
Subj: Theatre

RICHARD ADAMIAK — Mail Order-Antiquarian
1700 E 56th St, No 3604, 60637-1936. Tel 312-955-4571
Estab 1971. 4000 Vols. Cat ann
Types: Hb, 1st ed, fine bnd, out of print, old & rare
Subj: Econ, law, philos, polit sci

ANTIQUARIAN BOOKS — Mail Order-Antiquarian
2248 N Kedvale Ave, 60639. Tel 312-235-2326
10,000 Titles. 10,000 Vols. Cat 4x ann
Types: Hb, juvenile, mass mkt papbk, used, out of print, papbk, 1st ed, facsimile editions, illus bk, ltd ed, remainders
Subj: Amer, art

HERBERT BIBLO BOOKSELLER — Mail Order-Antiquarian
5225 Blackstone Ave, 60615. Tel 312-643-2363
5000 Vols. Cat
Types: Out of print
Subj: Africa, black studies, presidents & presidency

THE BLACKSTAR BOOKSTORE, CAFE & THEATER — Used
6544 N Sheridan, 60626. Tel 312-743-6685
Estab 1981. 60,000 Titles. 75,000 Vols. 4000 sq ft
Types: Old & rare, out of print
Subj: Philos, rel, lit, Eur hist

BOOKLEGGER'S — Antiquarian-Americana
6743 N Sheridan Rd, 60626. Tel 312-743-4195
Estab 1980. 7000 Vols. 600 sq ft
Types: 1st ed, hb, illus bk, juvenile, ltd ed, old & rare, out of print, papbk, used
Subj: Amer, Am hist & lit, sci fiction & fantasy

BOOKMAN'S CORNER — Used
2959 N Clark St, 60657. Tel 312-929-8298
Estab 1975. 25,000 Vols. 1400 sq ft
Types: Out of print, remainders
Subj: Art, hist, nonfiction, scholarly

BOOKSELLERS ROW INC — Used
2445 N Lincoln, 60614. Tel 312-348-1170
Estab 1978. 30,000 Titles. 30,000 Vols. 2200 sq ft
Types: 1st ed, hb, old & rare, out of print, papbk, used, fine bnd
Subj: Art, scholarly lit

THE BOOKWORKS — Antiquarian
3444 N Clark, 60657. Tel 312-871-5318
20,000 Vols. 1200 sq ft
Types: Illus bk, fine bnd, 1st ed, hb, juvenile, ltd ed, old & rare, out of print, papbk, used

CHICAGO LAW BOOK CO — Law
4814 S Pulaski Rd, 60632-4194. Tel 312-376-1711
Mgr, Bernadine Dziedzic
Estab 1940. 11,000 Titles. 150,000 Vols. Cat 4x ann
Types: Col text, hb, high priced papbk, used, out of print, old & rare, leather antiquarian bks
Subj: Antq, criminology, econ, law, law enforcement, real estate, criminal justice, law-related police

THE CHILDRENS BOOKSTORE — Juvenile
2465 N Lincoln Ave, 60614. Tel 312-248-2665
Mgr, Christine Blum
Types: Hb, papbk, used, imp, for lang, out of print

CREEDMOOR BOOKSTORE* — Antiquarian
2323 W Foster, 60625. Tel 312-769-4232
Estab 1974. 12,000 Vols
Types: Hb, new & used, out of print, papbk, remainders
Subj: Hunting & fishing, natural hist, guns, Chicago hist

STEPHEN DAITER BOOKS — Mail Order
5423 S Eastview Park, 60615. Tel 312-947-0295
Estab 1985. 800 Titles. 1000 Vols
Types: Out of print, 1st ed, hb, ltd ed, old & rare
Subj: Photog, arts & crafts

N FAGIN BOOKS — Anthropology
1039 W Grand Ave, 60622. Tel 312-829-5252
Estab 1980. 5000 Vols. 800 sq ft. Cat 2x ann
Types: Hb, out of print, high priced papbk, new & used, journals
Subj: Botany, nature & environ, zool, archaeol, anthrop

FRANK'S BOOKS — Mail Order
952 W Dickens, 60614. Tel 312-281-9204
Estab 1973. 10,000 Vols
Types: For lang, hb, high priced papbk, out of print, old & rare, 1st ed

GALLERY BOOK & MAGAZINE SHOP — Used
1833 W Irving Park Rd, 60613. Tel 312-528-0747
Types: Hb, out of print, papbk

GUSTAFSON BOOKS & ANTIQUES — Used
6962 N Clark St, 60626. Tel 312-761-0904
Estab 1955. 25,000 Vols. 2000 sq ft
Types: For lang, hb, juvenile, out of print, papbk
Subj: Local hist, Amer, hist, class studies, natural hist, sci-tech

THOMAS J JOYCE AND CO — Antiquarian
411 S Sangamon No 1D, 60607-3527. Tel 312-738-1933
Estab 1975. 5000 Vols. 2000 sq ft. Cat 4x ann
Types: Fine bnd, 1st ed, hb, illus bk, juvenile, ltd ed, old & rare, out of print, pvt presses, used
Subj: Amer, mod lit, sci fiction & fantasy, Western Amer, law, Chicago

CHARLES H KERR PUBLISHING, CO — Mail Order-Antiquarian
1740 W Greenleaf Ave, 60626. Tel 312-465-7774
Mgr, Joseph Giganti; Buyer, M Lenoir
Estab 1886. 15,000 Titles. 150,000 Vols. 10,000 sq ft. Cat 3x ann
Types: For lang, Fr lang, Ger lang, Ital lang, papbk, remainders, col text, used, facsimile editions, 1st ed, old & rare, out of print
Subj: Socialism, anarchism, utopias, humor, radical & labor history, US popular culture

KROCH'S & BRENTANO'S INC GENERAL OFFICES & MAIN STORE — General
29 S Wabash Ave, 60603. Tel 312-332-7500. WATS 800-523-5083
Pres, William Rickman; Trade Buyer, Ray Carroll; Papbk Buyer, Sandy Popik; Mgr, John S Judd; Dir of Marketing, Doris Laufer; Remd Buyer, Philip Anderson; Tech & Sci Buyer, Harlan Smith; Asst Trade Buyer, John Norris
Estab 1907. 100,000 Titles. 30,000 sq ft. Cat Bi-monthly
Types: For lang, imp, juvenile, out of print, papbk, remainders
Subj: Art, music, psychol, rel, sci-tech
See Also: Aurora, Calumet City, Evanston, Evergreen Park, Matteson, Mount Prospect, Oak Brook, Oak Park, Orland Park, Rockford, Shaumburg, Skokie, Vernon Hills

LARRY LAWS BOOKSTORE — Mail Order-Antiquarian
831 Cornelia, 60657. Tel 312-477-9247
Estab 1975. 25,000 Titles. 100,000 Vols. 5000 sq ft. Cat 4x ann
Types: Out of print, used, remainders
Subj: Dance, performing arts, films & filmmaking, fairs & expositions, nudist mags, Victorian mags, Naval Institute proceedings

ANNE W LEONARD BOOKS — Used
1935 W 95th St, 60643. Tel 312-239-7768
12,000 Titles. 12,000 Vols. 960 sq ft
Types: Juvenile, out of print

THE OCCULT BOOKSTORE — Metaphysics & Occult
3230 N Clark St, 60657. Tel 312-281-0599
Types: Hb, imp UK, imp India, out of print, papbk, used, facsimile editions, 1st ed, ltd ed, old & rare
Subj: Astrol, magic & conjuring
See Also: Prisca Magia Bookstore, Madison, WI

J E PEARSON -BOOKSELLER — Mail Order-Antiquarian
PO Box 446, 60690. Tel 312-776-9566
Estab 1967. 5000 Titles. 8000 Vols
Types: Facsimile editions, hb, ltd ed, new & used, old & rare, out of print, papbk
Subj: Railroadiana, aviation, military, buses, trolley coaches

ELSIE M PHALEN - OUT-OF-PRINT BOOKS — Antiquarian
2331 W Eastwood, 60625. Tel 312-561-0198
2000 Vols
Types: 1st ed, out of print, old & rare
Subj: Fiction, nonfiction

PRAIRIE AVENUE BOOKSHOP — Architecture
711 S Dearborn, 60605. Tel 312-922-8311
Estab 1963. 4000 Titles. 5000 Vols. 1500 sq ft. Cat ann
Types: Hb, imp, out of print, papbk
Subj: Urban design

A & A PROSSER BOOKSELLERS — Antiquarian
3118 N Keating Ave, 60641-5523. Tel 312-685-7680
Estab 1936. 12,000 Titles. 15,000 Vols. Cat ann
Types: Out of print, used, op Catholic bks
Subj: Chesterton & Belloc, pre-Vatican II Catholic authors

PSYCHOLOGY BOOKSTORE — Psychology
220 S State, 60605. Tel 312-341-3480
Mgr, Charles Depondt
Estab 1985. 900 Titles. 1200 Vols. 550 sq ft. Cat 2x ann
Types: Hb, mass mkt papbk, high priced papbk, col text, old & rare, out of print, new & used
Subj: Reference, testing & assessment, minority & women's issues

RAINBOW ISLAND BOOKS BOOKSELLER — Used
6011 W Belmont Ave, 60634. Tel 312-237-1133
Estab 1987. 35,000 Vols
Types: Out of print, papbk, hb

PAUL ROHE & SONS BOOKSELLERS — Used
3176 N Clark St, 60657. Tel 312-477-1999
Mgr, Christopher Rohe
Estab 1977. 20,000 Vols
Types: Old & rare, out of print, papbk, hb, fine bnd
Subj: Art, photog, illus, drama, tv, fiction, film

JOHN RYBSKI BOOKSELLER — Antiquarian
2319 W 47th Pl, 60609. Tel 312-847-5082
Estab 1968. 20,000 Vols. Cat 3x ann
Types: Hb, imp, out of print
Subj: Alaskana, Am hist & lit, Arctic, Civil War, Am Indian studies, Latin Am, Revolutionary War, Western Amer, Am bus hist, midwest

SEASON TO TASTE BOOKS LTD — Cooking & Nutrition
911 School St, 60657. Tel 312-327-0210
Estab 1988. 3000 Titles. 5000 Vols. 950 sq ft. Cat quarterly
Types: Out of print, high priced papbk, hb, imp, facsimile editions, 1st ed, ltd ed, old & rare, new
Subj: Food, wines

SELECTED WORKS — Antiquarian
3619 N Broadway, 60613. Tel 312-975-0002
Mgr, Keith Peterson
Estab 1984. 600 sq ft
Types: Hb, out of print, papbk, used
Subj: Philos, rel, hist

SULLIVAN SPORTING BOOKS — Mail Order-Antiquarian
3748 N Damen Ave, 60618. Tel 312-472-2638
Estab 1969. 2000 Vols
Types: Hb, old & rare, out of print
Subj: Sports

YESTERDAY — Antiquarian-Comics
1143 W Addison St (Mail add: 1771 W Cullom Ave, 60613). Tel 312-248-8087
Estab 1976. 750 Vols. 400 sq ft
Types: 1st ed, hb, illus bk, juvenile, out of print, old & rare, papbk, used
Subj: Biog, movies, baseball

CHILLICOTHE — 6176. Area code 309

THE AMERICAN BOTANIST, BOOKSELLERS — Horticulture
1103 W Truitt Ave, 61523-1403. Tel 309-274-5254
Office Mgr, Betsy Ferraro
Estab 1983. 3000 Titles. 3800 Vols. 700 sq ft. Cat 4x ann
Types: Out of print, remainders, hb, used, facsimile editions, fine bnd, 1st ed, illus bk, ltd ed, old & rare
Subj: Agr, botany, gardening, med botany, North Am

DEERFIELD — 17,430. Area code 312

NORMA K ADLER BOOKS — Mail Order-Antiquarian
59 Eastwood Dr, IL, 60015. Tel 312-945-8575
Estab 1977. 800 Titles. 800 Vols
Types: Fine bnd, 1st ed, hb, ltd ed, old & rare, out of print, remainders

DOWNERS GROVE — 39,274. Area code 312

THOMAS W BURROWS BOOKSELLER — Antiquarian
PO Box 400, 60515-0400. Tel 312-960-1028
Estab 1971. 15,000 Vols. Cat
Types: Hb, 1st ed, new & used, old & rare, out of print
Subj: Amer, bks on bks, bibliog, class studies, hist, humanities, rel-c,p, scholarly lit

ELMHURST — 44,251. Area code 312

YE OLDE BOOK WORM — General
161 N York, 60126. Tel 312-279-0123
Estab 1973. 50,000 Titles. 60,000 Vols. 1800 sq ft
Types: Juvenile, new, out of print, papbk, used, hb
Subj: Amer, art, biog, fiction, metaphys & occult, sci fiction & fantasy, travel, sports

EVANSTON — 73,706. Area code 312

ABRAHAM'S BOOKS — General
613 Dempster St, 60201. Tel 312-475-1777
Estab 1979. 8000 Vols. 600 sq ft
Types: Facsimile editions, fine bnd, 1st ed, hb, out of print, old & rare, remainders, used
Subj: Art, hist, philos, psychol, scholarly lit, sociol, photog

THE ALEPH — Antiquarian-Science Fiction & Fantasy
831 Main St, 60202. Tel 312-869-6410
Estab 1988. 4000 Titles. 5000 Vols
Types: 1st ed, hb, out of print, papbk
Subj: Sci fiction & fantasy, horror

ALKAHEST BOOKSHOP — Antiquarian
1814 Central St, 60201. Tel 312-475-0990
Estab 1970. 5000 Vols. 600 sq ft. Cat 4x ann
Types: Hb, illus bk, out of print, old & rare, remainders, used, fine bnd
Subj: Amer, art, drama, films & filmmaking, fine arts, music, literary criticism, photog, fantasy

RICHARD S BARNES & CO, BOOKS — Mail Order-Antiquarian
1745 Hinman Ave, 60201. Tel 312-869-2272
Owners, Richard S & Patricia N Barnes
Estab 1951. 25,000 Vols
Types: Fine bnd, 1st ed, hb, juvenile, out of print, old & rare, used
Subj: Biog, hist, mod lit, art, travel, Amer

BOOKMAN'S ALLEY — Antiquarian
1712 (Rear) Sherman Ave, 60201. Tel 312-869-6999
Estab 1980. 20,000 Vols. 4000 sq ft
Types: 1st ed, hb, illus bk, juvenile, ltd ed, old & rare, out of print, used
Subj: Drama, humor, mod lit, poetry, Am hist, Chicago

BOOKNOOK PARNASSUS — Used
2000 Maple, 60201. Tel 312-475-3445
Estab 1980. 12,000 Vols. 900 sq ft
Types: 1st ed, facsimile editions, fine bnd, hb, illus bk, juvenile, ltd ed, out of print, old & rare, papbk, remainders, used
Subj: Art, class studies, drama, metaphys & occult, music, philos, psychol, rel, sci fiction & fantasy, Judaica

CHICAGO HISTORICAL BOOKWORKS — Used
831 Main St, 60202. Tel 312-869-6410
Estab 1984. 5000 Titles. 7000 Vols. Cat 5x ann
Types: 1st ed, hb, old & rare, out of print, papbk
Subj: Archit, poetry, Chicago authors, crime, politics, WPA & lakeside classics

HOLDEN'S — Mail Order
1628 Keeney St (Mail add: PO Box 1456, 60204). Tel 312-491-1680
Estab 1988. 100 Titles
Types: Hb, out of print, papbk, remainders
Subj: Bus & mgt, nonfiction, photog, self-develop, success, retailing

KENNEDY'S BOOKS* — Mail Order-Antiquarian
PO Box 191, 60204. Tel 312-475-2481 (appt only)
Estab 1962. 10,000 Vols. 1000 sq ft
Types: 1st ed, hb, out of print, old & rare, used
Subj: Sci-tech

KROCH'S & BRENTANO'S INC — General
1711 Sherman Ave, 60201. Tel 312-328-7220
Mgr, Tom Anderson
Estab 1950. 35,000 Titles Buys through hq
Types: Hb, imp, juvenile, out of print, papbk, remainders, for lang
Subj: Art, music, psychol, rel, sci-tech

PRESERVATION BOOKSHOP — Used
1911 Central, 60201. Tel 312-864-4449
Estab 1960. 8000 Titles. 10,000 Vols
Types: Hb, out of print, papbk
Subj: Hist

GEORGE RITZLIN BOOKS & MAPS — Antiquarian
Box 6060, 60204. Tel 312-328-1966
Mgr, Mary McMichael
Estab 1977. 1200 Titles. 1200 Vols. Cat
Types: Old & rare, out of print
Subj: Cartography, cartographic ref, maps

PHYLLIS THOLIN BOOKS — Antiquarian
PO Box 5408, 60204. Tel 312-475-1174 (by appt)
Estab 1979. 3000 Titles. 3000 Vols. Cat 3x ann
Types: Hb, old & rare, out of print, used
Subj: Women's studies, Chicagoana

EVERGREEN PARK — 22,260. Area code 312

KROCH'S & BRENTANO'S INC — General
J-6 Evergreen Plaza, 60642. Tel 312-424-9550
Mgr, Dave Bukwa
Estab 1963. 35,000 Titles Buys through hq
Types: Hb, imp, juvenile, out of print, papbk, remainders, for lang
Subj: Art, music, psychol, rel, sci-tech

FORSYTH — 1072. Area code 217

OLD BOOK BARN — Used
Rt 51, 62535. Tel 217-875-0222
Estab 1981. 150,000 Vols. 16,000 sq ft
Types: Hb, juvenile, out of print, papbk, mag, pamphlets

GALENA — 3876. Area code 815

ANNA'S GATE BOOKSHOP — Used
204 Hill St, 61036. Tel 815-777-3885
Estab 1984. 2500 Titles. 3000 Vols. 700 sq ft. Cat ann
Types: Juvenile, out of print, papbk, high priced papbk, remainders, illus bk, hb
Subj: Psychol, women's studies, Jungian, inner development

GREAT LAKES — Area code 312

GALAXY OF BOOKS — Used
Great Lakes Depot, Rte 137 & Sheridan Rd, 60064. Tel 312-473-1099
Types: Mass mkt papbk, comics, out of print

HIGHLAND PARK — 30,611. Area code 312

ORT ALLEY BOOKSHOP — Used
1905 Sheridan Rd, 60035. Tel 312-433-1172
Owner, Lake County Region, Women's American ORT; Mgr, Jackie Wilkins
Estab 1972. 5000 Titles. 50,000 Vols
Types: Out of print, papbk, hb

LA GRANGE — 15,681. Area code 312

JOHN WILLIAM MARTIN - BOOKSELLER — Antiquarian-English Hist & Lit
231 S La Grange Rd, 60525. Tel 312-352-8115
Estab 1973. 9000 Titles. 10,000 Vols. 1000 sq ft. Cat 5x ann
Types: Facsimile editions, fine bnd, 1st ed, hb, old & rare, out of print
Subj: Bks on bks, Am & Brit lit & criticism 1550-1980

LAKE FOREST — 15,245. Area code 312

D J FLYNN -BOOKS — Mail Order-Antiquarian
421 E Westleigh Rd, 60045. Tel 312-234-1146
Estab 1974. 9000 Titles. 9000 Vols
Types: Hb, used, out of print, 1st ed, illus bk
Subj: Bks with fore-edge paintings

LIBERTYVILLE — 16,520. Area code 312

COGITATOR BOOKS* — Antiquarian
PO Box 405, 60048. Tel 312-362-4676
Estab 1963. 5000 Vols
Types: 1st ed, juvenile, illus bk, out of print, pvt presses

LINCOLN — 16,327. Area code 217

YESTERYEAR — Antiquarian
420 Lincoln Ave, 62656. Tel 217-732-6474
Estab 1972. 10,000 Titles. 12,000 Vols
Types: Hb, out of print
Subj: Amer, Am Indian studies, Civil War

MARTINTON — 363. Area code 815

LEONARD HOFFNUNG BOOKS — Antiquarian
RR1 Box 148A, 60951. Tel 815-486-7281
Estab 1977. 15,000 Vols. Cat Monthly
Types: 1st ed, old & rare, out of print
Subj: Bibliog, bks on bks, scholarly lit

MATTESON — 10,223. Area code 312

KROCH'S & BRENTANO'S INC — General
159 Lincoln Mall, 60443. Tel 312-481-6140
Mgr, Mark Heroldt
Estab 1973. 35,000 Titles Buys through hq
Types: Hb, imp, juvenile, out of print, papbk, remainders, for lang
Subj: Art, music, psychol, rel, sci-tech

MATTOON — 19,787. Area code 217

MUNSON BOOKS — Mail Order
3436 Willow Dr, 61938-4799. Tel 217-234-8465
Estab 1974. Cat 4x ann
Types: Col & el-hi text, hb, out of print, papbk, used

MOUNT PROSPECT — 52,634. Area code 312

CROWN BOOKS — Mail Order-Science Fiction
1016 S Elmhurst Rd, 60056. Tel 312-439-1180
Mgr, James Cozzarelli
Estab 1983. 11,000 Titles. 20,000 Vols. Cat 3x ann
Types: Hb, out of print, mass mkt papbk, papbk, 1st ed, illus bk, imp UK, ltd ed, new, old & rare, remainders, used

JACK'S USED BOOKS — Used
718 East Northwest Hwy, 60056. Tel 312-398-7767
Estab 1975. 30,000 Vols. 2000 sq ft
Types: 1st ed, hb, illus bk, old & rare, papbk, out of print
Subj: Hist, mystery & detective, Am hist & lit, Eur studies, military, sci fiction & fantasy, mod 1st editions, Stephen King 1st editions

KROCH'S & BRENTANO'S INC — General
Randhurst Ctr, 999 Elmhurst Rd, 60056. Tel 312-259-5510
Mgr, Pat Pistone
Estab 1974. 35,000 Titles Buys through hq
Types: Hb, imp, juvenile, out of print, papbk, remainders, for lang
Subj: Art, music, psychol, rel, sci-tech

OAK BROOK — 6651. Area code 312

KROCH'S & BRENTANO'S INC — General
80 Oak Brook Ctr, 60521. Tel 312-574-0340
Mgr, Don Hailman
Estab 1961. 35,000 Titles Buys through hq
Types: Hb, imp, juvenile, out of print, papbk, remainders, for lang
Subj: Art, music, psychol, rel, sci-tech

OAK FOREST — 26,096. Area code 312

ROBERT & PHYLLIS WEINBERG BOOKS — Mail Order-Science Fiction
15145 Oxford Dr, 60452. Tel 312-687-5765
Mgr, Phyllis Weinberg
Estab 1973. 10,000 Vols
Types: Hb, papbk, out of print
Subj: Mystery & detective

OAK PARK — 54,887. Area code 312

THE BOOKSMITH — Used
108 S Marion St, 60302. Tel 312-383-8734
Estab 1974. 8000 Vols. 750 sq ft. Cat 2x ann
Types: Out of print, remainders
Subj: Biog, fiction, hist

OWEN DAVIES BOOKSELLER — Railroadiana
200 W Harrison St, 60304. Tel 312-848-1186
Estab 1929. 7200 Vols. Cat 4x ann
Types: Out of print, new, imp Eng, Jap, Fr, imp Ger, imp Switz
Subj: Transp, maritime hist

KROCH'S & BRENTANO'S INC — General
1028 Lake St, 60301. Tel 312-848-9003
Mgr, William Skoda
Estab 1965. 35,000 Titles Buys through hq
Types: Hb, imp, juvenile, out of print, papbk, remainders, for lang
Subj: Music, psychol, rel, sci-tech

LEFT BANK BOOKSTALL — Used
104 S Oak Park Ave, 60302. Tel 312-383-4700
Estab 1978. 15,000 Titles. 15,000 Vols. 1000 sq ft. Cat ann
Types: Out of print, remainders, small presses
Subj: Rel

THOMAS & THOMAS BOOKSELLERS — Mail Order
1138 Erie St, 60302-1940. Tel 312-848-9620
Estab 1982. 2700 Titles. 3000 Vols. Cat ann
Types: Hb, new & used, out of print, old & rare
Subj: Wines, cooking

ORLAND PARK — 23,045. Area code 312

KROCH'S & BRENTANO'S INC — General
100 Orland Sq, 151st St & Rte 45, 60462. Tel 312-349-0676
Mgr, Michelle Kopp
Estab 1976. 35,000 Titles Buys through hq
Types: Hb, imp, juvenile, out of print, papbk, remainders, for lang
Subj: Art, music, psychol, rel, sci-tech

PARK FOREST — 26,222. Area code 312

TATTERED PAGES — Used
204 Blackhawk Dr, 60466. Tel 312-481-8850
Estab 1972. 25,000 Titles. 1000 sq ft. Cat 4x ann
Types: Imp Ger, out of print, facsimile editions, fine bnd, 1st ed, hb, illus bk, juvenile, ltd ed, old & rare
Subj: Medieval studies

PEORIA — 124,160. Area code 309

BOOKMAN — Antiquarian
Illinois Antique Center, 100 Walnut (Mail add: 1009F Northmoor, 61614)
2000 Titles
Types: Hb, juvenile, old & rare, out of print, papbk, used
Subj: Judaica, psychol

PRINCETON — 7342. Area code 815

VILLAGE BOOKS — Used
614 S Pleasant, 61356. Tel 815-875-4652
Estab 1968. 4000 Titles. 4000 Vols
Types: Out of print, juvenile
Subj: Fiction, needlecrafts

ROCKFORD — 139,712. Area code 815

BOOKSTALL OF ROCKFORD — Used
1032 Crosby St, 61107. Tel 815-963-1671
Estab 1980. 10,000 Vols. 2000 sq ft
Types: 1st ed, hb, illus bk, juvenile, old & rare, out of print, used
Subj: Amer, military, sci-tech

KROCH'S & BRENTANO'S INC — General
E-108 The Mall at Cherryvale, 61112. Tel 815-332-2405
Mgr, Jamie Yardlimek
Estab 1974. 35,000 Titles Buys through hq
Types: Hb, imp, juvenile, out of print, papbk, remainders, for lang
Subj: Art, music, psychol, rel, sci-tech

SAINT CHARLES — 17,492. Area code 312

JAMES DOWD BOOKSELLER — Mail Order-Antiquarian
38 W 281 Toms Trail Dr, 60174. Tel 312-584-1930
Estab 1980. 5000 Vols. Cat
Types: 1st ed, facsimile editions, fine bnd, hb, juvenile, ltd ed, new & used, old & rare, out of print
Subj: Civil War, Illinoisiana, local hist, Western Amer

SEVEN OAKS PRESS — Used
405 S Seventh St, 60174. Tel 312-584-0187
Estab 1969. 5000 Vols. Cat 3x ann
Types: Facsimile editions, fine bnd, 1st ed, illus bk, ltd ed, hb, incunab, papbk, imp, juvenile, new & used, old & rare, out of print, remainders

SCHAUMBURG — 52,319. Area code 312

KROCH'S & BRENTANO'S INC — General
J-108 Woodfield Mall, 60173. Tel 312-884-0888
Mgr, David Plath
Estab 1974. 30,000 Vols Buys through hq
Types: Hb, imp, juvenile, out of print, papbk, remainders, for lang
Subj: Art, music, psychol, rel, sci-tech

SKOKIE — 60,278. Area code 312

ARTICLES OF WAR LTD — Military
8806 N Bronx, 60077-1823. Tel 312-674-7445
Estab 1971. 5000 Titles. 12,000 Vols. Cat 4-5x ann
Types: Hb, imp, out of print, remainders, used
Subj: Hist

KROCH'S & BRENTANO'S INC — General
7550 N Keeler, 60076. Tel 312-675-7550
Mgr, Maureen Como
Estab 1956. 35,000 Titles Buys through hq
Types: Hb, imp, juvenile, out of print, papbk, remainders, for lang
Subj: Art, music, psychol, rel, sci-tech

PASSING THE BOOK INC — Paperback
3423 Church St, 60203. Tel 312-673-3423
Estab 1988. 15,000 Titles. 16,000 Vols. 1000 sq ft
Types: Hb, juvenile, out of print, mass mkt papbk, remainders, used, 1st ed, new, old & rare

SPRINGFIELD — 99,637. Area code 217

FOLLETT'S LAKESIDE BOOKSTORE — College
Sangamon State Univ, 62703. Tel 217-786-6766. Telex 40-4451
Mgr, Lu Ann Johnson
Estab 1972. 10,000 Vols. 2700 sq ft
Types: Juvenile, out of print, papbk, remainders, used
Subj: Bus & mgt, econ, psychol, sci-tech, math, sci fiction & fantasy, feminism

SYCAMORE — 9219. Area code 815

STOREYBOOK ANTIQUES & BOOKS — Antiquarian
1325 E State St, 60178-9538. Tel 815-895-5910
Estab 1972. 8000 Titles. 8000 Vols
Types: 1st ed, fine bnd, hb, illus bk, juvenile, ltd ed, out of print, old & rare, used
Subj: Finance, polit sci, rel, sexuality, christmas, gerontology

TREMONT — 2096. Area code 309

ALLENTOWN BOOKSTORE, ENIGMA BOOKS — Mail Order
RR 1 Box 85, 61568. Tel 309-925-3907
Mgr, Dan Dexter
Estab 1987. 200 Titles. 4000 Vols. Cat 6x ann
Types: Out of print, mass mkt papbk, high priced papbk, used
Subj: New age

URBANA — 35,798. Area code 217

BURKWOOD BOOKS — Antiquarian
PO Box 172, 61801. Tel 217-344-1419
Estab 1973. 6000 Vols. 1500 sq ft. Cat
Types: Fine bnd, 1st ed, hb, illus bk, ltd ed, old & rare, out of print
Subj: Am hist & lit, Amer, Western Amer

VERNON HILLS — 9827. Area code 312

KROCH'S & BRENTANO'S INC — General
106 Hawthorn Ctr, 60061. Tel 312-367-0141
Mgr, Pam Kowalski
Estab 1973. 35,000 Vols Buys through hq
Types: Hb, imp, juvenile, out of print, papbk, remainders, for lang
Subj: Art, music, psychol, rel, sci-tech

MARSHALL FIELD & CO BOOK DEPT — Dept Store
One Hawthorn Ctr, 60061. Tel 312-367-1234
Mgr, Bob Aruda Buys through hq & indep
Types: Hb, juvenile, out of print, papbk, remainders
Subj: Cooking

WALNUT — 1513. Area code 815

BOOK BARN — Antiquarian
RR 1, 61376. Tel 815-379-2581
Estab 1980. 16,000 Vols. 800 sq ft. Cat
Types: Facsimile editions, 1st ed, hb, ltd ed, old & rare, out of print, used
Subj: Civil War, fiction, local hist, Amer

WAUKEGAN — 67,653. Area code 312

WAUKEGAN DUPLICATE CLUB — Bridge
927 Grand Ave, 60085. Tel 312-662-7204
2000 Titles. 10,000 Vols. 7500 sq ft. Cat 4x ann
Types: Out of print, used
Subj: Games, bks on playing cds

WHEATON — 43,043. Area code 312

EX LIBRIS THEOLOGICAL BOOKS — Religious-C, J, P
1022 College Av, 60187. Tel 312-690-3456
Estab 1982. 10,000 Titles. 1000 sq ft
Types: Out of print, used, old & rare, Fr, Ger & Latin

RICHARD OWEN ROBERTS BOOKSELLERS — Antiquarian-Theology
Box 21, 60189. Tel 312-584-8069
Estab 1961. 50,000 Vols. 3000 sq ft. Cat 4x ann
Types: Facsimile editions, fine bnd, 1st ed, hb, incunab, illus bk, bibles, imp, ltd ed, new & used, old & rare, out of print, papbk
Subj: Biog, hist, philos, psychol, rel studies

WINTHROP HARBOR — 5438. Area code 312

LEEKLEY BOOK SEARCH — Mail Order-Antiquarian
PO Box 337, 60096. Tel 312-872-2311
Estab 1964. 5000 Titles. 5000 Vols. Cat 3x ann
Types: 1st ed, hb, out of print, old & rare, used
Subj: Humanities, mod lit, hist, scholarly lit, soc sci, soc movements

WOODSTOCK — 11,725. Area code 815

HEARTLAND BOOKS — Used
PO Box 1094, 60098. Tel 815-338-5272
Estab 1986. 7000 Titles. 7000 Vols. Cat 6x ann
Types: 1st ed, old & rare, out of print
Subj: Hunting & fishing, Civil War, mystery & detective, Western Amer

ZION — 17,861. Area code 312

GALAXY OF BOOKS — Used
1908 Sheridan Rd (Mail add: PO Box 153, 60099). Tel 312-872-3313
Estab 1976. 35,000 Vols. 1200 sq ft
Types: Hb, juvenile, out of print, mass mkt papbk
Subj: Art, cooking, hunting & fishing, military, nautical, natural hist, exploration
See Also: Great Lakes

INDIANA

ANDERSON — 64,695. Area code 317

BOOK WORLD* — Used
2206 E Tenth St, 46012. Tel 317-642-0776
Gen Mgr, Enola Hensley
Types: Out of print, papbk, comics
See Also: Indianapolis

AUBURN — 8122. Area code 219

WAANDER'S BOOKMART — General
108 E Seventh St, 46706. Tel 219-925-2330
Estab 1985
Types: Hb, juvenile, out of print, papbk
Subj: Indiana auth

BLOOMINGTON — 51,646. Area code 812

ALMAGRE BOOKS — Antiquarian-Western Americana
4615 Cranbrook Rd, 47401. Tel 812-334-0465
Proprietor, William Wroth
Estab 1979. 4000 Titles. 4000 Vols. Cat 12x ann
Types: Out of print, rare
Subj: Western Amer, art, photog

BETWEEN THE LINES — Antiquarian
1400 E Third St, 47401. Tel 812-332-4440
Estab 1981. 50,000 Vols. 2400 sq ft
Types: Hb, out of print, papbk, used
Subj: Humanities, scholarly lit

CAVEAT EMPTOR — Antiquarian
208 S Dunn St, 47401. Tel 812-332-9995
Owner, Caveat Emptor, Inc; Mgr, Janet Starcs
Estab 1971. 40,000 Vols. 1300 sq ft. Cat
Types: Hb, juvenile, out of print, papbk, used
Subj: Sci fiction & fantasy, soc sci, scholarly lit

FRIENDS OF ART BOOKSHOP — Museum
Indiana University - Fine Arts Bldg, 47405. Tel 812-335-1333
Merch Mgr, Susan S Shelden
Estab 1968. 7000 Titles. 20,000 Vols. 1000 sq ft
Types: Col text, hb, high priced papbk, juvenile, remainders, out of print, used, imp Fr, Ger, Nigeria, Port, UK, Netherlands, Italy
Subj: Fine arts, arts & crafts, photog, travel

G JAY RAUSCH BOOKSELLER — Mail Order-Antiquarian
PO Box 2346, 47402. Tel 812-333-1178
Estab 1981. 11,000 Titles. 14,000 Vols. Cat 5x ann
Types: Imp UK, out of print
Subj: Biog, literary criticism

TIS INC — College
1302 E Third St (Mail add: PO Box 669, 47402). Tel 812-332-3306
Mgr, Gregory L Lloyd
Estab 1974. 50,000 Titles. Cat
Types: Hb, juvenile, out of print, mass mkt papbk, remainders, used, text bks
Subj: Fr, Ger & Sp lang, law, music

25TH CENTURY FIVE & DIME PAPER AND INC — Mystery & Detective
106 E Kirkwood (Mail add: PO Box 7, 47402). Tel 812-332-0011
Mgr, Michael Redman
Estab 1984. 20,000 Vols. 1200 sq ft
Types: Hb, imp, juvenile, out of print, papbk, used, comics
Subj: Mystery & detective, sci fiction & fantasy

ELBERFELD — 640. Area code

LARRY SCHNELL'S PAPERTIQUES — Mail Order-Antiquarian
Third & Mulberry, Box 252, 47613. Tel 812-983-4009
Types: Fine bnd, 1st ed, hb, used, ltd ed, illus bk, old & rare, out of print

ELKHART — 41,305. Area code 219

BOOKS & BEYOND — Used
51533 State Rd 19 N, 45614-5814. Tel 219-262-1798
Estab 1986. 17,000 Titles. 20,000 Vols. 875 sq ft
Types: Out of print, papbk, remainders, el-hi text, used, juvenile, new, old & rare
Subj: Sci fiction & fantasy, mystery & detective, nonfiction, hist fict, role playing game bks

THE BOOKSTACK — Antiquarian
112 W Lexington Ave, 46516. Tel 219-293-3815
Mgr, George A Foster Jr
Estab 1975. 25,000 Vols. 1000 sq ft. Cat 2x ann
Types: Facsimile editions, 1st ed, hb, illus bk, juvenile, old & rare, out of print, papbk, remainders, used
Subj: Amer, hist, hunting & fishing, nature & environ, horticulture

EVANSVILLE — 130,496. Area code 812

THE BOOK BROKER — Used
2127 S Weinbach, 47714-4207. Tel 812-479-5647
Estab 1975. 140,000 Vols. 6000 sq ft
Types: Hb, papbk, out of print, illus bk, juvenile, old & rare, comics

THE BOOKSELLER — Used
2922 Broadway, 47712. Tel 812-424-7472
Mgr, Betty Robertson
Estab 1982. 21,000 Titles. 45,000 Vols
Types: Papbk, hb, juvenile, 1st ed, old & rare, out of print
Subj: Fiction, rel, regional authors

CAMPFIRE BOOKS — Mail Order-Antiquarian
6016 Sarabeth, 47712-3626. Tel 812-425-8549
Estab 1981. 3500 Vols. 500 sq ft. Cat ann
Types: Hb, ltd ed, new, old & rare, out of print
Subj: Hunting & fishing, Alaskana, guns

FORT WAYNE — 172,196. Area code 219

CHANTICLEER BOOKS — Used
1120 Michigan Ave, 46802. Tel 219-424-0746
Mgr, R W Clark
Estab 1976. 7000 Vols. 1000 sq ft
Types: Out of print, papbk
Subj: Indianiana

FOREST PARK BOOKSHOP — Used
1412 Delaware Ave, 46805-4597. Tel 219-424-1058
Estab 1970. 7500 Titles. 8000 Vols. 800 sq ft
Types: 1st ed, hb, illus bk, juvenile, old & rare, out of print, papbk, remainders
Subj: Mystery & detective, Amer, Indianiana

GRIFFITH — 17,026. Area code 219

BRANCHES & ROOTS — General
246 S Broad, PO Box 596, 46319. Tel 219-924-4050
Estab 1966. 35,000 Titles. 50,000 Vols
Types: For lang, hb, papbk, juvenile, out of print, used, 1st ed, illus bk, ltd ed, old & rare

HAMMOND — 93,714. Area code 219

CALUMET CAMPUS SHOP — College
Purdue Univ Calumet, 2233 171st St, 46323. Tel 219-844-1081
Mgr & Buyer, Paul McKita
Estab 1976Buys indep & thru hq
Types: Hb, juvenile, out of print, papbk, remainders, used

HOBART — 22,987. Area code 219

FRIENDLY FRANK'S COMICS — Comics
220 Main St, 46342. Tel 219-942-6020
Mgr, Clarence D Thurmond
Estab 1982. 3000 Titles. 100,000 sq ft
Types: New & used, out of print

INDIANAPOLIS — 700,807. Area code 317

THE ABSTRACT — General
5538 N Pennsylvania St, 46220. Tel 317-259-1654
Mgr, Pat Koerber
Estab 1980. 4500 Titles. 4600 Vols
Types: 1st ed, hb, illus bk, juvenile, out of print, used, old & rare

BARNETT & PATTON LAW BOOKSTORE — Law
312 Ober Bldg, 38 N Pennsylvania St, 46204. Tel 317-635-6896
Estab 1920. 15,000 Vols
Types: Hb, out of print, col text, new & used
Subj: Hist

THE BOOK NOOK — Religious-LDS
5685 Terrytown Pkwy, 46254. Tel 317-299-5185
Estab 1981. 1200 Titles. 3000 Vols
Types: Hb, juvenile, out of print, papbk

BOOKS UNLIMITED — General
922 E Washington St, 46202. Tel 317-634-0949
Mgr, Mike Stafford
Estab 1978. 5000 Titles. 50,000 Vols. 2400 sq ft. Cat 2x ann
Types: Hb, out of print, papbk, used, comics
Subj: Rel, nat sci, cookbks

BROAD RIPPLE BOOKSHOP — Used
6407 Ferguson, 46220. Tel 317-259-1980
Estab 1975. 60,000 Vols
Types: Old & rare, out of print
Subj: Amer, art, natural hist, philos, typography, Indianiana

COMIC CARNIVAL & NOSTALGIA EMPORIUM — Science Fiction & Fantasy
6265 N Carrollton Ave, 46220. Tel 317-253-8882
Estab 1977. 150,000 Vols. 1200 sq ft
Types: 1st ed, hb, ltd ed, out of print, papbk, used
Subj: Comedy

FLO SILVER BOOKS — Mail Order
8442 Oakwood Ct N, 46260. Tel 317-255-5118
Estab 1987. 2500 Titles. Cat 4x ann
Types: Out of print, used, facsimile editions, 1st ed, hb, ltd ed, old & rare
Subj: Latin Am

HOOSIER BOOKSHOP — Mail Order-Antiquarian
3820 E 61st St, 46220. Tel 317-257-0888
Cat 4x ann
Types: 1st ed, out of print, old & rare
Subj: Indianiana, Midwest Amer

WILLIAM S JOHNSON BOOKS — Mail Order-Antiquarian
829 E Drive, Woodruff Pl, 46201. Tel 317-639-1256
5000 Vols
Types: Hb, out of print
Subj: Literary criticism, Russ lang, World Wars I & II, Chinese art

THE MUSEUM SHOP — Museum
202 N Alabama St, 46204. Tel 317-632-5007
Owner, Indiana State Museum Society; Mgr, Vanessa Wright
Estab 1970. Cat ann
Types: Hb, out of print, high priced papbk
Subj: Hist, humanities, Indianiana, natural hist

ODDS & EADS BOOKSELLERS — Used
1127 Prospect St, 46203-1936. Tel 317-635-2592
Estab 1979. 350,000 Vols. 9500 sq ft
Types: Col & el-hi text, hb, juvenile, out of print, papbk, remainders
Subj: Fiction, nonfiction

ELEANOR PASOTTI — Mail Order-Antiquarian
5939 Evanston Ave, 46220. Tel 317-255-2079
5000 Vols
Types: Hb, juvenile, old & rare, out of print, used

LAFAYETTE — 43,011. Area code 317

NEW CONCEPT BOOKSTORE — Used
402 N Earl, 47905. Tel 317-448-1305
Mgr, Carole Gibson
Estab 1975. 50,000 Titles. 150,000 Vols. 4000 sq ft
Types: Juvenile, out of print, new
Subj: Comedy
See Also: Terre Haute

LA PORTE — 21,796. Area code 219

A HOOSIER SCHOOLMASTER'S BOOKS — Mail Order-Antiquarian
1228 Michigan Ave, 46350-3584
Estab 1960. 45,000 Titles. 50,000 Vols. Cat 6x ann
Types: Fine bnd, 1st ed, hb, illus bk, ltd ed, new, old & rare, out of print, papbk, used
Subj: Indianiana, Am hist & lit, US Presidents

MONTICELLO — 5162. Area code 219

AUTONOMY HOUSE PUBLICATIONS — Antiquarian
417 N Main St, 47960-1934. Tel 219-583-8593
1000 Titles. 1500 Vols
Types: Out of print, new & used, facsimile editions, illus bk, old & rare
Subj: Antique stoves

MUNCIE — 77,216. Area code 317

THE MELANCHOLY LOBSTER — Mail Order
2605 W Berkshire, 47304. Tel 317-284-8295
Estab 1985. 3000 Vols
Types: Used, out of print

SOUTH BEND — 109,727. Area code 219

ERASMUS BOOKS — Used
1027 E Wayne, 46617. Tel 219-232-8444
Estab 1978. 30,000 Vols. 1800 sq ft
Types: Fine bnd, 1st ed, hb, illus bk, imp, juvenile, ltd ed, old & rare, out of print, papbk, remainders

GRIFFON BOOKSTORE — General
121 W Colfax, 46601. Tel 219-287-5533
Estab 1976. 20,000 Vols
Types: Hb, new & used, out of print, old & rare, papbk
Subj: Games, reference, sci fiction & fantasy, rel-c,j,p

TERRE HAUTE — 61,125. Area code 812

THE BOOK BUNGALOW — Used
2940 S Seventh St, 47802. Tel 812-238-2665
Estab 1987. 15,000 Titles. 2000 sq ft
Types: Used, 1st ed, hb, illus bk, juvenile, old & rare, out of print, papbk, used

VALPARAISO — 22,247. Area code 219

UNIVERSITY BOOK CENTER College
Valparaiso University, Union Bldg, 46383. Tel 219-464-5421
Dir, Garth Grover
Estab 1973. 4000 Titles. 7000 Vols. 8000 sq ft Buys indep
Types: Hb, juvenile, out of print, papbk, remainders, used
Subj: Reference

WABASH — 12,985. Area code 219

READING ROOM BOOKS Antiquarian
264 S Wabash St, 46992. Tel 219-563-6421
Estab 1974. 108,000 Titles. 132,000 Vols. 4400 sq ft. Cat monthly
Types: 1st ed, fine bnd, hb, juvenile, ltd ed, old & rare, out of print, papbk, used
Subj: Natural hist, Indianiana, military, theol

WEST LAFAYETTE — 21,247. Area code 317

MIDNIGHT BOOKMAN Antiquarian-Books On Books
237 Schilling, 47906-2448. Tel 317-743-1790
Estab 1970. 5000 Vols. 450 sq ft. Cat Monthly
Types: 1st ed, fine bnd, hb, illus bk, ltd ed, old & rare, out of print, used
Subj: Calligraphy, collecting, illus, typography, papermaking, printing, publ hist

CEDAR RAPIDS — 110,243. Area code 319

EL-ZAR HORSE BOOK BAR — Mail Order-Horses
PO Box 9064, 52409. Tel 319-396-3444
Estab 1969. 300 Titles. Cat 4x ann
Types: Hb, imp UK, out of print, new
Subj: Horsemanship

CHARLES CITY — 8778. Area code 515

GONE TO MARKET — Gift Shop
201 N Main St, 50616. Tel 515-228-7322
Types: Hb, out of print, papbk

DAVENPORT — 103,264. Area code 319

AVATAR BOOKS — Antiquarian
2212 E 12th St, Suite 206, 52803. Tel 319-322-4159
Estab 1982. 20,000 Vols. 1300 sq ft
Types: Out of print
Subj: Amer, Civil War

BRICKHOUSE BOOKSTORE — Used
528 E Third St, 52807. Tel 319-386-0949
Estab 1986. 15,000 Titles. 15,000 Vols. 1200 sq ft
Types: Out of print, used, old & rare, papbk

PETERSEN BOOK CO — Mail Order-Antiquarian
235 McClellan Blvd (Mail add: PO Box 966, 52805). Tel 319-355-7051
Estab 1944. 1800 Titles. 2000 Vols. 450 sq ft. Cat 2x ann
Types: Col text, hb, out of print, papbk, used, imp SAm, imp UK, imp Central Am
Subj: Natural hist, ornith

THE SOURCE BOOKSTORE — Antiquarian
232 W Third St, 52801. Tel 319-324-8941
Estab 1939. 200,000 Vols
Types: 1st ed, hb, new & used, old & rare, out of print, papbk, remainders
Subj: Amer, biog, chiropractic, class studies, Iowiana, travel, jazz mus, Lincoln

DES MOINES — 191,003. Area code 515

BOB'S BOOKS — Used
2429 University Ave, PO Box 1171, 50311. Tel 515-279-4417
Spec Sales Martha J Fowler
Estab 1981. 125,000 Titles. 125,000 Vols. 1500 sq ft
Types: Hb, out of print, papbk
Subj: Rel, hist, literary criticism

DIFFERENT DRUMMER BOOKS — Mail Order-Used
PO Box 1008, 50311. Tel 515-279-0717
Estab 1978. 3500 Titles. 5000 Vols. 800 sq ft. Cat bi-monthly
Types: Hb, out of print, papbk, remainders, small presses
Subj: Fiction, hist, philos, poetry

FAIRFIELD — 9428. Area code 515

BROKEN KETTLE BOOKS — Used
702 E Madison, 52556. Tel 712-568-2114
50,000 Vols. Cat
Types: Out of print, old & rare, used, trade
Subj: Farm machinery

INDIANOLA — 10,843. Area code 515

BOOKS & MUSIC LTD — Music
801 E Salem Ave, 50125-2733. Tel 515-961-3734
Owner, Carroll M Proctor
10,000 Titles. 10,000 Vols. Cat 12x ann
Types: Fr, Ger & It lang, imp, out of print, col text, used
Subj: Biog, classical singing instr, biogs of classical singers, vocal lit in re-sale condition, bks on pedagogy

IOWA CITY — 50,508. Area code 319

AMARANTH BOOKS — Antiquarian
332 E Washington St, 52240. Tel 319-354-0722
Estab 1987. 12,000 Titles. 12,000 Vols. Cat 4x ann
Types: Used, 1st ed, hb, old & rare, out of print
Subj: Natural hist, Amer, sci-tech, lit

KARL M ARMENS BOOKS — Mail Order-Antiquarian
740 Juniper Dr, 52245-6925. Tel 319-337-7755
Estab 1973. 15,000 Vols. Cat
Types: 1st ed, out of print, used
Subj: Amer, nonfiction, sci fiction & fantasy, mystery & detective, Eng lit, Am lit, 1st ed

THE BOOKERY — Antiquarian-General
116 S Linn, 52240. Tel 319-351-3510
Estab 1985. 12,000 Titles. 12,000 Vols. 1600 sq ft
Types: Fine bnd, 1st ed, hb, illus bk, juvenile, old & rare, out of print, papbk, remainders, used
Subj: Amer, military, Eastern philos, mythology

WILLIAM A GRAF - BOOKS — Mail Order
717 Clark St, 52240. Tel 319-337-7748
Estab 1969. Cat 11x ann
Types: Facsimile editions, 1st ed, hb, new & used, old & rare, out of print, pvt presses, remainders
Subj: Bks on bks, Iowiana, railroadiana, hist of US Army, ptg

HAUNTED BOOKSHOP ON-THE-CREEK — Used
520 Washington, 52240. Tel 319-337-2996
Estab 1978. 30,000 Titles. 30,000 Vols. Cat
Types: Fine bnd, 1st ed, hb, illus bk, imp, juvenile, old & rare, out of print, papbk, used
Subj: Antq, Fr & Span lang, mod lit, philos, photog, metaphysics, sci fiction & fantasy, Eastern rel, John Steinbeck

THE LEGACY COMPANY — Used
Box 1303, 52244. Tel 319-337-9914
Estab 1984. 15,000 Titles. 20,000 Vols. Cat 6x ann
Types: Used, fine bnd, 1st ed, illus bk, ltd ed, old & rare, out of print
Subj: Art, archit, illus, photog, hist, medicine

MURPHY-BROOKFIELD BOOKS — Used
219 N Gilbert, 52245. Tel 319-338-3077
Estab 1980. 26,000 Vols. 1000 sq ft
Types: Hb, out of print, papbk
Subj: Hist, philos, soc sci, women's studies, Eng hist & lit, Irish hist & lit

MAQUOKETA — 6313. Area code 319

ANDROMEDA BOOKSHOP — Antiquarian
PO Box 1076, 52060. Tel 319-652-6455
Estab 1976. 20,000 Vols. 200 sq ft
Types: 1st ed, facsimile editions, fine bnd, hb, illus bk, juvenile, new & used, out of print, old & rare, papbk
Subj: Sci fiction & fantasy

MARSHALLTOWN — 26,938. Area code 515

GALE BOOKS — Antiquarian
1149 Sanford Ave, RR One, Box 61, 50158. Tel 515-366-2474
Estab 1967. 2000 Titles. 2000 Vols
Types: 1st ed, juvenile, out of print, used
Subj: Biog, educ, fiction, Iowiana, rel studies

NEWTON — 15,292. Area code 515

MATTINGLY'S — General
113 W Second St N, 50208. Tel 515-792-3250
Mgr, Joan Mattingly
Estab 1965. 20,000 Titles. 25,000 Vols
Types: Fr, Ger & Sp lang, out of print, papbk, mass mkt papbk, facsimile editions, fine bnd, 1st ed, hb, illus bk, ltd ed, old & rare, remainders, new & used

WILTON — 2502. Area code 319

DONALD R DOERRES — Mail Order-Antiquarian
503 E Third St (Mail add: PO Box 676, 52778-0676). Tel 319-732-2874
1000 Vols
Types: 1st ed, new & used, out of print
Subj: Iowiana, radio, railroadiana, locks & locksmithing, Mississippi River hist, steam boat & engines, zeppelin, mercenaries, weapons & armored vehicle manuals, mountain men

IOLA — 6938. Area code 316

SAMFORD'S BOOK NOOK — Religious
115 W Madison (Mail add: PO Box 256, 66749). Tel 316-365-2673
Estab 1966
Types: Hb, juvenile, out of print, papbk, remainders, used

LAWRENCE — 52,738. Area code 913

DAVID DARY WESTERN BOOKS — Antiquarian-Western Americana
1101 W 27th St, 66046. Tel 913-843-5268
Estab 1981. 5000 Titles. 5000 Vols. Cat 4x ann
Types: Facsimile editions, 1st ed, ltd ed, new & used, old & rare, out of print
Subj: Ranching, Kansasana, cattle trade, range life, lawmen, overland, narratives, Santa Fe & Oregon trails, Great Plains

J HOOD BOOKSELLER — Antiquarian
1401 Massachusetts, 66044. Tel 913-841-4644
Estab 1974. 75,000 Vols. 2500 sq ft
Types: Out of print, used
Subj: Art, psychol, math, scholarly lit, linguistics

HARRIET S WILSON OUT OF PRINT BOOKS — Mail Order-Antiquarian
3027 University Dr, 66044. Tel 913-842-3095
Estab 1980. 500 Titles. 200 sq ft
Types: 1st ed, hb, illus bk, juvenile, old & rare, out of print, used
Subj: Western Amer

MANHATTAN — 32,644. Area code 913

THE DUSTY BOOKSHELF — General
612 N 12th St, 66502. Tel 913-539-2839
Estab 1985. 25,000 Titles. 24,000 Vols
Types: Used, 1st ed, papbk, hb, out of print

VARNEY'S BOOKSTORE INC — College
623 N Manhattan Ave, 66502. Tel 913-539-0511
Mgr, Jon Levin
Estab 1916. 2000 Titles. 9000 Vols
Types: Hb, imp, juvenile, out of print, papbk, remainders, used

OVERLAND PARK — 81,784. Area code 913

CLINT'S BOOKS & COMICS — Comics
9601 B Metcalf, 66212. Tel 913-381-4213
Mgr, Tom Small
100,000 Vols
Types: Out of print, papbk, remainders
Subj: Sci fiction & fantasy

SALINA — 41,843. Area code 913

PAT'S BOOK NOOK-OLD & NEW — Used
135 S Fourth, 67401. Tel 913-823-6577
Estab 1977. 15,000 Titles. 25,000 Vols
Types: Out of print, papbk, old & rare
Subj: Cooking, rel

TOPEKA — 115,266. Area code 913

FLINT HILLS BOOKS — Antiquarian-Kansasana
Main St (Mail add: RR 1, Box 161, Eskridge, 66423). Tel 913-775-6237
Estab 1982. 4000 Vols. 1250 sq ft
Types: 1st ed, hb, remainders, old & rare, used, out of print
Subj: Kansasana

WATERVILLE — 694. Area code 913

THE BOOK LADY — Antiques
PO Box 62, 66548-0062. Tel 913-785-2412
Estab 1966. 3000 Titles. 800 sq ft. Cat ann
Types: Hb, imp, out of print, papbk, remainders, high priced papbk
Subj: Collectibles

WICHITA — 279,272. Area code 316

BEBBAH BOOKS — Antiquarian
149 N Broadway, Suite 203 (Mail add: PO Box 37, Andover, 67002). Tel 316-686-9713, 264-8008
Estab 1986. 4000 Titles. 4000 Vols. 550 sq ft. Cat 2-3x ann
Types: 1st ed, hb, illus bk, old & rare, out of print, used, univ presses
Subj: Amer, fiction, juv

THE BOOK MARK — Used
2073 N W St, 67203. Tel 316-943-9323
Estab 1986. 12,000 Titles. 16,000 Vols. 800 sq ft
Types: 1st ed, old & rare, out of print, papbk
Subj: Women's studies

GREEN DRAGON BOOKSTORE — Antiquarian
2730 Boulevard Plaza, PO Box 17338, 67217. Tel 316-681-0746
Estab 1975. 50,000 Vols. 2500 sq ft. Cat
Types: Facsimile editions, fine bnd, 1st ed, hb, illus bk, out of print, remainders, used
Subj: Aviation, biog, Southwestern Amer, art

KENTUCKY

BARDSTOWN — 6155. Area code 502

T T FOLEY ANTIQUARY BOOKSELLER — Mail Order-Antiquarian
203 E Stephen Foster Ave, 40004. Tel 502-348-6208
1000 Vols
Types: New, out of print, remainders, used
Subj: Antq, art, interior design

BEREA — 8226. Area code 606

APPALACHIAN MOUNTAIN BOOKS — General
123 Walnut St, 40403. Tel 606-986-1663
Estab 1982. 3000 Titles. 10,000 Vols. Cat 12x ann
Types: 1st ed, hb, illus bk, juvenile, ltd ed, new, old & rare, out of print, papbk, remainders, used
Subj: Southern Appalachian Mountains

COVINGTON — 49,013. Area code 606

T & S BOOKS — Antiquarian
1545 Scott Blvd, PO Box 14077, 41014. Tel 606-261-6435
Estab 1978. 25,000 Vols. 1600 sq ft. Cat
Types: Hb, juvenile, papbk, out of print, facsimile editions, fine bnd, 1st ed, illus bk, imp, ltd ed, old & rare, used
Subj: Kentuckiana, hunting & fishing, mil hist

ELIZABETHTOWN — 15,380. Area code 502

SICKLE BOOKSTORE — Religious
E-Town Walmart Plaza, 42701. Tel 502-765-2354
Estab 1975. 1800 sq ft
Types: Hb, juvenile, papbk, out of print
Subj: Biog, family studies, fiction, metaphys & occult, psychol, theol, Holy Spirit, marriage

FLORENCE — 15,586. Area code 606

WALDENBOOKS — General
1034 Florence Mall, 41042. Tel 606-371-0216
Estab 1976. 20,000 Vols. 3000 sq ft Buys indep & through hq
Types: Hb, juvenile, papbk, remainders, out of print

HOPKINSVILLE — 27,318. Area code 502

PENNYROYAL BOOKS — Mail Order-Antiquarian
2538 Cox Mill Rd, 42240. Tel 502-885-9609
Estab 1962. 750 Vols. 308 sq ft
Types: Used, old & rare, out of print, remainders
Subj: Hist, Kentuckiana, Tennesseeana, rel, philos

LEXINGTON — 204,165. Area code 606

BLACK SWAN BOOKS — Antiquarian
505 E Maxwell St (Mail add: PO Box 22804, 40522). Tel 606-252-7255
Estab 1986. 10,000 Titles. 15,000 Vols. Cat 4x ann
Types: Facsimile editions, 1st ed, hb, illus bk, juvenile, old & rare, out of print, used
Subj: Kentuckiana, horses, lit

CARAWAY BOOK CO — Antiquarian
3516 Castlegate E Wynd, 40502. Tel 606-266-9412
Estab 1984. 3500 Titles. 10,000 Vols. 1200 sq ft
Types: Used, hb, juvenile, fine bnd, 1st ed, illus bk, old & rare, out of print
Subj: Novels

GLOVER'S BOOKERY — Used
862 S Broadway, 40504. Tel 606-253-0614
Estab 1978. 30,000 Vols. 2000 sq ft. Cat 4x ann
Types: Old & rare, out of print, used, remainders, hb
Subj: Amer, horses, Kentuckiana, Civil War, local hist, natural hist, military, art, fiction

THE SAIL LOFT — Used
269 Cassidy Ave, 40502. Tel 606-266-6348
Estab 1934. 6000 Vols. 800 sq ft. Cat
Types: Hb, juvenile, out of print, 1st ed, illus bk, ltd ed
Subj: Natural hist, nonfiction, walking canes, pewter

LOUISVILLE — 298,451. Area code 502

THE COOKBOOK COTTAGE — Cooking & Nutrition
1279 Bardstown Rd, 40204-1303. Tel 502-458-5227
Estab 1987. 6000 Titles. 1500 sq ft
Types: Hb, out of print, papbk, col text, used, new

HAWLEY - COOKE BOOKSELLERS INC — General
Shelbyville Rd Plaza, 40207. Tel 502-893-0133
Mgr, Thomas Crabb
Estab 1978. 70,000 Titles. 90,000 Vols. 11,800 sq ft
Types: Hb, juvenile, out of print, papbk, remainders

LEGACY BOOK STORE — Used
1916 Bardstown Rd, 40205. Tel 502-454-0690
Estab 1984. 20,000 Vols. 800 sq ft
Types: Hb, out of print, used
Subj: Genealogy, Kentuckiana

MARATHON BOOKSHELF — Antiquarian-General
PO Box 33008, 40232
Estab 1971. 200,000 Vols. 6000 sq ft
Types: Hb, papbk, juvenile, out of print, remainders, used, imp
Subj: Poetry, cooking, self-develop, Appalachia, Kentuckiana

NUBIAN BOOKSTORE INC — General
2109 W Broadway, 40211. Tel 502-772-1627
Estab 1986. 600 Titles. 800 Vols. 300 sq ft. Cat 4x ann
Types: Hb, imp, juvenile, out of print, papbk, mass mkt papbk, high priced papbk, Swahili lang
Subj: Black studies, Africa

OLD LOUISVILLE BOOKS — Antiquarian
426 W Oak St, 40203. Tel 502-637-6411, 451-1130 (evenings)
Estab 1975. 20,000 Titles. 25,000 Vols. Cat
Types: 1st ed, hb, illus bk, juvenile, old & rare, out of print, used, letters, doc, scarce pb
Subj: Amer, Kentuckiana, rel, antq, Western Amer, Jesse Stuart, local authors

PHILATELIC BIBLIOPOLE — Mail Order-Philately
1819 Gresham Rd (Mail add: PO Box 36006, 40233-6006). Tel 502-451-0317
Mgr, Mary Jule Hartmann
Estab 1965. 3000 sq ft. Cat ann
Types: Facsimile editions, fine bnd, 1st ed, hb, incunab, imp, ltd ed, old & rare, out of print, used
Subj: Postal hist

PRESTONSBURG — 4011. Area code 606

BOOKWORM — General
No 2 N Arnold Ave (Mail add: PO Box 174, 41653). Tel 606-886-8228
Estab 1986. 1000 Titles. 3000 Vols. 250 sq ft
Types: Hb, juvenile, out of print, papbk, illus bk, new

BATON ROUGE — 219,486. Area code 504

CLAITOR'S LAW BOOKS & PUBLISHING DIVISION — Law
3165 S Acadian Thruway at I-10 (Mail add: PO Box 3333, 70821). Tel 504-344-0476. WATS 800-535-8141
Estab 1922. 4000 Titles. 250,000 Vols. Cat ann
Types: Facsimile editions, 1st ed, hb, imp, new & used, out of print, papbk, old & rare, remainders
Subj: Law, taxation

COTTONWOOD BOOKS — General
3054 Perkins Rd, 70808. Tel 504-343-1266
Estab 1978. 10,000 Vols. 1400 sq ft
Types: New & used, out of print, papbk
Subj: Fiction, liberal arts

BLANCHARD —1128. Area code 318

RED RIVER BOOKS — Mail Order-Antiquarian
Drawer RRB, 71009-1059. Tel 318-929-7520
Estab 1979. 10,000 Titles. 10,000 Vols. 665 sq ft. Cat 2x ann
Types: New & used, out of print
Subj: Petroleum, Louisianiana, guns, sporting bks

GRETNA — 20,615 area code 504

BAYOU BOOKS INC — Antiquarian-Louisianiana
1005 Monroe St, 70053. Tel 504-368-1171
Mgr, Lota Sparkman
Estab 1961. 20,000 Vols
Types: Hb, juvenile, out of print, new & used, papbk, remainders
Subj: Louisianiana

KINDER — 2603. Area code 318

THE SON SHINE SHOP — Religious
PO Drawer 1580, 70648. Tel 318-738-5659
Mgr, Betty Beniot
Types: Bibles, hb, juvenile, out of print, study bks

LAFAYETTE — 81,961. Area code 318

G & C ENTERPRISES — Antiquarian
612 Alonda Dr, 70503. Tel 318-984-9305
Estab 1980. 1000 Vols
Types: Out of print
Subj: Photog, recreation, wines, scouting, viticulture

LAKE CHARLES — 75,051. Area code 318

THE WORD SHOPPE — Religious
Rte 7, Box 1045, Long Dr, 70601. Tel 318-855-7562
Estab 1981. 900 sq ft
Types: Hb, out of print, papbk

Subj: Church hist

NEW ORLEANS — 557,482. Area code 504

ARCADIAN BOOKS & PRINTS DBA LA LIBRARIE D'ARCADE — Antiquarian-General
714 Orleans, 70116. Tel 504-523-4138
Estab 1981. 1000 sq ft
Types: Fr lang, hb, fine bnd, 1st ed, imp, new, old & rare, out of print, papbk, used

BOOK SEARCH SERVICE — Mail Order-Antiquarian
4532 Providence Pl, 70126. Tel 504-288-9706, 601-798-9211
Estab 1953. 1000 Titles. 1000 Vols. Cat 4x ann
Types: Facsimile editions, fine bnd, 1st ed, hb, new, old & rare, out of print
Subj: Music & hymnology

GEO HERGET BOOKS — Antiquarian
3109 Magazine St, 70115. Tel 504-891-5595
Buyer, Jean Nosich
Estab 1978. 15,000 Titles. 24,000 Vols. 1400 sq ft
Types: Out of print, used
Subj: Fiction, Louisianiana, music, military, Wagner

LIBRAIRIE BOOKSHOP — Antiquarian
823 Chartres St, 70116. Tel 504-525-4837
Estab 1967. 25,000 Vols
Types: Hb, out of print, old & rare, used
Subj: Louisianiana
Branches:
— BECKHAM'S BOOKSHOP
228 Decatur St, 70130. Tel 504-522-9875
Estab 1972. 50,000 Vols. 3500 sq ft
Types: Hb, old & rare, out of print, used

R & R CO — Mail Order-Antiquarian
1309 Seventh St, 70115. Tel 504-891-6508
Estab 1975
Types: Old & rare, out of print

J RAYMOND SAMUEL LTD — Antiquarian-Southern Americana
2727 Prytania St, 70130. Tel 504-891-9061
Estab 1981. 500 Vols. 700 sq ft
Types: Fine bnd, 1st ed, illus bk, hb, imp, old & rare, out of print, used
Subj: Hist, local hist, Mississippi River, steamboats

SHREVEPORT — 205,815. Area code 318

CITY BOOK & COIN STORE — Used
1917 Creswell St, 71104. Tel 318-425-5142
Mgr & Buyer, Vida Payton
Estab 1959. 3000 sq ft
Types: Out of print, papbk, new
Subj: Metaphys & occult, sci-tech, parapsychol

MAINE

BANGOR — 31,643. Area code 207

BILL LIPPINCOTT BOOKS — Antiquarian
624 Hammond St, 04401. Tel 207-942-4398
Estab 1974. 15,000 Vols. 900 sq ft
Types: Papbk, old & rare, juvenile, out of print, hb, used, Fr & Sp lang, fine bnd, 1st ed, illus bk, comics
Subj: Sci fiction & fantasy, Maineana, local hist, hunting & fishing, mystery & detective, boys' series

PRO LIBRIS BOOKSHOP — Antiquarian
Ten Third St, 04401. Tel 207-942-3019
Estab 1980. 15,000 Titles. 25,000 Vols. 800 sq ft
Types: Out of print, papbk
Subj: Biog, mystery & detective, romance, sci fiction & fantasy

BETHEL — 2340. Area code 207

BETHEL BOOK BARN — Used
Lower Main St, Box 353, 04217. Tel 207-824-3145
Estab 1981. 15,000 Titles. 900 sq ft
Types: Hb, out of print, papbk, mass mkt papbk, used
Subj: Hist, biog, art, philos

BREWER — 9017. Area code 207

MBS-MARITIME BOOKSHOP — Antiquarian-Nautical
PO Box 447, 04412. Tel 207-942-3882
Estab 1976. 950 Titles. 2000 Vols. Cat 4x ann
Types: Hb, out of print, new & used
Subj: Yachting, merchant sail

BROOKS —Area code 207

MILITARY HISTORY BOOKSHOP — Mail Order
PO Box 97, 04921-0097. Tel 207-722-3620
Mgr, Andrea L McGuire
Estab 1968. 15,000 Titles. 15,000 Vols. Cat 4x ann
Types: 1st ed, hb, illus bk, imp, ltd ed, old & rare, out of print, used
Subj: Military, aeronaut, naval, China & Far East

BRUNSWICK — 17,366. Area code 207

CROSS HILL BOOKS — Antiquarian-Nautical
9 Noble St, PO Box 798, 04011. Tel 207-729-8531
Estab 1977. 1000 Vols. Cat
Types: Fine bnd, 1st ed, hb, old & rare, out of print, used
Subj: Nautical

ROBERT E DYSINGER - BOOKS — Antiquarian-Americana
5 Stanwood St, 04011. Tel 207-729-1229
Mgr, Mary L Jordan
Estab 1981. 3000 Titles. 3000 Vols. Cat
Types: Fine bnd, 1st ed, old & rare, out of print, used

GORDON'S BOOKSHOP — Antiquarian
14 Center St, 04011. Tel 207-725-2500
Estab 1983. 5500 Vols. 300 sq ft
Types: Hb, papbk, old & rare, out of print
Subj: Maineana, Arctic, Orientalia, travel, natural sci

OLD BOOKS — Used
136 Maine St, 04011. Tel 207-725-4524
Estab 1977. 15,000 Vols. 750 sq ft
Types: Hb, juvenile, out of print
Subj: Women's studies, lit

BUCKFIELD — 1333. Area code 207

PATRICIA LEDLIE - BOOKSELLER — Mail Order-Antiquarian
One Bean Rd, PO Box 90, 04220-0090. Tel 207-336-2778
Cat 5x ann
Types: New, out of print, old & rare
Subj: Natural hist

CAMDEN — 4584. Area code 207

DOLPHIN BOOKSTORE — Antiquarian
78 Elm St, PO Box 582, 04843-0582. Tel 207-236-3283
Estab 1976. 10,000 Vols. 1000 sq ft
Types: Juvenile, hb, imp, out of print, 1st ed, illus bk, ltd ed, old & rare, juvenile, used, antique prints
Subj: Fiction, Maineana, music, drama, art, illus

CASCO — 2243. Area code 207

VARNEY'S VOLUMES — Antiquarian
Quaker Ridge Rd (Mail add: Box 1175, RFD 2, 04015). Tel 207-655-4605
Estab 1978. 7500 Titles. 7500 Vols. 480 sq ft. Cat
Types: Hb, juvenile, old & rare, out of print, used

CASTINE — 1304. Area code 207

BARBARA FALK BOOKSELLER — General
Rte 166A, PO Box 356, 04421. Tel 207-326-4036
Types: Out of print

CUNDY'S HARBOR — area code 207

BOOK PEDLARS — Antiquarian
Holbrook St, RFD 2, 04011-2422. Tel 207-729-0087 (by appt)
Estab 1980. 3200 Titles. 5000 Vols
Types: Out of print, illus bk, juvenile
Subj: Amer, Maineana, children's illus

DEXTER — 4286. Area code 207

FREDERICA DE BEURS BOOKS — Antiquarian
Upper Garland Rd, RFD 1, Box 2880, 04930. Tel 207-924-7474 (by appt)
Estab 1980. 4000 Vols. 400 sq ft
Types: 1st ed, hb, illus bk, juvenile, old & rare, out of print, papbk, used
Subj: Maineana, sci-tech, art, Dutch lang, Netherlands

DRESDEN — 998. Area code 207

THE MATHOM BOOKSHOP & BINDERY — Antiquarian
Blinn Hill Rd off Rte 27, PO Box 161, 04342. Tel 207-737-8806 (summer), 315-343-4851 (winter)
Estab 1979. 3000 Titles. 3000 Vols. 375 sq ft
Types: Facsimile editions, fine bnd, 1st ed, hb, illus bk, juvenile, ltd ed, new, old & rare, out of print, remainders, used
Subj: Amer, poetry, scholarly lit

ELLSWORTH — 5179. Area code 207

BIG CHICKEN BARN - BOOKS & ANTIQUES — Antiquarian
Rt 3 Box 150A, 04605. Tel 207-667-7308
Estab 1978. 110,000 Vols
Types: 1st ed, hb, illus bk, juvenile, ltd ed, out of print,

old & rare, papbk, used
Subj: Hunting & fishing, Maineana, natural hist, rel, Amer, marine, western

FAIRFIELD — 6113. Area code 207

THISTLE'S BOOKS & COLLECTIBLES — Antiquarian-General
16 Main St, 04937. Tel 207-453-9817
Estab 1984. 18,000 Titles. 12,000 Vols. 1000 sq ft
Types: 1st ed, hb, illus bk, juvenile, old & rare, out of print, used, old & rare
Subj: New England, hunting & fishing, Amer

FALMOUTH — 6853. Area code 207

THE BOOK REVIEW — General
Falmouth S/Ctr, US Rte 1, 04105. Tel 207-781-4808
Vpres, Stephen Fournier
Estab 1980. 15,000 Vols
Types: Hb, out of print, papbk

GARDINER — 6485. Area code 207

BUNKHOUSE BOOKS — Antiquarian-Maineana
Lewiston Rd-126, Rte 5A, 04345. Tel 207-582-2808
Estab 1975. 15,000 Vols. Cat 2x ann
Types: 1st ed, old & rare, out of print, used
Subj: Hunting & fishing, local hist, sports

JAY — 5080. Area code 207

RIVER OAKS BOOKS — Used
R F D 2, Box 5505, Jay Bridge Circle, 04239-9658. Tel 207-897-3734
Estab 1976. 35,000 Titles. 40,000 Vols. Cat 6x ann
Types: Hb, illus bk, juvenile, old & rare, out of print, used, vintage papbk
Subj: Amer, Maineana, mystery & detective, illus, Can

KEZAR FALLS — Area code 207

PILLSBURY PAPERBACK EXCHANGE — Used Paperback
Rte 25, PO Box 33, 04047. Tel 207-625-8684
Estab 1977. 100,000 Vols
Types: Out of print

LUBEC — 2045. Area code 207

BOBROVNIKOFF BOOKS — Antiquarian
Rte 2, PO Box 273, 04652. Tel 207-733-4773
Estab 1983. 2000 Titles. 2000 Vols. 200 sq ft. Cat 4x ann
Types: Facsimile editions, fine bnd, 1st ed, hb, incunab, illus bk, ltd ed, old & rare, out of print
Subj: Amer, bibliog

MADISON — 4367. Area code 207

BOOKS BOUGHT & SOLD, RECORDS TOO — Antiquarian
125 Main St, 04950-1224. Tel 207-696-8361
Estab 1981. 10,000 Titles. Cat
Types: Used, out of print
Subj: Hist, mystery & detective, Maineana, belles lettres, nonfiction

MANCHESTER — 1949. Area code 207

CHARLES ROBINSON RARE BOOKS — Antiquarian
The Pond Rd, Box 299, 04351. Tel 207-622-1885
Estab 1975. 5000 Vols. 1100 sq ft. Cat
Types: Fine bnd, 1st ed, hb, illus bk, ltd ed, old & rare, out of print, used
Subj: Natural hist, travel, sci-tech, medicine

NEWBURGH — area code 207

GARY W WOOLSON BOOKSELLER — Mail Order-Remainder
Rte Nine (Mail add: RFD One, Box 1576, Hampden, 04444). Tel 207-234-4931
Estab 1967. 10,000 Titles. 10,000 Vols. 500 sq ft. Cat 4x ann
Types: Facsimile editions, 1st ed, hb, incunab, illus bk, ltd ed, old & rare, out of print, remainders, used
Subj: Art, hist, Maineana, natural sci

NEW GLOUCESTER — 3180. Area code 207

DONALD C CHANDLER BOOKS — Antiquarian
Lower Gloucester Rd, 04260. Tel 207-926-4653
Estab 1960. 5000 Vols
Types: Out of print
Subj: Amer, Maineana

NEW SHARON — 969. Area code 207

ATTIC OWL BOOKS — Mail Order
RFD No 1, Box 1802, 04955. Tel 207-778-2006
Estab 1986. 3000 Titles. 3000 Vols. Cat 6x ann
Types: Hb, out of print, old & rare, remainders, used
Subj: Philos

NORRIDGEWOCK — 2552. Area code 207

SNOWBOUND BOOKS — Mail Order-Antiquarian
PO Box 458, 04957-0458. Tel 207-634-4398
Types: Used, old & rare, out of print, juvenile, 1st ed
Subj: Maineana, military, children's series bks

NORTHEAST HARBOR — Area code 207

WIKHEGAN BOOKS — Antiquarian
Main St (Mail add: PO Box 370, Mount Desert, 04660). Tel 207-276-5079, 244-7060
Estab 1970. 10,000 Titles. Cat
Types: Fine bnd, 1st ed, hb, illus bk, ltd ed, old & rare, out of print, used
Subj: Am Indian studies, local hist, Amer decorative arts, maritime

NORTH VASSALBORO — Area code 207

BANCROFT'S BOOKS — Used
RFD 1, Box 1680, 04962. Tel 207-968-2495
Estab 1982. 4000 Titles. 4000 Vols
Types: Fine bnd, 1st ed, hb, juvenile, ltd ed, old & rare, out of print, signed editions

OGUNQUIT — 1492. Area code 207

FRANK MICHELLI BOOKS — Antiquarian
Box 627, 03907. Tel 207-646-3886
15,000 Vols
Types: Out of print, used
See Also: Newark, NJ

ORONO — 10,578. Area code 207

UNIVERSITY OF MAINE BOOKSTORE — College
University of Maine, 04469. Tel 207-581-1700. Telex 94-4400
Mgr, Sharon Cole; Asst Mgr Wendy Gavett
27,000 Titles
Types: Hb, juvenile, out of print, papbk, remainders
See Also: Augusta

PARIS — 4168. Area code 207

HAUNTED BOOKSHOP — Used
Paris Hill, 04271-0034. Tel 207-743-6216
Estab 1978. 5000 Vols
Types: Out of print, old & rare

POLAND SPRING — Area code 207

UNITED SOCIETY OF SHAKERS — Museum
RR 1, Box 640, 04274. Tel 207-926-4391
Owner, United Society of Shakers; Mgr & Buyer, David Richards
Estab 1783. 181 Vols. 150 sq ft. Cat 3x ann
Types: Hb, juvenile, out of print, papbk, remainders
Subj: Arts & crafts, nature & environ, country ways & rural life, Shaker culture & hist, NE Amer hist
See Also: Wholesale section

PORTLAND — 61,572. Area code 207

CARLSON & TURNER BOOKS — Antiquarian
241 Congress St, 04101. Tel 207-773-4200
Estab 1972. 50,000 Vols. 2500 sq ft. Cat
Types: Old & rare, out of print
Subj: Graphic arts, Leonard Baskin, Rockwell Kent

NATHAN COPELAND BOOKSELLER — Antiquarian
72 Groveside Rd, 04102. Tel 207-773-3647
Estab 1962. 5000 Vols
Types: 1st ed, hb, old & rare, out of print, used
Subj: Maineana, travel, maritime communications

CUNNINGHAM BOOKS — Antiquarian
762 Congress St (Mail add: PO Box 3756, 04104). Tel 207-775-2246
Estab 1980. 20,000 Titles. 20,000 Vols. 1000 sq ft
Types: 1st ed, hb, out of print, papbk, remainders, used

FLYNN BOOKS — Mail Order
466 Ocean Ave, 04103. Tel 207-772-2685
Estab 1970. 10,000 Titles. 800 sq ft
Types: Facsimile editions, fine bnd, 1st ed, hb, illus bk, ltd ed, old & rare, out of print, used

F M O'BRIEN ANTIQUARIAN BOOKSELLER — Antiquarian
38 High St, 04101. Tel 207-774-0931
Estab 1934. 100,000 Vols. Cat
Types: Used, out of print, old & rare, remainders
Subj: Amer, Maineana, Am hist & lit

PORTLAND MUSEUM OF ART SHOP — Museum
7 Congress Square, 04101-0218. Tel 207-775-6148
Sales Mgr Robin Stidworthy
Estab 1983. 800 Titles. 600 sq ft
Types: Hb, papbk, out of print, juvenile
Subj: Archit, arts & crafts, photog, art, decorative arts

SACO — 12,921. Area code 207

F P WOOD BOOKS — Antiquarian
48 Ferry Rd, 04072. Tel 207-282-2278
Estab 1979. 3000 Vols. Cat 4x ann
Types: 1st ed, hb, illus bk, juvenile, old & rare, out of print, remainders, used
Subj: Amer, Maineana, utopias

SANFORD — 18,020. Area code 207

BOOK ADDICT — Used
Pine Tree Dr, RR 1 Box 1281, 04073. Tel 207-324-2243
Estab 1978. 4000 Vols
Types: Fine bnd, 1st ed, illus bk, old & rare, papbk, out of print
Subj: Amer, hist, nature & environ, sports, fiction

SKOWHEGAN — 8098. Area code 207

RED HERRING BOOKS* — Antiquarian
329 Water St, US Rt 2, 04976. Tel 207-474-3403
Estab 1978. 9000 Titles. 13,500 Vols. Cat bi-monthly
Types: Hb, papbk, out of print
Subj: Mystery & detective, fiction, nonfiction

SOUTH CHINA — area code 207

GRAY MATTER SERVICE — Antiquarian
Box 381, 04358. Tel 207-445-2245
Estab 1968. 30,000 Vols
Types: Old & rare, out of print, used, hb, juvenile, fine bnd

SOUTH PORTLAND — 22,712. Area code 207

J GLATTER BOOKS — Antiquarian
146 Ocean St (Mail add: PO Box 214, Cumberland Center, 04021-0214). Tel 207-799-7283, 829-5408
Estab 1984. 14,000 Titles. 14,000 Vols. 700 sq ft
Types: For lang, hb, juvenile, out of print, papbk, high priced papbk, used

SPRINGVALE — 2914. Area code 207

HARLAND H EASTMAN BOOKS — Antiquarian-Maineana
66 Main St, PO Box 276, 04083. Tel 207-324-2797
Estab 1979. 6000 Vols. 1125 sq ft
Types: Facsimile editions, fine bnd, 1st ed, hb, illus bk, juvenile, old & rare, out of print, used
Subj: Local hist

SPRUCE HEAD — Area code 207

LOBSTER LANE BOOKSHOP — Used
04859. Tel 207-594-7520
Estab 1964. 50,000 Vols
Types: Hb, out of print, papbk, remainders

STEEP FALLS — Area code 207

WARD'S BOOKBARN — Used
Box 6, 04085. Tel 207-675-3348
Estab 1970. 25,000 Titles. 25,000 Vols. 2000 sq ft
Types: Out of print, 1st ed, hb, illus bk, juvenile, old & rare, Victorian bks
Subj: Fiction

STOCKTON SPRINGS — 1230. Area code 207

VICTORIAN HOUSE BOOK BARN — Antiquarian
PO Box 397, E Main St, 04981-0097. Tel 207-567-3351
Estab 1960. 30,000 Titles. 30,000 Vols. 3200 sq ft. Cat
Types: 1st ed, hb, out of print, old & rare, used, papbk
Subj: Amer, mystery & detective, Maine

WELLS — 8211. Area code 207

THE BOOK BARN — Mail Order-Antiquarian
PO Box 557, Rte 1, 04090. Tel 207-646-4926
Estab 1985. 4000 Titles. 20,000 Vols. 1500 sq ft
Types: Out of print, mass mkt papbk, high priced papbk, remainders, used, facsimile editions, fine bnd, 1st ed, hb, illus bk, juvenile, ltd ed, old & rare, comics

EAST COAST BOOKS — Antiquarian
Depot St & Rte 109, PO Box 849, 04090. Tel 207-646-3584
Estab 1976. 20,000 Titles. 20,000 Vols. Cat 5x ann
Types: Remainders, out of print, used
Subj: Maineana, art

A DAVID PAULHUS OLD BOOKS & PAINTINGS — Antiquarian
Burnt Mill Rd, PO Box 501, 04090. Tel 207-646-7022
10,000 Vols. Cat 2x ann
Types: Out of print, used

SNUG HARBOR BOOKS — Antiquarian
Rte 1, PO Box 160, 04090. Tel 207-646-4124
Mgr, Karen Flanders Austin
Estab 1981. 20,000 Vols. 1200 sq ft
Types: Facsimile editions, fine bnd, 1st ed, illus bk, ltd ed, hb, juvenile, papbk, old & rare, out of print, remainders, used
Subj: Amer, art, antq, New England

MARYLAND

ANNAPOLIS — 31,740. Area code 301

CHARING CROSS BOOKSHOP INC — General
88 Maryland Ave, 21401. Tel 301-268-1440
Estab 1981. 5000 Vols. 1000 sq ft
Types: Hb, imp UK, out of print, papbk, remainders, used
Subj: Archit, humanities, mystery & detective, travel

CIRCLE WEST BOOKSELLERS — Used
38 West St, 21401. Tel 301-267-8761
Owner, Books Plus Corporation; Mgr, Jeffrey Gordon
Estab 1977. 150,000 Titles. 150,000 Vols. 2600 sq ft
Types: Hb, out of print, papbk
Subj: Art, fiction, for lang, medicine, poetry, travel, mystery & detective, sci fiction & fantasy, nautical, metaphys & occult

DRAGOMAN BOOKS — Used
680 Americana Dr - 38, 21403. Tel 301-263-2757
Estab 1977. 3000 Titles. 5000 Vols. 2600 sq ft. Cat
Types: Facsimile editions, fine bnd, 1st ed, hb, illus bk, juvenile, ltd ed, old & rare, out of print, used
Subj: Archaeol, for lang, poetry

BALDWIN — Area code 301

B R ARTCRAFT CO — Mail Order-Arts & Crafts
6701 Cherry Hill Rd, 21013. Tel 301-592-2847
Estab 1934. 15,000 Vols. Cat ann
Types: Hb, imp, out of print, papbk, remainders, used
Subj: Archit, fine arts

BALTIMORE — 736,775. Area code 301

AUTOBOOKS INC-THE AUTOBOOKMEN — Automobiles
6119 Oakleaf Ave, 21215. Tel 301-358-4545. WATS 800-638-1830
Pres, Lee Sacks
Estab 1974. 700 Titles. 10,000 Vols. 1500 sq ft
Types: Hb, imp, out of print, papbk, remainders, used
Subj: Bicycles, motorcycles & trucks

SHIRLEY BALSER 16TH-20TH CENTURY PAINTINGS, PRINTS & BOOKS — Antiquarian
PO Box 5803, 21208. Tel 301-484-0880
Estab 1961. 15,000 Vols. 900 sq ft. Cat
Types: 1st ed, fine bnd, illus bk, ltd ed, out of print, old & rare, art & illus bks
Subj: Art, Amer, Marylandiana, hist, photog, lit, sci

BUTTERNUT & BLUE — Civil War
3411 Northwind Rd, 21234. Tel 301-256-9220
Mgr & Merch Mgr, James McLean
Estab 1984. 1500 Titles. 2000 Vols. Cat 6x ann
Types: 1st ed, hb, ltd ed, new, out of print

CHIRURGICAL BOOKSHOP — Mail Order-Antiquarian
1211 Cathedral St, 21201. Tel 301-539-0872
Owner, Maryland Medical & Chirurgical Faculty; Mgr, William Sleeman
Estab 1980. Cat 2x ann
Types: Facsimile editions, fine bnd, 1st ed, hb, illus bk, incunab, imp, ltd ed, old & rare, out of print, used
Subj: Medicine

DRUSILLA'S BOOKS — Antiquarian
859 N Howard St, 21201-4696. Tel 301-225-0277
Estab 1977. 3000 Titles. 3000 Vols. Cat 2x ann
Types: 1st ed, hb, illus bk, juvenile, old & rare, out of print, used

GOODWILL BOOK NOOK — General
525 N Charles St, 21201. Tel 301-837-5068
Owner, Goodwill Industries of Baltimore, Inc; Mgr, Nancy Ledden
Estab 1977. 10,000 Vols. 100 sq ft
Types: For lang, hb, juvenile, out of print, papbk, remainders, col text, used

HARDFORD COIN CO, INC — Antiquarian
2160 E Joppa Rd, 21234. Tel 301-665-1814
Estab 1961. 1600 Vols. 1200 sq ft. Cat ann
Types: For lang, hb, imp, old & rare, out of print, remainders, used
Subj: Numismatics, finance

HARRIS AUCTION GALLERIES — Antiquarian
875 N Howard St, 21201. Tel 301-728-7040
Estab 1951. 1000 Titles. 1000 Vols. Cat 6-8x ann
Types: Facsimile editions, fine bnd, 1st ed, hb, incunab, illus bk, imp, juvenile, ltd ed, old & rare, out of print, used

JOHNS HOPKINS UNIVERSITY -BOOK CENTER — College
Charles & 34th St, 21218. Tel 301-338-8317. Telex 8-7994
Mgr, Paul Lynch
20,000 Titles. 17,000 Vols. Cat 1-2x ann
Types: Fr, Ger & Sp lang, Ital lang, hb, imp, juvenile, out of print, papbk, remainders, used
Subj: Philos, literary criticism, class studies, poetry, reference

KELMSCOTT BOOKSHOP — Antiquarian
32 W 25th St, 21218. Tel 301-235-6810
Estab 1978. 25,000 Vols. 1500 sq ft
Types: Fine bnd, 1st ed, hb, illus bk, juvenile, ltd ed, old & rare, out of print, used, rare
Subj: Eng hist & lit, Marylandiana, travel

LOYOLA COLLEGE BOOKSTORE — College
4501 N Charles St, 21210. Tel 301-433-3332
Mgr, John Resseger
Estab 1967
Types: Hb, juvenile, out of print, remainders, papbk, used

MINDBRIDGE LTD — Collecting
1786 Merritt Blvd, 21222. Tel 301-284-7880
Mgrs, Rick & Sue Shanklin
Estab 1976. 250,000 Vols. 1200 sq ft. Cat
Types: Hb, imp UK, ltd ed, old & rare, out of print, papbk, used, juvenile, coloring bks
Subj: Advertising, art, comedy, mystery & detective, romance, sci fiction & fantasy
See Also: Perry Hall

NEW ERA BOOKSHOP INC — Paperback
408 Park Ave, 21201. Tel 301-539-6364
Mgr & Buyer, Fred Marks
Estab 1963. 300 sq ft
Types: Col text, hb, juvenile, out of print, used, peace bks
Subj: Black studies, cooking, art, hist, lang arts, philos, poetry, polit sci, sci-tech, arts & crafts, Africa, Asian studies, US govt, socialism, Leninism, Marxism

THE RUG BOOKSHOP — Mail Order-Antiquarian
2603 Talbot Rd, 21216. Tel 301-367-8194
Estab 1976. 750 Titles. 7500 Vols. 300 sq ft. Cat 2x ann
Types: Imp UK, hb, new & used, out of print, high priced papbk, old & rare, imp Ger, imp Ital
Subj: Oriental rugs & textiles, Navajo rugs

CECIL ARCHER RUSH — Antiquarian
1410 Northgate Rd, 21218. Tel 301-323-7767, 467-2622
Vpres, Gordon Rush
Estab 1942. 3000 Vols. Cat ann

Types: Facsimile editions, hb, imp, incunab, new & used, out of print, old & rare, ltd ed
Subj: Orientalia, India, China, erotic art, Japan, Tibet

SHERLOCK BOOK DETECTIVE — Mail Order-Antiquarian
PO Box 1174, 21203. Tel 301-235-2326
Types: Out of print, used

TIBER BOOKSHOP — Used
Eight W 25th St, 21218. Tel 301-243-2789
Estab 1987. 50,000 Titles. 50,000 Vols. 2500 sq ft
Types: Fine bnd, 1st ed, hb, illus bk, juvenile, ltd ed, old & rare, out of print, papbk, remainders

BETHESDA — 71,621. Area code 301

AOC BOOKS — Mail Order-Antiquarian
6601 Lybrook Ct, 20817. Tel 301-469-9000
1500 Titles. 1500 Vols
Types: Illus bk, out of print, fine bnd
Subj: Art, hist, travel

ASHE & DEANE FINE BOOKS — Antiquarian
4931 Cordell Ave, Ste A, 20814. Tel 301-652-6680
Estab 1987. 7000 Titles. 7500 Vols. 6500 sq ft. Cat
Types: Hb, old & rare, out of print
Subj: Poetry, hist, Amer, literary criticism, art, travel, lit

BARTLEBY'S BOOKSHOP — General
7704 Woodmont Ave, 20814. Tel 301-654-4373
Estab 1984. 20,000 Vols. 1750 sq ft
Types: Out of print, used, scholarly
Subj: Humanities, philos, sci-tech, hist, music

LEONARD S BLONDES USED LAW BOOKS — Law
7100 Crail Dr, 20817. Tel 301-229-7102
Owner, Shellenard, Inc
Estab 1951
Types: Used, out of print

THE BOOK CELLAR — Used
8227 Woodmont Ave, 20814. Tel 301-654-1898
Estab 1976. 45,000 Titles. 45,000 Vols. 1400 sq ft
Types: For lang, hb, imp, juvenile, out of print, high priced papbk
Subj: Amer, art, belles lettres, Civil War, cooking, hist, law, linguistics, math, medicine, military, music, nature & environ, performing arts, philos, psychol, sci-tech, travel, jazz & classical

CONTINENTAL DIVIDE TRAIL SOCIETY — Antiquarian-Western Americana
PO Box 30002, 20814-0002. Tel 301-493-4080
Dir, James R Wolf
Estab 1978. 500 Titles. 1000 Vols. Cat
Types: Out of print
Subj: Materials related to continental divide

GEORGETOWN BOOKSHOP — Used
7770 Woodmont Ave, 20814. Tel 301-907-6923
Mgr, Geoff Germond
Estab 1984. 10,000 Titles. 1000 sq ft
Types: Out of print, remainders, 1st ed, hb, old & rare
Subj: Hist, military, art, photog, Soviet military

BOWIE — 33,695. Area code 301

THE MAGIC PAGE — Used
7416 Laurel-Bowie Rd, 20715. Tel 301-262-4735
Pres, George C Bridgers; Mgr, Janice M Bridgers
Estab 1982. 3000 Vols Buys through hq
Types: Hb, out of print, papbk
Subj: Fiction, nonfiction

BRINKLOW — Area code 301

OLD HICKORY BOOKSHOP LTD — Antiquarian
20225 New Hampshire Ave, Box 36, 20862. Tel 301-924-2225
Estab 1940. 20,000 Vols. Cat 4x ann
Types: Old & rare, out of print
Subj: Dentistry, medicine, sci-tech

CAMP SPRINGS — 22,776. Area code 301

ENCORE BOOK STORE INC — General
7120 Temple Hills Rd, 20734. Tel 301-292-0333, 292-0552
Estab 1983. 30,000 Titles. 50,000 Vols. 2000 sq ft
Types: For lang, hb, imp UK, juvenile, out of print, papbk, mass mkt papbk, high priced papbk, remainders, used, 1st ed
Subj: Mystery & detective, sci fiction & fantasy, romance, polit sci, nonfiction, Victorian poetry

STEWART'S USED BOOKSTORE — Used
6504 Old Branch Ave, 20748. Tel 301-449-6766
Estab 1975. 30,000 Vols. 800 sq ft
Types: Hb, out of print
Subj: Military

CENTREVILLE — 2018. Area code 301

GARY YOUNG — Antiques
128 S Commerce, 21617. Tel 301-758-2132
Estab 1972. 1500 Vols. 225 sq ft
Types: Fine bnd, hb, out of print, old & rare, used
Subj: Antq, local hist, decorative arts, early Am imprints

COCKEYSVILLE — 2601. Area code 301

THE BOOK RACK — Paperback
12 Scott Adam Rd, 21030. Tel 301-667-6897
Estab 1980. 20,000 Vols Buys indep
Types: New & used, out of print
Subj: Fiction

COLLEGE PARK — 23,614. Area code 301

MARY CHAPMAN BOOKSELLER — Mail Order-Antiquarian
PO Box 304, 20740-0304. Tel 301-490-5432
Buyer, David Kueker
Estab 1975. 4000 Vols. Cat ann
Types: Old & rare, out of print
Subj: Needlecrafts, textiles, weaving, lace

JEFF DYKES WESTERN BOOKSCOUT — Antiquarian-Western Americana
Box 38, 20740. Tel 301-864-0666
Estab 1965. 400 Titles. 500 Vols. Cat
Types: Hb, out of print
Subj: Western Amer, range livestock industry, Western illustrators, gunners

COLUMBIA — 8815. Area code 301

CULPEPPER, HUGHES & HEAD — Mail Order-Black Studies
9770 Basket Ring Rd, 21045. Tel 301-730-1484
Estab 1984. 2000 Titles. 100,000 Vols. Cat 4x ann
Types: New, old & rare, out of print, remainders, used
Subj: Africa, black studies, Caribbean hist

DARNESTOWN — Area code 301

STEVEN C BERNARD FIRST EDITIONS — Mail Order-Antiquarian
15011 Plainfield Lane, 20874. Tel 301-948-8423
Estab 1974. 6000 Titles. 6000 Vols. Cat 6x ann
Types: 1st ed, hb, illus bk, ltd ed, old & rare, out of print, used
Subj: Mod lit, sci fiction & fantasy, mystery & detective

EDGEWOOD — 8551. Area code 301

CAROL'S USED BOOKSHOP — Used
2002 Pulaski Hwy, 21040. Tel 301-676-3560
Mgr, Nancy Ioht
Estab 1977. 25,000 Vols
Types: For lang, hb, juvenile, out of print, papbk
Subj: Mod lit, mystery & detective, romance, sci fiction & fantasy, comedy

ELKTON — 6468. Area code 301

STONE HOUSE BOOKS — Antiquarian
71 Stone House Lane, 21921. Tel 301-398-6835
Estab 1975. 3500 Vols. 1000 sq ft. Cat
Types: Old & rare, out of print, used
Subj: Delawariana, hort, illus, mystery & detective, natural hist

ELLICOTT CITY — 9506. Area code 301

DEEDS BOOKSHOP — Used
8012 Main St, PO Box 85, 21043. Tel 301-465-9419
Estab 1971. 9000 Vols
Types: Out of print, juvenile, hb, old & rare, remainders, illus bk, 1st ed

FREDERICK — 27,557. Area code 301

ODDS & ENDS SHOP — Antiquarian
South & Carroll Sts, 21701. Tel 301-662-5388
Estab 1973. 10,000 Vols. 200 sq ft
Types: Out of print, used, papbk

GAITHERSBURG — 26,424. Area code 301

OLDE SOLDIER BOOK — Antiquarian
18779 B N Frederick Ave, 20879. Tel 301-963-2929
Estab 1976. 2500 Vols. Cat 3-4x ann
Types: New & used, old & rare, out of print, remainders
Subj: Civil War

HAGERSTOWN — 34,132. Area code 301

BARNWOOD BOOKS — Used
103 S Potomac St, 21740. Tel 301-790-0606
Estab 1979. 40,000 Titles. 50,000 Vols. 2100 sq ft
Types: Fr, Ger & Sp lang, hb, juvenile, out of print, papbk, used

HYATTSVILLE — 12,709. Area code 301

HIRAM LAREW BOOKS — Mail Order-Antiquarian
3312 Gumwood Dr, 20783. Tel 301-422-2738
Estab 1984. 300 Titles. 300 Vols
Types: 1st ed, out of print, used
Subj: Am hist & lit, natural hist

KENSINGTON — 1822. Area code 301

KENSINGTON USED BOOKSHOP — Used
10417 Armory Ave, 20895. Tel 301-949-9411
Estab 1972. 25,000 Vols. 600 sq ft
Types: For lang, hb, juvenile, old & rare, out of print, papbk

JOHN C RATHER — Mail Order
PO Box 273, 20895. Tel 301-942-0515
Estab 1976. 7,500 Vols. Cat 2-3x ann
Types: Illus bk, old & rare, out of print
Subj: Chess, photog, magic & conjuring, art hist, mountaineering

LA PLATA — 2484. Area code 301

SAMUEL WARD — Mail Order-Govt Publications
PO Box 309, 20646. Tel 301-934-8298
Estab 1938. Cat
Types: Out of print

LAUREL — 12,103. Area code 301

ATTIC BOOKS — Used
357 Main St, 20707. Tel 301-725-3725
Estab 1970. 20,000 Titles. 25,000 Vols
Types: Out of print, old & rare
Subj: Military, mystery & detective, sci fiction & fantasy

LEXINGTON PARK — 9136. Area code 301

BOWES BOOKS — General
718 Great Mills Rd, 20653. Tel 301-863-6200
25,000 Vols. 3000 sq ft
Types: Hb, papbk, out of print, old & rare
Subj: Art, music, sci-tech

LINTHICUM — area code 301

THE PAPER DOOR — General
607 Camp Meade Rd, 21090. Tel 301-850-0688
Mgr, Charles Thomas
Estab 1988. 4000 Titles. 5000 Vols. 800 sq ft
Types: Hb, papbk, juvenile, out of print
Subj: Fine arts, philos, rel

MONKTON — Area code 301

CHARLOTTE'S WEB ANTIQUES* — Antiquarian
1901 Monkton Rd (Mail add: c/o Eleanor C Weller, 16135 Old York Rd, 21111). Tel 301-771-4239, 771-4753
Mgr, Joan Wilhelm & Suzette Power
Estab 1981. 1000 Vols
Types: Facsimile editions, fine bnd, 1st ed, hb, illus bk, imp, new & used, old & rare, out of print, remainders
Subj: Antq, archit, art, gardening, sports, travel, flower arranging, landscaping

MOUNT AIRY — 2450. Area code 301

B & B SMITH - BOOKSELLERS — Classical Studies
14008 E Annapolis Ct (Mail add: PO Box 158, 21771-0158). Tel 301-549-1227
Estab 1980. 4000 Titles. 6000 Vols. 800 sq ft. Cat 4x ann
Types: Hb, ltd ed, new & used, old & rare, out of print, papbk, remainders, imp EEur
Subj: Hist, ancient hist & lit, archaeol

OAKLAND — 1994. Area code 301

APPALACHIAN BOOKSHOP — Used
301 S Second St, 21550-1816
Estab 1971. 15,000 Titles. 2000 sq ft
Types: Juvenile, out of print, mass mkt papbk, used, 1st ed, hb, old & rare
Subj: Massachusettsana, genealogy, West Virginiana, Marylandiana, local hist, rural, agr topics

OLNEY — 2138. Area code 301

THIS 'N' THAT ANTIQUES — Antiquarian
16650 Georgia Ave, 20832-9998. Tel 301-774-6991
Owner, Michael Plant
Estab 1973. 400 Titles. 400 Vols
Types: Out of print, old & rare
Subj: Amer, biog

PERRY HALL — Area code 301

MINDBRIDGE LTD II* — Collecting
9847 Belair Rd, 21128. Tel 301-256-7880
Buyer, Rick Shanklin; Mgr, Walt Hovatter
Estab 1984. 30,000 Vols Buys through hq

Types: Hb, papbk, used, out of print, ltd ed, old & rare, imp UK, juvenile, comics, coloring bks
Subj: Art, mystery & detective, romance, sci fiction & fantasy, advertising, comedy, horror

POOLESVILLE — 3428. Area code 301

WILLIS VAN DEVANTER BOOKS — Antiquarian
PO Box 277, 20837. Tel 301-972-7298
Estab 1973. 4500 Vols
Types: Old & rare, out of print
Subj: Black studies, cooking, biking

PORT TOBACCO — Area code 301

OLD QUENZEL STORE — Antiquarian
Town Square, PO Box 326, 20677-0326. Tel 301-934-8045
Estab 1973. 5000 Vols. 900 sq ft. Cat 7x ann
Types: Facsimile editions, hb, out of print, old & rare
Subj: Civil War, hist, Lincoln

ROCKVILLE — 43,811. Area code 301

Q M DABNEY & CO — Mail Order-Antiquarian
11910 Parklawn Dr (Mail add: PO Box 42026, Washington, DC, 20015). Tel 301-881-1470
Gen Mgr, Michael Schnitter
Cat 20x ann
Types: Facsimile editions, 1st ed, hb, illus bk, ltd ed, old & rare, out of print, remainders, used
Subj: Govt publn, humanities, law, military, soc sci, hist, Amer, Eur studies

ROBERT A MADLE SF-FANTASY BOOKS — Mail Order-Antiquarian
4406 Bestor Dr, 20853. Tel 301-460-4712
8000 Titles. 6000 Vols. 450 sq ft. Cat 2x ann
Types: New, old & rare, out of print, used
Subj: Sci fiction & fantasy

QUILL & BRUSH BOOKSTORE — Antiquarian
Box 5365, 20851. Tel 301-460-3700
Estab 1976. 5000 Titles. 6000 Vols. 1700 sq ft. Cat monthly
Types: 1st ed, illus bk, ltd ed, old & rare, out of print
Subj: Amer, art, travel, 20th century authors

YAK & YETI BOOKS — Mail Order-Antiquarian
PO Box 5736, 20855. Tel 301-977-7285
Estab 1982. 750 Titles. 1000 Vols. Cat 4x ann
Types: Hb, used, old & rare, out of print
Subj: Mountaineering, Himalayas, Tibet, Central Asia

SALISBURY — 16,429. Area code 301

HENRIETTA'S ATTIC — Antiquarian-Americana
PO Box 907, 21801. Tel 301-546-3700
Estab 1980. 5000 Titles. 8000 Vols. 3000 sq ft. Cat 12x ann
Types: 1st ed, hb, illus bk, juvenile, out of print, old & rare, papbk, used
Subj: Fiction, rel, Marylandiana, Delawariana, art

SILVER SPRING — 77,496. Area code 301

BONIFANT BOOKS — Used
11240 Georgia Ave, 20902. Tel 301-946-1526
Mgr, Steven Des Roches
Estab 1986. 60,000 Titles. 70,000 Vols. 2333 sq ft
Types: Hb, illus bk, juvenile, old & rare, out of print, papbk, remainders, comics, for lang, sci-fict, mil
See Also: Samuel Yudkin & Associates, Alexandria, VA, wholesale section

HIRSCHTRITT'S "1712" — Mail Order-Antiquarian
1712 Republic Rd, 20902. Tel 301-649-5393
Estab 1970. 2000 Vols. Cat
Types: 1st ed, hb, illus bk, ltd ed, old & rare, out of print
Subj: Amer, Orientalia

IMAGINATION BOOKS — Antiquarian
946 Sligo Ave, 20910. Tel 301-589-2223
Estab 1973. 75,000 Vols. 2000 sq ft
Types: 1st ed, hb, illus bk, imp, juvenile, ltd ed, old & rare, out of print, papbk, used
Subj: Class studies, metaphys & occult, music, mystery & detective, philos, sci fiction & fantasy, World Wars I & II

FRANK & LAURESE KATEN — Numismatics
708 Cloverly St, 20904. Tel 301-384-9444, 384-9449. Cable: KATENCOIN
Mgr, Larry K Pusey
Estab 1938. 10,000 Titles. 25,000 Vols. Cat 2-3X ann
Types: Imp, out of print, old & rare
Subj: Archaeol, bibliog, hist, philately, finance

PETER KOFFSKY — Mail Order-Antiquarian
1708 Glenkarney Pl, 20902. Tel 301-649-6105
Estab 1980. 3000 Titles
Types: Out of print
Subj: Hist

TANEYTOWN — Area code 301

TANEYTOWN ANTIQUE SHOPPES — Antiques
Seven Frederick St, 21787. Tel 301-756-4262
Estab 1984. 6000 Vols. 3000 sq ft
Types: Ger lang, juvenile, out of print, old & rare, used, fine bnd, 1st ed, hb
Subj: Agr, biog, fiction, medicine, nature & environ, polit sci

TOWSON — 77,809. Area code 301

GREETINGS & READINGS — General
809 Taylor Ave, 21204. Tel 301-825-4225
Buyer, Dee Peeler
Estab 1969. 22,000 Titles. 75,000 Vols. 25,000 sq ft. Cat 5x ann
Types: Col & el-hi text, hb, juvenile, out of print, papbk, remainders
Subj: Computer sci, travel, reference, cooking

JEAN-MAURICE POITRAS & SONS — Mail Order-Medicine
107 Edgerton Rd, 21204. Tel 301-821-6284
40,000 Vols
Types: Old & rare, facsimile editions, fine bnd, 1st ed, hb, incunab, out of print, used
Subj: Med hist

TRAPPE — 739. Area code 301

UNICORN BOOKSHOP — Used
PO Box 154, Rte 50, 21673. Tel 301-476-3838
Estab 1975. 1200 Vols. 1200 sq ft
Types: 1st ed, hb, illus bk, old & rare, out of print
Subj: Art, auto, Marylandiana, natural hist, sailing

WHEATON — 66,247. Area code 301

THE BARBARIAN BOOKSHOP INC — Used
11254 Triangle Lane, 20902. Tel 301-946-4184
Pres, George C Bridgers
Estab 1973. 40,000 Vols. 1300 sq ft
Types: Hb, out of print, papbk
Subj: Fiction, nonfiction
See Also: The Magic Page, Bowie

BOOKS OF COLONIAL AMERICA — Mail Order-Antiquarian
3611 Janet Rd, 20906-4353. Tel 301-946-6490
Estab 1981. 2000 Vols. 200 sq ft
Types: Hb, old & rare, out of print, used
Subj: Amer, hist, Marylandiana, New Yorkiana, Pennsylvaniana, meteorology, climatology

AMHERST — 33,229. Area code 413

BOOK MARKS — Antiquarian
Carriage Shops, 1 E Pleasant St, 01002. Tel 413-549-6136
Estab 1982. 8000 Titles. 8000 Vols. 600 sq ft
Types: Hb, facsimile editions, 1st ed, juvenile, ltd ed, old & rare, out of print, used
Subj: Art, music, photog, poetry

NATIONAL YIDDISH BOOK CENTER — Mail Order-Used
Old East Street School (Mail add: PO Box 969, 01004). Tel 413-256-1241
Mgr, Aaron Lansky; Merch Mgr, Nansi Glick
Estab 1980. 15,000 Titles. 17,000 sq ft. Cat bi-monthly
Types: Old & rare, out of print
Subj: Yiddish lang

ANDOVER — Area code 508

ANDOVER ANTIQUARIAN BOOKS & GALLERY — Mail Order-Antiquarian
68 Park St, 01810. Tel 617-475-1645
Estab 1977. 5000 Titles. 5000 Vols. 600 sq ft. Cat ann
Types: Facsimile editions, fine bnd, 1st ed, hb, incunab, illus bk, imp, juvenile, ltd ed, old & rare, out of print, remainders, used
Subj: Gardening

ARLINGTON — 48,219. Area code 617

SCIENTIA BOOKS — General
432A Massachusetts Ave, Box 433, 02174. Tel 617-643-5725, 646-7336
Estab 1985. 5000 Titles. 5000 Vols. Cat 2x ann
Types: Hb, 1st ed, facsimile editions, illus bk, old & rare, out of print
Subj: Medicine, sci, hist of med, hist of sci

ASHFIELD — 1458. Area code 413

YESTERDAY'S BOOKS — Used
Baptist Corner Rd, 01330. Tel 413-628-3249
3000 Vols
Types: Out of print, used

ATTLEBORO — 34,196. area code 508

C CONWAY — Mail Order
PO Box 102, 02703
Estab 1970. 100 Titles. 5000 Vols. Cat weekly
Types: 1st ed, old & rare, out of print
Subj: Auto

AUBURN — 14,845. Area code 508

KENNETH ANDERSEN BOOKS — Mail Order-Antiquarian
PO Box H, 01501. Tel 508-832-3524
Cat 3x ann
Types: 1st ed, hb, illus bk, old & rare, out of print, used
Subj: Hunting & fishing, golf, tennis, mountaineering

BELLINGHAM — 14,300. Area code 508

THE CATHOLIC BOOK COLLECTOR — Antiquarian
381 Wrentham Rd, 02019. Tel 508-883-4344
Estab 1974. 23,500 Titles. 25,000 Vols. 1000 sq ft
Types: 1st ed, hb, out of print, old & rare, papbk, used
Subj: Theol, rel-c

BERNARDSTON — 1750. Area code 413

ASTRONOMY BOOKS — Antiquarian
Huckle Hill Rd (Mail add: PO Box 217, 01337-0217). Tel 413-648-9500
Estab 1975. 750 Vols. 500 sq ft. Cat 4-5x ann
Types: 1st ed, hb, illus bk, old & rare, out of print, used
Subj: Astron, optics, physics, hist of sci

BERNARDSTON BOOKS — Used
503 South St (Mail add: PO Box 484, 01337). Tel 413-643-9864
Mgr, A L Fullerton
Estab 1986. 20,000 Titles. 20,000 Vols. 3500 sq ft
Types: For lang, out of print
Subj: Art, biog, hist, literary criticism, military, philos, rel

BEVERLY — 37,655. Area code 508

JEAN S MCKENNA OLD, SCARCE, OUT-OF-PRINT BOOKS — Antiquarian
PO Box 190, 01915-0697. Tel 508-927-3067
Estab 1976. 7000 Vols. 600 sq ft
Types: 1st ed, hb, illus bk, juvenile, old & rare, out of print, used
Subj: Local hist, juv

BLANDFORD — 1038. Area code 413

ROBERT F LUCAS — Antiquarian
Main St (Mail add: PO Box 63, 01008). Tel 413-848-2061
Owner, Robert F Lucas
Estab 1977. 2000 Vols. 400 sq ft. Cat 2-4x ann
Types: Out of print
Subj: Amer, whales & whaling, Thoreau, transcendentalism, Poe

LYMAN BOOKS-THEATRE — Mail Order-Antiquarian
Moreau Rd (Mail add: PO Box 853, East Otis, 01029). Tel 413-269-6311
3000 Titles. Cat 2x ann
Types: Used, 1st ed, hb, out of print
Subj: Drama, circus, theatre, vaudeville

BOSTON — 562,994. Area code 617

ATLANTIC BOOK SERVICE — Antiquarian
PO Box 218, Charlestown Sta, 02129. Tel 617-242-0188
Cat
Types: 1st ed, hb, incunab, new & used, out of print, old & rare
Subj: Oceanog

AVENUE VICTOR HUGO BOOKSHOP — Used
339 Newbury St, 02115. Tel 617-266-7746
Owner, Avenue Victor Hugo, Inc; Mgr & Buyer, Vincent McCaffrey
Estab 1975. 30,000 Titles. 1500 sq ft. Cat 10-12x ann
Types: 1st ed, hb, illus bk, imp, juvenile, ltd ed, mass mkt papbk, new & used, out of print, comics
Subj: Archit, art, photog, sci fiction & fantasy

BARNES & NOBLE BOOKSTORE DISCOUNT — General
607 Boylston St, 02116. Tel 617-236-1308. Telex 94-0823
Mgrs, Heidi Lemmerhirt-Lane & Rich Dean
Estab 1976. 30,000 sq ft
Types: Col & el-hi text, hb, imp, for lang, juvenile, papbk, out of print, remainders, used

BOSTON BOOK ANNEX — Antiquarian
906 Beacon St, 02215. Tel 617-266-1090
Estab 1979. 50,000 Titles. 60,000 Vols. 2000 sq ft. Cat 3x ann
Types: Facsimile editions, fine bnd, 1st ed, hb, juvenile, ltd ed, out of print, old & rare, papbk, used
Subj: 19th & 20th century literary 1st ed

BRATTLE BOOK SHOP — Used
9 West St, 02111. Tel 617-542-0210. WATS 800-447-9595
Estab 1948. 350,000 Vols. 6000 sq ft
Types: Facsimile editions, fine bnd, 1st ed, hb, incunab, illus bk, imp, juvenile, ltd ed, old & rare, out of print, papbk

CHOREOGRAPHICA — Antiquarian
82 Charles St, 02114. Tel 617-227-4780
Estab 1964. 6000 Vols
Types: 1st ed, fine bnd, hb, illus bk, juvenile, ltd ed, old & rare, out of print, used
Subj: Dance, art, illus

THE COMPUTER MUSEUM STORE — Computers
300 Congress St, 02210. Tel 617-426-2800
Owner, The Computer Museum
Estab 1982. 600 Titles. 2000 Vols. 780 sq ft. Cat ann
Types: Hb, imp UK, out of print, papbk, col text, used, young adult
Subj: Computer graphics

GOODSPEED'S BOOKSHOP INC — Antiquarian
7 Beacon St, 02108. Tel 617-523-5970
Owner, Goodspeed's Bookshop Inc; Treas G T Goodspeed
Estab 1898. Cat
Types: 1st ed, incunab, out of print, old & rare, used
Subj: Amer, genealogy, local hist

LAURIAT'S INC — General
30 Franklin St, 02110. Tel 617-482-2850
Mgr, Jean Licht Buys through hq
Types: Hb, out of print, papbk, remainders

SAMUEL L LOWE JR ANTIQUES, INC — Antiquarian-Nautical
80 Charles St, 02114. Tel 617-742-0845
Mgr, Fred Campbell
Estab 1964. 800 Vols
Types: 1st ed, hb, incunab, out of print, old & rare, used
Subj: Hist, discovery & explor, whales & whaling, nautical archit, navigation, scrimshaw, China trade porcelain

THE NOSTALGIA FACTORY — Antiquarian
144 Kneeland St, 02111. Tel 617-482-8803
Estab 1988. 2000 Vols
Types: Illus bk, old & rare, out of print
Subj: Archit, tennis, golf

EDWARD T POLLACK — Mail Order-Antiquarian
236 Beacon St, 02116. Tel 617-437-1095
4500 Titles. 4500 Vols. Cat 4x ann
Types: Out of print, illus bk, 1st ed, hb, juvenile, ltd ed, old & rare, remainders, used
Subj: Art, archit, photog, fine arts

RALPH KRISTIANSEN BOOKSELLER — Mail Order-Antiquarian
PO Box 524, Kenmore Station, 02215. Tel 617-424-1527
5000 Vols. Cat
Types: 1st ed, old & rare, out of print
Subj: Films & filmmaking, sci fiction & fantasy, mystery & detective, literature

SPENSER'S MYSTERY BOOKSHOP — Mystery & Detective
314 Newbury St, 02115. Tel 617-262-0880
Estab 1983. 15,000 Vols
Types: Hb, out of print, papbk, remainders, used

IVAN STORMGART BOOKS — Antiquarian
PO Box 1232 GMF, 02205. Tel 617-268-3942
Estab 1977. 10,000 Titles. Cat 4x ann
Types: 1st ed, hb, imp Fr, illus bk, imp Ger, imp Den, ltd ed, old & rare, out of print, papbk, used
Subj: Sexuality, sexology, curiosa

CHARLES B WOOD III INC, ANTIQUARIAN BOOKSELLERS — Mail Order-Antiquarian
PO Box 310, 02117. Tel 617-247-7844
Estab 1967. 3000 Titles. Cat 2x ann
Types: Out of print, old & rare
Subj: Archit, art, sci-tech, photog

BOXBOROUGH — 3126. Area code 508

KEMPTON J C SMITH BOOKSELLER — Mail Order
140 Waite Rd, 01719. Tel 508-369-9562
Types: Out of print

BRAINTREE — 36,337. Area code 617

ORGAN LITERATURE FOUNDATION — Mail Order
45 Norfolk Rd, 02184-5915. Tel 617-848-1388
Estab 1950. 3073 Titles. 25,000 Vols. Cat ann
Types: Hb, imp, out of print, papbk, remainders, used
Subj: Hist, organ bldg, tuning, new organ bks

XANADU BOOK SEARCH — Mail Order-Antiquarian
PO Box 91, 02184. Tel 617-848-8584
Types: Out of print, out of print

BREWSTER — 5226. Area code 508

CAPE COD MUSEUM OF NATURAL HISTORY — Museum
Rte 6A (Mail add: PO Drawer R, 02631). Tel 508-896-3867
Buyer, Kathy Schrock
Estab 1955. 1000 Titles. 732 sq ft
Types: Hb, juvenile, out of print, high priced papbk
Subj: Natural hist

THE PUNKHORN BOOKSHOP — Antiquarian-General
672 Main St, 02631. Tel 508-896-2114
Estab 1987. 25,000 Titles. 15,000 Vols. 1500 sq ft
Types: Hb, for lang, imp, juvenile, out of print, papbk, remainders, used, old & rare

BROCKTON — 95,712. Area code 508

ALL PHOTOGRAPHY BOOKS — Mail Order-Photography
40 Reservoir St, No 510, 02401. Tel 508-587-6074
Estab 1973. 2500 Vols. Cat 1-2x ann
Types: Hb, imp, old & rare, out of print, papbk, remainders, used
Subj: Photog

BROOKLINE — 55,062. Area code 617

ROBERT H RUBIN BOOKS — Mail Order-Antiquarian
PO Box 267, 02146. Tel 617-277-7677
Estab 1978. Cat 4x ann
Types: Old & rare, out of print
Subj: Amer, econ, law, philos, soc sci

BUZZARDS BAY — 2422. Area code 508

HORIZON BOOKS — General
61 Main St (Mail add: PO Box 282, 61 Main St, 02532). Tel 508-759-1549
Buyer, Sharon Lee Spieldenner
Estab 1985. 10,000 Titles. 11,000 Vols. 1000 sq ft
Types: Juvenile, out of print, remainders, high priced papbk, mass mkt papbk only, hb, text bks, used, imp Fr, China & Jap
Subj: Antq, art, hist

CAMBRIDGE — 95,322. Area code 617

ROBIN BLEDSOE BOOKSELLER — Used
1640 Massachusetts Ave (Mail add: 65 Mt Auburn St, 02138). Tel 617-576-3634
Estab 1973. 3000 Vols. 600 sq ft. Cat 6x ann
Types: Hb, illus bk, old & rare, out of print
Subj: Archit, archaeol, horses, scholarly art hist

THE BOOK CASE INC — Used
42 Church St, 02138. Tel 617-876-0832
Treas, Colman Johnson
Estab 1965. 100,000 Vols
Types: Hb, out of print, papbk, used
Subj: Hist, scholarly lit

BRYN MAWR BOOKSALE — Used
373 Huron Ave, 02138. Tel 617-661-1770
Chairperson, Joan Shurcliff
Estab 1971. 720 sq ft
Types: Out of print

GROLIER BOOK SHOP — Poetry
6 Plympton St, 02138-6606. Tel 617-547-4648. WATS 800-234-POEM
Estab 1927. 9000 Vols. 392 sq ft. Cat 2x ann
Types: Small presses, hb, imp, high priced papbk, out of print

HURST GALLERY — Antiquarian
53 Mt Auburn St, 02138. Tel 617-491-6888
750 sq ft. Cat
Types: Fine bnd, 1st ed, hb, old & rare, out of print
Subj: Art, travel, ethnography

KATE'S MYSTERY BOOKS MURDER UNDER COVER, INC — Mystery & Detective
2211 Massachusetts Ave, 02140. Tel 617-491-2660
Estab 1983. 9000 Titles. 18,000 Vols. 500 sq ft. Cat
Types: Hb, imp, juvenile, out of print, papbk, remainders, used
Subj: Women detectives, New England authors

PANGLOSS BOOKSHOP — Antiquarian
65 Mount Auburn St, 02138. Tel 617-354-4003
Estab 1950. 50,000 Vols
Types: 1st ed, out of print, hb, old & rare, remainders, used
Subj: Humanities, soc sci, scholarly bks

STARR BOOKSHOP INC — Used
29 Plympton St, 02138. Tel 617-547-6864
Estab 1930. 150,000 Vols. Cat
Types: Out of print, used, remainders, review copies
Subj: Am hist & lit, art, Eng hist & lit, philos, class studies, soc sci, sci-tech, natural hist, medieval studies, Latin lang

CANTON — 18,182. Area code 617

ISHTAR BOOKS — Antiquarian
318 Sherman St, 02021. Tel 617-828-2753 (by appt)
Cat ann
Types: Out of print, old & rare
Subj: Arabian horses

CHATHAM — 6071. Area code 508

PAPYRUS BOOKS — General
Main St, Rte 28 (Mail add: Shop Ahoy Plaza, Box 451, 02633). Tel 617-945-5903
Mgr, Claire Nolan Ford
Estab 1986. 4000 Titles. 4000 Vols. 350 sq ft
Types: Fr lang, Gr lang, imp UK, out of print, papbk, mass mkt papbk, high priced papbk, remainders, 1st ed, illus bk, juvenile, used, Latin lang
Subj: Biog, mystery & detective, psychol, Am & Eng lit

CHESTNUT HILL — Area code 617

BOOK & TACKLE SHOP — Antiquarian
29 Old Colony Rd, 02167. Tel 617-965-0459
Estab 1953. 15 Titles. 25,000 Vols. Cat 3x ann
Types: 1st ed, hb, juvenile, new & used, old & rare, out of print, papbk
Subj: Amer, art, cooking, feminism, hunting & fishing, medicine, nature & environ
See Also: Watch Hill, RI

LAURIAT'S INC — General
Chestnut Hill Mall, Hammond Pond Pkwy, 02167. Tel 617-965-1481Buys through hq
Types: Hb, out of print, papbk, remainders

CONCORD — 16,293. Area code 508

BOOKS WITH A PAST INC — Used
17 Walden St, 01742. Tel 617-371-0180
Estab 1981. 10,000 Titles. 10,000 Vols
Types: Fine bnd, 1st ed, hb, illus bk, juvenile, old & rare, out of print, papbk
Subj: Local authors, music, Thoreau, Alcotts, Emerson, Hawthorne

MALCOLM M FERGUSON — Mail Order-Antiquarian
1489 Main St, 01742. Tel 508-369-2898
Mgr, Malcolm M Ferguson
Estab 1945. 8000 Vols
Types: Hb, illus bk, old & rare, out of print, used
Subj: Sci fiction & fantasy, Thoreau

THE THOREAU LYCEUM BOOKSHOP — Museum
156 Belknap St, 01742. Tel 508-369-5912
Owner, The Thoreau Society, Inc; Curator, Anne R McGrath
Estab 1968. 225 Titles. 5000 Vols. 200 sq ft. Cat 4x ann
Types: Hb, out of print, used, papbk
Subj: Nature & environ, Concord authors & hist; Henry D Thoreau, the transcendentalists

CONWAY — 1213. Area code 413

SOUTHPAW BOOKS — Mail Order-Antiquarian
Box 155, 01341. Tel 413-369-4406
Mgr, Eugine Povirk
Estab 1982. 13,000 Titles. Cat 4x ann
Types: 1st ed, hb, illus bk, out of print, papbk, used, modern 1st ed
Subj: Indust & labor, radical polit, feminism

DANVERS — Area area code 508

CAPE ANN ANTIQUES — Mail Order
15 Mildred Rd (Mail add: P O Box 3502, Peabody, 01960). Tel 617-777-3011
Estab 1980. 500 Titles. 1000 Vols. Cat 4x ann
Types: 1st ed, hb, out of print, papbk, old & rare
Subj: Drug related

DEERFIELD — 4517. Area code 413

M DOUGLAS SACKMAN — Mail Order-Antiquarian
PO Box 308, 24 Meadow Wood, 01342. Tel 413-665-3401
Cat 2x ann
Types: Hb, out of print, old & rare, used
Subj: Amer, genealogy, Massachusettsana

DUXBURY — 11,807. Area code 617

MATTAKEESETT BOOKS — Mail Order-Used
65 Bay View Rd, 02332. Tel 617-934-5564
Estab 1986. 600 Titles. 600 Vols. Cat 2x ann
Types: Fine bnd, hb, 1st ed, ltd ed, old & rare, out of print, papbk, used
Subj: J D Salinger, Robert Frost, S King

EAST ARLINGTON — Area code 617

HENRY DEEKS — Antiquarian-Civil War
PO Box 1500, 02174
200 Titles. 200 Vols
Types: Old & rare, out of print
Subj: Civil War

EAST LONGMEADOW — 12,905. Area code 413

W D HALL — Mail Order-Antiquarian
99 Maple St, 01028. Tel 413-525-3064
Estab 1965. 6000 Vols. Cat 12x ann
Types: Hb, old & rare, out of print, used
Subj: Amer, art, Civil War, nature & environ, nautical, travel, ephemera

EAST SANDWICH — Area code 617

TITCOMB'S BOOKSHOP — Antiquarian
432 Rte 6-A (Mail add: PO Box 45, 02537). Tel 508-888-2331
Estab 1966. 13,000 Titles. 15,000 Vols
Types: Hb, new, old & rare, out of print
Subj: Amer, New England, nonfiction

FALL RIVER — 92,574. Area code 508

BOOKHAVEN BOOKSTORE — General
1749 N Main, 02720. Tel 508-679-0188
Estab 1978. 19,000 Vols
Types: Fine bnd, hb, illus bk, juvenile, out of print, old & rare, used
Subj: Whales & whaling, military

TASTE OF HONEY BOOKSTORE — Antiquarian
1755 N Main St, 02720. Tel 508-679-8844
Estab 1972. 10,000 Vols. 1000 sq ft. Cat ann
Types: Fine bnd, 1st ed, hb, illus bk, old & rare, out of print, papbk, used
Subj: New England, Rhode Islandana, local hist

FOXBOROUGH — 14,148. Area code 508

IBIS BOOKS — Mail Order-Natural History
28 Cocassett St, 02035. Tel 508-543-3512
Estab 1978. 2000 Vols. 800 sq ft. Cat 4x ann
Types: Hb, illus bk, new & used, old & rare, out of print, remainders

FRAMINGHAM — 65,113. Area code 508

MIRIAM REDLO BOOKS — Mail Order-Antiquarian
11 Forest Ave, 01701-6369. Tel 617-872-0297
Estab 1983. 10,000 Titles. 10,000 Vols
Types: Hb, juvenile, out of print, remainders, illus bk, used
Subj: Psychol

GARDNER — 17,900. Area code 508

IRENE'S BOOKSHOP — Used
49 W Broadway, 01440. Tel 617-632-5574
Estab 1967. 30,000 Vols. 1600 sq ft. Cat 6x ann
Types: Fine bnd, 1st ed, hb, illus bk, juvenile, ltd ed, out of print, old & rare

GEORGETOWN — 5687. Area code 508

JANE FIELD BOOKS — Used
14 North St, 01833-2018. Tel 508-352-6641
Estab 1960. 7800 Titles. 8000 Vols. 900 sq ft
Types: Out of print, hb, juvenile, papbk, remainders
Subj: Hist, military, nonfiction

GLOUCESTER — 27,768. Area code 508

THE ENGLISH BOOKSHOP — Used
22 Rocky Neck Ave, 01930. Tel 617-283-8981
Owner, Peggy Sibley; Mgr, Margaret Sibley
Estab 1956. 5000 Vols
Types: Juvenile, illus bk, hb, imp, old & rare, out of print, new, children's illus classics imp
Subj: Nautical, women's studies, Great Britain

TEN POUND ISLAND BOOK CO — Antiquarian
3 Center St, 01930. Tel 617-283-5299
Estab 1976. 5000 Vols. 500 sq ft. Cat 12x ann
Types: Facsimile editions, 1st ed, hb, illus bk, juvenile, ltd ed, old & rare, out of print
Subj: Amer, local hist, nautical, fine arts, art, maritime

GREAT BARRINGTON — 7405. Area code 413

J & J LUBRANO — Antiquarian
39 Hollenbeck Ave, 01230. Tel 413-528-5799
Estab 1977. 6000 Vols. 250 sq ft. Cat 2x ann
Types: Facsimile editions, hb, illus bk, old & rare, out of print, used
Subj: Dance, music, theatre

GREENFIELD — 18,116. Area code 413

STEVE FINER - BOOKS — Mail Order-Antiquarian
PO Box 758, 01302. Tel 413-773-5811
Estab 1979. 7500 Vols. Cat 6x ann
Types: Fine bnd, 1st ed, hb, illus bk, old & rare, out of print, used
Subj: Games, horses, magic & conjuring, New England, photog, sci-tech

ROBERT GEAR — Agriculture
PO Box 1137, 01302. Tel 413-772-6576
450 Vols. Cat 12x ann
Types: Hb, out of print, imp UK, high priced papbk
Subj: Hort, agr, horses

HADLEY — 4125. Area code 413

KEN LOPEZ BOOKSELLER — Antiquarian
51 Huntington Rd, 01035. Tel 413-584-4827
Estab 1981. 10,000 Titles. 10,000 Vols. Cat 6x ann
Types: 1st ed, hb, ltd ed, new & used, old & rare, out of print, remainders
Subj: Latin Am, mod lit, nature & environ, poetry, fiction, advance galleys, proofs, signed books, Am Indian lit, essays, Vietnam War lit

HINGHAM — 20,339. Area code 617

INDIAN FORT BOOK HOUSE — Antiquarian
99 Fort Hills St, 02043. Tel 617-749-1651, 749-2728
Estab 1944. 4500 Titles. 5000 Vols
Types: Out of print, facsimile editions, fine bnd, 1st ed, hb, incunab, illus bk, imp, juvenile, ltd ed, new, old & rare, used

HULL — 9714. Area code 617

UNIVERSITY BOOK RESERVE — Mail Order-Antiquarian
75 Main St, 02045-0905. Tel 617-925-0570
Estab 1941. 100,000 Vols. 4823 sq ft. Cat
Types: 1st ed, hb, old & rare, out of print, used
Subj: Philos, rel studies, soc sci, general lit

HUNTINGTON — 1804. Area code 413

PAULSON BOOKS — Antiquarian
Allen Coit Rd, 01050. Tel 413-667-3208
10,000 Titles. 10,000 Vols. 1500 sq ft
Types: 1st ed, hb, illus bk, juvenile, ltd ed, old & rare, out of print, used
Subj: Massachusettsana, mystery & detective, sci fiction & fantasy, Rockwell Kent, victorian ephemera

HYANNIS — 6847. Area code 508

WAKE-BROOK HOUSE BOOKS — Antiquarian
PO Box 153, 02601. Tel 508-775-5860
Estab 1968. 2000 Vols. Cat
Types: 1st ed, hb, out of print, old & rare
Subj: New England, Joseph C Lincoln, Thornton W Burgess

LANESBOROUGH — 3131. Area code 413

SECOND LIFE BOOKS INC — Antiquarian
Quarry Rd, PO Box 242, 01237. Tel 413-447-8010
Estab 1972. 30,000 Titles. 30,000 Vols. 1500 sq ft. Cat 4x ann
Types: Fine bnd, hb, illus bk, imp, juvenile, ltd ed, old & rare, out of print, used
Subj: Polit sci, hist, agr, hort, women's studies, lit, signed bks

LEXINGTON — 29,418. Area code 617

EVA AROND BOOKS — Antiquarian
52 Turning Mill Road, 02173. Tel 617-862-6379
Estab 1981. 7500 Vols. 375 sq ft
Types: Juvenile, out of print, used
Subj: Feminism

LITTLETON — 6970 Area code 508

PEACOCK BOOKS — Antiquarian-Ornithology
PO Box 2024, 01460. Tel 508-456-8404
Estab 1982. 600 Titles. 750 Vols. Cat 3x ann
Types: Out of print
Subj: Falconry

MARBLEHEAD — 20,126. Area code 617

IRVING GALIS — Mail Order-Antiquarian
357 Atlantic Ave, 01945. Tel 617-631-5351
5000 Vols
Types: 1st ed, hb, illus bk, ltd ed, old & rare, out of print, remainders, used, imp Eng
Subj: Biog, Eng hist & lit, military, polit sci, US presidents & presidency, JFK assassination, Richard Nixon, Watergate, World War II, military unit histories

MUCH ADO — Used
7 Pleasant St, 01945. Tel 617-639-0400
Estab 1984. 24,000 Titles. 24,000 Vols. Cat
Types: Hb, juvenile, out of print, fine bnd, 1st ed, illus bk, ltd ed, old & rare
Subj: New England, nautical, fiction

MARSHFIELD — 20,916. Area code 617

LORD RANDALL BOOK & PRINT SHOP — Antiquarian
22 Main St, 02050. Tel 617-837-1400
Estab 1972. 20,000 Vols
Types: Out of print, old & rare
Subj: Amer, art, local hist

MASHPEE — 3700. Area code 508

CAPE COD BOOK CENTER INC — General
Rte 28, PO Box 1380, 02649. Tel 508-477-9903
Estab 1974. 20,000 Vols. 2000 sq ft
Types: Hb, out of print, old & rare, papbk, remainders, new & used, juvenile
Subj: Hunting & fishing, military hist, Cape Cod hist

MELROSE — 30,055. Area code 617

STARR BOOK CO, INC — Antiquarian
44 W Wyoming Ave, 02176-3745. Tel 617-662-2580
Estab 1930. 300,000 Vols. 3000 sq ft
Types: Out of print
Subj: Drama, feminism, fiction, mystery & detective, nautical, nonfiction, philos, psychol, hist

METHUEN — 36,701. Area code 508

LAURIAT'S INC — General
Methuen Mall, Howe St, 01844. Tel 508-682-3287
Mgr, Cynthia Robbins Buys through hq
Types: Hb, out of print, papbk, remainders

MONTAGUE — 8011. Area code 413

PETER L MASI - BOOKS — Antiquarian
17 Central St, PO Box B, 01351. Tel 413-367-2628
Asst Mgr, Deborah M Masi
Estab 1979. 8000 Titles. 8000 Vols. 1000 sq ft. Cat 6x ann
Types: Out of print, used
Subj: Agr, cooking, sci-tech, archit, bus & mgt, photog, Amer

NANTUCKET — 5087. Area code 508

ISLAND ATTIC INDUSTRIES — Antiques
91 Humock Pond Rd, 02554. Tel 508-228-9405
Estab 1977
Types: Juvenile, out of print, papbk, used
Subj: Nantucket

LITTORAL BOOKS — Antiquarian
11 Vestal St, 02554. Tel 508-228-2202
Estab 1983. 4000 Vols. 240 sq ft. Cat
Types: Out of print
Subj: Travel, oceanog, archit, Nantuckiana

NEEDHAM — 27,901. Area code 617

ESTHER TUVESON OUT OF PRINT BOOKS & EPHEMERA — Antiquarian
30 Brookside Rd, 02192. Tel 617-444-5533
Types: Juvenile, hb, out of print, used, facsimile editions, 1st ed, illus bk, ltd ed, old & rare
Subj: Illus, art, biog, nonfiction

NEW BEDFORD — 98,478. Area code 508

SALTMARSH'S — Dept Store
777 Purchase St, 02740. Tel 508-997-0061
Mgr, Robert J Saltmarsh
Estab 1864
Types: El-hi text, hb, juvenile, out of print, papbk, remainders, used
Subj: Art, rel-c,j,p

NEWBURYPORT — 15,900. Area code 508

FRANK E REYNOLDS BOOKSELLER — Antiquarian-Civil War
PO Box 805, 01950-5505. Tel 617-462-1524
Estab 1968. 750 Titles. 1000 Vols. 300 sq ft. Cat 6x ann
Types: Hb, old & rare, out of print, remainders, used
Subj: Abraham Lincoln

NEW SALEM — 688. Area code 508

COMMON READER BOOKSHOP — Antiquarian-Women's Studies
Old Main St (Mail add: Box 32, 01355). Tel 508-544-3002, 544-7039
Estab 1977. 5000 Vols. 300 sq ft
Types: 1st ed, hb, illus bk, old & rare, out of print

QUABBIN BOOKS — Mail Order-Antiquarian
W Main St (Mail add: Box 14, 01355). Tel 508-544-7141
1500 Vols. Cat 4x ann
Types: Hb, new, old & rare, out of print, papbk, used
Subj: Anthrop, archaeol, ethnology

NEWTON — 83,622. Area code 617

THE BOOK COLLECTOR — Antiquarian
375 Elliot St, 02164. Tel 617-964-3599
Estab 1972. 28,000 Titles. 30,000 Vols. 1200 sq ft
Types: 1st ed, facsimile editions, fine bnd, hb, illus bk, imp, juvenile, ltd ed, old & rare, out of print, papbk, used, for lang

HARD-TO-FIND NEEDLEWORK BOOKS — Needlecrafts
96 Roundwood Rd, 02164. Tel 617-969-0942
Estab 1979. 8000 Titles. 10,000 Vols. 500 sq ft. Cat 4x ann
Types: Hb, out of print, remainders, used, imp UK, imp Jap, Sp lang, Fr, Ger & It lang
Subj: Costuming, lace, quilting, knitting, crocheting, needlepoint

SUZANNE SCHLOSSBERG — Antiquarian-Juvenile
529 Ward St, 02159. Tel 617-964-0213
Estab 1975. 1500 Vols. Cat
Types: Fine bnd, 1st ed, hb, illus bk, ltd ed, old & rare, out of print
Subj: Illus

NEWTON CENTER — Area code 617

A BOY'S WILL BOOKS — Antiquarian
33 Paul St, 02159. Tel 617-964-5046
Estab 1980. 5000 Vols. 250 sq ft. Cat 2x ann
Types: Facsimile editions, fine bnd, 1st ed, illus bk, ltd ed, hb, juvenile, old & rare, out of print, new & used
Subj: Poetry, class studies

EDWARD MORRILL & SON — Antiquarian
27 Country Club Rd, 02159-3021. Tel 617-527-7448
Estab 1939. Cat 7x ann
Types: Out of print, old & rare
Subj: Amer, arts & crafts

NEWTON HIGHLANDS — Area code 617

JESSICA'S BISCUIT — Mail Order
82 Needham St, 02161. Tel 617-965-0530
1000 Titles. 1000 Vols. Cat ann
Types: Hb, papbk, out of print
Subj: Cooking

NORTHAMPTON — 29,286. Area code 413

AMERICAN DECORATIVE ARTS — Used
9 1/2 Market St (Mail add: PO Box 751, 01061-0751). Tel 413-584-6804
Estab 1981. 500 Titles. 600 Vols. 600 sq ft. Cat 2x ann
Types: Hb, old & rare, out of print, used
Subj: Modern design, modern glass, furniture, ceramics

LUNARIA, A FEMINIST BOOKSTORE — Feminism
90 King St, 01060. Tel 413-586-7851
Estab 1988
Types: Hb, juvenile, mass mkt papbk, remainders, text bks, used, imp, out of print, 1st ed, new, old & rare
Subj: Music

OAK BLUFFS — 1984. Area code 508

BOOK DEN EAST — Used
New York Ave, Box 721, 02557. Tel 508-693-3946
Estab 1977. 20,000 Vols. Cat
Types: Out of print

ORLEANS — 5306. Area code 508

THE HAUNTED BOOKSHOP — Antiquarian
14 Cove Rd, PO Box 558, 02653. Tel 617-255-3780
Estab 1985. 10,000 Titles. 10,000 Vols. 338 sq ft
Types: Hb, facsimile editions, fine bnd, 1st ed, illus bk, juvenile, ltd ed, old & rare, out of print, papbk
Subj: Art, archaeol, scholarly lit, mystery & detective, sci fiction & fantasy, biol, New England, Amer, poetry

FRANC LADNER — Mail Order
45 West Rd Unit 1F, PO Box 653, 02653-0653. Tel 508-255-3466
Estab 1983. 1000 Vols
Types: Out of print, used, general
Subj: Fiction

PEABODY — 45,976. Area code 508

LAURIAT'S INC — General
N Shore S/Ctr, Rtes 128 & 114, 01960. Tel 508-531-3255
Mgr, Rick Dunavan Buys through hq
Types: Hb, out of print, papbk, remainders

PLYMOUTH — 35,913. Area code 508

THE SECOND TIME AROUND BOOKSTORE — Used
186 Water St, 02360. Tel 508-746-1336
Mgr, Mary Newton
Estab 1982. 10,000 Titles. 20,000 Vols
Types: Hb, out of print, papbk, mass mkt papbk, comics

YANKEE BOOK EXCHANGE — Antiquarian
10 North St, 02360. Tel 508-747-2691
Estab 1982. 7000 Vols. 650 sq ft
Types: 1st ed, hb, illus bk, ltd ed, out of print, old & rare, fine bnd, exploration
Subj: Genealogy, local hist, performing arts

PROVINCETOWN — 3536. Area code 508

BRYANT'S — Antiquarian
467 Commercial St, 02657. Tel 508-487-0134
Mgr, George D Bryant
Estab 1837. 5000 Vols
Types: Illus bk, new, old & rare, out of print
Subj: Fiction, nonfiction, fishing indust, marine transp, lifesaving, lighthouses, Provincetown & Cape Cod

READING — 22,678. Area code 617

PAGES BOOKSHOP OF READING — Antiquarian
25 Harnden St, 01867. Tel 617-944-9613
Estab 1985. 10,000 Vols. 1000 sq ft
Types: Out of print, mass mkt papbk, remainders, used, comics
Subj: Collecting, sports, travel

SALEM — 38,220. Area code 508

NORTH SALEM BOOKS — Used
243 North St, 01970. Tel 508-741-4670
Estab 1986. 4000 Titles. 4000 Vols. 200 sq ft
Types: Juvenile, papbk, remainders, out of print
Subj: Massachusettsana, biog, auto

PEABODY MUSEUM OF SALEM BOOKSTORE — Museum
161 Essex, 01970. Tel 508-745-1876
Dir, Peter Fetchko; Mgr, Daniele Lambrechts
Estab 1950. 1000 Titles. 2000 Vols
Types: Hb, juvenile, high priced papbk, out of print, remainders, used
Subj: Maritime, nat hist & ethnol of non-Europ peoples

SANDWICH — 8727. Area code 508

RETLOKS BOOKSTORE — Used
37 Merchants Sq, 02563. Tel 508-888-8437
Estab 1987. 12,000 Titles. 12,000 Vols. 800 sq ft. Cat 4x ann
Types: Facsimile editions, fine bnd, 1st ed, hb, incunab, illus bk, imp, juvenile, ltd ed, old & rare, out of print
Subj: Nautical, concord authors

SHARON — 13,601. Area code 508

ANTIQUARIAN BOOKWORM — Mail Order-Antiquarian
22 Sentry Hill Rd, 02067. Tel 617-784-9411
Cat 3x ann
Types: Used, out of print, old & rare
Subj: Amer, archit, Civil War, Western Amer, medicine, travel

PEPPER & STERN — Mail Order-Antiquarian
PO Box 357, 02067. Tel 617-784-7618
Estab 1972. 5000 Titles. 6000 Vols. Cat 8x ann
Types: 1st ed, old & rare, out of print
Subj: Fiction, mystery & detective

SOMERVILLE — 77,372. Area code 617

SUN SIGNS & SCOPES — Astrology
54 Putnam Rd, 02145. Tel 617-625-8816
Types: Hb, out of print, papbk, remainders, used

ZEMBLA BOOKS — Used
93 Holland St, 02144. Tel 617-625-6640
Types: Out of print

SOUTHAMPTON — 4137. Area code 413

HERITAGE BOOKS — Mail Order-Antiquarian
College Hwy, PO Box 48, 01073. Tel 413-527-6200
Mgr, Rosmarie Coombs
Cat
Types: Hb, papbk, juvenile, out of print, illus bk

SOUTHBRIDGE — 16,665. Area code 508

THE BOOKIES' INC — Paperback
918 Main St, 01550. Tel 617-764-8040
Mgr, Linda McDonald
Estab 1980. 40,000 Titles. 60,000 Vols. 1600 sq ft
Types: Juvenile, out of print, new & used, old & rare, books-on-tape
Subj: Fiction, nonfiction, educ, sci fiction & fantasy

SOUTH EGREMONT — Area code 413

BRUCE & SUSAN GVENTER "BOOKS" — Antiquarian
Rte 23 & Tyrrel Rd (Mail add: PO Box 298, 01258-0298). Tel 413-528-2327; 528-9499 (home)
Mgr, Bruce Gventer
Estab 1980. 15,000 Titles. 15,000 Vols. Cat 4x ann
Types: 1st ed, hb, illus bk, juvenile, ltd ed, new, old & rare, out of print, papbk, remainders, used
Subj: Biog, fashion, costuming, hand color plate bks, manuscripts, early 19th century color illustrations, early printing

SOUTH HAMILTON — Area code 508

ELMCRESS BOOKS — Antiquarian
161 Bay Rd, 01982. Tel 508-468-3261
Estab 1978. 5000 Vols. 1000 sq ft. Cat 6x ann
Types: Facsimile editions, fine bnd, 1st ed, hb, illus bk, juvenile, ltd ed, old & rare, out of print, used
Subj: Bibliog, nautical, bks on bks, natural hist, Mod British royal family

SOUTH HARWICH — Area code 617

THE CAPE COLLECTOR — Antiquarian
1012 Main St, Rte 28, Cape Cod, 02661-0096. Tel 508-432-3701
Estab 1969. 35,000 Vols
Types: Used, juvenile, out of print, hb
Subj: New England, nautical, art, sports, nature & environ, hist, biog, fiction, rel, hobbies, Cape Cod, maritime

SPENCER — 10,774. Area code 508

SUNFLOWER BOOKS — Used
4 Mechanic St, PO Box 405, 01562-2202. Tel 508-885-9983
Papbk Buyer, Lois Y Mortell
Estab 1984. 15,000 Titles. 15,000 Vols. 580 sq ft. Cat ann
Types: Juvenile, out of print, mass mkt papbk, high priced papbk
Subj: Fiction, nonfiction, romance, sci fiction & fantasy

SPRINGFIELD — 152,319. Area code 413

FRANCIS JOHN BRECK JR BOOKSELLER — Antiquarian-Metaphys & Occult
52 Mountainview St, 01108. Tel 413-733-3523
Estab 1982. 2000 Titles. 7000 Vols. Cat 3x ann
Types: Facsimile editions, fine bnd, 1st ed, hb, incunab, illus bk, ltd ed, old & rare, out of print, remainders, Fr & Sp lang

JOHNSON'S INC — General
1379 Main St, 01103-1692. Tel 413-732-6222
Mgr, Mary Senecal
Estab 1893. 75,000 Vols
Types: Hb, juvenile, new & used, out of print, papbk

RED BRICK BOOKS — Used
797 Page Blvd, 01104. Tel 413-732-2213
Estab 1981. 20,000 Vols. 800 sq ft
Types: Hb, juvenile, out of print, papbk, new

STOUGHTON — 26,710. Area code 508

HENRY J VICKEY — Mail Order-Antiquarian
Nine Brook, PO Box 268, 02072. Tel 617-344-3649
Estab 1945. 4000 Vols
Types: Out of print, used

WESTERN HEMISPHERE INC — Mail Order-Antiquarian
144 West St (Mail add: PO Box 178, 02072). Tel 617-344-8200
Estab 1967. 7500 Titles. 7500 Vols. Cat monthly
Types: Out of print, old & rare
Subj: Econ, govt publn, law, soc sci, bus & mgt, polit sci

STOW — 5144. Area code 508

YANKEE PACKET BOOKS — Antiquarian-General
531 Great Rd, 01775. Tel 617-897-1746
Estab 1981. 15,000 Titles. 14,000 Vols. 1200 sq ft
Types: Fine bnd, 1st ed, hb, illus bk, juvenile, ltd ed, old & rare, out of print, used
Subj: Nautical, nature & environ, graphic arts, travel, archit, maritime, tech

SUDBURY — 14,027. Area code 508

WATER ROW BOOKS INC — Mail Order
PO Box 438, 01776. Tel 508-443-8910
Mgr, Rooster Kirschbaum
Estab 1970. 10,000 Vols. Cat 6x ann
Types: Facsimile editions, fine bnd, 1st ed, hb, papbk, ltd ed, old & rare, out of print
Subj: Mod first ed

WALTHAM — 58,200. Area code 617

BURSTEIN & COMPANY — Mail Order-Antiquarian
36 Riverside Dr, 02154. Tel 617-893-7974
Mgr, Michael D Burstein
Estab 1954. Cat 3x ann
Types: 1st ed, juvenile, old & rare, out of print
Subj: Am hist & lit, Amer, bibliog

JOHN O JOHNSON JR — Mail Order-Antiquarian
1106 Trapelo Rd, 02154-3236. Tel 617-893-8861
Estab 1970
Types: Hb, illus bk, old & rare, out of print, used
Subj: Philately, postal hist

WAYLAND — 12,170. Area code 508

ROGER F CASAVANT — Mail Order-Antiquarian
88 Dudley Rd, 01778. Tel 508-653-4104
10,000 Vols. Cat
Types: Out of print, 1st ed, hb, illus bk, juvenile, ltd ed, old & rare, fine bnd
Subj: Amer, Am & Eng hist & lit

WELLESLEY — 27,709. Area code 617

MEDALLION BOOKS — General
555 Washington St, 02181. Tel 617-237-5152
Estab 1979. 312 sq ft. Cat 3x ann
Types: Hb, out of print, old & rare, collectibles

TERRAMEDIA BOOKS — Mail Order-Antiquarian
19 Homestead Rd, 02181-6923. Tel 617-237-6485
Mgr, Elias Saad
Estab 1980. 2500 Titles. 2500 Vols. Cat 12x ann
Types: Out of print, fine bnd, old & rare
Subj: Africa, Middle East, discovery & explor, natural hist, Orientalia

WELLFLEET — 2209. Area code 508

TWICE SOLD TALES — General
W Main St (Mail add: PO Box 725, 02667). Tel 508-349-9829
Estab 1978. 5000 Vols. Cat
Types: 1st ed, illus bk, juvenile, ltd ed, out of print, old & rare, new & used, hb, papbk
Subj: Feminism, folklore, women's studies

WEST BRIDGEWATER — 6359. Area code 508

THE BOOKSTORE OF WEST BRIDGEWATER — Antiquarian-General
222 N Main St, 02379. Tel 508-588-4774
Estab 1972. 50,000 Vols. 2000 sq ft. Cat 4x ann
Types: Fine bnd, 1st ed, hb, illus bk, ltd ed, new & used, old & rare, out of print, papbk

WEST FALMOUTH — Area code 508

AFRICAN & CARIBBEAN IMPRINT LIBRARY SERVICES — Mail Order
410 W Falmouth Hwy (Mail add: PO Box 350, 02574). Tel 508-540-5378. WATS 800-227-4835
Dir, Dir Allen R Boyd; Managing Dir, Christopher Boyd
Estab 1970. 130,000 Titles. 6000 sq ft. Cat
Types: Col & el-hi text, for lang, hb, imp, juvenile, mass mkt papbk, out of print, papbk, used, imp Afr & Caribbean lang, business directories

WESTFIELD — 36,465. Area code 413

GUSTAVE H SUHM BOOK-TIQUE — Mail Order-Antiquarian
81 Llewellyn Dr, 01085-2513. Tel 413-568-5627 (by appt only)
Estab 1978. 5000 Vols. Cat 2x ann
Types: 1st ed, hb, illus bk, ltd ed, old & rare, out of print, used
Subj: Guns, hunting & fishing, general

WESTON — 11,169. Area code 617

JANE CHORAS BOOKS — Antiquarian
225 Winter St, 02193. Tel 617-237-9828
Estab 1985. 2000 Titles. 2500 Vols. 416 sq ft
Types: 1st ed, hb, illus bk, juvenile, mass mkt papbk only, out of print, papbk, remainders
Subj: Sci fiction & fantasy

WESTPORT — 13,763. Area code 508

PHILIP LOZINSKI SCHOLARLY BOOKS — Mail Order-Antiquarian
PO Box 3097, 02790. Tel 508-636-2567
Estab 1960. 10,000 Vols. Cat monthly
Types: Facsimile editions, hb, imp, old & rare, out of print, reprint
Subj: For lang, hist, humanities, Orientalia, slavica
See Also: Philip Lozinski, Canadian Branch Reg'd, Saint Bruno, Q

WEST STOCKBRIDGE — 1280. Area code 413

DOROTHY ELSBERG — Antiquarian-Music
Box 178, 01266. Tel 413-232-8560
Cat 4x ann
Types: Old & rare, out of print

WILLIAMSTOWN — 8741. Area code 413

SETH NEMEROFF ANTIQUARIAN BOOKS INC — Antiquarian
PO Box 606, 35 Spring St, 2nd Floor, 01267. Tel 413-458-9212
Estab 1984. 5000 Vols
Types: Old & rare, out of print, new & used, illus bk, imp UK, for lang
Subj: Psychol, theol, mythology, philos, literary criticism, travel, illus, Classical, Medieval & Oriental studies, scholarly humanities & sci, Western & Eastern art hist & theory, bk arts & bk hist, classical tradition, personal growth

WORCESTER — 161,799 Area code 508

MANASHA BILSEY — Antiquarian
Seven E Kendall St, 01605. Tel 508-754-0278
Estab 1984. 5000 Titles
Types: Hb, used, facsimile editions, fine bnd, 1st ed, illus bk, juvenile, old & rare, out of print, papbk, remainders
Subj: Amer, cooking, hist, metaphys & occult

FABULOUS FICTION BOOKSTORE — Science Fiction & Fantasy
587 Park Ave, 01603. Tel 508-754-8826
Estab 1979. 65,000 Vols. 5500 sq ft. Cat 2x ann
Types: Hb, juvenile, out of print, papbk, new & used
Subj: Sci fiction & fantasy

PHENOMENOLOGICA — Mail Order-Antiquarian
PO Box 27, West Side Station, 01602-0027. Tel 508-757-9155
Consultants, Peter Wackell & Mark S Roberts
10000 Vols. Cat
Types: 1st ed, old & rare, out of print, new & used
Subj: Philos, psychiat

THE TATNUCK BOOKSELLER — General
647 Chandler St, 01602. Tel 508-756-7644
Estab 1975. 40,000 Vols. 1900 sq ft
Types: Hb, juvenile, out of print, papbk, remainders, used
See Also: wholesale section

ISAIAH THOMAS BOOKS & PRINTS INC — Antiquarian
980 Main St, 01603. Tel 508-754-0750
Estab 1970. 50,000 Vols. Cat
Types: Fine bnd, 1st ed, hb, illus bk, juvenile, ltd ed, old & rare, out of print, remainders, used

ADRIAN — 21,186. Area code 517

BOOK OP SHOP — Mail Order
64 Swan Lake Dr, 49221. Tel 517-423-4467
Mgr, John Nolan
Types: Hb, used, facsimile editions, 1st ed, juvenile, old & rare, out of print, illus bk
Subj: Cooking, art, scouting, gardening, hist, travel, music, decorating

ANN ARBOR — 107,316. Area code 313

DAVID'S BOOKS — General
622 E Liberty, 48104. Tel 313-665-8017
Estab 1977. 40,000 Vols. 1600 sq ft
Types: For lang, hb, juvenile, out of print, papbk, used
Subj: Humanities, sci-tech, chess, fiction

THE DAWN TREADER BOOKSHOP — Antiquarian
525 E Liberty, 48104. Tel 313-995-1008
Estab 1978. 55,000 Vols. 2800 sq ft. Cat 3x ann
Types: Fine bnd, 1st ed, hb, illus bk, ltd ed, old & rare, out of print, papbk, used
Subj: Folklore, natural hist, mystery & detective, sci fiction & fantasy, psychol, art, voyages, 19th-20th century 1st ed
See Also: The Classic Bookshop, Royal Oak

ERIC & GALE EKLUND BOOKSELLERS — Used
3160 Saline Rd, Ann Arbor Rd, 48103. Tel 313-663-4614
Estab 1981. 15,000 Vols. 2000 sq ft
Types: Out of print
Subj: Music, nonfiction

HARTFIELD FINE & RARE BOOKS — Used
117 Dixboro Rd, 48105. Tel 313-662-6035
Estab 1970. 10,000 Titles. 10,000 Vols. 1000 sq ft. Cat 4x ann
Types: Fine bnd, 1st ed, hb, illus bk, ltd ed, old & rare, out of print, fine press
Subj: Eng hist & lit, 18th & early 19th century lit

KERAMOS — Antiquarian
PO Box 7500, 48107-7500. Tel 313-429-7864
Mgr, Marjorie E Uren
Estab 1972. Cat
Types: For lang, fine bnd, hb, illus bk, imp, incunab, ltd ed, new, old & rare, out of print
Subj: Asian studies, ceramics, Oriental art
See Also: wholesale section

LEAVES OF GRASS — Mail Order-Antiquarian
2433 Whitmore Lake Rd, 48103. Tel 313-995-2300
Estab 1973. 10,000 Vols. Cat 3x ann
Types: Fine bnd, 1st ed, hb, illus bk, ltd ed, old & rare, out of print, used
Subj: Am hist & lit, Amer, bks on bks, Eng hist & lit

THE SCIENCE BOOKSHELF — Mail Order-Antiquarian
Box 8183, 48107. Tel 313-665-0537
4000 Vols
Types: 1st ed, hb, old & rare, out of print, used
Subj: Medicine, natural hist, sci fiction & fantasy, sci-tech, mystery & detective

STATE STREET BOOKSHOP — Antiquarian
316 S State St, 48104. Tel 313-994-4041
Estab 1975. 25,000 Vols. 2000 sq ft. Cat
Types: 1st ed, hb, illus bk, imp, old & rare, out of print, used
Subj: Philos, linguistics, anthrop, Fr, Ger & It lang, Sp lang, humanities, nat sci, angling

WEST SIDE BOOKSHOP — Antiquarian
113 W Liberty, 48104. Tel 313-995-1891
Estab 1975. 15,000 Vols. 1000 sq ft. Cat 4x ann
Types: Fine bnd, 1st ed, hb, illus bk, juvenile, ltd ed, old & rare, out of print, used
Subj: Nautical, photog, polar exploration

THE WINE & FOOD LIBRARY — Antiquarian
1207 W Madison, 48103-4929. Tel 313-663-4894
Estab 1973. 15,000 Vols. 1100 sq ft. Cat 2x ann
Types: Facsimile editions, fine bnd, 1st ed, hb, incunab, illus bk, imp, ltd ed, new & used, old & rare, out of print
Subj: Cooking, food, gardening, hort, wines, beverages, gastronomy, decorative arts, herbs & spices

WOODEN SPOON BOOKS — Used
200 N Fourth Ave, 48104. Tel 313-769-4775
Types: Hb, out of print, papbk
See Also: Wooden Spoon West, Carlsbad, NM

AUBURN HILLS — Area code 313

GUNNERMAN BOOKS — Mail Order-Antiquarian
Box 4292, 48057. Tel 313-879-2779
Estab 1978. 10,000 Vols. Cat 3x ann
Types: Old & rare, out of print, remainders, used
Subj: Hunting & fishing

MARION THE ANTIQUARIAN LIBRARIAN — Mail Order-Antiquarian
3668 S Shimmons Circle, 48057-1140. Tel 313-373-8414
Estab 1979. 1500 Vols. 130 sq ft. Cat
Types: 1st ed, hb, illus bk, juvenile, ltd ed, old & rare, out of print
Subj: Automobilia

BATTLE CREEK — 35,724. Area code 616

MEMORY AISLE — Used
1162 W Columbia Ave, 49015. Tel 616-964-4293
Estab 1972. 26,000 Vols. 1000 sq ft. Cat
Types: Old & rare, new & used, papbk, hb, juvenile, out of print
Subj: Metaphysics, Michiganiana, rel-Seventh Day Adventist, Western Amer, Battle Creek ephemera

BIRMINGHAM — 21,689. Area code 313

HALSTED GALLERY INC - BOOK DEPT — Art Gallery
560 N Woodward Ave, 48009. Tel 313-644-8284
Mgr, Melanie Johns
Types: Hb, papbk, old & rare, out of print
Subj: Photog

BLOOMFIELD HILLS — 3985. Area code 313

CRANBROOK ACADEMY OF ART MUSEUM BOOKSTORE — Museum
500 Lone Pine Rd, PO Box 801, 48013. Tel 313-645-3325
Mgr, Debra Jonas
Estab 1976. 750 Titles. 2500 Vols. Cat
Types: Hb, juvenile, out of print, papbk
Subj: Archit, art, design, graphic arts

BURTON — 29,976. Area code 517

WOOTEN'S BOOKS — Used
G 3311 Cheyenne, 48529. Tel 313-744-1987
10,000 Titles. 10,000 Vols
Types: Out of print, juvenile, illus bk, 1st ed
Subj: Hist, Amer, cooking

DECATUR — 1915. Area code 616

BOHLING BOOK CO — Mail Order-Antiquarian
PO Box 204, 49045-0204. Tel 616-423-8786
Estab 1967. 9500 Titles. 25,000 Vols. 3000 sq ft. Cat 8-10x ann
Types: Hb, old & rare, out of print
Subj: Amer, local hist, Old Northwest US

DETROIT — 1,203,339. Area code 313

THE CELLAR BOOK SHOP — Mail Order-Antiquarian
18090 Wyoming, 48221. Tel 313-861-1776
Managing Partner Petra F Netzorg
Estab 1946. 10,000 Titles. Cat
Types: Old & rare, out of print, new, imp Southeast Asia & Pacific Islands
Subj: Southeast Asia, Pacific Islands

GRUB STREET - A BOOKERY — Antiquarian
17194 E Warren, 48224. Tel 313-882-7143
Estab 1977. 30,000 Titles. 30,000 Vols. 2600 sq ft. Cat 6x ann
Types: Facsimile editions, fine bnd, 1st ed, hb, illus bk, juvenile, ltd ed, old & rare, out of print, papbk, remainders, used, small presses
Subj: Art, class studies, photog, Amer, Civil War

JOHN K KING BOOKS — Antiquarian
901 W Lafayette Blvd (Mail add: PO Box 33363, 48232-5363). Tel 313-961-0622
Mgr, Thomas R Schlientz
Estab 1965. 500,000 Titles. 500,000 Vols. 30,000 sq ft. Cat 24x ann
Types: Hb, out of print, old & rare, papbk, used
Subj: Autg, Civil War, Michiganiana

KSIEGARNIA LUDOWA PEOPLES BOOK STORE — General
5347 Chene St, 48211-2790. Tel 313-921-2479
Mgr, Florence Dombrowski; Buyer, John Zukowski; Papbk Buyer, Bill Pishalski; Text Buyer, Janice Street; Juv Buyer, Ursula Zaryszny; Juv Buyer, Keith Love
Estab 1920. 2000 Vols. 150 sq ft. Cat 3x ann
Types: Imp Pol, out of print, papbk, Pol lang
Subj: Rel-c

EAST LANSING — 48,309. Area code 517

CURIOUS BOOK SHOP — Antiquarian
307 E Grand River Ave, 48823. Tel 517-332-0112
Estab 1970. 65,000 Vols. 3700 sq ft. Cat 3x ann
Types: Fine bnd, 1st ed, hb, illus bk, juvenile, ltd ed, new & used, out of print, old & rare, papbk, remainders
Subj: Illus, Michiganiana, nostalgia, sci fiction & fantasy, mystery & detective, Amer
See Also: Argos Used Bookshop, Grand Rapids

BENJAMIN DE WIT BOOKSELLER — Mail Order
709 Lantern Hill Dr, 48823. Tel 517-351-2648 (by appt only)
Estab 1981. 25,000 Vols. 800 sq ft. Cat 6x ann
Types: Hb, out of print, papbk, used
Subj: Theol, philos, sci-tech, linguistics, bus & mgt, econ, scholarly lit, medieval studies, psychol, law, criminology, politics

EATON RAPIDS — 4510. Area code 517

ALBERT G CLEGG — Geology
PO Box 306, 48827-0306. Tel 517-663-8428
Estab 1962. 6000 Titles. 12,000 Vols. 500 sq ft. Cat 5x ann
Types: Hb, out of print, used
Subj: Hydrol, paleontology

FARMINGTON — 11,022. Area code 313

BOOKS ABOUND — General
33336 Grand River Ave, 48024. Tel 313-477-8777
Estab 1984. 25,000 Titles. 25,900 Vols. 1700 sq ft
Types: Out of print, hb, juvenile, old & rare, remainders, new & used

FARMINGTON HILLS — 58,056. Area code 313

GEORGE BARRY BOOKS — Antiquarian
31160 Orchard Lake Rd, 48018. Tel 313-737-8099
Estab 1988. 7500 Titles
Types: Facsimile editions, fine bnd, 1st ed, hb, incunab, illus bk, juvenile, ltd ed, old & rare, out of print, papbk, used
Subj: Illus

FERNDALE — 26,227. Area code 313

A-ALBIONIC RESEARCH — Mail Order
626 Flowerdale (Mail add: PO Box 20273, 48220). Tel 313-291-4028
Estab 1984. 200 Titles. 4000 Vols
Types: New, old & rare, out of print, remainders, used
Subj: Hist, biog of rich & powerful, conspiracy, assassination

FLUSHING — 8624. Area code 313

RICHARD C WERTZ BOOKSELLER — Used
3009 Pinehill, 48433. Tel 313-732-6976
Estab 1981. 4200 Titles. 4000 Vols. 200 sq ft. Cat
Types: Hb, out of print
Subj: Great Lakes, local authors, Michiganiana, military, travel, liberal rel

GRAND RAPIDS — 181,843. Area code 616

ARGOS USED BOOKSHOP — Used
1405 Robinson Rd SE, 49506. Tel 616-454-0111
Estab 1975. 22,500 Vols Buys through hq
Types: Hb, new & used, papbk, out of print
Subj: Nostalgia, sci fiction & fantasy

BAKER BOOK HOUSE — Religious-P
2768 E Paris Rd, PO Box 6287, 49506. Tel 616-957-3110
Mgr & Buyer, Gary Popma
Estab 1939. 50,000 Vols. Cat
Types: Hb, out of print, papbk, remainders, used
See Also: Grandville, Holland

KREGEL'S BOOKSTORE — Religious-P
525 Eastern Ave SE, PO Box 2607, 49501-2607. Tel 616-459-9444
Owner, Kregel, Inc; Pres, Robert L Kregel; Mgr & Buyer, Gary Courtright; Used Bk Buyer Kenneth L Kregel
Estab 1910. 100,000 Vols. 6000 sq ft. Cat 3x ann
Types: Hb, juvenile, new & used, out of print, papbk, remainders

MEMORY AISLE II — Antiquarian
1509 Lake Dr SE, 49506. Tel 616-456-5908
Assoc Dealer Frank Mercantante
Estab 1983. 15,000 Vols. 2400 sq ft. Cat
Types: Facsimile editions, fine bnd, 1st ed, hb, illus bk, juvenile, ltd ed, new, old & rare, out of print, papbk,

remainders, used
Subj: Western Amer, hunting & fishing, metaphysics, Michigan esp Grand Rapids

POOR RICHARD'S BOOKS — Mail Order-Antiquarian
PO Box 68032, 49516-8032. Tel 616-458-6337
Estab 1984. 500 Titles. 550 Vols. Cat ann
Types: Out of print, juvenile, hb, mass mkt papbk, new & used
Subj: Hist, folklore, Amer, colonial & early Am hist, living hist

TARDY'S C C INC — Comics
2009 Eastern Ave SE, 49507. Tel 616-247-7828
Mgr, Chris Alexander
Estab 1979. 10,000 Titles. 100,000 Vols. Cat
Types: New, out of print, comics
See Also: Kentwood

RICHARD WEIDERMAN — Mail Order
1259 Franklin SE, 49506. Tel 616-245-8812
Estab 1971. Cat 2x ann
Types: Facsimile editions, 1st ed, hb, new & used, out of print, papbk, old & rare, remainders
Subj: Jack London

GROSSE POINTE PARK — 13,639. Area code 313

JAMES A MONNIG BOOKSELLER — General
15133 Kercheval, 48230. Tel 313-331-2238
Estab 1975. 40,000 Titles. 50,000 Vols. 1600 sq ft
Types: Hb, juvenile, out of print

HARSENS ISLAND — Area code 313

JAMES M BABCOCK BOOKSELLER — Antiquarian
PO Box 160, 48028. Tel 313-748-9779
Estab 1973. 20,000 Vols. 800 sq ft. Cat 4x ann
Types: Facsimile editions, fine bnd, 1st ed, hb, incunab, illus bk, juvenile, ltd ed, old & rare, out of print
Subj: Am Indian studies, genealogy, Michiganiana

HILLSDALE — 7432. Area code 517

VOLUME I BOOKS & RECORDS — General
3 Union St, 49242. Tel 517-437-2228
23,000 Vols. 1200 sq ft
Types: Hb, out of print, papbk, remainders, used
Subj: Radical polit, women's studies

HOLLAND — 26,281. Area code 616

J E SHELDON FINE BOOKS — Antiquarian
1 E Eighth St, 49423. Tel 616-396-5542
Estab 1974. 8500 Vols. 1200 sq ft. Cat 3x ann
Types: 1st ed, hb, illus bk, juvenile, old & rare, out of print, used
Subj: Civil War, Michiganiana, A Conan Doyle

JACKSON — 39,739. Area code 517

BARGAIN BOOK SERVICE — General
1011 E McDevitt, 49203. Tel 517-782-8195
Estab 1979. 6000 Titles. 10,000 Vols. 2000 sq ft. Cat 12x ann
Types: Facsimile editions, fine bnd, 1st ed, hb, illus bk, imp, juvenile, new & used, papbk, out of print, old & rare
Subj: Fiction, health, medicine, rel

GEORGE TRAMP - BOOKS — Antiquarian
709 Second St, 49203. Tel 517-784-1057 (by appt)
Estab 1975. 25,000 Vols. 588 sq ft. Cat 4x ann
Types: Old & rare, out of print, used, hb, juvenile
Subj: Hist, natural hist, biog, anthrop, sci fiction & fantasy, rel, class studies, Latin Am, Arctic, black studies, Can, Michiganiana, poetry, Revolutionary & Civil War, ships & sea lit, German, Irish & England

KALAMAZOO — 79,722. Area code 616

BICENTENNIAL BOOKSHOP — Antiquarian
820 S Westnedge, 49008. Tel 616-345-5987
Estab 1975. 30,000 Vols. 3000 sq ft
Types: Hb, out of print, used
Subj: Golf, Amer

CALL ME ISHMAEL BOOKSTORE — Mail Order-Antiquarian
2425 Mt Olivet, 49004. Tel 616-344-2697
Estab 1977. 800 Titles. 800 Vols. Cat 4xann
Types: Used, out of print
Subj: Michiganiana, Great Lakes

OLD & RARE LITERATURE — Antiquarian
211 Woodward Ave, 49007. Tel 616-344-8869
Estab 1981. 1000 Vols
Types: 1st ed, illus bk, ltd ed, old & rare, out of print

KENTWOOD — 30,438. Area code 616

TARDY'S C C INC NO 2 — Comics
4301 Kalamazoo St, 49508. Tel 616-455-3380
Mgr, Kirby J Tardy
Types: Comics, out of print, new

LIVONIA — 104,814. Area code 313

THE OPEN BOOK — General
Wonderland Mall, 29661 Plymouth Rd, 48150. Tel 313-525-3530
Estab 1974. 4000 Vols
Types: Hb, juvenile, papbk, out of print

MARQUETTE — 23,288. Area code 906

SNOWBOUND BOOKS — Antiquarian-General
118 N Third St, 49855. Tel 906-228-4448
Estab 1984. 14,000 Titles. 18,250 Vols
Types: Used, 1st ed, hb, out of print, old & rare, used, papbk
Subj: Mining, sci fiction & fantasy, local hist, Michiganiana

MUSKEGON — 40,823. Area code 616

THE BOOK TRADER — Used
1347 Peck St, 49441. Tel 616-728-3181
Estab 1984. 30,000 Titles
Types: For lang, hb, imp, juvenile, out of print, mass mkt papbk, high priced papbk, facsimile editions, fine bnd, 1st ed, illus bk, ltd ed, old & rare, used

MUSKEGON HEIGHTS — 14,611. Area code 616

FIRST EDITION BOOKSTORE — General
7 Center St, 49444. Tel 616-733-2176
Estab 1979. 20,000 Vols. 2800 sq ft
Types: Hb, juvenile, out of print, papbk, remainders, new, used
Subj: Fiction, Great Lakes, Michiganiana

NILES — 13,115. Area code 616

CASPERSON BOOKS — General
1303 Niles-Buchanan Rd (Mail add: PO Box 634, 49120-0634). Tel 616-683-2888
Estab 1970. 50,000 Titles. 80,000 Vols. 2300 sq ft
Types: Fine bnd, hb, out of print, old & rare, papbk, used, antiquarian

OAK PARK — 31,537. Area code 313

YESTERDAY'S BOOKS — Antiquarian
25222 Greenfield Rd, 48237. Tel 313-968-1510
Estab 1980. 75,000 Vols. 1600 sq ft. Cat 4x ann
Types: Fine bnd, 1st ed, hb, illus bk, juvenile, ltd ed, old & rare, out of print, papbk, used
Subj: Sci fiction & fantasy, mod mystery, mod 1st ed

OKEMOS — 7770. Area code 517

EINER NISULA RARE BOOKS — Mail Order-Antiquarian
1931 Osage Dr, 48864. Tel 517-349-0495
Cat 4x ann
Types: 1st ed, fine bnd, incunab, illus bk, ltd ed, old & rare, out of print
Subj: Philos

PETOSKEY — 6097. Area code 616

BOOK STOP — Used
301 W Mitchell, 49770. Tel 616-347-4400
Estab 1975. 20,000 Vols
Types: Hb, juvenile, out of print, papbk

PONTIAC — 76,715. Area code 313

FORGOTTEN LORE — Mail Order-Antiquarian
670 E Mansfield, 48055
Types: Out of print, old & rare, facsimile editions, fine bnd, 1st ed

POTTERVILLE — 1502. Area code 517

DOWNEY-LEPCZY BOOK DEPT* — Mail Order-Numismatics
5586 Nixon, 48876. Tel 517-645-2150
Estab 1972. 4000 Vols. 1000 sq ft. Cat 2x ann
Types: For lang, used, old & rare, out of print
Subj: Coin bks

PULLMAN — Area code 616

RUSSIAN LANGUAGE SPECIALTIES — Russian Lang
PO Box 196, 49450. Tel 616-236-5880
Estab 1961. 3800 Titles. 50,000 Vols. Cat 6x ann
Types: Col text, hb, out of print, papbk, imp Russ

ROCHESTER — 7203. Area code 313

TREASURES FROM THE CASTLE — Mail Order-Antiquarian
1720 N Livernois, 48064. Tel 313-651-7317 (by appt)
Estab 1981. Cat 2x ann
Types: Juvenile, out of print

DALE WEBER BOOKS — Mail Order-Antiquarian
5740 Livernois, 48064. Tel 313-651-3177
Estab 1975. 1000 Vols. Cat 2x ann
Types: Facsimile editions, fine bnd, 1st ed, hb, ltd ed, out of print, old & rare
Subj: Poe, Churchill, Agatha Christie, Roycroft Press

ROYAL OAK — 70,893. Area code 313

METROPOLIS ART BOOKS — Art
1323 N Vermont, 48067. Tel 313-543-2872
Estab 1985. 4500 Titles. Cat 4x ann
Types: Out of print, old & rare
Subj: Fine arts, archit, photog, reference, decorative arts

SAGINAW — 77,508. Area code 517

CORA DUNCAN BOOKS — Antiquarian
1737 Gratiot Ave, 48602. Tel 517-790-1109
Types: Juvenile, out of print, hb, fine bnd, facsimile editions, 1st ed, illus bk, ltd ed, old & rare, used
Subj: Great Lakes, Michiganiana

SCOTTVILLE — 1241. Area code 616

WEST SHORE COMMUNITY COLLEGE CAMPUS BOOKSTORE — College
3000 N Stiles Rd (Mail add: PO Box 277, 49454). Tel 616-845-6211
Mgr & Buyer, Margaret Adamski
Estab 1970
Types: Hb, out of print, papbk, used, col text

SOUTHFIELD — 75,568. Area code 313

MUCH LOVED BOOKS — Antiquarian
PO Box 2005, 48037. Tel 313-355-2040
Estab 1978. 10,000 Vols. Cat
Types: Fine bnd, 1st ed, illus bk, ltd ed, out of print, old & rare, pvt presses
Subj: Amer, autg, bibliog, Michiganiana, New Jerseyana, New Yorkiana

STEVENSVILLE — 1268. Area code 616

BIBLIOTIQUES — General
7622 Red Arrow Hwy, 49127. Tel 616-465-5091
Estab 1965. 10,000 Titles
Types: Fine bnd, 1st ed, hb, illus bk, juvenile, ltd ed, old & rare, out of print, used
Subj: Amer, illus

SUTTONS BAY — 504. Area code 616

SUTTONS BAY BOOKSTORE — Antiquarian
100 A Cedar St, PO Box 669, 49682. Tel 616-271-3923
Types: Hb, juvenile, out of print, papbk, used
Subj: Michiganiana, Michigan authors, Hemingway

THREE OAKS — 1774. Area code 616

OLD MUSIC SHOP — Antiquarian-Music
208 Chicago, PO Box 3, 49128. Tel 616-756-9218
Estab 1960. 100,000 Vols. 1000 sq ft. Cat
Types: Old & rare, out of print

TRAVERSE CITY — 15,516. Area code 616

ARNOLD'S OF MICHIGAN — Antiquarian
511 S Union St, 49684. Tel 616-946-9212
Estab 1931. 40,000 Titles. Cat
Types: Fine bnd, 1st ed, out of print, used
Subj: Michiganiana, Great Lakes & regional Amer

HIGHWOOD BOOKSHOP — Antiquarian-Sports
Box 1246, 49685-1246. Tel 616-271-3898
Estab 1970. 15,000 Vols. 3000 sq ft. Cat 1-2x ann
Types: Hb, illus bk, ltd ed, old & rare, out of print
Subj: Hunting & fishing, dogs, guns

PENINSULA BOOKS — Mail Order-Antiquarian
323 W 11th St, 49684. Tel 616-941-8745
Estab 1985. 6000 Titles. 6000 Vols. Cat 4x ann
Types: Hb, old & rare, out of print, used
Subj: Michiganiana, Great Lakes

UTICA — 5282. Area code 313

THE PAPERBACK OUTLET — Paperback
52132 Van Dyke, 48087. Tel 313-731-6601
Mgrs, Joyce Lamoreau & Pat Franks
Estab 1980. 1500 Titles. 3000 Vols
Types: Mass mkt papbk, juvenile, hb, used, remainders, out of print, young adult, comics
Subj: Romance, nonfiction, fiction, mystery & detective, sci fiction & fantasy

WARREN — 161,134. Area code 313

EXNOWSKI ENTERPRISES — Mail Order-Antiquarian
31512 Reid Dr, 48092. Tel 313-264-1686
Estab 1971. 450 Vols. Cat quarterly
Types: Facsimile editions, 1st ed, hb, incunab, new & used, old & rare, pvt presses, out of print, high priced papbk, remainders, imp Poland, UK, Hungary, Ger, Jap & Neth
Subj: Amer, art, arts & crafts, bibliog, biog, Civil War, ethnic studies, hist, Michiganiana, reference, World Wars I & II, erotica, new age

WEST BLOOMFIELD — 41,962. Area code 313

BOOKPEOPLE — General
6399 Orchard Lake Rd, 48322. Tel 313-851-9150
Estab 1973. 30,000 Vols. 4000 sq ft
Types: Hb, juvenile, out of print, papbk, remainders
Subj: Art, cooking

WESTLAND — 84,603. Area code 313

PAPERBACKS & THINGS — Paperback
8044 N Wayne Rd, 48185. Tel 313-522-8018
Buyer, Robert J Adis; Merch Mgr, Theresa Farley
Estab 1984. 20,000 Titles. 20,000 Vols. 1500 sq ft. Cat
Types: For lang, hb, imp, juvenile, out of print, mass mkt papbk, new & used

YPSILANTI — 24,031. Area code 313

WEEKEND BOOKSHOP — Antiquarian-Americana
PO Box 464, 48197. Tel 313-482-1760 (by appt only)
Types: Hb, old & rare, out of print

O.P. Resources

ALBERT LEA — 19,190. Area code 507

THE CONSTANT READER — Used
238 S Broadway, 56007. Tel 507-373-6512
Estab 1988. 1400 sq ft
Types: Juvenile, hb, out of print, mass mkt papbk, remainders, new & used, high priced papbk
Subj: Romance, mystery & detective, how-to, hist, biog, fiction, nonfiction

ANOKA — 15,634. Area code 612

J & J O'DONOGHUE BOOKS — Juvenile
1926 Second Ave S, 55303. Tel 612-427-4320
Estab 1972. 25,000 Vols. 2000 sq ft
Types: Hb, juvenile, out of print, papbk, remainders, new & used
Subj: Fiction, mystery & detective, nonfiction, sci fiction & fantasy

BEMIDJI — 10,949. Area code 218

CATALYST BOOKSTORE — Antiquarian-General
403 America Ave NW, 56601. Tel 218-759-1402
Estab 1982. 15,000 Titles. 16,000 Vols. 750 sq ft
Types: Remainders, out of print, hb, papbk, used, 1st ed
Subj: Minnesotiana

DETROIT LAKES — 7106. Area code 218

DUANE JOHNSON BOOKSELLER — Used
107 Pioneer, 56501. Tel 218-847-2535
Types: Hb, out of print, col text, for lang, comics, juvenile
Subj: Rel, philos, soc sci, humanities, fiction, Irish hist & lit

DULUTH — 92,811. Area code 218

BIG LEAGUE GAME CO — Mail Order-Sports
321 E Superior St, 55802. Tel 218-722-1275
Estab 1968. 40,000 Vols. Cat 4x ann
Types: Hb, juvenile, new & used, out of print, papbk, remainders
Subj: Hist, military, sci fiction & fantasy, sports
Branches:
— WORLD BOOK
209 E Superior St, 55802
Estab 1975. 10,000 Vols. 2400 sq ft
Types: New, out of print, papbk, used

BOOKS BOUND — Used
2109 E Superior, 55812. Tel 218-722-1419
Estab 1987. 10,000 Titles. 10,000 Vols. 350 sq ft
Types: Juvenile, out of print, facsimile editions, fine bnd, 1st ed, hb, illus bk, ltd ed, old & rare

PAGE ONE — Antiquarian
Hwy 53, Orr, 55771. Tel 218-757-3907 (by appt only)
2000 Vols
Types: 1st ed, ltd ed, hb, juvenile, old & rare, out of print

EAGAN — 20,532. Area code 612

MICHAEL K KENNON OLD BOOKS & MAPS — Antiquarian-Minnesotiana
1741 Meadowlark Rd, 55122-1721. Tel 612-688-6690
Estab 1982. 600 Titles. Cat 6x ann
Types: Old & rare, out of print

EXCELSIOR — 2523. Area code 612

MELVIN MCCOSH BOOKSELLER — Mail Order-Antiquarian
26500 Edgewood Road, 55331. Tel 612-474-8084
Estab 1952. Cat
Types: 1st ed, hb, out of print, remainders, used
Subj: Bibliog, hist, literary criticism, philos

GRAND MARAIS — 1289. Area code 218

WALT CHADDE BOOKSELLER — Mail Order
Rte 3, Box 629, 55604. Tel 218-387-2220
Estab 1974. 25,000 Vols. 3600 sq ft. Cat 4x ann
Types: Hb, out of print, papbk, used
Subj: Fiction, lit, op fict

HUTCHINSON — 9244. Area code 612

B J BOOKSELLERS INC — General
1060 S R Hwy 15 S, 55350. Tel 612-587-7609
Estab 1986. 5000 Titles. 7500 Vols. 1320 sq ft
Types: Remainders, for lang, hb, juvenile, out of print, papbk, high priced papbk

MANKATO — 28,651. Area code 507

ONCE READ BOOK EXCHANGE — Used Paperback
629 S Front St, 56001. Tel 507-388-8144
Estab 1975. 5000 Vols
Types: Out of print
Subj: Minnesotiana

MINNEAPOLIS — 370,951. Area code 612

ARCH BOOKS — Antiquarian-Juvenile
5916 Drew Ave S, 55410. Tel 612-927-0298
Estab 1980. 30,000 Titles. 30,000 Vols
Types: 1st ed, hb, illus bk, old & rare, out of print, used, bibles, informational bks, series bks, anthologies, shape bks, coloring bks, pop-ups
Subj: Sci fiction & fantasy, mythology, poetry, biog, cooking, class studies, reference, fairy tales, fables, mod & hist fict, minority lit, animal stories, ABC bks, toys

BATTLEFIELD MILITARY ANTIQUES & BOOKSTORE — Military
1600-B W Lake St, 55408. Tel 612-823-3711
Mgr, Robert Johnson
Estab 1976. 5000 Titles. 10,000 Vols. Cat ann
Types: Fr lang, Ger lang, hb, used, out of print, papbk, Imports Europe & Australia
Subj: Aviation, mil, nav hist

BIERMAIER'S B H BOOKS — Antiquarian
809 SE Fourth St, 55414. Tel 612-378-0129
Owner, Biermaier & Hanson; Merch Mgr & Buyer, William Biermaier
Estab 1930. 100,000 Vols
Types: 1st ed, hb, juvenile, old & rare, out of print, papbk, used

THE BOOK HOUSE BOOKSELLERS — Antiquarian
429 SE 14th Ave, 55414. Tel 612-331-1430
Estab 1976. 100,000 Vols. Cat
Types: Hb, out of print, old & rare, used, scholarly
Subj: Hist, mythology, folklore, humanities, sci-tech, psychol, rel, philos

THE BOOK HOUSE IN DINKYTOWN — Antiquarian-Scholarly Lit
429 SE 14th Ave, 55414
Mgr, Jim Cummings Jr
Estab 1976. 100000 Titles. 3000 sq ft
Types: Old & rare, out of print
Subj: Scholarly lit

CALHOUN BOOKSTORE — Antiquarian
2645 Lyndale Ave S, 55408. Tel 612-871-1941
Estab 1950. 20,000 Titles. 30,000 Vols
Types: Hb, new & used, out of print, remainders, univ presses
Subj: Nonfiction

CHINA BOOK GALLERY — Mail Order-Antiquarian
PO Box 19324, 55419. Tel 612-926-6887
Estab 1978. 35,000 Titles. 40,000 Vols. 4200 sq ft. Cat 4x ann
Types: Hb, imp China, new, old & rare, out of print, papbk, remainders, used, serials
Subj: Chinese lang, China, Japan, SE Asia

DINKYTOWN ANTIQUARIAN BOOKSTORE — Antiquarian
1316 SE Fourth St, 55414. Tel 612-378-1286
Estab 1971. 30,000 Vols. 1800 sq ft. Cat 8x ann
Types: 1st ed, ltd ed, old & rare, out of print, papbk, remainders, used
Subj: Fine arts, belles lettres

DREAMHAVEN — Science Fiction & Fantasy
1300 Fourth St SE, 55414-2029. Tel 612-379-8924
Estab 1982. 6000 Titles. 20,000 Vols. Cat 4x ann
Types: 1st ed, illus bk, juvenile, out of print, old & rare, new & used, hb, papbk
Subj: Art, comedy, mystery & detective

ENIGMA BOOKSTORE — Antiquarian
307 SE Oak St, 55414. Tel 612-379-9472
Estab 1970. 20,000 Titles
Types: 1st ed, hb, ltd ed, new, old & rare, out of print, for lang
Subj: Medicine, art, reference

GREGORY C GAMRADT — Mail Order-Antiquarian
PO Box 22694, 55422. Tel 612-537-0359
Estab 1980. 3500 Titles. 4000 Vols. Cat 2-4x ann
Types: 1st ed, illus bk, new & used, old & rare, out of print, imp Fr, imp Ger, imp UK
Subj: China, Mongolia, Himalayas, Tibet, Japan

LIEN'S BOOK SHOP — Antiquarian
57 S Ninth St, 55402. Tel 612-332-7081
Buyer, Leland N Lien
Estab 1955. 50,000 Vols. Cat 4x ann
Types: Out of print, fine bnd, 1st ed, hb, incunab, illus bk, old & rare, used
Subj: Am hist & lit, Amer, Western Amer, European hist & lit

MINNEHAHA BOOKSTORE — Antiquarian
4901 39th Ave S, 55417. Tel 612-722-3630
Estab 1973. 12,000 Titles
Types: Out of print, hb
Subj: Hist, metaphys & occult, lit

UNCLE HUGO'S SCIENCE FICTION BOOKSTORE — Science Fiction & Fantasy
2864 Chicago Ave S, 55407. Tel 612-824-6347
Mgr, Scott Imes
Estab 1974. 6000 Vols. 2800 sq ft. Cat
Types: Hb, imp UK, juvenile, out of print, remainders, used, papbk

NORTHFIELD — 12,562. Area code 507

SEVEN GABLES BOOKS & ANTIQUES — Nature & Environment
313 Washington, 55057. Tel 507-645-8572
Estab 1984. 8000 Titles. Cat ann
Types: For lang, hb, juvenile, out of print, papbk, 1st ed, illus bk, old & rare, remainders, used
Subj: Dogs, cats, horses, nature & environ

RICHFIELD — 37,851. Area code 612

BOOKSTORE INC — Paperback
7332 Elliot Ave S, 55423. Tel 612-869-0549
Estab 1975. 12,000 Vols. 900 sq ft
Types: Out of print, remainders, used, new, juvenile
Subj: Mystery & detective, reference, sci fiction & fantasy

SAINT PAUL — 270,230. Area code 612

J A BAUMHOFER FINE BOOKS — Mail Order
PO Box 65493, 55165. Tel 612-698-7151
Types: 1st ed, hb, old & rare, out of print, used

BOOKSELLERS, ET AL — Antiquarian
167 Snelling Ave N, 55104. Tel 612-647-1471
Estab 1983. 75,000 Titles. 75,000 Vols. 4000 sq ft
Types: Facsimile editions, fine bnd, 1st ed, hb, illus bk, juvenile, ltd ed, new, old & rare, out of print, papbk, remainders, used
Subj: Rel, philos, films & filmmaking, hist

CURTIS BOOKS — Used
892 Rice St, 55117. Tel 612-488-4978
Mgr, Melissa Londroche; Merch Mgr, Andy Decker
Estab 1986. 25,000 Titles. 30,000 Vols. 600 sq ft
Types: For lang, hb, juvenile, out of print, papbk, remainders, col & el-hi text, used
Subj: Sci fiction & fantasy, Western Amer, rel studies, biog, warfare, mystery & detective, fiction

G R GOODMAN BOOKSELLER — Antiquarian
1209 Arcade St, 55106. Tel 612-778-1781
Estab 1982. 8000 Titles. 8000 Vols. 1000 sq ft. Cat 2x ann
Types: 1st ed, illus bk, new & used, hb, papbk, juvenile, remainders, old & rare, out of print
Subj: Amer, biog, Minnesotiana, World War II

GREEN LION BOOKS — Mail Order
2402 University Ave W, Suite 409, 55114. Tel 612-644-9070
Mgr & Buyer, Mark Goodman
Estab 1986. 40,000 Titles. 40,000 Vols. 1000 sq ft. Cat 3x ann
Types: New & used, papbk, hb, juvenile, mass mkt papbk, out of print, old & rare, 1st ed, vintage paperbk-pre-1960
Subj: Mystery & detective, sci fiction & fantasy, movies, tv, horror, general lit, westerns

HAROLD'S BOOKSHOP — Antiquarian
186 W Seventh St, 55102. Tel 612-222-4524
Estab 1949. 40,000 Titles. 40,000 Vols. 2500 sq ft
Types: 1st ed, hb, out of print, old & rare, used
Subj: Minnesotiana, mil hist, WW II

JAMES & MARY LAURIE BOOKSELLERS — Antiquarian
251 S Snelling, 55105. Tel 612-699-1114
Estab 1978. 20,000 Vols. Cat 6x ann
Types: 1st ed, small presses, ltd ed, old & rare, out of print, used
Subj: Am hist & lit, literary criticism, bibliog, bks on bks, typography

THE E M LOHMANN CO — Religious-C, P
89 E Seventh St, 55101. Tel 612-222-6801. WATS 800-792-1028, 328-1602, 792-1603
Mgr & Buyer, Stefan Czyzewski
Estab 1860. 8500 Vols. Cat ann
Types: Hb, imp, juvenile, out of print, papbk, remainders

LUTHER NORTHWESTERN SEMINARY BOOKSTORE — Religious-P
2375 Como Ave W, 55108. Tel 612-641-3440
Mgr, W Jennings Mergenthal; Asst Mgr, Terry Borhlkis
30,000 Vols
Types: Hb, juvenile, out of print, papbk, remainders, used, imp Belgium, Eng, Ger, Hong Kong, India, Jap, Neth, Swed, Switz, Fr, Afr, Isr, Can, Nor

MIDWAY BOOKSTORE INC — Antiquarian
1579 University Ave, 55104. Tel 612-644-7605
Pres, Thomas Stransky
Estab 1965
Types: 1st ed, juvenile, ltd ed, old & rare, out of print, comics, used, pulps
Subj: Hist, art, sci fiction & fantasy, photog

S & S BOOKS — Mail Order-Antiquarian
80 N Wilder, 55104-5895. Tel 612-645-5962
Estab 1971. 8000 Titles. 10,000 Vols. 600 sq ft. Cat
Types: 1st ed, hb, imp, juvenile, new & used, out of print, papbk, old & rare, remainders, ltd ed
Subj: Fiction, inspirational, metaphys & occult, mystery & detective, rel studies, sci fiction & fantasy, computer sci

TINSELTOWN TITLES — Used
167 N Snelling Ave N, 55104. Tel 612-647-1471
Estab 1983. 75,000 Titles. 2200 sq ft
Types: Out of print, used, fine bnd, ltd ed, hb, illus bk, juvenile, old & rare, papbk
Subj: Films & filmmaking, cooking, rel, Western Am, mil hist, true crime

SPRING GROVE — 1275. Area code 507

FIVE QUAIL BOOKS — Mail Order-Antiquarian
PO Box 278, 55974-0278. Tel 507-498-3346
Estab 1978. 5000 Vols. Cat 2-4x ann
Types: 1st ed, hb, illus bk, ltd ed, out of print, old & rare, used
Subj: Angling, Colorado River, Grand Canyon, Am deserts, Baja California, US govt publn pre 1900

STILLWATER — 12,290. Area code 612

JAMES CUMMINGS BOOKSELLERS — Antiquarian
303 N Fourth St, 55082. Tel 612-439-8944
Estab 1959. 50,000 Titles. 50,000 Vols. Cat 6x ann
Types: Hb, used, out of print
Subj: Folklore, diaries, literary criticism, bks on bks, biog, scholarly lit, 19th century Am lit, 18th cent Eng lit, novel as lit genre, festschriften

LOOME THEOLOGICAL BOOKSELLERS — Antiquarian-Theology
Old Swedish Covenant Church, 320 N Fourth St, 55082. Tel 612-430-1092
Types: Old & rare, out of print, 1st ed, fine bnd, facsimile editions, for lang, devotional, hymnals, liturgical texts
Subj: Theol, rel-c,p, philos, Catholic & Protestant religious biography, lives of the saints, ecclesiastical music, history & art

VIRGINIA — 11,056. Area code 218

DALE SEPPA BOOKSELLER — Antiquarian
103 Sixth Ave N, 55792. Tel 218-749-8108
Mgr, Carmen Arroyo
Estab 1979. 5000 Vols. 550 sq ft. Cat 4x ann
Types: Hb, imp, Sp lang, high priced papbk, new & used, remainders, old & rare, illus bk, facsimile editions, out of print
Subj: Hist, finance, numismatics, Latin Am, holocaust

BILOXI — 49,311. Area code 601

KINGS X STORE — Mail Order-Paperback
2803A Paso Rd, 39531. Tel 601-374-6632
Mgr & Buyer, Sharon Zocchi
Estab 1986. 1500 Titles. 1600 sq ft
Types: Papbk, mass mkt papbk, high priced papbk, used, imp Eng, Jap, Fr, imp Ger, imp Ital, out of print, hb, illus bk, imp, ltd ed, new, old & rare
Subj: Hist, sci fiction & fantasy

CARLISLE —Area code 601

JAMES A DILLON -BOOKS — Mail Order
Star Rte, Box 23, 39049. Tel 601-535-2946
Types: Out of print, papbk, high priced papbk, used
Subj: Civil War, Mississippi non-fiction, authors, poets & artists

JACKSON — 202,895. Area code 601

CHOCTAW BOOKS — Used
406 Manship St, 39202. Tel 601-352-7281
Mgr & Buyer, Fred C Smith
Estab 1982. 35,00 Titles. 38,000 Vols. Cat 2x ann
Types: 1st ed, hb, illus bk, juvenile, ltd ed, old & rare, out of print
Subj: Mississippiana, Civil War, mystery & detective, local authors, Amer

BOB LURATE DBA CARROB INC — Civil War
5455 Hartsdale Dr (Mail add: PO Box 13333, 39211). Tel 601-956-6487
Estab 1982. 1500 Titles. 1500 Vols. Cat quarterly
Types: Out of print, used, 1st ed
Subj: Virginiana, Southern Amer

NOUVEAU RARE BOOKS — Mail Order-Antiquarian
5005 Meadow Oaks Park Dr, PO Box 12471, 39236. Tel 601-956-9950 (by appt)
Estab 1981. 3700 Titles. 4500 Vols. Cat 4x ann
Types: Fine bnd, 1st ed, hb, imp, ltd ed, out of print, used
Subj: Poetry, drama, literary criticism, fiction, essays

STAR STORE — Comics
4212 N State St, 39206. Tel 601-362-8001
Mgr, Curtis L Collins
Estab 1978. 1400 sq ft Buys indep & through hq
Types: Out of print, used
Subj: Sci fiction & fantasy

MISSISSIPPI STATE — Area code 601

MISSISSIPPI STATE UNIVERSITY BOOKSTORE — College
Box BS, 39762. Tel 601-325-2244. Telex 5-3882
Dir, Steve Word
Estab 1965. 2000 Titles. Cat 2x ann
Types: Hb, imp, juvenile, out of print, papbk, remainders, used
Subj: Art

OCEAN SPRINGS — 14,504. Area code 601

SPANISH TRAIL BOOKS — Antiquarian
1006 Thorn Ave, 39564. Tel 601-875-1144
Estab 1985. 15,000 Vols
Types: 1st ed, hb, illus bk, imp, old & rare, out of print, used, comics, papbk
Subj: Hist, philos, mystery & detective, sci fiction & fantasy

TUPELO — 23,905. Area code 601

THE COTTAGE BOOKSHOP — Used
214 N Madison, 38801. Tel 601-844-1553
Estab 1984. 5000 Titles. 5000 Vols. 1200 sq ft
Types: Hb, out of print, fine bnd, 1st ed, illus bk, imp, juvenile, ltd ed, old & rare
Subj: Mississippiana, Civil War, hist, biog, Southern Lit, Mississippi authors

WISE OWL BOOKSTORE — General
2301 W Main, 38801. Tel 601-842-6500
Estab 1983. 24,000 Vols. 2200 sq ft
Types: Fr & Sp lang, hb, papbk, juvenile, out of print, remainders, col & el-hi text, new & used, facsimile editions, fine bnd, 1st ed, illus bk, imp, ltd ed, old & rare
Subj: Fiction

CARTHAGE — 11,104. Area code 417

MOSTLY BOOKS — Antiquarian
Garland Bldg, 328 Grant, 64836. Tel 417-358-7999
Estab 1978. 40,000 Titles. 40,000 Vols. 20,000 sq ft. Cat 6x ann
Types: Facsimile editions, fine bnd, 1st ed, hb, incunab, illus bk, imp, juvenile, ltd ed, old & rare, out of print, used
Subj: Western Amer, local hist

COLUMBIA — 62,061. Area code 314

ACORN BOOKSHOP — Used
211 S Ninth, 65201. Tel 314-449-8030
Estab 1986. 30,000 Titles. 32,000 Vols. 1200 sq ft
Types: Fr, Ger & Sp lang, hb, juvenile, mass mkt papbk, out of print, used, 1st ed, illus bk, old & rare

I C ADAMS — Used
16 N Glenwood, 65203. Tel 314-442-7989
Estab 1946. 40,000 Vols
Types: Hb, out of print, papbk

COLUMBIA BOOKS — Antiquarian
13 N 9th, PO Box 27, 65201. Tel 314-449-7417
Estab 1977. 25,000 Titles. 25,000 Vols. 1700 sq ft
Types: Facsimile editions, fine bnd, 1st ed, hb, illus bk, juvenile, ltd ed, old & rare, out of print, remainders, used
Subj: Art, mod lit, illus, scholarly

COLUMBIA COLLEGE BOOKSTORE — College
Eighth & Rogers, 65201. Tel 314-875-7340, 7341
Mgr, Norma Katt
Types: Hb, juvenile, out of print, papbk

DC BOOK SERVICE — Mail Order-Railroadiana
PO Box 122, 65205-0122. Tel 314-442-0001
Estab 1954. 750 Vols. Cat
Types: Hb, out of print, used
Subj: Western Amer, Missouriana

FLORISSANT — 55,372. Area code 314

BOOK BROKERS UNLIMITED — General
12 Paddock Hills Plaza, 63033. Tel 314-838-8111
Estab 1976. 27,000 Vols. 1600 sq ft. Cat ann
Types: Hb, juvenile, out of print, papbk, remainders, used
Subj: Computer sci, for lang

GREENWOOD — 1315. Area code 816

HENDERSON & PARK BOOKSHOP — Nature & Environment
500 Main, 64034-0303. Tel 816-537-6388
Estab 1942. 8500 Titles. 16,000 Vols. 1100 sq ft. Cat 4x ann
Types: Hb, new, out of print, old & rare, papbk
Subj: Natural hist, art, hunting & fishing, country living

HANNIBAL — 18,811. Area code 314

BECKY THATCHER BOOKS & GIFTS — Juvenile
209-211 Hill St, 63401. Tel 314-221-0822
Estab 1947. 1000 Titles. 8000 Vols. 600 sq ft
Types: Hb, out of print, papbk, remainders, used
Subj: How-to, Mark Twain

IRONTON — 1743. Area code 314

BOYCE MCCASLIN BOOKS — Mail Order-Used
HCR 69, Box 1580, 63650. Tel 314-546-7923
Estab 1977. 2000 Titles. 200 Vols
Types: Remainders, fine bnd, 1st ed, hb, illus bk, ltd ed, old & rare, out of print
Subj: Amer, Western Amer, illus, Twain, Faulkner

JOPLIN — 38,893. Area code 417

BOOK BARN — Used Paperback
1202 Main, 64801. Tel 417-782-2778
Estab 1980. 20,000 Vols. 1100 sq ft
Types: Hb, juvenile, out of print, papbk, used

MCDEE'S BOOKSTORE — Used
618 Jacksonon, 64801. Tel 417-782-1263
Mgr, JoAnn McDowell
Estab 1980. 40,000 Vols. 900 sq ft
Types: Col text, 1st ed, hb, juvenile, old & rare, out of print, papbk

KANSAS CITY — 448,159. Area code 816

CLINT'S BOOKS & COMICS — Comics
3943 Main St, PO Box 10275, 64111. Tel 816-561-2848
Mgr, Rick Jarvis
Estab 1967. 100,000 Vols. Cat
Types: Out of print, papbk, remainders
Subj: Sci fiction & fantasy
See Also: Overland Park, KS; Fort Worth, Hurst, Richardson, TX

GLENN BOOKS — Antiquarian
323 E 55th St, 64113. Tel 816-444-4447
Estab 1933. 10,000 Vols. 1200 sq ft. Cat
Types: Fine bnd, 1st ed, hb, incunab, illus bk, imp, ltd ed, old & rare, out of print, used
Subj: Antq, hist, scholarly lit, Western Amer, printing hist

KLAUS GRUNEWALD - BOOKDEALER — Antiquarian-General
807 W 87 Terrace, 64114. Tel 816-333-7799
20,000 Vols. Cat 20-30x ann
Types: Facsimile editions, fine bnd, 1st ed, hb, illus bk, juvenile, ltd ed, old & rare, out of print, remainders, used
Subj: Kansasana, Missouriana, philos, illus

THE MAGICK LANTERN — Metaphysics & Occult
1715 Westport Rd, 64111. Tel 816-531-7265
Estab 1984. 1500 Titles. 1400 sq ft
Types: Hb, imp UK, juvenile, out of print, mass mkt papbk, high priced papbk

RED BRIDGE BOOKS — General
230 W 75th St, 64114. Tel 816-523-1449
Estab 1976. 80,000 Titles. 80,000 Vols. 4200 sq ft
Types: Used, out of print, hb, illus bk, ltd ed
Subj: Fine arts, hist, lit

ROYAL BOOKSTORE — Paperback
206 E16, 64108. Tel 816-842-0291
Estab 1935. 50,000 Vols
Types: 1st ed, hb, juvenile, out of print, used, comics
Subj: Civil War, railroadiana, nostalgia

WESTPORT BOOKSTORE — Used
14 Westport Rd, 64111. Tel 816-931-9822
Estab 1968. 30,000 Titles
Types: Hb, juvenile, out of print, papbk
Subj: Art, sci fiction & fantasy, mystery & detective, hist, Amer, natural sci

WHISTLER'S BOOKS — General
427 Westport Rd, 64111. Tel 816-531-5959
Mgrs, Joann & Michael Chafee
Estab 1982. 20,000 Titles. 50,000 Vols. 2800 sq ft
Types: Col text, hb, juvenile, out of print, papbk, remainders, Fr, Ger & Sp lang
Subj: Archit, art, dance, music, philos, photog, poetry

O'FALLON — 8654. Area code 314

ROSE'S BOOKHOUSE — Paperback
411 Hwy 175, 63366. Tel 314-272-5857
Estab 1980. 40,000 Vols. 1600 sq ft
Types: Hb, juvenile, out of print, new & used
Subj: Cooking, fiction, health

OVERLAND — 19,620. Area code 314

ALCHEMIST SHOP — Metaphysics & Occult
2521 Woodson Rd, 63114. Tel 314-423-2711
Estab 1976. 1200 Vols. 1000 sq ft. Cat 2x ann
Types: Hb, imp, out of print, papbk, used
Subj: Astrol, magic & conjuring, philos, rel, herbology, witchcraft

SAINT LOUIS — 453,085. Area code 314

ADVENTURE BOOKS — Antiquarian-Juvenile
427 Graeser Rd, 63141. Tel 314-872-7783
Estab 1978. 4000 Vols
Types: Out of print, used
Subj: Irish hist & lit, nautical, Edgar Rice Burroughs

THE BOOK HOUSE — Antiquarian
9719 Manchester, Rock Hill, 63119. Tel 314-968-4491
Estab 1978. 35,000 Vols. 1500 sq ft
Types: Old & rare, hb, papbk, out of print, juvenile, used
Subj: Sci fiction & fantasy, natural hist, metaphysics

R DUNAWAY BOOKSELLER — Antiquarian
6138 Delmar Blvd, 63112. Tel 314-725-1581
Estab 1965. 50,000 Vols. 600 sq ft. Cat 10x ann
Types: Hb, remainders, fine bnd, 1st ed, illus bk, ltd ed, new, old & rare, out of print
Subj: Hist

ELIZABETH F DUNLAP BOOKS & MAPS — Mail Order
6063 Westminster Pl, 63112. Tel 314-863-5068
Estab 1955. 2000 Vols. Cat 2x ann
Types: Hb, out of print, old & rare, used
Subj: Western Amer, Missouriana, Illinoisiana, Amer, Abraham Lincoln

ANTHONY GARNETT - FINE BOOKS — Antiquarian
PO Box 4918, 63108. Tel 314-367-8080
Estab 1967. 25,000 Vols. Cat
Types: 1st ed, hb, illus bk, ltd ed, old & rare, out of print
Subj: Art, hist, philos, Eng lit 17th-20th century

FRANCIS T GUELKER BOOKSELLER — Antiquarian
9420 Mackenzie Circle Ct, 63123. Tel 314-544-4433
Estab 1978. 2500 Vols. 1000 sq ft
Types: Hb, 1st ed, hb, illus bk, imp, ltd ed, old & rare, out of print, used
Subj: Bks on bks, bookbindings, papermaking

D HALLORAN BOOKS — Antiquarian-Hunting & Fishing
7629 Wydown Blvd, 63105. Tel 314-863-1690
Estab 1976. 3000 Vols
Types: Fine bnd, 1st ed, hb, illus bk, juvenile, ltd ed, out of print, old & rare
Subj: Hunting & fishing

HIRSCHFELD GALLERIES INC — Used
234 N Euclid Ave, 63108. Tel 314-454-0500
Estab 1931. 10,000 Vols. 3000 sq ft
Types: Facsimile editions, fine bnd, 1st ed, hb, incunab, illus bk, imp, ltd ed, old & rare, out of print

Eugene M Hughes — Antiquarian
6518 Parkwood Pl, 63116
Estab 1978. 2000 Vols. Cat ann
Types: Out of print, used

READMORE BOOKS — Used
3607 Meramec St, 63116. Tel 314-352-3769
Estab 1978. 15,000 Vols
Types: Hb, juvenile, out of print, papbk

THE WEBSTER GROVES BOOKSHOP — General
100 W Lockwood, 63119. Tel 314-968-1185
Estab 1965. 30,000 Vols. 2600 sq ft. Cat ann
Types: Hb, juvenile, out of print, papbk, remainders
Subj: Antq, biog, cooking, nature & environ, juv

SPRINGFIELD — 133,116. Area code 417

ABC BOOKS — Antiquarian
2109J N Glenstone, 65803. Tel 417-831-3523
Estab 1961. 92,000 Vols
Types: 1st ed, fine bnd, hb, illus bk, juvenile, out of print, old & rare, remainders, used
Subj: Amer, Civil War, military, nostalgia, rel

ADDISON'S BOOKSTORE — Antiquarian
314 E Commercial, 65803. Tel 417-862-8460
Estab 1952. 20,000 Vols
Types: 1st ed, out of print, used, hb, old & rare, papbk
Subj: Biog, fiction, hist, rel, 1st ed Am & Eng novels & poetry

HOOKED ON BOOKS — Used
2756 S Campbell, 65807. Tel 417-882-3397
Estab 1984. 35,000 Titles. 50,000 Vols. 1600 sq ft
Types: Hb, juvenile, out of print, papbk, mass mkt papbk, used, fine bnd, 1st ed, illus bk, ltd ed, old & rare, remainders
Subj: Sci fiction & fantasy, hist, class studies, arts & crafts, cookbks

SHIRLEY'S OLD BOOKSHOP — Antiquarian
1950-V S Glenstone, 65804-2305. Tel 417-882-3734
Estab 1979.
Types: 1st ed, hb, illus bk, juvenile, ltd ed, old & rare, papbk, remainders, used, for lang, out of print

UNIVERSITY CITY — 42,738. Area code 314

A COLLECTOR'S BOOKSHOP — Used
6275 Delmar, 63130. Tel 314-721-6127
Estab 1987. 30,000 Vols
Types: Old & rare, out of print, fine bnd, 1st ed, hb, papbk, univ presses
Subj: Rel, local hist, art, hist, philos, entertainment

DELMAR BOOKSHOP — General
6273 Delmar, 63130. Tel 314-725-5640
Estab 1985. 25,000 Titles. 35,000 Vols. 1600 sq ft
Types: Used, remainders, high priced papbk, hb, imp, for lang, out of print, fine bnd, 1st ed, illus bk, old & rare
Subj: Class studies, hist, philos, sci fiction & fantasy, mystery & detective

WESTON —Area code 816

BOOKENDERS — General
517 Main, 64098-0279. Tel 816-386-5800
150,000 Titles. 200,000 Vols. 7000 sq ft. Cat ann
Types: 1st ed, hb, illus bk, juvenile, ltd ed, old & rare, out of print, used, fine bnd

MONTANA

ALBERTON — 368. Area code 406

MONTANA VALLEY BOOKSTORE — General
512 Railroad Ave, 59820. Tel 406-722-4950
Estab 1978. 50,000 Titles. 50,000 Vols. 5000 sq ft
Types: 1st ed, hb, imp, out of print, papbk, used

BILLINGS — 66,798. Area code 406

THE BOOK SHELF — Used
113 N 30th St, 59101. Tel 406-248-1850
Estab 1970. 20,000 Titles. 30,000 Vols
Types: Papbk, high priced papbk, 1st ed, new, out of print, juvenile, want lists, best sellers
Subj: Romance, mystery & detective, sci fiction & fantasy, nonfiction, adventure, westerns, horror

THOMAS MINCKLER ART & BOOKS — Antiquarian-Western Americana
2907 Second Ave N, 59101. Tel 406-245-2969
Estab 1977. 5000 Vols. Cat ann
Types: Fine bnd, 1st ed, hb, illus bk, ltd ed, old & rare, out of print, used
Subj: Montaniana, scholarly lit, Amer

BOZEMAN — 21,645. Area code 406

JANE GRAHAM TREASURED BOOKS FROM THE TREASURE STATE — Antiquarian-Western Americana
109 S Fourth Ave, 59715. Tel 406-586-7449
Estab 1975. 3200 Titles. 3800 Vols. 560 sq ft. Cat 4x ann
Types: Hb, out of print, old & rare, used
Subj: Montaniana, Western fict, Yellowstone Park

VARGO'S BOOKS — Antiquarian
One E Main, 59715. Tel 406-587-5383
Estab 1984. 30,000 Titles. 31,000 Vols
Types: Hb, out of print, papbk, used, 1st ed, juvenile, new & used, old & rare
Subj: Western Amer, Montaniana, hunting & fishing

HAVRE — 10,891. Area code 406

THE BOOKSTORE — General
301 Third Ave (Mail add: PO Box 31, 59501). Tel 406-265-7066
Estab 1985. 6000 Titles. 10,000 Vols. 2300 sq ft. Cat 2-3x ann
Types: Juvenile, hb, out of print, high priced papbk, papbk, remainders
Subj: Regional-west

HELENA — 23,938. Area code 406

BOOKS FROM YESTERDAY — Antiquarian
125 S Howie St & 1212 Cedar, PO Box 6, 59624-0006. Tel 406-442-3887, 442-7950
Mgr, Walter & Dorothy Coslet
Estab 1948. 1000 Vols
Types: Old & rare, out of print, bibles, new & used
Subj: Sci fiction & fantasy, gardening, rel

GOLDEN HILL ANTIQUARIAN BOOKS — Antiquarian
2119 Livingston, 56901. Tel 406-443-0678
Estab 1977. 2000 Titles. Cat 2x ann
Types: Out of print, 1st ed, hb, illus bk, juvenile, old & rare, used
Subj: Amer, Montaniana

THE MONTANA GALLERY & BOOKSHOPPE — Art Gallery
2301 Colonial Dr, 59601. Tel 406-442-3820
Estab 1971. 4000 Vols. Cat
Types: Hb, juvenile, out of print, papbk, remainders, used
Subj: Western Amer

KALISPELL — 10,648. Area code 406

BLACKTAIL MOUNTAIN BOOKS — Antiquarian
42 First Ave W, 59901. Tel 406-257-5573
Estab 1976. 50,000 Vols. 2000 sq ft. Cat 2x ann
Types: New & used, out of print
Subj: Montaniana, sports, big game hunting, firearms

MISSOULA — 33,388. Area code 406

BIRD'S NEST INC — Western Americana
219 N Higgins, PO Box 8809, 59807-8809. Tel 406-721-1125
Estab 1975. 45 Titles. 60,000 Vols. 3000 sq ft. Cat 2x ann
Types: Hb, out of print, old & rare, used, papbk
Subj: Montaniana, new Amer

THE BOOK EXCHANGE — Used
Holiday Village S/Ctr, 59801. Tel 406-728-6342
Mgr, Rebecca L Haddad
Estab 1979. 31,400 Vols. 1200 sq ft
Types: Fine bnd, 1st ed, hb, illus bk, imp, juvenile, ltd ed, new, old & rare, out of print, papbk, remainders
Subj: Montaniana, Northwest hist, Lewis & Clark
See Also: Spokane, WA

SIDNEY'S USED BOOKS — Used
518 S Fourth W, 59801. Tel 406-543-5343
5000 Vols. Cat 2x ann
Types: Hb, papbk, out of print
Subj: Montaniana, Western Amer, mod lit, humanities, liberal arts

PLAINS — 1116. Area code 406

DAVID A LAWYER BOOKSELLER — Used
Rte 2, Box 95, 59859-9706. Tel 406-826-3229
Merch Mgr, Stanley Noble; Buyer, Esther M Lawyer
Estab 1930. 250,000 Vols. 320 sq ft
Types: Hb, imp, out of print, papbk, remainders, col text
Subj: Sci-tech, Fr & Ger lang

AMES — Area code 402

RESEARCH UNLIMITED, BOOK DEPT — Western Americana
210 N Main St, 68621. Tel 402-721-8588
Buyer, J D Tainter
Estab 1965. 950 Titles. 15,000 Vols. Cat 2x ann
Types: Facsimile editions, hb, imp, out of print, papbk, remainders
Subj: Amer, biog, engineering, mining, prospecting, self-develop, treasure hunting, Western Amer, survival, dowsing

CHADRON — 5933. Area code 308

EAGLE BOOKSTORE — College
Chadron State College, Campus Ctr, 69337. Tel 308-432-2200
Mgr, Annette Dix; Asst Mgr, Kathy Phillips
14,000 Vols Buys indep
Types: Hb, juvenile, out of print, papbk, remainders, used
Subj: Art, music

FREMONT — 23,979. Area code 402

C NELSON BOOKS — Antiquarian-Mystery & Detective
2318 E Third, 68025. Tel 402-727-1727
Estab 1982. 250 Titles. 250 Vols. Cat 4x ann
Types: 1st ed, hb, old & rare, out of print, used
Subj: Fiction

GRAND ISLAND — 33,180. Area code 308

AISLE-LAND BOOKS — Used
1007 W Second, 68801. Tel 308-384-5575
Types: Out of print, hb, papbk, comics

KEARNEY — 21,158. Area code 308

COLLEGE BOOKSTORE & MARKET — College
Nebraskan Bldg, Kearney State College, 68849. Tel 308-234-3030
Mgr, Eric Fields
Estab 1958Buys indep
Types: Hb, juvenile, out of print, papbk, remainders, used

DONNA'S BOOK NOOK — Used
2215 Ave G, 68847. Tel 308-234-4044
Estab 1981. 33,000 Vols. 1600 sq ft
Types: Papbk, out of print, comics

LINCOLN — 171,932. Area code 402

BLUESTEM BOOKS — Antiquarian
712 O St, 68508. Tel 402-435-7120
Estab 1975. 25,000 Vols
Types: 1st ed, hb, old & rare, out of print, used
Subj: Nebraskana

J & L LEE BOOKSELLERS — General
East Park Plaza, 66th & O St (Mail add: PO Box 5575, 68505). Tel 402-467-4416
Juv Buyer, Linda Hillegass; Mgr, Terry Phillips
Estab 1969. 22,000 Titles. 2750 sq ft. Cat 2x ann
Types: For lang, hb, juvenile, out of print, papbk, remainders
Subj: Bus & mgt, cooking, gardening, psychol, sci fiction & fantasy, travel, nutrition

LONG'S BOOKSTORE — Used
1907 O St (Mail add: PO Box 81704, 68501-1704). Tel 402-474-4697
Estab 1914. 30,000 Vols
Types: Hb, out of print, papbk, old & rare, el-hi text
Subj: Western Amer, Nebraskana

OMAHA — 311,681. Area code 402

THE ANTIQUARIUM — Antiquarian
1215 Harney St, 68102. Tel 402-341-8077
Estab 1969. 350,000 Vols. 25,000 sq ft. Cat
Types: 1st ed, hb, illus bk, ltd ed, old & rare, out of print, papbk, used
Subj: Am hist & lit, Amer, medicine, psychol

DICKEY BOOKS — Antiquarian
2104 S 135th St, 68144-2406. Tel 402-330-3256
Estab 1981. 10,000 Vols. 900 sq ft. Cat 2x ann
Types: 1st ed, hb, out of print, old & rare, remainders, used
Subj: Philos, genealogy, 20th century Amer poetry & fiction

D N DUPLEY BOOK DEALER — Mail Order-Antiquarian
9118 Pauline St, 68124. Tel 402-393-2906
Estab 1964. 4000 Vols
Types: Hb, old & rare, out of print, used
Subj: Western Amer, Nebraskana

PERU — 998. Area code 402

BOBCAT BOOKSTORE — College
Student Ctr, Peru State College, 68421. Tel 402-872-3815, Ext 254
Owner, Peru State Advancement, Inc; Mgr, Christina Joy
100 Titles. 60 Vols
Types: Hb, juvenile, out of print, papbk, remainders, used

SOUTH SIOUX CITY — 9339. Area code 402

BOOK BARN — Mail Order-Antiquarian
RR 1 Box 304-H, 68776
Estab 1977. 60,000 Vols
Types: Illus bk, juvenile, out of print, old & rare, used, mag
Subj: Art, archit, auto, autg, Civil War, music, poetry, travel, Western Amer, cooking, geol, gardening, mystery & detective, magic & conjuring, Amer, fashion, photog, Indians, mil foreign countries, animals, med, stocks & bonds

SYRACUSE — 1638. Area code 402

WORDSMITH STORES — Antiquarian-Nebraskana
495 Midland St, 68446. Tel 402-269-2991
Estab 1982. 15,000 Titles. 15,000 Vols. 2000 sq ft. Cat 10x ann
Types: 1st ed, hb, juvenile, old & rare, out of print, new & used
Subj: Nebraskana, Western Amer, Nebraska authors, original art

NEVADA

LAS VEGAS — 164,674. Area code 702

AMBER UNICORN — Antiquarian
2202 W Charleston Blvd, Suite 2, 89102. Tel 702-384-5838
Estab 1981. 48,000 Titles. 47,000 Vols. 2550 sq ft. Cat 2-4x ann
Types: Facsimile editions, fine bnd, 1st ed, hb, illus bk, juvenile, ltd ed, old & rare, out of print, used, new, cookbooks, new age
Subj: Nonfiction, sci fiction & fantasy, Western Amer, metaphys & occult

K APPEL - BOOKS — Judaica
PO Box 85003, 89185
Estab 1979. 4000 Vols
Types: Imp Isr, out of print, mass mkt papbk, used, Ger lang, Hebr lang
Subj: Bibliog, Hebraica

BOOK STOP III — Antiquarian-General
1440 E Charleston Blvd, 89104. Tel 702-386-4858
Estab 1973. 1200 sq ft
Types: 1st ed, hb, illus bk, juvenile, ltd ed, old & rare, out of print, papbk, used
Subj: Metaphys & occult, psychol, sci fiction & fantasy, classical lit

BOOK TRADERS — General
4180 S Sandhill Rd, B6, 89121. Tel 702-454-3212
Types: Hb, papbk, out of print

M F DUFFY BOOKS — Antiquarian-Americana
6650 W Flamingo Rd, 89103. Tel 702-365-6862
Types: 1st ed, old & rare, out of print
Subj: Am biog, western bks

GAMBLER'S BOOK CLUB — Gambling
630 S 11th St (Mail add: PO Box 4115, 89127). Tel 702-382-7555. WATS 800-634-6243
Dir, Howard Schwartz
Estab 1971. 900 Titles. 50,000 Vols. 6600 sq ft. Cat ann
Types: Hb, imp, out of print, papbk, remainders, col text, used
Subj: Biog, games, how-to, psychol, sports

GAMBLER'S GENERAL STORE — Gambling
800 S Main St, 89101. Tel 702-382-9903. WATS 800-322-2447. FAX 702-366-0329
Estab 1986. 700 Titles. 10,000 Vols. 2000 sq ft. Cat ann
Types: Hb, 1st ed, new, out of print, papbk, remainders, used

NOVEL IDEA — Used
6680 W Flamingo No 10 (Mail add: PO Box 80153, Flamingo Plaza, 89180-0153). Tel 702-873-2665
Estab 1988. 15,000 Titles. 975 sq ft
Types: Hb, juvenile, out of print, high priced papbk, mass mkt papbk only, text bks, new & used
Subj: Romance, Western Amer, mystery & detective, sci fiction & fantasy

SOLOMON GUNDY'S BOOK WORLD — General
1442 E Charleston Blvd, 89104. Tel 702-385-6043
Estab 1978. 10,000 Vols. 1600 sq ft
Types: Out of print, papbk, used, for lang, hb, juvenile

RENO — 100,756. Area code 702

PAPERBACK EXCHANGE — Used Paperback
131 Vesta, 89502. Tel 702-322-8822
Estab 1974. 70,000 Vols. 1400 sq ft
Types: Out of print, mass mkt papbk, used, large print

SPARKS — 40,780. Area code 702

THE BOOK GALLERY — General
1203 N Rock Blvd, 89431. Tel 702-356-8900
Mgr, Dianne Custer
Estab 1988. 20000 Titles. 21000 Vols. 1000 sq ft
Types: Hb, papbk, juvenile, for lang, imp, out of print, remainders, text bks, used, facsimile editions, fine bnd, old & rare, 1st ed
Subj: Metaphysics, geol, Nevadiana

ANDOVER — 1587. Area code 603

CILLEYVILLE BOOKSTORE — General
PO Box 127 Rte 11, 03216. Tel 603-735-5667
Estab 1977. 45,000 Vols
Types: Imp Fr, imp Ger, imp Sp, imp Ital, juvenile, out of print, papbk, col & el-hi text, used, 1st ed, illus bk, old & rare

ASHLAND — 1807. Area code 603

BUMP'S BARN BOOKSHOP — Mail Order-Antiquarian
23 Depot St, Box 531, 03217. Tel 603-968-3354
Estab 1958. 10,000 Vols. 2000 sq ft. Cat ann
Types: Hb, mag & newspr, out of print, papbk, used
Subj: Hypnosis, metaphys & occult, photog, health, dolls, macrobiotics

BRADFORD — 1115. Area code 603

KALONBOOKS — Antiquarian
Rte 114, Box 16, 03221. Tel 603-938-2380
Estab 1977. 8000 Titles. 11,000 Vols
Types: Out of print, remainders, used, papbk
Subj: Am hist & lit, sci fiction & fantasy

CANTERBURY — 1410. Area code 603

CRABTREE'S COLLECTION — Nature & Environment
310 Baptist Rd, 03224. Tel 603-783-9394
Estab 1983. 6000 Titles. 6000 Vols. Cat
Types: Juvenile, out of print, used, 1st ed, old & rare
Subj: Hunting & fishing

CONCORD — 30,400. Area code 603

APPLE TREE BOOK SHOP — General
24 Warren St, 03301. Tel 603-228-8451
Estab 1927. 5000 Titles. 10,000 Vols
Types: Hb, juvenile, out of print, papbk, remainders

THE BOOK BIN — Mail Order
4 Roger Ave, 03301. Tel 603-224-5609
Mgrs, Dot & Jim O'Neill
Estab 1967. 5000 Vols
Types: Hb, out of print, used
Subj: New England, New Hampshireana, early fiction

THE OLD ALMANACK SHOP — Mail Order-Antiquarian
5 S State St, 03301. Tel 603-225-5411
Estab 1975. 8500 Titles. 8500 Vols
Types: Facsimile editions, fine bnd, 1st ed, hb, illus bk, juvenile, ltd ed, old & rare, out of print, papbk, used
Subj: Hist, art, natural hist, science

CONTOOCOOK — Area code 603

CHURCHILL BOOKS — Mail Order-Antiquarian
Burrage Rd RFD No 1, 03229. Tel 603-746-5606
Estab 1981. 350 Titles. 1000 Vols. 300 sq ft. Cat 3x ann
Types: Facsimile editions, fine bnd, 1st ed, illus bk, hb, imp UK, ltd ed, new, old & rare, out of print, papbk, used
Subj: Sir Winston Churchill

EMERY'S BOOK AUCTIONS — Mail Order-Antiquarian
Rte 2, Duston Rd, 03229. Tel 603-746-5787
Estab 1975. 5000 Vols. Cat 2-4x ann
Types: Facsimile editions, fine bnd, 1st ed, hb, illus bk, juvenile, ltd ed, old & rare, out of print, used
Subj: Amer, art, Eng hist & lit, sci-tech, travel, bks before 1800

CONWAY — 7158. Area code 603

LA TIENDA EL QUETZAL — Mail Order-Antiquarian
PO Box 298, 03818-0298. Tel 603-447-5584
Estab 1977. 300 Titles. 1500 Vols. 150 sq ft. Cat
Types: Facsimile editions, 1st ed, hb, illus bk, imp, new, old & rare, out of print, papbk, used
Subj: William Walker

DERRY — 18,875. Area code 603

BERT BABCOCK - BOOKSELLER — Mail Order-Antiquarian
9 E Derry Rd (Mail add: PO Box 1140, 03038). Tel 603-432-9142
Estab 1976. 4000 Titles. 6000 Vols. 1200 sq ft. Cat 10x ann
Types: 1st ed, hb, imp, ltd ed, new & used, old & rare, out of print
Subj: Fiction, poetry

DOVER — 20,377. Area code 603

M H LACY CO-DBA LACY'S LINES & LYRICS — General
436 Central Ave, 03820. Tel 603-742-2775
Mgr, Alan Gluck; Merch Mgr & Buyer, Lisa Morin
Estab 1986. 14,000 Titles. 30,000 Vols. 3600 sq ft
Types: For lang, hb, juvenile, out of print, papbk, mass mkt papbk

EXETER — 11,024. Area code 603

A THOUSAND WORDS — General
65 Water St, 03833. Tel 603-778-1991
Estab 1985. 4000 Titles. 4000 Vols. 1000 sq ft
Types: Juvenile, out of print, remainders, used, wholesale used
Subj: Mountains, Western Amer, hist, natural & physical sci

COLOPHON BOOKSHOP — Antiquarian
117 Water St, 03833. Tel 603-772-8443
Estab 1971
Types: Hb, used, out of print, 1st ed
Subj: Biog, bks on bks, 19th & 20th century Am & Eng lit

EXETER OLD BOOK BARN — Antiquarian
200 High St, 03833. Tel 603-772-8356
Estab 1984. 3000 Titles. 3000 Vols. Cat 6x ann
Types: Fine bnd, 1st ed, hb, ltd ed, old & rare, out of print, remainders, used
Subj: Gardening, Scotland

LANDSCAPE BOOKS — Mail Order-Antiquarian
PO Box 483, 03833. Tel 603-964-9333
Estab 1972. 2000 Titles. 3000 Vols. Cat 2x ann
Types: Hb, imp, new & used, out of print, old & rare, remainders
Subj: Gardening, archit, landscape archit

FARMINGTON — 4630. Area code 603

THE BOOKERY — Antiquarian
62 N Main St, 03835. Tel 603-755-4471
Estab 1975. 5000 Titles. 5000 Vols. 4500 sq ft. Cat
Types: Hb, out of print, 1st ed, new & used
Subj: Biog, hist, Amer, nonfiction, military

FRANCESTOWN — 830. Area code 603

THE TYPOGRAPHEUM BOOKSHOP — Mail Order-Antiquarian
Bennington Rd, 03043
Estab 1976. 3000 Titles. Cat 4x ann
Types: 1st ed, fine bnd, ltd ed, old & rare, out of print, pvt presses

GOSHEN — 549. Area code 603

AND USED BOOKS — Used
Brook Rd (Mail add: RR 2 Box 212, Newport, 03773). Tel 603-863-4394
Estab 1974. 25,000 Titles. 25,000 Vols
Types: Juvenile, out of print, papbk, remainders, used
Subj: Arts & crafts, illus, New England

NELSON CRAFTS & USED BOOKS — Used
Brook Rd (Mail add: RR 2 Box 212, Newport, 03773). Tel 603-863-4394
Estab 1973. 25,000 Titles. 25,000 Vols
Types: 1st ed, hb, illus bk, juvenile, old & rare, out of print, papbk, remainders

GREENLAND — 2129. Area code 603

WILLIAM J THOMPSON ANTIQUARIAN BOOKSELLER — Used
10 Tide Mill Rd, 03840. Tel 603-431-2369
4000 Titles. 4000 Vols. 200 sq ft
Types: Used, out of print
Subj: Amer, Civil War, natural hist, nonfiction, sporting

HENNIKER — 3246. Area code 603

BOOK FARM — Antiquarian
Concord Rd, Box 515, 03242. Tel 603-428-3429
Estab 1970. 30,000 Vols. Cat 6x ann
Types: 1st ed, hb, out of print, old & rare, remainders, used
Subj: Amer, biog, class studies, New England, poetry, lit

HOPKINTON — 3861. Area code 603

WOMEN'S WORDS BOOKS — Antiquarian
R R 4, Box 322, 03229. Tel 603-228-8000
Estab 1977. 3000 Vols. Cat 4x ann
Types: 1st ed, hb, illus bk, ltd ed, old & rare, out of print, papbk, remainders, used
Subj: Feminism, metaphysics, women's studies

JAFFREY — 4349. Area code 603

JAFFREY BIBLE HOUSE — Religious
Silver Ranch (Mail add: PO Box 475, 03452-0475). Tel 603-532-7297
Estab 1960. 2500 Vols
Types: Bibles, hb, juvenile, out of print, papbk

JAFFREY CENTER — Area code 603

R B STEPHENSON - BOOKS — Antiquarian-Travel
Box 67, 03454-0067. Tel 603-532-6066
Estab 1969. 10,000 Titles. 1000 sq ft. Cat
Types: 1st ed, hb, used, out of print, old & rare
Subj: Local & nat'l hist

LACONIA — 15,571. Area code 603

LEE BURT BARN LOFT BOOKSHOP — Antiquarian
96 Woodland Ave, 03246. Tel 603-524-4839
Estab 1978. 8000 Titles. 8000 Vols
Types: 1st ed, hb, illus bk, juvenile, out of print, used
Subj: New England, local hist

LANCASTER — 3401. Area code 603

ELM STREET & STOLCRAFT NEW BOOKS USED — General
20 Elm St, 03584. Tel 603-788-4844
Estab 1983. 100,000 Titles. 150,000 Vols. 1500 sq ft
Types: For lang, hb, imp, juvenile, out of print, mass mkt papbk, papbk, used, facsimile editions, fine bnd, 1st ed, illus bk, ltd ed, new, old & rare, remainders
Subj: Hist

LITTLETON — 5558. Area code 603

ANDY'S BOOK SHOP INC — Used
78 Main St, 03561. Tel 603-444-7740
Estab 1986. 12,000 Titles. 12,000 Vols. 750 sq ft. Cat 2x ann
Types: Juvenile, hb, out of print, mass mkt papbk, used, fine bnd, 1st ed, illus bk, ltd ed, old & rare
Subj: Geol, mineralogy, New Hampshireana, white mountains

MANCHESTER — 90,936. Area code 603

LAURIAT'S INC — General
1000 Elm St, 03105. Tel 603-669-2273
Mgr, John Angeb Buys through hq
Types: Hb, out of print, papbk, remainders

MARLBOROUGH — 1846. Area code 603

HOMESTEAD BOOKSHOP — Used
Rte 101, E Main St (Mail add: PO Box 90, 03455). Tel 603-876-4213
Estab 1970. 45,000 Vols. 1500 sq ft. Cat
Types: 1st ed, hb, illus bk, juvenile, ltd ed, old & rare, out of print, papbk
Subj: Fiction

MEREDITH — 4646. Area code 603

MARY ROBERTSON, BOOKS — Used
US Rte 3, PO Box 296, 03253. Tel 603-279-8750
Estab 1981
Types: Hb, high priced papbk, juvenile, out of print, remainders
Subj: Antq, art, arts & crafts, cooking, gardening, nature & environ, regional Amer

MERIDEN — 300. Area code 603

1791 HOUSE BOOKS — Mail Order-Antiquarian
Main St, P O Box 115, 03770. Tel 603-469-3636
Estab 1982. 30,000 Titles. 30,000 Vols. 1200 sq ft. Cat
Types: Facsimile editions, fine bnd, 1st ed, hb, incunab, illus bk, juvenile, old & rare, out of print, used
Subj: Photog, baseball, British Royalty, Lewis & Clarke expedition

NASHUA — 67,865. Area code 603

PAUL HENDERSON BOOKS — Antiquarian
50 Berkeley St, 03060. Tel 603-883-8918
Cat ann
Types: Old & rare, out of print
Subj: Genealogy, local hist

NEWINGTON — 716. Area code 603

LAURIAT'S INC — General
Fox Run Mall, 03801. Tel 603-431-1918
Mgr, Janice Cunningham
Cat annBuys through hq
Types: Hb, out of print, papbk, remainders

PETERBOROUGH — 4895. Area code 603

CALLAHAN & CO BOOKSELLERS — Antiquarian
Box 505, 03458. Tel 603-924-3726
Cat 6x ann
Types: Out of print, old & rare
Subj: Hunting & fishing, natural hist

THE TOADSTOOL INC, A BOOKSHOP — General
Three Main St, 03458. Tel 603-924-3543
Buyer, Willard Williams
Estab 1972. 20,000 Titles. 40,000 Vols. 1500 sq ft
Types: Hb, juvenile, out of print, papbk, remainders
See Also: Keene

PIKE — area code 603

THE BRASS HAT — Military
Cutting Hill Rd, RR2 Box 197A, 03780. Tel 603-989-5697
Estab 1975. 5000 Titles. 10,000 Vols. 1200 sq ft. Cat 4 ann
Types: Out of print, used
Subj: Military hist

PORTSMOUTH — 26,254. Area code 603

THE ANTIQUARIAN BOOKSTORE — Antiquarian-General
1070 Lafayette Rd, 03801. Tel 603-436-7250
Estab 1973. 100,000 Vols
Types: Out of print, old & rare
Subj: Erotica

BOOK GUILD OF PORTSMOUTH — Antiquarian
58 State St, 03801. Tel 603-436-1758
Mgr, Doug Robertson
Estab 1982. 20,000 Titles. 25,000 Vols. Cat 4x ann
Types: Fine bnd, 1st ed, hb, illus bk, juvenile, ltd ed, old & rare, out of print, used
Subj: New England, maritime

NEW ENGLAND LIT — New England
58 Ceres St, 03801. Tel 603-436-2278
Estab 1987. 2500 Titles. 3500 Vols. 510 sq ft
Types: Hb, imp, imp UK, juvenile, out of print, papbk, high priced papbk, mass mkt papbk, remainders, imp Can

RICHMOND — 518. Area code 603

NORTH COUNTRY BOOKSHOP — Antiquarian
Rte 119 (Mail add: RFD 3, Four Corners, 03470). Tel 603-239-6547
Estab 1981. 540 sq ft. Cat ann
Types: Facsimile editions, fine bnd, 1st ed, illus bk, ltd ed, hb, new & used, old & rare, out of print, imp, juvenile, 1st ed papbk, softbound op
Subj: Sci-tech, biog, Amer, railroadiana, nautical, theol, military, polit, foreign

STODDARD — 482. Area code 603

THE BOOKMAN OF ARCADY — Mail Order-Search Service
HCR 32, Box 501, 03464-9701
Estab 1980. 900 Titles. 1000 Vols
Types: Fine bnd, 1st ed, hb, ltd ed, out of print
Subj: Poetry, fine press

STRATHAM — 2507. Area code 603

ABBOTT & ABBOTT BOOKS — Mail Order-Used
58 River Rd, 03885. Tel 603-772-4464
3000 Titles. 3000 Vols
Types: Hb, out of print, used, 1st ed, new, old & rare, out of print
Subj: Aviation, natural hist, birds

WEARE — 3232. Area code 603

SYKES & FLANDERS ANTIQUARIAN BOOKSELLERS — Antiquarian
Rte 77 N, PO Box 86, 03281. Tel 603-529-7432
Estab 1975. 5000 Vols. Cat 4x ann
Types: Out of print, old & rare, 1st ed
Subj: Amer, discovery & explor, illus, mystery & detective, travel, New Hampshireana, white mountains

WESTMORELAND — 1452. Area code 603

HURLEY BOOKS — Antiquarian-Agriculture
Rte 12, RR 1, Box 160, 03467-9736. Tel 603-399-4342
Estab 1966. 10,000 Titles. 25,000 Vols. Cat 6x ann
Types: 1st ed, out of print, old & rare, used
Subj: Amer, gardening, theol

NEW JERSEY

ASBURY PARK — 17,015. Area code 201

WHITE'S GALLERIES INC, BOOK DEPT — General
607 Lake Ave, 07712. Tel 201-774-9300, 531-4535
Estab 1967. 100,000 Titles. 150,000 Vols
Types: New & used, old & rare, hb, papbk, out of print, 1st ed
Subj: New Jerseyana, Amer, music, biog, rel, fiction

ATLANTIC CITY — 40,199. Area code 609

PRINCETON ANTIQUES BOOKSERVICE — Mail Order
2915-17-31 Atlantic Ave, 08401-6395. Tel 609-344-1943
Estab 1974. 175,000 Titles
Types: Out of print
Subj: Antq, art, sci-tech

BERKELEY HEIGHTS — 12,549. Area code 201

PAPER & INK BOOKSHOP — Mail Order-Antiquarian
44 Beech Ave, 07922
1000 Vols. Cat
Types: Hb, old & rare, out of print
Subj: New Jersey Hist, Eastern Amer

BRIELLE — 4068. Area code 201

THE ESCARGOT USED BOOK SHOP — Used
503 Rte 71, 08730. Tel 201-528-5955
Mgr, Richard S Weiner
25,000 Vols
Types: Out of print

CHERRY HILL — 64,395. Area code 609

CANEY BOOKSELLERS — Mail Order-Used
PO Box 4435, Suite 600, 08034. Tel 609-424-0888
3000 Titles. 3000 Vols. Cat quarterly
Types: Out of print, old & rare, 1st ed, hb, ltd ed, illus bk
Subj: Photog, mod lit

COLLINGSWOOD — 15,838. Area code 609

BETWEEN THE COVERS — Mail Order-Antiquarian
575 Collings Ave, 08107. Tel 609-869-0512
Estab 1986. 20,000 Titles. 20,000 Vols. 1000 sq ft. Cat 6x ann
Types: Used, out of print, fine bnd, 1st ed, hb, illus bk, imp, juvenile, ltd ed, old & rare
Subj: Fine arts, photog, Am hist & lit, Eng hist & lit, mystery & detective, sci fiction & fantasy

CRANBURY — 1927. Area code 609

CRANBURY BOOK WORM — Used
54 N Main, 08512. Tel 609-655-3815
Estab 1974. 80,000 Vols. 28,000 sq ft
Types: Out of print

CRANFORD — 24,573. Area code 201

CRANFORD ANTIQUE BOOK-SELLERS — Antiquarian-Juvenile
9 Columbia Ave, 07016. Tel 201-272-3999
Estab 1965. 4000 Vols. 5000 sq ft
Types: 1st ed, illus bk, juvenile, ltd ed, old & rare, out of print
Subj: New Jerseyana

CRESSKILL — 7609. Area code 201

VERONICA K RONYETS BOOKS — Mail Order-Antiquarian
300 County Rd, 07626. Tel 201-894-1836
Estab 1963. 3000 Vols. 8500 sq ft
Types: Fine bnd, 1st ed, for lang, hb, illus bk, imp, juvenile, ltd ed, new & used, old & rare, out of print, remainders
Subj: Poetry, antq, collecting, bks on bks

DOVER — 14,681. Area code 201

LEO LOEWENTHAL — Mail Order
PO Box 938, 07801-0938. Tel 201-328-7196
5000 Titles. Cat
Types: Hb, out of print
Subj: Archit, art, dance, films & filmmaking, performing arts, photog, poetry, cooking

EAST ORANGE — 77,025. Area code 201

THOMAS KELLY* — Antiquarian
227 Midland Ave, 07017. Tel 201-746-7884
Estab 1950. 100,000 Vols
Types: Hb, out of print
Subj: Art, biog, hist

EDISON — 70,193. Area code 201

EDISON HALL BOOKS — Mail Order-Antiquarian
Five Ventnor Dr, 08820. Tel 201-548-4455
10,000 Titles. 10,000 Vols. Cat
Types: Fine bnd, 1st ed, hb, illus bk, imp Ger, imp UK, juvenile, ltd ed, old & rare, out of print, papbk, used, bibles
Subj: Fiction, New Yorkiana, New Jerseyana, Amer, biog, metaphys & occult, educ, illus, teacher preparation, westerns, UFO's, Thomas A Edison, Tarzan, Kerouac, children's art

EGG HARBOR CITY — 4618. Area code 609

EGG HARBOR BOOKS — Antiquarian
612 White Horse Pike, 08215. Tel 609-965-1708
Mgr, Norman Arrington
Estab 1978. 30,000 Vols. 1200 sq ft
Types: 1st ed, hb, illus bk, out of print, papbk, used

HEINOLDT BOOKS — Antiquarian-Americana
1325 W Central Ave, 08215. Tel 609-965-2284
Estab 1959. 7000 Vols. 800 sq ft. Cat 2x ann
Types: Out of print, old & rare
Subj: Am Indian studies, discovery & explor, local hist, Revolutionary War, Am hist

ELMWOOD PARK — 18,377. Area code 201

RELIABLE BOOK SERVICE — Mail Order
19 Orange Ave (Mail add: PO Box 2033, Paterson, 07509). Tel 201-791-7018
Estab 1936. 100,000 Vols
Types: Used, out of print, 1st ed, hb, old & rare, papbk
Subj: Art, sci fiction & fantasy, fiction, nonfiction, military, cinema, theatre

ENGLEWOOD — 23,701. Area code 201

THE BOOK STORE AT DEPOT SQUARE — Antiquarian-General
8 Depot Sq, 07631. Tel 201-568-6563
Estab 1978. 30,000 Vols. 2000 sq ft. Cat
Types: Fine bnd, 1st ed, hb, old & rare, out of print, used
Subj: Cooking, New Jerseyana, Federal Writers Project

RUTH WOODS ORIENTAL BOOKS & ART — Mail Order
266 Arch Rd, 07631. Tel 201-567-0149. FAX 201-567-1419
Estab 1983. 1000 Titles. 1000 Vols. Cat 2x ann
Types: Hb, illus bk, old & rare, out of print, used
Subj: Art, philos, folklore, arts & crafts, music, sci-tech, China, Jap, Tib, Kor, Asia lang arts, lit

ENGLEWOOD CLIFFS — 5698. Area code 201

S GEORGE GREENSPAN CO — Social Science
580 Sylvan Ave, 07632. Tel 201-569-8777
Estab 1960. 1000 Vols. Cat ann
Types: Hb, imp, out of print, high priced papbk, col & el-hi text, used
Subj: Bus & mgt, soc sci

FLEMINGTON — 4132. Area code 201

THE PEOPLE'S BOOKSHOP — Antiquarian
160 Main St, 08822. Tel 201-788-4953
Mgr, Rosemarie Beardsley
Estab 1979. 7000 Titles. 6000 Vols. 950 sq ft
Types: Imp, used, juvenile, out of print, papbk, fine bnd, 1st ed, hb, incunab, illus bk, ltd ed, old & rare
Subj: Early fiction

FORT LEE — 32,449. Area code 201

VATHEK BOOKS — Mail Order-Antiquarian
250 Slocum Way, 07024. Tel 201-585-1760
Estab 1983. 40,000 Vols
Types: Out of print, used, col text, 1st ed, hb, incunab, illus bk, imp, juvenile, old & rare, papbk
Subj: Fiction, Roman & early eastern hist

FREEHOLD — 10,020. Area code 201

C M C MYRIFF BOOKSELLER — Mail Order-Military
82 Townsend Dr, 07728. Tel 201-431-1785
100,000 Vols. Cat 3x ann
Types: Out of print, used, old & rare
Subj: Military

RARE BOOK CO — Antiquarian
PO Box 957, 07728. Tel 201-780-1393
Estab 1920. 20,000 Vols. 1000 sq ft. Cat ann
Types: Facsimile editions, 1st ed, hb, imp, new & used, out of print, papbk, old & rare
Subj: Rel-Christian Sci

HADDONFIELD — 12,337. Area code 609

RAY BOAS BOOKSELLER — Mail Order-Antiquarian
Five Roberts Ave, 08033-1319. Tel 609-429-9240
Estab 1982. 1000 Titles. 2500 Vols. Cat 4x ann
Types: Old & rare, out of print, used, hb
Subj: Bus & mgt, finance, hist, biog

OLD COOKBOOKS - H T HICKS — Antiquarian
PO Box 462, 08033. Tel 609-854-2844
Estab 1979. 2000 Titles. 2000 Vols. 400 sq ft. Cat quarterly
Types: Old & rare, out of print, pre-1918
Subj: Cooking, gastronomy

HIGHLAND PARK — 13,396. Area code 201

RUTGERS BOOK CENTER — Mail Order-Arms & Armor
127 Raritan Ave, 08904. Tel 201-545-4344
Owner, Gun Room Press
Estab 1962. 6000 Titles. 500,000 Vols. 15,000 sq ft. Cat 3x ann
Types: Hb, out of print, remainders, used, new
Subj: Antq, hunting & fishing, military, railroadiana, warfare, Western Amer, mil hist, big game hunting

HILLSDALE — 10,495. Area code 201

THE BOOK SHOP — Used
430 Hillsdale Ave, 07642. Tel 201-391-9101
Estab 1984. 6000 Titles. 8000 Vols. 250 sq ft
Types: Out of print
Subj: Mystery & detective, nonfiction, hist, philos, cooking, theater

HOBOKEN — 42,460. Area code 201

LITERARY SHOP — Used
736 Washington St, 07030. Tel 201-420-7917
Estab 1982. 20,000 Vols. 480 sq ft
Types: Out of print, papbk, mass mkt papbk, hb, new, old & rare, remainders, new & used comic bks

HOPEWELL — 2001. Area code 609

LA SCALA AUTOGRAPHS INC — Antiquarian-Performing Arts
PO Box 368, 08525. Tel 609-799-8523
Estab 1975. 1000 Vols. Cat
Types: Facsimile editions, new & used, out of print
Subj: Performing arts

ELISABETH WOODBURN — Mail Order-Antiquarian
Booknoll Farm, PO Box 398, 08525. Tel 609-466-0522
Estab 1946. 12,500 Titles. 13,000 Vols. Cat 2x ann
Types: Hb, imp, new & used, out of print, remainders, reprints
Subj: Agr, hort

IMLAYSTOWN — Area code 609

THE EDENITE SOCIETY INC — Mail Order
Rte 526, 08526. Tel 609-259-7517
Dir, Frank Muccie Jr
Estab 1976
Types: Facsimile editions, hb, old & rare, out of print
Subj: Health & diet, Dead Sea Scrolls, Essene, Gnostic rel

KENDALL PARK — Area code 201

RICHARD P DEVICTOR — Mail Order
Three Dov Place, 08824. Tel 201-297-0296
4000 Titles. 4000 Vols. Cat 12x ann
Types: Juvenile, out of print, illus bk, used
Subj: Amer, Western

KENILWORTH — 8221. Area code 201

OZ & ENDS BOOK SHOPPE — Antiquarian
14 Dorset Dr, 07033. Tel 201-276-8368
Estab 1978. 300 Titles. 1000 Vols. 200 sq ft. Cat
Types: 1st ed, juvenile, old & rare, out of print, used, reprints
Subj: Oziana & other bks by Oz auth & illust

LAMBERTVILLE — 2044. Area code 609

PHOENIX BOOKS — Used
49 N Union St, PO Box 367, 08530. Tel 609-397-4960
Estab 1987. 20,000 Titles. 20,000 Vols. 1100 sq ft
Types: Out of print
Subj: Fiction, natural hist, sci-tech, art hist, film & lit criticism

LEDGEWOOD — 1500. Area code 201

BOOKTOWN — General
Rte 10 Ledgewood Mall, 07852. Tel 201-927-0044
Mgr, Selim Uzel
Estab 1987. 50,000 Titles. 250,000 Vols. 2000 sq ft
Types: Hb, juvenile, out of print, papbk, remainders, col & el-hi text
Subj: Art, hist, computer sci, sci-tech, lit

LINCROFT — Area code 201

PAST HISTORY — Mail Order-Antiquarian
136 Parkview Terr, 07738. Tel 201-842-4545
Estab 1962. 25,000 Vols. 3000 sq ft. Cat 6x ann
Types: Facsimile editions, hb, out of print, old & rare, 1st ed
Subj: Amer, Am hist & lit, New Jerseyana

MADISON — 15,357. Area code 201

THE CHATHAM BOOKSELLER — Antiquarian
8 Green Village Rd, 07940. Tel 201-822-1361
70,000 Vols
Types: Hb, out of print, papbk, used

MATAWAN — 8837. Area code 201

TRANSATLANTIC BOOKS — Importer
19 Noble Pl (Mail add: PO Box 44, 07747-0044). Tel 201-566-8689
Estab 1955. 2000 Vols
Types: Hb, high priced papbk, imp UK, out of print, remainders

METUCHEN — 13,762. Area code 201

BEL CANTO BOOKS — Mail Order-Antiquarian
PO Box 55, Metuchen, 08840. Tel 201-548-7371
Estab 1956. 5000 Titles. 7500 Vols. 300 sq ft. Cat 2x ann
Types: 1st ed, facsimile editions, hb, illus bk, imp, new & used, old & rare, out of print, papbk
Subj: Dance, music, musicians

SIGN OF THE DOVE — Religious-Christian
178 Main St, 08840. Tel 201-494-2530
Mgr, Jo Navatkoski
Estab 1983. 3000 Titles. 12,000 Vols. 1500 sq ft
Types: 1st ed, hb, new, juvenile, out of print, papbk

MIDLAND PARK — 7381. Area code 201

CHRISTIAN GROWTH MINISTRIES BOOKSTORE OF NEW JERSEY — Religious-P
80 Van Biarcom Ave (Mail add: 183 Godwin Ave, 07432). Tel 201-445-8906
Owner, Midland Park Christian Reformed Church; Mgr, Angie Haan
Estab 1977. 2000 sq ft
Types: Hb, papbk, juvenile, out of print, bibles

MILLVILLE — 24,815. Area code 609

SOUTH JERSEY MAGAZINE — Mail Order-Antiquarian
PO Box 847, 24 Westwood Terrace, 08332. Tel 609-825-1615
Estab 1972
Types: Old & rare, out of print
Subj: Diaries, New Jerseyana, nostalgia, railroadiana

MONTCLAIR — 38,321. Area code 201

SIMON GALLERY OF PHOTOGRAPHY BOOKSHOP — Art Gallery
15 Union St, 07042. Tel 201-783-5480
Estab 1981. 25 Titles. 100 Vols
Types: Hb, out of print, papbk, remainders
Subj: Hist, literary criticism, photog

PATTERSON SMITH — Antiquarian
23 Prospect Terrace, 07042. Tel 201-744-3291
Estab 1955. 50,000 Vols. 4000 sq ft
Types: Out of print, old & rare, used
Subj: Criminology, sociol, gambling

WANGNER'S BOOKSHOP & BOOK SEARCH — Antiquarian
9 Midland Ave, 07042. Tel 201-744-4211
Estab 1977. 25,000 Vols. 1200 sq ft
Types: Facsimile editions, fine bnd, 1st ed, hb, incunab, illus bk, juvenile, ltd ed, old & rare, out of print, used

MONTVALE — 7318. Area code 201

WHITNEY MCDERMUT — Mail Order-Books On Books
49 Spring Valley Rd, 07645. Tel 201-391-5905
6000 Vols
Types: Old & rare, out of print, used
Subj: New Jerseyana

MORRISTOWN — 16,614. Area code 201

OLD BOOKSHOP — Antiquarian
4 John St, 07960. Tel 201-538-1210
Estab 1945. 25,000 Vols. Cat
Types: 1st ed, hb, old & rare, out of print, papbk, used
Subj: Amer

MOUNTAIN LAKES — 4153. Area code 201

THE BOOKFACTORY-XTRA EFFORT — Mail Order
11 Hillcrest Rd, PO Box 72, 07046. Tel 201-334-1189
Estab 1976
Types: Hb, papbk, facsimile editions, old & rare, out of print
Subj: Poetry, cooking

NETCONG —3557. Area code 201

BOOKS OF YESTERYEAR — Used
39 Ledgewood Ave, Rte 183 N (Mail add: PO Box 38, 07857). Tel 201-691-8214
Estab 1975. 70,000 Titles. 70,000 Vols. 2000 sq ft
Types: Juvenile, out of print, old & rare
Subj: Fiction, mystery & detective

NEWARK — 329,248. Area code 201

FRANK MICHELLI BOOKS — Used
45 Halsey St, 07102. Tel 201-623-4289
Estab 1952. 20,000 Vols
Types: Hb, out of print

NEW BRUNSWICK — 41,442. Area code 201

OLD YORK BOOKS — Antiquarian-General
122 French St, 08901. Tel 201-249-0430
Proprietor E T Cecile Hopkins
Estab 1965. 65,000 Titles. 90,000 Vols. Cat
Types: Out of print, hb, papbk, 1st ed, scholarly bks
Subj: Poetry, for lang, philos

NORTH BERGEN — 47,019. Area code 201

BOOK HUNTERS — Mail Order-Antiquarian
802 74th St (Mail add: Box 7519, 07047). Tel 201-869-8786
Estab 1958
Types: Out of print

LARRY SMITH BOOKS — Mail Order-Antiquarian
9060 Palisade Ave, 07047-6148. Tel 201-854-3288
Cat 2x ann
Types: Hb, out of print, used
Subj: Psychol

NORWOOD — 4413. Area code 201

WALTER J JOHNSON INC — Mail Order-Antiquarian
355 Chestnut St, 07648-2090. Tel 201-767-1303. Telex 13-5393
Head of Acct Patricia Fiorino
Types: Facsimile editions, imp, new & used, out of print, old & rare
Subj: Humanities, medicine, sci-tech, soc sci

OCEAN CITY — 13,949. Area code 609

NORTHEAST BOOK & RECORD SHOP — Antiquarian
411 E Eighth St, 08226. Tel 609-399-9086
Estab 1984. 10,000 Titles. 11,000 Vols. 600 sq ft. Cat 3x ann
Types: Fine bnd, 1st ed, hb, illus bk, juvenile, old & rare, out of print, used, remainders
Subj: Nonfiction

PARSIPPANY — 49,868. Area code 201

ABOUT BOOKS — Used
PO Box 5717, 07054. Tel 201-515-4591
Estab 1982. 10,000 Vols. Cat 4x ann
Types: Hb, out of print, remainders, 1st ed, modern 1st ed
Subj: Bks on bks, bibliog, Amer

PASSAIC — 52,463. Area code 201

PASSAIC BOOK CENTER — General
594 Main Ave, 07055. Tel 201-778-6646
Mgr, Peter Ryby
Estab 1965. 100,000 Vols. Cat
Types: Hb, out of print, papbk, new & used, comics
Subj: Mystery & detective, romance, sci fiction & fantasy
See Also: Montclair Book Center, Montclair

PLAINFIELD — 45,555. Area code 201

BLACK GOLD CULTURAL ARTS CENTER, BOOK DEPT — Black Studies
500 Wachung Ave, 07060. Tel 201-755-9888
Mgr, Tyrone Laws
Estab 1979
Types: Illus bk, juvenile, papbk, fine bnd, out of print, old & rare, imp Afr
Subj: Cooking, health, poetry, rel, philos, Egyptology

P M BOOKSHOP — Antiquarian
321 Park Ave, 07060. Tel 201-754-3900
Estab 1940. 100,000 Vols
Types: 1st ed, facsimile editions, hb, incunab, old & rare, out of print, papbk, remainders, used

PRINCETON — 12,035. Area code 609

BRYN MAWR BOOKSHOP — Used
Arts Council Bldg, 102 Witherspoon St, 08542. Tel 609-921-6813
Owner, Bryn Mawr Club of Princeton; Co-Chmn, Margery R Claghorn
Estab 1986. 6000 Vols
Types: Out of print, old & rare

JOSEPH J FELCONE INC, RARE BOOKS — Antiquarian
PO Box 366, 08540. Tel 609-924-0539
Bibliographer G Scott Clemons; Bookbinder Anne Krawitz
Estab 1972. 10,000 Vols. Cat 6x ann
Types: Old & rare, out of print
Subj: Am hist & lit, bks on bks, New Jerseyana, sports, travel

PRINCETON UNIVERSITY STORE — College
36 University Pl, 08540. Tel 609-921-8500
VP Books, H Pierce; Buyers, C Van Dyk & C Harlich; Text Buyer, J Scott
Estab 1902. 75,000 Titles. 42,000 sq ft. Cat 2x ann
Types: For lang, hb, imp, juvenile, out of print, mass mkt papbk, high priced papbk
See Also: The Jigger Shop, Lawrenceville

ROLAND ROBERGE BOOKSELLER — Antiquarian
491 Rosedale Rd, 08540. Tel 609-924-6329
Estab 1984. 2000 Titles. 2000 Vols. Cat 4x ann
Types: Hb, illus bk, old & rare, out of print, used
Subj: Art

WITHERSPOON ART & BOOKSTORE — Antiquarian
12 Nassau St, 08542. Tel 609-924-3582
Estab 1925. 30,000 Vols. Cat
Types: 1st ed, facsimile editions, incunab, ltd ed, old & rare, out of print

RANCOCAS — Area code 609

SPORTING BOOK SERVICE — Mail Order
PO Box 177, 08073. Tel 609-267-5506
7000 Vols. Cat 4x ann
Types: Facsimile editions, 1st ed, hb, imp, incunab, new & used, out of print, papbk, old & rare, remainders
Subj: Hunting & fishing, horses, arms & armor, natural hist, dogs

RED BANK — 12,031. Area code 201

KEITH LIBRARY — Antiquarian
217 W Front, 07701. Tel 201-842-7377
Asst Maureen Hanisch
Estab 1955. 9000 Titles. 10,000 Vols. 400 sq ft
Types: Fr lang, hb, imp Fr, imp UK, juvenile, out of print, remainders, facsimile editions, fine bnd, 1st ed, illus bk, ltd ed, old & rare, scholarly lit
Subj: New Jerseyana, art, travel, military, Am hist & lit, Eng hist & lit, Britain

TIME AGAIN BOOKS, PRINTS & COLLECTIBLES — Antiquarian
PO Box 8655, 60 Ambassador Dr, 07701. Tel 201-842-4412
Estab 1980. 10,000 Titles
Types: Out of print, used, fine bnd, 1st ed, hb, illus bk, ltd ed

RIDGEWOOD — 25,208. Area code 201

BROWN'S BOOKSHOP — Used
10 Garber Sq, 07450. Tel 201-445-3910
Estab 1982. 20,000 Titles. 20,000 Vols
Types: Out of print, papbk, remainders, old & rare, hb

CUMBERLAND BOOKS — Mail Order-Poetry
575 Grove St, 07450. Tel 201-652-0185
Estab 1983. 10 Titles. 500 Vols. Cat ann
Types: Fine bnd, 1st ed, hb, ltd ed, out of print
Subj: Mod lit, broadsides, fine press, poetry, rare

RINGWOOD — 12,625. Area code 201

KIRKSCO INDUSTRIES — Mail Order
70-220 Cedar Rd, 07456. Tel 201-962-6519
Estab 1970. 6000 Vols. 900 sq ft
Types: Hb, juvenile, out of print, high priced papbk, remainders, col text, used
Subj: How-to, sci-tech

RIVERDALE — 2530. Area code 201

CENTURY HOUSE ANTIQUE & BOOKSHOP — Antiques
47 Newark Pompton Turnpike, 07457. Tel 201-835-4635
Estab 1947. 3000 Titles. 3000 Vols. 400 sq ft
Types: Out of print, new & used, juvenile, old
Subj: Military, hist, poetry, travel, western

ROCKAWAY — 6852. Area code 201

RAY & JUDY'S BOOK STOP — Used
40 W Main St, 07866. Tel 201-586-9182
Vpres, Judith Sedivec
Estab 1982. 50,000 Vols. 1200 sq ft
Types: Juvenile, out of print, remainders, col & el-hi text, comics
Subj: New Jerseyana, Morris County hist bks

SADDLE RIVER — 2763. Area code 201

GERRY & HELEN DE LA REE SCIENTIFANTASY SPECIALISTS — Science Fiction & Fantasy
7 Cedarwood Lane, 07458. Tel 201-327-6621
Estab 1950. 1000 Vols. Cat monthly
Types: Hb, new & used, old & rare, out of print
Subj: Sci fiction & fantasy

SUMMIT — 21,071. Area code 201

ERNEST S HICKOK — Antiquarian
382 Springfield Ave, 07901. Tel 201-277-1427
Mgr, Henie
Estab 1958. 5000 Vols. Cat
Types: Hb, out of print
Subj: Hunting & fishing, Am paintings & prints

UPPER MONTCLAIR — Area code 201

THE BOOK CORNER — General
211 Bellevue Ave, 07043. Tel 201-746-5951
Estab 1968. 20,000 Titles. 35,000 Vols. Cat
Types: Hb, juvenile, papbk, out of print
Subj: Louisianiana

LITTLE MERMAID BOOK — Antiquarian
411 Park St, 07043
Estab 1984. 9000 Titles. 10,000 Vols. 8500 sq ft
Types: Used, juvenile, hb, text bks, old & rare, ltd ed, out of print, facsimile editions, fine bnd, 1st ed, illus bk
Subj: Polit sci, law, hist, performing arts, music, Ireland & Irish auth

WALDWICK — 10,802. Area code 201

HAROLD NESTLER — Mail Order-Antiquarian
13 Pennington Ave, 07463. Tel 201-444-7413
Estab 1952. 3800 Vols. Cat 8x ann
Types: Old & rare, out of print
Subj: New Yorkiana, Revolutionary War, early Am indust

WAYNE — 46,474. Area code 201

THE BAGGAGE CAR — Mail Order-Antiquarian
128 Lake Dr E, 07470. Tel 201-694-6749
Estab 1981. 700 Titles. 1400 Vols. Cat 3x ann
Types: 1st ed, hb, juvenile, old & rare, out of print, used
Subj: Railroadiana, nautical, aviation, trolleys, automobiles

WESTFIELD — 30,447. Area code 201

HOBBIT RARE BOOKS — Antiquarian
305 W South Ave, 07090. Tel 201-654-4115
Estab 1969. 5000 Vols. 800 sq ft
Types: Facsimile editions, fine bnd, 1st ed, hb, incunab, illus bk, juvenile, ltd ed, old & rare, out of print
Subj: Art

WEST ORANGE — 39,510. Area code 201

ALBERT SAIFER — Mail Order-Antiquarian
102 Longview St, 07052. Tel 201-731-5701
Estab 1932. 20,000 Vols. Cat 12x ann
Types: Facsimile editions, fine bnd, 1st ed, hb, incunab, ltd ed, old & rare, out of print, remainders, used

WILDWOOD — 4913. Area code 609

HOLLY BEACH BOOK SHOP — General
3314 Pacific Ave, 08260. Tel 609-522-5463
Types: Hb, papbk, juvenile, remainders, used, out of print, mag

ALAMOGORDO — 24,024. Area code 505

SCHAAF'S — Southwestern Americana
907 New York Ave (Mail add: PO Box 1765, 88310). Tel 505-437-0404
Types: Hb, old & rare, out of print
Subj: Amer, New Mexicana, Texana

ALBUQUERQUE — 331,767. Area code 505

THE BOOK ADDICT — Mail Order-Antiquarian
PO Box 9134, 87119-9134
Estab 1978. 5000 Titles. 5000 Vols. 400 sq ft
Types: Hb, new & used, old & rare, out of print, remainders
Subj: Mayan & Mexican archaeol, Himalayan mountaineering, Antarctic exploration

BOOK FARE - FOOD FOR THOUGHT — General
5901 Wyoming NE, 87109. Tel 505-821-6758
Estab 1980. 2450 sq ft. Cat ann
Types: New, hb, papbk, juvenile, out of print
Subj: Bus & mgt, horses, Southwestern Amer, pets, reference, livestock, nature

BOOKS-BY-MAIL — Antiquarian
1833 Central Ave NW, 87104. Tel 505-247-3043
Estab 1959
Types: Facsimile editions, 1st ed, hb, new & used, out of print, papbk
Subj: Archaeol, Southwestern Amer

BOOKSTOP ALBUQUERQUE — Antiquarian
University Area Store, 112 Hermosa SE, 87108. Tel 505-268-8898
Estab 1979. 40,000 Vols. 3000 sq ft
Types: 1st ed, hb, illus bk, old & rare, out of print, papbk, used

TOM DAVIES BOOKSHOP — Antiquarian-Humanities
414 Central SE, 87102. Tel 505-247-2072
Estab 1956. 5000 Vols. 700 sq ft
Types: Hb, out of print, old & rare, used, fine press
Subj: Am Indian studies, art, class studies, Southwestern Amer, antq

DON'S PAPERBACK BOOKS — Paperback
1013 San Mateo Blvd SE, 87108. Tel 505-268-0520
Estab 1971. 130,000 Vols. 1800 sq ft
Types: New, out of print
Subj: Sci fiction & fantasy

HUMMINGBIRD BOOKS — Antiquarian-Philosophy
2400 Hannett NE, 87106. Tel 505-268-6277 (by appt)
Estab 1978. 4000 Vols. Cat
Types: 1st ed, hb, new, old & rare, out of print, remainders, used, pvt presses
Subj: Philos, travel, Am lit, women writers

LITERARY TIMES BOOKSTORE — General
Suite D 5809 Juan Tabo NE, 87111. Tel 505-293-4803
Types: Hb, papbk, juvenile, out of print, 1st ed
Subj: Twentieth century

MURDER UNLIMITED — Paperback
2510 San Mateo Pl NE, 87110. Tel 505-884-5491
Estab 1977. 4000 Titles. 8000 Vols. 750 sq ft. Cat 4x ann
Types: Out of print, mass mkt papbk, high priced papbk, used, imp UK
Subj: Mystery & detective, true crime

PRAYING HANDS — Religious-Christian
4212 Fourth St NW, 87107. Tel 505-345-4673
Types: Hb, Navajo lang, Sp lang, juvenile, out of print, papbk, col text, used, bibles

JACK D RITTENHOUSE BOOKS — Antiquarian
PO Box 4422, 87196-4422. Tel 505-255-2479
Estab 1951. 10,000 Vols. 700 sq ft. Cat 4x ann
Types: Hb, new, out of print, old & rare
Subj: Western Amer

JANE ZWISOHN BOOKS — Mail Order-Antiquarian
524 Solano Dr NE, 87108. Tel 505-255-4080
Estab 1981. 1000 Vols. Cat 2x ann
Types: 1st ed, old & rare, out of print
Subj: Latin Am, travel, Western Amer

CARLSBAD — 25,496. Area code 505

WOODEN SPOON WEST — Used
306 W Luckey St, 88220. Tel 505-887-5313
Estab 1976. 4000 Vols Buys indep
Types: Hb, out of print, papbk
Subj: Arts & crafts, fine arts, humanities, natural hist, self-develop, Western Amer, Western artists

CORRALES — 2791. Area code 505

PEGGY & HAROLD SAMUELS — Mail Order-Antiquarian
Star Rte, Box 1281, 87048. Tel 505-898-7258
Estab 1970. 6000 Vols
Types: Out of print
Subj: Amer art; Frederic Remington, Rough Riders, Blakelock, Henry Adams

LAS CRUCES — 45,086. Area code 505

COAS BOOKS — General
535 S Melendres, 88005
150,000 Titles. 250,000 Vols
Types: New & used, for lang, hb, imp, juvenile, out of print, papbk, remainders, text bks, imp Alb, fine bnd, 1st ed, ltd ed
Subj: Anthrop, Western Amer, hist

LAS VEGAS — 14,322. Area code 505

LA GALERIA DE LOS ARTESANOS — Western Americana
220 N Plaza, PO Box 1657, 87701. Tel 505-425-8331
Estab 1950. 26,000 Titles. 30,000 Vols
Types: Out of print, used, old & rare, juvenile, papbk, hb
Subj: New Mexicana, archaeol, military, hist preservation, poetry, music, folklore, fiction, railroadiana, anthrop, New Mexicana, Southwestern Amer, Western Amer, women of the West, cattle, outlaws, mountain men & fur trade, Sp & Eng lit

RATON — 8225. Area code 505

ABC BOOK & GIFT SHOP — General
205 Park Ave (Mail add: PO Box 115, 87740). Tel 505-445-8454
Estab 1971. 5000 Vols. 600 sq ft
Types: Hb, juvenile, out of print, papbk, remainders, bibles
Subj: Cooking, rel studies, Southwestern Amer

ROSWELL — 39,676. Area code 505

CLASSIC NEWS AGENCY — Paperback
129 East Third, PO Box 487, 88202. Tel 505-622-0121
Types: Hb, papbk, out of print, for lang

COBEAN STATIONERY CO, BOOK DEPT — Stationers
320 N Richardson (Mail add: PO Box 1598, 88201). Tel 505-622-1922
Mgr, Donna Groseclose; Secy & Treas Ruth C McPherson
Estab 1916. 10,000 Vols
Types: Hb, juvenile, out of print, high priced papbk, remainders, bibles
Subj: Cooking, gardening, rel, Western Amer, art, hobbies

RUIDOSO — 4260. Area code 505

THE ASPEN TREE — General
2340 Sudderth Dr (Mail add: PO Box 367, 88345). Tel 505-257-4088
Estab 1977. 4000 Vols. 600 sq ft
Types: Hb, juvenile, out of print, papbk, remainders
Subj: Fiction, nonfiction, Southwestern Amer, hummingbirds

SANTA FE — 48,899. Area code 505

ABACUS BOOKS — Mail Order-Antiquarian
1896 Lorca Dr, PO Box 5555, 87502-5555. Tel 505-983-6434
Estab 1970. 5000 Vols. 600 sq ft
Types: 1st ed, out of print, old & rare
Subj: Bks on bks, Southwestern Amer

BOOKS & MORE BOOKS — General
1341 Cerrillos, 87501. Tel 505-983-5438
Estab 1988. 22,000 Titles. 25,000 Vols. 1000 sq ft
Types: Out of print, high priced papbk, remainders, used, hb, juvenile
Subj: Western Amer, philos, rel studies, art, fiction

GREAT SOUTHWEST BOOKS — Antiquarian-Southwestern Americana
PO Box 2247, 87504. Tel 505-983-1680
Estab 1976. 5000 Titles. 5000 Vols. 1000 sq ft
Types: 1st ed, hb, illus bk, ltd ed, old & rare, out of print
Subj: New Mexicana, Rydal Press

R T LINCOLN BOOK SEARCH SERVICE — Mail Order-Antiquarian
Rte 9, Box 16T, 87505. Tel 505-471-2821
Estab 1985
Types: Out of print

NUMISMATIC ARTS OF SANTE FE — Mail Order-Antiquarian
Box 9712, 87504. Tel 505-982-8792
Estab 1987. 5000 Titles. 10,000 Vols. Cat 2x ann
Types: Facsimile editions, fine bnd, 1st ed, hb, incunab, illus bk, imp, ltd ed, new & used, old & rare, out of print
Subj: Numismatics, philatelics

PARKER BOOKS OF THE WEST — Antiquarian-Western Americana
142 W Palace Ave (Mail add: PO Box 8390, 87504-8390). Tel 505-988-1076
Estab 1980. 15,000 Titles. 15,000 Vols. 1200 sq ft. Cat 1-3x ann
Types: Hb, old & rare, out of print, used
Subj: Am hist & lit

NICHOLAS POTTER BOOKSELLER — Antiquarian
203 E Palace Ave, 87501. Tel 505-983-5434
Estab 1969. 7500 Vols. 1200 sq ft
Types: Fine bnd, 1st ed, hb, illus bk, juvenile, ltd ed, old & rare, out of print, used
Subj: Photog, Southwestern Amer, mod lit

THE SANTA FE BOOKSELLER — Art
203 W San Francisco St, 87501. Tel 505-983-5278
Estab 1979. 30,000 Vols. 1900 sq ft. Cat 4x ann
Types: Hb, old & rare, out of print
Subj: Art, Southwestern Amer

SANTE FE HOUSE OF BOOKS — Antiquarian-Western Americana
Santa Fe House of Books, PO Box 503, 87504-0503. Tel 505-473-5161
CEO S S Margolis
Estab 1983. 4000 Titles. 6000 Vols. Cat 4x ann
Types: Hb, out of print, 1st ed, new, old & rare, papbk, remainders
Subj: Am Indian studies, arts & crafts, ethnic studies, Southwestern Amer, fiction, Western Amer

TAOS — 3369. Area code 505

HIGHER GROUND BOOK STORE — Mail Order-Metaphys & Occult
33 Bent St (Mail add: PO Box 698, Ranchos De Taos, 87557). Tel 505-758-9251
Estab 1986. 1000 Titles. 400 sq ft. Cat ann
Types: Hb, papbk, mass mkt papbk, high priced papbk, juvenile, out of print, used, illus bk, new, old & rare
Subj: Astrol, natural healing, magic & conjuring, self-develop, East & West spirituality

KIT CARSON HOME & MUSEUM BOOK DEPT — Museum
Old Kit Carson Rd, Drawer CCC, 87571. Tel 505-758-4741
Owner, Kit Carson Memorial Foundation, Inc; Dir, Niel Poese
Estab 1956. 1000 Vols. 320 sq ft
Types: Hb, juvenile, out of print, papbk, used
Subj: New Mexicana, Am Indian studies, Southwestern Amer, fur trade

T N LUTHER BOOKS — Antiquarian
PO Box 429, 87571-0429. Tel 505-776-8117
Estab 1962. 8000 Vols. Cat 4x ann
Types: Old & rare, out of print, 1st ed, hb, papbk, remainders
Subj: Western Amer, archaeol, ethnic studies, Am Indian studies, Indian artifacts

THE TAOS BOOKSHOP INC — General
122-D Kit Carson, 87571. Tel 505-758-3733
Mgr, Mimi Meck
Estab 1947. 6000 Vols. Cat 2x ann
Types: Hb, juvenile, papbk, out of print, remainders
Subj: Am Indian studies, Southwestern Amer, local hist, DH Lawrence, Southwestern art

10 DIRECTIONS BOOKS — Used
PO Box 330, 87571. Tel 505-758-2725
Estab 1985. 10,000 Titles. 10,000 Vols. 900 sq ft
Types: Hb, remainders, used, out of print
Subj: Art, biog, metaphys & occult, rel, Southwestern Amer, Am hist & lit, nonfiction

ALBANY — 101,727. Area code 518

BRYN MAWR BOOKSHOP — Used
One Spring St, 12210. Tel 518-465-8126
Owner, Bryn Mawr College Scholarship Fund; Mgrs, Barbara C M Dudley & Virginia B Bennett
Estab 1968. 40,000 Vols. 3000 sq ft
Types: Juvenile, hb, for lang, out of print, mass mkt papbk, old & rare
Subj: Amer, lang arts, music, soc sci, travel

CAPITAL BOOKSTORE — Used
402 Broadway, 12207. Tel 518-434-4927
Estab 1959. 20,000 Vols
Types: Out of print, mass mkt papbk, text bks, used, 1st ed, hb, old & rare
Subj: Hist, biog

NELSON'S BOOKSTORES — Used
26 Central Ave, 12210. Tel 518-463-1023
Estab 1971. 100,000 Vols. 1250 sq ft. Cat 4x ann
Types: For lang, hb, out of print, papbk, remainders
Subj: Military, sports, art, lit, Beat Generation auth
See Also: Schenectady, Troy

TOM SHAW BOOKS — General
11 Albright Ave, 12203. Tel 518-456-5905
Estab 1960. 15,000 Vols. 200 sq ft. Cat 15x ann
Types: Hb, juvenile, out of print, used
Subj: Mystery & detective, fiction

STATE UNIVERSITY OF NEW YORK AT ALBANY BOOKSTORE — General
1400 Washington Ave, 12222. Tel 518-442-5690. Telex 145-486
Mgr, John Styles
12,000 Vols. 9000 sq ft
Types: Col text, for lang, hb, out of print, papbk, remainders, used

ALBERTSON — 6792. Area code 516

SANDYS — Antiquarian
PO Box 181, 11507. Tel 516-484-4299
2000 Titles. 2000 Vols
Types: Out of print, illus bk, old & rare, used
Subj: Amer, sports, military, early periodicals

AMHERST — 108,706. Area code 716

VILLAGE GREEN BOOKSTORE — General
1089 Niagara Falls Blvd, 14226. Tel 716-836-8960
Vpres, Jessie Marvin; Mgr, Lisa Carter; Merch Buyer John Borek
Estab 1973. 50,000 Titles. 150,000 Vols. 16,000 sq ft Buys through hq
Types: For lang, hb, imp, juvenile, papbk, out of print

AMSTERDAM — 21,872. Area code 518

DISCOUNT BOOK CENTER — General
Amsterdam Mall, 12010. Tel 518-843-4423
Mgr, Barbara Sprouse
Estab 1985. 6000 Titles. 20,000 Vols. Cat 3x annBuys indep & through hq
Types: For lang, hb, juvenile, out of print, papbk, remainders, used

RESTON'S BOOKNOOK — Antiquarian
59 Rockton St, 12010. Tel 518-843-1601
Estab 1965. 1200 Vols. Cat 4x ann
Types: 1st ed, incunab, juvenile, old & rare, out of print, used
Subj: New Yorkiana, sci fiction & fantasy

ANCRAMDALE — Area code 518

JOHN F SCHULTZ ANCRAMDALE BOOK BARN — Mail Order-Antiquarian
Woods Dr, 12503. Tel 518-329-0193
Estab 1965. 15,000 Vols
Types: Out of print, used

AURORA — 926. Area code 315

TALBOTHAYS BOOKS — Antiquarian
Black Rock Rd (Mail add: PO Box 118, 13026-0118). Tel 315-364-7550
6000 Titles. 7000 Vols. Cat 3-5x ann
Types: 1st ed, hb, out of print, old & rare
Subj: Amer, military

BAYPORT —Area code 516

MAESTRO BOOKS — Mail Order-Antiquarian
344 Middle Rd, PO Box 848, 11705. Tel 516-472-1222
Types: Juvenile, for lang, out of print, used, illus bk, 1st ed, hb

BAY SHORE — 11,119. Area code 516

FRIAR TUCK BOOKSHOP — General
Gardiner Manor Mall, 836-6 Sunrise Hwy, 11706. Tel 516-666-0010
Mgr, Mary Infante
Estab 1979. 6000 Titles. 20,000 Vols. Cat 3x annBuys indep & through hq
Types: For lang, hb, juvenile, out of print, papbk, remainders, used

BAYSIDE — Area code 718

THE BOOK SHOP — Paperback
214-05 41st Ave, 11361. Tel 718-225-8275
Estab 1980. 20,000 Vols
Types: Juvenile, out of print, papbk, used

HERBERT A LUFT* — Mail Order
69-11 229th St (Mail add: PO Box 91, Oakland Gardens, 11364-0091). Tel 718-428-2770
Estab 1950. 150 Titles. 4000 Vols. Cat
Types: Hb, out of print, high priced papbk, remainders, col text, used, imp Fr, imp Ger, imp UK
Subj: Astron

BAYVILLE — 7034. Area code 516

THOMOLSEN BOOKS — Mail Order
10 Deans Lane (Mail add: PO Box 24, 11709). Tel 516-628-8819
3000 Titles. 3000 Vols. Cat 2x ann
Types: Out of print, used
Subj: Mystery & detective, true crime

BOICEVILLE — Area code 914

EDITIONS — Mail Order-Antiquarian
Rte 28A, 12412-0168. Tel 914-657-7000

Estab 1948. 100,000 Vols. Cat monthly
Types: Hb, out of print, old & rare, used
Subj: Art, fiction, hist, philos, soc sci

BREWSTER — 1650. Area code 914

OLANA GALLERY — Mail Order-Antiquarian
Two Carillon Rd, 10509. Tel 914-279-8077
Estab 1971. 9000 Vols. 3500 sq ft. Cat 4x ann
Types: Facsimile editions, ltd ed, new, old & rare, out of print, used
Subj: Am art

BRIARCLIFF — Area code 914

J H FABER — Mail Order-Antiquarian
89 Fuller Rd, 10510. Tel 914-762-2656
Estab 1981. 3000 Titles. 4000 Vols. Cat 4x ann
Types: Hb, imp, out of print, used
Subj: Military, world hist, aviation, naval

BROCKPORT — 9776. Area code 716

BEECH & CROW BOOKS — Used
121 Park Ave, 14420. Tel 716-637-7150
Mgr, Michael Hopkins
Estab 1987. 7000 Titles. 7000 Vols
Types: Out of print, used, juvenile
Subj: Biog, anthrop, art, cooking, fiction, hist, music, mythology, natural hist, philos, poetry, psychol, rel, sci-tech, sociol, occult

BRONX — 1,169,115. Area code 212

ABBOT BOOKS — Business & Management
100-26L Benchley Pl, 10475. Tel 212-671-9800
Estab 1978. 2000 Titles
Types: 1st ed, hb, old & rare, out of print, used
Subj: Railroadiana, Amer, Wall St

CHARLES BARON — Mail Order-Antiquarian
55 Knolls Crescent, 10463. Tel 212-548-3951
Estab 1936. 1000 Vols
Types: 1st ed, out of print, used
Subj: Amer

H CELNICK — General
2144 Muliner Ave, 10462-2003. Tel 212-823-5731
Estab 1942. 20,000 Vols
Types: Hb, imp, out of print, papbk, remainders, used
Subj: Econ, health & phys educ, hort, medicine, metaphys & occult, natural healing, natural hist, theol, chiropractic, freethought, Judaica-in-English

J M COHEN RARE BOOKS — Mail Order-Antiquarian
PO Box 542, 10463-0542. Tel 212-548-7160
Estab 1982. 5000 Vols. Cat 6x ann
Types: Old & rare, out of print, used
Subj: Fashion, textiles, jewelry, furniture, design, decorative & applied arts

DENBRY BOOKS — Antiquarian
3555 Rochambeau Ave, 10467. Tel 212-881-7459
Types: 1st ed, hb, illus bk, juvenile, ltd ed, old & rare, out of print, used

BROOKLYN — 2,230,936. Area code 718

AVERY BOOKSTORES INC — General
308 Livingston St, 11217. Tel 718-858-3606
Estab 1953. 50,000 Vols
Types: Hb, juvenile, out of print, papbk, col & el-hi text, used, old & rare

BIBLO BOOKS — General
48 Hicks, 11201. Tel 718-596-1623
Estab 1980
Types: Out of print, used, old & rare
Subj: Art, scholarly lit

BINKIN'S BOOK CENTER — Antiquarian-General
54 Willoughby St, 11201. Tel 718-855-7813
Estab 1939.
Types: Old & rare, out of print, used, facsimile editions, fine bnd, 1st ed, hb, incunab, illus bk, ltd ed, remainders

NORMAN BLAUSTEIN UNCOMMON BOOKS — General
646 Vanderbilt Ave, 11238. Tel 718-783-8574
Estab 1986. 25,000 Titles. 25,000 Vols. 7500 sq ft. Cat 6x ann
Types: Used, facsimile editions, hb, illus bk, ltd ed, old & rare, out of print

CALEB BOOKSELLERS — Religious
414 53rd St, 11220. Tel 718-439-6268
Types: Fr & Sp lang, dictionaries, hb, papbk, juvenile, out of print, bibles
Subj: Theol, rel-evangelical, reformers, commentaries, Lutheran, Calvinism

THE DANCE MART — Mail Order-Dance
Box 48, Homecrest Sta, 11229. Tel 718-627-0477
Estab 1950. 2000 Vols. Cat 2x ann
Types: Hb, imp, out of print, papbk, remainders, col text, used

ENCHANTED BOOKS — Antiquarian
2435 Ocean Ave Apt 6J, 11229. Tel 718-891-5241
Estab 1985. 4000 Titles. 4000 Vols. Cat
Types: Illus bk, juvenile, out of print, old & rare, juv

FRANCES KLENETT — Mail Order-Antiquarian
13 Cranberry St, 11201. Tel 718-852-2424
Owner, Klenett Worldwide Books
Estab 1955
Types: Out of print, used

MAIN STREET BOOKSELLERS — Antiquarian
PO Box 103, Vanderveer Sta, 11210-0103. Tel 718-275-0331
Estab 1968. 5000 Titles. 10,000 Vols. 1500 sq ft. Cat 2x ann
Types: 1st ed, hb, illus bk, juvenile, ltd ed, old & rare, out of print, dictionaries
Subj: Chess, fiction, reference

H C ROSEMAN BOOKSELLER — Mail Order-Antiquarian
85 Livingston St, 11201. Tel 718-834-8928
Cat 2x ann
Types: Imp, new, out of print, papbk, old & rare
Subj: Amer, biog, Brazil, dance, films & filmmaking, econ, Caribbean, ballroom dancing

SANGRAAL INC — Mail Order-Antiquarian
189 23rd St, 11232. Tel 718-499-6189. 499-1465
Mgr & Buyer, Richard Russel
5000 Titles. 8000 Vols. 400 sq ft. Cat 8x ann
Types: Facsimile editions, 1st ed, hb, ltd ed, old & rare, out of print, used
Subj: Sci fiction & fantasy, metaphys & occult, poetry, belles lettres, religious philos

C J SCHEINER BOOKS — Mail Order-Antiquarian
275 Linden Blvd, 11226. Tel 718-469-1089
Estab 1977. 4000 Vols. 500 sq ft. Cat 2x ann
Types: Facsimile editions, fine bnd, 1st ed, hb, illus bk, ltd ed, old & rare, out of print, papbk, imp Eur
Subj: Curiosa, erotica, sexology

RONA SCHNEIDER FINE PRINTS & RARE BOOKS — Mail Order-Graphic Arts
12 Monroe Pl, 11201. Tel 718-858-9297
200 Titles. 200 Vols
Types: Out of print, old & rare
Subj: Amer art

BUFFALO — 357,870. Area code 716

THE HAUNTED BOOKSHOP — Used
100 Elmwood Ave, 14201. Tel 716-882-9273
Estab 1985. Cat
Types: Facsimile editions, fine bnd, 1st ed, hb, illus bk, juvenile, ltd ed, old & rare, out of print, papbk, used
Subj: Mystery & detective, horror

WILLIAM S HEIN & CO, INC* — Law
1285 Main St, 14209. Tel 716-882-2600
Exec Dir, Kevin Marmion; Merch Mgr, Peter Glose
Estab 1961. 100,000 sq ft
Types: Out of print, col text, used, hb, papbk, new & used, library bound, looseleaf with binders
Subj: Law, govt publn, medicine, international

CLAUDE HELD — Mail Order-Antiquarian
PO Box 515, 14225
Estab 1942. 8000 Vols. Cat 4x ann
Types: Imp, out of print, old & rare, Sunday comic pages
Subj: Sci fiction & fantasy, mystery & detective, E R Burroughs, G A Henty

OLGA HOEFLIGER'S BOOKCORNER — Mail Order-Antiquarian
438 Vermont St, 14213. Tel 716-886-1898
Estab 1976. 6000 Titles. 4000 Vols. Cat 2x ann
Types: Fine bnd, 1st ed, hb, illus bk, juvenile, ltd ed, old & rare, out of print, used
Subj: Latin Am, SAm

OLD EDITIONS BOOKSHOP — Antiquarian
3124 Main St, 14214. Tel 716-836-7354
Estab 1976. 40,000 Vols. 2500 sq ft
Types: Fine bnd, 1st ed, hb, illus bk, out of print, used, papbk
Subj: Art, chess, hist

CANAAN — 1654. Area code 518

SYDNEY R SMITH SPORTING BOOKS — Mail Order
12029. Tel 518-794-8998
Estab 1939. Cat
Types: Hb, imp, new & used, out of print, old & rare
Subj: Dogs, horses, hunting & fishing

CANTON — 7055. Area code 315

JENISON'S BOOKS — Mail Order-Antiquarian
23 Gouveneur St, 13617. Tel 315-386-3022
Estab 1975. 15,000 Titles. 15,000 Vols. Cat
Types: Fine bnd, hb, illus bk, old & rare, out of print, trade
Subj: Amer, general

CARMEL — 27,948. Area code 914

THE BOOK & RECORD — General
Putnam Plaza, 10512. Tel 914-225-6556
Mgr, Karen Yzelac Buys indep & through hq
Types: Hb, out of print, papbk, remainders

CASTILE — 1135. Area code 716

THE LOON PEOPLE — Mail Order
6353 Burke Hill Rd, Perry, NY, 14530. Tel 716-786-2319
Types: Old & rare, out of print, 1st ed, hb
Subj: Natural sci, E T Seton, wolves, coyotes, loons

CATSKILL — 4718. Area code 518

CATTAIL BOOKS & COLLECTIBLES — Used
340 Main St, PO Box 433, 12414. Tel 518-943-6517
Estab 1986. 20,000 Titles. 25,000 Vols. 800 sq ft. Cat 4x ann
Types: Hb, juvenile, out of print, 1st ed, illus bk, old & rare
Subj: Railroadiana, mystery & detective, fiction, New Yorkiana, Hudson River Valley hist, juvenilia

PAN BOOKS & GRAPHICS — Antiquarian
401 Main St, 12414. Tel 518-943-4771
20,000 Vols. 2000 sq ft. Cat 24x ann
Types: Hb, juvenile, out of print, used, old & rare
Subj: Graphic arts, photog, New Yorkiana, autg, art, illus, scholarly lit

CATTARAUGUS — 1200. Area code 716

ROCKLAND BOOKMAN — Antiquarian
Washington St, 14719. Tel 716-257-5121
Estab 1970. 15,000 Titles. 15,000 Vols. Cat 3x ann
Types: 1st ed, hb, illus bk, out of print, old & rare, used
Subj: Amer, archaeol, art, Am Indian, Am imprints, mss

CELERON — area code 716

OLD & RARE LOVE AFFAIR — Search Service
PO Box 459, 14720-0459. Tel 716-483-1373
Estab 1983. 1000 Titles. 1000 Vols. Cat
Types: 1st ed, hb, illus bk, juvenile, old & rare, out of print, used
Subj: New Yorkiana, Issac Asimov

CIRCLEVILLE — Area code 914

NICHOLAS J CERTO BOOKS — Mail Order
PO Box 322, 10919. Tel 914-361-1190
Estab 1987. 5000 Titles. 12,000 Vols. Cat 12x ann
Types: Hb, imp, out of print, used, 1st ed, ltd ed
Subj: Sci fiction & fantasy, mystery & detective

CLINTON — 2107. Area code 315

BLUE FOX USED BOOKS — Antiquarian
34 College St, 13323. Tel 315-853-6494
Estab 1985. 35,000 Titles. 40,000 Vols. Cat
Types: Juvenile, out of print, old & rare, hb
Subj: Fiction, hist, poetry, drama, philos, belles lettres, travel, classics

CLINTON CORNERS —Area code 914

SEABOOK SEARCH — Antiquarian-Nautical
PO Box 239, 12514-0239. Tel 914-266-5800
Types: Hb, out of print

COLD SPRING HARBOR — 5498. Area code 516

NOSEGAY ANTIQUARIAN BOOKS — Mail Order-Antiquarian
46 Glen Way, 11724. Tel 516-692-4315
Estab 1978. 3000 Titles. 6000 Vols. 500 sq ft
Types: 1st ed, hb, illus bk, juvenile, out of print, used, rare
Subj: Art, biog, humor, poetry, travel, drama, gardening, antq collecting, London, roses

COLONIE — 8869. Area code 518

DISCOUNT BOOK CENTER — General
Northway Mall, 1440 Central Ave, 12205. Tel 518-482-3300
Mgr, Sue Robertson
Estab 1982. 6000 Titles. 20,000 Vols. Cat 3x annBuys indep & through hq
Types: For lang, hb, juvenile, papbk, remainders, used, out of print

COOPERSTOWN — 2342. Area code 607

ARTBOOKS — Mail Order-Antiquarian
107 Pioneer St (Mail add: PO Box 665, 13326-0665). Tel 607-547-9448
Estab 1983. 1500 Titles. 1500 Vols. Cat 2x ann
Types: New, out of print
Subj: Fine arts, Eur studies, Amer, decorative arts

PAULA CRONIN BOOKS — Mail Order-Antiquarian
RD Two, Box 110, 13326. Tel 607-547-6137
Estab 1982. Cat 12x ann
Types: 1st ed, old & rare, out of print
Subj: Medicine, natural hist, sci-tech, dogs, wolves

WILLIS MONIE BOOKS — Antiquarian
139 Main St, 13326. Tel 607-547-8363. WATS 800-322-2995
Estab 1979. 25,000 Vols. Cat monthly
Types: 1st ed, old & rare, out of print
Subj: Amer, New Yorkiana, theol

CORNING — 12,953. Area code 607

THE BOOK EXCHANGE — Used
90 W Market St, 14830. Tel 607-936-8536
Mgr, J T Iraggi; Juv Buyer, Melissa Iraggi
Estab 1977. 5000 Vols. 1500 sq ft. Cat 2x ann
Types: Hb, out of print, papbk
Subj: Glass ref mat

CRAGSMOOR — Area code 914

CRAGSMOOR BOOKS — Mail Order-Antiquarian
PO Box 66, 12420-0066. Tel 914-647-5588
Estab 1969. 10,000 Titles. 12,000 Vols. Cat 4x ann
Types: 1st ed, hb, illus bk, imp Fr, imp Ger, old & rare, out of print, remainders, used, Ital lang, Sp lang, Russ lang
Subj: Literary criticism, soc sci, hist, women's studies

CROTON-ON-HUDSON — 6889. Area code 914

THE BOOK & RECORD — General
Shop Rite Plaza, 10520. Tel 914-271-8700Buys indep & through hq
Types: Hb, out of print, papbk, remainders

CROTON BOOK SERVICE-SPORTSMANS BOOK SERVICE — Mail Order-Antiquarian
PO Box 131, 10520-0131. Tel 914-271-6575
Estab 1966
Types: Hb, juvenile, papbk, old & rare, out of print
Subj: Military, Hudson River, Croton Dam & Aqueduct, West Point & US Military Academy
Branches:
— SPORTMAN'S BOOK SERVICE
PO Box 131, 10520-0131. Tel 914-271-6575
Estab 1974
Types: New, old & rare, out of print

OLD BOOK ROOM — Antiquarian
111 Grand St, 10520. Tel 914-271-6802
Estab 1978. 5000 Titles. 5000 Vols. 2000 sq ft. Cat ann
Types: Used, out of print, juvenile
Subj: Local hist, New Yorkiana, art, Amer, biog, food, scholarly lit, travel, Hudson River, radical writers & artists

DEANSBORO — Area code 315

BERRY HILL BOOKSHOP — Antiquarian
Rte 12-B, Box 118, 13328. Tel 315-821-6188
Estab 1968. 80,000 Titles. 80,000 Vols. 1500 sq ft. Cat
Types: 1st ed, hb, illus bk, juvenile, out of print

DIX HILLS — 9840. Area code 516

GOLDEN AGE — Antiquarian
81 Buttonwood Dr, 11746. Tel 516-499-6112
Estab 1983. 10,000 Vols
Types: Hb, fine bnd, 1st ed, illus bk, juvenile, ltd ed, out of print, old & rare
Subj: Hist, biog, Judaica, discovery & explor, military, golf, nautical, antq, 19th century lit, adventure

DOBBS FERRY — 10,053. Area code 914

FREDERICK ARONE RAILROAD ITEMS — Antiquarian-Railroadiana
377 Ashford Ave, 10522. Tel 914-693-5858
Estab 1956. 20,000 Vols. 1600 sq ft. Cat 8x ann
Types: 1st ed, facsimile editions, hb, illus bk, new, out of print, old & rare, used

BROWN BAG BOOKSTORE — Used
127A Main St (Mail add: Box 276, 10522). Tel 914-693-2322
Estab 1984. 14,000 Titles. 15,000 Vols. 600 sq ft
Types: Remainders, hb, juvenile, out of print, used, 1st ed, illus bk, ltd ed, new, old & rare, papbk
Subj: Biog, Am hist & lit

EAST CHATHAM — Area code 518

LIBRARIUM — Antiquarian
Black Bridge Rd, Rd 190, 12060-9730. Tel 518-392-5209
Mgr & Buyer, Sharon S Lips
Estab 1979. 20,000 Vols. 480 sq ft
Types: 1st ed, hb, juvenile, out of print, papbk

EASTCHESTER — 32,648. Area code 914

JERRY ALPER INC — Mail Order-Antiquarian
271 Main St, PO Box 218, 10707. Tel 914-793-2100. TWX 710-562-0119
Mgr, Ken Hoch
Estab 1981. Cat ann
Types: Old & rare, out of print, used

EAST HAMPTON — 1886. Area code 516

LVIS BARGAIN BOOKS — General
95 Main St, 11937. Tel 516-324-1821
Estab 1967. 10,000 Titles. 12,500 Vols
Types: Juvenile, used, 1st ed, illus bk, ltd ed, used, old & rare, Fr lang, Ger lang, out of print
Subj: Biog, drama, fiction, mystery & detective

EAST MEADOW — 46,252. Area code 516

THE BOOK STOP — Paperback
384 E Meadow Ave, 11554. Tel 516-794-9129
Estab 1974. 100,000 Titles. 150,000 Vols
Types: New & used, out of print, for lang, juvenile, collectible comics
Subj: Romance, sci fiction & fantasy, mystery & detective

EAST NORTHPORT — Area code 516

FISHER OF BOOKS — Mail Order-Antiquarian
75 Cedar Rd, 11731. Tel 516-368-7396
5000 Titles. 5000 Vols
Types: Fine bnd, 1st ed, hb, illus bk, juvenile, ltd ed, old & rare, out of print
Subj: Amer, travel, New Yorkiana, exploration, Long Island

EDMESTON — 1732. Area code 607

INGEBORG QUITZAU — Mail Order-Antiquarian
Rt 80, PO Box 5160, 13335. Tel 607-965-8605
Estab 1971. 10,000 Vols. Cat 12x ann
Types: 1st ed, hb, illus bk, juvenile, ltd ed, old & rare, out of print, used, miniature bks
Subj: Bks on bks, mod lit, Ger hist & lit

ELIZABETHTOWN — 659. Area code 518

L W CURREY RARE BOOKS, INC — Mail Order-Antiquarian
Church St, PO Box 187, 12932. Tel 518-873-6477 (by appt only)
Estab 1967. 30,000 Vols. Cat 8x ann
Types: Hb, imp, new & used, old & rare, out of print, 1st ed, fine printing
Subj: Am hist & lit, mod lit, sci fiction & fantasy

ELMA — 10,574. Area code 716

AS YOU LIKE IT BOOKSHOP — Used
Bullis & Bowen Rds, 14059. Tel 716-652-0060
Estab 1976. 10,000 Titles. 5000 Vols. 450 sq ft
Types: Hb, fine bnd, 1st ed, illus bk, juvenile, old & rare, out of print, papbk
Subj: Art, nature & environ, sci fiction & fantasy, sci-tech, travel, polit hist

ELMHURST — Area code 718

ELYSIAN FIELDS BOOKSELLERS — Homosexuality
80-50 Baxter Ave, Suite 339, 11373. Tel 718-424-2789
Estab 1973. 10,000 Vols. Cat 3x ann
Types: 1st ed, hb, ltd ed, new & used, out of print, papbk
Subj: Homosexuality, gay lit

ANTON GUD — Mail Order-Antiquarian
41-22 Judge St, 11373. Tel 718-898-2316
Estab 1935. 10,000 Vols. Cat
Types: Facsimile editions, 1st ed, hb, illus bk, imp, new & used, out of print, papbk, old & rare, remainders, fine press
Subj: Amer, sci fiction & fantasy

V JANTA — Mail Order-Antiquarian
88-28 43rd Ave, 11373. Tel 718-898-6917 (by appt)
Estab 1974. 10,000 Vols
Types: Out of print, old & rare, rare Polish bks

ENDICOTT — 14,457. Area code 607

RICHARD E DONOVAN ENTERPRISES — Antiquarian
305 Massachusetts Ave, PO Box 7070, 13760-7070. Tel 607-785-5874
Cat 4x ann
Types: New, out of print, old & rare, used
Subj: Golf

FARMINGDALE — 7946. Area code 516

PRELUDE BOOK SHOP — Antiquarian-General
455 Main St, 11735. Tel 516-752-7062
Estab 1983. 20,000 Titles. 20,000 Vols. 1000 sq ft. Cat
Types: Hb, juvenile, out of print, papbk, remainders, used, 1st ed, ltd ed, new, old & rare, modern 1st ed
Subj: Humanities, hist

SCITECH BOOKS INC — Mail Order-Science-Technology
40 Motor Ave, PO Box 250, 11735. Tel 516-293-1771
Estab 1986. 30,000 Titles. 35,000 Vols. Cat
Types: New, used, out of print
Subj: Chem, engineering, math, metallurgy, medicine, for lang, electronics, computer sci, physics, scientifics

FLUSHING — Area code 718

HAITIAN BOOK CENTRE — French Lang
PO Box 324, 11369-0324. Tel 718-528-6543
Estab 1977. 1000 Vols. Cat 3x ann
Types: For lang, imp, out of print
Subj: Anthrop, art, Haiti, hist, lang arts, political thought, sociol, creole lang

M & M HALPERN BOOKDEALERS — Mail Order-Antiquarian
67-32 136th St, 11367. Tel 718-544-3885
Types: Out of print, 1st ed, illus bk, juvenile
Subj: Fiction, photog, cinema

NIPPAN DAIDO USA INC — General
137-80 Northern Blvd, 11354. Tel 718-961-1550
Mgr, Mr Kawamura
Types: Jap lang, hb, juvenile, papbk, out of print
See Also: White Plains; Chamblee, GA; Fort Lee, NJ; Houston, TX

FOREST HILLS — Area code 718

BIBLION INC — Mail Order-Antiquarian
PO Box 9, 11375. Tel 718-263-3910
Mgr, Ludwig Gottschalk
Estab 1948. 15,000 Vols. Cat
Types: Incunab, old & rare, out of print
Subj: Medicine, sci-tech

HENRY FELDSTEIN - PHOTOGRAPHY BOOKS — Mail Order-Antiquarian
107-40 Queens Blvd (Mail add: PO Box 398, 11375). Tel 718-544-3002
2000 Vols. 500 sq ft. Cat 4x ann
Types: 1st ed, out of print
Subj: Photog

FREEVILLE —449. Area code 607

THE PHOENIX USED & RARE BOOKS — Used
1608 Dryden Rd, Rte 13 (Mail add: PO Box 230, 13068). Tel 607-347-4767
Estab 1985. 50,000 Titles. 50,000 Vols. 2000 sq ft
Types: Hb, out of print, used, 1st ed, old & rare
Subj: Sci-tech, soc sci, hist, philos, math, fiction, literary criticism

GARDINER — 3552. Area code 914

BOOKWAYS — General
RD 1 Box 256, 12525. Tel 914-255-1959
Estab 1977. 8500 Vols. 1200 sq ft
Types: Hb, juvenile, out of print, papbk
Subj: Fiction, nonfiction, sci fiction & fantasy

GENESEO — 6746. Area code 716

LESLIE POSTE — Mail Order-Antiquarian
Lakeville Rd (Mail add: PO Box 68, 14454). Tel 716-243-3246
Estab 1971. 10,000 Vols. 600 sq ft
Types: 1st ed, out of print, old & rare
Subj: Scholarly lit

STATE UNIVERSITY OF NEW YORK COLLEGE AT GENESEO BOOKSTORE — College
College Union Bldg, 14454. Tel 716-245-5866. Telex 978433
Mgr, Diedre Staley
Estab 1959. 10,000 Vols. 5400 sq ft. Cat
Types: Hb, juvenile, out of print, papbk, remainders, used
Subj: Fiction, hobbies, literary criticism, nonfiction, reference, sci-tech

O.P. Resources

GENEVA — 15,133. Area code 315

THE BOOK FINDER Used
207 Lyons Rd, 14456-3417. Tel 315-789-9388
Estab 1978. 18,000 Vols
Types: 1st ed, hb, out of print, papbk, used
Subj: Humanities

CALHOUN'S BOOKS Antiquarian
1510 Rts 5 & 20 W, 14456-9106. Tel 315-789-8599
Estab 1981. 10,000 Vols. 1000 sq ft. Cat 6x ann
Types: Fine bnd, 1st ed, hb, illus bk, old & rare, out of print, juvenile, used
Subj: Aviation, Civil War, hunting & fishing, photog, New Yorkiana, navigation, black Amer, women's hist

GLEN HEAD — 4000. Area code 516

XERXES FINE AND RARE BOOKS AND DOCUMENTS Mail Order-Antiquarian
PO Box 428, 11545-0428. Tel 516-671-6235
Estab 1980. 20,000 Vols. Cat 6x ann
Types: Out of print, old & rare, sixteenth thru nineteenth century bks
Subj: Orientalia, travel, rel, Amer, medicine, sci-tech, Latin Am, hist doc

GLEN OAKS — Area code 516

SEA HERITAGE Antiquarian
254-26 75th Ave, 11004. Tel 718-343-9575
Mgr & Buyer, Bernard Klay
1500 Titles. 1500 Vols. Cat 8x ann
Types: Out of print, fine bnd, 1st ed, ltd ed, old & rare
Subj: Marine art & history, wreck diving, pirates

GREENWICH — 1955. Area code 518

OWL PEN - BOOKS Antiquarian
Rte 2 Box 202, 12834. Tel 518-692-7039
Estab 1960. 75,000 Vols. Cat
Types: Out of print, used, hb, juvenile
Subj: Natural hist

HARRIMAN — 796. Area code 914

HARRIMAN BOOKSHOP Antiquarian-Americana
PO Box 316, Harriman Sq, 10926. Tel 914-782-4338
Estab 1985. 10,000 Titles. 10,000 Vols
Types: Old & rare, out of print, used
Subj: New Jerseyana, New Yorkiana, Hudson River

HASTINGS-ON-HUDSON — 8573. Area code 914

RIVERRUN Antiquarian
7 Washington Ave, 10706. Tel 914-478-4307
Mgr, Frank Scioscia
Estab 1977. 150,000 Vols. 5000 sq ft
Types: 1st ed, hb, out of print, used
Subj: Fiction, mod lit, art

CHRISTOPHER P STEPHENS Antiquarian
7 Terrace Dr, 10706. Tel 914-478-2522 (by appt)
Estab 1973. 40,000 Vols. 1000 sq ft. Cat 8x ann
Types: 1st ed, out of print, illus bk, ltd ed, old & rare, fine presses
Subj: Fiction, mystery & detective, poetry, sci fiction & fantasy, Latin Am, author collec, translations, letters, scholarly symposia & scientific conferences

HAUPPAUGE — 13,957. Area code 516

H & R SALERNO Antiquarian
One Given Ct, 11788. Tel 516-724-8795, 265-3008
Estab 1977. Cat
Types: 1st ed, hb, illus bk, juvenile, ltd ed, old & rare, out of print, used
Subj: Art, mystery & detective, photog, sci fiction & fantasy, Long Island hist

HEMPSTEAD — 40,404. Area code 516

HOFSTRA UNIVERSITY BOOKSTORE College
1000 Fulton Ave, 11550. Tel 516-560-6654. Telex 96-7803. Easylink: 62045569
Mgr, Elaine Malnichuck; Asst Mgr, Michelle Feigenvaum; Text Mgr, Michele Guinta; Merch Buyer, Laura Martin
Types: Hb, juvenile, out of print, papbk, col text
Subj: Art, black studies, law, music, rel-c,j,p, sci-tech

LONG ISLAND BOOK CENTER Antiquarian
193 Front St, 11550. Tel 516-483-6527
Types: New & used, out of print, fine bnd, old & rare
Subj: General

WOMRATH COUNTY BOOKSHOP General
229 Fulton Ave, 11550. Tel 516-483-6338
Mgrs, Abraham Thomas
Estab 1955. 4000 Titles. 8000 Vols
Types: Col & el-hi text, hb, juvenile, out of print, papbk, remainders
Subj: Auto, bus & mgt, how-to, medicine, metaphys & occult, military, nursing, rel, civil serv

HILLSDALE — 1648. Area code 518

MAUREEN RODGERS BOOK BARN Used
Rodman Rd, 12529. Tel 518-325-3610
Estab 1971. 50,000 Vols
Types: Hb, out of print, papbk, juvenile

HOLBROOK — 12,103. Area code 516

HERPETOLOGICAL BOOKSELLERS Mail Order
15 Goodwill Lane, 11741. Tel 516-585-6539
Estab 1982. 3000 Titles. Cat 2x ann
Types: Hb, papbk, imp, for lang, out of print, remainders, used, 1st ed, illus bk, ltd ed, new, old & rare
Subj: Reptiles, amphibians

HOOSICK FALLS — 3609. Area code 518

FRANCIS PAUL GEOSCIENCE LITERATURE Mail Order
50 Church St, 12090-1691. Tel 518-686-7986
Types: Illus bk, old & rare, out of print
Subj: Geol, mineralogy, paleontology, US geological survey

HUDSON FALLS — 7419. Area code 518

THE VILLAGE BOOKSMITH Antiquarian
223 Main St, 12839. Tel 518-747-3261
Estab 1976. 45,000 Titles. 55,000 Vols. 2000 sq ft
Types: Out of print, new & used
Subj: Magic & conjuring, Amer, New Yorkiana, behavioral sci

HUNTINGTON — 201,512. Area code 516

COLLECTRIX Antiques
389 New York Ave, 11743. Tel 516-424-6479
Estab 1982. 1000 Vols. Cat 2x ann
Types: New, papbk, out of print
Subj: Collecting

POLYANTHOS BOOKS INC — Antiquarian
8 Green St (Mail add: PO Box 343, 11743). Tel 516-271-5558
Estab 1984. 25,000 Vols. Cat 3x ann
Types: Used, fine bnd, 1st ed, hb, illus bk, juvenile, ltd ed, old & rare, out of print, papbk, mod 1st ed

HUNTINGTON STATION — 28,817. Area code 516

WOMANKIND BOOKS INC — Mail Order-Women's Studies
5 Kivy St, 11746. Tel 516-427-1289
Estab 1979. 10,000 Vols. Cat 4x ann
Types: Col text, hb, out of print, remainders, juvenile
Subj: Health, psychol, non-sexist, lesbian fict & nonfict

HYDE PARK — 20,768. Area code 914

THE BOOK & RECORD — General
Mall at Hyde Park, 12538. Tel 914-229-5505
Estab 1970Buys indep & through hq
Types: Hb, out of print, papbk, remainders

ITHACA — 28,732. Area code 607

THE BOOKERY — General
Dewitt Mall, 215 N Cayuga St, 14850. Tel 607-273-5055
Mgr, Jack R Goldman
Estab 1975. 15,000 Titles. 20,000 Vols. Cat
Types: Fr & Sp lang, new & used, out of print, old & rare
Subj: Archit, linguistics, philos, New Yorkiana, sci-tech, math, art, anthrop, fiction, hist, scholarly lit, travel, natural science, history of science

JAMAICA — 100,000 Area code 718

CARAVAN-MARITIME BOOKS — Mail Order-Antiquarian
87-06 168th Pl, 11432. Tel 718-526-1380
Estab 1947. 8000 Titles. 14,0000 Vols. Cat 4x ann
Types: Illus bk, out of print, used, pamphlets
Subj: Maritime subjects only

JAMAICA BOOK CENTER — Antiquarian-General
146-16 Jamaica Ave, 11435. Tel 718-658-2500
Estab 1936. 50,000 Titles. 400,000 Vols. Cat
Types: Hb, juvenile, out of print, papbk, col text, used, new, encyclopedias, rare
Subj: Computer sci, tech

JOHNSON CITY — 17,126. Area code 607

FAT CAT BOOKS — Science Fiction & Fantasy
263 Main St, 13790. Tel 607-797-9111
Mgr, Tawna Lewis
Estab 1976. 2500 Titles. 8000 Vols. 1200 sq ft. Cat
Types: 1st ed, hb, ltd ed, new & used, old & rare, out of print, papbk, remainders, comics
Subj: Mystery & detective, horror

JOHNSTOWN — 9360. Area code 518

TRYON COUNTY BOOKSHOP — Used
RD One, Rte 29, Box 207, 12095. Tel 518-762-1060
5000 Vols. Cat
Types: Out of print
Subj: Hunting & fishing, wildlife, Africa, mil hist

KATONAH — Area code 914

KATONAH BOOK SCOUT — Mail Order-Antiquarian
75 Meadow Ln, 10536. Tel 914-232-5768
Estab 1980. 8000 Titles. Cat ann black studies
Types: Used, out of print, 1st ed, illus bk, hb, ltd ed, old & rare, juvenile
Subj: Fiction, performing arts, military, nautical, black studies, sports, biog, travel, mystery & detective

KEW GARDENS — Area code 718

AUSTIN BOOKSHOP — Antiquarian
Box 36, 11415. Tel 718-441-1199, 7014
75,000 Vols. Cat 2x ann
Types: 1st ed, imp, out of print, old & rare, remainders, used
Subj: Women's studies, ethnic studies, hist, immigration, law, Judaica, Am hist & lit, baseball, lit, holocaust

KINDERHOOK — 1377. Area code 518

L E GOBRECHT BOOKS — Antiquarian
Kinderhook Antiques Ctr, Rte 9H, PO Box 531, 12106. Tel 518-758-7939, 758-3431
Estab 1978. 5000 Titles. 400 sq ft
Types: 1st ed, hb, illus bk, old & rare, out of print, used
Subj: Am hist & lit, archit, local hist, Am decorative arts

LAFAYETTE — 4488. Area code 315

HAROLD J SHOEBRIDGE ANTIQUARIAN BOOKS — Mail Order-Used
Maple Hill, Berry Rd, 13084. Tel 315-677-3056
Estab 1980. 500 Vols. Cat
Types: Fine bnd, 1st ed, hb, illus bk, ltd ed, old & rare, out of print, used, signed copies
Subj: Bks on bks, New Yorkiana, binding

LAKE PLACID — 2490. Area code 518

WITH PIPE & BOOK — Antiquarian
91 Main St, 12946-1301. Tel 518-523-9096
Estab 1977. 20,000 Titles. 20,000 Vols. 1400 sq ft. Cat 2x ann
Types: 1st ed, hb, old & rare, out of print, used, papbk
Subj: Adirondacks, skating, tobacco

LANSINGBURG — Area code 518

WARREN F BRODERICK BOOKS — Mail Order-Used
695 Fourth Ave, PO Box 124, 12182. Tel 518-235-4041
Estab 1977. 4000 Vols
Types: Facsimile editions, hb, illus bk, imp UK, new, old & rare, out of print, remainders
Subj: Gardening, hort

LARCHMONT — 6308. Area code 914

F A BERNETT INC — Antiquarian
2001 Palmer Ave (Mail add: PO Box 948, 10538). Tel 914-834-3026
Estab 1944. 5000 Titles. 6000 Vols. Cat 6x ann
Types: Out of print, old & rare
Subj: Archaeol, art, archit

WILD MUSE — Mail Order
PO Box 509, 10538. Tel 212-320-1394
Estab 1985. 10,000 Titles. 10,000 Vols. Cat 4x ann
Types: Out of print, 1st ed, hb, old & rare
Subj: Lit 1st ed

LATHAM — 9661. Area code 518

DISCOUNT BOOK CENTER — General
New Loudon Plaza, Rte 9, 12210. Tel 518-783-6352
Mgr, Melissa Amsden
Estab 1983. 6000 Titles. 20,000 Vols. Cat 3x annBuys indep & through hq
Types: For lang, hb, juvenile, out of print, papbk, remainders, used

LEWISTON — 3326. Area code 716

BROADWATER BOOKS — Antiquarian
PO Box 278, 14092. Tel 716-754-8145
Estab 1948. 7500 Vols. Cat ann
Types: Out of print, used
Subj: Natural hist

LIMA — 2025. Area code 716

MAXWELL'S TREASURES, FINE BOOKS & EPHEMERA — Antiquarian-General
7303 E Main St (Mail add: 11 Quaker Dr, Rochester, 14623). Tel 716-624-4550
Estab 1981. 5000 Titles. 800 sq ft. Cat ann
Types: Hb, old & rare, out of print, imp UK, facsimile editions, fine bnd, 1st ed, illus bk, juvenile, ltd ed, used
Subj: Amer, ethnology

LINDENHURST — 26,919. Area code 516

HERPETOLOGICAL SEARCH SERVICE & EXCHANGE* — Mail Order-Natural History
117 E Santa Barbara Rd, 11757. Tel 516-957-3624
Cat ann
Types: Out of print, papbk

LIVINGSTON — 3087. Area code 518

HOWARD FRISCH — Antiquarian
PO Box 75, Old Post Rd, 12541-0075. Tel 518-851-7493
Estab 1954. 10,000 Vols. Cat 2x ann
Types: Hb, juvenile, out of print
Subj: Amer
See Also: New York

LONG ISLAND CITY — Area code 718

BILL THE BOOKY — Antiquarian
30-91 Crescent St (Mail add: PO Box 6228, 11106). Tel 718-728-4791
Owners, Bill Epstein & Irma Epstein
Cat 3-4x ann
Types: Out of print, used, 1st ed, old & rare
Subj: Caricature bks, cartoon bks, original cartoon art, journalism

LOUDONVILLE — 9299. Area code 518

MICHAEL HUXLEY BOOKSELLER — Mail Order-Antiquarian
355 Loudon Rd, 12211. Tel 518-449-7280
Estab 1981. 3000 Titles. 3500 Vols. Cat 3x ann
Types: Facsimile editions, 1st ed, hb, illus bk, imp, juvenile, ltd ed, old & rare, out of print, remainders, used
Subj: Africa, natural hist, travel

MAMARONECK — 17,616. Area code 914

ARMCHAIR SAILOR — Nautical
157 Mamaroneck Ave, 10543. Tel 914-381-6030
Mgr, E Chester Peet Jr
Types: Hb, out of print, papbk, remainders, col text
Subj: Marine, navigation

R A GOODKIND — Mail Order-Antiquarian
151 Fenimore Rd 63 B, 10543. Tel 914-698-7854
Mgr, Rachel A Goodkind
Estab 1930. 2000 Vols
Types: Out of print, old & rare
Subj: Music, cellos, violas, violins & their bows, vegetarianism

YESTERDAYS BOOKS — Antiquarian
124 Palmer Ave, 10543. Tel 914-834-6630
Estab 1984. 15,000 Titles. 16,000 Vols. 850 sq ft
Types: Fine bnd, 1st ed, hb, illus bk, juvenile, ltd ed, old & rare, out of print, remainders
Subj: Military, Amer, antq & art ref

MANHASSET — 8541. Area code 516

MANHASSET BOOK CO — General
365 Plandome Rd, 11030. Tel 516-365-5775
Types: Hb, juvenile, out of print, papbk, remainders, used, dictionaries

MASSAPEQUA PARK — 19,779. Area code 516

AMERICAN CROSSWORD FEDERATION — Mail Order-Antiquarian
113 Kings Walk, 11762. Tel 516-795-8823
Estab 1983. 1000 Titles
Types: Out of print, used

MIDDLETOWN — 21,454. Area code 914

THE BOOK & RECORD — General
Orange Plaza, 10940. Tel 914-343-3593Buys indep & through hq
Types: Out of print, papbk, remainders

QUALITY BOOK SERVICE - T EMMETT HENDERSON — Antiquarian
130 W Main St, 10940. Tel 914-343-1038
Asst Mgr Barbara Lynn Henderson
Estab 1954. 7000 Vols. Cat ann
Types: 1st ed, hb, new & used, out of print, papbk, old & rare, remainders
Subj: Amer, early sci

MILLBROOK — 1343. Area code 914

COPPER FOX FARM BOOKS — Used
Box 763, 12545. Tel 914-677-3013
Estab 1968. 50,000 Titles. 55,000 Vols. Cat
Types: Facsimile editions, 1st ed, hb, illus bk, juvenile, ltd ed, old & rare, out of print, papbk
Subj: Gardening, natural hist, antq, military, horses, dogs

MILTON — 12,876. Area code 914

PALENQUE BOOKS — Antiquarian
RR-1 Box 12, 12547. Tel 914-795-5266
Mgr, William Stickle
5000 Titles. 5000 Vols
Types: Out of print, used, hb
Subj: F D Roosevelt, New Deal

MOUNT KISCO — 8025. Area code 914

PAGES — Mail Order-Antiquarian
16 Dakin Ave, 10549. Tel 914-666-8281
Estab 1981. 10,000 Vols. 205 sq ft. Cat bi-ann
Types: 1st ed, hb, illus bk, juvenile, ltd ed, out of print, old & rare, used
Subj: Art, Hudson River, Westchester

NEVERSINK — Area code 914

WANTAGH RARE BOOK CO — Mail Order-Americana
Myers Rd, PO Box 605, 12765-0605. Tel 914-985-7482
Estab 1966. Cat 6x ann
Types: Hb, out of print, old & rare, used, juvenile
Subj: Am hist & lit, Amer

NEWBURGH — 23,438. Area code 914

CLOUGH'S BOOKSHOP — Used
159 Liberty, 12550. Tel 914-561-5522
Estab 1984. 25,000 Titles. 35,000 Vols. 700 sq ft. Cat
Types: Out of print, remainders, 1st ed, hb, illus bk, juvenile, new, papbk, old & rare
Subj: Natural hist, New Yorkiana

NEW PALTZ — 4941. Area code 914

THE BOOK & RECORD — Gift Shop
New Paltz Plaza, 12561. Tel 914-255-7575
Mgr, Diane Donohue Buys indep & through hq
Types: Hb, out of print, papbk, remainders

GORDON & GORDON BOOKSELLERS — Antiquarian
Cherry Hill Center, 12561. Tel 914-255-1529
Estab 1987. 10,000 Titles. 10,000 Vols. Cat 2x ann
Types: Imp UK, out of print, fine bnd, 1st ed, hb, illus bk, old & rare, ltd ed
Subj: 19th century private press bks, radical

NEW YORK — 7,071,030. Area code 212

ABRAHAM'S MAGAZINE SERVICE — Mail Order-Antiquarian
56 E 13th St, 10003. Tel 212-777-4700
Mgr, Stephen J Baron
Estab 1889. Cat
Types: Facsimile editions, imp, new & used, out of print, old & rare
See Also: Wholesale section

ACANTHUS BOOKS — Antiquarian
48 W 22nd St, 10010. Tel 212-463-0750. by appt
Estab 1982. 1000 Vols. Cat 4x ann
Types: Old & rare, out of print
Subj: Archit, antq, decorative arts

A PHOTOGRAPHER'S PLACE — Photography
133 Mercer St, 10012. Tel 212-431-9358
Estab 1979. 4000 Titles. 9000 Vols. 1200 sq ft. Cat 6x ann
Types: Hb, imp, out of print, papbk, remainders, used
Subj: Sci-tech, collecting

THE APOTHECARY — Mail Order-Medicine
Drawer F, Lenox Hill Station, 10021. Tel 215-294-9036
Estab 1958. 5000 Vols. Cat
Types: Out of print, used
Subj: Pharmacy

ARGOSY BOOKSTORE INC — Antiquarian
116 E 59th St, 10022. Tel 212-753-4455
Estab 1924. 400,000 Titles. 500,000 Vols. Cat 10x ann
Types: 1st ed, out of print, used
Subj: Amer, art, medicine

ART OF READING — General
206 Mercer St, 10012. Tel 212-673-1860
Estab 1985. 10,000 Titles. 25,000 Vols. 1400 sq ft
Types: Hb, high priced papbk, remainders, col text, used, out of print
Subj: Art, medicine, computer sci, sci-tech

ASIAN RARE BOOKS INC — Antiquarian-Orientalia
234 Fifth Ave, (3/F), 10001. Tel 718-259-3732. Cable: Asianrare
Assoc Dir, Stephen Feldman
Estab 1976. Cat 10x ann
Types: Out of print, old & rare
Subj: Asian studies, Middle East

ASIA SOCIETY BOOKSTORE — Museum
725 Park Ave, 10021. Tel 212-288-6400
Mgr, Warren Gunderson
Estab 1981. 5000 Vols. 600 sq ft. Cat 4x ann
Types: Col text, hb, imp, juvenile, out of print, papbk, remainders
Subj: Asian studies

THE BALLET SHOP — Dance
1887 Broadway, 10023. Tel 212-581-7990
Mgr & Buyer, Tobias Leibovitz
Estab 1974. 500 Titles
Types: Hb, imp, out of print, mass mkt papbk, used
Subj: Opera, performing arts, ballet

C VIRGINIA BARNES - BOOKSELLER — Antiquarian
2 Fifth Ave, 16M, 10011
Estab 1954. Cat
Types: Facsimile editions, 1st ed, hb, imp, incunab, juvenile, new & used, out of print, old & rare, papbk, remainders
Subj: Genealogy, magic & conjuring, Pennsylvaniana, Southern Amer, memory, mnemonics

C RICHARD BECKER — Mail Order-Antiques
238 W 14th St, 10011-7217. Tel 212-243-3789
3000 Titles. 4000 Vols. Cat 4x ann
Types: Fine bnd, 1st ed, hb, illus bk, ltd ed, old & rare, out of print
Subj: Fine arts, decorative arts

BIOGRAPHY HOUSE — Antiquarian-Biography
547 W 27th St, 10001. Tel 212-714-2004
Estab 1986. 22,000 Titles. 26,000 Vols. 800 sq ft
Types: Hb, out of print, old & rare

BLOCH PUBLISHING CO, INC — Religious-J
37 W 26th St, 10010. Tel 212-532-3977
Estab 1854. 100 Titles. 1200 sq ft. Cat
Types: Col & el-hi text, imp UK, imp Isr, juvenile, out of print, papbk, remainders
Subj: Hist, Judaica

THE BOOK CHEST — Antiquarian-Humor
125 E 87th St, 10128. Tel 212-410-4711
Estab 1972. 1200 Titles. 1200 Vols. Cat 1-2x ann
Types: Hb, out of print, old & rare
Subj: Humor, comedy, colorplate, satire, 15th-20th century humor

BOOKFINDERS GENERAL INC — Mail Order-Antiquarian
PO Box 837, Madison Square Station, 10159-0837. Tel 212-689-0772
Cat 3x ann
Types: Out of print, old & rare
Subj: Medicine, genealogy

BOOK RANGER* — Mail Order
105 Charles, 10014. Tel 212-924-4957
Estab 1973
Types: 1st ed, hb, illus bk, ltd ed, out of print, used

BOOKS-N-THINGS — Used
64 E Seventh St, 10003. Tel 212-533-2320
Estab 1941. 10,000 Vols
Types: 1st ed, hb, juvenile, out of print, papbk
Subj: Dance, literary criticism, music, poetry, films & filmmaking, art, photog, theater

BRAZEN HEAD BOOKSTORE — Antiquarian
235 E 84th St, 10028. Tel 212-879-9830
10,000 Vols
Types: Hb, papbk, 1st ed, old & rare, out of print, used
Subj: Biog, hist

E W BRILL -ANTIQUARIAN BOOKS — Mail Order
249 W 34th St, Rm 707, 10001. Tel 212-864-1269, 695-1996. WATS 800-562-9911
Types: Out of print
Subj: Hebraica, Judaica

BROUDE BROTHERS LIMITED — Music
170 Varick St, 10013. Tel 212-242-7001. WATS 800-225-3197
Mgr, M R Roberts
Estab 1939. Cat
Types: Col text, hb, imp, out of print
Subj: Art, scholarly lit

BURLINGTON BOOKSHOP — General
1082 Madison Ave, 10028. Tel 212-288-7420
Estab 1930. 4000 Titles. 10,000 Vols

Types: Hb, papbk, out of print
Subj: Art, cooking, fiction, mystery & detective, nonfiction

CAMEL BOOK COMPANY — Mail Order-Antiquarian
PO Box 1936, Cathedral Sta, 10025-1936
Estab 1985. 2000 Titles. 2000 Vols. Cat 2x ann
Types: Used, Arabic lang, hb, illus bk, old & rare, out of print, imp Arab countries & Israel
Subj: Judaica, Middle East, Islam, lit, Judaica

CARLTON PRESS INC — General
11 West 32nd St, 10001. Tel 212-714-0300
Dir Publicity, Alan Young
600 Titles
Types: Hb, out of print, remainders, text bks
Subj: Fiction, nonfiction, sports, military, biog, poetry

JAMES F CARR — Antiquarian
220 E 81st St, 10028. Tel 212-535-8110
Mgr, L E Piasecki
Estab 1959. 40,000 Vols. 2000 sq ft. Cat
Types: Used, papbk, hb, Fr lang, out of print, old & rare, fine bnd

CFM — French Lang
138 W 17th St, 10011. Tel 212-929-4001
Estab 1986. 200 Titles. 300 Vols
Types: Fr lang, fine bnd, 1st ed, illus bk, imp Fr, ltd ed, out of print

CHARTWELL BOOKSELLERS — General
Park Ave Plaza, 55 E 52nd St, 10055. Tel 212-308-0643
Estab 1983. 7500 Titles. 10,000 Vols. 685 sq ft. Cat ann
Types: Hb, imp UK, out of print, juvenile
Subj: Art, fashion, photog, archit, interior design, travel, gardening, cooking, bus & mgt, finance, Winston Churchill, fly fishing, jazz

CHIP'S BOOKSEARCH — Antiquarian
PO Box 123 Planetarium Station, 10024. Tel 212-362-9336
Estab 1957. Cat 2x ann
Types: Hb, old & rare, out of print, 1st ed
Subj: Literary criticism, belles lettres, Conrad

CHIP'S BOOKSHOP INC — Mail Order-Antiquarian
Box 639-Cooper Sta, 10003
5000 Vols. Cat 2x ann
Types: 1st ed, hb, imp, out of print, used
Subj: Art, humanities, literary criticism

COLLECTORS' EDITIONS — Mail Order
PO Box 20422, Cherokee Sta, 10028-9991. Tel 212-288-3649
Estab 1977. 2000 Titles. 2000 Vols. Cat
Types: Out of print, rare
Subj: Photog, art, decorative arts, bk arts, trade catalogues

CONTINENTAL BOOK SEARCH — Mail Order
PO Box 1163, 10009. Tel 212-254-8719
10,000 Titles. Cat
Types: Out of print
Subj: Nonfiction, anthrop, philos

HOWARD C DAITZ PHOTOGRAPHICA — Antiquarian-Photography
328 W 20th St (Mail add: Box 530, Old Chelsea Station, 10011). Tel 212-929-8987
3000 Vols
Types: Old & rare, out of print
Subj: 19th or 20th century bks or photographs

A DIFFERENT LIGHT — Homosexuality
548 Hudson St, 10014. Tel 212-989-4850. WATS 800-343-4002
Owners, Androgyny Books Inc & Norman Laurila; Mgr & Buyer, Jim Vivyan
Estab 1984. 7000 Titles. 6000 Vols. 750 sq ft. Cat 4x ann
Types: Fr, Ger & Sp lang, hb, juvenile, papbk, remainders, col text, out of print, imp Can, Australia, UK, Fr, Ger, Sp, Ital, Neth
Subj: Gay & lesbian lit
See Also: Los Angeles, San Francisco, CA

DONAN BOOKS INC — Used
220 E 82nd St, 10028. Tel 212-734-0707
Estab 1969. 20,000 Titles. 20,000 Vols. 1500 sq ft
Types: Hb, out of print

EL CASCAJERO, THE OLD SPANISH BOOK MINE — Antiquarian
506 La Guardia Pl, 10012-2501. Tel 212-254-0905
Estab 1956. 10,000 Vols. Cat 2x ann
Types: 1st ed, hb, imp, old & rare, out of print
Subj: Hispanica

ELLIOT GORDON BOOKS — Art
150 E 69th St, 8-H, 10021. Tel 212-861-2892
1500 Titles
Types: Out of print, used, illus bk, old & rare
Subj: Reference, scholarly lit, art hist

EX LIBRIS — Antiquarian-Art
160A E 70th St, 10021. Tel 212-249-2618
Mgr, W Michael Sheehe
Estab 1974. 5000 Titles. 5000 Vols. Cat 4-6x ann
Types: 1st ed, hb, illus bk, for lang, ltd ed, new, old & rare, out of print
Subj: Graphic arts, photog, 20th Century archit, Russ avant-garde, surrealism, Vienna secession

FANTASY ARCHIVES — Antiquarian-Science Fiction & Fantasy
71 Eighth Ave, 10014. Tel 212-929-5391
Estab 1980. 20,000 Titles. 20,000 Vols. 1000 sq ft. Cat
Types: Hb, 1st ed, fine bnd, illus bk, imp UK, juvenile, ltd ed, new & used, old & rare, out of print, papbk
Subj: Horror bestsellers

BOB FEIN BOOKS — Antiquarian-Am Indians
150 Fifth Ave, Room 623, 10011. Tel 212-807-0489
Estab 1980. 3000 Titles. 4000 Vols. 400 sq ft. Cat 10x ann
Types: Old & rare, out of print, used
Subj: NAmer, SAm, Eskimo art & culture, pre-Columbian art, African & Egyptian art & archeology, Mexican muralists

PETER THOMAS FISHER - BOOKSELLER — Mail Order
41 Union Square W, 10003. Tel 212-255-6789
Estab 1976. 10,000 Vols. Cat 4x ann
Types: For lang, hb, fine bnd, 1st ed, incunab, illus bk, imp, juvenile, old & rare, out of print, used, Ger lang
Subj: Ger lang, Stefan Zwieg

HOWARD FRISCH NEW & ANTIQUARIAN BOOKS — Mail Order-Antiquarian
PO Box 128, Village Sta, 10014. Tel 212-243-6188
Estab 1954. 10,000 Vols. Cat 2x annBuys indep & thourgh hq
Types: Hb, juvenile, out of print
Subj: Amer

RALPH D GARDNER — Mail Order-Antiquarian
135 Central Park W, 10023. Tel 212-877-6820
Types: 1st ed, hb, juvenile, new & used, out of print, old & rare, papbk

GENERAL MEDICAL BOOK CO — Medicine
310 E 26th St, 10010. Tel 212-532-0756, 532-9822
Owner, Univ Book Co; Mgr, Ricki Applebaum
Estab 1918. 3500 Vols. Cat
Types: Hb, out of print
Subj: Dentistry, nursing, vet med

V F GERMACK, PROFESSIONAL PHOTOGRAPHY COLLECTORS — Antiquarian-Photography
1199 Park Ave, 10028. Tel 212-289-8411 (by appt only)
Estab 1978
Types: Old & rare, out of print

GOLDEN GRIFFIN BOOKSHOP — Antiquarian
PO Box 748 FDR Sta, 10150-0748. Tel 914-337-6969
Owner, Arts Inc; Mgr, J Vanos
Estab 1952. 6000 Vols
Types: Hb, Fr lang, Gr lang, juvenile, out of print, papbk
Subj: Art

GOTHAM BOOK MART & GALLERY INC — Modern Literature
41 W 47th St, 10036. Tel 212-719-4448
Mgr & Buyer, Philip Lyman
Estab 1920. 400,000 Vols
Types: 1st ed, hb, high priced papbk, out of print, used, small presses
Subj: Philos, poetry, class studies, cinema, theater

GRAMERCY BOOK SHOP — Mail Order-Antiquarian
22 E 17th St, 10003-3289. Tel 212-255-5568
Mgr, R Wilbur
Estab 1940. 8500 Vols. Cat 3-4x ann
Types: 1st ed, hb, out of print, old & rare, remainders, used
Subj: Poetry, drama, biog, literary criticism, American & English lit

V L GREEN BOOKSELLERS — Mail Order
19 E 76th St, 10021. Tel 212-439-9194
Estab 1987. 8000 Titles. 7500 Vols. 800 sq ft. Cat 4x ann
Types: Hb, out of print, imp Fr, imp Ital, imp Ger, imp UK, old & rare
Subj: Art, archaeol, decorative art

GRYPHON BOOKSHOP — Used
2246 Broadway, 10024. Tel 212-362-0706
Estab 1974. 50,000 Vols
Types: Fine bnd, 1st ed, illus bk, juvenile, ltd ed, old & rare, out of print
Subj: Performing arts, illus, Oz

J N HERLIN INC — Antiquarian
40 Harrison St, Apt 85D, 10013. Tel 212-732-1086
Estab 1972. 10,000 Vols. 350 sq ft
Types: Out of print
Subj: Photog, 20th century art

HWK BOOKS — Antiquarian-Natural History
540 W 114th St, 10025. Tel 212-865-6202
Mgr, Herman W Kitchen
Estab 1972. 5000 Titles. 6000 Vols. 1200 sq ft. Cat 2x ann
Types: Hb, imp, out of print, used, fine bnd, incunab, illus bk, old & rare
Subj: Diaries, discovery & explor

IDEAL BOOKSTORE — Antiquarian
1125 Amsterdam Ave, 10025. Tel 212-662-1909
Estab 1931. 30,000 Titles. 45,000 Vols. 1200 sq ft. Cat 12x ann
Types: Imp, new & used, out of print, remainders
Subj: Humanities, soc sci

INTERNATIONAL CENTER OF PHOTOGRAPHY — Museum
1130 Fifth Ave, 10128. Tel 212-860-1751
Dir, Edna Ghertler
Estab 1974. 700 Titles. 700 Vols. Cat
Types: Hb, out of print, papbk
Subj: Photog

IRISH BOOKS & GRAPHICS — Antiquarian-Irish Hist & Lit
90 W Broadway, 10007. Tel 212-962-4237
Estab 1979. 300 sq ft
Types: New, out of print, Gaelic lang
Subj: Irish hist & lit

HARMER JOHNSON BOOKS, LTD — Antiquarian
38 E 64th St, Suite 3, 10021. Tel 212-752-1189
Owners, Harmer Johnson & Peter Sharrer
Estab 1977. 10,000 Vols. Cat 3x ann
Types: Facsimile editions, 1st ed, hb, illus bk, imp, ltd ed, old & rare, out of print
Subj: Art ref, colorplate bks (Egyptian, Roman & Gr antq, ethnographic art), ancient art, tribal art

ARNOLD B JOSEPH — Antiquarian-Transportation
1140 Broadway, Room 701, 10001-7504. Tel 212-532-0019
Estab 1978. 3500 Titles. 10,000 Vols. 500 sq ft
Types: Hb, papbk, new & used, out of print, illus bk, old & rare, imp UK, imp Can, used
Subj: Railroadiana, transp

YOSHIO KISHI — Mail Order
165 W 66 St, 10023. Tel 212-787-7954
Estab 1969. 10,000 Titles. 11,000 Vols. 500 sq ft. Cat
Types: 1st ed, hb, old & rare, out of print
Subj: Asians in North & South Am, North Pacific

JUDITH & PETER KLEMPERER — Antiquarian-New Yorkiana
400 Second Ave, 10010. Tel 212-684-5970
Estab 1975. 3000 Titles. 3000 Vols. Cat ann
Types: Hb, illus bk, juvenile, old & rare, out of print, used
Subj: New York City

THE LAWBOOK EXCHANGE LTD — Law
135 W 29th St, 10001-5104. Tel 212-594-4341. WATS 800-422-6686
Estab 1983. 25,000 Vols. 6000 sq ft. Cat 4x ann
Types: Used, facsimile editions, old & rare, out of print

LARRY LAWRENCE RARE SPORTS — Mail Order-Antiquarian
PO Box 756, Planetarium Sta, 10024. Tel 212-362-8593
Estab 1978. 500 Titles. 500 Vols. Cat 8x ann
Types: Out of print, old & rare
Subj: Sports, golf, baseball

JANET LEHR INC — Photography
PO Box 617, Gracie Sq Sta, 10028. Tel 212-288-1802
Estab 1966. 2500 Titles. 5000 Vols. 2000 sq ft. Cat 4x ann
Types: Out of print, photog illus bks
Subj: Asian studies, Western Amer, fashion, 19th & 20th cent travel

MAGAZINE CENTER — Mail Order-Antiquarian
1133 Broadway, Dept 451, 10010. Tel 212-929-5255
Estab 1974. Cat 4x ann
Types: Imp, out of print, old & rare
Subj: Art, fashion

ISAAC H MANN — Mail Order-Antiquarian
240 W 98th St, 10025. Tel 212-230-6712
Cat
Types: Out of print, used, Eng, Yiddish & Hebr lang
Subj: Judaica

M M EINHORN MAXWELL BOOKS - AT THE SIGN OF THE DANCING BEAR — Antiquarian
80 E 11th St, 10003. Tel 212-228-6767, 477-5066
Estab 1977. 10,000 Vols. Cat 4x ann
Types: Hb, imp, new & used, out of print, old & rare, remainders
Subj: Wines, cooking, gastronomy, hotels & restaurants

THE MILITARY BOOKMAN — Antiquarian
29 E 93rd St, 10128-0695. Tel 212-348-1280
Mgr, Jason Dubinman
Estab 1976. 10,000 Titles. 10,000 Vols. 750 sq ft. Cat 3x ann
Types: Out of print
Subj: Military, naval, aviation

ARTHUR H MINTERS INC — Antiquarian
39 W 14th St, Rm 401, 10011. Tel 212-989-0593
Estab 1957. 10,000 Vols. 2200 sq ft. Cat 6x ann
Types: Facsimile editions, 1st ed, hb, illus bk, old & rare, out of print, used, for lang, mod illus bks
Subj: Archit, art, films & filmmaking, graphic arts, mod lit, photog

JAMES C MOREL FINE BOOKS — Mail Order-Antiquarian
241 Central Park W, 10024. Tel 212-580-9140
Estab 1974. Cat ann
Types: 1st ed, illus bk, out of print
Subj: Mod lit, poetry

MURDER INK LTD — Mystery & Detective
271 W 87th St, 10024. Tel 212-362-8905
Estab 1972. 25,000 Vols. 400 sq ft. Cat 2x ann
Types: 1st ed, hb, imp UK, out of print, old & rare, papbk, used

MUSEUM BOOKS INC — Art
6 W 37th St, 10018. Tel 212-562-2770
Mgr, N Kosteas

Estab 1947. Cat
Types: Hb, imp, out of print, papbk
Subj: Calligraphy, design, typography, graphic design & technique, fiber arts, crafts, applied & decorative arts

THE MYSTERIOUS BOOKSHOP — Antiquarian-Mystery & Detective
129 W 56th St, 10019. Tel 212-765-0900
Mgr & Buyer, Michael Krugman
Estab 1979. 15,000 Titles. 40,000 Vols. Cat 2x ann
Types: Hb, imp, juvenile, out of print, papbk, used
Subj: Fiction, reference

NEW YORK BOUND BOOKSHOP — Antiquarian-New Yorkiana
29 E 11th St, 10003. Tel 212-245-8503
Estab 1976. 3000 Vols. Cat 4x ann
Types: Out of print, old & rare, used

NUDEL BOOKS — Antiquarian
135 Spring St, 10012. Tel 212-966-5624
Estab 1981. 20,000 Vols. 1000 sq ft. Cat 4x ann
Types: 1st ed, illus bk, ltd ed, old & rare, out of print
Subj: Photog, black lit

OCEANIE AFRIQUE NOIRE — Mail Order
9 E 38th St, 4th Fl, 10016. Tel 212-779-0486
Pres, Lynda Cunningham
Estab 1967. 10,000 Titles. 100,000 Vols. 4200 sq ft. Cat 4x ann
Types: Facsimile editions, fine bnd, 1st ed, for lang, hb, imp, new & used, old & rare, out of print, papbk, remainders
Subj: Africa, NAmer, ethnic studies, art, Oceania, SE Asia, tribal textiles & jewelry

PAGEANT BOOK AND PRINT SHOP — Antiquarian
109 E Ninth St, 10003. Tel 212-674-5296
Estab 1945. 250,000 Vols. Cat
Types: 1st ed, old & rare, out of print, used
Subj: Art, fiction, psychol, hist

FRED & ELIZABETH PAJERSKI — Photography
225 W 25th St, 4K, 10001. Tel 212-255-6501
Estab 1984. 1750 Titles. 5000 Vols. Cat 3x ann
Types: For lang, hb, imp, papbk, facsimile editions, 1st ed, illus bk, new, out of print, remainders, used
Subj: Photog in the 19th cent

PATHS UNTRODDEN BOOK SERVICE — Mail Order-Homosexuality
PO Box 459 Village Sta, 10014-0459. Tel 212-924-5421
Estab 1979. 2000 Titles. 3000 Vols. Cat ann
Types: Ger lang, hb, imp UK, imp Ger, out of print, remainders, used, 1st ed, illus bk, ltd ed, new, old & rare, papbk
Subj: Transvestism, gay liberation, erotica

POMANDER BOOKSHOP — Antiquarian
955 West End Ave, 10025. Tel 212-866-1777
Estab 1974. 10,000 Vols
Types: 1st ed, hb, out of print, used
Subj: Art, travel, lit

RICHARD C RAMER OLD & RARE BOOKS — Mail Order-Antiquarian
225 E 70th St, 10021. Tel 212-737-0222, 737-0223
Estab 1969. 10,000 Vols. Cat
Types: Out of print, old & rare
Subj: Amer, Asian studies, Brazil, Latin Am, Port lang, nautical, Sp lang, travel, cartography

REINHOLD-BROWN GALLERY — Mail Order-Antiquarian
26 E 78th St, 10021. Tel 212-734-7999
Cat
Types: Hb, imp, old & rare, out of print
Subj: Art, poster & graphic design

MARY S ROSENBERG INC — Importer
1841 Broadway, 10023. Tel 212-307-7733
Estab 1940. 100,000 Vols. 2700 sq ft. Cat 3x ann
Types: Hb, out of print, papbk, used
Subj: Fr lang, Ger lang

PAULETTE ROSE LTD — Antiquarian-Feminism
360 E 72nd St, 10021. Tel 212-861-5607
1000 Titles. 2000 Vols. Cat 2x ann
Types: 1st ed, imp Fr, old & rare, out of print
Subj: Feminism, women's studies, Fr lit, Eng lit

J B RUND — Mail Order-Antiquarian
PO BOX 1234, Old Chelsea Sta, 10113. Tel 212-620-4276
Estab 1967
Types: Facsimile editions, 1st ed, out of print, old & rare, used
Subj: Erotica

CHARLOTTE F SAFIR BOOKS — Mail Order-Antiquarian
1349 Lexington Ave, Apt 9B, 10128. Tel 212-534-7933
3500 Vols
Types: Juvenile, old & rare, out of print, used
Subj: Art, cooking, for lang, hist, Judaica

SALVATION ARMY SUPPLIES & PURCHASING — Religious
145 W 15th St, 10011. Tel 212-337-7200
Buyer, George Larson; Mgr, Clifford Hall
25,000 Vols. Cat 2x ann
Types: Hb, juvenile, out of print, papbk, remainders

THE SCIENCE FICTION SHOP — Science Fiction & Fantasy
56 Eighth Ave, 10014. Tel 212-741-0270
Mgr, Michael Franklin
Estab 1973. 6000 Titles. Cat 6x ann
Types: Hb, imp UK, out of print, papbk, used
Subj: Horror

S R SHAPIRO CO, BOOKS FOR LIBRARIES — Antiquarian
29 E Tenth St, 10003. Tel 212-673-0610
Mgr, A M Robinson
Estab 1935. 100,000 Vols. Cat monthly
Types: Facsimile editions, 1st ed, imp, incunab, new, out of print, old & rare
Subj: Africa, bibliog, fine arts, Latin Am, hist, Far, Near & Middle East, Slavic lands

SOMERVILLE & ROSS — Mail Order
PO Box 7272, FDR Station, 10150-1910. Tel 718-768-8211
Cat 4x ann
Types: Out of print, used, 1st ed
Subj: Women's lit, op novels, 19th & 20th century lit

SOUTH STREET SEAPORT MUSEUM BOOK & CHART STORE — Museum
209 Water St (Mail add: 19 Fulton St, Suite 303, 10038). Tel 212-669-9453
Mgr & Buyer, Michael Flynn
Estab 1970. 4000 Vols
Types: Hb, juvenile, out of print, papbk, remainders, used
Subj: Maritime & naval hist, New York City, boating magazines

SPERLING BOOKS — Mail Order
Madison Square Station, PO Box 1766, 10159. Tel 212-260-5949
Estab 1977. 20,000 Vols. Cat
Types: 1st ed, fine bnd, illus bk, old & rare, out of print, used, imp UK

RICHARD STODDARD PERFORMING ARTS BOOKS — Antiquarian-Performing Arts
18 E 16th St, Room 202, 10003. Tel 212-645-9576
Estab 1975. 8000 Vols. 500 sq ft. Cat 5x ann
Types: 1st ed, hb, ltd ed, new & used, old & rare, out of print, papbk
Subj: Circus, dance, films & filmmaking, music, theatre

STRAND BOOKSTORE — Antiquarian
828 Broadway, 10003. Tel 212-473-1452
Buyer, Marvin Mondlin
Estab 1929. 500,000 Titles. 2,000,000 Vols. 32,000 sq ft. Cat 8x ann
Types: 1st ed, facsimile editions, hb, imp, new & used, out of print, old & rare, remainders
Subj: Amer, art, hist, nature & environ, performing arts, soc sci, econ

STUBBS BOOKS & PRINTS INC — Antiquarian
28 E 18th St, 10003. Tel 212-982-8368
Mgr, Jane Stubbs

Estab 1981. 6000 Vols. 1500 sq ft. Cat 3x ann
Types: Fine bnd, 1st ed, hb, illus bk, imp, out of print, old & rare
Subj: Archit, Egyptology, archaeol, decorative arts, landscapes

SUPERSNIPE COMIC BOOK EUPHORIUM & ART GALLERY — Comics
PO Box 1102 Gracie Station, 10028. Tel 212-879-9628
Mgr, Deborah Coyne
Estab 1970. 300,000 Vols. 525 sq ft. Cat 2x ann
Types: 1st ed, hb, illus bk, imp UK, imp EEur, juvenile, ltd ed, out of print, papbk, new, old & rare
Subj: Illus, fantasy, orig comic art, comic stip anthologies, comic bk hist, animation art

THEATREBOOKS INC — Performing Arts
1600 Broadway, Rm 1009, 10019. Tel 212-757-2834
Estab 1979. 10,000 Vols
Types: New & used, out of print
Subj: Drama, theatre

UNION SQUARE ART BOOKS — Mail Order
33 Union Sq W, 10003. Tel 212-989-3083
Estab 1980. 3000 Titles. 3000 Vols. 1200 sq ft. Cat monthly
Types: Imp Ital, imp Fr, imp Sp, Fr, Ger & Sp lang, out of print, papbk, high priced papbk, illus bk, ltd ed, new, old & rare, Am titles
Subj: Art

UNIVERSITY PLACE BOOKSHOP — Antiquarian
821 Broadway, 10003. Tel 212-254-5998
Estab 1932. 60,000 Vols. 3000 sq ft. Cat 4x ann
Types: Hb, imp, incunab, out of print, old & rare, used, for lang
Subj: Africa, black studies, West Indies, chess

UNTITLED II INC — Art
680 Broadway, 10012. Tel 212-982-1145
Mgr, Bevan Davies
Estab 1984. 1000 Titles. 35,000 Vols. 1500 sq ft. Cat monthly
Types: Out of print, imp, ltd ed, new, used, imp Fr, imp Ital, imp Ger, Fr lang, Ital lang, Sp lang, Ger lang
Subj: Design, archit, photog

URBAN CENTER BOOKS — Architecture
457 Madison Ave, 10022. Tel 212-935-3592. FAX 212-753-1816
Owner, The Municipal Art Society; Mgr, John Frazier
Estab 1980. 4000 Titles. 16,000 Vols. 500 sq ft. Cat ann
Types: Hb, imp, juvenile, out of print, high priced papbk
Subj: Archit, design, hist preservation, urban planning

URSUS BOOKS & PRINTS — Antiquarian-Art
981 Madison Ave, 10021. Tel 212-772-8787
Estab 1972. 50,000 Vols. Cat 8x ann
Types: Out of print
Subj: Reference, fine arts, archit

ANDREW D WASHTON BOOKS ON THE FINE ARTS — Antiquarian-Art
411 E 83rd St (Mail add: PO Box 20062, Cherokee Station, 10028). Tel 212-861-0513
1000 Titles. Cat 3x ann
Types: For lang, hb, imp, out of print
Subj: Western Eur art through 1850

SAMUEL WEISER INC — Metaphysics
132 E 24th St, 10010. Tel 212-777-6363
Mgr, Henry Suzuki
Estab 1926. 75,000 Vols. 4000 sq ft. Cat 4x ann
Types: Hb, imp, out of print, papbk, used
Subj: Archaeol, Eastern philos, Orientalia, psychol, theol, esoteric

WEITZ WEITZ & COLEMAN — Antiquarian
1377 Lexington Ave, 10128. Tel 212-831-2213
Estab 1909. 15,000 Vols. Cat ann
Types: Imp, out of print, hb, juvenile, old & rare, used, fine bnd
Subj: Amer, art, bks on bks, hist

WEYHE ART BOOKS INC — Antiquarian
794 Lexington Ave, 10021. Tel 212-838-5466
Estab 1916
Types: Facsimile editions, 1st ed, hb, illus bk, incunab, new & used, out of print, papbk, old & rare, remainders, Dutch, Fr, Ger, It & Sp lang
Subj: Archit, fine arts, interior design

JONATHAN WHITE — Mail Order-Antiquarian
98 Riverside Dr 10G, 10024. Tel 212-496-8854
7500 Vols. Cat
Types: 1st ed, out of print, papbk, used, old & rare
Subj: Sci fiction & fantasy

PHILIP WILLIAMS POSTERS — Mail Order
60 Grand St, 10013. Tel 212-226-7830
Estab 1973. 100 Titles. Cat ann
Types: Hb, imp, papbk, mass mkt papbk, high priced papbk, out of print, remainders, Fr lang, new, old & rare

FRED WILSON BOOKS — Antiquarian-General
80 E 11th St, Suite 334, 10003. Tel 212-533-6381
Estab 1973. 3000 Vols. 130 sq ft. Cat 3x ann
Types: New & used, out of print, old & rare
Subj: Chess

THE WITKIN GALLERY — Antiquarian-Photography
415 West Broadway, 4th fl, 10012. Tel 212-925-5510
Dir, Evelyne Z Daitz
Estab 1969. 2000 Titles. Cat
Types: Old & rare, out of print, current
Subj: Photog

WITTENBORN ART BOOKS INC — Art
1018 Madison Ave, 10021. Tel 212-288-1558
Mgr, Patricia Strain
Estab 1937. 125,000 Vols. 10,000 sq ft. Cat 12x ann
Types: Hb, imp, out of print, high priced papbk
Subj: Archaeol, archit, design, for lang, typography, art, Far & Near East

WORD BIRD LINDA C FRANKLIN* — Mail Order-Antiquarian
PO Box 383, Murray Hill, 10156. Tel 212-679-6038
Types: Out of print, remainders
Subj: Antq, bks on bks, old kitchenwares, early tech

CHRISTINE YOUNG BOOKS — Mail Order
955 Park Ave, 10028. Tel 212-744-1469
Estab 1982. 900 Titles. 900 Vols. Cat 2x ann
Types: Fine bnd, facsimile editions, hb, illus bk, imp, old & rare, out of print
Subj: Art, archaeol of Indians of North & South Amer

ALFRED F ZAMBELLI — Mail Order-Antiquarian
156 Fifth Ave, 10010. Tel 212-734-2141
Estab 1949. 10,000 Vols. Cat 4x ann
Types: Old & rare, out of print
Subj: Bibliog, medieval studies, philos, rel studies, Renaissance & Reformation hist & lit, hist of ptg

IRVING ZUCKER ART BOOKS, INC — Antiquarian-Illustration
303 Fifth Ave, Rm 1503, 10016. Tel 212-679-6332
Owners, Irving & Janis Zucker
Estab 1940. 600 Titles. 600 Vols. 850 sq ft
Types: Illus bk, imp, out of print, old & rare
Subj: Art, archit, natural hist, fine arts

NORTHPORT — 7651. Area code 516

BAYVIEW BOOKS & BINDERY — Mail Order-Antiquarian
PO Box 710, 11768. Tel 516-757-3563
Estab 1980. 400 Titles. 1500 Vols. Cat 1-2x ann
Types: Fine bnd, 1st ed, hb, illus bk, old & rare, out of print
Subj: Discovery & explor, nautical, travel

NYACK — 6428. Area code 914

DEECEE BOOKS — Mail Order-Antiquarian
32 Washington St, PO Box 506, 10960. Tel 914-358-3989
Estab 1954. 34,000 Titles. 40,000 Vols. Cat
Types: 1st ed, out of print, old & rare, used
Subj: Soc sci, political thought, aviation, Africa, black studies, drama, art, movies, China, 19th & 20th century lit, Soviet Union

PICKWICK BOOKSHOP — General
8 S Broadway, 10960. Tel 914-358-9126
Types: Hb, juvenile, papbk, used, out of print
Subj: Hudson River

OLD FORGE — Area code 315

WILDWOOD BOOKS & PRINTS — Antiquarian
Rte 28 (Mail add: PO Box 560, 13420-0560). Tel 315-369-3397
Estab 1979. 10,000 Vols. 1000 sq ft
Types: 1st ed, hb, illus bk, new & used, old & rare, out of print
Subj: Amer, hunting & fishing, New Yorkiana, canoeing, Adirondackiana

ONEONTA — 14,933. Area code 607

CARNEY BOOKS — Mail Order-Antiquarian
44 Elm St, 13820-1833. Tel 607-432-5360
Estab 1978. 20,000 Vols. 1200 sq ft
Types: 1st ed, hb, illus bk, papbk, out of print, 1st ed, papbk, remainders, used

ROSE & LAUREL BOOKSHOP — General
One Dietz St, 13820. Tel 607-432-5604
Estab 1976. 4000 Titles. 1500 sq ft
Types: Juvenile, hb, high priced papbk, papbk, out of print
Subj: Mystery & detective, sci fiction & fantasy, fiction, local hist, natural hist, nature & environ, art, antq, cooking, humor, health, reference, home improvement

SERPENT & EAGLE BOOKS — Used
One Dietz St, 13820. Tel 607-432-5604
Estab 1979. 1500 Titles. 1500 Vols. Cat
Types: Old & rare, out of print
Subj: Folklore

OSSINING — 20,196. Area code 914

BEV CHANEY JR, BOOKS — Mail Order-Antiquarian
73 Croton Ave, 10562. Tel 914-271-8153, 941-1002
Estab 1973. 3500 Titles. 15,000 Vols. Cat 3 - 5x ann
Types: 1st ed, ltd ed, out of print
Subj: Bks on bks, mod lit, proofs

OWEGO — 4364. Area code 607

MRS KENNETH F COOPER — Antiquarian
Meadow Bank Farm (Mail add: Box 343, 13827). Tel 607-687-1422
Vpres, Marilyn J Cooper
Types: Out of print, used

RIVEROW BOOKSHOP — General
187 Front St, 13827. Tel 607-687-4094
Estab 1976. 15,000 Vols. 2500 sq ft. Cat 2x ann
Types: Fine bnd, 1st ed, hb, illus bk, juvenile, ltd ed, new & used, old & rare, out of print
Subj: Archit, art, cooking, hist, illus, nature & environ, New Yorkiana, aesthetic movement

OYSTER BAY — 305,750. Area code 516

PAUL ETTENSON - BOOK SCOUT — Mail Order-Antiquarian
68 School St, 11771. Tel 516-922-7754
Estab 1975. 10,000 Titles. 10,000 Vols
Types: High priced papbk, papbk, out of print
Subj: Films & filmmaking, fiction, military, biog, mystery & detective, Irish hist & lit

PALMYRA — 3729. Area code 315

K GEORGE ARTHURTON - BOOKS* — General
146 Cuyler St (Mail add: 1783 Maple Ave, 14522). Tel 315-597-2637
Estab 1985
Types: Used, hb, papbk, out of print

PAWLING — 1996. Area code 914

THE BOOK COVE — General
One Arch St, 12564. Tel 914-855-9590
Estab 1976. 3000 Titles. 8000 Vols. 800 sq ft
Types: Hb, juvenile, out of print, papbk
Subj: Reference, art, rel, cooking

PEEKSKILL — 18,236. Area code 914

CHANG TANG BOOKS — Dogs
35 Di Rubbo Dr (Mail add: Box 42, Hawthorne, 10532-0042). Tel 914-739-8167, 473-5838 (home)
Estab 1979. 1000 Vols. Cat
Types: Facsimile editions, 1st ed, illus bk, imp, old & rare, out of print, used
Subj: Dogs of Tibet and East Asia

TIMOTHY TRACE BOOKSELLERS — Mail Order-Antiquarian
Red Mill Rd, 10566. Tel 914-528-4074
7000 Vols. Cat
Types: Hb, imp, out of print, old & rare
Subj: Antq, archit, arts & crafts, trades

PIERMONT — 2269. Area code 914

PIER BOOKS INC — Antiquarian-Nautical
PO Box 5, 10968-0005. Tel 914-353-0232
Estab 1976. 4000 Titles. Cat ann
Types: Facsimile editions, fine bnd, 1st ed, hb, illus bk, imp, out of print, used, old & rare

PLAINVIEW — 10,759. Area code 516

BONMARK BOOKS INC — General
998 Old Country Rd, 11803. Tel 516-938-9000
Mgr, Mark Blinderman; Buyer, Abraham Blinderman
Estab 1983. 70,000 Vols
Types: Fine bnd, 1st ed, illus bk, hb, juvenile, ltd ed, old & rare, out of print, papbk, remainders, comics, new & used
Subj: Art, cooking, hist, sci fiction & fantasy, fiction

BENGTA WOO — Antiquarian-Mystery & Detective
1 Sorgi Ct, 11803. Tel 516-692-4426
Estab 1970. 9000 Vols
Types: 1st ed, hb, out of print, papbk, used
Subj: Romance, sci fiction & fantasy

PLANDOME — 1503. Area code 516

LEE & MIKE TEMARES — Antiquarian
50 Heights Rd, 11030. Tel 516-627-8688
Merch Mgr, Myron Temares
Estab 1972. 25,000 Vols. 900 sq ft
Types: 1st ed, hb, illus bk, juvenile, ltd ed, old & rare, out of print, used
Subj: Biog, art, rel-j, Judaica, Heritage Press, Limited Editions Club, children's series, mod 1st eds

PLATTSBURGH — 21,057. Area code 518

THE CORNER-STONE BOOKSHOP — Antiquarian
110 Margaret St, 12901. Tel 518-561-0520
Estab 1973. 50,000 Vols
Types: Hb, out of print, old & rare, papbk, used

PLEASANTVILLE — 6749. Area code 914

COLONIAL OUT-OF-PRINT BOOK SERVICE — Mail Order-Used
PO Box 451, 10570. Tel 914-769-1704
Estab 1934. 1000 Titles. 1000 Vols
Types: Out of print, used
Subj: Art, hist, music, philos, psychol, theol

PORT JEFFERSON — 6731. Area code 516

THE GOOD TIMES BOOKSHOP — Antiquarian
150 E Main St, 11777. Tel 516-928-2664
Estab 1972. 27,000 Titles. 30,000 Vols
Types: 1st ed, hb, ltd ed, old & rare, out of print, papbk, used
Subj: Scholarly lit, humanities

PORT WASHINGTON — 15,923. Area code 516

COLLECTORS ANTIQUES INC — Antiquarian
286 A Main St, 11050. Tel 516-883-2098
Estab 1964. 2000 Vols. 150 sq ft
Types: Fine bnd, 1st ed, hb, illus bk, incunab, juvenile, old & rare, out of print
Subj: Antq, hist

POUGHKEEPSIE — 29,757. Area code 914

ROBERT E UNDERHILL — Antiquarian
85 Underhill Rd, 12603. Tel 914-452-5986
Types: 1st ed, hb, imp, new & used, out of print, papbk, old & rare, remainders
Subj: Natural hist, hort, agr

REGO PARK — Area code 718

E-K BOOK SERVICE — Mail Order
64-44 Ellwell Cresent, PO Box 83, 11374. Tel 718-263-8980
Estab 1939. 10,000 Titles. 150,000 Vols. 750 sq ft
Types: Old & rare, out of print, papbk
Subj: Math, philos, physics, psychol, scholarly lit, sci-tech, educ

RENSSELAER — 9047. Area code 518

SCOTTISH ENTERPRISES — Mail Order-Antiquarian
PO Box 2, 12144
Estab 1985. 500 Titles. 500 Vols. Cat 5x ann
Types: Imp UK, 1st ed, old & rare, out of print, used
Subj: Scottish, early British & American

ROCHESTER — 241,741. Area code 716

ABACUS BOOKSHOP — Antiquarian
115 Park Ave, 14607. Tel 716-461-9341
Estab 1987. 5000 Titles. 5000 Vols. 400 sq ft
Types: Out of print, remainders, fine bnd, 1st ed, hb, illus bk, imp, juvenile, ltd ed, old & rare, used
Subj: Art, biog, hist, music, local hist, sci-tech, travel, lit, entertainment

ABRA-CADAVER THE HOUSE OF MYSTERY* — Mystery & Detective
110 Dunrovin Ln, 14618. Tel 716-244-7665, Ext 1
Estab 1970. 5000 Vols. 2000 sq ft. Cat 6x ann
Types: Col text, for lang, hb, juvenile, out of print, papbk, remainders, used, imp UK
Subj: Photog, mystery & detective, gambling

ANG & LILL'S COLLECTOR'S CORNER — Antiquarian
149 Stone Rd, 14616. Tel 716-621-8930
Estab 1971
Types: Facsimile editions, fine bnd, 1st ed, hb, illus bk, juvenile, ltd ed, old & rare, out of print, used

KURT FEUERHERM BOOKSELLER — Antiquarian
740 Monroe Ave, 14607. Tel 716-546-5513, 442-8040
Estab 1983. 5000 Titles. 650 Vols
Types: Hb, out of print, used, fine bnd, 1st ed, illus bk, juvenile, ltd ed, old & rare, ephemera
Subj: Art, photog, local hist, pre-1950 mag

GENESEE BOOKSHOP — Antiquarian
2420 Monroe Ave, 14618. Tel 716-442-3620
Types: 1st ed, hb, old & rare, out of print, papbk, used
Subj: Russ lang, Russian translations

GUTENBERG'S — Antiquarian
675 Monroe Ave, 14607. Tel 716-442-4620
Estab 1981. 10,000 Vols
Types: Out of print, illus bk
Subj: Art, hist, literary criticism, social hist, womens hist

C F HEINDL BOOKS — Mail Order-Antiquarian
PO Box 8345, 14618. Tel 716-271-1423
Estab 1975. 10,000 Vols. 800 sq ft
Types: 1st ed, old & rare, out of print
Subj: Charles Dickens

HOUSE OF SARAH BOOKS — Mail Order-Antiquarian
79 Arvine Heights, 14611. Tel 716-436-9564
Estab 1986. 2000 Titles. 2000 Vols. Cat 2x ann
Types: Hb, new & used, old & rare, out of print
Subj: Women-and-rel

PARK AVENUE BOOKSTORE — General
370 Park Ave, 14607. Tel 716-271-6120
Estab 1976. 15,000 Vols. 750 sq ft
Types: Hb, juvenile, out of print, papbk, remainders, new & used
Subj: Hist, Judaica, mystery & detective, scholarly bks

TERRA FIRMA BOOKS — Mail Order-Antiquarian
PO Box 10307, 14610. Tel 716-244-5546
Estab 1985. 1600 Titles. 1650 Vols. Cat 3x ann
Types: Out of print
Subj: Recorded sound, mechanical music devices, antique phonographs

YANKEE PEDDLER BOOKSHOP VOLUME II — Antiquarian
Peddlers Village, 274 Goodman St, 14607. Tel 716-271-5080
Mgr, Douglas Westerberg
Estab 1983. 12,000 Titles. 12,000 Vols Buys indep & through hq
Types: Facsimile editions, fine bnd, 1st ed, hb, illus bk, juvenile, ltd ed, new & used, old & rare, out of print, remainders
Subj: Amer, Can, aeronaut, travel, Am military hist, NYS photog

ROCKVILLE CENTRE — 25,405. Area code 516

ELGEN BOOKS — Mail Order-Antiquarian
336 DeMott Ave, 11570. Tel 516-536-6276
Estab 1977. 5000 Vols. Cat 1-2x ann
Types: Fine bnd, hb, old & rare, out of print, used
Subj: Math, medicine, sci-tech

DAVID M KING ROLLS-ROYCE ARCHIVES — Mail Order-Antiquarian
5 Brouwer Lane, 11570. Tel 516-766-1561
Estab 1978. 2000 Titles. Cat ann
Types: Fine bnd, 1st ed, hb, illus bk, ltd ed, old & rare, out of print, used
Subj: Auto, Rolls-Royce & Bentley cars, racing & hist, travel by automobile bks

ROME — 43,826. Area code 315

BRIDGMAN BOOKS — Mail Order-Used
906 Roosevelt Ave, 13440. Tel 315-337-7252
Estab 1978. 20,000 Titles. 20,000 Vols. Cat 8x ann
Types: Out of print

ROSLYN HEIGHTS — 7140. Area code 516

BOOKMARX INC — Antiquarian
28 Lincoln Ave, 11577. Tel 516-621-0095
Estab 1979. 12,000 Titles. 12,000 Vols. Cat ann
Types: Fine bnd, 1st ed, hb, illus bk, ltd ed, out of print, old & rare, papbk
Subj: Poetry, Judaica, New Yorkiana, sports

MNLD-BOOKS — Mail Order-Antiquarian
PO Box 155, 11577. Tel 516-621-5091
Estab 1984. 2500 Titles. 1500 Vols. Cat 2x ann
Types: For lang, used, old & rare, out of print, facsimile editions, 1st ed, illus bk, imp, ltd ed
Subj: Medicine, natural hist, art

SHELDON L TARAKAN ANTIQUARIAN BOOKS & AUTOGRAPHS — Antiquarian-Performing Arts
40 Holly Lane, 11577. Tel 516-621-2445 (by appt only). FAX 516-484-5217
Owner, Sheldon L Tarakan; Mgr, Sharen E Feldman
Estab 1979. 8000 Vols. 1500 sq ft. Cat 4x ann
Types: Hb, papbk, old & rare, out of print
Subj: Autg, auto, mythology, metaphysics, metaphys & occult, musicians, jazz, opera, English & Am lit

SAINT JAMES — 10,818. Area code 516

THE BOOK TRADER — General
532 N Country Rd, 11780. Tel 516-862-7982
Estab 1984. 2000 Titles. 75,000 Vols. 750 sq ft. Cat 4x ann
Types: 1st ed, hb, illus bk, juvenile, ltd ed, new, old & rare, out of print, papbk, used
Subj: Sci fiction & fantasy, psychol, horror, new age

J-J BOOKS — Antiquarian-Science Fiction & Fantasy
21 Hobson Ave, 11780. Tel 516-584-6858
Estab 1984. 6000 Titles. 8500 Vols
Types: Hb, 1st ed, ltd ed, old & rare, out of print, used
Subj: Mystery & detective

SALISBURY MILLS — Area code 914

DENNING HOUSE — Antiquarian
Orrs Mills Rd, Box 42, 12577. Tel 914-496-6771
Cat 15x ann
Types: Out of print, old & rare

SARATOGA SPRINGS — 23,906. Area code 518

THE ANGLICAN BIBLIOPOLE — Theology
858 Church St, 12866-9111. Tel 518-587-7470
Estab 1979. 8000 Vols. Cat 2x ann
Types: Hb, out of print, used
Subj: Biog, hist, music, theol, rel studies, rel-p, Anglican Church

HENNESSEY'S BOOKSTORE — Antiquarian-General
Fourth & Woodlawn, 12866. Tel 518-584-4921
Estab 1961. Cat ann
Types: 1st ed, old & rare, out of print, used
Subj: Sports, general dealer

LYRICAL BALLAD BOOKSTORE — Antiquarian-General
7 Phila St, 12866. Tel 518-584-8779
Estab 1971. 20,000 Vols. 1200 sq ft
Types: Fine bnd, 1st ed, hb, illus bk, juvenile, old & rare, out of print, used
Subj: Amer, dance, folklore, horses, local hist, mythology, New Yorkiana, Adirondacks & Saratoga Springs, thoroughbred racing

SOAVE FAIR INC — Art Gallery
449-451 Broadway, 12866. Tel 518-587-8448
Mgr, Steve Adkins
Estab 1973. 8000 Titles. 11,000 Vols. 10,000 sq ft. Cat ann
Types: Hb, imp Europe, imp Jap, juvenile, out of print, mass mkt papbk, remainders
Subj: Art, fiction, nonfiction, self-develop

SCARSDALE — 17,650. Area code 914

NANCY SCHECK ART REFERENCE BOOKS — Art
164 Boulevard, 10583. Tel 914-723-6974
Estab 1982. 1000 Titles. 1050 Vols. Cat 6x ann
Types: Hb, out of print, new, old & rare, papbk
Subj: Amer, bks on prints & printmaking

SCHENECTADY — 67,972. Area code 518

BIBLIOMANIA — Antiquarian
129 Jay St, 12305. Tel 518-393-8069
Estab 1981. 10,000 Titles. 12,000 Vols. 700 sq ft. Cat ann
Types: Facsimile editions, fine bnd, 1st ed, hb, illus bk, ltd ed, new & used, old & rare, out of print, remainders
Subj: Amer, art, local hist, mod lit, mystery & detective, photog, hunting & fishing, mountaineering

HAMMER MOUNTAIN BOOK HALLS — Antiquarian
841 Union St, 12308. Tel 518-393-5266
Estab 1971. 10,000 Vols. Cat 3x ann
Types: Out of print, old & rare, used
Subj: Humanities, soc sci

SEA CLIFF — 5364. Area code 516

SEA CLIFF BOOKS — Antiquarian
327 Sea Cliff Ave, 11579. Tel 516-676-6088
Estab 1952. 25,000 Vols. 1000 sq ft
Types: Fine bnd, 1st ed, hb, illus bk, ltd ed, old & rare, out of print, used, 19th cent prints
Subj: Fiction, performing arts, media, drugs, temperance

SETAUKET — 6857. Area code 516

CORNER BOOKSHOP — General
Rte 25A & Nicolls Rd, 11733. Tel 516-751-1904
Buyer, Nancy Mullen
Estab 1962
Types: Hb, juvenile, out of print, papbk, remainders, used

SHELTER ISLAND — 2071. Area code 516

PAUL OLINKIEWICZ, BOOKS & VIDEO — General
17 Grand Ave (Mail add: PO Box 636, 11965). Tel 516-749-8925
Mgr, Janet Olinkiewicz; Merch Mgr, Elizabeth Weslek
Estab 1980. 2300 Titles. 4000 Vols. 1000 sq ft. Cat
Types: Hb, papbk, mass mkt papbk, 1st ed, juvenile, new & used, old & rare, out of print
Subj: Local hist

SNYDER — Area code 716

KEVIN T RANSOM - BOOKSELLER — Mail Order-Antiquarian
116 Audubon Dr (Mail add: PO Box 176, Amherst, 14226). Tel 716-839-1510
Estab 1978. 8000 Vols. Cat 4x ann
Types: Facsimile editions, fine bnd, 1st ed, hb, illus bk, juvenile, ltd ed, old & rare, out of print
Subj: Mystery & detective, mod lit

SOUTHAMPTON — 42,849. Area code 516

ROBERT KEENE BOOKS — Antiquarian
21 S Main St, PO Drawer 0, 11968. Tel 516-283-1612
Estab 1950. 1000 Titles. 27,000 Vols. 2000 sq ft
Types: Facsimile editions, fine bnd, 1st ed, hb, illus bk, incunab, imp, juvenile, ltd ed, old & rare, out of print, remainders, used
Subj: T Capote, K Roberts, Long Island hist

SOUTH SHORE BOOK RESERVE — Antiquarian
Box 768, 11968. Tel 516-283-5347
2000 Vols. Cat ann
Types: Hb, new, old & rare, out of print
Subj: Archit, art

SPENCERPORT — 3424. Area code 716

BOOK CENTRE — Antiquarian
Village Plaza, 14559. Tel 716-352-1890
Types: Hb, papbk, remainders, juvenile, out of print, used

STATEN ISLAND — 352,121. Area code 718

CARMEL GIFT CENTER — Religious
10 Carmel Ave, 10314. Tel 718-761-8480
Estab 1980. 2000 Vols. 900 sq ft
Types: Juvenile, out of print, papbk
Subj: Hebraica, Judaica, rel-j

EUROPE UNIE BOOKS — German Lang
60 Reynolds St, 10305. Tel 718-273-0475
Estab 1975. 50,000 Vols. 1500 sq ft. Cat 3x ann
Types: Old & rare, out of print

GREAT EXPECTATIONS — Mail Order-Antiquarian
30 Barton Ave, 10306. Tel 718-351-5043
4000 Titles. Cat 2-3x ann
Types: Fine bnd, 1st ed, hb, illus bk, juvenile, old & rare, out of print, used
Subj: Amer, illus

STILLWATER — 1572. Area code 518

BOOK-IN-HAND — Antiquarian
Condon Rd, 12170. Tel 518-587-0040
Estab 1980. 12,500 Titles. 17,000 Vols. 1000 sq ft
Types: Fine bnd, 1st ed, hb, incunab, illus bk, juvenile, ltd ed, old & rare, out of print, used
Subj: New Yorkiana, Am Revolution, generalia, Adirondackiana

STONE RIDGE — Area code 914

RIDGE BOOKS — Mail Order-Antiquarian
Box 58, 12484. Tel 914-687-9774
Estab 1963. 3000 Vols. Cat 6x ann
Types: 1st ed, ltd ed, out of print
Subj: Fitzgerald, Hemingway, Albee, Tennesse Williams

STONY BROOK — 6391. Area code 516

HELEN KOLYER — Antiquarian
208 Christian Ave, 11790-0235. Tel 516-751-8888
Estab 1977. 2000 Vols. 600 sq ft. Cat ann
Types: Facsimile editions, 1st ed, hb, old & rare, out of print, used
Subj: Auto, aviation, clocks, watches

SWAN LAKE — Area code 914

MORRIS HELLER — Mail Order-Antiquarian
RD 1 Box 87, 12783. Tel 914-583-5879
Estab 1963. 4000 Vols. 800 sq ft. Cat 2x ann
Types: Hb, out of print, old & rare
Subj: Hunting & fishing, natural hist
See Also: Monticello

SYOSSET — 9970. Area code 516

CORNUCOPIA — Used
RD Box 2108, Edge Rd, 11791. Tel 516-921-4813
3000 Titles. 3000 Vols
Types: Hb, out of print, used
Subj: Cooking, needlecrafts, gardening, domestic hist, etiquette

SYRACUSE — 170,105. Area code 315

HORSE'S MOUTH BOOK STORE — General
214 Walton St, 13202. Tel 315-475-0388
Types: Hb, imp, Fr, Ger & Sp lang, new & used, fine bnd, 1st ed, incunab, illus bk, juvenile, ltd ed, old & rare, out of print, papbk, remainders
Subj: Natural hist, biblical studies, class studies, fiction

TWILIGHT BOOK & GAME EMPORIUM INC — Science Fiction & Fantasy
1401 N Salina St, 13208. Tel 315-471-3139
Estab 1982. 15,000 Titles. 30,000 Vols. 3000 sq ft. Cat ann
Types: Hb, imp, out of print, papbk, used, 1st ed, comics
Subj: Sci fiction & fantasy

THERESA — 827. Area code 315

CHRIS FESSLER BOOKSELLER — Mail Order-Antiquarian
RD One, PO Box 112 Poole Rd, 13691-9726. Tel 315-628-5560
5000 Vols. Cat 4x ann
Types: Facsimile editions, 1st ed, hb, ltd ed, old & rare, out of print, remainders, used, imp, imp Asia
Subj: Ancient hist & lit, anthrop, archaeol, class studies, Orientalia, philos, rel studies, travel, Am Indian studies, Amer, mod hist

TIVOLI — 711. Area code 914

RICHARD C WILES -BARN EAST BOOKS — Mail Order-Used
29 Montgomery St, 12583. Tel 914-757-4294
Estab 1976. 12,000 Titles. 12,000 Vols. 414 sq ft
Types: Facsimile editions, fine bnd, 1st ed, hb, illus bk, imp, ltd ed, old & rare, out of print
Subj: Local hist

TROY — 56,638. Area code 518

SUMAC BOOKS — Mail Order-Used
RD 1, Box 197, Smith Hill Rd, 12180. Tel 518-279-9638
Estab 1987. 8000 Titles. 13,000 Vols. 1000 sq ft
Types: Out of print, remainders, used, 1st ed, hb, old & rare
Subj: Communism, polit sci, socialism

TROJAN BOOKS — Antiquarian
182 River St, 12180. Tel 518-271-6925
Estab 1972. 2000 sq ft. Cat 3x ann
Types: Facsimile editions, fine bnd, ltd ed, hb, incunab, illus bk, juvenile, 1st ed, old & rare, out of print, papbk, used

TURNING OVER A NEW LEAF — Used
457 Broadway, 12180. Tel 518-273-8277
Mgr, John Horton
Estab 1981. 15,000 Titles. 20,000 Vols
Types: Out of print, old & rare
Subj: Sci-tech, polit sci

UPPER NYACK — 1906. Area code 914

THE BOOK NOOK — Antiquarian
366 Rte 9W, 10960. Tel 914-358-1114
Estab 1973. 10,000 Vols. 750 sq ft
Types: For lang, hb, juvenile, out of print, used, fine bnd, 1st ed, illus bk, old & rare
Subj: Military, art, music, mystery & detective, drama, biog, poetry, botany, Am hist & lit, sports, aviation, nautical

UTICA — 75,632. Area code 315

RAVENSWOOD INC — Used
1411 Oriskany St, 13502. Tel 315-735-3699
Mgr, Joseph Zogby
Estab 1983. 5000 Titles. 150,000 Vols. 800 sq ft
Types: Out of print, hb, imp Jap, juvenile, Fr & Sp lang, mass mkt papbk, high priced papbk, facsimile editions, 1st ed, illus bk, imp UK, ltd ed, old & rare, remainders

VAILS GATE — Area code 914

THE BOOK & RECORD — General
Big V Mall, Rte 32, 12584. Tel 914-561-7580Buys indep & through hq
Types: Hb, out of print, papbk, remainders

VALHALLA — Area code 914

EDUCO SERVICES INTERNATIONAL LTD — Antiquarian
75 N Kensico Ave, PO Box 226, 10595-1919. Tel 914-997-7044. Telex 64-6703
Cat ann
Types: 1st ed, illus bk, ltd ed, juvenile, hb, old & rare, out of print

VALLEY COTTAGE — 6007. Area code 914

ALEPH-BET BOOKS — Mail Order-Antiquarian
670 Waters Edge, 10989. Tel 914-268-7410
Estab 1978. 4000 Vols. Cat 4x ann
Types: Hb, illus bk, juvenile, old & rare, out of print, used

WARWICK — 4320. Area code 914

BOOK LOOK — Search Service
51 Maple Ave, 10990. Tel 914-986-2665, 986-1981
Estab 1964. 60,000 Vols. 20,000 sq ft. Cat
Types: Hb, papbk, out of print

WEBSTER — 5499. Area code 716

THE BACKROOM BOOKSTORE — Antiquarian-General
PO Box 223, 14580-0223. Tel 716-671-0437
Estab 1976. 10,000 Vols. Cat 4x ann
Types: Fine bnd, hb, juvenile, new & used, old & rare, out of print
Subj: Class studies, educ, philos, poetry, photog

WESTBURY — 13,871. Area code 516

C MOEBIUS FORD BOOKS — Mail Order
484 Winthrop St, 11590. Tel 516-333-3797
Mgr, Linda Geist
450 Titles. 2500 Vols. Cat 2x ann
Types: Out of print, hb, old & rare
Subj: Auto, Ford Motor Co, Henry Ford

WEST HEMPSTEAD — 20,375. Area code 516

OCEANSIDE BOOKS UNLIMITED (THE MYSTERY BOOKSTORE) — Antiquarian-Mystery & Detective
173A Woodfield Rd, 11552. Tel 516-565-4710
Estab 1973. 10,000 Vols. Cat 6-7x ann
Types: 1st ed, hb, out of print, old & rare, papbk
Subj: Bibliog

WHITE PLAINS — 46,999. Area code 914

AVONLEA BOOKS — Mail Order-Used
Box 74, Main Sta, 10602-0074. Tel 914-946-5923. WATS 800-423-0622
Estab 1979
Types: 1st ed, hb, illus bk, juvenile, old & rare, out of print, used
Subj: L M Montgomery

B K BOOKS — Mail Order-Antiquarian
PO Box 1681, Main Station, 10602
Types: Out of print
Subj: Hist, performing arts, black studies, Am hist & lit, ancient hist & lit, Eng hist & lit

BRYN MAWR BOOKSHOP — Used
170 Grand St, 10601. Tel 914-946-5356
Owner, Bryn Mawr Col Scholarship Fund; Mgr, Eleanor Forman
Estab 1975. 15,000 Vols. 600 sq ft
Types: Out of print, old & rare, used, papbk, for lang, cookbks
Subj: Collecting, sci fiction & fantasy, fiction, nonfiction

ALBERT J PHIEBIG INC — Antiquarian
5 Rutherford Ave (Mail add: PO Box 352, 10605). Tel 914-948-0138
Estab 1947
Types: Col text, hb, old & rare, out of print, papbk, used, for lang, imp

WILLIAMSON — 6319. Area code 716

YANKEE PEDDLER BOOKSHOP — Antiquarian
3895 Rte 104, 14589. Tel 315-589-2063
Mgr, John Westerberg
Estab 1970. 8000 Titles. 8000 Vols. 640 sq ft. Cat ann
Types: Facsimile editions, fine bnd, 1st ed, hb, illus bk, juvenile, ltd ed, new & used, old & rare, out of print, remainders
Subj: World Wars I & II, Amer, Can, Civil War, New Yorkiana, Western Amer, photog, aeronaut

WOODSIDE — Area code 718

RICHARD T JORDAN ANTIQUARIAN — Mail Order-Antiquarian
PO Box 807, 11377. Tel 212-382-3535
Estab 1977. 15,000 Titles. 20,000 Vols. 2000 sq ft. Cat ann
Types: 1st ed, hb, new & used, out of print, old & rare, papbk, remainders
Subj: Archit, art, feminism, films & filmmaking, performing arts, reference, sociol, theol, Vietnam, deforestation, environ conf & tech reports, Greenhouse Effect, Black hist, op mus pubns, peace & non-violence, rainforests

WOODSTOCK — 6804. Area code 914

NATHANIEL COWEN — Mail Order-Antiquarian
16 Schoonmaker Lane, 12498. Tel 914-679-6475
Associate Florence M Cowen
Estab 1933.
Types: Hb, out of print
Subj: Am hist & lit, art, Eng hist & lit

YORKTOWN HEIGHTS — 6805. Area code 914

VERMONT RARE BOOKS — Antiquarian-Vermontiana
1042 Barberry Rd, 10598. Tel 914-245-2361
4000 Titles. 4000 Vols. Cat
Types: Used, hb, illus bk, imp, out of print, fine bnd, 1st ed

NORTH CAROLINA

ASHEVILLE — 53,281. Area code 704

THE BOOK MART — Used
7 Biltmore Plaza, Box 5094, 28813-5094. Tel 704-274-2241
Estab 1947. 20,000 Vols. 900 sq ft
Types: Hb, juvenile, out of print, old & rare
Subj: Appalachia, North Carolinana, rel-p, South Carolinana

CAPTAIN'S BOOKSHELF INC — General
26 1/2 Battery Park Ave, 28801. Tel 704-253-6631
Estab 1976. 10,000 Vols. 1100 sq ft. Cat 4x ann
Types: Out of print, old & rare, 1st ed, secondhand
Subj: Art, photog

LITTLE PROFESSOR BOOK CENTER — General
Biltmore Pkwy Centre, 1378 Hendersonville Rd (Mail add: PO Box 1814, Weaverville, 28787-1814). Tel 704-274-0990
Estab 1988. 7000 Titles. 15,000 Vols. 1550 sq ft. Cat 7x ann
Types: Hb, papbk, juvenile, out of print

SUPER GIANT BOOKS — Used
344 Merrimon Ave, 28801-1222. Tel 704-253-2103
Estab 1977. 12,000 Vols. 1200 sq ft. Cat
Types: Hb, out of print, papbk, used
Subj: Sci fiction & fantasy

E N TREVERTON — Used
115 Cisco Rd, 28805. Tel 704-298-1882
Estab 1984. 6000 Titles. 6500 Vols. 500 sq ft
Types: Out of print, remainders, hb, 1st ed
Subj: Antq, Civil War, North Carolinana, geol, archaeol, art, photog, mining

ATLANTIC BEACH — 941. Area code 919

KNOWLEDGE OF CHRIST BOOKSTORE — Religious
PO Box 114, Atlantic Station S/Ctr, 28512. Tel 919-726-7370
Mgr, Doris Hollowell
Estab 1981
Types: Juvenile, out of print, papbk

BOONE — 10,191. Area code 704

APPALACHIAN STATE UNIVERSITY BOOKSTORE — College
210 College St, 28607. Tel 704-262-3070
Mgr, Roby L Triplett
Types: Hb, papbk, juvenile, out of print, mass mkt papbk, text bks, used, col text
Subj: Art, sci-tech, bus

CARTHAGE — 925. Area code 919

PERRY'S BOOKS — Antiquarian
RD 2 Box 348 A, 28327. Tel 919-947-2209
Estab 1981. 16,000 Vols. 750 sq ft
Types: Facsimile editions, fine bnd, hb, illus bk, juvenile, ltd ed, old & rare, out of print, papbk, used
Subj: North Carolinana

CHAPEL HILL — 32,421. Area code 919

MICHAEL E BERNHOLZ ANTIQUES & BOOKS — Antiquarian-Southern Americana
One Sycamore Dr, 27514. Tel 919-929-3533
Estab 1970. 10,000 Titles. 10,000 Vols. 6000 sq ft
Types: Facsimile editions, fine bnd, 1st ed, hb, illus bk, incunab, imp, juvenile, ltd ed, old & rare, out of print
Subj: Fiction, medicine, military

THE BOOKSHOP INC — Used
400 W Franklin St, 27516. Tel 919-942-5178
Secy Linda Saaremaa
Estab 1979. 100,000 Titles. 150,000 Vols. 6000 sq ft. Cat 6x ann
Types: Hb, juvenile, out of print, papbk
Subj: Mystery & detective, fiction, nonfiction, North Carolinana

CHARLOTTE — 314,447. Area code 704

CAROLINA BOOKSHOP — Antiquarian-Southern Americana
1601 E Independence Blvd, 28205. Tel 704-375-7305
Estab 1975. 10,000 Vols. 2000 sq ft. Cat 8x ann
Types: Fine bnd, 1st ed, hb, juvenile, ltd ed, old & rare, out of print, papbk, used
Subj: Amer, Civil War, North Carolinana, masonry

DILWORTH BOOKS — General
2238-A Park Rd, 28203
Estab 1987. 50,000 Titles. 50,000 Vols. 1400 sq ft
Types: Out of print, mass mkt papbk only, hb, used, illus bk, juvenile, old & rare, ltd ed, 1st ed

NEWSSTAND INTERNATIONAL — Paperback
Providence Sq S/Ctr, 28226. Tel 704-365-0910
Estab 1977. 8000 Titles. 10,000 Vols
Types: Hb, imp, imp UK, Ital lang, juvenile, out of print, papbk, remainders, hb

POPLAR STREET BOOKS — Used
226 W Tenth St, 28202. Tel 704-372-9146
Estab 1983. 20,000 Vols. 900 sq ft
Types: For lang, facsimile editions, 1st ed, illus bk, new & used, remainders, out of print, hb, high priced papbk, juvenile
Subj: Poetry, sci fiction & fantasy, rel, biog, art, hist, mystery & detective, philos, cookbks

DURHAM — 100,831. Area code 919

BELL BOOK & COFFEE — Used
802 W Main St, 27705. Tel 919-683-3211
Estab 1987. 25,000 Titles. 1800 sq ft
Types: For lang, juvenile, out of print, papbk
Subj: Fiction, scholarly lit, sci fiction & fantasy

BOOKS DO FURNISH A ROOM — General
1809 W Markham Ave, 27705-4806. Tel 919-286-1076
Estab 1983. 14,000 Titles. 15,000 Vols. 1200 sq ft
Types: Hb, out of print, high priced papbk, remainders, used, comics
Subj: Hist, poetry, music

CHELSEA ANTIQUES — Antiquarian
905 W Main, 27701. Tel 919-683-1865
Estab 1982. 2000 Vols
Types: Out of print, old & rare, juvenile, fine bnd, 1st ed, hb, illus bk, ltd ed, imp
Subj: Class studies, North Carolinana, medicine

WENTWORTH & LEGGETT RARE BOOKS — Antiquarian
Brightleaf Sq, 905 W Main St, 27701. Tel 919-688-5311
Estab 1977. 7000 Vols. Cat 1-2x ann
Types: Fine bnd, 1st ed, illus bk, juvenile, old & rare, out of print
Subj: Amer, antq, art, black studies, Civil War, cooking, gardening, golf, medicine, mystery & detective, performing arts, rel studies, sci-tech, travel

ELIZABETH CITY — 13,784. Area code 919

OXENA NEWS STAND — Newsdealer
104 108A N McMorrine St, 27909. Tel 919-338-6962
Mgr, George E McPherson
Estab 1952
Types: Hb, juvenile, out of print, papbk, remainders

FAIRMONT — 2658. Area code 919

THE BOOK TRADER — Antiquarian
304 S Main, PO Box 603, 28340-0603. Tel 919-628-0945
9000 Vols. Cat 3x ann
Types: Hb, juvenile, new & used, old & rare, out of print, papbk, remainders
Subj: North Carolinana, South Carolinana

GREENSBORO — 155,642. Area code 919

THE BROWSERY — Used
506 S Elm, 27403. Tel 919-273-7259
Estab 1976. 100,000 Vols. 5000 sq ft
Types: Hb, old & rare, out of print, papbk, illus bk, 1st ed, juvenile
Subj: Biog, drama, fiction, hist, philos, poetry

JOHN NEAL BOOKSELLER — Calligraphy
1833 Spring Garden, 27403. Tel 919-272-7604
Estab 1981. 500 Titles. 10,000 Vols. 950 sq ft. Cat 6x ann
Types: Ger lang, hb, imp UK, imp Ger, imp Hungary, juvenile, out of print, papbk, remainders, col text
Subj: Calligraphy, illumination, bk arts

ALICE ROBBINS BOOKSELLER — General
3002 Round Hill Rd, 27408. Tel 919-282-1964
Cat
Types: Out of print, 1st ed, ltd ed, old & rare, mod 1st ed

HICKORY — 20,757. Area code 704

C-2 BOOKS & COMICS — General
Hickory Corners S/Ctr, Hwy 64-70 SE, 28602. Tel 704-322-6560
Estab 1982. 3200 Titles
Types: Hb, out of print, papbk, mass mkt papbk
Subj: Christian, secular

JAMESTOWN — 2148. Area code 919

PACIFICANA — Mail Order-Antiquarian
PO Box 398, 27282. Tel 919-454-4938, 454-3534
Estab 1971. 4000 Vols. Cat 4x ann
Types: Facsimile editions, 1st ed, hb, illus bk, imp, juvenile, ltd ed, new, old & rare, out of print, papbk, remainders, used
Subj: Pacific Islands

LITTLE SWITZERLAND — area code 704

GRASSY MOUNTAIN SHOP — Used
Rte 226A (Mail add: PO Box 448, 28749). Tel 704-765-9070
Estab 1987. 10,000 Vols
Types: Illus bk, 1st ed, hb, old & rare, out of print, ltd ed, juvenile

MORGANTON — 13,763. Area code 704

CHRIS HARTMANN BOOKSELLER — Mail Order-Used
Rte 10, Box 120, 28655. Tel 704-433-5478
Estab 1979. 7000 Vols. 800 sq ft. Cat 6x ann
Types: 1st ed, hb, out of print, remainders, old & rare
Subj: Amer, art, natural hist, Southern Amer, Civil War

MURPHY — 2070. Area code 704

THE BOOK & CARD SHOP — Paperback
200 Valley River Ave, 28906. Tel 704-837-7685
Mgr, Edward Brumby
Estab 1977. 3000 Titles. 5000 Vols. 1000 sq ft
Types: Hb, juvenile, out of print, used, mass mkt papbk, high priced papbk
Subj: Sci fiction & fantasy, mystery & detective, regional

NORTH WILKESBORO — 3260. Area code 919

RHOADES BOOKSTORE — General
217 Ninth St, 28659. Tel 919-838-3156
Papbk Buyer, Vernell Rhoades
Estab 1964. 40,000 Vols. 2800 sq ft. Cat ann
Types: Hb, illus bk, imp, juvenile, new, out of print, papbk, remainders
Subj: Music

PINNACLE —Area code 919

BOLINGBROKE BOOKS — Mail Order
PO Box 153, 27043-0153. Tel 919-325-2210
Estab 1984. 10,000 Titles. 10,000 Vols. Cat 4x ann
Types: Used, hb, imp UK, fine bnd, 1st ed, old & rare, out of print, new
Subj: Political thought, SAm, conservative auths

PITTSBORO — 1332. Area code 919

H E TURLINGTON BOOKS — Antiquarian
Rte 4, PO Box 146, 27312. Tel 919-542-3403
Mgr, H E Turlington
Estab 1979. 2500 Vols. 800 sq ft. Cat 6x ann
Types: 1st ed, hb, ltd ed, out of print, used
Subj: 19th & 20th cent lit, Southern fict & poetry

RALEIGH — 149,771. Area code 919

LUCY'S BOOK EXCHANGE — Used
6701-103 North Blvd, 27604. Tel 919-878-0625
Estab 1983. 17,000 Titles. 32,000 Vols. 1500 sq ft
Types: Hb, juvenile, out of print, papbk, mass mkt papbk, remainders, old & rare, westerns
Subj: Fiction, mystery & detective, sci fiction & fantasy

OCTOBER FARM — Antiquarian-Horses
Rte 2, Box 183-C, 27610. Tel 919-772-0482 (by appt only)
Estab 1977. 2500 Vols. Cat 2-3x ann
Types: 1st ed, hb, illus bk, juvenile, old & rare, out of print, used
Subj: Horses

RALEIGH CREATIVE COSTUMES — Performing Arts
616 Saint Mary's St, 27605. Tel 919-834-0061
Estab 1979. 1000 Titles. 1000 Vols. 300 sq ft. Cat ann
Types: Hb, out of print, papbk, remainders, used
Subj: Drama, scripts

TROY — 2702. Area code 919

GRANDPA'S HOUSE — Antiquarian
Hwy 27 West, Rt 3, Box 292, 27371. Tel 919-572-3484
Estab 1963. 1500 sq ft
Types: 1st ed, hb, illus bk, juvenile, out of print, old & rare, used

WAKE FOREST — 3780. Area code 919

STEVENS BOOKSHOP — Used
245 E Roosevelt Ave, PO Box 1977, 27587. Tel 919-556-3830
Estab 1954. 200,000 Vols. 8000 sq ft. Cat monthly
Types: 1st ed, hb, juvenile, old & rare, out of print, papbk,

remainders, biblical searches
Subj: Biog, fiction, hist, North Carolinana, Southern Amer, theol, biblical studies, church hist, psychol, rel studies
See Also: Raleigh

WINSTON-SALEM — 131,885. Area code 919

THE COLLEGE BOOKSTORE — College
Wake Forest University, PO Box 7717, Reynolda Sta, 27109-7717. Tel 919-761-5599
Dir Richard T Clay; Book Mgr David O Dyer Sr; Asst Dir Richard Whisnant
Estab 1956. 16,000 Vols
Types: Hb, juvenile, out of print, new & used, papbk, remainders
Subj: Art, black studies, rel-c,j,p

LOVETT & LOVETT BOOKSELLERS — Antiquarian
110 N Hawthorne Rd, 27104. Tel 919-722-5499
Estab 1986. 5000 Titles. 5000 Vols. 1000 sq ft. Cat 5x ann
Types: Out of print, 1st ed, hb, illus bk, ltd ed, old & rare, used, juvenile, mod 1st ed

DUANE JOHNSON BOOKSELLER — Used
506 Broadway, 58102. Tel 701-232-0178
Associate Mgr Steve Illg
Estab 1982. 50,000 Titles. 50,000 Vols. 2000 sq ft
Types: For lang, hb, out of print, papbk, col text, comics, juvenile
Subj: Rel, philos, soc sci, humanities, fiction
See Also: Grand Forks; Detroit Lakes, MN

ALLEN J PETERSEN BOOKS — Mail Order-Antiquarian
809-20th ST S, 58103. Tel 701-280-0538
5000 Vols. Cat 4x ann
Types: Out of print, hb, used
Subj: North Dakotana

R B BOOKS — Used
313 N P Ave (Mail add: PO Box 1524, 58107). Tel 701-234-0954
Estab 1986. 15,000 Titles. 20,000 Vols. 3000 sq ft
Types: Juvenile, hb, out of print, papbk, high priced papbk
Subj: Hist, travel, natural hist, belles lettres, Amer

GRAND FORKS — 43,765. Area code 701

COLLECTOR'S CORNER — Comics
306 N 4th St (Mail add: PO Box 101, 58206-0101). Tel 701-772-2518
Estab 1982. 200,000 Titles. 200,000 Vols
Types: Out of print, new & used, comics
Subj: Marvel, DC

DUANE JOHNSON BOOKSELLER — Used
16 N Fourth St, 58201. Tel 701-772-6931
Estab 1982. 50,000 Titles. 50,000 Vols. 2000 sq ft
Types: Hb, out of print, papbk, col text, for lang, comics, juvenile
Subj: Rel, philos, soc sci, humanities, fiction

NECHE — 471. Area code 204

PANDORA'S BOOKS LTD — Mail Order-Antiquarian
Box 54, 58265. Tel 204-324-8548
Estab 1973. 120,000 Vols. Cat monthly
Types: 1st ed, hb, imp, ltd ed, new & used, old & rare, out of print, papbk
Subj: Can, hist, mystery & detective, sci fiction & fantasy

AKRON — 237,177. Area code 216

AKRON ANTIQUARIAN BOOKS — Antiquarian
500 W Exchange St, 44302-1428. Tel 216-434-8808, 867-8118
Estab 1983. 21,000 Titles. 19,000 Vols. 2000 sq ft. Cat
Types: Fine bnd, hb, illus bk, juvenile, new, old & rare, out of print, used
Subj: Ancient hist & lit, local hist

THE BOOKSELLER INC — Antiquarian
521 W Exchange St, 44302. Tel 216-762-3101
Buyer, Andrea Klein
Estab 1948. 29,000 Titles. 30,000 Vols. 2600 sq ft. Cat 4x ann
Types: 1st ed, hb, old & rare, out of print, papbk, used
Subj: Aviation, military, Ohioana, lighter-than-air bindings

MURDER BY THE BOOK — Mystery & Detective
500 W Exchange St (Mail add: PO Box 231, Main St Sta, 44308-0231). Tel 216-434-2112
Estab 1981. 15,000 Titles. 20,000 Vols. 15,000 sq ft. Cat 6x ann
Types: Hb, juvenile, out of print, mass mkt papbk, high priced papbk, used, 1st ed, ltd ed, new, old & rare, remainders
Subj: Sherlockiana, true crime

BAY VILLAGE — 17,846. Area code 216

BAY BOOKS — Mail Order
PO Box 40306, 44140
Estab 1986. 15,550 Titles. 16,000 Vols. 2500 sq ft
Types: Remainders, out of print, hb, old & rare, new & used, ltd ed
Subj: Amer, archit, Ohioana, nature & environ, reference, transp, travel, Western Amer, atlases pre 1915, trade cat

BOWLING GREEN — 25,728. Area code 419

RYAN D TWENEY BOOKSELLER — Antiquarian-Scholarly Lit
413 Sand Ridge, 43402. Tel 419-352-6771
Estab 1973. 4000 Vols. Cat 2x ann
Types: 1st ed, old & rare, out of print, used
Subj: Philos, psychiat, psychol, medicine, sci-tech, neuroscience

BURTON — 1401. Area code 216

THE ASPHODEL BOOKSHOP — Antiquarian
17192 Ravenna Rd, Rte 44, 44021. Tel 216-834-4775
Estab 1963. 6000 Vols. Cat 6x ann
Types: 1st ed, imp, new, out of print, old & rare
Subj: 20th century lit

CANFIELD — 5535. Area code 216

THE CANFIELD BOOKSTORE — General
46 S Broad St, 44406. Tel 216-533-4800
Estab 1987. 2000 Titles. 3000 Vols. 400 sq ft
Types: Hb, juvenile, out of print, papbk, used, best sellers
Subj: Class studies, classics

CAREY — 3674. Area code 419

ROBERT G HAYMAN ANTIQUARIAN BOOKS — Antiquarian
575 West St (Mail add: Box 188, 43316-0188). Tel 419-396-6933
Estab 1963. 10,000 Vols. Cat 5x ann
Types: Out of print, old & rare
Subj: Amer, local hist

CENTERVILLE — 18,886. Area code 513 and 614

CENTERVILLE BIBLE COLLEGE BOOKSTORE — College
38 N Main St, 45459. Tel 513-433-5021
Owner, First Baptist Church of Centerville; Mgr, Michael B DeLong
Estab 1978. 50 Titles. 300 Vols. 225 sq ft
Types: Papbk, out of print, for lang, hb, Sp lang, Gr lang
Subj: Theol, music, rel, biblical studies

CINCINNATI — 385,457. Area code 513

BARBARA AGRANOFF BOOKS & OLD POSTCARDS — Mail Order-Antiquarian
4025 Paddock Rd, Apt 501 (Mail add: PO Box 6501, 45206). Tel 513-281-5095
Estab 1972. 4000 Vols. Cat
Types: Fine bnd, 1st ed, hb, incunab, illus bk, juvenile, ltd ed, old & rare, out of print, used
Subj: Amer, illus, natural hist, trades, sports, archit, art, performing arts, photog, medicine, transp

DUTTENHOFER'S BOOK TREASURES — Antiquarian
214 W McMillan St, 45219. Tel 513-381-1340
Estab 1975. 40,000 Vols. 5000 sq ft
Types: 1st ed, for lang, hb, illus bk, ltd ed, old & rare, out of print, papbk, used
Subj: Biog, metaphys & occult, poetry, sci fiction & fantasy

MRS TROLLOPE'S BAZAAR — Mail Order-Antiquarian
6428 Westover Circle (Mail add: PO Box 1302, 45201-1302). Tel 513-891-7823
Estab 1975. 300 Titles. 1000 Vols. Cat ann
Types: Facsimile editions, fine bnd, 1st ed, hb, illus bk, imp, ltd ed, new & used, old & rare, out of print, papbk, remainders
Subj: Anthony, Thomas Adolphus & Frances Trollope, Benjamin Disraeli, H Rider Haggard

OHIO BOOKSTORE — Antiquarian
726 Main St, 45202. Tel 513-621-5142
Mgr, Dick Baringhaus
Estab 1941. 200,000 Vols. Cat monthly
Types: New & used, old & rare, out of print, papbk, remainders
Subj: Amer, local hist

POSITIVE LIVING CENTER BOOKSTORE — Metaphysics & Occult
Positive Living Ctr, 8425 Vine St, 45216. Tel 513-761-3763
Mgr & Buyer, Rene Steinkamp
Estab 1977. 2000 Titles. Cat
Types: Hb, imp India, papbk, mass mkt papbk, out of print, bibles
Subj: Self-develop, metaphysics, health, reincarnation, pyramids, spirituality, new age

SHEPPARD BOOKS & SERVICE — Mail Order-Search Service
1243 Ida St, 45202. Tel 513-241-0001
Estab 1972. 2400 sq ft
Types: Hb, imp, juvenile, out of print
Subj: Art, hist, medicine, law

SIGNIFICANT BOOKS — Antiquarian
3053 Madison Rd, 45209. Tel 513-321-7567
16,000 Vols
Types: Out of print, old & rare, used
Subj: Art, hist, medicine, sci-tech

CLEVELAND — 573,822. Area code 216

BOOKSTORE ON W 25TH — General
1921 W 25th St, 44113. Tel 216-566-8897
Mgr & Buyer, Mike O'Brien
Estab 1976. 70,000 Vols. 2475 sq ft
Types: Hb, new & used, out of print, papbk, juvenile, remainders, small presses
Subj: Feminism, black studies, homosexuality, philos, poetry, class studies

SUSAN HELLER BOOKS - PAGES FOR SAGES — Antiquarian
22611 Halburton Rd (Mail add: PO Box 2200 E, 44122). Tel 216-283-2665
Estab 1974. 40,000 Titles. 40,000 Vols. 1000 sq ft. Cat 4x ann
Types: Fine bnd, illus bk, juvenile, ltd ed, old & rare, out of print, signed bks, mod 1st ed
Subj: Fine arts, natural hist, nautical, photog, art, Amer, discovery & explor, travel, scholarly lit, mod lit, bks on bks, sporting

PUBLIX BOOK MART — General
2037 E 14th St, 44115. Tel 216-621-6624
Mgr, Nina T Bailey
Estab 1937. 10,000 Titles. 40,000 Vols. 4000 sq ft. Cat
Types: Hb, juvenile, out of print, papbk, facsimile editions, fine bnd, 1st ed, ltd ed, old & rare
Subj: Cooking, mystery & detective, travel

JOHN T ZUBAL INC — Antiquarian
2969 W 25th St, 44113. Tel 216-241-7640. Telex 29-8256. FAX 216-241-6966
Estab 1965. 180,000 Titles. 200,000 Vols. 65,000 sq ft. Cat 10x ann
Types: Out of print, used
Subj: Hist, literary criticism, philos, polit sci, art, archaeol, anthrop

CLEVELAND HEIGHTS — 56,438. Area code 216

ATTENSON ANTIQUES & BOOKS — Antiquarian-General
1771 Coventry Rd, 44118. Tel 216-321-2515
Estab 1981. 10,000 Vols. 1500 sq ft
Types: Fine bnd, illus bk, old & rare, out of print

COLUMBUS — 564,871. Area code 614

BOOKS & BUTTONS — Mail Order
PO Box 3228, 43210
Types: Out of print, old & rare
Subj: Natural hist, button collecting & manufacturing, antq clothes & buttons, med hist

HOFFMAN'S BOOKSHOP — Photography
211 E Arcadia Ave, 43202. Tel 614-267-0203
Mgrs, Ed & Tina Hoffman; Merch Mgr & Buyer, Ed Hoffman
Estab 1982. 20,000 Titles. 20,000 Vols. 2000 sq ft. Cat 8x ann
Types: Out of print, 1st ed, hb, illus bk, used
Subj: Photog, art, military, antq, Ohioana, Thurber

MIRAN ARTS & BOOKS — Antiquarian
2824 Elm Ave, 43209. Tel 614-258-6687, 236-0002
Estab 1975. 6000 Titles. 7000 Vols. 2000 sq ft. Cat
Types: 1st ed, hb, illus bk, juvenile, ltd ed, old & rare, out of print, 1st ed out of print
Subj: Medicine, photog

PAUL H NORTH JR — Antiquarian
81 Bullitt Park Pl, 43209. Tel 614-252-1826
Estab 1948. 20,000 Vols. Cat
Types: 1st ed, out of print, old & rare, used
Subj: Amer, antq

THE OHIO STATE UNIVERSITY BOOKSTORE — College
154 N Oval, Derby Hall, 43210. Tel 614-292-2991
Dir, Robert Carlson; Merch Mgr, Jim Deerhake; Text Buyer, Tom Hayward; Operations Supvr, Barbara Osborne
Estab 1927. 25,000 Titles. 40,000 Vols. 50,000 sq ft
Types: For lang, hb, imp, juvenile, out of print, papbk, remainders, used
Subj: Reference, sci-tech, graduate, review
See Also: Lima, Mansfield, Marion, Newark, Wooster

PENGWYN BOOKS LTD — Used
2518 N High St, 43202. Tel 614-267-6711
Estab 1977. 20,000 Titles. 25,000 Vols. 1500 sq ft
Types: Hb, juvenile, facsimile editions, fine bnd, 1st ed, illus bk, ltd ed, old & rare, out of print, remainders, used, Ger, Fr, Sp, Latin, Ger & Russ langs, trade
Subj: Philos, rel, drama, natural hist, sci-tech, sci fiction & fantasy, bibliog, mystery & detective, archaeol, anthrop, fine arts, Amer, women's studies, travel, Orientalia, reference, medieval studies, Renaissance hist & lit, definitive lit texts, mil hist

L J RYAN - SCHOLARLY BOOKS — Mail Order-Antiquarian
PO Box 243, 43216. Tel 614-252-4469
Estab 1972. Cat
Types: 1st ed, hb, old & rare, out of print
Subj: Amer, art, communism, folklore, hist, soc sci, women's studies, rel, int relations, scholarly lit, psychol, Far East

KAREN WICKLIFF BOOKS — Antiquarian
2579 N High St, 43202. Tel 614-263-2903
Estab 1976. 35,000 Titles. 35,000 Vols. 2800 sq ft. Cat 6x ann
Types: 1st ed, hb, juvenile, old & rare, out of print, papbk, used, for lang
Subj: Fine arts, sci-tech, rel, scholarly lit, nature & environ, hist, medicine, philos, soc sci
See Also: Bookhaven of Springfield, Springfield

DAYTON — 203,588. Area code 513

THE DRAGON'S LAIR INC — General
110 W 5th, 45402. Tel 513-222-1479
Estab 1974. 250,000 Vols. 12,000 sq ft
Types: Hb, juvenile, out of print, papbk, used, comics
Subj: Mystery & detective, nonfiction, sci fiction & fantasy

MORNINGSIDE BOOKSHOP — Mail Order
260 Oak St (Mail add: PO Box 1087, 45410). Tel 513-461-6736
Mgr, Robert Younger
Estab 1969. 200 Titles. 20,000 Vols. Cat 4x ann
Types: Hb, old & rare, out of print, papbk, reprints
Subj: Civil War

PROFESSIONAL BOOKS SERVICE — Law
PO Box 366, 45401. Tel 513-223-3734. WATS 800-538-4984
Mgr, Kevin Mayl
Estab 1962. 30,000 Vols. Cat 12x ann
Types: Imp, out of print, used
Subj: Law, medicine, bus & mgt, tech
See Also: Los Angeles, CA

EAST LIVERPOOL — 16,687. Area code 216

BEST LITTLE BOOK HOUSE — Used Paperback
49083 Foulks Dr Calcutta, 43920. Tel 216-385-3969
Types: Out of print

ELYRIA — 57,504. Area code 216

THE ELYRIA BAZAAR — Used
333 Broad St, 44035. Tel 216-323-4430
Estab 1972. 25,000 Vols. 410 sq ft
Types: Hb, juvenile, out of print, papbk
Subj: Biog, hist, metaphys & occult, philos, poetry, rel, self-develop, cooking, arts & crafts, music

FOWLER — area code 216

ALICE'S BOOK SHELF — Mail Order
5053 Wilson-Sharpsville Rd (Mail add: PO Box 120, 44418). Tel 216-637-1766
Types: Out of print

GREENSBURG — Area code 216

RON-DOT BOOKFINDERS — Antiquarian
4700 Massillon Rd (Mail add: PO Box 44, 44232). Tel 216-896-3482
Estab 1976. 20,000 Vols. 576 sq ft. Cat
Types: 1st ed, hb, illus bk, out of print, old & rare, papbk, used

HAMILTON — 63,189. Area code 513

HAMILTON BOOK EXCHANGE — Used Paperback
90 Brookwood Ave, 45013. Tel 513-894-7445
Estab 1982. 40,000 Titles. 70,000 Vols. 2500 sq ft
Types: Papbk, juvenile, new, old & rare, out of print, remainders
Subj: Comedy

HILLIARD — 8008. Area code 614

BOOKPHIL BOOK SEARCH SERVICE — Search Service
3987 Main St (Mail add: PO Box 706, 43026). Tel 614-876-0442
Estab 1972. 18,000 Titles. 20,000 Vols
Types: Hb, juvenile, out of print, used
Subj: Biog, hist, military, Eng hist & lit, Am auth, Ger & Russ hist & lit, espionage, Nat Geographic bks, Her Majesty's stationery Office Books

KENT — 26,164. Area code 216

ARCHER'S USED & RARE BOOKS — Used
164 E Main St, 44240. Tel 216-673-0945
Estab 1986. 12,000 Titles. 12,000 Vols. Cat 5x ann
Types: Out of print
Subj: Amer, mystery & detective, baseball

LANCASTER — 34,953. Area code 614

THE PAPERBACK EXCHANGE — Used Paperback
120 N Columbus St, 43130. Tel 614-654-5856
Estab 1979. 10,000 Vols. 800 sq ft
Types: Hb, papbk, juvenile, remainders, text bks, out of print

MARYSVILLE — 7414. Area code 513

CHARLES D DYER BOOKS — Used
13904 Fairway Dr, 43040. Tel 513-644-0285
Estab 1981. 11,000 Titles. 12,000 Vols. Cat 4x ann
Types: Out of print, new
Subj: Mountaineering & exploration

MEDINA — 15,268. Area code 216

COTSWOLD CORNER BOOKS — Antiquarian
538 Granger Road, 44256. Tel 216-239-2222
Estab 1980. 10,000 Titles. 10,000 Vols. 500 sq ft. Cat 2-3x ann
Types: Fine bnd, 1st ed, hb, illus bk, imp UK, juvenile, old & rare, out of print, used
Subj: Eng hist & lit, cooking, James Boswell, Samuel Johnson, Thomas Wolfe

MENTOR — 42,065. Area code 216

HILO FARM ANTIQUES — Mail Order-Antiquarian
9058 Little Mountain Rd, 44060. Tel 216-255-9530
Estab 1958. 7000 Vols
Types: 1st ed, old & rare, out of print, used
Subj: Amer

MAGGIE MCGIGGLES ANTIQUES — Antiquarian
8627 Mentor Ave, 44060. Tel 216-255-1623
Estab 1978. 510 sq ft
Types: Juvenile, out of print, hb, used, for lang, old & rare
Subj: Civil War, medicine, cooking

REREADABLES — Antiquarian
8674 Mentor Ave, 44060. Tel 216-255-4996
Estab 1980. 10,000 Titles. 10,000 Vols. 1000 sq ft
Types: 1st ed, hb, old & rare, out of print, used

MIAMISBURG — 15,304. Area code 513

GLENN ARMITAGE — Mail Order-Antiquarian
108 Fifth Ave, 45342
Estab 1960. 4900 Titles. 5000 Vols. Cat
Types: Fine bnd, 1st ed, hb, illus bk, imp, ltd ed, old & rare, out of print, papbk, remainders, used
Subj: Fine arts, literary criticism, 20th Century lit

MONTPELIER — 4431. Area code 419

JERRY RAY BOOKS — Used
321 Iuka, 43543. Tel 419-485-3602
Estab 1973. 16,000 Titles. 18,000 Vols. Cat 4x ann
Types: Hb, old & rare, out of print
Subj: Anthrop, evolution, psychol, sci-tech, sociol, creation, Jehovah's witness, sci

MOUNT VERNON — 14,380. Area code 614

OWL CREEK BOOKSHOP — Used
309 W Vine St, 43050. Tel 614-397-9337
Estab 1968. 11,000 Titles. 12,000 Vols. 700 sq ft
Types: 1st ed, hb, illus bk, juvenile, ltd ed, old & rare, out of print

NORWALK — 14,358. Area code 419

RICHARD P GERMANN — Mail Order-Antiquarian
Six Vinewood Dr, 44857. Tel 419-668-9640
Mgr, Richard P Germann
Estab 1955. 3000 Vols. Cat
Types: New & used, out of print, papbk
Subj: Astrol, metaphys & occult, palmistry, sci before 1800

IRVING M ROTH ANTIQUES — Mail Order-Antiquarian
89 Whittlesey Ave, 44857. Tel 419-668-2893
Estab 1946. 20,000 Vols
Types: Out of print, old & rare
Subj: Amer, antq, Civil War, numismatics, Ohioana, Am expositions, freemasonry

OBERLIN — 8660. Area code 216

MIRANDA BOOKS — Used
PO Box 306, 44074. Tel 216-775-1296
Estab 1983. 20,000 Titles. Cat 2x ann
Types: Hb, out of print, mass mkt papbk, high priced papbk, used
Subj: Biog

PROSPECT —1159. Area code 614

LOIS WARD BOOKS — Antiquarian
502 North St (Mail add: PO Box 368, 43342-0368). Tel 614-494-2117
Estab 1974. 6000 Vols. Cat 2x ann
Types: Used, out of print, old & rare
Subj: Cooking, mystery & detective, rel studies, theol

SOUTH EUCLID — 25,713. Area code 216

PAPER PEDDLERS — Antiquarian
4425 Mayfield Rd, 44121-3633. Tel 216-382-6383
Estab 1974. 10,000 Vols. 750 sq ft
Types: 1st ed, hb, illus bk, old & rare, out of print, juvenile
Subj: Performing arts

SPRINGFIELD — 72,563. Area code 513

BOOKHAVEN OF SPRINGFIELD — General
1549 Commerce Rd, 45504. Tel 513-322-9021
Mgr, Penny Gaber
Estab 1973. 15,000 Titles. 15,000 Vols. 3000 sq ft
Types: Hb, papbk, juvenile, remainders, used, out of print, comics
Subj: Fiction, hist, art, military, sci-tech

PHILLIPS BOOK STORE — Religious-P
32 E Washington St, 45502. Tel 513-322-6716
Estab 1947. 5000 Vols. 3800 sq ft. Cat ann
Types: Hb, juvenile, out of print, papbk, remainders

STEUBENVILLE — 26,400. Area code 614

THE BISHOP OF BOOKS LTD — Antiquarian-Americana
328 Market St, PO Box 579, 43952-2153. Tel 614-283-2665, 264-5120
Estab 1977. 30,000 Vols. Cat 12x ann
Types: Fine bnd, 1st ed, hb, illus bk, ltd ed, old & rare, out of print, papbk
Subj: Ohioana, Pennsylvaniana, West Virginiana, Western Amer, autg, fiction, alcoholism, 20th century Am auth

TOLEDO — 354,635. Area code 419

ACE DRUGS INC, BOOK DEPT — Drug Store
3047 W Bancroft St, 43606. Tel 419-535-5777
Mgr & Papbk Buyer, R Moses; Papbk Buyer & Text Buyer, R A Moses
Estab 1957. 650 Vols. 3000 sq ft. Cat 2x ann
Types: Papbk, juvenile, out of print

GEORGE D BROWN BOOKS — Antiquarian
7001 Bancroft St, 43617. Tel 419-841-4979
Estab 1967. 15,000 Titles. 20,000 Vols
Types: Hb, out of print, old & rare, bibles
Subj: Archaeol, archit, art, aviation, cooking, gardening, Great Lakes, how-to, Indianiana, Michiganiana, natural hist, Ohioana, railroadiana, hunting & fishing, glass

HOLLYWOOD DREAM FACTORY BOOK DEPT — Films & Filmmaking
1842 W Sylvania Ave, 43613. Tel 419-474-3065. FAX: 419-474-9740
Owner, Hollywood Dream Factory, Inc; Mgr, Marilyn Anderson
Estab 1981. 1000 Titles. 1000 Vols. Cat 4x ann
Types: Hb, papbk, for lang, juvenile, used, out of print
Subj: Films & filmmaking, biog

THE LIBRARY NEWS & SMOKE SHOP — Used
53 Franklin Park Mall, 43623. Tel 419-472-0775
Owner, Burley & Books Inc; Pres & Mgr, Michael W Lora
Estab 1973. 1000 Titles. 1500 Vols. 876 sq ft
Types: Out of print, hb, illus bk
Subj: Bks on bks, bibliog, Sherlock Holmes, bk collecting, bk arts, hiking & camping before 1960, mod British & Amer fict

TROY — 19,086. Area code 513

MARKET STREET BOOKSELLERS — General
Five S Market St, 45373. Tel 513-335-3737
Mgr, Margaret Begg
15,000 Titles. 28,000 Vols
Types: Juvenile, out of print, papbk, remainders, text bks

WARREN — 56,629. Area code 216

MCCLINTOCK'S BOOKS — Antiquarian
522-A High St NE (Mail add: PO Box 1949, 44482-1949). Tel 216-394-3398
Estab 1976. 10,000 Vols. 765 sq ft. Cat 10x ann
Types: Fine bnd, 1st ed, hb, illus bk, ltd ed, new & used, out of print, old & rare, op papbk
Subj: Amer, mystery & detective, scholarly lit, sci fiction & fantasy

WAUSEON — 6173. Area code 419

NAPOLEON BOOKSELLERS — Antiquarian
Wauseon Antique Mall-Booth 15, 117 S Fulton (Mail add: PO Box 251, Napolean, 43545)
Estab 1987. 6000 Titles
Types: Out of print
Subj: Amer, Ohioana, biblical studies

WESTERVILLE — 23,414. Area code 614

THE BOOK HARBOR — Antiquarian
32 W College Av, 43081. Tel 614-895-3788
Merch Mgr, George Spurgeon
Estab 1987. 20,000 Titles. 20,000 Vols. 1000 sq ft
Types: Out of print, remainders
Subj: Art, military, poetry, biog, transp, mystery & detective, sci fiction & fantasy

WILLOWICK — 17,834. Area code 216

RADIOGRAPHICS BOOKS — Mail Order-Antiquarian
Box 5483, 44094. Tel 216-943-6374
Estab 1974. 9000 Vols. Cat 8x ann
Types: 1st ed, fine bnd, hb, new & used, old & rare, out of print, papbk
Subj: Radio, electricity, telegraphy

WORTHINGTON — 15,016. Area code 614

THE LOOKING GLASS — Mail Order-Antiquarian
5584 Morning St, 43085. Tel 614-848-5600
Estab 1975. 10,000 Vols. Cat ann
Types: 1st ed, hb, illus bk, ltd ed, out of print, old & rare, used
Subj: Can, military, poetry, Canadian authors

XENIA — 24,653. Area code 513

JERRY MERKEL BOOKSELLER — Antiquarian
2281 Spahr Rd, 45385-9315. Tel 513-848-2359
Estab 1973. 40,000 Titles. 40,000 Vols. Cat 4x ann
Types: Hb, out of print, used, fine bnd, 1st ed, old & rare
Subj: Amer, biog, literary criticism, nonfiction, scholarly lit, humor, publ hist

YOUNGSTOWN — 115,436. Area code 216

CAROL BUTCHER — Mail Order-Hunting & Fishing
3955 New Rd, 44515. Tel 216-793-6832
Cat
Types: Out of print, old & rare, used
Subj: Dogs, rel-c

LYN'S BOOKS & MINIATURES — Paperback
108 E Midlothian Blvd, 44507. Tel 216-783-1235
Estab 1980. 12,000 Titles. 40,000 Vols. 1000 sq ft
Types: Hb, juvenile, out of print, used
Subj: Fiction, antq

REDEEMED BOOKS — Used
2615 Market St, 44507. Tel 216-788-8848
Mgr, Richard M Judy Jr
Estab 1987. 8000 Titles. 10,000 Vols. 900 sq ft. Cat Quarterly
Types: Out of print, mass mkt papbk, high priced papbk, hb
Subj: Rel studies, sci fiction & fantasy, church hist

JOSEPH F SCHEETZ - ANTIQUARIAN BOOKS* — Mail Order-Antiquarian
6236 Foxridge Dr, 44512. Tel 216-758-0427
Estab 1968. 5000 Vols. Cat
Types: 1st ed, hb, out of print, old & rare, used, pvt press
Subj: Amer, Ohioana

ZANESVILLE — 28,655. Area code 614

THE BOOKSHELF — Antiquarian-Am Hist & Lit
25 N Fifth St, PO Box 1162, 43702-1162. Tel 614-455-3922
Estab 1983. 10,000 Vols. 2000 sq ft. Cat 4x ann
Types: 1st ed, illus bk, hb, papbk, used, old & rare, out of print
Subj: Amer, hist, class studies

ADA — 15,902. Area code 405

ADA BOOK STALL — Used
301 W 12th, 74820. Tel 405-332-8062
Owner, Oklahoma Bk Traders Ltd; Mgr, Teri L Gross
Estab 1974. 15,000 Vols. 1400 sq ft Buys indep & through hq
Types: Facsimile editions, fine bnd, 1st ed, hb, illus bk, juvenile, ltd ed, old & rare, out of print, papbk, remainders
Subj: Comedy

BARTLESVILLE — 34,568. Area code 918

DEWAYNE DICK — General
4808 Carole Ct, 74006-3711. Tel 918-335-2179
Estab 1987. 10,000 Vols. Cat 2x ann
Types: Out of print, papbk, used, imp UK, 1st ed, old & rare
Subj: Sci fiction & fantasy, mystery & detective, horror

BROKEN ARROW — 35,761. Area code 918

AMERICAN INDIAN BOOKS — Antiquarian-Am Indians
PO Box 1000, 74013-1000. Tel 918-455-4194
Estab 1972. 5000 Vols. 800 sq ft. Cat
Types: Hb, juvenile, out of print, high priced papbk
Subj: Western Amer

CLAREMORE — 12,085. Area code 918

THE BOOKSTORE & MORE — General
973 W Will Rogers, 74017. Tel 918-342-4744
Estab 1984. 4000 Titles. 1200 sq ft
Types: For lang, hb, imp, juvenile, out of print, mass mkt papbk, papbk
Subj: Fiction, cats, Oklahomana, local hist

EDMOND — 34,637. Area code 405

RON BEVER — Mail Order-Antiquarian
Rte 3, Box 243-B, 73013. Tel 405-478-0125
Estab 1977. 13,500 Vols. Cat 4x ann
Types: Hb, old & rare, out of print, used
Subj: Oklahomana, rel, Western Amer, stock market & commodity

LAWTON — 80,054. Area code 405

LAWTON BOOK STALL — Antiquarian
1832 NW 52nd, Regency Sq S/Ctr, 73505. Tel 405-248-3111
Owner, Oklahoma Book Traders, Ltd; Mgr, Melanie Griffith
Estab 1980. 25,000 Vols. 1500 sq ft Buys indep & through hq
Types: Hb, out of print, illus bk, imp, juvenile, ltd ed, old & rare, 1st ed, papbk, remainders, used, comics
Subj: Southwestern Amer

BRYAN WAID - BOOK COLLECTOR & TRADER — General
702 Euclid, 73501. Tel 405-353-8199
600 Titles. 2500 Vols. Cat ann
Types: 1st ed, hb, papbk, used, out of print
Subj: Western Amer, Oklahomana, Am Indian studies, biog, fiction

NORMAN — 68,020. Area code 405

THE BOOK STALL — Used
300 W Gray, Suite 108, 73069-7113. Tel 405-329-6787
Owner, Oklahoma Bk Traders Ltd; Mgr, Cathy Ball
Estab 1972. 12,000 Titles. 25,000 Vols. 1500 sq ft
Types: Facsimile editions, fine bnd, 1st ed, hb, illus bk, juvenile, ltd ed, old & rare, out of print, papbk, remainders
Subj: Hist, biog, Amer, poetry
See Also: Ada Book Stall, Ada, Lawton Book Stall, Lawton, Del City Book Stall, Midwest City, Shawnee Book Stall, Shawnee

OKLAHOMA CITY — 403,213. Area code 405

ALADDIN BOOK SHOPPE — Antiquarian
2037 NW 23rd, 73106. Tel 405-528-0814
Estab 1930. 40,000 Vols. 2800 sq ft
Types: Fine bnd, 1st ed, hb, incunab, illus bk, juvenile, ltd ed, old & rare, out of print, papbk, remainders, used
Subj: Oklahomana, Southwestern Amer

ARCANE BOOKS — Mail Order-Antiquarian
3120 Harvey Pkwy, 73118. Tel 405-525-6260
Estab 1972. 5000 Titles. 10,000 Vols
Types: Fine bnd, 1st ed, hb, old & rare, remainders, used, out of print
Subj: Discovery & explor, Irish hist & lit, travel

ARROWHEAD SUPPLY — Gemology
330 SW 28th St, 73109. Tel 405-634-7128
Types: Hb, juvenile, imp, out of print, papbk, col text
Subj: Antq, arms & armor, sci-tech

MICHAEL'S BOOKSTORE — Used
925 NW 23rd St, 73113. Tel 405-525-0123
Estab 1963. 20,000 Vols. 3600 sq ft
Types: 1st ed, hb, old & rare, out of print, papbk
Subj: Southwestern Amer

SHAWNEE — 26,506. Area code 405

SHAWNEE BOOK STALL — Used
702-B W Ayre, 74801. Tel 405-275-5714
Owner, Oklahoma Bk Traders Ltd; Mgr, Cindy Hamilton
Estab 1976. 15,000 Vols Buys indep & through hq
Types: Facsimile editions, fine bnd, 1st ed, hb, illus bk, juvenile, ltd ed, old & rare, out of print, papbk, remainders
Subj: Philos, rel studies, hist, Amer, poetry

TULSA — 360,919. Area code 918

THE FIRST EDITION BOOKSHOP — General
1502 E 15th St, 74120. Tel 918-582-1967
Mgr, Marilyn D McCulloch
Estab 1981. 50,000 Titles. 50,000 Vols. 3700 sq ft
Types: For lang, out of print, illus bk, ltd ed, old & rare, remainders, used
Subj: Art, Amer, rel, Oklahomana, collecting

STEVE'S SUNDRY BOOKS & RECORDS — General
2612 S Harvard, 74114. Tel 918-743-3544
Estab 1947. 30,000 Titles. 4500 Vols. 288 sq ft
Types: Hb, juvenile, out of print, papbk, remainders

OREGON

ASHLAND — 19,943. Area code 503

BLUE DRAGON BOOK SHOP — Antiquarian
283 E Main St, PO Box 216, 97520. Tel 503-482-2142
Estab 1983. 15,000 Titles. 800 sq ft. Cat 2-3x ann
Types: Facsimile editions, fine bnd, 1st ed, hb, incunab, illus bk, imp, juvenile, ltd ed, old & rare, out of print, papbk, remainders, used
Subj: Metaphysics, Orientalia, Western Amer, theatre, polar regions

BAKER — 9471. Area code 503

BETTY'S BOOKS — General
1813 Main St, 97814. Tel 503-523-7551
Mgr, Betty Kuhl
Estab 1979. 10,000 Vols. 1200 sq ft
Types: Hb, juvenile, out of print, papbk, remainders, used
Subj: Amer

BEAVERTON — 30,582. Area code 503

BOOK VAULT INC — General
Bernard-Beaverton Mall, 3125 SW Cedar Hills Blvd, 97005. Tel 503-646-8119
Estab 1968. 2500 sq ft
Types: Hb, juvenile, out of print, papbk, remainders

BEND — 17,263. Area code 503

PEGASUS BOOKS OF BEND — Science Fiction & Fantasy
105 NW Minnesota, 97701. Tel 503-388-4588
Owners, Duncan McGeary & Linda McGeary; Mgr, Duncan McGeary
Estab 1979. 5000 Titles. 1250 sq ft
Types: Hb, imp, out of print, papbk, juvenile, comics
Subj: Graphic arts, mystery & detective

TWICE TOLD TALES — Mail Order-Antiquarian
61587 Rockway Terrace, 97702. Tel 503-382-3244
Estab 1983. Cat 2x ann
Types: 1st ed, hb, out of print, old & rare, used
Subj: Fiction

CORVALLIS — 40,960. Area code 503

AVOCET USED BOOKS — Antiquarian
614 SW Third, 97333. Tel 503-753-4119
Estab 1979. 40,000 Vols. 1000 sq ft
Types: Used, hb, papbk, out of print, juvenile, for lang
Subj: Fiction, nonfiction, sci fiction & fantasy, metaphys & occult, cooking, lit

DALLAS — 8530. Area code 503

ALLEN A DUNN — Mail Order
1255 Oak Villa Rd, 97338. Tel 503-623-5136
3000 Vols
Types: Hb, out of print, remainders, used
Subj: Natural hist, Western Amer, hunting dogs, hunting

DUNDEE — 1223. Area code 503.

AUTHORS OF THE WEST — Mail Order-Antiquarian
191 Dogwood Dr, 97115. Tel 503-538-8132
Estab 1973. Cat 2x ann
Types: 1st ed, fine bnd, hb, illus bk, ltd ed, new, old & rare, out of print, remainders, used
Subj: Fiction, poetry, Western Amer

ELGIN — 1701. Area code 503

JOY A WHEELER BOOKS — Mail Order-Antiquarian
Rte 1, Box 49K, 97827. Tel 503-437-8641
2000 Titles. 2000 Vols. Cat 6-12x ann
Types: Facsimile editions, 1st ed, hb, illus bk, juvenile, old & rare, out of print, used
Subj: Fiction, nonfiction, Oregoniana

ENTERPRISE — 2003. Area code 503

THE BOOKLOFT — General
107 E Main St, 97828. Tel 503-426-3351
Estab 1976. 6000 Vols. 850 sq ft. Cat 2 x ann
Types: Hb, juvenile, mass mkt papbk, out of print
Subj: Western Amer, adjacent art

EUGENE — 105,624. Area code 503

BACKSTAGE BOOKS — Mail Order-Performing Arts
PO Box 3676, 97403-3676
Estab 1977. 15,000 Vols. Cat 2x ann
Types: Old & rare, out of print, used
Subj: Theatre related titles including plays

BOOK FAIR — Used
1409 Oak St, 97401. Tel 503-343-3033
Estab 1966. 40,000 Vols. 1100 sq ft
Types: Col text, for lang, hb, juvenile, out of print, papbk, remainders, used
Subj: Amer, bus & mgt, comedy, cooking, rel, sci fiction & fantasy, drama

CELLAR OF BOOKS — Mail Order-Antiquarian
PO Box 10863, 97440. Tel 503-343-0262
Estab 1979. 9000 Titles. 10,000 Vols. Cat quarterly
Types: 1st ed, illus bk, juvenile, ltd ed, old & rare, juvenile, out of print
Subj: Cooking, music, rel studies, NW Amer

J MICHAELS BOOKS — Antiquarian
160 E Broadway, 97401. Tel 503-342-2002
Estab 1973. 100,000 Titles. 120,000 Vols. 2500 sq ft. Cat ann
Types: 1st ed, out of print, old & rare, remainders, used
Subj: Art, archit, photog, Western Amer, class studies, general lit

GRANDE RONDE — 300. Area code 503

JIM'S TRADING POST — General
29335 Salmon River Hwy, 97347. Tel 503-879-5411
Estab 1958. 100,000 Vols. 5000 sq ft
Types: Hb, juvenile, new & used, old & rare, out of print, papbk, remainders

GRANTS PASS — 14,997. Area code 503

ERNEST L SACKETT — Mail Order-Antiquarian
100 Waverly Dr, 97526. Tel 503-476-6404
Estab 1970. 500 Vols. Cat ann
Types: 1st ed, hb, illus bk, juvenile, ltd ed, old & rare, out of print, used, pvt presses
Subj: Hunting & fishing, NAmer, rel-p, Western Amer

YELLOW PAGES USED BOOKS — Used
111 SE G St, 97526. Tel 503-474-5514
Estab 1981. 35,000 Vols. 600 sq ft
Types: 1st ed, juvenile, papbk, out of print
Subj: Hist, psychol, rel, hunting & fishing, pets, metaphysics

JACKSONVILLE — 2030. Area code 503

JACKSONVILLE BOOKS — Antiquarian-Western Americana
120 E California St, PO Box 716, 97530-0716. Tel 503-899-8520
Estab 1982. 5000 Titles. 4000 Vols. 1000 sq ft. Cat triann
Types: New & used, out of print, 1st ed, hb, juvenile, old & rare
Subj: Nonfiction, North Amer Indian

KLAMATH FALLS — 16,661. Area code 503

SHAW STATIONERY CO — Stationers
729 Main St, 97601. Tel 503-882-2586
Mgr, David S Drew
Types: Hb, juvenile, out of print, papbk
Subj: Amer, cooking, fiction, nonfiction, travel

LA GRANDE — 11,354. Area code 503

BIBLIOTHECA MILITARIANA — Mail Order-Military
Rte 2, PO Box 2610, 97850. Tel 503-963-9107
Estab 1981. 2500 Vols. 400 sq ft. Cat 1-4x ann
Types: Hb, imp Russ, out of print, high priced papbk, remainders, used, imp UK
Subj: Martial arts

MONMOUTH — 5594. Area code 503

THE WESTERN BOOKSTORE WESTERN OREGON STATE COLLEGE BOOKSTORE — College
Western Oregon State College, 345 N Monmouth, 97361. Tel 503-838-1220, Ext 300
Owner, State of Oregon; Mgr, Charles A Chance; Text Buyer, Florine Dixon
Estab 1921. 2000 Titles. 4000 Vols. 4800 sq ft
Types: Hb, juvenile, out of print, papbk

NEWBERG — 10,394. Area code 503

THE KEN-L-QUESTOR — Antiquarian
32255 N Hwy 99W, 97132. Tel 503-538-2051
Estab 1935. 4000 Titles. 5000 Vols. 400 sq ft. Cat
Types: Facsimile editions, fine bnd, 1st ed, hb, illus bk, imp, old & rare, out of print, remainders, new & used
Subj: Dogs, botany, cacti, lilies, mushrooms

NEW PINE CREEK — Area code 503

GARDEN OF BOOKS — General
PO Box 39, 97635-0039. Tel 503-947-3411
Estab 1978. 12,500 Titles. 15,000 Vols. Cat
Types: New & used, ltd ed, hb, papbk, juvenile, imp, out of print, remainders, facsimile editions, fine bnd, 1st ed, illus bk
Subj: Natural hist, agr, hort, metaphys & occult, medicine, back-to-the-earth, health, pets, environmental sci

NOTI — Area code 503

ANTIQUES & ARTIFACTS — Mail Order-Railroadiana
20457 Hwy 126, 97461-9708. Tel 503-935-1619
Estab 1971. 640 Titles. 2700 Vols. Cat 8x ann
Types: Facsimile editions, 1st ed, hb, illus bk, ltd ed, new & used, old & rare, out of print, papbk, remainders
Subj: Railroadiana, transp, express, telegraphs, telephones

PORTLAND — 366,383. Area code 503

APACHE BOOKS — Comics
3652 SE Division, 97202. Tel 503-235-4590
Mgr, Sandra Monical
Estab 1971. 15,000 Vols. 1000 sq ft
Types: New & used, out of print, papbk
Subj: Sci fiction & fantasy

ARMCHAIR FAMILY BOOKSTORE — General
3205 SE Milwaukie Ave, PO Box 42555, 97242. Tel 503-238-6680
Estab 1969. 25,000 Titles. 35,000 Vols. 2500 sq ft. Cat 2x ann
Types: Hb, out of print, old & rare, papbk, used, comics

CAROL BARNETT BOOKS — Mail Order-Antiquarian
3128 SE Alder Ct, 97214. Tel 503-239-5745
Estab 1983. 2000 Vols. Cat 4x ann
Types: Facsimile editions, illus bk, old & rare, out of print, used, hb
Subj: Hort, natural hist

BEAVER BOOKSTORE — Used
3747 SE Hawthorne Blvd, 97214-5145. Tel 503-238-1668
Estab 1956. 50,000 Titles. 70,000 Vols
Types: Hb, papbk, juvenile, out of print, remainders

CAMERON'S BOOKSTORE — Used
336 SW Third Ave, 97204. Tel 503-228-2391
25,000 Vols. 1800 sq ft
Types: Hb, out of print, papbk

CHRISTIAN SUPPLY BOOKSTORE — Religious-P
10209 SE Division St, 97266. Tel 503-256-4520
Owner, Multnomah School of the Bible; Mgr, Judy Garrett
Estab 1973. 25,000 Vols
Types: Col & el-hi text, hb, imp, juvenile, mass mkt papbk, out of print, remainders, used
See Also: Beaverton, Oregon City

GREAT NORTHWEST BOOKSTORE — General
1001 SW Tenth Ave, 97205. Tel 503-223-8098
Estab 1977. 75,000 Titles. 75,000 Vols. Cat 4-5x ann
Types: Hb, juvenile, papbk, used, out of print, rare
Subj: Mystery & detective, sci fiction & fantasy, Southwestern Amer, NW Amer

HAWTHORNE BLVD BOOKS — Antiquarian-Americana
3129 SE Hawthorne Blvd, 97214. Tel 503-236-3211
Mgr, Roger Roberts
Estab 1985. 25,000 Titles. 30,000 Vols. Cat 2x ann
Types: Used, remainders, out of print, facsimile editions, fine bnd, 1st ed, hb, illus bk, imp, juvenile, ltd ed, old & rare
Subj: Amer

HOLLAND'S BOOKSTORE — Antiquarian
527 SW 12th, 97205. Tel 503-224-4242
Estab 1979. 15,000 Vols. 1200 sq ft
Types: 1st ed, hb, out of print, old & rare, used
Subj: Amer, hist, humanities, metaphys & occult, philos, sci-tech, socialism, social theory

RAYMOND KIMELDORF — Mail Order-Antiquarian
1925 SE 59th Ave, 97215-3432. Tel 503-236-1848
Estab 1984. 3000 Titles. 3000 Vols
Types: Hb, used, 1st ed, illus bk, juvenile, old & rare, out of print, papbk
Subj: Judaica

LONGFELLOW'S BOOKS — Used
6229-31 SE Milwaukee Ave, 97202-5416. Tel 503-239-5222
Estab 1981. 30,000 Titles. 45,000 Vols. 2000 sq ft. Cat
Types: Hb, out of print, old & rare, 1st ed, used, Academic-Collectibles, curiousa
Subj: Am hist & lit, Oregoniana, cooking, military, Northwest Amer, National Geographic Society bks, monographs & reports

MCDUFFIE'S OLD BOOKS & PICTURES — Used
PO Box 42448, 97242-0448. Tel 503-232-0322
Estab 1953. Cat 6x ann
Types: Old & rare, out of print
Subj: Alaskana, medicine, sci-tech, geol, mining, Amer, med & sci since 1800

MURDER BY THE BOOK — Mystery & Detective
3729 SE Hawthorne, 97214. Tel 503-232-9995
Estab 1983. 15,000 Vols. 800 sq ft. Cat 3x ann
Types: Juvenile, papbk, out of print, hb
Subj: Horror

NORTHWEST FARMS — Mail Order-Wildlife
Box 3003, 97208. Tel 503-771-0628
Buyer, Dorothy V Burmester
Estab 1958. Cat
Types: Hb, imp, out of print, papbk
Subj: Ornith

OLD OREGON BOOKSTORE — Antiquarian
1128 SW Alder St, 97205. Tel 503-227-2742
Estab 1949. 50,000 Titles. 50,000 Vols. 3000 sq ft. Cat 2x ann
Types: Imp, out of print, old & rare, remainders, used
Subj: Art, Western Amer, Am, Eng & Russ hist & lit

THE PAPER MOON — Used
1852 SE Hawthorne, 97215. Tel 503-236-5195
Estab 1978. 50,000 Vols. 2000 sq ft
Types: 1st ed, illus bk, old & rare, out of print, used, juvenile, papbk
Subj: Photog, poetry, scholarly lit

POWELL'S BOOKS INC — General
1005 W Burnside, 97209. Tel 503-228-4651
Adv & Publicity Dir, Joanna Knapp; Mgr, Miriam Sontz
Estab 1971. 558,000 Titles. 900,000 Vols
Types: Hb, new & used, out of print, old & rare, papbk
Subj: Scholarly lit, nonfiction
See Also: Beaverton

SECOND STORY BOOKS — Used
3530 SE Hawthorne (Mail add: 1633 SE Main, 97214). Tel 503-234-0343
Estab 1988
Types: Imp, high priced papbk, out of print, juvenile, hb, trade

TOM STEWART SPORTING BOOKS — Mail Order-Antiquarian
PO Box 5998, 97228-5998. Tel 503-775-6411
Estab 1980. 3000 Titles. 5000 Vols. Cat ann
Types: Fine bnd, 1st ed, hb, illus bk, ltd ed, old & rare, out of print, used
Subj: Guns, hunting & fishing, shooting, Derrydale press

USA BOOK CO — General
13611 NW Cornell Rd, 97229. Tel 503-626-4743
Owner, Harold Walkup
Estab 1983. 30,000 Titles. 43,500 Vols. 1400 sq ft. Cat
Types: For lang, hb, juvenile, out of print, papbk, mass mkt papbk, remainders, col text, used, new
Subj: Regional northwest

REEDSPORT — 4984. Area code 503

HOLE IN THE WALL BOOKSTORE — General
439 Fir Ave, 97467. Tel 503-271-4761
20,000 Vols. 1600 sq ft
Types: Hb, juvenile, out of print, papbk, used, new, old
Subj: Fiction, nonfiction, biog, sci fiction & fantasy, how-to, local hist, Oregoniana, cooking, cookbks

SALEM — 89,233. Area code 503

DOUG BEARCE — Scouting
315 Khartoum SE (Mail add: PO Box 4742, 97302). Tel 503-393-1767, 399-9872
1000 Vols. Cat 4-5x ann
Types: Facsimile editions, hb, juvenile, out of print
Subj: Scouting

BOOKS WELRED — Used
3070 N River Rd, 97303. Tel 503-371-6525
Estab 1979. 171,000 Vols. 5000 sq ft
Types: Hb, papbk, out of print, comics

LARRY'S BOOKS — General
PO Box 5073, 97304. Tel 503-363-1927
Estab 1973. 3500 Vols. 1589 sq ft
Types: Hb, out of print, papbk
Subj: Rel

SEASIDE — 5193. Area code 503

TURNAROUND BOOKS — General
111 Broadway #3, 97138. Tel 503-738-3211
Estab 1978. 10,000 Titles. 30,000 Vols. 1200 sq ft
Types: Hb, imp UK, juvenile, out of print, papbk, remainders, used, Fr, Ger & Sp lang
Subj: Art, travel, regional

SISTERS — 696. Area code 503

LONESOME WATER BOOKS — Used
161 N Elm (Mail add: Box 1268, 97759-1268). Tel 503-549-9460
Estab 1988. 7000 Titles. 7000 Vols. 800 sq ft. Cat 2x ann
Types: Hb, juvenile, out of print, used, facsimile editions, fine bnd, 1st ed, illus bk, ltd ed, old & rare
Subj: Western Amer

SUBLIMITY — 1,077. Area code 503

OREGON TERRITORIAL BOOKS — Antiquarian
Po Box 22, 97385. Tel 503-769-7356
Estab 1982. 8000 Vols. Cat 8x ann
Types: 1st ed, hb, old & rare, out of print
Subj: Western Amer, fur trade

WOODBURN — 11,196. Area code 503

99-E ANTIQUE-USED — Antiquarian
17207 Hwy 99-E, 97071. Tel 503-981-0200
Estab 1978. 5000 Vols
Types: 1st ed, hb, illus bk, juvenile, ltd ed, old & rare, out of print, papbk, used
Subj: Auto, cooking, sci fiction & fantasy, warfare, Western Amer

ADAH — Area code 412

PAULINE C HULL BOOKSELLER — Mail Order-Antiquarian
Rd 1, Box 83-C, 15410. Tel 412-246-2854
Estab 1977. 40,000 Vols
Types: Hb, juvenile, out of print, used, 1st ed, illus bk, old & rare
Subj: Arctic, Amer, hist, poetry

ALLENTOWN — 103,758. Area code 215

BOOKS 'N MORE — Paperback
1409 N Cedar Crest Blvd, 18104. Tel 215-767-2349
Mgr, Victoria A Zsilavecz
Estab 1986. 3000 Titles. 15,000 Vols. 800 sq ft
Types: Juvenile, remainders, used, new, old & rare, out of print

THE OCCULT EMPORIUM — Metaphysics & Occult
102 N 9 St, 18102. Tel 215-433-3610
Estab 1979. 700 Titles. 3000 Vols. 900 sq ft. Cat ann
Types: Hb, imp UK, out of print, mass mkt papbk, remainders, used, facsimile editions, fine bnd, 1st ed, illus bk, ltd ed, new, old & rare
Subj: Magic & conjuring, witchcraft, demonology, esoterica

ALLENWOOD — Area code 717

OTZINACHSON BOOKSHOP — Antiquarian
RR 1, Box 30, 17810. Tel 717-538-1800
Estab 1977. 20,000 Vols. Cat
Types: Hb, out of print

BALA-CYNWYD — 6483. Area code 215

RABBI PIOTRKOWSKI'S JUDAICA CENTER — Religious-J
289 Montgomery Ave, 19004. Tel 215-664-1303
Mgr, Madelyn Heyman
Types: Hebr lang, imp Isr, juvenile, out of print, papbk, col & el-hi text, bibles
Subj: Music, Judaica, Isr, kosher cookbks

BARTONSVILLE —Area code 717

RIMROCK STUDIOS-GALLERIES AKA VAL D ROBBINS — Antiquarian
PO Box 44, Rimrock Dr, 18321. Tel 717-629-3200
Estab 1958. 10,000 Titles. 2500 sq ft
Types: Fine bnd, 1st ed, hb, illus bk, old & rare, out of print, used
See Also: Rimrock West, Tucson, AZ

BLOOMSBURG — 11,717. Area code 717

BOOKS & BOUTIQUES — General
221 Ctr St, 17815. Tel 717-784-3765
Estab 1975. 15,000 Vols. 1200 sq ft
Types: Hb, juvenile, out of print, papbk, remainders, col text, used

BRYN MAWR — 5737. Area code 215

THE EPISTEMOLOGIST SCHOLARLY BOOKS — Mail Order-Antiquarian
PO Box 63, 19010. Tel 215-527-1065
Estab 1972. 3000 Vols. 200 sq ft. Cat 4x ann
Types: Hb, old & rare, out of print, used
Subj: Psychol, philos, psychiat, sci-tech

THE OWL BOOKSHOP — Used
801 Yarrow St, 19010. Tel 215-525-6117
Owner, Bryn Mawr College Alumnae Regional Scholarship Fund; Coordinator, Shirley Baird
Estab 1971. 50,000 Vols
Types: Old & rare, out of print, used

THE TITLE PAGE — Antiquarian
24 Summit Grove Ave, 19010. Tel 215-527-1772
Estab 1982. 17,000 Titles. 20,000 Vols. 1300 sq ft
Types: Old & rare, out of print, fine bnd, illus bk, imp, juvenile, papbk, used, scholarly
Subj: Amer, art, archit, hist, lit

CARLISLE — 18,314. Area code 717

THE ANGLERS ART BOOKS FOR FLY FISHERMEN — Mail Order-Antiquarian
R D Nine, Box 203, 17013. Tel 717-243-9721
Estab 1973. 1000 Titles. 10,000 Vols. Cat 2x ann
Types: New & used, imp, hb, remainders, facsimile editions, fine bnd, 1st ed, illus bk, ltd ed, old & rare, out of print
Subj: Fly fishing only

KENT BOOKS — Used
1202 Harrisburg Pike, PO Box 614, 17013. Tel 717-243-1600
Estab 1937. 20,000 Vols. Cat
Types: Out of print
Subj: Rel, military, Pennsylvaniana

CHAMBERSBURG — 16,174. Area code 717

GEORGE HALL JR BOOKS — Antiquarian
1441 Lincoln Way E, 17201. Tel 717-263-4388
Estab 1975. 3000 Vols. Cat ann
Types: Old & rare, out of print
Subj: Nonfiction

CESI KELLINGER, BOOKSELLER — Mail Order-Antiquarian
735 Philadelphia Ave, 17201. Tel 717-263-4474
Mgr, Cesi Kellinger
Estab 1974. 15,000 Vols. Cat 2x ann
Types: 1st ed, old & rare, out of print
Subj: Amer, fine arts, mod dance

COLUMBIA — 10,466. Area code 717

UNDERWOOD-MILLER — General
515 Chestnut St, 17512-1233. Tel 717-684-7335
Mgr & Buyer, Chuck Miller
Estab 1975. 500 Titles. 10,000 Vols. Cat 4x ann
Types: Hb, imp, papbk, mass mkt papbk, 1st ed, illus bk, ltd ed, old & rare, out of print, new & used
Subj: Sci fiction & fantasy, romance

DILLSBURG — 1733. Area code 717

BOOK HOUSE — General
Rte 15 N, 17019. Tel 717-432-2720
Estab 1976
Types: Hb, juvenile, papbk, out of print, remainders, used, 1st ed
Subj: Antq, local hist, mystery & detective, sci fiction & fantasy, Civil War

DUNCANSVILLE — area code 814

PAPER AMERICANA — General
1301 3rd Avenue, 16635. Tel 814-696-4293
Estab 1978
Types: Used, juvenile, out of print, old & rare, illus bk

EASTON — 26,027. Area code 215

HIVE OF INDUSTRY BOOKSELLERS — Mail Order-Antiquarian
201 Alpha Bldg, PO Box 602, 18042. Tel 215-258-6663
Estab 1960. 10,000 Vols. Cat 12x ann
Types: Out of print, used
Subj: Bus & mgt, soc sci, psychol, sci-tech, econ

EPHRATA — 11,095. Area code 717

AVOCATIONAL — Mail Order-Antiquarian
PO Box 41, 17522. Tel 717-738-2932
10,000 Vols
Types: Hb, out of print, old & rare, used
Subj: Amer, fiction, nonfiction, Pennsylvaniana

ERIE — 119,123. Area code 814

THE ERIE BOOKSPACE — General
717 French St, 16501. Tel 814-452-3354
Estab 1921. 2000 sq ft
Types: Hb, juvenile, out of print, papbk, remainders, used

EXPORT — 1143. Area code 412

WILLIAM H POWERS — Mail Order-Antiquarian
RD 3, 15632. Tel 412-327-6886
Mgr, William Powers
Estab 1969. 8000 Vols. 800 sq ft. Cat 4x ann
Types: Hb, new & used, old & rare, out of print
Subj: Civil War, military, Amer, Pennsylvaniana, hunting & fishing, firearms

FERNDALE — 2204. Area code 215

THE GATEWAY — Mail Order-Antiquarian
18921. Tel 215-847-5644
Estab 1930. 10,000 Vols. 1500 sq ft. Cat
Types: 1st ed, hb, new & used, old & rare, out of print, papbk
Subj: Metaphys & occult, mysticism, Orientalia

FRAZER —1509. Area code 215

CHESTER VALLEY OLD BOOKS — Used
489 Lancaster Ave, 19355. Tel 215-251-9500
Estab 1967. 50,000 Vols. 2000 sq ft
Types: 1st ed, hb, imp, out of print, papbk

GETTYSBURG — 7194. Area code 717

DR WALTER L POWELL ANTIQUARIAN BOOKMAN — Mail Order-Antiquarian
201 Ewell Ave, 17325. Tel 717-334-7036
Estab 1983. 2000 Titles. 2000 Vols. 400 sq ft. Cat 2x ann
Types: Hb, old & rare, out of print, used
Subj: Civil War, Am hist & lit, Am mus

GLEN ROCK — 1662. Area code 717

THE FAMILY ALBUM — Antiquarian
RD 1, Box 42, 17327-9707. Tel 717-235-2134
Estab 1969. 25,000 Vols. 2000 sq ft. Cat 4x ann
Types: Fine bnd, 1st ed, hb, incunab, illus bk, imp, ltd ed, old & rare, out of print, used
Subj: Pennsylvaniana, early imprints, rare photog

GREENCASTLE — 3679. Area code 717

MICHAEL T SHILLING BOOKMAN — Mail Order-Antiquarian
152 S Washington St, 17225. Tel 717-597-8007
Estab 1980. 15,000 Titles. Cat 3x ann
Types: 1st ed, hb, illus bk, juvenile, old & rare, out of print, used
Subj: Children's illus

HARRISBURG — 53,264. Area code 717

THE BOOKWORM — Antiquarian
4335 Crestview Rd, 17112. Tel 717-657-8563
Estab 1980. 50,000 Titles. 50,000 Vols
Types: 1st ed, hb, old & rare, out of print, papbk
Subj: Biog, military, general
See Also: The Book Bin, Lancaster

HATFIELD — 2533. Area code 215

JEAN'S BOOKS — Mail Order-Antiquarian
School St, Box 264, 19440. Tel 215-362-0732
Estab 1976. 6500 Titles. 4500 Vols. Cat
Types: Hb, old & rare, out of print, acct bks
Subj: Amer, diaries, domestic craft rec

HERSHEY — 7407. Area code 717

R F SELGAS SPORTING BOOKS — Mail Order-Antiquarian
PO Box 227, 17033-0227. Tel 717-533-5594
200 Vols
Types: 1st ed, ltd ed, old & rare, out of print, used
Subj: Hunting & fishing

JENKINTOWN — 4942. Area code 215

THE BOOKSTORE — General
Jenkintown Sq, 19046. Tel 215-884-3134
Mgr, Mrs E Parry; Buyer, Mrs E Perloff
Estab 1958
Types: Hb, juvenile, out of print, papbk, remainders

HOBSON'S CHOICE — Mail Order-Antiquarian
511 Runnymede, 19046. Tel 215-884-4853
2500 Titles. 3000 Vols. 1000 sq ft. Cat occasionally
Types: Fine bnd, 1st ed, hb, illus bk, juvenile, ltd ed, old & rare, out of print, pvt presses
Subj: Fiction, poetry, antq, art, drama, music, Eng & Amer lit, Philadelphia, childrens' illustration

KANE — 4916. Area code 814

STEPHEN SHUART PHOTOGRAPHIC BOOKS — Antiquarian-Photography
109 S Edgar St (Mail add: PO Box 419, 16735-0419). Tel 814-837-7786. WATS 800-458-6092
Estab 1969. 1000 Titles. 10,000 Vols. 1000 sq ft
Types: Facsimile editions, old & rare, out of print, remainders, used, imp
Subj: Collecting, guns

KENNETT SQUARE — 4715. Area code 215

THOMAS MACALUSO RARE & FINE BOOKS — Antiquarian
111 S Union St, 19348. Tel 215-444-1063
Estab 1973. 7000 Titles. 7000 Vols. Cat 3x ann
Types: Facsimile editions, fine bnd, 1st ed, hb, illus bk, incunab, ltd ed, old & rare, out of print
Subj: Amer, art, Eng hist & lit, geosci

KIMBERTON — Area code 215

SEVEN STARS SHOP — Museum
West Seven Stars Rd, 19442. Tel 215-933-3635
Owners, Kimberton Farms School Inc; Mgr & Buyer, Peg Savage
Estab 1979. 1600 Titles
Types: Hb, juvenile, out of print, papbk, mass mkt papbk, imp Ger, imp Switz, imp UK
Subj: Art, Rudolf Steiner, Waldorf educ, biodynamics, homeopathy

KUTZTOWN — 4040. Area code 215

THE USED BOOKSTORE — Antiquarian
474 W Main St, 19530. Tel 215-683-9055
Estab 1979. 39,000 Titles. 40,000 Vols. 1700 sq ft
Types: Hb, juvenile, old & rare, out of print, papbk, used
Subj: Biog, fiction, hist, humanities, mystery & detective, philos, sci fiction & fantasy, soc sci

LANCASTER — 54,725. Area code 717

ALEXIA BOOKS — General
154 N Prince St, 17603. Tel 717-393-0227
Buyer, Anne-Tracy Barros-Ruof
Estab 1985. 6000 Titles. 8000 Vols
Types: Hb, juvenile, out of print, mass mkt papbk, high priced papbk, remainders
Subj: Fiction, art, nonfiction, films & filmmaking, music, poetry, literary criticism, biog, drama, folklore

THE BOOK BIN — Antiquarian
27 N Prince St, 17603. Tel 717-392-6434
Estab 1988. 20,000 Titles. 20,000 Vols
Types: 1st ed, hb, old & rare, out of print, papbk
Subj: Art, biog, hist, music, poetry, lit

BOOK HAVEN — Antiquarian
146 N Prince St, 17603. Tel 717-393-0920
Asst Mgr, Kelly Rock
Estab 1978. 30,000 Vols. 1750 sq ft
Types: Fine bnd, 1st ed, hb, illus bk, old & rare, out of print, juvenile
Subj: Pennsylvaniana, illus, Civil War, early Am imprints

FRANKLIN & MARSHALL COLLEGE BOOKSHOP — College
PO Box 3003, Steinman College Ctr, 17604-3003. Tel 717-291-4093
Mgr, Mike Small
Estab 1787. 10,000 Titles. 12,000 Vols. 4500 sq ft
Types: Hb, juvenile, out of print, papbk
Subj: Art, black studies, music, sci-tech

LEBANON — 25,711. Area code 717

JOHNSON & ROTH USED BOOKS — Used
121 E Cumberland St, 17042. Tel 717-272-2511
Estab 1981. 20,000 Titles. 20,000 Vols. 1200 sq ft. Cat
Types: Hb, juvenile, papbk, remainders, col text, out of print
Subj: Philos, hist, military, Pennsylvaniana, metaphysics, rel, arts & crafts, music, natural hist, fiction, class studies

LUMBERVILLE — Area code 215

GEOFFREY STEELE INC — Mail Order-Antiquarian
Fleecydale Rd, 18933. Tel 215-297-5187
Types: Imp, out of print, old & rare
Subj: Design, archit, fine arts

MANCHESTER — area code 717

BOOKS & BIRDS — Antiquarian
519 East Middle Tpk, Rt 30, 06040. Tel 203-649-3449
Estab 1980. 15,000 Vols. 1000 sq ft
Types: Hb, juvenile, out of print, papbk, used, old & rare
Subj: Art, military, natural hist, ornith, hunting & fishing, Amer, cooking, gardening

MECHANICSBURG — 9487. Area code 717

WILLIAM THOMAS - BOOKSELLER — Mail Order-Antiquarian
Box 331, 17055. Tel 717-766-7778
Estab 1970. 5000 Vols. Cat 2x ann
Types: Old & rare, out of print, used
Subj: Amer, Pennsylvaniana

MERCERSBURG — 1617. Area code 717

LIGHT OF PARNELL BOOKSHOP — Antiquarian
3511 Mercersburg Rd, 17236. Tel 717-328-3478
Estab 1972. 10,000 Vols. 1000 sq ft
Types: 1st ed, hb, old & rare, out of print, used
Subj: Amer, local hist, Pennsylvaniana, Civil War

MESHOPPEN — 571. Area code 717

BIG JOHN'S BOOKROOM — Mail Order-Antiquarian
RD 2, PO Box 329B, 18630. Tel 717-833-5323
Mgr, Aileen Wiles
Estab 1970. 9000 Vols. 600 sq ft
Types: Hb, old & rare, out of print, used
Subj: Biog, hist, mystery & detective

MORGANTOWN — Area code 215

BRIGHT BOOKS — Antiquarian
Joanna Rd (Mail add: PO Box 420, Elverson, 19520). Tel 215-286-6537
Estab 1984. 5000 Titles. 5000 Vols. Cat 4x ann
Types: Juvenile, out of print, used, imp UK
Subj: Horses, hunting & fishing, dogs, sports, fox hunting, beagling, hounds-dogs, shooting, sporting art

NEW HOPE — 1473. Area code 215

BRIDGE STREET OLD BOOKS — General
129 W Bridge St, 18938. Tel 215-862-0615
Estab 1986. 10,000 Titles
Types: Out of print, used, no papbks
Subj: Amer, art, collecting, hist, law, medicine, music, natural hist, rel, sci-tech, sports, travel

NEWTOWN SQUARE — Area code 215

S & C NAJARIAN — Antiquarian
852 Milmar Rd, 19073
Types: Old & rare, out of print
Subj: 19th century sh mus

OREFIELD — Area code 215

THE REFERENCE RACK INC — Mail Order-Antiques
PO Box 445Z, 18069. Tel 215-395-0004
Pres, J M Johnston
Estab 1975. 2500 Titles. 10,000 Vols. Cat
Types: Hb, papbk, out of print
Subj: Collecting, antq

PAOLI — 5835. Area code 215

JOHN E NORRIS — Antiquarian
Box 442, 19301-0442. Tel 215-644-5957
Estab 1972. 1000 Vols. 400 sq ft. Cat 8x ann
Types: Old & rare, out of print
Subj: Pigeons, poultry

PARKESBURG — 2578. Area code 215

JAMES W BEATTIE BOOKS — Mail Order-Used
RD 1, Box 242, Box 242, 19365. Tel 215-857-5686
Estab 1978. 4000 Titles. 4300 Vols. 1200 sq ft. Cat 18x ann
Types: Fine bnd, hb, illus bk, old & rare, out of print
Subj: Art, travel, medicine, sci-tech, vet med

PHILADELPHIA — 1,688,210. Area code 215

WILLIAM H ALLEN BOOKSELLER, INC — Antiquarian
2031 Walnut St, 19103. Tel 215-563-3398
Estab 1918. 30,000 Vols. Cat 4x ann
Types: Hb, imp, out of print, old & rare, used
Subj: Africa, Orientalia, philos, Am, Eng, Latin, Gr & Medieval hist & lit, Mod Eur lang & hist

BOOK MARK — Antiquarian
2049 Rittenhouse Sq W, 19103. Tel 215-735-5546
Estab 1976. 10,000 Vols. 1000 sq ft
Types: Fine bnd, 1st ed, hb, illus bk, ltd ed, old & rare, out of print, used
Subj: Archit

THE BOOK TRADER — Used
501 South St, 19147. Tel 215-925-0219
Mgr & Buyer, Ralph Young
Estab 1975. 70,000 Titles. 200,000 Vols. 4500 sq ft. Cat ann
Types: 1st ed, hb, ltd ed, out of print, papbk, old & rare

ART CARDUNER — Antiquarian
6228 Greene St, 19144-2618. Tel 215-843-6071
Estab 1950. 30,000 Vols. 3000 sq ft. Cat 4x ann
Types: Out of print, used, 1st ed, old & rare
Subj: Amer, drama, poetry, scholarly lit, mil hist

MIRIAM I & WILLIAM H CRAWFORD BOOKS — Mail Order
PO Box 7928, 19101
Estab 1986. Cat ann
Types: Hb, imp Russ, juvenile, out of print, papbk, remainders, used, 1st ed, illus bk, ltd ed, new, old & rare, pamphlets
Subj: Amer, biog, fiction, Pennsylvaniana, Afro-Am, left & Marxist bks, lit

FACTOTUM BOOKS — Used
1709 South, 19146. Tel 215-985-1929
Estab 1986. 20,000 Titles. 20,000 Vols. 1500 sq ft
Types: Imp UK, out of print, remainders, hb, fine bnd, 1st ed
Subj: Mod lit, fine arts, Philadelphia hist

GIOVANNI'S ROOM — Homosexuality
345 S 12th, 19107. Tel 215-923-2960
Estab 1973. 22,000 Titles. 1500 sq ft. Cat monthly
Types: For lang, hb, imp, juvenile, mass mkt papbk, old & rare, out of print, papbk, remainders, used
Subj: Feminism, sexual polit

DAVID & LUBA HAYNES BOOKS — Mail Order-Antiquarian
2210 Trenton Ave, 19125. Tel 215-426-2108
Cat 3X ann
Types: Fine bnd, 1st ed, illus bk, juvenile, old & rare, out of print, used, bibles
Subj: Biblical studies, reference, theol, rel

LAME DUCK USED BOOKS — Used
218 S 45th St, 19104. Tel 215-387-3130
Estab 1984. 34,000 Titles. 42,000 Vols. 1800 sq ft
Types: Out of print, high priced papbk, 1st ed, papbk, hb
Subj: Philos, rel studies, math, sci-tech, hist, soc sci, lang arts, literary criticism, social sci, lit

GEORGE S MACMANUS CO — Antiquarian
1317 Irving St, 19107. Tel 215-735-4456
Cat 4x ann
Types: 1st ed, out of print, old & rare
Subj: Amer, Delawariana, New Jerseyana, Pennsylvaniana, Am & Eng lit

THE PHILADELPHIA PRINT SHOP LTD — General
8441 Germantown Ave, 19118. Tel 215-242-4750
Estab 1982. 2000 Titles. 3000 Vols
Types: Fine bnd, illus bk, out of print, hb

KATHLEEN RAIS & CO — Antiquarian-Dogs
One Longford St, 19136. Tel 215-332-6066
Estab 1978. Cat 4x ann
Types: 1st ed, hb, illus bk, ltd ed, old & rare, out of print
Subj: Albert Payson Terhune, cynogetica

REEDMOR MAGAZINE CO, INC — Used
1229 Walnut St, 19107. Tel 215-922-6643
Pres & Buyer, David Bagelman; Buyer, Elaine Bagelman
Estab 1927
Types: Hb, out of print, old & rare, remainders
Subj: Sci fiction & fantasy

RITTENHOUSE BOOKSTORE — Health
1706 Rittenhouse Sq, 19103. Tel 215-545-6072
Mgr, C Hazell
Estab 1946. 7500 Titles. 8500 Vols. 900 sq ft. Cat 10x ann
Types: New, old & rare, out of print, current med
Subj: Dentistry, health, medicine, vet med

SCHUYLKILL BOOK & CURIO SHOP — Antiquarian
873 Belmont Ave, 19104. Tel 215-473-4769
Estab 1945. Cat
Types: Bibles, 1st ed, illus bk, incunab, out of print, old & rare
Subj: Medicine, sci-tech, scholarly lit, reference, art

CARMEN D VALENTINO — Antiquarian-Americana
2956 Richmond St, 19134. Tel 215-739-6056
Estab 1978. 4500 Titles. 5000 Vols. Cat
Types: Fine bnd, hb, illus bk, out of print, old & rare, used, trade cat
Subj: Local hist, nonfiction

PITTSBURGH — 423,938. Area code 412

BRETT'S BOOKS — Mail Order-Used
5548 Wellesley Ave, 15206. Tel 412-361-7582
Estab 1972. 16,000 Titles
Types: Hb, old & rare, out of print, used

BRYN MAWR - VASSAR BOOKSTORE INC — Used
4612 Winthrop St, 15213. Tel 412-687-3433
Owner, Bryn Mawr College Scholarship Fund
Estab 1972. 7500 Vols. 600 sq ft
Types: For lang, hb, imp, juvenile, out of print, papbk, remainders, col & el-hi text

CITY BOOKS INC — General
1111 E Carson St, 15203. Tel 412-481-7555
Estab 1986. 25,000 Titles. 40,000 Vols. 1600 sq ft
Types: Juvenile, out of print, remainders, used, high priced papbk, hb, juvenile

ELLEN'S BOOK EXCHANGE — Used
626 California Ave, 15202. Tel 412-761-2280
Mgr, Ellen Mitchell
Types: Papbk, out of print

ARTHUR SCHARF TRAVEL BOOKS — Mail Order-Antiquarian
5040 Carolyn Dr, 15236. Tel 412-653-4402
Estab 1970. 5500 Titles. 6000 Vols. 500 sq ft. Cat 2x ann
Types: Hb, imp, out of print
Subj: Travel, WPA Writers' Project, Central Asia, Central Afr, Latin Am

SCHOYER'S BOOKS Antiquarian
1404 S Negley Ave, 15217. Tel 412-521-8464
Estab 1952. 20,000 Titles. 21,000 Vols. Cat 6x ann
Types: 1st ed, juvenile, ltd ed, out of print, old & rare, children's
Subj: Local hist, Amer, travel, discovery & explor, regional hist

FRANK W SKLEDER - BOOKS General
240 Forbes Ave, 15222. Tel 412-261-1890
Estab 1961. 100,000 Vols. 2400 sq ft
Types: New, used, out of print, remainders, papbk

THE TUCKERS Antiquarian
2236 Murray Ave, 15217-2396. Tel 412-521-0249
Estab 1972. 10,000 Vols. 750 sq ft. Cat 6-12x ann
Types: Facsimile editions, fine bnd, 1st ed, hb, illus bk, juvenile, old & rare, out of print
Subj: Pennsylvaniana

POCONO PINES — Area code 717

GRAVESEND BOOKS Mail Order-Antiquarian
PO Box 235, Park Ave Ext, 18350. Tel 717-646-3317
Estab 1971. 7500 Titles. 8000 Vols. Cat 4x ann
Types: Out of print, 1st ed, hb, imp, ltd ed, new & used, old & rare, papbk
Subj: Mystery & detective, Sherlockiana, John Buchan, Woolrich, Starrett

POTTSTOWN — 22,729. Area code 215

THE AMERICANIST Antiquarian
1525 Shenkel Rd, 19464. Tel 215-323-5289
Estab 1954. 25,000 Vols. Cat
Types: 1st ed, hb, juvenile, out of print, old & rare
Subj: Amer, sci-tech, Am & for lit

S F COLLINS' BOOKCELLAR Mail Order
266 Concord Dr, 19464. Tel 215-323-2495
3500 Titles. 3500 Vols
Types: Illus bk, juvenile, out of print
Subj: Rackham, Nielson, J W Smith, Baumiana, Nicholson, Newell

FRANKLIN M ROSHON Antiquarian
378 Buchert Rd, 19464. Tel 215-323-6047
Types: Out of print, old & rare
Subj: Arms & armor, hunting & fishing, trades

READING — 78,686. Area code 215

DELL'S OUTLET Used
1018 Windsor St, 19612-3156. Tel 215-376-7957
Estab 1978. 40,000 Vols. 10,000 sq ft
Types: Hb, papbk, 1st ed, out of print, comics
Subj: Sci fiction & fantasy

LARRY W SOLTYS Mail Order-Antiquarian
330 S 17 1/2 St, 19602. Tel 215-372-7670
Types: Used, hb, out of print, 1st ed, illus bk, old & rare
Subj: Pennsylvaniana, local authors, local hist, Berks County

REBERSBURG — area code 814

LAMPLIGHT BOOKSHOP Used
Rte 192 E (Mail add: PO Box 143, 16872). Tel 814-349-8160
Estab 1987. 2700 Vols. 270 sq ft
Types: Out of print, remainders, used, hb, juvenile, old & rare, out of print, papbk, remainders, used

REVERE — Area code 215

J HOWARD WOOLMER - RARE BOOKS Mail Order-Antiquarian
Marienstein Rd, 18953. Tel 215-847-5074
Estab 1961. Cat 2x ann
Types: 1st ed, hb, imp, out of print, old & rare, used

RILLTON — Area code 412

HOFFMAN RESEARCH SERVICES Science-Technology
Seven Howell Rd, PO Box 342, 15678-0342. Tel 412-446-3374
Estab 1965. 25,000 Vols. Cat 6x ann
Types: Facsimile editions, 1st ed, hb, imp, new & used, out of print, papbk, old & rare, remainders
Subj: Sci-tech, medicine, criminology, Pennsylvaniana, Amer, soc sci, sports, Western Amer, psychiat, psychol, sociol, bus & mgt

SAXTON — 814. Area code 814

BRANDYWINE BOOKS Mail Order-Antiquarian
715 Spring St, 16678. Tel 814-635-2874
Estab 1963. 70,000 Vols. 11,500 sq ft. Cat 4x ann
Types: Out of print, used
Subj: Bus & mgt, law, military, Pennsylvaniana, hist, polit sci

SELINSGROVE — 5227. Area code 717

D J ERNST BOOKS Used
27 N Market St, 17870. Tel 717-374-9461
Estab 1975. 10,000 Vols. 1000 sq ft
Types: Facsimile editions, fine bnd, 1st ed, hb, incunab, illus bk, juvenile, old & rare, out of print, papbk
Subj: Pennsylvania hist

SHIPPENSBURG — 5261. Area code 717

DALE W STARRY SR - BOOKSELLER Used
115 N Washington St, 17257. Tel 717-532-2690
Estab 1965. 3000 Titles. 10,000 Vols. 800 sq ft
Types: 1st ed, hb, illus bk, juvenile, out of print
Subj: Biog, fiction, nonfiction

STATE COLLEGE — 36,130. Area code 814

MICHAEL GIBBS BOOKS Mail Order-Antiquarian
PO Box 883, 16804. Tel 814-234-1745
Estab 1978. 3000 Vols. Cat 4x ann
Types: Old & rare, out of print
Subj: Southwestern Amer, Texana, Western Amer, J Evetts Haley, oil hist

UNIVERSITY BOOK CENTRE College
206 E College Ave, 16801. Tel 814-238-0524. Telex 84-2519
Mgr, Stephen R Long Buys indep
Types: Hb, juvenile, out of print, papbk, remainders, used

SWARTHMORE — 5950. Area code 215

BOOKSOURCE LTD General
15 S Chester Rd (Mail add: PO Box 43, 19081). Tel 215-328-5083
Estab 1976. 10,000 Titles. 20,000 Vols. 1800 sq ft
Types: Out of print, used

F THOMAS HELLER INC Antiquarian
435 Riverview Rd, PO Box 356, 19081-0356. Tel 215-543-3582
Mgr, Christopher Wolfe
Estab 1943. 2500 Vols. Cat 2x ann
Types: 1st ed, illus bk, incunab, old & rare, out of print
Subj: Medicine, philos, psychiat, sci-tech, psychol, metaphys & occult

TITUSVILLE — 6884. Area code 814

GARY K OLSEN — Mail Order-Antiquarian
116 E Spruce St, 16354-1835
Estab 1967. 5000 Titles. 500 sq ft
Types: Old & rare, out of print, used

WARMINSTER — 3000. Area code 215

VOLUME CONTROL — Mail Order
955 Sandy Lane, 18974-2643. Tel 215-674-0217
Estab 1984. 3000 Titles. 3000 Vols. Cat 6x ann
Types: For lang, hb, imp Australia, imp Fr, imp Gr, imp UK, out of print, remainders, used
Subj: Warfare, WWII, mil hist, Third Reich

WASHINGTON — 18,363. Area code 412

ROSEMARY SULLIVAN RARE & OP BOOKS — Mail Order-Antiquarian
52 S Wade, PO Box 1596, 15301. Tel 412-225-1964
Estab 1977. 20,000 Titles. 22,000 Vols. Cat 5x ann
Types: Hb, juvenile, out of print, illus bk, new, old & rare, mag, used
Subj: Amer, genealogy, hist, Revolutionary War, Civil War, nature & environ

WAYNE — 1020. Area code 215

THE BOOK SHELF — General
Four Louella Ct, 19087. Tel 215-688-1446
Estab 1936. 2500 Vols. 600 sq ft
Types: Hb, juvenile, papbk, used, out of print
Subj: Nature & environ, cook bks

KONIGSMARK BOOKS — Mail Order-Antiquarian
309 Midland Ave, 19087. Tel 215-687-5965
Estab 1980. 5000 Titles. 5000 Vols. Cat
Types: Facsimile editions, fine bnd, 1st ed, hb, illus bk, juvenile, ltd ed, old & rare, out of print, remainders, used
Subj: Art, lit, Jane Austin

WELLSBORO — 3805. Area code 717

EMERSON CO — Mail Order-Antiquarian
36 East Ave, 16901. Tel 712-724-3139
Estab 1985. 1000 Titles
Types: 1st ed, hb, illus bk, old & rare, used, out of print
Subj: Eng hist & lit

WEST CHESTER — 17,435. Area code 215

ELIZABETH L MATLAT — Antiques
PO Box 3511, 19381. Tel 215-358-0359
Estab 1969
Types: Hb, new & used, out of print, papbk
Subj: Archit, antq

WILLIAMSPORT — 33,401. Area code 717

THE LAST HURRAH BOOKSHOP — Used
937 Memorial Ave, 17701. Tel 717-327-9338
Estab 1982. 20,000 Vols. 400 sq ft. Cat 2x ann
Types: Out of print, papbk, hb, 1st ed, illus bk, ltd ed, old & rare, remainders
Subj: Polit assassinations, hist, criminology, 19th & 20th century Am polit, Kennedy conspiracy, 19th century Amer

WILLOW STREET — Area code 717

GAME BAG BOOKS — Antiquarian-Hunting & Fishing
2704 Ship Rock Rd, 17584. Tel 717-464-2941
Estab 1974. 2000 Titles. Cat 2x ann
Types: Old & rare, out of print
Subj: Guns

YORK — 44,619. Area code 717

MARIE FETROW — Mail Order-Antiquarian
1777 W Market St, 17404. Tel 717-843-0290
Types: 1st ed, hb, illus bk, imp, juvenile, old & rare, out of print, remainders, used

FIRST CAPITOL ANTIQUARIAN BOOK & PAPER MARKET — Antiquarian
343 W Market St, 17401. Tel 717-846-2866
Estab 1984. 100,000 Titles. 150,000 Vols. 5000 sq ft
Types: Out of print, used, 1st ed, hb, illus bk, juvenile, old & rare
Subj: Nonfiction, Pennsylvaniana, travel

CRANSTON — 71,992. Area code 401

THE OWL AT THE BRIDGE — Mail Order-Foreign Lang
25 Berwick Lane, 02905-3708. Tel 401-467-7362
Estab 1981. 5000 Vols
Types: Incunab, new, old & rare, out of print, imp Ital
Subj: Art, Renaissance hist & lit, silver

EAST GREENWICH — 10,211. Area code 401

DON E BURNETT — Mail Order-Antiquarian
PO Box 178, 02818. Tel 401-884-6181
Estab 1934. 10,000 Vols. 1200 sq ft. Cat
Types: 1st ed, hb, juvenile, out of print, old & rare, used
Subj: Amer, juvenile 1790-1880, archit 1835-1925

LIMITED EDITION BOOKSTORE — General
232 Main St, 02818. Tel 401-884-3211
Estab 1983. 4000 Titles. 7000 Vols
Types: Hb, juvenile, out of print, papbk, remainders, old & rare, used

FOSTER — 3370. Area code 401

LINCOLN BOOK SHOPPE INC & LINCOLN OUT-OF-PRINT BOOK SEARCH LTD — Mail Order-Antiquarian
Mt Hygeia Rd, 02825. Tel 401-647-2825
Estab 1931. 75,000 Vols. 2000 sq ft
Types: Old & rare, out of print
Subj: Econ, fine arts, hist, literary criticism, soc sci

NEWPORT — 29,259. Area code 401

ANCHOR & DOLPHIN BOOKS — Antiquarian-Architecture
30 Franklin St (Mail add: PO Box 823, 02840-0823). Tel 401-846-6890
Estab 1979. 2500 Vols. 400 sq ft. Cat 4x ann
Types: Fine bnd, 1st ed, illus bk, ltd ed, old & rare, out of print
Subj: Gardening, archit, design, landscape archit, garden hist

ARMCHAIR SAILOR BOOKSTORE — Nautical
Lee's Wharf, 02840. Tel 401-847-4252
Estab 1979. 8000 Titles. 2300 sq ft. Cat 4x ann
Types: Hb, out of print, papbk, remainders, new & used, Fr lang, juvenile, imp UK, imp Australian, New Zealand
Subj: Natural hist

CORNER BOOKSHOP — General
418 Spring St, 02840. Tel 401-846-8406
Estab 1962. 6000 Vols
Types: New & used, out of print, old & rare, papbk
Subj: Rhode Islandana, Newport

THE NOSTALGIA FACTORY — Antiquarian
Brick Market Pl, 221 Goddard Row, 02840. Tel 401-849-3441
Estab 1971. 1000 Titles. 1000 Vols. Cat 2x ann
Types: Illus bk, old & rare, out of print
Subj: Archit, tennis, golf, world exhibitions
See Also: Boston, MA

PROVIDENCE — 156,804. Area code 401

CELLAR STORIES — Used
190 Mathewson, 02903. Tel 401-521-2665
Estab 1982. 40,000 Vols. 1500 sq ft
Types: Juvenile, hb, papbk, out of print
Subj: Fiction, sci fiction & fantasy, mystery & detective, military, hist, cooking, arts & crafts, local hist

CORNERSTONE BOOKSTORE — Black Studies
236 Meeting St, 02906. Tel 401-331-1340
Estab 1983. 6000 Titles. 800 sq ft. Cat 4x ann
Types: Hb, used, fine bnd, 1st ed, incunab, illus bk, imp, ltd ed, old & rare, out of print, papbk, Ital lang
Subj: Black studies, Rhode Islandana, black lit, modern first editions

SEWARD'S FOLLY, BOOKS — Antiquarian
139 Brook St, 02906. Tel 401-272-4454
Estab 1976. 15,000 Vols
Types: 1st ed, fine bnd, hb, illus bk, imp, old & rare, out of print, papbk, remainders, used
Subj: Scholarly lit

TYSON BOOKS — General
334 Westminster Mall, Third Floor, 02903. Tel 401-421-3939
Estab 1930. 25,000 Titles. 8000 Vols. Cat
Types: Hb, out of print, old & rare, used, 1st ed
Subj: Amer, Rhode Islandana, Am hist & lit, fine arts

SMITHFIELD — 16,886. Area code 401

SMITHFIELD RARE BOOKS — Mail Order
Red 4, Deer Run Trail, 02917. Tel 401-231-8225
Estab 1986. 1000 Titles. 1200 Vols. 400 sq ft. Cat 6x ann
Types: Out of print, 1st ed, hb, illus bk, old & rare, out of print
Subj: Sci-tech, medicine, natural hist

WARWICK — 87,123. Area code 401

BUR-LIN BOOKS — Mail Order-Antiquarian
3 Colgate St, 02888. Tel 401-467-3364
Mgr, Jeremy W Morritt
Estab 1976. 500 Vols
Types: Out of print, used
Subj: T W Burges, J C Lincoln

FORTUNATE FINDS BOOKSTORE — Antiquarian
16 W Natick Rd, 02886-1180. Tel 401-737-8160
Estab 1955. 10,000 Vols. Cat 4x ann
Types: Out of print, old & rare, juvenile
Subj: Genealogy, hist, art, archit, trades, Rhode Islandana

WATCH HILL — Area code 401

BOOK & TACKLE SHOP — General
Seven Bay St (Mail add: PO Box 462, Westerly, 02891). Tel 401-596-0700
Estab 1953. 15 Titles. 25,000 Vols. Cat 3x annBuys through hq
Types: Hb, juvenile, out of print, papbk, remainders, col & el-hi text, used
Subj: Hist, hunting & fishing, medicine, sci-tech, sea

WESTERLY — 18,850. Area code 401

THE NEW AGE METAPHYSICAL BOOKSHOP — Antiquarian-Metaphys & Occult
30 Canal St, 02891. Tel 401-596-2879
Estab 1973. 3000 Vols
Types: Out of print, old & rare, new & used, used, rare
Subj: Astrol, parapsychol, numerology, nature & environ, yoga, healing, meditation, new thought, color, gems

THE WAYSIDE BOOKSHOP — Antiquarian
Langworthy Rd, RR 3, Box 501, 02891. Tel 401-322-1698
Estab 1974. 3500 Vols. Cat
Types: 1st ed, hb, illus bk, juvenile, ltd ed, old & rare, out of print, juvenile
Subj: Women's studies, hort, Amer, floriculture

SOUTH CAROLINA

ANDERSON — 27,313. Area code 803

ANDERSON BOOK NOOK — General
3438 Cinema Center, 29622-2426. Tel 803-231-9221
Mgr, R E Bowie
Estab 1986. 14,000 Titles. 750 sq ft
Types: New & used, old & rare, out of print, papbk, high priced papbk, remainders

BEAUFORT — 8634. Area code 803

BEAUFORT BOOK CO — Mail Order
PO Box 1127, 29901. Tel 803-524-4666
5 Titles
Types: Hb, old & rare, out of print, remainders
Subj: South Carolinana

CHARLESTON — 69,510. Area code 803

ATLANTIC BOOKS — Mail Order-Antiquarian
363 King St, 29401. Tel 803-723-4751
Estab 1978. 19,000 Titles. 20,000 Vols. 1400 sq ft. Cat
Types: Remainders, used, hb, 1st ed, new, old & rare, out of print, papbk
Subj: Southern Amer, Civil War, Southern auth

HOPPIN' JOHN'S — Food
30 Pinckney St, 29401. Tel 803-577-6404
Estab 1986. 3000 Titles. 3500 Vols. 400 sq ft
Types: Hb, imp, out of print, mass mkt papbk, high priced papbk, remainders, col text
Subj: Hunting & fishing, gardening, wines

PALMETTO BOOKS — South Carolinana
1811 Kempton Ave, PO Box 12753, 29412. Tel 803-795-1996
Estab 1983. 1500 Vols. 200 sq ft. Cat 10x ann
Types: Out of print, old & rare
Subj: Hunting & fishing, Civil War

CLEMSON — 8118. Area code 803

THE BOOK CELLAR — Used
102-4 Earle St, 29631. Tel 803-654-3603
Estab 1977. 17,000 Vols. 600 sq ft
Types: Out of print, papbk
Subj: Mystery & detective, nonfiction, romance, sci fiction & fantasy, Western Amer

COLUMBIA — 99,296. Area code 803

THE BOOK DISPENSARY INC — General
Boozer S/Ctr, 1600 Broad River Rd, 29210. Tel 803-798-4739
Mgr, Mike Wadsworth
Estab 1975. 80,000 Vols. 5000 sq ft
Types: Hb, papbk, out of print, collectible bks

BOOK PLACE — Used
3129 Millwood Ave, 29205. Tel 803-799-6561
Estab 1976. 20,000 Vols. 1500 sq ft. Cat
Types: Out of print
Subj: Fiction, nonfiction, Civil War, South Carolinana

ST ANDREWS BOOKS — Mail Order-Used
PO Box 210756, 29221. Tel 803-772-4551
Estab 1985. 3000 Titles. 3000 Vols. Cat
Types: Out of print, facsimile editions, 1st ed, hb, old & rare, new & used
Subj: Ship model, scale modeling, Virginia Woolf

GREENVILLE — 58,242. Area code 803

ROBBINS RARITIES INC — Used
2038-C Laurens Rd, 29607. Tel 803-297-7948
Estab 1985. 5000 Titles. 5500 Vols. 1200 sq ft
Types: Out of print, facsimile editions, fine bnd, 1st ed, hb, illus bk, old & rare, juvenile, incunab
Subj: Civil War, military, illus

VOLUME I BOOKS — Antiquarian-General
407 Augusta St, 29601. Tel 803-235-6419
Mgr, Dianne G Bailey
Estab 1974. 15,000 Titles. 20,000 Vols
Types: Hb, juvenile, papbk, new & used, out of print
Subj: South Carolinana

GREENWOOD — 21,163. Area code 803

NOAH'S ARK BOOK ATTIC — Antiquarian
Stony Point, Rte 2, 29649. Tel 803-229-1022
Estab 1954. 85,000 Vols. Cat 8x ann
Types: Bibles, imp, incunab, out of print, old & rare
Subj: Theol
See Also: The Attic Inc, Hodges

HODGES — 154. Area code 803

THE ATTIC INC — Antiquarian
PO Box 100, 29653. Tel 803-229-1022
Pres, Donald Hawthorne
Estab 1961. 65,000 Vols. Cat 2x ann
Types: Imp, out of print, old & rare
Subj: South Carolinana

MYRTLE BEACH — 18,758. Area code 803

LETTY WILDER BOOKS — Used
212 Highland Blvd, 29577. Tel 803-449-3466
Types: Out of print
Subj: North Carolinana, South Carolinana

NEWBERRY — 9866. Area code 803

HAMPTON BOOKS — Antiquarian
Rte 1, Box 202, 29108. Tel 803-276-6870
Mgr, Muriel Price Hamilton
Estab 1946. 2400 sq ft. Cat
Types: Facsimile editions, imp, out of print, old & rare, juvenile, 1st ed
Subj: Golf, hunting & fishing, photog, Southern auth, cinema

ROCK HILL — 35,344. Area code 803

JAMES S PIPKIN OLD & RARE BOOKS — Mail Order-Antiquarian
2324-A Rosewood Dr, 29730. Tel 803-366-3839
Estab 1968. 12,000 Vols
Types: 1st ed, hb, illus bk, juvenile, out of print, old & rare, used
Subj: Amer, Civil War, fiction, mystery & detective, rel studies, South Carolinana, World Wars I & II

SPARTANBURG — 43,968. Area code 803

NORM BURLESON BOOKSELLER — Antiquarian-Religious Studies
104 First Ave, PO Box 15007, 29302-0201. Tel 803-583-8845
Estab 1979. 500 Titles. 1500 Vols. Cat ann
Types: Hb, imp, old & rare, out of print, new
Subj: Biblical studies, sermons, outlines, commentaries

CHRISTIAN SUPPLY SHOPPE INC — Religious-P
303 E Wood St, 29303. Tel 803-585-5436
Merch Mgr & Buyer, Norman Burleson; Juv Buyer, Audrey Horton
Estab 1953. 50,000 Vols. 15,000 sq ft. Cat ann
Types: Hb, juvenile, out of print, papbk, remainders, used

KITEMAUG BOOKS — Mail Order-Antiquarian
229 Mohawk Dr, 29301. Tel 803-576-3338
Estab 1959. 700 Vols. Cat
Types: Facsimile editions, 1st ed, hb, new & used, old & rare, out of print, papbk, pvt presses, remainders
Subj: Nautical, Amer, Navy, submarines

RAPID CITY — 46,492. Area code 605

AGAPE BOOK SHOPPE — Inspirational
4220 Brookside Dr, 57702. Tel 605-342-6998
Estab 1979. 600 Titles. 3000 Vols
Types: Out of print
Subj: Metaphysics, self-develop, theosophy

SIOUX FALLS — 81,343. Area code 605

KOLBE'S BOOKS PHOTOS & MAPS — Used
1301 S Duluth St, 57105. Tel 605-332-9662
Estab 1972. 400 sq ft
Types: Out of print
Subj: Western Amer, SDak

VERMILLION — 9582. Area code 605

BUTEO BOOKS — Natural History
PO Box 481, 57069-0481. Tel 605-624-4343
Estab 1971. 10,000 Vols. 1000 sq ft. Cat 4x ann
Types: Hb, imp, out of print, papbk, remainders, col text, used
Subj: Ornith, discovery & explor

BUCHANAN —2871. Area code 901

FIRST FOLIO — Antiquarian
RR 1, Box 127A, 38222. Tel 901-644-9940
Co-Owner Dennis Hatman
Estab 1983. 10,000 Titles. 10,000 Vols. Cat
Types: Fine bnd, 1st ed, hb, illus bk, juvenile, ltd ed, old & rare, out of print, juvenile
Subj: Art

CLEVELAND — 26,415. Area code 615

BADEN BADEN BOOKSHOP — Used
PO Box 2424, 37320-2424. Tel 615-476-2921
Estab 1967. 25,000 Vols. Cat 2x ann
Types: Hb, juvenile, out of print, papbk, remainders
Subj: Alt life styles, rel-j, rel-Rosicrucian, Masonic, mystery & detective

THE BOOK SHELF — Tennesseeana
3765 Hillsdale Dr NE, 37312-5133. Tel 615-472-8408
Estab 1974. 1000 Titles. 3000 Vols. 600 sq ft. Cat 4x ann
Types: 1st ed, facsimile editions, hb, new, old & rare, out of print
Subj: Alabamana, genealogy, Southern Amer

COLUMBIA — 25,767. Area code 615

THE VILLAGE BOOK STORE — General
311 W Eighth, 38401-3198. Tel 615-381-9525
Estab 1969. 8000 Vols. 2200 sq ft. Cat ann
Types: Hb, juvenile, out of print, papbk, remainders, bibles
Subj: Rel studies, hist

JOHNSON CITY — 39,753. Area code 615

THE BOOKSHELF — Comics
2254 N Roan, 37604. Tel 615-282-8090
Estab 1980. 15,000 Vols. 600 sq ft
Types: New & used, out of print, hb

KINGSPORT — 32,027. Area code 615

THE BOOK WAREHOUSE — General
4320 Allendale Market Place, 37660. Tel 615-245-5057
Owner, Chapters Inc; Mgr, Virgil Starnes
Estab 1987. 7000 Titles. 25,000 Vols. 4800 sq ft
Types: Hb, papbk, juvenile, remainders, for lang, out of print

HILLS BOOKS — Mail Order-Antiquarian
1012 Ransome Lane, 37662. Tel 615-247-8704
Merch Mgr, Mrs F M Hill
Estab 1959. 25,000 Vols. Cat 8x ann
Types: 1st ed, hb, out of print, old & rare, used
Subj: Appalachia, Civil War, hunting & fishing, Southern Amer, Tennesseeana, genealogy

WINTER GALLEY BOOKS — Antiquarian
Rt 1, 37660. Tel 615-323-4320 (by appt)
Estab 1980. 200 Vols
Types: Out of print
Subj: Dogs

KNOXVILLE — 183,139. Area code 615

R R ALLEN - BOOKS — Mail Order-Antiquarian
5300 Bluefield Rd, 37921. Tel 615-584-4487
Estab 1962. 7500 Titles. 7500 Vols. Cat 2x ann
Types: Old & rare, out of print
Subj: Amer, Tennesseeana

ANDOVER SQUARE BOOKS — Mail Order-Antiquarian
Kingston Pike Antq Mall, 5404 Kingston Pike (Mail add: 805 Norgate Rd, 37919). Tel 615-693-8984
Mgrs, M R & G A Yeomans
Estab 1978. 8000 Titles. 10,000 Vols. Cat 12x ann
Types: 1st ed, illus bk, ltd ed, old & rare, out of print, used
Subj: Civil War

DONALDSON'S BOOKS — Mail Order-Antiquarian
600 Inskip Rd Apt A102, 37912. Tel 615-687-8872
Estab 1977. 10,000 Vols
Types: 1st ed, hb, illus bk, juvenile, old & rare, out of print, used
Subj: Natural hist, Amer, belles lettres

MADISON — Area code 615

BOOK ATTIC — Used
The Shoppes At Rivergate, 2142 N Gallatin Rd, 37115. Tel 615-859-7219
Estab 1987. 17,000 Titles. 30,000 Vols. 1250 sq ft
Types: Hb, papbk, juvenile, used, for lang, text bks, remainders, out of print

FOX BOOKS — Mail Order
1420 Neely's Bend Rd, 37115. Tel 615-868-2078
Types: Out of print
Subj: Tennesseeana

MEMPHIS — 646,356. Area code 901

BURKE'S BOOKSTORE INC — Antiquarian
1719 Poplar Ave, 38104. Tel 901-278-7484
Estab 1875. 20,000 Vols. 3000 sq ft. Cat ann
Types: Out of print, el-hi text, used, old & rare, 1st ed
Subj: Hist, local authors, sci-tech, Civil War

MEMPHIS COMICS & RECORDS — Comics
665 S Highland Dr, 38111. Tel 901-452-1304
Types: 1st ed, illus bk, ltd ed, old & rare, out of print, papbk, collector comic bks, pulps
Subj: Amateur publ
See Also: Star Store, Jackson, MS

MID-AMERICA BOOKS — General
571 S Highland, 38111. Tel 901-452-0766
Estab 1981. 40,000 Titles. 2000 sq ft. Cat 4x ann
Types: 1st ed, hb, illus bk, juvenile, old & rare, out of print, papbk, used
Subj: Hist, rel, class studies, mystery & detective, sci fiction & fantasy, pulps

W E OATES GALLERY — General
97 N Tillman St, 38111. Tel 901-323-5659
Estab 1965. 100 Titles. 200 Vols
Types: Out of print

SUPERSEARCH BOOK SERVICE — Mail Order-Antiquarian
Box 241484, 38124-1484. Tel 901-725-0815
1000 Titles. 1000 Vols. Cat
Types: Used, out of print, old & rare, hb, 1st ed, fine bnd
Subj: Anthrop, art, reference, underwater archaeol, lit

XANADU BOOKSTORE — General
7235 Winchester Rd, 38125. Tel 901-757-9885
Mgr, Beverly Nickey Lowe
Types: Hb, juvenile, out of print, papbk, used

MILAN — 8083. Area code 901

FMS INC THE CHRISTIAN BOOKSTORES & GIFTSHOPS — Religious
103 Adobe Sq, 38358. Tel 901-686-3075
Types: Bibles, hb, papbk, juvenile, out of print

NASHVILLE — 455,651. Area code 615

THE BATTERY BOOK PRESS INC — Mail Order-Military
PO Box 3107, Uptown Station, 37219. Tel 615-298-1401
Estab 1976. 110 Titles. 5000 Vols. Cat ann
Types: Facsimile editions, fine bnd, 1st ed, for lang, hb, illus bk, ltd ed, new, old & rare, out of print, papbk, used
Subj: Military

THE BOOK TREASURY — Mail Order-Antiquarian
2216 Eighth Ave S, 37204. Tel 615-269-3358
Estab 1984. 8000 Titles. 8000 Vols. 2800 sq ft. Cat ann
Types: Fine bnd, 1st ed, illus bk, juvenile, ltd ed, old & rare, out of print

DAD'S OLD BOOKSTORE — Used
4004 Hillsboro Pke, 37215. Tel 615-298-5880
Estab 1985. 20,000 Titles. 20,000 Vols. 2000 sq ft
Types: Fine bnd, 1st ed, hb, illus bk, juvenile, ltd ed, old & rare, out of print

ELDER'S BOOKSTORE — Mail Order-Antiquarian
2115 Elliston Pl, 37203. Tel 615-327-1867
Mgr, Randy Elder
Estab 1951. 40,000 Titles. 4200 sq ft
Types: Hb, used, facsimile editions, fine bnd, 1st ed, illus bk, juvenile, ltd ed, new, old & rare, out of print, incunab
Subj: Civil War, local hist, Tennesseeana, Southern lit

FUGITIVE BOOKS — Mail Order-Antiquarian
Belle Meade Station, P O Box 50293, 37205. Tel 615-356-1350
Mgr, Pamela Chenery
Estab 1986. 1500 Titles. 5000 Vols. Cat 6x ann
Types: Hb, old & rare, out of print, used, 1st ed
Subj: Civil War, 20th cent Southern lit

RIPLEY — 6366. Area code 901

ENTERPRISE BOOKS — Antiquarian
PO Box 289, 38063-0289. Tel 901-635-1771
Estab 1965. 15,000 Titles. 18,000 Vols. 4000 sq ft
Types: Hb, out of print, remainders, old & rare, used, papbk
Subj: Bks on bks, printing, papermaking

SIGNAL MOUNTAIN — 5818. Area code 615

CRABTREE BOOKSELLERS — Antiquarian-General
3500 Taft Hwy, PO Box 366, 37377. Tel 615-886-5944
30,000 Vols. 2000 sq ft
Types: Hb, out of print, remainders
Subj: Biog, hist, philos, rel

TULLAHOMA — 15,800. Area code 615

BARCLAY BOOKS & SECRETARIAL SERVICE — Antiquarian
100 S Jackson St (Mail add: PO Box 357, 37388). Tel 615-455-8882
Estab 1985. 3000 Titles. 3000 Vols. 510 sq ft. Cat
Types: Facsimile editions, fine bnd, 1st ed, hb, illus bk, imp, juvenile, ltd ed, old & rare, out of print, used
Subj: Aviation, women's studies

CENTAUR BOOKS & COMICS — Antiquarian-Comics
509-C N Jackson, 37388. Tel 615-455-2196
15,000 Vols. 840 sq ft
Types: Illus bk, out of print, remainders, used, papbk, new
Subj: Sci fiction & fantasy

AMARILLO — 149,230. Area code 806

HASTINGS BOOKS & RECORDS — General
Western Plaza, No 15, 79109. Tel 806-355-0061, 355-8471
Owner, Western Merchandising; Mgr, Mark Gongare
Estab 1969
Types: Hb, juvenile, out of print, papbk, remainders
For location of branches in other cities, see index

TIME & AGAIN — Antiquarian
3207 W Sixth St, 79106. Tel 806-371-0271
Estab 1978. 7500 Titles. 8000 Vols. 800 sq ft. Cat 4x ann
Types: Used, out of print, fine bnd, 1st ed, hb, illus bk, juvenile, ltd ed, old & rare
Subj: Texana, Western Amer

ANDREWS — 11,061. Area code 915

BOY SCOUT MEMORABILIA BOOK HOUSE — Used
1400 NW Ninth St, 79714. Tel 915-523-2902
Estab 1969. 5000 Titles. 8000 Vols. 1200 sq ft. Cat 4x ann
Types: Imp, out of print, juvenile
Subj: Hist

ARLINGTON — 160,123. Area code 817

THE BOOK RACK — Used Paperback
2304 W Park Row Dr, 76013. Tel 817-274-1717
Estab 1975Buys Indep
Types: Juvenile, out of print, papbk, Fr lang, contemp novels, non-fic
Subj: Western Amer, sci fiction & fantasy, mystery & detective, romance, warfare

GENERALBOOK STORE — General
604-J Doug Russell Rd, 76010. Tel 817-265-0351
Estab 1963. 50,000 Vols. 1900 sq ft. Cat ann
Types: Col & el-hi text, juvenile, ltd ed, out of print, remainders, used, papbk
Subj: Mystery & detective, romance, sci fiction & fantasy, bus & mgt, how-to

LONE STAR COMICS & SCIENCE FICTION INC — Science Fiction & Fantasy
511 E Abram St, 76010. Tel 817-265-0491
Buyer, Steve Schiavo
Estab 1977. 1000 Titles. 3000 Vols. 2350 sq ft
Types: Hb, imp UK, out of print, papbk, used, comics
See Also: Dallas, Irving, Mesquite

AUSTIN — 345,496. Area code 512

ALPHA MUSIC CENTER — Music
611 W 29th St, 78705. Tel 512-477-5009
Estab 1976. 10,000 Titles. 7500 Vols. 1200 sq ft
Types: Out of print, new & used, Western Europe
Subj: Class studies, hard-to-find & current popular music of all eras

ATTALS SOUTHWEST GALLERY — Used
3310 Red River, 78705. Tel 512-476-3634
Estab 1964. 10,000 Vols. 2000 sq ft
Types: Fine bnd, 1st ed, hb, illus bk, juvenile, ltd ed, old & rare, out of print
Subj: Civil War, Texana

CONGRESS AVENUE BOOKSELLERS — General
718 Congress Ave, 78701. Tel 512-478-1157, 478-1241
Owner, Cochran Corp; Mgr, Jill Miller
Estab 1973. 25,000 Titles. 2250 sq ft
Types: Hb, juvenile, papbk, remainders, out of print
Subj: Bus & mgt, polit sci, sci fiction & fantasy, Texana, contemporary lit

HALF PRICE BOOKS, RECORDS & MAGAZINES — Used
3110 Guadalupe, 78705. Tel 512-451-4463
Estab 1975. 80,000 Vols. 9000 sq ft Buys indep & through hq
Types: Hb, old & rare, out of print, papbk, remainders, for lang, imp, col & el-hi text

MACK LEE BOOK FAIRS — Mail Order-Antiquarian
2000 Palo Duro Rd, 78757. Tel 512-451-3631
Estab 1981. 1200 Titles. 1500 Vols. Cat 2x ann
Types: 1st ed, ltd ed, out of print, used, inprint

PHOTO-EYE — Mail Order-Photography
1818 W 11th (Mail add: PO Box 1504, 78767-1504). Tel 512-480-8409
Estab 1979. 1400 Titles. 6500 Vols. Cat 6x ann
Types: Hb, imp Fr, imp Gr, out of print, imp
Subj: Photog, art, archit

K B SLOCUM - BOOKS — Mail Order
11201 Yucca Dr, Suite 620 (Mail add: PO Box 10998 No 620, 78759). Tel 512-258-7442
Estab 1966. 25,000 Vols. Cat 3x ann
Types: Hb, high priced papbk, out of print, remainders
Subj: Antq, collecting, hist, local hist

STATE HOUSE BOOKS — Antiquarian
1604 S Congress, 78704. Tel 512-448-0700
Estab 1983. 8500 Vols
Types: Out of print, old & rare, new & used, hb
Subj: Military, Texana, Western Amer, guns, hunting & fishing

TEXAS TEXTBOOKS INC — College
2323 San Antonio St, 78705. Tel 512-478-9833
Estab 1978. 15,000 Titles. 40,000 Vols. 12,500 sq ft
Types: Hb, new & used, out of print, papbk, remainders

BAYTOWN — 59,923. Area code 713

BOOK BARN — Used
222 E Texas Ave, 77520. Tel 713-428-1645
Mgr, Harley L Ashley
Estab 1983. 8000 Titles. 20,000 Vols
Types: Out of print, mass mkt papbk
Subj: Romance, sci fiction & fantasy, mystery & detective, warfare, rel, Texana, espionage

BEAUMONT — 118,102. Area code 409

THE BOOK GALLERY — Used
2227 Calder Ave, 77701. Tel 409-835-2665
Estab 1988. 7000 Titles. 7000 Vols. 1000 sq ft
Types: Hb, out of print, old & rare, new, 1st ed
Subj: Biog, fiction, hist

BELLAIRE — 14,950. Area code 713

KENDRICK BOOK STORE — Antiquarian
6605 South Rice Ave, 77401. Tel 713-669-8668
Estab 1961. 22,000 Vols
Types: 1st ed, new & used, out of print, old & rare
Subj: Texana, Civil War, biog, American wars

BLANCO — 1179. Area code 512

MAGGIE LAMBETH BOOKS — Antiquarian-Western Americana
Star Rt 4, Box 361, 78606. Tel 512-833-5252 (by appt only)
Estab 1980. 8000 Titles. 8000 Vols. Cat 3x ann
Types: Fine bnd, 1st ed, illus bk, ltd ed, hb, juvenile, used, old & rare, out of print
Subj: Hist, Texana, Southwestern Amer, Mex, agr

BRYAN — 44,337. Area code 409

FRONTIER AMERICA CORPORATION — Mail Order-Antiquarian
PO Box 3698, 77805-3698. Tel 409-846-4462
Owner, Fred White Jr
Estab 1967. 7000 Titles. 75,000 Vols. Cat 3x ann
Types: Hb, old & rare, out of print, fine bnd
Subj: Mex, photog, Texana, Western Amer

HALF PRICE BOOKS, RECORDS & MAGAZINES — Used
3828 S Texas, 77801. Tel 409-846-2738Buys indep & through hq
Types: Col & el-hi text, for lang, hb, imp, juvenile, old & rare, out of print, papbk, remainders

CANYON — 10,724. Area code 806

BUFFALO BOOKSTORE INC — College
2318 Fourth Ave, 79015. Tel 806-655-4632
Estab 1962
Types: Hb, out of print, papbk, remainders, col text

CLEBURNE — 19,218. Area code 817

BILL'S BOOKS — General
116 S Main St, PO Box 592, 76031. Tel 817-645-7591
Estab 1980. 60,000 Titles. 200,000 Vols. 2500 sq ft
Types: Hb, juvenile, out of print, mass mkt papbk, high priced papbk, remainders, used

COLLEGE STATION — 37,272. Area code 409

CGT CO - BOOKS — Mail Order-Antiquarian
1115 Langford St, 77840. Tel 409-693-2707
Estab 1982. 3000 Vols. Cat
Types: Out of print, old & rare
Subj: Amer, archaeol, discovery & explor, medicine, sci-tech, travel

CONROE — 18,034. Area code 409

GIERSPECK & ROPER BOOKSELLERS INC — General
1132 W Dallas, 77301. Tel 409-756-9142
Estab 1976. 24,000 Vols. 1875 sq ft
Types: Hb, out of print, papbk

CORPUS CHRISTI — 231,999. Area code 512

L V BOLING BOOKS — Mail Order
3413 Tiger Lane, 78415. Tel 512-852-1131
Estab 1964. 2000 Titles. 5000 Vols. Cat 12-24x ann
Types: Hb, imp Mex, out of print, used
Subj: Mex, Southwestern Amer, Texana

HALF PRICE BOOKS, RECORDS & MAGAZINES — Used
5821 Weber Sq S/Ctr, 78413. Tel 512-852-2199
Estab 1982. 60,000 Titles. 70,000 Vols Buys indep & through hq
Types: Col & el-hi text, for lang, hb, imp, juvenile, old & rare, out of print, papbk, remainders, comics

SOUTHERN MAJESTY BOOKS — Mail Order
6402 Meadow Circle, 78413. Tel 512-991-9150, 883-9030
Estab 1986. 2000 Titles. 2200 Vols. Cat 1-2x ann
Types: Hb, out of print, used, 1st ed, ltd ed, new
Subj: Amer, Southern Amer, Southwestern Amer, Texana, Southern women

DALLAS — 904,078. Area code 214

THE AFTERIMAGE PHOTOGRAPH GALLERY — Art Gallery
The Quadrangle, Suite 250 (Mail add: 2800 Routh St, 250, 75201). Tel 214-871-9140
Estab 1971. 300 Titles. 450 Vols. 1200 sq ft
Types: Hb, imp, out of print, high priced papbk, remainders, col text, used
Subj: Photog

ALDREDGE BOOKSTORE — Used
2909-1A Maple Ave, 75201. Tel 214-871-3333
Estab 1947. 10,000 Vols. Cat 4x ann
Types: Hb, out of print
Subj: Texana

BIG D BOOKS & COMICS — Comics
1516 Centerville, 75228. Tel 214-328-0130
Estab 1978. 2000 sq ft. Cat ann
Types: Illus bk, juvenile, old & rare, out of print, papbk, used, comics, collectable comics
Subj: Comedy, sci fiction & fantasy

THE BOOK TREE — Used
43 Richardson Heights village, 75080. Tel 214-437-4337
Estab 1986. 2300 Vols. 1400 sq ft
Types: Hb, 1st ed, old & rare, remainders, out of print, papbk
Subj: Fiction, military, Texana, hist, biog

BYGONE BOOKS — Used
PO Box 25042 (Mail add: Antique World, 9101 John Carpenter Freeway, 75225). Tel 214-373-0218
Estab 1973. 10,000 Vols
Types: Used, juvenile, out of print, old & rare
Subj: Texana, Southwestern Amer, art, antq, Civil War, military, cooking

THE DALLAS INSTITUTE OF HUMANITIES & CULTURE BOOKSTORE — Humanities
2719 Routh St, 75201-1927. Tel 214-871-2440
Mgr, Frank Lukner
Estab 1982. 1500 Titles. 3500 Vols
Types: Hb, imp UK, out of print, used
Subj: Literary criticism, psychol, poetry, Jungian psychol, archetypal

FINDERS KEEPERS — Mail Order
PO Box 820247, 75382-0247. Tel 214-341-3961
Estab 1983. 1500 Titles. 1500 Vols
Types: Out of print, used

DAVID GROSSBLATT BOOKSELLER — Antiquarian
PO Box 25042 (Mail add: Antique World, 9101 John Carpenter Freeway, 75225). Tel 214-263-1444
Estab 1973. 30,000 Vols. 5000 sq ft. Cat 3x ann
Types: Fine bnd, 1st ed, hb, illus bk, ltd ed, new, old & rare, out of print
Subj: Amer, Texana, Western Amer

HALF PRICE BOOKS, RECORDS & MAGAZINES INC — Used
5915 E Northwest Hwy, 75231. Tel 214-363-8374
Vpres, Nando Arduini II; Mgr, Sharon Anderson; Treas, Pat Anderson
Estab 1972. 500,000 Vols. 14,000 sq ft
Types: Col & el-hi text, for lang, hb, imp, juvenile, old & rare, out of print, papbk, remainders
See Also: Arlington, Austin, Bedford, Bryan, Corpus Christi, Fort Worth, Garland, Houston, Richardson, San Antonio, Waco; Berkeley, CA: Saint Louis Park, Saint Paul, MN; Columbus, OH; Bellevue, WA; Madison, Milwaukee, WI; Texas Bookman, wholesale section

GEORGE OWEN BOECKSTARR — Used
PO Box 29633, 75229. Tel 214-357-3431
Estab 1978. 25,000 Titles. 30,000 Vols. Cat 4x ann
Types: Out of print, used

QUEST FOR EXCELLENCE — Self-Development
2636 Walnut Hill Lane, Suite 115, 75229. Tel 214-350-1802
Types: Hb, papbk, juvenile, out of print

REMEMBER WHEN — Nostalgia
2431 Valwood Pkwy, 75234. Tel 214-243-3439
Mgr, Sandra Williams
Estab 1978. 1500 Vols. 2400 sq ft
Types: Hb, out of print, papbk, used, imp UK
Subj: Sci fiction & fantasy, comic & fantasy art, movies

THE TRACERY — Antiquarian
6027 Glendora, PO Box 670236, 75367-0236. Tel 214-361-5269
Estab 1975. 3000 Vols. Cat 4x ann
Types: Hb, imp, juvenile, out of print, remainders, used
Subj: Texana, World Wars I & II, hist of Christmas lore & legends

DEL RIO — 30,034. Area code 512

THE BOOKSHOP — Antiquarian-Western Americana
1808 N Main, 78840-3334. Tel 512-775-5935
Mgr, Sue Croom
Estab 1977. 5000 Vols. 200 sq ft
Types: Hb, juvenile, papbk, remainders, out of print, old & rare
Subj: Mex, Texana, Amer, Sp lang

DENISON — 23,884. Area code 214

SIMPSON'S BOOKS — Used
1113 S Armstrong, 75020. Tel 214-463-2629
Estab 1972. 16,000 Vols. 2000 sq ft
Types: Hb, juvenile, new & used, out of print, papbk, remainders, comics

DENTON — 48,063. Area code 817

ATTIC BOOKS & PRINTS — Mail Order-Antiquarian
PO Box 1279, 76202-1279. Tel 817-497-5138
Estab 1983. 30,000 Titles. 30,000 Vols. 1000 sq ft. Cat monthly
Types: 1st ed, old & rare, out of print, children's
Subj: Amer, mystery & detective, warfare, Western Amer, mod 1st ed, photos, vintage paperbks

DICKINSON — 7505. Area code 713

SCHROEDER'S BOOK HAVEN — Antiquarian
Rte 1, Box 2820, 77539. Tel 713-337-1002
Estab 1968. 110,000 Vols. 3000 sq ft
Types: Hb, out of print, remainders, used
Subj: Texana

EL PASO — 425,259. Area code 915

HI BOOKS — Antiquarian-Southwestern Americana
6509 N Mesa, 79912. Tel 915-581-3900
Estab 1985. 20,000 Titles. 20,000 Vols. 2000 sq ft
Types: 1st ed, illus bk, hb, juvenile, ltd ed, out of print, old & rare, used
Subj: Amer, Texana, art, military, Am Indian studies, travel, photog, hist, aviation, biog, 20th century lit, nat sci

FORT DAVIS — 1212. Area code 915

EL CERRO ANTIQUES & BOOKS — Antiques
PO Box 1458, 79734
Estab 1979. 150 Titles. 1000 Vols
Types: Juvenile, old & rare, out of print
Subj: Southwestern Amer, Texana

FORT WORTH — 385,141. Area code 817

BARBER'S BOOKSTORE INC — General
215 W Eighth St, 76102-6105. Tel 817-335-5469
Estab 1925. 50,000 Titles. 65,000 Vols. 3000 sq ft. Cat
Types: Out of print, juvenile, hb, papbk, remainders, used, new
Subj: Amer, aviation, military, Texana, Western Amer, maritime

THE BOOK CELLAR — General
400 Main, 76102. Tel 817-332-2072
Estab 1978. 20,000 Vols. 5200 sq ft
Types: Hb, papbk, out of print
Subj: Literary criticism, poetry, Texana

EVERGREEN BOOKS — Used
1500 W Magnolia Ave, 76104. Tel 817-335-1911
Estab 1976. 30,000 Vols. 1000 sq ft
Types: 1st ed, illus bk, juvenile, old & rare, out of print
Subj: Literary criticism

GUILDHALL INC — Mail Order
2535 Weisenberger, 76107. Tel 817-332-6733. WATS 800-356-6733
Estab 1979. 4000 Titles. 6000 Vols. 2000 sq ft. Cat
Types: Hb, out of print, remainders, col text, used, ltd ed, old & rare
Subj: Art, hist, bus & mgt, biog, rel, tv, Jap art, hist & culture, Amer culture, christianity, communications, native Am art

HALF PRICE BOOKS, RECORDS & MAGAZINES — Used
6207 Sunset, 76116. Tel 817-732-4111
Estab 1978. 50,000 Vols Buys indep & through hq
Types: Col & el-hi text, for lang, hb, imp, juvenile, old & rare, out of print, papbk, remainders

OVERLOOK BOOKS — Mail Order
3309 Winthrop, Suite 77 (Mail add: PO Box 121444, 76116). Tel 817-275-0344
Estab 1981. 1500 Titles. 1550 Vols. Cat 3x ann
Types: Hb, imp UK, out of print, fine bnd, 1st ed, ltd ed, old & rare
Subj: Sci fiction & fantasy, horror

THOMPSON BOOKSTORES — General
900 Houston, 76102. Tel 817-332-0326
Estab 1936. 300,000 Vols
Types: Col & el-hi text, for lang, hb, juvenile, out of print, papbk, remainders, used, illus bk

FREDERICKSBURG — 6412. Area code 512

PEDDLER'S WAGON — Mail Order-Used
515 W Austin (Mail add: PO Box 903, 78624-0903). Tel 512-997-8437
Estab 1985. Cat quarterly
Types: Juvenile, papbk, out of print
Subj: Needlecrafts, illus

GARLAND — 138,857. Area code 214

HALF PRICE BOOKS, RECORDS & MAGAZINES — Used
1560 NW Hwy, Suite 104, 75041. Tel 214-681-3348
Estab 1979. 40,000 Vols
Types: Col & el-hi text, for lang, hb, imp, juvenile, old & rare, out of print, papbk, remainders

GLEN ROSE — 2075. Area code 817

LIMESTONE HILLS BOOK SHOP — Mail Order-Antiquarian
Box 1125, 76043. Tel 817-897-4991
Estab 1975. 5000 Vols. Cat 2x ann
Types: Facsimile editions, fine bnd, 1st ed, hb, illus bk, juvenile, old & rare, out of print, papbk, used
Subj: Mystery & detective, bks on bks, 19th & 20th century Eng & Am lit

GONZALES — 7152. Area code 512

GONZALES CHRISTIAN GENERAL STORE — Religious-Christian
303 St James St, 78629. Tel 512-672-6217
Estab 1981. 1800 sq ft
Types: Hb, juvenile, out of print, papbk, col text, used, Sp lang, Hebr lang, Gr lang
Subj: Texana, travel

GREENVILLE — 22,161. Area code 214

STILLMEADOW ANTIQUES & BOOKS — Juvenile
PO Box 1432, 3504 Johnson St, 75401. Tel 214-455-9545
3000 Titles. 3000 Vols. Cat 4x ann
Types: Out of print, hb, illus bk, imp, old & rare, used, juvenile

GROVES — 17,090. Area code 409

CAPTAIN VAN INC — Mail Order-Nautical
5548 Beaumont Ave, 77619-5606. Tel 409-962-2225
Office Mgr R Block
Estab 1917. 3000 Vols. 1600 sq ft. Cat ann
Types: Col & el-hi text, hb, high priced papbk, out of print, imp UK
Subj: Mod lit, govt publn, navigation, marine eng license exam prep-courses

HOUSTON — 1,594,086. Area code 713

A BOOK BUYERS SHOP — Used
1305 S Shepherd, 77019. Tel 713-529-1059
Mgr & Buyer, Chester Doby
Estab 1980. 20,000 Vols. 2400 sq ft. Cat 2x ann
Types: Hb, juvenile, imp, mass mkt papbk, used, facsimile editions, fine bnd, 1st ed, illus bk, ltd ed, old & rare, out of print
Subj: Western Amer

A FEW BOOKS & RECORDS — Antiquarian
11330 Beechnut (Mail add: PO Box 695, Alief, 77411). Tel 713-933-6629
Mgr, Mrs Few
Estab 1978. 10,000 Titles. 10,000 Vols
Types: Hb, papbk, new & used, out of print, comics

BOOK CASE* — General
2419 S Sheperd Dr, 77019. Tel 713-524-9825
Estab 1974. 35,000 Vols. 1250 sq ft
Types: For lang, hb, imp, juvenile, out of print, papbk, used
Subj: Biog, fiction, hist, sci fiction & fantasy, sci-tech, Texana, Judaica

BOOKED UP — Antiquarian
711 Studewood, 77007. Tel 713-868-3910
Estab 1980. 24,000 Titles. 24,500 Vols. 1200 sq ft. Cat 4x ann
Types: Out of print, 1st ed, hb, illus bk, ltd ed, old & rare, used
Subj: Bks on bks, Texana

THE BOOKSHELF — Law
1207 Cullen Blvd, 77023. Tel 713-225-4738
Estab 1930. 20,000 Vols
Types: Bibles, for lang, hb, imp, out of print, papbk
Subj: Law, rel studies

THE CHRISTIAN CORNER — Religious-Christian
10620 Westheimer, 77042
Types: Hb, papbk, juvenile, for lang, used, imp, out of print

COLLEEN'S BOOKS & THINGS — Used
6880-C Telephone Rd, 77061-2888. Tel 713-641-1753. WATS 800-553-1753
Estab 1971. 80,000 Vols. 3100 sq ft. Cat ann
Types: Facsimile editions, fine bnd, 1st ed, hb, incunab, imp Eng, Jap, Fr, ltd ed, new & used, out of print, old & rare
Subj: Hist, military, biog, Texana, Southwestern Amer, space & flight

GRUETZMACHER BOOKS* — Mail Order-Used
1937 W McKinney, 77019. Tel 713-528-7804
Estab 1985. 5000 Titles. 5000 Vols. Cat 4x ann
Types: 1st ed, hb, old & rare, out of print
Subj: Texana

HALF PRICE BOOKS, RECORDS & MAGAZINES — Used
2410 Waugh, 77006. Tel 713-520-1084
100,000 Vols. 5000 sq ft
Types: Col & el-hi text, for lang, hb, imp, juvenile, old & rare, out of print, papbk, remainders

HAND N HAND — Religious-Christian
12651-D Memorial Dr, 77024. Tel 713-468-4343
Types: Hb, papbk, juvenile, out of print

MCLAREN BOOKS — Mail Order-Antiquarian
10935 Creektree, 77070. Tel 713-469-1484
Estab 1982. 4000 Titles. 4000 Vols. Cat 2x ann
Types: Used, hb, 1st ed, illus bk, old & rare, out of print
Subj: Texana, humor

MONTROSE BOOKSHOP* — Mail Order-Antiquarian
PO Box 66265, 77006. Tel 713-522-1713
Estab 1968. 5000 Vols
Types: 1st ed, ltd ed, old & rare, out of print
Subj: Eng hist & lit, cooking

RUPPERT BOOKS — Used
1186 Meyerland Plaza at Antique World (Mail add: 5909 Darnell, 77074). Tel 713-666-1344, 774-2202
Estab 1982. 4000 Titles. 6000 Vols. 1000 sq ft
Types: Hb, juvenile, out of print, early illus juv bks
Subj: Biog, nonfiction, Texana

SACCO CHURCH SUPPLIES — General
2323 San Jacinto, 77002. Tel 713-659-4709
Mgr, Grady Sacco
Estab 1953. 500 Titles. 12,500 sq ft. Cat ann
Types: Juvenile, out of print, high priced papbk, Sp lang, imp

THIRD PLANET — Science Fiction & Fantasy
2339 Bissonnet, 77005. Tel 713-528-1067
Mgr, Scott Whitt; Warehouse Mgr, Kim Trybula
Estab 1977. 5000 Titles. 1,000,000 Vols. 2000 sq ft. Cat 2x ann
Types: Out of print, papbk, new & used, hb, 1st ed, illus bk, imp UK, ltd ed, old & rare
Subj: Nostalgia, sci fiction & fantasy

TRACKSIDE BOOKS — Antiquarian-Railroadiana
8819 Mobud Dr (Mail add: PO Box 770264, 77215-0264). Tel 713-772-8107
Buyer, Kathleen M Madole
Estab 1964. 6200 Vols. 4000 sq ft. Cat 4x ann
Types: Facsimile editions, 1st ed, hb, imp, ltd ed, new & used, old & rare, out of print, papbk, remainders

HURST — 31,420. Area code 817

INFINITE POTENTIAL BOOKS — New Age
236-2 Bedford Euless Rd, 76053. Tel 817-282-2220
Mgr, Ellen Davis
Types: Hb, juvenile, out of print, papbk, used

IRVING — 109,943. Area code 214

SILVERBEAR BOOKS — General
4020 N Macarthur Blvd, #132, 75038
Mgr, Dean Meadors
Types: Hb, juvenile, out of print, papbk, used

KINGSVILLE — 28,808. Area code 512

MARGE'S KRAZY KORNER BOOKS — Used Paperback
1422 S 14th (Mail add: 4710 Middlecoff Rd, Apt C-73, Corpus Christi, 78413). Tel 512-595-0004, 852-0161
Estab 1982. 40,000 Vols. 1250 sq ft
Types: Hb, juvenile, remainders, out of print, old & rare, 1st ed, new

LOCKHART — 7953. Area code 512

THE BOOK STALL — General
Rte 3, Box 64, 78644. Tel 512-398-6642
Estab 1979. 10,000 Vols. 1000 sq ft
Types: Juvenile, imp, hb, for lang, out of print, papbk, used
Subj: Fiction, unicorns

LONGVIEW — 62,762. Area code 214

EDDIE WOODS BOOKS — Used
208 N Center, 75601. Tel 214-757-6254
Estab 1976. 1000 sq ft
Types: 1st ed, hb, juvenile, new & used, old & rare, out of print

LUBBOCK — 173,979. Area code 806

THE BOOK INN — Used
6401C University, 79413. Tel 806-793-0342
Estab 1983. 25,000 Titles. 25,500 Vols. 2000 sq ft
Types: For lang, hb, imp, juvenile, out of print, mass mkt papbk, high priced papbk

STAR BOOKS & COMICS — Paperback
2014 34th St, 79411. Tel 806-744-9150
Estab 1977. 10,000 Vols. 1200 sq ft
Types: New & used, out of print
Subj: Sci fiction & fantasy, Western Amer, Am auth

MESQUITE — 67,053. Area code 214

GEOGRAPHIC ENTERPRISES — Mail Order-Antiquarian
1930 Wilkinson Rd (Mail add: PO Box 246, 75149). Tel 214-289-7107
Estab 1981. 2000 Titles. 100,000 Vols. 2000 sq ft. Cat ann
Types: 1st ed, hb, old & rare, out of print, used

MIDLAND — 70,525. Area code 915

BOOK & THINGS — Religious-LDS
2928 W Louisiana No 101, 79701. Tel 915-682-1428
Estab 1973. 1700 Titles. 5000 Vols. 150 sq ft
Types: Hb, papbk, juvenile, illus bk, out of print, new

NACOGDOCHES — 27,149. Area code 409

VIEW FROM ORBIT BOOKS — Mail Order-Antiquarian
905 E Main, 75961. Tel 409-564-5818
Estab 1984. 100,000 Titles. 100,000 Vols. 1200 sq ft. Cat 3x ann
Types: Hb, juvenile, out of print, mass mkt papbk, high priced papbk, el-hi text, used, 1st ed, incunab, new, old & rare

ORANGE — 23,628. Area code 409

MUSEUM SHOP — Museum
Stark Museum of Art, 712 Green Ave (Mail add: PO Box 1897, 77630-0051). Tel 409-883-6661
Owner, Nelda & H J Lutcher Stark Foundation; Mgr, Dorothy Hane
Estab 1978. 400 Vols
Types: Hb, juvenile, out of print, papbk, remainders
Subj: Western artists

PARIS — 25,498. Area code 214

FAMILY BOOKS & GIFTS — Religious-P
Five E Plaza, 75460. Tel 214-785-7693
Estab 1980. 15,000 Vols. 2200 sq ft
Types: Bibles, hb, juvenile, out of print, papbk, remainders
Subj: Christian

PLANO — 72,331. Area code 214

BOOK NOOK — Used
2109 W Parker Rd, Suite 216, 75023. Tel 214-867-4550
Mgr, Alice Lancaster
Estab 1982. 40,000 Titles
Types: Out of print, papbk, mass mkt papbk, 1st ed, comics
Subj: Fiction, sci fiction & fantasy, Western Amer

RICHARDSON — 72,496. Area code 214

HALF PRICE BOOKS, RECORDS & MAGAZINES — Used
2100 Alamo, 75080. Tel 214-234-4286
Estab 1976. 40,000 Vols Buys indep & through hq
Types: Col & el-hi text, for lang, hb, imp, juvenile, old & rare, out of print, papbk, remainders

ROCKPORT — 3686. Area code 512

PAUL ANTHONY BOOKSELLER — Mail Order-Antiquarian
PO Box 2124, 78382. Tel 512-729-7768
Estab 1985
Types: 1st ed, hb, illus bk, out of print, used
Subj: Nautical, gardening

SALADO — Area code 512 and 817

FLETCHER'S BOOKS — Antiquarian
Main St, Box 65, 76571. Tel 817-947-5414
Estab 1930. 250 Titles. 5000 Vols
Types: 1st ed, hb, new & used, out of print
Subj: Texana

SAN ANGELO — 73,240. Area code 915

INFO BOOKS — Mail Order
3222 N Oakes St (Mail add: Box 5200, 76902). Tel 915-653-1795
Estab 1965. 5000 Vols
Types: Col text, hb, out of print, mass mkt papbk, remainders, used
Subj: Nature & environ, agr, fish farming

SAN ANTONIO — 785,410. Area code 512

ALL POINTS OF VIEW — Mail Order-Sociology
Box 321, 78292-0321. Tel 512-732-6660
Estab 1961. 12,000 Vols
Types: Hb, juvenile, out of print, papbk
Subj: Afro-Am, Chicano, Marxist-Leninist studies

BOOKETERIA — Antiquarian
3323 Fredericksburg Rd, 78201. Tel 512-734-8760
Mgr, Carol Harwell
Estab 1976. 150,000 Vols. 1400 sq ft. Cat
Types: Fine bnd, hb, old & rare, out of print, papbk, used
Subj: Texana, military, rel

THE BOOK WORM — Used
4707 Blanco Rd, 78212. Tel 512-342-4258
Estab 1979. 100,000 Vols. 2000 sq ft
Types: For lang, hb, juvenile, out of print, papbk, used, 1st ed

DUNGEON BOOK & COMIC STORE — Science Fiction & Fantasy
3700 Fredericksburg Rd, Suite 105, 78201. Tel 512-732-2272
Estab 1981. 7500 Vols. 2500 sq ft
Types: Hb, papbk, out of print, comics
Subj: Am Indian studies, performing arts

HALF PRICE BOOKS, RECORDS & MAGAZINES — Used
3207 Broadway, 78209. Tel 512-822-4597
Estab 1979. 100,000 Vols. 6000 sq ft Buys indep & through hq
Types: Col & el-hi text, for lang, hb, imp, juvenile, old & rare, out of print, papbk, remainders

ROSENGREN'S — General
801 Garraty, 78209. Tel 512-826-0946
Buyer, Camille Rosengren
Estab 1919. 4000 Titles. 4000 Vols. Cat
Types: Out of print, old & rare, hb, papbk
Subj: Art, Texana

TEXANA BOOKS — Mail Order
4810 Rockford, 78249. Tel 512-696-7538
Estab 1980. 500 Titles. 500 Vols. Cat
Types: 1st ed, hb, ltd ed, old & rare, out of print
Subj: Texana

TAFT — 3686. Area code 512

COLLECTOR'S MUSEUM & MARKET — Mail Order-Antiquarian
113 Green Ave, 78390. Tel 512-528-3353
Estab 1977. 12,000 Titles. 15,000 Vols. 6000 sq ft
Types: 1st ed, hb, juvenile, ltd ed, new & used, old & rare, out of print, papbk
Subj: Autg, comedy, fiction, metaphys & occult, nonfiction, sci fiction & fantasy, hist

TEMPLE — 42,483. Area code 817

BOOK CELLAR — Used
Two S Main, 76501. Tel 817-773-7545
Estab 1978. 100,000 Vols. 3000 sq ft
Types: Fine bnd, 1st ed, hb, illus bk, juvenile, old & rare, out of print, papbk, used
Subj: Poetry, Texana

TERRELL — 13,225. Area code 214

DSHAMS - BOOKS & TREASURES — Horses
628 County Rd 234, 75160. Tel 214-563-7853
Estab 1984. 500 Titles. 2000 Vols. Cat 4x ann
Types: Hb, out of print, remainders, used, imp UK, imp Ger, 1st ed, juvenile, ltd ed, new, old & rare
Subj: Stud bks, riding & training (all disciplines), fict, breeding, health care, all breeds of horses

VICTORIA — 50,695. Area code 512

JOE PETTY - BOOKS — Antiquarian
1704 Park Ave, 77901. Tel 512-573-3320
Estab 1940. 4000 Vols
Types: 1st ed, hb, imp, out of print, old & rare, used
Subj: Bks on bks, Texana

WACO — 101,261. Area code 817

HALF PRICE BOOKS, RECORDS & MAGAZINES — Used
807 N Valley Mills Dr, 76710. Tel 817-776-0249
Estab 1974. 40,000 Vols Buys indep & through hq
Types: Col & el-hi text, for lang, hb, imp, juvenile, old & rare, out of print, remainders

RED INK PUBLICATIONS BOOKSTORE — General
Rte 7, Box 471 B, 76705. Tel 817-863-5915
Estab 1987. 100 Titles. 250 Vols
Types: Hb, out of print, papbk, col text, used
Subj: Rel

WAXAHACHIE — 14,624. Area code 214

THE WRIGHT COLLECTION — Antiquarian
333 Harbin St, 75165. Tel 214-937-6502
Estab 1945. 3000 Titles. 6000 Vols. 1200 sq ft. Cat 4x ann
Types: 1st ed, old & rare, out of print, used, remainders
Subj: Latin Am, Southwestern Amer, Texana, Western Amer, horses, cattle, outlaws

WICHITA FALLS — 94,201. Area code 817

MICRO EDUCATION BOOKSTORE LTD — College
4512 Allendale Rd, 76310. Tel 817-691-0814
Owner, Trinity Foundation; Gen Mgr, Alan D Martin
Estab 1967. 4000 Titles. 7000 Vols. 2100 sq ft
Types: Hb, juvenile, out of print, papbk, remainders, used
Subj: Bus & mgt, how-to, nonfiction, rel studies, self-develop, sci fiction & fantasy, computer sci

WIMBERLEY — 350. Area code 512

RICHERSON'S BOOKS — General
1156 Buzzard High Rd (Mail add: PO Box 181, Blanco, 78606). Tel 512-833-5350
Estab 1987. Cat 4x ann
Types: Hb, papbk, mass mkt papbk, high priced papbk, juvenile, out of print, remainders, used
Subj: Texana, women's studies, lit

CEDAR CITY — 10,972. Area code 801

AMERICAN WEST ARCHIVES — Western Americana
339 W 1725 N (Mail add: PO Box 100, 84720). Tel 801-586-9497
Cat 6x ann
Types: Old & rare, out of print, used
Subj: Biog, mining, signed autobiographies

GRANTSVILLE —4419. Area code 801

THE BOOKSTORE ETC — General
168 E Main, 84029. Tel 801-884-6393
Mgr, Kathleen H Day
Estab 1982. 4000 Titles. 1000 sq ft
Types: Hb, illus bk, new & used, old & rare, out of print, papbk, LDS

OGDEN — 64,407. Area code 801

LINDA'S BOOK & FLORAL — General
1150 Washington Blvd, 84404. Tel 801-399-5844
Estab 1978. 3050 sq ft
Types: For lang, hb, juvenile, out of print, papbk
Subj: Rel studies

PROVO — 73,907. Area code 801

WALT WEST BOOKS — Antiquarian-Western Americana
1355 Riverside Ave, 84604. Tel 801-377-1298
Estab 1979. 20,000 Titles. 25,000 Vols. 1100 sq ft
Types: 1st ed, hb, illus bk, old & rare, out of print, used
Subj: Mormon

SALT LAKE CITY — 163,033. Area code 801

BRENNAN BOOKS — Mail Order-Antiquarian
PO Box 9002, 84109-0002. Tel 801-278-7946
Estab 1978. 7800 Titles. 8000 Vols. 1500 sq ft
Types: Old & rare, out of print
Subj: Redevelopment of Trans-Mississippi West

CBC — General
320 N 3700 W, No 22552, North Ogden, 84122. Tel 801-543-9007
Mgr, Joe Jason
Estab 1974. 2500 Titles. 10,000 Vols. Cat 4x ann
Types: For lang, hb, imp, juvenile, out of print, papbk
Subj: Rel, music, improvement

COSMIC AEROPLANE BOOKS — General
258 E First St, 84111. Tel 801-533-9409
Trade Buyer, Bob Ormsby; Papbk Buyer, Joe Knighton
Estab 1976. 60,000 Vols. 4500 sq ft
Types: Hb, juvenile, out of print, old & rare, papbk, remainders, used, small presses, rare bks
Subj: Alt life styles, art, metaphys & occult, poetry, rel-lds, sci fiction & fantasy, Utahiana, Western Amer

SCALLAWAGIANA BOOKS — Mail Order-Antiquarian
1513 South 1500 East (Mail add: PO Box 2441, 84110). Tel 801-467-3011
Estab 1980. 3000 Titles. 4000 Vols. 200 sq ft. Cat 4x ann
Types: 1st ed, hb, ltd ed, out of print, old & rare, hermetica
Subj: Utahiana, Western Amer, metaphys & occult, Mormons, Vardis Fisher, Wallace Stegner, free masonry, anti-masonry

UNIVERSITY BOOKSTORE — College
University of Utah Campus, 84112. Tel 801-581-6325
Gen Book Mgr & Buyer Deborah Hunter
Estab 1899. 45,000 Titles. 45,000 sq ft
Types: Hb, imp, juvenile, out of print, papbk, remainders

SAM WELLER'S ZION BOOKSTORE INC — General
254 S Main St, 84101. Tel 801-328-2586
Merch Mgr, Jean McGean; Mgr, Used & Rare Books, Joan Nay
Estab 1929. 1,000,000 Vols. 15,000 sq ft. Cat
Types: Hb, juvenile, out of print, papbk, remainders, new & used, facsimile editions, fine bnd, 1st ed, illus bk, ltd ed, old & rare
Subj: Rel-lds, Western Amer, Utahiana
See Also: Bountiful, Midvale

VERMONT

BELLOWS FALLS — 3456. Area code 802

ARCHBRIDGE BOOKSHOP* — Antiquarian
142 Westminster St, 2nd Floor, 05101. Tel 802-463-9395
Estab 1976. 8500 Vols. Cat 3-4x ann
Types: 1st ed, hb, old & rare, out of print, papbk, used
Subj: Civil War, World Wars I & II, travel, New England, railroadiana, Western Amer, military hist
See Also: Quechee Books, Quechee

BENNINGTON — 15,815. Area code 802

BRADFORD BOOKS — Used
West Road, 05201. Tel 802-447-0387
Estab 1973. 10,000 Vols
Types: Out of print, juvenile
Subj: Hist, bridge, biog, art, cooking, art, Vermontiana

NEW ENGLANDIANA — Antiquarian
121 Benmont Ave, PO Box 589, 05201-0589. Tel 802-447-1695
Estab 1961. 7500 Vols. Cat 4x ann
Types: Out of print, old & rare, remainders, used

NOW AND THEN BOOKS — Antiquarian-General
439 Main St, 05201. Tel 802-447-1470
Types: Out of print, hb, papbk, juvenile, used
Subj: Cooking, aviation, World War II

BRATTLEBORO — 11,886. Area code 802

THE BOOK CELLAR — General
120 Main St, 05301. Tel 802-254-6026
Estab 1948
Types: Hb, juvenile, out of print, papbk, remainders, small presses
Subj: Poetry, Vermontiana

BRISTOL —1793. Area code 802

TERRY HARPER BOOKSELLER — Antiquarian
PO Box 37, 05443-0037. Tel 802-453-5088
7000 Vols. Cat 4-6x ann
Types: Fine bnd, 1st ed, hb, illus bk, juvenile, ltd ed, old & rare, out of print, used
Subj: Amer, discovery & explor, natural hist, travel

BURLINGTON — 37,712. Area code 802

BYGONE BOOKS INC — Antiquarian
31 Main, 05401. Tel 802-862-4397
Pres, P Welsh
Estab 1978. 10,000 Vols. 1000 sq ft
Types: Facsimile editions, fine bnd, 1st ed, hb, illus bk, imp, juvenile, ltd ed, old & rare, out of print, papbk, remainders, used
Subj: Vermontiana

CODEX BOOKS — Antiquarian
30 Elmwood Ave, 05401. Tel 802-862-6413
Estab 1980. 15,000 Vols. 1000 sq ft. Cat monthly
Types: Facsimile editions, fine bnd, 1st ed, hb, illus bk, old & rare, out of print, used, imp UK, imp Fr, imp Ger, used
Subj: Hist of ideas, philos, theol, class studies, reference, early printing

THE DUSTY COVER — Used
18 N Winooski Ave, 05401. Tel 802-862-6088
Estab 1982. 10,000 Vols. 1000 sq ft
Types: Hb, papbk, out of print, used
Subj: Sci fiction & fantasy, fiction, soc sci, rel, humanities, psychol

FRASER PUBLISHING CO — Mail Order
309 S Willard (Mail add: PO Box 494, 05402). Tel 802-658-0322
Owner, Fraser Management Associates; Mgr, Karla Ferrelli
Estab 1965. 60 Titles. 2000 Vols. Cat ann
Types: Hb, out of print, papbk, used
Subj: Econ, finance, contrary opinion thinking, speculation, stock market

CUTTINGSVILLE — Area code 802

HAUNTED MANSION BOOKSHOP — Antiquarian
05738-0388. Tel 802-492-3462
Estab 1966. 50,000 Vols. 2400 sq ft
Types: Old & rare, out of print
Subj: Amer, Vermontiana

FAIRFAX — 1805. Area code 802

THE BOOKSTORE — Used
Main St (Mail add: RFD No 1, 140 Huntville Rd, 05454). Tel 802-849-2209
Mgr, Louise Wold
Estab 1979.
Types: Hb, juvenile, out of print, papbk

GREENSBORO — 677. Area code 802

RECOVERY BOOKS THE ROBERT FROST BOOK SHOP — Used
PO Box 232, 05841. Tel 802-586-2846
Estab 1981. 3000 Titles. 3000 Vols. 300 sq ft. Cat monthly
Types: Out of print, 1st ed, ltd ed, old & rare
Subj: Robert Frost

LYNDONVILLE — 1401. Area code 802

GREEN MOUNTAIN BOOKS & PRINTS — Antiquarian-General
100 Broad St, 05851. Tel 802-626-5051
Mgr, Ellen Doyle
Estab 1977. 80,000 Vols. Cat 5-6x ann
Types: Fine bnd, 1st ed, hb, old & rare, out of print, papbk, remainders, new & used
Subj: Amer

MIDDLEBURY — 7574. Area code 802

POOR RICHARD'S USED BOOKS — Used
56 Main St, Box 67, 05753. Tel 802-388-3241
Estab 1980. 8500 Vols. 1600 sq ft
Types: For lang, hb, juvenile, out of print, papbk

THE VERMONT BOOKSHOP INC — General
38 Main St, 05753-1416. Tel 802-388-2061
Mgr, Grant W Novak
Estab 1949. 28,500 Titles. 1700 sq ft. Cat ann
Types: Hb, out of print, papbk, remainders
Subj: Vermontiana, Alexander Botts, Robert Frost

MORRISVILLE — 2074. Area code 802

BRICK HOUSE BOOKSHOP — Antiquarian-General
RFD 3 Box 3020, Morristown Corners, 05661. Tel 802-888-4300
Estab 1976. 30,000 Titles. 30,000 Vols. 1600 sq ft
Types: Fine bnd, hb, illus bk, juvenile, ltd ed, old & rare, out of print, papbk, used
Subj: Fiction, nonfiction, Vermontiana

NEWFANE — 1129. Area code 802

NU-TIQUE SHOPPE — Antiquarian
PO Box 35, 05345. Tel 802-365-7677
Estab 1971. 20,000 Vols. 1500 sq ft
Types: Juvenile, 1st ed, illus bk, out of print
Subj: Amer, poetry, warfare, biog, rel, autobiog

NEWPORT — 4756. Area code 802

MICHAEL DUNN BOOKS — Mail Order-Antiquarian
PO Box 436, 05855-0436. Tel 802-334-2768
Estab 1978. 5000 Vols. 500 sq ft. Cat 5-6x ann
Types: Old & rare, out of print, used
Subj: Amer, Can, hunting & fishing, Vermontiana, mountaineering

NORTH BENNINGTON — 1685. Area code 802

JOHN JOHNSON NATURAL HISTORY BOOKS — Antiquarian-Natural History
RR No1 Box 513, 05257-9743. Tel 802-442-6738
Estab 1949. 20,000 Vols. 2000 sq ft. Cat 4x ann
Types: Hb, illus bk, old & rare, out of print, used
Subj: Botany, natural hist, zool, birds, mammals, insects, fish, reptiles, paleontology, naturalist travels, voyages & exploration, invertebrates

PLAINFIELD — 1549. Area code 802

THE COUNTRY BOOKSHOP — Antiquarian
Village Sq, RFD 2, 05667. Tel 802-454-8439
Estab 1973. 10,000 Titles. 10,000 Vols. 1000 sq ft. Cat 2x ann
Types: 1st ed, hb, old & rare, out of print, used
Subj: Folklore, travel, bells, folk music

RUTLAND — 18,436. Area code 802

F P ELWERT — Mail Order-Antiquarian
Box 254, 05701. Tel 802-773-3417
Estab 1965. 3000 Vols. Cat 4x ann
Types: Illus bk, out of print, old & rare, used
Subj: Archit, indust archaeol, tech

TUTTLE ANTIQUARIAN BOOKS INC — Antiquarian
28 S Main, PO Box 541, 05701-0541. Tel 802-773-8930; 773-8229
Estab 1832. 25,000 Vols. 1200 sq ft. Cat
Types: 1st ed, imp, new, old & rare, out of print
Subj: Genealogy, local hist, Vermontiana

SHELBURNE — 5000. Area code 802

WILLIAM L PARKINSON BOOKS — Antiquarian-Vermontiana
RR 1 Box 1330, 05482. Tel 802-482-3113 (by appt only)
Estab 1980. 10,000 Vols. 576 sq ft. Cat 12x ann
Types: Fine bnd, 1st ed, illus bk, hb, old & rare, out of print, used
Subj: Vermontiana

VILLAGE BOOK SHOP OF SHELBURNE — Paperback
RR4 Box 4000-20, 05482. Tel 802-985-8868
Types: Used, out of print
Subj: Vermontiana, authors, illustrators, publishers

SOUTH ROYALTON — Area code 802

BOOKS AT CHELSEA STREET — Used
204 Chelsea St (Mail add: PO Box 425, 05068)
Estab 1987. 20,000 Titles
Types: Out of print, 1st ed, hb, illus bk, old & rare
Subj: Nature & environ, rel studies, hist, nonfiction

SPRINGFIELD — 10,190. Area code 802

ABATIS BOOKS — Mail Order
PO Box 451, 05156-0451. Tel 802-885-3151
Estab 1978
Types: Hb, out of print, used

WAITSFIELD — 1300. Area code 802

RARE & WELL-DONE BOOKS — Antiquarian
Rte 100 (Mail add: PO Box 292, Warren, 05674). Tel 802-496-2791
Estab 1982. 5000 Titles. 5000 Vols
Types: 1st ed, hb, illus bk, ltd ed, old & rare, out of print
Subj: Belles lettres, evolution

VIRGINIA

ALEXANDRIA — 103,217. Area code 703

AIR, LAND & SEA — Mail Order-Aviation
1215 King St, 22314. Tel 703-684-5118
Estab 1983. 1200 Titles. 3500 Vols. 1200 sq ft. Cat 4x ann
Types: Out of print, hb, imp, old & rare, papbk, used
Subj: Military, nautical

THE BOOK NICHE & CAPITAL COMICS CENTER — Used
2008 Mount Vernon Ave, 22301. Tel 703-548-3466
Estab 1976. 20,000 Vols. 400 sq ft
Types: Hb, juvenile, out of print, old & rare, papbk
Subj: Art, biog, comedy, sci fiction & fantasy, films & filmmaking, hist, hort, metaphys & occult, mystery & detective, music, nature & environ, North Dakotana, Western Amer, cartoon, classic bks, game bks, graphic novels

FROM OUT OF THE PAST — Used
6440 Richmond Hwy, 22306. Tel 703-768-7827
50,000 Vols. 4000 sq ft
Types: 1st ed, hb, illus bk, juvenile, ltd ed, old & rare, out of print

JENNIE'S BOOK NOOK — Mail Order-Antiquarian
15 W Howell Ave, 22301. Tel 703-683-0694
Estab 1976. 2500 Vols. Cat bi-ann
Types: Hb, old & rare, out of print
Subj: Biog, fiction, genealogy, hist, poetry, Virginiana, Robert E Lee

DONNA LEE'S BOOKS — General
206 Queen St, 22314. Tel 703-548-5830
Mgr, F L Opie
Estab 1980. 5000 Titles. 5000 Vols. 3000 sq ft. Cat 4x ann
Types: Illus bk, 1st ed, hb, old & rare, out of print, used
Subj: Amer, Civil War, the west

OLD MILL BOOKS — Mail Order-Antiquarian
PO Box 21561, 22320. Tel 703-683-1831
Cat 6x ann
Types: Out of print
Subj: South Pacific, SE Asia, Antarctica

ARLINGTON — 174,284. Area code 703

BOOK ENDS — Antiquarian
2710 Washington Blvd, 22201. Tel 703-524-4976
Estab 1979. 30,000 Vols. 1200 sq ft
Types: Hb, illus bk, juvenile, old & rare, out of print, papbk, used

BOOKHOUSE — Antiquarian
805 N Emerson St, 22205. Tel 703-527-7797
Estab 1969. 40,000 Vols. 1200 sq ft
Types: Fine bnd, illus bk, out of print
Subj: Amer, art, military, natural hist

EVANGELICAL USED BOOKS — Religious-P
1815 N Nelson St, 22207. Tel 703-522-0596
Estab 1978. 10,000 Vols
Types: Out of print, papbk, used

ATLANTIC —Area code 804

IRENE ROUSE - BOOKSELLER — Antiquarian-Folklore
Box 310, 23303. Tel 804-824-4090, 824-5626
Estab 1972. 36,000 Vols. Cat 6x ann
Types: Hb, out of print, old & rare, used
Subj: Amer, fiction, poetry, music

BERRYVILLE — 1752. Area code 703

VIRGINIA BOOK COMPANY — Mail Order-Virginiana
114 S Church St (Mail add: PO Box 431, 22611). Tel 703-955-1428
Mgr, L F Myers
Estab 1950. 10,000 Vols. Cat
Types: Out of print, old & rare, reprints

BRISTOL — 19,042. Area code 703

TAUSCHER BOOKS — Mail Order-Antiquarian
102 Norwood Dr, 24201. Tel 703-669-2994
Estab 1977. 20,000 Vols
Types: Out of print, used, 1st ed, hb, old & rare, papbk
Subj: Southern Amer, Civil War, Am Indian studies, sci fiction & fantasy, hunting & fishing

CHARLOTTESVILLE — 45,010. Area code 804

ABINTRA, THE BOOKSELLER — Mail Order
412 First St N, 22901. Tel 804-295-4378
Estab 1986. 800 Titles. 1000 Vols. Cat 6x ann
Types: Used, old & rare, out of print
Subj: Folklore, rel-Eastern, mysticism, mythology

CLOVER HILL BOOKS — Mail Order-Antiquarian
PO Box 6278, 22906. Tel 804-973-1506
Estab 1983. 2000 Titles. 2000 Vols. Cat 2x ann
Types: Fine bnd, 1st ed, audio visual mat, new, out of print, old & rare, imp UK
Subj: 20th cent Amer & Eng lit

HEARTWOOD BOOKS INC — Antiquarian
Five & Nine Elliewood Ave, 22903. Tel 804-295-7083
Rare Bks Mgr, J M Evans
Estab 1975. 50,000 Vols. Cat 2x ann
Types: Out of print, old & rare, remainders
Subj: Scholarly lit

NEWCOMB HALL BOOKSTORE — College
University of Virginia, 22901. Tel 804-924-3721
Estab 1962. 25,000 Titles
Types: Hb, juvenile, out of print, papbk, remainders
Subj: Hist, Virginiana, literary criticism

CHESAPEAKE — 114,226. Area code 804

GREAT BRIDGE BOOKS LTD — Antiquarian
404 Woodford Dr, 23320. Tel 804-482-1666
Estab 1975. 10,000 Titles. 8000 Vols. 1000 sq ft
Types: Fine bnd, 1st ed, hb, illus bk, juvenile, ltd ed, old & rare, out of print, papbk, used
Subj: Virginiana

FAIRFAX — 19,390. Area code 703

NOVEL IDEAS — Used
3940 Old Lee Hwy, 22030. Tel 703-385-5951
Estab 1982. 12,000 Vols. 800 sq ft
Types: Hb, juvenile, out of print, papbk

FALLS CHURCH — 9515. Area code 703

HOLE IN THE WALL BOOKS — Antiquarian
905 W Broad St, 22046. Tel 703-536-2511
Estab 1979. 50,000 Vols. 1000 sq ft. Cat 2x ann
Types: Hb, illus bk, juvenile, new, out of print, papbk, used
Subj: Sci fiction & fantasy, mystery & detective, horror

FARMVILLE — 6067. Area code 804

THE GOOD OL' GIRL BOOKSTORE — Used
115 N Main St, 23901. Tel 804-392-1638
Mgr, Al H Millette
Estab 1988. 40,000 Vols. 2600 sq ft
Types: Hb, out of print, remainders, col text, used

FRONT ROYAL — 11,126. Area code 703

ROYAL OAK BOOKSHOP INC — General
207 S Royal Ave, 22630. Tel 703-635-7070
Mgr, Maryann Rankin
Estab 1975. 10,000 Vols
Types: Hb, out of print, papbk, new & used
Subj: Civil War, Virginiana, May Sarton

LEXINGTON — 7292. Area code 703

BEST SELLER — General
29 W Nelson St, 24450. Tel 703-463-4647
Estab 1975. 5000 Vols. 1200 sq ft
Types: Hb, juvenile, papbk, used, out of print

CHRISTIANSEN'S BOOKS — General
Old Main St Mall, 29 N Main St, 24450. Tel 703-291-3154
Estab 1988. 4500 Titles. 4500 Vols
Types: 1st ed, hb, illus bk, ltd ed, old & rare, out of print

LYNCHBURG — 66,743. Area code 804

GIVENS BOOKS INC — General
2345 Lakeside Dr, 24501. Tel 804-237-3440
Estab 1975. 80,000 Vols. 5000 sq ft
Types: Out of print, papbk, remainders, new, old & rare, used
Subj: Amer, biog, rel, class studies
See Also: Salem

MC DOWELL — Area code 703

JACK R LEVIEN — Mail Order-Antiquarian
PO Box 31, 24458. Tel 703-396-3345
Estab 1962. 3000 Vols. 170 sq ft
Types: Out of print, used
Subj: Horses, miniature bks

MC LEAN — 17,698. Area code 703

AAPH BOOK SERVICES — Mail Order
PO Box 731, 22101-0731. Tel 703-631-1810
Types: Used, hb, old & rare, out of print
Subj: Hypnosis, hypnotherapy, unusual or unorthodox forms of healing, unusual rel

NEWPORT NEWS — 144,903. Area code 804

HILTON VILLAGE BOOKSHOP — Antiquarian
10375 Warwick Blvd, 23601. Tel 804-595-5866
Estab 1980. 10,000 Titles. 10,000 Vols. 1000 sq ft
Types: 1st ed, fine bnd, hb, out of print, illus bk, juvenile, ltd ed, old & rare
Subj: Antq, art, Civil War, hunting & fishing, nautical, travel, Virginiana, World Wars I & II, rel studies, Amer

NORFOLK — 266,979. Area code 804

JOHN LYNCH BOOKS — General
2370 E Little Creek Rd, 23518. Tel 804-588-0699
Mgr, Marie Rouka
Estab 1984. 24,000 Titles. 91,000 Vols. 1400 sq ft
Types: Hb, imp, juvenile, out of print, papbk, high priced papbk, fine bnd, 1st ed, illus bk, ltd ed, new, old & rare, remainders

WARDS CORNER BOOK SHOP INC — General
7524 Granby St, 23505-3485. Tel 804-587-3303
Pres, Harvey D Eluto
Estab 1965. 22,000 Titles. 225,000 Vols. 3000 sq ft
Types: Col text, 1st ed, hb, juvenile, ltd ed, out of print, mass mkt papbk, new & used, old & rare, papbk, remainders
Subj: Civil War, Southern Amer, Virginiana, sci fiction & fantasy

PETERSBURG — 41,055. Area code 804

BOOK SEARCH — Antiquarian
1741 Fairfax St, 23805-1647. Tel 804-862-2288
Accountant, R Black
Estab 1972
Types: Old & rare, out of print, used

LOUIS GINSBERG - BOOKS & PRINTS — Mail Order-Antiquarian
1642 Avon Way, 23805. Tel 804-732-8188
Estab 1955. 10,000 Vols. Cat 12x ann
Types: 1st ed, imp, out of print, old & rare, used, old cookbks
Subj: Black studies, bks on bks, Civil War, Judaica, law, medicine, military, photog, rel, SAm, Southern Amer, Southwestern Amer, travel, wines, local hist, bees, coal & oil, Mormons, Cuba, Caribbean Islands

SECOND CORPS BOOKSHOP — Mail Order-Civil War
209 High St, 23803. Tel 804-861-1863
Estab 1987. 2000 Titles. 2000 Vols. Cat 5x ann
Types: Out of print, used, hb
Subj: Am Civil War

RESTON — 5723. Area code 703

ANTIQUARIAN TOBACCIANA — Mail Order-Antiquarian
11505 Turnbridge Lane, 22094. Tel 703-435-8133
Estab 1976. 1000 Titles. 2000 Vols. Cat 4x ann
Types: For lang, facsimile editions, fine bnd, 1st ed, illus bk, ltd ed, hb, papbk, used, remainders, imp, old & rare, out of print
Subj: Tobacco & smoking

W B O'NEILL - OLD & RARE BOOKS — Mail Order-Middle East
11609 Hunters Green Ct, 22091. Tel 703-860-0782
Estab 1951. 2000 Vols. 450 sq ft. Cat ann
Types: Hb, used, 1st ed, old & rare, out of print, for lang, travel guides
Subj: Hist, Middle East, military, travel, Armenia, Lebanon, Cyprus, modern Greece, Turkey, Palestine

RICHMOND — 219,214. Area code 804

COLLECTORS' OLD BOOKSHOP — Antiquarian
15 S Fifth St, 23219. Tel 804-644-2097
Estab 1945. 15,000 Vols. 1400 sq ft
Types: 1st ed, imp, out of print, old & rare, used, hb
Subj: Amer, Civil War, Virginiana

FIRST EDITIONS BOOKSHOP & PRESS — Antiquarian
4040 MacArthur Ave, 23227. Tel 804-264-7276
Estab 1973. 10,000 Vols. Cat 2-4x ann
Types: 1st ed, ltd ed, old & rare, out of print
Subj: Bks on bks, mystery & detective, Virginiana, hunting & fishing, sports

THE FOUNTAIN BOOKSTORE INC — General
1312 E Cary St, 23219. Tel 804-788-1594
Buyer, Molly Smythe; Mgr, Louise Smythe
Estab 1978. 4000 Titles. 5320 Vols. Cat
Types: Hb, juvenile, out of print, papbk, remainders
Subj: Bus & mgt, corporate & govt training programs

NOVEL FUTURES INC — Science Fiction & Fantasy
402 N Robinson St, 23220. Tel 804-353-0573
Estab 1988. 2000 Titles. 4000 Vols. 1200 sq ft
Types: Hb, imp UK, juvenile, out of print, papbk, used, remainders
Subj: Related nonfict

OLD FAVORITES BOOKSHOP Antiquarian
610 N Sheppard St, 23221. Tel 804-355-2437
Estab 1982. 15,000 Vols. 680 sq ft. Cat 4x ann
Types: Juvenile, out of print, remainders, used
Subj: Civil War, sci fiction & fantasy

RELIGIOUS GOODS SHOP INC Religious-C
20 N Belmont, 23221-3099. Tel 804-355-6634
Mgr, Taylor F Campbell
Estab 1945. 1200 Vols. 1400 sq ft
Types: Hb, papbk, out of print

RICHMOND BOOKSHOP INC Used
808 W Broad St, 23220. Tel 804-644-9970
Cataloging, bibliography & appraisals, A P Hubbard
30,000 Vols. Cat
Types: Hb, out of print, papbk, remainders, old & rare
Subj: Virginiana, mystery & detective, fic 1840-1940

ROANOKE — 100,427. Area code 703

NELSON BOND Mail Order-Antiquarian
4724 Easthill Dr, 24018. Tel 703-774-2674
Estab 1967. 7500 Vols. Cat 8x ann
Types: Old & rare, out of print, used
Subj: Bks by & about James Branch Cabell

DAN WHEELER OLD AND RARE BOOKS Used
120A E Campbell Ave (Mail add: PO Box 6503, 24017). Tel 703-344-1592
Estab 1985. 30,000 Vols. Cat monthly
Types: Old & rare, out of print
Subj: Am hist & lit

SALEM — 23,958. Area code 703

GIVENS BOOKS Used
1641 E Main St, 24153. Tel 703-986-1103
Estab 1983. 15,000 Titles. 15,000 Vols. 1200 sq ft
Types: Hb, juvenile, out of print, papbk, mass mkt papbk, 1st ed, new
Subj: Class studies, hist, poetry, drama, gardening

SPRINGFIELD — 11,613. Area code 703

SPORTS BOOKS ETC Sports
5224 Port Royal Rd, 22151. Tel 703-321-8660
Estab 1984. 5000 Titles. 8000 Vols. 2000 sq ft. Cat 4x ann
Types: Hb, juvenile, out of print, papbk, mass mkt papbk, remainders, col text, used, imp UK, mag & newspr

VIRGINIA BEACH — 262,199. Area code 804

BARGAIN BOOKS OF VIRGINIA, INC DBA BARGAIN BOOKS - GIANT SQUARE General
Giant Sq S/Ctr, 737 Independence Blvd, 23455-6205. Tel 804-499-3303
Owner, Bargain Books of Virginia, Inc
Estab 1986. 25,000 Titles. 250,000 Vols
Types: Hb, out of print, papbk, remainders, mass mkt papbk, ltd ed, new & used, old & rare, juvenile, 1st ed, col text
Subj: Sci fiction & fantasy, Civil War, Virginiana, Southern Amer

WILLIAMSBURG — 9870. Area code 804

THE BOOKPRESS LTD Antiquarian
411 W Duke of Gloucester St, PO Box KP, 23187. Tel 804-229-1260
Mgr, Archie Fincher
Estab 1973. 7000 Vols. 2700 sq ft. Cat 5x ann
Types: Fine bnd, 1st ed, hb, illus bk, old & rare, out of print
Subj: Amer, archit, bks on bks, travel, archit, hist & technique of printing, 18th & 19th century binding, color printing

HAMILTON'S BOOKSTORE Antiquarian
1784 Jamestown Rd, 23185. Tel 804-220-3000
Estab 1980. 25,000 Titles. 25,000 Vols. 5000 sq ft. Cat
Types: Hb, 1st ed, illus bk, out of print, old & rare, fine bnd
Subj: Civil War, Virginiana, Amer, rel studies, nautical, natural hist, cooking, art, archit, archaeol, Western Amer

WYTHEVILLE — 7135. Area code 703

BOOKWORM & SILVERFISH Antiquarian
PO Box 639, 24382. Tel 703-686-5813
Estab 1972. 10,000 Titles. 4000 sq ft. Cat 10x ann
Types: Hb, old & rare, out of print
Subj: Civil War, Southern Appalachia, 19th-Century technology

ANACORTES — 9013. Area code 206

THE BUSINESS — Used
1717 Commercial, 98221. Tel 206-293-9788
Estab 1978. 30,000 Vols. 1600 sq ft. Cat
Types: Out of print

AUBURN — 26,417. Area code 206

COMSTOCK'S BINDERY & BOOKSHOP — Antiquarian
257 E Main St, 98002. Tel 206-939-8770
Estab 1968. 46,000 Vols. 3400 sq ft
Types: Out of print, used, remainders, juvenile, spec interest biper
Subj: Alaskana, art, auto, aviation, food, military, mystery & detective, natural hist, nautical, photog, railroadiana, reference, rel, sci fiction & fantasy, sci-tech, naval, Pac NW

BELLEVUE — 73,903. Area code 206

EVANGEL INC — Religious-P
127-106th Ave NE, 98004. Tel 206-454-3991
Estab 1967. 10,000 Titles. 12,000 sq ft
Types: 1st ed, hb, new, out of print, mass mkt papbk, comics
Subj: Amer, art, class studies, cooking, metaphys & occult, poetry, rel studies, travel, self-develop, fiction, class studies
See Also: Seattle

P T MALLAHAN BOOKSELLER — Mail Order-Antiquarian
307 130th Ave SE, 98005. Tel 206-454-1663
5000 Vols
Types: Out of print
Subj: Imperial Russia, World War I

BELLINGHAM — 45,794. Area code 206

AMERICAN EAGLES — Military
1213 1/2 Cornwall St, 98225. Tel 206-671-1913
Mgr, Stacey Block
Types: Hb, imp UK, imp Ger, out of print, papbk
Subj: Aviation, hist, hobbies, military

MICHAEL'S BOOKS — Used
109 Grand St, 98225. Tel 206-733-6272
Estab 1983. 100,000 Titles. 140,000 Vols
Types: Fr, Ger & Sp lang, Chinese lang, Russ lang, hb, papbk, mass mkt papbk, used, imp UK, fine bnd, 1st ed, old & rare, out of print

BREMERTON — 36,208. Area code 206

INTERIM BOOKS — Antiquarian
615 4th St, 98310. Tel 206-377-4343
Estab 1981. 7500 Vols. 600 sq ft
Types: 1st ed, hb, illus bk, juvenile, old & rare, out of print, papbk
Subj: Aviation, military, nautical, travel, mod firsts

CENTRALIA — 10,809. Area code 206

BLUE ROSE BOOKS ETC — Antiques
Centralia Square Antique Mall, 205 S Pearl (Mail add: 1119 Borthwick, 98531). Tel 206-736-0370
Estab 1986. 300 Titles. 350 Vols. 100 sq ft
Types: Remainders, used, new & used, hb, old & rare, out of print, papbk
Subj: Collecting

CHENEY — 7630. Area code 509

FISHERS OF MEN BIBLE BOOKSTORE — Religious-Christian
401 First St, 99004. Tel 509-235-8044
Estab 1985. 3000 Titles. 1000 sq ft
Types: Hb, juvenile, mass mkt papbk, illus bk, new, out of print, bibles, remainders, trade papbk

CLARKSTON — 6903. Area code 509

PEGGATTY BOOKS INC — Antiquarian
609 Maple St, 99403. Tel 509-758-9517
Estab 1975. 20,000 Vols
Types: Fine bnd, 1st ed, hb, illus bk, juvenile, ltd ed, new, old & rare, out of print, papbk, used

DES MOINES — 7378. Area code 206

RICHARD T KENNEDY - BOOKS — Mail Order-Antiquarian
1017 S 251st St, 98198-8548. Tel 206-824-2635
Estab 1978. 1200 Titles. 150 Vols
Types: Out of print
Subj: National Geographic Society publications

EDMONDS — 27,526. Area code 206

EDMONDS OLDE BOOKSTORE — General
9679 Firdale Village, 98020. Tel 206-542-8636
Estab 1983. 40,000 Vols. 1000 sq ft. Cat
Types: Papbk, out of print, old & rare
Subj: Alaskana, nautical, Northwest Amer

J D HOLMES BOOKSELLER — Mail Order-Antiquarian
PO Box 623, 98020-0623. Tel 206-771-2701
4000 Titles. 600 sq ft. Cat 10X ann
Types: Facsimile editions, hb, imp, old & rare, out of print, used
Subj: Orientalia, metaphysics, travel, rel, Egyptology, occult, Japanese theater & film

EVERETT — 54,413. Area code 206

EVERETT COMMUNITY COLLEGE BOOKSTORE — College
Everett Community College, 801 Wetmore Ave, 98201-1327. Tel 206-259-7151, Ext 413, 414, 415
Mgr & Buyer, Charles Morrison
Estab 1966. 4500 Titles. 10,000 Vols. 3500 sq ft
Types: Hb, juvenile, out of print, papbk, used

FRIDAY HARBOR — 1200. Area code 206

GRIFFIN BAY BOOKSTORE — General
PO Box 1669, 98250. Tel 206-378-5511
Estab 1979. 6000 Titles. 12000 Vols. Cat ann
Types: Hb, juvenile, papbk, out of print, books-on-tape
Subj: Gardening, marine, PNW outdoor guides

GIG HARBOR — 2429. Area code 206

MOSTLY BOOKS — General
3126 Harborview Dr, PO Box 428, 98335. Tel 206-851-3219
Estab 1969. 8000 Titles. 1500 sq ft
Types: Hb, juvenile, out of print, papbk, remainders, used
Subj: Arts & crafts, biog, nature & environ, nautical, railroadiana, Indians, NW hist

HADLOCK — 500. Area code 206

UNICORNS, TOO — General
1895 Irondale Rd (Mail add: PO Box 149, 98339). Tel 206-385-4841
Buyer & Text Buyer, Lisa Ferenz
60,000 Vols. 1200 sq ft
Types: Hb, juvenile, out of print, papbk, new & used, col text, facsimile editions, 1st ed, illus bk, ltd ed, old collector papbk
Subj: Comedy, cooking

KENNEWICK — 34,397. Area code 509

CIPRIANO'S BOOKS — Mail Order-Antiquarian
2109 S Ledbetter, 99336. Tel 509-582-4971
Estab 1961. 1500 Vols
Types: Out of print, old & rare, used
Subj: Art, photog, fine press

KENT — 23,152. Area code 206

BOOKWORLD — Remainder
23406 Pacific Hwy S, 98032. Tel 206-824-9422
Estab 1972. 100,000 Titles. 100,000 Vols. 13,000 sq ft
Types: Hb, new & used, out of print, papbk, comics, ltd ed, remainders, juvenile
Subj: Comedy, sci fiction & fantasy

KIRKLAND — 18,779. Area code 206

FORTUNA BOOKS — Antiquarian
113 Lake St, 98033. Tel 206-827-7294
Estab 1984. 17,500 Titles. 950 sq ft
Types: 1st ed, hb, juvenile, old & rare, out of print, papbk, used
Subj: Art, for lang

MOUNT VERNON — 13,009. Area code 206

EASTON'S BOOKS — Used
223 S First, 98273. Tel 206-336-2066
Estab 1976. 30,000 Titles. 30,000 Vols. 1800 sq ft
Types: Hb, out of print, papbk, used
Subj: Northwest

OLYMPIA — 27,447. Area code 206

AERO LITERATURE — Mail Order-Aviation
PO Box 1441, 98507-1441. Tel 206-357-8713
Estab 1967. 800 Titles. 1200 Vols. 400 sq ft. Cat 1-2x ann
Types: Hb, out of print, used, facsimile editions, fine bnd, 1st ed, illus bk, old & rare

BOOKPRESS BOOKS — Mail Order
2210 Black Lake Blvd, 98502. Tel 206-866-1323
Estab 1980. 2500 Titles. 1500 Vols. Cat 3x ann
Types: Hb, illus bk, out of print, remainders, used

BROWSERS' BOOKSHOP — Used
107 N Capitol Way, 98501. Tel 206-357-7462
Estab 1929. 12,000 Vols
Types: Hb, papbk, out of print

DOHM'S EX LIBRIS — Mail Order-Antiquarian
625 S Foote St, 98502
Estab 1976. 2500 Titles. 2000 Vols. Cat
Types: Juvenile, out of print, used, foreign picture books

EURO-FILES — Travel
2406 18th Ave NW, PO Box 6262, 98502-4119. Tel 206-786-8888
Mgr, Stephen Beck
Estab 1983. 850 Titles. 4000 Vols. 462 sq ft. Cat 2x ann
Types: Imp, out of print, papbk, used
Subj: European travel

PORT ANGELES — 17,311. Area code 206

GRANDMA'S ATTIC — Used
321 W Eighth St, 98362. Tel 206-452-1230
Estab 1981. 10,000 Titles. 6000 Vols. 250 sq ft
Types: Papbk, juvenile, remainders, out of print
Subj: Hodgepodge

PORT TOWNSEND — 6067. Area code 206

WILLIAM JAMES BOOKSELLER — General
829 Water St (Mail add: PO Box 1578, 98368). Tel 206-385-7313
Estab 1987. 12,000 Titles. 13,000 Vols. 750 sq ft. Cat
Types: Hb, out of print, mass mkt papbk, high priced papbk, remainders, used
Subj: Rel, nautical, Washingtoniana, Olympic Peninsula, boat building

PULLMAN — 23,579. Area code 509

BRUSED BOOKS — Used
N 105 Grand, 99163. Tel 509-334-7898
Estab 1981. 30,000 Titles. 40,000 Vols. 1300 sq ft
Types: Hb, papbk, out of print

RENTON — 30,612. Area code 206

PARKS OP BOOK SERVICE — Mail Order
PO Box 11, 98057. Tel 206-631-2902
25,000 Titles. 25,000 Vols
Types: Hb, papbk, juvenile, old & rare, out of print, used, 1st ed, ltd ed, incunab
Subj: Auto, biog

RICHLAND — 33,578. Area code 509

THE BOOKWORM — Paperback
1908-D George Washington Way, 99352. Tel 509-946-0898
Estab 1974. 50,000 Vols. 1000 sq ft
Types: Hb, imp UK, juvenile, new & used, out of print
Subj: Sci fiction & fantasy, comedy, cooking
See Also: Kennewick,The Bookery, Walla Walla

WESTGATE BOOK NOOK — General
2143 Van Giesen, 99352. Tel 509-946-2477
Estab 1985. 25,000 Titles. 1600 sq ft
Types: Used, hb, juvenile, out of print, papbk, high priced papbk
Subj: Mystery & detective, art, hunting & fishing, Western Amer

SEATTLE — 493,846. Area code 206

AMERICAN EAGLES INC, MILITARY HOBBIES DIVISION — Hobbies
2220 NW Market St, 98107. Tel 206-782-8448
Estab 1969. 1500 Titles. 2700 Vols. Cat
Types: Hb, imp UK, imp Ger, out of print, papbk
Subj: Aviation, hist, hobbies, military
See Also: Bellingham

ANTIQUES & ART ASSOCIATES — Antiquarian
2113 Third Ave, 98121. Tel 206-728-2113
Estab 1972
Types: 1st ed, hb, juvenile, illus bk, ltd ed, out of print, old & rare
Subj: Northwest United States hist

BAUER BOOKS: THE CREATIVE AWARENESS BOOK EXCHANGE — General
714 N 34th St, 98103-8801. Tel 206-547-2665
Mgr, Bob Bauer
Estab 1976. 40,000 Vols. 1250 sq ft
Types: New & used, used, for lang, hb, out of print, mass mkt papbk, high priced papbk
Subj: Feminism, fiction, hist, mod lit, sci fiction & fantasy, self-develop, sociol, counseling, psychotherapy

BEAUTY & THE BOOKS — Antiquarian
4213 University Way NE, 98105. Tel 206-632-8510
Estab 1975. 180,000 Titles. 200,000 Vols. 4000 sq ft
Types: Hb, imp, juvenile, out of print, papbk, mass mkt papbk, books-on-tape, used, fine bnd, 1st ed, illus bk, ltd ed, new, old & rare, remainders, Fr lang, Ger lang, Jap lang
Subj: Art, metaphys & occult, sci fiction & fantasy, philos, photog, true crime, boating, lit

BIBELOTS & BOOKS INC — Antiquarian-Juvenile
112 E Lynn St, 98102. Tel 206-329-6676
Owner & Vpres, Shirley Schneider
Estab 1977. 10,000 Vols. 1200 sq ft
Types: Facsimile editions, fine bnd, 1st ed, hb, illus bk, imp, used, old & rare, out of print, papbk
Subj: Mystery & detective, illus

M TAYLOR BOWIE BOOKSELLER — Antiquarian
2613 Fifth Ave, 98121. Tel 206-441-5363
Estab 1976. 10,000 Vols. 550 sq ft. Cat 1-2x ann
Types: 1st ed, hb, illus bk, old & rare, out of print
Subj: Discovery & explor, fine arts, mod lit, travel, bks on bks

ROBERT L BROWN BOOKMONGER — Mail Order-Antiquarian
1832 N 52nd St, 98103. Tel 206-632-8507
Estab 1976. 3000 Vols. 100 sq ft. Cat 2x ann
Types: Fine bnd, 1st ed, hb, ltd ed, old & rare, out of print, used
Subj: Mod lit, mystery & detective, sci fiction & fantasy, hunting & fishing

CINEMA BOOKS — Films & Filmmaking
4753 Roosevelt Way N E, 98105. Tel 206-547-7667
Estab 1977. 23,000 Vols. 1000 sq ft. Cat 12x ann
Types: Hb, out of print, papbk, remainders, used, imp Jap, imp UK
Subj: Drama, tv

COLLINS RARE BOOKS — Antiquarian
1211 E Denny Way, 98122. Tel 206-323-3999
Estab 1984. 5000 Titles. Cat 6x ann
Types: 1st ed, hb, illus bk, old & rare, out of print
Subj: Anthrop, archaeol

THE COMIC CHARACTER SHOP — Antiquarian-Comics
110 Alaskan Way S, Box 99142, 98199. Tel 206-283-0532
Owner, Dennis Books
Estab 1978. 2500 sq ft. Cat ann
Types: Illus bk, juvenile, old & rare, out of print, used
Subj: Antq, art, comedy

FILLIPI BOOK & RECORD SHOP — Used
1351 E Olive Way, 98122. Tel 206-682-4266
Estab 1935. 35,000 Vols
Types: Hb, out of print
Subj: Art, literary criticism, hist, lit

FLORA & FAUNA BOOKS & PRINTS — Antiquarian-Natural History
121 First Ave S, 98104. Tel 206-623-4727
Estab 1983. 10,000 Titles. 25,000 Vols. Cat ann
Types: Papbk, used, col text, facsimile editions, fine bnd, 1st ed, hb, illus bk, imp, ltd ed, new, out of print, old & rare
Subj: Botany, hort, ornith, physics, Alaskana, geol, astron, zool, gardening, limnology, entomology, reptiles, mammology, expedition

GALLERY BOOKSTORE — Museum
Henry Art Gallery, University of Washington, DE-15, 98195. Tel 206-543-1544
Owner, Henry Art Gallery; Mgr, Paul Cabarga
Estab 1980. 1500 Titles. 3000 Vols. 300 sq ft
Types: Hb, out of print, papbk
Subj: Art

DAVID ISHII BOOKSELLER — Antiquarian
212 First Ave S, 98104. Tel 206-622-4719
Estab 1972. 5000 Vols. 800 sq ft. Cat
Types: Fine bnd, 1st ed, hb, illus bk, juvenile, ltd ed, old & rare, out of print, used
Subj: Asia-Am, fly fishing, baseball

MAGUS INC — Antiquarian
1408 NE 42nd, 98105. Tel 206-633-1800
Estab 1974. 60,000 Vols. 1750 sq ft
Types: Facsimile editions, fine bnd, 1st ed, hb, illus bk, ltd ed, old & rare, out of print, papbk, remainders, used

MANDALA BOOKS AND GALLERIE — Mail Order
918 N E 64th St, 98115. Tel 206-527-2979. WATS 800-843-1170
Owner, Free Daist Communion; Mgr, Bill Smails
Estab 1972. 3000 Vols. 2000 sq ft. Cat 2x ann
Types: Hb, high priced papbk, imp India, juvenile, mass mkt papbk, out of print, remainders
Subj: Spiritual lit

ROBERT W MATTILA BOOKSELLER — Antiquarian
Pioneer Sq Sta, PO Box 4038, 98104. Tel 206-622-9455
2500 Vols. Cat 6x ann
Types: Out of print, old & rare, used
Subj: Alaskana, Arctic, music, Antarctic, Northwest Amer, WPA guides

PETER MILLER BOOKS — Architecture
1930 First Ave, 98101. Tel 206-441-4114
Cat 2x ann
Types: For lang, out of print
Subj: Design

W O MOYE BOOKSELLER — Mail Order-Antiquarian
7717 Aurora Ave N, 98103. Tel 206-783-8103
Cataloger Ross Bowman
Estab 1946. 10,000 Titles. 10,000 Vols. 1500 sq ft. Cat 5x ann
Types: 1st ed, hb, juvenile, ltd ed, old & rare, out of print, used
Subj: Natural hist, travel, wines, literary criticism, antq

SIMON OTTENBERG BOOKSELLERS — Antiquarian-Africa
PO Box 15509, 98115. Tel 206-322-5398
Estab 1968. 3500 Titles. 3500 Vols. 100 sq ft. Cat 2x ann
Types: 1st ed, hb, old & rare, out of print, papbk, used
Subj: Afr art

PEGASUS BOOK EXCHANGE — Used
4823 California Ave SW, 98116. Tel 206-937-5410
Estab 1979. 35,000 Titles. 50,000 Vols
Types: Out of print, juvenile, hb, mass mkt papbk, high priced papbk
Subj: Sci fiction & fantasy, mystery & detective, metaphysics, nonfiction, hist romance

RAVENNA RARE BOOKS — Antiquarian
5639 University Way NE, 98105. Tel 206-525-3737
Mgr, B Cutts
Estab 1971. 30,000 Vols. 1500 sq ft
Types: Fine bnd, 1st ed, hb, incunab, illus bk, old & rare, out of print, used
Subj: Art

SEATTLE BOOK CENTER — Mail Order-Antiquarian
2231 Second Ave, 98121. Tel 206-443-1533
Estab 1978. 4000 Vols. Cat 5x ann
Types: 1st ed, hb, old & rare, out of print, used
Subj: Natural hist, sci fiction & fantasy, travel

THE SHOREY BOOKSTORE — Antiquarian
110 Union St, 98101. Tel 206-624-0221
Estab 1890. 1,250,000 Vols. Cat 6x ann
Types: New & used, out of print, papbk, rare
Subj: Alaskana, Arctic, natural hist, Western Amer, fiction, marine voyages

TWELFTH AVENUE BOOKS — Used
1830 12th Ave, 98122. Tel 206-323-6719
Estab 1984. 15,000 Titles. 15,000 Vols. 550 sq ft
Types: Out of print, mass mkt papbk, high priced papbk
Subj: Cooking, humanities, Amer, natural hist

GEORGE H TWENEY, BOOKS — Antiquarian-Western Americana
16660 Marine View Dr SW, 98166. Tel 206-243-8243
Estab 1969. 3000 Vols. 2500 sq ft. Cat
Types: 1st ed, ltd ed, hb, imp, new & used, out of print,

old & rare
Subj: Alaskana, Am hist & lit, bibliog, travel, discovery & explor, Western Amer

THE WHALER BOOKSTORE — Used Paperback
213 SW 152nd St, 98166. Tel 206-246-5265
Estab 1982. 20,000 Titles. 20,000 Vols. 1500 sq ft
Types: For lang, hb, juvenile, out of print, mass mkt papbk, comics, mod first ed
Subj: Mystery & detective, westerns

SILVERDALE — Area code 206

PAGES BOOKS — Used
Kitsap Place, PO Box 3159, 98383. Tel 206-692-3352
Estab 1987. 15,000 Titles. 25,000 Vols. 1000 sq ft
Types: Hb, juvenile, papbk, high priced papbk, mass mkt papbk, out of print
Subj: Sci fiction & fantasy

SOUTHWORTH — area code 206

R M WEATHERFORD - BOOKS — Antiquarian-Western Americana
PO Box 5, 98386. Tel 206-871-3617
Assoc N Ross Bowman
Estab 1980. 8000 Titles. 8000 Vols. Cat 6x ann
Types: Fine bnd, 1st ed, hb, illus bk, old & rare, out of print
Subj: Alaskana, Am Indian studies, Amer, NAmer, Pacific, sci-tech, anthrop, geol, discovery & explor, ethnology, primitive art

SPOKANE — 171,300. Area code 509

THE BOOK EXCHANGE — Antiquarian
University City E, E 10812 Sprague Ave, 99206. Tel 509-928-4073
Mgr, Richard Allen
Estab 1981. 29,000 Vols. 1400 sq ft
Types: Fine bnd, 1st ed, hb, illus bk, imp, juvenile, ltd ed, new & used, old & rare, out of print, papbk, remainders

CLARK'S OLD BOOKSTORE — Used
W 318 Sprague Ave, 99204. Tel 509-624-1846
Estab 1910. 20,000 Vols
Types: Hb, juvenile, out of print, papbk, comics
Subj: Art, sci-tech, Western Amer, nature & environ, gardening, poetry, cookbks, classics

FORGET ME NOT ANTIQUES — Antiquarian
PO Box 14992, 99214. Tel 509-926-3854
Estab 1975. 5000 Vols
Types: Fine bnd, 1st ed, hb, illus bk, ltd ed, out of print, used, comics, pre-1950 children's bks
Subj: Cooking, Northwest hist

INLAND BOOKSTORE — Used
W 411 First Ave, 99204. Tel 509-624-9064
Estab 1955. 30,000 Vols
Types: 1st ed, fine bnd, hb, illus bk, juvenile, out of print, papbk, remainders, used, imp UK, Ireland
Subj: Anthrop, art, aviation, guns, hist, hunting & fishing, military, natural hist, philos, poetry, Alaskana, Arctic, Am & British lit, sea & ships

SPOKANE BOOK CENTER — Used
N626 Monroe, 99201. Tel 509-328-2332
Estab 1984. 20,000 Titles. 20,000 Vols
Types: Hb, for lang, juvenile, out of print, high priced papbk
Subj: Photog, rel studies, World Wars I & II, Western Amer, metaphys & occult, natural hist, and others

STANWOOD — 2744. Area code 206

THE SNOW GOOSE — General
8716 - 271st NW, 98292. Tel 206-629-3631
Mgr, Elaine J Walters
Types: Hb, papbk, juvenile, out of print
Subj: Cooking

SUNNYSIDE — 9225. Area code 509

HOPFENGARTEN GALLERY & BOOKSHOP — Collecting
Mini Mall, 214 S 6th St (Mail add: PO Box 100, Mabton, 98935-0335). Tel 509-837-6936
Owner, L O Gannon & Son, Inc; Dir, R M Anderson
Estab 1957. 6000 Vols. 1000 sq ft
Types: Hb, juvenile, out of print, papbk, remainders, used
Subj: Antq, art, reference, militaria, Indian relics, primitive tribal arts

TACOMA — 158,501. Area code 206

FOX BOOK CO — Antiquarian
737 Saint Helens St, 98402. Tel 206-627-2223
Estab 1935. 250,000 Vols. Cat 3x ann
Types: 1st ed, fine bnd, old & rare, out of print, remainders
Subj: Fiction, nonfiction, NW Am

J & J MAREK BOOKS — Mail Order-Antiquarian
6412 Fairlawn Dr SW, 98499. Tel 206-582-4575
Estab 1975. 3000 Titles. 3000 Vols. Cat
Types: Out of print
Subj: Amer, scholarly lit, hist, math, Eng hist & lit, sci-tech, hist of sci

O'LEARY'S BOOKS — Antiquarian
3828 100th SW, 98499. Tel 206-588-2503
Estab 1975. 100,000 Vols. 6000 sq ft. Cat
Types: Hb, juvenile, out of print, mass mkt papbk, used, comics, new & used mag
Subj: Military, sci fiction & fantasy, Northwest Amer

PLASTICS AND TACTICS — Military
5435 S Tacoma Hwy, 98409. Tel 206-474-7944
Mgr, Al Davis
Types: Hb, imp UK, imp Ger, out of print, papbk
Subj: Aviation, hist, military hobby ref

TACOMA BOOK CENTER — General
116 S 9th, 98402. Tel 206-572-8248
Estab 1985. 70,000 Titles. 60,000 Vols. 1100 sq ft
Types: Hb, juvenile, papbk, high priced papbk, used, out of print, facsimile editions, fine bnd, 1st ed, illus bk, ltd ed, old & rare, remainders
Subj: Class studies, mystery & detective, sci fiction & fantasy, hist

VANCOUVER — 42,834. Area code 206

GARY L ESTABROOK - BOOKS — Antiquarian
PO Box 61453, 98666. Tel 206-699-5454
Estab 1974. 6000 Vols. Cat 4x ann
Types: 1st ed, fine bnd, hb, ltd ed, old & rare, out of print, used
Subj: Hunting & fishing

DICK PERIER BOOKS — Mail Order-Antiquarian
PO Box 1, 98666. Tel 206-696-2033
Estab 1982. 5000 Titles. 5000 Vols. Cat 6x ann
Types: Out of print
Subj: Cooking, West, America

SPENCER'S BOOKSTORE — Used
10415 NE Fourth Plain Rd, 98662. Tel 206-892-9862
Estab 1981. 30,000 Vols. 1200 sq ft
Types: Mass mkt papbk, out of print

WENATCHEE — 17,257. Area code 509

THE HOMESTEADER-BOOKS — General
26 N Wenatchee Ave, 98801-2257. Tel 509-662-7988
Estab 1978. 12,000 Titles. 15,000 Vols. 3000 sq ft
Types: Hb, juvenile, new & used, out of print, papbk, remainders
Subj: Fiction, how-to, Northwest regional, cookbks

YAKIMA — 49,826. Area code 509

THE BOOK NOOK — General
722 Summit, 98902. Tel 509-453-3762
Owners, Dorothy Emmert & Marion Kelly
Estab 1974. 2000 Titles. 5000 Vols
Types: Hb, juvenile, out of print, papbk, remainders
Subj: Health, self-develop, metaphysics, women's studies, chemical dependency

CHESHIRE BOOKS — Antiquarian
310 E Yakima Ave, 98901. Tel 509-457-0930
Estab 1983. 30,000 Vols. 2700 sq ft. Cat 4x ann
Types: Papbk, used, fine bnd, 1st ed, out of print, old & rare, juvenile
Subj: Washingtoniana, Western Amer, Pacific Northwest

CHURCHILL'S BOOK LOVERS' HAUNT — General
125 S Second St, 98901-2882. Tel 509-453-8207
Estab 1968
Types: Hb, juvenile, mass mkt papbk, new & used, out of print
Subj: NW hist, reg hist

PIED PIPER — Juvenile
1605 Summitview, 98902. Tel 509-248-7628
Juv Buyer, Judy Harmon
Estab 1984. 4000 Titles. 9000 Vols. 1000 sq ft. Cat ann
Types: Hb, papbk, out of print
Subj: Fiction, nonfiction

JAY WOODS CONSULTANT — History
1 Bohoskey Dr, 98901. Tel 509-457-3724
Estab 1979. 20,000 Titles. 23,000 Vols. 4,000 sq ft. Cat ann
Types: Facsimile editions, new & used, out of print, old & rare
Subj: Computer sci, medieval studies, sci fiction & fantasy, taxonomy

WEST VIRGINIA

BLUEFIELD — 16,060. Area code 304

APPALACHIAN BOOKSHOP — Antiquarian
1316 Pen Mar Ave, 24701. Tel 304-327-5493
Estab 1972. 20,000 Vols. 2000 sq ft. Cat
Types: Hb, old & rare, out of print, papbk, remainders, used
Subj: Civil War, genealogy, mountain culture

BRUCETON MILLS — 296. Area code 304

UNICORN LIMITED INC — Mail Order
Sandy Acres Rd (Mail add: PO Box 397, 26525). Tel 304-379-8803
Estab 1979. 500 Titles. 3000 Vols. Cat 6x ann
Types: Gaelic lang, imp UK, juvenile, remainders, out of print, papbk, new & used
Subj: Hist, genealogy, music, ethnic Scottish, Celtic, Viking, Norse

CHARLESTON — 63,968. Area code 304

TRANS ALLEGHENY BOOKS INC — Used
114 Capitol St, 25301. Tel 304-346-0551
Mgr, Gordon Simmons
Estab 1988. 25,000 Titles. 500 sq ft
Types: Out of print, remainders, used, hb, new, old & rare, papbk
Subj: Appalachia

LEWISBURG — 3065. Area code 304

BOOKSTORE — General
104 S Jefferson, 24901. Tel 304-645-6910
Buyer, Darlene Fife
Estab 1977. 5000 Titles. 5000 Vols. Cat
Types: For lang, hb, imp, juvenile, out of print, papbk, mass mkt papbk, 1st ed, ltd ed, old & rare, remainders, new & used
Subj: Philos, poetry, West Virginiana, Civil War, Chesapeake & Ohio railroadiana

MIDDLEBOURNE — 941. Area code 304

WOODEN PORCH BOOKS — Antiquarian
Rt 1, Box 262, 26149. Tel 304-386-4434
Estab 1980. 4300 Titles. 6000 Vols. Cat 8x ann
Types: Hb, illus bk, old & rare, out of print, used
Subj: Textiles, fashion, costumes, steamboats & rivers

MORGANTOWN — 27,605. Area code 304

PINOCCHIO'S BOOKS & TOYS — Juvenile
245 Walnut St, 26505. Tel 304-296-2332
Estab 1979. 2600 Vols. 920 sq ft
Types: Hb, out of print, papbk

WOLF'S HEAD BOOKS — Antiquarian
198 Foundry St, PO Box 1020, 26507-1020. Tel 304-296-0706
Mgr, Barbara E Nailler
Estab 1980. 50,000 Titles. 50,000 Vols. 3520 sq ft. Cat 5x ann
Types: Hb, papbk, 1st ed, juvenile, used, out of print, old & rare
Subj: Amer, Appalachia, military, West Virginiana, fiction, art, archit, mysticism
See Also: St Augustine, FL

MOUNT NEBO —Area code 304

SEBERT'S BOOKS — Mail Order-Antiquarian
Rte 3 Box 325, 26679. Tel 304-438-8180
Estab 1965. 4600 Titles
Types: Hb, juvenile, papbk, used, old & rare, out of print

PARKERSBURG — 39,967. Area code 304

TRANS ALLEGHENY BOOKS INC — Antiquarian
Carnegie Library Bldg, Eighth & Green St, 26101. Tel 304-422-4499
Estab 1974. 35,000 Vols. Cat 8x ann
Types: Old & rare, out of print, used
Subj: Amer, fiction, Ohioana, Pennsylvaniana, West Virginiana, Civil War, Western Amer, Appalachia, Ohio River & Valley
See Also: Charleston

SPENCER — 2799. Area code 304

IMAGINATION — General
314 Market St, 25276. Tel 304-927-4866
Mgr, Paul Geismar
Types: Hb, juvenile, out of print, papbk, used, comics
Subj: Hobbies, children's activities

WHEELING — 43,010. Area code 304

RICHARD A HAND BOOKS — Mail Order
81 Lynwood Ave, 26003. Tel 304-242-8853
Estab 1986. 600 Titles. 600 Vols. Cat 2x ann
Types: Facsimile editions, 1st ed, old & rare, out of print, used
Subj: Am Indian studies, archaeol, Western Amer

WILLIAMSBURG — 1409. Area code 304

STOUD BOOKSELLERS — Antiquarian-Theology
Star Rte, Box 94, Pembroke Rd, 24991. Tel 304-645-7169
Estab 1975. 5000 Titles. 5000 Vols. Cat 10x ann
Types: Old & rare, out of print, used
Subj: Biblical studies, church hist, missionaries, hort, gardening, agr

ALTOONA — 4393. Area code 715

AVIAN PUBLICATIONS — Mail Order
3311 W Country Club Lane, 54720. Tel 715-835-6806
Estab 1977. 225 Titles. 500 Vols. Cat 2x ann
Types: Hb, new, papbk, out of print
Subj: Bird textbks, care & mgmt

APPLETON — 59,032. Area code 414

OCTOBER BOOKS — Used
606 N Lawe, 54911. Tel 414-735-0700
Estab 1979. 4000 Titles. 1250 sq ft
Types: Hb, old & rare, out of print, papbk

BROOKFIELD — 34,035. Area code 414

LITTLEWOOD'S BOOKS — Used
PO Box 681, 53008-0681. Tel 414-797-9045
Estab 1971. 5000 Vols. Cat quarterly
Types: Fine bnd, 1st ed, hb, old & rare, out of print
Subj: Amer, hist, nature & environ, bus hist, sci hist

DELAVAN — 5684. Area code 414

OLD DELAVAN BOOK CO, INC — Antiquarian
67 E Walworth Ave, 53115. Tel 414-728-6988
Estab 1976. 100,000 Vols
Types: Out of print, old & rare
Subj: Amer, cats, railroadiana, juv

DE PERE — 14,892. Area code 414

SADLON'S LTD — Antiquarian
109 N Broadway, 54115. Tel 414-336-6665
Estab 1981. 2900 Vols. 2940 sq ft. Cat 2x ann
Types: Fine bnd, hb, illus bk, imp, ltd ed, out of print, old & rare, 1st ed
Subj: Discovery & explor, hist, travel, Amer, lit

ELM GROVE — 6735. Area code 414

WEST'S BOOKING AGENCY — Antiquarian-Mystery & Detective
Box 406, 53122. Tel 414-786-8420
Estab 1975. 5000 Vols. Cat 2x ann
Types: 1st ed, hb, illus bk, imp, juvenile, ltd ed, new, out of print, old & rare
Subj: Fiction

GENOA CITY — 1202. Area code 414

FAIR CHASE INC — Mail Order-Antiquarian
9310 402nd Ave (Mail add: Box 838, Twin Lakes, 53181). Tel 414-279-5478
Estab 1982. 750 Titles. 2000 Vols. Cat 8x ann
Types: Out of print, old & rare, hb, high priced papbk, fine bnd, 1st ed, used
Subj: Hunting & fishing, archery, nature, decoys, woodcarving, big game

LAKE DELTON — 1158. Area code 608

WISE OWL BOOKSHOP — Antiquarian
Burritt St, Box 377, 53940. Tel 608-254-2092
Estab 1970. 12,000 Vols. 600 sq ft
Types: 1st ed, hb, illus bk, juvenile, old & rare, out of print, papbk, used
Subj: Wisconsinana

MADISON — 170,616. Area code 608

G F GLAEVE ART & BOOKS — Antiquarian
6654 Odana RD, 53719-1012. Tel 608-833-3113
5000 Vols. 1000 sq ft
Types: Out of print, remainders, used, hb, old & rare
Subj: Antq, art, midwest regional

PAUL'S BOOKSTORE — Used
670 State St, 53703. Tel 608-257-2968
Estab 1954
Types: Hb, out of print, papbk

SHAKTI BOOKSHOP — New Age
320 State St, 53703. Tel 608-255-5007
Mgr, John Lindgren
Estab 1972. 5000 Vols
Types: Hb, imp UK, imp India, out of print, papbk, remainders
Subj: Eastern philos, health & phys educ, rel studies, homoeopathy, western psychol, new age

SPAIGHTWOOD GALLERIES — Art Gallery
1150 Spaight St, 53703. Tel 608-255-3043
Estab 1980. 2000 Vols
Types: Facsimile editions, incunab, illus bk, imp Fr, imp Sp, ltd ed, new, old & rare, out of print, used

20TH CENTURY BOOKS — Used
108 King St, 53703-3314. Tel 608-251-6226
Estab 1979. 20,000 Titles. 30,000 Vols. 1500 sq ft. Cat 2x ann
Types: Hb, juvenile, out of print, papbk, remainders
Subj: Mystery & detective, sci fiction & fantasy, comedy, humor, music, movies

MARSHFIELD — 18,290. Area code 715

W BRUCE FYE ANTIQUARIAN MEDICAL BOOKS — Mail Order-Medicine
1607 N Wood Ave, 54449. Tel 715-384-8128
Mgr & Buyer, W Bruce Fye
Estab 1973. 10,000 Titles. 15,000 Vols. 1500 sq ft. Cat 4x ann
Types: Facsimile editions, fine bnd, 1st ed, hb, illus bk, ltd ed, old & rare, out of print, remainders, used
Subj: Hist of med

MILWAUKEE — 636,212. Area code 414

THE BOOK TRADER — Paperback
3172 S 27 St, 53215. Tel 414-645-9666
Estab 1980. 180,000 Titles. 4000 sq ft. Cat
Types: Out of print, new & used, juvenile, quality
Subj: Mystery & detective, sci fiction & fantasy, romance, nonfiction, class studies, suspense, westerns
See Also: Glendale

CASANOVA GUNS INC, BOOK DEPT — Sports
1601 W Greenfield Ave, 53204. Tel 414-672-3040. WATS 800-627-4570
Vpres, Pierre Casanova
Estab 1968. 14,000 Titles. 28,000 Vols. 5000 sq ft. Cat ann
Types: Hb, out of print, remainders, used, imp Jap, imp UK, imp Fr, imp Ger
Subj: Auto, aviation, hunting & fishing, railroadiana, rel studies, guns, weapons, Navy, armored vehicle, air guns

CONSTANT READER BOOKSHOP LTD — Antiquarian-General
1625-27 E Irving Pl, 53202-1415. Tel 414-291-0452
Mgr, John Esser; Merch Mgr & Buyer, David Hurlbutt
Estab 1979. 25,000 Titles. 4000 sq ft. Cat bi-monthly
Types: 1st ed, facsimile editions, fine bnd, hb, juvenile, ltd ed, old & rare, used, out of print
Subj: Art, biog, fiction, literary criticism, military, nautical, philos, rel studies, nature & environ, Amer, drama, music, mystery & detective, sci fiction & fantasy, show business

RAYMOND DWORCZYK RARE BOOKS — Mail Order-Antiquarian
2114 W Rogers St, 53204. Tel 414-383-2659
Estab 1962. 100,000 Vols. Cat
Types: Facsimile editions, fine bnd, 1st ed, hb, incunab, juvenile, new & used, out of print, old & rare, remainders
Subj: Amer, Africa, Asian studies, scholarly lit, warfare, early tools

JUST BOOKS — Antiquarian
845 N Marshall St, 53202. Tel 414-278-8478
Estab 1973. 7000 Vols. 500 sq ft
Types: Fine bnd, hb, old & rare, out of print

J & J PENN CO — Mail Order-Antiquarian
3955 S First Pl, 53207. Tel 414-483-7306
Estab 1960. 5000 Vols. Cat
Types: New & used, out of print, remainders
Subj: Aviation

RENAISSANCE BOOKSHOP INC — General
834 N Plankinton, 53203. Tel 414-271-6850
Vpres, Robert John
Estab 1960. 250,000 Vols
Types: Facsimile editions, 1st ed, for lang, hb, juvenile, ltd ed, new & used, old & rare, out of print, papbk
Subj: Biog, cooking, fiction, local hist, medicine, military, nonfiction, rel-c,j,p, psychol, sci fiction & fantasy, soc sci, sports

SPECTRUM BOOKS & RECORDS — Antiquarian
2110 W Wells, 53233. Tel 414-344-5522
Estab 1972. 10,000 Vols. 800 sq ft
Types: Old & rare, out of print, papbk, used
Subj: Fiction, hist, philos, sci fiction & fantasy, comedy

WOODLAND PATTERN INC — Poetry
720 E Locust, PO Box 92081, 53202. Tel 414-263-5001
Mgr, Anne Kingsbury
Estab 1979. 6000 Titles. 8000 Vols. 1000 sq ft
Types: Hb, out of print, remainders, small presses
Subj: Mod lit

YESTERDAY'S MEMORIES BOOK & OLD RECORD SHOP — Used
5406 W Center St, 53210. Tel 414-444-6210
Mgr, Ken Freck
Estab 1976. 10,000 Titles. 10,000 Vols. 1000 sq ft
Types: Old & rare, out of print
Subj: Judaica, music, military, drama, cooking, art, show bus memorabilia & mus nostalgia, Wisconsin history

MINERAL POINT — 2259. Area code 608

THE CORNISH MINER — General
231 High St, 53565. Tel 608-987-2642
Estab 1983. 3000 Titles. 6500 Vols. 1750 sq ft. Cat 4x ann
Types: Hb, imp UK, juvenile, used, remainders, out of print
Subj: Wisconsinana, Cornwall, England; Wales

NECEDAH — 773. Area code 608

BOOKSEARCH OF NECEDAH — Used
Rt 1, Box 315 (Mail add: POB 369, 54646). Tel 608-565-2822
Estab 1980. 18,000 Titles. 21,000 Vols. 900 sq ft. Cat 2x ann
Types: Out of print
Subj: Rel-c, nonfiction, juv Cath

NEW MINER TRADING POST — Used
PO Box 188, 54646. Tel 608-565-2822
Estab 1976. 15,000 Titles. 18,000 Vols. Cat
Types: Hb, juvenile, out of print, old & rare
Subj: Rel-c, hist, church hist

NEW BERLIN — 30,529. Area code 414

MEANDAUR BOOKSELLER — Antiquarian
17125 W Cleveland, 53151. Tel 414-786-6650
Vpres & Mgr, Ann Findley
Estab 1979. 5800 Titles. 6000 Vols. Cat 2x ann
Types: 1st ed, juvenile, out of print
Subj: Nature narratives, fairy tales, 1800-1930

OSHKOSH — 49,678. Area code 414

UNIVERSITY BOOKSTORE — College
University of Wisconsin-Oshkosh, Blackhawk Commons, 54901. Tel 414-424-2385
Dir, Sue M Neabling
Estab 1970. 50,000 Titles. 725,000 Vols
Types: Hb, imp, juvenile, papbk, remainders, used, out of print

RACINE — 85,725. Area code 414

THE OLD BOOK CORNER — Antiquarian
312 Sixth St (Mail add: 1747 College Ave, 53403). Tel 414-632-5195
Owner, Andrew McLean
Estab 1980. 6000 Vols. 250 sq ft. Cat
Types: 1st ed, fine bnd, hb, juvenile, old & rare, out of print, used
Subj: Literary criticism, rel, military

SISTER BAY — 564. Area code 414

WM CAXTON BOOKS — Used
Box 709, 54234. Tel 312-475-1800
Estab 1986. 25,000 Titles. 40,000 Vols. 1400 sq ft
Types: Hb, remainders, out of print, old & rare
Subj: Anthrop, hist, literary criticism, philos

SPRING GREEN — 1265. Area code 608

THE WINSTED SHOP — Gift Shop
140 S Winsted St (Mail add: Box 9, 53588). Tel 608-588-7544
Estab 1968. 1200 sq ft
Types: Hb, papbk, juvenile, out of print, used
Subj: Wisconsinana, Frank Lloyd Wright

WATERLOO — 2393. Area code 414

JAMES HYER BOOKSELLER — Mail Order-Antiquarian
N7609 Airport Rd, 53594. Tel 414-478-3644
15,000 Vols
Types: Out of print
Subj: Wisconsinana

THE UNTAMED SHREW-BOOKS — Mail Order-Feminism
N 7609 Airport Rd, 53594. Tel 414-478-3644
Mgr, Joan Hyer
Estab 1982. 4000 Titles. 4000 Vols. Cat 2-3x ann
Types: Out of print, used, 1st ed, hb, imp, ltd ed, old & rare, remainders
Subj: Women's studies, fiction, nonfiction, poetry

WAUKESHA — 50,319. Area code 414

PIC-A-BAC PAPERBACK EXCHANGE — Used Paperback
317 W Saint Paul Ave, 53188. Tel 414-549-1587
Estab 1979. 40,000 Titles. 100,000 Vols. 1700 sq ft

Types: Out of print, mass mkt papbk, used
Subj: Rel studies, poetry, short stories, class studies, self-develop, sports, nonfiction, romance, fiction, hist, warfare, sci fiction & fantasy, humor, mystery & detective, autobio, westerns, horror, Gothic, plays, young adult

WEST SALEM — 3276. Area code 608

HISTORIC SALEM
Mail Order-Antiques
99 Jefferson St, PO Box 884, 54669-0884. Tel 608-786-1675
Estab 1986. 20,000 Titles. 22,000 Vols
Types: Hb, papbk, juvenile, out of print, 1st ed, old & rare, used
Subj: Biog, hist

WYOMING

SUMMERHOUSE BOOKS — Antiquarian-Western Americana
PO Box 66, 82836. Tel 307-655-2367, 655-9714
5000 Titles. 5000 Vols
Types: 1st ed, hb, illus bk, incunab, juvenile, out of print, old & rare, used
Subj: Wyomingana

GLENROCK — 2736. area code 307

GENERATION III — General
313 W Birch St, Glenrock, 82637-1351. Tel 307-436-9545
Estab 1981. Cat ann
Types: Papbk, hb, new & used, out of print, old & rare, juvenile
Subj: Lit

LARAMIE — 24,410. Area code 307

HIGH COUNTRY BOOKS — General
306 S Second, 82070. Tel 307-742-5640
Estab 1972. 30,000 Vols. 16,000 sq ft
Types: Hb, juvenile, out of print, papbk, used
Subj: Art, cooking, philos, Western Amer, recreation, nature & environ

UNIVERSITY OF WYOMING BOOKSTORE — College
University Sta, Box 3255, 82071-3255. Tel 307-766-3264
Mgr, Peggy L Falgien; Text Buyer, Nancy Gillen; Trade & Juv Buyer Loretta Herman
Estab 1921
Types: Hb, juvenile, out of print, papbk, remainders, used
Subj: Art

SHERIDAN — 15,146. Area code 307

THE BOOKSHOP — General
122 N Main St, 82801. Tel 307-672-6505
Estab 1976. 5000 Titles. 1400 sq ft
Types: Hb, juvenile, out of print, papbk, remainders

SUNDANCE — 1087. Area code 307

BACKPOCKET RANCH BOOKSHOP — General
364 Farrall Rd, 82729. Tel 307-283-2665
Mgr & Buyer, Gaydell Collier
Estab 1977. 2000 Vols. 300 sq ft. Cat 2x ann
Types: Hb, juvenile, papbk, remainders, used, out of print, imp horse bks from Eng
Subj: Horses, local authors, nature & environ, ranching, Western Amer, Wyomingana, agr, rural living

Puerto Rico

HATO REY — Area code 809

BOOK WORLD* — General
149 Plaza Las Americas, 00919. Tel 809-753-7140
Mgr & Buyer, Miguel Garcia
Estab 1979. 70,000 Vols. Cat
Types: Audio visual mat, hb, mass mkt papbk, out of print, papbk, Sp lang, trade

Virgin Islands

SAINT CROIX — 31,779. Area code 809

JELTRUPS' BOOKS — General
51 ABC Company St, Christiansted, 00820. Tel 809-773-1018
Estab 1960. 500 sq ft
Types: Hb, juvenile, out of print, papbk, old & rare, new & used
Subj: Virgin Islands, Caribbean

SAINT THOMAS — 28,960. Area code 809

DOCKSIDE BOOKSHOP INC — General
PO Box 8648, 00801-8648. Tel 809-774-4937
Mgr, Erland Jonathan Gjessing
Estab 1978. 10,000 Titles. 20,000 Vols. 1200 sq ft. Cat ann
Types: Hb, juvenile, papbk, remainders, out of print
Subj: Art, hobbies, cooking, nautical, photog, how-to, bus & mgt, West Indies, lang ref

CANADA

ALBERTA

CALGARY — 560,618. Area code 403

AQUILA BOOKS — General
1009 16th Ave (Mail add: PO Box 3331, Station B, T2M 4L8). Tel 403-282-5832
Estab 1984. 20,000 Vols. Cat ann
Types: Out of print, old & rare
Subj: Astron, Western Canadiana, polar exploration

OWLS' ROOK BOOKS LTD — Used
139 16th Ave NW, T2M 0H3. Tel 403-277-2595
Estab 1980. 50,000 Vols. 1000 sq ft
Types: Juvenile, hb, imp, for lang, out of print, papbk, remainders
Subj: Sci fiction & fantasy

TRAINS & SUCH LTD, BOOK DEPT — Railroadiana
4127 Fourth St NW, T2K 1A3. Tel 403-282-2442
Estab 1972. 300 Vols
Types: New & used, out of print

TOM WILLIAMS BOOKS — Antiquarian
Box 4126, Sta C, T2T 5M9. Tel 403-264-0184
Estab 1958. 48,000 Titles. 50,000 Vols. Cat
Types: Hb, old & rare, out of print
Subj: Can, Arctic, petroleum, aviation, dance, mountaineering, ice hockey, big game hunting

CANMORE — 3166. Area code 403

ROBIN'S ROOST BOOKS & PAPERY — General
713 Eighth St, T0L 0M0. Tel 403-678-2002
Estab 1985. 4500 Titles. 6000 Vols. 1000 sq ft
Types: Hb, juvenile, out of print, papbk, remainders, used

CARDSTON — 3043. Area code 403

CARDSTON BOOK SHOP — Religious
220 Main St, Box 1150, T0K 0K0. Tel 403-653-4222
2000 Titles. 8000 Vols. 1800 sq ft
Types: Juvenile, mass mkt papbk, out of print, remainders

CLARESHOLM — 3425. Area code 403

WHITE RABBIT BOOKS AND TOYS — General
4815 Second St W (Mail add: PO Box 848, T0L 0T0). Tel 403-625-4304
Estab 1988. 2000 Titles. 8000 Vols. 400 sq ft
Types: Fr & Sp lang, hb, juvenile, mass mkt papbk, out of print
Subj: Local hist, fiction, humor, reference

EDMONTON — 505,773. Area code 403

ABACUS BOOKS — Antiquarian
10449-124th St, T5N 1R7. Tel 403-488-9758
Estab 1985. 12,000 Vols. 1000 sq ft
Types: Out of print, used, facsimile editions, fine bnd, 1st ed, incunab, illus bk, imp, juvenile, ltd ed, old & rare
Subj: Can

THE EDMONTON BOOKSTORE LTD — Antiquarian
8530 109th St, T6G 1E5. Tel 403-433-1781
Mgr & Buyer, Barbara Ellis
Estab 1965. 30,000 Vols. 1200 sq ft. Cat 2x ann
Types: Col text, ltd ed, old & rare, out of print, used
Subj: Can, hist, Arctic, flora & fauna

REGINALD SMITH BOOKS — Used
80 McCauley Plaza, 10025 Jasper Ave, T5J 1S5. Tel 403-425-9135
Estab 1986. 9000 Titles. 12,000 Vols. 1000 sq ft
Types: Papbk, out of print
Subj: Hist, natural hist, mystery & detective, fiction

F SPEUR -BOOKS — Antiquarian-General
10824A-82(Whyte) Ave, T6E 2B3. Tel 403-439-4195
Estab 1985. 15,000 Titles. 20,000 Vols. 1000 sq ft. Cat 3x ann
Types: Hb, used, for lang, out of print, Fr lang, Ger lang, facsimile editions, fine bnd, 1st ed, illus bk, old & rare
Subj: Belles lettres, art, hist, philos, rel, travel

BRITISH COLUMBIA

COQUITLAM — 62,000. Area code 604

AUSTIN BOOKS — Newsdealer
1105 Austin Ave, V3K 3P4. Tel 604-939-4114
Estab 1972. 10,000 Titles. 1000 sq ft
Types: Mass mkt papbk, new, out of print, used
Subj: Sci fiction & fantasy

GANGES — Area code 604

JENNIFER INDERWICK — Mail Order
Salt Spring Island, PO Box 1526, V0S 1E0. Tel 604-537-4204
Estab 1987. 50,000 Titles. Cat 4x ann
Types: Out of print, remainders, study guides
Subj: Natural hist

NORTH VANCOUVER — 63,471. Area code 604

STEPHEN C LUNSFORD BOOKS — Mail Order-Antiquarian
PO Box 86773, V7L 4L3. Tel 604-681-6830
5000 Vols. Cat 4x ann
Types: Old & rare, out of print
Subj: Can, Western Amer, Indians of N Amer

PACIFIC BOOKS — Used
1135 Lonsdale, V7M 2H4. Tel 604-980-2121
Estab 1973. 1000 sq ft
Types: Out of print, remainders
Subj: Art, humanities

TOFINO — 612. Area code 604

VENKATESA BOOKS — Mail Order-Antiquarian
Box 524, V0R 2Z0. Tel 604-725-4222
Estab 1979. 1200 Titles. 1200 Vols. Cat 2x ann
Types: Fine bnd, 1st ed, hb, illus bk, juvenile, ltd ed, old & rare, out of print, used, small press publishing
Subj: Oz memorabilia
See Also: Capitola, CA

VANCOUVER — 410,188. Area code 604

ASHLEY'S BOOKS — Modern Literature
3712 W Tenth Ave, V6R 2G4. Tel 604-228-1180
Estab 1973. 10,000 Vols
Types: 1st ed, hb, high priced papbk, out of print, used
Subj: Art, Can, hist, humanities, mod lit, music, philos, psychol

BETTER BUY BOOKS — General
4443 W Tenth Ave, V6R 2H8. Tel 604-224-4144
Estab 1959. 20,000 Titles. 50,000 Vols
Types: Col text, hb, papbk, out of print, remainders
Subj: Fiction, mystery & detective, nonfiction, sci fiction & fantasy, sci-tech

BOND'S BOOKSHOP — Antiquarian
319 W Hastings, PO Box 3166, V6B 3X6. Tel 604-688-5227
Estab 1932. 80,000 Vols. 4500 sq ft. Cat 4x ann
Types: Out of print, hb
Subj: Alaskana, Arctic, art, Can, children's, exploration

BOOK WAREHOUSE — Remainder
632 W Broadway, V5Z 1G1. Tel 604-872-5711
Mgr, Gary Crompton
Estab 1980. 10,000 Titles. 100,000 Vols. 4000 sq ft
Types: Col & el-hi text, hb, imp, juvenile, out of print, papbk, best sellers
Subj: Art, cooking

COLOPHON BOOKS — Antiquarian
407 W Cordova St, V6B 1E7. Tel 604-685-4138
Estab 1978. 25,000 Vols. 1600 sq ft. Cat 3x ann
Types: Hb, out of print
Subj: Can art

THE COMICS SHOP — Comics
2089 W Fourth Ave, V6J 1N3. Tel 604-738-8122
Estab 1974. 100,000 Vols. 4000 sq ft. Cat 3x ann
Types: Hb, imp Fr, out of print, papbk, remainders, used
Subj: Sci fiction & fantasy

REGINALD LISSEL BOOKSELLER — General
434 Homer St, V6B 2V5. Tel 604-682-8061
Estab 1983. 3500 Vols. 600 sq ft
Types: For lang, hb, high priced papbk, remainders, out of print, used
Subj: Archit, photog, philos

WILLIAM HOFFER BOOKSELLER — Antiquarian
58-60 Powell St, V6A 1E7. Tel 604-683-3022
Estab 1969. 25,000 Vols. Cat 4x ann
Types: Out of print, pvt presses
Subj: Anthrop, humanities, Can lit & hist

KESTREL BOOKS — Antiquarian
144 E Broadway, V5T 1V9. Tel 604-872-2939
Estab 1985. 15,000 Titles. 20,000 Vols. 750 sq ft
Types: Used, facsimile editions, fine bnd, 1st ed, hb, illus bk, juvenile, ltd ed, old & rare, out of print, papbk, remainders
Subj: Natural hist

LAWRENCE BOOKS — Used
5579 Dunbar St, V6N 1W5. Tel 604-261-3812
Estab 1981. 30,000 Titles. 30,000 Vols. 1500 sq ft. Cat
Types: Hb, out of print, juvenile, fine bnd, 1st ed, illus bk, old & rare
Subj: Military, hist, lit

SHALOM BOOKS & GIFTS GALORE — Religious-J
3712 Oak St, V6H 2M3. Tel 604-734-1106
Estab 1979. 1000 Titles. 4000 Vols. 800 sq ft
Types: Juvenile, out of print, mass mkt papbk, Hebr lang, Yiddish lang

MICHAEL THOMPSON BOOKSELLER — Mail Order-Used
434 W Pender St, V6B 1T5. Tel 604-682-6885
Estab 1986. 20,000 Titles. 20,000 Vols. 1400 sq ft. Cat 2x ann
Types: Old & rare, out of print, fine bnd, 1st ed, illus bk, ltd ed, papbk
Subj: Mystery & detective, sci fiction & fantasy, horror

WEST COAST BOOKS LTD — Used
3209 W Broadway, V6K 2H5. Tel 604-732-6311
Mgr, Michael Price
Estab 1980. 15,000 Titles. 15,000 Vols
Types: Out of print, antiquarian
Subj: Art, humanities
See Also: Burnaby Books, Burnaby

VICTORIA — 62,551. Area code 604

THE HAUNTED BOOKSHOP — General
13-560 Johnson St, V8W 3C6. Tel 604-382-1427
Estab 1947. 20,000 Vols. Cat
Types: 1st ed, out of print, used
Subj: Biog, Can

ISLAND FANTASY COMIC SERVICE — Comics
29 Market Sq, 560 Johnson St, V8W 3C6. Tel 604-381-1134
Mgr, Pattie Whitehouse
Estab 1979. 2400 sq ft. Cat ann
Types: Hb, juvenile, imp UK, mass mkt papbk, high priced papbk, out of print, remainders, imp US & Eur
Subj: Comic bk related mat, movie mat, fantasy art & gaming

PICKWICK'S USED BOOKS — Used
1610 Island Hwy, V9B 1H8. Tel 604-474-2042
Estab 1982. 22,000 Titles. 35,000 Vols. 850 sq ft
Types: 1st ed, illus bk, juvenile, out of print, papbk, antiquarian
Subj: All subjects

RENAISSANCE BOOKS — Humanities
1016 A Fort St, V8V 3K4. Tel 604-381-6469
Estab 1980. 10,000 Vols
Types: Hb, papbk, out of print, used, 1st ed, illus bk, imp
Subj: Art

WEST VANCOUVER — 37,144. Area code 604

THE BOOKSTALL — General
1425 Clyde St, V7T 1E9. Tel 604-926-2425
Owner, West Vancouver Book Ltd; Mgr, David A Moon; Asst Mgr, Robert Carfrae
Estab 1960. 125,000 Vols. Cat
Types: Hb, papbk, out of print, out of print per
Subj: Can, natl geog, gov't reports

MANITOBA

GIMLI — 1659. Area code 204

SHELEMY'S BOOK NOOK — Used Paperback
38 Centre & Third Ave, R0C 1B0. Tel 204-642-8330
Estab 1981. 10,000 Titles. 270 sq ft
Types: Juvenile, out of print, papbk, new
Subj: Nonfiction, rel studies, auto, biol

WINNIPEG — 610,000. Area code 204

THE BOOKSHELF — Used
3042-B Portage Ave, R3K 0Y1. Tel 204-889-6270
Estab 1980. 30,000 Vols. 800 sq ft
Types: Juvenile, out of print, papbk
Subj: Fiction, nonfiction, class studies

BURTON LYSECKI BOOKS — Antiquarian
527 Osborne St, R3L 2B2. Tel 204-284-4546
Estab 1971. 30,000 Vols. 900 sq ft
Types: 1st ed, fine bnd, hb, illus bk, old & rare, out of print, papbk, used
Subj: Biog, Can

RED RIVER BOOKSHOP — General
93 King St, R3B 1T3. Tel 204-943-9788
Owner, Dennis Boyko
Estab 1974. 50,000 Vols. Cat
Types: 1st ed, new, old & rare, out of print
Subj: Art, Can, mystery & detective, comedy, sci fiction & fantasy, mystery

WINNIPEG, MANITOBA

ERNEST SHAPIRO -FINE BOOKS — Antiquarian
222-167 Lombard Ave, R3B 0T6. Tel 204-943-2116
Mgr, Zave J Shapiro
Estab 1984. 3500 Titles. 3500 Vols. 400 sq ft. Cat 2x ann
Types: Hb, 1st ed, old & rare, out of print, used
Subj: Adult educ, gerontology

NEW BRUNSWICK

SAINT ANDREWS — 1711. Area code 506

KATHLEEN & MICHAEL LAZARE — Antiquarian
59 Carleton St, E0G 2X0. Tel 506-529-3834
Estab 1980. 10,000 Vols
Types: 1st ed, hb, illus bk, juvenile, old & rare, out of print

NOVA SCOTIA

HALIFAX — 117,882. Area code 902

ATTIC OWL BOOKSHOP — Antiquarian
5802 South St, B3H 1S5. Tel 902-422-2433
Estab 1985. 10,000 Titles. 10,000 Vols. 500 sq ft
Types: For lang, hb, imp, juvenile, out of print, mass mkt papbk, high priced papbk, used, facsimile editions, 1st ed, illus bk, ltd ed
Subj: Can

BACK PAGES USED BOOKS — Used
1520 Queen, B3J 2H8. Tel 902-423-4750
Estab 1979. 13,000 Titles. 12,000 Vols. Cat ann
Types: Hb, out of print, papbk, old & rare
Subj: Can, local hist

NAUTICA BOOKSELLERS — Antiquarian-Nautical
1579 Dresden Row, B3J 2K4. Tel 902-429-2741
Estab 1975. 5500 Titles. 8000 Vols. Cat 3x ann
Types: Out of print, 1st ed, facsimile editions, fine bnd, hb, incunab, ltd ed
Subj: Exclusively nautical & maritime

SCHOONER BOOKS STORE LTD — Antiquarian
5378 Inglis St, B3H 1J5. Tel 902-423-8419
Estab 1975. 30,000 Vols. 1200 sq ft. Cat 2x ann
Types: Hb, out of print, old & rare
Subj: Can, Canadian Maritime Prov

WINDSOR — 3702. Area code 902

BETWEEN THE PAGES BOOK SHOPPE — General
Box 2618, B0N 2T0. Tel 902-798-8280
Mgr, Suzanne Pelham
Types: Hb, juvenile, out of print, papbk

WOLFVILLE — 3073. Area code 902

THOTH'S BOOKSHOPS LTD — Antiquarian
12 Gaspereau Ave (Mail add: Box 749, B0P 1X0). Tel 902-542-2640
Estab 1979. 10,000 Vols. Cat
Types: 1st ed, hb, juvenile, out of print, old & rare, papbk, univ presses, used
Subj: Can, metaphys & occult, philos, sci fiction & fantasy, theol

ONTARIO

AMHERSTBURG — 5836. Area code 519

PAST & PRESENT BOOKS — Antiquarian
169 Lowe's Side Rd, N9V 1S4. Tel 519-736-4126
Estab 1972. 8000 Titles. 8000 Vols. 900 sq ft. Cat 4x ann
Types: Juvenile, out of print, used, hb, illus bk, old & rare
Subj: Can, music, hist of 19th cent

BOLTON — Area code 416

GREAT NORTHWEST BOOK CO — Antiquarian
255 King St E, L7E 3J7. Tel 416-857-3010
Estab 1977. 20,000 Vols. 1000 sq ft. Cat
Types: 1st ed, hb, illus bk, new & used, out of print
Subj: Arctic, art, biog, Can, drama, ethnic studies, local hist, poetry, transp

BRAMPTON — 129,188. Area code 416

THE UNIVERSE BOOKSTORE — Metaphysics & Occult
Ten George St N, L6X 1R2. Tel 416-454-4523
Estab 1982. 4500 Titles. 2200 sq ft. Cat 5x ann
Types: Out of print, mass mkt papbk, high priced papbk, facsimile editions, hb, used
Subj: Astrol, mythology, health, philos, biblical studies, symbolism, Healing, ancient rel & wisdom

COBALT — 1777. Area code 705

HIGHWAY BOOK SHOP — General
11 Hwy S, P0J 1C0. Tel 705-679-8375. FAX 705-679-8511
Estab 1957. 100,000 Vols. 6000 sq ft
Types: Fr lang, hb, juvenile, out of print, papbk, used, new
Subj: Can

COMBERMERE — 214. Area code 613

MADONNA HOUSE BOOKSHOP — Antiquarian
K0J 1L0. Tel 613-756-3149
Mgr, Karen Van DeLoop
Estab 1975. 35,000 Vols. Cat 3-4x ann
Types: 1st ed, hb, out of print, used
Subj: Can, rel-c

DELHI — 14,931. Area code 519

IVIX BOOKS — Used
159 Queen St, N4B 2K4. Tel 519-582-1794
Estab 1987. 6000 Titles. 6000 Vols. 150 sq ft
Types: Hb, for lang, imp, juvenile, out of print, papbk, mass mkt papbk, high priced papbk, remainders, col text
Subj: Can, travel, exploration

DUNDAS — 19,266. Area code 416

JOHN C STIRLING GALLERY BOOKSHOP — Antiquarian-Art
212 Hatt St, L9H 2G8. Tel 416-627-5008
Estab 1981. 2200 Titles. 3000 Vols
Types: Remainders, for lang, used, out of print, 1st ed, Eng lang
Subj: Art, medicine, Can, re portrait miniature painting & painters

FORT ERIE — 23,808. Area code 416

WILLIAM MATTHEWS BOOKSELLER — Antiquarian-General
16 Jarvis St, L2A 2S1. Tel 416-871-7859
Estab 1976. 25,000 Titles. 25,000 Vols. 2500 sq ft. Cat 4x ann
Types: 1st ed, hb, ltd ed, old & rare, out of print, papbk, used
Subj: Sci fiction & fantasy

GEORGETOWN — 17,053. Area code 416

OXBOW BOOKS — General
102 Main St S, L7G 3E4. Tel 416-877-8861
7500 Vols
Types: New, out of print, old & rare
Subj: Biog, discovery & explor, geol, military, polit sci, travel, geography, mountaineering

GUELPH — 71,408. Area code 519

NOSTALGIA BOOKS — Mail Order-Antiquarian
PO Box 1442, N1H 6N9. Tel 519-821-9580
Estab 1979. 4000 Titles. 4000 Vols. Cat 2x ann
Types: 1st ed, hb, fine bnd, ltd ed, old & rare, out of print, used, illus bk
Subj: Can, art, antq, archit, printed ephemera

HAMILTON — 306,538. Area code 416

A G GIBSON BOOKS — Metaphysics & Occult
331 Main St W, L8L 4Y1. Tel 416-521-8976
Estab 1987. 1000 Titles. 300 sq ft
Types: Hb, out of print, papbk, high priced papbk, remainders, new, ltd ed, facsimile editions, fine bnd, 1st ed
Subj: Philos, new age, radial sci & medicine, hermetica, alchemy

HOLY ROSARY RELIGIOUS GOODS — Religious
245 King St E, L8N 1B6. Tel 416-528-4754
Types: Bibles, out of print, papbk, hb

JOHN RUSH BOOKS — Mail Order-Antiquarian
116 Eastbourne Ave, L8M 2M8. Tel 416-545-0661
Cat 12x ann
Types: 1st ed, hb, old & rare, out of print, used
Subj: Can

HANOVER — 5786. Area code 519

WILLIAMS BOOKSELLERS — General
211 10th St, N4N 1N8. Tel 519-364-3778
Estab 1987. 70,000 Titles. 1200 sq ft
Types: Hb, imp, juvenile, out of print, papbk, remainders, text bks, used, facsimile editions, fine bnd, 1st ed, illus bk, ltd ed, new

HIGHLAND CREEK — 1724. Area code 416

ALBION BOOK SHOP — General
376 Old Kingston Rd, M1C 1B6. Tel 416-284-4801
Estab 1978
Types: Col text, Fr lang, juvenile, out of print, imp UK, papbk, hb
Subj: Arts & crafts

KINGSTON — 61,088. Area code 613

THE BOOK BIN — General
225 Princess St, K7L 1B3. Tel 613-548-4871
Estab 1972. 50,000 Vols. Cat ann
Types: Hb, juvenile, out of print, papbk, used, 1st ed, old & rare
Subj: Military, travel, art

IDEA FACTORY — Used
370 Barrie, K7K 3T3. Tel 613-546-7056
Mgr, Rose E Deshaw
Estab 1979. 30,000 Titles. 30,000 Vols
Types: Out of print
Subj: Math, mystery & detective, philos, sci-tech

THE KINGSTON BOOK EXCHANGE — Paperback
12 Montreal St, K7L 3G6. Tel 613-544-5705
Estab 1982. 12,000 Titles. 18,000 Vols. 1200 sq ft
Types: For lang, juvenile, out of print, used

WAYFARER BOOKS — Used
85 Princess St, K7L 1A6. Tel 613-542-8615
Estab 1975. 40,000 Vols
Types: Fr lang, Ger lang, papbk, remainders, hb, out of print
Subj: Can, art, literary criticism, philos, biog, hist, Amer

KITCHENER — 136,091. Area code 519

C & E BOOKS — Antiquarian
Box 2744 Station B, N2H 6N3. Tel 519-745-8272
Estab 1980. 400 Titles. 10,000 Vols. Cat 6x ann
Types: Hb, old & rare, out of print, used, papbk
Subj: Can, local hist, genealogy

GAIL WILSON BOOKSELLER INC — Used
91 King St W, N2G 1A7. Tel 416-744-2166
Estab 1978. 25,000 Vols. 1200 sq ft
Types: Hb, out of print, old & rare, papbk
Subj: Agr, fashion, sci-tech, belles lettres, domestic econ

LOCUST HILL — 89. Area code 416

OLD FAVORITES BOOKSHOP LTD — Antiquarian-General
RR 1, Hwy 7, Green River, L0H 1J0. Tel 416-294-4298, 294-3865
Gen Mgr, Joy Saunders
Estab 1979. 10,000 Vols
Types: Hb, used, out of print

LONDON — 256,789. Area code 519

CITY LIGHTS BOOKSHOP — Used
356 Richmond St, N6A 3C3. Tel 519-679-8420
Estab 1972. 110,000 Vols. 4000 sq ft
Types: Fine bnd, 1st ed, hb, illus bk, ltd ed, juvenile, old & rare, out of print, papbk, Fr, Ger & Sp lang, imp Russ, imp UK, Dutch lang
Subj: Local hist

WOMANSLINE BOOKS — Feminism
711 Richmond St, N6A 3H1. Tel 519-679-3416
Estab 1986. 5500 Titles. 10,000 Vols
Types: Hb, juvenile, out of print, papbk
Subj: Hist, fiction, nonfiction, women's biog, gay & lesbian fiction

MANOTICK — 1410. Area code 613

SPORTSMAN'S CABINET — Antiquarian-Hunting & Fishing
Box 15, K0A 2N0. Tel 613-692-3618
Estab 1973. 5000 Vols. 1000 sq ft. Cat 4x ann
Types: 1st ed, hb, old & rare, out of print, used, illus bk, ltd ed, new, remainders
Subj: Hunting & fishing, dogs

MISSISSAUGA — 283,429. Area code 416

BOOK — Mail Order
PO Box 547, Streetsville, L5M 2C1
Estab 1976. 5000 Vols. Cat 4x ann
Types: Out of print, remainders, used
Subj: Sports, aircraft, maritime, ice hockey

MORRISBURG — 2301. Area code 613

OLD AUTHORS' FARM — Used
K0C 1X0. Tel 613-543-3337
Estab 1933. 35,000 Vols. Cat 4x ann
Types: Old & rare, out of print
Subj: Can, Amer

NIAGARA FALLS — 70,771. Area code 416

PAGE ONE BOOKS — General
4552 Queen St, L2E 2L5. Tel 416-354-9761
Mgr & Buyer, Marv Sommer
Estab 1964. 50,000 Titles. 100,000 Vols. 1200 sq ft. Cat 4x ann
Types: Remainders, used, imp, out of print, papbk, high priced papbk, mass mkt papbk, hb, 1st ed, ltd ed, old & rare
Subj: Sci fiction & fantasy, military, mystery & detective

NIAGARA ON THE LAKE — 12,307. Area code 416

D W GOUDY BOOKS — Mail Order-Used
8 Luther Ave (Mail add: PO Box 1650, L0S 1J0). Tel 416-468-7890
Estab 1982. 1800 Titles. 4000 Vols. Cat 5x ann
Types: Imp Fr, out of print, facsimile editions, fine bnd, 1st ed, hb, incunab, illus bk, juvenile, ltd ed, new, old & rare, used
Subj: Napoleon Bonaparte, French Revolution & War of 1812

NORTH BAY — 50,417. Area code 705

ALLISON THE BOOKMAN — Used
342 Main St E, P1B 1B4. Tel 705-476-1450
Mgr, Christine Cramer
Estab 1973. 94,000 Vols. 4000 sq ft
Types: Hb, juvenile, out of print, papbk
Subj: Can

NORTH YORK — 559,521. Area code 416

LARRY BECKER'S COLLECTIBLES WAREHOUSE — Antiquarian
438 Limestone Crescent (Mail add: PO Box 1011, M2K 2T6). Tel 416-661-3175. FAX 416-663-6727; Telex 06-218921
Owner, North Toronto Coins Ltd; Pres, Larry Becker
Estab 1965. 5000 Titles. 1600 Vols. 800 sq ft
Types: 1st ed, hb, incunab, juvenile, ltd ed, old & rare, out of print, papbk, used
Subj: Advertising, Can, military, transp, antq, local hist

OHSWEKEN — Area code 519

IROQRAFTS LTD, BOOK DEPT — American Indian Studies
RR 2, N0A 1M0. Tel 416-765-4206. FAX 416-765-4206
Estab 1959. 225 Titles. 18,531 Vols. 100 sq ft. Cat ann
Types: Hb, imp, out of print, papbk, remainders, used
Subj: Iroquois Indians

ORANGEVILLE — 13,034. Area code 519

SUMMIT BOOKS — Used
Mono Plaza, Hwy 10 N, L9W 2Z1. Tel 519-942-0498
Estab 1986. 10,000 Titles. 10,000 Vols. 750 sq ft
Types: Hb, out of print, papbk, high priced papbk, mass mkt papbk, 1st ed, new & used, text bks
Subj: Fiction, biog, rel, Can, psychol, polit sci, bus & mgt, hist

ORLEANS — Area code 613

BOOK HEAVEN — General
2297 St Joseph Blvd, K1C 1E7. Tel 613-830-3365
Estab 1986. 50,000 Titles. 70,000 Vols. 1800 sq ft
Types: Remainders, used, new, hb, imp, juvenile, out of print, papbk, mass mkt papbk, high priced papbk, books-on-tape
Subj: Fiction, mystery & detective, sci fiction & fantasy

OSHAWA — 115,197. Area code 416

MORGAN SELF LTD — Used
84 Simcoe St S, L1H 4G6. Tel 416-723-7621
Estab 1970. 175,000 Vols. 1700 sq ft. Cat
Types: Hb, out of print, papbk, remainders

OTTAWA — 303,070. Area code 613

MRS A L ASHTON — Mail Order-Antiquarian
49 Birch Ave, K1K 3G5. Tel 613-749-1741
10,000 Vols
Types: Fine bnd, 1st ed, hb, illus bk, juvenile, ltd ed, old & rare, out of print
Subj: Can, mod lit, nonfiction, poetry, pre 18th century exploration

BIBLIO SERVICES — Mail Order-Antiquarian
360 Frank St, Suite 104 (Mail add: Box 3327, Station D, K1P 6H8). Tel 613-235-8200
Mgr, A W Warkentin
Estab 1969. 10,000 Vols. 1200 sq ft
Types: Hb, out of print, remainders
Subj: Bus & mgt, bibliog, econ, transp

BOOK BAZAAR — Antiquarian
755 Bank St, K1S 3V3. Tel 613-233-4380
Estab 1974. 10,000 Vols
Types: Hb, juvenile, out of print, old & rare, papbk, used
Subj: Can, music, art

THE BOOKERY OF OTTAWA, LTD — Juvenile
541 Sussex Dr, K1N 6Z6. Tel 613-238-1428
Estab 1975. 1100 sq ft. Cat 2x ann
Types: Papbk, hb, out of print, used
Subj: Educ, parenting, Fr lang

DYMENT BOOKS-SCHOLARS' BOOKSTORE — Antiquarian-Philosophy
319 Wilbrod St, K1N 6M4. Tel 613-235-0565
Estab 1967. 25,000 Vols. Cat 6x ann
Types: Fine bnd, 1st ed, hb, juvenile, used, out of print, old & rare, papbk, col text
Subj: Philos, soc sci, political thought, academic

SHIRLEY LEISHMAN BOOKS LTD — General
Westgate Mall, Lower Concourse, Carling Ave, K1Z 5L7. Tel 613-722-8313, 8314
Mgr, Diane Walker; Asst Mgr Shelagh Cunnington
Estab 1961. 6000 sq ft
Types: Hb, juvenile, out of print, papbk, remainders
Subj: Can

PATRICK MCGAHERN - BOOKS, INC — Antiquarian
783 Bank St, K1S 3V5. Tel 613-233-2215
Estab 1969. 25,000 Vols. 1200 sq ft. Cat 6-8x ann
Types: Old & rare, out of print, used
Subj: Can, Irish hist & lit, travel, Arctic

THE OLD BOOK CELLAR — Antiquarian
238 Dalhousie, K1N 7E2. Tel 613-232-2121
Mgr, Lea Dunning
Estab 1982. 15,000 Titles. 15,000 Vols. 500 sq ft. Cat 4x ann
Types: 1st ed, hb, illus bk, old & rare, out of print, papbk, used
Subj: Art, hist, biog, Can

PARKHILL — 1375. Area code 519

ATTIC BOOKS — Antiquarian
206 Main St, N0M 2K0. Tel 519-294-6516
Mgr, Nancy Buckingham
Estab 1976. 20,000 Titles. 20,000 Vols. 2000 sq ft. Cat 4x ann
Types: Fine bnd, 1st ed, hb, illus bk, juvenile, ltd ed, old & rare, out of print, papbk, used
Subj: Can, medicine, illus, sci-tech, true crime, mod lit

PETERBOROUGH — 59,981. Area code 705

MARK JOKINEN BOOKS — Used
382 Water, K9H 3L6. Tel 705-742-4514
Estab 1988. 15,000 Titles. 15,000 Vols. 600 sq ft
Types: Hb, high priced papbk, col text, used, out of print
Subj: Can, literary criticism, sci fiction & fantasy, foreign authors in translation

PORT COLBORNE — 19,449. Area code 416

THE ALPHABET BOOKSHOP — Antiquarian
145 Main St W, L3K 3V3. Tel 416-534-5323
Estab 1977. 10,000 Vols. 3000 sq ft. Cat 6x ann
Types: 1st ed, hb, out of print
Subj: Can, fiction, poetry, Am & Brit lit, 19th & 20th cent; mod 1st ed

PORT HOPE — 9992. Area code 416

BLUESTONE HOUSE — General
21 Dorser St E, L1A 1E2
Mgr, Joan Rumgay
Types: Hb, remainders, imp, out of print, mag
Subj: Antq, cooking, gardening, home
See Also: Home & Garden Bookstore, Port Hope

ROCKTON — Area code 519

POMONA BOOK EXCHANGE — Antiquarian
Hwy 52, L0R 1X0. Tel 519-621-8897
Estab 1972. 4000 Vols. Cat 3x ann
Types: Facsimile editions, hb, illus bk, ltd ed, new, out of print, old & rare, remainders, used
Subj: Agr, botany, food, hort

SAINT CATHARINES — 123,956. Area code 416

HEADLEY HANNELORE OLD & FINE BOOKS — Antiquarian
71 Queen St, L2R 5G9. Tel 416-684-6145
Estab 1972. 30,000 Vols
Types: 1st ed, hb, illus bk, old & rare, out of print, used
Subj: Art, Can, local hist, military

STOUFFVILLE — Area code 416

JOHN LORD'S BOOKSLTD — General
29 Main E, PO Box 453, L4A 7Z7. Tel 416-640-3579
Estab 1974. 30,000 Titles. 40,000 Vols. Cat ann
Types: New & used, hb, papbk, juvenile, out of print, old & rare
Subj: Can, horses

THORNHILL — 1135. Area code 416

BEN ABRAHAM BOOKS — Antiquarian
97 Donnamora Crescent, L3T 4K6. Tel 416-886-0534
Mgr, Charles Taylor
Estab 1981. 5500 Vols. 1500 sq ft. Cat 4x ann
Types: Facsimile editions, fine bnd, 1st ed, hb, incunab, illus bk, imp, ltd ed, new, old & rare, out of print, papbk, remainders, used
Subj: Metaphys & occult, astrol, rel studies, Judaica, magic & conjuring, theosophy, Alchemy, Arthurian legend, Assyriology, Atlantis & Lemuria, William Blake & his circle, Celtic studies & Druidism, Aleister Crowley & Thelema, cult fiction, dark fantasy, occult fiction, demonology, satanism, Eastern religions & mysticism, Free Masonary & secret society, ghost, Gnosticism, Graecio-Roman mythology & mystery, Guredjess & his circle, herbs, healing, Kabbalah, palmistry, spiritualism, tarot, theosophy, witchcraft & paganism, psychial research
See Also: wholesale section

TORONTO — 642,449. Area code 416

ABOUT BOOKS — Antiquarian
280 Queen St W, M5V 2A1. Tel 416-593-0792
Estab 1957. 30,000 Vols. 1500 sq ft. Cat
Types: 1st ed, hb, imp, ltd ed, out of print, old & rare, papbk, remainders, used
Subj: Dogs, scholarly lit, mountaineering

ANNEX BOOKS — Used
1083 Bathurst, M5R 3G8. Tel 416-537-1852
Estab 1984. 14,000 Titles. 15,000 Vols. 1000 sq ft. Cat 3x ann
Types: Fr lang, hb, old & rare, juvenile, out of print, mass mkt papbk, used, 1st ed, ltd ed
Subj: Poetry, Can

ANN'S BOOKS & MOSTLY MYSTERIES — Antiquarian-Mystery & Detective
225 Carlton St, M5A 2L2. Tel 416-964-6470
Estab 1979. 30,000 Titles. 30,000 Vols. 5000 sq ft. Cat 4x ann
Types: Hb, imp, used, 1st ed, out of print
Subj: Cooking, hort, Can, anthrop, archaeol, folklore, literary criticism, mod lit, gardening, crime fiction, true crime, 19th century lit, Sherlockiana

ANOTHER MAN'S POISON — General
161 John St, M5T 1X3. Tel 416-593-6451
Estab 1983. 4000 Titles
Types: New, out of print, hb, papbk, juvenile
Subj: Design, antq, collectibles

BAKKA SCIENCE FICTION BOOKSTORE — Science Fiction & Fantasy
282 Queen St W, M5V 2A1. Tel 416-596-8161
Estab 1972. 1200 sq ft. Cat 4x ann
Types: Hb, imp, out of print, papbk, 1st ed, used

BATTA BOOKSTORE — Used
710 The Queensway, M8Y 1L3. Tel 416-259-2618
Estab 1965. 50,000 Vols. 2500 sq ft
Types: 1st ed, hb, out of print, papbk, remainders
Subj: Biog, Can, fiction, hist, mod lit, mystery & detective, travel

THE BOOK BARREL INC — General
2284 Bloor St W, M6S 1N9. Tel 416-767-7417
Estab 1973. 40,000 Vols. 800 sq ft
Types: Hb, imp, juvenile, papbk, out of print, remainders, imp Ger
Subj: Ger hist & lit, fiction, nonfiction

BROADWAY & HOLLYWOOD BOOKS — Used
PO Box 1277, Station F, M4Y 2V8. Tel 416-926-8992
Mgr & Buyer, S Stern
Estab 1985. 5000 Titles. 700 sq ft. Cat 6x ann
Types: Hb, imp UK, out of print, high priced papbk, remainders, 1st ed, new, imp USA
Subj: Stage & screen

CANADIANA HOUSE — Mail Order-Antiquarian
121 Admiral Rd (Mail add: PO Box 306, Postal Sta F, M4Y 2L7). Tel 416-924-6577
Estab 1961. 25,000 Vols. Cat 6-8x ann
Types: Fine bnd, 1st ed, hb, juvenile, ltd ed, old & rare, out of print, remainders, used
Subj: Arctic, Amer, Can, travels, voyages

EDWARDS BOOKS & ART — General
356 Queen St W, M5V 2A2. Tel 416-593-0126
Estab 1979. 30,000 Vols. 2000 sq ft
Types: Col text, hb, imp, juvenile, out of print, papbk, remainders, used
Subj: Art, photog

FRIENDS OF TERPSICHORE — Dance
396 Dundas St E (Mail add: Box 563 Postal Sta Q, M4T 2N4). Tel 416-960-5817
Estab 1981. 1000 Titles. 2500 Vols. Cat
Types: For lang, juvenile, out of print, papbk, used, facsimile editions, fine bnd, 1st ed, hb, illus bk, imp, ltd ed, new, old & rare, remainders
Subj: Performing arts, photog

HADJI & SHERLOCK BOOKS — Mail Order
1600 Bloor St W, M6P 1A7. WATS 416-534-6586
Estab 1970. 10,000 Vols. 1500 sq ft. Cat 4x ann
Types: 1st ed, hb, papbk, juvenile, ltd ed, old & rare, out of print, remainders, used, general
Subj: Sci fiction & fantasy, mystery & detective, folklore, supernatural lit, magic realism, surreal art

J L H LAW BOOKS LTD — Law
66 Isabella St, Suite 105, M4Y 1N3. Tel 416-926-0643
Mgr, Krista Chiu
Estab 1982. 4000 Titles. 15,000 Vols. 800 sq ft. Cat ann
Types: Fr lang, imp UK, imp Can, out of print, used, new, old & rare, hb, high priced papbk
Subj: Law, true crime
See Also: Delta, BC, wholesale section

J A MARTIN BOOKS — Antiquarian
55 Maitland St, Suite 1108 (Mail add: Box 1115, Station F, M4Y 2T8). Tel 416-967-9352
Estab 1983. Cat 4x ann
Types: Hb, old & rare, out of print, used
Subj: Hunting & fishing, mountain climbing

DAVID MASON BOOKS — Antiquarian
342 Queen St W, 2nd floor, M5V 2A2. Tel 416-598-1015
Estab 1968. 35,000 Vols. Cat 4x ann
Types: Fine bnd, 1st ed, hb, illus bk, incunab, juvenile, ltd ed, out of print, used
Subj: 19th century Am & Eng lit

DAVID MIRVISH BOOKS ON ART — Art
596 Markham St, M6G 2L8. Tel 416-531-9975
Mgr, Eleanor Johnston
Estab 1972. Cat
Types: Hb, imp, ltd ed, out of print, papbk, remainders
Subj: Archit, cats, photog, Can

OLD FAVORITES BOOKSHOP LTD — Antiquarian-General
250 Adelaide St W, M5H 1X8. Tel 416-977-2944
Estab 1954. 300,000 Vols. 10,000 sq ft. Cat 2x ann
Types: Fine bnd, 1st ed, hb, incunab, illus bk, juvenile, ltd ed, old & rare, out of print, papbk, used
Subj: Auto, aviation, Can, horses, fiction
See Also: Locust Hill

JOSEPH PATRICK BOOKS — Used
PO Box 100, Sta V, M6R 3A4. Tel 416-531-1891
Asst Mgr, Warren Wiles
Estab 1958. 20,000 Vols. 1500 sq ft. Cat 8x ann
Types: Facsimile editions, fine bnd, 1st ed, illus bk, ltd ed, old & rare, out of print, hb, juvenile, used
Subj: Arctic, Can, discovery & explor, rel, Catholica

STEVEN TEMPLE BOOKS — Antiquarian
483 Queen St W, M5V 2A9. Tel 416-865-9908
Asst Anne Larsson
Estab 1974. 15,000 Vols. Cat 2x ann
Types: 1st ed, hb, old & rare, out of print, used
Subj: Mod 1st ed

TEN EDITIONS BOOKS — Antiquarian
698 Spadina Ave, M6S 1N7. Tel 416-964-3803
Estab 1980. 800 sq ft. Cat 3x ann
Types: Out of print
Subj: Amer

VILLAGE BOOKSTORE — Antiquarian
239 Queen St W, M5V 1Z4. Tel 416-598-4097
Estab 1961. 20,000 Vols. 3000 sq ft
Types: Fine bnd, 1st ed, illus bk, ltd ed, out of print, old & rare, papbk, remainders, used
Subj: Antq, bks on bks, Can art

ARTHUR WHARTON BOOKS — Antiquarian-Science Fiction & Fantasy
652 Queen St W, M6J 1E5. Tel 416-865-9907
Estab 1979. 15,000 Vols. 1100 sq ft. Cat 5x ann
Types: 1st ed, old & rare, out of print
Subj: Philos, sci fiction & fantasy, soc sci, scholarly lit, hist of sci

WESTON — Area code 416

PETER L JACKSON - MILITARY BOOKS & PRINTS — Antiquarian
23 Castle Green Crescent, M9R 1N5. Tel 416-249-4796
Estab 1970. 3000 Vols. Cat 3x ann
Types: Hb, illus bk, old & rare, out of print, used, imp British & European
Subj: Military

PRINCE EDWARD ISLAND

CHARLOTTETOWN — 17,063. Area code 902

THE BOOK COLLECTOR — Antiquarian
118 Euston St, C1A 1W3. Tel 902-892-8338
Estab 1973. 14,000 Vols. 600 sq ft
Types: 1st ed, hb, juvenile, new & used, out of print, old & rare, papbk

QUEBEC

MAGOG — 13,300. Area code 819

STANLEY VAN ZUIDEN BOOKS — Mail Order-Antiquarian
795 Pine St, J1X 2J5. Tel 819-843-4529
Estab 1981. 10,000 Titles. 10,000 Vols
Types: Hb, illus bk, old & rare, out of print, used
Subj: Art, Can, Fr hist & lit

MONTREAL — 1,069,700. Area code 514

AEROPLANE BOOKS & RECORDS — Used
5900 Sherbrooke W, H4A 1X7. Tel 514-481-9398
Estab 1985. 9500 Titles. 10,000 Vols. 1200 sq ft
Types: Fr lang, hb, out of print, high priced papbk, remainders, imp UK
Subj: Philos, rel, music, fine arts, anthrop, psychol, hist, sci

CIRCUM BOOKS — General
1946 Catherine W St, H3H 1M4. Tel 514-933-9598
Mgr, Diane Blount
Estab 1986. 15,000 Titles. 20,000 Vols
Types: Hb, out of print, papbk, used, remainders
Subj: Philos, lit

CARON LIBRAIRE BOOKSELLER — General
251 Ste Catherine St E, H2X 1L5. Tel 514-845-5698
Estab 1969. 75,000 Titles. 200 Vols. 9000 sq ft
Types: Old & rare, used, Fr lang, out of print, imp Europe
Subj: Can

LIBRAIRIE DE SEVIGNE — General
200 Ouest Dorchester MH, H2Z 1X4. Tel 514-844-6655
Mgr & Buyer, Nathalie Ouellette
Estab 1984
Types: For lang, hb, imp Fr, juvenile, papbk, high priced papbk, mass mkt papbk, best sellers, facsimile editions, fine bnd, 1st ed, illus bk, ltd ed, new, out of print
Subj: Medicine

LIBRAIRIE ENCYCLOPEDIQUE — Antiquarian
1272 est rue Sainte-Catherine, H2L 2H2. Tel 514-521-2398
Estab 1970. 25,000 Vols. 800 sq ft. Cat 2x ann
Types: Out of print, old & rare
Subj: Can, Fr hist & lit

LIBRAIRIE KEBUK — Used
2048 Sainte Denis, H2X 3K7. Tel 514-842-6971
Estab 1978. 22,000 Vols. Cat 2x ann
Types: Hb, old & rare, out of print, papbk, used
Subj: Art, music, nature & environ, photog, Fr hist & lit, Eng, Fr, & Sp lang

LIBRAIRIE LAS AMERICAS INC — Spanish Lang
2075 Blvd St-Laurent, H2X 2T3. Tel 514-844-5994. FAX 514-284-2282
Estab 1968. 65,000,000 Titles. 200,000 Vols. 5000 sq ft. Cat ann
Types: Col & el-hi text, hb, imp Sp, juvenile, out of print, papbk, remainders, imp Cuba, dictionaries, encyclopedias, imp Latin Am, Sp text lang bks
Subj: Sp hist & lit, soc sci

RUSSELL BOOKS THE BOOK NOOK — Antiquarian
275 St Antoine Ouest, H2Z 1H5. Tel 514-866-0564
Mgr, John Russell
Estab 1961. 250,000 Vols. 10,000 sq ft
Types: Used, out of print, remainders
See Also: Ages Fine Books & Print, Westmount

S W WELCH BOOKSELLER — Used
5673 Sherbrooke W, H4A 1W6. Tel 514-488-5943
Estab 1983. 20,000 Titles. 20,000 Vols. 1000 sq ft
Types: Fine bnd, hb, illus bk, ltd ed, old & rare, out of print, papbk

THE WORD BOOKSTORE — Used
469 Milton St, H2X 1W3. Tel 514-845-5640
Estab 1975. 10,000 Vols. 600 sq ft
Types: Col text, out of print, remainders
Subj: Art, philos, scholarly lit

QUEBEC

QUEBEC — 177,082. Area code 418

JEAN GAGNON — Antiquarian
402-764, St Joseph St E (Mail add: PO Box 653 HV, G1R 4S2). Tel 418-523-6760
Estab 1955. Cat 10x ann
Types: Out of print, old & rare
Subj: Can

LIBRAIRIE DU FAUBOURG — French Lang
718 rue St Jean, G1R 1P9. Tel 418-529-8287
Estab 1978. 25,000 Titles. 28,000 Vols. 1200 sq ft
Types: Used, facsimile editions, fine bnd, 1st ed, hb, incunab, illus bk, ltd ed, old & rare, out of print, papbk
Subj: Rel-c, theol, philos, Fr hist & lit, hagiography

MICHEL VILLENEUVE LIBRAIREENR — Antiquarian
1138, 3e Ave, G1L 2X6. Tel 418-648-6148
Mgr, Michel Villeneuve
Estab 1982. 10,000 Titles. 20,000 Vols. 1000 sq ft. Cat 3-5x ann
Types: 1st ed, ltd ed, old & rare, out of print
Subj: Can hist

SAINT BRUNO — 2299. Area code 514

LIBRA BOOKSTORE — Used Paperback
Saint Bruno S/Ctr, 67 Seigneuriale, J3V 2G9. Tel 514-653-1652
Estab 1976. 30,000 Titles. 50,000 Vols. 1200 sq ft
Types: Fr lang, hb, imp Fr, imp UK, juvenile, out of print, remainders
Subj: Fiction

PHILIP LOZINSKI CANADIAN BRANCH REG'D — Mail Order-Antiquarian
1175 rue Wolfe, J3V 3K7. Tel 514-653-8890
Estab 1964. 4000 Titles. 17,000 Vols. 1800 sq ft. CatBuys indep
Types: Out of print, old & rare, used
Subj: Can, for lang, Slavic lang

WESTMOUNT — 21,006. Area code 514

AGES FINE BOOKS & PRINT — Antiquarian
360 Victoria, Suite 303, H3Z 2N4. Tel 514-487-2828
Estab 1986. 5000 Titles. 5000 Vols
Types: Remainders, out of print, 1st ed, hb, incunab, illus bk, juvenile, ltd ed, new, old & rare

SASKATCHEWAN

ARELEE — 60. Area code 306

RENALDO'S SUPPLY — Trades
PO Box 64, S0K 0H0. Tel 306-237-9585
Buyer, Valerie Dawson
Estab 1972. 1000 Vols. 400 sq ft
Types: Out of print, hb
Subj: Woodworking

REGINA — 149,593. Area code 306

RICHARD SPAFFORD BOOKSELLER — Antiquarian-General
3036 13th Ave, S4T 1N9. Tel 306-757-0844
Estab 1969. 20,000 Vols. 1600 sq ft. Cat
Types: Out of print, used
Subj: Can, econ, polit sci

SASKATOON — 133,750. Area code 306

EIGHTH STREET BOOKS — Antiquarian
1010 Eighth St E, S7H 0R9. Tel 306-343-6624
Mgr, Dave Muttart
Estab 1983. 75,000 Titles. 123,000 Vols. 1500 sq ft
Types: 1st ed, hb, illus bk, ltd ed, new & used, out of print, papbk, remainders, small presses
Subj: Western Canadiana

NORTHLAND BOOKS — Antiquarian
813 Broadway Ave, S7N 1B5. Tel 306-242-9466
Estab 1968. 30,000 Vols. 4000 sq ft. Cat 1-2x ann
Types: 1st ed, hb, illus bk, juvenile, ltd ed, old & rare, out of print, used
Subj: Biog, Can, fiction, local hist, reference, soc sci, natural sci, Western & Northern Canada

O.P-O.S.I. WHOLESALERS

CALIFORNIA

BEVERLY HILLS — 32,367. Area code 213

ERIC CHAIM KLINE BOOKSELLER
2221 Benedict Canyon Dr, 90210. Tel 213-395-4745
Estab 1985
Imp & exp
Types: Out of print
Subj: Judaica

ELKGROVE — 17,327. Area code 916

SHUEY BOOK SEARCH
8886 Sharkey Ave, 95624. Tel 916-685-3044
Estab 1978
Cat ann. Imp & exp
Types: Hb, out of print
Subj: Nonfiction, Sp & Latin Am lit

ENCINO — Area code 818

TROPHY ROOM BOOKS, BIG GAME HUNTING BOOKS
PO Box 3041, 91301. Tel 818-889-2469
Estab 1976
Cat 3-4x ann
Types: Ltd ed, out of print, old & rare, used, color plate bks
Subj: Africa, Asia & N Amer Big game exploration, hunting & studies, Central Asia travel & exploration, Richard Burton 1st ed

FREMONT — 131,945. Area code 415

CAL WILSON FINE NUMISMATIC LITERATURE
4501 Eggers Dr, Suite C, 94536. Tel 415-792-4133
Estab 1981
Cat 4x ann. Imp & exp
Types: Out of print, antiquarian numismatic books, catalogues & periodicals
Subj: Numismatics

MORONGO VALLEY —Area code 619

SAGEBRUSH PRESS
PO Box 87, 92256. Tel 619-363-7398
Cat 1-2x ann. Exp on order only
Types: Hb, out of print, used, 1st ed, ltd ed, old & rare, high priced papbk
Subj: Nonfiction, Western Amer

OAKLAND — 339,288. Area code 415

GULL BOOK SHOP
1547 San Pablo Ave, 94612. Tel 415-836-9141
Estab 1962
Cat
Types: 1st ed, hb, illus bk, ltd ed, old & rare, out of print, papbk, used
Subj: Fiction, photog, juv

SAN BERNARDINO — 118,057. Area code 714

THE UNICORN BOOK SHOP
393 W Athol, Unit 4, 92401. Tel 714-885-4905
Mgr, Curt Norman
Estab 1972
Types: Used, out of print, hb, illus bk, ltd ed, old & rare

SAN FRANCISCO — 678,974. Area code 415

LIBERTY TREE NETWORK
350 Sansome St, 94104. Tel 415-981-1326
Estab 1986
Cat 3x ann. Imp & exp
Types: Hb, mass mkt papbk only, juvenile, remainders, out of print, imp UK
Subj: Hist, philos, polit sci, econ, educ, self-develop, bus & mgt, political thought, pub relations, self defense, freedom US govt, personal investment
See Also: retail section, Gilroy

SAN LUIS OBISPO — 34,252. Area code 805

SQUARE DEAL RECORDS BOOK DEPT
50 Prado Rd, 93401-1002. Tel 805-543-3636
Estab 1971
Cat 2x ann. Exp & imp
Types: Remainders, out of print, spec priced imp
Subj: Music

CONNECTICUT

STRATFORD — 50,541. Area code 203

SPECIALIZED BOOK SERVICE INC
1418 Barnum Ave, 06497-5403. Tel 203-377-6510. TWX 510-601-5355. FAX: 203-377-6510
Field reps 3
Estab 1956
Cat. Imp & exp
Types: Hb, out of print, mass mkt papbk, text bks
Subj: Computer sci, engineering, chem, tech, research

FLORIDA

BONITA SPRINGS — 1932. Area code 813

JEAN COHEN BOOKS
PO Box 654, 33959. Tel 813-992-1262
Estab 1968
Cat 25x ann
Types: Hb, out of print, used

SARASOTA — 48,868. Area code 813

CHRISTINE PEGRAM BOOKS
4391 Pasadena Circle, 34233. Tel 813-921-2467
Estab 1984
Types: 1st ed, hb, illus bk, out of print, remainders, used
Subj: Arctic, Floridiana, nonfiction, Marilyn Monroe

WESTVILLE —343. Area code 904

ALEC R ALLENSON INC
PO Box 447, 32464
Pres, Robert D Allenson
Estab 1924.
Cat
Types: Old & rare, out of print
Subj: Rel, philos, hist, bibliog

HAWAII

KAILUA KONA — 3365. Area code 808

CONCORD BOOKS
PO Box 3380, 96740. Tel 808-326-2514
Mgr & Buyer, Evelyn Davis. Field reps 1
Estab 1972.
Cat 3x ann. Exp
Types: Hb, out of print, mass mkt papbk, new & used
Subj: Econ, hist, how-to, survival, educ, polit sci

INDIANA

GARY — 151,953. Area code 219

FRIENDLY FRANK'S DISTRIBUTION, INC
3990 Broadway, 46408. Tel 219-884-5052
Pres & Gen Mgr, Frank W Mangiaracina
Types: New & used, out of print, imp UK, comics

IOWA

MARION — 19,474. Area code 319

O G WAFFLE BOOK CO
897 13th St, 52302. Tel 319-373-1832
Field reps 1
Estab 1883
Types: Hb, illus bk, out of print, new & used, mass mkt papbk, high priced papbk
Subj: Juvenile

MAINE

POLAND SPRING — Area code 207

UNITED SOCIETY OF SHAKERS
RR 1, Box 640, 04274. Tel 207-926-4391
Mgr & Buyer, David Richards
Estab 1783
Cat 3x ann
Types: Hb, juvenile, out of print, papbk, remainders
Subj: Arts & crafts, nature & environ, country ways & rural life, Shaker culture & hist, NE Am hist
See Also: Retail section

MARYLAND

GERMANTOWN — Area code 301

LIBRARY SYSTEMS & SERVICES INC BOOKSTORE
20251 Century Blvd, 20874-1162. Tel 301-428-3400
Mgr, Judy Pezzanite; Merch Mgr, Sally Shipp. Field reps 3
Estab 1981
Imp & exp
Types: Hb, high priced papbk, mag & newspr, mass mkt papbk, out of print

WESTMINSTER — 8804. Area code 301

CHRISTIAN CLASSICS INC
PO Box 30, 21157. Tel 301-848-3065. WATS 800-888-3065
Dir, John J McHale
Estab 1966
Cat 2x ann. Imp & exp
Types: Hb, imp, new & used, out of print, papbk
Subj: Rel-c

NEW HAMPSHIRE

NORTHFIELD — area code 603

YANKEE PAPERBACK
38 Summer St, 03276. Tel 603-286-4840
Estab 1983
Types: Col & el-hi text, hb, high priced papbk, mass mkt papbk, new & used, out of print, children's, el-hi-col wkbks
Subj: Sci-tech

NEW JERSEY

BLACKWOOD — Area code 609

BLACKWELL NORTH AMERICA INC
1001 Fries Mill Rd, 08012. Tel 609-629-0700. Telex 83-1663
VPres Eastern Operations, Bob Sochurek; Mgr, Don Federico
Estab 1975
Types: Hb, papbk, out of print

FAIRVIEW — 10,519. Area code 201

JUNIUS BOOK DISTRIBUTORS INC
PO Box 85, 07022. Tel 201-868-7725
Estab 1975
Cat 4x ann. Imp
Types: Facsimile editions, fine bnd, 1st ed, hb, old & rare, out of print, remainders, used, reference
Subj: Medicine, scholarly lit, sociol

NEW YORK

BROOKLYN — 2,230,936. Area code 718

CITY WIDE BOOK & PREMIUM CO
159 Manhattan Ave (Mail add: Box 211 WMBG Sta, 11211-0211). Tel 718-388-0037
Estab 1936
Cat 2x ann. Exp
Types: For lang, hb, imp, out of print, mass mkt papbk, remainders, used
Subj: Biol, hist, juv

NEW YORK

ITHACA — 28,732. Area code 607

THE BOOKERY
Dewitt Bldg, 14850. Tel 607-273-5055. Telex 32-3960
Mgr, Jack Goldman
Estab 1975
Cat 2x ann. Imp
Types: For lang, new & used, out of print, old & rare, remainders
Subj: Archit, Eng hist & lit, Fr, Ger & Sp lang, linguistics, philos, New Yorkiana, sci-tech, Cornelliana

NEW YORK — 7,071,030. Area code 212

RUSSICA BOOK & ART SHOP INC
799 Broadway, 10003. Tel 212-473-7480. FAX 212-473-7480
Mgr, David A Daskal; Merch Mgr, Irina Kuharets
Estab 1976
Cat 8x ann. Imp & exp
Types: Col & el-hi text, hb, imp Fr, out of print, papbk, remainders, Russ lang, used
Subj: Russ lang, juvenile

POUGHKEEPSIE — 29,757. Area code 914

APOLLO BOOK
Five School House Lane, 12603-4907. Tel 914-462-0040. WATS 800-431-5003. NY WATS 800-942-8222
Field reps 1
Estab 1977
Cat ann. Imp & exp
Types: Hb, high priced papbk, fine bnd, out of print
Subj: Art, antq, reference, movies, dance, drama, archit, gardening, last-copy art bks

NORTH CAROLINA

ASHEVILLE — 53,281. Area code 704

THE BOOK MART
7 Billmore Plaza, Box 5094, 28803-5094. Tel 704-274-2241
Estab 1947
Types: Hb, juvenile, out of print, old & rare
Subj: Appalachia, North Carolinana, rel-p, South Carolinana
See Also: Retail section

WINSTON-SALEM — 131,885. Area code 919

LARRY LASTER OLD & RARE BOOKS & PRINTS
2416 Maplewood Ave, 27103. Tel 919-724-7544
Estab 1985
Imp only
Types: Used, out of print, fine bnd, 1st ed, hb, incunab, illus bk, imp, old & rare

OREGON

LAKE OSWEGO — 22,868. Area code 503

BLACKWELL NORTH AMERICA
6024 SW Jean Rd, Bldg G, 97035. Tel 503-684-1140. Telex 15-1234
Owner, B H Blackwell Ltd & Blackwell Scientific Publ; Pres, Charles Marshall; Dir Publ Relations, Oliver Sitea; Chmn, Per Saugman; VPres Western Opers, Bob Sochurek. Field reps 15
Estab 1975
Cat. Imp & exp
Types: Hb, papbk, out of print
See Also: Blackwood, NJ

PENNSYLVANIA

SAYRE — 6951. Area code 717

VALLEY BOOKS
111 S Elmer Ave, 18840. Tel 717-888-9785
Estab 1979
Types: Illus bk, juvenile, ltd ed, out of print, used
Subj: Archit, photog, illust

VIRGINIA

ALEXANDRIA — 103,217. Area code 703

SAMUEL YUDKIN & ASSOCIATES
2109 Popkin's Lane, 22307. Tel 703-768-1858
Estab 1970
Cat 6x ann
Types: 1st ed, hb, juvenile, new & used, out of print, papbk, old & rare, remainders

WEST VIRGINIA

MARTINSBURG — 13,063. Area code 304

JOHN JUSTICE BOOK WHOLESALERS
110 Exchange Pl, 25401. Tel 304-263-3399
Field reps 2
Estab 1978
Cat 5x ann
Types: Facsimile editions, 1st ed, hb, illus bk, imp, ltd ed, new, out of print, remainders
Subj: Amer, aviation, Civil War, military, nautical

WISCONSIN

BUTLER — 2059. Area code 414

CLERGY BOOK SERVICE
12855 W Silver Spring Dr, 53007. Tel 414-781-1234. WATS 800-558-0580
Owner, Priests of the Sacred Heart; Mgr, John Timmerman
Estab 1968
Cat ann. Imp
Types: Col & el-hi text, hb, papbk, out of print
Subj: Rel-c,p

ONTARIO

THORNHILL — 1135. Area code 416

BEN ABRAHAM BOOKS*
97 Donnamora Cres, L3T 4K6. Tel 416-886-0534
Mgr, Charles Taylor
Estab 1981
Cat 4 x ann
Types: Facsimile editions, fine bnd, 1st ed, hb, incunab, illus bk, imp, ltd ed, new, out of print, papbk, remainders, used
Subj: Metaphysics, astrol, rel studies, Judaica, magic & conjuring, theosophy
See Also: Retail section

WHOLESALE REMAINDER DEALERS

Adler, Marion F., Out of Print Children's Bks., Box 744, Stockbridge, MA 01262 (SAN 680-4586) Tel 413-298-3559. Free worldwide search for out-of-print children's books, if not in stock. Personal service, no obligation. Open by appointment for buying, selling or browsing.

American Media Corp., 219 N. Milwaukee St., Milwaukee, WI 53202 (SAN 695-698X) Tel 414-272-3355. Specializes in juveniles.

Antiquarian Bk. Fair, Old Service Village, Old Sturbridge, MA 01566 (SAN 682-1065).

Atlanta News Agency, Inc. *See* **Smith, W. H., Pubs., Inc.**

BDD Promotional Bk. Co., Inc., Div. of Bantam, Doubleday, Dell Publishing Group, Inc., *(BDD Promo Bk; 0-7924),* 666 Fifth Ave., 21st Flr., New York, NY 10103 (SAN 251-0650) Tel 212-492-9621; Toll free: 800-223-6834; Orders to: 1905 S. Mt. Prospect at Howard St., Des Plaines, IL 60018 (SAN 251-2874).

Baker & Taylor Bks., A Grace Distribution Co., Div. of W. R. Grace, *(0-8480),* Corporate Hdqtrs., 652 E. Main St., Bridgewater, NJ 08807 (SAN 169-5606) Tel 201-218-0400; Toll free: 800-526-3811; 800-526-3825; 800-435-5111; 800-241-6004; 800-648-3540; 800-892-1892 (in Illinois); 800-282-6854 (in Georgia); 800-524-2486 (in Canada); Eastern Div., 50 Kirby Ave., Somerville, NJ 08876-0734 (SAN 169-4901) Tel 201-722-8000; Midwestern Div., 501 S. Gladiolus St., Momence, IL 60954-2444 (SAN 169-2100) Tel 815-472-2444; Southern Div., Mt. Olive Rd., Commerce, GA 30599-9988 (SAN 169-1503) Tel 404-335-5000; Western Div., 380 Edison Way, Reno, NV 89564 (SAN 169-4464) Tel 702-786-6700.

Barbour & Co., Inc., Affil. of Book Bargains, Inc., *(Barbour & Co; 0-916441; 1-55748),* 164 Mill St., P.O. Box 1219, Westwood, NJ 07675 (SAN 295-7094) Tel 201-664-0577; Toll free: 800-221-2648; Dist. by: Spring Arbor Distributors, 10885 Textile Rd., Belleville, MI 48111 (SAN 158-9016) Tel 313-481-0900; Toll free: 800-521-3690; Dist. by: Ingram Bk. Co., 1125 Heilquaker Blvd., La Vergne, TN 37086 (SAN 169-7978) Tel 615-793-5000; Toll free: 800-251-5902; 800-251-5900 (orders only); Dist. by: Baker & Taylor Bks., Eastern Div., 50 Kirby Ave., Somerville, NJ 08876 (SAN 169-4901) Tel 201-722-8000; Toll free: 800-435-1845; 800-352-4833 (in New Jersey); Dist. by: Riverside/World, 1500 Riverside Dr., P.O. Box 370, Iowa Falls, IA 50126 (SAN 169-2666) Tel 515-648-4269; Toll free: 800-247-5111; Dist. by: Living Bks., Inc., 12155 Magnolia Ave., Bldg. 11-B, Riverside, CA 92503 (SAN 169-006X) Tel 714-354-7330; Toll free: 800-854-4746; 800-922-0047 (in California); Dist. by: Cicero Bible Pr., 1901 Airport Rd., Harrison, AR 72601 (SAN 170-3692) Tel 501-741-3400; Toll free: 800-643-9780.

Barnett Bks., 150 N. Plains Industrial Rd., Wallingford, CT 06492 Tel 203-288-5715.

Beekman Pubs., Inc., *(Beekman Pubs; 0-8464),* P.O. Box 888, Woodstock, NY 12498 (SAN 170-1622) Tel 914-679-2300.

Book Essentials, Inc., *(Book Essentials; 0-933895),* 151 E. 31st St., Suite 10J, New York, NY 10016 (SAN 692-7122) Tel 212-951-4813.

Book Sales, Inc., *(Bk Sales Inc; 0-89009; 1-55521),* 110 Enterprise Ave., Secaucus, NJ 07094-1995 (SAN 169-488X) Tel 201-864-6341; Toll free: 800-526-7257; 276 Fifth Ave., New York, NY 10001.

Booksmith Promotional Co., 432 Park Ave., S., New York, NY 10016 (SAN 169-5681) Tel 718-782-0405; 100 Paterson Plank Rd., Jersey City, NJ 07307 (SAN 664-5364) Tel 201-659-2768. Remainders & promotional assortments to trade & institutional markets. Specializes in art, juveniles, quality paperbacks, textbooks, psychology & general nonfiction titles.

Buckley-Little Bk. Catalogue Co., Inc., *(Buckley-Little; 0-916667),* P.O. Box 1062, Lenox Hill Sta., New York, NY 10021 (SAN 297-0104); Toll free: 800-223-8323.

Camex, Inc., *(Camex; 0-932565),* 535 Fifth Ave., New York, NY 10017 (SAN 687-4746) Tel 212-682-8400.

Chamalian, P.O. Box 387, Crompond, NY 10517 (SAN 682-1022). Offers information on approximately 100,000 out-of-print novels. Fast service from stock.

Chicago Bk. Mart, P.O. Box 595Y, Batavia, IL 60510 (SAN 682-1014). Free search service.

Cuson News Agency, 1118 Union St., Monroe, MI 48161 (SAN 169-3913) Tel 313-242-2319.

Daedalus Bks., 4601 Decatur St., Hyattsville, MD 20781 (SAN 158-9202) Tel 301-779-4102. Trade & scholarly remainders.

Donan Bks., Inc., 220 E. 82nd St., New York, NY 10028 (SAN 680-4527) Tel 212-734-0707. Large stock of out-of-print titles. Free search service worldwide.

Faro Hse., Ltd., 26 E. 33rd St., New York, NY 10016 (SAN 246-3148) Tel 212-684-3872; Orders to: P.O. Box 215, WVS, Binghamton, NY 13905 Tel 607-729-3988.

Galahad Bks., Div. of LDAP, Inc., *(0-88365),* 166 Fifth Ave., New York, NY 10010 (SAN 169-5762) Tel 212-691-4688.

Gordon's Bks., Inc., 2323 Delgany St., Denver, CO 80216 (SAN 169-0531) Tel 303-296-1830; Toll free: 800-525-6979 (west of the Mississippi).

H. F. Sales, Inc., 8136 Miramar Rd., San Diego, CA 92126 Tel 619-566-0222.

Horizon Bk. Promotions, Inc., 230 Fifth Ave., Suite 1907, New York, NY 10001 (SAN 107-7198) Tel 212-696-9171. Remainder dealer.

International Service Co., 333 Fourth Ave., Indialantic, FL 32903 (SAN 169-5134).

Karr, Jean, & Co., 10116 Crestbury Pl., Bethesda, MD 20817 (SAN 169-0922) Tel 202-529-6789. Specialize in juvenile titles.

LBC Bks., Box 4991, 185 Main St., Holyoke, MA 01040 (SAN 246-3121) Tel 413-532-7862.

Landmark Bk. Co., *(Landmark NY; 0-929194),* 260 Fifth Ave., New York, NY 10001 (SAN 169-5843) Tel 212-696-5430.

Leighton Bks., P.O. Box 16347, Baltimore, MD 21210 (SAN 680-4667). Mail order sales of out-of-print hard cover detective, espionage, & suspense books. Will try to locate specific titles, but not an organized search service.

Lescron Enterprises, P.O. Box B, Johnson City, NY 13790 (SAN 169-538X); Toll free: 800-847-1669. All types of remainders & promotionals; cloth & paper, adult fiction & non-fiction, juvenile, mass market paper, quality trade paper, scholarly, art, educational, cookbooks & reference books.

Lewis, Stanley, & Assocs., 35 W. 92nd St., New York, NY 10025 (SAN 135-020X) Tel 212-932-3134.

Little Dania's Juvenile Promotions, Div. of Booksmith Promotional Co., *(Little Danias)*, 149 Madison Ave., New York, NY 10016 (SAN 169-5681) Tel 201-659-2768. Juvenile remainders & promotional assortments.

Love, Abel, Inc., P.O. Box 2250, Newport News, VA 23602 (SAN 158-4081) Tel 804-877-2939.

Marboro Bks., *(Marboro Bks; 0-88029)*, 1 Pond Rd., Rockleigh, NJ 07647 (SAN 150-8059) Tel 201-767-6660. Publishers' remainders (primarily hardcover) & hardcover reprints to trade, institutional & foreign markets. Specialize in art, biography, history, literature & quality fiction.

Merchandise Dynamics, Inc., *(Merchandise Dyn)*, 184 Fifth Ave., New York, NY 10010 (SAN 287-668X); Toll free: 800-221-1928. Trade, general, children's books & textbooks; cloth, paper & mass market paperbacks.

Michelli, Frank, Bks., 45 Halsey St., Newark, NJ 07102 (SAN 695-7889) Tel 201-623-4289. Search service. General stock of 20,000 books, mostly out-of-print.

Military Bookman, The, 29 E. 93rd St., New York, NY 10128 (SAN 680-4543) Tel 212-348-1280. Military, naval, & aviation history books. Subscription catalogue three times yearly, lists over 2500 titles. Select war arts.

Milligan News Co., Inc., 150 N. Autumn St., San Jose, CA 95110 (SAN 169-0272) Tel 408-286-7604.

Moneysworth Bks., Subs. of Avant-Garde Media Inc., *(Moneysworth Bks)*, 555 W. 57th St., New York, NY 10019 (SAN 287-6698) Tel 212-581-2000. One million nonfiction books in stock.

Motorbooks International, Pubs. & Wholesalers, Inc., *(Motorbooks Intl; 0-87938)*, 729 Prospect Ave., Osceola, WI 54020 (SAN 169-9164) Tel 715-294-3345; Toll free: 800-458-0454 (except in Wisconsin & Alaska); Orders to: Box 2, Osceola, WI 54020 (SAN 699-5462).

National Learning Corp., *(Natl Learning; 0-8373; 0-8293)*, 212 Michael Dr., Syosset, NY 11791 (SAN 206-8869) Tel 516-921-8888; Toll free: 800-645-6337. Educational, commercial, industrial & government sales.

Northwoods Bks., P.O. Box 23435, Santa Barbara, CA 93121 (SAN 695-6882) Tel 805-962-2812. Mail order dealer. Issues a quarterly catalogue. Deals in antiquarian and out-of-print children's and illustrated books.

Out-of-State Bk. Service, P.O. Box 3253D, San Clemente, CA 92672 (SAN 680-4616) Tel 714-492-2976. National & international search service for out-of-print books. No obligation. General stock of out-of-print books.

Outlet Bk. Co., Affil. of Crowns Pubs., Inc., *(Outlet Bk Co; 0-87000)*, 225 Park Ave., S., New York, NY 10003 (SAN 200-2620) Tel 212-254-1600; Toll free: 800-526-4264; 800-726-0600 (customer service); Orders to: Random House, Inc., 400 Hahn Rd., Westminster, MD 21157 (SAN 202-5507) Tel 301-848-1900; Toll free: 800-733-3000. Promotional books of all kinds; remainders, reprints, imports, original publications.

Past History Rare & Old Bks., 136 Parkview Terr., Lincroft, NJ 07738 (SAN 680-456X) Tel 201-842-4545. Large stock of rare and old books. Specializing in general Americana with special emphasis on New Jersey. Free search.

Peninsula Booksearch, P.O. Box 1305, Burlingame, CA 94011-1305 (SAN 695-6874). Offers free out-of-print book search. Satisfaction is guaranteed for all books purchased. Full refund on returns (any reason) within 10 days of receipt. Payment methods: check, money order, Visa, Mastercard. In business since 1978.

Pop-M Co., 65 Richard Rd., Ivyland, PA 18974 (SAN 106-7788) Tel 215-674-5410.

Princeton Antiques Bookshop, 2915-17 Atlantic Ave., Atlantic City, NJ 08401 (SAN 280-1876) Tel 609-344-1943. Out of print stock of 200,000 different hardback titles, indexed by author, title, & subject. Full-time staff searches worldwide for individual titles, authors, or subjects.

Probook, Div. of KBP Co., Inc., Box 1722, Paramus, NJ 07653 (SAN 246-3105) Tel 201-664-9652.

Publishers Marketing Enterprises, Inc., *(Pubs Marketing)*, 386 Park Ave., S., Suite 500, New York, NY 10016 (SAN 159-141X) Tel 212-686-8000; Toll free: 800-462-2665.

Quality Bks., Inc., *(Quality Bks IL; 0-89196)*, 918 Sherwood Dr., Lake Bluff, IL 60044-2204 (SAN 169-2127) Tel 312-295-2010; Toll free: 800-323-4241 (Libraries Only).

Reliable Bk. Service, P.O. Box 2033, Paterson, NJ 07509 (SAN 680-4608) Tel 201-791-7018. If titles cannot be supplied from comprehensive stock, free search service is available for fiction, history, military, biography, cinema, theatre, classical and scholarly books, published from 1880 to 1983. Established 1935.

S & L Sales Co., P.O. Box 2067, Industrial Blvd., Waycross, GA 31502 (SAN 107-413X) Tel 912-283-0210; Toll free: 800-243-3699 (orders only).

School Aid Co., *(Sch Aid; 0-87385)*, 911 Colfax Dr., P.O. Box 123, Danville, IL 61832 (SAN 158-3719) Tel 217-442-6855; Toll free: 800-447-2665.

Seven Hills Bks. *See* **Seven Hills Bk. Distributors**

Seven Hills Bk. Distributors, Div. of Books for the Decorative Arts, Inc., *(Seven Hills Bk Dists; 0-911403)*, 49 Central Ave., Cincinnati, OH 45202 (SAN 169-6629) Tel 513-381-3881; Toll free: 800-545-2005.

Sharpe, John K., Inc., *(J K Sharpe Inc)*, Box 442, Wilmette, IL 60091 (SAN 276-9395) Tel 312-295-1024.

Silver, Robert, Assocs., *(R Silver; 0-937414)*, 307 E. 37th St., New York, NY 10016 (SAN 241-5801) Tel 212-686-5630.

Smith, W. H., Pubs., Inc., Subs. of W. H. Smith & Son, Ltd., *(Smith Pubs; 0-8317)*, 112 Madison Ave., New York, NY 10016 (SAN 216-3241) Tel 212-532-6600; Toll free: 800-932-0070 (in New Jersey); 800-645-9990 (in New York); 80 Distribution Blvd., Edison, NJ 08817 (SAN 658-1625) Tel 201-287-3550; Wholesale Offices: 4070 Shirley Dr., SW, Atlanta, GA 30336 (SAN 169-1384) Tel 404-691-2800; 12 Interchange Dr., Savannah, GA 31402 (SAN 169-1554) Tel 912-234-3429.

Tainters, P.O. Box 36, Temple, NH 03084 (SAN 682-1049).

Texas Bookman, The, 2703 W. Mockingbird Ln., Dallas, TX 75235 (SAN 106-875X) Tel 214-350-6648.

True Remainders, Inc., Box 770, 240 Portage Rd., Lewiston, NY 14092 (SAN 246-313X) Tel 716-284-7784.

Western Bk. Distributors, 2970 San Pablo Ave., Berkeley, CA 94702 (SAN 158-4332) Tel 415-849-0100; Toll free: 800-825-0100. Remainders by title & promotional assortments; half-price paperback promotions.

Wilshire Bk. Co., *(Wilshire; 0-87980)*, 12015 Sherman Rd., North Hollywood, CA 91605-3781 (SAN 168-9932) Tel 213-875-1711.

X-S Bks., Inc., 725 Dell Rd., Carlstadt, NJ 07072 (SAN 169-4634) Tel 201-935-4493. Remainders & promotional books to trade & institutional markets; specializes in art & general trade titles, juveniles, songbooks, texts, clothbound & paperback; title-by-title & promotional assortments.

Yellow Pages Used Bks., 111 SE G St., Grants Pass, OR 97526 (SAN 680-4659) Tel 503-474-5514. Free computerized out-of-print search. In-house inventory of over 75,000 books, catalogs used. Has a selection of back issues of science fiction & fantasy magazines. Write for current catalogs. Buys, sells, and trades libraries or small lots.

ON DEMAND PUBLISHERS

AMS Pr., Inc., *(AMS Pr; 0-404),* 56 E. 13th St., New York, NY 10003 (SAN 106-6706) Tel 212-777-4700.

Anacomp Microprinting, *(A N A C O M P),* 1245 Forest Ave., Suite 12, Des Plaines, IL 60018 (SAN 287-6787) Tel 312-296-0310. Commercial, high technology, industrial, databases, consumer publications, publications, library reference.

Abraham's Magazine Service *See* **AMS Pr., Inc.**

American Institute of Physics, *(Am Inst Physics; 0-88318),* 335 E. 45th St., New York, NY 10017 (SAN 201-162X) Tel 212-661-9404; Toll free: 800-247-7497. Publishes scholarly journals, books & databases in physics & related sciences in hardcopy, 16mm & 35mm microfilm, reel & cartridge, videocassettes & microfiche. North American distributor of journals from the Institute of Physics (UK), Annals of the Israel Physical Society, Physics Briefs from the Fachinformationszentrum (West Germany), & Physica Scripta (Royal Swedish Academy of Sciences). Distributes & markets videocassettes on a variety of physics topics.

American Jewish Periodical Ctr., 3101 Clifton Ave., Cincinnati, OH 45220 (SAN 267-0097) Tel 513-221-1875. Microfilm of American-Jewish serials only.

American Theological Library Assn., Board of Microtext, *(0-7905),* 1118 E. 54th Pl., Chicago, IL 60615 (SAN 210-3850) Tel 312-643-7470. Microfilm (35mm) of newspapers, periodicals, religious monographs; microfiche collections of religious & theological monographs.

Andronicus Publishing Co., Subs. of Haldi Assocs., Inc., *(Andronicus Pub Co),* 680 Fifth Ave., 11th Flr., New York, NY 10019 (SAN 287-6795).

Art Dealers Assn. of America, *(Art Dlrs Assn Amer),* 575 Madison Ave., New York, NY 10022 (SAN 224-6260) Tel 212-940-8590.

BIOSIS, *(BIOSIS; 0-916246),* 2100 Arch St., Philadelphia, PA 19103 (SAN 287-6809) Tel 215-587-4800; Toll free: 800-523-4806. Biological Abstracts & Biological Abstracts 5-Year Collective Indexes on microfilm (Collective Indexes also on microfiche). Biological Abstracts/RRM (Reports, Reviews, Meetings) 5-Year Collective Indexes on microfiche.

Balch Institute Pr., *(Balch IES Pr; 0-937437; 0-944190),* 18 S. Seventh St., Philadelphia, PA 19106 (SAN 695-7838) Tel 215-925-8090; Dist. by: Associated University Presses, 440 Forsgate Dr., Cranbury, NJ 08512 (SAN 281-2959) Tel 609-655-4770.

Bell & Howell, Pubn. Systems Div., *(Bell & Howell; 0-934425),* Old Mansfield Rd., Wooster, OH 44691-9050 (SAN 208-4635) Tel 216-264-6666. Micropublishing: American & foreign newspapers on 35mm microfilm, periodicals & telephone directories on microfiche, newspaper indexes, microform reading equipment. Career & occupational information service. Free catalogs.

BioSciences Information Services *See* **BIOSIS**

Books on Demand, Div. of University Microfilms, International, *(Bks Demand UMI; 0-8357),* 300 N. Zeeb Rd., Ann Arbor, MI 48106-1346 (SAN 212-2464) Tel 313-761-4700; Toll free: 800-521-0600. On-demand reprints of out-of-print books reproduced by xerography & bound in paper covers (cloth covers are available for 6.00 additional). Imprint of University Microfilms International.

Brookhaven Pr., *(Brookhaven Pr),* 2004 Kramer St., Box 2287, La Crosse, WI 54602-2287 (SAN 287-6817) Tel 608-781-0850. Government documents (national & international), periodicals, newspapers, statistics, research collections, reference & source publications, scholarly projects (all subjects), manuscript & archival materials. Formats: 16mm & 35mm microfilm & 4 x 6 microfiche. Agent for several micropublishers.

Canner, J. S., & Co., Inc., Subs. of Plenum Publishing Corp., *(Canner; 0-910324),* 10 Charles St., Needham Heights, MA 02194 (SAN 202-5094) Tel 617-449-9103. Microcards; also microfilm of Plenum journals only.

Chadwyck-Healey Inc., *(Chadwyck-Healey; 0-914146; 0-89887; 0-85964),* 1101 King St., Alexandria, VA 22314 (SAN 282-3306) Tel 703-683-4890.

Clearwater Publishing Co., Inc. *See* **Ross, Norman, Publishing, Inc.**

Congressional Information Service, Inc., Subs. of Elsevier US Holdings, Inc., *(Cong Info; 0-912380; 0-88692),* 4520 East-West Hwy., Suite 800, Bethesda, MD 20814 (SAN 206-345X) Tel 301-654-1550; Toll free: 800-638-8380. Federal, state, municipal, foreign & international government documents; documents from non-government sources; statistical data, legislative histories; indexes, abstracts, online & microfiche.

Dakota Graphics Inc., *(Dakota Graph),* 9655 W. Colfax Ave., Lakewood, CO 80215 (SAN 287-685X) Tel 303-237-0408. Roll microfilm only of German music books.

Disclosure, Inc., *(Disclosure),* 5161 River Rd., Bethesda, MD 20816 (SAN 287-6868) Tel 301-951-1413. On-line microfiche & paper copy of SEC reports.

ERIC Clearinghouse on Counseling & Personnel, *(ERIC Clearinghouse),* Univ. of Michigan, Schl. of Education Bldg., Rm. 2108, Ann Arbor, MI 48109 (SAN 287-6876) Tel 313-764-9492. Articles, research papers & reports on microfiche.

ERIC Document Reproduction Service, Box 190, Arlington, VA 22210 (SAN 695-8192).

Empire Microfilm Co., 2300 Valley View Ln., Suite 300, Dallas, TX 75234 (SAN 246-3113) Tel 214-243-6173.

Fairchild Bks., Div. of Fairchild Pubns., *(Fairchild; 0-87005),* 7 E. 12th St., New York, NY 10003 (SAN 201-470X) Tel 212-741-4280.

General Microfilm Co., 70 Coolidge Hill Rd., Watertown, MA 02172 (SAN 695-7846) Tel 617-926-5557.

Godfrey Memorial Library, *(Godfrey Mem),* 134 Newfield St., Middletown, CT 06457 (SAN 287-6884) Tel 203-346-4375. Microfiche editions of corporate annual reports, genealogical materials & other publications.

Health, Physical Education & Recreation Microform Pubns., *(Health Physical),* 1477 Moss St., Eugene, OR 97403 (SAN 287-6892) Tel 503-686-4117.

High Density Systems, Inc., *(High Density),* Box 175, Inwood Sta., New York, NY 10034 (SAN 287-6914) Tel 212-569-5340. Microfiche & 16mm roll microfilm in high-density formats in the fine arts, music & humanities. Contract micropublications, master microfiche creation, microfiche duplication, distribution & consultation.

Hoover Institution Pr., Affil. of Hoover Institution, *(Hoover Inst Pr; 0-8179),* Stanford Univ., Stanford, CA 94305-6010 (SAN 202-3024) Tel 415-723-3373.

Information Handling Services, *(IHS; 0-910972; 0-89847),* 15 Inverness Way E., P.O. Box 1154, Englewood, CO 80150 (SAN 203-7254) Tel 303-790-0600; Toll free: 800-525-7052. Prepackaged & custom services on 8mm & 16mm roll microfilm & 24X & 48X microfiche with accompanying hard copy. Products include federal & military specifications & standards, Industry standards, government procurement packages, product & vendor catalog data, & educational materials.

Inprint Pubs., Inc., 1701 Blount Rd., Section C, Pompano Beach, FL 33069 (SAN 665-9705) Tel 305-979-3277.

Institute for Scientific Information, *(Inst Sci Info; 0-941708),* 3501 Market St., Philadelphia, PA 19104 (SAN 239-2348) Tel 215-386-0100; Toll free: 800-523-4092.

JA Micropublishing, Inc., *(JA Micropublishing; 0-912127),* 271 Main St., Box 218, Eastchester, NY 10707 (SAN 264-6730) Tel 914-793-2130; Toll free: 800-227-2477.

Jai Pr., Inc., *(Jai Pr; 0-89232; 1-55938),* 55 Old Post Rd., No. 2, P.O. Box 1678, Greenwich, CT 06836 (SAN 208-4082) Tel 203-661-7602.

Johnson Reprint Corp., Subs. of Harcourt, Brace, Jovanovich, Inc., *(Johnson Repr; 0-384),* 111 Fifth Ave., New York, NY 10003 (SAN 285-0362) Tel 212-614-3000; Toll free: 800-543-1918.

Kraus Microform, Div. of Kraus-Thomson Organization, Ltd., *(Kraus Micro),* Rte. 100, Millwood, NY 10546 (SAN 287-6930) Tel 914-762-2200. Thirty-Five mm microfilm & microfiche of journals, newspapers, foreign official gazettes, curriculum guides, census reports, scholarly research collections & government archives.

Law Journal Seminars-Pr., Div. of New York Law Publishing Co., *(Law Journal),* 111 Eighth Ave., New York, NY 10011 (SAN 287-7023) Tel 212-741-8300. Microfilm & microfiche.

Library Microfilms, Div. of Bay Microfilm Inc., *(Lib Micro),* 1115 E. Arques Ave., Sunnyvale, CA 94086 (SAN 287-6957) Tel 408-736-7444. Microfilm, microfiche, photofiche, supplies & equipment; publications on microfilm & microfiche, library union catalogs.

Massachusetts Historical Society, *(Mass Hist Soc; 0-934909),* 1154 Boylston St., Boston, MA 02215 (SAN 202-2133) Tel 617-536-1608; Dist. by: Northeastern Univ. Pr., 360 Huntington Ave., Huntington Plaza, Suite 272, Boston, MA 02115 (SAN 205-3764) Tel 617-437-5480; Dist. by: University Microfilms, Inc., 300 N. Zeeb Rd., Ann Arbor, MI 48106 (SAN 212-2464) Tel 313-761-4700; Toll free: 800-521-0600.

Micro Media, Inc., *(Micro Media Inc),* P.O. Box 95, North Branford, CT 06471 (SAN 287-6965) Tel 203-785-0000. Microfiche, 16mm & 35mm microfilming, readers & supplies, equipment, hard copy, reproductions, microfilm & microfiche duplicating; micropublishing; 105mm fiche; engineering drawing.

Microfiche Pubns., Div. of Microfiche Systems Corp., *(Microfiche Pubns),* Box 3513, Grand Central Sta., New York, NY 10163 (SAN 287-6973); 248 Hempstead Tpke., West Hempstead, NY 11552 (SAN 244-822X) Tel 516-481-2300. Public Papers of the Presidents: microfiche collection of public statements, news conferences & speeches of Truman, Eisenhower, Kennedy & Johnson. Language & Linguistics: microfiche series containing 4300 titles in 16 subject categories. National Auxiliary Publications Service (NAPS) : operated for ASIS; over 4000 deposits in scientific journals.

Microforms International Marketing Corp., Subs. of Pergamon Pr., Inc., *(Microforms Intl; 0-8277),* Fairview Park, Elmsford, NY 10523 (SAN 287-6981) Tel 914-592-7700. Micropublishing of scientific & scholarly journals, including all Pergamon Press journals & selected GPO serials on 16mm & 35mm microfilm & microfiche. Historical files of HMSO British parliamentary debates & of annual reports of major American companies, with updating. Gauthier-Villars journals on microfilm. Microform annuals covering 140 major micropublishers; Masson & Cie journals, American Psychological Association journals, New York Stock Exchange listing applications, History of Economics series.

Microplex, Inc., Subs. of West Canadian Graphic Industries, Ltd., *(Microplex Inc),* 14875 Landmark Blvd., Suite 400, Dallas, TX 75240 (SAN 287-699X) Tel 214-352-3400. Microfilm, microfiche & source document conversion service.

NCR Corp., Law Dept., Intellectual Property Section, *(NCR Law; 0-925738),* 1700 S. Patterson Blvd., Dayton, OH 45479 (SAN 287-7015) Tel 513-445-1291. No longer produces software.

National Archives & Records Administration, *(Natl Archives & Records; 0-911333),* Pubns. Div., Seventh St. & Pennsylvania Ave., NW, Rm. G9, Washington, DC 20408 (SAN 210-363X) Tel 202-523-5611. Official records of the federal government on microfilm; facsimiles & reproductions of important historical documents, census records from 1790 to 1910 on microfilm. Catalog of National Archives Microfilm Publications, Black Studies, Indian Studies, immigration, & genealogical records. Catalogs of Federal Population Census, 1790 to 1910. Books & guides on the preservation & use of federal records.

National Auxiliary Pubns. Service, Microfiche Pubns., *(Natl Aux Pubns),* P.O. Box 3513, Grand Central Sta., New York, NY 10163 (SAN 287-7007) Tel 516-481-2300. Depository for information that is supplemental to published journal articles or monographs & for full-length works accompanied by footnotes. Twenty-four hour reproduction service in microfilm or photocopy form. Operated for ASIS.

National Technical Information Service, U. S. Dept. of Commerce, *(Natl Tech Info; 0-934213),* 5285 Port Royal Rd., Springfield, VA 22161 (SAN 205-7255) Tel 703-487-4805.

NCR Corp., Source Document Service Div. *See* **NCR Corp., Law Dept., Intellectual Property Section**

New York Public Library, Photographic Service, Fifth Ave. & 42nd St., Rm. 313, New York, NY 10018 (SAN 278-0569) Tel 212-930-0814. Microfilm & microfiche.

New York Times, *(NY Times),* 229 W. 43rd St., New York, NY 10036 (SAN 208-3027) Tel 212-556-3664; Toll free: 800-631-2580.

Newsbank, Inc., 58 Pine St., New Canaan, CT 06840 (SAN 695-7900) Tel 203-966-1100.

Princeton Microfilm Corp., *(Princeton Microfilm),* 43 Hightstown Rd., Princeton Junction, NJ 08550 (SAN 287-7031) Tel 609-452-2066; Toll free: 800-257-9502.

Professional Data Services, c/o Congressional Information Services, 450 East-West Hwy., Suite 800, Bethesda, MD 20814 (SAN 695-8206).

Readex Bks., Div. of Readex Microprint Corp., *(Readex Bks; 0-918414),* 58 Pine St., New Canaan, CT 06840 (SAN 209-9926) Tel 203-966-5906; Toll free: 800-223-4739. Conventional reference works & bibliographies, research & reference collections in Microprint (opaque), microfiche & reel Microfilm.

Research Pubns., Inc., Subs. of International Thomson Organization, Inc., *(Res Pubns CT; 0-89235),* 12 Lunar Dr., Drawer AB, Woodbridge, CT 06525 (SAN 238-2717) Tel 203-397-2600; Toll free: 800-732-2477.

Ross, Norman, Publishing, Inc., *(N Ross; 0-8287; 0-88354),* 1995 Broadway, New York, NY 10023 (SAN 201-8969) Tel 212-873-2100. Primarily microfilm & microfiche; also: audiocassettes & videocassettes. Microform distributor for ACRPP, Alpha COM, C. H. Beck Verlag, Bibliotheque Nationale, Emmett Microforms, Hachette Microeditions, Inter Documentation Co. (IDC), Irish Times, Microform Academic Pubs., Mikropress GmbH, Mindata Ltd., Georg Olms Verlag, Oxford Univ. Pr., Microfiche, World Microfilms Pubns., Yushodo Booksellers, & others.

Rothman, Fred B., & Co., *(Rothman; 0-8377),* 10368 W. Centennial Rd., Littleton, CO 80127 (SAN 159-9437) Tel 303-979-5657; Toll free: 800-457-1986. Acquired Rothman Reprints.

Saur, K. G., Subs. of R. R. Bowker Co., *(K G Saur; 0-89664; 0-86291; 3-598; 3-7940),* 245 W. 17th St., New York, NY 10011 (SAN 214-1191) Tel 212-337-7023; Toll free: 800-521-8110; 800-537-8416 (in Canada).

Scholarly Resources, Inc., *(Scholarly Res Inc; 0-8420),* 104 Greenhill Ave., Wilmington, DE 19805 (SAN 203-2619) Tel 302-654-7713; Toll free: 800-772-8937. Monographs, reference books & text books. Subjects: genealogy, history, law, military studies & political science. Government documents, documents, journals, manuscript collections & newspapers.

Teleprint Publishing, Inc., 7 Elliewood Ave., Charlottesville, VA 22903 (SAN 684-5266); Toll free: 800-582-0026.

Tennessee Microfilms, P.O. Box 1096, Nashville, TN 37202 (SAN 695-8168).

Trans Media/The Oceana Group, *(Trans Media Oceana),* 75 Main St., Dobbs Ferry, NY 10522 (SAN 287-7082) Tel 914-693-5944. Publishes documentary & legal microfilm.

Univelt, Inc., *(Univelt Inc; 0-912183; 0-87703),* P.O. Box 28130, San Diego, CA 92128 (SAN 170-3099); 740 Metcalf St., Suite 13, Escondido, CA 92025 (SAN 658-2095) Tel 619-746-4005.

University Microfilms, Inc., Div. of Bell & Howell, *(Univ Microfilms; 0-8357),* 300 N. Zeeb Rd., Ann Arbor, MI 48106 (SAN 212-2464) Tel 313-761-4700; Toll free: 800-521-0600; 800-343-5299 (in Canada); Orders to: P.O. Box 1307, Ann Arbor, MI 48106 (SAN 241-8797). Serials & newspapers in microform, reprints of articles & issues, dissertations published & available on demand. Imprints: Books on Demand (reprints out-of-print books), & UMI Research Pr. (scholarly & professional book publisher).

University Music Editions, Div. of High Density Systems Inc., *(Univ Mus Ed),* Box 175, Inwood Sta., New York, NY 10034 (SAN 287-7139) Tel 212-569-5393; Orders to: 4712A Broadway, New York, NY 10040 (SAN 287-7147). Publish music on microfiche & roll-film, collected anthologies, editions of complete works of master composers, historical sets & music literature. Publish all microfiche titles in patented binder-with-index format.

Univ. of Chicago Pr., Div. of Univ. of Chicago, *(U of Chicago Pr; 0-226),* 5801 Ellis Ave., 4th Flr., Chicago, IL 60637 (SAN 202-5280) Tel 312-702-7700; Toll free: 800-621-2736; Orders to: 11030 S. Langley Ave., Chicago, IL 60628 (SAN 202-5299) Tel 312-568-1550.

Univ. of Florida, Libraries, *(Univ Florida Lib; 0-929595),* Gainesville, FL 32611 (SAN 287-7104) Tel 904-392-0341. 35mm microfilm of Florida & of Carribean & Latin American newspapers. Request through Inter-Library Loan Office.

Univ. of Michigan, Harlan Hatcher Graduate Library, Interlibrary Lending, Circulation Dept., Ann Arbor, MI 48109-1205 (SAN 695-8214) Tel 313-764-0400.

Univ. of Wisconsin Library, Interlibrary Loan Dept., 728 State St., Madison, WI 53706 (SAN 695-8222) Tel 608-262-3193.

Updata Pubns., Inc., *(Updata Pubns; 0-9607840),* 1746 Westwood Blvd., Los Angeles, CA 90024 (SAN 238-2067) Tel 213-829-5090. Consultants for all types of micropublishing. Micropublishers in all formats. Collections: National Advisory Committee for Aeronautics, 1915-1958; U.S. Bureau of Mines, from 1910; DMIC Metallurgy, 1952-1971; U.S. Dept. of the Army, Foreign Area Studies; Mine Safety & Health Administration; Cranfield College of Aeronautics; National Research Council (Canada), 1951-1977; Institute of Aerospace Studies (Univ. of Toronto) 1948-1977; Central Intelligence Agency; U.S. Dept. of Agriculture; U.S. Geological Survey, Water Supply Papers, 1896-date; all U.S. Dept. of Agriculture documents from inception to date; all U.S. Bureau National Marine Fisheries Service (NOAA) & its predecessors, 1871-date; U.S. Bureau of Labor Statistics Bulletins & reports, 1866-date.

SEARCH SERVICES

Adler, Marion F., Out of Print Children's Bks., Box 744, Stockbridge, MA 01262 (SAN 680-4586) Tel 413-298-3559. Free worldwide search for out-of-print children's books, if not in stock. Personal service, no obligation. Open by appointment for buying, selling or browsing.

Art Bk. Finders, Box 156, Purchase, NY 10577 (SAN 695-6815). Free search service for out-of-print art books.

Avonlea Bks., P.O. Box 74, Main Sta., White Plains, NY 10602 (SAN 680-4446) Tel 914-946-5923. Worldwide mail order search service for out-of-print books of all categories. Phone requests accepted. Serves individuals, corporations, libraries, & many bookstores.

Better Bk. Getter, 118 W. 72nd St., New York, NY 10023 (SAN 680-4462) Tel 212-877-6018. A book search and book appraisal service.

Bibliofile Bk. Search, 1346 20th Ave., San Francisco, CA 94122 (SAN 664-5380) Tel 415-540-8223.

Book Assocs., P.O. Box 687, Orange, CT 06477 (SAN 664-5054) Tel 203-795-3107.

Book Quest, 175 Fifth Ave., Suite 3201, New York, NY 10010 (SAN 680-4489) Tel 212-677-4564. Offers free out-of-print search service. Stock includes biography, illustrated books and others. Ships worldwide.

Book Ranger, 105 Charles St., New York, NY 10012 (SAN 680-4500) Tel 212-924-4957. Searches for out-of-print books. Specializes in Americana.

Book Services International, 425 Asylum St., Bridgeport, CT 06610-9990 (SAN 157-9541) Tel 203-334-2165; Toll free: 800-243-2790. All available titles from any publisher, government agency or nonprofit organization from any country; out-of-print book search; paperbacks converted to hardbound; rush, continuation & standing orders; online order capability via UTLAS.

Book Tracers, P.O. Box 114, Fords, NJ 08863 (SAN 682-1057). Free search. Reasonable quotes.

Books-on-Call, P.O. Box 41471, Memphis, TN 38174 (SAN 664-5372) Tel 901-278-7917.

Booksearch, 105 W. Third St., Winona, MN 55987 (SAN 695-6823) Tel 507-454-6954. Out-of-print book locating company.

Booksearch San Francisco, P.O. Box 210265, San Francisco, CA 94121 (SAN 664-5356) Tel 415-221-5575.

Brennan Bks., P.O. Box 9002, Salt Lake City, UT 84109-0002 (SAN 680-4519) Tel 801-278-7946. International out-of-print search service.

Continental Bk. Search, P.O. Box 1163, New York, NY 10009 (SAN 680-473X) Tel 212-254-8719. Bookfinder specializing in elusive titles, either out-of-print or otherwise hard-to-find. Free search. Customer pays only for books ordered. Satisfaction guaranteed. Mail order only.

Dickens, C., Out-of-Print Bks., Lenox Sq., 3393 Peachtree Rd., NE, Atlanta, GA 30326 (SAN 664-2926) Tel 404-231-3825.

Donan Bks., Inc., 220 E. 82nd St., New York, NY 10028 (SAN 680-4527) Tel 212-734-0707. Large stock of out-of-print titles. Free search service worldwide.

Elliot's Bks., *(Elliots Bks; 0-911830),* P.O. Box 6, Northford, CT 06472 (SAN 204-1529) Tel 203-484-2184.

Fourth Avenue Booksellers, Box 456, Cooper Sta., New York, NY 10276 (SAN 675-7413). Provides a search service.

International Bookfinders, Inc., Box 1, Pacific Palisades, CA 90272 (SAN 695-7870). Free search service for out-of-print books. Want lists invited. Mail order only. Member, ABAA. Founded 1950.

International Service Co., 333 Fourth Ave., Indialantic, FL 32903 (SAN 169-5134).

J & J Hse. Booksellers, 632 Broadway, San Diego, CA 92101 (SAN 664-5410) Tel 619-232-8331.

Klenett, Frances, Bk. Service, 13 Cranberry St., Brooklyn Heights, NY 11201 (SAN 680-4535) Tel 718-852-2424. Search service for out-of-print and hard-to-find books.

Leekley Bk. Search, P.O. Box 337, Winthrop Harbor, IL 60096 (SAN 249-9266) Tel 312-872-2311.

Michelli, Frank, Bks., 45 Halsey St., Newark, NJ 07102 (SAN 695-7889) Tel 201-623-4289. Search service. General stock of 20,000 books, mostly out-of-print.

Out-of-State Bk. Service, P.O. Box 3253D, San Clemente, CA 92672 (SAN 680-4616) Tel 714-492-2976. National & international search service for out-of-print books. No obligation. General stock of out-of-print books.

Past History Rare & Old Bks., 136 Parkview Terr., Lincroft, NJ 07738 (SAN 680-456X) Tel 201-842-4545. Large stock of rare and old books. Specializing in general Americana with special emphasis on New Jersey. Free search.

Peninsula Booksearch, P.O. Box 1305, Burlingame, CA 94011-1305 (SAN 695-6874). Offers free out-of-print book search. Satisfaction is guaranteed for all books purchased. Full refund on returns (any reason) within 10 days of receipt. Payment methods: check, money order, Visa, Mastercard. In business since 1978.

Phoenix Bookfinders, 17 Sheridan Ct., Plainview, NY 11803 (SAN 680-4683) Tel 516-938-8192. Search service is limited exclusively to the locating of rare, hard-to-find, and out-of-print books. Free quotes. "Want" lists are available on request.

Princeton Antiques Bookshop, 2915-17 Atlantic Ave., Atlantic City, NJ 08401 (SAN 280-1876) Tel 609-344-1943. Out of print stock of 200,000 different hardback titles, indexed by author, title, & subject. Full-time staff searches worldwide for individual titles, authors, or subjects.

Ralston Popular Fiction, P.O. Box 4174, Fullerton, CA 92634 (SAN 695-7854) Tel 714-990-0432. Issues booklists. Stock includes first editions in all areas of fiction. Will provide search service.

Reed Bks., Box 55893B, Birmingham, AL 35255 (SAN 664-5046) Tel 205-871-9239.

Reliable Bk. Service, P.O. Box 2033, Paterson, NJ 07509 (SAN 680-4608) Tel 201-791-7018. If titles cannot be supplied from comprehensive stock, free search service is available for fiction, history, military, biography, cinema, theatre, classical and scholarly books, published from 1880 to 1983. Established 1935.

Rinen, A., Bks., 105 E. 2nd St., New York, NY 10009 (SAN 680-4748) Tel 212-777-1468. Free search. Catalogues free.

School Aid Co., *(Sch Aid; 0-87385),* 911 Colfax Dr., P.O. Box 123, Danville, IL 61832 (SAN 158-3719) Tel 217-442-6855; Toll free: 800-447-2665.

Scribe's Perch Search Service, 62-64 Thames St., Newport, RI 02840 (SAN 695-703X) Tel 401-849-8426; Toll free: 800-242-5461. Free search service for out-of-print books.

Transbooks, Box 44-RB, Matawan, NJ 07747 (SAN 695-7048). Specializes in locating & supplying out-of-print American & British books.

Treasures from the Castle, 1720 N. Livernois, Rochester, MI 48064 (SAN 695-7862) Tel 313-651-7317. Search service for out-of-print children's books. Issues (sells) book lists.

Vathek Bks., 250 Slocum Way, Ft. Lee, NJ 07024 (SAN 680-4721) Tel 201-585-1760. Out-of-print searches by telephone or mail. Purchases books on the Roman Empire and ancient Near East.

Viewpoint, 41 Union Sq. W., New York, NY 10003 (SAN 664-5038) Tel 212-242-5478.

Vroman's, A. C., 695 E. Colorado Blvd., Pasadena, CA 91101 (SAN 169-0027) Tel 818-449-5320.

Yellow Pages Used Bks., 111 SE G St., Grants Pass, OR 97526 (SAN 680-4659) Tel 503-474-5514. Free computerized out-of-print search. In-house inventory of over 75,000 books, catalogs used. Has a selection of back issues of science fiction & fantasy magazines. Write for current catalogs. Buys, sells, and trades libraries or small lots.

O.P. Resources